COLLINS

Concise
Dictionary

Collins

An Imprint of HarperCollins*Publishers*

HarperCollins Publishers

PO Box, Glasgow G4 0NB

First Edition 1982
Second Edition 1988
Third Edition 1992
Revised Third Edition 1995
Fourth Edition 1999

© HarperCollins Publishers 1982, 1988, 1992, 1995, 1999
1 2 3 4 5 6 7 8 9 10

Standard Edition	ISBN 0 00 472257 4
Thumb-indexed Edition	ISBN 0 00 472258 2
Australian Edition	ISBN 0 00 472396 1

Collins® is a registered trademark of
HarperCollins Publishers Limited

The HarperCollins website address is
www.fireandwater.com

A catalogue record for this book is
available from the British Library.

This edition prepared in conjunction with Market House Books Ltd, Aylesbury, England

Typeset by Market House Books Ltd, Aylesbury, England
Printed and bound in Great Britain by Caledonian International Book Manufacturing Ltd,
Glasgow

Collins concise dictionary.
4th ed.
ISBN 0 00 472396 1.
1 English language – Dictionaries. 2. English language –
Australia – Dictionaries.

423

Corpus Acknowledgments

We would like to thank those authors and publishers who kindly gave permission for copyright
material to be used in the Bank of English. We would also like to thank Times Newspapers Ltd
for providing valuable data.

COLLINS
Concise
Dictionary

General Consultant

J M Sinclair

Formerly Professor, Department of English Language
and Literature
University of Birmingham

For Australian Edition

G A Wilkes

Challis Professor of English Literature
University of Sydney

W A Krebs

Associate Professor in Literature
and Communications
Bond University, Queensland

Contents

General Consultant

J M Sinclair
Formerly Professor, Department of English Language and
Literature
University of Birmingham

Special Consultants

AUSTRALIAN ENGLISH
G A Wilkes
Challis Professor of English
Literature
University of Sydney

W A Krebs
Associate Professor in
Literature and Communications
Bond University, Queensland

W S Ramson
Reader in English
Australian National University

BRITISH REGIONAL ENGLISH,
URBAN DIALECTS
Harold Orton
Professor Emeritus, Department
of English
University of Leeds

CANADIAN ENGLISH
R J Gregg
Formerly Professor, Department
of Linguistics
University of British Columbia

Patrick Drysdale
Editor, *A Dictionary of
Canadianisms on
Historical Principles*

James Arthurs
Professor, Department of
Linguistics
University of Victoria

CARIBBEAN ENGLISH
S R R Allsopp
Coordinator, Caribbean
Lexicography Project
University of the West Indies,
Barbados

EAST AFRICAN ENGLISH
J Kalema
Department of Linguistic Science
University of Reading

INDIAN ENGLISH
R K Bansal
Professor, Department of
Phonetics and Spoken English
Central Institute of English and
Foreign Languages, Hyderabad

IRISH ENGLISH
R J Gregg
Formerly Professor, Department
of Linguistics
University of British
Columbia

T de Bhaldraithe
Professor, Department of Irish
Dialectology
University College, Dublin

NEW ZEALAND ENGLISH
Ian A Gordon
Professor Emeritus
University of Wellington

SCOTTISH ENGLISH
A J Aitken
Department of English Language
University of Edinburgh
Formerly Editor, *Dictionary of the
Older Scottish Tongue*

SOUTH AFRICAN ENGLISH
L W Lanham
Professor, Department of
Phonetics and General
Linguistics
University of the Witwatersrand

M V Aldridge
Professor, Department of
Phonetics and General
Linguistics
University of the Witwatersrand

Geoffrey Hughes
Professor, Department of English
University of the Witwatersrand

WEST AFRICAN ENGLISH
J Spencer
Director, Institute of Modern
English Language Studies
University of Leeds

PRONUNCIATION
A C Gimson
Formerly Professor, Department
of Phonetics and Linguistics
University College
University of London

Specialist Contributors

AERONAUTICS
T C Wooldridge, Angus Boyd
Senior Lecturer in Aerodynamics,
The College of Aeronautics,
Cranfield

ARCHITECTURE; CIVIL
ENGINEERING
Bruce Martin

AUSTRALIAN ENGLISH
Steve Higgs
Melbourne Grammar School

BIOGRAPHIES, PLACES
Market House Books
Aylesbury

BROADCASTING, FILM, ETC.
Patrick Leggatt
Chief Engineer,
External Relations,
British Broadcasting
Corporation

BUSINESS
Alan Isaacs

CHEMISTRY
John Daintith

COMPUTERS
Richard Fryer
Department of Computer Science,
University of Strathclyde

CONSTRUCTION
M J Walker
Construction Industry
Research and Information
Association

Specialist Contributors

EARTH SCIENCES
Peter J Smith
Reader in Earth Sciences,
The Open University

ECONOMICS
P Donaldson
Ruskin College, Oxford

EDUCATION
Catherine Playford
Head Teacher of English,
Priestnall School

ENGINEERING
J P Quayle
Editor, *Kempe's Engineering
Year-Book*

INDUSTRIAL RELATIONS
Professor Angela M Bowey
Strathclyde Business School,
University of Strathclyde
Alexander Purdie
Scottish College of Textiles,
Galashiels

INFORMATION
TECHNOLOGY
Professor Thomas Carbery
Andrew Doswell
Catherine M Young
Department of Information
Science,
University of Strathclyde

JUDAISM
Ephraim Borowski
Department of Philosophy,
University of Glasgow

LANGUAGES & PEOPLES
David Kilby
Formerly, Department of
Language and Linguistics,
University of Essex

LAW
Richard Latham
Barrister-at-Law
Brian Russell Davis
Barrister-at-Law
Sandra Clarke

LIFE SCIENCES
Miranda Robertson
Life Sciences Editor, *Nature*
Dr W Gratzer
MRC Cell Biophysics Unit

LINGUISTICS
Professor Yorick Wilks
New Mexico State University

LINGUISTICS AND GRAMMAR
Lloyd Humberstone

LOGIC
Ephraim Borowski
Department of Philosophy,
University of Glasgow

MALAYSIAN ENGLISH
U Yong-ee

MARKETING
Professor M Christopher
Department of Marketing and
Logistics Systems,
Cranfield School of
Management

METALLURGY
Stanley White

MILITARY
Major S R Elliot
Colonel Andrew Duncan
The International Institute for
Strategic Studies

MILITARY AND NAUTICAL
TERMS
Cmdr I Johnston RN

PHILOSOPHY
Christopher Sion
Ephraim Borowski
Department of Philosophy,
University of Glasgow

PHYSICAL SCIENCES
R Cutler

PHYSICS
J W Warren
Department of Physics,

Brunel University

PIDGINS AND CREOLES
Loreto Todd
The School of English,
University of Leeds

PLANTS
Sandra Holmes

POP MUSIC
Ingrid von Essen

PRINTING
C H Parsons
Laurence Chizlett

PSYCHOLOGY
Dr Eric Taylor
Professor Stuart Sutherland
Director, Centre for Research
on Perception and Cognition,
University of Sussex

RAILWAYS
James Barnes

RELIGION
The Rev D Lancashire
University of Essex

RELIGIOUS TERMS
David Bourke
Rev Canon D W Gundry
Chancellor of Leicester Cathedral

SOCIAL WELFARE
Bob Marsden
Harrow Social Services Department

SPORT
Stuart Bathgate
Freelance Journalist

STATISTICS
Ephraim Borowski
Department of Philosophy,
University of Glasgow

TOOLS
N J Small
Associate of the Institute of
Marine Engineers

Other Contributors

Jane Bartholomew ANIMALS
Jenny Baster COOKERY; CLOTHING
　AND FASHION; TEXTILES
Denise Bown PLACE NAMES
Ron Brown JAZZ
Daphne Butler CHEMISTRY
Christopher L Clarke HOROLOGY
Brian Dalgleish METALLURGY
Carolyn Eardley ANTIQUES; FURNI-
　TURE; TEXTILES
R J Edwards PSYCHOLOGY
Dennis Exton FILMS, TV, AND RADIO

Rosalind Fergusson BIOGRAPHIES
Ian Fuller PSYCHOLOGY
C Gallon PLANTS
Robert Hine BIOGRAPHIES
Amanda Isaacs BIOGRAPHIES
Cherry McDonald-Taylor
　EDUCATION; LIBRARY SCIENCE
David Martin PSYCHOLOGY
Mary Marshall CARDS; DANCING AND
　BALLET
Peter Miller SPORTS
Stewart Murray METALLURGY

Serena Penman ART
H G Procter PSYCHOLOGY
Mark Salad PLACE NAMES
David H Shaw ENGINEERING
Brian Street ANTHROPOLOGY
Andrew Treacher PSYCHOLOGY
Ralph Tyler FILMS, TV, AND RADIO;
　LITERATURE; MYTHOLOGY; THEATRE;
　BIOGRAPHIES
Jennifer Wearden ARCHAEOLOGY
Irene Wise BIOCHEMISTRY

BANK of ENGLISH

This dictionary has been compiled by referring to the Bank of English, a unique database of the English language with examples of over 323 million words enabling Collins lexicographers to analyse how English is actually used today and how it is changing. This is the evidence on which the changes in this dictionary are based.

The Bank of English was set up as a joint initiative by HarperCollins Publishers and Birmingham University to be a resource for language research and lexicography. It contains a very wide range of material from books, newspapers, radio, TV, magazines, letters, and talks reflecting the whole spectrum of English today. Its size and range make it an unequalled resource and the purpose-built software for its analysis is unique to Collins Dictionaries.

This ensures that Collins Dictionaries accurately reflect English as it is used today in a way that is most helpful to the dictionary user as well as including the full range of rarer and historical words and meanings.

Foreword

The fourth edition of Collins Concise Dictionary offers, in its new extended length, an even more wide-ranging and up-to-date survey of the English language as it is used in Britain and around the world approaching the millennium. Continuing from the success of the last edition, it also includes entries for people and places; household names in all fields from arts to sport, both past and present; as well as essential facts about countries, cities, and towns the world over. This combination makes it an especially handy reference book for the home, college, or office, whether you are studying, writing, or just keeping up with the news.

Research shows that spelling is the most frequent reason for checking a dictionary and Collins Concise Dictionary is exceptionally helpful for this because it contains all the spelling forms you might want spelt out in full (no cryptic abbreviations) so you can be absolutely confident. Meanings are numbered and explained clearly and precisely with numerous examples. The modern core meaning is shown first and technical and specialist meanings are clearly labelled.

Deciding what is "correct English" can often pose problems, so Collins Concise Dictionary gives guidance on those knotty points of language by referring to current usage (as evidenced in the Bank of English) and pointing out where traditional preferences may differ. These helpful notes appear in boxes at the end of many entries.

As language use changes, so do the meanings and the very words we use. Collins Concise Dictionary covers a host of new words and meanings from all sorts of subjects like Computing, Marketing, Finance and Politics, and ranging in style from the most technical to the most informal. Collins lexicographers and Collins special subject and language consultants are constantly monitoring language change in Britain and around the world wherever English is spoken. This enables us to provide a truly international survey of English as a world language. In this Collins has the special advantage of the Bank of English which enables us to check an enormous number of examples of a word from an enormous range of sources. You will find more about this unique resource on page vii.

All this wealth of information is presented in a new layout designed to make the Dictionary quick and easy to use as well as a pleasure to browse. The new edition of Collins Concise Dictionary provides essential, up-to-date reference for everyone whether reading, writing, or studying, and is an essential resource for all who love the English language.

Guide to the Text

Headword

Pronunciation

Part of speech

Subject-field label

Cross-reference

bugle² ('bju:gʰl) *n* any of several Eurasian plants having small blue or white flowers. [C13: from LL *bugula*, from ?]

bugle³ ('bju:gʰl) *n* a tubular glass or plastic bead sewn onto clothes for decoration. [C16: from ?]

bugloss ('bju:glɒs) *n* any of various hairy Eurasian plants having clusters of blue flowers. [C15: from L, from Gk *bouglōssos* ox-tongued]

bugong ('bu:gɒn) *n* another name for **bogong**.

buhl (bu:l) *adj, n* a variant spelling of **boulle**.

build (bɪld) *vb* builds, building, built. **1** to make, construct, or form by joining parts or materials: *to build a house*. **2** (*tr*) to order the building of: *the government builds most of our hospitals*. **3** (foll. by *on* or *upon*) to base; found: *his theory was not built on facts*. **4** (*tr*) to establish and develop: *it took ten years to build a business*. **5** (*tr*) to make in a particular way or for a particular purpose: *the car was not built for speed*. **6** (*intr;* often foll. by *up*) to increase in intensity. ♦ *n* **7** physical form, figure, or proportions: *a man with an athletic build*. [OE *byldan*]

builder ('bɪldə) *n* a person who builds, esp. one who contracts for and supervises the construction or repair of buildings.

building ('bɪldɪn) *n* **1** something built with a roof and walls. **2** the act, business, occupation, or art of building houses, boats, etc.

building society *n* a cooperative banking enterprise financed by deposits on which interest is paid and from which mortgage loans are advanced on homes and real property; many now offer a range of banking services.

build up *vb* (*adv*) **1** (*tr*) to construct gradually, systematically, and in stages. **2** to increase, accumulate, or strengthen, esp. by degrees: *the murmur built up to a roar*. **3** (*tr*) to improve the health or physique of (a person). **4** (*intr*) to prepare for or gradually approach a climax. ♦ *n* **build-up. 5** progressive increase in number, size, etc.: *the build-up of industry*. **6** a gradual approach to a climax. **7** extravagant publicity or praise, esp. in the form of a campaign. **8** *Mil.* the process of attaining the required strength of forces and equipment.

built (bɪlt) *vb* the past tense and past participle of **build**.

built-in *adj* **1** made or incorporated as an integral part: *a built-in cupboard*. **2** essential; inherent. ♦ *n* **3** *Austral*. a built-in cupboard.

built-in obsolescence *n* See **planned obsolescence**.

built-up *adj* **1** having many buildings (esp. in **built-up area**). **2** increased by the addition of parts: *built-up heels*.

Buitenzorg ★ (*Dutch* 'bœitənzɔrx) *n* the former name of **Bogor**.

Bujumbura ★ (,bu:dʒəm'buərə) *n* the capital of Burundi, a port at the NE end of Lake Tanganyika. Pop.: 300 000 (1994 est.). Former name: **Usumbura**.

Bukavu ★ (bu:'kɑːvu:) *n* a port in E Democratic Republic of the Congo (formerly Zaïre), on Lake Kivu: commercial and industrial centre. Pop.: 201 569 (1994 est.). Former name (until 1966): **Costermansville**.

Bukhara *or* **Bokhara** ★ (bʊ'xɑːrə) *n* **1** a city in S Uzbekistan: capital of the former emirate of Bukhara. Pop.: 236 000 (1993 est.). **2** a former emirate of central Asia: a powerful kingdom and centre of Islam; became a territory of the Soviet Union (1920) and was divided between the former Uzbek, Tajik, and Turkmen SSRs.

Bukovina *or* **Bucovina** ★ (,bu:kə'vi:nə) *n* a region of E central Europe, part of the NE Carpathians: the north was seized by the Soviet Union (1940) and later became part of the Ukraine; the south remained Romanian.

Bulawayo ★ (,bʊlə'weɪəʊ) *n* a city in SW Zimbabwe founded (1893) on the site of the kraal of Lobengula, the last Matabele king; the country's main industrial centre. Pop.: 620 936 (1992).

bulb (bʌlb) *n* **1** a rounded organ of vegetative reproduction in plants such as the tulip and onion: a flattened stem bearing a central shoot surrounded by fleshy nutritive inner leaves and thin brown outer leaves. **2** a plant, such as a hyacinth or daffodil, that grows from a bulb. **3** See **light bulb**. **4** any bulb-shaped thing. [C16: from L *bulbus*, from Gk *bolbos* onion]
▶ **'bulbous** *adj*

Inflected forms

Grammatical information

Definition

Sense number

x

Guide to the Text

Etymology

People and Places

Derived words

Example

Usage note

Related adjective

Idiom or phrase

Usage label

bulbil ('bʌlbɪl) *n* **1** a small bulb produced from a parent bulb. **2** a bulblike reproductive organ in a leaf axil of certain plants. **3** any small bulblike structure in an animal. [C19: from NL *bulbillus* BULB]

bulbul ('bʊlbʊl) *n* a songbird of tropical Africa and Asia having brown plumage and, in many species, a distinct crest. [C18: via Persian from Ar.]

Bulg. *abbrev. for* Bulgaria(n).

Bulgakov ★ (*Russian* bul'gakəf) *n* **Mikhail Afanaseyev** (mixaʼil afaʼnasjɪf). 1891–1940, Soviet writer; his novels include *The Master and Margarita* (1966–67).

Bulganin ★ (*Russian* bul'ganin) *n* **Nikolai Aleksandrovich** (nikaʼlaj alɪkʼsandrəvitʃ). 1895–1975, Soviet statesman and military leader.

Bulgaria ★ (bʌlˈgeərɪə, bʊl-) *n* a republic in SE Europe, on the Balkan Peninsula on the Black Sea: under Turkish rule from 1395 until 1878; became an independent kingdom in 1908 and a Communist republic in 1946; in 1990 free elections ousted the Communist Party. Consists chiefly of the Danube valley in the north, the Balkan Mountains in the central part, separated from the Rhodope Mountains of the south by the valley of the Maritsa River. Language: Bulgarian. Religion: Christian (Bulgarian Orthodox) majority. Currency: lev. Capital: Sofia. Pop.: 8 329 000 (1997). Area: 110 911 sq. km (42 823 sq. miles).
▸ **Bulˈgarian** *adj, n*

bulge (bʌldʒ) *n* **1** a swelling or an outward curve. **2** a sudden increase in number, esp. of population. ◆ *vb* **bulges, bulging, bulged. 3** to swell outwards. [C13: from OF *bouge*, from L *bulga* bag, prob. of Gaulish origin]
▸ **ˈbulging** *adj* ▸ **ˈbulgy** *adj*

bulgur ('bʌlgə) *n* cracked wheat that has been hulled, steamed, and roasted so that it requires little or no cooking. [C20: from Ar. *burghul*]

bulimia (bjuːˈlɪmɪə) *n* **1** pathologically insatiable hunger. **2** Also called: **bulimia nervosa.** a disorder characterized by compulsive overeating followed by vomiting. [C17: from NL, from Gk *bous* ox + *limos* hunger]

bulk (bʌlk) *n* **1** volume, size, or magnitude, esp. when great. **2** the main part: *the bulk of the work is repetitious.* **3** a large body, esp. of a person. **4** the part of food which passes unabsorbed through the digestive system. **5 in bulk. 5a** in large quantities. **5b** (of a cargo, etc.) unpackaged. ◆ *vb* **6** to cohere or cause to cohere in a mass. **7 bulk large.** to be or seem important or prominent. [C15: from ON *bulki* cargo]

> **USAGE NOTE** The use of a plural noun after *bulk* was formerly considered incorrect, but is now acceptable.

bulk buying *n* the purchase of goods in large amounts, often at reduced prices.

bulkhead ('bʌlk,hɛd) *n* any upright wall-like partition in a ship, aircraft, etc. [C15: prob. from *bulk* projecting framework from ON *bálkr* +HEAD]

bulk modulus *n* a coefficient of elasticity of a substance equal to the ratio of the applied stress to the resulting fractional change in volume.

bulky ('bʌlkɪ) *adj* **bulkier, bulkiest.** very large and massive, esp. so as to be unwieldy.
▸ **ˈbulkily** *adv* ▸ **ˈbulkiness** *n*

bull[1] (bʊl) *n* **1** any male bovine animal, esp. one that is sexually mature. Related adj: **taurine. 2** the male of various other animals including the elephant and whale. **3** a very large, strong, or aggressive person. **4** *Stock Exchange.* **4a** a speculator who buys in anticipation of rising prices in order to make a profit on resale. **4b** (*as modifier*): *a bull market.* Cf. **bear**[2] (sense 5). **5** *Chiefly Brit.* short for **bull's-eye** (senses 1, 2). **6** *Sl.* short for **bullshit. 7 a bull in a china shop.** a clumsy person. **8 take the bull by the horns.** to face and tackle a difficulty without shirking. ◆ *adj* **9** male; masculine: *a bull elephant.* **10** large; strong. [OE *bula*]

Editorial Staff

For the Fourth Edition

Guide to the Use of the Dictionary

Collins Concise Dictionary is designed to be easy to use so that you can go straight to the word you want. The Guide that follows sets out the main principles on which the Dictionary is arranged and enables you to make full use of the Dictionary by showing the range of information that it contains.

HEADWORD

All main entries, including place names, biographies, abbreviations, prefixes, and suffixes, are printed in large boldface type and are listed in strict alphabetical order. This applies even if the headword consists of more than one word.

Order of entries

Words that have the same spelling but are derived from different sources (homographs) are entered separately with superscript numbers after the headwords.

> **saw**[1] (sɔː) *n* **1** any of various hand tools ...
> **saw**[2] (sɔː) *vb* the past tense of **see**[1].
> **saw**[3] (sɔː) *n* a wise saying, maxim, or proverb. ...

A word with a capital initial letter, if entered separately, follows the lower-case form. For example, **Arras** follows **arras**.

Place names

If a place has more than one name, its main entry is given at the name most often used in modern English, with a cross-reference at other names. Thus, the main entry for the capital of Bavaria is at **Munich**, with a cross-reference at **München**. If a place name has no current anglicized form, its main entry is at the form of the name used in the official language of the area. Thus, the main entry is at **Brno**, with a cross-reference at **Brünn**. Historical names of importance are also given, with dates where these can be ascertained.

> **Paris**[1] ★ ('pærɪs; *French* pari) *n* ... Ancient name: **Lutetia**.

> **Volgograd** ★ (*Russian* vəlgaˈgrat; *English* ˈvɒlgəˌgræd) *n* ...
> Former names: **Tsaritsyn** (until 1925), **Stalingrad** (1925–61).

Statistical information about places has been obtained from the most up-to-date and reliable sources available. Population figures have been compiled from the most recent census available at the time of going to press. The date of the census is always given.

Biographical entries

Biographical entries are entered separately from and immediately following place names of the same spelling. They are entered at the surname of the subject or at his or her title if that is the name by which he or she is better known and are grouped under one headword when the spelling of the surname (or title) is identical.

Abbreviations, acronyms, and symbols

Abbreviations, acronyms, and symbols are entered as headwords in the main alphabetical list. In line with modern practice, full stops are generally not used but it can be assumed that nearly all abbreviations are equally acceptable with or without stops.

Prefixes, suffixes, and combining forms

Prefixes (e.g. **in-**, **pre-**, **sub-**), suffixes (e.g. **-able**, **-ation**, **-ity**), and combining forms (e.g. **psycho-**, **-iatry**) have been entered as headwords if they are still used freely to produce new words in English.

Variant spellings

Common acceptable variant spellings of English words are given as alternative forms of the headword.

> **capitalize** *or* **capitalise** ('kæpɪtəˌlaɪz) *vb* ...

US spellings

Where it is different, the US spelling of a word is also recorded in the headword.

> **centre** *or US* **center** ('sɛntə) *n*

PRONUNCIATION

Pronunciations of words in this Dictionary represent those that are common in educated British English speech. They are transcribed in the International Phonetic Alphabet (IPA). *A Key to the Pronunciation Symbols* is printed at the end of this Guide. The pronunciation is normally given in brackets immediately after the headword.

> **abase** (əˈbeɪs) *vb* **abases, abasing, abased.** (*tr*) **1** to humble ...

The stress pattern is marked by the symbols ' for primary stress and ‚ for secondary stress. The stress mark precedes the syllable to which it applies.

Variant pronunciations

When a headword has an acceptable variant pronunciation or stress pattern, the variant is given by repeating only the syllable or syllables that change.

Guide to the Use of the Dictionary

economic (ˌiːkəˈnɒmɪk, ˌɛkə-) *adj* **1** of or relating to ...

Pronunciations with different parts of speech

When two or more parts of speech of a word have different pronunciations, the pronunciations are shown in brackets before the relevant group of senses.

record *n* ('rɛkɔːd). **1** an account in permanent form, ... ♦ *vb* (rɪˈkɔːd). (*mainly tr*) **18** to set down in some permanent form ...

Pronunciation of individual senses

If one sense of a headword has a different pronunciation from that of the rest, the pronunciation is given in brackets after the sense number.

conjure ('kʌndʒə) *vb* conjures, conjuring, conjured. **1** (*intr*) to practise conjuring. **2** (*intr*) to call upon supposed supernatural forces by spells and incantations. **3** (kənˈdʒʊə). (*tr*) to appeal earnestly to: *I conjure you to help me.* ...

INFLECTED FORMS

Inflected forms are shown for the following:

Nouns and verbs whose inflections involve a change in internal spelling.

goose[1] (guːs) *n, pl* geese. ...

drive (draɪv) *vb* drives, driving, drove, driven. ...

Nouns, verbs, and adjectives that end in a consonant plus -*y*, where *y* is changed to *i* before inflectional endings.

augury ('ɔːgjʊrɪ) *n, pl* auguries. ...

Nouns having identical singular and plural forms.

sheep (ʃiːp) *n, pl* sheep. ...

Nouns that closely resemble others but form their plurals differently.

mongoose ('mɒŋˌguːs) *n, pl* mongooses. ...

Nouns that end in -*ful*, -*o*, and -*us*.

handful ('hændfʊl) *n, pl* handfuls. ...
tomato (təˈmɑːtəʊ) *n, pl* tomatoes. ...
prospectus (prəˈspɛktəs) *n, pl* prospectuses. ...

Nouns whose plurals are not regular English inflections.

basis ('beɪsɪs) *n, pl* bases (-siːz) ...

Plural nouns whose singulars are not regular English forms.

bacteria (bækˈtɪərɪə) *pl n, sing* bacterium. ...

Nouns whose plurals have regular spellings but involve a change in pronunciation.

house *n* (haʊs), *pl* houses ('haʊzɪz). ...

Multiword nouns when it is not obvious which word takes a plural inflection.

attorney-at-law *n, pl* attorneys-at-law. ...

Adjectives that change their roots to form comparatives and superlatives.

good (gʊd) *adj* better, best. ...

Adjectives and verbs that double their final consonant before adding endings.

fat (fæt) ... ♦ *adj* fatter, fattest. ...
control (kənˈtrəʊl) *vb* controls, controlling, controlled. ...

Verbs that are regular and do not (as might be expected) double their final consonant before adding endings.

rivet ('rɪvɪt) ... ♦ *vb* rivets, riveting, riveted. ...

Verbs and adjectives that end in a vowel plus -*e*.

canoe (kəˈnuː) ... ♦ *vb* canoes, canoeing, canoed. ...
free (friː) *adj* freer, freest. ... ♦ *vb* frees, freeing, freed. ...

Verbs that end in -*e*.

pace[1] (peɪs) ... ♦ *vb* paces, pacing, paced. ...

PARTS OF SPEECH

A part-of-speech label in italics precedes the sense or senses relating to that part of speech.

Standard parts of speech

The standard parts of speech, with the abbreviations used, are as follows:

adjective (*adj*), adverb (*adv*), conjunction (*conj*), interjection (*interj*), noun (*n*), preposition (*prep*), pronoun (*pron*), verb (*vb*).

Less traditional parts of speech

Certain other less traditional parts of speech have been used in this Dictionary.

determiner. This denotes such words as *the, a, some, any, that, this,* as well as the numerals, and possessives such as *my* and *your*. Many determiners can have a pronoun function without change of meaning:

some (sʌm; *unstressed* səm) *determiner* ... **2a** an unknown or unspecified quantity or amount of: *there's some rice on the table; he owns some horses.* **2b** (*as pron; functioning as sing or pl*): *we'll buy some.* ...

sentence connector. This description replaces the traditional classification of certain words, such as *therefore* and *however*, as adverbs or conjunctions. These words link sentences together rather in the manner of conjunctions; however, they are not confined to the first position in a clause as conjunctions are.

sentence substitute. Sentence substitutes are words such as *yes, no, perhaps, definitely,* and *maybe.* They can stand as meaningful utterances by themselves.

Words used as more than one part of speech

If a word can be used as more than one part of speech, the senses of one part of speech are separated from the others by a lozenge (♦).

lure (lʊə) *vb* **lures, luring, lured.** (*tr*) ... **2** *Falconry.* to entice (a hawk or falcon) from the air to the falconer by a lure. ♦ *n* **3** a person or thing that lures. ...

GRAMMATICAL INFORMATION

Grammatical information is provided in brackets and typically in italics to distinguish it from other types of information.

Adjectives and determiners

Some adjectives and determiners are restricted by usage to a particular position relative to the nouns they qualify. This is indicated by the following labels:

postpositive (used predicatively or after the noun, but not before the noun):

ablaze (ə'bleɪz) *adj* (*postpositive*), *adv* **1** on fire; burning. ...

immediately postpositive (always used immediately following the noun qualified and never used predicatively):

galore (gə'lɔː) *determiner* (*immediately postpositive*) in great numbers or quantity: *there were daffodils galore in the park.* ...

prenominal (used before the noun, and never used predicatively):

chief (tʃiːf) ... ♦ *adj* **4** (*prenominal*) **4a** most important; principal. ...

Intensifiers

Adjectives and adverbs that perform an exclusively intensifying function, with no addition of meaning, are described as (intensifier) without further explanation.

blooming ('bluːmɪŋ) *adv, adj Brit. inf.* (intensifier): *a blooming genius; blooming painful.*

Conjunctions

Conjunctions are divided into two classes, marked by the following labels:

coordinating. Coordinating conjunctions connect words, phrases, or clauses that perform an identical function and are not dependent on each other. They include *and, but,* and *or.*

subordinating. Subordinating conjunctions introduce clauses that are dependent on a main clause in a complex sentence. They include *where, until,* and *if.*

Some conjunctions, such as *while* and *whereas,* can function as either coordinating or subordinating conjunctions.

Singular and plural labelling of nouns

Headwords and senses that are apparently plural in form but that take a singular verb, etc., are marked '*functioning as sing*'

physics ('fɪzɪks) *n* (*functioning as sing*) **1** the branch of science ...

Headwords and senses that appear to be singular, such as collective nouns, but that take a plural verb, etc., are marked '*functioning as pl*'

cattle ('kætᵊl) *n* (*functioning as pl*) **1** bovid mammals of the tribe *Bovini* ...

Headwords and senses that may take either a singular or a plural verb, etc., are marked '*functioning as sing or pl*'

bellows ('beləuz) *n* (*functioning as sing or pl*) **1** Also: **pair of bellows.** an instrument consisting of an air chamber ...

Modifiers

A noun that is commonly used as if it were an adjective is labelled *modifier.* If the sense of the modifier can be understood from the sense of the noun, the modifier is shown without further explanation, with an example to illustrate its use. Otherwise its meaning and/or usage is explained separately.

key[1] (kiː) *n* ... **8** (*modifier*) of great importance: *a key issue.*

Verbs

The principal parts given are: 3rd person singular of the present tense; present participle; past tense; past participle if different from the past tense.

Intransitive and transitive verbs

When a sense of a verb (*vb*) is restricted to transitive use, it is labelled (*tr*); if it is intransitive only, it is labelled (*intr*). If all the senses of a verb are transitive or all are intransitive, the appropriate label appears before the first numbered sense and is not repeated.

Absence of a label is significant: it indicates that the sense may be used both transitively and intransitively.

If nearly all the senses of a verb are transitive, the label (*mainly tr*) appears immediately before the first numbered sense. This indicates that, unless otherwise labelled, any given sense of the verb is transitive. Similarly, all the senses of a verb may be labelled (*mainly intr*).

Copulas

A verb that takes a complement is labelled copula.

> **seem** (siːm) *vb* (*may take an infinitive*) **1** (*copula*) to appear to the mind or eye; look: *the car seems to be running well.* ...

Phrasal verbs

Verbal constructions consisting of a verb and a prepositional or an adverbial particle are given headword status if the meaning of the phrasal verb cannot be deduced from the separate meanings of the verb and the particle.

Phrasal verbs are labelled to show four possible distinctions: a transitive verb with an adverbial particle (*tr, adv*); a transitive verb with a prepositional particle (*tr, prep*); an intransitive verb with an adverbial particle (*intr, adv*); an intransitive verb with a prepositional particle (*intr, prep*):

> **turn on** ... **4** (*tr, adv*) *Inf.* to produce (charm, tears, etc.) suddenly or automatically.

> **take for** *vb* (*tr, prep*) *Inf.* to consider or suppose to be, esp. mistakenly: *the fake coins were taken for genuine; who do you take me for?*

> **break off** ... **3** (*intr, adv*) to stop abruptly: *he broke off in the middle of his speech.*

> **turn on** ... **2** (*intr, prep*) to depend or hinge on: *the success of the party turns on you.*

The absence of a label is significant. If there is no label (*tr*) or (*intr*), the verb may be used either transitively or intransitively. If there is no label (*adv*) or (*prep*), the particle may be either adverbial or prepositional.

Any noun, adjective, or modifier formed from a phrasal verb is entered under the phrasal-verb headword. In some cases, where the noun or adjective is more common than the verb, the phrasal verb is entered after the noun or adjective form:

> **breakaway** ('breɪkəˌweɪ) *n* **1a** loss or withdrawal of a group of members from an association, club, etc. **1b** (*as modifier*): *a breakaway faction.* ... ◆ *vb* **break away.** (*intr, adv*) **3** (often foll. by *from*) to leave hastily or escape. **4** to withdraw or secede.

RESTRICTIVE LABELS

If a particular sense is restricted as to appropriateness, connotation, subject field, etc., an italic label is placed immediately before the relevant definition.

> **hang on** *vb* (*intr*) ... **5** (*adv*) *Inf.* to wait: *hang on for a few minutes.*

If a label applies to all senses of one part of speech, it is placed immediately after the part-of-speech label.

> **assured** (əˈʃʊəd) *adj* ... ◆ *n* **4** *Chiefly Brit.* **4a** the beneficiary under a life assurance policy. **4b** the person whose life is insured. ...

If a label applies to all senses of a headword, it is placed immediately after the pronunciation (or inflections).

> **con**[1] (kɒn) *Inf.* ◆ *n* **1a** short for **confidence trick. 1b** (*as modifier*): *con man.* ◆ *vb* **cons, conning, conned. 2** (*tr*) to swindle ...

Usage labels

Sl. (*Slang*). Refers to words or senses that are informal and restricted in context, for example, to members of a particular social or cultural group. Slang words are inappropriate in formal speech or writing.

Inf. (*Informal*). Applies to words or senses that may be widely used, especially in conversation, letter-writing, etc., but that are not common in formal writing. Such words are subject to fewer contextual restrictions than slang words.

Taboo. Indicates words that are not acceptable in polite use.

Offens. (*Offensive*). Indicates that a word might be regarded as offensive by the person described or referred to, even if the speaker uses the word without any malicious intention.

Derog. (*Derogatory*). Implies that the connotations of a word are unpleasant with intent on the part of the speaker or writer.

Not standard. Indicates words or senses that are frequently encountered but widely regarded as incorrect.

Arch. (*Archaic*). Denotes a word or sense that is no longer in common use but that may be found in literary works or used to impart a historical colour to contemporary writing.

Obs. (*Obsolete*). Denotes a word or sense that is no longer in use. In specialist or technical fields the label often implies that the term has been superseded.

The word 'formerly' is placed in brackets before a sense when the practice, concept, etc., being described, rather than the word itself, is obsolete or out-of-date.

A number of other usage labels, such as *Ironic*, *Facetious*, and *Euphemistic*, are used where appropriate.

More extended help on usage is provided in usage notes after certain entries.

Subject-field labels A number of italic labels are used to indicate that a word or sense is used in a particular specialist or technical field.

MEANING

The meaning of each headword in this Dictionary is explained in one or more definitions, together with information about context and typical use.

Order of senses As a general rule, where a headword has more than one sense, the first sense given is the one most common in current usage.

> **complexion** (kəm'plɛkʃən) *n* **1** the colour and general appearance of a person's skin, esp. of the face. **2** aspect or nature: *the general complexion of a nation's finances.* **3** *Obs.* temperament. ...

Where the lexicographers consider that a current sense is the 'core meaning' in that it illuminates the meaning of other senses, the core meaning may be placed first.

> **competition** (,kɒmpɪ'tɪʃən) *n* **1** the act of competing. **2** a contest in which a winner is selected from among two or more entrants. **3** a series of games, sports events, etc. **4** the opposition offered by competitors....

Subsequent senses are arranged so as to give a coherent account of the meaning of a headword. If a word is used as more than one part of speech, all the senses of each part of speech are grouped together in a single block. Within a part-of-speech block, closely related senses are grouped together; technical senses generally follow general senses; archaic and obsolete sense follow technical senses; idioms and fixed phrases are generally placed last.

Scientific and technical definitions *Units, physical quantities, formulas, etc.* In accordance with the recommendations of the International Standards Organization, all scientific measurements are expressed in SI units (*Système International d'Unités*). Measurements and quantities in more traditional units are often given as well as SI units. The entries for chemical compounds give the systematic names as well as the more familiar popular names.

CROSS-REFERENCES

Cross-references introduced by the words 'See also' or 'Compare' refer the reader to additional information elsewhere in the Dictionary. If the cross-reference is preceded by a lozenge (♦), it applies to all senses of the headword that have gone before it, unless otherwise stated. If there is no lozenge, the cross-reference applies only to the sense immediately preceding it.

Variant spellings

Variant spellings (e.g. **foetus**...a variant spelling of **fetus**) are generally entered as cross-references if their place in the alphabetical list is more than ten entries distant from the main entry.

Alternative names

Alternative names or terms are printed in boldface type and introduced by the words 'Also' or 'Also called'. If the alternative name or term is preceded by a lozenge, it applies to the entire entry.

RELATED ADJECTIVES

Certain nouns, especially of Germanic origin, have related adjectives that are derived from Latin or French. For example, *mural* (from Latin) is an adjective related in meaning to *wall*. Such adjectives are shown in a number of cases after the sense (or part-of-speech block) to which they are related.

> **wall** (wɔːl) *n* **1a** a vertical construction made of stone, brick, wood, etc. ... Related adj: **mural**. ...

IDIOMS

Fixed noun phrases, such as **dark horse**, and certain other idioms are given full headword status. Other idioms are placed under the key word of the idiom, as a separate sense, generally at the end of the appropriate part-of-speech block.

> **ground**[1] (graund) *n* ... **17 break new ground.** to do something that has not been done before. ...

ETYMOLOGIES

Etymologies are placed in bold square brackets after the definition. They are given for all headwords except those that are derivative forms (consisting of a base word and a suffix or prefix), compound words, inflected forms, and proper names.

Many headwords, such as **enlighten** and **prepossess**, consist of a prefix and a base word and are not accompanied by etymologies since the essential etymological information is shown for the component parts, all of which are entered in the Dictionary as headwords in their own right.

The purpose of the etymologies is to trace briefly the history of the word back from the present day, through its first recorded appearance in English, to its origin, often in some source language other than English. The etymologies show the history of the word both in English (wherever there has been significant change in form or sense) and in its pre-English source languages.

Words printed in SMALL CAPITALS refer to other headwords where relevant or additional information, either in the definition or in the etymology, may be found.

Dating

The etymology records the first known occurrence (a written citation) of a word in English. Words first appearing in the language during the Middle English period or later are dated by century, abbreviated **C**.

> **mantis** ('mæntɪs) ... [C17: NL, from Gk: prophet, alluding to its praying posture]

This indicates that there is a written citation for **mantis** in the seventeenth century. The absence of a New Latin or Greek form in the etymology means that the form of the word was the same in those languages as in English.

Old English

Native words from Old English are not dated, written records of Old English being scarce, but are simply identified as being of Old English origin.

DERIVED WORDS

Words derived from a base word by the addition of suffixes such as *-ly*, *-ness*, etc., are entered in boldface type immediately after the etymology or after the last definition if there is no etymology. They are preceded by an arrow head (▸). The meanings of such words may be deduced from the meanings of the suffix and the headword.

USAGE NOTES

A brief note introduced by the label **USAGE NOTE** has been added at the end of a number of entries in order to comment on matters of usage.

List of Abbreviations used in the Dictionary

abbrev. abbreviation
Abor. Aboriginal
adj adjective
adv adverb(ial)
Afrik. Afrikaans
Amerind American Indian
Anat. Anatomy
approx. approximate(ly)
Ar. Arabic
Arch. Archaic
Archaeol. Archaeology
Archit. Architecture
Astrol. Astrology
Astron. Astronomy
Austral. Australian

Biol. Biology
Bot. Botany
Brit. Britain; British

C century (e.g. **C14** = 14th century)
°C degrees Celsius
Canad. Canadian
cap. capital
cf. compare
Chem. Chemistry
comp. comparative
conj conjunction

Derog. Derogatory
dim. diminutive
Du. Dutch

E east(ern); (in etymologies) English
Econ. Economics
e.g. for example
esp. especially
est. estimate

F French
fem feminine
foll. followed
ft foot *or* feet

G German
Geog. Geography
Geol. Geology
Geom. Geometry
Gk Greek
Gmc Germanic

Heb. Hebrew

i.e. that is
imit. of imitative origin
in. inch(es)
Inf. Informal
infl. influence(d)
interj interjection
intr intransitive
It. Italian

km kilometre(s)

L Late; Latin
lit. literally
LL Late Latin

m metre(s)
M Middle
masc masculine
Maths Mathematics
Med. Medicine; (in etymologies) Medieval
MHG Middle High German
Mil. Military
Mod. Modern
Myth. Mythology

n noun
N north(ern)
Naut. Nautical
NE northeast(ern)
NL New Latin
no. number
NW northwest(ern)
NZ New Zealand

O Old
Obs. Obsolete
Offens. Offensive

OHG Old High German
ON Old Norse
orig. originally

Photog. Photography
pl plural
pop. population
Port. Portuguese
p.p. past participle
prep preposition(al)
prob. probably
pron pronoun
Psychol. Psychology
pt. point
p.t. past tense

rel. related

S south(ern)
S. African South African
Sansk. Sanskrit
Scand. Scandinavian
Scot. Scottish; Scots
SE southeast(ern)
sing singular
Sl. slang
Sp. Spanish
sq. square
sup. superlative
SW southwest(ern)

Theol. Theology
tr transitive

ult. ultimately
US United States

var. variant
vb verb
vol. volume

W west(ern)
wt. weight

Zool. Zoology

? in etymologies indicates "query"

Pronunciation Key

The symbols used in the pronunciation transcriptions are those of the International Phonetic Alphabet. The following consonant symbols have their usual English values: *b, d, f, h, k, l, m, n, p, r, s, t, v, w, z*. The remaining symbols and their interpretations are listed below.

English Sounds

ɑ: as in *father* ('fɑːðə), *alms* (ɑːmz), *clerk* (klɑːk), *heart* (hɑːt), *sergeant* ('sɑːdʒənt)

æ as in *act* (ækt), *Caedmon* ('kædmən), *plait* (plæt)

aɪ as in *dive* (daɪv), *aisle* (aɪl), *guy* (gaɪ), *might* (maɪt), *rye* (raɪ)

aɪə as in *fire* ('faɪə), *buyer* ('baɪə), *liar* ('laɪə), *tyre* ('taɪə)

au as in *out* (aut), *bough* (bau), *crowd* (kraud), *slouch* (slautʃ)

auə as in *flour* ('flauə), *cower* ('kauə), *flower* ('flauə), *sour* ('sauə)

ε as in *bet* (bεt), *ate* (εt), *bury* ('bεrɪ), *heifer* ('hεfə), *said* (sεd), *says* (sεz)

eɪ as in *paid* (peɪd), *day* (deɪ), *deign* (deɪn), *gauge* (geɪdʒ), *grey* (greɪ), *neigh* (neɪ)

εə as in *bear* (bεə), *dare* (dεə), *prayer* (prεə), *stairs* (stεəz), *where* (wεə)

g as in *get* (gεt), *give* (gɪv), *ghoul* (guːl), *guard* (gɑːd), *examine* (ɪg'zæmɪn)

ɪ as in *pretty* ('prɪtɪ), *build* (bɪld), *busy* ('bɪzɪ), *nymph* (nɪmf), *pocket* ('pɒkɪt), *sieve* (sɪv), *women* ('wɪmɪn)

iː as in *see* (siː), *aesthete* ('iːsθiːt), *evil* ('iːvᵊl), *magazine* (ˌmægə'ziːn), *receive* (rɪ'siːv), *siege* (siːdʒ)

ɪə as in *fear* (fɪə), *beer* (bɪə), *mere* (mɪə), *tier* (tɪə)

j as in *yes* (jεs), *onion* ('ʌnjən), *vignette* (vɪ'njεt)

ɒ as in *pot* (pɒt), *botch* (bɒtʃ), *sorry* ('sɒrɪ)

əu as in *note* (nəut), *beau* (bəu), *dough* (dəu), *hoe* (həu), *slow* (sləu), *yeoman* ('jəumən)

ɔ: as in *thaw* (θɔː), *broad* (brɔːd), *drawer* ('drɔːə), *fault* (fɔːlt), *halt* (hɔːlt), *organ* ('ɔːgən)

ɔɪ as in *void* (vɔɪd), *boy* (bɔɪ), *destroy* (dɪ'strɔɪ)

u as in *pull* (pul), *good* (gud), *should* (ʃud), *woman* ('wumən)

uː as in *zoo* (zuː), *do* (duː), *queue* (kjuː), *shoe* (ʃuː), *spew* (spjuː), *true* (truː), *you* (juː)

uə as in *poor* (puə), *skewer* (skjuə), *sure* (ʃuə)

ə as in *potter* ('pɒtə), *alone* (ə'ləun), *furious* ('fjuərɪəs), *nation* ('neɪʃən), *the* (ðə)

ɜ: as in *fern* (fɜːn), *burn* (bɜːn), *fir* (fɜː), *learn* (lɜːn), *term* (tɜːm), *worm* (wɜːm)

ʌ as in *cut* (kʌt), *flood* (flʌd), *rough* (rʌf), *son* (sʌn)

ʃ as in *ship* (ʃɪp), *election* (ɪ'lεkʃən), *machine* (mə'ʃiːn), *mission* ('mɪʃən), *pressure* ('prεʃə), *schedule* ('ʃεdjuːl), *sugar* ('ʃugə)

ʒ as in *treasure* ('trεʒə), *azure* ('æʒə), *closure* ('kləuʒə), *evasion* (ɪ'veɪʒən)

tʃ as in *chew* (tʃuː), *nature* ('neɪtʃə)

dʒ as in *jaw* (dʒɔː), *adjective* ('ædʒɪktɪv), *lodge* (lɒdʒ), *soldier* ('səuldʒə), *usage* ('juːsɪdʒ)

θ as in *thin* (θɪn), *strength* (strεŋθ), *three* (θriː)

ð as in *these* (ðiːz), *bathe* (beɪð), *lather* ('lɑːðə)

ŋ as in *sing* (sɪŋ), *finger* ('fɪŋgə), *sling* (slɪŋ)

ᵊ indicates that the following consonant (*l* or *n*) is syllabic, as in *bundle* ('bʌndᵊl), *button* ('bʌtᵊn)

Foreign Sounds

The symbols above are also used to represent foreign sounds where these are similar to English sounds. However, certain common foreign sounds require symbols with markedly different values, as follows:

a *a* in French *ami*, German *Mann*, Italian *pasta*: a sound between English (æ) and (ɑː), similar to the vowel in Northern English *cat* or London *cut*.

ɑ *a* in French *bas*: a sound made with the tongue position similar to that of English (ɑː), but shorter.

e *é* in French *été*, *eh* in German *sehr*, *e* in Italian *che*: a sound similar to the first part of the English diphthong (eɪ) in *day* or to the Scottish vowel in *day*.

i *i* in French *il*, German *Idee*, Spanish *filo*, Italian *signor*: a sound made with a tongue position similar to that of English (iː), but shorter.

ɔ *o* in Italian *no*, French *bonne*, German *Sonne*: a vowel resembling English (ɒ), but with a higher tongue position and more rounding of the lips.

o *o* in French *rose*, German *so*, Italian *voce*: a sound between English (ɔː) and (uː) with closely rounded lips, similar to the Scottish vowel in *so*.

u *ou* in French *genou*, *u* in German *kulant*,

Spanish *puna*: a sound made with a tongue position similar to that of English (uː), but shorter.

y *u* in French *tu*, *ü* in German *über* or *fünf*: a sound made with a tongue position similar to that of English (iː), but with closely rounded lips.

ø *eu* in French *deux*, *ö* in German *schön*: a sound made with the tongue position of (e), but with closely rounded lips.

œ *œu* in French *œuf*, *ö* in German *zwölf*: a sound made with a tongue position similar to that of English (ɛ), but with open rounded lips.

~ above a vowel indicates nasalization, as in French *un* (œ̃), *bon* (bɔ̃), *vin* (vɛ̃), *blanc* (blɑ̃).

χ *ch* in Scottish *loch*, German *Buch*, *j* in Spanish *Juan*.

ç *ch* in German *ich*: a (j) sound as in *yes*, said without voice; similar to the first sound in *huge*.

β *b* in Spanish *Habana*: a voiced fricative sound similar to (v), but made by the two lips.

ʎ *ll* in Spanish *llamar*, *gl* in Italian *consiglio*: similar to the (lj) sequence in *million*, but with the tongue tip lowered and the sounds said simultaneously.

ɥ *u* in French *lui*: a short (y).

ɲ *gn* in French *vigne*, Italian *gnocchi*, *ñ* in Spanish *España*: similar to the (nj) sequence in *onion*, but with the tongue tip lowered and the two sounds said simultaneously.

ɣ *g* in Spanish *luego*: a weak (g) made with voiced friction.

Length

The symbol : denotes length and is shown together with certain vowel symbols when the vowels are typically long.

Stress

Three grades of stress are shown in the transcriptions by the presence or absence of marks placed immediately *before* the affected syllable. Primary or strong stress is shown by ', while secondary or weak stress is shown by ˌ. Unstressed syllables are not marked. In *photographic* (ˌfəʊtəˈgræfɪk), for example, the first syllable carries secondary stress and the third primary stress, while the second and fourth are unstressed.

Notes

(i) Though words like *castle*, *path*, and *fast* are shown as pronounced with an /ɑː/ sound, many speakers use an /æ/. Such variations are acceptable and are to be assumed by the reader.

(ii) The letter "r" in some positions is not sounded in the speech of Southern England and elsewhere. However, many speakers in other areas do sound the "r" in such positions with varying degrees of distinctness. Again such variations are to be assumed, and in such words as *fern*, *fear*, and *arm* the reader will sound or not sound the "r" according to his or her speech habits.

(iii) Though the widely received pronunciation of words like *which* and *why* is with a simple /w/ sound and is so shown in the dictionary, many speakers in Scotland and elsewhere preserve an aspirated sound: /hw/. Once again this variation is to be assumed.

A DICTIONARY
OF THE
ENGLISH LANGUAGE

Aa

a or **A** (eɪ) *n, pl* **a's, A's,** or **As. 1** the first letter and first vowel of the English alphabet. **2** any of several speech sounds represented by this letter, as in *take, bag,* or *calm.* **3** Also called: **alpha.** the first in a series, esp. the highest mark. **4 from A to Z.** from start to finish.

a¹ (ə; *emphatic* eɪ) *determiner* (*indefinite article;* used before an initial consonant. Cf. **an¹**) **1** used preceding a singular countable noun, not previously specified: *a dog; a great pity.* **2** used preceding a noun or determiner of quantity: *a dozen eggs; a great many; to read a lot.* **3** (preceded by *once, twice, several times,* etc.) each or every; per: *once a day.* **4** a certain; one: *a Mr Jones called.* **5** (preceded by *not*) any at all: *not a hope.* ◆ Cf. **the¹.**

a² *symbol for:* **1** acceleration. **2** are(s) (metric measure of area). **3** atto-.

A *symbol for:* **1** *Music.* **1a** the sixth note of the scale of C major. **1b** the major or minor key having this note as its tonic. **2** a human blood type of the ABO group, containing the A antigen. **3** (in Britain) a major arterial road. **4** ampere(s). **5** absolute (temperature). **6** area. **7** (*in combination*) atomic: *an A-bomb; an A-plant.* **8a** a person whose job is in top management, or who holds a senior administrative or professional position. **8b** (*as modifier*): *an A worker.* ◆ See also **occupation groupings.**

Å *symbol for* angstrom unit.

a. *abbrev. for:* **1** acre(s). **2** Also: **A.** alto.

A. *abbrev. for:* **1** acre(s). **2** America(n). **3** answer.

a-¹ or *before a vowel* **an-** *prefix* not; without; opposite to: *atonal; asocial.* [from Gk *a-, an-* not, without]

a-² *prefix* **1** on; in; towards: *aground; aback.* **2** in the state of: *afloat; asleep.*

A1, A-1, or **A-one** (ˈeɪˈwʌn) *adj* **1** physically fit. **2** *Inf.* first class; excellent. **3** (of a vessel) in first-class condition.

A4 *n* a standard paper size, 297 × 210 mm.

AA *abbrev. for:* **1** Alcoholics Anonymous. **2** anti-aircraft. **3** (in Britain) Automobile Association.

AAA *abbrev. for:* **1** (formerly) *Brit.* Amateur Athletic Association. **2** *US.* Automobile Association of America.

Aachen ★ (ˈɑːkən; *German* ˈaːxən) *n* a city and spa in W Germany, in North Rhine-Westphalia: the northern capital of Charlemagne's empire. Pop.: 247 113 (1995 est.). French name: **Aix-la-Chapelle.**

Aalborg or **Ålborg** ★ (*Danish* ˈɔlbɔr) *n* a city and port in Denmark, in N Jutland. Pop.: 159 056 (1995 est.).

Aalesund ★ (*Norwegian* ˈoːləsun) *n* a variant spelling of **Ålesund.**

Aalto ★ (*Finnish* ˈɑːlto) *n* **Alvar** (ˈalvar). 1898–1976, Finnish architect and furniture designer, noted particularly for his public and industrial buildings, in which wood is much used. He invented bent plywood furniture (1932).

A & E *abbrev. for* Accident and Emergency (in hospitals).

A & R *abbrev. for* artists and repertoire.

AAP *abbrev. for:* **1** Australian Associated Press. **2** (in US) affirmative action programme.

Aarau ★ (*German* ˈaːrau) *n* a town in N Switzerland, capital of Aargau canton: capital of the Helvetic Republic from 1798 to 1803. Pop.: 15 881 (1990).

aardvark (ˈɑːdˌvɑːk) *n* a nocturnal burrowing African mammal that has long ears and snout and feeds on termites. Also called: **ant bear.** [C19: from obs. Afrik., from *aarde* earth + *varken* pig]

aardwolf (ˈɑːdˌwʊlf) *n, pl* **aardwolves.** a nocturnal mammal of the hyena family that inhabits the plains of southern Africa and feeds on termites and insect larvae. [C19: from Afrik., from *aarde* earth + *wolf* wolf]

Aargau ★ (*German* ˈaːrgau) *n* a canton in N Switzerland.

Capital: Aarau. Pop.: 523 114 (1995 est.). Area: 1404 sq. km (542 sq. miles). French name: **Argovie.**

Aarhus or **Århus** ★ (*Danish* ˈɔrhuːs) *n* a city and port in Denmark, in E Jutland. Pop.: 277 477 (1995 est.).

Aaron ★ (ˈɛərən) *n Old Testament.* the first high priest of the Israelites, brother of Moses (Exodus 4:14).

Aaron's beard *n* another name for **rose of Sharon.**

Aaron's rod *n* a widespread Eurasian plant having tall erect spikes of yellow flowers.

A'asia *abbrev. for* Australasia.

AB *abbrev. for:* **1** Also: **a.b.** able-bodied seaman. **2** Alberta. **3** (in the US) Bachelor of Arts. ◆ **4** *symbol for* a human blood type of the ABO group, containing both the A antigen and the B antigen.

ab-¹ *prefix* away from; opposite to: *abnormal.* [from L *ab* away from]

ab-² *prefix* a cgs unit of measurement in the electromagnetic system: *abampere, abwatt, abvolt.* [from ABSOLUTE]

aba (ˈæbə) *n* **1** a type of cloth from Syria, made of goat or camel hair. **2** a sleeveless outer garment of such cloth. [from Ar.]

abaca (ˈæbəkə) *n* **1** a Philippine plant, the source of Manila hemp. **2** another name for **Manila hemp.** [via Sp. from Tagalog *abaká*]

aback (əˈbæk) *adv* **taken aback. a** startled or disconcerted. **b** *Naut.* (of a vessel or sail) having the wind against the forward side so as to prevent forward motion. [OE *on bæc* to the back]

abacus (ˈæbəkəs) *n, pl* **abaci** (-ˌsaɪ) or **abacuses. 1** a counting device that consists of a frame holding rods on which a number of beads are free to move. **2** *Archit.* the flat upper part of the capital of a column. [C16: from L, from Gk *abax* board covered with sand, from Heb. *ābhāq* dust]

Abaddon ★ (əˈbædⁿn) *n* **1** the Devil (Revelation 9:11). **2** (in rabbinical literature) a part of Gehenna; Hell. [Heb., lit.: destruction]

abaft (əˈbɑːft) *Naut.* ◆ *adv, adj* (*postpositive*) **1** closer to the stern than to another place on a vessel. ◆ *prep* **2** behind; aft of. [C13: *on baft; baft* from OE *beæftan,* from *be* by + *æftan* behind]

Abakan ★ (*Russian* abaˈkan) *n* a city in S central Russia, capital of the Khakass Republic, at the confluence of the Yenisei and Abakan Rivers. Pop.: 161 000 (1995 est.).

abalone (ˌæbəˈləʊnɪ) *n* an edible marine mollusc having an ear-shaped shell perforated with a row of respiratory holes and lined with mother-of-pearl. Also called: **ear shell.** [C19: from American Sp. *abulón*]

abandon (əˈbændən) *vb* (*tr*) **1** to forsake completely; desert; leave behind. **2** to give up completely: *to abandon hope.* **3** to give up (something begun) before completion: *the game was abandoned.* **4** to surrender (oneself) to emotion without restraint. **5** to give (insured property that has suffered partial loss or damage) to the insurers in order that a claim for a total loss may be made. ◆ *n* **6** freedom from inhibitions, restraint, or worry: *she danced with abandon.* [C14: *abandounen* (vb), from OF, from *a bandon* under one's control, from *a* at, to + *bandon* control]
► a'bandonment *n*

abandoned (əˈbændənd) *adj* **1** deserted: *an abandoned hut.* **2** forsaken: *an abandoned child.* **3** uninhibited.

abase (əˈbeɪs) *vb* **abases, abasing, abased.** (*tr*) **1** to humble or belittle (oneself, etc.). **2** to lower or reduce, as in rank. [C15 *abessen,* from OF *abaissier* to make low. See BASE²]
► a'basement *n*

abash (əˈbæʃ) *vb* (*tr; usually passive*) to cause to feel ill at

ease, embarrassed, or confused. [C14: from OF *esbair* to be astonished, from *es-* out + *bair* to gape]
▸ a'bashed *adj*

abate (ə'beɪt) *vb* abates, abating, abated. 1 to make or become less in amount, intensity, degree, etc. 2 (*tr*) *Law*. 2a to suppress or terminate (a nuisance). 2b to suspend or extinguish (a claim or action). 2c to annul (a writ). 3 (*intr*) *Law*. (of a writ, etc.) to become null and void. [C14: from OF *abatre* to beat down]
▸ a'batement *n*

abatis or **abattis** ('æbətɪs) *n* 1 a rampart of felled trees with their branches outwards. 2 a barbed-wire entanglement before a position. [C18: from F, from *abattre* to fell]

abattoir ('æbə,twɑː) *n* another name for **slaughterhouse**. [C19: F, from *abattre* to fell]

Abba ★ ('æbə) *n* 1 *New Testament*. father (used of God). 2 a title given to bishops and patriarchs in the Syrian, Coptic, and Ethiopian Churches. [from Aramaic]

abbacy ('æbəsɪ) *n, pl* **abbacies**. the office, term of office, or jurisdiction of an abbot or abbess. [C15: from Church L *abbātia*, from *abbāt-* ABBOT]

Abbado ★ (ə'bɑːdəʊ) *n* Claudio. born 1933, Italian conductor.

abbatial (ə'beɪʃəl) *adj* of an abbot, abbess, or abbey. [C17: from Church L *abbātiālis*, from *abbāt-* ABBOT]

Abbe ★ ('æbə; *German* 'abə) *n* Ernst. 1840–1905, German physicist, noted for his work in optics and the microscope condenser known as the **Abbe condenser**.

abbé ('æbeɪ) *n* 1 a French abbot. 2 a title used in addressing any other French cleric, such as a priest.

abbess ('æbɪs) *n* the female superior of a convent. [C13: from OF, from Church L *abbātissa*]

Abbevillian (æb'vɪlɪən) *Archaeol*. ◆ *n* 1 the period represented by Lower Palaeolithic European sites containing the earliest hand axes. ◆ *adj* 2 of this period. [C20: after *Abbeville*, N France, where the stone tools were discovered]

abbey ('æbɪ) *n* 1 a building inhabited by a community of monks or nuns. 2 a church built in conjunction with such a building. 3 a community of monks or nuns. [C13: via OF *abeie* from Church L *abbātia* ABBACY]

abbot ('æbət) *n* the superior of an abbey of monks. [OE *abbod*, from Church L *abbāt-* (stem of *abbas*), ult. from Aramaic *abbā* father]
▸ 'abbotship or 'abbotcy *n*

abbreviate (ə'briːvɪ,eɪt) *vb* abbreviates, abbreviating, abbreviated. (*tr*) 1 to shorten (a word or phrase) by contraction or omission of some letters or words. 2 to cut short; curtail. [C15: from p.p. of LL *abbreviāre*, from L *brevis* brief]

abbreviation (ə,briːvɪ'eɪʃən) *n* 1 a shortened or contracted form of a word or phrase. 2 the process or result of abbreviating.

ABC[1] *n* 1 (*pl in US*) the rudiments of a subject. 2 an alphabetical guide. 3 (*often pl in US*) the alphabet.

ABC[2] *abbrev. for:* 1 American Broadcasting Company. 2 Australian Broadcasting Corporation.

Abdias ★ (æb'daɪəs) *n Bible*. the Douay form of **Obadiah**.

abdicate ('æbdɪ,keɪt) *vb* abdicates, abdicating, abdicated. to renounce (a throne, rights, etc.), esp. formally. [C16: from L *abdicāre* to disclaim]
▸ ,abdi'cation *n* ▸ 'abdi,cator *n*

abdomen ('æbdəmən) *n* 1 the region of the body of a vertebrate that contains the viscera other than the heart and lungs. 2 the front or surface of this region; belly. 3 (in arthropods) the posterior part of the body behind the thorax. [C16: from L; from ?]
▸ abdominal (æb'dɒmɪn°l) *adj*

abduct (æb'dʌkt) *vb* (*tr*) 1 to remove (a person) by force or cunning; kidnap. 2 (of certain muscles) to pull (a leg, arm, etc.) away from the median axis of the body. [C19: from L *abdūcere* to lead away]
▸ ab'duction *n* ▸ ab'ductor *n*

Abdul-Hamid II ★ (,æbdul'hæmɪd) *n* 1842–1918, sultan of Turkey (1876–1909), deposed by the Young Turks,

noted for his brutal suppression of the Armenian revolt (1894–96).

abeam (ə'biːm) *adv, adj* (*postpositive*) at right angles to the length of a vessel or aircraft. [C19: A-[2] + BEAM]

abed (ə'bɛd) *adv Arch*. in bed.

Abednego ★ (ə'bɛdnɪ,gəʊ) *n Old Testament*. one of Daniel's three companions who, together with Shadrach and Meshach, was miraculously saved from destruction in Nebuchadnezzar's fiery furnace (Daniel 3:12–30).

Abel ★ ('eɪb°l) *n Old Testament*. the second son of Adam and Eve, a shepherd, murdered by his brother Cain (Genesis 4:1–8).

Abelard ★ ('æbə,lɑːd) *n* Peter. French name *Pierre Abélard*. 1079–1142, French philosopher and theologian whose works include *Historia Calamitatum* and *Sic et Non* (1121). His love for Héloïse is recorded in their correspondence.

Abeokuta ★ (,æbɪəʊ'kuːtə) *n* a town in W Nigeria, capital of Ogun state. Pop.: 416 800 (1994 est.).

Aberdare ★ (,æbə'dɛə) *n* a town in South Wales, in Rhondda, Cynon, Taff county borough. Pop.: 29 040 (1991).

Aberdeen[1] ★ (,æbə'diːn) 1 *n* a city in NE Scotland: centre for processing North Sea oil and gas; university (1494). Pop.: 217 260 (1996 est.). 2 **City of.** a council area in NE Scotland, established in 1996. Pop.: 219 100 (1995 est.). Area: 186 sq. km (72 sq. miles).
▸ Aberdonian (,æbə'dəʊnɪən) *n, adj*

Aberdeen[2] ★ (,æbə'diːn) *n* George Hamilton-Gordon, 4th Earl of. 1784–1860, British statesman. He was foreign secretary under Wellington (1828) and Peel (1841–46); became prime minister of a coalition ministry in 1852 but was compelled to resign after mismanagement of the Crimean War (1855).

Aberdeen Angus *n* a black hornless breed of beef cattle originating in Scotland.

Aberdeenshire ★ (,æbə'diːn,ʃɪə, -ʃə) *n* a council area and historic county of N Scotland: part of Grampian region (1975–96). Administrative centre: Aberdeen. Pop.: 227 430 (1996 est.). Area 6319 sq. km (2439 sq. miles).

Aberfan ★ (,æbə'væn) *n* a village in S Wales, in Merthyr Tydfil county borough, formerly a coal-mining village: scene of a disaster in 1966 when a slag heap collapsed onto part of the village killing 144 people (including 116 children).

aberrant (æ'bɛrənt) *adj* 1 deviating from the normal or usual type. 2 behaving in an abnormal or untypical way. 3 deviating from morality. [rare before C19: from L *aberrāre* to wander away]
▸ ab'errance or ab'errancy *n*

aberration (,æbə'reɪʃən) *n* 1 deviation from what is normal, expected, or usual. 2 departure from truth, morality, etc. 3 a lapse in control of one's mental faculties. 4 *Optics*. a defect in a lens or mirror that causes either a distorted image or one with coloured fringes. 5 *Astron*. the apparent displacement of a celestial body due to the motion of the observer with the earth.

Aberystwyth ★ (,æbə'rɪstwɪθ) *n* a resort and university town in Wales, in Ceredigion on Cardigan Bay. Pop.: 11 154 (1991).

abet (ə'bɛt) *vb* abets, abetting, abetted. (*tr*) to assist or encourage, esp. in wrongdoing. [C14: from OF *abeter* to lure on, from *beter* to bait]
▸ a'betment *n* ▸ a'better or (*esp. Law*) a'bettor *n*

abeyance (ə'beɪəns) *n* 1 (usually preceded by *in* or *into*) a state of being suspended or put aside temporarily. 2 (usually preceded by *in*) *Law*. an indeterminate state of ownership. [C16–17: from Anglo-F, from OF *abeance* expectation, lit. a gaping after]

ABH *abbrev. for* actual bodily harm.

abhor (əb'hɔː) *vb* abhors, abhorring, abhorred. (*tr*) to detest vehemently; find repugnant. [C15: from L *abhorrēre*, from *ab-* away from + *horrēre* to shudder]
▸ ab'horrer *n*

abhorrence (əb'hɒrəns) *n* 1 a feeling of extreme loathing or aversion. 2 a person or thing that is loathsome.

abhorrent (əb'hɒrənt) *adj* 1 repugnant; loathsome. 2 (when *postpositive*, foll. by *of*) feeling extreme aversion

★ people and places

(for): *abhorrent of vulgarity*. **3** (usually *postpositive* and foll. by *to*) conflicting (with): *abhorrent to common sense*.

Abia ★ (æb'iːə) *n* a state of SE Nigeria. Capital: Umuahia. Pop.: 2 297 978 (1991). Area (including Imo state): 11 850 sq. km (4575 sq. miles).

abide (ə'baɪd) *vb* **abides, abiding, abode** *or* **abided. 1** (*tr*) to tolerate; put up with. **2** (*tr*) to accept or submit to. **3** (*intr*; foll. by *by*) **3a** to comply (with): *to abide by the decision*. **3b** to remain faithful (to): *to abide by your promise*. **4** (*intr*) to remain or continue. **5** (*intr*) *Arch*. to dwell. **6** (*tr*) *Arch*. to await in expectation. [OE *ābīdan*, from *a-* (intensive) + *bīdan* to wait]
▸ **a'bider** *n*

abiding (ə'baɪdɪŋ) *adj* permanent; enduring: *an abiding belief*.

Abidjan ★ (ˌæbɪ'dʒɑːn; *French* abidʒã) *n* a port in the Côte d'Ivoire, on the Gulf of Guinea: the legislative capital (Yamoussoukro became the administrative capital in 1983). Pop.: 2 797 000 (1995 est.).

Abigail ★ ('æbɪˌɡeɪl) *n Old Testament*. the woman who brought provisions to David and his followers and subsequently became his wife (I Samuel 25:1–42).

ability (ə'bɪlɪtɪ) *n, pl* **abilities. 1** possession of necessary skill, competence, or power. **2** considerable proficiency; natural capability: *a man of ability*. **3** (*pl*) special talents. [C14: from OF from L *habilitās* aptitude, from *habilis* ABLE]

Abingdon ★ ('æbɪŋdən) *n* a market town in S England, in Oxfordshire. Pop.: 35 234 (1991).

ab initio Latin. (æb ɪ'nɪʃɪˌəʊ) from the start.

abiogenesis (ˌeɪbaɪəʊ'dʒɛnɪsɪs) *n* the hypothetical process by which living organisms arise from inanimate matter. Also called: **spontaneous generation**. [C19: NL, from A-¹ + BIO- + GENESIS]

abject ('æbdʒɛkt) *adj* **1** utterly wretched or hopeless. **2** forlorn; dejected. **3** submissive: *an abject apology*. **4** contemptible; despicable: *an abject liar*. [C14 (in the sense: rejected, cast out): from L *abjectus* thrown away, from *abjicere*, from *ab-* away + *jacere* to throw]
▸ **ab'jection** *n* ▸ **'abjectly** *adv* ▸ **'abjectness** *n*

abjure (əb'dʒʊə) *vb* **abjures, abjuring, abjured.** (*tr*) **1** to renounce or retract, esp. formally or under oath. **2** to abstain from. [C15: from OF *abjurer* or L *abjurāre* to deny on oath]
▸ **ˌabju'ration** *n* ▸ **ab'jurer** *n*

Abkhazia ★ (æb'kɑːzɪə) *n* an administrative division of NW Georgia, between the Black Sea and the Caucasus Mountains: a subtropical region, with narrow coastal lowlands and mountains rising over 3900 m (13 000 ft). Capital: Sukhumi. Pop.: 516 600 (1993 est.). Area: 8600 sq. km (3320 sq. miles). Also called: **Abkhaz Autonomous Republic** ('æbkæz).

ablation (æb'leɪʃən) *n* **1** the surgical removal of an organ, structure, or part. **2** the melting or wearing away of a part, such as the heat shield of a space re-entry vehicle on passing through the earth's atmosphere. **3** the wearing away of a rock or glacier. [C15: from LL *ablatiōn-*, from L *auferre* to carry away]
▸ **ablate** (æb'leɪt) *vb*

ablative ('æblətɪv) *Grammar*. ◆ *adj* **1** (in certain inflected languages such as Latin) denoting a case of nouns, pronouns, and adjectives indicating the agent, or the instrument, manner, or place of the action. ◆ *n* **2** the ablative case or a speech element in it.

ablaut ('æblaʊt) *n Linguistics*. vowel gradation, esp. in Indo-European languages. See **gradation** (sense 5). [G, coined 1819 by Jakob Grimm from *ab* off + *Laut* sound]

ablaze (ə'bleɪz) *adj* (*postpositive*), *adv* **1** on fire; burning. **2** brightly illuminated. **3** emotionally aroused.

able ('eɪb°l) *adj* **1** (*postpositive*) having the necessary power, resources, skill, opportunity, etc., to do something. **2** capable; talented. **3** *Law*. competent or authorized. [C14: ult. from L *habilis* easy to hold, manageable, from *habēre* to have + *-ilis* -ILE]

-able *suffix forming adjectives*. **1** capable of or deserving of (being acted upon as indicated): *enjoyable; washable*. **2** in-

clined to; able to; causing: *comfortable; variable*. [via OF from L *-ābilis, -ībilis*, forms of *-bilis*, adjectival suffix]
▸ **-ably** *suffix forming adverbs*. ▸ **-ability** *suffix forming nouns*.

able-bodied *adj* physically strong and healthy; robust.

able-bodied seaman *n* a seaman, esp. one in the merchant navy, who has been trained in certain skills. Also: **able seaman**. Abbrev.: **AB, a.b.**

abled ('eɪb°ld) *adj* having a range of physical powers as specified (esp. in **less abled, differently abled**).

ableism ('eɪb°lˌɪzəm) *n* discrimination against disabled or handicapped people.

able rating *n* (esp. in the Royal Navy) a rating who is qualified to perform certain duties of seamanship.

abloom (ə'bluːm) *adj* (*postpositive*) in flower; blooming.

ablution (ə'bluːʃən) *n* **1** the ritual washing of a priest's hands or of sacred vessels. **2** (*often pl*) the act of washing: *perform one's ablutions*. **3** (*pl*) *Mil. inf.* a washing place. [C14: ult. from L *ablūere* to wash away]
▸ **ab'lutionary** *adj*

ably ('eɪblɪ) *adv* in a competent or skilful manner.

ABM *abbrev. for* antiballistic missile.

abnegate ('æbnɪˌɡeɪt) *vb* **abnegates, abnegating, abnegated.** (*tr*) to deny to oneself; renounce. [C17: from L *abnegāre* to deny]
▸ **ˌabne'gation** *n* ▸ **'abneˌgator** *n*

abnormal (æb'nɔːməl) *adj* **1** not normal; deviating from the usual or typical. **2** concerned with abnormal behaviour: *abnormal psychology*. **3** *Inf.* odd; strange. [C19: AB-¹ + NORMAL, replacing earlier *anormal* from Med. L *anormalus*, a blend of LL *anōmalus* ANOMALOUS + L *abnormis* departing from a rule]
▸ **ab'normally** *adv*

abnormality (ˌæbnɔː'mælɪtɪ) *n, pl* **abnormalities. 1** an abnormal feature, event, etc. **2** a physical malformation. **3** deviation from the usual.

Abo ('æbəʊ) *n, pl* **Abos.** (*sometimes not cap*.) *Austral. inf., often derog.* short for **Aborigine** (sense 1).

Åbo ★ ('oːbuː) *n* the Swedish name for **Turku**.

aboard (ə'bɔːd) *adv, adj* (*postpositive*), *prep* **1** on, in, onto, or into (a ship, train, etc.). **2** *Naut.* alongside. **3 all aboard!** a warning to passengers to board a vehicle, ship, etc.

abode¹ (ə'bəʊd) *n* a place in which one lives; one's home. [C17: n formed from ABIDE]

abode² (ə'bəʊd) *vb* a past tense and past participle of **abide**.

abolish (ə'bɒlɪʃ) *vb* (*tr*) to do away with (laws, regulations, customs, etc.). [C15: from OF, ult. from L *abolēre* to destroy]
▸ **a'bolishable** *adj* ▸ **a'bolisher** *n* ▸ **a'bolishment** *n*

abolition (ˌæbə'lɪʃən) *n* **1** the act of abolishing or the state of being abolished; annulment. **2** (*often cap*.) (in British territories) the ending of the slave trade (1807) or of slavery (1833). **3** (*often cap*.) (in the US) the emancipation of slaves, by the Emancipation Proclamation (1863, ratified 1865). [C16: from L *abolitio*, from *abolēre* to destroy]
▸ **ˌabo'litionary** *adj* ▸ **ˌabo'litionism** *n* ▸ **ˌabo'litionist** *n, adj*

abomasum (ˌæbə'meɪsəm) *n* the fourth and last compartment of the stomach of ruminants. [C18: NL, from AB-¹ + *omāsum* bullock's tripe]

A-bomb *n* short for **atomic bomb**.

abominable (ə'bɒmɪnəb°l) *adj* **1** offensive; loathsome; detestable. **2** *Inf.* very bad or inferior: *abominable workmanship*. [C14: from L, from *abōmināri* to ABOMINATE]
▸ **a'bominably** *adv*

abominable snowman *n* a large manlike or apelike creature alleged to inhabit the Himalayas. Also called: **yeti**. [translation of Tibetan *metohkangmi*, from *metoh* foul + *kangmi* snowman]

abominate (ə'bɒmɪˌneɪt) *vb* **abominates, abominating, abominated.** (*tr*) to dislike intensely; detest. [C17: from L *abōmināri* to regard as an ill omen, from *ab-* away from + *ōmin-*, from OMEN]
▸ **a'bomiˌnator** *n*

abomination (əˌbɒmɪ'neɪʃən) *n* **1** a person or thing that is disgusting or loathsome. **2** an action that is vicious, vile, etc. **3** intense loathing or disgust.

aboriginal (ˌæbəˈrɪdʒɪnᵊl) *adj* existing in a place from the earliest known period; indigenous.
▶ ˌaboˈriginally *adv*

Aboriginal (ˌæbəˈrɪdʒɪnᵊl) *adj* **1** of, relating to, or characteristic of the native peoples of Australia. ♦ *n* **2** another word for **Aborigine** (sense 1).
▶ ˌAboˌrigiˈnality *n*

aborigine (ˌæbəˈrɪdʒɪnɪ) *n* an original inhabitant of a country or region. [C16: back formation from *aborigines*, from L: inhabitants of Latium in pre-Roman times, associated in folk etymology with *ab origine* from the beginning]

Aborigine (ˌæbəˈrɪdʒɪnɪ) *n* **1** Also called: **native Australian, Aboriginal.** a member of a dark-skinned hunting and gathering people who were living in Australia when European settlers arrived. **2** any of the languages of this people.

abort (əˈbɔːt) *vb* **1** to undergo or cause (a woman) to undergo the termination of pregnancy before the fetus is viable. **2** (*tr*) to cause (a fetus) to be expelled from the womb before it is viable. **3** (*intr*) to fail to come to completion. **4** (*tr*) to stop the development of; cause to be abandoned. **5** (*intr*) to give birth to a dead or nonviable fetus. **6** (of a space flight or other undertaking) to fail or terminate prematurely. **7** (*intr*) (of an organism or part of an organism) to fail to develop into the mature form. ♦ *n* **8** the premature termination or failure of (a space flight, etc.). [C16: from L *abortāre*, from *aborīrī* to miscarry, from *ab-* wrongly + *orīrī* to be born]

abortifacient (əˌbɔːtɪˈfeɪʃənt) *adj* **1** causing abortion. ♦ *n* **2** a drug or agent that causes abortion.

abortion (əˈbɔːʃən) *n* **1** an operation or other procedure to terminate pregnancy before the fetus is viable. **2** the premature termination of pregnancy by spontaneous or induced expulsion of a nonviable fetus from the uterus. **3** an aborted fetus. **4** a failure to develop to completion or maturity. **5** a person or thing that is deformed.

abortionist (əˈbɔːʃənɪst) *n* a person who performs abortions, esp. illegally.

abortion pill *n* a drug, such as mifepristone (RU 486), used to terminate a pregnancy in its earliest stage.

abortive (əˈbɔːtɪv) *adj* **1** failing to achieve a purpose; fruitless. **2** (of organisms) imperfectly developed. **3** causing abortion.

ABO system *n* a system for classifying human blood on the basis of the presence or absence of two antigens in the red cells: there are four such blood types (A, B, AB, and O).

Aboukir Bay *or* **Abukir Bay** ★ (ˌæbuːˈkɪə) *n* a bay on the N coast of Egypt, where the Nile enters the Mediterranean: site of the Battle of the Nile (1798), in which Nelson defeated the French fleet. Arabic name: **Abu Qîr** (abuˈkiːr).

aboulia (əˈbuːlɪə, -ˈbjuː-) *n* a variant spelling of **abulia.**

abound (əˈbaʊnd) *vb* (*intr*) **1** to exist or occur in abundance. **2** (foll. by *with* or *in*) to be plentifully supplied (with): *the fields abound in corn.* [C14: via OF from L *abundāre* to overflow, from *undāre* to flow, from *unda* wave]

about (əˈbaʊt) *prep* **1** relating to; concerning. **2** near or close to. **3** carried on: *I haven't any money about me.* **4** on every side of. **5** active in or engaged in. ♦ *adv* **6** near in number, time, degree, etc.: *about 50 years old.* **7** nearby. **8** here and there: *walk about to keep warm.* **9** all around; on every side. **10** in or to the opposite direction. **11** in rotation or revolution: *turn and turn about.* **12** used in informal phrases to indicate understatement: *it's about time you stopped.* **13** *Arch.* around. **14 about to. 14a** on the point of; intending to: *she was about to jump.* **14b** (with a negative) determined not to: *nobody is about to miss it.* ♦ *adj* **15** (*predicative*) active; astir after sleep: *up and about.* **16** (*predicative*) in existence, current, or in circulation: *there aren't many about nowadays.* [OE *abūtan, onbūtan*, from ON + *būtan* outside]

about turn *or US* **about face** *sentence substitute.* **1** a military command to a formation of men to reverse the direction in which they are facing. ♦ *n* **about-turn** *or US* **about-face.** **2** a complete change of opinion, direction, etc. ♦ *vb* **about-turn** *or US* **about-face.** **3** (*intr*) to perform an about-turn.

above (əˈbʌv) *prep* **1** on top of or higher than; over. **2** greater than in quantity or degree: *above average.* **3** superior to or prior to: *to place honour above wealth.* **4** too high-minded for: *above petty gossiping.* **5** too respected for; beyond: *above suspicion.* **6** too difficult to be understood by: *the talk was above me.* **7** louder or higher than (other noise). **8** in preference to. **9** north of. **10** upstream from. **11 above all.** most of all; especially. **12 above and beyond.** in addition to. ♦ *adv* **13** in or to a higher place: *the sky above.* **14a** in a previous place (in something written). **14b** (*in combination*): *the above-mentioned clause.* **15** higher in rank or position. **16** in or concerned with heaven. ♦ *n* **17 the above.** something previously mentioned. ♦ *adj* **18** appearing in a previous place (in something written). [OE *abufan*, from *a-* on + *bufan* above]

above board *adj* (**aboveboard** when prenominal), *adv* in the open; without dishonesty, concealment, or fraud.

abracadabra (ˌæbrəkəˈdæbrə) *interj* **1** a spoken formula, used esp. by conjurors. ♦ *n* **2** a word used in incantations, etc., considered to possess magic powers. **3** gibberish. [C17: magical word used in certain Gnostic writings, ? rel. to Gk *Abraxas*, a Gnostic deity]

abrade (əˈbreɪd) *vb* **abrades, abrading, abraded.** (*tr*) to scrape away or wear down by friction. [C17: from L *abrādere*, from AB-¹ + *rādere* to scrape]
▶ aˈbrader *n*

Abraham ★ (ˈeɪbrəˌhæm, -həm) *n* **1** *Old Testament.* the first of the patriarchs, the father of Isaac and the founder of the Hebrew people (Genesis 11–25). **2** *Abraham's bosom.* the place where the just repose after death (Luke 16:22).

abranchiate (əˈbræŋkɪɪt, -ˌeɪt) *or* **abranchial** *adj Zool.* having no gills. [C19: A-¹ + BRANCHIATE]

abrasion (əˈbreɪʒən) *n* **1** the process of scraping or wearing down by friction. **2** a scraped area or spot; graze. **3** *Geog.* the effect of mechanical erosion of rock, esp. a river bed, by rock fragments scratching and scraping it. [C17: from Med. L *abrāsiōn-*, from L *abrādere* to ABRADE]

abrasive (əˈbreɪsɪv) *n* **1** a substance or material such as sandpaper, pumice, or emery, used for cleaning, smoothing, or polishing. ♦ *adj* **2** causing abrasion; rough. **3** irritating in manner or personality.

abreaction (ˌæbrɪˈækʃən) *n Psychoanal.* the release and expression of emotional tension associated with repressed ideas by bringing those ideas into consciousness.

abreast (əˈbrɛst) *adj* (*postpositive*) **1** alongside each other and facing in the same direction. **2** (foll. by *of* or *with*) up to date (with).

abridge (əˈbrɪdʒ) *vb* **abridges, abridging, abridged.** (*tr*) **1** to reduce the length of (a written work) by condensing. **2** to curtail. [C14: via OF *abregier* from LL *abbreviāre* to shorten]
▶ aˈbridgable *or* aˈbridgeable *adj* ▶ aˈbridger *n*

abridgment *or* **abridgement** (əˈbrɪdʒmənt) *n* **1** a shortened version of a written work. **2** the act of abridging or state of being abridged.

abroad (əˈbrɔːd) *adv, adj* (*postpositive*). **1** to or in a foreign country or countries. **2** (of rumours, etc.) in general circulation. **3** out in the open. **4** over a wide area. [C13: from A-² + BROAD]

abrogate (ˈæbrəʊˌɡeɪt) *vb* **abrogates, abrogating, abrogated.** (*tr*) to cancel or revoke formally or officially. [C16: from L *abrogātus* repealed, from AB-¹ + *rogāre* to propose (a law)]
▶ ˌabroˈgation *n* ▶ ˈabroˌgator *n*

abrupt (əˈbrʌpt) *adj* **1** sudden; unexpected. **2** brusque or brief in speech, manner, etc. **3** (of a style of writing or speaking) disconnected. **4** precipitous; steep. **5** *Bot.* truncate. **6** *Geol.* (of strata) cropping out suddenly. [C16: from L *abruptus* broken off, from AB-¹ + *rumpere* to break]
▶ abˈruptly *adv* ▶ abˈruptness *n*

Abruzzi ★ (*Italian* aˈbruttsi) *n* a region of S central Italy, between the Apennines and the Adriatic: separated from the former administrative region **Abruzzi e Molise** in 1965.

★ people and places

Capital: Aquila. Pop.: 1 262 948 (1994 est.). Area: 10 794 sq. km (4210 sq. miles).

Absalom ★ ('æbsələm) *n Old Testament.* the third son of David, who rebelled against his father and was eventually killed by Joab (II Samuel 15–18).

ABS brake *n* another name for **antilock brake**. [from G *Antiblockiersystem*]

abscess ('æbsɛs) *n* **1** a localized collection of pus formed as the product of inflammation. ◆ *vb* **2** (*intr*) to form such a collection of pus. [C16: from L *abscessus*, from *abscēdere* to go away]
► 'abscessed *adj*

abscissa (æb'sɪsə) *n, pl* **abscissas** or **abscissae** (-'sɪsiː). the horizontal or *x*-coordinate of a point in a two-dimensional system of Cartesian coordinates. It is the distance from the *y*-axis measured parallel to the *x*-axis. Cf. **ordinate**. [C17: NL, orig. *linea abscissa* a cut-off line]

abscission (æb'sɪʒən) *n* **1** the separation of leaves, branches, flowers, and bark from plants. **2** the act of cutting off. [C17: from L, from AB-[1] + *scissiō* a cleaving]

abscond (əb'skɒnd) *vb* (*intr*) to run away secretly, esp. to avoid prosecution or punishment. [C16: from L *abscondere*, from abs- AB-[1] + *condere* to stow]
► ab'sconder *n*

abseil ('æbsaɪl) *Mountaineering.* ◆ *vb* (*intr*) **1** to descend a steep slope or vertical drop by a rope secured from above and coiled around one's body. ◆ *n* **2** an instance or the technique of abseiling. [C20: from G *abseilen*, from *ab-* down + *Seil* rope]

absence ('æbsəns) *n* **1** the state of being away. **2** the time during which a person or thing is away. **3** the fact of being without something; lack. [C14: via OF from L *absentia*, from *absēns* a being away]

absent *adj* ('æbsənt). **1** away or not present. **2** lacking. **3** inattentive. ◆ *vb* (æb'sɛnt). **4** (*tr*) to remove (oneself) or keep away. [C14: from L *absent-*, from *abesse* to be away]
► ab'senter *n*

absentee (,æbsən'tiː) *n* **a** a person who is absent. **b** (*as modifier*): *an absentee landlord.*

absenteeism (,æbsən'tiːɪzəm) *n* persistent absence from work, school, etc.

absent-minded *adj* preoccupied; forgetful.
► ,absent-'mindedly *adv* ► ,absent-'mindedness *n*

absinthe or **absinth** ('æbsɪnθ) *n* **1** a potent green alcoholic drink, originally having high wormwood content. **2** another name for **wormwood** (the plant). [C15: via F and L from Gk *apsinthion* wormwood]

absolute ('æbsə,luːt) *adj* **1** complete; perfect. **2** free from limitations, restrictions, or exceptions. **3** despotic: *an absolute ruler.* **4** undoubted; certain: *the absolute truth.* **5** not dependent on, conditioned by, or relative to anything else; independent: *absolute humidity; absolute units.* **6** pure; unmixed: *absolute alcohol.* **7** (of a grammatical construction) syntactically independent of the main clause, as for example the construction *Joking apart* in the sentence *Joking apart, we'd better leave now.* **8** *Grammar.* (of a transitive verb) used without a direct object, as the verb *intimidate* in the sentence *His intentions are good, but his rough manner tends to intimidate.* **9** *Grammar.* (of an adjective) used as a noun, as for instance *young* and *aged* in the sentence *The young care little for the aged.* ◆ *n* **10** something that is absolute. [C14: from L *absolūtus* unconditional, from *absolvere.* See ABSOLVE]

Absolute ('æbsə,luːt) *n* (*sometimes not cap.*) *Philosophy.* **1** the ultimate basis of reality. **2** that which is totally unconditioned, unrestricted, pure, perfect, or complete.

absolutely (,æbsə'luːtlɪ) *adv* **1** in an absolute manner, esp. completely or perfectly. ◆ *sentence substitute.* **2** yes; certainly.

absolute magnitude *n* the magnitude a given star would have if it were 10 parsecs (32.6 light years) from earth.

absolute majority *n* a number of votes totalling over 50 per cent, such as the total number of votes or seats obtained by a party that beats the combined opposition.

absolute pitch *n* **1** Also called: **perfect pitch.** the ability to identify the pitch of a note, or to sing a given note,

without reference to one previously sounded. **2** the exact pitch of a note determined by vibration per second.

absolute temperature *n* another name for **thermodynamic temperature.**

absolute value *n* **1** the positive real number equal to a given real but disregarding its sign: written | *x* |. Where *x* is positive, | *x* | = *x* = | –*x* |. **2** Also called: **modulus.** a measure of the magnitude of a complex number.

absolute zero *n* the lowest temperature theoretically attainable, at which the particles constituting matter would be at rest: equivalent to –273.15°C or –459.67°F.

absolution (,æbsə'luːʃən) *n* **1** the act of absolving or the state of being absolved; release from guilt, obligation, or punishment. **2** *Christianity.* **2a** a formal remission of sin pronounced by a priest in the sacrament of penance. **2b** the form of words granting such a remission. [C12: from L *absolūtiōn-* acquittal, from *absolvere* to ABSOLVE]

absolutism ('æbsəluː,tɪzəm) *n* the principle or practice of a political system in which unrestricted power is vested in a monarch, dictator, etc.; despotism.
► abso'lutist *n, adj*

absolve (əb'zɒlv) *vb* **absolves, absolving, absolved.** (*tr*) **1** (usually foll. by *from*) to release from blame, sin, obligation, or responsibility. **2** to pronounce not guilty. [C15: from L *absolvere*, from AB-[1] + *solvere* to make loose]
► ab'solver *n*

absorb (əb'sɔːb) *vb* (*tr*) **1** to soak or suck up (liquids). **2** to engage or occupy (the interest or time) of (someone). **3** to receive or take in (the energy of an impact). **4** *Physics.* to take in (all or part of incident radiated energy) and retain it. **5** to take in or assimilate; incorporate. **6** to pay for as part of a commercial transaction: *the distributor absorbed the cost of transport.* **7** *Chem.* to cause to undergo a process in which one substance permeates into or is dissolved by a liquid or solid: *porous solids absorb water.* [C15: via OF from L *absorbēre*, from AB-[1] + *sorbēre* to suck]
► ab,sorba'bility *n* ► ab'sorbable *adj*

absorbed (əb'sɔːbd) *adj* engrossed; deeply interested.

absorbed dose *n* the amount of energy transferred by radiation to a unit mass of absorbing material.

absorbent (əb'sɔːbənt) *adj* **1** able to absorb. ◆ *n* **2** a substance that absorbs.
► ab'sorbency *n*

absorbing (əb'sɔːbɪŋ) *adj* occupying one's interest or attention.
► ab'sorbingly *adv*

absorptance (əb'sɔːptəns) *or* **absorption factor** *n* *Physics.* the ability of an object to absorb radiation, measured as the ratio of absorbed flux to incident flux. [C20: from ABSORPTION + -ANCE]

absorption (əb'sɔːpʃən) *n* **1** the process of absorbing or the state of being absorbed. **2** *Physiol.* **2a** normal assimilation by the tissues of the products of digestion. **2b** the process of taking up various fluids, drugs, etc., through the mucous membranes or skin. [C16: from L *absorptiōn-*, from *absorbēre* to ABSORB]
► ab'sorptive *adj*

absorption spectrum *n* the characteristic pattern of dark lines or bands that occurs when electromagnetic radiation is passed through an absorbing medium into a spectroscope. See also **emission spectrum.**

abstain (əb'steɪn) *vb* (*intr;* usually foll. by *from*) **1** to choose to refrain. **2** to refrain from voting, esp. in a committee, legislature, etc. [C14: via OF from L *abstinēre*, from abs- AB-[1] + *tenēre* to hold]
► ab'stainer *n*

abstemious (əb'stiːmɪəs) *adj* sparing, esp. in the consumption of alcohol or food. [C17: from L *abstēmius*, from abs- AB-[1] + *tēm-*, from *tēmētum* intoxicating drink]
► ab'stemiously *adv* ► ab'stemiousness *n*

abstention (əb'stɛnʃən) *n* **1** the act of refraining or abstaining. **2** the act of withholding one's vote. [C16: from LL *abstentiōn;* see ABSTAIN]

abstinence ('æbstɪnəns) *n* the act or practice of refraining from some action or from the use of something, esp.

alcohol. [C13: via OF from L *abstinentia*, from *abstinēre* to ABSTAIN]
▶ **'abstinent** *adj*

abstract *adj* (æbstrækt). **1** having no reference to material objects or specific examples. **2** not applied or practical; theoretical. **3** hard to understand. **4** denoting art characterized by geometric, formalized, or otherwise nonrepresentational qualities. ◆ *n* ('æbstrækt). **5** a condensed version of a piece of writing, speech, etc.; summary. **6** an abstract term or idea. **7** an abstract painting, sculpture, etc. **8 in the abstract.** without reference to specific circumstances. ◆ *vb* (æb'strækt). (*tr*) **9** to regard theoretically. **10** to form a general idea of (something) by abstraction. **11** ('æbstrækt). (*also intr*) to summarize. **12** to remove or extract. [C14 (in the sense: extracted): from L *abstractus* drawn off, from *abs-* AB-[1] + *trahere* to draw]

abstracted (æb'stræktɪd) *adj* **1** lost in thought; preoccupied. **2** taken out or separated.
▶ **ab'stractedly** *adv*

abstract expressionism *n* a school of painting in the 1940s that combined the spontaneity of expressionism with abstract forms in apparently random compositions.

abstraction (æb'strækʃən) *n* **1** preoccupation. **2** the process of formulating generalized concepts by extracting common qualities from specific examples. **3** a concept formulated in this way: *good and evil are abstractions*. **4** an abstract painting, sculpture, etc.
▶ **ab'stractive** *adj*

abstract noun *n* a noun that refers to an abstract concept, as for example *peace, joy,* etc.

abstract term *n* in traditional logic, the name of an attribute of many individuals: *humanity is an abstract term*.

abstruse (əb'struːs) *adj* not easy to understand. [C16: from L *abstrūsus*, from *abs-* AB-[1] + *trūdere* to thrust]
▶ **ab'strusely** *adv* ▶ **ab'struseness** *n*

absurd (əb'sɜːd) *adj* **1** at variance with reason; manifestly false. **2** ludicrous; ridiculous. [C16: via F from L *absurdus*, from AB-[1] (intensive) + *surdus* dull-sounding]
▶ **ab'surdity** *or* **ab'surdness** *n* ▶ **ab'surdly** *adv*

ABTA ('æbtə) *n acronym for* Association of British Travel Agents.

Abu Dhabi ★ ('æbuː 'dɑːbɪ) *n* a sheikhdom (emirate) of SE Arabia, on the S coast of the Persian Gulf: the chief sheikhdom and capital of the United Arab Emirates, consisting principally of the port of Abu Dhabi and a desert hinterland; contains major oilfields. Pop.: 871 000 (1993). Area: 67 350 sq. km (25 998 sq. miles).

Abuja ★ (ə'buːdʒə) *n* the federal capital of Nigeria: the seat of government since 1991. Pop.: 339 100 (1995 est.).

Abukir Bay ★ (ˌæbuːˈkɪə) *n* a variant spelling of **Aboukir Bay.**

abulia *or* **aboulia** (ə'buːlɪə, -'bjuː-) *n Psychiatry*. a pathological inability to take decisions. [C19: NL, from Gk *aboulia* lack of resolution, from A-[1] + *boulē* will]

abundance (ə'bʌndəns) *n* **1** a copious supply; great amount. **2** fullness or benevolence: *from the abundance of my heart*. **3** degree of plentifulness: *the abundance of uranium-235 in natural uranium*. **4** Also: **abondance**. a call in solo whist undertaking to make nine tricks. **5** affluence. [C14: via OF from L, from *abundāre* to ABOUND]

abundant (ə'bʌndənt) *adj* **1** existing in plentiful supply. **2** (*postpositive*; foll. by *in*) having a plentiful supply (of). [C14: from L *abundant-*, p.p. of *abundāre* to ABOUND]
▶ **a'bundantly** *adv*

abuse *vb* (ə'bjuːz), **abuses, abusing, abused.** (*tr*) **1** to use incorrectly or improperly; misuse. **2** to maltreat, esp. physically or sexually. **3** to speak insultingly or cruelly to. ◆ *n* (ə'bjuːs). **4** improper, incorrect, or excessive use. **5** maltreatment of a person; injury. **6** insulting or coarse speech. **7** an evil, unjust, or corrupt practice. **8** See **child abuse. 9** *Arch*. a deception. [C14 (vb): via OF from L *abūsus*, p.p. of *abūtī* to misuse, from AB-[1] + *ūtī* to USE]
▶ **a'buser** *n*

Abu Simbel ★ (ˌæbuː 'sɪmbᵊl) *n* a former village in S

Egypt: site of two temples of Rameses II, which were moved to higher ground (1966–67) before the area behind the Aswan High Dam was flooded. Also called: **Ipsambul.**

abusive (ə'bjuːsɪv) *adj* **1** characterized by insulting or coarse language. **2** characterized by maltreatment. **3** incorrectly used.
▶ **a'busively** *adv* ▶ **a'busiveness** *n*

abut (ə'bʌt) *vb* **abuts, abutting, abutted.** (usually foll. by *on, upon,* or *against*) to adjoin, touch, or border on (something) at one end. [C15: from OF *abouter* to join at the ends; infl. by *abuter* to touch at an end]

abutment (ə'bʌtmənt) *or* **abuttal** *n* **1** the state or process of abutting. **2a** something that abuts. **2b** the thing on which something abuts. **2c** the point of junction between them. **3** a construction that supports the end of a bridge.

abutter (ə'bʌtə) *n Property law*. the owner of adjoining property.

abuzz (ə'bʌz) *adj* (*postpositive*) humming, as with conversation, activity, etc.; buzzing.

Abydos ★ (ə'baɪdɒs) *n* **1** an ancient town in central Egypt: site of many temples and tombs. **2** an ancient Greek colony on the Asiatic side of the Dardanelles (Hellespont): scene of the legend of Hero and Leander.

abysm (ə'bɪzəm) *n* an archaic word for **abyss.** [C13: via OF from Med. L *abysmus* ABYSS]

abysmal (ə'bɪzməl) *adj* **1** immeasurable; very great. **2** *Inf*. extremely bad.
▶ **a'bysmally** *adv*

abyss (ə'bɪs) *n* **1** a very deep gorge or chasm. **2** anything that appears to be endless or immeasurably deep, such as time, despair, or shame. **3** hell. [C16: via LL from Gk *abussos* bottomless, from A-[1] + *bussos* depth]

abyssal (ə'bɪsəl) *adj* **1** of or relating to an abyss. **2** of or belonging to the ocean depths, esp. below 2000 metres (6500 ft): *abyssal zone*.

Abyssinia ★ (ˌæbɪ'sɪnɪə) *n* a former name for **Ethiopia.**
▶ **ˌAbys'sinian** *adj, n*

Ac the chemical symbol for actinium.

AC *abbrev. for:* **1** Air Corps. **2** alternating current. Cf. **DC. 3** ante Christum. [L: before Christ] **4** athletic club. **5** Companion of the Order of Australia.

a/c *Book-keeping. abbrev. for:* **1** account. **2** account current.

acacia (ə'keɪʃə) *n* **1** a tropical or subtropical shrub or tree, having small yellow or white flowers. In Australia, the term is applied esp. to the wattle. **2 false acacia.** another name for **locust** (senses 2, 3). **3 gum acacia.** another name for **gum arabic.** [C16: from L, from Gk *akakia*, ? rel. to *akē* point]

academe ('ækəˌdiːm) *n Literary*. any place of learning, such as a college or university. [C16: first used by Shakespeare in *Love's Labour's Lost* (1594); see ACADEMY]

academic (ˌækə'dɛmɪk) *adj* **1** belonging or relating to a place of learning, esp. a college, university, or academy. **2** of purely theoretical or speculative interest. **3** (esp. of pupils) having an aptitude for study. **4** excessively concerned with intellectual matters. **5** conforming to set rules and traditions: *an academic painter*. **6** relating to studies such as languages and pure science rather than technical, applied, or professional studies. ◆ *n* **7** a member of a college or university.
▶ **ˌaca'demically** *adv*

academician (əˌkædə'mɪʃən) *n* a member of an academy (senses 1, 2).

academy (ə'kædəmɪ) *n, pl* **academies. 1** an institution or society for the advancement of literature, art, or science. **2** a school for training in a particular skill or profession: *a military academy*. **3** a secondary school, esp. in Scotland: now only used as part of a name. [C16: via L from Gk *akadēmeia* the grove where Plato taught, named after the legendary hero *Akadēmos*]
▶ **ˌaca'demical** *adj*

Academy Award *n* the official name for an **Oscar.**

Acadia ★ (ə'keɪdɪə) *n* **1a** the Atlantic Provinces of Canada. **1b** the French-speaking areas of these provinces. **2** (formerly) a French colony in the present-day

★ **people and places**

Atlantic Provinces: ceded to Britain in 1713. ◆ French name: **Acadie** (akadi).
▶ **A'cadian** *adj, n*

acanthus (ə'kænθəs) *n, pl* **acanthuses** *or* **acanthi** (-θaɪ). **1** a shrub or herbaceous plant, native to the Mediterranean region but widely cultivated as an ornamental plant, having large spiny leaves and spikes of white or purplish flowers. **2** a carved ornament based on the leaves of the acanthus plant, esp. as used on the capital of a Corinthian column. [C17: NL, from Gk *akanthos*, from *akantha* thorn, spine]

a cappella (ɑː kə'pɛlə) *adj, adv Music.* without instrumental accompaniment. [It.: lit., according to (the style of the) chapel]

Acapulco ★ (ˌækə'pʊlkəʊ; *Spanish* aka'pulko) *n* a port and resort in SW Mexico, in Guerrero state. Pop.: 515 374 (1990). Official name: **Acapulco de Juárez** (*Spanish* de 'xwares).

acariasis (ˌækə'raɪəsɪs) *n* infestation with mites or ticks. [C19: NL: see ACARID, -IASIS]

acarid ('ækərɪd) *or* **acaridan** (ə'kærɪdᵊn) *n* any of an order of small arachnids that includes the ticks and mites. [C19: from Gk *akari* a small thing, mite]

acarpous (eɪ'kɑːpəs) *adj* (of plants) producing no fruit. [from Gk *akarpos*, from A-¹ + *karpos* fruit]

ACAS *or* **Acas** ('eɪkæs) *n* (in Britain) *acronym for* Advisory Conciliation and Arbitration Service.

acc. *abbrev. for:* **1** accompanied. **2** according. **3** *Bookkeeping.* account. **4** *Grammar.* accusative.

Accad ★ ('ækæd) *n* a variant spelling of **Akkad.**

accede (æk'siːd) *vb* **accedes, acceding, acceded.** (*intr*; usually foll. by *to*) **1** to assent or give one's consent. **2** to enter upon or attain (to an office, right, etc.): *the prince acceded to the throne.* **3** *International law.* to become a party (to an agreement between nations, etc.). [C15: from L *accēdere*, from *ad-* to + *cēdere* to yield]
▶ **ac'cedence** *n*

accelerando (æk,sɛlə'rændəʊ) *adj, adv Music.* (to be performed) with increasing speed. [It.]

accelerate (æk'sɛlə,reɪt) *vb* **accelerates, accelerating, accelerated. 1** to go, occur, or cause to go or occur more quickly; speed up. **2** (*tr*) to cause to happen sooner than expected. **3** (*tr*) to increase the velocity of (a body, reaction, etc.). [C16: from L *accelerātus*, from *accelerāre*, from *ad-* (intensive) + *celerāre* to hasten, from *celer* swift]
▶ **ac'celerative** *adj*

acceleration (æk,sɛlə'reɪʃən) *n* **1** the act of accelerating or the state of being accelerated. **2** the rate of increase of speed or the rate of change of velocity. **3** the power to accelerate.

acceleration of free fall *n* the acceleration of a body falling freely in a vacuum in the earth's gravitational field. Symbol: *g* Also called: **acceleration due to gravity.**

accelerator (æk'sɛlə,reɪtə) *n* **1** a device for increasing speed, esp. a pedal for controlling the fuel intake in a motor vehicle; throttle. **2** *Physics.* a machine for increasing the kinetic energy of subatomic particles or atomic nuclei. **3** Also: **accelerant.** *Chem.* a substance that increases the speed of a chemical reaction; catalyst.

accelerometer (æk,sɛlə'rɒmɪtə) *n* an instrument for measuring acceleration, esp. of an aircraft or rocket.

accent *n* ('æksənt). **1** the characteristic mode of pronunciation of a person or group, esp. one that betrays social or geographical origin. **2** the relative prominence of a spoken or sung syllable, esp. with regard to stress or pitch. **3** a mark (such as ´ , ˌ , ˆ , or ˋ) used in writing to indicate the stress or prominence of a syllable. **4** any of various marks or symbols conventionally used in writing certain languages to indicate the quality of a vowel. See **acute** (sense 8), **grave**² (sense 5), **circumflex. 5** rhythmic stress in verse or prose. **6** *Music.* **6a** stress placed on certain notes in a piece of music, indicated by a symbol printed over the note concerned. **6b** the rhythmic pulse of a piece or passage, usually represented as the stress on the first beat of each bar. **7** a distinctive characteristic of anything, such as taste, pattern, style, etc. **8** particular attention or emphasis: *an accent on learning.* **9** a strongly contrasting detail. ◆ *vb* (æk'sɛnt). (*tr*) **10** to mark with an accent in writing, speech, music, etc. **11** to lay particular emphasis or stress on. [C14: via OF from L *accentus*, from *ad-* to + *cantus* chant]

accentor (æk'sɛntə) *n* a small sparrow-like songbird, which inhabits mainly mountainous regions of Europe and Asia. See also **hedge sparrow.**

accentual (æk'sɛntʃʊəl) *adj* **1** of, relating to, or having accents; rhythmic. **2** *Prosody.* of or relating to verse based on the number of stresses in a line.
▶ **ac'centually** *adv*

accentuate (æk'sɛntʃʊ,eɪt) *vb* **accentuates, accentuating, accentuated.** (*tr*) to stress or emphasize.
▶ **ac,centu'ation** *n*

accept (ək'sɛpt) *vb* (*mainly tr*) **1** to take or receive (something offered). **2** to give an affirmative reply to. **3** to take on the responsibilities, duties, etc., of: *he accepted office.* **4** to tolerate. **5** to consider as true or believe in (a philosophy, theory, etc.). **6** (*may take a clause as object*) to be willing to believe: *you must accept that he lied.* **7** to receive with approval or admit, as into a community, group, etc. **8** *Commerce.* to agree to pay (a bill, draft, etc.). **9** to receive as adequate or valid. [C14: from L *acceptāre*, from *ad-* to + *capere* to take]
▶ **ac'cepter** *n*

acceptable (ək'sɛptəbᵊl) *adj* **1** satisfactory; adequate. **2** pleasing; welcome. **3** tolerable.
▶ **ac,cepta'bility** *or* **ac'ceptableness** *n* ▶ **ac'ceptably** *adv*

acceptance (ək'sɛptəns) *n* **1** the act of accepting or the state of being accepted or acceptable. **2** favourable reception. **3** (often foll. by *of*) belief (in) or assent (to). **4** *Commerce.* a formal agreement by a debtor to pay a draft, bill, etc. **5** (*pl*) *Austral. & NZ.* a list of horses accepted as starters in a race.

acceptation (ˌæksɛp'teɪʃən) *n* the accepted meaning, as of a word, phrase, etc.

accepted (ək'sɛptɪd) *adj* commonly approved or recognized; customary; established.

acceptor (ək'sɛptə) *n* **1** *Commerce.* the person or organization on which a draft or bill of exchange is drawn. **2** *Electronics.* an impurity, such as gallium, added to a semiconductor material to increase its p-type semiconductivity.

access ('æksɛs) *n* **1** the act of approaching or entering. **2** the condition of allowing entry, esp. (of a building, etc.) entry by prams, wheelchairs, etc. **3** the right or privilege to approach, enter, or make use of something. **4** a way or means of approach or entry. **5** the opportunity or right to see or approach someone: *my ex-wife sabotages my access to the children.* **6** (*modifier*) designating programmes made by the general public: *access television.* **7** a sudden outburst or attack, as of rage or disease. ◆ *vb* (*tr*) **8** *Computing.* **8a** to obtain or retrieve (information) from a storage device. **8b** to place (information) in a storage device. **9** to gain access to; make accessible or available. [C14: from OF or from L *accessus*, from *accēdere* to ACCEDE]

accessible (ək'sɛsəbᵊl) *adj* **1** easy to approach, enter, or use. **2 accessible to.** likely to be affected by. **3** obtainable; available.
▶ **ac,cessi'bility** *n*

accession (ək'sɛʃən) *n* **1** the act of attaining to an office, right, condition, etc. **2** an increase due to an addition. **3** an addition, as to a collection. **4** *Property law.* an addition to land or property by natural increase or improvement. **5** *International law.* the formal acceptance of a convention or treaty. **6** agreement. ◆ *vb* **7** (*tr*) to make a record of (additions to a collection).
▶ **ac'cessional** *adj*

accessory (ək'sɛsərɪ) *n, pl* **accessories. 1** a supplementary part or object, as of a car, appliance, etc. **2** (*often pl*) a small accompanying item of dress, esp. of women's dress. **3** (formerly) a person involved in a crime although absent during its commission. ◆ *adj* **4** supplementary; additional. **5** assisting in or having knowledge of an act, esp. a crime. [C17: from LL *accessōrius*: see ACCESS]
▶ **accessorial** (ˌæksɛ'sɔːrɪəl) *adj* ▶ **ac'cessorily** *adv*

access road *n* a road giving entry to a region or, esp., a motorway.

access time *n Computing.* the time required to retrieve a piece of stored information.

acciaccatura (ə,tʃækə'tuərə) *n, pl* **acciaccaturas** *or* **acciaccature** (-reɪ). a small grace note melodically adjacent to a principal note and played simultaneously with or immediately before it. [C18: It.: lit., a crushing sound]

accidence ('æksɪdəns) *n* the part of grammar concerned with changes in the form of words for the expression of tense, person, case, number, etc. [C15: from L *accidentia* accidental matters, from *accidere* to happen. See ACCIDENT]

accident ('æksɪdənt) *n* **1** an unforeseen event or one without an apparent cause. **2** anything that occurs unintentionally or by chance: *I met him by accident.* **3** a misfortune or mishap, esp. one causing injury or death. **4** *Geol.* a surface irregularity in a natural formation. [C14: via OF from L *accident-*, from the p.p. of *accidere* to happen, from *ad-* to + *cadere* to fall]

accidental (,æksɪ'dɛntᵊl) *adj* **1** occurring by chance, unexpectedly, or unintentionally. **2** nonessential; incidental. **3** *Music.* denoting sharps, flats, or naturals that are not in the key signature of a piece. ◆ *n* **4** an incidental or supplementary circumstance, factor, or attribute. **5** *Music.* a symbol denoting a sharp, flat, or natural that is not a part of the key signature.
▸ ,acci'dentally *adv*

accident-prone *adj* liable to become involved in accidents.

accidie ('æksɪdɪ) *or* **acedia** *n* spiritual sloth; apathy; indifference. [in use C13 to C16 and revived C19: via LL from Gk *akēdia*, from A-¹ + *kēdos* care]

accipiter (æk'sɪpɪtə) *n* any of a genus of hawks having short rounded wings and a long tail. [C19: NL, from L: hawk]
▸ ac'cipitrine *adj*

acclaim (ə'kleɪm) *vb* **1** (*tr*) to acknowledge publicly the excellence of (a person, act, etc.). **2** to applaud. **3** (*tr*) to acknowledge publicly: *they acclaimed him king.* ◆ *n* **4** an enthusiastic expression of approval, etc. [C17: from L *acclāmāre*, from *ad-* to + *clāmāre* to shout]
▸ ac'claimer *n*

acclamation (,æklə'meɪʃən) *n* **1** an enthusiastic reception or exhibition of welcome, approval, etc. **2** an expression of approval with shouts or applause. **3** *Canad.* an instance of electing or being elected without opposition.
▸ acclamatory (ə'klæmətərɪ) *adj*

acclimatize *or* **acclimatise** (ə'klaɪmə,taɪz) *vb* **acclimatizes, acclimatizing, acclimatized** *or* **acclimatises, acclimatising, acclimatised.** to adapt or become accustomed to a new climate or environment.
▸ ac'clima,tizable *or* ac'clima,tisable *adj* ▸ ac,climati-'zation *or* ac,climati'sation *n*

acclivity (ə'klɪvɪtɪ) *n, pl* **acclivities.** an upward slope, esp. of the ground. Cf. **declivity.** [C17: from L, from *acclīvis* sloping up]
▸ ac'clivitous *adj*

accolade ('ækə,leɪd) *n* **1** strong praise or approval. **2** an award or honour. **3** the ceremonial gesture used to confer knighthood, a touch on the shoulder with a sword. **4** a rare word for **brace** (sense 6). [C17: via F & It. from Vulgar L *accollāre* (unattested) to hug; rel. to L *collum* neck]

accommodate (ə'kɒmə,deɪt) *vb* **accommodates, accommodating, accommodated.** **1** (*tr*) to supply or provide, esp. with lodging. **2** (*tr*) to oblige or do a favour for. **3** to adapt. **4** (*tr*) to bring into harmony. **5** (*tr*) to allow room for. **6** (*tr*) to lend money to. [C16: from L *accommodāre*, from *ad-* to + *commodus* having the proper measure]

accommodating (ə'kɒmə,deɪtɪŋ) *adj* willing to help; kind; obliging.

accommodation (ə,kɒmə'deɪʃən) *n* **1** lodging or board and lodging. **2** adjustment, as of differences or to new circumstances; settlement or reconciliation. **3** something fulfilling a need, want, etc. **4** *Physiol.* the automatic or voluntary adjustment of the thickness of the lens of the eye for far or near vision. **5** willingness to help or oblige. **6** *Commerce.* a loan.

accommodation address *n* an address on letters, etc., to a person or business that does not wish or is not able to receive post at a permanent or actual address.

accommodation ladder *n Naut.* a flight of stairs or a ladder for lowering over the side of a ship for access to and from a small boat, pier, etc.

accompaniment (ə'kʌmpənɪmənt) *n* **1** something that accompanies or is served or used with something else. **2** *Music.* a subordinate or supporting part for an instrument, voices, or an orchestra.

accompanist (ə'kʌmpənɪst) *n* a person who plays a musical accompaniment for another performer.

accompany (ə'kʌmpənɪ) *vb* **accompanies, accompanying, accompanied.** **1** (*tr*) to go along with, so as to be in company with. **2** (*tr*; foll. by *with*) to supplement. **3** (*tr*) to occur or be associated with. **4** to provide a musical accompaniment for (a soloist, etc.). [C15: from OF *accompaignier*, from *compaing* COMPANION¹]

accomplice (ə'kɒmplɪs, ə'kʌm-) *n* a person who has helped another in committing a crime. [C15: from *a complice*, interpreted as *ac* complice, from OF, from LL *complex* partner, from L *complicāre* to COMPLICATE]

accomplish (ə'kɒmplɪʃ, ə'kʌm-) *vb* (*tr*) **1** to manage to do; achieve. **2** to complete. [C14: from OF *acomplir*, ult. from L *complēre* to fill up. See COMPLETE]

accomplished (ə'kɒmplɪʃt, ə'kʌm-) *adj* **1** successfully completed; achieved. **2** expert; proficient.

accomplishment (ə'kɒmplɪʃmənt, ə'kʌm-) *n* **1** the act of achieving. **2** something successfully completed. **3** (*often pl*) skill or talent. **4** (*often pl*) social grace and poise.

accord (ə'kɔːd) *n* **1** agreement; accordance (esp. in **in accord with**). **2** concurrence of opinion. **3** **with one accord.** unanimously. **4** pleasing relationship between sounds, colours, etc. **5 of one's own accord.** voluntarily. ◆ *vb* **6** to be or cause to be in harmony or agreement. **7** (*tr*) to grant; bestow. [C12: via OF from L *ad-* to + *cord-*, stem of *cor* heart]

accordance (ə'kɔːdəns) *n* conformity; agreement; accord (esp. in **in accordance with**).

according (ə'kɔːdɪŋ) *adj* **1** (foll. by *to*) in proportion. **2** (foll. by *to*) as stated (by). **3** (foll. by *to*) in conformity (with). **4** (foll. by *as*) depending (on whether).

accordingly (ə'kɔːdɪŋlɪ) *adv* **1** in an appropriate manner; suitably. ◆ *sentence connector.* **2** consequently.

accordion (ə'kɔːdɪən) *n* **1** a portable box-shaped instrument consisting of metallic reeds that are made to vibrate by air from a set of bellows controlled by the player's hands. Notes are produced by means of studlike keys. **2** short for **piano accordion.** [C19: from G, from *Akkord* harmony]
▸ ac'cordionist *n*

accordion pleats *pl n* tiny knife pleats.

accost (ə'kɒst) *vb* (*tr*) to approach, stop, and speak to (a person), as to ask a question, solicit sexually, etc. [C16: from LL *accostāre*, from L *costa* side, rib]
▸ ac'costable *adj*

accouchement *French.* (akuʃmɑ̃) *n* childbirth or the period of confinement. [C19: from *accoucher* to put to bed. See COUCH]

account (ə'kaʊnt) *n* **1** a verbal or written report, description, or narration of some occurrence, event, etc. **2** an explanation of conduct, esp. one made to someone in authority. **3** basis; consideration: *on this account.* **4** importance, consequence, or value: *of little account.* **5** assessment; judgment. **6** profit or advantage: *to good account.* **7** part or behalf (only in **on one's** *or* **someone's account**). **8** *Finance.* **8a** a business relationship between a bank, department store, etc., and a depositor, customer, or client permitting the latter certain banking or credit services. **8b** the sum of money deposited at a bank. **8c** the amount of credit available to the holder of an account. **8d** a record of these. **9** a statement of monetary transactions with the resulting balance. **10** (formerly, on the London Stock Exchange) the period, ordinarily of a fortnight's duration, at the end of which settlements were made.

★ people and places

11a a regular client or customer. **11b** an area of business assigned to another: *they transferred their publicity account to a new agent.* **12 call** (or **bring**) **to account. 12a** to insist on explanation. **12b** to reprimand. **12c** to hold responsible. **13** give a good (bad, etc.) **account of oneself.** to perform well (badly, etc.). **14** on account. **14a** on credit. **14b** Also: **to account.** as partial payment. **15 on account of.** (*prep*) because of. **16** take account of or take into account. to take into consideration; allow for. **17** settle or square accounts with. **17a** to pay or receive a balance due. **17b** to get revenge on (someone). **18** See bank account. ◆ *vb* **19** (*tr*) to consider or reckon: *he accounts himself poor.* [C13: from OF *acont*, from *conter* to COUNT[1]]

accountable (əˈkaʊntəb°l) *adj* **1** responsible to someone or for some action. **2** able to be explained.
▸ ac,counta'bility *n* ▸ ac'countably *adv*

accountancy (əˈkaʊntənsɪ) *n* the profession or business of an accountant.

accountant (əˈkaʊntənt) *n* a person concerned with the maintenance and audit of business accounts.

account executive *n* an executive in an advertising agency or public relations firm who manages a client's account.

account for *vb* (*intr, prep*) **1** to give reasons for (an event, act, etc.). **2** to make or provide a reckoning of (expenditure, etc.). **3** to be responsible for destroying or putting (people, aircraft, etc.) out of action.

accounting (əˈkaʊntɪŋ) *n* **a** the skill or practice of maintaining and auditing accounts and preparing reports on the assets, liabilities, etc., of a business. **b** (*as modifier*): *an accounting period.*

accoutre or *US* **accouter** (əˈkuːtə) *vb* **accoutres, accoutring, accoutred** or *US* **accouters, accoutering, accoutered.** (*tr; usually passive*) to provide with equipment or dress, esp. military. [C16: from OF *accoustrer*, ult. rel. to L *consuere* to sew together]

accoutrement (əˈkuːtrəmənt, əˈkuːtə-) or *US* **accouterment** (əˈkuːtərmənt) *n* **1** equipment worn by soldiers in addition to their clothing and weapons. **2** (*usually pl*) clothing, equipment, etc.; trappings: *the correct accoutrements for any sport.*

Accra ★ (əˈkrɑː) *n* the capital of Ghana, a port on the Gulf of Guinea: built on the site of three 17th-century trading fortresses founded by the English, Dutch, and Danish. Pop.: 949 113 (1988 est.).

accredit (əˈkrɛdɪt) *vb* (*tr*) **1** to ascribe or attribute. **2** to give official recognition to. **3** to certify as meeting required standards. **4** (often foll. by *at* or *to*) **4a** to send (an envoy, etc.) with official credentials. **4b** to appoint (someone) as an envoy, etc. **5** to believe. **6** *NZ.* to pass (a candidate) for university entrance on school recommendation, without external examination. [C17: from F *accréditer*, from *mettre à crédit* to put to CREDIT]
▸ ac,credi'tation *n*

accredited (əˈkrɛdɪtɪd) *adj* **1** officially authorized; recognized. **2** (of milk, cattle, etc.) certified as free from disease; meeting certain standards. **3** *NZ.* accepted for university entrance on school recommendation, without external examination.

accrete (əˈkriːt) *vb* **accretes, accreting, accreted. 1** to grow or cause to grow together. **2** to make or become bigger, as by addition. [C18: back formation from ACCRETION]

accretion (əˈkriːʃən) *n* **1** any gradual increase in size, as through growth or external addition. **2** something added, esp. extraneously, to cause growth or an increase in size. **3** the growing together of normally separate plant or animal parts. [C17: from L *accretiō* increase, from *accrēscere*. See ACCRUE]
▸ ac'cretive *adj*

accrual (əˈkruːəl) *n* **1** the act of accruing. **2** something that has accrued. **3** *Accounting* a charge incurred in one accounting period that has not been paid by the end of it.

accrue (əˈkruː) *vb* **accrues, accruing, accrued.** (*intr*) **1** to increase by growth or addition, esp. (of capital) to increase by periodic addition of interest. **2** (often foll. by *to*) to fall naturally (to). [C15: from OF *accreue*, ult. from L *accrēscere*, from *ad-* to, in addition + *crēscere* to grow]

acct *Book-keeping. abbrev. for* account.

acculturate (əˈkʌltʃəˌreɪt) *vb* **acculturates, acculturating, acculturated.** (of a cultural or social group) to assimilate the cultural traits of another group. [C20: from AD- + CULTURE + -ATE[1]]
▸ ac,cultur'ation *n*

accumulate (əˈkjuːmjʊˌleɪt) *vb* **accumulates, accumulating, accumulated.** to gather or become gathered together in an increasing quantity; collect. [C16: from L *accumulāre* to heap up, from *cumulus* a heap]
▸ ac'cumulable *adj* ▸ ac'cumulative *adj*

accumulation (əˌkjuːmjʊˈleɪʃən) *n* **1** the act or process of collecting together or becoming collected. **2** something that has been collected, gathered, heaped, etc. **3** *Finance.* the continuous growth of capital by retention of interest or earnings.

accumulator (əˈkjuːmjʊˌleɪtə) *n* **1** Also called: **battery, storage battery.** a rechargeable device for storing electrical energy in the form of chemical energy. **2** *Horse racing, Brit.* a collective bet on successive races, with both stake and winnings being carried forward to accumulate progressively. **3** a register in a calculator or computer used for holding the results of a computation or data transfer.

accuracy (ˈækjʊrəsɪ) *n, pl* **accuracies.** faithful measurement or representation of the truth; correctness; precision.

accurate (ˈækjʊrɪt) *adj* **1** faithfully representing or describing the truth. **2** showing a negligible or permissible deviation from a standard: *an accurate ruler.* **3** without error; precise. **4** *Maths.* (of a number) correctly represented to a specified number of decimal places or significant figures. [C16: from L *accūrāre* to perform with care, from *cūra* care]
▸ 'accurately *adv*

accursed (əˈkɜːsɪd, əˈkɜːst) or **accurst** (əˈkɜːst) *adj* **1** under or subject to a curse. **2** (*prenominal*) hateful; detestable. [OE *ācursod*, p.p. of *ācursian* to put under a CURSE]
▸ accursedly (əˈkɜːsɪdlɪ) *adv* ▸ ac'cursedness *n*

accusation (ˌækjuːˈzeɪʃən) *n* **1** an allegation that a person is guilty of some fault or crime. **2** a formal charge brought against a person.

accusative (əˈkjuːzətɪv) *adj* **1** *Grammar.* denoting a case of nouns, pronouns, and adjectives in inflected languages that is used to identify the direct object of a finite verb, of certain prepositions, and for certain other purposes. **2** another word for **accusatorial.** ◆ *n* **3** *Grammar.* the accusative case or a speech element in it. [C15: from L; in grammar, from *cāsus accūsātīvus* accusative case, a mistaken translation of Gk *ptōsis aitiatikē* the case indicating causation. See ACCUSE]
▸ accusatival (əˌkjuːzəˈtaɪv°l) *adj* ▸ ac'cusatively *adv*

accusatorial (əˌkjuːzəˈtɔːrɪəl) or **accusatory** (əˈkjuːzətərɪ) *adj* **1** containing or implying blame or strong criticism. **2** *Law.* denoting a legal system in which the defendant is prosecuted before a judge in public. Cf. **inquisitorial.**

accuse (əˈkjuːz) *vb* **accuses, accusing, accused.** to charge (a person or persons) with some fault, offence, crime, etc. [C13: via OF from L *accūsāre* to call to account, from *ad-* to + *causa* lawsuit]
▸ ac'cuser *n* ▸ ac'cusing *adj* ▸ ac'cusingly *adv*

accused (əˈkjuːzd) *n* (preceded by *the*) *Law.* the defendant or defendants on a criminal charge.

accustom (əˈkʌstəm) *vb* (*tr; usually foll. by to*) to make (oneself) familiar (with) or used (to), as by habit or experience. [C15: from OF *acostumer*, from *costume* CUSTOM]

accustomed (əˈkʌstəmd) *adj* **1** usual; customary. **2** (*postpositive; foll. by to*) used (to). **3** (*postpositive; foll. by to*) in the habit (of).

AC/DC *adj Inf.* (of a person) bisexual. [C20: humorous reference to electrical apparatus that is adaptable for ALTERNATING CURRENT and DIRECT CURRENT]

ace (eɪs) *n* **1** any die, domino, or any of four playing cards with one spot. **2** a single spot or pip on a playing card, die, etc. **3** *Tennis.* a winning serve that the opponent fails to reach. **4** a fighter pilot accredited with destroying several enemy aircraft. **5** *Inf.* an expert: *an ace at driving.* **6 an ace up one's sleeve.** a hidden and powerful advantage.

◆ *adj* **7** *Inf.* superb; excellent. [C13: via OF from L *as* a unit]

-acea *suffix forming plural proper nouns.* denoting animals belonging to a class or order: *Crustacea* (class); *Cetacea* (order). [NL, from L, neuter pl of *-āceus* -ACEOUS]

-aceae *suffix forming plural proper nouns.* denoting plants belonging to a family: *Liliaceae.* [NL, from L, fem pl of *-āceus* -ACEOUS]

acedia (ə'siːdɪə) *n* another word for **accidie.**

ACE inhibitor *n* any one of a class of drugs, including captopril and enalpapril, that cause the arteries to widen by preventing the synthesis of angiotensin: used to treat high blood pressure and heart failure. [C20: from *a(ngiotensin-)c(onverting) e(nzyme) inhibitor*]

-aceous *suffix forming adjectives.* relating to, having the nature of, or resembling: *herbaceous.* [NL, from L *-āceus* of a certain kind; rel. to *-āc, -āx,* adjectival suffix]

acephalous (ə'sefələs) *adj* having no head or one that is reduced and indistinct, as certain insect larvae. [C18: via Med. L from Gk *akephalos.* See A-¹, -CEPHALIC]

acer ('eɪsə) *n* any tree or shrub of the genus *Acer,* often cultivated for their brightly coloured foliage. See also **maple.**

acerbate ('æsə,beɪt) *vb* **acerbates, acerbating, acerbated.** (*tr*) **1** to embitter or exasperate. **2** to make sour or bitter. [C18: from L *acerbāre* to make sour]

acerbic (ə'sɜːbɪk) *adj* harsh, bitter, or astringent; sour. [C17: from L *acerbus* sour, bitter]

acerbity (ə'sɜːbɪtɪ) *n, pl* **acerbities. 1** vitriolic or embittered speech, temper, etc. **2** sourness or bitterness of taste.

acetabulum (,æsɪ'tæbjʊləm) *n, pl* **acetabula** (-lə) the deep cuplike cavity on the side of the hipbone that receives the head of the thighbone. [L: vinegar cup, hence a cuplike cavity, from *acētum* vinegar + *-abulum,* suffix denoting a container]

acetal ('æsɪ,tæl) *n* **1** a type of organic compound formed by addition of an alcohol to an aldehyde or ketone. **2** a colourless pleasant-smelling volatile liquid used in perfumes. Formula: $CH_3CH(OC_2H_5)_2$. Systematic name: **diethoxyethane.** [C19: from G *Azetal,* from ACETO- + ALCOHOL]

acetaldehyde (,æsɪ'tældɪ,haɪd) *n* a colourless volatile pungent liquid, used in the manufacture of organic compounds and as a solvent. Formula: CH_3CHO. Systematic name: **ethanal.**

acetanilide (,æsɪ'tænɪ,laɪd) *n* a white crystalline powder used in the manufacture of dyes and as an analgesic in medicine. Formula: $C_6H_5NH(COCH_3)$. Systematic names: **N-phenylethanamide, phenylacetamide.** [C19: from ACETO- + ANILINE + -IDE]

acetate ('æsɪ,teɪt) *n* **1** any salt or ester of acetic acid. Systematic name: **ethanoate. 2** short for **acetate rayon** or **cellulose acetate. 3** an audio disc with an acetate lacquer coating: used for demonstration purposes, etc. [C19: from ACETIC + -ATE¹]

acetate rayon *n* a synthetic textile fibre made from cellulose acetate.

acetic (ə'siːtɪk) *adj* of, containing, producing, or derived from acetic acid or vinegar. [C19: from L *acētum* vinegar]

acetic acid *n* a colourless pungent liquid widely used in the manufacture of plastics, pharmaceuticals, dyes, etc. Formula: CH_3COOH. Systematic name: **ethanoic acid.** See also **vinegar.**

acetify (ə'setɪ,faɪ) *vb* **acetifies, acetifying, acetified.** to become or cause to become acetic acid or vinegar.
▸ a,cetifi'cation *n*

aceto- *or before a vowel* **acet-** *combining form.* containing an acetyl group or derived from acetic acid: *acetone.* [from L *acētum* vinegar]

acetone ('æsɪ,təʊn) *n* a colourless volatile pungent liquid used in the manufacture of chemicals and as a solvent for paints, varnishes, and lacquers. Formula: CH_3COCH_3. Systematic name: **propanone.** [C19: from G *Azeton,* from ACETO- + -ONE]

acetous ('æsɪtəs) *or* **acetose** ('æsɪ,təʊs) *adj* **1** producing or resembling acetic acid or vinegar. **2** tasting like vinegar. [C18: from LL *acētōsus* vinegary, from *acētum* vinegar]

acetyl ('æsɪ,taɪl, ə'siːtaɪl) *n* (*modifier*) of or containing the monovalent group CH_3CO-. [C19: from ACET(IC) + -YL]

acetylcholine (,æsɪtaɪl'kəʊliːn, -lɪn) *n* a chemical substance secreted at the ends of many nerve fibres, responsible for the transmission of nervous impulses.

acetylene (ə'setɪ,liːn) *n* **1** a colourless soluble flammable gas used in the manufacture of organic chemicals and in cutting and welding metals. Formula: C_2H_2. Systematic name: **ethyne. 2** another name for **alkyne.**

acetylene series *n* another name for **alkyne series.**

acetylsalicylic acid (,æsɪtaɪl,sælɪ'sɪlɪk) *n* the chemical name for **aspirin.**

Achaea (ə'kiːə) *or* **Achaia** (ə'kaɪə) *n* **1** a department of Greece, in the N Peloponnese. Capital: Patras. Pop.: 300 078 (1991). Area: 3209 sq. km (1239 sq. miles). Modern Greek name: **Akhaïa. 2** a province of ancient Greece, in the N Peloponnese on the Gulf of Corinth: enlarged as a Roman province in 27 B.C.

Achaean (ə'kiːən) *or* **Achaian** (ə'kaɪən) *n* **1** a member of a principal Greek tribe in the Mycenaean era. ◆ *adj* **2** of or relating to the Achaeans.

Achates ★ (ə'keɪtiːz) *n* **1** *Classical myth.* Aeneas' faithful companion in Virgil's *Aeneid.* **2** a loyal friend.

ache (eɪk) *vb* **aches, aching, ached.** (*intr*) **1** to feel, suffer, or be the source of a continuous dull pain. **2** to suffer mental anguish. ◆ *n* **3** a continuous dull pain. [OE *ācan* (vb), *æce* (n), ME *aken* (vb), *ache* (n)]
▸ 'aching *adj*

Achebe ★ (ə'tʃeɪbɪ) *n* Chinua. born 1930, Nigerian novelist. His works include *Things Fall Apart* (1958), *A Man of the People* (1966), and *Anthills of the Savannah* (1987).

Achelous ★ (,ækɪ'ləʊəs) *n Classical myth.* a river god who changed into a snake and a bull while fighting Hercules but was defeated when Hercules broke off one of his horns.

achene (ə'kiːn) *n* a dry one-seeded indehiscent fruit with the seed distinct from the fruit wall. [C19: from NL *achaenium* that which does not open, from A-¹ + Gk *khainein* to yawn]

Acheron ★ ('ækə,rɒn) *n Greek myth.* **1** one of the rivers in Hades over which the souls of the dead were ferried by Charon. Cf. **Styx. 2** the underworld or Hades.

Acheson ★ ('ætʃɪsªn) *n* Dean (Gooderham). 1893–1971, US lawyer and statesman: secretary of state (1949–53).

Acheulian *or* **Acheulean** (ə'ʃuːlɪən) *Archaeol.* ◆ *n* **1** (in Europe) the period in the Lower Palaeolithic following the Abbevillian, represented by the use of soft hammerstones in hand-axe production. **2** (in Africa) the period represented by every stage of hand-axe development. ◆ *adj* **3** of or relating to this period. [C20: after *St Acheul,* town in N France]

achieve (ə'tʃiːv) *vb* **achieves, achieving, achieved.** (*tr*) **1** to bring to a successful conclusion. **2** to gain as by hard work or effort: *to achieve success.* [C14: from OF *achever* to bring to an end, from a *chef* to a head]
▸ a'chievable *adj* ▸ a'chiever *n*

achievement (ə'tʃiːvmənt) *n* **1** something that has been accomplished, esp. by hard work, ability, or heroism. **2** successful completion; accomplishment.

achillea (,ækɪ'liːə) *n* any of several cultivated varieties of yarrow. [NL, from Gk *akhilleios* plant used medicinally by ACHILLES]

Achilles ★ (ə'kɪliːz) *n Greek myth.* Greek hero, the son of Peleus and the sea goddess Thetis: in the *Iliad* the foremost of the Greek warriors at the siege of Troy. While he was a baby his mother plunged him into the river Styx making his body invulnerable except for the heel by which she held him. After slaying Hector, he was killed by Paris who wounded him in the heel.
▸ **Achillean** (,ækɪ'liːən) *adj*

Achilles heel *n* a small but fatal weakness.

Achilles tendon *n* the fibrous cord that connects the muscles of the calf to the heelbone.

★ people and places

Achill Island ★ (ˈækɪl) *n* an island in the Republic of Ireland, off the W coast of Co. Mayo. Pop.: 2853 (1991). Area: 148 sq. km (57 sq. miles).

Achitophel ★ (əˈkɪtəˌfɛl) *n Bible.* the Douay spelling of **Ahithophel.**

achromat (ˈækrəˌmæt) *or* **achromatic lens** *n* a lens designed to reduce chromatic aberration.

achromatic (ˌækrəˈmætɪk) *adj* **1** without colour. **2** capable of reflecting or refracting light without chromatic aberration. **3** *Music.* involving no sharps or flats. ▸ ˌachroˈmatically *adv* ▸ **achromatism** (əˈkrəʊməˌtɪzəm) *or* achromaticity (əˌkrəʊməˈtɪsɪtɪ) *n*

acid (ˈæsɪd) *n* **1** any substance that dissociates in water to yield a sour corrosive solution containing hydrogen ions, and turning litmus red. **2** a sour-tasting substance. **3** a slang name for **LSD.** ◆ *adj* **4** *Chem.* **4a** of, derived from, or containing acid. **4b** being or having the properties of an acid. **5** sharp or sour in taste. **6** cutting, sharp, or hurtful in speech, manner, etc. [C17: from F *acide* or L *acidus*, from *acēre* to be sour] ▸ **ˈacidly** *adv* ▸ **ˈacidness** *n*

acid-fast *adj* (of bacteria and tissues) resistant to decolorization by mineral acids after staining.

Acid House *or* **Acid** *n* a dance music dominated by beat and bass line, created with synthesizers and digital sampling; popular in the late 1980s. [C20: from ACID (LSD) + HOUSE (MUSIC)]

acidic (əˈsɪdɪk) *adj* another word for **acid.**

acidify (əˈsɪdɪˌfaɪ) *vb* **acidifies, acidifying, acidified.** to convert into or become acid. ▸ **aˈcidiˌfiable** *adj* ▸ **aˌcidifiˈcation** *n*

acidity (əˈsɪdɪtɪ) *n, pl* **acidities. 1** the quality or state of being acid. **2** the amount of acid present in a solution.

acidosis (ˌæsɪˈdəʊsɪs) *n* a condition characterized by an abnormal increase in the acidity of the blood. ▸ **acidotic** (ˌæsɪˈdɒtɪk) *adj*

acid rain *n* rain containing pollutants, chiefly sulphur dioxide and nitrogen oxide, released into the atmosphere by burning coal or oil.

acid rock *n* rock music characterized by bizarre amplified instrumental effects. [C20: from ACID (LSD)]

acid test *n* a rigorous and conclusive test to establish worth or value. [C19: from the testing of gold with nitric acid]

acidulate (əˈsɪdjʊˌleɪt) *vb* **acidulates, acidulating, acidulated.** (*tr*) to make slightly acid or sour. [C18: ACIDULOUS + -ATE¹] ▸ **aˌciduˈlation** *n*

acidulous (əˈsɪdjʊləs) *or* **acidulent** *adj* **1** rather sour. **2** sharp or sour in speech, manner, etc.; acid. [C18: from L *acidulus* sourish, dim. of *acidus* sour]

acinus (ˈæsɪnəs) *n, pl* **acini** (-ˌnaɪ). **1** *Anat.* any of the terminal saclike portions of a compound gland. **2** *Bot.* any of the small drupes that make up the fruit of the raspberry, etc. **3** *Bot., obs.* a collection of berries, such as a bunch of grapes. [C18: NL, from L: grape, berry]

Acis ★ (ˈeɪsɪs) *n Greek myth.* a Sicilian shepherd and the lover of the nymph Galatea. In jealousy, Polyphemus crushed him with a huge rock, and his blood was turned by Galatea into a river.

ack-ack (ˈækˌæk) *n Mil.* **a** anti-aircraft fire. **b** (*as modifier*): *ack-ack guns.* [C20: British Army World War I phonetic alphabet for AA, abbrev. of *anti-aircraft*]

acknowledge (əkˈnɒlɪdʒ) *vb* **acknowledges, acknowledging, acknowledged.** (*tr*) **1** (*may take a clause as object*) to recognize or admit the existence, truth, or reality of. **2** to indicate recognition or awareness of, as by a greeting, glance, etc. **3** to express appreciation or thanks for. **4** to make the receipt of known: *to acknowledge a letter.* **5** to recognize, esp. in legal form, the authority, rights, or claims of. [C15: prob. from earlier *knowledge*, on the model of OE *oncnāwan*, ME *aknowen* to confess, recognize] ▸ **acˈknowledgeable** *adj*

acknowledgment *or* **acknowledgement** (əkˈnɒlɪdʒmənt) *n* **1** the act of acknowledging or state of being acknowledged. **2** something done or given as an expres-

sion of thanks. **3** (*pl*) an author's statement acknowledging his use of the works of other authors.

aclinic line (əˈklɪnɪk) *n* another name for **magnetic equator.** [C19 *aclinic*, from Gk *aklinēs* not bending, from A-¹ + *klinein* to bend]

acme (ˈækmɪ) *n* the culminating point, as of achievement or excellence. [C16: from Gk *akmē*]

acne (ˈæknɪ) *n* a chronic skin disease common in adolescence, characterized by pustules on the face. [C19: NL, from a misreading of Gk *akmē* eruption on the face. See ACME]

acolyte (ˈækəˌlaɪt) *n* **1** a follower or attendant. **2** *Christianity.* an officer who assists a priest. [C16: via OF & Med. L from Gk *akolouthos* a follower]

Aconcagua ★ (*Spanish* akonˈkaɣwa) *n* a mountain in W Argentina: the highest peak in the Andes and in the W Hemisphere. Height: 6960 m (22 835 ft).

aconite (ˈækəˌnaɪt) *n* **1** any of a genus of N temperate plants, such as monkshood and wolfsbane, many of which are poisonous. Cf. **winter aconite. 2** the dried poisonous root of many of these plants, sometimes used as a narcotic. [C16: via OF or L from Gk *akoniton* aconite] ▸ **aconitic** (ˌækəˈnɪtɪk) *adj*

Açôres ★ (əˈsoreʃ) *n* the Portuguese name for (the) **Azores.**

acorn (ˈeɪkɔːn) *n* the fruit of the oak tree, consisting of a smooth thick-walled nut in a woody scaly cuplike base. [C16: var. (infl. by *corn*) of OE *æcern* the fruit of a tree, acorn]

acoustic (əˈkuːstɪk) *or* **acoustical** *adj* **1** of or related to sound, hearing, or acoustics. **2** designed to respond to or absorb sound: *an acoustic tile.* **3** (of a musical instrument or recording) without electronic amplification: *an acoustic guitar.* [C17: from Gk *akoustikos*, from *akouein* to hear] ▸ **aˈcoustically** *adv*

acoustics (əˈkuːstɪks) *n* **1** (*functioning as sing*) the scientific study of sound and sound waves. **2** (*functioning as pl*) the characteristics of a room, auditorium, etc., that determine the fidelity with which sound can be heard within it.

acquaint (əˈkweɪnt) *vb* (*tr*) (foll. by *with* or *of*) to make (a person) familiar (with). [C13: via OF & Med. L from L *accognitus*, from *accognōscere* to know perfectly, from *ad-* (intensive) + *cognōscere* to know]

acquaintance (əˈkweɪntəns) *n* **1** a person whom one knows but who is not a close friend. **2** knowledge of a person or thing, esp. when slight. **3 make the acquaintance of.** to come into social contact with. **4** those persons collectively whom one knows. ▸ **acˈquaintanceship** *n*

acquainted (əˈkweɪntɪd) *adj* (*postpositive*) **1** (sometimes foll. by *with*) on terms of familiarity but not intimacy. **2** (foll. by *with*) familiar (with).

acquiesce (ˌækwɪˈɛs) *vb* **acquiesces, acquiescing, acquiesced.** (*intr*) often foll. by *in* or *to*) to comply (with); assent (to) without protest. [C17: from L *acquiēscere*, from *ad-* at + *quiēscere* to rest, from *quiēs* QUIET] ▸ **ˌacquiˈescence** *n* ▸ **ˌacquiˈescent** *adj*

> **USAGE NOTE** The use of *to* after *acquiesce* was formerly regarded as incorrect, but is now acceptable.

acquire (əˈkwaɪə) *vb* **acquires, acquiring, acquired.** (*tr*) to get or gain (something, such as an object, trait, or ability). [C15: via OF from L *acquīrere*, from *ad-* in addition + *quaerere* to get, seek] ▸ **acˈquirable** *adj* ▸ **acˈquirement** *n*

acquired behaviour *n Psychol.* the behaviour of an organism resulting from the effects of the environment.

acquired characteristic *n* a characteristic of an organism resulting from the effects of the environment.

acquired immune deficiency syndrome *or* **acquired immunodeficiency syndrome** *n* the full name for **AIDS.**

acquired immunity *n* the immmunity produced by

exposure of an organism to antigens, which stimulates the production of antibodies.

acquired taste n 1 a liking for something at first considered unpleasant. 2 the thing liked.

acquisition (ˌækwɪˈzɪʃən) n 1 the act of acquiring or gaining possession. 2 something acquired. 3 a person or thing of special merit added to a group. [C14: from L *acquisītiōn-*, from *acquīrere* to ACQUIRE]

acquisitive (əˈkwɪzɪtɪv) adj inclined or eager to acquire things, esp. material possessions.
▸ acˈquisitively adv ▸ acˈquisitiveness n

acquit (əˈkwɪt) vb **acquits, acquitting, acquitted.** (tr) 1 (foll. by *of*) 1a to free or release (from a charge of crime). 1b to pronounce not guilty. 2 (foll. by *of*) to free or relieve (from an obligation, duty, etc.). 3 to repay or settle (a debt or obligation). 4 to conduct (oneself). [C13: from OF *aquiter*, from *quiter* to release, QUIT]
▸ acˈquittal n ▸ acˈquitter n

acquittance (əˈkwɪtəns) n 1 a release from or settlement of a debt, etc. 2 a record of this, such as a receipt.

acre (ˈeɪkə) n 1 a unit of area used in certain English-speaking countries, equal to 4840 square yards or 4046.86 square metres. 2 (pl) 2a land, esp. a large area. 2b Inf. a large amount. 3 **farm the long acre.** NZ. to graze stock on the grass along a highway. [OE *æcer* field, acre]

Acre ★ n 1 (ˈɑːkrə). a state of W Brazil: mostly unexplored tropical forests; acquired from Bolivia in 1903. Capital: Rio Branco. Pop.: 455 200 (1995 est.). Area: 152 589 sq. km (58 899 sq. miles). 2 (ˈeɪkə, ˈɑːkə). a city and port in N Israel, strategically situated on the **Bay of Acre** in the E Mediterranean: taken and retaken during the Crusades (1104, 1187, 1191, 1291), taken by the Turks (1517), by Egypt (1832), and by the Turks again (1839). Pop.: 40 500 (1989 est.). Old Testament name: **Accho** (ˈækəʊ). Arabic name: **'Akka** (ˈækɑː). Hebrew name: **'Akko** (ˈækəʊ).

acreage (ˈeɪkərɪdʒ) n 1 land area in acres. ◆ adj 2 Austral. of or relating to a large residential block of land, esp. in a rural area.

acrid (ˈækrɪd) adj 1 unpleasantly pungent or sharp to the smell or taste. 2 sharp or caustic, esp. in speech or nature. [C18: from L *ācer* sharp, sour; prob. infl. by ACID]
▸ **acridity** (əˈkrɪdɪtɪ) n ▸ ˈacridly adv

acridine (ˈækrɪˌdiːn) n a colourless crystalline solid used in the manufacture of dyes.

acriflavine (ˌækrɪˈfleɪvɪn) n a brownish or orange-red powder used in medicine as an antiseptic. [C20: from ACRIDINE + FLAVIN]

acriflavine hydrochloride n a red crystalline substance obtained from acriflavine and used as an antiseptic.

Acrilan (ˈækrɪˌlæn) n Trademark. an acrylic fibre or fabric, characterized by strength and resistance to creasing and used for clothing, carpets, etc.

acrimony (ˈækrɪmənɪ) n, pl **acrimonies.** bitterness or sharpness of manner, speech, temper, etc. [C16: from L *ācrimōnia*, from *ācer* sharp, sour]
▸ **acrimonious** (ˌækrɪˈməʊnɪəs) adj

acro- combining form. 1 denoting something at a height, top, beginning, or end: *acropolis*. 2 denoting an extremity of the human body: *acromegaly*. [from Gk *akros* extreme, topmost]

acrobat (ˈækrəˌbæt) n 1 an entertainer who performs acts that require skill, agility, and coordination, such as swinging from a trapeze or walking a tightrope. 2 a person noted for his frequent and rapid changes of position or allegiance. [C19: via F from Gk *akrobatēs*, one who walks on tiptoe, from ACRO- + *bat-*, from *bainein* to walk]
▸ ˌacroˈbatic adj ▸ ˌacroˈbatically adv

acrobatics (ˌækrəˈbætɪks) pl n 1 the skills or feats of an acrobat. 2 any activity requiring agility and skill: *mental acrobatics*.

acrogen (ˈækrədʒən) n any flowerless plant, such as a fern or moss, in which growth occurs from the tip of the main stem.
▸ **acrogenous** (əˈkrɒdʒɪnəs) adj

acromegaly (ˌækrəʊˈmegəlɪ) n a chronic disease characterized by enlargement of the bones of the head, hands,

and feet, and swelling and enlargement of soft tissue. It is caused by excessive secretion of growth hormone by the pituitary gland. [C19: from F *acromégalie*, from ACRO- + Gk *megal-*, stem of *megas* big]
▸ **acromegalic** (ˌækrəʊmɪˈgælɪk) adj, n

acronym (ˈækrənɪm) n a pronounceable name made from a series of initial letters or parts of a group of words; for example, *UNESCO* for the *United Nations Educational, Scientific, and Cultural Organization*. [C20: from ACRO- + -ONYM]

acrophobia (ˌækrəˈfəʊbɪə) n abnormal fear or dread of being at a great height. [C19: from ACRO- + -PHOBIA]
▸ ˌacroˈphobic adj, n

acropolis (əˈkrɒpəlɪs) n the citadel of an ancient Greek city. [C17: from Gk, from ACRO- + *polis* city]

Acropolis ★ (əˈkrɒpəlɪs) n the citadel of Athens on which the Parthenon stands.

across (əˈkrɒs) prep 1 from one side to the other side of. 2 on or at the other side of. 3 so as to transcend the boundaries or barriers of: *across religious divisions*. ◆ adv 4 from one side to the other. 5 on or to the other side. [C13 *on croice, acros*, from OF *a croix* crosswise]

across-the-board adj (**across the board** when postpositive) (of salary increases, taxation cuts, etc.) affecting all levels or classes equally.

acrostic (əˈkrɒstɪk) n a number of lines of writing, such as a poem, certain letters of which form a word, proverb, etc. A **single acrostic** is formed by the initial letters of the lines, a **double acrostic** by the initial and final letters, and a **triple acrostic** by the initial, middle, and final letters. [C16: via F from Gk, from ACRO- + *stikhos* line of verse]

acrylic (əˈkrɪlɪk) adj 1 of, derived from, or concerned with acrylic acid. ◆ n 2 short for **acrylic fibre, acrylic resin.** [C20: from L *ācer* sharp + *olēre* to smell + -IC]

acrylic acid n a colourless corrosive pungent liquid, used in the manufacture of acrylic resins. Formula: CH_2:CHCOOH. Systematic name: **propenoic acid.**

acrylic fibre n a man-made fibre used in blankets, knitwear, etc.

acrylic resin n any of a group of polymers of acrylic acid, its esters, or amides, used as synthetic rubbers, paints, and as plastics such as Perspex.

act (ækt) n 1 something done or performed. 2 the performance of some physical or mental process; action. 3 (cap. when part of a name) the formally codified result of deliberation by a legislative body. 4 (often pl) a formal written record of transactions, proceedings, etc., as of a society, committee, or legislative body. 5 a major division of a dramatic work. 6a a short performance of skill, a comic sketch, dance, etc. 6b those giving such a performance. 7 an assumed attitude or pose, esp. one intended to impress. 8 **get in on the act.** Inf. to become involved in a profitable situation in order to share in the benefit. 9 **get one's act together.** Inf. to organize oneself. ◆ vb 10 (intr) to do something. 11 (intr) to operate; react: *his mind acted quickly*. 12 to perform (a part or role) in a play, etc. 13 (tr) to present (a play, etc.) on stage. 14 (intr; usually foll. by *for* or *as*) to be a substitute (for). 15 (intr; foll. by *as*) to serve the function or purpose (of). 16 (intr) to conduct oneself or behave (as if one were): *she usually acts like a lady*. 17 (intr) to behave in an unnatural or affected way. 18 (copula) to play the part of: *to act the fool*. 19 (copula) to behave in a manner appropriate to: *to act one's age*. ◆ See also **act on, act up.** [C14: from L *actus* a doing, & *actum* a thing done, from the p.p. of *agere* to do]
▸ ˈactable adj ▸ ˌactaˈbility n

ACT abbrev. for: 1 Australian Capital Territory. 2 advance corporation tax.

Actaeon ★ (ækˈtiːən, ˈæktɪən) n Greek myth. a hunter of Boeotia who, having accidentally seen Artemis bathing, was turned into a stag and torn apart by his own hounds.

ACTH n adrenocorticotrophic hormone; a hormone, secreted by the anterior lobe of the pituitary gland, that stimulates growth of the adrenal gland. It is used in treating rheumatoid arthritis, allergic and skin diseases, etc.

acting (ˈæktɪŋ) adj (prenominal) 1 taking on duties tempo-

★ people and places

rarily, esp. as a substitute for another. **2** performing the duties of though not yet holding the rank of: *acting lieutenant*. **3** operating or functioning. **4** intended for stage performance; provided with directions for actors: *an acting version of "Hedda Gabler"*. ◆ *n* **5** the art or profession of an actor.

actinia (æk'tɪnɪə) *n, pl* **actiniae** (-'tɪnɪ,iː) *or* **actinias**. a sea anemone common in rock pools. [C18: NL, lit.: things having a radial structure]

actinic (æk'tɪnɪk) *adj* (of radiation) producing a photochemical effect. [C19: from ACTINO- + -IC]
▸ **ac'tinically** *adv* ▸ **'actin,ism** *n*

actinide series ('æktɪ,naɪd) *n* a series of 15 radioactive elements with increasing atomic numbers from actinium to lawrencium.

actinium (æk'tɪnɪəm) *n* a radioactive element of the actinide series, occurring as a decay product of uranium. It is used in neutron production. Symbol: Ac; atomic no.: 89; half-life of most stable isotope, ^{227}Ac: 22 years. [C19: NL, from ACTINO- + -IUM]

actino- *or before a vowel* **actin-** *combining form.* **1** indicating a radial structure: *actinomorphic*. **2** indicating radioactivity or radiation: *actinometer*. [from Gk, from *aktis* ray]

actinobiology (,æktɪnəʊbaɪ'ɒlədʒɪ) *n* the branch of biology concerned with the effects of radiation on living organisms.

actinoid ('æktɪ,nɔɪd) *adj* having a radiate form, as a sea anemone or starfish.

actinometer (,æktɪ'nɒmɪtə) *n* an instrument for measuring the intensity of radiation, esp. of the sun's rays.

actinomycin (,æktɪnəʊ'maɪsɪn) *n* any of several toxic antibiotics obtained from soil bacteria, used in treating some cancers.

actinozoan (,æktɪnəʊ'zəʊən) *n, adj* another word for **anthozoan**.

action ('ækʃən) *n* **1** the state or process of doing something or being active. **2** something done, such as an act or deed. **3** movement or posture during some physical activity. **4** activity, force, or energy: *a man of action.* **5** (*usually pl*) conduct or behaviour. **6** *Law.* a legal proceeding brought by one party against another; lawsuit. **7** the operating mechanism, esp. in a piano, gun, watch, etc. **8** the force applied to a body. **9** the way in which something operates or works. **10** **out of action.** not functioning. **11** the events that form the plot of a story, play, or other composition. **12** *Mil.* **12a** a minor engagement. **12b** fighting at sea or on land: *he saw action in the war.* **13** *Inf.* the profits of an enterprise or transaction (esp. in **a piece of the action**). **14** *Sl.* the main activity, esp. social activity. **15** short for **industrial action.** ◆ *vb* (*tr*) **16** to put into effect; take action concerning. ◆ *sentence substitute.* **17** a command given by a film director to indicate that filming is to begin. [C14 *accioun*, ult. from L *āctiōn-*, from *agere* to do]

actionable ('ækʃənəb°l) *adj Law.* affording grounds for legal action.
▸ **'actionably** *adv*

action committee *or* **group** *n* a committee or group formed to pursue an end, usually political, using petitions, marches, etc.

action painting *n* a development of abstract expressionism characterized by accidental effects of thrown, smeared, dripped, or spattered paint. Also called: **tachisme.**

action replay *n* the rerunning of a small section of a television film or tape of a match or other sporting contest, often in slow motion.

action stations *pl n* **1** *Mil.* the positions taken up by individuals in preparation for or during a battle. ◆ *sentence substitute.* **2** a command to take up such positions. **3** *Inf.* a warning to get ready for something.

Actium ★ ('æktɪəm) *n* a town of ancient Greece that overlooked the naval battle in 31 B.C. at which Octavian's fleet under Agrippa defeated that of Mark Antony and Cleopatra.

activate ('æktɪ,veɪt) *vb* **activates, activating, activated.** (*tr*) **1** to make active or capable of action. **2** *Physics.* to make ra-

dioactive. **3** *Chem.* to increase the rate of (a reaction). **4** to purify (sewage) by aeration. **5** *US mil.* to mobilize or organize (a unit).
▸ **,acti'vation** *n* ▸ **'acti,vator** *n*

activated carbon *n* a highly adsorptive form of carbon used to remove colour or impurities from liquids and gases.

activated sludge *n* a mass of aerated precipitated sewage added to untreated sewage to bring about purification by hastening bacterial decomposition.

active ('æktɪv) *adj* **1** moving, working, or doing something. **2** busy or involved: *an active life.* **3** physically energetic. **4** effective: *an active ingredient.* **5** *Grammar.* denoting a voice of verbs used to indicate that the subject of a sentence is performing the action or causing the event or process described by the verb, as *kicked* in *The boy kicked the football.* **6** being fully engaged in military service. **7** (of a volcano) erupting periodically; not extinct. **8** *Astron.* (of the sun) exhibiting a large number of sunspots, solar flares, etc., and a marked variation in intensity and frequency of radio emission. ◆ *n* **9** *Grammar.* **9a** the active voice. **9b** an active verb. [C14: from L *āctivus.* See ACT, -IVE]
▸ **'actively** *adv* ▸ **'activeness** *n*

active list *n Mil.* a list of officers available for full duty.

activism ('æktɪ,vɪzəm) *n* a policy of taking direct and often militant action to achieve an end, esp. a political or social one.
▸ **'activist** *n*

activity (æk'tɪvɪtɪ) *n, pl* **activities.** **1** the state or quality of being active. **2** lively action or movement. **3** any specific action, pursuit, etc.: *recreational activities.* **4** the number of disintegrations of a radioactive substance in a given unit of time. **5** *Chem.* a measure of the ability of a substance to take part in a chemical reaction.

act of God *n Law.* a sudden and inevitable occurrence caused by natural forces, such as a flood or earthquake.

act on *or* **upon** *vb* (*intr, prep*) **1** to regulate one's behaviour in accordance with (advice, information, etc.). **2** to have an effect on (illness, a part of the body, etc.).

actor ('æktə) *or* (*fem*) **actress** ('æktrɪs) *n* a person who acts in a play, film, broadcast, etc.

actual ('æktʃʊəl) *adj* **1** existing in reality or as a matter of fact. **2** real or genuine. **3** existing at the present time; current. ◆ See also **actuals.** [C14 *actuel* existing, from LL, from L *āctus* ACT]

> **USAGE NOTE** The excessive use of *actual* and *actually* should be avoided. They are unnecessary in sentences such as *in actual fact, he is forty-two,* and *he did actually go to the play but did not enjoy it.*

actual bodily harm *n Criminal law.* injury caused by one person to another that is less serious than grievous bodily harm. Abbrev.: **ABH.**

actuality (,æktʃʊ'ælɪtɪ) *n, pl* **actualities.** **1** true existence; reality. **2** (*sometimes pl*) a fact or condition that is real.

actualize *or* **actualise** ('æktʃʊə,laɪz) *vb* **actualizes, actualizing, actualized** *or* **actualises, actualising, actualised.** (*tr*) **1** to make actual or real. **2** to represent realistically.
▸ **,actuali'zation** *or* **,actuali'sation** *n*

actually ('æktʃʊəlɪ) *adv* **1a** as an actual fact; really. **1b** (*as sentence modifier*): *actually, I haven't seen him.* **2** at present.

actuals ('æktʃʊəlz) *pl n Commerce.* commodities that can be purchased and used, as opposed to those bought and sold in a futures market. Also called: **physicals.**

actuarius (,æktʃʊ'ɛərɪəs) *n S. African history.* an official of the synod of a Dutch Reformed Church. [from L; see ACTUARY]

actuary ('æktʃʊərɪ) *n, pl* **actuaries.** a person qualified to calculate commercial risks and probabilities involving uncertain future events, esp. in such contexts as life assurance. [C16 (meaning: registrar): from L *āctuārius* one who keeps accounts, from *actum* public business, & *acta* documents]
▸ **actuarial** (,æktʃʊ'ɛərɪəl) *adj*

actuate ('æktʃʊ,eɪt) *vb* **actuates, actuating, actuated.** (*tr*) **1** to put into action or mechanical motion. **2** to motivate: *actuated by unworthy desires.* [C16: from Med. L *actuātus*, from *actuāre* to incite to action, from L *āctus* ACT]
▶ ,actu'ation *n* ▶ 'actu,ator *n*

act up *vb* (*intr, adv*) *Inf.* to behave in a troublesome way: *the engine began to act up.*

acuity (ə'kjuːɪtɪ) *n* keenness or acuteness, esp. in vision or thought. [C15: from OF, from L *acūtus* ACUTE]

aculeus (ə'kjuːlɪəs) *n* **1** a prickle, such as the thorn of a rose. **2** a sting. [C19: from L, dim. of *acus* needle]
▶ a'culeate *adj*

acumen ('ækjʊ,mɛn, ə'kjuːmən) *n* the ability to judge well; insight. [C16: from L: sharpness, from *acuere* to sharpen]
▶ a'cuminous *adj*

acuminate *adj* (ə'kjuːmɪnɪt). **1** narrowing to a sharp point, as some types of leaf. ◆ *vb* (ə'kjuːmɪ,neɪt), **acuminates, acuminating, acuminated.** **2** (*tr*) to make pointed or sharp. [C17: from L *acūmināre* to sharpen]
▶ a,cumi'nation *n*

acupoint ('ækjʊ,pɔɪnt) *n* any of the specific points on the body into which a needle is inserted in acupuncture or onto which pressure is applied in shiatsu. [C19: from ACU(PUNCTURE) + POINT]

acupressure ('ækjʊ,prɛʃə) *n* another name for **shiatsu**. [C19: from ACU(PUNCTURE) + PRESSURE]

acupuncture ('ækjʊ,pʌŋktʃə) *n* the insertion of the tips of needles into the skin at specific points for the purpose of treating various disorders by stimulating nerve impulses. [C17: from L *acus* needle + PUNCTURE]
▶ 'acu,puncturist *n*

acute (ə'kjuːt) *adj* **1** penetrating in perception or insight. **2** sensitive to details; keen. **3** of extreme importance; crucial. **4** sharp or severe; intense. **5** having a sharp end or point. **6** *Maths.* (of an angle) less than 90°. **7** (of a disease) **7a** arising suddenly and manifesting intense severity. **7b** of relatively short duration. **8** *Phonetics.* of or relating to an accent (´) placed over vowels, denoting that the vowel is pronounced with higher musical pitch (as in ancient Greek) or with certain special quality (as in French). **9** (of a hospital, hospital bed, or ward) intended to accommodate short-term patients. ◆ *n* **10** an acute accent. [C14: from L *acūtus*, p.p. of *acuere* to sharpen, from *acus* needle]
▶ a'cutely *adv* ▶ a'cuteness *n*

acute accent *n* the diacritical mark (´), used in some languages to indicate that the vowel over which it is placed has a special quality (as in French *été*) or that it receives the strongest stress in the word (as in Spanish *hablé*).

acute dose *n* a fatal dose of radiation.

ad (æd) *n Inf.* short for **advertisement.**

A.D. *or* **AD** (indicating years numbered from the supposed year of the birth of Christ) *abbrev. for* anno Domini: *70* A.D. [L: in the year of the Lord]

> **USAGE NOTE** In strict usage, A.D. is only employed with specific years: *he died in 1621* A.D., but *he died in the 17th century* (and not *the 17th century* A.D.). Formerly the practice was to write A.D. preceding the date (A.D. *1621*), and it is also strictly correct to omit *in* when A.D. is used, since this is already contained in the meaning of the Latin *anno Domini* (in the year of Our Lord), but this is no longer general practice. B.C. is used with both specific dates and indications of the period: *Heraclitus was born about 540* B.C.; *the battle took place in the 4th century* B.C.

ad- *prefix* **1** to; towards: *adsorb.* **2** near; next to: *adrenal.* [from L: towards. As a prefix in words of L origin, *ad-* became *ac-, af-, ag-, al-, an-, acq-, ar-, as-,* and *at-* before *c, f, g, l, n, q, r, s,* and *t,* and became *a-* before *gn, sc, sp, st*]

adage ('ædɪdʒ) *n* a traditional saying that is accepted by many as true; proverb. [C16: via OF from L *adagium*; rel. to *āio* I say]

adagio (ə'dɑːdʒɪ,əʊ) *Music.* ◆ *adj, adv* **1** (to be performed) slowly. ◆ *n, pl* **adagios.** **2** a movement or piece to be performed slowly. [C18: It., from *ad* + *agio* ease]

Adam[1] ★ ('ædəm) *n* **1** *Bible.* the first man, created by God (Genesis 2–3). **2 not know (someone) from Adam.** to have no knowledge of or acquaintance with someone. **3 Adam's ale** *or* **wine.** water.

Adam[2] ★ ('ædəm) *n* **1** (*French* adã). **Adolphe** (adɔlf). 1803–56, French composer, best known for his ballet *Giselle* (1841). **2 Robert.** 1728–92, Scottish neoclassical architect and furniture designer. Assisted by his brother, **James,** 1730–94. ◆ *adj* **3** in the neoclassical style made popular by Robert Adam.

adamant ('ædəmənt) *adj* **1** unshakable in determination, purpose, etc.; inflexible. **2** unbreakable; impenetrable. ◆ *n* **3** any extremely hard substance. **4** a legendary stone said to be impenetrable. [OE: from L *adamas*, from Gk, lit.: unconquerable, from A-[1] + *daman* to conquer]
▶ ,ada'mantine *adj*

Adams[1] ★ ('ædəmz) *n* a mountain in SW Washington, in the Cascade Range. Height: 3751 m (12 307 ft).

Adams[2] ★ ('ædəmz) *n* **1 Ansel** ('ænsᵊl). 1902–84, US photographer. **2 Gerard,** known as **Gerry.** born 1948, Irish politician; president of Sinn Féin from 1983. **3 Henry (Brooks).** 1838–1918, US historian and writer. His works include *Mont Saint Michel et Chartres* (1913) and his autobiography *The Education of Henry Adams* (1918). **4 John.** 1735–1826, second president of the US (1797–1801); US ambassador to Great Britain (1785–88). **5 John Couch.** 1819–92, British astronomer who deduced the existence and position of the planet Neptune. **6 John Quincy,** son of John Adams. 1767–1848, sixth president of the US (1825–29); secretary of state (1817–25). **7 Richard.** born 1920, British author, noted for his novels *Watership Down* (1972), *The Plague Dogs* (1977), and *The Girl in a Swing* (1980). **8 Samuel.** 1722–1803, American revolutionary leader; one of the organizers of the Boston Tea Party; a signatory of the Declaration of Independence.

Adam's apple *n* the visible projection of the thyroid cartilage of the larynx at the front of the neck.

Adana ★ ('ædənə) *n* a city in S Turkey, capital of Adana province. Pop.: 1 047 300 (1994 est.). Also called: **Seyhan.**

adapt (ə'dæpt) *vb* **1** (often foll. by *to*) to adjust (someone or something) to different conditions. **2** (*tr*) to fit, change, or modify to suit a new or different purpose. [C17: from L *adaptāre*, from *ad-* + *aptāre* to fit]
▶ a'daptable *adj* ▶ a,dapta'bility *n* ▶ a'daptive *adj*

adaptation (,ædəp'teɪʃən) *n* **1** the act or process of adapting or the state of being adapted. **2** something that is produced by adapting something else. **3** something that is changed or modified to suit new conditions. **4** *Biol.* a modification in organisms that makes them better suited to survive and reproduce in a particular environment.

adaptor *or* **adapter** (ə'dæptə) *n* **1** a person or thing that adapts. **2** any device for connecting two parts, esp. ones that are of different sizes. **3a** a plug used to connect an electrical device to a mains supply when they have different types of terminals. **3b** a device used to connect several electrical appliances to a single socket.

ADC *abbrev. for:* **1** aide-de-camp. **2** analogue-digital converter.

add (æd) *vb* **1** to combine (two or more numbers or quantities) by addition. **2** (*tr;* foll. by *to*) to increase (a number or quantity) by another number or quantity using addition. **3** (*tr;* often foll. by *to*) to join (something) to something else in order to increase the size, effect, or scope: *to add insult to injury.* **4** (*intr;* foll. by *to*) to have an extra and increased effect (on). **5** (*tr*) to say or write further. **6** (*tr;* foll. by *in*) to include. ◆ See also **add up.** [C14: from L *addere,* from *ad-* to + *-dere, dare* to put]

ADD *abbrev. for* attention deficit disorder.

Addams ★ ('ædəmz) *n* **Jane.** 1860–1935, US social re-

> ★ people and places

former, feminist, and pacifist, who founded Hull House, a social settlement in Chicago: Nobel peace prize 1931.

addax ('ædæks) *n* a large light-coloured antelope having ribbed loosely spiralled horns and inhabiting desert regions in N Africa. [C17: L, from an unidentified ancient N African language]

addend ('ædɛnd) *n* any of a set of numbers that is to be added. [C20: short for ADDENDUM]

addendum (ə'dɛndəm) *n*, *pl* **addenda** (-də). **1** something added; an addition. **2** a supplement or appendix to a book, magazine, etc. [C18: from L, gerundive of *addere* to ADD]

adder ('ædə) *n* **1** Also called: **viper.** a common viper that is widely distributed in Europe, including Britain, and Asia and is dark grey with a black zigzag pattern along the back. **2** any of various similar venomous or nonvenomous snakes. ◆ See also **death adder, puff adder.** [OE *nǣdre* snake; in ME *a naddre* was mistaken for *an addre*]

adder's-tongue *n* any of several ferns that grow in the N hemisphere and have a narrow spore-bearing body that sticks out like a spike from the leaf.

addict *vb* (ə'dɪkt). **1** (*tr; usually passive; often foll. by to*) to cause (someone or oneself) to become dependent (on something, esp. a narcotic drug). ◆ *n* ('ædɪkt). **2** a person who is addicted, esp. to narcotic drugs. **3** *Inf.* a person devoted to something: *a jazz addict.* [C16 (as adj and as vb; n use C20): from L *addictus* given over, from *addīcere*, from *ad-* to + *dīcere* to say]
▸ **ad'diction** *n* ▸ **ad'dictive** *adj*

Addington ★ ('ædɪŋtən) *n* **Henry,** 1st Viscount Sidmouth. 1757–1844, British statesman; prime minister (1801–04) and Home Secretary (1812–21).

Addis Ababa ★ ('ædɪs 'æbəbə) *n* the capital of Ethiopia, on a central plateau 2400 m (8000 ft) above sea level: founded in 1887; became capital in 1896. Pop.: 2 316 400 (1994 est.).

Addison ★ ('ædɪs°n) *n* **Joseph.** 1672–1719, English essayist and poet who, with Richard Steele, founded *The Spectator* (1711–14) and contributed most of its essays, including the *de Coverley Papers.*

Addison's disease *n* a disease characterized by bronzing of the skin, anaemia, and extreme weakness, caused by underactivity of the adrenal glands. [C19: after Thomas *Addison* (1793–1860), E physician who identified it]

addition (ə'dɪʃən) *n* **1** the act, process, or result of adding. **2** a person or thing that is added or acquired. **3** a mathematical operation in which the sum of two numbers or quantities is calculated. Usually indicated by the symbol +. **4** *Obs.* a title. **5 in addition.** (*adv*) also; as well. **6 in addition to.** (*prep*) besides; as well as. [C15: from L *additiōn-*, from *addere* to ADD]
▸ **ad'ditional** *adj*

additionality (ə,dɪʃə'nælɪtɪ) *n* (in the European Union) the principle that the EU contributes to the funding of a project in a member country provided that the member country also contributes.

Additional Member System *n* a system of voting in which people vote separately for the candidate and the party of their choice. Parties are allocated extra seats if the number of constituencies they win does not reflect their overall share of the vote. See also **proportional representation.**

additive ('ædɪtɪv) *adj* **1** characterized or produced by addition. ◆ *n* **2** any substance added to something to improve it, prevent deterioration, etc. **3** short for **food additive.** [C17: from LL *additīvus*, from *addere* to ADD]

addle ('æd°l) *vb* **addles, addling, addled.** **1** to make or become confused or muddled. **2** to make or become rotten. ◆ *adj* **3** (*in combination*) indicating a confused or muddled state: *addle-brained.* [C18 (vb), back formation from *addled*, from C13 *addle* rotten, from OE *adela* filth]

add-on *n* a feature that can be added to a standard model or package to give increased benefits.

address (ə'drɛs) *n* **1** the conventional form by which the location of a building is described. **2** the written form of

this, as on a letter or parcel. **3** the place at which someone lives. **4** a speech or written communication, esp. one of a formal nature. **5** skilfulness or tact. **6** *Arch.* manner of speaking. **7** *Computing.* a number giving the location of a piece of stored information. **8** (*usually pl*) expressions of affection made by a man in courting a woman. ◆ *vb* (*tr*) **9** to mark (a letter, parcel, etc.) with an address. **10** to speak to, refer to in speaking, or deliver a speech to. **11** (used reflexively; foll. by *to*) **11a** to speak or write to. **11b** to apply oneself to: *he addressed himself to the task.* **12** to direct (a message, warning, etc.) to the attention of. **13** to adopt a position facing (the ball in golf, etc.). [C14 (in the sense: to make right, adorn) and C15 (in the modern sense: to direct words): via OF from Vulgar L *addrictiāre* (unattested), from L *ad-* to + *dīrectus* DIRECT]
▸ **ad'dresser** *or* **ad'dressor** *n*

addressee (,ædrɛ'siː) *n* a person or organization to whom a letter, etc., is addressed.

adduce (ə'djuːs) *vb* **adduces, adducing, adduced.** (*tr*) to cite (reasons, examples, etc.) as evidence or proof. [C15: from L *addūcere* to lead to]
▸ **ad'ducent** *adj* ▸ **ad'ducible** *adj* ▸ **adduction** (ə'dʌkʃən) *n*

adduct (ə'dʌkt) *vb* (*tr*) **1** (of a muscle) to draw or pull (a leg, arm, etc.) towards the median axis of the body. ◆ *n* **2** *Chem.* a compound formed by direct combination of two or more different compounds or elements. [C19: from L *addūcere*; see ADDUCE]
▸ **ad'duction** *n* ▸ **ad'ductor** *n*

add up *vb* (*adv*) **1** to find the sum (of). **2** (*intr*) to result in a correct total. **3** (*intr*) *Inf.* to make sense. **4** (*intr*; foll. by *to*) to amount to.

-ade *suffix forming nouns.* a sweetened drink made of various fruits: *lemonade.* [from F, from L *-āta* made of, fem p.p. of verbs ending in *-āre*]

Adelaide ★ ('ædɪ,leɪd) *n* the capital of South Australia: **Port Adelaide,** 11 km (7 miles) away on St Vincent Gulf, handles the bulk of exports. Pop.: 1 081 000 (1995 est.).

Aden ★ ('eɪd°n) *n* **1** the main port and commercial capital of Yemen, on the N coast of the **Gulf of Aden,** an arm of the Indian Ocean at the entrance to the Red Sea: capital of South Yemen until 1990: formerly an important port of call on shipping routes to the East. Pop.: 562 000 (1995 est.). **2** a former British colony and protectorate on the S coast of the Arabian Peninsula: became part of South Yemen in 1967, now part of Yemen. Area: 195 sq. km (75 sq. miles).

Adenauer ★ (*German* 'aːdənauər) *n* **Konrad** ('kɔnraːt). 1876–1967, German statesman; chancellor of West Germany (1949–63).

adenine ('ædənɪn) *n* a purine base present in animal and plant tissues as a constituent of the nucleic acids DNA and RNA.

adeno- *or before a vowel* **aden-** *combining form.* gland or glandular: *adenoid; adenology.* [NL, from Gk *adēn* gland]

adenoidal (,ædɪ'nɔɪd°l) *adj* **1** having the nasal tones or impaired breathing of one with enlarged adenoids. **2** of adenoids.

adenoids ('ædɪ,nɔɪdz) *pl n* a mass of lymphoid tissue at the back of the throat behind the uvula: when enlarged it often restricts nasal breathing, esp. in young children. [C19 : from Gk *adenoeidēs*. See ADENO-, -OID]

adenoma (,ædɪ'nəumə) *n*, *pl* **adenomas** *or* **adenomata** (-mətə). **1** a tumour occurring in glandular tissue. **2** a tumour having a glandlike structure.

adenopathy (,ædɪ'nɒpəθɪ) *n Pathol.* **1** enlargement of the lymph nodes. **2** enlargement of a gland.

adenosine (æ'dɛnə,siːn) *n Biochem.* a compound formed by the condensation of adenine and ribose. It is present in all living cells in a combined form. See also **ADP**[1], **AMP, ATP.** [C20: a blend of ADENINE + RIBOSE]

adept *adj* (ə'dɛpt). **1** proficient in something requiring skill or manual dexterity. **2** expert. ◆ *n* ('ædɛpt). **3** a person who is skilled or proficient in something. [C17: from Med. L *adeptus*, from L *adipiscī*, from *ad-* to + *apiscī* to attain]
▸ **a'deptness** *n*

adequate ('ædɪkwɪt) *adj* able to fulfil a need without being abundant, outstanding, etc.   [C17: from L *adaequāre*, from *ad-* to + *aequus* EQUAL]
▸ **adequacy** ('ædɪkwəsɪ) *n* ▸ **'adequately** *adv*

à deux *French.* (a dø) *adj, adv* of or for two persons.

ADFA *abbrev. for* Australian Defence Force Academy.

ADH *abbrev. for* antidiuretic hormone. See **vasopressin.**

adhere (əd'hɪə) *vb* **adheres, adhering, adhered.** (*intr*) **1** (usually foll. by *to*) to stick or hold fast. **2** (foll. by *to*) to be devoted (to a political party, religion, etc.). **3** (foll. by *to*) to follow exactly.   [C16: via Med. L, from L *adhaerēre* to stick to]

> **USAGE NOTE**   See at **adhesion.**

adherent (əd'hɪərənt) *n* **1** (usually foll. by *of*) a supporter or follower.   ♦ *adj* **2** sticking, holding fast, or attached.
▸ **ad'herence** *n*

adhesion (əd'hiːʒən) *n* **1** the quality or condition of sticking together or holding fast. **2** ability to make firm contact without slipping. **3** attachment, as to a political party, cause, etc. **4** an attraction or repulsion between the molecules of unlike substances in contact. **5** *Pathol.* abnormal union of structures or parts.   [C17: from L *adhaesiōn-* a sticking. See ADHERE]

> **USAGE NOTE**   *Adhesion* is the preferred term when talking about sticking or holding fast in a physical sense. *Adherence* is preferred when talking about attachment to a political party, cause, etc.

adhesive (əd'hiːsɪv) *adj* **1** able or designed to adhere: *adhesive tape.* **2** tenacious or clinging.   ♦ *n* **3** a substance used for sticking, such as glue or paste.
▸ **ad'hesively** *adv* ▸ **ad'hesiveness** *n*

ad hoc (æd 'hɒk) *adj, adv* for a particular purpose only: *an ad hoc committee.*   [L, lit.: to this]

ad hominem *Latin.* (æd 'hɒmɪˌnɛm) *adj, adv* directed against a person rather than his arguments.   [lit.: to the man]

adiabatic (ˌædɪə'bætɪk) *adj* **1** (of a thermodynamic process) taking place without loss or gain of heat.   ♦ *n* **2** a curve on a graph representing the changes in a system undergoing an adiabatic process.   [C19: from Gk, from A-[1] + *diabatos* passable]

Adie ★ ('eɪdɪ) *n* **Kathryn,** known as *Kate.* born 1945, British television journalist.

adieu (ə'djuː) *sentence substitute, n, pl* **adieus** *or* **adieux** (ə'djuːz). goodbye.   [C14: from OF, from *a* to + *dieu* God]

ad infinitum (æd ˌɪnfɪ'naɪtəm) *adv* without end; endlessly; to infinity. Abbrev.: **ad inf.**   [L]

ad interim (æd 'ɪntərɪm) *adj, adv* for the meantime: *ad interim measures.* Abbrev.: **ad int.**   [L]

adipocere (ˌædɪpəʊ'sɪə) *n* a waxlike fatty substance sometimes formed during the decomposition of corpses.   [C19: from NL *adiposus* fat + F *cire* wax]

adipose ('ædɪˌpəʊs) *adj* **1** of, resembling, or containing fat; fatty.   ♦ *n* **2** animal fat.   [C18: from NL *adiposus,* from L *adeps* fat]

Adirondack Mountains (ˌædɪ'rɒndæk) *or* **Adirondacks** ★ *pl n* a mountain range in NE New York State. Highest peak: Mount Marcy, 1629 m (5344 ft).

adit ('ædɪt) *n* an almost horizontal shaft into a mine, for access or drainage.   [C17: from L *aditus,* from *adīre,* from *ad-* towards + *īre* to go]

adj. *abbrev. for:* **1** adjective. **2** adjunct. **3** Also: **adjt.** adjutant.

adjacent (ə'dʒeɪsᵊnt) *adj* being near or close, esp. having a common boundary; contiguous.   [C15: from L *adjacēre,* from *ad-* near + *jacēre* to lie]
▸ **ad'jacency** *n* ▸ **ad'jacently** *adv*

adjacent angles *pl n* two angles having the same vertex and a side in common.

adjective ('ædʒɪktɪv) *n* **1a** a word imputing a characteristic to a noun or pronoun. **1b** (*as modifier*): *an adjective phrase.* Abbrev.: **adj.**   ♦ *adj* **2** additional or dependent.   [C14: from LL, from L from *adjicere,* from *ad-* to + *jacere* to throw]
▸ **adjectival** (ˌædʒɪk'taɪvᵊl) *adj*

adjoin (ə'dʒɔɪn) *vb* **1** to be next to (an area of land, etc.). **2** (*tr;* foll. by *to*) to join; attach.   [C14: via OF from L, from *ad-* to + *jungere* to join]
▸ **ad'joining** *adj*

adjourn (ə'dʒɜːn) *vb* **1** (*intr*) (of a court, etc.) to close at the end of a session. **2** to postpone or be postponed, esp. temporarily. **3** (*tr*) to put off (a problem, discussion, etc.) for later consideration. **4** (*intr*) *Inf.* to move elsewhere: *let's adjourn to the kitchen.*   [C14: from OF *ajourner* to defer to an arranged day, from *a-* to + *jour* day, from LL *diurnum,* from L *diēs* day]
▸ **ad'journment** *n*

adjudge (ə'dʒʌdʒ) *vb* **adjudges, adjudging, adjudged.** (*tr; usually passive*) **1** to pronounce formally; declare. **2a** to judge. **2b** to decree: *he was adjudged bankrupt.* **2c** to award (costs, damages, etc.). **3** *Arch.* to condemn.   [C14: via OF from L *adjūdicāre.* See ADJUDICATE]

adjudicate (ə'dʒuːdɪˌkeɪt) *vb* **adjudicates, adjudicating, adjudicated.** **1** (when *intr,* usually foll. by *upon*) to give a decision (on), esp. a formal or binding one. **2** (*intr*) to serve as a judge or arbiter, as in a competition.   [C18: from L *adjūdicāre,* from *ad-* to + *jūdicāre* to judge, from *jūdex* judge]
▸ **adˌjudiˈcation** *n* ▸ **adˈjudiˌcator** *n*

adjunct ('ædʒʌŋkt) *n* **1** something incidental or not essential that is added to something else. **2** a person who is subordinate to another. **3** *Grammar.* **3a** part of a sentence other than the subject or the predicate. **3b** a modifier.   ♦ *adj* **4** added or connected in a secondary position.   [C16: from L *adjunctus,* p.p. of *adjungere* to ADJOIN]
▸ **adjunctive** (ə'dʒʌŋktɪv) *adj* ▸ **'adjunctly** *adv*

adjure (ə'dʒʊə) *vb* **adjures, adjuring, adjured.** (*tr*) **1** to command, often by exacting an oath. **2** to appeal earnestly to.   [C14: from L *adjūrāre,* from *ad-* to + *jūrāre* to swear, from *jūs* oath]
▸ **adjuration** (ˌædʒʊə'reɪʃən) *n* ▸ **ad'juratory** *adj* ▸ **ad'jurer** *or* **ad'juror** *n*

adjust (ə'dʒʌst) *vb* **1** (*tr*) to alter slightly, esp. to achieve accuracy. **2** to adapt, as to a new environment, etc. **3** (*tr*) to put into order. **4** (*tr*) *Insurance.* to determine the amount payable in settlement of (a claim).   [C17: from OF *adjuster,* from *ad-* to + *juste* right, JUST]
▸ **ad'justable** *adj* ▸ **ad'juster** *n*

adjustment (ə'dʒʌstmənt) *n* **1** the act of adjusting or state of being adjusted. **2** a control for regulating.

adjutant ('ædʒətənt) *n* an officer who acts as administrative assistant to a superior officer.   [C17: from L *adjūtāre* to AID]
▸ **'adjutancy** *n*

adjutant bird *or* **stork** *n* either of two large carrion-eating storks which are similar to the marabou and occur in S and SE Asia. [so called for its supposedly military gait]

adjutant general *n, pl* **adjutants general. 1** *Brit. Army.* a member of the Army Board responsible for personnel and administrative functions. **2** *US Army.* the adjutant of a military unit with general staff.

adjuvant ('ædʒəvənt) *adj* **1** aiding or assisting.   ♦ *n* **2** something that aids or assists; auxiliary.   [C17: from L *adjuvāre,* from *juvāre* to help]

Adler ★ *n* **1** (*German* 'aːdlər). **Alfred** ('alfreːt). 1870–1937, Austrian psychiatrist, noted for his descriptions of inferiority feelings. **2** ('ædlə). **Larry,** full name *Lawrence Cecil Adler.* born 1914, US harmonica player.

Adlerian (æd'lɪərɪən) *adj* of or relating to the work of Alfred Adler.

ad-lib (æd'lɪb) *vb* **ad-libs, ad-libbing, ad-libbed. 1** to improvise and deliver spontaneously (a speech, etc.).   ♦ *adj* (**ad lib** *when predicative*) **2** improvised.   ♦ *adv* **ad lib. 3** spontaneously; freely.   ♦ *n* **4** an improvised performance, often humorous.   [C18: short for L *ad libitum,* lit.: according to pleasure]

> ★ people and places

ad libitum (ˌæd ˈlɪbɪtəm) *adv, adj Music.* at the performer's discretion. [L.: see AD-LIB]

Adm. *abbrev. for:* **1** Admiral. **2** Admiralty.

adman (ˈædˌmæn) *n, pl* **admen.** *Inf.* a man who works in advertising.

admass (ˈædmæs) *n* the section of the public that is susceptible to advertising, etc., and the processes involved in influencing them. [C20: from AD + MASS]

admeasure (ædˈmɛʒə) *vb* **admeasures, admeasuring, admeasured.** to measure out (land, etc.) as a share; apportion. [C14 *amesuren,* from OF, from *mesurer* to MEASURE; the modern form derives from AD- + MEASURE]

Admetus ★ (ædˈmiːtəs) *n Greek myth.* a king of Thessaly, one of the Argonauts, who was married to Alcestis.

admin (ˈædmɪn) *n Inf.* short for **administration.**

administer (ədˈmɪnɪstə) *vb* (*mainly tr*) **1** (*also intr*) to direct or control (the affairs of a business, etc.). **2** to dispense: *administer justice.* **3** (when *intr,* foll. by *to*) to give or apply (medicine, etc.). **4** to supervise the taking of (an oath, etc.). **5** to manage (an estate, property, etc.). [C14 *amynistre* via OF from L, from *ad-* to + *ministrāre* to MINISTER]

administrate (ədˈmɪnɪˌstreɪt) *vb* **administrates, administrating, administrated.** to manage or direct (the affairs of a business, institution, etc.).

administration (ədˌmɪnɪˈstreɪʃən) *n* **1** management of the affairs of an organization, such as a business or institution. **2** the duties of an administrator. **3** the body of people who administer an organization. **4** the conduct of the affairs of government. **5** term of office: used of governments, etc. **6** the government as a whole. **7** (*often cap.*) *Chiefly US.* the political executive, esp. of the US. **8** *Property law.* **8a** the conduct or disposal of the estate of a deceased person. **8b** the management by a trustee of an estate. **9a** the administering of something, such as a sacrament or medical treatment. **9b** the thing that is administered.
▶ ad'ministrative *adj* ▶ ad'ministratively *adv*

administration order *n Law.* **1** an order by a court appointing a person to manage a company that is in financial difficulty. **2** an order by a court for the administration of the estate of a debtor who has been ordered by the court to pay money that he owes.

administrator (ədˈmɪnɪˌstreɪtə) *n* **1** a person who administers the affairs of an organization, official body, etc. **2** *Property law.* a person authorized to manage an estate.

admirable (ˈædmərəbᵊl) *adj* deserving or inspiring admiration; excellent.
▶ 'admirably *adv*

admiral (ˈædmərəl) *n* **1** the supreme commander of a fleet or navy. **2** Also called: **admiral of the fleet, fleet admiral.** a naval officer of the highest rank. **3** a senior naval officer entitled to fly his own flag. See also **rear admiral, vice admiral.** **4** *Chiefly Brit.* the master of a fishing fleet. **5** any of various brightly coloured butterflies, esp. the red admiral or white admiral. [C13 *amyral,* from OF *amiral* emir, & from Med. L *admīrālis* (spelling prob. infl. by *admīrābilis* admirable; both from Ar. *amīr* emir, commander, esp. in *amīr-al* commander of]
▶ 'admiralship *n*

admiralty (ˈædmərəltɪ) *n, pl* **admiralties. 1** the office or jurisdiction of an admiral. **2** jurisdiction over naval affairs.

Admiralty Board *n* **the.** a department of the British Ministry of Defence, responsible for the administration of the Royal Navy.

Admiralty House *n* the official residence of the Governor General of Australia, in Sydney.

Admiralty Islands ★ *pl n* a group of about 40 volcanic and coral islands in the SW Pacific, part of Papua New Guinea, in the Bismarck Archipelago: main island: Manus. Pop.: 35 200 (1995). Area: about 2000 sq. km (800 sq. miles). Also called: **Admiralties.**

Admiralty Range ★ *n* a mountain range in Antarctica, on the coast of Victoria Land, northwest of the Ross Sea.

admiration (ˌædməˈreɪʃən) *n* **1** pleasurable contemplation or surprise. **2** a person or thing that is admired.

admire (ədˈmaɪə) *vb* **admires, admiring, admired.** (*tr*) **1** to regard with esteem, approval, or pleased surprise. **2** *Arch.* to wonder at. [C16: from L *admīrārī,* from *ad-* to, at + *mīrārī* to wonder]
▶ ad'mirer *n* ▶ ad'miring *adj* ▶ ad'miringly *adv*

admissible (ədˈmɪsəbᵊl) *adj* **1** able or deserving to be considered or allowed. **2** deserving to be allowed to enter. **3** *Law.* (esp. of evidence) capable of being admitted in a court of law.
▶ ad,missi'bility *n*

admission (ədˈmɪʃən) *n* **1** permission to enter or the right to enter. **2** the price charged for entrance. **3** acceptance for a position, etc. **4** a confession, as of a crime, etc. **5** an acknowledgment of the truth of something. [C15: from L *admissiōn-,* from *admittere* to ADMIT]
▶ ad'missive *adj*

admit (ədˈmɪt) *vb* **admits, admitting, admitted.** (*mainly tr*) **1** (*may take a clause as object*) to confess or acknowledge (a crime, mistake, etc.). **2** (*may take a clause as object*) to concede (the truth of something). **3** to allow to enter. **4** (foll. by *to*) to allow participation (in) or the right to be part (of). **5** (when *intr,* foll. by *of*) to allow (of). [C14: from L *admittere,* from *ad-* to + *mittere* to send]

admittance (ədˈmɪtᵊns) *n* **1** the right or authority to enter. **2** the act of giving entrance. **3** *Electricity.* the reciprocal of impedance.

admittedly (ədˈmɪtɪdlɪ) *adv* (*sentence modifier*) willingly conceded: *admittedly I am afraid.*

admix (ədˈmɪks) *vb* (*tr*) *Rare.* to mix or blend. [C16: back formation from obs. *admixt,* from L *admīscēre* to mix with]

admixture (ədˈmɪkstʃə) *n* **1** a less common word for **mixture. 2** an ingredient.

admonish (ədˈmɒnɪʃ) *vb* (*tr*) **1** to reprove firmly but not harshly. **2** to warn; caution. [C14: via OF from Vulgar L *admonestāre* (unattested), from L *admonēre,* from *monēre* to advise]
▶ **admonition** (ˌædməˈnɪʃən) *n* ▶ ad'monitory *adj*

ad nauseam (æd ˈnɔːzɪˌæm) *adv* to a disgusting extent. [L: to (the point of) nausea]

ado (əˈduː) *n* bustling activity; fuss; bother; delay (esp. in *without more ado,* *with much ado*). [C14: from *at do* a to-do, from ON *at* (marking the infinitive) + DO[1]]

adobe (əˈdəʊbɪ) *n* **1** a sun-dried brick used for building. **2** a building constructed of such bricks. **3** the clayey material from which such bricks are made. [C19: from Sp.]

adolescence (ˌædəˈlɛsəns) *n* the period in human development that occurs between the beginning of puberty and adulthood. [C15: via OF from L, from *adolēscere* to grow up]

adolescent (ˌædəˈlɛsᵊnt) *adj* **1** of or relating to adolescence. **2** *Inf.* behaving in an immature way. ◆ *n* **3** an adolescent person.

Adonai ★ (ˌædɒˈnaɪ, -ˈneɪaɪ) *n Judaism.* a name for God. [C15: from Heb.: lord; cf. ADONIS]

Adonis ★ (əˈdəʊnɪs) *n* **1** *Greek myth.* a handsome youth loved by Aphrodite. **2** a handsome young man. [C16: from L via Gk from Phoenician *adōni* my lord; rel. to Heb. *Adonai* Lord]

adopt (əˈdɒpt) *vb* (*tr*) **1** *Law.* to take (another's child) as one's own child. **2** to choose and follow (a plan, method, etc.). **3** to take over (an idea, etc.) as if it were one's own. **4** to assume: *to adopt a title.* **5** to accept (a report, etc.). [C16: from L *adoptāre,* from *optāre* to choose]
▶ ,adop'tee *n* ▶ a'doption *n*

adopted (əˈdɒptɪd) *adj* having been adopted.

adoptive (əˈdɒptɪv) *adj* **1** acquired or related by adoption: *an adoptive father.* Cf. **adopted. 2** of or relating to adoption.

adorable (əˈdɔːrəbᵊl) *adj* **1** very attractive; lovable. **2** *Becoming rare.* deserving adoration.
▶ a'dorably *adv*

adoration (ˌædəˈreɪʃən) *n* **1** deep love or esteem. **2** the act of worshipping.

adore (əˈdɔː) *vb* **adores, adoring, adored. 1** (*tr*) to love intensely or deeply. **2** to worship (a god) with religious

rites. **3** (*tr*) *Inf.* to like very much. [C15: via F from L *adōrāre*, from *ad-* to + *ōrāre* to pray]
▸ **a'dorer** *n* ▸ **a'doring** *adj* ▸ **a'doringly** *adv*

adorn (ə'dɔːn) *vb* (*tr*) **1** to decorate. **2** to increase the beauty, distinction, etc., of. [C14: via OF from L *adōrnāre*, from *ōrnāre* to furnish]
▸ **a'dornment** *n*

Adowa ★ ('ɑːdɪ,wɑː) *n* a variant spelling of **Aduwa**.

ADP *n Biochem.* adenosine diphosphate; a substance derived from ATP with the liberation of energy that is then used in the performance of muscular work.

Adrastus ★ (ə'dræstəs) *n Greek myth.* a king of Argos and leader of the Seven against Thebes of whom he was the sole survivor.

ad rem *Latin.* (æd 'rɛm) *adj, adv* to the point; without digression.

adrenal (ə'driːnᵊl) *adj* **1** on or near the kidneys. **2** of or relating to the adrenal glands or their secretions. ◆ *n* **3** an adrenal gland. [C19: from AD- (near) + RENAL]

adrenal gland *n* an endocrine gland at the anterior end of each kidney. It secretes adrenaline. Also called: **suprarenal gland.**

adrenaline *or* **adrenalin** (ə'drɛnəlɪn) *n* a hormone that is secreted by the adrenal medulla in response to stress and increases heart rate, pulse rate, and blood pressure. It is extracted from animals or synthesized for medical use. US name: **epinephrine.**

Adrian IV ★ *n* original name *Nicholas Breakspear.* ?1100–59, the only English pope (1154–59).

Adrianople (,eɪdrɪə'nəʊpᵊl) *or* **Adrianopolis** ★ (,eɪdrɪə'nɒpəlɪs) *n* former names of **Edirne.**

Adriatic (,eɪdrɪ'ætɪk) *adj* **1** of or relating to the Adriatic Sea, or to the inhabitants of its coast or islands. ◆ *n* **2** the. short for the **Adriatic Sea.**

Adriatic Sea ★ *n* an arm of the Mediterranean between Italy and the Balkan Peninsula.

adrift (ə'drɪft) *adj* (*postpositive*), *adv* **1** floating without steering or mooring; drifting. **2** without purpose; aimless. **3** *Inf.* off course.

adroit (ə'drɔɪt) *adj* **1** skilful or dexterous. **2** quick in thought or reaction. [C17: from F *à droit* rightly]
▸ **a'droitly** *adv* ▸ **a'droitness** *n*

adsorb (əd'sɔːb) *vb* to undergo or cause to undergo a process in which a substance, usually a gas, accumulates on the surface of a solid forming a thin film. [C19: AD- + -*sorb* as in ABSORB]
▸ **ad'sorbable** *adj* ▸ **ad'sorbent** *adj* ▸ **ad'sorption** *n*

adsorbate (əd'sɔːbeɪt) *n* a substance that has been or is to be adsorbed.

ADT (in the US and Canada) *abbrev.* for Atlantic Daylight Time.

adulate ('ædjʊ,leɪt) *vb* **adulates, adulating, adulated.** (*tr*) to flatter or praise obsequiously. [C17: back formation from C15 *adulation*, from L *adūlāri* to flatter]
▸ **,adu'lation** *n* ▸ **'adu,lator** *n* ▸ **adulatory** (,ædjʊ'leɪtərɪ) *adj*

adult ('ædʌlt, ə'dʌlt) *adj* **1** having reached maturity; fully developed. **2** of or intended for mature people: *adult education.* **3** suitable only for adults because of being pornographic. ◆ *n* **4** a person who has attained maturity. **5** a mature fully grown animal or plant. **6** *Law.* a person who has attained the age of legal majority. [C16: from L *adultus*, from *adolēscere* to grow up]
▸ **a'dulthood** *n*

adulterant (ə'dʌltərənt) *n* **1** a substance that adulterates. ◆ *adj* **2** adulterating.

adulterate *vb* (ə'dʌltə,reɪt), **adulterates, adulterating, adulterated.** **1** (*tr*) to debase by adding inferior material: *to adulterate milk with water.* ◆ *adj* (ə'dʌltərɪt). **2** debased or impure. [C16: from L *adulterāre* to corrupt, commit adultery, prob. from *alter* another]
▸ **a,dulter'ation** *n* ▸ **a'dulter,ator** *n*

adulterer (ə'dʌltərə) *or* (*fem*) **adulteress** *n* a person who has committed adultery. [C16: orig. also *adulter*, from L *adulter*, back formation from *adulterāre* to ADULTERATE]

adulterous (ə'dʌltərəs) *adj* of, characterized by, or inclined to adultery.
▸ **a'dulterously** *adv*

adultery (ə'dʌltərɪ) *n, pl* **adulteries.** voluntary sexual intercourse between a married man or woman and a partner other than the legal spouse. [C15 *adulterie*, altered from C14 *avoutrie*, via OF from L *adulterium*, from *adulter*, back formation from *adulterāre*. See ADULTERATE]

adumbrate ('ædʌm,breɪt) *vb* **adumbrates, adumbrating, adumbrated.** (*tr*) **1** to outline; give a faint indication of. **2** to foreshadow. **3** to obscure. [C16: from L *adumbrāre* to cast a shadow on, from *umbra* shadow]
▸ **,adum'bration** *n* ▸ **adumbrative** (æd'ʌmbrətɪv) *adj*

Aduwa *or* **Adowa** ★ ('ɑːdʊ,wɑː) *n* a town in N Ethiopia: Emperor Menelik II defeated the Italians here in 1896. Pop.: 17 476 (1989 est.). Italian name: **Adua** (a'dua).

adv. *abbrev. for:* **1** adverb. **2** adverbial. **3** adversus. [L: against] **4** advertisement. **5** advocate.

ad valorem (æd və'lɔːrəm) *adj, adv* (of taxes) in proportion to the estimated value of the goods taxed. Abbrev.: **ad val., a.v., A/V.** [from L]

advance (əd'vɑːns) *vb* **advances, advancing, advanced.** **1** to go or bring forward in position. **2** (foll. by *on*) to move (towards) in a threatening manner. **3** (*tr*) to present for consideration. **4** to improve; further. **5** (*tr*) to cause (an event) to occur earlier. **6** (*tr*) to supply (money, goods, etc.) beforehand, either for a loan or as an initial payment. **7** to increase (a price, etc.) or (of a price, etc.) to be increased. **8** (*intr*) to be promoted. ◆ *n* **9** forward movement; progress in time or space. **10** improvement; progress in development. **11** *Commerce.* **11a** the supplying of commodities or funds before receipt of an agreed consideration. **11b** the commodities or funds supplied in this manner. **12** Also called: **advance payment.** a money payment made before it is legally due: *this is an advance on your salary.* **13** a loan of money. **14** an increase in price, etc. **15 in advance.** beforehand: *payment in advance.* **15b** (foll. by *of*) ahead in time or development: *ideas in advance of the time.* **16** (*modifier*) forward in position or time: *advance booking.* ◆ See also **advances.** [C15 *advauncen*, altered from C13 *avauncen*, via OF from L *abante*, from *ab-* away + *ante* before]
▸ **ad'vancer** *n*

advance corporation tax *n* a British tax in which a company paying a dividend must deduct the basic rate of income tax from the grossed-up value of the dividend and pay it to the Inland Revenue. Abbrev.: **ACT.**

advanced (əd'vɑːnst) *adj* **1** being ahead in development, knowledge, progress, etc. **2** having reached a comparatively late stage: *a man of advanced age.* **3** ahead of the times.

advanced gas-cooled reactor *n* a nuclear reactor using carbon dioxide as the coolant, and ceramic uranium dioxide cased in stainless steel as the fuel. Abbrev.: **AGR.**

advance directive *n* another name for **living will.**

Advanced level *n* a formal name for **A level.**

advancement (əd'vɑːnsmənt) *n* **1** promotion in rank, status, etc. **2** a less common word for **advance** (senses 9, 10).

advances (əd'vɑːnsɪz) *pl n* (*sometimes sing; often foll. by to or towards*) overtures made in an attempt to become friendly, etc.

advantage (əd'vɑːntɪdʒ) *n* **1** (often foll. by *over* or *of*) a more favourable position; superiority. **2** benefit or profit (esp. **in** *to one's advantage*). **3** *Tennis.* the point scored after deuce. **4 take advantage of. 4a** to make good use of. **4b** to impose upon the weakness, good nature, etc., of. **4c** to seduce. **5 to advantage.** to good effect. ◆ *vb* **advantages, advantaging, advantaged. 6** (*tr*) to put in a better position; favour. [C14 *avantage* (later altered to *advantage*), from OF *avant* before, from L *abante* from before. See ADVANCE]

advantageous (,ædvən'teɪdʒəs) *adj* producing advantage.
▸ **,advan'tageously** *adv*

advection (əd'vɛkʃən) *n* the transference of heat energy in a horizontal stream of gas, esp. of air. [C20: from L *advectiō*, from *advehere*, from *ad-* to + *vehere* to carry]

★ people and places

dvent ('ædvɛnt, -vənt) *n* an arrival or coming, esp. one which is awaited. [C12: from L *adventus*, from *advenīre*, from *ad-* to + *venīre* to come]

Advent ('ædvɛnt) *n* the season including the four Sundays preceding Christmas.

Advent calendar *n* a large card with small numbered doors for children to open on each of the days of Advent, revealing pictures beneath them.

Adventist ('ædvɛntɪst) *n* a member of a Christian group that holds that the Second Coming of Christ is imminent.

dventitious (ˌædvɛn'tɪʃəs) *adj* 1 added or appearing accidentally. 2 (of a plant or animal part) developing in an abnormal position. [C17: from L *adventīcius* coming from outside, from *adventus* a coming]
▸ ˌadven'titiously *adv*

dventure (əd'vɛntʃə) *n* 1 a risky undertaking of unknown outcome. 2 an exciting or unexpected event or course of events. 3 a hazardous financial operation.
◆ *vb* **adventures, adventuring, adventured.** 4 to take a risk or put at risk. 5 (*intr*; foll. by *into, on,* or *upon*) to dare to enter (into a place, dangerous activity, etc.). 6 to dare to say (something): *he adventured his opinion.* [C13 *aventure* (later altered to *adventure*), via OF ult. from L *advenīre* to happen to (someone), arrive]

adventure playground *n Brit.* a playground for children that contains building materials, etc., used to build with, climb on, etc.

adventurer (əd'vɛntʃərə) *or* (*fem*) **adventuress** *n* 1 a person who seeks adventure, esp. one who seeks success or money through daring exploits. 2 a person who seeks money or power by unscrupulous means. 3 a speculator.

adventurism (əd'vɛntʃəˌrɪzəm) *n* recklessness, esp. in politics and finance.
▸ ad'venturist *n*

adventurous (əd'vɛntʃərəs) *adj* 1 Also: **adventuresome.** daring or enterprising. 2 dangerous; involving risk.

adverb ('ædˌvɜːb) *n* a a word or group of words that serves to modify a whole sentence, a verb, another adverb, or an adjective; for example, *easily, very,* and *happily* respectively in the sentence *They could easily envy the very happily married couple.* b (*as modifier*): *an adverb marker.* Abbrev.: **adv.** [C15–C16: from L *adverbium* adverb, lit.: added word]
▸ ad'verbial *adj*

adversarial (ˌædvɜː'sɛərɪəl) *adj* (of political parties) hostile to and opposing each other on party lines; antagonistic.

adversary ('ædvəsəri) *n, pl* **adversaries.** 1 a person or group that is hostile to someone. 2 an opposing contestant in a sport. [C14: from L *adversārius,* from *adversus* against]

adversative (əd'vɜːsətɪv) *Grammar.* ◆ *adj* 1 (of a word, phrase, or clause) implying opposition. *But* and *although* are adversative conjunctions. ◆ *n* 2 an adversative word or speech element.

adverse ('ædvɜːs) *adj* 1 antagonistic; hostile: *adverse criticism.* 2 unfavourable to one's interests: *adverse circumstances.* 3 contrary or opposite: *adverse winds.* [C14: from L *adversus,* from *advertere,* from *ad-* towards + *vertere* to turn]
▸ ad'versely *adv* ▸ ad'verseness *n*

adversity (əd'vɜːsɪtɪ) *n, pl* **adversities.** 1 distress; affliction; hardship. 2 an unfortunate event.

advert[1] (əd'vɜːt) *vb* (*intr*; foll. by *to*) to draw attention (to). [C15: from L *advertere* to turn one's attention to]

advert[2] ('ædvɜːt) *n Brit. inf.* short for **advertisement.**

advertise *or US* (*sometimes*) **advertize** ('ædvəˌtaɪz) *vb* **advertises, advertising, advertised** *or US* (*sometimes*) **advertizes, advertizing, advertized.** 1 to present or praise (goods, a service, etc.) to the public, esp. in order to encourage sales. 2 to make (a vacancy, article for sale, etc.) publicly known: *to advertise a job.* 3 (*intr*; foll. by *for*) to make a public request (for): *she advertised for a cook.* [C15: from OF *avertir,* ult. from L *advertere* to turn one's attention to. See ADVERSE]
▸ 'adverˌtiser *or US* (*sometimes*) 'adverˌtizer *n*

advertisement *or US* (*sometimes*) **advertizement** (əd'vɜːtɪsmənt) *n* any public notice, as a printed display in a newspaper, short film on television, etc., designed to sell goods, publicize an event, etc.

advertising *or US* (*sometimes*) **advertizing** ('ædvəˌtaɪzɪŋ) *n* 1 the promotion of goods or services for sale through impersonal media such as television. 2 the business that specializes in creating such publicity. 3 advertisements collectively.

Advertising Standards Authority *n* (in Britain) an independent body set up by the advertising industry to ensure that all advertisements comply with the British Code of Advertising Practice. Abbrev.: **ASA.**

advertorial (ˌædvɜː'tɔːrɪəl) *n* 1 advertising presented under the guise of editorial material. ◆ *adj* 2 presented in such a manner. [C20: from blend of ADVERT[2] + EDITORIAL]

advice (əd'vaɪs) *n* 1 recommendation as to appropriate choice of action. 2 (*sometimes pl*) formal notification of facts. [C13 *avis* (later *advise*), via OF from Vulgar L, from L *ad* to + *vīsum* view]

advisable (əd'vaɪzəb°l) *adj* worthy of recommendation; prudent.
▸ ad'visably *adv* ▸ adˌvisa'bility *or* ad'visableness *n*

advise (əd'vaɪz) *vb* **advises, advising, advised.** (*when tr, may take a clause as object or an infinitive*) 1 to offer advice (to a person or persons): *he advised caution.* 2 (*tr*; sometimes foll. by *of*) to inform or notify. 3 (*intr*; foll. by *with*) *Chiefly US, obs.* in Britain. to consult. [C14: via OF from Vulgar L *advīsāre* (unattested), from L *ad-* to + *vidēre* to see]

advised (əd'vaɪzd) *adj* resulting from deliberation. See also **ill-advised, well-advised.**
▸ **advisedly** (əd'vaɪzɪdlɪ) *adv*

adviser *or* **advisor** (əd'vaɪzə) *n* 1 a person who advises. 2 *Education.* a person responsible for advising students on career guidance, etc. 3 *Brit. education.* a subject specialist who advises on current teaching methods and facilities.

advisory (əd'vaɪzərɪ) *adj* 1 empowered to make recommendations: *an advisory body.* ◆ *n, pl* **advisories.** 2 a statement issued to give advice, recommendations, or a warning: *a travel advisory.* 3 a person or organization with an advisory function: *the Prime Minister's media advisory.*

advocaat ('ædvəuˌkɑː) *n* a liqueur having a raw egg base. [C20: Du.]

advocacy ('ædvəkəsɪ) *n, pl* **advocacies.** active support, esp. of a cause.

advocate *vb* ('ædvəˌkeɪt), **advocates, advocating, advocated.** 1 (*tr; may take a clause as object*) to support or recommend publicly. ◆ *n* ('ædvəkɪt). 2 a person who upholds or defends a cause. 3 a person who intercedes on behalf of another. 4 a person who pleads his client's cause in a court of law. 5 *Scots Law.* the usual word for **barrister.** [C14: via OF from L *advocātus* legal witness, from *advocāre,* from *vocāre* to call]

advowson (əd'vauz°n) *n English ecclesiastical law.* the right of presentation to a vacant benefice. [C13: via OF from L *advocātiōn-,* from *advocāre* to summon]

advt *abbrev. for* advertisement.

Adygei Republic (ˌɑːdɪ'geɪ) *or* **Adygea ★** (ˌɑːdɪ'geɪə; *Russian* adɪ'geja) *n* a constituent republic of SW Russia, bordering on the Caucasus Mountains: chiefly agricultural but with some mineral resources. Capital: Maikop. Pop.: 450 000 (1995 est.). Area: 7600 sq. km (2934 sq. miles).

adze *or US* **adz** (ædz) *n* a hand tool with a steel blade attached at right angles to a wooden handle, used for dressing timber. [OE *adesa*]

Adzhar Autonomous Republic (ə'dʒɑː) *or* **Adzharia ★** (ə'dʒɑːrɪə) *n* an administrative division of SW Georgia, on the Black Sea: part of Turkey from the 17th century until 1878; mostly mountainous, reaching 2805 m (9350 ft), with a subtropical coastal strip. Capital: Batumi. Pop.: 386 700 (1993 est.). Area: 3000 sq. km (1160 sq. miles).

★ people and places

AEA (in Britain) *abbrev. for* Atomic Energy Authority.

AEC (in the US) *abbrev. for* Atomic Energy Commission.

aedes (eɪˈiːdiːz) *n* a mosquito of tropical and subtropical regions which transmits yellow fever. [C20: NL, from Gk *aēdēs* unpleasant, from A-¹ + *ēdos* pleasant]

aedile *or US (sometimes)* **edile** (ˈiːdaɪl) *n* a magistrate of ancient Rome in charge of public works, games, buildings, and roads. [C16: from L *aedīlis*, from *aedēs* a building]

Aeëtes ★ (iːˈiːtiːz) *n Greek myth.* a king of Colchis, father of Medea and keeper of the Golden Fleece.

AEEU (in Britain) *abbrev. for* Amalgamated Engineering and Electrical Union.

Aegean (iːˈdʒiːən) *adj* of or relating to the Aegean Sea or Islands.

Aegean Islands ★ *pl n* the islands of the Aegean Sea, including the Cyclades, Dodecanese, Euboea, and Sporades. The majority are under Greek administration.

Aegean Sea ★ *n* an arm of the Mediterranean between Greece and Turkey.

Aegeus ★ (iːˈdʒiːuːs, ˈiːdʒɪəs) *n Greek myth.* an Athenian king and father of Theseus.

Aegina ★ (iːˈdʒaɪnə) *n* **1** an island in the Aegean Sea, in the Saronic Gulf. Area: 85 sq. km (33 sq. miles). **2** a town on the coast of this island: a city-state of ancient Greece. **3 Gulf of.** another name for the **Saronic Gulf.** ◆ Greek name: **Aíyina.**

Aegir ★ (ˈiːdʒɪə) *n Norse myth.* the god of the sea.

aegis *or US (sometimes)* **egis** (ˈiːdʒɪs) *n* **1** sponsorship or protection (esp. in **under the aegis of**). **2** *Greek myth.* the shield of Zeus. [C18: from L, from Gk *aigis* shield of Zeus]

Aegisthus ★ (iːˈdʒɪsθəs) *n Greek myth.* a cousin to and the murderer of Agamemnon, whose wife Clytemnestra he had seduced. He usurped the kingship of Mycenae until Orestes, Agamemnon's son, returned home and killed him.

Aegospotami ★ (ˌiːɡəsˈpɒtəˌmaɪ) *n* a river of ancient Thrace that flowed into the Hellespont. At its mouth the Spartan fleet under Lysander defeated the Athenians in 405 B.C., ending the Peloponnesian War.

aegrotat (ˈaɪɡrəʊˌtæt, ˈiː-) *n* **1** (in British and certain other universities, and, sometimes, schools) a certificate allowing a candidate to pass an examination although he has missed all or part of it through illness. **2** a degree or other qualification obtained in such circumstances. [C19: L, lit.: he is ill]

Ælfric ★ (ˈælfrɪk) *n* called *Grammaticus.* ?955–?1020, English abbot, writer, and grammarian.

-aemia, -haemia, *or US* **-emia, -hemia** *n combining form.* denoting blood, esp. a specified condition of the blood in diseases: *leukaemia.* [NL, from Gk, from *haima* blood]

Aeneas ★ (ɪˈniːəs) *n Classical myth.* a Trojan prince, the son of Anchises and Aphrodite, who escaped the sack of Troy and sailed to Italy via Carthage and Sicily. After seven years, he and his followers established themselves near the site of the future Rome.

Aeneid (ɪˈniːɪd) *n* an epic poem in Latin by Virgil relating the experiences of Aeneas after the fall of Troy.

aeolian harp (iːˈəʊlɪən) *n* a stringed instrument that produces a musical sound when wind passes over the strings. Also called: **wind harp.** [after AEOLUS]

Aeolian Islands ★ *pl n* another name for the **Lipari Islands.**

Aeolis (ˈiːəlɪs) *or* **Aeolia** ★ (iːˈəʊlɪə) *n* the ancient name for the coastal region of NW Asia Minor, including the island of Lesbos, settled by the Aeolian Greeks (about 1000 B.C.).

aeolotropic (ˌiːələʊˈtrɒpɪk) *adj* a less common word for **anisotropic.** [C19: from Gk *aiolos* fickle + -TROPIC] ► **aeolotropy** (ˌiːəˈlɒtrəpɪ) *n*

Aeolus ★ (ˈiːələs, iːˈəʊləs) *n Greek myth.* **1** the god of the winds. **2** the founding king of the Aeolians in Thessaly.

aeon *or esp. US* **eon** (ˈiːən, ˈiːɒn) *n* **1** an immeasurably long period of time. **2** *Astron.* a period of one thousand million years. [C17: from Gk *aiōn* an infinitely long time]

aerate (ˈɛəreɪt) *vb* **aerates, aerating, aerated.** (*tr*) **1** to charge (a liquid) with a gas, as in the manufacture of effervescent drink. **2** to expose to the action or circulation of the air.
► **aerˈation** *n* ► **ˈaerator** *n*

aeri- *combining form.* a variant of **aero-**.

aerial (ˈɛərɪəl) *adj* **1** of or resembling air. **2** existing, moving, or operating in the air: *aerial cable car.* **3** ethereal, light and delicate. **4** imaginary. **5** extending high into the air. **6** of or relating to aircraft: *aerial combat.* ◆ *n* Also called: **antenna.** the part of a radio or television system by means of which radio waves are transmitted or received. [C17: via L from Gk *aērios*, from *aēr* air]

aerialist (ˈɛərɪəlɪst) *n* a trapeze artist or tightrope walker.

aerie (ˈɛərɪ) *n* a variant spelling (esp. US) of **eyrie.**

aeriform (ˈɛərɪˌfɔːm) *adj* **1** having the form of air; gaseous. **2** unsubstantial.

aero (ˈɛərəʊ) *n (modifier)* of or relating to aircraft or aeronautics: *an aero engine.*

aero-, aeri-, *or before a vowel* **aer-** *combining form.* **1** denoting air, atmosphere, or gas: *aerodynamics.* **2** denoting aircraft: *aeronautics.* [ult. from Gk *aēr* air]

aerobatics (ˌɛərəʊˈbætɪks) *n (functioning as sing or pl)* spectacular or dangerous manoeuvres, such as loops or rolls, performed in an aircraft or glider. [C20: from AERO- + (ACRO)BATICS]

aerobe (ˈɛərəʊb) *or* **aerobium** (ɛəˈrəʊbɪəm) *n, pl* **aerobes** *or* **aerobia** (-ˈəʊbɪə). an organism that requires free oxygen or air for respiration. [C19: from AERO- + Gk *bios* life]

aerobic (ɛəˈrəʊbɪk) *adj* **1** (of an organism or process) depending on free oxygen or air. **2** of or relating to aerobes. **3** designed for or relating to aerobics: *aerobic shoes; aerobic dances.*

aerobics (ɛəˈrəʊbɪks) *n (functioning as sing)* any system of exercises designed to increase the amount of oxygen in the blood.

aerodrome (ˈɛərəˌdrəʊm) *n* a landing area that is smaller than an airport.

aerodynamic braking *n* **1** the use of aerodynamic drag to slow spacecraft re-entering the atmosphere. **2** the use of airbrakes to retard flying vehicles or objects. **3** the use of a parachute or reversed thrust to decelerate an aircraft before landing.

aerodynamics (ˌɛərəʊdaɪˈnæmɪks) *n (functioning as sing)* the study of the dynamics of gases, esp. of the forces acting on a body passing through air.
► **ˌaerodyˈnamic** *adj* ► **ˌaerodyˈnamically** *adv* ► **aerodyˈnamicist** *n*

aeroembolism (ˌɛərəʊˈɛmbəˌlɪzəm) *n* the presence in the blood of nitrogen bubbles, caused by an abrupt reduction in atmospheric pressure. See **decompression sickness.**

aero engine *n* an engine for powering an aircraft.

aerofoil (ˈɛərəʊˌfɔɪl) *n* a cross section of a wing, rotor blade, etc.

aerogram *or* **aerogramme** (ˈɛərəˌɡræm) *n* an airmail letter written on a single sheet of lightweight paper that folds and is sealed to form an envelope. Also called: **air letter.**

aerolite (ˈɛərəˌlaɪt) *n* a stony meteorite consisting of silicate minerals.

aerology (ɛəˈrɒlədʒɪ) *n* the study of the atmosphere, including its upper layers.
► **aerological** (ˌɛərəˈlɒdʒɪkˀl) *adj* ► **aerˈologist** *n*

aeromechanics (ˌɛərəʊmɪˈkænɪks) *n (functioning as sing)* the mechanics of gases, esp. air.
► **ˌaeromeˈchanical** *adj*

aeronautics (ˌɛərəˈnɔːtɪks) *n (functioning as sing)* the study or practice of all aspects of flight through the air.
► **ˌaeroˈnautical** *adj*

aeropause (ˈɛərəˌpɔːz) *n* the region of the upper atmosphere above which aircraft cannot fly.

aeroplane (ˈɛərəˌpleɪn) *or US* **airplane** (ˈɛəˌpleɪn) *n* a heavier-than-air powered flying vehicle with fixed wings. [C19: from F *aéroplane*, from AERO- + Gk *-planos* wandering]

erosol ('ɛərə,sɒl) *n* **1** a colloidal dispersion of solid or liquid particles in a gas. **2** a substance, such as a paint or insecticide, dispensed from a small metal container by a propellant under pressure. **3** Also called: **air spray.** such a substance together with its container. [C20: from AERO- + SOL(UTION)]

erospace ('ɛərə,speɪs) *n* **1** the atmosphere and space beyond. **2** (*modifier*) of rockets, missiles, space vehicles, etc.: *the aerospace industry.*

erostat ('ɛərə,stæt) *n* a lighter-than-air craft, such as a balloon. [C18: from F *aérostat*, from AERO- + Gk *-statos* standing]
▶ ,aero'static *adj*

erostatics (,ɛərə'stætɪks) *n* (*functioning as sing*) **1** the study of gases in equilibrium and bodies held in equilibrium in gases. Cf. **aerodynamics. 2** the study of lighter-than-air craft, such as balloons.

erugo (ɪ'ruːgəu) *n* (esp. of old bronze) another name for **verdigris.** [C18: from L, from *aes* copper, bronze]
▶ **aeruginous** (ɪ'ruːdʒɪnəs) *adj*

ery ('ɛərɪ) *n, pl* **aeries.** a variant of **eyrie.**

Aeschylus ★ ('iːskələs) *n* ?525–?456 B.C., Greek dramatist, regarded as the father of Greek tragedy. His plays include *Seven Against Thebes, Prometheus Bound,* and the trilogy of the *Oresteia.*
▶ **Aeschylean** (,iːskə'liːən)*adj*

Aesculapius ★ (,iːskju'leɪpɪəs) *n* the Roman god of medicine or healing. Greek counterpart: **Asclepius.**
▶ ,Aescu'lapian *adj*

Aesir ★ ('eɪsɪə) *pl n* the chief gods of Norse mythology dwelling in Asgard. [ON, lit.: gods]

Aesop ★ ('iːsɒp) *n* ?620–564 B.C., Greek author of fables in which animals are given human characters and used to satirize human failings.
▶ **Ae'sopian** *or* **Ae'sopic** *adj*

aesthesia *or US* **esthesia** (iːs'θiːzɪə) *n* the normal ability to experience sensation. [C20: back formation from ANAESTHESIA]

aesthete *or US* **esthete** ('iːsθiːt) *n* a person who has or who affects a highly developed appreciation of beauty. [C19: back formation from AESTHETICS]

aesthetic (iːs'θɛtɪk, ɪs-) *or US* (*sometimes*) **esthetic** *adj also* **aesthetical** *or US* (*sometimes*) **esthetical. 1** connected with aesthetics. **2a** relating to pure beauty rather than to other considerations. **2b** artistic: *an aesthetic consideration.* ◆ *n* **3** a principle of taste or style adopted by a particular person, group, or culture: *the Bauhaus aesthetic of functional modernity.* [C19: from Gk *aisthētikos*, from *aisthanesthai* to perceive, feel]
▶ **aes'thetically** *or US* (*sometimes*) **es'thetically** *adv* ▶ **aes-'theti,cism** *or US* (*sometimes*) **es'theti,cism** *n*

aesthetics *or US* (*sometimes*) **esthetics** (iːs'θɛtɪks) *n* (*functioning as sing*) **1** the branch of philosophy concerned with the study of such concepts as beauty, taste, etc. **2** the study of the rules and principles of art.

aestival *or US* **estival** (iː'staɪvᵊl) *adj Rare.* of or occurring in summer. [C14: from F, from LL *aestīvālis*, from L *aestās* summer]

aestivate *or US* **estivate** ('iːstɪ,veɪt) *vb* **aestivates, aestivating, aestivated** *or US* **estivates, estivating, estivated.** (*intr*) **1** to pass the summer. **2** (of animals) to pass the summer or dry season in a dormant condition. [C17: from L, from *aestīvāre*, from *aestās* summer]
▶ ,aesti'vation *or US* ,esti'vation *n*

aet. *or* **aetat.** *abbrev. for* aetatis. [L: at the age of]

Ethelbert ★ ('æθəl,bɜːt) *n* a variant of **Ethelbert.**

Ethelred ★ ('æθəl,rɛd) *n* a variant of **Ethelred.**

aether ('iːθə) *n* a variant spelling of **ether** (senses 3, 4).

aetiology *or* **etiology** (,iːtɪ'ɒlədʒɪ) *n, pl* **aetiologies** *or* **etiologies. 1** the philosophy or study of causation. **2** the study of the causes of diseases. **3** the cause of a disease. [C16: from LL *aetologia*, from Gk *aitiologia*, from *aitia* cause]
▶ ,aetio'logical *or* ,etio'logical *adj* ▶ ,aetio'logically *or* ,etio'logically *adv* ▶ ,aeti'ologist *or* ,eti'ologist *n*

Aetna ★ ('ɛtnə) *n* the Latin name for Mount **Etna.**

Aetolia ★ (iː'təulɪə) *n* a mountainous region forming (with the region of Acarnania) a department of W central Greece, north of the Gulf of Patras: a powerful federal state in the 3rd century B.C. Chief city: Missolonghi. Pop. (with Acarnania): 228 180 (1991). Area: 5461 sq. km (2108 sq. miles).

AEU (in Britain) *abbrev. for* Amalgamated Engineering Union.

Af. *abbrev. for* Africa(n).

a.f. *abbrev. for* audio frequency.

afar (ə'fɑː) *adv* **1** at, from, or to a great distance. ◆ *n* **2** a great distance (esp. in **from afar**). [C14 *a fer*, altered from earlier *on fer* & *of fer*; see A-², FAR]

Afars and the Issas ★ ('ɑːfɑːz, 'iːsɑːs) *n* **Territory of the.** a former name (1967–77) of **Djibouti.**

AFC *abbrev. for:* **1** Air Force Cross. **2** Association Football Club. **3** automatic frequency control.

afeard *or* **afeared** (ə'fɪəd) *adj* (*postpositive*) an archaic or dialect word for **afraid.** [OE *āfǣred*, from *afǣran* to frighten]

affable ('æfəbᵊl) *adj* **1** showing warmth and friendliness. **2** easy to converse with; approachable. [C16: from L *affābilis*, from *affārī*, from *ad-* to + *fārī* to speak]
▶ ,affa'bility *n* ▶ 'affably *adv*

affair (ə'fɛə) *n* **1** a thing to be done or attended to; matter. **2** an event or happening: *a strange affair.* **3** (*qualified by an adjective or descriptive phrase*) something previously specified: *our house is a tumbledown affair.* **4** a sexual relationship between two people who are not married to each other. [C13: from OF, from *à faire* to do]

affairs (ə'fɛəz) *pl n* **1** personal or business interests. **2** matters of public interest: *current affairs.*

affect¹ *vb* (ə'fɛkt). (*tr*) **1** to act upon or influence, esp. in an adverse way. **2** to move or disturb emotionally or mentally. **3** (of pain, disease, etc.) to attack. ◆ *n* ('æfɛkt). **4** *Psychol.* the emotion associated with an idea or set of ideas. [C17: from L *affectus*, p.p. of *afficere*, from *ad-* to + *facere* to do]

affect² (ə'fɛkt) *vb* (*mainly tr*) **1** to put on an appearance or show of: *to affect ignorance.* **2** to imitate or assume, esp. pretentiously. **3** to have or use by preference. **4** to adopt the character, manner, etc., of. **5** to incline habitually towards. [C15: from L *affectāre* to strive after; rel. to *afficere* to AFFECT¹]

affectation (,æfɛk'teɪʃən) *n* **1** an assumed manner of speech, dress, or behaviour, esp. one that is intended to impress others. **2** (*often foll. by of*) deliberate pretence. [C16: from L *affectātiōn-*, from *affectāre*; see AFFECT²]

affected¹ (ə'fɛktɪd) *adj* (*usually postpositive*) **1** deeply moved, esp. by sorrow or grief. **2** changed, esp. detrimentally. [C17: from AFFECT¹]

affected² (ə'fɛktɪd) *adj* **1** behaving, speaking, etc., in an assumed way, esp. in order to impress others. **2** feigned: *affected indifference.* [C16: from AFFECT²]
▶ af'fectedly *adv*

affecting (ə'fɛktɪŋ) *adj* evoking feelings of pity; moving.
▶ af'fectingly *adv*

affection (ə'fɛkʃən) *n* **1** a feeling of fondness or tenderness for a person or thing. **2** (*often pl*) emotion, feeling, or sentiment: *to play on a person's affections.* **3** *Pathol.* any disease or pathological condition. **4** the act of affecting or the state of being affected. [C13: from L *affectiōn-*, from *afficere* to AFFECT¹]
▶ af'fectional *adj*

affectionate (ə'fɛkʃənɪt) *adj* having or displaying tender feelings, affection, or warmth.
▶ af'fectionately *adv*

affective (ə'fɛktɪv) *adj* concerned with the emotions or affection.
▶ affectivity (,æfɛk'tɪvɪtɪ) *n*

affective disorder *n* any mental disorder, such as depression or mania, that is characterized by abnormal disturbances of mood.

affectless ('æfɛkt,lɪs, ə'fɛktlɪs) *adj* **a** showing no emotion or concern for others. **b** not giving rise to any emotion or feeling: *an affectless novel.* [C20: from AFFECT[1] (sense 4) + -LESS]

afferent ('æfərənt) *adj* bringing or directing inwards to a part or an organ of the body, esp. towards the brain or spinal cord. [C19: from L *afferre*, from *ad-* to + *ferre* to carry]

affiance (ə'faɪəns) *vb* **affiances, affiancing, affianced.** (*tr*) to bind (a person or oneself) in a promise of marriage; betroth. [C14: via OF from Med. L *affīdāre* to trust (oneself) to, from *fīdāre* to trust]

affidavit (,æfɪ'deɪvɪt) *n Law.* a declaration in writing made upon oath before a person authorized to administer oaths. [C17: from Med. L, lit.: he declares on oath, from *affīdāre*; see AFFIANCE]

affiliate *vb* (ə'fɪlɪ,eɪt), **affiliates, affiliating, affiliated. 1** (*tr;* foll. by *to* or *with*) to receive into close connection or association (with a larger body, group, organization, etc.). **2** (foll. by *with*) to associate (oneself) or be associated, esp. as a subordinate or subsidiary. ♦ *n* (ə'fɪlɪt). **3a** a person or organization that is affiliated with another. **3b** (*as modifier*): *an affiliate member.* [C18: from Med. L *affīliātus* adopted as a son, from *affīliāre*, from L *filius* son]
► af,fili'ation *n*

affiliation order *n Law.* an order that a man adjudged to be the father of an illegitimate child shall contribute towards the child's maintenance.

affine ('æfaɪn) *adj Maths.* denoting transformations which preserve collinearity, esp. those of translation, rotation, and reflection. [C16: from F: see AFFINITY]

affinity (ə'fɪnɪtɪ) *n, pl* **affinities. 1** a natural liking, taste, or inclination for a person or thing. **2** the person or thing so liked. **3** a close similarity in appearance or quality. **4** relationship by marriage. **5** similarity in structure, form, etc., between different animals, plants, or languages. **6** *Chem.* chemical attraction. **7** *Immunol.* a measure of the degree of interaction between an antigen and an antibody. [C14: via OF from L *affīnitāt-*, from *affīnis* bordering on, related]
► af'finitive *adj*

affinity card *n* a credit card issued by a bank or credit-card company, which donates a small percentage of the money spent using the card to a specified charity.

affirm (ə'fɜːm) *vb* (*mainly tr*) **1** (*may take a clause as object*) to declare to be true. **2** to uphold, confirm, or ratify. **3** (*intr*) *Law.* to make an affirmation. [C14: via OF from L *affirmāre*, from *ad-* to + *firmāre* to make FIRM[1]]
► af'firmer *or* af'firmant *n*

affirmation (,æfə'meɪʃən) *n* **1** the act of affirming or the state of being affirmed. **2** a statement of the truth of something; assertion. **3** *Law.* a solemn declaration permitted on grounds of conscientious objection to taking an oath.

affirmative (ə'fɜːmətɪv) *adj* **1** confirming or asserting something as true or valid. **2** indicating agreement or assent. **3** *Logic.* (of a categorical proposition) affirming the satisfaction by the subject of the predicate, as in the proposition *some men are married.* ♦ *n* **4** a positive assertion. **5** a word or phrase stating agreement or assent, such as *yes: to answer in the affirmative.* ♦ *sentence substitute.* **6** *Mil., etc.* a signal codeword used to express assent or confirmation.
► af'firmatively *adv*

affix *vb* (ə'fɪks). (*tr;* usually foll. by *to* or *on*) **1** to attach, fasten, join, or stick. **2** to add or append: *to affix a signature to a document.* **3** to attach or attribute (guilt, blame, etc.). ♦ *n* ('æfɪks). **4** a linguistic element added to a word or root to produce a derived or inflected form, as *-ment* in *establishment.* See also **prefix, suffix, infix. 5** something fastened or attached. [C15: from Med. L *affixāre*, from *ad-* to + *fixāre* to FIX]
► **affixture** (ə'fɪkstʃə) *n*

afflatus (ə'fleɪtəs) *n* an impulse of creative power or inspiration considered to be of divine origin. [C17: L, from *afflātus*, from *afflāre*, from *flāre* to blow]

afflict (ə'flɪkt) *vb* (*tr*) to cause suffering or unhappiness to; distress greatly. [C14: from L *afflictus*, p.p. of *afflīgere* to knock against, from *flīgere* to strike]
► af'flictive *adj*

affliction (ə'flɪkʃən) *n* **1** a condition of great distress o suffering. **2** something responsible for physical or men tal suffering.

affluence ('æfluəns) *n* **1** an abundant supply of money goods, or property; wealth. **2** *Rare.* abundance or profu sion.

affluent ('æfluənt) *adj* **1** rich; wealthy. **2** abundant; cop ous. **3** flowing freely. ♦ *n* **4** a tributary stream. [C1! from L *affluent-*, present participle of *affluere*, from *fluel* to flow]

affluent society *n* a society in which the material ber efits of prosperity are widely available.

afflux ('æflʌks) *n* a flowing towards a point: *an afflux blood to the head.* [C17: from L *affluxus*, from *fluxus* FLUX]

afford (ə'fɔːd) *vb* **1** (preceded by *can, could,* etc.) to be abl to do or spare something, esp. without incurring finan cial difficulties or without risk of undesirable conse quences. **2** to give, yield, or supply. [OE *geforthian* t further, promote, from *forth* FORTH]
► af'fordable *adj* ► af,forda'bility *n*

afforest (ə'fɒrɪst) *vb* (*tr*) to plant trees on. [C15: fron Med. L *afforestāre*, from *forestis* FOREST]
► af'forest'ation *n*

affranchise (ə'fræntʃaɪz) *vb* **affranchises, affranchisinç affranchised.** (*tr*) to release from servitude or an obliga tion. [C15: from OF *afranchir*]
► af'franchisement *n*

affray (ə'freɪ) *n* a fight, noisy quarrel, or disturbance be tween two or more persons in a public place. [C14: vi OF from Vulgar L *exfrīdāre* (unattested) to break th peace]

affricate ('æfrɪkɪt) *n* a composite speech sound consist ing of a stop and a fricative articulated at the same point such as the sound written *ch,* as in *chair.* [C19: from . *affricāre,* from *fricāre* to rub]

affright (ə'fraɪt) *Arch. or poetic.* ♦ *vb* **1** (*tr*) to frighten ♦ *n* **2** a sudden terror. [OE *āfyrhtan,* from *a-* + *fyrhtan* t FRIGHT]

affront (ə'frʌnt) *n* **1** a deliberate insult. ♦ *vb* (*tr*) **2** to in sult, esp. openly. **3** to offend the pride or dignity of [C14: from OF *afronter* to strike in the face, from L *a. frontem* to the face]

Afg. *or* **Afgh.** *abbrev.* for Afghanistan.

afghan ('æfgæn, -gən) *n* **1** a knitted or crocheted woo blanket or shawl, esp. one with a geometric pattern. **2** sheepskin coat, often embroidered. [from AFGHANISTAN]

Afghan ('æfgæn) *or* **Afghani** (æf'gænɪ) *n* **1** a native, cit izen, or inhabitant of Afghanistan. **2** another name fo Pashto (the language). ♦ *adj* **3** denoting Afghanistan, it people, or their language.

Afghan hound *n* a tall graceful breed of hound with long silky coat.

Afghanistan ★ (æf'gænɪ,stɑːn, -,stæn) *n* a republic ir central Asia: became independent in 1919; occupied b Soviet troops 1979–89; Islamic fundamentalist factiona fighting followed, the Taliban taking control in 1996 generally arid and mountainous, with the Hindu Kush range rising over 7500 m (25 000 ft) and fertile valleys o the Amu Darya, Helmand, and Kabul Rivers. Languages Pashto, Dari (Persian), and Tajik. Religion: Muslim. Cur rency: afghani. Capital: Kabul. Pop.: 23 738 000 (1997) Area: 657 500 sq. km (250 000 sq. miles).

aficionado (ə,fɪʃjə'nɑːdəʊ) *n, pl* **aficionados. 1** an ardent supporter or devotee: *a jazz aficionado.* **2** a devotee o bullfighting. [Sp., from *aficionar,* from *aficion* AFFECTION]

afield (ə'fiːld) *adv, adj* (*postpositive*) **1** away from one' usual surroundings or home (esp. in **far afield**). **2** off the subject (esp. in **far afield**). **3** in or to the field.

afire (ə'faɪə) *adv, adj* (*postpositive*) **1** on fire. **2** intensely in terested or passionate: *he was afire with enthusiasm for the new plan.*

aflame (ə'fleɪm) *adv, adj* (*postpositive*) **1** in flames. **2** deeply aroused, as with passion: *he was aflame with desire.*

aflatoxin (,æflə'tɒksɪn) *n* a toxin produced by a fungus growing on peanuts, maize, etc., causing liver disease (esp. cancer) in man. [C20: from L name of fungus *A(spergillus) fla(vus)* + TOXIN]

★ people and places

afloat (ə'fləʊt) *adj* (*postpositive*), *adv* **1** floating. **2** aboard ship; at sea. **3** covered with water. **4** aimlessly drifting. **5** in circulation: *nasty rumours were afloat.* **6** free of debt.

aflutter (ə'flʌtə) *adj* (*postpositive*), *adv* in or into a nervous or excited state.

AFM *abbrev. for* Air Force Medal.

afoot (ə'fʊt) *adj* (*postpositive*), *adv* **1** in operation; astir: *mischief was afoot.* **2** on or by foot.

afore (ə'fɔː) *adv, prep, conj* an archaic or dialect word for **before.**

aforementioned (ə'fɔːˌmɛnʃənd) *adj* (*usually prenominal*) (chiefly in legal documents) stated or mentioned before.

aforesaid (ə'fɔːˌsɛd) *adj* (*usually prenominal*) (chiefly in legal documents) spoken of or referred to previously.

aforethought (ə'fɔːˌθɔːt) *adj* (*immediately postpositive*) premeditated (esp. in **malice aforethought**).

a fortiori ('eɪ ˌfɔːtɪ'ɔːraɪ) *adv* for similar but more convincing reasons. [L]

afp *abbrev. for* alpha-fetoprotein.

Afr. *abbrev. for* Africa(n).

afraid (ə'freɪd) *adj* (*postpositive*) **1** (often foll. by *of*) feeling fear or apprehension. **2** reluctant (to do something), as through fear or timidity. **3** (often foll. by *that*; used to lessen the effect of an unpleasant statement) regretful: *I'm afraid that I shall have to tell you to go.* [C14 *affraied*, p.p. of AFFRAY (*obs.*) to frighten]

afreet *or* **afrit** ('æfriːt, ə'friːt) *n in Arabian myth.* a powerful evil demon. [C19: from Ar. *'ifrīt*]

afresh (ə'frɛʃ) *adv* once more; again; anew.

Africa ★ ('æfrɪkə) *n* the second largest of the continents, on the Mediterranean in the north, the Atlantic in the west, and the Red Sea, Gulf of Aden, and Indian Ocean in the east. The Sahara desert divides the continent unequally into North Africa (an early centre of civilization, in close contact with Europe and W Asia, now inhabited chiefly by Arabs) and Africa south of the Sahara (relatively isolated from the rest of the world until the 19th century and inhabited chiefly by Negroid peoples). It was colonized mainly in the 18th and 19th centuries by Europeans and now comprises independent nations. The largest lake is Lake Victoria and the chief rivers are the Nile, Niger, Congo, and Zambezi. Pop.: 720 363 000 (1996 est.). Area: about 30 300 000 sq. km (11 700 000 sq. miles).

African ('æfrɪkən) *adj* **1** denoting or relating to Africa or any of its peoples, languages, nations, etc. ◆ *n* **2** a native or inhabitant of any of the countries of Africa. **3** a member or descendant of any of the peoples of Africa, esp. a Black person.

Africana (ˌæfrɪ'kɑːnə) *n* objects of cultural or historical interest of southern African origin.

African-American *or* **Afro-American** *n* **1** an American of African descent. ◆ *adj* **2** of or relating to Americans of African descent.

Africander (ˌæfrɪ'kændə) *n* a breed of hump-backed beef cattle originally raised in southern Africa. [C19: from South African Du., formed on the model of *Hollander*]

African National Congress *n* (in South Africa) a political party, founded in 1912 in South Africa as an African nationalist movement and banned from 1960 until 1990 because of its opposition to apartheid. In 1994 the ANC won South Africa's first multiracial elections. Abbrev.: **ANC.**

African violet *n* a tropical African plant cultivated as a house plant, with violet, white, or pink flowers and hairy leaves.

Afrikaans (ˌæfrɪ'kɑːns, -'kɑːnz) *n* one of the official languages of the Republic of South Africa, closely related to Dutch. Sometimes called: **South African Dutch.** [C20: from Du.: African]

Afrikaner (ˌæfrɪ'kɑːnə) *n* a White native of the Republic of South Africa whose mother tongue is Afrikaans. See also **Boer.**

afrit ('æfriːt, ə'friːt) *n* a variant spelling of **afreet.**

Afro ('æfrəʊ) *n, pl* **Afros.** a hairstyle in which the hair is shaped into a wide frizzy bush. [C20: independent use of AFRO-]

Afro- *combining form.* indicating Africa or African: *Afro-Asiatic.*

Afro-American *n, adj* another word for **African-American.**

Afro-Caribbean *adj* **1** denoting or relating to Caribbean people of African descent or their culture. ◆ *n* **2** a Caribbean of African descent.

afrormosia (ˌæfrɔː'məʊzɪə) *n* a hard teaklike wood obtained from a genus of tropical African trees. [C20: from AFRO- + Ormosia (genus name)]

aft (ɑːft) *adv, adj Chiefly naut.* towards or at the stern or rear: *the aft deck.* [C17: ? shortened from earlier ABAFT]

after ('ɑːftə) *prep* **1** following in time; in succession to: *after dinner.* **2** following; behind. **3** in pursuit or search of: *he's only after money.* **4** concerning: *to inquire after his health.* **5** considering: *after what you have done, you shouldn't complain.* **6** next in excellence or importance to. **7** in imitation of; in the manner of. **8** in accordance with or in conformity to: *a man after her own heart.* **9** with a name derived from. **10** *US.* past (the hour of): *twenty after three.* **11 after all. 11a** in spite of everything: *it's only a game after all.* **11b** in spite of expectations, efforts, etc. **12 after you.** please go, enter, etc., before me. ◆ *adv* **13** at a later time; afterwards. **14** coming afterwards. **15** *Naut.* further aft. ◆ *conj* **16** (*subordinating*) at a time later than that at which. ◆ *adj* **17** *Naut.* further aft: *the after cabin.* [OE *æfter*]

afterbirth ('ɑːftəˌbɜːθ) *n* the placenta and fetal membranes expelled from the uterus after the birth of offspring.

afterburner ('ɑːftəˌbɜːnə) *n* **1** a device in the exhaust system of an internal-combustion engine for removing dangerous exhaust gases. **2** a device in an aircraft jet engine to produce extra thrust by igniting additional fuel.

aftercare ('ɑːftəˌkeə) *n* **1** support services by a welfare agency for a person discharged from a hospital, prison, etc. **2** *Med.* the care of a patient after a serious illness or operation. **3** any system of maintenance or upkeep of an appliance or product: *contact-lens aftercare.*

afterdamp ('ɑːftəˌdæmp) *n* a poisonous gas, consisting mainly of carbon monoxide, formed after the explosion of firedamp in coal mines.

aftereffect ('ɑːftərɪˌfɛkt) *n* any result occurring some time after its cause.

afterglow ('ɑːftəˌgləʊ) *n* **1** the glow left after a light has disappeared, such as that sometimes seen after sunset. **2** the glow of an incandescent metal after the source of heat has been removed.

afterimage ('ɑːftərˌɪmɪdʒ) *n* a sustained or renewed sensation, esp. visual, after the original stimulus has ceased.

afterlife ('ɑːftəˌlaɪf) *n* life after death or at a later time in a person's lifetime.

aftermath ('ɑːftəˌmɑːθ) *n* **1** signs or results of an event or occurrence considered collectively: *the aftermath of war.* **2** *Agriculture.* a second crop of grass from land that has already yielded one crop earlier in the same year. [C16: AFTER + *math* a mowing, from OE *mæth*]

aftermost ('ɑːftəˌməʊst) *adj* closer or closest to the rear or (in a vessel) the stern; last.

afternoon (ˌɑːftə'nuːn) *n* **1a** the period between noon and evening. **1b** (*as modifier*): *afternoon tea.* **2** a later part: *the afternoon of life.*

afternoons (ˌɑːftə'nuːnz) *adv Inf.* during the afternoon, esp. regularly.

afterpains ('ɑːftəˌpeɪnz) *pl n* cramplike pains caused by contraction of the uterus after childbirth.

afters ('ɑːftəz) *n* (*functioning as sing or pl*) *Brit. inf.* dessert; sweet.

aftershave lotion ('ɑːftəˌʃeɪv) *n* a lotion, usually perfumed, for application to the face after shaving. Often shortened to **aftershave.**

aftertaste ('ɑːftəˌteɪst) *n* **1** a taste that lingers on after eating or drinking. **2** a lingering impression or sensation.

afterthought ('ɑːftə,θɔːt) *n* **1** a comment, reply, etc., that occurs to one after the opportunity to deliver it has passed. **2** an addition to something already completed.

afterwards ('ɑːftəwədz) *or* **afterward** *adv* after an earlier event or time. [OE æfterweard, æfteweard, from AFT + WARD]

Ag *the chemical symbol for* silver. [from L *argentum*]

AG *abbrev. for:* **1** Adjutant General. **2** Attorney General.

aga *or* **agha** ('ɑːgə) *n* (in the Ottoman Empire) a title of respect, often used with the title of a senior position. [C17: Turkish, lit.: lord]

Agadir ★ (,ægə'dɪə) *n* a port in SW Morocco, which became the centre of an international crisis (1911), when a gunboat arrived to protect German interests. Britain issued a strong warning to Germany but the French negotiated and war was averted. In 1960 the town was virtually destroyed by an earthquake, about 10 000 people being killed. Pop.: 137 000 (1993 est.).

again (ə'gen, ə'geɪn) *adv* **1** another or a second time: *he had to start again*. **2** once more in a previously experienced state or condition: *he is ill again*. **3** in addition to the original amount, quantity, etc. (esp. in **as much again; half as much again**). **4** (*sentence modifier*) on the other hand. **5** besides; also. **6** *Arch.* in reply; back: *he answered again*. **7** **again and again**. continuously; repeatedly. ◆ *sentence connector*. **8** moreover; furthermore. [OE *ongegn* opposite to, from A-² + *gegn* straight]

against (ə'genst, ə'geɪnst) *prep* **1** opposed to; in conflict or disagreement with. **2** standing or leaning beside: *a ladder against the wall*. **3** coming in contact with. **4** in contrast to: *silhouettes are outlines against a light background*. **5** having an unfavourable effect on: *the system works against small companies*. **6** as a protection from: *a safeguard against contaminated water*. **7** in exchange for or in return for. **8** *Now rare.* in preparation for: *he gave them warm clothing against their journey*. **9** **as against**. as opposed to or as compared with. [C12 *ageines*, from *again*, *ageyn*, etc. AGAIN + *-es*, genitive ending]

Aga Khan ('ɑːgə 'kɑːn) *n* the hereditary title of the head of the Ismaili Islamic sect.

Aga Khan IV ★ *n* Prince **Karim** (kə'riːm). born 1936, spiritual leader of the Ismaili sect of Muslims from 1957.

Agamemnon ★ (,ægə'mɛmnɒn) *n Greek myth.* a king of Mycenae who led the Greeks at the siege of Troy. On his return home he was murdered by his wife Clytemnestra and her lover Aegisthus. See also **Menelaus**.

agamic (ə'gæmɪk) *adj* asexual; occurring or reproducing without fertilization. [C19: from Gk *agamos* unmarried, from A-¹ + *gamos* marriage]

agamogenesis (,ægəməʊ'dʒɛnɪsɪs) *n* asexual reproduction, such as fission or parthenogenesis. [C19: AGAMIC + GENESIS]

Agaña ★ (ə'gɑːnjə) *n* the capital of the Pacific island of Guam, on its W coast. Pop.: 1139 (1990).

agapanthus (,ægə'pænθəs) *n* a South African plant with blue funnel-shaped flowers, widely cultivated for ornament. [C19: NL, from Gk *agape* love + *anthos* flower]

agape (ə'geɪp) *adj* (*postpositive*) **1** (esp. of the mouth) wide open. **2** very surprised, expectant, or eager. [C17: A-² + GAPE]

Agape ('ægəpɪ) *n* **1** Christian love, esp. as contrasted with erotic love; charity. **2** a communal meal in the early Church in commemoration of the Last Supper. [C17: Gk *agapē* love]

agar ('eɪgə) *n* a gelatinous carbohydrate obtained from seaweeds, used as a culture medium for bacteria, as a laxative, a thickening agent (**E406**) in food, etc. Also called: **agar-agar**. [C19: Malay]

agaric ('ægərɪk) *n* a fungus having gills on the underside of the cap. The group includes the edible mushrooms and poisonous forms such as the fly agaric. [C16: via L from Gk *agarikon*]

Agartala ★ (ʌgətə,lɑː) *n* a city in NE India, capital of the state of Tripura. Pop.: 157 636 (1991).

agate ('ægɪt) *n* **1** an impure form of quartz consisting of a variegated, usually banded chalcedony, used as a gemstone and in making pestles and mortars. **2** a playing marble of this quartz or resembling it. [C16: via F from L, from Gk *akhatēs*]

agave (ə'geɪvɪ) *n* a plant native to tropical America with tall flower stalks rising from thick fleshy leaves. Some species are the source of fibres such as sisal. [C18: NL, from Gk *agauē*, fem. of *agauos* illustrious]

age (eɪdʒ) *n* **1** the period of time that a person, animal, or plant has lived or is expected to live. **2** the period of existence of an object, material, group, etc.: *the age of this table is 200 years*. **3a** a period or state of human life: *he should know better at his age*. **3b** (*as modifier*): *age group*. **4** the latter part of life. **5a** a period of history marked by some feature or characteristic. **5b** (*cap. when part of a name*): *the Middle Ages*. **6** generation: *the Edwardian age*. **7** *Geol., palaeontol.* **7a** a period of the earth's history distinguished by special characteristics: *the age of reptiles*. **7b** a subdivision of an epoch. **8** (*often pl*) *Inf.* a relatively long time: *I've been waiting ages*. **9** *Psychol.* the level in years that a person has reached in any area of development, compared with the normal level for his chronological age. **10 of age**. adult and legally responsible for one's actions (usually at 18 years). ◆ *vb* **ages, ageing** *or* **aging, aged**. **11** to become or cause to become old or aged. **12** (*intr*) to begin to seem older: *to have aged a lot in the past year*. **13** *Brewing.* to mature or cause to mature. [C13: via OF from Vulgar L, from L *aetās*]

-age *suffix forming nouns.* **1** indicating a collection, set, or group: *baggage*. **2** indicating a process or action or the result of an action: *breakage*. **3** indicating a state or relationship: *bondage*. **4** indicating a house or place: *orphanage*. **5** indicating a charge or fee: *postage*. **6** indicating a rate: *dosage*. [from OF, from LL *-āticum* belonging to]

aged ('eɪdʒɪd) *adj* **1a** advanced in years; old. **1b** (*as collective n*; preceded by *the*): *the aged*. **2** of, connected with, or characteristic of old age. **3** (eɪdʒd). (*postpositive*) having the age of: *a woman aged twenty*.

Agee ★ ('eɪdʒiː) *n James.* 1909–55, US novelist, poet, and film critic. His works include the autobiographical novel *A Death in the Family* (1957).

ageing *or* **aging** ('eɪdʒɪŋ) *n* **1** the process of growing old or developing the appearance of old age. ◆ *adj* **2** becoming or appearing older: *an ageing car*. **3** giving the appearance of elderliness: *that dress is really ageing*.

ageism *or* **agism** ('eɪdʒɪzəm) *n* discrimination against people on the grounds of age.
▸ **'ageist** *or* **'agist** *adj*

ageless ('eɪdʒlɪs) *adj* **1** apparently never growing old. **2** timeless; eternal: *an ageless quality*.

agency ('eɪdʒənsɪ) *n, pl* **agencies**. **1** a business or other organization providing a specific service: *an employment agency*. **2** the place where an agent conducts business. **3** the business, duties, or functions of an agent. **4** action, power, or operation: *the agency of fate*. [C17: from Med. L *agentia*, from L *agere* to do]

agenda (ə'dʒɛndə) *n* **1** (*functioning as sing*) Also: **agendum**. a schedule or list of items to be attended to. **2** (*functioning as pl*) Also: **agendas, agendums**. matters to be attended to, as at a meeting. [C17: L, lit.: things to be done, from *agere* to do]

agent ('eɪdʒənt) *n* **1** a person who acts on behalf of another person, business, government, etc. **2** a person or thing that acts or has the power to act. **3** a substance or organism that exerts some force or effect: *a chemical agent*. **4** the means by which something occurs or is achieved. **5** a person representing a business concern, esp. a travelling salesman. [C15: from L *agent-*, noun use of the present participle of *agere* to do]
▸ **agential** (eɪ'dʒɛnʃəl) *adj*

agent-general *n, pl* **agents-general**. a representative in London of a Canadian province or an Australian state.

Agent Orange *n* a highly poisonous herbicide used as a spray for defoliation and crop destruction, esp. by US forces during the Vietnam War. [C20: named after the identifying colour stripe on its container]

agent provocateur *French.* (aʒã prɔvɔkatœr) *n, pl*

agents provocateurs (aʒɑ̃ prɔvɔkatœr). a secret agent employed to provoke suspected persons to commit illegal acts and so be discredited or liable to punishment.

age of consent *n* **1** the age at which a person, esp. a female, is considered legally competent to consent to marriage or sexual intercourse. **2** the age at which a person can enter into a legally binding contract.

Age of Reason *n* (usually preceded by *the*) the 18th century in W Europe. See also **Enlightenment.**

age-old *or* **age-long** *adj* very old or of long duration; ancient.

ageratum (ˌædʒə'reɪtəm) *n* a tropical American plant with thick clusters of purplish-blue flowers. [C16: NL, via L from Gk *agēraton* that does not age, from A-^{1} + *gērat-*, stem of *gēras* old age]

agglomerate *vb* (ə'glɒmə,reɪt), **agglomerates, agglomerating, agglomerated. 1** to form or be formed into a mass or cluster. ◆ *n* (ə'glɒmərɪt, -,reɪt). **2** a confused mass. **3** a volcanic rock consisting of angular fragments within a groundmass of lava. ◆ *adj* (ə'glɒmərɪt, -,reɪt). **4** formed into a mass. [C17: from L *agglomerāre*, from *glomerāre* to wind into a ball]
▶ **ag,glomer'ation** *n* ▶ **ag'glomerative** *adj*

agglutinate (ə'gluːtɪ,neɪt) *vb* **agglutinates, agglutinating, agglutinated. 1** to adhere or cause to adhere, as with glue. **2** *Linguistics.* to combine or be combined by agglutination. **3** (*tr*) to cause (bacteria, red blood cells, etc.) to clump together. [C16: from L *agglūtināre* to glue to, from *gluten* glue]
▶ **ag'glutinable** *adj* ▶ **ag'glutinant** *adj*

agglutination (ə,gluːtɪ'neɪʃən) *n* **1** the act or process of agglutinating. **2** a united mass of parts. **3** *Chem.* the formation of clumps of particles in a suspension. **4** *Immunol.* the formation of a mass of particles, such as red blood cells, by the action of antibodies. **5** *Linguistics.* the building up of words from component morphemes in such a way that these undergo little or no change of form or meaning.

aggrandize *or* **aggrandise** (ə'grændaɪz) *vb* **aggrandizes, aggrandizing, aggrandized** *or* **aggrandises, aggrandising, aggrandised.** (*tr*) **1** to increase the power, wealth, prestige, scope, etc., of. **2** to cause (something) to seem greater. [C17: from OF *aggrandiss-*, stem of *aggrandir*, from L *grandis* GRAND]
▶ **aggrandizement** *or* **aggrandisement** (ə'grændɪzmənt) *n* ▶ **'aggran,dizer** *or* **'aggran,diser** *n*

aggravate ('ægrə,veɪt) *vb* **aggravates, aggravating, aggravated.** (*tr*) **1** to make (a disease, situation, problem, etc.) worse. **2** *Inf.* to annoy. [C16: from L *aggravāre* to make heavier, from *gravis* heavy]
▶ **'aggra,vating** *adj* ▶ **,aggra'vation** *n*

aggregate *adj* ('ægrɪgɪt). **1** formed of separate units collected into a whole. **2** (of fruits and flowers) composed of a dense cluster of florets. ◆ *n* ('ægrɪgɪt, -,geɪt). **3** a sum or assemblage of many separate units. **4** *Geol.* a rock, such as granite, consisting of a mixture of minerals. **5** the sand and stone mixed with cement and water to make concrete. **6 in the aggregate.** taken as a whole. ◆ *vb* ('ægrɪ,geɪt). **7** to combine or be combined into a body, etc. **8** (*tr*) to amount to (a number). [C16: from L *aggregāre* to add to a flock or herd, from *grex* flock]
▶ **,aggre'gation** *n* ▶ **aggregative** ('ægrɪ,geɪtɪv) *adj*

aggress (ə'grɛs) *vb* (*intr*) to attack first or begin a quarrel. [C16: from Med. L *aggressāre*, from L *aggredī* to attack]
▶ **aggressor** (ə'grɛsə) *n*

aggression (ə'grɛʃən) *n* **1** an attack or harmful action, esp. an unprovoked attack by one country against another. **2** any offensive activity, practice, etc. **3** *Psychol.* a hostile or destructive mental attitude. [C17: from L *aggression-*, from *aggredī* to attack]

aggressive (ə'grɛsɪv) *adj* **1** quarrelsome or belligerent. **2** assertive; vigorous.
▶ **ag'gressively** *adv* ▶ **ag'gressiveness** *n*

aggrieve (ə'griːv) *vb* **aggrieves, aggrieving, aggrieved.** (*tr*) **1** (*often impersonal or passive*) to grieve; distress; afflict. **2** to injure unjustly, esp. by infringing a person's legal rights. [C14 *agreven*, via OF from L *aggravāre* to AGGRAVATE]
▶ **ag'grieved** *adj* ▶ **aggrievedly** (ə'griːvɪdlɪ) *adv*

aggro ('ægrəʊ) *n Brit. sl.* aggressive behaviour. [C20: from AGGRAVATION]

aghast (ə'gɑːst) *adj* (*postpositive*) overcome with amazement or horror. [C13 *agast*, from OE *gæstan* to frighten]

agile ('ædʒaɪl) *adj* **1** quick in movement; nimble. **2** mentally quick or acute. [C15: from L *agilis*, from *agere* to do, act]
▶ **'agilely** *adv* ▶ **agility** (ə'dʒɪlɪtɪ) *n*

agin (ə'gɪn) *prep Inf. or dialect.* against. [C19: from obs. *again* AGAINST]

Agincourt ('ædʒɪn,kɔːt; *French* aʒɛ̃kur) *n* a battle fought in 1415 near the village of Azincourt, N France: a decisive victory for English longbowmen under Henry V over French forces vastly superior in number.

agio ('ædʒɪəʊ) *n, pl* **agios. a** the difference between the nominal and actual values of a currency. **b** the charge payable for conversion of the less valuable currency. [C17: from It., lit.: ease]

agitate ('ædʒɪ,teɪt) *vb* **agitates, agitating, agitated. 1** (*tr*) to excite, disturb, or trouble (a person, the mind or feelings). **2** (*tr*) to shake, stir, or disturb. **3** (*intr;* often foll. by *for* or *against*) to attempt to stir up public opinion for or against something. [C16: from L *agitātus*, from *agitāre* to set into motion, from *agere* to act]
▶ **'agi,tated** *adj* ▶ **'agi,tatedly** *adv* ▶ **,agi'tation** *n*

agitato (,ædʒɪ'tɑːtəʊ) *adj, adv Music.* (to be performed) in an agitated manner.

agitator ('ædʒɪ,teɪtə) *n* **1** a person who agitates for or against a cause, etc. **2** a device for mixing or shaking.

agitprop ('ædʒɪt,prɒp) *n* **a** any promotion, as in the arts, of political propaganda, esp. of a Communist nature. **b** (*as modifier*): *agitprop theatre.* [C20: short for Russian *Agitpropbyuro*]

Aglaia ★ (ə'glaɪə) *n Greek myth.* one of the three Graces. [Gk: splendour, from *aglaos* splendid]

agleam (ə'gliːm) *adj* (*postpositive*) glowing; gleaming.

aglet ('æglɪt) *or* **aiglet** *n* **1** a metal sheath or tag at the end of a shoelace, ribbon, etc. **2** a variant spelling of **aiguillette.** [C15: from OF *aiguillette* a small needle]

agley (ə'gleɪ, ə'gliː, ə'glaɪ) *or* **aglee** (ə'gliː) *adv, adj Scot.* awry; askew. [from *gley* squint]

aglitter (ə'glɪtə) *adj* (*postpositive*) sparkling; glittering.

aglow (ə'gləʊ) *adj* (*postpositive*) glowing.

aglu *or* **agloo** ('ægluː) *n Canad.* a breathing hole made in ice by a seal. [C19: from Eskimo]

AGM *abbrev. for* annual general meeting.

agnail ('æg,neɪl) *n* another name for **hangnail.**

agnate ('ægneɪt) *adj* **1** related by descent from a common male ancestor. **2** related in any way. ◆ *n* **3** a male or female descendant by male links from a common male ancestor. [C16: from L *agnātus* born in addition, from *agnāsci*, from *ad-* in addition + *gnāsci* to be born]

Agnes ★ ('ægnɪs) *n Saint.* ?292–?304 A.D., Christian child martyr under Diocletian. Feast day: Jan. 21.

Agnesi ★ (*Italian* aɲ'ɲeːze) *n* **Maria (Gaetana).** 1718–99, Italian mathematician and philosopher, noted for her work on differential calculus.

Agnew ★ ('ægnjuː) *n* **Spiro (Theodore).** 1918–96, US Republican politician; vice president (1969–73).

Agni ★ ('ʌgnɪ) *n Hinduism.* the god of fire, one of the three chief deities of the Vedas. [Sansk.: fire]

agnostic (æg'nɒstɪk) *n* **1** a person who holds that knowledge of a Supreme Being, ultimate cause, etc., is impossible. Cf. **atheist, theist. 2** a person who claims, with respect to any particular question, that the answer cannot be known with certainty. ◆ *adj* **3** of or relating to agnostics. [C19: coined 1869 by T. H. Huxley from A-^{1} + GNOSTIC]
▶ **ag'nosti,cism** *n*

Agnus Dei ('ægnʊs 'deɪɪ) *n* **1** the figure of a lamb bearing a cross or banner, emblematic of Christ. **2** a chant beginning with these words or a translation of them, forming part of the Roman Catholic Mass. [L: Lamb of God]

★ people and places

ago (ə'gəʊ) *adv* in the past: *five years ago; long ago.* [C14 *ago*, from OE *āgān* to pass away]

> **USAGE NOTE** The use of *ago* with *since* (*it's ten years ago since he wrote the novel*) is redundant and should be avoided: *it is ten years since he wrote the novel.*

agog (ə'gɒg) *adj* (*postpositive*) eager or curious. [C15: ?from OF *en gogues* in merriments]

-agogue *or esp. US* **-agog** *n combining form.* indicating a person or thing that leads or incites to action: *demagogue.* [via LL from Gk *agōgos*, from *agein* to lead] ▸ **-agogic** *adj combining form.* ▸ **-agogy** *n combining form.*

agonic (ə'gɒnɪk) *adj* forming no angle. [C19: from Gk *agōnos*, from A-¹ + *gōnia* angle]

agonic line *n* an imaginary line on the surface of the earth connecting points of zero magnetic declination.

agonize *or* **agonise** ('ægə,naɪz) *vb* **agonizes, agonizing, agonized** *or* **agonises, agonising, agonised.** **1** to suffer or cause to suffer agony. **2** (*intr*) to struggle; strive. [C16: via Med. L from Gk *agōnizesthai* to contend for a prize, from *agōn* contest] ▸ **'ago,nizingly** *or* **'ago,nisingly** *adv*

agony ('ægənɪ) *n, pl* **agonies.** **1** acute physical or mental pain; anguish. **2** the suffering or struggle preceding death. [C14: via LL from Gk *agōnia* struggle, from *agōn* contest]

agony aunt *n* (*sometimes cap.*) a person who replies to readers' letters in an agony column.

agony column *n* **1** a newspaper or magazine feature offering sympathetic advice to readers on their personal problems. **2** *Inf.* a newspaper or magazine column devoted to advertisements relating esp. to personal problems.

agora ('ægərə) *n, pl* **agorae** (-riː, -raɪ) *or* **agoras.** (*often cap.*) **a** the marketplace in Athens, used for popular meetings in ancient Greece. **b** the meeting itself. [from Gk, from *agorein* to gather]

agoraphobia (,ægərə'fəʊbɪə) *n* a pathological fear of being in public spaces. ▸ **,agora'phobic** *adj, n*

agouti (ə'guːtɪ) *n, pl* **agoutis** *or* **agouties.** a rodent of Central and South America and the Caribbean. Agoutis are agile and long-legged, with hooflike claws, and are valued for their meat. [C18: via F & Sp. from Guarani]

AGR *abbrev. for* advanced gas-cooled reactor.

Agra ★ ('ɑːgrə) *n* a city in N India, in W Uttar Pradesh on the Jumna River: a capital of the Mogul empire until 1658; famous for its Mogul architecture, esp. the Taj Mahal. Pop.: 899 195 (1991).

Agram ★ ('ɑːgram) *n* the German name for **Zagreb.**

agrarian (ə'grɛərɪən) *adj* **1** of or relating to land or its cultivation. **2** of or relating to rural or agricultural matters. ◆ *n* **3** a person who favours the redistribution of landed property. [C16: from L *agrārius*, from *ager* field, land] ▸ **a'grarian,ism** *n*

agree (ə'griː) *vb* **agrees, agreeing, agreed.** (*mainly intr*) **1** (often foll. by *with*) to be of the same opinion. **2** (*also tr;* when *intr*, often foll. by *to;* when *tr*, takes a clause as object *or an infinitive*) to give assent; consent. **3** (*also tr;* when *intr*, foll. by *on* or *about;* when *tr, may take a clause as object*) to come to terms (about). **4** (foll. by *with*) to be similar or consistent; harmonize. **5** (foll. by *with*) to be agreeable or suitable (to one's health, etc.). **6** (*tr; takes a clause as object*) to concede: *they agreed that the price was too high.* **7** *Grammar.* to undergo agreement. [C14: from OF *agreer*, from *a gre* at will or pleasure]

agreeable (ə'grɪəbᵊl) *adj* **1** pleasing; pleasant. **2** prepared to consent. **3** (foll. by *to* or *with*) in keeping. **4** (foll. by *to*) to one's liking. ▸ **a'greeableness** *n* ▸ **a'greeably** *adv*

agreed (ə'griːd) *adj* **1** determined by common consent: *the agreed price.* ◆ *sentence substitute.* **2** an expression of consent or agreement.

agreement (ə'griːmənt) *n* **1** the act of agreeing. **2** a settlement, esp. one that is legally enforceable. **3** a contract or document containing such a settlement. **4** the state of being of the same opinion. **5** the state of being similar or consistent. **6** *Grammar.* the determination of the inflectional form of one word by some grammatical feature, such as number or gender, of another word. [C14: from OF]

agribusiness ('ægrɪ,bɪznɪs) *n* the various businesses that process and distribute farm products. [C20: from AGRI(CULTURE) + BUSINESS]

Agricola ★ (ə'grɪkələ) *n* **Gnaeus Julius** ('niːəs 'dʒuːlɪəs). 40–93 A.D., Roman general; governor of Britain who advanced Roman rule north to the Firth of Forth.

agriculture ('ægrɪ,kʌltʃə) *n* the science or occupation of cultivating land and rearing crops and livestock; farming. [C17: from L *agricultūra*, from *ager* field, land + *cultūra* CULTURE] ▸ **,agri'cultural** *adj* ▸ **,agri'culturist** *or* **,agri'culturalist** *n*

Agrigento ★ (*Italian* agri'dʒɛnto) *n* a town in Italy, in SW Sicily: site of six Greek temples. Pop.: 56 372 (1990). Former name (until 1927): **Girgenti** (gɜ:'gɛntɪ).

agrimony ('ægrɪmənɪ) *n* **1** any of various plants of the rose family, which have compound leaves, long spikes of small yellow flowers, and bristly burlike fruits. **2** any of several other plants, such as hemp agrimony. [C15: via OF from L, from Gk *argemōnē* poppy]

Agrippa ★ (ə'grɪpə) *n* **Marcus Vipsanius** ('mɑːkəs vɪp'seɪnɪəs). 63–12 B.C., Roman general: chief adviser and later son-in-law of Augustus.

Agrippina ★ (,ægrɪ'piːnə) *n* **1** called *the Elder.* c. 14 B.C.–33 A.D., Roman matron: mother of Caligula and Agrippina the Younger. **2** called *the Younger.* 15–59 A.D., mother of Nero, who put her to death after he became emperor.

agro- *combining form.* denoting fields, soil, or agriculture: *agrobiology.* [from Gk *agros* field]

agrobiology (,ægrəʊbaɪ'ɒlədʒɪ) *n* the science of plant growth and nutrition in relation to agriculture.

agroforestry (,ægrəʊ'fɒrɪstrɪ) *n* a method of farming integrating herbaceous and tree crops.

agronomics (,ægrə'nɒmɪks) *n* (*functioning as sing*) the branch of economics dealing with the distribution, management, and productivity of land. ▸ **,agro'nomic** *adj*

agronomy (ə'grɒnəmɪ) *n* the science of cultivation of land, soil management, and crop production. ▸ **a'gronomist** *n*

agrostemma (,ægrəʊ'stɛmə) *n* any cultivated variety of corncockle. [NL, from Gk *agros* field + *stemma* wreath]

aground (ə'graʊnd) *adv, adj* (*postpositive*) on or onto the ground or bottom, as in shallow water.

agterskot ('axtə,skɒt) *n* (in South Africa) the final payment to a farmer for crops. Cf. **voorskot.** [C20: Afrikaans *agter* after + *skot* shot, payment]

Aguascalientes ★ (*Spanish* ,aɣwaska'ljentes) *n* **1** a state in central Mexico. Pop.: 862 335 (1995 est.). Area: 5471 sq. km (2112 sq. miles). **2** a city in central Mexico, capital of Aguascalientes state, about 1900 m (6200 ft) above sea level, with hot springs. Pop.: 440 425 (1990).

ague ('eɪgjuː) *n* **1** malarial fever with successive stages of fever and chills. **2** a fit of shivering. [C14: from OF (*fievre*) *ague* acute fever; see ACUTE] ▸ **'aguish** *adj*

ah (ɑː) *interj* an exclamation expressing pleasure, pain, sympathy, etc., according to the intonation of the speaker.

AH (indicating years in the Muslim system of dating, numbered from the Hegira (622 A.D.)) *abbrev. for* anno Hegirae. [L]

aha (ɑː'hɑː) *interj* an exclamation expressing triumph, surprise, etc., according to the intonation of the speaker.

Ahab ★ ('eɪhæb) *n Old Testament.* the king of Israel from approximately 869 to 850 B.C. and husband of Jezebel: rebuked by Elijah (I Kings 16:29–22:40).

Ahasuerus ★ (ə,hæzjuː'ɪərəs) *n Old Testament.* a king of

> | ★ people and places |

ancient Persia and husband of Esther, generally identified with Xerxes.

ahead (ə'hɛd) *adj* **1** (*postpositive*) in front; in advance. ◆ *adv* **2** at or in the front; before. **3** forwards: *go straight ahead.* **4 ahead of. 4a** in front of; at a further advanced position than. **4b** *Stock Exchange.* in anticipation of: *the share price rose ahead of the annual figures.* **5 be ahead.** *Inf.* to have an advantage; be winning. **6 get ahead.** to attain success.

ahem (ə'hɛm) *interj* a clearing of the throat, used to attract attention, express doubt, etc.

Ahern ★ (ə'hɜːn) *n* **Bertie.** born 1951, Irish politician; prime minister of the Republic of Ireland from 1997.

ahimsa (ɑː'hɪmsɑː) *n* (in Hindu, Buddhist, and Jainist philosophy) the law of reverence for, and nonviolence to, every form of life. [Sansk., from *a* without + *himsā* injury]

Ahithophel (ə'hɪθə,fɛl) or **Achitophel** ★ *n Old Testament.* a member of David's council, who became one of Absalom's advisers in his rebellion and hanged himself when his advice was overruled (II Samuel 15:12–17:23).

Ahmedabad or **Ahmadabad** ★ ('ɑːmədə,bɑːd) *n* a city in W India, in Gujarat: famous for its mosque. Pop.: 2 872 865 (1991).

Ahmednagar or **Ahmadnagar** ★ (,ɑːməd'nʌɡə) *n* a city in W India, in Maharashtra: formerly one of the kingdoms of Deccan. Pop.: 181 015 (1991).

ahoy (ə'hɔɪ) *interj Naut.* a hail used to call a ship or to attract attention.

Ahriman ★ ('ɑːrɪmən) *n Zoroastrianism.* the supreme evil spirit and diabolical opponent of Ormazd.

Ahura Mazda ★ (ə'hʊərə 'mæzdə) *n Zoroastrianism.* another name for **Ormazd.**

Ahvenanmaa ★ ('ɑhvenɑmmɑː) *n* the Finnish name for the Åland Islands.

Ahwaz (ɑː'wɑːz) or **Ahvaz** ★ (ɑː'vɑːz) *n* a town in SW Iran, on the Karun River. Pop.: 724 653 (1991).

ai ('ɑːɪ) *n, pl* **ais.** another name for **three-toed sloth** (see **sloth** (sense 1)). [C17: from Port., from Tupi]

AI *abbrev. for:* **1** Amnesty International. **2** artificial insemination. **3** artificial intelligence.

aid (eɪd) *vb* **1** to give support to (someone to do something); help or assist. **2** (*tr*) to assist financially. ◆ *n* **3** assistance; help; support. **4** a person, device, etc., that helps or assists. **5** *Mountaineering.* a device such as a piton when used as a direct help in the ascent. **6** (in medieval Europe) a feudal payment made to the king or any lord by his vassals on certain occasions such as the knighting of an eldest son. [C15: via OF *aidier* from L *adjūtāre*, from *juvāre* to help] ▸ **'aider** *n*

Aid or **-aid** *n combining form.* denoting a charitable organization or function that raises money for a cause: *Band Aid; Ferryaid.*

AID *abbrev. for:* **1** *US.* Agency for International Development. **2** artificial insemination (by) donor: former name for donor insemination (DI).

Aidan ★ ('eɪdən) *n Saint.* died 651 A.D., Irish missionary in Northumbria, who founded the monastery at Lindisfarne (635). Feast day: Aug. 31.

aide (eɪd) *n* **1** an assistant. **2** short for **aide-de-camp.**

aide-de-camp or **aid-de-camp** ('eɪd də 'kɒŋ) *n, pl* **aides-de-camp** or **aids-de-camp.** a military officer serving as personal assistant to a senior. Abbrev.: **ADC.** [C17: from F: camp assistant]

aide-mémoire ('eɪdmɛm'wɑː) *n, pl* **aides-mémoire** ('eɪdzmɛm'wɑː). **1** a note serving as a reminder. **2** a summarized diplomatic communication. [F, from *aider* to help + *mémoire* memory]

Aidin ★ ('aɪdɪn) *n* a variant spelling of **Aydin.**

AIDS or **Aids** (eɪdz) *n acronym for* acquired immune (or immuno-) deficiency syndrome: a condition, caused by a virus, in which the body loses its ability to resist infection. AIDS is transmitted by sexual intercourse, through infected blood and blood products, and through the placenta.

AIDS-related complex *n* See **ARC.**

AIF (formerly) *abbrev. for* Australian Imperial Force.

aiglet ('eɪɡlɪt) *n* a variant of **aglet.**

aigrette or **aigret** ('eɪɡrɛt) *n* **1** a long plume worn on hats or as a headdress, esp. one of long egret feathers. **2** an ornament in imitation of a plume of feathers. [C17: from F; see EGRET]

aiguille (eɪ'ɡwiːl) *n* **1** a rock mass or peak shaped like a needle. **2** an instrument for boring holes in rocks or masonry. [C19: F, lit.: needle]

aiguillette (,eɪɡwɪ'lɛt) *n* **1** an ornamentation worn by certain military officers, consisting of cords with metal tips. **2** a variant of **aglet.** [C19: F; see AGLET]

AIH *abbrev. for* artificial insemination (by) husband.

aikido (aɪ'kiːdəʊ) *n* a Japanese system of self-defence employing similar principles to judo, but including blows from the hands and feet. [from Japanese, from *ai* to join, receive + *ki* spirit, force + *do* way]

ail (eɪl) *vb* **1** (*tr*) to trouble; afflict. **2** (*intr*) to feel unwell. [OE *eglan*, from *egle* painful]

ailanthus (eɪ'lænθəs) *n, pl* **ailanthuses.** an E Asian deciduous tree having pinnate leaves, small greenish flowers, and winged fruits. Also called: **tree of heaven.** [C19: NL, from native name in the Moluccas in the Indian and Pacific Oceans]

aileron ('eɪlərɒn) *n* a flap hinged to the trailing edge of an aircraft wing to provide lateral control. [C20: from F, dim. of *aile* wing]

ailing ('eɪlɪŋ) *adj* unwell or unsuccessful, esp. over a long period.

ailment ('eɪlmənt) *n* a slight but often persistent illness.

aim (eɪm) *vb* **1** to point (a weapon, missile, etc.) or direct (a blow) at a particular person or object. **2** (*tr*) to direct (satire, criticism, etc.) at a person, object, etc. **3** (*intr;* foll. by *at* or an infinitive) to propose or intend. **4** (*intr;* often foll. by *at* or *for*) to direct one's efforts or strive (towards). ◆ *n* **5** the action of directing something at an object. **6** the direction in which something is pointed: *to take aim.* **7** the object at which something is aimed. **8** intention; purpose. [C14: via OF *aesmer* from L *aestimāre* to ESTIMATE]

AIM *abbrev. for* Alternative Investment Market.

aimless ('eɪmlɪs) *adj* having no purpose or direction. ▸ **'aimlessly** *adv* ▸ **'aimlessness** *n*

Ain ★ (*French* ɛ̃) *n* **1** a department in E central France, in Rhône-Alpes region. Capital: Bourg. Pop.: 497 943 (1994 est.). Area: 5785 sq. km (2256 sq. miles). **2** a river in E France, rising in the Jura Mountains and flowing south to the Rhône. Length: 190 km (118 miles).

ain't (eɪnt) *Not standard. contraction of* am not, is not, are not, have not, or has not: *I ain't seen it.*

Aintree ★ ('eɪntrɪ) *n* a suburb of Liverpool, in Merseyside: site of the racecourse over which the Grand National steeplechase has been run since 1839.

Ainu ('aɪnuː) *n* (*pl* **Ainus** or **Ainu**) **1** a member of the aboriginal people of Japan. **2** the language of this people, sometimes tentatively associated with Altaic, still spoken in parts of Hokkaido. [Ainu: man]

air (ɛə) *n* **1** the mixture of gases that forms the earth's atmosphere. It consists chiefly of nitrogen, oxygen, argon, and carbon dioxide. **2** the space above and around the earth; sky. Related adj: **aerial. 3** breeze; slight wind. **4** public expression; utterance. **5** a distinctive quality: *an air of mystery.* **6** a person's distinctive appearance, manner, or bearing. **7** *Music.* a simple tune for either vocal or instrumental performance. **8** transportation in aircraft (esp. in **by air**). **9** an archaic word for **breath** (senses 1–3). **10 in the air. 10a** in circulation; current. **10b** unsettled. **11 into thin air.** leaving no trace behind. **12 on** (*or* **off**) **the air.** (not) in the act of broadcasting or (not) being broadcast on radio or television. **13 take the air.** to go out of doors, as for a short walk. **14 up in the air. 14a** uncertain. **14b** *Inf.* agitated or excited. **15** (*modifier*) *Astrol.* of or relating to a group of three signs of the zodiac, Gemini, Libra, and Aquarius. ◆ *vb* **16** to expose or be exposed to the air so as to cool or freshen. **17** to expose or be exposed to warm or heated air so as to dry: *to air linen.* **18** (*tr*) to make known publicly: *to air one's opinions.* **19** (*intr*) (of a television or radio programme) to be broadcast. ◆ See also **airs.** [C13: via OF & L from Gk *aēr* the lower atmosphere]

Aïr ★ (ˈɑːɪə) *n* a mountainous region of N central Niger, in the Sahara, rising to 1500 m (5000 ft): a former native kingdom. Area: about 77 700 sq. km (30 000 sq. miles). Also called: **Asben, Azbine.**

air bag *n* a safety device in a car, consisting of a bag that inflates automatically in an accident and prevents the passengers from being thrown forwards.

air base *n* a centre from which military aircraft operate.

air bladder *n* **1** an air-filled sac, lying above the alimentary canal in bony fishes, that regulates buoyancy at different depths by a variation in the pressure of the air. **2** any air-filled sac, such as one in seaweeds.

airborne (ˈɛəˌbɔːn) *adj* **1** conveyed by or through the air. **2** (of aircraft) flying; in the air.

air brake *n* **1** a brake operated by compressed air, esp. in heavy vehicles and trains. **2** an articulated flap or small parachute for reducing the speed of an aircraft.

airbrick (ˈɛəˌbrɪk) *n Chiefly Brit.* a brick with holes in it, put into the wall of a building for ventilation.

airbrush (ˈɛəˌbrʌʃ) *n* **1** an atomizer for spraying paint or varnish by means of compressed air. ◆ *vb* (*tr*) **2** to paint or varnish (something) by using an airbrush. **3** to improve the image of (a person or thing) by concealing defects beneath a bland exterior: *an airbrushed version of the government's record.*

air chief marshal *n* a senior officer of the Royal Air Force and certain other air forces, of equivalent rank to admiral in the Royal Navy.

air cleaner *n* a filter that prevents dust and other particles from entering the air intake of an internal-combustion engine. Also called: **air filter.**

air commodore *n* a senior officer of the Royal Air Force and certain other air forces, of equivalent rank to brigadier in the Army.

air conditioning *n* a system or process for controlling the temperature and sometimes the humidity of the air in a house, etc. ▸ ˈair-conˌdition *vb* (*tr*) ▸ **air conditioner** *n*

air-cool *vb* (*tr*) to cool (an engine) by a flow of air. Cf. **water-cool.**

aircraft (ˈɛəˌkrɑːft) *n, pl* **aircraft.** any machine capable of flying by means of buoyancy or aerodynamic forces, such as a glider, helicopter, or aeroplane.

aircraft carrier *n* a warship with an extensive flat deck for the launch of aircraft.

aircraftman (ˈɛəˌkrɑːftmən) *n, pl* **aircraftmen.** a serviceman of the most junior rank in the Royal Air Force. ▸ ˈaircraftˌwoman *fem n*

air curtain *n* an air stream across a doorway to exclude draughts, etc.

air cushion *n* **1** an inflatable cushion. **2** the pocket of air that supports a hovercraft.

Airdrie ★ (ˈɛədrɪ; *Scot.* ˈerdrɪ) *n* a town in W central Scotland in North Lanarkshire, E of Glasgow. Pop.: 36 998 (1991).

airdrop (ˈɛəˌdrɒp) *n* **1** a delivery of supplies, troops, etc., from an aircraft by parachute. ◆ *vb* **airdrops, airdropping, airdropped.** **2** (*tr*) to deliver (supplies, etc.) by an airdrop.

Aire ★ (ɛə) *n* a river in N England rising in the Pennines and flowing southeast to the Ouse. Length: 112 km (70 miles).

Airedale (ˈɛəˌdeɪl) *n* a large rough-haired tan-coloured breed of terrier with a black saddle-shaped patch covering most of the back. Also called: **Airedale terrier.** [C19: from district in Yorkshire]

air engine *n* **1** an engine that uses the expansion of heated air to drive a piston. **2** a small engine that uses compressed air to drive a piston.

airfield (ˈɛəˌfiːld) *n* a landing and taking-off area for aircraft.

air filter *n* another name for **air cleaner.**

airfoil (ˈɛəˌfɔɪl) *n* the US and Canad. name for **aerofoil.**

air force *n* **a** the branch of a nation's armed services primarily responsible for air warfare. **b** (*as modifier*): *an air force base.*

airframe (ˈɛəˌfreɪm) *n* the body of an aircraft, excluding its engines.

air guitar *n* an imaginary guitar played while miming to rock music.

air gun *n* a gun discharged by means of compressed air.

airhead (ˈɛəˌhɛd) *n Sl.* a stupid or simple-minded person; idiot. [C20: from AIR + HEAD]

air hole *n* **1** a hole that allows the passage of air, esp. for ventilation. **2** a section of open water in a frozen surface.

air hostess *n* a stewardess on an airliner.

airily (ˈɛərɪlɪ) *adv* **1** in a jaunty or high-spirited manner. **2** in a light or delicate manner.

airiness (ˈɛərɪnɪs) *n* **1** the quality or condition of being fresh, light, or breezy. **2** gaiety.

airing (ˈɛərɪŋ) *n* **1a** exposure to air or warmth, as for drying or ventilation. **1b** (*as modifier*): *airing cupboard.* **2** an excursion in the open air. **3** exposure to public debate.

airless (ˈɛəlɪs) *adj* **1** lacking fresh air; stuffy or sultry. **2** devoid of air. ▸ ˈairlessness *n*

air letter *n* another name for **aerogram.**

airlift (ˈɛəˌlɪft) *n* **1** the transportation by air of passengers, troops, cargo, etc., esp. when other routes are blocked. ◆ *vb* **2** (*tr*) to transport by an airlift.

airline (ˈɛəˌlaɪn) *n* **1a** a system or organization that provides scheduled flights for passengers or cargo. **1b** (*as modifier*): *an airline pilot.* **2** a hose or tube carrying air under pressure.

airliner (ˈɛəˌlaɪnə) *n* a large passenger aircraft.

airlock (ˈɛəˌlɒk) *n* **1** a bubble in a pipe causing an obstruction. **2** an airtight chamber with regulated air pressure used to gain access to a space that has air under pressure.

airmail (ˈɛəˌmeɪl) *n* **1** the system of conveying mail by aircraft. **2** mail conveyed by aircraft. ◆ *adj* **3** of or for airmail.

airman (ˈɛəmən) *n, pl* **airmen.** a man who serves in his country's air force.

air marshal *n* **1** a senior Royal Air Force officer of equivalent rank to a vice admiral in the Royal Navy. **2** a Royal Australian Air Force officer of the highest rank. **3** a Royal New Zealand Air Force officer of the highest rank when chief of defence forces.

air mass *n* a large body of air having characteristics of temperature, moisture, and pressure that are approximately uniform horizontally.

Air Miles *pl n* points awarded by certain companies to purchasers of flight tickets and some other products that may be used to pay for other flights.

air miss *n* a situation in which two aircraft pass very close to one another in the air; near miss.

airplane (ˈɛəˌpleɪn) *n* the US and Canad. name for **aeroplane.**

airplay (ˈɛəˌpleɪ) *n* (of recorded music) radio exposure.

air pocket *n* a localized region of low air density or a descending air current, causing an aircraft to suffer an abrupt decrease in height.

airport (ˈɛəˌpɔːt) *n* a landing and taking-off area for civil aircraft, usually with runways and aircraft maintenance and passenger facilities.

air power *n* the strength of a nation's air force.

air pump *n* a device for pumping air into or out of something.

air raid *n* **a** an attack by hostile aircraft or missiles. **b** (*as modifier*): *an air-raid shelter.*

air-raid warden *n* a member of a civil defence organization responsible for enforcing regulations, etc., during an air attack.

air rifle *n* a rifle discharged by compressed air.

airs (ɛəz) *pl n* affected manners intended to impress others: *to give oneself airs; put on airs.*

★ people and places

air sac *n* any of the membranous air-filled extensions of the lungs of birds, which increase the efficiency of respiration.

airscrew ('ɛə,skruː) *n Brit.* an aircraft propeller.

air-sea rescue *n* an air rescue at sea.

air shaft *n* a shaft for ventilation, esp. in a mine or tunnel.

airship ('ɛə,ʃɪp) *n* a lighter-than-air self-propelled craft. Also called: **dirigible.**

airshow ('ɛə,ʃəʊ) *n* an occasion when an air base is open to the public and a flying display and, usually, static exhibitions are held.

airsick ('ɛə,sɪk) *adj* nauseated from travelling in an aircraft.

airside ('ɛə,saɪd) *n* the part of an airport nearest the aircraft, the boundary of which is the security check, customs, passport control, etc. Cf. **landside** (sense 1).

airspace ('ɛə,speɪs) *n* the atmosphere above the earth or part of the earth, esp. the atmosphere above a particular country.

airspeed ('ɛə,spiːd) *n* the speed of an aircraft relative to the air in which it moves.

airstrip ('ɛə,strɪp) *n* a cleared area for the landing and taking-off of aircraft; runway. Also called: **landing strip.**

air terminal *n Brit.* a building in a city from which air passengers are taken to an airport.

airtight ('ɛə,taɪt) *adj* 1 not permitting the passage of air. 2 having no weak points; rigid or unassailable.

air-to-air *adj* operating between aircraft in flight.

air-traffic control *n* an organization that determines the altitude, speed, and direction at which planes fly in a given area, giving instructions to pilots by radio.
▶ **air-traffic controller** *n*

air vice-marshal *n* 1 a senior Royal Air Force officer of equivalent rank to a rear admiral in the Royal Navy. 2 a Royal Australian Air Force officer of the second highest rank. 3 a Royal New Zealand Air Force officer of the highest rank.

airwaves ('ɛə,weɪvz) *pl n Inf.* radio waves used in radio and television broadcasting.

airway ('ɛə,weɪ) *n* 1 an air route, esp. one that is fully equipped with navigational aids, etc. 2 a passage for ventilation, esp. in a mine. 3 the passage of air from the nose or mouth to the lungs. 4 *Med.* a tubelike device inserted via the throat to keep open the airway of an unconscious patient.

air waybill *n* a document made out by the consigner of goods by air freight giving details of the goods and the name of the consignee.

airworthy ('ɛə,wɜːðɪ) *adj* (of an aircraft) safe to fly.

airy ('ɛərɪ) *adj* **airier, airiest.** 1 abounding in fresh air. 2 spacious or uncluttered. 3 nonchalant. 4 visionary; fanciful: *airy promises.* 5 of or relating to air. 6 weightless and insubstantial. 7 light and graceful in movement. 8 high up in the air.

Aisha *or* **Ayesha** ★ ('ɑːiː,ʃɑː) *n* ?613–678 A.D., the favourite wife of Mohammed; daughter of Abu-Bekr.

aisle (aɪl) *n* 1 a passageway separating seating areas in a theatre, church, etc. 2 a lateral division in a church flanking the nave or chancel. [C14 *ele* (later *aile, aisle,* through confusion with *isle*), via OF from L *āla* wing]
▶ **aisled** *adj*

Aisne ★ (eɪn; *French* ɛn) *n* 1 a department of NE France, in Picardy region. Capital: Laon. Pop.: 539 097 (1994 est.). Area: 7428 sq. km (2897 sq. miles). 2 a river in N France, rising in the Argonne Forest and flowing northwest and west to the River Oise: scene of a major Allied offensive in 1918 which turned the tide finally against Germany in World War I. Length: 282 km (175 miles).

ait (eɪt) *or* **eyot** *n Dialect.* an islet, esp. in a river. [OE *ȳgett* small island, from *ieg* ISLAND]

aitch (eɪtʃ) *n* the letter *h* or the sound represented by it. [C16: a phonetic spelling]

aitchbone ('eɪtʃ,bəʊn) *n* 1 the rump bone in cattle. 2 a cut of beef from or including the rump bone. [C15 *hach-*

boon, altered from earlier *nache-bone* (a *nache* mistaken for *an ache, an aitch*); *nache* buttock, via OF from LL *natica,* from L *natis* buttock]

Aitken ★ ('eɪtkən) *n* **1 Robert Grant.** 1864–1951, US astronomer who discovered over three thousand double stars. **2 William Maxwell.** See **Beaverbrook.**

Aix-en-Provence ★ (*French* ɛksɑ̃prɔvɑ̃s) *n* a city and spa in SE France: the medieval capital of Provence. Pop.: 126 854 (1990). Also called: **Aix.**

Aix-la-Chapelle ★ (*French* ɛkslaʃapɛl) *n* the French name for **Aachen.**

Aix-les-Bains ★ (*French* ɛkslebɛ̃) *n* a town in E France: a resort with sulphurous springs. Pop.: 24 830 (1990).

Aíyina ★ ('ejina) *n* transliteration of the Modern Greek name for **Aegina.**

Ajaccio ★ (əˈdʒætsɪˌəʊ, -ˈdʒeɪ-) *n* the capital of Corsica, a port on the W coast. Pop.: 55 279 (1990).

ajar (əˈdʒɑː) *adj* (*postpositive*), *adv* (esp. of a door) slightly open. [C18: altered form of obs. *on char,* lit.: on the turn; from OE *cierran* to turn]

Ajax ★ ('eɪdʒæks) *n Greek myth.* **1** the son of Telamon; a Greek hero of the Trojan War who killed himself in vexation when Achilles' armour was given to Odysseus. **2** called *Ajax the Lesser,* a Locrian king, a swift-footed Greek hero of the Trojan War.

Ajmer ★ (ʌdʒˈmɪə) *n* a city in NW India, in Rajasthan: textile centre. Pop.: 402 700 (1991).

AK *abbrev.* for Alaska.

AK-47 *n Trademark.* a type of Kalashnikov.

a.k.a. *or* **AKA** *abbrev. for* also known as.

Akbar ★ ('ækbɑː) *n* called *Akbar the Great.* 1542–1605, Mogul emperor of India (1556–1605), who extended the Mogul empire to include N India.

akene (əˈkiːn) *n* a variant spelling of **achene.**

Akhaïa ★ (əˈxaːja) *n* transliteration of the modern Greek name for **Achaea.**

Akhenaten *or* **Akhenaton** ★ (,ækəˈnɑːtᵊn) *n* original name *Amenhotep IV.* died ?1358 B.C., king of Egypt, of the 18th dynasty; he moved his capital from Thebes to Tell El Amarna and introduced the cult of Aten.

Akhmatova ★ (*Russian* axˈmatəvə) *n* **Anna** ('annə). pseudonym of *Anna Gorenko.* 1889–1966, Russian poet.

Akihito ★ (,ækɪˈhiːtəʊ) *n* born 1933, Emperor of Japan from 1989.

akimbo (əˈkɪmbəʊ) *adj, adv* (**with**) **arms akimbo.** with hands on hips and elbows out. [C15 *in kenebowe,* lit.: in keen bow, that is, in a sharp curve]

akin (əˈkɪn) *adj* (*postpositive*) **1** related by blood. **2** (often foll. by *to*) having similar characteristics, properties, etc.

Akkad *or* **Accad** ★ ('ækæd) *n* **1** a city on the Euphrates in N Babylonia, the centre of a major empire and civilization (2360–2180 B.C.). Ancient name: **Agade** (əˈɡɑːdɪ, əˈɡeɪdɪ). **2** an ancient region lying north of Babylon, from which the Akkadian language and culture is named.

Akkadian *or* **Accadian** (əˈkeɪdɪən) *n* **1** a member of an ancient Semitic people who lived in Mesopotamia in the third millennium B.C. **2** the extinct language of this people.

Akkerman ★ (*Russian* akɪrˈman) *n* the former name (until 1944) of **Byelgorod-Dnestrovski.**

Akmola ★ (*Kazakh* akmɔˈla) *n* the former name (1994–98) of **Astana.**

Aktyubinsk ★ (*Russian* akˈtjubinsk) *n* the former name (until 1991) of **Aqtöbe.**

Akure ★ (əˈkuːre) *n* a city in SW Nigeria, capital of Ondo state: agricultural trade centre. Pop.: 158 200 (1995 est.).

Al *the chemical symbol for* aluminium.

AL *abbrev. for:* **1** Alabama. **2** Anglo-Latin.

-al[1] *suffix forming adjectives.* of; related to: *functional; sectional; tonal.* [from L *-ālis*]

-al[2] *suffix forming nouns.* the act or process of doing what is indicated by the verb stem: *renewal.* [via OF *-aille, -ail,* from L *-ālia,* neuter pl used as substantive, from *-ālis* -AL[1]]

★ people and places

-al[3] *suffix forming nouns.* **1** (*not used systematically*) indicating any aldehyde: *ethanal.* **2** indicating a pharmaceutical product: *phenobarbital.* [shortened from ALDEHYDE]

ala ('eɪlə) *n, pl* **alae** ('eɪliː). **1** *Zool.* a wing or flat winglike process or structure. **2** *Bot.* a winglike part, such as one of the wings of a sycamore seed. [C18: from L *āla* a wing]

à la (ɑː lɑː) *prep* **1** in the manner or style of. **2** as prepared in (a particular place) or by or for (a particular person). [C17: from F, short for *à la mode de* in the style of]

Ala. *abbrev. for* Alabama.

Alabama ★ (ˌæləˈbæmə) *n* **1** a state in the southeastern US, on the Gulf of Mexico: consists of coastal and W lowlands crossed by the Tombigbee, Black Warrior, and Alabama Rivers, with parts of the Tennessee Valley and Cumberland Plateau in the north; noted for producing cotton and white marble. Capital: Montgomery. Pop.: 4 273 084 (1996 est.). Area: 131 333 sq. km (50 708 sq. miles). Abbrevs.: **Ala.** or (with zip code) **AL** **2** a river in Alabama, flowing southwest to the Mobile and Tensaw Rivers. Length: 507 km (315 miles).
▸ ˌAla'bamian *adj*

alabaster ('æləˌbɑːstə) *n* **1** a fine-grained usually white, opaque, or translucent variety of gypsum. **2** a variety of hard semitranslucent calcite. ◆ *adj* **3** of or resembling alabaster. [C14: from OF *alabastre*, from L *alabaster*, from Gk *alabastros*]
▸ ˌala'bastrine *adj*

à la carte (ɑː lɑː 'kɑːt) *adj, adv* (of a menu) having dishes listed separately and individually priced. Cf. **table d'hôte.** [C19: from F, lit.: according to the card]

alack (ə'læk) *or* **alackaday** (ə'lækəˌdeɪ) *interj* an archaic or poetic word for **alas.** [C15: from *a* ah! + *lack* loss, LACK]

alacrity (ə'lækrɪtɪ) *n* liveliness or briskness. [C15: from L, from *alacer* lively]

Ala Dağ *or* **Ala Dagh** ★ (Turkish ɑ'lɑ dɑː) *n* **1** the E part of the Taurus Mountains, in SE Turkey, rising over 3600 m (12 000 ft). **2** a mountain range in E Turkey, rising over 3300 m (11 000 ft). **3** a mountain range in NE Turkey, rising over 3000 m (10 000 ft).

Alagez *or* **Alagöz** ★ (ɑlɑ'gœz) *n* the Turkish name for (Mount) **Aragats.**

Alagoas ★ (Portuguese ɑlɑ'goːɑʃ) *n* a state in NE Brazil, on the Atlantic coast. Capital: Maceió. Pop.: 2 685 400 (1995 est.). Area: 30 776 sq. km (11 031 sq. miles).

Alai ★ (ɑː'laɪ) *n* a mountain range in central Asia, in SW Kyrgyzstan running from the Tian Shan range in China into Tajikistan. Average height: 4800 m (16 000 ft), rising over 5850 m (19 500 ft).

Alain-Fournier ★ (French alɛ̃furnje) *n* real name *Henri-Alban Fournier.* 1886–1914, French novelist; author of *Le Grand Meaulnes* (1913; translated as *The Lost Domain*, 1959).

Alamein ★ ('æləˌmeɪn) *n* See **El Alamein.**

Alamo ★ (ˈæləˌməʊ) *n* **the.** a mission in San Antonio, Texas, the site of a siege and massacre in 1836 by Mexican forces under Santa Anna of a handful of American rebels fighting for Texan independence from Mexico.

à la mode (ɑː lɑː 'məʊd) *adj* **1** fashionable in style, design, etc. **2** (of meats) braised with vegetables in wine. [C17: from F: according to the fashion]

Alanbrooke ★ ('ælənˌbrʊk) *n* **Alan Francis Brooke,** 1st Viscount. 1883–1963, British field marshal; chief of Imperial General Staff (1941–46).

Åland Islands ★ ('ɔːlənd, 'ɔːlənd; Swedish 'oːland) *pl n* a group of over 6000 islands under Finnish administration, in the Gulf of Bothnia. Capital: Mariehamn. Pop.: 24 847 (1992). Finnish name: **Ahvenanmaa.**

Al-Anon ('æləˌnɒn) *n* an association for the families and friends of alcoholics to give mutual support.

alar ('eɪlə) *adj* relating to, resembling, or having wings or alae. [C19: from L *āla* a wing]

Alar ('eɪlɑː) *n* a chemical sprayed on cultivated apple trees in certain countries to increase fruit set; daminozide.

Alarcón ★ (Spanish alar'kon) *n* **Pedro Antonio de** ('peðro an'tonjo de). 1833–91, Spanish writer, noted for his *The Three-Cornered Hat* (1874).

Alaric ★ ('ælərɪk) *n* ?370–410 A.D., king of the Visigoths who served under the Roman emperor Theodosius I but later invaded Greece and Italy, capturing Rome in 410.

alarm (ə'lɑːm) *vb* (*tr*) **1** to fill with apprehension, anxiety, or fear. **2** to warn about danger; alert. **3** to fit or activate a burglar alarm on (a house, car, etc.). ◆ *n* **4** fear or terror aroused by awareness of danger. **5** apprehension or uneasiness. **6** a noise, signal, etc., warning of danger. **7** any device that transmits such a warning: *a burglar alarm.* **8a** the device in an alarm clock that triggers off the bell or buzzer. **8b** short for **alarm clock. 9** *Arch.* a call to arms. [C14: from OF *alarme*, from OIt. *all'arme* to arms; see ARM²]
▸ a'larming *adj*

alarm clock *n* a clock with a mechanism that sounds at a set time: used esp. for waking a person up.

alarmist (ə'lɑːmɪst) *n* **1** a person who alarms or attempts to alarm others needlessly. **2** a person who is easily alarmed. ◆ *adj* **3** characteristic of an alarmist.

alarum (ə'lærəm, -'lɑːr-) *n* **1** *Arch.* an alarmist, esp. a call to arms. **2** (used as a stage direction, esp. in Elizabethan drama) a loud disturbance or conflict (esp. in **alarums and excursions**). [C15: var. of ALARM]

alas (ə'læs) *sentence connector.* **1** unfortunately; regrettably: *there were, alas, none left.* ◆ *interj* **2** *Arch.* an exclamation of grief or alarm. [C13: from OF *ha las!* oh wretched!; *las* from L *lassus* weary]

Alas. *abbrev. for* Alaska.

Alaska ★ (ə'læskə) *n* **1** the largest state of the US, in the extreme northwest of North America: the aboriginal inhabitants are Eskimos; the earliest White settlements were made by the Russians; it was purchased by the US from Russia in 1867. It is mostly mountainous and volcanic, rising over 6000 m (20 000 ft), with the Yukon basin in the central region; large areas are covered by tundra; it has important mineral resources (chiefly coal, oil, and natural gas). Capital: Juneau. Pop.: 607 007 (1996 est.). Area: 1 530 694 sq. km (591 004 sq. miles). Abbrevs.: **Alas.** or (with zip code) **AK** **2 Gulf of.** the N part of the Pacific, between the Alaska Peninsula and the Alexander Archipelago.
▸ A'laskan *adj, n*

Alaska Highway ★ *n* a road extending from Dawson Creek, British Columbia, to Fairbanks, Alaska: built by the US Army (1942). Length: 2452 km (1523 miles). Originally called: **Alcan Highway.**

Alaska Peninsula ★ *n* an extension of the mainland of SW Alaska between the Pacific and the Bering Sea, ending in the Aleutian Islands. Length: about 644 km (400 miles).

Alaska Range ★ *n* a mountain range in S central Alaska. Highest peak: Mount McKinley, 6194 m (20 320 ft).

alate ('eɪleɪt) *adj* having wings or winglike extensions. [C17: from L, from *āla* wing]

alb (ælb) *n Christianity.* a long white linen vestment with sleeves worn by priests and others. [OE *albe*, from Med. L *alba* (*vestis*) white (clothing)]

Alb. *abbrev. for* Albania(n).

Alba ★ (Spanish 'alβa) *n* See (Duke of) **Alva.**

albacore ('ælbəˌkɔː) *n* a tunny occurring mainly in warm regions of the Atlantic and Pacific. It has very long pectoral fins and is a valued food fish. [C16: from Port., from Ar.]

Alba Longa ★ ('ælbə 'lɒŋɡə) *n* a city of ancient Latium, southeast of modern Rome: the legendary birthplace of Romulus and Remus.

Alban ★ ('ɔːlbən) *n* **Saint.** 3rd century A.D., the first English martyr. He was beheaded by the Romans on the site on which St Alban's Abbey now stands, for admitting his conversion to Christianity. Feast day: June 17.

Albania ★ (æl'beɪnɪə) *n* a republic in SE Europe, on the Balkan Peninsula: became independent in 1912 after more than four centuries of Turkish rule; established as a republic (1946) under Communist rule. A noncommunist government was elected in 1992. It is generally mountainous, rising over 2700 m (9000 ft), with exten-

★ people and places

sive forests. Language: Albanian. Religion: Muslim majority. Currency: lek. Capital: Tirana. Pop.: 3 293 000 (1997). Area: 28 749 sq. km (11 100 sq. miles).

Albany ★ ('ɔːlbənɪ) n **1** a city in E New York State, on the Hudson River: the state capital. Pop.: 104 828 (1994 est.). **2** a river in central Canada, flowing east and northeast to James Bay. Length: 982 km (610 miles).

Ibatross ('ælbə,trɒs) n **1** a large bird of cool southern oceans, with long narrow wings and a powerful gliding flight. See also **wandering albatross. 2** a constant and inescapable burden or handicap. **3** *Golf.* a score of three strokes under par for a hole. [C17: from Port. *alcatraz* pelican, from Ar., from *al* the + *ghattās* white-tailed sea eagle; infl. by L *albus* white: C20 in sense 2, from Coleridge's poem *The Rime of the Ancient Mariner* (1798)]

Ibedo (æl'biːdəʊ) n the ratio of the intensity of light reflected from an object, such as a planet, to that of the light it receives from the sun. [C19: from Church L: whiteness, from L *albus* white]

Albee ★ ('ɔːlbiː) n Edward. born 1928, US dramatist. His plays include *Who's Afraid of Virginia Woolf?* (1962), *Seascape* (1975), and *The Play about the Baby* (1998).

Ibeit (ɔːl'biːɪt) *conj* even though. [C14 *al be it*, that is, although it be (that)]

Albemarle Sound ★ ('ælbə,mɑːl) n an inlet of the Atlantic in NE North Carolina. Length: about 96 km (60 miles).

Alberich ★ (*German* 'albərɪç) n (in medieval German legend) the king of the dwarfs and guardian of the treasures of the Nibelungs.

Albers ★ ('ælbəz) n Josef. 1888–1976, US painter and poet, born in Germany.

albert ('ælbət) n a kind of watch chain usually attached to a waistcoat. [C19: after Prince ALBERT, who was presented with one by the jewellers of Birmingham in 1845]

Albert[1] ★ ('ælbət) n Lake. a former name for (**Lake**) **Mobutu.**

Albert[2] ★ ('ælbət) n Prince. full name *Albert Francis Charles Augustus Emmanuel of Saxe-Coburg-Gotha.* 1819–61, Prince Consort of Queen Victoria of Great Britain and Ireland.

Albert I ★ n **1** *c.* 1255–1308, king of Germany (1298–1308). **2** 1875–1934, king of the Belgians (1909–34). **3** called *Albert the Bear. c.* 1100–70, German military leader: first margrave of Brandenburg.

Albert II ★ n full name *Albert Felix Humbert Theodore Christian Eugene Marie.* born 1934, king of Belgium from 1993.

Alberta ★ (æl'bɜːtə) n a province of W Canada: mostly prairie, with the Rocky Mountains in the southwest. Capital: Edmonton. Pop.: 2 747 000 (1995 est.). Area: 661 188 sq. km (255 285 sq. miles). Abbrevs.: **Alta, AB**

Albert Edward ★ n a mountain in SE New Guinea, in the Owen Stanley Range. Height: 3993 m (13 100 ft).

Alberti ★ (*Italian* al'bɛrti) n **1** Domenico (do'meːniko). *c.* 1710–40, Italian composer of harpsichord sonatas. **2** Leon Battista (le'ɔn bat'tista). 1404–72, Italian Renaissance architect and painter.

Albertus Magnus ★ (æl'bɜːtəs 'mæɡnəs) n Saint. original name *Albert, Count von Böllstadt.* ?1193–1280, German scholastic philosopher; teacher of Thomas Aquinas and commentator on Aristotle. Feast day: Nov. 15.

albescent (æl'bɛs°nt) *adj* shading into or becoming white. [C19: from L *albēscere*, from *albus* white]
▸ al'bescence n

Albi ★ (*French* albi) n a town in S France: connected with the Albigensian heresy and the crusade against it. Pop.: 48 700 (1990).

Albigenses (,ælbɪ'dʒɛnsiːz) *pl n* members of a Manichean sect that flourished in S France from the 11th to the 13th century. [from Med. L: inhabitants of ALBI]
▸ ,Albi'gensian *adj* ▸ ,Albi'gensian,ism n

albino (æl'biːnəʊ) n, *pl* albinos. **1** a person with congenital absence of pigmentation in the skin, eyes, and hair. **2** any animal or plant that is deficient in pigment. [C18: via Port. & Sp. from L *albus* white]
▸ albinism ('ælbɪ,nɪzəm) n ▸ albinotic (,ælbɪ'nɒtɪk) *adj*

Albinoni ★ (*Italian* albi'noːni) n Tomaso (to'maːzo). 1671–1750, Italian composer.

Albinus ★ (æl'biːnəs) n another name for **Alcuin.**

Albion ★ ('ælbɪən) n Arch. or poetic. Britain or England. [C13: from L, of Celtic origin]

albite ('ælbaɪt) n a white, bluish-green, or reddish-grey feldspar mineral used in the manufacture of glass and as a gemstone. [C19: from L *albus* white]

Ålborg ★ (*Danish* 'ɔlbɔr) n a variant spelling of **Aalborg.**

album ('ælbəm) n **1** a book or binder consisting of blank pages, for keeping photographs, stamps, autographs, etc. **2** one or more long-playing CDs, cassettes, or records released as a single item. **3** a booklike holder containing sleeves for gramophone records. **4** *Chiefly Brit.* anthology. [C17: from L: blank tablet, from *albus* white]

albumen ('ælbjumɪn) n **1** the white of an egg; the nutritive substance that surrounds the yolk. **2** a variant spelling of **albumin.** [C16: from L: white of an egg, from *albus* white]

albumin *or* **albumen** ('ælbjumɪn) n any of a group of simple water-soluble proteins that are found in blood plasma, egg white, etc. [C19: from ALBUMEN + -IN]
▸ al'buminous *adj*

albuminoid (æl'bjuːmɪ,nɔɪd) *adj* **1** resembling albumin.
♦ n **2** another name for **scleroprotein.**

albuminuria (æl,bjuːmɪ'njʊərɪə) n the presence of albumin in the urine. Also called: **proteinuria.**

Albuquerque[1] ★ ('ælbə,kɜːkɪ) n a city in central New Mexico, on the Rio Grande. Pop.: 366 750 (1986 est.).

Albuquerque[2] ★ ('ælbə,kɜːkɪ; *Portuguese* albu'kɛrkə) n Afonso de (ə'fõsu də). 1453–1515, Portuguese navigator who established Portuguese colonies in the East by conquering Goa, Ceylon, Malacca, and Ormuz.

alburnum (æl'bɜːnəm) n a former name for **sapwood.** [C17: from L: sapwood, from *albus* white]

Albury-Wodonga ★ ('ɔːlbərɪ, -brɪ ,wʌ'dɒŋə) n a city in SE Australia, in S central New South Wales, on the Murray River: commercial centre of an agricultural region. Pop.: 63 610 (1991).

Alcaeus ★ (æl'siəs) n 7th century B.C., Greek lyric poet who wrote hymns, love songs, and political odes.

Alcaic (æl'keɪɪk) *adj* **1** of a metre used by Alcaeus, consisting of a strophe of four lines each with four feet. ♦ n **2** (*usually pl*) verse written in the Alcaic form. [C17: from LL *Alcaicus* of ALCAEUS]

alcalde (æl'kældɪ) *or* **alcade** (æl'keɪd) n (in Spain and Spanish America) the mayor or chief magistrate in a town. [C17: from Sp., from Ar. *al-qādī* the judge]

Alcan Highway ★ ('ælkæn) n original name of the Alaska Highway.

Alcatraz ★ ('ælkə,træz) n an island in W California, in San Francisco Bay: a federal prison until 1963.

alcazar (,ælkə'zɑː; *Spanish* al'kaθar) n any of various palaces or fortresses built in Spain by the Moors. [C17: from Sp., from Ar. *al-qasr* the castle]

Alcazar de San Juan ★ (,ælkə,zɑː; *Spanish* al'kaθar) n a town in S central Spain: associated with Cervantes and Don Quixote. Pop.: 25 679 (1991).

Alcestis ★ (æl'sɛstɪs) n Greek myth. the wife of king Admetus of Thessaly. To save his life, she died in his place, but was rescued from Hades by Hercules.

alchemist ('ælkəmɪst) n a person who practises alchemy.

alchemize *or* **alchemise** ('ælkə,maɪz) *vb* alchemizes, alchemizing, alchemized *or* alchemises, alchemising, alchemised. (*tr*) to alter (an element, metal, etc.) by alchemy.

alchemy ('ælkəmɪ) n, *pl* alchemies. **1** the pseudoscientific predecessor of chemistry that sought a method of transmuting base metals into gold, and an elixir to prolong life indefinitely. **2** a power like that of alchemy: *her beauty had a potent alchemy.* [C14 *alkamye*, via OF from Med. L, from Ar., from *al* the + *kīmiyā'* transmutation, from LGk *khēmeia* the art of transmutation]
▸ alchemic (æl'kɛmɪk) *or* al'chemical *adj*

★ people and places

alcheringa (ˌæltʃəˈrɪŋgə) *n* another name for **Dreamtime**. [from Abor., lit.: dream time]

Alchevsk ★ (ælˈtʃɛvsk) *n* a city in E Ukraine. Pop.: 124 000 (1996 est.). Former name (until 1992): **Kommunarsk**.

Alcibiades ★ (ˌælsɪˈbaɪəˌdiːz) *n* 450–404 B.C., Athenian statesman and general in the Peloponnesian War: brilliant, courageous, and unstable, he defected to the Spartans in 415, but returned and led the Athenian victories at Abydos (411) and Cyzicus (410).
▸ ˌAlciˌbiaˈdean *adj*

Alcides ★ (ælˈsaɪdiːz) *n* another name for **Hercules** (sense 1).

Alcinoüs ★ (ælˈsɪnəʊəs) *n* (in Homer's *Odyssey*) a Phaeacian king at whose court the shipwrecked Odysseus told of his wanderings. See also **Nausicaä**.

ALCM *abbrev. for* air-launched cruise missile: a type of cruise missile that can be launched from an aircraft.

Alcock ★ (ˈɔːlkɒk) *n* Sir **John William**. 1892–1919, English aviator who with A.W. Brown made the first nonstop flight across the Atlantic (1919).

alcohol (ˈælkəˌhɒl) *n* **1** a colourless flammable liquid, the active principle of intoxicating drinks, produced by the fermentation of sugars. Formula: C_2H_5OH. Also called: **ethanol, ethyl alcohol**. **2** a drink or drinks containing this substance. **3** *Chem.* any one of a class of organic compounds that contain one or more hydroxyl groups bound to carbon atoms that are not part of an aromatic ring. Cf. **phenol** (sense 2). [C16: via NL from Med. L, from Ar. *al-kuhl* powdered antimony]

alcohol-free *adj* **1** (of beer or wine) containing only a trace of alcohol. Cf. **low-alcohol**. **2** (of a period of time) during which no alcoholic drink is consumed: *there should be one or two alcohol-free days per week.*

alcoholic (ˌælkəˈhɒlɪk) *n* **1** a person affected by alcoholism. ♦ *adj* **2** of, relating to, containing, or resulting from alcohol.

Alcoholics Anonymous *n* an association of alcoholics who try, esp. by mutual assistance, to overcome alcoholism.

alcoholism (ˈælkəhɒˌlɪzəm) *n* a condition in which dependence on alcohol harms a person's health, family life, etc.

alcoholize *or* **alcoholise** (ˈælkəhɒˌlaɪz) *vb* **alcoholizes, alcoholizing, alcoholized** *or* **alcoholises, alcoholising, alcoholised**. (*tr*) to turn into alcoholic drink, as by fermenting or mixing with alcohol.
▸ ˌalcoˌholiˈzation *or* ˌalcoˌholiˈsation *n*

alcopop (ˈælkəʊˌpɒp) *n Inf.* an alcoholic drink that tastes like a soft drink. [C20: from ALCO(HOL) + POP[1] (sense 11)]

Alcoran *or* **Alkoran** (ˌælkɒˈrɑːn) *n* another name for the **Koran**.
▸ ˌAlcoˈranic *or* ˌAlkoˈranic *adj*

Alcott ★ (ˈɔːlkət) *n* **Louisa May**. 1832–88, US novelist, noted for her children's books, esp. *Little Women* (1869).

alcove (ˈælkəʊv) *n* **1** a recess or niche in the wall of a room, as for a bed, books, etc. **2** any recessed usually vaulted area, as in a garden wall. **3** any covered or secluded spot. [C17: from F, from Sp. *alcoba*, from Ar. *al-qubbah* the vault]

Alcuin (ˈælkwɪn) *or* **Albinus** ★ *n* 735–804 A.D., English scholar and theologian; friend and adviser of Charlemagne.

Aldabra ★ (ælˈdæbrə) *n* an island group in the Indian Ocean: part of the British Indian Ocean Territory (1965–76); now administratively part of the Seychelles.

Aldan ★ (*Russian* alˈdan) *n* a river in E Russia in SE Sakha Republic, rising in the **Aldan Mountains** and flowing north and west to the Lena River. Length: about 2700 km (1700 miles).

Aldeburgh ★ (ˈɔːlbərə) *n* a small resort in SE England, in Suffolk: site of an annual music festival established in 1948 by Benjamin Britten. Pop.: 2654 (1991).

aldehyde (ˈældɪˌhaɪd) *n* **1** any organic compound containing the group -CHO. Aldehydes are oxidized to carboxylic acids. **2** (*modifier*) consisting of, containing,

or concerned with the group -CHO. [C19: from N *al*(*cohol*) *dehyd*(*rogenātum*) dehydrogenated alcohol]
▸ **aldehydic** (ˌældəˈhɪdɪk) *adj*

al dente (ˌæl ˈdɛntɪ) *adj* (of pasta) still firm after cooking [It., lit: to the tooth]

alder (ˈɔːldə) *n* **1** a shrub or tree of the birch family, having toothed leaves and conelike fruits. The wood is use for bridges, etc., because it resists underwater rot. **2** any of several similar trees or shrubs. [OE *alor*]

alderman (ˈɔːldəmən) *n, pl* **aldermen**. **1** (in England an Wales until 1974) one of the senior members of a loca council, elected by other councillors. **2** (in the US, Car ada, Australia, etc.) a member of the governing body of municipality. **3** *History*. a variant spelling of **ealdorma** [OE *aldormann*, from *ealdor* chief (comp. of *eald* OLD) *mann* MAN]
▸ **aldermanic** (ˌɔːldəˈmænɪk) *adj*

Aldermaston ★ (ˈɔːldəˌmɑːstən) *n* a village in S Eng land, in Berkshire SW of Reading: site of the Atomi Weapons Research Establishment and starting point o the Aldermaston marches (1958–63), organized by th Campaign for Nuclear Disarmament. Pop.: 2200 (lates est.).

Alderney ★ (ˈɔːldənɪ) *n* **1** one of the Channel Islands, i the English Channel: separated from the French coas by a dangerous tidal channel (the **Race of Alderney**). Pop. 2375 (1994 est.). Area: 8 sq. km (3 sq. miles). Frencl name: **Aurigny** (oriɲi). **2** any of a breed of dairy cattle orig inating from the island of Alderney.

Aldershot ★ (ˈɔːldəˌʃɒt) *n* a town in S England, in Hamp shire: site of a large military camp. Pop.: 51 356 (1991)

Aldington ★ (ˈɔːldɪŋtən) *n* **Richard**. 1892–1962, Englisl poet, novelist, and biographer. His novels include *Deati of a Hero* (1929) and *The Colonel's Daughter* (1931), whicl reflect postwar disillusion following World War I.

Aldis lamp (ˈɔːldɪs) *n* a portable signalling lamp. [C20 after its inventor A.C.W. *Aldis*]

Aldiss ★ (ˈɔːldɪs) *n* **Brian W**(ilson). born 1925, British sci ence fiction writer. His works include *Non-Stop* (1958) *Somewhere East of Life* (1994), and *The Detached Retine* (1995).

Aldridge-Brownhills ★ (ˈɔːldrɪdʒˈbraʊnˌhɪlz) *n* a towr in central England, in Walsall unitary authority, Wes Midlands: formed by the amalgamation of neighbour ing towns in 1966. Pop.: 37 444 (1991).

aldrin (ˈɔːldrɪn) *n* a poisonous crystalline solid, mostly $C_{12}H_8Cl_6$, used as an insecticide. [C20: after K. *Alde* (1902–58), G chemist]

Aldrin ★ (ˈɔːldrɪn) *n* **Edwin Eugene Jr.**, known as *Buzz*. borr 1930, US astronaut; the second man to set foot on the moon.

Aldus Manutius ★ (ˈɔːldəs məˈnjuːʃɪəs) *n* 1450–1515 Italian printer, noted for his fine editions of the classics He introduced italic type.

ale (eɪl) *n* **1** a beer fermented in an open vessel using yeasts that rise to the top of the brew. Compare **beer lager. 2** (formerly) an alcoholic drink made by fermentl ing a cereal, esp. barley, but differing from beer by being unflavoured by hops. **3** *Chiefly Brit.* another word fo **beer**. [OE *alu, ealu*]

aleatory (ˈeɪlɪətərɪ) *or* **aleatoric** (ˌeɪlɪəˈtɒrɪk) *adj* **1** de pendent on chance. **2** (esp. of a musical composition) in volving elements chosen at random by the performer. [C17: from L, from *āleātor* gambler, from *ālea* game of chance]

Alecto ★ (əˈlɛktəʊ) *n Greek myth.* one of the three Furies; the others are Megaera and Tisiphone.

alee (əˈliː) *adv, adj* (*postpositive*) *Naut.* on or towards the lee: *with the helm alee.*

alehouse (ˈeɪlˌhaʊs) *n* **1** *Arch.* a place where ale was sold; tavern. **2** *Inf.* a pub.

Aleichem ★ (ɑːˈleɪçəm) *n* **Sholom** (ˈʃɒləm), real name Solomon Rabinowitz. 1859–1916, US Jewish writer, borr in Russia. His works include *Tevye the Milkman*, adapted for the musical *Fiddler on the Roof*.

Aleksandropol ★ (*Russian* alɪksanˈdrɔpəlj) *n* the former name (from 1837 until after the Revolution) of **Leninakan**.

Aleksandrovsk ★ (*Russian* alɪk'sandrəfsk) *n* the former name (until 1921) of **Zaporozhye**.

Alembert, d' ★ (*French* dalɑ̃bɛr) *n* **Jean Le Rond** (ʒɑ̃ lə rɔ̃). 1717–83, French mathematician, noted for his *Traité de dynamique* (1743).

alembic (ə'lɛmbɪk) *n* **1** an obsolete type of retort used for distillation. **2** anything that distils or purifies. [C14: from Med. L, from Ar. *al-anbīq* the still, from Gk *ambix* cup]

Alençon ★ (*French* alɑ̃sɔ̃) *n* a town in NW France: early lace-manufacturing centre. Pop.: 31 140 (1990).

aleph ('ɑːlɪf; *Hebrew* 'alɛf) *n* the first letter in the Hebrew alphabet. [Heb.: ox]

aleph-null *or* **aleph-zero** *n* the smallest infinite cardinal number; the cardinal number of the set of positive integers.

Aleppo ★ (ə'lɛpəu) *n* an ancient city in NW Syria: industrial and commercial centre. Pop.: 1 591 400 (1994 est.). French name: **Alep** (alɛp). Arabic name: **Haleb** ('halɛp).

alert (ə'lɜːt) *adj* (*usually postpositive*) **1** vigilantly attentive: *alert to the problems*. **2** brisk, nimble, or lively. ◆ *n* **3** an alarm or warning. **4** the period during which such a warning remains in effect. **5 on the alert. 5a** on guard against danger, attack, etc. **5b** watchful; ready. ◆ *vb* (*tr*) **6** to warn or signal (troops, police, etc.) to prepare for action. **7** to warn of danger, an attack, etc. [C17: from It. *all'erta* on the watch, from *erta* lookout post]
▶ a'lertly *adv* ▶ a'lertness *n*

Alessandria ★ (*Italian* ales'sandrja) *n* a town in NW Italy, in Piedmont. Pop.: 93 866 (1990).

Ålesund *or* **Aalesund** ★ (*Norwegian* 'oːləsun) *n* a port and market town in W Norway, on an island between Bergen and Trondheim: fishing and sealing fleets. Pop.: 35 862 (1990).

aleurone (ə'luərən) *or* **aleuron** (ə'luərɒn) *n* a protein that occurs in the form of storage granules in plant cells, esp. in seeds such as maize. [C19: from Gk *aleuron* flour]

Aleut (æ'luːt) *n* **1** a member of a people inhabiting the Aleutian Islands and SW Alaska, related to the Eskimos. **2** the language of this people, related to Eskimo. [from Russian *aleút*, prob. of native origin]
▶ Aleutian (ə'luːʃən) *n, adj*

Aleutian Islands ★ *n* a chain of over 150 volcanic islands, extending southwestwards from the Alaska Peninsula between the N Pacific and the Bering Sea.

A level *n Brit.* **1a** the advanced level of a subject taken for the General Certificate of Education. **1b** (*as modifier*): *A-level maths*. **2** a pass in a subject at A level: *he has two A levels*.

alewife ('eɪl,waɪf) *n, pl* **alewives**. a North American fish similar to the herring. [C19: ?from F *alose* shad]

Alexander ★ (,ælɪg'zɑːndə) *n* **Harold** (**Rupert Leofric George**), **Earl Alexander of Tunis**. 1891–1969, British field marshal in World War II, who commanded in North Africa (1943) and Sicily and Italy (1944–45); governor general of Canada (1946–52); British minister of defence (1952–54).

Alexander I ★ *n* **1** *c.* 1080–1124, king of Scotland (1107–24), son of Malcolm III. **2** 1777–1825, tsar of Russia (1801–25), who helped defeat Napoleon and formed the Holy Alliance (1815).

Alexander II ★ *n* **1** 1198–1249, king of Scotland (1214–49), son of William I. **2** 1818–81, tsar of Russia (1855–81), son of Nicholas I; assassinated by the Nihilists.

Alexander III ★ *n* **1** 1241–86, king of Scotland (1249–86), son of Alexander II. **2** original name *Orlando Bandinelli*. died 1181, pope (1159–81), who excommunicated Barbarossa. **3** 1845–94, tsar of Russia (1881–94), son of Alexander II.

Alexander VI ★ *n* original name *Rodrigo Borgia*. 1431–1503, pope (1492–1503): noted for his extravagance and patronage of the arts.

Alexander Archipelago ★ *n* a group of over 1000 islands along the coast of SE Alaska.

Alexander I Island ★ *n* an island of Antarctica, west of Palmer Land, in the Bellingshausen Sea. Length: about 378 km (235 miles).

Alexander Nevski ★ ('nɛvski, 'nɛf-; *Russian* 'njefskij) *n* **Saint**. ?1220–63, Russian prince and military leader, who defeated the Swedes at the River Neva (1240) and the Teutonic knights at Lake Peipus (1242).

Alexander technique *n* a technique for developing awareness of one's posture and movement in order to improve it. [C20: named after Frederick Matthias *Alexander* (d. 1955), Australian actor who originated it]

Alexander the Great ★ *n* 356–323 B.C., king of Macedon, who conquered Greece (336), Egypt (331), and the Persian Empire (328), and founded Alexandria.

Alexandra ★ (,ælɪg'zɑːndrə) *n* **1** 1844–1925, queen consort of Edward VII of Great Britain and Ireland. **2** 1872–1918, the wife of Nicholas II of Russia; her misrule while Nicholas was supreme commander of the Russian forces during World War I precipitated the Russian Revolution.

Alexandretta ★ (,ælɪgzɑːn'drɛtə) *n* the former name of **Iskenderun**.

Alexandria ★ (,ælɪg'zændrɪə, -'zɑːn-) *n* the chief port of Egypt, on the Nile Delta: cultural centre of ancient times, founded by Alexander the Great (332 B.C.). Pop.: 3 382 000 (1994 est.). Arabic name: **El Iskandariyah**.
▶ ,Alex'andrian *adj, n*

Alexandrine (,ælɪg'zændraɪn) *n* **1** a line of verse having six iambic feet, usually with a caesura after the third foot. ◆ *adj* **2** of or written in Alexandrines. [C16: from F, from *Alexandre*, 15th-cent. poem in this metre]

alexandrite (,ælɪg'zændraɪt) *n* a green variety of chrysoberyl used as a gemstone. [C19: after ALEXANDER I of Russia; see -ITE[1]]

Alexandroúpolis ★ (*Greek* alɛksan'ðrupɔlis) *n* a port in NE Greece, in W Thrace. Pop.: 39 283 (1991 est.). Former name (until the end of World War I): **Dedéagach**.

alexia (ə'lɛksɪə) *n* a disorder of the central nervous system characterized by impaired ability to read. [C19: from NL, from A-[1] + Gk *lexis* speech]

Alexis Mikhailovich ★ (ə'lɛksɪs mɪ'kaɪlə,vɪtʃ) *n* 1629–76, tsar of Russia (1645–76); father of Peter the Great.

alfalfa (æl'fælfə) *n* a leguminous plant of Europe and Asia, widely cultivated for forage. Also called: **lucerne**. [C19: from Sp., from Ar. *al-fasfasah*]

Alfonso VI ★ (*Spanish* al'fonso) *n* died 1109, king of Léon (1065–1109) and of Castile (1072–1109). He appointed his vassal, the Spanish hero El Cid, ruler of Valencia.

Alfonso XIII ★ (*Spanish* al'fonso) *n* 1886–1941, king of Spain (1886–1931): abdicated on the establishment of the republic.

Alfred the Great ★ ('ælfrɪd) *n* 849–99, king of Wessex (871–99) and overlord of England, who defeated the Danes.

alfresco (æl'frɛskəu) *adj, adv* in the open air. [C18: from It.: in the cool]

Alfvén ★ (al'ven) *n* **Hannes Olaf Gösta** ('hannes 'uːlaf 'jøsta). 1908–95, Swedish physicist, noted for his research on magnetohydrodynamics; shared the Nobel prize for physics 1970.

alg. *abbrev. for* algebra *or* algebraic.

Alg. *abbrev. for* Algeria(n).

algae ('ældʒiː) *pl n, sing* **alga** ('ælgə). unicellular or multicellular organisms formerly classified as plants, occurring in water or moist ground, that have chlorophyll but lack true stems, roots, and leaves. [C16: from L, pl of *alga* seaweed, from ?]
▶ **algal** ('ælgəl) *or* **algoid** ('ælgɔɪd) *adj*

Algarve ★ (æl'gɑːv) *n* **the**. an area in the south of Portugal, on the Atlantic; it approximately corresponds to the administrative district of Faro: fishing and tourism important.

algebra ('ældʒɪbrə) *n* **1** a branch of mathematics in which arithmetical operations and relationships are generalized by using symbols to represent numbers. **2**

any abstract calculus, a formal language in which functions and operations can be defined and their properties studied. [C14: from Med. L, from Ar. *al-jabr* the bone-setting, mathematical reduction]
‣ **algebraic** (ˌældʒɪˈbreɪɪk) *or* ˌalgeˈbraical *adj* ‣ **algebraist** (ˌældʒɪˈbreɪɪst) *n*

Algeciras ★ (ˌældʒɪˈsɪərəs; *Spanish* alxeˈθiras) *n* a port and resort in SW Spain, on the Strait of Gibraltar: scene of a conference of the Great Powers in 1906. Pop.: 103 787 (1994 est.).

Algeria ★ (ælˈdʒɪərɪə) *n* a republic in NW Africa, on the Mediterranean: became independent in 1962, after more than a century of French rule; one-party constitution adopted in 1976; religious extremists began a campaign of violence in 1988; consists chiefly of the N Sahara, with the Atlas Mountains in the north, and contains rich deposits of oil and natural gas. Official language: Arabic; French and Berber also widely spoken. Religion: Muslim. Currency: dinar. Capital: Algiers. Pop.: 29 476 000 (1997). Area: about 2 382 800 sq. km (920 000 sq. miles). French name: **Algérie** (alʒeri).
‣ **Al'gerian** *or* **Algerine** (ˈældʒəˌriːn) *adj, n*

-algia *n combining form.* denoting pain in the part specified: *neuralgia; odontalgia.* [from Gk *algos* pain]
‣ **-algic** *adj combining form.*

algid (ˈældʒɪd) *adj Med.* chilly or cold. [C17: from L *algidus*, from *algēre* to be cold]
‣ **al'gidity** *n*

Algiers ★ (ælˈdʒɪəz) *n* the capital of Algeria, an ancient port on the Mediterranean; up to 1830 a centre of piracy. Pop.: 2 168 000 (1985 est.). Arabic name: **Al-Jezair** (ˌældʒɛˈzɑːɪə). French name: **Alger** (alʒe).

alginate (ˈældʒɪˌneɪt) *n* a salt or ester of alginic acid.

alginic acid (ælˈdʒɪnɪk) *n* a white or yellowish powdery substance having hydrophilic properties. Extracted from kelp, it is used mainly in the food and textile industries.

Algol (ˈælgɒl) *n* a computer-programming language designed for mathematical and scientific purposes. [C20: *alg(orithmic) o(riented) l(anguage)*]

algolagnia (ˌælgəˈlægnɪə) *n* sexual pleasure got from suffering or inflicting pain. [ML, from Gk *algos* pain + *lagneiā* lust]

Algonquian (ælˈgɒŋkɪən, -kwɪ-) *or* **Algonkian** *n* **1** a widespread family of North American Indian languages. **2** (*pl* **Algonquians** *or* **Algonquian**) a member of any of the North American Indian peoples that speak any of these languages. ◆ *adj* **3** denoting or relating to this linguistic family or its speakers.

Algonquin (ælˈgɒŋkɪn, -kwɪn) *or* **Algonkin** (ælˈgɒŋkɪn) *n* **1** (*pl* **Algonquins, Algonquin** *or* **Algonkins, Algonkin**) a member of a North American Indian people formerly living along the St Lawrence and Ottawa Rivers in Canada. **2** The language of this people, a dialect of Ojibwa. ◆ *n, adj* **3** a variant of **Algonquian**. [C17: from Canad. F., earlier written as *Algoumequin*; perhaps rel. to Micmac *algoomaking* at the fish-spearing place]

algorism (ˈælgəˌrɪzəm) *n* **1** the Arabic or decimal system of counting. **2** the skill of computation. **3** an algorithm. [C13: from OF, from Med. L, from Ar., from the name of abu-Ja'far Mohammed ibn-Mūsa *al-Khuwārizmi*, 9th-cent. Persian mathematician]

algorithm (ˈælgəˌrɪðəm) *n* **1** a logical arithmetical or computational procedure that if correctly applied ensures the solution of a problem. **2** *Logic, maths.* a recursive procedure whereby an infinite sequence of terms can be generated. ◆ Also called: **algorism**. [C17: changed from ALGORISM, infl. by Gk *arithmos* number]
‣ ˌalgo'rithmic *adj*

Algren ★ (ˈɔːlgrən) *n* **Nelson**. 1909–81, US novelist. His novels, mostly set in Chicago, include *Never Come Morning* (1942) and *The Man with the Golden Arm* (1949).

Alhambra ★ (ælˈhæmbrə) *n* a citadel and palace in Granada, Spain, built for the Moorish kings during the 13th and 14th centuries: noted for its rich ornamentation.
‣ **Alhambresque** (ˌælhæmˈbrɛsk) *adj*

Al Hijrah *or* **Al Hijra** (æl ˈhɪdʒrə) *n* an annual Muslim

festival marking the beginning of the Muslim year: commemorates Mohammed's move from Mecca to M dina. See also **Hegira**. [from Ar. *hijrah* emigration flight]

Al Hufuf *or* **Al Hofuf** ★ (æl huˈfuːf) *n* a town in E Sau Arabia: a trading centre with nearby oilfields and oase Pop.: 102 000 (latest est.).

Ali ★ (ˈɑːliː) *n* **1** ?600–661 A.D., fourth caliph of Islam (65ᵉ 61 A.D.), considered the first caliph by the Shiites: cousi and son-in-law of Mohammed. **2 Mehemet**. See **Mehem** **Ali**. **3 Muhammad**. See **Muhammad Ali**.

alias (ˈeɪlɪəs) *adv* **1** at another time or place known as ᵉ named: *Dylan, alias Zimmerman.* ◆ *n, pl* **aliases**. **2** an ᵃ sumed name. [C16: from L *aliās* (adv) otherwise, froᵐ *alius* other]

aliasing (ˈeɪlɪəsɪŋ) *n Radio & TV.* the error in a vision ᵒ sound signal arising from limitations in the system thᵃ generates or processes the signal.

alibi (ˈælɪˌbaɪ) *n, pl* **alibis**. **1** *Law.* **1a** a defence by an aᶜ cused person that he was elsewhere at the time the criᵐ was committed. **1b** the evidence given to prove this. *Inf.* an excuse. ◆ *vb* **alibis, alibiing, alibied**. **3** (*tr*) to proviᶜ with an alibi. [C18: from L *alibī* elsewhere, from *aliᵘ* other + -*bī* as in *ubī* where]

Alicante ★ (ˌælɪˈkænti) *n* a port in SE Spain: commerciᵃ centre. Pop.: 274 964 (1994 est.).

Alice (ˈælɪs) *or* **the Alice** ★ *n Austral. sl.* short for **Aliᶜ Springs**.

Alice band *n* an ornamental band worn across the froᵐ of the hair to hold it back from the face.

Alice-in-Wonderland *adj* fantastic; irrational. [C2ᵉ alluding to the absurdities of Wonderland in Lewⁱ Carroll's book]

Alice Springs ★ *n* a town in central Australia, in thᵉ Northern Territory, in the Macdonnell Ranges: capitᵃ of the former territory of Central Australia. Pop.: 24 85ᵉ (1994). Former name (until 1931): **Stuart**.

alicyclic (ˌælɪˈsaɪklɪk, -ˈsɪk-) *adj* (of an organic comᵖ pound) having essentially aliphatic properties, in spit ᵒ of the presence of a ring of carbon atoms. [C19: froᵐ ALI(PHATIC) + CYCLIC]

alidade (ˈælɪˌdeɪd) *or* **alidad** (ˈælɪˌdæd) *n* **1** a surveyinᵍ instrument used for drawing lines of sight on a distaᵣ object and taking angular measurements. **2** the uppᵉ rotatable part of a theodolite. [C15: from F, from Meᵈ L, from Ar. *al-'idāda* the revolving radius of a circle]

alien (ˈeɪlɪən) *n* **1** a person owing allegiance to a countᵣ other than that in which he lives. **2** any being or thinᵍ foreign to its environment. **3** (in science fiction) a beiⁿ from another world. ◆ *adj* **4** unnaturalized; foreign. ⁵ having foreign allegiance: *alien territory.* **6** unfamiliar: ᵃ *alien quality.* **7** (*postpositive*; foll. by *to*) repugnant or opᵖ posed (to): *war is alien to his philosophy.* **8** (in science fiᶜ tion) of or from another world. [C14: from L *aliēnuᵐ* foreign, from *alius* other]

alienable (ˈeɪlɪənəbᵊl) *adj Law.* (of property) transferablᵉ to another owner.
‣ ˌaliena'bility *n*

alienate (ˈeɪlɪəˌneɪt) *vb* **alienates, alienating, alienated**. (*tr*) to cause (a friend, etc.) to become unfriendly or hostilᵉ **2** to turn away: *to alienate the affections of a person.* **3** *Laⁱ* to transfer the ownership of (property, etc.) to anothᵉ person.
‣ ˌalien'ation *n* ‣ 'alienˌator *n*

alienee (ˌeɪlɪəˈniː) *n Law.* a person to whom a transfer ᵒ property is made.

alienist (ˈeɪlɪənɪst) *n US.* a psychiatrist who specializes iⁿ the legal aspects of mental illness.

alienor (ˈeɪlɪənə) *n Law.* a person who transfers propertⁱ to another.

aliform (ˈælɪˌfɔːm) *adj* wing-shaped. [C19: from Nᴸ *āliformis*, from L *āla* a wing]

Aligarh ★ (ˌɑːlɪˈɡɑː, ˌælɪ-) *n* a city in N India, in W Uttaᵣ Pradesh, with a famous Muslim university (1920). Pop.ᵗ 480 520 (1991).

alight¹ (əˈlaɪt) *vb* **alights, alighting, alighted** *or* **alit**. (*intr*) ¹ (usually foll. by *from*) to step out (of): *to alight from a taxi*

★ people and places

2 to come to rest; land: *a thrush alighted on the wall.* [OE *ālīhtan*, from A-[2] + *līhtan* to make less heavy]

alight[2] (ə'laɪt) *adj* (*postpositive*), *adv* **1** burning; on fire. **2** illuminated. [OE, from *ālīhtan* to light up]

align (ə'laɪn) *vb* **1** to place or become placed in a line. **2** to bring (components or parts) into proper coordination or relation. **3** (*tr;* usually foll. by *with*) to bring (a person, country, etc.) into agreement with the policy, etc., of another. [C17: from OF, from *à ligne* into line]

alignment (ə'laɪnmənt) *n* **1** arrangement in a straight line. **2** the line or lines formed in this manner. **3** alliance with a party, cause, etc. **4** proper coordination or relation of components. **5** a ground plan of a railway, road, etc.

alike (ə'laɪk) *adj* (*postpositive*) **1** possessing the same or similar characteristics: *they all look alike.* ◆ *adv* **2** in the same or a similar manner or degree: *they walk alike.* [OE *gelīc*]

aliment ('ælɪmənt) *n* something that nourishes or sustains the body or mind. [C15: from L *alimentum* food, from *alere* to nourish]
▸ ˌali'mental *adj*

alimentary (ˌælɪ'mɛntərɪ) *adj* **1** of or relating to nutrition. **2** providing sustenance or nourishment.

alimentary canal *n* the tubular passage extending from the mouth to the anus, through which food is passed and digested.

alimentation (ˌælɪmɛn'teɪʃən) *n* **1** nourishment. **2** sustenance; support.

alimony ('ælɪmənɪ) *n Law.* (formerly) an allowance paid under a court order by one spouse to another when they are separated but not divorced. See also **maintenance**. [C17: from L, from *alere* to nourish]

A-line ('eɪˌlaɪn) *adj* (of garments) flaring out slightly from the waist or shoulders.

Ali Pasha ★ ('ɑːliː 'pɑːʃə) *n* known as *the Lion of Janina.* 1741–1822, Turkish pasha and ruler of Albania (1787–1820), who was deposed and assassinated after intriguing against Turkey.

aliphatic (ˌælɪ'fætɪk) *adj* (of an organic compound) not aromatic, esp. having an open chain structure. [C19: from Gk *aleiphat-, aleiphar* oil]

aliquant ('ælɪkwənt) *adj Maths.* of or signifying a quantity or number that is not an exact divisor of a given quantity or number: *5 is an aliquant part of 12.* [C17: from NL, from L *aliquantus* somewhat, a certain quantity of]

aliquot ('ælɪˌkwɒt) *adj Maths.* of or signifying an exact divisor of a quantity or number: *3 is an aliquot part of 12.* [C16: from L: several, a few]

A list *n* a the most socially desirable category. **b** (*as modifier*): *an A-list event.* ◆ Cf. **B list**.

alit (ə'lɪt) *vb* a rare past tense and past participle of **alight**[1].

aliterate (eɪ'lɪtərɪt) *n* **1** a person who is able to read but disinclined to do so. ◆ *adj* **2** of or relating to aliterates.

alive (ə'laɪv) *adj* (*postpositive*) **1** living; having life. **2** in existence; active: *they kept hope alive.* **3** (*immediately postpositive*) now living: *the happiest woman alive.* **4** full of life; lively. **5** (usually foll. by *with*) animated: *a face alive with emotion.* **6** (foll. by *to*) aware (of); sensitive (to). **7** (foll. by *with*) teeming (with): *the mattress was alive with fleas.* **8** *Electronics.* another word for **live**[2] (sense 11). [OE *on līfe* in LIFE]

alizarin (ə'lɪzərɪn) *n* a brownish-yellow powder or orange-red crystalline solid used as a dye. [C19: prob. from F, from Ar. *al-ʿasārah* the juice, from *ʿasara* to squeeze]

alkali ('ælkəˌlaɪ) *n, pl* **alkalis** or **alkalies. 1** *Chem.* a soluble base or a solution of a base. **2** a soluble mineral salt that occurs in arid soils. [C14: from Med. L, from Ar. *al-qili* the ashes (of saltwort)]

alkali metal *n* any of the monovalent metals lithium, sodium, potassium, rubidium, caesium, and francium.

alkaline ('ælkəˌlaɪn) *adj* having the properties of or containing an alkali.
▸ **alkalinity** (ˌælkə'lɪnɪtɪ) *n*

alkaline earth *n* **1** Also called: **alkaline earth metal, alkaline earth element.** any of the divalent electropositive metals beryllium, magnesium, calcium, strontium, barium, and radium. **2** an oxide of one of the alkaline earth metals.

alkalize or **alkalise** ('ælkəˌlaɪz) *vb* **alkalizes, alkalizing, alkalized** or **alkalises, alkalising, alkalised.** (*tr*) to make alkaline.
▸ 'alkaˌlizable or 'alkaˌlisable *adj*

alkaloid ('ælkəˌlɔɪd) *n* any of a group of nitrogenous compounds found in plants. Many are poisonous and some are used as drugs.

alkane ('ælkeɪn) *n* any saturated aliphatic hydrocarbon with the general formula C_nH_{2n+2}. Former name: **paraffin**.

alkane series *n* a homologous series of saturated hydrocarbons starting with methane and having the general formula C_nH_{2n+2}. Also called: **methane series**.

alkanet ('ælkəˌnɛt) *n* **1** a European plant, the roots of which yield a red dye. **2** the dye obtained. [C14: from Sp., from Med. L, from Ar. *al* the + *hinnā'* henna]

alkene ('ælkiːn) *n* any unsaturated aliphatic hydrocarbon with the general formula C_nH_{2n}. Former name: **olefine**.

alkene series *n* a homologous series of unsaturated hydrocarbons starting with ethylene (ethene) and having the general formula C_nH_{2n}. Also called: **ethylene series, ethene series.**

Alkmaar ★ (*Dutch* 'ɑlkmɑːr) *n* a city in the W Netherlands, in North Holland. Pop.: 92 962 (1994).

Alkoran or **Alcoran** (ˌælkɒ'rɑːn) *n* a less common name for the **Koran**.

alkyd resin ('ælkɪd) *n* any of several synthetic resins made from a dicarboxylic acid, used in paints and adhesives.

alkyl ('ælkɪl) *n* (*modifier*) of or containing the monovalent group C_nH_{2n+1}: *alkyl radical.* [C19: from G, from *Alk(ohol)* ALCOHOL + -YL]

alkylating agent ('ælkɪˌleɪtɪŋ) *n* any cytotoxic drug containing alkyl groups that acts by damaging DNA; widely used in chemotherapy.

alkyne ('ælkaɪn) *n* any unsaturated aliphatic hydrocarbon with the general formula C_nH_{2n-2}.

alkyne series *n* a homologous series of unsaturated hydrocarbons starting with acetylene (ethyne) and having the general formula C_nH_{2n-2}. Also called: **acetylene series.**

all (ɔːl) *determiner* **1a** the whole quantity or amount of; everyone of a class: *all the rice; all men are mortal.* **1b** (*as pronoun; functioning as sing or pl*): *all of it is nice; all are welcome.* **1c** (*in combination with a noun used as a modifier*): *an all-night sitting; an all-ticket match.* **2** the greatest possible: *in all earnestness.* **3** any whatever: *beyond all doubt.* **4** (*as pronoun*): *all along. all the time.* **5 all but.** nearly: *all but dead.* **6 all of.** no less or smaller than: *she's all of thirteen years.* **7 all over. 7a** finished. **7b** everywhere (in, on, etc.): *all over England.* **7c** *Inf.* typically (in *that's me* (**him**, etc.) **all over). 7d** unduly effusive towards. **8 all in all. 8a** everything considered: *all in all, it was a great success.* **8b** the object of one's attention: *you are my all in all.* **9 all the.** (foll. by a comp. adj or adv) so much (more or less) than otherwise: *we must work all the faster now.* **10 all too.** definitely but regrettably: *it's all too true.* **11 at all. 11a** (used with a negative or in a question) in any way or to any degree: *I didn't know that at all.* **11b** anyway: *I'm surprised you came at all.* **12 be all for.** *Inf.* to be strongly in favour of. **13 for all. 13a** in so far as: *for all anyone knows, he was a baron.* **13b** notwithstanding: *for all my pushing, I still couldn't move it.* **14 for all that.** in spite of that: *he was a nice man for all that.* **15 in all.** altogether: *there were five in all.* ◆ *adv* **16** (in scores of games) apiece; each: *the score was three all.* ◆ *n* **17** (preceded by *my, his,* etc.) (one's) complete effort or interest: *to give your all.* **18** totality or whole. [OE *eall*]

all- *combining form.* a variant of **allo-** before a vowel.

alla breve ('ælə 'breɪvɪ) *Music.* ◆ *adj, adv* **1** with two beats to the bar instead of four, i.e. twice as fast as written. ◆ *n* **2** (formerly) a time of two or four minims to the bar. Symbol: ₵ [C19: It., lit.: according to the breve]

Allah ('ælə) *n* the name of God in Islam. [C16: from Ar., from *al* the + *Ilāh* god]

Allahabad ★ (ˌæləhəˈbæd, -ˈbɑːd) *n* a city in N India, in SE Uttar Pradesh at the confluence of the Ganges and Jumna Rivers: Hindu pilgrimage centre. Pop.: 792 858 (1991).

all-American *adj US*. **1** representative of the whole of the United States. **2** composed exclusively of American members. **3** (of a person) typically American.

allantois (əˈlæntəʊɪs, əˈlæntɔɪs) *n* a membranous sac growing out of the ventral surface of the hind gut of embryonic reptiles, birds, and mammals. [C17: NL, from Gk *allantoeidēs* sausage-shaped]
▶ **allantoic** (ˌælənˈtəʊɪk) *adj*

allay (əˈleɪ) *vb* **1** to relieve (pain, grief, etc.) or be relieved. **2** (*tr*) to reduce (fear, anger, etc.). [OE *ālecgan* to put down]

All Blacks *pl n the.* the international Rugby Union football team of New Zealand. [so named because of the players' black strip]

all clear *n* **1** a signal indicating that some danger, such as an air raid, is over. **2** permission to proceed.

all-dayer (ˌɔːlˈdeɪə) *n* an entertainment, such as a pop concert or film screening, that lasts all day.

allegation (ˌælɪˈɡeɪʃən) *n* **1** the act of alleging. **2** an unproved assertion, esp. an accusation.

allege (əˈledʒ) *vb* **alleges, alleging, alleged.** (*tr; may take a clause as object*) **1** to state without or before proof: *he alleged malpractice.* **2** to put forward (an argument or plea) for or against an accusation, claim, etc. [C14 *aleggen*, ult. from L *allēgāre* to dispatch on a mission, from *lēx* law]

alleged (əˈledʒd) *adj* (*prenominal*) **1** stated to be such: *the alleged murderer.* **2** dubious: *an alleged miracle.*
▶ **allegedly** (əˈledʒɪdlɪ) *adv*

Allegheny Mountains (ˌælɪˈɡeɪnɪ) *or* **Alleghenies** ★ *pl n* a mountain range in Pennsylvania, Maryland, Virginia, and West Virginia: part of the Appalachian system; rising from 600 m (2000 ft) to over 1440 m (4800 ft).

allegiance (əˈliːdʒəns) *n* **1** loyalty, as of a subject to his sovereign. **2** (in feudal society) the obligations of a vassal to his liege lord. [C14: from OF, from *lige* LIEGE]

allegorical (ˌælɪˈɡɒrɪkᵊl) *or* **allegoric** *adj* used in, containing, or characteristic of allegory.

allegorize *or* **allegorise** (ˈælɪɡəˌraɪz) *vb* **allegorizes, allegorizing, allegorized** *or* **allegorises, allegorising, allegorised.** **1** to transform (a story, fable, etc.) into or compose in the form of allegory. **2** (*tr*) to interpret allegorically.
▶ **allegori'zation** *or* **allegori'sation** *n*

allegory (ˈælɪɡərɪ) *n, pl* **allegories. 1** a poem, play, picture, etc., in which the apparent meaning of the characters and events is used to symbolize a moral or spiritual meaning. **2** use of such symbolism. **3** anything used as a symbol. [C14: from OF, from L, from Gk, from *allēgorein* to speak figuratively, from *allos* other + *agoreuein* to make a speech in public]
▶ **'allegorist** *n*

allegretto (ˌælɪˈɡretəʊ) *Music.* ◆ *adj, adv* **1** (to be performed) fairly quickly or briskly. ◆ *n, pl* **allegrettos. 2** a piece or passage to be performed in this manner. [C19: dim. of ALLEGRO]

Allegri ★ (*Italian* alˈleːɡri) *n* **Gregorio** (ɡreˈɡɔrjo). 1582–1652, Italian composer and singer.

allegro (əˈleɪɡrəʊ, -ˈleɡ-) *Music.* ◆ *adj, adv* **1** (to be performed) in a brisk lively manner. ◆ *n, pl* **allegros. 2** a piece or passage to be performed in this manner. [C17: from It.: cheerful, from L *alacer* brisk, lively]

allele (əˈliːl) *n* any of two or more genes that are responsible for alternative characteristics, such as smooth or wrinkled seeds in peas. Also called: **allelomorph** (əˈliːləˌmɔːf). [C20: from G *Allel*, from *Allelomorph*, from Gk *allēl-* one another + *morphē* form]

alleluia (ˌælɪˈluːjə) *interj* praise the Lord! Used in liturgical contexts in place of *hallelujah*. [C14: via Med. L from Heb. *hallelūyāh*]

allemande (ˈælɪmænd) *n* **1** the first movement of the classical suite, composed in a moderate tempo. **2** any of several German dances. **3** a figure in country dancing or square dancing by which couples change position in the set. [C17: from F *danse allemande* German dance]

Allen[1] ★ (ˈælən) *n* **1 Bog of.** a region of peat bogs in central Ireland, west of Dublin. Area: over 10 sq. km (3.75 sq. miles). **2 Lough.** a lake in Ireland, in county Leitrim.

Allen[2] ★ (ˈælən) *n* **1 Ethan.** 1738–89, American soldier during the War of Independence who led the Green Mountain Boys of Vermont. **2 Woody.** real name *Allen Stewart Konigsberg.* born 1935, US film comedian, screenwriter, and director. His films as actor and director include *Annie Hall* (1977), *Manhattan* (1979), *Hannah and Her Sisters* (1986), and *Celebrity* (1998).

Allenby ★ (ˈælənbɪ) *n* **Edmund Henry Hynman,** 1st Viscount Allenby. 1861–1936, British field marshal who captured Palestine and Syria from the Turks in 1918; high commissioner in Egypt (1919–25).

Allende ★ (*Spanish* aˈʎende) *n* **Salvador** (salβaˈðor). 1908–73, Chilean Marxist politician; president of Chile (1970–73): killed by army.

allergen (ˈæləˌdʒen) *n* any substance capable of inducing an allergy.
▶ **ˌaller'genic** *adj*

allergic (əˈlɜːdʒɪk) *adj* **1** of, having, or caused by an allergy. **2** (*postpositive; foll. by to*) *Inf.* having an aversion (to): *allergic to work.*

allergist (ˈælədʒɪst) *n* a physician skilled in the treatment of allergies.

allergy (ˈælədʒɪ) *n, pl* **allergies. 1** a hypersensitivity to a substance that causes the body to react to any contact with it. Hay fever is an allergic reaction to pollen. **2** *Inf.* an aversion. [C20: from G *Allergie* (indicating a changed reaction), from Gk *allos* other + *ergon* activity]

alleviate (əˈliːvɪˌeɪt) *vb* **alleviates, alleviating, alleviated.** (*tr*) to make (pain, sorrow, etc.) easier to bear; lessen. [C15: from LL, from L *levis* light]
▶ **alˌleviˈation** *n* ▶ **alˈleviˌator** *n*

USAGE NOTE See at **ameliorate.**

---

alley[1] (ˈælɪ) *n* **1** a narrow passage, esp. one between or behind buildings. **2** See **bowling alley. 3** *Tennis, chiefly US.* the space between the singles and doubles sidelines. **4** a walk in a garden, esp. one lined with trees. **5 up** (*or* **down**) **one's alley.** *Sl.* suited to one's abilities or interests. [C14: from OF, from *aler* to go, ult. from L *ambulāre* to walk]

alley[2] (ˈælɪ) *n* a large playing marble. [C18: shortened and changed from ALABASTER]

alleyway (ˈælɪˌweɪ) *n* a narrow passage; alley.

All Fools' Day *n* another name for **April Fools' Day** (see **April fool**).

all found *adj* (of charges for accommodation) inclusive of meals, heating, etc.

all hail *sentence substitute.* an archaic greeting or salutation. [C14, lit.: all health (to someone)]

Allhallows (ˌɔːlˈhæləʊz) *n* a less common term for **All Saints' Day.**

alliaceous (ˌælɪˈeɪʃəs) *adj* **1** of or relating to a genus of plants that have a strong smell and often have bulbs. The genus occurs in the N hemisphere and includes onion and garlic. **2** tasting or smelling like garlic or onions. [C18: from L *allium* garlic]

alliance (əˈlaɪəns) *n* **1** the act of allying or state of being allied; union. **2** a formal agreement, esp. a military one, between two or more countries. **3** the countries involved. **4** a union between families through marriage. **5** affinity or correspondence in characteristics. **6** *Bot.* a taxonomic category consisting of a group of related families. [C13: from OF, from *alier* to ALLY]

allied (əˈlaɪd, ˈælaɪd) *adj* **1** joined, as by treaty or marriage; united. **2** of the same type or class.

Allied (ˈælaɪd) *adj* of or relating to the Allies.

Allier ★ (*French* alje) *n* **1** a department of central France, in Auvergne region. Capital: Moulins. Pop.: 352 970

(1994 est.). Area: 7382 sq. km (2879 sq. miles). **2** a river in S central France, rising in the Cévennes and flowing north to the Loire. Length: over 403 km (250 miles).

Allies ('ælaɪz) *pl n* **1** (in World War I) the powers of the Triple Entente (France, Russia, and Britain) together with the nations allied with them. **2** (in World War II) the countries that fought against the Axis and Japan, esp. Britain and the Commonwealth countries, the US, the Soviet Union, China, Poland, and France.

alligator ('ælɪˌgeɪtə) *n* **1** a large crocodilian of the southern US, having powerful jaws but differing from the crocodiles in having a shorter and broader snout. **2** a similar but smaller species occurring in China. **3** any of various tools or machines having adjustable toothed jaws. [C17: from Sp. *el lagarto* the lizard, from L *lacerta*]

alligator pear *n* another name for **avocado**.

all-important *adj* crucial; vital.

all in *adj* **1** (*postpositive*) *Inf.* completely exhausted. ♦ *adv, adj* (**all-in** *when prenominal*). **2** with all expenses included: *one hundred pounds a week all in.* **3** (of wrestling) in freestyle.

Allingham ★ ('ælɪŋəm) *n* **Margery.** 1904–66, British author of detective stories, featuring Albert Campion. Her works include *Tiger in the Smoke* (1952) and *The Mind Readers* (1965).

alliterate (ə'lɪtəˌreɪt) *vb* **alliterates, alliterating, alliterated. 1** to contain or cause to contain alliteration. **2** (*intr*) to speak or write using alliteration.

alliteration (əˌlɪtə'reɪʃən) *n* the use of the same consonant (**consonantal alliteration**) or of a vowel (**vocalic alliteration**), at the beginning of each word or stressed syllable in a line of verse, as in *around the rock the ragged rascal ran.* [C17: from L *litera* letter]
▸ al'literative *adj*

allium ('ælɪəm) *n* a genus of liliaceous plants that includes the onion, garlic, shallot, leek, and chive. [C19: from L: garlic]

all-nighter (ˌɔːl'naɪtə) *n* an entertainment, such as a pop concert or film screening, that lasts all night.

allo- *or before a vowel* **all-** *combining form.* indicating difference, variation, or opposition: *allopathy; allomorph.* [from Gk *allos* other, different]

Alloa ★ ('æləʊə) *n* a town in E central Scotland, the administrative centre of Clackmannanshire: brewing. Pop.: 18 842 (1991).

allocate ('æləˌkeɪt) *vb* **allocates, allocating, allocated.** (*tr*) **1** to assign for a particular purpose. **2** a less common word for **locate** (sense 2). [C17: from Med. L, from L *locus* a place]
▸ 'allo,catable *adj* ▸ ,allo'cation *n*

allocution (ˌælə'kjuːʃən) *n Rhetoric.* a formal or authoritative speech or address. [C17: from LL *allocūtiō*, from L *alloquī* to address]

allomerism (ə'lɒməˌrɪzəm) *n* similarity of crystalline structure in substances of different chemical composition.
▸ ,allo'meric (ˌælə'mɛrɪk) *or* al'lomerous *adj*

allomorph ('æləˌmɔːf) *n* **1** *Linguistics.* any of the representations of a single morpheme. For example, the final (s) and (z) sounds of *bets* and *beds* are allomorphs. **2** any of the different crystalline forms of a chemical compound, such as a mineral.
▸ ,allo'morphic *adj*

allopath ('æləˌpæθ) *or* **allopathist** (ə'lɒpəθɪst) *n* a person who practises or is skilled in allopathy.

allopathy (ə'lɒpəθɪ) *n* the usual method of treating disease, by inducing a condition different from the cause of the disease. Cf. **homeopathy.**
▸ ,allo'pathic (ˌælə'pæθɪk) *adj*

allophone ('æləˌfəʊn) *n* **1** any of several speech sounds regarded as variants of the same phoneme. In English the aspirated initial (p) in *pot* and the unaspirated (p) in *spot* are allophones of the phoneme /p/. **2** *Canad.* a Canadian whose native language is neither French nor English.
▸ ,allo'phonic (ˌælə'fɒnɪk) *adj*

All-Ordinaries Index *n* an index of share prices on the Australian Stock Exchange giving a weighted arithmetic average of 245 ordinary shares.

allot (ə'lɒt) *vb* **allots, allotting, allotted.** (*tr*) **1** to assign or distribute (shares, etc.). **2** to designate for a particular purpose; apportion: *we allotted two hours to the case.* [C16: from OF, from *lot* portion]

allotment (ə'lɒtmənt) *n* **1** the act of allotting. **2** a portion or amount allotted. **3** *Brit.* a small piece of land rented by an individual for cultivation.

allotrope ('æləˌtrəʊp) *n* any of two or more physical forms in which an element can exist.

allotropy (ə'lɒtrəpɪ) *or* **allotropism** *n* the existence of an element in two or more physical forms.
▸ allotropic (ˌælə'trɒpɪk) *adj*

all-out *Inf.* ♦ *adj* **1** using one's maximum powers: *an all-out effort.* ♦ *adv* **all out. 2** to one's maximum capacity: *he went all out.*

allow (ə'laʊ) *vb* **1** (*tr*) to permit (to do something). **2** (*tr*) to set aside: *five hours were allowed to do the job.* **3** (*tr*) to let enter or stay: *they don't allow dogs.* **4** (*tr*) to acknowledge (a point, claim, etc.). **5** (*tr*) to let have: *he was allowed few visitors.* **6** (*intr;* foll. by *for*) to take into account. **7** (*intr;* often foll. by *of*) to permit: *a question that allows of only one reply.* **8** (*tr; may take a clause as object*) *US dialect.* to assert; maintain. [C14: from OF, from LL *allaudāre* to extol, infl. by Med. L *allocāre* to assign]
▸ al'lowable *adj* ▸ al'lowably *adv*

allowance (ə'laʊəns) *n* **1** an amount of something, esp. money or food, given at regular intervals. **2** a discount, as in consideration for something given in part exchange; rebate. **3** (in Britain) an amount of a person's income that is not subject to income tax. **4** a portion set aside to cover special expenses. **5** admission; concession. **6** the act of allowing; toleration. **7 make allowances** (*or* **allowance**). (usually foll. by *for*) **7a** to take mitigating circumstances into account. **7b** to allow (for). ♦ *vb* **allowances, allowancing, allowanced.** (*tr*) **8** to supply (something) in limited amounts.

Alloway ★ ('æləˌweɪ) *n* a village in Scotland, in South Ayrshire, S of Ayr: birthplace of Robert Burns.

allowedly (ə'laʊɪdlɪ) *adv* (*sentence modifier*) by general admission or agreement; admittedly.

alloy *n* ('ælɔɪ, ə'lɔɪ). **1** a metallic material, such as steel, consisting of a mixture of two or more metals or of metallic with nonmetallic elements. **2** something that impairs the quality of the thing to which it is added. ♦ *vb* (ə'lɔɪ). (*tr*) **3** to add (one metal or element to another) to obtain a substance with a desired property. **4** to debase (a pure substance) by mixing with an inferior element. **5** to diminish or impair. [C16: from OF *aloi* a mixture, from *aloier* to combine, from L *alligāre*]

all-purpose *adj* useful for many things.

all right *adj* (*postpositive except in slang use*), *adv* **1** adequate; satisfactory. **2** unharmed; safe. **3 all-right.** *US sl.* acceptable; reliable. ♦ *sentence substitute.* **4** very well: used to express assent. ♦ *adv* **5** satisfactorily: *the car goes all right.* **6** without doubt. ♦ Also **alright.**

USAGE NOTE See at **alright.**

---

all-round *adj* **1** efficient in all respects, esp. in sport: *an all-round player.* **2** comprehensive; many-sided: *an all-round education.*

all-rounder *n* a versatile person, esp. in a sport.

All Saints' Day *n* a Christian festival celebrated on Nov. 1 to honour all the saints.

all-singing all-dancing *adj* having every desirable feature possible: *an all-singing all-dancing computer.*

All Souls' Day *n RC Church.* a day of prayer (Nov. 2) for the dead in purgatory.

allspice ('ɔːlˌspaɪs) *n* **1** a tropical American tree, having small white flowers and aromatic berries. **2** the seeds of this berry used as a spice, having a flavour said to resemble a mixture of cinnamon, cloves, and nutmeg. ♦ Also called: **pimento.**

all-star *adj* (*prenominal*) consisting of star performers.

all-time adj (prenominal) Inf. unsurpassed.

all told adv (sentence modifier) in all: we were seven all told.

allude (ə'luːd) vb alludes, alluding, alluded. (intr; foll. by to) 1 to refer indirectly. 2 (loosely) to mention. [C16: from L allūdere, from lūdere to sport, from lūdus a game]

> USAGE NOTE Avoid confusion with **elude**.

allure (ə'luə) vb allures, alluring, allured. 1 (tr) to entice or tempt (someone); attract. ◆ n 2 attractiveness; appeal. [C15: from OF alurer, from lure bait]
▸ al'lurement n ▸ al'luring adj

allusion (ə'luːʒən) n 1 the act of alluding. 2 a passing reference. [C16: from LL allūsiō, from L allūdere to sport with]

allusive (ə'luːsɪv) adj containing or full of allusions.
▸ al'lusiveness n

alluvial (ə'luːvɪəl) adj 1 of or relating to alluvium. ◆ n 2 another name for **alluvium**.

alluvion (ə'luːvɪən) n 1a the wash of the sea or a river. 1b a flood. 1c sediment; alluvium. 2 Law. the gradual formation of new land, as by the recession of the sea. [C16: from L alluviō an overflowing, from luere to wash]

alluvium (ə'luːvɪəm) n, pl alluviums or alluvia (-vɪə). a fine-grained fertile soil consisting of mud, silt, and sand deposited by flowing water. [C17: from L; see ALLUVION]

ally vb (ə'laɪ), allies, allying, allied. (usually foll. by or with) 1 to unite or be united, esp. formally, as by treaty. 2 (tr; usually passive) to be related, as through being similar. ◆ n ('ælaɪ), pl allies. 3 a country, person, or group allied with another. 4 a plant, animal, etc., closely related to another in characteristics or form. [C14: from OF alier to join, from L ligāre to bind]

allyl resin ('ælɪl) n any of several thermosetting synthetic resins, containing the CH_2:$CHCH_2$– group, used as adhesives. [C19: from L allium garlic + -YL]

Alma-Ata ★ (Russian al'maa'ta) n the Russian name for **Almaty**.

Almada ★ (Portuguese ɑl'mɑːdə) n a town in S central Portugal, on the S bank of the Tagus estuary opposite Lisbon: statue of Christ 110 m (360 ft) high, erected 1959. Pop.: 153 189 (1991).

Al Madinah ★ (ˌæl mæ'diːnə) n the Arabic name for **Medina**.

alma mater ('ælmə 'mɑːtə, 'meɪtə) n (often caps.) one's school, college, or university. [C17: from L: bountiful mother]

almanac ('ɔːlmə,næk) n a yearly calendar giving statistical information, such as the phases of the moon, tides, anniversaries, etc. Also (archaic): **almanack**. [C14: from Med. L almanachus, ?from LGk almenikhiaka]

almandine ('ælməndɪn) n a deep violet-red garnet. [C17: from F, from Med. L, from Alabanda, ancient city of Asia Minor where these stones were cut]

Al Mansûrah ★ (ˌæl mæn'suərə) n a variant of **El Mansûra**.

Al Marj ★ (æl 'mɑːdʒ) n an ancient town in N Libya: founded in about 550 B.C. Pop.: 25 166 (latest est.). Italian name: **Barce**.

Alma-Tadema ★ ('ælmə'tædɪmə) n Sir **Lawrence**. 1836–1912, Dutch-English painter.

Almaty ★ (æl'mɑːtɪ) n a city in SE Kazakhstan, the capital until 1997; an important trading centre with many historic buildings. Pop.: 1 150 500 (1995 est.). Former name (until 1927): **Verny**. Russian name **Alma-Ata**.

almighty (ɔːl'maɪtɪ) adj 1 omnipotent. 2 Inf. (intensifier): an almighty row. ◆ adv 3 Inf. (intensifier): an almighty loud bang.

Almighty ★ (ɔːl'maɪtɪ) n the. another name for **God**.

almond ('ɑːmənd) n 1 a small widely cultivated rosaceous tree that is native to W Asia and has pink flowers and an edible nutlike seed. 2 the seed, which has a yellowish-brown shell. 3 (modifier) made of or containing almonds: almond cake. [C13: from OF almande, ult. from Gk amugdalē]

almond-eyed adj having narrow oval eyes.

almoner ('ɑːmənə) n 1 Brit. a former name for a trained hospital social worker. 2 (formerly) a person who distributes charity on behalf of a household or institution. [C13: from OF, from almosne alms, ult. from L eleēmosyna]

almost ('ɔːlməust) adv very nearly.

alms (ɑːmz) pl n charitable donations of money or goods to the poor or needy. [OE ælmysse, from LL, from Gk eleēmosunē pity]

almshouse ('ɑːmz,haus) n Brit. history. a privately supported house offering accommodation to the aged or needy.

almucantar or **almacantar** (ˌælmə'kæntə) n 1 a circle on the celestial sphere parallel to the horizon. 2 an instrument for measuring altitudes. [C14: from F, from Ar. almukantarāt sundial]

aloe ('æləu) n, pl aloes. 1 any plant of the genus Aloe, chiefly native to southern Africa, with fleshy spiny-toothed leaves. 2 American aloe. Also called: century plant. a tropical American agave which blooms only once in 10 to 30 years. [C14: from L aloē, from Gk]

aloes ('æləuz) n (functioning as sing) a bitter purgative drug made from the leaves of several species of aloe. Also called: **bitter aloes**.

aloe vera ('vɪərə) n 1 a plant of the species Aloe vera, the leaves of which yield a juice used as an emollient. 2 the juice of this plant, used in skin and hair preparations.

aloft (ə'lɒft) adv, adj (postpositive) 1 in or into a high or higher place. 2 Naut. in or into the rigging of a vessel. [C12: from ON ā lopt in the air]

alone (ə'ləun) adj (postpositive), adv 1 apart from another or others. 2 without anyone or anything else: one man alone could lift it. 3 without equal: he stands alone in the field of microbiology. 4 to the exclusion of others: she alone believed him. 5 leave or let alone. to refrain from annoying or interfering with. 6 leave well alone. to refrain from interfering with something that is satisfactory. 7 let alone. not to mention; much less: he can't afford beer, let alone whisky. [OE al one, lit.: all (entirely) one]

along (ə'lɒŋ) prep 1 over or for the length of: along the road. ◆ adv 2 continuing over the length of some specified thing. 3 together with some specified person or people: he'd like to come along. 4 forward: the horse trotted along. 5 to a more advanced state: he got the work moving along. 6 along with. together with: consider the advantages along with the disadvantages. [OE andlang, from and- against + lang LONG¹]

> USAGE NOTE See at **plus**.

alongshore (ə,lɒŋ'ʃɔː) adv, adj (postpositive) close to, by, or along a shore.

alongside (ə'lɒŋ,saɪd) prep 1 (often foll. by of) close beside: alongside the quay. ◆ adv 2 near the side of something: come alongside.

aloof (ə'luːf) adj distant, unsympathetic, or supercilious in manner. [C16: from A-¹ + loof, var. of LUFF]
▸ a'loofly adv ▸ a'loofness n

alopecia (ˌælə'piːʃɪə) n baldness. [C14: from L, from Gk alōpekia, orig.: mange in foxes]

aloud (ə'laud) adv, adj (postpositive) 1 in a normal voice. 2 in a spoken voice; not silently.

Aloysius ★ (ˌæləu'ɪʃəs) n Saint. full name Aloysius Luigi Gonzaga. 1568–91, Italian Jesuit who died nursing plague victims; the patron saint of youth. Feast day: June 21.

alp (ælp) n 1 (in Switzerland) a mountain pasture. 2 a high mountain. 3 the Alps. a high mountain range in S central Europe. [C16: from L Alpes]

ALP abbrev. for Australian Labor Party.

alpaca (æl'pækə) n 1 a domesticated South American mammal related to the llama, with dark shaggy hair. 2 the cloth made from the wool of this animal. 3 a glossy

> ★ people and places

fabric simulating this. [C18: via Sp. from Aymara *allpaca*]

lpenhorn ('ælpən,hɔːn) *n* another name for **alphorn**.

lpenstock ('ælpən,stɒk) *n* a stout stick with an iron tip used by hikers, mountain climbers, etc. [C19: from G, from *Alpen* Alps + *Stock* STICK¹]

Alpes-de-Haute-Provence ★ (*French* alpdəotprɔvɑ̃s) *n* a department of SE France in Provence-Alpes-Côte-d'Azur region. Capital: Digne. Pop.: 137 903 (1994 est.). Area: 6988 sq. km (2725 sq. miles). Former name: **Basses-Alpes**.

Alpes Maritimes ★ (*French* alp maritim) *n* a department of the SE corner of France in Provence-Alpes-Côte-d'Azur region. Capital: Nice. Pop.: 1 010 196 (1994 est.). Area: 4298 sq. km (1676 sq. miles).

alpha ('ælfə) *n* **1** the first letter in the Greek alphabet (A, α). **2** *Brit.* the highest grade or mark, as in an examination. **3** (*modifier*) **3a** involving helium nuclei. **3b** denoting an isomeric or allotropic form of a substance. [via L from Gk, of Phoenician origin]

alpha and omega *n* the first and last, a phrase used in Revelation 1:8 to signify God's eternity.

alphabet ('ælfə,bɛt) *n* **1** a set of letters or other signs used in a writing system, each letter or sign being used to represent one or sometimes more than one phoneme in the language being transcribed. **2** any set of characters, esp. one representing sounds of speech. **3** basic principles or rudiments. [C15: from LL, from the first two letters of the Gk alphabet; see ALPHA, BETA]

alphabetical (,ælfə'bɛtɪk³l) *or* **alphabetic** *adj* **1** in the conventional order of the letters of an alphabet. **2** of or expressed by an alphabet.
▸ ,alpha'betically *adv*

alphabetize *or* **alphabetise** ('ælfəbə,taɪz) *vb* **alphabetizes, alphabetizing, alphabetized** *or* **alphabetises, alphabetising, alphabetised.** (*tr*) **1** to arrange in conventional alphabetical order. **2** to express by an alphabet.
▸ ,alphabeti'zation *or* ,alphabeti'sation *n*

alpha-blocker *n* any of a class of drugs that prevent the stimulation of alpha receptors, a type of receptor in the sympathetic nervous system, by adrenaline and that therefore cause widening of blood vessels: used in the treatment of high blood pressure.

alpha decay *n* the radioactive decay process resulting in emission of alpha particles.

alpha-fetoprotein (,ælfə,fiːtəʊ'prəutiːn) *n* a protein that forms in the liver of the human fetus; excessive quantities in the amniotic fluid may indicate spina bifida in the fetus; low levels may point to Down's syndrome. Abbrev.: **afp**.

alphanumeric (,ælfənjuː'mɛrɪk) *or* **alphameric** *adj* (of a character set or file of data) consisting of alphabetical and numerical symbols.

alpha particle *n* a helium nucleus, containing two neutrons and two protons, emitted during some radioactive transformations.

alpha ray *n* ionizing radiation consisting of a stream of alpha particles.

alpha rhythm *or* **wave** *n Physiol.* the normal bursts of electrical activity from the cerebral cortex of a person at rest. See also **brain wave**.

alpha stock *n* any of the most active securities on the London stock exchange of which there are between 100 and 200.

Alpheus ★ (æl'fiːəs) *n Greek myth.* a river god, lover of the nymph Arethusa. She changed into a spring to evade him, but he changed into a river and mingled with her.

alphorn ('ælp,hɔːn) *or* **alpenhorn** *n* a wind instrument used in the Swiss Alps, made from a very long tube of wood. [C19: from G: Alps horn]

alpine ('ælpaɪn) *adj* **1** of or relating to high mountains. **2** (of plants) growing on mountains above the limit for tree growth. **3** connected with mountaineering. **4** *Skiing.* of racing events on steep prepared slopes, such as the slalom and downhill. Cf. **nordic**. ◆ *n* **5** a plant grown in or native to high altitudes.

Alpine ('ælpaɪn) *adj* of or relating to the Alps or their inhabitants.

alpinist ('ælpɪnɪst) *n* a mountain climber.

Alps ★ (ælps) *pl n* **1** a mountain range in S central Europe, extending over 1000 km (650 miles) from the Mediterranean coast of France and NW Italy through Switzerland, N Italy, and Austria to NW Slovenia. Highest peak: Mont Blanc, 4807 m (15 771 ft). **2** a range of mountains in the NW quadrant of the moon, which is cut in two by a straight fracture, the **Alpine Valley**.

already (ɔːl'rɛdɪ) *adv* **1** by or before a stated or implied time: *he is already here.* **2** at a time earlier than expected: *is it ten o'clock already?*

alright (ɔːl'raɪt) *adv, sentence substitute, adj* a variant spelling of **all right**.

> **USAGE NOTE** The form *alright*, though very common, is still considered by many people to be wrong or less acceptable than *all right*.

Alsace ★ (æl'sæs; *French* alzas) *n* a region and former province of NE France, between the Vosges mountains and the Rhine: famous for its wines. Area: 8280 sq. km (3196 sq. miles). Ancient name: **Alsatia**. German name: **Elsass**.

Alsace-Lorraine ★ *n* an area of NE France, comprising the modern regions of Alsace and Lorraine: under German rule 1871–1919 and 1940–44. Area: 14 522 sq. km (5607 sq. miles). German name: **Elsass-Lothringen**.

Alsatia ★ (æl'seɪʃə) *n* **1** the ancient name for **Alsace**. **2** an area around Whitefriars, London, in the 17th century, which was a sanctuary for criminals and debtors.

Alsatian (æl'seɪʃən) *n* **1** Also called: **German shepherd** (dog). a large wolflike breed of dog often used as a guard dog and by the police. **2** a native or inhabitant of Alsace. ◆ *adj* **3** of or relating to Alsace or its inhabitants.

also ('ɔːlsəʊ) *adv* **1** (*sentence modifier*) in addition; as well; too. ◆ *sentence connector.* **2** besides; moreover. [OE *alswā*; see ALL, SO¹]

also-ran *n* **1** a contestant, horse, etc., failing to finish among the first three. **2** a loser.

alstroemeria (,ælstrəʊ'mɪərɪə) *n* any of several plants with fleshy roots and brightly coloured flowers in summer, esp. the Peruvian lily. [C18: NL, after Claude *Alstroemer* (1736–96), Swedish naturalist]

alt. *abbrev. for:* **1** alternate. **2** altitude. **3** alto.

Alta. *abbrev. for* Alberta.

Altaic (æl'teɪɪk) *n* **1** a postulated family of languages of Asia and SE Europe, including the Turkic, Tungusic, and Mongolic subfamilies. See also **Ural-Altaic**. ◆ *adj* **2** denoting or relating to this linguistic family or its speakers.

Altai Mountains ★ (ɑːl'taɪ) *pl n* a mountain system of central Asia, in W Mongolia, W China, and S Russia. Highest peak: Belukha, 4506 m (14 783 ft).

Altai Republic ★ *n* another name for **Gorno-Altai Republic**.

Altamira ★ (*Spanish* alta'mira) *n* a cave in N Spain, SW of Santander, noted for Old Stone Age wall drawings.

altar ('ɔːltə) *n* **1** a raised place or structure where sacrifices are offered and religious rites performed. **2** (in Christian churches) the communion table. **3** a step in the wall of a dry dock. [OE, ult. from L *altus* high]

altar boy *n RC Church, Church of England.* a boy serving as an acolyte.

altarpiece ('ɔːltə,piːs) *n* a work of art set above and behind an altar; a reredos.

altazimuth (æl'tæzɪməθ) *n* an instrument for measuring the altitude and azimuth of a celestial body. [C19: from ALT(ITUDE) + AZIMUTH]

altazimuth mounting *n* a telescope mounting that allows motion of the telescope about a vertical axis (in altitude) and a horizontal axis (in azimuth).

Altdorf ★ (*German* 'altdɔrf) *n* a town in central Switzerland, capital of Uri canton: setting of the William Tell legend. Pop.: 8150 (1990).

alter ('ɔːltə) *vb* **1** to make or become different in some respect; change. **2** (*tr*) *Inf., chiefly US.* a euphemistic word for **castrate** or **spay**. [C14: from OF, ult. from L *alter* other] ▸ **'alterable** *adj*

alteration (ˌɔːltə'reɪʃən) *n* **1** a change or modification. **2** the act of altering.

alterative ('ɔːltərətɪv) *adj* **1** likely or able to produce alteration. **2** (of a drug) able to restore health. ◆ *n* **3** such a drug.

altercate ('ɔːltəˌkeɪt) *vb* **altercates, altercating, altercated.** (*intr*) to argue, esp. heatedly; dispute. [C16: from L *altercārī* to quarrel with another, from *alter* other]

altercation (ˌɔːltə'keɪʃən) *n* an angry or heated discussion or quarrel; argument.

alter ego ('æltər 'iːgəʊ, 'egəʊ) *n* **1** a second self. **2** a very close friend. [L: other self]

alternate *vb* ('ɔːltəˌneɪt), **alternates, alternating, alternated. 1** (often foll. by *with*) to occur or cause to occur by turns: *day and night alternate.* **2** (*intr*; often foll. by *between*) to swing repeatedly from one condition, action, etc., to another. **3** (*tr*) to interchange regularly or in succession. **4** (*intr*) (of an electric current, voltage, etc.) to reverse direction or sign at regular intervals. ◆ *adj* (ɔːl'tɜːnɪt). **5** occurring by turns: *alternate feelings of love and hate.* **6** every other or second one of a series: *he came on alternate days.* **7** being a second choice; alternative: *alternate director.* **8** *Bot.* (of leaves, flowers, etc.) arranged singly at different heights on either side of the stem. ◆ *n* ('ɔːltənɪt, ɔːl'tɜːnɪt). **9** *US & Canad.* a person who substitutes for another; stand-in. [C16: from L *alternāre* to do one thing and then another, ult. from *alter* other] ▸ ˌalter'nation *n*

alternate angles *pl n* two angles at opposite ends and on opposite sides of a transversal cutting two lines.

alternately (ɔːl'tɜːnɪtlɪ) *adv* in an alternating sequence or position.

alternating current *n* an electric current that periodically reverses direction. Abbrev.: **AC.**

alternation of generations *n* the occurrence in the life cycle of many plants and lower animals of alternating sexual and asexual reproductive forms.

alternative (ɔːl'tɜːnətɪv) *n* **1** a possibility of choice, esp. between two things. **2** either of such choices: *we took the alternative of walking.* ◆ *adj* **3** presenting a choice, esp. between two possibilities only. **4** (of two things) mutually exclusive. **5** denoting a lifestyle, culture, art form, etc., that is regarded as preferable to that of contemporary society because it is less conventional, materialistic, or institutionalized. ▸ **al'ternatively** *adv*

alternative curriculum *n Brit. education.* any course of study offered as an alternative to the National Curriculum.

alternative energy *n* a form of energy derived from a natural source, such as the sun, wind, tides, or waves. Also called: **renewable energy.**

Alternative Investment Market *n* a market on the London Stock Exchange for small companies that want to avoid the expenses of a main-market listing. Abbrev.: **AIM.**

alternative medicine *n* the treatment or alleviation of disease by techniques such as osteopathy and acupuncture, allied with attention to a person's general wellbeing. Also called: **complementary medicine.**

alternative society *n* a group of people who agree in rejecting the traditional values of the society around them.

Alternative Vote *n* (*modifier*) of or relating to a system of voting in which voters list the candidates in order of preference. If no candidate obtains more than 50% of first-preference votes, the votes for the bottom candidate are redistributed according to the voters' next preference. See **proportional representation.**

alternator ('ɔːltəˌneɪtə) *n* an electrical machine that generates an alternating current.

althaea or *US* **althea** (æl'θiːə) *n* any Eurasian plant of the genus *Althaea*, such as the hollyhock, having tall spikes of showy flowers. [C17: from L, from Gk *althaia* marsh mallow]

althorn ('ælt,hɔːn) *n* a valved brass musical instrument belonging to the saxhorn family.

Althorp House ★ ('ɔːlθɔːp, -θrʌp) *n* a mansion in Northamptonshire: seat of the Earls Spencer since 1508. Diana, Princess of Wales is buried on Round Oval Island in Althorp Park.

although (ɔːl'ðəʊ) *conj* (*subordinating*) even though: *although she was ill, she worked hard.*

altimeter (æl'tɪmɪtə, 'æltɪˌmiːtə) *n* an instrument that indicates height above sea level, esp. one based on an aneroid barometer and fitted to an aircraft. [C19: from L *altus* high + -METER]

Altiplano ★ (*Spanish* alti'plano) *n* a plateau of the Andes covering two thirds of Bolivia and extending into S Peru: contains Lake Titicaca. Height: 3000 m (10 000 ft) to 3900 m (13 000 ft).

altitude ('æltɪˌtjuːd) *n* **1** the vertical height of an object, esp. above sea level. **2** *Geom.* the perpendicular distance from the vertex to the base of a geometrical figure or solid. **3** Also called: **elevation.** *Astron., navigation.* the angular distance of a celestial body from the horizon. **4** *Surveying.* the angle of elevation of a point above the horizontal plane of the observer. **5** (*often pl*) a high place or region. [C14: from L *altus* high, deep]

alto ('æltəʊ) *n, pl* **altos. 1** (in choral singing) short for **contralto. 2** the highest adult male voice; countertenor. **3** a singer with such a voice. **4** a flute, saxophone, etc., that is the third or fourth highest instrument in its group. ◆ *adj* **5** denoting such an instrument. [C18: from It.: high, from L *altus*]

alto clef *n* the clef that establishes middle C as being on the third line of the staff.

altocumulus (ˌæltəʊ'kjuːmjʊləs) *n, pl* **altocumuli** (-laɪ). a globular cloud at an intermediate height of about 2400 to 6000 m (8000 to 20 000 ft).

altogether (ˌɔːltə'geðə, 'ɔːltəˌgeðə) *adv* **1** with everything included: *altogether he owed me sixty pounds.* **2** completely; utterly: *altogether mad.* **3** on the whole: *altogether it was very good.* ◆ *n* **4 in the altogether.** *Inf.* naked.

altoist ('æltəʊɪst) *n* a person who plays the alto saxophone.

altostratus (ˌæltəʊ'streɪtəs, -'strɑː-) *n, pl* **altostrati** (-taɪ). a layer cloud at an intermediate height of about 2400 to 6000 m (8000 to 20 000 ft).

altricial (æl'trɪʃəl) *adj* **1** denoting birds whose young, after hatching, are naked, blind, and dependent on the parents for food. ◆ *n* **2** an altricial bird. ◆ Cf. **precocial.** [C19: from NL, from L *altrix* a nurse]

Altrincham ★ ('ɔːltrɪŋəm) *n* a residential town in NW England, in Trafford unitary authority, Greater Manchester. Pop.: 40 042 (1991).

altruism ('æltruːˌɪzəm) *n* unselfish concern for the welfare of others. [C19: from F, from It. *altrui* others, from L] ▸ **'altruist** *n* ▸ ˌaltru'istic *adj* ▸ ˌaltru'istically *adv*

ALU *Computing.* abbrev. for arithmetical and logical unit.

alum ('æləm) *n* **1** a colourless soluble hydrated double sulphate of aluminium and potassium used in manufacturing and in medicine. Formula: $K_2SO_4.Al_2(SO_4)_3.24H_2O$. **2** any of a group of similar hydrated double sulphates of a monovalent metal or group and a trivalent metal. [C14: from OF, from L *alūmen*]

alumina (ə'luːmɪnə) *n* another name for **aluminium oxide.** [C18: from NL, pl of L *alūmen* ALUM]

aluminium (ˌæljʊ'mɪnɪəm) or *US & Canad.* **aluminum** (ə'luːmɪnəm) *n* a light malleable silvery-white metallic element that resists corrosion; the third most abundant element in the earth's crust, occurring as a compound, principally in bauxite. Symbol: Al; atomic no.: 13; atomic wt.: 26.981.

aluminium oxide *n* a powder occurring naturally as corundum and used in the production of aluminium, abrasives, glass, and ceramics. Formula: Al_2O_3. Also called: **alumina.**

aluminize or **aluminise** (ə'luːmɪˌnaɪz) *vb* **aluminizes,**

★ people and places

aluminizing, aluminized or **aluminises, aluminising, aluminised.** (tr) to cover with aluminium or aluminium paint.

aluminous (ə'lu:mɪnəs) adj resembling aluminium.

alumnus (ə'lʌmnəs) or (fem) **alumna** (ə'lʌmnə) n, pl **alumni** (-naɪ) or **alumnae** (-ni:). Chiefly US & Canad. a graduate of a school, college, etc. [C17: from L: nursling, pupil, from alere to nourish]

Alva or **Alba** ★ ('ælvə; Spanish 'alβa) n **Duke of,** title of Fernando Alvarez de Toledo. 1508–82, Spanish general and statesman who suppressed the Protestant revolt in the Netherlands (1567–72) and conquered Portugal (1580).

Alvarez ★ ('ælvərez) n **Luis Walter.** 1911–88, US physicist. He measured the neutron's magnetic moment (1939). Nobel prize for physics 1968.

alveolar (æl'vɪələ, ,ælvɪ'əʊlə) adj 1 Anat. of an alveolus. 2 denoting the part of the jawbone containing the roots of the teeth. 3 (of a consonant) articulated with the tongue in contact with the part of the jawbone immediately behind the upper teeth. ◆ n 4 an alveolar consonant, such as t, d, and s in English.

alveolate (æl'vɪəlɪt, -,leɪt) adj having many small cavities. [C19: from LL alveolātus hollowed, from L: ALVEOLUS]
▸ ,alveo'lation n

alveolus (æl'vɪələs) n, pl **alveoli** (-,laɪ). any small pit, cavity, or saclike dilation, such as a honeycomb cell, a tooth socket, or the tiny air sacs in the lungs. [C18: from L: a little hollow, dim. of alveus]

always ('ɔ:lweɪz) adv 1 without exception; every time: he always arrives on time. 2 continually; repeatedly. 3 in any case: you could always take a day off work. ◆ Also (archaic): **alway.** [C13 alles weiss, from OE ealne weg, lit.: all the way]

Alwyn ★ ('ɔ:lwɪn) n **William.** 1905–85, British composer. His works include the oratorio The Marriage of Heaven and Hell (1936) and the Suite of Scottish Dances (1946).

alyssum ('ælɪsəm) n a widely cultivated herbaceous garden plant, having clusters of small yellow or white flowers. [C16: from NL, from Gk alusson, from alussos (adj) curing rabies]

Alzheimer's disease ('ælts,haɪməz) n a disorder of the brain resulting in progressive decline and eventual dementia. Often shortened to **Alzheimer's.** [C20: after A. Alzheimer (1864–1915), G physician who first identified it]

am (æm; unstressed əm) vb (used with I) a form of the present tense of **be.** [OE eam]

Am the chemical symbol for americium.

AM abbrev. for: 1 Also: **am.** amplitude modulation. 2 US. Master of Arts. 3 Member of the Order of Australia.

Am. abbrev. for America(n).

a.m., A.M., am, or **AM** (indicating the period from midnight to midday) abbrev. for ante meridiem. [L: before noon]

amabokoboko (ama'bɒkɒbɒkɒ) pl n S. African. an African name for the **Springbok** rugby team. [C20: from Nguni ama, a plural prefix + bokoboko, from bok a diminutive of SPRINGBOK]

Amadhlozi or **Amadlozi** (,æmæ'hlɒʒi:) pl n S. African. the ancestral spirits. [from Zulu, pl. amadlozi]

amadoda (,æmæ'dɒdə) pl n S. African. grown men. [from Nguni ama, a plural prefix + doda men]

amadou ('æmə,du:) n a spongy substance got from some fungi, used (formerly) as tinder, a styptic, and by fishermen to dry flies. [C18: from F, from Provençal: lover, from L amāre to love (because easily set alight)]

amah ('ɑ:mə) n (in the East, esp. formerly) a nurse or maidservant. [C19: from Port. ama nurse]

amain (ə'meɪn) adv Arch. or poetic. with great strength or haste. [C16: from A-² + MAIN¹]

Amalfi ★ (ə'mælfɪ) n a town in SW Italy: a major Mediterranean port from the 10th to the 18th century, now a resort.

amalgam (ə'mælgəm) n 1 an alloy of mercury with another metal, esp. silver: dental amalgam. 2 a blend or combination. [C15: from Med. L amalgama, from ?]

amalgamate (ə'mælgə,meɪt) vb **amalgamates, amalgamating, amalgamated.** 1 to combine or cause to combine; unite. 2 to alloy (a metal) with mercury.

amalgamation (ə,mælgə'meɪʃən) n 1 the process of amalgamating. 2 the state of being amalgamated. 3 a method of extracting precious metals by treatment with mercury. 4 a merger.

amanuensis (ə,mænjʊ'ɛnsɪs) n, pl **amanuenses** (-si:z). a person employed to take dictation or to copy manuscripts. [C17: from L, from servus ā manū slave at hand (that is, handwriting)]

Amanullah Khan ★ (,æmə'nʊlə 'kɑ:n) n 1892–1960, emir (1919–26) and king (1926–29) of Afghanistan; he obtained Afghan independence from Britain (1919).

Amapá ★ (Portuguese ama'pa) n a state of N Brazil, on the Amazon delta. Capital: Macapá. Pop.: 326 200 (1995 est.). Area: 143 716 sq. km (55 489 sq. miles).

amaranth ('æmə,rænθ) n 1 Poetic. an imaginary flower that never fades. 2 any of numerous plants having tassel-like heads of small green, red, or purple flowers. 3 a synthetic red food colouring (**E123**), used in packet soups, cake mixes, etc. [C17: from L amarantus, from Gk, from A-¹ + marainein to fade]

amaretto (,æmə'retəʊ) n an Italian liqueur with a flavour of almonds. [C20: from It. amaro bitter]

amaryllis (,æmə'rɪlɪs) n 1 a plant native to southern Africa having large lily-like reddish or white flowers. 2 any of several related plants. [C18: from NL, from L: after Amaryllis, Gk conventional name for a shepherdess]

amass (ə'mæs) vb 1 (tr) to accumulate or collect (esp. riches, etc.). 2 to gather in a heap. [C15: from OF, from masse MASS]
▸ a'masser n

amateur ('æmətə) n 1 a person who engages in an activity, esp. a sport, as a pastime rather than for gain. 2 a person unskilled in a subject or activity. 3 a person who is fond of or admires something. 4 (modifier) of or for amateurs: an amateur event. ◆ adj 5 not professional or expert: an amateur approach. [C18: from F, from L amātor lover, from amāre to love]
▸ 'amateurism n

amateurish ('æmətərɪʃ) adj lacking professional skill or expertise.
▸ 'amateurishly adv

Amati ★ n 1 (Italian a'ma:ti). a family of Italian violin makers, active in Cremona in the 16th and 17th centuries, esp. **Nicolò** (niko'lò), 1596–1684, who taught Guarneri and Stradivari. 2 (ə'mɑ:tɪ). (pl **Amatis**) a violin or other stringed instrument made by any member of this family.

amative ('æmətɪv) adj a rare word for **amorous.** [C17: from Med. L, from L amāre to love]

amatory ('æmətərɪ) or **amatorial** (,æmə'tɔ:rɪəl) adj of, relating to, or inciting sexual love or desire. [C16: from L amātōrius, from amāre to love]

amaurosis (,æmɔ:'rəʊsɪs) n blindness, esp. when occurring without observable damage to the eye. [C17: via NL from Gk: darkening, from amauroun to dim]
▸ amaurotic (,æmɔ:'rɒtɪk) adj

amaze (ə'meɪz) vb **amazes, amazing, amazed.** (tr) 1 to fill with incredulity or surprise; astonish. ◆ n 2 an archaic word for **amazement.** [OE āmasian]
▸ a'mazing adj

amazement (ə'meɪzmənt) n incredulity or great astonishment; complete wonder.

Amazon¹ ★ ('æməz°n) n 1 Greek myth. one of a race of women warriors of Scythia. 2 (often not cap.) any tall, strong, or aggressive woman. [C14: via L from Gk Amazōn, from ?]
▸ **Amazonian** (,æmə'zəʊnɪən) adj

Amazon² ★ ('æməz°n) n a river in South America, rising in the Peruvian Andes and flowing east through N Brazil to the Atlantic: in volume, the largest river in the world; navigable for 3700 km (2300 miles). Length: over 6440 km (4000 miles). Area of basin: over 5 827 500 sq. km (2 250 000 sq. miles).
▸ **Amazonian** (,æmə'zəʊnɪən) adj

★ people and places

Amazonas ★ (ˌæməˈzəʊnəs) n a state of W Brazil, consisting of the central Amazon basin: vast areas of unexplored tropical rainforest. Capital: Manaus. Pop.: 2 320 200 (1995 est.). Area: 1 542 277 sq. km (595 474 sq. miles).

Amazonia ★ (æməˈzəʊnɪə) n the land around the Amazon river.

Ambala ★ (əmˈbɑːlə) n a city in N India, in Haryana: site of archaeological remains of a prehistoric Indian civilization: grain, cotton, food processing. Pop.: 119 338 (1991).

ambassador (æmˈbæsədə) n 1 a diplomat of the highest rank, accredited as permanent representative to another country. **2 ambassador extraordinary.** a diplomat of the highest rank sent on a special mission. **3 ambassador plenipotentiary.** a diplomat of the first rank with treaty-signing powers. **4 ambassador-at-large.** US. an ambassador with special duties who may be sent to more than one government. **5** an authorized representative or messenger. [C14: from OF, from It., from OProvençal ambaisador, from ambaisa (unattested) mission, errand] ▸ **amˈbassadress** fem n ▸ **ambassadorial** (æmˌbæsəˈdɔːrɪəl) adj ▸ **amˈbassadorˌship** n

amber (ˈæmbə) n 1 a yellow translucent fossil resin derived from extinct coniferous trees and often containing trapped insects. **2a** a brownish-yellow colour. **2b** (as adj): an amber dress. **3** an amber traffic light used as a warning between red and green. [C14: from Med. L ambar, from Ar. ˈanbar ambergris]

amber gambler n Brit. inf. a driver who races through traffic lights when they are at amber.

ambergris (ˈæmbəˌgriːs, -grɪs) n a waxy substance secreted by the intestinal tract of the sperm whale and often found floating in the sea: used in the manufacture of some perfumes. [C15: from OF ambre gris grey amber]

amberjack (ˈæmbəˌdʒæk) n any of several large fishes occurring in tropical and subtropical Atlantic waters. [C19: from AMBER + JACK]

ambi- combining form. indicating both: ambidextrous; ambivalence. [from L: round, on both sides, both, from ambo both]

ambidextrous (ˌæmbɪˈdɛkstrəs) adj 1 equally expert with each hand. **2** Inf. skilled or adept. **3** underhanded. ▸ **ambidexterity** (ˌæmbɪdɛkˈstɛrɪtɪ) or ˌambiˈdextrousness n

ambience or **ambiance** (ˈæmbɪəns) n the atmosphere of a place. [C19: from F, from ambiant surrounding]

ambient (ˈæmbɪənt) adj 1 surrounding. **2** creating a relaxing atmosphere: ambient music. [C16: from L ambiēns going round, from AMBI- + īre to go]

ambiguity (ˌæmbɪˈɡjuːɪtɪ) n, pl ambiguities. **1** the possibility of interpreting an expression in more than one way. **2** an instance or example of this, as in the sentence they are cooking apples. **3** vagueness or uncertainty of meaning.

ambiguous (æmˈbɪɡjʊəs) adj 1 having more than one possible interpretation. **2** difficult to understand; obscure. [C16: from L ambiguus going here and there, uncertain, from ambigere to go around] ▸ **amˈbiguously** adv ▸ **amˈbiguousness** n

ambisexual (ˌæmbɪˈsɛksjʊəl) or **ambosexual** adj Biol. relating to or affecting both the male and female sexes.

ambit (ˈæmbɪt) n 1 scope or extent. **2** limits or boundary. [C16: from L ambitus a going round, from ambīre to go round]

ambition (æmˈbɪʃən) n 1 strong desire for success or distinction. **2** something so desired; goal. [C14: from OF, from L ambitiō a going round (of candidates), from ambīre to go round]

ambitious (æmˈbɪʃəs) adj 1 having a strong desire for success or achievement. **2** necessitating extraordinary effort or ability: an ambitious project. **3** (often foll. by of) having a great desire (for something or to do something). ▸ **amˈbitiousness** n

ambivalence (æmˈbɪvələns) or **ambivalency** n the coexistence of two opposed and conflicting emotions etc. ▸ **amˈbivalent** adj

amble (ˈæmbəl) vb ambles, ambling, ambled. (intr) **1** to walk at a leisurely relaxed pace. **2** (of a horse) to move, lifting both legs on one side together. **3** to ride a horse at an amble. ◆ n **4** a leisurely motion in walking. **5** a leisurely walk. **6** the ambling gait of a horse. [C14: from OF, from L ambulāre to walk]

Ambler ★ (ˈæmblə) n Eric. 1909–98, British novelist. His thrillers include The Mask of Dimitrios (1939), Journey into Fear (1940), A Kind of Anger (1964), and Doctor Frigo (1974).

Ambleside ★ (ˈæmbəlˌsaɪd) n a town in NW England, in Cumbria: a tourist centre for the Lake District. Pop.: 2905 (1991).

amblyopia (ˌæmblɪˈəʊpɪə) n impaired vision with no discernible damage to the eye or optic nerve. [C18: NL, from Gk ambluōpia, from amblus dull, dim + ōps eye] ▸ **amblyopic** (ˌæmblɪˈɒpɪk) adj

Amboina ★ (æmˈbɔɪnə) n 1 an island in Indonesia, in the Moluccas. Capital: Amboina. Area: 1000 sq. km (386 sq. miles). **2** Also called: **Ambon** (ˈɑːmbɒn). a port in the Moluccas, the capital of Amboina island.

Amboise ★ (French ɑ̃bwaz) n a town in NW central France, on the River Loire: famous castle, a former royal residence. Pop.: 11 415 (1982).

amboyna or **amboina** (æmˈbɔɪnə) n the mottled curly-grained wood of an Indonesian tree, used in making furniture.

Ambrose ★ (ˈæmbrəʊz) n Saint. ?340–397 A.D., bishop of Milan; built up the secular power of the early Christian Church; also wrote music and Latin hymns. Feast day: Dec. 7 or April 4. ▸ **Amˈbrosian** adj

ambrosia (æmˈbrəʊzɪə) n 1 Classical myth. the food of the gods, said to bestow immortality. Cf. **nectar** (sense 2). **2** anything particularly delightful to taste or smell. **3** another name for **beebread**. [C16: via L from Gk: immortality, from A-¹ + brotos mortal] ▸ **amˈbrosial** or **amˈbrosian** adj

ambry (ˈæmbrɪ) or **aumbry** (ˈɔːmbrɪ) n, pl ambries or aumbries. **1** a recessed cupboard in the wall of a church near the altar, used to store sacred vessels, etc. **2** Obs. a small cupboard. [C14: from OF almarie, ult. from L armārium chest for storage, from arma arms]

ambulance (ˈæmbjʊləns) n a motor vehicle designed to carry sick or injured people. [C19: from F, based on (hôpital) ambulant mobile or field (hospital), from L ambulāre to walk]

ambulance chaser n US sl. a lawyer who seeks to encourage and profit from the lawsuits of accident victims. ▸ **ambulance chasing** n

ambulance stocks pl n high-performance stocks and shares recommended by a broker to a dissatisfied client to improve their relationship.

ambulant (ˈæmbjʊlənt) adj 1 moving about from place to place. **2** Med. another word for **ambulatory** (sense 3).

ambulate (ˈæmbjʊˌleɪt) vb ambulates, ambulating, ambulated. (intr). to wander about or move from place to place. [C17: from L ambulāre to walk] ▸ ˌambuˈlation n

ambulatory (ˈæmbjʊlətərɪ) adj 1 of or designed for walking. **2** changing position; not fixed. **3** Also: **ambulant**. able to walk. ◆ n, pl ambulatories. **4** a place for walking, such as an aisle or a cloister.

ambuscade (ˌæmbəˈskeɪd) n 1 an ambush. ◆ vb ambuscades, ambuscading, ambuscaded. **2** to ambush or lie in ambush. [C16: from F, from OIt. imboscata, prob. of Gmc origin; cf. AMBUSH]

ambush (ˈæmbʊʃ) n 1 the act of waiting in a concealed position in order to launch a surprise attack. **2** a surprise attack from such a position. **3** the concealed position from which such an attack is launched. **4** the person or persons waiting to launch such an attack. ◆ vb **5** to lie in wait (for). **6** (tr) to attack suddenly from a concealed position. [C14: from OF embuschier to position in ambush, from em- IM- + -buschier, from busche piece of firewood, prob. of Gmc origin]

meba (ə'miːbə) *n, pl* **amebae** (-biː) *or* **amebas**. the usual US spelling of **amoeba**.
▶ a'**mebic** *adj*

ameer (ə'mɪə) *n* a variant spelling of **emir**.

ameliorate (ə'miːljə,reɪt) *vb* **ameliorates, ameliorating, ameliorated**. to make or become better. [C18: from F *améliorer* to improve, from OF, from *meillor* better, from L *melior*]
▶ a,melio'**ration** *n* ▶ a'**meliorative** *adj* ▶ a'**melio,rator** *n*

> **USAGE NOTE** *Ameliorate* is often wrongly used where *alleviate* is proper. *Ameliorate* is properly used to mean 'improve', not 'make easier to bear', so one should talk about *alleviating* pain or hardship, not *ameliorating* it.

amen (,eɪ'mɛn, ,ɑː'mɛn) *sentence substitute*. **1** so be it!: a term used at the end of a prayer. ◆ *n* **2** the use of the word *amen*. [C13: via LL via Gk from Heb. *āmēn* certainly]

Amen ★ ('ɑːmən) *n Egyptian myth.* a local Theban god, having a ram's head and symbolizing life and fertility, identified by the Egyptians with the national deity Amen-Ra.

amenable (ə'miːnəb°l) *adj* **1** likely to listen, cooperate, etc. **2** accountable to some authority; answerable. **3** capable of being tested, judged, etc. [C16: from Anglo-F, from OF, from L *mināre* to drive (cattle), from *minārī* to threaten]
▶ a,mena'**bility** *or* a'**menableness** *n* ▶ a'**menably** *adv*

amend (ə'mɛnd) *vb (tr)* **1** to improve; change for the better. **2** to correct. **3** to alter or revise (legislation, etc.) by formal procedure. [C13: from OF, from L *ēmendāre* to EMEND]
▶ a'**mendable** *adj* ▶ a'**mender** *n*

amendment (ə'mɛndmənt) *n* **1** correction. **2** an addition or alteration to a document, etc.

amends (ə'mɛndz) *n (functioning as sing)* recompense or compensation for some injury, insult, etc.: *to make amends*. [C13: from OF, from *amende* compensation, from *amender* to EMEND]

Amenhotep III (,æmɛn'həʊtɛp) *or* **Amenhotpe III** ★ (,æmɛn'hɒtpɪ) *n* Greek name *Amenophis*. ?1411–?1375 B.C., Egyptian pharaoh who erected many buildings.

amenity (ə'miːnɪtɪ) *n, pl* **amenities**. **1** (*often pl*) a useful or pleasant facility: *a swimming pool was one of the amenities*. **2** the fact or condition of being agreeable. **3** (*usually pl*) a social courtesy. [C14: from L, from *amoenus* agreeable]

amenorrhoea *or esp. US* **amenorrhea** (æ,mɛnə'rɪə, eɪ-) *n* abnormal absence of menstruation. [C19: from A-¹ + MENO- + -RRHOEA]

Amen-Ra ★ (,ɑːmən'rɑː) *n Egyptian myth.* the sun-god; the principal deity during the period of Theban hegemony.

ament ('æmənt) *n* another name for **catkin**. Also called: **amentum** (ə'mɛntəm). [C18: from L *āmentum* thong]
▶ ,amen'**taceous** *adj*

amentia (ə'mɛnʃə) *n* severe mental deficiency, usually congenital. [C14: from L: insanity, from *āmēns* mad, from *mēns* mind]

Amer. *abbrev. for* America(n).

amerce (ə'mɜːs) *vb* **amerces, amercing, amerced**. *(tr) Obs.* **1** *Law.* to punish by a fine. **2** to punish with any arbitrary penalty. [C14: from Anglo-F, from OF *à merci* at the mercy; see MERCY]
▶ a'**mercement** *n*

America ★ (ə'mɛrɪkə) *n* **1** short for the **United States of America**. **2** Also called: **the Americas**. the American continent, including North, South, and Central America. [C16: from *Americus*, L form of *Amerigo*; see VESPUCCI]

American (ə'mɛrɪkən) *adj* **1** of or relating to the United States of America, its inhabitants, or their form of English. **2** of or relating to the American continent. ◆ *n* **3** a native or citizen of the US. **4** a native or inhabitant of any country of North, Central, or South America. **5** the English language as spoken or written in the United States.

Americana (ə,mɛrɪ'kɑːnə) *pl n* objects, such as documents, relics, etc., relating to America.

American aloe *n* See **aloe** (sense 2).

American Civil War *n* see **Civil War** (sense 2).

American Dream *n* **the**. the notion that the American social, economic, and political system makes success possible for every individual.

American football *n* **1** a team game similar to rugby, with 11 players on each side. **2** the oval-shaped inflated ball used in this game.

American Indian *n* **1** Also called: **Indian, Amerindian, Native American**. a member of any of the indigenous peoples of America, typically having straight black hair and a yellow-to-brown skin. ◆ *adj* **2** Also called: **Amerindian**. of or relating to any of these peoples, their languages, or their cultures.

Americanism (ə'mɛrɪkə,nɪzəm) *n* **1** a custom, linguistic usage, or other feature peculiar to or characteristic of the United States. **2** loyalty to the United States.

Americanize *or* **Americanise** (ə'mɛrɪkə,naɪz) *vb* **Americanizes, Americanizing, Americanized** *or* **Americanises, Americanising, Americanised**. to make or become American in outlook, attitudes, etc.
▶ A,mericani'**zation** *or* A,mericani'**sation** *n*

American Revolution *n* the usual US term for **War of American Independence**.

American Samoa ★ *n* the part of the Samoa Islands that is administered by the US. Capital: Pago Pago. Pop.: 52 860 (1993 est.). Area: 197 sq. km (76 sq. miles).

americium (,æmə'rɪsɪəm) *n* a white metallic transuranic element artificially produced from plutonium. It is used as an alpha-particle source. Symbol: Am; atomic no.: 95; half-life of most stable isotope, ^{243}Am: 7.4×10^3 years. [C20: from AMERICA (where it was first produced) + -IUM]

Amerigo Vespucci ★ (*Italian* ame'riːgo ves'puttʃi) *n* See **Vespucci**.

Amerindian (,æmə'rɪndɪən) *n also* **Amerind** ('æmərɪnd), *adj* another word for **American Indian**.
▶ ,Amer'**indic** *adj*

amethyst ('æmɪθɪst) *n* **1** a purple or violet variety of quartz used as a gemstone. **2** a purple variety of sapphire. **3a** the purple colour of amethyst. **3b** (*as adj*): *amethyst shadow*. [C13: from OF, from L, from Gk *amethustos*, lit.: not drunken, from A-¹ + *methuein* to make drunk; from the belief that the stone could prevent intoxication]
▶ **amethystine** (,æmɪ'θɪstaɪn) *adj*

Amex ('æmɛks) *n acronym for* **1** *Trademark*. American Express. **2** American Stock Exchange.

AMF *abbrev. for* Australian Military Forces.

Amhara ★ (æm'hɑːrə) *n* **1** a region of NW Ethiopia: formerly a kingdom. **2** an inhabitant of the former kingdom of Amhara.

Amharic (æm'hærɪk) *n* **1** the official language of Ethiopia. ◆ *adj* **2** denoting this language.

Amherst ★ ('æmhɜːst) *n* **Jeffrey**, 1st Baron Amherst. 1717–97, British general who defeated the French in Canada (1758–60): governor general of British North America (1761–63).

amiable ('eɪmɪəb°l) *adj* having or displaying a pleasant or agreeable manner; friendly. [C14: from OF, from LL *amīcābilis* AMICABLE]
▶ ,amia'**bility** *or* '**amiableness** *n* ▶ '**amiably** *adv*

amianthus (,æmɪ'ænθəs) *n* any of the fine silky varieties of asbestos. [C17: from L *amiantus*, from Gk *amiantos* unsullied, from A-¹ + *miainein* to pollute]

amicable ('æmɪkəb°l) *adj* characterized by friendliness: *an amicable agreement*. [C15: from LL *amīcābilis*, from L *amīcus* friend]
▶ ,amica'**bility** *or* '**amicableness** *n* ▶ '**amicably** *adv*

amice ('æmɪs) *n Christianity*. a rectangular piece of white linen worn by priests around the neck and shoulders

amicus curiae (ə'miːkʊs 'kjuərɪˌiː) n, pl **amici curiae** (æ'miːkaɪ) Law. a person, not directly engaged in a case, who advises the court. [L, lit.: friend of the court]

amid (ə'mɪd) or **amidst** prep in the middle of; among. [OE on middan in the middle]

amide ('æmaɪd) n 1 any organic compound containing the group -CONR₂, where R denotes a hydrogen atom or a hydrocarbon group. 2 (modifier) containing the group -CONR₂: amide group or radical. 3 an inorganic compound containing the NH_2^- ion and having the general formula $M(NH_2)_n$, where M is a metal atom. [C19: from AM(MONIA) + -IDE]

amidships (ə'mɪdʃɪps) adv, adj (postpositive) Naut. at, near, or towards the centre of a vessel.

Amiens ★ ('æmɪənz; French amjɛ̃) n a city in N France: its Gothic cathedral is the largest church in France. Pop.: 136 234 (1990).

amigo (æ'miːgəu, ə-) n, pl **amigos**. a friend; comrade. [Sp., from L amicus]

Amin¹ ★ (æ'miːn, ɑː-) n **Lake**. a former official name for (Lake) **Edward**.

Amin² ★ (æ'miːn, ɑː-) n **Idi** ('iːdiː). born 1925, Ugandan dictator (1971–79). Notorious for his brutality; overthrown and exiled.

amine (ə'miːn, 'æmɪn) n an organic base formed by replacing one or more of the hydrogen atoms of ammonia by hydrocarbon groups. [C19: from AM(MONIUM) + -INE²]

amino (ə'miːnəu) n (modifier) of or containing the group of atoms -NH₂: amino radical.

amino acid n 1 any of a group of organic compounds containing one or more amino groups, -NH₂, and one or more carboxyl groups, -COOH. 2 any of a group of organic nitrogenous compounds that form the component molecules of proteins.

amino resin n a thermosetting synthetic resin used as an adhesive and coating for paper and textiles.

amir (ə'mɪə) n a variant spelling of **emir**. [C19: from Ar., var. of EMIR]
▶ **a'mirate** n

Amis ★ ('eɪmɪs) n 1 Sir **Kingsley**. 1922–95, British writer, noted for his novels Lucky Jim (1954), Stanley and the Women (1984), and The Folks that Live on the Hill (1990). 2 his son, **Martin**. born 1949, British novelist. His works include The Rachel Papers (1974), Time's Arrow (1991), and Night Train (1997).

Amish ('æmɪʃ, 'ɑː-) adj of a US and Canadian Mennonite sect. [C19: from G Amisch, after Jakob Amman, 17th-cent. Swiss Mennonite bishop]

amiss (ə'mɪs) adv 1 in an incorrect or defective manner. 2 take (something) amiss. to be annoyed or offended by (something). ◆ adj 3 (postpositive) wrong or faulty. [C13 a mis, from mis wrong]

amitosis (ˌæmɪ'təusɪs) n a form of cell division in which the nucleus and cytoplasm divide without the formation of chromosomes. [C20: from A-¹ + MITOSIS]
▶ **amitotic** (ˌæmɪ'tɒtɪk) adj

amity ('æmɪtɪ) n, pl **amities**. friendship; cordiality. [C15: from OF amité, ult. from L amīcus friend]

Amman ★ (ə'mɑːn) n the capital of Jordan, northeast of the Dead Sea: ancient capital of the Ammonites, rebuilt by Ptolemy in the 3rd century B.C. Pop.: 963 490 (1994). Ancient names: **Rabbath Ammon, Philadelphia**.

ammeter ('æmˌmiːtə) n an instrument for measuring an electric current in amperes. [C19: AM(PERE) + -METER]

ammo ('æməu) n Inf. short for **ammunition**.

Ammon¹ ★ ('æmən) n Old Testament. the ancestor of the Ammonites.

Ammon² ★ ('æmən) n Myth. the classical name of the Egyptian god Amen, identified by the Greeks with Zeus and by the Romans with Jupiter.

ammonia (ə'məunɪə) n 1 a colourless pungent gas used in the manufacture of fertilizers and as a refrigerant and solvent. Formula: NH₃. 2 a solution of ammonia in water, containing ammonium hydroxide. [C18: from NL, from L (sal) ammōniacus (sal) AMMONIAC]

ammoniac (ə'məunɪˌæk) n a gum resin obtained from the stems of an Asian plant and formerly used as a stimulant, perfume, and in porcelain cement. Also called **gum ammoniac**. [C14: from L, from Gk ammōniakos belonging to Ammon (apparently the gum resin was extracted from plants found in Libya near the temple of Ammon)]

ammoniacal (ˌæmə'naɪəkᵊl) adj of, containing, or resembling ammonia.

ammoniate (ə'məunɪˌeɪt) vb **ammoniates, ammoniating, ammoniated**. to unite or treat with ammonia.
▶ **am,moni'ation** n

ammonify (ə'mɒnɪˌfaɪ) vb **ammonifies, ammonifying, ammonified**. to treat or impregnate with ammonia or compound of ammonia.
▶ **am,monifi'cation** n

ammonite ('æməˌnaɪt) n 1 any extinct marine cephalopod mollusc of the order Ammonoidea, which were common in Mesozoic times and had a coiled partitioned shell. 2 the shell of any of these animals, commonly occurring as a fossil. [C18: from L corn Ammōnis, lit.: horn of Ammon]

ammonium (ə'məunɪəm) n (modifier) of or containing the monovalent group NH₄₋ or the ion NH₄⁺: ammonium compounds.

ammonium chloride n a white soluble crystalline solid used as an electrolyte in dry batteries. Formula: NH₄Cl. Also called: **sal ammoniac**.

ammonium hydroxide n a compound existing in solution when ammonia is dissolved in water. Formula: NH₄OH.

ammonium sulphate n a white soluble crystalline solid used mainly as a fertilizer and in water purification. Formula: (NH₄)₂SO₄.

ammunition (ˌæmju'nɪʃən) n 1 any projectiles, such as bullets, rockets, etc., that can be discharged from a weapon. 2 bombs, missiles, chemicals, etc., capable of use as weapons. 3 any means of defence or attack, as in an argument. [C17: from obs. F amunition, by mistaken division from earlier la munition; see MUNITION]

amnesia (æm'niːzjə, -ʒjə, -zɪə) n a defect in memory, esp one resulting from a pathological cause. [C19: via NL from Gk: forgetfulness, prob. from amnēstia oblivion]
▶ **amnesiac** (æm'niːzɪˌæk) or **amnesic** (æm'niːsɪk, -zɪk) adj, n

amnesty ('æmnɪstɪ) n, pl **amnesties**. 1 a general pardon esp. for offences against a government. 2 a period during which a law is suspended to allow offenders to admit their crime without fear of prosecution. ◆ vb **amnesties, amnestying, amnestied**. 3 (tr) to overlook or forget (an offence). [C16: from L amnēstia, from Gk: oblivion, from A-¹ + -mnēstos, from mnasthai to remember]

Amnesty International n an international organization that works to secure the release of people imprisoned for their beliefs, to ban the use of torture, and to abolish the death penalty. Abbrev.: **AI**.

amniocentesis (ˌæmnɪəusən'tiːsɪs) n, pl **amniocenteses** (-siːz). removal of amniotic fluid for diagnostic purposes by the insertion into the womb of a hollow needle. [C20: from AMNION + centesis from Gk kentēsis from kentein to prick]

amnion ('æmnɪən) n, pl **amnions** or **amnia** (-nɪə). the innermost of two membranes enclosing an embryonic reptile, bird, or mammal. [C17: via NL from Gk: a little lamb, from amnos a lamb]
▶ **amniotic** (ˌæmnɪ'ɒtɪk) adj

amniotic fluid n the fluid surrounding the fetus in the womb.

amoeba or US **ameba** (ə'miːbə) n, pl **amoebae** (-biː) or **amoebas** or US **amebae** (-biː) or **amebas**. any of a phylum of protozoans able to change shape because of the movements of cell processes. They live in fresh water or soil or as parasites in man and animals. [C19: from NL, from Gk, from ameibein to change, exchange]
▶ **a'moebic** or US **a'mebic** adj

mok (ə'mʌk, ə'mɒk) *or* **amuck** (ə'mʌk) *n* **1** a state of murderous frenzy. ◆ *adv* **2 run amok.** to run about as with a frenzied desire to kill. [C17: from Malay *amoq* furious assault]

mong (ə'mʌŋ) *or* **amongst** *prep* **1** in the midst of: *he lived among the Indians.* **2** to each of: *divide the reward among yourselves.* **3** in the group, class, or number of: *among the greatest writers.* **4** taken out of (a group): *he is one among many.* **5** with one another within a group: *decide it among yourselves.* **6** in the general opinion or practice of: *accepted among experts.* [OE *amang*, contracted from *on gemang* in the group of, from ON + *gemang* crowd]

> **USAGE NOTE** See at **between.**

montillado (ə,mɒntɪ'lɑːdəʊ) *n* a medium-dry sherry. [C19: from Sp. *vino amontillado* wine of *Montilla*, town in Spain]

moral (,eɪ'mɒrəl) *adj* **1** having no moral quality; nonmoral. **2** without moral standards or principles.
▸ **amorality** (,eɪmɒ'rælɪtɪ) *n*

> **USAGE NOTE** *Amoral* is often wrongly used where *immoral* is meant. *Immoral* is properly used to talk about the breaking of moral rules, *amoral* about people who have no moral code or about places or situations where moral considerations do not apply.

morist ('æmərɪst) *n* a lover or a writer about love.

moroso (,æmə'rəʊsəʊ) *adj*, *adv* **1** *Music.* (to be played) tenderly. ◆ *n* **2** a rich sweet sherry. [from It. & Sp.: AMO- ROUS]

morous ('æmərəs) *adj* **1** inclined towards or displaying love or desire. **2** in love. **3** of or relating to love. [C14: from OF, from Med. L, from L *amor* love]
▸ **'amorously** *adv* ▸ **'amorousness** *n*

morphous (ə'mɔːfəs) *adj* **1** lacking a definite shape. **2** of no recognizable character or type. **3** (of rocks, etc.) not having a crystalline structure. [C18: from NL, from Gk, from A-¹ + *morphē* shape]
▸ **a'morphism** *n* ▸ **a'morphousness** *n*

mortize *or* **amortise** (ə'mɔːtaɪz) *vb* **amortizes, amortiz- ing, amortized** *or* **amortises, amortising, amortised.** (*tr*) **1** *Fi- nance.* to liquidate (a debt, mortgage, etc.) by payments or by periodic transfers to a sinking fund. **2** to write off (a wasting asset) by transfers to a sinking fund. **3** *Property law.* (formerly) to transfer (lands, etc.) in mortmain. [C14: from Med. L, from OF *amortir* to reduce to the point of death, ult. from L *ad* to + *mors* death]
▸ **a,morti'zation** *or* **a,morti'sation** *n*

Amos ★ ('eɪmɒs) *n Old Testament.* **1** a Hebrew prophet of the 8th century B.C. **2** the book containing his oracles.

mount (ə'maʊnt) *n* **1** extent; quantity. **2** the total of two or more quantities. **3** the full value or significance of something. **4** a principal sum plus the interest on it, as in a loan. ◆ *vb* **5** (*intr*; usually foll. by *to*) to be equal or add up. [C13: from OF *amonter* to go up, from *amont* up- wards, from *a* to + *mont* mountain (from L *mōns*)]

> **USAGE NOTE** The use of a plural noun after *amount of* (*an amount of bananas; the amount of ref- ugees*) should be avoided: *a quantity of bananas; the number of refugees.*

amount of substance *n* a measure of the number of entities (atoms, molecules, ions, electrons, etc.) present in a substance, expressed in moles.

amour (ə'mʊə) *n* a love affair, esp. a secret or illicit one. [C13: from OF, from L *amor* love]

amour-propre French. (amurprɔprə) *n* self-respect.

Amoy ★ (ə'mɔɪ) *n* **1** a port in SE China, in Fujian prov- ince on **Amoy Island,** at the mouth of the Jiu-long River

opposite Taiwan: one of the first treaty ports opened to European trade (1842). Pop.: 368 786 (1990 est.). Mod- ern Chinese name: **Xiamen. 2** the dialect of Chinese spo- ken in Amoy, Taiwan, and elsewhere: a Min dialect.

amp (æmp) *n* **1** an ampere. **2** *Inf.* an amplifier.

AMP *n Biochem.* adenosine monophosphate; a substance produced by hydrolysis of ATP with the liberation of en- ergy. The cyclic form (**cyclic AMP**) acts as a messenger in many hormone-induced biochemical reactions.

ampelopsis (,æmpɪ'lɒpsɪs) *n* any of a genus of woody climbing plants of tropical and subtropical Asia and America. [C19: from NL, from Gk *ampelos* grapevine]

amperage ('æmpərɪdʒ) *n* the strength of an electric cur- rent measured in amperes.

ampere ('æmpeə) *n* **1** the basic SI unit of electric current; the constant current that, when maintained in two par- allel conductors of infinite length and negligible cross section placed 1 metre apart in free space, produces a force of 2×10^{-7} newton per metre between them. **2** a former unit of electric current (**international ampere**); the current that, when passed through a solution of silver nitrate, deposits silver at the rate of 0.001118 gram per second. ◆ Abbrev.: **amp.** Symbol: A [C19: after A. M. AMPÈRE]

Ampère ★ ('æmpeə; *French* ɑ̃pɛr) *n* **André Marie** (ɑ̃dre mari). 1775–1836, French physicist who made major discoveries in magnetism and electricity.

ampere-turn *n* a unit of magnetomotive force; the magnetomotive force produced by a current of 1 ampere passing through one complete turn of a coil.

ampersand ('æmpə,sænd) *n* the character (&), meaning and: *John Brown & Co.* [C19: shortened from *and per se and*, that is, the symbol & by itself (represents) *and*]

amphetamine (æm'fetə,miːn) *n* a synthetic colourless liquid used medicinally as the white crystalline sul- phate, mainly for its stimulant action on the central ner- vous system. [C20: from A(LPHA) + M(ETHYL) + PH(ENYL) + ET(HYL) + AMINE]

amphi- *prefix* **1** on both sides; at both ends; of both kinds: *amphipod; amphibious.* **2** around: *amphibole.* [from Gk]

amphibian (æm'fɪbɪən) *n* **1** any cold-blooded vertebrate of the class *Amphibia,* typically living on land but breed- ing in water. The class includes newts, frogs, and toads. **2** an aircraft able to land and take off from both water and land. **3** any vehicle able to travel on both water and land. ◆ *adj* **4** another word for **amphibious. 5** of or be- longing to the class *Amphibia.*

amphibious (æm'fɪbɪəs) *adj* **1** able to live both on land and in the water, as frogs, etc. **2** designed for operation on or from both water and land. **3** relating to military forces and operations launched from the sea against an enemy shore. **4** having a dual or mixed nature. [C17: from Gk *amphibios,* lit.: having a double life, from AMPHI- + *bios* life]
▸ **am'phibiousness** *n*

amphibole ('æmfɪ,bəʊl) *n* any of a large group of miner- als consisting of the silicates of calcium, iron, magne- sium, sodium, and aluminium, which are common constituents of igneous rocks. [C17: from F, from Gk *amphibolos* uncertain; so called from the large number of varieties in the group]

amphibology (,æmfɪ'bɒlədʒɪ) *or* **amphiboly** (æm'fɪb- əlɪ) *n, pl* **amphibologies** *or* **amphibolies.** ambiguity of expres- sion, esp. when due to a grammatical construction, as in *save rags and waste paper.* [C14: from LL, ult. from Gk *amphibolos* ambiguous]

amphimixis (,æmfɪ'mɪksɪs) *n, pl* **amphimixes** (-'mɪksiːz). true sexual reproduction, esp. the fusion of gametes from two organisms. [C19: from AMPHI- + Gk *mixis* a blending]
▸ **amphimictic** (,æmfɪ'mɪktɪk) *adj*

amphioxus (,æmfɪ'ɒksəs) *n, pl* **amphioxi** (-'ɒksaɪ) *or* **amphioxuses.** another name for the **lancelet.** [C19: from NL, from AMPHI- + Gk *oxus* sharp]

amphipod ('æmfɪ,pɒd) *n* **1** any marine or freshwater crustacean of the order *Amphipoda,* such as the sand hop-pers, in which the body is laterally compressed. ◆ *adj* **2** of or belonging to the *Amphipoda*.

amphiprostyle (æm'frprə,staɪl) *adj* **1** (esp. of a classical temple) having a set of columns at both ends but not at the sides. ◆ *n* **2** a temple of this kind.

amphisbaena (æmfɪs'biːnə) *n, pl* **amphisbaenae** (-niː) *or* **amphisbaenas**. **1** a genus of wormlike lizards of tropical America. **2** *Classical myth*. a fabulous serpent with a head at each end. [C16: from L, from Gk *amphisbaina*, from *amphis* both ways + *bainein* to go]

amphitheatre *or US* **amphitheater** ('æmfɪ,θɪətə) *n* **1** a building, usually circular or oval, in which tiers of seats rise from a central open arena. **2** a place where contests are held. **3** any level circular area of ground surrounded by higher ground. **4** a gallery in a theatre. **5** a lecture room in which seats are tiered away from a central area.

Amphitrite ★ (,æmfɪ'traɪtɪ) *n Greek myth*. a sea goddess, wife of Poseidon and mother of Triton.

amphora ('æmfərə) *n, pl* **amphorae** (-fə,riː) *or* **amphoras**. a Greek or Roman two-handled narrow-necked jar for oil, etc. [C17: from L, from Gk, from AMPHI- + *phoreus* bearer, from *pherein* to bear]

amphoteric (,æmfə'tɛrɪk) *adj Chem*. able to function as either a base or an acid. [C19: from Gk *amphoteros* each of two (from *amphō* both) + -IC]

ampicillin (,æmpɪ'sɪlɪn) *n* a form of penicillin used to treat various infections.

ample ('æmpᵊl) *adj* **1** more than sufficient: *an ample helping*. **2** large: *of ample proportions*. [C15: from OF, from L *amplus* spacious]
▶ '**ampleness** *n*

amplification (,æmplɪfɪ'keɪʃən) *n* **1** the act or result of amplifying. **2** material added to a statement, story, etc., to expand or clarify it. **3** a statement, story, etc., with such additional material. **4** *Electronics*. the increase in strength of an electrical signal by means of an amplifier.

amplifier ('æmplɪ,faɪə) *n* **1** an electronic device used to increase the strength of the current fed into it, esp. one for the amplification of sound signals in a radio, record player, etc. **2** *Photog*. an additional lens for altering focal length. **3** a person or thing that amplifies.

amplify ('æmplɪ,faɪ) *vb* **amplifies, amplifying, amplified**. **1** (*tr*) to increase in size, extent, effect, etc., as by the addition of extra material. **2** *Electronics*. to produce amplification of (electrical signals). **3** (*intr*) to expand a speech, narrative, etc. [C15: from OF, ult. from L *amplificāre* to enlarge, from *amplus* spacious + *facere* to make]

amplitude ('æmplɪ,tjuːd) *n* **1** greatness of extent; magnitude. **2** abundance. **3** breadth or scope, as of the mind. **4** *Astron*. the angular distance along the horizon measured from true east or west to the point of intersection of the vertical circle passing through a celestial body. **5** *Physics*. the maximum displacement from the zero or mean position of a periodic motion. [C16: from L, from *amplus* spacious]

amplitude modulation *n* one of the principal methods of transmitting information using radio waves, the relevant signal being superimposed onto a radio-frequency carrier wave. The frequency of the carrier wave remains unchanged but its amplitude is varied in accordance with the amplitude of the input signal. Cf. **frequency modulation**.

amply ('æmplɪ) *adv* fully; generously.

ampoule ('æmpuːl, -pjuːl) *or esp. US* **ampule** *n Med*. a small glass vessel in which liquids for injection are hermetically sealed. [C19: from F, from L: see AMPULLA]

ampulla (æm'pʊlə) *n, pl* **ampullae** (-'pʊliː). **1** *Anat*. the dilated end part of certain ducts or canals. **2a** *Christianity*. a vessel for the wine and water used at the Eucharist. **2b** a small flask for consecrated oil. **3** a Roman two-handled bottle for oil, wine, or perfume. [C16: from L, dim. of AMPHORA]

amputate ('æmpju,teɪt) *vb* **amputates, amputating, amputated**. *Surgery*. to remove (all or part of a limb). [C17: from L, from *am-* around + *putāre* to trim, prune]
▶ ,**ampu'tation** *n*

amputee (,æmpju'tiː) *n* a person who has had a limb amputated.

Amritsar ★ (æm'rɪtsə) *n* a city in India, in NW Punjab: centre of the Sikh religion; site of a massacre in 1919 of unarmed supporters of Indian self-government by British troops; in 1984 the Golden Temple, fortified by Sikhs, was attacked by Indian troops with the loss of many Sikh lives. Pop.: 708 835 (1991).

Amsterdam ★ (,æmstə'dæm; *Dutch* ɑmstər'dɑm) *n* the commercial capital of the Netherlands, a major industrial centre and port on the IJsselmeer, connected with the North Sea by canal: built on about 100 islands within a network of canals. Pop.: 722 245 (1995 est.).

amu *abbrev. for* atomic mass unit.

amuck (ə'mʌk) *n, adv* a variant spelling of **amok**.

Amu Darya ★ (*Russian* a'mu darj'ja) *n* a river in central Asia, rising in the Pamirs and flowing northwest through the Hindu Kush and across Turkmenistan and Uzbekistan to its delta in the Aral Sea: forms much of the N border of Afghanistan. Length: 2400 km (1500 miles). Ancient name: **Oxus**.

amulet ('æmjʊlɪt) *n* a trinket or piece of jewellery worn as a protection against evil; charm. [C17: from L *amulētum*, from ?]

Amundsen ★ (*Norwegian* 'aːmunsən) *n* **Roald** ('rɔald) 1872–1928, Norwegian explorer and navigator, who was the first man to reach the South Pole (1911).

Amundsen Sea ★ ('ɑːmundsən) *n* a part of the South Pacific Ocean, in Antarctica off Byrd Land.

Amur ★ (ə'mʊə) *n* a river in NE Asia, rising in N Mongolia as the Argun and flowing southeast, then northeast to the Sea of Okhotsk: forms the boundary between Manchuria and Russia. Length: about 4350 km (2700 miles). Modern Chinese name: **Heilong Jiang**.

amuse (ə'mjuːz) *vb* **amuses, amusing, amused**. (*tr*) **1** to entertain; divert. **2** to cause to laugh or smile. [C15: from OF *amuser* to cause to be idle, from *muser* to MUSE[1]]

amusement (ə'mjuːzmənt) *n* **1** something that amuses, such as a game or pastime. **2** a mechanical device used for entertainment, as at a fair. **3** the act of amusing or the state or quality of being amused.

amusement arcade *n Brit*. a covered area having coin-operated game machines.

amusing (ə'mjuːzɪŋ) *adj* entertaining; causing a smile or laugh.
▶ a'**musingly** *adv*

amygdalin (ə'mɪgdəlɪn) *n* a white soluble bitter-tasting glycoside extracted from bitter almonds. [C17: from Gk: ALMOND + -IN]

amyl ('æmɪl) *n* (*modifier*) (no longer in technical usage) of or containing any of eight isomeric forms of the monovalent group C_5H_{11}–: *amyl group or radical*. [C19: from L: AMYLUM]

amylaceous (,æmɪ'leɪʃəs) *adj* of or resembling starch.

amyl alcohol *n* **1** any of eight isomeric alcohols with the general formula $C_5H_{11}OH$. **2** a mixture of these alcohols, used in preparing amyl nitrite.

amylase ('æmɪ,leɪz) *n* any of several enzymes that hydrolyse starch and glycogen to simple sugars, such as glucose.

amyl nitrite *n* an ester of amyl alcohol and nitrous acid, used as a vasodilator, esp. to treat angina.

amyloid ('æmɪ,lɔɪd) *n* **1** any substance resembling starch. ◆ *adj* **2** starchlike.

amylopsin (,æmɪ'lɒpsɪn) *n* an enzyme of the pancreatic juice that converts starch into sugar; pancreatic amylase. [C19: from AMYL + (PE)PSIN]

amylum ('æmɪləm) *n* another name for **starch** (sense 1,2). [L, from Gk *amulon* fine meal, starch]

amyotrophic lateral sclerosis (,æmɪəu'trɒfɪk) *n* a form of motor neurone disease in which degeneration of motor tracts in the spinal cord causes progressive muscular paralysis starting in the limbs. Also called: **Lou Gehrig's disease**.

Amytal ('æmɪ,tæl) *n Trademark*. sodium amytal, used as a sedative and hypnotic.

an[1] (æn; *unstressed* ən) *determiner* (*indefinite article*) a form of **a**[1], used before an initial vowel sound: *an old car; an elf; an hour.* [OE *ān* ONE]

> **USAGE NOTE**   *An* was formerly often used before words that begin with *h* and are unstressed on the first syllable: *an hotel; an historic meeting.* Sometimes the initial *h* was not pronounced. This usage is now becoming obsolete.

an[2] or **an'** (æn; *unstressed* ən) *conj* (*subordinating*) an obsolete or dialect word for **if**. See **and** (sense 8).

An[1] ★ (ɑːn) *n Myth.* the Sumerian sky god. Babylonian counterpart: **Anu.**

An[2] *the chemical symbol for* actinon.

an. *abbrev. for* anno. [L: in the year]

an- *or before a consonant* **a-** *prefix* not; without: *anaphrodisiac.* [from Gk]

-an, -ean, *or* **-ian** *suffix* **1** (*forming adjectives and nouns*) belonging to; coming from; typical of; adhering to: *European; Elizabethan; Christian.* **2** (*forming nouns*) a person who specializes or is expert in: *dietitian.* [from L *-ānus,* suffix of adjectives]

ana- *or before a vowel* **an-** *prefix* **1** up; upwards: *anadromous.* **2** again: *anagram.* **3** back; backwards: *anapaest.* [from Gk *ana*]

-ana *or* **-iana** *suffix forming nouns.* denoting a collection of objects or information relating to a particular individual, subject or place: *Victoriana, Americana.* [NL, from L *-āna,* lit.: matters relating to, neuter pl of *-ānus;* see **-AN**]

Anabaptist (ˌænəˈbæptɪst) *n* **1** a member of any of various Protestant movements, esp. of the 16th century, that rejected infant baptism, insisted that adults be rebaptized, and sought to establish Christian communism. ◆ *adj* **2** of these sects or their doctrines. [C16: from Ecclesiastical L, from *anabaptīzāre* to baptize again, from LGk *anabaptizein*]
▶ ˌAnaˈbaptism *n*

anabas (ˈænəˌbæs) *n* any of several freshwater fishes, esp. the climbing perch, that can travel on land. [C19: from NL, from Gk *anabainein* to go up]

anabasis (əˈnæbəsɪs) *n, pl* **anabases** (-ˌsiːz). **1** the march of Cyrus the Younger from Sardis to Cunaxa in Babylonia in 401 B.C., described by Xenophon in his *Anabasis.* **2** any military expedition, esp. one from the coast to the interior. [C18: from Gk: a going up, from *anabainein* to go up]

anabatic (ˌænəˈbætɪk) *adj Meteorol.* (of air currents) rising upwards. [C19: from Gk *anabatikos* relating to ascents, from *anabainein* to go up]

anabiosis (ˌænəbaɪˈəʊsɪs) *n* the ability to return to life after apparent death; suspended animation. [C19: via NL from Gk, from *anabioein* to come back to life]
▶ **anabiotic** (ˌænəbaɪˈɒtɪk) *adj*

anabolic steroid *n* any of a group of synthetic steroid hormones (androgens) used to stimulate muscle and bone growth for athletic or therapeutic purposes.

anabolism (əˈnæbəˌlɪzəm) *n* a metabolic process in which complex molecules are synthesized from simpler ones with the storage of energy; constructive metabolism. [C19: from ANA- + (META)BOLISM]
▶ **anabolic** (ˌænəˈbɒlɪk) *adj*

anachronism (əˈnækrəˌnɪzəm) *n* **1** the representation of an event, person, or thing in a historical context in which it could not have occurred or existed. **2** a person or thing that belongs or seems to belong to another time. [C17: from L, from Gk *anakhronismos* a mistake in chronology, from ANA- + *khronos* time]
▶ aˌnachroˈnistic *adj* ▶ aˌnachroˈnistically *adv*

anacoluthon (ˌænəkəˈluːθɒn) *n, pl* **anacolutha** (-θə). a construction that involves the change from one grammatical sequence to another within a single sentence. [C18: from LL, from Gk, from *anakolouthos* not consistent, from AN- + *akolouthos* following]

anaconda (ˌænəˈkɒndə) *n* a very large nonvenomous arboreal and semiaquatic snake of tropical South America, which kills its prey by constriction. [C18: prob.

changed from Sinhalese *henakandayā* whip snake; orig. referring to a snake of Sri Lanka]

Anacreon ★ (əˈnækrɪˌɒn, -ən) *n* ?572–?488 B.C., Greek lyric poet.
▶ **A,nacreˈontic** *adj, n*

anacrusis (ˌænəˈkruːsɪs) *n, pl* **anacruses** (-siːz). **1** *Prosody.* one or more unstressed syllables at the beginning of a line of verse. **2** *Music.* an unstressed note or group of notes immediately preceding the strong first beat of the first bar. [C19: from Gk, from *anakrouein* to strike up, from ANA- + *krouein* to strike]

anadromous (əˈnædrəməs) *adj* (of fishes such as the salmon) migrating up rivers from the sea in order to breed. [C18: from Gk *anadromos* running upwards]

Anadyr ★ (*Russian* aˈnadir) *n* **1** a town in Russia, in NE Siberia at the mouth of the Anadyr River. Pop.: 6586 (1993 est.). **2** a mountain range in Russia, in NE Siberia, rising over 1500 m (5000 ft). **3** a river in Russia, rising in mountains on the Arctic Circle, south of the Anadyr Range, and flowing east to the Gulf of Anadyr. Length: 725 km (450 miles). **4 Gulf of.** an inlet of the Bering Sea, off the coast of NE Russia.

anaemia *or US* **anemia** (əˈniːmɪə) *n* a deficiency in the number of red blood cells or in their haemoglobin content, resulting in pallor and lack of energy. [C19: from NL, from Gk *anaimia* lack of blood, from AN- + *haima* blood]

anaemic *or US* **anemic** (əˈniːmɪk) *adj* **1** relating to or suffering from anaemia. **2** pale and sickly looking; lacking vitality.

anaerobe (æˈnɛərəʊb, ˈænərəʊb) *or* **anaerobium** (ˌænɛəˈrəʊbɪəm) *n, pl* **anaerobes** *or* **anaerobia** (-ˈəʊbɪə). an organism that does not require, or requires the absence of, free oxygen or air.
▶ ˌanaerˈobic *adj*

anaesthesia *or US* **anesthesia** (ˌænɪsˈθiːzɪə) *n* **1** loss of bodily sensation, esp. of touch, as the result of nerve damage or other abnormality. **2** loss of sensation, esp. of pain, induced by drugs: called **general anaesthesia** when consciousness is lost and **local anaesthesia** when only a specific area of the body is involved. [C19: from NL, from Gk *anaisthēsia* absence of sensation]

anaesthetic *or US* **anesthetic** (ˌænɪsˈθɛtɪk) *n* **1** a substance that causes anaesthesia. ◆ *adj* **2** causing or characterized by anaesthesia.

anaesthetics (ˌænɪsˈθɛtɪks) *n* (*functioning as sing*) the science of anaesthesia and its application. US name: **anesthesiology.**

anaesthetist (əˈniːsθətɪst) *n* **1** *Brit.* a doctor specializing in the administration of anaesthetics. US name: **anesthesiologist. 2** *US.* See **anesthetist.**

anaesthetize, anaesthetise, *or US* **anesthetize** (əˈniːsθəˌtaɪz) *vb* **anaesthetizes, anaesthetizing, anaesthetized** *or* **anaesthetises, anaesthetising, anaesthetised** *or US* **anesthetizes, anesthetizing, anesthetized.** (*tr*) to render insensible to pain by administering an anaesthetic.
▶ aˌnaesthetiˈzation, aˌnaesthetiˈsation, *or US* aˌnestheti-ˈzation *n*

anaglyph (ˈænəˌglɪf) *n* **1** *Photog.* a stereoscopic picture consisting of two images of the same object, taken from slightly different angles, in two complementary colours. When viewed through coloured spectacles, the images merge to produce a stereoscopic sensation. **2** anything cut to stand in low relief, such as a cameo. [C17: from Gk *anagluphē* carved in low relief, from ANA- + *gluphē* carving, from *gluphein* to carve]
▶ ˌanaˈglyphic *adj*

Anaglypta (ˌænəˈglɪptə) *n Trademark.* a type of thick embossed wallpaper designed to be painted. [C19: from Gk *anagluptos;* see ANAGLYPH]

anagram (ˈænəˌgræm) *n* a word or phrase the letters of which can be rearranged into another word or phrase. [C16: from NL, from Gk, from *anagrammatizein* to transpose letters, from ANA- + *gramma* a letter]
▶ **anagrammatic** (ˌænəgrəˈmætɪk) *or* ˌanagramˈmatical *adj*

anagrammatize *or* **anagrammatise** (ˌænə-ˈgræməˌtaɪz) *vb* **anagrammatizes, anagrammatizing,**

anagrammatized or **anagrammatises, anagrammatising, anagrammatised.** to arrange into an anagram.

anal ('eɪnºl) adj **1** of or near the anus. **2** Psychoanal. relating to a stage of psychosexual development during which the child's interest is concentrated on the anal region and excremental functions. [C18: from NL ānālis; see ANUS]
▸ 'anally adv

analects ('ænə,lekts) or **analecta** (,ænə'lektə) pl n selected literary passages from one or more works. [C17: via L from Gk, from analegein to collect up, from legein to gather]

analeptic (,ænº'leptɪk) adj **1** (of a drug, etc.) restorative or invigorating. ◆ n **2** a restorative remedy or drug. [C17: from NL, from Gk analēptikos stimulating, from analambanein to take up]

anal fin n an unpaired fin between the anus and tail fin in fishes that maintains equilibrium.

analgesia (,ænºl'dʒiːzɪə) or **analgia** (æn'ældʒɪə) n inability to feel pain. [C18: via NL from Gk: insensibility, from AN- + algēsis sense of pain]

analgesic (,ænºl'dʒiːzɪk) adj **1** of or causing analgesia. ◆ n **2** a substance that produces analgesia.

analog ('ænə,lɒg) n a variant spelling of **analogue.**

USAGE NOTE The spelling analog is a US variant of analogue in all its senses, and is also the generally preferred spelling in the computer industry.

analog computer n a computer that performs arithmetical operations using a variable physical quantity, such as mechanical movement or voltage, to represent numbers.

analogize or **analogise** (ə'nælə,dʒaɪz) vb **analogizes, analogizing, analogized** or **analogises, analogising, analogised. 1** (intr) to make use of analogy, as in argument. **2** (tr) to make analogous or reveal analogy in.

analogous (ə'næləgəs) adj **1** similar or corresponding in some respect. **2** Biol. (of organs and parts) having the same function but different evolutionary origin. **3** Linguistics. formed by analogy: an analogous plural. [C17: from L, from Gk analogos proportionate, from ANA- + logos speech, ratio]

USAGE NOTE The use of with after analogous should be avoided: swimming has no event that is analogous to (not with) the 100 metres in athletics.

analogue or US (sometimes) **analog** ('ænº,lɒg) n **1a** a physical object or quantity used to measure or represent another quantity. **1b** (as modifier): analogue watch; analogue recording. **2** something analogous to something else. **3** Biol. an analogous part or organ.

USAGE NOTE See at analog.

analogue recording n a sound recording process in which an audio input is converted into an analogous electrical waveform.

analogy (ə'nælədʒɪ) n, pl **analogies. 1** agreement or similarity, esp. in a limited number of features. **2** a comparison made to show such a similarity: an analogy between an atom and the solar system. **3** Biol. the relationship between analogous organs or parts. **4** Logic, maths, philosophy. a form of reasoning in which a similarity between two or more things is inferred from a known similarity between them in other respects. **5** Linguistics. imitation of existing models or regular patterns in the formation of words, etc.: a child may use "sheeps" as the plural of "sheep" by analogy with "cat", "cats", etc. [C16: from Gk analogia correspondence, from analogos ANALOGOUS]
▸ **analogical** (,ænə'lɒdʒɪk'l) adj

anal retentive Psychoanal. ◆ n **1** a person who exhibits

anal personality traits, such as orderliness, meanness, stubbornness, etc. ◆ adj **anal-retentive. 2** exhibiting anal personality traits, such as orderliness, meanness, stubbornness, etc.

analysand (ə'nælɪ,sænd) n any person who is undergoing psychoanalysis. [C20: from ANALYSE + -and, on the model of multiplicand]

analyse or US **analyze** ('ænº,laɪz) vb **analyses, analysing, analysed** or US **analyzes, analyzing, analyzed.** (tr) **1** to examine in detail in order to discover meaning, essential features, etc. **2** to break down into components or essential features. **3** to make a mathematical, chemical, etc., analysis of. **4** another word for **psychoanalyse.** [C17: back formation from ANALYSIS]
▸ 'ana,lyser or US 'ana,lyzer n

analysis (ə'nælɪsɪs) n, pl **analyses** (-,siːz). **1** the division of a physical or abstract whole into its constituent parts to examine or determine their relationship. **2** a statement of the results of this. **3** short for **psychoanalysis. 4** Chem. **4a** the decomposition of a substance in order to determine the kinds of constituents present (qualitative analysis) or the amount of each constituent (quantitative analysis). **4b** the result obtained by such a determination. **5** Linguistics. the use of word order together with word function to express syntactic relations in a language, as opposed to the use of inflections. **6** Maths. the branch of mathematics principally concerned with the properties of functions. **7 in the last, final,** or **ultimate analysis.** after everything has been given due consideration. [C16: from NL, from Gk analusis, lit.: a dissolving, from ANA- + luein to loosen]

analysis of variance n Statistics. a technique for analysing the total variation of a set of observations as measured by the variance of the observations multiplied by their number.

analyst ('ænəlɪst) n **1** a person who analyses or is skilled in analysis. **2** short for **psychoanalyst.**

analytic (,ænə'lɪtɪk) or **analytical** adj **1** relating to analysis. **2** capable of or given to analysing: an analytic mind. **3** Linguistics. denoting languages characterized by analysis. **4** Logic. (of a proposition) true or false by virtue of the meanings of the words alone: all spinsters are unmarried is analytically true. [C16: via LL from Gk analutikos, from analuein to dissolve, break down]
▸ ,ana'lytically adv ▸ analyticity (,ænəlɪ'tɪsɪtɪ) n

analytical geometry n the branch of geometry that uses algebraic notation to locate a point; coordinate geometry.

analytic philosophy n See **philosophical analysis.**

Anambra ★ (ə'næmbrə) n a state of S Nigeria, formed in 1976 from part of East-Central State. Capital: Enugu. Pop.: 2 850 940 (1992 est.). Area: 4844 sq. km (1870 sq. miles).

Ananda ★ (ə'nændə) n 5th century B.C., the first cousin, favourite disciple, and personal attendant of the Buddha.

anandrous (æn'ændrəs) adj (of flowers) having no stamens. [C19: from Gk anandros lacking males, from AN- + anēr man]

Ananias ★ (,ænə'naɪəs) n **1** New Testament. a Jewish Christian of Jerusalem who was struck dead for lying (Acts 5). **2** a liar.

anapaest or **anapest** ('ænəpest, -,piːst) n Prosody. a metrical foot of three syllables, the first two short, the last long (˘˘–). [C17: via L from Gk anapaistos reversed, from ana- back + paiein to strike]
▸ ,ana'paestic or ,ana'pestic adj

anaphora (ə'næfərə) n **1** Grammar. the use of a word such as a pronoun to avoid repetition, as for example one in He offered me a drink but I didn't want one. **2** Rhetoric. the repetition of a word or phrase at the beginning of successive clauses. [C16: via L from Gk: repetition, from ANA- + pherein to bear]

anaphrodisiac (,ænæfrə'dɪzɪ,æk) adj **1** tending to lessen sexual desire. ◆ n **2** an anaphrodisiac drug.

anaphylaxis (,ænəfɪ'læksɪs) n extreme sensitivity to an injected antigen following a previous injection. [C20: from ANA- + (PRO)PHYLAXIS]

★ people and places

anaplasmosis (ˌænəplæz'məʊsɪs) *n* another name for **gallsickness**.

anaptyxis (ˌænæp'tɪksɪs) *n, pl* **anaptyxes** (-'tɪksiːz). the insertion of a short vowel between consonants in order to make a word more easily pronounceable. [C19: via NL from Gk *anaptuxis*, from *anaptussein* to unfold, from ANA- + *ptussein* to fold]

Anapurna ★ (ˌænə'pʊənə) *n* a variant spelling of **Annapurna**.

anarchism ('ænəˌkɪzəm) *n* 1 *Political theory*. a doctrine advocating the abolition of government. 2 the principles or practice of anarchists.

anarchist ('ænəkɪst) *n* 1 a person who advocates a society based on voluntary cooperation and the abolition of government. 2 a person who causes disorder or upheaval.
▶ **anarchic** (æn'ɑːkɪk) *or* **an'archical** *adj*

anarchy ('ænəkɪ) *n* 1 general lawlessness and disorder, esp. when thought to result from an absence or failure of government. 2 the absence of government. 3 the absence of any guiding or uniting principle; chaos. 4 political anarchism. [C16: from Med. L, from Gk, from *anarkhos* without a ruler, from AN- + *arkh-* leader, from *arkhein* to rule]

Anastasia ★ (ˌænə'stɑːzɪə, -'steɪ-) *n* **Grand Duchess**. 1901–?18, daughter of Tsar Nicholas II, believed to have been executed by the Bolsheviks in 1918, although several women subsequently claimed to be her.

anastigmat (æ'næstɪɡmæt, ˌænə'stɪɡmæt) *n* a lens system designed to be free of astigmatism. [C19: from AN- + ASTIGMATIC]
▶ ˌanastig'matic *adj*

anastomose (ə'næstəˌməʊz) *vb* **anastomoses, anastomosing, anastomosed.** to join (two parts of a blood vessel, etc.) by anastomosis.

anastomosis (əˌnæstə'məʊsɪs) *n, pl* **anastomoses** (-siːz). 1 a natural connection between two tubular structures, such as blood vessels. 2 the union of two hollow parts that are normally separate. [C16: via NL from Gk: opening, from *anastomoun* to equip with a mouth, from *stoma* mouth]

anastrophe (ə'næstrəfɪ) *n Rhetoric*. another term for **inversion** (sense 3). [C16: from Gk, from *anastrephein* to invert]

anathema (ə'næθəmə) *n, pl* **anathemas**. 1 a detested person or thing: *he is anathema to me*. 2 a formal ecclesiastical excommunication, or denunciation of a doctrine. 3 the person or thing so cursed. 4 a strong curse. [C16: via Church L from Gk: something accursed, from *anatithenai* to dedicate, from ANA- + *tithenai* to set]

anathematize *or* **anathematise** (ə'næθɪməˌtaɪz) *vb* **anathematizes, anathematizing, anathematized** *or* **anathematises, anathematising, anathematised.** to pronounce an anathema (upon a person, etc.); curse.

Anatolia ★ (ˌænə'təʊlɪə) *n* the Asian part of Turkey, occupying the peninsula between the Black Sea, the Mediterranean, and the Aegean: consists of a plateau, largely mountainous, with salt lakes in the interior. Historical name: **Asia Minor**.
▶ ˌAna'tolian *adj, n*

anatomical (ˌænə'tɒmɪkᵃl) *adj* of anatomy.

anatomist (ə'nætəmɪst) *n* an expert in anatomy.

anatomize *or* **anatomise** (ə'nætəˌmaɪz) *vb* **anatomizes, anatomizing, anatomized** *or* **anatomises, anatomising, anatomised.** (*tr*) 1 to dissect (an animal or plant). 2 to examine in minute detail.

anatomy (ə'nætəmɪ) *n, pl* **anatomies**. 1 the science concerned with the physical structure of animals and plants. 2 the physical structure of an animal or plant or any of its parts. 3 a book or treatise on this subject. 4 dissection of an animal or plant. 5 any detailed analysis: *the anatomy of a crime*. 6 *Inf*. the human body. [C14: from L, from Gk *anatomē*, from ANA- + *temnein* to cut]

anatto (ə'nætəʊ) *n, pl* **anattos**. a variant spelling of **annatto**.

Anaxagoras ★ (ˌænæk'sæɡərəs) *n* ?500–428 B.C., Greek philosopher who maintained that all things were composed of minute particles.

Anaximander ★ (əˌnæksɪ'mændə) *n* 611–547 B.C., Greek philosopher, astronomer, and mathematician.

ANC *abbrev. for* African National Congress.

-ance *or* **-ancy** *suffix forming nouns*. indicating an action, state or condition, or quality: *resemblance; tenancy*. [via OF from L *-antia*]

ancestor ('ænsestə) *n* 1 a person from whom another is directly descended; forefather. 2 an early animal or plant from which a later type has evolved. 3 a person or thing regarded as a forerunner: *the ancestor of the modern camera*. [C13: from OF, from LL *antecessor* one who goes before, from L *antecēdere*]
▶ 'ancestress *fem n*

ancestral (æn'sestrəl) *adj* of or inherited from ancestors.

ancestry ('ænsestrɪ) *n, pl* **ancestries**. 1 lineage or descent, esp. when noble or distinguished. 2 ancestors collectively.

Anchises ★ (æn'kaɪsiːz) *n Classical myth*. a Trojan prince and father of Aeneas. In the *Aeneid*, he is rescued by his son at the fall of Troy and dies in Sicily.

anchor ('æŋkə) *n* 1 a device attached to a vessel by a cable and dropped overboard so as to grip the bottom and restrict movement. 2 an object used to hold something else firmly in place: *the rock provided an anchor for the rope*. 3 a source of stability or security. 4 short for **anchorman** *or* **anchorwoman**. 5 **cast, come to**, *or* **drop anchor**. to anchor a vessel. 6 **ride at anchor**. to be anchored. ◆ *vb* 7 to use an anchor to hold (a vessel) in one place. 8 to fasten or be fastened securely; fix or become fixed firmly. ◆ See also **anchors**. [OE *ancor*, from L, from Gk *ankura*]

anchorage ('æŋkərɪdʒ) *n* 1 the act of anchoring. 2 any place where a vessel is anchored. 3 a place designated for vessels to anchor. 4 a fee imposed for anchoring. 5 anything used as an anchor. 6 a source of security or strength.

Anchorage ★ ('æŋkərɪdʒ) *n* the largest city in Alaska, a port in the south, at the head of Cook Inlet. Pop.: 253 649 (1994 est.).

anchorite ('æŋkəˌraɪt) *n* a person who lives in seclusion, esp. a religious recluse; hermit. [C15: from Med. L, from LL, from Gk, from *anakhōrein* to retire, from *khōra* a space]
▶ 'anchoress *fem n*

anchorman ('æŋkəmæn) *n, fem* **anchorwoman** ('æŋkəwʊmæn) *pl* **anchormen, anchorwomen**. 1 *Sport*. the last person in a team to compete, esp. in a relay race. 2 (in broadcasting) a person in a central studio who links up and maintains contact with various outside camera units, reporters, etc.

anchors ('æŋkəz) *pl n Sl*. the brakes of a motor vehicle: *he rammed on the anchors*.

anchovy ('æntʃəvɪ) *n, pl* **anchovies** *or* **anchovy**. any of various small marine food fishes which have a salty taste and are often tinned or made into a paste or essence. [C16: from Sp. *anchova*, ? ult. from Gk *aphuē* small fish]

anchusa (æŋ'kjuːsə) *n* any of several Eurasian plants having rough hairy stems and leaves and blue flowers. [C18: from L]

anchylose ('æŋkɪˌləʊz) *vb* a variant spelling of **ankylose**.

ancien régime *French*. (ɑ̃sjɛ̃ reʒim) *n, pl* **anciens régimes** (ɑ̃sjɛ̃ reʒim). the political and social system of France before the Revolution of 1789. [lit.: old regime]

ancient ('eɪnʃənt) *adj* 1 dating from very long ago: *ancient ruins*. 2 very old. 3 of the far past, esp. before the collapse of the Western Roman Empire (476 A.D.). ◆ *n* 4 (*often pl*) a member of a civilized nation in the ancient world, esp. a Greek or Roman. 5 (*often pl*) one of the classical authors of Greek or Roman antiquity. 6 *Arch*. an old man. [C14: from OF *ancien*, from Vulgar L *anteanus* (unattested), from L *ante* before]
▶ 'ancientness *n*

ancient lights *n* (*usually functioning as sing*) the legal right to receive, by a particular window or windows, adequate and unobstructed daylight.

anciently ('eɪnʃəntlɪ) *adv* in ancient times.

Ancient of Days *n* a name for God, originating in the Authorized Version of the Old Testament (Daniel 7:9).

★ people and places

ancillary (æn'sɪlərɪ) *adj* **1** subsidiary. **2** auxiliary; supplementary: *ancillary services.* ◆ *n, pl* **ancillaries. 3** a subsidiary or auxiliary thing or person. [C17: from L *ancillāris* concerning maidservants, ult. from *ancūla* female servant]

Ancohuma ★ (ˌæŋkəʊ'uːmə) *n* one of the two peaks of (Mount) Sorata.

ancon ('æŋkɒn) *or* **ancone** ('æŋkəʊn) *n, pl* **ancones** (æŋ'kəʊniːz). *Architect.* a projecting bracket or console supporting a cornice. [C18: from Gk *ankōn* a bend]

Ancona ★ (*Italian* aŋ'koːna) *n* a port in Central Italy, on the Adriatic, capital of the Marches: founded by Greeks from Syracuse in about 390 B.C. Pop.: 100 597 (1994 est.)

-ancy *suffix forming nouns.* a variant of **-ance**, indicating condition or quality: *poignancy.*

ancylostomiasis (ˌænsɪˌlɒstə'maɪəsɪs) *or* **ankylostomiasis** (ˌæŋkɪˌlɒstə'maɪəsɪs) *n* infestation of the intestine with blood-sucking hookworms; hookworm disease. [from NL, ult. from Gk *ankulos* hooked + *stoma* mouth]

and (ænd; *unstressed* ənd, ən) *conj* (*coordinating*) **1** in addition to: *boys and girls.* **2** as a consequence: *he fell down and cut his knee.* **3** afterwards: *we pay and go through that door.* **4** plus: *two and two equals four.* **5** used to give emphasis or indicate repetition or continuity: *it rained and rained.* **6** used to express a contrast between instances of what is named: *there are jobs and jobs.* **7** *Inf.* used in place of *to* in infinitives after verbs such as *try, go,* and *come: try and see it my way.* **3** an obsolete word for **if**: *and it please you.* [OE *and*]

> **USAGE NOTE** See at **to.**

-and *or* **-end** *suffix forming nouns.* indicating a person or thing that is to be dealt with in a specified way: *dividend; multiplicand.* [from L gerundives ending in *-andus, -endus*]

Andalusia ★ (ˌændə'luːzɪə) *n* a region of S Spain, on the Mediterranean and the Atlantic, with the Sierra Morena in the north, the Sierra Nevada in the southeast, and the Guadalquivir River flowing over fertile lands between them; a centre of Moorish civilization; it became an autonomous region in 1981. Area: about 87 280 sq. km (33 700 sq. miles). Spanish name: **Andalucía** (andalu'θia).

Andaman and Nicobar Islands ★ ('ændəmən; 'nɪkəʊˌbɑː) *pl n* a territory of India, in the E Bay of Bengal, consisting of two groups of over 200 islands. Capital: Port Blair. Pop.: 322 000 (1994 est.). Area: 8140 sq. km (3143 sq. miles).

Andaman Islands ★ *pl n* a group of islands in the E Bay of Bengal, part of the Indian territory of the Andaman and Nicobar Islands. Pop.: 240 089 (1991 est.). Area: 6408 sq. km (2474 sq. miles).

Andaman Sea ★ *n* part of the Bay of Bengal, between the Andaman and Nicobar Islands and the Malay Peninsula.

andante (æn'dæntɪ) *Music.* ◆ *adj, adv* **1** (to be performed) at a moderately slow tempo. ◆ *n* **2** a passage or piece to be performed in this manner. [C18: from It., from *andare* to walk, from L *ambulāre*]

andantino (ˌændæn'tiːnəʊ) *Music.* ◆ *adj, adv* **1** (to be performed) slightly faster or slower than andante. ◆ *n, pl* **andantinos. 2** a passage or piece to be performed in this manner. [C19: dim. of ANDANTE]

AND circuit *or* **gate** (ænd) *n Computing.* a logic circuit that has a high-voltage output signal if and only if all input signals are at a high voltage simultaneously. Cf. NAND circuit, NOR circuit, OR circuit. [C20: from similarity of operation of *and* in logical conjunctions]

Andean (æn'diːən, 'ændɪən) *adj* of, relating to, or resembling the Andes.

Andersen ★ ('ændəsⁿn) *n* Hans Christian. 1805–75, Danish author of fairy tales.

Andersen Nexø ★ ('anərsen) *n* See (Martin Andersen) Nexø.

Anderson[1] ★ ('ændəsⁿn) *n* a river in N Canada, in the Northwest Territories, rising in lakes north of Great Bear Lake and flowing west and north to the Beaufort Sea. Length: about 580 km (360 miles).

Anderson[2] ★ ('ændəsⁿn) *n* **1 Carl David.** 1905–91, US physicist, who discovered the positron in cosmic rays (1932): Nobel prize for physics 1936. **2 Elizabeth Garrett.** 1836–1917, British physician: campaigned for the admission of women to the professions. **3** Dame **Judith,** real name *Frances Margaret Anderson.* 1898–1992, Australian actress. **4 Lindsay (Gordon).** 1923–94, British film director: his films include *This Sporting Life* (1963) and *If* (1968). **5 Marian.** 1902–93, US contralto, the first Black permanent member of the Metropolitan Opera Company, New York. **6 Philip Warren.** 1923–96, US physicist, noted for his work on solid-state physics. Nobel prize for physics 1977. **7 Sherwood.** 1874–1941, US writer, best known for *Winesburg Ohio* (1919).

Andes ★ ('ændiːz) *pl n* a major mountain system of South America, extending for about 7250 km (4500 miles) along the entire W coast, with several parallel ranges or cordilleras and many volcanic peaks: rich in minerals, including gold, silver, copper, iron ore, and nitrates. Average height: 3900 m (13 000 ft). Highest peak: Aconcagua, 6960 m (22 835 ft).

Andhra Pradesh ★ ('ændrə prɑː'deʃ) *n* a state of SE India, on the Bay of Bengal: formed in 1953 from parts of Madras and Hyderabad states. Capital: Hyderabad. Pop.: 71 800 000 (1994 est.). Area: 275 068 sq. km (106 204 sq. miles).

andiron ('ændˌaɪən) *n* either of a pair of metal stands for supporting logs in a hearth. [C14: from OF *andier,* from ?; infl. by IRON]

Andong ★ ('æn'dʊŋ) *n* a port in E China, in Liaoning province at the mouth of the Yalu River. Pop.: 188 452 (1995). Also called: **Tan-tung.**

and/or *conj* (*coordinating*) used to join terms when either one or the other or both is indicated: *passports and/or other means of identification.*

> **USAGE NOTE** Many people think that *and/or* is only acceptable in legal and commercial contexts. In other contexts, it is better to use *or* both: *some alcoholics lose their jobs or their driving licences or both* (not *their jobs and/or their driving licences*).

Andorra ★ (æn'dɔːrə) *n* a mountainous principality in SW Europe, between France and Spain: according to tradition, given independence by Charlemagne in the 9th century for helping to fight the Moors; placed under the joint sovereignty of the Comte de Foix and the Spanish bishop of Urgel in 1278; under the joint overlordship of the French head of state and the bishop of Urgel from the 16th century. Languages: Catalan, French, and Spanish. Religion: Roman Catholic. Currency: French franc and Spanish peseta. Capital: Andorra la Vella. Pop.: 64 600 (1997). Area: 464 sq. km (179 sq. miles). Official name: **Principat d'Andorra.**
▶ **An'dorran** *adj, n*

Andorra la Vella ★ (*Spanish* an'dɔrra la 'beʎa) *n* the capital of Andorra, situated in the west of the principality. Pop.: 22 821 (1994 est.). French name: **Andorre la Vieille** (ɑ̃dɔr la vjɛj).

Andrássy ★ (æn'dræsɪ; *Hungarian* 'ɔndrɑːʃi) *n* Count **Gyula** ('djulɔ). 1823–90, Hungarian statesman; the first prime minister of Hungary under the Dual Monarchy of Austria-Hungary (1867).

Andrea del Sarto ★ (*Italian* an'drea del 'sarto) *n* See **Sarto.**

Andreanof Islands ★ (ˌændrɪ'ɑːnɒf) *pl n* a group of islands in the central Aleutian Islands, Alaska. Area: 3710 sq. km (1432 sq. miles).

Andrew ★ ('ændruː) *n* Saint. *New Testament.* one of the twelve apostles of Jesus; the brother of Peter; patron saint of Scotland. Feast day: Nov. 30.

Andrewes ★ ('ændruːz) *n* Lancelot. 1555–1626, English bishop and theologian.

> ★ people and places

Andrews ★ ('ændru:z) *n* **Thomas**. 1813–85, Irish physical chemist, noted for his work on the liquefaction of gases.

Andrić ★ (*Serbo-Croat* 'andritʃ) *n* **Ivo** ('i:vɔ). 1892–1975, Serbian novelist; author of *The Bridge on the Drina* (1945): Nobel prize for literature 1961.

andro- *or before a vowel* **andr-** *combining form*. **1** male; masculine: *androsterone*. **2** (in botany) stamen or anther: *androecium*. [from Gk *anēr* (genitive *andros*) man]

Androcles ('ændrə,kli:z) *or* **Androclus** ★ ('ændrəkləs) *n* (in Roman legend) a slave whose life was spared in the arena by a lion from whose paw he had once extracted a thorn.

androecium (æn'dri:sɪəm) *n, pl* **androecia** (-sɪə). the stamens of a flowering plant collectively. [C19: from NL, from ANDRO- + Gk *oikion* a little house]

androgen ('ændrədʒən) *n* any of several steroids that promote development of male sexual characteristics.
▸ **androgenic** (,ændrə'dʒɛnɪk) *adj*

androgyne ('ændrə,dʒaɪn) *n* another word for **hermaphrodite**. [C17: from OF, via L from Gk *androgunos*, from *anēr* man + *gunē* woman]

androgynous (æn'drɒdʒɪnəs) *adj* **1** *Bot*. having male and female flowers in the same inflorescence. **2** having male and female characteristics; hermaphrodite.
▸ **an'drogyny** *n*

android ('ændrɔɪd) *n* **1** (in science fiction) a robot resembling a human being. ◆ *adj* **2** resembling a human being. [C18: from LGk *androeidēs* manlike; see ANDRO-, -OID]

andrology (æn'drɒlədʒɪ) *n* the branch of medicine concerned with diseases in men, esp. of the reproductive organs. [C20: from ANDRO- + -LOGY]
▸ **an'drologist** *n*

Andromache ★ (æn'drɒməkɪ) *n Greek myth*. the wife of Hector.

Andromeda ★ (æn'drɒmɪdə) *n Greek myth*. the wife of Perseus, who saved her from a sea monster.

Andropov[1] ★ (æn'drɒpɒv; *Russian* ən'drɔ:pəf) *n* a former name (1984–91) for **Rybinsk**.

Andropov[2] ★ (æn'drɒpɒv; *Russian* ən'drɔ:pəf) *n* **Yuri Vladimirovich**. 1914–84, Soviet statesman; president of the Soviet Union (1983–84).

Andros ★ ('ændrəs) *n* **1** an island in the Aegean Sea, the northernmost of the Cyclades: long famous for wine. Capital: Andros. Pop.: 8155 (1990). Area: about 311 sq. km (120 sq. miles). **2** an island in the N Caribbean, the largest of the Bahamas. Pop.: 8177 (1990). Area: 4144 sq. km (1600 sq. miles).

androsterone (æn'drɒstə,rəun) *n* an androgenic steroid hormone produced in the testes.

-androus *adj combining form*. (in botany) indicating number or type of stamens: *diandrous*. [from NL, from Gk *-andros*, from *anēr* man]

Andvari ★ (æn'dwɑ:rɪ) *n Norse myth*. a dwarf who possessed a treasure hoard, which was robbed by Loki.

ane (eɪn) *determiner, pron, n* a Scottish word for **one**.

-ane *suffix forming nouns*. indicating a hydrocarbon of the alkane series: *hexane*. [coined to replace *-ene*, *-ine*, and *-one*]

anecdotage ('ænɪk,dəʊtɪdʒ) *n Humorous*. garrulous old age. [from ANECDOTE + -AGE, with play on *dotage*]

anecdote ('ænɪk,dəʊt) *n* a short usually amusing account of an incident. [C17: from Med. L, from Gk *anekdotos* unpublished, from AN- + *ekdotos* published]
▸ ,anec'dotal *or* ,anec'dotic *adj* ▸ ,anec'dotalist *or* 'anec,dotist *n*

anechoic (,ænɪ'kəʊɪk) *adj* having a low degree of reverberation: *an anechoic recording studio*.

Aneirin ★ (ə'naɪ°rɪn) *n* 6th century A.D., Welsh poet. His *Y Gododdin*, preserved in *The Book of Aneirin* (?1250), is one of the earliest surviving Welsh poems.

anemia (ə'ni:mɪə) *n* the usual US spelling of **anaemia**.
▸ **anemic** (ə'ni:mɪk) *adj*

anemo- *combining form*. indicating wind: *anemometer*; *anemophilous*. [from Gk *anemos* wind]

anemograph (ə'nɛməʊ,grɑ:f) *n* a self-recording anemometer.

anemometer (,ænɪ'mɒmɪtə) *n* an instrument for recording the speed and often the direction of winds. Also called: **wind gauge**.
▸ ,ane'mometry *n* ▸ **anemometric** (,ænɪməʊ'mɛtrɪk) *adj*

anemone (ə'nɛmənɪ) *n* any woodland plant of the genus *Anemone* of N temperate regions, such as the white-flowered **wood anemone** or **windflower**. Some cultivated anemones have coloured flowers. [C16: via L from Gk: windflower, from *anemos* wind]

anemophilous (,ænɪ'mɒfɪləs) *adj* (of flowering plants such as grasses) pollinated by the wind.
▸ ,ane'mophily *n*

anent (ə'nɛnt) *prep Arch. or Scot*. **1** lying against; alongside. **2** concerning; about. [OE *on efen*, lit.: on even (ground)]

aneroid barometer ('ænə,rɔɪd) *n* a device for measuring atmospheric pressure without the use of fluids. It consists of a partially evacuated chamber, the lid of which is displaced by variations in air pressure. This displacement is magnified by levers and made to operate a pointer. [C19 *aneroid*, from F, from AN- + Gk *nēros* wet + -OID]

anesthesia (,ænɪs'θi:zɪə) *n* the usual US spelling of **anaesthesia**.

anesthesiologist (,ænɪs,θi:zɪ'ɒlədʒɪst) *n* the US name for an **anaesthetist**.

anesthesiology (,ænɪs,θi:zɪ'ɒlədʒɪ) *n* the US name for **anaesthetics**.

anesthetic (,ænɪs'θɛtɪk) *n, adj* the usual US spelling of **anaesthetic**.

anesthetist (ə'nɛsθətɪst) *n* (in the US) a person qualified to administer anaesthesia, often a nurse or someone other than a physician.

Aneto ★ (*Spanish* a'neto) *n* **Pico de** ('piko de). a mountain in N Spain, near the French border: the highest in the Pyrenees. Height: 3404 m (11 168 ft).

aneurysm *or* **aneurism** ('ænjə,rɪzəm) *n* a sac formed by abnormal dilation of the weakened wall of a blood vessel. [C15: from Gk *aneurusma*, from *aneurunein* to dilate]

anew (ə'nju:) *adv* **1** once more. **2** in a different way; afresh. [OE *of nīwe*; see OF, NEW]

Anfinsen ★ ('ænfɪnsᵊn) *n* **Christian Boehmer** ('beɪmə). 1916–95, US biochemist, noted for his research on the structure of enzymes. Nobel prize for chemistry 1972.

Angara ★ (*Russian* anga'ra) *n* a river in S Russia, in Siberia, flowing from Lake Baikal north and west to the Yenisei River: important for hydroelectric power. Length: 1840 km (1150 miles).

angary ('æŋgərɪ) *n Law*. the right of a belligerent state to use the property of a neutral state or to destroy it subject to payment of compensation to the owners. [C19: from F, from LL *angaria* enforced service, from Gk *angaros* courier]

angel ('eɪndʒəl) *n* **1** one of a class of spiritual beings attendant upon God. In medieval angelology they are divided by rank into nine orders. **2** a divine messenger from God. **3** a guardian spirit. **4** a conventional representation of any of these beings, depicted in human form with wings. **5** *Inf*. a person who is kind, pure, or beautiful. **6** *Inf*. an investor, esp. in a theatrical production. **7** Also called: **angel-noble**. a former English gold coin with a representation of the archangel Michael on it. **8** *Inf*. an unexplained signal on a radar screen. [OE, from LL *angelus*, from Gk *angelos* messenger]

angel cake *or esp. US* **angel food cake** *n* a very light sponge cake made without egg yolks.

angel dust *n* a slang name for **PCP**.

Angel Falls ★ *n* a waterfall in SE Venezuela, on the Caroní River. Height (probably the highest in the world): 979 m (3211 ft).

angelfish ('eɪndʒəl,fɪʃ) *n, pl* **angelfish** *or* **angelfishes**. **1** any of various small tropical marine fishes which have a deep flattened brightly coloured body. **2** a South American freshwater fish having a compressed body and large dorsal and anal fins: a popular aquarium fish. **3** a shark with flattened pectoral fins.

angelic (æn'dʒɛlɪk) adj **1** of or relating to angels. **2** Also: **angelical**. resembling an angel in beauty, etc.
▸ **an'gelically** adv

angelica (æn'dʒɛlɪkə) n **1** an umbelliferous plant, the aromatic seeds, leaves, and stems of which are used in medicine and cookery. **2** the candied stems of this plant, used for decorating and flavouring sweet dishes. [C16: from Med. L (*herba*) *angelica* angelic (herb)]

Angelico ★ (*Italian* an'dʒeːliko) n **Fra** (fra), original name *Guido di Pietro;* monastic name *Fra Giovanni da Fiesole.* ?1400–55, Italian fresco painter and Dominican friar.

Angell ★ ('eɪndʒəl) n Sir **Norman**, real name *Ralph Norman Angell Lane.* 1874–1967, British writer and economist, noted for his work on the economic futility of war, *The Great Illusion* (1910): Nobel peace prize 1933.

Angelou ★ ('ændʒə,luː) n **Maya** ('maɪə), real name *Marguerite Johnson.* born 1928, US Black writer. Her works include the novel *I Know Why the Caged Bird Sings* (1970) and its sequels and *Phenomenal Woman* (1995).

Angelus ('ændʒɪləs) n *RC Church.* **1** a series of prayers recited in the morning, at midday, and in the evening. **2** the bell (**Angelus bell**) signalling the times of these prayers. [C17: L, from *Angelus domini nuntiavit Mariae* the angel of the Lord brought tidings to Mary]

anger ('æŋɡə) n **1** a feeling of great annoyance or antagonism as the result of some real or supposed grievance; rage; wrath. ♦ vb (*tr*) **2** to make angry; enrage. [C12: from ON *angr* grief]

Angers ★ (*French* ɑ̃ʒe) n a city in W France, on the river Maine. Pop.: 146 163 (1990).

Angevin ('ændʒɪvɪn) n **1** a native or inhabitant of Anjou. **2** *History.* a member of the Plantagenet royal line, esp. one of the kings of England from Henry II to John (1154–1216). ♦ adj **3** of Anjou or its inhabitants. **4** of the Plantagenet kings of England between 1154 and 1216.

angina (æn'dʒaɪnə) n **1** any disease marked by painful attacks of spasmodic choking. **2** Also called: **angina pectoris** ('pɛktərɪs). a sudden intense pain in the chest, caused by momentary lack of adequate blood supply to the heart muscle. [C16: from L: quinsy, from Gk *ankhonē* a strangling]

angio- *or before a vowel* **angi-** *combining form.* indicating a blood or lymph vessel; seed vessel. [from Gk *angeion* vessel]

angioma (,ændʒɪ'əumə) n, pl **angiomas** or **angiomata** (-mətə). a tumour consisting of a mass of blood vessels or a mass of lymphatic vessels.

angioplasty ('ændʒɪə,plæstɪ) n a surgical technique for restoring normal blood flow through an artery narrowed or blocked by atherosclerosis, either by inserting a balloon into it or by using a laser beam.

angiosperm ('ændʒɪə,spɜːm) n any seed-bearing plant in which the ovules are enclosed in an ovary which develops into the fruit after fertilization; any flowering plant. Cf. **gymnosperm**.
▸ ,angio'spermous adj

Angkor ★ ('æŋkɔː) n a large area of ruins in NW Cambodia, containing **Angkor Thom** (tɔːm), the capital of the former Khmer Empire, and **Angkor Wat** (wɒt), a three-storey temple, which were overgrown with dense jungle from the 14th to 19th centuries.

angle[1] ('æŋɡ°l) n **1** the space between two straight lines or two planes that extend from a common point. **2** the shape formed by two such lines or planes. **3** the extent to which one such line or plane diverges from the other, measured in degrees or radians. **4** a recess; corner. **5** point of view: *look at the question from another angle.* **6** See **angle iron**. ♦ vb **angles, angling, angled. 7** to move in or bend into angles or an angle. **8** (*tr*) to produce (an article, statement, etc.) with a particular point of view. **9** (*tr*) to present or place at an angle. **10** (*intr*) to turn in a different direction. [C14: from F, from OL *angulus* corner]

angle[2] ('æŋɡ°l) vb **angles, angling, angled.** (*intr*) **1** to fish with a hook and line. **2** (often foll. by *for*) to attempt to get: *he* angled for a compliment. ♦ n **3** *Obs.* a fish-hook. [OE *angul* fish-hook]

Angle ('æŋɡ°l) n a member of a people from N Germany who invaded and settled large parts of E and N England in the 5th and 6th centuries A.D. [from L *Anglus,* of Gmc origin, an inhabitant of *Angul,* a district in Schleswig, a name identical with OE *angul* hook, ANGLE[2], referring to its shape]
▸ 'Anglian adj, n

angle iron n an iron or a steel structural bar that has an L-shaped cross section. Also called: **angle, angle bar.**

angle of incidence n **1** the angle that a line or beam of radiation makes with a line perpendicular to the surface at the point of incidence. **2** the angle between the chord line of an aircraft wing or tailplane and the aircraft's longitudinal axis.

angle of reflection n the angle that a beam of reflected radiation makes with the normal to a surface at the point of reflection.

angle of refraction n the angle that a refracted beam of radiation makes with the normal to the surface between two media at the point of refraction.

angle of repose n the maximum angle to the horizontal at which rock, soil, etc., will remain without sliding.

angler ('æŋɡlə) n **1** a person who fishes with a hook and line. **2** Also called: **angler fish.** any of various spiny-finned fishes which live at the bottom of the sea and typically have a long movable dorsal fin with which they lure their prey.

Anglesey ★ ('æŋɡlsɪ) n an island and county of N Wales, formerly part of Gwynedd (1974–96), separated from the mainland by the Menai Strait. Administrative centre: Llangefni. Pop.: 68 400 (1994 est.). Area: 720 sq. km (278 sq. miles). Welsh name: **Ynys Môn.**

Anglia ★ ('æŋɡlɪə) n a Latin name for **England.**

Anglican ('æŋɡlɪkən) adj **1** denoting or relating to the Church of England or one of the churches in communion with it. ♦ n **2** a member of the Anglican Church. [C17: from Med. L, from *Anglicus* English, from L *Anglī* the Angles]
▸ 'Anglican,ism n

Anglicism ('æŋɡlɪ,sɪzəm) n **1** a word, or idiom peculiar to the English language, esp. as spoken in England. **2** an English mannerism, custom, etc. **3** the fact of being English.

anglicize or **anglicise** ('æŋɡlɪ,saɪz) vb **anglicizes, anglicizing, anglicized** or **anglicises, anglicising, anglicised.** (*sometimes cap.*) to make or become English in outlook, form, etc.

angling ('æŋɡlɪŋ) n the art or sport of catching fish with a baited hook or other lure, such as a fly; fishing.

Anglo ('æŋɡləu) n, pl **Anglos. 1** *US.* a White inhabitant of the US who is not of Latin extraction. **2** *Canad.* an English-speaking Canadian, esp. one of Anglo-Celtic origin; an Anglo-Canadian.

Anglo- *combining form.* denoting English or England: *Anglo-Saxon.* [from Med. L *Anglī*]

Anglo-American adj **1** of relations between England and the United States. ♦ n **2** *Chiefly US.* an inhabitant of the United States who was or whose ancestors were born in England.

Anglo-Catholic adj **1** of or relating to a group within the Anglican Church that emphasizes the Catholic elements in its teaching and practice. ♦ n **2** a member of this group.
▸ ,Anglo-Ca'tholi,cism n

Anglo-Egyptian Sudan ★ n the former name (1899–1956) of the **Sudan.**

Anglo-French adj **1** of England and France. **2** of Anglo-French. ♦ n **3** the Norman-French language of medieval England.

Anglo-Indian adj **1** of England and India. **2** denoting or relating to Anglo-Indians. **3** (of a word) introduced into English from an Indian language. ♦ n **4** a person of mixed English and Indian descent. **5** an English person who lives or has lived for a long time in India.

★ people and places

Anglomania (ˌæŋgləʊˈmeɪnɪə) *n* excessive respect for English customs, etc.
▸ ˌAngloˈmaniˌac *n*

Anglo-Norman *adj* **1** relating to the Norman conquerors of England, their society, or their language. ◆ *n* **2** a Norman inhabitant of England after 1066. **3** the Anglo-French language.

Anglophile (ˈæŋgləʊfɪl, -ˌfaɪl) *or* **Anglophil** *n* a person having admiration for England or the English.

Anglophobe (ˈæŋgləʊˌfəʊb) *n* **1** a person who hates or fears England or its people. **2** *Canad.* a person who hates or fears Canadian Anglophones.

Anglophone (ˈæŋgləˌfəʊn) (*often not cap.*) ◆ *n* **1** a person who speaks English. ◆ *adj* **2** speaking English.

Anglo-Saxon *n* **1** a member of any of the West Germanic tribes that settled in Britain from the 5th century A.D. **2** the language of these tribes. See **Old English. 3** any White person whose native language is English. **4** *Inf.* plain blunt English. ◆ *adj* **5** forming part of the Germanic element in Modern English: *"forget" is an Anglo-Saxon word.* **6** of the Anglo-Saxons or the Old English language. **7** of the White Protestant culture of Britain, Australia, and the US.

Angola ★ (æŋˈgəʊlə) *n* a republic in SW Africa, on the Atlantic: includes the enclave of Cabinda, north of the River Congo; a Portuguese possession from 1575 until its independence in 1975; factional violence. It consists of a narrow coastal plain with a large fertile plateau in the east. Currency: kwanza. Religion: Christian majority. Capital: Luanda. Pop.: 10 624 000 (1997). Area: 1 246 693 sq. km (481 351 sq. miles).
▸ **An'golan** *adj, n*

angora (æŋˈgɔːrə) *n* (*sometimes cap.*) **1** the long soft hair of the Angora goat or the fur of the Angora rabbit. **2** yarn, cloth, or clothing made from this hair or fur. **3** (*as modifier*): *an angora sweater.* ◆ See also **mohair.** [from *Angora*, former name of Ankara, in Turkey]

Angora goat (æŋˈgɔːrə) *n* a breed of domestic goat with long soft hair.

Angora rabbit *n* a breed of rabbit with long silky fur.

Angostura ★ (*Spanish* aŋgɒsˈtura) *n* the former name (1764–1846) for **Ciudad Bolívar.**

angostura bark (ˌæŋgəˈstjʊərə) *n* the bitter aromatic bark of certain South American trees, formerly used to reduce fever. [C18: from ANGOSTURA]

angostura bitters *pl n* (*often cap.*) *Trademark.* a bitter aromatic tonic, used as a flavouring in alcoholic drinks.

angry (ˈæŋgrɪ) *adj* **angrier, angriest. 1** feeling or expressing annoyance, animosity, or resentment. **2** suggestive of anger: *angry clouds.* **3** severely inflamed: *an angry sore.*
▸ ˈangrily *adv*

> **USAGE NOTE** It was formerly considered incorrect to talk about being *angry at* a person, but this use is now acceptable.

angst (æŋst) *n* an acute but nonspecific sense of anxiety or remorse. [G]

angstrom (ˈæŋstrəm) *n* a unit of length equal to 10^{-10} metre, used principally to express the wavelengths of electromagnetic radiations. Symbol: Å or A Also called: **angstrom unit.** [C20: after Anders J. ÅNGSTRÖM]

Ångström ★ (ˈæŋstrəm; *Swedish* ˈɒŋstrœm) *n* **Anders Jonas** (ˈandərs ˈjuːnas). 1814–74, Swedish physicist, noted for his work on spectroscopy, solar physics, and geomagnetism.

Anguilla ★ (æŋˈgwɪlə) *n* an island in the Caribbean, in the Leeward Islands, a United Kingdom overseas territory: part of the British associated state of St Kitts-Nevis-Anguilla from 1967 until 1980, when it reverted to the status of a British dependency. Pop.: 8960 (1992). Area: 90 sq. km (35 sq. miles).

anguine (ˈæŋgwɪn) *adj* of or similar to a snake. [C17: from L *anguīnus*, from *anguis* snake]

anguish (ˈæŋgwɪʃ) *n* **1** extreme pain or misery; mental or physical torture; agony. ◆ *vb* **2** to afflict or be afflicted with anguish. [C13: from OF *angoisse* a strangling, from L, from *angustus* narrow]
▸ ˈanguished *adj*

angular (ˈæŋgjʊlə) *adj* **1** lean or bony. **2** awkward or stiff. **3** having an angle or angles. **4** placed at an angle. **5** measured by an angle or by the rate at which an angle changes; *angular momentum; angular velocity.* [C15: from L *angulāris*, from *angulus* ANGLE[1]]

angularity (ˌæŋgjʊˈlærɪtɪ) *n, pl* **angularities. 1** the condition of being angular. **2** an angular shape.

Angus ★ (ˈæŋgəs) *n* a council area and historic county of E Scotland, on the North Sea: part of Tayside region (1975–96). Administrative centre: Forfar. Pop.: 111 020 (1996 est.). Area: 2181 sq. km (842 sq. miles).

Angus Og ★ (əug) *n Irish myth.* the god of love and beauty.

Anhalt ★ (*German* ˈanhalt) *n* a former duchy and state of central E Germany, now part of the state of Saxony-Anhalt: part of East Germany until 1990.

anhedral (ænˈhiːdrəl) *n* the downward inclination of an aircraft wing in relation to the lateral axis.

Anhui *or* **Anhwei** ★ (ˈænˈweɪ) *n* a province of E China, crossed by the Yangtze River. Capital: Hefei. Pop.: 59 550 000 (1995 est.). Area: 139 860 sq. km (54 000 sq. miles).

anhydride (ænˈhaɪdraɪd) *n* **1** a compound that has been formed from another compound by dehydration. **2** a compound that forms an acid or base when added to water. [C19: from ANHYDR(OUS) + -IDE]

anhydrous (ænˈhaɪdrəs) *adj* containing no water, esp. no water of crystallization. [C19: from Gk *anudros*; see AN-, HYDRO-]

Aniakchak ★ (ˌænɪˈæktʃæk) *n* an active volcanic crater in SW Alaska, on the Alaska Peninsula: the largest explosion crater in the world. Height: 1347 m (4420 ft). Diameter: 9 km (6 miles).

anil (ˈænɪl) *n* a leguminous West Indian shrub which is a source of indigo. Also called: **indigo.** [C16: from Port., from Ar. *an-nīl*, the indigo]

aniline (ˈænɪlɪn, -ˌliːn) *n* a colourless oily poisonous liquid used in the manufacture of dyes, plastics, and explosives. Formula: $C_6H_5NH_2$.

aniline dye *n* any synthetic dye originally made from aniline, obtained from coal tar.

anima (ˈænɪmə) *n* (in Jungian psychology) **a** the feminine principle as present in the male unconscious. **b** the inner personality. [L: air, breath, spirit, fem of ANIMUS]

animadversion (ˌænɪmædˈvɜːʃən) *n* criticism or censure.

animadvert (ˌænɪmædˈvɜːt) *vb* (*intr*) **1** (usually foll. by *on* or *upon*) to comment with strong criticism (upon); make censorious remarks (about). **2** to make an observation or comment. [C16: from L *animadvertere* to notice, from *animus* mind + *advertere* to turn to]

animal (ˈænɪməl) *n* **1** *Zool.* any living organism characterized by voluntary movement, the possession of specialized sense organs enabling rapid response to stimuli, and the ingestion of complex organic substances. **2** any mammal, esp. except man. **3** a brutish person. **4** *Facetious.* a person or thing (esp. in **no such animal**). ◆ *adj* **5** of, relating to, or derived from animals. **6** of or relating to physical needs or desires; carnal; sensual. [C14: from L, from *animālis* (adj) living, breathing; see ANIMA]

animalcule (ˌænɪˈmælkjuːl) *n* a microscopic animal such as an amoeba or rotifer. [C16: from NL *animalculum* a small animal]
▸ ˌaniˈmalcular *adj*

animal husbandry *n* the science of breeding, rearing, and caring for farm animals.

animalism (ˈænɪməˌlɪzəm) *n* **1** preoccupation with physical matters; sensuality. **2** the doctrine that man lacks a spiritual nature. **3** a mode of behaviour typical of animals.

animality (ˌænɪˈmælɪtɪ) *n* **1** the animal side of man, as

★ people and places

opposed to the intellectual or spiritual. **2** the characteristics of an animal.

animalize or **animalise** ('ænɪmə,laɪz) vb **animalizes, animalizing, animalized** or **animalises, animalising, animalised.** (tr) to rouse to brutality or sensuality or make brutal or sensual.
▶ ,animali'zation or ,animali'sation n

animal magnetism n **1** the quality of being attractive, esp. to members of the opposite sex. **2** Obs. hypnotism.

animal rights pl n a the rights of animals to be protected from exploitation and abuse by humans. **b** (as modifier): the animal-rights lobby.

animal spirits pl n boisterous exuberance. [from a vital force once supposed to be dispatched by the brain to all points of the body]

animate vb ('ænɪ,meɪt), **animates, animating, animated.** (tr) **1** to give life to or cause to come alive. **2** to make energetic or lively. **3** to encourage or inspire. **4** to impart motion to. **5** to record on film or video tape so as to give movement to. ◆ adj ('ænɪmɪt). **6** having life. **7** spirited or lively. [C16: from L animāre to make alive, from anima breath, spirit]
▶ 'ani,matedly adv

animated cartoon n a film produced by photographing a series of gradually changing drawings, etc., which give the illusion of movement when the series is projected rapidly.

animation (,ænɪ'meɪʃən) n **1** vivacity. **2** the condition of being alive. **3** the techniques used in the production of animated cartoons.

animato (,ænɪ'mɑːtəʊ) adj, adv Music. lively; animated. [It.]

animatronics (,ænɪmə'trɒnɪks) n (functioning as sing) a branch of film and theatre technology that combines traditional puppetry techniques with electronics to create lifelike animated effects. [C20: from ANIMA(TION) + (ELEC)TRONICS]

animé ('ænɪ,meɪ, -mɪ) n any of various resins, esp. that obtained from a tropical American leguminous tree. [F: from ?]

animism ('ænɪ,mɪzəm) n **1** the belief that natural objects have desires and intentions. **2** (in the philosophies of Plato and Pythagoras) the hypothesis that there is an immaterial force that animates the universe. [C19: from L anima vital breath, spirit]
▶ animistic (,ænɪ'mɪstɪk) adj

animosity (,ænɪ'mɒsɪtɪ) n, pl animosities. a powerful and active dislike or hostility. [C15: from LL animōsitās, from ANIMUS]

animus ('ænɪməs) n **1** intense dislike; hatred; animosity. **2** motive or purpose. **3** (in Jungian psychology) the masculine principle present in the female unconscious. [C19: from L: mind, spirit]

anion ('æn,aɪən) n a negatively charged ion; an ion that is attracted to the anode during electrolysis. Cf. **cation.** [C19: from ANA- + ION]
▶ anionic (,ænaɪ'ɒnɪk) adj

anise ('ænɪs) n a Mediterranean umbelliferous plant having clusters of small yellowish-white flowers and liquorice-flavoured seeds. [C13: from OF anis, via L from Gk anison]

aniseed ('ænɪ,siːd) n the liquorice-flavoured aromatic seeds of the anise plant, used medicinally for expelling intestinal gas and in cookery.

anisette (,ænɪ'zɛt, -'sɛt) n a liquorice-flavoured liqueur made from aniseed. [C19: from F]

anisotropic (æn,aɪsəʊ'trɒpɪk) adj **1** having different physical properties in different directions: anisotropic crystals. **2** (of a plant) responding unequally to an external stimulus in different parts.
▶ an,iso'tropically adv ▶ anisotropy (,ænaɪ'sɒtrəpɪ) n

Anjou ★ (French ɑ̃ʒu) n a former province of W France, in the Loire valley: a medieval countship from the 10th century, belonging to the English crown from 1154 until 1204; annexed by France in 1480.

Ankara ★ ('æŋkərə) n the capital of Turkey: an ancient city in the Anatolian highlands: first a capital in the 3rd

century B.C., in the Celtic kingdom of Galatia. Pop.: 2 782 200 (1994 est.). Ancient name: **Ancyra.** Former name (until 1930): **Angora.**

ankh (æŋk) n a tau cross with a loop on the top, symbolizing eternal life: often appearing in Egyptian personal names, such as Tutankhamen. [from Egyptian 'nh life, soul]

Anking ★ ('ɑːn'kɪŋ) n a variant transliteration of the Chinese name for **Anqing.**

ankle ('æŋkʰl) n **1** the joint connecting the leg and the foot. **2** the part of the leg just above the foot. [C14: from ON]

ankle biter n Austral. sl. a child.

anklebone ('æŋkʰl,bəʊn) n the nontechnical name for **talus**[1].

anklet ('æŋklɪt) n an ornamental chain worn around the ankle.

ankylose or **anchylose** ('æŋkɪ,ləʊz) vb **ankyloses, ankylosing, ankylosed** or **anchyloses, anchylosing, anchylosed.** (of bones in a joint, etc.) to fuse or stiffen by ankylosis.

ankylosis or **anchylosis** (,æŋkɪ'ləʊsɪs) n abnormal adhesion or immobility of the bones in a joint, as by a fibrous growth of tissues within the joint. [C18: from NL, from Gk ankuloun to crook]
▶ ankylotic or anchylotic (,æŋkɪ'lɒtɪk) adj

anna ('ænə) n a former Indian coin, worth one sixteenth of a rupee. [C18: from Hindi ānā]

Annaba ★ ('ænəbə) n a port in NE Algeria: site of the Roman city of Hippo Regius. Pop.: 222 518 (1987). Former name: **Bône.**

annals ('ænʰlz) pl n **1** yearly records of events. **2** history in general. **3** regular reports of the work of a society, learned body, etc. [C16: from L (librī) annālēs yearly (books), from annus year]
▶ 'annalist n ▶ annal'istic adj

Annan ★ ('ænæn) n Kofi ('kəʊfɪ). born 1938, Ghanaian international civil servant; secretary-general of the United Nations from 1997.

Annapolis ★ (ə'næpəlɪs) n the capital of Maryland, near the mouth of the Severn River on Chesapeake Bay: site of the US Naval Academy. Pop.: 33 187 (1990).

Annapolis Royal ★ n a town in SE Canada in W Nova Scotia on an arm of the Bay of Fundy: the first settlement in Canada (1605). Pop.: 633 (1991). Former name (until 1710): **Port Royal.**

Annapurna or **Anapurna** ★ (,ænə'pʊənə) n a massif of the Himalayas, in Nepal. Highest peak: 8078 m (26 502 ft).

Ann Arbor ★ (æn 'ɑːbə) n a city in SE Michigan: seat of the University of Michigan. Pop.: 108 817 (1994 est.).

annates ('æneɪts, -əts) pl n RC Church. the first year's revenue of a see, etc., paid to the pope. [C16: from F, from Med. L annāta, from L annus year]

annatto or **anatto** (ə'nætəʊ) n, pl annattos or anattos. **1** a small tropical American tree having pulpy seeds that yield a dye. **2** the yellowish-red dye obtained from the seeds of this tree, used for colouring fabrics, butter, varnish, etc. [from Carib]

Anne ★ (æn) n **1** Princess, the Princess Royal. born 1950, daughter of Elizabeth II of Great Britain and Northern Ireland; a noted horsewoman and president of the Save the Children Fund. **2** Queen. 1665–1714, queen of Great Britain and Ireland (1702–14), daughter of James II. **3** Saint. (in Christian tradition) the mother of the Virgin Mary. Feast day: July 26 or 25.

anneal (ə'niːl) vb **1** to temper or toughen (something) by heat treatment to remove internal stress, crystal defects, and dislocations. **2** (tr) to toughen or strengthen (the will, determination, etc.). ◆ n **3** an act of annealing. [OE onǣlan, from ON + ǣlan to burn, from āl fire]
▶ an'nealer n

Anne Boleyn ★ n See (Anne) **Boleyn.**

Annecy ★ (French ansi) n **1** a city and resort in E France, on Lake Annecy. Pop.: 51 143 (1990). **2 Lake.** a lake in E France, in the Alps.

annelid ('ænəlɪd) n **1** a worm in which the body is di-

★ people and places

vided into segments both externally and internally, as the earthworms. ◆ *adj* **2** of such worms. [C19: from NL *Annelida*, from OF, ult. from L *ānulus* ring]
▶ **annelidan** (ə'nɛlɪdən) *n*, *adj*

Anne of Austria ★ *n* 1601–66, wife of Louis XIII of France and daughter of Philip III of Spain: regent of France (1643–61) for her son Louis XIV.

Anne of Cleves ★ (kliːvz) *n* 1515–57, the fourth wife of Henry VIII of England; their marriage (1540) was annulled.

annex *vb* (æ'nɛks). (*tr*) **1** to join or add, esp. to something larger. **2** to add (territory) by conquest or occupation. **3** to add or append as a condition, etc. **4** to appropriate without permission. ◆ *n* ('ænɛks). **5** a variant spelling (esp. US) of **annexe**. [C14: from Med. L, from L *annectere* to attach to, from *nectere* to join]
▶ **an'nexable** *adj* ▶ **ˌannex'ation** *n*

annexe *or esp. US* **annex** ('ænɛks) *n* **1a** an extension to a main building. **1b** a building used as an addition to a main one nearby. **2** something added, esp. a supplement to a document.

Annigoni ★ (*Italian* anni'goːni) *n* Pietro ('pjɛːtro). 1910–88, Italian painter; noted esp. for his portraits.

annihilate (ə'naɪəˌleɪt) *vb* **annihilates, annihilating, annihilated.** (*tr*) **1** to destroy completely; extinguish. **2** *Inf.* to defeat totally, as in argument. [C16: from LL, from L *nihil* nothing]
▶ **anˌnihi'lation** *n* ▶ **an'nihiˌlator** *n*

anniversary (ˌænɪ'vɜːsərɪ) *n*, *pl* **anniversaries. 1** the date on which an event occurred in some previous year: *a wedding anniversary.* **2** the celebration of this. **3** of or relating to an anniversary. [C13: from L *anniversārius* returning every year, from *annus* year + *vertere* to turn]

anno Domini ('ænəʊ 'dɒmɪˌnaɪ, -ˌniː) **1** the full form of **A.D.** ◆ *n* **2** *Inf.* advancing old age. [L: in the year of our Lord]

annotate ('ænəʊˌteɪt, 'ænəˌteɪt) *vb* **annotates, annotating, annotated.** to supply (a written work) with critical or explanatory notes. [C18: from L *annotāre*, from *nota* mark]
▶ **'annoˌtative** *adj* ▶ **'annoˌtator** *n*

annotation (ˌænəʊ'teɪʃən, ˌænə'teɪʃən) *n* **1** the act of annotating. **2** a note added in explanation, etc., esp. of some literary work.

announce (ə'naʊns) *vb* **announces, announcing, announced. 1** (*tr*; *may take a clause as object*) to make known publicly. **2** (*tr*) to declare the arrival of: *to announce a guest.* **3** (*tr*; *may take a clause as object*) to presage: *the dark clouds announced rain.* **4** (*intr*) to work as an announcer, as on radio or television. [C15: from OF, from L *annuntiāre*, from *nuntius* messenger]
▶ **an'nouncement** *n*

announcer (ə'naʊnsə) *n* a person who announces, esp. one who reads the news, etc., on radio or television.

annoy (ə'nɔɪ) *vb* **1** to irritate or displease. **2** to harass with repeated attacks. [C13: from OF, from LL *inodiāre* to make hateful, from L *in odiō (esse)* (to be) hated, from *odium* hatred]
▶ **an'noyer** *n* ▶ **an'noying** *adj* ▶ **an'noyingly** *adv*

annoyance (ə'nɔɪəns) *n* **1** the feeling of being annoyed. **2** the act of annoying. **3** a person or thing that annoys.

annual ('ænjʊəl) *adj* **1** occurring, done, etc., once a year or every year; yearly: *an annual income.* **2** lasting for a year: *an annual subscription.* ◆ *n* **3** a plant that completes its life cycle in one year. **4** a book, magazine, etc., published once every year. [C14: from LL, from L *annuus* yearly, from *annus* year]
▶ **'annually** *adv*

annual general meeting *n* the statutory meeting of the directors and shareholders of a company or of the members of a society, held once every financial year. Abbrev.: **AGM.**

annualize *or* **annualise** ('ænjʊəˌlaɪz) *vb* **annualizes, annualizing, annualized** *or* **annualises, annualising, annualised.** (*tr*) to convert (a rate of interest) to an annual rate when it is quoted for a period less than a year: *an annualized percentage rate.*

annual percentage rate *n* the annual equivalent of a

rate of interest when the rate is quoted more frequently than annually, usually monthly. Abbrev.: **APR.**

annual ring *n* a ring indicating one year's growth, seen in the transverse section of stems and roots of woody plants. Also called: **tree ring.**

annuitant (ə'njuːɪtənt) *n* a person in receipt of or entitled to an annuity.

annuity (ə'njuːɪtɪ) *n*, *pl* **annuities.** a fixed sum payable at specified intervals over a period, such as the recipient's life, or in perpetuity, in return for a premium paid either in instalments or in a single payment. [C15: from F, from Med. L *annuitās*, from L *annuus* ANNUAL]

annul (ə'nʌl) *vb* **annuls, annulling, annulled.** (*tr*) to make (something, esp. a law or marriage) void; abolish. [C14: from OF, from LL *adnullāre* to bring to nothing, from L *nullus* not any]
▶ **an'nullable** *adj*

annular ('ænjʊlə) *adj* ring-shaped. [C16: from L *annulāris*, from *annulus, ānulus* ring]

annular eclipse *n* an eclipse of the sun in which the moon does not cover the entire disc of the sun, so that a ring of sunlight surrounds the shadow of the moon.

annular ligament *n Anat.* any of various ligaments that encircle a part, such as the wrist.

annulate ('ænjʊlɪt, -ˌleɪt) *adj* having, composed of, or marked with rings. [C19: from L *ānulātus*, from *ānulus* a ring]
▶ **ˌannu'lation** *n*

annulet ('ænjʊlɪt) *n* **1** *Archit.* a moulding in the form of a ring. **2** *Heraldry.* a ring-shaped device on a shield. **3** a little ring. [C16: from L *ānulus* ring + -ET]

annulment (ə'nʌlmənt) *n* **1** a formal invalidation, as of a marriage, judicial proceeding, etc. **2** the act of annulling.

annulus ('ænjʊləs) *n*, *pl* **annuli** (-ˌlaɪ) *or* **annuluses. 1** the area between two concentric circles. **2** a ring-shaped part. [C16: from L, var. of *ānulus* ring]

annunciate (ə'nʌnsɪˌeɪt, -ʃɪ-) *vb* **annunciates, annunciating, annunciated.** (*tr*) a less common word for **announce.** [C16: from Med L from L *annuntiāre*; see ANNOUNCE]

Annunciation (əˌnʌnsɪ'eɪʃən) *n* **1** the. the announcement of the Incarnation by the angel Gabriel to the Virgin Mary (Luke 1:26–38). **2** Also called: **Annunciation Day.** the festival commemorating this, on March 25 (Lady Day).

annunciator (ə'nʌnsɪˌeɪtə) *n* **1** a device that gives a visual indication as to which of a number of electric circuits has operated, such as an indicator showing in which room a bell has been rung. **2** a device giving an audible signal indicating the position of a train. **3** an announcer.

annus horribilis ('ænʊs hɒ'rɪːbɪlɪs) *n* a terrible year. [C20: from L, modelled on ANNUS MIRABILIS, first used by Elizabeth II of the year 1992]

annus mirabilis ('ænʊs mɪ'ræbɪlɪs) *n*, *pl* **anni mirabiles** ('ænaɪ mɪ'ræbɪliːz). a year of wonders, catastrophes, or other notable events. [L: wonderful year]

anoa (ə'nəʊə) *n* the smallest of the cattle tribe, having small straight horns and inhabiting the island of Celebes in Indonesia. [from a native name in Celebes]

anode ('ænəʊd) *n* **1** the positive electrode in an electrolytic cell or in an electronic valve. **2** the negative terminal of a primary cell. Cf. **cathode.** [C19: from Gk *anodos* way up, from *hodos* a way; alluding to the movement of the current]
▶ **anodal** (eɪ'nəʊdˀl) *or* **anodic** (ə'nɒdɪk) *adj*

anodize *or* **anodise** ('ænəˌdaɪz) *vb* **anodizes, anodizing, anodized** *or* **anodises, anodising, anodised.** to coat (a metal, such as aluminium) with a protective oxide film by electrolysis.

anodyne ('ænəˌdaɪn) *n* **1** a drug that relieves pain. **2** anything that alleviates mental distress. ◆ *adj* **3** capable of relieving pain or distress. [C16: from L, from Gk *anōdunos* painless, from AN- + *odunē* pain]

anoint (ə'nɔɪnt) *vb* (*tr*) **1** to smear or rub over with oil. **2** to apply oil to as a sign of consecration or sanctification.

[C14: from OF, from L *inunguere*, from IN-² + *unguere* to smear with oil]
‣ a'**nointer** *n* ‣ a'**nointment** *n*

anointing of the sick *n RC Church.* a sacrament in which a person who is seriously ill or dying is anointed by a priest with consecrated oil. Former name: **extreme unction.**

anomalistic (ə,nɒmə'lɪstɪk) *adj* **1** *Astron.* **1a** (of a month) measured between successive perigees of the moon. **1b** (of a year) between successive perihelia of the earth. **2** anomalous.

anomalous (ə'nɒmələs) *adj* deviating from the normal or usual order, type, etc. [C17: from LL, from Gk *anōmalos* uneven, inconsistent, from AN- + *homalos* even, from *homos* one and the same]
‣ a'**nomalousness** *n*

anomaly (ə'nɒməlɪ) *n, pl* **anomalies. 1** something anomalous. **2** deviation from the normal; irregularity. **3** *Astron.* the angle between a planet, the sun, and the previous perihelion of the planet.

anomie *or* **anomy** ('ænəʊmɪ) *n Sociol.* lack of social or moral standards in an individual or society. [from Gk *anomia* lawlessness, from A-¹ + *nomos* law]
‣ **anomic** (ə'nɒmɪk) *adj*

anon (ə'nɒn) *adv Arch. or literary.* **1** soon. **2** ever and anon. now and then. [OE *on āne*, lit.: in one, that is, immediately]

anon. *abbrev. for* anonymous.

anonym ('ænənɪm) *n* **1** a less common word for **pseudonym. 2** an anonymous person or publication.

anonymize *or* **anonymise** (ə'nɒnɪ,maɪz) *vb* **anonymizes, anonymizing, anonymized** *or* **anonymises, anonymising, anonymised.** (*tr*) to carry out or organize in such a way as to preserve anonymity: *anonymized AIDS screening.*

anonymous (ə'nɒnɪməs) *adj* **1** from or by a person, author, etc., whose name is unknown or withheld. **2** having no known name. **3** lacking individual characteristics. **4** (*often cap.*) denoting an organization which provides help to applicants who remain anonymous: *Alcoholics Anonymous.* [C17: via LL from Gk *anōnumos*, from AN- + *onoma* name]
‣ **anonymity** (,ænə'nɪmɪtɪ) *n*

anopheles (ə'nɒfɪ,liːz) *n, pl* **anopheles.** any of various mosquitoes constituting the genus *Anopheles,* some species of which transmit the malaria parasite to man. [C19: via NL from Gk *anóphelēs* useless, from AN- + *ōphelein* to help]

anorak ('ænə,ræk) *n* **1** a warm waterproof hip-length jacket usually with a hood. **2** *Inf.* a boring or socially inept person. [from Eskimo *ánorâq*]

anorexia (,ænə'rɛksɪə) *n* **1** loss of appetite. **2** Also called: **anorexia nervosa** (nɜː'vəʊsə). a disorder characterized by fear of becoming fat and refusal of food, leading to debility and even death. [C17: via NL from Gk, from AN- + *orexis* appetite]
‣ ,ano'**rectic** *or* ,ano'**rexic** *adj, n*

anosmia (æn'ɒzmɪə, -'ɒs-) *n* loss of the sense of smell. [C19: from NL, from AN- + Gk *osmē* smell]
‣ **anosmatic** (,ænɒz'mætɪk) *or* an'**osmic** *adj*

another (ə'nʌðə) *determiner* **1a** one more: *another chance.* **1b** (*as pron*): *help yourself to another.* **2a** a different: *another era from ours.* **2b** (*as pron*): *to try one, then another.* **3a** a different example of the same sort. **3b** (*as pron*): *we got rid of one, but I think this is another.* [C14: orig. *an other*]

A.N. Other *n Brit.* an unnamed person: used in team lists, etc., to indicate a place that remains to be filled.

Anouilh ★ (*French* anuj) *n* **Jean** (ʒɑ̃). 1910–87, French dramatist, noted for his reinterpretations of Greek myths: his works include *Eurydice* (1942), *Antigone* (1944), and *Becket* (1959).

anoxia (æn'ɒksɪə) *n* lack or deficiency of oxygen. [C20: from AN- + OX(YGEN) + -IA]
‣ an'**oxic** *adj*

Anqing ('ɑːn'tʃɪŋ) *or* **Anking** ★ *n* a city in E China, in SW Anhui province on the Yangtze River: famous seven-storeyed pagoda. Pop.: 250 718 (1990 est.).

Anschluss ('ænʃlʊs) *n* a political or economic union, esp. the annexation of Austria by Nazi Germany (1938). [G, from *anschliessen* to join]

Anselm ★ ('ænselm) *n* **Saint.** 1033–1109, Italian Benedictine monk; archbishop of Canterbury (1093–1109): one of the founders of scholasticism; author of *Cur Deus Homo?* (*Why did God become Man?*). Feast day: Aug. 21.

anserine ('ænsə,raɪn) *adj* of or resembling a goose. [C19: from L *anserīnus,* from *anser* goose]

Ansermet ★ (*French* ɑ̃sɛrmɛ) *n* **Ernest** (ɛrnɛst). 1883–1969, Swiss orchestral conductor; principal conductor of Diaghilev's Ballet Russe.

answer ('ɑːnsə) *n* **1** a reply, either spoken or written, as to a question, request, letter, or article. **2** a reaction or response: *drunkenness was his answer to disappointment.* **3** a solution, esp. of a mathematical problem. ♦ *vb* **4** (when *tr, may take a clause as object*) to reply or respond (to) by word or act: *to answer a question; to answer the door.* **5** (*tr*) to reply correctly to; solve: *I could answer only three questions.* **6** (*intr;* usually foll. by *to*) to respond or react: *the steering answers to the slightest touch.* **7a** (when *intr,* often foll. by *for*) to meet the requirements (of); be satisfactory (for): *this will answer his needs.* **7b** to be responsible (to a person or for a thing). **8** (when *intr,* foll. by *to*) to match or correspond (esp. in **answer** (*or* **answer to**) **the description**). **9** (*tr*) to give a defence or refutation of (a charge) or in (an argument). [OE *andswaru* an answer; see SWEAR]

answerable ('ɑːnsərəb°l) *adj* **1** (*postpositive*; foll. by *for* or *to*) responsible or accountable: *answerable to one's boss.* **2** able to be answered.

answer back *vb* (*adv*) to reply rudely to (a person, esp. someone in authority) when one is expected to remain silent.

answering machine *n* a device by which a telephone call is answered automatically and the caller leaves a recorded message. In full: **telephone answering machine.** Also called: **answerphone.**

ant (ænt) *n* **1** a small social insect of a widely distributed hymenopterous family, typically living in highly organized colonies of winged males, wingless sterile females (workers), and fertile females (queens). Related adj: **formic. 2 white ant.** another name for a **termite.** [OE *æmette*]

-ant *suffix forming adjectives and nouns.* causing or performing an action or existing in a certain condition: *pleasant; deodorant; servant.* [from L *-ant,* ending of present participles of the first conjugation]

antacid (ænt'æsɪd) *n* **1** a substance used to treat acidity, esp. in the stomach. ♦ *adj* **2** having the properties of this substance.

Antaeus ★ (æn'tiːəs) *n Greek myth.* an African giant who was invincible as long as he touched the ground, but was lifted into the air by Hercules and crushed to death.

antagonism (æn'tægə,nɪzəm) *n* **1** openly expressed and usually mutual opposition. **2** the inhibiting or nullifying action of one substance or organism on another.

antagonist (æn'tægənɪst) *n* **1** an opponent or adversary. **2** any muscle that opposes the action of another. **3** a drug that counteracts the effects of another drug.
‣ an,tago'**nistic** *adj* ‣ an,tago'**nistically** *adv*

antagonize *or* **antagonise** (æn'tægə,naɪz) *vb* **antagonizes, antagonizing, antagonized** *or* **antagonises, antagonising, antagonised.** (*tr*) **1** to make hostile; annoy or irritate. **2** to act in opposition to or counteract. [C17: from Gk, from ANTI- + *agōnizesthai* to strive, from *agōn* contest]
‣ an,tago'**nization** *or* an,tago'**nisation** *n*

Antakiya ★ (,æntɑ:'ki:jə) *n* the Arabic name for **Antioch.**

Antakya ★ (ɑn'takja) *n* the Turkish name for **Antioch.**

antalkali (ænt'ælkə,laɪ) *n, pl* **antalkalis** *or* **antalkalies.** a substance that neutralizes alkalis.

Antananarivo ★ (,æntə,nænə'ri:vəʊ) *n* the capital of Madagascar, on the central plateau: founded in the 17th century by a Hova chief; university (1961). Pop.: 1 052 835 (1993). Former name: **Tananarive.**

Antarctic ★ (ænt'ɑːktɪk) *n* **1 the.** Also called: **Antarctic Zone.** Antarctica and the surrounding waters. ♦ *adj* **2** of or relating to the south polar regions. [C14: via L from Gk *antarktikos;* see ANTI-, ARCTIC]

★ people and places

Antarctica ★ (ænt'ɑːktɪkə) *n* a continent around the South Pole: consists of an ice-covered plateau, 1800–3000 m (6000 ft to 10 000 ft) above sea level, and mountain ranges rising to 4500 m (15 000 ft) with some volcanic peaks; average temperatures all below freezing and human settlement is confined to research stations.

Antarctic Archipelago ★ *n* the former name of the **Palmer Archipelago.**

Antarctic Circle *n* the imaginary circle around the earth, parallel to the equator, at latitude 66° 32′ S.

Antarctic Ocean ★ *n* the sea surrounding Antarctica, consisting of the most southerly parts of the Pacific, Atlantic, and Indian Oceans. Also called: **Southern Ocean.**

Antarctic Peninsula ★ *n* the largest peninsula of Antarctica, between the Weddell Sea and the Pacific: consists of Graham Land in the north and the Palmer Peninsula in the south. Former name (until 1964): **Palmer Peninsula.**

ant bear *n* another name for **aardvark.**

ante ('æntɪ) *n* **1** the gaming stake put up before the deal in poker by the players. **2** *Inf.* a sum of money representing a person's share, as in a syndicate. **3 up the ante.** *Inf.* to increase the costs, risks, or considerations involved in taking an action or reaching a conclusion. ◆ *vb* **antes, anteing, anted** *or* **anteed. 4** to place (one's stake) in poker. **5** (usually foll. by *up*) *Inf.* to pay.

ante- *prefix* before in time or position: *antedate; antechamber.* [from L]

anteater ('ænt,iːtə) *n* any of several toothless mammals having a long tubular snout used for eating termites.

antebellum (,æntɪ'bɛləm) *adj* of or during the period before a war, esp. the American Civil War. [L *ante bellum,* lit.: before the war]

antecede (,æntɪ'siːd) *vb* **antecedes, anteceding, anteceded.** (*tr*) to go before; precede. [C17: from L *antecēdere,* from *cēdere* to go]

antecedent (,æntɪ'siːdᵊnt) *n* **1** an event, etc., that happens before another. **2** *Grammar.* a word or phrase to which a pronoun refers. In "People who live in glass houses shouldn't throw stones," *people* is the antecedent of *who.* **3** *Logic.* the first hypothetical clause in a conditional statement. ◆ *adj* **4** preceding in time or order; prior.
▶ ,ante'cedence *n*

antecedents (,æntɪ'siːdᵊnts) *pl n* **1** ancestry. **2** a person's past history.

antechamber ('æntɪ,tʃeɪmbə) *n* an anteroom. [C17: from OF, from It. *anticamera;* see ANTE-, CHAMBER]

antedate ('æntɪ,deɪt) *vb* (*tr*) **1** to be or occur at an earlier date than. **2** to affix or assign a date to (a document, event, etc.) that is earlier than the actual date. **3** to cause to occur sooner. ◆ *n* **4** an earlier date.

antediluvian (,æntɪdɪ'luːvɪən) *adj* **1** of the ages before the biblical Flood. **2** old-fashioned. ◆ *n* **3** an antediluvian person or thing. [C17: from ANTE- + L *dīluvium* flood]

antelope ('æntɪ,ləup) *n, pl* **antelopes** *or* **antelope.** any of a group of mammals of Africa and Asia. They are typically graceful, having long legs and horns, and include the gazelles, springbok, impala, and dik-diks. [C15: from OF, from Med. L, from LGk *antholops* a legendary beast]

antemeridian (,æntɪmə'rɪdɪən) *adj* before noon; in the morning. [C17: from L]

ante meridiem ('æntɪ mə'rɪdɪəm) the full form of **a.m.** [L, from ANTE- + *merīdiēs* midday]

antenatal (,æntɪ'neɪtᵊl) *adj* occurring or present before birth; during pregnancy.

antenna (æn'tɛnə) *n* **1** (*pl* **antennae** (-niː)) one of a pair of mobile appendages on the heads of insects, crustaceans, etc., that often respond to touch and taste but may be specialized for swimming. **2** (*pl* **antennas**) an aerial. [C17: from L: sail yard, from ?]
▶ an'tennal *or* an'tennary *adj*

antenuptial contract (,æntɪ'nʌpʃəl) *n* (in South Africa) a marriage contract effected prior to the wedding giving each partner control over his or her property.

antependium (,æntɪ'pɛndɪəm) *n, pl* **antependia** (-dɪə). a covering hung over the front of an altar. [C17: from Med. L, from L ANTE- + *pendēre* to hang]

antepenult (,æntɪpɪ'nʌlt) *n* the third last syllable in a word. [C16: shortened from L (*syllaba*) *antepaenultima;* see ANTE-, PENULT]

antepenultimate (,æntɪpɪ'nʌltɪmɪt) *adj* **1** third from last. ◆ *n* **2** anything that is third from last.

ante-post *adj Brit.* (of a bet) placed before the runners in a race are confirmed.

anterior (æn'tɪərɪə) *adj* **1** at or towards the front. **2** earlier. **3** *Zool.* of or near the head end. **4** *Bot.* (of part of a flower or leaf) farthest away from the main stem. [C17: from L, comp. of *ante* before]

anteroom ('æntɪ,ruːm, -,rʊm) *n* a room giving entrance to a larger room, often used as a waiting room.

anthelion (æn'θiːlɪən) *n, pl* **anthelia** (-lɪə). **1** a faint halo sometimes seen in high altitude regions around a shadow cast onto fog. **2** a white spot occasionally appearing at the same height as and opposite to the sun. [C17: from LGk, from *anthēlios* opposite the sun, from ANTE- + *hēlios* sun]

anthelmintic (,ænθɛl'mɪntɪk) *or* **anthelminthic** (,ænθɛl'mɪnθɪk) *n Med.* another name for **vermifuge.**

anthem ('ænθəm) *n* **1** a song of loyalty: *a national anthem.* **2** a musical composition for a choir, usually set to words from the Bible. **3** a religious chant sung antiphonally. [OE *antemne,* from LL *antiphōna* ANTIPHON]

anthemis (æn'θiːmɪs) *n* any of several cultivated varieties of camomile. [NL, from L, from Gk *anthos* flower]

anther ('ænθə) *n* the terminal part of a stamen consisting of two lobes each containing two sacs in which the pollen matures. [C18: from NL, from L, from Gk *anthēros* flowery, from *anthos* flower]

antheridium (,ænθə'rɪdɪəm) *n, pl* **antheridia** (-ɪə). the male sex organ of algae, fungi, mosses, etc. [C19: from NL, dim. of *anthēra* ANTHER]

ant hill *n* a mound of soil, leaves, etc., near the entrance of an ants' or termites' nest, deposited there by the ants or termites while constructing the nest.

anthologize *or* **anthologise** (æn'θɒlə,dʒaɪz) *vb* **anthologizes, anthologizing, anthologized** *or* **anthologises, anthologising, anthologised.** to compile or put into an anthology.

anthology (æn'θɒlədʒɪ) *n, pl* **anthologies. 1** a collection of literary passages, esp. poems, by various authors. **2** any printed collection of literary pieces, songs, etc. [C17: from Med. L, from Gk, lit.: a flower gathering, from *anthos* flower + *legein* to collect]
▶ an'thologist *n*

Anthony ★ ('æntənɪ) *n* **Saint.** ?251–?356 A.D., Egyptian hermit, commonly regarded as the founder of Christian monasticism. Feast day: Jan. 17.

Anthony of Padua ★ *n* **Saint.** 1195–1231, Franciscan friar, who preached in France and Italy. Feast day: June 13.

anthozoan (,ænθə'zəuən) *n* **1** any of the sessile marine coelenterates of the class *Anthozoa,* including corals and sea anemones, in which the body is in the form of a polyp. ◆ *adj* also: **actinozoan. 2** of or relating to these.

anthracene ('ænθrə,siːn) *n* a colourless crystalline solid, used in the manufacture of chemicals and as crystals in scintillation counters. [C19: from ANTHRAX + -ENE]

anthracite ('ænθrə,saɪt) *n* a hard coal that burns slowly with a nonluminous flame giving out intense heat. Also called: **hard coal.** [C19: from L, from Gk *anthrakītēs* coal-like, from *anthrax* coal]
▶ **anthracitic** (,ænθrə'sɪtɪk) *adj*

anthracosis (,ænθrə'kəusɪs) *n* a lung disease due to inhalation of coal dust.

anthrax ('ænθræks) *n, pl* **anthraces** (-θrə,siːz). **1** a highly infectious bacterial disease of animals, esp. cattle and sheep, which can be transmitted to man. **2** a pustule caused by this disease. [C19: from LL, from Gk: carbuncle]

anthropic principle *n Astron.* the cosmological theory

that the presence of life in the universe limits the ways in which the very early universe could have evolved.

anthropo- *combining form.* indicating man or human: *anthropology.* [from Gk *anthrōpos*]

anthropocentric (ˌænθrəpəʊˈsɛntrɪk) *adj* regarding humans as the central factor in the universe.

anthropogenesis (ˌænθrəpəʊˈdʒɛnɪsɪs) *or* **anthropogeny** (ˌænθrəˈpɒdʒɪnɪ) *n* the study of the origins of humans.

anthropoid (ˈænθrəˌpɔɪd) *adj* 1 resembling humans. 2 resembling an ape; apelike. ♦ *n* 3 any primate of the suborder *Anthropoidea,* including monkeys, apes, and humans.

anthropoid ape *n* any of a group of primates having no tail, elongated arms, and a highly developed brain, including gibbons, orang-utans, chimpanzees, and gorillas.

anthropology (ˌænθrəˈpɒlədʒɪ) *n* the study of human beings, their origins, institutions, religious beliefs, social relationships, etc.
▸ ˌanthropoˈlogical *adj* ▸ ˌanthroˈpologist *n*

anthropometry (ˌænθrəˈpɒmɪtrɪ) *n* the comparative study of sizes and proportions of the human body.
▸ ˌanthropoˈmetric *or* ˌanthropoˈmetrical *adj*

anthropomorphic (ˌænθrəpəˈmɔːfɪk) *adj* 1 of or relating to anthropomorphism. 2 resembling the human form.
▸ ˈanthropoˌmorph *n* ▸ ˌanthropoˈmorphically *adv*

anthropomorphism (ˌænθrəpəˈmɔːfɪzəm) *n* the attribution of human form or behaviour to a deity, animal, etc.

anthropomorphous (ˌænθrəpəˈmɔːfəs) *adj* 1 shaped like a human being. 2 another word for **anthropomorphic.**

anthropophagi (ˌænθrəˈpɒfəˌɡaɪ) *pl n, sing* **anthropophagus** (-ɡəs). cannibals. [C16: from L, from Gk *anthrōpophagos;* see ANTHROPO-, -PHAGE]

anthroposophy (ˌænθrəˈpɒsəfɪ) *n* the spiritual and mystical teachings of Rudolph Steiner, based on the belief that creative activities are psychologically valuable, esp. for educational and therapeutic purposes.
▸ ˌanthropoˈsophic *adj*

anti (ˈæntɪ) *Inf.* ♦ *adj* 1 opposed to a party, policy, attitude, etc. ♦ *n* 2 an opponent.

anti- *prefix* 1 against; opposing: *anticlerical.* 2 opposite to: *anticlimax.* 3 rival; false: *antipope.* 4 counteracting or neutralizing: *antifreeze; antihistamine.* 5 designating the antiparticle of the particle specified: *antineutron.* [from Gk *anti*]

anti-aircraft (ˌæntɪˈɛəkrɑːft) *n (modifier)* of or relating to defence against aircraft attack: *anti-aircraft batteries.*

anti-apartheid *adj* opposed to a policy of racial segregation.

antiar (ˈæntɪˌɑː) *n* another name for **upas** (senses 1, 2). [from Javanese]

antiballistic missile (ˌæntɪbəˈlɪstɪk) *n* a ballistic missile designed to destroy another ballistic missile in flight.

Antibes ★ *(French* ɑ̃tib*) n* a port and resort in SE France, on the Mediterranean: an important Roman town. Pop.: 60 000 (latest est.).

antibiosis (ˌæntɪbaɪˈəʊsɪs) *n* an association between two organisms, esp. microorganisms, that is harmful to one of them.

antibiotic (ˌæntɪbaɪˈɒtɪk) *n* 1 any of various chemical substances, such as penicillin, produced by microorganisms, esp. fungi, or made synthetically, and capable of destroying microorganisms, esp. bacteria. ♦ *adj* 2 of or relating to antibiotics.

antibody (ˈæntɪˌbɒdɪ) *n, pl* **antibodies.** any of various proteins produced in the blood in response to an antigen. By becoming attached to antigens on infectious organisms antibodies can render them harmless.

antic (ˈæntɪk) *Arch.* ♦ *n* 1 an actor in a ludicrous or grotesque part; clown. ♦ *adj* 2 fantastic; grotesque. ♦ See also **antics.** [C16: from It. *antico* something grotesque

(from its application to fantastic carvings found in ruins of ancient Rome)]

anticathode (ˌæntɪˈkæθəʊd) *n* the target electrode for the stream of electrons in a vacuum tube, esp. an X-ray tube.

Antichrist ★ (ˈæntɪˌkraɪst) *n* 1 *Bible.* the antagonist of Christ, expected by early Christians to appear and reign over the world until overthrown at Christ's Second Coming. 2 *(sometimes not cap.)* an enemy of Christ or Christianity.

anticipant (ænˈtɪsɪpənt) *adj* 1 operating in advance. ♦ *n* 2 a person who anticipates.

anticipate (ænˈtɪsɪˌpeɪt) *vb* **anticipates, anticipating, anticipated.** *(mainly tr)* 1 *(may take a clause as object)* to foresee and act in advance of; forestall: *I anticipated his punch.* 2 *(also intr)* to mention (something) before its proper time: *don't anticipate the climax of the story.* 3 *(may take a clause as object)* to regard as likely; expect. 4 to make use of in advance of possession: *he anticipated his salary in buying a leather jacket.* [C16: from L *anticipāre* to take before, from *anti-* + *capere* to take]
▸ anˈticiˌpator *n* ▸ anˈticiˌpatory *or* anˈticipative *adj*

> **USAGE NOTE** The use of *anticipate* to mean *expect* should be avoided.

anticipation (ænˌtɪsɪˈpeɪʃən) *n* 1 the act of anticipating; expectation, premonition, or foresight. 2 *Music.* an unstressed, usually short note introduced before a downbeat.

anticlerical (ˌæntɪˈklɛrɪkˀl) *adj* 1 opposed to the power and influence of the clergy, esp. in politics. ♦ *n* 2 a supporter of an anticlerical party.
▸ ˌantiˈclericalism *n*

anticlimax (ˌæntɪˈklaɪmæks) *n* 1 a disappointing or ineffective conclusion to a series of events, etc. 2 a sudden change from a serious subject to one that is disappointing or ludicrous.
▸ **anticlimactic** (ˌæntɪklaɪˈmæktɪk) *adj*

anticline (ˈæntɪˌklaɪn) *n* a formation of stratified rock raised up, by folding, into a broad arch so that the strata slope down on both sides from a common crest.
▸ ˌantiˈclinal *adj*

anticlockwise (ˌæntɪˈklɒkˌwaɪz) *adv, adj* in the opposite direction to the rotation of the hands of a clock. US equivalent: **counterclockwise.**

anticoagulant (ˌæntɪkəʊˈæɡjʊlənt) *adj* 1 acting to prevent or retard coagulation, esp. of blood. ♦ *n* 2 an agent that prevents or retards coagulation.

anti-Communist *adj* opposed to Communism or its principles.

anticonvulsant (ˌæntɪkənˈvʌlsənt) *n* 1 any of a class of drugs used to relieve convulsions. ♦ *adj* 2 of or relating to such drugs.

Anticosti ★ (ˌæntɪˈkɒstɪ) *n* an island of E Canada, in the Gulf of St Lawrence; part of Quebec. Area: 7881 sq. km (3043 sq. miles).

antics (ˈæntɪks) *pl n* absurd acts or postures.

anticyclone (ˌæntɪˈsaɪkləʊn) *n Meteorol.* a body of moving air of higher pressure than the surrounding air, in which the pressure decreases away from the centre. Also called: **high.**
▸ **anticyclonic** (ˌæntɪsaɪˈklɒnɪk) *adj*

antidazzle mirror (ˌæntɪˈdæzˀl) *n* a rear-view mirror for road vehicles that only partially reflects headlights behind.

antidepressant (ˌæntɪdɪˈprɛsˀnt) *n* 1 any of a class of drugs used to alleviate depression. ♦ *adj* 2 of this class of drugs.

antidiuretic hormone (ˌæntɪˌdaɪjʊˈrɛtɪk) *n* another name for **vasopressin.** Abbrev.: **ADH.**

antidote (ˈæntɪˌdəʊt) *n* 1 *Med.* a drug or agent that counteracts or neutralizes the effects of a poison. 2 anything that counteracts or relieves a harmful condition. [C15:

★ people and places

from L, from Gk *antidoton* something given as a counter-measure, from ANTI- + *didonai* to give]
▸ ˌanti'dotal *adj*

antiemetic (ˌæntɪ'mɛtɪk) *adj* **1** preventing vomiting.
♦ *n* **2** any antiemetic drug, such as promethazine.

antifreeze ('æntɪˌfriːz) *n* a liquid, usually ethylene glycol (ethanediol), added to water to lower its freezing point, esp. for use in an internal-combustion engine.

antifungal (ˌæntɪ'fʌŋgᵊl) *adj* **1** inhibiting the growth of fungi. **2** (of a drug) possessing antifungal activity and therefore used to treat fungal infections. ♦ Also: **antimycotic.**

antigen ('æntɪdʒən, -ˌdʒɛn) *n* a substance, usually a toxin produced by a bacterium, that stimulates the production of antibodies. [C20: from ANTI(BODY) + -GEN]

Antigone ★ (æn'tɪgənɪ) *n Greek myth.* daughter of Oedipus and Jocasta, who was condemned to death for cremating the body of her brother Polynices in defiance of an edict of her uncle, King Creon of Thebes.

Antigua ★ (æn'tiːgə) *n* an island in the Caribbean, one of the Leeward Islands: a British colony, with its dependency Barbuda, until 1967, when it became a British associated state; it became independent in 1981 as part of the state of Antigua and Barbuda. Area: 279 sq. km (108 sq. miles).
▸ An'tiguan *adj, n*

Antigua and Barbuda ★ *n* a state in the Caribbean, comprising the islands of Antigua, Barbuda, and Redonda: gained independence in 1981: a member of the Commonwealth. Official language: English. Religion: Christian majority. Currency: East Caribbean dollar. Capital: St John's. Pop.: 64 500 (1997). Area: 442 sq. km (171 sq. miles).

antihero ('æntɪˌhɪərəʊ) *n, pl* **antiheroes.** a central character in a novel, play, etc., who lacks the traditional heroic virtues.

antihistamine (ˌæntɪ'hɪstəˌmiːn, -mɪn) *n* any drug that neutralizes the effects of histamine, used esp. in the treatment of allergies.

anti-inflammatory *adj* **1** reducing inflammation. ♦ *n*, *pl* **anti-inflammatories. 2** any anti-inflammatory drug, such as cortisone, aspirin, or ibuprofen.

anti-inflationary *adj* (of an economic policy) designed to reduce or counteract the effects of inflation.

antiknock (ˌæntɪ'nɒk) *n* a compound, such as lead tetraethyl, added to petrol to reduce knocking in the engine.

Anti-Lebanon ★ *n* a mountain range running north and south between Syria and Lebanon, east of the Lebanon Mountains. Highest peak: Mount Hermon, 2814 m (9232 ft).

Antilles ★ (æn'tɪliːz) *pl n* **the.** a group of islands in the Caribbean consisting of the **Greater Antilles** and the **Lesser Antilles.**

antilock brake (ˌæntɪ'lɒk) *n* a brake fitted to some road vehicles that prevents skidding and improves control by sensing and compensating for overbraking. Also called: **ABS brake.**

antilogarithm (ˌæntɪ'lɒgəˌrɪðəm) *n* a number whose logarithm to a given base is a given number: *100 is the antilogarithm of 2 to base 10.* Often shortened to **antilog.**
▸ ˌanti,loga'rithmic *adj*

antilogy (æn'tɪlədʒɪ) *n, pl* **antilogies.** a contradiction in terms. [C17: from Gk *antilogia*]

antimacassar (ˌæntɪmə'kæsə) *n* a cloth covering the back and arms of chairs, etc., to prevent soiling. [C19: from ANTI- + MACASSAR (OIL)]

antimagnetic (ˌæntɪmæg'nɛtɪk) *adj* of a material that does not acquire permanent magnetism when exposed to a magnetic field.

antimalarial (ˌæntɪmə'lɛərɪəl) *adj* **1** effective in the treatment of malaria. ♦ *n* **2** an antimalarial drug or agent.

antimasque ('æntɪˌmɑːsk) *n* a comic dance, presented between the acts of a masque.

antimatter ('æntɪˌmætə) *n* a form of matter composed of antiparticles, such as antihydrogen, consisting of antiprotons and positrons.

antimetabolite (ˌæntɪmɪ'tæbəˌlaɪt) *n* any drug that acts by disrupting the normal growth of a cell. Antimetabolites are used in cancer treatment.

antimissile (ˌæntɪ'mɪsaɪl) *adj* **1** relating to defensive measures against missile attack: *an antimissile system.* ♦ *n* **2** Also called: **antimissile missile.** a defensive missile used to intercept and destroy attacking missiles.

antimony ('æntɪmənɪ) *n* a toxic metallic element that exists in two allotropic forms and is added to alloys to increase their strength and hardness. Symbol: Sb; atomic no.: 51; atomic wt.: 121.75. [C15: from Med. L *antimōnium*, from ?]
▸ **antimonial** (ˌæntɪ'məʊnɪəl) *adj*

antimuon (ˌæntɪ'mjuːɒn) *n* the antiparticle of a muon.

antimycotic (ˌæntɪmaɪ'kɒtɪk) *adj* another word for **antifungal.**

anti-Nazi *adj* opposed to Nazism or its principles.

antinoise ('æntɪˌnɔɪz) *n* sound generated so that it is out of phase with a noise, such as that made by an engine, in order to reduce the noise level by interference.

antinomian (ˌæntɪ'nəʊmɪən) *adj* **1** relating to the doctrine that by faith a Christian is released from the obligation of adhering to any moral law. ♦ *n* **2** a member of a Christian sect holding such a doctrine.
▸ ˌanti'nomianism *n*

antinomy (æn'tɪnəmɪ) *n, pl* **antinomies. 1** opposition of one law, principle, or rule to another. **2** *Philosophy.* contradiction existing between two apparently indubitable propositions. [C16: from L, from Gk: conflict between laws, from ANTI- + *nomos* law]
▸ **antinomic** (ˌæntɪ'nɒmɪk) *adj*

antinovel ('æntɪˌnɒvᵊl) *n* a type of prose fiction in which conventional or traditional novelistic elements are rejected.

antinuclear (ˌæntɪ'njuːklɪə) *adj* opposed to nuclear weapons or nuclear power.

Antioch ★ ('æntɪˌɒk) *n* a city in S Turkey, on the Orontes River: ancient commercial centre and capital of Syria (300–64 B.C.); early centre of Christianity. Pop.: 137 200 (1994 est.). Arabic name: **Antakiya.** Turkish name: **Antakya.**

Antiochus III ★ (æn'taɪəkəs) *n* known as *Antiochus the Great.* 242–187 B.C., king of Syria (223–187), who was forced (190) to surrender most of Asia Minor to the Romans.

Antiochus IV ★ *n* ?215–164 B.C., Seleucid king of Syria (175–164), who attacked the Jews and provoked the revolt of the Maccabees.

antioxidant (ˌæntɪ'ɒksɪdənt) *n* **1** any substance that retards deterioration by oxidation, esp. of fats, oils, foods, or rubber. **2** *Biol.* a substance, such as vitamin C, vitamin E, or beta carotene, that counteracts the damaging effects of oxidation in a living organism.

antiparticle ('æntɪˌpɑːtɪkᵊl) *n* any of a group of elementary particles that have the same mass as their corresponding particle but have a charge of equal magnitude but opposite sign. When a particle collides with its antiparticle mutual annihilation occurs.

antipasto (ˌæntɪ'pɑːstəʊ, -'pæs-) *n, pl* **antipastos.** a course of hors d'oeuvres in an Italian meal. [It.: before food]

antipathetic (ˌæn,tɪpə'θɛtɪk, ˌæntɪpə-) *or* **antipathical** *adj* (often foll. by *to*) having or arousing a strong aversion.

antipathy (æn'tɪpəθɪ) *n, pl* **antipathies. 1** a feeling of dislike or hostility. **2** the object of such a feeling. [C17: from L, from Gk, from ANTI- + *patheia* feeling]

antipersonnel (ˌæntɪˌpɜːsə'nɛl) *adj* (of weapons, etc.) designed to cause casualties to personnel rather than to destroy equipment.

antiperspirant (ˌæntɪ'pɜːspərənt) *n* **1** a substance applied to the skin to reduce or prevent perspiration. ♦ *adj* **2** reducing perspiration.

antiphlogistic (ˌæntɪflə'dʒɪstɪk) *adj* **1** of or relating to the prevention or alleviation of inflammation. ◆ *n* **2** an antiphlogistic drug.

antiphon ('æntɪfən) *n* **1** a short passage, usually from the Bible, recited or sung as a response after certain parts of a liturgical service. **2** a psalm, hymn, etc., chanted or sung in alternate parts. **3** any response. [C15: from LL *antiphōna* sung responses, from LGk, pl of *antiphōnon* (something) responsive, from ANTI- + *phōnē* sound]
▸ **antiphonal** (æn'tɪfənəl) *adj*

antiphonary (æn'tɪfənərɪ) *n*, *pl* **antiphonaries.** a bound collection of antiphons.

antiphony (æn'tɪfənɪ) *n*, *pl* **antiphonies. 1** antiphonal singing. **2** any musical or other sound effect that answers or echoes another.

antipode ('æntɪpəʊd) *n* the exact or direct opposite.
▸ **antipodal** (æn'tɪpəd'l) *adj*

antipodes (æn'tɪpə‚diːz) *pl n* **1** either or both of two places that are situated diametrically opposite one another on the earth's surface. **2** the people who live there. **3** (*often cap.*) **the.** Australia and New Zealand. [C16: via LL from Gk, pl of *antipous* having the feet opposite, from ANTI- + *pous* foot]
▸ **antipodean** (æn‚tɪpə'diːən) *adj*

Antipodes Islands ★ *pl n* **the.** a group of small uninhabited islands in the South Pacific, southeast of and belonging to New Zealand. Area: 62 sq. km (24 sq. miles).

antipope ('æntɪ‚pəʊp) *n* a rival pope elected in opposition to one who has been canonically chosen.

anti-Protestant *adj* opposed to Protestantism.

antipsychotic (‚æntɪsaɪ'kɒtɪk) *adj* **1** preventing or treating psychosis. ◆ *n* **2** any antipsychotic drug, such as chlorpromazine: used to treat such conditions as schizophrenia.

antipyretic (‚æntɪpaɪ'rɛtɪk) *adj* **1** preventing or alleviating fever. ◆ *n* **2** an antipyretic remedy or drug.

antiquarian (‚æntɪ'kwɛərɪən) *adj* **1** concerned with the study of antiquities or antiques. ◆ *n* **2** a less common name for **antiquary.**
▸ ‚**anti'quarianism** *n*

antiquark ('æntɪ‚kwɑːk) *n* the antiparticle of a quark.

antiquary ('æntɪkwərɪ) *n*, *pl* **antiquaries.** a person who collects, deals in, or studies antiques or ancient works of art. Also called: **antiquarian.**

antiquate ('æntɪ‚kweɪt) *vb* **antiquates, antiquating, antiquated.** (*tr*) to make obsolete or old-fashioned. [C15: from L *antīquāre* to make old, from *antīquus* ancient]
▸ '**anti‚quated** *adj*

antique (æn'tiːk) *n* **1a** a decorative object, piece of furniture, or other work of art created in an earlier period, that is valued for its beauty, workmanship, and age. **1b** (*as modifier*): *an antique shop.* **2** any object made in an earlier period. **3** **the.** the style of ancient art, esp. Greek or Roman. ◆ *adj* **4** made in or in the style of an earlier period. **5** of or belonging to the distant past, esp. of ancient Greece or Rome. **6** *Inf.* old-fashioned. **7** *Arch.* aged or venerable. ◆ *vb* **antiques, antiquing, antiqued. 8** (*tr*) to give an antique appearance to. [C16: from L *antīquus* ancient, from *ante* before]

antiquities (æn'tɪkwɪtɪz) *pl n* remains or relics, such as statues, buildings, or coins, that date from ancient times.

antiquity (æn'tɪkwɪtɪ) *n*, *pl* **antiquities. 1** the quality of being ancient: *a vase of great antiquity.* **2** the far distant past, esp. preceding the Middle Ages. **3** the people of ancient times collectively.

antiracism (‚æntɪ'reɪsɪzəm) *n* the policy of challenging racism and promoting racial tolerance.
▸ ‚**anti'racist** *n*, *adj*

anti-riot *adj* designed for or employed in controlling crowds: *anti-riot police.*

anti-roll bar *n* a crosswise rubber-mounted bar in the suspension of a motor vehicle, which counteracts the movement downwards on one side when cornering.

antirrhinum (‚æntɪ'raɪnəm) *n* any plant of the genus *Antirrhinum*, esp. the snapdragon, which has two-lipped flowers of various colours. [C16: via L from Gk *antirrhinon*, from ANTI- (imitating) + *rhis* nose]

Antisana ★ (*Spanish* anti'sana) *n* a volcano in N central Ecuador, in the Andes. Height: 5756 m (18 885 ft).

antiscorbutic (‚æntɪskɔː'bjuːtɪk) *adj* **1** preventing or curing scurvy. ◆ *n* **2** an antiscorbutic agent.

anti-Semite *n* a person who persecutes or discriminates against Jews.
▸ ‚**anti-Se'mitic** *adj* ▸ ‚**anti-'Semitism** *n*

antisepsis (‚æntɪ'sɛpsɪs) *n* **1** destruction of undesirable microorganisms, such as those that cause disease or putrefaction. **2** the state of being free from such microorganisms.

antiseptic (‚æntɪ'sɛptɪk) *adj* **1** of or producing antisepsis. **2** entirely free from contamination. **3** *Inf.* lacking spirit or excitement. ◆ *n* **4** an antiseptic agent.
▸ ‚**anti'septically** *adv*

antiserum (‚æntɪ'sɪərəm) *n*, *pl* **antiserums** or **antisera** (-rə). blood serum containing antibodies against a specific antigen, used to treat or provide immunity to a disease.

antisocial (‚æntɪ'səʊʃəl) *adj* **1** avoiding the company of other people; unsociable. **2** contrary or injurious to the interests of society in general.

antispasmodic (‚æntɪspæz'mɒdɪk) *adj* **1** preventing or arresting spasms. ◆ *n* **2** an antispasmodic drug.

antistatic (‚æntɪ'stætɪk) *adj* (of a substance, textile, etc.) retaining sufficient moisture to provide a conducting path, thus avoiding the effects of static electricity.

antistrophe (æn'tɪstrəfɪ) *n* (in ancient Greek drama) **a** the second of two movements made by a chorus during the performance of a choral ode. **b** the second part of a choral ode sung during this movement. ◆ See **strophe** [C17: via LL from Gk *antistrophē* an answering turn, from ANTI- + *strophē* a turning]
▸ **antistrophically** (‚æntɪ'strɒfɪkəlɪ) *adv*

antitank (‚æntɪ'tæŋk) *adj* designed to immobilize or destroy armoured vehicles.

antithesis (æn'tɪθɪsɪs) *n*, *pl* **antitheses** (-‚siːz). **1** the exact opposite. **2** contrast or opposition. **3** *Rhetoric.* the juxtaposition of contrasting ideas or words to produce an effect of balance, such as *my words fly up, my thoughts remain* below. [C15: via L from Gk: a setting against, from ANTI- + *tithenai* to place]
▸ **antithetical** (‚æntɪ'θɛtɪk'l) *adj*

antitoxin (‚æntɪ'tɒksɪn) *n* **1** an antibody that neutralizes a toxin. **2** blood serum that contains a specific antibody.
▸ ‚**anti'toxic** *adj*

antitrades ('æntɪ‚treɪdz) *pl n* winds in the upper atmosphere blowing in the opposite direction from and above the trade winds.

antitrust (‚æntɪ'trʌst) *n* (*modifier*) *Chiefly US.* regulating or opposing trusts, monopolies, cartels, or similar organizations.

antitussive (‚æntɪ'tʌsɪv) *n* **1** any of a class of drugs used to suppress or alleviate coughing. ◆ *adj* **2** of or relating to such drugs. [from ANTI- + L *tussis* a cough]

antitype ('æntɪ‚taɪp) *n* **1** a person or thing that is foreshadowed or represented by a type or symbol. **2** an opposite type.
▸ **antitypical** (‚æntɪ'tɪpɪk'l) *adj*

antivenin (‚æntɪ'vɛnɪn) or **antivenene** (‚æntɪvɪ'niːn) *n* an antitoxin that counteracts a specific venom, esp. snake venom. [C19: from ANTI- + VEN(OM) + -IN]

antiviral (‚æntɪ'vaɪrəl) *adj* **1** inhibiting the growth of viruses. ◆ *n* **2** any antiviral drug.

antler ('æntlə) *n* one of a pair of bony outgrowths on the heads of male deer and some related species of either sex. [C14: from OF *antoillier*]
▸ '**antlered** *adj*

antlion ('ænt‚laɪən) *n* **1** any of various insects which resemble dragonflies and are most common in tropical regions. **2** the larva of this insect, which buries itself in the sand to await its prey.

Antoinette ★ (*French* ãtwanɛt) *n* See **Marie Antoinette.**

Antonello da Messina ★ (‚æntə'nɛləʊ) *n* ?1430–?79 Italian painter, born in Sicily.

Antonescu ★ (‚æntɒ'nɛskjuː) *n* **Ion.** 1882–1946, Romanian general and statesman; appointed prime minister (1940) by King Carol II: executed for war crimes.

Antonine Wall ★ ('æntənaın) *n* a Roman frontier defence work across S Scotland, extending between the River Clyde and the Firth of Forth. It was built in 142 A.D. on the orders of Antoninus Pius.

Antoninus ★ (ˌæntə'naınəs) *n* See **Marcus Aurelius Antoninus.**

Antoninus Pius ★ *n* 86–161 A.D., emperor of Rome (138–161); adopted son and successor of Hadrian.

Antonioni ★ (ˌæntəʊnɪ'əʊnɪ) *n* **Michelangelo** (mike'lan-dʒelo). born 1912, Italian film director; his films include *Blow-Up* (1966), *Zabriskie Point* (1970), and *Beyond the Clouds* (1995).

antonomasia (ˌæntənə'meɪzɪə) *n* **1** the substitution of a title or epithet for a proper name, such as *his highness*. **2** the use of a proper name for an idea: *he is a Daniel come to judgment*. [C16: via L from Gk, from *antonomazein* to name differently, from *onoma* name]

Antony ★ ('æntənɪ) *n* **Mark**. Latin name *Marcus Antonius*. ?83–30 B.C., Roman general who served under Julius Caesar and became a member of the second triumvirate (43). He defeated Brutus and Cassius at Philippi (42) but having repudiated his wife for Cleopatra, he was defeated by Octavian (Augustus) at Actium (31).

antonym ('æntənɪm) *n* a word that means the opposite of another. [C19: from Gk, from ANTI- + *onoma* name]
▸ **antonymous** (æn'tɒnɪməs) *adj*

Antrim ★ ('æntrɪm) *n* **1** a historic county of NE Northern Ireland, famous for the Giant's Causeway on the N coast: in 1973 it was replaced for administrative purposes by local government districts. Area: 3046 sq. km (1176 sq. miles). **2** a district in E Northern Ireland, bordering the NE shore of Lough Neagh: livestock, synthetic fibres. Administrative centre: Antrim. Pop.: 44 516 (1991). Area: 562 sq. km (217 sq. miles).

antrum ('æntrəm) *n, pl* **antra** (-trə) *Anat.* a natural cavity, hollow, or sinus, esp. in a bone. [C14: from L: cave, from Gk *antron*]
▸ **'antral** *adj*

Antung ★ ('æn'tʊŋ) *n* a variant transliteration of the Chinese name for **Andong.**

Antwerp ★ ('æntwɜːp) *n* **1** a province of N Belgium. Pop.: 1 628 710 (1995 est.). Area: 2859 sq. km (1104 sq. miles). **2** a port in N Belgium, capital of Antwerp province, on the River Scheldt: a major European port. Pop.: 459 072 (1995 est.). Flemish name: **Antwerpen** ('ɒntwɛrpən). French name: **Anvers.**

Anu ★ ('ɑːnuː) *n* Babylonian myth. the sky god.

ANU *abbrev.* for Australian National University.

Anubis ★ (ə'njuːbɪs) *n* Egyptian myth. a deity, a son of Osiris, who conducted the dead to judgment. He is represented as having a jackal's head and was identified by the Greeks with Hermes.

Anuradhapura ★ (ə'nʊərədəˌpʊərə, ˌʌnʊ'rɑːdə-) *n* a town in Sri Lanka: ancient capital of Ceylon; site of the sacred bo tree and place of pilgrimage for Buddhists. Pop.: 42 600 (1995 est.).

anuresis (ˌænjuˈriːsɪs) *n* inability to urinate. [C20: NL, from AN- + Gk *ouresis* urination]

anus ('eɪnəs) *n* the excretory opening at the end of the alimentary canal. [C16: from L]

Anvers ★ (ɑ̃vɛr) *n* the French name for **Antwerp.**

anvil ('ænvɪl) *n* **1** a heavy iron or steel block on which metals are hammered during forging. **2** any part having a similar shape or function, such as the lower part of a telegraph key. **3** *Anat.* the nontechnical name for **incus.** [OE *anfealt*]

anxiety (æŋ'zaɪɪtɪ) *n, pl* **anxieties. 1** a state of uneasiness or tension caused by apprehension of possible misfortune, danger, etc. **2** intense desire; eagerness. **3** *Psychol.* a state of intense apprehension, common in mental illness or after a very distressing experience. [C16: from L *anxietas*]

anxiety disorder *n* any of various mental disorders characterized by extreme anxiety.

anxious ('æŋkʃəs, 'æŋʃəs) *adj* **1** worried and tense because of possible misfortune, danger, etc. **2** causing anxiety; worrying; distressing: *an anxious time.* **3** intensely desirous: *anxious for promotion.* [C17: from L *anxius*; rel. to L *angere* to torment]
▸ **'anxiously** *adv* ▸ **'anxiousness** *n*

any ('ɛnɪ) *determiner* **1a** one, some, or several, as specified, no matter how much, what kind, etc.: *you may take any clothes you like.* **1b** (*as pron; functioning as sing or pl*): *take any you like.* **2** (*usually used with a negative*) **2a** even the smallest amount or even one: *I can't stand any noise.* **2b** (*as pron; functioning as sing or pl*): *don't give her any.* **3** whatever or whichever: *any dictionary will do.* **4** an indefinite or unlimited (amount or number): *any number of friends.*
◆ *adv* **5** (*usually used with a negative*) (foll. by a comp. adj) to even the smallest extent: *it isn't any worse.* [OE *ænig*]

Anyang ★ ('ɑːn'jɑːŋ) *n* a town in E China, in Henan province: archaeological site and capital of the Shang dynasty. Pop.: 590 996 (1995).

anybody ('ɛnɪˌbɒdɪ) *pron* **1** any person; anyone. **2** (*usually used with a negative or a question*) a person of any importance: *he isn't anybody.* ◆ *n, pl* **anybodies. 3** (*often preceded by just*) any person at random.

anyhow ('ɛnɪˌhaʊ) *adv* **1** in any case. **2** by any means whatever. **3** carelessly.

any more or esp. US **anymore** (ˌɛnɪ'mɔː) *adv* any longer; still; nowadays.

anyone ('ɛnɪˌwʌn) *pron* **1** any person; anybody. **2** (*used with a negative or a question*) a person of any importance: *is he anyone?* **3** (often preceded by *just*) any person at random.

anyplace ('ɛnɪˌpleɪs) *adv* US & Canad. inf. anywhere.

anything ('ɛnɪˌθɪŋ) *pron* **1** any object, event, action, etc., whatever: *anything might happen.* ◆ *n* **2** a thing of any kind: *have you anything to declare?* ◆ *adv* **3** in any way: *he wasn't anything like his father.* **4** anything but. not in the least: *she was anything but happy.* **5** like anything. (intensifier): *he ran like anything.*

anyway ('ɛnɪˌweɪ) *adv* **1** in any case; at any rate; nevertheless. **2** in a careless manner. **3** Usually **any way.** in any manner.

anywhere ('ɛnɪˌwɛə) *adv* **1** in, at, or to any place. **2** get anywhere. to be successful.

anywise ('ɛnɪˌwaɪz) *adv* Chiefly US. in any way.

ANZAAS ('ænzəs, -zæs) *n* acronym for Australian and New Zealand Association for the Advancement of Science.

Anzac ('ænzæk) *n* **1** (in World War I) a soldier serving with the Australian and New Zealand Army Corps. **2** (now) any Australian or New Zealand soldier. **3** the Anzac landing at Gallipoli in 1915.

Anzac Day *n* April 25, a public holiday in Australia and New Zealand commemorating the Anzac landing at Gallipoli in 1915.

Anzio ★ ('ænzɪˌəʊ; *Italian* 'antsjo) *n* a port and resort on the W coast of Italy: site of Allied landings in World War II. Pop.: 32 383 (1991 est.).

ANZUS ('ænzəs) *n* acronym for Australia, New Zealand, and the United States, with reference to the security alliance between them.

AO *abbrev.* for Officer of the Order of Australia.

A/O or **a/o** (accounting, etc.) *abbrev.* for account of.

AOB or **a.o.b.** *abbrev.* for any other business.

AOC *abbrev.* for appellation d'origine contrôlée: the highest French wine classification; indicates that the wine meets strict requirements concerning area of production, strength, etc. Cf. **VDQS, vin de pays.**

AONB (in England and Wales) *abbrev.* for area of outstanding natural beauty: an area officially designated as requiring protection to conserve and enhance its natural beauty.

Aorangi-Mount Cook ★ (ˌeɪəʊ'ræŋgɪ) *n* the official name for Mount **Cook.**

aorist ('eɪərɪst, 'eərɪst) *n* Grammar. a tense of the verb, esp. in classical Greek, indicating past action without reference to whether the action involved was momentary or continuous. [C16: from Gk *aoristos* not limited, from A-[1] + *horistos*, from *horizein* to define]

aorta (eɪˈɔːtə) *n, pl* **aortas** *or* **aortae** (-tiː). the main vessel in the arterial network, which conveys oxygen-rich blood from the heart. [C16: from NL, from Gk *aortē*, lit.: something lifted, from *aeirein* to raise]
▸ a**'ortic** *or* a**'ortal** *adj*

Aosta ★ (*Italian* aˈɔsta) *n* a town in NW Italy, capital of Valle d'Aosta region: Roman remains. Pop.: 36 339 (1990).

Aotearoa ★ (ˌæʊˌtɪəˈrəʊə) *n NZ.* the Maori name for New Zealand. [Maori: the long white cloud]

aoudad (ˈɑːuˌdæd) *n* a wild mountain sheep of N Africa. Also called: **Barbary sheep**. [from F, from Berber *audad*]

Aouita ★ (auˈiːtə) *n* **Saïd** (saɪˈiːd). born 1960, Moroccan middle-distance runner: world record holder in the 2000 m (1987–95), 5000 m (1987–94), and 1500 m events (1987–93).

ap (æp) son of: occurring as part of some surnames of Welsh origin: *ap Thomas*. [from Welsh *mab* son]

apace (əˈpeɪs) *adv* quickly; rapidly. [C14: prob. from OF *à pas*, at a (good) pace]

apache (əˈpæʃ) *n* a Parisian gangster or ruffian. [from F: APACHE]

Apache (əˈpætʃɪ) *n* **1** (*pl* **Apaches** *or* **Apache**) a member of a North American Indian people inhabiting the southwestern US and N Mexico. **2** the language of this people. [from Mexican Sp.]

apanage (ˈæpənɪdʒ) *n* a variant spelling of **appanage**.

apart (əˈpɑːt) *adj* (*postpositive*), *adv* **1** to or in pieces: *he had the television apart.* **2** placed or kept separately or for a particular purpose, etc.; aside (esp. in **set** *or* **put apart**). **3** separate in time, place, or position: *he stood apart from the group.* **4** not being taken into account: *these difficulties apart, the project ran smoothly.* **5** individual; distinct: *a race apart.* **6** separately or independently: *considered apart, his reasoning was faulty.* **7 apart from.** (*prep*) besides. ◆ See also **take apart, tell apart.** [C14: from OF *a part* at (the) side]

apartheid (əˈpɑːthaɪt, -heɪt) *n* (formerly, in South Africa) the government policy of racial segregation; officially renounced in 1992. [C20: Afrik., from *apart* APART + *-heid* -HOOD]

apartment (əˈpɑːtmənt) *n* **1** (*often pl*) any room in a building, usually one of several forming a suite, used as living accommodation, offices, etc. **2a** another name (esp. US and Canad.) for **flat**[2]. **2b** (*as modifier*): *apartment house.* [C17: from F *appartement*, from It., from *appartare* to separate]

apathetic (ˌæpəˈθetɪk) *adj* having or showing little or no emotion or interest. [C18: from APATHY + PATHETIC]
▸ ˌapa**'thetically** *adv*

apathy (ˈæpəθɪ) *n* **1** absence of interest in or enthusiasm for things generally considered interesting or moving. **2** absence of emotion. [C17: from L, from Gk *apatheia*, from A-[1] + *pathos* feeling]

apatite (ˈæpəˌtaɪt) *n* a common naturally occurring mineral consisting basically of calcium fluorophosphate. It is a source of phosphorus and is used in fertilizers. [C19: from G *Apatit*, from Gk *apatē* deceit; from its misleading similarity to other minerals]

ape (eɪp) *n* **1** any of various primates in which the tail is very short or absent. **2** (not in technical use) any monkey. **3** an imitator; mimic. ◆ *vb* **apes, aping, aped. 4** (*tr*) to imitate. [OE *apa*]
▸ ˈape**ˌlike** *adj*

APEC *Canad. abbrev.* for Atlantic Provinces Economic Council.

Apeldoorn ★ (ˈæpʰlˌdɔːn; *Dutch* ˈaːpəldoːrn) *n* a town in the Netherlands, in Gelderland province: nearby is the summer residence of the Dutch royal family. Pop.: 149 904 (1995 est.).

Apelles ★ (əˈpeliːz) *n* 4th century B.C., Greek painter of mythological subjects, none of whose work survives, his fame resting on the testimony of Pliny and other writers.

apeman (ˈeɪpˌmæn) *n, pl* **apemen.** any of various extinct apelike primates thought to have been the forerunner▪ of modern man.

Apennines ★ (ˈæpəˌnaɪnz) *pl n* **1** a mountain range in Italy, extending over 1250 km (800 miles) from the northwest to the southernmost tip of the peninsula Highest peak: Monte Corno, 2912 m (9554 ft). **2** a mountain range lying in the N quadrants of the moon extending over 950 km along the SE border of the Mare Imbrium and rising to 6200 m.

aperçu *French.* (apersy) *n* **1** an outline. **2** an insight [from *apercevoir* to PERCEIVE]

aperient (əˈpɪərɪənt) *Med.* ◆ *adj* **1** laxative. ◆ *n* **2** a mild laxative. [C17: from L *aperīre* to open]

aperiodic (ˌeɪpɪərɪˈɒdɪk) *adj* **1** not periodic; not occurring at regular intervals. **2** *Physics.* **2a** (of a system or instrument) being damped sufficiently to reach equilibrium without oscillation. **2b** (of an oscillation or vibration) not having a regular period. **2c** (of an electrical circuit) not having a measurable resonant frequency.
▸ **aperiodicity** (ˌeɪpɪərɪəˈdɪsɪtɪ) *n*

apéritif (əˌperiˈtiːf) *n* an alcoholic drink before a meal to whet the appetite. [C19: from F, from Med. L, from L *aperīre* to open]

aperture (ˈæpətʃə) *n* **1** a hole; opening. **2** *Physics.* a usually circular and often variable opening in an optical instrument or device that controls the quantity of radiation entering or leaving it. [C15: from LL *apertūra* opening, from *aperīre* to open]

apetalous (eɪˈpetələs) *adj* (of flowering plants such as the wood anemone) having no petals. [C18: from NL, see A-[1], PETAL]

apex (ˈeɪpeks) *n, pl* **apexes** *or* **apices. 1** the highest point, vertex. **2** the pointed end or tip of something. **3** a high point, as of a career. [C17: from L: point]

APEX (ˈeɪpeks) *n acronym for:* **1** Advance Purchase Excursion, a reduced airline or long-distance rail fare that must be paid a specified number of days in advance. **2** Association of Professional, Executive, Clerical, and Computer Staff.

Apex Club (ˈeɪpeks) *n* (in Australia) an association of business and professional men to promote community welfare.
▸ **Apexian** (eɪˈpeksɪən) *adj, n*

apgar score *or* **rating** (ˈæpgɑː) *n* a system for determining the condition of an infant at birth by allotting a maximum of 2 points to each of the following: heart rate, breathing effort, muscle tone, response to stimulation, and colour. [C20: after V. Apgar (1909–74), US anaesthetist]

aphaeresis *or* **apheresis** (əˈfɪərɪsɪs) *n* the omission of a letter or syllable at the beginning of a word. [C17: via LL from Gk, from *aphairein* to remove]

aphasia (əˈfeɪzɪə) *n* a disorder of the central nervous system characterized by loss of the ability to communicate, esp. in speech. [C19: via NL from Gk, from A-[1] + *-phasia*, from *phanai* to speak]

aphelion (æpˈhiːlɪən, əˈfiː-) *n, pl* **aphelia** (-lɪə). the point in its orbit when a planet or comet is at its greatest distance from the sun. [C17: from NL *aphēlium*, from AP(O)- + Gk *hēlios* sun]

aphesis (ˈæfɪsɪs) *n* the gradual disappearance of an unstressed vowel at the beginning of a word, as in *squire* from *esquire*. [C19: from Gk, from *aphienai* to set free]
▸ **aphetic** (əˈfetɪk) *adj*

aphid (ˈeɪfɪd) *n* any of the small homopterous insects of the family Aphididae, which feed by sucking the juices from plants. [C19: from *aphides*, pl. of APHIS]

aphis (ˈeɪfɪs) *n, pl* **aphides** (ˈeɪfɪˌdiːz). any of a genus of aphids, such as the blackfly. [C18: from NL (coined by Linnaeus for obscure reasons)]

aphonia (əˈfəʊnɪə) *or* **aphony** (ˈæfənɪ) *n* loss of voice caused by damage to the vocal tract. [C18: NL, from Gk, from A-[1] + *phōnē* sound]

aphorism (ˈæfəˌrɪzəm) *n* a short pithy saying expressing a general truth; maxim. [C16: from LL, from Gk *aphorismos*, from *aphorizein* to define]
▸ **'aphorist** *n* ▸ ˌapho**'ristic** *adj*

aphrodisiac (ˌæfrəˈdɪzɪæk) *n* **1** a drug, food, etc., that excites sexual desire. ◆ *adj* **2** exciting sexual desire. [C18: from Gk, from *aphrodisios* belonging to *Aphrodite*, goddess of love]

Aphrodite ★ (ˌæfrəˈdaɪtɪ) *n Greek myth.* the goddess of love and beauty, daughter of Zeus. Roman counterpart: **Venus**. Also called: **Cytherea**.

aphyllous (əˈfɪləs) *adj* (of plants) having no leaves. [C19: from NL, from Gk A-¹ + *phullon* leaf]

apian (ˈeɪpɪən) *adj* of, relating to, or resembling bees. [C19: from L *apiānus*, from *apis* bee]

apiarist (ˈeɪpɪərɪst) *n* a person who studies or keeps bees.

apiary (ˈeɪpɪərɪ) *n, pl* **apiaries.** a place where bees are kept. [C17: from L *apiārium*, from *apis* bee]

apical (ˈæpɪkˀl, ˈeɪ-) *adj* of, at, or being the apex. [C19: from NL *apicālis*]
▸ **'apically** *adv*

apices (ˈæpɪˌsiːz, ˈeɪ-) *n* a plural of **apex.**

apiculture (ˈeɪpɪˌkʌltʃə) *n* the breeding and care of bees. [C19: from L *apis* bee + CULTURE]
▸ ˌapi'cultural *adj* ▸ ˌapi'culturist *n*

apiece (əˈpiːs) *adv* (*postpositive*) for, to, or from each one: *they were given two apples apiece.*

Apis ★ (ˈɑːpɪs) *n* (in ancient Egypt) a sacred bull worshipped at Memphis.

apish (ˈeɪpɪʃ) *adj* **1** stupid; foolish. **2** resembling an ape. **3** slavishly imitative.
▸ **'apishly** *adv* ▸ **'apishness** *n*

aplanatic (ˌæpləˈnætɪk) *adj* (of a lens or mirror) free from spherical aberration. [C18: from Gk *aplanetos* free from error, from A-¹ + *planaein* to wander]

aplenty (əˈplɛntɪ) *adj* (*postpositive*), *adv* in plenty.

aplomb (əˈplɒm) *n* equanimity, self-confidence, or self-possession. [C18: from F: uprightness, from *à plomb* according to the plumb line]

apnoea *or US* **apnea** (æpˈnɪə) *n* a temporary inability to breathe. [C18: from NL, from Gk *apnoia*, from A-¹ + *pnein* to breathe]

Apo ★ (ˈɑːpəʊ) *n* the highest mountain in the Philippines, on SE Mindanao: active volcano with three peaks. Height: 2954 m (9690 ft).

apo- *or* **ap-** *prefix* **1** away from; off: *apogee.* **2** separation of: *apocarpous.* [from Gk *apo* away, off]

Apoc. *abbrev. for:* **1** Apocalypse. **2** Apocrypha *or* Apocryphal.

apocalypse (əˈpɒkəlɪps) *n* **1** a prophetic disclosure or revelation. **2** an event of great importance, violence, etc., like the events described in the Apocalypse. [C13: from LL *apocalypsis*, from Gk, from APO- + *kaluptein* to hide]
▸ aˌpocaˈlyptic *adj*

Apocalypse (əˈpɒkəlɪps) *n Bible.* another name for the Book of Revelation.

apocarpous (ˌæpəˈkɑːpəs) *adj* (of the ovaries of flowering plants) consisting of separate carpels. [C19: from NL, from Gk APO- + *karpos* fruit]

apochromat (ˌæpəˈkrəʊmæt) *or* **apochromatic lens** (ˌæpəkrəˈmætɪk) *n* a lens system designed to bring trichromatic light to a single focus and reduce chromatic aberration.

apocope (əˈpɒkəpɪ) *n* omission of the final sound or sounds of a word. [C16: via LL from Gk, from *apokoptein* to cut off]

apocrine (ˈæpəkraɪn, -krɪn) *adj* losing cellular tissue in the process of secreting, as in mammary glands. Cf. **eccrine.** [C20: from APO- + *-crine*, from Gk *krinein* to separate]

Apocrypha (əˈpɒkrɪfə) *n* **the.** (*functioning as sing or pl*) the 14 books included as an appendix to the Old Testament in the Septuagint and the Vulgate but not in the Hebrew canon. [C14: via LL *apocrypha* (*scripta*) hidden (writings), from Gk, from *apokruptein* to hide away]

apocryphal (əˈpɒkrɪfəl) *adj* **1** of questionable authenticity. **2** (*sometimes cap.*) of or like the Apocrypha. **3** untrue; counterfeit.

apodal (ˈæpədˀl) *or* **apodous** (ˈæpədəs) *adj* without feet; having no pelvic fins. [C18: from Gk A-¹ + *pous* foot]

apodosis (əˈpɒdəsɪs) *n, pl* **apodoses** (-ˌsiːz). *Logic, grammar.* the consequent of a conditional statement, as *I won't go* in *if it rains I won't go.* [C17: via LL from Gk, from *apodidonai* to give back]

apogee (ˈæpəˌdʒiː) *n* **1** the point in its orbit around the earth when the moon or an artificial satellite is at its greatest distance from the earth. **2** the highest point. [C17: from NL, from Gk, from *apogaios* away from the earth]
▸ ˌapoˈgean *adj*

apolitical (ˌeɪpəˈlɪtɪkˀl) *adj* politically neutral; without political attitudes, content, or bias.

Apollinaire ★ (*French* apɔlinɛr) *n* **Guillaume** (gijom), real name *Wilhelm Apollinaris de Kostrowitzki.* 1880–1918, French poet, novelist, and dramatist, regarded as a precursor of surrealism; author of *Alcoöls* (1913) and *Calligrammes* (1918).

Apollo ★ (əˈpɒləʊ) *n Classical myth.* the god of light, poetry, music, healing, and prophecy: son of Zeus and Leto.

Apollyon (əˈpɒljən) *n* the destroyer, a name given to the Devil (Revelation 9:11). [C14: via LL from Gk, from *apollunai* to destroy totally]

apologetic (əˌpɒləˈdʒɛtɪk) *adj* **1** expressing or anxious to make apology; contrite. **2** defending in speech or writing.
▸ aˌpoloˈgetically *adv*

apologetics (əˌpɒləˈdʒɛtɪks) *n* (*functioning as sing*) **1** the branch of theology concerned with the rational justification of Christianity. **2** a defensive method of argument.

apologia (ˌæpəˈləʊdʒɪə) *n* a formal written defence of a cause or one's beliefs or conduct.

apologist (əˈpɒlədʒɪst) *n* a person who offers a defence by argument.

apologize *or* **apologise** (əˈpɒləˌdʒaɪz) *vb* **apologizes, apologizing, apologized** *or* **apologises, apologising, apologised.** (*intr*) **1** to express or make an apology; acknowledge faults. **2** to make a formal defence.

apologue (ˈæpəˌlɒg) *n* an allegory or moral fable. [C17: from L, from Gk *apologos*]

apology (əˈpɒlədʒɪ) *n, pl* **apologies.** **1** a verbal or written expression of regret or contrition for a fault or railing. **2** a poor substitute. **3** another word for **apologia.** [C16: from OF, from LL, from Gk: a verbal defence, from APO- + *logos* speech]

apophthegm *or* **apothegm** (ˈæpəˌθɛm) *n* a short remark containing some general or generally accepted truth; maxim. [C16: from Gk *apophthegma*, from *apophthengesthai* to speak frankly]

apoplectic (ˌæpəˈplɛktɪk) *adj* **1** of apoplexy. **2** *Inf.* furious.
▸ ˌapoˈplectically *adv*

apoplexy (ˈæpəˌplɛksɪ) *n* sudden loss of consciousness, often followed by paralysis, caused by rupture or occlusion of a blood vessel in the brain. [C14: from OF *apoplexie*, from LL, from Gk, from *apoplēssein* to cripple by a stroke]

aport (əˈpɔːt) *adv, adj* (*postpositive*) *Naut.* on or towards the port side: *with the head aport.*

apostasy (əˈpɒstəsɪ) *n, pl* **apostasies.** abandonment of one's religious faith, party, a cause, etc. [C14: from Church L *apostasia*, from Gk *apostasis* desertion]

apostate (əˈpɒsteɪt, -tɪt) *n* **1** a person who abandons his religion, party, etc. ◆ *adj* **2** guilty of apostasy.
▸ **apostatical** (ˌæpəˈstætɪkˀl) *adj*

apostatize *or* **apostatise** (əˈpɒstəˌtaɪz) *vb* **apostatizes, apostatizing, apostatized** *or* **apostatises, apostatising, apostatised.** (*intr*) to abandon one's belief, faith, or allegiance.

a posteriori (eɪ pɒsˌtɛrɪˈɔːraɪ, -rɪ; ɑː) *adj Logic.* **1** relating to inductive reasoning from particular facts to a general principle. **2** derived from or requiring evidence for its validation; empirical. [C18: from L, lit.: from the latter]

★ people and places

apostle (ə'pɒsᵊl) n **1** (often cap.) one of the 12 disciples chosen by Christ to preach his gospel. **2** any prominent Christian missionary, esp. one who first converts a people. **3** an ardent early supporter of a cause, movement, etc. [OE apostol, from Church L, from Gk apostolos a messenger]

Apostles' Creed n a concise statement of Christian beliefs dating from about 500 A.D., traditionally ascribed to the Apostles.

apostolate (ə'pɒstəlɪt, -ˌleɪt) n the office, authority, or mission of an apostle.

apostolic (ˌæpə'stɒlɪk) adj **1** of or relating to the Apostles or their teachings or practice. **2** of or relating to the pope as successor of the Apostles.
▶ **apos'tolical** adj

Apostolic See (ˌæpə'stɒlɪk) n the see of the pope.

Apostolic succession n the doctrine that the authority of Christian bishops derives from the Apostles through an unbroken line of consecration.

apostrophe[1] (ə'pɒstrəfɪ) n the punctuation mark ' used to indicate the omission of a letter or number, such as he's for he has or he is, also used in English to form the possessive, as in John's father. [C17: from LL, from Gk apostrophos mark of elision, from apostrephein to turn away]

apostrophe[2] (ə'pɒstrəfɪ) n Rhetoric. a digression from a discourse, esp. an address to an imaginary or absent person or a personification. [C16: from L apostrophē, from Gk: a turning away]

apostrophize or **apostrophise** (ə'pɒstrəˌfaɪz) vb **apostrophizes, apostrophizing, apostrophized** or **apostrophises, apostrophising, apostrophised.** (tr) to address an apostrophe to.

apothecaries' measure n a system of liquid volume measure used in pharmacy in which 20 fluid ounces equal 1 pint.

apothecaries' weight n a system of weights formerly used in pharmacy based on the Troy ounce.

apothecary (ə'pɒθɪkərɪ) n, pl **apothecaries. 1** an archaic word for **chemist. 2** Law. a chemist licensed by the Society of Apothecaries of London to prescribe, prepare, and sell drugs. [C14: from OF, from LL, from Gk apothēkē storehouse]

apothegm ('æpəˌθɛm) n a variant spelling of **apophthegm.**

apothem ('æpəˌθɛm) n the perpendicular from the centre of a regular polygon to any of its sides. [C20: from APO- + Gk thema, from tithenai to place]

apotheosis (əˌpɒθɪ'əʊsɪs) n, pl **apotheoses** (-siːz). **1** elevation to the rank of a god; deification. **2** glorification of a person or thing. **3** a glorified ideal. [C17: via LL from Gk: deification]

apotheosize or **apotheosise** (ə'pɒθɪəˌsaɪz) vb **apotheosizes, apotheosizing, apotheosized** or **apotheosises, apotheosising, apotheosised.** (tr) **1** to deify. **2** to glorify or idealize.

app. abbrev. for: **1** apparatus. **2** appendix (of a book). **3** applied. **4** appointed. **5** apprentice. **6** approved. **7** approximate.

appal or US **appall** (ə'pɔːl) vb **appals, appalling, appalled** or US **appalls, appalling, appalled.** (tr) to fill with horror; shock or dismay. [C14: from OF appalir to turn pale]

Appalachia ★ (ˌæpə'leɪtʃɪə) n a highland region of the eastern US, containing the Appalachian Mountains, extending from Pennsylvania to Alabama.
▶ ˌAppa'lachian adj

Appalachian Mountains or **Appalachians** ★ pl n a mountain system of E North America, extending from Quebec province in Canada to central Alabama in the US: contains rich deposits of anthracite, bitumen, and iron ore. Highest peak: Mount Mitchell, 2038 m (6684 ft).

appalling (ə'pɔːlɪŋ) adj **1** causing dismay, horror, or revulsion. **2** Inf. very bad.
▶ **ap'pallingly** adv

Appaloosa (ˌæpə'luːsə) n a breed of horse, originally from America, having a spotted rump. [C19: ?from Palouse, river in Idaho]

appanage or **apanage** ('æpənɪdʒ) n **1** land or other provision granted by a king for the support of esp. a younger son. **2** a customary accompaniment or perquisite, as to a job or position. [C17: from OF, from Med. L, from appānāre to provide for, from L pānis bread]

apparatchik (ˌæpə'rɑːtʃɪk) n **1** a member of a Communist Party organization. **2** a bureaucrat in any organization. [C20: from Russian, from apparat apparatus, instrument + -ckik, suffix denoting agent]

apparatus (ˌæpə'reɪtəs, -'rɑːtəs) n, pl **apparatus** or **apparatuses. 1** a collection of equipment used for a particular purpose. **2** a machine having a specific function: breathing apparatus. **3** the means by which something operates; organization. **4** Anat. any group of organs having a specific function. [C17: from L, from apparāre to make ready]

apparel (ə'pærəl) n **1** Arch. clothing. **2** Naut. a vessel's gear and equipment. ◆ vb **apparels, apparelling, apparelled** or US **apparels, appareling, appareled. 3** (tr) Arch. to clothe, adorn, etc. [C13: from OF apareillier to make ready, from Vulgar L appariculāre (unattested), from L parāre to prepare]

apparent (ə'pærənt) adj **1** readily seen or understood; obvious. **2** (usually prenominal) seeming, as opposed to real: his apparent innocence. **3** Physics. as observed but ignoring such factors as the motion of the observer, etc. [C14: from L appārēns, from appārēre to APPEAR]
▶ **ap'parently** adv

apparent magnitude n See **magnitude** (sense 4).

apparition (ˌæpə'rɪʃən) n **1** an appearance, esp. of a ghost or ghostlike figure. **2** the figure so appearing; spectre. **3** the act of appearing. [C15: from LL appāritiō, from L appārēre to APPEAR]

appassionato (əˌpæsjə'nɑːtəu) adj, adv Music. (to be performed) with passion. [It.]

appeal (ə'piːl) n **1** a request for relief, aid, etc. **2** the power to attract, please, stimulate, or interest. **3** an application or resort to another authority, esp. a higher one, as for a decision. **4** Law. **4a** the judicial review by a superior court of the decision of a lower tribunal. **4b** a request for such review. **5** Cricket. a request to the umpire to declare a batsman out. ◆ vb **6** (intr) to make an earnest request. **7** (intr) to attract, please, stimulate, or interest. **8** Law. to apply to a superior court to review (a case or issue decided by a lower tribunal). **9** (intr) to resort (to), as for a decision. **10** (intr) Cricket. to ask the umpire to declare a batsman out. **11** (intr) to challenge the umpire's or referee's decision. [C14: from OF appeler, from L appellāre to entreat, from pellere to drive]
▶ **ap'pealable** adj ▶ **ap'pealer** n ▶ **ap'pealing** adj ▶ **ap'pealingly** adv

appear (ə'pɪə) vb (intr) **1** to come into sight. **2** (copula; may take an infinitive) to seem: the evidence appears to support you. **3** to be plain or clear, as after further evidence, etc.: it appears you were correct after all. **4** to develop; occur: faults appeared during testing. **5** to be published: his biography appeared last month. **6** to perform: he has appeared in many London productions. **7** to be present in court before a magistrate or judge: he appeared on two charges of theft. [C13: from OF aparoir, from L appārēre to become visible, attend upon, from pārēre to appear]

appearance (ə'pɪərəns) n **1** the act or an instance of appearing. **2** the outward aspect of a person or thing. **3** an outward show; pretence: he gave an appearance of working hard. **4 keep up appearances.** to maintain the public impression of wellbeing or normality. **5 put in** or **make an appearance.** to attend briefly, as out of politeness. **6 to all appearances.** apparently.

appearance money n money paid by a promoter of an event to a particular celebrity in order to ensure that the celebrity takes part in the event.

appease (ə'piːz) vb **appeases, appeasing, appeased.** (tr) **1** to calm or pacify, esp. by acceding to the demands of. **2** to satisfy or quell (a thirst, etc.). [C16: from OF apaisier, from pais peace, from L pax]
▶ **ap'peaser** n

appeasement (ə'piːzmənt) n **1** the policy of acceding to the demands of a potentially hostile nation in the hope of maintaining peace. **2** the act of appeasing.

Appel ★ (*Dutch* 'ɑpəl) *n* **Karel** ('kɑːrəl). born 1921, Dutch abstract expressionist painter.

appellant (ə'pɛlənt) *n* **1** a person who appeals. **2** *Law.* the party who appeals to a higher court from the decision of a lower tribunal. ◆ *adj* **3** *Law.* another word for **appellate**. [C14: from OF; see APPEAL]

appellate (ə'pɛlɪt) *adj Law.* **1** of appeals. **2** (of a tribunal) having jurisdiction to review cases on appeal. [C18: from L *appellātus* summoned, from *appellāre* to APPEAL]

appellation (ˌæpɪ'leɪʃən) *n* **1** a name or title. **2** the act of naming.

appellative (ə'pɛlətɪv) *n* **1** a name or title. **2** *Grammar.* another word for **common noun**. ◆ *adj* **3** of or relating to a name. **4** (of a proper noun) used as a common noun.

append (ə'pɛnd) *vb* (*tr*) **1** to add as a supplement: *to append a footnote.* **2** to attach; hang on. [C15: from LL *appendere* to hang (something) from, from L *pendere* to hang]

appendage (ə'pɛndɪdʒ) *n* an ancillary or secondary part attached to a main part; adjunct, such as an organ that projects from the trunk of an animal.

appendant (ə'pɛndənt) *adj* **1** attached or added. **2** attendant or associated as an accompaniment or result. ◆ *n* **3** a person or thing attached or added.

appendicectomy (əˌpɛndɪ'sɛktəmɪ) *or esp. US & Canad.* **appendectomy** (ˌæpən'dɛktəmɪ) *n, pl* **appendicectomies** *or* **appendectomies**. surgical removal of any appendage, esp. the vermiform appendix.

appendicitis (əˌpɛndɪ'saɪtɪs) *n* inflammation of the vermiform appendix.

appendix (ə'pɛndɪks) *n, pl* **appendices** (-dɪˌsiːz) *or* **appendixes**. **1** a body of separate additional material at the end of a book, etc. **2** any part that is dependent or supplementary. **3** *Anat.* See **vermiform appendix**. [C16: from L: an appendage, from *appendere* to APPEND]

Appenzell ★ (*German* apən'tsɛl, 'apəntsɛl) *n* **1** a canton of NE Switzerland, divided in 1597 into the Protestant demicanton of **Appenzell Outer Rhodes** and the Catholic demicanton of **Appenzell Inner Rhodes**. Capitals: Herisau and Appenzell. Pop.: 54 227 and 14 742 (1995 est.) respectively. Areas: 243 sq. km (94 sq. miles) and 171 sq. km (66 sq. miles) respectively. **2** a town in NE Switzerland, capital of Appenzell Inner Rhodes demicanton. Pop.: 5157 (1990).

apperceive (ˌæpə'siːv) *vb* **apperceives, apperceiving, apperceived.** (*tr*) **1** to be aware of perceiving. **2** *Psychol.* to comprehend by assimilating (a perception) to ideas already in the mind. [C19: from OF, from L *percipere* to PERCEIVE]

apperception (ˌæpə'sɛpʃən) *n* **1** *Psychol.* the attainment of full awareness of a sensation or idea. **2** the act of apperceiving.
▸ ˌapper'ceptive *adj*

appertain (ˌæpə'teɪn) *vb* (*intr;* usually foll. by *to*) to belong (to) as a part, function, right, etc.; relate (to) or be connected (with). [C14: from OF *apertenir*, from LL, from L AD- + *pertinēre* to PERTAIN]

appetence ('æpɪtəns) *or* **appetency** *n, pl* **appetences** *or* **appetencies**. **1** a craving or desire. **2** an attraction or affinity. [C17: from L *appetentia*, from *appetere* to crave]

appetite ('æpɪˌtaɪt) *n* **1** a desire for food or drink. **2** a desire to satisfy a bodily craving, as for sexual pleasure. **3** (usually foll. by *for*) a liking or willingness: *a great appetite for work.* [C14: from OF *apetit*, from L, from *appetere* to desire ardently]
▸ **appetitive** (ə'pɛtɪtɪv) *adj*

appetizer *or* **appetiser** ('æpɪˌtaɪzə) *n* **1** a small amount of food or drink taken to stimulate the appetite. **2** any stimulating foretaste.

appetizing *or* **appetising** ('æpɪˌtaɪzɪŋ) *adj* pleasing or stimulating to the appetite; delicious; tasty.

Appian Way ★ ('æpɪən) *n* a Roman road in Italy, extending from Rome to Brindisi: begun in 312 B.C. by Appius Claudius Caecus. Length: about 560 km (350 miles).

applaud (ə'plɔːd) *vb* **1** to indicate approval of (a person, performance, etc.) by clapping the hands. **2** (*usually tr*) to express approval or praise of: *I applaud your decision.* [C15: from L *applaudere*, from *plaudere* to beat, applaud]

applause (ə'plɔːz) *n* appreciation or praise, esp. as shown by clapping the hands.

apple ('æp°l) *n* **1** a rosaceous tree, widely cultivated in temperate regions in many varieties. **2** the fruit of this tree, having red, yellow, or green skin and crisp whitish flesh. **3** the wood of this tree. **4** any of several unrelated trees that have fruit similar to the apple. **5 apple of one's eye.** a person or thing that is very much loved. [OE *æppel*]

apple green *n* **a** a bright light green. **b** (*as adj*): *an apple-green carpet.*

Apple Isle ★ *n* **the.** *Austral. inf.* Tasmania.
▸ **Apple Islander** *n*

apple-pie bed *n Brit.* a bed made with the sheets folded so as to prevent the person from entering it.

apple-pie order *n Inf.* perfect order or condition.

applet ('æplɪt) *n Computing.* a computer program that runs within a page on the World Wide Web. [C20: from APP(LICATION) + -LET]

Appleton ★ ('æp°ltən) *n* Sir **Edward** (**Victor**). 1892–1965, English physicist, noted particularly for his research on the ionosphere: Nobel prize for physics 1947.

appliance (ə'plaɪəns) *n* **1** a machine or device, esp. an electrical one used domestically. **2** any piece of equipment having a specific function. **3** another name for a **fire engine**.

applicable ('æplɪkəb°l, ə'plɪkə-) *adj* being appropriate or relevant; able to be applied; fitting.
▸ ˌapplica'bility *n* ▸ 'applicably *adv*

applicant ('æplɪkənt) *n* a person who applies, as for a job, grant, support, etc.; candidate. [C15: from L *applicāns*, from *applicāre* to APPLY]

application (ˌæplɪ'keɪʃən) *n* **1** the act of applying to a particular use. **2** relevance or value: *the practical applications of space technology.* **3** the act of asking for something. **4** a written request, as for a job, etc. **5** diligent effort: *a job requiring application.* **6** something, such as a lotion, that is applied, esp. to the skin.

applicator ('æplɪˌkeɪtə) *n* a device, such as a spatula or rod, for applying a medicine, glue, etc.

applicatory ('æplɪkətərɪ) *adj* suitable for application.

applied (ə'plaɪd) *adj* put to practical use: *applied mathematics.* Cf. **pure** (sense 5).

appliqué (æ'pliːkeɪ) *n* **1** a decoration of one material sewn or fixed onto another. **2** the practice of decorating in this way. ◆ *vb* **appliqués, appliquéing, appliquéd.** **3** (*tr*) to sew or fix (a decoration) on as an appliqué. [C18: from F, lit.: applied]

apply (ə'plaɪ) *vb* **applies, applying, applied.** **1** (*tr*) to put to practical use; employ. **2** (*intr*) to be relevant or appropriate. **3** (*tr*) to cause to come into contact with. **4** (*intr;* often foll. by *for*) to put in an application or request. **5** (*tr;* often foll. by *to*) to devote (oneself or one's efforts) with diligence. **6** (*tr*) to bring into use: *the police only applied the law to aliens.* [C14: from OF *aplier*, from L *applicāre* to attach to]
▸ ap'plier *n*

appoggiatura (əˌpɒdʒə'tʊərə) *n, pl* **appoggiaturas** *or* **appoggiature** (-reɪ). *Music.* an ornament consisting of a nonharmonic note preceding a harmonic one either before or on the stress. [C18: from It., lit.: a propping]

appoint (ə'pɔɪnt) *vb* (*mainly tr*) **1** (*also intr*) to assign officially, as to a position, responsibility, etc. **2** to establish by agreement or decree. **3** to prescribe: *laws appointed by tribunal.* **4** *Property law.* to nominate (a person) to take an interest in property. **5** to equip with usual features; furnish: *a well-appointed hotel.* [C14: from OF *apointer* to put into a good state]
▸ **appoin'tee** *n* ▸ ap'pointer *n*

appointive (ə'pɔɪntɪv) *adj Chiefly US.* filled by appointment: *an appointive position.*

appointment (ə'pɔɪntmənt) *n* **1** an arrangement to meet a person or be at a place at a certain time. **2** the act of placing in a job or position. **3** the person who receives such a job. **4** the job or position to which such a person is appointed. **5** (usually pl) a fixture or fitting.

apportion (ə'pɔːʃən) vb (tr) to divide, distribute, or assign shares of; allot proportionally.
▸ ap'portionable adj ▸ ap'portionment n

appose (ə'pəʊz) vb **apposes, apposing, apposed.** (tr) **1** to place side by side. **2** (usually foll. by to) to place (something) near or against another thing. [C16: from OF apposer, from poser to put, from L pōnere]
▸ ap'posable adj

apposite ('æpəzɪt) adj appropriate; apt. [C17: from L appositus, from appōnere, from pōnere to put]
▸ 'appositely adv ▸ 'appositeness n

apposition (ˌæpə'zɪʃən) n **1** a putting into juxtaposition. **2** a grammatical construction in which a word, esp. a noun, is placed after another to modify its meaning.
▸ ˌappo'sitional adj

appositive (ə'pɒzɪtɪv) Grammar. ◆ adj **1** in, of, or relating to apposition. ◆ n **2** an appositive word or phrase.
▸ ap'positively adv

appraisal (ə'preɪzəl) or **appraisement** n **1** an assessment of the worth or quality of a person or thing. **2** a valuation.

appraise (ə'preɪz) vb **appraises, appraising, appraised.** (tr) **1** to assess the worth, value, or quality of. **2** to make a valuation of, as for taxation. [C15: from OF, from prisier to PRIZE²]
▸ ap'praisable adj ▸ ap'praiser n

> **USAGE NOTE** *Appraise* is sometimes wrongly used where *apprise* is meant: *they had been apprised* (not *appraised*) *of my arrival.*

appreciable (ə'priːʃəbəl) adj sufficient to be easily measured or noticed.
▸ ap'preciably adv

appreciate (ə'priːʃɪˌeɪt, -sɪ-) vb **appreciates, appreciating, appreciated.** (mainly tr) **1** to feel thankful or grateful for. **2** (may take a clause as object) to take sufficient account of: to appreciate a problem. **3** to value highly. **4** (usually intr) to increase in value. [C17: from Med. L appretiāre to value, from L pretium PRICE]
▸ ap'preci₁ator n

appreciation (əˌpriːʃɪ'eɪʃən, -sɪ-) n **1** thanks or gratitude. **2** assessment of the true worth of persons or things. **3** perceptive recognition of qualities, as in art. **4** an increase in value. **5** a review of a book, etc., esp. when favourable.

appreciative (ə'priːʃɪətɪv) or **appreciatory** adj feeling or expressing appreciation.
▸ ap'preciatively adv ▸ ap'preciativeness n

apprehend (ˌæprɪ'hɛnd) vb **1** (tr) to arrest and escort into custody. **2** to grasp mentally; understand. **3** to await with fear or anxiety. [C14: from L apprehendere to lay hold of]

apprehensible (ˌæprɪ'hɛnsɪbəl) adj capable of being comprehended or grasped mentally.
▸ ˌappre₁hensi'bility n

apprehension (ˌæprɪ'hɛnʃən) n **1** anxiety over what may happen. **2** the act of arresting. **3** understanding. **4** a notion or conception.

apprehensive (ˌæprɪ'hɛnsɪv) adj **1** fearful or anxious. **2** (usually postpositive and foll. by of) Arch. intelligent, perceptive.
▸ ˌappre'hensively adv ▸ ˌappre'hensiveness n

apprentice (ə'prɛntɪs) n **1** someone who works for a skilled or qualified person in order to learn a trade, esp. for a recognized period. **2** any beginner or novice. ◆ vb **apprentices, apprenticing, apprenticed.** **3** (tr) to take, place, or bind as an apprentice. [C14: from OF aprentis, from aprendre to learn, from L apprehendere to APPREHEND]
▸ ap'prenticeship n

apprise or **apprize** (ə'praɪz) vb **apprises, apprising, apprised** or **apprizes, apprizing, apprized.** (tr; often foll. by of) to make aware; inform. [C17: from F appris, from apprendre to teach; learn]

> **USAGE NOTE** See at **appraise.**

appro ('æprəʊ) n an informal shortening of **approval:** on appro.

approach (ə'prəʊtʃ) vb **1** to come nearer in position, time, quality, character, etc., to (someone or something). **2** (tr) to make a proposal or suggestion to. **3** (tr) to begin to deal with. ◆ n **4** the act of drawing close or closer. **5** a close approximation. **6** the way or means of entering or leaving. **7** (often pl) an overture to a person. **8** a means adopted in tackling a problem, job of work, etc. **9** Also called: **approach path.** the course followed by an aircraft preparing for landing. **10** Also called: **approach shot.** Golf. a shot made to or towards the green after a tee shot. [C14: from OF aprochier, from LL appropiāre to draw near, from L prope near]
▸ ap'proachable adj ▸ apˌproacha'bility n

approbation (ˌæprə'beɪʃən) n **1** commendation; praise. **2** official recognition.
▸ 'appro₁bative or 'appro₁batory adj

appropriate adj (ə'prəʊprɪɪt). **1** right or suitable; fitting. ◆ vb (ə'prəʊprɪˌeɪt), **appropriates, appropriating, appropriated.** (tr) **2** to take for one's own use, esp. illegally. **3** to put aside (funds, etc.) for a particular purpose or person. [C15: from LL appropriāre to make one's own, from L proprius one's own]
▸ ap'propriately adv ▸ ap'propriateness n ▸ ap'propri₁ator n

appropriation (əˌprəʊprɪ'eɪʃən) n **1** the act of setting apart or taking for one's own use. **2** a sum of money set apart for a specific purpose.

approval (ə'pruːvəl) n **1** the act of approving. **2** formal agreement. **3** a favourable opinion. **4 on approval.** (of articles for sale) for examination with an option to buy or return.

approve (ə'pruːv) vb **approves, approving, approved.** **1** (when intr, often foll. by of) to consider fair, good, or right. **2** (tr) to authorize or sanction. [C14: from OF aprover, from L approbāre to approve, from probāre to test, PROVE]

approved school n (in Britain) a former name for **community home.**

approx. abbrev. for approximate(ly).

approximate adj (ə'prɒksɪmɪt). **1** almost accurate or exact. **2** inexact; rough; loose. **3** much alike; almost the same. **4** near; close together. ◆ vb (ə'prɒksɪˌmeɪt), **proximates, approximating, approximated.** **5** (usually foll. by to) to come or bring near or close; be almost the same (as). **6** Maths. to find an expression for (some quantity) accurate to a specified degree. [C15: from LL approximāre, from L proximus nearest]
▸ ap'proximately adv

approximation (əˌprɒksɪ'meɪʃən) n **1** the process or result of making a rough calculation, estimate, or guess. **2** an imprecise or unreliable record or version. **3** Maths. an inexact number, relationship, or theory that is sufficiently accurate for a specific purpose.

appurtenance (ə'pɜːtɪnəns) n **1** a less significant thing or part. **2** (pl) accessories. **3** Property law. a minor right, interest, or privilege. [C14: from Anglo-F apurtenance, from OF apartenance, from apartenir to APPERTAIN]

APR abbrev. for annual percentage rate.

Apr. abbrev. for April.

apraxia (ə'præksɪə) n a disorder of the central nervous system characterized by impaired ability to carry out certain purposeful muscular movements. [C19: via NL from Gk: inactivity, from A-¹ + praxis action]

après-ski (ˌæpreɪ'skiː) n **a** a social activity following a day's skiing. **b** (as modifier): an après-ski outfit. [F, lit.: after ski]

apricot ('eɪprɪˌkɒt) n **1** a tree native to Africa and W Asia, but widely cultivated for its edible fruit. **2** the yellow juicy fruit of this tree, which resembles a small peach.

> ★ people and places

[C16: from Port., from Ar., from LGk, from L *praecox* early-ripening]

April ('eɪprəl) *n* the fourth month of the year, consisting of 30 days. [C14: from L *Aprīlis*]

April fool *n* a victim of a practical joke performed on the first of April (**April Fools' Day** *or* **All Fools' Day**).

a priori (eɪ praɪ'ɔːraɪ, ɑː prɪ'ɔːrɪ) *adj* **1** *Logic*. relating to or involving deductive reasoning from a general principle to the expected facts or effects. **2** known to be true independently of experience of the subject matter. [C18: from L, lit.: from the previous]
▸ **apriority** (,eɪpraɪ'ɒrɪtɪ) *n*

apron ('eɪprən) *n* **1** a protective or sometimes decorative garment worn over the front of the body and tied around the waist. **2** the part of a stage extending in front of the curtain. **3** a hard-surfaced area in front of an aircraft hangar, terminal building, etc. **4** a continuous conveyor belt composed of metal slats. **5** a protective plate screening the operator of a machine, artillery piece, etc. **6** *Geol*. a sheet of sand, gravel, etc., deposited at the front of a moraine. **7** another name for **skirt** (sense 3). **8** **tied to someone's apron strings.** dominated by someone, esp. a mother or wife. ◆ *vb* **9** (*tr*) to protect or provide with an apron. [C16: mistaken division of *a napron*, from OF, from L *mappa* napkin]

apron stage *n* a stage that projects into the auditorium so that the audience sits on three sides of it.

apropos (,æprə'pəʊ) *adj* **1** appropriate. ◆ *adv* **2** appropriately. **3** by the way; incidentally. **4** **apropos of.** (*prep*) in respect of. [C17: from F *à propos* to the purpose]

apse (æps) *n* a domed or vaulted semicircular or polygonal recess, esp. at the east end of a church. Also called: **apsis**. [C19: from L *apsis*, from Gk: a fitting together, from *haptein* to fasten]
▸ **'apsidal** *adj*

apsis ('æpsɪs) *n, pl* **apsides** (æp'saɪdiːz). either of two points lying at the extremities of an eccentric orbit of a planet, satellite, etc. Also called: **apse**. [C17: via L from Gk; see APSE]
▸ **apsidal** ('æpsɪd°l) *adj*

apt (æpt) *adj* **1** suitable; appropriate. **2** (*postpositive; foll. by an infinitive*) having a tendency (to behave as specified). **3** having the ability to learn and understand easily. [C14: from L *aptus* fitting, from *apere* to fasten]
▸ **'aptly** *adv* ▸ **'aptness** *n*

APT *abbrev. for* Advanced Passenger Train.

apterous ('æptərəs) *adj* **1** (of insects) without wings, as silverfish. **2** without winglike expansions, as some seeds and fruits. [C18: from Gk, from A-¹ + *pteron* wing]
▸ **'apter,ism** *n*

apteryx ('æptərɪks) *n* another name for **kiwi** (the bird). [C19: from NL; see APTEROUS]

aptitude ('æptɪ,tjuːd) *n* **1** inherent or acquired ability. **2** ease in learning or understanding. **3** the quality of being apt. [C15: via OF from LL, from L *aptus* APT]

Apuleius ★ (,æpjʊ'liːəs) *n* **Lucius** ('luːsɪəs). 2nd century A.D., Roman writer, noted for his romance *The Golden Ass*.

Apulia ★ (ə'pjuːljə) *n* a region of SE Italy, on the Adriatic. Capital: Bari. Pop.: 4 065 603 (1994 est.). Area: 19 223 sq. km (7422 sq. miles). Italian name: **Puglia**.

Aqaba *or* **Akaba** ★ ('ækəbə) *n* the only port in Jordan, in the southwest, on the **Gulf of Aqaba**. Pop.: 46 090 (1990 est.).

Aqtöbe ★ (æk'tjuːbɪ; *Kazakh* ɑktø'be) *n* an industrial city in W Kazakhstan. Pop.: 258 900 (1995 est.). Former name (until 1991): **Aktyubinsk**.

aqua ('ækwə) *n, pl* **aquae** ('ækwiː) *or* **aquas**. **1** water: used in compound names of certain liquid substances or solutions of substances in water. ◆ *n, adj* **2** short for **aquamarine** (the colour). [L: water]

aquaculture ('ækwə,kʌltʃə) *or* **aquiculture** *n* the cultivation of freshwater and marine organisms for human consumption or use.

aquaerobics *or* **aquarobics** (,ækwə'rəʊbɪks) *n* (*functioning as sing*) the practice of exercising to music in a swimming pool. [C20: from L *aqua* water + AEROBICS]

aqua fortis ('fɔːtɪs) *n* an obsolete name for **nitric acid**. [C17: from L, lit.: strong water]

aqualung ('ækwə,lʌŋ) *n* breathing apparatus used by divers, etc., consisting of a mouthpiece attached to air cylinders strapped to the back.

aquamarine (,ækwəmə'riːn) *n* **1** a pale greenish-blue transparent variety of beryl used as a gemstone. **2a** a pale blue to greenish-blue colour. **2b** (*as adj*): *an aquamarine dress*. [C19: from NL, from L: sea water (referring to the gem's colour)]

aquanaut ('ækwənɔːt) *n* a person who works, swims, or dives underwater. [C20: from AQUA + *-naut*, as in ASTRONAUT]

aquaplane ('ækwə,pleɪn) *n* **1** a board on which a person stands and is towed by a motorboat. ◆ *vb* **aquaplanes, aquaplaning, aquaplaned.** (*intr*) **2** to ride on an aquaplane. **3** (of a motor vehicle travelling at high speeds on wet roads) to rise up onto a thin film of water so that contact with the road is lost.

aqua regia ('riːdʒɪə) *n* a mixture of nitric acid and hydrochloric acid. [C17: from NL: royal water; referring to its use in dissolving gold, the royal metal]

aquarist ('ækwərɪst) *n* **1** the curator of an aquarium. **2** a person who studies aquatic life.

aquarium (ə'kweərɪəm) *n, pl* **aquariums** *or* **aquaria** (-rɪə). **1** a tank, bowl, or pool in which aquatic animals and plants are kept for pleasure, study, or exhibition. **2** a building housing a collection of aquatic life, as for exhibition. [C19: from L *aquārius* relating to water, on the model of VIVARIUM]

Aquarius (ə'kweərɪəs) *n, Latin genitive* **Aquarii** (ə'kweərɪ,aɪ). **1** *Astron*. a S constellation. **2** *Astrol*. also called: the **Water Carrier**. the eleventh sign of the zodiac. The sun is in this sign between about Jan. 20 and Feb. 18. [L]

aquatic (ə'kwætɪk) *adj* **1** growing, living, or found in water. **2** *Sport*. performed in or on water. ◆ *n* **3** a marine animal or plant. [C15: from L *aquāticus*, from *aqua* water]

aquatics (ə'kwætɪks) *pl n* sports or pastimes performed in or on the water.

aquatint ('ækwə,tɪnt) *n* **1** a technique of etching copper with acid to produce an effect resembling watercolour. **2** an etching made in this way. ◆ *vb* **3** (*tr*) to etch (a block, etc.) in aquatint. [C18: from It. *acqua tinta* dyed water]

aquavit ('ækwə,vɪt) *n* a grain- or potato-based spirit flavoured with aromatic seeds. Also called: **akvavit**. [of Scandinavian origin: see AQUA VITAE]

aqua vitae ('viːtaɪ, 'vaɪtiː) *n* an archaic name for **brandy**. [Med. L: water of life]

aqueduct ('ækwɪ,dʌkt) *n* **1** a conduit used to convey water over a long distance. **2** a structure, often a bridge, that carries such a conduit or a canal across a valley or river. **3** a channel or conduit in the body. [C16: from L *aquaeductus*, from *aqua* water + *dūcere* to convey]

aqueous ('eɪkwɪəs) *adj* **1** of, like, or containing water. **2** dissolved in water: *aqueous ammonia*. **3** (of rocks, etc.) formed from material laid down in water. [C17: from Med. L *aqueus*, from L *aqua* water]

aqueous humour *n Physiol.* the watery fluid within the eyeball between the cornea and the lens.

aquiculture ('eɪkwɪ,kʌltʃə, 'ækwɪ-) *n* **1** another name for **hydroponics. 2** a variant of **aquaculture.**
▸ **'aqui,culturist** *n* ▸ **'aqui,cultural** *adj*

aquifer ('ækwɪfə) *n* a deposit or rock, such as a sandstone, containing water that can be tapped to supply wells.

Aquila ('ækwɪlə; *Italian* 'aːkwila) *or* **l'Aquila** ★ *n* a city in central Italy, capital of Abruzzi region. Pop.: 67 820 (1990). Official name: **Aquila degli Abruzzi** ('deʎʎi a'bruttsi).

aquilegia (,ækwɪ'liːdʒɪə) *n* another name for **columbine**. [C19: from Med. L, from ?]

aquiline ('ækwɪ,laɪn) *adj* **1** (of a nose) having the curved shape of an eagle's beak. **2** of or like an eagle. [C17: from L, from *aquila* eagle]

Aquinas ★ (ə'kwaɪnəs) *n* **Saint Thomas**. 1225–74, Italian theologian, scholastic philosopher, and Dominican friar, whose works include *Summa contra Gentiles* (1259–64) and *Summa Theologiae* (1267–73). Feast day: Jan. 28. See also **Thomism**.

Aquino ★ (əˈkiːnəu) *n* **Corazón**, known as **Cory**. born 1933, Philippine stateswoman: president (1986–92).

Aquitaine ★ (ˌækwɪˈteɪn; *French* akitɛn) *n* a region of SW France, on the Bay of Biscay: a former Roman province and medieval duchy. It is generally flat in the west, rising to the slopes of the Massif Central in the northeast and the Pyrenees in the south; mainly agricultural. Ancient name: **Aquitania** (ˌækwɪˈteɪnɪə).

Ar *the chemical symbol for* argon.

ar. *abbrev. for:* **1** arrival. **2** arrive(s).

Ar. *abbrev. for:* **1** Arabia(n). **2** Also: **Ar** Arabic. **3** Aramaic.

a.r. *abbrev. for* anno regni. [L: in the year of the reign]

-ar *suffix forming adjectives.* of; belonging to; like: *linear; polar.* [via OF *-er* from L *-āris*]

ARA *abbrev. for:* **1** (in Britain) Associate of the Royal Academy. **2** (in New Zealand) Auckland Regional Authority.

Arab (ˈærəb) *n* **1** a member of a Semitic people originally inhabiting Arabia. **2** a small breed of horse, used for riding. **3** (*modifier*) of or relating to the Arabs. [C14: from L, from Gk *Araps*, from Ar. *'Arab*]

arabesque (ˌærəˈbɛsk) *n* **1** *Ballet.* a classical position in which the dancer has one leg raised behind. **2** *Music.* a piece or movement with a highly ornamented melody. **3** *Arts.* a type of curvilinear decoration in painting, metalwork, etc., with intricate intertwining designs. [C18: from F, from It. *arabesco* in the Arabic style]

Arabia ★ (əˈreɪbɪə) *n* a great peninsula of SW Asia, between the Red Sea and the Persian Gulf: consists chiefly of a desert plateau, with mountains rising over 3000 m (10 000 ft) in the west and scattered oases; includes the present-day countries of Saudi Arabia, Yemen, Oman, Bahrain, Qatar, Kuwait, and the United Arab Emirates. Area: about 2 600 000 sq. km (1 000 000 sq. miles).

Arabian (əˈreɪbɪən) *adj* **1** of or relating to Arabia or the Arabs. ◆ *n* **2** another word for **Arab**.

Arabian camel *n* a domesticated camel with one hump on its back, used as a beast of burden in the deserts of N Africa and SW Asia.

Arabian Desert ★ *n* **1** a desert in E Egypt, between the Nile, the Gulf of Suez, and the Red Sea: mountainous parts rise over 1800 m (6000 ft). Area: about 220 000 sq. km (85 000 sq. miles). **2** a desert, mainly in Saudi Arabia, that forms the desert area of the Arabian Peninsula, esp. in the north. Area: about 2 330 000 sq. km (900 000 sq. miles).

Arabian Sea ★ *n* the NW part of the Indian Ocean, between Arabia and India.

Arabic (ˈærəbɪk) *n* **1** the Semitic language of the Arabs, which has its own alphabet and is spoken in Algeria, Egypt, Iraq, Jordan, Saudi Arabia, Syria, Tunisia, etc. ◆ *adj* **2** denoting or relating to this language, any of the peoples that speak it, or the countries in which it is spoken.

arabica bean (əˈræbɪkə) *n* a high-quality coffee bean, obtained from the tree *Coffea arabica*.

Arabic numeral *n* one of the numbers 0, 1, 2, 3, 4, 5, 6, 7, 8, 9. Cf. **Roman numerals**.

arabis (ˈærəbɪs) *n* any of several trailing plants having pink or white flowers in spring. Also called: **rock cress**. [C16: from Med. L, from Gk *arabis*, ult. from *Arābios* Arabian, prob. from growing in sandy or stony soil]

Arabist (ˈærəbɪst) *n* a student of Arabic culture, language, history, etc.

arable (ˈærəbəl) *adj* **1** (of land) being or capable of being tilled for the production of crops. **2** of, relating to, or using such land. [C15: from L *arābilis*, from *arāre* to plough]

Araby ★ (ˈærəbɪ) *n* an archaic or poetic name for Arabia.

Aracajú ★ (*Portuguese* ərəkəˈʒu) *n* a port in E Brazil, capital of Sergipe state. Pop.: 401 676 (1991).

Arachne ★ (əˈræknɪ) *n Greek myth.* a maiden changed into a spider for having presumptuously challenged Athena to a weaving contest. [from Gk *arakhnē* spider]

arachnid (əˈræknɪd) *n* any of a class of arthropods characterized by simple eyes and four pairs of legs, including the spiders, scorpions, and ticks. [C19: from NL *Arachnida*, from Gk *arakhnē* spider]
▶ a**'rachnidan** *adj, n*

arachnoid (əˈræknɔɪd) *n* **1** the middle one of three membranes that cover the brain and spinal cord. ◆ *ad,* **2** of or relating to this membrane. **3** *Bot.* consisting of or covered with soft fine hairs or fibres.

arachnophobia (əˌræknəˈfəubɪə) *n* an abnormal fear of spiders. [C20: from Gk *arakhnē* + -PHOBIA]

Arafat ★ (ˈærəfæt) *n* **Yasser** (ˈjæsə). born 1929, Palestinian leader; cofounder of Al Fatah (1956); leader of the Palestine Liberation Organization from 1969 and chairman of the Palestine National Authority from 1994; shared Nobel peace prize 1994.

Arafura Sea ★ (ˌærəˈfuərə) *n* a part of the W Pacific Ocean, between N Australia and SW New Guinea.

Aragats ★ (*Russian* ˌaraˈgats) *n* **Mount.** a volcanic mountain in NW Armenia. Height: 4090 m (13 419 ft). Turkish name: **Alagez**.

Aragon[1] ★ (ˈærəgən) *n* an autonomous region of NE Spain: independent kingdom from the 11th century until 1479, when it was united with Castile to form modern Spain. Pop.: 1 183 576 (1994 est.). Area: 47 609 sq. km (18 382 sq. miles).
▶ **Aragonese** (ˌærəgəˈniːz) *n, adj*

Aragon[2] ★ (*French* aragɔ̃) *n* **Louis** (lwi). 1897–1982, French writer. His works include the verse collections *Le Crève-Coeur* (1941) and *Les Yeux d'Elsa* (1942) and the series of novels *Le Monde réel* (1933–51).

Araguaia or **Araguaya** ★ (ˌɑːrəˈgwaɪə) *n* a river in central Brazil, rising in S Mato Grosso state and flowing north to the Tocantins River. Length: over 1771 km (1100 miles).

arak (ˈærək) *n* a variant spelling of **arrack**.

Arakan Yoma ★ (ˌɑːrɑːˈkɑːn ˈjəumɑː) *n* a mountain range in Myanmar, between the Irrawaddy River and the W coast: forms a barrier between Myanmar and India. teak forests.

Araks (aˈraks) *n* the Russian name for the **Aras**.

Araldite (ˈærəldaɪt) *n Trademark.* an epoxy resin used as a glue for mending glass, plastic, and china.

Aral Sea ★ (ˈærəl) *n* a lake in Kazakhstan and Uzbekistan, east of the Caspian Sea, formerly the fourth largest lake in the world: shallow and saline, now badly polluted. Use of its source waters for irrigation led to a loss of 40% of its area between 1967 and 1987. Area: about 64 750 sq. km (25 000 sq. miles). Also called: **Lake Aral**.

Aram ★ (ˈɛəræm, -rəm) *n* the biblical name for ancient Syria.
▶ **Aramaean** or **Aramean** (ˌærəˈmiːən) *adj, n*

Aram. *abbrev. for* Aramaic.

Aramaic (ˌærəˈmeɪɪk) *n* **1** an ancient Semitic language of the Middle East, still spoken in parts of Syria and the Lebanon. ◆ *adj* **2** of, relating to, or using this language.

Aran (ˈærən) *adj* **1** of or relating to the Aran Islands. **2** made of thick natural wool: *an Aran sweater*.

Aran Islands ★ *pl n* a group of three islands in the Atlantic, off the W coast of the Republic of Ireland: Aranmore or Inishmore (the largest), Inishmaan, and Inisheer. Pop.: 1000 (latest est.). Area: 46 sq. km (18 sq. miles).

Ararat ★ (ˈærəˌræt) *n* an extinct volcanic mountain massif in E Turkey: two main peaks; **Great Ararat** 5155 m (16 916 ft), said to be the resting place of Noah's Ark after the Flood (Genesis 8:4), and **Little Ararat** 3914 m (12 843 ft).

Aras ★ (æˈræs) *n* a river rising in Turkish Armenia and flowing east to the Caspian Sea: forms part of the E border of Turkey and the N border of Iran. Length: about 1100 km (660 miles). Ancient name: **Araxes**. Russian name: **Araks**.

★ people and places

Araucania ★ (ˌærɔːˈkeɪnɪə; *Spanish* arauˈkanja) *n* a region of central Chile, inhabited by Araucanian Indians.
▶ ˌArauˈcanian *adj, n*

araucaria (ˌærɔːˈkɛərɪə) *n* any of a group of coniferous trees of South America, Australia, and Polynesia, such as the monkey puzzle. [C19: from NL (*arbor*) *Araucaria* (tree) from *Arauco,* a province in Chile]

arbalest *or* **arbalist** (ˈɑːbəlɪst) *n* a large medieval crossbow, usually cocked by mechanical means. [C11: from OF, from LL *arcuballista,* from L *arcus* bow + BALLISTA]

Arbela ★ (ɑːˈbiːlə) *n* an ancient city in Assyria, near which the **Battle of Arbela** took place (331 B.C.), in which Alexander the Great defeated the Persians. Modern name: **Erbil**.

Arber ★ (ˈɑːbə) *n* **Werner** (ˈvɛːnə). born 1929, Swiss microbiologist, noted for his work on restriction enzymes. Nobel prize for physiology or medicine 1978.

Arbil ★ (ˈɑːbɪl) *n* a variant spelling of **Erbil**.

arbiter (ˈɑːbɪtə) *n* **1** a person empowered to judge in a dispute; referee. **2** a person having control of something. [C15: from L, from ?]
▶ ˈarbitress *fem n*

arbitrament (ɑːˈbɪtrəmənt) *n* **1** the decision or award made by an arbitrator upon a disputed matter. **2** another word for **arbitration**.

arbitrary (ˈɑːbɪtrərɪ) *adj* **1** founded on or subject to personal whims, prejudices, etc. **2** not absolute. **3** (of a government, ruler, etc.) despotic or dictatorial. **4** *Law.* (esp. of a penalty) within the court's discretion. [C15: from L *arbitrārius* arranged through arbitration]
▶ ˈarbitrarily *adv* ▶ ˈarbitrariness *n*

arbitrate (ˈɑːbɪˌtreɪt) *vb* **arbitrates, arbitrating, arbitrated. 1** to achieve a settlement between parties. **2** to submit to or settle by arbitration. [C16: from L *arbitrāri* to give judgment]
▶ ˈarbiˌtrator *n*

arbitration (ˌɑːbɪˈtreɪʃən) *n* the hearing and determination of a dispute, esp. an industrial one, by an impartial referee selected or agreed upon by the parties concerned.

Arblay, d' ★ (ˈdɑːbleɪ; *French* darblɛ) *n* **Madame.** the married name of (Fanny) **Burney**.

arbor[1] (ˈɑːbə) *n* the US spelling of **arbour**.

arbor[2] (ˈɑːbə) *n* **1** a rotating shaft in a machine on which a milling cutter or grinding wheel is fitted. **2** a rotating shaft. [C17: from L: tree]

arboraceous (ˌɑːbəˈreɪʃəs) *adj Literary.* **1** resembling a tree. **2** wooded.

arboreal (ɑːˈbɔːrɪəl) *adj* **1** of or resembling a tree. **2** living in or among trees.

arborescent (ˌɑːbəˈrɛsᵊnt) *adj* having the shape or characteristics of a tree.
▶ ˌarboˈrescence *n*

arboretum (ˌɑːbəˈriːtəm) *n, pl* **arboreta** (-tə) *or* **arboretums.** a place where trees or shrubs are cultivated. [C19: from L, from *arbor* tree]

arboriculture (ˈɑːbərɪˌkʌltʃə) *n* the cultivation of trees or shrubs.
▶ ˌarboriˈculturist *n*

arbor vitae (ˈɑːbɔː ˈviːtaɪ, ˈvaɪtiː) *n* any of several Asian and North American evergreen coniferous trees having tiny scalelike leaves and egglike cones. [C17: from NL, lit.: tree of life]

arbour (ˈɑːbə) *n* a leafy glade or bower shaded by trees, vines, shrubs, etc. [C14 *erber,* from OF, from L *herba* grass]

Arbroath ★ (ɑːˈbrəʊθ) *n* a port and resort in E Scotland, in Angus council area: scene of the barons of Scotland's declaration of independence to Pope John XXII in 1320. Pop.: 23 474 (1991).

Arbus ★ (ˈɑːbəs) *n* **Diane,** original name *Diane Nemerov.* 1923–71, US photographer.

Arbuthnot ★ (ɑːˈbʌθnɒt) *n* **John.** 1667–1735, Scottish physician and satirist: author of *The History of John Bull* (1712) and, with others, of the *Memoirs of Martinus Scriblerus* (1741).

arbutus (ɑːˈbjuːtəs) *n, pl* **arbutuses.** any of a genus of

shrubs having clusters of white or pinkish flowers, broad evergreen leaves, and strawberry-like berries. [C16: from L; rel. to *arbor* tree]

arc (ɑːk) *n* **1** something curved in shape. **2** part of an unbroken curved line. **3** a luminous discharge that occurs when an electric current flows between two electrodes separated by a small gap. **4** *Maths.* a section of a curve, graph, or geometric figure. ◆ *vb* **arcs, arcing, arced** *or* **arcs, arcking, arcked.** *5 (intr)* to form an arc. ◆ *adj* **6** *Maths.* specifying an inverse trigonometric function: *arcsin, arccos, arctan.* [C14: from OF, from L *arcus* bow, arch]

ARC *abbrev. for* AIDS-related complex: a condition in which a person infected with the AIDS virus suffers from relatively mild symptoms, such as loss of weight, fever, etc.

arcade (ɑːˈkeɪd) *n* **1** a set of arches and their supporting columns. **2** a covered and sometimes arched passageway, usually with shops on one or both sides. [C18: from F, from It. *arcata,* from L *arcus* bow, arch]

Arcadia ★ (ɑːˈkeɪdɪə) *n* **1** a department of Greece, in the central Peloponnese. Capital: Tripolis. Pop.: 105 309 (1991). Area: 4367 sq. km (1686 sq. miles). **2** *Also called* (*poetic*): **Arcady** (ˈɑːkədɪ). the traditional idealized rural setting of Greek and Roman bucolic poetry and later in the literature of the Renaissance.

Arcadian (ɑːˈkeɪdɪən) *adj* **1** of the idealized Arcadia of pastoral poetry. **2** rustic or bucolic. ◆ *n* **3** a person who leads a quiet simple rural life.
▶ Arˈcadianism *n*

arcane (ɑːˈkeɪn) *adj* requiring secret knowledge to be understood; esoteric. [C16: from L *arcānus* secret, from *arcēre* to keep safe]

arcanum (ɑːˈkeɪnəm) *n, pl* **arcana** (-nə). (*sometimes pl*) a secret or mystery. [C16: from L; see ARCANE]

Arc de Triomphe ★ (ˈɑːk də ˈtriːəʊmf; *French* ark də trijɔ̃f) *n* the triumphal arch in Paris begun by Napoleon I to commemorate his victories of 1805–6 and completed in 1836.

arch[1] (ɑːtʃ) *n* **1** a curved structure that spans an opening. **2** *Also called:* **archway.** a structure in the form of an arch that serves as a gateway. **3** something curved like an arch. **4** any of various parts or structures of the body having a curved or archlike outline, such as the raised vault formed by the tarsal and metatarsal bones (**arch of the foot**). ◆ *vb* **5** *(tr)* to span (an opening) with an arch. **6** to form or cause to form an arch or a curve resembling that of an arch. **7** *(tr)* to span or extend over. [C14: from OF *arche,* from L *arcus* bow, ARC]

arch[2] (ɑːtʃ) *adj* **1** (*prenominal*) chief; principal; leading. **2** (*prenominal*) expert: *an arch criminal.* **3** knowing or superior; coyly playful: *an arch look.* [C16: independent use of ARCH-]
▶ ˈarchly *adv* ▶ ˈarchness *n*

arch. *abbrev. for:* **1** archaic. **2** archaism. **3** archipelago. **4** architect. **5** architectural. **6** architecture.

arch- *or* **archi-** *combining form.* **1** chief; principal: *archbishop.* **2** eminent above all others of the same kind: *archenemy.* [ult. from Gk *arkhi-,* from *arkhein* to rule]

-arch *n combining form.* leader; ruler; chief: *patriarch; monarch.* [from Gk *arkhēs,* from *arkhein* to rule]

Archaean *or esp. US* **Archean** (ɑːˈkiːən) *adj* of the metamorphosed rocks formed in the early Precambrian era.

archaeology *or* **archeology** (ˌɑːkɪˈɒlədʒɪ) *n* the study of man's past by scientific analysis of the material remains of his cultures. [C17: from LL, from Gk *arkhaiologia* study of what is ancient, from *arkhē* beginning]
▶ archaeological *or* archeological (ˌɑːkɪəˈlɒdʒɪkᵊl) *adj* ▶ ˌarchaeˈologist *or* ˌarcheˈologist *n*

archaeopteryx (ˌɑːkɪˈɒptərɪks) *n* any of several extinct primitive birds which occurred in Jurassic times and had teeth, a long tail, and well-developed wings. [C19: from Gk *arkhaios* ancient + *pterux* winged creature]

archaic (ɑːˈkeɪɪk) *adj* **1** belonging to or characteristic of a much earlier period. **2** out of date; antiquated. **3** (of vocabulary, etc.) characteristic of an earlier period of a lan-

guage. [C19: from F, from Gk *arkhaïkos*, from *arkhaios* ancient, from *arkhē* beginning, from *arkhein* to begin]
▶ ar'chaically *adv*

archaism ('ɑːkeɪˌɪzəm) *n* **1** the adoption or imitation of archaic words or style. **2** an archaic word, style, etc. [C17: from NL, from Gk, from *arkhaizein* to model one's style upon that of ancient writers; see ARCHAIC]
▶ 'archaist *n* ▶ ˌarcha'istic *adj*

archangel ('ɑːkˌeɪndʒəl) *n* a principal angel.
▶ archangelic (ˌɑːkæn'dʒɛlɪk) *adj*

Archangel ★ ('ɑːkˌeɪndʒəl) *n* a port in NW Russia, on the Dvina River: major centre for the timber trade and White Sea fisheries. Pop.: 374 000 (1995 est.). Russian name: **Arkhangelsk**.

archbishop ('ɑːtʃ'bɪʃəp) *n* a bishop of the highest rank. Abbrev.: **abp, Abp, Arch., Archbp.**

archbishopric ('ɑːtʃ'bɪʃəprɪk) *n* the rank, office, or jurisdiction of an archbishop.

archdeacon ('ɑːtʃ'diːkən) *n* **1** an Anglican clergyman ranking just below a bishop. **2** a clergyman of similar rank in other Churches.
▶ 'arch'deaconry *n*

archdiocese (ˌɑːtʃ'daɪəˌsiːs) *n* the diocese of an archbishop.
▶ archdiocesan (ˌɑːtʃdaɪ'ɒsɪsᵊn) *adj*

archducal ('ɑːtʃ'djuːkᵊl) *adj* of or relating to an archduke, archduchess, or archduchy.

archduchess ('ɑːtʃ'dʌtʃɪs) *n* **1** the wife or widow of an archduke. **2** (since 1453) a princess of the Austrian imperial family.

archduchy ('ɑːtʃ'dʌtʃɪ) *n, pl* **archduchies**. the territory ruled by an archduke or archduchess.

archduke ('ɑːtʃ'djuːk) *n* a chief duke, esp. (since 1453) a prince of the Austrian imperial dynasty.

Archean (ɑː'kiːən) *adj* a variant spelling (esp. US) of **Archaean**.

archegonium (ˌɑːkɪ'gəʊnɪəm) *n, pl* **archegonia** (-nɪə). a female sex organ, occurring in mosses, ferns, etc. [C19: from NL, from Gk, from *arkhe*- chief, first + *gonos* seed, race]

archenemy ('ɑːtʃ'ɛnɪmɪ) *n, pl* **archenemies**. **1** a chief enemy. **2** (*often cap.*; preceded by *the*) the devil.

archeology (ˌɑːkɪ'ɒlədʒɪ) *n* a variant of **archaeology**.

archer ('ɑːtʃə) *n* a person skilled in the use of a bow and arrow. [C13: from OF, from LL, from L *arcus* bow]

Archer[1] ('ɑːtʃə) *n* **the**. the constellation Sagittarius.

Archer[2] ★ ('ɑːtʃə) *n* **1** Frederick Scott. 1813–57, British inventor and sculptor. He developed (1851) the wet collodion photographic process, enabling multiple copies of pictures to be made. **2** Jeffrey (Howard), Baron Archer of Weston-Super-Mare. born 1940, British novelist and Conservative politician; MP from 1969 until 1974. His works include *Kane and Abel* (1979) and *The Fourth Estate* (1996). **3** William. 1856–1924, Scottish critic and dramatist: made the first English translations of Ibsen.

archerfish ('ɑːtʃəˌfɪʃ) *n, pl* **archerfish** or **archerfishes**. a freshwater fish, related to the perch, of SE Asia and Australia, that catches insects by spitting water at them.

archery ('ɑːtʃərɪ) *n* **1** the art or sport of shooting with bows and arrows. **2** archers or their weapons collectively.

archetype ('ɑːkɪˌtaɪp) *n* **1** a perfect or typical specimen. **2** an original model; prototype. **3** *Psychoanal.* one of the inherited mental images postulated by Jung. **4** a recurring symbol or motif in literature, etc. [C17: from L *archetypum* an original, from Gk, from *arkhetupos* first-moulded; see ARCH-, -TYPE]
▶ ˌarche'typal *adj*

archfiend ('ɑːtʃ'fiːnd) *n* (*often cap.*) **the**. the devil; Satan.

archidiaconal (ˌɑːkɪdaɪ'ækənᵊl) *adj* of or relating to an archdeacon or his office.
▶ ˌarchidi'aconate *n*

archiepiscopal (ˌɑːkɪɪ'pɪskəpᵊl) *adj* of or associated with an archbishop.
▶ ˌarchie'piscopate *n*

archil ('ɑːtʃɪl) *n* a variant of **orchil**.

archimandrite (ˌɑːkɪ'mændraɪt) *n* *Greek Orthodox Church*. the head of a monastery. [C16: from LL, from LGk *arkhimandritēs*, from ARCHI- + *mandra* monastery]

Archimedes ★ (ˌɑːkɪ'miːdiːz) *n* ?287–212 B.C., Greek mathematician of Syracuse, noted for his work in geometry, hydrostatics, and mechanics.
▶ ˌArchi'medean *adj*

Archimedes' principle *n* a law of physics stating that the apparent loss in weight of a body immersed in a fluid is equal to the weight of the displaced fluid.

Archimedes' screw or **Archimedean screw** *n* an ancient water-lifting device using a spiral passage in an inclined cylinder.

archipelago (ˌɑːkɪ'pɛləˌgəʊ) *n, pl* **archipelagos** or **archipelagoes**. **1** a group of islands. **2** a sea studded with islands. [C16 (meaning: the Aegean Sea): from It., from L *pelagus*, from Gk, from ARCH- + *pelagos* sea]
▶ archipelagic (ˌɑːkɪpɪ'lædʒɪk) *adj*

architect ('ɑːkɪˌtɛkt) *n* **1** a person qualified to design buildings and to supervise their erection. **2** a person similarly qualified in another form of construction: *a naval architect*. **3** any planner or creator. [C16: from F, from L, from Gk *arkhitektōn* director of works, from ARCHI- + *tektōn* workman; rel. to *tekhnē* art, skill]

architectonic (ˌɑːkɪtɛk'tɒnɪk) *adj* **1** denoting, relating to, or having architectural qualities. **2** *Metaphysics*. of the systematic classification of knowledge. [C16: from LL *architectonicus* concerning architecture; see ARCHITECT]

architectonics (ˌɑːkɪtɛk'tɒnɪks) *n* (*functioning as sing*) **1** the science of architecture. **2** *Metaphysics*. the scientific classification of knowledge.

architecture ('ɑːkɪˌtɛktʃə) *n* **1** the art and science of designing and superintending the erection of buildings, etc. **2** a style of building or structure. **3** buildings or structures collectively. **4** the structure or design of anything.
▶ ˌarchi'tectural *adj*

architrave ('ɑːkɪˌtreɪv) *n* *Archit.* **1** the lowest part of an entablature that bears on the columns. **2** a moulding around a doorway, window opening, etc. [C16: via F from It., from ARCHI- + *trave* beam, from L *trabs*]

archive ('ɑːkaɪv) *n* (*often pl*) **1** a collection of records of an institution, family, etc. **2** a place where such records are kept. **3** *Computing*. data transferred to a tape or disk for long-term storage rather than frequent use. ◆ *vb* (*tr*) to store (documents, data, etc.) in an archive or other repository. [C17: from LL, from Gk *arkheion* repository of official records, from *arkhē* government]
▶ ar'chival *adj*

archivist ('ɑːkɪvɪst) *n* a person in charge of archives.

archon ('ɑːkɒn) *n* (in ancient Athens) one of the nine chief magistrates. [C17: from Gk *arkhōn* ruler, from *arkhein* to rule]
▶ 'archonˌship *n*

archpriest ('ɑːtʃ'priːst) *n* **1** (formerly) a chief assistant to a bishop. **2** a senior priest.

archway ('ɑːtʃˌweɪ) *n* a passageway or entrance under an arch or arches.

-archy *n combining form*. government; rule: *anarchy; monarchy*. [from Gk *-arkhia*; see -ARCH]

arc light *n* a light source in which an arc between two electrodes produces intense white illumination. Also called: **arc lamp**.

arctic ('ɑːktɪk) *adj* **1** of or relating to the Arctic. **2** *Inf.* cold; freezing. ◆ *n* **3** (*modifier*) suitable for conditions of extreme cold: *arctic clothing*. [C14: from L *arcticus*, from Gk *arktikos* northern, lit.: pertaining to (the constellation of) the Bear, from *arktos* bear]

Arctic ★ ('ɑːktɪk) *n* **1** **the**. Also called: **Arctic Zone**. the regions north of the Arctic Circle. ◆ *adj* **2** of or relating to the regions north of the Arctic Circle.

Arctic Circle *n* the imaginary circle round the earth, parallel to the equator, at latitude 66° 32′ N.

arctic hare *n* a large hare of the Canadian Arctic whose fur is white in winter.

Arctic Ocean ★ *n* the ocean surrounding the North Pole, north of the Arctic Circle. Area: about 14 100 000 sq. km (5 440 000 sq. miles).

★ people and places

arctic willow *n.* a low-growing shrub of the Canadian tundra.

Arcturus (ɑːkˈtjʊərəs) *n* the brightest star in the constellation Boötes: a red giant. [C14: from L, from Gk *Arktouros*, from *arktos* bear + *ouros* guard, keeper]

arcuate (ˈɑːkjʊɪt) *adj* shaped or bent like an arc or bow. [C17: from L *arcuāre*, from *arcus* ARC]

arc welding *n* a technique in which metal is welded by heat generated by an electric arc.
▶ **arc welder** *n*

-ard or **-art** *suffix forming nouns.* indicating a person who does something, esp. to excess: *braggart; drunkard.* [via OF, of Gmc origin]

Ardèche ★ *(French* ardɛʃ) *n* a department of S France, in Rhône-Alpes region. Capital: Privas. Pop.: 282 432 (1994 est.). Area: 5556 sq. km (2167 sq. miles).

Arden[1] ★ (ˈɑːdᵊn) *n* **Forest of.** a region of N Warwickshire, part of a former forest: scene of Shakespeare's *As You Like It.*

Arden[2] ★ (ˈɑːdᵊn) *n* **John.** born 1930, British dramatist and novelist. His plays include *Serjeant Musgrave's Dance* (1959), *The Workhouse Donkey* (1963), and *A Suburban Suicide* (1994): often works with Margaretta D'Arcy.

Ardennes ★ (ɑːˈdɛn; *French* arden) *n* **1** a department of NE France, in Champagne-Ardenne region. Capital: Mézières. Pop.: 292 642 (1994 est.). Area: 5253 sq. km (2049 sq. miles). **2 the.** a wooded plateau in SE Belgium, Luxembourg, and NE France: scene of heavy fighting in both World Wars.

ardent (ˈɑːdᵊnt) *adj* **1** expressive of or characterized by intense desire or emotion. **2** intensely enthusiastic; eager. **3** glowing or shining: *ardent eyes.* **4 ardent spirits.** alcoholic drinks. [C14: from L *ārdēre* to burn]
▶ **'ardency** *n* ▶ **'ardently** *adv*

ardour or US **ardor** (ˈɑːdə) *n* **1** feelings of great intensity and warmth. **2** eagerness; zeal. [C14: from OF, from L *ārdor*, from *ārdēre* to burn]

Ards ★ (ɑːdz) *n* a district of E Northern Ireland, on the Irish Sea and Strangford Lough: agriculture. Administrative centre: Newtownards. Pop.: 64 764 (1991). Area: 361 sq. km (139 sq. miles).

arduous (ˈɑːdjuːəs) *adj* **1** difficult to accomplish; strenuous. **2** hard to endure; harsh. **3** steep or difficult: *an arduous track.* [C16: from L *arduus* steep, difficult]
▶ **'arduously** *adv* ▶ **'arduousness** *n*

are[1] (ɑː; *unstressed* ə) *vb* the plural form of the present tense of **be** and the singular form used with *you.* [OE *aron*, second person pl of *bēon* to BE]

are[2] (ɑː) *n* a unit of area equal to 100 square metres. [C19: from F, from L *ārea* piece of ground; see AREA]

area (ˈɛərɪə) *n* **1** any flat, curved, or irregular expanse of a surface. **2a** the extent of a two-dimensional surface: *the area of a triangle.* **2b** the two-dimensional extent of a plane or surface: *the area of a sphere.* **3** a section or part. **4** region; district. **5a** a geographical division of administrative responsibility. **5b** *(as modifier): area manager.* **6** a part or section, as of a building, town, etc., having some specified function: *reception area; commercial area.* **7** the range or scope of anything. **8** a subject field or field of study. **9** Also called: **areaway.** a sunken area, usually enclosed, giving light, air, and sometimes access to a cellar basement. [C16: from L: level ground, threshing-floor; rel. to *ārēre* to be dry]
▶ **'areal** *adj*

arena (əˈriːnə) *n* **1** an enclosure or platform, usually surrounded by seats, in which sports events, entertainments, etc., take place: *a boxing arena.* **2** the central area of an ancient Roman amphitheatre, in which gladiatorial contests were held. **3** a sphere of intense activity: *the political arena.* [C17: from L *harēna* sand, place where sand was strewn for the combats]

arenaceous (ˌærɪˈneɪʃəs) *adj* **1** (of sedimentary rocks) composed of sand. **2** (of plants) growing in a sandy soil. [C17: from L *harēnāceus* sandy, from *harēna* sand]

Arendt ★ (ˈɛərənt) *n* **Hannah.** 1906–75, US political philosopher, born in Germany. Her publications include

The Origins of Totalitarianism (1951) and *Eichmann in Jerusalem* (1961).

aren't (ɑːnt) **1** *contraction of* are not. **2** *Inf., chiefly Brit.* (used in interrogative sentences) *contraction of* am not.

areola (əˈrɪələ) *n, pl* **areolae** (-ˌliː) *or* **areolas.** *Anat.* any small circular area, such as the pigmented ring around the human nipple. [C17: from L: dim. of AREA]
▶ **a'reolar** *or* **areolate** (əˈrɪəlɪt, -ˌleɪt) *adj*

areole (ˈærɪəʊl) *n* **1** *Biol.* a space outlined on a surface, such as an area between veins on a leaf. **2** a sunken area on a cactus from which spines, hairs, etc., arise.
▶ **'areo,late** *adj*

Areopagus (ˌærɪˈɒpəgəs) *n* **1a** the hill to the northwest of the Acropolis in Athens. **1b** (in ancient Athens) the judicial council whose members (Areopagites) met on this hill. **2** *Literary.* any high court. [via L from Gk *Areiopagus*, contracted from *Areios pagos*, hill of Ares]
▶ **Areopagite** (ˌærɪˈɒpəˌdʒaɪt) *n*

Arequipa ★ (ˌærɪˈkiːpə; *Spanish* areˈkipa) *n* a city in S Peru, at an altitude of 2250 m (7500 ft): founded in 1540 on the site of an Inca city. Pop.: 725 838 (1995).

Ares ★ (ˈɛəriːz) *n* *Greek myth.* the god of war, born of Zeus and Hera. Roman counterpart: **Mars.**

arête (əˈreɪt, əˈrɛt) *n* a sharp ridge that separates glacial valleys. [C19: from F: fishbone, ridge, from L *arista* ear of corn, fishbone]

Arethusa (ˌærɪˈθjuːzə) *n* *Greek myth.* a nymph who was changed into a spring on the island of Ortygia to escape the amorous advances of the river god Alpheus.

Arezzo ★ (əˈretsəʊ; *Italian* aˈrettso) *n* a city in central Italy, in E Tuscany. Pop.: 91 527 (1990). Ancient Latin name: **Arretium.**

Arg. *abbrev. for* Argentina.

argal (ˈɑːɡəl) *n* another name for **argol.**

argali (ˈɑːɡəlɪ) *or* **argal** *n, pl* **argali** *or* **argals.** a wild sheep, with massive horns in the male, inhabiting semidesert regions in central Asia. [C18: from Mongolian]

argent (ˈɑːdʒənt) *n* **a** an archaic or poetic word for **silver. b** *(as adj; often postpositive, esp. in heraldry): a bend argent.* [C15: from OF, from L]

Argenteuil ★ *(French* arʒɑ̃tœj) *n* a suburb of Paris, France, with a convent (656) that became famous when Héloïse was abbess (12th century). Pop.: 93 096 (1990).

argentiferous (ˌɑːdʒənˈtɪfərəs) *adj* containing or bearing silver.

Argentina ★ (ˌɑːdʒənˈtiːnə) *n* a republic in southern South America: colonized by the Spanish from 1516 onwards; gained independence in 1816 and became a republic in 1852; consists chiefly of subtropical plains and forests (the Chaco) in the north, temperate plains (the pampas) in the central parts, the Andes in the west, and an infertile plain extending to Tierra del Fuego in the south (Patagonia); an important meat producer. Language: Spanish. Religion: Roman Catholic. Currency: peso. Capital: Buenos Aires. Pop.: 35 409 000 (1997). Area: 2 776 653 sq. km (1 072 067 sq. miles). Also called: **the Argentine.**

argentine (ˈɑːdʒənˌtaɪn) *adj* **1** of or resembling silver. ◆ *n* **2** a small marine fish characterized by a long silvery body.

Argentine ★ (ˈɑːdʒənˌtiːn, -ˌtaɪn) *n* **1 the.** another name for **Argentina. 2** a native or inhabitant of Argentina. ◆ *adj* **3** of or relating to Argentina. ◆ Also (for senses 2, 3): **Argentinian** (ˌɑːdʒənˈtɪnɪən).

argillaceous (ˌɑːdʒɪˈleɪʃəs) *adj* (of sedimentary rocks) composed of very fine-grained material, such as clay. [C18: from L *argilla* white clay, from Gk, from *argos* white]

Argive (ˈɑːdʒaɪv, -ɡaɪv) *adj* **1** of or relating to Argos. **2** a literary word for **Greek.** ◆ *n* **3** an ancient Greek, esp. one from Argos.

Argo ★ (ˈɑːɡəʊ) *n* *Greek myth.* the ship in which Jason sailed in search of the Golden Fleece.

argol (ˈɑːɡɒl) *or* **argal** (ˈɑːɡəl) *n* crude potassium hydrogentartrate. [C14: from Anglo-F *argoil*, from ?]

Argolis ★ (ˈɑːɡəlɪs) *n* **1** a department and ancient region of Greece, in the NE Peloponnese. Capital: Nauplion. Pop.: 97 636 (1991). Area: 2261 sq. km (873 sq. miles). **2 Gulf of.** an inlet of the Aegean Sea, in the E Peloponnese.

argon ('ɑːgɒn) *n* an unreactive colourless odourless element of the rare gas series that forms almost 1 per cent of the atmosphere. It is used in electric lights. Symbol: Ar; atomic no.: 18; atomic wt.: 39.95. [C19: from Gk, from *argos* inactive, from A-¹ + *ergon* work]

Argonaut ★ ('ɑːgə,nɔːt) *n* **1** *Greek myth.* one of the heroes who sailed with Jason in quest of the Golden Fleece. **2** a person who took part in the Californian gold rush of 1849. **3** (*not cap.*) another name for the **paper nautilus.** [C16: from Gk *Argonautēs*, from *Argō* the name of Jason's ship + *nautēs* sailor]
▸ ,Argo'nautic *adj*

Argonne ★ ('ɑːgɒn; *French* argɔn) *n* **the.** a wooded region of NE France: scene of major battles in both World Wars.

Argos ★ ('ɑːgɒs, -gəs) *n* an ancient city in SE Greece, in the NE Peloponnese: one of the oldest Greek cities, it dominated the Peloponnese in the 7th century B.C. Pop.: 22 000 (1995 est.).

argosy ('ɑːgəsı) *n, pl* **argosies.** *Arch. or poetic.* a large abundantly laden merchant ship, or a fleet of such ships. [C16: from It. *Ragusea* (*nave*) (ship) of Ragusa]

argot ('ɑːgəʊ) *n* slang or jargon peculiar to a particular group, esp. (formerly) a group of thieves. [C19: from F, from ?]

Argovie ★ (argɔvi) *n* the French name for **Aargau.**

arguable ('ɑːgjʊəb²l) *adj* **1** capable of being disputed. **2** plausible; reasonable.
▸ 'arguably *adv*

argue ('ɑːgjuː) *vb* **argues, arguing, argued. 1** (*intr*) to quarrel; wrangle. **2** (*intr*; often foll. by *for* or *against*) to present supporting or opposing reasons or cases in a dispute. **3** (*tr; may take a clause as object*) to try to prove by presenting reasons. **4** (*tr; often passive*) to debate or discuss. **5** (*tr*) to persuade. **6** (*tr*) to suggest: *her looks argue despair.* [C14: from OF *arguer* to assert, from L *arguere* to make clear, accuse]
▸ 'arguer *n*

argufy ('ɑːgjʊ,faɪ) *vb* **argufies, argufying, argufied.** *Facetious or dialect.* to argue or quarrel, esp. over something trivial.

argument ('ɑːgjʊmənt) *n* **1** a quarrel; altercation. **2** a discussion in which reasons are put forward; debate. **3** (*sometimes pl*) a point or series of reasons presented to support or oppose a proposition. **4** a summary of the plot or subject of a book, etc. **5** *Logic.* **5a** a process of reasoning in which the conclusion can be shown to be true or false. **5b** the middle term of a syllogism. **6** *Maths.* another name for **independent variable** of a function.

argumentation (,ɑːgjʊmen'teɪʃən) *n* **1** the process of reasoning methodically. **2** argument; debate.

argumentative (,ɑːgjʊ'mentətɪv) *adj* **1** given to arguing. **2** characterized by argument; controversial.

Argus ★ ('ɑːgəs) *n* **1** *Greek myth.* a giant with a hundred eyes who was made guardian of the heifer Io. **2** a vigilant person.

Argus-eyed *adj* observant; vigilant.

argy-bargy *or* **argie-bargie** ('ɑːdʒɪ'bɑːdʒɪ) *n, pl* **argy-bargies.** *Brit. inf.* a wrangling argument or verbal dispute. [C19: from Scot., from dialect *argle*, prob. from ARGUE]

Argyll and Bute ★ (ɑː'gaɪl) *n* a council area in W Scotland on the Atlantic Ocean: in 1975 the historic counties of Argyllshire and Bute became part of Strathclyde region; in 1996 they were reinstated as a single unitary authority. Administrative centre: Lochgilphead. Pop.: 90 550 (1996 est.). Area: 6930 sq. km (2676 sq. miles).

Argyllshire ★ (ɑː'gaɪl,ʃɪə, -ʃə) *n* a historic county of W Scotland, part of Strathclyde region (1975–96), now part of Argyll and Bute.

Århus ★ (*Danish* 'ɔrhuːs) *n* a variant spelling of **Aarhus.**

aria ('ɑːrɪə) *n* an elaborate accompanied song for solo voice from a cantata, opera, or oratorio. [C18: from It.: tune, AIR]

Ariadne ★ (,ærɪ'ædnɪ) *n Greek myth.* daughter of Minos and Pasiphaë: she gave Theseus the thread with which he found his way out of the Minotaur's labyrinth.

Arian ('ɛərɪən) *adj* **1** of or relating to Arius or to Arianism. ◆ *n* **2** an adherent of Arianism.

-arian *suffix forming nouns.* indicating a person or thing that advocates, believes, or is associated with something: *vegetarian; librarian.* [from L *-ārius* -ARY + -AN]

Arianism ('ɛərɪə,nɪzəm) *n* the doctrine of Arius, declared heretical, which asserted that Christ was not of one substance with the Father.

Arias Sánchez ★ ('ærɪæs 'sæntʃez) *n* Oscar. born 1940, Costa Rican statesman; president (1986–90); Nobel peace prize 1987.

Arica ★ (ə'riːkə; *Spanish* a'rika) *n* a port in extreme N Chile: awarded to Chile in 1929 after the lengthy Tacna-Arica dispute with Peru; outlet for Bolivian and Peruvian trade. Pop.: 173 336 (1995 est.). See also **Tacna-Arica.**

arid ('ærɪd) *adj* **1** having little or no rain; dry. **2** devoid of interest. [C17: from L *āridus*, from *ārēre* to be dry]
▸ **aridity** (ə'rɪdɪtɪ) *or* 'aridness *n*

arid zone *n* either of the zones of latitude 15–30° N and S, with low rainfall and desert or semidesert terrain.

Ariège ★ (*French* arjɛʒ) *n* a department of SW France, in Midi-Pyrénées region. Capital: Foix. Pop.: 136 667 (1994 est.). Area: 4903 sq. km (1912 sq. miles).

Aries ('ɛəriːz) *n, Latin genitive* **Arietis** (ə'raɪɪtɪs). **1** *Astron.* a N constellation. **2** *Astrol.* Also called: the **Ram.** the first sign of the zodiac. The sun is in this sign between about March 21 and April 19. [C14: from L: ram]

aright (ə'raɪt) *adv* correctly; rightly; properly.

aril ('ærɪl) *n* an additional covering formed on certain seeds, such as those of the yew and nutmeg, after fertilization. [C18: from NL, from Med. L *arilli* raisins, pips of grapes]
▸ 'aril,late *adj*

Arimathea *or* **Arimathaea** ★ (,ærɪmə'θiːə) *n* a town in ancient Palestine: location unknown.

Ariminum ★ (ə'rɪmɪnəm) *n* the ancient name of **Rimini.**

arioso (,ɑːrɪ'əʊzəʊ) *n, pl* **ariosos** *or* **ariosi** (-siː). *Music.* a recitative with the lyrical quality of an aria. [C18: from It., from ARIA]

Ariosto ★ (*Italian* a'rjɔsto) *n* **Ludovico** (ludo'viːko). 1474–1533, Italian poet, famous for his romantic epic *Orlando Furioso* (1516).

arise (ə'raɪz) *vb* **arises, arising, arose, arisen** (ə'rɪz²n). (*intr*) **1** to come into being; originate. **2** (foll. by *from*) to proceed as a consequence. **3** to get or stand up, as from a sitting or lying position. **4** to come into notice. **5** to ascend. [OE *ārīsan*]

aristo ('ærɪstəʊ, ə'rɪstəʊ) *n, pl* **aristos.** *Inf.* short for **aristocrat.**

aristocracy (,ærɪ'stɒkrəsɪ) *n, pl* **aristocracies. 1** a privileged class of people usually of high birth; the nobility. **2** such a class as the ruling body of a state. **3** government by such a class. **4** a state governed by such a class. **5** a class of people considered to be outstanding in a sphere of activity. [C16: from LL, from Gk *aristokratia* rule by the best-born, from *aristos* best; see -CRACY]

aristocrat ('ærɪstə,kræt) *n* **1** a member of the aristocracy. **2** a person who has the manners or qualities of a member of a privileged class. **3** a supporter of aristocracy as a form of government.

aristocratic (,ærɪstə'krætɪk) *adj* **1** relating to or characteristic of aristocracy or an aristocrat. **2** elegant or stylish in appearance and behaviour.
▸ ,aristo'cratically *adv*

Aristophanes ★ (,ærɪ'stɒfə,niːz) *n* ?448–?380 B.C., Greek comic dramatist, who satirized leading contemporary figures such as Socrates and Euripides. Eleven of his plays are extant, including *The Clouds, The Frogs, The Birds,* and *Lysistrata.*

Aristotelian (,ærɪstə'tiːlɪən) *adj* **1** of or relating to Aristotle or to his philosophy. ◆ *n* **2** a follower of Aristotle.

Aristotelian logic *n* **1** traditional logic, esp. relying on the theory of syllogism. **2** the logical method of Aristotle, esp. as developed in the Middle Ages.

Aristotle ★ ('ærɪ,stɒt²l) *n* 384–322 B.C., Greek philosopher; pupil of Plato, tutor of Alexander the Great, and founder of the Peripatetic school at Athens; author of works on logic, ethics, politics, poetics, rhetoric, biology, zoology, and metaphysics. His works influenced Muslim philosophy and science and medieval scholastic philosophy.

arithmetic *n* (ə'rɪθmətɪk). **1** the branch of mathematics concerned with numerical calculations, such as addition, subtraction, multiplication, and division. **2** calculations involving numerical operations. **3** knowledge of or skill in using arithmetic. ♦ *adj* (ˌærɪθ'mɛtɪk) *also* **arithmetical**. **4** of, relating to, or using arithmetic. [C13: from L, from Gk *arithmētikē*, from *arithmein* to count, from *arithmos* number]
▶ ˌarith'metically *adv* ▶ aˌrithme'tician *n*

arithmetic mean *n* the average value of a set of terms or quantities, expressed as their sum divided by their number: *the arithmetic mean of 3, 4, and 8 is 5*. Also called: **average**.

arithmetic progression *n* a sequence, each term of which differs from the succeeding term by a constant amount, such as 3,6,9,12.

-arium *suffix forming nouns*. indicating a place for or associated with something: *aquarium; solarium*. [from L *-ārium*, neuter of *-ārius* -ARY]

Arius ★ ('ɛərɪəs) *n* ?250–336 A.D., Greek Christian theologian, originator of the doctrine of Arianism.

Ariz. *abbrev. for* Arizona.

Arizona ★ (ˌærɪ'zəʊnə) *n* a state of the southwestern US: consists of the Colorado plateau in the northeast, including the Grand Canyon, divided from desert in the southwest by mountains rising over 3750 m (12 500 ft). Capital: Phoenix. Pop.: 4 428 068 (1996 est.). Area: 293 750 sq. km (113 417 sq. miles). Abbrevs.: **Ariz.** or (with zip code) **AZ**

Arjuna ★ ('ɑːdʒʊnə) *n Hindu myth*. the most important of the five princes in the *Mahabharata*. Krishna served as his charioteer in the battle with the Kauravas.

ark (ɑːk) *n* **1** the vessel that Noah built which survived the Flood (Genesis 6–9). **2** a place or thing offering shelter or protection. **3** *Dialect*. a box. [OE *arc*, from L *arca* box, chest]

Ark (ɑːk) *n Judaism*. **1** Also called: **Holy Ark**. the cupboard in a synagogue in which the Torah scrolls are kept. **2** Also called: **Ark of the Covenant**. the most sacred symbol of God's presence among the Hebrew people, carried in their journey from Sinai to the Promised Land (Canaan).

Ark. *abbrev. for* Arkansas.

Arkansas ★ *n* **1** ('ɑːkənˌsɔː). a state of the southern US: mountainous in the north and west, with the alluvial plain of the Mississippi in the east; has the only diamond mine in the US; the chief US producer of bauxite. Capital: Little Rock. Pop.: 2 509 793 (1996 est.). Area: 134 537 sq. km (51 945 sq. miles). Abbrevs.: **Ark.** or (with zip code) **AR 2** (ɑː'kænzəs). a river in the S central US, rising in central Colorado and flowing east and southeast to join the Mississippi in Arkansas. Length: 2335 km (1450 miles).
▶ **Arkansan** (ɑː'kænzən) *n, adj*

Arkhangelsk ★ (ar'xangɪljsk) *n* the Russian name for **Archangel**.

Arkwright ★ ('ɑːkraɪt) *n* Sir **Richard**. 1732–92, English cotton manufacturer: inventor of the spinning frame (1769) which produced cotton thread strong enough to be used as a warp.

Arles ★ (ɑːlz; *French* arl) *n* **1** a city in SE France, on the Rhône: Roman amphitheatre. Pop.: 52 593 (1990). **2 Kingdom of.** a kingdom in SE France which had dissolved by 1378: known as the Kingdom of Burgundy until about 1200.

Arlington ★ ('ɑːlɪŋtən) *n* a county of N Virginia: site of **Arlington National Cemetery**.

Arlon ★ (*French* arlɔ̃) *n* a town in SE Belgium, capital of Luxembourg province. Pop.: 17 000 (1991 est.).

arm[1] (ɑːm) *n* **1** (in man) either of the upper limbs from the shoulder to the wrist. Related adj: **brachial**. **2** the part of either of the upper limbs from the elbow to the wrist;

forearm. **3a** the corresponding limb of any other vertebrate. **3b** an armlike appendage of some invertebrates. **4** an object that covers or supports the human arm, esp. the sleeve of a garment or the side of a chair, etc. **5** anything considered to resemble an arm in appearance, function, etc.: *an arm of the sea; the arm of a record player*. **6** an administrative subdivision of an organization: *an arm of the government*. **7** power; authority: *the arm of the law*. **8 arm in arm**. with arms linked. **9 at arm's length**. at a distance. **10 in the arms of Morpheus**. sleeping. **11 with open arms**. with great warmth and hospitality. [OE]

arm[2] (ɑːm) *vb* **1** to equip with weapons as a preparation for war. **2** (*tr*) to provide (a person or thing) with something that strengthens, protects, or increases efficiency. **3a** (*tr*) to activate (a fuse) so that it will explode at the required time. **3b** to prepare (an explosive device) for use by introducing a detonator, etc. ♦ *n* **4** (*usually pl*) a weapon, esp. a firearm. [C14: from OF *armes*, from L *arma* arms, equipment]

Arm. *abbrev. for:* **1** Armenia(n). **2** Armoric *or* Armorican.

armada (ɑː'mɑːdə) *n* **1** a large number of ships or aircraft. **2** (*cap.*) **the.** Also called: **Spanish Armada**. the great fleet sent by Philip II of Spain against England in 1588. [C16: from Sp., from Med. L *armāta* fleet, armed forces, from L *armāre* to provide with arms]

armadillo (ˌɑːmə'dɪləʊ) *n, pl* **armadillos**. a burrowing mammal of Central and South America with a covering of strong horny plates over most of the body. [C16: from Sp., dim. of *armado* armed (man), from L *armātus* armed; cf. ARMADA]

Armageddon (ˌɑːmə'ged³n) *n* **1** *New Testament*. the final battle between good and evil at the end of the world. **2** a catastrophic and extremely destructive conflict. [C19: from LL, from Gk, from Heb. *har megiddōn*, mountain district of *Megiddo* (in N Palestine)]

Armagh ★ (ɑː'mɑː) *n* **1** a historic county of S Northern Ireland: in 1973 its administrative functions were given to local government districts. Area: 1326 sq. km (512 sq. miles). **2** a district of SE Northern Ireland, bordering the Irish Republic: fruit growing, light industry. Administrative centre: Armagh. Area: 676 sq. km (261 sq. miles). Pop.: 51 817 (1991). **3** a city in S Northern Ireland, in the district of Armagh: seat of Roman Catholic and Protestant archbishops. Pop.: 14 640 (1991).

Armalite ('ɑːməlaɪt) *n Trademark*. a lightweight high-velocity rifle of various calibres, capable of automatic and semiautomatic operation. [C20: from *Armalite* Division, Fairchild Engine and Airplane Company, manufacturers]

armament ('ɑːməmənt) *n* **1** (*often pl*) the weapon equipment of a military vehicle, ship, or aircraft. **2** a military force raised and armed ready for war. **3** preparation for war. [C17: from L *armāmenta* utensils, from *armāre* to equip]

Armani ★ (ɑː'mɑːnɪ; *Italian* ar'maːni) *n* **Giorgio** ('dʒɔrdʒo). born 1936, Italian fashion designer, noted for his restrained classical style.

armature ('ɑːmətjʊə) *n* **1** a revolving structure in an electric motor or generator, wound with the coils that carry the current. **2** any part of an electric machine or device that moves under the influence of a magnetic field or within which an electromotive force is induced. **3** Also called: **keeper**. a soft iron or steel bar placed across the poles of a magnet to close the magnetic circuit. **4** *Sculpture*. a framework to support the clay or other material used in modelling. **5** the protective outer covering of an animal or plant. [C15: from L *armātūra* armour, equipment, from *armāre* to furnish with equipment]

armchair ('ɑːmˌtʃɛə) *n* **1** a chair, esp. an upholstered one, that has side supports for the arms or elbows. **2** (*modifier*) taking or involving no active part: *an armchair strategist*.

armed[1] (ɑːmd) *adj* **1** equipped with or supported by arms, armour, etc. **2** prepared for conflict or any difficulty. **3** (of an explosive device) prepared for use. **4** (of plants) having the protection of thorns, spines, etc.

armed[2] (ɑːmd) *adj* **a** having an arm or arms. **b** (*in combination*): *long-armed; one-armed*.

armed forces *pl n* the military forces of a nation or nations, including the army, navy, air force, marines, etc.

Armenia ★ (ɑːˈmiːnɪə) *n* **1** a republic in W Asia: originally part of the Armenian kingdom; acquired by Russia in 1828: became the Armenian Soviet Socialist Republic in 1936; gained independence in 1991. It is mountainous, rising over 4000 m (13 000 ft). Language: Armenian. Religion: Christian majority. Currency: dram. Capital: Yerevan. Pop.: 3 773 000 (1997). Area: 29 800 sq km (11 490 sq. miles). **2** a former kingdom in W Asia, between the Black Sea and the Caspian Sea, south of Georgia. **3** a town in central Colombia: centre of a coffee-growing district. Pop.: 283 842 (1997 est.).
▸ **Arˈmenian** *adj, n*

Armentières ★ (ˈɑːmənˌtɪəz; *French* armɑ̃tjɛr) *n* a town in N France: site of battles in both World Wars. Pop.: 26 240 (1990).

armful (ˈɑːmfʊl) *n, pl* **armfuls.** the amount that can be held by one or both arms.

armhole (ˈɑːmˌhəʊl) *n* the opening in an article of clothing through which the arm passes.

Armidale ★ (ˈɑːmɪˌdeɪl) *n* a town in Australia, in NE New South Wales: a centre for tourism. Pop.: 21 606 (1991 est.).

armillary sphere (ɑːˈmɪlərɪ) *n* a model of the celestial sphere formerly used in fixing the positions of heavenly bodies.

Arminian (ɑːˈmɪnɪən) *adj* denoting, relating to, or believing in the Protestant doctrines of Jacobus Arminius, which rejected absolute predestination and stressed free will in man.
▸ **Arˈminianˌism** *n*

armistice (ˈɑːmɪstɪs) *n* an agreement between opposing armies to suspend hostilities; truce. [C18: from NL, from L *arma* arms + *sistere* to stop]

Armistice Day (ˈɑːmɪstɪs) *n* the anniversary of the signing of the armistice that ended World War I, on Nov. 11, 1918. See also **Remembrance Sunday.**

armlet (ˈɑːmlɪt) *n* **1** a small arm, as of a lake. **2** a band or bracelet worn round the arm.

armoire (ɑːmˈwɑː) *n* a large cabinet, originally used for storing weapons. [C16: from F, from OF *armaire*, from L *armārium* chest, closet; see AMBRY]

armorial (ɑːˈmɔːrɪəl) *adj* of or relating to heraldry or heraldic arms.

armour *or US* **armor** (ˈɑːmə) *n* **1** any defensive covering, esp. that of metal, chain mail, etc., worn by medieval warriors. **2** the protective metal plates on a tank, warship, etc. **3** *Mil.* armoured fighting vehicles in general. **4** any protective covering, such as the shell of certain animals. **5** heraldic insignia; arms. ♦ *vb* **6** (*tr*) to equip or cover with armour. [C13: from OF *armure*, from L *armātūra* armour, equipment]

armoured *or US* **armored** (ˈɑːməd) *adj* **1** having a protective covering. **2** comprising units making use of armoured vehicles: *an armoured brigade.*

armourer *or US* **armorer** (ˈɑːmərə) *n* **1** a person who makes or mends arms and armour. **2** a person employed in the maintenance of small arms and weapons in a military unit.

armour plate *n* a tough heavy steel often hardened on the surface, used for protecting warships, tanks, etc.

armoury *or US* **armory** (ˈɑːmərɪ) *n, pl* **armouries** *or* **armories.** **1** a secure place for the storage of weapons. **2** armour generally; military supplies. **3** resources, such as arguments, on which to draw: *a few choice terms from her armoury of invective.*

armpit (ˈɑːmˌpɪt) *n* **1** the small depression beneath the arm where it joins the shoulder. Technical name: **axilla.** **2** *Sl.* an extremely unpleasant place: *the armpit of the Middle West.*

armrest (ˈɑːmˌrɛst) *n* the part of a chair, sofa, etc., that supports the arm. Sometimes shortened to **arm.**

arms (ɑːmz) *pl n* **1** weapons collectively. See also **small arms. 2** military exploits: *prowess in arms.* **3** the official heraldic symbols of a family, state, etc. **4** bear arms. **4a** to carry weapons. **4b** to serve in the armed forces. **4c** to

have a coat of arms. **5 in** *or* **under arms.** armed and prepared for war. **6 lay down one's arms.** to stop fighting; surrender. **7 take (up) arms.** to prepare to fight. **8 up in arms.** indignant; prepared to protest strongly. [C13: from OF, from L *arma*; see ARM²]

Armstrong ★ (ˈɑːmˌstrɒŋ) *n* **1 Edwin Howard.** 1890–1954, US electrical engineer; invented the superheterodyne radio receiver and the FM radio. **2 Gillian,** born 1950, Australian film director; her films include *My Brilliant Career* (1978) and *Little Women* (1994). **3 (Daniel) Louis,** known as **Satchmo.** 1900–71, US jazz trumpeter and bandleader. **4 Neil (Alden).** born 1930, US astronaut; commanded Apollo 11 on the first manned lunar landing during which he became the first man to set foot on the moon on July 20, 1969.

arm wrestling *n* a contest of strength in which two people rest the elbow of one arm on a flat surface, grasp each other's hand, and try to force their opponent's forearm down flat.

army (ˈɑːmɪ) *n, pl* **armies. 1** the military land forces of a nation. **2** a military unit usually consisting of two or more corps with supporting arms and services. **3** (*modifier*) of or characteristic of an army. **4** any large body of people united for some specific purpose. **5** a large number of people, animals, etc. [C14: from OF, from Med. L *armāta* armed forces]

army ant *n* any of various tropical American predatory ants which travel in vast hordes preying on other animals. Also called: **legionary ant.**

army worm *n* a type of caterpillar which travels in vast hordes and is a serious pest of cereal crops.

Arnaud ★ (ˈɑːnəʊ; *French* arno) *n* **Yvonne.** 1892–1958, French actress, who was well known on the London stage and in British films. A theatre in Guildford is named after her.

Arne ★ (ɑːn) *n* **Thomas (Augustine).** 1710–78, English composer, noted for his setting of Shakespearean songs and for his song *Rule Britannia.*

Arnhem ★ (ˈɑːnəm) *n* a city in the E Netherlands, capital of Gelderland province, on the Rhine: site of a World War II battle. Pop.: 134 499 (1995 est.).

Arnhem Land ★ *n* a region of N Australia, in the N Northern Territory, large areas of which are reserved for aboriginal Australians.

arnica (ˈɑːnɪkə) *n* **1** any of a genus of N temperate or arctic plants having yellow flowers. **2** the tincture of the dried flower heads of any of these plants, used in treating bruises. [C18: from NL, from ?]

Arnim ★ (*German* ˈarnɪm) *n* **Achim von** (ˈaxɪm fɔn). 1781–1831, German romantic poet. He published, with Clemens Brentano, the collection of folk songs, *Des Knaben Wunderhorn* (1805–08).

Arno ★ (ˈɑːnəʊ) *n* a river in central Italy, rising in the Apennines and flowing through Florence and Pisa to the Ligurian Sea. Length: about 240 km (150 miles).

Arnold[1] ★ (ˈɑːnˀld) *n* a town in N central England, in S Nottinghamshire. Pop.: 37 646 (1991).

Arnold[2] ★ (ˈɑːnˀld) *n* **1 Sir Malcolm.** born 1921, English composer, esp. of orchestral works in a traditional idiom. **2 Matthew.** 1822–88, English poet, essayist, and literary critic, noted particularly for his poems *Sohrab and Rustum* (1853) and *Dover Beach* (1867), and for his *Essays in Criticism* (1865) and *Culture and Anarchy* (1869). **3** his father, **Thomas.** 1795–1842, English historian and educationalist, headmaster of Rugby School, noted for his reforms in public-school education.

aroha (ˈɑːrɒhə) *n NZ.* love, compassion, or affectionate regard. [Maori]

aroid (ˈærɔɪd, ˈɛər-) *adj* of or relating to a plant family that includes the arum, calla, and anthurium. [C19: from ARUM + -OID]

aroint thee *or* **ye** (əˈrɔɪnt) *sentence substitute. Arch.* away! begone! [C17: from ?]

aroma (əˈrəʊmə) *n* **1** a distinctive usually pleasant smell, esp. of spices, wines, and plants. **2** a subtle pervasive quality or atmosphere. [C18: via L from Gk: spice]

aromatherapy (əˌrəʊməˈθɛrəpɪ) *n* the use of fragrant es-

★ people and places

sential oils as a treatment in alternative medicine to relieve tension and cure certain minor ailments.
▸ a,roma'therapist n

aromatic (,ærə'mætɪk) adj **1** having a distinctive, usually fragrant smell. **2** (of an organic compound) having an unsaturated ring, esp. containing a benzene ring. Cf. **aliphatic.** ◆ n **3** something, such as a plant or drug, giving off a fragrant smell.
▸ ,aro'matically adv ▸ a,roma'ticity n

aromatize or **aromatise** (ə'rəʊmə,taɪz) vb **aromatizes, aromatizing, aromatized** or **aromatises, aromatising, aromatised.** (tr) to make aromatic.
▸ a,romati'zation or a,romati'sation n

arose (ə'rəʊz) vb the past tense of **arise.**

around (ə'raʊnd) prep **1** situated at various points in: a lot of shelves around the house. **2** from place to place in: driving around Ireland. **3** somewhere in or near. **4** approximately in: it happened around 1957. ◆ adv **5** in all directions from a point of reference: he owns the land for ten miles around. **6** in the vicinity, esp. restlessly but idly: to stand around. **7** in no particular place or direction: dotted around. **8** Inf. (of people) active and prominent in a particular area or profession. **9** Inf. present in some place (the exact location being unknown or unspecified). **10** Inf. in circulation; available: that type of phone has been around for some years now. **11** Inf. to many places, so as to have gained considerable experience, often of a worldly or social nature: I've been around. [C17: (rare earlier): from A-² + ROUND]

USAGE NOTE In American English, *around* is usually used instead of *round* in adverbial and prepositional senses, except in a few fixed phrases such as *all year round*. The use of *around* in adverbial senses is less common in British English.

arouse (ə'raʊz) vb **arouses, arousing, aroused. 1** (tr) to evoke or elicit (a reaction, emotion, or response). **2** to awaken from sleep.
▸ a'rousal n ▸ a'rouser n

Arp ★ (French arp) n **Jean** (ʒɑ̃) or **Hans** (hans). 1887–1966, Alsatian sculptor, painter, and poet, cofounder of the Dada movement in Zürich, noted particularly for his abstract organic sculptures based on natural forms.

arpeggio (ɑ:'pɛdʒɪəʊ) n, pl **arpeggios.** a chord whose notes are played or sung in rapid succession rather than simultaneously. [C18: from It., from arpeggiare to perform on the harp, from arpa HARP]

arquebus (ɑ:'kwɪbəs) or **harquebus** n a portable long-barrelled gun dating from the 15th century. [C16: via OF from MDu. hakebusse, lit.: hook gun, from the shape of the butt, from hake hook + busse box, gun, from LL busis box]

arr. abbrev. for: **1** arranged (by). **2** arrival. **3** arrive(d).

arrack or **arak** ('ærək) n a coarse spirit distilled in various Eastern countries from grain, rice, sugar cane, etc. [C17: from Ar. 'araq sweat, sweet juice, liquor]

arraign (ə'reɪn) vb (tr) **1** to bring (a prisoner) before a court to answer an indictment. **2** to call to account; accuse. [C14: from OF, from Vulgar L ratiōnāre (unattested) to talk, argue, from L ratiō a reasoning]
▸ ar'raigner n ▸ ar'raignment n

Arran ★ ('ærən) n an island off the SW coast of Scotland, in the Firth of Clyde. Pop.: 4000 (latest est.). Area: 427 sq. km (165 sq. miles).

arrange (ə'reɪndʒ) vb **arranges, arranging, arranged. 1** (tr) to put into a proper or systematic order. **2** (tr; may take a clause as object or an infinitive) to arrive at an agreement about. **3** (when intr, often foll. by for; when tr, may take a clause as object or an infinitive) to make plans or preparations in advance (for something): we arranged for her to be met. **4** (tr) to adapt (a musical composition) for performance in a different way, esp. on different instruments. **5** (intr; often foll. by with) to come to an agreement. [C14: from OF arangier, from A-² + rangier to put in a row, RANGE]
▸ ar'rangeable adj ▸ ar'ranger n

arrangement (ə'reɪndʒmənt) n **1** the act of arranging or being arranged. **2** the form in which things are arranged. **3** a thing composed of various ordered parts: a flower arrangement. **4** (often pl) a preparation. **5** an understanding. **6** an adaptation of a piece of music for performance in a different way, esp. on different instruments.

arrant ('ærənt) adj utter; out-and-out: an arrant fool. [C14: var. of ERRANT (wandering, vagabond)]
▸ 'arrantly adv

arras ('ærəs) n a wall hanging, esp. of tapestry.

Arras ★ ('ærəs; French aras) n a town in N France: formerly famous for tapestry; severely damaged in both World Wars. Pop.: 42 715 (1990).

Arrau ★ (ə'raʊ) n **Claudio.** 1903–91, Chilean pianist.

array (ə'reɪ) n **1** an impressive display or collection. **2** an orderly arrangement, esp. of troops in battle order. **3** Poetic. rich clothing. **4** Maths. a set of numbers or symbols arranged in rows and columns, as in a determinant or matrix. **5** Law. a panel of jurors. **6** Computing. a regular data structure in which elements may be located by reference to index numbers. ◆ vb (tr) **7** to dress in rich attire. **8** to arrange in order (esp. troops for battle). **9** Law. to draw up (a panel of jurors). [C13: from OF, from arayer to arrange, of Gmc origin]
▸ ar'rayal n

arrears (ə'rɪəz) n (sometimes sing) **1** Also called: **arrearage.** something outstanding or owed. **2 in arrears** or **arrear.** late in paying a debt or meeting an obligation. [C18: from obs. arrear (adv) behindhand, from OF, from Med. L adretrō, from L ad to + retrō backwards]

arrest (ə'rɛst) vb (tr) **1** to deprive (a person) of liberty by taking him into custody, esp. under lawful authority. **2** to seize (a ship) under lawful authority. **3** to slow or stop the development of (a disease, growth, etc.). **4** to catch and hold (one's attention, etc.). ◆ n **5** the act of taking a person into custody, esp. under lawful authority. **6** the act of seizing and holding a ship under lawful authority. **7** the state of being held: under arrest. **8** the slowing or stopping of something: a cardiac arrest. [C14: from OF, from Vulgar L arrestāre (unattested), from L ad at, to + restāre to stand firm, stop]

arresting (ə'rɛstɪŋ) adj attracting attention; striking.
▸ ar'restingly adv

Arretium ★ (æ'ri:tɪəm, -'rɛt-) n the ancient Latin name of Arezzo.
▸ **Arretine** ('ærɪ,taɪn) adj

arrhythmia (ə'rɪðmɪə) n any variation from the normal rhythm in the heartbeat. [C19: NL, from Gk arrhuthmia, from A-¹ + rhuthmos RHYTHM]

arrière-pensée French. (arjɛrpɑ̃se) n an unrevealed thought or intention. [C19: lit.: behind thought]

Ar Rimal ★ (ɑ:r rɪ'mɑ:l) n another name for **Rub' al Khali.**

arris ('ærɪs) n, pl **arris** or **arrises.** a sharp edge at the meeting of two surfaces at an angle with one another. [C17: from OF areste beard of grain, sharp ridge; see ARÊTE]

arrival (ə'raɪv³l) n **1** the act or time of arriving. **2** a person or thing that arrives or has arrived.

arrive (ə'raɪv) vb **arrives, arriving, arrived.** (intr) **1** to come to a certain place during or after a journey. **2** to reach: to arrive at a decision. **3** to occur eventually: the moment arrived when pretence was useless. **4** Inf. (of a baby) to be born. **5** Inf. to attain success. [C13: from OF, from Vulgar L arrīpāre (unattested) to land, reach the bank, from L ad to + rīpa river bank]

arrivederci Italian. (arrive'dertʃi) sentence substitute. goodbye.

arriviste (,ærɪ'vi:st) n a person who is unscrupulously ambitious. [F: see ARRIVE, -IST]

arrogant ('ærəgənt) adj having or showing an exaggerated opinion of one's own importance, merit, ability, etc.: an arrogant assumption. [C14: from L arrogāre to claim as one's own; see ARROGATE]
▸ 'arrogance n ▸ 'arrogantly adv

arrogate ('ærə,geɪt) vb **arrogates, arrogating, arrogated.** (tr) **1** to claim or appropriate for oneself without justification. **2** to attribute or assign to another without justification. [C16: from L arrogāre, from rogāre to ask]
▸ ,arro'gation n ▸ **arrogative** (ə'rɒgətɪv) adj

★ people and places

arrondissement (*French* arɔ̃dismã) *n* (in France) **1** the largest subdivision of a department. **2** a municipal district of large cities, esp. Paris. [C19: from *arrondir* to make round]

arrow ('ærəʊ) *n* **1** a long slender pointed weapon, usually having feathers fastened at the end as a balance, that is shot from a bow. **2** any of various things that resemble an arrow in shape, function, or speed. [OE *arwe*]

arrowhead ('ærəʊ,hɛd) *n* **1** the pointed tip of an arrow, often removable from the shaft. **2** something that resembles the head of an arrow in shape. **3** an aquatic herbaceous plant having arrow-shaped leaves.

arrowroot ('ærəʊ,ruːt) *n* **1** a white-flowered West Indian plant, whose rhizomes yield an easily digestible starch. **2** the starch obtained from this plant.

arroyo (ə'rɔɪəʊ) *n, pl* **arroyos**. *Chiefly southwestern US.* a steep-sided stream bed that is usually dry except after heavy rain. [C19: from Sp.]

Arru Islands ★ ('ɑːruː) *pl n* a variant spelling of **Aru Islands.**

arse (ɑːs) *or US & Canad.* **ass** *n Taboo.* **1** the buttocks. **2** the anus. **3** a stupid person; fool. ◆ Also called (for senses 2, 3): **arsehole,** (US & Canad.) **asshole.** [OE]

arsenal ('ɑːsən°l) *n* **1** a store for arms, ammunition, and other military items. **2** a workshop that produces munitions. **3** a store of anything regarded as weapons. [C16: from It. *arsenale* dockyard, from Ar., from *dār* house + *siñ'ah* manufacture]

arsenate ('ɑːsə,neɪt, -nɪt) *n* a salt or ester of arsenic acid.

arsenic *n* ('ɑːsnɪk). **1** a toxic metalloid element used in transistors, lead-based alloys, and high-temperature brasses. Symbol: As; atomic no.: 33; atomic wt.: 74.92. **2** a nontechnical name for **arsenic trioxide** (As_2O_3), used as rat poison and an insecticide. ◆ *adj* (ɑː'sɛnɪk). **3** of or containing arsenic, esp. in the pentavalent state; designating an arsenic(V) compound. [C14: from L, from Gk *arsenikon* yellow arsenic ore, from Syriac *zarnīg* (infl. by Gk *arsenikos* virile)]

arsenic acid *n* a white poisonous soluble crystalline solid used in the manufacture of insecticides.

arsenical (ɑː'sɛnɪk°l) *adj* **1** of or containing arsenic. ◆ *n* **2** a drug or insecticide containing arsenic.

arsenious (ɑː'siːnɪəs) *or* **arsenous** ('ɑːsɪnəs) *adj* of or containing arsenic in the trivalent state; designating an arsenic(III) compound.

arson ('ɑːs°n) *n Criminal law.* the act of intentionally or recklessly setting fire to property for some improper reason. [C17: from OF, from Med. L *ārsiō*, from L *ārdēre* to burn]
  ▸ **'arsonist** *n*

art[1] (ɑːt) *n* **1a** the creation of works of beauty or other special significance. **1b** (*as modifier*): *an art movement.* **2** the exercise of human skill (as distinguished from *nature*). **3** imaginative skill as applied to representations of the natural world or figments of the imagination. **4a** works of art collectively, esp. of the visual arts. **4b** (*as modifier*): *an art gallery.* **5** any branch of the visual arts, esp. painting. **6a** any field using the techniques of art to display artistic qualities. **6b** (*as modifier*): *art film.* **7** method, facility, or knack: *the art of threading a needle.* **8** skill governing a particular human activity: *the art of government.* **9** cunning. **10 get something down to a fine art.** to become highly proficient at something through practice. ◆ *See also* **arts.** [C13: from OF, from L *ars* craftsmanship]

art[2] (ɑːt) *vb Arch.* (used with the pronoun *thou*) a singular form of the present tense of **be.** [OE *eart*, part of *bēon* to BE]

art. *abbrev. for:* **1** article. **2** artificial. **3** Also: **arty.** artillery.

-art *suffix forming nouns.* a variant of **-ard.**

Artaud ★ (*French* arto) *n* **Antonin** (ãtɔnɛ̃). 1896–1948, French stage director and dramatist, noted for his concept of the theatre of cruelty, esp. *Manifeste du théâtre de la cruauté* (1932).

Artaxerxes II ★ *n* died ?358 B.C., king of Persia (?404–?358). He defeated his brother Cyrus the Younger at Cunaxa (401).

Art Deco ('dɛkəʊ) *n* a style of interior decoration, architecture, etc., at its height in the 1930s and characterized by geometrical shapes. [C20: from *art décoratif*, after the *Exposition des arts décoratifs* held in Paris in 1925]

art director *n* a person responsible for the sets and costumes in a film.

artefact *or* **artifact** ('ɑːtɪ,fækt) *n* **1** something made or given shape by man, such as a tool or a work of art, esp. an object of archaeological interest. **2** anything manmade, such as a spurious experimental result. **3** *Cytology.* a structure seen in dead tissue that is not normally present in the living tissue. [C19: from L *arte factum*, from *ars* skill + *facere* to make]

artel (ɑː'tɛl) *n* (in the former Soviet Union) a cooperative union or organization, esp. of producers, such as peasants. [from Russian *artel'*, from It. *artieri* artisans, from *arte* work, from L *ars* ART[1]]

Artemis ★ ('ɑːtɪmɪs) *n Greek myth.* the virgin goddess of the hunt and the moon: the twin sister of Apollo. Roman counterpart: **Diana.** Also called: **Cynthia.**

arterial (ɑː'tɪərɪəl) *adj* **1** of or affecting an artery or arteries. **2** denoting or relating to the bright red reoxygenated blood that circulates in the arteries. **3** being a major route, esp. one with many minor branches.
  ▸ **ar'terially** *adv*

arterialize *or* **arterialise** (ɑː'tɪərɪə,laɪz) *vb* **arterializes, arterializing, arterialized** *or* **arterialises, arterialising, arterialised.** (*tr*) **1** to change (venous blood) into arterial blood by replenishing the depleted oxygen. **2** to provide with arteries.
  ▸ **ar,teriali'zation** *or* **ar,teriali'sation** *n*

arteriole (ɑː'tɪərɪ,əʊl) *n Anat.* any of the small subdivisions of an artery that form the final vessels ending in capillaries. [C19: from NL, from L *artēria* ARTERY]

arteriosclerosis (ɑː,tɪərɪəʊsklɪə'rəʊsɪs) *n, pl* **arterioscleroses** (-siːz). a thickening and loss of elasticity of the walls of the arteries. Nontechnical name: **hardening of the arteries.**
  ▸ **arteriosclerotic** (ɑː,tɪərɪəʊsklɪə'rɒtɪk) *adj*

artery ('ɑːtərɪ) *n, pl* **arteries. 1** any of the tubular thick-walled muscular vessels that convey oxygenated blood from the heart to various parts of the body. Cf. **pulmonary artery, vein. 2** a major road or means of communication. [C14: from L *artēria*, rel. to Gk *aortē* the great artery, AORTA]

artesian well (ɑː'tiːzɪən) *n* a well sunk through impermeable strata into strata receiving water from an area at a higher altitude than that of the well, so the water is forced to flow upwards. [C19: from F, from OF *Arteis* Artois, old province, where such wells were common]

Artex ('ɑːtɛks) *n Trademark.* a textured coating for walls and ceilings.

art form *n* **1** an accepted mode of artistic composition, such as the sonnet, symphony, etc. **2** a recognized medium of artistic expression.

artful ('ɑːtfʊl) *adj* **1** cunning or tricky. **2** skilful in achieving a desired end.
  ▸ **'artfully** *adv* ▸ **'artfulness** *n*

art house *n* **1** a cinema that specializes in showing films that are not part of the commercial mainstream. ◆ *adj* **2** of or relating to such films or a cinema that specializes in showing them.

arthralgia (ɑː'θrældʒə) *n Pathol.* pain in a joint.
  ▸ **ar'thralgic** *adj*

arthritis (ɑː'θraɪtɪs) *n* inflammation of a joint or joints characterized by pain and stiffness of the affected parts. [C16: via L from Gk *arthron* joint + -ITIS]
  ▸ **arthritic** (ɑː'θrɪtɪk) *adj, n*

arthropod ('ɑːθrə,pɒd) *n* an invertebrate having jointed limbs, a segmented body, and an exoskeleton made of chitin, as the crustaceans, insects, arachnids, and centipedes. [C19: from NL, from Gk *arthron* joint + *-podus* footed, from *pous* foot]

Arthur ★ ('ɑːθə) *n* **1** a legendary king of the Britons in the sixth century A.D., who led Celtic resistance against the Saxons: possibly based on a historical figure; represented as leader of the Knights of the Round Table at

★ people and places

Camelot. **2 Chester Alan.** 1830–86, 21st president of the US (1881–85).

Arthurian ★ (ɑː'θjʊərɪən) *adj* of or relating to King Arthur and his Knights of the Round Table.

artic (ɑː'tɪk) *n Inf.* short for **articulated lorry.**

artichoke ('ɑːtɪ,tʃəʊk) *n* **1** Also called: **globe artichoke.** a thistle-like Eurasian plant, cultivated for its large edible flower head. **2** the unopened flower head of this plant, which can be cooked and eaten. **3** See **Jerusalem artichoke.** [C16: from It., from OSp., from Ar. *al-kharshūf*]

article ('ɑːtɪkəl) *n* **1** one of a class of objects; item. **2** an unspecified or previously named thing, esp. a small object. **3** a written composition on a subject, often being one of several found in a magazine, newspaper, etc. **4** *Grammar.* a kind of determiner, occurring in many languages including English, that lacks independent meaning. See also **definite article, indefinite article. 5** a clause or section in a written document. **6** *(often cap.)* Christianity. See **Thirty-nine Articles.** ◆ *vb* **articles, articling, articled.** *(tr)* **7** to bind by a written contract, esp. one that governs a period of training: *an articled clerk.* [C13: from OF, from L *articulus* small joint, from *artus* joint]

articular (ɑː'tɪkjʊlə) *adj* of or relating to joints or to the structural components in a joint. [C15: from L *articulāris* concerning the joints, from *articulus* small joint]

articulate *adj* (ɑː'tɪkjʊlɪt). **1** able to express oneself fluently and coherently. **2** having the power of speech. **3** distinct, clear, or definite: *an articulate document.* **4** *Zool.* (of arthropods and higher vertebrates) possessing joints or jointed segments. ◆ *vb* (ɑː'tɪkjʊ,leɪt), **articulates, articulating, articulated. 5** to speak or enunciate (words, syllables, etc.) clearly and distinctly. **6** *(tr)* to express coherently in words. **7** *(intr) Zool.* to be jointed or form a joint. [C16: from L *articulāre* to divide into joints]
▶ ar'ticulately *adv* ▶ ar'ticulateness *n* ▶ ar'ticu,lator *n*

articulated lorry *n* a large lorry made in two separate sections, a tractor and a trailer, connected by a pivoted bar.

articulation (ɑː,tɪkjʊ'leɪʃən) *n* **1** the act or process of speaking or expressing in words. **2a** the process of articulating a speech sound. **2b** the sound so produced, esp. a consonant. **3** the act or the state of being jointed together. **4** *Zool.* **4a** a joint such as that between bones or arthropod segments. **4b** the way in which jointed parts are connected. **5** *Bot.* the part of a plant at which natural separation occurs.

artifact ('ɑːtɪ,fækt) *n* a variant spelling of **artefact.**

artifice ('ɑːtɪfɪs) *n* **1** a clever expedient. **2** crafty or subtle deception. **3** skill; cleverness. **4** a skilfully contrived device. [C16: from OF, from L *artificium* skill, from *artifex* one possessed of a specific skill, from *ars* skill + *-fex*, from *facere* to make]

artificer (ɑː'tɪfɪsə) *n* **1** a skilled craftsman. **2** a clever or inventive designer. **3** a serviceman trained in mechanics.

artificial (,ɑːtɪ'fɪʃəl) *adj* **1** produced by man; not occurring naturally. **2** made in imitation of a natural product: *artificial cream.* **3** pretended; insincere. **4** lacking in spontaneity; affected: *an artificial laugh.* [C14: from L *artificiālis* belonging to art, from *artificium* skill, ARTIFICE]
▶ artificiality (,ɑːtɪ,fɪʃɪ'ælɪtɪ) *n* ▶ ,arti'ficially *adv*

artificial daylight *n Physics.* artificial light having approximately the same spectral characteristics as natural daylight.

artificial disintegration *n Physics.* radioactive transformation of a substance by bombardment with high-energy particles, such as alpha particles or neutrons.

artificial insemination *n* introduction of spermatozoa into the vagina or uterus by means other than sexual union.

artificial intelligence *n* the ability of a machine, such as a computer, to imitate intelligent human behaviour.

artificial respiration *n* **1** any of various methods of restarting breathing after it has stopped. **2** any method of maintaining respiration, as by use of an iron lung.

artillery (ɑː'tɪlərɪ) *n* **1** guns, cannon, mortars, etc., of cali-

bre greater than 20mm. **2** troops or military units specializing in using such guns. **3** the science dealing with the use of guns. [C14: from OF, from *artillier* to equip with weapons, from ?]

artiodactyl (,ɑːtɪəʊ'dæktɪl) *n* an ungulate with an even number of toes, as pigs, camels, deer, cattle, etc. [C19: from Gk *artios* even-numbered + *daktulos* finger]
▶ ,artio'dactylous *adj*

artisan ('ɑːtɪ,zæn, ,ɑːtɪ'zæn) *n* a skilled workman; craftsman. [C16: from F, from OIt. *artigiano,* from *arte* ART[1]]
▶ artisanal (ɑː'tɪzənˀl, 'ɑːtɪzənˀl) *adj*

artist ('ɑːtɪst) *n* **1** a person who practises or is skilled in an art, esp. painting, drawing, or sculpture. **2** a person who displays in his work qualities required in art, such as sensibility and imagination. **3** a person whose profession requires artistic expertise. **4** a person skilled in some task or occupation. **5** *Sl.* a person devoted to or proficient in something: *a con artist; a booze artist.*
▶ ar'tistic *adj* ▶ ar'tistically *adv*

artiste (ɑː'tiːst) *n* **1** an entertainer, such as a singer or dancer. **2** a person who is highly skilled in some occupation: *a hair artiste.* [F]

artistry ('ɑːtɪstrɪ) *n* **1** artistic workmanship, ability, or quality. **2** artistic pursuits. **3** great skill.

artless ('ɑːtlɪs) *adj* **1** free from deceit; ingenuous: *an artless remark.* **2** natural; unpretentious. **3** without art or skill.
▶ 'artlessly *adv*

Art Nouveau (ɑː nuː'vəʊ; *French* ar nuvo) *n* a style of art and architecture of the 1890s, characterized by sinuous outlines and stylized natural forms. [F, lit.: new art]

art paper *n* a high-quality type of paper having a smooth coating of china clay or similar substance on it.

arts (ɑːts) *pl n* **1a the.** imaginative, creative, and nonscientific branches of knowledge considered collectively, esp. as studied academically. **1b** *(as modifier): an arts degree.* **2** See **fine art. 3** cunning actions or schemes.

Arts and Crafts *pl n* decorative handicraft and design, esp. that of the **Arts and Crafts movement,** in late nineteenth-century Britain, which sought to revive medieval craftsmanship.

art union *n Austral. & NZ.* an officially approved lottery for prizes other than cash (formerly works of art).

arty ('ɑːtɪ) *adj* **artier, artiest.** *Inf.* having an affected interest in artists or art.
▶ 'artiness *n*

Aruba ★ (ə'ruːbə; *Dutch* ɑ'ryːbɑ) *n* an island in the Caribbean, off the NW coast of Venezuela, a dependency of the Netherlands with special status; part of the Netherlands Antilles until 1986. Chief town: Oranjestad. Pop.: 68 897 (1991). Area: about 181 sq. km (70 sq. miles).

arugula (ə'ruːgjʊlə) *n* a Mediterranean plant of the mustard family with yellowish-white flowers and pungent leaves that are used as a salad; rocket. See also **rocket**[2] (sense 1). [C20: from N It. dialect]

Aru Islands *or* **Arru Islands** ★ ('ɑːruː) *pl n* a group of islands in Indonesia, in the SW Moluccas. Area: about 8500 sq. km (3300 sq. miles).

arum ('ɛərəm) *n* **1** any of various aroid plants of Europe and the Mediterranean region, having arrow-shaped leaves and a typically white spathe, such as the cuckoo-pint. **2 arum lily.** another name for **calla** (sense 1). [C16: from L, var. of *aros* wake-robin, from Gk *aron*]

Arunachal Pradesh ★ (,ɑːrə'nɑːkˀl prə'deʃ) *n* a state in NE India, formed in 1986 from the former Union Territory. Capital: Itanagar. Pop.: 965 000 (1994 est.). Area: 83 743 sq. km (32 648 sq. miles). Former name (until 1972): **North East Frontier Agency.**

Arundel ★ ('ærəndəl) *n* a town in S England, in West Sussex: 11th-century castle. Pop.: 3033 (1991).

arvo ('ɑːvəʊ) *n Austral. inf.* afternoon.

-ary *suffix.* **1** *(forming adjectives)* of; related to; belonging to: *cautionary.* **2** *(forming nouns)* a person or thing connected with: *missionary; aviary.* [from L *-ārius, -āria, -ārium*]

Aryan ('ɛərɪən) *n* **1** (in Nazi ideology) a Caucasian of non-Jewish descent. **2** a member of any of the peoples supposedly descended from the Indo-Europeans. ◆ *adj* **3** of or characteristic of an Aryan or Aryans. ◆ *adj, n* **4** *Arch.* Indo-European. [C19: from Sansk. *ārya* of noble birth]

as[1] (æz; *unstressed* əz) *conj* (*subordinating*) **1** (often preceded by *just*) while; when: *he caught me as I was leaving.* **2** in the way that: *dancing as only she can.* **3** that which; what: *I did as I was told.* **4** (of) which fact, event, etc. (referring to the previous statement): *to become wise, as we all know, is not easy.* **5** as it were. in a way; as if it were really so. **6** since; seeing that. **7** in the same way that: *he died of cancer, as his father had done.* **8** for instance: *capital cities, as London.* ◆ *adv, conj* **9a** used to indicate identity of extent, amount, etc.: *she is as heavy as her sister.* **9b** used with this sense after a noun phrase introduced by *the same: same height as her sister.* ◆ *prep* **10** in the role of; being: *as his friend, I am probably biased.* **11** as for or to. with reference to: *as for my past, I'm not telling you anything.* **12 as if** or **though.** as it would be if: *he talked as if he knew all about it.* **13 as (it) is.** in the existing state of affairs. **14 as was.** in a previous state. [OE *alswā* likewise]

USAGE NOTE See at **like.**

---

as[2] (æs) *n* **1** an ancient Roman unit of weight approximately equal to 1 pound Troy (373 grams). **2** a copper coin of ancient Rome. [C17: from L *ās* unity]

As *symbol for:* **1** altostratus. **2** *Chem.* arsenic.

AS *abbrev. for:* **1** Also: **A.S.** Anglo-Saxon. **2** antisubmarine.

ASA *abbrev. for:* **1** (in Britain) Amateur Swimming Association. **2** (in Britain) Advertising Standards Authority. **3** (in the US) American Standards Association.

ASA/BS *abbrev.* an obsolete expression of the speed of a photographic film, replaced by the ISO rating. [C20: from *American Standards Association/British Standard*]

asafoetida *or* **asafetida** (ˌæsəˈfɛtɪdə) *n* a bitter resin with an unpleasant onion-like smell, obtained from the roots of some umbelliferous plants: formerly used to treat flatulence, etc. [C14: from Med. L, from *asa* gum (cf. Persian *azā* mastic) + L *foetidus* evil-smelling]

a.s.a.p. *abbrev. for* as soon as possible.

Asben ★ (æsˈben) *n* another name for **Aïr** (region of the Sahara).

asbestos (æsˈbɛstɒs) *n* **a** any of the fibrous amphibole minerals that are incombustible and resistant to chemicals. It was formerly widely used in the form of fabric or board as a heat-resistant structural material. **b** (*as modifier*): *asbestos matting.* [C14: via L from Gk: from *asbestos* inextinguishable, from A-[1] + *shennunai* to extinguish]

asbestosis (ˌæsbɛsˈtəʊsɪs) *n* inflammation of the lungs resulting from chronic inhalation of asbestos particles.

Ascanius ★ (æˈskeɪnɪəs) *n Roman myth.* the son of Aeneas and Creusa; founder of Alba Longa, mother city of Rome. Also called: **Iulus.**

ascarid (ˈæskərɪd) *n* a parasitic nematode worm such as the common roundworm of man and pigs. [C14: from NL, from Gk *askarides*, pl. of *askaris*]

ascend (əˈsɛnd) *vb* **1** to go or move up (a ladder, hill, slope, etc.) **2** (*intr*) to slope or incline upwards. **3** (*intr*) to rise to a higher point, level, etc. **4** to trace (a genealogy, etc.) back in time. **5** to sing or play (a scale, etc.) from the lower to higher notes. **6 ascend the throne.** to become king or queen. [C14: from L *ascendere*, from *scandere*]

ascendancy, ascendency (əˈsɛndənsɪ) *or* **ascendance, ascendence** *n* the condition of being dominant.

ascendant *or* **ascendent** (əˈsɛndənt) *adj* **1** proceeding upwards; rising. **2** dominant or influential. ◆ *n* **3** a position or condition of dominance. **4** *Astrol.* (*sometimes cap.*) **4a** a point on the ecliptic that rises on the eastern horizon at a particular moment. **4b** the sign of the zodiac containing this point. **5 in the ascendant.** increasing in influence, etc.

ascender (əˈsɛndə) *n* **1** *Printing.* the part of certain lower-

---

case letters, such as *b* or *h*, that extends above the body of the letter. **2** a person or thing that ascends.

ascension (əˈsɛnʃən) *n* the act of ascending.
 ► **as'censional** *adj*

Ascension[1] (əˈsɛnʃən) *n Bible.* the passing of Jesus Christ from earth into heaven (Acts 1:9).

Ascension[2] ★ (əˈsɛnʃən) *n* an island in the S Atlantic, northwest of St Helena: uninhabited until claimed by Britain in 1815. Pop.: 1117 (1993). Area: 88 sq. km (34 sq. miles).

Ascension Day *n* the 40th day after Easter, when the Ascension of Christ into heaven is celebrated.

ascent (əˈsɛnt) *n* **1** the act of ascending; upward movement. **2** an upward slope. **3** movement back through time (esp. in **line of ascent**).

ascertain (ˌæsəˈteɪn) *vb* (*tr*) **1** to determine definitely. **2** *Arch.* to make certain. [C15: from OF *acertener* to make certain]
 ► ˌascer'tainable *adj* ► ˌascer'tainment *n*

ascetic (əˈsɛtɪk) *n* **1** a person who practises great self-denial and abstains from worldly comforts and pleasures, esp. for religious reasons. ◆ *adj also* **ascetical.** **2** rigidly abstinent or abstemious. **3** of or relating to ascetics or asceticism. [C17: from Gk *askētikos*, from *askētēs*, from *askein* to exercise]
 ► as'cetically *adv* ► a'sceti,cism *n*

Asch ★ (æʃ) *n Sholem* (ˈʃəʊləm). 1880–1957, US writer, born in Poland, who wrote in Yiddish.

Aschaffenburg ★ (*German* aˈʃafənburk) *n* a city in Germany, on the River Main in Bavaria: seat of the Imperial Diet (1447); ceded to Bavaria in 1814. Pop.: 62 050 (1989 est.).

Ascham ★ (ˈæskəm) *n Roger.* ?1515–68, English humanist writer and classical scholar: he was tutor to Queen Elizabeth I.

ascidian (əˈsɪdɪən) *n* any of a class of minute marine invertebrate animals, such as the sea squirt, the adults of which are degenerate and sedentary.

ascidium (əˈsɪdɪəm) *n, pl* **ascidia** (-ˈsɪdɪə). part of a plant that is shaped like a pitcher, such as the modified leaf of the pitcher plant. [C18: from NL, from Gk *askidion* a little bag, from *askos* bag]

Asclepius ★ (əˈskliːpɪəs) *n Greek myth.* a god of healing; son of Apollo. Roman counterpart: **Aesculapius** (ˌiːskjuˈleɪpɪəs).

ascomycete (ˌæskəmaɪˈsiːt) *n* any of a phylum of fungi in which the spores (ascospores) are formed inside a club-shaped cell (ascus). The group includes yeast, penicillium, and certain mildews.
 ► ˌascomy'cetous *adj*

ascorbic acid (əˈskɔːbɪk) *n* a white crystalline vitamin present in plants, esp. citrus fruits, tomatoes, and green vegetables. A deficiency in the diet of man leads to scurvy. Also called: **vitamin C.**

Ascot ★ (ˈæskət) *n* a town in S England, in Berkshire: noted for its horse-race meetings, esp. **Royal Ascot,** a four-day meeting held in June. Pop.: 13 500 (latest est.).

ascribe (əˈskraɪb) *vb* **ascribes, ascribing, ascribed.** (*tr*) **1** to credit or assign, as to a particular origin or period. **2** to consider as belonging to: *to ascribe beauty to youth.* [C15: from L *ascrībere* to enrol, from *ad* in addition + *scrībere* to write]
 ► as'cribable *adj*

USAGE NOTE *Ascribe* is sometimes wrongly used where *subscribe* is meant: *I do not subscribe* (not *ascribe*) *to this view.*

---

ascription (əˈskrɪpʃən) *n* **1** the act of ascribing. **2** a statement ascribing something to someone. [C16: from L *ascriptiō*, from *ascrībere* to ASCRIBE]

asdic (ˈæzdɪk) *n* an early form of **sonar.** [C20: from *A*(*nti*)*S*(*ubmarine*) *D*(*etection*) *I*(*nvestigation*) *C*(*ommittee*)]

-ase *suffix forming nouns.* indicating an enzyme: *oxidase.* [from DIASTASE]

★ people and places

ASEAN ('æsɪˌæn) n acronym for Association of South-East Asian Nations.

asepsis (ə'sɛpsɪs, eɪ-) n 1 the state of being free from living pathogenic organisms. 2 the methods of achieving a germ-free condition.
▸ **a'septic** adj

asexual (eɪ'sɛksjʊəl) adj 1 having no apparent sex or sex organs. 2 (of reproduction) not involving the fusion of male and female gametes. Cf.: sexual (sense 2).
▸ ˌasexu'ality n ▸ a'sexually adv

Asgard ('æsgɑːd) or **Asgarth** ★ ('æsgɑːθ) n Norse myth. the dwelling place of the principal gods, the Aesir.

ash[1] (æʃ) n 1 the residue formed when matter is burnt. 2 fine particles of lava thrown out by an erupting volcano. 3 a light silvery-grey colour. ♦ See also **ashes**. [OE æsce]

ash[2] (æʃ) n 1 a tree having compound leaves, clusters of small greenish flowers, and winged seeds. 2 the wood of this tree, used for tool handles, etc. 3 any of several trees resembling the ash, such as the mountain ash. 4 Austral. any of various eucalypts. [OE æsc]

ash[3] (æʃ) n the digraph æ, as in Old English, representing a vowel approximately like that of the a in Modern English hat.

ASH (æʃ) n (in Britain) acronym for Action on Smoking and Health.

ashamed (ə'ʃeɪmd) adj (usually postpositive) 1 overcome with shame or remorse. 2 (foll. by of) suffering from feelings of shame in relation to (a person or deed). 3 (foll. by to) unwilling through fear of humiliation, shame, etc. [OE āscamod, p.p. of āscamian to shame, from scamu SHAME]
▸ **ashamedly** (ə'ʃeɪmɪdlɪ) adv

Ashanti (ə'ʃæntɪ) n 1 an administrative region of central Ghana: former native kingdom, suppressed by the British in 1900 after four wars. Capital: Kumasi. Pop.: 2 485 766 (1991 est.). Area: 24 390 sq. km (9417 sq. miles). 2 (pl **Ashanti** or **Ashantis**) a native or inhabitant of Ashanti.

A shares pl n ordinary shares in a company which carry restricted voting rights.

ash can n a US word for **dustbin**. Also called: **garbage can, ash bin, trash can**.

Ashcroft ★ ('æʃkrɒft) n Dame **Peggy**. 1907–91, English stage and film actress.

Ashdod ★ ('æʃdɒd) n a town in central Israel, on the Mediterranean coast: an important city in the Philistine Empire, with its artificial harbour (1961) it is now a major port. Pop.: 137 100 (1997 est.).

Ashdown ★ ('æʃdaʊn) n **Paddy**, real name Jeremy John Durham Ashdown. born 1941, British politician; leader of the Liberal Democrats (1988–99).

Ashe ★ (æʃ) n Arthur (Robert). 1943–93, US tennis player: US champion 1968; Wimbledon champion 1975.

ashen[1] ('æʃən) adj 1 drained of colour. 2 consisting of or resembling ashes. 3 of a pale greyish colour.

ashen[2] ('æʃən) adj of, relating to, or made from the ash tree or its timber.

Asher ★ ('æʃə) n the son of Jacob and ancestor of one of the 12 tribes of Israel.

ashes ('æʃɪz) pl n 1 ruins or remains, as after burning. 2 the remains of a human body after cremation.

Ashes ('æʃɪz) pl n the. a cremated cricket stump constituting a trophy competed for by England and Australia in test cricket since 1882. [from a mock obituary of English cricket after a great Australian victory]

Ashford ★ ('æʃfəd) n a market town in SE England, in central Kent. Pop.: 52 002 (1991).

Ashkenazi (ˌæʃkə'nɑːzɪ) n, pl **Ashkenazim** (-zɪm). 1 (modifier) of or relating to the Jews of Germany and E Europe. 2 a Jew of German or E European descent. Cf. **Sephardi**. [C19: LHeb., from Heb. Ashkenaz, the son of Gomer (Genesis 10:3; I Chronicles 1:6)]

Ashkenazy ★ (ˌæʃkə'nɑːzɪ) n Vladimir. born 1937, Soviet-born pianist and conductor, living in Iceland.

Ashkhabad (Russian aʃxa'baɪt) or **Ashgabat** ★ ('ɑːʃgəbæt; Turkmen aʃgɑ'bɑt) n the capital of Turkmenistan. Pop.: 518 000 (1994 est.).

ashlar or **ashler** ('æʃlə) n 1 a square block of hewn stone for use in building. 2 a thin dressed stone with straight edges, used to face a wall. 3 masonry made of ashlar. [C14: from OF aisselier crossbeam, from ais board, from L axis axletree]

Ashley ★ ('æʃlɪ) n Laura. 1925–85, British fashion designer.

ashore (ə'ʃɔː) adv 1 towards or onto land from the water. ♦ adj (postpositive), adv 2 on land: a day ashore before sailing.

ashram ('æʃrəm) n a religious retreat or community where a Hindu holy man lives. [from Sansk. āśrama, from ā- near + śrama religious exertion]

Ashton ★ ('æʃtən) n Sir **Frederick**. 1906–88, British ballet dancer and choreographer. His ballets include Façade (1931) and A Month in the Country (1976).

Ashton-under-Lyne ★ (laɪn) n a town in NW England, in Tameside unitary authority, Greater Manchester. Pop.: 43 906 (1991).

Ashtoreth ★ ('æʃtəˌrɛθ) n Old Testament. an ancient Semitic fertility goddess, identified with Astarte and Ishtar.

ashtray ('æʃˌtreɪ) n a receptacle for tobacco ash, cigarette butts, etc.

Ashur ★ ('æʃʊə) n a variant spelling of **Assur**.

Ash Wednesday n the first day of Lent, named from the Christian custom of sprinkling ashes on penitents' heads.

ashy ('æʃɪ) adj ashier, ashiest. 1 of a pale greyish colour; ashen. 2 consisting of, covered with, or resembling ash.

'Asi ★ ('æsɪ) n the Arabic name for the **Orontes**.

Asia ★ ('eɪʃə, 'eɪʒə) n the largest of the continents, bordering on the Arctic Ocean, the Pacific Ocean, the Indian Ocean, and the Mediterranean and Red Seas in the west. It includes the large peninsulas of Asia Minor, India, Arabia, and Indochina and the island groups of Japan, Indonesia, the Philippines, and Sri Lanka; contains the mountain ranges of the Hindu Kush, Himalayas, Pamirs, Tian Shan, Urals, and Caucasus, the great plateaus of India, Iran, and Tibet, vast plains and deserts, and the valleys of many large rivers including the Mekong, Irrawaddy, Indus, Ganges, Tigris, and Euphrates. Pop.: 3 499 626 (1996 est.). Area: 44 391 162 sq. km (17 139 445 sq. miles).

Asia Minor ★ n the historical name for **Anatolia**.

Asian ('eɪʃən, 'eɪʒən) adj 1 of or relating to Asia or to any of its peoples or languages. 2 Brit. of or relating to natives of the Indian subcontinent or their descendants, esp. when living in Britain. ♦ n 3 a native or inhabitant of Asia or a descendant of one. 4 Brit. a native of the Indian subcontinent or a descendant of one.

> **USAGE NOTE** The use of Asian or Asiatic as a noun can be offensive and should be avoided.

Asian flu n a type of influenza caused by a virus which apparently originated in China in 1957.

Asian pear n a variety of pear, apple-shaped with crisp juicy flesh.

Asiatic (ˌeɪʃɪ'ætɪk, -zɪ-) n, adj another word for **Asian**.

> **USAGE NOTE** See at **Asian**.

Asiatic cholera n another name for **cholera**.

aside (ə'saɪd) adv 1 on or to one side. 2 out of hearing; in or into seclusion. 3 away from oneself: he threw the book aside. 4 out of mind or consideration: he put aside all fears. 5 in or into reserve: to put aside money for old age. ♦ n 6 something spoken by an actor, intended to be heard by the audience, but not by the others on stage. 7 any confidential statement spoken in undertones. 8 an incidental remark, note, etc.

★ people and places

A-side *n* the side of a gramophone record regarded as more important.

Asimov ★ ('æzɪmɒf) *n* **Isaac.** 1920–92, US writer and biochemist, born in Russia. His science-fiction works include *Foundation Trilogy* (1951–53; sequel 1982) and the collection of stories *I, Robot* (1950).

asinine ('æsɪˌnaɪn) *adj* **1** obstinate or stupid. **2** resembling an ass. [C16: from L *asinīnus*, from *asinus* ASS[1]]
▸ **'asi,ninely** *adv* ▸ **asininity** (ˌæsɪ'nɪnɪtɪ) *n*

ASIO *abbrev. for* Australian Security Intelligence Organization.

Asir ★ (æ'sɪə) *n* a region of SW Saudi Arabia, in the Southern Province on the Red Sea: under Turkish rule until 1933. Area: 81 000 sq. km (31 000 sq. miles).

ask (ɑːsk) *vb* **1** (often foll. by *about*) to put a question (to); request an answer (from). **2** (*tr*) to inquire about: *she asked the way.* **3** (*tr*) to direct or put (a question). **4** (*may take a clause as object or an infinitive; often foll. by for*) to make a request or demand: *they asked for a deposit.* **5** (*tr*) to demand or expect (esp. in **ask a lot of, ask too much of**). **6** (*tr*) Also: **ask out, ask over.** to request (a person) politely to come or go to a place: *he asked her to the party.* [OE *āscian*]
▸ **'asker** *n*

Ask ★ (ɑːsk) *n Norse myth.* the first man, created by the gods from an ash tree.

ask after *vb* (*prep*) to make inquiries about the health of (someone): *he asked after her mother.*

askance (ə'skæns) *or* **askant** (ə'skænt) *adv* **1** with an oblique glance. **2** with doubt or mistrust. [C16: from ?]

askew (ə'skjuː) *adv, adj* at an oblique angle; towards one side; awry.

Askey ★ ('æskɪ) *n* **Arthur.** 1900–82, British comedian.

ask for *vb* (*prep*) **1** to try to obtain by requesting. **2** (*intr*) *Inf.* to behave in a provocative manner that is regarded as inviting (trouble, etc.): *you're asking for it.*

asking price *n* the price suggested by a seller but usually considered to be subject to bargaining.

Askja ★ ('ɑːskjə) *n* a volcano in E central Iceland: active in 1961; largest crater in Iceland. Height: 1510 m (4954 ft). Area of crater: 88 sq. km (34 sq. miles).

aslant (ə'slɑːnt) *adv* **1** at a slant. ◆ *prep* **2** at a slant across or athwart.

asleep (ə'sliːp) *adj* (*postpositive*) **1** in or into a state of sleep. **2** in or into a dormant or inactive state. **3** (of limbs) numb; lacking sensation. **4** *Euphemistic.* dead.

ASLEF ('æzlɛf) *n* (in Britain) *acronym for* Associated Society of Locomotive Engineers and Firemen.

AS level *n Brit.* **1a** an advanced level of a subject taken for the General Certificate of Education, with a smaller course content than an A level. **1b** (*as modifier*): *AS-level English.* **2** a pass in a subject at AS level: *I've got three AS levels.*

ASM *abbrev. for:* **1** air-to-surface missile. **2** *Theatre.* assistant stage manager.

Asmara ★ (æs'mɑːrə) *n* the capital of Eritrea. Pop.: 367 300 (1991 est.).

Asnières ★ (*French* anjɛr) *n* a suburb of Paris, France, on the Seine. Pop.: 72 250 (1990).

Aso ★ ('ɑːsəʊ) *n* a group of five volcanic cones in Japan on central Kyushu, one of which, Naka-dake, has the largest crater in the world, between 16 km (10 miles) and 24 km (15 miles) in diameter. Highest cone: 1592 m (5223 ft). Also called: **Asosan** (ˌɑːsəʊ'sɑːn).

asocial (eɪ'səʊʃəl) *adj* **1** avoiding contact. **2** unconcerned about the welfare of others. **3** hostile to society.

asp (æsp) *n* **1** the venomous snake that caused the death of Cleopatra. **2** Also called: **asp viper.** a viper that occurs in S Europe and is very similar to but smaller than the adder. **3 horned asp.** another name for **horned viper.** [C15: from L *aspis*, from Gk]

asparagus (ə'spærəgəs) *n* **1** a plant of the lily family, having small scaly or needle-like leaves. **2** the succulent young shoots, which may be cooked and eaten. **3 asparagus fern.** a fernlike species of asparagus, native to southern Africa. [C15: from L, from Gk *asparagos*, from ?]

aspartame (ə'spɑːˌteɪm) *n* an artificial sweetener produced from a nonessential amino acid. [C20: from *aspart(ic acid)* + *(phenyl)a(lanine)* *m(ethyl)* *e(ster)*]

aspect ('æspɛkt) *n* **1** appearance to the eye; visual effect. **2** a distinct feature or element in a problem, situation, etc.; facet. **3** the way in which a problem, idea, etc., may be considered. **4** a facial expression: *a severe aspect.* **5** a position facing a particular direction: *the southern aspect of a house.* **6** a view in a certain direction. **7** *Astrol.* any of several specific angular distances between two planets. **8** *Grammar.* a category of verbal inflections that expresses such features as the continuity, repetition, or completedness of the action described. [C14: from L *aspectus* a sight, from *ad-* to, at + *specere* to look]

aspect ratio *n* **1** the ratio of width to height of a picture on a television or cinema screen. **2** *Aeronautics.* the ratio of the span of a wing to its mean chord.

aspen ('æspən) *n* a kind of poplar tree in which the leaves are attached to the stem by long flattened stalks so that they quiver in the wind. [OE *æspe*]

Asperger's syndrome ('æspəgəz) *n* a form of autism in which the sufferer has limited but obsessive interests and has difficulty relating to other people. [C20: after Hans *Asperger* (20th century), Austrian physician who first described it]

asperity (æ'spɛrɪtɪ) *n, pl* **asperities.** **1** roughness or sharpness of temper. **2** roughness or harshness of a surface, sound, etc. **3** *Physics.* the elongated compressed region of contact between two surfaces caused by the normal force. [C16: from L *asperitās*, from *asper* rough]

asperse (ə'spɜːs) *vb* **asperses, aspersing, aspersed.** (*tr*) to spread false rumours about; defame. [C15: from L *aspersus*, from *aspergere* to sprinkle]
▸ **as'perser** *n* ▸ **as'persive** *adj*

aspersion (ə'spɜːʃən) *n* **1** a disparaging or malicious remark (esp. in **cast aspersions (on)**). **2** the act of defaming.

asphalt ('æsfælt) *n* **1** any of several black semisolid substances composed of bitumen and inert mineral matter. They occur naturally and as a residue from petroleum distillation. **2** a mixture of this substance with gravel, used in road-surfacing and roofing materials. **3** (*modifier*) containing or surfaced with asphalt. ◆ *vb* **4** (*tr*) to cover with asphalt. [C14: from LL *aspaltus*, from Gk *asphaltos*, prob. from A-[1] + *sphallein* to cause to fall; referring to its use as a binding agent]
▸ **as'phaltic** *adj*

asphodel ('æsfəˌdɛl) *n* **1** any of various S European plants of the lily family having clusters of white or yellow flowers. **2** an unidentified flower of Greek legend said to cover the Elysian fields. [C16: from L *asphodelus*, from Gk *asphodelos*, from ?]

asphyxia (æs'fɪksɪə) *n* lack of oxygen in the blood due to restricted respiration; suffocation. [C18: from NL, from Gk *asphuxia* a stopping of the pulse, from A-[1] + *sphuxis* pulse, from *sphuzein* to throb]
▸ **as'phyxial** *adj* ▸ **as'phyxiant** *adj*

asphyxiate (æs'fɪksɪˌeɪt) *vb* **asphyxiates, asphyxiating, asphyxiated.** to cause asphyxia in or undergo asphyxia; smother; suffocate.
▸ **as,phyxi'ation** *n* ▸ **as'phyxi,ator** *n*

aspic ('æspɪk) *n* a savoury jelly based on meat or fish stock, used as a relish or as a mould for meat, vegetables, etc. [C18: from F: aspic (jelly), asp]

aspidistra (ˌæspɪ'dɪstrə) *n* a popular house plant of the lily family with long tough evergreen leaves. [C19: from NL, from Gk *aspis* shield, on the model of *Tupistra*, genus of liliaceous plants]

aspirant ('æspɪrənt) *n* **1** a person who aspires, as to a high position. ◆ *adj* **2** aspiring.

aspirate *vb* ('æspɪˌreɪt), **aspirates, aspirating, aspirated.** (*tr*) **1** *Phonetics.* **1a** to articulate (a stop) with some force, so that breath escapes audibly. **1b** to pronounce (a word or syllable) with an initial *h*. **2** to remove by inhalation or suction, esp. to suck (air or fluid) from a body cavity. **3** to supply air to (an internal-combustion engine). ◆ *n* ('æspɪrɪt). **4** *Phonetics.* **4a** a stop pronounced with an audible release of breath. **4b** the glottal fricative represented in English and several other languages as *h*. ◆ *adj* ('æspɪrɪt). **5** *Phonetics*. (of a stop) pronounced with a forceful expulsion of breath.

aspiration (ˌæspɪ'reɪʃən) *n* **1** strong desire to achieve something, such as success. **2** the aim of such desire. **3** the act of breathing. **4** *Phonetics*. **4a** the pronunciation of an aspirated consonant. **4b** an aspirated consonant. **5** *Med*. **5a** the sucking of fluid or foreign matter into the air passages of the body. **5b** the removal of air or fluid from the body by suction.
▸ ˌaspi'rational *adj* ▸ aspiratory (ə'spaɪrətərɪ) *adj*

aspirator ('æspɪˌreɪtə) *n* a device employing suction, such as a jet pump or one for removing fluids from a body cavity.

aspire (ə'spaɪə) *vb* aspires, aspiring, aspired. (*intr*) **1** (usually foll. by *to* or *after*) to yearn (for), desire, or hope (to do or be something): *to aspire to be a great leader*. **2** to rise to a great height. [C15: from L *aspīrāre* to breathe upon, from *spīrāre* to breathe]
▸ as'piring *adj*

aspirin ('æsprɪn) *n*, *pl* aspirin *or* aspirins. **1** a white crystalline compound widely used in the form of tablets to relieve pain, fever, and colds. Chemical name: **acetylsalicylic acid**. **2** a tablet of aspirin. [C19: from G, from *A*(*cetyl*) + *Spir*(*säure*) spiraeic acid (modern salicylic acid) + -IN]

Aspirin ('æsprɪn) *n* (in Canada) a trademark for **aspirin**.

asquint (ə'skwɪnt) *adv*, *adj* (*postpositive*) with a glance from the corner of the eye, esp. a furtive one. [C13: ?from Du. *schuinte* slant, from ?]

Asquith ★ ('æskwɪθ) *n* Herbert Henry, 1st Earl of Oxford and Asquith. 1852–1928, British statesman; prime minister (1908–16); leader of the Liberal Party (1908–26).

ass[1] (æs) *n* **1** a mammal related to the horse. It is hardy and sure-footed, having longer ears than the horse. **2** (not in technical use) the donkey. **3** a foolish or ridiculously pompous person. [OE *assa*, prob. from OIrish *asan*, from L *asinus*; rel. to Gk *onos* ass]

ass[2] (æs) *n* the usual US and Canad. word for **arse**. [OE *ærs*]

Assad ★ ('asat) *n* Hafezal ('hafɛzal). born 1928, Syrian statesman and general; president of Syria from 1971.

assagai ('æsəˌgaɪ) *n*, *pl* assagais. a variant spelling of **assegai**.

assai (æ'saɪ) *adv Music*. (usually preceded by a musical direction) very: *allegro assai*. [It.: enough]

assail (ə'seɪl) *vb* (*tr*) **1** to attack violently; assault. **2** to criticize or ridicule vehemently. **3** to beset or disturb: *his mind was assailed by doubts*. **4** to encounter with the intention of mastering. [C13: from OF *asalir*, from L *assilīre*, from *salīre* to leap]
▸ as'sailable *adj* ▸ as'sailer *n*

assailant (ə'seɪlənt) *n* a person who attacks another, either physically or verbally.

Assam ★ (æ'sæm) *n* a state of NE India, situated in the central Brahmaputra valley: tropical forest, with the heaviest rainfall in the world; produces large quantities of tea. Capital: Dispur. Pop.: 24 200 000 (1994 est.). Area: 78 438 sq. km (30 285 sq. miles).
▸ ˌAssa'mese *adj*, *n*

assassin (ə'sæsɪn) *n* a murderer, esp. one who kills a prominent political figure. [C16: from Med. L *assassīnus*, from Ar. *hashshāshīn*, pl. of *hashshāsh* one who eats HASHISH]

assassinate (ə'sæsɪˌneɪt) *vb* assassinates, assassinating, assassinated. (*tr*) **1** to murder (a political figure). **2** to ruin or harm (a person's reputation, etc.) by slander.
▸ asˌsassi'nation *n*

assault (ə'sɔːlt) *n* **1** a violent attack, either physical or verbal. **2** *Law*. an act that threatens violence to another. **3a** the culmination of a military attack. **3b** (*as modifier*): *assault troops*. **4** rape or attempted rape. ◆ *vb* (*tr*) **5** to make an assault upon. **6** to rape or attempt to rape. [C13: from OF *asaut*, from Vulgar L, from *assalīre* (unattested) to leap upon; see ASSAIL]
▸ as'saultive *adj*

assault and battery *n Criminal law*. a threat of attack to another person followed by actual attack.

assault course *n* an obstacle course designed to give soldiers practice in negotiating hazards.

assay *vb* (ə'seɪ). **1** to subject (a substance, such as silver or gold) to chemical analysis, as in the determination of the amount of impurity. **2** (*tr*) to attempt (something or to do something). ◆ *n* (ə'seɪ, 'æseɪ). **3a** an analysis, esp. a determination of the amount of metal in an ore or the amounts of impurities in a precious metal. **3b** (*as modifier*): *an assay office*. **4** a substance undergoing an analysis. **5** a written report on the results of an analysis. **6** a test. [C14: from OF *assai*; see ESSAY]
▸ as'sayer *n*

assegai *or* **assagai** ('æsəˌgaɪ) *n*, *pl* assegais *or* assagais. **1** a southern African tree, the wood of which is used for making spears. **2** a sharp light spear. [C17: from Port. *azagaia*, from Ar. *az zaghāyah*, from *al* the + *zaghāyah* assegai, from Berber]

assemblage (ə'semblɪdʒ) *n* **1** a number of things or persons assembled together. **2** the act of assembling or the state of being assembled. **3** (ˌæsəm'blɑːʒ). a three-dimensional work of art that combines various objects.

assemble (ə'sembəl) *vb* assembles, assembling, assembled. **1** to come or bring together; collect or congregate. **2** to fit or join together (the parts of something, such as a machine). [C13: from OF *assembler*, from Vulgar L *assimulāre* (unattested) to bring together, from L *simul* together]

assembler (ə'semblə) *n* **1** a person or thing that assembles. **2** a computer program that converts a program written in assembly language into machine code. Cf. **compiler**. **3** another name for **assembly language**.

assembly (ə'semblɪ) *n*, *pl* assemblies. **1** a number of people gathered together, esp. for a formal meeting held at regular intervals. **2** the act of assembling or the state of being assembled. **3** the process of putting together a number of parts to make a machine. **4** *Mil*. a signal for personnel to assemble.

Assembly (ə'semblɪ) *n*, *pl* Assemblies. **1** the lower chamber in various state legislatures, esp. in Australia and America. See also **House of Assembly, legislative assembly**. **2** *NZ*. short for **General Assembly**.

assembly language *n Computing*. a low-level programming language that allows a programmer complete control of the machine code to be generated.

assembly line *n* a sequence of machines, tools, operations, workers, etc., in a factory, arranged so that at each stage a further process is carried out.

Assen ★ (*Dutch* 'ɑsə) *n* a city in the N Netherlands, capital of Drenthe province. Pop.: 52 268 (1994).

assent (ə'sent) *n* **1** agreement, as to a statement, proposal, etc. **2** compliance. ◆ *vb* (*intr*; usually foll. by *to*) **3** to agree or express agreement. [C13: from OF *assenter*, from L *assentīrī*, from *sentīre* to think]

assert (ə'sɜːt) *vb* (*tr*) **1** to insist upon (rights, etc.). **2** (*may take a clause as object*) to state to be true; declare. **3** to put (oneself) forward in an insistent manner. [C17: from L *asserere* to join to oneself, from *serere* to join]
▸ as'serter *or* as'sertor *n*

assertion (ə'sɜːʃən) *n* **1** a positive statement, usually made without evidence. **2** the act of asserting.

assertion sign *n* a sign ⊢ used in symbolic logic to introduce the conclusion of a valid argument: often read as "therefore."

assertive (ə'sɜːtɪv) *adj* **1** confident and direct in dealing with others. **2** given to making assertions; dogmatic or aggressive.
▸ as'sertively *adv* ▸ as'sertiveness *n*

assess (ə'ses) *vb* (*tr*) **1** to evaluate. **2** (foll. by *at*) to estimate the value of (income, property, etc.) for taxation purposes. **3** to determine the amount of (a fine, tax, etc.). **4** to impose a tax, fine, etc., on (a person or property). [C15: from OF *assesser*, from L *assidēre* to sit beside, from *sedēre* to sit]
▸ as'sessable *adj*

assessment (ə'sesmənt) *n* **1** the act of assessing, esp. (in

Britain) the evaluation of a student's achievement on a course. **2** an amount determined as payable. **3** a valuation set on taxable property, etc. **4** evaluation.

assessment tests *pl n Brit. education.* nationally standardized tests for pupil assessment based on attainment targets in the National Curriculum. Formal name: **standard assessment tasks, SATs.**

assessor (ə'sɛsə) *n* **1** a person who evaluates the merits of something. **2** a person who values property for taxation. **3** a person who estimates the value of damage to property for insurance purposes. **4** a person with technical expertise called in to advise a court.
▸ **assessorial** (ˌæsɛ'sɔːrɪəl) *adj*

asset ('æsɛt) *n* anything valuable or useful. [C19: back formation from ASSETS]

assets ('æsɛts) *pl n* **1** *Accounting.* the property and claims against debtors that are shown balanced against liabilities. **2** *Law.* the property available to an executor for settling a deceased person's estate. **3** any property owned by a person or firm. [C16: from OF *asez* enough, from Vulgar L *ad satis* (unattested) from L *ad* up to + *satis* enough]

asset-stripping *n Commerce.* the practice of taking over a failing company at a low price and then selling the assets piecemeal.
▸ **'asset-ˌstripper** *n*

asset value *n* the value of a share in a company calculated by dividing the difference between the total of its assets and its liabilities by the number of ordinary shares issued.

asseverate (ə'sɛvəˌreɪt) *vb* **asseverates, asseverating, asseverated.** (*tr*) to declare solemnly. [C18: from L *assevērāre* to do (something) earnestly, from *sevērus* SEVERE]
▸ **asˌseverˈation** *n*

Asshur ★ ('æʃʊə) *n* a variant spelling of **Assur.**

assibilate (ə'sɪbɪˌleɪt) *vb* **assibilates, assibilating, assibilated.** (*tr*) *Phonetics.* to pronounce (a speech sound) with or as a sibilant. [C19: from LL *assībīlāre* to hiss at, from *sībilāre* to hiss]
▸ **asˌsibiˈlation** *n*

assiduity (ˌæsɪ'djuːɪtɪ) *n, pl* **assiduities. 1** constant and close application. **2** (*often pl*) devoted attention.

assiduous (ə'sɪdjʊəs) *adj* **1** hard-working; persevering. **2** undertaken with perseverance and care. [C16: from L, from *assidēre* to sit beside, from *sedēre* to sit]
▸ **asˈsiduousness** *n*

assign (ə'saɪn) *vb* (*mainly tr*) **1** to select for and appoint to a post, etc. **2** to give out or allot (a task, problem, etc.). **3** to set apart (a place, person, time, etc.) for a particular function or event: *to assign a day for the meeting.* **4** to attribute to a specified cause, origin, or source. **5** to transfer (one's right, interest, or title to property) to someone else. ◆ *n* **6** *Law.* a person to whom property is assigned; assignee. [C14: from OF, from L *assignāre*, from *signāre* to mark out]
▸ **asˈsignable** *adj* ▸ **asˈsigner** *or* ˌassignˈor *n*

assignation (ˌæsɪg'neɪʃən) *n* **1** a secret or forbidden arrangement to meet, esp. one between lovers. **2** the act of assigning; assignment. [C14: from OF, from L *assignātiō* a marking out]

assignee (ˌæsaɪ'niː) *n Law.* a person to whom some right, interest, or property is transferred.

assignment (ə'saɪnmənt) *n* **1** something that has been assigned, such as a mission or task. **2** a position or post to which a person is assigned. **3** the act of assigning or state of being assigned. **4** *Law.* **4a** the transfer to another of a right, interest, or title to property. **4b** the document effecting such a transfer.

assimilate (ə'sɪmɪˌleɪt) *vb* **assimilates, assimilating, assimilated. 1** (*tr*) to learn (information, etc.) and understand it thoroughly. **2** (*tr*) to absorb (food). **3** (*intr*) to become absorbed, incorporated, or learned and understood. **4** (usually foll. by *into* or *with*) to adjust or become adjusted: *the new immigrants assimilated easily.* **5** (usually foll. by *to* or *with*) to become or cause to become similar. **6** (usually foll. by *to*) *Phonetics.* to change (a consonant) or (of a consonant) to be changed into another under the influ-

ence of one adjacent to it. [C15: from L *assimilāre* to make one thing like another, from *similis* like, SIMILAR]
▸ **asˈsimilable** *adj* ▸ **asˌsimiˈlation** *n* ▸ **asˈsimilative** *or* asˈsimilatory *adj* ▸ **asˈsimiˌlator** *n*

Assiniboine ★ (ə'sɪnɪˌbɔɪn) *n* a river in W Canada, rising in E Saskatchewan and flowing southeast and east to the Red River at Winnipeg. Length: over 860 km (500 miles).

Assisi ★ (*Italian* as'si:zi) *n* a town in central Italy, in Umbria: birthplace of St Francis, who founded the Franciscan religious order here in 1208. Pop.: 24 790 (1990).

assist (ə'sɪst) *vb* **1** to give help or support to (a person, cause, etc.). **2** to work or act as an assistant or subordinate to (another). ◆ *n* **3** *US.* the act of helping. [C15: from F, from L *assistere* to stand by, from *sistere* to cause to stand, from *stāre* to stand]
▸ **asˈsister** *n*

assistance (ə'sɪstəns) *n* **1** help; support. **2** the act of assisting. **3** *Brit. inf.* See **national assistance.**

assistant (ə'sɪstənt) *n* **1a** a person who assists, esp. in a subordinate position. **1b** (*as modifier*): *assistant manager.* **2** See **shop assistant.**

assistant referee *n Soccer.* the official name for **linesman** (sense 1).

assize (ə'saɪz) *n Scots Law.* **a** a trial by a jury. **b** a jury. [C13: from OF *assise* session, from *asseoir* to seat, from L *assidēre* to sit beside]

assizes (ə'saɪzɪz) *pl n* (formerly in England and Wales) the sessions of the principal court in each county, exercising civil and criminal jurisdiction: replaced in 1971 by crown courts.

assoc. *abbrev. for:* **1** associate(d). **2** association.

associate *vb* (ə'səʊʃɪˌeɪt, -sɪ-). (usually foll. by *with*) **associates, associating, associated. 1** (*tr*) to link or connect in the mind or imagination. **2** (*intr*) to mix socially: *to associate with writers.* **3** (*intr*) to form or join an association, group, etc. **4** (*tr; usually passive*) to consider in conjunction: *rainfall is associated with humidity.* **5** (*tr*) to bring (a person, esp. oneself) into friendship, partnership, etc. **6** (*tr; often passive*) to express agreement (with): *Bertrand Russell was associated with the CND movement.* ◆ *n* (ə'səʊʃɪɪt, -sɪ-). **7** a person joined with another or others in an enterprise, business, etc. **8** a companion or friend. **9** something that usually accompanies another thing. **10** a person having a subordinate position in or admitted to only partial membership of an institution, association, etc. ◆ *adj* (ə'səʊʃɪɪt, -sɪ-). (*prenominal*) **11** joined with another or others in an enterprise, business, etc.: *an associate director.* **12** having partial rights or subordinate status: *an associate member.* **13** accompanying; concomitant. [C14: from L *associāre* to ally with, from *sociāre* to join, from *socius* an ally]
▸ **asˈsociable** *adj* ▸ **asˈsociˌator** *n* ▸ **asˈsociateˌship** *n*

association (əˌsəʊsɪ'eɪʃən, -ʃɪ-) *n* **1** a group of people having a common purpose or interest; a society or club. **2** the act of associating or the state of being associated. **3** friendship or companionship: *their association will not last.* **4** a mental connection of ideas, feelings, or sensations. **5** *Chem.* the formation of groups of molecules and ions held together by weak chemical bonds. **6** *Ecology.* a group of similar plants that grow in a uniform environment.

association football *n* a more formal name for **soccer.**

associative (ə'səʊʃɪətɪv, -sɪ-) *adj* **1** of, relating to, or causing association or union. **2** *Maths, logic.* **2a** of an operation, such as multiplication or addition, in which the answer is the same regardless of the way in which the elements are grouped: $(2 \times 3) \times 4 = 2 \times (3 \times 4)$. **2b** referring to this property: *the associative laws of arithmetic.*

assonance ('æsənəns) *n* **1** the use of the same vowel sound with different consonants or the same consonant with different vowels, as in a line of verse. Examples are *time* and *light* or *mystery* and *mastery.* **2** partial correspondence. [C18: from F, from L *assonāre* to sound, from *sonāre* to sound]
▸ **'assonant** *adj, n*

assort (ə'sɔːt) *vb* **1** (*tr*) to arrange or distribute into groups

---

★ people and places

of the same type; classify. **2** (*intr*; usually foll. by *with*) to fit or fall into a class or group. **3** (*tr*) to supply with an assortment of merchandise. **4** (*tr*) to put in the same category as others. [C15: from OF *assorter*, from *sorte* SORT]
▶ **as'sortative** *adj*

assorted (ə'sɔːtɪd) *adj* **1** consisting of various kinds mixed together. **2** classified: *assorted categories*. **3** matched (esp. in **well-assorted**, **ill-assorted**).

assortment (ə'sɔːtmənt) *n* **1** a collection or group of various things or sorts. **2** the act of assorting.

ASSR (formerly) *abbrev. for* Autonomous Soviet Socialist Republic.

asst *abbrev. for* assistant.

assuage (ə'sweɪdʒ) *vb* **assuages, assuaging, assuaged.** (*tr*) **1** to soothe, moderate, or relieve (grief, pain, etc.). **2** to give relief to (thirst, etc.). **3** to pacify; calm. [C14: from OF, from Vulgar L *assuāviāre* (unattested) to sweeten, from L *suāvis* pleasant]
▶ **as'suagement** *n* ▶ **as'suager** *n*

Assuan *or* **Assouan** ★ (ɑːs'wɑːn) *n* variant spellings of **Aswan**.

assume (ə'sjuːm) *vb* **assumes, assuming, assumed.** (*tr*) **1** (*may take a clause as object*) to take for granted; suppose. **2** to undertake or take on or over (a position, responsibility, etc.): *to assume office*. **3** to pretend to; feign: *he assumed indifference*. **4** to take or put on; adopt: *the problem assumed gigantic proportions*. **5** to appropriate or usurp (power, control, etc.). [C15: from L *assūmere* to take up, from *sūmere* to take up, from SUB- + *emere* to take]
▶ **as'sumable** *adj* ▶ **as'sumer** *n*

assumed (ə'sjuːmd) *adj* **1** false; fictitious: *an assumed name*. **2** taken for granted. **3** usurped.

assuming (ə'sjuːmɪŋ) *adj* **1** expecting too much; presumptuous. ♦ *conj* **2** (often foll. by *that*) if it is assumed or taken for granted.

assumption (ə'sʌmpʃən) *n* **1** the act of taking something for granted or something that is taken for granted. **2** an arrogation of power or possession. **3** presumption. **4** *Logic*. a statement that is used as the premise of a particular argument but may not be otherwise accepted. [C13: from L *assūmptiō* a taking up, from *assūmere* to ASSUME]
▶ **as'sumptive** *adj*

Assumption (ə'sʌmpʃən) *n Christianity.* **1** the taking up of the Virgin Mary (body and soul) into heaven when her earthly life was ended. **2** the feast commemorating this.

Assur, Asur ('æsə), **Asshur,** *or* **Ashur** ★ ('æʃʊə) *n* **1** the supreme national god of the ancient Assyrians, chiefly a war god, whose symbol was an archer within a winged disc. **2** one of the chief cities of ancient Assyria, on the River Tigris about 100 km (60 miles) downstream from the present-day city of Mosul.

assurance (ə'ʃʊərəns) *n* **1** a statement, assertion, etc., intended to inspire confidence. **2** a promise or pledge of support. **3** freedom from doubt; certainty. **4** forwardness; impudence. **5** *Chiefly Brit.* insurance providing for certainties such as death as contrasted with fire.

assure (ə'ʃʊə) *vb* **assures, assuring, assured.** (*tr; may take a clause as object*) **1** to convince: *to assure a person of one's love*. **2** to promise; guarantee. **3** to state positively. **4** to make (an event) certain. **5** *Chiefly Brit.* to insure against loss, esp. of life. [C14: from OF, from Med. L *assēcūrāre* to secure or make sure, from *sēcūrus* SECURE]
▶ **as'surable** *adj* ▶ **as'surer** *n*

assured (ə'ʃʊəd) *adj* **1** sure; guaranteed. **2** self-assured. **3** *Chiefly Brit.* insured. ♦ *n* **4** *Chiefly Brit.* **4a** the beneficiary under a life assurance policy. **4b** the person whose life is insured.
▶ **assuredly** (ə'ʃʊərɪdlɪ) *adv*

asswipe ('æs,waɪp) *n US sl.* a despicable or stupid person. [C20: orig.: toilet paper, from ASS² + WIPE]

Assyria ★ (ə'sɪrɪə) *n* an ancient kingdom of N Mesopotamia: it established an empire that stretched from Egypt to the Persian Gulf, reaching its greatest extent between 721 and 633 B.C. Its chief cities were Assur and Nineveh.
▶ **A'ssyrian** *adj, n*

AST *abbrev. for* Atlantic Standard Time.

Astaire ★ (ə'steə) *n* **Fred,** real name *Frederick Austerlitz.* 1899–1987, US dancer and actor whose films include *Top Hat* (1935) and *The Band Wagon* (1953).

Astana ★ (æ'stænə) *n* the capital of Kazakhstan: an important railway junction. Pop.: 280 200 (1995 est.). Former names: **Akmolinsk** (until 1961), **Tselinograd** (1961–94), **Akmola** (1994–98).

Astarte ★ (æ'stɑːtɪ) *n* a fertility goddess worshipped by the Phoenicians: identified with Ashtoreth of the Hebrews and Ishtar of the Babylonians and Assyrians.

astatic (æ'stætɪk, eɪ-) *adj* **1** not static; unstable. **2** *Physics*. having no tendency to assume any particular position or orientation. [C19: from Gk *astatos* unsteady]
▶ **a'statically** *adv*

astatine ('æstə,tiːn) *n* a radioactive element that occurs naturally in minute amounts and is artificially produced by bombarding bismuth with alpha particles. Symbol: At; atomic no.: 85; half-life of most stable isotope, ^{210}At: 8.1 hours. [C20: from Gk *astatos* unstable]

Astbury ★ ('æstbərɪ) *n* **John.** 1688–1743, English potter; earliest of the great Staffordshire potters.

aster ('æstə) *n* **1** a plant having white, blue, purple, or pink daisy-like flowers. **2 China aster.** a related Chinese plant widely cultivated for its showy brightly coloured flowers. [C18: from NL, from L *aster* star, from Gk]

-aster *suffix forming nouns.* a person or thing that is inferior to what is specified: *poetaster*. [from L]

asterisk ('æstərɪsk) *n* **1** a star-shaped character (*) used in printing or writing to indicate a cross-reference to a footnote, an omission, etc. ♦ *vb* **2** (*tr*) to mark with an asterisk. [C17: from LL *asteriscus* a small star, from Gk, from *astēr* star]

asterism ('æstə,rɪzəm) *n* **1** three asterisks arranged in a triangle (⁂ or ⸪), to draw attention to the text that follows. **2** a cluster of stars or a constellation. [C16: from Gk *asterismos* arrangement of constellations, from *astēr* star]

astern (ə'stɜːn) *adv, adj (postpositive) Naut.* **1** at or towards the stern. **2** with the stern first: *full speed astern!* **3** aft of the stern of a vessel.

asteroid ('æstə,rɔɪd) *n* **1** Also called: **minor planet, planetoid.** any of numerous small celestial bodies that move around the sun mainly between the orbits of Mars and Jupiter. **2** a starfish. ♦ *adj also* ,**aste'roidal. 3** of a starfish. **4** shaped like a star. [C19: from Gk *asteroeidēs* starlike, from *astēr* a star]

asthenia (æs'θiːnɪə) *n Pathol.* an abnormal loss of strength; debility. [C19: via NL from Gk *astheneia* weakness, from A-¹ + *sthenos* strength]

asthenic (æs'θɛnɪk) *adj* **1** of or having asthenia; weak. **2** referring to a physique characterized by long limbs and a small trunk. ♦ *n* **3** a person with long limbs and a small trunk.

asthma ('æsmə) *n* a respiratory disorder, often of allergic origin, characterized by difficulty in breathing. [C14: from Gk: laborious breathing, from *azein* to breathe hard]

asthmatic (æs'mætɪk) *adj* **1** of or having asthma. ♦ *n* **2** a person who has asthma.
▶ **asth'matically** *adv*

Asti ★ ('æstɪ) *n* a town in NW Italy: famous for its sparkling wine, **Asti spumante** (spuː'mæntɪ). Pop.: 74 649 (1990).

astigmatic (,æstɪg'mætɪk) *adj* relating to or affected with astigmatism. [C19: from A-¹ + Gk *stigmat-, stigma* spot, focus]
▶ ,**astig'matically** *adv*

astigmatism (ə'stɪgmə,tɪzəm) *or* **astigmia** (ə'stɪgmɪə) *n* **1** a defect of a lens resulting in the formation of distorted images, caused by light rays not meeting at a single focal point. **2** faulty vision resulting from defective curvature of the cornea or lens of the eye.

astilbe (ə'stɪlbɪ) *n* any perennial plant of the genus *Astilbe*, cultivated for its spikes of ornamental pink or white flowers. [C19: NL, from Gk A-¹ + *stilbē*, from *stilbein* to glitter; referring to its inconspicuous individual flowers]

astir (ə'stɜ:) *adj* (*postpositive*) **1** awake and out of bed. **2** in motion; on the move.

Astolat ★ ('æstəʊˌlæt) *n* a town in Arthurian legend: location unknown.

Aston ★ ('æstən) *n* **Francis William.** 1877–1945, British physicist and chemist, who developed the first mass spectrograph: Nobel prize for chemistry 1922.

astonish (ə'stɒnɪʃ) *vb* (*tr*) to fill with amazement; surprise greatly. [C15: from earlier *astonyen*, from OF, from Vulgar L *extonāre* (unattested) to strike with thunder, from L *tonāre* to thunder]
▸ a'**stonishing** *adj*

astonishment (ə'stɒnɪʃmənt) *n* **1** extreme surprise; amazement. **2** a cause of amazement.

Astor ★ ('æstə) *n* **1 John Jacob**, 1st Baron Astor of Hever. 1886–1971, British proprietor of *The Times* (1922–66). **2 Nancy** (**Witcher**), Viscountess, original name *Nancy Langhorne*. 1879–1964, British Conservative politician, born in the US; the first woman MP.

astound (ə'staʊnd) *vb* (*tr*) to overwhelm with amazement; bewilder. [C17: from *astoned* amazed, from OF, from *estoner* to ASTONISH]
▸ a'**stounding** *adj*

astraddle (ə'strædᵊl) *adj* **1** (*postpositive*) with a leg on either side of something. ♦ *prep* **2** astride.

astragal ('æstrəgᵊl) *n* **1** *Archit.* Also called: **bead.** a small convex moulding, usually with a semicircular cross section. **2** *Anat.* the ankle or anklebone. [C17: from L, from Gk *astragalos* anklebone, hence, small round moulding]

astragalus (æ'strægələs) *n, pl* **astragali** (-ˌlaɪ). *Anat.* another name for **talus¹**. [C16: via NL from L: ASTRAGAL]

astrakhan (ˌæstrə'kæn) *n* **1** a fur, usually black or grey, made of the closely curled wool of lambs from Astrakhan. **2** a cloth with curled pile resembling this. **3** (*modifier*) made of such fur or cloth.

Astrakhan ★ (ˌæstrə'kæn, -'kɑːn; *Russian* 'astrəxənj) *n* a city in SE Russia, on the delta of the Volga River, 21 m (70 ft) below sea level. Pop.: 486 000 (1995 est.).

astral ('æstrəl) *adj* **1** relating to or resembling the stars. **2** *Theosophy.* relating to a supposed supersensible substance taking the form of an aura discernible to certain gifted individuals. [C17: from LL *astrālis*, from L *astrum* star, from Gk *astron*]

astray (ə'streɪ) *adj* (*postpositive*), *adv* **1** out of the correct path or direction. **2** out of the right or expected way. [C13: from OF, from *estraier* to STRAY]

astride (ə'straɪd) *adj* (*postpositive*) **1** with a leg on either side. **2** with the legs far apart. ♦ *prep* **3** with a leg on either side of. **4** with a part on both sides of; spanning.

astringent (ə'strɪndʒənt) *adj* **1** severe; harsh. **2** sharp or invigorating. **3** causing contraction of body tissues, checking blood flow; styptic. ♦ *n* **4** an astringent drug or lotion. [C16: from L *astringēns* drawing together]
▸ a'**stringency** *n* ▸ a'**stringently** *adv*

astro- *combining form.* indicating a star or star-shaped structure: *astrology*. [from Gk, from *astron* star]

astrobiology (ˌæstrəʊbaɪ'ɒlədʒɪ) *n* the branch of biology that investigates the possibility of life on other planets.

astrochemistry (ˌæstrəʊ'kemɪstrɪ) *n* the study of the chemistry of celestial bodies and space.

astrodome ('æstrəˌdəʊm) *n* a transparent dome on the top of an aircraft, through which observations can be made.

astrol. *abbrev. for:* **1** astrologer. **2** astrological. **3** astrology.

astrolabe ('æstrəˌleɪb) *n* an instrument used by early astronomers to measure the altitude of stars and planets and also as a navigational aid. [C13: via OF & Med. L from Gk, from *astrolabos*, from *astron* star + *lambanein* to take]

astrology (ə'strɒlədʒɪ) *n* **1** the study of the motions and relative positions of the planets, sun, and moon, interpreted in terms of human characteristics and activities. **2** primitive astronomy. [C14: from OF, from L *astrologia*,

from Gk, from *astrologos* (orig.: astronomer); see ASTRO-, -LOGY]
▸ as'**trologer** *or* as'**trologist** *n* ▸ **astrological** (ˌæstrə'lɒdʒɪkᵊl) *adj*

astron. *abbrev. for:* **1** astronomer. **2** astronomical. **3** astronomy.

astronaut ('æstrəˌnɔːt) *n* a person trained for travelling in space. See also **cosmonaut**. [C20: from ASTRO- + *-naut*, from Gk *nautēs* sailor, on the model of *aeronaut*]

astronautics (ˌæstrə'nɔːtɪks) *n* (*functioning as sing*) the science and technology of space flight.
▸ ˌastro'**nautical** *adj*

Astronomer Royal *n* an honorary title awarded to an eminent British astronomer: until 1972, the Astronomer Royal was also director of the Royal Greenwich Observatory.

astronomical (ˌæstrə'nɒmɪkᵊl) *or* **astronomic** *adj* **1** enormously large. **2** of or relating to astronomy.
▸ ˌastro'**nomically** *adv*

astronomical clock *n* **1** a complex clock showing astronomical phenomena, such as the phases of the moon. **2** any clock showing sidereal time used in observatories.

astronomical unit *n* a unit of distance used in astronomy equal to the mean distance between the earth and the sun. 1 astronomical unit is equivalent to 1.495×10^{11} metres.

astronomy (ə'strɒnəmɪ) *n* the scientific study of the individual celestial bodies (excluding the earth) and of the universe as a whole. [C13: from OF, from L *astronomia*, from Gk; see ASTRO-, -NOMY]
▸ as'**tronomer** *n*

astrophysics (ˌæstrəʊ'fɪzɪks) *n* (*functioning as sing*) the branch of physics concerned with the physical and chemical properties of the celestial bodies.
▸ ˌastro'**physicist** *n*

Astroturf ('æstrəʊˌtɜːf) *n Trademark.* a type of grasslike artificial surface used for playing fields and lawns. [C20: from *Astro*(*dome*) the baseball stadium in Texas where it was first used + *turf*]

Asturias¹ ★ (æ'stʊərɪˌæs) *n* a region and former kingdom of NW Spain, consisting of a coastal plain and the Cantabrian Mountains: a Christian stronghold against the Moors (8th to 13th centuries); rich mineral resources.

Asturias² ★ (æ'stʊərɪˌæs) *n* **Miguel Ángel.** 1899–1974, Guatemalan novelist and poet. His novels include *El Señor Presidente* (1946). Nobel prize for literature 1967.

astute (ə'stjuːt) *adj* having insight or acumen; perceptive; shrewd. [C17: from L *astūtus* cunning, from *astus* (n) cleverness]
▸ as'**tutely** *adv* ▸ as'**tuteness** *n*

Asunción ★ (*Spanish* asun'sjon) *n* the capital and chief port of Paraguay, on the Paraguay River, 1530 km (950 miles) from the Atlantic. Pop.: 502 426 (1992).

asunder (ə'sʌndə) *adv, adj* (*postpositive*) in or into parts or pieces; apart: *to tear asunder.* [OE *on sundran* apart]

Asur ★ ('æsə) *n* a variant spelling of **Assur**.

Aswan, Assuan, *or* **Assouan** ★ (ɑː'swɑːn) *n* an ancient town in SE Egypt, on the Nile, just below the First Cataract. Pop.: 220 000 (1992 est.). Ancient name: **Syene.**

Aswan High Dam ★ *n* a dam on the Nile forming a reservoir (Lake Nasser) extending 480 km (300 miles) from the First to the Third Cataracts: opened in 1971, it was built 6 km (4 miles) upstream from the old **Aswan Dam** (built in 1902 and twice raised). Height of dam: 109 m (365 ft).

asylum (ə'saɪləm) *n* **1** shelter; refuge; sanctuary. **2** a safe or inviolable place of refuge, esp. as formerly offered by the Christian Church. **3** *International law.* refuge afforded to a person whose extradition is sought by a foreign government: *political asylum.* **4** an institution for the care or confinement of individuals, esp. (formerly) a mental hospital. [C15: via L from Gk *asulon* refuge, from A-¹ + *sulon* right of seizure]

asymmetric (ˌæsɪ'metrɪk, ˌeɪ-) *or* **asymmetrical** *adj* **1**

★ people and places

not symmetrical; lacking symmetry; misproportioned. **2** *Logic, maths.* (of a relation) never holding between a pair of values *x* and *y* when it holds between *y* and *x*, as in *John is the father of David*.
> ▸ ˌasym'metrically *adv*

asymmetric bars *pl n Gymnastics.* **a** (*functioning as pl*) a pair of wooden or fibreglass bars placed parallel to each other but set at different heights, for various exercises. **b** (*functioning as sing*) an event in a gymnastic competition in which competitors exercise on such bars.

asymmetry (æ'sɪmɪtrɪ, eɪ-) *n* lack or absence of symmetry.

asymptomatic (ˌeɪsɪmptə'mætɪk) *adj* not showing any symptoms of disease.

asymptote ('æsɪmˌtəʊt) *n* a straight line that is closely approached by a curve so that the distance between them decreases to zero as the distance from the origin increases to infinity. [C17: from Gk *asumptōtos* not falling together, from A-[1] + SYN- + *ptōtos* inclined to fall, from *piptein* to fall]
> ▸ **asymptotic** (ˌæsɪm'tɒtɪk) *or* ˌasymp'totical *adj*

asystole (ə'sɪstəlɪ) *n Pathol.* the absence of heartbeat; cardiac arrest.
> ▸ **asystolic** (ˌæsɪs'tɒlɪk) *adj*

at (æt) *prep* **1** used to indicate location or position: *are they at the table?* **2** towards; in the direction of: *looking at television.* **3** used to indicate position in time: *come at three o'clock.* **4** engaged in; in a state of (being): *children at play.* **5** (in expressions concerned with habitual activity) during the passing of: *he used to work at night.* **6** for; in exchange for: *it's selling at four pounds.* **7** used to indicate the object of an emotion: *shocked at his behaviour.* **8** where it's at. *SI.* the real place of action. [OE æt]

At the chemical symbol for astatine.

AT *Brit. education. abbrev. for* attainment target.

at. *abbrev. for:* **1** atmosphere (unit of pressure). **2** atomic.

Atacama Desert ★ (*Spanish* ata'kama) *n* a desert region along the W coast of South America, mainly in N Chile: a major source of nitrates. Area: about 80 000 sq. km (31 000 sq. miles).

Atahualpa (ˌætə'wɑːlpə) *or* **Atabalipa** ★ (ˌætə'bɑːlɪpə) *n* ?1500–33, the last Inca emperor of Peru (1525–33), who was put to death by the Spanish under Pizarro.

Atalanta ★ (ˌætə'læntə) *n Greek myth.* a maiden who agreed to marry any man who could defeat her in a running race. She lost to Hippomenes when she paused to pick up three golden apples that he had deliberately dropped.

ataractic (ˌætə'ræktɪk) *or* **ataraxic** (ˌætə'ræksɪk) *adj* **1** able to calm or tranquillize. ◆ *n* **2** an ataractic drug.

ataraxia (ˌætə'ræksɪə) *or* **ataraxy** ('ætəˌræksɪ) *n* calmness or peace of mind; emotional tranquillity. [C17: from Gk: serenity, from A-[1] + *tarassein* to trouble]

Atatürk ★ ('ætəˌtɜːk) *n* **Kemal** (kɛ'mɑːl), real name *Mustafa Kemal.* 1881–1938, Turkish general and statesman; founder of the Turkish republic and president of Turkey (1923–38), who westernized and secularized the country.

atavism ('ætəˌvɪzəm) *n* **1** the recurrence in a plant or animal of certain primitive characteristics that were present in an ancestor but have not occurred in intermediate generations. **2** reversion to a former type. [C19: from F, from L *atavus* strictly: great-grandfather's grandfather, prob. from *atta* daddy + *avus* grandfather]
> ▸ ˌata'vistic *adj*

ataxia (ə'tæksɪə) *or* **ataxy** (ə'tæksɪ) *n Pathol.* lack of muscular coordination. [C17: via NL from Gk: lack of coordination, from A-[1] + *-taxia*, from *tassein* to put in order]
> ▸ a'taxic *adj*

ATB *abbrev. for* Advanced Technology Bomber.

Atbara ★ ('ætbərə, æt'bɑː-) *n* **1** a town in NE Sudan. Pop.: 73 000 (latest est.). **2** a river in NE Africa, rising in N Ethiopia and flowing through E Sudan to the Nile at Atbara. Length: over 800 km (500 miles).

ATC *abbrev. for:* **1** air-traffic control. **2** (in Britain) Air Training Corps.

ate (ɛt, eɪt) *vb* the past tense of **eat**.

Ate ★ ('eɪtɪ, 'ɑːtɪ) *n Greek myth.* a goddess who makes men blind so that they will blunder into guilty acts. [C16: via L from Gk *atē* a rash impulse]

-ate[1] *suffix.* **1** (*forming adjectives*) having the appearance or characteristics of: *fortunate.* **2** (*forming nouns*) a chemical compound, esp. a salt or ester of an acid: *carbonate.* **3** (*forming nouns*) the product of a process: *condensate.* **4** forming verbs from nouns and adjectives: *hyphenate.* [from L *-ātus*, p.p. ending of verbs ending in *-āre*]

-ate[2] *suffix forming nouns.* denoting office, rank, or a group having a certain function: *episcopate.* [from L *-ātus*, suffix of collective nouns]

atelier ('ætəlˌjeɪ) *n* an artist's studio or workshop. [C17: from OF, from *astele* chip of wood, from L *astula* splinter, from *assis* board]

a tempo (ɑː 'tɛmpəʊ) *Music.* ◆ *adj, adv* **1** to the original tempo. ◆ *n* **2** a passage thus marked. ◆ Also: **tempo primo.** [It.: in (the original) time]

Aten *or* **Aton** ★ ('ɑːtªn) *n* (in ancient Egypt) the solar disc worshipped as the sole god in the reign of Akhenaten.

Atget ★ (*French* adʒe) *n* (**Jean**) **Eugène** (**Auguste**) (øʒɛn). 1856–1927, French photographer.

Athabaska *or* **Athabasca** ★ (ˌæθə'bæskə) *n* **1** Lake. a lake in W Canada, in NW Saskatchewan and NE Alberta. Area: about 7770 sq. km (3000 sq. miles). **2** a river in W Canada, rising in the Rocky Mountains and flowing northeast to Lake Athabaska. Length: 1230 km (765 miles).

Athanasian Creed (ˌæθə'neɪʃən) *n Christianity.* a profession of faith widely used in the Western Church which, though formerly attributed to Athanasius, probably originated in Gaul between 381 and 428 A.D.

Athanasius ★ (ˌæθə'neɪʃəs) *n* **Saint.** ?296–373 A.D., patriarch of Alexandria who championed Christian orthodoxy against Arianism. Feast day: May 2.
> ▸ ˌAtha'nasian *adj*

Athapascan, Athapaskan (ˌæθə'pæskən) *or* **Athabascan, Athabaskan** (ˌæθə'bæskən) *n* a group of North American Indian languages including Apache and Navaho. [from Cree *athapaskaaw* scattered grass]

atheism ('eɪθɪˌɪzəm) *n* rejection of belief in God or gods. [C16: from F, from Gk *atheos* godless, from A-[1] + *theos* god]
> ▸ 'atheist *n, adj* ▸ ˌathe'istic *adj*

Athelstan ★ ('æθəlstən) *n* ?895–939 A.D., king of Wessex and Mercia (924–939 A.D.), who extended his kingdom to include most of England.

athematic (ˌæθɪ'mætɪk) *adj* **1** *Music.* not based on themes. **2** *Linguistics.* (of verbs) having a suffix attached with no intervening vowel.

Athena (ə'θiːnə) *or* **Athene** ★ (ə'θiːnɪ) *n Greek myth.* a virgin goddess of wisdom, practical skills, and prudent warfare. She was born, fully armed, from the head of Zeus. Also called: **Pallas Athena, Pallas.** Roman counterpart: **Minerva.**

athenaeum *or US* **atheneum** (ˌæθɪ'niːəm) *n* **1** an institution for the promotion of learning. **2** a building containing a reading room or library. [C18: from LL, from Gk *Athēnaion* temple of Athene, frequented by poets and teachers]

Athenian (ə'θiːnɪən) *n* **1** a native or inhabitant of Athens. ◆ *adj* **2** of or relating to Athens.

Athens ★ ('æθɪnz) *n* the capital of Greece, in the southeast near the Saronic Gulf: became capital after independence in 1834; ancient city-state, most powerful in the 5th century B.C.; contains the hill citadel of the Acropolis. Pop.: 772 072 (1991). Greek name: **Athinai** (a'θine).

atherosclerosis (ˌæθərəʊsklɪə'rəʊsɪs) *n, pl* **atheroscleroses** (-siːz). a degenerative disease of the arteries characterized by thickening of the arterial walls, caused by deposits of fatty material. [C20: from NL, from Gk *athērōma* tumour full of grainy matter + SCLEROSIS]
> ▸ **atherosclerotic** (ˌæθərəʊsklɪə'rɒtɪk) *adj*

athirst (ə'θɜːst) *adj* (*postpositive*) **1** (often foll. by *for*) having an eager desire; longing. **2** *Arch.* thirsty.

athlete ('æθliːt) *n* **1** a person trained to compete in sports or exercises. **2** a person who has a natural aptitude for physical activities. **3** *Chiefly Brit.* a competitor in track and field events. [C18: from L via Gk, from *athlein* to compete for a prize, from *athlos* a contest]

athlete's foot *n* a fungal infection of the skin of the foot, esp. between the toes and on the soles.

athletic (æθ'letɪk) *adj* **1** physically fit or strong. **2** of, relating to, or suitable for an athlete or for athletics.
▸ ath'letically *adv* ▸ ath'leticism *n*

athletics (æθ'letɪks) *n* (*functioning as sing or pl*) **1** *Chiefly Brit.* **1a** track and field events. **1b** (*as modifier*): *an athletics meeting.* **2** sports or exercises engaged in by athletes.

athletic support *n* a more formal term for **jockstrap**.

at-home *n* **1** a social gathering in a person's home. **2** another name for **open day**.

-athon *suffix forming nouns.* a variant of **-thon**.

Athos ★ ('æθɒs, 'eɪ-) *n* Mount. a mountain in NE Greece, in Macedonia Central region: site of the Monastic Republic of Mount Athos, autonomous since 1927; inhabited by Greek Orthodox Basilian monks in 20 monasteries founded in the 10th century. Pop.: 1557 (1991). Area: 336 sq. km (130 sq. miles).

athwart (ə'θwɔːt) *adv* **1** transversely; from one side to another. ◆ *prep* **2** across the path or line of (esp. a ship). **3** in opposition to; against. [C15: from A-² + THWART]

-atic *suffix forming adjectives.* of the nature of the thing specified: *problematic.* [from F, from Gk *-atikos*]

-ation *suffix forming nouns.* indicating an action, process, state, condition, or result: *arbitration; hibernation.* [from L *-ātiōn-*, suffix of abstract nouns]

-ative *suffix forming adjectives.* of, relating to, or tending to: *authoritative; informative.* [from L *-ātīvus*]

Atkinson ★ ('ætkɪnsᵊn) *n* Sir **Harry Albert.** 1831–92, New Zealand statesman, born in England: prime minister of New Zealand (1876–77; 1883–84; 1887–91).

Atlanta ★ (ət'læntə) *n* a city in N Georgia: the state capital. Pop.: 396 052 (1994 est.).

Atlantean (ˌætlæn'tiːən) *adj Literary.* of, relating to, or like Atlas; prodigiously strong.

Atlantic (ət'læntɪk) *n* **1** the. short for the **Atlantic Ocean**. ◆ *adj* **2** of, relating to, or bordering the Atlantic Ocean. **3** of or relating to Atlas or the Atlas Mountains. [C15: from L, from Gk (*pelagos*) *Atlantikos* (the sea) of Atlas (so called because it lay beyond the Atlas Mountains)]

Atlantic City ★ *n* a resort in SE New Jersey on Absecon Beach, an island on the Atlantic coast. Pop.: 37 986 (1990).

Atlantic Intracoastal Waterway ★ *n* a system of inland and coastal waterways along the Atlantic coast of the US from Cape Cod to Florida Bay. Length: 2495 km (1550 miles).

Atlanticism (ət'læntɪˌsɪzəm) *n* advocacy of close cooperation in military, political, and economic matters between Western Europe, esp. the UK, and the US.
▸ At'lanticist *n*

Atlantic Ocean ★ *n* the world's second largest ocean, bounded in the north by the Arctic, in the south by the Antarctic, in the west by North and South America, and in the east by Europe and Africa. Greatest depth: 9220 m (30 246 ft). Area: about 81 585 000 sq. km (31 500 000 sq. miles).

Atlantic Provinces ★ *pl n* the. certain of the Canadian provinces with coasts facing the Gulf of St Lawrence or the Atlantic: New Brunswick, Nova Scotia, Prince Edward Island, and Newfoundland.

Atlantis ★ (ət'læntɪs) *n* (in ancient legend) a continent said to have sunk beneath the Atlantic west of Gibraltar.

atlas ('ætləs) *n* **1** a collection of maps, usually in book form. **2** a book of charts, graphs, etc.: *an anatomical atlas.* **3** *Anat.* the first cervical vertebra, supporting the skull in man. **4** (*pl* **atlantes**) *Archit.* another name for **telamon**. [C16: via L from Gk; first applied to maps from depictions of Atlas supporting the heavens in 16th-cent. books of maps]

Atlas ★ ('ætləs) *n Greek myth.* **1** a Titan compelled to support the sky on his shoulders as punishment for rebelling against Zeus. **2** a US intercontinental ballistic missile, also used in launching spacecraft.

Atlas Mountains ★ *pl n* a mountain system of N Africa, between the Mediterranean and the Sahara. Highest peak: Mount Toubkal, 4165 m (13 664 ft).

Atli ★ ('ɑːtlɪ) *n Norse legend.* a king of the Huns who married Gudrun for her inheritance and was slain by her after he killed her brothers.

ATM *abbrev. for* automated teller machine.

atm. *abbrev. for:* **1** atmosphere (unit of pressure). **2** atmospheric.

atman ('ɑːtmən) *n Hinduism.* **1** the personal soul or self. **2** Brahman considered as the Universal Soul. [from Sansk. *ātman* breath]

atmolysis (æt'mɒlɪsɪs) *n, pl* **atmolyses** (-ˌsiːz). the separation of gases by differential diffusion through a porous substance.

atmosphere ('ætməsˌfɪə) *n* **1** the gaseous envelope surrounding the earth or any other celestial body. **2** the air or climate in a particular place. **3** a general pervasive feeling or mood. **4** the prevailing tone or mood of a novel, symphony, painting, etc. **5** any local gaseous environment or medium: *an inert atmosphere.* **6** Abbrev.: **at., atm.** a unit of pressure; the pressure that will support a column of mercury 760 mm high at 0°C at sea level.
▸ **atmospheric** (ˌætməs'ferɪk) *adj* ▸ ˌatmos'pherically *adv*

atmospheric pressure *n* the pressure exerted by the atmosphere at the earth's surface. It has an average value of 1 atmosphere.

atmospherics (ˌætməs'ferɪks) *pl n* radio interference, heard as crackling or hissing in receivers, caused by electrical disturbance.

at. no. *abbrev. for* atomic number.

atoll ('ætɒl) *n* a circular coral reef or string of coral islands surrounding a lagoon. [C17: from *atollon*, native name in the Maldive Islands]

atom ('ætəm) *n* **1a** the smallest quantity of an element that can take part in a chemical reaction. **1b** this entity as a source of nuclear energy: *the power of the atom.* **2** the hypothetical indivisible particle of matter postulated by certain ancient philosophers. **3** a very small amount or quantity: *to smash something to atoms.* [C16: via OF & L, from Gk, from *atomos* (adj) that cannot be divided, from A-¹ + *temnein* to cut]

atomic (ə'tɒmɪk) *adj* **1** of, using, or characterized by atomic bombs or atomic energy: *atomic warfare.* **2** of or comprising atoms: *atomic hydrogen.*
▸ a'tomically *adv*

atomic bomb *or* **atom bomb** *n* a type of bomb in which the energy is provided by nuclear fission. Also called: **A-bomb, fission bomb.** Cf. **fusion bomb.**

atomic clock *n* an extremely accurate clock in which an electrical oscillator is controlled by the natural vibrations of an atomic or molecular system such as caesium or ammonia.

atomic energy *n* another name for **nuclear energy**.

atomicity (ˌætə'mɪsɪtɪ) *n* **1** the state of being made up of atoms. **2** the number of atoms in the molecules of an element. **3** a less common name for **valency**.

atomic mass unit *n* a unit of mass used to express atomic and molecular weights that is equal to one-twelfth of the mass of an atom of carbon-12. Abbrev.: **amu.**

atomic number *n* the number of protons in the nucleus of an atom of an element. Abbrev.: **at. no.**

atomic pile *n* the original name for a **nuclear reactor**.

atomic sentence *n Logic.* a sentence consisting of one predicate and a finite number of terms: *"it is raining"* is an *atomic sentence.*

atomic structure *n* the concept of an atom as a central positively charged nucleus consisting of protons and neutrons surrounded by a number of electrons. The number of electrons is equal to the number of protons: the whole entity is thus electrically neutral.

atomic theory *n* **1** any theory in which matter is re-

★ people and places

garded as consisting of atoms. **2** the current concept of the atom as an entity with a definite structure. See **atomic structure.**

tomic weight *n* the former name for **relative atomic mass.** Abbrev.: **at. wt.**

tomize *or* **atomise** ('ætə,maɪz) *vb* **atomizes, atomizing, atomized** *or* **atomises, atomising, atomised. 1** to separate or be separated into free atoms. **2** to reduce (a liquid or solid) to fine particles or spray or (of a liquid or solid) to be reduced in this way. **3** (*tr*) to destroy by weapons, esp. nuclear weapons.

tomizer *or* **atomiser** ('ætə,maɪzə) *n* a device for reducing a liquid to a fine spray, such as a bottle with a fine outlet used to spray perfumes.

tom smasher *n Physics.* the nontechnical name for **accelerator** (sense 2).

tomy ('ætəmɪ) *n, pl* **atomies.** *Arch.* a minute particle or creature. [C16: from L *atomi* atoms, used as sing]

Aton ★ ('ɑ:t°n) *n* a variant spelling of **Aten.**

tonal (eɪ'təʊn°l) *adj Music.* having no established key.

tonality (,eɪtəʊ'nælɪtɪ) *n* **1** absence of or disregard for an established musical key in a composition. **2** the principles of composition embodying this.

tone (ə'təʊn) *vb* **atones, atoning, atoned.** (*intr;* foll. by *for*) to make amends or reparation (for a crime, sin, etc.). [C16: back formation from ATONEMENT]
► a'**toner** *n*

tonement (ə'təʊnmənt) *n* **1** satisfaction, reparation, or expiation given for an injury or wrong. **2** (*often cap.*) *Christian theology.* **2a** the reconciliation of man with God through the sacrificial death of Christ. **2b** the sufferings and death of Christ. [C16: from ME *at onement* in harmony]

tonic (eɪ'tɒnɪk, æ-) *adj* **1** (of a syllable, word, etc.) carrying no stress; unaccented. **2** lacking body or muscle tone. ◆ *n* **3** an unaccented or unstressed syllable, word, etc. [C18: from L, from Gk *atonos* lacking tone]

top (ə'tɒp) *adv* **1** on top; at the top. ◆ *prep* **2** on top of; at the top of.

ator *suffix forming nouns.* a person or thing that performs a certain action: *agitator; radiator.* [from L -*ātor*]

atory *suffix forming adjectives.* of, relating to, characterized by, or serving to: *circulatory; explanatory.* [from L -*ātōrius*]

ATP *n* adenosine triphosphate; a substance found in all plant and animal cells. It is the major source of energy for cellular reactions.

atrabilious (,ætrə'bɪlɪəs) *or* **atrabiliar** *adj Rare.* irritable or gloomy. [C17: from L *ātra bīlis* black bile, from *āter* black + *bīlis* BILE¹]
► ,atra'**biliousness** *n*

atrazine ('ætrəzi:n) *n* a white crystalline compound widely used as a weedkiller. Formula: $C_8H_{14}N_5Cl$. [C20: from A(MINO) *tr(i)azine*]

Atreus ★ ('eɪtrɪ,u:s, 'eɪtrɪəs) *n Greek myth.* a king of Mycenae, son of Pelops, father of Agamemnon and Menelaus, and member of the family known as the **Atreids** ('eɪtrɪɪdz).

atrium ('eɪtrɪəm, 'ɑ:-) *n, pl* **atria** ('eɪtrɪə, 'ɑ:-). **1** the open main court of a Roman house. **2** a central often glass-roofed hall that extends through several storeys in a building, such as a shopping centre or hotel. **3** a court in front of an early Christian or medieval church. **4** *Anat.* a cavity or chamber in the body, esp. the upper chamber of each half of the heart. [C17: from L; rel. to *āter* black]
► 'atrial *adj*

atrocious (ə'trəʊʃəs) *adj* **1** extremely cruel or wicked: *atrocious deeds.* **2** horrifying or shocking. **3** *Inf.* very bad: *atrocious writing.* [C17: from L *ātrōx* dreadful, from *āter* black]
► a'**trociousness** *n*

atrocity (ə'trɒsɪtɪ) *n, pl* **atrocities. 1** behaviour or an action that is wicked or ruthless. **2** the fact or quality of being atrocious. **3** (*usually pl*) acts of extreme cruelty.

atrophy ('ætrəfɪ) *n, pl* **atrophies. 1** a wasting away of an organ or part, or a failure to grow to normal size. **2** any

degeneration or diminution. ◆ *vb* **atrophies, atrophying, atrophied. 3** to waste away or cause to waste away. [C17: from LL, from Gk, from *atrophos* ill-fed, from A-¹ + -*trophos,* from *trephein* to feed]
► **atrophic** (ə'trɒfɪk) *adj*

atropine ('ætrə,pi:n) *n* a poisonous alkaloid obtained from the deadly nightshade, used to treat peptic ulcers, biliary and renal colic, etc. [C19: from NL *atropa* deadly nightshade, from Gk *atropos* unchangeable, inflexible]

Atropos ★ ('ætrə,pɒs) *n Greek myth.* the one of the three Fates who severs the thread of life. [Gk, from *atropos* that may not be turned, from A-¹ + -*tropos* from *trepein* to turn]

attach (ə'tætʃ) *vb* (*mainly tr*) **1** to join, fasten, or connect. **2** (*reflexive or passive*) to become associated with or join. **3** (*intr;* foll. by *to*) to be connected (with): *responsibility attaches to the job.* **4** to attribute or ascribe. **5** to include or append: *a proviso is attached to the contract.* **6** (*usually passive*) *Mil.* to place on temporary duty with another unit. **7** to appoint officially. **8** *Law.* to arrest or take (a person, property, etc.) with lawful authority. [C14: from OF *atachier* to fasten, changed from *estachier* to fasten with a stake]
► at'**tachable** *adj* ► at'**tacher** *n*

attaché (ə'tæʃeɪ) *n* a specialist attached to a diplomatic mission: *military attaché.* [C19: from F: someone attached (to a mission)]

attaché case *n* a small flat rectangular briefcase used for carrying documents, papers, etc.

attached (ə'tætʃt) *adj* **1** (foll. by *to*) fond (of). **2** married, engaged, or associated in an exclusive sexual relationship.

attachment (ə'tætʃmənt) *n* **1** a fastening. **2** (often foll. by *to*) affection or regard (for). **3** an object to be attached: *an attachment for an electric drill.* **4** the act of attaching or the state of being attached. **5a** the lawful seizure of property and placing of it under control of a court. **5b** a writ authorizing such seizure.

attack (ə'tæk) *vb* **1** to launch a physical assault (against) with or without weapons. **2** (*intr*) to take the initiative in a game, sport, etc. **3** (*tr*) to criticize or abuse vehemently. **4** (*tr*) to turn one's mind or energies to (a job, problem, etc.). **5** (*tr*) to begin to injure or affect adversely: *rust attacked the metal.* ◆ *n* **6** the act or an instance of attacking. **7** strong criticism or abuse. **8** an offensive move in a game, sport, etc. **9 the attack.** *Ball games.* the players in a team whose main role is to attack the opponents. **10** commencement of a task, etc. **11** any sudden and usually severe manifestation of a disease or disorder: *a heart attack.* **12** *Music.* **12a** decisiveness in beginning a passage, movement, or piece. **12b** (in electronic instruments) the time between the start of a note and its maximum volume. [C16: from F, from OIt. *attaccare* to attack, attach, from *estaccare* to attach]
► at'**tacker** *n*

attain (ə'teɪn) *vb* **1** (*tr*) to achieve or accomplish (a task, aim, etc.). **2** (*tr*) to reach in space or time. **3** (*intr;* often foll. by *to*) to arrive (at) with effort or exertion. [C14: from OF, from L *attingere* to reach, from *tangere* to touch]
► at'**tainable** *adj* ► at,taina'**bility** *or* at'**tainableness** *n*

attainder (ə'teɪndə) *n* (formerly) the extinction of a person's civil rights resulting from a sentence of death or outlawry on conviction for treason or felony. [C15: from Anglo-F *attaindre* to convict, from OF *ateindre* to AT-TAIN]

attainment (ə'teɪnmənt) *n* an achievement or the act of achieving; accomplishment.

attainment target *n Brit. education.* a general defined level of ability that a pupil is expected to achieve in every subject at each key stage in the National Curriculum. Abbrev.: **AT.**

attaint (ə'teɪnt) *vb* (*tr*) *Arch.* **1** to pass judgment of death or outlawry upon (a person). **2** (of sickness) to affect or strike (somebody). ◆ *n* **3** a less common word for **attainder.** [C14: from OF *ateint* convicted, from *ateindre* to AT-TAIN]

attar ('ætə), **otto** ('ɒtəʊ), *or* **ottar** ('ɒtə) *n* an essential oil from flowers, esp. the damask rose: *attar of roses*. [C18: from Persian, from *'itr* perfume, from Ar.]

attempt (ə'tɛmpt) *vb* (*tr*) **1** to make an effort (to do something) or to achieve (something); try. **2** to try to surmount (an obstacle). **3** to try to climb. ◆ *n* **4** an endeavour to achieve something; effort. **5** a result of an attempt or endeavour. **6** an attack, esp. with the intention to kill. [C14: from OF, from L *attemptāre* to strive after, from *tentāre* to try]
▸ at'temptable *adj*

> USAGE NOTE *Attempt* should not be used in the passive when followed by an infinitive: *attempts were made to find a solution* (not *a solution was attempted to be found*).

Attenborough ★ ('ætʰnbʰrə) *n* **1** Sir **David**. born 1926, British naturalist and broadcaster. **2** his brother **Richard**, Baron Attenborough. born 1923, British film actor, director, and producer; noted for the films *Gandhi* (1982), *Cry Freedom* (1987), and *Shadowlands* (1993).

attend (ə'tɛnd) *vb* **1** to be present at (an event, etc.). **2** (when *intr*, foll. by *to*) to give care (to); minister (to). **3** (when *intr*, foll. by *to*) to pay attention. **4** (*tr*; *often passive*) to accompany or follow: *a high temperature attended by a severe cough*. **5** (*intr*; foll. by *on* or *upon*) to follow as a consequence (of). **6** (*intr*; foll. by *to*) to apply oneself: *to attend to the garden*. **7** (*tr*) to escort or accompany. **8** (*intr*; foll. by *on* or *upon*) to provide for the needs (of): *to attend on a guest*. [C13: from OF, from L *attendere* to stretch towards, from *tendere* to extend]

attendance (ə'tɛndəns) *n* **1** the act or state of attending. **2** the number of persons present.

attendant (ə'tɛndənt) *n* **1** a person who accompanies or waits upon another. **2** a person employed to assist, guide, or provide a service for others. **3** a person who is present. ◆ *adj* **4** being in attendance. **5** associated: *attendant problems*.

attendee (ə,tɛn'di:) *n* a person who is present at a specified event.

attention (ə'tɛnʃən) *n* **1** concentrated direction of the mind, esp. to a problem or task. **2** consideration, notice, or observation. **3** detailed care or special treatment: *to pay attention to one's appearance*. **4** (*usually pl*) an act of courtesy or gallantry indicating affection or love. **5** the motionless position of formal military alertness, an upright position with legs and heels together. ◆ *sentence substitute*. **6** the order to be alert or to adopt a position of formal military alertness. [C14: from L, from *attendere* to apply the mind to]

attention deficit disorder *n* a disorder, particularly of children, characterized by excessive activity and inability to concentrate on one task for any length of time. Abbrev.: **ADD**.

attentive (ə'tɛntɪv) *adj* **1** paying attention; listening carefully. **2** (*postpositive*; often foll. by *to*) careful to fulfil the needs or wants (of).
▸ at'tentively *adv* ▸ at'tentiveness *n*

attenuate *vb* (ə'tɛnjʊˌeɪt) **attenuates, attenuating, attenuated**. **1** to weaken or become weak. **2** to make or become thin or fine; extend. ◆ *adj* (ə'tɛnjʊɪt, -ˌeɪt). **3** weakened or reduced. **4** *Bot*. tapering. [C16: from L *attenuāre* to weaken, from *tenuis* thin]
▸ at,tenu'ation *n*

attest (ə'tɛst) *vb* **1** (*tr*) to affirm the correctness or truth of. **2** (when *intr*, usually foll. by *to*) to witness (an act, event, etc.) or bear witness (to an act, event, etc.). **3** (*tr*) to make evident; demonstrate. **4** (*tr*) to provide evidence for. [C16: from L, from *testārī* to bear witness, from *testis* a witness]
▸ at'testable *adj* ▸ at'testant, at'tester *or esp. in legal usage* at'testor *n* ▸ attestation (ˌætɛ'steɪʃən) *n*

attested (ə'tɛstɪd) *adj Brit*. (of cattle, etc.) certified to be free from a disease, esp. from tuberculosis.

attic ('ætɪk) *n* **1** a space or room within the roof of a house. **2** *Archit*. a storey or low wall above the cornice of

a classical façade. [C18: special use of ATTIC, from use o Attic-style pilasters on façade of top storey]

Attic ('ætɪk) *adj* **1** of or relating to Attica, its inhabitants or the dialect of Greek spoken there. **2** (*often not cap.* classically elegant, simple, or pure. ◆ *n* **3** the dialect o Ancient Greek spoken and written in Athens.

Attica ★ ('ætɪkə) *n* a region and department of E centra Greece: in ancient times the territory of Athens. Capital Athens. Pop.: 3 523 407 (1991). Area: 14 157 sq. km (5466 sq. miles).

Atticism ('ætɪˌsɪzəm) *n* **1** the idiom or character of the Attic dialect of Ancient Greek. **2** an elegant, simple expression.

Attic salt *or* **wit** *n* refined incisive wit.

Attila ★ (ə'tɪlə) *n* ?406–453 A.D., king of the Huns, who devastated much of the Roman Empire, invaded Gaul in 451 A.D., but was defeated by the Romans and Visigoths at Châlons-sur-Marne.

attire (ə'taɪə) *vb* **attires, attiring, attired**. **1** (*tr*) to dress, esp. in fine elegant clothes; array. ◆ *n* **2** clothes or garments, esp. if fine or decorative. [C13: from OF *atirier* to put in order, from *tire* row]

attitude ('ætɪˌtjuːd) *n* **1** the way a person views something or tends to behave towards it, often in an evaluative way. **2** a theatrical pose created for effect (esp. in **strike an attitude**). **3** a position of the body indicating mood or emotion. **4** *Inf*. a hostile manner: *don't give me attitude, my girl*. **5** the orientation of an aircraft's axes or a spacecraft in relation to some plane or the direction of motion. [C17: from F, from It. *attitudine* disposition, from LL *aptitūdō* fitness, from L *aptus* APT]
▸ ˌatti'tudinal *adj*

attitudinize *or* **attitudinise** (ˌætɪ'tjuːdɪˌnaɪz) *vb* **attitudinizes, attitudinizing, attitudinized** *or* **attitudinises, attitudinising, attitudinised**. (*intr*) to adopt a pose or opinion for effect; strike an attitude.

Attlee ★ ('ætlɪ) *n* **Clement Richard**, 1st Earl Attlee. 1883–1967, British statesman; prime minister (1945–51); leader of the Labour party (1935–55).

attn *abbrev. for* attention.

atto- *prefix denoting* 10^{-18}: *attotesla*. Symbol: a [from Norwegian & Danish *atten* eighteen]

attorney (ə'tɜːnɪ) *n* **1** a person legally appointed or empowered to act for another. **2** *US*. a lawyer qualified to represent clients in legal proceedings. [C14: from OF, from *atourner* to direct to, from *tourner* to TURN]
▸ at'torneyˌship *n*

attorney-at-law *n*, *pl* **attorneys-at-law**. *Law, now chiefly US*. a lawyer.

attorney general *n*, *pl* **attorneys general** *or* **attorney generals**. a chief law officer and senior legal adviser of some national and state governments.

attract (ə'trækt) *vb* (*mainly tr*) **1** to draw (notice, a crowd of observers, etc.) to oneself (esp. in **attract attention**). **2** (*also intr*) to exert a force on (a body) that tends to oppose a separation: *the gravitational pull of the earth attracts objects to it*. **3** to possess some property that pulls or draws (something) towards itself. **4** (*also intr*) to exert a pleasing or fascinating influence (upon). [C15: from L *attrahere* to draw towards, from *trahere* to pull]
▸ at'tractable *adj* ▸ at'tractor *n*

attraction (ə'trækʃən) *n* **1** the act or quality of attracting. **2** a person or thing that attracts or is intended to attract. **3** a force by which one object attracts another: *magnetic attraction*.

attractive (ə'træktɪv) *adj* **1** appealing to the senses or mind through beauty, form, character, etc. **2** arousing interest: *an attractive opportunity*. **3** possessing the ability to draw or pull: *an attractive force*.
▸ at'tractively *adv*

attrib. *abbrev. for*: **1** attribute. **2** attributive.

attribute *vb* (ə'trɪbjuːt). **attributes, attributing, attributed**. **1** (*tr*; usually foll. by *to*) to regard as belonging (to), produced (by), or resulting (from): *to attribute a painting to Picasso*. ◆ *n* ('ætrɪˌbjuːt). **2** a property, quality, or feature belonging to or representative of a person or thing. **3** an object accepted as belonging to a particular office or po-

sition. **4** *Grammar.* **4a** an adjective or adjectival phrase. **4b** an attributive adjective. **5** *Logic.* the property or feature that is affirmed or denied concerning the subject of a proposition. [C15: from L *attribuere* to associate with, from *tribuere* to give]
► at'tributable *adj* ► attribution (ˌætrɪ'bjuːʃən) *n*

attributive (ə'trɪbjutɪv) *adj* **1** relating to an attribute. **2** *Grammar.* (of an adjective or adjectival phrase) preceding the noun modified. Cf. **predicative**. **3** *Philosophy.* relative to an understood domain, as *small* in *that elephant is small*.

attrition (ə'trɪʃən) *n* **1** the act of wearing away or the state of being worn away, as by friction. **2** constant wearing down to weaken or destroy (often in **war of attrition**). **3** *Geog.* the grinding down of rock particles by friction. **4** *Theol.* sorrow for sin arising from fear of damnation, esp. as contrasted with contrition. [C14: from LL *attrītiō* a rubbing against something, from L *atterere* to weaken, from *terere* to rub]

Attu ★ ('ætuː) *n* the westernmost of the Aleutian Islands, off the coast of SW Alaska: largest of the Near Islands.

attune (ə'tjuːn) *vb* **attunes, attuning, attuned.** (*tr*) to adjust or accustom (a person or thing); acclimatize.

ATV *abbrev. for* all-terrain vehicle.

at. vol. *abbrev. for* atomic volume.

Atwood ★ ('æt,wud) *n* **Margaret (Eleanor).** born 1939, Canadian writer. Her novels include *Lady Oracle* (1976), *The Handmaid's Tale* (1986), and *Alias Grace* (1996).

at. wt. *abbrev. for* atomic weight.

atypical (eɪ'tɪpɪkᵊl) *adj* not typical; deviating from or not conforming to type.
► a'typically *adv*

Au *the chemical symbol for* gold. [from NL *aurum*]

aubade (əu'bɑːd) *n* a poem or short musical piece to greet the dawn. [C19: F, from OProvençal *auba* dawn, ult. from L *albus* white]

Aube ★ (*French* ob) *n* **1** a department of N central France, in Champagne-Ardenne region. Capital: Troyes. Pop.: 292 765 (1994 est.). Area: 6026 sq. km (2350 sq. miles). **2** a river in N central France, flowing northwest to the Seine. Length: about 225 km (140 miles).

aubergine ('əubəˌʒiːn) *n* **1** *Chiefly Brit.* a tropical Old World plant widely cultivated for its egg-shaped typically dark purple fruit. US, Canad., and Austral. name: **eggplant. 2** the fruit of this plant, which is cooked and eaten as a vegetable. **3a** a dark purple colour. **3b** (*as adj*): *an aubergine dress.* [C18: from F, from Catalan *alberginia*, from Ar. *al-bādindjān*, ult. from Sansk. *vatin-ganah*, from ?]

Aubrey ★ ('ɔːbrɪ) *n* **John.** 1626–97, English antiquary noted for his *Brief Lives* (edited 1898).

aubrietia, aubrietia, *or* **aubretia** (ɔː'briːʃə) *n* a trailing purple-flowered plant native to European mountains but widely planted in rock gardens. [C19: from NL, after Claude *Aubriet*, 18th-cent. F painter of flowers and animals]

auburn ('ɔːbᵊn) *n* **a** a moderate reddish-brown colour. **b** (*as adj*): *auburn hair.* [C15 (orig. meaning: blond): from OF *alborne* blond, from Med. L, from L *albus* white]

Aubusson ★ (*French* obysɔ̃) *n* **1** a town in central France, in the Creuse department: a centre for flat-woven carpets and for tapestries since the 16th century. Pop.: 5000 (latest est.). ◆ *adj* **2** denoting or relating to these carpets or tapestries.

Auckland ★ ('ɔːklənd) *n* the chief port of New Zealand, in the northern part of North Island: former capital of New Zealand (1840–65). Pop. (urban area): 353 670 (1996).

Auckland Islands ★ *pl n* a group of six uninhabited islands, south of New Zealand. Area: 611 sq. km (234 sq. miles).

au courant *French.* (o kurɑ̃) *adj* up-to-date, esp. in knowledge of current affairs. [lit.: in the current]

auction ('ɔːkʃən) *n* **1** a public sale of goods or property in which prospective purchasers bid until the highest price is reached. **2** the competitive calls made in bridge before play begins. ◆ *vb* **3** (*tr*; often foll. by *off*) to sell by auc-

tion. [C16: from L *auctiō* an increasing, from *augēre* to increase]

auction bridge *n* a variety of bridge in which all the tricks made score towards game.

auctioneer (ˌɔːkʃə'nɪə) *n* **1** a person who conducts an auction. ◆ *vb* **2** (*tr*) to sell by auction.

auctorial (ɔːk'tɔːrɪəl) *adj* of or relating to an author. [C19: from L *auctor* AUTHOR]

audacious (ɔː'deɪʃəs) *adj* **1** recklessly bold or daring. **2** impudent or presumptuous. [C16: from L *audāx* bold, from *audēre* to dare]
► au'daciousness *or* audacity (ɔː'dæsɪtɪ) *n*

Aude ★ (*French* od) *n* a department of S France on the Gulf of Lions, in Languedoc-Roussillon region. Capital: Carcassonne. Pop.: 304 707 (1994 est.). Area: 6342 sq. km (2473 sq. miles).

Auden ★ ('ɔːdᵊn) *n* **W(ystan) H(ugh).** 1907–73, US poet and dramatist, born in Britain.

audible ('ɔːdɪbᵊl) *adj* perceptible to the hearing; loud enough to be heard. [C16: from LL, from L *audīre* to hear]
► ˌaudi'bility *or* 'audibleness *n* ► 'audibly *adv*

audience ('ɔːdɪəns) *n* **1** a group of spectators or listeners, esp. at a concert or play. **2** the people reached by a book, film, or radio or television programme. **3** the devotees or followers of a public entertainer, etc. **4** a formal interview with a monarch or head of state. [C14: from L *audientia* a hearing, from *audīre* to hear]

audio ('ɔːdɪəu) *n* (*modifier*) **1** of or relating to sound or hearing: *audio frequency.* **2** relating to or employed in the transmission or reproduction of sound. [C20: from L *audīre* to hear]

audio book *n* a reading of a book recorded on tape.

audio frequency *n* a frequency in the range 20 hertz to 20 000 hertz. A sound wave of this frequency would be audible to the human ear.

audiology (ˌɔːdɪ'ɒlədʒɪ) *n* the scientific study of hearing, often including the treatment of persons with hearing defects.
► ˌaudi'ologist *n*

audiometer (ˌɔːdɪ'ɒmɪtə) *n* an instrument for testing hearing.
► ˌaudi'ometrist *n* ► ˌaudi'ometry *n*

audiophile ('ɔːdɪəu,faɪl) *n* a person who has a great interest in high-fidelity sound reproduction.

audiotypist ('ɔːdɪəu,taɪpɪst) *n* a typist trained to type from a dictating machine.
► 'audio,typing *n*

audiovisual (ˌɔːdɪəu'vɪʒuəl) *adj* (esp. of teaching aids) involving or directed at both hearing and sight.
► ˌaudio'visually *adv*

audit ('ɔːdɪt) *n* **1a** an inspection, correction, and verification of business accounts, conducted by an independent qualified accountant. **1b** (*as modifier*): *audit report.* **2** *US.* an audited account. **3** any thoroughgoing examination or check. ◆ *vb* **audits, auditing, audited. 4** to inspect, correct, and certify (accounts, etc.). [C15: from L *audītus* a hearing, from *audīre* to hear]

audition (ɔː'dɪʃən) *n* **1** a test at which a performer or musician is asked to demonstrate his ability for a particular role, etc. **2** the act or power of hearing. ◆ *vb* **3** to judge by means of or be tested in an audition. [C16: from L *audītiō* a hearing, from *audīre* to hear]

auditor ('ɔːdɪtə) *n* **1** a person qualified to audit accounts. **2** a person who hears or listens. [C14: from OF, from L *audītor* a hearer]
► ˌaudi'torial *adj*

Auditor General *n* (in Canada) an officer appointed by the Governor General to audit the accounts of the Federal Government and report to Parliament.

auditorium (ˌɔːdɪ'tɔːrɪəm) *n, pl* **auditoriums** *or* **auditoria** (-'tɔːrɪə). **1** the area of a concert hall, theatre, etc., in which the audience sits. **2** *US & Canad.* a building for public meetings. [C17: from L: a judicial examination]

auditory ('ɔːdɪtərɪ) *adj* of or relating to hearing or the sense of hearing. [C14: from L *audītōrius* relating to hearing, from *audīre* to hear]

Audubon ★ ('ɔːdə,bɒn) *n* **John James**. 1785–1851, US naturalist and artist, noted for his paintings of birds.

Auerbach ★ ('auə,bɑːk) *n* **Frank (Helmuth)**. born 1931, British painter, born in Germany.

au fait French. (o fɛ) *adj* fully informed; in touch or expert. [C18: lit.: to the point]

au fond French. (o fɔ̃) *adv* fundamentally; essentially. [lit.: at the bottom]

auf Wiedersehen German. (auf 'viːdərzeːən) *sentence substitute*. goodbye, until we see each other again.

Aug. *abbrev. for* August.

Augean (ɔː'dʒiːən) *adj* extremely dirty or corrupt. [C16: from *Augeas*, in Gk myth., king whose filthy stables Hercules cleaned in one day]

augend ('ɔːdʒɛnd, ɔː'dʒɛnd) *n* a number to which another number, the addend, is added. [from L *augendum*, from *augēre* to increase]

auger ('ɔːgə) *n* **1** a hand tool with a bit shaped like a corkscrew, for boring holes in wood. **2** a larger tool of the same kind for boring holes in the ground. [C15: *an augur*, mistaken division of *a nauger*, from OE *nafugār* nave (of a wheel) spear, from *nafu* NAVE² + *gār* spear]

aught *or* **ought** (ɔːt) (*used with a negative or in conditional or interrogative sentences or clauses*) Arch. or literary. ▷ *pron* **1** anything whatever (esp. in **for aught I know**). ◆ *adv* **2** Dialect. to any degree. [OE *āwiht*, from *ā* ever, + *wiht* thing]

augment (ɔːg'mɛnt) *vb* to make or become greater in number, strength, etc. [C15: from LL, from *augmentum* growth, from L *augēre* to increase]
▶ aug'mentable *adj* ▶ aug'menter *n*

augmentation (,ɔːgmɛn'teɪʃən) *n* **1** the act of augmenting or the state of being augmented. **2** the amount by which something is increased.

augmentative (ɔːg'mɛntətɪv) *adj* **1** tending or able to augment. **2** Grammar. denoting an affix that may be added to a word to convey the meaning *large* or *great*: for example, the suffix *-ote* in Spanish, where *hombre* means man and *hombrote* big man.

augmented (ɔːg'mɛntɪd) *adj* **1** Music. (of an interval) increased from being perfect or major by the raising of the higher note or the dropping of the lower note by one semitone: *C to G sharp is an augmented fifth*. **2** having been increased, esp. in number: *an augmented orchestra*.

au gratin (*French* o gratɛ̃) *adj* covered and cooked with browned breadcrumbs and sometimes cheese. [F, lit.: with the grating]

Augsburg ★ (*German* 'auksbʊrk) *n* a city in S Germany, in Bavaria: founded by the Romans in 14 B.C.; site of the diet that produced the **Peace of Augsburg** (1555), which ended the struggles between Lutherans and Catholics in the Holy Roman Empire and established the principle that each ruler should determine the form of worship in his lands. Pop.: 262 110 (1995 est.). Roman name: **Augusta Vindelicorum** (au'guːstə vɪn'dɛlɪ,kəurəm).

augur ('ɔːgə) *n* **1** (in ancient Rome) a religious official who observed and interpreted omens and signs. **2** any prophet or soothsayer. ◆ *vb* **3** to predict (some future event), as from signs or omens. **4** (*tr; may take a clause as object*) to be an omen (of). **5** (*intr*) to foreshadow future events: *this augurs well for us*. [C14: from L: a diviner, ?from *augēre* to increase]
▶ augural ('ɔːgjurəl) *adj*

augury ('ɔːgjurɪ) *n, pl* **auguries**. **1** the art of or a rite conducted by an augur. **2** a sign or portent; omen.

august (ɔː'gʌst) *adj* **1** dignified or imposing. **2** of noble birth or high rank: *an august lineage*. [C17: from L *augustus*; rel. to *augēre* to increase]
▶ au'gustness *n*

August ('ɔːgəst) *n* the eighth month of the year, consisting of 31 days. [OE, from L, after the emperor AUGUSTUS]

Augusta ★ (ɔː'gʌstə) *n* **1** a town in the US, in Georgia. Pop.: 44 639 (1990). **2** a port in S Italy, in E Sicily. Pop.: 38 900 (latest est.). **3** a city in the US, the state capital of

Maine: founded (1628) as a trading post; timber industry. Pop.: 21 325 (1990).

Augustan (ɔː'gʌstən) *adj* **1** characteristic of or relating to the Roman emperor Augustus Caesar, his period, or the poets writing during his reign. **2** of or characteristic of any literary period noted for refinement and classicism, esp. the 18th century in England. ◆ *n* **3** an author in an Augustan Age.

Augustine ★ (ɔː'gʌstɪn) *n* **1** Saint. 354–430 A.D., one of the Fathers of the Christian Church; bishop of Hippo in North Africa (396–430), noted for his *Confessions* and *De Civitate Dei*. Feast day: Aug. 28. **2** Saint. died 604 A.D., Roman monk, sent to Britain (597 A.D.) to convert the Anglo-Saxons: first archbishop of Canterbury (601–604). Feast day: May 26 or 27. **3** a member of an Augustinian order.

Augustinian (,ɔːgʌ'stɪnɪən) *adj* **1** of Saint Augustine of Hippo, his doctrines, or the Christian religious orders founded on his doctrines. ◆ *n* **2** a member of any of several religious orders that are governed by the rule of Saint Augustine. **3** a person who follows the doctrines of Saint Augustine.

Augustus ★ (ɔː'gʌstəs) *n* original name *Gaius Octavianus*; after his adoption by Julius Caesar (44 B.C.) known as *Gaius Julius Caesar Octavianus*. 63 B.C.–14 A.D., Roman statesman, a member of the second triumvirate (43 B.C.). After defeating Mark Antony at Actium (31 B.C.), he became first emperor of Rome, adopting the title Augustus (27 B.C.).

auk (ɔːk) *n* **1** a diving bird of northern oceans having a heavy body, short tail, narrow wings, and a black-and-white plumage. See also **great auk, razorbill**. **2 little auk**. a small short-billed auk, abundant in Arctic regions. [C17: from ON *ālka*]

au lait (əu 'leɪ) *adj* prepared or served with milk. [F, lit.: with milk]

auld (ɔːld) *adj* a Scottish word for **old**. [OE *āld*]

auld lang syne ('ɔːld læŋ 'saɪn) *n* times past, esp. those remembered with nostalgia. [Scot., lit.: old long since]

Auld Reekie ★ ('riːkɪ) *n* Scot. a nickname for **Edinburgh**[1]. [lit.: Old Smoky]

Aulis ★ ('ɔːlɪs) *n* an ancient town in E central Greece, in Boeotia: traditionally the harbour from which the Greeks sailed at the beginning of the Trojan war.

aumbry ('ɔːmbrɪ) *n, pl* **aumbries**. a variant of **ambry**.

au naturel French. (o natyrɛl) *adj, adv* **1** naked; nude. **2** uncooked or plainly cooked. [lit.: in (a) natural (condition)]

Aung San Suu Kyi ★ ('auŋ 'sæn 'suː 'kiː) *n* born 1945, Burmese politician; cofounder (1988) and general secretary (1988–91 and from 1995) of the National League for Democracy: Nobel peace prize 1991.

aunt (ɑːnt) *n* (*often cap., esp. as a term of address*) **1** a sister of one's father or mother. **2** the wife of one's uncle. **3** a term of address used by children for a female friend of the parents. **4 my (sainted) aunt!** an exclamation of surprise. [C13: from OF, from L *amita* a father's sister]

auntie *or* **aunty** ('ɑːntɪ) *n, pl* **aunties**. a familiar or diminutive word for **aunt**.

Auntie ('ɑːntɪ) *n Brit. inf.* the BBC.

Aunt Sally ('sælɪ) *n, pl* **Aunt Sallies**. Brit. **1** a figure of an old woman used in fairgrounds and fêtes as a target. **2** any person who is a target for insults or criticism.

au pair (əu 'pɛə) *n* **a** a young foreigner, usually a girl, who undertakes housework in exchange for board and lodging, esp. in order to learn the language. **b** (*as modifier*): *an au pair girl*. [C20: from F: on an equal footing]

aura ('ɔːrə) *n, pl* **auras** *or* **aurae** ('ɔːriː). **1** a distinctive air or quality considered to be characteristic of a person or thing. **2** any invisible emanation, esp. surrounding a person or object. **3** Pathol. strange sensations, such as noises in the ears or flashes of light, that immediately precede an attack, esp. of epilepsy. [C18: via L from Gk: breeze]

aural ('ɔːrəl) *adj* of or relating to the sense or organs of hearing; auricular. [C19: from L *auris* ear]
▶ 'aurally *adv*

★ people and places

ureate ('ɔːrɪɪt) *adj* **1** covered with gold; gilded. **2** (of a style of writing or speaking) excessively elaborate. [C15: from LL, from L *aureus* golden, from *aurum* gold]

Aurelian ★ (ɔːˈriːlɪən) *n* Latin name *Lucius Domitius Aurelianus.* ?212–275 A.D., Roman emperor (270–275), who conquered Palmyra (273) and restored political unity to the Roman Empire.

Aurelius ★ (ɔːˈriːlɪəs) *n* See **Marcus Aurelius Antoninus.**

aureole ('ɔːrɪˌəʊl) *or* **aureola** (ɔːˈriːələ) *n* **1** a border of light or radiance enveloping the head of a figure represented as holy. **2** a less common word for **halo. 3** another name for **corona** (sense 2). [C13: from OF, from Med. L (*corōna*) *aureola* golden (crown), from L, from *aurum* gold]

au revoir French. (o rəvwar) *sentence substitute.* goodbye. [lit.: to the seeing again]

auric ('ɔːrɪk) *adj* of or containing gold, esp. in the trivalent state; designating a gold(III) compound. [C19: from L *aurum* gold]

Auric ★ (*French* ɔrik) *n* **Georges** (ʒɔrʒ). 1899–1983, French composer; one of *les Six.*

auricle ('ɔːrɪkʰl) *n* **1** the upper chamber of the heart; atrium. **2** Also called: **pinna.** *Anat.* the external part of the ear. **3** *Biol.* an ear-shaped part or appendage. [C17: from L *auricula* the external ear, from *auris* ear]
▸ **'auricled** *adj*

auricula (ɔːˈrɪkjʊlə) *n, pl* **auriculae** (-ˌliː) *or* **auriculas. 1** Also called: **bear's-ear.** a widely cultivated alpine primrose with leaves shaped like a bear's ear. **2** another word for **auricle** (sense 3). [C17: from NL, from L; see AURICLE]

auricular (ɔːˈrɪkjʊlə) *adj* **1** of, relating to, or received by the sense or organs of hearing; aural. **2** shaped like an ear. **3** of or relating to an auricle of the heart.

auriferous (ɔːˈrɪfərəs) *adj* (of rock) containing gold; gold-bearing. [C18: from L, from *aurum* gold + *ferre* to bear]

Aurignacian (ˌɔːrɪgˈneɪʃən) *adj* of or produced during a flint culture of the Upper Palaeolithic type characterized by the use of bone and antler tools, and also by cave art. [C20: after *Aurignac*, France, near the cave where remains were discovered]

Auriol ★ (*French* ɔrjɔl) *n* **Vincent** (vɛ̃sã). 1884–1966, French statesman; president of the Fourth Republic (1947–54).

aurochs ('ɔːrɒks) *n, pl* **aurochs.** a recently extinct member of the cattle tribe that inhabited forests in N Africa, Europe, and SW Asia. Also called: **urus.** [C18: from G, from OHG *ūrohso*, from *ūro* bison + *ohso* OX]

aurora (ɔːˈrɔːrə) *n, pl* **auroras** *or* **aurorae** (-riː). **1** an atmospheric phenomenon consisting of bands, curtains, or streamers of light, that move across the sky. **2** *Poetic.* the dawn. [C14: from L: dawn]
▸ **au'roral** *adj*

Aurora[1] ★ (ɔːˈrɔːrə) *n* **1** the Roman goddess of the dawn. Greek counterpart: **Eos. 2** the dawn or rise of something.

Aurora[2] ★ (ɔːˈrɔːrə) *n* another name for **Maewo.**

aurora australis (ɒˈstreɪlɪs) *n* (*sometimes cap.*) the aurora seen around the South Pole. Also called: **southern lights.** [NL: southern aurora]

aurora borealis (ˌbɔːrɪˈeɪlɪs) *n* (*sometimes cap.*) the aurora seen around the North Pole. Also called: **northern lights.** [C17: NL: northern aurora]

aurous ('ɔːrəs) *adj* of or containing gold, esp. in the monovalent state; designating a gold(I) compound. [C19: from F *aureux*, LL *aurōsus* gold-coloured, from L *aurum* gold]

Aus. *abbrev. for:* **1** Australia(n). **2** Austria(n).

Auschwitz ★ (*German* ˈaʊʃvɪts) *n* an industrial town in S Poland; site of a Nazi concentration camp during World War II. Pop.: 45 400 (1989 est.). Polish name: **Oświęcim.**

auscultation (ˌɔːskəlˈteɪʃən) *n* **1** the diagnostic technique in medicine of listening to the various internal sounds made by the body, usually with the aid of a stethoscope. **2** the act of listening. [C19: from L, from *auscultāre* to listen attentively; rel. to L *auris* ear]
▸ **'auscul,tate** *vb* ▸ **auscultatory** (ɔːˈskʌltətərɪ) *adj*

auspice ('ɔːspɪs) *n* **1** (*usually pl*) patronage (esp. in **under the auspices of**). **2** (*often pl*) an omen, esp. one that is favourable. [C16: from L *auspicium* augury from birds]

auspicious (ɔːˈspɪʃəs) *adj* **1** favourable or propitious. **2** *Arch.* fortunate.
▸ **aus'piciously** *adv* ▸ **aus'piciousness** *n*

> **USAGE NOTE** The use of *auspicious* to mean 'very special' (as in *this auspicious occasion*) should be avoided.

Aussie ('ɒzɪ) *n, adj Inf.* Australian.

Aust. *abbrev. for:* **1** Australia(n). **2** Austria(n).

Austen ★ ('ɒstɪn, 'ɔː-) *n* **Jane.** 1775–1817, English novelist, noted particularly for the insight and delicate irony of her portrayal of middle-class families. Her completed novels are *Sense and Sensibility* (1811), *Pride and Prejudice* (1813), *Mansfield Park* (1814), *Emma* (1816), *Northanger Abbey* (1818), and *Persuasion* (1818).

austere (ɒˈstɪə) *adj* **1** stern or severe in attitude or manner. **2** grave, serious, or serious. **3** self-disciplined, abstemious, or ascetic: *an austere life.* **4** severely simple or plain: *an austere design.* [C14: from OF, from L *austērus* sour, from Gk *austēros* astringent; rel. to Gk *hauein* to dry]
▸ **aus'terely** *adv*

austerity (ɒˈstɛrɪtɪ) *n, pl* **austerities. 1** the state or quality of being austere. **2** (*often pl*) an austere habit, practice, or act. **3a** reduced availability of luxuries and consumer goods. **3b** (*as modifier*): *an austerity budget.*

Austerlitz ★ ('ɔːstəlɪts) *n* a town in the Czech Republic, in Moravia: site of Napoleon's victory over the Russian and Austrian armies in 1805. Pop.: 4800 (latest est.). Czech name: **Slavkov.**

Austin[1] ★ ('ɒstɪn, 'ɔː-) *n* a city in central Texas, on the Colorado River: state capital since 1845. Pop.: 514 013 (1994 est.).

Austin[2] ★ ('ɒstɪn, 'ɔː-) *n* **1 Herbert,** 1st Baron. 1866–1941, British automobile engineer. **2 John.** 1790–1859, British jurist, noted for *The Province of Jurisprudence Determined* (1832). **3 J(ohn) L(angshaw).** 1911–60, British philosopher, noted for his posthumous *Sense and Sensibilia* (1962).

austral[1] ('ɔːstrəl) *adj* of or coming from the south: *austral winds.* [C14: from L *austrālis*, from *auster* the south wind]

austral[2] (auˈstrɑːl) *n, pl* **australes** (-ˈstrɑːles). a former monetary unit of Argentina. [from Sp.; see AUSTRAL[1]]

Austral. *abbrev. for:* **1** Australasia. **2** Australia(n).

Australasia ★ (ˌɒstrəˈleɪzɪə) *n* **1** Australia, New Zealand, and neighbouring islands in the S Pacific Ocean. **2** (loosely) the whole of Oceania.
▸ **ˌAustra'lasian** *adj*

Australia ★ (ɒˈstreɪlɪə) *n* a country and the smallest continent, situated between the Indian Ocean and the Pacific: a former British colony, now an independent member of the Commonwealth, constitutional links with Britain formally abolished in 1986; consists chiefly of a low plateau, mostly arid in the west, with the basin of the Murray River and the Great Dividing Range in the east and the Great Barrier Reef off the NE coast. Language: English. Currency: dollar. Capital: Canberra. Pop.: 18 508 000 (1997). Area: 7 682 300 sq. km (2 966 150 sq. miles).
▸ **Aus'tralian** *adj, n*

Australiana (ɒ,streɪlɪˈɑːnə) *pl n* objects, books, documents, etc. relating to Australia and its history and culture.

Australian Alps ★ *pl n* a mountain range in SE Australia, in E Victoria and SE New South Wales. Highest peak: Mount Kosciusko, 2195 m (7316 ft).

Australian Antarctic Territory ★ *n* the area of Antarctica, other than Adélie Land, that is administered by Australia, lying south of latitude 60°S and between longitudes 45°E and 160°E.

Australian Capital Territory ★ *n* a territory of SE Australia, within New South Wales: consists of two

---

★ people and places

exclaves, one containing Canberra, the capital of Australia, and one at Jervis Bay. Pop.: 306 400 (1996 est.). Area: 2432 sq. km (939 sq. miles). Former name: **Federal Capital Territory.**

Australian Rules n (*functioning as sing*) a game resembling rugby, played in Australia between teams of 18 men each on an oval pitch, with a ball resembling a large rugby ball. Players attempt to kick the ball between posts (without crossbars) at either end of the pitch.

Austral Islands ★ ('ɔːstrəl) pl n another name for the **Tubuai Islands.**

Australoid ('ɒstrə,lɔɪd) adj **1** denoting, relating to, or belonging to a racial group that includes the native Australians and certain other peoples of southern Asia and the Pacific islands. ◆ n **2** any member of this racial group.

australopithecine (,ɒstrələʊ'pɪθɪ,siːn) n any of various extinct apelike primates whose remains have been found in southern and E Africa. Some species are estimated to be over 4.5 million years old. [C20: from NL, from L *austrālis* southern + Gk *pithēkos* ape]

Australorp ('ɒstrə,lɔːp) n a heavy black breed of domestic fowl laying brown eggs. [shortened from *Austral(ian Black) Orp(ington)*]

Austrasia ★ (ɒ'streɪʒə, -ʃə) n the eastern region of the kingdom of the Merovingian Franks that had its capital at Metz and lasted from 511 A.D. until 814 A.D. It covered the area now comprising NE France, Belgium, and western Germany.

Austria ★ ('ɒstrɪə) n a republic in central Europe: ruled by the Hapsburgs from 1282 to 1918; formed a dual monarchy with Hungary in 1867 and became a republic in 1919; a member of the European Union; contains part of the Alps, the Danube basin in the east, and extensive forests. Language: German. Religion: chiefly Roman Catholic. Currency: schilling and euro. Capital: Vienna. Pop.: 8 087 000 (1997). Area: 83 849 sq. km (32 374 sq. miles). German name: **Österreich.**
▸ **'Austrian** adj, n

Austrian blind n a window blind consisting of rows of vertically gathered fabric that may be drawn up to form a series of ruches.

Austro-[1] ('ɒstrəʊ) *combining form.* southern: *Austro-Asiatic.* [from L *auster* the south wind]

Austro-[2] ('ɒstrəʊ) *combining form.* Austrian: *Austro-Hungarian.*

Austronesia ★ (,ɒstrəʊ'niːʒə, -ʃə) n the islands of the central and S Pacific, including Indonesia, Melanesia, Micronesia, and Polynesia.
▸ **,Austro'nesian** adj, n

AUT (in Britain) abbrev. for Association of University Teachers.

autarchy ('ɔːtɑːkɪ) n, pl **autarchies.** unlimited rule; autocracy. [C17: from Gk *autarkhia*, from *autarkhos* autocratic]
▸ **au'tarchic** or **au'tarchical** adj

autarky ('ɔːtɑːkɪ) n, pl **autarkies.** (esp. of a political unit) a system or policy of economic self-sufficiency. [C17: from Gk *autarkeia*, from *autarkēs* self-sufficient, from AUTO- + *arkein* to suffice]
▸ **au'tarkic** adj ▸ **'autarkist** n

auteur (ɔː'tɜː) n a director whose creative influence on a film is so great as to be considered its author. [Fr: author]
▸ **au'teurism** n ▸ **au'teurist** n

authentic (ɔː'θɛntɪk) adj **1** of undisputed origin or authorship; genuine. **2** trustworthy; reliable: *an authentic account.* **3** (of a deed, etc.) duly executed. **4** *Music.* **4a** using period instruments and historically researched scores and playing techniques. **4b** (*in combination*): *an authentic-instrument performance.* **5** *Music.* commencing on the perfect and ending an octave higher. Cf. **plagal.** [C14: from LL *authenticus* coming from the author, from Gk, from *authentēs* one who acts independently, from AUTO- + *hentēs* a doer]
▸ **au'thentically** adv ▸ **authenticity** (,ɔːθɛn'tɪsɪtɪ) n

authenticate (ɔː'θɛntɪ,keɪt) vb **authenticates, authenticat-**

ing, authenticated. (*tr*) **1** to establish as genuine or valid. **2** to give authority or legal validity to.
▸ **au,thenti'cation** n ▸ **au'thenti,cator** n

author ('ɔːθə) n **1** a person who composes a book, article or other written work. Related adj: **auctorial. 2** a person who writes books as a profession; writer. **3** an originator or creator: *the author of this plan.* ◆ vb (*tr*) **4** to write or originate. [C14: from OF, from L *auctor* author, from *augēre* to increase]
▸ **authorial** (ɔː'θɔːrɪəl) adj

authoritarian (ɔː,θɒrɪ'tɛərɪən) adj **1** favouring or characterized by strict obedience to authority. **2** favouring or relating to government by a small elite. **3** dictatorial; domineering. ◆ n **4** a person who favours or practises authoritarian policies.

authoritative (ɔː'θɒrɪtətɪv) adj **1** recognized or accepted as being true or reliable. **2** commanding: *an authoritative manner.* **3** possessing or supported by authority; official.
▸ **au'thoritatively** adv ▸ **au'thoritativeness** n

authority (ɔː'θɒrɪtɪ) n, pl **authorities. 1** the power or right to control, judge, or prohibit the actions of others. **2** (*often pl*) a person or group of people having this power, such as a government, police force, etc. **3** a position that commands such a power or right (often in **in authority**). **4** such a power or right delegated: *she has his authority.* **5** the ability to influence or control others. **6** an expert or an authoritative written work in a particular field. **7** evidence or testimony. **8** confidence resulting from great expertise. **9** (*cap. when part of a name*) a public board or corporation exercising governmental authority: *Advertising Standards Authority.* [C14: from OF, from L, from *auctor* author]

authorize or **authorise** ('ɔːθə,raɪz) vb **authorizes, authorizing, authorized** or **authorises, authorising, authorised.** (*tr*) **1** to confer authority upon (someone to do something). **2** to permit (someone to do or be something) with official sanction.
▸ **,authori'zation** or **,authori'sation** n

Authorized Version n **the.** an English translation of the Bible published in 1611 under James I. Also called: **King James Version.**

authorship ('ɔːθə,ʃɪp) n **1** the origin or originator of a written work, plan, etc. **2** the profession of writing books.

autism ('ɔːtɪzəm) n *Psychiatry.* abnormal self-absorption, usually affecting children, characterized by lack of response to people and limited ability to communicate. [C20: from Gk *autos* self + -ISM]
▸ **au'tistic** adj

auto ('ɔːtəʊ) n, pl **autos.** US & Canad. inf. **a** short for **automobile. b** (*as modifier*): *auto parts.*

auto. abbrev. for: **1** automatic. **2** automobile. **3** automotive.

auto- or sometimes before a vowel **aut-** combining form. **1** self; same; of or by the same one: *autobiography.* **2** self-caused: *autohypnosis.* **3** self-propelling: *automobile.* [from Gk *autos* self]

autobahn ('ɔːtə,bɑːn) n a motorway in German-speaking countries. [C20: from G from *Auto* car + *Bahn* road, track]

autobiography (,ɔːtəʊbaɪ'ɒgrəfɪ) n, pl **autobiographies.** an account of a person's life written or otherwise recorded by that person.
▸ **,autobi'ographer** n ▸ **autobiographical** (,ɔːtə,baɪə'græfɪk[ə]l) adj

autocephalous (,ɔːtəʊ'sɛfələs) adj (of an Eastern Christian Church) governed by its own national synods and appointing its own patriarchs or prelates.

autochthon (ɔː'tɒkθən) n, pl **autochthons** or **autochthones** (-θə,niːz). **1** (*often pl*) one of the earliest known inhabitants of any country. **2** an animal or plant that is native to a particular region. [C17: from Gk *autokhthōn* from the earth itself, from AUTO- + *khthōn* the earth]
▸ **au'tochthonous** adj

autoclave ('ɔːtə,kleɪv) n **1** a strong sealed vessel used for chemical reactions at high pressure. **2** an apparatus for sterilizing objects (esp. surgical instruments) by means

---

★ people and places

of steam under pressure. [C19: from F AUTO- + -*clave*, from L *clāvis* key]

autocracy (ɔːˈtɒkrəsɪ) *n, pl* **autocracies. 1** government by an individual with unrestricted authority. **2** a country, society, etc., ruled by an autocrat.

autocrat (ˈɔːtəˌkræt) *n* **1** a ruler who possesses absolute and unrestricted authority. **2** a domineering or dictatorial person.
▸ ˌauto'cratic *adj* ▸ ˌauto'cratically *adv*

autocross (ˈɔːtəʊˌkrɒs) *n* a motor sport in which cars race over a half-mile circuit of rough grass.

autocue (ˈɔːtəʊˌkjuː) *n Trademark.* an electronic television prompting device whereby a script, unseen by the audience, is displayed for the speaker.

auto-da-fé (ˌɔːtəʊdəˈfeɪ) *n, pl* **autos-da-fé. 1** *History.* a ceremony of the Spanish Inquisition including the pronouncement and execution of sentences passed on sinners and heretics. **2** the burning to death of people condemned as heretics by the Inquisition. [C18: from Port., lit.: act of the faith]

autoeroticism (ˌɔːtəʊɪˈrɒtɪˌsɪzəm) *or* **autoerotism** (ˌɔːtəʊˈɛrəˌtɪzəm) *n Psychol.* the arousal and use of one's own body as a sexual object.
▸ ˌautoe'rotic *adj*

autoexposure (ˌɔːtəʊɪkˈspəʊʒə) *n* another name for **automatic exposure.**

autofocus (ˈɔːtəʊˌfəʊkəs) *n* another name for **automatic focus.**

autogamy (ɔːˈtɒgəmɪ) *n* self-fertilization.
▸ au'togamous *adj*

autogenic training (ˌɔːtəʊˈdʒɛnɪk) *n* a technique for reducing stress through mental exercises. Also called: **autogenics.**

autogenous (ɔːˈtɒdʒɪnəs) *adj* **1** originating within the body. **2** self-produced. **3** denoting a weld in which the filler metal and the parent metal are of similar composition.
▸ au'togenously *adv*

autogiro *or* **autogyro** (ˌɔːtəʊˈdʒaɪrəʊ) *n, pl* **autogiros** *or* **autogyros.** a self-propelled aircraft supported in flight mainly by unpowered rotating horizontal blades. [C20: orig. a trademark]

autograph (ˈɔːtəˌgrɑːf) *n* **1a** a handwritten signature, esp. that of a famous person. **1b** (*as modifier*): *an autograph album.* **2** a person's handwriting. **3a** a book, document, etc., handwritten by its author. **3b** (*as modifier*): *an autograph letter.* ◆ *vb* (*tr*) **4** to write one's signature on or in; sign. **5** to write with one's own hand.
▸ autographic (ˌɔːtəˈgræfɪk) *adj* ▸ ˌauto'graphically *adv*

autohypnosis (ˌɔːtəʊhɪpˈnəʊsɪs) *n Psychol.* the process or result of self-induced hypnosis.

autoimmune (ˌɔːtəʊɪˈmjuːn) *adj* (of a disease) caused by the action of antibodies produced against substances normally present in the body.
▸ ˌautoim'munity *n*

autointoxication (ˌɔːtəʊɪnˌtɒksɪˈkeɪʃən) *n* self-poisoning caused by toxic products originating within the body.

autologous (ɔːˈtɒləgəs) *adj* (of a tissue graft, blood transfusion, etc.) originating from the recipient rather than from a donor.

Autolycus ★ (ɔːˈtɒlɪkəs) *n Greek myth.* a thief who stole cattle from his neighbour Sisyphus and prevented him from recognizing them by making them invisible.

autolysis (ɔːˈtɒlɪsɪs) *n* the destruction of cells and tissues of an organism by enzymes produced by the cells themselves.
▸ autolytic (ˌɔːtəˈlɪtɪk) *adj*

automat (ˈɔːtəˌmæt) *n* another name, esp. US, for **vending machine.**

automate (ˈɔːtəˌmeɪt) *vb* **automates, automating, automated.** to make (a manufacturing process, factory, etc.) automatic, or (of a manufacturing process, etc.) to be made automatic.

automated teller machine *n* a computerized cash dispenser. Abbrev.: **ATM.**

automatic (ˌɔːtəˈmætɪk) *adj* **1** performed from force of habit or without conscious thought: *an automatic smile.* **2a** (of a device, mechanism, etc.) able to activate, move, or regulate itself. **2b** (of an act or process) performed by such automatic equipment. **3** (of the action of a muscle, etc.) involuntary or reflex. **4** occurring as a necessary consequence: *promotion is automatic after a year.* **5** (of a firearm) utilizing some of the force of each explosion to eject the empty shell, replace it with a new one, and fire continuously until release of the trigger. ◆ *n* **6** an automatic firearm. **7** a motor vehicle having automatic transmission. **8** a machine that operates automatically. [C18: from Gk *automatos* acting independently]
▸ ˌauto'matically *adv*

automatic door *n* a self-opening door.

automatic exposure *n* the automatic adjustment of the lens aperture and shutter speed of a camera by a control mechanism. Also called: **autoexposure.**

automatic focus *n* **a** a system in a camera that automatically adjusts the lens so that the object being photographed is in focus. **b** (*as modifier*): *automatic-focus lens.* Also called: **autofocus.**

automatic gain control *n* a control of a radio receiver which adjusts the magnitude of the input so that the output (or volume) remains approximately constant.

automatic pilot *n* **1** a device that automatically maintains an aircraft on a preset course. **2** *Inf.* a state of mind in which a person performs familiar tasks automatically: *I was on automatic pilot all day.* ◆ Also called: **autopilot.**

automatic transmission *n* a transmission system in a motor vehicle in which the gears change automatically.

automation (ˌɔːtəˈmeɪʃən) *n* **1** the use of methods for controlling industrial processes automatically, esp. by electronically controlled systems. **2** the extent to which a process is so controlled.

automatism (ɔːˈtɒməˌtɪzəm) *n* **1** the state or quality of being automatic; mechanical or involuntary action. **2** *Psychol.* the performance of actions, such as sleepwalking, without conscious knowledge or control.
▸ au'tomatist *n*

automatize *or* **automatise** (ɔːˈtɒməˌtaɪz) *vb* **automatizes, automatizing, automatized** *or* **automatises, automatising, automatised.** to make (a process, etc.) automatic or (of a process, etc.) to be made automatic.
▸ auˌtomati'zation *or* auˌtomati'sation *n*

automaton (ɔːˈtɒmətən) *n, pl* **automatons** *or* **automata. 1** a mechanical device operating under its own hidden power. **2** a person who acts mechanically. [C17: from L, from Gk, from *automatos* spontaneous]

automobile (ˈɔːtəməˌbiːl) *n* another word (esp. US) for **car** (sense 1).
▸ ˌauto'mobilist *n*

automobilia (ˌɔːtəməˈbiːlɪə) *pl n* items connected with cars and motoring that are of interest to the collector.

automotive (ˌɔːtəˈməʊtɪv) *adj* **1** relating to motor vehicles. **2** self-propelling.

autonomic (ˌɔːtəˈnɒmɪk) *adj* **1** occurring spontaneously. **2** of or relating to the autonomic nervous system. **3** Also: **autonomous.** (of plant movements) occurring as a result of internal stimuli.
▸ ˌauto'nomically *adv*

autonomic nervous system *n* the section of the nervous system of vertebrates that controls the involuntary actions of the smooth muscles, heart, and glands.

autonomics (ˌɔːtəˈnɒmɪks) *n* (*functioning as sing*) *Electronics.* the study of self-regulating systems for process control.

autonomous (ɔːˈtɒnəməs) *adj* **1** (of a community, country, etc.) possessing a large degree of self-government. **2** of or relating to an autonomous community. **3** independent of others. **4** *Biol.* existing as an organism independent of other organisms or parts. [C19: from Gk *autonomos* living under one's own laws, from AUTO- + *nomos* law]
▸ au'tonomously *adv*

★ people and places

autonomy (ɔː'tɒnəmɪ) *n, pl* **autonomies. 1** the right or state of self-government, esp. when limited. **2** a state or individual possessing autonomy. **3** freedom to determine one's own actions, behaviour, etc. **4** *Philosophy.* the doctrine that the individual human will is, or ought to be, governed only by its own principles and laws. [C17: from Gk *automonia* freedom to live by one's own laws]

autopilot (ˌɔːtə'paɪlət) *n* short for **automatic pilot.**

autopsy ('ɔːtəpsɪ, ɔː'tɒp-) *n, pl* **autopsies. 1** Also called: **postmortem examination.** dissection and examination of a dead body to determine the cause of death. **2** an eyewitness observation. **3** any critical analysis. [C17: from NL, from Gk: seeing with one's own eyes, from AUTO- + *opsis* sight]

autoroute ('ɔːtəuˌruːt) *n* a motorway in French-speaking countries. [C20: from F from *auto* car + *route* road]

autostrada ('ɔːtəuˌstrɑːdə) *n* a motorway in Italian-speaking countries. [C20: from It. from *auto* car + *strada* road]

autosuggestion (ˌɔːtəusə'dʒestʃən) *n* a process of suggestion in which the person unconsciously supplies the means of influencing his own behaviour or beliefs.

autotelic (ˌɔːtəu'telɪk) *adj* being or having an end or justification in itself. [C20: from AUTO- + Gk *telos* end]

autotomy (ɔː'tɒtəmɪ) *n, pl* **autotomies.** the casting off by an animal of a part of its body, to facilitate escape when attacked.
► **autotomic** (ˌɔːtə'tɒmɪk) *adj*

autotrophic (ˌɔːtə'trɒfɪk) *adj* (of organisms such as green plants) capable of manufacturing complex organic nutritive compounds from simple inorganic sources.
► **'auto,troph** *n*

autumn ('ɔːtəm) *n* **1** (*sometimes cap.*) **1a** Also called (esp. US): **fall.** the season of the year between summer and winter, astronomically from the September equinox to the December solstice in the N hemisphere and from the March equinox to the June solstice in the S hemisphere. **1b** (*as modifier*): *autumn leaves.* **2** a period of late maturity, esp. one followed by a decline. [C14: from L *autumnus*]
► **autumnal** (ɔː'tʌmnᵊl) *adj*

autumn crocus *n* a plant of the lily family having pink or purplish autumn flowers, found in Europe and N Africa.

Auvergne ★ (əu'veən, əu'vɜːn; *French* overɲ) *n* a region of S central France: largely mountainous, rising over 1800 m (6000 ft).

aux. *abbrev. for* auxiliary.

auxanometer (ˌɔːksə'nɒmɪtə) *n* an instrument that measures the linear growth of plant shoots. [C19: from Gk *auxanein* to increase + -METER]

Aux Cayes ★ (əu 'keɪ; *French* o kɑj) *n* the former name of **Les Cayes.**

Auxerre ★ (*French* osɛr) *n* a town in central France, capital of the Yonne department; Gothic cathedral. Pop.: 40 600 (1990).

auxiliaries (ɔːg'zɪljərɪz, -'zɪlə-) *pl n* foreign troops serving another nation; mercenaries.

auxiliary (ɔːg'zɪljərɪ, -'zɪlə-) *adj* **1** secondary or supplementary. **2** supporting. ◆ *n, pl* **auxiliaries. 3** a person or thing that supports or supplements. **4** *Naut.* **4a** a sailing vessel with an engine. **4b** the engine of such a vessel. [C17: from L, from *auxilium* help, from *augēre* to increase, strengthen]

auxiliary rotor *n* the tail rotor of a helicopter, used for directional and rotary control.

auxiliary verb *n* a verb used to indicate the tense, voice, or mood of another verb where this is not indicated by inflection, such as English *will* in *he will go.*

auxin ('ɔːksɪn) *n* a plant hormone that promotes growth. [C20: from Gk *auxein* to grow]

AV *abbrev. for* Authorized Version (of the Bible).

av. *abbrev. for:* **1** average. **2** avoirdupois.

Av. *or* **av.** *abbrev. for* avenue.

a.v. *or* **A/V** *abbrev. for* ad valorem.

avadavat (ˌævədə'væt) *or* **amadavat** (ˌæmədə'væt) *n* either of two Asian weaverbirds having a red plumage: often kept as cagebirds. [C18: from *Ahmadabad,* Indian city from which these birds were brought to Europe]

avail (ə'veɪl) *vb* **1** to be of use, advantage, profit, or assistance (to). **2 avail oneself of.** to make use of to one's advantage. ◆ *n* **3** use or advantage (esp. in **of no avail, to little avail**). [C13 *availen,* from OF *valoir,* from L *valēre* to be strong]

available (ə'veɪləbᵊl) *adj* **1** obtainable or accessible; capable of being made use of. **2** *Arch.* advantageous.
► **a,vaila'bility** *or* **a'vailableness** *n* ► **a'vailably** *adv*

avalanche ('ævəˌlɑːntʃ) *n* **1a** a fall of large masses of snow and ice down a mountain. **1b** a fall of rocks, sand, etc. **2** a sudden or overwhelming appearance of a large quantity of things. ◆ *vb* **avalanches, avalanching, avalanched. 3** to come down overwhelmingly (upon) [C18: from F, by mistaken division from *la valanche,* from *valanche,* from dialect *lavantse*]

Avalon ★ ('ævəˌlɒn) *n Celtic myth.* an island paradise in the western seas: in Arthurian legend it is where King Arthur was taken after he was mortally wounded. [from Med L *insula avallonis* island of Avalon, from O Welsh *aballon* apple]

avant- ('ævɒŋ) *prefix* of or belonging to the avant-garde of a specified field.

avant-garde (ˌævɒŋ'gɑːd) *n* **1** those artists, writers, musicians, etc., whose techniques and ideas are in advance of those generally accepted. ◆ *adj* **2** of such artists, etc., their ideas, or techniques. [from F: VANGUARD]

avarice ('ævərɪs) *n* extreme greed for riches. [C13: from OF, from L, from *avārus* covetous, from *avēre* to crave]
► **avaricious** (ˌævə'rɪʃəs) *adj*

avast (ə'vɑːst) *sentence substitute. Naut.* stop! cease! [C17 ?from Du. *hou'vast* hold fast]

avatar ('ævəˌtɑː) *n* **1** *Hinduism.* the manifestation of a deity in human or animal form. **2** a visible manifestation of an abstract concept. [C18: from Sansk. *avatāra* a going down, from *ava* down + *tarati* he passes over]

avaunt (ə'vɔːnt) *sentence substitute. Arch.* go away! depart [C15: from OF *avant!* forward! from LL *ab ante* forward, from L *ab* from + *ante* before]

avdp. *abbrev. for* avoirdupois.

ave ('ɑːvɪ, 'ɑːveɪ) *sentence substitute.* welcome or farewell. [L]

Ave[1] ('ɑːvɪ) *n RC Church.* short for **Ave Maria**: see **Hail Mary.** [C13: from L: hail!]

Ave[2] *or* **ave** *abbrev. for* avenue.

Avebury ★ ('eɪvbərɪ) *n* a village in Wiltshire, site of an extensive neolithic stone circle.

Aveiro ★ (*Portuguese* ə've:iru) *n* a port in N central Portugal, on the **Aveiro lagoon**: ancient Roman town; linked by canal with the Atlantic Ocean. Pop.: 35 250 (1991). Ancient name: **Talabriga** (ˌtælə'briːgə).

Ave Maria (mə'riːə) *n* another name for **Hail Mary.** [C14: from Med L: hail, Mary!]

avenge (ə'vendʒ) *vb* **avenges, avenging, avenged.** (*usually tr*) to inflict a punishment in retaliation for (harm, injury, etc.) done to (a person or persons): *to avenge a crime; to avenge a murdered friend.* [C14: from OF, from *vengier,* from L *vindicāre;* see VENGEANCE, VINDICATE]
► **a'venger** *n*

USAGE NOTE The use of *avenge* with a reflexive pronoun was formerly considered incorrect, but is now acceptable: *she avenged herself on the man who killed her daughter.*

avens ('ævɪnz) *n, pl* **avens.** (*functioning as sing*) **1** any of a genus of plants, such as **water avens,** which has a purple calyx and orange-pink flowers. **2 mountain avens.** a trailing evergreen white-flowered shrub that grows on mountains in N temperate regions. [C15: from OF, from Med. L *avencia* variety of clover]

★ people and places

Aventine ★ ('ævən,taɪn, -tɪn) *n* one of the seven hills on which Rome was built.

aventurine (ə'ventjurɪn) *or* **avanturine** (ə'væntjurɪn) *n* **1** a dark-coloured glass, usually green or brown, spangled with fine particles of gold, copper, or some other metal. **2** a variety of quartz containing red or greenish particles of iron oxide or mica. [C19: from F, from It., from *avventura* chance; so named because usually found by accident]

avenue ('ævɪnjuː) *n* **1a** a broad street, often lined with trees. **1b** (*cap. as part of a street name*) a road, esp. in a built-up area. **2** a main approach road, as to a country house. **3** a way bordered by two rows of trees. **4** a line of approach: *explore every avenue.* [C17: from F, from *avenir* to come to, from L, from *venīre* to come]

aver (ə'vɜː) *vb* **avers, averring, averred.** (*tr*) **1** to state positively. **2** *Law.* to allege as a fact or prove to be true. [C14: from OF, from Med. L *advērāre*, from L *vērus* true]
▸ **a'verment** *n*

average ('ævərɪdʒ, 'ævrɪdʒ) *n* **1** the typical or normal amount, quality, degree, etc.: *above average in intelligence.* **2** Also called: **arithmetic mean.** the result obtained by adding the numbers or quantities in a set and dividing the total by the number of members in the set: *the average of 3, 4, and 8 is 5.* **3** a similar mean for continuously variable ratios, such as speed. **4** *Maritime law.* **4a** a loss incurred or damage suffered by a ship or its cargo at sea. **4b** the equitable apportionment of such loss among the interested parties. **5 on (the *or* an) average.** usually; typically. ◆ *adj* **6** usual or typical. **7** mediocre or inferior: *his performance was only average.* **8** constituting a numerical average: *an average speed.* **9** approximately typical of a range of values: *the average contents of a matchbox.* ◆ *vb* **averages, averaging, averaged.** **10** (*tr*) to obtain or estimate a numerical average of. **11** (*tr*) to assess the general quality of. **12** (*tr*) to perform or receive a typical number of: *to average eight hours' work a day.* **13** (*tr*) to divide up proportionately. **14** to amount to or be on average: *the children averaged 15 years of age.* [C15 *averay* loss arising from damage to ships, from OIt. *avaria*, ult. from Ar. *awār* damage, blemish]
▸ **'averagely** *adv*

Averno ★ (*Italian* a'vɛrno) *n* a crater lake in Italy, near Naples: in ancient times regarded as an entrance to hell. Latin name: *Avernus* (ə'vɜːnəs). [from L, from Gk *aornos* without birds, from A-¹ + *ornis* bird; referring to the legend that the lake's sulphurous exhalations killed birds]

Averroës ★ (ə'vɛrəu,iːz) *n* Arabic name *ibn-Rushd.* 1126–88, Arab philosopher and physician in Spain, noted particularly for his attempts to reconcile Aristotelian philosophy with Islamic religion, which profoundly influenced Christian scholasticism.

averse (ə'vɜːs) *adj* (*postpositive; usually foll. by to*) opposed, disinclined, or loath. [C16: from L, from *āvertere* to turn from, from *vertere* to turn]
▸ **a'versely** *adv* ▸ **a'verseness** *n*

aversion (ə'vɜːʃən) *n* **1** (usually foll. by *to* or *for*) extreme dislike or disinclination. **2** a person or thing that arouses this: *he is my pet aversion.*

aversion therapy *n Psychiatry.* a way of suppressing an undesirable habit, such as smoking, by associating an unpleasant effect, such as an electric shock, with the habit.

avert (ə'vɜːt) *vb* (*tr*) **1** to turn away or aside: *to avert one's gaze.* **2** to ward off: *to avert danger.* [C15: from OF, from L *āvertere; see* AVERSE]
▸ **a'vertible** *or* **a'vertable** *adj*

Avesta (ə'vestə) *n* a collection of sacred writings of Zoroastrianism, including the Songs of Zoroaster.

Avestan (ə'vestən) *n* **1** the earliest recorded form of the Iranian language, formerly called **Zend.** ◆ *adj* **2** of the Avesta or its language.

Aveyron ★ (*French* averõ) *n* a department of S France in Midi-Pyrénées region. Capital: Rodez. Pop.: 266 849 (1994 est.). Area: 8771 sq. km (3421 sq. miles).

avian ('eɪvɪən) *adj* of, relating to, or resembling a bird. [C19: from L *avis* bird]

aviary ('eɪvjərɪ) *n, pl* **aviaries.** a large enclosure in which birds are kept. [C16: from L, from *aviārius* concerning birds, from *avis* bird]

aviation (,eɪvɪ'eɪʃən) *n* **1** the art or science of flying aircraft. **2** the design, production, and maintenance of aircraft. [C19: from F, from L *avis* bird]

aviator ('eɪvɪ,eɪtə) *n Old-fashioned.* the pilot of an aeroplane or airship; flyer.
▸ **'avi,atrix** *or* **'avi,atress** *fem n*

Avicenna ★ (,ævɪ'senə) *n* Arabic name *ibn-Sina.* 980–1037, Arab philosopher and physician whose philosophical writings, which combined Aristotelianism with neo-Platonist ideas, greatly influenced scholasticism, and whose medical work *Qanun* was the greatest single influence on medieval medicine.

avid ('ævɪd) *adj* **1** very keen; enthusiastic: *an avid reader.* **2** (*postpositive; often foll. by for or of*) eager (for): *avid for revenge.* [C18: from L, from *avēre* to long for]
▸ **avidity** (ə'vɪdɪtɪ) *n* ▸ **'avidly** *adv*

Aviemore ★ (,ævɪ'mɔː) *n* a winter sports resort in Scotland, in Moray between the Monadhliath and Cairngorm Mountains. Pop.: 2214 (1991).

avifauna (,eɪvɪ'fɔːnə) *n* all the birds in a particular region.
▸ **,avi'faunal** *adj*

Avignon ★ (*French* aviɲõ) *n* a city in SE France, on the Rhône: seat of the papacy (1309–77); famous 12th-century bridge, now partly destroyed. Pop.: 181 136 (1990).

Ávila ★ (*Spanish* 'aβila) *n* a city in central Spain: 11th-century granite walls and Romanesque cathedral. Pop.: 45 092 (1988 est.).

avionics (,eɪvɪ'ɒnɪks) *n* **1** (*functioning as sing*) the science and technology of electronics applied to aeronautics. **2** (*functioning as pl*) the electronic circuits and devices of an aerospace vehicle. [C20: from *avi(ation electr)onics*]
▸ **,avi'onic** *adj*

avitaminosis (æ,vɪtəmɪn'əusɪs) *n, pl* **avitaminoses** (-siːz). any disease caused by a vitamin deficiency in the diet.

Avlona ★ (æv'ləunə) *n* the ancient name for **Vlorë.**

avocado (,ævə'kɑːdəu) *n, pl* **avocados.** **1** a pear-shaped fruit having a leathery green or blackish skin, a large stony seed, and a greenish-yellow edible pulp. **2** the tropical American tree that bears this fruit. **3a** a dull greenish colour. **3b** (*as adj*): *an avocado bathroom suite.* ◆ Also called (*for senses 1 & 2*): **avocado pear, alligator pear.** [C17: from Sp. *aguacate*, from Nahuatl *ahuacatl* testicle, alluding to the shape of the fruit]

avocation (,ævə'keɪʃən) *n* **1** *Formal.* a minor occupation undertaken as a diversion. **2** *Not standard.* a person's regular job. [C17: from L, from *āvocāre* to distract, from *vocāre* to call]

avocet ('ævə,set) *n* a long-legged shore bird having black-and-white plumage and a long slender upward-curving bill. [C18: from F, from It. *avocetta*, from ?]

Avogadro ★ (,ævə'gɑːdrəu; *Italian* avo'ga:dro) *n* **Amedeo** (ame'deːo), *Conte di Quaregna.* 1776–1856, Italian physicist, noted for his work on gases.

Avogadro constant *or* **number** *n* the number of atoms or molecules in a mole of a substance, equal to 6.02252×10^{23} per mole.

Avogadro's law *or* **hypothesis** *n* the principle that equal volumes of all gases contain the same number of molecules at the same temperature and pressure.

avoid (ə'vɔɪd) *vb* (*tr*) **1** to keep out of the way of. **2** to refrain from doing. **3** to prevent from happening: *to avoid damage to machinery.* **4** *Law.* to invalidate; quash. [C14: from Anglo-F, from OF *esvuidier*, from *vuidier* to empty]
▸ **a'voidable** *adj* ▸ **a'voidably** *adv* ▸ **a'voidance** *n* ▸ **a'voider** *n*

avoirdupois *or* **avoirdupois weight** (,ævədə'pɔɪz) *n* a system of weights used in many English-speaking countries. It is based on the pound, which contains 16 ounces or 7000 grains. [C14: from OF *aver de peis* goods of weight]

Avon¹ ★ ('eɪvᵊn) *n* **1** a former county of SW England, created in 1974 from parts of N Somerset and S Gloucestershire: replaced in 1996 by unitary authorities.

2 a river in central England, rising in Northamptonshire and flowing southwest through Stratford-on-Avon to the River Severn at Tewkesbury. Length: 154 km (96 miles). **3** a river in SW England, rising in Gloucestershire and flowing south and west through Bristol to the Severn estuary at **Avonmouth**. Length: 120 km (75 miles). **4** a river in S England, rising in Wiltshire and flowing south to the English Channel. Length: about 96 km (60 miles).

Avon[2] ★ ('eɪv⁰n) n **Earl of**. title of (Anthony) **Eden**.

avouch (ə'vautʃ) vb (tr) Arch. **1** to vouch for; guarantee. **2** to acknowledge. **3** to assert. [C16: from OF avouchier to summon, call on, from L advocāre; see ADVOCATE]
▸ a'**vouchment** n

avow (ə'vau) vb (tr) **1** to state or affirm. **2** to admit openly. [C13: from OF avouer to confess, from L advocāre to appeal to, call upon]
▸ a'**vowal** n ▸ a'**vowed** adj ▸ **avowedly** (ə'vauɪdlɪ) adv ▸ a'**vower** n

avuncular (ə'vʌŋkjulə) adj **1** of or concerned with an uncle. **2** resembling an uncle; friendly. [C19: from L avunculus (maternal) uncle, dim. of avus grandfather]

AWACS or **Awacs** ('eɪwæks) n acronym for Airborne Warning and Control System.

await (ə'weɪt) vb **1** (tr) to wait for. **2** (tr) to be in store for. **3** (intr) to wait, esp. with expectation.

awake (ə'weɪk) vb **awakes**, **awaking**, **awoke** or **awaked**, **awoken** or **awaked**. **1** to emerge or rouse from sleep. **2** to become or cause to become alert. **3** (usually foll. by to) to become or make aware (of). **4** Also: **awaken**. (tr) to arouse (feelings, etc.) or cause to remember (memories, etc.). ◆ adj (postpositive) **5** not sleeping. **6** (sometimes foll. by to) lively or alert. [OE awacian, awacan]

USAGE NOTE   See at **wake**[1].

---

award (ə'wɔːd) vb (tr) **1** to give (something due), esp. as a reward for merit: to award prizes. **2** Law. to declare to be entitled, as by decision of a court or an arbitrator. ◆ n **3** something awarded, such as a prize or medal. **4** Austral. & NZ. the amount of an **award wage** (esp. in **above award**). **5** Law. **5a** the decision of an arbitrator. **5b** a grant made by a court of law. [C14: from Anglo-F awarder, from OF eswarder to decide after investigation, from es- EX-[1] + warder to observe]
▸ a'**warder** n

award wage n (in Australia and New Zealand) statutory minimum pay for a particular group of workers. Sometimes shortened to **award**.

aware (ə'weə) adj **1** (postpositive; foll. by of) having knowledge: aware of his error. **2** informed of current developments: politically aware. [OE gewær]
▸ a'**wareness** n

awash (ə'wɒʃ) adv, adj (postpositive) Naut. **1** level with the surface of the sea. **2** washed over by the waves.

away (ə'weɪ) adv **1** from a particular place: to swim away. **2** in or to another, a usual, or a proper place: to put toys away. **3** apart; at a distance: to keep away from strangers. **4** out of existence: the music faded away. **5** indicating motion, displacement, transfer, etc., from a normal or proper place: to turn one's head away. **6** indicating activity that is wasteful or designed to get rid of something: to sleep away the hours. **7** continuously: laughing away. **8 away with**. a command for a person to go or be removed: away with him to prison! ◆ adj (usually postpositive) **9** not present: away from school. **10** distant: he is a good way away. **11** having started; released: he was away before sunrise. **12** (also prenominal) Sport. played on an opponent's ground. ◆ n **13** Sport. a game played or won at an opponent's ground. ◆ sentence substitute. **14** an expression of dismissal. [OE on weg on way]

awayday (ə'weɪˌdeɪ) n a day trip taken for pleasure, relaxation, etc.; day excursion. [C20: from awayday ticket, name applied to some special-rate railway day returns]

awe (ɔː) n **1** overwhelming wonder, respect, or dread. **2** Arch. power to inspire fear or reverence. ◆ vb **awes**,

awing, **awed**. **3** (tr) to inspire with reverence or dread. [C13: from ON agi]

aweigh (ə'weɪ) adj (postpositive) Naut. (of an anchor) no longer hooked into the bottom; hanging by its rope or chain.

awe-inspiring adj causing or worthy of admiration or respect; amazing or magnificent.

awesome ('ɔːsəm) adj **1** inspiring or displaying awe. **2** Sl. excellent or outstanding.
▸ '**awesomely** adv ▸ '**awesomeness** n

awestruck or **awe-stricken** adj overcome or filled with awe.

awful ('ɔːful) adj **1** very bad; unpleasant. **2** Arch. inspiring reverence or dread. **3** Arch. overcome with awe. ◆ adv **4** Not standard. (intensifier): an awful cold day. [C13: see AWE, -FUL]
▸ '**awfulness** n

awfully ('ɔːfəlɪ) adv **1** in an unpleasant, bad, or reprehensible manner. **2** Inf. (intensifier): I'm awfully keen to come. **3** Arch. so as to express or inspire awe.

awhile (ə'waɪl) adv for a brief period.

awkward ('ɔːkwəd) adj **1** lacking dexterity, proficiency, or skill; clumsy. **2** ungainly or inelegant in movements or posture. **3** unwieldy; difficult to use. **4** embarrassing: an awkward moment. **5** embarrassed: he felt awkward about leaving. **6** difficult to deal with; requiring tact: an awkward customer. **7** deliberately unhelpful. **8** dangerous or difficult. [C14: awk, from ON öfugr turned the wrong way round + -WARD]
▸ '**awkwardly** adv ▸ '**awkwardness** n

awl (ɔːl) n a pointed hand tool with a fluted blade used for piercing wood, leather, etc. [OE æl]

awn (ɔːn) n any of the bristles growing from the flowering parts of certain grasses and cereals. [OE agen ear of grain]
▸ **awned** adj

awning ('ɔːnɪŋ) n a roof of canvas or other material supported by a frame to provide protection from the weather, esp. one placed over a doorway or part of a deck of a ship. [C17: from ?]

awoke (ə'wəuk) vb a past tense and (now rare or dialectal) past participle of **awake**.

AWOL ('eɪwɒl) or **A.W.O.L.** adj Mil. absent without leave but without intending to desert.

awry (ə'raɪ) adv, adj (postpositive) **1** with a slant or twist to one side; askew. **2** away from the appropriate or right course; amiss. [C14 on wry; see A-[2], WRY]

axe or US **ax** (æks) n, pl **axes**. **1** a hand tool with one side of its head forged and sharpened to a cutting edge, used for felling trees, splitting timber, etc. **2 an axe to grind. 2a** an ulterior motive. **2b** a grievance. **2c** a pet subject. **3** the **axe**. Inf. **3a** dismissal, esp. from employment (esp. in **get the axe**). **3b** Brit. severe cutting down of expenditure, esp. in a public service. ◆ vb **axes**, **axing**, **axed**. (tr) **4** to chop or trim with an axe. **5** Inf. to dismiss (employees), restrict (expenditure or services), or terminate (a project, etc.). [OE æx]

axel ('æksəl) n Skating. a jump of one and a half, two and a half, or three and a half turns, taking off from the forward outside edge of one skate and landing on the back-ward outside edge of the other. [C20: after Axel Paulsen (d. 1938), Norwegian skater]

axeman ('æksmən) n, pl **axemen**. **1** a man who wields an axe, esp. to cut down trees. **2** a person who makes cuts in expenditure or services, esp. on behalf of another: the chancellor's axeman.

axes[1] ('æksiːz) n the plural of **axis**[1].

axes[2] ('æksɪz) n the plural of **axe**.

axial ('æksɪəl) adj **1** forming or characteristic of an axis. **2** situated in, on, or along an axis.
▸ ˌaxi'**ality** n ▸ '**axially** adv

axil ('æksɪl) n the upper angle between a branch or leafstalk and the stem from which it grows. [C18: from L axilla armpit]

axilla (æk'sɪlə) n, pl **axillae** (-liː). **1** the technical name for

★ people and places

the **armpit. 2** the area under a bird's wing corresponding to the armpit. [C17: from L: armpit]

axillary (æk'sɪlərɪ) *adj* **1** of, relating to, or near the armpit. **2** *Bot.* growing in or related to the axil. ♦ *n, pl* **axillaries. 3** (*usually pl*) Also called: **axillar** (æk'sɪlə). one of the feathers growing from the axilla of a bird's wing.

axiom ('æksɪəm) *n* **1** a generally accepted proposition or principle, sanctioned by experience. **2** a universally established principle or law that is not a necessary truth. **3** a self-evident statement. **4** *Logic, maths.* a statement that is stipulated to be true for the purpose of a chain of reasoning. [C15: from L *axiōma* a principle, from Gk, from *axioun* to consider worthy, from *axios* worthy]

axiomatic (,æksɪə'mætɪk) *adj* **1** self-evident. **2** containing maxims; aphoristic.
▸ ,axio'matically *adv*

axis[1] ('æksɪs) *n, pl* **axes. 1** a real or imaginary line about which a body, such as an aircraft, can rotate or about which an object, form, composition, or geometrical construction is symmetrical. **2** one of two or three reference lines used in coordinate geometry to locate a point in a plane or in space. **3** *Anat.* the second cervical vertebra. **4** *Bot.* the main central part of a plant, typically consisting of the stem and root. **5** an alliance between a number of states to coordinate their foreign policy. **6** Also called: **principal axis.** *Optics.* the line of symmetry of an optical system, such as the line passing through the centre of a lens. [C14: from L: axletree, earth's axis; rel. to Gk *axōn* axis]

axis[2] ('æksɪs) *n, pl* **axises.** a S Asian deer with a reddish-brown white-spotted coat and slender antlers. [C18: from L: Indian wild animal, from ?]

Axis ('æksɪs) *n* **a the.** the alliance (1936) of Nazi Germany and Fascist Italy, later joined by Japan and other countries, and lasting until their defeat in World War II. **b** (*as modifier*): *the Axis powers.*

axle ('æksəl) *n* a bar or shaft on which a wheel, pair of wheels, or other rotating member revolves. [C17: from ON *öxull*]

axletree ('æksəl,triː) *n* a bar fixed across the underpart of a wagon or carriage that has rounded ends on which the wheels revolve.

Axminster carpet ('æks,mɪnstə) *n* a type of patterned carpet with a cut pile. Often shortened to **Axminster.** [after *Axminster* in Devon]

axolotl (,æksə'lɒt°l) *n* an aquatic salamander of N America, such as the **Mexican axolotl,** in which the larval form (including external gills) is retained throughout life under natural conditions. [C18: from Nahuatl, from *atl* water + *xolotl* servant, doll]

axon ('æksɒn) *n* the long threadlike extension of a nerve cell that conducts nerve impulses from the cell body. [C19: via NL from Gk: axis, axle, vertebra]

ay[1] *or* **aye** (eɪ) *adv Arch.* poetic always.

ay[2] (aɪ) *sentence substitute, n* a variant spelling of **aye.**

Ayacucho ★ (*Spanish* aja'kutʃo) *n* a city in SE Peru: nearby is the site of the battle (1824) that won independence for Peru. Pop.: 105 918 (1993).

ayah ('aɪə) *n* (in parts of the former British Empire) a native maidservant or nursemaid. [C18: from Hindi *āyā*, from Port. *aia*, from L *avia* grandmother]

ayatollah (,aɪə'tɒlə) *n* one of a class of Shiite religious leaders in Iran. [via Persian from Ar., from *aya* creation + ALLAH]

Ayckbourn ★ ('eɪkbɔːn) *n* Sir **Alan.** born 1939, British dramatist. His plays include *Absurd Person Singular* (1973), the trilogy *The Norman Conquests* (1974) and *Things We Do for Love* (1998).

Aycliffe ★ ('eɪklɪf) *n* a town in Co. Durham: founded as a new town in 1947. Pop.: 40 000 (latest est.).

Aydin *or* **Aidin** ★ ('aɪdɪn) *n* a town in SW Turkey: an ancient city of Lydia. Pop.: 121 200 (1994 est.). Ancient name: **Tralles.**

aye *or* **ay** (aɪ) *sentence substitute.* **1** yes: archaic or dialectal except in voting by voice. ♦ *n* **2a** a person who votes in the affirmative. **2b** an affirmative vote. ♦ Cf. **nay.** [C16: prob. from pron *I*, expressing assent]

aye-aye ('aɪ,aɪ) *n* a rare nocturnal arboreal primate of Madagascar related to the lemurs. It has long bony fingers and rodent-like incisor teeth. [C18: from F, from Malagasy *aiay*, prob. imit.]

Ayer ★ (ɛə) *n* Sir **Alfred Jules.** 1910–89, British positivist philosopher, noted for *Language, Truth, and Logic* (1936).

Ayers Rock ★ (ɛəz) *n* the former name for **Uluru.**

Ayesha ★ ('ɑːiː,ʃɑː) *n* a variant spelling of **Aisha.**

Aylesbury ★ ('eɪlzbərɪ, -brɪ) *n* a town in SE central England, administrative centre of Buckinghamshire. Pop.: 58 058 (1991).

Aylward ★ ('eɪlwəd) *n* **Gladys.** 1903–70, British missionary in China.

Aymara (,aɪmə'rɑː) *n* **1** (*pl* **-ras** *or* **-ra**) a member of a S American Indian people of Bolivia and Peru. **2** the language of this people. [from Sp. *aimará*, from Amerind]

Ayodha ★ (aɪ'jəʊdɑː) *n* an ancient town in N India, in Uttar Pradesh state: sacred to Hindus and a Buddhist centre. Also called: **Awadh** (ə'wɒd), **Oudh** (aʊd).

Ayr ★ (ɛə) *n* a port in SW Scotland, in South Ayrshire. Pop.: 47 962 (1991).

Ayrshire ('ɛəʃə) *n* any one of a hardy breed of brown-and-white dairy cattle. [from *Ayrshire,* former Scot. county]

Ayub Khan ★ (aɪ'juːb 'kɑːn) *n* **Mohammed.** 1907–74, Pakistani field marshal; president of Pakistan (1958–69).

Ayutthaya ★ (ɑː'juːtəjə) *n* a city in S Thailand, on the Chao Phraya River: capital of the country until 1767; noted for its canals and ruins. Pop.: 61 185 (1990). Also called: **Ayudhya** (ɑː'juːdjə), **Ayuthia** (ɑː'juːθɪə).

AZ *abbrev. for* Arizona.

azalea (ə'zeɪljə) *n* an ericaceous plant cultivated for its showy pink or purple flowers. [C18: via NL from Gk, from *azaleos* dry; from its supposed preference for a dry situation]

Azaña ★ (*Spanish* a'θaɲa) *n* **Manuel** (ma'nwel). 1880–1940, Spanish statesman; president of the Spanish Republic (1936–39) until overthrown by Franco.

Azania ★ (ə'zɑːnɪə, ə'zɑːnjə) *n* another name (used esp. by many Black political activists) for **South Africa.** [perhaps from Arabic *Adzan* East Africa]
▸ A'zanian *n, adj*

Azbine ★ (æz'biːn) *n* another name for **Aïr.**

azeotrope (ə'ziːə,trəʊp) *n* a mixture of liquids that boils at a constant temperature, at a given pressure, without change of composition. [C20: from A-[1] + *zeo-*, from Gk *zein* to boil + -TROPE]
▸ azeotropic (,eɪzɪə'trɒpɪk) *adj*

Azerbaijan ★ (,æzəbaɪ'dʒɑːn) *n* **1** a republic in NW Asia: the region was acquired by Russia from Persia in the early 19th century; became the Azerbaijan Soviet Socialist Republic in 1936; gained independence in 1991; consists of dry subtropical steppes around the Aras and Kura Rivers, surrounded by the Caucasus; contains the extensive Baku oilfields. Language: Azerbaijani. Currency: manat. Capital: Baku. Pop.: 7 617 000 (1997). Area: 86 600 sq. km (33 430 sq. miles). **2** a mountainous region of NW Iran, separated from the republic of Azerbaijan by the Aras River: divided administratively into **Eastern Azerbaijan** and **Western Azerbaijan.** Capitals: Tabriz and Rezaiyeh. Pop.: 5 562 926 (1991).
▸ ,Azerbai'jani *adj, n*

azerty *or* **AZERTY keyboard** (ə'zɜːtɪ) *n* a common European version of typewriter keyboard layout with the characters a, z, e, r, t, and y positioned at the top left of the keyboard.

azide ('eɪzaɪd) *n* **a** an acyl derivative or salt of hydrazoic acid, used as a coating to enhance electron emission. **b** (*as modifier*): *an azide group or radical.*

Azikiwe ★ (,ɑːziː'kiːweɪ) *n* **Nnamdi** (°n'næmdɪ). 1904–96, Nigerian statesman; first president of Nigeria (1963–66).

Azilian (ə'zɪlɪən) *n* **1** a Palaeolithic culture of Spain and SW France that can be dated to the 10th millennium B.C., characterized by flat bone harpoons and schematically painted pebbles. ♦ *adj* **2** of or relating to this culture.

★ people and places

azimuth ('æzɪməθ) n **1** Astron., navigation. the angular distance usually measured clockwise from the south point of the horizon in astronomy or from the north point in navigation to the intersection with the horizon of the vertical circle passing through a celestial body. **2** Surveying. the horizontal angle of a bearing clockwise from north. [C14: from OF azimut, from Ar. as-sumūt, pl. of as-samt the path, from L semita path]
▸ **azimuthal** (ˌæzɪˈmʌθəl) adj

azine ('eɪziːn) n an organic compound having a six-membered ring with at least one nitrogen atom, the other atoms in the ring being carbon atoms.

azo ('eɪzəʊ, 'æ-) adj of, consisting of, or containing the divalent group -N:N-: an azo group or radical. See also **diazo**. [from F azote nitrogen, from Gk azōos lifeless]

azoic (əˈzəʊɪk) adj without life; characteristic of the ages that have left no evidence of life in the form of organic remains. [C19: from Gk azōos lifeless]

Azores ★ (əˈzɔːz) pl n **the**. three groups of volcanic islands in the N Atlantic, since 1976 autonomous region of Portugal; includes the districts of Angra do Heroísmo, Horta, and Ponta Delgada. Capital: Ponta Delgada (on São Miguel). Pop.: 236 500 (1992 est.). Area: 2335 sq. km (901 sq. miles). Portuguese name: **Açôres**.

[C19: after Mas d'Azil, France, where artefacts were found]

Azorín ★ (Spanish aθoˈrin) n real name José Martínez Ruiz. 1874–1967, Spanish writer.

Azov ★ ('ɑːzɒv) n **Sea of**. a shallow arm of the Black Sea, to which it is connected by the Kerch Strait: almost entirely landlocked; fed chiefly by the River Don. Area: about 37 500 sq. km (14 500 sq. miles).

AZT abbrev. for azidothymidine: another name for **zidovudine**.

Aztec ('æztɛk) n **1** a member of a Mexican Indian people who established a great empire, centred on the valley of Mexico, that was overthrown by Cortés in the early 16th century. **2** the language of the Aztecs. See also **Nahuatl**. ◆ adj also **Aztecan**. **3** of, relating to, or characteristic of the Aztecs, their civilization, or their language. [C18: from Sp., from Nahuatl Aztecatl, from Aztlan, their traditional place of origin, lit.: near the cranes]

azure ('æʒə, 'eɪ-) n **1** a deep blue similar to the colour of a clear blue sky. **2** Poetic. a clear blue sky. ◆ adj **3** of the colour azure. **4** (usually postpositive) Heraldry. of the colour blue. [C14: from OF, from OSp., from Ar. lāzaward lapis lazuli, from Persian lāzhuward]

azurite ('æʒʊˌraɪt) n a deep blue mineral consisting of hydrated basic copper carbonate. It is used as an ore of copper and as a gemstone.

azygous ('æzɪgəs) adj Biol. developing or occurring singly. [C17: via NL from Gk azugos, from A-[1] + zugon YOKE]

Bb

b or **B** (biː) *n*, *pl* **b's**, **B's**, or **Bs**. **1** the second letter of the English alphabet. **2** a speech sound represented by this letter **3** Also: **beta**. the second in a series, class, or rank.

b *symbol for:* **1** *Music.* **1a** the seventh note of the scale of C major. **1b** the major or minor key having this note as its tonic. **2** the less important of two things. **3** a human blood type of the ABO group, containing the B antigen. **4** (in Britain) a secondary road. **5** *Chem.* boron. **6** magnetic flux density. **7** *Chess.* bishop. **8** (on Brit. pencils, signifying degree of softness of lead) black. **9** Also: **b** *Physics.* bel. **10** *Physics.* baryon number. **11a** a person whose job is in middle management, or who holds an intermediate administrative or professional position. **11b** (*as modifier*): *a B worker.* ◆ See also **occupation groupings.**

b. *abbrev. for:* **1** born. **2** *Cricket.* **2a** bowled. **2b** bye.

b. or **B.** *abbrev. for:* **1** *Music.* bass or basso. **2** billion. **3** book. **4** breadth.

B. *abbrev. for:* **1** (on maps, etc.) bay. **2** Bible.

B- (of US military aircraft) *abbrev. for* bomber.

Ba[1] *the chemical symbol for* barium.

Ba[2] ★ (bɑː) *n Egyptian myth.* the soul, represented as a bird with a human head.

BA *abbrev. for:* **1** Bachelor of Arts. **2** British Academy. **3** British Airways. **4** British Association (for the Advancement of Science). **5** British Association screw thread.

baa (bɑː) *vb* **baas, baaing, baaed.** **1** (*intr*) to make the cry of a sheep; bleat. ◆ *n* **2** the cry made by sheep.

BAA *abbrev. for* British Airports Authority.

Baader-Meinhof Gang (*German* 'bɑːdər 'mainhoːf) *n* **the.** a group of West German guerrillas dedicated to the violent overthrow of capitalist society. Also called: **Red Army Faction.** [C20: named after its leading members, Andreas *Baader* (1943–77) and Ulrike *Meinhof* (1934–76).]

Baal ★ (bɑːl) *n* **1** any of several ancient Semitic fertility gods. **2** *Phoenician myth.* the sun god and supreme national deity. **3** (*sometimes not cap.*) any false god or idol. [from Heb. *báʿal* lord, master]

Baalbek ★ ('bɑːlbɛk) *n* a town in E Lebanon: an important city in Phoenician and Roman times; extensive ruins. Pop.: 15 600 (1995 est.). Ancient name: **Heliopolis.**

Baal Shem Tov or **Baal Shem Tob** ★ (bɑːl 'ʃɛm tɒv, 'ʃɑːm) *n* original name *Israel ben Eliezer.* ?1700–60, Jewish religious leader in Poland: founder of modern Chassidism.

baas (bɑːs) *n* a South African word for **boss**[1] (sense 1): used by Africans and Coloured people in addressing European managers or overseers. [C17: from Afrik., from MDu. *baes* master]

baaskap or **baasskap** ('bɑːsˌkap) *n* (*sometimes cap.*) (in South Africa) control by Whites of non-Whites. [from Afrik., from BAAS + -*skap* -SHIP]

Bab ★ (bɑːb) *n* **the.** title of *Mirza Ali Mohammed.* 1819–50, Persian religious leader: founded Babism; executed as a heretic of Islam. [from Persian *bāb* gate, from Ar.]

baba ('bɑːbɑː) *n* a small cake, usually soaked in rum (**rum baba**). [C19: from F, from Polish, lit.: old woman]

babalas ('bæbəˌlæs) *n S. African.* a hangover. [from Zulu *ibhabhalasi*]

Babar ★ ('bɑːbə) *n* a variant spelling of **Baber.**

Babbage ★ ('bæbɪdʒ) *n* **Charles.** 1792–1871, British mathematician, who built a calculating machine.

babbitt ('bæbɪt) *vb* (*tr*) to line (a bearing) or face (a surface) with Babbitt metal.

Babbitt ('bæbɪt) *n US derog.* a narrow-minded and complacent member of the middle class. [C20: after George *Babbitt,* central character in the novel *Babbitt* (1922) by Sinclair Lewis]
► **'Babbittry** *n*

Babbitt metal *n* any of a number of alloys originally based on tin, antimony, and copper but now often including lead: used esp. in bearings. [C19: after Isaac *Babbitt* (1799–1862), US inventor]

babble ('bæbᵊl) *vb* **babbles, babbling, babbled.** **1** to utter (words, sounds, etc.) in an incoherent jumble. **2** (*intr*) to talk foolishly, incessantly, or irrelevantly. **3** (*tr*) to disclose (secrets, etc.) carelessly. **4** (*intr*) (of streams, birds, etc.) to make a low murmuring sound. ◆ *n* **5** incoherent or foolish speech. **6** a murmuring sound. [C13: prob. imit.]

babbler ('bæblə) *n* **1** a person or thing that babbles. **2** any of various birds of the Old World tropics and subtropics having an incessant song.

babe (beɪb) *n* **1** a baby. **2** *Inf.* a naive or gullible person. **3** *Sl.* a girl or young woman, esp. an attractive one.

Babel[1] ('beɪbᵊl) *n* **1** *Old Testament.* Also called: **Tower of Babel.** a tower presumptuously intended to reach from earth to heaven, the building of which was frustrated when Jehovah confused the language of the builders (Genesis 11:1–10). **2** (*often not cap.*) **2a** a confusion of noises or voices. **2b** a scene of noise and confusion. [from Heb. *Bābhél,* from Akkadian *Bāb-ilu,* lit.: gate of God]

Babel[2] ★ (*Russian* 'babɪl) *n* **Isaak Emmanuilovich** (i'sak imənu'iləvitʃ). 1894–1941, Russian writer, whose works include *Red Cavalry* (1926).

Bab el Mandeb ★ ('bæb ɛl 'mændɛb) *n* a strait between SW Arabia and E Africa, connecting the Red Sea with the Gulf of Aden.

Baber, Babar, or **Babur** ★ ('bɑːbə) *n* original name *Zahir ud-Din Mohammed.* 1483–1530, founder of the Mogul Empire: conquered India in 1526.

Babeuf ★ (*French* babœf) *n* **François Noël** (frɑ̃swa nɔɛl). 1760–97, French political agitator: plotted unsuccessfully to destroy the Directory and establish a communistic system.

Babington ★ ('bæbɪŋtən) *n* **Anthony.** 1561–86, English conspirator, executed for unsuccessful plot (1586) to assassinate Elizabeth I.

babirusa (ˌbɑːbɪ'ruːsə) *n* a wild pig of Indonesia. It has an almost hairless wrinkled skin and enormous curved canine teeth. [C17: from Malay, from *bābī* hog + *rūsa* deer]

Babism ('bɑːbɪzəm) *n* a pantheistic Persian religious sect, founded in 1844, forbidding polygamy, concubinage, begging, trading in slaves, and indulgence in alcohol and drugs. [C19: from the BAB]

baboon (bə'buːn) *n* any of several medium-sized Old World monkeys. They have an elongated muzzle, large teeth, and a fairly long tail. [C14 *babewyn* gargoyle, later, baboon, from OF]

babu ('bɑːbuː) *n* (in India) **1** a form of address more or less equivalent to *Mr.* **2** (formerly) an Indian clerk who could write English. [Hindi, lit.: father]

Babur ★ ('bɑːbə) *n* a variant spelling of **Baber.**

babushka (bə'buːʃkə) *n* **1** a headscarf tied under the chin, worn by Russian peasant women. **2** (in Russia) an old woman. [Russian: grandmother, from *baba* old woman]

baby ('beɪbɪ) *n*, *pl* **babies.** **1a** a newborn child; infant. **1b** (*as modifier*): *baby food.* **2** an unborn child; fetus. **3** the youngest or smallest of a family or group. **4** a newborn or recently born animal. **5** *Usually derog.* an immature person. **6** *Sl.* a young woman or sweetheart. **7** a project of personal concern. **8 be left holding the baby.** to be left with the responsibility. ◆ *adj* **9** (*prenominal*) comparatively small of its type: *a baby car.* ◆ *vb* **babies, babying, babied.** **10** (*tr*) to treat with love and attention. **11** to treat (some-

one) like a baby; pamper or overprotect. [C14: prob. childish reduplication]
▶ **'baby,hood** n ▶ **'babyish** adj

baby bonus n Canad. inf. Family Allowance.

baby boomer n a person born during a **baby boom**, a sharp increase in the birth rate, esp. (in Britain and the US) one born during the years 1945–55.

baby buggy n **1** Brit. Trademark. a child's pushchair. **2** US & Canad. inf. a small pram.

baby carriage n the US and Canad. name for **pram**[1].

Babylon ★ ('bæbɪlən) n **1** the chief city of ancient Mesopotamia: first settled around 3000 B.C. See also **Hanging Gardens of Babylon**. **2** Derog. (in Protestant polemic) the Roman Catholic Church, regarded as the seat of luxury and corruption. **3** Derog. any society or group in a society considered as corrupt or as a place of exile by another society or group, esp. White Britain as viewed by some Rastafarians. [via L and Gk from Heb. Bābhel; see BABEL[1]]
▶ **Babylonian** (,bæbɪ'ləʊnɪən) adj, n

Babylonia ★ (,bæbɪ'ləʊnɪə) n the southern kingdom of ancient Mesopotamia: a great empire from about 2200–538 B.C., when it was conquered by the Persians.

baby-sit vb **baby-sits, baby-sitting, baby-sat**. (intr) to act or work as a baby-sitter.
▶ **'baby-,sitting** n, adj

baby-sitter n a person who takes care of a child or children while the parents are out.

baby snatcher n Inf. **1** a person who steals a baby from its pram. **2** someone who marries or has an affair with a much younger person.

baby wipe n a disposable moistened medicated paper towel used for cleaning babies.

Bacău ★ (bə'kaʊ) n a city in E Romania on the River Bistrila: oil refining, textiles, paper. Pop.: 206 995 (1993 est.).

baccalaureate (,bækə'lɔːrɪɪt) n the university degree of Bachelor of Arts. [C17: from Med. L baccalaureātus, from baccalaureus advanced student from baccalārius BACHELOR]

baccarat ('bækə,rɑː, ,bækə'rɑː) n a card game in which two or more punters gamble against the banker. [C19: from F baccara from ?]

baccate ('bækeɪt) adj Bot. **1** like a berry. **2** bearing berries. [C19: from L bāca berry]

Bacchae ★ ('bækiː) pl n the priestesses or female devotees of Bacchus. [L, from Gk Bakkhai, plural of Bakkhē priestess of BACCHUS]

bacchanal ('bækən°l) n **1** a follower of Bacchus. **2** a drunken and riotous celebration. **3** a participant in such a celebration. ◆ adj **4** of or relating to Bacchus. [C16: from L Bacchānālis]

bacchanalia (,bækə'neɪlɪə) pl n **1** (often cap.) orgiastic rites associated with Bacchus. **2** any drunken revelry.
▶ **,baccha'nalian** adj, n

bacchant ('bækənt) or (fem) **bacchante** (bə'kæntɪ) n, pl **bacchants** or **bacchantes** (bə'kæntɪz). **1** a priest, priestess, or votary of Bacchus. **2** a drunken reveller. [C17: from L bacchāns, from bacchārī to celebrate the BACCHANALIA]

Bacchic ('bækɪk) adj **1** of or relating to Bacchus. **2** (often not cap.) riotously drunk.

Bacchus ★ ('bækəs) n (in ancient Greece and Rome) a god of wine and giver of ecstasy, identified with Dionysus. [C15: from L, from Gk Bakkhos; related to L bāca small round fruit, berry]

baccy ('bækɪ) n a Brit. informal name for **tobacco**.

bach (bætʃ) NZ. ◆ n **1** a seaside, bush, or country cottage. ◆ vb **2** a variant spelling of **batch**[2].

Bach ★ (German bax) n **1 Johann Christian** (jo'han 'krɪstjan), 11th son of J. S. Bach. 1735–82, German composer, called the English Bach, resident in London from 1762. **2 Johann Christoph** ('krɪstɔf). 1642–1703, German composer: wrote oratorios, cantatas, and motets, some of which were falsely attributed to J. S. Bach, of whom he was a distant relative. **3 Johann Sebastian** (zeˈbastjan). 1685–1750, German composer: musical director for Prince Leopold of Köthen (1717–28); musical director for the city of Leipzig (1728–50). His works include can-

tatas and oratorios, settings of the Passion according to S John (1723) and St Matthew (1729), the six Brandenbur Concertos (1720–21), the 48 preludes and fugues, and th Mass in B Minor (1733–38). **4 Karl** (or **Carl**) **Philipp Emanue** (karl 'fiːlɪp eˈmaːnuel), 3rd son of J. S. Bach. 1714–88 German composer, chiefly of symphonies, sonatas, an church music. **5 Wilhelm Friedemann** ('vɪlhelm 'friːdəman) eldest son of J. S. Bach. 1710–84, German composer works include nine symphonies.

bachelor ('bætʃələ, 'bætʃlə) n **1a** an unmarried man. **1** (as modifier): a bachelor flat. **2** a person who holds the de gree of Bachelor of Arts, Bachelor of Education, Bachelo of Science, etc. **3** (in the Middle Ages) a young knigh serving a great noble. **4 bachelor seal**. a young male sea that has not yet mated. [C13: from OF bacheler youth squire, from Vulgar L baccalāris (unattested) farm worker]
▶ **'bachelor,hood** n

bachelor girl n a young unmarried woman, esp. on who is self-supporting.

Bachelor of Arts n **1** a degree conferred on a person who has successfully completed undergraduate studie in the liberal arts or humanities. **2** a person who hold this degree.

Bachelor of Science n **1** a degree conferred on a per son who has successfully completed undergraduate studies in a science. **2** a person who holds this degree.

bachelor's-buttons n (functioning as sing or pl) any o various plants with button-like flower heads, esp. a dou ble-flowered buttercup.

Bach flower remedy (bɑːx) n Trademark. an alterna tive medicine consisting of a distillation from various flowers, supposed to counteract negative states of min and restore emotional balance. [C20: after Dr E. Bac (1886–1936), homeopath who developed this system]

bacillary (bə'sɪlərɪ) or **bacillar** (bə'sɪlə) adj **1** of, relating to, or caused by bacilli. **2** Also: **bacilliform** (bə'sɪlɪ,fɔːm) shaped like a short rod.

bacillus (bə'sɪləs) n, pl **bacilli** (-'sɪlaɪ). **1** any rod-shaped bacterium. **2** any of various rodlike spore-producing bac teria constituting the family Bacillaceae. [C19: from L from baculum walking stick]

back (bæk) n **1** the posterior part of the human body from the neck to the pelvis. **2** the corresponding o upper part of an animal. **3** the spinal column. **4** the par or side of an object opposite the front. **5** the part or side of anything less often seen or used. **6** the part or side o anything that is furthest from the front or from a specta tor: the back of the stage. **7** something that supports, cov ers, or strengthens the rear of an object. **8** Ball games. **8a** mainly defensive player behind a forward. **8b** the posi tion of such a player. **9** the part of a book to which the pages are glued or that joins the covers. **10 at the back o one's mind**. not in one's conscious thoughts. **11 back o Bourke**. Austral. a remote or backward place. **12 behind one's back**. secretly or deceitfully. **13 break one's back**. to overwork or work very hard. **14 break the back of**. to com plete the greatest or hardest part of (a task). **15 get off someone's back**. Inf. to stop criticizing or pestering some one. **16 put one's back into**. to devote all one's strength to (a task). **17 put** (or **get**) **someone's back up**. to annoy some one. **18 the back of beyond**. a very remote place. **19 turn one's back on**. **19a** to turn away from in anger or con tempt. **19b** to refuse to help; abandon. ◆ vb (mainly tr **20** (also intr) to move or cause to move backwards. **21 back water**. to reverse the direction of a boat, esp. to push the oars of a rowing boat. **22** to provide support, money, or encouragement for (a person, enterprise, etc.). **23** to bet on the success of: to back a horse. **24** to provide with a back, backing, or lining. **25** to provide with a musical ac companiment. **26** to countersign or endorse. **27** (intr; foll. by on or onto) to have the back facing (towards): the house backs onto a river. **28** (intr) (of the wind) to change direction anticlockwise. Cf. **veer** (sense 3). ◆ adj (prenominal) **29** situated behind: a back lane. **30** of the past: back issues of a magazine. **31** owing from an earlier date: back rent. **32** remote: a back road. **33** Phonetics. of or denoting a vowel articulated with the tongue retracted towards the soft palate, as for the vowels in English hard,

★ people and places

fall, hot, full, fool. ◆ *adv* **34** at, to, or towards the rear; behind. **35** in, to, or towards the original starting point, place, or condition: *to go back home; put the book back.* **36** in or into the past: *to look back on one's childhood.* **37** in reply, repayment, or retaliation: *to hit someone back.* **38** in check: *the dam holds back the water.* **39** in concealment; in reserve: *to keep something back.* **40 back and forth.** to and fro. **41 back to front. 41a** in reverse. **41b** in disorder. ◆ See also **back down, back off, back out, back up.** [OE *bæc*]

backbencher ('bæk'bentʃə) *n Brit., Austral., NZ., etc.* a Member of Parliament who does not hold office in the government or opposition.

backbite ('bæk,baɪt) *vb* **backbites, backbiting, backbit; backbitten** *or* **backbit.** to talk spitefully about (an absent person).
▸ '**back,biter** *n*

backboard ('bæk,bɔːd) *n* **1** a board that is placed behind something to form or support its back. **2** a board worn to straighten or support the back, as after surgery. **3** (in basketball) a flat upright surface supported on a high frame, under which the basket is attached.

back boiler *n* a tank or series of pipes at the back of a fireplace for heating water.

backbone ('bæk,bəʊn) *n* **1** a nontechnical name for **spinal column**. **2** something that resembles the spinal column in function, position, or appearance. **3** strength of character; courage.

backbreaking ('bæk,breɪkɪŋ) *adj* exhausting.

backburn ('bæk,bɜːn) *Austral. & NZ.* ◆ *vb* **1** (*tr*) to clear (an area of scrub, bush, etc.) by creating a new fire that burns in the opposite direction to the line of advancing fire. ◆ *n* **2** the act or result of backburning.

back-calculate *vb* **back-calculates, back-calculating, back-calculated.** to estimate (the probable amount of alcohol in a person's blood) at an earlier time than that at which the blood test was taken, based on an average rate at which alcohol leaves the bloodstream: used to determine whether a driver had more than the legal limit of alcohol at the time of an accident.
▸ '**back-,calcu'lation** *n*

back catalogue *n* the recordings that a musician has made in the past, as distinct from his or her current recording: *favourites from his back catalogue.*

backchat ('bæk,tʃæt) *n Inf.* the act of answering back, esp. impudently.

backcloth ('bæk,klɒθ) *n* a painted curtain at the back of a stage set. Also called: **backdrop.**

backcomb ('bæk,kəʊm) *vb* to comb the under layers of (the hair) towards the roots to give more bulk to a hairstyle. Also: **tease.**

back country *n Austral. & NZ.* land remote from settled areas.

backdate (,bæk'deɪt) *vb* **backdates, backdating, backdated.** (*tr*) to make effective from an earlier date.

back door *n* **1** a door at the rear or side of a building. **2** a means of entry to a job, etc., that is secret or obtained through influence.

back down *vb* **1** (*intr, adv*) to withdraw an earlier claim. ◆ *n* **backdown. 2** abandonment of an earlier claim.

backed (bækt) *adj* **a** having a back or backing. **b** (*in combination*): *high-backed; black-backed.*

backer ('bækə) *n* **1** a person who gives financial or other support. **2** a person who bets on a competitor or contestant.

backfield ('bæk,fiːld) *n American football.* **1** (usually preceded by *the*) the quarterback and running backs in a team. **2** the area behind the line of scrimmage from which the backfield begin each play.

backfill ('bæk,fɪl) *vb* (*tr*) to refill an excavated trench, esp. (in archaeology) at the end of an investigation.

backfire (,bæk'faɪə) *vb* **backfires, backfiring, backfired.** (*intr*) **1** (of an internal-combustion engine) to emit a loud noise as a result of an explosion in the exhaust system. **2** to fail to have the desired effect, and, instead, recoil upon the originator. **3** to start a controlled fire in order to halt an advancing forest or prairie fire by creating a barren area. ◆ *n* **4** (in an internal-combustion engine)

an explosion of unburnt gases in the exhaust system. **5** a controlled fire started to create a barren area that will halt an advancing forest or prairie fire.

back formation *n* **1** the invention of a new word on the assumption that a familiar word is derived from it. The verbs *edit* and *burgle* in English were so created from *editor* and *burglar.* **2** a word formed by this process.

backgammon ('bæk,gæmən) *n* **1** a game for two people played on a board with pieces moved according to throws of the dice. **2** the most complete form of win in this game. [C17: BACK + *gammon*, var. of GAME¹]

background ('bæk,graund) *n* **1** the part of a scene furthest from the viewer. **2a** an inconspicuous or unobtrusive position (esp. in **in the background**). **2b** (*as modifier*): *a background influence.* **3** the plane or ground in a picture upon which all other planes or forms appear superimposed. **4** a person's social class, education, or experience. **5a** the circumstances that lead up to or help to explain something. **5b** (*as modifier*): *background information.* **6a** a low level of sound, lighting, etc., whose purpose is to be an unobtrusive accompaniment to something else. **6b** (*as modifier*): *background music.* **7** Also called: **background radiation.** *Physics.* low-intensity radiation from small amounts of radioisotopes in soil, air, etc. **8** *Electronics.* unwanted effects, such as noise, occurring in a measuring instrument, electronic device, etc.

backhand ('bæk,hænd) *n* **1** *Tennis, etc.* a stroke made across the body with the back of the hand facing the direction of the stroke. **2** the side on which backhand strokes are made. **3** handwriting slanting to the left. ◆ *adv* **4** with a backhand stroke.

backhanded (,bæk'hændɪd) *adj* **1** (of a blow, shot, etc.) performed with the arm moving across the body. **2** double-edged; equivocal: *a backhanded compliment.* **3** (of handwriting) slanting to the left. ◆ *adv* **4** in a backhanded manner.

backhander ('bæk,hændə) *n* **1** a backhanded stroke or blow. **2** *Inf.* an indirect attack. **3** *Sl.* a bribe.

backing ('bækɪŋ) *n* **1** support. **2** a body of supporters. **3** something that forms, protects, or strengthens the back of something. **4** musical accompaniment, esp. for a pop singer. **5** *Meteorol.* an anticlockwise change in wind direction.

backing dog *n NZ.* a dog that moves a flock of sheep by jumping on their backs.

backlash ('bæk,læʃ) *n* **1** a sudden and adverse reaction. **2** a reaction or recoil between interacting worn or badly fitting parts in a mechanism. **3** the excessive play between such parts.

backlog ('bæk,lɒg) *n* an accumulation of uncompleted work, unsold stock, etc., to be dealt with.

back marker *n* a competitor who is at the back of a field in a race.

back matter *n* the parts of a book, such as the index and appendices, that follow the text.

backmost ('bæk,məʊst) *adj* furthest back.

back number *n* **1** an issue of a newspaper, magazine, etc., that appeared on a previous date. **2** *Inf.* a person or thing considered to be old-fashioned.

back off *vb* (*adv*) *Inf.* **1** (*intr*) to retreat. **2** (*tr*) to abandon (an intention, objective, etc.).

back out *vb* (*intr, adv*; often foll. by *of*) to withdraw (from an agreement, etc.).

backpack ('bæk,pæk) *n* **1** a rucksack. **2** a pack carried on the back of an astronaut, containing oxygen cylinders, etc. ◆ *vb* (*intr*) **3** to travel about with a backpack.

back passage *n* the rectum.

back-pedal *vb* **back-pedals, back-pedalling, back-pedalled** *or US* **back-pedals, back-pedaling, back-pedaled.** (*intr*) **1** to turn the pedals of a bicycle backwards. **2** to retract or modify a previous opinion, principle, etc.

back projection *n* a method of projecting pictures onto a translucent screen so that they are viewed from the opposite side, used esp. in films to create the illusion that the actors in the foreground are moving.

Back River ★ *n* a river in N Canada, rising in the Northwest Territories and flowing northeast to the Arctic Ocean. Length: about 966 km (600 miles).

back room n a a place where important and usually secret research or planning is done. b (as modifier): back-room boys.

Backs ★ (bæks) pl n the. the grounds between the River Cam and certain Cambridge colleges.

back seat n 1 a seat at the back, esp. of a vehicle. 2 Inf. a subordinate or inconspicuous position (esp. in **take a back seat**).

back-seat driver n Inf. 1 a passenger in a car who offers unwanted advice to the driver. 2 a person who offers advice on or tries to direct matters that are not his or her concern.

backsheesh ('bækʃiːʃ) n a variant spelling of **baksheesh.**

back shift n Brit. 1 a group of workers who work a shift from late afternoon to midnight in an industry or occupation where a day or a night shift is also worked. 2 the period worked. ◆ US and Canad. name: **swing shift.**

backside (,bæk'saɪd) n Inf. the buttocks.

backslide (,bæk'slaɪd) vb **backslides, backsliding, backslid.** (intr) to relapse into former bad habits.
▸ ,**back'slider** n

backspace ('bæk,speɪs) vb **backspaces, backspacing, backspaced.** to move (a typewriter carriage, etc.) backwards.

backspin ('bæk,spɪn) n Sport. a backward spin imparted to a ball to reduce its speed at impact.

backstage (,bæk'steɪdʒ) adv 1 behind the part of the theatre in view of the audience. 2 towards the rear of the stage. ◆ adj 3 situated backstage. 4 Inf. away from public view.

backstairs (,bæk'stɛəz) pl n 1 a secondary staircase in a house, esp. one originally for the use of servants. ◆ adj also **backstair.** 2 underhand: backstairs gossip.

backstay ('bæk,steɪ) n Naut. a stay leading aft from the upper mast to the deck or stern.

backstreet ('bæk,striːt) n 1 a street in a town remote from the main roads. 2 (modifier) denoting illicit activities regarded as likely to take place in such a street: a backstreet abortion.

backstroke ('bæk,strəʊk) n Swimming. a stroke performed on the back, using backward circular strokes of each arm and flipper movements of the feet. Also called: **back crawl.**

back-to-back adj (usually postpositive) 1 facing in opposite directions, often with the backs touching. 2 Chiefly Brit. (of urban houses) built so that their backs are joined or separated only by a narrow alley.

backtrack ('bæk,træk) vb (intr) 1 to return by the same route by which one has come. 2 to retract or reverse one's opinion, policy, etc.

back up vb (adv) 1 (tr) to support. 2 (intr) Cricket. (of a nonstriking batsman) to move down the wicket in readiness for a run as a ball is bowled. 3 (of water) to accumulate. 4 (of traffic) to become jammed behind an accident or other obstruction. 5 Computing. to make a copy of (a data file), esp. as a security copy. 6 (intr; usually foll. by on) Austral. to repeat an action immediately. ◆ n **backup.** 7 a support or reinforcement. 8a a substitute. 8b (as modifier): a backup copy. 9 the overflow from a blocked drain or pipe.

backward ('bækwəd) adj 1 (usually prenominal) directed towards the rear: a backward glance. 2 retarded in physical, material, or intellectual development. 3a conservative or reactionary. 3b (in combination): backward-looking. 4 reluctant or bashful: a backward lover. ◆ adv 5 a variant of **backwards.**
▸ '**backwardness** n

backwardation (,bækwə'deɪʃən) n 1 the difference between the spot price for a commodity, including rent and interest, and the forward price. 2 (formerly, on the Stock Exchange) postponement of delivery by a seller of securities until the next settlement period.

backwards ('bækwədz) or **backward** adv 1 towards the rear. 2 with the back foremost. 3 in the reverse of usual order or direction. 4 to or towards the past. 5 into a worse state. 6 towards the point of origin. 7 **bend, lean,** or

fall over backwards. Inf. to make a special effort, esp. in order to please.

backwash ('bæk,wɒʃ) n 1 water washed backwards by the motion of oars or other propelling devices. 2 the backward flow of air set up by aircraft engines. 3 a repercussion.

backwater ('bæk,wɔːtə) n 1 a body of stagnant water connected to a river. 2 an isolated or backward place or condition.

backwoods ('bækwʊdz) pl n 1 partially cleared, sparsely populated forests. 2 any remote sparsely populated place. 3 (modifier) of or like the backwoods. 4 (modifier) uncouth; rustic.
▸ '**back,woodsman** n

backword ('bæk,wɜːd) n Dialect. a failure to keep a promise.

back yard n 1 a yard at the back of a house, etc. 2 **in one's own back yard.** 2a close at hand. 2b involving or implicating one.

baclava ('bɑːklə,vɑː) n a variant spelling of **baklava.**

Bacolod ★ (bə'kɒləd) n a town in the Philippines, on the NW coast of Negros Island. Pop.: 343 048 (1994 est.).

bacon ('beɪkən) n 1 meat from the back and sides of a pig, dried, salted, and usually smoked. 2 **bring home the bacon.** Inf. 2a to achieve success. 2b to provide material support. 3 **save (someone's) bacon.** Brit. inf. to help (someone) to escape from danger. [C12: from OF bacon, from OHG bahho]

Bacon ★ ('beɪkən) n 1 **Francis,** Baron Verulam, Viscount St Albans. 1561–1626, English philosopher and statesman; his works include The Advancement of Learning (1605) and Novum Organum (1620). 2 **Francis.** 1909–92, Irish painter. 3 **Roger.** ?1214–92, English Franciscan monk and scientist. His Opus Majus (1266) is a compendium of all the sciences of his age.

Baconian (beɪ'kəʊnɪən) adj 1 of or relating to Francis Bacon, the philosopher, or his inductive method of reasoning. ◆ n 2 a follower of Bacon's philosophy. 3 one who believes that plays attributed to Shakespeare were written by Bacon.

BACS (bæks) n acronym for Bankers Automated Clearing System; a method of making payments direct to a creditor's bank without using a cheque.

bacteria (bæk'tɪərɪə) pl n, sing **bacterium.** a large group of typically unicellular microorganisms, many of which cause disease. [C19: NL, from Gk baktērion, from baktron rod, staff]
▸ bac'**terial** adj ▸ bac'**terially** adv

bactericide (bæk'tɪərɪ,saɪd) n a substance able to destroy bacteria.
▸ bac,**teri'cidal** adj

bacterio-, bacteri-, or sometimes before a vowel **bacter-** combining form. indicating bacteria or an action or condition relating to bacteria: bacteriology; bactericide.

bacteriology (bæk,tɪərɪ'ɒlədʒɪ) n the study of bacteria.
▸ **bacteriological** (bæk,tɪərɪə'lɒdʒɪk²l) adj ▸ bac,teri'**ologist** n

bacteriophage (bæk'tɪərɪə,feɪdʒ) n a virus that is parasitic in a bacterium and destroys its host. Often shortened to **phage.**

bacterium (bæk'tɪərɪəm) n the singular of **bacteria.**

Bactria ★ ('bæktrɪə) n an ancient country of SW Asia, between the Hindu Kush mountains and the Oxus River: forms the present Balkh region in N Afghanistan.
▸ '**Bactrian** adj, n

Bactrian camel n a two-humped camel, used in the cold deserts of central Asia.

bad¹ (bæd) adj **worse, worst.** 1 not good; of poor quality; inadequate. 2 (often foll. by at) lacking skill or talent; incompetent. 3 (often foll. by for) harmful. 4 immoral; evil. 5 naughty; mischievous. 6 rotten; decayed: a bad egg. 7 severe; intense: a bad headache. 8 incorrect; faulty: bad pronunciation. 9 ill or in pain (esp. in **feel bad**). 10 sorry or upset (esp. in **feel bad about**). 11 unfavourable; distressing: bad news. 12 offensive; unpleasant: bad language; bad temper. 13 not valid or sound: a bad cheque. 14 not recoverable: a bad debt. 15 (**badder, baddest**) Sl. good, excellent. 16

go bad. to putrefy; spoil. **17 in a bad way.** *Inf.* **17a** seriously ill. **17b** in trouble. **18 make the best of a bad job.** to manage as well as possible in unfavourable circumstances. **19 not bad** *or* **not so bad.** *Inf.* passable; fairly good. **20 too bad.** *Inf.* (often used dismissively) regrettable. ◆ *n* **21** unfortunate or unpleasant events (often in **take the bad with the good**). **22** an immoral or degenerate state (often in **go to the bad**). **23** the debit side of an account: *£200 to the bad.* **24 go from bad to worse.** to deteriorate even more. ◆ *adv* **25** *Not standard.* badly: *to want something bad.* [C13: prob. from *bæd-*, as the first element of OE *bæddel* hermaphrodite]
▶ '**baddish** *adj* ▶ '**badness** *n*

> **USAGE NOTE**   See at **good.**

bad[2] (bæd) *vb* a variant spelling of **bade.**

Badajoz ★ ('bædə,hɒz; *Spanish* ba'ðaxoθ) *n* a city in SW Spain: strategically positioned near the frontier with Portugal. Pop.: 130 153 (1994 est.).

Badalona ★ (*Spanish* baða'lona) *n* a port in NE Spain: an industrial suburb of Barcelona. Pop.: 219 340 (1994 est.).

bad blood *n* a feeling of intense hatred or hostility; enmity.

baddie *or* **baddy** ('bædɪ) *n, pl* **baddies.** *Inf.* a bad character in a film, etc., esp. an opponent of the hero.

bade (bæd, beɪd) *or* **bad** *vb* past tense of **bid.**

Baden ★ ('ba:dən) *n* a former state of SW Germany and West Germany, now part of Baden-Württemberg.

Baden-Baden ★ *n* a spa in SW Germany, in Baden-Württemberg. Pop.: 52 520 (1991).

Baden-Powell ★ ('beɪdⁿn'pəʊəl, -'paʊəl) *n* **Robert Stephenson Smyth** (smɪθ, smaɪθ), 1st Baron Baden-Powell. 1857–1941, British general, noted for his defence of Mafeking (1899–1900); founder of the Boy Scouts (1908) and (with his sister Agnes) the Girl Guides (1910).

Baden-Württemberg ★ *n* a state of SW Germany. Capital: Stuttgart. Pop.: 10 272 100 (1995 est.). Area: 35 742 sq. km (13 800 sq. miles).

Bader ★ ('ba:də) *n* Sir **Douglas.** 1910–82, British fighter pilot. Despite losing both legs, he became a national hero in World War II.

badge (bædʒ) *n* **1** a distinguishing emblem or mark worn to signify membership, employment, achievement, etc. **2** any revealing feature or mark. [C14: from OF *bage*]

badger ('bædʒə) *n* **1** any of various stocky omnivorous mammals occurring in Europe, Asia, and N America. They are large burrowing animals, with strong claws and a thick coat striped black and white on the head. ◆ *vb* **2** (*tr*) to pester or harass. [C16: var. of *badgeard*, prob. from BADGE (from the white mark on its forehead) + -ARD]

Bad Godesberg ★ (*German* ba:t 'gɔ:dəsberk) *n* the official name for **Godesberg.**

bad hair day *n Inf.* **1** a day on which one's hair is untidy and unmanageable. **2** a day of mishaps and general irritation.

badinage ('bædɪ,nɑ:ʒ) *n* playful or frivolous repartee or banter. [C17: from F, from *badiner* to jest]

badlands ('bæd,lændz) *pl n* any deeply eroded barren area.

Bad Lands ★ *pl n* a deeply eroded barren region of SW South Dakota and NW Nebraska.

badly ('bædlɪ) *adv* **worse, worst. 1** poorly; defectively; inadequately. **2** unfavourably; unsuccessfully: *our scheme worked out badly.* **3** severely; gravely: *badly hurt.* **4** incorrectly or inaccurately: *to speak German badly.* **5** improperly; wickedly: *to behave badly.* **6** cruelly: *to treat badly.* **7** very much (esp. in **need badly, want badly**). **8** regretfully: *he felt badly about it.* **9 badly off.** poor.

badminton ('bædmɪntən) *n* **1** a game played with rackets and a shuttlecock which is hit back and forth across a high net. **2** Also called: **badminton cup.** a long drink of claret with soda water and sugar. [from *Badminton House, Glos*]

Badminton ★ ('bædmɪntən) *n* a village in SW England,

in Gloucestershire: site of Badminton House, seat of the Duke of Beaufort; annual horse trials.

bad-mouth *vb* (*tr*) *Sl., chiefly US & Canad.* to speak unfavourably about.

bad-tempered *adj* angry; irritable.

BAe *abbrev. for* British Aerospace.

Baedeker ('beɪdɪkə) *n* any of a series of travel guidebooks issued by the German publisher Karl Baedeker (1801–59) or his firm.

Baez ★ ('baɪez) *n* **Joan.** born 1941, US rock and folk singer.

BAF *abbrev. for* British Athletics Federation.

Baffin Bay ★ ('bæfɪn) *n* part of the Northwest Passage, situated between Baffin Island and Greenland. [after William *Baffin*, 17th-century English navigator]

Baffin Island ★ *n* the largest island of the Canadian Arctic, between Greenland and Hudson Bay. Area: 476 560 sq. km (184 000 sq. miles). [see BAFFIN BAY]

baffle ('bæfⁿl) *vb* **baffles, baffling, baffled.** (*tr*) **1** to perplex; bewilder; puzzle. **2** to frustrate (plans, efforts, etc.). **3** to check, restrain, or regulate (the flow of a fluid or the emission of sound or light). ◆ *n* **4** Also called: **baffle board, baffle plate.** a plate or mechanical device to restrain or regulate the flow of fluid, light, or sound, esp. in a loudspeaker or microphone. [C16: ?from Scot. dialect *bachlen* to condemn publicly]
▶ '**bafflement** *n* ▶ '**baffler** *n* ▶ '**baffling** *adj* ▶ '**bafflingly** *adv*

BAFTA ('bæftə) *n acronym for* British Academy of Film and Television Arts.

bag (bæg) *n* **1** a flexible container with an opening at one end. **2** Also: **bagful.** the contents of or amount contained in such a container. **3** a piece of portable luggage. **4** short for **handbag. 5** anything that sags, or is shaped like a bag, such as a loose fold of skin under the eyes. **6** any pouch or sac forming part of the body of an animal. **7** the quantity of quarry taken in a single hunting trip or by a single hunter. **8** *Derog. sl.* an ugly or bad-tempered woman or girl (often in **old bag**). **9 bag and baggage.** *Inf.* **9a** with all one's belongings. **9b** entirely. **10 bag of bones.** a lean creature. **11 in the bag.** *Sl.* almost assured of succeeding or being obtained. **12 rough as bags.** *Austral. sl.* **12a** uncouth. **12b** shoddy. ◆ *vb* **bags, bagging, bagged. 13** (*tr*) to put into a bag. **14** to bulge or cause to bulge. **15** (*tr*) to capture or kill, as in hunting. **16** (*tr*) to catch, seize, or steal. **17** (*intr*) to hang loosely; sag. **18** (*tr*) *Brit. & Austral. inf.* to secure the right to do or to have: *he bagged the best chair.* **19** (*tr*) to achieve or accomplish: *she bagged seven birdies.* ◆ See also **bags.** [C13: prob. from ON *baggi*]

bagasse (bə'gæs) *n* the dry pulp remaining after the extraction of juice from sugar cane or similar plants: used as fuel, for making fibreboard, etc. [C19: from F, from Sp. *bagazo* dregs]

bagatelle (,bægə'tel) *n* **1** something of little value. **2** a board game in which balls are struck into holes, with pins as obstacles. **3** a short light piece of music. [C17: from F, from It. *bagatella*, from (dialect) *bagatta* a little possession]

Bagdad ★ (bæg'dæd) *n* a variant spelling of **Baghdad.**

Bagehot ★ ('bædʒət) *n* **Walter.** 1826–77, British economist, author of *The English Constitution* (1867) and *Lombard Street* (1873).

bagel *or* **beigel** ('beɪgⁿl) *n* a hard ring-shaped bread roll. [C20: from Yiddish *beygel*]

baggage ('bægɪdʒ) *n* **1** suitcases, bags, etc., packed for a journey; luggage. **2** an army's portable equipment. **3** *Inf., old-fashioned.* **3a** a pert young woman. **3b** an immoral woman. **4** *Irish inf.* a cantankerous old woman. **5** *Inf.* previous knowledge and experience that a person may use or be influenced by in new circumstances: *cultural baggage.* [C15: from OF *bagage*, from *bague* a bundle]

baggy ('bægɪ) *adj* **baggier, baggiest.** (of clothes) hanging loosely; puffed out.
▶ '**baggily** *adv* ▶ '**bagginess** *n*

Baghdad *or* **Bagdad** ★ (bæg'dæd) *n* the capital of Iraq, on the River Tigris: capital of the Abbasid Caliphate (762–1258). Pop.: 4 478 000 (1995 est.).

bag lady *n* a homeless woman who wanders city streets with all her possessions in shopping bags.

bagman ('bægmən) *n, pl* **bagmen. 1** *Brit. inf.* a travelling salesman. **2** *Sl., chiefly US.* a person who collects or distributes money for racketeers. **3** *Austral.* a tramp or swagman, esp. one on horseback. **4** *Inf., chiefly Canad.* a person who solicits money for a political party.

bagnio ('baːnjəʊ) *n, pl* **bagnios. 1** a brothel. **2** *Obs.* an oriental prison for slaves. **3** *Obs.* an Italian or Turkish bathhouse. [C16: from It. *bagno*, from L *balneum* bath]

Bagnold ★ ('bægnəʊld) *n* **Enid** (**Algerine**). 1889–1981, British writer; her works include the novel *National Velvet* (1935) and the play *The Chalk Garden* (1955).

bagpipes ('bæg,paɪps) *pl n* any of a family of musical wind instruments in which sounds are produced in reed pipes by air from a bag inflated either by the player's mouth or by arm-operated bellows.

bags (bægz) *pl n* **1** *Inf.* a lot. **2** *Brit. inf.* trousers. ◆ *interj* **3** Also: **bags I.** *Children's sl., Brit. & Austral.* an indication of the desire to do, be, or have something.

baguette *or* **baguet** (bæ'gɛt) *n* **1** a narrow French stick loaf. **2** a small gem cut as a long rectangle. **3** *Archit.* a small moulding having a semicircular cross section. [C18: from F, from It. *bacchetta* a little stick, from *bacchio* rod]

Baguio ★ ('bægɪ,əʊ) *n* a city in the N Philippines, on N Luzon: summer capital of the Republic. Pop.: 169 565 (1994 est.).

bah (baː, bæ) *interj* an expression of contempt or disgust.

Bahá'í (bə'haːɪ) *n* **1** an adherent of the Bahá'í Faith. ◆ *adj* **2** of or relating to the Bahá'í Faith. [from Persian *bahā'ī*, lit.: of glory]

Bahá'í Faith *or* **Bahí'í** *n* a religious system founded in 1863, based on Babism and emphasizing the value of all religions and the spiritual unity of mankind.

Bahá'ísm (bə'haː,ɪzəm) *n* another name, not in Bahá'í use, for the **Bahá'í Faith.**

Bahamas (bə'haːməz) *or* **Bahama Islands** ★ *pl n* the. a group of over 700 coral islands (about 20 of which are inhabited) in the Caribbean: a British colony (1783–1964); an independent nation within the Commonwealth from 1973. Language: English. Currency: Bahamian dollar. Capital: Nassau. Pop.: 287 000 (1997). Area: 13 939 sq. km (5381 sq. miles).
▸ **Bahamian** (bə'heɪmɪən, -'haː-) *adj, n*

Bahawalpur ★ (,bæhə'wʊlpə) *n* an industrial city in Pakistan: cotton, soap. Pop.: 180 000 (latest est.).

Bahia ★ (bə'hiːə; *Portuguese* bɐ'iːɐ) *n* **1** a state of E Brazil, on the Atlantic coast. Capital: Salvador. Pop.: 12 646 000 (1995 est.). Area: about 562 000 sq. km (217 000 sq. miles). **2** the former name of **San Salvador.**

Bahía Blanca ★ (*Spanish* ba'ia 'blanka) *n* a port in E Argentina. Pop.: 260 096 (1991).

Bahia de los Cochinos ★ (ba'ia de los ko'tʃinos) *n* the Spanish name for the **Bay of Pigs.**

Bahrain *or* **Bahrein** ★ (baː'reɪn) *n* an independent sheikhdom on the Persian Gulf, consisting of several islands: under British protection until the declaration of independence in 1971. It has large oil reserves. Language: Arabic. Religion: Muslim. Currency: dinar. Capital: Manama. Pop.: 620 000 (1997). Area: 678 sq. km (262 sq. miles).
▸ **Bah'raini** *or* **Bah'reini** *adj, n*

Baikal ★ (baɪ'kaːl, -'kæl) *n* **Lake.** a lake in Russia, in SE Siberia: the largest freshwater lake in Eurasia and the deepest in the world. Greatest depth: over 1500 m (5000 ft). Area: about 33 670 sq. km (13 000 sq. miles).

bail¹ (beɪl) *Law.* ◆ *n* **1** a sum of money by which a person is bound to take responsibility for the appearance in court of another person or himself, forfeited if the person fails to appear. **2** the person or persons so binding themselves; surety. **3** the system permitting release of a person from custody where such security has been taken: *he was released on bail.* **4 jump bail** *or* (*formal*) **forfeit bail.** to fail to appear in court to answer to a charge. **5 stand** *or* **go bail.** to act as surety (for someone). ◆ *vb* (*tr*) **6** (often foll. by *out*) to release or obtain the release of (a person) from custody, security having been made. [C14: from OF: custody, from *baillier* to hand over, from L *bāiulāre* to carry burdens]

bail² *or* **bale** (beɪl) *vb* **bails, bailing, bailed** *or* **bales, baling baled.** (often foll. by *out*) to remove (water) from (a boat) See also **bail out.** [C13: from OF *baille* bucket, from L *bāiulus* carrier]
▸ **'bailer** *or* **'baler** *n*

bail³ (beɪl) *n* **1** *Cricket.* either of two small wooden bars across the tops of the stumps. **2** a partition between stalls in a stable or barn. **3** *Austral. & NZ.* a framework in a cowshed used to secure the head of a cow during milking. **4** a movable bar on a typewriter that holds the paper against the platen. ◆ *vb* **5** See **bail up.** [C18: from OF *baile* stake fortification, prob. from L *baculum* stick]

bail⁴ *or* **bale** (beɪl) *n* the semicircular handle of a kettle, bucket, etc. [C15: prob. of Scand. origin]

bailey ('beɪlɪ) *n* the outermost wall or court of a castle [C13: from OF *baille* enclosed court, from *bailler* to enclose]

Bailey ★ ('beɪlɪ) *n* **1 David.** born 1938, British photographer. **2 Nathan** *or* **Nathaniel.** died 1742, British lexicographer.

Bailey bridge ('beɪlɪ) *n* a temporary bridge made of prefabricated steel parts that can be rapidly assembled. [C20: after Sir Donald Coleman *Bailey* (1901–85), its Brit. designer]

bailie ('beɪlɪ) *n* (in Scotland) a municipal magistrate. [C13: from OF *bailli*, from earlier *baillif* BAILIFF]

bailiff ('beɪlɪf) *n* **1** *Brit.* the agent of a landlord or landowner. **2** a sheriff's officer who serves writs and summonses, makes arrests, and ensures that the sentences of the court are carried out. **3** *Chiefly Brit.* (formerly) a high official having judicial powers. **4** *Chiefly US.* an official having custody of prisoners appearing in court. [C13: from OF *baillif*, from *bail* custody; see BAIL¹]

bailiwick ('beɪlɪwɪk) *n* **1** *Law.* the area over which a bailiff has jurisdiction. **2** a person's special field of interest. [C15: from BAILIE + WICK²]

bail out *or* **bale out** *vb* (*adv*) **1** (*intr*) to make an emergency parachute jump from an aircraft. **2** (*tr*) *Inf.* to help (a person, organization, etc.) out of a predicament.

bail up *vb* (*adv*) **1** *Austral. & NZ.* to confine (a cow) or (of a cow) to be confined by the head in a bail. See **bail**³ (sense 3). **2** (*tr*) *Austral.* (of a bushranger) to hold under guard in order to rob. **3** (*intr*) *Austral.* to submit to robbery without offering resistance. **4** (*tr*) *Austral. inf.* to accost or detain, esp. in conversation.

Bainbridge ★ ('beɪn,brɪdʒ) *n* **Beryl.** born 1934, British writer. Her novels include *The Dressmaker* (1973), *Injury Time* (1977), *Every Man for Himself* (1996), and *Master Georgie* (1998); plays include *It's a Lovely Day Tomorrow* (1977).

bain-marie *French.* (bɛ̃mari) *n, pl* **bains-marie** (bɛ̃mari). a vessel for holding hot water, in which sauces and other dishes are gently cooked or kept warm. [C19: from F, from Med. L *balneum Mariae*, lit.: bath of Mary, inaccurate translation of Med. Gk *kaminos Marios*, lit.: furnace of *Miriam*, alleged author of a treatise on alchemy]

Bairam (baɪ'ræm, 'baɪræm) *n* either of two Muslim festivals, one (**Lesser Bairam**) at the end of Ramadan, the other (**Greater Bairam**) at the end of the Islamic year. [from Turkish *bayrām*]

Baird ★ (bɛəd) *n* **John Logie** ('ləʊgɪ). 1888–1946, Scottish engineer: inventor of a television system, later replaced.

bairn (bɛən) *n Scot. & N English.* a child. [OE *bearn*]

bait¹ (beɪt) *n* **1** something edible fixed to a hook or in a trap to attract fish or animals. **2** an enticement; temptation. **3** a variant spelling of **bate**². **4** *Arch.* a short stop for refreshment during a journey. ◆ *vb* **5** (*tr*) to put a piece of food on or in (a hook or trap). **6** (*tr*) to persecute or tease. **7** (*tr*) to entice; tempt. **8** (*tr*) to set dogs upon (a bear, etc.). **9** (*intr*) *Arch.* to stop for rest and refreshment during a journey. [C13: from ON *beita* to hunt]

★ people and places

ait² (beɪt) *vb* a variant spelling of **bate**².

aize (beɪz) *n* a woollen fabric resembling felt, usually green, used mainly for the tops of billiard tables. [C16: from OF *baies*, pl. of *baie* baize, from *bai* reddish brown, BAY³]

aja ('bæhə) **California Norte** ★ ('nɔː teɪ) *n* **1** a state of NW Mexico, in the N part of the Lower California peninsula. Capital: Mexicali. Pop.: 2 108 118 (1995 est.). Area: about 71 500 sq. km (27 600 sq. miles). **2** the Spanish name for **Lower California (North).**

aja California Sur ★ *n* a state of NW Mexico, in the S part of the Lower California peninsula. Capital: La Paz. Pop.: 375 450 (1995 est.). Area: 73 475 sq. km (28 363 sq. miles).

ake (beɪk) *vb* **bakes, baking, baked.** **1** (*tr*) to cook by dry heat as in an oven. **2** (*intr*) to cook bread, pastry, etc. **3** to make or become hardened by heat. **4** (*intr*) *Inf.* to be extremely hot. ♦ *n* **5** a batch of things baked at one time. **6** *Caribbean.* a small flat fried cake. [OE *bacan*]

aked Alaska (əˈlæskə) *n* a dessert made of cake and ice cream covered with meringue and cooked very quickly.

aked beans *pl n* haricot beans, baked and tinned in tomato sauce.

Bakelite ('beɪkə,laɪt) *n Trademark.* any one of a class of thermosetting resins used as electric insulators and for making plastic ware, etc. [C20: after L. H. *Baekeland* (1863–1944), Belgian-born US inventor]

aker ('beɪkə) *n* a person whose business or employment is to make or sell bread, cakes, etc.

Baker ★ ('beɪkə) *n* **1** Sir **Benjamin.** 1840–1907, British engineer who, with Sir John Fowler, designed much of the London underground railway and the first Aswan Dam. **2** James (**Addison**). born 1930, US Republican politician; Secretary of State from 1988. **3** Dame **Janet.** born 1933, British mezzo-soprano. **4** Sir **Samuel White.** 1821–93, British explorer: discovered Lake Albert (1864).

aker's dozen *n* thirteen. [C16: from the bakers' former practice of giving thirteen rolls where twelve were requested, to protect themselves against accusations of giving light weight]

akery ('beɪkərɪ) *n, pl* **bakeries.** **1** a room or building equipped for baking. **2** a shop in which bread, cakes, etc., are sold.

Bakewell ★ ('beɪkwel) *n* **Robert.** 1725–95, British agriculturist; radically improved livestock breeding.

Bakhtaran ★ (,bæktəˈrɑːn, -ˈræn) *n* a city in W Iran, in the valley of the Qareh Su: oil refinery. Pop.: 624 084 (1991). Former name (until 1987): **Kermanshah.**

baking powder *n* a powdered mixture that contains sodium bicarbonate and one or more acidic compounds, such as cream of tartar: used in baking as a raising agent.

baklava *or* **baclava** ('bɑːklə,vɑː) *n* a rich cake consisting of thin layers of pastry filled with nuts and honey. [from Turkish]

baksheesh *or* **backsheesh** ('bækʃiːʃ) *n* (in some Eastern countries, esp. formerly) money given as a tip, a present, or alms. [C17: from Persian *bakhshīsh*, from *bakhshīdan* to give]

Bakst ★ (*Russian* bakst) *n* **Leon Nikolayevich** (lɪˈɒn nikaˈlajɪvɪtʃ). 1866–1924, Russian painter and stage designer, noted particularly for his richly coloured sets for Diaghilev's *Ballet Russe* (1909–21).

Baku ★ (*Russian* ba'ku) *n* the capital of Azerbaijan, a port on the Caspian Sea: important for its extensive oilfields. Pop.: 1 087 000 (1994 est.).

Bakunin ★ (*Russian* baˈkunin) *n* **Mikhail** (mixaˈil). 1814–76, Russian anarchist and writer: a prominent member of the First International, expelled from it after conflicts with Marx.

bal. *Book-keeping. abbrev. for* balance.

Bala ★ ('bælə) *n* **Lake.** a narrow lake in Gwynedd: the largest natural lake in Wales. Length: 6 km (4 miles).

Balaam ★ ('beɪlæm) *n Old Testament.* a Mesopotamian diviner who, when summoned to curse the Israelites, prophesied future glories for them instead, after being reproached by his ass (Numbers 22–23).

Balaclava *or* **Balaclava helmet** (,bælə'klɑːvə) *n* (*often not caps.*) a close-fitting woollen hood that covers the ears and neck, as originally worn by soldiers in the Crimean War. [C19: from BALAKLAVA]

Balakirev ★ (*Russian* ba'lakɪrɪf) *n* **Mily Alexeyevich** ('milij alɪk'sjejɪvɪtʃ). 1837–1910, Russian composer, whose works include two symphonic poems and two symphonies.

Balaklava *or* **Balaclava** ★ (,bælə'klɑːvə; *Russian* bəla-'klavə) *n* a small port in the Ukraine, in S Crimea: scene of an inconclusive battle (1854), which included the charge of the Light Brigade, during the Crimean War.

balalaika (,bælə'laɪkə) *n* a Russian plucked musical instrument, usually having a triangular body and three strings. [C18: from Russian]

balance ('bæləns) *n* **1** a weighing device, generally consisting of a horizontal beam pivoted at its centre, from the ends of which two pans are suspended. The substance to be weighed is placed in one pan and weights are placed in the other until the beam returns to the horizontal. **2** a state of equilibrium. **3** something that brings about such a state. **4** equilibrium of the body; steadiness: *to lose one's balance.* **5** emotional stability. **6** harmony in the parts of a whole. **7** the act of weighing factors, quantities, etc., against each other. **8** the power to influence or control: *the balance of power.* **9** something that remains: *the balance of what you owe.* **10** *Accounting.* **10a** equality of debit and credit totals in an account. **10b** a difference between such totals. **11 in the balance.** in an uncertain or undecided condition. **12 on balance.** after weighing up all the factors. **13 strike a balance.** to make a compromise. ♦ *vb* **balances, balancing, balanced.** **14** (*tr*) to weigh in or as if in a balance. **15** (*intr*) to be or come into equilibrium. **16** (*tr*) to bring into or hold in equilibrium. **17** (*tr*) to compare the relative weight, importance, etc., of. **18** (*tr*) to be equal to. **19** (*tr*) to arrange so as to create a state of harmony. **20** (*tr*) *Accounting.* **20a** to compare the credit and debit totals of (an account). **20b** to equalize the credit and debit totals of (an account) by making certain entries. **20c** to settle or adjust (an account) by paying any money due. **21** (*intr*) (of a balance sheet, etc.) to have the debit and credit totals equal. [C13: from OF, from Vulgar L *bilancia* (unattested), from LL *bilanx* having two scales, from BI- + *lanx* scale]
▶ 'balanceable *adj* ▶ 'balancer *n*

Balance ('bæləns) *n* **the.** the constellation Libra, the seventh sign of the zodiac.

balance of payments *n* the difference over a given time between total payments to foreign nations and total receipts from foreign nations.

balance of power *n* the distribution of power among countries so that no one nation can seriously threaten another.

balance of trade *n* the difference in value between total exports and total imports of goods.

balance sheet *n* a statement that shows the financial position of a business by listing the asset balances and the claims on such assets.

balance wheel *n* a wheel oscillating against the hairspring of a timepiece, regulating its beat.

Balanchine ★ ('bælən,tʃiːn, ,bælən'tʃiːn) *n* **George.** 1904–83, US choreographer, born in Russia.

balata ('bælətə) *n* **1** a tropical American tree, yielding a latex-like sap. **2** a rubber-like gum obtained from this sap: a substitute for gutta-percha. [from American Sp., of Carib origin]

Balaton ★ (*Hungarian* 'bɔlɔton) *n* **Lake.** a large shallow lake in W Hungary. Area: 689 sq. km (266 sq. miles).

Balboa¹ ★ (bæl'bəʊə; *Spanish* bal'βoa) *n* **Vasco Núñez de** ('basko 'nuɲeθ de). ?1475–1519, Spanish explorer, who discovered the Pacific Ocean in 1513.

Balboa² ★ (bæl'bəʊə; *Spanish* bal'βoa) *n* a port in Panama at the Pacific end of the Panama Canal: the administrative centre of the former Canal Zone. Pop.: 2750 (1990).

Balcon ★ (*'bɔːlkən*) *n* Sir **Michael.** 1896–1977, British film producer; his Ealing Studio films include *Kind Hearts and Coronets* (1949).

balcony ('bælkənı) *n, pl* **balconies. 1** a platform projecting from a building with a balustrade along its outer edge, often with access from a door or window. **2** a gallery in a theatre, above the dress circle. **3** *US & Canad.* any circle in a theatre. [C17: from It. *balcone*, prob. from OHG *balko* beam]
▶ '**balconied** *adj*

bald (bɔːld) *adj* **1** having no hair or fur, esp. (of a man) having no hair on the scalp. **2** lacking natural growth or covering. **3** plain or blunt: *a bald statement.* **4** bare or unadorned. **5** Also: **baldfaced.** (of birds and animals) having white markings on the head and face. **6** (of a tyre) having a worn tread. [C14 *ballede* (lit.: having a white spot)]
▶ '**baldish** *adj* ▶ '**baldly** *adv* ▶ '**baldness** *n*

baldachin *or* **baldaquin** ('bɔːldəkɪn) *n* **1** a richly ornamented brocade. **2** a canopy over an altar, shrine, or throne or carried in Christian religious processions over an object of veneration. [OE *baldekin*, from It. *baldacchino*, lit.: stuff from Baghdad]

bald eagle *n* a large eagle of North America, having a white head and tail. It is the US national bird.

Balder ★ ('bɔːldə) *n Norse myth.* a god, son of Odin and Frigg, noted for his beauty and sweet nature. He was killed by a bough of mistletoe thrown by the blind god Höd, misled by the malicious Loki.

balderdash ('bɔːldə,dæʃ) *n* stupid or illogical talk; senseless rubbish. [C16: from ?]

balding ('bɔːldɪŋ) *adj* somewhat bald or becoming bald.

baldric ('bɔːldrɪk) *n* a sash or belt worn over the right shoulder to the left hip for carrying a sword, etc. [C13: from OF *baudrei*, of Frankish origin]

Baldwin ★ ('bɔːldwɪn) *n* **1 James (Arthur).** 1924–87, US writer, whose works include the novel *Go Tell it on the Mountain* (1954). **2 Stanley,** 1st Earl Baldwin of Bewdley. 1867–1947, British Conservative statesman: prime minister (1923–24, 1924–29, 1935–37).

Baldwin I ★ *n* 1058–1118, crusader and first king of Jerusalem (1100–18), who captured Acre (1104), Beirut (1109), and Sidon (1110).

baldy ('bɔːldɪ) *Inf.* ◆ *adj* **1** bald. ◆ *n, pl* **baldies. 2** a bald person.

bale[1] (beɪl) *n* **1** a large bundle, package, or carton of goods bound by ropes, wires, etc., for storage or transportation. **2** *US.* 500 pounds of cotton. ◆ *vb* **bales, baling, baled. 3** to make (hay, etc.) or put (goods) into a bale or bales. [C14: prob. from OF *bale*, from OHG *balla* BALL[1]]

bale[2] (beɪl) *n Arch.* **1** evil; injury. **2** woe; suffering; pain. [OE *bealu*]

bale[3] (beɪl) *vb* a variant spelling of **bail**[2].

bale[4] (beɪl) *n* a variant spelling of **bail**[4].

Bâle ★ (bɑl) *n* the French name for **Basel.**

Balearic Islands ★ (,bælɪ'ærɪk) *pl n* a group of islands in the W Mediterranean, consisting of Majorca, Minorca, Ibiza, Formentera, Cabrera, and 11 islets: a province of Spain. Capital: Palma, on Majorca. Pop.: 736 865 (1994 est.). Area: 5012 sq. km (1935 sq. miles). Spanish name: **Baleares** (bale'ares).

baleen (bə'liːn) *n* whalebone. [C14: from L *bālaena* whale]

baleen whale *n* another name for **whalebone whale.**

baleful ('beɪlful) *adj* harmful, menacing, or vindictive.
▶ '**balefully** *adv* ▶ '**balefulness** *n*

Balenciaga ★ (*Spanish* balen'θjaγa) *n* **Cristóbal** (kris-'toβal). 1895–1972, Spanish couturier.

baler ('beɪlə) *n* a machine for making bales of hay, etc. Also called: **baling machine.**

Balfour ★ ('bælfɔː, -fə, -fʊə) *n* **Arthur James,** 1st Earl of Balfour. 1848–1930, British Conservative statesman: prime minister (1902–05); foreign secretary (1916–19).

Bali ★ ('bɑːlɪ) *n* an island in Indonesia, east of Java: mountainous, rising over 3000 m (10 000 ft). Capital: Denpasar. Pop.: 2 902 200 (1995 est.). Area: 5558 sq. km (2146 sq. miles).
▶ ,**Bali'nese** *adj, n*

Balikpapan ★ (,bɑːlɪk'pɑːpɑːn) *n* a city in Indonesia, on the SE coast of Borneo. Pop.: 309 492 (1990).

Baliol *or* **Balliol** ★ ('beɪlɪəl) *n* **1 Edward.** ?1283–1364 king of Scotland (1332, 1333–56). **2 John.** 1249–1315 king of Scotland (1292–96): imprisoned by Edward (1296).

balk *or* **baulk** (bɔːk, bɔːlk) *vb* **1** (*intr;* usually foll. by *at*) t stop short; jib: *the horse balked at the jump.* **2** (*intr;* foll. b *at*) to recoil: *he balked at the idea of murder.* **3** (*tr*) to thwart check, or foil: *he was balked in his plans.* ◆ *n* **4** a roughl squared heavy timber beam. **5** a timber tie beam of roof. **6** an unploughed ridge between furrows. **7** an ob stacle; hindrance; disappointment. **8** *Baseball.* an illega motion by a pitcher. ◆ See also **baulk.** [OE *balca*]

Balkan ('bɔːlkən) *adj* of, denoting, or relating to the Bal kan States or their inhabitants, the Balkan Peninsula, o the Balkan Mountains.

Balkan Mountains ★ *pl n* a mountain range extending across Bulgaria from the Black Sea to the western border Highest peak: Mount Botev, 2376 m (7793 ft).

Balkan Peninsula ★ *n* a large peninsula in SE Europe between the Adriatic and Aegean Seas.

Balkan States ★ *pl n* the countries of the Balkan Penin sula: the former Yugoslav Republic, Romania, Bulgaria Albania, Greece, and the European part of Turkey. Als called: **the Balkans.**

Balkh ★ (bɑːlk) *n* a region of N Afghanistan, correspond ing to ancient Bactria. Chief town: Mazar-i-Sharif.

Balkhash ★ (*Russian* bal'xaʃ) *n* **Lake.** a salt lake in S Kazakhstan. Area: about 1800 sq. km (7000 sq. miles).

balky *or* **baulky** ('bɔːkɪ, 'bɔːlkɪ) *adj* **balkier, balkiest** *o* **baulkier, baulkiest.** inclined to stop abruptly and unex pectedly: *a balky horse.*

ball[1] (bɔːl) *n* **1** a spherical or nearly spherical body o mass. **2** a round or roundish body, of a size and composi tion suitable for any of various games. **3** a ball propelle in a particular way: *a high ball.* **4** any rudimentary gam with a ball: *to play ball.* **5** a single delivery of the ball i cricket and other games. **6a** a solid nonexplosive projec tile for a firearm, cannon, etc. **6b** such projectiles collec tively. **7** any more or less rounded part: *the ball of the foot* **8** ball of muscle. *Austral.* a very strong, fit person. **9 have th ball at one's feet.** to have the chance of doing something **10 keep the ball rolling.** to maintain the progress of a pro ject, plan, etc. **11 on the ball.** *Inf.* alert; informed. **12 play ball.** *Inf.* to cooperate. **13 set** *or* **start the ball rolling.** to initi ate an action, discussion, etc. ◆ *vb* **14** to make, form wind, gather, etc., into a ball or balls. ◆ See also **balls balls-up.** [C13: from ON *böllr*]

ball[2] (bɔːl) *n* **1** a social function for dancing, esp. one that is lavish or formal. **2** *Inf.* a very enjoyable time (esp. i **have a ball).** [C17: from F *bal* (n), from OF *baller* (vb) from LL *ballāre* to dance]

Ball ★ (bɔːl) *n* **John.** died 1381, English priest: executed a one of the leaders of the Peasants' Revolt (1381).

ballad ('bæləd) *n* **1** a narrative song with a recurrent re frain. **2** a narrative poem in short stanzas of popular ori gin. **3** a slow sentimental song, esp. a pop song. [C15 from OF *balade*, from OProvençal *balada* song accompa nying a dance]

ballade (bæ'lɑːd) *n* **1** *Prosody.* a verse form consisting o three stanzas and an envoy, all ending with the same line. **2** *Music.* an instrumental composition based on o intended to evoke a narrative.

balladeer (,bælə'dɪə) *n* a singer of ballads.

Ballance ★ ('bæləns) *n* **John.** 1839–93, New Zealand statesman, born in Northern Ireland: prime ministe (1891–93).

ball-and-socket joint *n* *Anat.* a joint in which a rounded head fits into a rounded cavity, allowing a wide range of movement.

Ballarat ★ ('bælə,ræt, ,bælə'ræt) *n* a town in SE Australia, in S central Victoria: originally a gold-mining region Pop.: 64 980 (1991).

Ballard ★ ('bælɑːd) *n* **J(ames) G(raham).** born 1930, Brit ish novelist, born in China; his books include *Crash* (1973), *Empire of the Sun* (1984), and *Cocaine Nights* (1996).

ballast ('bæləst) *n* **1** any heavy material used to stabilize

★ people and places

a vessel, esp. one that is not carrying cargo. **2** crushed rock, broken stone, etc., used for the foundation of a road or railway track or in making concrete. **3** anything that provides stability or weight. **4** *Electronics.* a device for maintaining the current in a circuit. ◆ *vb* (*tr*) **5** to give stability or weight to. [C16: prob. from Low G]

ball bearing *n* **1** a bearing consisting of steel balls rolling between a metal sleeve fitted over the rotating shaft and an outer sleeve held in the bearing housing, so reducing friction. **2** a metal ball, esp. one used in such a bearing.

ball boy *or* (*fem*) **ball girl** *n* (esp. in tennis) a person who retrieves balls that go out of play.

ballbreaker ('bɔːl,breɪkə) *n Sl.* someone, esp. a woman, whose behaviour may be regarded as threatening a man's sense of power. [C20: from BALLS (in the sense: testicles) + BREAKER]

ball cock *n* a device for regulating the flow of a liquid into a tank, cistern, etc., consisting of a floating ball mounted at one end of an arm and a valve on the other end that opens and closes as the ball falls and rises.

ballerina (,bælə'riːnə) *n* a female ballet dancer. [C18: from It., fem of *ballerino* dancing master, from *ballare* to dance]

Ballesteros ★ (,bælɛ'stɛrɒs; *Spanish* baʎes'terɔs) *n* **Severiano** (seve'rjano). born 1957, Spanish professional golfer: won the British Open Championship (1979; 1984; 1988).

ballet ('bæleɪ, bæ'leɪ) *n* **1** a classical style of expressive dancing based on precise conventional steps. **2** a theatrical representation of a story or theme performed by ballet dancers. **3** a troupe of ballet dancers. **4** music written for a ballet. [C17: from F, from It. *balletto*, lit.: a little dance, from *ballare* to dance] ► **balletic** (bæ'lɛtɪk) *adj*

balletomane ('bælɪtəʊ,meɪn) *n* a ballet enthusiast.

balletomania (,bælɪtəʊ'meɪnɪə) *n* passionate enthusiasm for ballet.

ball game *n* **1** any game played with a ball. **2** *US & Canad.* a game of baseball. **3** *Inf.* a situation; state of affairs (esp. in **a whole new ball game**).

Balliol ★ ('beɪlɪəl) *n* See **Baliol**.

ballista (bə'lɪstə) *n, pl* **ballistae** (-tiː). an ancient catapult for hurling stones, etc. [C16: from L, ult. from Gk *ballein* to throw]

ballistic (bə'lɪstɪk) *adj* **1** of or relating to ballistics. **2** denoting or relating to the flight of projectiles moving under their own momentum and the force of gravity. **3** (of a measurement or measuring instrument) depending on a brief impulse or current that causes a movement related to the quantity to be measured: *a ballistic pendulum.* **4 go ballistic.** *Inf.* to become enraged or frenziedly violent. ► **bal'listically** *adv*

ballistic missile *n* a missile that has no wings or fins and that follows a ballistic trajectory when its propulsive power is discontinued.

ballistics (bə'lɪstɪks) *n* (*functioning as sing*) **1** the study of the flight dynamics of projectiles. **2** the study of the effects of firing on firearms and their projectiles.

ball lightning *n Meteorol.* a luminous ball occasionally seen during electrical storms.

ballocks ('bɒləks) *pl n, interj* a variant spelling of **bollocks**.

ball of fire *n Inf.* a very lively person.

balloon (bə'luːn) *n* **1** an inflatable rubber bag used as a plaything or party decoration. **2** a large bag inflated with a lighter-than-air gas, designed to rise and float in the atmosphere. It may have a basket or gondola for carrying passengers, etc. **3** an outline containing the words or thoughts of a character in a cartoon. **4** a large rounded brandy glass. **5** *Commerce.* **5a** a large sum paid as an irregular instalment of a loan repayment. **5b** (*as modifier*): *a balloon loan.* **6** *Surgery.* **6a** an inflatable plastic tube used for dilating obstructed blood vessels or parts of the alimentary canal. **6b** (*as modifier*): *balloon angioplasty.* **7 go balloon** *or* **lead a lead balloon.** to prove unsuccessful or unpopular; fail: *the suggestion that the chairman should get a 77% pay rise went down like a lead balloon.* **8 when the balloon goes**

up. *Inf.* when the action starts. ◆ *vb* **9** (*intr*) to go up or fly in a balloon. **10** to inflate or be inflated: *the wind ballooned the sails.* **11** (*intr*) to increase or expand significantly and rapidly: *losses ballooned to £278 million.* **12** (*tr*) *Brit.* to propel (a ball) high into the air. [C16 (in the sense: ball, ball game): from It. dialect *ballone*] ► **bal'loonist** *n* ► **bal'loon-,like** *adj*

balloon loan *n* a loan in respect of which interest and capital are paid off in instalments at regular intervals.

ballot ('bælət) *n* **1** the practice of selecting a representative, course of action, etc., by submitting the options to a vote of all qualified persons. **2** an instance of voting, usually in secret. **3** a list of candidates standing for office. **4** the number of votes cast in an election. ◆ *vb* **ballots**, **balloting**, **balloted.** **5** to vote or elicit a vote from: *we balloted the members on this issue.* **6** (*tr*; usually foll. by *for*) to vote for or decide on by lot or ballot. [C16: from It. *ballotta*, lit.: a little ball]

ballot box *n* a box into which ballot papers are dropped after voting.

ballotini (,bælə'tiːnɪ) *pl n* small glass beads used in reflective paints. [from Italian *ballotini* small balls]

ballot paper *n* a paper used for voting.

ballpark ('bɔːl,pɑːk) *n* **1** *US & Canad.* a stadium used for baseball games. **2** *Inf.* **2a** approximate range: *in the right ballpark.* **2b** (*as modifier*): *a ballpark figure.* **3** *Inf.* a situation; state of affairs: *it's a whole new ballpark.*

ball-peen hammer *n* a hammer with one end of the head rounded for beating metal.

ballpoint *or* **ballpoint pen** ('bɔːl,pɔɪnt) *n* a pen having a small ball bearing as a writing point.

ballroom ('bɔːl,ruːm, -,rʊm) *n* a large hall for dancing.

ballroom dancing *n* social dancing, popular since the beginning of the 20th century, to dances in conventional rhythms (**ballroom dances**).

balls (bɔːlz) *Taboo sl.* ◆ *pl n* **1** the testicles. **2** nonsense; rubbish. **3** courage; determination. ◆ *interj* **4** an exclamation of disagreement, contempt, etc.

balls-up *Taboo sl.* ◆ *n* **1** something botched or muddled. ◆ *vb* **balls up. 2** (*tr, adv*) to muddle or botch.

ballsy ('bɔːlzɪ) *adj* **ballsier, ballsiest.** *Sl., chiefly US.* showing courage or determination; bold. [C20: from BALLS (sense 3) + -Y¹] ► **'ballsiness** *n*

bally ('bælɪ) *adj, adv* (intensifier) *Brit. sl.* a euphemistic word for **bloody** (sense 5).

ballyhoo (,bælɪ'huː) *Inf.* ◆ *n* **1** a noisy, confused, or nonsensical situation. **2** sensational or blatant advertising or publicity. ◆ *vb* **ballyhoos, ballyhooing, ballyhooed. 3** (*tr*) *Chiefly US.* to advertise by sensational or blatant methods. [C19: from ?]

Ballymena ★ (,bælɪ'miːnə) *n* a district in central Northern Ireland: agriculture, textiles. Pop.: 56 641 (1991). Area: 634 sq. km (247 sq. miles).

Ballymoney ★ (,bælɪ'mʌnɪ) *n* a district of N Northern Ireland: agriculture. Pop.: 24 198 (1991). Area: 418 sq. km (161 sq. miles).

balm (bɑːm) *n* **1** any of various oily aromatic substances obtained from certain tropical trees and used for healing and soothing. See also **balsam** (sense 1). **2** any plant yielding such a substance, esp. the balm of Gilead. **3** something comforting or soothing. **4** Also called: **lemon balm.** an aromatic Eurasian plant, having clusters of small fragrant white flowers. **5** a pleasant odour. [C13: from OF *basme*, from L *balsamum* BALSAM]

Balmain ★ (*French* balmɛ̃) *n* **Pierre Alexandre** (pjɛr alɛksɑ̃drə). 1914–82, French couturier.

balm of Gilead ('gɪlɪ,æd) *n* **1** any of several trees of Africa and W Asia that yield a fragrant oily resin. **2** the resin exuded by these trees. **3** a North American poplar tree. **4** a fragrant resin obtained from the balsam fir.

Balmoral¹ (bæl'mɒrəl) *n* (*sometimes not cap.*) **1** a laced walking shoe. **2** a Scottish brimless hat usually with a cockade and plume. [from BALMORAL Castle]

Balmoral² ★ (bæl'mɒrəl) *n* a castle in NE Scotland, in SW

Aberdeenshire: a private residence of the British sovereign.

balmy ('bɑːmɪ) *adj* **balmier, balmiest. 1** (of weather) mild and pleasant. **2** having the qualities of balm; fragrant or soothing. **3** a variant spelling of **barmy.**
► **'balmily** *adv* ► **'balminess** *n*

balneology (ˌbælnɪ'ɒlədʒɪ) *n* the branch of medical science concerned with the therapeutic value of baths, esp. with natural mineral waters. [C19: from L *balneum* bath]
► **balneological** (ˌbælnɪə'lɒdʒɪk°l) *adj* ► **ˌbalne'ologist** *n*

baloney *or* **boloney** (bə'ləʊnɪ) *n Inf.* foolish talk; nonsense. [C20: from *Bologna* (sausage)]

BALPA ('bælpə) *n acronym for* British Airline Pilots' Association.

balsa ('bɔːlsə) *n* **1** a tree of tropical America. **2** Also called: **balsawood.** the very light wood of this tree, used for making rafts, etc. **3** a light raft. [C18: from Sp.: raft]

balsam ('bɔːlsəm) *n* **1** any of various fragrant oleoresins, such as balm, obtained from any of several trees and shrubs and used as a base for medicines and perfumes. **2** any of various similar substances used as ointments. **3** any of certain aromatic resinous turpentines. See **Canada balsam. 4** any plant yielding balsam. **5** Also called: **busy Lizzie.** any of several plants of the genus *Impatiens*. **6** anything healing or soothing. [C15: from L *balsamum*, from Gk *balsamon*, from Heb. *bāśām* spice]
► **balsamic** (bɔːl'sæmɪk) *adj*

balsam fir *n* a fir tree of NE North America, that yields Canada balsam.

Balthazar ★ ('bælθə,zɑː, bæl'θæzə) *n* one of the Magi, the others being Caspar and Melchior.

Balthus ★ (*French* baltys) *n*   real name *Balthasar Klossowski de Rola*. born 1908, French painter of Polish descent.

balti ('bɔːltɪ, 'bæltɪ) *n* **a** a spicy Indian dish, stewed until most of the liquid has evaporated, and served in a woklike pot. **b** (*as modifier*): *a balti house.* [C20: from ?]

Baltic ('bɔːltɪk) *adj* **1** denoting or relating to the Baltic Sea or the Baltic states. **2** of or characteristic of Baltic as a group of languages. ♦ *n* **3** a branch of the Indo-European family of languages consisting of Lithuanian, Latvian, and Old Prussian. **4** Also called: **Baltic Exchange.** a commodity and freight-chartering market in the City of London.

Baltics ★ ('bɔːltɪks) *pl n* **the.** another name for the **Baltic States.**

Baltic Sea ★ *n* a sea in N Europe, connected with the North Sea by the Skaggerak, Kattegat, and Öresund; shallow, with low salinity and small tides.

Baltic Shield ★ *n* the wide area of ancient rock in Scandinavia. Also called: **Scandinavian Shield.** See **shield** (sense 6).

Baltic States ★ *pl n* the independent republics of Estonia, Latvia, and Lithuania; constituent republics of the Soviet Union (1940–91). Sometimes shortened to **Baltics.**

Baltimore[1] ★ ('bɔːltɪ,mɔː) *n* a port in N Maryland, on Chesapeake Bay. Pop.: 702 979 (1994 est.).

Baltimore[2] ★ ('bɔːltɪ,mɔː) *n* **1** David. born 1938, US molecular biologist: shared the Nobel prize for physiology or medicine (1975) for his discovery of reverse transcriptase. **2** Lord. See (Sir George) **Calvert.**

Baluchistan (bəˈluːtʃɪˌstɑːn, -ˌstæn) *or* **Balochistan** ★ (bəˈlɒtʃɪˌstɑːn, -ˌstæn) *n* **1** a mountainous region of SW Asia, in SW Pakistan and SE Iran. **2** a province of SW Pakistan: a former territory of British India (until 1947). Capital: Quetta. Pop.: 6 341 000 (1995 est.).

baluster ('bæləstə) *n* any of a set of posts supporting a rail or coping. [C17: from F *balustre*, from It. *balaustro* pillar resembling a pomegranate flower, ult. from Gk *balaustion*]

balustrade ('bælə,streɪd) *n* an ornamental rail or coping with its supporting set of balusters. [C17: from F, from *balustre* BALUSTER]

Balzac ★ ('bælzæk; *French* balzak) *n* **Honoré de** (ɔnɔre də). 1799–1850, French novelist: author of a collection of novels *La Comédie humaine*.

Bamako ★ (ˌbæmæ'kəʊ) *n* the capital of Mali, in the south, on the River Niger. Pop.: 800 000 (1995 est.).

Bamberg ★ ('bæmbɜːg; *German* 'bamberk) *n* a town in S Germany, in N Bavaria: seat of independent prince-bishops of the Holy Roman Empire (1007–1802). Pop.: 70 690 (1991).

bambino (bæm'biːnəʊ) *n, pl* **bambinos** *or* **bambini** (-niː). *Inf.* a young child, esp. Italian. [C18: from It.]

bamboo (bæm'buː) *n* **1** a tall treelike tropical or semi-tropical grass having hollow stems with ringed joints. **2** the stem, used for building, poles, and furniture. [C16: prob. from Malay *bambu*]

bamboozle (bæm'buːz°l) *vb* **bamboozles, bamboozling, bamboozled.** (*tr*) *Inf.* **1** to cheat; mislead. **2** to confuse. [C18: from ?]
► **bam'boozlement** *n* ► **bam'boozler** *n*

ban (bæn) *vb* **bans, banning, banned. 1** (*tr*) to prohibit, esp. officially, from action, display, entrance, sale, etc.; forbid. ♦ *n* **2** an official prohibition or interdiction. **3** a public proclamation, esp. of outlawry. **4** *Arch.* a curse; imprecation. [OE *bannan* to proclaim]

Banaba ★ (bə'nɑːbə) *n* an island in the SW Pacific, in the Republic of Kiribati. Phosphates were mined by Britain (1900–79). Area: about 5 sq. km (2 sq. miles). Pop.: 284 (1990). Also called: **Ocean Island.**
► **Ba'naban** *adj, n*

banal (bə'nɑːl) *adj* lacking force or originality; trite; commonplace. [C18: from OF: relating to compulsory feudal service, hence common to all, commonplace]
► **banality** (bə'nælɪtɪ) *n* ► **ba'nally** *adv*

banana (bə'nɑːnə) *n* **1** any of several tropical and sub-tropical treelike plants, esp. a widely cultivated species having hanging clusters of edible fruit. **2** the crescent-shaped fruit of any of these plants. [C16: from Sp. or Port., of African origin]

banana republic *n Inf. & derog.* a small country, esp. in Central America, that is politically unstable and has an economy dominated by foreign interest, usually dependent on one export.

banana skin *n* **1** the soft outer covering of a banana. **2** *Inf.* something unforeseen that causes an obvious and embarrassing mistake. [sense 2 from the common slapstick joke of slipping on a banana skin]

Banaras ★ (bə'nɑːrəz) *n* a variant spelling of **Benares.**

Banat ★ ('bænɪt, 'bɑːnɪt) *n* a fertile plain extending through Hungary, Romania, and Yugoslavia.

Banbridge ★ ('bænbrɪdʒ) *n* a district of SE Northern Ireland: agriculture, linen, footwear. Administrative centre: Banbridge. Pop.: 33 880 (1992). Area: 445 sq. km (172 sq. miles).

Banbury ★ ('bænbərɪ) *n* a town in central England, in N Oxfordshire. Pop.: 39 906 (1991).

band[1] (bænd) *n* **1** a company of people having a common purpose; group: *a band of outlaws.* **2** a group of musicians playing either brass and percussion instruments only (**brass band**) or brass, woodwind, and percussion instruments (**concert band** or **military band**). **3** a group of musicians who play popular music, jazz, etc., often for dancing. ♦ *vb* **4** (usually foll. by *together*) to unite; assemble. [C15: from F *bande*, prob. from OProvençal *banda*, of Gmc origin]

band[2] (bænd) *n* **1** a thin flat strip of some material, used esp. to encircle objects and hold them together: *a rubber band.* **2a** a strip of fabric or other material used as an ornament or to reinforce clothing. **2b** (*in combination*): *waistband; hatband.* **3** a stripe of contrasting colour or texture. **4** a driving belt in machinery. **5** a range of values that are close or related in number, degree, or quality. **6** *Physics.* a range of frequencies or wavelengths between two limits. **7** short for **energy band. 8** *Computing.* one or more tracks on a magnetic disk or drum. **9** *Anat.* any structure resembling a ribbon or cord that connects, encircles, or binds different parts. **10** *Archit.* a strip of flat panelling, such as a fascia, usually attached to a wall. **11** either of a pair of hanging extensions of the collar, forming part of academic, legal, or (formerly) clerical dress. ♦ *vb* (*tr*) **12** to fasten or mark with a band. [C15: from F *bende*, of Gmc origin]

Banda ★ ('bændə) *n* **Hastings Kamuzu** (kæ'muːzuː). 1906–97, Malawi statesman; first prime minister of Nyasaland (1963–64); president of Malawi (1966–94).

bandage ('bændɪdʒ) *n* **1** a piece of material used to dress a wound, bind a broken limb, etc. ◆ *vb* **bandages, bandaging, bandaged. 2** to cover or bind with a bandage. [C16: from F, from *bande* strip, BAND²]

bandanna *or* **bandana** (bæn'dænə) *n* a large silk or cotton handkerchief or neckerchief. [C18: from Hindi *bāndhnū* tie-dyeing]

Bandaranaike ★ (ˌbændərə'naɪkə) *n* **1 Chandrika.** See Chandrika **Kumaratunga. 2** Mrs **Sirimavo** (ˌsɪrɪ'mɑːvəu). born 1916, prime minister of Sri Lanka, formerly Ceylon (1960–65; 1970–77; 1994–). **3** her husband, **Solomon.** 1899–1959, prime minister of Ceylon (1956–59); assassinated.

Bandar Seri Begawan ★ ('bɑːndɑː 'serɪ bə'gɑːwən) *n* the capital of Brunei. Pop.: 21 484 (1991). Former name: **Brunei.**

Banda Sea ★ *n* a part of the Pacific in Indonesia, between Sulawesi and New Guinea.

B & B *abbrev. for* bed and breakfast.

bandbox ('bændˌbɒks) *n* a lightweight usually cylindrical box for small articles, esp. hats.

bandeau ('bændəu) *n, pl* **bandeaux** (-dəuz). a narrow band of ribbon, velvet, etc., worn round the head. [C18: from F, from OF *bandel* a little BAND²]

banderole *or* **banderol** ('bændəˌrəul) *n* **1** a long narrow flag, usually with forked ends, esp. one attached to the mast of a ship. **2** a ribbon-like scroll or sculptured band bearing an inscription. [C16: from OF, from It. *banderuola,* lit.: a little banner]

bandicoot ('bændɪˌkuːt) *n* **1** an agile terrestrial marsupial of Australia and New Guinea with a long pointed muzzle and a long tail. Also called: **mole rat. 2 bandicoot rat.** any of three burrowing rats of S and SE Asia. [C18: from Telugu *pandikokku*]

banding ('bændɪŋ) *n Brit.* the practice of putting schoolchildren into ability groups to ensure a balanced intake to secondary school.

bandit ('bændɪt) *n, pl* **bandits** *or* **banditti** (bæn'dɪtɪ). a robber, esp. a member of an armed gang. [C16: from It. *bandito,* from *bandire* to proscribe, from *bando* edict]
▶ **'banditry** *n*

Bandjarmasin *or* **Bandjermasin** ★ (ˌbændʒə'mɑːsɪn) *n* variant spellings of **Banjarmasin.**

bandmaster ('bændˌmɑːstə) *n* the conductor of a band.

Band of Hope *n* a society devoted to abstinence from alcohol.

bandolier *or* **bandoleer** (ˌbændə'lɪə) *n* a soldier's broad shoulder belt having small pockets or loops for cartridges. [C16: from OF *bandouliere*]

band-pass filter *n* **1** *Electronics.* a filter that transmits only currents having frequencies within specified limits. **2** an optical device for transmitting waves of predetermined wavelengths.

band saw *n* a power-operated saw consisting of an endless toothed metal band running over and driven by two wheels.

bandsman ('bændzmən) *n, pl* **bandsmen.** a player in a musical band, esp. a brass or military band.

bandstand ('bændˌstænd) *n* a platform for a band, usually out of doors and roofed.

band theory *n* the theory that electrons in solids have a range of energies falling into allowed bands, between which are forbidden bands.

Bandung ★ ('bænduŋ) *n* a city in Indonesia, in SW Java. Pop.: 2 026 893 (1990).

bandwagon ('bændˌwægən) *n* **1** *US.* a wagon for the band in a parade. **2 jump, climb,** *or* **get on the bandwagon.** to join or support a party or movement that seems assured of success.

bandwidth ('bændˌwɪdθ) *n* the range of frequencies within a given waveband used for a particular radio transmission.

bandy ('bændɪ) *adj* **bandier, bandiest. 1** Also: **bandy-legged.**

having legs curved outwards at the knees. **2** (of legs) curved thus. ◆ *vb* **bandies, bandying, bandied.** (*tr*) **3** to exchange (words) in a heated or hostile manner. **4** to give and receive (blows). **5** (often foll. by *about*) to circulate (a name, rumour, etc.). [C16: prob. from OF *bander* to hit the ball back and forth at tennis]

bane (beɪn) *n* **1** a person or thing that causes misery or distress (esp. in **bane of one's life**). **2** something that causes death or destruction. **3a** a fatal poison. **3b** (*in combination*): ratsbane. **4** *Arch.* ruin or distress. [OE *bana*]
▶ **'baneful** *adj*

baneberry ('beɪnbərɪ) *n, pl* **baneberries. 1** Also called: **herb Christopher** (Brit.). a plant which has small white flowers and red or white poisonous berries. **2** the berry.

Banff ★ (bæmf) *n* **1** a town in Canada, in SW Alberta, in the Rocky Mountains: surrounded by **Banff National Park.** Pop.: 5700 (1991). **2** a town in NE Scotland, in Aberdeenshire. Pop.: 6230 (1991).

Banffshire ★ ('bæmfˌʃɪə, -ʃə) *n* (until 1975) a county of NE Scotland, now part of Aberdeenshire.

bang¹ (bæŋ) *n* **1** a short loud explosive noise, as of the report of a gun. **2** a hard blow or knock, esp. a noisy one. **3** *Sl.* an injection of heroin or other narcotic. **4** *Taboo sl.* an act of sexual intercourse. **5 with a bang.** successfully: *the party went with a bang.* ◆ *vb* **6** to hit or knock, esp. with a loud noise. **7** to move noisily or clumsily: *to bang about the house.* **8** to close (a door, window, etc.) or (of a door, etc.) be closed noisily; slam. **9** (*tr*) to cause to move by hitting vigorously: *he banged the ball over the fence.* **10** to make or cause to make a loud noise, as of an explosion. **11** *Taboo sl.* to have sexual intercourse (with). **12** (*intr*) *Sl.* to inject heroin, etc. **13 bang one's head against a brick wall.** to try to achieve something impossible. ◆ *adv* **14** with a sudden impact or effect: *the car drove bang into a lamppost.* **15** precisely: *bang in the middle.* **16 go bang.** to burst, shut, etc., with a loud noise. [C16: from ON *bang, banga* hammer]

bang² (bæŋ) *n* **1** (*usually pl*) a section of hair cut straight across the forehead. ◆ *vb* (*tr*) **2** to cut (the hair) in such a style. **3** to dock (the tail of a horse, etc.). [C19: prob. short for *bangtail* short tail]

Bangalore ★ (ˌbæŋgə'lɔː) *n* a city in S India, capital of Karnataka state: printing, textiles, pharmaceuticals. Pop.: 2 660 088 (1991).

banger ('bæŋə) *n Brit.* **1** *Sl.* a sausage. **2** *Inf.* an old decrepit car. **3** a firework that explodes loudly.

Bangka *or* **Banka** ★ ('bæŋkə) *n* an island in Indonesia, separated from Sumatra by the **Bangka Strait.** Chief town: Pangkalpinang. Area: about 11 914 sq. km (4600 sq. miles).

Bangkok ★ ('bæŋkɒk, bæŋ'kɒk) *n* the capital and chief port of Thailand, on the Chao Phraya River: became a royal city and the capital in 1782. Pop.: 5 584 228 (1993 est.). Thai name: **Krung Thep** ('kruŋ 'teɪp).

Bangla ('bæŋglə) *n* another name for **Bengali** (sense 2).

Bangladesh ★ (ˌbɑːŋglə'deʃ, ˌbæŋ-) *n* a republic in S Asia: formerly the Eastern Province of Pakistan; became independent in 1971 after civil war and the defeat of Pakistan by India; consists of the plains and vast deltas of the Ganges and Brahmaputra Rivers; a member of the Commonwealth: economy based on jute and jute products (over 80 per cent of world production). Language: Bengali. Religion: Muslim. Currency: taka. Capital: Dhaka. Pop.: 125 340 000 (1997). Area: 142 797 sq. km (55 126 sq. miles).
▶ ˌBangla'deshi *adj, n*

bangle ('bæŋg°l) *n* a bracelet, usually without a clasp, often worn round the arm or sometimes round the ankle. [C19: from Hindi *bangrī*]

bang on *adj, adv Brit. inf.* **1** with absolute accuracy. **2** excellent or excellently.

Bangor ★ ('bæŋgɔː, -gə) *n* **1** a university town in NW Wales, in Gwynedd, on the Menai Strait. Pop.: 12 330 (1991). **2** a town in SE Northern Ireland, in Co. Down, on Belfast Lough. Pop.: 52 437 (1991).

bangtail ('bæŋˌteɪl) *n* **1** a horse's tail cut straight across but not through the bone. **2** a horse with a tail cut in this way. [C19: from *bangtail* short tail]

★ people and places

Bangui ★ (French băgi) n the capital of the Central African Republic, in the south part, on the Ubangi River. Pop.: 524 000 (1994 est.).

Bangweulu ★ (ˌbæŋwɪˈuːlu) n **Lake**. a shallow lake in NE Zambia, discovered by David Livingstone, who died there in 1873. Area: about 9850 sq. km (3800 sq. miles), including swamps.

banian ('bænjən) n a variant spelling of **banyan**.

banish ('bænɪʃ) vb (tr) **1** to expel from a place, esp. by an official decree as a punishment. **2** to drive away: to banish gloom. [C14: from OF banir, of Gmc origin]
▶ **'banishment** n

banisters or **bannisters** ('bænɪstəz) pl n the railing and supporting balusters on a staircase; balustrade. [C17: altered from BALUSTER]

Banja Luka ★ (Serbo-Croat 'baːnja: ˌluːka) n a city in NW Bosnia-Herzegovina, on the Vrbas River: scene of battles between the Austrians and Turks in 1527, 1688, and 1737; besieged by Serb forces (1992–95). Pop.: 195 139 (1991).

Banjarmasin, Banjermasin, Bandjarmasin or **Bandjermasin** ★ (ˌbændʒəˈmɑːsɪn) n a port in Indonesia, in SW Borneo. Pop.: 443 738 (1990).

banjo ('bændʒəʊ) n, pl **banjos** or **banjoes**. a stringed musical instrument with a long neck and a circular drumlike body overlaid with parchment, plucked with the fingers or a plectrum. [C18: var. (US Southern pronunciation) of earlier bandore, ult. from Gk pandora]
▶ **'banjoist** n

Banjul ★ (bæn'dʒuːl) n the capital of The Gambia, a port at the mouth of the Gambia River. Pop.: 42 407 (1993). Former name (until 1973): **Bathurst**.

bank[1] (bæŋk) n **1** an institution offering certain financial services, such as the safekeeping of money and lending of money at interest. **2** the building used by such an institution. **3** a small container used at home for keeping money. **4** the funds held by a banker or dealer in some gambling games. **5** (in various games) **5a** the stock, as of money, etc., on which players may draw. **5b** the player holding this stock. **6** any supply, store, or reserve: a data bank. ◆ vb **7** (tr) to deposit (cash, cheques, etc.) in a bank. **8** (intr) to transact business with a bank. **9** (intr) to engage in banking. ◆ See also **bank on**. [C15: prob. from It. banca bench, moneychanger's table, of Gmc origin]

bank[2] (bæŋk) n **1** a long raised mass, esp. of earth; ridge. **2** a slope, as of a hill. **3** the sloping side of any hollow in the ground, esp. when bordering a river. **4** the ground beside a river or canal. **5a** an elevated section of the bed of a sea, lake, or river. **5b** (in combination): sandbank. **6** the face of a body of ore in a mine. **7** the lateral inclination of an aircraft about its longitudinal axis during a turn. **8** a bend on a road, athletics track, etc., having the outside built higher than the inside to reduce the effects of centrifugal force on vehicles, runners, etc., rounding it at speed. Also called: **camber, superelevation**. ◆ vb **9** (when tr, often foll. by up) to form into a bank or mound. **10** (tr) to border or enclose (a road, etc.) with a bank. **11** (tr; sometimes foll. by up) to cover (a fire) with ashes, fresh fuel, etc., so that it will burn slowly. **12** to cause (an aircraft) to tip laterally about its longitudinal axis or (of an aircraft) to tip in this way, esp. while turning. [C12: of Scand. origin]

bank[3] (bæŋk) n **1** an arrangement of similar objects in a row or in tiers: a bank of dials. **2** a tier of oars in a galley. ◆ vb **3** (tr) to arrange in a bank. [C17: from OF banc bench, of Gmc origin]

Banka ★ ('bæŋkə) n a variant spelling of **Bangka**.

bankable ('bæŋkəb°l) adj **1** appropriate for receipt by a bank. **2** dependable or reliable: a bankable promise. **3** (esp. of a star) likely to ensure the financial success of a film.
▶ ˌbanka'bility n

bank account n **1** an account created by the deposit of money at a bank by a customer. **2** the amount credited to a depositor at a bank.

bank bill n **1** Also called: **bank draft**. a bill of exchange drawn by one bank on another. **2** US. a banknote.

bankbook ('bæŋkˌbʊk) n a book held by depositors at certain banks, in which the bank enters a record of deposits, withdrawals, and earned interest. Also called: **passbook**.

bank card or **banker's card** n any plastic card issued by a bank, such as a cash card or cheque card.

bank draft n a cheque drawn by a bank on itself, which is bought by a person to pay a supplier unwilling to accept a normal cheque. Also called: **banker's cheque**.

banker[1] ('bæŋkə) n **1** a person who owns or is an executive in a bank. **2** an official or player in charge of the bank in various games. **3** a result that has been forecast identically in a series of entries on a football pool coupon. **4** a person whose performance can be relied on.

banker[2] ('bæŋkə) n Austral. & NZ inf. a stream almost overflowing its banks (esp. in **run a banker**).

banker's order n another name for **standing order** (sense 1).

Bankhead ★ ('bæŋkˌhɛd) n **Tallulah (Brockman)**. 1902–68, US stage and film actress.

bank holiday n (in Britain) any of several weekdays on which banks are closed by law and which are observed as national holidays.

banking ('bæŋkɪŋ) n the business engaged in by a bank.

bank manager n a person who directs the business of a local branch of a bank.

banknote ('bæŋkˌnəʊt) n a promissory note, esp. one issued by a central bank, serving as money.

Bank of England n the central bank of the United Kingdom, which acts as banker to the government and the commercial banks.

bank on vb (intr, prep) to expect or rely with confidence on: you can bank on him.

bankroll ('bæŋkˌrəʊl) Chiefly US & Canad. ◆ n **1** a roll of currency notes. **2** the financial resources of a person, organization, etc. ◆ vb **3** (tr) Sl. to provide the capital for; finance.

bankrupt ('bæŋkrʌpt, -rəpt) n **1** a person adjudged insolvent by a court, his property being administered for the benefit of his creditors. **2** any person unable to discharge all his debts. **3** a person whose resources in a certain field are exhausted: a spiritual bankrupt. ◆ adj **4** adjudged insolvent. **5** financially ruined. **6** depleted in resources: spiritually bankrupt. **7** (foll. by of) Brit. lacking: bankrupt of intelligence. ◆ vb **8** (tr) to make bankrupt. [C16: from OF banqueroute, from OIt. bancarotta, from banca BANK[1] + rotta broken, from L ruptus]
▶ **'bankruptcy** n

Banks ★ (bæŋks) n Sir **Joseph**. 1743–1820, British botanist and explorer: circumnavigated the world with James Cook (1768–71).

banksia ('bæŋksɪə) n any shrub or tree of the Australian genus Banksia, having dense cylindrical heads of flowers that are often yellowish. [C19: NL, after Sir Joseph BANKS]

Banks Island ★ n **1** an island of N Canada, in the Northwest Territories: the westernmost island of the Arctic Archipelago. Area: about 67 340 sq. km (26 000 sq. miles). **2** an island of W Canada, off British Columbia. Length: about 72 km (45 miles).

bank statement n a statement of transactions in a bank account, esp. one of a series sent at regular intervals to the depositor.

banner ('bænə) n **1** a long strip of material displaying a slogan, advertisement, etc. **2** a placard carried in a procession or demonstration. **3** something that represents a belief or principle. **4** the flag of a nation, army, etc. **5** Also called: **banner headline**. a large headline in a newspaper, etc., extending across the page. [C13: from OF baniere, of Gmc origin]
▶ **'bannered** adj

Bannister ★ ('bænɪstə) n Sir **Roger (Gilbert)**. born 1929, British athlete and doctor: first to run a four minute mile (1954).

bannisters ('bænɪstəz) pl n a variant spelling of **banisters**.

bannock ('bænək) n a round flat cake originating in Scotland, made from oatmeal or barley and baked on a griddle. [OE bannuc]

★ people and places

Bannockburn ★ ('bænək,bɜːn) n a village in central Scotland, south of Stirling: nearby is the site of a victory (1314) of the Scots, led by Robert the Bruce, over the English. Pop.: 2675 (1991).

banns or **bans** (bænz) pl n 1 the public declaration of an intended marriage, usually on three successive Sundays in the parish churches of the betrothed. 2 **forbid the banns.** to raise an objection to a marriage announced in this way. [C14: pl of bann proclamation]

banquet ('bæŋkwɪt) n 1 a sumptuous meal; feast. 2 a ceremonial meal for many people. ◆ vb **banquets, banqueting, banqueted.** 3 (intr) to hold or take part in a banquet. 4 (tr) to entertain (a person) with a banquet. [C15: from OF, from It. banchetto, from banco a table, of Gmc origin] ▸ **'banqueter** n

banquette (bæŋ'kɛt) n 1 an upholstered bench. 2 (formerly) a raised part behind a parapet. [C17: from F, from Provençal banqueta, lit.: a little bench]

banshee ('bænʃiː, bæn'ʃiː) n (in Irish folklore) a female spirit whose wailing warns of impending death. [C18: from Irish Gaelic bean sídhe, lit.: woman of the fairy mound]

Banstead ★ ('bæn,stɛd) n a town in S England, in NE Surrey: a dormitory town for London. Pop.: 37 245 (1991).

bantam ('bæntəm) n 1 any of various very small breeds of domestic fowl. 2 a small but aggressive person. 3 Boxing. short for **bantamweight.** [C18: after Bantam, village in Java, said to be the original home of this fowl]

bantamweight ('bæntəm,weɪt) n 1a a professional boxer weighing 112–118 pounds (51–53.5 kg). 1b an amateur boxer weighing 51–54 kg (112–119 pounds). 2 an amateur wrestler weighing usually 52–57 kg (115–126 pounds).

banter ('bæntə) vb 1 to speak or tease lightly or jokingly. ◆ n 2 teasing or joking language or repartee. [C17: from ?] ▸ **'banterer** n

Banting ★ ('bæntɪŋ) n Sir **Frederick Grant.** 1891–1941, Canadian physiologist: discovered the insulin treatment for diabetes with Best and Macleod (1922) and shared the Nobel prize for physiology or medicine (1923).

Bantock ★ ('bæntɒk) n Sir **Granville.** 1868–1946, British composer. His works include the Hebridean Symphony (1915), five ballets, and three operas.

Bantu ('bɑːntuː) n 1 a group of languages of Africa, including most of the principal languages spoken from the equator to the Cape of Good Hope. 2 (pl **Bantu** or **Bantus**) Derog. a Black speaker of a Bantu language. ◆ adj 3 of or relating to this group of peoples or their languages. [C19: from Bantu Ba-ntu people]

Bantustan ('bɑːntuˌstɑːn) n Derog. (formerly, in South Africa) an area reserved for occupation by a Black African people, with limited self-government; abolished in 1993. Official name: **homeland.** [from BANTU + Hindi -stan country of]

banyan or **banian** ('bænjən) n 1 an Indian tree with aerial roots that grow down into the soil forming additional trunks. 2 a member of the Hindu merchant caste of India. 3 a loose-fitting shirt, or robe, worn originally in India. [C16: from Hindi baniyā, from Sansk. vānija merchant]

banzai ('bɑːnzaɪ, bɑːn'zaɪ) interj a patriotic cheer, battle cry, or salutation. [Japanese: lit.: (may you live for) ten thousand years]

baobab ('beɪəu,bæb) n a tree native to Africa and N Australia that has a very thick trunk, angular branches, and a gourdlike fruit with an edible pulp. [C17: prob. from a native African word]

Baoding ('bau'dɪŋ), **Paoting,** or **Pao-ting** ★ n a city in NE China, in N Hebei province. Pop.: 483 155 (1990 est.). Former name: **Tsingyuan** or **Ch'ing-yüan.**

BAOR abbrev. for British Army of the Rhine.

Baotou ('bau'tu:) or **Paotow** ★ n an industrial city in N China, in the central Inner Mongolia AR on the Yellow River. Pop.: 1 200 000 (1991 est.).

bap (bæp) n Brit. a large soft bread roll. [from ?]

baptism ('bæp,tɪzəm) n a Christian religious rite consisting of immersion in or sprinkling with water as a sign that the subject is cleansed from sin and constituted as a member of the Church.
▸ **bap'tismal** adj ▸ **bap'tismally** adv

baptism of fire n 1 a soldier's first experience of battle. 2 any initiating ordeal.

Baptist ('bæptɪst) n 1 a member of any of various Christian sects that affirm the necessity of baptism (usually of adults and by immersion). 2 **the Baptist.** John the Baptist, the cousin and forerunner of Jesus, whom he baptized. ◆ adj 3 denoting or characteristic of any Christian sect of Baptists.

baptistry or **baptistery** ('bæptɪstrɪ) n, pl **baptistries** or **baptisteries.** 1 a part of a Christian church in which baptisms are carried out. 2 a tank in a Baptist church in which baptisms are carried out.

baptize or **baptise** (bæp'taɪz) vb **baptizes, baptizing, baptized** or **baptises, baptising, baptised.** 1 Christianity. to immerse (a person) in water or sprinkle water on (a person) as part of the rite of baptism. 2 (tr) to give a name to; christen. [C13: from LL baptizāre, from Gk, from baptein to bathe, dip]

bar¹ (bɑː) n 1 a rigid usually straight length of metal, wood, etc., used esp. as a barrier or as a structural part: a bar of a gate. 2 a solid usually rectangular block of any material: a bar of soap. 3 anything that obstructs or prevents. 4 an offshore ridge of sand, mud, or shingle across the mouth of a river, bay, or harbour. 5 a counter or room where alcoholic drinks are served. 6 a counter, room, or establishment where a particular range of goods, food, services, etc., are sold: a coffee bar; a heel bar. 7 a narrow band or stripe, as of colour or light. 8 a heating element in an electric fire. 9 See **Bar.** 10 the place in a court of law where the accused stands during his trial. 11 a particular court of law. 12 Brit. (in Parliament) the boundary where nonmembers wishing to address either House appear and where persons are arraigned. 13 a plea showing that a plaintiff has no cause of action. 14 anything referred to as an authority or tribunal: the bar of decency. 15 Music. a group of beats that is repeated with a consistent rhythm throughout a piece of music. The number of beats in the bar is indicated by the time signature. Also called: **measure.** 16a Brit. insignia added to a decoration indicating a second award. 16b US. a strip of metal worn with uniform, esp. to signify rank or as an award for service. 17 Football, etc. See **crossbar.** 18 Gymnastics. See **horizontal bar.** 19 Heraldry. a narrow horizontal line across a shield. 20 **behind bars.** in prison. 21 **won't have a bar of.** Austral. & NZ inf. cannot tolerate; dislikes. ◆ vb **bars, barring, barred.** (tr) 22 to secure with a bar: to bar the door. 23 to shut in or out with or as if with barriers: to bar the entrances. 24 to obstruct: the fallen tree barred the road. 25 (usually foll. by from) to prohibit; forbid: to bar a couple from meeting. 26 (usually foll. by from) to keep out; exclude: to bar a person from membership. 27 to mark with a bar or bars. 28 Law. to prevent or halt (an action) by showing that the plaintiff has no cause. ◆ prep 29 except for. without exception. [C12: from OF barre, from Vulgar L barra (unattested) bar, rod, from ?]

bar² (bɑː) n a cgs unit of pressure equal to 10^6 dynes per square centimetre. [C20: from Gk baros weight]

Bar (bɑː) n the. 1 (in England and elsewhere) barristers collectively. 2 US. the legal profession collectively. 3 **be called to the Bar.** Brit. to become a barrister. 4 **be called within the Bar.** Brit. to be appointed as a Queen's Counsel.

bar. abbrev. for: 1 barometric. 2 barrel. 3 barrister.

Barabbas ★ (bə'ræbəs) n New Testament. a condemned robber who was released at the Passover instead of Jesus (Matthew 27:16).

Baranof Island ★ ('bærənəf) n an island off SE Alaska, in the western part of the Alexander Archipelago. Area: 4162 sq. km (1607 sq. miles).

barathea (,bærə'θɪə) n a fabric made of silk and wool or cotton and rayon. [C19: from ?]

barb¹ (bɑːb) n 1 a point facing in the opposite direction to the main point of a fish-hook, harpoon, etc., intended to make extraction difficult. 2 any of various pointed parts. 3 a cutting remark. 4 any of the hairlike filaments

that form the vane of a feather. **5** a beardlike growth, hair, or projection. ◆ vb **6** (tr) to provide with a barb or barbs. [C14: from OF *barbe* beard, point, from L *barba* beard]
► **barbed** adj

barb² (bɑːb) n a breed of horse of North African origin, similar to the Arab but less spirited. [C17: from F *barbe*, from It. *barbero* a Barbary (horse)]

Barbados ★ (bɑːˈbeɪdəʊs, -dəʊz, -dɒs) n an island in the Caribbean, in the E Lesser Antilles: a British colony from 1628 to 1966, now an independent state within the Commonwealth. Language: English. Currency: Barbados dollar. Capital: Bridgetown. Pop.: 265 000 (1997). Area: 430 sq. km (166 sq. miles).
► **Bar'badian** adj, n

barbarian (bɑːˈbɛərɪən) n **1** a member of a primitive or uncivilized people. **2** a coarse or uncultured person. **3** a vicious person. ◆ adj **4** of an uncivilized culture. **5** uncultured or brutal. [C16: see BARBAROUS]

barbaric (bɑːˈbærɪk) adj **1** of or characteristic of barbarians. **2** primitive; unrestrained. **3** brutal. [C15: from L *barbaricus* outlandish; see BARBAROUS]
► **bar'barically** adv

barbarism (ˈbɑːbəˌrɪzəm) n **1** a brutal, coarse, or ignorant act. **2** the condition of being backward, coarse, or ignorant. **3** a substandard word or expression; solecism. **4** any act or object that offends against accepted taste. [C16: from L *barbarismus* error of speech, from Gk *barbarismos*, from *barbaros* BARBAROUS]

barbarity (bɑːˈbærɪtɪ) n, pl **barbarities. 1** the state of being barbaric or barbarous. **2** a vicious act.

barbarize or **barbarise** (ˈbɑːbəˌraɪz) vb **barbarizes, barbarizing, barbarized** or **barbarises, barbarising, barbarised. 1** to make or become barbarous. **2** to use barbarisms in (language).
► **ˌbarbari'zation** or **ˌbarbari'sation** n

Barbarossa ★ (ˌbɑːbəˈrɒsə) n **1** the nickname of the Holy Roman Emperor **Frederick I.** See **Frederick Barbarossa. 2** real name *Khair ed-Din. c.* 1465–1546, Turkish pirate and admiral: conquered Tunis for the Ottomans (1534).

barbarous (ˈbɑːbərəs) adj **1** uncivilized; primitive. **2** brutal or cruel. **3** lacking refinement. [C15: via L from Gk *barbaros* barbarian, non-Greek, imit. of incomprehensible speech]
► **'barbarously** adv ► **'barbarousness** n

Barbary ★ (ˈbɑːbərɪ) n a region of N Africa, extending from W Egypt to the Atlantic and including the former **Barbary States** of Tripolitania, Tunisia, Algeria, and Morocco.

Barbary ape n a tailless macaque that inhabits NW Africa and Gibraltar.

Barbary Coast ★ n the. the Mediterranean coast of North Africa: a centre of piracy against European shipping from the 16th to the 19th centuries.

barbate (ˈbɑːbeɪt) adj Biol. having tufts of long hairs; bearded. [C19: from L *barba* a beard]

barbecue (ˈbɑːbɪˌkjuː) n **1** a meal cooked out of doors over an open fire. **2** a grill or fireplace used in barbecuing. **3** the food so cooked. **4** a party or picnic at which barbecued food is served. ◆ vb **barbecues, barbecuing, barbecued.** (tr) **5** to cook (meat, fish, etc.) on a grill, usually over charcoal and often with a highly seasoned sauce. [C17: from American Sp. *barbacoa:* frame made of sticks]

barbed wire n strong wire with sharply pointed barbs at close intervals.

barbel (ˈbɑːbᵊl) n **1** any of several slender tactile spines or bristles that hang from the jaws of certain fishes, such as the carp. **2** any of several cyprinid fishes that resemble the carp. [C14: from OF, from LL from L *barba* beard]

barbell (ˈbɑːˌbɛl) n a long metal rod to which heavy discs are attached at each end for weightlifting.

barber (ˈbɑːbə) n **1** a person whose business is cutting men's hair and shaving beards. ◆ vb (tr) **2** to cut the hair of. [C13: from OF *barbeor*, from *barbe* beard, from L *barba*]

Barber ★ (ˈbɑːbə) n **Samuel.** 1910–81, US composer: his

works include an *Adagio for Strings* and the opera *Vanessa* (1958).

barberry (ˈbɑːbərɪ) n, pl **barberries.** any spiny Asian shrub of the genus *Berberis,* having clusters of yellow flowers and orange or red berries. [C15: from OF *berberis,* from Ar. *barbāris*]

barbershop (ˈbɑːbəˌʃɒp) n **1** Now chiefly US. the premises of a barber. **2** (modifier) denoting a type of close four-part harmony for male voices: *a barbershop quartet.*

barber's pole n a barber's sign consisting of a pole painted with red-and-white spiral stripes.

barbican (ˈbɑːbɪkən) n **1** a walled outwork to protect a gate or drawbridge of a fortification. **2** a watchtower projecting from a fortification. [C13: from OF *barbacane* from Med. L, from ?]

Barbican ★ (ˈbɑːbɪkən) n the. a building complex in the City of London: includes residential developments and the Barbican Arts Centre (completed 1982) housing concert and exhibition halls, theatres, cinemas, etc.

barbicel (ˈbɑːbɪˌsɛl) n Ornithol. any of the minute hooks on the barbules of feathers that interlock with those on adjacent barbules. [C19: from NL *barbicella,* lit.: a small beard]

Barbirolli ★ (ˌbɑːbəˈrɒlɪ) n Sir **John.** 1899–1970, British conductor of the Hallé Orchestra (1943–68).

barbitone (ˈbɑːbɪˌtəʊn) or US **barbital** (ˈbɑːbɪˌtæl) n a long-acting barbiturate. [C20: from BARBIT(URIC ACID) + -ONE]

barbiturate (bɑːˈbɪtjʊrɪt, -ˌreɪt) n a derivative of barbituric acid, such as barbitone, used in medicine as a sedative or hypnotic.

barbituric acid (ˌbɑːbɪˈtjʊərɪk) n a white crystalline solid used in the preparation of barbiturate drugs. [C19: partial translation of G *Barbitursäure*]

Barbour jacket or **Barbour** (ˈbɑːbə) n Trademark. a hard-wearing waterproof waxed jacket.

Barbuda ★ (bɑːˈbuːdə) n a coral island in the E Caribbean, in the Leeward Islands: part of the independent state of Antigua and Barbuda. Area: 160 sq. km (62 sq. miles).

barbule (ˈbɑːbjuːl) n Ornithol. any of the minute hairs that project from a barb and in some feathers interlock. [C19: from L *barbula* a little beard]

Barbusse ★ (French barbys) n **Henri** (ɑ̃ri). 1873–1935, French novelist and poet. His novels include *L'Enfer* (1908) and *Le Feu* (1916).

barcarole or **barcarolle** (ˈbɑːkəˌrəʊl, -ˌrɒl; ˌbɑːkəˈrəʊl) n **1** a Venetian boat song. **2** an instrumental composition resembling this. [C18: from F, from It. *barcarola,* from *barcaruolo* boatman, from *barca* boat]

Barce (ˈbɑːtʃe) or **Barca** ★ (ˈbɑːka) n the Italian name for **Al Marj.**

Barcelona ★ (ˌbɑːsɪˈləʊnə) n the chief port of Spain, on the NE Mediterranean coast: seat of the Republican government during the Civil War (1936–39); the commercial capital of Spain. Pop.: 1 630 867 (1994 est.). Ancient name: **Barcino** (bɑːˈsiːnəʊ).

bar chart n another term for **bar graph.**

Barclay de Tolly ★ (ˈbɑːklɪ də ˈtɒlɪ; Russian barˈklai də ˈtɔlj) n Prince **Mikhail** (mixaˈil). 1761–1818, Russian field marshal: commander in chief against Napoleon in 1812.

bar code n Commerce. a machine-readable arrangement of numbers and parallel lines printed on a package, which can be electronically scanned at a checkout to register the price of the goods and to activate computer stock checking and reordering.

Barcoo River ★ (bɑːˈkuː) n a river in E Central Australia, in SW Queensland: joins with the Thomson River to form Cooper Creek.

bard¹ (bɑːd) n **1a** (formerly) one of an ancient Celtic order of poets. **1b** a poet who wins a verse competition at a Welsh eisteddfod. **2** Arch. or literary. any poet. [C14: from Scot. Gaelic]
► **'bardic** adj

bard² (bɑːd) n **1** a piece of bacon or pork fat placed on meat during roasting to prevent drying out. ◆ vb (tr) **2**

★ people and places

to place a bard on. [C15: from OF *barde*, from OIt. *barda*, from Ar. *barda'ah* packsaddle]

Bard ★ (baːd) *n* **the.** an epithet of (William) **Shakespeare.**

Bardeen ★ (,baː'diːn) *n* **John.** 1908–91, US physicist and electrical engineer, noted for his research on electrical conduction in solids; shared the Nobel prize for physics 1956 for the invention of the transistor and shared Nobel prize for physics 1972 for work on superconductivity.

bardie ('baːdɪ) *n* **1** an edible white wood-boring grub of Australia. **2 starve the bardies!** *Austral.* an exclamation of surprise or protest. [from Abor.]

Bardot ★ (*French* bardo) *n* **Brigitte** (briʒit). born 1934, French film actress.

bare[1] (beə) *adj* **1** unclothed: used esp. of a part of the body. **2** without the natural, conventional, or usual covering. **3** lacking appropriate furnishings, etc. **4** unembellished; simple: *the bare facts.* **5** (*prenominal*) just sufficient: *the bare minimum.* **6 with one's bare hands.** without a weapon or tool. ◆ *vb* **bares, baring, bared. 7** (*tr*) to make bare; uncover. [OE *bær*]
▶ **'bareness** *n*

bare[2] (beə) *vb Arch.* a past tense of **bear**[1].

bareback ('beə,bæk) *or* **barebacked** *adj, adv* (of horse-riding) without a saddle.

barefaced ('beə,feɪst) *adj* unconcealed or shameless: *a barefaced lie.*
▶ **barefacedly** ('beə,feɪsɪdlɪ) *adv* ▶ **'bare,facedness** *n*

barefoot ('beə,fʊt) *or* **barefooted** *adj, adv* **1** with the feet uncovered. ◆ *adj* **2** denoting a worker with basic training sent to help people in remote rural areas, esp. of developing countries: *barefoot doctor.*

bareheaded (,beə'hedɪd) *adj, adv* with the head uncovered.

Bareilly ★ (bə'reɪlɪ) *n* a city in N India, in N central Uttar Pradesh. Pop.: 587 211 (1991).

bare-knuckle *adj* **1** without boxing gloves: *a bare-knuckle fighter.* **2** aggressive; without civilized restraint: *a bare-knuckle confrontation.*

barely ('beəlɪ) *adv* **1** only just: *barely enough.* **2** *Inf.* not quite: *barely old enough.* **3** scantily: *barely furnished.* **4** *Arch.* openly.

USAGE NOTE See at **hardly.**

Barenboim ★ ('bærən,bɔɪm) *n* **Daniel.** born 1942, Israeli concert pianist and conductor, born in Argentina.

Barents Sea ★ ('bærənts) *n* a part of the Arctic Ocean, bounded by Norway, Russia, and the islands of Novaya Zemlya, Spitsbergen, and Franz Josef Land. [after Willem *Barents* (1550–97), Dutch navigator and explorer who discovered it in 1596]

barf (baːf) *vb* (*intr*) *Sl.* to vomit. [C20: prob. imit.]

bargain ('baːgɪn) *n* **1** an agreement establishing what each party will give, receive, or perform in a transaction. **2** something acquired or received in such an agreement. **3a** something bought or offered at a low price. **3b** (*as modifier*): *a bargain price.* **4 into the bargain.** in excess; besides. **5 make** *or* **strike a bargain.** to agree on terms. ◆ *vb* **6** (*intr*) to negotiate the terms of an agreement, transaction, etc. **7** (*tr*) to exchange, as in a bargain. **8** to arrive at (an agreement or settlement). [C14: from OF *bargaigne*, from *bargaignier* to trade, of Gmc origin]
▶ **'bargainer** *n*

bargain away *vb* (*tr, adv*) to lose (rights, etc.) in return for something valueless.

bargain for *vb* (*intr, prep*) to expect; anticipate: *he got more than he bargained for.*

bargain on *vb* (*intr, prep*) to rely or depend on (something): *he bargained on her support.*

barge (baːdʒ) *n* **1** a vessel, usually flat-bottomed and with or without its own power, used for transporting freight, esp. on canals. **2** a vessel, often decorated, used in pageants, etc. **3** *Navy.* a boat allocated to a flag officer, used esp. for ceremonial occasions. ◆ *vb* **barges, barging,**

barged. **4** (*intr;* foll. by *into*) *Inf.* to bump (into). **5** *Inf.* to push (someone or one's way) violently. **6** (*intr;* foll. by *into* or *in*) *Inf.* to interrupt rudely or clumsily: *to barge into a conversation.* [C13: from OF, from Med. L *barga*, prob. from LL *barca* a small boat]

bargeboard ('baːdʒ,bɔːd) *n* a board, often decorated, along the gable end of a roof.

bargee (baː'dʒiː) *n* a person employed on or in charge of a barge.

bargepole ('baːdʒ,pəʊl) *n* **1** a long pole used to propel a barge. **2 not touch with a bargepole.** *Inf.* to refuse to have anything to do with.

bar graph *n* a graph consisting of vertical or horizontal bars whose lengths are proportional to amounts or quantities.

Bari ★ ('baːrɪ; *Italian* 'baːri) *n* a port in SE Italy, capital of Apulia, on the Adriatic coast. Pop.: 338 949 (1994 est.).

bariatrics (,bærɪ'ætrɪks) *n* (*functioning as sing*) the branch of medicine concerned with the treatment of obese people. [C20: from Gk *baros* weight + -IATRICS]

Baring ★ ('beərɪŋ) *n* **Evelyn,** 1st Earl of Cromer. 1841–1917, British administrator. As consul general he controlled the Egyptian government (1883–1907).

barite ('beəraɪt) *n* the usual US and Canad. name for **barytes.** [C18: from BAR(IUM) + -ITE[1]]

baritone ('bærɪ,təʊn) *n* **1** the second lowest adult male voice. **2** a singer with such a voice. **3** the second lowest instrument in the families of the saxophone, horn, oboe, etc. ◆ *adj* **4** relating to or denoting a baritone. [C17: from It., from Gk, from *barus* heavy, low + *tonos* TONE]

barium ('beərɪəm) *n* a soft silvery-white metallic element of the alkaline earth group. Symbol: Ba; atomic no.: 56; atomic wt.: 137.34. [C19: from BAR(YTA) + -IUM]

barium meal *n* a preparation of barium sulphate, which is opaque to X-rays, swallowed by a patient before X-ray examination of the upper part of his or her alimentary canal.

bark[1] (baːk) *n* **1** the loud abrupt usually harsh cry of a dog or certain other animals. **2** a similar sound, such as one made by a person, gun, etc. **3 his bark is worse than his bite.** he is bad-tempered but harmless. ◆ *vb* **4** (*intr*) (of a dog, etc.) to make its typical cry. **5** (*intr*) (of a person, gun, etc.) to make a similar loud harsh sound. **6** to say or shout in a brusque or angry tone: *he barked an order.* **7 bark up the wrong tree.** *Inf.* to misdirect one's attention, efforts, etc.; be mistaken. [OE *beorcan*]

bark[2] (baːk) *n* **1** a protective layer of dead corky cells on the outside of the stems of woody plants. **2** any of several varieties of this, used in tanning, dyeing, or in medicine. ◆ *vb* (*tr*) **3** to scrape or rub off skin, as in an injury. **4** to remove the bark or a circle of bark from (a tree). **5** to tan (leather), principally by the tannins in barks. [C13: from ON *börkr*]

bark[3] (baːk) *n* a variant spelling of **barque.**

barkentine ('baːkən,tiːn) *n* the usual US and Canad. spelling of **barquentine.**

barker ('baːkə) *n* **1** an animal or person that barks. **2** a person at a fair booth, etc., who loudly addresses passers-by to attract customers.

Barker ★ ('baːkə) *n* **1 George (Granville).** 1913–91, British poet: author of *Calamiterror* (1937). **2 Howard.** born 1946, British playwright: his plays include *The Castle* (1985) and *A Hard Heart* (1992). **3 Ronnie,** full name *Ronald William George Barker.* born 1929, British comedian: known for his partnership with Ronnie Corbett (born 1930).

barking ('baːkɪŋ) *Sl.* ◆ *adj* **1** mad; crazy. ◆ *adv* **2** (intensifier): *barking mad.*

Barking and Dagenham ★ ('baːkɪŋ, 'dægənəm) *n* a borough of E Greater London. Pop.: 143 180 (1991). Area: 34 sq. km (13 sq. miles).

Bar Kochba *or* **Bar Kosba** ★ (baː 'kɒxbə, 'kɒs-) *n* **Simeon.** died 135 AD. Jewish leader who led an unsuccessful revolt against the Romans in Palestine.

Barletta ★ (*Italian* bar'letta) *n* a port in SE Italy, in Apulia. Pop.: 88 750 (1990).

barley ('bɑːlɪ) *n* **1** any of various annual temperate grasses that have dense bristly flower spikes and are widely cultivated for grain and forage. **2** the grain of any of these grasses, used in making beer and whisky and for soups, puddings, etc. [OE *bærlīc* (adj); rel. to *bere* barley]

barleycorn ('bɑːlɪ,kɔːn) *n* **1** a grain of barley, or barley itself. **2** an obsolete unit of length equal to one third of an inch.

barley sugar *n* a brittle clear amber-coloured sweet.

barley water *n* a drink made from an infusion of barley.

barm (bɑːm) *n* **1** the yeasty froth on fermenting malt liquors. **2** an archaic or dialect word for **yeast**. [OE *bearm*]

barmaid ('bɑː,meɪd) *n* a woman who serves in a pub.

barman ('bɑːmən) *n*, *pl* **barmen**. a man who serves in a pub.

Barmecide ('bɑːmɪ,saɪd) *adj* lavish in imagination only; illusory; sham: *a Barmecide feast*. [C18: from a prince in the *Arabian Nights' Entertainment* who served empty plates to beggars, alleging that they held sumptuous food]

Bar Mitzvah (bɑː 'mɪtsvə) (*sometimes not caps.*) *Judaism.* ◆ *adj* **1** (of a Jewish boy) having assumed full religious obligations, being at least thirteen years old. ◆ *n* **2** the occasion or celebration of this. **3** the boy himself. [Heb.: son of the law]

barmy ('bɑːmɪ) *adj* **barmier, barmiest.** *Sl.* insane. [C16: orig., full of BARM, hence frothing, excited]

barn[1] (bɑːn) *n* **1** a large farm outbuilding, chiefly for storing grain, etc., but also for livestock. **2** *US & Canad.* a large shed for railroad cars, trucks, etc. **3** any large building, esp. an unattractive one. **4** (*modifier*) relating to a system of poultry farming in which birds are allowed to move freely within a barn: *barn eggs*. [OE *beren*, from *bere* barley + *ærn* room]

barn[2] (bɑːn) *n* a unit of nuclear cross section equal to 10^{-28} square metres. Symbol: b [C20: from BARN[1]; so called because of the relatively large cross section]

Barnabas ★ ('bɑːnəbəs) *n* **Saint.** *New Testament.* original name *Joseph.* a Cypriot Levite who supported Saint Paul in his apostolic work (Acts 4:36,37). Feast day: June 11.

barnacle ('bɑːnəkʰl) *n* **1** any of various marine crustaceans that, as adults, live attached to rocks, ship bottoms, etc. **2** a person or thing that is difficult to get rid of. [C16: from earlier *bernak*, from OF *bernac*, from LL, from ?]
▸ **'barnacled** *adj*

barnacle goose *n* a N European goose that has a black-and-white head and body. [C13 *bernekke*: it was formerly believed that the goose developed from a shellfish]

Barnard ★ ('bɑːnɑːd) *n* **1 Christiaan (Neethling).** born 1923, South African surgeon, who performed the first human heart transplant (1967). **2 Edward Emerson.** 1857–1923, US astronomer: noted for his discovery of the fifth satellite of Jupiter.

Barnardo ★ (bəˈnɑːdəʊ, bɑː-) *n* **Dr Thomas John.** 1845–1905, British philanthropist, who founded homes for destitute children.

Barnaul ★ (*Russian* bərnaˈul) *n* a city in S Russia, on the River Ob. Pop.: 596 000 (1995 est.).

barn dance *n* **1** *Brit.* a progressive round country dance. **2** *Brit.* a disco or party held in a barn. **3** *US & Canad.* a party with hoedown music and square-dancing.

Barnet ★ ('bɑːnɪt) *n* a borough of N Greater London: scene of a Yorkist victory (1471) in the Wars of the Roses. Pop.: 292 783 (1991). Area: 89 sq. km (34 sq. miles).

barney ('bɑːnɪ) *Inf.* ◆ *n* **1** a noisy fight or argument. ◆ *vb* **2** (*intr*) *Chiefly Austral. & NZ.* to argue or quarrel. [C19: from ?]

barn owl *n* an owl with a pale brown and white plumage and a heart-shaped face.

Barnsley ★ ('bɑːnzlɪ) *n* **1** an industrial town in N England, in South Yorkshire. Pop.: 75 120 (1991). **2** a uni-

tary authority in N England, in South Yorkshire. Pop.: 224 800 (1992 est.). Area: 329 sq. km (127 sq. miles).

Barnstaple ★ ('bɑːnstəpʰl) *n* a town in SW England, in Devon, on the estuary of the River Taw: tourism, agriculture. Pop.: 27 691 (1991).

barnstorm ('bɑːn,stɔːm) *vb* (*intr*) **1** to tour rural districts putting on shows. **2** *Chiefly US & Canad.* to tour rural districts making speeches in a political campaign.
▸ **'barn,storming** *n*, *adj*

Barnum ★ ('bɑːnəm) *n* **P(hineas) T(aylor).** 1810–91, US showman, who with J. A. Bailey founded the Barnum and Bailey Circus (1881).

barnyard ('bɑːn,jɑːd) *n* **1** a yard adjoining a barn. **2** (*modifier*) characteristic of a barnyard. **3** (*modifier*) crude or earthy.

baro- *combining form.* indicating weight or pressure: *barometer*. [from Gk *baros* weight]

baroceptor ('bærəʊ,septə) *n* another name for **baroreceptor**.

Baroda ★ (bəˈrəʊdə) *n* **1** a former state of W India, part of Gujarat since 1960. **2** the former name (until 1976) of **Vadodara.**

barogram ('bærə,græm) *n Meteorol.* the record of atmospheric pressure traced by a barograph or similar instrument.

barograph ('bærə,grɑːf) *n Meteorol.* a self-recording aneroid barometer.
▸ **barographic** (,bærəˈgræfɪk) *adj*

Baroja ★ (*Spanish* baˈroxa) *n* **Pio** ('pio). 1872–1956, Spanish Basque novelist, who wrote nearly 100 novels.

barometer (bəˈrɒmɪtə) *n* **1** an instrument for measuring atmospheric pressure, usually to determine altitude or weather changes. **2** anything that shows change.
▸ **barometric** (,bærəˈmetrɪk) *or* ,**baro'metrical** *adj* ▸ ba'**rometry** *n*

baron ('bærən) *n* **1** a member of a specific rank of nobility, esp. the lowest rank in the British Isles. **2** (in Europe from the Middle Ages) originally any tenant-in-chief of a king or other overlord. **3** a powerful businessman or financier: *a press baron*. [C12: from OF, of Gmc origin]

baronage ('bærənɪdʒ) *n* **1** barons collectively. **2** the rank or dignity of a baron.

baroness ('bærənɪs) *n* **1** the wife or widow of a baron. **2** a woman holding the rank of baron.

baronet ('bærənɪt, -,net) *n* (in Britain) a commoner who holds the lowest hereditary title of honour, ranking below a baron. Abbrev.: **Bart, Bt.**
▸ **'baronetage** *n* ▸ **'baronetcy** *n*

baronial (bəˈrəʊnɪəl) *adj* of, relating to, or befitting a baron or barons.

baron of beef *n* a cut of beef consisting of a double sirloin joined at the backbone.

barony ('bærənɪ) *n*, *pl* **baronies. 1a** the domain of a baron. **1b** (in Ireland) a division of a county. **1c** (in Scotland) a large estate or manor. **2** the rank or dignity of a baron.

baroque (bəˈrɒk, bəˈrəʊk) *n* (*often cap.*) **1** a style of architecture and decorative art in Europe from the late 16th to the early 18th century, characterized by extensive ornamentation. **2** a 17th-century style of music characterized by extensive use of ornamentation. **3** any ornate or heavily ornamented style. ◆ *adj* **4** denoting, in, or relating to the baroque. **5** (of pearls) irregularly shaped. [C18: from F, from Port. *barroco* a rough or imperfectly shaped pearl]

baroreceptor ('bærəʊrɪ,septə) *or* **baroceptor** *n* a collection of sensory nerve endings, principally in the carotid sinuses and the aortic arch, that monitor blood-pressure changes in the body.

baroscope ('bærə,skəʊp) *n* any instrument for measuring atmospheric pressure.
▸ **baroscopic** (,bærəˈskɒpɪk) *adj*

barouche (bəˈruːʃ) *n* a four-wheeled horse-drawn carriage, popular in the 19th century, having a retractable hood over the rear half. [C19: from G (dialect) *Barutsche*, from It. *baroccio*, from LL *birotus*, from BI- + *rota* wheel]

Barozzi ★ (*Italian* ba'rottsi) *n* See (Giacomo Barozzi da) **Vignola**.

barperson ('bɑː,pɜːs°n) *n*, *pl* **barpersons**. a person who serves in a pub: used esp. in advertisements.

barque (bɑːk) *n* **1** a sailing ship of three or more masts having the foremasts rigged square and the aftermast rigged fore-and-aft. **2** *Poetic*. any boat. [C15: from OF, from OProvençal *barca*]

barquentine or **barquantine** ('bɑːkən,tiːn) *n* a sailing ship of three or more masts rigged square on the foremast and fore-and-aft on the others. [C17: from BARQUE + (BRIG)ANTINE]

Barquisimeto ★ (*Spanish* barkisi'meto) *n* a city in NW Venezuela. Pop.: 625 450 (1990).

Barra ★ ('bærə) *n* an island in NW Scotland, in the Outer Hebrides: fishing, crofting, tourism. Pop.: 1200 (latest est.).

barrack[1] ('bærək) *vb* to house (soldiers, etc.) in barracks.

barrack[2] ('bærək) *vb Brit., Austral., & NZ inf.* **1** to criticize loudly or shout against (a team, speaker, etc.); jeer. **2** (*intr;* foll. by *for*) to shout support (for). [C19: from Irish: to boast]

barrack-room lawyer *n* a person who freely offers opinions, esp. in legal matters, that he is unqualified to give.

barracks ('bærəks) *pl n* (*sometimes sing; when pl, sometimes functions as sing*) **1** a building or group of buildings used to accommodate military personnel. **2** any large building used for housing people, esp. temporarily. **3** a large and bleak building. [C17: from F *baraque*, from OCatalan *barraca* hut, from ?]

barracouta (,bærə'kuːtə) *n* a large predatory Pacific fish. [C17: var. of BARRACUDA]

barracuda (,bærə'kjuːdə) *n*, *pl* **barracuda** or **barracudas**. a predatory marine mostly tropical fish, which attacks man. [C17: from American Sp., from ?]

barrage ('bærɑːʒ) *n* **1** *Mil*. the firing of artillery to saturate an area, either to protect against an attack or to support an advance. **2** an overwhelming and continuous delivery of something, as questions. **3** a construction across a watercourse, esp. one to increase the depth. [C19: from F, from *barrer* to obstruct; see BAR[1]]

barrage balloon *n* one of a number of tethered balloons with cables or net suspended from them, used to deter low-flying air attack.

barramundi (,bærə'mʌndɪ) *n*, *pl* **barramundis, barramundies, barramundi**. a large edible Australian estuary fish of the perch family. [from Abor.]

Barranquilla ★ (*Spanish* barran'kiʎa) *n* a port in N Colombia, on the Magdalena River. Pop.: 1 064 255 (1995 est.).

barratry or **barretry** ('bærətrɪ) *n* **1** *Criminal law*. (formerly) the vexatious stirring up of quarrels or bringing of lawsuits. **2** *Maritime law*. a fraudulent practice committed by the master or crew of a ship to the prejudice of the owner. **3** the purchase or sale of public or Church offices. [C15: from OF *baraterie* deception, from *barater* to BARTER] ▸ **'barratrous** or **'barretrous** *adj* ▸ **'barrator** *n*

Barrault ★ (*French* baro) *n* **Jean-Louis** (ʒɑ̃lwi). 1910–94, French actor and director, noted as a mime.

barre *French*. (bar) *n* a rail at hip height used for ballet practice and leg exercises. [lit.: bar]

barrel ('bærəl) *n* **1** a cylindrical container usually bulging outwards in the middle and held together by metal hoops. **2** Also called: **barrelful**. the amount that a barrel can hold. **3** a unit of capacity of varying amount in different industries. **4** a thing shaped like a barrel, esp. a tubular part of a machine. **5** the tube through which the projectile of a firearm is discharged. **6** the trunk of a four-legged animal: *the barrel of a horse*. **7 over a barrel**. *Inf*. powerless. **8 scrape the barrel**. *Inf*. to be forced to use one's last and weakest resource. ◆ *vb* **barrels, barrelling, barrelled** or *US* **barrels, barreling, barreled**. **9** (*tr*) to put into a barrel or barrels. [C14: from OF *baril*, ?from *barre* BAR[1]]

barrel-chested *adj* having a large rounded chest.

barrel organ *n* an instrument consisting of a cylinder turned by a handle and having pins on it that interrupt

the air flow to certain pipes or pluck strings, thereby playing tunes.

barrel roll *n* a flight manoeuvre in which an aircraft rolls about its longitudinal axis while following a spiral course in line with the direction of flight.

barrel vault *n Archit*. a vault in the form of a half cylinder.

barren ('bærən) *adj* **1** incapable of producing offspring, seed, or fruit; sterile. **2** unable to support the growth of crops, etc.: *barren land*. **3** lacking in stimulation; dull. **4** not producing worthwhile results; unprofitable: *a barren period*. **5** (foll. by *of*) devoid (of): *barren of wit*. **6** (of rock strata) having no fossils. [C13: from OF *brahain*, from ?] ▸ **'barrenness** *n*

Barren Lands ★ *pl n* **the**. a sparsely inhabited region of tundras in N Canada, extending westwards from Hudson Bay. Also called: **Barren Grounds**.

barricade (,bærɪ'keɪd, 'bærɪ,keɪd) *n* **1** a barrier for defence, esp. one erected hastily, as during street fighting. ◆ *vb* **barricades, barricading, barricaded**. (*tr*) **2** to erect a barricade across (an entrance, etc.) or at points of access to (a room, district, etc.). [C17: from OF, from *barriquer* to barricade, from *barrique* a barrel, from Sp. *barrica*, from *barril* BARREL]

Barrie ★ ('bærɪ) *n* Sir **James Matthew**. 1860–1937, Scottish writer, noted for his plays *The Admirable Crichton* (1902) and *Peter Pan* (1904).

barrier ('bærɪə) *n* **1** anything serving to obstruct passage or to maintain separation, such as a fence or gate. **2** anything that prevents progress. **3** anything that separates or hinders union: *a language barrier*. [C14: from OF *barriere*, from *barre* BAR[1]]

barrier cream *n* a cream used to protect the skin, esp. the hands.

barrier-nurse *vb* (*tr*) to tend (infectious patients) in isolation, to prevent the spread of infection. ▸ **barrier nursing** *n*

barrier reef *n* a long narrow coral reef near the shore, separated from it by deep water.

barring ('bɑːrɪŋ) *prep* unless (something) occurs; except for.

barrister ('bærɪstə) *n* **1** Also called: **barrister-at-law**. (in England) a lawyer who has been called to the bar and is qualified to plead in the higher courts. Cf. **solicitor**. **2** (in Canada) a lawyer who pleads in court **3** *US*. a less common word for **lawyer**. [C16: from BAR[1]]

barrow[1] ('bærəʊ) *n* **1** See **wheelbarrow, handbarrow**. **2** Also called: **barrowful**. the amount contained in or on a barrow. **3** *Chiefly Brit*. a handcart with a canvas roof, used esp. by street vendors. [OE *bearwe*]

barrow[2] ('bærəʊ) *n* a heap of earth placed over one or more prehistoric tombs, often surrounded by ditches. [OE *beorg*]

Barrow ★ ('bærəʊ) *n* **1** a river in SE Ireland, rising in the Slieve Bloom Mountains and flowing south to Waterford Harbour. Length: about 193 km (120 miles). **2** See **Barrow-in-Furness** and **Barrow Point**.

barrow boy *n Brit*. a man who sells his wares from a barrow; street vendor.

Barrow-in-Furness ★ *n* an industrial town in NW England, in S Cumbria. Pop.: 48 947 (1991).

Barrow Point ★ *n* the northernmost tip of Alaska, on the Arctic Ocean.

Barry[1] ★ ('bærɪ) *n* a port in SE Wales, on the Bristol Channel. Pop.: 49 887 (1991).

Barry[2] ★ ('bærɪ) *n* **1** Sir **Charles**. 1795–1860, British architect: designer, assisted by Pugin, of the Houses of Parliament in London. **2** (*French* bari). **Comtesse du**. See **du Barry**.

Barrymore ★ ('bærɪ,mɔː) *n* a US family of actors, esp. **Ethel** (1879–1959), **John** (1882–1942), and **Lionel** (1878–1954).

Barry Mountains ★ *pl n* a mountain range in SE Australia, in E Victoria: part of the Australian Alps.

bar sinister *n* **1** (not in heraldic usage) another name for **bend sinister**. **2** the condition or stigma of being of illegitimate birth.

Bart ★ (bɑːt) *n* **Lionel.** 1930–99, British composer and playwright. His musicals include *Oliver* (1960).

Bart. *abbrev. for* Baronet.

bartender ('bɑː,tendə) *n* another name (esp. US and Canad.) for **barman** or **barmaid.**

barter ('bɑːtə) *vb* **1** to trade (goods, services, etc.) in exchange for other goods, services, etc., rather than for money. **2** (*intr*) to haggle over such an exchange; bargain. ◆ *n* **3** trade by the exchange of goods. [C15: from OF *barater* to cheat]

Barth ★ *n* **1** (*German* bart). **Heinrich.** ('haɪnrɪç). 1821–65, German explorer: author of *Travels and Discoveries in North and Central Africa* (1857–58). **2** (bɑːθ). **John** (**Simmons**). born 1930, US novelist; his novels include *Giles Goat-Boy* (1966) and *Once Upon a Time* (1994). **3** (*German* bart). **Karl** (karl). 1886–1968, Swiss Protestant theologian.
  ▸ **Barthian** ('bɑːtɪən, -θɪən) *adj, n*

Barthes ★ (*French* bart) *n* **Roland** (rɔlɑ̃). 1915–80, French writer and critic, who applied structuralist theory to literature: his books include *Mythologies* (1957) and *Elements of Semiology* (1964).

Bartholdi ★ (*French* bartɔldi) *n* **Frédéric August** (frederik ogyst). 1834–1904, French sculptor and architect, who designed (1884) the Statue of Liberty.

Bartholomew ★ (bɑː'θɒlə,mjuː) *n* **Saint.** *New Testament.* one of the twelve apostles (Matthew 10:3). Feast day: Aug. 24 or June 11.

bartizan ('bɑːtɪzən, ,bɑːtɪ'zæn) *n* a small turret projecting from a wall, parapet, or tower. [C19: var. of *bertisene*, erroneously for *bretising*, from *bretasce* parapet; see BRATTICE]
  ▸ **bartizaned** ('bɑːtɪzənd, ,bɑːtɪ'zænd) *adj*

Bartók ★ ('bɑːtɒk; *Hungarian* 'bɔrtoːk) *n* **Béla** ('beːlɔ). 1881–1945, Hungarian composer and pianist. His works include six string quartets, three piano concertos, ballets (including *The Miraculous Mandarin*, 1919), and the opera *Bluebeard's Castle* (produced 1918).

Bartolommeo ★ (*Italian* bartolom'meo) *n* **Fra.** original name *Baccio della Porta.* 1472–1517, Italian painter.

Barton ★ ('bɑːtⁿn) *n* **1** Sir **Derek** (**Harold Richard**). 1918–98, British chemist: shared the Nobel prize for chemistry (1969) for his work on conformational analysis. **2** Sir **Edmund.** 1849–1920, Australian statesman; first prime minister of Australia (1901–03). **3** Elizabeth, known as the *Maid of Kent.* ?1506–34, English nun; executed for criticizing Henry VIII's attempt to annul his first marriage.

Baruch ★ ('bɛəruk, 'bɑː-) *n* **Bible.** **a** a disciple of Jeremiah (Jeremiah 32–36). **b** the book of the Apocrypha said to have been written by him.

baryon ('bærɪ,ɒn) *n* any of a class of elementary particles that have a mass greater than or equal to that of the proton. Baryons are either nucleons or hyperons. The **baryon number** is the number of baryons in a system minus the number of antibaryons. [C20: from Gk *barus* heavy + -ON]
  ▸ ,bary'onic *adj*

Baryshnikov ★ (bə'rɪʃnɪ,kɒf) *n* **Mikhail** (mɪ'kaɪ⁸l). born 1948, Soviet-born ballet dancer, who defected (1974) to the West while on tour with the Kirov Ballet: director (1980–90) of the American Ballet Theatre.

baryta (bə'raɪtə) *n* another name for barium oxide or barium hydroxide. [C19: NL, from Gk *barutēs* weight, from *barus* heavy]

barytes (bə'raɪtiːz) *n* a colourless or white mineral occurring in sedimentary rocks and with sulphide ores: a source of barium. [C18: from Gk *barus* heavy + -*itēs* -ITE¹]

basal ('beɪs⁸l) *adj* **1** at, of, or constituting a base. **2** of or constituting a basis; fundamental.

basal metabolism *n* the amount of energy required by an individual in the resting state, for such functions as breathing and blood circulation.

basalt ('bæsɔːlt) *n* **1** a dark basic igneous rock: the most common volcanic rock. **2** a form of black unglazed pottery resembling basalt. [C18: from LL *basaltēs*, var. of *basanitēs*, from Gk *basanitēs* touchstone]
  ▸ ba'saltic *adj*

bascule ('bæskjuːl) *n* **1** a bridge with a movable section hinged about a horizontal axis and counterbalanced by a weight. **2** a movable roadway forming part of such a bridge. [C17: from F: seesaw, from *bas* low + *cul* rump]

base¹ (beɪs) *n* **1** the bottom or supporting part of any thing. **2** the fundamental principle or part. **3a** a centre of operations, organization, or supply. **3b** (*as modifier*): *base camp.* **4** starting point: *the new discovery became the base for further research.* **5** the main ingredient of a mixture: *to use rice as a base in cookery.* **6** a chemical compound that combines with an acid to form a salt and water. A solution of a base in water turns litmus paper blue and produces hydroxyl ions. **7** a medium such as oil or water in which the pigment is dispersed in paints, inks, etc. **8** *Biol.* the point of attachment of an organ or part. **9** the bottommost layer or part of anything. **10** *Archit.* the part of a column between the pedestal and the shaft. **11** the lower side or face of a geometric construction. **12** *Maths.* the number of units in a counting system that is equivalent to one in the next higher counting place: *10 is the base of the decimal system.* **13** *Maths.* the number that when raised to a certain power has a logarithm (based on that number) equal to that power: *the logarithm to the base 10 of 1000 is 3.* **14** *Linguistics.* a root or stem. **15** *Electronics.* the region in a transistor between the emitter and collector. **16** a starting or finishing point in any of various games. ◆ *vb* **bases, basing, based. 17** (*tr;* foll. by *on* or *upon*) to use as a basis (for); found (on). **18** (often foll. by *at* or *in*) to station, post, or place (a person or oneself). [C14: from OF, from L *basis* pedestal; see BASIS]

base² (beɪs) *adj* **1** devoid of honour or morality; contemptible. **2** of inferior quality or value. **3** debased; alloyed; counterfeit: *base currency.* **4** *English history.* (of land tenure) held by villein or other ignoble service. **5** *Arch.* born of humble parents. **6** *Arch.* illegitimate. [C14: from OF *bas*, from LL *bassus* of low height]
  ▸ 'baseness *n*

baseball ('beɪs,bɔːl) *n* **1** a team game with nine players on each side, played on a field with four bases connected to form a diamond. The object is to score runs by batting the ball and running round the bases. **2** the hard raw-hide-covered ball used in this game.

baseball cap *n* a close-fitting thin cap with a deep peak.

baseborn ('beɪs,bɔːn) *adj Arch.* **1** born of humble parents. **2** illegitimate.

base hospital *n Austral.* a hospital serving a large rural area.

Basel ('bɑːz⁸l) *or* **Basle** ★ (bɑːl) *n* **1** a canton of NW Switzerland, divided into the demicantons of **Basel-Land** and **Basel-Stadt.** Pops.: 251 229 and 197 054 (1995 est.). Areas: 427 sq. km (165 sq. miles) and 36 sq. km (14 sq. miles) respectively. **2** a city in NW Switzerland, capital of Basel canton, on the Rhine: oldest university in Switzerland. Pop.: 175 561 (1995 est.). French name: **Bâle.**

baseless ('beɪslɪs) *adj* not based on fact; unfounded.
  ▸ 'baselessness *n*

baseline ('beɪs,laɪn) *n* **1** *Surveying.* a measured line through a survey area from which triangulations are made. **2** a line at each end of a tennis court that marks the limit of play.

basement ('beɪsmənt) *n* **1a** a partly or wholly underground storey of a building, esp. one used for habitation rather than storage. **1b** (*as modifier*): *a basement flat.* **2** the foundation of a wall or building.

base metal *n* any of certain common metals, such as copper and lead, as distinct from precious metals.

basenji (bə'sendʒɪ) *n* a small African breed of dog that is unable to bark. [C20: from Bantu]

base rate *n* **1** *Brit.* the rate of interest used by individual commercial banks as a basis for their lending rates. **2** *Brit. inf.* the rate at which the Bank of England lends to the discount houses, which effectively controls the interest rates charged throughout the banking system. **3** *Statistics.* the average number of times an event occurs divided by the average number of times on which it might occur.

bases¹ ('beɪsiːz) *n* the plural of **basis.**

bases² ('beɪsɪz) *n* the plural of **base.**

★ people and places

ase unit *n Physics.* any of the fundamental units in a system of measurement. The base SI units are the metre, kilogram, second, ampere, kelvin, candela, and mole.

ash (bæʃ) *Inf.* ◆ *vb* **1** (*tr*) to strike violently or crushingly. **2** (*tr; often foll. by* *in, down,* etc.) to smash, break, etc., with a crashing blow. **3** (*intr; foll. by* *into*) to crash (into); collide (with). **4** to dent or be dented. ◆ *n* **5** a heavy blow. **6** a party. **7 have a bash.** *Inf.* to make an attempt. [C17: from ?]

ashful ('bæʃful) *adj* **1** shy or modest; diffident. **2** indicating or characterized by shyness or modesty. [C16: from *bash,* short for ABASH + -FUL]
▶ 'bashfully *adv* ▶ 'bashfulness *n*

bashing *n and adj combining form.* **a** indicating a malicious attack on members of a particular group: *union-bashing.* **b** indicating any of various other activities: *Bible-bashing.*
▶ -**basher** *n combining form.*

Bashkir Republic ★ (bæʃˈkɪə) *n* a constituent republic of E central Russia, in the S Urals: established as the first Soviet autonomous republic in 1919; rich mineral resources. Capital: Ufa. Pop.: 4 080 000 (1995 est.). Area: 143 600 sq. km (55 430 sq. miles). Also called: **Bashkiria** (bæʃˈkɪərɪə), **Bashkortostan** (bæʃˈkɔːtɔːˌstɑːn; *Russian* baʃkortɔˈstaːn).

basho ('bæʃəʊ) *n, pl* **basho.** a grand tournament in sumo wrestling. [C20: from Japanese, lit.: place]

Basho ★ (bɑːˈʃɔ) *n* full name **Matsuo Basho,** originally *Matsuo Munefusa.* 1644–94, Japanese poet and travel writer.

asic ('beɪsɪk) *adj* **1** of, relating to, or forming a base or basis; fundamental. **2** elementary or simple: *a few basic facts.* **3** excluding additions or extras: *basic pay.* **4** *Chem.* of, denoting, or containing a base; alkaline. **5** *Metallurgy.* of or made by a process in which the furnace or converter is made of a basic material, such as magnesium oxide. **6** (of such igneous rocks as basalt) containing between 52 and 45 per cent silica. ◆ *n* **7** (*usually pl*) a fundamental principle, fact, etc.
▶ 'basically *adv*

BASIC *or* **Basic** ('beɪsɪk) *n* a computer programming language that uses common English terms. [C20: *b*(eginner's) *a*(ll-purpose) *s*(ymbolic) *i*(nstruction) *c*(ode)]

Basic Curriculum *n Brit. education.* the National Curriculum plus religious education.

asic English *n* a simplified form of English with a vocabulary of approximately 850 common words, intended as an international language.

basic industry *n* an industry which is highly important in a nation's economy.

basicity (beɪˈsɪsɪtɪ) *n Chem.* **a** the state of being a base. **b** the number of molecules of acid required to neutralize one molecule of a given base.

basic slag *n* a slag produced in steel-making, containing calcium phosphate.

basic wage *n* **1** a person's wage excluding overtime, bonuses, etc. **2** *Austral.* the statutory minimum wage for any worker.

oasidiomycete (bæˌsɪdɪəʊmaɪˈsiːt) *n* any of a class of fungi, including puffballs and rusts, which produce spores at the tips of slender projecting stalks. [C19: see BASIS, -MYCETE]
▶ ba,sidiomy'cetous *adj*

Basie ★ ('beɪsɪ) *n* **William,** known as *Count Basie.* 1904–84, US jazz pianist, bandleader, and composer.

basil ('bæzˀl) *n* a Eurasian plant having spikes of small white flowers and aromatic leaves used as herbs for seasoning. Also called: **sweet basil.** [C15: from OF *basile,* from LL, from Gk *basilikos* royal]

Basil ★ ('bæzˀl) *n* **Saint,** called *the Great.* ?329–379 A.D., Greek patriarch: one of the founders of monasticism. Feast day: Jan. 2, June 14, or Jan. 1.

Basilan ★ (bəˈsiːlɑːn, bæˈsiːlæn) *n* **1** a group of islands in the Philippines, SW of Mindanao. **2** the main island of this group, separated from Mindanao by the **Basilan Strait.** Area: 1282 sq. km (495 sq. miles). **3** a city on Basilan Island. Pop.: 201 407 (1980).

basilar ('bæsɪlə) *adj Chiefly anat.* of or at a base. Also: **basilary** ('bæsɪlərɪ, -sɪlrɪ). [C16: from NL *basilaris*]

Basildon ★ ('bæzɪldən) *n* a town in SE England, in S Essex: designated a new town in 1955. Pop.: 100 924 (1991).

basilica (bəˈzɪlɪkə) *n* **1** a Roman building, used for public administration, having a large rectangular central nave with an aisle on each side and an apse at the end. **2** a Christian church of similar design. **3** a Roman Catholic church having special ceremonial rights. [C16: from L, from Gk, from *basilikē oikia* the king's house]
▶ ba'silican *or* ba'silic *adj*

Basilicata ★ (*Italian* bazilɪˈkata) *n* a region of S Italy, between the Tyrrhenian Sea and the Gulf of Taranto. Capital: Potenza. Pop.: 611 155 (1994 est.). Area: 9985 sq. km (3855 sq. miles).

basilisk ('bæzɪˌlɪsk) *n* **1** (in classical legend) a serpent that could kill by its breath or glance. **2** a small semiaquatic lizard of tropical America. The males have an inflatable head crest, used in display. [C14: from L *basiliscus,* from Gk *basiliskos* royal child]

basin ('beɪsˀn) *n* **1** a round container open and wide at the top with sides sloping inwards towards the bottom. **2** Also called: **basinful.** the amount a basin will hold. **3** a washbasin or sink. **4** any partially enclosed or sheltered area where vessels may be moored. **5** the catchment area of a particular river and its tributaries. **6** a depression in the earth's surface. **7** *Geol.* a part of the earth's surface consisting of rock strata that slope down to a common centre. [C13: from OF *bacin,* from LL *bacchinon*]

Basingstoke ★ ('beɪzɪŋˌstəʊk) *n* a town in S England, in N Hampshire. Pop.: 77 837 (1991).

basis ('beɪsɪs) *n, pl* **bases** (-siːz). **1** something that underlies, supports, or is essential to something else, esp. an idea. **2** a principle on which something depends or from which something has issued. [C14: via L from Gk: step]

bask (bɑːsk) *vb* (*intr; usually foll. by* *in*) **1** to lie in or be exposed to pleasant warmth, esp. that of the sun. **2** to flourish or feel secure under some benevolent influence or favourable condition. [C14: from ON *bathask* to BATHE]

basket ('bɑːskɪt) *n* **1** a container made of interwoven strips of pliable materials, such as cane, and often carried by a handle. **2** Also called: **basketful.** the amount a basket will hold. **3** something resembling such a container, such as the structure suspended from a balloon. **4** *Basketball.* **4a** the hoop fixed to the backboard, through which a player must throw the ball to score points. **4b** a point or points scored in this way. **5** a group of similar or related things: *a basket of currencies.* **6** *Inf.* a euphemism for **bastard** (senses 1–3). [C13: prob. from OF *baskot* (unattested), from L *bascauda* wickerwork holder]

basketball ('bɑːskɪtˌbɔːl) *n* **1** a game played by two teams of five men (or six women), usually on an indoor court. Points are scored by throwing the ball through an elevated horizontal hoop. **2** the ball used in this game.

basket case *n Sl.* **1** *Chiefly US & Canad.* a person who has had both arms and both legs amputated. **2** a person who is suffering from extreme nervous strain; nervous wreck. **3a** someone or something that is incapable of functioning effectively. **3b** (*as modifier*): *a basket-case economy.*

basket chair *n* a chair made of wickerwork.

basketry ('bɑːskɪtrɪ) *n* **1** the art or practice of making baskets. **2** baskets collectively.

basket weave *n* a weave of yarns, resembling that of a basket.

basketwork ('bɑːskɪtˌwɜːk) *n* another word for **wickerwork.**

basking shark *n* a very large plankton-eating shark, often floating at the sea surface.

Basle ★ (bɑːl) *n* a variant spelling of **Basel.**

basmati rice (bəzˈmætɪ) *n* a variety of long-grain rice with slender aromatic grains, used for savoury dishes. [from Hindi, lit.: aromatic]

basophil ('beɪsəfɪl) *or* **basophile** *adj also* **basophilic** (ˌbeɪsəˈfɪlɪk). **1** (of cells or cell contents) easily stained by basic dyes. ◆ *n* **2** a basophil cell, esp. a leucocyte. [C19: from Gk; see BASIS, -PHILE]

Basotho-Qwaqwa ★ (bəˈsuːtuːˈkwɑːkwə, -ˈsəʊtəʊ-) *n* (formerly) a Bantu homeland in South Africa; reintegrated into South Africa in 1994. Also called: **Qwaqwa**. Former name (until 1972): **Basotho-Ba-Borwa**.

basque (bæsk) *n* a type of tight-fitting bodice for women. [from F, from BASQUE]

Basque (bæsk, bɑːsk) *n* **1** a member of a people living around the W Pyrenees in France and Spain. **2** the language of this people, of no known relationship with any other language. ◆ *adj* **3** of or relating to this people or their language. [C19: from F, from L *Vascō* a Basque]

Basque Provinces ★ *n* an autonomous region of N Spain, comprising the provinces of Álava, Guipúzcoa, and Viscaya: inhabited mainly by Basques, who retained virtual autonomy from the 9th to the 19th century. Pop.: 2 075 561 (1994 est.). Area: about 7250 sq. km (2800 sq. miles).

Basra, Basrah (ˈbæzrə), **Busra**, *or* **Busrah** ★ (ˈbʌsrə) *n* a port in SE Iraq, on the Shatt-al-Arab. Pop.: 406 296 (1987).

bas-relief (ˌbɑːrɪˈliːf, ˈbæsrɪˌliːf) *n* sculpture in low relief, in which the forms project slightly from the background. [C17: from F, from It. *basso rilievo* low relief]

Bas-Rhin ★ (*French* bɑrɛ̃) *n* a department of NE France in Alsace region. Capital: Strasbourg. Pop.: 990 724 (1994 est.). Area: 4793 sq. km (1869 sq. miles).

bass[1] (beɪs) *n* **1** the lowest adult male voice. **2** a singer with such a voice. **3 the bass.** the lowest part in a piece of harmony. **4** *Inf.* short for **bass guitar, double bass**. **5a** the low-frequency component of an electrical audio signal, esp. in a record player or tape recorder. **5b** the knob controlling this. ◆ *adj* **6** relating to or denoting the bass. [C15 *bas* BASE[1]; modern spelling infl. by BASSO]

bass[2] (bæs) *n* **1** any of various sea perches. **2** a European spiny-finned freshwater fish. **3** any of various predatory North American freshwater fishes. [C15: from BASE[2], infl. by It. *basso* low]

bass clef (beɪs) *n* the clef that establishes F a fifth below middle C on the fourth line of the staff.

bass drum (beɪs) *n* a large drum of low pitch.

Bassein ★ (bɑːˈseɪn) *n* a city in Myanmar, on the Irrawaddy delta: a port on the **Bassein River** (the westernmost distributary of the Irrawaddy). Pop.: 150 000 (latest est.).

Basse-Normandie ★ (*French* bɑsnɔrmɑ̃di) *n* a region of NW France, on the English Channel: consists of the Cherbourg peninsula in the west rising to the Normandy hills in the east; mainly agricultural.

Bassenthwaite ★ (ˈbæsˌⁿθˌweɪt) *n* a lake in NW England, in Cumbria near Keswick. Length: 6 km (4 miles).

Basses-Alpes ★ (*French* bɑsalp) *n* the former name for **Alpes-de-Haute-Provence**.

Basses-Pyrénées ★ (*French* bɑspirene) *pl n* the former name for **Pyrénées (Atlantiques)**.

basset (ˈbæsɪt) *n* a smooth-haired breed of hound with short legs and long ears. Also: **basset hound**. [C17: from F, from *basset* short, from *bas* low]

Basseterre ★ (bæsˈtɛə; *French* bɑstɛr) *n* a port in St Kitts in the Leeward Islands: the capital of St Kitts-Nevis. Pop.: 14 107 (1990).

Basse-Terre ★ (ˈbæsˈtɛə; *French* bɑstɛr) *n* **1** a mountainous island in the Caribbean, in the Leeward Islands, comprising part of Guadeloupe. Area: 848 sq. km (327 sq. miles). **2** a port in W Guadeloupe, on Basse-Terre Island: the capital of the French Overseas Department of Guadeloupe. Pop.: 29 522 (1994 est.).

basset horn *n* an obsolete woodwind instrument. [C19: prob. from G *Bassetthorn*, from It. *bassetto*, dim. of BASSO + HORN]

bass guitar (beɪs) *n* a guitar that has the same pitch and tuning as a double bass, usually electrically amplified.

bassinet (ˌbæsɪˈnɛt) *n* a wickerwork or wooden cradle or pram, usually hooded. [C19: from F: little basin; associated in folk etymology with F *barcelonnette* a little cradle]

bassist (ˈbeɪsɪst) *n* a player of a double bass or bass guitar.

basso (ˈbæsəʊ) *n*, *pl* **bassos** *or* **bassi** (-sɪ). (esp. in operatic or solo singing) a singer with a bass voice. [C19: from It., from LL *bassus* low; see BASE[2]]

bassoon (bəˈsuːn) *n* **1** a woodwind instrument, the tenor of the oboe family. **2** an orchestral musician who plays the bassoon. [C18: from F *basson*, from It., from *basso* deep] ▸ bas'soonist *n*

basso rilievo (*Italian* ˈbasso riˈljɛːvo) *n*, *pl* **basso rilievos** Italian name for **bas-relief**.

Bass Strait ★ (bæs) *n* a channel between mainland Australia and Tasmania, linking the Indian Ocean and the Tasman Sea.

bass viol (beɪs) *n* **1** another name for **viola da gamba**. **2** US a less common name for **double bass** (sense 1).

bast (bæst) *n* **1** *Bot.* another name for **phloem**. **2** fibrous material obtained from the phloem of jute, flax, etc: used for making rope, matting, etc. [OE *bæst*]

bastard (ˈbɑːstəd, ˈbæs-) *n* **1** *Inf., offens.* an obnoxious or despicable person. **2** *Inf.* a person, esp. a man: *luck bastard*. **3** *Inf.* something extremely difficult or unpleasant. **4** *Arch. or offens.* a person born of parents not married to each other. **5** something irregular, abnormal, or inferior. **6** a hybrid, esp. an accidental or inferior one. ◆ *adj* (*prenominal*) **7** *Arch. or offens.* illegitimate by birth. **8** irregular, abnormal, or inferior. **9** resembling a specified thing, but not actually being such: *a bastard cedar*. **10** counterfeit; spurious. **11** hybrid. [C13: from OF *bastart*, ?from *fils de bast* son of the packsaddle] ▸ 'bastardy *n*

bastardize *or* **bastardise** (ˈbɑːstəˌdaɪz, ˈbæs-) *vb* **bastardizes, bastardizing, bastardized** *or* **bastardises, bastardising, bastardised**. (*tr*) **1** to debase. **2** *Arch.* to declare illegitimate.

baste[1] (beɪst) *vb* **bastes, basting, basted**. (*tr*) to sew with loose temporary stitches. [C14: from OF *bastir* to build, of Gmc origin] ▸ 'basting *n*

baste[2] (beɪst) *vb* **bastes, basting, basted**. (*tr*) to moisten (meat) during cooking with hot fat and the juices produced. [C15: from ?]

baste[3] (beɪst) *vb* **bastes, basting, basted**. (*tr*) to beat thoroughly; thrash. [C16: prob. from ON *beysta*]

Bastia ★ (ˈbɑːstjə) *n* a port in NE Corsica: the main commercial and industrial town of the island: capital of Haute-Corse department. Pop.: 38 728 (1990).

Bastille (bæˈstiːl) *n* a fortress in Paris: a prison until its destruction in 1789, at the beginning of the French Revolution. [C14: from OF *bastille* fortress, from OProvençal *bastida*, from *bastir* to build]

bastinado (ˌbæstɪˈneɪdəʊ) *n*, *pl* **bastinadoes**. **1** punishment or torture in which the soles of the feet are beaten with a stick. ◆ *vb* **bastinadoes, bastinadoing, bastinadoed**. **2** (*tr*) to beat (a person) thus. [C16: from Sp. *bastonada*, from *baston* stick]

bastion (ˈbæstɪən) *n* **1** a projecting part of a fortification designed to permit fire to the flanks along the the face of the wall. **2** any fortified place. **3** a thing or person regarded as defending a principle, etc. [C16: from F, from earlier *bastillon* bastion, from *bastille* BASTILLE]

Bastogne ★ (bæˈstəʊn; *French* bastɔɲ) *n* a town in SE Belgium: of strategic importance to Allied defences during the Battle of the Bulge; besieged by the Germans during the winter of 1944–45. Pop.: 7000 (1991 est.).

Basutoland ★ (bəˈsuːtəʊˌlænd) *n* the former name (until 1966) of **Lesotho**.

bat[1] (bæt) *n* **1** any of various types of club with a handle used to hit the ball in certain sports, such as cricket. **2** a flat round club with a short handle used by a man on the ground to guide the pilot of an aircraft when taxiing. **3** *Cricket*. short for **batsman**. **4** *Inf.* a blow from a stick. **5** *Sl.* speed; pace: *they went at a fair bat*. **6** carry one's bat. *Cricket* (of an opening batsman) to reach the end of an innings without being dismissed. **7** off one's own bat. **7a** of one's own accord. **7b** by one's own unaided efforts. ◆ *vb* **bats, batting, batted**. **8** (*tr*) to strike with or as if with a bat. **9** (*intr*)

Cricket, etc. (of a player or a team) to take a turn at batting. [OE *batt* club, prob. of Celtic origin]

oat[2] (bæt) *n* **1** a nocturnal mouselike animal flying with a pair of membranous wings. **2** *Sl.* an irritating or eccentric woman. **3 blind as a bat.** having extremely poor eyesight. **4 have bats in the** (*or* **one's**) **belfry.** *Inf.* to be mad or eccentric. [C14 *bakke*, prob. of Scand. origin]

oat[3] (bæt) *vb* **bats, batting, batted.** (*tr*) **1** to wink or flutter (one's eyelids). **2 not bat an eye** (*or* **eyelid**). *Inf.* to show no surprise or concern. [C17: prob. var. of BATE[2]]

Bataan ★ (bə'tæn, -'tɑːn) *n* a peninsula in the Philippines, in W Luzon: scene of the surrender of US and Philippine forces to the Japanese during World War II, later retaken by American forces.

Batangas ★ (bə'tæŋgæs) *n* a port in the Philippines, in SW Luzon. Pop.: 190 627 (1994 est.).

Batan Islands ★ (bə'tɑːn) *pl n* a group of islands in the Philippines, north of Luzon. Capital: Basco. Pop.: 12 091 (1980). Area: 197 sq. km (76 sq. miles).

Batavia ★ (bə'teɪvɪə) *n* **1** an ancient district of the Netherlands, on an island at the mouth of the Rhine. **2** an archaic or literary name for **Holland**[1] (sense 1). **3** a former name for **Jakarta.**
▸ **Ba'tavian** *adj, n*

batch[1] (bætʃ) *n* **1** a group or set of usually similar objects or people, esp. if sent off, handled, or arriving at the same time. **2** the bread, cakes, etc., produced at one baking. **3** the amount of a material needed for an operation. ◆ *vb* **4** to group (items) for efficient processing. **5** to handle by batch processing. [C15 *bache*; rel. to OE *bacan* to BAKE]

batch[2] *or* **bach** (bætʃ) *vb* (*intr*) *Austral. & NZ inf.* (of a man) to do his own cooking and housekeeping.

batch processing *n* a system by which the computer programs of a number of individual users are submitted as a single batch.

bate[1] (beɪt) *vb* **bates, bating, bated.** **1** another word for **abate.** **2 with bated breath.** in suspense or fear.

bate[2] (beɪt) *vb* **bates, bating, bated.** (*intr*) (of a hawk) to jump violently from a perch or the falconer's fist, often hanging from the leash while struggling to escape. [C13: from OF *batre* to beat]

bate[3] (beɪt) *n Brit. Sl.* a bad temper or rage. [C19: from BAIT[1], alluding to the mood of a person who is being baited]

bateau (bæ'təʊ) *n, pl* **bateaux** (-'təʊz). a light flat-bottomed boat used on rivers in Canada and the northern US. [C18: from F: boat]

bateleur eagle ('bætələː) *n* an African short-tailed bird of prey. [C19: from F *bateleur* juggler]

Bates ★ (beɪts) *n* **1 Alan** (**Arthur**). born 1934, British actor. **2 H(erbert) E(rnest).** 1905–74, British writer, noted for the novels *The Darling Buds of May* (1958) and *The Triple Echo* (1970).

bath (bɑːθ) *n, pl* **baths** (bɑːðz). **1** a large container used for washing the body. **2** the act or an instance of washing in such a container. **3** the amount of liquid contained in a bath. **4** (*usually pl*) a place having baths or a swimming pool for public use. **5a** a vessel in which something is immersed to maintain it at a constant temperature, to process it photographically, etc., or to lubricate it. **5b** the liquid used in such a vessel. ◆ *vb* **6** *Brit.* to wash in a bath. [OE *bæth*]

Bath ★ (bɑːθ) *n* a city in SW England, in Bath and North East Somerset unitary authority on the River Avon: famous for its hot springs; a fashionable spa in the 18th century; Roman remains, notably the baths. Pop.: 85 202 (1991). Latin name: **Aquae Sulis** ('ækwɪ'suːlɪs).

Bath and North East Somerset ★ *n* a unitary authority in SW England; formerly (1974–96) part of the county of Avon. Pop.: 158 692 (1996). Area: 351 sq. km (136 sq. miles).

Bath bun (bɑːθ) *n Brit.* a sweet bun containing spices and dried fruit.

Bath chair *n* a wheelchair for invalids.

bath cube *n* a cube of soluble scented material for use in a bath.

bathe (beɪð) *vb* **bathes, bathing, bathed.** **1** (*intr*) to swim in a body of open water, esp. for pleasure. **2** (*tr*) to apply liquid to (skin, a wound, etc.) in order to cleanse or soothe. **3** to immerse or be immersed in a liquid. **4** *Chiefly US & Canad.* to wash in a bath. **5** (*tr, often passive*) to suffuse. ◆ *n* **6** *Brit.* a swim in a body of open water. [OE *bathian*]
▸ **'bather** *n*

bathers ('beɪðəz) *pl n Austral.* a swimming costume.

bathhouse ('bɑːθ,haʊs) *n* a building containing baths, esp. for public use.

bathing cap ('beɪðɪŋ) *n* a tight rubber cap worn by a swimmer to keep the hair dry.

bathing costume ('beɪðɪŋ) *n* another name for **swimming costume.**

bathing machine ('beɪðɪŋ) *n* a small hut, on wheels so that it could be pulled to the sea, used in the 18th and 19th centuries for bathers to change their clothes.

bathing suit ('beɪðɪŋ) *n* a garment worn for bathing, esp. an old-fashioned one that covers much of the body.

batho- *combining form.* a variant of **bathy-.**

batholith (,bæθəlɪθ) *or* **batholite** ('bæθə,laɪt) *n* a very large irregular-shaped mass of igneous rock, esp. granite, formed from an intrusion of magma at great depth, esp. one exposed after erosion of less resistant overlying rocks.
▸ **,batho'lithic** *or* **batholitic** (,bæθə'lɪtɪk) *adj*

Bath Oliver ('ɒlɪvə) *n Brit.* a kind of unsweetened biscuit [C19: after William *Oliver* (1695–1764), a physician at Bath]

bathometer (bə'θɒmɪtə) *n* an instrument for measuring the depth of water.
▸ **bathometric** (,bæθə'mɛtrɪk) *adj* ▸ **ba'thometry** *n*

bathos ('beɪθɒs) *n* **1** a sudden ludicrous descent from exalted to ordinary matters or style in speech or writing. **2** insincere or excessive pathos. [C18: from Gk: depth]
▸ **ba'thetic** *adj*

bathrobe ('bɑːθ,rəʊb) *n* **1** a loose-fitting garment of towelling, for wear before or after a bath or swimming. **2** *US & Canad.* a dressing gown.

bathroom ('bɑːθ,ruːm, -,rʊm) *n* **1** a room containing a bath or shower and usually a washbasin and lavatory. **2** *US & Canad.* another name for **lavatory.**

bath salts *pl n* soluble scented salts for use in a bath.

Bathsheba ★ (bæθ'ʃiːbə, 'bæθʃɪbə) *n Old Testament.* the wife of Uriah, who committed adultery with David and later married him and became the mother of his son Solomon (II Samuel 11–12).

bathtub ('bɑːθ,tʌb) *n* a bath, esp. one not permanently fixed.

Bathurst ★ ('bæθəst) *n* **1** a city in SE Australia, in E New South Wales: scene of a gold rush in 1851. Pop.: 24 682 (1991). **2** a port in E Canada, in NE New Brunswick: rich mineral resources discovered in 1953. Pop.: 15 890 (1991). **3** the former name (until 1973) of **Banjul.**

bathy- *or* **batho-** *combining form.* indicating depth: *bathysphere.* [from Gk *bathus* deep]

bathyscaph ('bæθɪ,skæf), **bathyscaphe** ('bæθɪ,skeɪf, -,skæf), *or* **bathyscape** ('bæθɪ,skeɪp) *n* a submersible vessel with an observation capsule underneath, capable of reaching ocean depths of over 10 000 metres. [C20: from BATHY- + Gk *skaphē* light boat]

bathysphere ('bæθɪ,sfɪə) *n* a strong steel deep-sea diving sphere, lowered by cable.

batik ('bætɪk) *n* **a** a process of printing fabric in which parts not to be dyed are covered by wax. **b** fabric printed in this way. [C19: via Malay from Javanese: painted]

Batista ★ (*Spanish* ba'tista) *n* **Fulgencio** (ful'xenθjo), full name *Batista y Zaldívar.* 1901–73, Cuban military leader and dictator: president of Cuba (1940–44, 1952–59); overthrown by Fidel Castro.

batiste (bæ'tiːst) *n* a fine plain-weave cotton. [C17: from F, prob. after *Baptiste* of Cambrai, 13th-cent. F weaver, its reputed inventor]

Batley ★ ('bætlɪ) *n* a town in N England, in Kirklees unitary authority, in West Yorkshire. Pop.: 48 030 (1991).

batman ('bætmən) *n, pl* **batmen.** an officer's servant in the armed forces. [C18: from OF *bat, bast,* from Med. L *bastum* packsaddle]

baton ('bætən) *n* **1** a thin stick used by the conductor of an orchestra, choir, etc. **2** *Athletics.* a short bar carried by a competitor in a relay race and transferred to the next runner at the end of each stage. **3** a long stick with a knob on one end, carried, twirled, and thrown up and down by a drum major or majorette, esp. at the head of a parade. **4** a police truncheon (esp. in **baton charge**). **5** a staff or club carried as a symbol of authority. [C16: from F *bâton,* from LL *bastum* rod]

Baton Rouge ★ ('bæt°n 'ruːʒ) *n* the capital of Louisiana, in the SE part on the Mississippi River. Pop.: 227 482 (1994 est.).

baton round *n* the official name for **plastic bullet.**

batrachian (bə'treɪkɪən) *n* **1** any amphibian, esp. a frog or toad. ◆ *adj* **2** of or relating to the frogs and toads. [C19: from NL *Batrachia,* from Gk *batrakhos* frog]

bats (bæts) *adj Inf.* mad or eccentric.

batsman ('bætsmən) *n, pl* **batsmen. 1** *Cricket, etc.* **1a** a person who bats or whose turn it is to bat. **1b** a player who specializes in batting. **2** a person on the ground who uses bats to guide the pilot of an aircraft when taxiing.

battalion (bə'tæljən) *n* **1** a military unit comprised of three or more companies or formations of similar size. **2** (*usually pl*) any large army. [C16: from F *bataillon,* from OIt., from *battaglia* company of soldiers, BATTLE]

batten[1] ('bæt°n) *n* **1** a sawn strip of wood used in building, to cover joints, support lathing, etc. **2** a long narrow board used for flooring. **3** a lath used for holding a tarpaulin along the side of a hatch on a ship. **4** *Theatre.* **4a** a row of lights. **4b** the bar supporting them. ◆ *vb* **5** (*tr*) to furnish or strengthen with battens. **6 batten down the hatches. 6a** to use battens in securing a tarpaulin over a hatch on a ship. **6b** to prepare for action, a crisis, etc. [C15: from F *bâton* stick; see BATON]

batten[2] ('bæt°n) *vb* (*intr*) (usually foll. by *on*) to thrive, esp. at the expense of someone else. [C16: prob. from ON *batna* to improve]

Batten ★ ('bæt°n) *n* **Jean.** 1909–82, New Zealand aviator: the first woman to fly from Australia to Britain (1935).

batter[1] ('bætə) *vb* **1** to hit (someone or something) repeatedly using heavy blows, as with a club. **2** (*tr; often passive*) to damage or injure, as by blows, heavy wear, etc. **3** (*tr*) to subject (a person, esp. a close relative) to repeated physical violence. [C14: *bateren,* prob. from *batten* to BAT[1]]
▶ '**batterer** *n* ▶ '**battering** *n*

batter[2] ('bætə) *n* a mixture of flour, eggs, and milk, used to make cakes, pancakes, etc., and to coat certain foods before frying. [C15 *bater,* prob. from *bateren* to BATTER[1]]

batter[3] ('bætə) *n Baseball, etc.* a player who bats.

batter[4] ('bætə) *n* **1** the slope of the face of a wall that recedes gradually backwards and upwards. ◆ *vb* **2** (*intr*) to have such a slope. [C16 (vb: to incline): from ?]

battered[1] ('bætəd) *adj* subjected to persistent physical violence, esp. by a close relative living in the house: *a battered baby.*

battered[2] ('bætəd) *adj* coated in batter: *battered cod.*

battering ram *n* (esp. formerly) a large beam used to break down fortifications.

Battersea ('bætəsɪ) *n* a district in London, in Wandsworth: noted for its dogs' home, power station (being developed into a leisure centre), and park.

battery ('bætərɪ) *n, pl* **batteries. 1** two or more primary cells connected, usually in series, to provide a source of electric current. **2** another name for **accumulator** (sense 1). **3** a number of similar things occurring together: *a battery of questions.* **4** *Criminal law.* unlawful beating or wounding of a person or mere touching in a hostile or offensive manner. **5** a fortified structure on which artillery is mounted. **6** a group of guns, missile launchers, etc, operated as a single entity. **7** a small unit of artillery. **8** *Chiefly Brit.* **8a** a large group of cages for intensive rearing of poultry and other farm animals. **8b** (*as modifier*): *battery hens.* **9** *Baseball.* the pitcher and the catcher considered together. [C16: from OF *batterie* beating, from *battre* to beat, from L *battuere*]

batting ('bætɪŋ) *n* **1** cotton or woollen wadding used in quilts, etc. **2** the action of a person or team that hits with a bat.

battle ('bæt°l) *n* **1** a fight between large armed forces military or naval engagement. **2** conflict; struggle. **3 do give,** or **join battle.** to engage in conflict or competition. ◆ *vb* **battles, battling, battled. 4** (when *intr,* often foll. by *against, for,* or *with*) to fight in or as if in military combat contend (with): *shop stewards battling to improve conditions at work.* **5** to struggle: *he battled through the crowd.* **6** (*intr Austral.* to scrape a living. [C13: from OF *bataile,* from LL *battālia* exercises performed by soldiers, from *battuere* to beat]
▶ '**battler** *n*

Battle[1] ('bæt°l) ★ *n* a town in SE England, in East Sussex site of the Battle of Hastings (1066); medieval abbey Pop.: 5235 (1991).

Battle[2] ('bæt°l) ★ *n* **Kathleen.** born 1948, US opera singer.

battle-axe *n* **1** (formerly) a large broad-headed axe. **2** *Inf.* an argumentative domineering woman.

battle-axe block *n Austral.* a block of land behind another, with access from the street through a narrow drive.

battle cruiser *n* a high-speed warship of battleship size but with lighter armour.

battle cry *n* **1** a shout uttered by soldiers going into battle. **2** a slogan used to rally the supporters of a campaign movement, etc.

battledore ('bæt°l,dɔː) *n* **1** Also called: **battledore and shuttlecock.** an ancient racket game. **2** a light racket used in this game. **3** (formerly) a wooden utensil used for beating clothes, in baking, etc. [C15 *batyldoure,* ?from OProvençal *batedor* beater, from OF *battre* to beat]

battledress ('bæt°l,drɛs) *n* the ordinary uniform of a soldier.

battle fatigue *n Psychol.* mental disorder, characterized by anxiety and depression, caused by the stress of warfare. Also: **combat fatigue.**

battlefield ('bæt°l,fiːld) *or* **battleground** ('bæt°l,graʊnd) *n* the place where a battle is fought.

battlement ('bæt°lmənt) *n* a parapet or wall with indentations or embrasures, originally for shooting through [C14: from OF *batailles,* pl. of *bataille* BATTLE]
▶ '**battlemented** *adj*

battle royal *n* **1** a fight, esp. with fists or cudgels, involving more than two combatants; melee. **2** a long violent argument.

battleship ('bæt°l,ʃɪp) *n* a heavily armoured warship of the largest type.

batty ('bætɪ) *adj* **battier, battiest.** *Sl.* **1** insane; crazy. **2** odd; eccentric. [C20: from BAT[2]]

Batum (bɑː'tuːm) *or* **Batumi** ★ (bɑː'tuːmɪ) *n* a city in Georgia: capital of the Adzhar Autonomous Republic; a major Black Sea port. Pop.: 137 500 (1991 est.).

batwoman ('bæt,wʊmən) *n, pl* **batwomen.** a female servant in any of the armed forces.

bauble ('bɔːb°l) *n* **1** a trinket of little value. **2** (formerly) a mock staff of office carried by a jester. [C14: from OF *baubel* plaything, from ?]

Bauchi ★ ('baʊtʃɪ) *n* **1** a state of N Nigeria: formed in 1976 from part of North-Eastern State; tin mining. Capital: Bauchi. Pop.: 4 423 246 (1992 est.). Area: 64 605 sq. km (24 944 sq. miles). **2** a town in N central Nigeria, capital of Bauchi state. Pop.: 76 070 (1991 est.).

baud (bɔːd) *n* a unit used to measure the speed of electronic code transmissions. [after J. M. E. *Baudot* (1845–1903), Fr inventor]

Baudelaire ★ (*French* bodlɛr) *n* **Charles Pierre** (ʃarl pjɛr). 1821–67, French poet, noted for *Les fleurs du mal* (1857).

Baudouin I ★ (*French* bodwɛ̃) *n* 1930–93, king of Belgium (1951–93).

bauera ('baʊərə) *n* a small evergreen Australian shrub with pink or purple flowers. [C19: after Franz & Ferdinand *Bauer,* 19th-cent. Austrian botanical artists]

★ people and places

Bauhaus ('bau,haus) *n* a German school of functionalist architecture and applied arts founded in 1919. [G, lit.: building house]

bauhinia (bɔː'hɪnɪə, bəu-) *n* a climbing leguminous plant of tropical and warm regions, cultivated for ornament. [C18: NL, after Jean & Gaspard *Bauhin*, 16th-cent. F herbalists]

baulk (bɔːk; *usually for sense 1* bɔːlk) *n* **1** Also: **balk**. *Billiards.* the space between the baulk line and the bottom cushion. **2** *Archaeol.* a strip of earth left between excavation trenches for the study of the complete stratigraphy of a site. ◆ *vb*, *n* **3** a variant spelling of **balk**.

baulk line *or* **balk line** *n Billiards.* a straight line across a billiard table behind which the cue balls are placed at the start of a game. Also: **string line**.

baulky ('bɔːkɪ, 'bɔːlkɪ) *adj* a variant of **balky**.

Bautzen ★ ('bautsən) *n* a city in E Germany, in Saxony: site of an indecisive battle in 1813 between Napoleon's army and an allied army of Russians and Prussians. Pop.: 52 390 (1989 est.).

bauxite ('bɔːksaɪt) *n* an amorphous claylike substance consisting of hydrated alumina with iron and other impurities: the chief source of alumina and aluminium and also used as an abrasive and catalyst. [C19: from F, from (*Les*) *Baux* in southern France, where orig. found]

Bav. *abbrev. for* Bavaria(n).

Bavaria ★ (bə'vɛərɪə) *n* a state of S Germany: a former duchy and kingdom; mainly wooded highland, with the Alps in the south. Capital: Munich. Pop.: 11 921 900 (1995 est.) Area: 70 531 sq. km (27 232 sq. miles). German name: **Bayern**.
► **Ba'varian** *adj*, *n*

bawd (bɔːd) *n Arch.* **1** a person who runs a brothel, esp. a woman. **2** a prostitute. [C14: from OF *baude*, fem. of *baud* merry]

bawdy ('bɔːdɪ) *adj* **bawdier, bawdiest. 1** (of language, plays, etc.) containing references to sex, esp. to be humorous. ◆ *n* **2** obscenity or eroticism, esp. in writing or drama.
► **'bawdily** *adv* ► **'bawdiness** *n* ► **bawdry** ('bɔːdrɪ) *n*

bawdyhouse ('bɔːdɪ,haus) *n* an archaic word for **brothel**.

bawl (bɔːl) *vb* **1** (*intr*) to utter long loud cries, as from pain or frustration; wail. **2** to shout loudly, as in anger. ◆ *n* **3** a loud shout or cry. [C15: imit.]
► **'bawler** *n* ► **'bawling** *n*

bawl out *vb* (*tr, adv*) *Inf.* to scold loudly.

Bax ★ (bæks) *n* Sir **Arnold** (**Edward Trevor**). 1883–1953, British composer; his works include seven symphonies and the tone poem *Tintagel* (1917).

Baxter ★ ('bækstə) *n* **1 James** (**Keir**). 1926–72, New Zealand poet. His works include *The Fallen House* (1953). **2 Richard.** 1615–91, English Puritan devotional writer.

bay[1] (beɪ) *n* **1** a wide semicircular indentation of a shoreline, esp. between two headlands. **2** an extension of lowland into inlets that partly surround it. [C14: from OF *baie*, ?from OF *baer* to gape, from Med. L *batāre* to yawn]

bay[2] (beɪ) *n* **1** an alcove or recess in a wall. **2** any partly enclosed compartment. **3** See **bay window**. **4** an area off a road in which vehicles may park or unload. **5** a compartment in an aircraft: *the bomb bay*. **6** *Naut.* a compartment in the forward part of a ship between decks, often used as the ship's hospital. **7** *Brit.* a tracked recess in the platform of a railway station, esp. one forming the terminus of a branch line. [C14: from OF *baee* gap, from *baer* to gape; see BAY[1]]

bay[3] (beɪ) *n* **1** a deep howl, esp. of a hound on the scent. **2 at bay. 2a** forced to turn and face attackers: *the dogs held the deer at bay*. **2b** at a distance. **3 bring to bay.** to force into a position from which retreat is impossible. ◆ *vb* **4** (*intr*) to howl (at) in deep prolonged tones. **5** (*tr*) to utter in a loud prolonged tone. **6** (*tr*) to hold at bay. [C13: from OF, imit.]

bay[4] (beɪ) *n* **1** a Mediterranean laurel. See **laurel** (sense 1). **2** any of several magnolias. See **sweet bay. 3** any of certain other trees or shrubs, esp. bayberry. **4** (*pl*) a wreath of bay leaves. [C14: from OF *baie* laurel berry, from L *bāca* berry]

bay[5] (beɪ) *n, adj* **1** (of) a reddish-brown colour. ◆ *n* **2** an animal of this colour. [C14: from OF *bai*, from L *badius*]

Bayamón ★ (*Spanish* baja'mon) *n* a city in NE central Puerto Rico, south of San Juan. Pop.: 231 334 (1995 est.).

bayberry ('beɪbərɪ) *or* **bay** *n, pl* **bayberries. 1** any of several North American aromatic shrubs or small trees that bear grey waxy berries. **2** a tropical American tree that yields an oil used in making bay rum. **3** the fruit of any of these plants.

Bayern ★ ('baɪərn) *n* the German name for **Bavaria**.

Bayeux ★ (*French* bajø) *n* a town in NW France, on the River Aure: its museum houses the Bayeux tapestry and there is a 13th-century cathedral: dairy foods, plastic. Pop.: 14 704 (1990).

bay leaf *n* a leaf, usually dried, of the Mediterranean laurel, used in cooking to flavour soups and stews.

Baylis ★ ('beɪlɪs) *n* **Lillian Mary.** 1874–1937, British theatre manager: founded the Old Vic (1912) and the Sadler's Wells company for opera and ballet (1931).

Bay of Pigs ★ *n* a bay on the SW coast of Cuba: scene of an unsuccessful invasion of Cuba by US-backed troops (April 17, 1961). Spanish name: **Bahía de los Cochinos**.

bayonet ('beɪənɪt) *n* **1** a blade for stabbing that can be attached to the muzzle of a firearm. **2** a type of fastening in which a cylindrical member is inserted into a socket against spring pressure and turned so that pins on its side engage in slots in the socket. ◆ *vb* **bayonets, bayoneting, bayoneted** *or* **bayonets, bayonetting, bayonetted. 3** (*tr*) to stab or kill with a bayonet. [C17: from F *baïonnette*, from BAYONNE]

Bayonne ★ (*French* bajɔn) *n* a port in SW France: a commercial centre for the Basque region. Pop.: 41 846 (1990).

bayou ('baɪjuː) *n* (in the southern US) a sluggish marshy tributary of a lake or river. [C18: from Louisiana F, from Amerind *bayuk*]

Bayreuth ★ (*German* baɪ'rɔyt) *n* a city in E Germany, in NE Bavaria: home and burial place of Richard Wagner; annual festivals of his music. Pop.: 72 780 (1991).

bay rum *n* an aromatic liquid, used in medicines and cosmetics, originally obtained by distilling the leaves of the bayberry tree with rum: now also synthesized.

bay window *n* a window projecting from a wall and forming an alcove of a room.

bazaar *or* **bazar** (bə'zɑː) *n* **1** (esp. in the Orient) a market area, esp. a street of small stalls. **2** a sale in aid of charity, esp. of second-hand or handmade articles. **3** a shop where a variety of goods is sold. [C16: from Persian *bāzār*]

bazooka (bə'zuːkə) *n* a portable tubular rocket-launcher, used by infantrymen as a short-range antitank weapon. [C20: after a comic pipe instrument]

BB *abbrev. for:* **1** Boys' Brigade. **2** (on British pencils, signifying degrees of softness of lead) double black.

BBC *abbrev. for* British Broadcasting Corporation.

bbl. *abbrev. for* barrel (container or measure).

BBQ *abbrev. for* barbecue.

BC *abbrev. for* British Columbia.

B.C. *or* **BC** *abbrev. for* (indicating years numbered back from the supposed year of the birth of Christ) before Christ.

USAGE NOTE See at **A.D.**

BCE *abbrev. for:* **1** Before Common Era (used, esp. by non-Christians, in numbering years B.C.). **2** *Brit.* Board of Customs and Excise.

BCG *abbrev. for* Bacillus Calmette-Guérin (antituberculosis vaccine).

BCNZ *abbrev. for* Broadcasting Corporation of New Zealand.

B complex *n* short for **vitamin B complex**.

BD *abbrev. for* Bachelor of Divinity.

bdellium ('dɛlɪəm) *n* **1** any of several African or W Asian trees that yield a gum resin. **2** the aromatic gum resin produced by any of these trees. [C16: from L, from Gk *bdellion*, ? from Heb. *bĕdhōlah*]

BDS *abbrev. for* Bachelor of Dental Surgery.

be (bi:; *unstressed* bɪ) *vb present sing 1st person* **am**; *2nd person* **are**; *3rd person* **is**. *present pl* **are**. *past sing 1st person* **was**; *2nd person* **were**; *3rd person* **was**. *past pl* **were**. *present participle* **being**. *past participle* **been**. (*intr*) **1** to have presence in perceived reality; exist; live: *I think, therefore I am*. **2** (*used in the perfect tenses only*) to pay a visit; go: *have you been to Spain?* **3** to take place: *my birthday was last Thursday*. **4** (*copula*) used as a linking verb between the subject of a sentence and its noun or adjective complement. In this case **be** expresses relationship of equivalence or identity (*John is a man; John is a musician*) or specifies an attribute (*honey is sweet; Susan is angry*). It is also used with an adverbial complement to indicate a relationship in space or time (*Bill is at the office; the party is on Saturday*). **5** (*takes a present participle*) forms the progressive present tense: *the man is running*. **6** (*takes a past participle*) forms the passive voice of all transitive verbs: *a good film is being shown on television tonight*. **7** (*takes an infinitive*) expresses intention, expectation, or obligation: *the president is to arrive at 9.30*. [OE *bēon*]

Be *the chemical symbol for* beryllium.

BE *abbrev. for:* **1** bill of exchange. **2** Bachelor of Education. **3** Bachelor of Engineering.

be- *prefix forming transitive verbs*. **1** (*from nouns*) to surround or cover: *befog*. **2** (*from nouns*) to affect completely: *bedazzle*. **3** (*from nouns*) to consider as or cause to be: *befriend*. **4** (*from nouns*) to provide or cover with: *bejewel*. **5** (*from verbs*) at, for, against, on, or over: *bewail; berate*. [OE *be-*, *bi-*, unstressed var. of *bī* BY]

beach (bi:tʃ) *n* **1** an area of sand or shingle sloping down to a sea or lake, esp. the area between the high- and low-water marks on a seacoast. ◆ *vb* **2** to run or haul (a boat) onto a beach. [C16: perhaps rel. to OE *bæce* river]

beachcomber ('bi:tʃ,kəumə) *n* **1** a person who searches shore debris for anything of worth. **2** a long high wave rolling onto a beach.

beachhead ('bi:tʃ,hɛd) *n Mil.* an area on a beach that has been captured from the enemy and on which troops and equipment are landed.

Beachy Head ★ ('bi:tʃɪ) *n* a headland in East Sussex, on the English Channel, consisting of chalk cliffs 171 m (570 ft) high.

beacon ('bi:kən) *n* **1** a signal fire or light on a hill, tower, etc., esp. formerly as a warning of invasion. **2** a hill on which such fires were lit. **3** a lighthouse, signalling buoy, etc. **4** short for **radio beacon**. **5** a radio or other signal marking a flight course in air navigation. **6** short for **Belisha beacon**. **7** a person or thing that serves as a guide, inspiration, or warning. [OE *beacen* sign]

Beaconsfield[1] ★ ('bekənz,fi:ld, 'bi:k-) *n* a town in SE England, in Buckinghamshire: a residential centre for London. Pop.: 12 292 (1991).

Beaconsfield[2] ★ ('bi:kənz,fi:ld, 'bɛk-) *n* **1st Earl of.** title of (Benjamin) **Disraeli.**

bead (bi:d) *n* **1** a small pierced usually spherical piece of glass, wood, plastic, etc., which may be strung with others to form a necklace, etc. **2 tell one's beads.** to pray with a rosary. **3** a small drop of moisture. **4** a small bubble in or on a liquid. **5** a small metallic knob acting as the sight of a firearm. **6 to draw** *or* **hold a bead on.** to aim a rifle or pistol at. **7** *Archit., furniture*. a small convex moulding having a semicircular cross section. ◆ *vb* **8** (*tr*) to decorate with beads. **9** to form into beads or drops. [OE *bed* prayer]
▸ **'beaded** *adj*

beading ('bi:dɪŋ) *n* **1** another name for **bead** (sense 7). **2** Also called: **beadwork** ('bi:d,wɜːk). a narrow strip of some material used for edging or ornamentation.

beadle ('bi:dᵊl) *n* **1** *Brit.* (formerly) a minor parish official who acted as an usher and kept order. **2** *Judaism*. a synagogue attendant. **3** *Scot.* a church official who attends the minister. **4** an official in certain British institutions. [OE *bydel*]
▸ **'beadleship** *n*

beadsman *or* **bedesman** ('bi:dzmən) *n, pl* **beadsmen** *or*

bedesmen. *Arch*. **1** a person who prays for another's soul: esp. one paid or fed for doing so. **2** a person kept in an almshouse.

beady ('bi:dɪ) *adj* **beadier, beadiest**. **1** small, round, and glittering (esp. in **beady eyes**). **2** resembling or covered with beads.
▸ **'beadiness** *n*

beagle ('bi:gᵊl) *n* **1** a small sturdy breed of hound. **2** *Arch*. a spy. ◆ *vb* **beagles, beagling, beagled**. **3** (*intr*) to hunt with beagles. [C15: from ?]

Beaglehole ★ ('bi:gᵊl,həul) *n* **John.** 1901–71, New Zealand historian. His works include *The Journals of James Cook* (1955).

beak[1] (bi:k) *n* **1** the projecting jaws of a bird, covered with a horny sheath. **2** any beaklike mouthpart in other animals. **3** *Sl.* a person's nose. **4** any projecting part, such as the pouring lip of a bucket. **5** *Naut.* another word for **ram** (sense 5). [C13: from OF *bec*, from L *beccus*, of Gaulish origin]
▸ **beaked** *adj* ▸ **'beaky** *adj*

beak[2] (bi:k) *n a Brit.* slang word for **judge, magistrate, headmaster**, or **schoolmaster**. [C19: orig. thieves' jargon]

beaker ('bi:kə) *n* **1** a cup usually having a wide mouth. **2** a cylindrical flat-bottomed container used in laboratories, usually made of glass and having a pouring lip. [C14: from ON *bikarr*]

Beaker folk ('bi:kə) *n* a prehistoric people inhabiting Europe and Britain during the second millennium B.C. [after beakers found among their remains]

Beale ★ (bi:l) *n* **Dorothea.** 1831–1906, British champion of women's education and suffrage; principal of Cheltenham Ladies' College (1858–1906).

be-all and end-all *n Inf.* the ultimate aim or justification.

beam (bi:m) *n* **1** a long thick piece of wood, metal, etc., esp. one used as a horizontal structural member. **2** the breadth of a ship or boat taken at its widest part. **3** a ray or column of light, as from a beacon. **4** a broad smile. **5** one of two cylindrical rollers on a loom, which hold the warp threads and the finished work. **6** the main stem of a deer's antler. **7** the central shaft of a plough to which all the main parts are attached. **8** a narrow unidirectional flow of electromagnetic radiation or particles: *an electron beam*. **9** the horizontal centrally pivoted bar in a balance. **10 beam in one's eye.** a fault or grave error greater in oneself than in another person. **11 broad in the beam.** *Inf.* having wide hips. **12 off (the) beam.** *Inf.* **12a** not following a radio beam to maintain a course. **12b** *Inf.* mistaken or irrelevant. **13 on the beam. 13a** following a radio beam to maintain a course. **13b** *Inf.* correct, relevant, or appropriate. ◆ *vb* **14** to send out or radiate. **15** (*tr*) to divert or aim (a radio signal, light, etc.) in a certain direction: *to beam a programme to Tokyo*. **16** (*intr*) to smile broadly. [OE]
▸ **'beaming** *adj*

beam-ends *pl n* **1 on her beam-ends.** (of a vessel) heeled over through an angle of 90°. **2 on one's beam-ends.** out of resources; destitute.

bean (bi:n) *n* **1** any of various leguminous plants producing edible seeds in pods. **2** any of various other plants whose seeds are produced in pods or podlike fruits. **3** the seed or pod of any of these plants. **4** any of various beanlike seeds, as coffee. **5** *US & Canad. sl.* another word for **head. 6 full of beans.** *Inf.* full of energy and vitality. **7 not have a bean.** *Sl.* to be without money. [OE *bēan*]

beanbag ('bi:n,bæg) *n* **1** a small cloth bag filled with dried beans and thrown in games. **2** a very large cushion filled with foam rubber or polystyrene granules and used as a seat.

bean counter *n Inf.* an accountant.

bean curd *n* another name for **tofu.**

beanfeast ('bi:n,fi:st) *n Brit. inf.* **1** an annual dinner given by employers to employees. **2** any festive or merry occasion.

beano ('bi:nəu) *n, pl* **beanos.** *Brit. sl.* a celebration, party, or other enjoyable time.

beanpole ('bi:n,pəul) *n* **1** a tall stick used to support bean plants. **2** *Sl.* a tall thin person.

★ people and places

bean sprout n the sprout of a newly germinated mung bean, eaten esp. in Chinese dishes.

beanstalk ('biːnˌstɔːk) n the stem of a bean plant.

bear[1] (bɛə) vb **bears, bearing, bore, borne.** (*mainly tr*) **1** to support or hold up. **2** to bring: *to bear gifts*. **3** to accept or assume the responsibility of: *to bear an expense*. **4** (**born** in passive use except when followed by *by*) to give birth to: *to bear children*. **5** (*also intr*) to produce as by natural growth: *to bear fruit*. **6** to tolerate or endure. **7** to admit of; sustain: *his story does not bear scrutiny*. **8** to hold in the mind: *to bear a grudge*. **9** to show or be marked with: *he still bears the scars*. **10** to render or supply (esp. in **bear witness**). **11** to conduct (oneself, the body, etc.). **12** to have, be, or stand in (relation or comparison): *his account bears no relation to the facts*. **13** (*intr*) to move or lie in a specified direction. **14 bear a hand.** to give assistance. **15 bring to bear.** to bring into operation or effect. ♦ See also **bear down, bear on,** etc. [OE *beran*]

bear[2] (bɛə) n, pl **bears** or **bear.** **1** a plantigrade mammal typically having a large head, a long shaggy coat, and strong claws. **2** any of various bearlike animals, such as the koala. **3** a clumsy, churlish, or ill-mannered person. **4** a teddy bear. **5** *Stock Exchange*. **5a** a speculator who sells in anticipation of falling prices to make a profit on repurchase. **5b** (*as modifier*): *a bear market*. Cf. **bull**[1] (sense 4). ♦ vb **bears, bearing, beared. 6** (*tr*) to lower or attempt to lower the price or prices of (a stock market or a security) by speculative selling. [OE *bera*]

Bear (bɛə) n *the.* **1** the English name for either Ursa Major (Great Bear) or Ursa Minor (Little Bear). **2** an informal name for Russia.

bearable ('bɛərəb°l) adj endurable; tolerable.

bear-baiting n (formerly) an entertainment in which dogs attacked a chained bear.

beard (bɪəd) n **1** the hair growing on the lower parts of a man's face. **2** any similar growth in animals. **3** a tuft of long hairs in plants such as barley; awn. **4** a barb, as on a fish-hook. ♦ vb (*tr*) **5** to oppose boldly or impertinently. [OE *beard*]
▶ **'bearded** adj

beardless ('bɪədlɪs) adj **1** without a beard. **2** too young to grow a beard; immature.

bear down vb (*intr, adv; often foll. by on or upon*) **1** to press or weigh down. **2** to approach in a determined or threatening manner.

Beardsley ★ ('bɪədzlɪ) n **Aubrey (Vincent)**. 1872–98, British illustrator: noted for his stylized black-and-white illustrations.

bearer ('bɛərə) n **1** a person or thing that bears, presents, or upholds. **2** a person who presents a note or bill for payment. **3** (in Africa, India, etc., formerly) a native porter or servant. **4** (*modifier*) *Finance*. payable to the person in possession: *bearer bonds*.

bear garden n **1** (formerly) a place where bear-baiting took place. **2** a scene of tumult.

bear hug n **1** a wrestling hold in which the arms are locked tightly round an opponent's chest and arms. **2** any similar tight embrace. **3** *Commerce*. an approach to the board of one company by another to indicate that an offer is to be made for their shares.

bearing ('bɛərɪŋ) n **1** a support for a rotating or reciprocating mechanical part. **2** (foll. by *on* or *upon*) relevance (to): *it has no bearing on this problem*. **3** a person's general social conduct. **4** the act, period, or capability of producing fruit or young. **5** anything that carries weight or acts as a support. **6** the angular direction of a point or course measured from a known position. **7** (*usually pl*) the position, as of a ship, fixed with reference to two or more known points. **8** (*usually pl*) a sense of one's relative position; orientation (esp. in **lose, get,** or **take one's bearings**). **9** *Heraldry*. **9a** a device on a heraldic shield. **9b** another name for **coat of arms**.

bearing rein n *Chiefly Brit*. a rein from the bit to the saddle, designed to keep the horse's head in the desired position.

bearish ('bɛərɪʃ) adj **1** like a bear; rough; clumsy; churlish. **2** *Stock Exchange*. causing, expecting, or characterized by a fall in prices: *a bearish feel to the market*.
▶ **'bearishness** n

bear on vb (*intr, prep*) **1** to be relevant to; relate to. **2** to be burdensome to or afflict.

bear out vb (*tr, adv*) to show to be true or truthful; confirm: *the witness will bear me out*.

bear raid n an attempt to force down the price of a security or commodity by sustained selling.

bearskin ('bɛəˌskɪn) n **1** the pelt of a bear, esp. when used as a rug. **2** a tall helmet of black fur worn by certain British Army regiments.

bear up vb (*intr, adv*) to endure cheerfully.

bear with vb (*intr, prep*) to be patient with.

beast (biːst) n **1** any animal other than man, esp. a large wild quadruped. **2** savage nature or characteristics: *the beast in man*. **3** a brutal, uncivilized, or filthy person. [C13: from OF *beste*, from L *bestia*, from ?]

beastly ('biːstlɪ) adj **beastlier, beastliest. 1** *Inf*. unpleasant; disagreeable. **2** *Obs*. of or like a beast; bestial. ♦ adv **3** *Inf*. (intensifier): *the weather is so beastly hot*.
▶ **'beastliness** n

beast of burden n an animal, such as a donkey or ox, used for carrying loads.

beast of prey n any animal that hunts other animals for food.

beat (biːt) vb **beats, beating, beat; beaten** or **beat. 1** (when *intr*, often foll. by *against, on*, etc.) to strike with or as if with a series of violent blows. **2** (*tr*) to punish by striking; flog. **3** to move up and down; flap: *the bird beat its wings heavily*. **4** (*intr*) to throb rhythmically; pulsate. **5** (*tr*; sometimes foll. by *up*) *Cookery*. to stir or whisk vigorously. **6** (*tr*; sometimes foll. by *out*) to shape, thin, or flatten (metal) by repeated blows. **7** (*tr*) *Music*. to indicate (time) by one's hand, baton, etc., or by a metronome. **8** (when *tr*, sometimes foll. by *out*) to produce (a sound or signal) by or as if by striking a drum. **9** to overcome; defeat. **10** (*tr*) to form (a path, track, etc.) by repeatedly walking or riding over it. **11** (*tr*) to arrive, achieve, or finish before (someone or something). **12** (*tr*; often foll. by *back, down, off*, etc.) to drive, push, or thrust. **13** to scour (woodlands or undergrowth) so as to rouse game for shooting. **14** (*tr*) *Sl*. to puzzle or baffle: *it beats me*. **15** (*intr*) *Naut*. to steer a sailing vessel as close as possible to the direction from which the wind is blowing. **16 beat a retreat.** to withdraw in haste. **17 beat it.** *Sl.* (*often imperative*) to go away. **18 beat the bounds.** *Brit*. (formerly) to define the boundaries of a parish by making a procession around them and hitting the ground with rods. **19 can you beat it** or **that?** *Sl*. an expression of surprise. ♦ n **20** a stroke or blow. **21** the sound made by a stroke or blow. **22** a regular throb. **23a** an assigned or habitual round or route, as of a policeman. **23b** (*as modifier*): *beat police officers.* **24** the basic rhythmic unit in a piece of music. **25a** pop or rock music characterized by a heavy rhythmic beat. **25b** (*as modifier*): *a beat group.* **26** *Physics*. one of the regular pulses produced by combining two sounds or electrical signals that have similar frequencies. **27** *Prosody*. the accent or stress in a metrical foot. **28** (*modifier*) (*often cap*.) of, characterized by, or relating to the Beat Generation. ♦ adj **29** (*postpositive*) *Sl*. totally exhausted. ♦ See also **beat down, beat up.** [OE *bēatan*]
▶ **'beatable** adj

beatbox ('biːtˌbɒks) n another name for **drum machine**.

beat down vb (*adv*) **1** (*tr*) *Inf*. to force or persuade (a seller) to accept a lower price. **2** (*intr*) (of the sun) to shine intensely.

beaten ('biːt°n) adj **1** defeated or baffled. **2** shaped or made thin by hammering: *beaten gold*. **3** much travelled; well trodden. **4 off the beaten track. 4a** in unfamiliar territory. **4b** out of the ordinary; unusual. **5** (of food) mixed by beating; whipped. **6** tired out; exhausted.

beater ('biːtə) n **1** a person who beats or hammers: *a panel beater*. **2** a device used for beating: *a carpet beater*. **3** a person who rouses wild game.

Beat Generation n (*functioning as sing or pl*) **1** members of the generation that came to maturity in the 1950s, whose rejection of the social and political systems of the West was expressed through contempt for regular work, possessions, traditional dress, etc. **2** a group of US writers, notably Jack Kerouac, Allen Ginsberg, and William Burroughs, who emerged in the 1950s.

beatific (ˌbiːəˈtɪfɪk) *adj* **1** displaying great happiness, calmness, etc. **2** of or conferring a state of celestial happiness. [C17: from LL *beātificus*, from L *beātus*, from *beāre* to bless + *facere* to make]
▶ ˌbea'tifically *adv*

beatify (brˈætɪˌfaɪ) *vb* **beatifies, beatifying, beatified.** (*tr*) **1** *RC Church.* (of the pope) to declare formally that (a deceased person) showed a heroic degree of holiness in life and is worthy of veneration: the first step towards canonization. **2** to make extremely happy. [C16: from OF *beatifier*; see BEATIFIC]
▶ **beatification** (brˌætɪfɪˈkeɪʃən) *n*

beating ('biːtɪŋ) *n* **1** a whipping or thrashing. **2** a defeat or setback. **3 take some** or **a lot of beating.** to be difficult to improve upon.

beatitude (brˈætɪˌtjuːd) *n* **1** supreme blessedness or happiness. **2** an honorific title of the Eastern Christian Church, applied to those of patriarchal rank. [C15: from L *beātitūdō*, from *beātus* blessed; see BEATIFIC]

Beatitude (brˈætɪˌtjuːd) *n Christianity.* any of eight sayings of Jesus in the Sermon on the Mount (Matthew 5:3 –11) in which he declares that the poor, the meek, etc., will, in various ways, receive the blessings of heaven.

Beatles ★ ('biːtⁿlz) *pl n* **the.** British rock group (1961–70): comprised John Lennon, Paul McCartney, George Harrison (born 1943), and Ringo Starr (real name *Richard Starkey*, born 1940). See also (John Winston Ono) **Lennon,** (Paul) **McCartney.**

beatnik ('biːtnɪk) *n* **1** a member of the Beat Generation (sense 1). **2** *Inf.* any person with long hair and shabby clothes. [C20: from BEAT (n) + -NIK]

Beaton ('biːtⁿn) *n* Sir **Cecil (Walter Hardy)**. 1904–80, British photographer.

Beatrix ★ ('biːətrɪks) *n* full name *Beatrix Wilhelmina Armgard.* born 1938, queen of the Netherlands from 1980.

Beatty ★ ('biːtɪ) *n* **David,** 1st Earl Beatty. 1871–1936, British admiral of the fleet in World War I.

beat up *Inf.* ◆ *vb* **1** (*tr, adv*) to strike or kick repeatedly, so as to inflict severe physical damage. ◆ *adj* **beat-up. 2** worn-out; dilapidated.

beau (bəʊ) *n, pl* **beaux** (bəʊ, bəʊz) or **beaus** (bəʊz). **1** a man who is greatly concerned with his clothes and appearance; dandy. **2** *Chiefly US.* a boyfriend; sweetheart. [C17: from F, from OF *biau,* from L *bellus* handsome]

Beaufort ★ ('bəʊfət) *n* **1 Henry.** ?1374–1447, English cardinal, half-brother of Henry IV; chancellor (1403–04, 1413–17, 1424–26). **2** Lady **Margaret,** Countess of Richmond and Derby. ?1443–1509, mother of Henry VII.

Beaufort scale *n Meteorol.* an international scale of wind velocities from 0 (calm) to 12 (hurricane) (0 to 17 in the US). [C19: after Sir Francis *Beaufort* (1774–1857), Brit. admiral and hydrographer who devised it]

Beaufort Sea ★ *n* part of the Arctic Ocean off the N coast of North America.

beau geste *French.* (bo ʒɛst) *n, pl* **beaux gestes** (bo ʒɛst). a noble or gracious gesture or act. [lit.: beautiful gesture]

Beauharnais ★ (*French* boarnɛ) *n* **1 Alexandre** (alɛksādr), Vicomte de. 1760–94, French general; first husband of Empress Joséphine: guillotined. **2** his son, **Eugène de** (øʒɛn də). 1781–1824, viceroy of Italy (1805–14) for his stepfather Napoleon I. **3** (**Eugénie**) **Hortense de** (øʒeni ɔrtãs də). 1783–1837, queen of Holland (1806–10) as wife of Louis Bonaparte; daughter of Alexandre Beauharnais; mother of Napoleon III. **4 Joséphine de** (ʒozefin də). See (Empress) **Joséphine.**

beaujolais ('bəʊʒəˌleɪ) *n* (*sometimes cap.*) a popular fresh-tasting red or white wine from southern Burgundy in France.

Beaulieu ★ ('bjuːlɪ) *n* a village in S England, in Hampshire: site of Palace House, seat of Lord Montagu and once the gatehouse of the ruined 13th-century abbey; the National Motor Museum is in its grounds. Pop.: 1200 (latest est.).

Beaumarchais ★ (*French* bomarʃɛ) *n* **Pierre Augustin Caron de** (pjɛr ogystɛ karɔ̃ də). 1732–99, French dramatist, noted for his comedies *The Barber of Seville* (1775) and *The Marriage of Figaro* (1784).

Beaumaris ★ (bəʊˈmærɪs) *n* a resort in N Wales, on the island of Anglesey: 13th-century castle. Pop.: 1561 (1991).

beau monde ('bəʊ 'mɒnd) *n* the world of fashion and society. [C18: F, lit.: fine world]

Beaumont[1] ★ ('bəʊmɒnt) *n* a city in SE Texas. Pop.: 115 022 (1994 est.).

Beaumont[2] ★ ('bəʊmɒnt) *n* **Francis.** 1584–1616, English dramatist, who collaborated with John Fletcher on plays including *The Maid's Tragedy* (1611).

Beaune ★ (bəʊn) *n* **1** a city in E France, near Dijon: an important trading centre for Burgundy wines. Pop.: 22 170 (1990). **2** a wine produced in this district.

beaut (bjuːt) *Sl., chiefly Austral. & NZ.* ◆ *n* **1** an outstanding person or thing. ◆ *adj, interj* **2** excellent.

beauteous ('bjuːtɪəs) *adj* a poetic word for **beautiful.**
▶ 'beauteousness *n*

beautician (bjuːˈtɪʃən) *n* a person who works in or manages a beauty salon.

beautiful ('bjuːtɪful) *adj* **1** possessing beauty; aesthetically pleasing. **2** highly enjoyable; very pleasant.
▶ 'beautifully *adv*

beautify ('bjuːtɪˌfaɪ) *vb* **beautifies, beautifying, beautified.** to make or become beautiful.
▶ **beautification** (ˌbjuːtɪfɪˈkeɪʃən) *n* ▶ 'beautiˌfier *n*

beauty ('bjuːtɪ) *n, pl* **beauties. 1** the combination of all the qualities of a person or thing that delight the senses and mind. **2** a very attractive woman. **3** *Inf.* an outstanding example of its kind. **4** *Inf.* an advantageous feature: *one beauty of the job is the short hours.* ◆ *interj* **5** (*NZ* 'bjuːdɪ). *Austral. & NZ sl.* an expression of approval or agreement. [C13: from OF *biauté,* from *biau* beautiful; see BEAU]

beauty queen *n* an attractive young woman, esp. one who has won a beauty contest.

beauty salon or **parlour** *n* an establishment providing services such as hairdressing, facial treatment, and massage.

beauty sleep *n Inf.* sleep, esp. sleep before midnight.

beauty spot *n* **1** a place of outstanding beauty. **2** a mole or other similar natural mark on the skin. **3** (esp. in the 18th century) a small dark-coloured patch or spot worn on a lady's face as an adornment.

Beauvais ★ (*French* bovɛ) *n* a market town in N France, 64 km (40 miles) northwest of Paris. Pop.: 56 280 (1990).

Beauvoir ★ (*French* bovwar) *n* **Simone de** (simɔn də). 1908–86, French writer, whose works include *Le deuxième sexe* (1949), and *Les mandarins* (1954).

beaux (bəʊ, bəʊz) *n* a plural of **beau.**

beaux-arts (bəʊˈzɑː) *pl n* **1** another word for **fine art. 2** (*modifier*) relating to the classical decorative style, esp. that of the École des Beaux-Arts in Paris: *beaux-arts influences.* [F]

beaver[1] ('biːvə) *n* **1** a large amphibious rodent of Europe, Asia, and North America. It has soft brown fur, a broad flat hairless tail, and webbed hind feet, and constructs complex dams and houses (lodges) in rivers. **2** its fur. **3** a tall hat of beaver fur worn during the 19th century. **4** a woollen napped cloth resembling beaver fur. **5** *Obs.* a full beard. **6** a bearded man. **7** (*modifier*) made of beaver fur or similar material. ◆ *vb* **8** (*intr*; usually foll. by *away*) to work industriously or steadily. [OE *beofor*]

beaver[2] ('biːvə) *n* a movable piece on a medieval helmet used to protect the lower face. [C15: from OF *baviere,* from *baver* to dribble]

Beaverbrook ★ ('biːvəˌbrʊk) *n* **1st Baron,** title of *William Maxwell Aitken.* 1879–1964, British newspaper proprietor and Conservative politician, born in Canada. Minister of information (1918); minister of aircraft production (1940–41).

Bebington ★ ('bɛbɪŋtən) *n* a town in NW England, in Wirral unitary authority, Merseyside: docks and chemical works. Pop.: 60 148 (1991).

★ people and places

bebop ('bi:bɒp) *n* the full name for **bop** (sense 1). [C20: imit. of the rhythm]
► **'bebopper** *n*

becalmed (bɪ'kɑːmd) *adj* (of a sailing boat or ship) motionless through lack of wind.

became (bɪ'keɪm) *vb* the past tense of **become**.

because (bɪ'kɒz, -'kəz) *conj* **1** (*subordinating*) on account of the fact that; since: *because it's so cold we'll go home*. **2 because of.** (*prep*) on account of: *I lost my job because of her*. [C14 *bi cause*, from *bi* BY + CAUSE]

USAGE NOTE See at **reason.**

béchamel sauce (,beɪʃə'mɛl) *n* a thick white sauce flavoured with onion and seasonings. [C18: after the Marquis of *Béchamel*, its F inventor]

Béchar ★ (*French* beʃar) *n* a city in NW Algeria: an oasis. Pop.: 107 311 (1987). Former name: **Colomb-Béchar.**

bêche-de-mer (,beʃdə'mɛə) *n*, *pl* **bêches-de-mer** (,beʃdə'mɛə) *or* **bêche-de-mer.** another name for **trepang.** [C19: quasi-F, from earlier E *biche de mer*, from Port. *bicho do mar* worm of the sea]

Bechet ★ ('beʃeɪ) *n* **Sidney** (**Joseph**). 1897–1959, US jazz soprano saxophonist and clarinettist.

Bechstein ★ (*German* 'beçʃtaɪn) *n* **Karl** (karl). 1826–1900, German piano maker; founder (1853) of the Bechstein company of piano manufacturers in Berlin.

Bechuana (beˈtʃwɑːnə; ,bekjuˈɑːnə) *n*, *pl* **Bechuana** *or* **Bechuanas.** a former name for a Bantu of Botswana.

Bechuanaland ★ (beˈtʃwɑːnəˌlænd; ,betʃuˈɑːnəˌlænd, ,bekjuˈ-) *n* the former name (until 1966) of **Botswana.**

beck[1] (bek) *n* **1** a nod, wave, or other gesture. **2 at (someone's) beck and call.** subject to (someone's) slightest whim. [C14: short for *becnen* to BECKON]

beck[2] (bek) *n* (in N England) a stream. [OE *becc*]

Beckenbauer ★ ('bekən,bauə) *n* **Franz.** born 1945, German footballer: team captain when West Germany won the World Cup (1974): manager of West Germany (1984–90).

Becker ★ ('bekə) *n* **Boris** ('bɒrɪs). born 1967, German tennis player: Wimbledon champion 1985, 1986, and 1989.

Becket ★ ('bekɪt) *n* **Saint Thomas à.** 1118–70, English prelate; chancellor (1155–62) to Henry II; archbishop of Canterbury (1162–70): murdered. Feast day: Dec. 29 or July 7.

Beckett ★ ('bekɪt) *n* **1 Margaret Mary.** born 1943, British Labour politician; president of the board of trade and secretary of state for trade and industry from 1997. **2 Samuel.** 1906–89, Irish dramatist and novelist writing in French and English, whose works include the plays *Waiting for Godot* (1952), *Endgame* (1957), and the novel *Malone Dies* (1951): Nobel prize for literature 1969.

Beckford ★ ('bekfəd) *n* **William.** 1759–1844, British writer; author of the oriental romance *Vathek* (1787).

Beckmann ★ (*German* 'bekman) *n* **1 Ernst Otto** (ɛrnst 'ɔto). 1853–1923, German chemist: devised the **Beckmann thermometer.** **2 Max** (maks). 1884–1950, German expressionist painter.

beckon ('bekən) *vb* **1** to summon with a gesture of the hand or head. **2** to entice or lure. ◆ *n* **3** a summoning gesture. [OE *biecnan*, from *bēacen* sign]
► **'beckoner** *n* ► **'beckoning** *adj*

becloud (bɪ'klaud) *vb* (*tr*) **1** to cover or obscure with a cloud. **2** to confuse or muddle.

become (bɪ'kʌm) *vb* **becomes, becoming, became, become.** (*mainly intr*) **1** (*copula*) to come to be; develop or grow into: *he became a monster*. **2** (foll. by *of*; *usually used in a question*) to happen (to): *what became of him?* **3** (*tr*) to suit: *that dress becomes you*. **4** (*tr*) to be appropriate; to befit: *it ill becomes you to complain*. [OE *becuman* to happen]

becoming (bɪ'kʌmɪŋ) *adj* suitable; appropriate.
► **be'comingly** *adv* ► **be'comingness** *n*

becquerel (,bekə'rɛl) *n* the SI unit of activity of a radioactive source. [after A. H. BECQUEREL]

Becquerel ★ (*French* bɛkrɛl) *n* **Antoine Henri** (ɑ̃twan ɑ̃ri). 1852–1908, French physicist, who instigated the study of radioactivity: Nobel prize for physics 1903.

bed (bed) *n* **1** a piece of furniture on which to sleep. **2** the mattress and bedclothes: *an unmade bed*. **3** sleep or rest: *time for bed*. **4** any place in which a person or animal sleeps or rests. **5** *Med.* a unit of potential occupancy in a hospital or residential institution. **6** *Inf.* sexual intercourse. **7** a plot of ground in which plants are grown. **8** the bottom of a river, lake, or sea. **9** a part of this used for cultivation of a plant or animal: *oyster beds*. **10** any underlying structure or part. **11** a layer of rock, esp. sedimentary rock. **12 go to bed. 12a** (often foll. by *with*) to have sexual intercourse (with). **12b** *Journalism, printing.* (of a newspaper, etc.) to go to press; start printing. **13 in bed with.** *Inf.* cooperating closely with (another person, organization, government, etc.), esp. covertly. **14 put to bed.** *Journalism.* to finalize work on (a newspaper, etc.) so that it is ready to go to press. **15 take to one's bed.** to remain in bed, esp. because of illness. ◆ *vb* **beds, bedding, bedded. 16** (usually foll. by *down*) to go to or put into a place to sleep or rest. **17** (*tr*) to have sexual intercourse with. **18** (*tr*) to place firmly into position; embed. **19** *Geol.* to form or be arranged in a distinct layer; stratify. **20** (*tr*; often foll. by *out*) to plant in a bed of soil. [OE *bedd*]

BEd *abbrev.* for Bachelor of Education.

bed and board *n* sleeping accommodation and meals.

bed and breakfast *n Chiefly Brit.* **1** (in a hotel, boarding house, etc.) overnight accommodation and breakfast. **2** the selling of shares after hours one evening on a stock exchange and buying them back the next morning, in order to establish a loss for capital-gains tax purposes.

bedaub (bɪ'dɔːb) *vb* (*tr*) **1** to smear all over with something thick, sticky, or dirty. **2** to ornament in a gaudy or vulgar fashion.

bedazzle (bɪ'dæzəl) *vb* **bedazzles, bedazzling, bedazzled.** (*tr*) to dazzle or confuse, as with brilliance.
► **be'dazzlement** *n*

bed bath *n* another name for **blanket bath.**

bedbug ('bed,bʌg) *n* any of several bloodsucking wingless insects of temperate regions, infesting dirty houses.

bedchamber ('bed,tʃeɪmbə) *n* an archaic word for **bedroom.**

bedclothes ('bed,kləuðz) *pl n* sheets, blankets, and other coverings for a bed.

beddable ('bedəbəl) *adj* sexually attractive.

bedding ('bedɪŋ) *n* **1** bedclothes, sometimes considered with a mattress. **2** litter, such as straw, for animals. **3** a foundation, such as mortar under a brick. **4** the stratification of rocks.

bedding plant *n* an immature plant that may be planted out in a garden bed.

Beddoes ★ ('bedəuz) *n* **Thomas Lovell.** 1803–49, British poet, noted for his macabre imagery, esp. in *Death's Jest-Book* (1850).

Bede ★ (bi:d) *n* **Saint**, known as *the Venerable Bede*. ?673–735 A.D., English monk, scholar, historian, and theologian, noted for his Latin *Ecclesiastical History of the English People* (731). Feast day: May 27 or 25.

bedeck (bɪ'dek) *vb* (*tr*) to cover with decorations; adorn.

bedevil (bɪ'dɛvəl) *vb* **bedevils, bedevilling, bedevilled** *or US* **bedevils, bedeviling, bedeviled.** (*tr*) **1** to harass or torment. **2** to throw into confusion. **3** to possess, as with a devil.
► **be'devilment** *n*

bedew (bɪ'djuː) *vb* (*tr*) to wet as with dew.

bedfellow ('bed,feləu) *n* **1** a person with whom one shares a bed. **2** a temporary ally or associate.

Bedford[1] ★ ('bedfəd) *n* **1** a town in SE central England, administrative centre of Bedfordshire, on the River Ouse. Pop.: 73 917 (1991). **2** short for **Bedfordshire.**

Bedford[2] ★ ('bedfəd) *n* **1 David.** born 1937, British composer, influenced by rock music. **2 Duke of,** title of *John of Lancaster.* 1389–1435, son of Henry IV of England: protector of England and regent of France (1422–35).

★ people and places

Bedfordshire ★ ('bɛdfəd,ʃɪə, -ʃə) n a county of S central England: mainly low-lying, with the Chiltern Hills in the south. Administrative centre: Bedford. Pop. (including Luton): 543 100 (1994 est.). Area (including Luton): 1235 sq. km (477 sq. miles). Abbrev.: **Beds**.

bedight (bɪ'daɪt) Arch. ◆ vb bedights, bedighting, bedight or bedighted. 1 (tr) to array or adorn. ◆ adj 2 (p.p.) adorned or bedecked. [C14: from DIGHT]

bedim (bɪ'dɪm) vb bedims, bedimming, bedimmed. (tr) to make dim or obscure.

Bedivere ★ ('bɛdɪ,vɪə) n Sir. (in Arthurian legend) a knight who took the dying King Arthur to the barge in which he was carried to Avalon.

bedizen (bɪ'daɪz°n, -'dɪz°n) vb (tr) Arch. to dress or decorate gaudily or tastelessly. [C17: from BE- + obs. dizen to dress up, from ?]
▸ be'dizenment n

bed jacket n a woman's short upper garment worn over a nightgown when sitting up in bed.

bedlam ('bɛdləm) n 1 a noisy confused situation. 2 Arch. a madhouse. [C13 bedlem, bethlem, from Hospital of St Mary of Bethlehem in London]

bed linen n sheets, pillowcases, etc., for a bed.

Bedloe's Island ('bɛdləʊz) or **Bedloe Island** ★ n the former name (until 1956) of **Liberty Island**.

Bedouin or **Beduin** ('bɛduɪn) n 1 (pl Bedouins, Bedouin or Beduins, Beduin) a nomadic Arab tribesman of the deserts of Arabia, Jordan, and Syria. 2 a wanderer. ◆ adj 3 of or relating to the Bedouins. 4 wandering. [C14: from OF beduin, from Ar. badāwi, pl. of badwi, from badw desert]

bedpan ('bɛd,pæn) n a vessel used by a bedridden patient to collect faeces and urine.

bedraggle (bɪ'dræg°l) vb bedraggles, bedraggling, bedraggled. (tr) to make (hair, clothing, etc.) limp, untidy, or dirty, as with rain or mud.
▸ be'draggled adj

bedridden ('bɛd,rɪd°n) adj confined to bed because of illness, esp. for a long or indefinite period. [OE bedreda]

bedrock ('bɛd,rɒk) n 1 the solid rock beneath the surface soil, etc. 2 basic principles or facts. 3 the lowest point, level, or layer.

bedroll ('bɛd,rəʊl) n a portable roll of bedding.

bedroom ('bɛd,ruːm, -,rʊm) n 1 a room used for sleeping. 2 (modifier) containing references to sex: a bedroom comedy.

Beds (bɛdz) abbrev. for Bedfordshire.

bedside ('bɛd,saɪd) n a the space beside a bed, esp. a sickbed. b (as modifier): a bedside lamp.

bedsit ('bɛd,sɪt) n a furnished sitting room containing sleeping accommodation. Also called: **bedsitting room**, **bedsitter**.

bedsore ('bɛd,sɔː) n a chronic ulcer on the skin of a bedridden person, caused by prolonged pressure.

bedspread ('bɛd,sprɛd) n a top cover on a bed.

bedstead ('bɛd,stɛd) n the framework of a bed.

bedstraw ('bɛd,strɔː) n any of numerous plants whicn have small white or yellow flowers and prickly or hairy fruits: formerly used as straw for beds.

bedtime ('bɛd,taɪm) n a the time when one usually goes to bed. b (as modifier): a bedtime story.

bed-wetting n the act of urinating in bed.

Bedworth ★ ('bɛdwəθ) n a town in central England, in N Warwickshire. Pop.: 31 932 (1991).

bee[1] (biː) n 1 any of various four-winged insects that collect nectar and pollen and make honey and wax. 2 **busy bee**. a person who is industrious as has many things to do. 3 **have a bee in one's bonnet**. to be obsessed with an idea. [OE bīo]

bee[2] (biː) n Chiefly US. a social gathering for a specific purpose, as to carry out a communal task: quilting bee. [?from dialect bean neighbourly help, from OE bēn boon]

Beeb (biːb) n the. an informal name for the **BBC**.

beebread ('biː,brɛd) n a mixture of pollen and nectar prepared by worker bees and fed to the larvae. Also called: **ambrosia**.

beech (biːtʃ) n 1 a European tree having smooth greyish bark. 2 a similar tree of temperate Australasia and South America. 3 the hard wood of either of these trees. 4 See copper beech. [OE bēce]
▸ 'beechen or 'beechy adj

Beecham ★ ('biːtʃəm) n Sir Thomas. 1879–1961, British conductor.

Beecher Stowe ★ n See (Harriet Elizabeth Beecher) Stowe.

beechnut ('biːtʃ,nʌt) n the small brown triangular edible nut of the beech tree, collectively often termed **beech mast**.

bee-eater n any of various insectivorous birds of the Old World tropics and subtropics.

beef (biːf) n 1 the flesh of various bovine animals, esp. the cow, when killed for eating. 2 (pl **beeves**) an adult ox, etc., reared for its meat. 3 Inf. human flesh, esp. when muscular. 4 (pl **beefs**) Sl. a complaint. ◆ vb 5 (intr) Sl. to complain, esp. repeatedly. 6 (tr; often foll. by up) Inf. to strengthen; reinforce. [C13: from OF boef, from L bōs ox]

beefburger ('biːf,bɜːgə) n a flat fried cake of minced beef; hamburger.

beefcake ('biːf,keɪk) n Sl. men displayed for their muscular bodies, esp. in photographs.

beefeater ('biːf,iːtə) n a nickname applied to the Yeomen of the Guard, and the Yeomen Warders at the Tower of London.

beef road n Austral. a road used for transporting cattle.

beefsteak ('biːf,steɪk) n a lean piece of beef that can be grilled, fried, etc.

beef tomato n a very large fleshy variety of tomato. Also called: **beefsteak tomato**.

beef tea n a drink made by boiling pieces of lean beef.

beefy ('biːfɪ) adj beefier, beefiest. 1 like beef. 2 Inf. muscular; brawny.
▸ 'beefiness n

beehive ('biː,haɪv) n 1 a man-made receptacle used to house a swarm of bees. 2 a dome-shaped structure. 3 a place where busy people are assembled. 4 the Beehive. the dome-shaped building which houses Parliament in Wellington, New Zealand.

beekeeper ('biː,kiːpə) n a person who keeps bees for their honey.
▸ 'bee,keeping n

beeline ('biː,laɪn) n the most direct route between two places (esp. in **make a beeline for**).

Beelzebub (bɪ'ɛlzɪ,bʌb) n Satan or any devil. [OE Belzebub, ult. from Heb. bá'al zebūb, lit.: lord of flies]

bee moth n any of various moths whose larvae live in the nests of bees or wasps, feeding on nest materials and host larvae.

been (biːn, bɪn) vb the past participle of **be**.

beep (biːp) n 1 a short high-pitched sound, as made by a car horn or by electronic apparatus. ◆ vb 2 to make or cause to make such a noise. [C20: imit.]
▸ 'beeper n

beer (bɪə) n 1 an alcoholic drink brewed from malt, sugar, hops, and water. 2 a slightly fermented drink made from the roots or leaves of certain plants: ginger beer. 3 (modifier) relating to beer: beer glass. 4 (modifier) in which beer is drunk, esp. (of licensed premises) having a licence to sell beer but not spirits: beer house; beer garden. [OE beor]

beer and skittles n (functioning as sing) Inf. enjoyment or pleasure.

Beerbohm ★ ('bɪəbəʊm) n Sir (Henry) Max(imilian). 1872–1956, British critic, and caricaturist, whose novels include Zuleika Dobson (1911).

beer parlour n Canad. a licensed place in which beer is sold to the public.

Beersheba ★ (bɪə'ʃiːbə) n a town in S Israel: commercial centre of the Negev. In biblical times it marked the southern limit of Palestine. Pop.: 152 600 (1996 est.).

★ people and places

beery ('bɪərɪ) *adj* **beerier, beeriest. 1** smelling or tasting of beer. **2** given to drinking beer.
▶ 'beerily *adv* ▶ 'beeriness *n*

bee's knees *n* the (*functioning as sing*) *Inf.* an excellent or ideally suitable person or thing.

beestings, biestings, beestings ('bi:stɪŋz) *n* *or US* (*functioning as sing*), the first milk secreted by a cow or similar animal after giving birth; colostrum. [OE *bȳsting*]

beeswax ('bi:z,wæks) *n* **1** a wax secreted by honeybees for constructing honeycombs. **2** this wax after refining, used in polishes, etc.

beeswing ('bi:z,wɪŋ) *n* a light filmy crust of tartar that forms in some wines after long keeping in the bottle.

beet (bi:t) *n* **1** a plant of a genus widely cultivated in such varieties as the sugar beet, mangelwurzel, and beetroot. **2** the leaves of any of several varieties of this plant, cooked and eaten as a vegetable. **3 red beet.** the US name for **beetroot**. [OE *bēte*, from L *bēta*]

Beethoven ★ ('beɪt,həʊv°n) *n* **Ludwig van** ('lu:tvɪç fan). 1770–1827, German composer. His works include nine symphonies, 32 piano sonatas, 16 string quartets, five piano concertos, a violin concerto, two masses, the opera *Fidelio* (1805), and choral music.

beetle[1] ('bi:t°l) *n* **1** an insect having biting mouthparts and forewings modified to form shell-like protective casings. **2** a game in which the players draw or assemble a beetle-shaped form. ◆ *vb* **beetles, beetling, beetled.** (*intr*; foll. by *along, off,* etc.) **3** *Inf.* to scuttle or scurry; hurry. [OE *bitela*]

beetle[2] ('bi:t°l) *n* **1** a heavy hand tool for pounding or beating. **2** a machine used to finish cloth by stamping it with wooden hammers. [OE *bīetel*, from *bēatan* to BEAT]

beetle[3] ('bi:t°l) *vb* **beetles, beetling, beetled. 1** (*intr*) to overhang; jut. ◆ *adj* **2** overhanging; prominent. [C14: ? rel. to BEETLE[1]]
▶ 'beetling *adj*

beetle-browed *adj* having bushy or overhanging eyebrows.

Beeton ★ ('bi:t°n) *n* **Isabella Mary,** known as *Mrs Beeton.* 1836–65, British cookery writer, author of *The Book of Household Management* (1861).

beetroot ('bi:t,ru:t) *n* a variety of the beet plant that has a bulbous dark red root that may be eaten as a vegetable, in salads, or pickled.

beet sugar *n* the sucrose obtained from sugar beet, identical in composition to cane sugar.

beeves (bi:vz) *n* the plural of **beef** (sense 2).

BEF *abbrev. for* British Expeditionary Force, the British army that served in France 1939-40.

befall (bɪ'fɔ:l) *vb* **befalls, befalling, befell, befallen.** *Arch. or literary.* **1** (*intr*) to take place. **2** (*tr*) to happen to. **3** (*intr*; usually foll. by *to*) to be due, as by right. [OE *befeallan*; see BE-, FALL]

befit (bɪ'fɪt) *vb* **befits, befitting, befitted.** (*tr*) to be appropriate to or suitable for. [C15: from BE- + FIT[1]]
▶ be'fitting *adj* ▶ be'fittingly *adv*

befog (bɪ'fɒg) *vb* **befogs, befogging, befogged.** (*tr*) **1** to surround with fog. **2** to make confused.

before (bɪ'fɔ:) *conj* (*subordinating*) **1** earlier than the time when. **2** rather than: *he'll resign before he agrees to it.* ◆ *prep* **3** preceding in space or time; in front of; ahead of: *standing before the altar.* **4** in the presence of: *to be brought before a judge.* **5** in preference to: *to put friendship before money.* ◆ *adv* **6** at an earlier time; previously. **7** in front. [OE *beforan*]

beforehand (bɪ'fɔ:,hænd) *adj* (*postpositive*), *adv* early; in advance; in anticipation.

befoul (bɪ'faʊl) *vb* (*tr*) to make dirty or foul.

befriend (bɪ'frɛnd) *vb* (*tr*) to be a friend to; assist; favour.

befuddle (bɪ'fʌd°l) *vb* **befuddles, befuddling, befuddled.** (*tr*) **1** to confuse. **2** to make stupid with drink.
▶ be'fuddlement *n*

beg (bɛg) *vb* **begs, begging, begged. 1** (when *intr*, often foll. by *for*) to solicit (for money, food, etc.), esp. in the street. **2** to ask formally, humbly, or earnestly: *I beg forgiveness; I*

beg to differ. **3** (*intr*) (of a dog) to sit up with forepaws raised expectantly. **4 beg the question. 4a** to evade the issue. **4b** to put forward an argument that assumes the very point it is supposed to establish or that depends on some other questionable assumption. **4c** to suggest that a question needs to be asked: *the firm's success begs the question: why aren't more companies doing the same?* **5 go begging.** to be unwanted or unused. ◆ See also **beg off.** [C13: prob. from OE *bedecian*]

USAGE NOTE The use of *beg the question* to mean that a question needs to be asked is considered by some people to be incorrect.

began (bɪ'gæn) *vb* the past tense of **begin.**

beget (bɪ'gɛt) *vb* **begets, begetting, begot** *or* **begat; begotten** *or* **begot.** (*tr*) **1** to father. **2** to cause or create. [OE *begietan;* see BE-, GET]
▶ be'getter *n*

beggar ('bɛgə) *n* **1** a person who begs, esp. one who lives by begging. **2** a person who has no money or resources; pauper. **3** *Chiefly Brit.* a fellow: *lucky beggar!* ◆ *vb* (*tr*) **4** to be beyond the resources of (esp. in **beggar description**). **5** to impoverish.
▶ 'beggardom *n*

beggarly ('bɛgəlɪ) *adj* meanly inadequate; very poor.
▶ 'beggarliness *n*

beggar-my-neighbour *n* a card game in which one player tries to win all the cards of the other player.

beggary ('bɛgərɪ) *n* extreme poverty or need.

begin (bɪ'gɪn) *vb* **begins, beginning, began, begun. 1** to start or cause to start (something or to do something). **2** to bring or come into being; arise or originate. **3** to start to say or speak. **4** (*with a negative*) to have the least capacity (to do something): *he couldn't begin to compete.* **5 to begin with.** in the first place. [OE *beginnan*]

Begin ★ ('beɪgɪn) *n* **Menachem** (mə'nɑ:kɪm). 1913–92, Israeli statesman, born in Poland. Prime minister of Israel (1977–83); Nobel peace prize jointly with Anwar Sadat of Egypt 1978, with whom he concluded the Camp David treaty.

beginner (bɪ'gɪnə) *n* a person who has just started to do or learn something; novice.

beginning (bɪ'gɪnɪŋ) *n* **1** a start; commencement. **2** (*often pl*) a first or early part or stage. **3** the place where or time when something starts. **4** an origin; source.

begird (bɪ'gɜ:d) *vb* **begirds, begirding, begirt** *or* **begirded.** (*tr*) *Poetic.* **1** to surround; gird around. **2** to bind. [OE *begierdan;* see BE-, GIRD[1]]

beg off *vb* (*intr, adv*) to ask to be released from an engagement, obligation, etc.

begone (bɪ'gɒn) *sentence substitute.* go away! [C14: from BE (imperative) + GONE]

begonia (bɪ'gəʊnjə) *n* a plant of warm and tropical regions, having ornamental leaves and waxy flowers. [C18: NL, after Michel *Bégon* (1638–1710), F patron of science]

begorra (bɪ'gɒrə) *interj* an emphatic exclamation, regarded as characteristic of Irishmen. [C19: from *by God!*]

begot (bɪ'gɒt) *vb* a past tense and past participle of **beget.**

begotten (bɪ'gɒt°n) *vb* a past participle of **beget.**

begrime (bɪ'graɪm) *vb* **begrimes, begriming, begrimed.** (*tr*) to make dirty; soil.

begrudge (bɪ'grʌdʒ) *vb* **begrudges, begrudging, begrudged.** (*tr*) **1** to give, admit, or allow unwillingly or with a bad grace. **2** to envy (someone) the possession of (something).
▶ be'grudgingly *adv*

beguile (bɪ'gaɪl) *vb* **beguiles, beguiling, beguiled.** (*tr*) **1** to charm; fascinate. **2** to delude; influence by slyness. **3** (often foll. by *of* or *out of*) to cheat (someone) of. **4** to pass pleasantly; while away.
▶ be'guilement *n* ▶ be'guiler *n* ▶ be'guiling *adj* ▶ be'guilingly *adv*

beguine (bɪ'gi:n) *n* **1** a dance of South American origin in

bolero rhythm. **2** a piece of music in the rhythm of this dance.   [C20: from Louisiana F, from F *béguin* flirtation]

begum ('beɪɡəm) *n* (in certain Muslim countries) a woman of high rank.   [C18: from Urdu *begam*, from Turkish *begim*; see BEY]

begun (bɪ'ɡʌn) *vb* the past participle of **begin**.

behalf (bɪ'hɑːf) *n* interest, part, benefit, or respect (only in **on (someone's) behalf, on** or US & Canad. **in behalf of, in this** (*or* **that**) **behalf**).   [OE *be halfe*, from *be* by + *halfe* side]

Behan ★ ('biːən) *n* Brendan. 1923–64, Irish writer, noted esp. for his plays *The Quare Fellow* (1954) and *The Hostage* (1958) and for *Borstal Boy* (1958).

behave (bɪ'heɪv) *vb* **behaves, behaving, behaved. 1** (*intr*) to act or function in a specified or usual way. **2** to conduct (oneself) in a specified way: *he behaved badly.* **3** to conduct (oneself) properly or as desired.   [C15: see BE-, HAVE]

behaviour *or* US **behavior** (bɪ'heɪvjə) *n* **1** manner of behaving. **2 on one's best behaviour.** behaving with careful good manners. **3** *Psychol.* the response of an organism to a stimulus. **4** the reaction or functioning of a machine, etc., under normal or specified circumstances.   [C15: from BEHAVE; infl. by ME *havior*, from OF *havoir*, from L *habēre* to have]
▸ **be'havioural** *or* US **be'havioral** *adj*

behavioural science *n* the scientific study of the behaviour of organisms.

behaviourism *or* US **behaviorism** (bɪ'heɪvjə,rɪzəm) *n* a school of psychology that regards objective observation of the behaviour of organisms as the only valid subject for study.
▸ **be'haviourist** *or* US **be'haviorist** *adj, n* ▸ **be,haviour'istic** *or* US **be,havior'istic** *adj*

behaviour therapy *n* any of various means of treating psychological disorders, such as aversion therapy, that depend on the patient systematically learning new behaviour.

behead (bɪ'hɛd) *vb* (*tr*) to remove the head from.   [OE *behēafdian*, from BE- + *heafod* HEAD]

beheld (bɪ'hɛld) *vb* the past tense and past participle of **behold**.

behemoth (bɪ'hiːmɒθ) *n* **1** *Bible.* a gigantic beast described in Job 40:15. **2** a huge or monstrous person or thing.   [C14: from Heb. *běhēmōth*, pl. of *běhēmāh* beast]

behest (bɪ'hɛst) *n* an order or earnest request.   [OE *behǣs*, from *behātan*; see BE-, HEST]

behind (bɪ'haɪnd) *prep* **1** in or to a position further back than. **2** in the past in relation to: *I've got the exams behind me now.* **3** late according to: *running behind schedule.* **4** concerning the circumstances surrounding: *the reasons behind his departure.* **5** supporting: *I'm right behind you in your application.* ◆ *adv* **6** in or to a position further back; following. **7** remaining after someone's departure: *he left his books behind.* **8** in debt; in arrears: *to fall behind with payments.* ◆ *adj* **9** (*postpositive*) in a position further back. ◆ *n* **10** *Inf.* the buttocks. **11** *Australian Rules football.* a score of one point made by kicking the ball over the **behind line** between a goalpost and one of the smaller outer posts (**behind posts**).   [OE *behindan*]

behindhand (bɪ'haɪnd,hænd) *adj* (*postpositive*), *adv* **1** remiss in fulfilling an obligation. **2** in arrears. **3** backward. **4** late.

Behistun (,beɪhɪ'stuːn), **Bisitun,** *or* **Bisutun ★** *n* a village in W Iran by the ancient road from Ecbatana to Babylon. On a nearby cliff is an inscription by Darius in Old Persian, Elamite, and Babylonian describing his enthronement.

Behn ★ (bɛn) *n* Aphra ('æfrə). 1640–89, English dramatist and novelist, best known for her play *The Rover* (1678) and her novel *Oroonoko* (1688).

behold (bɪ'həʊld) *vb* **beholds, beholding, beheld.** (often imperative) *Arch.* or *literary.* to look (at); observe.   [OE *bihealdan;* see BE-, HOLD¹]
▸ **be'holder** *n*

beholden (bɪ'həʊld³n) *adj* indebted; obliged.   [OE *behealden,* p.p. of *behealdan* to BEHOLD]

behoof (bɪ'huːf) *n, pl* **behooves.** *Rare.* advantage or profit.   [OE *behōf;* see BEHOVE]

behove (bɪ'həʊv) *vb* **behoves, behoving, behoved.** (*tr; impersonal*) *Arch.* to be necessary or fitting for: *it behoves me to arrest you.*   [OE *behōfian*]

Behrens ★ ('bɛərənz; *German* 'beːrəns) *n* Peter. 1868–1940, German architect.

Behring ★ *n* **1** (*German* 'beːrɪŋ), Emil (Adolf) von ('eːmɪl fɒn). 1854–1917, German bacteriologist, who discovered diphtheria and tetanus antitoxins: Nobel prize for physiology or medicine 1901. **2** ('bɛrɪŋ, 'bɛər-). See (Vitus) **Bering**.

Beiderbecke ★ ('baɪdə,bɛk) *n* Leon Bismarcke, known as **Bix.** 1903–31, US jazz cornettist, composer, and pianist.

beige (beɪʒ) *n* **1a** a very light brown, sometimes with a yellowish tinge. **1b** (*as adj*): *beige gloves.* **2** a fabric made of undyed or unbleached wool.   [C19: from OF, from ?]

Beijing ★ ('beɪ'dʒɪŋ) *n* the capital of the People's Republic of China, in the northeast in central Hebei province: dates back to the 12th century B.C.; consists of two central walled cities, the Outer City (containing the commercial quarter) and the Inner City, which contains the Imperial City, within which is the Purple or Forbidden City; three universities. Pop.: 7 000 000 (1991 est.). Former English name: **Peking**.

being ('biːɪŋ) *n* **1** the state or fact of existing; existence. **2** essential nature; self. **3** something that exists or is thought to exist: *a being from outer space.* **4** a person; human being.

Beira ★ ('baɪərə) *n* a port in E Mozambique: terminus of a transcontinental railway from Lobito, Angola, through the Democratic Republic of the Congo (formerly Zaïre), Zambia, and Zimbabwe. Pop.: 298 847 (1991 est.).

Beirut *or* **Beyrouth ★** (,beɪ'ruːt) *n* the capital of Lebanon, a port on the Mediterranean: part of the Ottoman Empire from the 16th century until 1918; four universities (Lebanese, American, French, and Arab). Pop.: 1 100 000 (1991 est.).

bejabers (bɪ'dʒeɪbəz) *or* **bejabbers** (bɪ'dʒæbəz) *interj* an exclamation of surprise, emphasis, etc., regarded as characteristic of Irishmen.   [C19: from *by Jesus!*]

bejewel (bɪ'dʒuːəl) *vb* **bejewels, bejewelling, bejewelled** *or* US **bejewels, bejeweling, bejeweled.** (*tr*) to decorate as with jewels.

Bekaa *or* **Beqaa ★** (bɪ'kɑː) *n* a broad valley in central Lebanon, between the Lebanon and Anti-Lebanon Mountains. Ancient name: **Coelesyria** (,siːliː'sɪrɪə).

bel (bɛl) *n* a unit for comparing two power levels, equal to the logarithm to the base ten of the ratio of the two powers.   [C20: after A. G. BELL]

Bel ★ (beɪl) *n* (in Babylonian and Assyrian mythology) the god of the earth.

belabour *or* US **belabor** (bɪ'leɪbə) *vb* (*tr*) **1** to beat severely; thrash. **2** to attack verbally.

Belarus ★ ('bɛlə,rʌs, -,rʊs) *n* a republic in E Europe; formerly a constituent republic of the Soviet Union (1919–91): mainly low-lying and forested. Languages: Belarussian, Russian. Religion: believers are mostly Christian. Currency: rouble. Capital: Minsk. Pop.: 10 360 000 (1997). Area: 207 600 sq. km (80 134 sq. miles). Also called: **Belorussia, Byelorussia, Byelorussian Republic, Bielorussia.** Former name: **White Russia.**

Belarussian *or* **Belarusian** (,bɛləʊ'rʌʃən) *adj* **1** of, relating to, or characteristic of Belarus, its people, or their language. ◆ *n* **2** the official language of Belarus. **3** a native or inhabitant of Belarus. Also: **Belorussian, Byelorussian, Bielorussian.**

belated (bɪ'leɪtɪd) *adj* late or too late: *belated greetings.*
▸ **be'latedly** *adv* ▸ **be'latedness** *n*

Belau ★ (bə'laʊ) *n* **Republic of.** a republic comprising a group of islands in the W Pacific, in the W Caroline Islands; administratively part of the UN Trust Territory of the Pacific Islands 1947–94; entered into an agreement of free association with the US (1980); became autonomous in 1981 and independent in 1994. Chief island: Babelthuap. Capital: Koror. Pop.: 14 106 (1988 est.). Area: 476 sq. km (184 sq. miles). Former names: **Pelew Islands,** (until 1981) **Palau Islands.**

belay *vb* (bɪ'leɪ) **belays, belaying, belayed. 1** *Naut.* to secure

---

★ people and places

(a line) to a pin, cleat, or bitt. **2** (*usually imperative*) *Naut.* to stop. **3** ('biː,leɪ). *Mountaineering.* to secure (a climber) by means of a belay. ◆ *n* ('biːl,eɪ). **4** *Mountaineering.* the attachment of a climber to a mountain by securing a rope round a rock, piton, etc., to safeguard the party in the event of a fall. [OE *belecgan*]

belaying pin *n Naut.* a cylindrical metal or wooden pin used for belaying.

bel canto (bɛl 'kæntəʊ) *n Music.* a style of singing characterized by beauty of tone rather than dramatic power. [It., lit.: beautiful singing]

belch (bɛltʃ) *vb* **1** (*usually intr*) to expel wind from the stomach noisily through the mouth. **2** to expel or be expelled forcefully from inside: *smoke belching from factory chimneys.* ◆ *n* **3** an act of belching. [OE *bialcan*]

beldam *or* **beldame** ('bɛldəm) *n Arch.* an old woman. [C15: from *bel-* grand (as in *grandmother*), from OF *bel* beautiful, + *dam* mother]

beleaguer (bɪ'liːgə) *vb* (*tr*) **1** to lay siege to. **2** to harass. [C16: from BE- + obs. *leaguer* a siege]

Belém ★ (*Portuguese* bə'lēi) *n* a port in N Brazil, the capital of Pará state, on the Pará River: major trading centre for the Amazon basin. Pop.: 765 476 (1991).

belemnite ('bɛləm,naɪt) *n* **1** an extinct marine mollusc related to the cuttlefish. **2** its long pointed conical internal shell: a common fossil. [C17: from Gk *belemnon* dart]

Belfast ★ ('bɛlfɑːst, bɛl'fɑːst) *n* the capital city and an administrative district of Northern Ireland; a port on Belfast Lough: became the centre of Irish Protestantism and of the linen industry in the 17th century. Pop.: 279 237 (1991). Area (district): 155 sq. km (44 sq. miles).

Belfort ★ (*French* bɛlfɔr) *n* **1** Territoire de (teritwar də). a department of E France: the only part of Alsace remaining to France after 1871. Capital: Belfort. Pop.: 136 795 (1990). Area: 608 sq. km (237 sq. miles). **2** a fortress town in E France: strategically situated in the **Belfort Gap** between the Vosges and the Jura mountains. Pop.: 50 125 (1990).

belfry ('bɛlfrɪ) *n, pl* **belfries**. **1** the part of a tower or steeple in which bells are hung. **2** a tower or steeple. [C13: from OF *berfrei*, of Gmc origin]

Belg. *or* **Bel.** *abbrev. for:* **1** Belgian. **2** Belgium.

Belgaum ★ (bɛl'gaum) *n* a city in India, in Karnataka: cotton, furniture, leather. Pop.: 326 399 (1991).

Belgian ('bɛldʒən) *n* **1** a native or inhabitant of Belgium. ◆ *adj* **2** of or relating to Belgium, the Belgians, or their languages.

Belgian Congo ★ *n* a former name (1908–60) of the Democratic Republic of the **Congo** (sense 2).

Belgian hare *n* a large red domestic rabbit.

Belgium ★ ('bɛldʒəm) *n* a federal kingdom in NW Europe: at various times under the rulers of Burgundy, Spain, Austria, France, and the Netherlands before becoming an independent kingdom in 1830. It formed the Benelux customs union with the Netherlands and Luxembourg in 1947 and was a founder member of the EEC (now the EU). It consists chiefly of a low-lying region of sand, woods, and heath (the Campine) in the north and west, and a fertile undulating central plain rising to the Ardennes Mountains in the southeast. Languages: French, Flemish (Dutch), and German. Religion: chiefly Roman Catholic. Currency: franc and euro. Capital: Brussels. Pop.: 10 189 000 (1997). Area: 30 513 sq. km (11 778 sq. miles).

Belgorod-Dnestrovski *or* **Byelgorod-Dnestrovski** ★ (*Russian* 'bjɛlgərətdnjɪ'strɔfskij) *n* a port in the SW Ukraine: belonged to Romania (1918–40) and the Soviet Union (1944–91). Pop.: 56 800 (1991 est.). Romanian name: **Cetatea Alba**. Former name: (until 1946): **Akkerman**.

Belgrade ★ (bɛl'greɪd, 'bɛlgreɪd) *n* the capital of Yugoslavia and of Serbia, in the E part at the confluence of the Danube and Sava Rivers: became the capital of Serbia in 1878 and of Yugoslavia in 1929. Pop.: 1 168 454 (1991). Serbo-Croat name: **Beograd**.

Belgravia ★ (bɛl'greɪvɪə) *n* a fashionable residential district of W central London, around Belgrave Square.

Belial ('biːlɪəl) *n* the devil or Satan. [C13: from Heb. *bəlīyya'al*, from *bəlīy* without + *ya'al* worth]

belie (bɪ'laɪ) *vb* **belies, belying, belied.** (*tr*) **1** to show to be untrue. **2** to misrepresent; disguise the nature of. **3** to fail to justify; disappoint. [OE *beléogan*; see BE-, LIE¹]

belief (bɪ'liːf) *n* **1** a principle, etc., accepted as true, esp. without proof. **2** opinion; conviction. **3** religious faith. **4** trust or confidence, as in a person's abilities, etc.

believe (bɪ'liːv) *vb* **believes, believing, believed.** **1** (*tr; may take a clause as object*) to accept (a statement or opinion) as true: *I believe God exists.* **2** (*tr*) to accept the statement or opinion of (a person) as true. **3** (*intr*; foll. by *in*) to be convinced of the truth or existence (of): *to believe in fairies.* **4** (*intr*) to have religious faith. **5** (when *tr, takes a clause as object*) to think, assume, or suppose. **6** (*tr*) to think that someone is able to do (a particular action): *I wouldn't have believed it of him.* [OE *beliefan*] ► **be'lievable** *adj* ► **be'liever** *n*

belike (bɪ'laɪk) *adv Arch.* perhaps; maybe.

Belisarius (,bɛlɪ'sɑːrɪəs) *n* ?505–565 A.D., Byzantine general under Justinian I. He recovered North Africa from the Vandals and Italy from the Ostrogoths and led forces against the Persians.

Belisha beacon (bə'liːʃə) *n Brit.* a flashing orange globe on a post, indicating a pedestrian crossing on a road. [C20: after L. Hore-*Belisha* (1893–1957), Brit. politician]

belittle (bɪ'lɪt°l) *vb* **belittles, belittling, belittled.** (*tr*) **1** to consider or speak of (something) as less important than it really is. **2** to make small; dwarf. ► **be'littlement** *n* ► **be'littler** *n*

Belitung ★ (bɪ'liːtʊŋ) *n* another name for **Billiton**.

Belize ★ (bə'liːz) *n* a state in Central America, on the Caribbean Sea: site of a Mayan civilization until the 9th century A.D.; colonized by the British from 1638; granted internal self-government in 1964; became an independent state within the Commonwealth in 1981. Official language: English; Carib and Spanish are also spoken. Currency: Belize dollar. Capital: Belmopan. Pop.: 228 000 (1997). Area: 22 965 sq. km (8867 sq. miles). Former name (until 1973): **British Honduras**. ► **Be'lizean** *adj, n*

Belize City ★ *n* a port in Belize: capital until 1973, when it was abandoned as hurricane-prone. Pop.: 48 655 (1994).

bell¹ (bɛl) *n* **1** a hollow, usually metal, cup-shaped instrument that emits a ringing sound when struck. **2** the sound made by such an instrument, as for marking the beginning or end of a period of time. **3** an electrical device that rings or buzzes as a signal. **4** something shaped like a bell, as the tube of certain musical wind instruments, or the corolla of certain flowers. **5** *Naut.* a signal rung on a ship's bell to count the number of half-hour intervals during each of six four-hour watches reckoned from midnight. **6** *Brit. sl.* a telephone call **7 bell, book, and candle.** **7a** instruments used formerly in excommunications and other ecclesiastical rites. **7b** *Inf.* the solemn ritual ratification of such acts. **8 ring a bell.** to sound familiar; recall something previously experienced. **9 sound as a bell.** in perfect condition. ◆ *vb* **10** to be or cause to be shaped like a bell. **11** (*tr*) to attach a bell or bells to. [OE *belle*]

bell² (bɛl) *n* **1** a bellowing or baying cry, esp. that of a stag in rut. ◆ *vb* **2** to utter (such a cry). [OE *bellan*]

Bell ★ (bɛl) *n* **1 Acton, Currer** ('kʌrə), and **Ellis.** pen names of the sisters Anne, Charlotte, and Emily **Brontë. 2 Alexander Graham.** 1847–1922, US scientist, born in Scotland, who invented the telephone (1876). **3 Sir Francis Henry Dillon.** 1851–1936, New Zealand statesman; prime minister (1925). **4 Gertrude (Margaret Lowthian).** 1868–1926, British writer and diplomat; secretary to the British High Commissioner in Baghdad (1917–26). **5 (Susan) Jocelyn.** married name *Jocelyn Burnell*, born 1943, British radio astronomer, who discovered the first pulsar.

belladonna (,bɛlə'dɒnə) *n* **1** either of two alkaloid drugs obtained from the leaves and roots of the deadly nightshade. **2** another name for **deadly nightshade**. [C16: from

It., lit.: beautiful lady; supposed to refer to its use as a cosmetic]

Bellamy ★ ('beləmɪ) n **David (James)**. born 1933, British botanist, writer, and broadcaster.

Bellarmine ★ ('belɑː,miːn) n **Saint Robert**. 1542–1621, Italian Jesuit theologian and cardinal.

Bellay ★ (French belɛ) n **Joachim du** (ʒɔaʃɛ̃ dy). 1522–60, French poet, a member of the Pléiade.

bellbird ('bel,bɜːd) n **1** any of several tropical American birds having a bell-like call. **2** either of two other birds with a bell-like call: an Australian flycatcher (**crested bellbird**) or a New Zealand honeyeater.

bell-bottoms pl n trousers that flare from the knee.
▸ '**bell-,bottomed** adj

bellboy ('bel,bɔɪ) n Chiefly US & Canad. a porter or page in a hotel, club, etc. Also called: **bellhop**.

bell buoy n a navigational buoy with a bell which strikes when the waves move the buoy.

belle (bel) n **1** a beautiful woman. **2** the most attractive woman at a function, etc. (esp. in **belle of the ball**). [C17: from F, fem of BEAU]

Belleau Wood ★ ('beləʊ; French belo) n a forest in N France: site of a battle (1918) in which the US Marines halted a German advance on Paris.

belle époque French. (bɛl epɔk) n the period of comfortable well-established life before World War I. [lit.: fine period]

Belle Isle ★ n an island in the Atlantic, at the N entrance to the **Strait of Belle Isle**, between Labrador and Newfoundland. Area: about 39 sq. km (15 sq. miles).

Bellerophon ★ (bə'lerə,fɒn) n Greek myth. a hero of Corinth who performed many deeds with the help of the winged horse Pegasus, notably the killing of the monster Chimera.

belles-lettres (French belletrə) n (functioning as sing) literary works, esp. essays and poetry, valued for their aesthetic content. [C17: from F: fine letters]
▸ **bel'letrist** n

bellflower ('bel,flaʊə) n another name for **campanula**.

bellfounder ('bel,faʊndə) n a foundry worker who casts bells.

bellicose ('belɪ,kəʊs, -,kəʊz) adj warlike; aggressive; ready to fight. [C15: from L bellicōsus, from bellum war]
▸ **bellicosity** (,belɪ'kɒsɪtɪ) n

belligerence (bɪ'lɪdʒərəns) n the act or quality of being belligerent or warlike; aggressiveness.

belligerency (bɪ'lɪdʒərənsɪ) n the state of being at war.

belligerent (bɪ'lɪdʒərənt) adj **1** marked by readiness to fight or argue; aggressive. **2** relating to or engaged in a war. ◆ n **3** a person or country engaged in war. [C16: from L belliger, from bellum war + gerere to wage]

Bellingshausen Sea ★ ('belɪŋz,haʊzᵊn) n an area of the S Pacific Ocean off the coast of Antarctica. [named after Fabian Gottlieb Bellingshausen (1778–1852), Russian explorer]

Bellini ★ (Italian bel'lini) n **1 Giovanni** (dʒo'vanni). ?1430–1516, Italian painter of the Venetian school. His father **Jacopo** (?1400–70) and his brother **Gentile** (?1429–1507) were also painters. **2 Vincenzo** (vin'tʃɛntso). 1801–35, Italian composer of operas, esp. La Sonnambula (1831) and Norma (1831).

Bellinzona ★ (Italian bellin'tsona) n a town in SE central Switzerland, capital of Ticino canton. Pop.: 35 860 (1990).

bell jar n a bell-shaped glass cover to protect flower arrangements, etc., or to cover apparatus in experiments. Also called: **bell glass**.

bellman ('belmən) n, pl **bellmen**. a man who rings a bell; (formerly) a town crier.

bell metal n an alloy of copper and tin, with some zinc and lead, used in casting bells.

Belloc ★ ('belɒk) n **Hilaire** ('hɪleə, hɪ'leə). 1870–1953, British writer, born in France, noted for his verse The Bad Child's Book of Beasts (1896) and Cautionary Tales (1907).

bellow ('beləʊ) vb **1** (intr) to make a loud deep cry like that of a bull; roar. **2** to shout (something) unrestrainedly, as in anger or pain. ◆ n **3** the characteristic noise of a bull. **4** a loud deep sound, as of pain or anger. [C14: prob. from OE bylgan]

Bellow ★ ('beləʊ) n **Saul**. born 1915, US novelist, born in Canada. His works include Dangling Man (1944), Herzog (1964), Humboldt's Gift (1975), and The Actual (1997): Nobel prize for literature 1976.

bellows ('beləʊz) n (functioning as sing or pl) **1** Also: **pair of bellows**. an instrument consisting of an air chamber with flexible sides that is used to create a stream of air, as for producing a draught for a fire or for sounding organ pipes. **2** a flexible corrugated part, as that connecting the lens system of some cameras to the body. [C16: from pl of OE belig BELLY]

bell pull n a handle, rope, or cord pulled to operate a doorbell or servant's bell.

bell push n a button pressed to operate an electric bell.

bell-ringer n a person who rings church bells or musical handbells.
▸ **'bell-,ringing** n

bells and whistles pl n additional features or accessories which are nonessential but very attractive. [C20: from the bells and whistles which used to decorate fairground organs]

bell tent n a cone-shaped tent having a single central supporting pole.

bellwether ('bel,wɛðə) n **1** a sheep that leads the herd, often bearing a bell. **2** a leader, esp. one followed blindly.

belly ('belɪ) n, pl **bellies**. **1** the lower or front part of the body of a vertebrate, containing the intestines and other organs; abdomen. **2** the stomach, esp. when regarded as the seat of gluttony. **3** a part that bulges deeply: the belly of a sail. **4** the inside or interior cavity of something. **5** the front, lower, or inner part of something. **6** the surface of a stringed musical instrument over which the strings are stretched. **7** Austral. & NZ. the wool from a sheep's belly. **8** Arch. the womb. **9 go belly up.** Inf. to die, fail, or come to an end. ◆ vb **bellies, bellying, bellied. 10** to swell out or cause to swell out; bulge. [OE belig]

bellyache ('belɪ,eɪk) n **1** an informal term for **stomachache**. ◆ vb **bellyaches, bellyaching, bellyached. 2** (intr) Sl. to complain repeatedly.
▸ **'belly,acher** n

bellyband ('belɪ,bænd) n a strap around the belly of a draught animal, holding the shafts of a vehicle.

bellybutton ('belɪ,bʌtᵊn) n an informal name for the navel. Also called: **tummy button**.

belly dance n **1** a sensuous dance of Middle Eastern origin, performed by women, with undulating movements of the abdomen. ◆ vb **belly-dance, belly-dances, belly-dancing, belly-danced. 2** (intr) to dance thus.
▸ **belly dancer** n

belly flop n **1** a dive into water in which the body lands horizontally. ◆ vb **belly-flop, belly-flops, belly-flopping, belly-flopped. 2** (intr) to perform a belly flop.

bellyful ('belɪ,fʊl) n **1** as much as one wants or can eat. **2** Sl. more than one can tolerate.

belly landing n the landing of an aircraft on its fuselage without use of its landing gear.

belly laugh n a loud deep hearty laugh.

Belmopan ★ (,belmə'pæn) n (since 1973) the capital of Belize, about 50 miles inland: founded in 1970. Pop.: 3927 (1994 est.).

Belo Horizonte ★ (Portuguese 'beːlori'zõːntə) n a city in SE Brazil, the capital of Minas Gerais state. Pop.: 1 529 566 (1991).

belong (bɪ'lɒŋ) vb (intr) **1** (foll. by to) to be the property or possession (of). **2** (foll. by to) to be bound (to) by ties of affection, allegiance, etc. **3** (foll. by to, under, with, etc.) to be classified (with): this plant belongs to the daisy family. **4** (foll. by to) to be a part or adjunct (of). **5** to have a proper or usual place. **6** Inf. to be acceptable, esp. socially. [C14 belongen, from BE- (intensive) + longen, from OE langian to belong]

belonging (bɪ'lɒŋɪŋ) n secure relationship; affinity (esp. in **a sense of belonging**).

belongings (bɪ'lɒŋɪŋz) *pl n* (*sometimes sing*) the things that a person owns or has with him.

Belorussia ★ (ˌbɛləʊ'rʌʃən) *n* a variant spelling of **Belarus**.
▶ ˌBelo'russian *n, adj*

Belostok ★ (bjɪla'stɔk) *n* transliteration of the Russian name for **Białystok**.

beloved (bɪ'lʌvɪd, -'lʌvd) *adj* **1** dearly loved. ◆ *n* **2** a person who is dearly loved.

Belovo ★ (*Russian* 'bjɛləvə) *n* a variant spelling of **Byelovo**.

below (bɪ'ləʊ) *prep* **1** at or to a position lower than; under. **2** less than. **3** south of. **4** downstream of. **5** unworthy of; beneath. ◆ *adv* **6** at or to a lower position. **7** at a later place (in something written). **8** *Arch.* on earth or in hell. [C14 *bilooghe*, from *bi* BY + *looghe* LOW¹]

Bel Paese ('bel pa:'eɪzɪ) *n* a mild creamy Italian cheese. [from It., lit.: beautiful country]

Belsen ★ ('belsᵊn; *German* 'bɛlzən) *n* a village in NE Germany: with Bergen, the site of a Nazi concentration camp (1943–45).

Belshazzar ★ (bɛl'ʃæzə) *n* 6th century B.C., the son of Nabonidus, coregent of Babylon with his father for eight years: referred to as king and son of Nebuchadnezzar in the Old Testament (Daniel 5:1, 17; 8:1); described as having received a divine message of doom written on a wall at a banquet (**Belshazzar's Feast**).

belt (belt) *n* **1** a band of cloth, leather, etc., worn, usually around the waist, to support clothing, carry weapons, etc., or as decoration. **2** a belt worn to show rank (as by a knight), to mark expertise (as in judo), or awarded as a prize (as in boxing). **3** a narrow band, circle, or stripe, as of colour. **4** an area where a specific thing is found; zone: *a belt of high pressure*. **5** See **seat belt**. **6** a band of flexible material between rotating shafts or pulleys to transfer motion or transmit goods: *a fan belt; a passenger belt*. **7** *Inf.* a sharp blow. **8 below the belt**. **8a** *Boxing*. below the waist. **8b** *Inf.* in an unscrupulous or cowardly way. **9 tighten one's belt**. to take measures to reduce expenditure. **10 under one's belt**. **10a** in one's stomach. **10b** as part of one's experience: *he had a degree under his belt*. ◆ *vb* **11** (*tr*) to fasten or attach with or as if with a belt. **12** (*tr*) to hit with a belt. **13** (*tr*) *Sl.* to give a sharp blow; punch. **14** (*intr*; often foll. by *along*) *Sl.* to move very fast, esp. in a car. **15** (*tr*) *Rare*. to encircle. [OE, from L *balteus*]
▶ 'belted *adj*

belt-and-braces *adj* providing double security, in case one security measure should fail: *a belt-and-braces policy*.

Beltane ('belteɪn, -tən) *n* an ancient Celtic festival with a sacrificial bonfire on May Day. [C15: from Scot. Gaelic *bealltainn*]

belter ('beltə) *n Sl.* **1** an event, person, quality, etc., that is admirable, outstanding, or thrilling: *a real belter of a match*. **2a** a rousing or spirited popular song that is sung loudly and enthusiastically. **2b** a person who sings popular songs in a loud and spirited manner.

belting ('beltɪŋ) *n* **1** material for belts. **2** belts collectively. **3** *Inf.* a beating.

belt man *n Austral. & NZ.* (formerly) the member of a beach life-saving team who swam out wearing a belt with a line attached.

belt out *vb* (*tr, adv*) *Inf.* to sing or emit sound loudly.

belt up *vb* (*adv*) **1** *Sl.* to stop talking: often imperative. **2** to fasten with a belt.

beluga (bɪ'lu:gə) *n* **1** a large white sturgeon of the Black and Caspian Seas: a source of caviar and isinglass. **2** another name for **white whale**. [C18: from Russian *byeluga*, from *byely* white]

belvedere ('belvɪˌdɪə, ˌbelvɪ'dɪə) *n* a building, such as a summerhouse, sited to command a fine view. [C16: from It.: beautiful sight]

Bembo ★ (*Italian* 'bembo) *n* Pietro ('pjɛːtro). 1470–1547, Italian scholar and cardinal (1539). Noted for his treatise *Prose della volgar lingua* (1525).

bemire (bɪ'maɪə) *vb* **bemires, bemiring, bemired**. (*tr*) **1** to soil as with mire. **2** (*usually passive*) to stick fast in mire.

bemoan (bɪ'məʊn) *vb* to mourn; lament (esp. in **bemoan one's fate**). [OE *bemǣnan*; see BE-, MOAN]

bemuse (bɪ'mju:z) *vb* **bemuses, bemusing, bemused**. (*tr*) to confuse; bewilder.

bemused (bɪ'mju:zd) *adj* preoccupied; lost in thought.

ben¹ (ben) *Scot.* ◆ *n* **1** an inner room in a cottage. ◆ *prep, adv* **2** in; within; inside. ◆ Cf. **but**². [OE *binnan*, from BE- + *innan* inside]

ben² (ben) *n Scot., Irish.* a mountain peak: *Ben Lomond*. [C18: from Gaelic *beinn*, from *beann*]

Benares (bɪ'nɑ:rɪz) *or* **Banaras** ★ *n* the former name of **Varanasi**.

Ben Bella ★ (ben 'belə) *n* Mohammed Ahmed ('ɑːmɪd). born 1916, Algerian statesman: first prime minister (1962–65) and president (1963–65) of independent Algeria: overthrown and imprisoned (1965–80).

Benbow ★ ('benbəʊ) *n* John. 1653–1702, English admiral killed during the War of the Spanish Succession.

bench (bentʃ) *n* **1** a long seat for more than one person, usually lacking a back. **2** a plain stout worktable. **3 the bench**. (*sometimes cap.*) **3a** a judge or magistrate sitting in court. **3b** judges or magistrates collectively. **4** a ledge in a mine or quarry from which work is carried out. **5** (in a gymnasium) a low table, which may be inclined, used for various exercises. **6** a platform on which dogs, etc., are exhibited at shows. **7** *NZ.* a hollow formed by sheep on a hillside. ◆ *vb* (*tr*) **8** to provide with benches. **9** to exhibit (a dog, etc.) at a show. **10** *US & Canad., Sports.* to take (a player) out of a game, often for disciplinary reasons. [OE *benc*]

bencher ('bentʃə) *n* (*often pl*) *Brit.* **1** a member of the governing body of one of the Inns of Court. **2** See **back-bencher**.

benchmark ('bentʃˌmɑːk) *n* **1** a mark on a stone post or other permanent feature, used as a reference point in surveying. **2** a criterion by which to measure something; reference point.

bench press *n* a weight-training exercise in which a person lies on a bench and pushes a barbell upwards with both hands from chest level until the arms are straight, then lowers it again.

bench test *n* the critical evaluation of a new or repaired component, device, apparatus, etc., prior to installation to ensure that it is in perfect condition.

bench warrant *n* a warrant issued by a judge or court directing that an offender be apprehended.

bend¹ (bend) *vb* **bends, bending, bent**. **1** to form or cause to form a curve. **2** to turn or cause to turn from a particular direction: *the road bends left*. **3** (*intr*; often foll. by *down*, etc.) to incline the body; stoop; bow. **4** to submit or cause to submit: *to bend before superior force*. **5** (*tr*) to turn or direct (one's eyes, steps, attention, etc.). **6** (*tr*) *Naut.* to attach or fasten, as a sail to a boom. **7 bend (someone's) ear**. to speak at length to an unwilling listener, esp. to voice one's troubles. **8 bend the rules**. *Inf.* to ignore rules or change them to suit one's own convenience. ◆ *n* **9** a curved part. **10** *Naut.* a knot in a line for joining it to another or to an object. **11** the act of bending. **12 round the bend**. *Brit. sl.* mad. [OE *bendan*]
▶ 'bendable *adj* ▶ 'bendy *adj*

bend² (bend) *n Heraldry.* a diagonal line traversing a shield. [OE *bend* BAND²]

bender ('bendə) *n Inf.* **1** a drinking bout. **2** a makeshift shelter constructed by placing tarpaulin or plastic sheeting over bent saplings or woven branches.

Bendigo ★ ('bendɪˌgəʊ) *n* a city in SE Australia, in central Victoria: founded in 1851 after the discovery of gold. Pop.: 57 427 (1991).

bends (bendz) *pl n* (*functioning as sing or pl*) **the**. a nontechnical name for **decompression sickness**.

bend sinister *n Heraldry.* a diagonal line bisecting a shield from the top right to the bottom left, typically indicating a bastard line.

beneath (bɪ'ni:θ) *prep* **1** below, esp. if covered, protected, or obscured by. **2** not as great or good as would be demanded by: *beneath his dignity*. ◆ *adv* **3** below; underneath. [OE *beneothan*, from BE- + *neothan* low]

benedicite (ˌbenɪ'daɪsɪtɪ) *n* (esp. in Christian religious orders) a blessing or grace. [C13: from L, from *benedīcere*, from *bene* well + *dīcere* to speak]

Benedict ★ (ˈbenɪˌdɪkt) *n* **Saint.** ?480–?547 A.D., Italian monk: founded the Benedictine order at Monte Cassino in Italy in about 540 A.D. His *Regula Monachorum* became the basis of the rule of all Western Christian monastic orders. Feast day: July 11 or March 14.

Benedict XV ★ *n* original name *Giacomo della Chiesa*. 1854–1922, pope (1914–22); noted for his repeated attempts to end World War I and for his organization of war relief.

Benedictine *n* **1** (ˌbenɪˈdɪktɪn, -taɪn). a monk or nun who is a member of the order of Saint Benedict. **2** (ˌbenɪˈdɪktiːn). a greenish-yellow liqueur first made at the Benedictine monastery at Fécamp in France in about 1510. ◆ *adj* (ˌbenɪˈdɪktɪn, -taɪn). **3** of or relating to Saint Benedict or his order.

benediction (ˌbenɪˈdɪkʃən) *n* **1** an invocation of divine blessing. **2** a Roman Catholic service in which the congregation is blessed with the sacrament. **3** the state of being blessed. [C15: from L *benedictio*, from *benedīcere* to bless; see BENEDICITE]
▸ ˌbeneˈdictory *adj*

Benedictus (ˌbenɪˈdɪktəs) *n* (*sometimes not cap.*) *Christianity.* **1** a canticle beginning *Benedictus qui venit in nomine Domini* in Latin and *Blessed is he that cometh in the name of the Lord* in English. **2** a canticle beginning *Benedictus Dominus Deus Israel* in Latin and *Blessed be the Lord God of Israel* in English.

benefaction (ˌbenɪˈfækʃən) *n* **1** the act of doing good, esp. by giving a donation to charity. **2** the donation or help given. [C17: from LL *benefactiō*, from L *bene* well + *facere* to do]

benefactor (ˈbenɪˌfæktə, ˌbenɪˈfæk-) *n* a person who supports or helps a person, institution, etc., esp. by giving money.
▸ ˈbeneˌfactress *fem n*

benefice (ˈbenɪfɪs) *n* **1** *Christianity.* an endowed Church office yielding an income to its holder; a Church living. **2** the property or revenue attached to such an office. [C14: from OF, from L *beneficium* benefit, from *bene* well + *facere* to do]
▸ ˈbeneficed *adj*

beneficent (bɪˈnefɪsᵊnt) *adj* charitable; generous. [C17: from L *beneficus*; see BENEFICE]
▸ beˈneficence *n*

beneficial (ˌbenɪˈfɪʃəl) *adj* **1** (sometimes foll. by *to*) advantageous. **2** *Law.* entitling a person to receive the profits or proceeds of property. [C15: from LL *beneficiālis*, from L *beneficium* kindness]

beneficiary (ˌbenɪˈfɪʃərɪ) *n*, *pl* **beneficiaries. 1** a person who gains or benefits. **2** *Law.* a person entitled to receive funds or other property under a trust, will, etc. **3** the holder of a benefice. **4** *NZ.* a person who receives government assistance: *social security beneficiary*. ◆ *adj* **5** of or relating to a benefice.

benefit (ˈbenɪfɪt) *n* **1** something that improves or promotes. **2** advantage or sake. **3** (*sometimes pl*) a payment or series of payments made by an institution or government to a person who is ill, unemployed, etc. **4** a theatrical performance, sports event, etc., to raise money for a charity. ◆ *vb* **benefits, benefiting, benefited** or *US* **benefits, benefitting, benefitted. 5** to do or receive good; profit. [C14: from Anglo-F *benfet*, from L *benefactum*, from *bene facere* to do well]

benefit in kind *n* a non-pecuniary benefit, such as a company car or medical insurance, given to an employee.

benefit of clergy *n* *Christianity.* **1** sanction by the church: *marriage without benefit of clergy*. **2** (in the Middle Ages) a privilege that placed the clergy outside the jurisdiction of secular courts.

benefit society *n* a US term for **friendly society.**

Benelux ★ (ˈbenɪˌlʌks) *n* **1** the customs union formed by Belgium, the Netherlands, and Luxembourg in 1948; became an economic union in 1960. **2** these countries collectively.

Beneš ★ (*Czech* ˈbenɛʃ) *n* **Eduard** (ˈeːduart). 1884–1948, Czech statesman; president of Czechoslovakia (1935–38; 1946–48) and of its government in exile (1939–45).

Benevento ★ (ˌbenəˈventəu) *n* a city in S Italy, in N Campania: at various times under Samnite, Roman, Lombard, Saracen, Norman, and papal rule. Pop.: 64 690 (1990). Ancient name: **Beneventum** (ˌbenəˈventum).

benevolence (bɪˈnevələns) *n* **1** inclination to do good; charity. **2** an act of kindness.

benevolent (bɪˈnevələnt) *adj* **1** intending or showing goodwill; kindly; friendly. **2** doing good rather than making profit; charitable: *a benevolent organization*. [C15: from L *benevolēns*, from *bene* well + *velle* to wish]

Benfleet ★ (ˈbenˌfliːt) *n* a town in SE England, in S Essex on an inlet of the Thames estuary. Pop.: 49 701 (1991).

BEng *abbrev.* for Bachelor of Engineering.

Bengal ★ (beŋˈgɔːl, beŋ-) *n* **1** a former province of NE India, in the great deltas of the Ganges and Brahmaputra Rivers: in 1947 divided into West Bengal (belonging to India) and East Bengal (Bangladesh). **2 Bay of.** a wide arm of the Indian Ocean, between India and Myanmar.

Bengali (beŋˈgɔːlɪ, beŋ-) *n* **1** a member of a people living chiefly in Bangladesh and in West Bengal. **2** Also called: **Bangla.** their language. ◆ *adj* **3** of or relating to Bengal, the Bengalis, or their language.

Bengal light *n* a firework or flare that burns with a bright blue light, formerly used as a signal.

Bengbu (ˈbeŋˈbuː), **Pengpu** or **Pang-fou** ★ *n* a city in E China, in Anhui province. Pop.: 449 245 (1990 est.).

Benghazi or **Bengasi** ★ (benˈgɑːzɪ) *n* a port in N Libya, on the Gulf of Sidra: centre of Italian colonization (1911–42); scene of much fighting in World War II. Pop.: 446 250 (1988 est.). Ancient names: **Hesperides, Berenice** (berəˈnaɪsɪ).

Benguela ★ (beŋˈgwelə) *n* a port in W Angola: founded in 1617; a terminus (with Lobito) of the railway that runs from Beira in Mozambique through the Copper Belt of Zambia and Zimbabwe. Pop.: 41 000 (latest est.).

Ben-Gurion ★ (benˈguərɪən) *n* **David**, original name *David Gruen*. 1886–1973, Israeli socialist statesman, born in Poland; first prime minister of Israel (1948–53, 1955–63).

Beni ★ (*Spanish* ˈbeni) *n* a river in N Bolivia, rising in the Cordillera of the Andes and flowing north to the Marmoré River. Length: over 1600 km (1000 miles).

benighted (bɪˈnaɪtɪd) *adj* **1** lacking cultural, moral, or intellectual enlightenment. **2** *Arch.* overtaken by night.
▸ beˈnightedness *n*

benign (bɪˈnaɪn) *adj* **1** showing kindliness; genial. **2** (of soil, climate, etc.) mild; gentle. **3** favourable; propitious. **4** *Pathol.* (of a tumour, etc.) not malignant. [C14: from OF *benigne*, from L *benignus*, from *bene* well + *gignere* to produce]
▸ beˈnignly *adv*

benignant (bɪˈnɪgnənt) *adj* **1** kind; gracious. **2** a less common word for **benign** (senses 3, 4).
▸ beˈnignancy *n*

benignity (bɪˈnɪgnɪtɪ) *n*, *pl* **benignities. 1** the quality of being benign. **2** a kind or gracious act.

Beni Hasan ★ (ˈbenɪ hæˈsɑːn) *n* a village in central Egypt, on the Nile, with cliff-cut tombs dating from 2000 B.C.

Benin ★ (beˈniːn) *n* **1** a republic in W Africa, on the **Bight of Benin**, a section of the Gulf of Guinea: in the early 19th century a powerful kingdom, famed for its women warriors; became a French colony in 1893, gaining independence in 1960. It consists chiefly of coastal lagoons and swamps in the south, a fertile plain and marshes in the centre, and the Atakora Mountains in the northwest. Official language: French. Religion: animist majority. Currency: franc. Capital: Porto Novo (the government sits in Cotonou). Pop.: 5 902 000 (1997). Area: 112 622 sq. km (43 474 sq. miles). Former name (until 1975): **Dahomey. 2** a former kingdom of W Africa, powerful from the 14th to the 17th centuries: now a province of S Nigeria: noted for its bronzes.
▸ Beˌniˈnese or Beninois (ˌbeniːˈnwɑː) *adj, n*

Benin City ★ *n* a city in S Nigeria: former capital of the kingdom of Benin. Pop.: 223 900 (1995 est.).

benison ('bɛnɪz°n, -s°n) *n Arch.* a blessing. [C13: from OF *beneison*, from L *benedictiō* BENEDICTION]

Benjamin[1] ★ ('bɛndʒəmɪn) *n* **1** *Old Testament.* **1a** the youngest and best-loved son of Jacob and Rachel (Genesis 35:16–18; 42:4). **1b** the tribe descended from this patriarch. **1c** the territory of this tribe, northwest of the Dead Sea. **2** *Arch.* a youngest and favourite son.

Benjamin[2] ★ *n* ('bɛndʒəmɪn). **Arthur**. 1893–1960, Australian composer. In addition to *Jamaican Rumba* (1938), he wrote five operas and a harmonica concerto (1953).

Ben Lomond ★ (bɛn 'ləʊmənd) *n* **1** a mountain in W central Scotland, on the E side of Loch Lomond. Height: 973 m (3192 ft). **2** a mountain in NE Tasmania. Height: 1527 m (5010 ft). **3** a mountain in SE Australia, in NE New South Wales. Height: 1520 m (4986 ft).

Benn ★ (bɛn) *n* **Antony (Neil) Wedgwood**, known as *Tony Benn.* born 1925, British left-wing Labour politician. He renounced (1963) the title of Viscount Stansgate.

Bennett ★ ('bɛnɪt) *n* **1 Alan.** born 1934, British actor and playwright. His plays include *Forty Years On* (1968) and *The Madness of George III* (1991). **2 (Enoch) Arnold.** 1867–1931, British novelist, noted for *The Old Wives' Tale* (1908) and *Clayhanger* (1910). **3 James Gordon.** 1837–1931, US newspaper editor, born in Scotland. He founded (1835) the *New York Herald*. **4 Jill.** 1931–90, British actress. **5 Richard Bedford**, 1st Viscount. 1870–1947, Canadian Conservative statesman; prime minister (1930–35). **6 Sir Richard Rodney.** born 1936, British composer, noted for his operas *The Mines of Sulphur* (1965) and *Victory* (1970).

Ben Nevis ★ (bɛn 'nɛvɪs) *n* a mountain in W Scotland, in the Grampian mountains: highest peak in Great Britain. Height: 1343 m (4406 ft).

Bennington ★ ('bɛnɪŋtən) *n* a town in SW Vermont: the site of a British defeat (1777) in the War of American Independence. Pop.: 16 451 (1990).

Benny ★ ('bɛnɪ) *n* **Jack**, real name *Benjamin Kubelsky.* 1894–1974, US comedian.

Benoît de Sainte-Maure ★ (*French* bənwa də sɛ̃tmɔr) *n* 12th-century French trouvère: author of the *Roman de Troie*, which contains the episode of Troilus and Cressida.

Benoni ★ (bɪ'nəʊnɪ) *n* a city in NE South Africa: gold mines. Pop.: 113 501 (1991).

bent[1] (bɛnt) *adj* **1** not straight; curved. **2** (foll. by *on*) resolved (to); determined (to). **3** *Sl.* **3a** dishonest; corrupt. **3b** (of goods) stolen. **3c** crazy. **3d** sexually deviant. ♦ *n* **4** personal inclination or aptitude. **5** capacity of endurance (esp. in **to the top of one's bent**).

bent[2] (bɛnt) *n* **1** short for **bent grass**. **2** *Arch.* any stiff grass or sedge. **3** *Arch. or dialect.* heath or moorland. [OE *bionot*]

bent grass *n* a perennial grass which has a spreading panicle of tiny flowers sometimes planted for hay or in lawns.

Bentham ★ ('bɛnθəm) *n* **Jeremy**. 1748–1832, British philosopher: a founder of utilitarianism. His works include *Introduction to the Principles of Morals and Legislation* (1789).

Benthamism ('bɛnθəmɪzəm) *n* the utilitarian philosophy of Jeremy Bentham, which holds that the ultimate goal of society should be to promote the greatest happiness of the greatest number.
▶ **'Benthamite** *n*, *adj*

benthos ('bɛnθɒs) *n* the animals and plants living at the bottom of a sea or lake. [C19: from Gk: depth; rel. to *bathus* deep]
▶ **'benthic** *adj*

Bentinck ★ ('bɛntɪŋk) *n* **Lord William Cavendish**. 1774–1839, British statesman, governor general of Bengal (1828–35).

Bentley ★ ('bɛntlɪ) *n* **Edmund Clerihew**. 1875–1956, British journalist, noted for his invention of the clerihew.

bentonite ('bɛntə,naɪt) *n* a clay that swells as it absorbs water: used as a filler in various industries. [after Fort *Benton*, Montana, USA, where found]

bentwood ('bɛnt,wʊd) *n* **a** wood bent in moulds after being heated by steaming, used mainly for furniture. **b** (*as modifier): a bentwood chair.*

Benue ★ ('bɛnʊ,eɪ) *n* **1** a state of SE Nigeria, formed in 1976 from part of Benue-Plateau state. Capital: Makurdi. Pop.: 2 863 810 (1992 est.). Area: 34 059 sq. km (13 150 sq. miles). **2** a river in W Africa, rising in N Cameroon and flowing west across Nigeria: chief tributary of the River Niger. Length: 1400 km (870 miles).

benumb (bɪ'nʌm) *vb* (*tr*) **1** to make numb or powerless; deaden, as by cold. **2** (*usually passive*) to stupefy (the mind, senses, will, etc.).

Benxi ('bɛn'ʃi), **Penchi**, *or* **Penki** ★ *n* an industrial city in SE China, in S Liaoning province. Pop.: 768 778 (1990 est.).

Benz ★ (bɛnz; *German* bɛnts) *n* **Karl (Friedrich)** (karl). 1844–1929, German engineer: designed the first car driven by an internal-combustion engine (1885).

Benzedrine ('bɛnzɪ,dri:n, -drɪn) *n* a trademark for **amphetamine**.

benzene ('bɛnzi:n) *n* a colourless flammable poisonous liquid used in the manufacture of styrene, phenol, etc., as a solvent for fats, resins, etc., and as an insecticide. Formula: C_6H_6.

benzene ring *n* the hexagonal ring of bonded carbon atoms in the benzene molecule.

benzine ('bɛnzi:n, bɛn'zi:n) *or* **benzin** ('bɛnzɪn) *n* a volatile mixture of the lighter hydrocarbon constituents of petroleum.

benzo- *or* **benz-** *combining form.* **1** indicating a fused benzene ring. **2** indicating derivation from benzene or benzoic acid or the presence of phenyl groups. [from BENZOIN]

benzoate ('bɛnzəʊ,eɪt, -ɪt) *n* a salt or ester of benzoic acid.

benzocaine ('bɛnzəʊ,keɪn) *n* a white crystalline ester used as a local anaesthetic.

benzodiazepine (,bɛnzəʊdaɪ'eɪzə,pi:n) *n* any of a group of chemical compounds that are used as minor tranquillizers, such as diazepam (Valium) and chlordiazepoxide (Librium). [C20: from BENZO- + DI-[1] + AZ(O)- + EP(OXY)- + -INE[2]]

benzoic (bɛn'zəʊɪk) *adj* of, containing, or derived from benzoic acid or benzoin.

benzoic acid *n* a white crystalline solid occurring in many natural resins, used in plasticizers and dyes and as a food preservative (**E210**).

benzoin ('bɛnzəɪn, -zəʊɪn) *n* a gum resin containing benzoic acid, obtained from various tropical Asian trees and used in ointments, perfume, etc. [C16: from F *benjoin*, from OCatalan *benjui*, from Ar. *lubān jāwī*, lit.: frankincense of Java]

benzol *or* **benzole** ('bɛnzɒl) *n* **1** a crude form of benzene obtained from coal tar or coal gas and used as a fuel. **2** an obsolete name for **benzene**.

Beograd ★ (be'ɔgrad) *n* the Serbo-Croat name for **Belgrade**.

bequeath (bɪ'kwi:ð, -'kwi:θ) *vb* (*tr*) **1** *Law.* to dispose of (property) by will. **2** to hand down; pass on. [OE *becwethan*]
▶ **be'queathal** *n*

bequest (bɪ'kwɛst) *n* **1** the act of bequeathing. **2** something that is bequeathed. [C14: BE- + OE *-cwiss* degree]

Berar ★ (be'rɑ:) *n* a region of W central India: part of Madhya Pradesh state since 1950; important for cotton growing.

berate (bɪ'reɪt) *vb* **berates**, **berating**, **berated**. (*tr*) to scold harshly.

Berber ('bɜ:bə) *n* **1** a member of a Caucasoid Muslim people of N Africa. **2** the language of this people. ♦ *adj* **3** of or relating to this people or their language.

Berbera ★ ('bɜ:bərə) *n* a port in N Somalia, on the Gulf of Aden. Pop.: 70 000 (latest est.).

berberis ('bɜːbərɪs) *n* any of a genus of mainly N temperate shrubs. See **barberry**. [C19: from Med. L, from ?]

berceuse (*French* bɛrsøz) *n* **1** a lullaby. **2** an instrumental piece suggestive of this. [C19: from F: lullaby]

Berchtesgaden ★ (*German* 'bɛrçtəsgaˌdən) *n* a town in Germany, in SE Bavaria: site of the mountain retreat of Adolf Hitler. Pop.: 7865 (1992 est.).

bereave (bɪˈriːv) *vb* **bereaves, bereaving, bereaved.** (*tr*) (usually foll. by *of*) to deprive (of) something or someone valued, esp. through death. [OE *bereafian*]
► **be'reaved** *adj* ► **be'reavement** *n*

bereft (bɪˈrɛft) *adj* (usually foll. by *of*) deprived; parted (from): *bereft of hope.*

beret ('bɛreɪ) *n* a round close-fitting brimless cap. [C19: from F *béret*, from OProvençal *berret*]

Berezina ★ (*Russian* bɪrɪziˈna) *n* a river in Belarus, rising in the north and flowing south to the River Dnieper: linked with the River Dvina and the Baltic Sea by the **Berezina Canal.** Length: 563 km (350 miles).

Berezniki ★ (*Russian* bɪrɪzniˈki) *n* a city in E Russia: chemical industries. Pop.: 184 000 (1995 est.).

berg[1] (bɜːg) *n* short for **iceberg**.

berg[2] (bɜːg) *n* a South African word for **mountain**.

Berg ★ (bɜːg; *German* bɛrk) *n* **1 Alban (Maria Johannes)** ('albaːn). 1885–1935, Austrian composer. His works include the operas *Wozzeck* (1921) and *Lulu* (1935), chamber works, and songs. **2 Paul.** born 1926, US molecular biologist, the first to identify transfer RNA (1956). Nobel prize for chemistry 1980.

Bergamo ★ (*Italian* 'bɛrgamo) *n* a walled city in N Italy, in Lombardy. Pop.: 115 889 (1994 est.).

bergamot ('bɜːgəˌmɒt) *n* **1** a small Asian tree having sour pear-shaped fruit. **2 essence of bergamot.** a fragrant essential oil extracted from the fruit rind of this plant, used in perfumery. **3** a Mediterranean mint that yields a similar oil. [C17: from F *bergamote*, from It. *bergamotta*, of Turkic origin]

Bergen ★ *n* **1** (*Norwegian* 'bærgən) a port in SW Norway: chief city in medieval times. Pop.: 223 100 (1996 est.). **2** ('bɛrxən). the Flemish name for **Mons.**

Bergerac (*French* bɛrʒərak) *n* See **Cyrano de Bergerac.**

bergie ('bɜːgiː) *n S. African inf.* a vagabond, esp. one living on the slopes of Table Mountain in SW South Africa. [from Afrik. *berg* mountain]

Bergius ★ (*German* 'bɛrgjus) *n* **Friedrich (Karl Rudolph)** ('friːdrɪç). 1884–1949, German chemist, who invented a process for producing oil from coal: Nobel prize for chemistry 1931.

Bergman ★ ('bɜːgmən) *n* **1** (**Ernst) Ingmar** ('ɪŋmɑː). born 1918, Swedish film director, whose films include *Wild Strawberries* (1957), *Autumn Sonata* (1978), and *Fanny and Alexander* (1982). **2 Ingrid.** 1915–82, Swedish actress, working in Hollywood 1938–48; noted for *Casablanca* (1942) and *The Inn of the Sixth Happiness* (1958).

bergschrund ('bɛrkʃrʊnt) *n* a crevasse at the head of a glacier. [C19: G: mountain crack]

Bergson ★ ('bɜːgsᵊn; *French* bɛrksɔn) *n* **Henri Louis** (ɑ̃ri lwi). 1859–1941, French philosopher, who sought to bridge the gap between metaphysics and science. His main works are *Memory and Matter* (1896, trans. 1911) and *Creative Evolution* (1907, trans. 1911): Nobel prize for literature 1927.
► **Bergsonian** (bɜːgˈsəʊnɪən) *adj,* *n* ► **'Bergsonˌism** *n*

bergwind ('bɜːxvənt) *n* a hot dry wind in South Africa blowing from the plateau down to the coast.

Beria ★ ('bɛrɪə; *Russian* 'bjerijə) *n* **Lavrenti Pavlovich** (laˈvrjentij 'pavləvitʃ). 1899–1953, Soviet chief of secret police; killed by his associates shortly after Stalin's death.

beriberi (ˌbɛrɪˈbɛrɪ) *n* a disease, endemic in E and S Asia, caused by dietary deficiency of thiamine (vitamin B_1). [C19: from Sinhalese, by reduplication from *beri* weakness]

Bering *or* **Behring** ★ ('bɛrɪŋ, 'bɛər-; *Danish* 'beːreŋ) *n* **Vitus** ('viːtus). 1681–1741, Danish navigator, who explored the N Pacific for the Russians and discovered Bering Island and the Bering Strait.

Bering Sea ★ *n* a part of the N Pacific Ocean, between NE Russia and Alaska. Area: about 2 275 000 sq. km (878 000 sq. miles).

Bering Strait ★ *n* a strait between Alaska and Russia, connecting the Bering Sea and the Arctic Ocean.

Beriosova ★ (bɛrɪˈəʊsəvə) *n* **Svetlana** (svɪtˈlanə). 1932–98, British ballet dancer, born in Lithuania.

berk *or* **burk** (bɜːk) *n Brit. sl.* a stupid person; fool. [C20: shortened from *Berkeley* or *Berkshire Hunt*, rhyming slang for *cunt*]

Berkeley[1] ★ ('bɜːklɪ) *n* a city in W California, on San Francisco Bay: seat of the University of California. Pop.: 99 830 (1994 est.).

Berkeley[2] ★ *n* **1** ('bɜːklɪ). **Busby.** real name *William Berkeley Enos.* 1895–1976, US dance director. **2** ('baːklɪ) **George.** 1685–1753, Irish idealist philosopher and Anglican bishop, noted for *A Treatise concerning the Principles of Human Knowledge* (1710) and his *Essay towards a New Theory of Vision* (1709). **3** ('baːklɪ). Sir **Lennox (Randal Francis)** 1903–89, British composer; his works include four symphonies, four operas, and the *Serenade for Strings* (1939).

berkelium (bɜːˈkiːlɪəm, 'bɜːklɪəm) *n* a radioactive transuranic element produced by bombardment of americium. Symbol: Bk; atomic no.: 97; half-life of most stable isotope, ^{247}Bk: 1400 years. [C20: after BERKELEY[1], where it was discovered]

Berks (baːks) *abbrev. for* Berkshire.

Berkshire ★ ('baːkʃɪə, -ʃə) *n* a historic county of S England: the River Thames marks the N boundary and the **Berkshire Downs** occupy central parts: for administrative purposes it was replaced by six unitary authorities in 1998. Abbrev.: **Berks.**

berley *or* **burley** ('bɜːlɪ) *Austral.* ◆ *n* **1** bait scattered on water to attract fish. **2** *Sl.* rubbish, nonsense. ◆ *vb* (*tr*) **3** to scatter (bait) on water. **4** to hurry (someone); urge on. [from ?]

berlin (bəˈlɪn, 'bɜːlɪn) *n* **1** (*sometimes cap.*) Also called: **berlin wool.** a fine wool yarn used for tapestry work, etc. **2** a four-wheeled two-seated covered carriage, popular in the 18th century. [after BERLIN[1]]

Berlin[1] ★ (bɜːˈlɪn; *German* berˈliːn) *n* the capital of Germany (1871–1945 and from 1990), formerly divided into the eastern sector, capital of East Germany, and the western sectors, which formed an exclave in East German territory closely affiliated politically and economically with West Germany: a wall dividing the sectors was built in 1961 by the East German authorities to stop the flow of refugees from east to west; demolition of the wall began in 1989 and the city was formally reunited in 1990: formerly (1618–1871) the capital of Brandenburg and Prussia. Pop.: 3 472 009 (1995 est.).
► **Ber'liner** *n*

Berlin[2] ★ (bɜːˈlɪn) *n* **1 Irving.** original name *Israel Baline.* 1888–1989, US composer and writer of lyrics, born in Russia. **2** Sir **Isaiah.** 1909–97, British philosopher and diplomat, born in Latvia. His books include *Historical Inevitability* (1954) and *The Magus of the North* (1993).

Berlioz ★ ('bɛəlɪˌəʊz; *French* bɛrljoz) *n* **Hector (Louis)** (ɛktɔr). 1803–69, French composer. His works include the cantata *La Damnation de Faust* (1846), the opera *Les Troyens* (1856–59), the *Symphonie fantastique* (1830), and the oratorio *L'Enfance du Christ* (1854).

berm *or* **berme** (bɜːm) *n* **1** a narrow path or ledge as at the edge of a slope, road, or canal. **2** *Mil.* a man-made ridge of sand or earth, used as an obstacle to tanks. **3** *NZ.* the grass verge of a suburban street, usually kept mown. [C18: from F *berme*, from Du. *berm*]

Bermejo ★ (*Spanish* berˈmexo) *n* a river in Argentina, rising in the northwest and flowing southeast to the Paraguay River. Length: about 1600 km (1000 miles).

Bermuda ★ (bəˈmjuːdə) *n* a United Kingdom overseas territory consisting of a group of over 150 coral islands (**the Bermudas**) in the NW Atlantic: discovered in about 1503, colonized by the British by 1612, acquired by the British crown in 1684. Capital: Hamilton. Pop.: 60 500 (1994). Area: 53 sq. km (20 sq. miles).
► **Ber'mudan** *or* **Ber'mudian** *n, adj*

★ people and places

Bermuda shorts *pl n* shorts that come down to the knees.

Bermuda Triangle ★ *n* an area in the Atlantic Ocean bounded by Bermuda, Puerto Rico, and Florida where ships and aeroplanes are alleged to have disappeared mysteriously.

Bern ★ (bɜːn; *German* bɛrn) *n* **1** the capital of Switzerland, in the W part, on the Aar River: entered the Swiss confederation in 1353 and became the capital in 1848. Pop.: 128 422 (1995 est.). **2** a canton of Switzerland, between the French frontier and the Bernese Alps. Capital: Bern. Pop.: 941 747 (1995 est.). Area: 6884 sq. km (2658 sq. miles). French name: **Berne** (bɛrn).

Bernadette of Lourdes ★ (ˌbɜːnəˈdɛt) *n* **Saint.** original name *Marie Bernarde Soubirous.* 1844–79, French peasant girl born in Lourdes, whose visions of the Virgin Mary there made it a centre of pilgrimage. Feast day: Feb. 18.

Bernadotte ★ *n* **1** (*Swedish* ˈbærnaˌdɔt). **Folke** (ˈfɔlkə), Count. 1895–1948, Swedish diplomat, noted for his work with the Red Cross during World War II and as United Nations mediator in Palestine (1948): assassinated by Jewish terrorists. **2** (ˈbɜːnəˌdɔt; *French* bɛrnadɔt). **Jean Baptiste Jules** (ʒɑ̃ batist ʒyl). 1764–1844, French marshal under Napoleon; king of Norway and Sweden (1818–44) as Charles XIV.

Bernard ★ *n* **1** (*French* bɛrnar). **Claude** (klod). 1813–78, French physiologist, noted for his research on the alimentary canal and the liver. **2** (ˈbɜːnəd). **Saint,** known as *Bernard of Menthon* and the *Apostle of the Alps.* 923–1008, French monk who founded hospices in the Alpine passes. Feast day: June 15.

Bernard of Clairvaux ★ (ˈbɜːnəd; klɛəˈvəu). *n* **Saint.** ?1090–1153, French theologian, who founded the stricter branch of the Cistercians in 1115. Feast day: Aug. 20.

Bernese Alps *or* **Oberland** ★ (ˈbɜːniːz) *n* a mountain range in SW Switzerland, the N central part of the Alps. Highest peak: Finsteraarhorn, 4274 m (14 022 ft).

Bernhardt ★ (ˈbɜːnhɑːt; *French* bɛrnar) *n* **Sarah.** original name *Rosine Bernard.* 1844–1923, French actress.

Bernina ★ (bəˈniːnə; *Italian* berˈniːna) *n* **Piz.** a mountain in SE Switzerland, the highest peak of the **Bernina Alps,** in the S Rhaetian Alps. Height: 4049 m (13 284 ft).

Bernina Pass ★ *n* a pass in the Alps between SE Switzerland and N Italy, east of Piz Bernina. Height: 2323 m (7622 ft).

Bernini ★ (*Italian* berˈniːni) *n* **Gian Lorenzo** (dʒan loˈrentso). 1598–1680, Italian painter, architect, and sculptor.

Bernoulli *or* **Bernouilli** ★ (*French* bɛrnuji; *German* berˈnʊli) *n* **1 Daniel** (danjɛl), son of Jean Bernoulli. 1700–82, Swiss mathematician and physicist, who developed an early form of the kinetic theory of gases and stated the principle of conservation of energy in fluid dynamics. **2 Jacques** (ʒɑk) *or* **Jakob** (ˈjaːkɔp). 1654–1705, Swiss mathematician, noted for his work on calculus and the theory of probability. **3** his brother, **Jean** (ʒɑ̃) *or* **Johann** (joˈhan). 1667–1748, Swiss mathematician who developed the calculus of variations.

Bernstein ★ (ˈbɜːnstaɪn, -stiːn) *n* **Leonard.** 1918–90, US conductor and composer, whose works include the score of the musical *West Side Story* (1957), and *Mass* (1971).

berretta (bɪˈrɛtə) *n* a variant spelling of **biretta.**

berry (ˈbɛrɪ) *n, pl* **berries. 1** any of various small edible fruits such as the blackberry and strawberry. **2** *Bot.* a fruit with two or more seeds and a fleshy pericarp, such as the grape or gooseberry. **3** any of various seeds or dried kernels, such as a coffee bean. **4** the egg of a lobster, crayfish, or similar animal. ◆ *vb* **berries, berrying, berried.** (*intr*) **5** to bear or produce berries. **6** to gather or look for berries. [OE *berie*]

Berry ★ *n* **1** (ˈbɛrɪ). **Chuck,** full name *Charles Edward Berry.* born 1926, US rock-and-roll guitarist, singer, and songwriter. **2** (*French* beri). **Jean de France** (ʒɑ̃ də frɑ̃s), Duc de. 1340–1416, French prince, son of King John II; coregent (1380–88) for Charles VI.

berserk (bəˈzɜːk, -ˈsɜːk) *adj* **1** frenziedly violent or destructive (esp. in **go berserk**). ◆ *n* **2** Also called: **berserker.**

one of a class of ancient Norse warriors who fought frenziedly. [C19: Icelandic *berserkr,* from *björn* bear + *serkr* shirt]

berth (bɜːθ) *n* **1** a bed or bunk in a vessel or train. **2** *Naut.* a place assigned to a ship at a mooring. **3** *Naut.* sufficient room for a ship to manoeuvre. **4 give a wide berth to.** to keep clear of. **5** *Inf.* a job, esp. as a member of a ship's crew. ◆ *vb* **6** (*tr*) *Naut.* to assign a berth to (a vessel). **7** *Naut.* to dock (a vessel). **8** (*tr*) to provide with a sleeping place. **9** (*intr*) *Naut.* to pick up a mooring in an anchorage. [C17: prob. from BEAR¹ + -TH¹]

bertha (ˈbɜːθə) *n* a wide deep collar, often of lace, usually to cover a low neckline. [C19: from F *berthe,* from *Berthe,* 8th-cent. Frankish queen]

Bertolucci ★ (*Italian* bertoˈluttʃi) *n* **Bernardo** (berˈnardo). born 1940, Italian film director: his films include *The Spider's Stratagem* (1970), *The Last Emperor* (1987), and *I Dance Alone* (1996).

Berwick ★ (ˈbɛrɪk) *n* **James Fitzjames,** Duke of Berwick. 1670–1734, marshal of France and illegitimate son of James II of England. He led French forces during the War of the Spanish Succession (1701–14).

Berwickshire ★ (ˈbɛrɪkˌʃɪə, -ʃə) *n* (until 1975) a county of SE Scotland, now part of Scottish Borders council area.

Berwick-upon-Tweed ★ (twiːd) *n* a town in N England, in N Northumberland at the mouth of the Tweed: much involved in border disputes between England and Scotland between the 12th and 16th centuries; neutral territory 1551–1885. Pop.: 13 544 (1991). Also called: **Berwick.**

beryl (ˈbɛrɪl) *n* a green, blue, yellow, pink, or white hard mineral consisting of beryllium aluminium silicate in hexagonal crystalline form. Emerald and aquamarine are transparent varieties. [C13: from OF, from L, from Gk *bērullos*]
▶ **'beryline** *adj*

beryllium (beˈrɪlɪəm) *n* a corrosion-resistant toxic silvery-white metallic element used mainly in X-ray windows and alloys. Symbol: Be; atomic no.: 4; atomic wt.: 9.012. [C19: from L, from Gk *bērullos*]

Berzelius ★ (bəˈziːlɪəs; *Swedish* bærˈseːlius) *n* Baron **Jöns Jakob** (ˈjœns ˈjɑːkɔp). 1779–1848, Swedish chemist, who invented the present system of chemical symbols and formulas, discovered several elements, and determined the atomic and molecular weight of many substances.

Besançon ★ (*French* bəzɑ̃sɔ̃) *n* a city in E France, on the Doubs River: university (1422). Pop.: 119 194 (1990).

Besant ★ (ˈbɛzᵊnt, bɪˈzænt) *n* **Annie,** *née* **Wood.** 1847–1933, British theosophist, writer, and political reformer in England and India.

beseech (bɪˈsiːtʃ) *vb* **beseeches, beseeching, besought** *or* **beseeched.** (*tr*) to ask (someone) earnestly (to do something or for something); beg. [C12: see BE-, SEEK]

beseem (bɪˈsiːm) *vb Arch.* to be suitable for or worthy of; befit.

beset (bɪˈsɛt) *vb* **besets, besetting, beset.** (*tr*) **1** (esp. of dangers or temptations) to trouble or harass constantly. **2** to surround or attack from all sides. **3** *Arch.* to cover with, esp. with jewels.

besetting (bɪˈsɛtɪŋ) *adj* tempting, harassing, or assailing (esp. in **besetting sin**).

beside (bɪˈsaɪd) *prep* **1** next to; at, by, or to the side of. **2** as compared with. **3** away from; wide of. **4** *Arch.* besides. **5 beside oneself.** (*postpositive;* often foll. by *with*) overwhelmed; overwrought: *beside oneself with grief.* ◆ *adv* **6** at, by, to, or along the side of something or someone. [OE *be sīdan;* see BY, SIDE]

besides (bɪˈsaɪdz) *prep* **1** apart from; even considering. ◆ *sentence connector.* **2** anyway; moreover. ◆ *adv* **3** as well.

besiege (bɪˈsiːdʒ) *vb* **besieges, besieging, besieged.** (*tr*) **1** to surround (a fortified area) with military forces to bring about its surrender. **2** to crowd round; hem in. **3** to overwhelm, as with requests.
▶ **be'sieger** *n*

besmear (bɪˈsmɪə) *vb* (*tr*) **1** to smear over; daub. **2** to sully; defile (often in **besmear (a person's) reputation**).

besmirch (bɪˈsmɜːtʃ) *vb* (*tr*) **1** to make dirty; soil. **2** to reduce the brightness of. **3** to sully (often in **besmirch (a person's) name**).

besom[1] (ˈbiːzəm) *n* a broom, esp. one made of a bundle of twigs tied to a handle. [OE *besma*]

besom[2] (ˈbiːzəm) *n Scot. & N English dialect.* a derogatory term for a **woman**. [?from OE *bysen* example; rel. to ON *bysn* wonder]

besotted (bɪˈsɒtɪd) *adj* **1** stupefied with drink. **2** infatuated; doting. **3** foolish; muddled.

besought (bɪˈsɔːt) *vb* a past tense and past participle of **beseech**.

bespangle (bɪˈspæŋɡᵊl) *vb* **bespangles, bespangling, bespangled.** (*tr*) to cover or adorn with or as if with spangles.

bespatter (bɪˈspætə) *vb* (*tr*) **1** to splash, as with dirty water. **2** to defile; besmirch.

bespeak (bɪˈspiːk) *vb* **bespeaks, bespeaking, bespoke; bespoken** *or* **bespoke.** (*tr*) **1** to engage or ask for in advance. **2** to indicate or suggest: *this act bespeaks kindness.* **3** *Poetic.* to address.

bespectacled (bɪˈspɛktəkᵊld) *adj* wearing spectacles.

bespoke (bɪˈspəʊk) *adj Chiefly Brit.* **1** (esp. of a suit, jacket, etc.) made to the customer's specifications. **2** making or selling such suits, jackets, etc.: *a bespoke tailor.*

besprinkle (bɪˈsprɪŋkᵊl) *vb* **besprinkles, besprinkling, besprinkled.** (*tr*) to sprinkle all over with liquid, powder, etc.

Bessarabia ★ (ˌbɛsəˈreɪbɪə) *n* a region of E Europe, mostly in Moldova and the Ukraine: long disputed by the Turks and Russians: a province of Romania from 1918 until 1940. Area: about 44 300 sq. km (17 100 sq. miles).

Bessel ★ (ˈbɛsᵊl) *n* Friedrich Wilhelm (ˈfriːdrɪç ˈvɪlhɛlm). 1784–1846, German astronomer and mathematician. He made the first measurement of a star's distance from the earth (1841) and devised mathematical Bessel functions, used in physics.

Bessemer process (ˈbɛsɪmə) *n* (formerly) a process for producing steel by blowing air through molten pig iron in a **Bessemer converter** (a refractory-lined furnace): impurities are removed and the carbon content is controlled. [C19: after Sir Henry *Bessemer* (1813–98), E engineer]

best (bɛst) *adj* **1** the superlative of **good. 2** most excellent of a particular group, category, etc. **3** most suitable, desirable, etc. **4 the best part of.** most of. ◆ *adv* **5** the superlative of **well**[1]. **6** in a manner surpassing all others; most excellently, attractively, etc. ◆ *n* **7 the best.** the most outstanding or excellent person, thing, or group in a category. **8** the utmost effort. **9** a winning majority. **10** Also: **all the best.** best wishes. **11** a person's smartest outfit of clothing. **12 at best.** in the most favourable interpretation. **12a** under the most favourable conditions. **13 for the best. 13a** for an ultimately good outcome. **13b** with good intentions. **14 get** *or* **have the best of.** to defeat or outwit. **15 give (someone) best.** to concede (someone's) superiority. **16 make the best of.** to cope as well as possible with. ◆ *vb* **17** (*tr*) to gain the advantage over or defeat. [OE *betst*]

Best ★ (bɛst) *n* **1 Charles Herbert.** 1899–1978, Canadian physiologist: associated with Banting and Macleod in their discovery of insulin in 1922. **2 George.** born 1946, Northern Ireland footballer.

bestead (bɪˈstɛd) *Arch.* ◆ *vb* **besteads, besteading, besteaded** *or* **bestead. 1** (*tr*) to help; avail. ◆ *adj also* **bested. 2** placed; situated. [C13: see BE-, STEAD]

bestial (ˈbɛstɪəl) *adj* **1** brutal or savage. **2** sexually depraved. **3** lacking in refinement; brutish. **4** of or relating to a beast. [C14: from LL *bestiālis*, from L *bestia* BEAST]

bestiality (ˌbɛstɪˈælɪtɪ) *n*, *pl* **bestialities. 1** bestial behaviour. **2** sexual activity between a person and an animal.

bestialize *or* **bestialise** (ˈbɛstɪəˌlaɪz) *vb* **bestializes, bestializing, bestialized** *or* **bestialises, bestialising, bestialised.** (*tr*) to make bestial or brutal.

bestiary (ˈbɛstɪərɪ) *n*, *pl* **bestiaries.** a moralizing medieval collection of descriptions of real and mythical animals.

bestir (bɪˈstɜː) *vb* **bestirs, bestirring, bestirred.** (*tr*) to cause (oneself) to become active; rouse.

best man *n* the male attendant of the bridegroom at a wedding.

bestow (bɪˈstəʊ) *vb* (*tr*) **1** to present (a gift) or confer (an honour). **2** *Arch.* to apply (energy, resources, etc.). **3** *Arch.* to house (a person) or store (goods).
▸ **beˈstowal** *n*

bestrew (bɪˈstruː) *vb* **bestrews, bestrewing, bestrewed; bestrewn** *or* **bestrewed.** (*tr*) to scatter or lie scattered over (a surface).

bestride (bɪˈstraɪd) *vb* **bestrides, bestriding, bestrode** *or* (*Arch.*) **bestrid; bestridden** *or* (*Arch.*) **bestrid.** (*tr*) **1** to have or put a leg on either side of. **2** to extend across; span. **3** to stride over or across.

bestseller (ˌbɛstˈsɛlə) *n* **1** a book or other product that has sold in great numbers. **2** the author of one or more such books, etc.
▸ **ˌbestˈselling** *adj*

bet (bɛt) *n* **1** an agreement between two parties that a sum of money or other stake will be paid by the loser to the party who correctly predicts the outcome of an event. **2** the stake risked. **3** the predicted result in such an agreement. **4** a person, event, etc., considered as likely to succeed or occur. **5** a course of action (esp. in **one's best bet**). **6** *Inf.* an opinion: *my bet is that you've been up to no good.* ◆ *vb* **bets, betting, bet** *or* **betted. 7** (when *intr* foll. by *on* or *against*) to make or place a bet with (a person or persons). **8** (*tr*) to stake (money, etc.) in a bet. **9** (*tr; may take a clause as object*) *Inf.* to predict (a certain outcome). **10 you bet.** *Inf.* of course; naturally. [C16: prob. short for ABET]

beta (ˈbiːtə) *n* **1** the second letter in the Greek alphabet (Β or β). **2** the second in a group or series. [from Gk *bēta*, from Heb.; see BETH]

beta-blocker *n* any of a class of drugs, such as propranolol, that decrease the activity of the heart: used in the treatment of high blood pressure and angina.

betacarotene (ˌbiːtəˈkærəˌtiːn) *n* the most important form of the plant pigment carotene, which occurs in milk, vegetables, and other foods and, when eaten by man and animals, is converted in the body to vitamin A.

beta decay *n* the radioactive change in an atomic nucleus accompanying the emission of an electron.

betake (bɪˈteɪk) *vb* **betakes, betaking, betook, betaken.** (*tr*) **betake oneself.** to go; move. **2** *Arch.* to apply (oneself) to.

beta particle *n* a high-speed electron or positron emitted by a nucleus during radioactive decay or nuclear fission.

beta ray *n* a stream of beta particles.

beta rhythm *or* **wave** *n Physiol.* the normal electrical activity of the cerebral cortex.

beta stock *n* any of the second rank of active securities on the London stock exchange, of which there are about 500. Continuous display of prices by market makers is required but not immediate publication of transactions.

betatron (ˈbiːtəˌtrɒn) *n* a type of particle accelerator for producing high-energy beams of electrons by magnetic induction.

betel (ˈbiːtᵊl) *n* an Asian climbing plant, the leaves of which are chewed by the peoples of SE Asia. [C16: from Port., from Malayalam *vettila*]

betel nut *n* the seed of the betel palm, chewed with betel leaves and lime by people in S and SE Asia as a digestive stimulant and narcotic.

betel palm *n* a tropical Asian feather palm.

bête noire *French.* (bɛt nwar) *n*, *pl* ***bêtes noires*** (bɛt nwar). a person or thing that one particularly dislikes or dreads. [lit.: black beast]

beth (bɛt) *n* the second letter of the Hebrew alphabet. [from Heb. *bēth-, bayith* house]

Bethany ★ (ˈbɛθənɪ) *n* a village in the West Bank, near Jerusalem at the foot of the Mount of Olives: in the New Testament, the home of Lazarus and the lodging place of Jesus during Holy Week.

Bethe ★ (ˈbeɪtə) *n* Hans Albrecht (hans ˈalbrɛçt). born 1906, US physicist, born in Germany; noted for his work on nuclear physics: Nobel prize for physics 1967.

Bethel ★ (ˈbɛθəl) *n* **1** an ancient town in the West Bank, near Jerusalem: in the Old Testament, the place where the dream of Jacob occurred (Genesis 28:19). **2** a chapel of any of certain Nonconformist Christian sects. **3** a seamen's chapel. [C17: from Heb. *bēth 'El* house of God]

Bethesda ★ (bə'θɛzdə) *n* **1** *New Testament.* a pool in Jerusalem reputed to have healing powers, where a paralytic was healed by Jesus (John 5:2). **2** a chapel of any of certain Nonconformist Christian sects.

bethink (bɪ'θɪŋk) *vb* **bethinks, bethinking, bethought.** *Arch.* or *dialect.* **1** to cause (oneself) to consider or meditate. **2** (*tr;* often foll. by *of*) to remind (oneself).

Bethlehem ★ ('bɛθlɪ,hɛm, -lɪəm) *n* a town in the West Bank, near Jerusalem: birthplace of Jesus and early home of King David.

Bethmann Hollweg ★ (*German* 'beːtman 'hɔlveːk) *n* **Theobald von** ('teːɔbalt fɔn). 1856–1921, chancellor of Germany (1909–17).

Bethsaida ★ (bɛθ'seɪdə) *n* a ruined town in N Israel, near the N shore of the Sea of Galilee.

betide (bɪ'taɪd) *vb* **betides, betiding, betided.** to happen or happen to (often in **woe betide (someone)**). [C13: from BE- + obs. *tide* to happen]

betimes (bɪ'taɪmz) *adv Arch.* **1** in good time; early. **2** soon. [C14 *bitimes;* see BY, TIME]

Betjeman ★ ('bɛtʃəmən) *n* Sir **John.** 1906–84, British poet, noted for his nostalgic verse. Poet laureate (1972–84).

betoken (bɪ'təʊkən) *vb* (*tr*) **1** to indicate; signify. **2** to portend; augur.

betony ('bɛtənɪ) *n, pl* **betonies. 1** a Eurasian plant with a spike of reddish-purple flowers, formerly used in medicine and dyeing. **2** any of several related plants. [C14: from OF, from L]

betray (bɪ'treɪ) *vb* (*tr*) **1** to hand over or expose (one's nation, friend, etc.) treacherously to an enemy. **2** to disclose (a secret, confidence, etc.) treacherously. **3** to break (a promise) or be disloyal to (a person's trust). **4** to show signs of; indicate. **5** to reveal unintentionally: *his grin betrayed his satisfaction.* [C13: from BE- + *trayen*, from OF, from L *trādere* to hand over]
▸ be'trayal *n* ▸ be'trayer *n*

betroth (bɪ'trəʊð) *vb* (*tr*) *Arch.* to promise to marry or to give in marriage. [C14 *betreuthen*, from BE- + *treuthe* TROTH, TRUTH]

betrothal (bɪ'trəʊðəl) *n* **1** engagement to be married. **2** a mutual promise to marry.

betrothed (bɪ'trəʊðd) *adj* **1** engaged to be married: *he was betrothed to her.* ◆ *n* **2** the person to whom one is engaged; fiancé or fiancée.

better ('bɛtə) *adj* **1** the comparative of **good. 2** more excellent than others. **3** more suitable, advantageous, attractive, etc. **4** improved or fully recovered in health. **5 better off.** in more favourable circumstances, esp. financially. **6 the better part of.** a large part of. ◆ *adv* **7** the comparative of **well**[1]. **8** in a more excellent manner; more advantageously, attractively, etc. **9** in or to a greater degree or extent; more. **10 had better.** would be wise, sensible, etc., to: *I had better be off.* **11 think better of. 11a** to change one's mind about (a course of action, etc.) after reconsideration. **11b** to rate more highly. ◆ *n* **12 the better.** something that is the more excellent, useful, etc., of two such things. **13** (*usually pl*) a person who is superior, esp. in social standing or ability. **14 for the better.** by way of improvement. **15 get the better of.** to defeat, outwit, or surpass. ◆ *vb* **16** to make or become better. **17** (*tr*) to improve upon; surpass. [OE *betera*]

better half *n Humorous.* one's spouse.

betterment ('bɛtəmənt) *n* **1** a change for the better; improvement. **2** *Property law.* an improvement effected on real property that enhances the value of the property.

betting shop *n* (in Britain) a licensed bookmaker's premises not on a racecourse.

between (bɪ'twiːn) *prep* **1** at a point or in a region intermediate to two other points in space, times, etc. **2** in combination: *between them, they saved enough money to buy a car.* **3** confined or restricted to: *between you and me.* **4** indicating a reciprocal relation or

comparison. **5** indicating two or more alternatives. ◆ *adv also* **in between. 6** between one specified thing and another. [OE *betwēonum;* see TWO, TWAIN]

> **USAGE NOTE** After *distribute* and words with a similar meaning, *among* should be used rather than *between*: *this enterprise issued shares which were distributed among its workers.*

betweentimes (bɪ'twiːn,taɪmz) *or* **betweenwhiles** *adv* between other activities; during intervals.

betwixt (bɪ'twɪkst) *prep, adv* **1** *Arch.* another word for **between. 2 betwixt and between.** in an intermediate or indecisive position. [OE *betwix*]

Betws-y-Coed ★ (,bɛtsɪ'kɔɪd) *n* a village in N Wales, in Conwy county borough on the River Conwy: noted for its scenery. Pop.: 2860 (1991).

Beulah ★ ('bjuːlə) *n Old Testament.* the land of Israel (Isaiah 62:4). [Heb., lit.: married woman]

Beuthen ★ ('bɔytən) *n* the German name for **Bytom.**

BeV (in the US) *abbrev. for* gigaelectronvolts (GeV). [C20: from *b(illion) e(lectron) v(olts)*]

Bevan ★ ('bɛvən) *n* **Aneurin** (ə'naɪərɪn), known as *Nye.* 1897–1960, British Labour statesman: as minister of health (1945–51) he introduced the National Health Service (1948).
▸ 'Bevan,ite *n, adj*

bevatron ('bɛvə,trɒn) *n* a synchrotron used to accelerate protons. [C20: from BeV + -TRON]

bevel ('bɛvəl) *n* **1** Also called: **cant.** a surface that meets another at an angle other than a right angle. ◆ *vb* **bevels, bevelling, bevelled** *or US* **bevels, beveling, beveled. 2** (*intr*) to be inclined; slope. **3** (*tr*) to cut a bevel on (a piece of timber, etc.). [C16: from OF, from *baer* to gape; see BAY[1]]

bevel gear *n* a gear having teeth cut into a conical surface. Two such gears mesh together to transmit power between two shafts at an angle.

bevel square *n* a tool with an adjustable arm that can be set to mark out an angle.

beverage ('bɛvərɪdʒ, 'bɛvrɪdʒ) *n* any drink, usually other than water. [C13: from OF *bevrage*, from *beivre* to drink, from L *bibere*]

beverage room *n Canad.* another name for **beer parlour.**

Beveridge ★ ('bɛvərɪdʒ) *n* **William Henry,** 1st Baron Beveridge. 1879–1963, British economist, whose *Report on Social Insurance and Allied Services* (1942) formed the basis of the welfare state.

Beverley ★ ('bɛvəlɪ) *n* a market town in NE England; administrative centre of the East Riding of Yorkshire. Pop.: 23 632 (1991).

Beverly Hills ★ ('bɛvəlɪ) *n* a city in SW California, near Los Angeles: famous as the home of film stars. Pop.: 31 970 (1990).

Bevin ★ ('bɛvɪn) *n* **Ernest.** 1881–1951, British Labour statesman, who was largely responsible for the creation of the Transport and General Workers' Union (1922): minister of labour (1940–45); foreign secretary (1945–51).

bevvy ('bɛvɪ) *n, pl* **bevvies.** *Dialect.* **1** a drink, esp. an alcoholic one. **2** a session of drinking. [prob. from OF *bevee*, *buvee* drinking]

bevy ('bɛvɪ) *n, pl* **bevies. 1** a flock of quails. **2** a group, esp. of girls. [C15: from ?]

bewail (bɪ'weɪl) *vb* to express great sorrow over (a person or thing); lament.
▸ be'wailer *n*

beware (bɪ'wɛə) *vb* (*usually used in the imperative or infinitive; often foll. by of*) to be cautious or wary (of); be on one's guard (against). [C13 *be war*, from BE (imperative) + *war* WARY]

Bewick ★ ('bjuːɪk) *n* **Thomas.** 1753–1828, British wood engraver; his best-known works are *Aesop's Fables* (1818) and the *History of British Birds* (1797–1804).

★ people and places

bewilder (bɪˈwɪldə) *vb* (*tr*) to confuse utterly; puzzle. [C17: see BE-, WILDER]
▸ be'wildering *adj* ▸ be'wilderingly *adv* ▸ be'wilderment *n*

bewitch (bɪˈwɪtʃ) *vb* (*tr*) **1** to attract and fascinate. **2** to cast a spell over. [C13 *bewicchen*; see BE-, WITCH¹]
▸ be'witching *adj*

bewray (bɪˈreɪ) *vb* (*tr*) an obsolete word for **betray**. [C13: from BE- + OE *wrēgan* to accuse]

Bexhill(-on-Sea) ★ (ˌbeksˈhɪl) *n* a resort in S England, in East Sussex on the English Channel. Pop.: 38 905 (1991).

Bexley ★ (ˈbekslɪ) *n* a borough of Greater London. Pop.: 210 257 (1991). Area: 61 sq. km (23 sq. miles).

bey (beɪ) *n* **1** (in the Ottoman Empire) a title given to provincial governors. **2** (in modern Turkey) a title of address, corresponding to *Mr*. ◆ Also called: **beg**. [C16: Turkish: lord]

Beyoğlu ★ (ˈbeɪɒːluː) *n* a district of Istanbul, north of the Golden Horn: the European quarter. Former name: **Pera**.

beyond (bɪˈjɒnd) *prep* **1** at or to a point on the other side of; at or to the further side of: *beyond those hills*. **2** outside the limits or scope of. ◆ *adv* **3** at or to the other or far side of something. **4** outside the limits of something. ◆ *n* **5 the beyond**. the unknown, esp. life after death in certain religious beliefs. [OE *begeondan*; see BY, YONDER]

Beyrouth ★ (beɪˈruːt, ˌbeɪruːt) *n* a variant spelling of **Beirut**.

Beza (*French* bəza) or **de Bèze** ★ (*French* də bez) *n* **Théodore** (teodɔr). 1519–1605, French Calvinist theologian and scholar, who lived in Switzerland. He succeeded Calvin as leader of the Swiss Protestants.

bezel (ˈbezˀl) *n* **1** the sloping face adjacent to the working edge of a cutting tool. **2** the upper oblique faces of a cut gem. **3** a grooved ring or part holding a gem, watch crystal, etc. **4** a retaining outer rim used in vehicle instruments such as tachometers and speedometers. **5** a small indicator light used in vehicle instrument panels. [C17: prob. from F *biseau*]

Béziers ★ (*French* bezje) *n* a city in S France: scene of a massacre (1209) during the Albigensian Crusade. It is a centre of the wine trade. Pop.: 70 996 (1990).

bezique (bɪˈziːk) *n* **1** a card game for two or more players using two packs with nothing below a seven. **2** (in this game) the queen of spades and jack of diamonds declared together. [C19: from F *bésigue*, from ?]

Bezwada ★ (ˈbeɪzˌwɑːdə) *n* the former name of Vijayawada.

B/F or **b/f** *Book-keeping. abbrev. for* brought forward.

BFPO *abbrev. for* British Forces Post Office.

Bhagalpur ★ (ˈbɑːɡəlˌpʊə) *n* a city in India, in Bihar: agriculture, textiles, university (1960). Pop.: 253 225 (1991).

bhaji (ˈbɑːdʒɪ) *n, pl* **bhaji, bhajis,** or **bhajia** (ˈbɑːdʒɪə). an Indian savoury made of chopped vegetables mixed in a spiced batter and deep-fried. [Hindi *bhājī* fried vegetables]

bhang or **bang** (bæŋ) *n* a preparation of the leaves and flower tops of Indian hemp having psychoactive properties: much used in India. [C16: from Hindi *bhāng*]

bhangra (ˈbæŋɡrə) *n* a type of Asian pop music that combines elements of traditional Punjabi music with Western pop. [C20: from Hindi]

bharal or **burhel** (ˈbʌrəl) *n* a wild Himalayan sheep with a bluish-grey coat. [Hindi]

Bharat ★ (ˈbʌrʌt) *n* transliteration of the Hindi name for **India**.

Bhatpara ★ (bɑːtˈpɑːrə) *n* a city in NE India, in West Bengal on the Hooghly River: jute and cotton mills. Pop.: 304 952 (1991).

Bhavnagar ★ (ˈbɑːvnəɡə) *n* a port in W India, in S Gujarat. Pop.: 402 338 (1991).

bhindi (ˈbɪndɪ) *n* the okra as used in Indian cooking. [Hindi]

Bhopal ★ (bəʊˈpɑːl) *n* a city in central India, the capital of Madhya Pradesh state: in 1984 2000 people were killed by poisonous gas, which leaked from a US-owned factory. Pop.: 1 062 771 (1991).

bhp *abbrev. for* brake horsepower.

BHP *Austral. abbrev. for* Broken Hill Proprietary.

Bhubaneswar ★ (ˌbʊbəˈneɪʃwə) *n* an ancient city in E India, the capital of Orissa state: many temples built between the 7th and 16th centuries. Pop.: 411 542 (1991).

Bhutan ★ (buːˈtɑːn) *n* a kingdom in central Asia: disputed by Tibet, China, India, and Britain since the 18th century, the conflict now being chiefly between China and India (which is responsible for Bhutan's external affairs); contains inaccessible stretches of the E Himalayas in the north. Official language: Dzongka; Nepali is also spoken. Official religion: Mahayana Buddhism. Currencies: ngultrum and Indian rupee. Capital: Thimbu. Pop.: 860 000 (1997). Area: about 46 600 sq. km (18 000 sq. miles).
▸ ˌBhutan'ese *n, adj*

Bhutto ★ (ˈbuːtəʊ) *n* **1 Benazir** (ˈbenəˌzɪə). born 1953, Pakistani stateswoman; prime minister (1988–90 and 1993–96). **2** her father, **Zulfikar Ali** (ˈzʊlfɪkə ˈɑːlɪ). 1928–79, Pakistani statesman; president (1971–73) and prime minister (1973–77): executed for the murder of a political rival.

Bi *the chemical symbol for* bismuth.

bi- *or sometimes before a vowel* **bin-** *combining form.* **1** two; having two: *bifocal.* **2** occurring every two; lasting for two: *biennial.* **3** on both sides, directions, etc.: *bilateral.* **4** occurring twice during: *biweekly.* **5a** denoting a compound containing two identical cyclic hydrocarbon systems: *biphenyl.* **5b** (rare in technical usage) indicating an acid salt of a dibasic acid: *sodium bicarbonate.* **5c** (not in technical usage) equivalent of **di-**¹ (sense 2). [from L, from *bis* TWICE]

Biafra ★ (bɪˈæfrə) *n* **1** a region of E Nigeria: seceded as an independent republic (1967–70) during the Civil War, but defeated by Nigerian government forces. **2 Bight of.** former name (until 1975) of (the Bight of) **Bonny**.
▸ Bi'afran *adj, n*

Biak ★ (biːˈjɑːk) *n* an island in Indonesia, north of West Irian: the largest of the Schouten Islands. Area: 2455 sq. km (948 sq. miles).

Białystok ★ (*Polish* bjaˈwistɔk) *n* a city in E Poland: belonged to Prussia (1795–1807) and to Russia (1807–1919). Pop.: 277 100 (1995 est.). Russian name: **Belostok**.

biannual (baɪˈænjʊəl) *adj* occurring twice a year. Cf. **biennial**.
▸ bi'annually *adv*

Biarritz ★ (ˈbɪərɪts, bɪəˈrɪts; *French* bjarits) *n* a town in SW France, on the Bay of Biscay: famous resort, patronized by Napoleon III and by Queen Victoria and Edward VII of Great Britain and Ireland. Pop.: 28 890 (1990).

bias (ˈbaɪəs) *n* **1** mental tendency or inclination, esp. irrational preference or prejudice. **2** a diagonal line or cut across the weave of a fabric. **3** *Electronics.* the voltage applied to an electrode of a transistor or valve to establish suitable working conditions. **4** *Bowls.* **4a** a bulge or weight inside one side of a bowl. **4b** the curved course of such a bowl. **5** *Statistics.* a latent influence that disturbs an analysis. ◆ *adv* **6** obliquely; diagonally. ◆ *vb* **biases, biasing, biased** or **biasses, biassing, biassed. 7** (*tr; usually passive*) to cause to have a bias; prejudice; influence. [C16: from OF *biais*]
▸ 'biased or 'biassed *adj*

bias binding *n* a strip of material cut on the bias, used for binding hems or for decoration.

biathlon (baɪˈæθlən, -lɒn) *n Sport.* a contest in which skiers with rifles shoot at four targets along a 20-kilometre (12.5-mile) cross-country course.

biaxial (baɪˈæksɪəl) *adj* (esp. of a crystal) having two axes.

bib (bɪb) *n* **1** a piece of cloth or plastic worn, esp. by babies, to protect their clothes while eating. **2** the upper front part of some aprons, dungarees, etc. **3** Also called: **pout, whiting pout.** a light brown European marine gadoid food fish with a barbel on its lower jaw. **4 stick one's bib in.** *Austral. inf.* to interfere. ◆ *vb* **bibs, bibbing, bibbed. 5** *Arch.*

★ people and places

to drink (something). [C14 *bibben* to drink, prob. from L *bibere*]

Bib. *abbrev. for:* **1** Bible. **2** Biblical.

bib and tucker *n Inf.* an outfit of clothes.

bibcock ('bɪbˌkɒk) *or* **bib** *n* a tap with a nozzle bent downwards from a horizontal pipe.

bibelot ('bɪbləʊ) *n* an attractive or curious trinket. [C19: from F, from OF *beubelet*]

bibl. *abbrev. for:* **1** bibliographical. **2** bibliography.

Bibl. *abbrev. for* Biblical.

Bible ('baɪbʰl) *n* **1a** *the.* the sacred writings of the Christian religion, comprising the Old and New Testaments. **1b** (*as modifier*): *a Bible reading.* **2** (*often not cap.*) the sacred writings of a religion. **3** (*usually not cap.*) a book regarded as authoritative. [C13: from OF, from Med. L *biblia* books, from Gk, dim. of *biblos* papyrus]

Bible Belt *n* those states of the S US where Protestant fundamentalism is dominant.

Bible-thumper *n Sl.* an enthusiastic or aggressive exponent of the Bible. Also: **Bible-basher.**
▶ 'Bible-ˌthumping *n, adj*

biblical ('bɪblɪkʰl) *adj* **1** of or referring to the Bible. **2** resembling the Bible in written style.

Biblicist ('bɪblɪsɪst) *or* **Biblist** *n* **1** a biblical scholar. **2** a person who takes the Bible literally.

biblio- *combining form.* indicating book or books: *bibliography.* [from Gk *biblion* book]

bibliography (ˌbɪblɪˈɒɡrəfɪ) *n, pl* **bibliographies. 1** a list of books on a subject or by a particular author. **2** a list of sources used in a book, thesis, etc. **3a** the study of the history, classification, etc., of literary material. **3b** a work on this subject.
▶ ˌbibliˈographer *n* ▶ bibliographic (ˌbɪblɪəʊˈɡræfɪk) *or* ˌbiblioˈgraphical *adj*

bibliomancy ('bɪblɪəʊˌmænsɪ) *n* prediction of the future by interpreting a passage chosen at random from a book, esp. the Bible.

bibliomania (ˌbɪblɪəʊˈmeɪnɪə) *n* extreme fondness for books.
▶ ˌbiblioˈmaniˌac *n, adj*

bibliophile ('bɪblɪəʊˌfaɪl) *or* **bibliophil** ('bɪblɪəfɪl) *n* a person who collects or is fond of books.
▶ bibliophilism (ˌbɪblɪˈɒfɪˌlɪzəm) *n* ▶ ˌbibliˈophily *n*

bibliopole ('bɪblɪəʊˌpəʊl) *or* **bibliopolist** (ˌbɪblɪˈɒpəlɪst) *n* a dealer in books, esp. rare or decorative ones. [C18: from L, from Gk, from BIBLIO- + *pōlein* to sell]
▶ ˌbibliˈopoly *n*

bibulous ('bɪbjʊləs) *adj* addicted to alcohol. [C17: from L *bibulus*, from *bibere* to drink]
▶ 'bibulously *adv* ▶ 'bibulousness *n*

bicameral (baɪˈkæmərəl) *adj* (of a legislature) consisting of two chambers. [C19: from BI- + L *camera* CHAMBER]
▶ biˈcameralˌism *n*

bicarb ('baɪkɑːb) *n* short for **bicarbonate of soda.**

bicarbonate (baɪˈkɑːbənɪt, -ˌneɪt) *n* a salt of carbonic acid.

bicarbonate of soda *n* sodium bicarbonate, esp. as medicine or a raising agent in baking.

bice (baɪs) *n* **1** Also called: **bice blue.** medium blue. **2** Also called: **bice green.** a yellowish green. [C14: from OF *bis* dark grey, from ?]

bicentenary (ˌbaɪsɛnˈtiːnərɪ) *or US* **bicentennial** (ˌbaɪsɛnˈtɛnɪəl) *adj* **1** marking a 200th anniversary. **2** occurring every 200 years. **3** lasting 200 years. ◆ *n, pl* **bicentenaries. 4** a 200th anniversary.

bicephalous (baɪˈsɛfələs) *adj* **1** *Biol.* having two heads. **2** crescent-shaped.

biceps ('baɪsɛps) *n, pl* **biceps.** *Anat.* any muscle having two heads or origins, esp. the muscle that flexes the forearm. [C17: from L, from BI- + *caput* head]

bichloride (baɪˈklɔːraɪd) *n* another name for **dichloride.**

bichloride of mercury *n* another name for **mercuric chloride.**

bichromate (baɪˈkrəʊˌmeɪt, -mɪt) *n* another name for **dichromate.**

bicker ('bɪkə) *vb* (*intr*) **1** to argue over petty matters; squabble. **2** *Poetic.* **2a** (esp. of a stream) to run quickly. **2b** to flicker; glitter. ◆ *n* **3** a squabble. [C13: from ?]
▶ 'bickerer *n*

bicolour ('baɪˌkʌlə), **bicoloured** *or US* **bicolor, bicolored** *adj* two-coloured.

biconcave (baɪˈkɒnkeɪv, ˌbaɪkɒnˈkeɪv) *adj* (of a lens) having concave faces on both sides.

biconditional (ˌbaɪkɒnˈdɪʃənʰl) *n* **1** *Logic, maths.* a relation, taken as meaning *if and only if,* between two propositions which are either both true or both false and such that each implies the other. **2** *Logic.* a logical connective between two propositions whose truth table is true only if both propositions are true or both false. ◆ Also called (esp. sense 1): **equivalence.**

biconvex (baɪˈkɒnvɛks, ˌbaɪkɒnˈvɛks) *adj* (of a lens) having convex faces on both sides.

bicuspid (baɪˈkʌspɪd) *or* **bicuspidate** (baɪˈkʌspɪˌdeɪt) *adj* **1** having two cusps or points. ◆ *n* **2** a bicuspid tooth; premolar.

bicycle ('baɪsɪkʰl) *n* **1** a vehicle with a tubular metal frame mounted on two spoked wheels, one behind the other. The rider sits on a saddle, propels the vehicle by means of pedals, and steers with handlebars on the front wheel. Often shortened to **bike** (inf.), **cycle.** ◆ *vb* **bicycles, bicycling, bicycled. 2** (*intr*) to ride a bicycle.
▶ 'bicyclist *or* 'bicycler *n*

bicycle clip *n* one of a pair of clips worn around the ankles by cyclists to keep the trousers tight and out of the chain.

bid (bɪd) *vb* **bids, bidding, bad, bade,** *or* (esp. for senses 1, 2, 5, 6) **bid; bidden** *or* (esp. for senses 1, 2, 5, 6) **bid. 1** (often foll. by *for* or *against*) to offer (an amount) in attempting to buy something. **2** *Commerce.* to respond to an offer by a seller stating (the more favourable terms) on which one is willing to make a purchase. **3** (*tr*) to say (a greeting, etc.): *to bid farewell.* **4** to order; command: *do as you are bid!* **5** (*intr*; usually foll. by *for*) to attempt to attain power, etc. **6** *Bridge, etc.* to declare before play how many tricks one expects to make. **7 bid defiance.** to resist boldly. **8 bid fair.** to seem probable. ◆ *n* **9a** an offer of a specified amount. **9b** the price offered. **10a** the quoting by a seller of a price. **10b** the price quoted. **11** *Commerce.* **11a** a statement by a buyer, in response to an offer by a seller, of the more favourable terms that would be acceptable. **11b** the price or other terms so stated. **12** an attempt, esp. to attain power. **13** *Bridge.* **13a** the number of tricks a player undertakes to make. **13b** a player's turn to make a bid. ◆ See also **bid up.** [OE *biddan*]
▶ 'bidder *n*

Bida ('baɪdɑː) *or* **El Beda** ★ (ɛl ˈbɛɪdɑː) *n* the former name of **Doha.**

biddable ('bɪdəbʰl) *adj* **1** having sufficient value to be bid on, as a hand at bridge. **2** docile; obedient.
▶ 'biddableness *n*

bidding ('bɪdɪŋ) *n* **1** an order; command. **2** an invitation; summons. **3** bids or the act of making bids.

biddy[1] ('bɪdɪ) *n, pl* **biddies.** a dialect word for **chicken** or **hen.** [C17: ? imit. of calling chickens]

biddy[2] ('bɪdɪ) *n, pl* **biddies.** *Inf.* a woman, esp. an old gossipy one. [C18: from pet form of *Bridget*]

biddy-biddy ('bɪdɪˌbɪdɪ) *n, pl* **biddy-biddies. 1** a low-growing rosaceous plant of New Zealand, having prickly burs. **2** the burs of this plant. ◆ Also: **bidgee-widgee** ('bɪdʒɪˌwɪdʒɪ). [from Maori *piripiri*]

bide (baɪd) *vb* **bides, biding, bided** *or* **bode, bided. 1** (*intr*) *Arch. or dialect.* to continue in a certain place or state; stay. **2** (*tr*) *Arch. or dialect.* to tolerate; endure. **3 bide one's time.** to wait patiently for an opportunity. [OE *bīdan*]

bidentate (baɪˈdɛnˌteɪt) *adj* having two teeth or toothlike parts or processes.

bidet ('biːdeɪ) *n* a small low basin for washing the genital area. [C17: from F: small horse]

bid up *vb* (*adv*) to increase the market price of (a commodity) by making artificial bids.

Biel ★ (biːl) *n* **1** a town in NW Switzerland, on Lake Biel. Pop.: 52 197 (1994). French name: **Bienne. 2 Lake.** a lake in NW Switzerland: remains of lake dwellings were discovered here in the 19th century. Area: 39 sq. km (15 sq. miles). German name: **Bielersee** ('bi:lərze:).

Bielefeld ★ (*German* 'bi:ləfɛlt) *n* a city in Germany, in NE North Rhine-Westphalia. Pop.: 324 067 (1995 est.).

Bielsko-Biała ★ (*Polish* 'bjelskɔ'bjawa) *n* a town in S Poland: created in 1951 by the union of Bielsko and Biala Krakowska; a leading textile centre since the 16th century. Pop.: 180 300 (1995 est.).

Bien Hoa ★ ('bjɛn 'həʊə) *n* a town in S Vietnam: a former capital of Cambodia. Pop.: 273 879 (1989).

Bienne ★ (bjɛn) *n* the French name for **Biel**.

biennial (baɪ'ɛnɪəl) *adj* **1** occurring every two years. **2** lasting two years. Cf. **biannual**. ◆ *n* **3** a plant that completes its life cycle in two years. **4** an event that takes place every two years.
▶ **bi'ennially** *adv*

bier (bɪə) *n* a platform or stand on which a corpse or a coffin containing a corpse rests before burial. [OE *bǣr*; rel. to *beran* to BEAR[1]]

Bierce ★ (bɪəs) *n* **Ambrose** (**Gwinett**). 1842–?1914, US journalist and author of *The Devil's Dictionary* (1906): he disappeared during a mission in Mexico (1913).

biestings ('bi:stɪŋz) *n* a variant spelling of **beestings**.

biff (bɪf) *Sl.* ◆ *n* **1** a blow with the fist. ◆ *vb* **2** (*tr*) to give (someone) such a blow. [C20: prob. imit.]

bifid ('baɪfɪd) *adj* divided into two lobes by a median cleft. [C17: from L, from BI- + *-fidus*, from *findere* to split]
▶ **bi'fidity** *n* ▶ **'bifidly** *adv*

bifocal (baɪ'fəʊkəl) *adj* **1** *Optics.* having two different focuses. **2** relating to a compound lens permitting near and distant vision.

bifocals (baɪ'fəʊkəlz) *pl n* a pair of spectacles with bifocal lenses.

BIFU (in Britain) *abbrev. for* Banking, Insurance and Finance Union.

bifurcate *vb* ('baɪfə,keɪt), **bifurcates, bifurcating, bifurcated. 1** to fork or divide into two branches. ◆ *adj* ('baɪfə,keɪt, -kɪt). **2** forked or divided into two branches. [C17: from Med. L, from L, from BI- + *furca* fork]
▶ **,bifur'cation** *n*

big (bɪg) *adj* **bigger, biggest. 1** of great or considerable size, height, weight, number, power, or capacity. **2** having great significance; important. **3** important through having power, influence, wealth, authority, etc. **4** *Inf.* considerable in extent or intensity (esp. in **in a big way**). **5a** elder: *my big brother.* **5b** grown-up. **6a** generous; magnanimous: *that's very big of you.* **6b** (*in combination*): *bighearted.* **7** extravagant; boastful: *big talk.* **8** **too big for one's boots** or **breeches**. conceited; unduly self-confident. **9** in an advanced stage of pregnancy (esp. in **big with child**). ◆ *adv Inf.* **10** boastfully; pretentiously (esp. in **talk big**). **11** in an exceptional way; well: *his talk went over big.* **12** on a grand scale (esp. in **think big**). ◆ See also **big up**. [C13: ?from ON]
▶ **'bigness** *n*

bigamy ('bɪgəmɪ) *n, pl* **bigamies**. the crime of marrying a person while still legally married to someone else. [C13: via F from Med. L; see BI-, -GAMY]
▶ **'bigamist** *n* ▶ **'bigamous** *adj*

Big Apple ★ *n* the. *Inf.* New York City. [C20: prob. from US jazzmen's earlier use to mean any big, esp. northern, city; from ?]

Big Bang *n* the reorganization of the London Stock Exchange that took effect in October 1986 when operations became fully computerized, fixed commissions were abolished, and the functions of jobbers and brokers were merged.

big-bang theory *n* a cosmological theory postulating that all the matter of the universe was hurled in all directions by a cataclysmic explosion and that the universe is still expanding. Cf. **steady-state theory**.

Big Brother *n* a person, organization, etc., that exercises total dictatorial control. [C20: from George Orwell's novel *1984* (1949)]

big business *n* large commercial organizations collec-

tively, esp. when considered as exploitative or socially harmful.

Big C *n* the. a euphemism for **cancer** (senses 1 and 2).

big deal *interj Sl.* an exclamation of scorn, derision, etc., used esp. to belittle a claim or offer.

big dipper *n* (in amusement parks) a narrow railway with open carriages that run swiftly over a route of sharp curves and steep inclines.

big end *n Brit.* the larger end of a connecting rod in an internal-combustion engine.

big game *n* large animals that are hunted or fished for sport.

big gun *n Inf.* an important person.

bighead ('bɪg,hed) *n Inf.* a conceited person.
▶ **,big'headed** *adj* ▶ **,big'headedness** *n*

bighorn ('bɪg,hɔːn) *n, pl* **bighorns** or **bighorn**. a large wild sheep inhabiting mountainous regions in North America.

bight (baɪt) *n* **1** a wide indentation of a shoreline, or the body of water bounded by such a curve. **2** the slack middle part or loop in a rope. [OE *byht*; see BOW[2]]

Bight ★ (baɪt) *n* the. the major indentation of the S coast of Australia. In full: **the Great Australian Bight**.

Big Mac (mæk) *n Trademark*. two hamburgers served with salad, dressing, and a pickle on a soft bread roll.

bigmouth ('bɪg,maʊθ) *n Sl.* a noisy, indiscreet, or boastful person.
▶ **'big-,mouthed** *adj*

big name *n Inf.* **a** a famous person. **b** (*as modifier*): *a big-name performer.*

big noise *n Brit. inf.* an important person.

bignonia (bɪg'nəʊnɪə) *n* a tropical American climbing shrub cultivated for its trumpet-shaped yellow or reddish flowers. [C19: from NL, after the Abbé Jean-Paul Bignon (1662–1743)]

big-note *vb* **big-notes, big-noting, big-noted.** (*tr*) *Austral. inf.* to boast about (oneself).

bigot ('bɪgət) *n* a person who is intolerant, esp. regarding religion, politics, or race. [C16: from OF: name applied contemptuously to the Normans by the French, from ?]
▶ **'bigoted** *adj* ▶ **'bigotry** *n*

big shot *n Inf.* an important person.

Big Smoke *n* the. *Inf.* a large city, esp. London.

big stick *n Inf.* force or the threat of force.

big time *n Inf.* **a** the. the highest level of a profession, esp. entertainment. **b** (*as modifier*): *a big-time comedian.*
▶ **'big-'timer** *n*

big top *n Inf.* **1** the main tent of a circus. **2** the circus itself.

big up *vb* **bigs, bigging, bigged.** (*tr, adv*) *Sl., chiefly Caribbean.* to make important, prominent, or famous: *we'll do our best to big you up.*

bigwig ('bɪg,wɪg) *n Inf.* an important person.

Bihar ★ (bɪ'hɑː) *n* a state of NE India: hilly in the south, with the Ganges plain in the north; important for rice and mineral resources, esp. coal. Capital: Patna. Pop.: 93 080 000 (1994 est.). Area: 174 038 sq. km (67 875 sq. miles).

Biisk ★ (*Russian* bjisk) *n* a variant spelling of **Biysk**.

Bijapur ★ (,bɪdʒə'pʊə) *n* an ancient city in W India, in N Mysore: capital of a former kingdom, which fell at the end of the 17th century: cotton. Pop.: 186 939 (1991).

bijou ('bi:ʒu:) *n, pl* **bijoux** (-ʒu:z). **1** something small and delicately worked. **2** (*modifier*) often ironic. small but tasteful: *a bijou residence.* [C19: from F, from Breton *bizou* finger ring, from *biz* finger]

bijugate ('baɪdʒʊ,geɪt, baɪ'dʒuːgeɪt) or **bijugous** *adj* (of compound leaves) having two pairs of leaflets.

Bikaner ★ ('bi:kə,nɪə) *n* a walled city in NW India, in Rajasthan: capital of the former state of Bikaner, on the edge of the Thar Desert. Pop.: 416 289 (1991).

bike (baɪk) *n* **1** *Inf.* short for **bicycle** or **motorcycle**. **2** *Sl.* a promiscuous woman. **3** **get off one's bike.** *Austral. & NZ sl.*

★ people and places

to lose one's self-control. ◆ vb **bikes, biking, biked. 4** (*intr*) *Inf.* to ride a cycle.

biker ('baɪkə) n a member of a motorcycle gang. Also called (*Austral.* and *NZ*): **bikie.**

biker jacket n a short, close-fitting leather jacket with zips and studs, often worn by motorcyclists.

bikini (bɪ'kiːnɪ) n a woman's very brief two-piece swimming costume. [C20: after *Bikini* atoll, from a comparison between the obvious and powerful effect of the atom-bomb test and the effect (on men) of women wearing bikinis]

Bikini ★ (bɪ'kiːnɪ) n an atoll in the N Pacific; one of the Marshall Islands: site of a US atom-bomb test in 1946.

Biko ★ ('biːkəʊ) n **Steven Bantu,** known as **Steve.** 1946–77, Black South African civil rights leader: founder of the South African Students Organization. His death in police custody caused worldwide concern.

bilabial (baɪ'leɪbɪəl) adj **1** of or denoting a speech sound articulated using both lips: (*p*) *is a bilabial stop.* ◆ n **2** a bilabial speech sound.

bilabiate (baɪ'leɪbɪˌeɪt, -ɪt) adj *Bot.* divided into two lips: *the snapdragon has a bilabiate corolla.*

bilateral (baɪ'lætərəl) adj **1** having or involving two sides. **2** affecting or undertaken by two parties; mutual. **3** having identical sides or parts on each side of an axis; symmetrical.

bilateral symmetry n symmetry in one plane only. Cf. **radial symmetry.**

Bilbao (bɪl'baːəʊ; *Spanish* bil'βau) n a port in N Spain, on the Bay of Biscay: famous since medieval times for the production of iron and steel goods, esp. swords; still contains the country's largest iron and steel works and exports iron ore. Pop.: 371 787 (1994 est.).

bilberry ('bɪlbərɪ) n, pl **bilberries. 1** any of several shrubs, such as the whortleberry, having edible blue or blackish berries. **2** the fruit of any of these plants. [C16: prob. of Scand. origin]

bilboes ('bɪlbəʊz) pl n a long iron bar with sliding shackles, for the ankles of a prisoner. [C16: ?from *Bilbao,* Spain]

Bildungsroman *German.* ('bɪldʊŋsroamaːn) n a novel about a person's formative years.

bile (baɪl) n **1** a bitter greenish to golden brown alkaline fluid secreted by the liver and stored in the gall bladder. It aids digestion of fats. **2** a health disorder due to faulty secretion of bile. **3** irritability or peevishness. [C17: from F, from L *bīlis*]

bilge (bɪldʒ) n **1** *Naut.* the parts of a vessel's hull where the sides curve inwards to form the bottom. **2** (*often pl*) the parts of a vessel between the lowermost floorboards and the bottom. **3** Also called: **bilge water.** the dirty water that collects in a vessel's bilge. **4** *Inf.* silly rubbish; nonsense. **5** the widest part of a cask. ◆ vb **bilges, bilging, bilged. 6** (*intr*) *Naut.* (of a vessel) to take in water at the bilge. **7** (*tr*) *Naut.* to damage (a vessel) in the bilge. [C16: prob. var. of BULGE]

bilharzia (bɪl'haːtsɪə) n **1** another name for a **schistosome. 2** another name for **schistosomiasis.** [C19: NL, after Theodor *Bilharz* (1825–62), G parasitologist who discovered schistosomes]

bilharziasis (ˌbɪlhaː'tsaɪəsɪs) or **bilharziosis** (bɪlˌhaːtsɪ'əʊsɪs) n another name for **schistosomiasis.**

biliary ('bɪlɪərɪ) adj of or relating to bile, the ducts that convey bile, or to the gall bladder.

bilingual (baɪ'lɪŋɡwəl) adj **1** able to speak two languages, esp. with fluency. **2** expressed in two languages. ◆ n **3** a bilingual person.
▸ **bi'lingual,ism** n

bilious ('bɪlɪəs) adj **1** of or relating to bile. **2** affected with or denoting any disorder related to secretion of bile. **3** *Inf.* bad-tempered; irritable. [C16: from L *bīliōsus* full of BILE]
▸ **'biliousness** n

bilk (bɪlk) vb (*tr*) **1** to balk; thwart. **2** (often foll. by *of*) to cheat or deceive, esp. to avoid making payment to. **3** to escape from; elude. ◆ n **4** a swindle or cheat. **5** a person who swindles or cheats. [C17: ? var. of BALK]
▸ **'bilker** n

bill[1] (bɪl) n **1** money owed for goods or services supplied. **2** a statement of money owed. **3** *Chiefly Brit.* such an account for food and drink in a restaurant, hotel, etc. **4** any list of items, events, etc., such as a theatre programme. **5** a statute in draft, before it becomes law. **6** a printed notice or advertisement. **7** *US & Canad.* a piece of paper money; note. **8** an obsolete name for **promissory note. 9** See **bill of exchange, bill of fare.** ◆ vb (*tr*) **10** to send or present an account for payment to (a person). **11** to enter (items, goods, etc.) on an account or statement. **12** to advertise by posters. **13** to schedule as a future programme. [C14: from Anglo-L *billa,* alteration of LL *bulla* document, BULL[3]]

bill[2] (bɪl) n **1** the projecting jaws of a bird, covered with a horny sheath; beak. **2** any beaklike mouthpart in other animals. **3** a narrow promontory. ◆ vb (*intr*) (esp. in **bill and coo**). **4** (of birds, esp. doves) to touch bills together. **5** (of lovers) to kiss and whisper amorously. [OE *bile*]

bill[3] (bɪl) n **1** a pike or halberd with a narrow hooked blade. **2** short for **billhook.** [OE *bill* sword]

billabong ('bɪləˌbɒŋ) n *Austral.* **1** a backwater channel that forms a lagoon or pool. **2** a branch of a river running to a dead end. [C19: from Abor., from *billa* river + *bong* dead]

billboard ('bɪlˌbɔːd) n *Chiefly US & Canad.* another name for **hoarding.** [C19: from BILL[1] + BOARD]

billet[1] ('bɪlɪt) n **1** accommodation, esp. for a soldier, in civilian lodgings. **2** the official requisition for such lodgings. **3** a space or berth in a ship. **4** *Inf.* a job. ◆ vb **5** (*tr*) to assign a lodging to (a soldier). **6** to lodge or be lodged. [C15: from OF *billette,* from *bulle* a document; see BULL[3]]

billet[2] ('bɪlɪt) n **1** a chunk of wood, esp. for fuel. **2** a small bar of iron or steel. [C15: from OF *billette* a little log, from *bille* log]

billet-doux (ˌbɪlɪ'duː) n, pl **billets-doux** (ˌbɪlɪ'duːz). *Old-fashioned or jocular.* a love letter. [C17: from F, lit.: a sweet letter]

billhook ('bɪlˌhʊk) n a tool with a curved blade terminating in a hook, used for pruning, chopping, etc. Also called: **bill.**

billiard ('bɪljəd) n (*modifier*) of or relating to billiards: *a billiard table; a billiard cue.*

billiards ('bɪljədz) n (*functioning as sing*) any of various games in which long cues are used to drive balls on a rectangular table covered with a smooth cloth and having raised cushioned edges. [C16: from OF *billard* curved stick, from *bille* log; see BILLET[2]]

billing ('bɪlɪŋ) n **1** *Theatre.* the relative importance of a performer or act as reflected in the prominence given in programmes, advertisements, etc. **2** *Chiefly US & Canad.* public notice or advertising.

billingsgate ('bɪlɪŋzˌɡeɪt) n obscene or abusive language. [C17: after BILLINGSGATE, notorious for such language]

Billingsgate ★ ('bɪlɪŋzˌɡeɪt) n the largest fish market in London, formerly on the N bank of the River Thames; moved to a new site on the Isle of Dogs in 1982.

Billings method ('bɪlɪŋz) n a natural method of birth control that involves examining the colour and viscosity of the cervical mucus to discover when ovulation is occurring. [C20: after Drs John and Evelyn *Billings*]

billion ('bɪljən) n, pl **billions** or **billion. 1** one thousand million: written as 1 000 000 000 or 10[9]. **2** (formerly, in Britain) one million million: it is written as 1 000 000 000 000 or 10[12]. US word: **trillion. 3** (*often pl*) any exceptionally large number. ◆ determiner **4** (preceded by *a* or a cardinal number) amounting to a billion. [C17: from F, from BI- + -*llion* as in *million*]
▸ **'billionth** adj, n

billionaire (ˌbɪljə'nɛə) n a person whose wealth exceeds a billion monetary units of his country.

Billiton ★ ('bɪlɪtɒn, bɪ'liːtɒn) n an island of Indonesia, in the Java Sea between Borneo and Sumatra. Chief town: Tandjungpandan. Area: 4833 sq. km (1866 sq. miles). Also called: **Belitung.**

bill of attainder n (formerly) a legislative act finding a person guilty without trial of treason or felony and declaring him attainted.

bill of exchange *n* (now chiefly in foreign transactions) a document, usually negotiable, instructing a third party to pay a stated sum at a designated future date or on demand.

bill of fare *n* another name for **menu**.

bill of health *n* **1** a certificate that attests to the health of a ship's company. **2 clean bill of health.** *Inf.* **2a** a good report of one's physical condition. **2b** a favourable account of a person's or a company's financial position.

bill of lading *n* (in foreign trade) a document containing full particulars of goods shipped.

bill of quantities *n* a document drawn up by a quantity surveyor providing details of the prices, dimensions, etc., of the materials required to build a large structure, such as a factory.

Bill of Rights *n* **1** an English statute of 1689 guaranteeing the rights and liberty of the individual subject. **2** the first ten amendments to the US Constitution which guarantee the liberty of the individual. **3** (*usually not caps.*) any charter of basic human rights.

bill of sale *n Law.* a deed transferring personal property.

billow ('bɪləʊ) *n* **1** a large sea wave. **2** a swelling or surging mass, as of smoke or sound. ◆ *vb* **3** to rise up, swell out, or cause to rise up or swell out. [C16: from ON *bylgja*]
▶ **'billowing** *adj, n* ▶ **'billowy** *adj* ▶ **'billowiness** *n*

billposter ('bɪl,pəʊstə) or **billsticker** *n* a person who sticks advertising posters to walls, etc.
▶ **'bill,posting** or **'bill,sticking** *n*

billy ('bɪlɪ) or **billycan** ('bɪlɪ,kæn) *n, pl* **billies** or **billycans.** **1** a metal can or pot for boiling water, etc., over a campfire. **2** *Austral. & NZ.* (*as modifier*): *billy-tea.* **3 boil the billy.** *Austral. & NZ. inf.* to make tea. [C19: from Scot. *billypot* cooking vessel]

billy goat *n* a male goat.

Billy the Kid ★ *n* nickname of *William H. Bonney.* 1859–81, US outlaw.

bilobate (baɪ'ləʊ,beɪt) or **bilobed** ('baɪ,ləʊbd) *adj* divided into or having two lobes.

biltong ('bɪl,tɒŋ) *n S. African.* strips of meat dried and cured in the sun. [C19: Afrik., from Du. *bil* buttock + *tong* TONGUE]

BIM *abbrev. for* British Institute of Management.

bimanous ('bɪmənəs, baɪ'meɪ-) *adj* (of man and the higher primates) having two hands distinct in form and function from the feet. [C19: from NL, from BI- + L *manus* hand]

bimanual (,baɪ'mænjʊəl) *adj* using both hands.

bimbo ('bɪmbəʊ) *n, pl* **bimbos.** *Derog. sl.* **1** an attractive but empty-headed young person, esp. a woman. **2** a fellow; a foolish or stupid person. [C20: from It.: little child, perhaps via Polari]

bimetallic (,baɪmɪ'tælɪk) *adj* **1** consisting of two metals. **2** of or based on bimetallism.

bimetallic strip *n* strips of two metals that expand differently welded together for use in a thermostat.

bimetallism (baɪ'metə,lɪzəm) *n* the use of two metals, esp. gold and silver, in fixed relative values as the standard of value and currency.
▶ **bi'metallist** *n*

bimonthly (baɪ'mʌnθlɪ) *adj, adv* **1** every two months. **2** twice a month. ◆ *n, pl* **bimonthlies.** **3** a periodical published every two months.

bimorph ('baɪmɔːf) or **bimorph cell** *n Electron.* two piezoelectric crystals cemented together so that their movement converts electrical signals into mechanical energy or vice versa: used in record-player pick-ups and loudspeakers.

bin (bɪn) *n* **1** a large container for storing something in bulk, such as coal, grain, or bottled wine. **2** Also called: **bread bin.** a small container for bread. **3** Also called: **dustbin, rubbish bin.** a container for rubbish, etc. ◆ *vb* **bins, binning, binned.** **4** to store in a bin. **5** to put in a wastepaper bin. [OE *binne* basket]

binary ('baɪnərɪ) *adj* **1** composed of or involving two;

dual. **2** *Maths, computing.* of or expressed in binary notation or binary code. **3** (of a compound or molecule) containing atoms of two different elements. ◆ *n, pl* **binaries. 4** something composed of two parts. **5** *Astron.* See **binary star.** [C16: from LL *bīnārius;* see BI-]

binary code *n Computing.* the representation of each one of a set of numbers, letters, etc., as a unique group of bits.

binary notation or **system** *n* a number system having a base of two, numbers being expressed by sequences of the digits 0 and 1: used in computing, as 0 and 1 can be represented electrically as *off* and *on*.

binary number *n* a number expressed in binary notation.

binary star *n* a double star system containing two associated stars revolving around a common centre of gravity in different orbits.

binary weapon *n* a chemical weapon containing two substances separately that mix to produce a lethal agent when the projectile is fired.

binate ('baɪ,neɪt) *adj Bot.* occurring in two parts or in pairs: *binate leaves.* [C19: from NL *bīnātus,* prob. from L *combīnātus* united]
▶ **'bi,nately** *adv*

binaural (baɪ'nɔːrəl, bɪn'ɔːrəl) *adj* **1** relating to, having, or hearing with both ears. **2** employing two separate channels for recording or transmitting sound.

bind (baɪnd) *vb* **binds, binding, bound. 1** to make or become fast or secure with or as if with a tie or band. **2** (*tr;* often foll. by *up*) to encircle or enclose with a band: *to bind the hair.* **3** (*tr*) to place (someone) under obligation; oblige. **4** (*tr*) to impose legal obligations or duties upon (a person). **5** (*tr*) to make (a bargain, agreement, etc.) irrevocable; seal. **6** (*tr*) to restrain or confine with or as if with ties, as of responsibility or loyalty. **7** (*tr*) to place under certain constraints; govern. **8** (*tr;* often foll. by *up*) to bandage. **9** to cohere or cause to cohere: *egg binds fat and flour.* **10** to make or become compact, stiff, or hard: *frost binds the earth.* **11** (*tr*) to enclose and fasten (the pages of a book) between covers. **12** (*tr*) to provide (a garment, hem, etc.) with a border or edging. **13** (*tr;* sometimes foll. by *out* or *over*) to employ as an apprentice; indenture. **14** (*intr*) *Sl.* to complain. ◆ *n* **15** something that binds. **16** *Inf.* a difficult or annoying situation. **17** a situation in which freedom of action is restricted. ◆ See also **bind over.** [OE *bindan*]

binder ('baɪndə) *n* **1** a firm cover or folder for holding loose sheets of paper together. **2** a material used to bind separate particles together. **3** a person who binds books, bookbinder. **4** something used to fasten or tie, such as rope or twine. **5** Also called: **reaper binder.** *Obs.* a machine for cutting grain and binding it into sheaves. **6** an informal agreement giving insurance coverage pending formal issue of a policy.

bindery ('baɪndərɪ) *n, pl* **binderies.** a place in which books are bound.

bindi-eye ('bɪndɪ,aɪ) *n Austral.* **1** any of various small weedy Australian herbaceous plants with burlike fruits. **2** any bur or prickle. [C20: ?from Abor.]

binding ('baɪndɪŋ) *n* **1** anything that binds or fastens. **2** the covering within which the pages of a book are bound. **3** the tape used for binding hems, etc. ◆ *adj* **4** imposing an obligation or duty. **5** causing hindrance; restrictive.

bind over *vb* (*tr, adv*) to place (a person) under a legal obligation, such as one to keep the peace.

bindweed ('baɪnd,wiːd) *n* any of various plants that twine around a support. See also **convolvulus.**

bine (baɪn) *n* the climbing or twining stem of any of various plants, such as the woodbine. [C19: var. of BIND]

Binet-Simon scale ('biːneɪ'saɪmən) *n Psychol.* a test used to determine the mental age of subjects. Also called: **Binet scale** or **test.** [C20: after Alfred Binet (1857–1911) + Théodore Simon (1873–1961), F psychologists]

binge (bɪndʒ) *Inf.* ◆ *n* **1** a bout of excessive drinking or eating. **2** excessive indulgence in anything. ◆ *vb* **binges, bingeing** or **binging, binged. 3** (*intr*) to indulge in a binge. [C19: prob. dial. *binge* to soak]

Bingen ★ ('bɪŋən) *n* a town in W Germany on the Rhine: wine trade and tourist centre. Pop.: 23 141 (1989 est.).

bingo ('bɪŋgəʊ) *n, pl* **bingos.** a gambling game, usually played with several people, in which random numbers are called out and the players cover the numbers on their individual cards. The first to cover a given arrangement of numbers is the winner. [C19: ?from *bing*, imit. of a bell ringing to mark the win]

binman ('bɪn,mæn, 'bɪnmən) *n, pl* **binmen.** *Inf.* another name for **dustman**.

binnacle ('bɪnək°l) *n* a housing for a ship's compass. [C17: changed from C15 *bitakle*, from Port. from LL *habitāculum* dwelling-place, from L *habitāre* to inhabit]

binocular (bɪ'nɒkjʊlə, baɪ-) *adj* involving, relating to, seeing with or intended for both eyes: *binocular vision*. [C18: from BI- + L *oculus* eye]

binoculars (bɪ'nɒkjʊləz, baɪ-) *pl n* an optical instrument for use with both eyes, consisting of two small telescopes joined together.

binomial (baɪ'nəʊmɪəl) *n* **1** a mathematical expression consisting of two terms, such as $3x + 2y$. **2** a two-part taxonomic name for an animal or plant indicating genus and species. ◆ *adj* **3** referring to two names or terms. [C16: from Med. L, from BI- + L *nōmen* name]
▶ bi'nomially *adv*

binomial distribution *n* a statistical distribution giving the probability of obtaining a specified number of independent trials of an experiment, with a constant probability of success in each.

binomial theorem *n* a general mathematical formula that expresses any power of a binomial without multiplying out, as in $(x+a)^n = x^n + nx^{n-1}a + [n(n-1)/2]x^{n-2}a^2 \ldots + a^n$.

bint (bɪnt) *n Sl.* a derogatory term for **girl** or **woman**. [C19: from Ar., lit.: daughter]

binturong ('bɪntjʊˌrɒŋ, bɪn'tjʊərɒŋ) *n* a long-bodied short-legged arboreal SE Asian mammal having shaggy black hair. [from Malay]

Binyon ★ ('bɪnjən) *n* (**Robert**) **Laurence.** 1869–1943, British poet, noted for his war poems "For the Fallen" (1914) and "The Burning of the Leaves" (1944).

bio- *or before a vowel* **bi-** *combining form.* **1** indicating or involving life or living organisms: *biogenesis.* **2** indicating a human life or career: *biography.* [from Gk *bios* life]

bioassay (ˌbaɪəʊ'æseɪ) *n* **1** a method of determining the concentration or effect of a drug, etc., by comparing its effect on living organisms with that of a standard preparation. ◆ *vb* (*tr*) **2** to subject to a bioassay.

bioastronautics (ˌbaɪəʊˌæstrə'nɔːtɪks) *n* (*functioning as sing*) the study of the effects of space flight on living organisms.

bioastronomy (ˌbaɪəʊə'strɒnəmɪ) *n* the branch of astronomy concerned with the search for life on other planets.

Bío-Bío ★ (*Spanish* 'biːoˈbiːo) *n* a river in central Chile, rising in the Andes and flowing northwest to the Pacific. Length: about 390 km (240 miles).

biochemical oxygen demand *n* a measure of the organic pollution of water; the number of milligrams of oxygen per litre of water absorbed in a given period. Abbrev.: **BOD**

biochemistry (ˌbaɪəʊ'kemɪstrɪ) *n* the study of the chemical compounds, reactions, etc., in living organisms.
▶ **biochemical** (ˌbaɪəʊ'kemɪk°l) *adj* ▶ ˌbio'chemist *n*

biocide ('baɪəˌsaɪd) *n* a chemical capable of killing living organisms.
▶ ˌbio'cidal *adj*

biocoenosis *or US* **biocenosis** (ˌbaɪəʊsɪ'nəʊsɪs) *n* the relationships between animals and plants subsisting together. [C19: NL from BIO- + Gk *koinōsis* sharing]

biodegradable (ˌbaɪəʊdɪ'greɪdəb°l) *adj* (of sewage, packaging, etc.) capable of being decomposed by bacteria or other biological means.
▶ **biodegradability** (ˌbaɪəʊdɪˌgreɪdə'bɪlɪtɪ) *n*

biodiversity (ˌbaɪəʊdaɪ'vɜːsɪtɪ) *n* the existence of a wide variety of plant and animal species in their natural environments, the maintaining of which is the aim of conservationists concerned about the indiscriminate destruction of rainforests and other habitats.

bioengineering (ˌbaɪəʊˌendʒɪ'nɪərɪŋ) *n* **1** the design and manufacture of aids, such as artificial limbs, to rectify defective body functions. **2** the design, manufacture, and maintenance of engineering equipment used in biosynthetic processes.
▶ ˌbioˌengi'neer *n*

bioethics (ˌbaɪəʊ'eθɪks) *n* (*functioning as sing*) the study of ethical problems arising from scientific advances, esp. in biology and medicine.

biofeedback (ˌbaɪəʊ'fiːdˌbæk) *n Physiol., psychol.* the technique of recording and presenting (usually visually) the activity of an autonomic function, such as the rate of heartbeat, in order to teach control of it.

biofuel ('baɪəʊˌfjuəl) *n* a substance of biological origin that is used as a fuel.

biog. *abbrev. for:* **1** biographical. **2** biography.

biogenesis (ˌbaɪəʊ'dʒenɪsɪs) *n* the principle that a living organism must originate from a parent organism similar to itself.
◆ ˌbioge'netic *or* ˌbioge'netical *adj*

biogenic (ˌbaɪəʊ'dʒenɪk) *adj* produced or originating from a living organism.

biography (baɪ'ɒgrəfɪ) *n, pl* **biographies.** **1** an account of a person's life by another. **2** such accounts collectively.
▶ bi'ographer *n* ▶ **biographical** (ˌbaɪə'græfɪk°l) *adj*

Bioko ★ (baɪ'əʊkəʊ) *n* an island in the Gulf of Guinea, off the coast of Cameroon: part of Equatorial Guinea. Capital: Malabo. Area: 2017 sq. km (786 sq. miles). Former names: **Fernando Po** (until 1973), **Macías Nguema** (1973–79).

biol. *abbrev. for:* **1** biological. **2** biology.

biological (ˌbaɪə'lɒdʒɪk°l) *adj* **1** of or relating to biology. **2** (of a detergent) containing enzymes for removing stains of organic origin from items to be washed. ◆ *n* **3** (*usually pl*) a drug derived from a living organism.

biological clock *n* **1** an inherent periodicity in the physiological processes of living organisms that is independent of external periodicity. **2** the hypothetical mechanism responsible for this. ◆ See also **circadian**.

biological control *n* the control of destructive organisms by nonchemical means, such as introducing the natural enemy of a pest.

biological warfare *n* the use of living organisms or their toxic products to induce death or incapacity in humans.

biology (baɪ'ɒlədʒɪ) *n* **1** the study of living organisms. **2** the animal and plant life of a particular region.
▶ bi'ologist *n*

bioluminescence (ˌbaɪəʊˌluːmɪ'nesəns) *n* the production of light by living organisms, such as the firefly.
▶ ˌbioˌlumi'nescent *adj*

biomass ('baɪəʊˌmæs) *n* the total number of living organisms in a given area, expressed in terms of living or dry weight per unit area.

biomathematics (ˌbaɪəʊˌmæθə'mætɪks, -ˌmæθ'mæt-) *n* (*functioning as sing*) the study of the application of mathematics to biology.

biomechanics (ˌbaɪəʊmɪ'kænɪks) *n* (*functioning as sing*) the study of the mechanics of the movement of living organisms.

biomedicine (ˌbaɪəʊ'medɪsɪn) *n* **1** the medical and biological study of the effects of unusual environmental stress, esp. in connection with space travel. **2** the study of herbal remedies.
▶ ˌbio'medical *adj*

biometry (baɪ'ɒmɪtrɪ) *or* **biometrics** (ˌbaɪə'metrɪks) *n* (*functioning as sing*) the study of biological data by means of statistical analysis.
▶ ˌbio'metric *adj*

bionic (baɪ'ɒnɪk) *adj* **1** of or relating to bionics. **2** (in science fiction) having physiological functions augmented by electronic equipment.

bionics (baɪ'ɒnɪks) *n* (*functioning as sing*) **1** the study of certain biological functions that are applicable to the development of electronic equipment designed to operate similarly. **2** the replacement of limbs or body parts by artificial limbs or parts that are electronically or mechanically powered.

bionomics (ˌbaɪə'nɒmɪks) n (functioning as sing) a less common name for **ecology**. [C19: from BIO- + nomics on pattern of ECONOMICS]
▶ ˌbio'nomic adj ▶ **bionomist** (baɪ'ɒnəmɪst) n

biophysics (ˌbaɪəʊ'fɪzɪks) n (functioning as sing) the physics of biological processes and the application of the methods used in physics to biology.
▶ ˌbio'physical adj ▶ ˌbio'physically adv ▶ **biophysicist** (ˌbaɪəʊ'fɪzɪsɪst) n

biopic ('baɪəʊˌpɪk) n Inf. a film based on the life of a famous person. [C20: from bio(graphical) + pic(ture)]

biopsy ('baɪɒpsɪ) n, pl **biopsies**. examination, esp. under a microscope, of tissue from a living body to determine the cause or extent of a disease. [C20: from BIO- + Gk opsis sight]

biorhythm ('baɪəʊˌrɪðəm) n a cyclically recurring pattern of physiological states, believed by some to affect a person's physical, emotional, and mental states and behaviour.

bioscope ('baɪəˌskəʊp) n **1** a kind of early film projector. **2** a South African word for **cinema**.

bioscopy (baɪ'ɒskəpɪ) n, pl **bioscopies**. examination of a body to determine whether it is alive.

-biosis n combining form. indicating a specified mode of life. [NL, from Gk biōsis; see BIO-, -OSIS]
▶ **-biotic** adj combining form.

biosphere ('baɪəˌsfɪə) n the part of the earth's surface and atmosphere inhabited by living things.

biosynthesis (ˌbaɪəʊ'sɪnθɪsɪs) n the formation of complex compounds from simple substances by living organisms.
▶ **biosynthetic** (ˌbaɪəʊsɪn'θetɪk) adj ▶ ˌbiosyn'thetically adv

biotech ('baɪəʊˌtek) n Inf. short for **biotechnology**.

biotechnology (ˌbaɪəʊtek'nɒlədʒɪ) n the use of microorganisms for beneficial effect, as in the processing of waste matter or (using genetic engineering) to produce antibiotics, hormones, vaccines, etc.

biotic (baɪ'ɒtɪk) adj of or relating to living organisms. [C17: from Gk biotikos, from bios life]

biotin ('baɪətɪn) n a vitamin of the B complex, abundant in egg yolk and liver. [C20: from Gk biotē life, way of life + -IN]

bipartisan (ˌbaɪpɑːtɪ'zæn, baɪ'pɑːtɪˌzæn) adj consisting of or supported by two political parties.
▶ ˌbiparti'sanship n

bipartite (baɪ'pɑːtaɪt) adj **1** consisting of or having two parts. **2** affecting or made by two parties. **3** Bot. (esp. of some leaves) divided into two parts almost to the base.
▶ bi'partitely adv ▶ **bipartition** (ˌbaɪpɑː'tɪʃən) n

biped ('baɪpɛd) n **1** any animal with two feet. ◆ adj also **bipedal** (baɪ'piːdˀl, -'pɛdˀl). **2** having two feet.

bipinnate (baɪ'pɪneɪt) adj (of compound leaves) having both the leaflets and the stems bearing them arranged pinnately.
▶ bi'pinnately adv

biplane ('baɪˌpleɪn) n a type of aeroplane having two sets of wings, one above the other.

bipolar (baɪ'pəʊlə) adj **1** having two poles: a bipolar dynamo. **2** of or relating to the North and South Poles. **3** having or characterized by two opposed opinions, etc. **4** (of a transistor) utilizing both majority and minority charge carriers.
▶ ˌbipo'larity n

biprism ('baɪˌprɪzəm) n Physics. a prism that has a highly obtuse angle to facilitate beam splitting.

biquadratic (ˌbaɪkwɒ'drætɪk) Maths. ◆ adj **1** of or relating to the fourth power. ◆ n **2** a biquadratic equation, such as $x^4 + x + 6 = 0$.

biracial (baɪ'reɪʃəl) adj of or for members of two races.
▶ bi'racialism n

birch (bɜːtʃ) n **1** any catkin-bearing tree or shrub having thin peeling bark. See also **silver birch**. **2** the hard close-grained wood of any of these trees. **3 the birch**. a bundle of birch twigs or a birch rod used, esp. formerly, for flogging offenders. ◆ adj **4** consisting of or made of birch. ◆ vb **5** (tr) to flog with a birch. [OE bierce]
▶ 'birchen adj

bird (bɜːd) n **1** any warm-blooded egg-laying vertebrate, characterized by a body covering of feathers and forelimbs modified as wings. **2** Inf. a person, as in **rare bird, wise bird, clever bird**. **3** Sl., chiefly Brit. a girl or young woman. **4** Sl. prison or a term in prison (esp. in **do bird**). **5 a bird in the hand**. something definite or certain. **6 birds of a feather**. people with the same characteristics, ideas, interests, etc. **7 get the bird**. Inf. **7a** to be fired or dismissed. **7b** (esp. of a public performer) to be hissed at. **8 kill two birds with one stone**. to accomplish two things with one action. **9 (strictly) for the birds**. Inf. deserving of disdain or contempt; not important. [OE bridd, from ?]

birdbath ('bɜːdˌbɑːθ) n a small basin or trough for birds to bath in, usually in a garden.

bird-brained adj Inf. silly; stupid.

birdcage ('bɜːdˌkeɪdʒ) n **1** a wire or wicker cage for captive birds. **2** Austral. & NZ. an area on a racecourse where horses parade before a race. **3** NZ inf. a second-hand car dealer's yard.

bird call n **1** the characteristic call or song of a bird. **2** an imitation of this.

birdie ('bɜːdɪ) n **1** Golf. a score of one stroke under par for a hole. **2** Inf. a bird, esp. a small bird. ◆ vb **3** (tr) Golf. to play (a hole) in one stroke under par.

birdlime ('bɜːdˌlaɪm) n **1** a sticky substance smeared on twigs to catch small birds. ◆ vb **birdlimes, birdliming, birdlimed**. **2** (tr) to smear (twigs) with birdlime to catch (small birds).

bird-nesting or **birds'-nesting** n searching for birds' nests as a hobby, often to steal the eggs.

bird of paradise n **1** any of various songbirds of New Guinea and neighbouring regions, the males having brilliantly coloured plumage. **2 bird-of-paradise flower**. any of various plants native to tropical southern Africa and South America that have purple bracts and large orange or yellow flowers resembling birds' heads.

bird of passage n **1** a bird that migrates seasonally. **2** a transient person.

bird of prey n a bird, such as a hawk or owl, that hunts other animals for food.

birdseed ('bɜːdˌsiːd) n a mixture of various kinds of seeds for feeding cagebirds.

bird's-eye adj **1a** seen or photographed from high above. **1b** summarizing (esp. in **bird's-eye view**). **2** having markings resembling birds' eyes.

bird's-foot or **bird-foot** n, pl **bird's-foots** or **bird-foots**. any of various plants whose flowers, leaves, or pods resemble a bird's foot or claw.

birdshot ('bɜːdˌʃɒt) n small pellets designed for shooting birds.

bird strike n a collision of an aircraft with a bird.

bird table n a table or platform in the open on which food for birds may be placed.

bird-watcher n a person who identifies and studies wild birds in their natural surroundings.
▶ 'bird-ˌwatching n

birefringence (ˌbaɪrɪ'frɪndʒəns) n another name for **double refraction**.
▶ ˌbire'fringent adj

bireme ('baɪriːm) n an ancient galley having two banks of oars. [C17: from L, from BI- + rēmus oar]

biretta or **berretta** (bɪ'rɛtə) n RC Church. a stiff square clerical cap. [C16: from It. berretta, from OProvençal, from LL birrus hooded cape]

Birgitta ★ (bɪə'gɪtə) n Saint. See (Saint) **Bridget** (sense 2).

Birkbeck ★ ('bɜːkˌbek) n George. 1776–1841, British educationist; founder of the London Mechanics Institute (1824), which later became Birkbeck College.

Birkenhead[1] ★ (ˌbɜːkən'hɛd) n a port in NW England, in

| ★ people and places |

Wirral unitary authority: former shipbuilding centre. Pop.: 93 087 (1991).

Birkenhead[2] ('bɜːkən,hɛd) ★ *n* **Frederick Edwin Smith**, 1st Earl of, known as *F. E. Smith*. 1872–1930, British Conservative statesman and lawyer.

birl (bɜːl) *vb* **1** *Scot.* to spin; twirl. **2** *US & Canad.* to cause (a floating log) to spin using the feet while standing on it, esp. as a sport among lumberjacks. ♦ *n* **3** a variant spelling of **burl**[2]. [C18: prob. imit. & infl. by WHIRL & HURL]

Birmingham ★ *n* **1** ('bɜːmɪŋəm) an industrial city in central England, in West Midlands: the second largest city in Great Britain. Pop.: 965 928 (1991). **2** a unitary authority in central England. Pop.: 1 008 400 (1994 est.). Area: 283 sq. km (109 sq. miles). **3** ('bɜːmɪŋ,hæm) an industrial city in N central Alabama: rich local deposits of coal, iron ore, and other minerals. Pop.: 264 527 (1994 est.).

Biro ('baɪrəʊ) *n, pl* **Biros**. *Trademark, Brit.* a kind of ballpoint. [C20: after Laszlo Bíró (1900–85), its Hungarian inventor]

Birobidzhan *or* **Birobijan** ★ (*Russian* birəbid'ʒan) *n* **1** a city in Russia, in SE Siberia: capital of the Jewish Autonomous Region. Pop.: 82 000 (1994). **2** another name for the **Jewish Autonomous Region**.

birth (bɜːθ) *n* **1** the process of bearing young; childbirth. **2** the act or fact of being born; nativity. **3** the coming into existence of something; origin. **4** ancestry; lineage: *of high birth*. **5** natural or inherited talent: *an artist by birth*. **6** **give birth (to)**. **6a** to bear (offspring). **6b** to produce or originate (an idea, plan, etc.). ♦ *vb* **7** (*tr*) *Rare.* to bear or bring forth (a child). [C12: from ON *byrth*]

birth certificate *n* an official form giving details of the time and place of a person's birth.

birth control *n* limitation of child-bearing by means of contraception.

birthday ('bɜːθ,deɪ) *n* **1a** an anniversary of the day of one's birth. **1b** (*as modifier*): *birthday present*. **2** the day on which a person was born.

birthing centre ('bɜːθɪŋ) *n* **NZ**. a private maternity hospital.

birthmark ('bɜːθ,mɑːk) *n* a blemish on the skin formed before birth; naevus.

birth mother *n* the woman who gives birth to a child, regardless of whether she is the genetic mother or subsequently brings up the child.

birthplace ('bɜːθ,pleɪs) *n* the place where someone was born or where something originated.

birth rate *n* the ratio of live births in a specified area, group, etc., to population, usually expressed per 1000 population per year.

birthright ('bɜːθ,raɪt) *n* **1** privileges or possessions that a person has or is believed to be entitled to as soon as he is born. **2** the privileges or possessions of a first-born son. **3** inheritance.

birthstone ('bɜːθ,stəʊn) *n* a precious or semiprecious stone associated with a month or sign of the zodiac and thought to bring luck if worn by a person born in that month or under that sign.

Birtwistle ★ ('bɜːt,wɪsᵊl) *n* **Sir Harrison**. born 1934, British composer, whose works include the operas *Punch and Judy* (1967) and *Exody* (1998).

biryani *or* **biriani** (,bɪrɪ'ɑːnɪ) *n* an Indian dish made with rice, highly flavoured and coloured, mixed with meat or fish. [from Urdu]

Bisayas ★ (bi'sajas) *pl n* the Spanish name for the **Visayan Islands**.

Biscay ★ ('bɪskeɪ, -kɪ) *n* **Bay of**. a large bay of the Atlantic Ocean between W France and N Spain: notorious for storms.

biscuit ('bɪskɪt) *n* **1** *Brit.* a small flat dry sweet or plain cake of many varieties. *US and Canad. word:* **cookie**. **2a** a pale brown or yellowish-grey colour. **2b** (*as adj*): *biscuit gloves*. **3** Also called: **bisque**. earthenware or porcelain that has been fired but not glazed. **4 take the biscuit**. *Brit.* to be regarded (by the speaker) as most surprising. [C14: from OF, from (*pain*) *bescuit* twice-cooked (bread), from *bes* twice + *cuire* to cook]

bise (biːz) *n* a cold dry northerly wind in Switzerland and parts of France and Italy. [C14: from OF, of Gmc origin]

bisect (baɪ'sɛkt) *vb* **1** (*tr*) *Maths.* to divide into two equal parts. **2** to cut or split into two. [C17: BI- + -*sect*, from L *secāre* to cut]
▸ **bisection** (baɪ'sɛkʃən) *n*

bisector (baɪ'sɛktə) *n* *Maths.* a straight line or plane that bisects an angle, etc.

bisexual (baɪ'sɛksjʊəl) *adj* **1** sexually attracted by both men and women. **2** showing characteristics of both sexes. **3** of or relating to both sexes. ♦ *n* **4** a bisexual organism; a hermaphrodite. **5** a bisexual person.
▸ **bisexuality** (,baɪsɛksjʊ'ælɪtɪ) *n*

Bishkek ★ (bɪʃ'kɛk) *n* the capital of Kyrgyzstan. Pop.: 597 000 (1994 est.). Also called: **Pishpek**. Former name (1926–91): **Frunze**.

bishop ('bɪʃəp) *n* **1** a clergyman having spiritual and administrative powers over a diocese. See also **suffragan**. Related adj: **episcopal**. **2** a chesspiece, capable of moving diagonally. **3** mulled wine, usually port, spiced with oranges, cloves, etc. [OE *biscop*, from LL, from Gk *episkopos*, from EPI- + *skopos* watcher]

Bishop Auckland ★ ('ɔːklənd) *n* a town in N England, in central Durham: seat of the bishops of Durham since the 12th century: light industries. Pop.: 23 154 (1991).

bishopric ('bɪʃəprɪk) *n* the see, diocese, or office of a bishop.

Bisitun ★ (,biːsɪ'tuːn) *n* another name for **Behistun**.

Bisk ★ (*Russian* bijsk) *n* a variant spelling of **Biysk**.

Biskra ★ ('bɪskrɑː) *n* a town and oasis in NE Algeria, in the Sahara. Pop.: 128 280 (1987).

Bisley ★ ('bɪzlɪ) *n* a village in SE England, in Surrey: annual meetings of the National Rifle Association.

Bismarck[1] ★ ('bɪzmɑːk) *n* a city in North Dakota, on the Missouri River: the state capital. Pop.: 49 256 (1990).

Bismarck[2] ★ (*German* 'bɪsmark) *n* **Prince Otto (Eduard Leopold) von** ('ɔtoː fɔn), called *the Iron Chancellor*. 1815–98, German statesman; prime minister of Prussia (1862–90). Under his leadership Prussia defeated Austria and France, and Germany was united. In 1871 he became the first chancellor of the German Reich.

Bismarck Archipelago ★ *n* a group of over 200 islands in the SW Pacific, northeast of New Guinea: part of Papua New Guinea. Main islands: New Britain, New Ireland, Lavongai, and the Admiralty Islands. Chief town: Rabaul, on New Britain. Pop.: 424 000 (1995 est.). Area: 49 658 sq. km (19 173 sq. miles).

bismuth ('bɪzməθ) *n* a brittle pinkish-white crystalline metallic element. It is widely used in alloys; its compounds are used in medicines. Symbol: Bi; atomic no.: 83; atomic wt.: 208.98. [C17: from NL *bisemūtum*, from G *Wismut*, from ?]

bison ('baɪsᵊn) *n, pl* **bison**. **1** Also called: **American bison, buffalo**. a member of the cattle tribe, formerly widely distributed over the prairies of W North America, with a massive head, shaggy forequarters, and a humped back. **2** Also called: **wisent, European bison**. a closely related and similar animal formerly widespread in Europe. [C14: from L *bisōn*, of Gmc origin]

bisque[1] (bɪsk) *n* a thick rich soup made from shellfish. [C17: from F]

bisque[2] (bɪsk) *n* **1a** a pink to yellowish tan colour. **1b** (*as adj*): *a bisque tablecloth*. **2** *Ceramics*. another name for **biscuit** (sense 3). [C20: shortened from BISCUIT]

bisque[3] (bɪsk) *n* *Tennis, golf, croquet*. an extra point, stroke, or turn allowed to an inferior player, usually taken when desired. [C17: from F, from ?]

Bissau (bɪ'saʊ) *or* **Bissão** ★ (*Portuguese* bi'sɐ̃u) *n* the capital of Guinea-Bissau, a port on the Atlantic: until 1974 the capital of Portuguese Guinea. Pop.: 197 610 (1991).

bistable (,baɪ'steɪbᵊl) *adj* **1** (of an electrical circuit switch, etc.) having two stable states. ♦ *n* **2** *Computing*. another name for **flip-flop** (sense 2).

bistort ('bɪstɔːt) *n* **1** Also called: **snakeweed**. a Eurasian plant having leaf stipules fused to form a tube around the stem and a spike of small pink flowers. **2** Also called:

snakeroot. a related plant of W North America, with oval clusters of pink or white flowers. **3** any of several similar plants. [C16: from F, from L *bis* twice + *tortus* from *torquēre* to twist]

bistoury ('bɪstərɪ) *n, pl* **bistouries.** a long narrow-bladed surgical knife. [C15: from OF *bistorie* dagger, from ?]

bistre *or US* **bister** ('bɪstə) *n* **1** a transparent water-soluble brownish-yellow pigment made by boiling the soot of wood. **2a** a yellowish-brown to dark brown colour. **2b** (*as adj*): *bistre paint*. [C18: from F, from ?]

bistro ('bi:strəʊ) *n, pl* **bistros.** a small restaurant. [F: ?from Russian *bistro* fast]

bisulphate (baɪ'sʌl,feɪt) *n* a salt or ester of sulphuric acid containing the monovalent group -HSO$_4$ or the ion HSO$_4^-$. Systematic name: **hydrogensulphate.**

bisulphide (baɪ'sʌlfaɪd) *n* another name for **disulphide.**

Bisutun ★ (,bi:su:'tu:n) *n* another name for **Behistun.**

bit[1] (bɪt) *n* **1** a small piece, portion, or quantity. **2** a short time or distance. **3** *US & Canad. inf.* the value of an eighth of a dollar: spoken of only in units of two: *two bits*. **4** any small coin. **5** short for **bit part. 6 a bit of.** rather; somewhat: *a bit dreary*. **7 a bit of. 7a** rather: *a bit of a dope*. **7b** a considerable amount: *it takes quite a bit of time*. **8 bit by bit.** gradually. **9 do one's bit.** to make one's expected contribution. [OE *bite* action of biting; see BITE]

bit[2] (bɪt) *n* **1** a metal mouthpiece on a bridle for controlling a horse. **2** anything that restrains or curbs. **3** a cutting or drilling tool, part, or head in a brace, drill, etc. **4** the part of a key that engages the levers of a lock. **5** the mouthpiece of a smoker's pipe. ♦ *vb* **bits, bitting, bitted.** (*tr*) **6** to put a bit in the mouth of (a horse). **7** to restrain; curb. [OE *bita*; rel. to OE *bītan* to BITE]

bit[3] (bɪt) *vb* the past tense of **bite.**

bit[4] (bɪt) *n Maths, computing.* **1** a single digit of binary notation, represented either by 0 or by 1. **2** the smallest unit of information, indicating the presence or absence of a single feature. [C20: from B(INARY + DIG)IT]

bitch (bɪtʃ) *n* **1** a female dog or other female canine animal, such as a wolf. **2** *Sl., derog.* a malicious, spiteful, or coarse woman. **3** *Inf.* a difficult situation or problem. ♦ *vb Inf.* **4** (*intr*) to complain; grumble. **5** to behave (towards) in a spiteful manner. **6** (*tr; often foll. by up*) to botch; bungle. [OE *bicce*]

bitchin' ('bɪtʃɪn) *or* **bitching** ('bɪtʃɪŋ) *US sl.* ♦ *adj* **1** wonderful or excellent. ♦ *adv* **2** extremely: *bitchin' good*.

bitchy ('bɪtʃɪ) *adj* **bitchier, bitchiest.** *Sl.* of or like a bitch; malicious; snide.
▶ **'bitchiness** *n*

bite (baɪt) *vb* **bites, biting, bit, bitten. 1** to grip, cut off, or tear as with the teeth or jaws. **2** (of animals, insects, etc.) to injure by puncturing or tearing (the skin or flesh) with the teeth, fangs, etc. **3** (*tr*) to cut or penetrate, as with a knife. **4** (of corrosive material such as acid) to eat away or into. **5** to smart or cause to smart; sting. **6** (*intr*) *Angling.* (of a fish) to take or attempt to take the bait or lure. **7** to take firm hold (of) or act effectively (upon). **8** (*tr*) *Sl.* to annoy or worry: *what's biting her?* **9** (*tr; often foll. by for*) *Austral. & NZ sl.* to ask (for); scrounge from. **10 bite the dust.** to fall down dead. **10b** to be rejected: *another good idea bites the dust*. ♦ *n* **11** the act of biting. **12** a thing or amount bitten off. **13** a wound, bruise, or sting inflicted by biting. **14** *Angling.* an attempt by a fish to take the bait or lure. **15** a light meal; snack. **16** a cutting, stinging, or smarting sensation. **17** *Dentistry.* the angle or manner of contact between the upper and lower teeth. **18 put the bite on.** *Sl.* to cadge or borrow from. [OE *bītan*]
▶ **'biter** *n*

Bithynia ★ (bɪ'θɪnɪə) *n* an ancient country on the Black Sea in NW Asia Minor.

biting ('baɪtɪŋ) *adj* **1** piercing; keen: *a biting wind*. **2** sarcastic; incisive.
▶ **'bitingly** *adv*

bitmap ('bɪt,mæp) *Computing.* ♦ *n* **1** a picture created on a visual display unit where each pixel corresponds to one or more bits in memory, the number of bits per pixel determining the number of available colours. ♦ *vb* **bitmaps, bitmapping, bitmapped. 2** (*tr*) to create a bitmap of.

Bitolj (*Serbo-Croat* 'bitolj) *or* **Bitola** ★ ('bi:təʊlə) *n* a city in SW Macedonia: under Turkish rule from 1382 until 1913. Pop.: 75 386 (1994).

bit part *n* a very small acting role with few lines to speak.

bitt (bɪt) *Naut.* ♦ *n* **1** one of a pair of strong posts on the deck of a ship for securing mooring and other lines. **2** another word for **bollard** (sense 1). ♦ *vb* **3** (*tr*) to secure (a line) by means of a bitt. [C14: prob. from ON]

bitten ('bɪt°n) *vb* the past participle of **bite.**

bitter ('bɪtə) *adj* **1** having or denoting an unpalatable harsh taste, as the peel of an orange. **2** showing or caused by strong unrelenting hostility or resentment. **3** difficult or unpleasant to accept or admit: *a bitter blow*. **4** cutting; sarcastic: *bitter words*. **5** bitingly cold: *a bitter night*. ♦ *adv* **6** very; extremely (esp. in **bitter cold**). ♦ *n* **7** a thing that is bitter. **8** *Brit.* beer with a slightly bitter taste. [OE *bitter*; rel. to *bītan* to BITE]
▶ **'bitterly** *adv* ▶ **'bitterness** *n*

bitter end *n* **1** *Naut.* the end of a line, chain, or cable. **2 to the bitter end. 2a** until the finish of a task, etc., however unpleasant or difficult. **2b** until final defeat or death. [C19: ?from BITT]

Bitter Lakes ★ *pl n* two lakes, the **Great Bitter Lake** and **Little Bitter Lake**, in NE Egypt: part of the Suez Canal.

bittern ('bɪtən) *n* a wading bird related and similar to the herons but with shorter legs and neck and a booming call. [C14: from OF *butor*, ?from L *būtiō* bittern + *taurus* bull]

bitters ('bɪtəz) *pl n* **1** bitter-tasting spirits of varying alcoholic content flavoured with plant extracts. **2** a similar liquid containing a bitter-tasting substance, used as a tonic.

bittersweet ('bɪtə,swi:t) *n* **1** any of several North American woody climbing plants having orange capsules that open to expose scarlet-coated seeds. **2** another name for **woody nightshade.** ♦ *adj* **3** tasting of or being a mixture of bitterness and sweetness. **4** pleasant but tinged with sadness.

bitty ('bɪtɪ) *adj* **bittier, bittiest. 1** lacking unity; disjointed. **2** containing bits, sediment, etc.
▶ **'bittiness** *n*

bitumen ('bɪtjʊmɪn) *n* **1** any of various viscous or solid impure mixtures of hydrocarbons that occur naturally in asphalt, tar, mineral waxes, etc.: used as a road surfacing and roofing material. **2 the bitumen.** *Austral. & NZ sl.* any road with a bitumen surface. [C15: from L *bitūmen*]
▶ **bituminous** (bɪ'tju:mɪnəs) *adj*

bituminize *or* **bituminise** (bɪ'tju:mɪ,naɪz) *vb* **bituminizes, bituminizing, bituminized** *or* **bituminises, bituminising, bituminised.** (*tr*) to treat with or convert into bitumen.

bituminous coal *n* a soft black coal that burns with a smoky yellow flame.

bivalent (baɪ'veɪlənt, 'bɪvə-) *adj* **1** *Chem.* another word for **divalent. 2** (of homologous chromosomes) associated together in pairs.
▶ **bi'valency** *n*

bivalve ('baɪ,vælv) *n* **1** a marine or freshwater mollusc, having a laterally compressed body, a shell consisting of two hinged valves, and gills for respiration. The group includes clams, cockles, oysters, and mussels. ♦ *adj* **2** of or relating to these molluscs. ♦ Also: **lamellibranch.**

bivouac ('bɪvʊ,æk, 'bɪvwæk) *n* **1** a temporary encampment, as used by soldiers, mountaineers, etc. ♦ *vb* **bivouacs, bivouacking, bivouacked. 2** (*intr*) to make such an encampment. [C18: from F *bivuac*, prob. from Swiss G *Beiwacht*, lit.: BY + WATCH]

biweekly (baɪ'wi:klɪ) *adj, adv* **1** every two weeks. **2** twice a week. See **bi-.** ♦ *n, pl* **biweeklies. 3** a periodical published every two weeks.

biyearly (baɪ'jɪəlɪ) *adj, adv* **1** every two years; biennial or biennially. **2** twice a year; biannual or biannually. See **bi-.**

Biysk, Biisk, *or* **Bisk** ★ (*Russian* bijsk) *n* a city in SW Russia, at the foot of the Altai Mountains. Pop: 228 000 (1995 est.).

biz (bɪz) *n Inf.* short for **business.**

bizarre (bɪ'zɑ:) *adj* odd or unusual, esp. in an interesting

or amusing way. [C17: from F, from It. *bizzarro* capricious, from ?]
▸ bi'zarreness *n*

Bizerte (bɪ'zɜːtə; *French* bizɛrt) *or* **Bizerta** ★ *n* a port in N Tunisia, on the Mediterranean at the canalized outlet of **Lake Bizerte**. Pop.: 98 900 (1994).

Bizet ★ ('biːzeɪ; *French* bizɛ) *n* **Georges** (ʒɔrʒ). 1838–75, French composer, whose works include the opera *Carmen* (1875) and incidental music to Daudet's *L'Arlésienne* (1872).

bizzy ('bɪzɪ) *n, pl* **bizzies**. *Brit. sl., chiefly Liverpudlian*. a policeman. [C20: from BUSY]

Björneborg ★ (bjœrnə'bɔrj) *n* the Swedish name for **Pori**.

bk *abbrev. for:* **1** bank. **2** book.

Bk *the chemical symbol for* berkelium.

bkg *abbrev. for* banking.

BL *abbrev. for:* **1** Bachelor of Law. **2** Bachelor of Letters. **3** Barrister-at-Law. **4** British Library.

B/L, b/l, *or* **b.l.** *pl* **Bs/L, bs/l,** *or* **bs.l.** *abbrev. for* bill of lading.

blab (blæb) *vb* **blabs, blabbing, blabbed. 1** to divulge (secrets, etc.) indiscreetly. **2** (*intr*) to chatter thoughtlessly; prattle. ◆ *n* **3** a less common word for **blabber.** [C14: of Gmc origin]

blabber ('blæbə) *n* **1** a person who blabs. **2** idle chatter. ◆ *vb* **3** (*intr*) to talk without thinking; chatter. [C15 *blabberen*, prob. imit.]

black (blæk) *adj* **1** of the colour of jet or carbon black, having no hue due to the absorption of all or nearly all incident light. **2** without light; completely dark. **3** without hope of alleviation; gloomy: *the future looked black.* **4** very dirty or soiled. **5** angry or resentful: *black looks.* **6** (of a play or other work) dealing with the unpleasant realities of life, esp. in a cynical or macabre manner: *black comedy.* **7** (of coffee or tea) served without milk or cream. **8a** wicked or harmful: *a black lie.* **8b** (*in combination*): *blackhearted.* **9** *Brit.* (of goods, jobs, works, etc.) being subject to boycott by trade unionists. ◆ *n* **10** a black colour. **11** a dye or pigment of or producing this colour. **12** black clothing, worn esp. as a sign of mourning. **13** *Chess, draughts.* a black or dark-coloured piece or square. **14** complete darkness: *the black of the night.* **15 in the black.** in credit or without debt. ◆ *vb* **16** another word for **blacken. 17** (*tr*) to polish (shoes, etc.) with blacking. **18** (*tr*) *Brit., Austral., & NZ.* (of trade unionists) to organize a boycott of (specified goods, jobs, work, etc.). ◆ *See also* **blackout.** [OE *blæc*]
▸ 'blackness *n*

Black[1] (blæk) *n* **1** *Sometimes derog.* a member of a dark-skinned race, esp. someone of Negroid or Australoid origin. ◆ *adj* **2** of or relating to a Black person or Black people.

Black[2] ★ (blæk) *n* **1** Sir **James** (**Whyte**). born 1924, British biochemist. He discovered beta-blockers and drugs for peptic ulcers: Nobel prize for physiology or medicine 1988. **2 Joseph.** 1728–99, Scottish physician and chemist, noted for his pioneering work on heat.

blackamoor ('blækə,mʊə, -,mɔː) *n Arch.* a Black or other person with dark skin. [C16: see BLACK[1], MOOR]

black-and-blue *adj* **1** (of the skin) discoloured, as from a bruise. **2** feeling pain or soreness, as from a beating.

Black and Tans *pl n* **the.** a specially recruited armed force sent to Ireland in 1921 by the British Government to combat Sinn Féin. [named after the colour of their uniforms]

black-and-white *n* **1a** a photograph, picture, sketch, etc., in black, white, and shades of grey rather than in colour. **1b** (*as modifier*): *black-and-white film.* **2 in black and white. 2a** in print or writing. **2b** in extremes: *he always saw things in black and white.*

black art *n* **the.** another name for **black magic.**

black-backed gull *n* either of two common black-and-white European coastal gulls, **lesser black-backed gull** and **great black-backed gull.**

blackball ('blæk,bɔːl) *n* **1** a negative vote or veto. **2** a black wooden ball used to indicate disapproval or to veto in a vote. ◆ *vb* (*tr*) **3** to vote against. **4** to exclude

(someone) from a group, profession, etc.; ostracize. [C18: from *black ball* used to veto]

black bean *n* an Australian leguminous tree: used in furniture manufacture. Also called: **Moreton Bay chestnut.**

black bear *n* **1 American black bear.** a bear inhabiting forests of North America. It is smaller and less ferocious than the brown bear. **2 Asiatic black bear.** a bear of central and E Asia, black with a pale V-shaped mark on the chest.

black belt *n Judo, karate, etc.* **a** a black belt worn by an instructor or expert. **b** a person entitled to wear this.

blackberry ('blækbərɪ) *n, pl* **blackberries. 1** Also called: **bramble.** any of several woody rosaceous plants that have thorny stems and black or purple edible berry-like fruits. **2** the fruit of any of these plants. ◆ *vb* **blackberries, blackberrying, blackberried. 3** (*intr*) to gather blackberries.

blackbird ('blæk,bɜːd) *n* **1** a common European thrush in which the male has black plumage and a yellow bill. **2** any of various American orioles having dark plumage. **3** (formerly) a person, esp. a South Sea Islander, who was kidnapped and sold as a slave, esp. in Australia. ◆ *vb* **4** (*tr*) (formerly) to kidnap and sell into slavery.

blackboard ('blæk,bɔːd) *n* a hard or rigid surface made of a smooth usually dark substance, used for writing or drawing on with chalk, esp. in teaching.

black body *n Physics.* a hypothetical body capable of absorbing all the electromagnetic radiation falling on it. Also called: **full radiator.**

black book *n* **1** a book containing the names of people to be punished, blacklisted, etc. **2 in someone's black books.** *Inf.* out of favour with someone.

black box *n* **1** a self-contained unit in an electronic or computer system whose circuitry need not be known to understand its function. **2** an informal name for **flight recorder.**

blackboy ('blæk,bɔɪ) *n* another name for **grass tree** (sense 1).

blackbuck ('blæk,bʌk) *n* an Indian antelope, the male of which has a dark back.

Blackburn ★ ('blækbɜːn) *n* **1** a city in NW England, in central Lancashire: textile industries. Pop: 105 994 (1991). **2 Mount.** a mountain in SE Alaska, the highest peak in the Wrangell Mountains. Height: 5037 m (16 523 ft).

Blackburn with Darwen ★ ('dɑːwen) *n* a unitary authority in NW England, in Lancashire. Pop.: 139 500 (1996).

blackbutt ('blæk,bʌt) *n* any of various Australian eucalyptus trees having rough fibrous bark and hard wood used as timber.

blackcap ('blæk,kæp) *n* a brownish-grey Old World warbler, the male of which has a black crown.

blackcock ('blæk,kɒk) *n* the male of the black grouse.

Black Country ★ *n* **the.** a formerly heavily industrialized region in the West Midlands of England.

blackcurrant (,blæk'kʌrənt) *n* **1** a N temperate shrub having red or white flowers and small edible black berries. **2** its fruit.

blackdamp ('blæk,dæmp) *n* air that is low in oxygen content and high in carbon dioxide as a result of an explosion in a mine. Also called: **chokedamp.**

Black Death *n* **the.** a form of bubonic plague pandemic in Europe and Asia during the 14th century. See **bubonic plague.**

black disc *n* a conventional black vinyl gramophone record as opposed to a compact disc.

black earth *n* another name for **chernozem.**

black economy *n* that portion of the income of a nation that remains illegally undeclared.

blacken ('blækən) *vb* **1** to make or become black or dirty. **2** (*tr*) to defame; slander (esp. in **blacken someone's name**).

Blackett ★ ('blækɪt) *n* **Patrick Maynard Stuart,** Baron. 1897–1974, British physicist, noted for his work on cosmic radiation; Nobel prize for physics 1948.

black eye *n* bruising round the eye.

black-eyed Susan ('suːzᵊn) *n* any of several North American plants having flower heads of orange-yellow rays and brown-black centres.

blackface ('blæk,feɪs) *n* **1** a variety of sheep with a black face. **2** the make-up used by a White performer imitating a Black person.

blackfish ('blæk,fɪʃ) *n, pl* **blackfish** *or* **blackfishes. 1** any of various dark fishes, esp. a common edible Australian estuary fish. **2** a female salmon that has recently spawned. Cf. **redfish** (sense 1).

black flag *n* another name for the **Jolly Roger.**

blackfly ('blæk,flaɪ) *n, pl* **blackflies.** a black aphid that infests beans, sugar beet, and other plants. Also called: **bean aphid.**

Black Forest ★ *n* **the.** a hilly wooded region of SW Germany, in Baden-Württemberg: a popular resort area. German name: **Schwarzwald.**

Black Friar *n* a Dominican friar.

black grouse *n* **1** a large N European grouse, the male of which has a bluish-black plumage. **2** a related and similar species of W Asia.

blackguard ('blægɑːd, -gəd) *n* **1** an unprincipled contemptible person; scoundrel. ◆ *vb* **2** (*tr*) to ridicule or denounce with abusive language. **3** (*intr*) to behave like a blackguard. [C16: see BLACK, GUARD]
▸ **'blackguardism** *n* ▸ **'blackguardly** *adj*

blackhead ('blæk,hed) *n* **1** a black-tipped plug of fatty matter clogging a pore of the skin. **2** any of various birds with black plumage on the head.

Blackheath ★ (,blæk'hiːθ) *n* a residential district in London, mainly in the borough of Lewisham and Greenwich: a large heath formerly notorious for highwaymen.

Black Hills ★ *pl n* a group of mountains in S South Dakota and NE Wyoming: famous for the gigantic sculptures of US presidents on the side of Mount Rushmore. Highest peak: Harney Peak, 2207 m (7242 ft).

black hole *n* **1a** *Astron.* a hypothetical region of space resulting from the gravitational collapse of a star and surrounded by a gravitational field so high that neither matter nor radiation could escape from it. **1b** a similar but much more massive region of space at the centre of a galaxy. **2** any place regarded as resembling a black hole in that items or information entering it cannot be retrieved.

black ice *n* a thin transparent layer of new ice on a road or similar surface.

blacking ('blækɪŋ) *n* any preparation for giving a black finish to shoes, metals, etc.

Black Isle ★ *n* **the.** a peninsula in NE Scotland, in Highland council area, between the Cromarty and Moray Firths. [so called because until the late 18th century much of it was uncultivated black moor]

blackjack[1] ('blæk,dʒæk) *Chiefly US & Canad.* ◆ *n* **1** a truncheon of leather-covered lead with a flexible shaft. ◆ *vb* (*tr*) **2** to hit as with a blackjack. **3** to compel (a person) by threats. [C19: from BLACK + JACK (implement)]

blackjack[2] ('blæk,dʒæk) *n* pontoon or any similar card game. [C20: from BLACK + JACK (the knave)]

black knight *n* *Commerce.* a person or firm that makes an unwelcome takeover bid for a company. Cf. **grey knight, white knight.**

black lead (led) *n* another name for **graphite.**

blackleg ('blæk,leg) *n* **1** Also called: **scab.** *Brit.* a person who acts against the interests of a trade union, as by continuing to work during a strike or taking over a striker's job. ◆ *vb* **blacklegs, blacklegging, blacklegged. 2** (*intr*) *Brit.* to act against the interests of a trade union, esp. by refusing to join a strike.

black light *n* the invisible electromagnetic radiation in the ultraviolet and infrared regions of the spectrum.

blacklist ('blæk,lɪst) *n* **1** a list of persons or organizations under suspicion, or considered untrustworthy, disloyal, etc. ◆ *vb* **2** (*tr*) to put on a blacklist.

black magic *n* magic used for evil purposes.

blackmail ('blæk,meɪl) *n* **1** the act of attempting to obtain money by intimidation, as by threats to disclose dis-

creditable information. **2** the exertion of pressure, esp. unfairly, in an attempt to influence someone. ◆ *vb* (*tr*) **3** to exact or attempt to exact (money or anything of value) from (a person) by threats or intimidation; extort. **4** to attempt to influence (a person), esp. by unfair pressure. [C16: from BLACK + OE *māl* terms]
▸ **'black,mailer** *n*

Black Maria (mə'raɪə) *n* a police van for transporting prisoners.

black mark *n* an indication of disapproval, failure, etc.

black market *n* **1** any system in which goods or currencies are sold and bought illegally, esp. in violation of controls or rationing. **2** the place where such a system operates. ◆ *vb* **black-market. 3** to sell (goods) on the black market.
▸ **black marketeer** *n*

black mass *n* (*sometimes caps.*) a blasphemous travesty of the Christian Mass, performed by practitioners of black magic.

black money *n* **1** that part of a nation's income that relates to its black economy. **2** any money that a person or organization acquires illegally, as by a means that involves tax evasion. **3** *US.* money to fund a government project that is concealed in the cost of some other project.

Blackmore ★ ('blæk,mɔː) *n* **R(ichard) D(oddridge).** 1825–1900, British novelist; author of *Lorna Doone* (1869).

Black Mountain ★ *n* **the.** a mountain range in S Wales, in E Carmarthenshire and W Powys. Highest peak: Carmarthen Van, 802 m (2632 ft).

Black Mountains ★ *pl n* a mountain range in S Wales and SW Hereford and Worcester, England. Highest peak: Waun Fach, 811 m (2660 ft).

Black Muslim *n* (esp. in the US) a member of an Islamic political movement of Black people who seek to establish a new Black nation.

black nightshade *n* a common poisonous weed in cultivated land, having white flowers and black berrylike fruits.

blackout ('blæk,aut) *n* **1** the extinguishing or hiding of all artificial light, esp. in a city visible to an air attack. **2** a momentary loss of consciousness, vision, or memory. **3** a temporary electrical power failure or cut. **4** the suspension of broadcasting, as by a strike or for political reasons. ◆ *vb* **black out. (adv) 5** (*tr*) to obliterate or extinguish (lights). **6** (*tr*) to create a blackout in (a city, etc.). **7** (*intr*) to lose vision, consciousness, or memory temporarily. **8** (*tr*) to stop (news, a television programme, etc.) from being broadcast.

black pepper *n* a pungent condiment made by grinding the dried unripe berries and husks of the pepper plant.

Blackpool ★ ('blæk,puːl) *n* a resort town and unitary authority in NW England, in Lancashire on the Irish Sea: famous for its tower, 158 m (518 ft) high, and its illuminations. Pop.: 146 262 (1991).

Black Power *n* a social, economic, and political movement of Black people, esp. in the US, to obtain equality with Whites.

Black Prince ★ *n* **the.** See **Edward**[2] (Prince of Wales).

black pudding *n* a kind of black sausage made from minced pork fat, pig's blood, and other ingredients. Also called: **blood pudding.**

Black Rod *n* (in Britain) an officer of the House of Lords and of the Order of the Garter, whose main duty is summoning the Commons at the opening and proroguing of Parliament.

Black Sea ★ *n* an inland sea between SE Europe and Asia: connected to the Aegean Sea by the Bosporus, the Sea of Marmara, and the Dardanelles, and to the Sea of Azov by the Kerch Strait. Area: about 415 000 sq. km (160 000 sq. miles). Also called: **Euxine Sea.** Ancient name: **Pontus Euxinus.**

black section *n* (in Britain) an unofficial group within the Labour Party in any constituency which represents the interests of local Black people.

★ people and places

black sheep *n* a person who is regarded as a disgrace or failure by his family or peer group.

Blackshirt ('blæk,ʃɜːt) *n* (in Europe) a member of a fascist organization, esp. the Italian Fascist party before and during World War II.

blacksmith ('blæk,smɪθ) *n* an artisan who works iron with a furnace, anvil, hammer, etc. [C14: see BLACK, SMITH]

black snake *n* **1** any of several Old World black venomous snakes, esp. the **Australian black snake**. **2** any of various dark nonvenomous snakes.

black spot *n* **1** a place on a road where accidents frequently occur. **2** any dangerous or difficult place. **3** a disease of roses that causes black blotches on the leaves.

black stump *n the. Austral.* an imaginary marker of the extent of civilization (esp. in **beyond the black stump**).

black tea *n* tea made from fermented tea leaves.

blackthorn ('blæk,θɔːn) *n* a thorny Eurasian shrub with black twigs, white flowers, and small sour plumlike fruits. Also called: **sloe**.

black tie *n* **1** a black bow tie worn with a dinner jacket. **2** (*modifier*) denoting an occasion when a dinner jacket should be worn.

blacktop ('blæk,tɒp) *n Chiefly US & Canad.* a bituminous mixture used for paving.

Black tracker *n Austral.* an Aboriginal tracker working for the police.

black velvet *n* a mixture of stout and champagne in equal proportions.

Black Volta ★ *n* a river in W Africa, rising in SW Burkina-Faso and flowing northeast, then south into Lake Volta: forms part of the border of Ghana with Burkina-Faso and with the Côte d'Ivoire. Length: about 800 km (500 miles).

Black Watch *n the.* the Royal Highland Regiment in the British Army.

blackwater fever ('blæk,wɔːtə) *n* a rare and serious complication of malaria, characterized by massive destruction of red blood cells, producing dark red or blackish urine.

black widow *n* an American spider, the female of which is highly venomous, and commonly eats its mate.

Blackwood[1] ('blæk,wʊd) *n Bridge.* a conventional bidding sequence of four and five no-trumps, which are requests to the partner to show aces and kings respectively. [C20: after E. F. *Blackwood*, its US inventor]

Blackwood[2] ('blæk,wʊd) ★ *n* **Algernon (Henry).** 1869–1951, British novelist and short-story writer.

bladder ('blædə) *n* **1** *Anat.* a distensible membranous sac, usually containing liquid or gas, esp. the urinary bladder. **2** an inflatable part of something. **3** a hollow saclike part in certain plants, such as the bladderwrack. [OE *blǣdre*]
▶ **'bladdery** *adj*

bladderwort ('blædə,wɜːt) *n* an aquatic plant some of whose leaves are modified as small bladders to trap minute aquatic animals.

bladderwrack ('blædə,ræk) *n* any of several seaweeds that grow in the intertidal regions of rocky shores and have branched brown fronds with air bladders.

blade (bleɪd) *n* **1** the part of a sharp weapon, tool, etc., that forms the cutting edge. **2** the thin flattish part of various tools, implements, etc., as of a propeller, turbine, etc. **3** the flattened expanded part of a leaf, sepal, or petal. **4** the long narrow leaf of a grass or related plant. **5** the striking surface of a bat, club, stick, or oar. **6** the metal runner on an ice skate. **7** the upper part of the tongue lying directly behind the tip. **8** *Arch.* a dashing or swaggering young man. **9** short for **shoulder blade**. **10** a poetic word for a **sword** or **swordsman**. [OE *blæd*]
▶ **'bladed** *adj*

blaeberry ('bleɪbərɪ) *n, pl* **blaeberries**. *Brit.* another name for **whortleberry** (senses 1, 2). [C15: from dialect *blae* bluish + BERRY]

Blaenau Gwent ★ ('blaɪ,naʊ 'gwɛnt) *n* a county borough of SE Wales. Administrative centre: Ebbw Vale. Pop.: 74 700 (1991 est.). Area: 109 sq. km (42 sq. miles).

blag (blæg) *Sl.* ◆ *n* **1** a robbery, esp. with violence. ◆ *vb* **blags, blagging, blagged.** (*tr*) **2** to obtain by wheedling or cadging: *she blagged free tickets from her mate.* **3** to snatch (wages, someone's handbag, etc.); steal. **4** to rob (esp. a bank or post office). [C19: from ?]
▶ **'blagger** *n*

Blagoveshchensk ★ (*Russian* bləgɐ'vjeʃtʃɪnsk) *n* a city in E Russia, on the Amur River. Pop.: 214 000 (1995 est.).

blah *or* **blah blah** (blɑː) *n Sl.* worthless or silly talk. [C20: imit.]

blain (bleɪn) *n* a blister, blotch, or sore on the skin. [OE *blegen*]

Blair ★ (blɛə) *n* **Tony,** full name *Anthony Charles Lynton Blair.* born 1953, British politician; leader of the Labour Party from 1994; prime minister from 1997.

Blairite ('blɛəraɪt) *adj* **1** of or relating to the modernizing policies of Tony Blair. ◆ *n* **2** a supporter of the modernizing policies of Tony Blair.

Blake ★ (bleɪk) *n* **1 Peter.** born 1932, British pop-art painter, a co-founder of the Brotherhood of Ruralists (1969). **2 Robert.** 1599–1657, English admiral, who commanded Cromwell's fleet against the Royalists, the Dutch, and the Spanish. **3 William.** 1757–1827, British poet and engraver. His literary works include *Songs of Innocence* (1789) and *Songs of Experience* (1794), and *Jerusalem* (1820). His engravings include illustrations for *The Book of Job* (1826) and for Dante's poems.

blame (bleɪm) *n* **1** responsibility for something that is wrong; culpability. **2** an expression of condemnation. ◆ *vb* **blames, blaming, blamed.** (*tr*) **3** (usually foll. by *for*) to attribute responsibility to: *I blame him for the failure.* **4** (usually foll. by *on*) to ascribe responsibility for (something) to: *I blame the failure on him.* **5** to find fault with. **6 be to blame.** to be at fault. [C12: from OF *blasmer*, ult. from LL *blasphēmāre* to blaspheme]
▶ **'blamable** *or* **'blameable** *adj* ▶ **'blamably** *or* **'blameably** *adv*

blameful ('bleɪmfʊl) *adj* deserving blame; guilty.
▶ **'blamefully** *adv* ▶ **'blamefulness** *n*

blameless ('bleɪmlɪs) *adj* free from blame; innocent.
▶ **'blamelessness** *n*

blameworthy ('bleɪm,wɜːðɪ) *adj* deserving censure.
▶ **'blame,worthiness** *n*

Blanc[1] ★ (*French* blɑ̃) *n* **1 Mont.** See **Mont Blanc. 2 Cape.** a headland in N Tunisia: the northernmost point of Africa. **3 Cape.** Also called: **Cape Blanco** ('blæŋkəʊ). a peninsula in Mauritania, on the Atlantic coast.

Blanc[2] ★ (*French* blɑ̃) *n* **(Jean Joseph Charles) Louis** (lwi). 1811–82, French socialist and historian: author of *L'Organisation du travail* (1840).

blanch (blɑːntʃ) *vb* (*mainly tr*) **1** to remove colour from; whiten. **2** (*usually intr*) to become or cause to become pale, as with sickness or fear. **3** to prepare (meat, green vegetables, nuts, etc.) by plunging them in boiling water. **4** to cause (celery, chicory, etc.) to grow free of chlorophyll by the exclusion of sunlight. [C14: from OF *blanchir*, from *blanc* white; see BLANK]

blancmange (blə'mɒnʒ) *n* a jelly-like dessert of milk, stiffened usually with cornflour. [C14: from OF *blanc manger*, lit.: white food]

bland (blænd) *adj* **1** devoid of distinctive or stimulating characteristics; uninteresting. **2** gentle and agreeable; suave. **3** mild and soothing. [C15: from L *blandus* flattering]
▶ **'blandly** *adv* ▶ **'blandness** *n*

blandish ('blændɪʃ) *vb* (*tr*) to seek to persuade or influence by mild flattery; coax. [C14: from OF *blandir*, from L *blandīrī*]

blandishments ('blændɪʃmənts) *pl n* (*rarely sing*) flattery intended to coax or cajole.

blank (blæŋk) *adj* **1** (of a writing surface) bearing no marks; not written on. **2** (of a form, etc.) with spaces left for details to be filled in. **3** without ornament or break. **4** not filled in; empty. **5** exhibiting no interest or expression: *a blank look.* **6** lacking understanding; confused: *he*

looked blank. **7** absolute; complete: *blank rejection.* **8** devoid of ideas or inspiration: *his mind went blank.* ◆ *n* **9** an emptiness; void; blank space. **10** an empty space for writing in. **11** a printed form containing such empty spaces. **12** something characterized by incomprehension or confusion: *my mind went a complete blank.* **13** a mark, often a dash, in place of a word, esp. a taboo word. **14** short for **blank cartridge**. **15** a piece of material prepared for stamping, punching, forging, or some other operation. **16 draw a blank.** to get no results from something. ◆ *vb (tr)* **17** (usually foll. by *out*) to cross out, blot, or obscure. [C15: from OF *blanc* white, of Gmc origin]
▶ '**blankness** *n*

blank cartridge *n* a cartridge containing powder but no bullet.

blank cheque *n* **1** a cheque that has been signed but on which the amount payable has not been specified. **2** complete freedom of action.

blanket ('blæŋkɪt) *n* **1** a large piece of thick cloth for use as a bed covering, animal covering, etc. **2** a concealing cover, as of smoke, leaves, or snow. **3** (*modifier*) applying to or covering a wide group or variety of people, conditions, situations, etc.: *blanket insurance against loss, injury, and theft.* **4 (born) on the wrong side of the blanket.** *Inf.* illegitimate. **5 on the blanket.** *Irish.* (of an imprisoned terrorist) wearing only a blanket instead of prison uniform, as a protest against not being recognized as a political prisoner. ◆ *vb (tr)* **6** to cover as with a blanket; overlie. **7** to cover a wide area; give blanket coverage. **8** (usually foll. by *out*) to obscure or suppress. [C13: from OF *blancquete*, from *blanc; see* BLANK]

blanket bath *n* an all-over wash given to a person confined to bed.

blanket bog *n* a very acid peat bog, low in nutrients, extending widely over a flat terrain, found in cold wet climates.

blanket stitch *n* a strong reinforcing stitch for the edges of blankets and other thick material.

blankety ('blæŋkɪtɪ) *adj, adv* a euphemism for any taboo word. [C20: from BLANK]

blank verse *n Prosody.* unrhymed verse, esp. in iambic pentameters.

Blantyre-Limbe ★ (blæn'taɪə'lɪmbeɪ) *n* a city in S Malawi: largest city in the country; formed in 1956 from the adjoining towns of Blantyre and Limbe. Pop.: 446 800 (1994 est.).

blare (bleə) *vb* **blares, blaring, blared. 1** to sound loudly and harshly. **2** to proclaim loudly and sensationally. ◆ *n* **3** a loud harsh noise. [C14: from MDu. *bleren;* imit.]

blarney ('blɑːnɪ) *n* **1** flattering talk. ◆ *vb* **2** to cajole with flattery; wheedle. [C19: after the *Blarney* Stone in SW Ireland, said to endow whoever kisses it with skill in flattery]

blasé ('blɑːzeɪ) *adj* **1** indifferent to something because of familiarity. **2** lacking enthusiasm; bored. [C19: from F, p.p. of *blaser* to cloy]

blaspheme (blæs'fiːm) *vb* **blasphemes, blaspheming, blasphemed. 1** (*tr*) to show contempt or disrespect for (God or sacred things), esp. in speech. **2** (*intr*) to utter profanities or curses. [C14: from LL, from Gk, from *blasphēmos* BLASPHEMOUS]
▶ blas'**phemer** *n*

blasphemous ('blæsfɪməs) *adj* involving impiousness or gross irreverence towards God or something sacred. [C15: via LL, from Gk *blasphēmos* evil-speaking, from *blapsis* evil + *phēmē* speech]

blasphemy ('blæsfɪmɪ) *n, pl* **blasphemies. 1** blasphemous behaviour or language. **2** Also called: **blasphemous libel.** *Law.* the crime committed if a person insults, offends, or vilifies the deity, Christ, or the Christian religion.

blast (blɑːst) *n* **1** an explosion, as of dynamite. **2** the rapid movement of air away from the centre of an explosion; shock wave. **3** the charge used in a single explosion. **4** a sudden strong gust of wind or air. **5** a sudden loud sound, as of a trumpet. **6** a violent verbal outburst, as of criticism. **7** a forcible jet of air, esp. one used to intensify the heating effect of a furnace. **8** any of several diseases of plants and animals. **9** *US sl.* a very enjoyable or thrill-

ing experience: *the party was a blast.* **10 (at) full blast.** at maximum speed, volume, etc. ◆ *interj* **11** *Sl.* an exclamation of annoyance. ◆ *vb* **12** (*tr*) to destroy or blow up with explosives, shells, etc. **13** to make or cause to make a loud harsh noise. **14** to wither or cause to wither; blight or be blighted. **15** (*tr*) to criticize severely. [OE *blæst*]
▶ '**blaster** *n*

-blast *n combining form.* (in biology) indicating an embryonic cell or formative layer: *mesoblast.* [from Gk *blastos* bud]

blasted ('blɑːstɪd) *adj* **1** blighted or withered. ◆ *adj* (*prenominal*), *adv* **2** *Sl.* (intensifier): *a blasted idiot.*

blast furnace *n* a vertical cylindrical furnace for smelting into which a blast of preheated air is forced.

blasto- *combining form.* indicating an embryo or bud. [see BLAST]

blastoff ('blɑːst,ɒf) *n* **1** the launching of a rocket under its own power. **2** the time at which this occurs. ◆ *vb* **blast off. 3** (*adv; when tr, usually passive*) to be launched.

blastula ('blæstjulə) *n, pl* **blastulas** or **blastulae** (-liː). an early form of an animal embryo that develops a sphere of cells with a central cavity. Also called: **blastosphere.** [C19: NL from Gk, from dim. of *blastos* bud]
▶ '**blastular** *adj*

blat (blæt) *n Sl.* a newspaper. [C20: from G *Blatt* leaf, sheet of paper]

blatant ('bleɪtᵊnt) *adj* **1** glaringly conspicuous or obvious: *a blatant lie.* **2** offensively noticeable; obtrusive. **3** offensively noisy. [C16: coined by Edmund Spenser; prob. infl. by L *blatīre* to babble]
▶ '**blatancy** *n*

blather ('blæðə) *vb, n* a variant of **blether.**

blatherskite ('blæðə,skaɪt) *n* **1** a talkative silly person. **2** foolish talk; nonsense. [C17: from BLATHER + Scot. & N English dialect *skate* fellow]

Blavatsky ★ (blə'vætskɪ) *n* Helena Petrovna (pɪ'trɒvnə), called *Madame Blavatsky.* 1831–91, Russian theosophist, cofounder (1875) of the Theosophical Society in New York; author of *The Secret Doctrine* (1888).

blaxploitation (ˌblæksplɔɪ'teɪʃən) *n* exploitative use of stereotypical images of Black people in films, books, etc. [C20: from BLACK¹ + EXPLOITATION]

Blaydon ★ ('bleɪdᵊn) *n* an industrial town in NE England, in Gateshead unitary authority. Pop: 15 510 (1991).

blaze¹ (bleɪz) *n* **1** a strong fire or flame. **2** a very bright light or glare. **3** an outburst (of passion, acclaim, patriotism, etc.). **4** brilliance; brightness. ◆ *vb* **blazes, blazing, blazed.** (*intr*) **5** to burn fiercely. **6** to shine brightly. **7** (often foll. by *up*) to become stirred, as with anger or excitement. **8** (usually foll. by *away*) to shoot continuously. ◆ See also **blazes.** [OE *blæse*]

blaze² (bleɪz) *n* **1** a mark, usually indicating a path, made on a tree. **2** a light-coloured marking on the face of a domestic animal. ◆ *vb* **blazes, blazing, blazed.** (*tr*) **3** to mark (a tree, path, etc.) with a blaze. **4 blaze a trail.** to explore new territories, areas of knowledge, etc., so that others can follow. [C17: prob. from MLow G *bles* white marking]

blaze³ (bleɪz) *vb* **blazes, blazing, blazed.** (*tr;* often foll. by *abroad*) to make widely known; proclaim. [C14: from MDu. *blāsen,* from OHG *blāsan*]

blazer ('bleɪzə) *n* a fairly lightweight jacket, often in the colours of a sports club, school, etc.

blazes ('bleɪzɪz) *pl n* **1** *Sl.* a euphemistic word for **hell. 2** *Inf.* (intensifier): *to run like blazes.*

blazon ('bleɪzᵊn) *vb* (*tr*) **1** (often foll. by *abroad*) to proclaim publicly. **2** *Heraldry.* to describe (heraldic arms) in proper terms. **3** to draw and colour (heraldic arms) conventionally. ◆ *n* **4** *Heraldry.* a conventional description or depiction of heraldic arms. [C13: from OF *blason* coat of arms]
▶ '**blazoner** *n*

blazonry ('bleɪzᵊnrɪ) *n, pl* **blazonries. 1** the art or process of describing heraldic arms in proper form. **2** heraldic arms collectively. **3** colourful or ostentatious display.

bldg *abbrev. for* building.

★ people and places

bleach (bliːtʃ) *vb* **1** to make or become white or colourless, as by exposure to sunlight, by the action of chemical agents, etc. ◆ *n* **2** a bleaching agent. **3** the act of bleaching. [OE *blǣcan*]
▶ **'bleacher** *n*

bleaching powder *n* a white powder consisting of chlorinated calcium hydroxide. Also called: **chloride of lime, chlorinated lime.**

bleak[1] (bliːk) *adj* **1** exposed and barren. **2** cold and raw. **3** offering little hope; dismal: *a bleak future.* [OE *blāc* bright, pale]
▶ **'bleakness** *n*

bleak[2] (bliːk) *n* any of various European cyprinid fishes occurring in slow-flowing rivers. [C15: prob. from ON *bleikja* white colour]

blear (blɪə) *Arch.* ◆ *vb* **1** (*tr*) to make (eyes or sight) dim as with tears; blur. ◆ *adj* **2** a less common word for **bleary.** [C13: *blere* to make dim]

bleary (ˈblɪərɪ) *adj* **blearier, bleariest. 1** (of eyes or vision) dimmed or blurred, as by tears or tiredness. **2** indistinct or unclear.
▶ **'bleariness** *n*

bleary-eyed *or* **blear-eyed** *adj* with eyes blurred, as with old age or after waking.

bleat (bliːt) *vb* **1** (*intr*) (of a sheep, goat, or calf) to utter its characteristic plaintive cry. **2** (*intr*) to speak with any similar sound. **3** to whine; whimper. ◆ *n* **4** the characteristic cry of sheep, goats, and calves. **5** any sound similar to this. **6** a weak complaint or whine. [OE *blǣtan*]
▶ **'bleater** *n* ▶ **'bleating** *n, adj*

bleb (bleb) *n* **1** a fluid-filled blister on the skin. **2** a small air bubble. [C17: var. of BLOB]

bleed (bliːd) *vb* **bleeds, bleeding, bled** (bled). **1** (*intr*) to lose or emit blood. **2** (*tr*) to remove or draw blood from (a person or animal). **3** (*intr*) to be injured or die, as for a cause. **4** (of plants) to exude (sap or resin), esp. from a cut. **5** (*tr*) *Inf.* to obtain money, etc., from, esp. by extortion. **6** (*tr*) to draw liquid or gas from (a container or enclosed system): *to bleed the hydraulic brakes.* **7** (*intr*) (of dye or paint) to run or become mixed, as when wet. **8** to print or be printed so that text, illustrations, etc., run off the trimmed page. **9 one's heart bleeds.** used to express sympathetic grief, often ironically. [OE *blēdan*]

bleeder (ˈbliːdə) *n* **1** *Sl.* **1a** *Derog.* a despicable person. **1b** any person. **2** *Pathol.* a nontechnical name for a **haemophiliac.**

bleeding (ˈbliːdɪŋ) *adj, adv Brit. sl.* (intensifier): *a bleeding fool.*

bleeding heart *n* **1** any of several plants, esp. a widely cultivated Japanese species which has heart-shaped nodding pink flowers. **2** *Inf.* **2a** an excessively softhearted person. **2b** (*as modifier*): *bleeding-heart liberals.*

bleep (bliːp) *n* **1** a single short high-pitched signal made by an electrical apparatus; beep. **2** another word for **bleeper.** ◆ *vb* **3** (*intr*) to make such a noise. **4** (*tr*) to call (somebody) by means of a bleeper. [C20: imit.]

bleeper (ˈbliːpə) *n* a small portable radio receiver, carried esp. by doctors, that sounds a coded bleeping signal to call the carrier. Also called: **bleep.**

blemish (ˈblemɪʃ) *n* **1** a defect; flaw; stain. ◆ *vb* **2** (*tr*) to flaw the perfection of; spoil; tarnish. [C14: from OF *blemir* to make pale]

blench (blentʃ) *vb* (*intr*) to shy away, as in fear; quail. [OE *blencan* to deceive]

blend (blend) *vb* **1** to mix or mingle (components) together thoroughly. **2** (*tr*) to mix (different grades or varieties of tea, whisky, etc.). **3** (*intr*) to look good together; harmonize. **4** (*intr*) (esp. of colours) to shade imperceptibly into each other. ◆ *n* **5** a mixture or type produced by blending. **6** the act of blending. **7** Also called: **portmanteau word.** a word formed by joining together the beginning and the end of two other words: *"brunch" is a blend of "breakfast" and "lunch."* [OE *blandan*]

blende (blend) *n* **1** another name for **sphalerite. 2** any of several sulphide ores. [C17: G, from *blenden* to deceive, BLIND; so called because it is easily mistaken for galena]

blender (ˈblendə) *n* **1** a person or thing that blends. **2** Also called: **liquidizer.** a kitchen appliance with blades used for puréeing vegetables, blending liquids, etc.

Blenheim ★ (ˈblenɪm) *n* a village in SW Germany, site of a victory of Anglo-Austrian forces under the Duke of Marlborough and Prince Eugène of Savoy that saved Vienna from the French and Bavarians (1704) during the War of the Spanish Succession. Modern name: **Blindheim.**

blenny (ˈblenɪ) *n, pl* **blennies.** any of various small fishes of coastal waters having a tapering scaleless body, a long dorsal fin, and long raylike pelvic fins. [C18: from L, from Gk *blennos* slime]

blent (blent) *vb Arch. or literary.* a past participle of **blend.**

blepharitis (ˌblefəˈraɪtɪs) *n* inflammation of the eyelids. [C19: from Gk *blephar(on)* eyelid + -ITIS]

Blériot ★ (*French* blerjo) *n* **Louis** (lwi). 1872–1936, French aviator: made the first flight across the English Channel (1909).

blesbok *or* **blesbuck** (ˈblesˌbʌk) *n, pl* **blesboks, blesbok** *or* **blesbucks, blesbuck.** an antelope of southern Africa. The coat is reddish brown with a white blaze between the eyes; the horns are lyre-shaped. [C19: Afrik., from Du. *bles* BLAZE[2] + *bok* BUCK[1]]

bless (bles) *vb* **blesses, blessing, blessed** *or* **blest.** (*tr*) **1** to consecrate or render holy by means of a religious rite. **2** to give honour or glory to (a person or thing) as holy. **3** to call upon God to protect; give a benediction to. **4** to worship or adore (God). **5** (*often passive*) to grant happiness, health, or prosperity to. **6** (*usually passive*) to endow with a talent, beauty, etc. **7** *Rare.* to protect against evil or harm. **8 bless you!** (*interj*) **8a** a traditional phrase said to a person who has just sneezed. **8b** an exclamation of well-wishing or surprise. **9 bless me!** *or* (*God*) **bless my soul!** (*interj*) an exclamation of surprise. [OE *blēdsian* to sprinkle with sacrificial blood]

blessed (ˈblesɪd, blest) *adj* **1** made holy; consecrated. **2** worthy of deep reverence or respect. **3** *RC Church.* (of a person) beatified by the pope. **4** characterized by happiness or good fortune. **5** bringing great happiness or good fortune. **6** a euphemistic word for **damned,** used in mild oaths: *I'm blessed if I know.*
▶ **'blessedly** *adv* ▶ **'blessedness** *n*

Blessed Sacrament *n Chiefly RC Church.* the consecrated elements of the Eucharist.

Blessed Virgin ★ *n Chiefly RC Church.* another name for **Mary** (sense 1a).

blessing (ˈblesɪŋ) *n* **1** the act of invoking divine protection or aid. **2** the words or ceremony used for this. **3** a short prayer before or after a meal; grace. **4** approval; good wishes. **5** the bestowal of a divine gift or favour. **6** a happy event.

blest (blest) *vb* a past tense and past participle of **bless.**

blether (ˈbleðə) *Scot.* ◆ *vb* **1** (*intr*) to speak foolishly. ◆ *n* **2** foolish talk; nonsense. [C16: from ON *blathr* nonsense]

blew (bluː) *vb* the past tense of **blow**[1] and **blow**[3].

Blida ★ (ˈbliːdə) *n* a city in N Algeria, on the edge of the Mitidja Plain. Pop.: 127 284 (1987).

Bligh ★ (blaɪ) *n* **William.** 1754–1817, British admiral; Governor of New South Wales (1806–9); commander of H.M.S. *Bounty* when the crew mutinied in 1789.

blight (blaɪt) *n* **1** any plant disease characterized by withering and shrivelling without rotting. **2** any factor that causes the symptoms of blight in plants. **3** a person or thing that mars or prevents growth. **4** an ugly urban district. ◆ *vb* **5** to cause or suffer a blight. **6** (*tr*) to frustrate or disappoint. **7** (*tr*) to spoil; destroy. [C17: ? rel. to OE *blǣce* rash]

blighter (ˈblaɪtə) *n Brit. inf.* **1** a fellow. **2** a despicable or irritating person or thing.

Blighty (ˈblaɪtɪ) *n* (*sometimes not cap.*) *Brit. sl.* (used esp. by troops serving abroad) **1** England; home. **2** (*pl* **Blighties**) Also called: **a blighty one.** (esp. in World War I) a wound that causes the recipient to be sent home to England. [C20: from Hindi *bilāyatī* foreign land, England, from Ar. *wilāyat* country]

blimey (ˈblaɪmɪ) *interj Brit. sl.* an exclamation of surprise or annoyance. [C19: short for *gorblimey* God blind me!]

blimp[1] (blɪmp) *n* **1** a small nonrigid airship. **2** *Films.* a soundproof cover fixed over a camera during shooting. [C20: prob. from (*type*) *B-limp*]

blimp[2] (blɪmp) *n* (*often cap.*) *Chiefly Brit.* a person, esp. a military officer, who is stupidly complacent and reactionary. Also called: **Colonel Blimp**. [C20: from a character created by David Low]
  ▶ 'blimpish *adj*

blind (blaɪnd) *adj* **1a** unable to see; sightless. **1b** (*as collective n*; preceded by *the*): *the blind*. **2** (usually foll. by *to*) unable or unwilling to understand or discern. **3** not determined by reason: *blind hatred*. **4** acting or performed without control or preparation. **5** done without being able to see, relying on instruments for information. **6** hidden from sight: *a blind corner*. **7** closed at one end: *a blind alley*. **8** completely lacking awareness or consciousness: *a blind stupor*. **9** *Inf.* very drunk. **10** having no openings or outlets: *a blind wall*. **11** (intensifier): *not a blind bit of notice*. ◆ *adv* **12** without being able to see ahead or using only instruments: *to drive blind*; *flying blind*. **13** without adequate knowledge or information; carelessly: *to buy a house blind*. **14 bake blind.** to bake (an empty pastry case) by half filling with dried peas, crusts, etc., to keep it in shape. ◆ *vb* (*mainly tr*) **15** to deprive of sight permanently or temporarily. **16** to deprive of good sense, reason, or judgment. **17** to darken; conceal. **18** (foll. by *with*) to overwhelm by showing detailed knowledge: *to blind somebody with science*. ◆ *n* **19** (*modifier*) for or intended to help the blind: *a blind school*. **20** a shade for a window, usually on a roller. **21** any obstruction or hindrance to sight, light, or air. **22** a person, action, or thing that serves to deceive or conceal the truth. **23** Also: **blinder**. *Brit. sl.* a drunken binge. [OE *blind*]
  ▶ 'blindly *adv* ▶ 'blindness *n*

blind alley *n* **1** an alley open at one end only; cul-de-sac. **2** *Inf.* a situation in which no further progress can be made.

blind date *n Inf.* a prearranged social meeting between a man and a woman who have not met before.

blinder ('blaɪndə) *n* **1** an outstanding performance in sport. **2** *Brit. sl.* another name for **blind** (sense 23).

blinders ('blaɪndəz) *pl n* the usual US & Canad. word for **blinkers.**

blindfold ('blaɪnd,fəuld) *vb* (*tr*) **1** to prevent (a person or animal) from seeing by covering (the eyes). ◆ *n* **2** a piece of cloth, bandage, etc., used to cover the eyes. ◆ *adj, adv* **3** having the eyes covered with a cloth or bandage. **4** rash; inconsiderate. [changed (C16) through association with FOLD[1] from OE *blindfellian* to strike blind; see BLIND, FELL[2]]

blind man's buff *n* a game in which a blindfolded person tries to catch and identify the other players. [C16: *buff*, ?from OF *buffe* a blow; see BUFFET[2]]

blind register *n* (in Britain) a list of those who are blind and are therefore entitled to financial and other benefits.

blindsight ('blaɪnd,saɪt) *n* the ability to respond to visual stimuli without having any conscious visual experience; it can occur after some forms of brain damage.

blind spot *n* **1** a small oval-shaped area of the retina, where the optic nerve enters, in which vision is not experienced. **2** a place or area where vision is obscured. **3** a subject about which a person is ignorant or prejudiced.

blind trust *n* a trust fund that manages the financial affairs of a person without informing him or her of any investments made, usually so that the beneficiary cannot be accused of using public office for private gain.

blindworm ('blaɪnd,wɜːm) *n* another name for **slowworm.**

blink (blɪŋk) *vb* **1** to close and immediately reopen (the eyes or an eye), usually involuntarily. **2** (*intr*) to look with the eyes partially closed. **3** to shine intermittently or unsteadily. **4** (*tr*; foll. by *away, from*, etc.) to clear the eyes of (dust, tears, etc.). **5** (when *tr*, usually foll. by *at*) to

be surprised or amazed. **6** (when *intr*, foll. by *at*) to pretend not to know or see (a fault, injustice, etc.). ◆ *n* **7** the act or an instance of blinking. **8** a glance; glimpse. **9** short for **iceblink** (sense 1). **10 on the blink.** *Sl.* not working properly. [C14: var. of BLENCH]

blinker[1] ('blɪŋkə) *n* **1** a flashing light for sending messages, as a warning device, etc., such as a direction indicator on a road vehicle. **2** (*often pl*) a slang word for **eye**[1] (sense 1).

blinker[2] ('blɪŋkə) *vb* (*tr*) **1** to provide (a horse) with blinkers. **2** to obscure or be obscured with or as with blinkers.
  ▶ 'blinkered *adj*

blinkers ('blɪŋkəz) *pl n* (*sometimes sing*) *Chiefly Brit.* leather sidepieces attached to a horse's bridle to prevent sideways vision.

blinking ('blɪŋkɪŋ) *adj, adv Inf.* (intensifier): *a blinking fool*; *a blinking good film*.

blip (blɪp) *n* **1** a repetitive sound, such as that produced by an electronic device. **2** Also called: **pip**. the spot of light on a radar screen indicating the position of an object. **3** a temporary irregularity recorded in the performance of something. ◆ *vb* **blips, blipping, blipped.** **4** (*intr*) to produce a blip. [C20: imit.]

bliss (blɪs) *n* **1** perfect happiness; serene joy. **2** the ecstatic joy of heaven. [OE *blīths*; rel. to *blīthe* BLITHE]

Bliss ★ (blɪs) *n* Sir **Arthur**. 1891–1975, British composer; Master of the Queen's Musick (1953–75). His works include the *Colour Symphony* (1922), film and ballet music, and a piano concerto (1938).

blissful ('blɪsfʊl) *adj* **1** serenely joyful or glad. **2 blissful ignorance.** unawareness or inexperience of something unpleasant.
  ▶ 'blissfully *adv* ▶ 'blissfulness *n*

B list *n* **a** a category considered to be slightly below the most socially desirable. **b** (*as modifier*): *B-list celebrities*. ◆ Cf. **A list.**

blister ('blɪstə) *n* **1** a small bubble-like elevation of the skin filled with serum, produced as a reaction to a burn, mechanical irritation, etc. **2** a swelling containing air or liquid, as on a painted surface. **3** *NZ sl.* **3a** a rebuke. **3b** a summons to court. ◆ *vb* **4** to have or cause to have blisters. **5** (*tr*) to attack verbally with great scorn or sarcasm. [C13: from OF *blestre*]
  ▶ 'blistered *adj*

blister pack *n* a type of pack for small goods, consisting of a transparent dome on a firm backing. Also called: **bubble pack.**

BLit *abbrev. for* Bachelor of Literature.

blithe (blaɪð) *adj* **1** very happy or cheerful; gay. **2** heedless; casual and indifferent. [OE *blīthe*]
  ▶ 'blithely *adv* ▶ 'blitheness *n*

blithering ('blɪðərɪŋ) *adj* **1** talking foolishly; jabbering. **2** *Inf.* stupid; foolish: *you blithering idiot*. [C19: var. of BLETHER + -ING[2]]

blithesome ('blaɪðsəm) *adj Literary.* cheery; merry.

BLitt *abbrev. for* Bachelor of Letters. [L *Baccalaureus Litterarum*]

blitz (blɪts) *n* **1** a violent and sustained attack, esp. with intensive aerial bombardment. **2** any sudden intensive attack or concerted effort. **3** *American football.* a defensive charge on the quarterback. ◆ *vb* **4** (*tr*) to attack suddenly and intensively. [C20: shortened from G *Blitzkrieg* lightning war]

Blitz (blɪts) *n* **the.** the systematic bombing of Britain in 1940–41 by the German Luftwaffe.

blitzkrieg ('blɪts,kriːg) *n* a swift intensive military attack designed to defeat the opposition quickly. [C20: from G: lightning war]

Blixen ★ ('blɪksən) *n* **Karen.** See (Isak) **Dinesen.**

blizzard ('blɪzəd) *n* a strong cold wind accompanied by widespread heavy snowfall. [C19: from ?]

bloat (bləut) *vb* **1** to swell or cause to swell, as with a liquid or air. **2** to become or cause to be puffed up, as with conceit. **3** (*tr*) to cure (fish, esp. herring) by half drying in smoke. [C17: prob. rel. to ON *blautr* soaked]
  ▶ 'bloated *adj*

★ people and places

bloater ('bləʊtə) *n* a herring that has been salted in brine, smoked, and cured.

blob (blɒb) *n* **1** a soft mass or drop. **2** a spot, dab, or blotch of colour, ink, etc. **3** an indistinct or shapeless form or object. [C15: ? imit.]

bloc (blɒk) *n* a group of people or countries combined by a common interest. [from F: BLOCK]

Bloch ★ (blɒk) *n* **1 Ernest.** 1880–1959, US composer, born in Switzerland: his works include the symphonies *Israel* (1916) and *America* (1926). **2 Felix.** 1905–83, US physicist, born in Switzerland: Nobel prize for physics (1952) for his work on the magnetic moments of atomic particles. **3 Konrad Emil.** born 1912, US biochemist, born in Germany: shared the Nobel prize for physiology or medicine in 1964 for his work on fatty-acid metabolism. **4** (*French* blɔk). **Marc** (mark). 1886–1944, French historian and Resistance fighter; author of *Feudal Society* (1935) and *Strange Defeat* (1940): killed by the Nazis.

block (blɒk) *n* **1** a large solid piece of wood, stone, or other material usually having at least one face fairly flat. **2** such a piece on which particular tasks may be done, as chopping, cutting, or beheading. **3** Also called: **building block.** one of a set of wooden or plastic cubes as a child's toy. **4** a form in which things are shaped: *a wig block.* **5** *Sl.* a person's head. **6 do one's block.** *Austral. & NZ sl.* to become angry. **7** a dull, unemotional, or hardhearted person. **8** a large building of offices, flats, etc. **9a** a group of buildings in a city bounded by intersecting streets on each side. **9b** the area or distance between such intersecting streets. **10** *Austral. & NZ.* an area of land for a house, farm, etc. **11** *NZ.* an area of bush reserved by licence for a trapper or hunter. **12** a piece of wood, metal, or other material having a design in relief, used for printing. **13** *Austral. & NZ.* a log, usually of willow, fastened to a timber base and used in a wood-chopping competition. **14** a casing housing one or more freely rotating pulleys. See also **block and tackle.** **15** an obstruction or hindrance. **16** *Pathol.* **16a** interference in the normal physiological functioning of an organ or part. **16b** See **heart block.** **16c** See **nerve block.** **17** *Psychol.* a short interruption of perceptual or thought processes. **18** obstruction of an opponent in a sport. **19a** a quantity handled or considered as a single unit. **19b** (*as modifier*): *a block booking.* **20** *Athletics.* short for **starting block.** ♦ *vb* (*mainly tr*) **21** (often foll. by *up*) to obstruct (a passage, channel, etc.) or prevent or impede the motion or flow of (something or someone) by introducing an obstacle: *to block the traffic; to block up a pipe.* **22** to impede, retard, or prevent (an action, procedure, etc.). **23** to stamp (a title, design, etc.) on (a book cover, etc.) esp. using gold leaf. **24** to shape by use of a block: *to block a hat.* **25** (*also intr*) *Sport.* to obstruct or impede movement by (an opponent). **26** to interrupt a physiological function, as by use of an anaesthetic. **27** (*also intr*) *Cricket.* to play (a ball) defensively. ♦ See also **block in, block out.** [C14: from OF *bloc*, from Du. *blok*]
► **'blocker** *n*

blockade (blɒ'keɪd) *n* **1** *Mil.* the interdiction of a nation's sea lines of communications, esp. of an individual port by the use of sea power. **2** something that prevents access or progress. **3** *Med.* the inhibition of the effect of a hormone or the action of a nerve by a drug. ♦ *vb* **blockades, blockading, blockaded.** (*tr*) **4** to impose a blockade on. **5** to obstruct the way to. [C17: from BLOCK + -*ade*, as in AMBUSCADE]
► **block'ader** *n*

blockage ('blɒkɪdʒ) *n* **1** the act of blocking or state of being blocked. **2** an object causing an obstruction.

block and tackle *n* a hoisting device in which a rope or chain is passed around a pair of blocks containing one or more pulleys.

blockboard ('blɒk,bɔːd) *n* a bonded board in which strips of soft wood are sandwiched between two layers of veneer.

blockbuster ('blɒk,bʌstə) *n Inf.* **1** a large bomb used to demolish extensive areas. **2** a very successful, effective, or forceful person, thing, etc. **3** a lavish film, show, novel, etc., that proves to be an outstanding popular success.

block diagram *n* **1** a diagram showing the interconnections between the parts of an industrial process. **2** *Computing.* a diagram showing the interconnections between electronic components or parts of a program.

blockhead ('blɒk,hɛd) *n Derog.* a stupid person.
► **'block,headed** *adj*

blockhouse ('blɒk,haʊs) *n* **1** (formerly) a wooden fortification with ports for defensive fire, observation, etc. **2** a concrete structure strengthened to give protection against enemy fire, with apertures to allow defensive gunfire. **3** a building constructed of logs or squared timber.

block in *vb* (*tr, adv*) to sketch or outline with little detail.

blockish ('blɒkɪʃ) *adj* lacking vivacity or imagination; stupid.
► **'blockishly** *adv*

block letter *n* **1** *Printing.* a less common name for **sans serif.** **2** Also called: **block capital.** a plain capital letter.

block out *vb* (*tr, adv*) **1** to plan or describe (something) in a general fashion. **2** to prevent the entry or consideration of (something).

block release *n Brit.* the release of industrial trainees from work for study at a college for several weeks.

block vote *n Brit.* (at a trade-union conference) the system whereby each delegate's vote has a value in proportion to the number of people he represents.

Bloemfontein ★ ('bluːmfɒn,teɪn) *n* a city in central South Africa: capital of Free State and judicial capital of South Africa. Pop.: 126 867 (1991).

Blois ★ (*French* blwa) *n* a city in N central France, on the Loire: 13th-century castle. Pop.: 51 550 (1990).

bloke (bləʊk) *n Brit. & Austral.* an informal word for **man.** [C19: from Shelta]

blokeish or **blokish** ('bləʊkɪʃ) *adj Brit. inf., sometimes derog.* denoting or exhibiting the characteristics believed typical of an ordinary man. Also: **blokey** ('bləʊkɪ).
► **'blokeishness** or **'blokishness** *n*

blonde or (*masc*) **blond** (blɒnd) *adj* **1** (of hair) of a light colour; fair. **2** (of people or a race) having fair hair, a light complexion, and, typically, blue or grey eyes. ♦ *n* **3** a person having light-coloured hair and skin. [C15: from OF *blond* (fem *blonde*), prob. of Gmc origin]
► **'blondeness** or **'blondness** *n*

Blondin ★ (*French* blɔ̃dɛ̃) *n* **Charles**, real name *Jean-François Gravelet.* 1824–97, French acrobat; best known for walking a tightrope across Niagara Falls (1859).

blood (blʌd) *n* **1** a reddish fluid in vertebrates that is pumped by the heart through the arteries and veins. **2** a similar fluid in invertebrates. **3** bloodshed, esp. when resulting in murder. **4** life itself; lifeblood. **5** relationship through being of the same family, race, or kind; kinship. **6 flesh and blood. 6a** near kindred or kinship, esp. that between a parent and child. **6b** human nature (esp. in *it's more than flesh and blood can stand*). **7 in one's blood.** as a natural or inherited characteristic or talent. **8 the blood.** royal or noble descent: *a prince of the blood.* **9** temperament; disposition; temper. **10a** good or pure breeding; pedigree. **10b** (*as modifier*): *blood horses.* **11** people viewed as members of a group, esp. as an invigorating force (**new blood, young blood**). **12** *Chiefly Brit., rare.* a dashing young man. **13 in cold blood.** showing no passion; deliberately; ruthlessly. **14 make one's blood boil.** to cause to be angry or indignant. **15 make one's blood run cold.** to fill with horror. ♦ *vb* (*tr*) **16** *Hunting.* to cause (young hounds) to taste the blood of a freshly killed quarry. **17** to initiate (a person) to war or hunting. [OE *blōd*]

blood-and-thunder *adj* denoting or relating to a melodramatic adventure story.

blood bank *n* a place where whole blood or blood plasma is stored until required in transfusion.

blood bath *n* indiscriminate slaughter; a massacre.

blood brother *n* **1** a brother by birth. **2** a man or boy who has sworn to treat another as his brother, often in a ceremony in which their blood is mingled.

blood count *n* determination of the number of red and white blood corpuscles in a specific sample of blood.

bloodcurdling ('blʌd,kɜːdlɪŋ) *adj* terrifying; horrifying.
► **'blood,curdlingly** *adv*

blood donor *n* a person who gives his blood to be used for transfusion.

blood doping *n* the illegal practice of removing a quantity of blood from an athlete long before a race and reinjecting it shortly before a race, so boosting oxygenation of the blood.

blooded ('blʌdɪd) *adj* **1** (of horses, cattle, etc.) of good breeding. **2** (*in combination*) having blood or temperament as specified: *hot-blooded, cold-blooded, warm-blooded, red-blooded*.

blood group *n* any one of the various groups into which human blood is classified on the basis of its specific agglutinating properties. Also called: **blood type**.

blood heat *n* the normal temperature of the human body, 98.4°F. or 37°C.

bloodhound ('blʌd,haʊnd) *n* a large breed of hound, formerly used in tracking and police work.

bloodless ('blʌdlɪs) *adj* **1** without blood. **2** conducted without violence (esp. in **bloodless revolution**). **3** anaemic-looking; pale. **4** lacking vitality; lifeless. **5** lacking in emotion; unfeeling.
▸ '**bloodlessly** *adv* ▸ '**bloodlessness** *n*

blood-letting ('blʌd,lɛtɪŋ) *n* **1** the therapeutic removal of blood. See also **phlebotomy. 2** bloodshed, esp. in a feud.

bloodline ('blʌd,laɪn) *n* all the members of a family group over generations, esp. regarding characteristics common to that group; pedigree.

blood money *n* **1** compensation paid to the relatives of a murdered person. **2** money paid to a hired murderer. **3** a reward for information about a criminal, esp. a murderer.

blood orange *n* a variety of orange all or part of the pulp of which is dark red when ripe.

blood poisoning *n* a nontechnical term for **septicaemia**.

blood pressure *n* the pressure exerted by the blood on the inner walls of the arteries, being relative to the elasticity and diameter of the vessels and the force of the heartbeat.

blood pudding *n* another name for **black pudding**.

blood relation *or* **relative** *n* a person related to another by birth, as distinct from one related by marriage.

bloodshed ('blʌd,ʃɛd) *n* slaughter; killing.

bloodshot ('blʌd,ʃɒt) *adj* (of an eye) inflamed.

blood sport *n* any sport involving the killing of an animal, esp. hunting.

bloodstain ('blʌd,steɪn) *n* a dark discoloration caused by blood, esp. dried blood.
▸ '**blood,stained** *adj*

bloodstock ('blʌd,stɒk) *n* thoroughbred horses.

bloodstone ('blʌd,stəʊn) *n* a dark green variety of chalcedony with red spots: used as a gemstone. Also called: **heliotrope**.

bloodstream ('blʌd,striːm) *n* the flow of blood through the vessels of a living body.

blood substitute *n* a mixture of plasma, albumin, and dextran used to replace lost blood or increase the blood volume.

bloodsucker ('blʌd,sʌkə) *n* **1** an animal that sucks blood, esp. a leech or mosquito. **2** *Inf.* a person or thing that preys upon another person, esp. by extorting money.
▸ '**blood,sucking** *adj*

blood sugar *n Med.* the glucose circulating in the blood: the normal fasting level is between 3·9 and 5·6 millimoles per litre.

bloodthirsty ('blʌd,θɜːstɪ) *adj* **bloodthirstier, bloodthirstiest. 1** murderous; cruel. **2** taking pleasure in bloodshed or violence. **3** describing or depicting killing and violence; gruesome.
▸ '**blood,thirstily** *adv* ▸ '**blood,thirstiness** *n*

blood type *n* another name for **blood group**.

blood vessel *n* an artery, capillary, or vein.

bloodwood ('blʌd,wʊd) *n* any of several species of Australian eucalyptus with red sap.

bloody ('blʌdɪ) *adj* **bloodier, bloodiest. 1** covered or stained with blood. **2** resembling or composed of blood. **3** marked by much killing and bloodshed: *a bloody war*. **4** cruel or murderous: *a bloody tyrant*. ◆ *adv, adj* **5** *Sl.* (intensifier): *a bloody fool*. ◆ *vb* **bloodies, bloodying, bloodied. 6** (*tr*) to stain with blood.
▸ '**bloodily** *adv* ▸ '**bloodiness** *n*

Bloody Mary *n* **1** nickname of **Mary I. 2** a drink consisting of tomato juice and vodka.

bloody-minded *adj Brit. inf.* deliberately obstructive and unhelpful.

bloom[1] (bluːm) *n* **1** a blossom on a flowering plant; a flower. **2** the state, time, or period when flowers open. **3** open flowers collectively. **4** a healthy, vigorous, or flourishing condition; prime. **5** youthful or healthy rosiness in the cheeks or face; glow. **6** a fine whitish coating on the surface of fruits, leaves, etc. **7** Also called: **chill**. a dull area on the surface of old gloss paint, lacquer, or varnish. **8** *Ecology*. a visible increase in the algal constituent of plankton, which may be due to excessive organic pollution. ◆ *vb* (*intr*) **9** (of flowers) to open; come into flower. **10** to bear flowers; blossom. **11** to flourish or grow. **12** to be in a healthy, glowing, or flourishing condition. [C13: of Gmc origin; cf. ON *blōm* flower]

bloom[2] (bluːm) *n* a rectangular mass of metal obtained by rolling or forging a cast ingot. [OE *blōma* lump of metal]

bloomer[1] ('bluːmə) *n* a plant that flowers, esp. in a specified way: *a night bloomer*.

bloomer[2] ('bluːmə) *n Brit. inf.* a stupid mistake; blunder. [C20: from BLOOMING]

bloomer[3] ('bluːmə) *n Brit.* a medium-sized loaf, glazed and notched on top. [C20: from?]

bloomers ('bluːməz) *pl n* **1** *Inf.* women's baggy knickers. **2** (formerly) loose trousers gathered at the knee worn by women for cycling, etc. **3** *History*. loose trousers gathered at the ankle and worn under a shorter skirt. [after Amelia *Bloomer* (1818–94), US social reformer]

Bloomfield ★ ('bluːm,fiːld) *n* Leonard. 1887–1949, US linguist, influential for his strictly scientific and descriptive approach to comparative linguistics; author of *Language* (1933).

blooming ('bluːmɪŋ) *adv, adj Brit. inf.* (intensifier): *a blooming genius; blooming painful*. [C19: euphemistic for BLOODY]

Bloomington ★ ('bluːmɪŋtən) *n* a city in central Indiana: seat of the University of Indiana (1820). Pop.: 60 633 (1990).

Bloomsbury ★ ('bluːmzbərɪ, -brɪ) *n* a district of central London in the borough of Camden: contains the British Museum.

Bloomsbury Group *n* a group of writers, artists, and intellectuals living and working in and around Bloomsbury from about 1907 to 1930. They included Leonard and Virginia Woolf, Roger Fry, E. M. Forster, Lytton Strachey, and John Maynard Keynes.

blossom ('blɒsəm) *n* **1** the flower or flowers of a plant, esp. producing edible fruit. **2** the time or period of flowering. ◆ *vb* (*intr*) **3** (of plants) to come into flower. **4** to develop or come to a promising stage. [OE *blōstm*]
▸ '**blossomy** *adj*

blot (blɒt) *n* **1** a stain or spot of ink, paint, dirt, etc. **2** something that spoils. **3** a blemish or stain on one's character or reputation. **4** *Austral. sl.* the anus. ◆ *vb* **blots, blotting, blotted. 5** (of ink, dye, etc.) to form spots or blobs on (a material) or (of a person) to cause such spots or blobs to form on (a material). **6** (*intr*) to stain or become stained or spotted. **7** (*tr*) to cause a blemish in or on; disgrace. **8** to soak up (excess ink, etc.) by using blotting paper. **9** (of blotting paper) to absorb (excess ink, etc.). **10** (*tr*; often foll. by *out*) **10a** to darken or hide completely; obscure; obliterate. **10b** to destroy; annihilate. [C14: prob. of Gmc origin]

blotch (blɒtʃ) *n* **1** an irregular spot or discoloration, esp. a dark and relatively large one. ◆ *vb* **2** to become or cause to become marked by such discoloration. [C17: prob. from BOTCH, infl. by BLOT]
▸ '**blotchy** *adj*

blotter ('blɒtə) *n* something used to absorb excess ink, esp. a sheet of blotting paper.

blotting paper *n* a soft absorbent unsized paper, used esp. for soaking up surplus ink.

blotto ('blɒtəu) *adj Sl.* unconscious, esp. through drunkenness. [C20: from BLOT (vb)]

blouse (blauz) *n* **1** a woman's shirtlike garment. **2** a waist-length belted jacket worn by soldiers. ◆ *vb* **blouses, blousing, bloused. 3** to hang or make so as to hang in full loose folds. [C19: from F, from ?]

blouson ('bluːzɒn) *n* a tight-waisted jacket or top that blouses out. [C20: from F]

blow[1] (bləu) *vb* **blows, blowing, blew, blown. 1** (of a current of air, the wind, etc.) to be or cause to be in motion. **2** (*intr*) to move or be carried by or as if by wind. **3** to expel (air, cigarette smoke, etc.) through the mouth or nose. **4** to force or cause (air, dust, etc.) to move (into, in, over, etc.) by using an instrument or by expelling breath. **5** (*intr*) to breathe hard; pant. **6** (sometimes foll. by *up*) to inflate with air or the breath. **7** (*intr*) (of wind, a storm, etc.) to make a roaring sound. **8** to cause (a whistle, siren, etc.) to sound by forcing air into it or (of a whistle, etc.) to sound thus. **9** (*tr*) to force air from the lungs through (the nose) to clear out mucus. **10** (often foll. by *up, down, in*, etc.) to explode, break, or disintegrate completely. **11** *Electronics.* to burn out (a fuse, valve, etc.) because of excessive current or (of a fuse, valve, etc.) to burn out. **12** (*tr*) to wind (a horse) by making it run excessively. **13** to cause (a wind instrument) to sound by forcing one's breath into the mouthpiece or (of such an instrument) to sound in this way. **14** (*intr*) (of flies) to lay eggs (in). **15** to shape (glass, ornaments, etc.) by forcing air or gas through the material when molten. **16** (*tr*) *Sl.* to spend (money) freely. **17** (*tr*) *Sl.* to use (an opportunity) ineffectively. **18** *Sl.* to go suddenly away (from). **19** (*tr*) *Sl.* to expose or betray (a secret). **20** (p.p. **blowed**). *Inf.* another word for **damn. 21 blow hot and cold.** *Inf.* to vacillate. **22 blow one's top.** *Inf.* to lose one's temper. ◆ *n* **23** the act or an instance of blowing. **24** the sound produced by blowing. **25** a blast of air or wind. **26a** *Brit.* a slang name for **cannabis** (sense 2). **26b** *US* a slang name for **cocaine. 27** *Austral. sl.* a brief rest; a breather. ◆ See also **blow away, blow in,** etc. [OE *blāwan*]

blow[2] (bləu) *n* **1** a powerful or heavy stroke with the fist, a weapon, etc. **2 at one** *or* **a blow.** by or with only one action. **3** a sudden setback. **4 come to blows.** to fight. **4b** to result in a fight. **5** an attacking action: *a blow for freedom.* **6** *Austral. & NZ.* a stroke of the shears in sheep-shearing. [C15: prob. of Gmc origin]

blow[3] (bləu) *vb* **blows, blowing, blew, blown. 1** (*intr*) (of a plant or flower) to blossom or open out. ◆ *n* **2** a mass of blossoms. **3** the state or period of blossoming. [OE *blōwan*]

blow away *vb* (*tr, adv*) *Sl., chiefly US.* **1** to kill (someone) by shooting. **2** to defeat decisively.

blow-by-blow *adj* (*prenominal*) explained in great detail: *a blow-by-blow account.*

blow-dry *vb* **blow-dries, blow-drying, blow-dried. 1** (*tr*) to style (the hair) while drying it with a hand-held hair dryer. ◆ *n* **2** this method of styling hair.

blower ('bləuə) *n* **1** a mechanical device, such as a fan, that blows. **2** a low-pressure compressor, esp. in a furnace or internal-combustion engine. **3** an informal name for **telephone.**

blowfish ('bləu,fɪʃ) *n, pl* **blowfish** *or* **blowfishes.** a popular name for **puffer** (sense 2).

blowfly ('bləu,flaɪ) *n, pl* **blowflies.** any of various flies that lay their eggs in rotting meat, dung, carrion, and open wounds. Also called: **bluebottle.**

blowgun ('bləu,gʌn) *n* the US word for **blowpipe** (sense 1).

blowhard ('bləu,hɑːd) *Inf.* ◆ *n* **1** a boastful person. ◆ *adj* **2** blustering or boastful.

blowhole ('bləu,həul) *n* **1** the nostril of whales, situated far back on the skull. **2** a hole in ice through which whales, seals, etc., breathe. **3** *Geol.* a hole in a cliff top leading to a sea cave through which air is forced by the

action of the sea. **4a** a vent for air or gas. **4b** *NZ.* a hole emitting gas or steam in a volcanic region.

blow in *Inf.* ◆ *vb* **1** (*intr, adv*) to arrive or enter suddenly. ◆ *n* **blow-in. 2** *Austral.* a newcomer.

blow job *Taboo.* a slang term for **fellatio.**

blowlamp ('bləu,læmp) *n* another name for **blowtorch.**

blown (bləun) *vb* the past participle of **blow**[1] and **blow**[3].

blow out *vb* (*adv*) **1** to extinguish (a flame, candle, etc.) or (of a flame, etc.) to become extinguished. **2** (*intr*) (of a tyre) to puncture suddenly, esp. at high speed. **3** (*intr*) (of a fuse) to melt suddenly. **4** (*tr; often reflexive*) to diminish or use up the energy of: *the storm blew itself out.* **5** (*intr*) (of an oil or gas well) to lose oil or gas in an uncontrolled manner. ◆ *n* **blowout. 6** the sudden melting of an electrical fuse. **7** a sudden burst in a tyre. **8** the uncontrolled escape of oil or gas from an oil or gas well. **9** *Sl.* a large filling meal or lavish entertainment.

blow over *vb* (*intr, adv*) **1** to cease or be finished: *the storm blew over.* **2** to be forgotten.

blowpipe ('bləu,paɪp) *n* **1** a long tube from which pellets, poisoned darts, etc., are shot by blowing. **2** Also called: **blow tube.** a tube for blowing air or oxygen into a flame to intensify its heat. **3** a long narrow iron pipe used to gather molten glass and blow it into shape.

blowsy *or* **blowzy** ('blauzɪ) *adj* **blowsier, blowsiest** *or* **blowzier, blowziest. 1** (esp. of a woman) untidy in appearance; slovenly or sluttish. **2** (of a woman) ruddy in complexion. [C18: from dialect *blowze* beggar girl, from ?]

blow through *vb* (*intr, adv*) *Austral. inf.* to leave; make off.

blowtorch ('bləu,tɔːtʃ) *n* a small burner that produces a very hot flame, used to remove paint, melt soft metal, etc.

blow up *vb* (*adv*) **1** to explode or cause to explode. **2** (*tr*) to increase the importance of (something): *they blew the whole affair up.* **3** (*intr*) to arise: *we lived very quietly before this affair blew up.* **4** (*intr*) to come into existence with sudden force: *a storm had blown up.* **5** (*intr*) *Inf.* to lose one's temper (with a person). **6** (*tr*) *Inf.* to reprimand. **7** (*tr*) *Inf.* to enlarge the size of (a photograph). ◆ *n* **blowup. 8** an explosion. **9** *Inf.* an enlarged photograph or part of a photograph. **10** *Inf.* a fit of temper.

blowy ('bləuɪ) *adj* **blowier, blowiest.** another word for **windy** (sense 1).

blub (blʌb) *vb* **blubs, blubbing, blubbed.** *Brit.* a slang word for **blubber** (senses 1–3).

blubber ('blʌbə) *vb* **1** to sob without restraint. **2** to utter while sobbing. **3** (*tr*) to make (the face) wet and swollen by crying. ◆ *n* **4** the fatty tissue of aquatic mammals such as the whale. **5** *Inf.* flabby body fat. **6** the act or an instance of weeping without restraint. ◆ *adj* **7** (*often in combination*) swollen or fleshy: *blubber-faced.* [C12: ?from Low G *blubbern* to BUBBLE, imit.]

▸ **'blubberer** *n* ▸ **'blubbery** *adj*

Blücher ★ (*German* 'blyçər) *n* **Gebhard Leberecht von** ('gephart 'leːbəreçt fɔn). 1742–1819, Prussian field marshal, who commanded the Prussian army against Napoleon at Waterloo (1815).

bludge (blʌdʒ) *Austral. & NZ inf.* ◆ *vb* **bludges, bludging, bludged. 1** (when *intr*, often foll. by *on*) to scrounge from (someone). **2** (*intr*) to skive. ◆ *n* **3** a very easy task. [C19: back formation from *bludger* pimp, from BLUDGEON]

bludgeon ('blʌdʒən) *n* **1** a stout heavy club, typically thicker at one end. **2** a person, line of argument, etc., that is effective but unsubtle. ◆ *vb* (*tr*) **3** to hit as with a bludgeon. **4** (often foll. by *into*) to force; bully; coerce. [C18: from ?]

bludger ('blʌdʒə) *n Austral. & NZ inf.* **1** a person who scrounges. **2** a person who avoids work. **3** a person in authority regarded as ineffectual by those working under him.

blue (bluː) *n* **1** any of a group of colours, such as that of a clear unclouded sky or the deep sea. **2** a dye or pigment of any of these colours. **3** blue cloth or clothing: *dressed in blue.* **4** a sportsman who represents or has represented Oxford or Cambridge University and has the right to wear the university colour. **5** *Brit.* an informal name for

Tory. **6** any of numerous small blue-winged butterflies. **7** a blue substance used in laundering. **8** *Austral. & NZ sl.* an argument or fight: *he had a blue with a taxi driver.* **9** Also: **bluey.** *Austral. & NZ sl.* a court summons. **10** *Austral. & NZ inf.* a mistake; error. **11 out of the blue.** apparently from nowhere; unexpectedly. ◆ *adj* **bluer, bluest. 12** of the colour blue. **13** (of the flesh) having a purple tinge, as from cold or contusion. **14** depressed, moody, or unhappy. **15** indecent, titillating, or pornographic: *blue films.* ◆ *vb* **blues, blueing** or **bluing, blued. 16** to make, dye, or become blue. **17** (*tr*) to treat (laundry) with blue. **18** (*tr*) *Sl.* to spend extravagantly or wastefully; squander. ◆ See also **blues.** [C13: from OF *bleu*, of Gmc origin]
▶ **'blueness** *n*

Blue (blu:) or **Bluey** ('blu:ɪ) *n Austral. inf.* a person with red hair.

blue baby *n* a baby born with a bluish tinge to the skin because of lack of oxygen in the blood.

Bluebeard ('blu:,bɪəd) *n* **1** a villain in European folk tales who marries several wives and murders them in turn. **2** a man who has had several wives.

bluebell ('blu:,bɛl) *n* **1** Also called: **wild** or **wood hyacinth.** a European woodland plant having a one-sided cluster of blue bell-shaped flowers. **2** a Scottish name for **harebell. 3** any of various other plants with blue bell-shaped flowers.

blueberry ('blu:bərɪ, -brɪ) *n, pl* **blueberries. 1** Also called: **huckleberry.** any of several North American ericaceous shrubs that have blue-black edible berries with tiny seeds. See also **bilberry. 2** the fruit of any of these plants.

bluebird ('blu:,bɜːd) *n* **1** a North American songbird of the thrush family having a blue or partly blue plumage. **2** any of various other birds having a blue plumage.

blue blood *n* royal or aristocratic descent. [C19: translation of Sp. *sangre azul*]
▶ ,blue-'blooded *adj*

bluebook ('blu:,bʊk) *n* **1** (in Britain) a government publication bound in a stiff blue paper cover: usually the report of a royal commission or a committee. **2** (in Canada) an annual statement of government accounts.

bluebottle ('blu:,bɒt°l) *n* **1** another name for the **blowfly. 2** any of various blue-flowered plants, esp. the cornflower. **3** *Brit.* an informal word for a **policeman. 4** *Austral. & NZ.* an informal name for **Portuguese man-of-war.**

blue button *n* a trainee market maker on the London stock exchange. [C20: from the *blue button* badge worn in the lapel]

blue cheese *n* cheese containing a blue mould, esp. Stilton, Roquefort, or Danish Blue.

blue chip *n* **1** a gambling chip with the highest value. **2** *Finance.* a stock considered reliable with respect to dividend income and capital value. **3** (*modifier*) denoting something considered to be a valuable asset.

blue-collar *adj* of or designating manual industrial workers. Cf. **white-collar.**

blue-eyed boy *n Inf., chiefly Brit.* the favourite or darling of a person or group.

bluefish ('blu:,fɪʃ) *n, pl* **bluefish** or **bluefishes. 1** Also called: **snapper.** a bluish marine food and game fish, related to the horse mackerel. **2** any of various other bluish fishes.

Blue Flag *n* an award given to a seaside resort that meets EU standards of cleanliness of beaches and purity of water in bathing areas.

blue fox *n* **1** a variety of the arctic fox that has a pale grey winter coat. **2** the fur of this animal.

blue funk *n Sl.* a state of great terror.

bluegrass ('blu:,grɑ:s) *n* **1** any of several North American bluish-green grasses, esp. **Kentucky bluegrass,** grown for forage. **2** a type of folk music originating in Kentucky.

blue-green algae *pl n* the former name for **cyanobacteria.**

blue ground *n Mineralogy.* another name for **kimberlite.**

blue gum *n* a tall fast-growing widely cultivated Australian eucalyptus, having bluish aromatic leaves containing a medicinal oil, bark that peels off in shreds, and hard timber.

blue heeler *n Austral.* a type of dog with dark speckled markings: used for herding cattle.

bluejacket ('blu:,dʒækɪt) *n* a sailor in the Navy.

blue jay *n* a common North American jay having bright blue plumage.

blue moon *n* **once in a blue moon.** *Inf.* very rarely; almost never.

blue mould *n* any fungus that forms a bluish mass on decaying food, leather, etc. Also called: **green mould.**

Blue Mountains ★ *pl n* **1** a mountain range in the US, in NE Oregon and SE Washington. Highest peak: Rock Creek Butte, 2773 m (9097 ft). **2** a mountain range in the Caribbean, in E Jamaica: Blue Mountain coffee is grown on its slopes. Highest peak: Blue Mountain Peak, 2256 m (7402 ft). **3** a plateau in SE Australia, in E New South Wales: part of the Great Dividing Range. Highest part: about 1134 m (3871 ft).

Blue Nile ★ *n* a river in E Africa, rising in central Ethiopia as the Abbai and flowing southeast, then northwest to join the White Nile. Length: about 1530 km (950 miles).

blue pencil *n* **1** deletion, alteration, or censorship of the contents of a book or other work. ◆ *vb* **blue-pencil, blue-pencils, blue-pencilling, blue-pencilled** or *US* **blue-pencils, blue-penciling, blue-penciled. 2** (*tr*) to alter or delete parts of (a book, film, etc.), esp. to censor.

blue peter *n* a signal flag of blue with a white square at the centre, displayed by a vessel about to leave port. [C19: from the name *Peter*]

blue pointer *n* a large shark of Australian coastal waters, having a blue back and pointed snout.

blueprint ('blu:,prɪnt) *n* **1** Also called: **cyanotype.** a photographic print of plans, technical drawings, etc., consisting of white lines on a blue background. **2** an original plan or prototype. ◆ *vb* **3** (*tr*) to make a blueprint of (a plan, etc.).

blue ribbon *n* **1** (in Britain) a badge of blue silk worn by members of the Order of the Garter. **2** a badge awarded as the first prize in a competition.

Blue Ridge Mountains ★ *pl n* a mountain range in the eastern US, extending from West Virginia into Georgia: part of the Appalachian mountains. Highest peak: Mount Mitchell, 2038 m (6684 ft).

blues (blu:z) *pl n* (*sometimes functioning as sing*) **the. 1** a feeling of depression or deep unhappiness. **2** a type of folk song devised by Black Americans, usually employing a basic 12-bar chorus and frequent minor intervals.

blue-sky *n* (*modifier*) of or denoting theoretical research without regard to any future application of its result: *a blue-sky project.*

bluestocking ('blu:,stɒkɪŋ) *n Usually disparaging.* a scholarly or intellectual woman. [from the blue worsted stockings worn by members of an 18th-cent. literary society]

bluestone ('blu:,stəʊn) *n* **1** a blue-grey sandstone containing much clay, used for building and paving. **2** the blue crystalline form of copper sulphate.

bluetit ('blu:,tɪt) *n* a common European tit having a blue crown, wings, and tail, yellow underparts, and a black-and-grey head.

blue whale *n* the largest mammal: a widely distributed bluish-grey whalebone whale, closely related and similar to the rorquals.

bluey ('blu:ɪ) *n Austral. inf.* **1** a blanket. **2** a swagman's bundle. **3 hump (one's) bluey.** to carry one's bundle; tramp. **4** a variant of **blue** (sense 9). **5** a cattle dog. [(for senses 1, 2, 4) C19: from BLUE (on account of their colour) + -Y²]

Bluey ('blu:ɪ) *n* a variant of **Blue.**

bluff¹ (blʌf) *vb* **1** to pretend to be confident about an uncertain issue in order to influence (someone). ◆ *n* **2** deliberate deception intended to create the impression of a stronger position than one actually has. **3 call someone's bluff.** to challenge someone to give proof of his claims. [C19: orig. US poker-playing term, from Du. *bluffen* to boast]
▶ **'bluffer** *n*

★ people and places

bluff² (blʌf) n **1** a steep promontory, bank, or cliff. **2** Canad. a clump of trees on the prairie; copse. ◆ adj **3** good-naturedly frank and hearty. **4** (of a bank, cliff, etc.) presenting a steep broad face. [C17 (in the sense: nearly perpendicular): ?from MDu. blaf broad]
▸ 'bluffly adv ▸ 'bluffness n

bluish or **blueish** ('bluːɪʃ) adj somewhat blue.

Blum ★ (bluːm) n **Léon** (leɔ̃). 1872–1950, French socialist statesman; premier of France (1936–37; 1938; 1946–47).

Blunden ★ ('blʌndən) n **Edmund** (**Charles**). 1896–1974, British writer, noted for Undertones of War (1928).

blunder ('blʌndə) n **1** a stupid or clumsy mistake. **2** a foolish tactless remark. ◆ vb (mainly intr) **3** to make stupid or clumsy mistakes. **4** to make foolish tactless remarks. **5** (often foll. by about, into, etc.) to act clumsily; stumble. **6** (tr) to mismanage; botch. [C14: of Scand. origin; cf. ON blunda to close one's eyes]
▸ 'blunderer n ▸ 'blundering n, adj

blunderbuss ('blʌndəˌbʌs) n an obsolete short musket with large bore and flared muzzle. [C17: changed (infl. by BLUNDER) from Du. donderbus; from donder THUNDER + obs. bus gun]

blunge (blʌndʒ) vb **blunges, blunging, blunged.** (tr) to mix (clay or a similar substance) with water in order to form a suspension for use in ceramics. [C19: prob. from BLEND + PLUNGE]
▸ 'blunger n

Blunkett ★ ('blʌŋkɪt) n **David.** born 1947, British Labour politician; secretary of state for education and employment from 1997.

blunt (blʌnt) adj **1** (esp. of a knife or blade) lacking sharpness or keenness; dull. **2** not having a sharp edge or point: a blunt instrument. **3** (of people, manner of speaking, etc.) straightforward and uncomplicated. ◆ vb (tr) **4** to make less sharp. **5** to diminish the sensitivity or perception of; make dull. [C12: prob. of Scand. origin]
▸ 'bluntly adv ▸ 'bluntness n

Blunt ★ (blʌnt) n **Anthony.** 1907–83, British art historian and Soviet spy.

blur (blɜː) vb **blurs, blurring, blurred. 1** to make or become vague or less distinct. **2** to smear or smudge. **3** (tr) to make (the judgment, memory, or perception) less clear; dim. ◆ n **4** something vague, hazy, or indistinct. **5** a smear or smudge. [C16: ? var. of BLEAR]
▸ **blurred** adj ▸ 'blurry adj

blurb (blɜːb) n a promotional description, as on the jackets of books. [C20: coined by G. Burgess (1866–1951), US humorist & illustrator]

blurt (blɜːt) vb (tr; often foll. by out) to utter suddenly and involuntarily. [C16: prob. imit.]

blush (blʌʃ) vb **1** (intr) to become suddenly red in the face from embarrassment, shame, modesty, or guilt; redden. **2** to make or become reddish or rosy. ◆ n **3** a sudden reddening of the face from embarrassment, shame, modesty, or guilt. **4** a rosy glow. **5** a cloudy area on the surface of freshly applied gloss paint. **6** another word for rosé. **7 at first blush.** when first seen; as a first impression. [OE blȳscan]

blusher ('blʌʃə) n a cosmetic applied to the cheeks to give a rosy colour.

bluster ('blʌstə) vb **1** to speak or say loudly or boastfully. **2** to act in a bullying way. **3** (tr; foll. by into) to force or attempt to force (a person) into doing something by behaving thus. **4** (intr) (of the wind) to be noisy or gusty. ◆ n **5** boisterous talk or action; swagger. **6** empty threats or protests. **7** a strong wind; gale. [C15: prob. from MLow G blüsteren to storm, blow violently]
▸ 'blusterer n ▸ 'blustery adj

Blvd abbrev. for Boulevard.

Blyth¹ ★ (blaɪð) n a port in N England, in SE Northumberland, on the North Sea. Pop.: 35 327 (1991).

Blyth² ★ (blaɪð) n Sir **Chay** (tʃeɪ). born 1940, British yachtsman, who sailed round the world alone (1970–71).

Blyton ★ ('blaɪtᵊn) n **Enid** (**Mary**). 1897–1968, British writer of children's books.

BM abbrev. for: **1** Bachelor of Medicine. **2** Surveying. benchmark. **3** British Museum.

BMA abbrev. for British Medical Association.

BMC abbrev. for British Medical Council.

B-movie n a film originally made (esp. in the 1940s and 50s) as a supporting film, now often considered as a genre in its own right.

BMus abbrev. for Bachelor of Music.

BMX 1 abbrev. for bicycle motocross: stunt riding over an obstacle course on a bicycle. ◆ n **2** a bicycle designed for bicycle motocross.

Bn abbrev. for: **1** Baron. **2** Battalion.

BNFL abbrev. for British Nuclear Fuels Limited.

bo or **boh** (bəʊ) interj an exclamation to startle or surprise someone, esp. a child in a game.

BO abbrev. for: **1** Inf. body odour. **2** box office.

b.o. abbrev. for: **1** back order. **2** branch office. **3** broker's order. **4** buyer's option.

boa ('bəʊə) n **1** any of various large nonvenomous snakes of Central and South America and the Caribbean. They kill their prey by constriction. **2** a woman's long thin scarf, usually of feathers or fur. [C19: from NL, from L]

boa constrictor n a very large snake of tropical America and the Caribbean that kills its prey by constriction.

Boadicea ★ (ˌbəʊədɪˈsiːə) n another name for **Boudicca**.

boar (bɔː) n **1** an uncastrated male pig. **2** See **wild boar**. [OE bār]

board (bɔːd) n **1** a long wide flat piece of sawn timber. **2a** a smaller flat piece of rigid material for a specific purpose: ironing board. **2b** (in combination): breadboard. **3** a person's meals, provided regularly for money. **4** Arch. a table, esp. when laden with food. **5a** (sometimes functioning as pl) a group of people who officially administer a company, trust, etc. **5b** (as modifier): a board meeting. **6** any other committee or council: a board of interviewers. **7** stiff cardboard or similar material, used for the outside covers of a book. **8** a flat thin rectangular sheet of composite material, such as plasterboard or chipboard. **9** Chiefly US. **9a** a list of stock-exchange prices. **9b** Inf. the stock exchange itself. **10** Naut. the side of a ship. **11** Austral. & NZ. the part of the floor of a sheep-shearing shed where the shearers work. **12** any of various portable surfaces specially designed for indoor games such as chess, backgammon, etc. **13 go by the board.** Inf. to be in disuse, neglected, or lost: in these days courtesy goes by the board. **14 on board.** on or in a ship, boat, aeroplane, or other vehicle. **15 the boards.** the stage. ◆ vb **16** to go aboard (a vessel, train, aircraft, or other vehicle). **17** to attack (a ship) by forcing one's way aboard. **18** (tr; often foll. by up, in, etc.) to cover or shut with boards. **19** (intr) to receive meals or meals and lodging in return for money. **20** (sometimes foll. by out) to arrange for (someone, esp. a child) to receive food and lodging away from home. **21** (in ice hockey and box lacrosse) to bodycheck an opponent against the boards. ◆ See also **boards**. [OE bord]

boarder ('bɔːdə) n **1** a pupil who lives at school during term time. **2** another word for **lodger**. **3** a person who boards a ship, esp. in an attack.

boarding ('bɔːdɪŋ) n **1** a structure of boards. **2** timber boards collectively. **3a** the act of embarking on an aircraft, train, ship, etc. **3b** (as modifier): a boarding pass. **4** (in ice hockey and box lacrosse) an act of bodychecking an opponent against the boards.

boarding house n a private house in which accommodation and meals are provided for paying guests.

boarding school n a school providing living accommodation for some or all of its pupils.

Board of Trade n (in Britain) a part of the Department of Trade and Industry responsible for the supervision of commerce and the promotion of export trade.

boardroom ('bɔːdˌruːm, -ˌrʊm) n a room where the board of directors of a company meets.

boards (bɔːdz) pl n a wooden wall about one metre high forming the enclosure in which ice hockey or box lacrosse is played.

board school n (formerly) a school managed by a board of local ratepayers.

★ people and places

boardwalk ('bɔːd,wɔːk) n US & Canad. a promenade, esp. along a beach, usually made of planks.

boast (bəʊst) vb **1** (intr; sometimes foll. by of or about) to speak in excessively proud terms of one's possessions, skills, or superior qualities; brag. **2** (tr) to possess (something to be proud of): the city boasts a fine cathedral. ◆ n **3** a bragging statement. **4** a possession, attribute, etc., that is or may be bragged about. [C13: from ?]
▶ 'boaster n ▶ 'boasting n, adj

boastful ('bəʊstfʊl) adj tending to boast; characterized by boasting.
▶ 'boastfully adv ▶ 'boastfulness n

boat (bəʊt) n **1** a small vessel propelled by oars, paddle, sails, or motor. **2** (not in technical use) another word for **ship. 3** a container for gravy, sauce, etc. **4 burn one's boats.** See burn¹ (sense 13). **5 in the same boat.** sharing the same problems. **6 miss the boat.** to lose an opportunity. **7 rock the boat.** Inf. to cause a disturbance in the existing situation. ◆ vb **8** (intr) to travel or go in a boat, esp. as a form of recreation. **9** (tr) to transport or carry in a boat. [OE bāt]

boater ('bəʊtə) n a stiff straw hat with a straight brim and flat crown.

boathook ('bəʊt,hʊk) n a pole with a hook at one end, used aboard a vessel for fending off other vessels or for catching a mooring buoy.

boathouse ('bəʊt,haʊs) n a shelter by the edge of a river, lake, etc., for housing boats.

boatie ('bəʊtɪ) n Austral. & NZ inf. a boating enthusiast.

boating ('bəʊtɪŋ) n rowing, sailing, or cruising in boats as a form of recreation.

boatload ('bəʊt,ləʊd) n the amount of cargo or number of people held by a boat or ship.

boatman ('bəʊtmən) n, pl **boatmen.** a man who works on, hires out, or repairs a boat or boats.

boatswain, bosun, or **bo's'n** ('bəʊs°n) n a petty officer or a warrant officer who is responsible for the maintenance of a ship and its equipment. [OE bātswegen; see BOAT, SWAIN]

boat train n a train scheduled to take passengers to or from a particular ship.

Boa Vista ★ (Portuguese 'boːə 'viʃtə) n a town in N Brazil, capital of the federal territory of Roraima, on the Rio Branco. Pop.: 118 928 (1991).

Boaz ★ (ˈbəʊæz) n Old Testament. a kinsman of Naomi, who married her daughter-in-law Ruth (Ruth 2–4); one of David's ancestors.

bob¹ (bɒb) vb **bobs, bobbing, bobbed. 1** to move or cause to move up and down repeatedly, as while floating in water. **2** to move or cause to move with a short abrupt movement, as of the head. **3** (intr; usually foll. by up) to appear or emerge suddenly. **4** (intr; usually foll. by for) to attempt to get hold of (a floating or hanging object, esp. an apple) in the teeth as a game. ◆ n **5** a short abrupt movement, as of the head. [C14: from ?]

bob² (bɒb) n **1** a hairstyle for women and children in which the hair is cut short evenly all round the head. **2** a dangling or hanging object, such as the weight on a pendulum or on a plumb line. **3** short for **bobsleigh. 4** a docked tail, esp. of a horse. ◆ vb **bobs, bobbing, bobbed. 5** (tr) to cut (the hair) in a bob. **6** (tr) to cut short (something, esp. the tail of an animal); dock or crop. **7** (intr) to ride on a bobsleigh. [C14 bobbe bunch of flowers]

bob³ (bɒb) n, pl **bob.** Brit. (formerly) an informal word for a shilling. [C19: from ?]

bobbejaan ('bɒbə,jɑːn) n S. African. **1** a baboon. **2** a large black spider. **3** a monkey wrench. [from Afrik., from MDu. babiaen]

bobbin ('bɒbɪn) n a spool or reel on which thread or yarn is wound. [C16: from OF bobine, from ?]

bobble ('bɒb°l) n **1** a short jerky motion, as of a cork floating on disturbed water; bobbing movement. **2** a tufted ball, usually for ornament, as on a knitted hat. ◆ vb **3** (intr) Sport. (of a ball) to bounce with a rapid, erratic motion due to an uneven playing surface. [C19: from BOB¹ (vb)]

bobby ('bɒbɪ) n, pl **bobbies.** Inf. a British policeman.

[C19: from Bobby, after Robert PEEL, who set up the Metropolitan Police Force in 1828]

bobby calf n an unweaned calf culled for slaughter.

bobby-dazzler n Dialect. anything outstanding, striking, or showy. [C19: expanded from dazzler something striking or attractive]

bobby pin n US, Canad., Austral., & NZ. a metal hairpin bent in order to hold the hair in place.

bobby socks pl n ankle-length socks worn by teenage girls, esp. in the US in the 1940s.

bobcat ('bɒb,kæt) n a North American feline mammal, closely related to but smaller than the lynx, having reddish-brown fur with dark spots or stripes, tufted ears, and a short tail. Also called: **bay lynx.** [C19: from BOB² + CAT¹]

Bobo-Dioulasso ★ ('bəʊbəʊdjuːˈlæsəʊ) n a city in W Burkina-Faso. Pop.: 300 000 (1993 est.).

bobolink ('bɒbə,lɪŋk) n an American songbird, the male of which has a white back and black underparts. [C18: imit.]

bobotie (bʊˈbʊtɪ) n a South African dish consisting of curried mincemeat with a topping of beaten egg baked to a crust. [C19: from Afrik., prob. from Malay]

Bobruisk or **Bobruysk** ★ (Russian baˈbruːjsk) n a port in Belarus on the River Berezina: engineering, timber, tyre manufacturing. Pop.: 227 100 (1996 est.).

bobsleigh ('bɒb,sleɪ) n **1** a racing sledge for two or more people, with a steering mechanism enabling the driver to direct it down a steeply banked ice-covered run. ◆ vb **2** (intr) to ride on a bobsleigh. ◆ Also called (esp. US and Canad.): **bobsled** ('bɒb,sled). [C19: BOB² + SLEIGH]

bobstay ('bɒb,steɪ) n a strong stay between a bowsprit and the stem of a vessel for holding down the bowsprit. [C18: ?from BOB¹ + STAY³]

bobsy-die ('bɒbzɪ,daɪ) n NZ inf. fuss; confusion (esp. in **kick up bobsy-die**). [from C19 Bob's a-dying]

bobtail ('bɒb,teɪl) n **1** a docked or diminutive tail. **2** an animal with such a tail. ◆ adj also **bobtailed. 3** having the tail cut short. ◆ vb (tr) **4** to dock the tail of. **5** to cut short; curtail.

Boccaccio ★ (Italian bokˈkattʃo) n **Giovanni** (dʒoˈvani). 1313–75, Italian poet and writer, noted for his Decameron (1349–51), a collection of 100 short stories.

Boccherini ★ (Italian bokkeˈrini) n **Luigi** (luˈidʒi). 1743–1805, Italian composer and cellist.

Boche (bɒʃ) n Derog. sl. (esp. in World Wars I and II) **1** a German, esp. a German soldier. **2 the.** (usually functioning as pl) Germans collectively, esp. German soldiers regarded as the enemy. [C20: from F, prob. shortened from alboche German, from allemand German + caboche pate]

Bochum ★ (German 'boːxʊm) n an industrial city in NW Germany, in W North Rhine-Westphalia: university (1965). Pop.: 401 129 (1995 est.).

bockedy ('bɒkədɪ) adj Irish. (of a structure, piece of furniture, etc.) unsteady. [from Irish Gaelic bacaideach limping]

bod (bɒd) n Inf. **1** a fellow; chap: he's a queer bod. **2** another word for **body** (sense 1). [C18: short for BODY]

BOD abbrev. for: biochemical oxygen demand.

bodacious (bəʊˈdeɪʃəs) adj Sl., chiefly US. impressive or remarkable; excellent. [C19: from E dialect; blend of BOLD and AUDACIOUS]

bode¹ (bəʊd) vb **bodes, boding, boded. 1** to be an omen of (good or ill, esp. of ill); portend; presage. **2** (tr) Arch. to predict; foretell. [OE bodian]
▶ 'bodement n

bode² (bəʊd) vb a past tense of **bide.**

bodega (bəʊˈdiːgə) n a shop selling wine and sometimes groceries, esp. in a Spanish-speaking country. [C19: from Sp., ult. from Gk apothēkē storehouse]

Bodensee ★ (German 'boːdənzeː) n the German name for (Lake) Constance.

bodge (bɒdʒ) vb **bodges, bodging, bodged.** Inf. to make a mess of; botch. [C16: changed from BOTCH]

★ people and places

bodgie ('bɒdʒɪ) *Austral. & NZ sl.* ◆ *n* 1 an unruly or un-couth young man, esp. in the 1950s. ◆ *adj* 2 false, fraudulent. [C20: from BODGE]

Bodh Gaya ★ ('bɒd gə'jɑː) *n* a variant spelling of **Buddh Gaya**.

Bodhidharma ★ (ˌbəʊdɪ'dɑːmə, ˌbɒd-) *n* 6th century A.D., Indian Buddhist monk, who taught in China (from 520): considered to be the founder of Zen Buddhism.

Bodhisattva (ˌbəʊdɪ'sætvə, -wə, ˌbɒd-) *n* (in Buddhism) a divine being worthy of nirvana who remains on the human plane to help men to salvation. [Sansk., from *bodhi* enlightenment + *sattva* essence]

bodice ('bɒdɪs) *n* 1 the upper part of a woman's dress, from the shoulder to the waist. 2 a tight-fitting corset worn laced over a blouse, or (formerly) as a woman's undergarment. [C16: orig. Scot. *bodies,* pl. of BODY]

bodice ripper *n Inf.* a romantic novel, usually on a historical theme, that involves some sex and violence.

-bodied *adj* (*in combination*) having a body or bodies as specified: *able-bodied; long-bodied*.

bodiless ('bɒdɪlɪs) *adj* having no body or substance; incorporeal or insubstantial.

bodily ('bɒdɪlɪ) *adj* 1 relating to or being a part of the human body. ◆ *adv* 2 by taking hold of the body: *he threw him bodily from the platform.* 3 in person; in the flesh.

bodkin ('bɒdkɪn) *n* 1 a blunt large-eyed needle. 2 *Arch.* a dagger. 3 *Arch.* a long ornamental hairpin. [C14: prob. of Celtic origin]

Bodmin ★ ('bɒdmɪn) *n* a market town in SW England, in Cornwall, near **Bodmin Moor**, a granite upland rising to 420 m (1375 ft). Pop.: 12 553 (1991).

body ('bɒdɪ) *n, pl* **bodies. 1a** the entire physical structure of an animal or human being. Related *adj*: **corporeal. 1b** (*as modifier*): *body odour.* 2 the trunk or torso. 3 a dead human or animal; corpse. 4 the flesh as opposed to the spirit. 5 the largest or main part of anything: *the body of a vehicle; the body of a plant.* 6 a separate or distinct mass of water or land. 7 a number of individuals regarded as a single entity; group. 8 fullness in the appearance of the hair. 9 the characteristic full quality of certain wines. 10 firmness, esp. of cloth. 11a the pigment contained in or added to paint, dye, etc. 11b the opacity of a paint. 11c (*as modifier*): *body colour.* 12 an informal or dialect word for a **person. 13** another word for **bodysuit** (sense 1). 14 **keep body and soul together.** to manage to keep alive; survive. ◆ *vb* **bodies, bodying, bodied.** (*tr*) 15 (usually foll. by *forth*) to give a body or shape to. [OE *bodig*]

body blow *n* 1 *Boxing.* a blow to an opponent's body. 2 a severe disappointment or setback.

body building *n* the practice of exercises to make the muscles of the body conspicuous.

bodycheck ('bɒdɪˌtʃɛk) *Ice hockey, etc.* ◆ *n* 1 obstruction of another player. ◆ *vb* 2 (*tr*) to deliver a bodycheck to (an opponent).

body double *n Films.* a person who substitutes for a star for the filming of a scene that involves shots of the body rather than the face.

bodyguard ('bɒdɪˌgɑːd) *n* a person or group of people who escort and protect someone.

body horror *n* a genre of horror film in which the main feature is the graphically depicted destruction or degeneration of a human body or bodies.

body language *n* the nonverbal imparting of information by means of conscious or subconscious bodily gestures, posture, etc.

body-line *adj Cricket.* denoting or relating to fast bowling aimed at the batsman's body.

body politic *n* **the.** the people of a nation or the nation itself considered as a political entity.

body search *n* 1 a form of search by police, customs officials, etc., that involves examination of a prisoner's or suspect's bodily orifices. ◆ *vb* **body-search.** 2 (*tr*) to search (a prisoner or suspect) in this manner.

body shop *n* a repair yard for vehicle bodywork.

body snatcher *n* (formerly) a person who robbed graves and sold the corpses for dissection.

body stocking *n* a one-piece undergarment for women, usually of nylon, covering the torso.

bodysuit ('bɒdɪˌsuːt, -ˌsjuːt) *n* 1 a woman's close-fitting one-piece garment for the torso. Sometimes shortened to **body.** 2 a one-piece undergarment for a baby.

body swerve *n* 1 *Sport.* (esp. in football games) the act or an instance of swerving past an opponent. 2 *Scot.* the act or an instance of avoiding (a situation considered unpleasant): *I think I'll give the meeting a body swerve.* ◆ *vb* **body-swerve, body-swerves, body-swerving, body-swerved. 3** *Sport.* (esp. in football games) to pass (an opponent) using a body swerve. 4 *Scot.* to avoid (a situation or person considered unpleasant).

body warmer *n* a sleeveless type of jerkin, usually quilted, worn as an outer garment.

bodywork ('bɒdɪˌwɜːk) *n* the external shell of a motor vehicle.

Boeotia ★ (bɪ'əʊʃɪə) *n* 1 a region of ancient Greece, northwest of Athens. It consisted of ten city-states, which formed the Boeotian League, led by Thebes: at its height in the 4th century B.C. 2 transliteration of the Modern Greek name for **Voiotia.**

Boeotian (bɪ'əʊʃɪən) *adj* 1 of Boeotia. 2 dull or stupid. ◆ *n* 3 a person from Boeotia. 4 a dull or stupid person.

Boer (bʊə) *n* a a descendant of any of the Dutch or Huguenot colonists who settled in South Africa. b (*as modifier*): *a Boer farmer.* [C19: from Du. *Boer*; see BOOR]

boerbul ('bʊəbəl) *n S. African.* a crossbred mastiff used esp. as a watchdog. [from Afrik. *boerboel,* from *boel* large dog]

boeremusiek ('bʊərəˌmœsɪk) *n S. African.* light music associated with the culture of the Afrikaners. [from Afrik. *boere* country, folk + *musiek* music]

boet (but) or **boetie** *n S. African inf.* a friend. [from Afrik.: brother]

Boethius ★ (bəʊ'iːθɪəs) *n* **Anicius Manlius Severinus** (ə'nɪsɪəs 'mænlɪəs ˌsevə'raɪnəs). ?480–?524 A.D., Roman philosopher and statesman, noted for *De Consolatione Philosophiae*: executed by Theodoric for treason.

boffin ('bɒfɪn) *n Brit. inf.* a scientist, esp. one carrying out military research. [C20: from ?]

boffo ('bɒfəʊ) *adj Sl.* very good; highly successful. [C20: from ?]

Bofors gun ('bəʊfəz) *n* an automatic 40 mm anti-aircraft gun, one or more of which are controlled by a radar-operated computer system mounted on a lightweight vehicle. [C20: after the Swedish armament firm that developed it]

bog (bɒg) *n* 1 wet spongy ground consisting of decomposing vegetation. 2 an area of such ground. 3 a slang word for **lavatory.** [C13: from Gaelic *bogach* swamp, from *bog* soft]
► **'boggy** *adj* ► **'bogginess** *n*

bogan ('bəʊgən) *n Canad.* (esp. in the Maritime Provinces) a sluggish side stream. Also called: **logan, pokelogan.** [of Algonquian origin]

Bogarde ★ ('bəʊgɑːd) *n* **Dirk,** real name *Derek Jules Gaspard Ulric Niven van den Bogaerde.* 1920–99, British film actor and writer: his films include *The Servant* (1963) and *Death in Venice* (1970). His writings include the autobiographical *A Postillion Struck by Lightning* (1977) and the novels *Jericho* (1992) and *A Period of Adjustment* (1994).

Bogart ★ ('bəʊgɑːt) *n* **Humphrey (DeForest).** nicknamed *Bogie.* 1899–1957, US film actor: his films include *High Sierra* (1941), *Casablanca* (1942), and *The Caine Mutiny* (1954).

Boğazköy ★ (*Turkish* bɔ:'ɑzkœi) *n* a village in central Asia Minor: site of the ancient Hittite capital.

bogbean ('bɒgˌbiːn) *n* another name for **buckbean.**

bog down *vb* **bogs, bogging, bogged.** (*adv*; when *tr, often passive*) to impede or be impeded physically or mentally.

bogey or **bogy** ('bəʊgɪ) *n* 1 an evil or mischievous spirit. 2 something that worries or annoys. 3 *Golf.* **3a** a score of one stroke over par on a hole. Cf. **par** (sense 5). **3b** *Obs.* a standard score for a hole or course, regarded as one that a good player should make. **4** *Sl.* a piece of dried mucus discharged from the nose. [C19: prob. rel. to obs. *bug* an evil spirit and BOGLE]

bogeyman ('bəʊgɪˌmæn) *n, pl* **bogeymen.** a person, real or imaginary, used as a threat, esp. to children.

boggle ('bɒgºl) *vb* **boggles, boggling, boggled.** (*intr;* often foll. by *at*) **1** to be surprised, confused, or alarmed (esp. in **the mind boggles**). **2** to hesitate or be evasive when confronted with a problem. [C16: prob. var. of BOGLE]

bogie *or* **bogy** ('bəʊgɪ) *n* **1** an assembly of four or six wheels forming a pivoted support at either end of a railway coach. **2** *Chiefly Brit.* a small railway truck of short wheelbase, used for conveying coal, ores, etc. [C19: from ?]

bogle ('bəʊgºl, 'bɒg-) *n* a dialect or archaic word for **bogey** (sense 1). [C16: from Scot. *bogill*]

bog myrtle *n* another name for **sweet gale.**

Bognor Regis ★ ('bɒgnə 'riːdʒɪs) *n* a resort in S England, in West Sussex on the English Channel: electronics industries. *Regis* was added to the name after King George V's convalescence there in 1929. Pop.: 56 744 (1991).

bog oak *n* oak found preserved in peat bogs.

bog off *Brit. sl.* ♦ *interj* **1** go away! ♦ *vb* **bogs, bogging, bogged. 2** (*intr, adv*) to go away.

bogong ('bəʊˌgɒŋ) *or* **bugong** ('buːˌgɒŋ) *n* an edible dark-coloured Australian noctuid moth.

Bogor ★ ('bəʊgɔː) *n* a city in Indonesia, in W Java: botanical gardens and research institutions. Pop.: 271 711 (1990). Former name: **Buitenzorg.**

Bogotá ★ (ˌbəʊgə'taː; *Spanish* boɣo'ta) *n* the capital of Colombia, on a central plateau of the E Andes: originally the centre of Chibcha civilization; founded as a city in 1538 by the Spaniards. Pop.: 5 237 635 (1995 est.).

bog-standard *adj Brit. & Irish sl.* completely ordinary; run-of-the-mill.

bogtrotter ('bɒgˌtrɒtə) *n* a derogatory term for an Irishman, esp. an Irish peasant.

bogus ('bəʊgəs) *adj* spurious or counterfeit; not genuine. [C19: from *bogus* apparatus for making counterfeit money]
► **'bogusly** *adv* ► **'bogusness** *n*

bogy ('bəʊgɪ) *n, pl* **bogies.** a variant spelling of **bogey** or **bogie.**

Bohai ('bɔː'haɪ) *or* **Pohai** ★ *n* a large inlet of the Yellow Sea on the coast of NE China. Also called: (Gulf of) **Chihli.**

bohea (bəʊ'hiː) *n* a black Chinese tea, once regarded as the choicest, but now as an inferior grade. [C18: from Chinese *Wu-i Shan,* range of hills on which this tea was grown]

Bohemia ★ (bəʊ'hiːmɪə) *n* **1** a former kingdom of central Europe, surrounded by mountains: independent from the 9th to the 13th century; belonged to the Hapsburgs from 1526 until 1918. **2** an area of the W Czech Republic, formerly a province (1918–49) of Czechoslovakia. From 1939 until 1945 it formed part of the German protectorate of **Bohemia-Moravia.** Czech name: **Čechy.** German name: **Böhmen** ('bøːmən). **3** a district frequented by unconventional people, esp. artists or writers.

Bohemian (bəʊ'hiːmɪən) *n* **1** a native or inhabitant of Bohemia; a Czech. **2** (*often not cap.*) a person, esp. an artist or writer, who lives an unconventional life. **3** the Czech language. ♦ *adj* **4** of, relating to, or characteristic of Bohemia, its people, or their language. **5** unconventional in appearance, behaviour, etc.

Bohemian Forest ★ *n* a mountain range between the SW Czech Republic and SE Germany. Highest peak: Arber, 1457 m (4780 ft). Czech name: **Český Les** ('tʃɛski: 'lɛs). German name: **Böhmerwald** ('bøːmər'valt).

Bohemianism (bəʊ'hiːmɪəˌnɪzəm) *n* unconventional behaviour or appearance, esp. of an artist.

Böhm ★ (*German* bøːm) *n* **Karl** (karl). 1894–1981, Austrian orchestral conductor.

Bohol ★ (bəʊ'hɔːl) *n* an island of the central Philippines.

Chief town: Tagbilaran. Pop.: 948 000 (1990). Area about 3900 sq. km (1500 sq. miles).

Bohr ★ (bɔː; *Danish* boːr) *n* **1 Aage Niels** ('ɔːɣə neːls). born 1922, Danish physicist, noted for his work on nuclear structure: shared the Nobel prize for physics 1975. **2** his father, **Niels** (**Henrik David**) (neːls). 1885–1962, Danish physicist, who applied the quantum theory to Rutherford's model of the atom: Nobel prize for physics 1922.

bohrium ('bɔːrɪəm) *n* a transuranic element artificially produced in minute quantities by bombarding [204]Bi atoms with [54]Cr nuclei. Symbol: Bh; atomic no.: 107. Former names: **element 107, unnilheptium.** [C20: after N. BOHR]

boil[1] (bɔɪl) *vb* **1** to change or cause to change from a liquid to a vapour so rapidly that bubbles of vapour are formed in the liquid. **2** to reach or cause to reach boiling point. **3** to cook or be cooked by the process of boiling. **4** (*intr*) to bubble and be agitated like something boiling; seethe: *the ocean was boiling.* **5** (*intr*) to be extremely angry or indignant. ♦ *n* **6** the state or action of boiling. ♦ See also **boil away, boil down, boil over.** [C13: from OF, from L, from *bulla* a bubble]

boil[2] (bɔɪl) *n* a red painful swelling with a hard pus-filled core caused by bacterial infection of the skin. Technical name: **furuncle.** [OE *bȳle*]

boil away *vb* (*adv*) **1** to cause (liquid) to evaporate completely by boiling or (of liquid) to evaporate completely.

boil down *vb* (*adv*) **1** to reduce or be reduced in quantity by boiling. **2 boil down to. 2a** (*intr*) to be the essential element in something. **2b** (*tr*) to summarize; reduce to essentials.

Boileau ★ (*French* bwalo) *n* **Nicolas** (nikɔla). full name *Nicolas Boileau-Despréaux.* 1636–1711, French poet; author of *L'Art poétique* (1674).

boiled shirt *n Inf.* a dress shirt with a stiff front.

boiler ('bɔɪlə) *n* **1** a closed vessel in which water is heated to supply steam or provide heat. **2** a domestic device to provide hot water, esp. for central heating. **3** a large tub for boiling laundry.

boilermaker ('bɔɪləˌmeɪkə) *n* a person who works with metal in heavy industry; plater or welder.

boilerplate ('bɔɪləˌpleɪt) *n* **1** a form of mild-steel plate used in the production of boiler shells. **2** a copy made with the intention of making other copies from it. **3** a set of instructions incorporated in several places in a computer program or a standard form of words used repeatedly in drafting contracts, guarantees, etc. **4** a draft contract that can be modified to cover various types of transaction.

boiler suit *n Brit.* a one-piece overall work garment.

boiling point *n* **1** the temperature at which a liquid boils at sea level. **2** *Inf.* the condition of being angered or highly excited.

boiling-water reactor *n* a nuclear reactor using water as coolant and moderator, steam being produced in the reactor itself. Abbrev.: **BWR.**

boil over *vb* (*adv*) **1** to overflow or cause to overflow while boiling. **2** (*intr*) to burst out in anger or excitement.

Bois de Boulogne ★ (*French* bwa də bulɔɲ) *n* a large park in W Paris, formerly a forest: includes the racecourses of Auteuil and Longchamp.

Boise *or* **Boise City** ★ ('bɔɪzɪ, -sɪ) *n* a city in SW Idaho: the state capital. Pop.: 145 987 (1994 est.).

Bois-le-Duc ★ (bwa lə dyk) *n* the French name for **'s Hertogenbosch.**

boisterous ('bɔɪstərəs, -strəs) *adj* **1** noisy and lively; unruly. **2** (of the wind, sea, etc.) stormy. [C13 *boistuous,* from ?]
► **'boisterously** *adv* ► **'boisterousness** *n*

Boito ★ (*Italian* 'bɔːito) *n* **Arrigo** (ar'riːgo). 1842–1918, Italian composer and librettist, whose works include the opera *Mefistofele* (1868) and the librettos for Verdi's *Otello* and *Falstaff.*

Bokassa I ★ (bə'kæsə) *n* original name *Jean Bedel Bokassa.* 1921–96, president of the Central African Republic (1972–76); emperor of the renamed Central African Empire from 1976 until overthrown in 1979.

ok choy ('bɒk 'tʃɔɪ) *n* a Chinese plant that is related to the cabbage and has edible stalks and leaves. Also called: **Chinese cabbage, Chinese leaf.** [from Chinese dialect, lit.: white vegetable]

okhara ★ (buˈxɑːrə) *n* a variant spelling of **Bukhara.**

ol. *abbrev. for* Bolivia(n).

ola ('bəʊlə) *or* **bolas** ('bəʊləs) *n, pl* **bolas** *or* **bolases.** a missile used by gauchos and Indians of South America, consisting of heavy balls on a cord. It is hurled at a running quarry, so as to entangle its legs. [Sp.: ball, from L *bulla* knob]

oland ★ ('bʊəlant) *n* an area of high altitude in SW South Africa.

olan Pass ★ (bəʊ'lɑːn) *n* a mountain pass in W central Pakistan through the Brahui Range, between Sibi and Quetta, rising to 1800 m (5900 ft).

old (bəʊld) *adj* **1** courageous, confident, and fearless; ready to take risks. **2** showing or requiring courage: *a bold plan.* **3** immodest or impudent: *she gave him a bold look.* **4** standing out distinctly; conspicuous: *a figure carved in bold relief.* **5** very steep: *the bold face of the cliff.* **6** imaginative in thought or expression. [OE *beald*]
▸ **'boldly** *adv* ▸ **'boldness** *n*

old face *Printing.* ◆ *n* **1** a weight of type characterized by thick heavy lines, as the entry words in this dictionary. ◆ *adj* **boldface. 2** (of type) having this weight.

oldrewood ★ ('bəʊldə,wʊd) *n* **Rolf,** real name *Thomas Alexander Browne.* 1826–1915, noted for his novels of the Australian outback, esp. *Robbery Under Arms* (1882–3).

ole (bəʊl) *n* the trunk of a tree. [C14: from ON *bolr*]

olero (bə'lɛərəʊ) *n, pl* **boleros. 1** a Spanish dance, usually in triple time. **2** a piece of music for or in the rhythm of this dance. **3** (*also* 'bɒlərəʊ). a short open bodice-like jacket not reaching the waist. [C18: from Sp.]

oleyn ★ (bə'lɪn, 'bʊlɪn) *n* **Anne.** 1507–36, second wife of Henry VIII of England; mother of Elizabeth I. She was executed on a charge of adultery.

olingbroke ★ ('bɒlɪŋ,brʊk) *n* **1** the surname of **Henry IV** of England. **2 Henry St John,** 1st Viscount Bolingbroke. 1678–1751, English politician; fled to France in 1714 and acted as secretary of state to the Old Pretender; returned to England in 1723.

olivar ★ ('bɒlɪ,vɑː; *Spanish* bo'liβar) *n* **Simon** (si'mon). 1783–1830, South American soldier, who drove the Spaniards from Venezuela, Colombia, Ecuador, and Peru hoping to set up a republican confederation, but was prevented by separatist movements in Venezuela and Colombia (1829–30). Upper Peru became a separate state, called Bolivia in his honour.

olivia ★ (bə'lɪvɪə) *n* an inland republic in central S America: original Aymará Indian population conquered by the Incas in the 13th century; colonized by Spain from 1538; became a republic in 1825; consists of low plains in the east, with ranges of the Andes rising to over 6400 m (21 000 ft) and the Altiplano, a plateau averaging 3900 m (13 000 ft) in the west; contains some of the world's highest inhabited regions; important producer of tin and other minerals. Official languages: Spanish, Quechua, and Aymara. Religion: Roman Catholic. Currency: boliviano. Capital: La Paz (administrative); Sucre (judicial). Pop.: 7 767 000 (1997). Area: 1 098 580 sq. km (424 260 sq. miles).
▸ **Bo'livian** *adj, n*

oliviano (bə,lɪvɪ'ɑːnəʊ; *Spanish* boli'βjano) **bolivianos** (-nəʊz; *Spanish* -nos). (until 1963 and from 1987) the standard monetary unit of Bolivia, equal to 100 centavos.

oll (bəʊl) *n* the fruit of such plants as flax and cotton, consisting of a rounded capsule containing the seeds. [C13: from Du. *bolle*; rel. to OE *bolla* BOWL[1]]

ollard ('bɒlɑːd, 'bɒləd) *n* **1** a strong wooden or metal post on a wharf, quay, etc., used for securing mooring lines. **2** *Brit.* a small post placed on a kerb or traffic island to make it conspicuous to motorists. [C14: ?from BOLE + -ARD]

bollocking ('bɒləkɪŋ) *n Sl.* a severe telling-off. [from *bollock* (vb) in the sense "to reprimand"]

bollocks ('bɒləks) *or* **ballocks** *Taboo sl.* ◆ *pl n* **1** another word for **testicles. 2** nonsense; rubbish. ◆ *interj* **3** an exclamation of annoyance, disbelief, etc. [OE *beallucas;* see BALL[1]]

boll weevil *n* a greyish weevil of the southern US and Mexico, whose larvae live in and destroy cotton bolls.

Bollywood ('bɒlɪ,wʊd) *n Inf.* **a** the Indian film industry. **b** (*as modifier*): *a Bollywood star.* [C20: from Bo(MBAY) + (Ho)LLYWOOD]

Bologna[1] ★ (bə'ləʊnjə; *Italian* bo'lɔɲɲa) *n* a city in N Italy, at the foot of the Apennines: became a free city in the Middle Ages; university (1088). Pop.: 394 969 (1994 est.). Ancient name: **Bononia** (bə'əʊnɪə).
▸ **Bolognese** (,bɒlə'niːz, -'neɪz) *adj, n*

Bologna[2] ★ (bə'ləʊnjə; *Italian* bo'lɔɲɲa) *n* **Giovanni da** (dʒo'vanni da). See **Giambologna.**

bologna sausage (bə'ləʊnjə) *n Chiefly US & Canad.* a large smoked sausage made of seasoned mixed meats. Also called: **baloney, boloney,** (esp. Brit.) **polony.**

bolometer (bəʊ'lɒmɪtə) *n* a sensitive instrument for measuring radiant energy. [C19: from Gk *bolē* ray of light, from *ballein* to throw + -METER]
▸ **bolometric** (,bəʊlə'metrɪk) *adj*

boloney (bə'ləʊnɪ) *n* **1** a variant of **baloney. 2** another name for **bologna sausage.**

Bolshevik ('bɒlʃɪvɪk) *n, pl* **Bolsheviks** *or* **Bolsheviki** (,bɒlʃɪ'viːkɪ). **1** (formerly) a Russian Communist. Cf. **Menshevik. 2** any Communist. **3** (*often not cap.*) *Inf. & derog.* any political radical, esp. a revolutionary. [C20: from Russian *Bol'shevik* majority, from *bol'shoi* great]
▸ **'Bolshe,vism** *n* ▸ **'Bolshevist** *adj, n*

bolshie *or* **bolshy** ('bɒlʃɪ) (*sometimes cap.*) *Brit. inf.* ◆ *adj* **1** difficult to manage; rebellious. **2** politically radical or left-wing. ◆ *n, pl* **bolshies. 3** *Derog.* any political radical. [C20: shortened from BOLSHEVIK]

bolster ('bəʊlstə) *vb* (*tr*) **1** (often foll. by *up*) to support or reinforce; strengthen: *to bolster morale.* **2** to prop up with a pillow or cushion. ◆ *n* **3** a long narrow pillow or cushion. **4** any pad or padded support. **5** a cold chisel used for cutting stone slabs, etc. [OE *bolster*]

bolt[1] (bəʊlt) *n* **1** a bar that can be slid into a socket to lock a door, gate, etc. **2** a bar or rod that forms part of a locking mechanism and is moved by a key or a knob. **3** a metal rod or pin that has a head and a screw thread to take a nut. **4** a sliding bar in a breech-loading firearm that ejects the empty cartridge, replaces it with a new one, and closes the breech. **5** a flash of lightning. **6** a sudden start or movement, esp. in order to escape. **7** a roll of something, such as cloth, wallpaper, etc. **8** an arrow, esp. for a crossbow. **9 a bolt from the blue.** a sudden, unexpected, and usually unwelcome event. **10 shoot one's bolt.** to exhaust one's efforts. ◆ *vb* **11** (*tr*) to secure or lock with or as with a bolt. **12** (*tr*) to eat hurriedly. **13** (*intr*; usually foll. *by from* or *out*) to move or jump suddenly: *he bolted from the chair.* **14** (*intr*) (esp. of a horse) to start hurriedly and run away without warning. **15** (*tr*) to roll (cloth, wallpaper, etc.) into bolts. **16** (*intr*) (of cultivated plants) to produce flowers and seeds prematurely. ◆ *adv* **17** stiffly, firmly, or rigidly (archaic except in **bolt upright**). [OE *bolt* arrow]
▸ **'bolter** *n*

bolt[2] *or* **boult** (bəʊlt) *vb* (*tr*) **1** to pass (a powder, etc.) through a sieve. **2** to examine and separate. [C13: from OF *bulter,* prob. of Gmc origin]
▸ **'bolter** *or* **'boulter** *n*

Bolt ★ (bəʊlt) *n* **Robert** (Oxton). 1924–95, British playwright. His plays include *A Man for All Seasons* (1960) and he wrote a number of screenplays.

bolt hole *n* a place of escape from danger.

Bolton ★ ('bəʊltən) *n* **1** a town in NW England: centre of the woollen trade since the 14th century; later important for cotton. Pop.: 139 020 (1991). **2** a unitary authority in NW England, in Greater Manchester. Pop.: 258 584 (1991 est.). Area: 140 sq. km (54 sq. miles).

★ people and places

boltrope ('bəʊlt,rəʊp) *n Naut.* a rope sewn to the foot or luff of a sail to strengthen it.

Boltzmann ★ (*German* 'bɒltsman) *n* **Ludwig** ('luːtvɪç). 1844–1906, Austrian physicist. He developed the kinetic theory of gases with J. C. Maxwell.

bolus ('bəʊləs) *n, pl* **boluses. 1** a small round soft mass, esp. of chewed food. **2** a large pill or tablet used in veterinary and clinical medicine. [C17: from NL, from Gk *bōlos* clod, lump]

Bolzano ★ (*Italian* bol'tsaːno) *n* a city in NE Italy, in Trentino-Alto Adige: belonged to Austria until 1919. Pop.: 100 380 (1990). German name: **Bozen.**

Boma ★ ('bəʊma) *n* a port in the Democratic Republic of the Congo (formerly Zaïre), capital (of the Belgian Congo) until 1926: forest products. Pop.: 135 284 (1994 est.).

bomb (bɒm) *n* **1a** a hollow projectile containing explosive, incendiary, or other destructive substance. **1b** (*as modifier*): *bomb disposal; a bomb bay.* **1c** (*in combination*): *bombproof.* **2** an object in which an explosive device has been planted: *a car bomb; a letter bomb.* **3** a round mass of volcanic rock, solidified from molten lava that has been thrown into the air. **4** *Med.* a container for radioactive material, applied therapeutically to any part of the body: *a cobalt bomb.* **5** *Brit. sl.* a large sum of money. **6** *US & Canad. sl.* a disastrous failure: *the new play was a total bomb.* **7** *Austral. & NZ sl.* an old or dilapidated motorcar. **8** *American football.* a very long high pass. **9 like a bomb.** *Brit. & NZ inf.* with great speed or success; very well. **10 the bomb.** a hydrogen or an atomic bomb considered as the ultimate destructive weapon. ◆ *vb* **11** to attack with or as if with a bomb or bombs; drop bombs (on). **12** (*intr*; often foll. by *off, along,* etc.) *Inf.* to move or drive very quickly. **13** (*intr*) *US sl.* to fail disastrously. [C17: from F, from It., from L, from Gk *bombos,* imit.]

bombard *vb* (bɒm'baːd). (*tr*) **1** to attack with concentrated artillery fire or bombs. **2** to attack with vigour and persistence. **3** to attack verbally, esp. with questions. **4** *Physics.* to direct high-energy particles or photons against (atoms, nuclei, etc.). ◆ *n* ('bɒmbaːd). **5** an ancient type of cannon that threw stone balls. [C15: from OF, from *bombarde* stone-throwing cannon, prob. from L *bombus* booming sound; see BOMB]
▸ **bom'bardment** *n*

bombardier (,bɒmbə'dɪə) *n* **1** the member of a bomber aircrew responsible for aiming and releasing the bombs. **2** *Brit.* a noncommissioned rank, below the rank of sergeant, in the Royal Artillery. [C16: from OF; see BOMBARD]

Bombardier (,bɒmbə'dɪə) *n Canad. trademark.* a snow tractor, usually having caterpillar tracks at the rear and skis at the front. [C20: after J. A. *Bombardier,* Canadian inventor and manufacturer]

bombast ('bɒmbæst) *n* pompous and grandiloquent language. [C16: from OF, from Med. L *bombāx* cotton]
▸ **bom'bastic** *adj* ▸ **bom'bastically** *adv*

Bombay ★ (bɒm'beɪ) *n* a port in W India, capital of Maharashtra state, on the Arabian Sea: ceded by Portugal to England in 1661 and of major importance in British India; commercial and industrial centre, esp. for cotton. Pop.: 9 925 891 (1991). Official and Hindi name: **Mumbai.**

Bombay duck *n* a fish that is eaten dried with curry dishes as a savoury. Also called: **bummalo.** [C19: changed from *bombil* through association with Bombay, from which it was exported]

bombazine *or* **bombasine** (,bɒmbə'ziːn, 'bɒmbə,ziːn) *n* a twilled fabric, esp. one of silk and worsted, formerly worn dyed black for mourning. [C16: from OF, from L, from *bombyx* silk]

bomber ('bɒmə) *n* **1** a military aircraft designed to carry out bombing missions. **2** a person who plants bombs.

bomber jacket *n* a short jacket finishing at the waist with an elasticated band, usually having a zip front.

bombora (bɒm'bɔːrə) *n Austral.* **1** a submerged reef. **2** a turbulent area of sea over such a reef. [from Abor.]

bombshell ('bɒm,ʃɛl) *n* **1** (esp. formerly) a bomb or artillery shell. **2** a shocking or unwelcome surprise.

bombsight ('bɒm,saɪt) *n* a mechanical or electronic device in an aircraft for aiming bombs.

Bomu ('bəʊmuː) *or* **Mbomu** ★ (ᵊm'bəʊmuː) *n* a river in central Africa, rising in the SE Central African Republic and flowing west into the Uele River, forming the Ubangi River. Length: about 800 km (500 miles).

Bon ★ (bɒn) *n* **Cape.** a peninsula of NE Tunisia.

Bona ★ ('bəʊnə) *n* **Mount.** a mountain in S Alaska, in the Wrangell Mountains. Height: 5005 m (16 420 ft).

bona fide ('bəʊnə 'faɪdɪ) *adj* **1** real or genuine: *a bona fide manuscript.* **2** undertaken in good faith: *a bona fide agreement.* [C16: from L]

bona fides ('bəʊnə 'faɪdiːz) *n Law.* good faith; honest intention. [L]

Bonaire ★ (bɒn'ɛə) *n* an island in the S Caribbean, in the E Netherlands Antilles: one of the Leeward Islands. Chief town: Kralendijk. Pop.: 12 533 (1994 est.). Area: about 288 sq. km (111 sq. miles).

bonanza (bə'nænzə) *n* **1** a source, usually sudden and unexpected, of luck or wealth. **2** *US & Canad.* a mine or vein rich in ore. [C19: from Sp., lit.: calm sea, hence good luck, from Med. L, from L *bonus* good + *malacia* calm, from Gk *malakia* softness]

Bonaparte ★ ('bəʊnə,paːt; *French* bɔnapart) *n* **1** See **Napoleon I. 2 Jérôme** (ʒerom), brother of Napoleon I. 1784–1860, king of Westphalia (1807–13). **3 Joseph** (ʒozef), brother of Napoleon I. 1768–1844, king of Naples (1806–08) and of Spain (1808–13). **4 Louis** (lwi), brother of Napoleon I. 1778–1846, king of Holland (1806–10). **5 Lucien** (lysjɛ̃), brother of Napoleon I. 1775–1840, prince of Canino.

Bonaventura (,bɒnəvɛn'tjʊərə) *or* **Bonaventure** ★ ('bɒnə,vɛntʃə) *n* **Saint,** called *the Seraphic Doctor.* 1221–74, Italian Franciscan monk, mystic, theologian, and philosopher. Feast day: July 14.

bonbon ('bɒnbɒn) *n* a sweet. [C19: from F, orig. a children's word from *bon* good]

bonce (bɒns) *n Brit. sl.* the head. [C19 (orig.: a large playing marble): from ?]

bond (bɒnd) *n* **1** something that binds, fastens, or holds together. **2** (*often pl*) something that brings or holds people together; tie: *a bond of friendship.* **3** (*pl*) something that restrains or imprisons; captivity or imprisonment. **4** a written or spoken agreement, esp. a promise. **5** *Finance.* a certificate of debt issued in order to raise funds. It is repayable with or without security at a specified future date. **6** *Law.* a written acknowledgment of an obligation to pay a sum or to perform a contract. **7** any of various arrangements of bricks or stones in a wall in which they overlap so as to provide strength. **8 chemical bond.** a mutual attraction between two atoms resulting from a redistribution of their outer electrons, determining chemical properties, shown in some formulae by a dot (.) or score (—). **9** See **bond paper. 10 in bond.** *Commerce.* deposited in a bonded warehouse. ◆ *vb* (*mainly tr*) **11** (*also intr*) to hold or be held together, as by a rope or an adhesive; bind; connect. **12** (*intr*) to become emotionally attached. **13** to put or hold (goods) in bond. **14** *Law.* to place under bond. **15** *Finance.* to issue bonds on; mortgage. [C13: from ON *band;* see BAND²]

Bond ★ (bɒnd) *n* **Edward.** born 1934, British dramatist: his plays include *Saved* (1965), *Restoration* (1981), and *In the Company of Men* (1990).

bondage ('bɒndɪdʒ) *n* **1** slavery or serfdom; servitude. **2** subjection to some influence or duty. **3** a sexual practice in which one participant is physically bound.

bonded ('bɒndɪd) *adj* **1** *Finance.* consisting of, secured by, or operating under a bond or bonds. **2** *Commerce.* deposited in a bonded warehouse.

bonded warehouse *n* a warehouse in which goods are deposited until duty is paid.

bondholder ('bɒnd,həʊldə) *n* an owner of bonds issued by a company or other institution.

Bondi¹ ★ ('bɒndɪ) *n* **Sir Hermann.** born 1919, British mathematician, born in Austria; originator (with Sir Fred Hoyle and Thomas Gold) of the steady-state theory of the universe.

ondi[2] ★ ('bɒndaɪ) *n* a beach in Sydney, Australia, popular with surfers.

onding ('bɒndɪŋ) *n* the process by which individuals become emotionally attached to one another.

ondmaid ('bɒnd,meɪd) *n* an unmarried female serf or slave.

ond paper *n* a superior quality of strong white paper, used esp. for writing and typing.

ondservant ('bɒnd,sɜːvənt) *n* a serf or slave.

ondsman ('bɒndzmən) *n*, *pl* **bondsmen.** 1 *Law.* a person bound by bond to act as surety for another. 2 another word for **bondservant.**

ond washing *n* a series of illegal deals in bonds made with the intention of avoiding taxation.

one (bəʊn) *n* 1 any of the various structures that make up the skeleton in most vertebrates. 2 the porous rigid tissue of which these parts are made. 3 something consisting of bone or a bonelike substance. 4 (*pl*) the human skeleton or body. 5 a thin strip of whalebone, plastic, etc., used to stiffen corsets and brassieres. 6 (*pl*) the essentials (esp. in **the bare bones**). 7 (*pl*) dice. 8 **close** *or* **near to the bone.** 8a risqué or indecent. 8b in poverty; destitute. 9 **feel in one's bones.** to have an intuition of. 10 **have a bone to pick.** to have grounds for a quarrel. 11 **make no bones about.** 11a to be direct and candid about. 11b to have no scruples about. 12 **point the bone.** (often foll. by *at*) *Austral.* 12a to wish bad luck (on). 12b to cast a spell (on) in order to kill. ◆ *vb* **bones, boning, boned.** (*mainly tr*) 13 to remove the bones from (meat for cooking, etc.). 14 to stiffen (a corset, etc.) by inserting bones. 15 *Brit.* a slang word for **steal.** ◆ See also **bone up.** [OE *bān*]
▸ 'boneless *adj*

ône ★ (*French* bon) *n* a former name of **Annaba.**

one ash *n* ash obtained when bones are burnt in air, consisting mainly of calcium phosphate.

one china *n* porcelain containing bone ash.

one-dry *adj Inf.* **a** completely dry: *a bone-dry well.* **b** (*postpositive*): *the well was bone dry.*

onehead ('bəʊn,hɛd) *n Sl.* a stupid or obstinate person.
▸ 'bone,headed *adj*

one idle *adj* very idle; extremely lazy.

one marrow *n* See **marrow** (sense 1).

one meal *n* dried and ground animal bones, used as a fertilizer or in stock feeds.

oner ('bəʊnə) *n Sl.* a blunder.

onesetter ('bəʊn,sɛtə) *n* a person who sets broken or dislocated bones, esp. one who has no formal medical qualifications.

oneshaker ('bəʊn,ʃeɪkə) *n* 1 an early type of bicycle having solid tyres and no springs. 2 *Sl.* any decrepit or rickety vehicle.

one up *vb* (*adv*; when *intr*, usually foll. by *on*) *Inf.* to study intensively.

onfire ('bɒn,faɪə) *n* a large outdoor fire. [C15: alteration (infl. by F *bon* good) of *bone-fire*; from the use of bones as fuel]

ong (bɒŋ) *n* 1 a deep reverberating sound, as of a large bell. ◆ *vb* 2 to make a deep reverberating sound. [C20: imit.]

ongo[1] ('bɒŋgəʊ) *n*, *pl* **bongo** *or* **bongos.** a rare spiral-horned antelope inhabiting forests of central Africa. The coat is bright red-brown with narrow vertical stripes. [of African origin]

ongo[2] ('bɒŋgəʊ) *n*, *pl* **bongos** *or* **bongoes.** a small bucket-shaped drum, usually one of a pair, played by beating with the fingers. [American Sp., prob. imit.]

onhoeffer ★ (*German* 'bɔːnhœfər) *n* **Dietrich** ('diːtrɪç). 1906–45, German theologian: executed by the Nazis.

onhomie ('bɒnəmiː) *n* exuberant friendliness. [C18: from F, from *bon* good + *homme* man]

oniface[1] ★ ('bɒnɪ,feɪs) *n* **Saint.** original name *Wynfrith.* ?680–?755 A.D. Anglo-Saxon missionary: archbishop of Mainz (746–755). Feast day: June 5.

oniface VIII ★ *n* original name *Benedict Caetano.* ?1234–1303, pope (1294–1303).

Bonington ★ ('bɒnɪŋtən) *n* 1 Sir **Chris(tian John Storey).** born 1934, British mountaineer; led 1970 Annapurna I and 1975 Everest expeditions, reached summit in 1985. 2 **Richard Parkes.** 1801–28, British painter.

Bonin Islands ★ ('bəʊnɪn) *pl n* a group of 27 volcanic islands in the W Pacific: occupied by the US after World War II; returned to Japan in 1968. Largest island: Chichijima. Area: 103 sq. km (40 sq. miles). Japanese name: **Ogasawara Gunto.**

bonito (bə'niːtəʊ) *n*, *pl* **bonitos.** any of various small tunny-like marine food fishes of warm Atlantic and Pacific waters. [C16: from Sp., from L *bonus* good]

bonk (bɒŋk) *vb Inf.* 1 (*tr*) to hit. 2 to have sexual intercourse. [C20: prob. imit.]
▸ 'bonking *n*

bonkbuster ('bɒŋk,bʌstə) *n Inf.* a novel characterized by graphic descriptions of the heroine's frequent sexual encounters. [C20: from BONK (sense 2) + (BLOCK)BUSTER]

bonkers ('bɒŋkəz) *adj Sl., chiefly Brit.* mad; crazy. [C20: from ?]

bon mot (*French* bɔ̃ mo) *n*, *pl* **bons mots** (bɔ̃ mo). a clever and fitting remark. [F, lit.: good word]

Bonn ★ (bɒn; *German* bɔn) *n* a city in W Germany, in North Rhine-Westphalia on the Rhine: the capital (1949–90) of the former West Germany; university (1786). Pop.: 293 072 (1995 est.).

Bonnard ★ (*French* bɔnar) *n* **Pierre** (pjɛr). 1867–1947, French painter.

bonnet ('bɒnɪt) *n* 1 any of various hats worn, esp. formerly, by women and girls, and tied with ribbons under the chin. 2 (in Scotland) Also: **bunnet. 2a** a soft cloth cap. 2b (formerly) a flat brimless cap worn by men. 3 the hinged metal part of a motor vehicle body that provides access to the engine. US name: **hood. 4** a cowl on a chimney. 5 *Naut.* a piece of sail laced to the foot of a foresail to give it greater area in light winds. 6 (in the US and Canada) a headdress of feathers worn by some tribes of American Indians. [C14: from OF *bonet*, from ?]

Bonnie Prince Charlie ★ ('bɒnɪ) *n* See (Charles Edward) **Stuart.**

bonny ('bɒnɪ) *adj* **bonnier, bonniest.** 1 *Scot. & N English dialect.* beautiful or handsome: *a bonny lass.* 2 good or fine. 3 (esp. of babies) plump. [C15: from OF *bon* good, from L *bonus*]

Bonny ★ ('bɒnɪ) *n* **Bight of.** a wide bay at the E end of the Gulf of Guinea off the coasts of Nigeria and Cameroon. Former name (until 1975): **Bight of Biafra.**

bonsai ('bɒnsaɪ) *n*, *pl* **bonsai.** 1 the art of growing dwarfed ornamental varieties of trees or shrubs in small shallow pots or trays by selective pruning, etc. 2 a tree or shrub grown by this method. [C20: from Japanese, from *bon* bowl + *sai* to plant]

bontebok ('bɒntɪ,bʌk) *n*, *pl* **bonteboks** *or* **bontebok.** an antelope of southern Africa, having a deep reddish-brown coat with a white blaze, tail, and rump patch. [C18: Afrik. from *bont* pied + *bok* BUCK[1]]

bonus ('bəʊnəs) *n* 1 something given, paid, or received above what is due or expected. 2 *Chiefly Brit.* an extra dividend allotted to shareholders out of profits. 3 *Insurance, Brit.* a dividend, esp. a percentage of net profits, distributed to policyholders. [C18: from L *bonus* (adj) good]

bonus issue *n Brit.* a free issue of shares distributed among shareholders pro rata with their holdings.

bon vivant *French.* (bɔ̃ vivɑ̃) *n*, *pl* **bons vivants** (bɔ̃ vivɑ̃). a person who enjoys luxuries, esp. good food and drink. Also called (but not in French): **bon viveur** (,bɒn viː'vɜː). [lit.: good-living (man)]

bon voyage (*French* bɔ̃ vwajaʒ) *sentence substitute.* a phrase used to wish a traveller a pleasant journey. [F, lit.: good journey]

bony ('bəʊnɪ) *adj* **bonier, boniest.** 1 resembling or consisting of bone. 2 having many bones. 3 having prominent bones. 4 thin or emaciated.

bony fish *n* any of a class of fishes, including most of the extant species, having a skeleton of bone rather than cartilage.

Bonynge ★ ('bɒnɪŋ) n **Richard.** born 1930, Australian conductor; married to the soprano Joan Sutherland.

bonze (bɒnz) n a Chinese or Japanese Buddhist priest or monk. [C16: from F, from Port. *bonzo*, from Japanese *bonsō*, from Sanskrit *bon* + *sō* priest or monk]

bonzer ('bɒnzə) adj Austral & NZ sl., arch. very good; excellent. [C20: ?from BONANZA]

boo (buː) interj **1** an exclamation uttered to startle or surprise someone, esp. a child. **2** a shout uttered to express disgust, dissatisfaction, or contempt. ◆ vb **boos, booing, booed. 3** to shout "boo" at (someone or something), esp. as an expression of disapproval.

boob (buːb) Sl. ◆ n **1** an ignorant or foolish person. **2** Brit. an embarrassing mistake; blunder. **3** a female breast. ◆ vb **4** (intr) Brit. to make a blunder. [C20: back formation from BOOBY]

boobialla (ˌbuːbɪˈælə) n Austral. **1** another name for **golden wattle** (sense 2). **2** any of various trees or shrubs of the genus *Myoporum*.

boo-boo n, pl **boo-boos.** an embarrassing mistake; blunder. [C20: ?from nursery talk]

boob tube Sl. **1** a close-fitting strapless top, worn by women. **2** Chiefly US & Canad. a television receiver.

booby ('buːbɪ) n, pl **boobies. 1** an ignorant or foolish person. **2** Brit. the losing player in a game. **3** any of several tropical marine birds related to the gannet. They have a straight stout bill and the plumage is white with darker markings. [C17: from Sp. *bobo*, from L *balbus* stammering]

booby prize n a mock prize given to the person having the lowest score.

booby trap n **1** a hidden explosive device primed in such a way as to be set off by an unsuspecting victim. **2** a trap for an unsuspecting person, esp. one intended as a practical joke. ◆ vb **booby-trap, booby-traps, booby-trapping, booby-trapped. 3** (tr) to set a booby trap in or on (a building or object) or for (a person).

boodle ('buːdˀl) n Sl. money or valuables, esp. when stolen, counterfeit, or used as a bribe. [C19: from Du. *boedel* possessions]

boogie ('buːgɪ) vb **boogies, boogieing, boogied.** (intr) Sl. **1** to dance to pop music. **2** to make love. [C20: orig. African-American slang, ?from Bantu *mbugi* devilishly good]

boogie-woogie ('bugɪˈwugɪ, 'buːgɪˈwuːgɪ) n a style of piano jazz using a dotted bass pattern, usually with eight notes in a bar and the harmonies of the 12-bar blues. [C20: ? imit.]

boohai (buːˈhaɪ) n **up the boohai.** NZ inf. thoroughly lost. [from the remote township of *Puhoi*]

boohoo (ˌbuːˈhuː) vb **boohoos, boohooing, boohooed.** (intr) **1** to sob or pretend to sob noisily. ◆ n, pl **boohoos. 2** (sometimes pl) distressed or pretended sobbing. [C20: nursery talk]

book (bʊk) n **1** a number of printed or written pages bound together along one edge and usually protected by covers. **2a** a written work or composition, such as a novel, technical manual, or dictionary. **2b** (as modifier): *book reviews.* **2c** (in combination): *bookseller; bookshop; bookshelf.* **3** a number of blank or ruled sheets of paper bound together, used to record lessons, keep accounts, etc. **4** (pl) a record of the transactions of a business or society. **5** the libretto of an opera, musical, etc. **6** a major division of a written composition, as of a long novel or of the Bible. **7** a number of tickets, stamps, etc., fastened together along one edge. **8** a record of betting transactions. **9** (in card games) the number of tricks that must be taken by a side or player before any trick has a scoring value. **10** strict or rigid rules or standards (esp. in **by the book**). **11** a source of knowledge or authority: *the book of life.* **12** **a closed book.** a person or subject that is unknown or beyond comprehension: *chemistry is a closed book to him.* **13** **an open book.** a person or subject that is thoroughly understood. **14** **bring to book.** to reprimand or require (someone) to give an explanation of his conduct. **15** **close the books.** Book-keeping. to balance accounts in order to prepare a statement or report. **16** **in someone's good (or bad) books.** regarded by someone with favour (or disfavour). **17** **keep the books.** to keep written records of the finances of a business. **18** **on the books. 18a** enrolled a member. **18b** recorded. **19** **the book.** (sometimes cap.) th Bible. **20** **throw the book at. 20a** to charge with every rel vant offence. **20b** to inflict the most severe punishment on. ◆ vb **21** to reserve (a place, passage, etc.) or engag the services of (a performer, driver, etc.) in advance. **2** (tr) to take the name and address of (a person guilty of minor offence) with a view to bringing a prosecution. **2** (tr) (of a football referee) to take the name of (a playe who grossly infringes the rules. **24** (tr) Arch. to record in book. ◆ See also **book in.** [OE *bōc;* see BEECH (its bark wa used as a writing surface)]

bookbinder ('bʊkˌbaɪndə) n a person whose business binding books.
▸ **'book,binding** n

bookbindery ('bʊkˌbaɪndərɪ) n, pl **bookbinderies.** a plac in which books are bound. Often shortened to **bindery.**

bookcase ('bʊkˌkeɪs) n a piece of furniture containin shelves for books.

book club n a club that sells books at low prices to mem bers, usually by mail order.

book end n one of a pair of usually ornamental support for holding a row of books upright.

Booker Prize ('bʊkə) n an annual prize for a work c British, Commonwealth, or Irish fiction of £20,00C awarded since 1969 by the Booker McConnell engineer ing company.

bookie ('bʊkɪ) n Inf. short for **bookmaker.**

book in vb (adv) **1** to reserve a room at a hotel. **2** Chief Brit. to register, esp. one's arrival at a hotel.

booking ('bʊkɪŋ) n **1** Chiefly Brit. a reservation, as of table, room, or seat. **2** Theatre. an engagement of an acto or company.

bookish ('bʊkɪʃ) adj **1** fond of reading; studious. **2** con sisting of or forming opinions through reading rathe than experience; academic. **3** of or relating to books.
▸ **'bookishness** n

book-keeping n the skill or occupation of systemati cally recording business transactions.
▸ **'book-,keeper** n

book-learning n knowledge gained from books rathe than from experience.

booklet ('bʊklɪt) n a thin book, esp. one having pape covers; pamphlet.

bookmaker ('bʊkˌmeɪkə) n a person who as an occupa tion accepts bets, esp. on horseraces, and pays out t winning betters.
▸ **'book,making** n

bookmark ('bʊkˌmɑːk) n **1** Also called: **bookmarker.** a strip of some material put between the pages of a book t mark a place. **2** Computing. an identifier put on a website that enables the user to return to it quickly and easily ◆ vb **3** (tr) Computing. to identify and store (a website) sc that one can return to it quickly and easily.

Book of Common Prayer n the official book o church services of the Church of England until 1980 when the Alternative Service Book was sanctioned.

bookplate ('bʊkˌpleɪt) n a label bearing the owner' name and a design, pasted into a book.

bookstall ('bʊkˌstɔːl) n a stall or stand where periodicals newspapers, or books are sold.

book token n Brit. a gift token to be exchanged fo books.

book value n **1** the value of an asset of a business ac cording to its books. **2** the net capital value of an enter prise as shown by the excess of book assets over book liabilities.

bookworm ('bʊkˌwɜːm) n **1** a person devoted to reading **2** any of various small insects that feed on the binding paste of books.

Boole ★ (buːl) n **George.** 1815–64, English mathemati cian. He applied mathematical formulae to logic, creat ing **Boolean** algebra, which is used in computers to codify nonmathematical logical operations.

boom[1] (buːm) vb **1** to make a deep prolonged resonant sound. **2** to prosper or cause to prosper vigorously and rapidly: *business boomed.* ◆ *n* **3** a deep prolonged resonant sound. **4** a period of high economic growth. **5** any similar period of high activity. **6** the activity itself: *a baby boom.* [C15: ?from Du. *bommen*, imit.]

oom² (bu:m) *n* **1** *Naut.* a spar to which a sail is fastened to control its position relative to the wind. **2** a pole carrying an overhead microphone and projected over a film or television set. **3** a barrier across a waterway, usually consisting of a chain of logs, to confine free-floating logs, protect a harbour from attack, etc. [C16: from Du. *boom* tree, BEAM]

oomer ('bu:mə) *n* **1** *Austral.* a large male kangaroo. **2** *Austral. & NZ inf.* anything exceptionally large.

oomerang ('bu:mə,ræŋ) *n* **1** a curved flat wooden missile of native Australians, which can be made to return to the thrower. **2** an action or statement that recoils on its originator. ◆ *vb* **3** (*intr*) (of a plan, etc.) to recoil or return unexpectedly, causing harm to its originator. [C19: from Abor.]

oomslang ('bu:m,slæŋ) *n* a large greenish venomous arboreal snake of southern Africa. [C18: from Afrik., from *boom* tree + *slang* snake]

oon¹ (bu:n) *n* **1** something extremely useful, helpful, or beneficial; a blessing or benefit. **2** *Arch.* a favour; request. [C12: from ON *bōn* request]

oon² (bu:n) *adj* **1** close, special, or intimate (in **boon companion**). **2** *Arch.* jolly or convivial. [C14: from OF *bon*, from L *bonus* good]

oondocks ('bu:n,dɒks) *pl n* **the**. *US & Canad. sl.* **1** wild, desolate, or uninhabitable country. **2** a remote rural or provincial area. [C20: from Tagalog *bundok* mountain]

oong (buŋ) *n Austral. offens.* a Black person. [C20: from Abor.]

oongary (bu:n'gɛərɪ) *n, pl* **-ries.** a tree kangaroo of NE Queensland. [from Abor.]

oor (buə) *n* an ill-mannered, clumsy, or insensitive person. [OE *gebūr* dweller, farmer; see NEIGHBOUR]
▸ '**boorish** *adj* ▸ '**boorishly** *adv* ▸ '**boorishness** *n*

oost (bu:st) *n* **1** encouragement, improvement, or help: *a boost to morale.* **2** an upward thrust or push. **3** an increase or rise. **4** the amount by which the induction pressure of a supercharged internal-combustion engine is increased. ◆ *vb* (*tr*) **5** to encourage, assist, or improve: *to boost morale.* **6** to lift by giving a push from below or behind. **7** to increase or raise: *to boost the voltage in an electrical circuit.* **8** to cause to rise; increase: *to boost sales.* **9** to advertise on a big scale. **10** to increase the induction pressure of (an internal-combustion engine); supercharge. [C19: from ?]

ooster ('bu:stə) *n* **1** a person or thing that supports, assists, or increases power. **2** Also called: **launch vehicle.** the first stage of a multistage rocket. **3** a radio-frequency amplifier to strengthen signals. **4** another name for **supercharger.** **5** short for **booster shot.**

ooster shot *n Inf.* a supplementary injection of a vaccine given to maintain the immunization provided by an earlier dose.

oot¹ (bu:t) *n* **1** a strong outer covering for the foot; shoe that extends above the ankle, often to the knee. **2** *Brit.* an enclosed compartment of a car for holding luggage, etc., usually at the rear. US and Canad. name: **trunk. 3** an instrument of torture used to crush the foot and lower leg. **4** *Inf.* a kick: *he gave the door a boot.* **5 boots and all.** *Austral. & NZ inf.* making every effort. **6 die with one's boots on.** to die while still active. **7 lick the boots of.** to be servile towards. **8 put the boot in.** *Sl.* **8a** to kick a person, esp. when he is already down. **8b** to harass someone. **8c** to finish off (something) with unnecessary brutality. **9 the boot.** *Sl.* dismissal from employment; the sack. **10 the boot is on the other foot** *or* **leg.** the situation is or has now reversed. ◆ *vb* (*tr*) **11** to kick. **12** to equip with boots. **13** *Inf.* **13a** (often foll. by *out*) to eject forcibly. **13b** to dismiss from employment. **14** to bootstrap (a computer system). [C14 *bote*, from OF, from ?]

oot² (bu:t) *vb* (*usually impersonal*) **1** *Arch.* to be of advantage or use to (a person): *what boots it to complain?* ◆ *n* **2** *Obs.* an advantage. **3 to boot.** as well; in addition. [OE *bōt* compensation]

bootblack ('bu:t,blæk) *n* (esp. formerly) a person who shines boots and shoes.

boot camp *n* **1** *US sl.* a basic training camp for new recruits to the US Navy or Marine Corps. **2** a centre for juvenile offenders with a strict disciplinary regime, hard physical exercise, and community labour programmes.

bootee ('bu:tɪ, bu:'tɪ) *n* **1** a soft shoe for a baby, esp. a knitted one. **2** a boot for women and children, esp. an ankle-length one.

Boötes (bəʊ'əʊtiːz) *n, Latin genitive* **Boötis** (bəʊ'əʊtɪs). a constellation in the N hemisphere containing the star Arcturus. [C17: via L from Gk: ploughman]

booth (bu:ð, bu:θ) *n, pl* **booths** (bu:ðz). **1** a stall, esp. a temporary one at a fair or market. **2** a small partially enclosed cubicle, such as one for telephoning (**telephone booth**) or for voting (**polling booth**). **3** two high-backed benches with a table between, used esp. in bars and restaurants. **4** (formerly) a temporary structure for shelter, dwelling, storage, etc. [C12: of Scand. origin]

Booth ★ (bu:ð) *n* **1 Edwin Thomas,** son of Junius Brutus Booth. 1833–93, US actor. **2 John Wilkes,** son of Junius Brutus Booth. 1838–65, US actor; assassin of Abraham Lincoln. **3 Junius Brutus** ('dʒu:nɪəs 'bru:təs). 1796–1852, US actor, born in England. **4 William.** 1829–1912, British religious leader; founder of the Salvation Army (1878).

Boothia Peninsula ★ ('bu:θɪə) *n* a peninsula of N Canada: the northernmost part of the mainland of North America, lying west of the **Gulf of Boothia,** an arm of the Arctic Ocean.

Boothroyd ★ ('bu:θrɔɪd) *n* **Betty.** born 1929, British politician; speaker of the House of Commons from 1992.

bootjack ('bu:t,dʒæk) *n* a device that grips the heel of a boot to enable the foot to be withdrawn easily.

Bootle ★ ('bu:tʰl) *n* a port in NW England, on the River Mersey adjoining Liverpool. Pop.: 65 454 (1991).

bootleg ('bu:t,lɛg) *vb* **bootlegs, bootlegging, bootlegged. 1** to make, carry, or sell (illicit goods, esp. alcohol). ◆ *n* **2** something made or sold illicitly, such as alcohol. **3** an illegally made copy of a CD, tape, etc. ◆ *adj* **4** produced, distributed, or sold illicitly. [C17: see BOOT¹, LEG; from smugglers carrying bottles of liquor concealed in their boots]
▸ '**boot,legger** *n*

bootless ('bu:tlɪs) *adj* of little or no use; vain; fruitless. [OE *bōtlēas*, from *bōt* compensation]

bootlicker ('bu:t,lɪkə) *n Inf.* one who seeks favour by servile or ingratiating behaviour towards (someone, esp. in authority); toady.

bootstrap ('bu:t,stræp) *n* **1** a loop on a boot for pulling it on. **2 by one's (own) bootstraps.** by one's own efforts; unaided. **3a** a technique for loading the first few program instructions into a computer main store to enable the rest of the program to be introduced from an input device. **3b** (*as modifier*): *a bootstrap loader.* **4** *Commerce.* an offer to purchase a controlling interest in a company, esp. with the intention of purchasing the remainder of the equity at a lower price. ◆ *vb* **bootstraps, bootstrapping, bootstrapped.** (*tr*) **5** to initiate (a computer system) by executing a bootstrap; boot.

booty ('bu:tɪ) *n, pl* **booties.** any valuable article or articles, esp. when obtained as plunder. [C15: from OF, from MLow G *buite* exchange]

booze (bu:z) *Inf.* ◆ *n* **1** alcoholic drink. **2** a drinking bout. ◆ *vb* **boozes, boozing, boozed. 3** (*usually intr*) to drink (alcohol), esp. in excess. [C13: from MDu. *būsen*]

boozer ('bu:zə) *n Inf.* **1** a person who is fond of drinking. **2** *Brit., Austral., & NZ.* a bar or pub.

booze-up *n Brit., Austral., & NZ sl.* a drinking spree.

boozy ('bu:zɪ) *adj* **boozier, booziest.** *Inf.* inclined to or involving excessive drinking of alcohol; drunken: *a boozy lecturer; a boozy party.*

bop (bɒp) *n* **1** a form of jazz originating in the 1940s, characterized by rhythmic and harmonic complexity and instrumental virtuosity. Originally called: **bebop.** ◆ *vb* **bops, bopping, bopped. 2** (*intr*) *Inf.* to dance to pop music. [C20: shortened from BEBOP]
▸ '**bopper** *n*

bo-peep (ˌbəʊ'piːp) *n* a game for very young children, in which one hides (esp. hiding one's face in one's hands) and reappears suddenly.

Bophuthatswana ★ (ˌbəʊpuːtɑːt'swɑːnə) *n* (formerly) a Bantu homeland in N South Africa: reintegrated into South Africa in 1994.

bora[1] ('bɔːrə) *n* (*sometimes cap.*) a violent cold north wind blowing from the Adriatic. [C19: from It. dialect., from L *borēas* the north wind]

bora[2] ('bɔːrə) *n* an initiation ceremony of native Australians, introducing youths to manhood. [from Abor.]

Bora Bora ★ ('bɔːrə 'bɔːrə) *n* an island in the S Pacific, in French Polynesia, in the Society Islands: one of the Leeward Islands. Area: 39 sq. km (15 sq. miles).

boracic (bə'ræsɪk) *adj* another word for **boric.**

borage ('bɒrɪdʒ, 'bʌrɪdʒ) *n* a Mediterranean plant with star-shaped blue flowers. The young leaves are sometimes used in salads. [C13: from OF, ?from Ar. *abū 'āraq*, lit.: father of sweat]

Borås ★ (*Swedish* bu'roːs) *n* a city in SW Sweden, chiefly producing textiles. Pop.: 96 123 (1994).

borate *n* ('bɔːreɪt, -ɪt). **1** a salt or ester of boric acid. ◆ *vb* ('bɔːreɪt), **borates, borating, borated. 2** (*tr*) to treat with borax, boric acid, or borate.

borax ('bɔːræks) *n, pl* **boraxes** *or* **boraces** (-rəˌsiːz). a soluble readily fusible white mineral in monoclinic crystalline form, occurring in alkaline soils and salt deposits. Formula: $Na_2B_4O_7.10H_2O$. [C14: from OF, from Med. L, from Ar., from Persian *būrah*]

borazon ('bɔːrəˌzɒn) *n* an extremely hard form of boron nitride. [C20: from BOR(ON) + AZO + -ON]

borborygmus (ˌbɔːbə'rɪgməs) *n, pl* **borborygmi** (-maɪ). rumbling of the stomach. [C18: from Gk]

Bordeaux ★ (bɔː'dəʊ; *French* bɔrdo) *n* **1** a port in SW France, on the River Garonne: a major centre of the wine trade. Pop.: 213 274 (1990). **2** any of several red, white, or rosé wines produced around Bordeaux.

Bordeaux mixture *n Horticulture.* a fungicide consisting of a solution of equal quantities of copper sulphate and quicklime.

border ('bɔːdə) *n* **1** a band or margin around or along the edge of something. **2** the dividing line or frontier between political or geographic regions. **3** a region straddling such a boundary. **4** a design around the edge of something. **5** a long narrow strip of ground planted with flowers, shrubs, etc.: *a herbaceous border.* ◆ *vb* **6** (*tr*) to provide with a border. **7** (when *intr*, foll. by *on* or *upon*) **7a** to be adjacent (to); lie along the boundary (of). **7b** to be nearly the same (as); verge (on): *his stupidity borders on madness.* [C14: from OF, from *bort* side of a ship, of Gmc origin]

Border[1] ★ ('bɔːdə) *n* **the. 1** (*often pl*) the area straddling the border between England and Scotland. **2** the area straddling the border between Northern Ireland and the Republic of Ireland. **3** the region in S South Africa around East London.

Border[2] ★ ('bɔːdə) *n* **Allan (Robert).** born 1955, Australian cricketer; captain of Australia (1985–94).

borderer ('bɔːdərə) *n* a person who lives in a border area.

borderland ('bɔːdəˌlænd) *n* **1** land located on or near a frontier or boundary. **2** an indeterminate state or condition.

borderline ('bɔːdəˌlaɪn) *n* **1** a border; dividing line. **2** an indeterminate position between two conditions: *the borderline between friendship and love.* ◆ *adj* **3** on the edge of one category and verging on another: *a borderline failure in the exam.*

Borders Region ★ *n* a former local government region in S Scotland; replaced in 1996 by Scottish Borders council area.

bore[1] (bɔː) *vb* **bores, boring, bored. 1** to produce (a hole) in (a material) by use of a drill, auger, or rotary cutting tool. **2** to increase the diameter of (a hole), as by turning. **3** (*tr*) to produce (a hole in the ground, tunnel, mine shaft, etc.) by digging, drilling, etc. **4** (*intr*) *Inf.* (of a horse or athlete in a race) to push other competitors out of the way. ◆ *n* **5** a hole or tunnel in the ground, esp. one drilled in search of minerals, oil, etc. **6** *Austral.* an artesian well. **7a** the hollow part of a tube or cylinder, esp. of a gun barrel. **7b** the diameter of such a hollow part; calibre. [OE *borian*]

bore[2] (bɔː) *vb* **bores, boring, bored. 1** (*tr*) to tire or make weary by being dull, repetitious, or uninteresting. ◆ *n* a dull or repetitious person, activity, or state. [C18: from ?]
▸ **bored** *adj* ▸ **'boring** *adj*

bore[3] (bɔː) *n* a high steep-fronted wave moving up a narrow estuary, caused by the tide. [C17: from ON *bār* wave, billow]

bore[4] (bɔː) *vb* the past tense of **bear**[1].

boreal ('bɔːrɪəl) *adj* of or relating to the north or the north wind. [C15: from L *boreās* the north wind]

Boreal ('bɔːrɪəl) *adj* of or denoting the coniferous forests in the north of the N hemisphere.

Boreas ★ ('bɔːrɪəs) *n Greek myth.* the god personifying the north wind. [C14: via L from Gk]

boredom ('bɔːdəm) *n* the state of being bored.

boree ('bɔːriː) *n Austral.* another name for **myall.** [from Abor.]

borer ('bɔːrə) *n* **1** a tool for boring holes. **2** any of various insects, insect larvae, molluscs, or crustaceans, that bore into plant material, esp. wood.

Borg ★ (bɔːg; *Swedish* bɔrj) *n* **Björn** (bjɔːn; *Swedish* bjœrn). born 1956, Swedish tennis player: Wimbledon champion 1976–80.

Borgerhout ★ (*Flemish* bɔrxər'hɔut) *n* a city in N Belgium, near Antwerp. Pop.: 44 000 (latest est.).

Borges ★ (*Spanish* 'borxes) *n* **Jorge Luis** ('xorxe lwis), 1899–1986, Argentinian poet and scholar. His short stories include *Ficciones* (1944).

Borgia ★ (*Italian* 'bordʒa) *n* **1 Cesare** ('tʃezare), son of Rodrigo Borgia (Pope Alexander VI). 1475–1507, Italian cardinal, politician, and military leader; model for Machiavelli's *The Prince.* **2** his sister, **Lucrezia** (lu'krettsja), daughter of Rodrigo Borgia. 1480–1519, Italian noblewoman. After her third marriage (1501), to the Duke of Ferrara, she became a patron of the arts and science. 3 **Rodrigo** (rod'rigo). See **Alexander VI.**

boric ('bɔːrɪk) *adj* of or containing boron. Also: **boracic.**

boric acid *n* a white soluble weakly acid crystalline solid used in the manufacture of heat-resistant glass and porcelain enamels, as a fireproofing material, and as a mild antiseptic. Formula: H_3BO_3. Also called: **orthoboric acid.** Systematic name: **trioxoboric(III) acid.**

borlotti bean (bɔː'lɒtɪ) *n* a variety of kidney bean with a pinkish-brown speckled skin that turns brown when cooked. [from It., plural of *borlotto* kidney bean]

Bormann ★ ('bɔːmən; *German* 'bɔrman) *n* **Martin.** 1900–45, German Nazi politician; Hitler's adviser and private secretary (1942–45): committed suicide.

born (bɔːn) *vb* **1** the past participle (in most passive uses) of **bear**[1] (sense 4). **2 not born yesterday.** not gullible or foolish. ◆ *adj* **3** possessing certain qualities from birth: *a born musician.* **4a** being at birth in a particular social status or other condition as specified: *ignobly born.* **4b** (*in combination*): *lowborn.* **5 in all one's born days.** *Inf.* so far in one's life.

> **USAGE NOTE** Care should be taken not to use *born* when *borne* is intended: *he had borne* (not *born*) *his ordeal with great courage; the following points should be borne in mind.*

Born ★ (bɔːn) *n* **Max.** 1882–1970, British nuclear physicist, born in Germany, noted for his fundamental contribution to quantum mechanics: Nobel prize for physics 1954.

born-again ('bɔːnəˌgɛn) *adj* **1** having experienced conversion, esp. to evangelical Christianity. **2** showing the enthusiasm of one newly converted to any cause: *a born again monetarist.* ◆ *n* **3** a person who shows fervent enthusiasm for a new-found cause, belief, etc.

orne (bɔːn) vb **1** the past participle of **bear**[1] (for all active uses of the verb; also for all passive uses except sense 4 unless foll. by *by*). **2 be borne in on** *or* **upon**. (of a fact, etc.) to be realized by (someone).

orneo ★ ('bɔːnɪˌəʊ) n an island in the W Pacific, between the Sulu and Java Seas, part of the Malay Archipelago: divided into Kalimantan (**Indonesian Borneo**), the Malaysian states of Sarawak and Sabah, and the British-protected sultanate of Brunei; mountainous and densely forested. Area: about 750 000 sq. km (290 000 sq. miles). ▶ '**Bornean** adj, n

ornholm ★ (*Danish* bɔrn'hɔlm) n an island in the Baltic Sea, south of Sweden: administratively part of Denmark. Chief town: Rønne. Pop.: 46 100 (1990). Area: 588 sq. km (227 sq. miles).

orno ★ ('bɔːnəʊ) n a state of NE Nigeria, on Lake Chad: the second largest state, formed in 1976 from part of North-Eastern State. Capital: Maiduguri. Pop.: 2 674 486 (1992 est.). Area: 70 898 sq. km (27 374 sq. miles).

orodin ★ ('bɒrədɪn; *Russian* bərɐ'din) n **Aleksandr Porfirevich** (alik'sandr pərfi'rjevitʃ). 1834–87, Russian composer, whose works include the unfinished opera *Prince Igor*, symphonies, songs, and chamber music.

orodino ★ (ˌbɒrɐ'diːnəʊ; *Russian* bərədi'nɔ) n a village in E central Russia, about 110 km (70 miles) west of Moscow: scene of a battle (1812) in which Napoleon defeated the Russians but irreparably weakened his army.

oron ('bɔːrɒn) n a very hard almost colourless crystalline metalloid element that in impure form exists as a brown amorphous powder. It occurs principally in borax and is used in hardening steel. Symbol: B; atomic no.: 5; atomic wt.: 10.81. [C19: from BOR(AX) + (CARB)ON]

oron carbide ★ n a black extremely hard inert substance used as an abrasive and in control rods in nuclear reactors. Formula: B_4C.

oronia (bə'rəʊnɪə) n any aromatic shrub of the Australian genus *Boronia*.

oron nitride n a white inert crystalline solid, used as a refractory, high-temperature lubricant and insulator, and heat shield.

orosilicate glass (ˌbɔːrəʊ'sɪlɪkɪt, -ˌkeɪt) n any of a range of heat- and chemical-resistant glasses, such as Pyrex, prepared by fusing together oxides of boron and silicon and, usually, a metal oxide.

orough ('bʌrə) n **1** a town, esp. (in Britain) one that forms the constituency of an MP or that was originally incorporated by royal charter. See also **burgh**. **2** any of the 32 constituent divisions of Greater London. **3** any of the five constituent divisions of New York City. **4** (in the US) a self-governing incorporated municipality. [OE *burg*]

orromini ★ (*Italian* borro'miːni) n **Francesco** (fran'tʃesko), original name *Francesco Castelli*. 1599–1667, Italian baroque architect, working in Rome.

orrow ('bɒrəʊ) vb **1** to obtain or receive (something, such as money) on loan for temporary use, intending to give it, or something equivalent, back to the lender. **2** to adopt (ideas, words, etc.) from another source; appropriate. **3** *Not standard*. to lend. **4** (*intr*) *Golf*. to putt the ball uphill of the direct path to the hole: *make sure you borrow enough*. [OE *borgian*] ▶ '**borrower** n

> **USAGE NOTE**   The use of *off* after *borrow* was formerly considered incorrect, but is now acceptable in informal contexts.

orrow ★ ('bɒrəʊ) n **George (Henry)**. 1803–81, British writer. His works include the semiautobiographical *Lavengro* (1851) and its sequel *The Romany Rye* (1857).

ors ★ (bɔːs) n **Sir**. (in Arthurian legend) **1** one the knights of the Round Table, nephew of Lancelot. **2** an illegitimate son of King Arthur.

borscht (bɔːʃt), **borsch**, (bɔːʃ), *or* **borshch** (bɔːʃtʃ) n a Russian and Polish soup based on beetroot. [from Russian *borshch*]

borscht belt n *Inf.*, *chiefly US*. a resort area of the Catskill

Mountains in New York State, popular with Jewish holiday-makers; its hotels and nightclubs (the **borscht circuit**) are regarded as a training ground for entertainers.

borstal ('bɔːstəl) n **1** (formerly, in Britain) an establishment in which offenders aged 15 to 21 could be detained for corrective training. Since 1982 they have been replaced by **young offender institutions**. **2** a similar establishment in Australia and New Zealand. [C20: after *Borstal*, village in Kent where the first institution was founded]

bort, boart (bɔːt), *or* **bortz** (bɔːts) n an inferior grade of diamond used for cutting and drilling or, in powdered form, as an industrial abrasive. [OE *gebrot* fragment]

borzoi ('bɔːzɔɪ) n, pl **borzois**. a tall fast-moving breed of dog with a long coat. Also called: **Russian wolfhound**. [C19: Russian, lit.: swift]

boscage *or* **boskage** ('bɒskɪdʒ) n *Literary*. a mass of trees and shrubs; thicket. [C14: from OF *bosc*, prob. of Gmc origin; see BUSH[1], -AGE]

Bosch ★ (bɒʃ) n **1 Carl**. 1874–1940, German chemist, who adapted the Haber process to produce ammonia. He shared the Nobel prize for chemistry 1931. **2 Hieronymus** (hɪ'rɒnɪməs), original name probably *Jerome van Aken* (or *Aeken*). ?1450–1516, Dutch painter, noted for his triptych *The Garden of Earthly Delights*.

Bose ★ (bəʊs) n **1** Sir **Jagadis Chandra** (dʒəgə'diːs 'tʃʌndrə). 1858–1937, Indian physicist and plant physiologist. **2 Satyendra Nath** (sə'tjendrə 'naːθ). 1894–1974, Indian physicist, who collaborated with Einstein in devising Bose-Einstein statistics. **3 Subhas Chandra** (sʊb'haːʃ 'tʃʌndrə), known as *Netaji*. 1897–1945, Indian nationalist leader; president of the Indian National Congress (1938–39); organized the Indian National Army, with Japanese support, in Singapore to free India from British Rule.

bosh (bɒʃ) n *Inf*. empty or meaningless talk or opinions; nonsense. [C19: from Turkish *boş* empty]

bosk (bɒsk) n *Literary*. a small wood of bushes and small trees. [C13: var. of *busk* BUSH[1]]

bosky ('bɒskɪ) adj **boskier, boskiest**. *Literary*. containing or consisting of bushes or thickets.

bo's'n ('bəʊsᵊn) n *Naut.* a variant spelling of **boatswain**.

Bosnia ★ ('bɒznɪə) n a region of Bosnia-Herzegovina: it has belonged to Turkey (1463–1878), to Austria-Hungary (1879–1918), and to Yugoslavia (1918–91). ▶ '**Bosnian** adj

Bosnia-Herzegovina, Bosnia-Hercegovina, *or esp. US* **Bosnia and Herzegovina** ★ n a country in SW Europe; a constituent republic of Yugoslavia until 1991; in a state of civil war also involving Serbian and Croatian forces (1992–95): mostly barren and mountainous, with forests in the east. Language: Serbo-Croat. Religion: Muslim, Serbian Orthodox, and Roman Catholic. Currency: dinar. Capital: Sarajevo. Pop.: 3 124 000 (1997). Area: 51 129 sq. km (19 737 sq. miles).

bosom ('bʊzəm) n **1** the chest or breast of a person, esp. the female breasts. **2** the part of a woman's dress, coat, etc., that covers the chest. **3** a protective centre or part: *the bosom of the family*. **4** the breast considered as the seat of emotions. **5** (*modifier*) very dear; intimate: *a bosom friend*. ♦ vb (*tr*) **6** to embrace. **7** to conceal or carry in the bosom. [OE *bōsm*]

bosomy ('bʊzəmɪ) adj (of a woman) having large breasts.

boson ('bəʊzɒn) n any of a group of elementary particles, such as a photon or pion, that has zero or integral spin and does not obey the Pauli exclusion principle. Cf. **fermion**. [C20: after S. N. BOSE; see -ON]

Bosporus ('bɒspərəs) *or* **Bosphorus** ★ ('bɒsfərəs) n **the**. a strait between European and Asian Turkey, linking the Black Sea and the Sea of Marmara.

boss[1] (bɒs) *Inf*. ♦ n **1** a person in charge of or employing others. **2** *Chiefly US*. a professional politician who controls a political organization, often using devious or illegal methods. ♦ vb (*tr*) **3** to employ, supervise, or be in charge of. **4** (usually foll. by *around* or *about*) to be domineering or overbearing towards (others). ♦ adj **5** *Sl.* excellent; fine: *a boss hand at carpentry; that's boss!* [C19: from Du. *baas* master]

boss[2] (bɒs) n **1** a knob, stud, or other circular rounded protuberance, esp. an ornamental one on a vault, a ceiling, or a shield. **2** an area of increased thickness, usually cylindrical, that strengthens or provides room for a locating device on a shaft, hub of a wheel, etc. **3** a rounded mass of igneous rock. ◆ *vb* (*tr*) **4** to ornament with bosses; emboss. [C13: from OF *boce*; rel. to It. *bozza* metal knob, swelling]

bossa nova ('bɒsə 'nəʊvə) *n* **1** a dance similar to the samba, originating in Brazil. **2** a piece of music composed for or in the rhythm of this dance. [C20: from Port., lit.: new voice]

bosset ('bɒsɪt) *n* either of the rudimentary antlers found in young deer. [C19: from F *bossette* a small protuberance, from *bosse* BOSS²]

bossy ('bɒsɪ) *adj* **bossier, bossiest.** *Inf.* domineering, overbearing, or authoritarian.
▸ **'bossily** *adv* ▸ **'bossiness** *n*

Boston ★ ('bɒstən) *n* **1** a port in E Massachusetts, the state capital. Pop.: 547 725 (1994 est.). **2** a port in E England, in SE Lincolnshire. Pop.: 34 606 (1991).

bosun ('bəʊsⁿn) *n Naut.* a variant spelling of **boatswain.**

Boswell ★ ('bɒzwəl) *n* **James.** 1740–95, Scottish author and lawyer, noted for his *Life of Samuel Johnson* (1791).
▸ **Boswellian** (bɒz'wɛlɪən) *adj*

Bosworth Field ★ ('bɒzwɜːθ, -wəθ) *n English history.* the site, two miles south of Market Bosworth in Leicestershire, of the battle that ended the Wars of the Roses (August, 1485). Richard III was killed and Henry Tudor was crowned king as Henry VII.

bot[1] *or* **bott** (bɒt) *n* **1** the larva of a botfly, which typically develops inside the body of a horse, sheep, or man. **2** any similar larva. [C15: prob. from Low G; rel. to Du. *bot*, from ?]

bot[2] (bɒt) *Austral. inf.* ◆ *vb* **bots, botting, botted. 1** to scrounge or borrow. ◆ *n* **2** a scrounger. **3 on the bot (for).** wanting to scrounge. [C20: ?from BOTFLY, alluding to its bite; see BITE (sense 9)]

bot. *abbrev. for:* **1** botanical. **2** botany. **3** bottle.

botanical (bə'tænɪkⁿl) *or* **botanic** *adj* **1** of or relating to botany or plants. ◆ *n* **2** any drug or pesticide that is made from parts of a plant. [C17: from Med. L, from Gk *botanē* plant, pasture]
▸ **bo'tanically** *adv*

botanize *or* **botanise** ('bɒtə,naɪz) *vb* **botanizes, botanizing, botanized** *or* **botanises, botanising, botanised. 1** (*intr*) to collect or study plants. **2** (*tr*) to explore and study the plants in (an area or region).

botany ('bɒtənɪ) *n, pl* **botanies. 1** the study of plants, including their classification, structure, physiology, ecology, and economic importance. **2** the plant life of a particular region or time. **3** the biological characteristics of a particular group of plants. [C17: from BOTANICAL; cf. ASTRONOMY, ASTRONOMICAL]
▸ **'botanist** *n*

Botany Bay ★ *n* **1** an inlet of the Tasman Sea, on the SE coast of Australia: surrounded by the suburbs of Sydney. **2** (in the 19th century) a British penal settlement that was in fact at Port Jackson, New South Wales.

Botany wool *n* a fine wool from the merino sheep. [C19: from BOTANY BAY, where the wool came from originally]

botch (bɒtʃ) *vb* (*tr*; often foll. by *up*) **1** to spoil through clumsiness or ineptitude. **2** to repair badly or clumsily. ◆ *n* **3** a badly done piece of work or repair (esp. in **make a botch of**). [C14: from ?]
▸ **'botcher** *n* ▸ **'botchy** *adj*

botfly ('bɒt,flaɪ) *n, pl* **botflies.** any of various stout-bodied hairy dipterous flies, the larvae of which are parasites of man, sheep, and horses.

both (bəʊθ) *determiner* **1a** the two; two considered together: *both dogs were dirty.* **1b** (*as pron*): *both are to blame.* ◆ *conj* **2** (*coordinating*) used preceding words, phrases, or clauses joined by *and*: *both Ellen and Keith enjoyed the play; both new and exciting.* [C12: from ON *bāthir*]

Botha ★ ('bəʊtə) *n* **1 Louis.** 1862–1919, South African statesman and general; first prime minister of the Union of South Africa (1910–19). **2 P(ieter) W(illem)** born 1916,

South African politician; defence minister (1965–78, prime minister (1978–84); state president (1984–89).

Botham ★ ('bəʊθəm) *n* **Ian (Terence).** born 1955, Englis. cricketer: played for Somerset (1973–86), Worcestershir (1987–91), and Durham (1991–93); captained Englanc (1980–81).

bother ('bɒðə) *vb* **1** (*tr*) to give annoyance, pain, or trou ble to. **2** (*tr*) to trouble (a person) by repeatedly disturb ing; pester. **3** (*intr*) to take the time or trouble; concerr oneself: *don't bother to come with me.* **4** (*tr*) to make (a per son) alarmed or confused. ◆ *n* **5** a state of worry, trou ble, or confusion. **6** a person or thing that causes fuss trouble, or annoyance. **7** *Inf.* a disturbance or fight; trou ble (esp. in **a spot of bother**). ◆ *interj* **8** *Chiefly Brit.* an ex clamation of slight annoyance. [C18: ?from Irish Gaeli *bodhar* deaf, vexed]

botheration (,bɒðə'reɪʃən) *n, interj Inf.* another word fo **bother** (senses 5, 8).

bothersome ('bɒðəsəm) *adj* causing bother; trouble some.

Bothnia ★ ('bɒθnɪə) *n* **Gulf of.** an arm of the Baltic Sea, ex tending north between Sweden and Finland.

Bothwell ★ ('bɒθwəl, 'bɒð-) *n* **Earl of,** title of *James Hep burn.* 1535–78, Scottish nobleman; third husband o Mary Queen of Scots.

bothy ('bɒθɪ) *n, pl* **bothies.** *Chiefly Scot.* **1** a cottage or hut. a farmworker's summer quarters. [C18: ? rel. to BOOTH]

bo tree (bəʊ) *n* another name for the **peepul.** [C19: from Sinhalese, from Pali *bodhitaru* tree of wisdom]

Botswana ★ (bʊ'tʃwɑːnə; bʊt'swɑːnə, bɒt-) *n* a republi in southern Africa: established as the British protector ate of Bechuanaland in 1885 as a defence against the Boers; became an independent state within the Commonwealth in 1966; consists mostly of a plateau averaging 1000 m (3300 ft), with the extensive Okavango swamps in the northwest and the Kalahar Desert in the southwest. Languages: English and Tswana. Religion: mostly animist. Currency: pula. Capi tal: Gaborone. Pop.: 1 501 000 (1997). Area: abou 570 000 sq. km (220 000 sq. miles).

bott (bɒt) *n* a variant spelling of **bot**[1].

Botticelli ★ (*Italian* bottiˈtʃɛlli) *n* **Sandro** ('sandro), origi nal name *Alessandro di Mariano Filipepi.* 1444–1510, Ital ian (Florentine) painter.

bottle ('bɒtⁿl) *n* **1a** a vessel, often of glass and typically cylindrical with a narrow neck, for containing liquids **1b** (*as modifier*): *a bottle rack.* **2** Also called: **bottleful.** the amount such a vessel will hold. **3** *Brit. sl.* courage; nerve initiative. **4 the bottle.** *Inf.* drinking of alcohol, esp. to ex cess. ◆ *vb* **bottles, bottling, bottled.** (*tr*) **5** to put or place in a bottle or bottles. **6** to store (gas) in a portable container under pressure. ◆ See also **bottle out, bottle up.** [C14: from OF *botaille*, from Med. L *butticula*, from LL *buttis* cask]

bottle bank *n* a large container into which the public may throw glass bottles for recycling.

bottlebrush ('bɒtⁿl,brʌʃ) *n* **1** a cylindrical brush on a thin shaft, used for cleaning bottles. **2** Also called: **cal listemon.** any of various Australian shrubs or trees having dense spikes of large red flowers with protruding brush like stamens.

bottled (*or* **bottle**) **gas** *n* butane or propane liquefied under pressure in portable metal containers for use in camping stoves, blowtorches, etc.

bottle-feed *vb* **bottle-feeds, bottle-feeding, bottle-fed.** to feed (a baby) with milk from a bottle.

bottle glass *n* glass used for making bottles, consisting of a silicate of sodium, calcium, and aluminium.

bottle green *n, adj* (of) a dark green colour.

bottle-jack *n NZ.* a large jack used for heavy lifts.

bottleneck ('bɒtⁿl,nɛk) *n* **1a** a narrow stretch of road or a junction at which traffic is or may be held up. **1b** the hold-up. **2** something that holds up progress.

bottlenose dolphin ('bɒtⁿl,nəʊz) *n* a type of dolphin with a bottle-shaped snout.

bottle out *vb* (*intr, adv*) *Brit. sl.* to lose one's nerve.

bottle party *n* a party to which guests bring drink.

★ people and places

ʙottler ('bɒt³lə) n Austral. & NZ inf. an exceptional or out-standing person or thing.

ʙottle shop n Austral. & NZ. a shop selling alcohol in unopened containers for consumption elsewhere. Also called (Austral.): **bottle store.**

ʙottle tree n any of several Australian trees that have a bottle-shaped swollen trunk.

ʙottle up vb (tr, adv) **1** to restrain (powerful emotion). **2** to keep (an army or other force) contained or trapped.

ʙottom ('bɒtəm) n **1** the lowest, deepest, or farthest re-moved part of a thing: the bottom of a hill. **2** the least im-portant or successful position: the bottom of a class. **3** the ground underneath a sea, lake, or river. **4** the inner depths of a person's true feelings (esp. in **from the bottom of one's heart**). **5** the underneath part of a thing. **6** Naut. the parts of a vessel's hull that are under water. **7** (in literary or commercial contexts) a boat or ship. **8** (often pl) US & Canad. the low land bordering a river. **9** (esp. of horses) staying power; stamina. **10** Inf. the buttocks. **11** impor-tance, seriousness, or influence: his views have weight and bottom. **12 at bottom.** in reality; basically. **13 be at the bottom of.** to be the ultimate cause of. **14 get to the bottom of.** to dis-cover the real truth about. ◆ adj (prenominal) **15** lowest or last. **16 bet** (or **put**) **one's bottom dollar on.** to be absolutely sure of. **17** of, relating to, or situated at the bottom. **18** fundamental; basic. ◆ vb **19** (tr) to provide (a chair, etc.) with a bottom or seat. **20** (tr) to discover the full facts or truth of; fathom. **21** (usually foll. by on or upon) to base or be founded (on an idea, etc.). [OE botm]

ʙottom drawer n Brit. a young woman's collection of linen, cutlery, etc., made in anticipation of marriage. US, Canad., and NZ equivalent: **hope chest.**

ʙottoming ('bɒtəmɪŋ) n the lowest level of foundation material for a road or other structure.

ʙottomless ('bɒtəmlɪs) adj **1** having no bottom. **2** un-limited; inexhaustible. **3** very deep.

ʙottom line n **1** the last line of a financial statement that shows the net profit or loss of a company or organi-zation. **2** the conclusion or main point of a process, dis-cussion, etc.

ʙottom out vb (intr, adv) to reach the lowest point and level out.

ʙottomry ('bɒtəmrɪ) n, pl **bottomries.** Maritime law. a con-tract whereby the owner of a ship borrows money to en-able the vessel to complete the voyage and pledges the ship as security for the loan. [C16: from Du. bodemerij, from bodem BOTTOM (hull of a ship) + -erij -RY]

ʙottom-up processing n a processing technique, ei-ther in the brain or in a computer, in which incoming information is analysed in successive steps and later-stage processing does not affect processing in earlier stages.

Bottrop ★ (German 'bɒtrɒp) n an industrial city in W Ger-many, in North Rhine-Westphalia in the Ruhr. Pop.: 119 669 (1995 est.).

botulism ('bɒtjʊˌlɪzəm) n severe, often fatal, poisoning resulting from the potent bacterial toxin, **botulin,** pro-duced in imperfectly preserved food, etc. [C19: from G Botulismus, lit.: sausage poisoning, from L botulus sau-sage]

Bouaké ★ (French bwake) n a market town in S central Côte d'Ivoire. Pop.: 329 850 (1988).

Boucher ★ (French buʃe) n **François** (frɑ̃swa). 1703–70, French rococo artist.

Bouches-du-Rhône ★ (French buʃdyron) n a depart-ment of S central France, in Provence-Alpes-Côte d'Azur region. Capital: Marseille. Pop.: 1 793 876 (1994 est.). Area: 5284 sq. km (2047 sq. miles).

bouclé ('buːkleɪ) n **1** a curled or looped yarn or fabric giv-ing a thick knobbly effect. ◆ adj **2** of or designating such a yarn or fabric. [C19: from F bouclé curly, from boucle a curl]

Boudicca ★ (bəʊˈdɪkə) n died 62 A.D., a queen of the Iceni, who led a revolt against Roman rule in Britain; after being defeated she poisoned herself. Also called: **Boadicea.**

Boudin ★ (French budɛ̃) n **Eugène** (øʒɛn). 1824–98, French painter.

boudoir ('buːdwɑː, -dwɔː) n a woman's bedroom or pri-vate sitting room. [C18: from F, lit.: room for sulking in, from bouder to sulk]

bouffant ('buːfɒŋ) adj **1** (of a hairstyle) having extra height and width through backcombing; puffed out. **2** (of sleeves, skirts, etc.) puffed out. [C20: from F, from bouffer to puff up]

Bougainville[1] ★ ('buːgənˌvɪl) n an island in the W Pa-cific, in Papua New Guinea: the largest of the Solomon Islands; unilaterally declared independence in 1990; oc-cupied by government troops in 1992. Chief town: Kieta. Pop.: 159 500 (1990 est.). Area: 10 049 sq. km (3880 sq. miles).

Bougainville[2] ★ (French bugɛ̃vil) n **Louis Antoine de** (lwi ɑ̃twan də). 1729–1811, French navigator.

bougainvillea (ˌbuːgənˈvɪlɪə) n a tropical woody climb-ing plant having inconspicuous flowers surrounded by showy red or purple bracts. [C19: NL, after L. A. de BOUGAINVILLE]

bough (baʊ) n any of the main branches of a tree. [OE bōg arm, twig]

bought (bɔːt) vb the past tense and past participle of **buy.**

bougie ('buːʒiː, buːˈʒiː) n Med. a slender semiflexible in-strument for inserting into body passages such as the rectum or urethra to introduce medication, etc. [C18: from F, orig. a wax candle from Bougie (Bujiya), Algeria]

bouillabaisse (ˌbuːjəˈbɛs) n a rich stew or soup of fish and vegetables. [C19: from F, from Provençal bouiabaisso, lit.: boil down]

bouillon ('buːjɒn) n a plain unclarified broth or stock. [C18: from F, from bouillir to BOIL[1]]

Boulanger ★ (French bulɑ̃ʒe) n **1 Georges** (ʒɔrʒ). 1837–91, French general and minister of war (1886–87). Accused of attempting a coup d'état, he fled to Belgium, where he committed suicide. **2 Nadia (Juliette)** (nadja). 1887–1979, French teacher of musical composition.

boulder ('bəʊldə) n a smooth rounded mass of rock that has been shaped by erosion. [C13: prob. from ON; cf. OSwedish bulder rumbling + sten STONE]

boulder clay n an unstratified glacial deposit consist-ing of fine clay, boulders, and pebbles.

Boulder Dam ★ n the former name (1933–47) of **Hoover Dam.**

boule ('buːliː) n **1** the senate of an ancient Greek city-state. **2** the parliament in modern Greece. [C19: from Gk boulē senate]

boules French. (bul) n (functioning as sing) a game, popular in France, in which metal bowls are thrown to land as near as possible to a target ball. [pl. of boule BALL[1]: see BOWL[2]]

boulevard ('buːlvɑː, -vɑːd) n a wide usually tree-lined road in a city. [C18: from F, from MDu. bolwerc BULWARK; so called because orig. often built on the ruins of an old rampart]

Boulez ★ ('buːlez; French bulɛ) n **Pierre** (pjɛr). born 1925, French composer and conductor, whose works employ total serialism.

boulle, boule, or buhl (buːl) adj **1** denoting or relating to a type of marquetry of patterned inlays of brass and tortoiseshell, etc. ◆ n **2** something ornamented with such marquetry. [C18: after A. C. Boulle (1642–1732), F cabinet-maker]

Boulogne ★ (bʊˈlɔɪn; French bulɔɲ) n a port in N France, on the English Channel. Pop.: 44 244 (1990). Official name: **Boulogne-sur-Mer** (French bulɔɲsyrmɛr).

Boulogne-Billancourt ★ (French bulɔɲbijɑ̃kur) n an industrial suburb of SW Paris. Pop.: 101 971 (1990). Also called: **Boulogne-sur-Seine** (French bulɔɲsyrsɛn).

boult (bəʊlt) vb a variant spelling of **bolt**[2].

Boult ★ (bəʊlt) n Sir **Adrian (Cedric).** 1889–1983, British conductor.

Boulton ★ ('bəʊlt³n) n **Matthew.** 1728–1809, British engi-neer and manufacturer, who financed Watt's steam en-gine and applied it to various industrial purposes.

★ people and places

Boumédienne ★ (buːˌmeɪdɪˈɛn) *n* **Houari** (ˈhaʊərɪ). 1927–78, Algerian statesman and soldier: prime minister of Algeria (1965–78) after overthrowing Ben Bella in a coup (1965).

bounce (baʊns) *vb* **bounces, bouncing, bounced**. **1** (*intr*) (of a ball, etc.) to rebound from an impact. **2** (*tr*) to cause (a ball, etc.) to hit a solid surface and spring back. **3** to move or cause to move suddenly, excitedly, or violently; spring. **4** *Sl.* (of a bank) to send (a cheque) back or (of a cheque) to be sent back by a bank to a payee unredeemed because of lack of funds in the drawer's account. **5** (*tr*) *Sl.* to force (a person) to leave a place or job; throw out; eject. ◆ *n* **6** the action of rebounding from an impact. **7** a leap; jump; bound. **8** the quality of being able to rebound; springiness. **9** *Inf.* vitality; vigour; resilience. **10** *Brit.* swagger or impudence. [C13: prob. imit.; cf. Low G *bunsen* to beat, Du. *bonken* to thump]

bounce back *vb* (*intr, adv*) to recover one's health, good spirits, confidence, etc., easily.

bouncer (ˈbaʊnsə) *n Sl.* a man employed at a club, disco, etc., to eject drunks or troublemakers.

bouncing (ˈbaʊnsɪŋ) *adj* (when *postpositive*, foll. by *with*) vigorous and robust (esp. in **a bouncing baby**).

bouncy (ˈbaʊnsɪ) *adj* **bouncier, bounciest**. **1** lively, exuberant, or self-confident. **2** having the capability or quality of bouncing: *a bouncy ball*. **3** responsive to bouncing; springy: *a bouncy bed*.

Bouncy Castle *n Trademark*. a large inflatable model, usually of a castle, on which children may bounce at fairs, etc.

bound[1] (baʊnd) *vb* **1** the past tense and past participle of **bind**. ◆ *adj* **2** in bonds or chains; tied as with a rope. **3** (*in combination*) restricted; confined: *housebound*. **4** (*postpositive*; foll. by an infinitive) destined; sure; certain: *it's bound to happen*. **5** (*postpositive*; often foll. by *by*) compelled or obliged. **6** *Rare*. constipated. **7** (of a book) secured within a cover or binding. **8** *Logic*. (of a variable) occurring within the scope of a quantifier. Cf. **free** (sense 18). **9 bound up with**. closely or inextricably linked with.

bound[2] (baʊnd) *vb* **1** to move forwards by leaps or jumps. **2** to bounce; spring away from an impact. ◆ *n* **3** a jump upwards or forwards. **4** a bounce, as of a ball. [C16: from OF *bond* a leap]

bound[3] (baʊnd) *vb* **1** (*tr*) to place restrictions on; limit. **2** (when *intr*, foll. by *on*) to form a boundary of. ◆ *n* **3** See **bounds**. [C13: from OF *bonde*, from Med. L *bodina*]

bound[4] (baʊnd) *adj* **a** (*postpositive*; often foll. by *for*) going or intending to go towards: *bound for Jamaica; homeward bound*. **b** (*in combination*): *northbound traffic*. [C13: from ON *buinn*, p.p. of *būa* to prepare]

boundary (ˈbaʊndərɪ, -drɪ) *n, pl* **boundaries**. **1** something that indicates the farthest limit, as of an area; border. **2** *Cricket*. **2a** the marked limit of the playing area. **2b** a stroke that hits the ball beyond this limit. **2c** the four or six runs scored with such a stroke.

boundary rider *n Austral.* an employee on a sheep or cattle station whose job is to maintain fences.

bounden (ˈbaʊndən) *adj* morally obligatory (arch. except in **bounden duty**). [arch. p.p. of BIND]

bounder (ˈbaʊndə) *n Old-fashioned Brit. sl.* a morally reprehensible person; cad.

boundless (ˈbaʊndlɪs) *adj* unlimited; vast: *boundless energy*.
▶ **ˈboundlessly** *adv*

bounds (baʊndz) *pl n* **1** (*sometimes sing*) a limit; boundary (esp. in **know no bounds**). **2** something that restrains or confines, esp. the standards of a society: *within the bounds of modesty*. ◆ See also **out of bounds**.

bounteous (ˈbaʊntɪəs) *adj Literary*. **1** giving freely; generous. **2** plentiful; abundant.
▶ **ˈbounteously** *adv* ▶ **ˈbounteousness** *n*

bountiful (ˈbaʊntɪful) *adj* **1** plentiful; ample (esp. in **a bountiful supply**). **2** giving freely; generous.
▶ **ˈbountifully** *adv*

bounty (ˈbaʊntɪ) *n, pl* **bounties**. **1** generosity; liberality. **2** a generous gift. **3** a payment made by a government, as, formerly, to a sailor on enlisting or to a soldier after a

campaign. **4** any reward or premium. [C13 (in th⟨e⟩ sense: goodness): from OF, from L, from *bonus* good]

bouquet (buːˈkeɪ) *n* **1** a bunch of flowers, esp. a larg⟨e⟩ carefully arranged one. **2** the characteristic aroma or fra⟨-⟩ grance of a wine or liqueur. **3** a compliment or expres⟨-⟩ sion of praise. [C18: from F: thicket, from OF *bosc* forest]

bouquet garni (ˈbuːkeɪ gɑːˈniː) *n, pl* **bouquets garni⟨s⟩** (ˈbuːkeɪz gɑːˈniː). a bunch of herbs tied together and use⟨d⟩ for flavouring soups, stews, etc. [C19: from F, lit.: gar⟨-⟩ nished bouquet]

bourbon (ˈbɜːbən) *n* a whiskey distilled, chiefly in th⟨e⟩ US, from maize, esp. one containing at least 51 per cen⟨t⟩ maize. [C19: after *Bourbon* county, Kentucky, where ⟨it⟩ was first made]

Bourbon ★ (ˈbʊəbən; *French* burbɔ̃) *n* **a** a member of th⟨e⟩ European royal line that ruled in France from 1589 t⟨o⟩ 1793 (when Louis XVI was executed by the revolution⟨-⟩ aries) and was restored in 1815, continuing to rule in it⟨s⟩ Orleans branch from 1830 until 1848. Bourbon dynas⟨-⟩ ties also ruled in Spain (1700–1808; 1813–1931) and Na⟨-⟩ ples and Sicily (1734–1806; 1815–1860). **b** (*as modifier*) *the Bourbon kings*.

bourdon (ˈbʊədən, ˈbɔːdən) *n* **1** a bass organ stop. **2** th⟨e⟩ drone of a bagpipe. [C14: from OF: drone (of a musica⟨l⟩ instrument), imit.]

bourgeois (ˈbʊəʒwɑː) *Often disparaging*. ◆ *n, pl* **bourgeois**. **1** a member of the middle class, esp. one regarded a⟨s⟩ being conservative and materialistic or capitalistic. **2** ⟨a⟩ mediocre, unimaginative, or materialistic person. ◆ *ad⟨j⟩* **3** characteristic of, relating to, or comprising the middl⟨e⟩ class. **4** conservative or materialistic in outlook. **5** (i⟨n⟩ Marxist thought) dominated by capitalists or capitalis⟨t⟩ interests. [C16: from OF *borjois, burgeis* burgher, citizen⟨;⟩ see BURGESS]
▶ **bourgeoise** (ˈbʊəʒwɑːz, bʊəˈʒwɑːz) *fem n*

bourgeoisie (ˌbʊəʒwɑːˈziː) *n* **the. 1** the middle classes. **2** (in Marxist thought) the capitalist ruling class. The bour⟨-⟩ geoisie owns the means of production, through which i⟨t⟩ exploits the working class.

bourgeon (ˈbɜːdʒən) *n, vb* a variant spelling of **burgeon**.

Bourges ★ (*French* burʒ) *n* a city in central France. Pop. 75 609 (1990).

Bourgogne ★ (burgɔɲ) *n* the French name for **Burgundy**.

Bourguiba ★ (bʊəˈɡiːbə) *n* **Habib ben Ali** (hæˈbɪb bɛn ˈɑːlɪ). born 1903, Tunisian statesman: president of Tunisia (1957–87).

bourn[1] *or* **bourne** (bɔːn) *n Arch.* **1** a destination; goal. **2** ⟨a⟩ boundary. [C16: from OF *borne*; see BOUND[3]]

bourn[2] (bɔːn) *n Chiefly southern Brit.* a stream. [C16: from OF *bodne* limit; see BOUND[3]]

Bournemouth ★ (ˈbɔːnməθ) *n* a resort and unitary au⟨-⟩ thority in S England, in SE Dorset, on the English Chan⟨-⟩ nel. Pop.: 160 900 (1995).

bourrée (ˈbʊəreɪ) *n* **1** a traditional French dance in fast duple time. **2** a piece of music in the rhythm of this dance. [C18: from F]

Bourse (bʊəs) *n* a stock exchange of continental Europe, esp. Paris. [C19: from F, lit.: purse, from Med. L *bursa*, ult. from Gk: leather]

boustrophedon (ˌbaʊstrəˈfiːdᵊn) *adj* having alternate lines written from right to left and from left to right. [C17: from Gk, lit.: turning as in ploughing with oxen, from *bous* ox + *strephein* to turn]

bout (baʊt) *n* **1a** a period of time spent doing something, such as drinking. **1b** a period of illness. **2** a contest or fight, esp. a boxing or wrestling match. [C16: var. of obs. *bought* turn]

boutique (buːˈtiːk) *n* **1** a shop, esp. a small one selling fashionable clothes and other items. **2** (*modifier*) of or denoting a small specialized producer or business: *a boutique operation*. [C18: from F, ult. from Gk *apothēkē* storehouse]

boutonniere (ˌbuːtɒnɪˈɛə) *n* the US name for **buttonhole** (sense 2). [C19: from F: buttonhole]

bouzouk⟨i⟩ (buːˈzuːkɪ) *n* a Greek long-necked stringed mu⟨-⟩ sical instrument related to the mandolin. [C20: from Mod. Gk, ?from Turkish *büjük* large]

★ people and places

ovine ('bəʊvaɪn) *adj* **1** of or relating to cattle. **2** (of people) dull; sluggish; stolid. [C19: from LL *bovīnus*, from L *bōs* ox, cow]
▶ '**bovinely** *adv*

ovine somatotrophin *n* the full name for **BST** (sense 1).

ovine spongiform encephalopathy *n* the full name for **BSE**.

Bovril ('bɒvrɪl) *n Trademark.* a concentrated beef extract, used for flavouring, as a stock, etc.

ovver ('bɒvə) *n Brit. sl.* **a** rowdiness, esp. caused by gangs of teenage youths. **b** (*as modifier*): *a bovver boy.* [C20: sl. pronunciation of BOTHER]

ow[1] (baʊ) *vb* **1** to lower (one's head) or bend (one's knee or body) as a sign of respect, greeting, assent, or shame. **2** to bend or cause to bend. **3** (*intr; usually foll. by to or before*) to comply or accept: *bow to the inevitable.* **4** (*tr; foll. by in, out, to*, etc.) to usher (someone) in or out with bows and deference. **5** (*tr; usually foll. by down*) to bring (a person, nation, etc.) to a state of submission. **6 bow and scrape.** to behave in an excessively deferential or obsequious way. ♦ *n* **7** a lowering or inclination of the head or body as a mark of respect, greeting, or assent. **8 take a bow.** to acknowledge or receive applause or praise. ♦ See also **bow out**. [OE *būgan*]

ow[2] (bəʊ) *n* **1** a weapon for shooting arrows, consisting of an arch of flexible wood, plastic, etc., bent by a string fastened at each end. **2a** a long stick across which are stretched strands of horsehair, used for playing the strings of a violin, viola, cello, etc. **2b** a stroke with such a stick. **3a** a decorative interlacing of ribbon or other fabrics, usually having two loops and two loose ends. **3b** the knot forming such an interlacing. **4** something that is curved, bent, or arched. ♦ *vb* **5** to form or cause to form a curve or curves. **6** to make strokes of a bow across (violin strings). [OE *boga* arch, bow]

bow[3] (baʊ) *n* **1** *Chiefly Naut.* **1a** (*often pl*) the forward end or part of a vessel. **1b** (*as modifier*): *the bow mooring line.* **2** *Rowing.* the oarsman at the bow. [C15: prob. from Low G *boog*]

bow compass (bəʊ) *n Geom.* a compass in which the legs are joined by a flexible metal bow-shaped spring rather than a hinge.

bowdlerize *or* **bowdlerise** ('baʊdlə,raɪz) *vb* **bowdlerizes, bowdlerizing, bowdlerized** *or* **bowdlerises, bowdlerising, bowdlerised.** (*tr*) to remove passages or words regarded as indecent from (a play, novel, etc.); expurgate. [C19: after Thomas *Bowdler* (1754–1825), E editor who expurgated Shakespeare]
▶ ,**bowdleri'zation** *or* ,**bowdleri'sation** *n* ▶ '**bowdlerism** *n*

bowel ('baʊəl) *n* **1** an intestine, esp. the large intestine in man. **2** (*pl*) innards; entrails. **3** (*pl*) the deep or innermost part (esp. in **the bowels of the earth**). [C13: from OF *bouel*, from L *botellus* a little sausage]

bowel movement *n* **1** the discharge of faeces; defecation. **2** the waste matter discharged; faeces.

Bowen ★ ('bəʊən) *n* **Elizabeth (Dorothea Cole).** 1899–1973, British writer, born in Ireland. Her novels include *The Death of the Heart* (1938) and *The Heat of the Day* (1949).

bower[1] ('baʊə) *n* **1** a shady leafy shelter or recess, as in a wood or garden; arbour. **2** *Literary.* a lady's bedroom or apartments; boudoir. [OE *būr* dwelling]

bower[2] ('baʊə) *n Naut.* a vessel's bow anchor. [C18: from BOW[3] + -ER[1]]

bowerbird ('baʊə,bɜːd) *n* **1** any of various songbirds of Australia and New Guinea. The males build bower-like display grounds to attract the females. **2** *Inf., chiefly Austral.* a collector of unconsidered trifles.

Bowery ★ ('baʊərɪ) *n* **the.** a street in New York City noted for its cheap hotels and bars, frequented by vagrants and drunks. [C17: from Du. *bouwerij*, from *bouwen* to farm + *erij* -ERY]

bowfin ('bəʊ,fɪn) *n* a primitive North American freshwater bony fish with an elongated body and a very long dorsal fin.

bowhead ('bəʊ,hed) *n* a large-mouthed arctic right whale. Also called: **Greenland whale.**

Bowie ★ *n* **1** ('baʊɪ, 'bəʊɪ) **David,** real name *David Jones.* born 1947, British rock singer and film actor. His recordings include "Space Oddity" (1969), *Let's Dance* (1983), and *Earthling* (1997). **2** ('bəʊɪ). **James,** known as *Jim Bowie.* 1796–1836, US frontiersman. A hero of the Texas Revolution, he died at the Battle of Alamo.

bowie knife ('bəʊɪ) *n* a stout hunting knife with a short hilt and a guard for the hand. [C19: named after Jim BOWIE, who popularized it]

bowl[1] (bəʊl) *n* **1** a round container open at the top, used for holding liquid, serving food, etc. **2** Also: **bowlful.** the amount a bowl will hold. **3** the rounded or hollow part of an object, esp. of a spoon or tobacco pipe. **4** any container shaped like a bowl, such as a sink or lavatory. **5** a bowl-shaped building or other structure, such as an amphitheatre. **6** *Chiefly US.* a bowl-shaped depression of the land surface. **7** *Literary.* a drinking cup. [OE *bolla*]

bowl[2] (bəʊl) *n* **1** a wooden ball used in the game of bowls, having one flattened side in order to make it run on a curved course. **2** a large heavy ball with holes for gripping, used in tenpin bowling. ♦ *vb* **3** to roll smoothly or cause to roll smoothly along the ground. **4** (*intr; usually foll. by along*) to move easily and rapidly, as in a car. **5** *Cricket.* **5a** to send (a ball) from one's hand towards the batsman. **5b** Also: **bowl out.** to dismiss (a batsman) by delivering a ball that breaks his wicket. **6** (*intr*) to play bowls or tenpin bowling. ♦ See also **bowl over, bowls.** [C15: from F *boule*, ult. from L *bulla* bubble]

bow legs (bəʊ) *pl n* a condition in which the legs curve outwards like a bow between the ankle and the thigh. Also called: **bandy legs.**
▶ **bow-legged** (bəʊ'legɪd, bəʊ'legd) *adj*

bowler[1] ('bəʊlə) *n* **1** one who bowls in cricket. **2** a player at the game of bowls.

bowler[2] ('bəʊlə) *n* a stiff felt hat with a rounded crown and narrow curved brim. US and Canad. name: **derby.** [C19: after John *Bowler*, 19th-cent. London hatter]

Bowles ★ ('bəʊlz) *n* **Paul.** born 1910, US writer and composer, living in Tangiers. His novels include *The Sheltering Sky* (1949) and *The Spider's House* (1955).

bowline ('bəʊlɪn) *n Naut.* **1** a line for controlling the weather leech of a square sail when a vessel is close-hauled. **2** a knot used for securing a loop that will not slip at the end of a piece of rope. [C14: prob. from MLow G *bōline*, equivalent to BOW[3] + LINE[1]]

bowling ('bəʊlɪŋ) *n* **1** any of various games in which a heavy ball is rolled down a special alley at a group of wooden pins. **2** the game of bowls. **3** *Cricket.* the act of delivering the ball to the batsman.

bowling alley *n* **1a** a long narrow wooden lane down which the ball is rolled in tenpin bowling. **1b** a similar lane or alley for playing skittles. **2** a building having lanes for tenpin bowling.

bowling crease *n Cricket.* a line marked at the wicket, over which a bowler must not advance fully before delivering the ball.

bowling green *n* an area of closely mown turf on which the game of bowls is played.

bowl over *vb* (*tr, adv*) **1** *Inf.* to surprise (a person) greatly, esp. in a pleasant way; astound; amaze. **2** to knock down.

bowls (bəʊlz) *n* (*functioning as sing*) **1** a game played on a bowling green in which a small bowl (the jack) is pitched from a mark and two opponents take turns to roll biased wooden bowls as near the jack as possible. **2** skittles or tenpin bowling.

bowman ('bəʊmən) *n, pl* **bowmen.** *Arch.* an archer.

bow out (baʊ) *vb* (*adv; usually tr; often foll. by of*) to retire or withdraw gracefully.

bowser ('baʊzə) *n* **1** a tanker containing fuel for aircraft, military vehicles, etc. **2** *Austral. & NZ obs.* a petrol pump at a filling station. [orig. a US proprietary name]

bowshot ('bəʊ,ʃɒt) *n* the distance an arrow travels from the bow.

bowsprit ('bəʊsprɪt) *n Naut.* a spar projecting from the bow of a vessel, esp. a sailing vessel. [C13: from MLow G, from *bōch* BOW[3] + *sprēt* pole]

★ people and places

bowstring ('bəʊˌstrɪŋ) n the string of an archer's bow.

bow tie (bəʊ) n a man's tie tied in a bow, now chiefly in plain black for formal evening wear.

bow window (bəʊ) n a bay window in the shape of a curve.

bow-wow ('baʊˌwaʊ, -'waʊ) n 1 a child's word for **dog. 2** an imitation of the bark of a dog. ◆ vb 3 (intr) to bark or imitate a dog's bark.

bowyangs ('bəʊjæŋz) pl n Austral. & NZ sl. a pair of strings or straps worn around the trouser leg below the knee, orig. esp. by agricultural workers. [C19: from E dialect bowy-yanks leggings]

box[1] (bɒks) n 1 a receptacle or container made of wood, cardboard, etc., usually rectangular and having a removable or hinged lid. 2 Also called: **boxful.** the contents of such a receptacle. 3 (often in combination) any of various small cubicles, kiosks, or shelters: a telephone box; a signal box. 4 a separate compartment in a public place for a small group of people, as in a theatre. 5 an enclosure within a courtroom: witness box. 6 a compartment for a horse in a stable or a vehicle. 7 Brit. a small country house occupied by sportsmen when following a field sport, esp. shooting. 8a a protective housing for machinery or mechanical parts. 8b (in combination): a gearbox. 9 a shaped device of light tough material worn by sportsmen to protect the genitals, esp. in cricket. 10 a section of printed matter on a page, enclosed by lines, a border, etc. 11 a central agency to which mail is addressed and from which it is collected or redistributed: a post-office box; a box number in a newspaper advertisement. 12 short for **penalty box. 13** the raised seat on which the driver sits in a horse-drawn coach. **14** Austral. & NZ. an accidental mixing of herds or flocks. **15** Brit. (esp. formerly) a present, esp. of money, given at Christmas to tradesmen, etc. **16** Austral. taboo sl. the female genitals. **17 out of the box.** Austral. inf. outstanding or excellent. **18 the box.** Brit. inf. television. ◆ vb **19** (tr) to put into a box. **20** (tr; usually foll. by in or up) to prevent from moving freely; confine. **21** (tr; foll. by in) Printing. to enclose (text) within a ruled frame. **22** Austral. & NZ. to mix (flocks or herds) or (of flocks) to become mixed accidentally. **23 box the compass.** Naut. to name the compass points in order. [OE box, from L buxus, from Gk puxos BOX³]
▶ 'box,like adj

box² (bɒks) vb **1** (tr) to fight (an opponent) in a boxing match. **2** (intr) to engage in boxing. **3** (tr) to hit (a person) with the fist. ◆ n **4** a punch with the fist, esp. on the ear. [C14: from ?]

box³ (bɒks) n **1** a slow-growing evergreen tree or shrub with small shiny leaves: used for hedges. **2** the wood of this tree. **3** any of several trees the timber or foliage of which resembles this tree, esp. various eucalyptus trees with rough bark. [OE, from L buxus, from Gk puxus]

box camera n a simple box-shaped camera having an elementary lens, shutter, and viewfinder.

box chronometer n Naut. a ship's chronometer, supported on gimbals in a wooden box.

boxer ('bɒksə) n **1** a person who boxes; pugilist. **2** a medium-sized smooth-haired breed of dog with a short nose and a docked tail.

Boxer ('bɒksə) n a member of a nationalistic Chinese secret society that led an unsuccessful rebellion in 1900 against foreign interests in China. [C18: rough translation of Chinese I Ho Ch'üan, lit.: virtuous harmonious fist]

boxer shorts pl n men's underpants shaped like shorts but having a front opening. Also called: **boxers.**

box girder n a girder that is hollow and square or rectangular in shape.

boxing ('bɒksɪŋ) n a the act, art, or profession of fighting with the fists. b (as modifier): a boxing enthusiast.

Boxing Day n Brit. the first day (traditionally and strictly, the first weekday) after Christmas, observed as a holiday. [C19: from the custom of giving Christmas boxes to tradesmen and staff on this day]

boxing glove n one of a pair of thickly padded mittens worn for boxing.

box junction n (in Britain) a road junction having yel low cross-hatching painted on the road surface. Vehicle may only enter the hatched area when their exit is clear

box kite n a kite with a boxlike frame open at both ends

box lacrosse n Canad. lacrosse played indoors. Als called: **boxla.**

box number n **1** the number of an individual pigeon hole at a newspaper to which replies to an advertise ment may be addressed. **2** the number of an individua pigeonhole at a post office from which mail may be col lected.

box office n **1** an office at a theatre, cinema, etc., wher tickets are sold. **2a** the public appeal of an actor or pro duction. **2b** (as modifier): a box-office success.

box pleat n a flat double pleat made by folding unde the fabric on either side of it.

boxroom ('bɒksˌruːm, -ˌrʊm) n a small room or large cupboard in which boxes, cases, etc., may be stored.

box seat n **1** a seat in a theatre box. **2 in the box seat.** Brit Austral., & NZ. in the best position.

box spanner n a spanner consisting of a steel cylinde with a hexagonal end that fits over a nut.

box spring n a coiled spring contained in a boxlik frame, used for mattresses, chairs, etc.

boxwood ('bɒksˌwʊd) n **1** the hard close-grained yellow wood of the box tree, used to make tool handles, etc. ʒ the box tree.

boxy ('bɒksɪ) adj squarish or chunky in style or appear ance: a boxy square-cut jacket.

boy (bɔɪ) n **1** a male child; lad; youth. **2** a man regarded a immature or inexperienced. **3 the boys.** Inf. a group o men, esp. a group of friends. **4** S. African derog. a Black male servant. **5 the boy.** Irish inf. the right tool for a partic ular task: that's the boy to cut it. ◆ interj **6** an exclamatior of surprise, pleasure, contempt, etc. [C13 (in the sense male servant; C14: young male): ?from Anglo-F abuié fet tered (unattested), from L boia fetter]
▶ 'boyish adj

Boyce ★ (bɔɪs) n **William.** ?1710–79, British composer, noted esp. for his church music and symphonies.

boycott ('bɔɪkɒt) vb **1** (tr) to refuse to have dealings with (a person, organization, etc.) or refuse to buy (a product) as a protest or means of coercion. ◆ n **2** an instance or the use of boycotting. [C19: after Captain C. C. Boycott (1832–97), Irish land agent, a victim of such practices for refusing to reduce rents]

Boycott ★ ('bɔɪkɒt) n **Geoff(rey).** born 1940, English cricketer: captained Yorkshire (1970–78); played for England (1964–74, 1977–82).

Boyd ★ (bɔɪd) n **1 Arthur.** born 1920, Australian painter and sculptor. **2 Martin (A'Beckett).** 1893–1972, Australian novelist, best known for The Montforts (1928). **3 William (Andrew Murray).** born 1953, British writer born in Ghana. His novels include An Ice-Cream War (1982).

Boyer ★ (French bwaje) n **Charles** (Jarl), known as the Great Lover. 1899–1978, French film actor.

boyfriend ('bɔɪˌfrɛnd) n a male friend with whom a person is romantically or sexually involved; sweetheart or lover.

boyhood ('bɔɪhʊd) n the state or time of being a boy.

Boyle ★ (bɔɪl) n **Robert.** 1627–91, Irish scientist who helped to dissociate chemistry from alchemy; author of The Sceptical Chymist (1661).

Boyle's law n the principle that the pressure of a gas varies inversely with its volume at constant temperature. [C18: after Robert BOYLE]

Boyne ★ (bɔɪn) n a river in the E Republic of Ireland, rising in the Bog of Allen and flowing northeast to the Irish Sea: William III of England defeated the deposed James II in a battle (**Battle of the Boyne**) on its banks in 1690, completing the overthrow of the Stuart cause in Ireland. Length: about 112 km (70 miles).

boyo ('bɔɪəʊ) n Brit. inf. a boy or young man: often used in direct address. [from Irish and Welsh]

Boyoma Falls ★ (bɔɪ'əʊmə) pl n a series of seven cataracts in the Democratic Republic of the Congo (formerly

Zaïre), on the upper River Congo: forms an unnavigable stretch of 90 km (56 miles), which falls 60 m (200 ft). Former name: **Stanley Falls.**

oy racer n Derog. sl. **a** a young man who drives a car irresponsibly and at high speeds. **b** (as modifier): boy-racer accessories.

oys' Brigade n (in Britain) an organization for boys, founded in 1883, with the aim of promoting discipline and self-respect.

oy scout n See **Scout.**

oysenberry ('bɔɪzᵊnbərɪ) n, pl **boysenberries.** **1** a type of bramble: a hybrid of the loganberry and various blackberries and raspberries. **2** the large red edible fruit of this plant. [C20: after Rudolph Boysen, American botanist]

oz ★ (bɒz) n pen name of (Charles) **Dickens.**

ozcaada ★ (ˌbɒzdʒaa'da) n the Turkish name for **Tenedos.**

ozen ★ ('bɔːtsən) n the German name for **Bolzano.**

p abbrev. for: **1** (of alcoholic density) below proof. **2** boiling point. **3** bishop. **4** Also: **B/P.** bills payable.

P abbrev. for: **1** blood pressure. **2** British Pharmacopoeia.

p. abbrev. for: **1** baptized. **2** birthplace.

/P or **bp** abbrev. for bills payable.

PC abbrev. for British Pharmaceutical Codex.

Phil abbrev. for Bachelor of Philosophy.

pi abbrev. for bits per inch (used of a computer tape).

PR abbrev. for business process re-engineering.

.pt. abbrev. for boiling point.

q Physics. symbol for becquerel.

r abbrev. for brother.

r **1** abbrev. for (in a religious order) Brother. ◆ **2** the chemical symbol for bromine.

R abbrev. for British Rail (British Railways).

r. abbrev. for: **1** branch. **2** bronze.

r. abbrev. for: **1** Breton. **2** Britain. **3** British.

ra (brɑː) n a woman's undergarment for covering and supporting the breasts. [C20: from BRASSIERE]

raai (braɪ) n short for **braaivleis.**

raaivleis (ˈbraɪˌfleɪs) n S. African. a barbecue. [from Afrik. braai grill + vleis meat]

rabant ★ (brə'bænt) n **1** a former duchy of W Europe: divided when Belgium became independent (1830), the south forming the Belgian provinces of Antwerp and Brabant and the north forming the province of North Brabant in the Netherlands. **2** a former province of central Belgium; replaced in 1995 by the provinces of **Flemish Brabant** and **Walloon Brabant.**

rabham ★ ('bræbəm) n Sir **John Arthur,** known as Jack. born 1926, Australian racing driver: world champion 1959, 1960, and 1966.

race (breɪs) n **1** a hand tool for drilling holes, with a socket to hold the drill on one end and a cranked handle by which the tool can be turned. See also **brace and bit. 2** something that steadies, binds, or holds up another thing. **3** a structural member, such as a beam or prop, used to stiffen a framework. **4** a pair, esp. of game birds. **5** either of a pair of characters, { }, used for connecting lines of printing or writing. **6** Also called: **accolade.** a line or bracket connecting two or more staves of music. **7** (often pl) an appliance of metal bands and wires for correcting uneven alignment of teeth. **8** Med. any of various appliances for supporting the trunk or a limb. **9** See **braces.** ◆ vb **braces, bracing, braced.** (mainly tr) **10** to provide, strengthen, or fit with a brace. **11** to steady or prepare (oneself or something) as before an impact. **12** (also intr) to stimulate; freshen; invigorate: sea air is bracing. [C14: from OF, from L brachia arms]

race and bit n a hand tool for boring holes, consisting of a cranked handle into which a drilling bit is inserted.

racelet ('breɪslɪt) n an ornamental chain worn around the arm or wrist. [C15: from OF, from L bracchium arm]

racelets ('breɪslɪts) pl n a slang name for **handcuffs.**

racer ('breɪsə) n **1** a person or thing that braces. **2** Inf. a tonic, esp. an alcoholic drink taken as a tonic.

braces ('breɪsɪz) pl n Brit. a pair of straps worn over the shoulders by men for holding up the trousers. US and Canad. word: **suspenders.**

brachial ('breɪkɪəl, 'bræk-) adj of or relating to the arm or to an armlike part or structure.

brachiate adj ('breɪkɪɪt, -ˌeɪt, 'bræk-). **1** Bot. having widely divergent paired branches. ◆ vb ('breɪkɪˌeɪt, 'bræk-), **brachiates, brachiating, brachiated. 2** (intr) (of some arboreal apes and monkeys) to swing by the arms from one hold to the next. [C19: from L bracchiātus with armlike branches]
▸ ˌbrachi'ation n

brachio- or before a vowel **brachi-** combining form. indicating a brachium: brachiopod.

brachiopod ('breɪkɪəˌpɒd, 'bræk-) n any marine invertebrate animal having a ciliated feeding organ and a shell consisting of dorsal and ventral valves. [C19: from NL Brachiopoda; see BRACHIUM, -POD]

brachiosaurus (ˌbreɪkɪə'sɔːrəs, ˌbræk-) n a dinosaur up to 30 metres long: the largest land animal ever known.

brachium ('breɪkɪəm, 'bræk-) n, pl **brachia** (-kɪə). **1** Anat. the arm, esp. the upper part. **2** a corresponding part in an animal. **3** Biol. a branching or armlike part. [C18: NL, from L bracchium arm]

brachy- combining form. indicating something short: brachycephalic. [from Gk brakhus short]

brachycephalic (ˌbrækɪsɪ'fælɪk) adj having a head nearly as broad from side to side as from front to back. Also: **brachycephalous** (ˌbrækɪ'sefələs).
▸ ˌbrachy'cephaly n

bracing ('breɪsɪŋ) adj **1** refreshing; stimulating; invigorating. ◆ n **2** a system of braces used to strengthen or support.

bracken ('brækən) n **1** Also called: **brake.** any of various large coarse ferns having small fronds with spore cases along the undersides. **2** a clump of any of these ferns. [C14: from ON]

bracket ('brækɪt) n **1** an L-shaped or other support fixed to a wall to hold a shelf, etc. **2** one or more wall shelves carried on brackets. **3** Archit. a support projecting from the side of a wall or other structure. **4** Also called: **square bracket.** either of a pair of characters, [ ], used to enclose a section of writing or printing. **5** a general name for **parenthesis** (sense 2), **square bracket,** and **brace** (sense 5). **6** a group or category falling within certain defined limits: the lower income bracket. **7** the distance between two preliminary shots of artillery fire in range-finding. ◆ vb **brackets, bracketing, bracketed.** (tr) **8** to fix or support by means of brackets. **9** to put (written or printed matter) in brackets. **10** to couple or join (two lines of text, etc.) with a brace. **11** (often foll. by with) to group or class together. **12** to adjust (artillery fire) until the target is hit. [C16: from OF braguette codpiece, from OProvençal braga, from L brāca breeches]

brackish ('brækɪʃ) adj (of water) slightly briny or salty. [C16: from MDu. brac salty; see -ISH]
▸ 'brackishness n

Bracknell ★ ('bræknəl) n a town in SE England, designated a new town in 1949. Pop.: 60 895 (1991).

Bracknell Forest ★ n a unitary authority in SE England. Pop.: 110 100 (1996).

bract (brækt) n a specialized leaf with a single flower or inflorescence growing in its axil. [C18: from L bractea thin metal plate, gold leaf, from ?]
▸ 'bracteal adj ▸ **bracteate** ('bræktɪɪt) adj

bracteole ('bræktɪˌəʊl) n a secondary or small bract. Also called: **bractlet.** [C19: from NL bracteola; see BRACT]

brad (bræd) n a small tapered nail with a small head. [OE brord point, prick]

bradawl ('bræd,ɔːl) n an awl used to pierce wood, leather, etc.

Bradbury ★ ('brædbərɪ) n **1 Malcolm (Stanley).** born 1932, British novelist and critic. His novels include The History Man (1975) and Doctor Criminale (1992). **2 Ray.** born 1920, US science-fiction writer. His novels include Fahrenheit 451 (1953), Death is a Lonely Business (1986), and A Graveyard for Lunatics (1990).

★ people and places

Bradford ★ ('brædfəd) *n* **1** an industrial city in N England, in West Yorkshire: a centre of the woollen industry from the 14th century and of the worsted trade from the 18th century. Pop.: 289 376 (1991). **2** a unitary authority in West Yorkshire. Pop.: 481 700 (1994 est.). Area: 370 sq. km (143 sq. miles).

Bradley ★ ('brædlɪ) *n* **1 Andrew Cecil.** 1851–1935, British critic; author of *Shakespearian Tragedy* (1904). **2 F(rancis) H(erbert).** 1846–1924, British idealist philosopher and metaphysical thinker; author of *Ethical Studies* (1876), *Principles of Logic* (1883), and *Appearance and Reality* (1893). **3 Henry.** 1845–1923, British lexicographer; one of the editors of the *Oxford English Dictionary*. **4 James.** 1693–1762, English astronomer, who discovered the aberration of light and the nutation of the earth's axis.

Bradman ★ ('brædmən) *n* (Sir) **Don(ald George).** born 1908, Australian cricketer.

Bradshaw ('bræd,ʃɔː) *n* a British railway timetable, published annually from 1839 to 1961. **[C19: after its original publisher, George *Bradshaw* (1801–53)]**

bradycardia (,brædɪ'kɑːdɪə) *n Pathol.* an abnormally slow heartbeat. **[C19: from Gk *bradus* slow + *kardia* heart]**

brae (breɪ) *n Scot.* **1** a hill or hillside **2** (*pl*) an upland area. **[C14 *bra*; rel to ON *brā* eyelash]**

Braemar ★ (,breɪ'mɑː) *n* a village in NE Scotland, in Aberdeenshire; Balmoral Castle is nearby: site of the Royal Braemar Gathering, an annual Highland Games meeting.

brag (bræg) *vb* **brags, bragging, bragged. 1** to speak arrogantly and boastfully. ◆ *n* **2** boastful talk or behaviour. **3** something boasted of. **4** a braggart; boaster. **5** a card game: an old form of poker. **[C13: from ?]**
▶ **'bragger** *n*

Braga ★ (*Portuguese* 'brɑːgə) *n* a city in N Portugal: capital of the Roman province of Lusitania; 12th-century cathedral, seat of the Primate of Portugal. Pop.: 90 535 (1991). Ancient name: **Bracara Augusta.**

Bragg ★ (bræg) *n* Sir **William Henry,** 1862–1942, and his son (**William**) **Lawrence,** 1890–1971, British physicists, who shared a Nobel prize for physics (1915) for their study of crystal structures by means of X-rays.

braggadocio (,brægə'dəʊtʃɪ,əʊ) *n, pl* **braggadocios. 1** vain empty boasting. **2** a person who boasts; braggart. **[C16: from *Braggadocchio*, a boastful character in Spenser's *Faerie Queene*; prob. from BRAGGART + It. *-occhio* (augmentative suffix)]**

braggart ('brægət) *n* **1** a person who boasts loudly or exaggeratedly; bragger. ◆ *adj* **2** boastful. **[C16: see BRAG]**

Bragi ('brɑːgɪ) *or* **Brage** ★ ('brɑːgə) *n Norse myth.* the god of poetry and music, son of Odin.

Brahe ★ (brɑː, 'brɑːhɪ; *Danish* 'brɑːə) *n* **Tycho** ('tyːço). 1546–1601, Danish astronomer, who supported Copernicus and worked with Kepler.

Brahma ('brɑːmə) *n* a Hindu god, the Creator. **[from Sansk., from *brahman* praise]**

Brahman ('brɑːmən) *n, pl* **Brahmans. 1** (*sometimes not cap.*) Also (esp. formerly): **Brahmin.** a member of the highest or priestly caste in the Hindu caste system. **2** another name for **Brahma. [C14: from Sansk. *brahman* prayer]**
▶ **Brahmanic** (brɑː'mænɪk) *or* **Brah'manical** *adj*

Brahmanism ('brɑːmə,nɪzəm) *or* **Brahminism** *n* (*sometimes not cap.*) the religious and social system of orthodox Hinduism.
▶ **'Brahmanist** *or* **'Brahminist** *n*

Brahmaputra ★ (,brɑːmə'puːtrə) *n* a river in S Asia, rising in SW Tibet as the Tsangpo and flowing through the Himalayas and NE India to join the Ganges at its delta in Bangladesh. Length: about 2900 km (1800 miles).

Brahmin ('brɑːmɪn) *n, pl* **Brahmin** *or* **Brahmins. 1** the older spelling of **Brahman** (a Hindu priest). **2** *US.* a highly intelligent or socially exclusive person.

Brahms ★ (brɑːmz) *n* **Johannes** (jo'hanəs). 1833–97, German composer. His works include four symphonies, four concertos, chamber music, and a requiem.

braid (breɪd) *vb* (*tr*) **1** to interweave (hair, thread, etc.);

plait. **2** to decorate with an ornamental trim or borde ◆ *n* **3** a length of hair, fabric, etc., that has been braide plait. **4** narrow ornamental tape of woven silk, wool, et **[OE *bregdan* to move suddenly, weave together]**
▶ **'braider** *n* ▶ **'braiding** *n*

Brăila ★ (*Romanian* brə'ila) *n* a port in E Romania: b longed to Turkey (1544–1828). Pop.: 236 344 (1993 est.

Braille[1] (breɪl) *n* **1** a system of writing for the blind con sisting of raised dots interpreted by touch. **2** any writin produced by this method. ◆ *vb* **Brailles, Brailling, Braille 3** (*tr*) to print or write using this method.

Braille[2] ★ (*French* braj) *n* **Louis** (lwi). 1809–52, French in ventor, musician, and teacher of the blind; blind fro the age of three, he devised the Braille system of writing

brain (breɪn) *n* **1** the soft convoluted mass of nervous ti sue within the skull of vertebrates that is the controllin and coordinating centre of the nervous system and th seat of thought, memory, and emotion. Related ad **cerebral. 2** (*often pl*) *Inf.* intellectual ability: *he's got brain* **3** *Inf.* shrewdness or cunning. **4** *Inf.* an intellectual or in telligent person. **5** (*usually pl; functioning as sing*) *Inf.* a pe son who plans and organizes. **6** an electronic device such as a computer, that performs similar functions t those of the human brain. **7 on the brain.** *Inf.* constantly i mind: *I had that song on the brain.* ◆ *vb* (*tr*) **8** to smash th skull of. **9** *Sl.* to hit hard on the head. **[OE *brægen*]**

brainchild ('breɪn,tʃaɪld) *n, pl* **brainchildren.** *Inf.* an idea c plan produced by creative thought.

braindead ('breɪn,dɛd) *adj* **1** having suffered brai death. **2** *Inf.* not using or showing intelligence; stupid.

brain death *n* irreversible cessation of respiration du to irreparable brain damage: widely considered as th criterion of death.

brain drain *n Inf.* the emigration of scientists, technolc gists, academics, etc.

Braine ★ (breɪn) *n* **John** (**Gerard**). 1922–86, British nove ist, whose works include *Room at the Top* (1957) and *Li at the Top* (1962).

brain fever *n* inflammation of the brain.

brainless ('breɪnlɪs) *adj* stupid or foolish.

brainpan ('breɪn,pæn) *n Inf.* the skull.

brainstem ('breɪn,stɛm) *n* the part of the brain that con trols such reflex actions as breathing and is continuou with the spinal cord.

brainstorm ('breɪn,stɔːm) *n* **1** a severe outburst of ex citement, often as the result of a transitory disturbanc of cerebral activity. **2** *Brit. inf.* a sudden mental aberra tion. **3** *US. & Canad. inf.* another word for **brainwave.**

brainstorming ('breɪn,stɔːmɪŋ) *n* intensive discussion to solve problems or generate ideas.

brains trust *n* a group of knowledgeable people whc discuss topics in public or on radio or television.

brain-teaser *or* **brain-twister** *n Inf.* a difficult prob lem.

brainwash ('breɪn,wɒʃ) *vb* (*tr*) to effect a radical change in the ideas and beliefs of (a person), esp. by method based on isolation, sleeplessness, etc.
▶ **'brain,washing** *n*

brainwave ('breɪn,weɪv) *n Inf.* a sudden idea or inspira tion.

brain wave *n* any of the fluctuations of electrical poten tial in the brain.

brainy ('breɪnɪ) *adj* **brainier, brainiest.** *Inf.* clever; intelli gent.
▶ **'braininess** *n*

braise (breɪz) *vb* **braises, braising, braised.** to cook (meat vegetables, etc.) by lightly browning in fat and ther cooking slowly in a closed pan with a small amount o liquid. **[C18: from F *braiser*, from OF *brese* live coals]**

brak (bræk) *n S. African.* a crossbred dog; mongrel. **[from Du. *brak* setter]**

brake[1] (breɪk) *n* **1** (*often pl*) a device for slowing or stop ping a vehicle, wheel, shaft, etc., or for keeping it sta tionary, esp. by means of friction. **2** a machine or tool for crushing or breaking flax or hemp to separate the fibres **3** Also called: **brake harrow.** a heavy harrow for breaking

up clods. **4** short for **shooting brake**. ◆ *vb* **brakes, braking, braked. 5** to slow down or cause to slow down, by or as if by using a brake. **6** (*tr*) to crush or break up using a brake. [C18: from MDu. *braeke*; rel. to *breken* to BREAK]
▸ **'brakeless** *adj*

rake[2] (breɪk) *n* an area of dense undergrowth, shrubs, brushwood, etc.; thicket. [OE *bracu*]

rake[3] (breɪk) *n* another name for **bracken** (sense 1).

rake[4] (breɪk) *vb Arch., chiefly biblical.* a past tense of **break**.

rake-fade *n* a decrease in the efficiency of the braking system of a motor vehicle as a result of overheating of the brakes.

rake horsepower *n* the rate at which an engine does work, expressed in horsepower. It is measured by the resistance of an applied brake. Abbrev.: **bhp.**

rake light *n* a red light or lights at the rear of a motor vehicle that light up when the brakes are applied.

rake lining *n* a renewable strip of asbestos riveted to a brake shoe.

rake pad *n* the flat metal casting, together with the attached friction material, in a disc brake.

rake shoe *n* **1** the curved metal casting to which the brake lining is riveted in a drum brake. **2** the curved metal casting together with the attached brake lining. ◆ Sometimes shortened (for both senses) to **shoe.**

rakesman ('breɪksmən) *n, pl* **brakesmen. 1** a pithead winch operator. **2** a brake operator on railway rolling stock.

rake van *n Railways, Brit.* the coach or vehicle from which the guard applies the brakes; guard's van.

rakpan ★ ('bræk,pæn) *n* a city in E South Africa: gold-mining centre. Pop.: 46 416 (1985).

ramante ★ (*Italian* bra'mante) *n* **Donato** (do'nato). ?1444–1514, Italian Renaissance architect and artist.

ramble ('bræmbəl) *n* **1** any of various prickly rosaceous plants or shrubs, esp. the blackberry. **2** any of several similar and related shrubs, such as the dog rose. **3** *Scot. & N English.* a blackberry. [OE *brǣmbel*]
▸ **'brambly** *adj*

rambling ('bræmblɪŋ) *n* a Eurasian finch with a speckled head and back and, in the male, a reddish-brown breast.

ran (bræn) *n* **1** husks of cereal grain separated from the flour. **2** food prepared from these husks. [C13: from OF, prob. of Gaulish origin]

ranagh ★ ('brænə) *n* **Kenneth.** born 1961, British actor and director, born in Northern Ireland.

ranch (brɑːntʃ) *n* **1** a secondary woody stem arising from the trunk or bough of a tree or the main stem of a shrub. **2** an offshoot or secondary part: *a branch of a deer's antlers.* **3a** a subdivision or subsidiary section of something larger or more complex: *branches of learning; branch of the family.* **3b** (*as modifier*): *a branch office.* **4** *US.* any small stream. ◆ *vb* **5** (*intr*) (of a tree or other plant) to produce or possess branches. **6** (*intr*; usually foll. by *from*) (of stems, roots, etc.) to grow and diverge (from another part). **7** to divide or be divided into subsidiaries or offshoots. **8** (*intr*; often foll. by *off*) to diverge from the main way, road, topic, etc. [C13: from OF *branche*, from LL *branca* paw, foot]
▸ **'branch,like** *adj*

ranchia ('brænkɪə) *n, pl* **branchiae** (-kɪ,iː). a gill in aquatic animals.
▸ **'branchial** *or* **'branchiate** *adj*

ranch out *vb* (*intr, adv*; often foll. by *into*) to expand or extend one's interests.

rancusi ★ (bræŋ'kuːzɪ; *Romanian* briŋ'kuʃj) *n* **Constantin** (konstan'tin). 1876–1957, Romanian sculptor.

rand (brænd) *n* **1** a particular product or a characteristic that identifies a particular producer. **2** a particular kind or variety. **3** an identifying mark made, usually by burning, on the skin of animals or (formerly) slaves or criminals, esp. as proof of ownership. **4** an iron heated and used for branding animals, etc. **5** a mark of disgrace or infamy; stigma. **6** a burning or burnt piece of wood, as in

a fire. **7** *Arch. or poetic.* **7a** a flaming torch. **7b** a sword. **8** a fungal disease of garden plants characterized by brown spots on the leaves. ◆ *vb* (*tr*) **9** to label, burn, or mark with or as with a brand. **10** to place indelibly in the memory: *the scene was branded in their minds.* **11** to denounce; stigmatize: *they branded him a traitor.* [OE *brand-*; see BURN[1]]
▸ **'brander** *n* ▸ **'branding** *n*

Brandenburg ★ ('brændən,bɜːɡ; *German* 'brandənburk) *n* **1** a state in NE Germany, part of East Germany until 1990. A former electorate, it expanded to become the kingdom of Prussia (1701). The district east of the Oder River became Polish in 1945. Capital: Potsdam. Pop.: 2 536 700 (1995 est.). Area: 29 481 sq. km (11 219 sq. miles). **2** a city in NE Germany: former capital of the Prussian province of Brandenburg. Pop.: 93 660 (1989 est.).

brandish ('brændɪʃ) *vb* **1** (*tr*) to wave or flourish (a weapon, etc.) in a triumphant, threatening, or ostentatious way. ◆ *n* **2** a threatening or defiant flourish. [C14: from OF *brandir*, of Gmc origin]
▸ **'brandisher** *n*

brand leader *n* the most widely sold brand of a particular product.

brandling ('brændlɪŋ) *n* a small red earthworm, found in manure and used as bait by anglers. [C17: from BRAND (n) + -LING[1]]

brand name *n* the name used for a particular make of a commodity.

brand-new *adj* absolutely new. [C16: from BRAND (n) + NEW, likened to newly forged iron]

Brando ★ ('brændəʊ) *n* **Marlon.** born 1924, US actor; his films include *On the Waterfront* (1954), *The Godfather* (1972), *Last Tango in Paris* (1972), and *The Island of Doctor Moreau* (1996).

Brandt ★ (brænt) *n* **1 Bill,** full name *William Brandt.* 1905–83, British photographer. His books include *The English at Home* (1936) and *Perspectives of Nudes* (1961). **2 Georg** (*Swedish* 'jeːɔrj). 1694–1768, Swedish chemist, who isolated cobalt (1742). **3** (*German* brant). **Willy** ('vɪlɪ). 1913–92, German statesman; socialist chancellor of West Germany (1969–74); chairman of the Social Democratic party (1964–87). Nobel peace prize 1971.

brandy ('brændɪ) *n, pl* **brandies. 1** an alcoholic spirit distilled from grape wine. **2** a distillation of wines made from other fruits: *plum brandy.* [C17: from earlier *brandewine*, from Du. *brandewijn* burnt (or distilled) wine]

brandy butter *n* butter and sugar creamed together with brandy and served with Christmas pudding, etc. Also called: **hard sauce.**

brandy snap *n* a crisp sweet biscuit, rolled into a cylinder and filled with whipped cream.

Branson ★ ('brænsən) *n* **Richard.** born 1950, British entrepreneur. Founder of a number of companies, including Virgin record company and Virgin airline. Made first Atlantic crossing by hot-air balloon (1987).

brant (brænt) *n, pl* **brants** *or* **brant.** another name (esp. US and Canad.) for **brent** (the goose).

Brantford ★ ('bræntfəd) *n* a city in central Canada, in SW Ontario. Pop.: 81 997 (1991).

bran tub *n Brit.* a tub containing bran in which small wrapped gifts are hidden.

Braque ★ (*French* brak) *n* **Georges** (ʒɔrʒ). 1882–1963, French cubist painter.

brash[1] (bræʃ) *adj* **1** tastelessly or offensively loud, showy, or bold. **2** hasty; rash. **3** impudent. [C19: ? infl. by RASH[1]]
▸ **'brashly** *adv* ▸ **'brashness** *n*

brash[2] (bræʃ) *n* loose rubbish, such as broken rock, hedge clippings, etc. [C18: from ?]
▸ **'brashy** *adj*

brasier ('breɪzɪə) *n* a less common spelling of **brazier.**

Brasil ★ (brə'ziːl) *n* the Portuguese spelling of **Brazil.**

Brasília ★ (brə'zɪljə; *Portuguese* brəzi'liːə) *n* the capital of Brazil (since 1960), on the central plateau: the former capital was Rio de Janeiro. Pop.: 1 778 000 (1995).

Braşov ★ (*Romanian* bra'ʃov) *n* an industrial city in central Romania: formerly a centre for expatriate Germans; ceded by Hungary to Romania in 1920. Pop.: 324 104 (1993 est.). Former name (1950–61): **Stalin**. German name: **Kronstadt**. Hungarian name: **Brassó**.

brass (brɑːs) n **1** an alloy of copper and zinc containing more than 50 per cent of copper. Cf. **bronze** (sense 1). **2** an object, ornament, or utensil made of brass. **3a** the large family of wind instruments including the trumpet, trombone, French horn, etc., made of brass. **3b** (*sometimes functioning as pl*) instruments of this family forming a section in an orchestra. **4** (*functioning as pl*) Inf. important or high-ranking officials, esp. military officers: *the top brass*. See also **brass hat**. **5** N English dialect. money. **6** Brit. an engraved brass memorial tablet or plaque in a church. **7** Inf. bold self-confidence; cheek; nerve. **8** (*modifier*) of, consisting of, or relating to brass or brass instruments: *a brass ornament; a brass band*. [OE *bræs*]

brassard ('bræsɑːd) or **brassart** ('bræsət) n an identifying armband or badge. [C19: from F, from *bras* arm]

brass band n See **band**[1] (sense 2).

brasserie ('bræsərɪ) n **1** a bar in which drinks and often food are served. **2** a small and usually cheap restaurant. [C19: from F, from *brasser* to stir]

brass hat n Brit. inf. a top-ranking official, esp. a military officer. [C20: from the gold decoration on the caps of officers of high rank]

brassica ('bræsɪkə) n any plant of the genus *Brassica*, such as cabbage, rape, turnip, and mustard. [C19: from L: cabbage]

brassie or **brassy** ('bræsɪ, 'brɑː-) n, pl **brassies**. Golf. a former name for a club, a No. 2 wood, originally having a brass-plated sole.

brassiere ('bræsɪə, 'bræz-) n the full name for **bra**. [C20: from 17th-cent. F: bodice, from OF *braciere* a protector for the arm]

Brassó ★ ('brɒʃʃɔː) n the Hungarian name for **Braşov**.

brass rubbing n **1** the taking of an impression of an engraved brass tablet or plaque by rubbing a paper placed over it with heelball, chalk, etc. **2** an impression made in this way.

brass tacks pl n Inf. basic realities; hard facts (esp. in **get down to brass tacks**).

brassy ('brɑːsɪ) adj **brassier, brassiest**. **1** insolent; brazen. **2** flashy; showy. **3** (of sound) harsh and strident. **4** like brass, esp. in colour. **5** decorated with or made of brass. ► '**brassily** adv ► '**brassiness** n

brat (bræt) n a child, esp. one who is ill-mannered or unruly. [C16: ?from earlier *brat* rag, from OE *bratt* cloak] ► '**bratty** adj

Bratislava ★ (ˌbrætɪ'slɑːvə) n the capital of Slovakia, a port on the River Danube; capital of Hungary (1541–1784) and seat of the Hungarian parliament until 1848. Pop.: 450 776 (1995 est.). German name: **Pressburg**. Hungarian name: **Pozsony**.

bratpack ('bræt,pæk) n **1** a group of precocious and successful young actors, writers, etc. **2** a group of ill-mannered young people. ► '**brat,packer** n

Brattain ★ ('bræt³n) n **Walter Houser**. 1902–87, US physicist, who shared the Nobel prize for physics (1956) for the invention of the transistor.

brattice ('brætɪs) n **1** a partition of wood or treated cloth used to control ventilation in a mine. **2** Medieval fortifications. a fixed wooden tower or parapet. [C13: from OF *bretesche* wooden tower]

Braun ★ (German braun) n **1** Eva ('eːfa). 1910–45, Adolf Hitler's mistress, whom he married shortly before their suicides in 1945. **2** Karl Ferdinand (karl 'fɛrdinənt). 1850–1918. German physicist, who invented crystal diodes and the oscilloscope. He shared the Nobel prize for physics (1909). **3** See (Wernher) von Braun.

Braunschweig ★ ('braunʃvaik) n the German name for **Brunswick**.

bravado (brə'vɑːdəʊ) n, pl **bravadoes** or **bravados**. vaunted display of courage or self-confidence; swagger. [C16: from Sp. *bravada*; see BRAVE]

brave (breɪv) adj **1a** having or displaying courage, resolu-

tion, or daring; not cowardly or timid. **1b** (*as collective* preceded by *the*): *the brave*. **2** fine; splendid: *a brave sigh* ♦ n **3** a warrior of a North American Indian tribe. ♦ **braves, braving, braved**. (tr) **4** to dare or defy: *to brave ti odds*. **5** to confront with resolution or courage: *to bra the storm*. [C15: from F, from It. *bravo* courageous, wild, ult. from L *barbarus* BARBAROUS] ► '**bravely** adv ► '**braveness** n ► '**bravery** n

bravo interj **1** (brɑː'vəʊ). well done! ♦ n **2** (brɑː'vəʊ) pl **bra vos**. a cry of "bravo". **3** ('brɑːvəʊ) pl **bravoes** or **bravos**. hired killer or assassin. [C18: from It.: splendid! se BRAVE]

bravura (brə'vjʊərə, -'vʊərə) n **1** a display of boldness daring. **2** Music. brilliance of execution. [C18: from It spirit, courage; see BRAVE]

braw (brɔː, brɑː) adj Chiefly Scot. fine or excellent, esp. appearance or dress. [C16: Scot. var. of BRAVE]

brawl (brɔːl) n **1** a loud disagreement or fight. **2** US sl. a uproarious party. ♦ vb (intr) **3** to quarrel or fight noisil squabble. **4** (esp. of water) to flow noisily. [C14: pro rel. to Du. *brallen* to boast, behave aggressively] ► '**brawler** n

brawn (brɔːn) n **1** strong well-developed muscles. **2** phy ical strength, esp. as opposed to intelligence. **3** Brit. a se soned jellied loaf made from the head of a pig or cal [C14: from OF *braon* slice of meat, of Gmc origin]

brawny ('brɔːnɪ) adj **brawnier, brawniest**. muscular an strong. ► '**brawniness** n

bray (breɪ) vb **1** (intr) (of a donkey) to utter its characteris tic loud harsh sound; heehaw. **2** (intr) to make a simila sound, as in laughing. **3** (tr) to utter with a loud harsh sound. ♦ n **4** the loud harsh sound uttered by a donkey **5** a similar loud cry or uproar. [C13: from OF *braire* prob. of Celtic origin]

Braz. abbrev. for Brazil(ian).

braze[1] (breɪz) vb **brazes, brazing, brazed**. (tr) **1** to decorat with or make of brass. **2** to make like brass, as in harc ness. [OE *bræsen*, from *bræs* BRASS]

braze[2] (breɪz) vb **brazes, brazing, brazed**. (tr) to make a join between (two metal surfaces) by fusing a layer of brass o high-melting solder between them. [C16: from OF: t burn, of Gmc origin; see BRAISE] ► '**brazer** n

brazen ('breɪz³n) adj **1** shameless and bold. **2** made of o resembling brass. **3** having a ringing metallic sound ♦ vb (tr) **4** (usually foll. by out or through) to face an overcome boldly or shamelessly. [OE *bræsen*, from *bræ* BRASS] ► '**brazenly** adv ► '**brazenness** n

brazier[1] or **brasier** ('breɪzɪə) n a person engaged i brass-working or brass-founding. [C14: from OE *bræsia* to work in brass + -ER[1]] ► '**braziery** n

brazier[2] or **brasier** ('breɪzɪə) n a portable metal recepta cle for burning charcoal or coal. [C17: from F *brasier* from *braise* live coals; see BRAISE]

brazil (brə'zɪl) n **1** Also called: **brazil wood**. the red woo obtained from various tropical trees of America: used fo cabinetwork. **2** the red or purple dye extracted from these woods. **3** short for **brazil nut**. [C14: from OSp., from *brasa* glowing coals, of Gmc origin; referring to the red ness of the wood]

Brazil ★ (brə'zɪl) n a republic in South America, compris ing about half the area and half the population of Sout America: colonized by the Portuguese from 1500 on wards; became independent in 1822 and a republic in 1889; consists chiefly of the tropical Amazon basin i the north, semiarid scrub in the northeast, and a vas central tableland; an important producer of coffee anc minerals, esp. iron ore. Official language: Portuguese Religion: chiefly Roman Catholic. Currency: cruzeirc real. Capital: Brasília. Pop.: 159 691 000 (1997). Area 8 511 957 sq. km (3 286 470 sq. miles). ► **Bra'zilian** adj, n

brazil nut n **1** a tropical South American tree producing large globular capsules, each containing several closely packed triangular nuts. **2** the nut, having an edible oily kernel and a woody shell. ◆ Often shortened to **brazil**.

Brazzaville ★ (French brazavil) n the capital of the Congo Republic, in the south on the River Congo. Pop.: 937 579 (1995 est.). [C19: named after Pierre de Brazza (1852–1905), F explorer]

BRCS abbrev. for British Red Cross Society.

breach (briːtʃ) n **1** a crack, break, or rupture. **2** a breaking, infringement, or violation of a promise, obligation, etc. **3** any severance or separation. ◆ vb (tr) **4** to break through or make an opening, hole, or incursion in. **5** to break a promise, law, etc. [OE bræc]

breach of promise n Law. (formerly) failure to carry out one's promise to marry.

breach of the peace n Law. an offence against public order causing an unnecessary disturbance of the peace.

bread (brɛd) n **1** a food made from a dough of flour or meal mixed with water or milk, usually raised with yeast or baking powder and then baked. **2** necessary food; nourishment. **3** Sl. money. **4 cast one's bread upon the waters.** to do good without expectation of advantage or return. **5 know which side one's bread is buttered.** to know what to do in order to keep one's advantages. **6 take the bread out of (someone's) mouth.** to deprive of a livelihood. ◆ vb **7** (tr) to cover with bread-crumbs before cooking. [OE brēad]

bread and butter Inf. ◆ n **1** a means of support or subsistence; livelihood. ◆ modifier. **bread-and-butter. 2a** providing a basic means of subsistence. **2b** expressing gratitude, as for hospitality (esp. in **bread-and-butter letter**).

breadbasket (ˈbrɛdˌbɑːskɪt) n **1** a basket for carrying bread or rolls. **2** Sl. stomach.

breadboard (ˈbrɛdˌbɔːd) n **1** a wooden board on which bread is sliced. **2** an experimental arrangement of electronic circuits.

breadfruit (ˈbrɛdˌfruːt) n, pl **breadfruits** or **breadfruit. 1** a tree of the Pacific Islands, having edible round, usually seedless, fruit. **2** the fruit, which is eaten baked or roasted and has a texture like bread.

breadline (ˈbrɛdˌlaɪn) n **1** a queue of people waiting for free food. **2 on the breadline.** impoverished; living at subsistence level.

breadth (brɛdθ, brɛtθ) n **1** the linear extent or measurement of something from side to side; width. **2** a piece of fabric, etc., having a standard or definite width. **3** distance, extent, size, or dimension. **4** openness and lack of restriction, esp. of viewpoint or interest; liberality. [C16: from obs. brēde (from OE brǣdu, from brād BROAD) + -TH[1]]

breadthways (ˈbrɛdθˌweɪz, ˈbrɛtθ-) or esp. US **breadthwise** (ˈbrɛdθˌwaɪz, ˈbrɛtθ-) adv from side to side.

breadwinner (ˈbrɛdˌwɪnə) n a person supporting a family with his or her earnings.

break (breɪk) vb **breaks, breaking, broke, broken. 1** to separate or become separated into two or more pieces. **2** to damage or become damaged so as to be inoperative: my radio is broken. **3** to crack or become cracked without separating. **4** to burst or cut the surface of (skin, etc.). **5** to discontinue or become discontinued: to break a journey. **6** to disperse or become dispersed: the clouds broke. **7** (tr) to fail to observe (an agreement, promise, law, etc.): to break one's word. **8** (foll. by with) to discontinue an association (with). **9** to disclose or be disclosed: he broke the news gently. **10** (tr) to fracture (a bone) in (a limb, etc.). **11** (tr) to divide (something complete or perfect): to break a set of books. **12** to bring or come to an end: the summer weather broke at last. **13** (tr) to bring to an end as by force: to break a strike. **14** (when intr, often foll. by out) to escape (from): he broke out of jail. **15** to weaken or overwhelm or be weakened or overwhelmed, as in spirit. **16** (tr) to cut through or penetrate: a cry broke the silence. **17** (tr) to improve on or surpass: to break a record. **18** (tr; often foll. by in) to accustom (a horse) to the bridle and saddle, to being ridden, etc. **19** (tr; often foll. by of) to cause (a person) to give up (a habit): this cure will break you of smoking. **20** (tr) to weaken the impact or force of: this net will break

his fall. **21** (tr) to decipher: to break a code. **22** (tr) to lose the order of: to break ranks. **23** (tr) to reduce to poverty or the state of bankruptcy. **24** (when intr, foll. by into) to obtain, give, or receive smaller units in exchange for; change: to break a pound note. **25** (tr) Chiefly mil. to demote to a lower rank. **26** (intr; often foll. by from or out of) to proceed suddenly. **27** (intr) to come into being: light broke over the mountains. **28** (intr; foll. by into or out into) **28a** to burst into song, laughter, etc. **28b** to change to a faster pace. **29** (tr) to open with explosives: to break a safe. **30** (intr) (of waves) **30a** (often foll. by against) to strike violently. **30b** to collapse into foam or surf. **31** (intr) (of prices, esp. stock exchange quotations) to fall sharply. **32** (intr) to make a sudden effort, as in running, horse racing, etc. **33** (intr) Cricket. (of a ball) to change direction on bouncing. **34** (intr) Snooker. to scatter the balls at the start of a game. **35** (intr) Boxing, wrestling. (of two fighters) to separate from a clinch. **36** (intr) (of the male voice) to undergo a change in register, quality, and range at puberty. **37** (tr) to open the breech of (certain firearms) by snapping the barrel away from the butt on its hinge. **38** (tr) to interrupt the flow of current in (an electrical circuit). **39** Inf., chiefly US. to become successful. **40 break camp.** to pack up and leave a camp. **41 break service.** Tennis. to win a game in which an opponent is serving. **42 break the bank.** to ruin financially or deplete the resources of a bank (as in gambling). **43 break the mould.** to make a change that breaks an established habit, pattern, etc. ◆ n **44** the act or result of breaking; fracture. **45** a crack formed as the result of breaking. **46** a brief respite. **47** a sudden rush, esp. to escape: to make a break for freedom. **48** a breach in a relationship. **49** any sudden interruption in a continuous action. **50** Brit. a short period between classes at school. **51** Inf. a fortunate opportunity, esp. to prove oneself. **52** Inf. a piece of good or bad luck. **53** (esp. in a stock exchange) a sudden and substantial decline in prices. **54** Billiards, snooker. a series of successful shots during one turn. **55** Billiards, snooker. the opening shot that scatters the placed balls. **56** Also called: **service break, break of serve.** Tennis. the act or an instance of breaking an opponent's service. **57a** Jazz. a short usually improvised solo passage. **57b** an instrumental passage in a pop song. **58** a discontinuity in an electrical circuit. **59** access to a radio channel by a citizens' band radio operator. **60 break of day.** the dawn. ◆ interj **61** Boxing, wrestling. a command by a referee for two opponents to separate. ◆ See also **breakaway, break down,** etc. [OE brecan]

breakable (ˈbreɪkəb°l) adj **1** capable of being broken. ◆ n **2** (usually pl) a fragile easily broken article.

breakage (ˈbreɪkɪdʒ) n **1** the act or result of breaking. **2** the quantity or amount broken. **3** compensation or allowance for goods damaged while in use, transit, etc.

breakaway (ˈbreɪkəˌweɪ) n **1a** loss or withdrawal of a group of members from an association, club, etc. **1b** (as modifier): a breakaway faction. **2** Austral. a stampede of animals, esp. at the smell of water. ◆ vb **break away.** (intr, adv) **3** (often foll. by from) to leave hastily or escape. **4** to withdraw or secede.

break dance n **1** an acrobatic dance style of the 1980s. ◆ vb **break-dance, break-dances, break-dancing, break-danced.** (intr) **2** to perform a break dance. ► **break dancer** n ► **break dancing** n

break down vb (adv) **1** (intr) to cease to function; become ineffective. **2** to yield or cause to yield, esp. to strong emotion or tears. **3** (tr) to crush or destroy. **4** (intr) to have a nervous breakdown. **5** to analyse or be subjected to analysis. **6** to separate or cause to separate into simpler chemical elements; decompose. **7 break it down.** Austral. & NZ inf. **7a** stop it. **7b** don't expect me to believe that; come off it. ◆ n **breakdown. 8** an act or instance of breaking down; collapse. **9** short for **nervous breakdown. 10** an analysis or classification of something into its component parts: he prepared a breakdown of the report. **11** a lively American country dance.

breaker (ˈbreɪkə) n **1** a person or thing that breaks something, such as a person or firm that breaks up old cars, etc. **2** a large wave with a white crest on the open sea or one that breaks into foam on the shore. **3** a citizens' band radio operator.

break even vb **1** (intr, adv) to attain a level of activity, as in commerce, or a point of operation, as in gambling, at which there is neither profit nor loss. ◆ *n* **breakeven. 2** *Accounting.* the level of commercial activity at which the total cost and total revenue of a business enterprise are equal.

breakfast ('brɛkfəst) *n* **1** the first meal of the day. **2** the food at this meal. ◆ *vb* **3** to eat or supply with breakfast. [C15: from BREAK + FAST²]
▶ **'breakfaster** *n*

break in *vb* (*adv*) **1** (sometimes foll. by *on*) to interrupt. **2** (*intr*) to enter a house, etc., illegally, esp. by force. **3** (*tr*) to accustom (a person or animal) to normal duties or practice. **4** (*tr*) to use or wear (shoes, new equipment, etc.) until comfortable or running smoothly. **5** *Austral.* to bring new land under cultivation. ◆ *n* **break-in. 6** the illegal entering of a building, esp. by thieves.

breaking and entering *n* (formerly) the gaining of unauthorized access to a building with intent to commit a crime.

breaking point *n* the point at which something or someone gives way under strain.

breakneck ('breɪk,nɛk) *adj* (*prenominal*) (of speed, pace, etc.) excessive and dangerous.

break off *vb* **1** to sever or detach or be severed or detached. **2** (*adv*) to end (a relationship, association, etc.) or (of a relationship, etc.) to be ended. **3** (*intr, adv*) to stop abruptly: *he broke off in the middle of his speech.*

break out *vb* (*intr, adv*) **1** to begin or arise suddenly. **2** to make an escape, esp. from prison. **3** (foll. by *in*) (of the skin) to erupt (in a rash, pimples, etc.). ◆ *n* **break-out. 4** an escape, esp. from prison or confinement.

break through *vb* **1** (*intr*) to penetrate. **2** (*intr, adv*) to achieve success, make a discovery, etc., esp. after lengthy efforts. ◆ *n* **breakthrough. 3** a significant development or discovery, esp. in science. **4** the penetration of an enemy's defensive position.

breakthrough bleeding ('breɪk,θruː) *n* vaginal bleeding that occurs other than at a menstrual period while a woman is using a low-dose oral contraceptive.

break up *vb* (*adv*) **1** to separate or cause to separate. **2** to put an end to (a relationship) or (of a relationship) to come to an end. **3** to dissolve or cause to dissolve; disrupt or be disrupted: *the meeting broke up at noon.* **4** (*intr*) *Brit.* (of a school) to close for the holidays. **5** *Inf.* to lose or cause to lose control of the emotions. **6** *Sl.* to be or cause to be overcome with laughter. ◆ *n* **break-up. 7** a separation or disintegration. **8a** in the Canadian north, the breaking up of the ice on a body of water that marks the beginning of spring. **8b** this season.

break-up value *n Commerce.* **1** the value of an organization assuming that it will not continue to trade. **2** the value of a share in a company based only on the value of its assets.

breakwater ('breɪk,wɔːtə) *n* **1** Also called: **mole.** a massive wall built out into the sea to protect a shore or harbour from the force of waves. **2** another name for **groyne.**

bream¹ (briːm; *Austral.* brɪm) *or Austral.* **brim** (brɪm) *n, pl* **bream** *or* **brim. 1** any of several Eurasian freshwater cyprinid fishes having a deep compressed body covered with silvery scales. **2** short for **sea bream. 3** *Austral.* any of various marine fishes. [C14: from OF *bresme,* of Gmc origin]

bream² (briːm) *vb Naut.* (formerly) to clean debris from (the bottom of a vessel) by heating to soften the pitch. [C15: prob. from MDu. *bremme* broom; from burning broom as a source of heat]

Bream ★ (briːm) *n* **Julian** (**Alexander**). born 1933, British guitarist and lutenist.

breast (brɛst) *n* **1** the front part of the body from the neck to the abdomen; chest. **2** either of the two soft fleshy milk-secreting glands on the chest in sexually mature human females. **3** a similar organ in certain other mammals. **4** anything that resembles a breast in shape or position: *the breast of the hill.* **5** a source of nourishment. **6** the source of human emotions. **7** the part of a garment that covers the breast. **8** a projection from the side of a wall, esp. that formed by a chimney. **9 beat one's breast.** to display guilt and remorse publicly or ostentatiously. **10 make a clean breast of.** to make a confession of. ◆ *vb* (*tr*) **11**

to confront boldly; face: *breast the storm.* **12** to oppo[se] with the breast or meet at breast level: *breasting the wave[s]*. **13** to reach the summit of: *breasting the mountain to[p]*. [OE *brēost*]

breastbone ('brɛst,bəun) *n* the nontechnical name f[or] sternum.

breast-feed *vb* **breast-feeds, breast-feeding, breast-fed.** [to] feed (a baby) with milk from the breast; suckle.

breastpin ('brɛst,pɪn) *n* a brooch worn on the breas[t] esp. to close a garment.

breastplate ('brɛst,pleɪt) *n* a piece of armour coverin[g] the chest.

breaststroke ('brɛst,strəuk) *n* a swimming stroke i[n] which the arms are extended in front of the head an[d] swept back on either side while the legs are drawn up b[e]neath the body and thrust back together.

breastwork ('brɛst,wɜːk) *n Fortifications.* a temporary de[-] fensive work, usually breast-high.

breath (brɛθ) *n* **1** the intake and expulsion of air durin[g] respiration. **2** the air inhaled or exhaled during respira[-]tion. **3** a single respiration or inhalation of air, etc. **4** the vapour, heat, or odour of exhaled air. **5** a slight gust o[f] air. **6** a short pause or rest. **7** a brief time. **8** a suggestio[n] or slight evidence; suspicion: *a breath of scandal.* **9** a whi[s]per or soft sound. **10** life, energy, or vitality: *the breath [of] new industry.* **11** *Phonetics.* the exhalation of air withou[t] vibration of the vocal cords, as in pronouncing fricative[s] such as (f) or (h) or stops such as (p) or (k). **12 catch one'[s] breath. 12a** to rest until breathing is normal, esp. after ex[-]ertion. **12b** to stop breathing momentarily from excite[-]ment, fear, etc. **13 in the same breath.** done or said at th[e] same time. **14 out of breath.** gasping for air after exertio[n] **15 save one's breath.** to refrain from useless talk. **16 tak[e] one's breath away.** to overwhelm with surprise, etc. **1[7] under** or **below one's breath.** in a quiet voice or whispe[r] [OE *brǣth*]

breathable ('briːðəb'l) *adj* **1** (of air) fit to be breathed. [2] (of a material) allowing air to pass through so that per[-] spiration can evaporate.

Breathalyser *or* **Breathalyzer** ('brɛθə,laɪzə) *n Trade[-] mark.* a device for estimating the amount of alcohol i[n] the breath: used in testing people suspected of drivin[g] under the influence of alcohol. [C20: BREATH + (AN)ALYSER]
▶ **'breatha,lyse** *or* **'breatha,lyze** *vb* (*tr*)

breathe (briːð) *vb* **breathes, breathing, breathed. 1** to take i[n] oxygen and give out carbon dioxide; respire. **2** (*intr*) t[o] exist; be alive. **3** (*intr*) to rest to regain breath, compo[-] sure, etc. **4** (*intr*) (esp. of air) to blow lightly. **5** (*intr*) *Ma[-] chinery.* to take in air, esp. for combustion. **6** (*tr*) *Phonetic[s]* to articulate (a speech sound) without vibration of th[e] vocal cords. **7** to exhale or emit: *the dragon breathed fire.* [8] (*tr*) to impart; instil: *to breathe confidence into the actors.* [9] (*tr*) to speak softly; whisper. **10** (*tr*) to permit to rest: *t[o] breathe a horse.* **11** (*tr*) (of a material) to allow air to pas[s] through so that perspiration can evaporate. **12 breath[e] again, freely,** or **easily.** to feel relief. **13 breathe one's last.** t[o] die or be finished or defeated. [C13: from BREATH]

breather ('briːðə) *n* **1** *Inf.* a short pause for rest. **2** a perso[n] who breathes in a specified way: *a deep breather.* **3** a ven[t] in a container to equalize internal and external pressure[.]

breathing ('briːðɪŋ) *n* **1** the passage of air into and out o[f] the lungs to supply the body with oxygen. **2** a singl[e] breath: *a breathing between words.* **3** *Phonetics.* **3a** expul[-] sion of breath (**rough breathing**) or absence of such expul[-] sion (**smooth breathing**) preceding the pronunciation o[f] an initial vowel or rho in ancient Greek. **3b** either of tw[o] symbols indicating this.

breathless ('brɛθlɪs) *adj* **1** out of breath; gasping, etc. [2] holding one's breath or having it taken away by excite[-] ment, etc. **3** (esp. of the atmosphere) motionless and sti[ll;] fling. **4** *Rare.* lifeless; dead.
▶ **'breathlessly** *adv* ▶ **'breathlessness** *n*

breathtaking ('brɛθ,teɪkɪŋ) *adj* causing awe or excite[-] ment.
▶ **'breath,takingly** *adv*

breath test *n Brit.* a chemical test of a driver's breath t[o] determine the amount of alcohol he has consumed.

breathy ('brɛθɪ) *adj* **breathier, breathiest. 1** (of the speaking voice) accompanied by an audible emission of breath. **2** (of the singing voice) lacking resonance.
▸ **'breathily** *adv* ▸ **'breathiness** *n*

reccia ('brɛtʃɪə) *n* a rock consisting of angular fragments embedded in a finer matrix. [C18: from It.]
▸ **'brecci,ated** *adj*

recht ★ (*German* brɛçt) *n* **Bertolt** ('bɛrtɔlt). 1898–1956, German dramatist. His early works include *The Threepenny Opera* (1928) and *Rise and Fall of the City of Mahagonny* (1930) (both with music by Kurt Weill). His later plays include *Mother Courage and her Children* (1941) and *The Caucasian Chalk Circle* (1955).
▸ **Brechtian** ('brɛktɪən) *adj, n*

recon ('brɛkən) *or* **Brecknock** ★ ('brɛknɒk) *n* **1** a town in SE Wales, in Powys: textile and leather industries. Pop.: 7523 (1991). **2** short for **Breconshire**.

reconshire ('brɛkənˌʃɪə, -ʃə) *or* **Brecknockshire** ★ ('brɛknɒkˌʃɪə, -ʃə) *n* (until 1974) a county of SE Wales, now mainly in Powys: over half its area forms the **Brecon Beacons National Park**.

red (brɛd) *vb* the past tense and past participle of **breed**.

reda ★ ('briːdə; *Dutch* breˈdaː) *n* a city in the S Netherlands, in North Brabant province: residence of Charles II of England during his exile. Pop.: 129 957 (1995 est.).

reech *n* (briːtʃ). **1** the buttocks; rump. **2** the lower part or bottom of something. **3** the part of a firearm behind the barrel or bore. ◆ *vb* (briːtʃ, brɪtʃ). (*tr*) **4** to fit (a gun) with a breech. **5** *Arch.* to clothe in breeches or any other clothing. [OE *brēc*, pl. of *brōc* leg covering]

> **USAGE NOTE** *Breech* is sometimes wrongly used as a verb where *breach* is meant: *the barrier/agreement was breached* (not *breeched*).

reechblock ('briːtʃˌblɒk) *n* a metal block in breech-loading firearms that is withdrawn to insert the cartridge and replaced before firing.

reech delivery *n* birth of a baby with the feet or buttocks appearing first.

reeches ('brɪtʃɪz, 'briː-) *pl n* **1** trousers extending to the knee or just below, worn for riding, etc. **2** *Inf. or dialect.* any trousers or pants, esp. extending to the knee.

reeches buoy *n* a ring-shaped life buoy with a support in the form of a pair of short breeches, in which a person is suspended for safe transfer from a ship.

reeching ('brɪtʃɪŋ, 'briː-) *n* the strap of a harness that passes behind a horse's haunches.

reech-loader ('briːtʃˌləʊdə) *n* a firearm that is loaded at the breech.
▸ **'breech-,loading** *adj*

reed (briːd) *vb* **breeding, bred. 1** to bear (offspring). **2** (*tr*) to bring up; raise. **3** to produce or cause to produce by mating; propagate. **4** to produce new or improved strains of (domestic animals and plants). **5** to produce or be produced; generate: *to breed trouble*. ◆ *n* **6** a group of organisms within a species, esp. domestic animals, having clearly defined characteristics. **7** a lineage or race. **8** a kind, sort, or group. [OE *brēdan*, of Gmc origin; rel. to BROOD]

reeder ('briːdə) *n* **1** a person who breeds plants or animals. **2** something that reproduces. **3** an animal kept for breeding purposes. **4** a source or cause: *a breeder of discontent*. **5** short for **breeder reactor**.

reeder reactor *n* a type of nuclear reactor that produces more fissionable material than it consumes.

reeding ('briːdɪŋ) *n* **1** the process of bearing offspring; reproduction. **2** the process of producing plants or animals by hybridization, inbreeding, or other methods of reproduction. **3** the result of good training, esp. the knowledge of correct social behaviour; refinement.

reed's Hill ★ (briːdz) *n* a hill in E Massachusetts, adjoining Bunker Hill: site of the Battle of Bunker Hill (1775).

breeze[1] (briːz) *n* **1** a gentle or light wind. **2** *Meteorol.* a wind of force two to six (4–31 mph) inclusive on the Beaufort scale. **3** *US & Canad. inf.* an easy task or state of ease. **4** *Inf., chiefly Brit.* a disturbance, esp. a lively quarrel. ◆ *vb* **breezes, breezing, breezed.** (*intr*) **5** to move quickly or casually: *he breezed into the room*. [C16: prob. from OSp. *briza* northeast wind]

breeze[2] (briːz) *n* ashes of coal, coke, or charcoal used to make breeze blocks. [C18: from F *braise* live coals; see BRAISE]

breeze block *n* a light building brick made from the ashes of coal, coke, etc., bonded together by cement.

breezeway ('briːzˌweɪ) *n* a roofed passageway connecting two buildings.

breezy ('briːzɪ) *adj* **breezier, breeziest. 1** fresh; windy. **2** casual or carefree; lively; light-hearted.
▸ **'breezily** *adv* ▸ **'breeziness** *n*

Bregenz ★ (*German* 'breːgɛnts) *n* a resort in W Austria, the capital of Vorarlberg province. Pop.: 26 730 (1989).

Bremen ★ ('breɪmən) *n* **1** a state of NW Germany, centred on the city of Bremen and its outport Bremerhaven; formerly in West Germany. Pop.: 680 000 (1995 est.). Area: 404 sq. km (156 sq. miles). **2** an industrial city and port in NW Germany, on the Weser estuary. Pop.: 549 182 (1995 est.).

Bremerhaven ★ (*German* breˈmərˈhaːfən) *n* a port in NW Germany. Pop.: 130 847 (1995 est.). Former name (until 1947): **Wesermünde**.

bremsstrahlung ('brɛmzˌʃtrɑːlʊŋ) *n* the x-radiation produced when an electrically charged particle, such as an electron, is slowed down by the electric field of an atomic nucleus. [G: braking radiation]

Brendel ★ (*German* 'brɛndəl) *n* **Alfred** ('alfreːt). born 1931, Austrian pianist and poet.

Bren gun (brɛn) *n* an air-cooled gas-operated light machine gun: used by the British in World War II. [C20: after *Br(no)*, now in the Czech Republic, where it was first made and *En(field)*, England, where manufacture was continued]

Brennan ★ ('brɛnən) *n* **Christopher John.** 1870–1932, Australian poet and classical scholar.

Brenner Pass ★ ('brɛnə) *n* a pass over the E Alps, between Austria and Italy. Highest point: 1372 m (4501 ft).

Brent ★ (brɛnt) *n* a borough of NW Greater London. Pop.: 244 500 (1994 est.). Area: 44 sq. km (17 sq. miles).

brent goose (brɛnt) *n* a small goose that has a dark grey plumage and short neck and occurs in most northern coastal regions. Also called: **brent**, (esp. US and Canad.) **brant**. [C16: ? of Scand. origin]

Brenton ★ ('brɛnt'n) *n* **Howard.** born 1942, British dramatist, author of such controversial plays as *The Romans in Britain* (1980), *Ugly Rumours* (1998), and (with David Hare) *Pravda* (1985).

Brentwood ★ ('brɛntˌwʊd) *n* a residential town in SE England, in SW Essex near London. Pop.: 49 463 (1991).

Brescia ★ (*Italian* 'brɛʃʃa) *n* a city in N Italy, in Lombardy: at its height in the 16th century. Pop.: 191 875 (1994 est.). Ancient name: **Brixia** ('brɪksɪə).

Breslau ★ ('brɛzlau) *n* the German name for **Wrocław**.

Brest ★ (brɛst) *n* **1** a port in NW France, in Brittany: chief naval station of the country, planned by Richelieu in 1631 and fortified by Vauban. Pop.: 153 099 (1990). **2** a city in SW Belarus: Polish until 1795 and from 1921 to 1945. Pop.: 293 000 (1996 est.). Former name (until 1921): **Brest Litovsk** (brɛst liˈtɔfsk). Polish name: **Brześć nad Bugiem.**

Bretagne ★ (brətaɲ) *n* the French name for **Brittany**.

brethren ('brɛðrɪn) *pl n Arch. except when referring to fellow members of a religion, society, etc.* a plural of **brother**.

Breton[1] ('brɛt'n) *adj* **1** of, relating to, or characteristic of Brittany, its people, or their language. ◆ *n* **2** a native or inhabitant of Brittany. **3** the Celtic language of Brittany.

Breton[2] ★ (*French* brətɔ̃) *n* **André** (ɑ̃dre). 1896–1966, French poet and art critic: founder and chief theorist of surrealism, publishing the first surrealist manifesto in 1924.

Breuer ★ ('brɔɪə) *n* **1 Josef** (*German* 'joːzɛf). 1842–1925,

Austrian physician and hypnotist. **2 Marcel Lajos** (mɑ:'sɛl 'lɒjəʊʃ). 1902–81, US architect and furniture designer, born in Hungary. He developed tubular metal furniture.

Breughel ★ ('brɔɪgˀl) n a variant spelling of **Brueghel.**

breve (bri:v) n **1** an accent, ˘ , placed over a vowel to indicate that it is short or is pronounced in a specified way. **2** *Music.* a note, now rarely used, equivalent to two semibreves. **3** *RC Church.* a less common word for **brief** (papal letter). [C13: from Med. L, from L *brevis* short]

brevet ('brɛvɪt) n **1** a document entitling a commissioned officer to hold temporarily a higher military rank without the appropriate pay and allowances. ◆ *vb* **brevets, brevetting, brevetted** or **brevets, breveting, breveted. 2** (*tr*) to promote by brevet. [C14: from OF, from *brief* letter; see BRIEF]
▸ 'brevetcy n

breviary ('bri:vjərɪ) n, pl **breviaries.** *RC Church.* a book of psalms, hymns, prayers, etc., to be recited daily by clerics and certain members of religious orders as part of the divine office. [C16: from L *breviārium* an abridged version, from *brevis* short]

brevity ('brɛvɪtɪ) n, pl **brevities. 1** conciseness of expression; lack of verbosity. **2** a short duration; brief time. [C16: from L, from *brevis* BRIEF]

brew (bru:) vb **1** to make (beer, ale, etc.) from malt and other ingredients by steeping, boiling, and fermentation. **2** to prepare (a drink, such as tea) by boiling or infusing. **3** (*tr*) to devise or plan: *to brew a plot.* **4** (*intr*) to be in the process of being brewed. **5** (*intr*) to be impending or forming: *there's a storm brewing.* ◆ n **6** a beverage produced by brewing, esp. tea or beer. **7** an instance or time of brewing: *last year's brew.* **8** a mixture. [OE *brēowan*]
▸ 'brewer n

brewery ('brʊərɪ) n, pl **breweries.** a place where beer, ale, etc., is brewed.

brewing ('bru:ɪŋ) n a quantity of a beverage brewed at one time.

Brezhnev ★ ('brɛʒnɛf; *Russian* 'brjɛʒnɪf) n **Leonid Ilyich** (lɪa'nit 'ilitʃ). 1906–82, Soviet statesman; president of the Soviet Union (1977–82); general secretary of the Soviet Communist Party (1964–82).

Brian ★ ('braɪən) n **Havergal** ('hævəgəl). 1876–1972, British composer, who wrote 32 symphonies.

Brian Boru ★ (bə'ru:) n ?941–1014, king of Ireland (1002–14): killed during the defeat of the Danes at the battle of Clontarf.

Briand ★ (*French* briɑ̃) n **Aristide** (aristid). 1862–1932, French socialist statesman: prime minister of France 11 times. Nobel peace prize 1926.

briar[1] or **brier** ('braɪə) n **1** Also called: **tree heath.** a shrub of S Europe, having a hard woody root (briarroot). **2** a tobacco pipe made from the root of this plant. [C19: from F *bruyère* heath]
▸ 'briary or 'briery adj

briar[2] or **brier** ('braɪə) n a variant spelling of **brier**[1].

Briareus ★ (braɪ'eərɪəs) n *Greek myth.* a giant with a hundred arms and fifty heads who aided Zeus and the Olympians against the Titans.
▸ Bri'arean adj

briarroot or **brierroot** ('braɪə,ru:t) n the hard woody root of the briar, used for making tobacco pipes. Also called: **briarwood, brierwood.**

bribe (braɪb) vb **bribes, bribing, bribed. 1** to promise, offer, or give something, often illegally, to (a person) to procure services or gain influence. ◆ n **2** a reward, such as money or favour, given or offered for this purpose. **3** any persuasion or lure. [C14: from OF *briber* to beg, from ?]
▸ 'bribery n

bric-a-brac ('brɪkə,bræk) n miscellaneous small objects, esp. furniture and curios, kept because they are ornamental or rare. [C19: from F]

brick (brɪk) n **1a** a rectangular block of clay mixed with sand and fired in a kiln or baked by the sun, used in building construction. **1b** (*as modifier*): *a brick house.* **2** the material used to make such blocks. **3** any rectangular block: *a brick of ice.* **4** bricks collectively. **5** *Inf.* a reliable, trustworthy, or helpful person. **6** *Brit.* a child's building

block. **7** **drop a brick.** *Brit. inf.* to make a tactless ◀ indiscreet remark. **8** **like a ton of bricks.** *Inf.* with grea force; severely. ◆ *vb* **9** (*tr*; usually foll. by *in, up,* or *over* to construct, line, pave, fill, or wall up with bricks: ▪ *brick up a window.* [C15: from OF *brique,* from MDu *bricke*]
▸ 'bricky adj

brickbat ('brɪk,bæt) n **1** a piece of brick or similar ma terial, esp. one used as a weapon. **2** blunt criticism [C16: BRICK + BAT[1]]

brickie ('brɪkɪ) n *Inf.* a bricklayer.

bricklayer ('brɪk,leɪə) n a person trained or skilled i laying bricks.
▸ 'brick,laying n

brick red n, adj (of) a reddish-brown colour.

brickwork ('brɪk,wɜ:k) n **1** a structure built of bricks. construction using bricks.

brickyard ('brɪk,jɑ:d) n a place in which bricks are made stored, or sold.

bricolage ('brɪkə,lɑ:ʒ; *French* brikəlaʒ) n *Archit.* a jumble effect produced by the close proximity of buildings fron different periods or in different styles. [F: odd jobs, dc it-yourself]

bridal ('braɪdˀl) adj of or relating to a bride or a wedding nuptial. [OE *brȳdealu,* lit.: "bride ale", that is, weddin feast]

bride (braɪd) n a woman who has just been or is about t be married. [OE *brȳd*]

Bride ★ (braɪd) n See (Saint) **Bridget.**

bridegroom ('braɪd,gru:m, -,grʊm) n a man who ha just been or is about to be married. [C14: change (through infl. of GROOM) from OE *brȳdguma,* from *brȳ* BRIDE + *guma* man]

bride price or **wealth** n (in some societies) money property, or services given by a bridegroom to the kins men of his bride.

bridesmaid ('braɪdz,meɪd) n a girl or young unmarrie woman who attends a bride at her wedding.

bridge[1] (brɪdʒ) n **1** a structure that spans and provides ▪ passage over a road, railway, river, or some other obsta cle. **2** something that resembles this in shape or func tion. **3** the hard ridge at the upper part of the nose formed by the underlying nasal bones. **4** the part of ▪ pair of glasses that rests on the nose. **5** Also called: **bridge work.** a dental plate containing one or more artificia teeth that is secured to the surrounding natural teeth. ▪ a platform from which a ship is piloted and navigated. ▪ a piece of wood, usually fixed, supporting the strings of ▪ violin, guitar, etc., and transmitting their vibrations te the sounding board. **8** Also called: **bridge passage.** a pas sage in a musical, literary, or dramatic work linking twe or more important sections. **9** Also called: **bridge circui** *Electronics.* any of several networks across which a devic is connected for measuring resistance, capacitance, etc **10** *Computing.* a device that connects networks and send packets between them. **11** *Billiards, snooker.* a support fo a cue. **12** **cross a bridge when** (**one**) **comes to it.** to deal with ▪ problem only when it arises. ◆ *vb* **bridges, bridging bridged.** (*tr*) **13** to build or provide a bridge over some thing; span: *to bridge a river.* **14** to connect or reduce the distance between: *let us bridge our differences.* [OE *brycg*]
▸ 'bridgeable adj

bridge[2] (brɪdʒ) n a card game for four players, based o whist, in which one hand (the dummy) is exposed and the trump suit decided by bidding between the players See also **contract bridge, auction bridge.** [C19: from ?]

Bridge ★ (brɪdʒ) n **Frank.** 1879–1941, British composer esp. of chamber music.

bridgehead ('brɪdʒ,hed) n **1** *Mil.* an area of ground se cured or to be taken on the enemy's side of an obstacle. **2** *Mil.* a fortified or defensive position at the end of ▪ bridge nearest to the enemy. **3** an advantageous positior gained for future expansion.

Bridgend ★ (,brɪdʒ'end) n a county borough in S Wales Pop.: 130 874 (1996 est.). Area: 264 sq. km (102 sq miles).

Bridge of Sighs ★ n a covered 16th-century bridge ir

Venice, between the Doge's Palace and the prisons, through which prisoners were formerly led to trial or execution.

Bridgeport ★ ('brɪdʒ,pɔːt) n a port in SW Connecticut, on Long Island Sound. Pop.: 132 919 (1994 est.).

bridge roll n a soft bread roll in a long thin shape. [C20: from BRIDGE² or ? BRIDGE¹]

Bridges ★ ('brɪdʒɪz) n Robert (Seymour). 1844–1930, British poet: poet laureate (1913–30).

Bridget ★ ('brɪdʒɪt) n Saint. 1 Also called: Bride, Brigid. 453–523 A.D., Irish abbess; a patron saint of Ireland. Feast day: Feb. 1. 2 Also called: Birgitta. ?1303-73, Swedish nun; patron saint of Sweden. Feast day: July 23.

Bridgetown ★ ('brɪdʒ,taun) n the capital of Barbados, a port on the SW coast. Pop.: 6070 (1990).

bridgework ('brɪdʒ,wɜːk) n a partial denture attached to the surrounding teeth.

bridging loan n a loan made to cover the period between two transactions, such as the buying of another house before the sale of the first is completed.

Bridgwater ★ ('brɪdʒ,wɔːtə) n a town in SW England, in central Somerset. Pop.: 34 610 (1991).

Bridie ★ ('braɪdɪ) n James, real name Osborne Henry Mavor. 1888–1951, Scottish physician and dramatist. His plays include The Anatomist (1930).

bridle ('braɪd°l) n 1 a headgear for a horse, etc., consisting of a series of buckled straps and a metal mouthpiece (bit) by which the animal is controlled through the reins. 2 something that curbs or restrains; check. 3 a Y-shaped cable, rope, or chain, used for holding, towing, etc. ◆ vb bridles, bridling, bridled. 4 (tr) to put a bridle on (a horse, mule, etc.). 5 (tr) to restrain; curb: he bridled his rage. 6 (intr; often foll. by at) to show anger, scorn, or indignation. [OE brigdels]

bridle path n a path suitable for riding or leading horses.

Brie (briː) n 1 a soft creamy white cheese. 2 a mainly agricultural area in N France, between the Rivers Marne and Seine: noted esp. for its cheese.

brief (briːf) adj 1 short in duration. 2 short in length or extent; scanty: a brief bikini. 3 abrupt in manner; brusque: the professor was brief with me. 4 terse or concise. ◆ n 5 a condensed statement or written synopsis; abstract. 6 Law. a document containing all the facts and points of law of a case by which a solicitor instructs a barrister to represent a client. 7 RC Church. a letter issuing from the Roman court written in modern characters, as contrasted with a papal bull; papal brief. 8 Also called: briefing. instructions. 9 hold a brief for. to argue for; champion. 10 in brief. in short; to sum up. ◆ vb (tr) 11 to prepare or instruct by giving a summary of relevant facts. 12 to make a summary or synopsis of. 13 English law. 13a to instruct (a barrister) by brief. 13b to retain (a barrister) as counsel. [C14: from OF bref, from L brevis]
► **'briefly** adv ► **'briefness** n

briefcase ('briːf,keɪs) n a flat portable case, often of leather, for carrying papers, books, etc.

briefing ('briːfɪŋ) n 1 a meeting at which information and instructions are given. 2 the facts presented at such a meeting.

briefless ('briːflɪs) adj (said of a barrister) without clients.

briefs (briːfs) pl n men's underpants or women's pants without legs.

brier¹ or **briar** ('braɪə) n any of various thorny shrubs or other plants, such as the sweetbrier. [OE brēr, brǣr, from ?]
► **'briery** or **'briary** adj

brier² ('braɪə) n a variant spelling of **briar¹**.

brierroot ('braɪə,ruːt) n a variant spelling of **briarroot**. Also called: **brierwood**.

brig¹ (brɪg) n 1 Naut. a two-masted square-rigger. 2 Chiefly US. a prison, esp. in a navy ship. [C18: shortened from BRIGANTINE]

brig² (brɪg) n a Scot. and N English word for a **bridge¹**.

Brig. abbrev. for Brigadier.

brigade (brɪ'geɪd) n 1 a military formation smaller than a division and usually commanded by a brigadier. 2 a group of people organized for a certain task: a rescue brigade. ◆ vb brigades, brigading, brigaded. (tr) 3 to organize into a brigade. [C17: from OF, from OIt., from brigare to fight; see BRIGAND]

brigadier (,brɪgə'dɪə) n 1 an officer of the British Army or Royal Marines junior to a major general but senior to a colonel, usually commanding a brigade. 2 an equivalent rank in other armed forces. [C17: from F, from BRIGADE]

brigalow ('brɪgələu) n Austral. a any of various acacia trees, forming dense scrub. b (as modifier): brigalow country. [C19: from Abor.]

brigand ('brɪgənd) n a bandit, esp. a member of a gang operating in mountainous areas. [C14: from OF, from OIt. brigante fighter, from briga strife]
► **'brigandage** or **'brigandry** n

brigantine ('brɪgən,tiːn, -,taɪn) n a two-masted sailing ship, rigged square on the foremast and fore-and-aft on the mainmast. [C16: from OIt. brigantino pirate ship, from brigante BRIGAND]

Briggs ★ (brɪgz) n Henry. 1561–1631, English mathematician: introduced common logarithms.

Brighouse¹ ('brɪg,haus) ★ n a town in N England, in Calderdale unitary authority, in West Yorkshire: machine tools, textiles, engineering. Pop.: 32 198 (1991).

Brighouse² ('brɪg,haus) ★ n Harold. 1882–1958, British writer, noted for his play Hobson's Choice (1915).

bright (braɪt) adj 1 emitting or reflecting much light; shining. 2 (of colours) intense or vivid. 3 full of promise: a bright future. 4 full of animation; cheerful: a bright face. 5 Inf. quick-witted or clever: a bright child. 6 magnificent; glorious. 7 polished; glistening. 8 (of a liquid) translucent and clear. 9 bright and early. very early in the morning. ◆ adv 10 brightly: the fire was burning bright. [OE beorht]
► **'brightly** adv ► **'brightness** n

Bright ★ (braɪt) n John. 1811–89, British liberal statesman, economist: with Richard Cobden he led the Anti-Corn-Law League (1838–46).

brighten ('braɪt°n) vb 1 to make or become bright or brighter. 2 to make or become cheerful.

brightening agent n a compound applied to a textile to increase its brightness by the conversion of ultraviolet radiation to visible (blue) light, used in detergents.

Brighton ★ ('braɪt°n) n a resort in S England, in Brighton and Hove unitary authority, in East Sussex: patronized by the Prince Regent, who had the Royal Pavilion built (1782); seat of the University of Sussex and the University of Brighton. Pop.: 124 851 (1991).

Brighton and Hove ★ (həuv) n a unitary authority in S England, in East Sussex. Pop.: 246 200 (1994 est.). Area: 72 sq. km (28 sq. miles).

Bright's disease (braɪts) n chronic inflammation of the kidneys; chronic nephritis. [C19: after Richard Bright (1789–1858), E physician]

brightwork ('braɪt,wɜːk) n shiny metal trimmings or fittings on ships, cars, etc.

Brigid ★ ('brɪdʒɪd) n See (Saint) **Bridget**.

brill¹ (brɪl) n, pl brill or brills. a European flatfish similar to the turbot. [C15: prob. from Cornish brȳthel mackerel, from OCornish brȳth speckled]

brill² (brɪl) adj Brit sl. excellent or wonderful. [C20: shortened form of BRILLIANT]

brilliance ('brɪljəns) or **brilliancy** n 1 great brightness; radiance. 2 excellence or distinction in physical or mental ability; exceptional talent. 3 splendour; magnificence.

brilliant ('brɪljənt) adj 1 shining with light; sparkling. 2 (of a colour) reflecting a considerable amount of light; vivid. 3 outstanding; exceptional: a brilliant success. 4 splendid; magnificent: a brilliant show. 5 of outstanding intelligence or intellect: a brilliant mind. ◆ n 6 Also called: brilliant cut. 6a a cut for diamonds and other gemstones in the form of two many-faceted pyramids joined

at their bases. **6b** a diamond of this cut. [C17: from F *brillant* shining, from It. *brillo* BERYL]
▸ **'brilliantly** *adv*

brilliantine ('brɪljən,tiːn) *n* a perfumed oil used to make the hair smooth and shiny. [C19: from F, from *brillant* shining]

brim (brɪm) *n* **1** the upper rim of a vessel: *the brim of a cup.* **2** a projecting rim or edge: *the brim of a hat.* **3** the brink or edge of something. ◆ *vb* **brims, brimming, brimmed. 4** to fill or be full to the brim: *eyes brimming with tears.* [C13: from MHG *brem*]
▸ **'brimless** *adj*

brimful *or* **brimfull** (ˌbrɪm'fʊl) *adj* (*postpositive*; foll. by *of*) filled up to the brim (with).

brimstone ('brɪm,stəʊn) *n* **1** an obsolete name for **sulphur. 2** a common yellow butterfly of N temperate regions of the Old World. [OE *brynstān*; see BURN[1], STONE]

Brindisi ★ (*Italian* 'brindizi) *n* a port in SE Italy, in SE Apulia: important naval base in Roman times and a centre of the Crusades in the Middle Ages. Pop.: 93 290 (1991). Ancient name: **Brundisium.**

brindle ('brɪnd°l) *n* **1** a brindled animal. **2** a brindled colouring. [C17: back formation from BRINDLED]

brindled ('brɪnd°ld) *adj* brown or grey streaked or patched with a darker colour: *a brindled dog.* [C17: changed from C15 *brended*, lit.: branded]

Brindley ★ ('brɪndlɪ) *n* **James.** 1716–72, British canal builder, who constructed (1759–61) the Bridgewater Canal, the first in England.

brine (braɪn) *n* **1** a strong solution of salt and water, used for salting and pickling meats, etc. **2** the sea or its water. ◆ *vb* **brines, brining, brined. 3** (*tr*) to soak in or treat with brine. [OE *brīne*]
▸ **'brinish** *adj*

bring (brɪŋ) *vb* **brings, bringing, brought.** (*tr*) **1** to carry, convey, or take (something or someone) to a designated place or person: *bring that book to me.* **2** to cause to happen or occur to (oneself or another): *to bring disrespect on oneself.* **3** to cause to happen as a consequence: *responsibility brings maturity.* **4** to cause to come to mind: *it brought back memories.* **5** to cause to be in a certain state, position, etc.: *the punch brought him to his knees.* **6** to force, persuade, or make (oneself): *I couldn't bring myself to do it.* **7** to sell for; fetch: *the painting brought 20 pounds.* **8** *Law.* **8a** to institute (proceedings, charges, etc.). **8b** to put (evidence, etc.) before a tribunal. **9 bring forth.** to give birth to. ◆ See also **bring about, bring down,** etc. [OE *bringan*]
▸ **'bringer** *n*

bring about *vb* (*tr, adv*) **1** to cause to happen. **2** to turn (a ship) around.

bring-and-buy sale *n Brit. & NZ.* an informal sale, often for charity, to which people bring items for sale and buy those that others have brought.

bring down *vb* (*tr, adv*) to cause to fall.

bring forward *vb* (*tr, adv*) **1** to present or introduce (a subject) for discussion. **2** *Book-keeping.* to transfer (a sum) to the top of the next page or column.

bring in *vb* (*tr, adv*) **1** to yield (income, profit, or cash). **2** to produce or return (a verdict). **3** to introduce (a legislative bill, etc.).

bring off *vb* (*tr, adv*) to succeed in achieving (something), esp. with difficulty.

bring out *vb* (*tr, adv*) **1** to produce or publish or have published. **2** to expose, reveal, or cause to be seen: *she brought out the best in me.* **3** (foll. by *in*) to cause (a person) to become covered (with spots, a rash, etc.). **4** *Brit.* to introduce (a girl) formally into society as a debutante.

bring over *vb* (*tr, adv*) to cause (a person) to change allegiances.

bring round *or* **around** *vb* (*tr, adv*) **1** to restore (a person) to consciousness, esp. after a faint. **2** to convince (another person, usually an opponent) of an opinion or point of view.

bring to *vb* (*tr, adv*) **1** to restore (a person) to consciousness. **2** to cause (a ship) to turn into the wind and reduce her headway.

bring up *vb* (*tr, adv*) **1** to care for and train (a child); rear.

2 to raise (a subject) for discussion; mention. **3** to vomi (food).

brinjal ('brɪndʒəl) *n* (in India and Africa) another nam for the **aubergine.** [C17: from Port. *berinjela*, from Ar.]

brink (brɪŋk) *n* **1** the edge, border, or verge of a steep place. **2** the land at the edge of a body of water. **3** th verge of an event or state: *the brink of disaster.* [C13: fron MDu. *brinc*, of Gmc origin]

brinkmanship ('brɪŋkmən,ʃɪp) *n* the art or practice o pressing a dangerous situation, esp. in international af fairs, to the limit of safety and peace in order to win a advantage.

briny ('braɪnɪ) *adj* **brinier, briniest. 1** of or resembling brine salty. ◆ *n* **2** (preceded by *the*) *Inf.* the sea.
▸ **'brininess** *n*

brio ('briːəʊ) *n* liveliness or vigour; spirit. See also **con brio** [C19: from It., of Celtic origin]

brioche ('briːəʊʃ, -ɒʃ) *n* a soft roll made from a very ligh yeast dough. [C19: from Norman dialect, from *brier* to knead, of Gmc origin]

briquette *or* **briquet** (brɪ'kɛt) *n* a small brick made o compressed coal dust, sawdust, charcoal, etc., used for fuel. [C19: from F: a little brick, from *brique* BRICK]

Brisbane ★ ('brɪzbən) *n* a port in E Australia, the capita of Queensland: founded in 1824 as a penal settlement vast agricultural hinterland. Pop.: 1 489 100 (1995 est.).

brisk (brɪsk) *adj* **1** lively and quick; vigorous: *a brisk walk* **2** invigorating or sharp: *brisk weather.* ◆ *vb* **3** (often foll by *up*) to enliven; make or become brisk. [C16: prob var. of BRUSQUE]
▸ **'briskly** *adv* ▸ **'briskness** *n*

brisket ('brɪskɪt) *n* **1** the breast of a four-legged animal. **2** the meat from this part, esp. of beef. [C14: prob. from ON]

brisling ('brɪslɪŋ) *n* another name for a **sprat.** [C20: from Norwegian; rel. to obs. Danish *bretling*]

bristle ('brɪs°l) *n* **1** any short stiff hair of an animal o plant, such as on a pig's back. **2** something resembling these hairs: *toothbrush bristle.* ◆ *vb* **bristles, bristling, bristled. 3** (when *intr*, often foll. by *up*) to stand up or cause to stand up like bristles. **4** (*intr*; sometimes foll. by *up*) to show anger, indignation, etc.: *she bristled at the suggestion.* **5** (*intr*) to be thickly covered or set: *the target bristled with arrows.* [C13 *bristil, brustel*, from earlier *brust*, from OE *byrst*]
▸ **'bristly** *adj*

Bristol ★ ('brɪst°l) *n* a port and industrial city and unitary authority in SW England, administrative centre of the county of Avon, on the River Avon seven miles from its mouth on the Bristol Channel: a major port, trading with America, in the 17th and 18th centuries: the modern port consists chiefly of docks at Avonmouth and Portishead; noted for the **Clifton Suspension Bridge** (designed by I. K. Brunel, 1834) over the Avon gorge; Bristol University (1909), University of the West of England. Pop.: 374 300 (1996 est.).

Bristol board *n* a heavy smooth cardboard of fine quality, used for drawing.

Bristol Channel ★ *n* an inlet of the Atlantic, between S Wales and SW England, merging into the Severn estuary. Length: about 137 km (85 miles).

Bristol fashion *adv, adj* (*postpositive*) in good order; efficiently arranged.

bristols ('brɪst°lz) *pl n Brit. sl.* a woman's breasts. [C20: short for *Bristol Cities*, rhyming slang for *titties*]

Brit (brɪt) *n Inf.* a British person.

Brit. *abbrev. for:* **1** Britain. **2** British.

Britain ★ ('brɪt°n) *n* another name for **Great Britain** or the **United Kingdom.**

Britannia (brɪ'tænɪə) *n* **1** a female warrior carrying a trident and wearing a helmet, personifying Great Britain or the British Empire. **2** (in the ancient Roman Empire) the S part of Great Britain. **3** short for **Britannia coin.**

Britannia coin *n* any of four British gold coins introduced in 1987 for investment purposes; their denominations are £100, £50, £25, and £10.

★ people and places

Britannia metal *n* an alloy of tin with antimony and copper: used for decorative purposes and for bearings.

Britannic (brɪˈtænɪk) *adj* of Britain; British (esp. in **His** *or* **Her Britannic Majesty**).

britches (ˈbrɪtʃɪz) *pl n* a variant spelling of **breeches**.

Briticism (ˈbrɪtɪˌsɪzəm) *n* a custom, linguistic usage, or other feature peculiar to Britain or its people. Also: **Britishism**.

British (ˈbrɪtɪʃ) *adj* **1** of or denoting Britain. **2** relating to, denoting, or characteristic of the inhabitants of Britain. **3** relating to or denoting the English language as spoken and written in Britain. **4** of or relating to the Commonwealth: *British subjects.* ◆ *n* **5 the British.** (*functioning as pl*) the natives or inhabitants of Britain.
▸ **'Britishness** *n*

British Antarctic Territory ★ *n* a United Kingdom overseas territory in the S Atlantic: created in 1962 and consisting of the South Shetland Islands, the South Orkney Islands, and Graham Land; formerly part of the Falkland Islands Dependencies.

British Cameroons ★ *pl n* a former British trust territory of West Africa. See **Cameroon**.

British Columbia ★ *n* a province of W Canada, on the Pacific coast: largely mountainous with extensive forests, rich mineral resources, and important fisheries. Capital: Victoria. Pop.: 3 766 000 (1995 est.). Area: 930 532 sq. km (359 279 sq. miles). Abbrev.: **BC**.
▸ **British Columbian** *n, adj*

British Council *n* an organization founded (1934) to extend the influence of British culture and education throughout the world.

British East Africa ★ *n* the former British possessions of Uganda, Kenya, Tanganyika, and Zanzibar, before their independence in the 1960s.

British Empire ★ *n* (formerly) the United Kingdom and the territories under its control, which reached its greatest extent at the end of World War I when it embraced over a quarter of the world's population and more than a quarter of the world's land surface.

Britisher (ˈbrɪtɪʃə) *n* (not used by the British) **1** a native or inhabitant of Great Britain. **2** any British subject.

British Guiana ★ *n* the former name (until 1966) of **Guyana**.

British Honduras ★ *n* the former name of **Belize**.

British India ★ *n* the 17 provinces of India formerly governed by the British under the British sovereign: ceased to exist in 1947 when the independent states of India and Pakistan were created.

British Indian Ocean Territory ★ *n* a United Kingdom overseas territory in the Indian Ocean: consists of the Chagos Archipelago (formerly a dependency of Mauritius) and formerly included (until 1976) Aldabra, Farquhar, and Des Roches, now administratively part of the Seychelles.

British Isles ★ *pl n* a group of islands in W Europe, consisting of Great Britain, Ireland, the Isle of Man, Orkney, the Shetland Islands, the Channel Islands belonging to Great Britain, and the islands adjacent to these.

Britishism (ˈbrɪtɪˌʃɪzəm) *n* a variant of **Briticism**.

British Legion *n Brit.* an organization founded in 1921 to provide services and assistance for former members of the armed forces.

British North America ★ *n* (formerly) Canada or its constituent regions or provinces that formed part of the British Empire.

British Somaliland ★ *n* a former British protectorate (1884–1960) in E Africa, on the Gulf of Aden: united with Italian Somaliland in 1960 to form the Somali Republic.

British thermal unit *n* a unit of heat in the fps system equal to the quantity of heat required to raise the temperature of 1 pound of water by 1°F. 1 British thermal unit is equivalent to 1055.06 joules. Abbrev.: **btu, BThU**.

British Virgin Islands ★ *pl n* a United Kingdom overseas territory in the Caribbean, consisting of 36 islands in the E Virgin Islands: formerly part of the Federation of the Leeward Islands (1871–1956). Capital: Road Town, on Tortola. Pop.: 17 000 (1993 est.). Area: 153 sq. km (59 sq. miles).

British West Africa ★ *n* the former British possessions of Nigeria, The Gambia, Sierra Leone, and the Gold Coast, and the former trust territories of Togoland and Cameroons.

British West Indies ★ *pl n* the states in the Caribbean that are members of the Commonwealth: Antigua and Barbuda, the Bahamas, Barbados, Dominica, Grenada, Jamaica, Saint Kitts-Nevis, Saint Lucia, Saint Vincent and the Grenadines, and Trinidad and Tobago.

Briton (ˈbrɪt°n) *n* **1** a native or inhabitant of Britain. **2** *History.* any of the early Celtic inhabitants of S Britain. [C13: from OF *Breton*, of Celtic origin]

Britpop (ˈbrɪtˌpop) *n* the characteristic pop music performed by some British bands of the mid 1990s.

Brittany ★ (ˈbrɪtənɪ) *n* a region of NW France, the peninsula between the English Channel and the Bay of Biscay: settled by Celtic refugees from Wales and Cornwall during the Anglo-Saxon invasions; disputed between England and France until 1364. Breton name: **Breiz** (braɪz). French name: **Bretagne**.

Britten ★ (ˈbrɪt°n) *n* (**Edward**) **Benjamin**, Baron Britten. 1913–76, British composer. His works include the operas *Peter Grimes* (1945) and *Billy Budd* (1951), choral works, and orchestral pieces.

brittle (ˈbrɪt°l) *adj* **1** easily cracked, snapped, or broken; fragile. **2** curt or irritable. **3** hard or sharp in quality. ◆ *n* **4** a crunchy sweet made with treacle and nuts: *peanut brittle.* [C14: ult. from OE *brēotan* to break]
▸ **'brittleness** *n*

brittle-star *n* an echinoderm occurring on the sea bottom and having long slender arms radiating from a small central disc.

Brno ★ (ˈbɜːnəʊ; *Czech* ˈbrnɔ) *n* a city in the Czech Republic, formerly the capital of Moravia: the country's second largest city. Pop.: 389 576 (1995 est.). German name: **Brünn**.

bro. *abbrev. for* brother.

broach (brəʊtʃ) *vb* (*tr*) **1** to initiate (a topic) for discussion. **2** to tap or pierce (a container) to draw off (a liquid): *to broach a cask.* **3** to open in order to begin to use. ◆ *n* **4** a tapered toothed cutting tool for enlarging holes. **5** a spit for roasting meat, etc. [C14: from OF *broche*, from L *brochus* projecting]

broad (brɔːd) *adj* **1** having relatively great breadth or width. **2** of vast extent; spacious: *a broad plain.* **3** (*postpositive*) from one side to the other: *four miles broad.* **4** of great scope or potential: *that invention had broad applications.* **5** not detailed; general: *broad plans.* **6** clear and open; full (esp. in **broad daylight**). **7** obvious or plain: *broad hints.* **8** liberal; tolerant: *a broad political stance.* **9** widely spread; extensive: *broad support.* **10** vulgar; coarse; indecent: *a broad joke.* **11** (of a dialect or pronunciation) consisting of a large number of speech sounds characteristic of a particular geographic area: *a broad Yorkshire accent.* **12** *Finance.* denoting an assessment of liquidity as including notes and coin in circulation with the public, banks' till money and balances, most private-sector bank deposits, and sterling bank-deposit certificates: *broad money.* Cf. **narrow** (sense 7). **13** *Phonetics.* the long vowel in English words such as *father, half,* as represented in Received Pronunciation. ◆ *n* **14** the broad part of something. **15** *Sl., chiefly US & Canad.* **15a** a girl or woman. **15b** a prostitute. **16** See **Broads**. [OE *brād*]
▸ **'broadly** *adv*

B-road *n* a secondary road in Britain.

broad arrow *n* **1** a mark shaped like a broad arrowhead designating British government property and formerly used on prison clothing. **2** an arrow with a broad head.

broad bean *n* **1** an erect annual Eurasian bean plant cultivated for its large edible flattened seeds. **2** the seed of this plant.

broadcast (ˈbrɔːdˌkɑːst) *vb* **broadcasts, broadcasting, broadcast** *or* **broadcasted**. **1** to transmit (announcements or programmes) on radio or television. **2** (*intr*) to take part in a radio or television programme. **3** (*tr*) to make widely known throughout an area: *to broadcast news.* **4** (*tr*) to scatter (seed, etc.) over an area, esp. by hand. ◆ *n* **5a** a transmission or programme on radio or television. **5b** (*as modifier*): *a broadcast signal.* **6** the act of scattering seeds. ◆ *adj* **7** dispersed over a wide area. ◆ *adv* **8** far and wide. ► **'broad,caster** *n* ► **'broad,casting** *n*

Broad Church *n* **1** a party within the Church of England which favours a broad and liberal interpretation of Anglican doctrine. **2** (*usually not caps.*) a group which embraces a wide and varied number of views and opinions. ◆ *adj* **Broad-Church. 3** of or relating to this party in the Church of England.

broadcloth ('brɔːˌklɒθ) *n* **1** fabric woven on a wide loom. **2** a closely woven fabric of wool, worsted, cotton, or rayon with lustrous finish, used for clothing.

broaden ('brɔːdᵊn) *vb* to make or become broad or broader; widen.

broad gauge *n* **1** a railway track with a greater distance between the lines than the standard gauge of 56½ inches (about 1·44 metres). ◆ *adj* **broad-gauge. 2** of or denoting a railway having this track.

broad-leaved *adj* denoting trees other than conifers; having broad rather than needle-shaped leaves.

broadloom ('brɔːdˌluːm) *n* (*modifier*) of or designating carpets woven on a wide loom.

broad-minded *adj* **1** tolerant of opposing viewpoints; not prejudiced; liberal. **2** not easily shocked by permissive sexual habits, pornography, etc. ► **,broad-'mindedly** *adv* ► **,broad-'mindedness** *n*

Broads ★ (brɔːdz) *pl n* **the.** a group of shallow navigable lakes, connected by a network of rivers, in E England, in Norfolk and Suffolk.

broadsheet ('brɔːdˌʃiːt) *n* **1** a newspaper having a large format, approximately 15 by 24 inches (38 by 61 centimetres). **2** another word for **broadside** (sense 4).

broadside ('brɔːdˌsaɪd) *n* **1** *Naut.* the entire side of a vessel. **2** *Naval.* **2a** all the armament fired from one side of a warship. **2b** the simultaneous discharge of such armament. **3** a strong or abusive verbal or written attack. **4** Also called: **broadside ballad.** a ballad or popular song printed on one side of a sheet of paper, esp. in 16th-century England. ◆ *adv* **5** with a broader side facing an object; sideways.

broad-spectrum *n* (*modifier*) effective against a wide variety of diseases or microorganisms: *a broad-spectrum antibiotic.*

broadsword ('brɔːdˌsɔːd) *n* a broad-bladed sword used for cutting rather than stabbing.

broadtail ('brɔːdˌteɪl) *n* **1** the highly valued black wavy fur obtained from the skins of newly born karakul lambs; caracul. **2** another name for **karakul.**

Broadway ★ ('brɔːdˌweɪ) *n* **1** a thoroughfare in New York City: the centre of the commercial theatre in the US. ◆ *adj* **2** of, relating to, or suitable for the commercial theatre, esp. on Broadway.

brocade (brəʊ'keɪd) *n* **1** a rich fabric woven with a raised design, often using gold or silver threads. ◆ *vb* **brocades, brocading, brocaded. 2** (*tr*) to weave with such a design. [C17: from Sp. *brocado*, from It. *broccato* embossed fabric, from L *brochus* projecting]

broccoli ('brɒkəlɪ) *n* **1** a cultivated variety of cabbage having branched greenish flower heads. **2** the flower head, eaten as a vegetable before the buds have opened. [C17: from It., pl of *broccolo* a little sprout, from *brocco* sprout]

broch (brɒk, brɒx) *n* (in Scotland) a prehistoric circular dry-stone tower large enough to serve as a fortified home. [C17: from ON *borg;* rel. to OE *burh* settlement, burgh]

brochette (brɒ'ʃɛt) *n* a skewer or small spit, used for holding pieces of meat, etc., while roasting or grilling. [C19: from OF *brochete* small pointed tool; see BROACH]

brochure ('brəʊʃjʊə, -ʃə) *n* a pamphlet or booklet, esp. one containing summarized or introductory information or advertising. [C18: from F, from *brocher* to stitch (a book)]

brock (brɒk) *n* a Brit. name for **badger** (sense 1). [OE *broc* of Celtic origin]

Brocken ★ (*German* 'brɔkən) *n* a mountain in central Germany: the highest peak of the Harz Mountains; important in German folklore. Height: 1142 m (3747 ft). The **Brocken Bow** or **Brocken Spectre** is an atmospheric phenomenon in which an observer, when the sun is low, may see his enlarged shadow against the clouds, often surrounded by coloured lights.

brocket ('brɒkɪt) *n* a small deer of tropical America, having small unbranched antlers. [C15: from Anglo-F *broquet*, from *broque* horn]

broderie anglaise ('brəʊdəri ɑːŋ'glɛz) *n* open embroidery on white cotton, fine linen, etc. [C19: from F: Eng lish embroidery]

Broederbond ('brudəˌbɔːnt, 'brudəˌbɒnt) *n* (in South Africa) a secret society of Afrikaner Nationalists. [Afrik. band of brothers]

Broglie ★ (brɔj) *n* **1** Prince **Louis Victor de** (lwi viktɔr də) 1892–1987, French physicist, noted for his development of wave mechanics: Nobel prize for physics 1929. **2** his brother, **Maurice** (mɔris), Duc de Broglie. 1875–1960 French physicist, noted for his research into X-ray spectra.

brogue[1] (brəʊg) *n* a broad gentle-sounding dialectal accent, esp. that used by the Irish in speaking English [C18: from ?]

brogue[2] (brəʊg) *n* **1** a sturdy walking shoe, often with ornamental perforations. **2** an untanned shoe worn formerly in Ireland and Scotland. [C16: from Irish Gaelic *bróg* shoe]

broil[1] (brɔɪl) *vb* **1** the usual US and Canad. word for **grill** (sense 1). **2** to become or cause to become extremely hot. **3** (*intr*) to be furious. [C14: from OF *bruillir* to burn]

broil[2] (brɔɪl) *Arch.* ◆ *n* **1** a loud quarrel or disturbance; brawl. ◆ *vb* **2** (*intr*) to brawl; quarrel. [C16: from OF *brouiller* to mix]

broiler ('brɔɪlə) *n* **1** a young tender chicken suitable for roasting. **2** a pan, grate, etc., for broiling food. **3** a very hot day.

broke (brəʊk) *vb* **1** the past tense of **break.** ◆ *adj* **2** *Inf.* having no money; bankrupt. **3** **go for broke.** *Sl.* to risk everything in a gambling or other venture.

broken ('brəʊkən) *vb* **1** the past participle of **break.** ◆ *adj* **2** fractured, smashed, or splintered: *a broken vase.* **3** interrupted; disturbed; disconnected: *broken sleep.* **4** intermittent or discontinuous: *broken sunshine.* **5** not functioning. **6** spoilt or ruined by divorce (esp. in **broken home, broken marriage**). **7** (of a trust, promise, contract, etc.) violated; infringed. **8** (of the speech of a foreigner) imperfect in grammar, vocabulary, and pronunciation: *broken English.* **9** Also: **broken-in.** made tame or disciplined by training. **10** exhausted or weakened, as through ill-health or misfortune. **11** irregular or rough; uneven: *broken ground.* **12** bankrupt. **13** (of colour) having a multicoloured decorative effect, as by stippling paint onto a surface. ► **'brokenly** *adv*

broken chord *n* another term for **arpeggio.**

broken-down *adj* **1** worn out, as by age or long use; dilapidated. **2** not in working order.

brokenhearted (ˌbrəʊkən'hɑːtɪd) *adj* overwhelmed by grief or disappointment. ► **,broken'heartedly** *adv*

Broken Hill ★ *n* a city in SE Australia, in W New South Wales: mining centre for lead, silver, and zinc. Pop.: 24 500 (1988 est.).

broken wind (wɪnd) *n* *Vet. science.* another name for **heaves.** ► **,broken'winded** *adj*

broker ('brəʊkə) *n* **1** an agent who, acting on behalf of a principal, buys or sells goods, securities, etc.: *insurance broker.* **2** short for **stockbroker. 3** a person who deals in second-hand goods. [C14: from Anglo-F *brocour* broacher (of casks, hence, one who sells, agent), from OF *broquier* to tap a cask]

★ people and places

brokerage ('brəʊkərɪdʒ) n **1** commission charged by a broker. **2** a broker's business or office.

brolga ('brɒlgə) n a large grey Australian crane having a red-and-green head and a trumpeting call. Also called: **native companion**. [C19: from Abor.]

brolly ('brɒlɪ) n, pl **brollies**. an informal Brit. name for **umbrella** (sense 1).

Bromberg ★ ('brɒmbɜːk) n the German name for **Bydgoszcz**.

bromeliad (brəʊ'miːlɪˌæd) n any of a family of tropical American plants, typically epiphytes with a rosette of fleshy leaves, such as the pineapple and Spanish moss. [C19: from NL, after Olaf Bromelius (1639–1705), Swedish botanist]

bromide ('brəʊmaɪd) n **1** any salt of hydrobromic acid. **2** any compound containing a bromine atom. **3** a dose of sodium or potassium bromide given as a sedative. **4a** a platitude. **4b** a boring person.

bromide paper n a type of photographic paper coated with an emulsion of silver bromide.

bromine ('brəʊmiːn, -mɪn) n a pungent dark red volatile liquid element that occurs in brine and is used in the production of chemicals. Symbol: Br; atomic no.: 35; atomic wt.: 79.91. [C19: from F brome bromine, from Gk brōmos bad smell, from ?]

Bromley ★ ('brɒmlɪ) n a borough of SE Greater London. Pop.: 293 000 (1994 est.). Area: 153 sq. km (59 sq. miles).

Bromsgrove ★ ('brɒmz,grəʊv) n a town in W central England, in NE Hereford and Worcester. Pop.: 26 366 (1991).

bronchi ('brɒŋkaɪ) n the plural of **bronchus**.

bronchial ('brɒŋkɪəl) adj of or relating to the bronchi or the bronchial tubes.
▶ 'bronchially adv

bronchial tubes pl n the bronchi or their smaller divisions.

bronchiectasis (,brɒŋkɪ'ɛktəsɪs) n chronic dilation and usually infection of the bronchi. [C19: from BRONCHO- + Gk ektasis a stretching]

bronchiole ('brɒŋkɪ,əʊl) n any of the smallest bronchial tubes. [C19: from NL; see BRONCHUS]
▶ ,bronchi'olar adj

bronchitis (brɒŋ'kaɪtɪs) n inflammation of the bronchial tubes, characterized by coughing, difficulty in breathing, etc.
▶ bronchitic (brɒŋ'kɪtɪk) adj, n

broncho- or before a vowel **bronch-** combining form. indicating or relating to the bronchi: bronchitis. [from Gk: BRONCHUS]

bronchodilator (,brɒŋkəʊdaɪ'leɪtə, -dɪ-) n any drug or other agent that causes dilation of the bronchial tubes by relaxing bronchial muscle: used, esp. in the form of aerosol sprays, for the relief of asthma and chronic bronchitis.

bronchopneumonia (,brɒŋkəʊnjuː'məʊnɪə) n inflammation of the lungs, starting in the bronchioles.

bronchoscope ('brɒŋkə,skəʊp) n an instrument for examining and providing access to the interior of the bronchial tubes.

bronchus ('brɒŋkəs) n, pl **bronchi**. either of the two main branches of the trachea. [C18: from NL, from Gk bronkhos windpipe]

bronco or **broncho** ('brɒŋkəʊ) n, pl **broncos** or **bronchos**. (in the US and Canada) a wild or partially tamed pony or mustang of the western plains. [C19: from Mexican Sp., from Sp.: rough, wild]

Brontë ★ ('brɒntɪ) n **1 Anne**, pen name Acton Bell. 1820–49, British novelist; author of The Tenant of Wildfell Hall (1847). **2** her sister, **Charlotte**, pen name Currer Bell. 1816–55, British novelist, author of Jane Eyre (1847), Villette (1853), and The Professor (1857). **3** her sister, **Emily (Jane)**, pen name Ellis Bell. 1818–48, British novelist and poet; author of Wuthering Heights (1847).

brontosaurus (,brɒntə'sɔːrəs) or **brontosaur** ('brɒntə,sɔː) n a very large herbivorous quadrupedal dinosaur, common in N America during late Jurassic times, having

a long neck and long tail. [C19: from NL, from Gk brontē thunder + sauros lizard]

Bronx ★ (brɒŋks) n **the.** a borough of New York City, on the mainland, separated from Manhattan by the Harlem River. Pop.: 1 203 789 (1990).

Bronx cheer n Chiefly US. a loud spluttering noise made with the lips and tongue and expressing derision or contempt; raspberry.

bronze (brɒnz) n **1** any hard water-resistant alloy consisting of copper and smaller proportions of tin and sometimes zinc and lead. **2** a yellowish-brown colour or pigment. **3** a statue, medal, or other object made of bronze. Cf. **bronze** (sense 1). ◆ adj **4** made of or resembling bronze. **5** of a yellowish-brown colour. ◆ vb **bronzes, bronzing, bronzed**. **6** (esp. of the skin) to make or become brown; tan. **7** (tr) to give the appearance of bronze to. [C18: from F, from It. bronzo]
▶ 'bronzy adj

Bronze Age n **a** a technological stage between the Stone and Iron Ages, beginning in the Middle East about 4500 B.C. and lasting in Britain from about 2000 to 500 B.C., during which weapons and tools were made of bronze. **b** (as modifier): a Bronze-Age tool.

bronze medal n a medal awarded to a competitor who comes third in a contest or race.

bronzing ('brɒnzɪŋ) n **1** blue pigment producing a metallic lustre when ground into paint media at fairly high concentrations. **2** the application of a mixture of powdered metal or pigments of a metallic lustre to a surface.

Bronzino, Il ★ (Italian bron'dziːno) n real name Agnolo di Cosimo di Mariano. 1503–72, Florentine mannerist painter.

brooch (brəʊtʃ) n an ornament with a hinged pin and catch, worn fastened to clothing. [C13: from OF broche; see BROACH]

brood (bruːd) n **1** a number of young animals, esp. birds, produced at one hatching. **2** all the offspring in one family: often used jokingly or contemptuously. **3** a group of a particular kind; breed. **4** (modifier) kept for breeding: a brood mare. ◆ vb **5** (of a bird) **5a** to sit on or hatch (eggs). **5b** (tr) to cover (young birds) protectively with the wings. **6** (when intr, often foll. by on, over, or upon) to ponder morbidly or persistently. [OE brōd]
▶ 'brooding n, adj

brooder ('bruːdə) n **1** a structure, usually heated, used for rearing young chickens or other fowl. **2** a person or thing that broods.

broody ('bruːdɪ) adj **broodier, broodiest**. **1** moody; introspective. **2** (of poultry) wishing to sit on or hatch eggs. **3** Inf. (of a woman) wishing to have a baby.
▶ 'broodiness n

brook¹ (brʊk) n a natural freshwater stream smaller than a river. [OE brōc]

brook² (brʊk) vb (tr) (usually used with a negative) to bear; tolerate. [OE brūcan]

Brooke ★ (brʊk) n **1 Alan Francis**. See (1st Viscount) **Alanbrooke**. **2 Sir James**. 1803–68, British soldier; first rajah of Sarawak (1841–63). **3 Rupert (Chawner)**. 1887–1915, British poet, noted for his war poetry.

brooklet ('brʊklɪt) n a small brook.

brooklime ('brʊk,laɪm) n either of two blue-flowered trailing plants, Veronica americana of North America or V. beccabunga of Europe and Asia, growing in moist places. See also **speedwell**. [C16: from BROOK¹ + -lime, from OE hleomoce]

Brooklyn ★ ('brʊklɪn) n a borough of New York City, on the SW end of Long Island. Pop.: 2 291 664 (1990).

Brookner ★ ('brʊknə) n **Anita**. born 1928, British writer. Her novels include Hotel du Lac (1984), which won the Booker Prize, Brief Lives (1990), and Falling Slowly (1998).

Brooks ★ (brʊks) n **Mel**, real name Melvyn Kaminsky. born 1926, US writer, actor, and film director. His films include Blazing Saddles (1974) and Dracula: Dead and Loving It (1996).

Brooks Range ★ (brʊks) n a mountain range in N Alaska. Highest peak: Mount Isto, 2761 m (9058 ft).

★ people and places

brook trout n a North American trout, valued as a food and game fish.

broom (bru:m, brʊm) n **1** an implement for sweeping consisting of a long handle to which is attached either a brush of straw or twigs, bound together, or a solid head into which are set tufts of bristles or fibres. **2** any of various yellow-flowered Eurasian leguminous shrubs. **3 new broom.** a newly appointed official, etc., eager to make changes. ◆ vb **4** (tr) to sweep with a broom. [OE brōm]

broomrape ('bru:m,reɪp, 'brʊm-) n any of a genus of leafless fleshy parasitic plants growing on the roots of other plants, esp. on broom. [C16: adaptation & partial translation of Med. L rāpum genistae tuber (hence: root nodule) of Genista (a type of broom plant)]

broomstick ('bru:m,stɪk, 'brʊm-) n the long handle of a broom.

bros. or **Bros.** abbrev. for brothers.

brose (brəʊz) n Scot. a porridge made by adding a boiling liquid to meal, esp. oatmeal. [C13 broys, from OF broez, from breu broth, of Gmc origin]

broth (brɒθ) n **1** a soup made by boiling meat, fish, vegetables, etc., in water. **2** another name for **stock** (sense 19). [OE broth]

brothel ('brɒθəl) n **1** a house where men pay to have sexual intercourse with prostitutes. **2** Austral. inf. any untidy place. [C16: short for brothel-house, from C14 brothel useless person, from OE brēothan to deteriorate]

brother ('brʌðə) n **1** a male person having the same parents as another person. **2a** a male person belonging to the same group, profession, nationality, trade union, etc., as another or others; fellow member. **2b** (as modifier): brother workers. **3** comrade; friend: used as a form of address. **4** Christianity. a member of a male religious order. ◆ Related adj: **fraternal.** [OE brōthor]

brotherhood ('brʌðə,hʊd) n **1** the state of being related as a brother or brothers. **2** an association or fellowship, such as a trade union. **3** all persons engaged in a particular profession, trade, etc. **4** the belief, feeling, or hope that all men should treat one another as brothers.

brother-in-law n, pl **brothers-in-law. 1** the brother of one's wife or husband. **2** the husband of one's sister. **3** the husband of the sister of one's husband or wife.

brotherly ('brʌðəlɪ) adj of, resembling, or suitable to a brother, esp. in showing loyalty and affection; fraternal. ▶ '**brotherliness** n

brougham ('bru:əm, bru:m) n **1** a four-wheeled horse-drawn closed carriage having a raised open driver's seat in front. **2** Obs. a large car with an open compartment at the front for the driver. **3** Obs. an early electric car. [C19: after Lord Brougham (1778–1868)]

brought (brɔ:t) vb the past tense and past participle of bring.

brouhaha ('bru:hɑ:hɑ:) n a loud confused noise; commotion; uproar. [F, imit.]

brow (braʊ) n **1** the part of the face from the eyes to the hairline; forehead. **2** short for **eyebrow. 3** the expression of the face; countenance: a troubled brow. **4** the jutting top of a hill, etc. [OE brū]

browbeat ('braʊ,bi:t) vb **browbeats, browbeating, browbeat, browbeaten.** (tr) to discourage or frighten with threats or a domineering manner; intimidate.

brown (braʊn) n **1** any of various dark colours, such as those of wood or earth. **2** a dye or pigment producing these colours. ◆ adj **3** of the colour brown. **4** (of bread) made from a flour that has not been bleached or bolted, such as wheatmeal or wholemeal flour. **5** deeply tanned or sunburnt. **6 in a brown study.** See **study** (sense 15). ◆ vb **7** to make (esp. food as a result of cooking) brown or (esp. of food) to become brown. [OE brūn]
▶ '**brownish** or '**browny** adj ▶ '**brownness** n

Brown ★ (braʊn) n **1** Sir **Arthur Whitten** ('wɪtᵊn). 1886–1948, British aviator who with J. W. Alcock made the first nonstop flight across the Atlantic (1919). **2 Ford Madox.** 1821–93, British Pre-Raphaelite painter. **3 George (Alfred),** Lord George-Brown. 1914–85, British Labour leader; deputy leader of the Labour party (1960–70); foreign secretary (1966–68). **4 George Mackay.** 1921–96,

Scottish poet, novelist, and short-story writer. **5 Gordo**[n] born 1951, British Labour politician; chancellor of th[e] exchequer from 1997. **6 Herbert Charles.** born 1912, U[S] chemist, who worked on the compounds of boro[n]; Nobel prize for chemistry, 1979. **7 James.** born 1928, U[S] soul singer and songwriter. **8 John.** 1800–59, US abol[i]tionist leader, hanged after leading an unsuccessful re[-] bellion of slaves at Harper's Ferry, Virginia. **9 Lancelo**[t], called Capability Brown. 1716–83, British landscape ga[r]dener. **10 Michael** (**Stuart**). born 1941, US physicia[n]; shared Nobel prize for physiology or medicine (1985) fo[r] work on cholesterol. **11 Robert.** 1773–1858, Scottish bota[-] nist who was the first to observe the Brownian move[-]ment in fluids.

brown bear n a large ferocious brownish bear inhabit[-]ing temperate forests of North America, Europe, an[d] Asia.

brown coal n another name for **lignite.**

brown dwarf n a type of celestial body midway in siz[e] between a large planet and a small star, thought to be one possible explanation of dark matter in the universe.

Browne ★ (braʊn) n **1 Coral** (**Edith**). 1913–91, Australia[n] actress. **2 Hablot Knight.** See **Phiz. 3** Sir **Thomas.** 1605–82[,] English physician and author. His works include Religi[o] Medici (1642).

browned-off adj Inf. thoroughly discouraged or dis[-]heartened; fed up.

brown fat n a dark form of adipose tissue that is readil[y] converted into energy.

brownfield ('braʊn,fi:ld) n (modifier) denoting or lo[-]cated in an urban area that has previously been built on[:] Hampshire has many brownfield developments.

Brownian movement ('braʊnɪən) n random move[-]ment of microscopic particles suspended in a fluid[,] caused by bombardment of the particles by molecules o[f] the fluid. [C19: after Robert Brown]

brownie ('braʊnɪ) n **1** (in folklore) an elf said to do help[-]ful work at night, esp. household chores. **2** a smal[l] square nutty chocolate cake. [C16: dim. of BROWN (tha[t] is, a small brown man)]

Brownie Guide or **Brownie** ('braʊnɪ) n a member o[f] the junior branch of the Guides.

Brownie point n a notional mark to one's credit fo[r] being seen to do the right thing. [C20: ?from the mis[-]taken notion that Brownie Guides earn points for goo[d] deeds]

browning ('braʊnɪŋ) n Brit. a substance used to darke[n] soups, gravies, etc.

Browning ★ ('braʊnɪŋ) n **1 Elizabeth Barrett.** 1806–61[,] British poet and critic; author of the Sonnets from the Por[-]tuguese (1850). **2** her husband, **Robert.** 1812–89, Britis[h] poet, noted for The Ring and the Book (1868–69).

brown paper n a kind of coarse unbleached paper use[d] for wrapping.

brown rice n unpolished rice, in which the grains retai[n] the outer yellowish-brown layer (bran).

Brown Shirt n **1** (in Nazi Germany) a storm trooper. **2** [a] member of any fascist party or group.

brownstone ('braʊn,stəʊn) n US. a reddish-brown iron[-]rich sandstone used for building.

brown sugar n sugar that is unrefined or only partiall[y] refined.

brown trout n a common brownish variety of the trou[t] that occurs in the rivers of N Europe.

browse (braʊz) vb **browses, browsing, browsed. 1** to look through (a book, articles for sale in a shop, etc.) in a ca[-]sual leisurely manner. **2** Computing. to read hypertext[,] esp. on the World Wide Web. **3** (of deer, goats, etc.) to feed upon (vegetation) by continual nibbling. ◆ n **4** the act or an instance of browsing. **5** the young twigs[,] shoots, leaves, etc., on which certain animals feed. [C15: from F broust, brost bud, of Gmc origin]

browser ('braʊzə) n **1** a person or animal that browses. **2** Computing. a software package that enables a user to read hypertext, esp. on the World Wide Web.

★ people and places

roz ★ (*Serbo-Croat* brɔːz) *n* **Josip** ('jɔsip). original name of (Marshal) **Tito**.

RS *abbrev. for* British Road Services.

rubeck ★ ('bruːbɛk) *n* **Dave**. born 1920, US modern jazz pianist and composer.

ruce[1] ★ (bruːs) *n* **1 James**. 1730–94, British explorer, who discovered the source of the Blue Nile (1770). **2 Lenny**. 1925–66, US comedian. **3 Robert the**. See **Robert I. 4 Stanley Melbourne**, 1st Viscount Bruce of Melbourne. 1883–1967, Australian prime minister (1923–29).

ruce[2] (bruːs) *n* **Brit**. a jocular name for an Australian man.

rucellosis (ˌbruːsɪˈləʊsɪs) *n* an infectious disease of cattle, goats, and pigs, caused by bacteria and transmittable to man. Also called: **undulant fever**. [C20: from NL *Brucella*, after Sir David *Bruce* (1855–1931), Australian bacteriologist & physician]

ruch ★ (*German* brux) *n* **Max** (maks). 1838–1920, German composer, noted for his three violin concertos.

ruckner ★ (*German* 'bruknər) *n* **Anton** ('antoːn). 1824–96, Austrian composer. His works include nine symphonies, four masses, and a Te Deum.

rudenell ★ ('bruːdənɛl) *n* **James Thomas**. See (7th Earl of) **Cardigan**.

rueghel, Bruegel, or **Breughel** ★ ('brɔɪgʰl; *Flemish* 'brøːxəl) *n* **1 Jan** (jɑn). 1568–1625, Flemish painter. **2** his father, **Pieter** ('piːtər), called *the Elder*. ?1525–69, Flemish painter. **3** his son, **Pieter**, called *the Younger*. ?1564–1637, Flemish painter.

ruges ★ (bruːʒ; *French* bryʒ) *n* a city in NW Belgium, capital of West Flanders province: centre of the medieval European wool and cloth trade. Pop.: 116 273 (1995 est.). Flemish name: **Brugge** ('bryxə).

ruin ('bruːɪn) *n* a name for a bear, used in children's tales, etc. [C17: from Du. *bruin* brown]

ruise (bruːz) *vb* **bruises, bruising, bruised**. (*mainly tr*) **1** (*also intr*) to injure (tissues) without breaking the skin, usually with discoloration, or (of tissues) to be injured in this way. **2** to offend or injure (someone's feelings). **3** to damage the surface of (something). **4** to crush (food, etc.) by pounding. ◆ *n* **5** a bodily injury without a break in the skin, usually with discoloration; contusion. [OE *brӯsan*]

ruiser ('bruːzə) *n Inf.* a strong tough person, esp. a boxer or a bully.

ruit (bruːt) *vb* **1** (*tr; often passive*; *usually foll. by about*) to report; rumour. ◆ *n* **2** *Arch.* **2a** a rumour. **2b** a loud outcry; clamour. [C15: via F from Med. L *brūgītus*, prob. from L *rugīre* to roar]

rumby ('brʌmbɪ) *n, pl* **brumbies**. *Austral*. **1** a wild horse, esp. one descended from runaway stock. **2** *Inf.* a wild or unruly person. [C19: from ?]

rume (bruːm) *n Poetic*. heavy mist or fog. [C19: from F: mist, winter, from L *brūma*, contracted from *brevissima diēs* the shortest day]

rummagem ★ ('brʌmədʒəm) *n* **1** an informal name for Birmingham. Often shortened to **Brum. 2** (*sometimes not cap.*) something that is cheap and flashy, esp. imitation jewellery. ◆ *adj* **3** (*sometimes not cap.*) cheap and gaudy; tawdry. [C17: from earlier *Bromecham*, local variant of BIRMINGHAM]

rummell ★ ('brʌmǝl) *n* **George Bryan**, called *Beau Brummell*. 1778–1840, British Regency dandy.

brunch (brʌntʃ) *n* a meal eaten late in the morning, combining breakfast with lunch. [C20: from BR(EAKFAST) + (L)UNCH]

rundisium ★ (brʌnˈdɪzɪəm) *n* the ancient name for **Brindisi**.

rundtland ★ ('brʌntlənd) *n* **Gro Harlem** (grəʊ 'hɑːləm). born 1939, Norwegian stateswoman: prime minister (1981 and from 1986).

runei ★ (bruːˈnaɪ, ˈbruːnaɪ) *n* **1** a sultanate in NW Borneo, consisting of two separate areas on the South China Sea, otherwise bounded by Sarawak: controlled all of Borneo and parts of the Philippines and the Sulu Islands in the 16th century; under British protection since 1888; internally self-governing since 1971; became independ-

ent in 1984 and is a member of the Commonwealth. The economy depends chiefly on oil and natural gas. Official language: Malay; English is also widely spoken. Religion: Muslim. Currency: Brunei dollar. Capital: Bandar Seri Begawan. Pop.: 308 000 (1997). Area: 5765 sq. km (2226 sq. miles). **2** the former name of **Bandar Seri Begawan**.

Brunel ★ (bruːˈnɛl) *n* **1 Isambard Kingdom** ('ɪzəmˌbɑːd). 1806–59, British engineer: designer of the Clifton Suspension Bridge (1828), railways, steamships, etc. **2** his father, Sir **Marc Isambard**. 1769–1849, French engineer in England.

Brunelleschi ★ (*Italian* brunelˈleski) *n* **Filippo** (fiˈlippo). 1377–1446, Italian Florentine architect.

brunette (bruːˈnɛt) *n* **1** a girl or woman with dark brown hair. ◆ *adj* **2** dark brown: *brunette hair*. [C17: from F, fem of *brunet* dark, brownish, from *brun* brown]

Brunhild ('brʊnhɪld, -hɪlt) or **Brünnhilde** ★ (*German* brynˈhɪldə) *n* (in the *Nibelungenlied*) a legendary queen won for King Gunther by the magic of Siegfried: corresponds to Brynhild in Norse mythology.

Brünn ★ (bryn) *n* the German name for **Brno**.

Bruno ★ (ˈbruːnəʊ) *n* **Franklin Roy**, known as *Frank*. born 1961, British heavyweight boxer.

Brunswick ★ ('brʌnzwɪk) *n* **1** a former duchy (1635–1918) and state (1918–46) of central Germany: now part of Lower Saxony. **2** a city in central Germany: formerly capital of the duchy and state of Brunswick. Pop.: 254 130 (1995 est.). German name: **Braunschweig**.

brunt (brʌnt) *n* the main force or shock of a blow, attack, etc. (esp. in **bear the brunt of**). [C14: from ?]

Brusa ★ (*Turkish* 'bruːsɑ) *n* the former name of **Bursa**.

brush[1] (brʌʃ) *n* **1** a device made of bristles, hairs, wires, etc., set into a firm back or handle: used to apply paint, clean or polish surfaces, groom the hair, etc. **2** the act or an instance of brushing. **3** a light stroke made in passing; graze. **4** a brief encounter or contact, esp. an unfriendly one; skirmish. **5** the bushy tail of a fox. **6** an electric conductor, esp. one made of carbon, that conveys current between stationary and rotating parts of a generator, motor, etc. ◆ *vb* **7** (*tr*) to clean, polish, scrub, paint, etc., with a brush. **8** (*tr*) to apply or remove with a brush or brushing movement. **9** (*tr*) to touch lightly and briefly. **10** (*intr*) to move so as to graze or touch something lightly. ◆ See also **brush aside, brush off, brush up**. [C14: from OF *broisse*, ?from *broce* BRUSH[2]]
► **'brusher** *n*

brush[2] (brʌʃ) *n* **1** a thick growth of shrubs and small trees; scrub. **2** land covered with such growth. **3** broken or cut branches or twigs; brushwood. **4** wooded sparsely populated country; backwoods. [C16 (dense undergrowth), C14 (cuttings of trees): from OF *broce*, from Vulgar L *bruscia* (unattested) brushwood]
► **'brushy** *adj*

brush aside or **away** *vb* (*tr, adv*) to dismiss without consideration; disregard.

brush discharge *n* a slightly luminous brushlike electrical discharge.

brushed (brʌʃt) *adj Textiles*. treated with a brushing process to raise the nap and give a softer and warmer finish: *brushed nylon*.

brushmark ('brʌʃˌmɑːk) *n* the indented lines sometimes left by the bristles of a brush on a painted surface.

brush off *Sl.* ◆ *vb* (*tr, adv*) **1** to dismiss and ignore (a person), esp. curtly. ◆ *n* **brushoff. 2** an abrupt dismissal or rejection.

brush turkey *n* any of several gallinaceous flightless birds of New Guinea and Australia, having a black plumage.

brush up *vb* (*adv*) **1** (*tr; often foll. by on*) to refresh one's knowledge, skill, or memory of (a subject). **2** to make (a person or oneself) clean or neat as after a journey. ◆ *n* **brush-up. 3** *Brit*. the act or an instance of tidying one's appearance (esp. in **wash and brush-up**).

brushwood ('brʌʃˌwʊd) *n* **1** cut or broken-off tree branches, twigs, etc. **2** another word for **brush**[2] (sense 1).

brushwork ('brʌʃˌwɜːk) *n* **1** a characteristic manner of applying paint with a brush: *Rembrandt's brushwork.* **2** work done with a brush.

brusque (bruːsk, brʊsk) *adj* blunt or curt in manner or speech. [C17: from F, from It. *brusco* sour, rough, from Med. L *bruscus* butcher's broom]
► **'brusquely** *adv* ► **'brusqueness** *n*

Brussels ★ ('brʌs°lz) *n* the capital of Belgium, in the central part: became capital of Belgium in 1830; seat of the European Commission. Pop.: 951 580 (1995 est.). Flemish name: **Brussel** ('brysəl). French name: **Bruxelles**.

Brussels carpet *n* a worsted carpet with a heavy pile formed by uncut loops of wool on a linen warp.

Brussels lace *n* a fine lace with a raised or appliqué design.

Brussels sprout *n* **1** a variety of cabbage, having a stout stem studded with budlike heads resembling tiny cabbages. **2** the head of this plant, eaten as a vegetable.

brut (bruːt) *adj* (of champagne or sparkling wine) very dry. [F, lit.: dry]

brutal ('bruːt°l) *adj* **1** cruel; vicious; savage. **2** extremely honest or coarse in speech or manner. **3** harsh; severe; extreme: *brutal cold.*
► **bru'tality** *n* ► **'brutally** *adv*

brutalism ('bruːtə,lɪzəm) *n* an austere style of architecture characterized by emphasis on such structural materials as undressed concrete and unconcealed service pipes. Also called: **new brutalism**.
► **'brutalist** *n, adj*

brutalize *or* **brutalise** ('bruːtə,laɪz) *vb* **brutalizes, brutalizing, brutalized** *or* **brutalises, brutalising, brutalised**. **1** to make or become brutal. **2** (*tr*) to treat brutally.
► ,**brutali'zation** *or* ,**brutali'sation** *n*

brute (bruːt) *n* **1a** any animal except man; beast; lower animal. **1b** (*as modifier*): *brute nature.* **2** a brutal person. ◆ *adj* (*prenominal*) **3** wholly instinctive or physical (esp. in **brute strength, brute force**). **4** without reason or intelligence. **5** coarse and grossly sensual. [C15: from L *brūtus* heavy, irrational]

brutish ('bruːtɪʃ) *adj* **1** of, relating to, or resembling a brute; animal. **2** coarse; cruel; stupid.
► **'brutishly** *adv* ► **'brutishness** *n*

Bruton ★ ('bruːt°n) *n* **John Gerard.** born 1947, Irish politician: leader of the Fine Gael party from 1990; prime minister of the Republic of Ireland (1994–97).

Brutus ★ ('bruːtəs) *n* **1 Lucius Junius** ('luːʃəs 'dʒuːnɪəs). late 6th century B.C., Roman statesman who ousted Tarquin (509) and helped found the Roman republic. **2 Marcus Junius** ('mɑːkəs 'dʒuːnɪəs) ?85–42 B.C., Roman statesman who, with Cassius, led the conspiracy to assassinate Caesar (44): committed suicide after defeat at Philippi (42).

Bruxelles ★ (brysɛl) *n* the French name for **Brussels**.

Bryansk ★ (brɪˈænsk; *Russian* brjansk) *n* a city in W Russia. Pop.: 462 000 (1995 est.).

Brynhild ★ ('brɪnhɪld) *n Norse myth.* a Valkyrie won as the wife of Gunnar by Sigurd who wakes her from an enchanted sleep: corresponds to Brunhild in the *Nibelungenlied.*

bryology (braɪˈɒlədʒɪ) *n* the branch of botany concerned with the study of bryophytes.
► **bryological** (,braɪəˈlɒdʒɪk°l) *adj* ► **bry'ologist** *n*

bryony *or* **briony** ('braɪənɪ) *n, pl* **bryonies** *or* **brionies**. any of several herbaceous climbing plants of Europe and N Africa. [OE *bryōnia*, from L, from Gk *bruōnia*]

bryophyte ('braɪə,faɪt) *n* any plant of the phylum *Bryophyta,* esp. mosses and liverworts. [C19: from Gk *bruon* moss + -PHYTE]
► **bryophytic** (,braɪəˈfɪtɪk) *adj*

bryozoan (,braɪəˈzəʊən) *n* any aquatic invertebrate animal forming colonies of polyps each having a ciliated feeding organ. Popular name: **sea mat**. [C19: from Gk *bruon* moss + *zōion* animal]

Brythonic (brɪˈθɒnɪk) *n* **1** the S group of Celtic languages, consisting of Welsh, Cornish, and Breton. ◆ *adj* **2** of or relating to this group of languages. [C19: from Welsh; see BRITON]

Brześć nad Bugiem ★ (bʒɛʃtʃ nad 'bugjɛm) *n* the Polish name for **Brest** (sense 2).

bs *abbrev. for:* **1** balance sheet. **2** bill of sale.

BS *abbrev. for* British Standard(s).

BSc *abbrev. for* Bachelor of Science.

BSE *abbrev. for* bovine spongiform encephalopathy: fatal slow-developing virus disease of cattle, affecting the nervous system. Informal name: **mad cow disease**.

BSI *abbrev. for* British Standards Institution.

B-side *n* the less important side of a gramophone record.

BST *abbrev. for:* **1** bovine somatotrophin: a growth hormone that can be used to increase milk production in dairy cattle. **2** British Summer Time.

Bt *abbrev. for* Baronet.

BT *abbrev. for* British Telecom. [C20: shortened from TELE-COMMUNICATIONS]

btu *or* **BThU** *abbrev. for* British thermal unit. US abbrev.: **BTU**.

bu. *abbrev. for* bushel.

bubble ('bʌb°l) *n* **1** a thin film of liquid forming a hollow globule around air or a gas: *a soap bubble.* **2** a small globule of air or a gas in a liquid or a solid. **3** the sound made by a bubbling liquid. **4** something lacking substance, stability, or seriousness. **5** an unreliable scheme or enterprise. **6** a dome, esp. a transparent glass or plastic one. ◆ *vb* **bubbles, bubbling, bubbled**. **7** to form or cause to form bubbles. **8** (*intr*) to move or flow with a gurgling sound. **9** (*intr*; often foll. by *over*) to overflow (with excitement, anger, etc.). [C14: prob. from ON; imit.]

bubble and squeak *n Brit. & Austral.* a dish of leftover boiled cabbage and potatoes fried together.

bubble bath *n* **1** a powder, liquid, or crystals used to scent, soften, and foam in bath water. **2** a bath to which such a substance has been added.

bubble car *n Brit.* (formerly) a small car with a transparent bubble-shaped top.

bubble chamber *n* a device that enables the tracks of ionizing particles to be photographed as a row of bubbles in a superheated liquid.

bubble gum *n* a type of chewing gum that can be blown into large bubbles.

bubble memory *n Computing.* a method of storing high volumes of data by using minute pockets of magnetism (bubbles) in a semiconducting material.

bubble point *n Chem.* the temperature at which bubbles just start to appear in a heated liquid mixture.

bubble wrap *n* a type of polythene wrapping containing many small air pockets, used as a protective covering when transporting breakable goods.

bubbly ('bʌblɪ) *adj* **bubblier, bubbliest**. **1** full of or resembling bubbles. **2** lively; animated; excited. ◆ *n* **3** *Inf.* champagne.

Buber ★ ('buːbə) *n* **Martin.** 1878–1965, Jewish theologian, existentialist philosopher, and scholar of Chassidism born in Austria, whose works include *I and Thou* (1923).

bubo ('bjuːbəʊ) *n, pl* **buboes**. *Pathol.* inflammation and swelling of a lymph node, esp. in the armpit or groin. [C14: from Med. L *bubo*, from Gk *boubōn* groin]
► **bubonic** (bjuːˈbɒnɪk) *adj*

bubonic plague *n* an acute infectious febrile disease characterized by chills, prostration, delirium, and formation of buboes: caused by the bite of an infected rat flea.

Bucaramanga ★ (*Spanish* bukaraˈmaŋga) *n* a city in N central Colombia, in the Cordillera Oriental: centre of a district growing coffee, tobacco, and cotton. Pop.: 351 737 (1995 est.).

buccal ('bʌk°l) *adj* **1** of or relating to the cheek. **2** of or relating to the mouth; oral. [C19: from L *bucca* cheek]

buccaneer (,bʌkəˈnɪə) *n* **1** a pirate, esp. one who preyed on Spanish shipping in the Caribbean in the 17th and 18th centuries. ◆ *vb* (*intr*) **2** to be or act like a buccaneer. [C17: from *boucan*, dried meat taken on long voyages, from F *boucaner* to smoke meat]

buccinator ('bʌksɪ,neɪtə) *n* either of two flat cheek muscles used in chewing. [C17: from L, from *buccina* a trumpet]

uchan ★ ('bʌkən) n **John**, 1st Baron Tweedsmuir. 1875–1940, Scottish statesman and writer of such adventure stories as *The Thirty-Nine Steps* (1915); governor general of Canada (1935–40).

uchanan ★ (bju:'kænən) n **1 George**. 1506–82, Scottish historian, who was tutor to Mary, Queen of Scots and James VI; author of *History of Scotland* (1582). **2 James**. 1791–1868, 15th president of the US (1857–61).

ucharest ★ (,bu:kə'rest, ,bju:-) n the capital of Romania, in the southeast. Pop.: 2 343 824 (1993 est.). Romanian name: **Bucureşti.**

uchenwald ★ (*German* 'bu:xənvalt) n a village in E central Germany, near Weimar; formerly in East Germany: site of a Nazi concentration camp (1937–45).

üchner ★ (*German* 'by:çnər) n **Georg** ('ge:ɔrk). 1813–37, German dramatist; author of *Woyzeck* (1837).

uck[1] (bʌk) n **1a** the male of various animals including the goat, hare, kangaroo, rabbit, and reindeer. **1b** (*as modifier*): *a buck antelope*. **2** *S. African*. an antelope or deer of either sex. **3** *Arch*. a robust sprightly young man. **4** the act of bucking. ◆ vb **5** (*intr*) (of a horse or other animal) to jump vertically, with legs stiff and back arched. **6** (*tr*) (of a horse, etc.) to throw (its rider) by bucking. **7** (when *intr*, often foll. by *against* or *at*) *Chiefly US, Canad., & Austral. inf.* to resist or oppose obstinately. **8** (*tr; usually passive*) *Inf.* to cheer or encourage: *I was very bucked at passing the exam.* ◆ See also **buck up.** [OE *bucca* he-goat]
▶ **'bucker** n

uck[2] (bʌk) n US, Canad., & Austral. inf. a dollar. [C19: from ?]

uck[3] (bʌk) n **1** *Poker*. a marker in the jackpot to remind the winner of some obligation when his turn comes to deal. **2 pass the buck**. *Inf*. to shift blame or responsibility onto another. [C19: prob. from *buckhorn knife*, placed before a player in poker to indicate that he was the next dealer]

uck ★ (bʌk) n **Pearl S**(ydenstricker). 1892–1973, US novelist, noted for her novel *The Good Earth* (1931): Nobel prize for literature 1938.

uckbean ('bʌk,bi:n) n a marsh plant with white or pink flowers. Also called: **bogbean.**

uckboard ('bʌk,bɔ:d) n US & Canad. an open four-wheeled horse-drawn carriage with the seat attached to a flexible board between the front and rear axles.

ucket ('bʌkɪt) n **1** an open-topped roughly cylindrical container; pail. **2** Also called: **bucketful.** the amount a bucket will hold. **3** any of various bucket-like parts of a machine, such as the scoop on a mechanical shovel. **4** *Chiefly US.* a turbine rotor blade. **5** *Austral.* a small container for ice cream. **6 kick the bucket.** *Sl.* to die. ◆ vb **buckets, bucketing, bucketed. 7** (*tr*) to carry in or put into a bucket. **8** (*intr*, often foll. by *down*) (of rain) to fall very heavily. **9** (*intr*, often foll. by *along*) *Chiefly Brit.* to travel or drive fast. **10** (*tr*) *Austral. sl.* to criticize severely. [C13: from Anglo-F *buket*, from OE *būc*]

ucket seat n a seat in a car, etc., having curved sides.

ucket shop n **1** an unregistered firm of stockbrokers that engages in fraudulent speculation. **2** *Chiefly Brit.* a firm specializing in cheap airline tickets.

uckeye ('bʌk,aɪ) n any of several North American trees of the horse chestnut family having erect clusters of white or red flowers and prickly fruits.

uckhorn ('bʌk,hɔ:n) n **a** a horn from a buck, used for knife handles, etc. **b** (*as modifier*): *a buckhorn knife.*

Buckingham[1] ★ ('bʌkɪŋəm) n a town in S central England, in Buckinghamshire; university (1975). Pop.: 2786 (1991).

Buckingham[2] ★ ('bʌkɪŋəm) n **1 George Villiers, 1st Duke of.** 1592–1628, English courtier and statesman; favourite of James I and Charles I. **2** his son, **George Villiers, 2nd Duke of.** 1628–87, English courtier; chief minister of Charles II and member of the Cabal (1667–73).

Buckingham Palace ★ n the London residence of the British sovereign: built in 1703, rebuilt by John Nash in

1821–36 and partially redesigned in the early 20th century.

Buckinghamshire ★ ('bʌkɪŋəm,ʃɪə, -ʃə) n a county in SE central England, containing the Vale of Aylesbury and parts of the Chiltern Hills. Administrative centre: Aylesbury. Pop. (including Milton Keynes): 658 400 (1994 est.). Area (including Milton Keynes): 1883 sq. km (727 sq. miles). Abbrev.: **Bucks.**

buckjumper ('bʌk,dʒʌmpə) n *Austral*. an untamed horse.

Buckland ★ ('bʌklənd) n **William**. 1784–1856, British geologist.

buckle ('bʌk°l) n **1** a clasp for fastening together two loose ends, esp. of a belt or strap, usually consisting of a frame with an attached movable prong. **2** an ornamental representation of a buckle, as on a shoe. **3** a kink, bulge, or other distortion. ◆ vb **buckles, buckling, buckled. 4** to fasten or be fastened with a buckle. **5** to bend or cause to bend out of shape. [C14: from OF, from L *buccula* a little cheek, hence, cheek strap of a helmet]

buckle down vb (*intr, adv*) *Inf.* to apply oneself with determination.

buckler ('bʌklə) n **1** a small round shield worn on the forearm. **2** a means of protection; defence. [C13: from OF *bocler*, from *bocle* shield boss]

Buckley's chance ('bʌklɪz) n *Austral. & NZ sl.* no chance at all. Often shortened to **Buckley's.** [C19: from ?]

buckminsterfullerene (,bʌkmɪnstə'fulə,ri:n) n a form of carbon that contains molecules with 60 carbon atoms arranged in a structure resembling a geodesic dome. Often shortened to: **fullerene.** [C20: after Buckminster FULLER]

bucko ('bʌkəu) n, pl **buckoes.** *Irish*. a lively young fellow: often a term of address.

buckram ('bʌkrəm) n **a** a cotton or linen cloth stiffened with size, etc., used in lining clothes, bookbinding, etc. **b** (*as modifier*): *a buckram cover.* [C14: from OF *boquerant*, ult. from BUKHARA, once important for textiles]

Bucks (bʌks) *abbrev. for* Buckinghamshire.

buckshee (,bʌk'ʃi:) adj Brit. sl. without charge; free. [C20: from BAKSHEESH]

buckshot ('bʌk,ʃɒt) n lead shot of large size used in shotgun shells, esp. for hunting game.

buckskin ('bʌk,skɪn) n **1** the skin of a male deer. **2a** a strong greyish-yellow suede leather, originally made from deerskin but now usually made from sheepskin. **2b** (*as modifier*): *buckskin boots.* **3** a stiffly starched cotton cloth. **4** a strong and heavy satin-woven woollen fabric.

buckthorn ('bʌk,θɔ:n) n any of several thorny small-flowered shrubs whose berries were formerly used as a purgative. [C16: from BUCK[1] (from the spiny branches resembling antlers) + THORN]

bucktooth ('bʌk,tu:θ) n, pl **buckteeth.** *Derog.* a projecting upper front tooth. [C18: from BUCK[1] (deer) + TOOTH]

buck up vb (*adv*) *Inf.* **1** to make or cause to make haste. **2** to make or become more cheerful, confident, etc.

buckwheat ('bʌk,wi:t) n **1** a cereal plant with fragrant white flowers, cultivated, esp. in the US, for its seeds. **2** the edible seeds of this plant, ground into flour or used as animal fodder. **3** the flour obtained from these seeds. [C16: from MDu. *boecweite*, from *boeke* BEECH + *weite* WHEAT, from the resemblance of the seeds to beechnuts]

buckyball ('bʌkɪ,bɔ:l) n *Inf.* a ball-like polyhedral carbon molecule, of the type found in buckminsterfullerene and other fullerenes.

buckytube ('bʌkɪ,tju:b) n a tube of carbon atoms structurally similar to buckminsterfullerene.

bucolic (bju:'kɒlɪk) adj also **bucolical. 1** of the countryside or country life; rustic. **2** of or relating to shepherds; pastoral. ◆ n **3** (*sometimes pl*) a pastoral poem. [C16: from L, from Gk, from *boukolos* cowherd, from *bous* ox]
▶ **bu'colically** adv

Bucovina ★ (,bu:kə'vi:nə) n a variant spelling of **Bukovina.**

Bucureşti ★ (buku'reʃtj) n the Romanian name for **Bucharest.**

bud (bʌd) n **1** a swelling on a plant stem consisting of overlapping immature leaves or petals. **2a** a partially opened flower. **2b** (in combination): rosebud. **3** any small budlike outgrowth: taste buds. **4** something small or immature. **5** an asexually produced outgrowth in simple organisms such as yeasts that develops into a new individual. **6 nip in the bud.** to put an end to (an idea, movement, etc.) in its initial stages. ◆ vb **buds, budding, budded. 7** (intr) (of plants and some animals) to produce buds. **8** (intr) to begin to develop or grow. **9** (tr) Horticulture. to graft (a bud) from one plant onto another. [C14 budde, of Gmc origin]

Budapest ★ (ˌbjuːdəˈpɛst; Hungarian ˈbudɔpɛʃt) n the capital of Hungary, in the central part, on the River Danube: formed in 1873 from the towns of Buda and Pest. Traditionally Buda, the old Magyar capital, was the administrative and Pest the trade centre: suffered severely in the Russian siege of 1945 and in the unsuccessful revolt against the Communist regime (1956). Pop.: 1 909 000 (1996 est.).

Buddha ★ (ˈbudə) n the. ?563–483 B.C., a title applied to Gautama Siddhartha, a religious teacher of N India regarded by his followers as the most recent rediscoverer of the path to enlightenment: the founder of Buddhism.

Buddh Gaya (ˈbud gəˈjɑː), **Buddha Gaya,** or **Bodh Gaya** ★ n a village in NE India, in Bihar: site of the sacred bo tree under which Gautama Siddhartha attained enlightenment and became the Buddha; pilgrimage centre. Pop.: 21 686 (1991 est.).

Buddhism (ˈbudɪzəm) n a religious teaching propagated by the Buddha and his followers, which declares that by destroying greed, hatred, and delusion, which are the causes of all suffering, man can attain perfect enlightenment.
▸ 'Buddhist n, adj

buddleia (ˈbʌdlɪə) n an ornamental shrub which has long spikes of mauve flowers. Also called: **butterfly bush.** [C19: after A. Buddle (died 1715), Brit. botanist]

buddy (ˈbʌdɪ) n, pl buddies. **1** Also (as a term of address): **bud.** Chiefly US & Canad. an informal word for **friend. 2** a volunteer who visits and gives help and support to a person suffering from AIDS. ◆ vb **buddies, buddying, buddied. 3** (intr) to act as a buddy to a person suffering from AIDS. [C19: prob. baby-talk var. (US) of BROTHER]

buddy-buddy adj Inf., chiefly US. on very friendly or intimate terms.

buddy movie or **film** n a genre of film dealing with the relationship and adventures of two friends.

budge (bʌdʒ) vb **budges, budging, budged.** (usually used with a negative) **1** to move, however slightly. **2** to change or cause to change opinions, etc. [C16: from OF bouger, from L bullīre to boil]

budgerigar (ˈbʌdʒərɪˌgɑː) n a small green Australian parrot: a popular cagebird bred in many different-coloured varieties. [C19: from Abor., from budgeri good + gar cockatoo]

budget (ˈbʌdʒɪt) n **1** an itemized summary of expected income and expenditure over a specified period. **2** (modifier) economical; inexpensive: budget meals for a family. **3** the total amount of money allocated for a specific purpose during a specified period. ◆ vb **budgets, budgeting, budgeted. 4** (tr) to enter or provide for in a budget. **5** to plan the expenditure of (money, time, etc.). **6** (intr) to make a budget. [C15 (meaning: leather pouch, wallet): from OF bougette, dim. of bouge, from L bulga]
▸ 'budgetary adj

Budget (ˈbʌdʒɪt) n the. an estimate of British government expenditures and revenues and the financial plans for the ensuing fiscal year presented annually to the House of Commons by the Chancellor of the Exchequer.

budget account n **1** an account with a department store, etc., enabling a customer to make monthly payments to cover his past and future purchases. **2** a bank account that allows the holder credit to pay certain bills in return for regular deposits.

budget deficit n the amount by which government expenditure exceeds income from taxation, customs duties, etc., in any one fiscal year.

budgie (ˈbʌdʒɪ) n Inf. short for **budgerigar.**

Buenaventura ★ (Spanish bwenaˈβenˈtura) n a majo port in W Colombia, on the Pacific coast. Pop.: 174 39 (1985).

Buena Vista ★ (Spanish ˈbwena ˈvista) n a village in N Mexico, near Saltillo: site of the defeat of the Mexican by US forces (1847).

Buenos Aires ★ (ˈbweɪnɒs ˈaɪrɪz; Spanish ˈbwenos ˈaires n the capital of Argentina, a major port and industri city on the Río de la Plata estuary: became capital i 1880; university (1821). Pop.: 2 988 006 (1995 est.).

buff[1] (bʌf) n **1a** a soft thick flexible undyed leather mad chiefly from the skins of buffalo, oxen, and elk. **1b** (a modifier): a buff coat. **2a** a dull yellow or yellowish-brow colour. **2b** (as adj): a buff envelope. **3** Also called: **buffer. 3a** cloth or pad of material used for polishing an object. **3** a disc or wheel impregnated with a fine abrasive for po ishing metals, etc. **4** Inf. one's bare skin (esp. in **in th buff**). ◆ vb **5** to clean or polish (a metal, floor, shoes, etc with a buff. **6** to remove the grain surface of (a leather [C16: from OF, from OIt. bufalo, from LL būfalus BUFFALO]

buff[2] (bʌf) n Arch. a blow or buffet (now only in **blin man's buff**). [C15: back formation from BUFFET[2]]

buff[3] (bʌf) n Inf. an expert on or devotee of a given sub ject. [C20: orig. US: an enthusiastic fire-watcher, fror the buff-coloured uniforms worn by volunteer fireme in New York City]

buffalo (ˈbʌfəˌləu) n, pl **buffaloes** or **buffalo. 1** a type of ca tle, mostly found in game reserves in southern and east ern Africa and having upward-curving horns. **2** short fo **water buffalo. 3** a US & Canad. name for **bison** (sense 1 [C16: from It. bufalo, from Gk bous ox]

Buffalo ★ (ˈbʌfəˌləu) n a port in W New York State, at th E end of Lake Erie. Pop.: 312 965 (1994 est.).

Buffalo Bill ★ n nickname of William Frederick Cody 1846–1917, US showman who toured Europe and the U with his Wild West Show.

buffalo grass n **1** a short grass growing on the dr plains of the central US. **2** Austral. a grass, Stenotaphrur americanum, introduced from North America.

buffel grass (ˈbʌfᵊl) n (in Australia) any of variou grasses used for grazing or fodder, originally introduce from Africa.

buffer[1] (ˈbʌfə) n **1** one of a pair of spring-loaded stee pads attached at both ends of railway vehicles and at th end of a railway track to reduce shock due to contact. **2** person or thing that lessens shock or protects from dam aging impact, circumstances, etc. **3** Chem. **3a** an ioni compound added to a solution to resist changes in it acidity or alkalinity and thus stabilize its pH. **3b** Als called: **buffer solution.** a solution containing such a com pound. **4** Computing. a memory device for temporaril storing data. ◆ vb (tr) **5** Chem. to add a buffer to (a solu tion). **6** to insulate against or protect from shock. [C19 from BUFF[2]]

buffer[2] (ˈbʌfə) n **1** any device used to shine, polish, etc. buff. **2** a person who uses such a device.

buffer[3] (ˈbʌfə) n Brit. inf. a stupid or bumbling man (esp in **old buffer**). [C18: ?from ME buffer stammerer]

buffer state n a small and usually neutral state betwee two rival powers.

buffer stock n Commerce. a stock of a commodity buil up by a government or trade organization with the ob ject of using it to stabilize prices.

buffet[1] n **1** (ˈbufeɪ). a counter where light refreshment are served. **2** (ˈbufeɪ). **2a** a meal at which guests hel themselves from a number of dishes. **2b** (as modifier): buffet lunch. **3** (ˈbʌfɪt, ˈbufeɪ). (formerly) a piece of furni ture used for displaying plate, etc., and typically com prising cupboards and open shelves. [C18: from F]

buffet[2] (ˈbʌfɪt) vb **buffets, buffeting, buffeted. 1** (tr) to knock against or about; batter. **2** (tr) to hit, esp. with the fist cuff. **3** to force (one's way), as through a crowd. **4** (intr) to struggle; battle. ◆ n **5** a blow, esp. with a fist or hand. **6** aerodynamic oscillation of an aircraft structure by sepa rated flows. [C13: from OF buffet a light blow]

Buffet ★ (*French* byfɛ) *n* **Bernard** (bɛrnar). born 1928, French painter.

buffet car ('bufeɪ) *n* Brit. a railway coach where light refreshments are served.

buffeting ('bʌfɪtɪŋ) *n* response of an aircraft structure to buffet, esp. an irregular oscillation of the tail.

bufflehead ('bʌfᵊl,hed) *n* a small North American diving duck: the male has black-and-white plumage and a fluffy head. [C17 *buffle*, from obs. *buffle* wild ox, referring to the duck's head]

buffo ('bufəu) *n*, *pl* **buffi** (-fɪ) *or* **buffos**. **1** (in Italian opera of the 18th century) a comic part, esp. one for a bass. **2** Also called: **buffo bass, basso buffo**. a bass singer who performs such a part. [C18: from It. (adj): comic, from *buffo* (n) BUFFOON]

buffoon (bə'fuːn) *n* **1** a person who amuses others by ridiculous or odd behaviour, jokes, etc. **2** a foolish person. [C16: from F *bouffon*, from It. *buffone*, from Med. L *būfō*, from L: toad]
► **buf'foonery** *n*

bug (bʌg) *n* **1** an insect having piercing and sucking mouthparts specialized as a beak. **2** *Chiefly US & Canad.* any insect. **3** *Inf.* **3a** a microorganism, esp. a bacterium, that produces disease. **3b** a disease, esp. a stomach infection, caused by a microorganism. **4** *Inf.* an obsessive idea, hobby, etc.; craze. **5** *Inf.* a person having such a craze. **6** (*often pl*) *Inf.* a fault, as in a machine. **7** *Inf.* a concealed microphone used for recording conversations, as in spying. ◆ *vb* **bugs, bugging, bugged**. *Inf.* **8** (*tr*) to irritate; bother. **9** (*tr*) to conceal a microphone in (a room, etc.). **10** (*intr*) US. (of eyes) to protrude. [C16: from ?]

Bug ★ (*Russian* buk) *n* **1** Also called: **Southern Bug**. a river in E Europe, rising in the W Ukraine and flowing southeast to the Black Sea. Length: 853 km (530 miles). **2** Also called: **Western Bug**. a river in E Europe, rising in the SW Ukraine and flowing northwest to the River Vistula in Poland, forming part of the border between Poland and the Ukraine. Length: 724 km (450 miles).

bugaboo ('bʌgə,buː) *n*, *pl* **bugaboos**. an imaginary source of fear; bugbear; bogey. [C18: prob. of Celtic origin; cf. Cornish *buccaboo* the devil]

Buganda ★ (buˈgændə) *n* a region of Uganda: a powerful Bantu kingdom from the 17th century.

Bugatti ★ (*Italian* buˈgatti) *n* **Ettore** (**Arco Isidoro**) ('ɛttore). 1881–1947, Italian car manufacturer.

bugbear ('bʌg,bɛə) *n* **1** a thing that causes obsessive anxiety. **2** (in English folklore) a goblin in the form of a bear. [C16: from obs. *bug* an evil spirit+ BEAR²]

bug-eyed *adj* having protruding eyes.

bugger ('bʌgə) *n* **1** a person who practises buggery. **2** *Taboo sl.* a person or thing considered to be contemptible, unpleasant, or difficult. **3** *Sl.* a humorous or affectionate term for a man or child: *a friendly little bugger.* **4 bugger all**. *Sl.* nothing. ◆ *vb* **5** to practise buggery (with). **6** (*tr*) *Sl., chiefly Brit.* to ruin, complicate, or frustrate. **7** (*tr*) *Sl.* to tire; weary. ◆ *interj* **8** *Taboo sl.* an exclamation of annoyance or disappointment. [C16: from OF *bougre*, from Med. L *Bulgarus* Bulgarian; from the condemnation of the Eastern Orthodox Bulgarians as heretics]

bugger about *or* **around** *vb* (*adv*) *Sl.* **1** (*intr*) to fool about and waste time. **2** (*tr*) to create difficulties for or complications for (a person).

bugger off *vb* (*intr*, *adv*) *Taboo sl.* to go away; depart.

buggery ('bʌgərɪ) *n* anal intercourse between a man and another man, a woman, or an animal.

buggy¹ ('bʌgɪ) *n*, *pl* **buggies**. **1** a light horse-drawn carriage having either four wheels (esp. in the US and Canada) or two wheels (esp. in Britain and India). **2** any small light cart or vehicle, such as a baby buggy. [C18: from ?]

buggy² ('bʌgɪ) *adj* **buggier, buggiest**. infested with bugs.

bugle¹ ('bjuːgᵊl) *n* **1** *Music.* a brass instrument similar to the cornet but usually without valves: used for military fanfares, signal calls, etc. ◆ *vb* **bugles, bugling, bugled**. **2** (*intr*) to play or sound (on) a bugle. [C14: short for *bugle horn* ox horn, from OF *bugle*, from L *būculus* young bullock, from *bōs* ox]
► **'bugler** *n*

bugle² ('bjuːgᵊl) *n* any of several Eurasian plants having small blue or white flowers. [C13: from LL *bugula*, from ?]

bugle³ ('bjuːgᵊl) *n* a tubular glass or plastic bead sewn onto clothes for decoration. [C16: from ?]

bugloss ('bjuːglɒs) *n* any of various hairy Eurasian plants having clusters of blue flowers. [C15: from L, from Gk *bouglōssos* ox-tongued]

bugong ('buːgɒŋ) *n* another name for **bogong**.

buhl (buːl) *adj*, *n* a variant spelling of **boulle**.

build (bɪld) *vb* **builds, building, built**. **1** to make, construct, or form by joining parts or materials: *to build a house.* **2** (*tr*) to order the building of: *the government builds most of our hospitals.* **3** (foll. by *on* or *upon*) to base; found: *his theory was not built on facts.* **4** (*tr*) to establish and develop: *it took ten years to build a business.* **5** (*tr*) to make in a particular way or for a particular purpose: *the car was not built for speed.* **6** (*intr*; often foll. by *up*) to increase in intensity. ◆ *n* **7** physical form, figure, or proportions: *a man with an athletic build.* [OE *byldan*]

builder ('bɪldə) *n* a person who builds, esp. one who contracts for and supervises the construction or repair of buildings.

building ('bɪldɪŋ) *n* **1** something built with a roof and walls. **2** the act, business, occupation, or art of building houses, boats, etc.

building society *n* a cooperative banking enterprise financed by deposits on which interest is paid and from which mortgage loans are advanced on homes and real property; many now offer a range of banking services.

build up *vb* (*adv*) **1** (*tr*) to construct gradually, systematically, and in stages. **2** to increase, accumulate, or strengthen, esp. by degrees: *the murmur built up to a roar.* **3** (*tr*) to improve the health or physique of (a person). **4** (*intr*) to prepare for or gradually approach a climax. ◆ *n* **build-up. 5** progressive increase in number, size, etc.: *the build-up of industry.* **6** a gradual approach to a climax. **7** extravagant publicity or praise, esp. in the form of a campaign. **8** *Mil.* the process of attaining the required strength of forces and equipment.

built (bɪlt) *vb* the past tense and past participle of **build**.

built-in *adj* **1** made or incorporated as an integral part: *a built-in cupboard.* **2** essential; inherent. ◆ *n* **3** *Austral.* a built-in cupboard.

built-in obsolescence *n* See **planned obsolescence**.

built-up *adj* **1** having many buildings (esp. in **built-up area**). **2** increased by the addition of parts: *built-up heels.*

Buitenzorg ★ (*Dutch* 'bœitənzɔrx) *n* the former name of **Bogor.**

Bujumbura ★ (ˌbuːdʒəm'buərə) *n* the capital of Burundi, a port at the NE end of Lake Tanganyika. Pop.: 300 000 (1994 est.). Former name: **Usumbura.**

Bukavu ★ (buːˈkɑːvuː) *n* a port in E Democratic Republic of the Congo (formerly Zaïre), on Lake Kivu: commercial and industrial centre. Pop.: 201 569 (1994 est.). Former name (until 1966): **Costermansville.**

Bukhara *or* **Bokhara** ★ (buˈxɑːrə) *n* **1** a city in S Uzbekistan: capital of the former emirate of Bukhara. Pop.: 236 000 (1993 est.). **2** a former emirate of central Asia: a powerful kingdom and centre of Islam; became a territory of the Soviet Union (1920) and was divided between the former Uzbek, Tajik, and Turkmen SSRs.

Bukovina *or* **Bucovina** ★ (ˌbuːkə'viːnə) *n* a region of E central Europe, part of the NE Carpathians: the north was seized by the Soviet Union (1940) and later became part of the Ukraine; the south remained Romanian.

Bulawayo ★ (ˌbulə'weɪəu) *n* a city in SW Zimbabwe founded (1893) on the site of the kraal of Lobengula, the last Matabele king; the country's main industrial centre. Pop.: 620 936 (1992).

bulb (bʌlb) *n* **1** a rounded organ of vegetative reproduction in plants such as the tulip and onion: a flattened stem bearing a central shoot surrounded by fleshy nutritive inner leaves and thin brown outer leaves. **2** a plant, such as a hyacinth or daffodil, that grows from a bulb. **3** See **light bulb. 4** any bulb-shaped thing. [C16: from L *bulbus*, from Gk *bolbos* onion]
► **'bulbous** *adj*

bulbil ('bʌlbɪl) *n* **1** a small bulb produced from a parent bulb. **2** a bulblike reproductive organ in a leaf axil of certain plants. **3** any small bulblike structure in an animal. [C19: from NL *bulbillus* BULB]

bulbul ('bʊlbʊl) *n* a songbird of tropical Africa and Asia having brown plumage and, in many species, a distinct crest. [C18: via Persian from Ar.]

Bulg. *abbrev. for* Bulgaria(n).

Bulgakov ★ (*Russian* bul'gakəf) *n* **Mikhail Afanaseyev** (mixa'il afa'nasjɪf). 1891–1940, Soviet writer; his novels include *The Master and Margarita* (1966–67).

Bulganin ★ (*Russian* bul'ganin) *n* **Nikolai Aleksandrovich** (nika'lai alık'sandrəvitʃ). 1895–1975, Soviet statesman and military leader.

Bulgaria ★ (bʌl'gɛərɪə, bʊl-) *n* a republic in SE Europe, on the Balkan Peninsula on the Black Sea: under Turkish rule from 1395 until 1878; became an independent kingdom in 1908 and a Communist republic in 1946; in 1990 free elections ousted the Communist Party. Consists chiefly of the Danube valley in the north, the Balkan Mountains in the central part, separated from the Rhodope Mountains of the south by the valley of the Maritsa River. Language: Bulgarian. Religion: Christian (Bulgarian Orthodox) majority. Currency: lev. Capital: Sofia. Pop.: 8 329 000 (1997). Area: 110 911 sq. km (42 823 sq. miles).
▶ **Bul'garian** *adj, n*

bulge (bʌldʒ) *n* **1** a swelling or an outward curve. **2** a sudden increase in number, esp. of population. ◆ *vb* **bulges, bulging, bulged. 3** to swell outwards. [C13: from OF *bouge*, from L *bulga* bag, prob. of Gaulish origin]
▶ **'bulging** *adj* ▶ **'bulgy** *adj*

bulgur ('bʌlgə) *n* cracked wheat that has been hulled, steamed, and roasted so that it requires little or no cooking. [C20: from Ar. *burghul*]

bulimia (bju:'lɪmɪə) *n* **1** pathologically insatiable hunger. **2** Also called: **bulimia nervosa.** a disorder characterized by compulsive overeating followed by vomiting. [C17: from NL, from Gk *bous* ox + *limos* hunger]

bulk (bʌlk) *n* **1** volume, size, or magnitude, esp. when great. **2** the main part: *the bulk of the work is repetitious.* **3** a large body, esp. of a person. **4** the part of food which passes unabsorbed through the digestive system. **5 in bulk. 5a** in large quantities. **5b** (of a cargo, etc.) unpackaged. ◆ *vb* **6** to cohere or cause to cohere in a mass. **7 bulk large.** to be or seem important or prominent. [C15: from ON *bulki* cargo]

> **USAGE NOTE** The use of a plural noun after *bulk* was formerly considered incorrect, but is now acceptable.

bulk buying *n* the purchase of goods in large amounts, often at reduced prices.

bulkhead ('bʌlk,hɛd) *n* any upright wall-like partition in a ship, aircraft, etc. [C15: prob. from *bulk* projecting framework from ON *bálkr* +HEAD]

bulk modulus *n* a coefficient of elasticity of a substance equal to the ratio of the applied stress to the resulting fractional change in volume.

bulky ('bʌlkɪ) *adj* **bulkier, bulkiest.** very large and massive, esp. so as to be unwieldy.
▶ **'bulkily** *adv* ▶ **'bulkiness** *n*

bull[1] (bʊl) *n* **1** any male bovine animal, esp. one that is sexually mature. Related adj: **taurine. 2** the male of various other animals including the elephant and whale. **3** a very large, strong, or aggressive person. **4** *Stock Exchange.* **4a** a speculator who buys in anticipation of rising prices in order to make a profit on resale. **4b** (*as modifier*): *a bull market.* Cf. **bear**[2] (sense 5). **5** *Chiefly Brit.* short for **bull's-eye** (senses 1, 2). **6** *Sl.* short for **bullshit. 7 a bull in a china shop.** a clumsy person. **8 take the bull by the horns.** to face and tackle a difficulty without shirking. ◆ *adj* **9** male; masculine: *a bull elephant.* **10** large; strong. [OE *bula*]

bull[2] (bʊl) *n* a ludicrously self-contradictory or inconsis‑ tent statement. [C17: from ?]

bull[3] (bʊl) *n* a formal document issued by the pope. [C1: from Med. L *bulla* seal attached to a bull, from L: roun‑ object]

Bull[1] (bʊl) *n* **the.** the constellation Taurus, the second sig‑ of the zodiac.

Bull[2] ★ (bʊl) *n* **1 John.** 1563–1628, English composer an‑ organist. **2** See **John Bull.**

Bullamakanka (,bu:ləmə'kæŋkə) *n Austral.* an imag‑ nary very remote place.

bull bars *pl n* a large protective metal grille on the fron‑ of some vehicles, esp. four-wheel-drive vehicles.

bulldog ('bʊl,dɒg) *n* a sturdy thickset breed of dog wit‑ an undershot jaw, broad head, and a muscular body.

bulldog clip *n* a clip for holding papers together, con‑ sisting of two T-shaped metal clamps held in place by cylindrical spring.

bulldoze ('bʊl,dəʊz) *vb* **bulldozes, bulldozing, bulldozed.** (*tr* **1** to move, demolish, flatten, etc., with a bulldozer. **2** *Inf* to force; push. **3** *Inf.* to intimidate or coerce. [C19: prob from BULL[1] + DOSE]

bulldozer ('bʊl,dəʊzə) *n* **1** a powerful tractor fitted wit‑ caterpillar tracks and a blade at the front, used for mov‑ ing earth, rocks, etc. **2** *Inf.* a person who bulldozes.

bull dust *n Austral.* **1** fine dust, as on roads in outbac‑ Australia. **2** *Sl.* nonsense.

bullet ('bʊlɪt) *n* **1a** a small metallic missile enclosed in ‑ cartridge, used as the projectile of a gun, rifle, etc. **1b** ‑ entire cartridge. **2** something resembling a bullet, esp. i‑ shape or effect. **3** *Stock Exchange.* a fixed interest securit‑ with a single maturity date. **4** *Commerce.* a security tha‑ offers a fixed interest and matures on a fixed date. ‑ *Commerce.* **5a** the final repayment of a loan that repa‑ the whole of the sum borrowed, as interim payment‑ have been for interest only. **5b** (*as modifier*): *a bullet loan‑* [C16: from F *boulette,* dim. of *boule* ball; see BOWL[2]]

bulletin ('bʊlɪtɪn) *n* **1** an official statement on a matter c‑ public interest. **2** a broadcast summary of the news. **3** ‑ periodical publication of an association, etc. ◆ *vb* **4** (*tr‑* to make known by bulletin. [C17: from F, from It., from‑ *bulletta,* dim. of *bulla* papal edict, BULL[3]]

bulletin board *n* **1** the US and Canad. name for **notic‑ board. 2** *Computing.* a facility on a computer network al‑ lowing any user to leave messages that can be read by‑ any other user, and to download software and informa‑ tion to the user's own computer.

bulletproof ('bʊlɪt,pru:f) *adj* **1** not penetrable by bullets‑ ◆ *vb* **2** (*tr*) to make bulletproof.

bulletwood ('bʊlɪt,wʊd) *n* the tough durable wood of ‑ tropical American tree, widely used for construction.

bullfight ('bʊl,faɪt) *n* a traditional Spanish, Portuguese‑ and Latin American spectacle in which a matador bait‑ and usually kills a bull in an arena.
▶ **'bull,fighter** *n* ▶ **'bull,fighting** *n*

bullfinch ('bʊl,fɪntʃ) *n* **1** a common European finch: th‑ male has a bright red throat and breast. **2** any of variou‑ similar finches. [C14: see BULL[1], FINCH]

bullfrog ('bʊl,frɒg) *n* any of various large frogs having ‑ loud deep croak, esp. the **American bullfrog.**

bullhead ('bʊl,hɛd) *n* any of various small norther‑ mainly marine fishes that have a large head covere‑ with bony plates and spines.

bull-headed *adj* blindly obstinate; stupid.
▶ **,bull-'headedly** *adv* ▶ **,bull-'headedness** *n*

bullhorn ('bʊl,hɔ:n) *n* the US and Canad. name for **loud‑ hailer.**

bullion ('bʊljən) *n* **1** gold or silver in mass. **2** gold or silve‑ in the form of bars and ingots, suitable for further pro‑ cessing. [C14: from Anglo-F: mint, prob. from OF‑ *bouillir* to boil, from L *bullīre*]

bullish ('bʊlɪʃ) *adj* **1** like a bull. **2** *Stock Exchange.* causing‑ expecting, or characterized by a rise in prices. **3** *Inf‑* cheerful and optimistic.
▶ **'bullishness** *n*

bull-necked *adj* having a short thick neck.

bullock ('bʊlək) n **1** a gelded bull; steer. ◆ vb **2** (intr) Austral. & NZ inf. to work hard and long. [OE bulluc; see BULL¹, -OCK]

bullocky ('bʊləkɪ) n, pl **bullockies**. Austral. & NZ. a bullock driver; teamster.

bullring ('bʊl,rɪŋ) n an arena for bullfighting.

bullroarer ('bʊl,rɔːrə) n a wooden slat attached to a thong that makes a roaring sound when the thong is whirled: used esp. by native Australians in religious rites.

bull's-eye n **1** the small central disc of a target, usually the highest valued area. **2** a shot hitting this. **3** Inf. something that exactly achieves its aim. **4** a small circular or oval window or opening. **5** a thick disc of glass set into a ship's deck, etc., to admit light. **6** the glass boss at the centre of a sheet of blown glass. **7a** a small thick planoconvex lens used as a condenser. **7b** a lamp containing such a lens. **8** a peppermint-flavoured boiled sweet.

bullshit ('bʊl,ʃɪt) Taboo sl. ◆ n **1** exaggerated or foolish talk; nonsense. **2** deceitful or pretentious talk. **3** (in the British Army) exaggerated zeal, esp. for ceremonial drill, cleaning, etc. Usually shortened to **bull**. ◆ vb **bullshits, bullshitting, bullshitted** or **bullshit**. **4** (intr) to talk in an exaggerated or foolish manner. **5** (tr) to talk bullshit to.

bull terrier n a breed of terrier having a muscular body and thick neck, with a short smooth coat. See also **pit bull terrier, Staffordshire bull terrier**.

bully ('bʊlɪ) n, pl **bullies**. **1** a person who hurts, persecutes, or intimidates weaker people. **2** a small New Zealand freshwater fish. ◆ vb **bullies, bullying, bullied**. **3** (when tr, often foll. by into) to hurt, intimidate, or persecute (a weaker or smaller person), esp. to make him do something. ◆ adj **4** dashing; jolly: my bully boy. **5** Inf. very good; fine. ◆ interj **6** Also: **bully for you, him**, etc. Inf. well done! bravo! [C16 (in the sense: sweetheart, hence fine fellow, hence swaggering coward): prob. from MDu. boele lover, from MHG buole]

bully beef n canned corned beef. Often shortened to **bully**. [C19 bully, anglicized version of F bouilli, from boeuf bouilli boiled beef]

bully-off Hockey. ◆ n **1** the method by which a game is restarted after a stoppage. Two opposing players stand with the ball between them and alternately strike their sticks together and against the ground three times before trying to hit the ball. ◆ vb **bully off**. **2** (intr, adv) to restart play with a bully-off. ◆ Often shortened to **bully**. [C19: from ?]

bullyrag ('bʊlɪ,ræg) vb **bullyrags, bullyragging, bullyragged**. (tr) to bully, esp. by means of cruel practical jokes. Also: **ballyrag**. [C18: from ?]

Bülow ★ (German 'byːlo) n Prince Bernhard von ('bɛrnhart fɔn). 1849–1929, chancellor of Germany (1900–09).

bulrush ('bʊl,rʌʃ) n **1** a popular name for **reed mace**. **2** a grasslike marsh plant used for making mats, chair seats, etc. **3** a biblical word for **papyrus** (the plant). [C15 bulrish, bul- ?from BULL¹ + rish RUSH²]

bulwark ('bʊlwək) n **1** a wall or similar structure used as a fortification; rampart. **2** a person or thing acting as a defence. **3** (often pl) Naut. a solid vertical fencelike structure along the outward sides of a deck. **4** a breakwater or mole. ◆ vb **5** (tr) to defend or fortify with or as if with a bulwark. [C15: via Du. from MHG bolwerk, from bol plank, BOLE + werk WORK]

Bulwer-Lytton ★ ('bʊlwə'lɪt³n) n See (1st Baron) **Lytton**.

bum¹ (bʌm) n Brit. sl. the buttocks or anus. [C14: from ?]

bum² (bʌm) Inf. ◆ n **1** a disreputable loafer or idler. **2** a tramp; hobo. ◆ vb **bums, bumming, bummed**. **3** (tr) to get by begging; cadge: to bum a lift. **4** (intr; often foll. by around) to live by begging or as a vagrant or loafer. **5** (intr; usually foll. by around) to spend time to no good purpose; loaf; idle. **6 bum (someone) off**. US & Canad. sl. to disappoint, annoy, or upset (someone). ◆ adj **7** (prenominal) of poor quality; useless. [C19: prob. shortened from earlier bummer a parasite, prob. from G bummeln to loaf]

bum bag n a small bag worn on a belt, round the waist.

bumbailiff (,bʌm'beɪlɪf) n Brit. derog. (formerly) an officer employed to collect debts and arrest debtors. [C17:

from BUM¹ + bailiff, so called because he follows hard behind debtors]

bumble ('bʌmb³l) vb **bumbles, bumbling, bumbled**. **1** to speak or do in a clumsy, muddled, or inefficient way. **2** (intr) to proceed unsteadily. [C16: ? a blend of BUNGLE + STUMBLE]
► **'bumbler** n ► **'bumbling** adj, n

bumblebee ('bʌmb³l,biː) or **humblebee** n any large hairy social bee of temperate regions. [C16: from bumble to buzz + BEE¹]

bumf or **bumph** (bʌmf) n Brit. **1** Inf., derog. official documents, forms, etc. **2** Sl. toilet paper. [C19: short for earlier bumfodder; see BUM¹]

bummer ('bʌmə) n Sl. a disappointing or unpleasant experience.

bump (bʌmp) vb **1** (when intr, usually foll. by against or into) to knock or strike with a jolt. **2** (intr; often foll. by along) to travel or proceed in jerks and jolts. **3** (tr) to hurt by knocking. **4** Cricket. to bowl (a ball) so that it bounces high on pitching or (of a ball) to bounce high when bowled. **5** (tr) Inf. to exclude (a ticket-holding passenger) from a flight as a result of overbooking. ◆ n **6** an impact; knock; jolt; collision. **7** a dull thud or other noise from an impact or collision. **8** the shock of a blow or collision. **9** a lump on the body caused by a blow. **10** a protuberance, as on a road surface. **11** any of the natural protuberances of the human skull, said by phrenologists to indicate underlying faculties and character. ◆ See also **bump into, bump off, bump up**. [C16: prob. imit.]

bumper¹ ('bʌmpə) n **1** a horizontal usually metal bar attached to the front or rear end of a car, lorry, etc., to protect against damage from impact. **2** Cricket. a ball bowled so that it bounces high on pitching; bouncer.

bumper² ('bʌmpə) n **1** a glass, tankard, etc., filled to the brim, esp. as a toast. **2** an unusually large or fine example of something. ◆ adj **3** unusually large, fine, or abundant: a bumper crop. [C17 (in the sense: a brimming glass): prob. from bump (obs. vb) to bulge; see BUMP]

bumph (bʌmf) n a variant spelling of **bumf**.

bump into vb (intr, prep) Inf. to meet by chance; encounter unexpectedly.

bumpkin ('bʌmpkɪn) n an awkward simple rustic person (esp. in **country bumpkin**). [C16: ?from Du. boomken small tree, or from MDu. boomekijn small barrel]

bump off vb (tr, adv) Sl. to murder; kill.

bumptious ('bʌmpʃəs) adj offensively self-assertive or conceited. [C19: ?from BUMP + FRACTIOUS]
► **'bumptiously** adv ► **'bumptiousness** n

bump up vb (tr, adv) Inf. to raise or increase.

bumpy ('bʌmpɪ) adj **bumpier, bumpiest**. **1** having an uneven surface. **2** full of jolts; rough.
► **'bumpily** adv ► **'bumpiness** n

bun (bʌn) n **1** a small roll, similar to bread but usually containing sweetening, currants, etc. **2** any of various small round cakes. **3** a hairstyle in which long hair is gathered into a bun shape at the back of the head. [C14: from ?]

bunch (bʌntʃ) n **1** a number of things growing, fastened, or grouped together: a bunch of grapes; a bunch of keys. **2** a collection; group: a bunch of queries. **3** Inf. a group or company: a bunch of boys. ◆ vb **4** (sometimes foll. by up) to group or be grouped into a bunch. [C14: from ?]

bunchy ('bʌntʃɪ) adj **bunchier, bunchiest**. **1** composed of or resembling bunches. **2** bulging.

buncombe ('bʌŋkəm) n a variant spelling (esp. US) of **bunkum**.

Bundaberg ★ ('bʌndə,bɜːg) n a city in E Australia, near the E coast of Queensland: centre of a sugar-growing area; with a nearby deep-water port. Pop.: 52 267 (1993).

Bundelkhand ★ (,bʌndəl'kʌnd, -'xʌnd) n a region of central India: formerly native states, now mainly part of Madhya Pradesh.

bundle ('bʌnd³l) n **1** a number of things or a quantity of material gathered or loosely bound together: a bundle of sticks. Related adj: **fascicular**. **2** something wrapped or tied for carrying; package. **3** Sl. a large sum of money. **4 go a bundle on**. Sl. to be extremely fond of. **5** Biol. a collec-

tion of strands of specialized tissue such as nerve fibres. **6** *Bot.* short for **vascular bundle. 7 drop one's bundle.** *Austral. & NZ sl.* to panic or give up hope. ◆ *vb* **bundles, bundling, bundled. 8** (*tr;* often foll. by *up*) to make into a bundle. **9** (foll. by *out, off, into,* etc.) to go or cause to go, esp. roughly or unceremoniously. **10** (*tr;* usually foll. by *into*) to push or throw, esp. quickly and untidily. **11** (*tr*) to give away (a relatively cheap product) when selling an expensive one to attract business: *software is often bundled with computers.* **12** (*intr*) to sleep or lie in one's clothes on the same bed as one's betrothed: formerly a custom in New England, Wales, and elsewhere. [C14: prob. from MDu. *bundel;* rel. to OE *bindele* bandage; see BIND, BOND]
▸ **'bundler** *n*

bundle up *vb* (*adv*) **1** to dress (somebody) warmly and snugly. **2** (*tr*) to make (something) into a bundle or bundles, esp. by tying.

bun fight *n Brit. sl.* **1** a tea party. **2** *Ironic.* an official function.

bung[1] (bʌŋ) *n* **1** a stopper, esp. of cork or rubber, for a cask, etc. **2** short for **bunghole.** ◆ *vb* (*tr*) **3** (often foll. by *up*) *Inf.* to close or seal with or as with a bung. **4** *Brit. sl.* to throw; sling. **5 bung it on.** *Austral. sl.* to behave in a pretentious manner. [C15: from MDu. *bonghe*]

bung[2] (bʌŋ) *adj Austral. & NZ inf.* **1** useless. **2 go bung. 2a** to fail or collapse. **2b** to die. [C19: from Abor.]

bungalow ('bʌŋgə,ləʊ) *n* a one-storey house, sometimes with an attic. [C17: from Hindi *banglā* (house) of the Bengal type]

bungee jumping *or* **bungy jumping** ('bʌndʒɪ) *n* a sport in which a participant jumps from a high bridge, building, etc., secured only by a rubber cord attached to the ankles. [C20: from *bungie,* slang for India rubber, of unknown origin]

bunghole ('bʌŋ,həʊl) *n* a hole in a cask, barrel, etc., through which liquid can be drained.

bungle ('bʌŋg°l) *vb* **bungles, bungling, bungled. 1** (*tr*) to spoil (an operation) through clumsiness, incompetence, etc. ◆ *n* **2** a clumsy or unsuccessful performance. [C16: ? of Scand. origin]
▸ **'bungler** *n* ▸ **'bungling** *adj, n*

bunion ('bʌnjən) *n* an inflamed swelling of the first joint of the big toe. [C18: ?from obs. *bunny* a swelling, from ?]

bunk[1] (bʌŋk) *n* **1** a narrow shelflike bed fixed along a wall. **2** short for **bunk bed. 3** *Inf.* any place where one sleeps. ◆ *vb* **4** (*intr;* often foll. by *down*) to prepare to sleep: *he bunked down on the floor.* **5** (*intr*) to occupy a bunk or bed. [C19: prob. short for BUNKER]

bunk[2] (bʌŋk) *n Inf.* short for **bunkum** (sense 1).

bunk[3] (bʌŋk) *n Brit. sl.* a hurried departure, usually under suspicious circumstances (esp. in **do a bunk**). [C19: ?from BUNK[1] (in the sense: to occupy a bunk, hence a hurried departure)]

bunk bed *n* one of a pair of beds constructed one above the other to save space.

bunker ('bʌŋkə) *n* **1** a large storage container or tank, as for coal. **2** Also called (esp. US and Canad.): **sand trap.** an obstacle on a golf course, usually a sand-filled hollow bordered by a ridge. **3** an underground shelter with a bank and embrasures for guns above ground. ◆ *vb* **4** (*tr*) *Golf.* **4a** to drive (the ball) into a bunker. **4b** (*passive*) to have one's ball trapped in a bunker. [C16 (in the sense: chest, box): from Scot. *bonkar,* from ?]

bunkhouse ('bʌŋk,haʊs) *n* (in the US and Canada) a building containing the sleeping quarters of workers on a ranch.

bunkum *or* **buncombe** ('bʌŋkəm) *n* **1** empty talk; nonsense. **2** *Chiefly US.* empty or insincere speechmaking by a politician. [C19: after *Buncombe,* a county in North Carolina, alluded to in an inane speech by its Congressional representative Felix Walker (about 1820)]

bunny ('bʌnɪ) *n, pl* **bunnies. 1** Also called: **bunny rabbit.** a child's word for **rabbit** (sense 1). **2** Also called: **bunny girl.** a night-club hostess whose costume includes rabbit-like tail and ears. **3** *Austral. sl.* a mug; dupe. [C17: from Scot. Gaelic *bun* scut of a rabbit]

Bunsen ★ ('bʌns°n; *German* 'bunzən) *n* Robert Wilhelm

('rɔːbert 'vɪlhelm). 1811–99, German chemist who with Kirchhoff developed spectrum analysis.

Bunsen burner *n* a gas burner consisting of a metal tube with an adjustable air valve at the base. [C19: after R. W. BUNSEN]

bunting[1] ('bʌntɪŋ) *n* **1** a coarse, loosely woven cotton fabric used for flags, etc. **2** decorative flags, pennants, and streamers. [C18: from ?]

bunting[2] ('bʌntɪŋ) *n* any of numerous seed-eating song birds of the Old World and North America having short stout bills. [C13: from ?]

buntline ('bʌntlɪn, -,laɪn) *n Naut.* one of several lines fastened to the foot of a square sail for hauling it up to the yard when furling. [C17: from *bunt* centre of a sail + LINE[1] (sense 11)]

Buñuel ★ (*Spanish* bu'ɲwel) *n* **Luis** (lwis). 1900–83, Spanish film director. He collaborated with Salvador Dali on the first surrealist film, *Un Chien Andalou* (1929). His later films include *The Discreet Charm of the Bourgeoisie* (1972).

bunya ('bʌnjə) *n* a tall dome-shaped Australian coniferous tree having edible cones (**bunya nuts**) and thickish flattened needles. Also called: **bunya-bunya.** [C19: from Abor.]

Bunyan ★ ('bʌnjən) *n* **John.** 1628–88, English preacher and writer, noted for *The Pilgrim's Progress* (1678).

bunyip ('bʌnjɪp) *n Austral.* a legendary monster said to inhabit swamps and lagoons. [C19: from Abor.]

Buonaparte ★ (bwɒnə'pɑːte) *n* the Italian spelling of **Bonaparte.**

Buonarroti ★ (*Italian* bwɒnar'rɔti) *n* See **Michelangelo.**

buoy (bɔɪ; *US* 'buːɪ) *n* **1** a distinctively shaped and coloured float, anchored to the bottom, for designating moorings, navigable channels, or obstructions in a body of water. See also **life buoy.** ◆ *vb* **2** (*tr;* usually foll. by *up,* to prevent from sinking: *the life belt buoyed him up.* **3** (*tr;* usually foll. by *up*) to raise the spirits of; hearten. **4** (*tr*) *Naut.* to mark (a channel or obstruction) with a buoy or buoys. **5** (*intr*) to rise to the surface; float. [C13: prob. of Gmc origin]

buoyancy ('bɔɪənsɪ) *n* **1** the ability to float in a liquid or to rise in liquid, air, or other gas. **2** the tendency of a fluid to keep a body afloat. **3** the ability to recover quickly after setbacks; resilience. **4** cheerfulness.

buoyant ('bɔɪənt) *adj* **1** able to float in or rise to the surface of a liquid. **2** (of a liquid or gas) able to keep a body afloat. **3** cheerful or resilient. [C16: prob. from Sp. *boyante,* from *boyar* to float]

BUPA ('buːpə) *n acronym for* The British United Provident Association Limited: a company which provides private medical insurance.

bupivacaine (bjuː'pɪvə,keɪn) *n* a local anaesthetic of long duration, used for nerve blocks. [C20: ?from BU(TYL) + *pi(pecoloxylidide)* + *-vacaine,* from (NO)VOCAINE]

bur (bɜː) *n* **1** a seed vessel or flower head having hooks or prickles. **2** any plant that produces burs. **3** a person or thing that clings like a bur. **4** a small surgical or dental drill. ◆ *vb* **burs, burring, burred. 5** (*tr*) to remove burs from. ◆ Also: **burr.** [C14: prob. from ON]

Buraydah *or* **Buraida** ★ (bu'raɪdə) *n* a town and oasis in central Saudi Arabia. Pop.: 69 940 (latest est.).

Burbage ★ ('bɜːbɪdʒ) *n* **1 James.** ?1530–97, English actor and theatre manager, who built (1576) the first public playhouse in England. **2** his son, **Richard.** ?1567–1619, English actor, closely associated with Shakespeare.

burble ('bɜːb°l) *vb* **burbles, burbling, burbled. 1** to make or utter with a bubbling sound; gurgle. **2** (*intr;* often foll. by *away* or *on*) to talk quickly and excitedly. ◆ *n* **3** a bubbling or gurgling sound. **4** a flow of excited speech. [C14: prob. imit.]
▸ **'burbler** *n*

burbot ('bɜːbət) *n, pl* **burbots** *or* **burbot.** a freshwater gadoid food fish that has barbels around its mouth and occurs in Europe, Asia, and North America. [C14: from OF *bourbotte,* from *bourbeter* to wallow in mud, from *bourbe* mud]

Burckhardt ★ (*German* 'burkhart) *n* **Jacob Christoph**

1818–97, Swiss historian; author of *The Civilisation of the Renaissance in Italy* (1860).

burden[1] ('bɜːd³n) *n* **1** something that is carried; load. **2** something that is exacting, oppressive, or difficult to bear. Related adj: **onerous. 3** *Naut.* **3a** the cargo capacity of a ship. **3b** the weight of a ship's cargo. ♦ *vb* (*tr*) **4** (sometimes foll. by *up*) to put or impose a burden on; load. **5** to weigh down; oppress. [OE *byrthen*]

burden[2] ('bɜːd³n) *n* **1** a line of words recurring at the end of each verse of a song; chorus or refrain. **2** the theme of a speech, book, etc. **3** another word for **bourdon.** [C16: from OF *bourdon* bass horn, droning sound, imit.]

burden of proof *n Law.* the obligation to provide evidence that will convince the court or jury of the truth of one's contention.

burdensome ('bɜːd³nsəm) *adj* hard to bear.

burdock ('bɜːˌdɒk) *n* a coarse weedy Eurasian plant having large heart-shaped leaves, tiny purple flowers surrounded by hooked bristles, and burlike fruits. [C16: from BUR + DOCK[4]]

bureau ('bjʊərəʊ) *n, pl* **bureaus** or **bureaux. 1** *Chiefly Brit.* a writing desk with pigeonholes, drawers, etc., against which the writing surface can be closed when not in use. **2** *US.* a chest of drawers. **3** an office or agency, esp. one providing services for the public. **4** a government department. [C17: from F, orig.: type of cloth used for covering desks, from OF *burel*]

bureaucracy (bjʊə'rɒkrəsɪ) *n, pl* **bureaucracies. 1** a system of administration based upon organization into bureaus, division of labour, a hierarchy of authority, etc. **2** government by such a system. **3** government or other officials collectively. **4** any administration in which action is impeded by unnecessary official procedures.

bureaucrat ('bjʊərəˌkræt) *n* **1** an official in a bureaucracy. **2** an official who adheres to bureaucracy, esp. rigidly.
▸ ˌbureau'cratic *adj* ▸ ˌbureau'cratically *adv*

bureaucratize or **bureaucratise** (bjʊə'rɒkrəˌtaɪz) *vb* **bureaucratizes, bureaucratizing, bureaucratized** or **bureaucratises, bureaucratising, bureaucratised.** (*tr*) to administer by or transform into a bureaucracy.
▸ bu,reaucrati'zation or bu,reaucrati'sation *n*

bureaux ('bjʊərəʊz) *n* a plural of **bureau.**

burette or *US* **buret** (bjʊ'rɛt) *n* a graduated glass tube with a stopcock on one end for dispensing and transferring known volumes of fluids, esp. liquids. [C15: from F, from OF *buire* ewer]

burg (bɜːɡ) *n* **1** *History.* a fortified town. **2** *US inf.* a town or city. [C18 (in the sense: fortress): from OHG *burg*]

burgage ('bɜːɡɪdʒ) *n History.* **1** (in England) tenure of land or tenement in a town or city, which originally involved a fixed money rent. **2** (in Scotland) the tenure of land direct from the crown in Scottish royal burghs in return for watching and warding. [C14: from Med. L *burgāgium*, from OE *burg*]

Burgas ★ (*Bulgarian* bur'gas) *n* a port in SE Bulgaria on an inlet of the Black Sea. Pop.: 199 470 (1996 est.).

Burgenland ★ (*German* 'burgən,lant) *n* a state of E Austria. Capital: Eisenstadt. Pop.: 273 613 (1994 est.). Area: 3965 sq. km (1531 sq. miles).

burgeon or **bourgeon** ('bɜːdʒən) *vb* **1** (often foll. by *forth* or *out*) (of a plant) to sprout (buds). **2** (*intr*; often foll. by *forth* or *out*) to develop or grow rapidly; flourish. [C13: from OF *burjon*]

burger ('bɜːɡə) *n Inf.* **a** short for **hamburger. b** (*in combination*): *a cheeseburger.*

burgess ('bɜːdʒɪs) *n* **1** (in England) a citizen, freeman, or inhabitant of a borough. **2** *English history.* a Member of Parliament from a borough, corporate town, or university. [C13: from OF *burgeis*; see BOROUGH]

Burgess ★ ('bɜːdʒɪs) *n* **1 Anthony**, real name *John Burgess Wilson.* 1917–93, British writer, whose novels include *A Clockwork Orange* (1962), *Earthly Powers* (1980), and *A Dead Man in Deptford* (1993). **2 Guy.** 1911–63, British spy, who fled to the Soviet Union in 1951.

burgh ('bʌrə) *n* **1** (in Scotland until 1975) a town, esp. one incorporated by charter, that enjoyed a degree of self-government. **2** an archaic form of **borough.** [C14: Scot. form of BOROUGH]
▸ burghal ('bɜːɡ³l) *adj*

burgher ('bɜːɡə) *n* **1** a member of the trading or mercantile class of a medieval city. **2** a respectable citizen; bourgeois. **3** *Arch.* a citizen or inhabitant of a corporate town, esp on the Continent. **4** *S. African history.* a citizen of the Cape Colony or of one of the Transvaal and Free State republics. [C16: from G *Bürger* or Du. *burger* freeman of a BOROUGH]

Burghley or **Burleigh** ★ ('bɜːlɪ) *n* **William Cecil**, 1st Baron Burghley. 1520–98, English statesman: chief adviser to Elizabeth I; secretary of state (1558–72) and Lord High Treasurer (1572–98).

burglar ('bɜːɡlə) *n* a person who commits burglary; housebreaker. [C15: from Anglo-F, from Med. L *burglātor*, prob. from *burgāre* to thieve]

burglary ('bɜːɡlərɪ) *n, pl* **burglaries.** the crime of entering a building as a trespasser to commit theft or another offence.
▸ burglarious (bɜː'ɡlɛərɪəs) *adj*

burgle ('bɜːɡ³l) *vb* **burgles, burgling, burgled.** to commit burglary upon (a house, etc.).

burgomaster ('bɜːɡəˌmɑːstə) *n* the chief magistrate of a town in Austria, Belgium, Germany, or the Netherlands; mayor. [C16: partial translation of Du. *burgemeester;* see BOROUGH, MASTER]

Burgos ★ (*Spanish* 'burɣos) *n* a city in N Spain, in Old Castile: cathedral. Pop.: 166 251 (1994 est.).

Burgoyne ★ (bɜː'ɡɔɪn) *n* **John.** 1722–92, British general in the War of American Independence, who was forced to surrender at Saratoga (1777).

Burgundy ★ ('bɜːɡəndɪ) *n, pl* **Burgundies. 1** a region of E France famous for its wines, lying west of the Saône: formerly a semi-independent duchy; annexed to France in 1482. French name: **Bourgogne. 2 Free County of.** another name for **Franche-Comté. 3** a monarchy (1384–1477) of medieval Europe, at its height including the Low Countries, the duchy of Burgundy, and Franche-Comté. **4 Kingdom of.** a kingdom in E France, established in the early 6th century A.D., eventually including the later duchy of Burgundy, Franche-Comté, and the Kingdom of Provence: known as the Kingdom of Arles from the 13th century. **5a** any red or white wine produced in the region of Burgundy, around Dijon. **5b** any heavy red table wine. **6** (*often not cap.*) a blackish-purple to purplish-red colour.
▸ Burgundian (bɜː'ɡʌndɪən) *adj, n*

burial ('bɛrɪəl) *n* the act of burying, esp. the interment of a dead body. [OE *byrgels* burial place, tomb; see BURY, -AL[2]]

burial ground *n* a graveyard or cemetery.

burin ('bjʊərɪn) *n* **1** a chisel of tempered steel used for engraving metal, wood, or marble. **2** *Archaeol.* a prehistoric flint tool. [C17: from F, ?from It. *burino*, of Gmc origin]

burk (bɜːk) *n* a variant spelling of **berk.**

Burke ★ (bɜːk) *n* **1 Edmund.** 1729–97, British Whig statesman, conservative political theorist, and orator, born in Ireland. **2 Robert O'Hara.** 1820–61, Irish explorer, who led the first expedition (1860–61) across Australia from south to north; died on return journey. **3 William.** 1792–1829, Irish murderer and body snatcher; associate of William Hare.

Burkina-Faso ★ (bɜː'kiːnə'fæsəʊ) *n* an inland republic in W Africa: dominated by Mossi kingdoms (10th–19th centuries); French protectorate established in 1896; became an independent republic in 1960; consists mainly of a flat savanna plateau. Official language: French; Mossi and other African languages also widely spoken. Religion: mostly animist, with a large Muslim minority. Currency: franc. Capital: Ouagadougou. Pop.: 10 891 000 (1997). Area: 273 200 sq. km (105 900 sq. miles). Former name (until 1984): **Upper Volta.**

burl[1] (bɜːl) *n* **1** a small knot or lump in wool. **2** a roundish warty outgrowth from certain trees. ♦ *vb* **3** (*tr*) to remove the burls from (cloth). [C15: from OF *burle* tuft of wool, prob. ult. from LL *burra* shaggy cloth]

burl[2] or **birl** (bɜːl) *n Inf.* **1** *Scot., Austral., & NZ.* an attempt;

try (esp. in **give it a burl**). **2** *Austral, & NZ*. a ride in a car. [C20: ?from BIRL in Scots sense: to spin or turn]

burlap ('bɜːlæp) *n* a coarse fabric woven from jute, hemp, or the like. [C17: from *borel* coarse cloth, from OF *burel* (see BUREAU) + LAP¹]

Burleigh ★ ('bɜːlɪ) *n* a variant spelling of **Burghley**.

burlesque (bɜːˈlesk) *n* **1** an artistic work, esp. literary or dramatic, satirizing a subject by caricaturing it. **2** a ludicrous imitation or caricature. **3** Also: **burlesk**. *US. & Canad. theatre*. a bawdy comedy show of the late 19th and early 20th centuries: the striptease eventually became one of its chief elements. ◆ *adj* **4** of, relating to, or characteristic of a burlesque. ◆ *vb* **burlesques, burlesquing, burlesqued. 5** to represent or imitate (a person or thing) in a ludicrous way; caricature. [C17: from F, from It., from *burla* a jest, piece of nonsense]
▸ bur'lesquer *n*

burley ('bɜːlɪ) *n* a variant spelling of **berley**.

Burlington ★ ('bɜːlɪŋtən) *n* **1** a city in S Canada on Lake Ontario, northeast of Hamilton. Pop.: 129 575 (1991). **2** a city in NW Vermont on Lake Champlain: largest city in the state; University of Vermont (1791). Pop.: 39 127 (1990).

burly ('bɜːlɪ) *adj* **burlier, burliest**. large and thick of build; sturdy. [C13: of Gmc origin]
▸ 'burliness *n*

Burma ★ ('bɜːmə) *n* the former name (until 1984) of **Myanmar**.

Burma Road ★ *n* the route extending from Lashio in (Myanmar) to Chongqing in China, which was used by the Allies during World War II to supply military equipment to Chiang Kai-shek's forces in China.

Burmese (bɜːˈmiːz) *adj also* **Burman**. **1** of or denoting Burma (Myanmar), or its inhabitants, their customs, etc. ◆ *n* **2** (*pl* **Burmese**) a native or inhabitant of Burma (Myanmar). **3** the language of the Burmese.

burn¹ (bɜːn) *vb* **burns, burning, burnt** *or* **burned. 1** to undergo or cause to undergo combustion. **2** to destroy or be destroyed by fire. **3** (*tr*) to damage, injure, or mark by heat: *he burnt his hand; she was burnt by the sun*. **4** to die or put to death by fire. **5** (*intr*) to be or feel hot: *my forehead burns*. **6** to smart or cause to smart: *brandy burns one's throat*. **7** (*intr*) to feel strong emotion, esp. anger or passion. **8** (*tr*) to use for the purposes of light, heat, or power: *to burn coal*. **9** (*tr*) to form by or as if by fire: *to burn a hole*. **10** to char or become charred: *the potatoes are burning*. **11** (*tr*) to brand or cauterize. **12** to produce by or subject to heat as part of a process: *to burn charcoal*. **13 burn one's bridges** *or* **boats**. to commit oneself to a particular course of action with no possibility of turning back. **14 burn one's fingers**. to suffer from having meddled or interfered. ◆ *n* **15** an injury caused by exposure to heat, electrical, chemical, or radioactive agents. **16** a mark, e.g. on wood, caused by burning. **17** a controlled use of rocket propellant, esp. for a course correction. **18** a hot painful sensation in a muscle, experienced during vigorous exercise. **19** *Sl*. tobacco or a cigarette. ◆ See also **burn out**. [OE *beornan* (intr), *bærnan* (tr)]

burn² (bɜːn) *n Scot. & N English*. a small stream; brook. [OE *burna*; rel. to ON *brunnr* spring]

Burne-Jones ★ ('bɜːn'dʒəʊnz) *n* Sir **Edward**. 1833–98, British Pre-Raphaelite painter and designer.

burner ('bɜːnə) *n* **1** the part of a stove, lamp, etc., that produces flame or heat. **2** an apparatus for burning something, as fuel or refuse.

burnet ('bɜːnɪt) *n* **1** a plant of the rose family which has purple-tinged green flowers and leaves. **2 burnet rose**. a very prickly Eurasian rose with white flowers and purplish-black fruits. **3** a moth with red-spotted dark green wings and antennae with enlarged tips. [C14: from OF *burnete*, var. of *brunete* BRUNETTE]

Burnet ★ (bə'net, 'bɜːnɪt) *n* Sir (**Frank**) **Macfarlane** (mək'faːlən). 1899–1985, Australian physician and virologist, who shared a Nobel prize for physiology or medicine in 1960 for work in immunology.

Burnett ★ (bɜː'net) *n* **Frances Hodgson** ('hɒdʒsən). 1849–1924, US novelist, born in England; author of *Little Lord Fauntleroy* (1886) and *The Secret Garden* (1911).

Burney ★ ('bɜːnɪ) *n* **Frances**. known as *Fanny*; married name *Madame D'Arblay*. 1752–1840, British novelist and diarist: author of *Evelina* (1778).

burning ('bɜːnɪŋ) *adj* **1** intense; passionate. **2** urgent; crucial: *a burning problem*.

burning bush *n* **1** any of several shrubs or trees that have bright red fruits or seeds. **2** any of several plants with a bright red autumn foliage. **3** *Bible*. the bush that burned without being consumed, from which God spoke to Moses (Exodus 3:2–4).

burning glass *n* a convex lens for concentrating the sun's rays to produce fire.

burnish ('bɜːnɪʃ) *vb* **1** to make or become shiny or smooth by friction; polish. ◆ *n* **2** a shiny finish; lustre. [C14 *burnischen*, from OF *brunir* to make brown, from *brun* BROWN]
▸ 'burnisher *n*

Burnley ★ ('bɜːnlɪ) *n* an industrial town in NW England, in E Lancashire. Pop.: 74 661 (1991).

burnoose, burnous, *or* **burnouse** (bɜː'nuːs, -'nuːz) *n* a long circular cloak with a hood attached, worn esp. by Arabs. [C20: via F *burnous* from Ar. *burnus*, from Gk *birros* cloak]

burn out *vb* (*adv*) **1** to become or cause to become inoperative as a result of heat or friction: *the clutch burnt out*. **2** (*intr*) (of a rocket, jet engine, etc.) to cease functioning as a result of exhaustion of the fuel supply. **3** (*tr; usually passive*) to destroy by fire. **4** to become or cause to become exhausted through overwork or dissipation.

Burns ★ (bɜːnz) *n* **Robert**. 1759–96, Scottish lyric poet. His verse, written mostly in dialect, includes love songs, nature poetry, and satires. *Auld Lang Syne* and *Tam o' Shanter* are among his best-known poems.

burnt (bɜːnt) *vb* **1** a past tense and past participle of **burn¹**. ◆ *adj* **2** affected by or as if by burning; charred.

burnt offering *n* a sacrificial offering burnt, usually on an altar, to honour, propitiate, or supplicate a deity.

burnt sienna *n* **1** a reddish-brown pigment obtained by roasting raw sienna. ◆ *n, adj* **2** (of) a reddish-brown colour.

burnt umber *n* **1** a brown pigment obtained by heating umber. ◆ *n, adj* **2** (of) a dark brown colour.

burp (bɜːp) *n* **1** *Inf*. a belch. ◆ *vb* **2** (*intr*) *Inf*. to belch. **3** (*tr*) to cause (a baby) to burp. [C20: imit.]

burr¹ (bɜː) *n* **1** a small power-driven hand-operated rotary file, esp. for removing burrs or for machining recesses. **2** a rough edge left on a workpiece after cutting, drilling, etc. **3** a rough or irregular protuberance, such as a burl on a tree. **4** a variant spelling of **bur**. [C14: var. of BUR]

burr² (bɜː) *n* **1** an articulation of (r) characteristic of certain English dialects, esp. the uvular fricative trill of Northumberland or the retroflex *r* of the West of England. **2** a whirring sound. ◆ *vb* **3** to pronounce (words) with a burr. **4** (*intr*) to make a whirring sound. [C18: either special use of BUR (in the sense: rough sound) or imit.]

Burren ★ ('bʌrən) *n* **the**. a limestone area on the North Clare coast in the Irish Republic, famous for its wild flowers, caves, and dolmens.

burrito (bə'riːtəʊ) *n, pl* **burritos**. *Mexican cookery*. a tortilla folded over a filling of minced beef, chicken, cheese, or beans. [C20: from Mexican Sp., from Sp.: literally, a young donkey]

burro ('bʊrəʊ) *n, pl* **burros**. a donkey, esp. one used as a pack animal. [C19: Sp., from Port., from *burrico*]

Burroughs ★ ('bʌrəʊz) *n* **1 Edgar Rice**. 1875–1950, US novelist, author of the *Tarzan* stories. **2 William S(eward)**. 1914–97, US novelist. His novels include *Junkie* (1953), *The Naked Lunch* (1959), and *Interzone* (1989).

burrow ('bʌrəʊ) *n* **1** a hole dug in the ground by a rabbit or other small animal. **2** a small snug place affording shelter or retreat. ◆ *vb* **3** to dig (a burrow) in, through, or under (ground). **4** (*intr*; often foll. by *through*) to move through by or as by digging. **5** (*intr*) to hide or live in a burrow. **6** (*intr*) to delve deeply: *he burrowed into his pockets*. **7** to hide (oneself). [C13: prob. var. of BOROUGH]
▸ 'burrower *n*

burry ('bɜːrɪ) *adj* **burrier**, **burriest**. **1** full of or covered in burs. **2** resembling burs; prickly.

bursa ('bɜːsə) *n, pl* **bursae** (-siː) *or* **bursas**. **1** *Anat.* a small fluid-filled sac that reduces friction, esp. at joints. **2** *Zool.* any saclike cavity or structure. [C19: from Med. L: bag, pouch, from Gk: skin, hide; see PURSE]
▸ **'bursal** *adj*

Bursa ★ ('bɜːsə) *n* a city in NW Turkey: founded in the 2nd century B.C.; seat of Bithynian kings. Pop.: 996 600 (1994 est.). Former name: **Brusa**.

bursar ('bɜːsə) *n* **1** a treasurer of a school, college, or university. **2** *Chiefly Scot. & NZ.* a student holding a bursary. [C13: from Med. L *bursārius* keeper of the purse, from *bursa* purse]

bursary ('bɜːsərɪ) *n, pl* **bursaries**. **1** Also called: **'bursar,ship.** a scholarship awarded esp. in Scottish and New Zealand schools and universities. **2** *Brit.* the treasury of a college, etc.
▸ **bursarial** (bɜːˈsɛərɪəl) *adj*

bursitis (bɜːˈsaɪtɪs) *n* inflammation of a bursa.

burst (bɜːst) *vb* **bursts**, **bursting**, **burst**. **1** to break or cause to break open or apart suddenly and noisily; explode. **2** (*intr*) to come, go, etc., suddenly and forcibly: *he burst into the room*. **3** (*intr*) to be full to the point of breaking open. **4** (*intr*) to give vent (to) suddenly or loudly: *to burst into song*. **5** (*tr*) to cause or suffer the rupture of: *to burst a blood vessel*. ◆ *n* **6** a sudden breaking open; explosion. **7** a break; breach; rupture. **8** a sudden display or increase of effort; spurt: *a burst of speed*. **9** a sudden and violent emission, occurrence, or outbreak: *a burst of applause*. **10** a volley of fire from a weapon. [OE *berstan*]

burthen ('bɜːðən) *n, vb* an archaic word for **burden**[1].
▸ **'burthensome** *adj*

burton ('bɜːtˀn) *n* **go for a burton**. *Brit. sl.* **a** to be broken, useless, or lost. **b** to die. [C20: from ?]

Burton ★ ('bɜːtˀn) *n* **1** Sir **Richard Francis**. 1821–90, English explorer, who discovered Lake Tanganyika (1858). **2** **Richard**, real name *Richard Jenkins*. 1925–84, Welsh actor: films include *Who's Afraid of Virginia Woolf?* (1966) and *Equus* (1977). **3** **Robert**, pen name *Democritus Junior*. 1577–1640, English clergyman, noted for his *Anatomy of Melancholy* (1621).

Burton-upon-Trent ★ *n* a town in W central England, in E Staffordshire: brewing. Pop.: 60 525 (1991).

Burundi ★ (bəˈrundɪ) *n* a republic in E central Africa: inhabited chiefly by the Hutu, Tutsi, and Twa; made part of German East Africa in 1899; part of the Belgian territory of Ruanda-Urundi from 1923 until it became independent in 1962; ethnic violence has persisted; consists mainly of high plateaus along the main Nile-Congo dividing range, dropping rapidly to the Great Rift Valley in the west. Official languages: Kirundi and French. Religion: Christian majority. Currency: Burundi franc. Capital: Bujumbura. Pop.: 6 053 000 (1997). Area: 27 731 sq. km (10 707 sq. miles). Former name (until 1962): **Urundi**.
▸ **Bu'rundian** *adj, n*

bury ('bɛrɪ) *vb* **buries**, **burying**, **buried**. (*tr*) **1** to place (a corpse) in a grave; inter. **2** to place in the earth and cover with soil. **3** to cover from sight; hide. **4** to embed; sink: *to bury a nail in plaster*. **5** to occupy (oneself) with deep concentration; engross: *to be buried in a book*. **6** to dismiss from the mind; abandon: *to bury old hatreds*. [OE *byrgan*]

Bury ★ ('bɛrɪ) *n* **1** a town in NW England, part of Greater Manchester: an early textile centre. Pop.: 62 633 (1991). **2** a unitary authority in NW England, in Greater Manchester. Pop.: 182 200 (1994 est.). Area: 99 sq. km (38 sq. miles).

Buryat Republic ★ (buəˈjɑːt, ˌbuərɪˈɑːt) *n* a constituent republic of SE central Russia, on Lake Baikal: mountainous and forested. Capital: Ulan-Ude. Pop.: 1 053 000 (1995 est.). Area: 351 300 sq. km (135 608 sq. miles). Also called: **Buryatia** (buˈrɪˈɑːtɪə; *Russian* buˈrja:tɪja).

Bury St Edmunds ★ ('bɛrɪ sənt 'ɛdməndz) *n* a market town in E England, in Suffolk. Pop.: 31 237 (1991).

bus (bʌs) *n, pl* **buses** *or* **busses**. **1** a large motor vehicle designed to carry passengers between stopping places along a regular route. More formal name: **omnibus**. **2** (*modifier*) of or relating to a bus or buses: *a bus driver; a bus*

station. **3** *Inf.* a car or aircraft, esp. one that is old and shaky. **4** *Electronics, computing.* short for **busbar**. **5** *Astronautics.* a platform in a space vehicle used for various experiments and processes. **6** **miss the bus**. to miss an opportunity. ◆ *vb* **buses**, **busing**, **bused** *or* **busses**, **bussing**, **bussed**. **7** to travel or transport by bus. **8** *Chiefly US & Canad.* to transport (children) by bus from one area to another in order to create racially integrated schools. [C19: short for OMNIBUS]

bus. *abbrev. for* business.

busbar ('bʌz,bɑː) *n* **1** an electrical conductor usually used to make a common connection between several circuits. **2** a group of such electrical conductors maintained at a low voltage, used for carrying data in binary form between the various parts of a computer or its peripherals.

busby ('bʌzbɪ) *n, pl* **busbies**. **1** a tall fur helmet worn by hussars. **2** (not in official usage) another name for **bearskin** (the hat). [C18: ?from a proper name]

Busby ★ ('bʌzbɪ) *n* Sir **Matthew**, known as *Matt*. 1909–94, British footballer. He played for Manchester City (1929–36) and for Liverpool (1936–39); he was manager of Manchester United (1946–69).

bush[1] (bʊʃ) *n* **1** a dense woody plant, smaller than a tree, with many branches arising from the lower part of the stem; shrub. **2** a dense cluster of such shrubs; thicket. **3** something resembling a bush, esp. in density: *a bush of hair*. **4** (often preceded by *the*) an uncultivated or sparsely settled area, covered with trees or shrubs, which can vary from open, shrubby country to dense rainforest. **5** a forested area; woodland. **6** *Canad.* Also called: **bush lot**, **woodlot**. an area on a farm on which timber is grown and cut. **7** (often preceded by *the*) *Inf.* the countryside, as opposed to the city: *out in the bush*. **8** *Obs.* a bunch of ivy hung as a vintner's sign in front of a tavern. **9** **beat about the bush**. to avoid the point at issue; prevaricate. ◆ *adj* **10** *Austral. & NZ inf.* rough-and-ready. **11** *US & Canad. inf.* unprofessional, unpolished, or second-rate. **12** **go bush**. *Inf.* **12a** *Austral. & NZ.* to abandon city amenities and live rough. **12b** *Austral.* to go into hiding. ◆ *vb* **13** (*intr*) to grow thick and bushy. **14** (*tr*) to cover, decorate, support, etc., with bushes. **15** **bush it**. *Austral.* to camp out in the bush. [C13: of Gmc origin]

bush[2] (bʊʃ) *n* **1** a thin metal sleeve or tubular lining serving as a bearing. ◆ *vb* **2** to fit a bush to (a bearing, etc.). [C15: from MDu. *busse* box, bush; rel. to LL *buxis* BOX[1]]

Bush ★ (bʊʃ) *n* **George**. born 1924, US Republican politician; vice president of the US (1981–89): 41st president of the US (1989–93). In 1993 he was awarded an honorary knighthood for his role in the Gulf War (1991).

bushbaby ('bʊʃ,beɪbɪ) *n, pl* **bushbabies**. an agile nocturnal arboreal primate occurring in Africa south of the Sahara. It has large eyes and ears and a long tail. Also called: **galago**.

bushbuck ('bʊʃ,bʌk) *or* **boschbok** ('bɒʃ,bʌk) *n, pl* **bushbucks**, **bushbuck** *or* **boschboks**, **boschbok**. a small nocturnal spiral-horned antelope of the bush and tropical forest of Africa.

bush carpenter *n Austral. & NZ sl.* a rough-and-ready unskilled workman.

bushed (bʊʃt) *adj Inf.* **1** (*postpositive*) extremely tired; exhausted. **2** *Canad.* mentally disturbed from living in isolation. **3** *Austral. & NZ.* lost or bewildered, as in the bush.

bushel ('bʊʃəl) *n* **1** a British unit of dry or liquid measure equal to 8 Imperial gallons. 1 Imperial bushel is equivalent to 0.036 37 cubic metres. **2** a US unit of dry measure equal to 64 US pints. 1 US bushel is equivalent to 0.035 24 cubic metres. **3** a container with a capacity equal to either of these quantities. **4** *US inf.* a large amount. **5** **hide one's light under a bushel**. to conceal one's abilities or good qualities. [C14: from OF *boissel*]

bushfire ('bʊʃ,faɪə) *n* an uncontrolled fire in the bush; a scrub or forest fire.

bushfly ('bʊʃ,flaɪ) *n pl* **bushflies**. any of various small black dipterous flies of Australia that breed in faeces and dung.

bush house *n Chiefly Austral.* a shed or hut in the bush or a garden.

Bushido (ˌbuːʃɪˈdəʊ) *n* (*sometimes not cap.*) the feudal code of the Japanese samurai. [C19: from Japanese *bushi* warrior + *dō* way]

bushie ('buʃɪ) *n* a variant spelling of **bushy²**.

bushing ('buʃɪŋ) *n* **1** another word for **bush²**. **2** an adaptor used to connect pipes of different sizes. **3** a layer of electrical insulation enabling a live conductor to pass through an earthed wall, etc.

Bushire ★ (bju:'ʃaɪə) *n* a port in SW Iran, on the Persian Gulf. Pop.: 133 000 (1991). Persian name: **Bushehr** (bu'ʃehr).

bush jacket *or* **shirt** *n* a casual jacket or shirt having four patch pockets and a belt.

bush lawyer *n Austral. & NZ.* **1** a trailing plant with sharp hooks. **2** *Inf.* a person who gives legal opinions but is not qualified to do so.

bush line *n* an airline operating in the bush country of Canada's northern regions.

bushman ('buʃmən) *n, pl* **bushmen**. *Austral. & NZ.* a person who lives or travels in the bush, esp. one versed in bush lore.

Bushman ('buʃmən) *n, pl* **Bushmen**. a member of a hunting and gathering people of southern Africa. [C18: from Afrik. *boschjesman*]

bushmaster ('buʃ,mɑːstə) *n* a large greyish-brown highly venomous snake of tropical America.

bush pilot *n Canad.* a pilot who operates in the bush country.

bushranger ('buʃ,reɪndʒə) *n* **1** *Austral.* (formerly) an outlaw living in the bush. **2** *US.* a person who lives away from civilization.

bush tea *n* **1** a leguminous shrub of southern Africa. **2** a beverage prepared from the dried leaves of such a plant.

bush telegraph *n* a means of spreading rumour, gossip, etc.

Bushveld ★ ('buʃ,felt, -,velt) *n* **the.** an area of low altitude in NE South Africa, having scrub vegetation. Also called: **Lowveld**.

bushwhack ('buʃ,wæk) *vb* **1** (*tr*) *US, Canad., & Austral.* to ambush. **2** (*intr*) *US, Canad., & Austral.* to cut or beat one's way through thick woods. **3** (*intr*) *US, Canad., & Austral.* to range or move around in woods or the bush. **4** (*intr*) *NZ.* to work in the bush. **5** (*intr*) *US & Canad.* to fight as a guerrilla in wild regions.

bushwhacker ('buʃ,wækə) *n* **1** *US, Canad., & Austral.* a person who travels around or lives in thinly populated woodlands. **2** *Austral. sl.* an unsophisticated person. **3** *NZ.* a person who works in the bush. **4** a Confederate guerrilla in the American Civil War. **5** *US.* any guerrilla.

bushy¹ ('buʃɪ) *adj* **bushier, bushiest. 1** covered or overgrown with bushes. **2** thick and shaggy.
▸ **'bushily** *adv* ▸ **'bushiness** *n*

bushy² *or* **bushie** ('buʃɪ) *n, pl* **bushies**. *Austral. inf.* **1** a person who lives in the bush. **2** an unsophisticated uncouth person.

business ('bɪznɪs) *n* **1** a trade or profession. **2** the purchase and sale of goods and services. **3** a commercial or industrial establishment. **4** commercial activity; dealings (esp. in **do business**). **5** volume of commercial activity: *business is poor today.* **6** commercial policy: *overcharging is bad business.* **7** proper or rightful concern or responsibility (often in **mind one's own business**). **8** a special task; assignment. **9** an affair; matter. **10** serious work or activity: *get down to business.* **11** a difficult or complicated matter. **12** *Theatre.* an incidental action performed by an actor for dramatic effect. **13 mean business.** to be in earnest. [OE *bisignis* solicitude, from *bisig* BUSY + -*nis* -NESS]

business college *n* a college providing courses in secretarial studies, business management, accounting, commerce, etc.

businesslike ('bɪznɪs,laɪk) *adj* efficient and methodical.

businessman ('bɪznɪs,mæn, -mən) *or* (*fem*) **businesswoman** *n, pl* **businessmen** *or* **businesswomen**. a person engaged in commercial or industrial business, esp. as an owner or executive.

business park *n* an area specially designated and landscaped to accommodate offices, warehouses, etc.

business plan *n* a detailed plan setting out the objectives of a business, the strategy and tactics planned to achieve them, and the expected profits.

business process re-engineering *n* restructuring an organization by means of a reassessment of its core processes and predominant competencies. Abbrev.: **BPR.**

business school *n* an institution that offers courses in aspects of business, such as marketing, finance, and law, designed to train managers in industry and commerce to do their jobs effectively.

busk (bʌsk) *vb* (*intr*) *Brit.* to make money singing, playing an instrument, performing, or dancing in public places. [C20: ?from Sp. *buscar* to look for]
▸ **'busker** *n*

buskin ('bʌskɪn) *n* **1** (formerly) a sandal-like covering for the foot and leg, reaching the calf. **2** a thick-soled laced half-boot worn esp. by actors of ancient Greece. **3** (usually preceded by *the*) *Chiefly literary.* tragic drama. [C16: ?from Sp. *borzeguí*; rel. to OF *bouzequin*]

busman's holiday ('bʌsmənz) *n Inf.* a holiday spent doing the same as one does at work. [C20: from a bus driver having a driving holiday]

Busra *or* **Busrah** ★ ('bʌsrə) *n* variant spellings of **Basra**.

buss (bʌs) *n, vb* an archaic or dialect word for **kiss**. [C16: prob. imit.]

Buss ★ (bʌs) *n* **Frances Mary**. 1827–94, British educationalist.

bust¹ (bʌst) *n* **1** the chest of a human being, esp. a woman's bosom. **2** a sculpture of the head, shoulders, and upper chest of a person. [C17: from F, from It. *busto* a sculpture, from ?]

bust² (bʌst) *Inf.* ◆ *vb* **busts, busting, busted** *or* **bust. 1** to burst or break. **2** to make or become bankrupt. **3** (*tr*) (of the police) to raid, search, or arrest. **4** (*tr*) *US & Canad.* to demote, esp. in military rank. ◆ *n* **5** a raid, search, or arrest by the police. **6** *Chiefly US.* a punch. **7** *US & Canad.* a failure, esp. bankruptcy. **8** a drunken party. ◆ *adj* **9** broken. **10** bankrupt. **11 go bust.** to become bankrupt. [C19: from a dialect pronunciation of BURST]

bustard ('bʌstəd) *n* a large terrestrial bird inhabiting open regions of the Old World. It has long strong legs, a heavy body, a long neck, and speckled plumage. [C15: from OF *bistarde*, from L *avis tarda* slow bird]

bustier ('buːstɪeɪ) *n* a type of close-fitting usually strapless top worn by women.

bustle¹ ('bʌs°l) *vb* **bustles, bustling, bustled. 1** (when *intr*, often foll. by *about*) to hurry or cause to hurry with a great show of energy or activity. ◆ *n* **2** energetic and noisy activity. [C16: prob. from obs. *buskle* to make energetic preparation]
▸ **'bustling** *adj*

bustle² ('bʌs°l) *n* a cushion or framework worn by women in the late 19th century at the back in order to expand the skirt. [C18: from ?]

bust-up *Inf.* ◆ *n* **1** a quarrel, esp. a serious one ending a friendship, etc. **2** *Brit.* a disturbance or brawl. ◆ *vb* **bust up** (*adv*) **3** (*intr*) to quarrel and part. **4** (*tr*) to disrupt (a meeting), esp. violently.

busy ('bɪzɪ) *adj* **busier, busiest. 1** actively or fully engaged; occupied. **2** crowded with or characterized by activity. **3** *Chiefly US & Canad.* (of a room, telephone line, etc.) in use; engaged. **4** overcrowded with detail: *a busy painting.* **5** meddlesome; inquisitive. ◆ *vb* **busies, busying, busied. 6** (*tr*) to make or keep (someone, esp. oneself) busy. [OE *bisig*]
▸ **'busily** *adv* ▸ **'busyness** *n*

busybody ('bɪzɪ,bɒdɪ) *n, pl* **busybodies**. a meddlesome, prying, or officious person.

busy Lizzie ('lɪzɪ) *n* a flowering plant that has pink, red, or white flowers and is often grown as a pot plant.

but¹ (bʌt; *unstressed* bət) *conj* (*coordinating*) **1** contrary to expectation: *he cut his knee but didn't cry.* **2** in contrast; on the contrary: *I like opera but my husband doesn't.* **3** (*usually used after a negative*) other than: *we can't do anything but wait.* ◆ *conj* (*subordinating*) **4** (*usually used after a negative*) without it happening: *we never go out but it rains.* **5** (foll. by *that*) except that: *nothing is impossible but that we live* forever. **6** *Arch.* if not; unless. ◆ *prep* **7** except; save: *they saved all but one.* **8 but for.** were it not for: *but for you, we couldn't have managed.* ◆ *adv* **9** just; merely: *he was but a child.* **10** *Dialect & Austral.* though; however: *it's a rainy day; warm, but.* ◆ *n* **11** an objection (esp. in **ifs and buts**). [OE *būtan* without, outside, except, from *be* BY + *ūtan* OUT]

but² (bʌt) *n Scot.* the outer room of a two-roomed cottage. Cf. **ben¹.** [C18: from *but* (adv) outside; see BUT¹]

butadiene (ˌbjuːtəˈdaɪiːn) *n* a colourless flammable gas used mainly in the manufacture of synthetic rubbers. Formula: CH₂:CHCH:CH₂. Systematic name: **buta-1,3-diene.** [C20: from BUTA(NE) + DI-¹ + -ENE]

butane (ˈbjuːteɪn, bjuːˈteɪn) *n* a colourless flammable gaseous alkane used mainly in the manufacture of rubber and fuels. Formula: C₄H₁₀. [C20: from BUT(YL) + -ANE]

butanoic acid (ˌbjuːtəˈnəʊɪk) *n* a carboxylic acid that produces the smell in rancid butter. Formula: CH₃(CH₂)₂COOH. Also called: **butyric acid.** [C20: from BUTAN(E) + -OIC]

butanol (ˈbjuːtəˌnɒl) *n* a colourless substance existing in four isomeric forms. The three liquid isomers are used as solvents and in the manufacture of organic compounds. Formula: C₄H₉OH. Also called: **butyl alcohol.**

butanone (ˈbjuːtəˌnəʊn) *n* a colourless flammable liquid used as a resin solvent, and paint remover, and in lacquers, adhesives, etc. Formula: CH₃COC₂H₅.

butch (bʊtʃ) *Sl.* ◆ *adj* **1** (of a woman or man) markedly or aggressively masculine. ◆ *n* **2** a lesbian who is noticeably masculine. **3** a strong rugged man. [C18: back formation from BUTCHER]

butcher (ˈbʊtʃə) *n* **1** a retailer of meat. **2** a person who slaughters or dresses meat. **3** an indiscriminate or brutal murderer. ◆ *vb* (*tr*) **4** to slaughter or dress (animals) for meat. **5** to kill indiscriminately or brutally. **6** to make a mess of; botch. [C13: from OF *bouchier*, from *bouc* he-goat]

butcherbird (ˈbʊtʃəˌbɜːd) *n* **1** a shrike, esp. of the genus *Lanius.* **2** any of several Australian magpies that impale their prey on thorns.

butcher's-broom *n* an evergreen shrub with stiff prickle-tipped flattened green stems, formerly used for making brooms.

butchery (ˈbʊtʃərɪ) *n, pl* **butcheries. 1** the business of a butcher. **2** wanton and indiscriminate slaughter. **3** a slaughterhouse.

Bute¹ ★ (bjuːt) *n* an island off the coast of SW Scotland, in the Firth of Clyde, separated from the Cowal peninsula by the **Kyles of Bute.** Chief town: Rothesay. Pop.: 8000 (latest est.). Area: 121 sq. km (47 sq. miles).

Bute² ★ (bjuːt) *n* **John Stuart,** 3rd Earl of Bute. 1713–92, British Tory statesman; prime minister (1762–63).

Butenandt ★ (*German* ˈbuːtənant) *n* **Adolf Johann** (ˈaːdɔlf). 1903–95, German organic chemist. He shared the Nobel prize for chemistry (1939) for his work on hormones.

Buteshire ★ (ˈbjuːtˌʃɪə, -ʃə) *n* (until 1975) a county of SW Scotland, now part of Argyll and Bute council area.

Buthelezi ★ (ˌbuːtəˈleɪzɪ) *n* **Mangosouthu Gatsha** (ˌmæŋɡəʊˈsuːtuː ˈɡætʃə), known as *Chief Buthelezi.* born 1928, Zulu leader; founder of the Inkatha movement.

butler (ˈbʌtlə) *n* the male servant of a household in charge of the wines, table, etc.: usually the head servant. [C13: from OF, from *bouteille* BOTTLE]

Butler ★ (ˈbʌtlə) *n* **1 Joseph.** 1692–1752, English theologian and author. **2 Josephine (Elizabeth).** 1828–1906, British social reformer. **3 Reg,** full name *Reginald Cotterell Butler.* 1913–81, British metal sculptor. **4 R(ichard) A(usten),** Baron Butler of Saffron Walden, known as *Rab Butler.* 1902–82, British Conservative politician: Chancellor of the Exchequer (1951–55); Home Secretary (1957–62); Foreign Secretary (1963–64). **5 Samuel.** 1612–80, English poet; author of *Hudibras* (1663–78). **6 Samuel.** 1835–1902, British novelist, noted for *Erewhon* (1872) and *The Way of All Flesh* (1903).

butlery (ˈbʌtlərɪ) *n, pl* **butleries. 1** a butler's room. **2** another name for **buttery².**

butt¹ (bʌt) *n* **1** the thicker or blunt end of something, such as the end of the stock of a rifle. **2** the unused end of something, esp. of a cigarette; stub. **3** *Inf., chiefly US &*

Canad. the buttocks. **4** *US.* a slang word for **cigarette. 5** *Building.* short for **butt joint.** [C15 (in the sense: thick end of something, buttock): rel. to OE *buttuc* end, ridge]

butt² (bʌt) *n* **1** a person or thing that is the target of ridicule, wit, etc. **2** *Shooting, archery.* **2a** a mound of earth behind the target that stops bullets or wide shots. **2b** the target itself. **2c** (*pl*) the target range. **3** a low barrier behind which sportsmen shoot game birds, esp. grouse. ◆ *vb* **4** (usually foll. by *on* or *against*) to lie or be placed end on to; abut. [C14 (in the sense: mark for archery practice): from OF *but*]

butt³ (bʌt) *vb* **1** to strike or push (something) with the head or horns. **2** (*intr*) to project; jut. **3** (*intr*; foll. by *in* or *into*) to intrude, esp. into a conversation; interfere. ◆ *n* **4** a blow with the head or horns. [C12: from OF *boter*, of Gmc origin]

butt⁴ (bʌt) *n* a large cask for storing wine or beer. [C14: from OF *botte*, from LL *buttis* cask]

butte (bjuːt) *n US & Canad.* an isolated steep flat-topped hill. [C19: F, from OF *bute* mound behind a target; see BUTT²]

butter (ˈbʌtə) *n* **1** an edible fatty whitish-yellow solid made from cream by churning. **2** any substance with a butter-like consistency, such as peanut butter. **3 look as if butter wouldn't melt in one's mouth.** to look innocent, although probably not so. ◆ *vb* (*tr*) **4** to put butter on or in. **5** to flatter. ◆ *See also* **butter up.** [OE *butere*, from L, from Gk *bouturon*, from *bous* cow + *turos* cheese]

butter bean *n* a variety of lima bean that has large pale flat edible seeds.

butterbur (ˈbʌtəˌbɜː) *n* a plant of the composite family with fragrant whitish or purple flowers, and large leaves formerly used to wrap butter.

buttercup (ˈbʌtəˌkʌp) *n* any of various yellow-flowered plants of the genus *Ranunculus* of Europe, Asia, and North America.

butterfat (ˈbʌtəˌfæt) *n* the fatty substance of milk from which butter is made, consisting of a mixture of glycerides.

Butterfield ★ (ˈbʌtəˌfiːld) *n* **William.** 1814–1900, British architect of the Gothic Revival: his buildings include Keble College, Oxford (1870).

butterfingers (ˈbʌtəˌfɪŋɡəz) *n* (*functioning as sing*) *Inf.* a person who drops things inadvertently or fails to catch things.
► ˈbutterˌfingered *adj*

butterfish (ˈbʌtəˌfɪʃ) *n, pl* **butterfish** *or* **butterfishes.** any of several species of fishes having a slippery skin.

butterflies (ˈbʌtəˌflaɪz) *pl n Inf.* tremors in the stomach region due to nervousness.

butterfly (ˈbʌtəˌflaɪ) *n, pl* **butterflies. 1** any diurnal insect that has a slender body with clubbed antennae and typically rests with the wings (often brightly coloured) closed over the back. **2** a person who never settles with one interest or occupation for long. **3** a swimming stroke in which the arms are plunged forward together in large circular movements. **4** *Commerce.* the simultaneous purchase and sale of traded call options, at different exercise prices or with different expiry dates, on a stock exchange or commodity market. [OE *buttorflēoge*]

butterfly collar *n* the Irish name for **wing collar.**

butterfly effect *n* the idea, used in chaos theory, that a very small difference in the initial state of a physical system can make a substantial difference to the state at some later time. [C20: from the theory that a butterfly flapping its wings in one part of the world might ultimately cause a hurricane in another part of the world]

butterfly nut *n* another name for **wing nut.**

Buttermere ★ (ˈbʌtəˌmɪə) *n* a lake in NW England, in Cumbria, in the Lake District, southwest of Keswick. Length: 2 km (1.25 miles).

buttermilk (ˈbʌtəˌmɪlk) *n* the sourish liquid remaining after the butter has been separated from milk.

butter muslin *n* a fine loosely woven cotton material originally used for wrapping butter.

butternut (ˈbʌtəˌnʌt) *n* **1** *Austral. & NZ.* a type of small edible pumpkin. **2a** a walnut tree of North America. **2b** its oily edible nut.

butterscotch ('bʌtə,skɒtʃ) *n* **1** a kind of hard brittle toffee made with butter, brown sugar, etc. **2** a flavouring made from these ingredients. [C19: ? first made in Scotland]

butter up *vb* (*tr, adv*) to flatter.

butterwort ('bʌtə,wɜːt) *n* a plant that grows in wet places and has violet-blue spurred flowers and fleshy greasy glandular leaves on which insects are trapped and digested.

Butterworth ★ ('bʌtəwəθ) *n* George. 1885–1916, British composer, noted for his settings of Housman's poems.

buttery[1] ('bʌtəri) *adj* containing, like, or coated with butter.
▶ '**butteriness** *n*

buttery[2] ('bʌtəri) *n, pl* **butteries**. **1** a room for storing foods or wines. **2** *Brit.* (in some universities) a room in which food and drink are supplied or sold to students. [C14: from Anglo-F *boterie*, prob. from L *butta* cask, BUTT[4]]

butt joint *n* a joint between two plates, planks, etc., fastened end to end without overlapping or interlocking. Sometimes shortened to **butt.**

buttock ('bʌtək) *n* **1** either of the two large fleshy masses of thick muscular tissue that form the human rump. See also **gluteus.** Related adj: **gluteal. 2** the analogous part in some mammals. [C13: ?from OE *buttuc* round slope]

button ('bʌt³n) *n* **1** a disc or knob of plastic, wood, etc., attached to a garment, etc., usually for fastening two surfaces together by passing it through a buttonhole or loop. **2** a small round object, such as any of various sweets, decorations, or badges. **3** a small disc that completes an electric circuit when pushed, as one that operates a machine. **4** *Biol.* any rounded knoblike part or organ, such as an unripe mushroom. **5** *Fencing.* the protective knob fixed to the point of a foil. **6** *Brit.* an object of no value (esp. in **not worth a button**). ◆ *vb* **7** to fasten with a button or buttons. **8** (*tr*) to provide with buttons. [C14: from OF *boton*, from *boter* to thrust, butt; see BUTT[3]]
▶ '**buttoner** *n* ▶ '**buttonless** *adj*

buttonhole ('bʌt³n,həʊl) *n* **1** a slit in a garment, etc., through which a button is passed to fasten two surfaces together. **2** a flower or small bunch of flowers worn pinned to the lapel or in the buttonhole, esp. at weddings. US name: **boutonniere.** ◆ *vb* **buttonholes, buttonholing, buttonholed.** (*tr*) **3** to detain (a person) in conversation. **4** to make buttonholes in.

buttonhook ('bʌt³n,hʊk) *n* a thin tapering hooked instrument formerly used for pulling buttons through the buttonholes of shoes.

button up *vb* (*tr, adv*) **1** to fasten (a garment) with a button or buttons. **2** *Inf.* to conclude (business) satisfactorily. **3 button up one's lip** *or* **mouth.** *Sl.* to be silent.

buttress ('bʌtrɪs) *n* **1** Also called: **pier.** a construction, usually of brick or stone, built to support a wall. **2** any support or prop. **3** something shaped like a buttress, such as a projection from a mountainside. ◆ *vb* (*tr*) **4** to support (a wall) with a buttress. **5** to support or sustain. [C13: from OF *bouterez*, from *bouter* to thrust, BUTT[3]]

butty[1] ('bʌtɪ) *n, pl* **butties.** *Chiefly N English dialect.* a sandwich: *a jam butty.* [C19: from *buttered* (bread)]

butty[2] ('bʌtɪ) *n, pl* **butties.** *English dialect.* (esp. in mining parlance) a friend or workmate. [C19: ?from obs. *booty* sharing, from BOOT[2]]

Butung ★ ('buːtʊŋ) *n* an island of Indonesia, southeast of Sulawesi: hilly and forested. Chief town: Baubau. Pop.: 317 124 (1980). Area: 4555 sq. km (1759 sq. miles).

butyl ('bjuː,taɪl, -tɪl) *n* (*modifier*) of or containing any of four isomeric forms of the group C_4H_9–: *butyl rubber.* [C19: from BUT(YRIC ACID) + -YL]

butyl alcohol *n* another name for **butanol.**

butyl rubber *n* a copolymer of isobutene and isoprene, used in tyres and as a waterproofing material.

butyric acid (bjuː'tɪrɪk) *n* another name for **butanoic acid.** [C19 *butyric,* from L *būtyrum* BUTTER]

buxom ('bʌksəm) *adj* **1** (esp. of a woman) healthily plump, attractive, and vigorous. **2** (of a woman) full-bosomed. [C12: *buhsum* compliant, pliant, from OE *būgan* to bend, BOW[1]]
▶ '**buxomness** *n*

Buxtehude ★ (*German* bʊkstə'huːdə) *n* Dietrich ('diːtrɪç). 1637–1707, Danish composer, in Germany from 1668.

Buxton ★ ('bʌkstən) *n* a town in N England, in NW Derbyshire in the Peak District: thermal springs. Pop.: 19 854 (1991).

buy (baɪ) *vb* **buys, buying, bought.** (*mainly tr*) **1** to acquire by paying or promising to pay a sum of money; purchase. **2** to be capable of purchasing: *money can't buy love.* **3** to acquire by any exchange or sacrifice: *to buy time by equivocation.* **4** to bribe or corrupt; hire by or as by bribery. **5** *Sl.* to accept as true, practical, etc. **6** (*intr;* foll. by *into*) to purchase shares of (a company). ◆ *n* **7** a purchase (often in **good** or **bad buy**). ◆ See also **buy in, buy into,** etc. [OE *bycgan*]

> **USAGE NOTE** The use of *off* after *buy* as in *I bought this off my neighbour* was formerly considered incorrect, but is now acceptable in informal contexts.

buy-back *n Commerce.* the repurchase by a company of some or all of its shares from an investor, who acquired them by putting venture capital into the company when it was formed.

buyer ('baɪə) *n* **1** a person who buys; customer. **2** a person employed to buy merchandise, materials, etc., as for a shop or factory.

buy in *vb* (*adv*) **1** (*tr*) to buy back for the owner (an item in an auction) at or below the reserve price. **2** (*intr*) to purchase shares in a company. **3** (*tr*) Also: **buy into.** *US inf.* to pay money to secure a position or place for (someone, esp. oneself) in some organization, esp. a business or club. **4** to purchase (goods, etc.) in large quantities. ◆ *n* **buy-in. 5** the purchase of a company by a manager or group who does not work for that company.

buy into *vb* (*intr, prep*) **1** to agree with or accept as valid (an argument, theory, etc.). **2** *Austral. & NZ inf.* to get involved in (an argument, fight, etc.).

buy off *vb* (*tr, adv*) to pay (a person or group) to drop a charge, end opposition, etc.

buy out *vb* (*tr, adv*) **1** to purchase the ownership, controlling interest, shares, etc., of (a company, etc.). **2** to gain the release of (a person) from the armed forces by payment. **3** to pay (a person) to give up ownership of (property, etc.). ◆ *n* **buy-out. 4** the purchase of a company, esp. by its former management or staff. See also **leveraged buyout, management buyout.**

buy up *vb* (*tr, adv*) **1** to purchase all, or all that is available, of (something). **2** to purchase a controlling interest in (a company, etc.).

buzz (bʌz) *n* **1** a rapidly vibrating humming sound, as of a bee. **2** a low sound, as of many voices in conversation. **3** a rumour; report; gossip. **4** *Inf.* a telephone call. **5** *Inf.* **5a** a pleasant sensation. **5b** a sense of excitement; kick. **6** (*modifier*) fashionable, trendy. ◆ *vb* **7** (*intr*) to make a vibrating sound like that of a prolonged *z.* **8** (*intr*) to talk or gossip with an air of excitement: *the town buzzed with the news.* **9** (*tr*) to utter or spread (a rumour). **10** (*intr;* often foll. by *about*) to move around quickly and busily. **11** (*tr*) to signal or summon with a buzzer. **12** (*tr*) *Inf.* to call by telephone. **13** (*tr*) *Inf.* to fly an aircraft very low over (an object). **14** (*tr*) (esp. of insects) to make a buzzing sound with (wings, etc.). [C16: imit.]

buzzard ('bʌzəd) *n* a diurnal bird of prey of the hawk family, typically having broad wings and tail and a soaring flight. [C13: from OF *buisard,* from L *būteō* hawk]

buzzer ('bʌzə) *n* **1** a device that produces a buzzing sound, esp. one similar to an electric bell. **2** *NZ.* a woodplaning machine.

buzz off *vb* (*intr, adv; often imperative*) *Inf., chiefly Brit.* to go away; leave; depart.

buzz word *n Inf.* a word, originally from a particular jargon, which becomes a popular vogue word. [C20: from ?]

★ people and places

BVM *abbrev. for* Beata Virgo Maria. [L: Blessed Virgin Mary]

bwana ('bwɑːnə) *n* (in E Africa) a master, often used as a form of address corresponding to *sir*. [Swahili, from Ar. *abūna* our father]

by (baɪ) *prep* **1** used to indicate the agent after a passive verb: *seeds eaten by the birds*. **2** used to indicate the person responsible for a creative work: *this song is by Schubert*. **3** via; through: *enter by the back door*. **4** foll. by a gerund to indicate a means used: *he frightened her by hiding behind the door*. **5** beside; next to; near: *a tree by the house*. **6** passing the position of; past: *he drove by the old cottage*. **7** not later than; before: *return the books by Tuesday*. **8** used to indicate extent, after a comparative: *it is hotter by five degrees*. **9** (esp. in oaths) invoking the name of: *I swear by all the gods*. **10** multiplied by: *four by three equals twelve*. **11** during the passing of (esp. in **by day, by night**). **12** placed between measurements of the various dimensions of something: *a pane four inches by seven*. ♦ *adv* **13** near: *the house is close by*. **14** away; aside: *he put some money by each week*. **15** passing a point near something; past: *he drove by*. ♦ *n, pl* **byes. 16** a variant spelling of **bye**[1]. [OE *bī*]

by- *or* **bye-** *prefix* **1** near: *bystander*. **2** secondary or incidental: *by-election; by-product*. [from BY]

by and by *adv* presently or eventually.

by and large *adv* in general; on the whole. [C17: orig. nautical: to the wind and off it]

Byatt ★ ('baɪət) *n* **A(ntonia) S(usan)**. born 1936, British writer. Her novels include *The Virgin in the Garden* (1978) and *Possession* (1990).

Bydgoszcz ★ (*Polish* 'bidgɔʃtʃ) *n* an industrial city and port in N Poland: under Prussian rule from 1772 to 1919. Pop.: 385 700 (1995 est.). German name: **Bromberg**.

bye[1] (baɪ) *n* **1** *Sport.* the situation in which a player or team wins a preliminary round by virtue of having no opponent. **2** *Golf.* one or more holes that are left unplayed after the match has been decided. **3** *Cricket.* a run scored off a ball not struck by the batsman. **4** something incidental or secondary. **5 by the bye**. incidentally; by the way. [C16: var. of BY]

bye[2] *or* **bye-bye** *sentence substitute. Brit. inf.* goodbye.

bye-byes *n* (*functioning as sing*) an informal word for **sleep**, used esp. to children (as in **go to bye-byes**).

by-election *or* **bye-election** *n* (in Great Britain and other countries of the Commonwealth) an election held during the life of a parliament to fill a vacant seat.

Byelgorod-Dnestrovski ★ (*Russian* 'bjɛlɡərət-dnjɪr'strɔfskij) *n* a variant spelling of **Belgorod-Dnestrovski**.

Byelorussia ★ (ˌbjɛləʊ'rʌʃə) *n* a variant spelling of **Belarus**.

▸ **Byelorussian** (ˌbjɛləʊ'rʌʃən) *adj, n*

Byelostok ★ (bjɪlə'stɔk) *n* a Russian name for **Białystok**.

Byelovo *or* **Belovo** ★ (*Russian* 'bjɛləvə) *n* a city in W central Russia. Pop.: 118 000 (1989).

bygone ('baɪˌɡɒn) *adj* **1** (*usually prenominal*) past; former. ♦ *n* **2** (*often pl*) a past occurrence. **3** an artefact, implement, etc., of former domestic or industrial use. **4 let bygones be bygones**. to agree to forget past quarrels.

bylaw *or* **bye-law** ('baɪˌlɔː) *n* **1** a rule made by a local authority. **2** a regulation of a company, society, etc. [C13: prob. of Scand. origin; cf. ON *bȳr* dwelling, town]

by-line *n* **1** a line under the title of a newspaper or magazine article giving the author's name. **2** another word for **touchline**.

Byng ★ (bɪŋ) *n* **1 George**, Viscount Torrington. 1663–1733, British admiral: defeated fleet of James Edward Stuart, the Old Pretender, off Scotland (1708); defeated Spanish fleet off Messina (1717). **2** his son **John**. 1704–57, British admiral: executed after failing to relieve Minorca. **3 Julian Hedworth George**, 1st Viscount Byng of Vimy. 1862–1935, British general in World War I; governor general of Canada (1921–26).

BYO(G) *n Austral. & NZ.* an unlicensed restaurant at which diners may drink their own wine, etc. [C20: from *bring your own* (*grog*)]

bypass ('baɪˌpɑːs) *n* **1** a main road built to avoid a city or other congested area. **2** a means of redirecting the flow of a substance around an appliance through which it would otherwise pass. **3** *Surgery.* **3a** the redirection of blood flow, either to avoid a diseased blood vessel or in order to perform heart surgery. See **coronary bypass. 3b** (*as modifier*): *bypass surgery*. **4** *Electronics.* an electrical circuit connected in parallel around one or more components, providing an alternative path for certain frequencies. ♦ *vb* (*tr*) **5** to go around or avoid (a city, obstruction, problem, etc.). **6** to cause (traffic, fluid, etc.) to go through a bypass. **7** to proceed without reference to (regulations, a superior, etc.); get round; avoid.

bypass engine *n* a gas turbine in which part of the compressor delivery bypasses the combustion zone, flowing directly into or around the exhaust to provide additional thrust.

bypath ('baɪˌpɑːθ) *n* a little-used path or track.

by-play *n* secondary action or talking carried on apart while the main action proceeds, esp. in a play.

by-product *n* **1** a secondary or incidental product of a manufacturing process. **2** a side effect.

Byrd ★ (bɜːd) *n* **1 Richard Evelyn**. 1888–1957, US rear admiral, aviator, and polar explorer. **2 William**. 1543–1623, English composer and organist.

Byrd Land ★ *n* a part of Antarctica, east of the Ross Ice Shelf and the Ross Sea: claimed for the US by Richard E. Byrd in 1929. Former name: **Marie Byrd Land**.

byre ('baɪə) *n Brit.* a shelter for cows. [OE *bȳre*; rel. to *būr* hut, cottage]

byroad ('baɪˌrəʊd) *n* a secondary or side road.

Byron ★ ('baɪərən) *n* **George Gordon**, 6th Baron. 1788–1824, British poet. His major works include *Childe Harold's Pilgrimage* (1812–18), and *Don Juan* (1819–24).

▸ **Byronic** (baɪ'rɒnɪk) *adj* ▸ **By'ronically** *adv* ▸ '**Byron,ism** *n*

byssinosis (ˌbɪsɪ'nəʊsɪs) *n* a lung disease caused by prolonged inhalation of fibre dust. [C19: from NL, from Gk *bussinos* of linen + -OSIS]

bystander ('baɪˌstændə) *n* a person present but not involved; onlooker; spectator.

byte (baɪt) *n Computing.* **1** a group of bits processed as one unit of data. **2** the storage space allocated to such a group of bits. **3** a subdivision of a word. [C20: prob. a blend of BIT[4] + BITE]

Bytom ★ (*Polish* 'bitɔm) *n* an industrial city in SW Poland, in Upper Silesia: under Prussian and German rule from 1742 to 1945. Pop.: 228 200 (1995 est.). German name: **Beuthen**.

byway ('baɪˌweɪ) *n* **1** a secondary or side road, esp. in the country. **2** an area, field of study, etc., that is very obscure or of secondary importance.

byword ('baɪˌwɜːd) *n* **1** a person or thing regarded as a perfect or proverbial example of something: *their name is a byword for good service*. **2** an object of scorn or derision. **3** a common saying; proverb. [OE *bīwyrde*; see BY, WORD]

Byzantine (bɪ'zæn,taɪn, -,tiːn, baɪ-; 'bɪzən,tiːn, -,taɪn) *adj* **1** of, characteristic of, or relating to Byzantium or the Byzantine Empire. **2** of, relating to, or characterizing the Orthodox Church or its rites and liturgy. **3** of or relating to the highly coloured stylized form of religious art developed in the Byzantine Empire. **4** of or relating to the style of architecture developed in the Byzantine Empire, characterized by massive domes with square bases, rounded arches, spires and minarets, and the extensive use of mosaics. **5** denoting the Medieval Greek spoken in the Byzantine Empire. **6** (of attitudes, etc.) inflexible or complicated. ♦ *n* **7** an inhabitant of Byzantium.

▸ **Byzantinism** (bɪ'zæntaɪ,nɪzəm, -tiː,; baɪ-; 'bɪzənti-,nɪzəm, -taɪ-) *n*

Byzantine Empire ★ *n* the continuation of the Roman Empire in the East, esp. after the deposition of the last emperor in Rome (476 A.D.). It was finally extinguished by the fall of Constantinople, its capital, in 1453.

Byzantium ★ (bɪ'zæntɪəm, baɪ-) *n* an ancient Greek city on the Bosphorus: founded about 660 B.C.; rebuilt by Constantine I in 330 A.D. and called Constantinople; present-day Istanbul.

Bz *or* **bz.** *abbrev. for* benzene.

★ people and places

Cc

c or **C** (siː) *n, pl* **c's, C's,** or **Cs. 1** the third letter of the English alphabet. **2** a speech sound represented by this letter, usually either as in *cigar* or as in *case*. **3** the third in a series, esp. the third highest grade in an examination. **4** something shaped like a C.

c *symbol for:* **1** centi-. **2** *Maths.* constant. **3** cubic. **4** cycle. **5** specific heat capacity. **6** the speed of light and other types of electromagnetic radiation in free space.

C *symbol for:* **1** *Music.* **1a** the first degree of a major scale containing no sharps or flats (**C major**). **1b** the major or minor key having this note as its tonic. **1c** a time signature denoting four crotchet beats to the bar. See also **alla breve** (sense 2), **common time. 2** *Chem.* carbon. **3** *Biochem.* cytosine. **4** capacitance. **5** heat capacity. **6** cold (water). **7** *Physics.* compliance. **8** Celsius. **9** centigrade. **10** century: C20. **11** coulomb. **12** *the Roman numeral for* 100. ◆ *n* **13** a type of high-level computer programming language.

c. *abbrev. for:* **1** carat. **2** carbon (paper). **3** *Cricket.* caught. **4** cent(s). **5** century *or* centuries. **6** (*pl* **cc.**) chapter. **7** (used esp. preceding a date) circa: *c. 1800*. [L: about] **8** colt. **9** contralto. **10** copyright. **11** coulomb.

C. *abbrev. for:* **1** (on maps as part of name) Cape. **2** Catholic. **3** Celtic. **4** Conservative. **5** Corps.

c/- (in Australia) *abbrev. for* care for.

C1 ('siː'wʌn) *n* **a** a person whose job is supervisory or clerical, or who works in junior management. **b** (*as adj*): *a C1 worker.* ◆ See also **occupation groupings.**

C2 ('siː'tuː) *n* **a** a skilled manual worker, or a manual worker with responsibility for other people. **b** (*as adj*): *a C2 worker.* ◆ See also **occupation groupings.**

Ca *the chemical symbol for* calcium.

CA *abbrev. for:* **1** California. **2** Central America. **3** chartered accountant. **4** Civil Aviation. **5** (in Britain) Consumers' Association.

ca. *abbrev. for* circa. [L: about]

CAA (in Britain) *abbrev. for* Civil Aviation Authority.

Caaba ('kɑːbə) *n* a variant spelling of **Kaaba.**

cab (kæb) *n* **1a** a taxi. **1b** (*as modifier*): *a cab rank.* **2** the enclosed compartment of a lorry, crane, etc., from which it is driven. **3** (formerly) a horse-drawn vehicle used for public hire. [C19: from CABRIOLET]

cabal (kə'bæl) *n* **1** a small group of intriguers, esp. one formed for political purposes. **2** a secret plot; conspiracy. **3** a clique. ◆ *vb* **cabals, caballing, caballed. 4** (*intr*) to form a cabal; plot. [C17: from F *cabale*, from Med. L *cabala*]

cabala (kə'bɑːlə) *n* a variant spelling of **cabbala.**

Caballé ★ (*Spanish* kaβa'ʎe) *n* **Montserrat** (monser'rat). born 1933, Spanish operatic soprano.

caballero (,kæbə'ljeərəʊ) *n, pl* **caballeros** (-rəuz). a Spanish gentleman. [C19: from Sp.: gentleman, from LL *caballārius* rider, from *caballus* horse]

cabana (kə'bɑːnə) *n Chiefly US.* a tent used as a dressing room by the sea. [from Sp. *cabaña*: CABIN]

cabaret ('kæbə,rei) *n* **1** a floor show of dancing, singing, etc., at a nightclub or restaurant. **2** *Chiefly US.* a nightclub or restaurant providing such entertainment. [C17: from Norman F: tavern, prob. from LL *camera* an arched roof]

cabbage ('kæbɪdʒ) *n* **1** Also called: **cole.** any of various cultivated varieties of a plant of the genus *Brassica* having a short thick stalk and a large head of green or reddish edible leaves. See also **brassica. 2a** the head of a cabbage. **2b** the edible leaf bud of the cabbage palm. **3** *Inf.* a dull or unimaginative person. **4** *Inf.* a person who has no mental faculties and is dependent on others. [C14: from Norman F *caboche* head]

cabbage palm *n* **1** a West Indian palm whose leaf buds are eaten like cabbage. **2** a similar Brazilian palm.

cabbage rose *n* a rose with a round compact full-petalled head.

cabbage tree *n* **1** a tall palmlike ornamental New Zealand tree. **2** a tall palm tree of Eastern Australia.

cabbage white *n* a large white butterfly, the larvae of which feed on the leaves of cabbages and related vegetables.

cabbala, cabala, kabbala, or **kabala** (kə'bɑːlə) *n* **1** an ancient Jewish mystical tradition. **2** any secret or occult doctrine. [C16: from Med. L, from Heb. *qabbālāh* tradition, from *qābal* to receive]
▸ **cabbalism, cabalism, kabbalism,** or **kabalism** ('kæbə,lɪzəm) *n* ▸ **'cabbalist, 'cabalist, 'kabbalist,** or **'kabalist** *n* ▸ ,cabba'listic, ,caba'listic, ,kabba'listic, or ,kaba'listic *adj*

cabbie or **cabby** ('kæbɪ) *n, pl* **cabbies.** *Inf.* a cab driver.

caber ('keɪbə) *n Scot.* a heavy section of trimmed tree trunk thrown in competition at Highland games (**tossing the caber**). [C16: from Gaelic *cabar* pole]

Cabernet Sauvignon ('kæbəneɪ 'səʊvɪnjɒn; *French* kabɛrnɛ soviɲɔ̃) *n* (*sometimes not caps.*) **1** a black grape grown in the Bordeaux area of France, Australia, California, Bulgaria, and elsewhere, used for making wine. **2** any of various red wines made from this grape. [F]

cabin ('kæbɪn) *n* **1** a small simple dwelling; hut. **2** a simple house providing accommodation for travellers or holiday-makers. **3** a room used as an office or living quarters in a ship. **4** a covered compartment used for shelter in a small boat. **5** *Brit.* another name for **signal box. 6a** the enclosed part of a light aircraft in which the pilot and passengers sit. **6b** the part of an aircraft for passengers or cargo. ◆ *vb* **7** (*tr*) to confine in a small space. [C14: from OF *cabane*, from OProvençal *cabana*, from LL *capanna* hut]

cabin boy *n* a boy who waits on the officers and passengers of a ship.

cabin cruiser *n* a power boat fitted with a cabin for pleasure cruising or racing.

Cabinda ★ (kə'biːndə) *n* an exclave of Angola, separated from the rest of the country by part of the Democratic Republic of the Congo (formerly Zaïre). Pop.: 174 000 (1993 est.). Area: 7270 sq. km (2807 sq. miles).

cabinet ('kæbɪnɪt) *n* **1** a piece of furniture containing shelves, cupboards, or drawers for storage or display. **2** the outer case of a television, radio, etc. **3a** (*often cap.*) the executive and policy-making body of a country, consisting of senior government ministers. **3b** (*sometimes cap.*) an advisory council to a president, governor, etc. **3c** (*as modifier*): *a cabinet reshuffle.* **4a** a standard size of paper, 6 × 4 inches (15 × 10 cm), for mounted photographs. **4b** (*as modifier*): *a cabinet photograph.* **5** *Arch.* a private room. [C16: from OF, dim. of *cabine*, from ?]

cabinet-maker *n* a craftsman specializing in making fine furniture.
▸ **'cabinet-,making** *n*

cabinetwork ('kæbɪnɪt,wɜːk) *n* **1** the making of furniture, esp. of fine quality. **2** an article made by a cabinet-maker.

cabin fever *n Canad.* acute depression resulting from being isolated or sharing cramped quarters in the wilderness.

cable ('keɪb°l) *n* **1** a strong thick rope, usually of twisted hemp or steel wire. **2** *Naut.* an anchor chain or rope. **3a** a unit of distance in navigation, equal to one tenth of a sea mile (about 600 ft). **3b** Also called: **cable length, cable's length.** a unit of length in nautical use that has various values, including 100 fathoms (600 ft). **4** a wire or bundle of wires that conducts electricity (see also *a submarine cable.* **5** Also called: **cablegram.** a telegram sent abroad by submarine cable, telephone line, etc. **6** Also called: **cable**

stitch. a knitting pattern resembling a twisted rope. ◆ vb **cables, cabling, cabled. 7** to send (a message) to (someone) by cable. **8** (tr) to fasten or provide with a cable or cables. **9** (tr) to supply (a place) with cable television. [C13: from OF, from LL *capulum* halter]

cable car n **1** a cabin suspended from and moved by an overhead cable in a mountain area. **P6.6D2** the passenger car on a **cable railway**, drawn along by a strong cable operated by a motor.

cable television n a television service in which the subscriber's television is connected to the supplier by cable, enabling a much greater choice of channels to be provided.

cabochon ('kæbə,ʃɒn) n a smooth domed gem, polished but unfaceted. [C16: from OF, from *caboche* head]

caboodle (kə'buːdᵊl) n Inf. a lot, bunch, or group (esp. in **the whole caboodle**). [C19: prob. contraction of KIT¹ & BOODLE]

caboose (kə'buːs) n **1** US inf. short for **calaboose. 2** Railways. US & Canad. a guard's van. **3a** a deckhouse for a galley aboard ship. **3b** Chiefly Brit. the galley itself. **4** Canad. **4a** a mobile bunkhouse used by lumbermen, etc. **4b** an insulated cabin on runners, equipped with a stove. [C18: from Du. *cabûse*, from ?]

Cabot ★ ('kæbət) n **1 John**, Italian name *Giovanni Caboto*. 1450–98, Italian explorer, who landed in North America in 1497, under patent from Henry VII of England. **2** his son, **Sebastian**. ?1476–1557, Italian navigator and cartographer who served the English and Spanish crowns: explored Brazil (1526–30).

cabotage ('kæbə,tɑːʒ) n **1** Naut. coastal navigation or shipping. **2** reservation to a country's carriers of its internal traffic, esp. air traffic. [C19: from F, from *caboter* to sail near the coast, apparently from Sp. *cabo* CAPE²]

Cabral ★ (Portuguese kə'bral) n **Pedro Álvarez** ('pɛːdru 'alvərəʒ). ?1460–?1526, Portuguese navigator: took possession of Brazil for Portugal in 1500.

cabriole ('kæbrɪ,əʊl) n a type of curved furniture leg, popular in the first half of the 18th century. Also called: **cabriole leg**. [C18: from F, from *cabrioler* to caper; from its being based on the leg of a capering animal]

cabriolet (,kæbrɪəʊ'leɪ) n **1** a small two-wheeled horse-drawn carriage with two seats and a folding hood. **2** a type of motorcar with a folding top. [C18: from F, lit.: a little skip, from L, from *caper* goat; referring to the lightness of movement]

cacao (kə'kɑːəʊ, -'keɪəʊ) n **1** a small tropical American evergreen tree having reddish-brown seed pods from which cocoa and chocolate are prepared. **2 cacao bean**. the seed pod; cocoa bean. **3 cacao butter**. another name for **cocoa butter**. [C16: from Sp., from Nahuatl *cacauatl* cacao beans]

cachalot ('kæʃə,lɒt) n another name for **sperm whale**. [C18: from F, from Port. *cachalote*, from ?]

cache (kæʃ) n **1** a hidden store of provisions, weapons, treasure, etc. **2** the place where such a store is hidden. **3** Computing. a small high-speed memory that improves computer performance. ◆ vb **caches, caching, cached. 4** (tr) to store in a cache. [C19: from F, from *cacher* to hide]

cachepot ('kæʃ,pɒt, kæʃ'pəʊ) n an ornamental container for a flowerpot. [F: pot-hider]

cachet ('kæʃeɪ) n **1** an official seal on a document, letter, etc. **2** a distinguishing mark. **3** prestige; distinction. **4** Philately. a mark stamped by hand on mail for commemorative purposes. **5** a hollow wafer, formerly used for enclosing an unpleasant-tasting medicine. [C17: from OF, from *cacher* to hide]

cachexia (kə'kɛksɪə) or **cachexy** n a weakened condition of body or mind resulting from any debilitating disease. [C16: from LL, from Gk, from *kakos* bad + *hexis* condition]

cachinnate ('kækɪ,neɪt) vb **cachinnates, cachinnating, cachinnated**. (intr) to laugh loudly. [C19: from L *cacchinâre*, prob. imit.]
▸ ,cachin'nation n ▸ ,cachin'natory adj

cachou ('kæʃuː, kæ'ʃuː) n **1** a lozenge eaten to sweeten the breath. **2** another name for **catechu**. [C18: via F from Port., from Malay *kâchu*]

cacique (kə'siːk) or **cazique** (kə'ziːk) n **1** an American Indian chief in a Spanish-speaking region. **2** (esp. in Spanish America) a local political boss. [C16: from Sp., of Amerind origin]

cack-handed (,kæk'hændɪd) adj Inf. **1** left-handed. **2** clumsy. [from dialect *cack* excrement]

cackle ('kækᵊl) vb **cackles, cackling, cackled. 1** (intr) (esp. of a hen) to squawk with shrill broken notes. **2** (intr) to laugh or chatter raucously. **3** (tr) to utter in a cackling manner. ◆ n **4** the noise or act of cackling. **5** noisy chatter. **6 cut the cackle**. Inf. to be quiet. [C13: prob. from MLow G *kâkelen*, imit.]

caco- combining form. bad, unpleasant, or incorrect: *cacophony*. [from Gk *kakos* bad]

cacodyl ('kækə,daɪl) n an oily poisonous liquid with a strong garlic smell; tetramethyldiarsine. [C19: from Gk, from *kakos* CACO- + *ozein* to smell + -YL]

cacoethes (,kækəʊ'iːθiːz) n an uncontrollable urge or desire: *a cacoethes for smoking*. [C16: from L *cacoēthes* malignant disease, from Gk, from *kakos* CACO- + *ēthos* character]

cacography (kæ'kɒgrəfɪ) n **1** bad handwriting. **2** incorrect spelling.
▸ **cacographic** (,kækə'græfɪk) adj

cacophony (kə'kɒfənɪ) n, pl **cacophonies**. harsh discordant sound.
▸ ca'cophonous adj

cactus ('kæktəs) n, pl **cactuses** or **cacti** (-taɪ). **1** any of a family of spiny succulent plants of the arid regions of America with swollen tough stems and leaves reduced to spines. **2 cactus dahlia**. a double-flowered variety of dahlia. [C17: from L: prickly plant, from Gk *kaktos* cardoon]
▸ **cactaceous** (kæk'teɪʃəs) adj

cacuminal (kæ'kjuːmɪnᵊl) Phonetics. ◆ adj **1** denoting a consonant articulated with the tip of the tongue turned back towards the hard palate. ◆ n **2** a consonant articulated in this manner. [C19: from L *cacūmen* point]

cad (kæd) n Brit. inf. old-fashioned. a man who does not behave in a gentlemanly manner towards others. [C18: from CADDIE]
▸ 'caddish adj

CAD (kæd) n acronym for computer-aided design.

cadaver (kə'deɪvə, -'dɑːv-) n Med. a corpse. [C16: from L, from *cadere* to fall]
▸ **cadaveric** (kə'dævərɪk) adj

cadaverous (kə'dævərəs) adj **1** of or like a corpse, esp. in being deathly pale. **2** thin and haggard.
▸ ca'daverousness n

Cadbury ★ ('kædbərɪ) n **George**. 1839–1922, British Quaker industrialist and philanthropist. He established, with his brother **Richard Cadbury** (1835–99), the chocolate-making company Cadbury Brothers and the garden village Bournville, near Birmingham, for their workers.

CADCAM ('kæd,kæm) n acronym for computer-aided design and manufacture.

caddie or **caddy** ('kædɪ) Golf. ◆ n, pl **caddies. 1** an attendant who carries clubs, etc., for a player. ◆ vb **caddies, caddying, caddied. 2** (intr) to act as a caddie. [C17 (C18 (Scot.): an errand-boy): from F CADET]

caddis fly n a small mothlike insect having two pairs of hairy wings and aquatic larvae (caddis worms). [C17: from ?]

caddis worm or **caddis** ('kædɪs) n the aquatic larva of a caddis fly, which constructs a protective case around itself made of silk, sand, stones, etc. Also called: **caseworm, strawworm**.

caddy¹ ('kædɪ) n, pl **caddies**. Chiefly Brit. a small container, esp. for tea. [C18: from Malay *kati*]

caddy² ('kædɪ) n, pl **caddies**, vb **caddies, caddying, caddied**. a variant spelling of **caddie**.

Cade ★ (keɪd) n **Jack**. died 1450, English leader of the Kentish rebellion.

cadence ('keɪdᵊns) _or_ **cadency** _n, pl_ **cadences** _or_ **cadencies. 1** the beat or measure of something rhythmic. **2** a fall in the pitch of the voice, as at the end of a sentence. **3** intonation. **4** rhythm in verse or prose. **5** the close of a musical phrase. [C14: from OF, from OIt. _cadenza_, lit.: a falling, from L _cadere_ to fall]

cadenza (kə'dɛnzə) _n_ a virtuoso solo passage occurring near the end of a piece of music, formerly improvised by the soloist. [C19: from It.; see CADENCE]

cadet (kə'dɛt) _n_ **1** a young person undergoing preliminary training, usually before full entry to the uniformed services, police, etc. **2** (in England and in France before 1789) a gentleman who entered the army to prepare for a commission. **3** a younger son. **4 cadet branch.** the family of a younger son. **5** (in New Zealand, formerly) a person learning sheep farming on a sheep station. [C17: from F, from dialect _capdet_ captain, ult. from L _caput_ head]
▸ **ca'detship** _n_

cadge (kædʒ) _vb_ **cadges, cadging, cadged. 1** to get (food, money, etc.) by sponging or begging. ◆ _n_ **2** _Brit._ a person who cadges. [C17: from ?]
▸ **'cadger** _n_

cadi _or_ **kadi** ('kɑːdɪ, 'keɪdɪ) _n, pl_ **cadis** _or_ **kadis.** a judge in a Muslim community. [C16: from Ar. _qāḍī_ judge]

Cádiz ★ (kə'dɪz; _Spanish_ 'kaðiθ) _n_ a port in SW Spain, on a narrow peninsula that forms the **Bay of Cádiz** at the E end of the **Gulf of Cádiz:** founded about 1100 B.C. as a Phoenician trading colony; centre of trade with America from the 16th to 18th centuries. Pop.: 155 438 (1994 est.).

Cadmean victory ('kædmɪən) _n_ another name for **Pyrrhic victory.**

cadmium ('kædmɪəm) _n_ a malleable bluish-white metallic element that occurs in association with zinc ores. It is used in electroplating and alloys. Symbol: Cd; atomic no.: 48; atomic wt.: 112.4. [C19: from NL, from L _cadmīa_ zinc ore, CALAMINE: both calamine and cadmium are found in the ore]

cadmium yellow _n_ an orange or yellow insoluble solid (cadmium sulphide) used as a pigment in paints, etc.

Cadmus ★ ('kædməs) _n Greek myth._ a Phoenician prince who killed a dragon and planted its teeth, from which sprang a multitude of warriors who fought among themselves until only five remained, who joined Cadmus to found Thebes.
▸ **'Cadmean** _adj_

cadre ('kɑːdə) _n_ **1** the nucleus of trained professional servicemen forming the basis for military expansion. **2** a group of activists, esp. in the Communist Party. **3** a basic unit or structure; nucleus. **4** a member of a cadre. [C19: from F, from It. _quadro_, from L _quadrum_ square]

caduceus (kə'djuːsɪəs) _n, pl_ **caducei** (-sɪ,aɪ). **1** _Classical myth._ a winged staff entwined with two serpents carried by Hermes (Mercury) as messenger of the gods. **2** an insignia resembling this staff used as an emblem of the medical profession. [C16: from L, from Doric Gk _karukeion_, from _karux_ herald]

caducous (kə'djuːkəs) _adj Biol._ (of parts of a plant or animal) shed during the life of the organism. [C17: from L, from _cadere_ to fall]

Cadwalader ★ (kæd'wɒlədə) _n_ 7th century A.D., legendary king of the Britons, probably a confusion of several historical figures.

caecilian (siː'sɪlɪən) _n_ a tropical limbless cylindrical amphibian resembling the earthworm and inhabiting moist soil. [C19: from L, from _caecus_ blind]

caecum _or US_ **cecum** ('siːkəm) _n, pl_ **caeca** _or US_ **ceca** (-kə). _Anat._ any structure that ends in a blind sac or pouch, esp. that at the beginning of the large intestine. [C18: short for L _intestinum caecum_ blind intestine, translation of Gk _tuphlon enteron_]
▸ **'caecal** _or US_ **'cecal** _adj_

Cædmon ★ ('kædmən) _n_ 7th century A.D., Anglo-Saxon poet and monk, the earliest English poet whose name survives.

Caelian ★ ('siːlɪən) _n_ the southeasternmost of the Seven Hills of Rome.

Caen ★ (kɒŋ; _French_ kã) _n_ an industrial city in NW France. Pop.: 115 624 (1990).

Caenozoic (,siːnə'zəʊɪk) _adj_ a variant spelling of **Cenozoic.**

Caernarfon, Caernarvon, _or_ **Carnarvon** ★ (kɑː'nɑːvᵊn) _n_ a port and resort in NW Wales, in Gwynedd on the Menai Strait: 13th-century castle. Pop.: 9695 (1991).

Caernarvonshire ★ (kɑː'nɑːvᵊn,ʃɪə, -ʃə) _n_ (until 1974) a county of NW Wales, now part of Gwynedd.

Caerphilly ★ (keə'fɪlɪ) _n_ **1** a market town in SE Wales, in SE Mid Glamorgan: site of the largest castle in Wales (13th–14th centuries). Pop.: 28 481 (1991). **2** a county borough in SE Wales, created in 1996 from parts of Mid Glamorgan and Gwent. Pop.: 170 000 (1996 est.). Area: 275 sq. km (106 sq. miles). **3** a creamy white mild-flavoured cheese.

Caesar ★ ('siːzə) _n_ **1 Gaius Julius** ('gaɪəs 'dʒuːlɪəs). 100–44 B.C., Roman general and historian. He formed the first triumvirate with Pompey and Crassus (60), conquered Gaul (58–50), invaded Britain (55–54), mastered Italy (49), and defeated Pompey (46): assassinated by Marcus Brutus and Cassius Longinus. **2** any Roman emperor. **3** (_sometimes not cap._) any emperor, autocrat, dictator, or other powerful ruler. **4** a title of the Roman emperors from Augustus to Hadrian. **5** (in the Roman Empire) **5a** a title borne by the imperial heir from the reign of Hadrian. **5b** the heir, deputy, and subordinate ruler to either of the two emperors under Diocletian's system of government.

Caesaraugusta ★ (,siːzərɔː'gʌstə) _n_ the Latin name for Zaragoza.

Caesarea ★ (,siːzə'rɪə) _n_ an ancient port in NW Israel, capital of Roman Palestine: founded by Herod the Great.

Caesarean, Caesarian, _or US_ **Cesarean, Cesarian** (sɪ'zɛərɪən) _adj_ **1** of or relating to any of the Caesars, esp. Julius Caesar. ◆ _n_ **2** (_sometimes not cap._) _Surgery._ **2a** a Caesarean section. **2b** (_as modifier_): _Caesarean operation._

Caesarean section _n_ surgical incision through the abdominal and uterine walls in order to deliver a baby. [C17: from the belief that Julius Caesar was so delivered, the name allegedly being derived from _caedere_ to cut]

caesious _or US_ **cesious** ('siːzɪəs) _adj Bot._ having a waxy bluish-grey coating. [C19: from L _caesius_ bluish grey]

caesium _or US_ **cesium** ('siːzɪəm) _n_ a ductile silvery-white element of the alkali metal group. It is used in photocells and in an atomic clock (**caesium clock**) that uses the frequency of radiation from changing the spin of electrons. The radioisotope **caesium-137,** with a half-life of 30.2 years, is used in radiotherapy. Symbol: Cs; atomic no.: 55; atomic wt.: 132.905.

caesura (sɪ'zjʊərə) _n, pl_ **caesuras** _or_ **caesurae** (-riː). **1** (in modern prosody) a pause, esp. for sense, usually near the middle of a verse line. **2** (in classical prosody) a break between words within a metrical foot. [C16: from L, lit.: a cutting, from _caedere_ to cut]
▸ **cae'sural** _adj_

Caetano ★ (kaɪ'tɑːnəʊ; _Portuguese_ kɑi'tɐnu) _n_ **Marcello** (mɑr'sɛlu). 1906–80, Portuguese statesman; prime minister (1968–74).

café ('kæfeɪ, 'kæfɪ) _n_ **1** a small or inexpensive restaurant serving light or easily prepared meals and refreshments. **2** _S. African._ a corner shop or grocer. [C19: from F: COFFEE]

café au lait _French._ (kafe o lɛ) _n_ **1** coffee with milk. **2a** a light brown colour. **2b** (_as adj_): _café au lait brocade._

café noir _French._ (kafe nwar) _n_ black coffee.

cafeteria (,kæfɪ'tɪərɪə) _n_ a self-service restaurant. [C20: from American Sp.: coffee shop]

caff (kæf) _n_ a slang word for **café.**

caffeine _or_ **caffein** ('kæfiːn) _n_ a white crystalline bitter alkaloid responsible for the stimulant action of tea, coffee, and cocoa. [C19: from G _Kaffein_, from _Kaffee_ COFFEE]

caftan ('kæf,tæn, -,tɑːn) _n_ a variant spelling of **kaftan.**

cage (keɪdʒ) _n_ **1a** an enclosure, usually made with bars or wire, for keeping birds, monkeys, etc. **1b** (_in combination_): _cagebird._ **2** a thing or place that confines. **3** something resembling a cage in function or structure: *the rib cage.* **4** the enclosed platform of a lift, esp. as used in a mine. ◆ *vb* **cages, caging, caged. 5** (*tr*) to confine in or as in a cage. [C13: from OF, from L *cavea* enclosure, from *cavus* hollow]

Cage ★ (keɪdʒ) *n* **John.** 1912–92, US composer of such experimental works as *Imaginary Landscape* (1951) and *Apartment Building 1776* (1976).

cagey *or* **cagy** ('keɪdʒɪ) *adj* **cagier, cagiest.** *Inf.* not frank; wary. [C20: from ?] ► **'caginess** *n*

Cagliari ★ (kæl'jɑːrɪ; *Italian* 'kaʎʎari) *n* a port in Italy, the capital of Sardinia, on the S coast. Pop.: 178 063 (1994 est.).

Cagney ★ ('kægnɪ) *n* **James.** 1899–1986, US actor, esp. in gangster roles; his films include *The Public Enemy* (1931) and *Yankee Doodle Dandy* (1942).

cagoule (kə'guːl) *n* a lightweight usually knee-length type of anorak. [C20: from F]

Cahokia Mounds ★ (kə'həʊkɪə) *pl n* the largest group of prehistoric Indian earthworks in the US, located northeast of East St Louis.

cahoots (kə'huːts) *pl n* (*sometimes sing*) *Inf.* **1** *US.* partnership; league. **2 in cahoots.** in collusion. [C19: from ?]

Caiaphas ★ ('kaɪəˌfæs) *n New Testament.* the high priest at the beginning of John the Baptist's preaching and during the trial of Jesus (Luke 3:2; Matthew 26).

Caicos Islands ★ ('keɪkəs) *pl n* a group of islands in the Caribbean: part of the British dependency of the **Turks and Caicos Islands.**

caiman ('keɪmən) *n, pl* **caimans.** a variant spelling of **cayman.**

Cain ★ (keɪn) *n* **1** the first son of Adam and Eve, who killed his brother Abel (Genesis 4:1–16). **2 raise Cain. 2a** to cause a commotion. **2b** to react or protest heatedly.

Caine ★ (keɪn) *n* **Michael.** real name *Maurice Micklewhite.* born 1933, British film actor. His films include *The Ipcress File* (1965) and *Little Voice* (1998).

Cainozoic (ˌkaɪnəʊ'zəʊɪk, ˌkeɪ-) *adj* a variant spelling of **Cenozoic.**

caïque (kaɪ'iːk) *n* **1** a long rowing skiff used on the Bosporus. **2** a sailing vessel of the E Mediterranean with a square topsail. [C17: from F, from It. *caicco,* from Turkish *kayik*]

Caird Coast ★ (kɛəd) *n* a region of Antarctica: a part of Coats Land on the SE coast of the Weddell Sea; now included in the British Antarctic Territory.

cairn (kɛən) *n* **1** a mound of stones erected as a memorial or marker. **2** Also called: **cairn terrier.** a small rough-haired breed of terrier orig. from Scotland. [C15: from Gaelic *carn*]

cairngorm (ˌkɛən'gɔːm) *n* a smoky yellow or brown variety of quartz, used as a gemstone. Also called: **smoky quartz.** [C18: from *Cairn Gorm* (lit.: blue cairn), mountain in Scotland]

Cairngorm Mountains ★ *pl n* a mountain range of NE Scotland: part of the Grampians. Highest peak: Ben Macdhui, 1309 m (4296 ft). Also called: **the Cairngorms.**

Cairo ★ ('kaɪrəʊ) *n* the capital of Egypt, on the Nile: the largest city in Africa and in the Middle East; industrial centre; site of the university and mosque of Al Azhar (founded in 972). Pop.: 6 849 000 (1994 est.). Arabic name: **El Qahira** (el 'kahiːrə). ► **'Cairene** *n, adj*

caisson (kə'suːn, 'keɪs³n) *n* **1** a watertight chamber open at the bottom and containing air under pressure, used to carry out construction work under water. **2** a watertight float filled with air, used to raise sunken ships. **3** a watertight structure placed across the entrance of a dry dock, etc., to exclude water. **4a** a box containing explosives formerly used as a mine. **4b** an ammunition chest. [C18: from F, assimilated to *caisse* CASE²]

caisson disease *n* another name for **decompression sickness.**

Caithness ★ (keɪθ'nɛs, 'keɪθnɛs) *n* (until 1975) a county of NE Scotland, now part of Highland.

caitiff ('keɪtɪf) *Arch. or poetic.* ◆ *n* **1** a cowardly or base person. ◆ *adj* **2** cowardly. [C13: from OF, from L *captīvus* CAPTIVE]

Caius ★ ('kaɪəs) *n* a variant of **Gaius.**

cajole (kə'dʒəʊl) *vb* **cajoles, cajoling, cajoled.** to persuade (someone) by flattery to do what one wants; wheedle; coax. [C17: from F *cajoler* to coax, from ?] ► **ca'jolement** *n* ► **ca'joler** *n* ► **ca'jolery** *n*

cake (keɪk) *n* **1** a baked food, usually in loaf or layer form, made from a mixture of flour, sugar, and eggs. **2** a flat thin mass of bread, esp. unleavened bread. **3** a shaped mass of dough or other food: *a fish cake.* **4** a mass, slab, or crust of a solidified substance, as of soap. **5 go** *or* **sell like hot cakes.** *Inf.* to be sold very quickly. **6 have one's cake and eat it.** to enjoy both of two desirable but incompatible alternatives. **7 piece of cake.** *Inf.* something that is easily achieved or obtained. **8 take the cake.** *Inf.* to surpass all others, esp. in stupidity, folly, etc. **9** the whole of something that is to be shared or divided: *a larger slice of the cake.* ◆ *vb* **cakes, caking, caked. 10** (*tr*) to encrust: *the hull was caked with salt.* **11** to form or be formed into a hardened mass. [C13: from ON *kaka*]

cakewalk ('keɪkˌwɔːk) *n* **1** a dance based on a march with intricate steps, orig. performed by African-Americans for the prize of a cake. **2** a piece of music for this dance. **3** *Inf.* an easy task.

CAL (kæl) *acronym for* computer-aided (*or* -assisted) learning.

cal. *abbrev. for:* **1** calendar. **2** calibre. **3** calorie (small).

Cal. *abbrev. for* Calorie (large).

Calabar ★ ('kæləˌbɑː) *n* a port in SE Nigeria, capital of Cross River state. Pop.: 170 000 (1995 est.).

calabash ('kæləˌbæʃ) *n* **1** Also called: **calabash tree.** a tropical American evergreen tree that produces large round gourds. **2** the gourd. **3** the dried hollow shell of a gourd used as the bowl of a tobacco pipe, a bottle, etc. **4 calabash nutmeg.** a tropical African shrub whose seeds can be used as nutmegs. [C17: from obs. F *calabasse* from Sp., ?from Ar., from *qar'ah* gourd + *yābisah* dry]

calaboose ('kæləˌbuːs) *n US inf.* a prison. [C18: from Creole F, from Sp. *calabozo* dungeon, from ?]

calabrese (ˌkæləˈbreɪz) *n* a variety of green sprouting broccoli. [C20: from It.: Calabrian]

Calabria ★ (kə'læbrɪə) *n* **1** a region of SW Italy: mostly mountainous and subject to earthquakes. Chief town: Reggio di Calabria. Pop.: 2 079 588 (1994 est.). Area: 15 080 sq. km (5822 sq. miles). **2** an ancient region of extreme SE Italy (3rd century B.C. to about 668 A.D.); now part of Apulia. ► **Ca'labrian** *adj, n*

Calais ★ ('kæleɪ, 'kælɪ; *French* kalɛ) *n* a port in N France, on the Strait of Dover: the nearest French port to England; belonged to England 1347–1558. Pop.: 75 309 (1990).

calamander ('kæləˌmændə) *n* the hard black-and-brown striped wood of several trees of India and Sri Lanka, used in making furniture. See also **ebony** (sense 2). [C19: metathetic var. of *coromandel* in COROMANDEL COAST]

calamine ('kæləˌmaɪn) *n* a pink powder consisting of zinc oxide and iron(III) oxide, used medicinally in the form of soothing lotions or ointments. [C17: from OF, from Med. L *calamīna,* from L *cadmīa;* see CADMIUM]

calamint ('kæləmɪnt) *n* an aromatic Eurasian plant having clusters of purple or pink flowers. [C14: from OF *calament,* from Med. L *calamentum,* from Gk *kalaminthē*]

calamitous (kə'læmɪtəs) *adj* causing, involving, or resulting in a calamity; disastrous.

calamity (kə'læmɪtɪ) *n, pl* **calamities. 1** a disaster or misfortune, esp. one causing distress or misery. **2** a state or feeling of deep distress or misery. [C15: from F *calamité,* from L *calamitās*]

Calamity Jane ★ *n* real name *Martha Canary.* ?1852–1903, US frontierswoman.

calamus ('kæləməs) *n, pl* **calami** (-ˌmaɪ). **1** any of a genus of tropical Asian palms, some of which are a source of rattan and canes. **2** another name for **sweet flag. 3**

Ornithol. a quill. [C14: from L, from Gk *kalamos* reed, stem]

calandria (kəˈlændrɪə) *n* a cylindrical vessel through which vertical tubes pass, esp. one forming part of a heat exchanger or nuclear reactor. [C20: arbitrarily named, from Sp., lit.: lark]

calash (kəˈlæʃ) *or* **calèche** *n* **1** a horse-drawn carriage with low wheels and a folding top. **2** a woman's folding hooped hood worn in the 18th century. [C17: from F, from G, from Czech *kolesa* wheels]

calcaneus (kælˈkeɪnɪəs) *or* **calcaneum** *n, pl* **calcanei** (-nɪˌaɪ). the largest tarsal bone, forming the heel in man. Nontechnical name: **heel bone.** [C19: from LL: heel, from L *calx* heel]

calcareous (kælˈkɛərɪəs) *adj* of, containing, or resembling calcium carbonate; chalky. [C17: from L *calcārius*, from *calx* lime]

calceolaria (ˌkælsɪəˈlɛərɪə) *n* a tropical American plant cultivated for its speckled slipper-shaped flowers. Also called: **slipperwort.** [C18: from L *calceolus* small shoe, from *calceus*]

calces (ˈkælsiːz) *n* a plural of **calx.**

calci- *or before a vowel* **calc-** *combining form.* indicating lime or calcium: *calcify.* [from L *calx, calc-* limestone]

calciferol (kælˈsɪfərɒl) *n* a fat-soluble steroid, found esp. in fish-liver oils and used in the treatment of rickets. Also called: **vitamin** D_2. [C20: from CALCIF(EROUS + ERGOST)EROL]

calciferous (kælˈsɪfərəs) *adj* producing salts of calcium, esp. calcium carbonate.

calcify (ˈkælsɪˌfaɪ) *vb* **calcifies, calcifying, calcified. 1** to convert or be converted into lime. **2** to harden or become hardened by impregnation with calcium salts.
► **ˌcalcifiˈcation** *n*

calcine (ˈkælsaɪn, -sɪn) *vb* **calcines, calcining, calcined. 1** (*tr*) to heat (a substance) so that it is oxidized, is reduced, or loses water. **2** (*intr*) to oxidize as a result of heating. [C14: from Med. L *calcināre* to heat, from L *calx* lime]
► **calcination** (ˌkælsɪˈneɪʃən) *n*

calcite (ˈkælsaɪt) *n* a colourless or white mineral consisting of crystalline calcium carbonate: the transparent variety is Iceland spar. Formula: $CaCO_3$.

calcium (ˈkælsɪəm) *n* a malleable silvery-white metallic element of the alkaline earth group, occurring esp. as forms of calcium carbonate. It is an essential constituent of bones and teeth. Symbol: Ca; atomic no.: 20; atomic wt.: 40.08. [C19: from NL, from L *calx* lime]

calcium antagonist *or* **blocker** *n* any drug that prevents the influx of calcium ions into cardiac and smooth muscle: used to treat high blood pressure and angina.

calcium carbide *n* a grey salt of calcium used in the production of acetylene. Formula: CaC_2. Sometimes shortened to **carbide.**

calcium carbonate *n* a white crystalline salt occurring in limestone, chalk, and pearl: used in the production of lime. Formula: $CaCO_3$.

calcium chloride *n* a white deliquescent salt occurring naturally in seawater and used in the de-icing of roads. Formula: $CaCl_2$.

calcium hydroxide *n* a white crystalline slightly soluble alkali with many uses, esp. in cement, water softening, and the neutralization of acid soils. Formula: $Ca(OH)_2$. Also called: **lime, slaked lime, caustic lime.**

calcium oxide *n* a white crystalline base used in the production of calcium hydroxide and in the manufacture of glass and steel. Formula: CaO. Also called: **lime, quicklime, calx.**

calcium phosphate *n* an insoluble nonacid calcium salt that occurs in bones and is the main constituent of bone ash. Formula: $Ca_3(PO_4)_2$

calcspar (ˈkælkˌspɑː) *n* another name for **calcite.** [C19: from Swedish *kalkspat*, from *kalk* lime (ult. from L *calx*) + *spat* SPAR[3]]

calculable (ˈkælkjʊləbᵊl) *adj* **1** that may be computed or estimated. **2** predictable.
► **ˌcalculaˈbility** *n* ► **ˈcalculably** *adv*

calculate (ˈkælkjʊˌleɪt) *vb* **calculates, calculating, calculated. 1** to solve (one or more problems) by a mathematical procedure. **2** (*tr; may take a clause as object*) to determine beforehand by judgment, etc.; estimate. **3** (*tr, usually passive*) to aim: *the car was calculated to appeal to women.* **4** (*intr;* foll. by *on* or *upon*) to rely. **5** (*tr; may take a clause as object*) *US dialect.* to suppose. [C16: from LL *calculāre*, from *calculus* pebble used as a counter]
► **calculative** (ˈkælkjʊlətɪv) *adj*

calculated (ˈkælkjʊˌleɪtɪd) *adj* (*usually prenominal*) **1** undertaken after considering the likelihood of success or failure. **2** premeditated: *a calculated insult.*

calculating (ˈkælkjʊˌleɪtɪŋ) *adj* **1** selfishly scheming. **2** shrewd.
► **ˈcalcuˌlatingly** *adv*

calculation (ˌkælkjʊˈleɪʃən) *n* **1** the act, process, or result of calculating. **2** a forecast. **3** careful planning, esp. for selfish motives.

calculator (ˈkælkjʊˌleɪtə) *n* **1** a device for performing mathematical calculations, esp. an electronic device that can be held in the hand. **2** a person or thing that calculates. **3** a set of tables used as an aid to calculations.

calculous (ˈkælkjʊləs) *adj Pathol.* of or suffering from a calculus.

calculus (ˈkælkjʊləs) *n, pl* **calculuses. 1** a branch of mathematics, developed independently by Newton and Leibnitz. Both **differential calculus** and **integral calculus** are concerned with the effect on a function of an infinitesimal change in the independent variable. **2** any mathematical system of calculation involving the use of symbols. **3** (*pl* **calculi** (-ˌlaɪ)). *Pathol.* a stonelike concretion of minerals found in organs of the body. [C17: from L: pebble, from *calx* small stone, counter]

Calcutta ★ (kælˈkʌtə) *n* a port in E India, capital of West Bengal state, on the Hooghly River: former capital of the country (1833–1912); major commercial and industrial centre; three universities. Pop.: 4 399 819 (1991).

Calder ★ (ˈkɔːldə) *n* **Alexander.** 1898–1976, US sculptor, who originated mobiles.

caldera (kælˈdɛərə) *n* a large basin-shaped crater at the top of a volcano, formed by the collapse of the cone. [C19: from Sp. *caldera*, lit.: CAULDRON]

Calderdale ★ (ˈkɔːldəˌdeɪl) *n* a unitary authority in N England, in West Yorkshire. Pop.: 193 600 (1994). Area: 364 sq. km (140 sq. miles).

caldron (ˈkɔːldrən) *n* a variant spelling of **cauldron.**

Caldwell ★ (ˈkɔːldwɛl, -wəl) *n* **Erskine** (ˈɜːskɪn). 1903–87, US novelist whose works include *Tobacco Road* (1933).

calèche (*French* kalɛʃ) *n* a variant of **calash.**

Caledonia ★ (ˌkælɪˈdəʊnɪə) *n* the Roman name for **Scotland.**

Caledonian (ˌkælɪˈdəʊnɪən) *adj* **1** relating to Scotland. **2** of a period of mountain building in NW Europe in the Palaeozoic era. ◆ *n* **3** *Literary.* a native or inhabitant of Scotland.

Caledonian Canal ★ *n* a canal in N Scotland, linking the Atlantic with the North Sea through the Great Glen: built 1803–47; now little used.

calefacient (ˌkælɪˈfeɪʃənt) *adj* **1** causing warmth. ◆ *n* **2** *Med.* an agent that warms, such as a mustard plaster. [C17: from L, from *calefacere* to heat]

calendar (ˈkælɪndə) *n* **1** a system for determining the beginning, length, and order of years and their divisions. **2** a table showing any such arrangement, esp. as applied to one or more successive years. **3** a list or schedule of pending court cases, appointments, etc. ◆ *vb* **calendars, calendaring, calendared. 4** (*tr*) to enter in a calendar; schedule. [C13: via Norman F from Med. L *kalendārium* account book, from *Kalendae* the CALENDS]
► **calendrical** (kæˈlɛndrɪkᵊl) *or* **caˈlendric** *adj*

calendar month *n* See **month** (sense 1).

calendar year *n* See **year** (sense 1).

calender (ˈkælɪndə) *n* **1** a machine in which paper or cloth is smoothed by passing between rollers. ◆ *vb* **2** (*tr*) to subject (material) to such a process. [C17: from F *calandre*, from ?]

calends *or* **kalends** ('kælındz) *pl n* the first day of each month in the ancient Roman calendar. [C14: from L *kalendae*]

calendula (kæ'lɛndjulə) *n* any of a genus of Eurasian plants, esp. the pot marigold, having orange-and-yellow rayed flowers. [C19: from Med. L, from L *kalendae* CALENDS]

calf[1] (kɑːf) *n, pl* **calves. 1** the young of cattle, esp. domestic cattle. **2** the young of certain other mammals, such as the buffalo and whale. **3** a large piece of ice detached from an iceberg, etc. **4 kill the fatted calf.** to celebrate lavishly, esp. as a welcome. [OE *cealf*]

calf[2] (kɑːf) *n, pl* **calves.** the thick fleshy part of the back of the leg between the ankle and the knee. [C14: from ON *kalfi*]

calf love *n* temporary infatuation of an adolescent for a member of the opposite sex.

calf's-foot jelly *n* a jelly made from the stock of boiled calves' feet and flavourings.

calfskin ('kɑːf,skɪn) *n* **1** the skin or hide of a calf. **2** Also called: **calf. 2a** fine leather made from this skin. **2b** (*as modifier*): *calfskin boots.*

Calgary ★ ('kælgərɪ) *n* a city in Canada, in S Alberta: centre of a large agricultural region; oilfields. Pop.: 710 677 (1991).

Calgon ('kælgɒn) *n Trademark.* a chemical compound, sodium hexametaphosphate, with water-softening properties, used in detergents.

calibrate ('kælɪ,breɪt) *vb* **calibrates, calibrating, calibrated.** (*tr*) **1** to measure the calibre of (a gun, etc.). **2** to mark (the scale of a measuring instrument) so that readings can be made in appropriate units. **3** to determine the accuracy of (a measuring instrument, etc.).
▸ ,cali'bration *n* ▸ 'cali,brator *n*

calibre *or US* **caliber** ('kælɪbə) *n* **1** the diameter of a cylindrical body, esp. the internal diameter of a tube or the bore of a firearm. **2** the diameter of a shell or bullet. **3** ability; distinction. **4** personal character: *a man of high calibre.* [C16: from OF, from It. *calibro*, from Ar. *qālib* shoemaker's last]
▸ 'calibred *or US* 'calibered *adj*

calices ('kælɪ,siːz) *n* the plural of **calix.**

calico ('kælɪ,kəʊ) *n, pl* **calicoes** *or* **calicos. 1** a white or unbleached cotton fabric. **2** *Chiefly US.* a coarse printed cotton fabric. [C16: based on *Calicut*, town in India]

calif ('keɪlɪf, 'kæl-) *n* a variant spelling of **caliph.**

Calif. *abbrev. for* California.

California ★ (,kælɪ'fɔːnɪə) *n* **1** a state on the W coast of the US: the third largest state in area and the largest in population; consists of a narrow, warm coastal plain rising to the Coast Range, deserts in the south, the fertile central valleys of the Sacramento and San Joaquin Rivers, and the mountains of the Sierra Nevada in the east; major industries include the growing of citrus fruits and grapes, fishing, oil production, computer technology, electronics, and films. Capital: Sacramento. Pop.: 31 878 234 (1996 est.). Area: 411 015 sq. km (158 693 sq. miles). Abbrevs.: **Cal., Calif.** or (with zip code) **CA 2 Gulf of.** an arm of the Pacific Ocean, between Sonora and Lower California.
▸ ,Cali'fornian *adj, n*

California poppy *n* a plant of the poppy family, native to the Pacific coast of North America, having yellow or orange flowers and finely dissected bluish-green leaves. Also called: **eschscholzia** *or* **eschscholtzia.**

californium (,kælɪ'fɔːnɪəm) *n* a transuranic element artificially produced from curium. Symbol: Cf; atomic no.: 98; half-life of most stable isotope, [251]Cf: 800 years (approx.). [C20: NL; discovered at the University of *California*]

Caligula ★ (kə'lɪgjulə) *n* original name *Gaius Caesar*, son of *Germanicus*. 12–41 A.D., Roman emperor (37–41), noted for his cruelty; assassinated.

calipash *or* **callipash** ('kælɪ,pæʃ) *n* the greenish glutinous edible part of the turtle found next to the upper shell. [C17: ? changed from Sp. *carapacho* CARAPACE]

calipee ('kælɪ,piː) *n* the yellow glutinous edible part of the turtle found next to the lower shell. [C17: ? a var. of CALIPASH]

caliper ('kælɪpə) *n* the usual US spelling of **calliper.**

caliph, calif, *or* **khalif** ('keɪlɪf, 'kæl-) *n Islam.* the title of the successors of Mohammed as rulers of the Islamic world. [C14: from OF, from Ar. *khalīfa* successor]

caliphate, califate *or* **khalifate** ('keɪlɪ,feɪt) *n* the office, jurisdiction, or reign of a caliph.

calisthenics (,kælɪs'θenɪks) *n* a variant spelling (esp. US) of **callisthenics.**

calix ('keɪlɪks, 'kæ-) *n, pl* **calices.** a cup; chalice. [C18: from L: CHALICE]

calk[1] (kɔːk) *vb* a variant spelling of **caulk.**

calk[2] (kɔːk) *or* **calkin** ('kɔːkɪn, 'kæl-) *n* **1** a metal projection on a horse's shoe to prevent slipping. ♦ *vb* (*tr*) **2** to provide with calks. [C17: from L *calx* heel]

call (kɔːl) *vb* **1** (often foll. by *out*) to speak or utter (words, sounds, etc.) loudly so as to attract attention: *he called out her name.* **2** (*tr*) to ask or order to come: *to call a policeman.* **3** (*intr*; sometimes foll. by *on*) to make a visit (to): *she called on him.* **4** (often foll. by *up*) to telephone (a person). **5** (*tr*) to summon to a specific office, profession, etc. **6** (of animals or birds) to utter (a characteristic sound or cry). **7** (*tr*) to summon (a bird or animal), as by imitating its cry. **8** (*tr*) to name or style: *they called the dog Rover.* **9** (*tr*) to designate: *they called him a coward.* **10** (*tr*) to regard in a specific way: *I call it a foolish waste of time.* **11** (*tr*) to attract (attention). **12** (*tr*) to read (a list, etc.) aloud to check for omissions or absentees. **13** (when *tr,* usually foll. by *for*) to give an account (for): *to call a strike.* **14** (*intr*) to try to predict the result of tossing a coin. **15** (*tr*) to awaken: *I was called early this morning.* **16** (*tr*) to cause to assemble. **17** (*tr*) *Sport.* (of an umpire, etc.) to pass judgment upon (a shot, etc.) with a call. **18** (*tr*) *Austral. & NZ.* to broadcast a commentary on (a horse race, etc.). **19** (*tr*) to demand repayment of (a loan, security, etc.). **20** (*tr*) *Brit.* to award (a student at an Inn of Court) the degree of barrister (esp. in **call to the bar**). **21** (*tr*) *Poker.* to demand that (a player) expose his hand, after equalling his bet. **22** (*intr*) *Bridge.* to make a bid. **23** (in square-dancing) to call out (instructions) to the dancers. **24a** (*intr*; foll. by *for*) **24a** to require: *this problem calls for study.* **24b** to come or go (for) in order to fetch. **25** (*intr*; foll. by *on* or *upon*) to make an appeal or request (to): *they called upon him to reply.* **26** **call into being.** to create. **27 call someone's bluff.** see **bluff**[1]. **28 call to mind.** to remember or cause to be remembered. ♦ *n* **29** a cry or shout. **30** the characteristic cry of a bird or animal. **31** a device, such as a whistle, intended to imitate the cry of a bird or animal. **32** a summons or invitation. **33** a summons or signal sounded on a horn, bugle, etc. **34** a short visit: *the doctor made six calls this morning.* **35** an inner urge to some task or profession; vocation. **36** allure or fascination, esp. of a place: *the call of the forest.* **37** need, demand, or occasion: *there is no call to shout.* **38** demand or claim (esp. in **the call of duty**). **39** *Theatre.* a notice to actors informing them of times of rehearsals. **40** a conversation or a request for a connection by telephone. **41** *Commerce.* **41a** a demand for repayment of a loan. **41b** (*as modifier*): *call money.* **42** *Finance.* a demand for redeemable bonds or shares to be presented for repayment. **43** *Poker.* a demand for a hand or hands to be exposed. **44** *Bridge.* a bid or a player's turn to bid. **45** *Sport.* a decision of an umpire or referee regarding a shot, pitch, etc. **46** *Austral.* a broadcast commentary on a horse race, etc. **47** Also called: **call option.** *Stock Exchange.* an option to buy a stated amount of securities at a specified price during a specified period. **48 on call. 48a** (of a loan, etc.) repayable on demand. **48b** available to be called for work outside normal working hours. **49 within call.** accessible. ♦ See also **call down, call forth,** etc. [OE *ceallian*]

calla ('kælə) *n* **1** Also called: **calla lily, arum lily.** a southern African plant which has a white funnel-shaped spathe enclosing a yellow spadix. **2** a plant that grows in wet places and has a white spathe and red berries. [C19: from NL, prob. from Gk *kalleia* wattles on a cock, prob. from *kallos* beauty]

Callaghan ★ ('kælə,hæn) *n* (**Leonard**) **James,** Baron Callaghan of Cardiff. born 1912, British Labour statesman; prime minister (1976–79).

Callanetics (ˌkælə'nɛtɪks) n (functioning as sing) Trademark. a system of exercise involving frequent repetition of small muscular movements and squeezes, designed to improve muscle tone. [C20: after Callan Pinckney (born 1939), its US inventor]

Callas ★ ('kæləs) n **Maria**, real name Maria Anna Cecilia Kalageropoulos. 1923–77, Greek soprano, born in the US.

call bird n Marketing. a cheap article displayed in a shop to attract custom, in the hope of selling expensive items.

call box n a soundproof enclosure for a public telephone. Also called: **telephone kiosk.**

callboy ('kɔːlˌbɔɪ) n a person who notifies actors when it is time to go on stage.

call centre n an office where staff carry out an organization's telephone transactions.

call down vb (tr, adv) to request or invoke: to call down God's anger.

caller ('kɔːlə) n **1** a person or thing that calls, esp. a person who makes a brief visit. **2** Austral. a racing commentator.

call forth vb (tr, adv) to cause (something) to come into action or existence.

call girl n a prostitute with whom appointments are made by telephone.

Callicrates ★ (kə'lɪkrəˌtiːz) n 5th century B.C., Greek architect: with Ictinus, designed the Parthenon.

calligraphy (kə'lɪgrəfɪ) n handwriting, esp. beautiful handwriting.
▶ cal'ligrapher or cal'ligraphist n ▶ calligraphic (ˌkælɪ'græfɪk) adj

Callimachus ★ (kə'lɪməkəs) n **1** late 5th century B.C., Greek sculptor, reputed to have invented the Corinthian capital. **2** ?305–?240 B.C., Greek poet of the Alexandrian School; author of hymns and epigrams.

call in vb (adv) **1** (intr; often foll. by on) to pay a visit, esp. a brief one: call in if you are in the neighbourhood. **2** (tr) to demand payment of: to call in a loan. **3** (tr) to take (something) out of circulation, because it is defective. **4** to summon to one's assistance: to call in a specialist.

calling ('kɔːlɪŋ) n **1** a strong inner urge to follow an occupation, etc.; vocation. **2** an occupation, profession, or trade.

calling card n the usual US and Canad. term for **visiting card.**

calliope (kə'laɪəpɪ) n US & Canad. a steam organ. [after CALLIOPE (lit.: beautiful-voiced)]

Calliope ★ (kə'laɪəpɪ) n Greek myth. the Muse of epic poetry.

calliper or US **caliper** ('kælɪpə) n **1** (often pl) Also called: **calliper compasses.** an instrument for measuring internal or external dimensions, consisting of two steel legs hinged together. **2** Also called: **calliper splint.** Med. a metal splint for supporting the leg. ◆ vb **3** (tr) to measure with callipers. [C16: var. of CALIBRE]

calliper rule n a measuring instrument having two parallel jaws, one fixed and the other sliding.

callistemon (kə'lɪstəmən) n another name for **bottlebrush** (sense 1).

callisthenics or **calisthenics** (ˌkælɪs'θɛnɪks) n **1** (functioning as pl) light exercises designed to promote general fitness. **2** (functioning as sing) the practice of callisthenic exercises. [C19: from Gk kalli- beautiful + sthenos strength]
▶ ˌcallis'thenic or ˌcalis'thenic adj

Callisto ★ (kə'lɪstəʊ) n Greek myth. a nymph who attracted the love of Zeus and was changed into a bear by Hera. Zeus then set her in the sky as the constellation Ursa Major.

call loan n a loan that is repayable on demand. Also called: **demand loan.**

call off vb (tr, adv) **1** to cancel or abandon: the game was called off. **2** to order (an animal or person) to desist: the man called off his dog. **3** to stop (something).

callose ('kæləʊz, -ləʊs) n a carbohydrate, a polymer of glucose, found in plants.

callosity (kə'lɒsɪtɪ) n, pl **callosities. 1** hard-heartedness. **2** a callus.

callous ('kæləs) adj **1** insensitive. **2** (of skin) hardened and thickened. ◆ vb **3** Pathol. to make or become callous. [C16: from L callōsus; see CALLUS]
▶ 'callously adv ▶ 'callousness n

call out vb (adv) **1** to utter aloud, esp. loudly. **2** (tr) to summon: call out the troops. **3** (tr) to order (workers) to strike. **4** (tr) to challenge to a duel.

callow ('kæləʊ) adj lacking experience of life; immature. [OE calu]
▶ 'callowness n

call sign n a group of letters and numbers identifying a radio transmitting station.

call up vb (tr, adv) **1** to summon to report for active military service, as in time of war. **2** to recall (something); evoke. **3** to bring or summon (people, etc.) into action. **4** to telephone. ◆ n **call-up. 5a** a general order to report for military service. **5b** the number of men so summoned.

callus ('kæləs) n, pl **calluses. 1** Also called: **callosity.** an area of skin that is hard or thick, esp. on the sole of the foot. **2** an area of bony tissue formed during the healing of a fractured bone. **3** Bot. a mass of hard protective tissue produced in woody plants at the site of an injury. [C16: from L, var. of callum hardened skin]

calm (kɑːm) adj **1** still: a calm sea. **2** Meteorol. without wind, or with wind of less than 1 mph. **3** not disturbed, agitated, or excited. **4** tranquil; serene: a calm voice. ◆ n **5** an absence of disturbance or rough motion. **6** absence of wind. **7** tranquillity. ◆ vb **8** (often foll. by down) to make or become calm. [C14: from OF calme, from OIt., from LL cauma heat, hence a rest during the heat of the day, from Gk, from kaiein to burn]
▶ 'calmly adv ▶ 'calmness n

calmative ('kælmətɪv, 'kɑːmə-) adj (of a remedy or agent) sedative.

caló (kə'ləʊ; Spanish ka'lo) n a form of Mexican Spanish incorporating many slang terms and English words: spoken esp. by Mexican Americans in the SW US.

calomel ('kæləˌmɛl, -məl) n a colourless tasteless powder consisting chiefly of mercurous chloride, used medicinally, esp. as a cathartic. [C17: ?from NL calomelas (unattested), lit.: beautiful black, from Gk kalos beautiful + melas black]

Calor Gas ('kælə) n Trademark. butane gas liquefied under pressure in portable containers for domestic use.

caloric (kə'lɒrɪk) adj **1** of or concerned with heat or calories. ◆ n **2** Obs. a hypothetical elastic fluid, the embodiment of heat.

calorie or **calory** ('kælərɪ) n, pl **calories.** a unit of heat, equal to 4.1868 joules (**International Table calorie**): formerly defined as the quantity of heat required to raise the temperature of 1 gram of water by 1°C. Abbrev.: **cal.** Also called: **small calorie.** [C19: from F, from L calor heat]

Calorie ('kælərɪ) n **1** Also called: **kilogram calorie, large calorie.** a unit of heat, equal to one thousand calories. Abbrev.: **Cal. 2** the amount of a specific food capable of producing one thousand calories of energy.

calorific (ˌkælə'rɪfɪk) adj of, concerning, or generating heat.
▶ ˌcalo'rifically adv

calorific value n the quantity of heat produced by the complete combustion of a given mass of a fuel.

calorimeter (ˌkælə'rɪmɪtə) n an apparatus for measuring amounts of heat, esp. to find calorific values, etc.
▶ calorimetric (ˌkælərɪ'mɛtrɪk) adj ▶ ˌcalo'rimetry n

calorize or **calorise** ('kæləˌraɪz) vb **calorizes, calorizing, calorized** or **calorises, calorising, calorised.** (tr) to coat (a ferrous metal) by spraying with aluminium powder and then heating.

Calpe ★ ('kælpɪ) n the ancient name for the (Rock of) **Gibraltar.**

calque (kælk) n another word for **loan translation.** [C20: from F: a tracing, from L calcāre to tread]

calumet ('kæljuˌmɛt) n the peace pipe. [C18: from Canad. F, from F: straw, from LL calamellus a little reed, from L: CALAMUS]

calumniate (kə'lʌmnɪ,eɪt) *vb* **calumniates, calumniating, calumniated.** (*tr*) to slander.
▸ ca,lumni'ation *n* ▸ ca'lumni,ator *n*

calumny ('kæləmnɪ) *n, pl* **calumnies.** **1** the malicious utterance of false charges or misrepresentation. **2** such a false charge or misrepresentation. [C15: from L *calumnia* deception, slander]
▸ **calumnious** (kə'lʌmnɪəs) *or* ca'lumniatory *adj*

Calvados ★ ('kælvə,dɒs) *n* **1** a department of N France in the Basse-Normandie region. Capital: Caen. Pop.: 632 462 (1994 est.). Area: 5693 sq. km (2198 sq. miles). **2** an apple brandy distilled from cider in this region.

Calvary ★ ('kælvərɪ) *n* the place just outside the walls of Jerusalem where Jesus was crucified. Also called: **Golgotha.** [from LL *Calvāria*, translation of Gk *kranion* skull, translation of Aramaic *gulgulta* Golgotha]

calve (kɑ:v) *vb* **calves, calving, calved.** **1** to give birth to (a calf). **2** (of a glacier or iceberg) to release (masses of ice) in breaking up.

Calvert ★ ('kælvət) *n* **1** Sir **George,** 1st Baron Baltimore. ?1580–1632, English statesman; founder of the colony of Maryland. **2** his son, **Leonard.** 1606–47, English statesman; first colonial governor of Maryland (1634–47).

calves (kɑ:vz) *n* the plural of **calf**[1] and **calf**[2].

Calvin ★ ('kælvɪn) *n* **1** **John,** original name *Jean Cauvin, Caulvin,* or *Chauvin.* 1509–64, French theologian: a leader of the Protestant Reformation, who established the first presbyterian government in Geneva; author of *Institutes of the Christian Religion* (1536). **2** **Melvin.** 1911–97, US chemist, noted for his research on photosynthesis: Nobel prize for chemistry 1961.

Calvin cycle *n Bot.* a series of reactions, occurring during photosynthesis, in which glucose is synthesized from carbon dioxide. [C20: named after M. CALVIN, who elucidated it]

Calvinism ('kælvɪ,nɪzəm) *n* the theological system of John Calvin and his followers, characterized by emphasis on predestination and justification by faith.
▸ 'Calvinist *n, adj* ▸ ,Calvin'istic *or* ,Calvin'istical *adj*

Calvino ★ (*Italian* kal'vi:no) *n* **Italo** ('i:talo). 1923–85, Italian writer. His works include *Our Ancestors* (1960) and *Invisible Cities* (1972).

calx (kælks) *n, pl* **calxes** *or* **calces. 1** the powdery metallic oxide formed when an ore or mineral is roasted. **2** calcium oxide. **3** *Anat.* the heel. [C15: from L: lime, from Gk *khalix* pebble]

calypso (kə'lɪpsəʊ) *n, pl* **calypsos.** a popular type of satirical West Indian ballad, esp. from Trinidad, usually extemporized to a syncopated accompaniment. [C20: prob. from CALYPSO]

Calypso ★ (kə'lɪpsəʊ) *n Greek myth.* (in Homer's *Odyssey*) a sea nymph who detained Odysseus on the island of Ogygia for seven years.

calyx ('keɪlɪks, 'kælɪks) *n, pl* **calyxes** *or* **calyces** ('kælɪ,si:z, 'keɪlɪ-). **1** the sepals of a flower collectively that protect the developing flower bud. **2** any cup-shaped cavity or structure. [C17: from L, from Gk *kalux* shell, from *kaluptein* to cover]

calzone (kæl'tsəʊnɪ) *n* a dish of Italian origin consisting of pizza dough folded over a filling of cheese and tomatoes, herbs, ham, etc. [C20: It., lit.: trouser leg, from *calzoni* COMRADE]

cam (kæm) *n* a slider or roller attached to a moving shaft to give a particular type of motion to a part in contact with it. [C16: from Du. *kam* comb]

Cam ★ (kæm) *n* a river in E England, in Cambridgeshire, flowing through Cambridge to the River Ouse. Length: about 64 km (40 miles).

CAM (kæm) *acronym for* computer-aided manufacture.

Camagüey ★ ('kæmə,gweɪ; *Spanish* kama'ɣwej) *n* a city in E central Cuba. Pop.: 293 961 (1994 est.).

camaraderie (,kæmə'rɑ:dərɪ) *n* a spirit of familiarity and trust existing between friends. [C19: from F, from *camarade* COMRADE]

Camargue ★ (kæ'mɑ:g) *n* **la** (la). a delta region in S France, between the channels of the Grand and Petit

Rhône: cattle, esp. bulls for the Spanish bullrings, and horses are reared.

camarilla (,kæmə'rɪlə) *n* a group of confidential advisers, esp. formerly, to the Spanish kings. [C19: from Sp., lit.: a little room]

Cambay ★ (kæm'beɪ) *n* **Gulf of.** an inlet of the Arabian Sea on the W coast of India, SE of the Kathiawar Peninsula.

camber ('kæmbə) *n* **1** a slight upward curve to the centre of the surface of a road, ship's deck, etc. **2** another name for **bank**[2] (sense 8). **3** an outward inclination of the front wheels of a road vehicle so that they are slightly closer together at the bottom. **4** aerofoil curvature expressed by the ratio of the maximum height of the aerofoil mean line to its chord. ◆ *vb* **5** to form or be formed with a surface that curves upwards to its centre. [C17: from OF *cambre* curved, from L *camurus*]

cambium ('kæmbɪəm) *n, pl* **cambiums** *or* **cambia** (-bɪə). *Bot.* a layer of cells that increases the girth of stems and roots. [C17: from Med. L: exchange, from LL *cambiāre* to exchange]
▸ 'cambial *adj*

Cambodia ★ (kæm'bəʊdɪə) *n* a country in SE Asia: became part of French Indochina in 1887; achieved self-government in 1949 and independence in 1953; civil war (1970–74) ended in victory for the Khmer Rouge, who renamed the country Kampuchea (1975); Vietnamese forces ousted the Khmer Rouge in 1979 and set up a pro-Vietnamese government who reverted (1981) to the name of Cambodia; in 1982 exiled factions formed the Coalition Government of Democratic Kampuchea (CGDK), which is recognized by the UN; after the Vietnamese withdrawal in 1989 CGDK guerrillas continued to engage government forces; in 1993 Sihanouk was restored to the throne: contains the central plains of the Mekong River and the Cardamom Mountains in the SW. Official language: Khmer; French is also widely spoken. Currency: riel. Capital: Phnom Penh. Pop.: 10 385 000 (1997). Area: 181 000 sq. km (69 895 sq. miles). See also **Kampuchea.**
▸ Cam'bodian *adj, n*

Cambrai ★ (*French* kɑ̃bre) *n* a town in NE France: textile industry: scene of a battle in which massed tanks were first used and broke through the German line (November, 1917). Pop.: 34 210 (1990).

Cambria ★ ('kæmbrɪə) *n* the Medieval Latin name for **Wales.**

Cambrian ('kæmbrɪən) *adj* **1** of or formed in the first 100 million years of the Palaeozoic era. **2** of or relating to Wales. ◆ *n* **3** the. the Cambrian period or rock system. **4** a Welshman.

Cambrian Mountains ★ *pl n* a mountain range in Wales, extending from Carmarthenshire in the S to Denbighshire in the N. Highest peak: Aran Fawddwy 891 m (2970 ft).

cambric ('keɪmbrɪk) *n* a fine white linen fabric. [C16: from Flemish *Kamerijk* CAMBRAI]

Cambridge ★ ('keɪmbrɪdʒ) *n* **1** a city in E England, administrative centre of Cambridgeshire, on the River Cam: centred around the university, founded in the 12th century. Pop.: 113 800 (1994 est.). Medieval Latin name: **Cantabrigia. 2** short for **Cambridgeshire. 3** a city in the US, in E Massachusetts: educational centre, with Harvard University (1636) and the Massachusetts Institute of Technology. Pop.: 99 890 (1994 est.).

Cambridgeshire ★ ('keɪmbrɪdʒ,ʃɪə, -ʃə) *n* a county of E England, in East Anglia: includes the former counties of the Isle of Ely and Huntingdon and lies largely in the Fens. Administrative centre: Cambridge. Pop.: 686 900 (1994 est.). Area: 3409 sq. km (1350 sq. miles).

Cambs *abbrev. for* Cambridgeshire.

Cambyses ★ (kæm'baɪsi:z) *n* died ?522 B.C., king of Persia (529–522 B.C.), who conquered Egypt (525); son of Cyrus the Great.

camcorder ('kæm,kɔ:də) *n* a video camera and recorder combined in a portable unit.

Camden[1] ★ ('kæmdən) *n* a borough of N Greater London. Pop.: 182 500 (1994 est.). Area: 21 sq. km (8 sq. miles).

Camden[2] ★ ('kæmdən) n **William**. 1551–1623, English antiquary; author of *Britannia* (1586).

came (keɪm) vb the past tense of **come**.

camel ('kæməl) n 1 either of two cud-chewing, humped mammals (see **Arabian camel, Bactrian camel**) that are adapted for surviving long periods without food or water in desert regions. 2 a float attached to a vessel to increase its buoyancy. 3a a fawn colour. 3b (*as adj*): *a camel coat*. [OE, from L, from Gk *kamēlos*, of Semitic origin]

cameleer (,kæmɪ'lɪə) n a camel driver.

camel hair or **camel's hair** n 1 the hair of the camel, used in rugs, etc. 2a soft cloth made of or containing this hair or a substitute, usually tan in colour. 2b (*as modifier*): *a camelhair coat*. 3a the hair of the squirrel's tail, used for paintbrushes. 3b (*as modifier*): *a camelhair brush*.

camellia (kə'miːlɪə) n any of a genus of ornamental shrubs having glossy evergreen leaves and showy white, pink, or red flowers. Also called: **japonica**. [C18: NL, after Georg Josef *Kamel* (1661–1706), Moravian Jesuit missionary]

camelopard ('kæmɪlə,pɑːd, kə'mɛl-) n an obsolete word for **giraffe**. [C14: from Med. L, from Gk, from *kamēlos* CAMEL + *pardalis* LEOPARD, because the giraffe was thought to have a head like a camel's and spots like a leopard's]

Camelot ★ ('kæmɪ,lɒt) n (in Arthurian legend) the English town where King Arthur's palace and court were situated.

Camembert ('kæməm,beə) n a soft creamy cheese. [F, from *Camembert*, a village in Normandy]

cameo ('kæmɪ,əʊ) n, pl **cameos**. 1 a medallion, as on a brooch or ring, with a profile head carved in relief. 2 an engraving upon a gem or other stone so that the background is of a different colour from the raised design. 3 a stone with such an engraving. 4a a brief dramatic scene played by a well-known actor or actress in a film or television play. 4b (*as modifier*): *a cameo performance*. 5 a short literary work. [C15: from It. *cammeo*, from ?]

camera ('kæmərə) n 1 an optical device consisting of a lens system set in a light-proof construction inside which a light-sensitive film or plate can be positioned. 2 *Television*. the equipment used to convert the optical image of a scene into the corresponding electrical signals. 3 (*pl* **camerae** (-ə,riː)): a judge's private room. 4 **in camera**. 4a *Law*. relating to a hearing from which members of the public are excluded. 4b in private. [C18: from L: vault, from Gk *kamara*]

cameraman ('kæmərə,mæn) n, pl **cameramen**. a person who operates a film or television camera.

camera obscura (ɒb'skjʊərə) n a darkened chamber with an aperture, in which images of outside objects are projected onto a flat surface. [NL: dark chamber]

Cameron ★ ('kæmərən) n 1 (**Mark**) **James** (**Walter**). 1911–85, British journalist. His books include *Witness in Vietnam* (1966). 2 **Julia Margaret**. 1815–79, British photographer, born in India.

Cameroon ★ (,kæmə'ruːn, 'kæmə,ruːn) n 1 a republic in West Africa, on the Gulf of Guinea: became a German colony in 1884; divided in 1919 into the **Cameroons** (administered by Britain) and **Cameroun** (administered by France); Cameroun and the S part of the Cameroons formed a republic in 1961 (the N part joined Nigeria); joined the Commonwealth in 1995. Official languages: French and English. Religions: Christian, Muslim, and animist. Currency: franc. Capital: Yaoundé. Pop.: 14 678 000 (1997). Area: 475 500 sq. km (183 591 sq. miles). French name: **Cameroun**. German name: **Kamerun**. 2 an active volcano in W Cameroon: the highest peak on the West African coast. Height: 4070 m (13 352 ft).

Cameroun ★ (kamrun) n the French name for **Cameroon**.

camiknickers ('kæmɪ,nɪkəz) pl n women's knickers attached to a camisole top.

camisole ('kæmɪ,səʊl) n 1 a woman's underbodice with shoulder straps, originally designed as a cover for a corset. 2 a woman's short negligee. [C19: from F, from Provençal *camisola*, from *camisa* shirt, from LL *camīsia*]

camomile or **chamomile** ('kæmə,maɪl) n 1 any of a genus of aromatic plants whose finely dissected leaves and daisy-like flowers are used medicinally. 2 any plant of a related genus such as **German** or **wild camomile. 3 camomile tea.** a herbal beverage made from the fragrant leaves and flowers of any of these plants. [C14: from OF, from Med. L, from Gk *khamaimēlon* lit., earth-apple (referring to the scent of the flowers)]

camouflage ('kæmə,flɑːʒ) n 1 the exploitation of natural surroundings or artificial aids to conceal or disguise the presence of military units, etc. 2 (*modifier*) (of fabric or clothing) having a design of irregular patches, in dull colours (such as browns and greens), as used in military camouflage. 3 the means by which animals escape the notice of predators. 4 a device or expedient designed to conceal or deceive. ◆ vb **camouflages, camouflaging, camouflaged.** 5 (*tr*) to conceal by camouflage. [C20: from F, from *camoufler*, from It. *camuffare* to disguise, from ?]

camp[1] (kæmp) n 1 a place where tents, cabins, etc. are erected for the use of military troops, etc. 2 tents, cabins, etc., used as temporary lodgings by holiday-makers, Scouts, Gypsies, etc. 3 the group of people living in such lodgings. 4 a group supporting a given doctrine: *the socialist camp*. 5 (*modifier*) suitable for use in temporary quarters, on holiday, etc.: *a camp bed; a camp chair*. 6 *S. African*. a field or pasture. 7 *Austral*. a place where sheep or cattle gather to rest. ◆ vb (*intr*) 8 (often foll. by *down*) to establish or set up a camp. 9 (often foll. by *out*) to live temporarily in or as if in a tent. [C16: from OF, ult. from L *campus* field]
  ▶ **'camping** n

camp[2] (kæmp) *Inf.* ◆ adj 1 effeminate; affected. 2 homosexual. 3 consciously artificial, vulgar, or mannered. ◆ vb 4 (*tr*) to perform or invest with a camp quality. 5 **camp it up. 5a** to overact. **5b** to flaunt one's homosexuality. [C20: from ?]
  ▶ **'campy** adj

Campagna ★ (kæm'pɑːnjə) n a low-lying plain surrounding Rome, Italy: once fertile, it deteriorated to malarial marshes; recently reclaimed. Area: about 2000 sq. km (800 sq. miles). Also called: **Campagna di Roma** (dɪ 'rəʊmə).

campaign (kæm'peɪn) n 1 a series of coordinated activities, such as public speaking, designed to achieve a social, political, or commercial goal: *a presidential campaign*. 2 *Mil.* a number of operations aimed at achieving a single objective. ◆ vb 3 (*intr*; often foll. by *for*) to conduct, serve in, or go on a campaign. [C17: from F *campagne* open country, from It., from LL, from L *campus* field]
  ▶ **cam'paigner** n

Campanella ★ (*Italian* kampa'nɛlla) n **Tommaso** (tom'maːzo). 1568–1639, Italian philosopher and Dominican friar, who wrote *La città del sole* (1599–1626), while imprisoned in Spain.

Campania ★ (kæm'peɪnɪə; *Italian* kam'paɲɲa) n a region of SW Italy: includes the islands of Capri and Ischia. Chief town: Naples. Pop.: 5 708 657 (1994 est.). Area: 13 595 sq. km (5248 sq. miles).

campanile (,kæmpə'niːlɪ) n (esp. in Italy) a bell tower, not usually attached to another building. [C17: from It., from *campana* bell]

campanology (,kæmpə'nɒlədʒɪ) n the art or skill of ringing bells. [C19: from NL, from LL *campāna* bell]
  ▶ **campanological** (,kæmpənə'lɒdʒɪk'l) adj ▶ **campa'nologist** or **,campa'nologer** n

campanula (kæm'pænjʊlə) n any of a genus of N temperate plants having blue or white bell-shaped flowers. Also called: **bellflower**. [C17: from NL: a little bell, from LL *campāna* bell]

Campbell ★ ('kæmb'l) n 1 Sir **Colin**, Baron Clyde. 1792–1863, British field marshal who relieved Lucknow for the second time (1857). 2 **Donald**. 1921–67, British water speed record-holder. 3 his father, Sir **Malcolm**. 1885–1948, British racing driver and land speed record-holder. 4 Mrs **Patrick**, original name *Beatrice Stella Tanner*. 1865–1940, British actress. 5 **Roy**. 1901–57, South African poet. His poetry includes *The Flaming Terrapin* (1924). 6 **Thomas**. 1777–1844, British poet, noted for his war poems *Ye Mariners of England*.

Campbell-Bannerman ★ ('kæmb'l'bænəmən) n Sir **Henry**. 1836–1908, British statesman and leader of the Liberal Party (1899–1908); prime minister (1905–08).

★ people and places

Camp David ★ *n* the US president's retreat in the Appalachian Mountains, Maryland: scene of the **Camp David Agreement** (Sept., 1978) between Anwar Sadat of Egypt and Menachem Begin of Israel, mediated by Jimmy Carter, outlining a framework for peace in the Middle East.

camp drafting *n Austral.* a competitive test of horsemen's skill in drafting cattle.

Campeche ★ (*Spanish* kam'petʃe) *n* **1** a state of SE Mexico, on the SW of the Yucatán peninsula: forestry and fishing. Capital: Campeche. Pop.: 642 082 (1995 est.). Area: 56 114 sq. km (21 666 sq. miles). **2** a port in SE Mexico, capital of Campeche state. Pop.: 150 518 (1990). **3 Bay of.** Also called: **Gulf of Campeche.** the SW part of the Gulf of Mexico.

camper ('kæmpə) *n* **1** a person who lives or temporarily stays in a tent, cabin, etc. **2** *US & Canad.* a vehicle equipped for camping out.

Campese ★ (kæm'peɪzɪ) *n* **David.** born 1962, Australian rugby union player.

camp follower *n* **1** any civilian, esp. a prostitute, who unofficially provides services to military personnel. **2** a nonmember who is sympathetic to a particular group, theory, etc.

camphor ('kæmfə) *n* a whitish crystalline aromatic ketone obtained from the wood of an Asian or Australian laurel (**camphor tree**): used in medicine as a liniment. [C15: from OF *camphre*, from Med. L *camphora*, from Ar. *kāfūr*, from Malay *kāpūr* chalk]
▶ **camphoric** (kæm'fɒrɪk) *adj*

camphorate ('kæmfə,reɪt) *vb* **camphorates, camphorating, camphorated.** (*tr*) to apply, treat with, or impregnate with camphor.

camphor ball *n* another name for **mothball** (sense 1).

camphor ice *n* an ointment consisting of camphor, white wax, spermaceti, and castor oil, used to treat skin ailments, esp. chapped skin.

camphor wood *n Austral.* a popular name for any of several trees with pungent smelling wood.

Campin ★ ('kæmpɪn) *n* **Robert.** 1379–1444, Flemish painter, noted esp. for his altarpieces: usually identified with the so-called Master of Flémalle.

campion ('kæmpɪən) *n* any of various plants related to the pink, having red, pink, or white flowers. [C16: prob. from *campion*, obs. var. of CHAMPION]

Campion ★ ('kæmpɪən) *n* **1 Saint Edmund.** 1540–81, English martyr. He joined the Jesuits in 1573 and returned to England (1580) as a missionary: charged with treason and hanged. **2 Thomas.** 1567–1620, English poet and musician, noted for his songs.

Campobello ★ (,kæmpə'beləu) *n* an island in the Bay of Fundy, off the coast of SE Canada: part of New Brunswick province. Area: about 52 sq. km (20 sq. miles). Pop.: 1317 (1991).

Campo Formio ★ (*Italian* 'kampo 'fɔrmjo) *n* a village in NE Italy, in Friuli-Venezia Giulia: scene of the signing of a treaty in 1797 that ended the war between revolutionary France and Austria. Modern name: **Campoformido** (kampo'formido).

Campo Grande ★ (*Portuguese* 'kəːmpu 'grəːndə) *n* a city in SW Brazil, capital of Mato Grosso do Sul state on the São Paulo–Corumbá railway: market centre. Pop.: 516 912 (1991).

camp oven *n Austral. & NZ.* a heavy metal pot or box with a lid, used for baking over an open fire.

camp pie *n Austral.* tinned meat.

camp site *n* an area on which holiday-makers may pitch a tent, etc. Also called: **camping site.**

campus ('kæmpəs) *n, pl* **campuses.** **1** the grounds and buildings of a university. **2** *Chiefly US.* the outside area of a college, etc. [C18: from L: field]

campylobacter ('kæmpɪləu,bæktə) *n* a rod-shaped bacterium that causes infections in animals and man; a common cause of gastroenteritis. [from Gk *kampulos* bent + BACTER(IUM)]

Cam Ranh ★ ('kæm 'ræn) *n* a port in SE Vietnam: large

natural harbour, in recent years used as a naval base by French, Japanese, US, and Russian forces successively. Pop.: 114 041 (1989).

camshaft ('kæm,ʃɑːft) *n* a shaft having one or more cams attached to it.

Camus ★ (*French* kamy) *n* **Albert** (albɛr). 1913–60, French writer, noted for the novels *L'Étranger* (1942) and *La Peste* (1947), the play *Caligula* (1946), and the essay *L'Homme révolté* (1951): Nobel prize for literature 1957.

can[1] (kæn; *unstressed* kən) *vb, past* **could.** (takes an infinitive without *to* or an implied infinitive) used as an auxiliary: **1** to indicate ability, skill, or fitness to perform a task: *I can run.* **2** to indicate permission or the right to do something: *can I have a drink?* **3** to indicate knowledge of how to do something: *he can speak three languages.* **4** to indicate the possibility, opportunity, or likelihood: *my trainer says I can win the race.* [OE *cunnan*]

> **USAGE NOTE** See at **may**[1].

can[2] (kæn) *n* **1** a container, esp. for liquids, usually of thin metal: *a petrol can.* **2** a tin (metal container): *a beer can.* **3** Also: **canful.** the contents of a can or the amount a can will hold. **4** a slang word for **prison. 5** *US & Canad.* a slang word for **toilet. 6** a shallow cylindrical metal container used for storing and handling film. **7 can of worms.** *Inf.* a complicated problem. **8 in the can. 8a** (of a film, piece of music, etc.) having been recorded, edited, etc. **8b** *Inf.* agreed: *the contract is in the can.* ◆ *vb* **cans, canning, canned. 9** to put (food, etc.) into a can or cans. [OE *canne*]
▶ **'canner** *n*

Can. *abbrev. for:* **1** Canada. **2** Canadian.

Cana ★ ('keɪnə) *n New Testament.* the town in Galilee, north of Nazareth, where Jesus performed his first miracle by changing water into wine (John 2:1, 11).

Canaan ★ ('keɪnən) *n* an ancient region between the River Jordan and the Mediterranean: the Promised Land of the Israelites.

Canaanite ('keɪnə,naɪt) *n* a member of an ancient Semitic people who occupied the land of Canaan before the Israelite conquest.

Canada ★ ('kænədə) *n* a country in North America: the second largest country in the world; first permanent settlements made by the French from 1605; ceded to Britain in 1763 after a series of colonial wars; established as the Dominion of Canada in 1867; a member of the Commonwealth. It consists generally of sparsely inhabited tundra regions, rich in natural resources, in the north, the Rocky Mountains in the west, the Canadian Shield in the east, and vast central prairies; the bulk of the population is concentrated along the US border and the Great Lakes in the south. Languages: English and French. Religion: Christian majority. Currency: Canadian dollar. Capital: Ottawa. Pop.: 30 287 000 (1997). Area: 9 976 185 sq. km (3 851 809 sq. miles).

Canada balsam *n* **1** a yellow transparent resin obtained from the balsam fir. Because its refractive index is similar to that of glass, it is used as a mounting medium for microscope specimens. **2** another name for **balsam fir.**

Canada Day *n* (in Canada) July 1, the anniversary of the day in 1867 when Canada received dominion status: a public holiday.

Canada goose *n* a large common greyish-brown North American goose with a black neck and head and a white throat patch.

Canada jay *n* a grey crestless jay, notorious in northern parts of N America for its stealing. Also called: **camp robber, whisky-jack.**

Canadian (kə'neɪdɪən) *adj* **1** of or relating to Canada or its people. ◆ *n* **2** a native, citizen, or inhabitant of Canada.

Canadiana (kə,neɪdɪ'ɑːnə; *Canad.* -'ænə) *n* objects, such as books, furniture, and antiques, relating to Canadian history and culture.

Canadian football *n* a game like American football played on a grass pitch between teams of 12 players.

Canadianism (kə'neɪdɪə,nɪzəm) n 1 the Canadian national character or spirit. 2 a linguistic usage, custom, or other feature peculiar to Canada, its people, or their culture.

Canadianize or **Canadianise** (kə'neɪdɪə,naɪz) vb **Canadianizes, Canadianizing, Canadianized** or **Canadianises, Canadianising, Canadianised.** to make or become Canadian by changing customs, ownership, character, content, etc.

Canadian River ★ n a river in the southern US, rising in NE New Mexico and flowing east to the Arkansas River in E Oklahoma. Length: 1458 km (906 miles).

Canadian Shield n the wide area of Precambrian rock extending over most of E and central Canada: rich in minerals. Also called: **Laurentian Shield.**

Canadien (French kanadjɛ̃; English kə,nædɪ'ɛn) or (fem) **Canadienne** (French kanadjɛn; English kə,nædɪ'ɛn) n a French Canadian.

canaille French. (kanɑj) n the masses; mob; rabble. [C17: from F, from It. canaglia pack of dogs]

canakin ('kænɪkɪn) n a variant spelling of **cannikin.**

canal (kə'næl) n 1 an artificial waterway constructed for navigation, irrigation, etc. 2 any of various passages or ducts: the alimentary canal. 3 any of various intercellular spaces in plants. 4 Astron. any of the indistinct surface features of Mars orig. thought to be a network of channels. ◆ vb **canals, canalling, canalled** or US **canals, canaling, canaled.** (tr) 5 to dig a canal through. 6 to provide with a canal or canals. [C15 (in the sense: pipe, tube): from L canālis channel, from canna reed]

canal boat n a long narrow boat used on canals, esp. for carrying freight.

Canaletto ★ (Italian kana'letto) n original name Giovanni Antonio Canale. 1697–1768, Venetian painter, noted also for his London views.

canaliculus (,kænə'lɪkjuləs) n, pl **canaliculi** (-,laɪ). a small channel or groove, as in some bones. [C16: from L: a little channel, from canālis CANAL]
▶ ,cana'licular or ,cana'liculate adj

canalize or **canalise** ('kænə,laɪz) vb **canalizes, canalizing, canalized** or **canalises, canalising, canalised.** (tr) 1 to provide with or convert into a canal or canals. 2 to give a particular direction to or provide an outlet for.
▶ ,canali'zation or ,canali'sation n

canal ray n Physics. a stream of positive ions produced in a discharge tube by allowing them to pass through holes in the cathode.

Canal Zone ★ n a former administrative region of the US, on the Isthmus of Panama around the Panama Canal: bordered on each side by the Republic of Panama, into which it was incorporated in 1979. Also called: **Panama Canal Zone.**

canapé ('kænəpɪ, -,peɪ) n a small piece of bread, toast, etc., spread with a savoury topping. [C19: from F: sofa]

Canara (kə'nɑːrə) n a variant spelling of **Kanara.**

canard (kæ'nɑːd) n 1 a false report; rumour or hoax. 2 an aircraft in which the tailplane is mounted in front of the wing. [C19: from F: a duck, from OF caner to quack, imit.]

canary (kə'nɛərɪ) n, pl **canaries. 1** a small finch of the Canary Islands and Azores: a popular cagebird noted for its singing. **2 canary yellow. 2a** a light yellow. **2b** (as adj): a canary-yellow car. **3** a sweet wine similar to Madeira. **4** Arch. a sweet wine from the Canary Islands. [C16: from OSp. canario of or from the Canary Islands]

Canary Islands or **Canaries** ★ pl n a group of mountainous islands in the Atlantic off the NW coast of Africa, forming an Autonomous Community of Spain. Pop.: 1 522 380 (1988 est.).

canasta (kə'næstə) n 1 a card game for two to six players who seek to amass points by declaring sets of cards. 2 Also called: **meld.** a declared set in this game, containing seven or more like cards. [C20: from Sp.: basket (because two packs of cards are required), from L canistrum; see CANISTER]

canaster ('kænəstə) n coarsely broken dried tobacco leaves. [C19: (meaning: basket in which tobacco was packed): from Sp.; see CANISTER]

Canaveral ★ (kə'nævərəl) n **Cape.** a cape on the E coast of Florida: site of the US Air Force Missile Test Centre, from which the majority of US space missions have been launched. Former name (1963–73): Cape **Kennedy.**

Canberra ★ ('kænbərə, -brə) n the capital of Australia, in Australian Capital Territory: founded in 1913 as a planned capital. Pop.: 303 700 (1995 est.).

cancan ('kæn,kæn) n a high-kicking dance performed by a female chorus, originating in the music halls of 19th-century Paris. [C19: from F, from ?]

cancel ('kænsᵊl) vb **cancels, cancelling, cancelled** or US **cancels, canceling, canceled.** (mainly tr) 1 to order (something already arranged, such as a meeting or event) to be postponed indefinitely; call off. 2 to revoke or annul: the order was cancelled. 3 to delete (writing, numbers, etc.); cross out. 4 to mark (a cheque, stamp, etc.) with an official stamp to prevent further use. 5 (also intr; usually foll. by out) to counterbalance: his generosity cancelled out his past unkindness. 6 Maths. to eliminate (numbers or terms) as common factors from both the numerator and denominator of a fraction or as equal terms from opposite sides of an equation. ◆ n 7 a new leaf or section of a book replacing one containing errors, or one that has been omitted. 8 a cancellation. 9 Music. a US word for **natural** (sense 16). [C14: from OF canceller, from Med. L, from LL: to make like a lattice, from L cancellī lattice]
▶ 'canceller or US 'canceler n

cancellate ('kænsɪ,leɪt) or **cancellated** adj 1 Anat. having a spongy internal structure: cancellate bones. 2 Bot. forming a network. [C17: from L cancellāre to make like a lattice]

cancellation (,kænsɪ'leɪʃən) n 1 the fact or an instance of cancelling. 2 something that has been cancelled, such as a theatre ticket: we have a cancellation in the stalls. 3 the marks made by cancelling.

cancer ('kænsə) n 1 any type of malignant growth or tumour, caused by abnormal and uncontrolled cell division. 2 the condition resulting from this. 3 an evil influence that spreads dangerously. [C14: from L: crab, a creeping tumour]
▶ 'cancerous adj

Cancer ('kænsə) n, Latin genitive **Cancri** ('kæŋkriː). 1 Astron. Also called: the **Crab.** a small N constellation. 2 Astrol. the fourth sign of the zodiac. The sun is in this sign between about June 21 and July 22. 3 **tropic of Cancer.** See **tropic** (sense 1).

cancerophobia (,kænsərəʊ'fəʊbɪə) n a morbid dread of being afflicted by cancer.

cancroid ('kæŋkrɔɪd) adj 1 resembling a cancerous growth. 2 resembling a crab. ◆ n 3 a skin cancer.

candela (kæn'diːlə, -'deɪlə) n the basic SI unit of luminous intensity; the intensity, in a perpendicular direction, of a surface of 1/600 000 square metre of a black body at the temperature of freezing platinum under a pressure of 101 325 newtons per square metre. Symbol: cd [C20: from L: CANDLE]

Candela ★ (kæn'diːlə) n **Felix.** born 1910, Mexican architect.

candelabrum (,kændɪ'lɑːbrəm) or **candelabra** n, pl **candelabra** (-brə), **candelabrums,** or **candelabras.** a large branched candleholder or holder for overhead lights. [C19: from L, from candēla CANDLE]

candescent (kæn'dɛsᵊnt) adj Rare. glowing or starting to glow with heat. [C19: from L, from candēre to be white, shine]
▶ can'descence n

c & f abbrev. for cost and freight.

C & G abbrev. for City and Guilds.

Candia ★ ('kandja) n the Italian name for **Iráklion.**

candid ('kændɪd) adj 1 frank and outspoken. 2 without partiality; unbiased. 3 unposed or informal: a candid photograph. [C17: from L, from candēre to be white]
▶ 'candidly adv ▶ 'candidness n

candida ('kændɪdə) n any of a genus of yeastlike parasitic fungi, esp. one that causes thrush (**candidiasis**).

candidate ('kændɪ,deɪt) n 1 a person seeking or nominated for election to a position of authority or selection for a job, etc. 2 a person taking an examination or test. 3 a person or thing regarded as suitable or likely for a particular fate or position. [C17: from L *candidātus* clothed in white (because the candidate wore a white toga), from *candidus* white]
► **candidacy** ('kændɪdəsɪ) or **candidature** ('kændɪdətʃə) n

candid camera n a small camera that may be used to take informal photographs of people.

candied ('kændɪd) adj impregnated or encrusted with or as if with sugar: *candied peel*.

candle ('kænd°l) n 1 a cylindrical piece of wax, tallow, or other fatty substance surrounding a wick, which is burned to produce light. 2 *Physics*. another name for **candela**. 3 **burn the candle at both ends**. to exhaust oneself by doing too much, esp. by being up late and getting up early to work. 4 **not hold a candle to**. *Inf*. to be inferior or contemptible in comparison with. 5 **not worth the candle**. *Inf*. not worth the price or trouble entailed. ♦ vb **candles, candling, candled. 6** (tr) to examine (eggs) for freshness or the likelihood of being hatched by viewing them against a bright light. [OE *candel*, from L *candēla*, from *candēre* to glitter]
► **'candler** n

candleberry ('kænd°lbərɪ) n, pl **candleberries**. another name for **wax myrtle**.

candlelight ('kænd°l,laɪt) n 1a the light from a candle or candles. 1b (as modifier): *a candlelight dinner*. 2 dusk; evening.

Candlemas ('kænd°lməs) n *Christianity*. Feb. 2, the Feast of the Purification of the Virgin Mary and the presentation of Christ in the Temple.

candlenut ('kænd°l,nʌt) n 1 a tree of tropical Asia and Polynesia. 2 the nut of this tree, which yields an oil used in paints. In their native regions the nuts are burned as candles.

candlepower ('kænd°l,paʊə) n the luminous intensity of a source of light in a given direction: now expressed in candelas.

candlestick ('kænd°l,stɪk) or **candleholder** ('kænd°l,həʊldə) n a holder, usually ornamental, with a spike or socket for a candle.

candlewick ('kænd°l,wɪk) n 1 unbleached cotton or muslin into which loops of yarn are hooked and then cut to give a tufted pattern. 2 (modifier) being or made of candlewick fabric.

C & M abbrev. for care and maintenance.

can-do adj confident and resourceful in the face of challenges: *a can-do attitude*.

Candolle ★ (French kɑ̃dɔl) n **Augustin Pyrame de** (ogystɛ piram də). 1778–1841, Swiss botanist; his *Théorie élémentaire de la botanique* (1813) introduced a new system of plant classification.

candour or US **candor** ('kændə) n 1 the quality of being open and honest; frankness. 2 fairness; impartiality. [C17: from L *candor*, from *candēre* to be white]

C & W abbrev. for country and western.

candy ('kændɪ) n, pl **candies**. 1 Chiefly US. & Canad. sweets, chocolate, etc. ♦ vb **candies, candying, candied. 2** to cause (sugar, etc.) to become crystalline or (of sugar) to become crystalline. 3 (tr) to preserve (fruit peel, ginger, etc.) by boiling in sugar. 4 (tr) to cover with any crystalline substance, such as ice or sugar. [C16: from OF *sucre candi* candied sugar, from Ar. *qandi* candied, from *qand* cane sugar]

candyfloss ('kændɪ,flɒs) n Brit. a very light fluffy confection made from coloured spun sugar, usually held on a stick. US and Canad. name: **cotton candy**. Austral. name: **fairyfloss**.

candy-striped adj (esp. of clothing fabric) having narrow coloured stripes on a white background.
► **candy stripe** n

candytuft ('kændɪ,tʌft) n either of two species of *Iberis* having clusters of white, red, or purplish flowers. [C17: *Candy*, obs. var. of CANDIA (town in Crete) + TUFT]

cane (keɪn) n 1a the long jointed pithy or hollow flexible stem of the bamboo, rattan, or any similar plant. 1b any plant having such a stem. 2a strips of such stems, woven or interlaced to make wickerwork, etc. 2b (as modifier): *a cane chair*. 3 the woody stem of a reed, blackberry, or loganberry. 4 a flexible rod with which to administer a beating. 5 a slender rod used as a walking stick. 6 See **sugar cane**. ♦ vb **canes, caning, caned.** (tr) 7 to whip or beat with or as if with a cane. 8 to make or repair with cane. 9 *Inf*. to defeat: *we got well caned in the match*. [C14: from OF, from L *canna*, from Gk *kanna*, of Semitic origin]
► **'caner** n

Canea ★ (kæ'nɪə) n the capital and chief port of Crete, on the NW coast. Pop.: 50 000 (latest est.). Also called: **Chania** ('hɑːnɪə). Greek name: **Khaniá**.

canebrake ('keɪn,breɪk) n US. a thicket of canes.

cane sugar n 1 the sucrose obtained from sugar cane. 2 another name for **sucrose**.

Canetti ★ (kə'netɪ) n **Elias**. 1905–94, British writer, born in Bulgaria; wrote chiefly in German. His works include the novel *Auto da Fé* (1935). Nobel prize for literature 1981.

cangue or **cang** (kæŋ) n (formerly in China) a large wooden collar worn by petty criminals as a punishment. [C18: from F, from Port. *canga* yoke]

canikin ('kænɪkɪn) n a variant spelling of **cannikin**.

canine ('keɪnaɪn, 'kæn-) adj 1 of or resembling a dog. 2 of or belonging to the Canidae, a family of mammals, including dogs, wolves, and foxes, typically having a bushy tail, erect ears, and a long muzzle. 3 of or relating to any of the four teeth, two in each jaw, situated between the incisors and the premolars. ♦ n 4 any animal of the family Canidae. 5 a canine tooth. [C17: from L *canīnus*, from *canis* dog]

caning ('keɪnɪŋ) n Inf. a severe defeat or punishment.

Canis Major ('keɪnɪs) n, Latin genitive **Canis Majoris** (mə'dʒɔːrɪs). a S constellation containing Sirius, the brightest star in the sky. Also called: the **Great Dog**. [L: the greater dog]

Canis Minor n, Latin genitive **Canis Minoris** (maɪ'nɔːrɪs). a small N constellation. Also called: the **Little Dog**. [L: the lesser dog]

canister ('kænɪstə) n 1 a container, usually made of metal, in which dry food, such as tea or coffee, is stored. 2 (formerly) 2a a type of shrapnel shell for firing from a cannon. 2b Also called: **canister shot**. the shot or shrapnel packed inside this. [C17: from L *canistrum* basket woven from reeds, from Gk, from *kanna* reed]

canker ('kæŋkə) n 1 an ulceration, esp. of the lips. 2 Vet. science. 2a a disease of horses in which the horn of the hoofs becomes spongy. 2b an ulcerative disease of the lining of the external ear, esp. in dogs and cats. 2c ulceration or abscess of the mouth, eyelids, ears, or cloaca of birds. 3 an open wound in the stem of a tree or shrub. 4 something evil that spreads and corrupts. ♦ vb 5 to infect or become infected with or as if with canker. [OE *cancer*, from L *cancer* cancerous sore]
► **'cankerous** adj

cankerworm ('kæŋkə,wɜːm) n the larva of either of two moths, which feed on and destroy fruit and shade trees in North America.

canna ('kænə) n any of a genus of tropical plants having broad leaves and red or yellow showy flowers. [C17: from NL CANE]

cannabis ('kænəbɪs) n 1 another name for **hemp** (the plant), esp. Indian hemp. 2 the drug obtained from the dried leaves and flowers of the hemp plant, which is smoked or chewed for its psychoactive properties. See also **hashish, marijuana. 3 cannabis resin**. a poisonous resin obtained from the hemp plant. [C18: from L, from Gk *kannabis*]

Cannae ★ ('kænɪ) n an ancient city in SE Italy: scene of a victory by Hannibal over the Romans (216 B.C.).

canned (kænd) adj 1 preserved and stored in airtight cans or tins. 2 Inf. prepared or recorded in advance: *canned music*. 3 Sl. drunk.

cannel coal or **cannel** ('kæn°l) n a dull coal burning with a smoky luminous flame. [C16: from N English dialect *cannel* candle]

cannelloni *or* **canneloni** (ˌkænɪˈləʊnɪ) *pl n* tubular pieces of pasta filled with meat or cheese. [It., pl of *cannellone*, from *cannello* stalk]

cannery (ˈkænərɪ) *n, pl* **canneries.** a place where foods are canned.

Cannes ★ (kæn, kænz; *French* kan) *n* a port and resort in SE France: developed in the 19th century from a fishing village; annual film festival. Pop.: 335 647 (1990).

cannibal (ˈkænɪbªl) *n* 1 a person who eats the flesh of other human beings. 2 an animal that feeds on the flesh of others of its kind. [C16: from Sp. *Canibales*, the name used by Columbus to designate the Caribs of Cuba and Haiti]
▸ ˈcannibaˌlism *n*

cannibalize *or* **cannibalise** (ˈkænɪbəˌlaɪz) *vb* **cannibalizes, cannibalizing, cannibalized** *or* **cannibalises, cannibalising, cannibalised.** (*tr*) to use (serviceable parts from one machine or vehicle) to repair another.
▸ ˌcannibaliˈzation *or* ˌcannibaliˈsation *n*

cannikin, canakin, *or* **canikin** (ˈkænɪkɪn) *n* a small can, esp. one used as a drinking vessel. [C16: from MDu. *kanneken*; see CAN², -KIN]

canning (ˈkænɪŋ) *n* the process or business of sealing food in cans or tins to preserve it.

Canning ★ (ˈkænɪŋ) *n* 1 **Charles John,** 1st Earl Canning. 1812–62, British statesman; governor general of India (1856–58) and first viceroy (1858–62). 2 his father, **George.** 1770–1827, British Tory statesman; foreign secretary (1822–27) and prime minister (1827).

Cannock ★ (ˈkænək) *n* a town in W central England, in S Staffordshire: **Cannock Chase** (a public area of heathland, once a royal preserve) is just to the E. Pop.: 60 106 (1991).

cannon (ˈkænən) *n, pl* **cannons** *or* **cannon.** 1 an automatic aircraft gun. 2 *History.* a heavy artillery piece consisting of a metal tube mounted on a carriage. 3 a heavy tube or drum, esp. one that can rotate freely. 4 See **cannon bone.** 5 *Billiards.* a shot in which the cue ball is caused to contact one object ball after another. Usual US and Canad. word: **carom.** ♦ *vb* 6 (*intr*) to rebound; collide (*with* into). 7 (*intr*) *Billiards.* to make a cannon. [C16: from OF *canon*, from It. *cannone* cannon, from *canna* tube]

cannonade (ˌkænəˈneɪd) *n* 1 an intense and continuous artillery bombardment. ♦ *vb* **cannonades, cannonading, cannonaded.** 2 to attack (a target) with cannon.

cannonball (ˈkænənˌbɔːl) *n* 1 a projectile fired from a cannon: usually a solid round metal shot. ♦ *vb* (*intr*) 2 (often foll. by *along*, etc.) to rush along. ♦ *adj* 3 very fast or powerful.

cannon bone *n* a bone in the legs of horses and other hoofed animals consisting of greatly elongated fused metatarsals or metacarpals.

cannoneer (ˌkænəˈnɪə) *n* (formerly) a soldier who served and fired a cannon; artilleryman.

cannon fodder *n* men regarded as expendable in war because they are part of a huge army.

cannot (ˈkænɒt, kæˈnɒt) *an* auxiliary verb expressing incapacity, inability, withholding permission, etc.; can not.

cannula *or* **canula** (ˈkænjʊlə) *n, pl* **cannulas, cannulae** (-ˌliː), *or* **canulas, canulae** (-ˌliː). *Surgery.* a narrow tube for draining fluid from or introducing medication into the body. [C17: from L: a small reed, from *canna* a reed]

canny (ˈkænɪ) *adj* **cannier, canniest.** 1 shrewd, esp. in business. 2 *Scot. & NE English dialect.* good or nice: used as a general term of approval. 3 *Scot.* lucky or fortunate. [C16: from CAN¹ (in the sense: to know how) + -Y¹]
▸ ˈcannily *adv* ▸ ˈcanniness *n*

canoe (kəˈnuː) *n* 1 a light narrow open boat, propelled by one or more paddles. ♦ *vb* **canoes, canoeing, canoed.** 2 to go in or transport by canoe. [C16: from Sp. *canoa*, of Carib origin]
▸ caˈnoeist *n*

canon¹ (ˈkænən) *n* 1 *Christianity.* a Church decree enacted to regulate morals or religious practices. 2 (*often pl*)

a general rule or standard, as of judgment, morals, etc. 3 (*often pl*) a principle or criterion applied in a branch of learning or art. 4 *RC Church.* the list of the canonized saints. 5 *RC Church.* Also called: **Eucharistic Prayer.** the prayer in the Mass in which the Host is consecrated. 6 a list of writings, esp. sacred writings, recognized as genuine. 7 a piece of music in which an extended melody in one part is imitated successively in one or more other parts. 8 a list of the works of an author that are accepted as authentic. [OE, from L, from Gk *kanōn* rule, rod for measuring]

canon² (ˈkænən) *n* 1 one of several priests on the permanent staff of a cathedral, who are responsible for organizing services, maintaining the fabric, etc. 2 *RC Church.* Also called: **canon regular.** a member of either of two religious orders living communally as monks but performing clerical duties.. [C13: from Anglo-F, from LL *canonicus* one living under a rule, from CANON¹]

canonical (kəˈnɒnɪkªl) *or* **canonic** *adj* 1 included in a canon of sacred or other officially recognized writings. 2 in conformity with canon law. 3 accepted; authoritative. 4 *Music.* in the form of a canon. 5 of or relating to a cathedral chapter. 6 of a canon (clergyman).
▸ caˈnonically *adv*

canonical hour *n* 1 *RC Church.* one of the seven prayer times appointed for each day by canon law. 2 *Church of England.* any time at which marriages may lawfully be celebrated.

canonicals (kəˈnɒnɪkªlz) *pl n* the vestments worn by clergy when officiating.

canonicity (ˌkænəˈnɪsɪtɪ) *n* the fact or quality of being canonical.

canonist (ˈkænənɪst) *n* a specialist in canon law.

canonize *or* **canonise** (ˈkænəˌnaɪz) *vb* **canonizes, canonizing, canonized** *or* **canonises, canonising, canonised.** (*tr*) 1 *RC Church.* to declare (a person) to be a saint. 2 to regard as a saint. 3 to sanction by canon law.
▸ ˌcanoniˈzation *or* ˌcanoniˈsation *n*

canon law *n* the codified body of laws enacted by the supreme authorities of a Christian Church.

canonry (ˈkænənrɪ) *n, pl* **canonries.** 1 the office, benefice, or status of a canon. 2 canons collectively. [C15: from CANON² + -RY]

canoodle (kəˈnuːdªl) *vb* **canoodles, canoodling, canoodled.** (*intr*; often by *with*) *Sl.* to kiss and cuddle. [C19: from ?]

Canopic jar, urn, *or* **vase** (kəˈnəʊpɪk) *n* (in ancient Egypt) one of four containers for holding the entrails of a mummy.

Canopus ★ (kəˈnəʊpəs) *n* a port in ancient Egypt east of Alexandria where granite monuments have been found inscribed with the name of Rameses II and written in languages similar to those of the Rosetta stone.
▸ Caˈnopic *adj*

canopy (ˈkænəpɪ) *n, pl* **canopies.** 1 an ornamental awning above a throne, bed, person, etc. 2 a rooflike covering over an altar, niche, etc. 3 a roofed structure serving as a sheltered passageway. 4 a large or wide covering: *the sky was a grey canopy.* 5 the hemisphere that forms the supporting surface of a parachute. 6 the transparent cover of an aircraft cockpit. 7 the highest level of foliage in a forest, formed by the crowns of the trees. ♦ *vb* **canopies, canopying, canopied.** 8 (*tr*) to cover with or as with a canopy. [C14: from Med. L *canōpeum* mosquito net, from L, from Gk *kōnōpeion* bed with protective net]

canst (kænst) *vb Arch.* the form of **can¹** used with the pronoun *thou* or its relative form.

cant¹ (kænt) *n* 1 insincere talk, esp. concerning religion or morals. 2 phrases that have become meaningless through repetition. 3 specialized vocabulary of a particular group, such as thieves, journalists, or lawyers. ♦ *vb* 4 (*intr*) to speak in or use cant. [C16: prob. via Norman F *canter* to sing, from L *cantāre*; used disparagingly, from the 12th cent., of chanting in religious services]
▸ ˈcantingly *adv*

cant² (kænt) *n* 1 inclination from a vertical or horizontal plane. 2 a sudden movement that tilts or turns something. 3 the angle or tilt thus caused. 4 a corner or outer angle. 5 an oblique or slanting surface, edge, or line.

◆ *vb* (*tr*) **6** to tip, tilt, or overturn. **7** to set in an oblique position. **8** another word for **bevel** (sense 1). ◆ *adj* **9** oblique; slanting. **10** having flat surfaces. [C14 (in the sense: edge): ?from L *canthus* iron hoop round a wheel, from ?]

Cant. *abbrev. for:* **1** Canterbury. **2** *Bible.* Canticles.

can't (kɑːnt) *contraction of* cannot.

Cantab. (kænˈtæb) *abbrev. for* Cantabrigiensis. [L: of Cambridge]

cantabile (kænˈtɑːbɪlɪ) *Music.* ◆ *adj, adv* **1** (to be performed) flowingly and melodiously. ◆ *n* **2** a piece or passage performed in this way. [It., from LL, from L *cantāre* to sing]

Cantabrian Mountains ★ (kænˈteɪbrɪən) *pl n* a mountain chain along the N coast of Spain, consisting of a series of high ridges that rise over 2400 m (8000 ft): rich in minerals (esp. coal and iron).

Cantabrigian (ˌkæntəˈbrɪdʒɪən) *adj* **1** of or characteristic of Cambridge or Cambridge University. ◆ *n* **2** a member or graduate of Cambridge University. **3** an inhabitant or native of Cambridge. [C17: from Med. L *Cantabrigia*]

Cantal ★ (*French* kɑtal) *n* **1** a department of S central France, in the Auvergne region. Capital: Aurillac. Pop.: 155 587 (1994 est.). Area: 5779 sq. km (2254 sq. miles). **2** a hard strong cheese made in this area.

cantaloupe *or* **cantaloup** (ˈkæntəˌluːp) *n* **1** a cultivated variety of muskmelon with ribbed warty rind and orange flesh. **2** any of several other muskmelons. [C18: from F, from *Cantaluppi*, near Rome, where first cultivated in Europe]

cantankerous (kænˈtæŋkərəs) *adj* quarrelsome; irascible. [C18: ?from C14 (obs.) *conteckour* a contentious person, from Anglo-F *contek* strife, from ?]
▶ **can'tankerously** *adv* ▶ **can'tankerousness** *n*

cantata (kænˈtɑːtə) *n* a musical setting of a text, esp. a religious text, consisting of arias, duets, and choruses. [C18: from It., from *cantare* to sing, from L]

canteen (kænˈtiːn) *n* **1** a restaurant attached to a factory, school, etc., providing meals for large numbers. **2a** a small shop that provides a limited range of items to a military unit. **2b** a recreation centre for military personnel. **3** a temporary or mobile stand at which food is provided. **4a** a box in which a set of cutlery is laid out. **4b** the cutlery itself. **5** a flask for carrying water or other liquids. [C18: from F, from It. *cantina* wine cellar, from *canto* corner, from L *canthus* iron hoop encircling chariot wheel]

Canteloube ★ (ˈkæntəˌluːb; *French* kãtlub) *n* (**Marie**) **Joseph** (*French* ʒɔzef). 1879–1957, French composer, best known for his *Chants d'Auvergne* (1923–30).

canter (ˈkæntə) *n* **1** a gait of horses, etc., between a trot and a gallop in speed. **2 at a canter.** easily; without effort. ◆ *vb* **2** to move or cause to move at a canter. [C18: short for *Canterbury trot,* the supposed pace at which pilgrims rode to Canterbury]

Canterbury ★ (ˈkæntəbərɪ, -brɪ) *n* **1** a city in SE England, in E Kent: starting point for St Augustine's mission to England (597 A.D.); cathedral where St Thomas à Becket was martyred (1170); seat of the archbishop and primate of England; seat of the University of Kent. Pop.: 36 464 (1991). Latin name: **Durovernum** (ˌduːrəʊˈvɜːnəm, ˌdjuə-). **2** a regional council of New Zealand, on E central South Island on **Canterbury Bight:** mountainous with coastal lowlands; agricultural. Chief town: Christchurch. Pop.: 477 667 (1996). Area: 43 371 sq. km (16 742 sq. miles).

Canterbury bell *n* a biennial European plant related to the campanula and widely cultivated for its blue, violet, or white flowers.

cantharides (kænˈθærɪˌdiːz) *pl n, sing* **cantharis** (ˈkæn-θərɪs). a diuretic and urogenital stimulant prepared from the dried bodies of Spanish fly. Also called: **Spanish fly.** [C15: from L, pl of *cantharis*, from Gk *kantharis* Spanish fly]

cant hook *or* **dog** *n Forestry.* a wooden pole with a blunt steel tip and an adjustable hook at one end, used for handling logs.

canthus (ˈkænθəs) *n, pl* **canthi** (-ˌθaɪ). the inner or outer

corner of the eye, formed by the natural junction of the eyelids. [C17: from NL, from L: iron tyre]

canticle (ˈkæntɪk°l) *n* a nonmetrical hymn, derived from the Bible and used in the liturgy of certain Christian churches. [C13: from L *canticulum*, dim. of *canticus* a song, from *canere* to sing]

cantilena (ˌkæntɪˈleɪnə) *n* a smooth flowing style in the writing of vocal music. [C18: It.]

cantilever (ˈkæntɪˌliːvə) *n* **1** a beam, girder, or structural framework that is fixed at one end only. **2** a part of a beam or a structure projecting outwards beyond its support. [C17: ?from CANT² + LEVER]

cantilever bridge *n* a bridge having spans that are constructed as cantilevers.

cantillate (ˈkæntɪˌleɪt) *vb* **cantillates, cantillating, cantillated. 1** to chant (passages of the Hebrew Scriptures) according to the traditional Jewish melody. **2** to intone or chant. [C19: from LL *cantillāre* to sing softly, from L *cantāre* to sing]
▶ **ˌcantilˈlation** *n*

cantle (ˈkænt°l) *n* **1** the back part of a saddle that slopes upwards. **2** a broken-off piece. [C14: from OF *cantel*, from *cant* corner]

canto (ˈkæntəʊ) *n, pl* **cantos.** a main division of a long poem. [C16: from It.: song, from L, from *canere* to sing]

canto fermo (ˈkæntəʊ ˈfɜːməʊ) *or* **cantus firmus** (ˈkæntəs ˈfɜːməs) *n* **1** a melody that is the basis to which other parts are added in polyphonic music. **2** the traditional Church plainchant as prescribed by use and regulation. [It., from Med L: fixed song]

canton *n* **1** (ˈkæntɒn, kænˈtɒn). a political division of Switzerland. **2** (ˈkæntən). *Heraldry.* a small square charge on a shield, usually in the top left corner. ◆ *vb* **3** (kænˈtɒn). (*tr*) to divide into cantons. **4** (kənˈtuːn). (esp. formerly) to allocate accommodation to (military personnel, etc.). [C16: from OF: corner, from It., from *canto* corner, from L *canthus* iron rim]
▶ **ˈcantonal** *adj*

Canton ★ *n* **1** (kænˈtɒn). a port in SE China, capital of Guangdong province, on the Zhu Jiang (Pearl River): the first Chinese port open to European trade. Pop.: 3 580 000 (1991 est.). Chinese names: **Guangzhou, Kwangchow. 2** (ˈkæntən). a city in the US, in NE Ohio. Pop.: 84 188 (1994 est.).

Cantonese (ˌkæntəˈniːz) *n* **1** the Chinese language spoken in the city of Canton, Guangdong and Guanxi provinces, Hong Kong, and elsewhere inside and outside China. **2** (*pl* **Cantonese**) a native or inhabitant of Canton city or Guangdong province. ◆ *adj* **3** of or relating to Canton or Guangdong or the Chinese language spoken there.

cantonment (kənˈtuːnmənt) *n Mil.* (esp. formerly) **1** a large training camp. **2** the winter quarters of a campaigning army. **3** *History.* a permanent military camp in British India.

Canton River ★ (kænˈtɒn) *n* another name for the **Zhu Jiang.**

cantor (ˈkæntɔː) *n* **1** *Judaism.* a man employed to lead synagogue services. **2** *Christianity.* the leader of the singing in a church choir. [C16: from L: singer, from *canere* to sing]

cantorial (kænˈtɔːrɪəl) *adj* **1** of a precentor. **2** (of part of a choir) on the same side of a cathedral, etc., as the precentor.

cantoris (kænˈtɔːrɪs) *adj* (in antiphonal music) to be sung by the cantorial side of a choir. Cf. **decani.** [L: genitive of *cantor* precentor]

Cantuar. (ˈkæntjʊˌɑː) *abbrev. for* Cantuariensis. [L: (Archbishop) of Canterbury]

Canuck (kəˈnʌk) *n, adj US & Canad. inf.* Canadian. [C19: from ?]

Canute, Cnut, *or* **Knut** ★ (kəˈnjuːt) *n* died 1035, Danish king of England (1016–35), Denmark (1018–35), and Norway (1028–35). He defeated Edmund II of England (1016), but divided the kingdom with him until Edmund's death. He invaded Scotland (1027) and drove Olaf II from Norway (1028).

canvas ('kænvəs) *n* **1a** a heavy cloth made of cotton, hemp, or jute, used for sails, tents, etc. **1b** (*as modifier*): *a canvas bag.* **2a** a piece of canvas, etc., on which a painting is done, usually in oils. **2b** an oil painting. **3** a tent or tents collectively. **4** *Naut.* the sails of a vessel collectively. **5** any coarse loosely woven cloth on which tapestry, etc., is done. **6** (preceded by *the*) the floor of a boxing or wrestling ring. **7** *Rowing.* the covered part at either end of a racing boat: *to win by a canvas.* **8 under canvas. 8a** in tents. **8b** *Naut.* with sails unfurled. [C14: from Norman F *canevas*, ult. from L *cannabis* hemp]

canvasback ('kænvəs,bæk) *n, pl* **canvasbacks** *or* **canvasback.** a North American diving duck, the male of which has a reddish-brown head.

canvass ('kænvəs) *vb* **1** to solicit votes, orders, etc., (from). **2** to determine the opinions of (voters before an election, etc.), esp. by conducting a survey. **3** to investigate (something) thoroughly, esp. by discussion. **4** *Chiefly US.* to inspect (votes) to determine their validity. ◆ *n* **5** a solicitation of opinions, votes, etc. [C16: prob. from obs. sense of CANVAS (to toss someone in a canvas sheet, hence, to criticize)]
► 'canvasser *n*

canyon *or* **cañon** ('kænjən) *n* a gorge or ravine, esp. in North America, usually formed by a river. [C19: from Sp., from *caña* tube, from L *canna* cane]

canzonetta (,kænzə'netə) *or* **canzonet** (,kænzə'net) *n* a short, lively song, typically of the 16th to 18th centuries. [C16: It.: dim. of *canzone*, from L *canere* to sing]

caoutchouc ('kautʃuk) *n* another name for **rubber**[1] (sense 1). [C18: from F, from obs. Sp., from Quechua]

cap (kæp) *n* **1** a covering for the head, esp. a small close-fitting one. **2** such a covering serving to identify the wearer's rank, occupation, etc.: *a nurse's cap.* **3** something that protects or covers: *lens cap.* **4** an uppermost surface or part: *the cap of a wave.* **5a** See **percussion cap. 5b** a small amount of explosive enclosed in paper and used in a toy gun. **6** *Sport, chiefly Brit.* **6a** an emblematic hat or beret given to someone chosen for a representative team. **6b** a player chosen for such a team. **7** any part like a cap in shape. **8** *Bot.* the pileus of a mushroom or toadstool. **9** *Hunting.* money contributed to the funds of a hunt by a follower who is neither a subscriber nor a farmer, in return for a day's hunting. **10** *Anat.* **10a** the natural enamel covering a tooth. **10b** an artificial protective covering for a tooth. **11** Also: **Dutch cap, diaphragm.** a contraceptive membrane placed over the mouth of the cervix. **12** an upper financial limit. **13** a mortarboard worn at an academic ceremony (esp. in **cap and gown**). **14** *Meteorol.* **14a** the cloud covering the peak of a mountain. **14b** the transient top of detached clouds above an increasing cumulus. **15 set one's cap at.** (of a woman) to be determined to win as a husband or lover. **16 cap in hand.** humbly, as when asking a favour. ◆ *vb* **caps, capping, capped.** (*tr*) **17** to cover, as with a cap: *snow capped the mountain tops.* **18** *Inf.* to outdo; excel. **19 cap it all.** to provide the finishing touch. **20** *Sport, Brit.* to select (a player) for a representative team. **21** to seal off (an oil or gas well). **22** to impose an upper limit on the level of increase of (a tax): *charge-cap.* **23** *Chiefly Scot. & NZ.* to award a degree to. [OE *cæppe*, from LL *cappa* hood, ?from L *caput* head]

CAP *abbrev. for:* Common Agricultural Policy: (in the EU) the system for supporting farm incomes at agreed levels.

cap. *abbrev. for:* **1** capacity. **2** capital. **3** capitalize. **4** capital letter.

Capa ★ ('kæpə) *n* **Robert**, real name *André Friedmann.* 1913–54, Hungarian photographer.

capability (,keɪpə'bɪlɪtɪ) *n, pl* **capabilities. 1** the quality of being capable; ability. **2** the quality of being susceptible to the use or treatment indicated: *the capability of a metal to be fused.* **3** (*usually pl*) potential aptitude.

Capablanca ★ (*Spanish* kapa'βlaŋka) *n* **José Raúl** (xo'se ra'ul), called *Capa* or the *Chess Machine.* 1888–1942, Cuban chess player; world champion 1921–27.

capable ('keɪpəb'l) *adj* **1** having ability; competent. **2** (*postpositive;* foll. by *of*) able or having the skill (to do something): *she is capable of hard work.* **3** (*postpositive;* foll.

by *of*) having the temperament or inclination (to do something): *he seemed capable of murder.* [C16: from F, from LL *capābilis* able to take in, from L *capere* to take]
► 'capableness *n* ► 'capably *adv*

capacious (kə'peɪʃəs) *adj* capable of holding much; roomy. [C17: from L, from *capere* to take]
► ca'paciously *adv* ► ca'paciousness *n*

capacitance (kə'pæsɪtəns) *n* **1** the property of a system that enables it to store electric charge. **2** a measure of this, equal to the charge that must be added to such a system to raise its electrical potential by one unit. Former name: **capacity.** [C20: from CAPACIT(Y) + -ANCE]
► ca'pacitive *adj*

capacitor (kə'pæsɪtə) *n* a device for accumulating electric charge, usually consisting of two conducting surfaces separated by a dielectric. Former name: **condenser.**

capacity (kə'pæsɪtɪ) *n, pl* **capacities. 1** the ability or power to contain, absorb, or hold. **2** the amount that can be contained: *a capacity of six gallons.* **3a** the maximum amount something can contain or absorb (esp. in **filled to capacity**). **3b** (*as modifier*): *a capacity crowd.* **4** the ability to understand or learn: *he has a great capacity for Greek.* **5** the ability to do or produce: *the factory's output was not at capacity.* **6** a specified position or function. **7** a measure of the electrical output of a piece of apparatus such as a generator or accumulator. **8** *Electronics.* a former name for **capacitance. 9** *Computing.* **9a** the number of words or characters that can be stored in a storage device. **9b** the range of numbers that can be processed in a register. **10** legal competence: *the capacity to make a will.* [C15: from OF *capacite*, from L, from *capāx* spacious, from *capere* to take]

cap and bells *n* the traditional garb of a court jester, including a cap with bells.

cap-a-pie (,kæpə'piː) *adv* (dressed, armed, etc.) from head to foot. [C16: from OF]

caparison (kə'pærɪsˀn) *n* **1** a decorated covering for a horse. **2** rich or elaborate clothing and ornaments. ◆ *vb* **3** (*tr*) to put a caparison on. [C16: via obs. F from OSp. *caparazón* saddlecloth, prob. from *capa* CAPE[1]]

cape[1] (keɪp) *n* a sleeveless garment like a cloak but usually shorter. [C16: from F, from Provençal *capa*, from LL *cappa;* see CAP]

cape[2] (keɪp) *n* a headland or promontory. [C14: from OF *cap*, from OProvençal, from L *caput* head]

Cape ★ (keɪp) *n* **the. 1** the SW region of South Africa, in Western Cape province. **2** See **Cape of Good Hope.**

Cape Breton Island ★ *n* an island off SE Canada, in NE Nova Scotia, separated from the mainland by the Strait of Canso: its easternmost point is **Cape Breton.** Pop.: 120 098 (1991). Area: 10 280 sq. km (3970 sq. miles).

Cape Cod ★ *n* a long sandy peninsula in SE Massachusetts, between **Cape Cod Bay** and the Atlantic.

Cape Colony ★ *n* the name from 1652 until 1910 of the former **Cape Province** of South Africa.

Cape Coloured *n* (in South Africa) another name for a **Coloured** (sense 2).

Cape doctor *n* S. African inf. a strong fresh SE wind blowing in the vicinity of Cape Town, esp. in the summer.

Cape Dutch *n* **1** (in South Africa) a distinctive style in furniture or buildings. **2** an obsolete name for **Afrikaans.**

Cape Flats ★ *pl n* the strip of low-lying land in South Africa joining the Cape Peninsula proper to the African mainland.

Cape gooseberry *n* another name for **strawberry tomato.**

Cape Horn ★ *n* a rocky headland on an island at the extreme S tip of South America, belonging to Chile. It is notorious for gales and heavy seas; until the building of the Panama Canal it lay on the only sea route between the Atlantic and the Pacific. Also called: **the Horn.**

Čapek ★ (*Czech* 'tʃapɛk) *n* **Karel** ('karɛl). 1890–1938, Czech writer; author of *R.U.R.* (1921), which introduced the word "robot", and *The Insect Play* (1921).

capelin ('kæpəlɪn) *or* **caplin** ('kæplɪn) *n* a small marine food fish of northern and Arctic seas. [C17: from F *capelan*, from OProvençal, lit.: chaplain]

:apellmeister *or* **kapellmeister** (kæ'pel,maɪstə) *n* a person in charge of an orchestra, esp. in an 18th-century princely household. [from G, from *Kapelle* chapel + *Meister* MASTER]

:ape of Good Hope ★ *n* a cape in SW South Africa south of Cape Town.

:ape Peninsula ★ *n* (in South Africa) the peninsula and the part of the mainland on which Cape Town and most of its suburbs are located.

:ape pigeon *n* a kind of petrel common in S Africa.

:ape Province ★ *n* a former province of S South Africa: replaced in 1994 by the new provinces of Northern Cape, Western Cape, Eastern Cape, and part of North-West. Official name: **Cape of Good Hope Province**. Former name (1652–1910): **Cape Colony**.

:aper[1] ('keɪpə) *n* **1** a playful skip or leap. **2** a high-spirited escapade. **3** cut a caper *or* capers. to skip, leap, or frolic. **4** *US & Canad. sl.* a crime. ◆ *vb* **5** (*intr*) to leap or dance about in a light-hearted manner. [C16: prob. from CAPRIOLE]

:aper[2] ('keɪpə) *n* **1** a spiny trailing Mediterranean shrub with edible flower buds. **2** its pickled flower buds, used in sauces. [C15: from earlier *capers, capres* (assumed to be pl), from L, from Gk *kapparis*]

:apercaillie *or* **capercailzie** (,kæpə'keɪljɪ) *n* a large European woodland grouse having a black plumage. [C16: from Scot. Gaelic *capull coille* horse of the woods]

:apernaum ★ (kə'pɜːnɪəm) *n* a ruined town in N Israel, on the NW shore of the Sea of Galilee: closely associated with Jesus Christ during his ministry.

:ape sparrow *n* a sparrow very common in southern Africa. Also called (esp. S. African): **mossie**.

:apet ★ ('kæpɪt, kæ'pet; *French* kapɛ) *n* **Hugh** *or* **Hugues** (yg). ?938–996 A.D., king of France (987–96); founder of the Capetian dynasty.
▶ **Capetian** (kə'piːʃən) *adj, n*

:ape Town ★ *n* the legislative capital of South Africa, situated in the southwest on Table Bay: founded in 1652, the first White settlement in southern Africa; important port. Pop.: 854 616 (1991).

:ape Verde ★ (vɜːd) *n* a republic in the Atlantic off the coast of West Africa, consisting of a group of ten islands and five islets: an overseas territory of Portugal until 1975, when the islands became independent. Official language: Portuguese. Religions: Roman Catholic and animist. Currency: Cape Verdean escudo. Capital: Praia. Pop.: 394 000 (1997). Area: 4033 sq. km (1557 sq. miles).
▶ **Cape Verdean** ('vɜːdɪən) *adj, n*

:ape York ★ *n* the northernmost point of the Australian mainland, in N Queensland on the Torres Strait at the tip of **Cape York Peninsula** (a peninsula between the Coral Sea and the Gulf of Carpentaria).

:ap-Haitien ★ (*French* kapaisjɛ̃, -tjɛ̃) *n* a port in N Haiti: capital during the French colonial period. Pop.: 100 638 (1995 est.). Also called: **le Cap** (lə kap).

:apias ('keɪpɪˌæs, 'kæp-) *n Law*. a writ directing a sheriff or other officer to arrest a named person. [C15: from L, lit.: you must take, from *capere*]

:apillarity (,kæpɪ'lærɪtɪ) *n* a phenomenon caused by surface tension and resulting in the elevation or depression of the surface of a liquid in contact with a solid. Also called: **capillary action**.

:apillary (kə'pɪlərɪ) *adj* **1** resembling a hair; slender. **2** (of tubes) having a fine bore. **3** *Anat*. of the delicate thin-walled blood vessels that interconnect between the arterioles and the venules. **4** *Physics*. of or relating to capillarity. ◆ *n, pl* **capillaries**. **5** *Anat*. any of the capillary blood vessels. [C17: from L *capillāris*, from *capillus* hair]

:apital[1] ('kæpɪt[l]) *n* **1a** the seat of government of a country. **1b** (*as modifier*): *a capital city*. **2** material wealth owned by an individual or business enterprise. **3** wealth available for or capable of use in the production of further wealth, as by industrial investment. **4** make capital (out) of. to get advantage from. **5** (*sometimes cap*.) the capitalist class or their interests: *capital versus labour*. **6** Ac-

counting. **6a** the ownership interests of a business as represented by the excess of assets over liabilities. **6b** the nominal value of the issued shares. **7** any assets or resources. **8a** a capital letter. Abbrev.: **cap. 8b** (*as modifier*): *capital B*. ◆ *adj* **9** (*prenominal*) *Law*. involving or punishable by death: *a capital offence*. **10** very serious: *a capital error*. **11** primary, chief, or principal: *our capital concern*. **12** of, relating to, or designating the large letter used chiefly as the initial letter in personal names and place names and often for abbreviations and acronyms. See also **upper case**. **13** *Chiefly Brit*. excellent; first-rate: *a capital idea*. [C13: from L *capitālis* (adj) concerning the head, from *caput* head]

capital[2] ('kæpɪt[l]) *n* the upper part of a column or pier that supports the entablature. [C14: from OF, from LL *capitellum*, dim. of *caput* head]

capital account *n* **1** *Econ*. that part of a balance of payments composed of movements of capital. **2** *Accounting*. a financial statement showing the net value of a company at a specified date.

capital expenditure *n* expenditure to increase fixed assets.

capital gain *n* the amount by which the selling price of a financial asset exceeds its cost.

capital gains tax *n* a tax on the profit made from sale of an asset.

capital goods *pl n Econ*. goods that are themselves utilized in the production of other goods.

capitalism ('kæpɪtə,lɪzəm) *n* an economic system based on the private ownership of the means of production, distribution, and exchange. Also called: **free enterprise, private enterprise**. Cf. **socialism** (sense 1).

capitalist ('kæpɪtəlɪst) *n* **1** a person who owns capital, esp. capital invested in a business. **2** *Politics*. a supporter of capitalism. ◆ *adj* **3** relating to capital, capitalists, or capitalism.
▶ ,**capital'istic** *adj*

capitalization *or* **capitalisation** (,kæpɪtəlaɪ'zeɪʃən) *n* **1a** the act of capitalizing. **1b** the sum so derived. **2** *Accounting*. the par value of the total share capital issued by a company. **3** the act of estimating the present value of future payments, etc.

capitalize *or* **capitalise** ('kæpɪtə,laɪz) *vb* **capitalizes, capitalizing, capitalized** *or* **capitalises, capitalising, capitalised**. (*mainly tr*) **1** (*intr*; foll. by *on*) to take advantage (of). **2** to write or print (text) in capital letters. **3** to convert (debt or earnings) into capital stock. **4** to authorize (a business enterprise) to issue a specified amount of capital stock. **5** to provide with capital. **6** *Accounting*. to treat (expenditures) as assets. **7a** to estimate the present value of (a periodical income). **7b** to compute the present value of (a business) from actual or potential earnings.

capitally ('kæpɪtəlɪ) *adv Chiefly Brit*. in an excellent manner; admirably.

capital punishment *n* the punishment of death for a crime; death penalty.

capital ship *n* one of the largest and most heavily armed ships in a naval fleet.

capital stock *n* **1** the par value of the total share capital that a company is authorized to issue. **2** the total physical capital existing in an economy at any moment of time.

capital transfer tax *n* (in Britain) a tax payable from 1974 to 1986 on the cumulative total of gifts of money or property made during the donor's lifetime or after his death. It was replaced by inheritance tax.

capitation (,kæpɪ'teɪʃən) *n* **1** a tax levied on the basis of a fixed amount per head. **2 capitation grant**. a grant of money given to every person who qualifies under certain conditions. [C17: from LL, from L *caput* head]

Capitol ★ ('kæpɪt[l]) *n* **1a** another name for the **Capitoline**. **1b** the temple on the Capitoline. **2 the**. the main building of the US Congress. **3** (*sometimes not cap*.) Also called: **statehouse**. (in the US) the building housing any state legislature. [C14: from Latin *Capitōlium*, from *caput* head]

Capitoline ★ ('kæpɪt[ə],laɪn, kə'pɪtəʊ-) *n* **1 the**. the most important of the Seven Hills of Rome. The temple of

Jupiter was on the southern summit and the ancient citadel on the northern summit. ◆ *adj* **2** of or relating to the Capitoline or the temple of Jupiter.

capitulate (kə'pɪtjʊˌleɪt) *vb* **capitulates, capitulating, capitulated.** (*intr*) to surrender, esp. under agreed conditions. [C16 (meaning: to draw up in order): from Med. L *capitulare* to draw up under heads, from *capitulum* CHAPTER]
▶ ca'pitu,lator *n*

capitulation (kəˌpɪtjʊ'leɪʃən) *n* **1** the act of capitulating. **2** a document containing terms of surrender. **3** a statement summarizing the main divisions of a subject.
▶ ca'pitulatory *adj*

capitulum (kə'pɪtjʊləm) *n, pl* **capitula** (-lə). an inflorescence in the form of a disc, the youngest at the centre. It occurs in the daisy and related plants. [C18: from L, lit.: a little head, from *caput* head]

capo ('kæpəʊ) *n, pl* **capos.** a device fitted across all the strings of a guitar, lute, etc., so as to raise the pitch of each string simultaneously. Also called: **capo tasto** ('tæstəʊ). [from It. *capo tasto* head stop]

capon ('keɪpən) *n* a castrated cock fowl fattened for eating. [OE *capun*, from L *cāpō* capon]
▶ 'capon,ize *or* 'capon,ise *vb*

Capone ★ (kə'pəʊn) *n* **Alphonse**, called *Al*. 1899–1947, US gangster in Chicago during Prohibition.

Caporetto ★ (kapo'retto) *n* the Italian name for **Kobarid**.

capote (kə'pəʊt) *n* a long cloak or soldier's coat, usually with a hood. [C19: from F: cloak, from *cape*]

Capote ★ (kə'pəʊtɪ) *n* **Truman**. 1924–84, US writer; his novels include *Other Voices, Other Rooms* (1948) and *In Cold Blood* (1964).

Capp ★ (kæp) *n* **Al**, full name *Alfred Caplin*. 1909–79, US cartoonist, noted for his comic strip *Li'l Abner*.

Cappadocia ★ (ˌkæpə'dəʊsɪə) *n* an ancient region of E Asia Minor famous for its horses.
▶ ˌCappa'docian *adj, n*

capping ('kæpɪŋ) *n Scot. & NZ.* **a** the act of conferring an academic degree. **b** (*as modifier*): *Capping Day.*

cappuccino (ˌkæpʊ'tʃiːnəʊ) *n, pl* **cappuccinos.** coffee with steamed milk, usually sprinkled with powdered chocolate. [It.: CAPUCHIN]

Capra ★ ('kæprə) *n* **Frank**. 1896–1991, US film director born in Italy. His films include *It Happened One Night* (1934) and a number of propaganda films during World War II.

Capri ★ (kə'priː; *Italian* 'kapri) *n* an island off W Italy, in the Bay of Naples: resort since Roman times. Pop.: 8000 (latest est.). Area: about 13 sq. km (5 sq. miles).

capriccio (kə'prɪtʃɪˌəʊ) *or* **caprice** *n, pl* **capriccios, capricci** (-'priːtʃɪ), *or* **caprices.** *Music.* a lively piece of irregular musical form. [C17: from It.: CAPRICE]

capriccioso (kəˌprɪtʃɪ'əʊzəʊ) *adv Music.* to be played in a free and lively style. [It.: from *capriccio* CAPRICE]

caprice (kə'priːs) *n* **1** a sudden change of attitude, behaviour, etc. **2** a tendency to such changes. **3** another word for **capriccio**. [C17: from F, from It. *capriccio*, from *capo* head + *riccio* lit.: hedgehog]

capricious (kə'prɪʃəs) *adj* characterized by or liable to sudden unpredictable changes in attitude or behaviour.
▶ ca'priciously *adv*

Capricorn ('kæprɪˌkɔːn) *n* **1** *Astrol.* Also called: the **Goat, Capricornus.** the tenth sign of the zodiac. The sun is in this sign between about Dec. 22 and Jan. 19. **2** *Astron.* a S constellation. **3** tropic of Capricorn. See **tropic** (sense 1). [C14: from L *Capricornus*, from *caper* goat + *cornū* horn]

Capricornia ★ (ˌkæprɪ'kɔːnɪə) *n* the regions of Australia in the tropic of Capricorn.

caprine ('kæpraɪn) *adj* of or resembling a goat. [C17: from L *caprīnus*, from *caper* goat]

capriole ('kæprɪˌəʊl) *n* **1** *Dressage.* a high upward but not forward leap made by a horse with all four feet off the ground. ◆ *vb* **caprioles, caprioling, caprioled. 2** (*intr*) to perform a capriole. [C16: from F, from OIt., from *capriolo* roebuck, from L *capreolus, caper* goat]

caps. *abbrev. for:* **1** capital letters. **2** capsule.

capsicum ('kæpsɪkəm) *n* **1** any of a genus of tropical American plants related to the potato, having mild or pungent seeds enclosed in a bell-shaped fruit. **2** the fruit of any of these plants, used as a vegetable or ground to produce a condiment. ◆ See also **pepper** (sense 4). [C18: from NL, from L *capsa* box]

capsid[1] ('kæpsɪd) *n* a bug related to the water bug that feeds on plant tissues, causing damage to crops. [C19: from NL *Capsus* (genus)]

capsid[2] ('kæpsɪd) *n* the outer protein coat of a mature virus. [C20: from F *capside*, from L *capsa* box]

capsize (kæp'saɪz) *vb* **capsizes, capsizing, capsized.** to overturn accidentally; upset. [C18: from ?]
▶ cap'sizal *n*

capstan ('kæpstən) *n* **1** a machine with a drum equipped with a ratchet, used for hauling in heavy ropes, etc. **2** the rotating shaft in a tape recorder that pulls the tape past the head. [C14: from OProvençal *cabestan*, from L *capistrum* a halter, from *capere* to seize]

capstan lathe *n* a lathe for repetitive work, having a rotatable turret to hold tools for successive operations. Also called: **turret lathe.**

capstone ('kæpˌstəʊn) *n* another word for **copestone** (sense 2).

capsule ('kæpsjuːl) *n* **1** a soluble case of gelatine enclosing a dose of medicine. **2** a thin metal cap, seal, or cover. **3** *Bot.* **3a** a dry fruit that liberates its seeds by splitting, as in the violet, or through pores, as in the poppy. **3b** the spore-producing organ of mosses and liverworts. **4** *Anat.* a membranous envelope surrounding any of certain organs or parts. **5** See **space capsule**. **6** an aeroplane cockpit that can be ejected in a flight emergency, complete with crew, instruments, etc. **7** (*modifier*) in a highly concise form: *a capsule summary.* [C17: from F, from L *capsula*, dim. of *capsa* box]
▶ 'capsu,late *adj*

capsulize *or* **capsulise** ('kæpsjʊˌlaɪz) *vb* **capsulizes, capsulizing, capsulized** *or* **capsulises, capsulising, capsulised.** (*tr*) **1** to state (information, etc.) in a highly condensed form. **2** to enclose in a capsule.

Capt. *abbrev. for* Captain.

captain ('kæptɪn) *n* **1** the person in charge of a vessel. **2** an officer of the navy who holds a rank junior to a rear admiral. **3** an officer of the army, certain air forces, and the marines who holds a rank junior to a major. **4** the officer in command of a civil aircraft. **5** the leader of a team in games. **6** a person in command over a group, organization, etc.: *a captain of industry.* **7** *US.* a policeman in charge of a precinct. **8** *US & Canad.* (formerly) a head waiter. ◆ *vb* **9** (*tr*) to be captain of. [C14: from OF, from LL *capitāneus* chief, from L *caput* head]
▶ 'captaincy *or* 'captainship *n*

Captain Cooker ('kʊkə) *n NZ.* a wild pig. [from Captain James COOK, who first released pigs in the New Zealand bush]

caption ('kæpʃən) *n* **1** a title, brief explanation, or comment accompanying an illustration. **2** a heading or title of a chapter, article, etc. **3** graphic material used in television presentation. **4** another name for **subtitle** (sense 2). **5** the formal heading of a legal document. ◆ *vb* **6** to provide with a caption or captions. [C14 (meaning: seizure): from L *captiō* a seizing, from *capere* to take]

captious ('kæpʃəs) *adj* apt to make trivial criticisms. [C14 (meaning: catching in error): from L *captiōsus*, from *captiō* a seizing]
▶ 'captiously *adv* ▶ 'captiousness *n*

captivate ('kæptɪˌveɪt) *vb* **captivates, captivating, captivated.** (*tr*) to hold the attention of by fascinating; enchant. [C16: from LL *captivāre*, from *captīvus* CAPTIVE]
▶ 'capti,vating *adj* ▶ ,capti'vation *n*

captive ('kæptɪv) *n* **1** a person or animal that is confined or restrained. **2** a person whose behaviour is dominated by some emotion: *a captive of love.* ◆ *adj* **3** held as prisoner. **4** held under restriction or control; confined. **5** captivated. **6** unable to avoid speeches, advertisements, etc.: *a captive audience.* [C14: from L *captīvus*, from *capere* to take]

captivity (kæp'tıvıtı) *n, pl* **captivities. 1** imprisonment. **2** the period of imprisonment.

captor ('kæptə) *n* a person or animal that holds another captive. [C17: from L, from *capere* to take]

capture ('kæptʃə) *vb* **captures, capturing, captured.** (*tr*) **1** to take prisoner or gain control over: *to capture a town.* **2** (in a game) to win possession of: *to capture a pawn in chess.* **3** to succeed in representing (something elusive): *the artist captured her likeness.* **4** *Physics.* (of an atom, etc.) to acquire (an additional particle). **5** to insert or transfer (data) into a computer. ♦ *n* **6** the act of taking by force. **7** the person or thing captured. **8** *Physics.* a process by which an atom, etc., acquires an additional particle. **9** *Geog.* the process by which the headwaters of one river are diverted into another. **10** *Computing.* the collection of data for processing. [C16: from L *captūra* a catching, that which is caught, from *capere* to take]
  ► **'capturer** *n*

Capua ★ ('kæ:pjuə; *Italian* 'ka:pwa) *n* a town in S Italy, in NW Campania: strategically important in ancient times, situated on the Appian Way. Pop.: 19 520 (1990).

Capuana ★ (*Italian* ka'pwa:na) *n* **Luigi** ('lwi:ʒi). 1839–1915, Italian realist novelist, dramatist, and critic. His works include the novel *Giacinta* (1879) and the play *Malia* (1895).

capuchin ('kæpjutʃin, -juʃin) *n* **1** an agile intelligent S American monkey having a cowl of thick hair on the top of the head. **2** a woman's hooded cloak. **3** (*sometimes cap.*) a variety of domestic fancy pigeon. [C16: from F, from It., from *cappuccio* hood]

Capuchin ('kæpjutʃin, -juʃin) *n* **1** a friar belonging to a branch of the Franciscan Order founded in 1525. ♦ *adj* **2** of or relating to this order. [C16: from F, from It. *cappuccio* hood]

capybara (,kæpı'bɑ:rə) *n* the largest rodent, resembling a guinea pig and native to Central and South America. [C18: from Port., from Tupi]

Caquetá ★ (*Spanish* kake'ta) *n* the Japurá River from its source in Colombia to the border with Brazil.

car (kɑ:) *n* **1a** Also called: **motorcar, automobile.** a self-propelled road vehicle designed to carry passengers, that is powered by an internal-combustion engine. **1b** (*as modifier*): *car coat.* **2** a conveyance for passengers, freight, etc., such as a cable car or the carrier of an airship or balloon. **3** *Brit.* a railway vehicle for passengers only. **4** *Chiefly US. & Canad.* a railway carriage or van. **5** a poetic word for **chariot.** [C14: from Anglo-F *carre*, ult. rel. to L *carra, carrum* two-wheeled wagon, prob. of Celtic origin]

CAR *abbrev. for* compound annual return.

carabineer *or* **carabinier** (,kærəbı'nıə) *n* variants of **carbineer.**

carabiner (,kærə'bi:nə) *n* a variant of **karabiner.**

caracal ('kærə,kæl) *n* **1** a lynxlike feline mammal inhabiting deserts of N Africa and S Asia, having a smooth coat of reddish fur. **2** this fur. [C18: from F, from Turkish *kara kūlāk*, lit.: black ear]

Caracalla ★ (,kærə'kælə) *n* real name *Marcus Aurelius Antoninus*, original name *Bassianus*. 188–217 A.D., Roman emperor (211–17): ruled with cruelty and extravagance; assassinated.

caracara (,kɑːrə'kɑːrə) *n* a large carrion-eating bird of prey of Central and South America, having long legs. [C19: from Sp. or Port., from Tupi: imit.]

Caracas ★ (kə'rækəs, -'rɑː-; *Spanish* ka'rakas) *n* the capital of Venezuela, in the north: founded in 1567; major industrial and commercial centre, notably for oil companies. Pop.: 1 822 465 (1990).

caracole ('kærə,kəul) *or* **caracol** ('kærə,kɒl) *Dressage.*
♦ *n* **1** a half turn to the right or left. ♦ *vb* **caracoles, caracoling, caracoled** *or* **caracols, caracoling, caracoled.** (*intr*) **2** to execute a half turn. [C17: from F, from Sp. *caracol* snail, spiral staircase]

Caractacus ★ (kə'ræktəkəs) *n* a variant of **Caratacus.**

caracul ('kærə,kʌl) *n* **1** Also called: **Persian lamb.** the black loosely curled fur obtained from the skins of newly born lambs of the karakul sheep. **2** a variant spelling of **karakul.**

carafe (kə'ræf, -'rɑ:f) *n* an open-topped glass container for serving water or wine at table [C18: from F, from It., from Sp., from Ar. *gharrāfah* vessel]

carageen ('kærə,gi:n) *n* a variant spelling of **carrageen.**

carambola (,kærəm'bəulə) *n* the yellow edible star-shaped fruit of a Brazilian tree, cultivated in the tropics, esp. SE Asia. Also called: **star fruit.** [Sp., from Port.]

caramel ('kærəməl) *n* **1** burnt sugar, used for colouring and flavouring food. **2** a chewy sweet made from sugar, milk, etc. [C18: from F, from Sp. *caramelo*, from ?]

caramelize *or* **caramelise** ('kærəmə,laız) *vb* **caramelizes, caramelizing, caramelized** *or* **caramelises, caramelising, caramelised.** to convert or be converted into caramel.

carapace ('kærə,peıs) *n* the thick hard shield that covers part of the body of crabs, tortoises, etc. [C19: from F, from Sp. *carapacho*, from ?]

carat ('kærət) *n* **1** a measure of the weight of precious stones, esp. diamonds, now standardized as 0.20 grams. **2** Usual US and Canad. spelling: **karat.** a measure of the gold in an alloy, expressed as the number of parts of gold in 24 parts of the alloy. [C16: from OF, from Med. L, from Ar. *qīrāt* weight of four grains, from Gk, from *keras* horn]

Caratacus (kə'rætəkəs), **Caractacus**, *or* **Caradoc** ★ (kə'rædək) *n* died ?54 A.D., British chieftain: led an unsuccessful resistance against the Romans (43–50).

Caravaggio ★ (*Italian* kara'vaddʒo) *n* **Michelangelo Merisi da** (mike'landʒelo me'ri:zi da). 1571–1610, Italian painter.

caravan ('kærə,væn) *n* **1a** a large enclosed vehicle capable of being pulled by a car and equipped to be lived in. US and Canad. name: **trailer.** **1b** (*as modifier*): *a caravan site.* **2** (esp. in some parts of Asia and Africa) a company of traders or other travellers journeying together. **3** a large covered vehicle, esp. a gaily coloured one used by Gypsies, circuses, etc. ♦ *vb* **caravans, caravanning, caravanned.** **4** (*intr*) *Brit.* to travel or have a holiday in a caravan. [C16: from It. *caravana*, from Persian *kārwān*]

caravanserai (,kærə'vænsə,raı) *or* **caravansary** (,kærə'vænsərı) *n, pl* **caravanserais** *or* **caravansaries.** (in some Eastern countries) a large inn enclosing a courtyard, providing accommodation for caravans. [C16: from Persian *kārwānsarāī* caravan inn]

caravel ('kærə,vel) *or* **carvel** *n* a two- or three-masted sailing ship used by the Spanish and Portuguese in the 15th and 16th centuries. [C16: from Port. *caravela*, dim. of *caravo* ship, ult. from Gk *karabos* crab]

caraway ('kærə,weı) *n* **1** an umbelliferous Eurasian plant having finely divided leaves and clusters of small whitish flowers. **2** **caraway seed.** the pungent aromatic fruit of this plant, used in cooking. [C14: prob. from Med. L *carvi*, from Ar. *karawyā*, from Gk *karon*]

carb (kɑ:b) *n Inf.* short for **carburettor.**

carbaryl ('kɑ:bərıl) *n* an organic compound of the carbamate group: used as an insecticide, esp. to treat head lice.

carbide ('kɑ:baıd) *n* **1** a binary compound of carbon with a metal. **2** See **calcium carbide.**

carbine ('kɑ:baın) *n* **1** a light automatic or semiautomatic rifle. **2** a light short-barrelled rifle formerly used by cavalry. [C17: from F *carabine*, from OF *carabin* carabineer]

carbineer (,kɑ:bı'nıə), **carabineer**, *or* **carabinier** (,kærəbı'nıə) *n* (formerly) a soldier equipped with a carbine.

carbo- *or before a vowel* **carb-** *combining form.* carbon: *carbohydrate; carbonate.*

carbocyclic (,kɑ:bəu'saıklık) *adj* (of a chemical compound) containing a closed ring of carbon atoms.

carbohydrate (,kɑ:bəu'haıdreıt) *n* any of a large group of organic compounds, including sugars and starch, that contain carbon, hydrogen, and oxygen, with the general formula $C_m(H_2O)_n$: a source of food and energy for animals.

carbolic acid (kɑ:'bɒlık) *n* another name for **phenol**, esp.

when used as a disinfectant. [C19: from CARBO- + -OL[1] + -IC]

carbon ('kɑ:b°n) n **1a** a nonmetallic element existing in three crystalline forms: graphite, diamond, and buckminsterfullerene: occurring in all organic compounds. The isotope **carbon-12** is the standard for atomic wt.; **carbon-14** is used in radiocarbon dating and as a tracer. Symbol: C; atomic no.: 6; atomic wt.: 12.011 15. **1b** (as modifier): a carbon compound. **2** short for **carbon paper** or **carbon copy**. **3** a carbon electrode used in a carbon-arc light. **4** a rod or plate, made of carbon, used in some types of battery. [C18: from F, from L carbō charcoal]

carbon-14 dating n another name for **carbon dating**.

carbonaceous (ˌkɑ:bə'neɪʃəs) adj of, resembling, or containing carbon.

carbonade (ˌkɑ:bə'neɪd, -'nɑ:d) n beef and onions stewed in beer. [C20: F]

carbonado (ˌkɑ:bə'neɪdəʊ) n, pl **carbonados** or **carbonadoes**. an inferior variety of diamond used in industry. Also called: **black diamond**. [Port., lit.: carbonated]

carbon arc n an electric arc between two carbon electrodes or between a carbon electrode and materials to be welded.

carbonate n ('kɑ:bəˌneɪt, -nɪt). **1** a salt or ester of carbonic acid. ♦ vb ('kɑ:bəˌneɪt), **carbonates, carbonating, carbonated**. **2** to turn into a carbonate. **3** (tr) to treat with carbon dioxide, as in the manufacture of soft drinks. [C18: from F, from carbone CARBON]

carbon black n a finely divided form of carbon produced by incomplete combustion of natural gas or petroleum: used in pigments and ink.

carbon brush n a small spring-loaded block of carbon used to convey current between the stationary and moving parts of an electric generator, motor, etc.

carbon copy n **1** a duplicate copy of writing, typewriting, or drawing obtained by using carbon paper. **2** Inf. a person or thing that is identical to another.

carbon dating n a technique for determining the age of organic materials, such as wood, based on their content of the radioisotope ^{14}C acquired from the atmosphere when they formed part of a living plant.

carbon dioxide n a colourless odourless incombustible gas present in the atmosphere and formed during respiration, etc.: used in fire extinguishers, and as dry ice for refrigeration. Formula: CO_2. Also called: **carbonic-acid gas**.

carbonette (ˌkɑ:bə'nɛt) n NZ. a ball of compressed coal dust used as fuel.

carbon fibre n a thread of pure carbon used because of its lightness and strength at high temperatures for reinforcing resins, ceramics, and metals, and for fishing rods.

carbonic (kɑ:'bɒnɪk) adj (of a compound) containing carbon, esp. tetravalent carbon.

carbonic acid n a weak acid formed when carbon dioxide combines with water. Formula: H_2CO_3.

carboniferous (ˌkɑ:bə'nɪfərəs) adj yielding coal or carbon.

Carboniferous (ˌkɑ:bə'nɪfərəs) adj **1** of, denoting, or formed in the fifth period of the Palaeozoic era during which coal measures were formed. ♦ n **2** the. the Carboniferous period or rock system divided into the **Upper Carboniferous** period and the **Lower Carboniferous** period.

carbonize or **carbonise** ('kɑ:bəˌnaɪz) vb **carbonizes, carbonizing, carbonized** or **carbonises, carbonising, carbonised**. **1** to turn or be turned into carbon as a result of heating, fossilization, chemical treatment, etc. **2** (tr) to coat (a substance) with carbon.
  ▸ ˌcarboni'zation or ˌcarboni'sation n

carbon monoxide n a colourless odourless poisonous gas formed when carbon compounds burn in insufficient air. Formula: CO.

carbon paper n a thin sheet of paper coated on one side with a dark waxy pigment, often containing carbon, that is transferred by pressure onto the copying surface below.

carbon tax n a tax on the emissions caused by the burning of coal, gas, and oil, aimed at reducing the production of greenhouse gases.

carbon tetrachloride n a colourless volatile nonflammable liquid made from chlorine and used as a solvent, cleaning fluid, and insecticide. Formula: CCl_4. Systematic name: **tetrachloromethane**.

car-boot sale n a sale of goods from car boots in a site hired for the occasion.

Carborundum (ˌkɑ:bə'rʌndəm) n Trademark. any of various abrasive materials, esp. one consisting of silicon carbide.

carboxyl group or **radical** (kɑ:'bɒksaɪl) n the monovalent group -COOH: the functional group in organic acids. [C19 carboxyl, from CARBO- + OXY-[2] + -YL]

carboxylic acid (ˌkɑ:bɒk'sɪlɪk) n any of a class of organic acids containing the carboxyl group. See also **fatty acid**.

carboy ('kɑ:ˌbɔɪ) n a large bottle, usually protected by a basket or box, used for containing corrosive liquids. [C18: from Persian qarāba]

carbuncle ('kɑ:ˌbʌŋk°l) n **1** an extensive skin eruption, similar to a boil, with several openings. **2** a rounded gemstone, esp. a garnet cut without facets. [C13: from L carbunculus, dim. of carbō coal]
  ▸ **carbuncular** (kɑ:'bʌŋkjulə) adj

carburation (ˌkɑ:bju'reɪʃən) n the process of mixing a hydrocarbon fuel with air to make an explosive mixture for an internal-combustion engine.

carburet ('kɑ:bjuˌrɛt, ˌkɑ:bju'rɛt) vb **carburets, carburetting, carburetted** or US **carburets, carbureting, carbureted**. (tr) to combine or mix (a gas, etc.) with carbon or carbon compounds. [C18: from CARB(ON) + -URET]

carburettor, carburetter (ˌkɑ:bə'rɛtə, 'kɑ:bəˌrɛtə), or US & Canad. **carburetor** ('kɑ:bəˌreɪtə) n a device used in some petrol engines for mixing atomized petrol with air, and regulating the intake of the mixture into the engine.

carcajou ('kɑ:kəˌdʒu:, -kəˌʒu:) n a North American name for **wolverine**. [C18: from Canad. F, from Algonquian karkajou]

carcass or **carcase** ('kɑ:kəs) n **1** the dead body of an animal, esp. one that has been slaughtered for food. **2** Inf., usually facetious or derog. a person's body. **3** the skeleton or framework of a structure. **4** the remains of anything when its life or vitality is gone. [C14: from OF carcasse, from ?]

Carcassonne ★ (French karkasɔn) n a city in SW France: extensive remains of medieval fortifications. Pop.: 44 990 (1990).

carcinogen (kɑ:'sɪnədʒən) n Pathol. any substance that produces cancer. [C20: from Gk karkinos CANCER + -GEN]
  ▸ ˌcarcino'genic adj

carcinogenesis (ˌkɑ:sɪnəʊ'dʒɛnɪsɪs) n Pathol. the development of cancerous cells from normal ones.

carcinoma (ˌkɑ:sɪ'nəʊmə) n, pl **carcinomas** or **carcinomata** (-mətə). Pathol. any malignant tumour derived from epithelial tissue. [C18: from L, from Gk, from karkinos CANCER]

card[1] (kɑ:d) n **1** a piece of stiff paper or thin cardboard, usually rectangular, with varied uses, as for bearing a written notice for display, etc. **2** such a card used for identification, reference, proof of membership, etc.: identity card. **3** such a card used for sending greetings, messages, or invitations: birthday card. **4a** one of a set of small pieces of cardboard, marked with figures, symbols, etc., used for playing games or for fortune-telling. See also **playing card**. **4b** (as modifier): a card game. **5** short for **cheque card** or **credit card**. **6** Inf. a witty or eccentric person. **7** See **compass card**. **8** Also called: **racecard**. Horse racing. a daily programme of all the races at a meeting. **9 a card up one's sleeve**. a thing or action used in order to gain an advantage, esp. one kept in reserve until needed. ♦ See also **cards**. [C15: from OF carte, from L charta leaf of papyrus, from Gk khartēs, prob. of Egyptian origin]

card[2] (kɑːd) *vb* **1** (*tr*) to comb out and clean (fibres of wool or cotton) before spinning. ♦ *n* **2** (formerly) a machine or comblike tool for carding fabrics or for raising the nap on cloth.   [C15: from OF *carde* card, teasel, from L *carduus* thistle]
▸ 'carder *n* ▸ 'carding *n*

cardamom ('kɑːdəməm) *or* **cardamon** ('kɑːdəmən) *n* **1** a tropical Asian plant that has large hairy leaves. **2** the seeds of this plant, used esp. as a spice or condiment.   [C15: from L, from Gk, from *kardamon* cress + *amōmon* an Indian spice]

cardboard ('kɑːd,bɔːd) *n* **1a** a thin stiff board made from paper pulp. **1b** (*as modifier*): *cardboard boxes*. ♦ *adj* **2** (*prenominal*) without substance.

cardboard city *n Inf.* an area of a city in which homeless people sleep rough, often in cardboard boxes.

card-carrying *adj* being an official member of an organization: *a card-carrying Communist*.

Cardenal ★ (*Spanish* karðe'nal) *n* **Ernesto** ('ɛrnɛs,təu). born 1925, Nicaraguan poet, revolutionary, and Roman Catholic priest.

cardiac ('kɑːdɪ,æk) *adj* **1** of or relating to the heart. **2** of or relating to the portion of the stomach connected to the oesophagus. ♦ *n* **3** a person with a heart disorder.   [C17: from L *cardiacus*, from Gk, from *kardia* heart]

cardiac arrest *n* failure of the pumping action of the heart, resulting in loss of consciousness and absence of pulse and breathing: a medical emergency requiring immediate resuscitative treatment.

cardie *or* **cardy** ('kɑːdɪ) *n, pl* **cardies**. *Inf.* short for **cardigan**.

Cardiff ★ ('kɑːdɪf) *n* **1** the capital of Wales, situated in the southeast: an important port. Pop.: 272 129 (1991). **2** a county borough in SE Wales. Pop.: 306 500 (1996 est.). Area: 139 sq. km (54 sq. miles).

cardigan ('kɑːdɪgən) *n* a knitted jacket or sweater with buttons up the front.   [C19: after 7th Earl of CARDIGAN]

Cardigan ★ ('kɑːdɪgən) *n* **7th Earl of**, title of *James Thomas Brudenell*. 1797–1868, British cavalry officer. He led the charge of the Light Brigade at Balaklava (1854).

Cardigan Bay ★ *n* an inlet of St George's Channel, on the W coast of Wales.

Cardiganshire ★ ('kɑːdɪgən,ʃɪə, -ʃə) *n* See **Ceredigion**.

Cardin ★ (*French* kardɛ̃) *n* **Pierre** (pjɛr). born 1922, French couturier, noted esp. for his collections for men.

cardinal ('kɑːdɪn°l) *n* **1** *RC Church.* any of the members of the Sacred College who elect the pope and act as his chief counsellors. **2** Also called: **cardinal red**. a deep red colour. **3** See **cardinal number**. **4** Also called (US): **redbird**. a crested North American bunting, the male of which has a bright red plumage. **5** a woman's hooded shoulder cape worn in the 17th and 18th centuries. ♦ *adj* **6** (*usually prenominal*) fundamentally important; principal. **7** of a deep red.   [C13: from L *cardinālis*, lit.: relating to a hinge, from *cardō* hinge]
▸ 'cardinally *adv*

cardinalate ('kɑːdɪn°l,eɪt) *or* **cardinalship** *n* **1** the rank, office, or term of office of a cardinal. **2** the cardinals collectively.

cardinal flower *n* a lobelia of E North America that has brilliant scarlet flowers.

cardinal number *or* **numeral** *n* a number denoting quantity but not order in a group. Sometimes shortened to **cardinal**. Cf. **ordinal number**.

cardinal points *pl n* the four main points of the compass: north, south, east, and west.

cardinal virtues *pl n* the most important moral qualities, traditionally justice, prudence, temperance, and fortitude.

cardinal vowels *pl n* a set of theoretical vowel sounds, based on the shape of the mouth needed to articulate them, that can be used to classify the vowel sounds of any speaker in any language.

card index *or* **file** *n* **1** an index in which each item is separately listed on systematically arranged cards. ♦ *vb* **card-index** *or* **card-file, card-indexes, card-indexing, card-**

indexed *or* **card-files, card-filing, card-filed**. (*tr*) **2** to make such an index of (a book, etc.).

cardio- *or before a vowel* **cardi-** *combining form.* heart: *cardiogram*.   [from Gk *kardia* heart]

cardiocentesis (,kɑːdɪəusɛn'tiːsɪs) *n Med.* surgical puncture of the heart.

cardiogram ('kɑːdɪəu,græm) *n* short for **electrocardiogram**. See **electrocardiograph**.

cardiograph ('kɑːdɪəu,grɑːf) *n* **1** an instrument for recording heart movements. **2** short for **electrocardiograph**.
▸ **cardiographer** (,kɑːdɪ'ɒgrəfə) *n* ▸ ,cardi'ography *n*

cardiology (,kɑːdɪ'ɒlədʒɪ) *n* the branch of medical science concerned with the heart and its diseases.
▸ ,cardi'ologist *n*

cardioplegia (,kɑːdɪəu'pliːdʒə) *n Med.* deliberate arrest of the action of the heart, as by hypothermia or the injection of chemicals, to enable complex heart surgery to be carried out.

cardiopulmonary resuscitation (,kɑːdɪəu'pʌl-mənərɪ, -'pul-) *n* an emergency measure to revive a patient whose heart has stopped beating, in which compressions applied with the hands to the patient's chest are alternated with mouth-to-mouth respiration. Abbrev.: **CPR**.

cardiovascular (,kɑːdɪəu'væskjulə) *adj* of or relating to the heart and the blood vessels.

cardoon (kɑː'duːn) *n* a thistle-like relative of the artichoke with an edible leafstalk.   [C17: from F, from L *carduus* thistle, artichoke]

cardphone ('kɑːdfəun) *n* a public telephone operated by the insertion of a phonecard instead of coins.

card punch *n* a device, no longer widely used, controlled by a computer, for transferring information from the central processing unit onto punched cards which can then be read by a **card reader**.

card reader *n* a device, no longer widely used, for reading information on a punched card and transferring it to a computer or storage device.

cards (kɑːdz) *n* **1** (*usually functioning as sing*) **1a** any game played with cards, esp. playing cards. **1b** the playing of such a game. **2** an employee's tax and national insurance documents or information held by the employer. **3 ask for** *or* **get one's cards**. to ask *or* be told to terminate one's employment. **4 on the cards**. possible. **5 play one's cards** (**right**). to manoeuvre (cleverly). **6 put** *or* **lay one's cards on the table**. to declare one's intentions, etc.

cardsharp ('kɑːd,ʃɑːp) *or* **cardsharper** *n* a professional card player who cheats.

Cardus ★ ('kɑːdəs) *n* **Sir Neville**. 1889–1975, British music critic and cricket writer.

card vote *n Brit.* a vote by delegates, esp. at a trade-union conference, in which each delegate's vote counts as a vote by all his constituents.

care (kɛə) *vb* **cares, caring, cared**. **1** (when *tr*, may take a clause as object) to be troubled or concerned: *he is dying, and she doesn't care*. **2** (*intr*; foll. by *for* or *about*) to have regard or consideration (for): *he cares more for his hobby than his job*. **3** (*intr*; foll. by *for*) to have a desire or taste (for): *would you care for tea?* **4** (*intr*; foll. by *for*) to provide physical needs, help, or comfort (for). **5** (*tr*) to agree or like (to do something): *would you care to sit down?* **6 for all I care** *or* **I couldn't care less**. I am completely indifferent. ♦ *n* **7** careful or serious attention: *he does his work with care*. **8** protective or supervisory control: *in the care of a doctor*. **9** (*often pl*) trouble; worry. **10** an object of or cause for concern. **11** caution: *handle with care*. **12 care of**. at the address of: written on envelopes. Usual abbrev.: **c/o**. **13 in** (*or* **into**) **care**. *Brit.* made the legal responsibility of a local authority by order of a court.   [OE *cearu* (n), *cearian* (vb), of Gmc origin]
▸ 'carer *n*

CARE (kɛə) *n acronym for:* **1** Cooperative for American Relief Everywhere. **2** communicated authenticity, regard, empathy: the three qualities believed to be essential in the therapist practising client-centred therapy.

care and maintenance *n Commerce.* the state of a building, ship, machinery, etc., that is not in current use although it is kept in good condition to enable it to be brought into service quickly if there is a demand for it. Abbrev.: **C & M.**

careen (kə'ri:n) vb **1** to sway or cause to sway over to one side. **2** (tr) Naut. to cause (a vessel) to keel over to one side, esp. in order to clean its bottom. **3** (intr) Naut. (of a vessel) to keel over to one side. [C17: from F, from It., from L carīna keel]
▶ **ca'reenage** n

career (kə'rɪə) n **1** a path through life or history. **2a** a profession or occupation chosen as one's life's work. **2b** (as modifier): a career diplomat. **3** a course or path, esp. a headlong one. ◆ vb **4** (intr) to rush in an uncontrolled way. [C16: from F, from LL carrāria carriage road, from L carrus two-wheeled wagon]

career girl or **woman** n a woman, often unmarried, who follows a profession.

careerist (kə'rɪərɪst) n a person who seeks to advance his career by any possible means.

carefree ('kɛə,fri:) adj without worry or responsibility.
▶ **'care,freeness** n

careful ('kɛəful) adj **1** cautious in attitude or action. **2** painstaking in one's work; exact and thorough. **3** (usually postpositive; foll. by of, in, or about) solicitous; protective. **4** Brit. mean or miserly.
▶ **'carefully** adv ▶ **'carefulness** n

careless ('kɛəlɪs) adj **1** done with or acting with insufficient attention. **2** (often foll. by in, of, or about) unconcerned in attitude or action. **3** (usually prenominal) carefree. **4** (usually prenominal) unstudied: careless elegance.
▶ **'carelessly** adv ▶ **'carelessness** n

Carême ★ (French karɛm) n **Marie Antonin**. 1784–1833, French chef, regarded as the founder of haute cuisine.

caress (kə'rɛs) n **1** a gentle touch or embrace, esp. one given to show affection. ◆ vb **2** (tr) to touch or stroke gently with or as with affection. [C17: from F, from It., from L cārus dear]

caret ('kærɪt) n a symbol (⁁) used to indicate the place in written or printed matter at which something is to be inserted. [C17: from L, lit.: there is missing, from carēre to lack]

caretaker ('kɛə,teɪkə) n **1** a person who looks after a place or thing, esp. in the owner's absence. **2** (modifier) interim: a caretaker government.

Carew ★ (kə'ru:) n **Thomas**. ?1595–?1639, English Cavalier poet.

careworn ('kɛə,wɔ:n) adj showing signs of care, stress, worry, etc.: a careworn face.

Carey ★ ('kɛərɪ) n **1 George** (**Leonard**). born 1935, British cleric, Archbishop of Canterbury from 1991. **2 William**. 1761–1834, British orientalist and pioneer Baptist missionary in India.

Carey Street ★ n **1** (formerly) the street in which the London bankruptcy court was situated. **2** the state of bankruptcy.

cargo ('kɑ:gəʊ) n, pl **cargoes** or esp. US **cargos**. **1a** goods carried by a ship, aircraft, or other vehicle; freight. **1b** (as modifier): a cargo vessel. **2** any load: a cargo of new arrivals. [C17: from Sp.: from cargar to load, from LL, from L carrus CAR]

Carib ('kærɪb) n **1** (pl **Caribs** or **Carib**) a member of a group of American Indian peoples of NE South America and the Lesser Antilles. **2** the family of languages spoken by these peoples. [C16: from Sp. Caribe, from Amerind]

Caribbean (,kærɪ'bɪən; US kə'rɪbɪən) adj **1** of or relating to the Caribbean Sea and its islands. **2** of or relating to the Carib or any of their languages. ◆ n **3 the.** short for the **Caribbean Sea. 4 the.** the states and islands of the Caribbean, esp. when considered as a geopolitical region. **5** a member of any of the peoples inhabiting the islands of the Caribbean Sea, such as a West Indian or a Carib.

Caribbean Sea ★ n an almost landlocked sea, part of the Atlantic Ocean, bounded by the Caribbean islands, Central America, and the N coast of South America. Area: 2 718 200 sq. km (1 049 500 sq. miles).

Caribbees ★ ('kærɪ,bi:z) pl n **the.** another name for the **Lesser Antilles.**

Cariboo ★ ('kærɪ,bu:) n **the.** Canad. a region in the W foothills of the Cariboo Mountains, scene of a gold rush beginning in 1860.

Cariboo Mountains ★ pl n a mountain range in SW Canada, in SE British Columbia. Highest peak: Mount Sir Wilfrid Laurier, 3582 m (11 750 ft).

caribou ('kærɪ,bu:) n, pl **caribou** or **caribous.** a large North American reindeer. [C18: from Canad. F, of Algonquian origin]

caricature ('kærɪkə,tjʊə) n **1** a pictorial, written, or acted representation of a person, which exaggerates his characteristic traits for comic effect. **2** an inadequate or inaccurate imitation. ◆ vb **caricatures, caricaturing, caricatured. 3** (tr) to represent in caricature or produce a caricature of. [C18: from It. caricatura a distortion, from caricare to load, exaggerate]
▶ **'carica,turist** n

CARICOM ('kærɪ,kɒm) n acronym for Caribbean Community and Common Market.

caries ('kɛəri:z) n, pl **caries.** progressive decay of a bone or a tooth. [C17: from L: decay]

carillon (kə'rɪljən) n Music. **1** a set of bells usually hung in a tower. **2** a tune played on such bells. **3** a mixture stop on an organ giving the effect of a bell. [C18: from F: set of bells, from OF quarregnon, ult. from L quattuor four]

carina (kə'ri:nə, -'raɪ-) n, pl **carinae** (-ni:) or **carinas.** a keellike part or ridge, as in the breastbone of birds or the fused lower petals of a leguminous flower. [C18: from L: keel]

carinate ('kærɪ,neɪt) or **carinated** adj Biol. having a keel or ridge. [C17: from L carīnāre, from carīna keel]

caring (kɛərɪŋ) adj **1** showing care and compassion: a caring attitude. **2** of or relating to professional social or medical care: nursing is a caring job. ◆ n **3** the practice of providing care.

Carinthia ★ (kə'rɪnθɪə) n a state of S Austria: an independent duchy from 976 to 1276; mainly mountainous, with many lakes and resorts. Capital: Klagenfurt. Pop.: 559 696 (1994 est.). Area: 9533 sq. km (3681 sq. miles). German name: **Kärnten.**

carioca (,kærɪ'əʊkə) n **1** a Brazilian dance similar to the samba. **2** a piece of music for this dance. [C19: from Brazilian Port.]

cariogenic (,kɛərɪəʊ'dʒɛnɪk) adj (of a substance) producing caries of the teeth.

cariole or **carriole** ('kærɪ,əʊl) n **1** a small open two-wheeled horse-drawn vehicle. **2** a covered cart. [C19: from F, ult. from L carrus; see CAR]

carious ('kɛərɪəs) or **cariose** ('kɛərɪ,əʊz) adj (of teeth or bone) affected with caries; decayed.

carjack ('kɑ:,dʒæk) vb (tr) to attack (a driver in a car) in order to rob the driver or steal the car for another crime. [C20: CAR + (HI)JACK]

carl or **carle** (kɑ:l) n Arch. or Scot. another word for **churl.** [OE, from ON karl]

Carl XVI Gustaf ★ (Swedish kɑ:rl 'gustav) n born 1946, king of Sweden from 1973.

Carlisle ★ (kɑ:'laɪl, 'kɑ:laɪl) n a city in NW England, administrative centre of Cumbria: industrial centre. Pop.: 72 439 (1991). Latin name: **Luguvallum** (,lu:gu:'væləm).

Carlos ★ ('kɑ:lɒs) n **Don.** full name Carlos María Isidro de Borbón. 1788–1855, second son of Charles IV: pretender to the Spanish throne and leader of the Carlists.

Carlota ★ (Spanish kar'lota) n original name Marie Charlotte Amélie Augustine Clémentine Léopoldine. 1840–1927, wife of Maximilian; empress of Mexico (1864–67).

Carlovingian (,kɑ:ləʊ'vɪndʒɪən) adj, n History. a variant of **Carolingian.**

Carlow ★ ('kɑ:ləʊ) n **1** a county of SE Republic of Ireland, in Leinster: mostly flat, with barren mountains in the southeast. County town: Carlow. Pop.: 40 942 (1991). Area: 896 sq. km (346 sq. miles). **2** a town in SE Republic

★ people and places

of Ireland, county town of Co. Carlow. Pop.: 11 275 (1991).

Carlyle ★ (kɑːˈlaɪl) n **Thomas**. 1795–1881, Scottish historian. His works include *Sartor Resartus* (1833–34), *The French Revolution* (1837), and lectures *On Heroes, Hero-Worship, and the Heroic in History* (1841).

carmagnole (ˌkɑːmənˈjəʊl) n **1** a dance and song popular during the French Revolution. **2** the costume worn by many French Revolutionaries. [C18: from F, prob. after *Carmagnola*, Italy]

Carmarthen ★ (kɑːˈmɑːðən) n a market town in S Wales, the administrative centre of Carmarthenshire: Norman castle. Pop.: 13 524 (1991).

Carmarthenshire ★ (kɑːˈmɑːðənˌʃɪə, -ʃə) n a county of S Wales, formerly part of Dyfed (1974–96). Administrative centre: Carmarthen. Pop.: 169 000 (1996 est.). Area: 2398 sq. km (926 sq. miles).

Carmel ★ (ˈkɑːməl) n **Mount**. a mountain ridge in NW Israel, extending from the Samarian Hills to the Mediterranean. Highest point: about 540 m (1800 ft).

Carmelite (ˈkɑːməˌlaɪt) n **RC Church**. **1** a member of an order of mendicant friars founded about 1154. **2** a member of a corresponding order of nuns founded in 1452, noted for its austere rule. ◆ adj **3** of or relating to either of these orders. [C14: from F, after Mount CARMEL, where the order was founded]

Carmichael ★ (kɑːˈmaɪkəl) n **Hoaglund Howard** (ˈhəʊglənd), known as **Hoagy**. 1899–1981, US pianist and composer of such songs as "Star Dust" (1929).

carminative (ˈkɑːmɪnətɪv) adj **1** able to relieve flatulence. ◆ n **2** a carminative drug. [C15: from F, from L *carmināre* to card wool]

carmine (ˈkɑːmaɪn) n **1a** a vivid red colour. **1b** (as adj): *carmine paint*. **2** a pigment of this colour obtained from cochineal. [C18: from Med. L *carmīnus*, from Ar. *qirmiz* KERMES]

Carnac ★ (ˈkɑːnæk) n a village in NW France: noted for its many megalithic monuments, including alignments of stone menhirs.

carnage (ˈkɑːnɪdʒ) n extensive slaughter. [C16: from F, from It., from Med. L, from L *carō* flesh]

carnal (ˈkɑːnəl) adj relating to the appetites and passions of the body. [C15: from LL, from L *carō* flesh]
▸ **car'nality** n ▸ **'carnally** adv

carnal knowledge n *Chiefly law*. sexual intercourse.

Carnap ★ (ˈkɑːnæp) n **Rudolf**. 1891–1970, US logical positivist philosopher, born in Germany.

Carnarvon ★ (kɑːˈnɑːvən) n a variant spelling of **Caernarfon**.

carnation (kɑːˈneɪʃən) n **1** Also called: **clove pink**. a Eurasian plant cultivated in many varieties for its white, pink, or red flowers, which have a fragrant scent of cloves. **2** the flower of this plant. **3a** a pink or reddish-pink colour. **3b** (as adj): *a carnation dress*. [C16: from F: flesh colour, from LL, from L *carō* flesh]

carnauba (kɑːˈnaʊbə) n **1** Also called: **wax palm**. a Brazilian fan palm. **2** Also called: **carnauba wax**. the wax obtained from the young leaves of this tree. [from Brazilian Port., prob. of Tupi origin]

Carné ★ (ˈkɑːneɪ; French karne) n **Marcel** (marsɛl). 1906–96, French film director. His films include *Le Jour se lève* (1939) and *Les Portes de la nuit* (1946).

Carnegie ★ (ˈkɑːnəgɪ, kɑːˈneɪ-) n **Andrew**. 1835–1919, US steel manufacturer and philanthropist, born in Scotland.

Carnegie Hall ★ (ˈkɑːnəgɪ) n a famous concert hall in New York (opened 1891); endowed by Andrew Carnegie.

carnelian (kɑːˈniːljən) n a reddish-yellow translucent variety of chalcedony, used as a gemstone. [C17: var. of *cornelian*, from OF, from ?]

carnet (ˈkɑːneɪ) n **1** a customs licence authorizing the temporary importation of a motor vehicle. **2** an official document permitting motorists to cross certain frontiers. [F: notebook, from OF, ult. from L *quaternī* four at a time]

Carniola ★ (ˌkɑːnɪˈəʊlə) n a region of N Slovenia: a former duchy and crownland of Austria (1335–1919); divided between Yugoslavia and Italy in 1919; part of Yugoslavia (1947–92). German name: **Krain** (kraɪn). Slovene name: **Kranj**.

carnival (ˈkɑːnɪvəl) n **1a** a festive period marked by merrymaking, etc.: esp. in some Roman Catholic countries, the period just before Lent. **1b** (as modifier): *a carnival atmosphere*. **2** a travelling fair having sideshows, rides, etc. **3** a show or display arranged as an amusement. **4** *Austral*. a sports meeting. [C16: from It., from OIt. *carnelevare* a removing of meat (referring to the Lenten fast)]

carnivore (ˈkɑːnɪˌvɔː) n **1** any of an order of mammals having large pointed canine teeth specialized for eating flesh. The order includes cats, dogs, bears, and weasels. **2** any other animal or any plant that feeds on animals. **3** *Inf*. an aggressively ambitious person. [C19: prob. back formation from CARNIVOROUS]

carnivorous (kɑːˈnɪvərəs) adj **1** (esp. of animals) feeding on flesh. **2** (of plants such as the pitcher plant and sundew) able to trap and digest insects. **3** of or relating to the carnivores. **4** *Inf*. aggressively ambitious or reactionary. [C17: from L, from *carō* flesh + *vorāre* to consume]
▸ **car'nivorousness** n

Carnot ★ (ˈkɑːnəʊ; French karno) n **1 Lazare (Nicolas Marguerite)** (laʒar), known as *the Organizer of Victory*. 1753–1823, French military engineer: organized the French Revolutionary army (1793–95). **2 Nicolas Léonard Sadi** (nikɔla leɔnar sadi). 1796–1832, French physicist, noted for his work on thermodynamics.

Caro ★ n **1** (ˈkærəʊ). **Sir Antony**. born 1924, British abstract sculptor. **2** (ˈkɑːrəʊ). **Joseph (ben Ephraim)**. 1488–1575, Jewish legal scholar, born in Spain; compiler of the *Shulhan Arukh* (1564–65).

carob (ˈkærəb) n **1** an evergreen Mediterranean tree with compound leaves and edible pods. **2** the long blackish sugary pod of this tree, used for animal fodder and sometimes for human food. [C16: from OF, from Med. L *carrūbium*, from Ar. *al kharrūbah*]

carol (ˈkærəl) n **1** a joyful hymn or religious song, esp. one (a **Christmas carol**) celebrating the birth of Christ. ◆ vb **carols**, **carolling**, **carolled** *or US* **carols**, **caroling**, **caroled**. **2** (intr) to sing carols at Christmas. **3** to sing (something) in a joyful manner. [C13: from OF, from ?]

Carol II ★ (ˈkærəl) n 1893–1953, king of Romania (1930–40), who was deposed by the Iron Guard.

Carolina ★ (ˌkærəˈlaɪnə) n a former English colony on the E coast of North America, first established in 1663: divided in 1729 into North and South Carolina, which are often referred to as **the Carolinas**.

Caroline (ˈkærəˌlaɪn) *or* **Carolean** (ˌkærəˈliːən) adj characteristic of or relating to Charles I or Charles II (kings of England, Scotland, and Ireland), the society over which they ruled, or their government. Also called: **Carolinian**.

Caroline Islands ★ pl n an archipelago of over 500 islands and islets in the W Pacific Ocean east of the Philippines, all are now part of the Federated States of Micronesia except for the Belau group: formerly part of the US Trust Territory of the Pacific Islands; centre of a typhoon zone.

Carolingian (ˌkærəˈlɪndʒɪən) adj **1** of or relating to the Frankish dynasty founded by Pepin the Short which ruled in France from 751–987 A.D. and in Germany until 911 A.D. ◆ n **2** a member of the dynasty of the Carolingian Franks. ◆ Also: **Carlovingian, Carolinian**.

Carolinian (ˌkærəˈlɪnɪən) adj, n a variant of **Caroline** or **Carolingian**.

carom (ˈkærəm) n *Billiards*. another word (esp. US & Canad.) for **cannon** (sense 5). [C18: from earlier *carambole* (taken as *carom ball*), from Sp. *carambola* CARAMBOLA]

carotene (ˈkærəˌtiːn) *or* **carotin** (ˈkærətɪn) n any of four orange-red isomers of a hydrocarbon present in many plants and converted to vitamin A in the liver. [C19 *carotin*, from L *carōta* CARROT]

carotenoid *or* **carotinoid** (kəˈrɒtɪˌnɔɪd) n any of a group of red or yellow pigments, including carotenes, found in plants and certain animal tissues.

carotid (kə'rɒtɪd) n **1** either of the two principal arteries that supply blood to the head and neck. ◆ adj **2** of either of these arteries. [C17: from F, from Gk, from *karoun* to stupefy; so named because pressure on them produced unconsciousness]

carousal (kə'raʊzᵊl) n a merry drinking party.

carouse (kə'raʊz) vb **carouses, carousing, caroused. 1** (intr) to have a merry drinking spree. ◆ n **2** another word for **carousal**. [C16: via F *carrousser* from G (*trinken*) *gar aus* (to drink) right out]
▶ **ca'rouser** n

carousel (ˌkærə'sɛl, -'zɛl) n **1** a circular tray in which slides for a projector are held in slots from which they can be released in turn. **2** a revolving luggage conveyor, as at an airport. **3** US and Canad. a merry-go-round. **4** History. a tournament in which horsemen took part in races. [C17: from F, from It. *carosello*, from ?]

carp[1] (kɑːp) n, pl **carp** or **carps. 1** a freshwater food fish having one long dorsal fin, and two barbels on each side of the mouth. **2** a cyprinid. [C14: from OF *carpe*, of Gmc origin]

carp[2] (kɑːp) vb (intr; often foll. by at) to complain or find fault. [C13: from ON *karpa* to boast]
▶ **'carper** n ▶ **'carping** adj, n

-carp n combining form. (in botany) fruit or a reproductive structure that develops into a particular part of the fruit: *epicarp*. [from NL -*carpium*, from Gk -*karpion*, from *karpos* fruit]

Carpaccio ★ (ˌkɑː'pætʃɪəʊ, -tʃəʊ; Italian kar'pattʃo) n **Vittore** (vit'toːre). ?1460–?1525, Venetian painter.

carpal ('kɑːpᵊl) n **a** any bone of the wrist. **b** (as modifier): *carpal bones*. [C18: from NL *carpālis*, from Gk *karpos* wrist]

car park n an area or building reserved for parking cars. Usual US and Canad. term: **parking lot**.

Carpathian Mountains (kɑː'peɪθɪən) or **Carpathians** ★ pl n a mountain system of central and E Europe, extending from Slovakia to central Romania: mainly forested, with rich iron ore resources. Highest peak: Gerlachovka, 2663 m (8788 ft).

Carpatho-Ukraine ★ (kɑː'peɪθəʊjuː'kreɪn) n another name for **Ruthenia**.

carpe diem Latin. ('kɑːpɪ 'diːɛm) sentence substitute. enjoy the pleasures of the moment, without concern for the future. [lit.: seize the day!]

carpel ('kɑːpᵊl) n the female reproductive organ of flowering plants, consisting of an ovary, style, and stigma. [C19: from NL *carpellum*, from Gk *karpos* fruit]
▶ **'carpellary** adj

Carpentaria ★ (ˌkɑːpən'tɛərɪə) n **Gulf of.** a shallow inlet of the Arafura Sea, in N Australia between Arnhem Land and Cape York Peninsula.

carpenter ('kɑːpɪntə) n **1** a person skilled in woodwork, esp. in buildings, ships, etc. ◆ vb **2** (intr) to do the work of a carpenter. **3** (tr) to make or fit together by or as if by carpentry. [C14: from Anglo-F, from L, from *carpentum* wagon]

Carpenter ★ ('kɑːpɪntə) n **John Alden.** 1876–1951, US composer: his works include the ballet *Skyscrapers* (1926) and the suite *Adventures in a Perambulator* (1915).

Carpentier ★ (French karpɑ̃tje) n **Georges** (ʒɔrʒ), known as *Gorgeous Georges.* 1894–1975, French boxer: world light-heavyweight champion (1920–22).

carpentry ('kɑːpɪntrɪ) n **1** the art or technique of working wood. **2** the work produced by a carpenter; woodwork.

carpet ('kɑːpɪt) n **1** a heavy fabric for covering floors. **2** a covering like a carpet: *a carpet of leaves*. **3 on the carpet.** Inf. **3a** before authority to be reproved. **3b** under consideration. ◆ vb **carpets, carpeting, carpeted.** (tr) **4** to cover with or as if with a carpet. **5** Inf. to reprimand. [C14: from OF, from OIt., from LL *carpeta*, from L *carpere* to pluck, card]

carpetbag ('kɑːpɪtˌbæg) n a travelling bag originally made of carpeting.

carpetbagger ('kɑːpɪtˌbægə) n **1** a politician who seeks public office in a locality where he has no real connections. **2** Brit. a person who makes a short-term investment in a mutual savings or life-assurance organization in order to benefit from free shares issued following the organization's conversion to a public limited company.

carpet beetle or US **carpet bug** n any of various beetles, the larvae of which feed on carpets, furnishing fabrics, etc.

carpet bombing n systematic intensive bombing of an area.

carpeting ('kɑːpɪtɪŋ) n carpet material or carpets in general.

carpet slipper n one of a pair of slippers, originally one made with woollen uppers resembling carpeting.

carpet snake or **python** n a large nonvenomous Australian snake having a carpet-like pattern on its back.

carpet-sweeper n a household device with a revolving brush for sweeping carpets.

car phone n a telephone that operates by cellular radio for use in a car.

carpo- combining form. (in botany) indicating fruit or a seed. [from Gk *karpos* fruit]

carport ('kɑːˌpɔːt) n a shelter for a car usually consisting of a roof built out from the side of a building and supported by posts.

-carpous or **-carpic** adj combining form. (in botany) indicating a certain kind or number of fruit: *apocarpous*. [from NL, from Gk *karpos* fruit]

carpus ('kɑːpəs) n, pl **carpi** (-paɪ). **1** the technical name for **wrist. 2** the eight small bones of the human wrist. [C17: NL, from Gk *karpos*]

Carracci ★ (kə'rɑːtʃɪ; Italian kar'rattʃi) n a family of Italian painters, born in Bologna: **Agostino** (agos'tiːno) (1557–1602); his brother, **Annibale** (an'niːbale) (1560–1609), noted for his frescoes, and their cousin, **Ludovico** (ludo'viːko) (1555–1619). They founded a teaching academy (1582) in Bologna.

carrack ('kærək) n a galleon sailed in the Mediterranean as a merchantman in the 15th and 16th centuries. [C14: from OF *caraque*, from OSp. *carraca*, from Ar. *qarāqīr* merchant ships]

carrageen, carragheen, or **carageen** ('kærəˌgiːn) n an edible red seaweed of North America and N Europe. Also called: **Irish moss.** [C19: from *Carragheen*, near Waterford, Ireland]

carrageenan, carragheenan, or **carageenan** (ˌkærə'giːnən) n a carbohydrate extracted from carrageen, used to make a beverage, medicine, and jelly, and as an emulsifying and gelling agent (**E407**) in various processed desserts and drinks.

Carrara ★ (kə'rɑːrə; Italian kar'raːra) n a town in NW Italy, in NW Tuscany: famous for its marble. Pop.: 68 480 (1990).

carrel or **carrell** ('kærəl) n a small individual study room or private desk, often in a library. [C20: from obs. *carrel* study area, var. of CAROL]

Carrel ★ (kə'rɛl, 'kærəl; French karɛl) n **Alexis** (ə'lɛksɪs; French aleksi). 1873–1944, French surgeon, active in the US (1905–39): developed a method of suturing blood vessels. Nobel prize for physiology or medicine 1912.

Carreras ★ (kə'rɛərəs) n **José** (həʊ'zeɪ). born 1947, Spanish tenor.

carriage ('kærɪdʒ) n **1** Brit. a railway coach for passengers. **2** the manner in which a person holds and moves his head and body. **3** a four-wheeled horse-drawn vehicle for persons. **4** the moving part of a machine that bears another part: *a typewriter carriage*. **5** ('kærɪdʒ, 'kærɪdʒ). **5a** the act of conveying. **5b** the charge made for conveying (esp. in **carriage forward,** when the charge is to be paid by the receiver, and **carriage paid**). [C14: from OF *cariage*, from *carier* to CARRY]

carriage clock n a portable clock, usually in a rectangular case, originally used by travellers.

carriage trade n trade from the wealthy part of society.

carriageway ('kærɪdʒˌweɪ) n Brit. the part of a road

★ people and places

along which traffic passes in a single line moving in one direction only: *a dual carriageway*.

Carrickfergus ★ (ˌkærɪkˈfɜːɡəs) *n* **1** a town in NE Northern Ireland, on Belfast Lough; historic settlement of Scottish Protestants; Norman castle. Pop.: 22 885 (1991). **2** a district of E Northern Ireland, on Belfast Lough N of Belfast: tourism. Administrative centre: Carrickfergus. Pop.: 32 750 (1991). Area: 77 sq. km (30 sq. miles).

carrier (ˈkærɪə) *n* **1** a person, thing, or organization employed to carry goods, etc. **2** a mechanism by which something is carried or moved, such as a device for transmitting rotation from the faceplate of a lathe to the workpiece. **3** *Pathol.* another name for **vector** (sense 3). **4** *Pathol.* a person or animal that, without having any symptoms of a disease, is capable of transmitting it to others. **5** Also called: **charge carrier**. *Physics.* an electron or hole that carries the charge in a conductor or semiconductor. **6** short for **carrier wave**. **7** *Chem.* **7a** an inert substance used to absorb a dyestuff, transport a sample through a gas chromatography column, contain a radioisotope for radioactive tracing, etc. **7b** a substance used to support a catalyst. **8** See **aircraft carrier**.

carrier bag *n Brit.* a large paper or plastic bag for carrying shopping, etc.

carrier pigeon *n* any homing pigeon, esp. one used for carrying messages.

carrier wave *n Radio.* a wave modulated in amplitude, frequency, or phase in order to carry a signal in radio transmission, etc.

Carrington ★ (ˈkærɪŋtən) *n* **1 Dora**, known as *Carrington*. 1893–1932, British painter; a member of the Bloomsbury Group. **2 Peter (Alexander Rupert)**, 6th Baron. born 1919, British Conservative politician: secretary of state for defence (1970–74); foreign secretary (1979–82); secretary general of NATO (1984–88).

carriole (ˈkærɪˌəʊl) *n* a variant spelling of **cariole**.

carrion (ˈkærɪən) *n* **1** dead and rotting flesh. **2** (*modifier*) eating carrion. **3** something rotten. [C13: from Anglo-F *caroine*, ult. from L *carō* flesh]

carrion crow *n* a common predatory and scavenging European crow similar to the rook but having a pure black bill.

Carroll ★ (ˈkærəl) *n* **Lewis**. real name *Charles Lutwidge Dodgson*. 1832–98, British writer; an Oxford mathematics don, he wrote *Alice's Adventures in Wonderland* (1865) and *Through the Looking-Glass* (1872).

carrot (ˈkærət) *n* **1** an umbelliferous plant with finely divided leaves. **2** the long tapering orange root of this plant, eaten as a vegetable. **3a** something offered as a lure or incentive. **3b** carrot and stick. reward and punishment as methods of persuasion. [C16: from OF *carotte*, from LL *carōta*, from Gk *karōton*]

carroty (ˈkærətɪ) *adj* **1** of a reddish or yellowish-orange colour. **2** having red hair.

carrousel (ˌkærəˈsel, -ˈzel) *n* a variant spelling of **carousel**.

carry (ˈkærɪ) *vb* **carries, carrying, carried**. (*mainly tr*) **1** (*also intr*) to take or bear (something) from one place to another. **2** to transfer for consideration: *he carried his complaints to her superior*. **3** to have on one's person: *he carries a watch*. **4** (*also intr*) to be transmitted or serve as a medium for transmitting: *sound carries over water*. **5** to bear or be able to bear the weight, pressure, or responsibility of: *her efforts carry the whole production*. **6** to have as an attribute or result: *this crime carries a heavy penalty*. **7** to bring or communicate: *to carry news*. **8** (*also intr*) to be pregnant with (young). **9** to bear (the head, body, etc.) in a specified manner: *she carried her head high*. **10** to conduct or bear (oneself) in a specified manner: *she carried herself well*. **11** to continue or extend: *the war was carried into enemy territory*. **12** to cause to move or go: *desire for riches carried him to the city*. **13** to influence, esp. by emotional appeal: *his words carried the crowd*. **14** to secure the passage of (a bill, motion, etc.). **15** to win (an election). **16** to obtain victory for (a candidate). **17** *Chiefly US*. to win a majority of votes in (a district, state, etc.): *the candidate carried 40 states*. **18** to capture: *our troops carried the town*. **19** (of communications media) to include as the con-

tent: *this newspaper carries no book reviews*. **20** Also (esp. US): **carry over**. *Book-keeping.* to transfer (an item) to another account, esp. to transfer to the following year's account: *to carry a loss*. **21** *Maths.* to transfer (a number) from one column of figures to the next. **22** (of a shop, trader, etc.) to keep in stock: *to carry confectionery*. **23** to support (a musical part or melody) against the other parts. **24** (*intr*) (of a ball, projectile, etc.) to travel through the air or reach a specified point: *his first drive carried to the green*. **25** *Inf.* to imbibe (alcoholic drink) without showing ill effects. **26** (*intr*) *Sl.* to have drugs on one's person. **27 carry all before** (**one**). to win unanimous support or approval for (oneself). **28 carry the can** (**for**). *Inf.* to take responsibility for some misdemeanour, etc. (on behalf of). **29 carry the day**. to be successful. ◆ *n, pl* **carries**. **30** the act of carrying. **31** *US & Canad.* a portion of land over which a boat must be portaged. **32** the range of a firearm or its projectile. **33** *Golf.* the distance from where the ball is struck to where it first touches the ground. ◆ See also **carry away**, **carry forward**, etc. [C14 *carien*, from OF *carier* to move by vehicle, from *car*, from L *carrum* transport wagon]

carryall (ˈkærɪˌɔːl) *n* the usual US and Canad. name for a **holdall**.

carry away *vb* (*tr, adv*) **1** to remove forcefully. **2** (*usually passive*) to cause (a person) to lose self-control. **3** (*usually passive*) to delight: *he was carried away by the music*.

carrycot (ˈkærɪˌkɒt) *n* a light cot with handles, similar to but smaller than the body of a pram.

carry forward *vb* (*tr, adv*) **1** *Book-keeping.* to transfer (a balance) to the next column, etc. **2** *Tax accounting.* to apply (a legally permitted credit, esp. an operating loss) to the taxable income of following years. ◆ Also: **carry over**.

carrying-on *n, pl* **carryings-on**. *Inf.* **1** unconventional behaviour. **2** excited or flirtatious behaviour.

carry off *vb* (*tr, adv*) **1** to remove forcefully. **2** to win. **3** to handle (a situation) successfully: *he carried off the introductions well*. **4** to cause to die: *he was carried off by pneumonia*.

carry on *vb* (*adv*) **1** (*intr*) to continue or persevere. **2** (*tr*) to conduct: *to carry on a business*. **3** (*intr*; often foll. by *with*) *Inf.* to have an affair. **4** (*intr*) *Inf.* to cause a fuss or commotion. ◆ *n* **carry-on. 5** *Inf.*, chiefly Brit. a fuss.

carry out *vb* (*tr, adv*) **1** to perform or cause to be implemented: *I wish he could afford to carry out his plan.* **2** to accomplish. ◆ *n* **carry-out**. *Chiefly Scot.* **3** alcohol bought at an off-licence, etc., for consumption elsewhere. **4a** a shop which sells hot cooked food for consumption away from the premises. **4b** (*as modifier*): *a carry-out shop*.

carry over *vb* (*tr, adv*) **1** to postpone or defer. **2** *Book-keeping, tax accounting.* another term for **carry forward**. ◆ *n* **carry-over. 3** something left over for future use, esp. goods to be sold. **4** *Book-keeping.* a sum or balance carried forward.

carry through *vb* (*tr, adv*) **1** to bring to completion. **2** to enable to endure (hardship, trouble, etc.); support.

carse (kɑːs) *n Scot.* a riverside area of flat fertile alluvium. [C14: from ?]

carsick (ˈkɑːˌsɪk) *adj* nauseated from riding in a car or other vehicle. ► **ˈcarˌsickness** *n*

Carson ★ (ˈkɑːsºn) *n* **1 Christopher**, known as *Kit Carson*. 1809–68, US frontiersman, trapper, scout, and Indian agent. **2 Edward Henry**, Baron. 1854–1935, Irish politician and lawyer; led northern Irish resistance to the British government's home rule for Ireland. **3 Rachel (Louise)**. 1907–64, US marine biologist and science writer; author of *Silent Spring* (1962). **4 Willie**, full name *William Hunter Fisher Carson*, born 1942, Scottish jockey; retired in 1997.

Carson City ★ *n* a city in W Nevada, capital of the state. Pop.: 46 770 (1995 est.).

Carstensz ★ (ˈkɑːstənz) *n* **Mount**. a former name of (Mount) **Jaya**.

cart (kɑːt) *n* **1** a heavy open vehicle, usually having two wheels and drawn by horses. **2** a light open horse-drawn vehicle for business or pleasure. **3** any small vehicle drawn or pushed by hand, such as a trolley. **4 in the cart**.

4a in an awkward situation. **4b** in the lurch. **5 put the cart before the horse.** to reverse the usual order of things. ◆ *vb* **6** (*usually tr*) to use or draw a cart to convey (goods, etc.). **7** (*tr*) to carry with effort: *to cart wood home.* [C13: from ON *kartr*]
▶ **'carter** *n*

cartage ('kɑːtɪdʒ) *n* the process or cost of carting.

Cartagena ★ (ˌkɑːtə'dʒiːnə; *Spanish* karta'xena) *n* **1** a port in NW Colombia, on the Caribbean: centre for the Inquisition and the slave trade in the 16th century; chief oil port of Colombia. Pop.: 745 689 (1995 est.). **2** a port in SE Spain, on the Mediterranean: important since Carthaginian and Roman times for its minerals. Pop.: 179 659 (1994 est.).

carte blanche ('kɑːt 'blɑːntʃ) *n, pl* **cartes blanches** ('kɑːts 'blɑːntʃ). complete discretion or authority: *the government gave their negotiator carte blanche.* [C18: from F: blank paper]

cartel (kɑː'tɛl) *n* **1** Also called: **trust.** a collusive association of independent enterprises formed to monopolize production and distribution of a product or service. **2** *Politics.* an alliance of parties to further common aims. [C20: from G *Kartell*, from F, from It. *cartello* public notice, dim. of *carta* CARD[1]]

Carter ★ ('kɑːtə) *n* **1 Angela.** 1940–92, British writer; her novels include *The Magic Toyshop* (1967) and *Nights at the Circus* (1984). **2 Elliot (Cook).** born 1908, US composer. His works include the *Piano Sonata* (1945–46), four string quartets, and orchestral pieces. **3 Howard.** 1873–1939, British Egyptologist: excavated the tomb of Tutankhamen. **4 James Earl,** known as *Jimmy.* born 1924, US Democratic statesman; 39th president of the US (1977–81).

Carteret ★ ('kɑːtərɪt) *n* **John,** 1st Earl Granville. 1690–1763, British statesman, who led the opposition to Walpole (1730–42), after whose fall he became secretary of state (1742–44).

Cartesian (kɑː'tiːzɪən) *adj* **1** of or relating to the works of Descartes. **2** of or used in Descartes' mathematical system.
▶ **Car'tesian,ism** *n*

Cartesian coordinates *pl n* a system of coordinates that defines the location of a point in space in terms of its perpendicular distance from each of a set of mutually perpendicular axes.

Carthage ★ ('kɑːθɪdʒ) *n* an ancient city state, on the N African coast near present-day Tunis. Founded about 800 B.C. by Phoenician traders, it grew into an empire dominating N Africa and the Mediterranean. Destroyed and then rebuilt by Rome, it was finally razed by the Arabs in 697 A.D.
▶ **Carthaginian** (ˌkɑːθə'dʒɪnɪən) *adj, n*

carthorse ('kɑːt,hɔːs) *n* a large heavily built horse kept for pulling carts or carriages.

Carthusian (kɑː'θjuːzɪən) *RC Church.* ◆ *n* **1** a member of a monastic order founded by Saint Bruno in 1084 near Grenoble, France. ◆ *adj* **2** of or relating to this order: *a Carthusian monastery.* [C14: from Med. L, from L *Carthusia* Chartreuse, near Grenoble]

Cartier ★ (*French* kartje) *n* **Jacques** (ʒak). 1491–1557, French navigator and explorer in Canada.

Cartier-Bresson ★ (*French* kartjebrɛsɔ̃) *n* **Henri** (ɑ̃ri). born 1908, French photographer.

cartilage ('kɑːtɪlɪdʒ) *n* a tough elastic tissue composing most of the embryonic skeleton of vertebrates. In the adults of higher vertebrates it is mostly converted into bone. Nontechnical name: **gristle.** [C16: from L *cartilāgō*]
▶ **cartilaginous** (ˌkɑːtɪ'lædʒɪnəs) *adj*

cartilaginous fish *n* any of a class of fish including the sharks and rays, having a skeleton composed entirely of cartilage.

Cartland ★ ('kɑːtlənd) *n* Dame **Barbara (Hamilton).** born 1901, British writer of popular fiction.

cartload ('kɑːt,ləʊd) *n* the amount a cart can hold.

cart off, away, or **out** *vb* (*tr, adv*) *Inf.* to carry or remove brusquely or by force.

cartogram ('kɑːtə,græm) *n* a map showing statistical in-

formation in diagrammatic form. [C20: from F *cartogramme,* from *carte* map, CHART]

cartography (kɑː'tɒɡrəfɪ) *n* the art, technique, or practice of compiling or drawing maps or charts. [C19: from F *cartographie,* from *carte* map, CHART]
▶ **car'tographer** *n* ▶ **cartographic** (ˌkɑːtə'ɡræfɪk) *or* **carto-'graphical** *adj*

carton ('kɑːt°n) *n* **1** a cardboard box for containing goods. **2** a container of waxed paper in which liquids, such as milk, are sold. [C19: from F, from It. *cartone* pasteboard, from *carta* CARD[1]]

cartoon (kɑː'tuːn) *n* **1** a humorous or satirical drawing, esp. one in a newspaper or magazine. **2** Also called: **comic strip.** a sequence of drawings in a newspaper, magazine, etc. **3** See **animated cartoon. 4** a full-size preparatory sketch for a fresco, tapestry, mosaic, etc. [C17: from It. *cartone* pasteboard]
▶ **car'toonist** *n*

cartouche *or* **cartouch** (kɑː'tuːʃ) *n* **1** a carved or cast ornamental tablet or panel in the form of a scroll. **2** an oblong figure enclosing characters expressing royal or divine names in Egyptian hieroglyphics. [C17: from F: scroll, cartridge, from It., from *carta* paper]

cartridge ('kɑːtrɪdʒ) *n* **1** a metal casing containing an explosive charge and often a bullet, for a rifle or other small arms. **2** a stylus unit of a record player, either containing a piezoelectric crystal (**crystal cartridge**) or an induction coil that moves in the field of a permanent magnet (**magnetic cartridge**). **3** an enclosed container of magnetic tape, photographic film, ink, etc., for insertion into a tape deck, camera, pen, etc. **4** *Computing.* a removable unit in a computer, such as an integrated circuit, containing software. [C16: from earlier *cartage,* var. of CARTOUCHE (cartridge)]

cartridge belt *n* a belt with pockets for cartridge clips or loops for cartridges.

cartridge clip *n* a metallic container holding cartridges for an automatic firearm.

cartridge paper *n* **1** an uncoated type of drawing or printing paper. **2** a heavy paper used in making cartridges or as drawing or printing paper.

cartwheel ('kɑːt,wiːl) *n* **1** the wheel of a cart, usually having wooden spokes. **2** an acrobatic movement in which the body makes a revolution supported by the hands with legs outstretched.

Cartwright ★ ('kɑːt,raɪt) *n* **Edmund.** 1743–1823, British clergyman, who invented the power loom.

caruncle ('kærəŋk°l, kə'rʌŋ-) *n* **1** a fleshy outgrowth on the heads of certain birds, such as a cock's comb. **2** an outgrowth near the hilum on the seeds of some plants. [C17: from obs. F *caruncule,* from L *caruncula* a small piece of flesh, from *carō* flesh]
▶ **caruncular** (kə'rʌŋkjʊlə) *or* **ca'runculous** *adj*

Caruso ★ (*Italian* ka'ruːso) *n* **Enrico** (en'riːko). 1873–1921, Italian tenor; one of the first to make records.

carve (kɑːv) *vb* **carves, carving, carved. 1** (*tr*) to cut or chip in order to form something: *to carve wood.* **2** to form (something) by cutting or chipping: *to carve statues.* **3** to slice (meat) into pieces. ◆ See also **carve out, carve up.** [OE *ceorfan*]

carvel ('kɑːv°l) *n* another word for **caravel.**

carvel-built *adj* (of a vessel) having a hull with planks made flush at the seams. Cf. **clinker-built.**

carven ('kɑːv°n) *vb* an archaic or literary past participle of **carve.**

carve out *vb* (*tr, adv*) *Inf.* to make or create (a career): *he carved out his own future.*

carver ('kɑːvə) *n* **1** a carving knife. **2** (*pl*) a large matched knife and fork for carving meat. **3** *Brit.* a chair having arms that forms part of a set of dining chairs.

carvery ('kɑːvərɪ) *n, pl* **carveries.** an eating establishment at which customers pay a set price for unrestricted helpings from a variety of meats, salads, etc.

carve up *vb* (*tr, adv*) **1** to cut (something) into pieces. **2** to divide (land, etc.). ◆ *n* **carve-up. 3** *Inf.* an act or instance of dishonestly prearranging the result of a competition. **4** *Sl.* the distribution of something.

★ people and places

carving ('kɑːvɪŋ) *n* a figure or design produced by carving stone, wood, etc.

carving knife *n* a long-bladed knife for carving cooked meat for serving.

Cary ★ ('kɛərɪ, 'kærɪ) *n* (**Arthur**) **Joyce** (**Lunel**). 1888–1957, British novelist; author of *Mister Johnson* (1939) and *The Horse's Mouth* (1944).

caryatid (,kærɪ'ætɪd) *n, pl* **caryatids** *or* **caryatides** (-ɪ,diːz). a column, used to support an entablature, in the form of a draped female figure. [C16: from L, from Gk *Karuatides* priestesses of Artemis at *Karuai* (Caryae), in Laconia]

Casablanca ★ (,kæsə'blæŋkə) *n* a port in NW Morocco, on the Atlantic: largest city in the country; industrial centre. Pop.: 2 943 000 (1993 est.).

Casals ★ (*Spanish* ka'sals) *n* **Pablo** ('paβlo). 1876–1973, Spanish cellist and composer.

Casanova ★ (,kæsə'nəʊvə) *n* **1 Giovanni Jacopo** (dʒo'vanni 'jaːkopo). 1725–98, Italian adventurer noted for his *Mémoires*, a vivid account of his sexual adventures. **2** any man noted for his amorous adventures; a rake.

casbah ('kæzbɑː) *n* (*sometimes cap.*) a variant spelling of **kasbah**.

cascade (kæs'keɪd) *n* **1** a waterfall or series of waterfalls over rocks. **2** something resembling this, such as folds of lace. **3** a consecutive sequence of chemical or physical processes. **4** a series of stages or devices in which each operates the next in turn. ◆ *vb* **cascades, cascading, cascaded. 5** (*intr*) to flow or fall in or like a cascade. [C17: from F, from It., ult. from L *cadere* to fall]

Cascade Range ★ *n* a chain of mountains in the US and Canada: a continuation of the Sierra Nevada range from N California through Oregon and Washington to British Columbia. Highest peak: Mount Rainier, 4392 m (14 408 ft).

cascara (kæs'kɑːrə) *n* **1** Also called: **cascara sagrada**. the dried bark of the cascara buckthorn, used as a laxative and stimulant. **2** Also called: **cascara buckthorn**. a shrub or small tree of NW North America. [C19: from Sp.: bark]

case[1] (keɪs) *n* **1** a single instance or example of something. **2** an instance of disease, injury, etc. **3** a question or matter for discussion. **4** a specific condition or state of affairs; situation. **5** a set of arguments supporting a particular action, cause, etc. **6a** a person attended or served by a doctor, social worker, solicitor, etc. **6b** (*as modifier): a case study.* **7a** an action or suit at law: *he has a good case.* **7b** the evidence offered in court to support a claim. **8** *Grammar.* **8a** a set of grammatical categories of nouns, pronouns, and adjectives indicating the relation of the noun, adjective, or pronoun to other words in the sentence. **8b** any one of these categories: *the dative case.* **9** *Inf.* an eccentric. **10 in any case.** (*adv*) no matter what. **11 in case.** (*adv*) **11a** in order to allow for eventualities. **11b** (*conj*) in order to allow for the possibility that: *take your coat in case it rains.* **12 in case of.** (*prep*) in the event of. **13 in no case.** (*adv*) under no circumstances. [OE *casus* (grammatical) case, associated also with OF *cas* a happening; both from L *cāsus*, a befalling, from *cadere* to fall]

case[2] (keɪs) *n* **1a** a container, such as a box or chest. **1b** (*in combination*): *suitcase.* **2** an outer cover, esp. for a watch. **3** a receptacle and its contents: *a case of ammunition.* **4** *Archit.* another word for **casing** (sense 3). **5** a cover ready to be fastened to a book to form its binding. **6** *Printing.* a tray in which a compositor keeps individual metal types of a particular size and style. Cases were originally used in pairs, one (the **upper case**) for capitals, the other (the **lower case**) for small letters. ◆ *vb* **cases, casing, cased.** (*tr*) **7** to put into or cover with a case. **8** *Sl.* to inspect carefully (esp. a place to be robbed). [C13: from OF *casse*, from L, from *capere* to take, hold]

casebook ('keɪs,bʊk) *n* a book in which records of legal or medical cases are kept.

case-harden *vb* (*tr*) **1** *Metallurgy.* to form a hard surface layer of high carbon content on (a steel component). **2** to make callous: *experience case-hardened the judge.*

case history *n* a record of a person's background, medical history, etc.

casein ('keɪsɪɪn, -siːn) *n* a protein, precipitated from milk by the action of rennin, forming the basis of cheese. [C19: from L *cāseus* cheese + -IN]

case law *n* law established by following judicial decisions given in earlier cases. Cf. **statute law.**

caseload ('keɪs,ləʊd) *n* the number of cases constituting the work of a doctor, social worker, solicitor, etc., over a specified period.

casemate ('keɪs,meɪt) *n* an armoured compartment in a ship or fortification in which guns are mounted. [C16: from F, from It. *casamatta*, ?from Gk *khasmata* apertures]

casement ('keɪsmənt) *n* **1** a window frame that is hinged on one side. **2** a window containing frames hinged at the side. **3** a poetic word for **window.** [C15: prob. from OF *encassement* frame, from *encasser* to encase, from *casse* framework]

Casement ★ ('keɪsmənt) *n* **Sir Roger** (**David**). 1864–1916, British diplomat and Irish nationalist: hanged by the British for seeking German support for Irish independence.

caseous ('keɪsɪəs) *adj* of or like cheese. [C17: from L *cāseus* CHEESE]

casern *or* **caserne** (kə'zɜːn) *n* (*formerly*) a billet or accommodation for soldiers in a town. [C17: from F *caserne*, from OProvençal *cazerna* group of four men, ult. from L *quattuor* four]

Caserta ★ (*Italian* ka'zɛrta) *n* a town in S Italy, in Campania: centre of Garibaldi's campaigns for the unification of Italy (1860); Allied headquarters in World War II. Pop.: 69 350 (1990).

casework ('keɪs,wɜːk) *n* social work based on close study of the personal histories and circumstances of individuals and families.
▸ **'case,worker** *n*

cash[1] (kæʃ) *n* **1** banknotes and coins, esp. when readily available. **2** immediate payment for goods or services (esp. in **cash down**). **3** (*modifier*) of, or paid by cash: *a cash transaction.* ◆ *vb* **4** (*tr*) to obtain or pay ready money for. ◆ See also **cash in, cash up.** [C16: from OIt. *cassa* money box, from L *capsa* CASE[2]]
▸ **'cashable** *adj*

cash[2] (kæʃ) *n, pl* **cash.** any of various Chinese or Indian coins of low value. [C16: from Port. *caixa*, from Tamil *kāsu*, from Sansk. *karsa* weight of gold]

Cash ★ (kæʃ) *n* **1 Johnny.** born 1932, US country-and-western singer and songwriter. His records include "A Boy named Sue" (1969). **2 Pat.** born 1965, Australian tennis player: Wimbledon champion 1987.

cash-and-carry *adj, adv* **1** sold or operated on a basis of cash payment for merchandise that is not delivered but removed by the purchaser. ◆ *n, pl* **cash-and-carries. 2** a wholesale store, esp. for groceries, that operates on this basis. **3** an operation on a commodities futures market in which spot goods are purchased for cash and sold at a profit on a futures contract, after paying interest and storage charges.

cashback ('kæʃ,bæk) *n* **1a** a discount offered in return for immediate payment. **1b** (*as modifier*): *cashback price £519.99– save £30!* **2a** a service provided by some supermarkets in which customers paying by debit card can draw cash. **2b** the cash so drawn.

cash-book *n* *Book-keeping.* a journal in which all receipts and disbursements are recorded.

cash card *n* a plastic card issued by a bank or building society enabling the holder to obtain cash from a cash dispenser.

cash cow *n* a product, acquisition, etc., that produces a steady flow of cash, esp. one with a well-known brand name commanding a high market share.

cash crop *n* a crop grown for sale rather than for subsistence.

cash desk *n* a counter or till in a shop where purchases are paid for.

cash discount *n* a discount granted to a purchaser who pays before a stipulated date.

cash dispenser *n* a computerized device outside a bank that supplies cash when the user inserts his cash card and keys in his identification number. Also called: **automated teller machine.**

cashew ('kæʃuː, kæ'ʃuː) n **1** a tropical American evergreen tree, bearing kidney-shaped nuts. **2** Also called: **cashew nut.** the edible nut of this tree. [C18: from Port. *cajú*, from Tupi *acajú*]

cash flow n **1** the movement of money into and out of a business. **2** a document that records or predicts this movement.

cashier[1] (kæ'ʃɪə) n **1** a person responsible for receiving payments for goods, services, etc., as in a shop. **2** an employee of a bank responsible for receiving deposits, cashing cheques, etc.: bank clerk. **3** any person responsible for handling cash in a business. [C16: from Du. or F, from *casse* money chest]

cashier[2] (kæ'ʃɪə) vb (tr) to dismiss with dishonour, esp. from the armed forces. [C16: from MDu., from OF, from L *quassāre* to QUASH]

cash in vb (adv) **1** (tr) to give (something) in exchange. **2** (intr; often foll. by *on*) *Inf.* **2a** to profit (from). **2b** to take advantage (of).

cashmere or **kashmir** ('kæʃmɪə) n **1** a fine soft wool from goats of the Kashmir area. **2a** cloth or knitted material made from this or similar wool. **2b** (as modifier): a *cashmere sweater.*

Cashmere ★ (kæʃ'mɪə) n a variant spelling of **Kashmir.**

cash on delivery n a service entailing cash payment to the carrier on delivery of merchandise. Abbrev.: **COD.**

cash point n **1** any retail outlet at which goods are bought for cash. **2** a cash dispenser.

cash register n a till with a keyboard that operates a mechanism for displaying and adding the amounts of cash received in individual sales.

cash up vb (intr, adv) *Brit.* (of cashiers, shopkeepers, etc.) to add up the money taken, esp. at the end of a working day.

casing ('keɪsɪŋ) n **1** a protective case or cover. **2** material for a case or cover. **3** Also called: **case.** a frame containing a door or window.

casino (kə'siːnəʊ) n, pl **casinos. 1** a public building or room in which gaming takes place. **2** a variant spelling of **cassino.** [C18: from It., dim. of *casa* house, from L]

cask (kɑːsk) n **1** a strong wooden barrel used mainly to hold alcoholic drink: *a wine cask.* **2** any barrel. **3** the quantity contained in a cask. **4** *Austral.* a lightweight cardboard container used to hold and serve wine. [C15: from Sp. *casco* helmet]

casket ('kɑːskɪt) n **1** a small box or chest for valuables, esp. jewels. **2** *Chiefly US.* another word for **coffin** (sense 1). [C15: prob. from OF *cassette* little box]

Caspar ('kæspə, 'kæspɑː) or **Gaspar** ★ n (in Christian tradition) one of the Magi, the other two being Melchior and Balthazar.

Caspian Sea ★ ('kæspɪən) n a salt lake between SE Europe and Asia: the largest inland sea in the world; fed mainly by the River Volga. Area: 394 299 sq. km (152 239 sq. miles).

casque (kæsk) n *Zool.* a helmet or a helmet-like structure, as on the bill of most hornbills. [C17: from F, from Sp. *casco*]
► **casqued** adj

Cassandra ★ (kə'sændrə) n **1** *Greek myth.* a daughter of Priam and Hecuba, endowed with the gift of prophecy but fated never to be believed. **2** anyone whose prophecies of doom are unheeded.

Cassatt ★ (kə'sæt) n **Mary.** 1845–1926, US impressionist painter, who lived in France.

cassava (kə'sɑːvə) n **1** Also called: **manioc.** any of various tropical plants, esp. the widely cultivated American species (**bitter cassava, sweet cassava**). **2** a starch derived from the root of this plant: a source of tapioca. [C16: from Sp. *cazabe* cassava bread, from Taino *caçábi*]

Cassel ★ (German 'kasəl) n a variant spelling of **Kassel.**

casserole ('kæsə,rəʊl) n **1** a covered dish of earthenware, glass, etc., in which food is cooked and served. **2** any food cooked and served in such a dish: *chicken casserole.*

♦ vb **casseroles, casseroling, casseroled. 3** to cook or be cooked in a casserole. [C18: from F, from OF *casse* ladle, from OProvençal, from LL *cattia* dipper, from Gk *kuathion*, dim. of *kuathos* cup]

cassette (kæ'sɛt) n **1a** a plastic container for magnetic tape, inserted into a tape deck to be played or used. **1b** (as modifier): *a cassette recorder.* **2** *Photog.* another term for **cartridge** (sense 3). **3** the injection of genes from one species into the fertilized egg of another species. [C18: from F: little box]

cassia ('kæsɪə) n **1** any of a genus of tropical plants whose pods yield **cassia pulp**, a mild laxative. See also **senna. 2** a lauraceous tree of tropical Asia. **3 cassia bark.** the cinnamon-like bark of this tree, used as a spice. [OE, from L *casia*, from Gk *kasia*, of Semitic origin]

Cassini ★ (French kasini) n **Giovanni Domenico** (ʒovani doːmeniko). 1625–1712, French astronomer, born in Italy. He discovered (1675) **Cassini's division**, the gap that divides Saturn's rings into two parts.

cassino or **casino** (kə'siːnəʊ) n a card game for two to four players in which players pair cards with those exposed on the table.

Cassiodorus ★ (,kæsɪəʊ'doːrəs) n **Flavius Magnus Aurelius** ('fleɪvɪəs 'mægnəs oː'riːlɪəs). ?490–?585 A.D., Roman statesman and monk; author of *Variae.*

Cassiopeia[1] ★ (,kæsɪə'piːə) n *Greek myth.* the wife of Cepheus and mother of Andromeda.

Cassiopeia[2] (,kæsɪə'piːə) n, *Latin genitive* **Cassiopeiae** (,kæsɪə'piːiː). a very conspicuous W-shaped constellation near the Pole Star.

Cassirer ★ (German ka'siːrər) n **Ernst** (ɛrnst). 1874–1945, German neo-Kantian philosopher, noted for *The Philosophy of Symbolic Forms* (1923–29).

cassis (kɑː'siːs) n a blackcurrant cordial. [C19: from F]

cassiterite (kə'sɪtə,raɪt) n a hard heavy brownish-black mineral, the chief ore of tin. Formula: SnO_2. Also called: **tinstone.** [C19: from Gk *kassiteros* tin]

Cassius Longinus ★ ('kæsɪəs lɒn'dʒaɪnəs) n **Gaius** ('gaɪəs). died 42 B.C., Roman general: led the conspiracy against Julius Caesar (44); defeated at Philippi by Mark Antony (42).

Cassivelaunus ★ (,kæsɪvə'loːnəs) n 1st century B.C., British chieftain, king of the Catuvellauni tribe, who organized resistance to Caesar's invasion of Britain (54 B.C.).

cassock ('kæsək) n an ankle-length garment, usually black, worn by Christian priests. [C16: from OF, from It. *casacca* a long coat, from ?]

Casson ★ ('kæs'n) n Sir **Hugh** (**Maxwell**). born 1910, British architect; president of the Royal Academy (1976–84).

cassowary ('kæsə,wɛərɪ) n, pl **cassowaries.** a large flightless bird inhabiting forests in NE Australia, New Guinea, and adjacent islands, having a horny head crest, black plumage, and brightly coloured neck. [C17: from Malay *kĕsuari*]

cast (kɑːst) vb **casts, casting, cast.** (mainly tr) **1** to throw or expel with force. **2** to throw off or away: *she cast her clothes to the ground.* **3** to reject: *he cast the idea from his mind.* **4** to shed or drop: *the horse cast a shoe.* **5** to cause to appear: *to cast a shadow.* **6** to express (doubts, etc.) or cause (them) to be felt. **7** to direct (a glance, etc.): *cast your eye over this.* **8** to place, esp. violently: *he was cast into prison.* **9** (also intr) *Angling.* to throw (a line) into the water. **10** to draw or choose (lots). **11** to give or deposit (a vote). **12** to select (actors) to play parts in (a play, etc.). **13a** to shape (molten metal, glass, etc.) by pouring into a mould. **13b** to make (an object) by such a process. **14** (also intr; often foll. by *up*) to compute (figures or a total). **15** *Astrol.* to draw on (a horoscope) details concerning the positions of the planets in the signs of the zodiac at a particular time for interpretation. **16** to contrive (esp. in **cast a spell**). **17** to formulate: *he cast his work in the form of a chart.* **18** (also intr) to twist or cause to twist. **19** (intr) (of birds of prey) to eject from the crop and bill a pellet consisting of the indigestible parts of birds or animals previously eaten. **20** *Printing.* to stereotype or electrotype. **21 be cast.** *NZ.* (of sheep) to have fallen and been unable to rise. ♦ n **22** the act of casting or throwing. **23a** Also called: **casting**. something that is shed, dropped, or egested, such as the coil of earth left by an earthworm. **23b** another name for **pellet** (sense 4). **24** the distance an object is or may be thrown. **25a** a throw at dice. **25b** the resulting number shown. **26** *Angling*. the act or an instance of casting a line. **27** the wide sweep made by a sheepdog to get behind a flock of sheep or by a hunting dog in search of a scent. **28a** the actors in a play collectively. **28b** (*as modifier*): *a cast list*. **29a** an object made of metal, glass, etc., that has been shaped in a molten state by being poured or pressed into a mould. **29b** the mould used to shape such an object. **30** form or appearance. **31** a sort, kind, or style. **32** a fixed twist or defect, esp. in the eye. **33** a distortion of shape. **34** *Surgery*. a rigid encircling casing, often made of plaster of Paris (**plaster cast**), for immobilizing broken bones while they heal. **35** a slight tinge or trace, as of colour. **36** fortune or stroke of fate. ◆ See also **cast about, castaway**, etc. [C13: from ON *kasta*]

ast about or **around** *vb* (*intr, adv*) to make a mental or visual search: *to cast about for a plot*.

astalia ★ (kæ'steɪlɪ) *n* a spring on Mount Parnassus: in ancient Greece sacred to Apollo and the Muses and believed to be a source of inspiration.
▶ **Cas'talian** *adj*

astanets (ˌkæstə'nɛts) *pl n* curved pieces of hollow wood, usually held between the fingers and thumb and made to click together: used esp. by Spanish dancers. [C17 *castanet*, from Sp. *castañeta*, dim. of *castaña* CHESTNUT]

astaway ('kɑːstəˌweɪ) *n* **1** a person who has been shipwrecked. ◆ *adj* (*prenominal*) **2** shipwrecked. **3** thrown away or rejected. ◆ *vb* **cast away**. **4** (*tr, adv; often passive*) to cause (a ship, person, etc.) to be shipwrecked.

ast back *vb* (*adv*) to turn (the mind) to the past.

ast down *vb* (*tr, adv*) to make (a person) discouraged or dejected.

aste (kɑːst) *n* **1a** any of the four major hereditary classes, namely the **Brahman, Kshatriya, Vaisya**, and **Sudra**, into which Hindu society is divided. **1b** Also called: **caste system**. the system or basis of such classes. **2** any social class or system based on such distinctions as heredity, rank, wealth, etc. **3** the position conferred by such a system. **4 lose caste**. *Inf*. to lose one's social position. **5** *Entomol*. any of various types of individual, such as the worker, in social insects. [C16: from Port. *casta* race, from *casto* pure, chaste, from L *castus*]

Castellammare di Stabia ★ (*Italian* kastɛllam'maːre di 'stabja) *n* a port and resort in SW Italy, in Campania on the Bay of Naples: site of the Roman resort of Stabiae, which was destroyed by the eruption of Vesuvius in 79 A.D. Pop.: 67 974 (1993 est.).

astellan ('kæstɪlən) *n Rare*. a keeper or governor of a castle. Also called: **chatelain**. [C14: from L *castellānus*, from *castellum* CASTLE]

astellated ('kæstɪˌleɪtɪd) *adj* **1** having turrets and battlements, like a castle. **2** having indentations similar to battlements: *a castellated nut*. [C17: from Med. L *castellātus*, from *castellāre* to fortify as a CASTLE]
▶ ˌcastel'lation *n*

aster ('kɑːstə) *n* **1** a person or thing that casts. **2** a bottle with a perforated top for sprinkling sugar, etc. **3** a small swivelled wheel fixed to a piece of furniture to enable it to be moved easily in any direction. ◆ Also (for senses 2, 3): **castor**.

caster sugar ('kɑːstə) *n* finely ground white sugar.

castigate ('kæstɪˌgeɪt) *vb* **castigates, castigating, castigated**. (*tr*) to rebuke or criticize in a severe manner. [C17: from L *castīgāre* to correct, from *castum* pure + *agere* to compel (to be)]
▶ ˌcasti'gation *n* ▶ 'castiˌgator *n*

Castiglione ★ (ˌkæstɪl'jəʊnɪ) *n* Count **Baldassare** (baldas'saːre). 1478–1529, Italian diplomat and writer, noted for *Il Libro del Cortegiano* (The Courtier) (1528).

Castile (kæ'stiːl) or **Castilla** ★ (*Spanish* kas'tiʎa) *n* a former kingdom comprising most of modern Spain: originally part of León, it became an independent kingdom in the 10th century and united with Aragon (1469), the first step in the formation of the Spanish state.

Castile soap *n* a hard soap made from olive oil and sodium hydroxide.

Castilian (kæ'stɪljən) *n* **1** the Spanish dialect of Castile; the standard form of European Spanish. **2** a native or inhabitant of Castile. ◆ *adj* **3** denoting or of Castile, its inhabitants, or the standard form of European Spanish.

Castilla la Vieja ★ (kas'tiʎa la 'bjexa) *n* the Spanish name for **Old Castile**.

casting ('kɑːstɪŋ) *n* **1** an object that has been cast, esp. in metal from a mould. **2** the process of transferring molten steel to a mould. **3** the choosing of actors for a production. **4** *Zool*. another word for **cast** (sense 23) or **pellet** (sense 4).

casting couch *n Inf*. a couch on which a casting director is said to seduce girls seeking a part in a film or play.

casting vote *n* the deciding vote used by the presiding officer of an assembly when votes cast on both sides are equal in number.

cast iron *n* **1** iron containing so much carbon that it cannot be wrought and must be cast into shape. ◆ *adj* **cast-iron**. **2** made of cast iron. **3** rigid or unyielding: *a cast-iron decision*.

castle ('kɑːsˀl) *n* **1** a fortified building or set of buildings as in medieval Europe. **2** any fortified place or structure. **3** a large magnificent house, esp. when the present or former home of a nobleman or prince. **4** *Chess*. another name for **rook**[2]. ◆ *vb* **castles, castling, castled. 5** *Chess*. to move (the king) two squares laterally on the first rank and place the nearest rook on the square passed over by the king. [C11: from L *castellum*, dim. of *castrum* fort]

Castlebar ★ (ˌkɑːsˀl'bɑː) *n* the county town of Co. Mayo, Republic of Ireland; site of the battle (1798) between the French and British known as Castlebar Races: bacon-curing. Pop.: 6070 (1991).

castle in the air or **in Spain** *n* a hope or desire unlikely to be realized; daydream.

Castlereagh[1] ★ ('kɑːsˀlˌreɪ) *n* a district of E Northern Ireland, SE of Belfast: a residential area for Belfast, whence it is administered. Pop.: 60 799 (1991). Area: 84 sq. km (33 sq. miles).

Castlereagh[2] ★ ('kɑːsˀlˌreɪ) *n* **Viscount**. title of *Robert Stewart*, Marquis of Londonderry. 1769–1822, British statesman: as foreign secretary (1812–22) led the Grand Alliance against Napoleon and attended the Congress of Vienna (1815).

Castner ★ ('kæstnə) *n* **Hamilton Young**. 1858–98, US chemist, who devised the **Castner process** for extracting sodium from sodium hydroxide.

cast-off *adj* **1** (*prenominal*) abandoned: *cast-off shoes*. ◆ *n* **castoff. 2** a person or thing that has been discarded or abandoned. **3** *Printing*. an estimate of the amount of space that a piece of copy will occupy. ◆ *vb* **cast off**. (*adv*) **4** to remove (mooring lines) that hold (a vessel) to a dock. **5** to knot (a row of stitches, esp. the final row) in finishing off knitted or woven material. **6** *Printing*. to estimate the amount of space that will be taken up by (a book, piece of copy, etc.).

cast on *vb* (*adv*) to form (the first row of stitches) in knitting and weaving.

castor[1] ('kɑːstə) *n* **1** the aromatic secretion of a beaver, used in perfumery and medicine. **2** the fur of the beaver. **3** a hat made of beaver or similar fur. [C14: from L, from Gk *kastōr* beaver]

castor[2] ('kɑːstə) *n* a variant spelling of **caster** (senses 2, 3).

Castor and Pollux ★ *n Classical myth*. the twin sons of Leda: Pollux was fathered by Zeus, Castor by the mortal Tyndareus. After Castor's death, Pollux spent half his days with his half-brother in Hades and half with the gods in Olympus.

castor oil *n* an oil obtained from the seeds of the castor-oil plant and used as a lubricant and cathartic.

castor-oil plant *n* a tall Indian plant cultivated for its poisonous seeds, from which castor oil is extracted.

castrate (kæ'streɪt) *vb* **castrates, castrating, castrated**. (*tr*) **1** to remove the testicles of. **2** to deprive of vigour, mascu-

linity, etc. **3** to remove the ovaries of; spay. [C17: from L *castrāre* to emasculate, geld]
▶ **cas'tration** *n*

castrato (kæ'strɑːtəu) *n, pl* **castrati** (-tɪ) *or* **castratos.** (in 17th- and 18th-century opera, etc.) a male singer whose testicles were removed before puberty, allowing the retention of a soprano or alto voice. [C18: from It., from L *castrātus* castrated]

Castries ★ (kæs'triːs) *n* the capital and chief port of St Lucia. Pop.: 13 615 (1992 est.).

Castro ★ ('kæstrəu; *Spanish* 'kastro) *n* **Fidel** (fi'del; *Spanish* fi'ðel). full name *Fidel Castro Ruz.* born 1927, Cuban statesman: communist prime minister from 1959 and president from 1976.

cast steel *n* steel containing varying amounts of carbon, manganese, etc., that is cast into shape rather than wrought.

cast stone *n Building trades.* a building component, such as a block or lintel, made from cast concrete with a facing that resembles natural stone.

casual ('kæʒjuəl) *adj* **1** happening by accident or chance. **2** offhand: *a casual remark.* **3** shallow or superficial: *a casual affair.* **4** being or seeming unconcerned or apathetic: *he assumed a casual attitude.* **5** (esp. of dress) for informal wear: *a casual coat.* **6** occasional or irregular: *a casual labourer.* ◆ *n* **7** (*usually pl*) an informal article of clothing or footwear. **8** an occasional worker. **9** (*usually pl*) a young man dressed in expensive casual clothes who goes to football matches in order to start fights. [C14: from LL *cāsuālis* happening by chance, from L *cāsus* event, from *cadere* to fall]
▶ **'casually** *adv* ▶ **'casualness** *n*

casualization *or* **casualisation** (ˌkæʒjuəlaɪ'zeɪʃən) *n* the altering of working practices so that regular workers are re-employed on a casual or short-term basis.

casualty ('kæʒjuəltɪ) *n, pl* **casualties. 1** a serviceman who is killed, wounded, captured, or missing as a result of enemy action. **2** a person who is injured or killed in an accident. **3** the hospital department treating victims of accidents. **4** anything that is lost, damaged, or destroyed as the result of an accident, etc.

casuarina (ˌkæʒjuə'riːnə) *n* any of a genus of trees of Australia and the East Indies, having jointed leafless branchlets. [C19: from NL, from Malay *kĕsuari* CASSOWARY, referring to the resemblance of the branches to the feathers of the cassowary]

casuist ('kæzjuɪst) *n* **1** a person, esp. a theologian, who attempts to resolve moral dilemmas by the application of general rules and the careful distinction of special cases. **2** a sophist. [C17: from F, from Sp. *casuista*, from L *cāsus* CASE¹]
▶ ˌ**casu'istic** *or* ˌ**casu'istical** *adj*

casuistry ('kæzjuɪstrɪ) *n, pl* **casuistries. 1** *Philosophy.* the resolution of particular moral dilemmas, esp. those arising from conflicting general moral rules, by the careful distinction of the cases to which these rules apply. **2** reasoning that is specious or oversubtle.

cat¹ (kæt) *n* **1** Also called: **domestic cat.** a small domesticated feline mammal having thick soft fur and occurring in many breeds in which the colour of the fur varies greatly: kept as a pet or to catch rats and mice. **2** Also called: **big cat.** any of the larger felines, such as a lion or tiger. **3** any wild feline mammal such as the lynx or serval, resembling the domestic cat. **4** *Inf.* a woman who gossips maliciously. **5** *Sl.* a man. **6** *Naut.* a heavy tackle for hoisting an anchor to the cathead. **7** *Austral. sl.* a coward. **8** short for **catboat. 9** *Inf.* short for **caterpillar** (the vehicle). **10** short for **cat-o'-nine-tails. 11 a bag of cats.** *Irish inf.* a bad-tempered person: *she's a real bag of cats this morning.* **12 fight like Kilkenny cats.** to fight until both parties are destroyed. **13 let the cat out of the bag.** to disclose a secret, often by mistake. **14 like a cat on a hot tin roof** *or* **on hot bricks.** in an uneasy or agitated state. **15 put, set,** etc., **the cat among the pigeons.** to introduce some violently disturbing new element. **16 rain cats and dogs.** to rain very heavily. ◆ *vb* **cats, catting, catted. 17** (*tr*) *Naut.* to hoist (an anchor) to the cathead. **18** (*intr*) *Sl.* to vomit. [OE *catte*, from L *cattus*]
▶ **'cat,like** *adj* ▶ **'cattish** *adj*

cat² (kæt) *adj* short for **catalytic:** *a cat cracker.*

CAT *abbrev. for* computer-assisted trading.

cat. *abbrev. for:* **1** catalogue. **2** catamaran.

cata-, kata-, *before an aspirate* **cath-,** *or before a vowe* **cat-** *prefix* **1** down; downwards; lower in position *catadromous.* **2** indicating reversal, opposition, degenera tion, etc.: *catatonia.* [from Gk *kata-*, from *kata.* In com pound words borrowed from Gk *kata-* means: down away, off, against, according to, and thoroughly]

catabolism *or* **katabolism** (kə'tæbə,lɪzəm) *n* a meta bolic process in which complex molecules are broken down into simple ones with the release of energy; de structive metabolism. [C19: from Gk *katabolē* a throw ing down, from *kata-* down + *ballein* to throw]
▶ **catabolic** *or* **katabolic** (ˌkætə'bɒlɪk) *adj*

catachresis (ˌkætə'kriːsɪs) *n* the incorrect use of words as *luxuriant* for *luxurious.* [C16: from L, from G *katakhrēsis* a misusing, from *khrēsthai* to use]
▶ **catachrestic** (ˌkætə'krestɪk) *adj*

cataclysm ('kætə,klɪzəm) *n* **1** a violent upheaval, esp. a political, military, or social nature. **2** a disastrous flood [C17: via F from L, from Gk, from *katakluzein* to flood from *kluzein* to wash]
▶ ˌ**cata'clysmic** *or* ˌ**cata'clysmal** *adj* ▶ ˌ**cata'clysmically** *adv*

catacomb ('kætə,kəum) *n* **1** (*usually pl*) an underground burial place, esp. in Rome, consisting of tunnels with niches leading off them for tombs. **2** a series of under ground tunnels or caves. [OE *catacumbe*, from L *catacumbas* (sing), name of the cemetery under the Basil ica of St Sebastian, near Rome; from ?]

catadioptric (ˌkætədaɪ'ɒptrɪk) *adj* involving a combina tion of reflecting and refracting components: *catadioptric telescope.* [C18: from CATA- + DIOPTRIC(S)]

catadromous (kə'tædrəməs) *adj* (of fishes such as the eel) migrating down rivers to the sea in order to breed. Cf. **anadromous.** [C19: from Gk, from *kata-* down + *dromos*, from *dremein* to run]

catafalque ('kætə,fælk) *n* a temporary raised platform on which a body lies in state before or during a funeral. [C17: from F, from It. *catafalco*, from ?]

Catalan ('kætə,læn) *n* **1** a language of Catalonia, closely related to Spanish and Provençal. **2** a native or inhabit ant of Catalonia. ◆ *adj* **3** denoting or characteristic of Catalonia, its inhabitants, or their language.

catalepsy ('kætə,lepsɪ) *n* a state of prolonged rigid pos ture, occurring for example in schizophrenia. [C16: from LL *catalēpsis*, from Gk *katalēpsis*, lit.: a seizing, from *kata-* down + *lambanein* to grasp]
▶ ˌ**cata'leptic** *adj*

catalogue *or* US **catalog** ('kætə,lɒg) *n* **1** a complete, usually alphabetical, list of items. **2** a book, usually illus trated, containing details of items for sale. **3** a list of all the books of a library. **4** *US and Canad.* a publication is sued by a university, college, etc., listing courses offered, regulations, services, etc. ◆ *vb* **catalogues, cataloguing, catalogued** *or* US **catalogs, cataloging, cataloged. 5** to compile a catalogue of (a library, etc.). **6** to add (books, items, etc.) to an existing catalogue. [C15: from LL *catalogus*, from Gk, from *katalegein* to list, from *kata-* completely + *legein* to collect]
▶ **'cata,loguer** *n*

Catalonia ★ (ˌkætə'ləunɪə) *n* a region of NE Spain, with a strong separatist tradition: became an autonomous re gion with its own parliament in 1979; an important ag ricultural and industrial region, with many resorts. Pop.: 6 090 107 (1994 est.). Area: 31 929 sq. km (12 328 sq. miles). Catalan name: **Catalunya** (ˌkatə'luːnɪə). Spanish name: **Cataluña** (kata'luɲa).

catalpa (kə'tælpə) *n* any of a genus of trees of North America and Asia, having large leaves, bell-shaped whit ish flowers, and long slender pods. [C18: NL, from Carolina Creek *kutuhlpa*, lit.: winged head]

catalyse *or* US **catalyze** ('kætə,laɪz) *vb* **catalyses, catalysing, catalysed** *or* US **catalyzes, catalyzing, catalyzed.** (*tr*) to influence (a chemical reaction) by catalysis.

catalysis (kə'tælɪsɪs) *n, pl* **catalyses** (-,siːz). acceleration of

---

a chemical reaction by the action of a catalyst. [C17: from NL, from Gk, from *kataluein* to dissolve]
► **catalytic** (ˌkætəˈlɪtɪk) *adj*

atalyst ('kætəlɪst) *n* **1** a substance that increases the rate of a chemical reaction without itself suffering any permanent chemical change. **2** a person or thing that causes a change.

atalytic converter *n* a device using three-way catalysts to reduce the poisonous products of combustion (mainly oxides of nitrogen, carbon monoxide, and unburnt hydrocarbons) from the exhaust of motor vehicles.

atalytic cracker *n* a unit in an oil refinery in which mineral oils with high boiling points are converted to fuels with lower boiling points by a catalytic process.

atamaran (ˌkætəməˈræn) *n* **1** a vessel, usually a sailing vessel, with twin hulls held parallel by a rigid framework. **2** a primitive raft made of logs lashed together. **3** *Inf.* a quarrelsome woman. [C17: from Tamil *kattumaram* tied timber]

atamite ('kætəˌmaɪt) *n* a boy kept for homosexual purposes. [C16: from L *Catamītus*, var. of *Ganymēdes* GANYMEDE]

atamount ('kætəˌmaʊnt) *or* **catamountain** *n* any of various felines, such as the puma or lynx. [C17: short for *cat of the mountain*]

atananche (kætənˈæŋkɪ) *n* any herb of the genus *Catananche*, having blue or yellow flowers. [C18: NL, from L, from Gk *kata* down + *anagkē* compulsion (from its use by ancient Greeks as a philtre)]

atania ★ (*Italian* kaˈtaːnja) *n* a port in E Sicily, near Mount Etna. Pop.: 327 163 (1994 est.).

ataplexy ('kætəˌplɛksɪ) *n* **1** sudden temporary paralysis, brought on by severe shock. **2** a state assumed by animals while shamming death. [C19: from Gk *kataplēxis* amazement, from *kataplēssein*, from *kata-* down + *plēssein* to strike]
► ˌcataˈplectic *adj*

atapult ('kætəˌpʌlt) *n* **1** a Y-shaped implement with a loop of elastic fastened to the ends of the prongs, used mainly by children for shooting stones, etc. US and Canad. name: **slingshot**. **2** a war engine used formerly for hurling stones, etc. **3** a device installed in warships to launch aircraft. ◆ *vb* **4** (*tr*) to shoot forth from or as if from a catapult. **5** (foll. by *over*, *into*, etc.) to move precipitately. [C16: from L, from Gk *katapeltēs*, from *kata-* down + *pallein* to hurl]

ataract ('kætəˌrækt) *n* **1** a large waterfall or rapids. **2** a downpour. **3** *Pathol.* **3a** partial or total opacity of the lens of the eye. **3b** the opaque area. [C15: from L, from Gk, from *katarassein* to dash down, from *arassein* to strike]

atarrh (kəˈtɑː) *n* inflammation of a mucous membrane with increased production of mucus, esp. affecting the nose and throat. [C16: via F from LL, from Gk, from *katarrhein* to flow down, from *kata-* down + *rhein* to flow]
► caˈtarrhal *adj*

atarrhine ('kætəˌraɪn) *adj* **1** (of apes and Old World monkeys) having the nostrils set close together and opening to the front of the face. ◆ *n* **2** an animal with this characteristic. [C19: ult. from Gk *katarrhin* having a hooked nose, from *kata-* down + *rhis* nose]

atastrophe (kəˈtæstrəfɪ) *n* **1** a sudden, extensive disaster or misfortune. **2** the denouement of a play. **3** a final decisive event, usually causing a disastrous end. [C16: from Gk, from *katastrephein* to overturn, from *strephein* to turn]
► **catastrophic** (ˌkætəˈstrɒfɪk) *adj* ► ˌcataˈstrophically *adv*

atastrophism (kəˈtæstrəˌfɪzəm) *n* **1** a former doctrine that the earth was formed by sudden divine acts rather than by evolutionary processes. **2** a modern doctrine that the evolutionary processes shaping the earth have in the past been supplemented by the effects of huge natural catastrophes.

atatonia (ˌkætəˈtəʊnɪə) *n* a form of schizophrenia characterized by stupor, with outbreaks of excitement. [C20: NL, from G *Katatonie*, from CATA- + Gk *tonos* tension]
► **catatonic** (ˌkætəˈtɒnɪk) *adj*, *n*

catbird ('kætˌbɜːd) *n* **1** any of several North American songbirds whose call resembles the mewing of a cat. **2** any of several Australian bowerbirds having a catlike call.

catboat ('kætˌbəʊt) *n* a sailing vessel with a single mast, set well forward, and a large sail. Shortened form: **cat**.

cat burglar *n* a burglar who enters buildings by climbing through upper windows, etc.

catcall ('kætˌkɔːl) *n* **1** a shrill whistle or cry expressing disapproval, as at a public meeting, etc. ◆ *vb* **2** to utter such a call (at).

catch (kætʃ) *vb* **catches, catching, caught. 1** (*tr*) to take hold of so as to retain or restrain. **2** (*tr*) to take or capture, esp. after pursuit. **3** (*tr*) to ensnare or deceive. **4** (*tr*) to surprise or detect in an act: *he caught the dog rifling the larder.* **5** (*tr*) to reach with a blow: *the stone caught him on the side of the head.* **6** (*tr*) to overtake or reach in time to board. **7** (*tr*) to see or hear; attend. **8** (*tr*) to be infected with: *to catch a cold.* **9** to hook or entangle or become hooked or entangled. **10** to fasten or be fastened with or as if with a latch or other device. **11** (*tr*) to attract: *she tried to catch his eye.* **12** (*tr*) to comprehend: *I didn't catch his meaning.* **13** (*tr*) to hear accurately: *I didn't catch what you said.* **14** (*tr*) to captivate or charm. **15** (*tr*) to reproduce accurately: *the painter managed to catch his model's beauty.* **16** (*tr*) to hold back or restrain: *he caught his breath in surprise.* **17** (*intr*) to become alight: *the fire won't catch.* **18** (*tr*) *Cricket.* to dismiss (a batsman) by intercepting and holding a ball struck by him before it touches the ground. **19** (*intr*; often foll. by *at*) **19a** to grasp or attempt to grasp. **19b** to take advantage (of): *he caught at the chance.* **20 catch it.** *Inf.* to be scolded or reprimanded. ◆ *n* **21** the act of catching or grasping. **22** a device that catches and fastens, such as a latch. **23** anything that is caught. **24** the amount or number caught. **25** *Inf.* an eligible matrimonial prospect. **26** a check or break in the voice. **27** *Inf.* **27a** a concealed, unexpected, or unforeseen drawback. **27b** (*as modifier*): *a catch question.* **28** *Cricket.* the catching of a ball struck by a batsman before it touches the ground, resulting in him being out. **29** *Music.* a type of round having a humorous text that is often indecent or bawdy and hard to articulate. ◆ See also **catch on, catch out, catch up.** [C13 *cacchen* to pursue, from OF *cachier*, from L *captāre* to snatch, from *capere* to seize]
► 'catchable *adj*

catch-22 *n* a situation in which a person is frustrated by a set of circumstances that preclude any attempt to escape from them. [C20: from the title of a novel (1961) by J. Heller]

catch-as-catch-can *n* a style of wrestling in which trips, holds below the waist, etc., are allowed.

catchfly ('kætʃˌflaɪ) *n, pl* **catchflies.** any of various plants that have sticky calyxes and stems on which insects are sometimes trapped.

catching ('kætʃɪŋ) *adj* **1** infectious. **2** attractive; captivating.

catching pen *n* *Austral. & NZ.* a pen adjacent to a shearer's stand containing the sheep ready for shearing.

catchment ('kætʃmənt) *n* **1** the act of catching or collecting water. **2** a structure in which water is collected. **3** the water so collected. **4** *Brit.* the intake of a school from one catchment area.

catchment area *n* **1** the area of land bounded by watersheds draining into a river, basin, or reservoir. **2** the area from which people are allocated to a particular school, hospital, etc.

catch on *vb* (*intr, adv*) *Inf.* **1** to become popular or fashionable. **2** to understand.

catch out *vb* (*tr, adv*) *Inf., chiefly Brit.* to trap (a person), esp. in an error.

catchpenny ('kætʃˌpɛnɪ) *adj* (*prenominal*) designed to have instant appeal, esp. in order to sell quickly: *catchpenny ornaments.*

catch phrase *n* a well-known frequently used phrase, esp. one associated with a particular group, etc.

catch up *vb* (*adv*) **1** (*tr*) to seize and take up (something) quickly. **2** (when *intr*, often foll. by *with*) to reach or pass (someone or something): *he caught him up.* **3** (*intr*; usually foll. by *on* or *with*) to make up for lost ground or deal with a backlog. **4** (*tr; often passive*) to absorb or involve: *she was caught up in her reading.* **5** (*tr*) to raise by or as if by fastening.

catchweight ('kætʃ,weɪt) *adj Wrestling.* of or relating to a contest in which normal weight categories have been waived by agreement.

catchword ('kætʃ,wɜːd) *n* **1** a word or phrase made temporarily popular; slogan. **2** a word printed as a running head in a book. **3** *Theatre.* an actor's cue to speak or enter. **4** the first word of a page repeated at the bottom of the page preceding.

catchy ('kætʃɪ) *adj* **catchier, catchiest. 1** (of a tune, etc.) pleasant and easily remembered. **2** deceptive: *a catchy question.* **3** irregular: *a catchy breeze.*

cat cracker *n* an informal name for **catalytic cracker.**

catechetical (,kætɪ'kɛtɪk°l) *or* **catechetic** *adj* of or relating to teaching by question and answer.
  ▶ ,cate'chetically *adv*

catechism ('kætɪ,kɪzəm) *n* instruction by a series of questions and answers, esp. a book containing such instruction on the religious doctrine of a Christian Church. [C16: from LL, ult. from Gk *katēkhizein* to CATE-CHIZE]
  ▶ ,cate'chismal *adj*

catechize *or* **catechise** ('kætɪ,kaɪz) *vb* **catechizes, catechizing, catechized** *or* **catechises, catechising, catechised.** (*tr*) **1** to teach or examine by means of questions and answers. **2** to give oral instruction in Christianity, esp. by using a catechism. **3** to put questions to (someone). [C15: from LL, from Gk *katēkhein*, from *katēkhein* to instruct orally, from *kata-* down + *ēkhein* to sound]
  ▶ 'catechist, 'cate,chizer *or* 'cate,chiser *n*

catechu ('kætɪ,tʃuː) *or* **cachou** *n* an astringent resinous substance obtained from certain tropical plants, and used in medicine, tanning, and dyeing. [C17: prob. from Malay *kachu*]

catechumen (,kætɪ'kjuːmɛn) *n Christianity.* a person, esp. in the early Church, undergoing instruction prior to baptism. [C15: via OF, from LL, from Gk *katēkhoumenos* one being instructed verbally]

categorial (,kætɪ'gɔːrɪəl) *adj* **1** of or relating to a category. **2** *Logic.* (of a statement) consisting of a subject, S, and a predicate, P, each of which denote a class, as in: *all S are P.*

categorical (,kætɪ'gɒrɪk°l) *or* **categoric** *adj* **1** unqualified; unconditional: *a categorical statement.* **2** relating to or included in a category. **3** another word for **categorial** (sense 2).
  ▶ ,cate'gorically *adv*

categorize *or* **categorise** ('kætɪgə,raɪz) *vb* **categorizes, categorizing, categorized** *or* **categorises, categorising, categorised.** (*tr*) to place in a category.
  ▶ ,categori'zation *or* ,categori'sation *n*

category ('kætɪgərɪ) *n, pl* **categories. 1** a class or group of things, people, etc., possessing some quality or qualities in common. **2** *Metaphysics.* one of the most basic classes into which objects and concepts can be analysed. **3a** (in the philosophy of Aristotle) any one of ten most fundamental modes of being, such as quantity, quality, and substance. **3b** (in the philosophy of Kant) one of twelve concepts required by human beings to interpret the empirical world. [C15: from LL, from Gk *katēgoria*, from *kategorein* to accuse, assert]

catena (kə'tiːnə) *n, pl* **catenae** (-niː). a connected series, esp. of patristic comments on the Bible. [C17: from L: chain]

catenaccio (*Italian* kate'nattʃo) *n Soccer.* an extremely defensive style of play. [C20: from L *catena* chain]

catenary (kə'tiːnərɪ) *n, pl* **catenaries. 1** the curve formed by a heavy uniform flexible cord hanging freely from two points. **2** the hanging cable between pylons along a railway track, from which the trolley wire is suspended.
  ◆ *adj* **3** of, resembling, relating to, or constructed using a catenary or suspended chain. [C18: from L *catēnārius* relating to a chain]

catenate ('kætɪ,neɪt) *vb* **catenates, catenating, catenated.**

Biol. to arrange or be arranged in a series of chains c rings. [C17: from L *catēnāre* to bind with chains]
  ▶ ,cate'nation *n*

cater ('keɪtə) *vb* **1** (*intr;* foll. by *for* or *to*) to provide what **i** required or desired (for). **2** (when *intr,* foll. by *for*) to pro vide food, services, etc. (for): *we cater for parties.* [C1**ɛ** from earlier *catour* purchaser, var. of *acatour*, from Anglc Norman *acater* to buy]
  ▶ 'catering *n*

cater-cornered ('kætə,kɔːnəd) *adj, adv US & Canad. in.** diagonal. Also: **catty-cornered, kitty-cornered.** [C16: fror dialect *cater* (adv) diagonally, from obs. *cater* (n) fou**r** spot of dice, from OF *quatre* four, from L *quattuor*]

caterer ('keɪtərə) *n* one who as a profession provide food for large social events, etc.

caterpillar ('kætə,pɪlə) *n* **1** the wormlike larva of butter flies and moths, having numerous pairs of legs and pow erful biting jaws. **2** *Trademark.* an endless track, driven b**y** sprockets or wheels, used to propel a heavy vehicle. **3** *Trademark.* a vehicle, such as a tractor, tank, etc., driven by such tracks. [C15 *catyrpel*, prob. from OF *catepelose* lit.: hairy cat]

caterwaul ('kætə,wɔːl) *vb* (*intr*) **1** to make a yowlin**g** noise, as a cat on heat. ◆ *n* **2** a yell made by or soundin**g** like a cat on heat. [C14: imit.]

Catesby ★ ('keɪtzbɪ) *n Robert.* 1573–1605, English leade of the Gunpowder Plot (1605): killed resisting arrest.

catfish ('kæt,fɪʃ) *n, pl* **catfish** *or* **catfishes. 1** any of numer ous mainly freshwater fishes having whisker-like barbel around the mouth. **2** another name for **wolffish.**

cat flap *or* **door** *n* a small flap or door in a larger doo through which a cat can pass.

catgut ('kæt,gʌt) *n* a strong cord made from the dried in testines of sheep and other animals that is used fo stringing certain musical instruments and sports rack ets.

Cath. *abbrev. for:* **1** Cathedral. **2** Catholic.

cath- *prefix* a variant of **cata-** before an aspirate: *cathode.*

Cathar ('kæθə) *or* **Catharist** ('kæθərɪst) *n, pl* **Cathars Cathari** (-əriː) *or* **Catharists.** a member of a Christian sect in Provence in the 12th and 13th centuries who believed the material world was evil and only the spiritual wa**s** good. [from Med. L, from Gk *katharoi* the pure]
  ▶ 'Cathar,ism *n*

catharsis (kə'θɑːsɪs) *n, pl* **catharses** (-siːz). **1** the purging or purification of the emotions through the evocation o**f** pity and fear, as in tragedy. **2** *Psychoanal.* the bringing o**f** repressed ideas or experiences into consciousness, thu**s** relieving tensions. **3** purgation, esp. of the bowels. [C19: NL, from Gk *katharsis*, from *katharein* to purge, pu rify]

cathartic (kə'θɑːtɪk) *adj* **1** purgative. **2** effecting cathar sis. ◆ *n* **3** a purgative drug or agent.
  ▶ ca'thartically *adv*

Cathay ★ (kæ'θeɪ) *n* a literary or archaic name for **China.** [C14: from Med. L *Cataya*]

cathead ('kæt,hɛd) *n* a fitting at the bow of a vessel for securing the anchor when raised.

cathedral (kə'θiːdrəl) *n* **a** the principal church of a dio cese, containing the bishop's official throne. **b** (*as modi fier*): *a cathedral city.* [C13: from LL (*ecclesia*) *cathedrālis* cathedral (church), from Gk *kathedra* seat]

Cather ★ ('kæðə) *n Willa* (**Sibert**). 1873–1947, US novelist, whose works include *O Pioneers!* (1913) and *My Antonia* (1918).

Catherine ★ ('kæθrɪn) *n Saint.* died 307 A.D., legendary Christian martyr of Alexandria, who was tortured on a spiked wheel and beheaded.

Catherine I ★ *n* ?1684–1727, second wife of Peter the Great, whom she succeeded as empress of Russia (1725– 27).

Catherine II ★ *n* known as *Catherine the Great.* 1729–96, empress of Russia (1762–96).

Catherine de' Medici *or* **de Médicis** ★ *n* 1519–89, queen of Henry II of France; mother of Francis II,

Charles IX, and Henry III of France; regent of France 1560–74).

atherine of Aragon ★ n 1485–1536, first wife of Henry VIII of England and mother of Mary I. The annulment of Henry's marriage to her (1533) marked an initial stage in the English Reformation.

atherine of Braganza ★ n 1638–1705, wife of Charles II of England, daughter of John IV of Portugal.

atherine of Siena ★ n Saint. 1347–80, Italian mystic; patron saint of the Dominican order. Feast day: April 29.

atherine wheel n 1 a firework which rotates, producing coloured flame. 2 a circular window having ribs radiating from the centre. [C16: after St CATHERINE of Alexandria]

atheter ('kæθɪtə) n Med. a long slender flexible tube for inserting into a bodily cavity for introducing or withdrawing fluid. [C17: from LL, from Gk kathetēr, from kathienai to insert]

atheterize or **catheterise** ('kæθɪtə,raɪz) vb catheterizes, catheterizing, catheterized or catheterises, catheterising, catheterised. (tr) to insert a catheter into.

athexis (kə'θeksɪs) n, pl cathexes (-'θeksi:z). Psychoanal. concentration of psychic energy on a single goal. [C20: from NL, from Gk kathexis, from katekhein to hold fast]

athode ('kæθəʊd) n 1 the negative electrode in an electrolytic cell. 2 the negatively charged electron source in an electronic valve. 3 the positive terminal of a primary cell. ◆ Cf. anode. [C19: from Gk kathodos a descent, from kata- down + hodos way]
▶ cathodal (kæ'θəʊd'l) or cathodic (kæ'θɒdɪk, -'θəʊ-) adj

athode rays pl n a stream of electrons emitted from the surface of a cathode in a vacuum tube.

athode-ray tube n a vacuum tube in which a beam of electrons is focused onto a fluorescent screen to give a visible spot of light. The device is used in television receivers, visual display units, etc.

atholic ('kæθəlɪk, 'kæθlɪk) adj 1 universal; relating to all men. 2 broad-minded; liberal. [C14: from L, from Gk katholikos universal, from kata- according to + holos whole]
▶ catholically or catholicly (kə'θɒlɪklɪ) adv

atholic ('kæθəlɪk, 'kæθlɪk) Christianity. ◆ adj 1 denoting or relating to the entire body of Christians, esp. to the Church before separation into the Eastern and Western Churches. 2 denoting or relating to the Latin or Western Church after this separation. 3 denoting or relating to the Roman Catholic Church. ◆ n 4 a member of the Roman Catholic Church.

atholicism (kə'θɒlɪ,sɪzəm) n 1 short for Roman Catholicism. 2 the beliefs, practices, etc., of any Catholic Church.

atholicity (,kæθə'lɪsɪtɪ) n 1 a wide range of interests, tastes, etc. 2 comprehensiveness.

atholicize or **catholicise** (kə'θɒlɪ,saɪz) vb catholicizes, catholicizing, catholicized or catholicises, catholicising, catholicised. 1 to make or become catholic. 2 (often cap.) to convert to or become converted to Catholicism.

atiline ★ ('kætɪ,laɪn) n Latin name Lucius Sergius Catilina. ?108–62 B.C., Roman politician: organized an unsuccessful conspiracy against Cicero (63–62).
▶ Catilinarian (,kætɪlɪ'neərɪən) adj

ation ('kætaɪən) n a positively charged ion; an ion that is attracted to the cathode during electrolysis. Cf. anion. [C19: from CATA- + ION]
▶ cationic (,kætaɪ'ɒnɪk) adj

atkin ('kætkɪn) n an inflorescence consisting of a hanging spike of much reduced flowers of either sex: occurs in birch, hazel, etc. [C16: from obs. Du. katteken kitten]

at litter n absorbent material used to line a receptacle in which a domestic cat can urinate and defecate.

atmint ('kæt,mɪnt) n a Eurasian plant having spikes of purple-spotted white flowers and scented leaves of which cats are fond. Also called: catnip.

atnap ('kæt,næp) n 1 a short sleep or doze. ◆ vb catnaps, catnapping, catnapped. 2 (intr) to sleep or doze for a short time or intermittently.

Cato ★ ('keɪtəʊ) n 1 Marcus Porcius ('mɑːkəs 'pɔːʃɪəs), known as Cato the Elder or the Censor. 234–149 B.C., Roman statesman, noted for his opposition to Carthage. 2 his great-grandson, Marcus Porcius, known as Cato the Younger or Uticensis. 95–46 B.C., Roman statesman and Stoic philosopher; opponent of Catiline and Caesar.

cat-o'-nine-tails n, pl cat-o'-nine-tails. a rope whip consisting of nine knotted thongs, used formerly to flog prisoners. Often shortened to cat.

CATS (kæts) n acronym for credit accumulation transfer scheme: a scheme enabling school-leavers and others to acquire transferable certificates for relevant work experience and study towards a recognized qualification.

CAT scanner (kæt) n former name for CT scanner. [C20: from Computerized Axial Tomography]

cat's cradle n a game played by making patterns with a loop of string between the fingers.

cat's-eye n any of a group of gemstones that reflect a streak of light when cut in a rounded unfaceted shape.

Catseye ('kætsaɪ) n Trademark, Brit. a glass reflector set into a small fixture, placed at intervals along roads to indicate traffic lanes at night.

Catskill Mountains ★ ('kætskɪl) pl n a mountain range in SE New York State: resort. Highest peak: Slide Mountain, 1261 m (4204 ft). Also called: Catskills.

cat's-paw n 1 a person used by another as a tool; dupe. 2 a pattern of ripples on the surface of water caused by a light wind. [(sense 1) C18: so called from the tale of the monkey who used a cat's paw to draw chestnuts out of a fire]

catsup ('kætsəp) n a variant spelling (esp. US) of ketchup.

cat's whisker n a pointed wire formerly used to make contact with the crystal in a crystal radio receiver.

cat's whiskers or **cat's pyjamas** n the. Sl. a person or thing that is excellent or superior.

Cattegat ★ ('kætɪ,gæt) n a variant spelling of Kattegat.

cattery ('kætərɪ) n, pl catteries. a place where cats are bred or looked after.

cattle ('kæt'l) n (functioning as pl) 1 bovid mammals of the tribe Bovini (bovines). 2 Also called: domestic cattle. any domesticated bovine mammals. [C13: from OF chatel CHATTEL]

cattle-cake n concentrated food for cattle in the form of cakes.

cattle-grid n a grid of metal bars covering a hole dug in a roadway intended to prevent the passage of livestock while allowing vehicles, etc., to pass unhindered.

cattleman ('kæt'lmən) n, pl cattlemen. 1 a person who breeds, rears, or tends cattle. 2 Chiefly US & Canad. a person who rears cattle on a large scale.

cattle market n 1 a place in which cattle are bought and sold. 2 Brit. sl. a situation or place in which women are on display and judged solely by their appearance.

cattle-stop n the New Zealand name for a cattle-grid.

catty ('kætɪ) or **cattish** adj cattier, cattiest. 1 Inf. spiteful: a catty remark. 2 of or like a cat.
▶ 'cattily or 'cattishly adv ▶ 'cattiness or 'cattishness n

Catullus ★ (kə'tʌləs) n Gaius Valerius ('gaɪəs və'lɪərɪəs). ?84–?54 B.C., Roman lyric poet.
▶ Catullan (kə'tʌlən) adj

CATV abbrev. for community antenna television.

catwalk ('kæt,wɔːk) n 1 a narrow ramp extending from the stage into the audience in a theatre etc., esp. as used by models in a fashion show. 2 a narrow pathway over the stage of a theatre, along a bridge, etc.

Cauca ★ (Spanish 'kauka) n a river in W Colombia, rising in the northwest and flowing north to the Magdalena River. Length: about 1350 km (840 miles).

Caucasia ★ (kɔː'keɪzɪə, -ʒə) n a region of SW Russia, Georgia, Armenia, and Azerbaijan, between the Caspian Sea and the Black Sea: contains the Caucasus Mountains, dividing it into Ciscaucasia in the north and Transcaucasia in the south; one of the most complex ethnic areas in the world, with over 50 different peoples. Also called: the Caucasus.

★ people and places

Caucasian (kɔː'keɪzɪən) *adj* **1** another word for **Caucasoid**. **2** of or relating to Caucasia or the Caucasus. ◆ *n* **3** a member of the Caucasoid race; a White person. **4** a native or inhabitant of Caucasia or the Caucasus.

Caucasoid ('kɔːkə,zɔɪd) *adj* **1** denoting or belonging to the light-complexioned racial group of mankind, which includes the peoples indigenous to Europe, N Africa, SW Asia, and the Indian subcontinent. ◆ *n* **2** a member of this racial group.

Caucasus ★ ('kɔːkəsəs) *n* **the. 1** Also called: **Caucasus Mountains.** a mountain range in SW Russia, in Caucasia between the Black Sea and the Caspian Sea: mostly over 2700 m (9000 ft). Highest peak: Mount Elbrus, 5642 m (18 510 ft). **2** another name for **Caucasia.**

Cauchy ★ ('kəʊʃɪ; *French* koʃi) *n* **Augustin Louis** (ogystɛ lwi), Baron Cauchy. 1789–1857, French mathematician, noted for his theory of functions.

caucus ('kɔːkəs) *n, pl* **caucuses. 1** *Chiefly US & Canad.* a closed meeting of the members of one party in a legislative chamber, etc., to coordinate policy, choose candidates, etc. **2** *Chiefly US.* a local meeting of party members. **3** *Brit.* a group or faction within a larger group, esp. a political party, who discuss tactics, choose candidates, etc. **4** *NZ.* a formal meeting of all MPs of one party. **5** *Austral.* a group of MPs from one party who meet to discuss tactics, etc. ◆ *vb* **6** (*intr*) to hold a caucus. [C18: prob. of Algonquian origin]

caudal ('kɔːd²l) *adj* **1** *Anat.* of the posterior part of the body. **2** *Zool.* resembling or in the position of the tail. [C17: from NL, from L *cauda* tail]
▸ **'caudally** *adv*

caudal fin *n* the tail fin of fishes and some other aquatic vertebrates, used for propulsion.

caudate ('kɔːdeɪt) *or* **caudated** *adj* having a tail or a tail-like appendage. [C17: from NL *caudātus,* from L *cauda* tail]
▸ **cau'dation** *n*

caudillo (kɔː'diːljəʊ) *n, pl* **caudillos** (-ljəʊz). (in Spanish-speaking countries) a military or political leader. [Sp., from LL *capitellum,* dim. of L *caput* head]

caudle ('kɔːd²l) *n* a hot spiced wine drink made with gruel, formerly used medicinally. [C13: from OF *caudel,* from Med. L, from L *calidus* warm]

caught (kɔːt) *vb* the past tense and past participle of **catch.**

caul (kɔːl) *n* *Anat.* a portion of the amniotic sac sometimes covering a child's head at birth. [C13: from OF *cale,* back formation from *calotte* close-fitting cap, of Gmc origin]

cauldron *or* **caldron** ('kɔːldrən) *n* a large pot used for boiling, esp. one with handles. [C13: from Anglo-F, from L *caldārium* hot bath, from *calidus* warm]

cauliflower ('kɒlɪ,flaʊə) *n* **1** a variety of cabbage having a large edible head of crowded white flowers on a very short thick stem. **2** the flower head of this plant, used as a vegetable. [C16: from It. *caoli fiori,* lit.: cabbage flowers]

cauliflower ear *n* permanent swelling and distortion of the external ear as the result of ruptures of the blood vessels: usually caused by blows received in boxing.

caulk *or* **calk** (kɔːk) *vb* **1** to stop up (cracks, crevices, etc.) with a filler. **2** *Naut.* to pack (the seams) between the planks of the bottom of (a vessel) with waterproof material to prevent leakage. [C15: from OF *cauquer* to press down, from L *calcāre* to trample, from *calx* heel]

causal ('kɔːz²l) *adj* **1** acting as or being a cause. **2** stating, involving, or implying a cause: *the causal part of the argument.*
▸ **'causally** *adv*

causality (kɔː'zælɪtɪ) *n, pl* **causalities. 1a** the relationship of cause and effect. **1b** the principle that nothing can happen without being caused. **2** causal agency or quality.

causation (kɔː'zeɪʃən) *n* **1** the production of an effect by a cause. **2** the relationship of cause and effect.
▸ **cau'sational** *adj*

causative ('kɔːzətɪv) *adj* **1** *Grammar.* relating to a form or class of verbs, such as *persuade,* that express causation. **2**

(*often postpositive* and foll. by *of*) producing an effect. ◆ **3** the causative form or class of verbs.
▸ **'causatively** *adv*

cause (kɔːz) *n* **1** a person, thing, event, state, or actic that produces an effect. **2** grounds for action; justific tion: *she had good cause to shout like that.* **3** the ideals, ete of a group or movement: *the Communist cause.* **4** the we fare or interests of a person or group in a dispute: *th fought for the miners' cause.* **5a** a ground for legal actio matter giving rise to a lawsuit. **5b** the lawsuit itself. *Arch.* a subject of debate or discussion. **7 make comm cause with.** to join with (a person, group, etc.) for a con mon objective. ◆ *vb* **causes, causing, caused. 8** (*tr*) to t the cause of; bring about. [C13: from L *causa* cause, re son, motive]
▸ **'causeless** *adj*

cause célèbre ('kɔːz sə'lɛbrə) *n, pl* **causes célèbres** ('kɔ sə'lɛbrəz). a famous lawsuit, trial, or controversy. [C1 from F: famous case]

causerie ('kəʊzərɪ) *n* an informal talk or conversation piece of writing. [C19: from F, from *causer* to chat]

causeway ('kɔːz,weɪ) *n* **1** a raised path or road crossin water, marshland, etc. **2** a paved footpath. [C *cauciwey* (from *cauci* + WAY); *cauci* paved road, from Me L, from L *calx* limestone]

caustic ('kɔːstɪk) *adj* **1** capable of burning or corrodir by chemical action: *caustic soda.* **2** sarcastic; cutting: *caustic reply.* ◆ *n* **3** Also called: **caustic surface.** a surfac that envelops the light rays reflected or refracted by curved surface. **4** Also called: **caustic curve.** a curv formed by the intersection of a caustic surface with plane. **5** *Chem.* a caustic substance, esp. an alkali. [C1 from L, from Gk *kaustikos,* from *kaiein* to burn]
▸ **'caustically** *adv* ▸ **causticity** (kɔː'stɪsɪtɪ) *n*

caustic potash *n* another name for **potassium hydroxide**

caustic soda *n* another name for **sodium hydroxide.**

cauterize *or* **cauterise** ('kɔːtə,raɪz) *vb* **cauterizes, caute izing, cauterized** *or* **cauterises, cauterising, cauterised.** (*t* (esp. in the treatment of a wound) to burn or sear (bod tissue) with a hot iron or caustic agent. [C14: from O from LL, from *cautērium* branding iron, from G *kautērion,* from *kaiein* to burn]
▸ **,cauteri'zation** *or* **,cauteri'sation** *n*

cautery ('kɔːtərɪ) *n, pl* **cauteries. 1** the coagulation o blood or destruction of body tissue by cauterizing. **2** a instrument or agent for cauterizing. [C14: from O *cautère,* from L *cautērium*]

caution ('kɔːʃən) *n* **1** care, forethought, or prudence, esp in the face of danger. **2** something intended or serving a a warning. **3** *Law, chiefly Brit.* a formal warning given to person suspected of an offence that his words will b taken down and may be used in evidence. **4** *Inf.* an amus ing or surprising person or thing. ◆ *vb* **5** (*tr*) to warn (person) to be careful. **6** (*tr*) *Law, chiefly Brit.* to give a cau tion to (a person). **7** (*intr*) to warn, urge, or advise: *he cau tioned against optimism.* [C13: from OF, from L *cautic* from *cavēre* to beware]

cautionary ('kɔːʃənərɪ) *adj* serving as a warning; in tended to warn: *a cautionary tale.*

cautious ('kɔːʃəs) *adj* showing or having caution.
▸ **'cautiously** *adv* ▸ **'cautiousness** *n*

Cavaco Silva ★ ('kavaku 'silvə) *n* **Aníbal** (a'nibal). born 1939, Portuguese statesman; prime minister (1985–95).

Cavafy ★ (kə'vɑːfɪ) *n* **Constantine.** Greek name *Kavafis* 1863–1933, Greek poet of Alexandria in Egypt.

cavalcade (,kævəl'keɪd) *n* **1** a procession of people or horseback, in cars, etc. **2** any procession. [C16: from F from It., from *cavalcare* to ride on horseback, from LL from *caballus* horse]

Cavalcanti ★ (*Italian* kaval'kanti) *n* **Guido** ('gwiːdo) ?1255–1300, Italian poet.

cavalier (,kævə'lɪə) *adj* **1** supercilious; offhand. ◆ *n* **2** courtly gentleman, esp. one acting as a lady's escort. *Arch.* a horseman, esp. one who is armed. [C16: from It. from OProvençal, from LL *caballārius* rider, from *caballu* horse, from ?]
▸ **,cava'lierly** *adv*

avalier (,kævə'lɪə) n a supporter of Charles I during the English Civil War.

avallini ★ (Italian kaval'li:ni) n **Pietro** ('pjɛ:tro). ?1250–1330, Italian fresco painter and mosaicist.

valry ('kævəlrɪ) n, pl **cavalries. 1** (esp. formerly) the part of an army composed of mounted troops. **2** the armoured element of a modern army. **3** (as modifier): a cavalry unit. [C16: from F cavallerie, from It., from cavaliere horseman]
  'cavalryman n

avan ★ ('kævᵊn) n **1** a county of north Republic of Ireland: hilly, with lakes and bogs. County town: Cavan. Pop.: 52 796 (1991). Area: 1890 sq. km (730 sq. miles). **2** a market town in north Republic of Ireland, county town of Co. Cavan. Pop.: 5000 (latest est.).

avatina (,kævə'ti:nə) n, pl **cavatine** (-nɪ). **1** a simple solo song. **2** an instrumental composition reminiscent of this. [C19: from It.]

ave[1] (keɪv) n **1** an underground hollow with access from the ground surface or from the sea. **2** Brit. history. a secession or a group seceding from a political party on some issue. **3** (modifier) living in caves. ◆ vb **caves, caving, caved. 4** (tr) to hollow out. [C13: from OF, from L cava, ol. of cavum cavity, from cavus hollow]

ave[2] ('keɪvɪ) Brit. school sl. ◆ n **1** lookout: keep cave. ◆ sentence substitute. **2** watch out! [from L cavē beware!]

aveat ('keɪvɪ,æt, 'kæv-) n **1** Law. a formal notice requesting the court not to take a certain action without warning the person lodging the caveat. **2** a caution. [C16: from L, lit.: let him beware]

aveat emptor ('emptɔ:) n the principle that the buyer must bear the risk for the quality of goods purchased. [L: let the buyer beware]

ave in vb (intr, adv) **1** to collapse; subside. **2** Inf. to yield completely, esp. under pressure. ◆ n **cave-in. 3** the sudden collapse of a roof, piece of ground, etc. **4** the site of such a collapse, as at a mine or tunnel.

avel ('keɪvᵊl) n NZ. a drawing of lots among miners for an easy and profitable place at the coalface. [C19: from E dialect cavel to cast lots, apportion]

avell ★ ('kævᵊl) n **Edith Louisa**. 1865–1915, British nurse: executed by the Germans in World War I for helping Allied prisoners to escape.

aveman ('keɪv,mæn) n, pl **cavemen. 1** a man of the Palaeolithic age; cave dweller. **2** Inf. a man who is primitive or brutal in behaviour, etc.

avendish ('kævəndɪʃ) n tobacco that has been sweetened and pressed into moulds to form bars. [C19: ?from the name of the first maker]

avendish ★ ('kævəndɪʃ) n **Henry**. 1731–1810, British physicist: recognized hydrogen and calculated the density of the earth.

avern ('kævᵊn) n **1** a cave, esp. when large. ◆ vb (tr) **2** to shut in or as if in a cavern. **3** to hollow out. [C14: from OF caverne, from L caverna, from cavus hollow]

avernous ('kævənəs) adj **1** suggestive of a cavern in vastness, etc.: cavernous eyes. **2** filled with small cavities. **3** (of rocks) containing caverns.

aviar or **caviare** ('kævɪ,ɑ:, ,kævɪ'ɑ:) n the salted roe of sturgeon, usually served as an hors d'oeuvre. [C16: from earlier cavery, from OIt. caviari, pl. of caviaro caviar, from Turkish havyār]

avil ('kævɪl) vb **cavils, cavilling, cavilled** or US **cavils, caviling, caviled. 1** (intr; foll. by at or about) to raise annoying petty objections. ◆ n **2** a trifling objection. [C16: from OF, from L cavillārī to jeer, from cavilla raillery]
  ▸ 'caviller n

aving ('keɪvɪŋ) n the sport of climbing in and exploring caves.
  ▸ 'caver n

avity ('kævɪtɪ) n, pl **cavities. 1** a hollow space. **2** Dentistry. a decayed area on a tooth. **3** any empty or hollow space within the body. [C16: from F, from LL cavitās, from L cavus hollow]

avity wall n a wall that consists of two separate walls with an airspace between them.

cavort (kə'vɔ:t) vb (intr) to prance; caper. [C19: ?from CURVET]
  ▸ ca'vorter n

Cavour ★ (Italian ka'vur) n **Conte Camillo Benso di** (ka'millo 'benzo di). 1810–61, Italian statesman and premier of Piedmont-Sardinia (1852–59; 1860–61): a leader of the movement for the unification of Italy.

cavy ('keɪvɪ) n, pl **cavies.** a small South American rodent having a thickset body and very small tail. See also **guinea pig.** [C18: from NL Cavia, from Carib cabiai]

caw (kɔ:) n **1** the cry of a crow, rook, or raven. ◆ vb **2** (intr) to make this cry. [C16: imit.]

Cawley ★ ('kɔ:lɪ) n **Evonne** (née Goolagong). born 1951, Australian tennis player: Wimbledon champion 1971 and 1980; Australian champion 1974–76.

Cawnpore (,kɔ:n'pɔ:) or **Cawnpur** ★ (,kɔ:n'puə) n the former name of **Kanpur.**

Caxton ★ ('kækstən) n **William.** ?1422–91, English printer; published, in Bruges, the first book printed in English (1475) and established the first press in England (1477).

cay (keɪ, ki:) n a small low island or bank composed of sand and coral fragments. [C18: from Sp. cayo, prob. from OF quai QUAY]

Cayenne ★ (keɪ'ɛn) n the capital of French Guiana, on an island at the mouth of the Cayenne River: French penal settlement from 1854 to 1938. Pop.: 41 659 (1990).

cayenne pepper (keɪ'ɛn) n a very hot red condiment made from the dried seeds of various capsicums. Often shortened to **cayenne.** Also called: **red pepper.** [C18: ult. from Tupi quinyha]

Cayes ★ (keɪ; French kaj) n short for **Les Cayes.**

Cayley ★ ('keɪlɪ) n **1 Arthur.** 1821–93, British mathematician, who invented matrices. **2 Sir George.** 1773–1857, British engineer and pioneer of aerial navigation.

cayman or **caiman** ('keɪmən) n, pl **caymans** or **caimans.** a tropical American crocodilian similar to alligators but with a more heavily armoured belly. [C16: from Sp. caimán, from Carib cayman]

Cayman Islands ★ ('keɪmən) pl n three coral islands in the Caribbean Sea northwest of Jamaica: a dependency of Jamaica until 1962, now a United Kingdom Overseas Territory. Capital: George Town. Pop.: 31 930 (1994). Area: about 260 sq. km (100 sq. miles).

CB abbrev. for: **1** Citizens' Band. **2** Companion of the (Order of the) Bath (a Brit. title). **3** County Borough.

CBC abbrev. for Canadian Broadcasting Corporation.

CBE abbrev. for Commander of the (Order of the) British Empire.

CBI abbrev. for: **1** US. Central Bureau of Investigation. **2** Confederation of British Industry.

CBT abbrev. for computer-based training.

cc or **c.c.** abbrev. for: **1** carbon copy or copies. **2** cubic centimetre(s).

CC abbrev. for: **1** City Council. **2** County Council. **3** Cricket Club.

cc. abbrev. for chapters.

c.c.c. abbrev. for cwmni cyfyngedig cyhoeddus; a public limited company in Wales.

C clef n Music. a symbol (𝄡), placed at the beginning of the staff, establishing the position of middle C: see **alto clef, soprano clef, tenor clef.**

CCTV abbrev. for closed-circuit television.

CCW abbrev. for Curriculum Council for Wales.

cd symbol for candela.

Cd the chemical symbol for cadmium.

CD abbrev. for: **1** compact disc. **2** Civil Defence (Corps). **3** Corps Diplomatique (Diplomatic Corps). **4** Conference on Disarmament: a United Nations standing conference, held in Geneva, to negotiate a global ban on chemical weapons.

CDE abbrev. for: compact disc erasable: a compact disc that can be used to record and rerecord. Cf. **CDR.**

CDI abbrev. for compact disc interactive.

★ people and places

Cdn *abbrev. for* Canadian.

cDNA *abbrev. for* complementary DNA.

CD player *n* a device for playing compact discs. In full: **compact-disc player**.

Cdr *Mil. abbrev. for* Commander.

CDR *abbrev. for* compact disc recordable: a compact disc that can be used to record only once. Cf. **CDE**.

CD-ROM (ˌsiːdiːˈrɒm) *abbrev. for* compact disc read only memory; a compact disc used for storing written information to be displayed on a visual-display unit.

CDT *abbrev. for:* **1** US & Canad. Central Daylight Time. **2** Craft, Design, and Technology: a subject on the GCSE syllabus, related to the National Curriculum.

CDV *abbrev. for* compact disc video.

CD-video *n* a compact-disc player that, when connected to a television and hi-fi, produces high-quality stereo sound and synchronized pictures from a disc resembling a compact audio disc. In full **compact-disc video**.

Ce *the chemical symbol for* cerium.

CE *abbrev. for:* **1** Church of England. **2** civil engineer. **3** Common Era.

Ceará ★ (*Portuguese* sjaˈra) *n* **1** a state of NE Brazil: sandy coastal plain, rising to a high plateau. Capital: Fortaleza. Pop.: 6 714 200 (1995 est.). Area: 150 630 sq. km (58 746 sq. miles). **2** another name for **Fortaleza**.

cease (siːs) *vb* **ceases, ceasing, ceased**. **1** (when *tr*, may take a gerund or an infinitive as object) to bring or come to an end. ◆ *n* **2 without cease**. without stopping. [C14: from OF, from L *cessāre*, frequentative of *cēdere* to yield]

ceasefire (ˈsiːsˌfaɪə) *Chiefly mil.* ◆ *n* **1** a period of truce, esp. one that is temporary. ◆ *sentence substitute, n* **2** the order to stop firing.

ceaseless (ˈsiːslɪs) *adj* without stop or pause; incessant. ▸ **ˈceaselessly** *adv*

Ceauşescu ★ (tʃaʊˈʃɛskuː) *n* **Nicolae** (ˌnɪkɒˈlaɪ). 1918–89, Romanian statesman; chairman of the state council (1967–89) and president (1974–89): deposed and executed.

Cebú ★ (sɪˈbuː) *n* **1** an island in the central Philippines. Pop.: 2 091 602 (1980). Area: 4422 sq. km (1707 sq. miles). **2** a port in the Philippines, on E Cebú island. Pop.: 688 196 (1994 est.).

Čechy ★ (ˈtʃɛxɪ) *n* the Czech name for **Bohemia**.

Cecil ★ (ˈsɛsᵊl, ˈsɪs-) *n* **1** Lord **David**. 1902–86, British biographer. **2 Robert**. See (3rd Marquess of) **Salisbury**. **3 William**. See (William Cecil) **Burghley**.

Cecilia ★ (sɪˈsiːljə) *n* **Saint**. died ?230 A.D., Roman martyr; patron saint of music. Feast day: Nov. 22.

cecum (ˈsiːkəm) *n, pl* **ceca** (-kə). *US*. a variant spelling of **caecum**. ▸ **ˈcecal** *adj*

cedar (ˈsiːdə) *n* **1** any of a genus of Old World coniferous trees having needle-like evergreen leaves, and erect barrel-shaped cones. See also **cedar of Lebanon, deodar**. **2** any of various other conifers, such as the red cedars and white cedars. **3** the wood of any of these trees. ◆ *adj* **4** made of the wood of a cedar tree. [C13: from OF, from L *cedrus*, from Gk *kedros*]

cedar of Lebanon (ˈlɛbənən) *n* a cedar of SW Asia with level spreading branches and fragrant wood.

cede (siːd) *vb* **cedes, ceding, ceded**. **1** (when *intr*, often foll. by *to*) to transfer, make over, or surrender (something, esp. territory or legal rights). **2** (*tr*) to allow or concede (a point in an argument, etc.). [C17: from L *cēdere* to yield] ▸ **ˈceder** *n*

cedilla (sɪˈdɪlə) *n* a character (ˌ) placed underneath a *c* before *a, o,* or *u*, esp. in French, Portuguese, or Catalan, denoting that it is to be pronounced (s), not (k). [C16: from Sp.: little *z*, from *ceda* zed, from LL *zeta*]

Ceefax (ˈsiːfæks) *n Trademark.* the BBC Teletext service. See **Teletext**.

CEGB (in Britain) *abbrev. for* Central Electricity Generating Board.

ceil (siːl) *vb* (*tr*) **1** to line (a ceiling) with plaster, etc. **2** to provide with a ceiling. [C15 *celen,* ? back formation from CEILING]

ceilidh (ˈkeɪlɪ) *n* (esp. in Scotland and Ireland) an informal social gathering with singing, dancing, and story telling. [C19: from Gaelic]

ceiling (ˈsiːlɪŋ) *n* **1** the inner upper surface of a room. **2** an upper limit, such as one set by regulation on prices or wages. **3** the upper altitude to which an aircraft can climb measured under specified conditions. **4** *Meteorol.* the highest level in the atmosphere from which the earth's surface is visible at a particular time, usually the base of a cloud layer. [C14: from ?]

Cela ★ (*Spanish* ˈθela) *n* **Camilo José** (kaˈmilo xoˈse). born 1916, Spanish novelist and essayist. His works include *The Family of Pascual Duarte* (1942), *La Colmena* (1951) and *Reloj de Sangre* (1989). Nobel prize for literature 1989.

celadon (ˈsɛləˌdɒn) *n* **1** a type of porcelain having a greyish-green glaze: mainly Chinese. **2a** a pale greyish-green colour. **2b** (*as adj*): *a celadon jar*. [C18: from F, from the name of the shepherd hero of *L'Astrée* (1610), a romance by Honoré d'Urfé]

Celan ★ (ˈsɛlæn) *n* **Paul**, real name *Paul Antschel*. 1920–71, Romanian Jewish poet, writing in German.

celandine (ˈsɛlənˌdaɪn) *n* either of two unrelated plants, **greater celandine** or **lesser celandine**, with yellow flowers. [C13: earlier *celydon*, from L, from Gk *khelidōn* swallow; the plant's season was believed to parallel the migration of swallows]

-cele *n combining form.* tumour or hernia: *hydrocele*. [from Gk *kēlē* tumour]

celeb (sɪˈlɛb) *n Inf.* a celebrity.

Celebes ★ (ˈsɛlɪbiːz, seˈliːbɪz) *n* the English name for **Sulawesi**.

Celebes Sea ★ *n* the part of the Pacific Ocean between Sulawesi, Borneo, and Mindanao.

celebrant (ˈsɛlɪbrənt) *n* a person participating in a religious ceremony, esp. at the Eucharist.

celebrate (ˈsɛlɪˌbreɪt) *vb* **celebrates, celebrating, celebrated**. **1** to rejoice in or have special festivities to mark (a happy day, event, etc.). **2** (*tr*) to observe (a birthday, anniversary, etc.). **3** (*tr*) to perform (a solemn or religious ceremony), esp. to officiate at (Mass). **4** (*tr*) to praise publicly; proclaim. [C15: from L, from *celeber* numerous, renowned] ▸ **ˌceleˈbration** *n* ▸ **ˈceleˌbrator** *n* ▸ **ˈceleˌbratory** *adj*

celebrated (ˈsɛlɪˌbreɪtɪd) *adj* (*usually prenominal*) famous: *a celebrated pianist*.

celebrity (sɪˈlɛbrɪtɪ) *n, pl* **celebrities**. **1** a famous person. **2** fame or notoriety.

celeriac (sɪˈlɛrɪˌæk) *n* a variety of celery with a large turnip-like root, used as a vegetable. [C18: from CELERY + -ac, from ?]

celerity (sɪˈlɛrɪtɪ) *n* rapidity; swiftness; speed. [C15: from OF *celerite*, from L *celeritās*, from *celer* swift]

celery (ˈsɛlərɪ) *n* **1** an umbelliferous Eurasian plant whose blanched leafstalks are used in salads or cooked as a vegetable. **2 wild celery**. a related and similar plant. [C17: from F *céleri*, from It. (Lombardy) dialect *selleri* (pl), from Gk *selinon* parsley]

celesta (sɪˈlɛstə) or **celeste** (sɪˈlɛst) *n Music.* a keyboard percussion instrument consisting of a set of steel plates of graduated length that are struck with key-operated hammers. [C19: from F, Latinized var. of *céleste* heavenly]

celestial (sɪˈlɛstɪəl) *adj* **1** heavenly; divine: *celestial peace*. **2** of or relating to the sky: *celestial bodies*. **3** of or connected with the celestial sphere: *celestial pole*. [C14: from Med. L, from L *caelestis*, from *caelum* heaven] ▸ **ceˈlestially** *adv*

Celestial Empire ★ *n* an archaic or literary name for the **Chinese Empire**.

celestial equator *n* the great circle lying on the celestial sphere the plane of which is perpendicular to the line joining the north and south celestial poles. Also called: **equinoctial, equinoctial circle**.

★ people and places

elestial mechanics *n* the study of the motion of celestial bodies under the influence of gravitational fields.

elestial sphere *n* an imaginary sphere of infinitely large radius enclosing the universe so that all celestial bodies appear to be projected onto its surface.

eliac ('si:lɪˌæk) *adj Anat.* the usual US spelling of **coeliac**.

elibate ('sɛlɪbɪt) *n* **1** a person who is unmarried, esp. one who has taken a religious vow of chastity. ◆ *adj* **2** abstaining from sexual intercourse. **3** unmarried. [C17: from L, from *caelebs* unmarried, from ?]
▶ **'celibacy** *n*

éline ★ *(French* selin*) n* **Louis-Ferdinand** (lwifɛrdinã), real name *Louis-Ferdinand Destouches.* 1894–1961, French novelist and physician; noted for his novel *Journey to the End of the Night* (1932).

ell (sɛl) *n* **1** a small simple room, as in a prison, convent, etc. **2** any small compartment: *the cells of a honeycomb.* **3** *Biol.* the smallest unit of an organism that is able to function independently. It consists of a nucleus, containing the genetic material, surrounded by the cytoplasm. **4** *Biol.* any small cavity, such as the cavity containing pollen in an anther. **5** a device for converting chemical energy into electrical energy, usually consisting of a container with two electrodes immersed in an electrolyte. See also **dry cell, fuel cell. 6** In full: **electrolytic cell.** a device in which electrolysis occurs. **7** a small religious house dependent upon a larger one. **8** a small group of persons operating as a nucleus of a larger organization: *Communist cell.* **9** the geographical area served by an individual transmitter in a cellular-radio network. [C12: from Med. L *cella* monk's cell, from L: room, storeroom]

ellar ('sɛlə) *n* **1** an underground room, or storey of a building, usually used for storage. **2** a place where wine is stored. **3** a stock of bottled wines. ◆ *vb* **4** (*tr*) to store in a cellar. [C13: from Anglo-F, from L *cellārium* foodstore, from *cella* cell]

ellarage ('sɛlərɪdʒ) *n* **1** an area of a cellar. **2** a charge for storing goods in a cellar, etc.

ellarer ('sɛlərə) *n* a monastic official responsible for food, drink, etc.

ellaret (ˌsɛlə'rɛt) *n* a cabinet or sideboard with compartments for holding wine bottles.

Cellini ★ (tʃɪ'li:nɪ; *Italian* tʃel'li:ni) *n* **Benvenuto** (benve'nu:to). 1500–71, Italian sculptor, goldsmith, and engraver, noted also for his autobiography.

ell line *n Biol.* a cell culture derived from a single cell and thus of invariable genetic make-up.

Cellnet ('sɛlˌnɛt) *n Trademark.* a British Telecom mobile phone.

ello ('tʃɛləʊ) *n, pl* **cellos.** *Music.* a bowed stringed instrument of the violin family. It has four strings, is held between the knees, and has a metal spike at the lower end, which acts as a support. Full name: **violoncello.**
▶ **'cellist** *n*

Cellophane ('sɛləˌfeɪn) *n Trademark.* a flexible thin transparent sheeting made from wood pulp and used as a moisture-proof wrapping. [C20: from CELLULOSE + -PHANE]

cellphone ('sɛlˌfəʊn) *n* a portable telephone operated by cellular radio. In full: **cellular telephone.**

ellular ('sɛljʊlə) *adj* **1** of, relating to, or composed of a cell or cells. **2** having cells or small cavities; porous. **3** divided into a network of cells. **4** *Textiles.* woven with an open texture: *a cellular blanket.* **5** designed for or involving cellular radio.

cellular radio *n* radio communication based on a network of transmitters each serving a small area known as a cell: used esp. in car phones in which the receiver switches frequencies automatically as it passes from one cell to another.

cellule ('sɛlju:l) *n* a very small cell. [C17: from L *cellula,* dim. of *cella* CELL]

cellulite ('sɛljʊˌlaɪt) *n* subcutaneous fat alleged to resist dieting.

cellulitis (ˌsɛljʊ'laɪtɪs) *n* inflammation of body tissue, with fever, pain, and swelling. [C19: from L *cellula* CELLULE + -ITIS]

celluloid ('sɛljʊˌlɔɪd) *n* **1** a flammable material consisting of cellulose nitrate and camphor: used in sheets, rods, etc. **2a** a cellulose derivative used for coating film. **2b** cinema film.

cellulose ('sɛljʊˌləʊz, -ˌləʊs) *n* a substance which is the main constituent of plant cell walls and used in making paper, rayon, and film. [C18: from F *cellule* cell (see CELLULE) + -OSE²]

cellulose acetate *n* nonflammable material used in the manufacture of film, dopes, lacquers, and artificial fibres.

cellulose nitrate *n* cellulose treated with nitric and sulphuric acids, used in plastics, lacquers, and explosives. See also **guncotton.**

Celsius ('sɛlsɪəs) *adj* denoting a measurement on the Celsius scale. Symbol: C [C18: after Anders *Celsius* (1701–44), Swedish astronomer who invented it]

Celsius scale *n* a scale of temperature in which 0° represents the melting point of ice and 100° represents the boiling point of water. See also **centigrade.** Cf. **Fahrenheit scale.**

celt (sɛlt) *n Archaeol.* a stone or metal axelike instrument. [C18: from LL *celtes* chisel, from ?]

Celt (kɛlt, sɛlt) *or* **Kelt** *n* **1** a person who speaks a Celtic language. **2** a member of an Indo-European people who in pre-Roman times inhabited Britain, Gaul, and Spain.

Celtic ('kɛltɪk, 'sɛl-) *or* **Keltic** *n* **1** a branch of the Indo-European family of languages that includes Gaelic, Welsh, and Breton. Modern Celtic is divided into the Brythonic (southern) and Goidelic (northern) groups. ◆ *adj* **2** of, relating to, or characteristic of the Celts or the Celtic languages.
▶ **Celticism** ('kɛltɪˌsɪzəm, 'sɛl-) *or* **'Kelti,cism** *n*

Celtic cross *n* a Latin cross with a broad ring surrounding the point of intersection.

cembalo ('tʃɛmbələʊ) *n, pl* **cembali** (-lɪ) *or* **cembalos.** another word for **harpsichord.** [C19: from It. *clavicembalo* from Med. L *clāvis* key + *cymbalum* CYMBAL]

cement (sɪ'mɛnt) *n* **1** a fine grey powder made of a mixture of limestone and clay, used with water and sand to make mortar, or with water, sand, and aggregate, to make concrete. **2** a binder, glue, or adhesive. **3** something that unites or joins. **4** *Dentistry.* any of various materials used in filling teeth. **5** another word for **cementum.** ◆ *vb* (*tr*) **6** to join, bind, or glue together with or as if with cement. **7** to coat or cover with cement. [C13: from OF, from L *caementum* stone from the quarry, from *caedere* to hew]

cementum (sɪ'mɛntəm) *n* a thin bonelike tissue that covers the dentine in the root of a tooth. [C19: NL, from L: CEMENT]

cemetery ('sɛmɪtrɪ) *n, pl* **cemeteries.** a place where the dead are buried, esp. one not attached to a church. [C14: from LL, from Gk *koimētērion,* from *koiman* to put to sleep]

-cene *n and adj combining form.* denoting a recent geological period. [from Gk *kainos* new]

Cenis ★ *(French* səni*) n* **Mont.** a pass over the Graian Alps in SE France, between Lanslebourg (France) and Susa (Italy): nearby tunnel, opened in 1871. Highest point: 2082 m (6831 ft). Italian name: **Monte Cenisio** ('monte tʃe'ni:zjo).

cenobite ('si:nəʊˌbaɪt) *n* a variant spelling of **coenobite.**

cenotaph ('sɛnəˌtɑːf) *n* a monument honouring a dead person or persons buried elsewhere. [C17: from L, from Gk, from *kenos* empty + *taphos* tomb]

Cenotaph ★ ('sɛnəˌtɑːf) *n* **the.** the monument in Whitehall, London, honouring the dead of both World Wars: designed by Sir Edwin Lutyens: erected in 1920.

Cenozoic, Caenozoic (ˌsiːnəʊ'zəʊɪk), *or* **Cainozoic** *adj* **1** of, denoting, or relating to the most recent geological era characterized by the development and increase of the mammals. ◆ *n* **2 the.** the Cenozoic era. [C19: from Gk *kainos* recent + *zōikos,* from *zōion* animal]

censer ('sɛnsə) *n* a container for burning incense. Also called: **thurible.**

censor ('sɛnsə) *n* **1** a person authorized to examine pub-

lications, films, letters, etc., in order to suppress in whole or part those considered obscene, politically unacceptable, etc. **2** any person who controls or suppresses the behaviour of others, usually on moral grounds. **3** (in republican Rome) either of two senior magistrates elected to keep the list of citizens up to date, and supervise public morals. **4** *Psychoanal.* the postulated factor responsible for regulating the translation of ideas and desires from the unconscious to the conscious mind. ◆ *vb* (*tr*) **5** to ban or cut portions of (a film, letter, etc.). **6** to act as a censor of (behaviour, etc.). [C16: from L, from *cēnsēre* to consider]
▸ **censorial** (sɛn'sɔːrɪəl) *adj*

censorious (sɛn'sɔːrɪəs) *adj* harshly critical; faultfinding.
▸ **cen'soriously** *adv*

censorship ('sɛnsə,ʃɪp) *n* **1** a policy or programme of censoring. **2** the act or system of censoring.

censure ('sɛnʃə) *n* **1** severe disapproval. ◆ *vb* **censures, censuring, censured. 2** to criticize (someone or something) severely. [C14: from L *censūra*, from *cēnsēre*: see CENSOR]
▸ **'censurable** *adj*

census ('sɛnsəs) *n, pl* **censuses. 1** an official periodic count of a population including such information as sex, age, occupation, etc. **2** any official count: *a traffic census.* **3** (in ancient Rome) a registration of the population and a property evaluation for taxation. [C17: from L, from *cēnsēre* to assess]

cent (sɛnt) *n* a monetary unit of Australia, Barbados, Canada, Cyprus, Dominica, Estonia, Ethiopia, Fiji, Grenada, Guyana, Jamaica, Kenya, Malaysia, New Zealand, Singapore, South Africa, Tanzania, Trinidad and Tobago, Uganda, the United States, etc. It is worth one hundredth of their respective standard units. [C16: from L *centēsimus* hundredth, from *centum* hundred]

cent. *abbrev. for:* **1** centigrade. **2** central. **3** century.

centaur ('sɛntɔː) *n Greek myth.* one of a race of creatures with the head, arms, and torso of a man, and the lower body and legs of a horse. [C14: from L, from Gk *kentauros*, from ?]

centaurea (sɛntɔː'rɪə, sɛn'tɔːrɪə) *n* any plant of the genus *Centaurea* which includes the cornflower and knapweed. [C19: ult. from Gk *Kentauros* the Centaur; see CENTAURY]

centaury ('sɛntɔːrɪ) *n, pl* **centauries. 1** any of a genus of Eurasian plants having purplish-pink flowers and formerly believed to have medicinal properties. **2** another name for **centaurea.** [C14: ult. from Gk *Kentauros* the Centaur; from the legend that Chiron the Centaur divulged its healing properties]

centavo (sɛn'tɑːvəʊ) *n, pl* **centavos.** a monetary unit of Argentina, Brazil, Colombia, Ecuador, El Salvador, Mexico, Nicaragua, the Philippines, Portugal, etc. It is worth one hundredth of their respective standard units. [Sp.: one hundredth part]

centenarian (,sɛntɪ'nɛərɪən) *n* **1** a person who is at least 100 years old. ◆ *adj* **2** being at least 100 years old. **3** of or relating to a centenarian.

centenary (sɛn'tiːnərɪ) *adj* **1** of or relating to a period of 100 years. **2** occurring once every 100 years. ◆ *n, pl* **centenaries. 3** a 100th anniversary or its celebration. [C17: from L, from *centēnī* a hundred each, from *centum* hundred]

centennial (sɛn'tɛnɪəl) *adj* **1** relating to or completing a period of 100 years. **2** occurring every 100 years. ◆ *n* **3** *US & Canad.* another name for **centenary.** [C18: from L *centum* hundred, on the model of BIENNIAL]

center ('sɛntə) *n, vb* the US spelling of **centre.**

centesimal (sɛn'tɛsɪməl) *n* **1** hundredth. ◆ *adj* **2** relating to division into hundredths. [C17: from L, from *centum* hundred]
▸ **cen'tesimally** *adv*

centesimo (sɛn'tɛsɪ,məʊ) *n, pl* **centesimos** *or* **centesimi.** a monetary unit of Italy, Panama, Uruguay, etc. It is worth one hundredth of their respective standard units. [C19: from Sp. & It., from L, from *centum* hundred]

centi- *or before a vowel* **cent-** *prefix* **1** denoting one hun-

dredth: *centimetre.* Symbol: c **2** *Rare.* denoting a hundred: *centipede.* [from F, from L *centum* hundred]

centiare ('sɛntɪ,ɛə) *or* **centare** ('sɛntɛə) *n* a unit of area equal to one square metre. [F, from CENTI- + *are* from *ārea*]

centigrade ('sɛntɪ,greɪd) *adj* **1** a former name for **Celsius** ◆ *n* **2** a unit of angle equal to one hundredth of a grade.

USAGE NOTE Although still used in meteorology, *centigrade*, when indicating the Celsius scale of temperature, is now usually avoided because of its possible confusion with the hundredth part of a grade.

centigram *or* **centigramme** ('sɛntɪ,græm) *n* one hundredth of a gram.

centilitre *or US* **centiliter** ('sɛntɪ,liːtə) *n* one hundredth of a litre.

centime ('sɒn,tiːm; *French* sɑ̃tim) *n* a monetary unit of Algeria, Belgium, the Central African Republic, France, Guinea, Haiti, Liechtenstein, Luxembourg, Mali, Switzerland, Togo, etc. It is worth one hundredth of their respective standard units. [C18: from F, from OF, from L from *centum* hundred]

centimetre *or US* **centimeter** ('sɛntɪ,miːtə) *n* one hundredth of a metre.

centimetre-gram-second *n* See **cgs units.**

céntimo ('sɛntɪ,məʊ) *n, pl* **céntimos.** a monetary unit of Costa Rica, Peru, Spain, Venezuela, etc. It is worth one hundredth of their respective standard currency units. [from Sp.; see CENTIME]

centipede ('sɛntɪ,piːd) *n* a carnivorous arthropod having a body of between 15 and 190 segments, each bearing one pair of legs.

cento ('sɛntəʊ) *n, pl* **centos.** a piece of writing, esp. a poem, composed of quotations from other authors. [C17: from L, lit.: patchwork garment]

CENTO ('sɛntəʊ) *n acronym for* Central Treaty Organization; an organization for military and economic cooperation formed in 1959 by the UK, Iran, Pakistan, and Turkey: disbanded 1979.

central ('sɛntrəl) *adj* **1** in, at, of, from, containing, or forming the centre of something: *the central street in a city.* **2** main, principal, or chief: *the central cause of a problem.*
▸ **centrality** (sɛn'trælɪtɪ) *n* ▸ **'centrally** *adv*

Central African Federation ★ *n* another name for the **Federation of Rhodesia and Nyasaland.**

Central African Republic ★ *n* a landlocked country of central Africa: joined with Chad as a territory of French Equatorial Africa in 1910; became an independent republic in 1960; a parliamentary monarchy (1976–79); consists of a huge plateau, mostly savanna, with dense forests in the south; drained chiefly by the Shari and Ubangi Rivers. Languages: French and Sangho. Religion: Christian and animist. Currency: franc. Capital: Bangui. Pop.: 3 342 000 (1997). Area: 622 577 sq. km (240 376 sq. miles). Former names: (until 1958) **Ubangi-Shari;** (1976–79) **Central African Empire.** French name: **République Centrafricaine** (repyblik sɑ̃trafrikɛn)

Central America ★ *n* an isthmus joining the continents of North and South America, extending from the S border of Mexico to the NW border of Colombia and consisting of Belize, Guatemala, Honduras, El Salvador, Nicaragua, Costa Rica, and Panama. Area: about 518 000 sq. km (200 000 sq. miles).
▸ **Central American** *adj*

central bank *n* a national bank that does business mainly with a government and with other banks: it regulates the volume of credit.

central heating *n* a system for heating the rooms of a building by means of radiators or air vents connected to a central source of heat.

Central India Agency ★ *n* a former group of 89 states in India, under the supervision of a British political

★ **people and places**

agent until 1947: most important were Indore, Bhopal, and Rewa.

entralism ('sɛntrə,lɪzəm) *n* the principle or act of bringing something under central control.
▶ '**centralist** *n, adj*

entralize *or* **centralise** ('sɛntrə,laɪz) *vb* **centralizes, centralizing, centralized** *or* **centralises, centralising, centralised.** 1 to draw or move (something) to or towards a centre. 2 to bring or come under central, esp. governmental, control.
▶ ,**centrali'zation** *or* ,**centrali'sation** *n*

:entral Karoo ★ (kə'ru:) *n* an arid plateau of S central South Africa, separated from the Little Karoo to the southwest by the Swartberg range. Average height: 750 m (2500 ft).

entral limit theorem *n Statistics.* the fundamental result that the sum of independent identically distributed random variables with finite variance approaches a normally distributed random variable as their number increases.

entral locking *n* a system by which all the doors of a motor vehicle can be locked simultaneously.

entral nervous system *n* the mass of nerve tissue that controls and coordinates the activities of an animal. In vertebrates it consists of the brain and spinal cord.

entral processing unit *n* the part of a computer that performs logical and arithmetical operations on the data. Abbrev.: **CPU.**

:entral Region ★ *n* a former local government region in central Scotland, replaced in 1996 by the council areas of Stirling, Falkirk, and Clackmannanshire.

:entral reserve *or* **reservation** *n Brit. & Austral.* the strip, often covered with grass, that separates the two sides of a motorway or dual carriageway.

:entral tendency *n Statistics.* the tendency of the values of a random variable to cluster around the mean, median, and mode.

:entre *or US* **center** ('sɛntə) *n* 1 *Geom.* 1a the midpoint of any line or figure, esp. the point within a circle or sphere that is equidistant from any point on the circumference or surface. 1b the point within a body through which a specified force may be considered to act, such as the centre of gravity. 2 the point, axis, or pivot about which a body rotates. 3 a point, area, or part that is approximately in the middle of a larger area or volume. 4 a place at which some specified activity is concentrated: a *shopping centre*. 5 a person or thing that is a focus of interest. 6 a place of activity or influence: *a centre of power*. 7 a person, group, or thing in the middle. 8 (*usually cap.*) *Politics.* a political party or group favouring moderation. 9 a bar with a conical point upon which a workpiece or part may be turned or ground. 10 *Football, hockey, etc.* 10a a player who plays in the middle of the forward line. 10b an instance of passing the ball from a wing to the middle of the field, etc. ◆ *vb* **centres, centring, centred** *or US* **centers, centering, centered.** 11 to move towards, mark, put, or be at a centre. 12 (*tr*) to focus or bring together: *to centre one's thoughts*. 13 (*intr*; often foll. by *on*) to have as a main theme: *the novel centred on crime*. 14 (*intr*; foll. by *on* or *round*) to have as a centre. 15 (*tr*) *Football, hockey, etc.* to pass (the ball) into the middle of the field or court. [C14: from L *centrum* the stationary point of a compass, from Gk *kentron* needle, from *kentein* to prick]

Centre ★ ('sɛntə) *n* **the.** the sparsely inhabited central region of Australia. Also called: **the Red Centre.**

centre bit *n* a drilling bit with a central point and two side cutters.

centreboard ('sɛntə,bɔ:d) *n* a supplementary keel for a sailing vessel.

centrefold *or US* **centerfold** ('sɛntə,fəʊld) *n* 1 a large coloured illustration folded so that it forms the central spread of a magazine. 2a a photograph of a nude or nearly nude woman (or man) in a magazine on such a spread. 2b the subject of such a photograph.

centre forward *n Soccer, hockey, etc.* the central forward in the attack.

centre half *or* **centre back** *n Soccer.* a defender who plays in the middle of the defence.

centre of gravity *n* the point through which the resultant of the gravitational forces on a body always acts.

centre pass *n Hockey.* a push or hit made in any direction to start the game or restart the game after a goal has been scored.

centrepiece ('sɛntə,pi:s) *n* an object used as the centre of something, esp. for decoration.

centre spread *n* 1 the pair of two facing pages in the middle of a magazine, newspaper, etc. 2a a photograph of a nude or nearly nude woman (or man) in a magazine on such pages. 2b the subject of such a photograph.

centri- *combining form.* a variant of **centro-.**

centric ('sɛntrɪk) *or* **centrical** *adj* 1 being central or having a centre. 2 relating to a nerve centre.
▶ **centricity** (sɛn'trɪsɪtɪ) *n*

-centric *suffix forming adjectives.* having a centre as specified: *heliocentric.* [abstracted from ECCENTRIC, CONCENTRIC, etc.]

centrifugal (sɛn'trɪfjugəl, 'sɛntrɪ,fju:gəl) *adj* 1 acting, moving, or tending to move away from a centre. Cf. **centripetal.** 2 of, concerned with, or operated by centrifugal force: *centrifugal pump.* [C18: from NL, from CENTRI- + L *fugere* to flee]
▶ **cen'trifugally** *adv*

centrifugal force *n* a fictitious force that can be thought of as acting outwards on any body that rotates or moves along a curved path.

centrifuge ('sɛntrɪ,fju:dʒ) *n* 1 any of various rotating machines that separate liquids from solids or other liquids by the action of centrifugal force. 2 any of various rotating devices for subjecting human beings or animals to varying accelerations. ◆ *vb* **centrifuges, centrifuging, centrifuged.** 3 (*tr*) to subject to the action of a centrifuge.
▶ **centrifugation** (,sɛntrɪfju'geɪʃən) *n*

centring ('sɛntrɪŋ) *or US* **centering** ('sɛntərɪŋ) *n* a temporary structure, esp. one made of timber, used to support an arch during construction.

centripetal (sɛn'trɪpɪtəl, 'sɛntrɪ,pi:təl) *adj* 1 acting, moving, or tending to move towards a centre. Cf. **centrifugal.** 2 of, concerned with, or operated by centripetal force. [C17: from NL *centripetus* seeking the centre]
▶ **cen'tripetally** *adv*

centripetal force *n* a force that acts inwards on any body that rotates or moves along a curved path.

centrist ('sɛntrɪst) *n* a person holding moderate political views.
▶ '**centrism** *n*

centro-, centri-, *or before a vowel* **centr-** *combining form.* denoting a centre: *centrosome; centrist.* [from Gk *kentron* CENTRE]

centrosome ('sɛntrə,səʊm) *n* a small protoplasmic body found near the cell nucleus.

centuplicate *vb* (sɛn'tju:plɪ,keɪt), **centuplicates, centuplicating, centuplicated.** 1 (*tr*) to increase 100 times. ◆ *adj* (sɛn'tju:plɪkɪt). 2 increased a hundredfold. ◆ *n* (sɛn'tju:plɪkɪt). 3 one hundredfold. ◆ Also **centuple** ('sɛntjup³l). [C17: from LL, from *centuplex* hundredfold, from L *centum* hundred + *-plex* -fold]

centurion (sɛn'tjʊərɪən) *n* the officer commanding a Roman century. [C14: from L *centuriō*, from *centuria* CENTURY]

century ('sɛntʃərɪ) *n, pl* **centuries.** 1 a period of 100 years. 2 one of the successive periods of 100 years dated before or after an epoch or event, esp. the birth of Christ. 3 a score or grouping of 100: *to score a century in cricket.* 4 (in ancient Rome) a unit of foot soldiers, originally consisting of 100 men. 5 (in ancient Rome) a division of the people for purposes of voting. [C16: from L *centuria*, from *centum* hundred]

cep (sɛp) *n* an edible woodland fungus with a brown shining cap and a rich nutty flavour. [C19: from F, from Gascon dialect *cep*, from L *cippus* stake]

cephalic (sɪ'fælɪk) *adj* 1 of or relating to the head. 2 situated in, on, or near the head.

-cephalic or **-cephalous** adj combining form. indicating skull or head; -headed: brachycephalic. [from Gk -kephalos]
▶ **-cephaly** or **-cephalism** n combining form

cephalic index n the ratio of the greatest width of the human head to its greatest length, multiplied by 100.

cephalo- or before a vowel **cephal-** combining form. indicating the head: cephalopod. [via L from Gk, from kephalē head]

Cephalonia ★ (ˌsɛfə'ləʊnɪə) n a mountainous island in the Ionian Sea, the largest of the Ionian Islands, off the W coast of Greece. Pop.: 32 474 (1991). Area: 935 sq. km (365 sq. miles). Modern Greek name: **Kephallinía.**

cephalopod ('sɛfələ,pɒd) n any of various marine molluscs, characterized by well-developed head and eyes and a ring of sucker-bearing tentacles, including the octopuses, squids, and cuttlefish.
▶ ,cepha'lopodan adj, n

cephalothorax (ˌsɛfələʊ'θɔːræks) n, pl **cephalothoraxes** or **cephalothoraces** (-rə,siːz). the anterior part of many crustaceans and some other arthropods consisting of a united head and thorax.

-cephalus n combining form. denoting a cephalic abnormality: hydrocephalus. [NL -cephalus; see -CEPHALIC]

Cepheid variable ('siːfɪɪd) n Astron. any of a class of variable stars with regular cycles of variations in luminosity, which are used for measuring distances.

Cepheus ★ ('siːfjuːs) n Greek myth. a king of Ethiopia, father of Andromeda and husband of Cassiopeia.

Ceram ★ (sɪ'ræm) n a variant spelling of **Seram.**

ceramic (sɪ'ræmɪk) n 1 a hard brittle material made by firing clay and similar substances. 2 an object made from such a material. ◆ adj 3 of or made from a ceramic. 4 of or relating to ceramics: ceramic arts. [C19: from Gk, from keramos potter's clay]

ceramic hob n (on an electric cooker) a flat ceramic cooking surface having heating elements fitted on the underside.

ceramic oxide n a compound of oxygen with nonorganic material: recently discovered to act as a high-temperature superconductor.

ceramics (sɪ'ræmɪks) n (functioning as sing) the art and techniques of producing articles of clay, porcelain, etc.
▶ ceramist ('sɛrəmɪst) n

Cerberus ★ ('sɜːbərəs) n 1 Greek myth. a dog, usually represented as having three heads, that guarded the entrance to Hades. 2 **a sop to Cerberus.** a bribe or something given to propitiate a potential source of danger or problems.
▶ **Cerberean** (sə'bɪərɪən) adj

cere (sɪə) n a soft waxy swelling, containing the nostrils, at the base of the upper beak, as in the parrot. [C15: from OF cire wax, from L cēra]

cereal ('sɪərɪəl) n 1 any grass that produces an edible grain, such as oat, wheat, rice, maize, and millet. 2 the grain produced by such a plant. 3 any food made from this grain, esp. breakfast food. 4 (modifier) of or relating to any of these plants or their products. [C19: from L cereālis concerning agriculture]

cerebellum (ˌsɛrɪ'bɛləm) n, pl **cerebellums** or **cerebella** (-lə). one of the major divisions of the vertebrate brain whose function is coordination of voluntary movements. [C16: from L, dim. of CEREBRUM]
▶ ,cere'bellar adj

cerebral ('sɛrɪbrəl; US also sə'riːbrəl) adj 1 of or relating to the cerebrum or to the entire brain. 2 involving intelligence rather than emotions or instinct. 3 Phonetics. another word for **cacuminal.**
▶ 'cerebrally adv

cerebral haemorrhage n bleeding from an artery in the brain, which in severe cases causes a stroke.

cerebral palsy n a nonprogressive impairment of muscular function and weakness of the limbs, caused by lack of oxygen to the brain immediately after birth, brain injury during birth, or viral infection.

cerebrate ('sɛrɪ,breɪt) vb **cerebrates, cerebrating, cere-** brated. (intr) Usually facetious. to use the mind; think; ponder; consider.
▶ ,cere'bration n

cerebro- or before a vowel **cerebr-** combining form. indicating the brain: cerebrospinal. [from CEREBRUM]

cerebrospinal (ˌsɛrɪbrəʊ'spaɪnᵊl) adj of or relating to the brain and spinal cord: cerebrospinal fluid.

cerebrovascular (ˌsɛrɪbrəʊ'væskjʊlə) adj of or relating to the blood vessels and the blood supply of the brain.

cerebrum ('sɛrɪbrəm) n, pl **cerebrums** or **cerebra** (-brə). 1 the anterior portion of the brain of vertebrates, consisting of two lateral hemispheres: the dominant part of the brain in man, associated with intellectual function, emotion, and personality. 2 the brain considered as a whole. [C17: from L: the brain]
▶ 'cerebric adj

cerecloth ('sɪə,klɒθ) n waxed waterproof cloth of a kind formerly used as a shroud. [C15: from earlier cered cloth from L cērāre to wax]

Ceredigion ★ (ˌkɛrə'dɪgjᵊn) n a county of W Wales, created in 1996: corresponds to the historic county of Cardiganshire, which ceased to have an administrative function in 1974. Administrative centre: Aberaeron. Pop.: 63 700 (1996 est.). Area: 1793 sq. km (692 sq. miles).

cerement ('sɪəmənt) n 1 cerecloth. 2 any burial clothes [C17: from F, from cirer to wax]

ceremonial (ˌsɛrɪ'məʊnɪəl) adj 1 involving or relating to ceremony or ritual. ◆ n 2 the observance of formality esp. in etiquette. 3 a plan for formal observances; ritual 4 Christianity. 4a the prescribed order of rites and ceremonies. 4b a book containing this.
▶ ,cere'monialism n ▶ ,cere'monialist n ▶ ,cere'monially adv

ceremonious (ˌsɛrɪ'məʊnɪəs) adj 1 especially or excessively polite or formal. 2 involving formalities.
▶ ,cere'moniously adv

ceremony ('sɛrɪmənɪ) n, pl **ceremonies.** 1 a formal act or ritual, often set by custom or tradition, performed in observation of an event or anniversary. 2 a religious rite or series of rites. 3 a courteous gesture or act: the ceremony of toasting the Queen. 4 ceremonial observances or gestures collectively. 5 **stand on ceremony.** to insist on or act with excessive formality. [C14: from Med. L, from L caerimōnia what is sacred]

Cerenkov ★ (Russian tʃɪˈrjɛnkəf) n See (Pavel Alekseyevich) **Cherenkov.**

Ceres ★ ('sɪəriːz) n the Roman goddess of agriculture. Greek counterpart: **Demeter.**

cerise (sə'riːz, -'riːs) n, adj (of) a moderate to dark red colour. [C19: from F: CHERRY]

cerium ('sɪərɪəm) n a malleable ductile steel-grey element of the lanthanide series of metals, used in lighter flints. Symbol: Ce; atomic no.: 58; atomic wt.: 140.12. [C19: NL, from Ceres (the asteroid) + -IUM]

CERN (sɜːn) n acronym for Conseil Européen pour la Recherche Nucléaire; an organization of European states with a centre in Geneva, for research in high-energy particle physics, now called the European Laboratory for Particle Physics.

Cernăuţi ★ (tʃɛrnə'utsj) n the Romanian name for **Chernovtsy.**

Cernuda ★ (Spanish θɛr'nuða) n **Luis** (lwiʃ). 1902–63, Spanish poet, noted for his Reality and Desire (1936–64).

cerography (sɪə'rɒgrəfɪ) n the art of engraving on a waxed plate on which a printing surface is created by electrotyping.

ceroplastic (ˌsɪərəʊ'plæstɪk) adj 1 relating to wax modelling. 2 modelled in wax.

Cerro de Pasco ★ (Spanish 'θɛrro ðe 'pasko) n a town in central Peru, in the Andes: one of the highest towns in the world, 4400 m (14 436 ft) above sea level; mining centre. Pop.: 62 749 (1993).

cert (sɜːt) n Inf. something that is a certainty, esp. a horse that is certain to win a race.

cert. abbrev. for: 1 certificate. 2 certification. 3 certified.

★ people and places

ertain ('sɜːt°n) adj **1** (postpositive) positive and confident about the truth of something; convinced: I am certain that he wrote a book. **2** (usually postpositive) definitely known: it is certain that they were on the bus. **3** (usually postpositive) sure; bound: he was certain to fail. **4** fixed: the date is already certain for the invasion. **5** reliable: his judgment is certain. **6** moderate or minimum: to a certain extent. **7 for certain.** without a doubt. ♦ determiner **8a** known but not specified or named: certain people. **8b** (as pron; functioning as pl): certain of the members have not paid. **9** named but not known: he had written to a certain Mrs Smith. [C13: from OF, from L certus sure, from cernere to decide]

ertainly ('sɜːt°nlɪ) adv **1** without doubt: he certainly rides very well. ♦ sentence substitute. **2** by all means; definitely.

ertainty ('sɜːt°ntɪ) n, pl **certainties. 1** the condition of being certain. **2** something established as inevitable. **3** for a certainty. without doubt.

ertEd (in Britain) abbrev. for Certificate in Education.

ertes ('sɜːtɪz) adv Arch. with certainty; truly. [C13: from OF, ult. from L certus CERTAIN]

ertificate n (sə'tɪfɪkɪt). **1** an official document attesting the truth of the facts stated, as of birth, death, completion of an academic course, ownership of shares, etc. ♦ vb (sə'tɪfɪ,keɪt), **certificates, certificating, certificated. 2** (tr) to authorize by or present with an official document. [C15: from OF, from certifier to CERTIFY]
▸ **cer'tificatory** adj

ertificate of Secondary Education n the full name for **CSE.**

ertification (,sɜːtɪfɪ'keɪʃən) n **1** the act of certifying or state of being certified. **2** Law. a document attesting the truth of a fact or statement.

ertified ('sɜːtɪ,faɪd) adj **1** holding or guaranteed by a certificate. **2** endorsed or guaranteed: a certified cheque. **3** (of a person) declared legally insane.

ertified accountant n (in Britain) a member of the Chartered Association of Certified Accountants, who is authorized to audit company accounts. Cf. **chartered accountant.**

ertify ('sɜːtɪ,faɪ) vb **certifies, certifying, certified. 1** to confirm or attest (to), usually in writing. **2** (tr) to endorse or guarantee that certain required standards have been met. **3** to give reliable information or assurances: he certified that it was Walter's handwriting. **4** (tr) to declare legally insane. [C14: from OF, from Med. L, from L certus CERTAIN + facere to make]
▸ **'certi,fiable** adj

ertiorari (,sɜːtɪɔː'reəraɪ) n Law. an order of a superior court directing that a record of proceedings in a lower court be sent up for review. [C15: from legal L: to be informed]

ertitude ('sɜːtɪ,tjuːd) n confidence; certainty. [C15: from Church L certitūdō, from L certus CERTAIN]

erulean (sɪ'ruːlɪən) n, adj (of) a deep blue colour. [C17: from L caeruleus, prob. from caelum sky]

erumen (sɪ'ruːmen) n the soft brownish-yellow wax secreted by glands in the external ear. Nontechnical name: **earwax.** [C18: from NL, from L cēra wax + ALBUMEN]
▸ **ce'ruminous** adj

Cervantes ★ (sə'væntɪːz; Spanish θer'βantes) n **Miguel de** (mi'ɣɛl ðe), full surname Cervantes Saavedra. 1547–1616, Spanish poet and writer, noted for his romance Don Quixote (1605).

ervelat ('sɜːvə,læt, -,lɑː) n a smoked sausage made from pork and beef. [C17: via obs. F from It. cervellata]

ervical (sə'vaɪk°l, 'sɜːvɪk°l) adj of or relating to the neck or cervix. [C17: from L cervīx neck]

ervical smear n Med. a smear taken from the neck (cervix) of the uterus for detection of cancer. See also **Pap test** or **smear.**

Cervin ★ (sɛrvɛ̃) n **Mont.** the French name for the **Matterhorn.**

ervine ('sɜːvaɪn) adj resembling or relating to a deer. [C19: from L cervīnus, from cervus a deer]

ervix ('sɜːvɪks) n, pl **cervixes** or **cervices** (sə'vaɪsiːz). **1** the technical name for **neck. 2** any necklike part, esp. the

lower part of the uterus that extends into the vagina. [C18: from L]

cesium ('siːzɪəm) n the usual US spelling of **caesium.**

Československo ★ ('tʃɛskɔslɔvɛnskɔ) n the Czech name for **Czechoslovakia.**

cess[1] (sɛs) n Brit. any of several special taxes, such as a land tax in Scotland. [C16: short for ASSESSMENT]

cess[2] (sɛs) n an Irish slang word for **luck** (esp. in **bad cess to you!**). [C19: prob. from CESS[1]]

cessation (sɛ'seɪʃən) n a ceasing or stopping; pause: temporary cessation of hostilities. [C14: from L, from cessāre to be idle, from cēdere to yield]

cession ('sɛʃən) n **1** the act of ceding. **2** something that is ceded, esp. land or territory. [C14: from L cessiō, from cēdere to yield]

cessionary ('sɛʃənərɪ) n, pl **cessionaries.** Law. a person to whom something is transferred.

cesspool ('sɛs,puːl) or **cesspit** ('sɛs,pɪt) n **1** Also called: **sink, sump.** a covered cistern, etc., for collecting and storing sewage or waste water. **2** a filthy or corrupt place: a cesspool of iniquity. [C17: ? changed from earlier cesperalle, from OF souspirail vent, air, from soupirer to sigh]

cestoid ('sɛstɔɪd) adj (esp. of tapeworms and similar animals) ribbon-like in form.

cesura (sɪ'zjʊərə) n, pl **cesuras** or **cesurae** (-riː). Prosody. a variant spelling of **caesura.**

cetacean (sɪ'teɪʃən) adj also **cetaceous. 1** of or belonging to an order of aquatic placental mammals having no hind limbs and a blowhole for breathing: includes toothed whales (dolphins, porpoises, etc.) and whalebone whales (rorquals, etc.). ♦ n **2** a whale. [C19: from NL, ult. from L cētus whale, from Gk kētos]

cetane ('siːteɪn) n a colourless insoluble liquid hydrocarbon used in the determination of the cetane number of diesel fuel. Also called: **hexadecane.** [C19: from L cētus whale + -ANE]

cetane number n a measure of the quality of a diesel fuel expressed as the percentage of cetane. Also called: **cetane rating.** Cf. **octane number.**

Cetatea Albă ★ (tʃe'tatea 'albə) n the Romanian name for **Byelgorod-Dnestrovski.**

Cetinje ★ (Serbo-Croat 'tsɛtinjɛ) n a city in S Yugoslavia, in SW Montenegro: former capital of Montenegro (until 1945); palace and fortified monastery, residences of Montenegrin prince-bishops. Pop.: 15 924 (1991).

cetrimide ('sɛtrɪ,maɪd) n an ammonium compound used as a detergent and, having powerful antiseptic properties, for sterilizing surgical instruments, cleaning wounds, etc.

Cetshwayo or **Cetewayo** ★ (Zulu kɛ'tʃwɑːjɔ) n ?1826–84, king of the Zulus (1873–79): defeated the British at Isandhlwana (1879) but was overwhelmed at Ulundi (1879); and reinstated as ruler of part of Zululand (1883).

Ceuta ★ (Spanish 'θeuta) n an enclave in Morocco on the Strait of Gibraltar, consisting of a port and military station: held by Spain since 1580. Pop.: 68 867 (1994 est.).

Cévennes ★ (French seven) n a mountain range in S central France, on the SE edge of the Massif Central. Highest peak: 1754 m (5755 ft).

Ceylon ★ (sɪ'lɒn) n **1** the former name (until 1972) of **Sri Lanka. 2** an island in the Indian Ocean, off the SE coast of India: consists politically of the republic of Sri Lanka. Area: 64 644 sq. km (24 959 sq. miles).
▸ **Ceylonese** (,selə'niːz, ,siːlə-) adj

Cézanne ★ (French sezan) n **Paul** (pɔl). 1839–1906, French postimpressionist painter, who was a major influence on modern art, esp. cubism, in stressing the structural elements latent in nature, such as the sphere and the cone.

Cf the chemical symbol for californium.

CF abbrev. for Canadian Forces.

cf. abbrev. for: **1** (in bookbinding, etc.) calfskin. **2** compare. [L: confer]

CFB abbrev. for Canadian Forces Base.

★ people and places

CFC *abbrev. for* chlorofluorocarbon.

CFL *abbrev. for* Canadian Football League.

CFS *abbrev. for* chronic fatigue syndrome.

cg *abbrev. for* centigram.

CGBR *abbrev. for* Central Government Borrowing Requirement.

cgs units *pl n* a metric system of units based on the centimetre, gram, and second. For scientific and technical purposes these units have been replaced by SI units.

CGT *abbrev. for* Capital Gains Tax.

CH 1 *abbrev. for* Companion of Honour (a Brit. title). ◆ **2** *international car registration for* Switzerland. [from F *Confédération Helvétique*]

ch. *abbrev. for:* **1** chain (unit of measure). **2** chapter. **3** *Chess.* check. **4** chief. **5** church.

Chablis ('ʃæblɪ) *n* (*sometimes not cap.*) a dry white wine made around Chablis, France.

Chabrier ★ ('ʃæbrɪeɪ, *French* ʃabrie) *n* (**Alexis**) **Emmanuel** (emanɥel). 1841–94, French composer; noted for the orchestral rhapsody *España* (1883).

Chabrol ★ (*French* ʃabrɔl) *n* **Claude** (klod). born 1930, French film director, whose films include *Les Biches* (1968) and *Rien Ne plus* (1998).

cha-cha-cha (ˌtʃɑːtʃɑːˈtʃɑː) *or* **cha-cha** *n* **1** a modern ballroom dance from Latin America with small steps and swaying hip movements. **2** a piece of music composed for this dance. ◆ *vb* (*intr*) **3** to perform this dance. [C20: from American (Cuban) Sp.]

Chaco ★ (*Spanish* 'tʃako) *n* See **Gran Chaco**.

chaconne (ʃəˈkɒn) *n* **1** a musical form consisting of a set of continuous variations upon a ground bass. **2** *Arch.* a dance in slow triple time probably originating in Spain. [C17: from F, from Sp. *chacona*]

Chad ★ (tʃæd) *n* **1** a republic in N central Africa: made a territory of French Equatorial Africa in 1910; became independent in 1960; contains much desert and the Tibesti Mountains, with Lake Chad in the west; produces chiefly cotton and livestock; has suffered intermittent civil war from 1963 and prolonged drought. Official languages: French and Arabic. Religion: chiefly Muslim, also animist and Christian. Currency: franc. Capital: Ndjamena. Pop.: 7 166 000 (1997). Area: 1 284 000 sq. km (495 750 sq. miles). French name: **Tchad. 2 Lake.** a lake in N central Africa: fed chiefly by the Shari River, it has no apparent outlet. Area: 10 000 to 26 000 sq. km (4000 to 10 000 sq. miles), varying seasonally.

Chadwick ★ ('tʃædwɪk) *n* **1** Sir **Edwin**. 1800–90, British social reformer. **2** Sir **James**. 1891–1974, British physicist: discovered the neutron (1932): Nobel prize for physics 1935. **3 Lynn** (**Russell**). born 1914, British sculptor in metal.

chafe (tʃeɪf) *vb* **chafes, chafing, chafed. 1** to make or become sore or worn by rubbing. **2** (*tr*) to warm (the hands, etc.) by rubbing. **3** to irritate or be irritated or impatient. **4** (*intr*; often foll. by *on*, *against*, etc.) to rub. ◆ *n* **5** a soreness or irritation caused by friction. [C14: from OF *chaufer* to warm, ult. from L, from *calēre* to be warm + *facere* to make]

chafer ('tʃeɪfə) *n* any of various beetles, such as the cockchafer. [OE *ceafor*]

chaff[1] (tʃɑːf) *n* **1** the mass of husks, etc., separated from the seeds during threshing. **2** finely cut straw and hay used to feed cattle. **3** something of little worth; rubbish: *to separate the wheat from the chaff.* **4** thin strips of metallic foil released into the earth's atmosphere to deflect radar signals and prevent detection. [OE *ceaf*]
▶ '**chaffy** *adj*

chaff[2] (tʃɑːf) *n* **1** light-hearted teasing or joking; banter. ◆ *vb* **2** to tease good-naturedly. [C19: prob. slang var. of CHAFE]
▶ '**chaffer** *n*

chaffer ('tʃæfə) *vb* **1** (*intr*) to haggle or bargain. **2** to chatter, talk, or say idly. ◆ *n* **3** haggling or bargaining. [C13 *chaffare*, from *chep* bargain + *fare* journey]
▶ '**chafferer** *n*

chaffinch ('tʃæfɪntʃ) *n* a European finch with black-an white wings and, in the male, a reddish body and blu grey head. [OE *ceaffinc*, from *ceaf* CHAFF[1] + *finc* FINCH]

chafing dish *n* a vessel with a heating apparatus b neath it, for cooking or keeping food warm at the table

Chagall ★ (*French* ʃagal) *n* **Marc** (mark). 1887–198 French painter, born in Russia: his work includes th decorations for the ceiling of the Paris Opera Hou (1964).

chagrin ('ʃægrɪn) *n* **1** a feeling of annoyance or morti cation. ◆ *vb* **2** to embarrass and annoy. [C17: from *chagrin, chagriner*, from ?]

chain (tʃeɪn) *n* **1** a flexible length of metal links, used fʋ confining, connecting, etc., or in jewellery. **2** (*usually p* anything that confines or restrains: *the chains of poverty.* (*usually pl*) a set of metal links that fit over the tyre of motor vehicle to reduce skidding on an icy surface. **4** series of related or connected facts, events, etc. **5** number of establishments such as hotels, shops, etc having the same owner or management. **5b** (*as modifiɛ* *a chain store*. **6** Also called: **Gunter's chain**. a unit of lengt equal to 22 yards. **7** Also called: **engineer's chain**. a unit length equal to 100 feet. **8** Also called: **nautical chain**. unit of length equal to 15 feet. **9** *Chem*. two or more atoms or groups bonded together so that the resultin molecule, ion, or radical resembles a chain. **10** *Geog.* a s ries of natural features, esp. mountain ranges. ◆ *vb* **1** (*tr*; often foll. by *up*) to confine, tie, or make fast with c as if with a chain. [C13: from OF, ult. from L; se CATENA]

Chain ★ (tʃeɪn) *n* Sir **Ernst Boris**. 1906–79, British biʋ chemist, born in Germany: purified penicillin for clin cal use; shared the Nobel prize for physiology medicine 1945.

chain gang *n* US. a group of convicted prisoneʳ chained together.

chain letter *n* a letter, often with a request for an promise of money, that is sent to many people who ad to or recopy it and send it on.

chain mail *n* **a** another term for **mail**[2] (sense 1). **b** (ʋ *modifier*): *a chain-mail hood*.

chain printer *n* a line printer in which the type is on continuous chain.

chain reaction *n* **1** a process in which a neutron collid ing with an atomic nucleus causes fission and the ejeʋ tion of one or more other neutrons. **2** a chemicaʳ reaction in which the product of one step is a reactant iʳ the following step. **3** a series of events, each of whicʰ precipitates the next.
▶ ˌ**chain-re'act** *vb* (*intr*)

chain saw *n* a motor-driven saw in which the cuttinɡ teeth form links in a continuous chain.

chain-smoke *vb* **chain-smokes, chain-smoking, chain** **smoked**. to smoke (cigarettes, etc.) continually, esp. light ing one from the preceding one.
▶ **chain smoker** *n*

chain stitch *n* **1** a looped embroidery stitch resemblinɡ the links of a chain. ◆ *vb* **chain-stitch**. **2** to sew (some thing) with this stitch.

chainwheel ('tʃeɪnˌwiːl) *n* (esp. on a bicycle) a tootheʋ wheel that transmits drive via the chain.

chair (tʃeə) *n* **1** a seat with a back on which one person sits, typically having four legs and often having arms. **2** an official position of authority. **3** the chairman of a de bate or meeting: *the speaker addressed the chair*. **4** a profes sorship. **5** *Railways*. an iron or steel cradle bolted to ʋ sleeper in which the rail is locked. **6** short for **sedan chaiⁱ** **7 take the chair**. to preside as chairman for a meeting, etc **8 the chair**. *Inf.* the electric chair. ◆ *vb* (*tr*) **9** to preside over (a meeting). **10** *Brit.* to carry aloft in a sitting posi tion after a triumph. **11** to provide with a chair or chairs **12** to install in a chair. [C13: from OF, from L *cathedra*, from Gk *kathedra*, from *kata-* down + *hedra* seat]

chairlift ('tʃeəˌlɪft) *n* a series of chairs suspended from ʋ power-driven cable for conveying people, esp. skiers, up a mountain.

chairman ('tʃeəmən) *n, pl* **chairmen**. a person who pre ides over a company's board of directors, a committee, debate, etc. Also: **chair, chairperson,** or (fem) **chairwoman.**

> **USAGE NOTE** *Chairman* can seem inappropriate when applied to a woman, while *chairwoman* can be offensive. *Chair* and *chairperson* can be applied to either a man or a woman; *chair* is generally preferred to *chairperson.*

aise (ʃeɪz) *n* **1** a light open horse-drawn carriage, esp. one with two wheels. **2** short for **post chaise** and **chaise ongue.** [C18: from F, var. of OF *chaiere* CHAIR]

aise longue (ˈʃeɪz ˈlɒŋ) *n, pl* **chaise longues** or **chaises ongues** (ˈʃeɪz ˈlɒŋ). a long low chair with a back and single armrest. [C19: from F: long chair]

haka ★ (ˈʃaka) *n* a variant spelling of **Shaka.**

akra (ˈtʃækrə, ˈtʃʌkrə) *n* (in yoga) any of the seven major energy centres in the human body. [C19: from Sansk. *cakra* wheel, circle]

alaza (kəˈleɪzə) *n, pl* **chalazas** or **chalazae** (-ziː). one of a pair of spiral threads holding the yolk of a bird's egg in position. [C18: NL, from Gk: hailstone]

alcedony (kælˈsɛdənɪ) *n, pl* **chalcedonies.** a form of quartz with crystals arranged in parallel fibres: a gemstone. [C15: from LL, from Gk *khalkēdōn* a precious stone, ? after *Khalkēdōn* Chalcedon, town in Asia Minor]
▶ **chalcedonic** (ˌkælsɪˈdɒnɪk) *adj*

halcidice ★ (kælˈsɪdɪsɪ) *n* a peninsula of N central Greece, in Macedonia Central, ending in the three promontories of Kassandra, Sithonia, and Akti. Area: 2945 sq. km (1149 sq. miles). Modern Greek name: **Khalkidíki.**

halcis ★ (ˈkælsɪs) *n* a city in SE Greece, at the narrowest point of the Euripus strait: important since the 7th century B.C., founding many colonies in ancient times. Pop.: 47 600 (1995 est.). Modern Greek name: **Khalkís.** Medieval English name: **Negropont.**

halcogen (ˈkælkəˌdʒən) *n* any of the elements oxygen, sulphur, selenium, tellurium, or polonium, of group 6A of the periodic table. [C20: from CHALCO(PYRITE) + -GEN]

halcolithic (ˌkælkəˈlɪθɪk) *adj Archaeol.* of or relating to the period in which both stone and bronze tools were used. [C19: from Gk *khalkos* copper + *lithos* stone]

halcopyrite (ˌkælkəˈpaɪraɪt) *n* a common ore of copper, a crystalline sulphide of copper and iron. Formula: CuFeS₂. Also called: **copper pyrites.**

haldea or **Chaldaea** ★ (kælˈdiːə) *n* **1** an ancient region of Babylonia; the land lying between the Euphrates delta, the Persian Gulf, and the Arabian desert. **2** another name for **Babylonia.**

haldron (ˈtʃɔːldrən) *n* a unit of capacity equal to 36 bushels. [C17: from OF *chauderon* CAULDRON]

halet (ˈʃæleɪ) *n* **1** a type of wooden house of Swiss origin, with wide projecting eaves. **2** a similar house used as a ski lodge, etc. [C19: from F (Swiss dialect)]

haliapin ★ (*Russian* ʃaˈljapin) *n* **Fyodor Ivanovich** (ˈfjɔdər iˈvanəvitʃ). 1873–1938, Russian operatic bass.

halice (ˈtʃælɪs) *n* **1** *Poetic.* a drinking cup; goblet. **2** *Christianity.* a gold or silver cup containing the wine at Mass. **3** a cup-shaped flower. [C13: from OF, from L *calix* cup]

halk (tʃɔːk) *n* **1** a soft fine-grained white sedimentary rock consisting of nearly pure calcium carbonate, containing minute fossil fragments of marine organisms. **2** a piece of chalk, or substance like chalk, often coloured, used for writing and drawing on blackboards. **3 as alike** (or different) **as chalk and cheese.** *Inf.* totally different or dissimilar. **4 by a long chalk.** *Brit. inf.* by far. **5 not by a long chalk.** *Brit. inf.* by no means. **6** (modifier) made of chalk. ◆ *vb* **7** to draw or mark (something) with chalk. **8** (tr) to mark, rub, or whiten with or as with chalk. [OE *cealc,* from L *calx* limestone, from Gk *khalix* pebble]
▶ ˈchalk, like *adj* ▶ ˈchalky *adj* ▶ ˈchalkiness *n*

halk out *vb* (tr, adv) to outline (a plan, scheme, etc.); sketch.

halkpit (ˈtʃɔːkˌpɪt) *n* a quarry for chalk.

chalk up *vb* (tr, adv) *Inf.* **1** to score or register (something). **2** to credit (money) to an account, etc. (esp. in **chalk it up**).

challenge (ˈtʃælɪndʒ) *vb* **challenges, challenging, challenged.** (mainly tr) **1** to invite or summon (someone to do something, esp. to take part in a contest). **2** (also intr) to call (something) into question. **3** to make demands on; stimulate: *the job challenges his ingenuity.* **4** to order (a person) to halt and be identified. **5** *Law.* to make formal objection to (a juror or jury). **6** to lay claim to (attention, etc.). **7** to inject (an experimental animal immunized with a test substance) with disease microorganisms to test for immunity to the disease. ◆ *n* **8** a call to engage in a fight, argument, or contest. **9** a questioning of a statement or fact. **10** a demanding or stimulating situation, career, etc. **11** a demand by a sentry, etc., for identification or a password. **12** *Law.* a formal objection to a person selected to serve on a jury or to the whole body of jurors. [C13: from OF *chalenge,* from L *calumnia* CALUMNY]
▶ ˈchallengeable *adj* ▶ ˈchallenger *n* ▶ ˈchallenging *adj*

challis (ˈʃælɪ, -lɪs) or **challie** (ˈʃælɪ) *n* a lightweight fabric of wool, cotton, etc., usually with a printed design. [C19: prob. from a surname]

Châlons-sur-Marne ★ (*French* ʃalɔ̃symarn) *n* a city in NE France, on the River Marne: scene of Attila's defeat by the Romans (451 A.D.). Pop.: 51 530 (1990). Shortened form: **Châlons.**

Chalon-sur-Saône ★ (*French* ʃalɔ̃syrson) *n* an industrial city in E central France, on the Saône River. Pop.: 54 575 (1990). Shortened form: **Chalon.**

chalybeate (kəˈlɪbɪɪt) *adj* containing or impregnated with iron salts. [C17: from NL *chalybeātus,* ult. from Gk *khalups* iron]

chamber (ˈtʃeɪmbə) *n* **1** a meeting hall, esp. one used for a legislative or judicial assembly. **2** a reception room in an official residence, palace, etc. **3** *Arch. or poetic.* a room in a private house, esp. a bedroom. **4a** a legislative, judicial, or administrative assembly. **4b** any of the houses of a legislature. **5** an enclosed space; compartment; cavity. **6** an enclosure for a cartridge in the cylinder of a revolver or for a shell in the breech of a cannon. **7** short for **chamber pot. 8** (modifier) of, relating to, or suitable for chamber music: *a chamber concert.* **9** (modifier) on a small, quasi-domestic scale. ◆ See also **chambers.** [C13: from OF, from LL *camera* room, L: vault, from Gk *kamara*]

chamberlain (ˈtʃeɪmbəlɪn) *n* **1** an officer who manages the household of a king. **2** the steward of a nobleman or landowner. **3** the treasurer of a municipal corporation. [C13: from OF *chamberlayn,* of Frankish origin]

Chamberlain ★ (ˈtʃeɪmbəlɪn) *n* **1** Sir (**Joseph**) **Austen.** 1863–1937, British Conservative statesman; foreign secretary (1924–29); Nobel peace prize for his negotiation of the Locarno Pact (1925). **2** his father, **Joseph.** 1836–1914, British statesman; originally a Liberal, he resigned in 1886 over Home Rule for Ireland and became leader of the Liberal Unionists. **3** his son, (**Arthur**) **Neville.** 1869–1940, British Conservative statesman; prime minister (1937–40): the failure of his policy of appeasement towards Germany led to World War II. **4 Owen.** born 1920, US physicist, who discovered the antiproton; shared Nobel prize for physics 1959.

chambermaid (ˈtʃeɪmbəˌmeɪd) *n* a woman employed to clean bedrooms, esp. in hotels.

chamber music *n* music for performance by a small group of instrumentalists.

chamber of commerce *n* (sometimes cap.) an organization composed mainly of local businessmen to promote, regulate, and protect their interests.

chamber orchestra *n* a small orchestra of about 25 players, used for the authentic performance of baroque and early classical music as well as modern music.

chamber pot *n* a vessel for urine, used in bedrooms.

chambers (ˈtʃeɪmbəz) *pl n* **1** a judge's room for hearing private cases not taken in open court. **2** (in England) the set of rooms occupied by barristers where clients are interviewed.

Chambéry ★ (*French* ʃɑ̃beri) *n* a city in SE France, in the

Alps: skiing centre; former capital of the duchy of Savoy. Pop.: 54 120 (1990).

chambray ('ʃæmbreɪ) *n* a smooth light fabric of cotton, linen, etc., with white weft and a coloured warp. [C19: after CAMBRAI]

chameleon (kə'miːlɪən) *n* **1** a lizard of Africa and Madagascar, having long slender legs, a prehensile tail and tongue, and the ability to change colour. **2** a changeable or fickle person. [C14: from L, from Gk *khamaileōn*, from *khamai* on the ground + *leōn* LION]
► **chameleonic** (kə,miːlɪ'ɒnɪk) *adj*

chamfer ('tʃæmfə) *n* **1** a narrow flat surface at the corner of a beam, post, etc. ♦ *vb* (*tr*) **2** to cut such a surface on (a beam, etc.). [C16: back formation from *chamfering*, from OF, from *chant* edge (see CANT²) + *fraindre* to break, from L *frangere*]

chamois ('ʃæmɪ; *for senses 1 and 4* 'ʃæmwɑː) *n, pl* **chamois.** **1** a sure-footed goat antelope of Europe and SW Asia, having vertical horns with backward-pointing tips. **2** a soft suede leather formerly made from this animal, now obtained from the skins of sheep and goats. **3** Also called: **chamois leather, shammy** (**leather**), **chammy** (**leather**). a piece of such leather or similar material used for polishing, etc. **4a** a greyish-yellow colour. **4b** (*as adj*): *a chamois stamp.* ♦ *vb* (*tr*) **5** to dress (leather or skin) like chamois. **6** to polish with a chamois. [C16: from OF, from LL *camox*, from ?]

chamomile ('kæmə,maɪl) *n* a variant spelling of **camomile.**

Chamonix ★ ('ʃæmənɪ; *French* ʃamɔni) *n* a town in SE France, in the Alps at the foot of Mont Blanc: skiing and tourist centre. Pop.: 9255 (latest est.).

champ¹ (tʃæmp) *vb* **1** to munch (food) noisily like a horse. **2** (when *intr*, often foll. by *on, at*, etc.) to bite (something) nervously or impatiently. **3 champ** (*or* **chafe**) **at the bit.** *Inf.* to be impatient to start work, a journey, etc. ♦ *n* **4** the act or noise of champing. [C16: prob. imit.]

champ² (tʃæmp) *n Inf.* short for **champion.**

champagne (ʃæm'peɪn) *n* **1** (*sometimes cap.*) a white sparkling wine produced around Reims and Épernay, France. **2** (loosely) any effervescent white wine. **3a** a pale tawny colour. **3b** (*as adj*): *champagne tights.* **4** (*modifier*) denoting a luxurious lifestyle: *a champagne capitalist.* [from *Champagne*, a region of NE France]

Champagne-Ardenne ★ (ʃæm'peɪnɑː'dɛn; *French* ʃapaɲardɛn) *n* a region of NE France: a countship and commercial centre in medieval times; it consists of a great plain, with sheep and dairy farms and many vineyards.

champagne socialist *n* a professed socialist who enjoys an extravagant lifestyle.

Champaigne ★ (ʃæm'peɪn; *French* ʃɑ̃pɛɲ) *n* **Philippe de** (filip də). 1602–74, French painter, born in Brussels.

champers ('ʃæmpəz) *n* (*functioning as sing*) *Sl.* champagne.

champerty ('tʃæmpətɪ) *n, pl* **champerties.** *Law.* (formerly) an illegal bargain between a party to litigation and an outsider whereby the latter agrees to pay for the action and thereby share in any proceeds recovered. [C14: from Anglo-F *champartie*, from OF *champart* share of produce, from *champ* field + *part* share]

Champigny-sur-Marne ★ (*French* ʃapiɲisyrmarn) *n* a suburb of Paris, on the River Marne. Pop.: 80 290 (latest est.).

champion ('tʃæmpɪən) *n* **1a** a person, plant, or animal that has defeated all others in a competition: *a chess champion.* **1b** (*as modifier*): *a champion team; a champion marrow.* **2** a person who defends a person or cause: *champion of the underprivileged.* **3** (formerly) a knight who did battle for another, esp. a king or queen. ♦ *adj* **4** *N English dialect.* excellent. ♦ *adv* **5** *N English dialect.* very well. ♦ *vb* (*tr*) **6** to support: *we champion the cause of liberty.* [C13: from OF, from LL *campiō*, from L *campus* field]

championship ('tʃæmpɪən,ʃɪp) *n* **1** (*sometimes pl*) any of various contests held to determine a champion. **2** the title of being a champion. **3** support for a cause, person, etc.

Champlain¹ ★ (ʃæm'pleɪn) *n* **Lake.** a lake in the nort eastern US, between the Green Mountains and t' Adirondack Mountains: linked by the **Champlain Canal** the Hudson River and by the Richelieu River to the Lawrence; a major communications route in colon times.

Champlain² ★ (ʃæm'pleɪn; *French* ʃɑ̃plɛ̃) *n* **Samuel** (samɥɛl də). ?1567–1635, French explorer; founder Quebec (1608) and governor of New France (1633–35

champlevé *French.* (ʃɑ̃lve) *adj* **1** of a process of enaml ling by which grooves are cut into a metal base and fill with enamel colours. ♦ *n* **2** an object enamelled by th process. [C19: from *champ* field (level surface) + *le* raised]

Champollion ★ (*French* ʃapɔljɔ̃) *n* **Jean François** (ʒ frɑ̃swa). 1790–1832, French Egyptologist, who de phered the hieroglyphics on the Rosetta stone.

Champs Elysées ★ (ʃɒnz eɪ'liːzeɪ; *French* ʃɑz elize) *n* major boulevard in Paris, leading from the Arc Triomphe: site of the Elysées Palace and government o fices.

Chanc. *abbrev. for:* **1** Chancellor. **2** Chancery.

chance (tʃɑːns) *n* **1a** the unknown and unpredictable el ment that causes an event to result in a certain wa rather than another, spoken of as a real force. **1b** (*modifier*): *a chance meeting.* Related adj: **fortuitous. 2** fo tune; luck; fate. **3** an opportunity or occasion. **4** a ris gamble. **5** the extent to which an event is likely to occu probability. **6** an unpredicted event, esp. a fortuna one. **7 by chance.** accidentally: *he slipped by chance.* **8 on tl** (**off**) **chance.** acting on the (remote) possibility. ♦ chances, chancing, chanced. **9** (*tr*) to risk; hazard. **10** (*intr*) happen by chance: *I chanced to catch sight of her.* **11 chanc on** (*or* **upon**). to come upon by accident. **12 chance one arm.** to attempt to do something although the chance success may be slight. [C13: from OF, from *cheoir* occur, from L *cadere*]
► 'chanceful *adj*

chancel ('tʃɑːnsəl) *n* the part of a church containing th altar, sanctuary, and choir. [C14: from OF, from *cancellī* (pl) lattice]

chancellery *or* **chancellory** ('tʃɑːnsələrɪ) *n, pl* **chance leries** *or* **chancellories. 1** the building or room occupied b a chancellor's office. **2** the position or office of a chance lor. **3** *US.* the office of an embassy or legation. [C1 from Anglo-F *chancellerie*, from OF *chancelier* CHANCELLOR

chancellor ('tʃɑːnsələ) *n* **1** the head of the governmen in several European countries. **2** *US.* the president of a university. **3** *Brit. & Canad.* the honorary head of a un versity. Cf. **vice chancellor. 4** *Christianity.* a clergyman act ing as the law officer of a bishop. [C11: from Anglo-F *chanceler*, from LL *cancellārius* porter, from L *cancellī* lav tice]
► 'chancellor,ship *n*

Chancellor of the Exchequer *n Brit.* the cabine minister responsible for finance.

chance-medley *n Law.* a sudden quarrel in which on party kills another. [C15: from Anglo-F *chance medle* mixed chance]

chancer ('tʃɑːnsə) *n Sl.* an unscrupulous or dishonest op portunist. [C19: from CHANCE + -ER¹]

chancery ('tʃɑːnsərɪ) *n, pl* **chanceries.** (*usually cap.*) **1** Als called: **Chancery Division.** (in England) the Lord Chance lor's court, now a division of the High Court of Justice. Also called: **court of chancery.** (in the US) a court of equity **3** *Brit.* the political section or offices of an embassy or le gation. **4** another name for **chancellery. 5** a court of publi records. **6** *Christianity.* a diocesan office under the super vision of a bishop's chancellor. **7 in chancery. 7a** *Law.* pending in a court of equity. **7b** in an awkward situ ation. [C14: shortened from CHANCELLERY]

chancre ('ʃæŋkə) *n Pathol.* a small hard growth, which i the first sign of syphilis. [C16: from F, from L: CANCER
► 'chancrous *adj*

chancroid ('ʃæŋkrɔɪd) *n* **1** a soft venereal ulcer, esp. o the male genitals. ♦ *adj* **2** relating to or resembling chancroid or chancre.

★ people and places

ancy or **chancey** ('tʃɑːnsɪ) *adj* chancier, chanciest. *Inf.* uncertain; risky.

andelier (,ʃændɪ'lɪə) *n* an ornamental hanging light with branches and holders for several candles or bulbs. [C17: from F: candleholder, from L CANDELABRUM]

andernagore ★ (,tʃʌndənə'gɔː) *n* a port in E India, in West Bengal on the Hooghly River: a former French settlement (1686–1950). Pop.: 120 378 (1991).

andigarh ★ (,tʃʌndɪ'gɑː) *n* a city and Union Territory of N India, joint capital of the Punjab and Haryana: modern city planned in the 1950s by Le Corbusier. Pop. of city): 504 094 (1991); (of union territory): 642 015 1991). Area (of union territory): 114 sq. km (44 sq. miles).

andler ('tʃɑːndlə) *n* 1 a dealer in a specified trade or merchandise: *ship's chandler.* 2 a person who makes or sells candles. [C14: from OF *chandelier* one who makes or deals in candles, from *chandelle* CANDLE]
► 'chandlery *n*

handler ★ ('tʃɑːndlə) *n* Raymond (Thornton). 1888–1959, US writer: created Philip Marlowe, an early detective hero.

handragupta ★ (,tʃʌndrə'guptə) *n* Greek name *Sandracottos.* died ?297 B.C., ruler of N India, who founded the Maurya dynasty (325) and defeated Seleucus (?305).

handrasekhar ★ (,tʃændrə'siːkə) *n* Subrahmanyan (,subrə'mænjən). 1910–95, US astronomer born in La-hore, India (now Pakistan): shared Nobel prize for phys-ics 1983.

handrasekhar limit *n Astron.* the upper limit to the mass of a white dwarf, equal to 1.44 solar masses. A star with greater mass will continue to collapse to form a neutron star. [C20: named after S. CHANDRASEKHAR]

hanel ★ (*French* ʃanɛl) *n* Gabrielle (gabriel), known as *Coco Chanel.* 1883–1971, French couturière and per-fumer, who created "the little black dress" and the per-fume Chanel No. 5.

hang ★ (tʃæŋ) *n* another name for the **Yangtze.**

hangan ★ ('tʃæŋɑːn) *n* a former name of **Xi An.**

hangchiakow or **Changchiak'ou** ★ ('tʃæŋ-'tʃjɑː'kəu) *n* a variant transliteration of the Chinese name for **Zhangjiakou.**

hangchow or **Ch'ang-chou** ★ ('tʃæŋ'tʃəu) *n* a vari-ant transliteration of the Chinese name for **Zhangzhou.**

hangchun or **Ch'ang Ch'un** ★ ('tʃæŋ'tʃun) *n* a city in NE China, capital of Jilin province: as **Hsinking,** capital of the Japanese state of Manchukuo (1932–45). Pop.: 2 110 000 (1991 est.).

hangde ('tʃæŋ'deɪ), **Changteh,** or **Ch'ang-te** ★ *n* a port in SE central China, in N Hunan province, near the mouth of the Yuan River: severely damaged by the Japa-nese in World War II. Pop.: 301 276 (1990 est.).

hange (tʃeɪndʒ) *vb* changes, changing, changed. 1 to make or become different; alter. 2 (*tr*) to replace with or ex-change for another: *to change one's name.* 3 (sometimes foll. by *to* or *into*) to transform or convert or be trans-formed or converted. 4 to give and receive (something) in return: *to change places.* 5 (*tr*) to give or receive (money) in exchange for the equivalent sum in a smaller denomi-nation or different currency. 6 (*tr*) to remove or replace the coverings of: *to change a baby.* 7 (when *intr,* may be foll. by *into* or *out of*) to put on other clothes. 8 to operate (the gear lever of a motor vehicle): *to change gear.* 9 to alight from (one bus, train, etc.) and board another. ◆ *n* 10 the act or fact of changing or being changed. 11 a variation or modification. 12 the substitution of one thing for another. 13 anything that is or may be substi-tuted for something else. 14 variety or novelty (esp. in **for a change**). 15 a different set, esp. of clothes. 16 money given or received in return for its equivalent in a larger denomination or in a different currency. 17 the balance of money when the amount tendered is larger than the amount due. 18 coins of a small denomination. 19 (*often cap.*) *Arch.* a place where merchants meet to transact business. 20 the act of passing from one state or phase to another. 21 the transition from one phase of the moon to the next. 22 the order in which a peal of bells may be

rung. 23 **get no change out of** (someone). *Sl.* not to be suc-cessful in attempts to exploit (someone). 24 **ring the changes.** to vary the manner or performance of an action that is often repeated. ◆ See also **change down, change-over, change up.** [C13: from OF, from L *cambīre* to ex-change, barter]
► 'changeful *adj* ► 'changeless *adj* ► 'changer *n*

changeable ('tʃeɪndʒəb°l) *adj* 1 able to change or be changed: *changeable weather.* 2 varying in colour as when viewed from different angles.
► ,changea'bility *n* ► 'changeably *adv*

change down *vb* (*intr, adv*) to select a lower gear when driving.

changeling ('tʃeɪndʒlɪŋ) *n* a child believed to have been exchanged by fairies for the parents' true child.

change of life *n* a nontechnical name for **menopause.**

changeover ('tʃeɪndʒ,əuvə) *n* 1 an alteration or com-plete reversal from one method, system, or product to another. 2 a reversal of a situation, attitude, etc. 3 *Sport.* the act of transferring to or being relieved by a team-mate in a relay race, as by handing over a baton, etc. ◆ *vb* **change over.** 4 to adopt (a different position or attitude): *the driver and navigator changed over.*

change-ringing *n* the art of bell-ringing in which a set of bells is rung in an established order which is then changed.

change up *vb* (*intr, adv*) to select a higher gear when driving.

Changsha or **Ch'ang-sha** ★ ('tʃæŋ'ʃɑː) *n* a port in SE China, capital of Hunan province, on the Xiang River. Pop.: 1 330 000 (1991 est.).

Changteh or **Ch'ang-te** ★ ('tʃæŋ'teɪ) *n* a variant trans-literation of the Chinese name for **Changde.**

Chania ★ ('hɑːnɪə) *n* a variant spelling of **Canea.**

channel ('tʃæn°l) *n* 1 a broad strait connecting two areas of sea. 2 the bed or course of a river, stream, or canal. 3 a navigable course through a body of water. 4 (*often pl*) a means or agency of access, communication, etc.: *through official channels.* 5 a course into which something can be directed or moved. 6 *Electronics.* 6a a band of radio fre-quencies assigned for a particular purpose, esp. the broadcasting of a television signal. 6b a path for an elec-trical signal: *a stereo set has two channels.* 7 a tubular pas-sage for fluids. 8 a groove, as in the shaft of a column. 9 *Computing.* 9a a path along which data can be transmit-ted. 9b one of the lines along the length of a paper tape on which information can be stored in the form of punched holes. ◆ *vb* **channels, channelling, channelled** *or US* **channels, channeling, channeled. 10** to make or cut chan-nels in (something). **11** (*tr*) to guide into or convey through a channel or channels: *information was chan-nelled through to them.* **12** to serve as a medium through whom the spirit of (a person of a former age) allegedly communicates with the living. **13** (*tr*) to form a groove or flute in (a column, etc.). [C13: from OF, from L *canālis* pipe, groove, conduit]

Channel ★ ('tʃæn°l) *n* the. short for **English Channel.**

Channel Country ★ *n* the. an area of E central Aus-tralia, in SW Queensland: crossed by intermittent rivers and subject to both flooding and long periods of drought.

channel-hop *vb* **channel-hops, channel-hopping, channel-hopped.** (*intr*) to change television channels repeatedly using a remote control device.

Channel Islands ★ *pl n* a group of islands in the Eng-lish Channel, off the NW coast of France, consisting of Jersey, Guernsey, Alderney, Brechou, Great Sark, Little Sark, Herm, Jethou, and Lihou (British crown dependen-cies), and the Roches Douvres and the Îles Chausey (which belong to France): the only part of the duchy of Normandy remaining to Britain. Pop.: 142 949 (1991). Area: 194 sq. km (75 sq. miles).

Channel Tunnel ★ *n* the Anglo-French railway tunnel that runs beneath the English Channel, between Folkestone and Coquelles, near Calais, opened in 1994. Also called: **Chunnel, Eurotunnel.**

chanson de geste *French.* (ʃɑ̃sɔ̃ də ʒɛst) *n* one of a genre of Old French epic poems, the most famous of which is the *Chanson de Roland*. [lit.: song of exploits]

chant (tʃɑːnt) *n* **1** a simple song. **2** a short simple melody in which several words or syllables are assigned to one note. **3** a psalm or canticle performed by using such a melody. **4** a rhythmic or repetitious slogan, usually spoken or sung, as by sports supporters, etc. ◆ *vb* **5** to sing or recite (a psalm, etc.) as a chant. **6** to intone (a slogan). [C14: from OF *chanter* to sing, from L *cantāre*, frequentative of *canere* to sing]
▶ 'chanting *n, adj*

chanter ('tʃɑːntə) *n* the pipe on a set of bagpipes on which the melody is played.

chanterelle (,tʃɑːntə'rɛl) *n* any of a genus of fungi having an edible yellow funnel-shaped mushroom. [C18: from F, from L *cantharus* drinking vessel, from Gk *kantharos*]

chanteuse (French ʃɑ̃tøz) *n* a female singer, esp. in a nightclub or cabaret. [F: singer]

chanticleer (,tʃæntɪ'klɪə) *n* a name for a cock, used esp. in fables. [C13: from OF, from *chanter cler* to sing clearly]

Chantilly ★ (ʃæn'tɪlɪ; *French* ʃɑtiji) *n* **1** a town in N France, near the **Forest of Chantilly:** formerly famous for lace and porcelain. Pop.: 11 341 (1990). ◆ *adj* **2** (of cream) lightly sweetened and whipped.

chantry ('tʃɑːntrɪ) *n, pl* **chantries.** *Christianity.* **1** an endowment for the singing of Masses for the soul of the founder. **2** a chapel or altar so endowed. [C14: from OF, from *chanter* to sing; see CHANT]

chanty ('ʃæntɪ, 'tʃæn-) *n, pl* **chanties.** a variant of **shanty**².

Chanukah *or* **Hanukkah** ('hɑːnəkə, -nʊ,kɑː) *n* the eight-day Jewish festival of lights commemorating the rededication of the temple by Judas Maccabaeus in 165 B.C. Also called: **Feast of Dedication, Feast of Lights.** [from Heb., lit.: a dedication]

Chaoan ★ ('tʃaʊ'ɑːn) *n* a city in SE China, in E Guangdong province, on the Han River: river port. Pop.: 313 469 (1990). Also called: **Chaochow.**

Chaochow ★ ('tʃaʊ'tʃəʊ) *n* another name for **Chaoan.**

chaology (keɪ'ɒlədʒɪ) *n* the study of chaos theory.
▶ cha'ologist *n*

chaos ('keɪɒs) *n* **1** (*usually cap.*) the disordered formless matter supposed to have existed before the ordered universe. **2** complete disorder; utter confusion. [C15: from L, from Gk *khaos*]
▶ **chaotic** (keɪ'ɒtɪk) *adj* ◆ cha'otically *adv*

chaos theory *n* a theory, applied in various branches of science, that apparently random phenomena have underlying order.

chap¹ (tʃæp) *vb* **chaps, chapping, chapped. 1** (of the skin) to make or become raw and cracked, esp. by exposure to cold. ◆ *n* **2** (*usually pl.*) a cracked patch on the skin. [C14: prob. of Gmc origin]

chap² (tʃæp) *n Inf.* a man or boy; fellow. [C16 (in the sense: buyer): shortened from CHAPMAN]

chap³ (tʃɒp, tʃæp) *n* a less common word for **chop**³.

chaparejos *or* **chaparajos** (,ʃæpə'reɪəʊs) *pl n* another name for **chaps.** [from Mexican Sp.]

chaparral (,tʃæpə'ræl, ,ʃæp-) *n* (in the southwestern US) a dense growth of shrubs and trees. [C19: from Sp., from *chaparra* evergreen oak]

chapati *or* **chapatti** (tʃə'pætɪ, -'pɑːtɪ) *n, pl* **chapati, chapatis, chapaties,** *or* **chapatti, chapattis, chapatties.** (in Indian cookery) a flat unleavened bread resembling a pancake. [from Hindi]

chapbook ('tʃæp,bʊk) *n* a book of popular ballads, stories, etc., formerly sold by chapmen.

chapel ('tʃæp°l) *n* **1** a place of Christian worship, esp. with a separate altar, in a church or cathedral. **2** a similar place of worship in a large house or institution, such as a college. **3** a church subordinate to a parish church. **4** (in Britain) **4a** a Nonconformist place of worship. **4b** Nonconformist religious practices or doctrine. **5a** the members of a trade union in a newspaper office, printing house, etc. **5b** a meeting of these members. [C13: from

OF, from LL *cappella*, dim. of *cappa* cloak (see CAP); o• the sanctuary where the cloak of St Martin was kept]

chaperon *or* **chaperone** ('ʃæpə,rəʊn) *n* **1** (esp. f• merly) an older or married woman who accompanies supervises a young unmarried woman on social oc• sions. ◆ *vb* **chaperons, chaperoning, chaperoned chaperones, chaperoning, chaperoned. 2** to act as a chaper to. [C14: from OF, from *chape* hood; see CAP]
▶ 'chaper,onage *n*

chapfallen ('tʃæp,fɔːlən) *or* **chopfallen** *adj* dejecte• downhearted. [C16: from CHOPS + FALLEN]

chaplain ('tʃæplɪn) *n* a Christian clergyman attached a chapel of an institution or ministering to a milita body, etc. [C12: from OF, from LL, from *cappella* CHAPE
▶ 'chaplaincy *n*

chaplet ('tʃæplɪt) *n* **1** an ornamental wreath of flow• worn on the head. **2** a string of beads. **3** *RC Church.* **3**• string of prayer beads constituting one third of the r• sary. **3b** the prayers counted on this string. **4** a narr• moulding in the form of a string of beads; astrag• [C14: from OF, from *chapel* hat]
▶ 'chapleted *adj*

Chaplin ★ ('tʃæplɪn) *n* Sir **Charles Spencer,** known Charlie Chaplin. 1889–1977, British comedian, fi• actor, and director. His films, mostly made in Holl• wood, include *The Gold Rush* (1924), *Modern Tim* (1936), and *The Great Dictator* (1940).
▶ ,Chaplin'esque *adj*

chapman ('tʃæpmən) *n, pl* **chapmen.** *Arch.* a trader, esp. • itinerant pedlar. [OE *cēapman*, from *cēap* buying a• selling]

Chapman ★ ('tʃæpmən) *n* **George.** 1559–1634, Engli• dramatist and poet, noted for his translation of Home

Chappell ★ ('tʃæp°l) *n* **Greg(ory Stephen).** born 1948, A• tralian cricketer.

chappie ('tʃæpɪ) *n Inf.* another word for **chap**².

chaps (tʃæps, ʃæps) *pl n* leather overleggings without seat, worn by cowboys. Also called: **chaparajos, chap• rejos.** [C19: shortened from CHAPAREJOS]

chapter ('tʃæptə) *n* **1** a division of a written work. **2** a s• quence of events: *a chapter of disasters.* **3** a period in a li• history, etc. **4** a numbered reference to that part of a p• liamentary session which relates to a specified Act • Parliament. **5** a branch of some societies, clubs, etc. **6** t• collective body or a meeting of the canons of a cathedr• or of the members of a monastic or knightly order. **chapter and verse.** exact authority for an action or stat• ment. ◆ *vb* **8** (*tr*) to divide into chapters. [C13: from C *chapitre*, from L *capitulum*, lit.: little head, hence, sectio• of writing, from *caput* head]

chapterhouse ('tʃæptə,haʊs) *n* **1** the building in whic• a chapter meets. See **chapter** (sense 6). **2** *US.* the meetin• place of a college fraternity or sorority.

char¹ (tʃɑː) *vb* **chars, charring, charred. 1** to burn or b• burned partially; scorch. **2** (*tr*) to reduce (wood) to cha• coal by partial combustion. [C17: short for CHARCOAL]

char² *or* **charr** (tʃɑː) *n, pl* **char, chars** *or* **charr, charrs.** any • various troutlike fishes occurring in cold lakes an• northern seas. [C17: from ?]

char³ (tʃɑː) *n* **1** *Inf.* short for **charwoman.** ◆ *vb* **chars, cha• ring, charred. 2** (*intr*) *Brit. inf.* to do cleaning as a job. [C1• from OE *cerran*]

char⁴ (tʃɑː) *n Brit.* a slang word for **tea.** [from Chines• ch'a]

charabanc ('ʃærə,bæŋ) *n Brit.* a coach, esp. for sightse• ing. [C19: from F: wagon with seats]

character ('kærɪktə) *n* **1** the combination of traits an• qualities distinguishing the individual nature of a pe• son or thing. **2** one such distinguishing quality; charac• teristic. **3** moral force: *a man of character.* **4a** a reputatio• esp. a good reputation. **4b** (*as modifier*): *character assass• nation.* **5** a person represented in a play, film, story, etc• role. **6** an outstanding person: *one of the great characters c• the century.* **7** *Inf.* an odd, eccentric, or unusual perso• *he's quite a character.* **8** an informal word for **person:** • *shady character.* **9** a symbol used in a writing system, suc• as a letter of the alphabet. **10** Also called: **sort.** *Printin•*

★ people and places

ny single letter, numeral, etc., cast as a type. **11** *Computing.* any letter, numeral, etc., which can be represented uniquely by a binary pattern. **12** a style of writing r printing. **13** *Genetics.* any structure, function, attribute, etc., in an organism that is determined by a gene or roup of genes. **14** a short prose sketch of a distinctive ype of person. **15 in** (*or* **out of**) **character.** typical (*or not* ypical) of the apparent character of a person. [C14: om L: distinguishing mark, from Gk *kharaktēr* enraver's tool]
> 'character**ful** *adj* ▸ 'character**less** *adj*

aracter actor *n* an actor who specializes in playing dd or eccentric characters.

aracter assassination *n* the act of deliberately attempting to destroy a person's reputation by defamatory emarks.

aracteristic (ˌkærɪktəˈrɪstɪk) *n* **1** a distinguishing quality, attribute, or trait. **2** *Maths.* **2a** the integral part of common logarithm: *the characteristic of 2.4771 is 2.* **2b** nother name for **exponent** (sense 4). ◆ *adj* **3** indicative of a distinctive quality, etc.; typical.
> ˌcharacter'istically *adv*

aracterize *or* **characterise** ('kærɪktəˌraɪz) *vb* char**acterizes, characterizing, characterized** *or* **characterises, characterising, characterised.** (*tr*) **1** to be a characteristic of. **2** to distinguish or mark as a characteristic. **3** to describe or portray the character of.
> ˌcharacteri'zation *or* ˌcharacteri'sation *n*

arade (ʃəˈrɑːd) *n* **1** an act in the game of charades. **2** *Chiefly Brit.* an absurd act; travesty.

arades (ʃəˈrɑːdz) *n* (*functioning as sing*) a parlour game in which one team acts out each syllable of a word, the other team having to guess the word. [C18: from F, from Provençal *charrado* chat, from *charra* chatter]

arcoal ('tʃɑːˌkəʊl) *n* **1** a black amorphous form of carbon made by heating wood or other organic matter in the absence of air. **2** a stick of this for drawing. **3** a drawing done in charcoal. **4** Also: **charcoal grey. 4a** a dark grey colour. **4b** (*as adj*): *a charcoal suit.* ◆ *vb* **5** (*tr*) to write, draw, or blacken with charcoal. [C14: from *char* (from ?) + COAL]

harcot ★ (*French* ʃarko) *n* **Jean Martin** (ʒɑ̃ martɛ̃). 1825–93, French neurologist, noted for his work on hysteria, which influenced Freud.

harcuterie (ʃɑːˈkuːtərɪ) *n* **1** cooked cold meats. **2** a shop selling cooked cold meats. [F]

hard (tʃɑːd) *n* a variety of beet with large succulent leaves and thick stalks, used as a vegetable. Also called: **Swiss chard.** [C17: prob. from F *carde*, ult. from L *carduus* thistle]

hardin ★ (*French* ʃardɛ̃) *n* **Jean-Baptiste Siméon** (ʒɑ̃batist simeɔ̃). 1699–1779, French genre painter.

hardonnay ('ʃɑːdəˌneɪ) *n* (*sometimes not cap.*) **1** a white grape grown in the Burgundy region of France, Australia, California, New Zealand and elsewhere, used for making wine. **2** any of various white wines made from this grape. [F]

hardonnet ★ (*French* ʃardɔnɛ) *n* (**Louis Marie**) **Hilaire Bernigaud** (iler bɛrnigo), **Comte de.** 1839–1924, French chemist and industrialist who produced rayon.

harente ★ (*French* ʃarɑ̃t) *n* **1** a department of W central France, in Poitou-Charentes region. Capital: Angoulême. Pop.: 341 383 (1994 est.). Area: 5972 sq. km (2329 sq. miles). **2** a river in W France, flowing west to the Bay of Biscay. Length: 362 km (225 miles).

harente-Maritime ★ (*French* ʃarɑ̃tmaritim) *n* a department of W France, in Poitou-Charentes region. Capital: La Rochelle. Pop.: 539 134 (1994 est.). Area: 7232 sq. km (2820 sq. miles).

harge (tʃɑːdʒ) *vb* **charges, charging, charged. 1** to set or demand (a price). **2** (*tr*) to enter a debit against a person or his account. **3** (*tr*) to accuse or impute a fault to (a person, etc.), as formally in a court of law. **4** (*tr*) to command; place a burden upon or assign responsibility for: *I was charged to take the message to headquarters.* **5** to make a rush at or sudden attack upon (a person or thing). **6** (*tr*) to fill (a receptacle) with the proper quantity. **7** (often foll. by *up*) to cause (an accumulator, capacitor, etc.) to

take or store electricity or (of an accumulator) to have electricity fed into it. **8** to fill or be filled with matter by dispersion, solution, or absorption: *to charge water with carbon dioxide.* **9** (*tr*) to fill or suffuse with feeling, emotion, etc.: *the atmosphere was charged with excitement.* **10** (*tr*) *Law.* (of a judge) to address (a jury) authoritatively. **11** (*tr*) to load (a firearm). **12** (*tr*) *Heraldry.* to paint (a shield, banner, etc.) with a charge. ◆ *n* **13** a price charged for some article or service; cost. **14** a financial liability, such as a tax. **15** a debt or a book entry recording it. **16** an accusation or allegation, such as a formal accusation of a crime in law. **17a** an onrush, attack, or assault. **17b** the call to such an attack in battle. **18** custody or guardianship. **19** a person or thing committed to someone's care. **20a** a cartridge or shell. **20b** the explosive required to discharge a firearm. **20c** an amount of explosive to be detonated at any one time. **21** the quantity of anything that a receptacle is intended to hold. **22** *Physics.* **22a** the attribute of matter responsible for all electrical phenomena, existing in two forms: *negative charge; positive charge.* **22b** an excess or deficiency of electrons in a system. **22c** a quantity of electricity determined by the product of an electric current and the time for which it flows, measured in coulombs. **22d** the total amount of electricity stored in a capacitor or an accumulator. **23** a load or burden. **24** a duty or responsibility; control. **25** a command, injunction, or order. **26** *Heraldry.* a design depicted on heraldic arms. **27 in charge.** in command. **28 in charge of. 28a** having responsibility for. **28b** *US.* under the care of. [C13: from OF *chargier* to load, from LL *carricāre*; see CARRY]

chargeable ('tʃɑːdʒəbᵊl) *adj* **1** liable to be charged. **2** liable to result in a legal charge.

chargeable asset *n* any asset that can give rise to assessment for capital gains tax on its disposal. Exempt assets include principal private residences, cars, investments held in a personal equity plan, and government securities.

charge account *n* another term for **credit account.**

charge-cap ('tʃɑːdʒˌkæp) *vb* **charge-caps, charge-capping, charge-capped.** (*tr*) (in Britain) to impose on (a local authority) an upper limit on the community charge it may levy.
> 'charge-ˌcapping *n*

charge card *n* a card issued by a chain store, shop, or organization, that enables customers to obtain goods and services for which they pay at a later date.

charge carrier *n* an electron, hole, or ion that transports the electric charge in an electric current.

chargé d'affaires ('ʃɑːʒeɪ dæˈfɛə) *n, pl* **chargés d'affaires** ('ʃɑːʒeɪ, -ʒeɪz). **1** the temporary head of a diplomatic mission in the absence of the ambassador or minister. **2** the head of a diplomatic mission of the lowest level. [C18: from F: (one) charged with affairs]

charge hand *n Brit.* a workman whose grade of responsibility is just below that of a foreman.

charge nurse *n Brit.* a nurse in charge of a ward in a hospital. Male equivalent of **sister.**

charger[1] ('tʃɑːdʒə) *n* **1** a person or thing that charges. **2** a horse formerly ridden into battle. **3** a device for charging an accumulator.

charger[2] ('tʃɑːdʒə) *n Antiques.* a large dish. [C14 *chargeour*, from *chargen* to CHARGE]

charge sheet *n Brit.* a document on which a police officer enters details of the charge against a prisoner and the court in which he will appear.

char-grilled *adj* (of food) grilled over charcoal.

Chari ('tʃɑːrɪ) *or* **Shari** ★ *n* a river in N central Africa, rising in the N Central African Republic and flowing north to Lake Chad. Length: about 2250 km (1400 miles).

charily ('tʃɛərɪlɪ) *adv* **1** cautiously; carefully. **2** sparingly.

chariness ('tʃɛərɪnɪs) *n* the state of being chary.

Charing Cross ★ ('tʃærɪŋ) *n* a district of London, in the city of Westminster: the modern cross (1863) in front of Charing Cross railway station replaces the one erected by Edward I (1290), the last of twelve marking the route of the funeral procession of his queen, Eleanor.

★ people and places

chariot ('tʃærɪət) n 1 a two-wheeled horse-drawn vehicle used in ancient wars, races, etc. 2 a light four-wheeled horse-drawn ceremonial carriage. 3 *Poetic*. any stately vehicle. [C14: from OF, augmentative of *char* CAR]

charioteer (ˌtʃærɪə'tɪə) n the driver of a chariot.

charisma (kə'rɪzmə) *or* **charism** ('kærɪzəm) n 1 a special personal quality or power making an individual capable of influencing or inspiring people. 2 a quality inherent in a thing, such as a particular type of car, which inspires great enthusiasm and devotion. 3 *Christianity*. a divinely bestowed power or talent. [C17: from Church L, from Gk *kharisma*, from *kharis* grace, favour]
▸ **charismatic** (ˌkærɪz'mætɪk) adj

charismatic movement n *Christianity*. any of various groups, within existing denominations, emphasizing the charismatic gifts of speaking in tongues, healing, etc.

charitable ('tʃærɪtəbəl) adj 1 generous in giving to the needy. 2 kind or lenient in one's attitude towards others. 3 of or for charity.
▸ **'charitableness** n ▸ **'charitably** adv

charitable trust n a trust set up for the benefit of a charity that complies with the regulations of the Charity Commissioners to enable it to be exempt from paying income tax.

charity ('tʃærɪtɪ) n, pl **charities**. 1a the giving of help, money, food, etc., to those in need. 1b (*as modifier*): a *charity show*. 2 an institution or organization set up to provide help, money, etc., to those in need. 3 the help, money, etc., given to the needy; alms. 4 a kindly attitude towards people. 5 love of one's fellow men. [C13: from OF, from L *cāritās* affection, from *cārus* dear]

charivari (ˌʃɑːrɪ'vɑːrɪ), **shivaree,** *or esp. US.* **chivaree** n 1 a discordant mock serenade to newlyweds, made with pans, kettles, etc. 2 a confused noise; din. [C17: from F, from LL, from Gk *karēbaria*, from *karē* head + *barus* heavy]

charlady ('tʃɑːˌleɪdɪ) n, pl **charladies**. another name for **charwoman**.

charlatan ('ʃɑːlətən) n someone who professes expertise, esp. in medicine, that he does not have; quack. [C17: from F, from It., from *ciarlare* to chatter]
▸ **'charlatan,ism** *or* **'charlatanry** n

Charlemagne ★ ('ʃɑːləˌmeɪn) n ?742–814 A.D., king of the Franks (768–814) and, as Charles I, Holy Roman Emperor (800–814). He conquered the Lombards (774), the Saxons (772–804), and the Avars (791–799).

Charles ★ (tʃɑːlz) n 1 *Prince of Wales*. born 1948, son of Elizabeth II; heir apparent to the throne of Great Britain and Northern Ireland. He married (1981) Lady Diana Spencer; they divorced in 1996. 2 **Ray**, real name *Ray Charles Robinson*. born 1930, US singer and songwriter, whose work spans jazz, blues, gospel, pop, and country music.

Charles I ★ n 1 title as Holy Roman Emperor of **Charlemagne**. 2 title as king of France of **Charles II** (Holy Roman Emperor). 3 title as king of Spain of **Charles V** (Holy Roman Emperor). 4 title of **Charles Stuart**. 1600–49, king of England, Scotland, and Ireland (1625–49); son of James I. He ruled for 11 years (1629–40) without parliament until rebellion broke out in Scotland. Conflict with the Long Parliament led to the Civil War and his defeat at Naseby (1645): executed by the English army under Cromwell (1647). 5 1887–1922, emperor of Austria, and, as Charles IV, king of Hungary (1916–18). The last ruler of the Austro-Hungarian monarchy; abdicated at the end of World War I.

Charles II ★ n 1 known as *Charles the Bald*. 823–877 A.D., Holy Roman Emperor (875–877) and, as Charles I, king of France (843–877). 2 the title as king of France of **Charles III** (Holy Roman Emperor). 3 1630–85, king of England, Scotland, and Ireland (1660–85) following the Restoration (1660); son of Charles I. 4 1661–1700, the last Hapsburg king of Spain: his reign saw the end of Spanish power in Europe.

Charles III ★ n 1 known as *Charles the Fat*. 839–888 A.D., Holy Roman Emperor (881–887) and, as Charles II, king of France (884–887). He briefly reunited the empire of

Charlemagne. 2 1716–88, king of Spain (1759–88), w curbed the power of the Church and tried to modern his country.

Charles IV ★ n 1 known as *Charles the Fair*. 1294–13 king of France (1322–28). 2 1316–78, king of Boher (1346–78) and Holy Roman Emperor (1355–78). 3 17 1819, king of Spain (1788–1808), whose reign saw domination of Spain by Napoleonic France: abdicated title as king of Hungary of **Charles I** (sense 5).

Charles V ★ n 1 known as *Charles the Wise*. 1337– king of France (1364–80) during the Hundred Yea War. 2 1500–58, Holy Roman Emperor (1519–56), ki of Burgundy and the Netherlands (1506–55), and, Charles I, king of Spain (1516–56): his reign saw the e pire threatened by Francis I of France, the Turks, and t spread of Protestantism; abdicated.

Charles VI ★ n 1 known as *Charles the Mad* or *Charles Well-Beloved*. 1368–1422, king of France (1380–142 defeated by Henry V of England at Agincourt (1415), was forced by the Treaty of Troyes (1420) to recogn Henry as his successor. 2 1685–1740, Holy Roman E peror (1711–40). His claim to the Spanish throne (17 led to the War of Spanish Succession.

Charles VII ★ n 1 1403–61, king of France (1422–6 son of Charles VI. He was excluded from the Fren throne by the Treaty of Troyes, but following Joan Arc's victory over the English at Orléans (1429), v crowned. 2 1697–1745, Holy Roman Emperor (1742– during the War of Austrian Succession.

Charles IX ★ n 1 1550–74, king of France (1560–74), s of Catherine de' Medici and Henry II: his reign w marked by war between Huguenots and Catholics.

Charles X ★ n 1 title of *Charles Gustavus*. 1622–60, ki of Sweden. 2 1757–1836, king of France (1824–30): l attempt to restore absolutism led to his enforced exil

Charles XIV ★ n the title as king of Sweden and N way of (Jean Baptiste Jules) **Bernadotte**.

Charles Edward Stuart ★ n See (Charles Edwa Stuart.

Charles Martel ★ (mɑː'tɛl) n grandfather Charlemagne. ?688–741 A.D., Frankish ruler of Austras (715–41), who checked the Muslim invasion of Euro by defeating the Moors at Poitiers (732).

Charles's Wain (weɪn) n another name for the Plou [OE *Carles wægn*, from *Carl* CHARLEMAGNE + *wægn* WAIN]

Charles the Great ★ n another name for **Charlemagn**

charleston ('tʃɑːlstən) n a fast rhythmic dance of th 1920s, characterized by kicking and by twisting of th legs from the knee down. [named after *Charlesto* South Carolina]

Charleston ★ ('tʃɑːlstən) n 1 a city in central West Vi ginia: the state capital. Pop.: 59 371 (1985 est.). 2 a po in SE South Carolina, on the Atlantic: scene of the fir action in the Civil War. Pop.: 76 854 (1994 est.).

Charleville-Mézières ★ (French ʃarləvilmezjɛr) n tw towns on opposite sides of the River Meuse in NE Franc Pop.: 59 440 (1990). See **Mézières**.

charley horse ('tʃɑːlɪ) n US & Canad. inf. cramp follov ing strenuous athletic exercise. [C19: from ?]

charlie ('tʃɑːlɪ) n Brit. inf. a silly person; fool.

charlock ('tʃɑːlɒk) n a weedy Eurasian plant with hai stems and foliage and yellow flowers. Also called: wi mustard. [OE *cerlic*, from ?]

charlotte ('ʃɑːlət) n 1 a dessert made with fruit and laye or a casing of bread or cake crumbs, sponge cake, etc apple charlotte. 2 short for **charlotte russe**. [C19: from from the name *Charlotte*]

Charlotte ★ ('ʃɑːlət) n a city in S North Carolina: th largest city in the state. Pop.: 437 797 (1994 est.).

Charlotte Amalie ★ ('ʃɑːlət ə'mɑːlɪə) n the capital the Virgin Islands of the United States, a port on Thomas Island. Pop.: 12 331 (1990). Former nam (1921–37): **Saint Thomas**.

Charlottenburg ★ (German ʃar'lɔtənburk) n a district Berlin (West Berlin until 1990), formerly an independe ent city. Pop.: 145 564 (1986 est.).

★ people and places

charlotte russe (ruːs) *n* a cold dessert made with sponge fingers enclosing a mixture of cream, custard, etc. [F.: Russian charlotte]

Charlottetown ★ ('ʃɑːlətˌtaʊn) *n* a port in SE Canada, capital of the province of Prince Edward Island. Pop.: 15 396 (1991).

Charlton ★ ('tʃɑːltᵊn) *n* **1** Bobby, full name *Sir Robert Charlton*. born 1937, English footballer; played for Manchester United and England. **2** his brother, **Jack**, full name *John Charlton*. born 1935, English footballer; played for Leeds United (1952–73) and England; manager of the Republic of Ireland soccer team (1986–95).

charm (tʃɑːm) *n* **1** the quality of pleasing, fascinating, or attracting people. **2** a pleasing or attractive feature. **3** a small object worn for supposed magical powers; amulet. **4** a trinket worn on a bracelet. **5** a magic spell. **6** a formula used in casting such a spell. **7** *Physics*. a property of certain elementary particles, used to explain some scattering experiments. **8 like a charm.** perfectly; successfully. ◆ *vb* **9** to attract or fascinate; delight greatly. **10** to cast a magic spell on. **11** to protect, influence, or heal, supposedly by magic. **12** (*tr*) to influence or obtain by personal charm. [C13: from OF, from L *carmen* song]
▸ '**charmer** *n*

charming ('tʃɑːmɪŋ) *adj* delightful; pleasant; attractive.
▸ '**charmingly** *adv*

charm offensive *n* a concentrated attempt to gain favour or respectability by conspicuously cooperative and obliging behaviour.

charnel ('tʃɑːnᵊl) *n* **1** short for **charnel house.** ◆ *adj* **2** ghastly; sepulchral; deathly. [C14: from OF: burial place, from L *carnālis* fleshly, CARNAL]

charnel house *n* (esp. formerly) a building or vault where corpses or bones are deposited.

Charnley ★ ('tʃɑːnlɪ) *n* Sir **John.** 1911–82, British surgeon noted for his hip-replacement surgery.

Charon ('kɛərən) *n Greek myth*. the ferryman who brought the dead across the rivers Styx or Acheron to Hades.

Charpentier ★ (*French* ʃarpɑ̃tje) *n* **1** Gustave (gystav). 1860–1956, French composer, noted for his opera *Louise* (1900). **2** Marc-Antoine (markɑ̃twan). ?1645–1704, French composer, noted for his sacred music, esp. his *Te Deum*.

chart (tʃɑːt) *n* **1** a map designed to aid navigation by sea or air. **2** an outline map, esp. one on which weather information is plotted. **3** a sheet giving graphical, tabular, or diagrammatical information. **4 the charts.** *Inf*. the lists produced weekly of the bestselling pop singles and albums or the most popular videos. ◆ *vb* **5** (*tr*) to make a chart of. **6** (*tr*) to plot or outline the course of. **7** (*intr*) (of a record) to appear in the charts. [C16: from L, from Gk *khartēs* papyrus]
▸ '**chartless** *adj*

charter ('tʃɑːtə) *n* **1** a formal document from the sovereign or state incorporating a city, bank, college, etc., and specifying its purposes and rights. **2** (*sometimes cap*.) a formal document granting or demanding certain rights or liberties. **3** a document issued by a society or an organization authorizing the establishment of a local branch or chapter. **4** a special privilege or exemption. **5** (*often cap*.) the fundamental principles of an organization; constitution. **6a** the hire or lease of transportation. **6b** (*as modifier*): *a charter flight.* ◆ *vb* (*tr*) **7** to lease or hire by charter. **8** to hire (a vehicle, etc.). **9** to grant a charter to (a group or person). [C13: from OF, from L *chartula*, dim. of *charta* leaf of papyrus; see CHART]
▸ '**charterer** *n*

chartered accountant *n* (in Britain) an accountant who has passed the examinations of the Institute of Chartered Accountants.

chartered bank *n Canad*. a privately owned bank that has been incorporated by Parliament to operate in the commercial banking system.

chartered librarian *n* (in Britain) a librarian who has obtained a qualification from the Library Association in addition to a degree or diploma in librarianship.

chartered surveyor *n* (in Britain) a member of the Royal Institution of Chartered Surveyors.

Charteris ★ ('tʃɑːtərɪs) *n* **Leslie**, original name *Leslie Charles Bowyer Yin*. 1907–93, British novelist, born in Singapore: created the character Simon Templar, known as The Saint.

Chartism ('tʃɑːtɪzəm) *n English history*. a movement (1838-48) to achieve certain political reforms, demand for which was embodied in charters presented to Parliament.
▸ '**Chartist** *n, adj*

Chartres ★ ('ʃɑːtrə, ʃɑːt; *French* ʃartrə) *n* a city in NW France: Gothic cathedral; market town. Pop.: 41 850 (1990).

chartreuse (ʃɑːˈtrɜːz; *French* ʃartrøz) *n* **1** either of two liqueurs, green or yellow, made from herbs. **2a** a yellowish-green colour. **2b** (*as adj*): *a chartreuse dress*. [C19: from F, after *La Grande Chartreuse*, monastery near Grenoble, where the liqueur is produced]

charwoman ('tʃɑːˌwʊmən) *n, pl* **charwomen**. *Brit*. a woman who is hired to clean a house.

chary ('tʃɛərɪ) *adj* **charier, chariest**. **1** wary; careful. **2** choosy; finicky. **3** shy. **4** sparing; mean. [OE *cearig*; rel. to *caru* CARE]

Charybdis (kəˈrɪbdɪs) *n* a ship-devouring monster in classical mythology, identified with a whirlpool off the coast of Sicily. Cf. **Scylla.**

chase[1] (tʃeɪs) *vb* **chases, chasing, chased. 1** to follow or run after (a person, animal, or goal) persistently or quickly. **2** (*tr*; often foll. by *out, away*, or *off*) to force to run (away); drive (out). **3** (*tr*) *Inf*. to court (a member of the opposite sex) in an unsubtle manner. **4** (*tr*; often foll. by *up*) *Inf*. to pursue persistently and energetically in order to obtain results, information, etc. **5** (*intr*) *Inf*. to hurry; rush. ◆ *n* **6** the act of chasing; pursuit. **7** any quarry that is pursued. **8** *Brit*. an unenclosed area of land where wild animals are preserved to be hunted. **9** *Brit*. the right to hunt a particular quarry over the land of others. **10 the chase.** the act or sport of hunting. **11** short for **steeplechase. 12 give chase.** to pursue (a person, animal, or thing) actively. [C13: from OF *chacier*, from Vulgar L *captiāre* (unattested), from L, from *capere* to take; see CATCH]

chase[2] (tʃeɪs) *n* **1** *Letterpress printing*. a rectangular steel frame into which metal type and blocks are locked for printing. **2** the part of a gun barrel from the trunnions to the muzzle. **3** a groove or channel, esp. to take a pipe, cable, etc. ◆ *vb* **chases, chasing, chased.** (*tr*) **4** Also: **chamfer.** to cut a groove, furrow, or flute in (a surface, column, etc.). [C17: prob. from F *châsse* frame, from OF *chas* enclosure, from LL *capsus* pen for animals; both from L *capsa* CASE[2]]

chase[3] (tʃeɪs) *vb* **chases, chasing, chased.** (*tr*) to ornament (metal) by engraving or embossing. Also: **enchase.** [C14: from OF *enchasser* ENCHASE]

chaser ('tʃeɪsə) *n* **1** a person or thing that chases. **2** a drink drunk after another of a different kind, as beer after spirits.

chasm ('kæzəm) *n* **1** a deep cleft in the ground; abyss. **2** a break in continuity; gap. **3** a wide difference in interests, feelings, etc. [C17: from L, from Gk *khasma*; rel. to *khainein* to gape]
▸ '**chasmal** ('kæzməl) *or* '**chasmic** *adj*

chasseur (ʃæˈsɜː) *n* **1** *French Army*. a member of a unit specially trained for swift deployment. **2** a uniformed attendant. ◆ *adj* **3** (*often postpositive*) designating or cooked in a sauce consisting of white wine and mushrooms. [C18: from F: huntsman]

Chassid *or* **Hassid** ('hæsɪd) *n pl* **Chassidim** *or* **Hassidim** ('hæsɪˌdiːm, -dɪm). **1** a sect of Jewish mystics founded in Poland about 1750, characterized by religious zeal and a spirit of prayer, joy, and charity. **2** a Jewish sect of the 2nd century B.C., formed to combat Hellenistic influences.
▸ **Chassidic** *or* **Hassidic** (həˈsɪdɪk) *adj*

chassis ('ʃæsɪ) *n, pl* **chassis** (-sɪz). **1** the steel frame, wheels, and mechanical parts of a motor vehicle. **2** *Electronics*. a mounting for the circuit components of an electrical or electronic device, such as a radio or television. **3** the landing gear of an aircraft. **4** the frame on which a cannon carriage moves. [C17 (meaning: window frame): from F *châssis,* from Vulgar L *capsicum* (unattested), ult. from L *capsa* CASE[2]]

chaste (tʃeɪst) *adj* **1** not having experienced sexual intercourse; virginal. **2** abstaining from unlawful sexual intercourse. **3** abstaining from all sexual intercourse. **4** (of conduct, speech, etc.) pure; decent; modest. **5** (of style) simple; restrained. [C13: from OF, from L *castus* pure]
▶ **'chastely** *adv* ▶ **'chasteness** *n*

chasten ('tʃeɪsᵊn) *vb* (*tr*) **1** to bring to submission; subdue. **2** to discipline or correct by punishment. **3** to moderate; restrain. [C16: from OF, from L *castigāre*; see CASTIGATE]
▶ **'chastener** *n*

chastise (tʃæs'taɪz) *vb* chastises, chastising, chastised. (*tr*) **1** to punish, esp. by beating. **2** to scold severely. [C14 *chastisen,* irregularly from *chastien* to CHASTEN]
▶ **chastisement** ('tʃæstɪzmənt, tʃæs'taɪz-) *n* ▶ **chas'tiser** *n*

chastity ('tʃæstɪtɪ) *n* **1** the state of being chaste; purity. **2** abstention from sexual intercourse; virginity or celibacy. [C13: from OF, from L, from *castus* CHASTE]

chasuble ('tʃæzjubᵊl) *n Christianity.* a long sleeveless outer vestment worn by a priest when celebrating Mass. [C13: from F, from LL *casubla* garment with a hood]

chat (tʃæt) *n* **1** informal conversation or talk in an easy familiar manner. **2** an Old World songbird of the thrush family, having a harsh chattering cry. **3** any of various North American warblers. **4** any of various Australian wrens. ◆ *vb* **chats, chatting, chatted. 5** (*intr*) to talk in an easy familiar way. ◆ See also **chat up.** [C16: short for CHATTER]

chateau *or* **château** ('ʃætəʊ) *n, pl* chateaux (-təʊ, -təʊz), chateaus *or* châteaux, châteaus. **1** a country house or castle, esp. in France. **2** (in the name of a wine) estate or vineyard. [C18: from F, from ML *castellum* CASTLE]

Chateaubriand ★ (*French* ʃatobriʒɑ̃) *n* **1** François René (frɑ̃swa rəne), Vicomte de Chateaubriand. 1768–1848, French writer and statesman: his works include *Le Génie du Christianisme* (1802) and *Mémoires d'outre-tombe* (1849–50). **2** a thick steak cut from the fillet of beef.

Châteauroux ★ (*French* ʃatoru) *n* a city in central France: tenth-century castle (**Château-Raoul**). Pop.: 52 950 (1990).

Château-Thierry ★ ('ʃætəʊ'tɪərɪ; *French* ʃatotjeri) *n* a town in N central France, on the River Marne: scene of the second battle of the Marne (1918) during World War I. Pop.: 15 830 (1990).

chatelaine ('ʃætəˌleɪn) *n* **1** (esp. formerly) the mistress of a castle or large household. **2** a chain or clasp worn at the waist by women in the 16th to the 19th centuries, with handkerchief, keys, etc., attached. [from F, from OF, ult. from L *castellum* CASTLE]

Chatham[1] ★ ('tʃætəm) *n* **1** a town in SE England, in N Kent on the River Medway: formerly royal naval dockyard. Pop.: 71 691 (1991). **2** a city in SE Canada, in SE Ontario on the Thames River. Pop.: 43 557 (1991).

Chatham[2] ★ ('tʃætəm) *n* **1st Earl of.** title of the elder (William) **Pitt.**

Chatham Island ★ *n* another name for **San Cristóbal** (sense 1).

Chatham Islands ★ *pl n* a group of islands in the S Pacific Ocean, forming a county of South Island, New Zealand: consists of the main islands of Chatham, Pitt, and several rocky islets. Chief settlement: Waitangi. Pop.: 769 (1991). Area: 963 sq. km (372 sq. miles).

chatline ('tʃætˌlaɪn) *n* a telephone service enabling callers to join in general conversation with each other.

chat show *n Brit.* a television or radio show in which guests are interviewed informally.

Chattanooga ★ (ˌtʃætᵊ'nuːgə) *n* a city in SE Tennessee, on the Tennessee River: scene of two battles during the Civil War, in which the North defeated the Confederates, cleared Tennessee, and opened the way to Georgia (1863). Pop.: 152 259 (1994 est.).

chattel ('tʃætᵊl) *n* **1** (*often pl*) *Property law.* **1a chattel personal.** an item of movable personal property, such as furniture, etc. **1b chattel real.** an interest in land less than a freehold. **2 goods and chattels.** personal property. [C13:

from OF *chatel* personal property, from Med. L *capit…* wealth]

chatter ('tʃætə) *vb* **1** to speak (about unimportant ma…ters) rapidly and incessantly. **2** (*intr*) (of birds, monkey… etc.) to make rapid repetitive high-pitched noises. **3** (*in…* (of the teeth) to click together rapidly through cold… fear. **4** (*intr*) to make rapid intermittent contact with… component, as in machining. ◆ *n* **5** idle or foolish ta… gossip. **6** the high-pitched repetitive noise made by… bird, monkey, etc. **7** the rattling of objects, such as pa… of a machine. [C13: imit.]
▶ **'chatterer** *n*

chatterbox ('tʃætəˌbɒks) *n Inf.* a person who talks co… stantly, esp. about trivial matters.

chattering classes *n Inf., often derog.* (usually p… ceded by *the*) those members of the educated sections… society who enjoy talking about politics, society, c… ture, etc.

Chatterton ★ ('tʃætətən) *n* **Thomas.** 1752–70, Briti… poet; author of spurious medieval verse: he committe… suicide at the age of 17.

chatty ('tʃætɪ) *adj* **chattier, chattiest. 1** full of trivial conve… sation; talkative. **2** informal and friendly; gossipy.
▶ **'chattily** *adv* ▶ **'chattiness** *n*

chat up *vb* (*tr, adv*) *Brit. inf.* **1** to talk flirtatiously… (someone) with a view to starting a romantic or sexu… relationship. **2** to talk persuasively to (a person), es… with an ulterior motive.

Chaucer ★ ('tʃɔːsə) *n* **Geoffrey.** ?1340–1400, English poe… noted for *The Canterbury Tales.* His other works inclu… *Troilus and Criseyde, The Legende of Good Women,* and *T…* *Parlement of Foules.*

chauffeur ('ʃəʊfə, ʃəʊ'fɜː) *n* **1** a person employed to dri… a car. ◆ *vb* **2** to act as driver for (a person, etc.): *he chau…* feured me to the stadium. [C20: from F, lit.: stoker, fro… *chauffer* to heat]
▶ **chauffeuse** (ʃəʊ'fɜːz) *fem n*

chaunt (tʃɔːnt) *n* a less common variant of **chant.**
▶ **'chaunter** *n*

chauvinism ('ʃəʊvɪˌnɪzəm) *n* **1** aggressive or fanatic… patriotism; jingoism. **2** enthusiastic devotion to a caus… **3** smug irrational belief in the superiority of one's ow… race, party, sex, etc.: *male chauvinism.* [C19: from F, aft… Nicolas *Chauvin,* F soldier under Napoleon, noted for h… unthinking patriotism]
▶ **'chauvinist** *n, adj* ▶ **ˌchauvin'istic** *adj* ▶ **ˌchauvi…** **'istically** *adv*

cheap (tʃiːp) *adj* **1** costing relatively little; inexpensive; … good value. **2** charging low prices: *a cheap hairdresser.* **3 …** poor quality; shoddy: *cheap furniture.* **4** worth relative… little: *promises are cheap.* **5** not worthy of respect; vulgar… ashamed; embarrassed: *to feel cheap.* **7** stingy; miserly… *Inf.* mean; despicable: *a cheap liar.* ◆ *n* **9 on the cheap.** Br… *inf.* at a low cost. ◆ *adv* **10** at very little cost. [OE c… barter, bargain, price, property]
▶ **'cheaply** *adv* ▶ **'cheapness** *n*

cheapen ('tʃiːpᵊn) *vb* **1** to make or become lower in rep… tation, quality, etc. **2** to make or become cheap c… cheaper.
▶ **'cheapener** *n*

cheap-jack *Inf.* ◆ *n* **1** a person who sells cheap an… shoddy goods. ◆ *adj* **2** shoddy or inferior. [C19: fro… CHEAP + JACK]

cheapo ('tʃiːpəʊ) *adj Inf.* very cheap and possibly shoddy…

cheapskate ('tʃiːpˌskeɪt) *n Inf.* a miserly person.

cheat (tʃiːt) *vb* **1** to deceive or practise deceit, esp. fo… one's own gain; trick or swindle (someone). **2** (*intr*) t… obtain unfair advantage by trickery, as in a game o… cards. **3** (*tr*) to escape or avoid (something unpleasan… by luck or cunning: *to cheat death.* **4** (when *intr,* usuall… foll. by *on*) *Inf.* to be sexually unfaithful to (one's wif… husband, etc.). ◆ *n* **5** a person who cheats. **6** a delib… erately dishonest transaction, esp. for gain; fraud. **7** *n… sham.* **8** *Law.* the obtaining of another's property b… fraudulent means. [C14: short for ESCHEAT]
▶ **'cheater** *n*

Cheb ★ (*Czech* xɛp) *n* a town in the W Czech Republic, i…

★ people and places

W Bohemia on the Ohře River: 12th-century castle where Wallenstein was murdered (1634); a centre of the Sudeten-German movement after World War I. Pop.: 31 847 (1991). German name: **Eger**.

heboksary ★ (*Russian* tʃıbak'sarı) *n* a port in W central Russia, on the River Volga: capital of the Chuvash Republic. Pop.: 450 000 (1995 est.).

hechenia (tʃı'tʃenɪə) *or* **Chechnya** ★ ('tʃetʃnjɑː) *n* a constituent republic of S Russia, on the N slopes of the Caucasus Mountains: part of the former Checheno-Ingush Autonomous Republic, which was split into Chechenia and Ingushetia in 1992; oil, gas, and mineral resources. Chechenia declared itself independent of Russia following the break-up of the Soviet Union in 1991; Russian troops fought separatists from 1994 to 1996. Capital: Grozny. Pop. (including Ingushetia): 1 234 000 (1995 est.). Area (including Ingushetia): 19 300 sq. km (7450 sq. miles).

heck (tʃek) *vb* **1** to pause or cause to pause, esp. abruptly. **2** (*tr*) to restrain or control: *to check one's tears*. **3** (*tr*) to slow the growth or progress of; retard. **4** (*tr*) to rebuke or rebuff. **5** (when *intr*, often foll. by *on* or *up on*) to examine, investigate, or make an inquiry into (facts, a product, etc.) for accuracy, quality, or progress. **6** (*tr*) *Chiefly US & Canad.* to mark off so as to indicate approval, correctness, or preference. **7** (*intr*; often foll. by *with*) *Chiefly US & Canad.* to correspond or agree: *this report checks with the other*. **8** (*tr*) *Chiefly US, Canad., & NZ.* to leave in or accept (property) for temporary custody. **9** *Chess.* to place (an opponent's king) in check. **10** (*tr*) to mark with a pattern of squares or crossed lines. **11** to crack or cause to crack. **12** (*tr*) *Ice hockey.* to impede an opponent. **13** (*intr*) *Hunting.* (of hounds) to pause while relocating a lost scent. ◆ *n* **14** a break in progress; stoppage. **15** a restraint or rebuff. **16** a person or thing that restrains, halts, etc. **17** a control, esp. a rapid or informal one, to ensure accuracy, progress, etc. **18** a means or standard to ensure against fraud or error. **19** the US word for **tick**[1] (senses 3, 6). **20** the US spelling of **cheque**. **21** *US & Canad.* the bill in a restaurant. **22** *Chiefly US & Canad.* a tag used to identify property deposited for custody. **23** a pattern of squares or crossed lines. **24** a single square in such a pattern. **25** fabric with a pattern of squares or crossed lines. **26** *Chess.* the state or position of a king under direct attack. **27** a small crack, as one that occurs in timber during drying. **28** a chip or counter used in some card and gambling games. **29** *Hunting.* a pause by the hounds owing to loss of the scent. **30** *Ice hockey.* the act of impeding an opponent with one's body or stick. **31 in check.** under control or restraint. ◆ *sentence substitute.* **32** *Chess.* a call made to an opponent indicating that his king is in check. **33** *Chiefly US & Canad.* an expression of agreement. ◆ See also **check in, check out, checkup**. [C14: from OF *eschec* a check at chess, via Ar. from Persian *shāh* the king]
► 'checkable *adj*

hecked (tʃekt) *adj* having a pattern of squares.

hecker[1] ('tʃekə) *n, vb* **1** the usual US spelling of **chequer**. ◆ *n* **2** *Textiles.* the US spelling of **chequer** (sense 2). **3** the US and Canad. name for **draughtsman** (sense 3).

hecker[2] ('tʃekə) *n Chiefly US.* **1** a cashier, esp. in a supermarket. **2** an attendant in a cloakroom, left-luggage office, etc.

heckerboard ('tʃekə,bɔːd) *n* the US and Canad. name for a **draughtboard**.

heckers ('tʃekəz) *n* (*functioning as sing*) the US and Canad. name for **draughts**.

heck in *vb* (*adv*) **1** (*intr*) to record one's arrival, as at a hotel or for work; sign in or report. **2** (*tr*) to register the arrival of (passengers, etc.). ◆ *n* **check-in. 3** the formal registration of arrival, as at an airport or a hotel. **4** the place where one registers arrival at an airport, etc.

heck list *n* a list of items, names, etc., to be referred to for identification or verification.

heckmate ('tʃek,meɪt) *n* **1** *Chess.* **1a** the winning position in which an opponent's king is under attack and unable to escape. **1b** the move by which this position is achieved. **2** utter defeat. ◆ *vb* **checkmates, checkmating, checkmated.** (*tr*) **3** *Chess.* to place (an opponent's king) in

checkmate. **4** to thwart or render powerless. ◆ *sentence substitute.* **5** *Chess.* a call made when placing an opponent's king in checkmate. [C14: from OF, from Ar. *shāh māt* the king is dead; see CHECK]

check out *vb* (*adv*) **1** (*intr*) to pay the bill and depart, esp. from a hotel. **2** (*intr*) to depart from a place; record one's departure from work. **3** (*tr*) to investigate or prove to be in order after investigation: *the police checked out all the statements*. **4** (*tr*) *Inf.* to have a look at; inspect: *check out the wally in the pink shirt*. ◆ *n* **checkout. 5** the latest time for vacating a room in a hotel, etc. **6** a counter, esp. in a supermarket, where customers pay.

checkpoint ('tʃek,pɔɪnt) *n* a place, as at a frontier, where vehicles or travellers are stopped for official identification, inspection, etc.

checkup ('tʃek,ʌp) *n* **1** an examination to see if something is in order. **2** *Med.* a medical examination, esp. one taken at regular intervals. ◆ *vb* **check up. 3** (*intr, adv*; sometimes foll. by *on*) to investigate or make an inquiry into (a person's character, evidence, etc.).

Cheddar ★ ('tʃedə) *n* **1** (*sometimes not cap.*) any of several types of smooth hard yellow or whitish cheese. **2** a village in SW England, in N Somerset: situated near **Cheddar Gorge**, a pass through the Mendip Hills renowned for its stalactitic caverns and rare limestone flora. Pop.: 4484 (1991).

cheek (tʃiːk) *n* **1** either side of the face, esp. that part below the eye. **2** *Inf.* impudence; effrontery. **3** (*often pl*) *Inf.* either side of the buttocks. **4** (*often pl*) a side of a door jamb. **5** one of the jaws of a vice. **6 cheek by jowl.** close together; intimately linked. **7 turn the other cheek.** to be submissive and refuse to retaliate. ◆ *vb* **8** (*tr*) *Inf.* to speak or behave disrespectfully to. [OE *ceace*]

cheekbone ('tʃiːk,bəʊn) *n* the nontechnical name for **zygomatic bone**.

cheeky ('tʃiːkɪ) *adj* **cheekier, cheekiest.** disrespectful in speech or behaviour; impudent.
► 'cheekily *adv* ► 'cheekiness *n*

cheep (tʃiːp) *n* **1** the short weak high-pitched cry of a young bird; chirp. ◆ *vb* **2** (*intr*) (of young birds) to utter such sounds.
► 'cheeper *n*

cheer (tʃɪə) *vb* **1** (usually foll. by *up*) to make or become happy or hopeful; comfort or be comforted. **2** to applaud with shouts. **3** (when *tr*, sometimes foll. by *on*) to encourage (a team, etc.) with shouts. ◆ *n* **4** a shout or cry of approval, encouragement, etc., often using **hurrah! 5 three cheers.** three shouts of hurrah given in unison to honour someone or celebrate something. **6** happiness; good spirits. **7** state of mind; spirits (archaic, except in **be of good cheer, with good cheer**). **8** *Arch.* provisions for a feast; fare. [C13 (in the sense: face, welcoming aspect): from OF *chere*, from LL *cara* face, from Gk *kara* head]

cheerful ('tʃɪəful) *adj* **1** having a happy disposition; in good spirits. **2** pleasantly bright: *a cheerful room*. **3** ungrudging: *cheerful help*.
► 'cheerfully *adv* ► 'cheerfulness *n*

cheerio (,tʃɪərɪ'əʊ) *Inf.* ◆ *sentence substitute. Chiefly Brit.* **1** a farewell greeting. **2** a drinking toast. ◆ *n, pl* **cheerios. 3** *NZ.* a type of small sausage.

cheerleader ('tʃɪə,liːdə) *n US & Canad.* a person who leads a crowd in cheers, esp. at sports events.

cheerless ('tʃɪəlɪs) *adj* dreary or gloomy.
► 'cheerlessly *adv* ► 'cheerlessness *n*

cheers (tʃɪəz) *sentence substitute. Inf., chiefly Brit.* **1** a drinking toast. **2** goodbye! cheerio! **3** thanks!

cheery ('tʃɪərɪ) *adj* **cheerier, cheeriest.** showing or inspiring cheerfulness.
► 'cheerily *adv* ► 'cheeriness *n*

cheese (tʃiːz) *n* **1** the curd of milk separated from the whey and variously prepared as a food. **2** a mass or cake of this substance. **3** any of various substances of similar consistency, etc.: *lemon cheese*. **4** *Sl.* an important person (esp. in **big cheese**). [OE *cēse*, from L *cāseus* cheese]

cheeseburger ('tʃiːz,bɜːgə) *n* a hamburger cooked with a slice of cheese on top of it.

cheesecake ('tʃiːz,keɪk) *n* **1** a rich tart filled with cheese, esp. cream cheese, cream, sugar, etc. **2** *Sl.* women displayed for their sex appeal, as in photographs in magazines or films.

cheesecloth ('tʃiːzˌklɒθ) *n* a loosely woven cotton cloth formerly used for wrapping cheese.

cheesed off *adj* (*usually postpositive*) *Brit. sl.* bored, disgusted, or angry. [C20: from ?]

cheeseparing ('tʃiːzˌpɛərɪŋ) *adj* **1** penny-pinching. ◆ *n* **2a** a paring of cheese rind. **2b** anything similarly worthless. **3** stinginess.

cheesy ('tʃiːzɪ) *adj* **cheesier, cheesiest. 1** like cheese in flavour, smell, or consistency. **2** *Inf.* (of a smile) broad but possibly insincere: *a big cheesy grin.* **3** *Inf.* banal or trite; in poor taste.
▸ 'cheesiness *n*

cheetah *or* **chetah** ('tʃiːtə) *n* a large feline of Africa and SW Asia: the swiftest mammal, having very long legs, and a black-spotted coat. [C18: from Hindi *cītā*, from Sansk. *citra* speckled]

Cheever ★ ('tʃiːvə) *n* **John.** 1912–82, US writer. His novels include *The Wapshot Chronicle* (1957) and *Bullet Park* (1969).

chef (ʃɛf) *n* a cook, esp. the principal cook in a restaurant. [C19: from F, from OF *chief* head, CHIEF]

chef-d'œuvre *French.* (ʃedœvrə) *n, pl* **chefs-d'œuvre** (ʃedœvrə). a masterpiece.

Chefoo ★ ('tʃiː'fuː) *n* another name for **Yantai.**

Che Guevara ★ (tʃeɪ ɡəˈvɑːrə; *Spanish* tʃe geˈβara) *n* See **Guevara.**

Cheiron ★ ('kaɪrɒn, -rən) *n* a variant spelling of **Chiron.**

Cheju ★ ('tʃeˈdʒuː) *n* a volcanic island in the N East China Sea, southwest of Korea: constitutes the province of Cheju-do in South Korea. Capital: Cheju. Pop.: 258 509 (1995). Area: 1792 sq. km (692 sq. miles). Also called: **Quelpart.**

Chekhov *or* **Chekov** ★ ('tʃɛkɒf; *Russian* 'tʃexəf) *n* **Anton Pavlovich** (anˈtɔn ˈpavləvitʃ). 1860–1904, Russian writer. His plays include *The Seagull* (1896), *Uncle Vanya* (1900), *The Three Sisters* (1901), and *The Cherry Orchard* (1904).
▸ **Chekhovian** *or* **Chekovian** (tʃeˈkəʊvɪən) *adj*

Chekiang ★ ('tʃeˈkjæŋ, -kaɪˈæŋ) *n* a variant transliteration of the Chinese name for **Zhejiang.**

chela[1] ('kiːlə) *n, pl* **chelae** (-liː). a large pincer-like claw of such arthropods as the crab and scorpion. [C17: NL, from Gk *khēlē* claw]

chela[2] ('tʃeɪlə) *n Hinduism.* a disciple of a religious teacher. [C19: from Hindi *celā*, from Sansk. *ceta* servant, slave]

chelate ('kiːleɪt) *n* **1** *Chem.* a chemical compound whose molecules contain a closed ring of atoms of which one is a metal atom. ◆ *adj* **2** *Zool.* of or possessing chelae. **3** *Chem.* of a chelate. ◆ *vb* **chelates, chelating, chelated. 4** (*intr*) *Chem.* to form a chelate. [C20: from CHELA[1]]
▸ che'lation *n*

chelicera (kɪˈlɪsərə) *n, pl* **chelicerae** (-əˌriː). one of a pair of appendages on the head of spiders and other arachnids: often modified as food-catching claws. [C19: from NL, from Gk *khēle* claw+ *keras* horn]

Chelmsford ★ ('tʃɛlmzfəd) *n* a town in SE England, administrative centre of Essex: market town. Pop.: 197 451 (1991).

cheloid ('kiːlɔɪd) *n Pathol.* a variant spelling of **keloid.**
▸ che'loidal *adj*

chelonian (kɪˈləʊnɪən) *n* **1** any reptile of the order *Chelonia*, including the tortoises and turtles, in which most of the body is enclosed in a bony capsule. ◆ *adj* **2** of or belonging to the *Chelonia*. [C19: from NL, from Gk *khelōnē* tortoise]

Chelsea ★ ('tʃɛlsɪ) *n* a residential district of SW London, in the Royal Borough of Kensington and Chelsea: site of the Chelsea Royal Hospital for old and invalid soldiers (**Chelsea Pensioners**).

Cheltenham ★ ('tʃɛltʰnəm) *n* **1** a town in W England, in central Gloucestershire: famous for its schools, racecourse, and saline springs (discovered in 1716). Pop.: 91 301 (1991). **2** a style of type.

Chelyabinsk ★ (*Russian* tʃɪrˈljabinsk) *n* a city in SW Ru• sia: a major industrial centre. Pop.: 1 086 000 (199• est.).

Chelyuskin ★ (*Russian* tʃɪrˈljuskin) *n* **Cape.** a cape in central Russia, in N Siberia at the end of the Taimyr Per• insula: the northernmost point of Asia.

chem. *abbrev. for:* **1** chemical. **2** chemist. **3** chemistry.

chem- *combining form.* a variant of **chemo-** before a vowel•

chemical ('kɛmɪkᵊl) *n* **1** any substance used in or resul• ing from a reaction involving changes to atoms or mo• ecules. ◆ *adj* **2** of or used in chemistry. **3** of, made fron• or using chemicals: *chemical fertilizer.*
▸ 'chemically *adv*

chemical engineering *n* the branch of engineerin• concerned with the design and manufacture of the pla• used in industrial chemical processes.
▸ **chemical engineer** *n*

chemical warfare *n* warfare using asphyxiating •• nerve gases, poisons, defoliants, etc.

chemiluminescence (ˌkɛmɪˌluːmɪˈnɛsəns) *n* the ph• nomenon in which a chemical reaction leads to th• emission of light without incandescence.
▸ ˌchemiˌlumi'nescent *adj*

chemin de fer (ʃəˈmæn də ˈfɛə) *n* a gambling game, variation of baccarat. [F: railway, referring to the fa• tempo of the game]

chemise (ʃəˈmiːz) *n* **1** an unwaisted loose-fitting dre• hanging straight from the shoulders. **2** a loose shirtlik• undergarment. ◆ Also called: **shift.** [C14: from OF: shir• from LL *camisa*]

chemist ('kɛmɪst) *n* **1** *Brit.* a shop selling medicines, co• metics, etc. **2** *Brit.* a qualified dispenser of prescribe• medicines. **3** a person studying, trained in, or engaged i• chemistry. [C16: from earlier *chimist*, from NL, shor• ened from Med. L *alchimista* ALCHEMIST]

chemistry ('kɛmɪstrɪ) *n, pl* **chemistries. 1** the branch •• physical science concerned with the composition, prop• erties, and reactions of substances. **2** the compositio• properties, and reactions of a particular substance. **3** th• nature and effects of any complex phenomenon: *th• chemistry of humour.* [C17: from earlier *chimistrie*, fron• *chimist* CHEMIST]

Chemnitz ★ (*German* 'kɛmnɪts) *n* a city in E Germany, i• Saxony at the foot of the Erzgebirge: textiles, engineer• ing. Pop.: 274 162 (1995 est.). Also called (1953–90)• **Karl-Marx-Stadt.**

chemo-, chemi-, *or before a vowel* **chem-** *combinin• form.* indicating that chemicals or chemical reactions ar• involved: *chemotherapy.* [NL, from LGk *khēmeia*; see A• CHEMY]

chemoreceptor (ˌkiːməʊrɪˈsɛptə) *or* **chemoceptor •** a sensory receptor in a biological cell membrane t• which an external molecule binds to generate a smell o• taste sensation.

chemosynthesis (ˌkiːməʊˈsɪnθɪsɪs) *n* the formation o• organic material by some bacteria using energy fron• simple chemical reactions.

chemotherapy (ˌkiːməʊˈθɛrəpɪ) *n* treatment of disease• esp. cancer, by means of chemical agents. Cf. **radio• therapy.**
▸ ˌchemo'therapist *n*

Chemulpo ★ (ˌtʃɛmʊlˈpəʊ) *n* a former name of **Inchon.**

chemurgy ('kɛmɜːdʒɪ) *n* the branch of chemistry con• cerned with the industrial use of organic raw materials• esp. of agricultural origin.
▸ chem'urgic *or* chem'urgical *adj*

Chenab ★ (tʃɪˈnæb) *n* a river rising in the Himalayas an• flowing southwest to the Sutlej River in Pakistan• Length: 1087 km (675 miles).

Cheng-chiang ★ ('tʃɛŋ'tʃæŋ) *n* a variant transliteratio• of the Chinese name for **Jinjiang.**

Chengchow *or* **Cheng-chou** ★ ('tʃɛŋ'tʃəʊ) *n* a varian• transliteration of the Chinese name for **Zhengzhou.**

Chengde, Chengteh, *or* **Ch'eng-te** ★ ('tʃɛŋ'teɪ) *n* a• city in NE China, in Hebei on the Luan River: summe•

residence of the Manchu emperors. Pop.: 246 799 (1990 est.).

hengdu, Chengtu, or **Ch'eng-tu** ★ ('tʃɛŋ'tuː) n a city in S central China, capital of Sichuan province. Pop.: 2 810 000 (1991 est.).

hénier ★ (French ʃenje) n **1 André (Marie de)** (ɑ̃dre). 1762–94, French poet; guillotined during the French Revolution. **2** his brother, **Marie-Joseph (Blaise de)** (mariʒozɛf). 1764–1811, French dramatist and politician.

henille (ʃə'niːl) n **1** a thick soft tufty silk or worsted velvet cord or yarn used in embroidery and for trimmings, etc. **2** a fabric of such yarn. **3** a carpet of such fabric. [C18: from F, lit.: hairy caterpillar, from L canicula, dim. of canis dog]

hennai ★ (tʃɪ'naɪ) n the official name for **Madras**.

heongsam (tʃɒŋ'sæm) n a straight dress with a stand-up collar and a slit in one side of the skirt, worn by Chinese women. [from Chinese ch'ang shan long jacket]

heops ★ ('kiːɒps) n original name Khufu. Egyptian king of the fourth dynasty (?2613–?2494 B.C.), who built the largest pyramid at El Gîza.

hepstow ★ ('tʃɛpstəu) n a town in S Wales, in Monmouthshire on the River Wye: tourism, light industry. Pop.: 9461 (1991).

heque or US **check** (tʃɛk) n **1** a bill of exchange drawn on a bank by the holder of a current account. **2** Austral. & NZ. the total sum of money received for contract work or a crop. **3** Austral. & NZ. wages. [C18: from CHECK, in the sense: means of verification]

heque account n an account at a bank or a building society upon which cheques can be drawn.

hequebook or US **checkbook** ('tʃɛk,buk) n a book of detachable blank cheques issued by a bank or building society to holders of cheque accounts.

hequebook journalism n the practice of securing exclusive rights to material for newspaper stories by paying a high price, regardless of any moral implications.

heque card n a card issued by a bank or building society, guaranteeing payment of a customer's cheques up to a stated value.

hequer or US **checker** ('tʃɛkə) n **1** any of the marbles, pegs, or other pieces used in the game of Chinese chequers. **2a** a pattern of squares. **2b** one of the squares in such a pattern. ◆ vb (tr) **3** to make irregular in colour or character; variegate. **4** to mark off with alternating squares of colour. ◆ See also **chequers**. [C13: chessboard, from Anglo-F escheker, from eschec CHECK]

hequered or esp. US **checkered** ('tʃɛkəd) adj marked by fluctuations of fortune (esp. in a **chequered career**).

hequers ('tʃɛkəz) n (functioning as sing) another name for **draughts**.

Chequers ★ ('tʃɛkəz) n an estate and country house in S England, in central Buckinghamshire: the official country residence of the British prime minister.

Cher ★ (French ʃer) n **1** a department of central France, in E Centre region. Capital: Bourges. Pop.: 320 174 (1982). Area: 7304 sq. km (2849 sq. miles). **2** a river in central France, rising in the Massif Central and flowing northwest to the Loire. Length: 354 km (220 miles).

Cherbourg ★ ('ʃɛəbuəg; French ʃerbur) n a port in NW France, on the English Channel. Pop.: 28 773 (1990).

Cherenkov or **Cerenkov** ★ (tʃɪ'rɛŋkɒf; Russian tʃɪr'rjɛnkəf) n **Pavel Alekseyevich** ('pavʲɪl alʲɪk'sjejɪvɪtʃ). 1904–90, Soviet physicist: noted for his work on the effects produced by high-energy particles: shared Nobel prize for physics 1958.

Cheribon ★ ('tʃɪərə,bɒn) n a variant spelling of **Tjirebon**.

cherish ('tʃɛrɪʃ) vb (tr) **1** to feel or show great tenderness or care for. **2** to cling fondly to (a hope, idea, etc.); nurse: to cherish ambitions. [C14: from OF, from cher dear, from L cārus]

Chernenko ★ (tʃɜː'njɛnkəu; Russian tʃɪr'nɪnkə) n **Konstantin (Ustinovich)** (kənstan'tin). 1911–85, Soviet statesman; general secretary of the Soviet Communist Party (1984–85).

Chernobyl ★ (tʃɜː'nəubʲl, -'nɒbʲl) n a town in the N

Ukraine; site of a nuclear power station accident in 1986.

Chernovtsy ★ (Russian tʃɪrnaf'tsi) n a city in the Ukraine on the Prut River: formerly under Polish, Austro-Hungarian, and Romanian rule; part of the Soviet Union (1947–91). Pop.: 261 000 (1996 est.). German name: **Czernowitz**. Romanian name: **Cernăuţi**.

chernozem ('tʃɜːnəu,zɛm) n a rich black soil found in temperate semiarid regions, such as the grasslands of Russia. [from Russian chernaya zemlya black earth]

Cherokee ('tʃɛrə,kiː) n **1** (pl **Cherokees** or **Cherokee**) a member of a North American Indian people formerly living in the Appalachian Mountains. **2** the Iroquois language of this people.

cheroot (ʃə'ruːt) n a cigar with both ends cut off squarely. [C17: from Tamil curuttu curl, roll]

cherry ('tʃɛrɪ) n, pl **cherries. 1** any of several trees of the genus Prunus, having a small fleshy rounded fruit containing a hard stone. **2** the fruit or wood of any of these trees. **3** any of various unrelated plants, such as the ground cherry and Jerusalem cherry. **4a** a bright red colour; cerise. **4b** (as adj): a cherry coat. **5** Taboo sl. virginity or the hymen as its symbol. [C14: back formation from OE ciris (mistakenly thought to be pl), ult. from LL ceresia, ?from L cerasus cherry tree, from Gk kerasios]

cherry tomato n a miniature tomato not much bigger than a cherry.

chert (tʃɜːt) n an impure black or grey microcrystalline variety of quartz that resembles flint. [C17: from ?]
▸ **'cherty** adj

Chertsey ★ ('tʃɜːtsɪ) n a town in S England, in N Surrey on the River Thames. Pop.: 11 786 (1991).

cherub ('tʃɛrəb) n, pl **cherubs** or (for sense 1) **cherubim** ('tʃɛrəbɪm, -ubɪm). **1** a member of the second order of angels, often represented as a winged child. **2** an innocent or sweet child. [OE, from Heb. kěrūbh]
▸ **cherubic** (tʃə'ruːbɪk) or **che'rubical** adj ▸ **che'rubically** adv

Cherubini ★ (,kɛru'biːnɪ) n **(Maria) Luigi (Carlo Zenobio Salvatore)** ('lwiːdʒɪ). 1760–1842, Italian composer, noted for his church music and his operas.

chervil ('tʃɜːvɪl) n an aromatic umbelliferous Eurasian plant with small white flowers and aniseed-flavoured leaves used as herbs in soups and salads. [OE cerfelle, from L, from Gk, from khairein to enjoy + phullon leaf]

Cherwell ★ ('tʃɜːwəl) n **Frederick Alexander Lindemann** ('lɪndəmən), Baron. 1886–1957, British physicist, born in Germany. He was scientific adviser to Winston Churchill during World War II.

Ches. abbrev. for Cheshire.

Chesapeake Bay ★ ('tʃɛsə,piːk) n the largest inlet of the Atlantic in the coast of the US: bordered by Maryland and Virginia.

Cheshire[1] ★ ('tʃɛʃə, 'tʃɛʃɪə) n a county of NW England: low-lying and undulating, bordering on the Pennines in the east; mainly agricultural. Administrative centre: Chester. Pop.: 975 600 (1994 est.). Area: 2328 sq. km (899 sq. miles). Abbrev.: **Ches.**

Cheshire[2] ★ ('tʃɛʃə) n **(Geoffrey) Leonard**, Baron. 1917–92, British philanthropist: awarded the Victoria Cross in World War II; founded the Leonard Cheshire Foundation Homes for the Disabled: married to Sue, Baroness Ryder.

Cheshire cheese n a mild-flavoured cheese with a crumbly texture, originally made in Cheshire.

chess (tʃɛs) n a game of skill for two players using a chessboard on which chessmen are moved. The object is to checkmate the opponent's king. [C13: from OF esches, pl. of eschec CHECK]

chessboard ('tʃɛs,bɔːd) n a square board divided into 64 squares of two alternating colours, used for playing chess or draughts.

chessman ('tʃɛs,mæn, -mən) n, pl **chessmen.** any of the pieces and pawns used in a game of chess. [C17: from chessmen, from ME chessemeyne chess company]

chest (tʃɛst) n **1a** the front part of the trunk from the neck to the belly. Related adj: **pectoral. 1b** (as modifier): a

chest cold. **2 get (something) off one's chest.** *Inf.* to unburden oneself of troubles, worries, etc., by talking about them. **3** a box used for storage or shipping: *a tea chest.* [OE *cest,* from L, from Gk *kistē* box]
▶ **'chested** *adj*

Chester ★ ('tʃɛstə) *n* a city in NW England, administrative centre of Cheshire, on the River Dee: intact surrounding walls; 16th- and 17th-century double-tier shops. Pop.: 80 110 (1991). Latin name: **Deva.**

chesterfield ('tʃɛstə,fiːld) *n* **1** a man's overcoat, usually with a velvet collar. **2** a large tightly stuffed sofa, with straight upholstered arms of the same height as the back. [C19: after a 19th-cent. Earl of *Chesterfield*]

Chesterfield[1] ★ ('tʃɛstə,fiːld) *n* an industrial town in N central England, in Derbyshire: famous 14th-century church with twisted spire. Pop.: 71 945 (1991).

Chesterfield[2] ★ ('tʃɛstə,fiːld) *n* Philip Dormer Stanhope, 4th Earl of Chesterfield. 1694–1773, British statesman and writer; author of *Letters to His Son* (1774).

Chesterton ★ ('tʃɛstət°n) *n* G(ilbert) K(eith). 1874–1936, British writer, noted for his Father Brown detective stories and his novels including *The Napoleon of Notting Hill* (1904).

chestnut ('tʃɛs,nʌt) *n* **1** a N temperate tree such as the **sweet** or **Spanish chestnut,** which produces flowers in long catkins and nuts in a prickly bur. Cf. **horse chestnut. 2** the edible nut of any of these trees. **3** the hard wood of any of these trees, used in making furniture, etc. **4a** a reddish-brown colour. **4b** *(as adj):* chestnut hair. **5** a horse of a golden-brown colour. **6** *Inf.* an old or stale joke. [C16: from earlier *chesten nut: chesten,* from OF, from L, from Gk *kastanea*]

chest of drawers *n* a piece of furniture consisting of a set of drawers in a frame.

chesty ('tʃɛstɪ) *adj* **chestier, chestiest.** *Inf.* **1** *Brit.* suffering from or symptomatic of chest disease: *a chesty cough.* **2** having a large well-developed chest or bosom.
▶ **'chestiness** *n*

cheval glass (ʃə'væl) *n* a full-length mirror mounted so as to swivel within a frame. [C19: from F *cheval* support (lit.: horse)]

chevalier (,ʃɛ'vælɪə) *n* **1** a member of certain orders of merit, such as the French Legion of Honour. **2** the lowest title of rank in the old French nobility. **3** an archaic word for **knight. 4** a chivalrous man; gallant. [C14: from OF, from Med. L *caballārius* horseman, CAVALIER]

Chevalier ★ *n* **1** (,ʃɛvə'lɪə). **Albert.** 1861–1923, British music-hall entertainer, remembered for his cockney songs. **2** (,ʃɛ'vælɪə; *French* ʃəvalje). **Maurice.** 1888–1972, French singer and film actor.

Cheviot ('tʃiːvɪət, 'tʃɛv–) *n* **1** a large British breed of sheep reared for its wool. **2** *(often not cap.)* a rough twill-weave woollen suiting fabric.

Cheviot Hills ★ *pl n* a range of hills on the border between England and Scotland, mainly in Northumberland.

chèvre ('ʃɛvrə) *n* any cheese made from goats' milk. [C20: from F, lit.: goat]

chevron ('ʃɛvrən) *n* **1** *Mil.* a badge or insignia consisting of one or more V-shaped stripes to indicate a noncommissioned rank or length of service. **2** *Heraldry.* an inverted V-shaped charge on a shield. **3** *(usually pl)* a pattern of horizontal black and white V-shapes on a road sign indicating a sharp bend. **4** any V-shaped pattern or device. [C14: from OF, ult. from L *caper* goat; cf. L *capreoli* pair of rafters (lit.: little goats)]

chevrotain ('ʃɛvrə,teɪn, -tɪn) *n* a small timid ruminant mammal of S and SE Asia. Also called: **mouse deer.** [C18: from F, from OF *chevrot* kid, from *chèvre* goat, ult. from L *caper* goat]

chevy ('tʃɛvɪ) *n, vb* a variant spelling of **chivy.**

chew (tʃuː) *vb* **1** to work the jaws and teeth in order to grind (food); masticate. **2** to bite repeatedly: *she chewed her nails anxiously.* **3** *(intr)* to use chewing tobacco. **4 chew the fat** or **rag.** *Sl.* **4a** to argue over a point. **4b** to talk idly; gossip. ◆ *n* **5** the act of chewing. **6** something that is chewed. [OE *ceowan*]
▶ **'chewable** *adj* ▶ **'chewer** *n*

chewing gum *n* a preparation for chewing, usual• made of flavoured and sweetened chicle or such subst• tutes as polyvinyl acetate.

chew over *vb* (*tr, adv*) to consider carefully.

chewy ('tʃuːɪ) *adj* **chewier, chewiest.** of a consistency r• quiring chewing.

Cheyenne ★ (ʃaɪ'æn, -'ɛn) *n* a city in SE Wyoming, cap• tal of the state. Pop.: 50 008 (1990).

chez *French.* (ʃe) *prep* **1** at the home of. **2** with, among, • in the manner of.

chi[1] (kaɪ) *n* the 22nd letter of the Greek alphabet (X, χ).

chi[2] *or* **ch'i** *or* **qi** (tʃiː) *n* (*sometimes cap.*) (in Oriental med• cine, martial arts, etc.) vital energy believed to circula• round the body in currents. [Chinese, lit.: energy]

chiack *or* **chyack** ('tʃaɪæk) *Austral inf.* ◆ *vb* (*tr*) **1** t• tease or banter. ◆ *n* **2** good-humoured banter. [C1• from *chi-hike,* a shout of greeting]

Chiang Ch'ing ★ ('tʃæŋ 'tʃɪŋ) *n* a variant transliteratio• of the Chinese name for **Jiang Qing.**

Chiang Ching-kuo ('tʃæŋ tʃɪŋ'kwəʊ) *or* **Jiang Jin• Guo** ★ *n* 1910–88, Chinese statesman; the son o• Chiang Kai-shek. He was prime minister of Taiwa• (1971–78); president (1978–88).

Chiang Kai-shek ('tʃæŋ kaɪ'ʃɛk) *or* **Jiang Jie Shi** ★ • original name *Chiang Chung-cheng,* 1887–1975, Chines• general: president of China (1928–31; 1943–49) and o• the Republic of China (Taiwan) (1950–75). As chairma• of the Kuomintang, he allied with the Communist• against the Japanese (1937–45), but in the Civil War tha• followed was forced to withdraw to Taiwan.

chianti (kɪ'æntɪ) *n* (*sometimes cap.*) a dry red wine pro• duced in Tuscany, Italy.

Chiapas ★ (*Spanish* 'tʃjapas) *n* a state of S Mexico: moun• tainous and forested; Maya ruins in the northeast; ric• mineral resources. Capital: Tuxtla Gutiérrez. Pop.• 3 606 828 (1995 est.). Area: 73 887 sq. km (28 816 sq• miles).

chiaroscuro (kɪ,ɑːrə'skʊərəʊ) *n, pl* **chiaroscuros. 1** the ar• tistic distribution of light and dark masses in a picture. **2** monochrome painting using light and dark only. [C17• from It., from *chiaro* CLEAR + *oscuro* OBSCURE]

chiasma (kaɪ'æzmə) *n, pl* **chiasmas, chiasmata** (-mətə) **1** *Cytology.* the cross-shaped connection produced by th• crossing over of pairing chromosomes during meiosis. **2** *Anat.* the crossing over of two parts or structures. [C19• from Gk *khiasma,* from *khi* CHI[1]]

chiasmus (kaɪ'æzməs) *n, pl* **chiasmi** (-maɪ). *Rhetoric.* re• versal of word order in the second of two paralle• phrases: *he came in triumph and in defeat departs.* [N• from Gk: see CHIASMA]
▶ **chiastic** (kaɪ'æstɪk) *adj*

Chiba ★ ('tʃiːbə) *n* an industrial city in central Japan, in• SE Honshu on Tokyo Bay. Pop.: 856 882 (1995).

chic (ʃiːk, ʃɪk) *adj* **1** (esp. of fashionable clothes, women• etc.) stylish or elegant. ◆ *n* **2** stylishness, esp. in dress• modishness; fashionable good taste. [C19: from F, from• ?]
▶ **'chicly** *adv*

Chicago ★ (ʃɪ'kɑːgəʊ) *n* a port in NE Illinois, on Lake• Michigan: the third largest city in the US; it is a• major railway and air traffic centre. Pop.: 2 731 743• (1994 est.).

chicane (ʃɪ'keɪn) *n* **1** a bridge or whist hand without• trumps. **2** *Motor racing.* a short section of sharp narrow• bends formed by barriers placed on a motor-racing cir• cuit. **3** a less common word for **chicanery.** ◆ *vb* **chicanes,• chicaning, chicaned. 4** (*tr*) to deceive or trick by chicanery.• **5** (*intr*) to use tricks or chicanery. [C17: from F *chicaner* to quibble, from ?]
▶ **chi'caner** *n*

chicanery (ʃɪ'keɪnərɪ) *n, pl* **chicaneries. 1** verbal decep• tion or trickery, dishonest or sharp practice. **2** a trick, de• ception, or quibble.

chicano (tʃɪ'kɑːnəʊ) *n, pl* **chicanos.** *US.* an American citi• zen of Mexican origin. [C20: from Sp. *mejicano* Mexi• can]

hichagof Island ★ ('tʃɪtʃə,gɔːf) *n* an island of Alaska, in the Alexander Archipelago. Area: 5439 sq. km (2100 sq. miles).

hichen Itzá ★ (*Spanish* tʃi'tʃen it'sa) *n* a village in Yucatán state in Mexico: site of important Mayan ruins.

hichester[1] ★ ('tʃɪtʃɪstə) *n* a city in S England, administrative centre of West Sussex: Roman ruins; 11th-century cathedral; Festival Theatre. Pop.: 26 572 (1991).

hichester[2] ★ ('tʃɪtʃɪstə) *n* **Sir Francis.** 1901–72, British yachtsman, who sailed alone round the world (1966–67).

hichi ('ʃiː,ʃiː) *adj* **1** affectedly pretty or stylish. ◆ *n* **2** the quality of being affectedly pretty or stylish. [C20: from F]

hichihaerh *or* **Ch'i-ch'i-haerh** ★ ('tʃiː,tʃiː'hɑː) *n* a variant transliteration of the Chinese name for **Qiqihar**.

hick (tʃɪk) *n* **1** the young of a bird, esp. of a domestic fowl. **2** *Sl.* a girl or young woman, esp. an attractive one. **3** a young child: used as a term of endearment. [C14: short for CHICKEN]

hickadee ('tʃɪkə,diː) *n* any of various small North American songbirds, typically having grey-and-black plumage. [C19: imit.]

hicken ('tʃɪkɪn) *n* **1** a domestic fowl bred for its flesh or eggs. **2** the flesh of such a bird used for food. **3** any of various similar birds, such as a prairie chicken. **4** *Sl.* a cowardly person. **5** *Sl.* a young inexperienced person. **6** *Inf.* any of various, often dangerous, games or challenges in which the object is to make one's opponent lose his nerve. **7** count one's chickens before they are hatched. to be over-optimistic in acting on expectations which are not yet fulfilled. ◆ *adj* **8** *Sl.* easily scared; cowardly; timid. [OE *ciecen*]

hicken feed *n Sl.* a trifling amount of money.

hicken-hearted *or* **chicken-livered** *adj* easily frightened; cowardly.

hicken out *vb* (*intr, adv*) *Inf.* to fail to do something through fear or lack of conviction.

hickenpox ('tʃɪkɪn,pɒks) *n* a highly communicable viral disease most commonly affecting children, characterized by slight fever and the eruption of a rash.

hicken wire *n* wire netting with a hexagonal mesh.

hickpea ('tʃɪk,piː) *n* **1** a bushy leguminous plant, cultivated for its edible pealike seeds. **2** the seed of this plant. [C16 *ciche peasen*, from *ciche* (from F, from L *cicer* chickpea) + *peasen*; see PEA]

hickweed ('tʃɪk,wiːd) *n* any of various plants of the pink family, esp. a common garden weed with small white flowers.

hiclayo ★ (*Spanish* tʃi'klajo) *n* a city in NW Peru. Pop.: 668 066 (1995).

hicle ('tʃɪkəl) *n* a gumlike substance obtained from the sapodilla; the main ingredient of chewing gum. [from Sp., from Nahuatl *chictli*]

hicory ('tʃɪkərɪ) *n, pl* **chicories. 1** a blue-flowered plant, cultivated for its leaves, which are used in salads, and for its roots. **2** the root of this plant, roasted, dried, and used as a coffee substitute. ◆ Cf. **endive.** [C15: from OF, from L *cichorium*, from Gk *kikhōrion*]

hide (tʃaɪd) *vb* **chides, chiding, chided** *or* **chid** (tʃɪd); **chided, chid** *or* **chidden** ('tʃɪdən). **1** to rebuke or scold. **2** (*tr*) to goad into action. [OE *cīdan*]
  ▸ '**chider** *n* ▸ '**chidingly** *adv*

hief (tʃiːf) *n* **1** the head or leader of a group or body of people. **2** *Heraldry.* the upper third of a shield. **3** in chief. primarily; especially. ◆ *adj* **4** (*prenominal*) **4a** most important; principal. **4b** highest in rank or authority. ◆ *adv* **5** *Arch.* principally. [C13: from OF, from L *caput* head]

hief executive *n* the person with overall responsibility for the efficient running of a company, organization, etc.

hief justice *n* **1** (in any of several Commonwealth countries) the judge presiding over a supreme court. **2** (in the US) the presiding judge of a court composed of a number of members. ◆ See also **Lord Chief Justice.**

chiefly ('tʃiːflɪ) *adv* **1** especially or essentially; above all. **2** in general; mainly; mostly. ◆ *adj* **3** of or relating to a chief or chieftain.

Chief of Staff *n* **1** the senior staff officer under the commander of a major military formation or organization. **2** the senior officer of each service of the armed forces.

chief petty officer *n* the senior naval rank for personnel without commissioned or warrant rank.

chieftain ('tʃiːftən, -tɪn) *n* the head or leader of a tribe or clan. [C14: from OF, from LL *capitāneus* commander; see CAPTAIN]
  ▸ '**chieftaincy** *or* '**chieftain,ship** *n*

chief technician *n* a noncommissioned officer in the Royal Air Force, junior to a flight sergeant.

chiffchaff ('tʃɪf,tʃæf) *n* a common European warbler with a yellowish-brown plumage. [C18: imit.]

chiffon (ʃɪ'fɒn, 'ʃɪfɒn) *n* **1** a fine almost transparent fabric of silk, nylon, etc. **2** (*often pl*) *Now rare.* feminine finery. ◆ *adj* **3** made of chiffon. **4** (of soufflés, pies, cakes, etc.) having a very light fluffy texture. [C18: from F, from *chiffe* rag]

chiffonier *or* **chiffonnier** (,ʃɪfə'nɪə) *n* **1** a tall, elegant chest of drawers. **2** a wide low open-fronted cabinet. [C19: from F, from *chiffon* rag]

Chifley ★ ('tʃɪflɪ) *n* **Joseph Benedict.** 1885–1951, Australian statesman; prime minister (1945–49).

chigetai (,tʃɪgɪ'taɪ) *n* a variety of the Asiatic wild ass of Mongolia. Also spelled: **dziggetai.** [from Mongolian *tchikhitei* long-eared, from *tchikhi* ear]

chigger ('tʃɪgə) *n* **1** *US & Canad.* the parasitic larva of a mite, which causes intense itching. **2** another name for **chigoe.**

chignon ('ʃiːnjɒn) *n* an arrangement of long hair in a roll or knot at the back of the head. [C18: from F, from OF *chaignon* link, from *chaine* CHAIN; infl. also by OF *tignon* coil of hair]

chigoe ('tʃɪgəʊ) *n* **1** a tropical flea, the female of which burrows into the skin of its host, which includes man. **2** another name for **chigger.** [C17: from Carib *chigo*]

Chigwell ★ ('tʃɪgwəl) *n* a town in S England, in W Essex. Pop.: 10 332 (1991).

Chihli ★ ('tʃiːliː) *n* **Gulf of.** another name for the **Bohai.**

Chihuahua ★ (tʃɪ'wɑːwɑː, -wə) *n* **1** a state of N Mexico: mostly high plateau; important mineral resources, with many silver mines. Capital: Chihuahua. Pop.: 2 792 989 (1995 est.). Area: 247 087 sq. km (153 194 sq. miles). **2** a city in N Mexico, capital of Chihuahua state. Pop.: 516 153 (1990). **3** a breed of tiny dog originally from Mexico, having short smooth hair, large erect ears, and protruding eyes.

chilblain ('tʃɪl,bleɪn) *n* (*usually pl*) an inflammation of the fingers or toes, caused by exposure to cold. [C16: from CHILL (n) + BLAIN]
  ▸ '**chil,blained** *adj*

child (tʃaɪld) *n, pl* **children. 1a** a boy or girl between birth and puberty. **1b** (*as modifier*): *child labour.* **2** a baby or infant. **3** an unborn baby. **4** with child. an old-fashioned term for **pregnant. 5** a human offspring; a son or daughter. Related adj: **filial. 6** a childish or immature person. **7** a member of a family or tribe; descendant: *a child of Israel.* **8** a person or thing regarded as the product of an influence or environment: *a child of nature.* [OE *cild*]
  ▸ '**childless** *adj* ▸ '**childlessness** *n*

child abuse *n* physical, sexual, or emotional ill-treatment of a child by its parents or other adults responsible for its welfare.

child-bearing *n* **a** the act or process of carrying and giving birth to a child. **b** (*as modifier*): *of child-bearing age.*

childbed ('tʃaɪld,bɛd) *n* (*often preceded by in*) the condition of giving birth to a child.

child benefit *n* (in Britain and New Zealand) a regular government payment to parents of children up to a certain age.

childbirth ('tʃaɪld,bɜːθ) *n* the act of giving birth to a child.

childcare ('tʃaɪld,keə) n Brit. **1** care provided for children without homes (or with a seriously disturbed home life) by a local authority. **2** care and supervision of children whose parents are working, provided by a childminder or local authority.

child endowment n (in Australia) a social security payment for dependent children.

Childers ★ ('tʃɪldəz) n (**Robert**) **Erskine.** 1870–1922, Irish politician, executed by the Irish Free State for his IRA activities: author of *The Riddle of the Sands* (1903).

childhood ('tʃaɪldhʊd) n the condition of being a child; the period of life before puberty.

childish ('tʃaɪldɪʃ) adj **1** in the manner of or suitable to a child. **2** foolish or petty: *childish fears.*
▶ '**childishly** adv ▶ '**childishness** n

childlike ('tʃaɪld,laɪk) adj like or befitting a child, as in being innocent, trustful, etc.

childminder ('tʃaɪld,maɪndə) n a person who looks after children, esp. those whose parents are working.

children ('tʃɪldrən) n the plural of **child.**

Children of Israel pl n the Jewish people or nation.

child-resistant adj (of packaging etc., esp. of drugs) designed to be difficult for children to open or tamper with. Also: **child-proof.**

child's play n Inf. something easy to do.

chile ('tʃɪlɪ) n a variant spelling of **chilli.**

Chile ★ ('tʃɪlɪ) n a republic in South America, on the Pacific, with a total length of about 4090 km (2650 miles) and an average width of only 177 km (110 miles): gained independence from Spain in 1818; the government of President Allende (elected 1970) attempted the implementation of Marxist policies within a democratic system until overthrown by a military coup (1973); democracy restored 1988. Chile consists chiefly of the Andes in the east, the Atacama Desert in the north, a central fertile region, and a huge S region of almost uninhabitable mountains, glaciers, fjords, and islands; an important producer of copper, iron ore, nitrates, etc. Language: Spanish. Religion: Roman Catholic. Currency: peso. Capital: Santiago. Pop.: 14 583 000 (1997). Area: 756 945 sq. km (292 256 sq. miles).
▶ '**Chilean** adj, n

Chile pine n another name for the **monkey puzzle.**

Chile saltpetre or **nitre** n a naturally occurring form of sodium nitrate.

chiliad ('kɪlɪ,æd) n **1** a group of one thousand. **2** one thousand years. [C16: from Gk, from *khilioi* a thousand]

chill (tʃɪl) n **1** a moderate coldness. **2** a sensation of coldness resulting from a cold or damp environment, or from a sudden emotional reaction. **3** a feverish cold. **4** a check on enthusiasm or joy. ◆ adj **5** another word for **chilly.** ◆ vb **6** to make or become cold. **7** (tr) to cool or freeze (food, drinks, etc.). **8** (tr) **8a** to depress (enthusiasm, etc.). **8b** to discourage. **9** (intr) Sl., chiefly US. to relax; calm oneself. ◆ See also **chill out.** [OE *ciele*]
▶ '**chilling** adj ▶ '**chillingly** adv ▶ '**chillness** n

chiller ('tʃɪlə) n **1** short for **spine-chiller. 2** NZ. a refrigerated storage area for meat.

chilli or **chili** ('tʃɪlɪ) n, pl **chillies** or **chilies.** the small red hot-tasting pod of a type of capsicum used for flavouring sauces, etc. [C17: from Sp., from Nahuatl *chilli*]

chilli con carne ('tʃɪlɪ kɒn 'kɑːnɪ) n a highly seasoned Mexican dish of meat, onions, beans, and chilli powder. [from Sp.: chilli with meat]

chilli dog n US. a frankfurter garnished with chilli con carne, served in a roll.

chilli powder n ground chilli blended with other spices.

chilli sauce n a highly seasoned sauce made of tomatoes cooked with chilli and other spices.

chill out Inf. ◆ vb **1** (intr, adv) to relax, esp. after energetic dancing at a rave. ◆ adj **chill-out. 2** suitable for relaxation after energetic dancing: *a chill-out area; chill-out music.*

chilly ('tʃɪlɪ) adj **chillier, chilliest. 1** causing or feeling cool

or moderately cold. **2** without warmth; unfriendly. **3** (of people) sensitive to cold.
▶ '**chilliness** n

chilly bin n NZ inf. a portable insulated container wit provision for packing food and drink in ice.

Chiloé Island ★ (,tʃɪləʊ'eɪ) n an island administered b Chile, off the W coast of South America in the Pacifi Ocean: timber. Pop.: 116 000 (1984 est.). Area: 8394 s km (3240 sq. miles).

Chilpancingo ★ (Spanish tʃilpan'θiŋgo) n a town in Mexico, capital of Guerrero state, in the Sierra Madre d Sur. Pop.: 136 243 (1990).

Chiltern Hills ★ ('tʃɪltən) pl n a range of low chalk hil in SE England extending northwards from the Tham valley. Highest point: 260 m (852 ft).

Chiltern Hundreds ('tʃɪltən) pl n (in Britain) short fo **Stewardship of the Chiltern Hundreds;** a nominal office tha an MP applies for in order to resign his seat.

Chilung or **Chi-lung** ★ ('tʃiː'lʊŋ) n a port in N Taiwa fishing and industrial centre. Pop.: 370 049 (1996 est. Also called: **Keelung, Kilung.**

Chimborazo ★ (,tʃɪmbə'rɑːzəʊ, -'reɪ-; Spanish tʃimbo 'raθo) n an extinct volcano in central Ecuador, in th Andes: the highest peak in Ecuador. Height: 6267 n (20 561 ft).

Chimbote ★ (Spanish tʃim'bote) n a port in N centra Peru: contains Peru's first steelworks (1958), using hy droelectric power from the Santa River. Pop.: 268 97 (1993).

chime[1] (tʃaɪm) n **1** an individual bell or the sound i makes when struck. **2** (often pl) the machinery employe to sound a bell in this way. **3** Also called: **bell.** a percus sion instrument consisting of a set of vertical meta tubes of graduated length, suspended in a frame an struck with a hammer. **4** agreement; concord. ◆ v **chimes, chiming, chimed. 5a** to sound (a bell) or (of a bell) t be sounded by a clapper or hammer. **5b** to produc (music or sounds) by chiming. **6** (tr) to indicate or sho (time or the hours) by chiming. **7** (intr; foll. by with) t agree or harmonize. [C13: prob. shortened from earlie *chymbe bell*, ult. from L *cymbalum* CYMBAL]
▶ '**chimer** n

chime[2], **chimb** (tʃaɪm), or **chine** n the projecting rin of a cask or barrel. [OE *cimb-*]

chime in vb (intr, adv) Inf. **1** to join in or interrupt (a con versation), esp. repeatedly and unwelcomely. **2** to voic agreement.

chimera or **chimaera** (kaɪ'mɪərə, kɪ-) n **1** a wild an unrealistic dream or notion. **2** (often cap.) Greek myth. fire-breathing monster with the head of a lion, body o goat, and tail of a serpent. **3** a fabulous beast made up o parts taken from various animals. **4** Biol. an organism consisting of at least two genetically different kinds o tissue as a result of mutation, grafting, etc. [C16: from L, from Gk *khimaira* she-goat]

chimerical (kaɪ'merɪk°l, kɪ-) or **chimeric** adj **1** wildly fanciful; imaginary. **2** given to or indulging in fantasies.
▶ chi'**merically** adv

Chimkent ★ (tʃim'kent) n a city in S Kazakhstan: a major railway junction. Pop.: 397 600 (1995 est.).

chimney ('tʃɪmnɪ) n **1** a vertical structure of brick, ma sonry, or steel that carries smoke or steam away from a fire, engine, etc. **2** another name for **flue** (sense 1). **3** shor for **chimney stack. 4** an open-ended glass tube fitting around the flame of an oil or gas lamp in order to ex clude draughts. **5** Brit. a fireplace, esp. an old and large one. **6** the vent of a volcano. **7** Mountaineering. a vertica fissure large enough for a person's body to enter. [C14 from OF *cheminée*, from LL *camīnāta*, from L *camīnus* fur nace, from Gk *kaminos* oven]

chimney breast n the wall or walls that surround the base of a chimney or fireplace.

chimneypot ('tʃɪmnɪ,pɒt) n a short pipe on the top of a chimney.

chimney stack n the part of a chimney that rises above the roof of a building.

★ people and places

himney sweep or **sweeper** n a person who cleans soot from chimneys.

himp (tʃɪmp) n Inf. short for **chimpanzee**.

himpanzee (ˌtʃɪmpæn'zi:) n a gregarious and intelligent anthropoid ape, inhabiting forests in central W Africa. [C18: from Central African dialect]

hin (tʃɪn) n **1** the protruding part of the lower jaw. **2** the front part of the face below the lips. **3 keep one's chin up.** Inf. to keep cheerful under difficult circumstances. **4 take it on the chin.** Inf. to face squarely up to a defeat, adversity, etc. ♦ vb **chins, chinning, chinned. 5** Gymnastics. to raise one's chin to (a horizontal bar, etc.) when hanging by the arms. [OE cinn]

hin. abbrev. for: **1** China. **2** Chinese.

hina ('tʃaɪnə) n **1** ceramic ware of a type originally from China. **2** any porcelain or similar ware. **3** cups, saucers, etc., collectively. **4** (modifier) made of china. [C16 chiny, from Persian chīnī]

hina ★ ('tʃaɪnə) n **1** People's Republic of. Also called: **Communist China, Red China.** a republic in E Asia: the third largest and the most populous country in the world; the oldest continuing civilization (beginning over 2000 years B.C.); republic established in 1911 after the overthrow of the Manchu dynasty by Sun Yat-sen; People's Republic formed in 1949; pro-democracy demonstrations violently suppressed in 1989: contains vast deserts, steppes, great mountain ranges (Himalayas, Kunlun, Tian Shan, and Nan Shan), a central rugged plateau, and intensively cultivated E plains. Language: Chinese in various dialects, the chief of which is Mandarin. Religion: nonreligious majority. Currency: yuan. Capital: Beijing. Pop.: 1 227 740 000 (1997). Area: 9 560 990 sq. km (3 691 502 sq. miles). **2 Republic of.** Also called: **Nationalist China, Taiwan.** a republic (recognized as an independent nation by 28 countries) in E Asia occupying the island of Taiwan, 13 nearby islands, and 64 islands of the Penghu (Pescadores) group: established in 1949 by the Nationalist government of China under Chiang Kaishek after its expulsion by the Communists from the mainland; under US protection 1954–79; lost its seat at the UN to the People's Republic of China in 1971; state of war with the People's Republic of China formally ended in 1991. Language: Mandarin Chinese. Religion: predominantly Buddhist and Taoist. Currency: New Taiwan dollar. Capital: Taipei. Pop.: 21 616 000 (1997). Area: 35 981 sq. km (13 892 sq. miles). Former name: **Formosa.** ♦ Related adj: **Sinitic.**

hina clay n another name for **kaolin.**

Chinagraph ('tʃaɪnəˌɡrɑːf) n Trademark. a coloured pencil used for writing on china, glass, etc.

Chinaman ('tʃaɪnəmən) n, pl **Chinamen. 1** Arch. or derog. a native or inhabitant of China. **2** (often not cap.) Cricket. a ball bowled by a left-handed bowler to a right-handed batsman that spins from off to leg.

Chinan or **Chi-nan** ★ ('tʃi:'næn) n a variant transliteration of the Chinese name for **Jinan.**

China Sea ★ n part of the Pacific Ocean off the coast of China: divided by Taiwan into the East China Sea in the north and the South China Sea in the south.

china stone n **1** a type of kaolinized granitic rock containing unaltered plagioclase. **2** any of certain limestones having a very fine grain and smooth texture.

Chinatown ('tʃaɪnəˌtaʊn) n a quarter of any city or town outside China with a predominantly Chinese population.

chinaware ('tʃaɪnəˌwɛə) n articles made of china, esp. those made for domestic use.

chincherinchee (ˌtʃɪntʃərɪn'tʃiː, -'rɪntʃɪ) n a bulbous South African liliaceous plant having long spikes of white or yellow long-lasting flowers. [from ?]

chinchilla (tʃɪn'tʃɪlə) n **1** a small gregarious rodent inhabiting mountainous regions of South America. It is bred in captivity for its soft silvery grey fur. **2** the highly valued fur of this animal. **3** a thick napped woollen cloth used for coats. [C17: from Sp., ?from Aymara]

chin-chin sentence substitute. Inf. a greeting or toast. [C18: from Chinese (Peking) ch'ing-ch'ing, please-please]

Chin-Chou or **Chin-chow** ★ ('tʃɪn'tʃaʊ) n a variant transliteration of the Chinese name for **Jinzhou.**

Chindit ('tʃɪndɪt) n a member of the Allied forces fighting behind the Japanese lines in Burma (1943–45). [C20: from Burmese chinthé a fabulous lion]

Chindwin ★ ('tʃɪn'dwɪn) n a river in N Myanmar, rising in the Kumôn Range and flowing northwest then south to the Irrawaddy, of which it is the main tributary. Length: about 966 km (600 miles).

chine[1] (tʃaɪn) n **1** the backbone. **2** the backbone of an animal with adjoining meat, cut for cooking. **3** a ridge or crest of land. ♦ vb **chines, chining, chined. 4** (tr) to cut (meat) along or across the backbone. [C14: from OF eschine, of Gmc origin; see SHIN]

chine[2] (tʃaɪn) n S English dialect. a deep fissure in the wall of a cliff. [OE cīnan to crack]

Chinese (tʃaɪ'niːz) adj **1** of, relating to, or characteristic of China, its people, or their languages. ♦ n **2** (pl **Chinese**) a native or inhabitant of China or a descendant of one. **3** any of the languages of China.

Chinese cabbage n **1** a Chinese plant that is related to the cabbage and has crisp edible leaves growing in a loose cylindrical head. **2** another name for **bok choy.**

Chinese chequers n (functioning as sing) a board game played with marbles or pegs.

Chinese Empire ★ n China as ruled by the emperors until the establishment of the republic in 1911–12.

Chinese gooseberry n another name for **kiwi fruit.**

Chinese lantern n **1** a collapsible lantern made of thin coloured paper. **2** an Asian plant, cultivated for its attractive orange-red inflated calyx.

Chinese leaf n another name for **bok choy.**

Chinese puzzle n **1** an intricate puzzle, esp. one consisting of boxes within boxes. **2** a complicated problem.

Chinese Turkestan ★ n the E part of the central Asian region of Turkestan: corresponds generally to the present-day Xinjiang Uygur Autonomous Region of China.

Chinese wall n (esp. in financial institutions) a notional barrier between departments in the same company in order to avoid conflicts of interest between them.

Chinghai or **Ch'ing-hai** ★ ('tʃɪŋ'haɪ) n a variant transliteration of the Chinese name for **Qinghai.**

Chingtao or **Ch'ing-tao** ★ ('tʃɪŋ'taʊ) n a variant transliteration of the Chinese name for **Qingdao.**

Ch'ing-yüan ★ ('tʃɪŋ'juːɑːn) n a former name of **Baoding.**

Chin-Hsien ★ ('tʃɪn'ʃjɛn) n the former name (1913–47) of **Jinzhou.**

chink[1] (tʃɪŋk) n **1** a small narrow opening, such as a fissure or crack. **2 chink in one's armour.** a small but fatal weakness. [C16: ? var. of earlier chine, from OE cine crack]

chink[2] (tʃɪŋk) vb **1** to make or cause to make a light ringing sound, as by the striking of glasses or coins. ♦ n **2** such a sound. [C16: imit.]

Chinkiang ★ ('tʃɪn'kjæŋ, -kaɪ'æŋ) n a variant transliteration of the Chinese name for **Jinjiang.**

chinless wonder ('tʃɪnlɪs) n Brit. inf. a person, esp. upper-class, lacking strength of character.

chinoiserie (ʃiːn,wɑːzə'riː, -'wɑːzərɪ) n **1** a style of decorative or fine art based on imitations of Chinese motifs. **2** an object or objects in this style. [F, from chinois CHINESE, -ERY]

chinook (tʃɪ'nuːk, -'nʊk) n **1** a warm dry southwesterly wind blowing down the eastern slopes of the Rocky Mountains. **2** a warm moist wind blowing onto the Washington and Oregon coasts from the sea. [C19: from Amerind]

Chinook (tʃɪ'nuːk, -'nʊk) n **1** (pl **Chinook** or **Chinooks**) a North American Indian people of the Pacific coast near the Columbia River. **2** the language of this people.

Chinook Jargon n a pidgin language containing elements of North American Indian languages, English, and French: formerly used among fur traders and Indians on the NW coast of North America.

Chinook salmon *n* a Pacific salmon valued as a food fish.

chinos ('tʃiːnəʊz) *pl n* trousers made of a durable cotton twill cloth. [C20: from *chino*, the cloth, from ?]

chintz (tʃɪnts) *n* a printed, patterned cotton fabric, with glazed finish. [C17: from Hindi *chīnt*, from Sansk. *citra* gaily-coloured]

chintzy ('tʃɪntsɪ) *adj* **chintzier, chintziest. 1** of, resembling, or covered with chintz. **2** *Brit. inf.* typical of the décor associated with the use of chintz soft furnishings.

chinwag ('tʃɪn,wæg) *n Brit. inf.* a chat.

Chios ★ ('kaɪɒs, -əʊs, 'kiː-) *n* **1** an island in the Aegean Sea, off the coast of Turkey: belongs to Greece. Capital: Chios. Pop.: 52 184 (1991). Area: 904 sq. km (353 sq. miles). **2** a port on the island of Chios: in ancient times, one of the 12 Ionian city-states. Pop.: 54 000 (1995 est.). Modern Greek name: **Khíos**.

chip (tʃɪp) *n* **1** a small piece removed by chopping, cutting, or breaking. **2** a mark left after a small piece has been broken off something. **3** (in some games) a counter used to represent money. **4** a thin strip of potato fried in deep fat. **5** the US, Canad. and Austral. name for **crisp** (sense 10). **6** *Sport.* a shot, kick, etc., lofted into the air, and travelling only a short distance. **7** *Electronics.* Also called: **microchip.** a tiny wafer of semiconductor material, such as silicon, processed to form a type of integrated circuit or component such as a transistor. **8** a thin strip of wood or straw used for making woven hats, baskets, etc. **9** *NZ.* a container for soft fruit, made of thin sheets of wood; punnet. **10 chip off the old block.** *Inf.* a person who resembles one of his or her parents in behaviour. **11 have a chip on one's shoulder.** *Inf.* to be aggressive or bear a grudge. **12 have had one's chips.** *Brit. inf.* to be defeated, condemned to die, killed, etc. **13 when the chips are down.** *Inf.* at a time of crisis. ◆ *vb* **chips, chipping, chipped. 14** to break small pieces from or become broken off in small pieces: *will the paint chip?* **15** (*tr*) to break or cut into small pieces: *to chip ice.* **16** (*tr*) to shape by chipping. **17** *Austral.* to dig or weed (a crop) with a hoe. **18** *Sport.* to strike or kick (a ball) in a high arc. [OE *cipp* (n), *cippian* (vb), from ?]

chip-based *adj* using or incorporating microchips in electronic equipment.

chipboard ('tʃɪp,bɔːd) *n* a thin rigid sheet made of compressed wood chips.

chip heater *n Austral. & NZ.* a domestic water heater that burns chips of wood.

chip in *vb* (*adv*) *Inf.* **1** to contribute (money, time, etc.) to a cause or fund. **2** (*intr*) to interpose a remark or interrupt with a remark.

chipmunk ('tʃɪp,mʌŋk) *n* a burrowing rodent of North America and Asia, typically having black-striped yellowish fur and cheek pouches for storing food. [C19: of Algonquian origin]

chipolata (,tʃɪpə'lɑːtə) *n Chiefly Brit.* a small sausage. [via F from It., from *cipolla* onion]

Chippendale ★ ('tʃɪp°n,deɪl) *n* **1 Thomas.** ?1718–79, English cabinet-maker and furniture designer. ◆ *adj* **2** (of furniture) designed by, made by, or in the style of Thomas Chippendale, characterized by the use of Chinese and Gothic motifs, cabriole legs, and massive carving.

chipper ('tʃɪpə) *adj Inf.* **1** cheerful; lively. **2** smartly dressed.

chippy[1] ('tʃɪpɪ) *n, pl* **chippies. 1** *Brit. inf.* a fish-and-chip shop. **2** *NZ.* a potato crisp.

chippy[2] ('tʃɪpɪ) *adj* **chippier, chippiest.** *Inf.* resentful or oversensitive about being perceived as inferior: *a chippy miner's son.* [C20: from CHIP (sense 11)]
▶ **'chippiness** *n*

chip shot *n Golf.* a short approach shot to the green, esp. one that is lofted.

Chirac ★ (*French* ʃirak) *n* **Jacques (René)** (ʒak). born 1932, French Gaullist politician: president of France from 1995; prime minister (1974–76 and 1986–88).

chiral ('kaɪrəl) *adj* relating to chirality. [C20: from CHIRO- + -AL[1]]

chirality (kaɪ'rælɪtɪ) *n* right- or left-handedness in an asymmetric molecule.

Chirico ★ (*Italian* 'kiːriko) *n* **Giorgio de** ('dʒɔrdʒo d[ɛ] 1888–1978, Italian artist born in Greece.

chiro- *or* **cheiro-** *combining form.* of or by means of t[he] hand: *chiromancy; chiropractic.* [via L from Gk *kh[eir]* hand]

chirography (kaɪ'rɒɡrəfɪ) *n* another name for **callig[ra]** phy.
▶ **chi'rographer** *n* ▶ **chirographic** (,kaɪrə'ɡræfɪk) *or* ,**chir[o]** 'graphical *adj*

chiromancy ('kaɪrə,mænsɪ) *n* another word for **pal[m]** istry.
▶ **'chiro,mancer** *n*

Chiron *or* **Cheiron** ★ ('kaɪrɒn, -rən) *n* **1** *Greek myth.* [a] wise and kind centaur who taught many great heroes [in] their youth, including Achilles, Actaeon, and Jason. **2** [a] minor planet, discovered by Charles Kowal in 1977, [re]volving round the sun between the orbits of Saturn an[d] Uranus.

chiropody (kɪ'rɒpədɪ) *n* the treatment of the feet, es[p.] corns, verrucas, etc.
▶ **chi'ropodist** *n*

chiropractic (,kaɪrə'præktɪk) *n* a system of treatin[g] bodily disorders by manipulation of the spine and oth[er] parts. [C20: from CHIRO- + Gk *praktikos* PRACTICAL]
▶ **'chiro,practor** *n*

chirp (tʃɜːp) *vb* (*intr*) **1** (esp. of some birds and insects) [to] make a short high-pitched sound. **2** to speak in a livel[y] fashion. ◆ *n* **3** a chirping sound. [C15 (as *chirpinge*, ge[r]und): imit.]
▶ **'chirper** *n*

chirpy ('tʃɜːpɪ) *adj* **chirpier, chirpiest.** *Inf.* cheerful; lively.
▶ **'chirpily** *adv* ▶ **'chirpiness** *n*

chirr *or* **churr** (tʃɜː) *vb* **1** (*intr*) (esp. of certain insect[s] such as crickets) to make a shrill trilled sound. ◆ *n* [2] such a sound. [C17: imit.]

chirrup ('tʃɪrəp) *vb* (*intr*) **1** (esp. of some birds) to chirp re[peatedly. **2** to make clucking sounds with the lips. ◆ *n* [3] such a sound. [C16: var. of CHIRUP]
▶ **'chirruper** *n* ▶ **'chirrupy** *adj*

chisel ('tʃɪz°l) *n* **1a** a hand tool for working wood, consis[t]ing of a flat steel blade with a handle. **1b** a similar too[l] without a handle for working stone or metal. ◆ *vb* **chis[el]els, chiselling, chiselled** *or US* **chisels, chiseling, chiseled. 2** t[o] carve (wood, stone, metal, etc.) or form (an engraving, [a] statue, etc.) with or as with a chisel. **3** *Sl.* to cheat or ob[tain by cheating. [C14: via OF, from Vulgar L *cīsellu[m]* (unattested), from L *caesus* cut]

chiseller ('tʃɪz°lə) *n* **1** a person who uses a chisel. **2** *Inf.* cheat. **3** *Dublin sl.* a child.

Chishima ★ (,tʃiːʃiː'ma) *n* the Japanese name for the **Kur[il]** **Islands.**

Chisimaio ★ (,kiːzɪ'mɑːjəʊ) *n* a port in S Somalia, on th[e] Indian Ocean. Pop.: 200 000 (1987 est.). Also calle[d] **Kismayu.**

Chişinău ★ (kiʃi'nəʊ) *n* the Romanian name for **Kishinev**[.]

chi-square distribution *n Statistics.* a continuous sin[gle-parameter distribution used esp. to measure good[ness of fit and to test hypotheses.

chi-square test *n Statistics.* a test derived from the ch[i-]square distribution to compare the goodness of fit o[f] theoretical and observed frequency distributions.

chit[1] (tʃɪt) *n* **1** a voucher for a sum of money owed, esp. fo[r] food or drink. **2** Also called: **chitty.** *Chiefly Brit.* **2a** a not[e] or memorandum. **2b** a requisition or receipt. [C18 from earlier *chitty*, from Hindi *cittha* note, from Sansk[.] *citra* marked]

chit[2] (tʃɪt) *n Facetious or derog.* a pert, impudent, or self[-]confident girl or child. [C14 (in the sense: young of a[n] animal, kitten): from ?]

Chita ★ (*Russian* tʃi'ta) *n* a city in SE Russia, on the Trans[-]Siberian railway: a major industrial centre. Pop.: 322 00[0] (1995 est.).

chital ('tʃiːt°l) *n* another name for **axis**[2] (the deer). [from Hindi]

itchat ('tʃɪt,tʃæt) n **1** gossip. ◆ vb **chitchats, chitchatting, chitchatted. 2** (intr) to gossip.

itin ('kaɪtɪn) n a polysaccharide that is the principal component of the exoskeletons of arthropods and of the bodies of fungi. [C19: from F, from Gk khitōn CHITON + -IN]
▷ **'chitinous** adj

iton ('kaɪtⁿn, -tɒn) n **1** (in ancient Greece) a loose woollen tunic worn by men and women. **2** any small primitive marine mollusc having an elongated body covered with eight overlapping shell plates. [C19: from Gk khitōn coat of mail]

ittagong ★ ('tʃɪtə,gɒŋ) n a port in E Bangladesh, on the Bay of Bengal: industrial centre. Pop.: 1 599 000 (1991).

itterlings ('tʃɪtəlɪŋz) or **chitlings** ('tʃɪtlɪŋz) pl n (sometimes sing) the intestines of a pig or other animal prepared as a dish. [C13: from ?]

iv (tʃɪv, ʃɪv) or **shiv** (ʃɪv) Sl. ◆ n **1** a knife. ◆ vb **chivs, chivving, chivved** or **shivs, shivving, shivved. 2** to stab (someone). [C17: ?from Romany chiv blade]

ivalrous ('ʃɪvəlrəs) adj **1** gallant; courteous. **2** involving chivalry. [C14: from OF, from CHEVALIER]
▷ **'chivalrously** adv ▷ **'chivalrousness** n

ivalry ('ʃɪvəlrɪ) n, pl **chivalries. 1** the combination of qualities expected of an ideal knight, esp. courage, honour, justice, and a readiness to help the weak. **2** courteous behaviour, esp. towards women. **3** the medieval system and principles of knighthood. **4** knights, noblemen, etc., collectively. [C13: from OF chevalerie, from CHEVALIER]
▷ **'chivalric** adj

ive (tʃaɪv) n a small Eurasian purple-flowered alliaceous plant, whose long slender hollow leaves are used in cooking. Also called: **chives.** [C14: from OF cive, ult. from L caepa onion]

ivy, chivvy ('tʃɪvɪ), or **chevy** Brit. ◆ vb **chivies, chivying, chivied, chivvies, chivvying, chivvied,** or **chevies, chevying, chevied. 1** (tr) to harass or nag. **2** (tr) to hunt. **3** (intr) to run about. ◆ n, pl **chivies, chivvies,** or **chevies. 4** a hunt. **5** Obs. a hunting cry. [C19: var. of chevy, prob. from Chevy Chase, title of a Scottish border ballad]

hkalov ★ (Russian 'tʃkaləf) n the former name (1938–57) of **Orenburg.**

hlamydia (klə'mɪdɪə) n any of a genus of virus-like bacteria responsible for such diseases as trachoma, psittacosis, and some sexually transmitted diseases. [C20: NL, from Gk khlamus mantle + -IA]

hloral ('klɔːrəl) n **1** a colourless oily liquid with a pungent odour, made from chlorine and acetaldehyde and used in preparing chloral hydrate and DDT. Formula: CCl₃CHO. **2** short for **chloral hydrate.**

hloral hydrate n a colourless crystalline soluble solid produced by the reaction of chloral with water and used as a sedative and hypnotic. Formula: CCl₃C(OH)₃.

hloramphenicol (,klɔːræm'fɛnɪ,kɒl) n a broad-spectrum antibiotic used esp. in treating typhoid fever and rickettsial infections. [C20: from CHLORO- + AM(IDE)- + PHE(NO)- + NI(TRO)- + (GLY)COL]

hlorate ('klɔːreɪt, -rɪt) n any salt of chloric acid, containing the monovalent ion ClO₃⁻.

hlordane ('klɔːdeɪn) or **chlordan** n a white insoluble toxic solid used as an insecticide. [C20: from CHLORO- + (IN)D(OLE + -ENE) + -ANE]

hlorhexidine (klɔː'hɛksɪdiːn) n an antiseptic compound used in skin cleansers, mouthwashes, etc. [C20: from CHLOR(O)- + HEX(ANE) + -I(DE) + (AM)INE]

hloric ('klɔːrɪk) adj of or containing chlorine in the pentavalent state.

hloric acid n a strong acid with a pungent smell, known only in solution and in the form of chlorate salts. Formula: HClO₃.

hloride ('klɔːraɪd) n **1** any salt of hydrochloric acid, containing the chloride ion Cl⁻. **2** any compound containing a chlorine atom, such as methyl chloride (chloromethane), CH₃Cl.

chloride of lime or **chlorinated lime** n another name for **bleaching powder.**

chlorinate ('klɔːrɪ,neɪt) vb **chlorinates, chlorinating, chlorinated.** (tr) **1** to combine or treat (a substance) with chlorine. **2** to disinfect (water) with chlorine.
▷ ,chlorin'ation n ▷ 'chlorin,ator n

chlorine ('klɔːriːn) or **chlorin** ('klɔːrɪn) n a toxic pungent greenish-yellow gas of the halogen group; occurring only in the combined state, mainly in common salt: used in the manufacture of many organic chemicals, in water purification, and as a disinfectant and bleaching agent. Symbol: Cl; atomic no.: 17; atomic wt.: 35.453. [C19 (coined by Sir Humphrey Davy): from CHLORO- + -INE², referring to its colour]

chlorite¹ ('klɔːraɪt) n any of a group of green soft secondary minerals consisting of the hydrated silicates of aluminium, iron, and magnesium. [C18: from L, from Gk, from khlōros greenish yellow]
▷ **chloritic** (klɔː'rɪtɪk) adj

chlorite² ('klɔːraɪt) n any salt of chlorous acid.

chloro- or before a vowel **chlor-** combining form. **1** indicating the colour green: chlorophyll. **2** chlorine: chloroform.

chlorofluorocarbon (,klɔːrə,flʊərəʊ'kɑːbⁿn) n Chem. any of various gaseous compounds of carbon, hydrogen, chlorine, and fluorine, used as refrigerants, aerosol propellants, solvents, and in foam: some cause a breakdown of ozone in the earth's atmosphere.

chloroform ('klɔːrə,fɔːm) n a heavy volatile liquid with a sweet taste and odour, used as a solvent and cleansing agent and in refrigerants: formerly used as an inhalation anaesthetic. Formula: CHCl₃. Systematic name: **trichloromethane.** [C19: from CHLORO- + formyl from FORMIC]

Chloromycetin (,klɔːrəʊmaɪ'siːtɪn) n Trademark. a brand of **chloramphenicol.**

chlorophyll or US **chlorophyl** ('klɔːrəfɪl) n the green pigment of plants, occurring in chloroplasts, that traps the energy of sunlight for photosynthesis: used as a colouring agent (E140) in medicines and food.
▷ **'chloro,phylloid** adj ▷ ,chloro'phyllous adj

chloroplast ('klɔːrəʊ,plæst) n a plastid containing chlorophyll and other pigments, occurring in plants that carry out photosynthesis.

chlorosis (klɔː'rəʊsɪs) n **1** Also called: **greensickness.** Pathol. a once-common iron-deficiency disease of adolescent girls, characterized by greenish-yellow skin colour, weakness, and palpitation. **2** Bot. a deficiency of chlorophyll in green plants caused by mineral deficiency, lack of light, disease, etc., the leaves appearing uncharacteristically pale. [C17: from CHLORO- + -OSIS]
▷ **chlorotic** (klɔː'rɒtɪk) adj

chlorous ('klɔːrəs) adj **1** of or containing chlorine in the trivalent state. **2** of or containing chlorous acid.

chlorous acid n an unstable acid that is a strong oxidizing agent. Formula: HClO₂.

chlorpromazine (klɔː'prɒmə,ziːn) n a drug used as a sedative and tranquilliser. [C20: from CHLORO- + PRO(PYL + A)M(INE) + AZINE]

chlortetracycline (klɔː,tɛtrə'saɪkliːn) n an antibiotic used in treating many bacterial and rickettsial infections and some viral infections.

chock (tʃɒk) n **1** a block or wedge of wood used to prevent the sliding or rolling of a heavy object. **2** Naut. **2a** a ringlike device with an opening at the top through which a rope is placed. **2b** a cradle-like support for a boat, barrel, etc. ◆ vb (tr) **3** (usually foll. by up) Brit. to cram full. **4** to fit with or secure by a chock. **5** to support (a boat, barrel, etc.) on chocks. ◆ adv **6** as closely or tightly as possible: chock against the wall. [C17: from ?; ? rel. to OF çoche log]

chock-a-block adj, adv **1** filled to capacity; in a crammed state. **2** Naut. with the blocks brought close together, as when a tackle is pulled as tight as possible.

chocker ('tʃɒkə) adj **1** Austral. & NZ inf. full up; packed. **2** Brit. sl. irritated; fed up. [C20: from CHOCK-A-BLOCK]

chock-full or **choke-full** adj (postpositive) completely full. [C17 choke-full; see CHOKE, FULL¹]

★ people and places

choco or **chocko** ('tʃɒkəʊ) *n, pl* **chocos** or **chockos.** *Austral. sl.* a conscript or militiaman. [from *chocolate soldier*]

chocolate ('tʃɒkəlɪt, 'tʃɒklɪt, -lət) *n* **1** a food preparation made from roasted ground cacao seeds, usually sweetened and flavoured. **2** a drink or sweetmeat made from this. **3a** a deep brown colour. **3b** (*as adj*): *a chocolate carpet.* [C17: from Sp., from Aztec *xocolatl*, from *xococ* sour + *atl* water]
▶ '**chocolaty** *adj*

chocolate-box *n* (*modifier*) *Inf.* sentimentally pretty or appealing.

Choctaw ('tʃɒktɔ:) *n* **1** (*pl* **-taws** or **-taw**) a member of a N American people originally of Alabama. **2** their language. [C18: from Choctaw *Chahta*]

choice (tʃɔɪs) *n* **1** the act or an instance of choosing or selecting. **2** the opportunity or power of choosing. **3** a person or thing chosen or that may be chosen: *he was a possible choice.* **4** an alternative action or possibility: *what choice did I have?* **5** a supply from which to select. ◆ *adj* **6** of superior quality; excellent: *choice wine.* **7** carefully chosen, appropriate: *a few choice words will do the trick.* **8** vulgar or rude: *choice language.* [C13: from OF, from *choisir* to CHOOSE]
▶ '**choicely** *adv* ▶ '**choiceness** *n*

choir ('kwaɪə) *n* **1** an organized group of singers, esp. for singing in church services. **2** the part of a cathedral, abbey, or church in front of the altar and used by the choir and clergy. **3** a number of instruments of the same family playing together: *a brass choir.* **4** Also called: **choir organ.** one of the manuals on an organ controlling a set of soft sweet-toned pipes. [C13 *quer,* from OF *cuer,* from L CHORUS]

choirboy ('kwaɪə,bɔɪ) *n* a young boy who sings the treble part in a church choir.

choir school *n* (in Britain) a school attached to a cathedral, college, etc., offering general education to boys whose singing ability is good.

Choiseul ★ (French ʃwazœl) *n* an island in the SW Pacific Ocean, in the Solomon Islands: hilly and densely forested. Area: 3885 sq. km (1500 sq. miles).

choke (tʃəʊk) *vb* **chokes, choking, choked. 1** (*tr*) to hinder or stop the breathing of (a person or animal), esp. by constricting the windpipe or by asphyxiation. **2** (*intr*) to have trouble or fail in breathing, swallowing, or speaking. **3** (*tr*) to block or clog up (a passage, pipe, street, etc.). **4** (*tr*) to retard the growth or action of: *the weeds are choking my plants.* **5** (*tr*) to enrich the petrol-air mixture by reducing the air supply to (a carburettor, petrol engine, etc.). ◆ *n* **6** the act or sound of choking. **7** a device in the carburettor of a petrol engine that enriches the petrol-air mixture by reducing the air supply. **8** any mechanism for reducing the flow of a fluid in a pipe, tube, etc. **9** Also called: **choke coil.** *Electronics.* an inductor having a relatively high impedance, used to prevent the passage of high frequencies or to smooth the output of a rectifier. [OE *ācēocian*]
▶ '**choky** or '**chokey** *adj*

choke back or **down** *vb* (*tr, adv*) to suppress (anger, tears, etc.).

choke chain *n* a collar and lead for a dog so designed that if the dog drags on the lead the collar tightens round its neck.

choked (tʃəʊkt) *adj Brit. inf.* annoyed or disappointed.

choker ('tʃəʊkə) *n* **1** a woman's high collar. **2** any neckband or necklace worn tightly around the throat. **3** a high clerical collar; stock. **4** a person who chokes. **5** something that causes a person to choke.

choke up *vb* (*tr, adv*) **1** to block (a drain, pipe, etc.) completely. **2** *Inf.* (*usually passive*) to overcome (a person) with emotion.

chokey or **choky** ('tʃəʊkɪ) *n Brit. sl.* prison. [C17: from Anglo-Indian, from Hindi *caukī* a lockup]

choko ('tʃəʊkəʊ) *n, pl* **chokos.** *Austral. & NZ.* the cucumber-like fruit of a tropical American vine: eaten as a vegetable in the Caribbean, Australia, and New Zealand. [C18: from Brazilian Indian]

cholangiography (kə,lændʒɪ'ɒɡrəfɪ) *n* radiographic

examination of the bile ducts after the introduction in them of a contrast medium.

chole- or before a vowel **chol-** *combining form.* bile or ga cholesterol. [from Gk *kholē*]

choler ('kɒlə) *n* **1** anger or ill humour. **2** *Arch.* one of t four bodily humours; yellow bile. [C14: from OF, fro Med. L, from L: jaundice, CHOLERA]

cholera ('kɒlərə) *n* an acute intestinal infection chara terized by severe diarrhoea, cramp, etc.: caused by inge tion of water or food contaminated with the bacteriu *Vibrio comma.* [C14: from L, from Gk *kholera* jaundice from *kholē* bile]
▶ **choleraic** (,kɒlə'reɪɪk) *adj*

choleric ('kɒlərɪk) *adj* **1** bad-tempered. **2** *Obs.* bilious causing biliousness.
▶ '**cholerically** *adv*

cholesterol (kə'lestə,rɒl) or **cholesterin** (kə'lestər *n* a sterol found in all animal tissues, blood, bile, and a imal fats. A high level of cholesterol is implicated some cases of atherosclerosis. [C19: from CHOLE- + (*stereos* solid]

choline ('kəʊli:n, -ɪn, 'kɒl-) *n* a colourless viscous solub alkaline substance present in animal tissues, esp. as constituent of lecithin. [C19: from CHOLE- + -INE²]

Cholula ★ (*Spanish* tʃo'lula) *n* a town in S Mexico, Puebla state: ancient ruins, notably a pyramid, 53 (177 ft) high. Pop.: 37 791 (1990).

chomp (tʃɒmp) or **chump** *vb* **1** to chew (food) noisil champ. ◆ *n* **2** the act or sound of chewing in this ma ner. [var. of CHAMP¹]

Chomsky ★ ('tʃɒmskɪ) *n* (**Avram**) **Noam** ('nəʊəm). bo 1928, US linguist, noted for his *Syntactic Structures* (195 on transformational grammar and his opposition to t Vietnam War.
▶ '**Chomskyan** or '**Chomsky,ite** *n, adj*

Chondokyo (,tʃɒndəʊ'kjəʊ) *n* an indigenous religion Korea, incorporating elements of Buddhism, Confucia ism, Christianity, and shamanism. Former nam **Tongchak.** [C20: from Korean: Religion of the Heaven Way]

chondrite ('kɒndraɪt) *n* a stony meteorite consistin mainly of silicate minerals in small spherical masses.

Chongqing ('tʃʊŋ'tʃɪŋ), **Chungking,** or **Ch'un ch'ing** ★ *n* a port in SW China, in Sichuan province the confluence of the Yangtze and Jialing rivers: site o city since the 3rd millennium B.C.; wartime capital o China (1938–45); major trade centre for W China. Po 2 980 000 (1991 est.). Also called: **Pahsien.**

choof off (tʃuf) *vb* (*intr, adv*) *Austral. sl.* to go away; mak off.

chook (tʃʊk) *n Inf., chiefly Austral. & NZ.* a hen or chicker Also called: **chookie.**

choose (tʃu:z) *vb* **chooses, choosing, chose, chosen. 1** to se lect (a person, thing, course of action, etc.) from a num ber of alternatives. **2** (*tr; takes a clause as object or a infinitive*) to consider it desirable or proper: *I don't choos to read that book.* **3** (*intr*) to like; please: *you may stand if yc choose.* [OE *ceosan*]
▶ '**chooser** *n*

choosy ('tʃu:zɪ) *adj* **choosier, choosiest.** *Inf.* particular i making a choice; difficult to please.

chop¹ (tʃɒp) *vb* **chops, chopping, chopped. 1** (often foll. b *down* or *off*) to cut (something) with a blow from an ax or other sharp tool. **2** (*tr*; often foll. by *up*) to cut int pieces. **3** (*tr*) *Brit. inf.* to dispense with or reduce. **4** (*intr*) t move quickly or violently. **5** *Tennis, cricket, etc.* to hit (ball) sharply downwards. **6** *Boxing, karate, etc.* to punc or strike (an opponent) with a short sharp blow. ◆ *n* **7** cutting blow. **8** the act or an instance of chopping. **9** piece chopped off. **10** a slice of mutton, lamb, or por generally including a rib. **11** *Austral. & NZ sl.* a share (esp in **get** or **hop in for one's chop**). **12** *Austral. & NZ.* a competi tion of skill and speed in chopping logs. **13** *Sport.* a shar downward blow or stroke. **14 not much chop.** *Austral. & N. inf.* not much good; poor. **15 the chop.** *Brit. & Austral. s. dismissal* from employment. [C16: var. of CHAP¹]

chop² (tʃɒp) *vb* **chops, chopping, chopped. 1** (*intr*) to chang direction suddenly; vacillate (esp. in **chop and change**). **2 chop logic.** use excessively subtle or involved argument. [OE *ceapian* to barter]

hop[3] (tʃɒp) *n* a design stamped on goods as a trademark, esp. in the Far East. [C17: from Hindi *chhāp*]

hop chop *adv* pidgin English for **quickly**. [C19: from Chinese dialect]

hophouse ('tʃɒp,haʊs) *n* a restaurant specializing in steaks, grills, chops, etc.

hopin ★ ('ʃɒpæn; *French* ʃɔpɛ̃) *n* **Frédéric (François)** (frederik). 1810–49, Polish composer and pianist active in France: noted for his piano music.

hopper ('tʃɒpə) *n* **1** *Chiefly Brit.* a small hand axe. **2** a butcher's cleaver. **3** a person or thing that cuts or chops. **4** an informal name for a **helicopter. 5** a device for periodically interrupting an electric current or beam of radiation to produce a pulsed current or beam. **6** a type of bicycle or motorcycle with very high handlebars. **7** *NZ.* a child's bicycle. **8** *Sl.*, *chiefly US.* a sub-machine-gun.

hoppy ('tʃɒpɪ) *adj* **choppier, choppiest**. (of the sea, weather, etc.) fairly rough.
  ▶ '**choppily** *adv* ▶ '**choppiness** *n*

hops (tʃɒps) *pl n* **1** the jaws or cheeks; jowls. **2** the mouth. **3 lick one's chops.** *Inf.* to anticipate with pleasure. [C16: from ?]

hopsticks ('tʃɒpstɪks) *pl n* a pair of thin sticks, of ivory, wood, etc., used for eating Chinese or other East Asian food. [C17: from pidgin E, from *chop* quick, from Chinese dialect + STICK[1]]

hop suey ('suːɪ) *n* a Chinese-style dish originating in the US, consisting of meat, bean sprouts, etc., served with rice. [C19: from Chinese *tsap sui* odds and ends]

horal ('kɔːrəl) *adj* relating to, sung by, or designed for a chorus or choir.
  ▶ '**chorally** *adv*

horale *or* **choral** (kɒ'rɑːl) *n* **1** a slow stately hymn tune. **2** *Chiefly US.* a choir or chorus. [C19: from G *Choralgesang*, translation of L *cantus chorālis* choral song]

hord[1] (kɔːd) *n* **1** *Maths.* a straight line connecting two points on a curve or curved surface. **2** *Engineering.* one of the principal members of a truss, esp. one that lies along the top or the bottom. **3** *Anat.* a variant spelling of **cord. 4** an emotional response, esp. one of sympathy: *the story struck the right chord.* [C16: from L, from Gk *khordē* gut, string; see CORD]

hord[2] (kɔːd) *n* **1** the simultaneous sounding of a group of musical notes, usually three or more in number. ◆ *vb* **2** (*tr*) to provide (a melodic line) with chords. [C15: short for ACCORD; spelling infl. by CHORD[1]]
  ▶ '**chordal** *adj*

hordate ('kɔːdeɪt) *n* **1** an animal with a backbone or notochord. ◆ *adj* **2** of or relating to the chordates. [C19: from Med. L *chordata*: see CHORD[1] & -ATE[1]]

hore (tʃɔː) *n* **1** a routine task. **2** a domestic one. **3** a boring task. [C19: from ME *chare*, from OE *cierr* a job]

chore *n combining form.* (in botany) indicating a plant that is distributed by a certain means: *anemochore.* [from Gk *khōrein* to move]
  ▶ -**chorous** *or* -**choric** *adj combining form.*

horea (kɒ'rɪə) *n* a disorder of the central nervous system characterized by uncontrollable irregular jerky movements. See **Huntington's disease, Sydenham's chorea.** [C19: from NL, from L: dance, from Gk *khoreia*; see CHORUS]

choreograph ('kɒrɪə,grɑːf) *vb* (*tr*) to compose the steps and dances for (a ballet, etc.)

horeography (,kɒrɪ'ɒgrəfɪ) *or* **choregraphy** (kɒ-'rɛgrəfɪ) *n* **1** the composition of dance steps and sequences for ballet and stage and film dancing. **2** the steps and sequences of a ballet or dance. **3** the notation representing such steps. **4** the art of dancing. [C18: from Gk *khoreia* dance + -GRAPHY]
  ▶ ,**chore**'**ographer** *or* **cho**'**regrapher** *n* ▶ **choreographic** (,kɒrɪə'græfɪk) *or* **choregraphic** (,kɒrə'græfɪk) *adj*
  ▶ ,**choreo**'**graphically** *or* ,**chore**'**graphically** *adv*

horic ('kɒrɪk) *adj* of, like, or for a chorus, esp. of singing, dancing, or the speaking of verse.

chorion ('kɔːrɪən) *n* the outer membrane surrounding an embryo. [C16: from Gk *khorion* afterbirth]
  ▶ **chorionic** (,kɔːrɪ'ɒnɪk) *adj*

chorionic gonadotrophin *n* a hormone, secreted by the placenta in mammals, that promotes the secretion of progesterone. See **HCG.**

chorionic villus sampling *n* a method of diagnosing genetic disorders early in pregnancy by the removal by catheter through the cervix of a tiny sample of tissue from the chorionic villi. Abbrev.: **CVS.**

chorister ('kɒrɪstə) *n* a singer in a choir, esp. a choirboy. [C14: from Med. L *chorista*]

Chorley ★ ('tʃɔːlɪ) *n* a town in NW England, in S Lancashire: cotton textiles. Pop.: 33 536 (1991).

choroid ('kɔːrɔɪd) *or* **chorioid** ('kɔːrɪˌɔɪd) *adj* **1** resembling the chorion, esp. in being vascular. ◆ *n* **2** the vascular membrane of the eyeball between the sclera and the retina. [C18: from Gk *khoroeidēs*, erroneously for *khorioeidēs*, from CHORION]

choropleth ('kɒrəˌplɛθ) *n* a symbol or marked area on a map denoting the distribution of some property. **b** (*as modifier*): *a choropleth map.* [C20: from Gk *khōra* place + *plēthos* multitude]

chortle ('tʃɔːt[ə]l) *vb* **chortles, chortling, chortled. 1** (*intr*) to chuckle gleefully. ◆ *n* **2** a gleeful chuckle. [C19: coined (1871) by Lewis Carroll; prob. a blend of CHUCKLE + SNORT]
  ▶ '**chortler** *n*

chorus ('kɔːrəs) *n*, *pl* **choruses. 1** a large choir of singers or a piece of music composed for such a choir. **2** a body of singers or dancers who perform together. **3** a section of a song in which a soloist is joined by a group of singers, esp. in a recurring refrain. **4** an intermediate section of a pop song, blues, etc., as distinct from the verse. **5** *Jazz.* any of a series of variations on a theme. **6** (in ancient Greece) **6a** a lyric poem sung by a group of dancers, originally as a religious rite. **6b** an ode or series of odes sung by a group of actors. **6c** the actors who sang the chorus and commented on the action of the play. **7a** (esp. in Elizabethan drama) the actor who spoke the prologue, etc. **7b** the part spoken by this actor. **8** a group of people or animals producing words or sounds simultaneously. **9** any speech, song, or utterance produced by a group of people or animals simultaneously: *the dawn chorus.* **10 in chorus.** in unison. ◆ *vb* **11** to speak, sing, or utter (words, sounds, etc.) in unison. [C16: from L, from Gk *khoros*]

chorus girl *n* a girl who dances or sings in the chorus of a musical comedy, revue, etc.

Chorzów ★ (*Polish* 'xɔʒuf) *n* an industrial city in SW Poland: under German administration from 1794 to 1921. Pop.: 126 500 (1995 est.). German name: **Königshütte.**

chose (tʃəʊz) *vb* the past tense of **choose.**

chosen ('tʃəʊz[ə]n) *vb* **1** the past participle of **choose.** ◆ *adj* **2** selected, esp. for some special quality.

Chosen ★ ('tʃəʊ'sɛn) *n* the official name for **Korea** as a Japanese province (1910–45).

Chosŏn ★ ('tʃəʊ'sɒn) *n* the Korean name for **North Korea.**

Chota Nagpur ★ ('tʃəʊtə 'nɑːgpʊə) *n* a plateau in E India, in Bihar state: forested, with rich mineral resources and much heavy industry; produces chiefly lac (world's leading supplier), coal (half India's total output), and mica.

Chou En-lai (en'laɪ) *or* **Zhou En Lai** ★ *n* 1898–1976, Chinese Communist statesman; foreign minister of the People's Republic of China (1949–58) and premier (1949–76).

chough (tʃʌf) *n* a large black passerine bird of parts of Europe, Asia, and Africa, with a long downward-curving red bill: family Corvidae (crows). [C14: from ?]

choux pastry (ʃuː) *n* a very light pastry made with eggs, used for éclairs, etc. [partial translation of F *pâte choux* cabbage dough]

chow (tʃaʊ) *n* **1** *Inf.* food. **2** short for **chow-chow** (sense 1).

chow-chow *n* **1** a thick-coated breed of dog with a curled tail, originally from China. Often shortened to **chow. 2** a Chinese preserve of ginger, orange peel, etc., in syrup. **3** a mixed vegetable pickle. [C19: from pidgin E, prob. based on Chinese *cha* miscellaneous]

chowder ('tʃaʊdə) *n Chiefly US & Canad.* a thick soup or stew containing clams or fish. [C18: from F *chaudière* kettle, from LL *caldāria;* see CAULDRON]

chow mein (meɪn) *n* a Chinese-American dish, consisting of mushrooms, meat, shrimps, etc., served with fried noodles. [from Chinese *ch'ao mien* fried noodles]

Chr. *abbrev. for:* **1** Christ. **2** Christian.

Chrétien ★ *(French* kretjɛ̃) *n* **(Joseph Jacques)** Jean (ʒã). born 1934, Canadian Liberal politician; prime minister of Canada from 1993.

Chrétien de Troyes ★ *(French* də trwa) *n* 12th century, French poet, who wrote five Arthurian romances (?1155–?1190).

chrism *or* **chrisom** ('krɪzəm) *n* a mixture of olive oil and balsam used for sacramental anointing in the Greek Orthodox and Roman Catholic Churches. [OE, from Med. L, from Gk, from *khriein* to anoint]
▸ **chrismal** ('krɪzməl) *adj*

Christ ★ (kraɪst) *n* **1** Jesus of Nazareth (Jesus Christ), regarded by Christians as fulfilling Old Testament prophecies of the Messiah. **2** the Messiah or anointed one of God as the subject of Old Testament prophecies. **3** an image or picture of Christ. ◆ *interj* **4** *Taboo sl.* an oath expressing anger, etc. ◆ See also **Jesus.** [OE *Crīst,* from L *Chrīstus,* from Gk *khristos* anointed one (from *khriein* to anoint), translating Heb. *māshīah* MESSIAH]
▸ **'Christly** *adj*

Christadelphian (ˌkrɪstəˈdɛlfɪən) *n* **1** a member of a Christian millenarian sect founded in the US about 1848, holding that only the just will enter eternal life, and that the ignorant and unconverted will not be raised from the dead. ◆ *adj* **2** of or relating to this body or its beliefs and practices. [C19: from LGk *khristadelphos, khristos* CHRIST + *adelpos* brother]

Christchurch ★ ('kraɪst,tʃɜːtʃ) *n* **1** a city in New Zealand, on E South Island: manufacturing centre of a rich agricultural region. Pop. (urban area): 313 969 (1996). **2** a town and resort in S England, in SE Dorset. Pop.: 36 379 (1991).

christen ('krɪsən) *vb (tr)* **1** to give a Christian name to in baptism as a sign of incorporation into a Christian Church. **2** another word for **baptize. 3** to give a name to anything, esp. with some ceremony. **4** *Inf.* to use for the first time. [OE *cristnian,* from *Crīst* CHRIST]
▸ **'christening** *n*

Christendom ('krɪsⁿndəm) *n* the collective body of Christians throughout the world.

Christian[1] ('krɪstʃən) *n* **1a** a person who believes in and follows Jesus Christ. **1b** a member of a Christian Church or denomination. **2** *Inf.* a person who possesses Christian virtues. ◆ *adj* **3** of, relating to, or derived from Jesus Christ, his teachings, example, or followers. **4** *(sometimes not cap.)* exhibiting kindness or goodness.
▸ **'christianly** *adj, adv*

Christian[2] ★ ('krɪstʃən) *n* **Charlie.** 1919–42, US modern-jazz guitarist.

Christian IV ★ *n* 1577–1648, king of Denmark and Norway (1588–1648).

Christian X ★ ('krɪstʃən; *Danish* 'kresdjan) *n* 1890–1947, king of Denmark (1912–47) and Iceland (1918–44).

Christian Democrat *n* a member or supporter of any of various right-of-centre political parties in Europe and Latin America that combine moderate conservatism with historical links to the Christian Church.
▸ **Christian Democracy** *n* ▸ **Christian Democratic** *adj*

Christian Era *n* the period beginning with the year of Christ's birth.

Christiania ★ (ˌkrɪstɪˈɑːnɪə) *n* a former name (1624–1877) of **Oslo.**

Christianity (ˌkrɪstɪˈænɪtɪ) *n* **1** the Christian religion. **2** Christian beliefs or practices. **3** a less common word for **Christendom.**

Christianize *or* **Christianise** ('krɪstʃəˌnaɪz) *vb* **Christianizes, Christianizing, Christianized** *or* **Christianises, Christianising, Christianised.** *(tr)* **1** to make Christian or con-

vert to Christianity. **2** to imbue with Christi... principles, spirit, or outlook.
▸ ˌChristiani'zation *or* ˌChristiani'sation *n* ▸ 'Christian,iz... *or* 'Christian,iser *n*

Christian name *n* a personal name formally given ... Christians at christening: loosely used to mean any pe... son's first name.

Christiansand ★ ('krɪstʃən,sænd; *Norwegian* kristia... 'san) *n* a variant spelling of **Kristiansand.**

Christian Science *n* the religious system of th... Church of Christ, Scientist, founded by Mary Baker Edd... (1879), emphasizing spiritual regeneration and heali... through prayer alone.
▸ **Christian Scientist** *n*

Christie ★ ('krɪstɪ) *n* **1** Dame **Agatha (Mary Clarissa).** 189... 1976, British author of detective stories, many featuri... Hercule Poirot, and several plays, including *The Mous... trap* (1952). **2** John **(Reginald Halliday).** 1898–1953, Briti... murderer: hanged. Confessed to murdering the baby ... Timothy Evans, for which Evans had already be... hanged. **3** Linford ('lɪnfəd). born 1960, British athlet... Commonwealth (1990) and Olympic (1992), 100 metr... gold medallist.

Christina ★ (krɪˈstiːnə) *n* 1626–89, queen of Swede... (1632–54), daughter of Gustavus Adolphus.

Christine de Pisan ★ *(French* kristin də pizã) *n* ?136... ?1430, French writer, born in Venice. Her works inclu... ballads, rondeaux, lays, and a biography of Charles V ... France.

Christingle (ˌkrɪsˈtɪŋgl) *n* (in Britain) a Christian servic... for children held shortly before Christmas, in whic... each child is given a decorated fruit with a lighted ca... dle in it. [C20: from CHRIST(MAS) + INGLE]

Christlike ('kraɪst,laɪk) *adj* resembling the spirit of Jesu... Christ.
▸ **'Christ,likeness** *n*

Christmas ('krɪsməs) *n* **1a** the annual commemoratio... by Christians of the birth of Jesus Christ, on Dec. 25. ... Also called: **Christmas Day.** Dec. 25, observed as a day ... secular celebrations when gifts and greetings are e... changed. **1c** *(as modifier): Christmas celebrations.* **2** Als... called: **Christmastide.** the season of Christmas extendin... from Dec. 24 (Christmas Eve) to Jan. 6 (the festival of th... Epiphany or Twelfth Night). [OE *Crīstes mæsse* MASS ... CHRIST]
▸ **'Christmassy** *adj*

Christmas box *n* a tip or present given at Christma... esp. to postmen, tradesmen, etc.

Christmas Eve *n* the evening or the whole day befor... Christmas Day.

Christmas Island ★ *n* **1** the former name (until 1981... of **Kiritimati. 2** an island in the Indian Ocean, south ... Java: administered by Singapore (1900–58), now by Aus... tralia; phosphate mining. Pop.: 2500 (1994 est.). Are... 135 sq. km (52 sq. miles).

Christmas pudding *n Brit.* a rich steamed puddin... containing suet, dried fruit, spices, etc. Also called: **plu... pudding.**

Christmas rose *n* an evergreen plant of S Europe an... W Asia with white or pinkish winter-blooming flowers... Also called: **hellebore, winter rose.**

Christmastide ('krɪsməs,taɪd) *n* another name fo... **Christmas** (sense 2).

Christmas tree *n* **1** an evergreen tree or an imitation o... one, decorated as part of Christmas celebrations. **2** Als... called: **Christmas bush.** *Austral.* any of various trees o... shrubs flowering at Christmas and used for decoration. ... *NZ.* another name for the **pohutukawa.**

Christoff ★ ('krɪstɒf) *n* **Boris.** 1919–93, Bulgarian bass... baritone.

Christopher ★ ('krɪstəfə) *n* **Saint.** 3rd century A.D., Chris... tian martyr; patron saint of travellers.

Christy *or* **Christie** ('krɪstɪ) *n, pl* **Christies.** *Skiing.* a tur... in which the body is swung sharply round with the ski... parallel: used for stopping or changing directio... quickly. [C20: from CHRISTIANIA]

chroma ('krəʊmə) *n* the attribute of a colour that enable...

★ people and places

an observer to judge how much chromatic colour it contains. See also **saturation** (sense 4). [C19: from Gk *khrōma* colour]

hromate ('krəʊmeɪt) *n* any salt or ester of chromic acid.

hromatic (krə'mætɪk) *adj* **1** of, relating to, or characterized by a colour or colours. **2** *Music.* **2a** involving the sharpening or flattening of notes or the use of such notes in chords and harmonic progressions. **2b** of or relating to the chromatic scale or an instrument capable of producing it. [C17: from Gk, from *khrōma* colour] ► **chro'matically** *adv* ► **chro'maticism** *n* ► **chromaticity** (ˌkrəʊmə'tɪsɪtɪ) *n*

hromatic aberration *n* a defect in a lens system in which different wavelengths of light are focused at different distances because they are refracted through different angles. It produces a blurred image with coloured fringes.

hromatics (krəʊ'mætɪks) *n* (*functioning as sing*) the science of colour.

hromatic scale *n* a twelve-note scale including all the semitones of the octave.

hromatin ('krəʊmətɪn) *n* the part of the nucleus that consists of DNA, RNA, and proteins, forms the chromosomes, and stains with basic dyes.

hromato- *or before a vowel* **chromat-** *combining form.* **1** indicating colour or coloured: *chromatophore.* **2** indicating chromatin: *chromatolysis.* [from Gk *khrōma, khrōmat-* colour]

hromatography (ˌkrəʊmə'tɒɡrəfɪ) *n* the technique of separating and analysing the components of a mixture of liquids or gases by selective adsorption.

hrome (krəʊm) *n* **1a** another word for **chromium**, esp. when present in a pigment or dye. **1b** (*as modifier*): *a chrome dye.* **2** anything plated with chromium. **3** a pigment or dye that contains chromium. ◆ *vb* **chromes, chroming, chromed. 4** to plate or be plated with chromium. **5** to treat or be treated with a chromium compound, as in dyeing or tanning. [C19: via F from Gk *khrōma* colour]

chrome *n and adj combining form.* colour, coloured, or pigment: *monochrome.* [from Gk *khrōma* colour]

hrome dioxide *n* another name for **chromium dioxide.**

hromel ('krəʊmel) *n* a nickel-based alloy containing about 10 per cent chromium, used in heating elements. [C20: from CHRO(MIUM) + ME(TA)L]

hrome steel *n* any of various hard rust-resistant steels containing chromium.

hrome yellow *n* any yellow pigment consisting of lead chromate.

hromic ('krəʊmɪk) *adj* **1** of or containing chromium in the trivalent state. **2** of or derived from chromic acid.

hromic acid *n* an unstable dibasic oxidizing acid known only in solution and as chromate salts. Formula: H_2CrO_4.

hromite ('krəʊmaɪt) *n* a brownish-black mineral consisting of a ferrous chromic oxide in crystalline form: the only commercial source of chromium. Formula: $FeCr_2O_4$.

hromium ('krəʊmɪəm) *n* a hard grey metallic element, used in steel alloys and electroplating to increase hardness and corrosion-resistance. Symbol: Cr; atomic no.: 24; atomic wt.: 51.996. [C19: from NL, from F: CHROME]

chromium dioxide *n* a chemical compound used as a magnetic coating on cassette tapes; chromium(IV) oxide. Formula: CrO_2. Also called (*not in technical usage*): **chrome dioxide.**

chromium steel *n* another name for **chrome steel.**

chromo ('krəʊməʊ) *n, pl* **chromos.** short for **chromolithograph.**

chromo- *or before a vowel* **chrom-** *combining form.* **1** indicating colour, coloured, or pigment: *chromogen.* **2** indicating chromium: *chromyl.* [from Gk *khrōma* colour]

chromolithograph (ˌkrəʊməʊ'lɪθəˌɡrɑːf) *n* a picture produced by chromolithography.

chromolithography (ˌkrəʊməʊlɪ'θɒɡrəfɪ) *n* the process of making coloured prints by lithography. ► ˌ**chromoli'thographer** *n* ► **chromolithographic** (ˌkrəʊməʊlɪθə'ɡræfɪk) *adj*

chromosome ('krəʊməˌsəʊm) *n* any of the microscopic rod-shaped structures that appear in a cell nucleus during cell division, consisting of nucleoprotein arranged into units (genes) that are responsible for the transmission of hereditary characteristics. ► ˌ**chromo'somal** *adj*

chromosome map *n* a graphic representation of the positions of genes on chromosomes, obtained by observation of stained chromosomes or by determining the degree of linkage between genes. See also **genetic map.** ► **chromosome mapping** *n*

chromosphere ('krəʊməˌsfɪə) *n* a gaseous layer of the sun's atmosphere extending from the photosphere to the corona. ► **chromospheric** (ˌkrəʊmə'sferɪk) *adj*

chromous ('krəʊməs) *adj* of or containing chromium in the divalent state.

chron. *or* **chronol.** *abbrev. for:* **1** chronological. **2** chronology.

Chron. *Bible. abbrev. for* Chronicles.

chronic ('krɒnɪk) *adj* **1** continuing for a long time; constantly recurring. **2** (of a disease) developing slowly, or of long duration. Cf. **acute** (sense 7). **3** inveterate; habitual: *a chronic smoker.* **4** *Inf.* **4a** very bad: *the play was chronic.* **4b** very serious: *he left her in a chronic condition.* [C15: from L, from Gk, from *khronos* time] ► ˈ**chronically** *adv* ► **chronicity** (krɒ'nɪsɪtɪ) *n*

chronic fatigue syndrome *n* a condition characterized by painful muscles and general weakness, sometimes persisting long after a viral illness. Also called: **myalgic encephalomyelitis, postviral syndrome.** Abbrev.: **CFS.**

chronicle ('krɒnɪk³l) *n* **1** a record or register of events in chronological order. ◆ *vb* **chronicles, chronicling, chronicled. 2** (*tr*) to record in or as if in a chronicle. [C14: from Anglo-F, via L *chronica* (pl) from Gk *khronika* annals; see CHRONIC] ► ˈ**chronicler** *n*

chrono- *or before a vowel* **chron-** *combining form.* time: *chronology.* [from Gk *khronos* time]

chronograph ('krɒnəˌɡrɑːf, 'krəʊnə-) *n* **1** an accurate instrument for recording small intervals of time. **2** any timepiece, esp. a wristwatch designed for maximum accuracy. ► **chronographic** (ˌkrɒnə'ɡræfɪk) *adj*

chronological (ˌkrɒnə'lɒdʒɪk³l, ˌkrəʊ-) *or* **chronologic** *adj* **1** (esp. of a sequence of events) arranged in order of occurrence. **2** relating to or in accordance with chronology. ► ˌ**chrono'logically** *adv*

chronology (krə'nɒlədʒɪ) *n, pl* **chronologies. 1** the determination of the proper sequence of past events. **2** the arrangement of dates, events, etc., in order of occurrence. **3** a table of events arranged in order of occurrence. ► **chro'nologist** *n*

chronometer (krə'nɒmɪtə) *n* a timepiece designed to be accurate in all conditions of temperature, pressure, etc., used esp. at sea. ► **chronometric** (ˌkrɒnə'metrɪk) *or* ˌ**chrono'metrical** *adj* ► ˌ**chrono'metrically** *adv*

chronometry (krə'nɒmɪtrɪ) *n* the science of measuring time with extreme accuracy.

chronon ('krəʊnɒn) *n* a unit of time equal to the time that a photon would take to traverse the diameter of an electron: about 10^{-24} seconds.

chrysalid ('krɪsəlɪd) *n* **1** another name for **chrysalis.** ◆ *adj* **2** of or relating to a chrysalis.

chrysalis ('krɪsəlɪs) *n, pl* **chrysalises** *or* **chrysalides** (krɪ'sælɪˌdiːz). **1** the pupa of a moth or butterfly, in a case or cocoon. **2** anything in the process of developing. [C17: from L, from Gk *khrusallis*, from *khrusos* gold]

chrysanthemum (krɪ'sænθəməm) *n* **1** any of various widely cultivated plants of the composite family, having brightly coloured showy flower heads in autumn. **2** any other plant of the genus *Chrysanthemum,* such as the oxeye daisy. [C16: from L: marigold, from Gk, from *khrusos* gold + *anthemon* flower]

chryselephantine (ˌkrɪselɪ'fæntɪn) *adj* (of ancient Greek statues, etc.) made of or overlaid with gold and ivory. [C19: from Gk, from *khrusos* gold + *elephas* ivory]

chrysoberyl ('krɪsə,berɪl) *n* a rare very hard greenish-yellow mineral consisting of beryllium aluminate: used as a gemstone. Formula: $BeAl_2O_4$. [C17: from L, from Gk, from *khrusos* gold + *berullos* beryl]

chrysolite ('krɪsə,laɪt) *n* a brown or yellowish-green olivine: used as a gemstone. [C14 *crisolite,* from OF, from L, from Gk, from *khrusos* gold + *lithos* stone]

chrysoprase ('krɪsə,preɪz) *n* an apple-green variety of chalcedony: used as a gemstone. [C13 *crisopace,* from OF, from L, from Gk, from *khrusos* gold + *prason* leek]

Chrysostom ★ ('krɪsəstəm) *n* Saint **John.** ?345–407 A.D., Greek patriarch; archbishop of Constantinople (398–404). Feast day: Sept. 13 or Nov. 13.

chthonian ('θəʊnɪən) *or* **chthonic** ('θɒnɪk) *adj* of or relating to the underworld. [C19: from Gk *khthonios* in or under the earth, from *khthōn* earth]

chub (tʃʌb) *n, pl* **chub** *or* **chubs. 1** a common European freshwater cyprinid game fish, having a dark greenish body. **2** any of various North American fishes, esp. certain whitefishes and minnows. [C15: from ?]

chubby ('tʃʌbɪ) *adj* **chubbier, chubbiest.** (esp. of the human form) plump. [C17: ?from CHUB]
▶ **'chubbiness** *n*

Chu Chiang ★ ('tʃuː 'kjæŋ, kaɪ'æŋ) *n* a variant transliteration of the Chinese name for the **Zhu Jiang.**

chuck[1] (tʃʌk) *vb* (*mainly tr*) **1** *Inf.* to throw. **2** to pat affectionately, esp. under the chin. **3** *Inf.* (sometimes foll. by *in* or *up*) to give up; reject: *he chucked up his job.* ◆ *n* **4** a throw or toss. **5** a pat under the chin. *Inf.* dismissal. ◆ See also **chuck in, chuck off, chuck out.** [C16: from ?]

chuck[2] (tʃʌk) *n* **1** Also called: **chuck steak.** a cut of beef from the neck to the shoulder blade. **2** a device that holds a workpiece in a lathe or tool in a drill. [C17: var. of CHOCK]

chuck[3] (tʃʌk) *n W Canad.* **1** a large body of water. **2** In full: **saltchuck.** the sea. [C19: from Chinook Jargon, of Amerind origin, from *chauk*]

chuck in *vb* (*adv*) **1** (*tr*) *Brit inf.* to abandon or give up: *to chuck in a hopeless attempt.* **2** (*intr*) *Austral. inf.* to contribute to the cost of something.

chuckle ('tʃʌkᵊl) *vb* **chuckles, chuckling, chuckled.** (*intr*) **1** to laugh softly or to oneself. **2** (of animals, esp. hens) to make a clucking sound. ◆ *n* **3** a partly suppressed laugh. [C16: prob. from *chuck* cluck + *le*]

chucklehead ('tʃʌkᵊl,hed) *n Inf.* a stupid person; dolt.

chuck off *vb* (*intr, adv;* often foll. by *at*) *Austral. & NZ inf.* to abuse or make fun of.

chuck out *vb* (*tr, adv;* often foll. by *of*) *Inf.* to eject forcibly (from); throw out (of).

Chudskoye Ozero ★ (*Russian* 'tʃutskəjɪ 'ɔzɪrə) *n* the Russian name for Lake **Peipus.**

chuff[1] (tʃʌf) *n* **1** a puffing sound as of a steam engine. ◆ *vb* **2** (*intr*) to move while emitting such sounds. [C20: imit.]

chuff[2] (tʃʌf) *vb* (*tr; usually passive*) *Brit. sl.* to please or delight: *he was chuffed by his pay rise.* [prob. from *chuff* (adj) pleased, happy]

chug (tʃʌg) *n* **1** a short dull sound, such as that made by an engine. ◆ *vb* **chugs, chugging, chugged. 2** (*intr*) (of an engine, etc.) to operate while making such sounds. [C19: imit.]

chukar (tʃʌ'kɑː) *n* a common Indian partridge having a red bill and black-barred sandy plumage. [from Hindi *cakor,* from Sansk. *cakora,* prob. imit.]

Chu Kiang ★ ('tʃuː 'kjæŋ, kaɪ'æŋ) *n* a variant transliteration of the Chinese name for the **Zhu Jiang.**

chukka *or US* **chukker** ('tʃʌkə) *n Polo.* a period of continuous play, generally lasting 7½ minutes. [C20: from Hindi *cakkar,* from Sansk. *cakra* wheel]

chukka boot ('tʃʌkə) *or* **chukka** *n* an ankle-high boo worn for playing polo. [C19: from CHUKKA]

chum (tʃʌm) *n* **1** *Inf.* a close friend. ◆ *vb* **chums, chummin chummed. 2** (*intr;* usually foll. by *up with*) to be or becom an intimate friend (of). [C17 (meaning: a person sha ing rooms with another): prob. shortened from *chamb fellow*]

chummy ('tʃʌmɪ) *adj* **chummier, chummiest.** *Inf.* friendly.
▶ **'chummily** *adv* ▶ **'chumminess** *n*

chump (tʃʌmp) *n* **1** *Inf.* a stupid person. **2** a thick heav block of wood. **3** the thick blunt end of anything, esp. c a piece of meat. **4** *Brit. sl.* the head (esp. in **off one's chump** [C18: ? a blend of CHUNK + LUMP]

chunder ('tʃʌndə) *Sl., chiefly Austral.* ◆ *vb* (*intr*) **1** t vomit. ◆ *n* **2** vomit. [C20: from ?]

Chungking ('tʃʊŋ'kɪŋ, 'tʃʌŋ-) *or* **Ch'ung-ch'ing** ('tʃʊŋ'tʃɪŋ, 'tʃʌŋ-) *n* a variant transliteration of the Ch nese name for **Chongqing.**

chunk (tʃʌŋk) *n* **1** a thick solid piece, as of meat, woo etc. **2** a considerable amount. [C17: var. of CHUCK[2]]

chunky ('tʃʌŋkɪ) *adj* **chunkier, chunkiest. 1** thick and short **2** containing thick pieces. **3** *Chiefly Brit.* (of clothes, es knitwear) made of thick bulky material.
▶ **'chunkiness** *n*

Chunnel ('tʃʌnᵊl) *n* an informal name for **Channel Tunne** [C20: from CH(ANNEL) + T(UNNEL)]

chunter ('tʃʌntə) *vb* (*intr;* often foll. by *on*) *Brit. inf.* t mutter or grumble incessantly in a meaningless fashion [C16: prob. imit.]

Chuquisaca ★ (*Spanish* tʃuki'saka) *n* the former nam (until 1839) of **Sucre**[1].

Chur ★ (*German* kuːr) *n* a city in E Switzerland, capital o Grisons canton. Pop.: 30 250 (1990). Ancient name: **Cu ria Rhaetorum** ('kuːrɪə riː'təʊrəm, 'kjuː:-). French name Coire.

church (tʃɜːtʃ) *n* **1** a building for public worship, esp Christian worship. **2** an occasion of public worship. **3** the clergy as distinguished from the laity. **4** (*usually cap.* institutionalized forms of religion as a political or socia force: *conflict between Church and State.* **5** (*usually cap.*) th collective body of all Christians. **6** (*often cap.*) a particula Christian denomination or group. **7** (*often cap.*) the Christian religion. ◆ Related adj: **ecclesiastical.** ◆ *v* (*tr*) **8** *Church of England.* to bring (someone, esp. a woma after childbirth) to church for special ceremonies. [O cirice,* from LGk, from Gk *kuriakon (dōma)* the Lord' (house), from *kurios* master, from *kuros* power]

Church Army *n* a voluntary Anglican organizatio founded to assist the parish clergy.

Church Commissioners *pl n Brit.* a group of repre sentatives of Church and State that administers th property of the Church of England.

churchgoer ('tʃɜːtʃ,gəʊə) *n* a person who attends churc regularly.
▶ **'church,going** *adj, n*

Churchill[1] ★ ('tʃɜːtʃɪl) *n* **1** a river in E Canada, rising in L Labrador and flowing north and southeast over Chur chill Falls, then east to the Atlantic. Length: about 100 km (600 miles). Former name: **Hamilton River. 2** a river i central Canada, rising in NW Saskatchewan and flowin east through several lakes to Hudson Bay. Length: abou 1600 km (1000 miles).

Churchill[2] ★ ('tʃɜːtʃɪl) *n* **1 Charles.** 1731–64, British poet noted for *The Rosciad* (1761) and *The Prophecy of Famin* (1763). **2 John.** See (1st Duke of) **Marlborough. 3** Lor **Randolph.** 1849–95, British Conservative politician: secre tary of state for India (1885–86) and chancellor of th Exchequer (1886). **4** his son, Sir **Winston** (**Leonard Spencer** 1874–1965, British Conservative statesman and write noted for his leadership during World War II. 1st Lord o the Admiralty (1911–15); prime minister (1940–45 1951–55). His writings include *Marlborough* (1933–38) *The Second World War* (1948–54), and *History of the Eng lish-Speaking Peoples* (1956–58): Nobel prize for literatur 1953.

Churchill Falls ★ *pl n* a waterfall in E Canada, in SW Labrador on the Churchill River: site of one of the larges hydroelectric power projects in the world. Height: 75 m (245 ft). Former name: **Grand Falls.**

churchly ('tʃɜːtʃlɪ) adj appropriate to or associated with the church.
▸ 'churchliness n

churchman ('tʃɜːtʃmən) n, pl churchmen. 1 a clergyman. 2 a male member of a church.

Church of Christ, Scientist n See **Christian Science.**

Church of England n the reformed established state Church in England, with the Sovereign as its temporal head.

Church of Jesus Christ of Latter-Day Saints n See **Mormon** (sense 1).

churchwarden (,tʃɜːtʃ'wɔːdᵊn) n 1 Church of England, Episcopal Church. one of two assistants of a parish priest who administer the secular affairs of the church. 2 a long-stemmed tobacco pipe made of clay.

churchwoman ('tʃɜːtʃ,wʊmən) n, pl churchwomen. a female member of a church.

churchyard ('tʃɜːtʃ,jɑːd) n the grounds round a church, used as a graveyard.

churinga (tʃə'rɪŋgə) n, pl churinga or churingas. a sacred amulet of the native Australians. [from Abor.]

churl (tʃɜːl) n 1 a surly ill-bred person. 2 Arch. a farm labourer. 3 Arch. a miserly person. [OE ceorl]
▸ 'churlish adj

churn (tʃɜːn) n 1 Brit. a large container for milk. 2 a vessel or machine in which cream or whole milk is vigorously agitated to produce butter. ◆ vb 3a to agitate (milk or cream) to make butter. 3b to make (butter) by this process. 4 (sometimes foll. by up) to move or cause to move with agitation. 5 (of a bank, broker, etc.) to encourage an investor or policyholder to change investments, endowment policies, etc., to increase commissions at the client's expense. 6 (of a government) to pay benefits to a wide category of people and claw it back by taxation from the well off. 7 to promote the turnover of existing subscribers leasing, and new subscribers joining, a cable television system. [OE ciern]
▸ 'churner n

churn out vb (tr, adv) Inf. 1 to produce (something) at a rapid rate: to churn out ideas. 2 to perform (something) mechanically: to churn out a song.

churr (tʃɜː) vb, n a variant spelling of **chirr.**

chute[1] (ʃuːt) n 1 an inclined channel or vertical passage down which water, parcels, coal, etc., may be dropped. 2 a steep slope, used as a slide as for toboggans. 3 a slide into a swimming pool. 4 a rapid or waterfall. [C19: from OF cheoite, fem. p.p. of cheoir to fall, from L cadere; in some senses, var. spelling of SHOOT]

chute[2] (ʃuːt) n, vb chutes, chuting, chuted. Inf. short for **parachute.**
▸ 'chutist n

Chu Teh ('tʃuː 'teɪ) or **Zhu De** ★ n 1886–1976, Chinese military leader and politician; commander in chief of the Red Army (1931) and was chairman of the Standing Committee of the National People's Congress of the People's Republic of China (1959–76).

chutney ('tʃʌtnɪ) n a pickle of Indian origin, made from fruit, vinegar, spices, sugar, etc.: mango chutney. [C19: from Hindi catni, from ?]

chutzpah ('xʊtspə) n US & Canad. inf. shameless audacity; impudence. [C20: from Yiddish]

Chuvash Republic ★ n (tʃu'vɑːʃ) n a constituent republic of W central Russia, in the middle Volga valley: generally low and undulating, with large areas of forest. Capital: Cheboksary. Pop.: 1 361 000 (1995 est.). Area: 18 300 sq. km (7064 sq. miles). Also called: **Chuvashia** (tʃuː'vɑːʃɪə).

chyack ('tʃaɪæk) vb, n a variant spelling of **chiack.**

chyle (kaɪl) n a milky fluid composed of lymph and emulsified fat globules, formed in the small intestine during digestion. [C17: from LL, from Gk khulos juice]
▸ **chylaceous** (kaɪ'leɪʃəs) or 'chylous adj

chyme (kaɪm) n the thick fluid mass of partially digested

food that leaves the stomach. [C17: from LL, from Gk khumos juice]
▸ 'chymous adj

chypre French. (ʃiprə) n a perfume made from sandalwood. [lit.: Cyprus, ? where it originated]

Ci symbol for curie.

CI abbrev. for Channel Islands.

CIA abbrev. for Central Intelligence Agency; a federal US bureau created in 1947 to coordinate and conduct espionage and intelligence activities.

ciabatta (tʃə'bætə) n a type of open-textured bread made with olive oil. [C20: from It., lit.: slipper]

Ciano ★ (Italian 'tʃaːno) n Galeazzo (gale'attso), full name Conte Galeazzo Ciano di Cortellazzo. 1903–44, Italian fascist politician; minister of foreign affairs (1936–43) and son-in-law of Mussolini: executed.

CIB abbrev. for Criminal Investigation Branch (of the New Zealand and Australian police).

Cibber ★ ('sɪbə) n Colley ('kɒlɪ). 1671–1757, English actor and dramatist; poet laureate (1730–57).

ciborium (sɪ'bɔːrɪəm) n, pl ciboria (-rɪə). Christianity. 1 a goblet-shaped lidded vessel used to hold consecrated wafers in Holy Communion. 2 a canopy fixed over an altar. [C17: from Med. L, from L, from Gk kibōrion cup-shaped seed vessel of the Egyptian lotus]

cicada (sɪ'kɑːdə) or **cicala** n, pl cicadas, cicadae (-diː) or cicale (-leɪ). any large broad insect, most common in warm regions, having membranous wings: the males produce a high-pitched drone by vibration of a pair of drumlike abdominal organs. [C19: from L]

cicatrix ('sɪkətrɪks) n, pl cicatrices (,sɪkə'traɪsiːz). 1 the tissue that forms in a wound during healing; scar. 2 a scar on a plant indicating the former point of attachment of a part, esp. a leaf. [C17: from L: scar, from ?]
▸ **cicatricial** (,sɪkə'trɪʃəl) adj

cicatrize or **cicatrise** ('sɪkə,traɪz) vb cicatrizes, cicatrizing, cicatrized or cicatrises, cicatrising, cicatrised. (of a wound or defect in tissue) to be closed by scar formation; heal.
▸ ,cicatri'zation or ,cicatri'sation n

cicely ('sɪsəlɪ) n, pl cicelies. short for **sweet cicely.** [C16: from L seselis, from Gk, from ?]

Cicero ★ (sɪsə,rəʊ) n Marcus Tullius ('maːkəs 'tʌlɪəs). 106–43 B.C., Roman consul and writer. He foiled Catiline's conspiracy (63) and was killed by Mark Antony's agents. Formerly known in English as **Tully.**

cicerone (,sɪsə'rəʊnɪ, ,tʃɪtʃ-) n, pl cicerones or ciceroni (-nɪ). a person who conducts and informs sightseers. [C18: from It.: antiquarian scholar, guide, after CICERO]

Cid ★ (sɪd; Spanish θið) n **El** or **the.** original name Rodrigo Diaz de Vivar. ?1043–99, Spanish soldier and hero of the wars against the Moors.

CID (in Britain) abbrev. for Criminal Investigation Department; the detective division of a police force.

-cide n combining form. 1 indicating a person or thing that kills: insecticide. 2 indicating a killing; murder: homicide. [from L -cīda (agent), and -cīdium (act), from caedere to kill]
▸ **-cidal** adj combining form.

cider or **cyder** ('saɪdə) n 1 an alcoholic drink made from the fermented juice of apples. 2 Also called: **sweet cider.** US & Canad. an unfermented drink made from apple juice. [C14: from OF, via Med. L, from LGk sikera strong drink, from Heb. shēkhār]

c.i.f. or **CIF** abbrev. for cost, insurance, and freight (included in the price quoted).

c.i.f.c.i. abbrev. for cost, insurance, freight, commission, and interest (included in the price quoted).

cig (sɪg) or **ciggy** ('sɪgɪ) n, pl cigs or ciggies. Inf. a cigarette.

cigar (sɪ'gɑː) n a cylindrical roll of cured tobacco leaves, for smoking. [C18: from Sp. cigarro]

cigarette or US (sometimes) **cigaret** (,sɪgə'rɛt) n a short tightly rolled cylinder of tobacco, wrapped in thin paper for smoking. [C19: from F, lit.: a little CIGAR]

cigarette card n a small picture card, formerly given away with cigarettes, now collected as a hobby.

★ people and places

cigarillo (ˌsɪgəˈrɪləʊ) *n, pl* **cigarillos.** a small cigar, often only slightly larger than a cigarette.

ciliary (ˈsɪlɪərɪ) *adj* of or relating to cilia.

ciliary body *n* the part of the eye that joins the choroid to the iris.

Cilician Gates ★ (sɪˈlɪʃɪən) *pl n* a pass in S Turkey, over the Taurus Mountains. Turkish name: **Gülek Bogaz.**

cilium (ˈsɪlɪəm) *n, pl* **cilia** (ˈsɪlɪə). **1** any of the short threads projecting from the surface of a cell, organism, etc., whose rhythmic beating causes movement. **2** the technical name for **eyelash.** [C18: NL, from L: (lower) eyelid, eyelash]
▶ **ciliate** (ˈsɪlɪɪt, -eɪt) *or* **ˈciliˌated** *adj*

Çiller ★ (ʃɪlə) *n* **Tansu** (ˈtænzuː). born 1945, Turkish politician; prime minister (1993–96).

Cimarosa ★ (*Italian* tʃimaˈroza) *n* **Domenico** (doˈmeːniko). 1749–1801, Italian composer, noted for his opera buffa *The Secret Marriage* (1792).

C in C *or* **C.-in-C.** *Mil. abbrev. for* Commander in Chief.

cinch (sɪntʃ) *n* **1** *Sl.* an easy task. **2** *Sl.* a certainty. **3** a US and Canad. name for **girth** (sense 2). **4** *US inf.* a firm grip. ◆ *vb* **5** (often foll. by *up*) *US & Canad.* to fasten a girth around (a horse). **6** (*tr*) *Inf.* to make sure of. **7** (*tr*) *Inf., chiefly US.* to get a firm grip on. [C19: from Sp., from L, from *cingere* to encircle]

cinchona (sɪŋˈkəʊnə) *n* **1** any tree or shrub of the South American genus *Cinchona,* having medicinal bark. **2** the dried bark of any of these trees, which yields quinine. **3** any of the drugs derived from cinchona bark. [C18: NL, after the Countess of *Chinchón* (1576–1639), vicereine of Peru]
▶ **cinchonic** (sɪŋˈkɒnɪk) *adj*

Cincinnati ★ (ˌsɪnsɪˈnætɪ) *n* a city in SW Ohio, on the Ohio River. Pop.: 358 170 (1994 est.).

Cincinnatus ★ (ˌsɪnsɪˈnɑːtəs) *n* **Lucius Quinctius** (ˈluːsɪəs ˈkwɪŋktɪəs). ?519–438 B.C., Roman general; dictator of Rome during two crises (458; 439).

cincture (ˈsɪŋktʃə) *n* something that encircles, esp. a belt or girdle. [C16: from L, from *cingere* to gird]

cinder (ˈsɪndə) *n* **1** a piece of incombustible material left after the combustion of coal, coke, etc.; clinker. **2** a piece of charred material that burns without flames; ember. **3** any solid waste from smelting or refining. **4** (*pl*) fragments of volcanic lava; scoriae. [OE *sinder*]
▶ **ˈcindery** *adj*

Cinderella (ˌsɪndəˈrɛlə) *n* **1** a girl who achieves fame after being obscure. **2** a poor, neglected, or unsuccessful person or thing. [C19: after *Cinderella,* the heroine of a fairy tale]

cine- *combining form.* indicating motion picture or cinema: *cine camera; cinephotography.*

cineaste (ˈsɪnɪˌæst) *n* an enthusiast for films. [C20: F]

cinema (ˈsɪnɪmə) *n* **1** *Chiefly Brit.* a place designed for the exhibition of films. **2 the cinema. 2a** the art or business of making films. **2b** films collectively. [C19 (earlier spelling: *kinema*): shortened from CINEMATOGRAPH]
▶ **cinematic** (ˌsɪnɪˈmætɪk) *adj* ▶ **ˌcineˈmatically** *adv*

cinematograph (ˌsɪnɪˈmætəˌgrɑːf) *Chiefly Brit.* ◆ *n* **1** a combined camera, printer, and projector. ◆ *vb* **2** to take (pictures) with a film camera. [C19 (earlier spelling: *kinematograph*): from Gk *kinēma* motion + -GRAPH]
▶ **cinematographer** (ˌsɪnɪməˈtogrəfə) *n* ▶ **cinematographic** (ˌsɪnɪˌmætəˈgræfɪk) *adj* ▶ **ˌcineˌmatoˈgraphically** *adv* ▶ **ˌcinemaˈtography** *n*

cinéma vérité (*French* sinema verite) *n* films characterized by subjects, actions, etc., that have the appearance of real life. [F, lit.: truth cinema]

cineraria (ˌsɪnəˈrɛərɪə) *n* a plant of the Canary Islands, widely cultivated for its blue, purple, red, or variegated daisy-like flowers. [C16: from NL, from L, from *cinis* ashes; from its downy leaves]

cinerarium (ˌsɪnəˈrɛərɪəm) *n, pl* **cineraria** (-ˈrɛərɪə). a place for keeping the ashes of the dead after cremation. [C19: from L, from *cinerārius* relating to ashes]
▶ **cinerary** (ˈsɪnərərɪ) *adj*

cinerator (ˈsɪnəˌreɪtə) *n Chiefly US.* a furnace for cremating corpses.
▶ **ˌcineˈration** *n*

cinnabar (ˈsɪnəˌbɑː) *n* **1** a heavy red mineral consisting of mercury(II) sulphide: the chief ore of mercury. Formula: HgS. **2** the red form of mercury(II) sulphide, esp. when used as a pigment. **3a** a bright red; vermilion. **3b** (*as adj*): *a cinnabar tint.* **4** a large red-and-black European moth. [C15: from OF, from L, from Gk *kinnabari,* of Oriental origin]

cinnamon (ˈsɪnəmən) *n* **1** a tropical Asian tree, having aromatic yellowish-brown bark. **2** the spice obtained from the bark of this tree, used for flavouring food and drink. **3a** a light yellowish brown. **3b** (*as adj*): *a cinnamon coat.* [C15: from OF, via L & Gk, from Heb. *qinnamown*]

cinque (sɪŋk) *n* the number five in cards, dice, etc. [C14: from OF *cinq* five]

cinquecento (ˌtʃɪŋkwɪˈtʃɛntəʊ) *n* the 16th century, esp. in reference to Italian art, architecture, or literature. [C18: It., shortened from *milcinquecento* 1500]

cinquefoil (ˈsɪŋkˌfɔɪl) *n* **1** any plant of the N temperate rosaceous genus *Potentilla,* typically having five-lobed compound leaves. **2** an ornamental carving in the form of five arcs arranged in a circle and separated by cusps. [C13 *sink foil,* from OF, from L *quinquefolium* plant with five leaves]

Cinque Ports (sɪŋk) *pl n* an association of ports on the SE coast of England, which from late Anglo-Saxon times until 1685 provided ships for the king's service in return for the profits of justice in their courts.

Cintra ★ (ˈsɪntrə) *n* the former name for **Sintra.**

cipher *or* **cypher** (ˈsaɪfə) *n* **1** a method of secret writing using substitution of letters according to a key. **2** a secret message. **3** the key to a secret message. **4** an obsolete name for **zero** (sense 1). **5** any of the Arabic numerals or the Arabic system of numbering. **6** a person or thing of no importance; nonentity. **7** a design consisting of interwoven letters; monogram. ◆ *vb* **8** to put (a message) into secret writing. **9** *Rare.* to perform (a calculation) arithmetically. [C14: from OF *cifre* zero, from Med. L, from Ar. *sifr* zero]

circa (ˈsɜːkə) *prep* (used with a date) at the approximate time of: *circa 1182 B.C.* Abbrev.: **c, ca.** [L: about]

circadian (sɜːˈkeɪdɪən) *adj* of or relating to biological processes that occur regularly at 24-hour intervals. See also **biological clock.** [C20: from L *circa* about + *diēs* day]

Circassia ★ (sɜːˈkæsɪə) *n* a region of S Russia, on the Black Sea north of the Caucasus Mountains.

Circe ★ (ˈsɜːsɪ) *n Greek myth.* an enchantress who detained Odysseus on her island and turned his men into swine.
▶ **Circean** (sɜːˈsɪən) *adj*

circle (ˈsɜːkəl) *n* **1** a closed plane curve every point of which is equidistant from a given fixed point, the centre. **2** the figure enclosed by such a curve. **3** *Theatre.* the section of seats above the main level of the auditorium, usually comprising the dress circle and the upper circle. **4** something formed or arranged in the shape of a circle. **5** a group of people sharing an interest, activity, upbringing, etc.; set: *golf circles; a family circle.* **6** an area of activity, interest, or influence. **7** a circuit. **8** a process or chain of events or parts that forms a connected whole; cycle. **9** a parallel of latitude. See also **great circle, small circle. 10** one of a number of Neolithic or Bronze Age rings of standing stones, such as Stonehenge. **11 come full circle.** to arrive back at one's starting point. See also **vicious circle.** ◆ *vb* **circles, circling, circled. 12** to move in a circle (around). **13** (*tr*) to enclose in a circle; encircle. [C14: from L *circulus,* from *circus* ring, circle]
▶ **ˈcircler** *n*

circlet (ˈsɜːklɪt) *n* a small circle or ring, esp. a circular ornament worn on the head. [C15: from OF *cerclet* a little CIRCLE]

circuit (ˈsɜːkɪt) *n* **1a** a complete route or course, esp. one that is curved or circular or that lies around an object. **1b** the area enclosed within such a route. **2** the act of following such a route: *we made three circuits of the course.* **3a** a complete path through which an electric current can

flow. **3b** (*as modifier*): *a circuit diagram*. **4a** a periodical journey around an area, as made by judges, salesmen, etc. **4b** the places visited on such a journey. **4c** the persons making such a journey. **5** an administrative division of the Methodist Church comprising a number of neighbouring churches. **6** a number of theatres, cinemas, etc., under one management. **7** *Sport.* **7a** a series of tournaments in which the same players regularly take part: *the international tennis circuit.* **7b** (usually preceded by *the*) the contestants who take part in such a series. **8** *Chiefly Brit.* a motor-racing track, usually of irregular shape. ◆ *vb* **9** to make or travel in a circuit around (something). [C14: from L *circuitus,* from *circum* around + *īre* to go]
▸ **'circuital** *adj*

circuit breaker *n* a device that under abnormal conditions, such as a short circuit, stops the flow of current in an electrical circuit.

circuitous (sə'kjuːɪtəs) *adj* indirect and lengthy; roundabout: *a circuitous route.*
▸ **cir'cuitously** *adv* ▸ **cir'cuitousness** *n*

circuitry ('sɜːkɪtrɪ) *n* **1** the design of an electrical circuit. **2** the system of circuits used in an electronic device.

circuity (sə'kjuːɪtɪ) *n, pl* **circuities**. (of speech, reasoning, etc.) a roundabout or devious quality.

circular ('sɜːkjʊlə) *adj* **1** of, involving, resembling, or shaped like a circle. **2** circuitous. **3** (of arguments) futile because the truth of the premises cannot be established independently of the conclusion. **4** travelling or occurring in a cycle. **5** (of letters, announcements, etc.) intended for general distribution. ◆ *n* **6** a printed advertisement or notice for mass distribution.
▸ **circularity** (,sɜːkjʊ'lærɪtɪ) *n* ▸ **'circularly** *adv*

circular breathing *n* a technique for sustaining a phrase on a wind instrument, using the cheeks to force air out of the mouth while breathing in through the nose.

circularize *or* **circularise** ('sɜːkjʊlə,raɪz) *vb* **circularizes, circularizing, circularized** *or* **circularises, circularising, circularised.** (*tr*) **1** to distribute circulars to. **2** to canvass or petition (people), for support, votes, etc., by distributing letters, etc. **3** to make circular.
▸ **,circulari'zation** *or* **,circulari'sation** *n*

circular saw *n* a power-driven saw in which a circular disc with a toothed edge is rotated at high speed.

circulate ('sɜːkjʊ,leɪt) *vb* **circulates, circulating, circulated. 1** to send, go, or pass from place to place or person to person: *don't circulate the news.* **2** to distribute or be distributed over a wide area. **3** to move or cause to move through a circuit, system, etc., returning to the starting point: *blood circulates through the body.* **4** to move in a circle. [C15: from L *circulāri,* from *circulus* CIRCLE]
▸ **'circulative** *adj* ▸ **'circu,lator** *n* ▸ **'circulatory** *adj*

circulating library *n* **1** another word (esp. US) for **lending library. 2** a small library circulated in turn to a group of institutions.

circulation (,sɜːkjʊ'leɪʃən) *n* **1** the transport of oxygenated blood through the arteries, and the return of oxygen-depleted blood through the veins to the heart, where the cycle is renewed. **2** the flow of sap through a plant. **3** any movement through a closed circuit. **4** the spreading or transmission of something to a wider group of people or area. **5** (of air and water) free movement within an area or volume. **6a** the distribution of newspapers, magazines, etc. **6b** the number of copies of an issue that are distributed. **7** in circulation. **7a** (of currency) serving as a medium of exchange. **7b** (of people) active in a social or business context.

circulatory system *n Anat., zool.* the system concerned with the transport of blood and lymph, consisting of the heart, blood vessels, lymph vessels, etc.

circum- *prefix* around; surrounding; on all sides: *circumlocution; circumpolar.* [from L *circum* around, from *circus* circle]

circumambient (,sɜːkəm'æmbɪənt) *adj* surrounding. [C17: from LL, from L CIRCUM- + *ambīre* to go round]
▸ **,circum'ambience** *or* **,circum'ambiency** *n*

circumambulate (,sɜːkəm'æmbjʊ,leɪt) *vb* **circumambulates, circumambulating, circumambulated. 1** to walk around

(something). **2** (*intr*) to avoid the point. [C17: from LL, from L CIRCUM- + *ambulāre* to walk]
▸ **,circum,ambu'lation** *n*

circumcise ('sɜːkəm,saɪz) *vb* **circumcises, circumcising, circumcised.** (*tr*) **1** to remove the foreskin of (a male). **2** to incise surgically the skin over the clitoris of (a female). **3** to remove the clitoris of (a female). **4** to perform such an operation as a religious rite on (someone). [C13: from L from CIRCUM- + *caedere* to cut]
▸ **circumcision** (,sɜːkəm'sɪʒən) *n*

circumference (sə'kʌmfərəns) *n* **1** the boundary of a specific area or figure, esp. of a circle. **2** the length of a closed geometric curve, esp. of a circle. [C14: from OF, from L from CIRCUM- + *ferre* to bear]
▸ **circumferential** (sə,kʌmfə'renʃəl) *adj* ▸ **cir,cumfer'entially** *adv*

circumflex ('sɜːkəm,fleks) *n* **1** a mark (^) placed over a vowel to show that it is pronounced with rising and falling pitch, as in ancient Greek, or as a long vowel, as in French. ◆ *adj* **2** (of nerves, arteries, etc.) bending or curving around. [C16: from L, from CIRCUM- + *flectere* to bend]
▸ **,circum'flexion** *n*

circumfuse (,sɜːkəm'fjuːz) *vb* **circumfuses, circumfusing, circumfused.** (*tr*) **1** to pour or spread (a liquid, powder, etc.) around. **2** to surround with a substance, such as a liquid. [C16: from L *circumfūsus,* from CIRCUM- + *fundere* to pour]
▸ **circumfusion** (,sɜːkəm'fjuːʒən) *n*

circumlocution (,sɜːkəmlə'kjuːʃən) *n* **1** an indirect way of expressing something. **2** an indirect expression.
▸ **circumlocutory** (,sɜːkəm'lɒkjətərɪ, -trɪ) *adj*

circumnavigate (,sɜːkəm'nævɪ,geɪt) *vb* **circumnavigates, circumnavigating, circumnavigated.** (*tr*) to sail or fly completely around.
▸ **,circum,navi'gation** *n* ▸ **,circum'navi,gator** *n*

circumscribe (,sɜːkəm'skraɪb, 'sɜːkəm,skraɪb) *vb* **circumscribes, circumscribing, circumscribed.** (*tr*) **1** to restrict within limits. **2** to mark or set the bounds of. **3** to draw a geometric construction around (another construction) so that the two are in contact but do not intersect. **4** to draw a line round. [C15: from L from CIRCUM- + *scrībere* to write]
▸ **,circum'scribable** *adj* ▸ **,circum'scriber** *n* ▸ **circumscription** (,sɜːkəm'skrɪpʃən) *n*

circumspect ('sɜːkəm,spekt) *adj* cautious, prudent, or discreet. [C15: from L, from CIRCUM- + *specere* to look]
▸ **,circum'spection** *n* ▸ **'circum,spectly** *adv*

circumstance ('sɜːkəmstəns) *n* **1** (*usually pl*) a condition of time, place, etc., that accompanies or influences an event or condition. **2** an incident or occurrence, esp. a chance one. **3** accessory information or detail. **4** formal display or ceremony (archaic except in **pomp and circumstance**). **5** under *or* in no circumstances. in no case; never. **6** under the circumstances. because of conditions; this being the case. ◆ *vb* **circumstances, circumstancing, circumstanced.** (*tr*) **7** to place in a particular condition or situation. [C13: from OF, from L *circumstantia,* from CIRCUM- + *stāre* to stand]

circumstantial (,sɜːkəm'stænʃəl) *adj* **1** of or dependent on circumstances. **2** fully detailed. **3** incidental.
▸ **,circum,stanti'ality** *n* ▸ **,circum'stantially** *adv*

circumstantial evidence *n* indirect evidence that tends to establish a conclusion by inference.

circumstantiate (,sɜːkəm'stænʃɪ,eɪt) *vb* **circumstantiates, circumstantiating, circumstantiated.** (*tr*) to support by giving particulars.
▸ **,circum,stanti'ation** *n*

circumvallate (,sɜːkəm'væleɪt) *vb* **circumvallates, circumvallating, circumvallated.** (*tr*) to surround with a defensive fortification. [C19: from L, from CIRCUM- + *vallum* rampart]
▸ **,circumval'lation** *n*

circumvent (,sɜːkəm'vent) *vb* (*tr*) **1** to evade or go around. **2** to outwit. **3** to encircle (an enemy) so as to intercept or capture. [C15: from L, from CIRCUM- + *venīre* to come]
▸ **,circum'vention** *n*

circus ('sɜːkəs) *n, pl* **circuses. 1** a travelling company of entertainers such as acrobats, clowns, trapeze artists, and trained animals. **2** a public performance given by such a company. **3** an arena, usually tented, in which such a performance is held. **4** a travelling group of professional sportsmen: *a cricket circus.* **5** (in ancient Rome) **5a** an open-air stadium, usually oval or oblong, for chariot races or public games. **5b** the games themselves. **6** *Brit.* **6a** an open place, usually circular, where several streets converge. **6b** (*cap. when part of a name*): *Piccadilly Circus.* **7** *Inf.* noisy or rowdy behaviour. **8** *Inf.* a group of people travelling together and putting on a display. [C16: from L, from Gk *kirkos* ring]

ciré ('sɪəreɪ) *adj* **1** (of fabric) treated with a heat or wax process to make it smooth. ◆ *n* **2** such a surface on a fabric. **3** a fabric having such a surface. [C20: F, from L *cēra* wax]

Cirencester ★ ('saɪrən,sestə) *n* a market town in S England, in Gloucestershire: Roman amphitheatre. Pop.: 15 221 (1991). Latin name: *Corinium.*

cirque (sɜːk) *n* a steep-sided semicircular or crescent-shaped depression found in mountainous regions. [C17: from F, from L *circus* ring]

cirrhosis (sɪ'rəʊsɪs) *n* any of various chronic progressive diseases of the liver, characterized by death of liver cells, irreversible fibrosis, etc. [C19: NL, from Gk *kirrhos* orange-coloured + -OSIS; referring to the appearance of the diseased liver]
> **cirrhotic** (sɪ'rɒtɪk) *adj*

cirripede ('sɪrɪ,piːd) *or* **cirriped** ('sɪrɪ,ped) *n* **1** any marine crustacean of the subclass *Cirripedia,* including the barnacles. ◆ *adj* **2** of, relating to, or belonging to the *Cirripedia.*

cirrocumulus (,sɪrəʊ'kjuːmjʊləs) *n, pl* **cirrocumuli** (-,laɪ). a high cloud of ice crystals grouped into small separate globular masses.

cirrostratus (,sɪrəʊ'strɑːtəs) *n, pl* **cirrostrati** (-taɪ). a uniform layer of cloud above about 6000 metres.

cirrus ('sɪrəs) *n, pl* **cirri** (-raɪ). **1** a thin wispy fibrous cloud at high altitudes, composed of ice particles. **2** a plant tendril or similar part. **3a** a slender tentacle or filament in barnacles and other marine invertebrates. **3b** any of various hairlike structures in other animals. [C18: from L: curl]

CIS *abbrev. for* Commonwealth of Independent States.

cis- *prefix* on this side of, as in **cismontane** on this side of the mountains. Often retains the original Latin sense of 'side nearest Rome', as in **cispadane** on this (the southern) side of the Po. [from L]

cisalpine (sɪs'ælpaɪn) *adj* on this (the southern) side of the Alps, as viewed from Rome.

Cisalpine Gaul ★ *n* (in the ancient world) that part of Gaul between the Alps and the Apennines.

Ciscaucasia ★ (,sɪskɔː'keɪzɪə, -ʒə) *n* the part of Caucasia north of the Caucasus Mountains.

cisco ('sɪskəʊ) *n, pl* **ciscoes** *or* **ciscos.** any of various whitefish, esp. the lake herring of cold deep lakes of North America. [C19: short for Canad. F *ciscoette,* of Algonquian origin]

Ciskei ★ ('sɪskaɪ) *n* (formerly) a Bantu homeland in SE South Africa; reintegrated into South Africa in 1994.

cislunar (sɪs'luːnə) *adj* of or relating to the space between the earth and the moon.

cisplatin (sɪs'plætɪn) *n* a cytotoxic drug that acts by preventing DNA replication and hence cell divisions, used in the treatment of tumours of the ovary and testis. [C20: from CIS- + PLATIN(UM)]

cissing ('sɪsɪŋ) *n* Building trades. the appearance of pinholes, craters, etc., in paintwork due to poor adhesion of the paint to the surface.

cissy ('sɪsɪ) *n, pl* **-sies.** a variant spelling of **sissy.**

cist[1] (sɪst) *n* a wooden box for holding ritual objects used in ancient Rome and Greece. [C19: from L *cista* box, from Gk *kistē*]

cist[2] (sɪst) *or* **kist** *n* a box-shaped burial chamber made from stone slabs or a hollowed tree trunk. [C19: from Welsh: chest, from L; see CIST[1]]

Cistercian (sɪ'stɜːʃən) *n* **1** Also called: **White Monk.** a member of a Christian order of monks and nuns founded in 1098, which follows an especially strict form of the Benedictine rule. ◆ *adj* **2** of or relating to this order. [C17: from F, from Med. L, from *Cistercium* (modern *Cîteaux*), original home of the order]

cistern ('sɪstən) *n* **1** a tank for the storage of water, esp. on or within the roof of a house or connected to a WC. **2** an underground reservoir for the storage of a liquid, esp. rainwater. **3** Also called: **cisterna.** *Anat.* a sac or partially enclosed space containing body fluid. [C13: from OF, from L *cisterna* underground tank, from *cista* box]

cistus ('sɪstəs) *n* any plant of the genus *Cistus.* See **rockrose.** [C16: NL, from Gk *kistos*]

citadel ('sɪtəd°l, -,del) *n* **1** a stronghold within or close to a city. **2** any strongly fortified building or place of safety; refuge. [C16: from OF, from OIt. *cittadella* a little city, from L *cīvitās*]

citation (saɪ'teɪʃən) *n* **1** the quoting of a book or author. **2** a passage or source cited. **3a** an official commendation or award, esp. for bravery or outstanding service. **3b** a formal public statement of this. **4** *Law.* **4a** an official summons to appear in court. **4b** the document containing such a summons.
> **citatory** ('saɪtətərɪ) *adj*

cite (saɪt) *vb* **cites, citing, cited.** (*tr*) **1** to quote or refer to (a passage, book, or author). **2** to mention or commend (a soldier, etc.) for outstanding bravery or meritorious action. **3** to summon to appear before a court of law. **4** to enumerate: *he cited the king's virtues.* [C15: from OF *citer* to summon, ult. from L *ciēre* to excite]
> **'citable** *or* **'citeable** *adj*

cithara ('sɪθərə) *or* **kithara** ('kɪθərə) *n* a stringed musical instrument of ancient Greece, similar to the lyre. [C18: from Gk *kithara*]

cither ('sɪθə) *or* **cithern** ('sɪθən) *n* a variant spelling of **cittern.** [C17: from L, from Gk *kithara*]

citified *or* **cityfied** ('sɪtɪ,faɪd) *adj Often derog.* having the customs, manners, or dress of city people.

citizen ('sɪtɪz°n) *n* **1** a native registered or naturalized member of a state, nation, or other political community. **2** an inhabitant of a city or town. **3** a civilian, as opposed to a soldier, public official, etc. [C14: from Anglo-F *citesein,* from OF *citeien,* from *cité* CITY]

citizenry ('sɪtɪzənrɪ) *n, pl* **citizenries.** citizens collectively.

Citizens' Band *n* a range of radio frequencies assigned officially for use by the public for private communication. Abbrev.: **CB**

Citizens' Charter *n* (in Britain) a government document setting out standards of service for various public and private sector companies.

citizenship ('sɪtɪzənʃɪp) *n* **1** the condition or status of a citizen, with its rights and duties. **2** a person's conduct as a citizen.

Citlaltépetl ★ (,siːtlɑːl'teɪpet°l) *n* a volcano in SE Mexico, in central Veracruz state: the highest peak in the country. Height: 5699 m (18 698 ft). Spanish name: **Pico de Orizaba** (piko de ori'saba).

citrate ('sɪtreɪt, -rɪt; 'saɪtreɪt) *n* any salt or ester of citric acid. [C18: from CITR(US) + -ATE[1]]

citric ('sɪtrɪk) *adj* of or derived from citrus fruits or citric acid.

citric acid *n* a water-soluble weak tribasic acid found in many fruits, esp. citrus fruits, and used in pharmaceuticals and as a flavouring (**E330**). Formula: $CH_2(COOH)C(OH)(COOH)CH_2COOH$.

citrine ('sɪtrɪn) *n* **1** a brownish-yellow variety of quartz: a gemstone; false topaz. **2a** the yellow colour of a lemon. **2b** (*as adj*): *citrine hair.*

citron ('sɪtrən) *n* **1** a small Asian tree, having lemon-like fruit with a thick aromatic rind. **2** the fruit of this tree. **3** the rind of this fruit candied and used for decoration and flavouring of foods. [C16: from OF, from L *citrus* citrus tree]

citronella (,sɪtrə'nelə) *n* **1** a tropical Asian grass with bluish-green lemon-scented leaves. **2** Also called: **citronella oil.** the yellow aromatic oil obtained from this grass, used

---

★ people and places

in insect repellents, soaps, perfumes, etc. [C19: NL, from F, from *citron* lemon]

citrus ('sɪtrəs) *n*, *pl* **citruses. 1** any tree or shrub of the tropical and subtropical genus *Citrus,* which includes the orange, lemon, and lime. ◆ *adj also* **citrous. 2** of or relating to the genus *Citrus* or to the fruits of plants of this genus. [C19: from L: citrus tree]

Città del Vaticano ★ (tʃit'ta del vati'ka:no) *n* the Italian name for **Vatican City.**

cittern ('sɪtɜːn), **cither,** *or* **cithern** *n* a medieval stringed instrument resembling a lute but having wire strings and a flat back. [C16: ? a blend of CITHER + GITTERN]

city ('sɪtɪ) *n*, *pl* **cities. 1** any large town or populous place. **2** (in Britain) a town that has received this title from the Crown: usually the seat of a bishop. **3** (in the US) an incorporated urban centre with its own government and administration established by state charter. **4** (in Canada) a similar urban municipality incorporated by the provincial government **5** the people of a city collectively. **6** (*modifier*) in or characteristic of a city: *city habits.* ◆ Related adjs.: **civic, urban, municipal.** [C13: from OF *cité,* from L *cīvitās* state, from *cīvis* citizen]

City ★ ('sɪtɪ) *n* **the. 1** short for **City of London:** the original settlement of London on the N bank of the Thames; a municipality governed by the Lord Mayor and Corporation. Resident pop.: 5893 (1981). **2** the area in central London in which the United Kingdom's major financial business is transacted. **3** the various financial institutions located in this area.

City and Guilds Institute *n* (in Britain) an examining body for technical and craft skills.

city chambers *n* (*functioning as sing*) (in Scotland) the municipal buildings of a city; town hall.

City Code *n* (in Britain) short for **City Code on Takeovers and Mergers:** a code laid down in 1968 (later modified) to control takeovers and mergers.

city desk *n* the editorial section of a newspaper dealing in Britain with financial news, in the US and Canada with local news.

city editor *n* (on a newspaper) **1** *Brit.* the editor in charge of financial and commercial news. **2** *US & Canad.* the editor in charge of local news.

city father *n* a person who is active or prominent in the public affairs of a city.

cityscape ('sɪtɪ,skeɪp) *n* an urban landscape; view of a city.

city-state *n Ancient history.* a state consisting of a sovereign city and its dependencies.

city technology college *n* (in Britain) a type of senior secondary school specializing in technological subjects, set up in inner-city areas with funding from industry as well as the government.

Ciudad Bolívar ★ (*Spanish* θiu'ðað bo'liβar) *n* a port in E Venezuela, on the Orinoco River: accessible to oceangoing vessels. Pop.: 225 340 (1990). Former name (1764–1846): **Angostura.**

Ciudad Guayana ★ (*Spanish* θiu'ðað gwa'jana) *n* an industrial conurbation in E Venezuela, on the River Orinoco: iron and steel processing, gold mining. Pop.: 453 047 (1990). Former name: **Santo Tomé de Guayana.**

Ciudad Juárez ★ (*Spanish* θiu'ðað 'xwareθ) *n* a city in N Mexico, in Chihuahua state on the Río Grande, opposite El Paso, Texas. Pop.: 789 522 (1990). Former name (until 1888): **El Paso del Norte** (el 'paso del 'nɔrte).

Ciudad Trujillo ★ (*Spanish* θiu'ðað tru'xiʎo) *n* the former name (1936–61) of **Santo Domingo.**

Ciudad Victoria ★ (*Spanish* θiu'ðað bik'torja) *n* a city in E central Mexico, capital of Tamaulipas state. Pop.: 194 996 (1990).

civet ('sɪvɪt) *n* **1** a catlike mammal of Africa and S Asia, typically having spotted fur and secreting a powerfully smelling fluid from anal glands. **2** the yellowish fatty secretion of such an animal, used as a fixative in the manufacture of perfumes. **3** the fur of such an animal. [C16: from OF, from It., from Ar. *zabād* civet perfume]

civic ('sɪvɪk) *adj* of or relating to a city, citizens, or citizenship. [C16: from L, from *cīvis* citizen] ▶ **'civically** *adv*

civic centre *n Brit.* the public buildings of a town, including recreational facilities and offices of local administration.

civics ('sɪvɪks) *n* (*functioning as sing*) the study of the rights and responsibilities of citizenship.

civies ('sɪvɪz) *pl n Inf.* a variant spelling of **civvies.** See **civvy** (sense 2).

civil ('sɪv³l) *adj* **1** of the ordinary life of citizens as distinguished from military, legal, or ecclesiastical affairs. **2** of or relating to the citizen as an individual: *civil rights.* **3** of or occurring within the state or between citizens: *civil strife.* **4** polite or courteous: *a civil manner.* **5** of or in accordance with Roman law. [C14: from OF, from L *cīvīlis,* from *cīvis* citizen] ▶ **'civilly** *adv*

civil defence *n* the organizing of civilians to deal with enemy attacks.

civil disobedience *n* a refusal to obey laws, pay taxes, etc.: a nonviolent means of protesting.

civil engineer *n* a person qualified to design and construct public works, such as roads, bridges, harbours, etc. ▶ **civil engineering** *n*

civilian (sɪ'vɪljən) *n* **a** a person whose occupation is civil or nonmilitary. **b** (*as modifier*): *civilian life.* [C14 (orig.: a practitioner of civil law): from *civile* (from L *jūs cīvīle* civil law) + -IAN]

civility (sɪ'vɪlɪtɪ) *n*, *pl* **civilities. 1** politeness or courtesy. **2** (*often pl*) an act of politeness.

civilization *or* **civilisation** (,sɪvɪlaɪ'zeɪʃən) *n* **1** a human society that has a complex cultural, political, and legal organization; an advanced state in social development. **2** the peoples or nations collectively who have achieved such a state. **3** the total culture and way of life of a particular people, nation, region, or period. **4** the process of bringing or achieving civilization. **5** intellectual, cultural, and moral refinement. **6** cities or populated areas, as contrasted with sparsely inhabited areas, deserts, etc.

civilize *or* **civilise** ('sɪvɪ,laɪz) *vb* **civilizes, civilizing, civilized** *or* **civilises, civilising, civilised.** (*tr*) **1** to bring out of savagery or barbarism into a state characteristic of civilization. **2** to refine, educate, or enlighten. ▶ **'civi,lizable** *or* **'civi,lisable** *adj* ▶ **'civi,lized** *or* **'civi,lised** *adj*

civil law *n* **1** the law of a state relating to private and civilian affairs. **2** the body of law in ancient Rome, esp. as applicable to private citizens. **3** law based on the Roman system as distinguished from common law and canon law.

civil liberty *n* the right of an individual to certain freedoms of speech and action.

civil list *n* (in Britain) the annuities voted by Parliament for the support of the royal household and the royal family.

civil marriage *n Law.* a marriage performed by an official other than a clergyman.

civil rights *pl n* **1** the personal rights of the individual citizen. **2** (*modifier*) of, relating to, or promoting equality in social, economic, and political rights.

civil servant *n* a member of the civil service.

civil service *n* **1** the service responsible for the public administration of the government of a country. It excludes the legislative, judicial, and military branches. **2** the members of the civil service collectively.

civil war *n* war between parties or factions within the same nation.

Civil War *n* **1** *English history.* the conflict between Charles I and the Parliamentarians resulting from disputes over their respective prerogatives. Parliament gained decisive victories at Marston Moor in 1644 and Naseby in 1645, and Charles was executed in 1649. **2** *US history.* the war fought from 1861 to 1865 between the North and the South, sparked off by Lincoln's election as president but with deep-rooted political and economic causes, exacerbated by the slavery issue. The advantages of the North in terms of population, finance, and communications brought about the South's eventual surrender at Appomattox.

civvy ('sɪvɪ) *n, pl* **civvies.** *Sl.* **1** a civilian. **2** (*pl*) Also: **civies.** civilian dress as opposed to uniform. **3 civvy street.** civilian life.

CJ *abbrev. for* Chief Justice.

CJA (in Britain) *abbrev. for* Criminal Justice Act.

CJD *abbrev. for* Creutzfeldt-Jakob disease.

Cl *the chemical symbol for* chlorine.

clachan (*Gaelic* 'klaxən; *English* 'klæ-) *n Scot. & Irish dialect.* a small village; hamlet. [C15: from Scot. Gaelic: prob. from *clach* stone]

clack (klæk) *vb* **1** to make or cause to make a sound like that of two pieces of wood hitting each other. **2** (*intr*) to jabber. ◆ *n* **3** a short sharp sound. **4** chatter. **5** Also called: **clack valve.** a simple nonreturn valve using a hinged flap or a ball. [C13: prob. from ON *klaka* to twitter, imit.]
▸ 'clacker *n*

Clackmannanshire ★ (klæk'mænən,ʃɪə, -ʃə) *n* a historic county and council area of central Scotland; part of Central region (1975–96). Administrative centre: Alloa. Pop.: 47 900 (1996 est.). Area: 142 sq. km (55 sq. miles).

Clacton *or* **Clacton-on-Sea** ★ ('klæktən) *n* a town and resort in SE England, in E Essex. Pop.: 43 571 (1981).

clad[1] (klæd) *vb* a past tense and past participle of **clothe.** [OE *clāthode* clothed, from *clāthian* to CLOTHE]

clad[2] (klæd) *vb* **clads, cladding, clad.** (*tr*) to bond a metal to (another metal), esp. to form a protective coating. [C14: special use of CLAD[1]]

cladding ('klædɪŋ) *n* **1** the process of protecting one metal by bonding a second metal to its surface. **2** the protective coating so bonded to metal. **3** the material used for the outside facing of a building, etc.

clade (kleɪd) *n Biol.* a group of organisms considered as having evolved from a common ancestor. [C20: from Gk *klados* branch, shoot]

cladistics (klə'dɪstɪks) *n* (*functioning as sing*) a method of grouping animals by measurable likenesses or homologues. [C20: NL from Gk *klados* branch, shoot]
▸ 'cladism ('klædɪzəm) *n* ▸ 'cladist ('klædɪst) *n*

claim (kleɪm) *vb* (*mainly tr*) **1** to demand as being due or as one's property; assert one's title or right to: *he claimed the record.* **2** (*takes a clause as object or an infinitive*) to assert as a fact; maintain against denial: *he claimed to be telling the truth.* **3** to call for or need; deserve: *this problem claims our attention.* **4** to take: *the accident claimed four lives.* ◆ *n* **5** an assertion of a right; a demand for something as due. **6** an assertion of something as true, real, or factual. **7** a right or just title to something; basis for demand: *a claim to fame.* **8** anything that is claimed, such as a piece of land staked out by a miner. **9a** a demand for payment in connection with an insurance policy, etc. **9b** the sum of money demanded. [C13: from OF *claimer* to call, from L *clāmāre* to shout]
▸ 'claimable *adj* ▸ 'claimant *or* 'claimer *n*

Clair ★ (*French* klɛr) *n* **René** (rəne), real name *René Chomette.* 1898–1981, French film director; noted for his comedies including *An Italian Straw Hat* (1928); later films include *Les Belles de nuit* (1952).

clairvoyance (kleə'vɔɪəns) *n* **1** the alleged power of perceiving things beyond the natural range of the senses. **2** keen intuitive understanding. [C19: from F: clearseeing, from *clair* clear + *voyance,* from *voir* to see]

clairvoyant (kleə'vɔɪənt) *adj* **1** of or possessing clairvoyance. **2** having great insight. ◆ *n* **3** a person claiming to have the power to foretell future events.
▸ clair'voyantly *adv*

clam (klæm) *n* **1** any of various burrowing bivalve molluscs. **2** the edible flesh of such a mollusc. **3** *Inf.* a reticent person. ◆ *vb* **clams, clamming, clammed. 4** (*intr*) *Chiefly US.* to gather clams. ◆ See also **clam up.** [C16: from earlier *clamshell,* that is, shell that clamps]

clamant ('kleɪmənt) *adj* **1** noisy. **2** calling urgently. [C17: from L, from *clāmāre* to shout]

clamber ('klæmbə) *vb* **1** (usually foll. by *up, over,* etc.) to climb (something) awkwardly, esp. by using both hands and feet. ◆ *n* **2** a climb performed in this manner. [C15: prob. var. of CLIMB]
▸ 'clamberer *n*

clammy ('klæmɪ) *adj* **clammier, clammiest. 1** unpleasantly sticky; moist. **2** (of the weather) close; humid. [C14: from OE *clǣman* to smear]
▸ 'clammily *adv* ▸ 'clamminess *n*

clamour *or US* **clamor** ('klæmə) *n* **1** a loud persistent outcry. **2** a vehement expression of collective feeling or outrage: *a clamour against higher prices.* **3** a loud and persistent noise: *the clamour of traffic.* ◆ *vb* **4** (*intr;* often foll. by *for* or *against*) to make a loud noise or outcry; make a public demand. **5** (*tr*) to move or force by outcry. [C14: from OF, from L, from *clāmāre* to cry out]
▸ 'clamorous *adj* ▸ 'clamorously *adv* ▸ 'clamorousness *n*

clamp[1] (klæmp) *n* **1** a mechanical device with movable jaws with which an object can be secured to a bench or with which two objects may be secured together. **2** See **wheel clamp.** ◆ *vb* (*tr*) **3** to fix or fasten with or as if with a clamp **4** to immobilize (a car) by means of a wheel clamp. **5** to inflict or impose forcefully: *they clamped a curfew on the town.* [C14: from Du. or Low G *klamp*]

clamp[2] (klæmp) *n* **1** a mound of a harvested root crop, covered with straw and earth to protect it from winter weather. ◆ *vb* **2** (*tr*) to enclose (a harvested root crop) in a mound. [C16: from MDu. *klamp* heap]

clamp down *vb* (*intr, adv;* often foll. by *on*) **1** to behave repressively; attempt to suppress something regarded as undesirable. ◆ *n* **clampdown. 2** a sudden restrictive measure.

clam up *vb* (*intr, adv*) *Inf.* to keep or become silent or withhold information.

clan (klæn) *n* **1** a group of people interrelated by ancestry or marriage. **2** a group of families with a common surname and a common ancestor, esp. among the Scots and the Irish. **3** a group of people united by common characteristics, aims, or interests. [C14: from Scot. Gaelic *clann* family, descendants, from L *planta* sprout]

clandestine (klæn'dɛstɪn) *adj* secret and concealed, often for illicit reasons; furtive. [C16: from L, from *clam* secretly]
▸ clan'destinely *adv*

clang (klæŋ) *vb* **1** to make or cause to make a loud resounding noise, as metal when struck. **2** (*intr*) to move or operate making such a sound. ◆ *n* **3** a resounding metallic noise. **4** the harsh cry of certain birds. [C16: from L *clangere*]

clanger ('klæŋə) *n* **1** *Inf.* a conspicuous mistake (esp. in **drop a clanger**). **2** something that clangs or causes a clang. [C20: from CLANG]

clangour *or US* **clangor** ('klæŋgə, 'klæŋə) *n* **1** a loud resonant often-repeated noise. **2** an uproar. ◆ *vb* **3** (*intr*) to make or produce a loud resonant noise.
▸ 'clangorous *adj* ▸ 'clangorously *adv*

clank (klæŋk) *n* **1** an abrupt harsh metallic sound. ◆ *vb* **2** to make or cause to make such a sound. **3** (*intr*) to move or operate making such a sound. [C17: imit.]
▸ 'clankingly *adv*

clannish ('klænɪʃ) *adj* **1** of or characteristic of a clan. **2** tending to associate closely within a group to the exclusion of outsiders; cliquish.
▸ 'clannishly *adv* ▸ 'clannishness *n*

clansman ('klænzmən) *or* (*fem*) **clanswoman** *n, pl* **clansmen** *or* **clanswomen.** a person belonging to a clan.

clap[1] (klæp) *vb* **claps, clapping, clapped. 1** to make or cause to make a sharp abrupt sound, as of two nonmetallic objects struck together. **2** to applaud (someone or something) by striking the palms of the hands together sharply. **3** (*tr*) to strike (a person) lightly with an open hand, in greeting, etc. **4** (*tr*) to place or put quickly or forcibly: *they clapped him into jail.* **5** (of certain birds) to flap (the wings) noisily. **6** (*intr;* foll. by *up* or *together*) to contrive or put together hastily. **7 clap eyes on.** *Inf.* to catch sight of. **8 clap hold of.** *Inf.* to grasp suddenly or forcibly. ◆ *n* **9** the sharp abrupt sound produced by striking the hands together. **10** the act of clapping, esp. in applause. **11** a sudden sharp sound, esp. of thunder. **12** a light blow. **13** *Arch.* a sudden action or mishap. [OE *clæppan;* imit.]

clap² (klæp) *n* (usually preceded by *the*) a slang word for **gonorrhoea**. [C16: from OF *clapoir* venereal sore, from *clapier* brothel, from ?]

clapboard ('klæp,bɔːd, 'klæbəd) *n* **1** a long thin timber board, used esp. in the US and Canada in wood-frame construction by lapping each board over the one below. ◆ *vb* **2** (*tr*) to cover with such boards. [C16: partial translation of Low G *klappholt,* from *klappen* to crack + *holt* wood]

clapped out *adj* (**clapped-out** *when prenominal*). *Inf.* **1** *Brit., Austral. & NZ.* worn out; dilapidated. **2** *Austral. & NZ.* extremely tired; exhausted.

clapper ('klæpə) *n* **1** a person or thing that claps. **2** *Also called:* **tongue.** a small piece of metal suspended within a bell that causes it to sound when made to strike against its side. **3 go** (**run, move**) **like the clappers.** *Brit. inf.* to move extremely fast.

clapperboard ('klæpə,bɔːd) *n* a pair of hinged boards clapped together during film shooting to aid in synchronizing sound and picture prints.

Clapton ★ ('klæptən) *n* **Eric.** born 1945, British rock guitarist, noted for his virtuoso style, his work with the Yardbirds (1963–65), Cream (1966–68), and, with Derek and the Dominos, the album *Layla* (1970).

claptrap ('klæp,træp) *n Inf.* **1** contrived but foolish talk. **2** insincere and pretentious talk: *politicians' claptrap.* [C18: from CLAP¹ + TRAP¹]

claque (klæk) *n* **1** a group of people hired to applaud. **2** a group of fawning admirers. [C19: from F, from *claquer* to clap, imit.]

Clare¹ ★ (klɛə) *n* a county of W Republic of Ireland, in Munster between Galway Bay and the Shannon estuary. County town: Ennis. Pop.: 90 918 (1991). Area: 3188 sq. km (1231 sq. miles).

Clare² ★ (klɛə) *n* **John.** 1793–1864, British poet, noted for *The Shepherd's Calendar* (1827) and *The Rural Muse* (1835). He was confined in a lunatic asylum from 1837.

Clarendon¹ ★ ('klærəndən) *n* a village near Salisbury in S England: site of a council held by Henry II in 1164 that produced a code of laws (the **Constitutions of Clarendon**) defining relations between church and state.

Clarendon² ★ ('klærəndən) *n* **1st Earl of,** title of *Edward Hyde.* 1609–74, English statesman and historian; chief adviser to Charles II (1660–67); author of *History of the Rebellion and Civil Wars in England* (1704–07).

Clare of Assisi ★ *n* **Saint.** 1194–1253, Italian nun; founder of the Franciscan Order of Poor Clares. Feast day: Aug. 11.

claret ('klærət) *n* **1** a red wine, esp. one from the Bordeaux district of France. **2a** a purplish-red colour. **2b** (*as adj*): *a claret football strip.* [C14: from OF (*vin*) *claret* clear (wine), from L *clārātum,* from L *clārus* clear]

clarify ('klærɪ,faɪ) *vb* **clarifies, clarifying, clarified. 1** to make or become clear or easy to understand. **2** to make or become free of impurities. **3** to make (fat, butter, etc.) clear by heating, etc., or (of fat, etc.) to become clear as a result of such a process. [C14: from OF, from LL, from L *clārus* clear + *facere* to make]
► ˌclarifiˈcation *n* ► ˈclariˌfier *n*

clarinet (ˌklærɪˈnɛt) *n Music.* **1** a keyed woodwind instrument with a cylindrical bore and a single reed. **2** an orchestral musician who plays the clarinet. [C18: from F, prob. from It., from *clarino* trumpet]
► ˌclariˈnettist *or US sometimes* ˌclariˈnetist *n*

clarion ('klærɪən) *n* **1** a stop of trumpet quality on an organ. **2** an obsolete, high-pitched, small-bore trumpet. **3** the sound of such an instrument or any similar sound. ◆ *adj* **4** (*prenominal*) clear and ringing; inspiring: *a clarion call to action.* ◆ *vb* **5** to proclaim loudly. [C14: from Med. L *clāriō* trumpet, from L *clārus* clear]

clarity ('klærɪtɪ) *n* **1** clearness, as of expression. **2** clearness, as of water. [C16: from L *clāritās,* from *clārus* clear]

Clark ★ (klɑːk) *n* **1 James,** known as *Jim.* 1936–68, Scottish racing driver; World Champion (1963, 1965). **2 (Charles)**

Joseph, known as *Joe.* born 1939, Canadian politician; prime minister (1979–80). **3 Kenneth,** Baron Clark of Saltwood. 1903–83, British art historian: his books include *Civilization* (1969). **4 William.** 1770–1838, US explorer and frontiersman: noted for his expedition to the Pacific Northwest (1804–06).

Clarke ★ (klɑːk) *n* **1** Sir **Arthur C(harles).** born 1917, British science-fiction writer. **2 Austin.** 1896–1974, Irish poet and verse dramatist. His work includes the poem *The Vengeance of Fionn* (1917) and the play *The Son of Learning* (1927). **3 Jeremiah.** ?1673–1707, English composer, noted for his *Trumpet Voluntary.* **4 Kenneth (Harry).** born 1940, British Conservative politician; home secretary (1992–93); chancellor of the exchequer (1993–97). **5 Marcus (Andrew Hislop).** 1846–81, Australian novelist born in England, noted for his novel *For the Term of His Natural Life* (1870–72) and *Old Tales of a Young Country* (1871).

clarkia ('klɑːkɪə) *n* any North American plant of the genus *Clarkia:* cultivated for their red, purple, or pink flowers. [C19: NL, after William CLARK]

Clarkson ★ ('klɑːksən) *n* **Thomas.** 1760–1846, British campaigner for the abolition of slavery.

clary ('klɛərɪ) *n, pl* **claries.** any of several European plants having aromatic leaves and blue flowers. [C14: from earlier *sclarreye,* from Med. L *sclareia,* from ?]

-clase *n combining form.* (in mineralogy) indicating a particular type of cleavage: *plagioclase.* [via F from Gk *klasis* a breaking]

clash (klæʃ) *vb* **1** to make or cause to make a loud harsh sound, esp. by striking together. **2** (*intr*) to be incompatible. **3** (*intr*) to engage together in conflict. **4** (*intr*) (of dates or events) to coincide. **5** (*intr*) (of colours) to look inharmonious together. ◆ *n* **6** a loud harsh noise. **7** a collision or conflict. [C16: imit.]
► ˈclasher *n*

clasp (klɑːsp) *n* **1** a fastening, such as a catch or hook, for holding things together. **2** a firm grasp or embrace. **3** *Mil.* a bar on a medal ribbon, to indicate either a second award or the battle, campaign, or reason for its award. ◆ *vb* (*tr*) **4** to hold in a firm grasp. **5** to grasp firmly with the hand. **6** to fasten together with or as if with a clasp. [C14: from ?]
► ˈclasper *n*

claspers ('klɑːspəz) *pl n Zool.* **1** a paired organ of male insects, used to clasp the female during copulation. **2** a paired organ of male sharks and related fish, used to assist the transfer of spermatozoa into the body of the female during copulation.

clasp knife *n* a large knife with one or more blades or other devices folding into the handle.

class (klɑːs) *n* **1** a collection or division of people or things sharing a common characteristic. **2** a group of persons sharing a similar social and economic position. **3a** the pattern of divisions that exist within a society on the basis of rank, economic status, etc. **3b** (*as modifier*): *the class struggle; class distinctions.* **4a** a group of pupils or students who are taught together. **4b** a meeting of a group of students for tuition. **5** *US.* a group of students who graduated in a specified year: *the class of '53.* **6** (*in combination and as modifier*) *Brit.* a grade of attainment in a university honours degree: *second-class honours.* **7** one of several standards of accommodation in public transport. **8** *Inf.* excellence or elegance, esp. in dress, design, or behaviour. **9** *Biol.* any of the taxonomic groups into which a phylum is divided and which contains one or more orders. **10** *Maths.* another name for **set²** (sense 3). **11 in a class of its own** *or* **in a class by oneself.** unequalled; unparalleled. ◆ *vb* **12** to have or assign a place within a group, grade, or class. [C17: from L *classis* class, rank, fleet]

class. *abbrev. for:* **1** classic(al). **2** classification. **3** classified.

class-conscious *adj* aware of belonging to a particular social rank.
► ˌclass-ˈconsciousness *n*

classic ('klæsɪk) *adj* **1** of the highest class, esp. in art or literature. **2** serving as a standard or model of its kind. **3** adhering to an established set of principles in the arts or sciences: *a classic proof.* **4** characterized by simplicity, balance, regularity, and purity of form; classical. **5** of lasting interest or significance. **6** continuously in fashion because of its simple style: *a classic dress.* ◆ *n* **7** an author, artist, or work of art of the highest excellence. **8** a creation or work considered as definitive. **9** *Horse racing.* any of the five principal races for three-year-old horses in Britain, namely the One Thousand Guineas, Two Thousand Guineas, Derby, Oaks, and Saint Leger. [C17: from L *classicus* of the first rank, from *classis* division, rank, class]

classical ('klæsɪk°l) *adj* **1** of, relating to, or characteristic of the ancient Greeks and Romans or their civilization. **2** designating, following, or influenced by the art or culture of ancient Greece or Rome: *classical architecture.* **3** *Music.* **3a** of, relating to, or denoting any music or its period of composition marked by stability of form, intellectualism, and restraint. Cf. **romantic** (sense 5). **3b** accepted as a standard: *the classical suite.* **3c** denoting serious art music in general. Cf. **pop**[2]. **4** denoting or relating to a style in any of the arts characterized by emotional restraint and conservatism: *a classical style of painting.* **5** (of an education) based on the humanities and the study of Latin and Greek. **6** *Physics.* not involving the quantum theory or the theory of relativity: *classical mechanics.*
▸ ˌclassiˈcality *or* ˈclassicalness *n* ▸ ˈclassically *adv*

Classical school *n* economic theory based on the works of Adam Smith and David Ricardo, which explains the creation of wealth and advocates free trade.

classic car *n Chiefly Brit.* a car that is more than twenty five years old. Cf. **veteran car, vintage car.**

classicism ('klæsɪˌsɪzəm) *or* **classicalism** ('klæsɪkəˌlɪzəm) *n* **1** a style based on the study of Greek and Roman models, characterized by emotional restraint and regularity of form; the antithesis of romanticism. **2** knowledge of the culture of ancient Greece and Rome. **3a** a Greek or Latin expression. **3b** an expression in a modern language that is modelled on a Greek or Latin form.
▸ ˈclassicist *n*

classicize *or* **classicise** ('klæsɪˌsaɪz) *vb* **classicizes, classicizing, classicized** *or* **classicises, classicising, classicised. 1** (*tr*) to make classic. **2** (*intr*) to imitate classical style.

classics ('klæsɪks) *n* **1 the.** a body of literature regarded as great or lasting, esp. that of ancient Greece or Rome. **2 the.** the ancient Greek and Latin languages. **3** (*functioning as sing*) ancient Greek and Roman culture as a subject for academic study.

classification (ˌklæsɪfɪˈkeɪʃən) *n* **1** systematic placement in categories. **2** one of the divisions in a system of classifying. **3** *Biol.* **3a** the placing of animals and plants in a series of increasingly specialized groups because of similarities in structure, origin, etc., that indicate a common relationship. **3b** the study of the principles and practice of this process; taxonomy. [C18: from F; see CLASS, -IFY, -ATION]
▸ ˈclassificatory *adj*

classified ('klæsɪˌfaɪd) *adj* **1** arranged according to some system of classification. **2** *Government.* (of information) not available to people outside a restricted group, esp. for reasons of national security. **3** *US & Canad. inf.* (of information) closely concealed or secret. **4** (of advertisements in newspapers, etc.) arranged according to type. **5** *Brit.* (of newspapers) containing sports results. **6** (of British roads) having a number in the national road system.

classify ('klæsɪˌfaɪ) *vb* **classifies, classifying, classified.** (*tr*) **1** to arrange or order by classes; categorize. **2** *Government.* to declare (information, documents, etc.) of possible aid to an enemy and therefore not available to people outside a restricted group. [C18: back formation from CLASSIFICATION]
▸ ˈclassiˌfiable *adj* ▸ ˈclassiˌfier *n*

class interval *n Statistics.* one of the intervals into which the range of a variable of a distribution is divided, esp. one of the divisions of the base line of a bar chart or histogram.

classless ('klɑːslɪs) *adj* **1** not belonging to a class. **2** characterized by the absence of economic and social distinctions.
▸ ˈclasslessness *n*

class list *n* (in Britain) a list categorizing students according to the class of honours they have obtained in their degree examination.

classmate ('klɑːsˌmeɪt) *n* a friend or contemporary of the same class in a school.

classroom ('klɑːsˌruːm, -ˌrʊm) *n* a room in which classes are conducted, esp. in a school.

class struggle *n* **the.** *Marxism.* the continual conflict between the capitalist and working classes for economic and political power.

classy ('klɑːsɪ) *adj* **classier, classiest.** *Sl.* elegant; stylish.
▸ ˈclassiness *n*

clatter ('klætə) *vb* **1** to make or cause to make a rattling noise, esp. as a result of movement. **2** (*intr*) to chatter. ◆ *n* **3** a rattling sound or noise. **4** a noisy commotion, such as loud chatter. [OE *clatrung* clattering (gerund)]
▸ ˈclatterer *n* ▸ ˈclatteringly *adv*

Claude Lorrain ★ (*French* klod lɔrɛ̃) *n* real name *Claude Gelée.* 1600–82, French painter.

Claudius ★ ('klɔːdɪəs) *n* full name *Tiberius Claudius Drusus Nero Germanicus.* 10 B.C.–54 A.D., Roman emperor (41–54); invaded Britain (43); poisoned by his fourth wife, Agrippina.

Claudius II ★ *n* full name *Marcus Aurelius Claudius,* called *Gothicus.* 214–270 A.D., Roman emperor (268–270).

clause (klɔːz) *n* **1** *Grammar.* a group of words, consisting of a subject and a predicate including a finite verb, that does not necessarily constitute a sentence. Cf. **phrase.** See also **main clause, subordinate clause. 2** a section of a legal document such as a contract, will, or draft statute. [C13: from OF, from Med. L *clausa* a closing (of a rhetorical period), from L, from *claudere* to close]
▸ ˈclausal *adj*

Clausewitz ★ (*German* ˈklauzəvɪts) *n* **Karl von** (karl fɔn). 1780–1831, Prussian general, noted for his works on military strategy, esp. *Vom Kriege* (1833).

Clausius ★ (*German* ˈklauzius) *n* **Rudolf Julius** ('ruːdɔlf ˈjuːlius). 1822–88, German physicist. He enunciated the second law of thermodynamics (1850) and developed the kinetic theory of gases.

claustrophobia (ˌklɔːstrəˈfəʊbɪə, ˌklɒs-) *n* an abnormal fear of being in a confined space. [C19: NL from L *claustrum* CLOISTER + -PHOBIA]
▸ ˈclaustroˌphobe *n* ▸ ˌclaustroˈphobic *adj*

clavate ('kleɪveɪt, -vɪt) *or* **claviform** ('klævɪˌfɔːm) *adj Biol.* shaped like a club. [C19: from L *clāva* club]
▸ ˈclavately *adv*

clave[1] (kleɪv, klɑːv) *n Music.* one of a pair of hardwood sticks struck together to make a hollow sound, esp. to mark the beat in Latin-American dance music. [C20: from American Sp., from L *clavis* key]

clave[2] (kleɪv) *vb Arch.* a past tense of **cleave.**

clavichord ('klævɪˌkɔːd) *n* a keyboard instrument consisting of a number of thin wire strings struck from below by brass tangents. [C15: from Med. L, from L *clāvis* key + *chorda* CHORD]

clavicle ('klævɪk°l) *n* **1** either of the two bones connecting the shoulder blades with the upper part of the breastbone. Nontechnical name: **collarbone. 2** the corresponding structure in other vertebrates. [C17: from Med. L *clāvicula,* from L *clāvis* key]
▸ **clavicular** (kləˈvɪkjʊlə) *adj*

clavier (kləˈvɪə, ˈklævɪə) *n* **a** any keyboard instrument. **b** the keyboard itself. [C18: from F: keyboard, from L *clāvis* key]

claw (klɔː) *n* **1** a curved pointed horny process on the end of each digit in birds, some reptiles, and certain mammals. **2** a corresponding structure in some invertebrates, such as the pincer of a crab. **3** a part or member like a claw in function or appearance. ◆ *vb* **4** to scrape, tear, or dig (something or someone) with claws, etc. **5** (*tr*) to create by scratching as with claws: *to claw an opening.* [OE *clawu*]
▸ ˈclawer *n*

claw back vb (tr, adv) **1** to get back (something) with difficulty. **2** to recover (a sum of money), esp. by taxation or a penalty. ◆ n **clawback**. **3** the recovery of a sum of money, esp. by taxation or a penalty. **4** the sum so recovered.

claw hammer n a hammer with a cleft at one end of the head for extracting nails.

clay (kleɪ) n **1** a very fine-grained material that occurs as sedimentary rocks, soils, and other deposits. It becomes plastic when moist but hardens on heating and is used in the manufacture of bricks, ceramics, etc. **2** earth or mud. **3** Poetic. the material of the human body. [OE clæg]
▸ **'clayey, 'clayish,** or **'clay,like** adj

Clay ★ (kleɪ) n **1 Cassius.** See **Muhammad Ali. 2 Henry.** 1777–1852, US statesman; secretary of state (1825–29).

claymore ('kleɪ,mɔː) n a large two-edged broadsword used formerly by Scottish Highlanders. [C18: from Gaelic claidheamh mōr great sword]

clay pigeon n a disc of baked clay hurled into the air from a machine as a target to be shot at.

clay road n NZ. an unmetalled road in a rural area.

CLC abbrev. for Canadian Labour Congress.

-cle suffix forming nouns. indicating smallness: cubicle; particle. [via OF from L -culus. See -CULE]

clean (kliːn) adj **1** without dirt or other impurities; unsoiled. **2** without anything in it or on it: a clean page. **3** recently washed; fresh. **4** without extraneous or foreign materials. **5** without defect, difficulties, or problems. **6** (of a nuclear weapon) producing little or no radioactive fallout or contamination. **7** (of a wound, etc.) having no pus or other sign of infection. **8** pure; morally sound. **9** without objectionable language or obscenity. **10** thorough or complete: a clean break. **11** dexterous or adroit: a clean throw. **12** Sport. played fairly and without fouls. **13** simple in design: a ship's clean lines. **14** Aeronautics. causing little turbulence; streamlined. **15** honourable or respectable. **16** habitually neat. **17** (esp. of a driving licence) showing or having no record of offences. **18** Sl. **18a** innocent; not guilty. **18b** not carrying illegal drugs, weapons, etc. ◆ vb **19** to make or become free of dirt, filth, etc.: the stove cleans easily. **20** (tr) to remove in making clean: to clean marks off the wall. **21** (tr) to prepare (fish, poultry, etc.) for cooking: to clean a chicken. ◆ adv **22** in a clean way; cleanly. **23** Not standard. (intensifier): clean forgotten. **24 come clean.** Inf. to make a revelation or confession. ◆ n **25** the act or an instance of cleaning: he gave his shoes a clean. **26 clean sweep.** See **sweep** (sense 28).
◆ See also **clean out, clean up.** [OE clǣne]
▸ **'cleanable** adj ▸ **'cleanness** n

clean-cut adj **1** clearly outlined; neat: clean-cut lines of a ship. **2** definite.

cleaner ('kliːnə) n **1** a person, device, chemical agent, etc., that removes dirt, as from clothes or carpets. **2** (usually pl) a shop, etc., that provides a dry-cleaning service. **3 take (a person) to the cleaners.** Inf. to rob or defraud (a person).

cleanly adv ('kliːnlɪ). **1** in a fair manner. **2** easily or smoothly. ◆ adj ('klɛnlɪ), **cleanlier, cleanliest. 3** habitually clean or neat.
▸ **cleanlily** ('klɛnlɪlɪ) adv ▸ **cleanliness** ('klɛnlɪnɪs) n

clean out vb (tr, adv) **1** (foll. by of or from) to remove (something) (from or away from). **2** Sl. to leave (someone) with no money. **3** Inf. to exhaust (stocks, goods, etc.) completely.

cleanse (klɛnz) vb **cleanses, cleansing, cleansed.** (tr) **1** to remove dirt, filth, etc., from. **2** to remove guilt from. **3** Arch. to cure. [OE clǣnsian; see CLEAN]

cleanser ('klɛnzə) n a cleansing agent.

clean-shaven adj (of men) having the facial hair shaved off.

clean sheet n Sport. an instance of conceding no goals or points in a match or competition (esp. in **keep a clean sheet**).

clean up vb (adv) **1** to rid (something) of dirt, filth, or other impurities. **2** to make (someone or something) orderly or presentable. **3** (tr) to rid (a place) of undesirable

people or conditions. **4** Inf., chiefly US & Canad. to make (a great profit). ◆ n **cleanup. 5** the process of cleaning up. **6** Inf., chiefly US. a great profit.

clear (klɪə) adj **1** free from darkness or obscurity; bright. **2** (of weather) free from dullness or clouds. **3** transparent. **4** even and pure in tone or colour. **5** without blemish: a clear skin. **6** easy to see or hear; distinct. **7** free from doubt or confusion. **8** (postpositive) certain in the mind; sure: are you clear? **9** (in combination) perceptive, alert: clear-headed. **10** evident or obvious: it is clear that he won't come now. **11** (of sounds or the voice) not harsh or hoarse. **12** serene; calm. **13** without qualification; complete: a clear victory. **14** free of suspicion, guilt, or blame: a clear conscience. **15** free of obstruction; open: a clear passage. **16** free from debt or obligation. **17** (of money, profits, etc.) without deduction; net. **18** emptied of freight or cargo. **19** Showjumping. (of a round) ridden without any points being lost. ◆ adv **20** in a clear or distinct manner. **21** completely or utterly. **22** (postpositive; often foll. by of) not in contact (with); free: stand clear of the gates. ◆ n **23** a clear space. **24 in the clear. 24a** free of suspicion, guilt, or blame. **24b** Sport. able to receive a pass without being tackled. ◆ vb **25** to make or become free from darkness, obscurity, etc. **26** (intr) **26a** (of the weather) to become free from dullness, fog, rain, etc. **26b** (of mist, fog, etc.) to disappear. **27** (tr) to free from impurity or blemish. **28** (tr) to free from doubt or confusion. **29** (tr) to rid of objects, obstructions, etc. **30** (tr) to make or form (a path, way, etc.) by removing obstructions. **31** (tr) to remove (a person or thing) from something, as of suspicion, blame, or guilt. **32** (tr) to move or pass by or over without contact: he cleared the wall easily. **33** (tr) to rid (the throat) of phlegm. **34** (tr) to make or gain (money) as profit. **35** (tr; often foll. by off) to discharge or settle (a debt). **36** (tr) to free (a debtor) from obligation. **37** (intr) (of a cheque) to pass through one's bank and be charged against one's account. **38** Banking. to settle accounts by exchanging (commercial documents) in a clearing house. **39** to permit (ships, aircraft, cargo, passengers, etc.) to unload, disembark, depart, etc., or (of ships, etc.) to be permitted to unload, etc. **40** to obtain or give (clearance). **41** (tr) to obtain clearance from. **42** (tr) to permit (a person, company, etc.) to see or handle classified information. **43** (tr) Mil., etc. to decode (a message, etc.). **44** (tr) Computing. to remove data from a storage device and revert to zero. **45 clear the air.** to dispel tension, confusion, etc., by settling misunderstandings, etc.
◆ See also **clear away, clear off,** etc. [C13: clere, from OF cler, from L clārus clear]
▸ **'clearer** n ▸ **'clearly** adv ▸ **'clearness** n

clearance ('klɪərəns) n **1a** the process or an instance of clearing: slum clearance. **1b** (as modifier): a clearance order. **2** space between two parts in motion or in relative motion. **3** permission for an aircraft, ship, passengers, etc., to proceed. **4** official permission to have access to secret information, projects, areas, etc. **5** Banking. the exchange of commercial documents drawn on the members of a clearing house. **6a** the disposal of merchandise at reduced prices. **6b** (as modifier): a clearance sale. **7** the act of clearing an area of land by mass eviction: the Highland Clearances.

clear away vb (adv) to remove (objects) from (the table) after a meal.

clear-cut adj (**clear cut** when postpositive). **1** definite; not vague: a clear-cut proposal. **2** clearly outlined.

clearing ('klɪərɪŋ) n an area with few or no trees or shrubs in wooded or overgrown land.

clearing bank n (in Britain) any bank that makes use of the central clearing house in London.

clearing house n **1** Banking. an institution where cheques and other commercial papers drawn on member banks are cancelled against each other so that only net balances are payable. **2** a central agency for the collection and distribution of information or materials.

clear off vb (intr, adv) Inf. to go away: often used imperatively.

clear out vb (adv) **1** (intr) Inf. to go away: often used imperatively. **2** (tr) to remove and sort the contents of (a room, etc.). **3** (*tr*) *Sl.* to leave (someone) with no money. **4** (*tr*) *Sl.* to exhaust (stocks, goods, etc.) completely.

clearstory ('klɪə,stɔːrɪ) *n* a variant of **clerestory**.

clear up *vb* (*adv*) **1** (*tr*) to explain or solve (a mystery, misunderstanding, etc.). **2** to put (a place or thing that is disordered) in order. **3** (*intr*) (of the weather) to become brighter.

clearway ('klɪə,weɪ) *n* **1** *Brit.* a stretch of road on which motorists may stop only in an emergency. **2** an area at the end of a runway over which an aircraft taking off makes its initial climb.

cleat (kliːt) *n* **1** a wedge-shaped block attached to a structure to act as a support. **2** a device consisting of two hornlike prongs projecting horizontally in opposite directions from a central base, used for securing lines on vessels, wharves, etc. ◆ *vb* (*tr*) **3** to supply or support with a cleat or cleats. **4** to secure (a line) on a cleat. [C14: of Gmc origin]

cleavage ('kliːvɪdʒ) *n* **1** *Inf.* the separation between a woman's breasts, esp. as revealed by a low-cut dress. **2** a division or split. **3** (of crystals) the act of splitting or the tendency to split along definite planes so as to yield smooth surfaces. **4** Also called: **segmentation.** (in animals) the repeated division of a fertilized ovum into a solid ball of cells. **5** the breaking of a chemical bond in a molecule to give smaller molecules or radicals. **6** *Geol.* the natural splitting of certain rocks, such as slates, into thin plates.

cleave[1] (kliːv) *vb* **cleaves, cleaving; cleft, cleaved,** *or* **clove; cleft, cleaved,** *or* **cloven. 1** to split or cause to split, esp. along a natural weakness. **2** (*tr*) to make by or as if by cutting: *to cleave a path.* **3** (when *intr*, foll. by *through*) to penetrate or traverse. [OE *clēofan*]
▸ **'cleavable** *adj*

cleave[2] (kliːv) *vb* **cleaves, cleaving, cleaved.** (*intr*; foll. by *to*) to cling or adhere. [OE *cleofian*]

cleaver ('kliːvə) *n* a heavy knife or long-bladed hatchet, esp. one used by butchers.

cleavers ('kliːvəz) *n* (*functioning as sing*) a Eurasian plant, having small white flowers and prickly stems and fruits. Also called: **goosegrass, hairif.** [OE *clīfe*; see CLEAVE[2]]

Cleese ★ (kliːz) *n* **John (Marwood).** born 1939, British writer, noted for the TV series *Monty Python's Flying Circus* (1969–74) and *Fawlty Towers* (1975, 1978); films include *Fierce Creatures* (1997).

Cleethorpes ★ ('kliːθɔːps) *n* a resort in E England, in NE Lincolnshire. Pop.: 32 719 (1991).

clef (klɛf) *n* one of several symbols placed on the left-hand side beginning of each stave indicating the pitch of the music written after it. [C16: from F: key, clef, from L *clāvis*]

cleft (klɛft) *vb* **1** a past tense and past participle of **cleave**[1]. ◆ *n* **2** a fissure or crevice. **3** an indentation or split in something, such as the chin, palate, etc. ◆ *adj* **4** split; divided. [OE *geclyft* (n); see CLEAVE[1]]

cleft palate *n* a congenital crack or fissure in the midline of the hard palate, often associated with a harelip.

cleg (klɛg) *n* another name for a **horsefly.** [C15: from ON *kleggi*]

Cleland ★ ('klɛlənd) *n* **John.** 1709–89, British writer, noted for his bawdy novel *Fanny Hill* (1748–49).

clematis ('klɛmətɪs, klə'meɪtɪs) *n* any N temperate climbing plant of the genus *Clematis*. Many species are cultivated for their large colourful flowers. [C16: from L, from Gk, from *klēma* vine twig]

Clemenceau ★ (*French* klemɑ̃so) *n* **Georges Eugène Benjamin** (ʒɔrʒ œʒɛn bẽʒamẽ). 1841–1929, French statesman; prime minister of France (1906–09; 1917–20); negotiated the Treaty of Versailles (1919).

clemency ('klɛmənsɪ) *n*, *pl* **clemencies. 1** mercy or leniency. **2** mildness, esp. of the weather. [C15: from L, from *clēmēns* gentle]

Clemens ★ ('klɛmənz) *n* **Samuel Langhorne.** See (Mark) Twain.

clement ('klɛmənt) *adj* **1** merciful. **2** (of the weather) mild. [C15: from L *clēmēns* mild]

Clement I ★ ('klɛmənt) *n* **Saint,** called *Clement of Rome,* pope (?88–?97 A.D.). Feast day: Nov. 23.

Clement V ★ *n* original name *Bertrand de Got.* ?1264–1314, pope (1305–14): removed the papal seat from Rome to Avignon in France (1309).

Clement VII ★ *n* original name *Giulio de' Medici.* 1478–1534, pope (1523–34): refused to authorize the annulment of the marriage of Henry VIII of England to Catherine of Aragon (1533).

clementine ('klɛmən,tiːn, -,taɪn) *n* a citrus fruit thought to be either a variety of tangerine or a hybrid between a tangerine and sweet orange. [C20: from F *clémentine*]

Clement of Alexandria ★ *n* **Saint.** original name *Titus Flavius Clemens.* ?150–?215 A.D., Greek Christian theologian: head of the catechetical school at Alexandria; teacher of Origen. Feast day: Dec. 5.

clench (klɛntʃ) *vb* (*tr*) **1** to close or squeeze together (the teeth, a fist, etc.) tightly. **2** to grasp or grip firmly. ◆ *n* **3** a firm grasp or grip. **4** a device that grasps or grips. **5** another word for **clinch.** [OE *beclencan*]

Cleon ★ ('kliːɒn) *n* died 422 B.C., Athenian demagogue and military leader.

Cleopatra ★ (,kliːə'pætrə, -'pɑː-) *n* ?69–30 B.C., queen of Egypt (51–30): the mistress of Julius Caesar and later of Mark Antony. She killed herself with an asp to avoid capture by Octavian (Augustus).

Cleopatra's Needle *n* either of two Egyptian obelisks, originally set up at Heliopolis about 1500 B.C.: one was moved to the Thames Embankment, London, in 1878, the other to Central Park, New York, in 1880.

clepsydra ('klɛpsɪdrə) *n*, *pl* **clepsydras** *or* **clepsydrae** (-,driː). an ancient device for measuring time by the flow of water or mercury through a small aperture. Also called: **water clock.** [C17: from L, from Gk, from *kleptein* to steal + *hudōr* water]

cleptomania (,klɛptəʊ'meɪnɪə) *n* a variant spelling of **kleptomania.**

clerestory *or* **clearstory** ('klɪə,stɔːrɪ) *n*, *pl* **clerestories** *or* **clearstories. 1** a row of windows in the upper part of the wall of a church that divides the nave from the aisle. **2** the part of the wall in which these windows are set. [C15: from CLEAR + STOREY]
▸ **'clere,storied** *or* **'clear,storied** *adj*

clergy ('klɜːdʒɪ) *n*, *pl* **clergies.** the collective body of men and women ordained as religious ministers, esp. of the Christian Church. [C13: from OF; see CLERK]

clergyman ('klɜːdʒɪmən) *n*, *pl* **clergymen.** a member of the clergy.

cleric ('klɛrɪk) *n* a member of the clergy. [C17: from Church L *clēricus* priest, CLERK]

clerical ('klɛrɪk°l) *adj* **1** relating to or associated with the clergy: *clerical dress.* **2** of or relating to office clerks or their work: *a clerical error.* **3** supporting or advocating clericalism.
▸ **'clerically** *adv*

clerical collar *n* a stiff white collar with no opening at the front that buttons at the back of the neck; the distinctive mark of the clergy in certain Churches. Informal name: **dog collar.**

clericalism ('klɛrɪk°,lɪzəm) *n* **1** a policy of upholding the power of the clergy. **2** the power of the clergy.
▸ **'clericalist** *n*

clericals ('klɛrɪk°lz) *pl n* the distinctive dress of a clergyman.

clerihew ('klɛrɪ,hjuː) *n* a form of comic or satiric verse consisting of two couplets of metrically irregular lines containing the name of a well-known person. [C20 after E. *Clerihew* BENTLEY, its inventor]

clerk (klɑːk; *US & Canad.* klɜːrk) *n* **1** a worker, esp. in an office, who keeps records, files, etc. **2** an employee of a court, legislature, board, corporation, etc., who keeps records and accounts, etc.: *a town clerk.* **3** Also called: **clerk in holy orders.** a cleric. **4** *US & Canad.* short for **saleclerk.** **5** Also called: **desk clerk.** *US & Canad.* a hotel receptionist. **6** *Arch.* a scholar. ◆ *vb* **7** (*intr*) to serve as a clerk. [OE *clerc*

★ people and places

from Church L *clēricus*, from Gk *klērikos* cleric, from *klēros* heritage]
▶ 'clerkess *fem n* (*chiefly Scot.*) ▶ 'clerkish *adj* ▶ 'clerkship *n*

clerk of works *n* an employee who supervises building work in progress.

Clermont-Ferrand ★ (*French* klɛrmɔ̃fɛrɑ̃) *n* a city in S central France: capital of Puy-de-Dôme department; industrial centre. Pop.: 140 167 (1990).

Cleveland[1] ★ ('kliːvlənd) *n* **1** a former county of NE England formed in 1974 from parts of E Durham and N Yorkshire; replaced in 1996 by four unitary authorities. **2** a port in NE Ohio, on Lake Erie: major heavy industries. Pop.: 492 901 (1994 est.). **3** a hilly region of NE England, extending from the **Cleveland Hills** to the River Tees.

Cleveland[2] ★ ('kliːvlənd) *n* **Stephen Grover.** 1837–1908, US Democratic politician; the 22nd and 24th president of the US (1885–89; 1893–97).

clever ('klɛvə) *adj* **1** displaying sharp intelligence or mental alertness. **2** adroit or dexterous, esp. with the hands. **3** smart in a superficial way. **4** *Brit. inf.* sly; cunning. [C13 *cliver* (in the sense: quick to seize, adroit), from ?]
▶ 'cleverly *adv* ▶ 'cleverness *n*

clevis ('klɛvɪs) *n* the U-shaped component of a shackle. [C16: rel. to CLEAVE[1]]

clew (kluː) *n* **1** a ball of thread, yarn, or twine. **2** *Naut.* either of the lower corners of a square sail or the after lower corner of a fore-and-aft sail. ◆ *vb* **3** (*tr*) to coil into a ball. [OE *cliewen* (vb)]

clianthus (klɪˈænθəs) *n* a leguminous plant of Australia and New Zealand with ornamental clusters of slender flowers. [C19: NL, prob. from Gk *klei-, kleos* glory + *anthos* flower]

cliché ('kliːʃeɪ) *n* **1** a word or expression that has lost much of its force through overexposure. **2** an idea, action, or habit that has become trite from overuse. **3** *Printing, chiefly Brit.* a stereotype or electrotype plate. [C19: from F, from *clicher* to stereotype; imit.]
▶ 'clichéd *or* 'cliché'd *adj*

click (klɪk) *n* **1** a short light often metallic sound. **2** the locking member of a ratchet mechanism, such as a pawl or detent. **3** *Phonetics.* any of various stop consonants that are produced by the suction of air into the mouth. ◆ *vb* **4** to make or cause to make a clicking sound: *to click one's heels.* **5** (usually foll. by *on*) *Computing.* to press and release (a button on a mouse) or to select (a particular function) by pressing and releasing a button on a mouse. **6** (*intr*) *Sl.* to be a great success: *that idea really clicked.* **7** (*intr*) *Inf.* to become suddenly clear: *it finally clicked.* **8** (*intr*) *Sl.* to get on well: *they clicked from their first meeting.* [C17: imit.]
▶ 'clicker *n*

client ('klaɪənt) *n* **1** a person, company, etc., that seeks the advice of a professional man or woman. **2** a customer. **3** a person for whom a social worker, etc., is responsible. **4** *Computing.* a program or work station that requests data or information from a server. [C14: from L *cliēns* retainer, dependent]
▶ 'cliental (klaɪˈɛnt'l) *adj*

clientele (ˌkliːɒnˈtɛl) *or* **clientage** ('klaɪəntɪdʒ) *n* customers or clients collectively. [C16: from L, from *cliēns* CLIENT]

cliff (klɪf) *n* a steep high rock face, esp. one that runs along the seashore. [OE *clif*]
▶ 'cliffy *adj*

cliffhanger ('klɪfˌhæŋə) *n* **1a** a situation of imminent disaster usually occurring at the end of each episode of a serialized film. **1b** the serialized film itself. **2** a situation that is dramatic or uncertain.
▶ 'cliff,hanging *adj*

climacteric (klaɪˈmæktərɪk, ˌklaɪmækˈtɛrɪk) *n* **1** a critical event or period. **2** another name for **menopause. 3** the period in the life of a man corresponding to the menopause, chiefly characterized by diminished sexual activity. ◆ *adj also* **climacterical** (ˌklaɪmækˈtɛrɪk°l). **4** involving a crucial event or period. [C16: from L, from Gk, from *klimakter* rung of a ladder from *klimax* ladder]

climactic (klaɪˈmæktɪk) *or* **climactical** *adj* consisting of, involving, or causing a climax.
▶ cliˈmactically *adv*

> **USAGE NOTE** See at **climate.**

climate ('klaɪmɪt) *n* **1** the long-term prevalent weather conditions of an area, determined by latitude, altitude, etc. **2** an area having a particular kind of climate. **3** a prevailing trend: *the political climate.* [C14: from LL, from Gk *klima* inclination, region]
▶ **climatic** (klaɪˈmætɪk), **cliˈmatical,** *or* 'climatal *adj* ▶ cliˈmatically *adv*

> **USAGE NOTE** *Climatic* is sometimes wrongly used where *climactic* is meant. *Climatic* is properly used to talk about things relating to climate; *climactic* is used to describe something which forms a climax.

climatic zone *n* any of the eight principal zones, roughly demarcated by lines of latitude, into which the earth can be divided on the basis of climate.

climatology (ˌklaɪməˈtɒlədʒɪ) *n* the study of climates.
▶ **climatologic** (ˌklaɪmətəˈlɒdʒɪk) *or* ˌclimatoˈlogical *adj* ▶ ˌclimaˈtologist *n*

climax ('klaɪmæks) *n* **1** the most intense or highest point of an experience or of a series of events: *the party was the climax of the week.* **2** a decisive moment in a dramatic or other work. **3** a rhetorical device by which a series of sentences, clauses, or phrases are arranged in order of increasing intensity. **4** *Ecology.* the stage in the development of a community during which it remains stable under the prevailing environmental conditions. **5** another word for **orgasm.** ◆ *vb* **6** to reach or bring to a climax. [C16: from LL, from Gk *klimax* ladder]

climb (klaɪm) *vb* (*mainly intr*) **1** (*also tr*; often foll. by *up*) to go up or ascend (stairs, a mountain, etc.). **2** (often foll. by *along*) to progress with difficulty: *to climb along a ledge.* **3** to rise to a higher point or intensity: *the temperature climbed.* **4** to incline or slope upwards: *the road began to climb.* **5** to ascend in social position. **6** (of plants) to grow upwards by twining, using tendrils or suckers, etc. **7** *Inf.* (foll. by *into*) to put (on) or get (into). **8** to be a climber or mountaineer. ◆ *n* **9** the act or an instance of climbing. **10** a place or thing to be climbed, esp. a route in mountaineering. [OE *climban*]
▶ 'climbable *adj*

climb down *vb* (*intr, adv*) **1** to descend. **2** (often foll. by *from*) to retreat (from an opinion, position, etc.). ◆ *n* **climb-down. 3** a retreat from an opinion, etc.

climber ('klaɪmə) *n* **1** a person or thing that climbs, esp. a mountaineer. **2** a plant that grows upwards by twining or clinging with tendrils and suckers. **3** *Chiefly Brit.* short for **social climber.**

clime (klaɪm) *n Poetic.* a region or its climate. [C16: from LL *clima*; see CLIMATE]

clinch (klɪntʃ) *vb* **1** (*tr*) to secure (a driven nail), by bending the protruding point over. **2** (*tr*) to hold together in such a manner. **3** (*tr*) to settle (something, such as an argument, bargain, etc.) in a definite way. **4** (*tr*) *Naut.* to fasten by means of a clinch. **5** (*intr*) to engage in a clinch, as in boxing or wrestling. ◆ *n* **6** the act of clinching. **7a** a nail with its point bent over. **7b** the part of such a nail, etc., that has been bent over. **8** *Boxing, wrestling, etc.* an act or an instance in which one or both competitors hold on to the other to avoid punches, regain wind, etc. **9** *Sl.* a lovers' embrace. **10** *Naut.* a loop or eye formed in a line. ◆ Also (for senses 1, 2, 4, 7, 8, 10): **clench.** [C16: var. of CLENCH]

clincher ('klɪntʃə) *n* **1** *Inf.* something decisive, such as a fact, score, etc. **2** a person or thing that clinches.

cline (klaɪn) *n* the range of variation of form within a species. [C20: from Gk *klinein* to lean]
▶ 'clinal *adj*

-cline *n combining form.* indicating a slope: *anticline.* [back formation from INCLINE]
▸ **-clinal** *adj combining form.*

cling ('klɪŋ) *vb* **clings, clinging, clung.** (*intr*) **1** (often foll. by *to*) to hold fast or adhere closely (to something), as by gripping or sticking. **2** (foll. by *together*) to remain in contact (with each other). **3** to be or remain physically or emotionally close. ◆ *n* **4** short for **clingstone.** [OE *clingan*]
▸ **'clinging** *adj* ▸ **'clingingly** *adv* ▸ **'clingy** *adj* ▸ **'clinginess** *or* **'clingingness** *n*

clingfilm ('klɪŋ,fɪlm) *n* a thin polythene material having the power to adhere closely: used for wrapping food.

clingstone ('klɪŋ,stəʊn) *n* **a** a fruit, such as certain peaches, in which the flesh adheres to the stone. **b** (*as modifier*): *a clingstone peach.*

clinic ('klɪnɪk) *n* **1** a place in which outpatients are given medical treatment or advice. **2** a similar place staffed by specialist physicians or surgeons: *eye clinic.* **3** *Brit.* a private hospital or nursing home. **4** the teaching of medicine to students at the bedside. **5** *Chiefly US & Canad.* a group or centre that offers advice or instruction. [C17: from L *clīnicus* one on a sickbed, from Gk, from *klinē* bed]

clinical ('klɪnɪk³l) *adj* **1** of or relating to a clinic. **2** of or relating to the observation and treatment of patients directly: *clinical medicine.* **3** scientifically detached; strictly objective: *a clinical attitude to life.* **4** plain, simple, and usually unattractive.
▸ **'clinically** *adv*

clinical thermometer *n* a thermometer for determining the temperature of the body.

clinician (klɪ'nɪʃən) *n* a physician, psychiatrist, etc., who specializes in clinical work as opposed to one engaged in experimental studies.

clink[1] (klɪŋk) *vb* **1** to make or cause to make a light and sharply ringing sound. ◆ *n* **2** such a sound. [C14: ?from MDu. *klinken*]

clink[2] (klɪŋk) *n* a slang word for **prison.** [C16: after *Clink*, a prison in Southwark, London]

clinker ('klɪŋkə) *n* **1** the ash and partially fused residues from a coal-fired furnace or fire. **2** a partially vitrified brick or mass of brick. **3** *Sl., chiefly US.* something of poor quality, such as a film. ◆ *vb* **4** (*intr*) to form clinker. [C17: from Du. *klinker* a type of brick, from *klinken* to CLINK[1]]

clinker-built *or* **clincher-built** *adj* (of a boat or ship) having a hull constructed with each plank overlapping that below. [C18 *clinker* a nailing together, prob. from CLINCH]

clinometer (klaɪ'nɒmɪtə) *n* an instrument used in surveying for measuring an angle of inclination.
▸ **clinometric** (,klaɪnə'mɛtrɪk) *or* ,**clino'metrical** *adj* ▸ **cli'nometry** *n*

Clinton ★ ('klɪntən) *n* **William Jefferson**, known as *Bill.* born 1946, US Democrat politician; 42nd president of the US from 1993.

Clio ★ ('klaɪəʊ) *n Greek myth.* the Muse of history. [C19: from L, from Gk *Kleiō*, from *kleein* to celebrate]

clip[1] (klɪp) *vb* **clips, clipping, clipped.** (*mainly tr*) **1** (*also intr*) to cut or trim with scissors or shears, esp. in order to shorten or remove a part. **2** *Brit.* to punch (a hole) in something, esp. a ticket. **3** to curtail. **4** to move a short section from (a film, etc.). **5** to shorten (a word). **6** *Inf.* to strike with a sharp, often slanting, blow. **7** *Sl.* to obtain (money) by deception or cheating. ◆ *n* **8** the act or process of clipping. **9** something clipped off. **10** a short extract from a film, etc. **11** *Inf.* a sharp, often slanting, blow. **12** *Inf.* speed: *a rapid clip.* **13** *Austral. & NZ.* the total quantity of wool shorn, as in one season, etc. **14** another word for **clipped form.** [C12: from ON *klippa* to cut]

clip[2] (klɪp) *n* **1** any of various small implements used to hold loose articles together or to attach one article to another. **2** an article of jewellery that can be clipped onto a dress, hat, etc. **3** short for **paperclip** or **cartridge clip.** ◆ *vb* **clips, clipping, clipped.** (*tr*) **4** to hold together tightly, as with a clip. [OE *clyppan* to embrace]

clipboard ('klɪp,bɔːd) *n* **1** a portable writing board with a clip at the top for holding paper. **2** *Computing.* a temporary storage area in desktop publishing and other programs where text or graphics are held when cut or copied.

clip joint *n Sl.* a place, such as a nightclub or restaurant in which customers are overcharged.

clipped (klɪpt) *adj* (of speech or tone of voice) abrupt, terse, and distinct.

clipped form *n* a shortened form of a word.

clipper ('klɪpə) *n* **1** any fast sailing ship. **2** a person or thing that cuts or clips.

clippers ('klɪpəz) *or* **clips** *pl n* **1** a hand tool for clipping fingernails, veneers, etc. **2** a hairdresser's tool for cutting short hair.

clippie ('klɪpɪ) *n Brit. inf.* a bus conductress.

clipping ('klɪpɪŋ) *n* **1** something cut out, esp. an article from a newspaper; cutting. **2** the distortion of an audio or visual signal in which the tops of peaks with a high amplitude are cut off, caused by, for example, overloading of amplifier circuits.

clique (kliːk, klɪk) *n* a small exclusive group of friends or associates. [C18: from F, ?from OF: latch, from *cliquer* to click]
▸ **'cliquey** *or* **'cliquy** *adj* ▸ **'cliquish** *adj* ▸ **'cliquishly** *adv* ▸ **'cliquishness** *n*

clitoridectomy (,klɪtərɪ'dɛktəmɪ) *n* surgical removal of the clitoris; a form of female circumcision, esp. practised as a religious or ethnic rite.

clitoris ('klɪtərɪs, 'klaɪ-) *n* a part of the female genitalia consisting of a small elongated highly sensitive erectile organ at the front of the vulva. [C17: from NL, from Gk *kleitoris*]
▸ **'clitoral** *adj*

Clive ★ (klaɪv) *n* **Robert**, Baron Clive of Plassey. 1725–74, British general and statesman, whose victory at Plassey (1757) strengthened British control in India.

Cllr *abbrev. for* Councillor.

cloaca (kləʊ'eɪkə) *n, pl* **cloacae** (-kiː). **1** a cavity in most vertebrates, except higher mammals, and certain invertebrates, into which the alimentary canal and the genital and urinary ducts open. **2** a sewer. [C18: from L sewer]
▸ **clo'acal** *adj*

cloak (kləʊk) *n* **1** a wraplike outer garment fastened at the throat and falling straight from the shoulders. **2** something that covers or conceals. ◆ *vb* (*tr*) **3** to cover with or as if with a cloak. **4** to hide or disguise. [C13: from OF *cloque*, from Med. L *clocca* cloak, bell]

cloak-and-dagger *n* (*modifier*) characteristic of or concerned with intrigue and espionage.

cloakroom ('kləʊk,ruːm, -rʊm) *n* **1** a room in which hats, coats, etc., may be temporarily deposited. **2** *Brit.* a euphemistic word for **toilet.**

clobber[1] ('klɒbə) *vb* (*tr*) *Sl.* **1** to batter. **2** to defeat utterly. **3** to criticize severely. [C20: from ?]

clobber[2] ('klɒbə) *n Brit. sl.* personal belongings, such as clothes. [C19: from ?]

clobbering machine *n NZ inf.* pressure to conform with accepted standards.

cloche (klɒʃ) *n* **1** a bell-shaped cover used to protect young plants. **2** a woman's close-fitting hat. [C19: from F: bell, from Med. L *clocca*]

clock[1] (klɒk) *n* **1** a timepiece having mechanically or electrically driven pointers that move constantly over a dial showing the numbers of the hours. Cf. **watch** (sense 7). **2** any clocklike device for recording or measuring, such as a taximeter or pressure gauge. **3** the downy head of a dandelion that has gone to seed. **4** short for **time clock.** **5** (usually preceded by *the*) an informal word for **speedometer** or **mileometer.** **6** *Brit.* a slang word for **face.** **around** *or* **round the clock.** all day and all night. ◆ *vb* (*tr*) **7** *Brit., Austral., & NZ sl.* to strike, esp. on the face or head. **8** to record time as with a stopwatch, esp. in the calculation of speed. **9** *Inf.* to turn back the mileometer on (a car) illegally so that its mileage appears less. [C14: from MDu. *clocke* clock, from Med. L *clocca* bell, ult. of Celtic origin]

.lock[2] (klɒk) *n* an ornamental design on the side of a stocking. [C16: see CLOCK[1]]

lock off *or* **out** *vb* (*intr, adv*) to depart from work, esp. when it involves registering the time of departure on a card.

lock on *or* **in** *vb* (*intr, adv*) to arrive at work, esp. when it involves registering the time of arrival on a card.

lock up *vb* (*tr, adv*) to record or register: *this car has clocked up 80 000 miles.*

:lock-watcher *n* an employee who frequently checks the time in anticipation of a break or of the end of the working day.

:lockwise ('klɒk,waɪz) *adv, adj* in the direction that the hands of a clock rotate; from top to bottom towards the right when seen from the front.

:lockwork ('klɒk,wɜːk) *n* **1** the mechanism of a clock. **2** any similar mechanism, as in a wind-up toy. **3 like clockwork.** with complete regularity and precision; smoothly.

:lod (klɒd) *n* **1** a lump of earth or clay. **2** earth, esp. when heavy or in hard lumps. **3** Also called: **clod poll, clodpate.** a dull or stupid person. [OE *clod-* (occurring in compound words) lump] ▸ **'cloddy** *adj* ▸ **'cloddish** *adj* ▸ **'cloddishly** *adv* ▸ **'clod-dishness** *n*

:lodhopper ('klɒd,hɒpə) *n Inf.* **1** a clumsy person; lout. **2** (*usually pl*) a large heavy shoe.

:log (klɒg) *vb* **clogs, clogging, clogged. 1** to obstruct or become obstructed with thick or sticky matter. **2** (*tr*) to encumber; hinder; impede. **3** (*intr*) to adhere or stick in a mass. ◆ *n* **4a** any of various wooden or wooden-soled shoes. **4b** (*as modifier*): *clog dance.* **5** a heavy block, esp. of wood, fastened to the leg of a person or animal to impede motion. **6** something that impedes motion or action; hindrance. [C14 (in the sense: block of wood): from ?] ▸ **'cloggy** *adj*

:loisonné (klwɑː'zɒneɪ) *n* **1a** a design made by filling in with coloured enamel an outline of flattened wire. **1b** the method of doing this. ◆ *adj* **2** of or made by cloisonné. [C19: from F, from *cloisonner* to divide into compartments, ult. from L *claudere* to close]

:loister ('klɔɪstə) *n* **1** a covered walk, usually around a quadrangle in a religious institution, having an open colonnade on the inside. **2** (*sometimes pl*) a place of religious seclusion, such as a monastery. **3** life in a monastery or convent. ◆ *vb* **4** (*tr*) to confine or seclude in or as if in a monastery. [C13: from OF *cloistre*, from Med. L *claustrum* monastic cell, from L *claudere* to close] ▸ **'cloistered** *adj* ▸ **'cloistral** *adj*

:lomb (kləum) *vb Arch.* a past tense and past participle of **climb.**

:lomp (klɒmp) *n, vb* a less common word for **clump** (senses 2, 7).

:lone (kləun) *n* **1** a group of organisms or cells of the same genetic constitution that are descended from a common ancestor by asexual reproduction, as by cuttings, grafting, etc. **2** Also called: **gene clone.** a segment of DNA that has been isolated and replicated by laboratory manipulation. **3** *Inf.* a person or thing that closely resembles another. **4** *Sl.* **4a** a mobile phone that has been given the electronic identity of an existing mobile phone, so that calls made on it are charged to the owner of that phone. **4b** any similar object, such as a credit card, that has been given the electronic identity of another device, usually in order to commit theft. ◆ *vb* **clones, cloning, cloned. 5** to produce or cause to produce a clone. **6** *Inf.* to produce near copies of (a person or thing). **7** (*tr*) *Sl.* to give (a mobile phone, etc.) the electronic identity of an existing mobile phone (or other device), so that calls, purchases, etc. made with it are charged to the original owner. [C20: from Gk *klōn* twig, shoot] ▸ **'cloning** *n*

:lonk (klɒŋk) *vb* **1** (*intr*) to make a loud dull thud. **2** (*tr*) *Inf.* to hit. ◆ *n* **3** a loud thud. [C20: imit.]

:lonmel ★ (klɒn'mel) *n* the county town of Co. Tipperary, Republic of Ireland; birthplace of Laurence Sterne; meat processing and enamelware. Pop.: 14 500 (1991).

clonus ('kləunəs) *n* a type of convulsion characterized by rapid contraction and relaxation of a muscle. [C19: from NL, from Gk *klonos* turmoil] ▸ **clonic** ('klɒnɪk) *adj* ▸ **clonicity** (klɒ'nɪsɪtɪ) *n*

clop (klɒp) *vb* **clops, clopping, clopped. 1** (*intr*) to make or move along with a sound as of a horse's hooves striking the ground. ◆ *n* **2** a sound of this nature. [C20: imit.]

close[1] (kləus) *adj* **1** near in space or time; in proximity. **2** having the parts near together; dense: *a close formation.* **3** near to the surface; short: *a close haircut.* **4** near in relationship: *a close relative.* **5** intimate: *a close friend.* **6** almost equal: *a close contest.* **7** not deviating or varying greatly from a model or standard: *a close resemblance; a close translation.* **8** careful, strict, or searching: *a close study.* **9** confined or enclosed. **10** shut or shut tight. **11** oppressive, heavy, or airless: *a close atmosphere.* **12** strictly guarded: *a close prisoner.* **13** neat or tight in fit. **14** secretive or reticent. **15** miserly; not generous, esp. with money. **16** (of money or credit) hard to obtain. **17** restricted as to public admission or membership. **18** hidden or secluded. **19** Also: **closed.** restricted or prohibited as to the type of game or fish able to be taken. ◆ *adv* **20** closely; tightly. **21** near or in proximity. **22 close to the wind.** *Naut.* sailing as nearly as possible towards the direction from which the wind is blowing. See also **wind**[1] (sense 23). [C13: from OF *clos*, from L *clausus*, from *claudere* to close] ▸ **'closely** *adv* ▸ **'closeness** *n*

close[2] (kləuz) *vb* **closes, closing, closed. 1** to put or be put in such a position as to cover an opening; shut: *the door closed behind him.* **2** (*tr*) to bar, obstruct, or fill up (an entrance, a hole, etc.): *to close a road.* **3** to bring the parts or edges of (a wound, etc.) together or (of a wound, etc.) to be brought together. **4** (*intr;* foll. by *on, over,* etc.) to take hold: *his hand closed over the money.* **5** to bring or be brought to an end; terminate. **6** (of agreements, deals, etc.) to complete or be completed successfully. **7** to cease or cause to cease to render service: *the shop closed at six.* **8** (*intr*) *Stock Exchange.* to have a value at the end of a day's trading, as specified: *steels closed two points down.* **9** (*tr*) *Arch.* to enclose or shut in. ◆ *n* **10** the act of closing. **11** the end or conclusion: *the close of the day.* **12** (kləus). *Brit.* a courtyard or quadrangle enclosed by buildings or an entry leading to such a courtyard. **13** (kləus). *Brit.* (*cap. when part of a street name*) a small quiet residential road: *Hillside Close.* **14** (kləus). the precincts of a cathedral or similar building. **15** (kləus). *Scot.* the entry from the street to a tenement building. ◆ See also **close down, close in,** etc. [C13: from OF *clos,* from L *clausus,* from *claudere* to close] ▸ **'closer** *n*

close company *n* a company that is controlled by its directors or by five or fewer participants.

closed (kləuzd) *adj* **1** blocked against entry; shut. **2** restricted; exclusive. **3** not open to question or debate. **4** (of a hunting season, etc.) close. **5** *Maths.* **5a** (of a curve or surface) completely enclosing an area or volume. **5b** (of a set) having members that can be produced by a specific operation on other members of the same set. **6** *Phonetics.* denoting a syllable that ends in a consonant. **7** not open to public entry or membership: *a closed society.*

closed chain *n Chem.* another name for **ring**[1] (sense 17).

closed circuit *n* a complete electrical circuit through which current can flow.

closed-circuit television *n* a television system in which signals are transmitted from the television camera to the receivers by cables or telephone links.

close down (kləuz) *vb* (*adv*) **1** to cease or cause to cease operations. **2** (*tr*) *Soccer.* to deny (an opposing player) space to run with the ball or to make or receive a pass. ◆ *n* **close-down. 3** a closure or stoppage, esp. in a factory. **4** *Brit. radio, television.* the end of a period of broadcasting, esp. late at night.

closed shop *n* (formerly) an industrial establishment in which there exists a contract between a trade union and the employer permitting the employment of the union's members only.

close-fisted (ˌkləʊsˈfɪstɪd) *adj* very careful with money; mean.
▶ ˌclose-ˈfistedness *n*

close harmony (kləʊs) *n* a type of singing in which all the parts except the bass lie close together.

close-hauled (ˌkləʊsˈhɔːld) *adj Naut.* with the sails flat, so as to sail as close to the wind as possible.

close in (kləʊz) *vb* (*intr, adv*) **1** (of days) to become shorter with the approach of winter. **2** (foll. by *on* or *upon*) to advance (on) so as to encircle or surround.

close out (kləʊz) *vb* (*adv*) to terminate (a client's or other account) usually by sale of securities to realize cash.

close punctuation (kləʊs) *n* punctuation in which many commas, full stops, etc., are used. Cf. **open punctuation**.

close quarters (kləʊs) *pl n* **1** a narrow cramped space or position. **2 at close quarters. 2a** engaged in hand-to-hand combat. **2b** in close proximity; very near together.

close season (kləʊs) *or* **closed season** *n* **1** the period of the year when it is prohibited to kill certain game or fish. **2** *Sport.* the period of the year when there is no domestic competition.

close shave (kləʊs) *n Inf.* a narrow escape.

closet (ˈklɒzɪt) *n* **1** a small cupboard or recess. **2** a small private room. **3** short for **water closet. 4** (*modifier*) private or secret. ◆ *vb* **closets, closeting, closeted. 5** (*tr*) to shut up or confine in a small private room, esp. for conference or meditation. [C14: from OF, from *clos* enclosure; see CLOSE¹]

close-up (ˈkləʊs,ʌp) *n* **1** a photograph or film or television shot taken at close range. **2** a detailed or intimate view or examination. ◆ *vb* **close up** (kləʊz). (*adv*) **3** to shut entirely. **4** (*intr*) to draw together: *the ranks closed up.* **5** (*intr*) (of wounds) to heal completely.

close with (kləʊz) *vb* (*intr, prep*) to engage in battle with (an enemy).

closure (ˈkləʊʒə) *n* **1** the act of closing or the state of being closed. **2** an end or conclusion. **3** something that closes or shuts, such as a cap or seal for a container. **4** Also called: **gag.** (in a deliberative body) a procedure by which debate may be halted and an immediate vote taken. ◆ *vb* **closures, closuring, closured. 5** (*tr*) (in a deliberative body) to end (debate) by closure. [C14: from OF, from LL, from L *claudere* to close]

clot (klɒt) *n* **1** a soft thick lump or mass. **2** *Brit. inf.* a stupid person; fool. ◆ *vb* **clots, clotting, clotted. 3** to form or cause to form into a soft thick lump or lumps. [OE *clott*, of Gmc origin]

cloth (klɒθ) *n, pl* **cloths** (klɒθs, klɒðz). **1a** a fabric formed by weaving, felting or knitting wool, cotton, etc. **1b** (*as modifier*): *a cloth bag.* **2** a piece of such fabric used for a particular purpose, as for a dishcloth. **3** (usually preceded by *the*) the clergy. [OE *clāth*]

clothe (kləʊð) *vb* **clothes, clothing, clothed** *or* **clad.** (*tr*) **1** to dress or attire (a person). **2** to provide with clothing. **3** to conceal or disguise. **4** to endow or invest. [OE *clāthian*, from *clāth* cloth]

clothes (kləʊðz) *pl n* **1** articles of dress. **2** *Chiefly Brit.* short for **bedclothes.** [OE *clāthas*, pl. of *clāth* cloth]

clotheshorse (ˈkləʊðz,hɔːs) *n* **1** a frame on which to hang laundry for drying or airing. **2** *Inf.* an excessively fashionable person.

clothesline (ˈkləʊðz,laɪn) *n* a piece of rope or wire on which clean washing is hung to dry.

clothes peg *n* a small wooden or plastic clip for attaching washing to a clothesline.

clothes pole *n* a post to which a clothesline is attached. Also called: **clothes post.**

clothes-press *n* a piece of furniture for storing clothes, usually containing wide drawers.

clothes prop *n* a long wooden pole with a forked end used to raise a line of washing to enable it to catch the breeze.

clothier (ˈkləʊðɪə) *n* a person who makes, sells, or deals in clothes or cloth.

clothing (ˈkləʊðɪŋ) *n* **1** garments collectively. **2** some thing that covers or clothes.

Clotho ★ (ˈkləʊθəʊ) *n Greek myth.* one of the three Fates spinner of the thread of life. [L, from Gk *Klōtho*, on who spins, from *klōthein* to spin]

cloth of gold *n* cloth woven from silk threads inter spersed with gold.

clotted cream *n Brit.* a thick cream made from scalde milk, esp. in SW England.

clotting factor *n* any one of a group of substances, in cluding factor VIII, the presence of which in the blood i essential for blood clotting to occur. Also called: **coagula tion factor.**

cloture (ˈkləʊtʃə) *n* **1** closure in the US Senate. ◆ *v* **clotures, cloturing, clotured. 2** (*tr*) to end (debate) by cloture [C19: from F *clôture*, from OF CLOSURE]

cloud (klaʊd) *n* **1** a mass of water or ice particles visible i the sky. **2** any collection of particles visible in the air esp. of smoke or dust. **3** a large number of insects o other small animals in flight. **4** something that darkens threatens, or carries gloom. **5** *Jewellery.* a cloudlike blem ish in a transparent stone. **6 in the clouds.** not in contac with reality. **7 on cloud nine.** *Inf.* elated; very happy. **under a cloud.** under reproach or suspicion. **8b** in a stat of gloom or bad temper. ◆ *vb* **9** (when *intr*, often foll. b *over* or *up*) to make or become cloudy, overcast, or indis tinct. **10** (*tr*) to make obscure; darken. **11** to make or be come gloomy or depressed. **12** (*tr*) to place under o render liable to suspicion or disgrace. **13** to render (li uids) milky or dull or (of liquids) to become milky o dull. [C13 (in the sense: a mass of vapour): from OE *clū* rock, hill]
▶ ˈcloudless *adj* ▶ ˈcloudlessly *adv* ▶ ˈcloudlessness *n*

cloudburst (ˈklaʊd,bɜːst) *n* a heavy downpour.

cloud chamber *n Physics.* an apparatus for detectin high-energy particles by observing their tracks throug a chamber containing a supersaturated vapour.

cloud-cuckoo-land *n* a realm of fantasy, dreams, o impractical notions.

cloudy (ˈklaʊdɪ) *adj* **cloudier, cloudiest. 1** covered wit cloud or clouds. **2** of or like clouds. **3** streaked or mottle like a cloud. **4** opaque or muddy. **5** obscure or unclear. troubled or gloomy.
▶ ˈcloudily *adv* ▶ ˈcloudiness *n*

clough (klʌf) *n Dialect.* a ravine. [OE *clōh*]

Clough ★ (klʌf) *n* **1 Arthur Hugh.** 1819–61, British poet, au thor of *Amours de Voyage* (1858) and *Dipsychus* (1865). **Brian.** born 1935, British footballer and manager.

clout (klaʊt) *n* **1** *Inf.* a blow with the hand or a hard ob ject. **2** power or influence, esp. political. **3** Also called **clout nail.** a short, flat-headed nail. **4** *Dialect.* **4a** a piece o cloth: *a dish clout.* **4b** a garment. ◆ *vb* (*tr*) **5** *Inf.* to give hard blow to, esp. with the hand. [OE *clūt* piece o metal or cloth, *clūtian* to patch (C14: to strike with th hand)]

clove¹ (kləʊv) *n* **1** a tropical evergreen tree of the myrtl family. **2** the dried unopened flower buds of this tree used as a pungent fragrant spice. [C14: from OF, *lit* nail of clove, *clou* from L *clāvus* nail + *girofle* clove tree]

clove² (kləʊv) *n* any of the segments of a compound bul that arise from the axils of the scales of a large bulb. [O *clufu* bulb; see CLEAVE¹]

clove³ (kləʊv) *vb* a past tense of **cleave**¹.

clove hitch *n* a knot or hitch used for securing a rope t a spar, post, or larger rope.

Clovelly ★ (klə'velɪ) *n* a village in SW England, in Devo on the Bristol Channel: noted for its steep cobble streets; tourism, fishing. Pop.: 500 (1989).

cloven (ˈkləʊvᵊn) *vb* **1** a past participle of **cleave**¹. ◆ *ad* split; cleft; divided.

cloven hoof *or* **foot** *n* **1** the divided hoof of a pig, goat cow, deer, or related animal. **2** the mark or symbol c Satan.
▶ ˌcloven-ˈhoofed *or* ˌcloven-ˈfooted *adj*

clove oil *n* a volatile pale-yellow aromatic oil obtaine from clove flowers, formerly much used in confectior ery, dentistry, and microscopy. Also called: **oil of cloves.**

★ people and places

clover ('kləʊvə) n **1** a leguminous fodder plant having trifoliate leaves and dense flower heads. **2** any of various similar or related plants. **3 in clover.** *Inf.* in a state of ease or luxury. [OE *clāfre*]

cloverleaf ('kləʊvə,liːf) n, pl **cloverleaves. 1** an arrangement of connecting roads, resembling a four-leaf clover in form, that joins two intersecting main roads. **2** (*modifier*) in the shape or pattern of a leaf of clover.

Clovis I ★ ('kləʊvɪs) n German name *Chlodwig.* ?466–511 A.D., king of the Franks (481–511).

clown (klaʊn) n **1** a comic entertainer, usually grotesquely costumed and made up, appearing in the circus. **2** a person who acts in a comic or buffoon-like manner. **3** a clumsy rude person; boor. **4** *Arch.* a countryman or rustic. ◆ *vb* (*intr*) **5** to perform as a clown. **6** to play jokes or tricks. **7** to act foolishly. [C16: ?from Low G]
▸ **'clownery** n ▸ **'clownish** adj ▸ **'clownishly** adv
▸ **'clownishness** n

cloy (klɔɪ) *vb* to make weary or cause weariness through an excess of something initially pleasurable or sweet. [C14 (orig.: to nail, hence, to obstruct): from earlier *acloyen*, from OF, from Med. L *inclavāre*, from L, from *clāvus* a nail]
▸ **'cloyingly** adv

cloze test (kləʊz) n a test of the ability to comprehend text in which the reader has to supply the missing words that have been removed from the text. [altered from *close* to complete a pattern (in Gestalt theory)]

club (klʌb) n **1** a stout stick, usually with one end thicker than the other, esp. one used as a weapon. **2** a stick or bat used to strike the ball in various sports, esp. golf. See **golf club. 3** short for **Indian club. 4** a group or association of people with common aims or interests. **5** the room, building, or facilities used by such a group. **6** a building in which elected, fee-paying members go to meet, dine, read, etc. **7** a commercial establishment in which people can drink and dance; disco. See also **nightclub. 8** *Chiefly Brit.* an organization, esp. in a shop, set up as a means of saving. **9** *Brit.* an informal word for **friendly society. 10a** the black trefoil symbol on a playing card. **10b** a card with one or more of these symbols or (*when pl*) the suit of cards so marked. **11 in the club.** *Brit. sl.* pregnant. ◆ *vb* **clubs, clubbing, clubbed. 12** (*tr*) to beat with or as if with a club. **13** (often foll. by *together*) to gather or become gathered into a group. **14** (often foll. by *together*) to unite or combine (resources, efforts, etc.) for a common purpose. [C13: from ON *klubba*, rel. to CLUMP]
▸ **'clubbing** n

clubbed (klʌbd) adj having a thickened end, like a club.

clubber ('klʌbə) n a person who regularly frequents nightclubs and similar establishments.

club class n a class of air travel that is less luxurious than first class but more luxurious than economy class. ◆ adj **club-class. 2** of or relating to this class of travel.

club foot n a congenital deformity of the foot, esp. one in which the foot is twisted so that most of the weight rests on the heel. Technical name: **talipes. 2** a foot so deformed.
▸ **,club-'footed** adj

clubhouse ('klʌb,haʊs) n the premises of a sports or other club, esp. a golf club.

clubman ('klʌbmən) or (*fem*) **clubwoman** n, pl **clubmen** or **clubwomen.** a person who is an enthusiastic member of a club or clubs.

club root n a fungal disease of cabbages and related plants, in which the roots become thickened and distorted.

cluck (klʌk) n **1** the low clicking sound made by a hen or any similar sound. ◆ *vb* **2** (*intr*) (of a hen) to make a clicking sound. **3** (*tr*) to call or express (a feeling) by making a similar sound. [C17: imit.]

clucky ('klʌkɪ) adj *Austral. inf.* **1** wanting to have a baby. **2** excessively protective towards children.

clue (kluː) n **1** something that helps to solve a problem or unravel a mystery. **2 not have a clue. 2a** to be completely baffled. **2b** to be ignorant or incompetent. ◆ *vb* **clues,**

cluing, clued. 3 (*tr;* usually foll. by *in* or *up*) to provide with helpful information. [C15: var. of CLEW]

clued-up adj *Inf.* shrewd; well-informed.

clueless ('kluːlɪs) adj *Sl.* helpless; stupid.

Cluj ★ (kluʃ, kluːʒ) n an industrial city in NW Romania, on the Someşul-Mic River: former capital of Transylvania. Pop.: 321 850 (1993 est.). German name: **Klausenburg.** Hungarian name: **Kolozsvár.**

clump (klʌmp) n **1** a cluster, as of trees or plants. **2** a dull heavy tread or similar sound. **3** an irregular mass. **4** an inactive mass of microorganisms, esp. a mass of bacteria produced as a result of agglutination. **5** an extra sole on a shoe. **6** *Sl.* a blow. ◆ *vb* **7** (*intr*) to walk or tread heavily. **8** to gather or be gathered into clumps, clusters, clots, etc. **9** to cause (bacteria, blood cells, etc.) to collect together or (of bacteria, etc.) to collect together. **10** (*tr*) *Sl.* to punch (someone). [OE *clympe*]
▸ **'clumpy** adj

clumsy ('klʌmzɪ) adj **clumsier, clumsiest. 1** lacking in skill or physical coordination. **2** awkwardly constructed or contrived. [C16 (in obs. sense: benumbed with cold; hence, awkward): ?from C13 dialect *clumse* to benumb, prob. of Scand. origin]
▸ **'clumsily** adv ▸ **'clumsiness** n

clung (klʌŋ) *vb* the past tense and past participle of **cling.**

clunk (klʌŋk) n **1** a blow or the sound of a blow. **2** a dull metallic sound. ◆ *vb* **3** to make or cause to make such a sound. [C19: imit.]

clunky ('klʌŋkɪ) adj **clunkier, clunkiest. 1** making a clunking noise. **2** clumsy or inelegant: *clunky ankle-strap shoes.* **3** awkward or unsophisticated: *then you guffaw at clunky dialogue.*

Cluny ★ ('kluːnɪ; *French* klyni) n a town in E central France: reformed Benedictine order founded here in 910; important religious and cultural centre in the Middle Ages. Pop.: 4724 (1990).
▸ **'Cluniac** adj

cluster ('klʌstə) n **1** a number of things growing, fastened, or occurring close together. **2** a number of persons or things grouped together. ◆ *vb* **3** to gather or be gathered in clusters. [OE *clyster*]
▸ **'clustered** adj ▸ **'clustery** adj

clutch[1] (klʌtʃ) *vb* **1** (*tr*) to seize with or as if with hands or claws. **2** (*tr*) to grasp or hold firmly. **3** (*intr;* usually foll. by *at*) to attempt to get hold or possession (of). ◆ *n* **4** a device that enables two revolving shafts to be joined or disconnected, esp. one that transmits the drive from the engine to the gearbox in a vehicle. **5** a device for holding fast. **6** a firm grasp. **7** a hand, claw, or talon in the act of clutching: *in the clutches of a bear.* **8** (*often pl*) power or control: *in the clutches of the Mafia.* [OE *clyccan*]

clutch[2] (klʌtʃ) n **1** a hatch of eggs laid by a particular bird or laid in a single nest. **2** a brood of chickens. **3** *Inf.* a group or cluster. ◆ *vb* **4** (*tr*) to hatch (chickens). [C17 (N English dialect): *cletch,* from ON *klekja* to hatch]

Clutha ★ ('kluːθə) n a river in New Zealand, the longest river in the South Island; rising in the Southern Alps it flows southeast to the Pacific. Length: 338 km (210 miles).

clutter ('klʌtə) *vb* **1** (*usually tr;* often foll. by *up*) to strew or amass (objects) in a disorderly manner. **2** (*intr*) to move about in a bustling manner. ◆ *n* **3** a disordered heap or mass of objects. **4** a state of disorder. **5** unwanted echoes that confuse the observation of signals on a radar screen. [C15 *clotter,* from *clotteren* to CLOT]

Clwyd ★ ('kluːɪd) n a former county in NE Wales, formed in 1974 from Flintshire, most of Denbighshire, and part of Merionethshire; replaced in 1996 as part of local government reorganization.

Clyde ★ (klaɪd) n **1 Firth of.** an inlet of the Atlantic in SW Scotland. Length: 103 km (64 miles). **2** a river in S Scotland, rising in South Lanarkshire and flowing northwest to the Firth of Clyde: formerly extensive shipyards. Length: 170 km (106 miles).

Clydebank ★ (,klaɪd'bæŋk, 'klaɪd,bæŋk) n a town in W Scotland, on the north bank of the River Clyde. Pop.: 29 171 (1991).

★ people and places

Clydesdale ('klaɪdz,deɪl) *n* a heavy powerful breed of carthorse, originally from Scotland.

clypeus ('klɪpɪəs) *n, pl* **clypei** ('klɪpɪ,aɪ). a cuticular plate on the head of some insects. [C19: from NL, from L *clipeus* round shield]
▸ 'clypeal *adj* ▸ clypeate ('klɪpɪ,eɪt) *adj*

Clytemnestra *or* **Clytaemnestra** ★ (,klaɪtɪm'nestrə) *n Greek myth.* the wife of Agamemnon, whom she killed on his return from the Trojan War.

cm *symbol for* centimetre.

Cm *the chemical symbol for* curium.

Cmdr *Mil. abbrev. for* Commander.

CMEA *abbrev. for* Council for Mutual Economic Assistance. See **Comecon**.

CMG *abbrev. for* Companion of St Michael and St George (a Brit. title).

CMOS ('si:mɒs) *adj Computing. acronym for* complementary metal oxide silicon: *CMOS memory.*

CMV *abbrev. for* cytomegalovirus.

CNAA *abbrev. for* Council for National Academic Awards.

CNAR *abbrev. for* compound net annual rate.

CND *Chiefly Brit. abbrev. for* Campaign for Nuclear Disarmament.

Cnossus ★ ('nɒsəs, 'knɒs-) *n* a variant spelling of **Knossos**.

Cnut ★ (kə'nju:t) *n* a variant spelling of **Canute**.

Co *the chemical symbol for* cobalt.

CO *abbrev. for:* **1** Commanding Officer. **2** conscientious objector.

Co. *or* **co.** *abbrev. for:* **1** (esp. in names of business organizations) Company. **2 and co.** (kəu) *Inf.* and the rest of them: *Harold and co.*

Co. *abbrev. for* County.

co- *prefix* **1** together; joint or jointly; mutual or mutually: *coproduction.* **2** indicating partnership or equality: *cofounder; copilot.* **3** to the same or a similar degree: *coextend.* **4** (in mathematics and astronomy) of the complement of an angle: *cosecant.* [from L, reduced form of COM-]

c/o *abbrev. for:* **1** care of. **2** *Book-keeping.* carried over.

coach (kəutʃ) *n* **1** a large vehicle for several passengers, used for transport over long distances, sightseeing, etc. **2** a large four-wheeled enclosed carriage, usually horsedrawn. **3** a railway carriage. **4** a trainer or instructor: *a drama coach.* **5** a tutor who prepares students for examinations. ◆ *vb* **6** to give tuition or instruction to (a pupil). **7** (*tr*) to transport in a bus or coach. [C16: from F *coche*, from Hungarian *kocsi szekér* wagon of Kocs, village in Hungary where coaches were first made]
▸ 'coacher *n*

coach-built *adj* (of a vehicle) having specially built bodywork.
▸ 'coach-,builder *n*

coachman ('kəutʃmən) *n, pl* **coachmen**. the driver of a coach or carriage.

coachwork ('kəutʃ,wɜːk) *n* **1** the design and manufacture of car bodies. **2** the body of a car.

coadjutor (kəu'ædʒutə) *n* **1** a bishop appointed as assistant to a diocesan bishop. **2** *Rare.* an assistant. [C15: via OF from L *co-* together + *adjūtor* helper, from *adjūtāre* to assist]

coagulate *vb* (kəu'ægju,leɪt), **coagulates, coagulating, coagulated.** **1** to cause (a fluid, such as blood) to change into a soft semisolid mass or (of such a fluid) to change into such a mass; clot; curdle. ◆ *n* (kəu'ægjulɪt, -,leɪt). **2** the solid or semisolid substance produced by coagulation. [C16: from L *coāgulāre*, from *coāgulum* rennet, from *cōgere* to drive together]
▸ co'agulant *or* co'agu,lator *n* ▸ co,agu'lation *n* ▸ coagulative (kəu'ægjulətɪv) *adj*

coagulation factor *n Med.* another name for **clotting factor.**

Coahuila ★ (*Spanish* koa'wila) *n* a state of N Mexico: mainly plateau, crossed by several mountain ranges that contain rich mineral resources. Capital: Saltillo. Pop.:

2 172 136 (1995 est.). Area: 151 571 sq. km (59 112 sq miles).

coal (kəul) *n* **1a** a compact black or dark brown carbonaceous rock consisting of layers of partially decomposed vegetation deposited in the Carboniferous period: a fuel and a source of coke, coal gas, and coal tar. **1b** (*as modifier*): *coal cellar; coal mine; coal dust.* **2** one or more lumps of coal. **3** short for **charcoal**. **4 coals to Newcastle.** something supplied where it is already plentiful. ◆ *vb* **5** to take in, provide with, or turn into coal. [OE *col*]
▸ 'coaly *adj*

coaler ('kəulə) *n* a ship, train, etc., used to carry or supply coal.

coalesce (,kəuə'les) *vb* **coalesces, coalescing, coalesced** (*intr*) to unite or come together in one body or mass; merge; fuse; blend. [C16: from L *co-* + *alēscere* to increase, from *alere* to nourish]
▸ ,coa'lescence *n* ▸ ,coa'lescent *adj*

coalface ('kəul,feɪs) *n* the exposed seam of coal in a mine.

coalfield ('kəul,fi:ld) *n* an area rich in deposits of coal.

coalfish ('kəul,fɪʃ) *n, pl* **coalfish** *or* **coalfishes.** a darkcoloured gadoid food fish occurring in northern seas Also called (Brit.): **saithe, coley.**

coal gas *n* a mixture of gases produced by the distillation of bituminous coal and used for heating and lighting.

coalition (,kəuə'lɪʃən) *n* **1a** an alliance between groups or parties, esp. some temporary and specific reason. **1b** (*as modifier*): *a coalition government.* **2** a fusion or merging into one body or mass. [C17: from Med. L *coalitiō*, from L *coalēscere* to COALESCE]
▸ ,coa'litionist *n*

Coal Measures *pl n* **the.** a series of coal-bearing rocks formed in the upper Carboniferous period.

coal miner's lung *n* an informal name for **anthracosis.**

coal scuttle *n* a container to supply coal to a domestic fire.

coal tar *n* a black tar, produced by the distillation of bituminous coal, that can be further distilled to yield benzene, toluene, etc.

coal tit *n* a small European songbird having a black head with a white patch on the nape.

coaming ('kəumɪŋ) *n* a raised frame round a ship's hatchway for keeping out water. [C17: from ?]

coarse (kɔːs) *adj* **1** rough in texture, structure, etc.; not fine: *coarse sand.* **2** lacking refinement or taste; indelicate; vulgar: *coarse jokes.* **3** of inferior quality. **4** (of a metal) not refined. [C14: from ?]
▸ 'coarsely *adv* ▸ 'coarseness *n*

coarse fish *n* a freshwater fish that is not of the salmon family.
▸ coarse fishing *n*

coarsen ('kɔːsᵊn) *vb* to make or become coarse.

coast (kəust) *n* **1** the line or zone where the land meets the sea. Related adj: **littoral**. **2** *Brit.* the seaside. **3** *US.* **3a** a slope down which a sledge may slide. **3b** the act or an instance of sliding down a slope. **4 the coast is clear.** *Inf.* the obstacles or dangers are gone. ◆ *vb* **5** to move or cause to move by momentum or force of gravity. **6** (*intr*) to proceed without great effort: *to coast to victory.* **7** to sail along (a coast). [C13: from OF *coste*, from L *costa* side, rib]
▸ 'coastal *adj*

coaster ('kəustə) *n* **1** *Brit.* a vessel engaged in coastal commerce. **2** a small tray for holding a decanter, wine bottle, etc. **3** a person or thing that coasts. **4** a protective mat for glasses. **5** *US.* short for **roller coaster.**

Coaster ('kəustə) *n NZ.* a person from the West Coast of the South Island, New Zealand.

coastguard ('kəust,gɑːd) *n* **1** a maritime force which aids shipping, saves lives at sea, prevents smuggling, etc **2** Also called: **coastguardsman.** a member of such a force.

coastline ('kəust,laɪn) *n* the outline of a coast.

Coast Mountains ★ *pl n* a mountain range in Canada on the Pacific coast of British Columbia. Highest peak Mount Waddington, 4043 m (13 266 ft).

★ people and places

coat (kəʊt) n **1** an outdoor garment with sleeves, covering the body from the shoulders to waist, knees, or feet. **2** any similar garment, esp. one forming the top to a suit. **3** a layer that covers or conceals a surface: *a coat of dust*. **4** the hair, wool, or fur of an animal. ♦ vb (tr) **5** (often foll. by *with*) to cover (with) a layer or covering. **6** to provide with a coat. [C16: from OF *cote*, of Gmc origin]

Coates (kəʊts) n **Joseph Gordon**. 1878–1943, New Zealand statesman; prime minister (1925–28).

coat hanger n a curved piece of wood, wire, etc., with a hook, used to hang up clothes.

coati (kəʊˈɑːtɪ), **coati-mondi**, or **coati-mundi** (kəʊˌɑːtɪˈmʌndɪ) n, pl **coatis**, **coati-mondis**, or **coati-mundis**. an omnivorous mammal of Central and South America, related to but larger than the raccoons, having a long flexible snout and a brindled coat. [C17: from Port., from Tupi, lit.: belt-nosed, from *cua* belt + *tim* nose]

coating (ˈkəʊtɪŋ) n **1** a layer or film spread over a surface. **2** fabric suitable for coats.

coat of arms n the heraldic bearings of a person, family, or corporation.

coat of mail n a protective garment made of linked metal rings or overlapping metal plates.

coat-tail n the long tapering tails at the back of a man's tailed coat.

coauthor (kəʊˈɔːθə) n **1** a person who shares the writing of a book, etc., with another. ♦ vb **2** (tr) to be the joint author of (a book, etc.).

coax (kəʊks) vb **1** to seek to manipulate or persuade (someone) by tenderness, flattery, pleading, etc. **2** (tr) to obtain by persistent coaxing. **3** (tr) to work on (something) carefully and patiently so as to make it function as desired: *he coaxed the engine into starting*. [C16: verb formed from obs. noun *cokes* fool, from ?]
► **'coaxer** n ► **'coaxingly** adv

coaxial (kəʊˈæksɪəl) or **coaxal** (kəʊˈæksəl) adj **1** having or mounted on a common axis. **2** *Geom.* (of a set of circles) having the same radical axis. **3** *Electronics.* formed from, using, or connected to a coaxial cable.

coaxial cable n a cable consisting of an inner insulated core of stranded or solid wire surrounded by an outer insulated flexible wire braid, used esp. as a transmission line for radio-frequency signals. Often shortened to **coax** (ˈkəʊæks).

cob (kɒb) n **1** a male swan. **2** a thickset type of riding and draught horse. **3** short for **corncob** or **cobnut**. **4** *Brit.* another name for **hazel** (sense 1). **5** a small rounded lump or heap of coal, ore, etc. **6** *Brit. & NZ.* a building material consisting of a mixture of clay and chopped straw. **7** *Brit.* a round loaf of bread. [C15: from ?]

cobalt (ˈkəʊbɔːlt) n a brittle hard silvery-white element that is a ferromagnetic metal: used in alloys. The radioisotope **cobalt-60** is used in radiotherapy and as a tracer. Symbol: Co; atomic no.: 27; atomic wt.: 58.933. [C17: G *Kobalt*, from MHG *kobolt* goblin; from the miners' belief that goblins placed it in the silver ore]

cobalt blue n **1** any greenish-blue pigment containing cobalt aluminate. **2a** a deep blue colour. **2b** (*as adj*): *a cobalt-blue car*.

cobalt bomb n **1** a cobalt-60 device used in radiotherapy. **2** a nuclear weapon consisting of a hydrogen bomb encased in cobalt, which releases large quantities of radioactive cobalt-60 into the atmosphere.

cobber (ˈkɒbə) n *Austral. arch. & NZ.* a friend; mate: used as a term of address to males. [C19: from E dialect *cob* to take a liking to someone]

Cobbett ★ (ˈkɒbɪt) n **William**. 1763–1835, British journalist and social reformer; founded *The Political Register* (1802); author of *Rural Rides* (1830).

cobble[1] (ˈkɒbəl) n **1** short for **cobblestone**. ♦ vb **cobbles**, **cobbling**, **cobbled**. **2** (tr) to pave (a road, etc.) with cobblestones. [C15 (in *cobblestone*): from COB]

cobble[2] (ˈkɒbəl) vb **cobbles**, **cobbling**, **cobbled**. (tr) **1** to make or mend (shoes). **2** to put together clumsily. [C15: back formation from COBBLER[1]]

cobbler[1] (ˈkɒblə) n a person who makes or mends shoes. [C13 (as surname): from ?]

cobbler[2] (ˈkɒblə) n **1** a sweetened iced drink, usually made from fruit and wine. **2** *Chiefly US.* a hot dessert made of fruit covered with a rich cakelike crust. [C19: (for sense 1) ? shortened from *cobbler's punch*]

cobblers (ˈkɒbləz) pl n *Brit. taboo sl.* **1** another word for **testicles**. **2** (**a load of old**) **cobblers**. rubbish; nonsense. [C20: from rhyming sl. *cobblers' awls* balls]

cobblestone (ˈkɒbəlˌstəʊn) n a rounded stone used for paving. Sometimes shortened to **cobble**.

Cobden ★ (ˈkɒbdən) n **Richard**. 1804–65, British economist and statesman: a leader of the campaign to abolish the Corn Laws (1846).

cobelligerent (ˌkəʊbɪˈlɪdʒərənt) n a country fighting in a war on the side of another country.

Cobham ★ (ˈkɒbəm) n **Lord**, title of (Sir John) **Oldcastle**.

Coblenz ★ (German ˈkoːblɛnts) n a variant spelling of **Koblenz**.

cobnut (ˈkɒbˌnʌt) or **cob** n other names for a **hazelnut**. [C16: from earlier *cobylle nut*]

COBOL or **Cobol** (ˈkəʊbɒl) n a high-level computer programming language designed for general commercial use. [C20: *co(mmon)* *b(usiness)* *o(riented)* *l(anguage)*]

cobra (ˈkəʊbrə) n any of several highly venomous snakes of tropical Africa and Asia. When alarmed they spread the skin of the neck region into a hood. [C19: from Port. *cobra (de capello)* snake (with a hood), from L *colubra* snake]

Coburg ★ (ˈkəʊbɜːg; German ˈkoːburk) n a city in E Germany, in N Bavaria. Pop.: 44 690 (1991).

cobweb (ˈkɒbˌwɛb) n **1** a web spun by certain spiders. **2** a single thread of such a web. **3** something like a cobweb, as in its flimsiness or ability to trap. [C14: *cob*, from OE *(ātor)coppe* spider]
► **'cob,webbed** adj ► **'cob,webby** adj

cobwebs (ˈkɒbˌwɛbz) pl n **1** mustiness, confusion, or obscurity. **2** *Inf.* stickiness of the eyelids experienced upon first awakening.

coca (ˈkəʊkə) n either of two shrubs, native to the Andes, the dried leaves of which contain cocaine and are chewed for their stimulating effects. [C17: from Sp., from Quechuan *kúka*]

Coca-Cola (ˌkəʊkəˈkəʊlə) n **1** *Trademark.* a carbonated soft drink flavoured with coca nuts, cola nuts, caramel, etc. **2** (*modifier*) denoting the spread of American culture and values to other parts of the world: *Coca-Cola generation*.

cocaine or **cocain** (kəˈkeɪn) n an addictive narcotic drug derived from coca leaves or synthesized, used medicinally as a topical anaesthetic. [C19: from COCA + -INE[1]]

coccus (ˈkɒkəs) n, pl **cocci** (-kaɪ, -ksaɪ). any spherical or nearly spherical bacterium, such as a staphylococcus. [C18: from NL, from Gk *kokkos* berry, grain]
► **'coccoid** or **'coccal** adj

coccyx (ˈkɒksɪks) n, pl **coccyges** (kɒkˈsaɪdʒiːz). a small triangular bone at the end of the spinal column in man and some apes. [C17: from NL, from Gk *kokkux* cuckoo, imit.; from its likeness to a cuckoo's beak]
► **coccygeal** (kɒkˈsɪdʒɪəl) adj

Cochin ★ (ˈkəʊtʃɪn, ˈkɒtʃ-) n **1** a region and former state of SW India: part of Kerala state since 1956. **2** a port in SW India, on the Malabar Coast: the first European settlement in India, founded by Vasco da Gama in 1502. Pop.: 564 589 (1991).

Cochin China ★ n a former French colony of Indochina (1862–1948): now the part of Vietnam that lies south of Phan Thiet.

cochineal (ˌkɒtʃɪˈniːl, ˈkɒtʃɪˌniːl) n **1** a Mexican insect that feeds on cacti. **2** a crimson substance obtained from the crushed bodies of these insects, used for colouring food and for dyeing. **3** the colour of this dye. [C16: from OSp. *cochinilla*, from L *coccineus* scarlet-coloured, from Gk *kokkos* kermes berry]

cochlea (ˈkɒklɪə) n, pl **cochleae** (-lɪ,iː). the spiral tube that forms part of the internal ear, converting sound vibrations into nerve impulses. [C16: from L: snail, spiral, from Gk *kokhlias*]
► **'cochlear** adj

cochlear implant ('kɒklɪə) *n* a device that stimulates the acoustic nerve in the inner ear in order to produce some form of hearing in people who are deaf from inner ear disease.

cochleate ('kɒklɪ,eɪt, -ɪt) *or* **cochleated** *adj Biol.* shaped like a snail's shell.

cock[1] (kɒk) *n* **1** the male of the domestic fowl. **2a** any other male bird. **2b** the male of certain other animals, such as the lobster. **2c** (*as modifier*): *a cock sparrow.* **3** short for **stopcock** or **weathercock**. **4** a taboo slang word for **penis**. **5a** the hammer of a firearm. **5b** its position when the firearm is ready to be discharged. **6** *Brit. inf.* a friend, mate, or fellow. **7** a jaunty or significant tilting upwards: *a cock of the head.* ◆ *vb* **8** (*tr*) to set the firing pin, hammer, or breech block of (a firearm) so that a pull on the trigger will release it and thus fire the weapon. **9** (*tr*; sometimes foll. by *up*) to raise in an alert or jaunty manner. **10** (*intr*) to stick or stand up conspicuously. ◆ See also **cockup**. [OE *cocc*, ult. imit.]

cock[2] (kɒk) *n* **1** a small, cone-shaped heap of hay, straw, etc. ◆ *vb* **2** (*tr*) to stack (hay, etc.) in such heaps. [C14: ? of Scand. origin]

cockabully (,kɒkə'bʊlɪ) *n, pl* **cockabullies**. any of several small freshwater fish of New Zealand. [Maori *kokopu*]

cockade (kɒ'keɪd) *n* a feather or ribbon worn on military headwear. [C18: changed from earlier *cockard*, from F, from *coq* COCK[1]]
▶ **cock'aded** *adj*

cock-a-doodle-doo (,kɒkə,duːd°l'duː) *interj* an imitation or representation of a cock crowing.

cock-a-hoop *adj* (*usually postpositive*) **1** in very high spirits. **2** boastful. **3** askew; confused. [C16: ?from *set the cock a hoop*: to put a cock on a *hoop*, a full measure of grain]

cockalorum (,kɒkə'lɔːrəm) *n* **1** a self-important little man. **2** bragging talk. [C18: from COCK[1] + *-alorum*, var. of L genitive pl ending; ? intended to suggest: the cock of all cocks]

cockamamie (,kɒkə'meɪmɪ) *adj Sl., chiefly US.* ridiculous or nonsensical: *a cockamamie story.* [C20: in an earlier sense: a paper transfer, prob. from DECALCOMANIA]

cock-and-bull story *n Inf.* an obviously improbable story, esp. one used as an excuse.

cockatoo (,kɒkə'tuː, 'kɒkə,tuː) *n, pl* **cockatoos. 1** any of a genus of parrots having an erectile crest and light-coloured plumage. **2** *Austral. & NZ.* a small farmer or settler. **3** *Austral. inf.* a lookout during some illegal activity. [C17: from Du., from Malay *kakatua*]

cockatrice ('kɒkətrɪs, -,traɪs) *n* **1** a legendary monster, part snake and part cock, that could kill with a glance. **2** another name for **basilisk** (sense 1). [C14: from OF, ult. from L *calcāre* to tread, from *calx* heel]

cockboat ('kɒk,bəʊt) *or* **cockleboat** *n* a ship's small boat. [C15 *cokbote*, ? ult. from LL *caudica* dugout canoe, from L *caudex* tree trunk]

cockchafer ('kɒk,tʃeɪfə) *n* any of various Old World beetles, whose larvae feed on crops and grasses. Also called: **May beetle, May bug**. [C18: from COCK[1] + CHAFER]

Cockcroft ★ ('kɒk,krɒft) *n* Sir **John Douglas**. 1897–1967, British nuclear physicist. Shared the Nobel prize for physics 1951, for his artificial transmutation of a nucleus.

cockcrow ('kɒk,krəʊ) *n* daybreak.

cocked hat *n* **1** a hat with brims turned up and caught together in order to give two points (bicorn) or three points (tricorn). **2 knock into a cocked hat** *Sl.* to outdo or defeat.

Cocker ★ ('kɒkə) *n* **1 Edward**. 1631–75, English arithmetician. **2 according to Cocker**. reliable or reliably; correct or correctly.

cockerel ('kɒkərəl, 'kɒkrəl) *n* a young domestic cock, less than a year old. [C15: dim. of COCK[1]]

Cockerell ★ ('kɒkərəl) *n* Sir **Christopher Sydney**. born 1910, British engineer who invented the hovercraft.

cocker spaniel ('kɒkə) *n* a small compact breed of spaniel. [C19: from *cocking* hunting woodcocks]

cockeyed ('kɒk,aɪd) *adj Inf.* **1** afflicted with strabismus or squint. **2** physically or logically abnormal, absurd, etc.; crooked; askew: *cockeyed ideas.* **3** drunk.

cockfight ('kɒk,faɪt) *n* a fight between two gamecocks fitted with sharp metal spurs.
▶ **'cock,fighting** *n*

cockhorse (,kɒk'hɔːs) *n* another name for **rocking horse** or **hobbyhorse**.

cockieleekie, cockyleeky, *or* **cock-a-leekie** ('kɒkə'liːkɪ) *n Scot.* a soup made from a fowl boiled with leeks.

cockle[1] ('kɒk°l) *n* **1** any edible sand-burrowing bivalve mollusc of Europe, typically having a rounded shell with radiating ribs. **2** any of certain similar or related molluscs. **3** short for **cockleshell** (sense 1). **4** a wrinkle or puckering. **5** one's deepest feelings (esp. in **warm the cockles of one's heart**). ◆ *vb* **cockles, cockling, cockled. 6** to contract or cause to contract into wrinkles. [C14: from OF *coquille* shell, from L *conchȳlium* shellfish, from Gk *konkhule* mussel; see CONCH]

cockle[2] ('kɒk°l) *n* any of several plants, esp. the corn cockle, that grow as weeds in cornfields.

cockleshell ('kɒk°l,ʃel) *n* **1** the shell of the cockle. **2** any of the shells of certain other molluscs. **3** any small light boat.

cockney ('kɒknɪ) (*often cap.*) ◆ *n* **1** a native of London, esp. of the East End, speaking a characteristic dialect of English. Traditionally defined as someone born within the sound of the bells of St Mary-le-Bow church. **2** the urban dialect of London or its East End. ◆ *adj* **3** characteristic of cockneys or their dialect of English. [C14: from *cokeney*, lit.: cock's egg, later applied contemptuously to townsmen, from *cokene*, genitive pl of *cok* COCK[1] + *ey* EGG[1]]
▶ **'cockneyish** *adj* ▶ **'cockney,ism** *n*

cock of the walk *n Inf.* a person who asserts himself in a strutting pompous way.

cockpit ('kɒk,pɪt) *n* **1** the compartment in a small aircraft in which the pilot, crew, and sometimes the passengers sit. Cf. **flight deck** (sense 1). **2** the driver's compartment in a racing car. **3** *Naut.* an enclosed or recessed area towards the stern of a small vessel from which it is steered. **4** the site of numerous battles or campaigns. **5** an enclosure used for cockfights.

cockroach ('kɒk,rəʊtʃ) *n* an insect having an oval flattened body with long antennae and biting mouthparts: a household pest. [C17: from Sp. *cucaracha*, from ?]

cockscomb *or* **coxcomb** ('kɒks,kəʊm) *n* **1** the comb of a domestic cock. **2** a garden plant with yellow, crimson, or purple feathery plumelike flowers in a broad spike resembling the comb of a cock. **3** *Inf.* a conceited dandy.

cockshy ('kɒk,ʃaɪ) *n, pl* **cockshies**. *Brit.* **1** a target aimed at in throwing games. **2** the throw itself. ◆ Often shortened to **shy**. [C18: from shying at a cock, the prize for the person who hit it]

cocksure (,kɒk'ʃʊə, -'ʃɔː) *adj* overconfident; arrogant. [C16: from ?]
▶ **,cock'sureness** *n*

cocktail ('kɒk,teɪl) *n* **1a** any mixed drink with a spirit base. **1b** (*as modifier*): *the cocktail hour.* **2** an appetizer of seafood, mixed fruits, etc. **3** any combination of diverse elements, esp. one considered potent. **4** (*modifier*) appropriate for formal occasions: *a cocktail dress.* [C19: from ?]

cockup ('kɒk,ʌp) *n* **1** *Brit. sl.* something done badly. ◆ *vb* **cock up**. (*tr, adv*) **2** (of an animal) to raise (its ears etc.), esp. in an alert manner. **3** *Brit. sl.* to botch.

cocky[1] ('kɒkɪ) *adj* **cockier, cockiest**. excessively proud of oneself.
▶ **'cockily** *adv* ▶ **'cockiness** *n*

cocky[2] ('kɒkɪ) *n, pl* **cockies**. *Austral. & NZ inf.* short for **cockatoo** (sense 2).

coco ('kəʊkəʊ) *n, pl* **cocos**. short for **coconut** or **coconut palm** [C16: from Port. *coco* grimace; from the likeness of the three holes of the nut to a face]

cocoa ('kəʊkəʊ) *or* **cacao** *n* **1** a powder made from cocoa beans after they have been roasted and ground. **2** a hot or cold drink made from cocoa and milk or water. **3a** a light to moderate brown colour. **3b** (*as adj*): *cocoa paint*. [C18: altered from CACAO]

cocoa bean *n* the seed of the cacao.

cocoa butter *n* a yellowish-white waxy solid that is obtained from cocoa beans and used for confectionery, soap, etc.

coconut *or* **cocoanut** ('kəʊkə,nʌt) *n* **1** the fruit of the coconut palm, consisting of a thick fibrous oval husk inside which is a thin hard shell enclosing edible white meat. The hollow centre is filled with a milky fluid (**coconut milk**). **2** the meat of the coconut, often shredded and used in cakes, curries, etc. [C18: see COCO]

coconut matting *n* a form of coarse matting made from the fibrous husk of the coconut.

coconut oil *n* the oil obtained from the meat of the coconut and used for making soap, etc.

coconut palm *n* a tall palm tree, widely planted throughout the tropics, having coconuts as fruits. Also called: **coco palm, coconut tree.**

cocoon (kə'kuːn) *n* **1** a silky protective envelope secreted by silkworms and certain other insect larvae, in which the pupae develop. **2** a protective spray covering used as a seal on machinery. **3** a cosy warm covering. ◆ *vb* **4** (*tr*) to wrap in a cocoon. [C17: from F, from Provençal *coucoun* eggshell, from *coco* shell]

cocopan ('kəʊkəʊ,pæn) *n* (in South Africa) a small wagon running on narrow-gauge railway lines used in mines. Also called: **hopper.** [C20: from Zulu *'ngkumbana* short truck]

Cocos Islands ★ ('kəʊkɒs, 'kəʊkəs) *pl n* a group of 27 coral islands in the Indian Ocean, southwest of Java: a Territory of Australia since 1955. Pop.: 593 (1993). Area: 13 sq. km (5 sq. miles). Also called: **Keeling Islands.**

cocotte (kəʊ'kɒt, kə-) *n* **1** a small fireproof dish in which individual portions of food are cooked and served. **2** a prostitute or promiscuous woman. [C19: from F, from fem of *coq* COCK[1]]

Cocteau ★ (*French* kɔkto) *n* **Jean** (ʒɑ̃). 1889–1963, French dramatist, novelist, poet, critic, designer, and film director. His works include the novel *Les Enfants terribles* (1929) and the play *La Machine infernale* (1934).

cod[1] (kɒd) *n, pl* **cod** *or* **cods. 1** any of the gadoid food fishes which occur in the North Atlantic and have a long body with three rounded dorsal fins. **2** any of various Australian fishes of fresh or salt water, such as the Murray cod or the red cod. [C13: prob. of Gmc origin]

cod[2] (kɒd) *n* **1** *Brit. & US dialect*. a pod or husk. **2** *Taboo*. an obsolete word for **scrotum.** [OE *codd* husk, bag]

cod[3] (kɒd) *Brit. sl.* ◆ *vb* **cods, codding, codded.** (*tr*) **1** to make fun of; tease. **2** to play a trick on; befool. ◆ *n* **3** a hoax or trick. [C19: ?from earlier *cod* a fool]

Cod ★ *n* Cape. See **Cape Cod.**

COD *abbrev. for:* **1** cash on delivery. **2** (in the US) collect on delivery.

coda ('kəʊdə) *n* **1** *Music*. the final passage of a musical structure. **2** a concluding part of a literary work that rounds off the main work but is independent of it. [C18: from It.: tail, from L *cauda*]

cod-act *vb* (*intr*) *Irish inf*. to play tricks; fool. [from COD[3] + ACT]

coddle ('kɒdᵊl) *vb* **coddles, coddling, coddled.** (*tr*) **1** to treat with indulgence. **2** to cook (something, esp. eggs) in water just below the boiling point. [C16: from ?; ? rel. to CAUDLE]
▶ **'coddler** *n*

code (kəʊd) *n* **1** a system of letters or symbols, by which information can be communicated secretly, briefly, etc.: *binary code; Morse code*. **2** a message in code. **3** a symbol used in a code. **4** a conventionalized set of principles or rules: *a code of behaviour*. **5** a system of letters or digits used for identification purposes. ◆ *vb* **codes, coding, coded.** (*tr*) **6** to translate or arrange into a code. [C14: from F, from L *cōdex* book, CODEX]
▶ **'coder** *n*

codeine ('kəʊdiːn) *n* a white crystalline alkaloid prepared mainly from morphine. It is used as an analgesic, a

sedative, and to relieve coughing. [C19: from Gk *kōdeia* head of a poppy, from *kōos* hollow place + -INE[2]]

Co. Derry *abbrev. for* County Londonderry.

codex ('kəʊdɛks) *n, pl* **codices** ('kəʊdɪ,siːz, 'kɒdɪ-). **1** a volume of manuscripts of an ancient text. **2** *Obs.* a legal code. [C16: from L: tree trunk, wooden block, book]

codfish ('kɒd,fɪʃ) *n, pl* **codfish** *or* **codfishes.** a cod.

codger ('kɒdʒə) *n Inf*. a man, esp. an old or eccentric one: often in **old codger.** [C18: prob. var. of CADGER]

codicil ('kɒdɪsɪl) *n* **1** *Law*. a supplement modifying a will or revoking some provision of it. **2** an additional provision; appendix. [C15: from LL dim. of CODEX]
▶ **,codi'cillary** *adj*

codify ('kəʊdɪ,faɪ, 'kɒ-) *vb* **codifies, codifying, codified.** (*tr*) to organize or collect together (laws, rules, procedures, etc.) into a system or code.
▶ **'codi,fier** *n* ▶ **,codifi'cation** *n*

codling[1] ('kɒdlɪŋ) *or* **codlin** ('kɒdlɪn) *n* **1** any of several varieties of long tapering apples. **2** any unripe apple. [C15 *querdlyng*, from ?]

codling[2] ('kɒdlɪŋ) *n* a codfish, esp. a young one.

cod-liver oil *n* an oil extracted from the livers of cod and related fish, rich in vitamins A and D.

codology (kɒd'ɒlədʒɪ) *n Irish inf*. the art or practice of bluffing or deception.

codpiece ('kɒd,piːs) *n* a bag covering the male genitals, attached to breeches: worn in the 15th and 16th centuries. [C15: from COD[2] + PIECE]

codswallop ('kɒdz,wɒləp) *n Brit. sl.* nonsense. [C20: from ?]

Co. Durham *abbrev. for* County Durham.

Cody ★ ('kəʊdɪ) *n* **William Frederick.** the real name of **Buffalo Bill.**

Coe ★ (kəʊ) *n* **Sebastian.** born 1956, British middle-distance runner and Conservative politician: winner of the 1500m in the 1980 and 1984 Olympic Games; held records at 800m, 1000m, 1500m, and a mile: member of parliament (1992–97).

co-ed (,kəʊ'ɛd) *adj* **1** coeducational. ◆ *n* **2** *US*. a female student in a coeducational college or university. **3** *Brit*. a school or college providing coeducation.

coeducation (,kəʊɛdjʊ'keɪʃən) *n* instruction in schools, colleges, etc., attended by both sexes.
▶ **,coedu'cational** *adj* ▶ **,coedu'cationally** *adv*

coefficient (,kəʊɪ'fɪʃənt) *n* **1** *Maths*. a numerical or constant factor in an algebraic term: *the coefficient of the term 3xyz is 3*. **2** *Physics*. a number that is the value of a given substance under specified conditions. [C17: from NL, from L *co-* together + *efficere* to EFFECT]

coefficient of variation *n Statistics*. a measure of the relative variation of distributions independent of the units of measurement; the standard deviation divided by the mean, sometimes expressed as a percentage.

coel- *prefix* indicating a cavity within a body or a hollow organ or part: *coelacanth; coelenterate*. [NL, from Gk *koilos* hollow]

coelacanth ('siːlə,kænθ) *n* a primitive marine bony fish, having fleshy limblike pectoral fins: thought to be extinct until a living specimen was discovered in 1938. [C19: from NL, from COEL- + Gk *akanthos* spine]

coelenterate (sɪ'lɛntə,reɪt, -rɪt) *n* any of various invertebrates having a saclike body with a single opening (mouth), such as jellyfishes, sea anemones, and corals. [C19: from NL *Coelenterata*, hollow-intestined (creatures)]

coeliac *or US* **celiac** ('siːlɪ,æk) *adj* of the abdomen. [C17: from L, from Gk, from *koilia* belly]

coeliac disease *n* an illness, esp. of children, in which the lining of the small intestine is sensitive to gluten in the diet, causing an impairment of food absorption.

coelom *or esp. US* **celom** ('siːləum, -ləm) *n* the body cavity of many multicellular animals, containing the digestive tract and other visceral organs. [C19: from Gk, from *koilos* hollow]
▶ **coelomic** *or esp. US* **celomic** (sɪ'lɒmɪk) *adj*

coeno- *or before a vowel* **coen-** *combining form.* common: *coenobite.* [NL, from Gk *koinos*]

coenobite *or* **cenobite** ('si:nəu,baɪt) *n* a member of a religious order following a communal rule of life. [C17: from OF or ecclesiastical L, from Gk *koinobion* convent, from *koinos* common + *bios* life]
▸ **coenobitic** (,si:nəu'bɪtɪk), **coeno'bitical** *or* ,ceno'bitic, ,ceno'bitical *adj*

coenzyme (kəu'enzaɪm) *n Biochem.* a nonprotein organic molecule that forms a complex with certain enzymes and is essential for their activity.

coequal (kəu'i:kwəl) *adj* **1** of the same size, rank, etc. ◆ *n* **2** a person or thing equal with another.
▸ **coequality** (,kəuɪ'kwɒlɪtɪ) *n*

coerce (kəu'ɜːs) *vb* **coerces, coercing, coerced.** (*tr*) to compel or restrain by force or authority without regard to individual wishes or desires. [C17: from L, from *co-* together + *arcēre* to enclose]
▸ **co'ercer** *n* ▸ **co'ercible** *adj*

coercion (kəu'ɜːʃən) *n* **1** the act or power of coercing. **2** government by force.
▸ **coercive** (kəu'ɜːsɪv) *adj* ▸ **co'ercively** *adv*

Coetzee ★ ('kɜːtzɪ) *n* J(ohn) M(ichael). born 1940, South African novelist.

Coeur ★ (kɜː; *French* kœr) *n* Jacques. ?1395–1456, French merchant; councillor and court banker to Charles VII of France.

coeval (kəu'i:vᵊl) *adj* **1** of or belonging to the same age or generation. ◆ *n* **2** a contemporary. [C17: from LL, from L *co-* + *aevum* age]
▸ **coevality** (,kəuɪ'vælɪtɪ) *n* ▸ **co'evally** *adv*

coexecutor (,kəuɪg'zekjutə) *n Law.* a person acting jointly with another or others as executor.

coexist (,kəuɪg'zɪst) *vb* (*intr*) **1** to exist together at the same time or in the same place. **2** to exist together in peace.
▸ ,**coex'istence** *n* ▸ ,**coex'istent** *adj*

coextend (,kəuɪk'stend) *vb* to extend or cause to extend equally in space or time.
▸ ,**coex'tension** *n* ▸ ,**coex'tensive** *adj*

C of C *abbrev. for* Chamber of Commerce.

C of E *abbrev. for* Church of England.

coffee ('kɒfɪ) *n* **1a** a drink consisting of an infusion of the roasted and ground seeds of the coffee tree. **1b** (*as modifier*): *coffee grounds.* **2** Also called: **coffee beans.** the beanlike seeds of the coffee tree, used to make this beverage. **3** the tree yielding these seeds. **4a** a light brown colour. **4b** (*as adj*): *a coffee carpet.* [C16: from It. *caffè*, from Turkish *kahve*, from Ar. *qahwah* coffee, wine]

coffee bar *n* a café; snack bar.

coffee cup *n* a small cup for serving coffee.

coffee house *n* a place where coffee is served, esp. one that was a fashionable meeting place in 18th-century London.

coffee mill *n* a machine for grinding roasted coffee beans.

coffeepot ('kɒfɪ,pɒt) *n* a pot in which coffee is brewed or served.

coffee shop *n* a shop where coffee is sold or drunk.

coffee table *n* a low table on which coffee may be served.

coffee-table book *n* a book, usually glossily illustrated, designed chiefly to be looked at, rather than read.

coffer ('kɒfə) *n* **1** a chest, esp. for storing valuables. **2** (*usually pl*) a store of money. **3** an ornamental sunken panel in a ceiling, dome, etc. **4** a watertight box or chamber. **5** short for **cofferdam.** ◆ *vb* (*tr*) **6** to store, as in a coffer. **7** to decorate (a ceiling, dome, etc.) with coffers. [C13: from OF *coffre*, from L, from Gk *kophinos* basket]

cofferdam ('kɒfə,dæm) *n* **1** a watertight structure that encloses an area under water, pumped dry to enable construction work to be carried out. **2** (on a ship) a compartment separating two bulkheads, as for insulation or to serve as a barrier against the escape of gas, etc. ◆ Often shortened to **coffer.**

coffin ('kɒfɪn) *n* **1** a box in which a corpse is buried or cremated. **2** the bony part of a horse's foot. ◆ *vb* **3** (*tr*) to place in or as in a coffin. [C14: from OF *cofin*, from L *cophinus* basket]

coffin nail *n* a slang term for **cigarette.**

coffle ('kɒfᵊl) *n* a line of slaves, beasts, etc., fastened together. [C18: from Ar. *qāfilah* caravan]

C of S *abbrev. for* Church of Scotland.

cog[1] (kɒg) *n* **1** any of the teeth or projections on the rim of a gearwheel. **2** a gearwheel, esp. a small one. **3** a person or thing playing a small part in a large organization or process. [C13: of Scand. origin]

cog[2] (kɒg) *n* **1** a tenon that projects from the end of a timber beam for fitting into a mortise. ◆ *vb* **cogs, cogging, cogged.** **2** (*tr*) to join (pieces of wood) with cogs. [C19: from ?]

cogent ('kəudʒənt) *adj* compelling belief or assent; forcefully convincing. [C17: from L *cōgent-, cōgēns*, from *co-* together + *agere* to drive]
▸ **'cogency** *n* ▸ **'cogently** *adv*

cogitate ('kɒdʒɪ,teɪt) *vb* **cogitates, cogitating, cogitated.** to think deeply about (a problem, possibility, etc.); ponder. [C16: from L, from *co-* (intensive) + *agitāre* to turn over]
▸ ,**cogi'tation** *n* ▸ **'cogitative** *adj* ▸ **'cogi,tator** *n*

Cognac ★ ('kɒnjæk; *French* kɔɲak) *n* **1** a town in SW France: centre of the district famed for its brandy. Pop. 21 000 (latest est.). **2** (*sometimes not cap.*) a high-quality grape brandy.

cognate ('kɒgneɪt) *adj* **1** akin; related: *cognate languages.* **2** related by blood or descended from a common maternal ancestor. ◆ *n* **3** something that is cognate with something else. [C17: from L, from *co-* same + *gnātus* born var. of *nātus*, p.p. of *nāscī* to be born]
▸ **'cognately** *adv* ▸ **'cognateness** *n* ▸ **cog'nation** *n*

cognition (kɒg'nɪʃən) *n* **1** the mental act or process by which knowledge is acquired, including perception, intuition, and reasoning. **2** the knowledge that results from such an act or process. [C15: from L, from *co-* (intensive) + *nōscere* to learn]
▸ **cog'nitional** *adj* ▸ **'cognitive** *adj*

cognitive therapy *n Psychol.* a form of psychotherapy in which the patient is encouraged to change the way he sees the world and himself: used particularly to treat depression.

cognizable *or* **cognisable** ('kɒgnɪzəbᵊl, 'kɒnɪ-) *adj* **1** perceptible. **2** *Law.* susceptible to the jurisdiction of a court.

cognizance *or* **cognisance** ('kɒgnɪzəns, 'kɒnɪ-) *n* **1** knowledge; acknowledgment. **2 take cognizance of.** to take notice of; acknowledge, esp. officially. **3** the range of scope of knowledge or perception. **4** *Law.* the right of a court to hear and determine a cause or matter. **5** *Heraldry* a distinguishing badge or bearing. [C14: from OF, from L *cognōscere* to learn; see COGNITION]

cognizant *or* **cognisant** ('kɒgnɪzənt, 'kɒnɪ-) *adj* (usually foll. by *of*) aware; having knowledge.

cognomen (kɒg'nəumen) *n, pl* **cognomens** *or* **cognomina** (-'nɒmɪnə, -'nəu-). (originally) an ancient Roman's third name or nickname, which later became his family name. [C19: from L: additional name, from *co-* together + *nōmen* name]
▸ **cognominal** (kɒg'nɒmɪn³l, -'nəu-) *adj*

cognoscenti (,kɒnjəu'ʃentɪ, ,kɒgnəu-) *or* **conoscenti** (,kɒnəu'ʃentɪ) *pl n, sing* **cognoscente** *or* **conoscente** (-tiː) (*sometimes sing*) people with informed appreciation of a particular field, esp. in the fine arts; connoisseurs. [C18: from obs. It., from L *cognōscere* to learn]

cogwheel ('kɒg,wiːl) *n* another name for **gearwheel.**

cohab ('kəu,hæb) *n* a sexual partner with whom one lives but to whom one is not married. [C20: a shortened form of *cohabitee*; see COHABIT]

cohabit (kəu'hæbɪt) *vb* (*intr*) to live together as husband and wife, esp. without being married. [C16: from L *co-* together + *habitāre* to live]
▸ ,**cohabi'tee, co'habitant,** *or* **co'habiter** *n*

cohabitation (kəu,hæbɪ'teɪʃən) *n* **1** the state or condition of living together as husband and wife without being married. **2** (of political parties) the state or condition...

tion of cooperating for specific purposes without forming a coalition.

coheir (kəʊ'ɛə) *n* a person who inherits jointly with others.
▶ **co'heiress** *fem n*

Cohen ★ ('kəʊən) *n* **Stanley**. born 1922, US biochemist: shared the Nobel prize for physiology or medicine 1986.

cohere (kəʊ'hɪə) *vb* **coheres, cohering, cohered**. (*intr*) 1 to hold or stick firmly together. 2 to be connected logically; be consistent. 3 *Physics*. to be held together by the action of molecular forces. [C16: from L *co-* together + *haerēre* to cling]

coherence (kəʊ'hɪərəns) *or* **coherency** *n* 1 logical or natural connection or consistency. 2 another word for **cohesion** (sense 1).

coherent (kəʊ'hɪərənt) *adj* 1 capable of intelligible speech. 2 logical; consistent and orderly. 3 cohering or sticking together. 4 *Physics*. (of two or more waves) having the same phase or a fixed phase difference: *coherent light*.
▶ **co'herently** *adv*

cohesion (kəʊ'hiːʒən) *n* 1 the act or state of cohering; tendency to unite. 2 *Physics*. the force that holds together the atoms or molecules in a solid or liquid, as distinguished from adhesion. 3 *Bot*. the fusion in some plants of flower parts, such as petals, that are usually separate. [C17: from L *cohaesus*, p.p. of *cohaerēre* to CO-HERE]
▶ **co'hesive** *adj*

coho ('kəʊhəʊ) *n, pl* **coho** *or* **cohos**. a Pacific salmon. Also called: **silver salmon**. [from ?]

cohort ('kəʊhɔːt) *n* 1 one of the ten units of an ancient Roman Legion. 2 any band of warriors or associates: *the cohorts of Satan*. 3 *Chiefly US*. an associate or follower. [C15: from L *cohors* yard, company of soldiers]

COHSE ('kəʊzɪ) *n* (formerly, in Britain) *acronym for* Confederation of Health Service Employees.

COI (in Britain) *abbrev. for* Central Office of Information.

coif (kɔɪf) *n* 1 a close-fitting cap worn under a veil in the Middle Ages. 2 a leather cap worn under a chain-mail hood. 3 (kwɑːf). a less common word for **coiffure** (sense 1). ◆ *vb* **coifs, coiffing, coiffed**. (*tr*) 4 to cover with or as if with a coif. 5 (kwɑːf). to arrange (the hair). [C14: from OF *coiffe*, from LL *cofea* helmet, cap, from ?]

coiffeur (kwɑː'fɜː) *n* a hairdresser.
▶ **coiffeuse** (kwɑː'fɜːz) *fem n*

coiffure (kwɑː'fjʊə) *n* 1 a hairstyle. 2 an obsolete word for headdress. ◆ *vb* **coiffures, coiffuring, coiffured**. 3 (*tr*) to dress or arrange (the hair).

coign of vantage (kɔɪn) *n* an advantageous position for observation or action.

coil[1] (kɔɪl) *vb* 1 to wind or gather (ropes, hair, etc.) into loops or (of ropes, hair, etc.) to be formed into such loops. 2 (*intr*) to move in a winding course. ◆ *n* 3 something wound in a connected series of loops. 4 a single loop of such a series. 5 an arrangement of pipes in a spiral or loop, as in a condenser. 6 an electrical conductor wound into the form of a spiral, to provide inductance or a magnetic field. 7 an intrauterine contraceptive device in the shape of a coil. 8 the transformer in a petrol engine that supplies the high voltage to the sparking plugs. [C16: from OF *coillir* to collect together; see CULL]

coil[2] (kɔɪl) *n* the troubles of the world (in Shakespeare's phrase **this mortal coil**). [C16: from ?]

Coimbra ★ (*Portuguese* 'kuimbrə) *n* a city in central Portugal: capital of Portugal from 1190 to 1260; seat of the country's oldest university. Pop.: 96 140 (1991).

coin (kɔɪn) *n* 1 a metal disc or piece used as money. 2 metal currency, as opposed to paper currency, etc. 3 *Archit*. a variant spelling of **quoin**. 4 **pay (a person) back in (his) own coin**. to treat (a person) in the way that he has treated others. ◆ *vb* (*tr*) 5 to make or stamp (coins). 6 to make into a coin. 7 to fabricate or invent (words, etc.). 8 *Inf*. to make (money) rapidly (esp. in **coin it in**). [C14: from OF: stamping die, from L *cuneus* wedge]

coinage ('kɔɪnɪdʒ) *n* 1 coins collectively. 2 the act of striking coins. 3 the currency of a country. 4 the act of

inventing something, esp. a word or phrase. 5 a newly invented word, phrase, usage, etc.

coincide (ˌkəʊɪn'saɪd) *vb* **coincides, coinciding, coincided**. (*intr*) 1 to occur or exist simultaneously. 2 to be identical in nature, character, etc. 3 to agree. [C18: from Med. L, from L *co-* together + *incidere* to occur, befall, from *cadere* to fall]

coincidence (kəʊ'ɪnsɪdəns) *n* 1 a chance occurrence of events remarkable either for being simultaneous or for apparently being connected. 2 the fact, condition, or state of coinciding. 3 (*modifier*) *Electronics*. of or relating to a circuit that produces an output pulse only when both its input terminals receive pulses within a specified interval: *coincidence gate*.

coincident (kəʊ'ɪnsɪdənt) *adj* 1 having the same position in space or time. 2 (usually *postpositive* and foll. by *with*) in exact agreement.
▶ **co,inci'dental** *adj* ▶ **co,inci'dentally** *adv*

coin-op ('kɔɪnˌɒp) *n* a launderette or other installation in which the machines are operated by the insertion of coins.
▶ **'coin-ˌoperˌated** *adj*

Cointreau ('kwɑːntrəʊ) *n Trademark*. a colourless liqueur with orange flavouring.

coir ('kɔɪə) *n* the fibre from the husk of the coconut, used in making rope and matting. [C16: from Malayalam *kāyar* rope, from *kāyaru* to be twisted]

Coire ★ (kwar) *n* the French name for **Chur**.

coitus ('kɔɪtəs) *or* **coition** (kəʊ'ɪʃən) *n* a technical term for **sexual intercourse**. [C18: from L, from *coīre* to meet, from *īre* to go]
▶ **'coital** *adj*

coke[1] (kəʊk) *n* 1 a solid-fuel product produced by distillation of coal to drive off its volatile constituents: used as a fuel. 2 the layer formed in the cylinders of a car engine by incomplete combustion of the fuel. ◆ *vb* **cokes, coking, coked**. 3 to become or convert into coke. [C17: prob. var. of C14 N English dialect *colk* core, from ?]

coke[2] (kəʊk) *n Sl*. short for **cocaine**.

Coke[1] (kəʊk) *n Trademark*. short for **Coca-Cola**.

Coke[2] ★ *n* 1 (kuk, kəʊk). Sir **Edward**. 1552–1634, English jurist: the Petition of Right (1628) was largely his work. 2 (kuk). **Thomas William**, 1st Earl of Leicester, known as *Coke of Holkham*. 1752–1842, British agriculturist.

col (kɒl) *n* 1 Also called: **saddle**. the lowest point of a ridge connecting two mountain peaks. 2 *Meteorol*. a low-pressure region between two anticyclones. [C19: from F: neck, col, from L *collum* neck]

Col. *abbrev. for:* 1 Colombia(n). 2 Colonel. 3 *Bible*. Colossians.

col- *prefix* a variant of **com-** before *l*: *collateral*.

cola *or* **kola** ('kəʊlə) *n* 1 either of two trees widely cultivated in tropical regions for their seeds (see **cola nut**). 2 a sweet carbonated drink flavoured with cola nuts. [C18: from *kola*, prob. var. of W African *kolo* nut]

colander ('kɒləndə, 'kʌl-) *or* **cullender** *n* a pan with a perforated bottom for straining or rinsing foods. [C14 *colyndore*, prob. from OProvençal *colador*, from LL, from L *cōlum* sieve]

cola nut *n* any of the seeds of the cola tree, which contain caffeine and theobromine and are used medicinally and in soft drinks.

Colbert ★ (*French* kɔlber) *n* 1 **Claudette** (klɔ'dɛt). real name *Lily Claudette Chauchoin*. 1903–96, US film actress, born in France. Her comedies include *It Happened One Night* (1934). 2 **Jean Baptiste** (ʒɑ̃ batist). 1619–83, French statesman: chief minister to Louis XIV.

Colchester ★ ('kəʊltʃɪstə) *n* a town in E England, in NE Essex. Pop.: 96 063 (1991). Latin name: **Camulodunum** (ˌkæmjʊləʊ'djuːnəm, ˌkæmʊləʊ'duːnəm).

colchicine ('kɒltʃɪˌsiːn, -sɪn, 'kɒlkɪ-) *n* a pale yellow crystalline alkaloid extracted from seeds or corms of the autumn crocus and used in the treatment of gout. [C19: from COLCHICUM + -INE[2]]

colchicum ('kɒltʃɪkəm, 'kɒlkɪ-) *n* 1 any Eurasian plant of the lily family, such as the autumn crocus. 2 the dried seeds or corms of the autumn crocus. [C16: from L, from Gk, from *kolkhikos* of COLCHIS]

Colchis ★ ('kɒlkɪs) *n* an ancient country on the Black Sea south of the Caucasus; the land of Medea and the Golden Fleece in Greek mythology.

cold (kəʊld) *adj* **1** having relatively little warmth; of a rather low temperature: *cold weather; cold hands.* **2** without proper warmth: *this meal is cold.* **3** lacking in affection or enthusiasm: *a cold manner.* **4** not affected by emotion: *cold logic.* **5** dead. **6** sexually unresponsive or frigid. **7** lacking in freshness: *a cold scent; cold news.* **8** chilling to the spirit; depressing. **9** (of a colour) having violet, blue, or green predominating; giving no sensation of warmth. **10** *Sl.* unconscious. **11** *Inf.* (of a seeker) far from the object of a search. **12** denoting the contacting of potential customers, voters, etc., without previously approaching them in order to establish their interest: *cold mailing.* **13** cold comfort. little or no comfort. **14** leave (someone) cold. *Inf.* to fail to excite: *the performance left me cold.* **15** throw cold water on. *Inf.* to be unenthusiastic about or discourage. ♦ *n* **16** the absence of heat regarded as a positive force: *the cold took away our breath.* **17** the sensation caused by loss or lack of heat. **18** (out) in the cold. *Inf.* neglected; ignored. **19** an acute viral infection of the upper respiratory passages characterized by discharge of watery mucus from the nose, sneezing, etc. **20** catch a cold. *Inf.* to make a financial loss. ♦ *adv* **21** *Inf.* without preparation: *he played his part cold.* [OE *ceald*]
  ► 'coldish *adj* ► 'coldly *adv* ► 'coldness *n*

cold-blooded *adj* **1** having or showing a lack of feeling or pity. **2** *Inf.* particularly sensitive to cold. **3** (of all animals except birds and mammals) having a body temperature that varies with that of the surroundings. Technical name: **poikilothermic**.
  ► ,cold-'bloodedly *adv* ► ,cold-'bloodedness *n*

cold cathode *n Electronics.* a cathode from which electrons are emitted at an ambient temperature.

cold chisel *n* a toughened steel chisel.

cold cream *n* an emulsion of water and fat used for softening and cleansing the skin.

cold cuts *pl n* cooked meats sliced and served cold.

cold feet *n Inf.* loss or lack of confidence.

cold frame *n* an unheated wooden frame with a glass top, used to protect young plants.

cold front *n Meteorol.* the boundary line between a warm air mass and the cold air pushing it from beneath and behind as it moves.

cold-hearted *adj* lacking in feeling or warmth; unkind.
  ► ,cold-'heartedly *adv* ► ,cold-'heartedness *n*

Colditz ★ ('kəʊldɪts) *n* a town in E Germany, on the River Mulde: during World War II its castle was used as a top-security camp for Allied prisoners of war; many daring escape attempts, some successful, were made.

cold-rolled *adj* (of metal sheets, etc.) having been rolled without heating, producing a smooth surface finish.

cold shoulder *Inf.* ♦ *n* **1** (often preceded by *the*) a show of indifference; a slight. ♦ *vb* **cold-shoulder.** (*tr*) **2** to treat with indifference.

cold sore *n* a cluster of blisters at the margin of the lips: a form of herpes simplex.

cold start *n Computing.* the reloading of a program or operating system.

cold storage *n* **1** the storage of things in an artificially cooled place for preservation. **2** *Inf.* a state of temporary suspension: *to put an idea into cold storage.*

Coldstream ★ ('kəʊld,stri:m) *n* a town in SE Scotland, on the English border: the Coldstream Guards were formed here (1660). Pop.: 1746 (1991).

cold sweat *n Inf.* a bodily reaction to fear or nervousness, characterized by chill and moist skin.

cold turkey *n Sl.* **1** a method of curing drug addiction by abrupt withdrawal of all doses. **2** the withdrawal symptoms, esp. nausea and shivering, brought on by this method.

cold war *n* a state of political hostility and military tension between two countries or power blocs, involving

propaganda, threats, etc., esp. that between the American and Soviet blocs after World War II (the **Cold War**).

cold wave *n* **1** *Meteorol.* a sudden spell of low temperatures over a wide area. **2** *Hairdressing.* a permanent wave made by chemical agents applied at normal temperatures.

cole (kəʊl) *n* any of various plants such as the cabbage and rape. Also called: **colewort.** [OE *cāl,* from L *caulis* cabbage]

Cole ★ (kəʊl) *n* **Nat 'King',** real name *Nathaniel Adams Cole.* 1917–65, US popular singer and jazz pianist.

Coleman ★ ('kəʊlmən) *n* **Ornette** (ɔ:'nɛt). born 1930, US avant-garde jazz saxophonist.

coleopter (,kɒlɪ'ɒptə) *n Aeronautics.* an aircraft that has an annular wing with the fuselage and engine on the centre line.

coleopteran (,kɒlɪ'ɒptərən) *n also* **coleopteron. 1** any of the order of insects in which the forewings are modified to form shell-like protective elytra. It includes the beetles and weevils. ♦ *adj also* **coleopterous. 2** of, relating to or belonging to this order. [C18: from NL, from Gk from *koleon* sheath + *pteron* wing]

Coleraine ★ (kəʊl'reɪn) *n* **1** a town in N Northern Ireland, in Co. Antrim, on the River Bann: light industries site of the New University of Ulster (1965). Pop.: 20 721 (1991). **2** a district of N Northern Ireland, on the Atlantic Ocean: agriculture, tourism. Administrative centre Coleraine. Area: 490 sq. km (189 sq. miles). Pop.: 50 438 (1991).

Coleridge ★ ('kəʊlərɪdʒ) *n* **Samuel Taylor.** 1772–1834, British poet, noted for *The Rime of the Ancient Mariner* (1798), *Kubla Khan* (1816), and *Christabel* (1816).

Coleridge-Taylor ★ (,kəʊlərɪdʒ'teɪlə) *n* **Samuel.** 1875–1912, British composer, best known for his oratorio *Song of Hiawatha* (1898–1900).

coleslaw ('kəʊl,slɔ:) *n* a salad of shredded cabbage, mayonnaise, carrots, onions, etc. [C19: from Du. *koolsla,* from *koolsalade,* lit.: cabbage salad]

colestipol (kə'lɛstɪ,pɒl) *n* a drug that reduces the level of cholesterol in the blood: used to prevent atherosclerosis

Colet ★ ('kɒlɪt) *n* **John.** ?1467–1519, English humanist and theologian; founder of St Paul's School, London (1509).

coletit ('kəʊltɪt) *n* another name for **coal tit.**

Colette ★ (kɒ'lɛt) *n* full name *Sidonie Gabrielle Claudine Colette.* 1873–1954, French novelist; her works include *Chéri* (1920), *Gigi* (1944), and the series of *Claudine* books.

coleus ('kəʊlɪəs) *n, pl* **coleuses.** any plant of the Old World genus *Coleus:* cultivated for their variegated leaves. [C19: from NL, from Gk, var. of *koleon* sheath]

coley ('kəʊlɪ, 'kɒlɪ) *n Brit.* any of various edible fishes, esp the coalfish.

colic ('kɒlɪk) *n* a condition characterized by acute spasmodic abdominal pain, esp. that caused by inflammation, distention, etc., of the gastrointestinal tract. [C15 from OF, from LL, from Gk *kōlon,* var. of *kolon* COLON²]
  ► 'colicky *adj*

coliform bacteria ('kɒlɪfɔ:m) *pl n* a large group of bacteria that inhabit the intestinal tract of man.

Coligny or **Coligni** ★ (French koliɲi) *n* **Gaspard de** (gaspardə), Seigneur de Châtillon. 1519–72, French Huguenot leader.

Colima ★ (Spanish ko'lima) *n* **1** a state of SW Mexico, on the Pacific coast: mainly a coastal plain, rising to the foothills of the Sierra Madre, with important mineral resources. Capital: Colima. Pop.: 487 324 (1995 est.). Area 5455 sq. km (2106 sq. miles). **2** a city in SW Mexico, capital of Colima state, on the Colima River. Pop.: 106 967 (1990). **3** Nevado de. a volcano in SW Mexico, in Jalisco state. Height: 4339 m (14 235 ft).

coliseum (,kɒlɪ'sɪəm) *or* **colosseum** (,kɒlə'sɪəm) *n* a large building, such as a stadium, used for entertainments, sports, etc. [C18: from Med. L, var. of COLOSSEUM]

colitis (kɒ'laɪtɪs) *n* inflammation of the colon.

collaborate (kə'læbə,reɪt) vb **collaborates, collaborating, collaborated.** (intr) **1** (often foll. by on, with, etc.) to work with another or others on a joint project. **2** to cooperate as a traitor, esp. with an enemy occupying one's own country. [C19: from LL, from L com- together + labōrāre to work]
▸ col,labo'ration n ▸ col'laborative adj ▸ col'labo,rator n

collage (kə'lɑːʒ, kɒ-) n **1** an art form in which compositions are made out of pieces of paper, cloth, photographs, etc., pasted on a dry ground. **2** a composition made in this way. **3** any work, such as a piece of music, created by combining unrelated styles. [C20: F, from colle glue, from Gk kolla]
▸ col'lagist n

collagen ('kɒlədʒən) n a fibrous protein of connective tissue and bones that yields gelatine on boiling. [C19: from Gk kolla glue + -GEN]

collapsar (kɒ'læpsɑː) n Astron. another name for **black hole.**

collapse (kə'læps) vb **collapses, collapsing, collapsed. 1** (intr) to fall down or cave in suddenly: the whole building collapsed. **2** (intr) to fail completely. **3** (intr) to break down or fall down from lack of strength. **4** to fold (furniture, etc.) compactly or (of furniture, etc.) to be designed to fold compactly. ♦ n **5** the act or instance of suddenly falling down, caving in, or crumbling. **6** a sudden failure or breakdown. [C18: from L, from collābī to fall in ruins, from lābī to fall]
▸ col'lapsible or col'lapsable adj ▸ col,lapsi'bility n

collar ('kɒlə) n **1** the part of a garment around the neck and shoulders, often detachable or folded over. **2** any band, necklace, garland, etc., encircling the neck. **3** a band or chain of leather, rope, or metal placed around an animal's neck. **4** Biol. a marking resembling a collar, such as that found around the necks of some birds. **5** a section of a shaft or rod having a locally increased diameter to provide a bearing seat or a locating ring. **6** a cut of meat, esp. bacon, taken from around the neck of an animal. ♦ vb (tr) **7** to put a collar on; furnish with a collar. **8** to seize by the collar. **9** Inf. to seize; arrest; detain. [C13: from L collāre neckband, from collum neck]

collarbone ('kɒlə,bəun) n the nontechnical name for **clavicle.**

collard ('kɒləd) n a variety of the cabbage, having a crown of edible leaves. See also **kale.** [C18: var. of colewort, from COLE + WORT]

collate (kɒ'leɪt, kə-) vb **collates, collating, collated.** (tr) **1** to examine and compare (texts, statements, etc.) in order to note points of agreement and disagreement. **2** to check the number and order of (the pages of a book). **3** Bookbinding. **3a** to check the sequence of (the sections of a book) after gathering. **3b** a nontechnical word for **gather** (sense 8). **4** (often foll. by to) Christianity. to appoint (an incumbent) to a benefice. [C16: from L, from com- together + lātus, p.p. of ferre to bring]
▸ col'lator n

collateral (kɒ'lætərəl, kə-) n **1a** security pledged for the repayment of a loan. **1b** (as modifier): a collateral loan. **2** a person, animal, or plant descended from the same ancestor as another but through a different line. ♦ adj **3** situated or running side by side. **4** descended from a common ancestor but through different lines. **5** serving to support or corroborate. [C14: from Med. L, from L com- together + laterālis of the side, from latus side]
▸ col'laterally adv

collateral damage n Mil. unintentional damage to civil property and civilian casualties, caused by military operations.

collation (kɒ'leɪʃən, kə-) n **1** the act or process of collating. **2** a description of the technical features of a book. **3** RC Church. a light meal permitted on fast days. **4** any light informal meal.

colleague ('kɒliːg) n a fellow worker or member of a staff, department, profession, etc. [C16: from F, from L collēga, from com- together + lēgāre to choose]

collect[1] (kə'lɛkt) vb **1** to gather together or be gathered together. **2** to accumulate (stamps, books, etc.) as a hobby or for study. **3** (tr) to call for or receive payment of

(taxes, dues, etc.). **4** (tr) to regain control of (oneself, one's emotions, etc.) as after a shock or surprise: he collected his wits. **5** (tr) to fetch: collect your own post. **6** (intr; sometimes foll. by on) Sl. to receive large sums of money. **7** (tr) Austral. & NZ inf. to collide with; be hit by. ♦ adv, adj **8** US. (of telephone calls, etc.) on a reverse-charge basis. [C16: from L, from com- together + legere to gather]

collect[2] ('kɒlɛkt) n Christianity. a short Church prayer in Communion and other services. [C13: from Med. L collecta (from ōrātiō ad collēctam prayer at the assembly), from L colligere to COLLECT[1]]

collectable or **collectible** (kə'lɛktəb°l) adj **1** (of antiques) of interest to a collector. ♦ n **2** (often pl) any object regarded as being of interest to a collector.

collected (kə'lɛktɪd) adj **1** in full control of one's faculties; composed. **2** assembled in totality or brought together into one volume or a set of volumes: the collected works of Dickens.
▸ col'lectedly adv ▸ col'lectedness n

collection (kə'lɛkʃən) n **1** the act or process of collecting. **2** a number of things collected or assembled together. **3** something gathered into a mass or pile; accumulation: a collection of rubbish. **4** a sum of money collected or solicited, as in church. **5** removal, esp. regular removal of letters from a postbox. **6** (often pl) (at Oxford University) a college examination or an oral report by a tutor.

collective (kə'lɛktɪv) adj **1** formed or assembled by collection. **2** forming a whole or aggregate. **3** of, done by, or characteristic of individuals acting in cooperation. ♦ n **4a** a cooperative enterprise or unit, such as a collective farm. **4b** the members of such a cooperative. **5** short for **collective noun.**
▸ col'lectively adv ▸ col'lectiveness n ▸ ,collec'tivity n

collective bargaining n negotiation between a trade union and an employer or an employers' organization on the incomes and working conditions of the employees.

collective noun n a noun that is singular in form but that refers to a group of people or things.

USAGE NOTE Collective nouns are usually used with singular verbs: the family is on holiday; General Motors is mounting a big sales campaign. In British usage, however, plural verbs are sometimes employed in this context, esp. where reference is being made to a collection of individual objects or people rather than to the group as a unit: the family are all on holiday. Care should be taken that the same collective noun is not treated as both singular and plural in the same sentence: the family is well and sends its best wishes or the family are all well and send their best wishes, but not the family is well and send their best wishes.

collective ownership n ownership by a group for the benefit of members of that group.

collective unconscious n (in Jungian psychological theory) a part of the unconscious mind incorporating patterns of memories, instincts, and experiences common to all mankind.

collectivism (kə'lɛktɪ,vɪzəm) n the principle of ownership of the means of production by the state or the people.
▸ col'lectivist n ▸ col,lectiv'istic adj

collectivize or **collectivise** (kə'lɛktɪ,vaɪz) vb **collectivizes, collectivizing, collectivized** or **collectivises, collectivising, collectivised.** (tr) to organize according to the principles of collectivism.
▸ col,lectivi'zation or col,lectivi'sation n

collector (kə'lɛktə) n **1** a person or thing that collects. **2** a person employed to collect debts, rents, etc. **3** a person who collects objects as a hobby. **4** (in India, formerly) the head of a district administration. **5** Electronics. the region in a transistor into which charge carriers flow from the base.

colleen ('kɒliːn, kɒ'liːn) n an Irish word for **girl**. [C19: from Irish Gaelic *cailín*]

college ('kɒlɪdʒ) n 1 an institution of higher education; part of a university. 2 a school or an institution providing specialized courses: *a college of music*. 3 the buildings in which a college is housed. 4 the staff and students of a college. 5 an organized body of persons with specific rights and duties: *an electoral college*. 6 a body organized within a particular profession, concerned with regulating standards. 7 *Brit.* a name given to some secondary schools. [C14: from L, from *collēga*; see COLLEAGUE]

College of Cardinals n *RC Church.* the collective body of cardinals having the function of electing and advising the pope.

college of education n *Brit.* a professional training college for teachers.

collegian (kə'liːdʒɪən) n a member of a college.

collegiate (kə'liːdʒɪt) adj 1 Also: **col'legial.** of or relating to a college or college students. 2 (of a university) composed of various colleges of equal standing.

collegiate church n 1 *RC Church, Church of England.* a church that has an endowed chapter of canons and prebendaries attached to it but that is not a cathedral. 2 *US Protestantism.* one of a group of churches presided over by a body of pastors. 3 *Scot. Protestantism.* a church served by two or more ministers.

col legno ('kɒl 'legnəʊ, 'leɪnjəʊ) adv *Music.* to be played (on a stringed instrument) with the back of the bow. [It.: with the wood]

Colles' fracture ('kɒlɪs) n a fracture of the radius just above the wrist with backward and outward displacement of the hand. [C19: after Abraham Colles (d. 1843), Irish surgeon]

collet ('kɒlɪt) n 1 (in a jewellery setting) a band or coronet-shaped claw that holds an individual stone. 2 *Mechanical engineering.* an externally tapered sleeve made in two or more segments and used to grip a shaft passed through its centre. 3 *Horology.* a small metal collar that supports the inner end of the hairspring. [C16: from OF: a little collar, from *col,* from L *collum* neck]

collide (kə'laɪd) vb **collides, colliding, collided.** (*intr*) 1 to crash together with a violent impact. 2 to conflict; clash; disagree. [C17: from L, from *com-* together + *laedere* to strike]

collider (kə'laɪdə) n *Physics.* a particle accelerator in which beams of particles are made to collide.

collie ('kɒlɪ) n any of several silky-coated breeds of dog developed for herding sheep and cattle. [C17: Scot., prob. from earlier *colie* black from *cole* coal]

collier ('kɒlɪə) n *Chiefly Brit.* 1 a coal miner. 2a a ship designed to transport coal. 2b a member of its crew. [C14: from COAL + -IER]

colliery ('kɒljərɪ) n, pl **collieries.** *Chiefly Brit.* a coal mine.

collimate ('kɒlɪ,meɪt) vb **collimates, collimating, collimated.** (*tr*) 1 to adjust the line of sight of (an optical instrument). 2 to use a collimator on (a beam of radiation). 3 to make parallel or bring into line. [C17: from NL *collimāre,* erroneously for L *collīneāre* to aim, from *com-* (intensive) + *līneāre,* from *līnea* line]
▸ **colli'mation** n

collimator ('kɒlɪ,meɪtə) n 1 a small telescope attached to a larger optical instrument as an aid in fixing its line of sight. 2 an optical system of lenses and slits producing a nondivergent beam of light. 3 any device for limiting the size and angle of spread of a beam of radiation or particles.

collinear (kɒ'lɪnɪə) adj lying on the same straight line.
▸ **collinearity** (,kɒlɪnɪ'ærɪtɪ) n

collins ('kɒlɪnz) n (*functioning as sing*) an iced drink made with gin, vodka, rum, etc., with fruit juice, soda water, and sugar. [C20: prob. from the name *Collins*]

Collins ★ ('kɒlɪnz) n 1 **Michael.** 1890–1922, Irish republican revolutionary: a leader of Sinn Féin. 2 (**William**) **Wilkie.** 1824–89, British author, noted particularly for his suspense novel *The Moonstone* (1868). 3 **William.** 1721–59, British poet.

collision (kə'lɪʒən) n 1 a violent impact of moving ob-

jects; crash. 2 the conflict of opposed ideas, wishes attitudes, etc. [C15: from LL, from L *collīdere* to COLLIDE]

collocate ('kɒlə,keɪt) vb **collocates, collocating, collocated** (*tr*) to group or place together in some system or order [C16: from L, from *com-* together + *locāre* to place]
▸ **collo'cation** n

collocutor ('kɒlə,kjuːtə) n a person who talks or engage in conversation with another.

collodion (kə'ləʊdɪən) or **collodium** (kə'ləʊdɪəm) n a syrupy liquid that consists of a solution of pyroxylin in ether and alcohol: used in medicine and in the manufacture of photographic plates, lacquers, etc. [C19: from NL, from Gk *kollōdēs* glutinous, from *kolla* glue]

collogue (kɒ'ləʊg) vb **collogues, colloguing, collogued.** (*intr* usually foll. by *with*) to confer confidentially; conspire [C16: ?from obs. *colleague* (vb) to conspire, infl. by L *colloquī* to talk with]

colloid ('kɒlɔɪd) n 1 a mixture having particles of one component suspended in a continuous phase of another component. The mixture has properties between those of a solution and a fine suspension. 2 *Physiol.* a gelatinous substance of the thyroid follicles that holds the hormonal secretions of the thyroid gland. [C19: from Gk *kolla* glue + -OID]
▸ **col'loidal** adj

collop ('kɒləp) n *Dialect.* 1 a slice of meat. 2 a small piece of anything. [C14: of Scand. origin]

colloq. *abbrev. for* colloquial(ly).

colloquial (kə'ləʊkwɪəl) adj 1 of or relating to conversation. 2 denoting or characterized by informal or conversational idiom or vocabulary.
▸ **col'loquially** adv ▸ **col'loquialness** n

colloquialism (kə'ləʊkwɪə,lɪzəm) n 1 a word or phrase appropriate to conversation and other informal situations. 2 the use of colloquial words and phrases.

colloquium (kə'ləʊkwɪəm) n, pl **colloquiums** or **colloqui** (-kwɪə). 1 a gathering for discussion. 2 an academic seminar. [C17: from L: COLLOQUY]

colloquy ('kɒləkwɪ) n, pl **colloquies.** 1 a formal conversation or conference. 2 an informal conference on religious or theological matters. [C16: from L *colloquium* from *com-* together + *loquī* to speak]
▸ **col'loquist** n

collotype ('kɒləʊ,taɪp) n 1 a method of lithographic printing (usually of high-quality reproductions) from a plate of hardened gelatine. 2 a print so made.

collude (kə'luːd) vb **colludes, colluding, colluded.** (*intr*) to conspire together, esp. in planning a fraud. [C16: from L, from *com-* together + *lūdere* to play]
▸ **col'luder** n

collusion (kə'luːʒən) n 1 secret agreement for a fraudulent purpose; conspiracy. 2 a secret agreement between opponents at law for some improper purpose. [C14 from L, from *collūdere* to COLLUDE]
▸ **col'lusive** adj

collywobbles ('kɒlɪ,wɒb°lz) pl n (usually preceded by *the*) *Sl.* 1 an upset stomach. 2 an intense feeling of nervousness. [C19: prob. from NL *cholera morbus*, infl through folk etymology by COLIC and WOBBLE]

Colmar ★ (*French* kɔlmar) n a city in NE France: annexed to Germany 1871–1919 and 1940–45; textile industry Pop.: 63 498 (1990). German name: **Kolmar.**

Colo. *abbrev. for* Colorado.

colobus ('kɒləbəs) n any leaf-eating arboreal Old World monkey of W and central Africa, having long silky fur and reduced or absent thumbs. [C19: NL, from Gk *kolobos* cut short; referring to its thumb]

cologarithm (kəʊ'lɒgə,rɪðəm) n the logarithm of the reciprocal of a number; the negative value of the logarithm: *the cologarithm of 4 is log ¼*. Abbrev.: **colog.**

cologne (kə'ləʊn) n a perfumed liquid or solid made of fragrant essential oils and alcohol. Also called: **Cologne water, eau de cologne.** [C18: *Cologne water* from COLOGNE where it was first manufactured (1709)]

Cologne ★ (kə'ləʊn) n an industrial city and river port in W Germany, in North Rhine-Westphalia on the Rhine important commercially since ancient times; university (1388). Pop.: 963 817 (1995 est.). German name: **Köln.**

:olomb-Béchar ★ (*French* kɔlɔ̃beʃar) *n* the former name of **Béchar.**

:olombes ★ (*French* kɔlɔ̃b) *n* an industrial and residential suburb of NW Paris, in France. Pop.: 79 060 (1990).

:olombia ★ (kəˈlɒmbɪə) *n* a republic in NW South America: inhabited by Chibchas and other Indians before Spanish colonization in the 16th century; independence won by Bolívar in 1819; became the Republic of Colombia in 1886. It consists chiefly of a hot swampy coastal plain, separated by ranges of the Andes from the pampas and the equatorial forests of the Amazon basin in the east. Language: Spanish. Religion: Roman Catholic majority. Currency: peso. Capital: Bogotá. Pop.: 36 200 000 (1997). Area: 1 138 908 sq. km (439 735 sq. miles).
▶ **Co'lombian** *adj, n*

:olombo ★ (kəˈlʌmbəʊ) *n* the capital and chief port of Sri Lanka, on the W coast, with one of the largest artificial harbours in the world. Pop.: 615 000 (1990 est.).

:olon¹ (ˈkəʊlən) *n, pl* **colons. 1** the punctuation mark : , usually preceding an explanation or an example, a list, or an extended quotation. **2** this mark used for certain other purposes, such as when a ratio is given in figures, as in 5:3. [C16: from L, from Gk *kōlon* limb, clause]

:olon² (ˈkəʊlən) *n, pl* **colons** or **cola** (-lə). the part of the large intestine between the caecum and the rectum. [C16: from L: large intestine, from Gk *kolon*]
▶ **colonic** (kəˈlɒnɪk) *adj*

:olón (kəʊˈləʊn; *Spanish* koˈlon) *n, pl* **colons** or **colones** (*Spanish* -ˈlones). **1** the standard monetary unit of Costa Rica, divided into 100 céntimos. **2** the standard monetary unit of El Salvador, divided into 100 centavos. [C19: American Sp., from Sp., after Cristóbal *Colón* Christopher Columbus]

:olón ★ (kɒˈlɒn; *Spanish* koˈlɔn) *n* **1** a port in Panama, at the Caribbean entrance to the Panama Canal. Chief Caribbean port. Pop.: 137 825 (1992 est.). **2 Archipiélago de** (ˌartʃiˈpjelaʝo ðe). the official name of the **Galápagos Islands.**

:olonel (ˈkɜːnᵊl) *n* an officer of land or air forces junior to a brigadier but senior to a lieutenant colonel. [C16: via OF, from OIt. *colonnello* column of soldiers, from *colonna* COLUMN]
▶ **'colonelcy** or **'colonelship** *n*

:olonial (kəˈləʊnɪəl) *adj* **1** of, characteristic of, relating to, possessing, or inhabiting a colony or colonies. **2** (*often cap.*) characteristic of or relating to the 13 British colonies that became the United States of America (1776). **3** (*often cap.*) of or relating to the colonies of the British Empire. **4** denoting or having the style of Neoclassical architecture used in the British colonies in America in the 17th and 18th centuries. **5** of or relating to the period of Australian history before federation (1901). **6** (of animals and plants) having become established in a community in a new environment. ◆ *n* **7** a native of a colony.
▶ **co'lonially** *adv*

:olonial goose *n* NZ. an old-fashioned name for stuffed roast mutton.

:olonialism (kəˈləʊnɪəˌlɪzəm) *n* the policy and practice of a power in extending control over weaker peoples or areas. Also called: **imperialism.**
▶ **co'lonialist** *n, adj*

:olonies (ˈkɒlənɪz) *pl n* **the. 1** Brit. the subject territories formerly in the British Empire. **2** US history. the 13 states forming the original United States of America when they declared their independence (1776).

:olonist (ˈkɒlənɪst) *n* **1** a person who settles or colonizes an area. **2** an inhabitant of a colony.

:olonize or **colonise** (ˈkɒləˌnaɪz) *vb* **colonizes, colonizing, colonized** or **colonises, colonising, colonised. 1** to send colonists to or establish a colony in (an area). **2** to settle in (an area) as colonists. **3** (*tr*) to transform (a commu-

nity, etc.) into a colony. **4** (of plants and animals) to become established in (a new environment).
▶ ˌ**coloni'zation** or ˌ**coloni'sation** *n* ▶ **'coloˌnizer** or **'coloˌniser** *n*

colonnade (ˌkɒləˈneɪd) *n* **1** a set of evenly spaced columns. **2** a row of regularly spaced trees. [C18: from F, from *colonne* COLUMN; on the model of It. *colonnato*]
▶ ˌ**colon'naded** *adj*

Colonsay ★ (ˈkɒlənseɪ, -zeɪ) *n* an island in W Scotland, in the Inner Hebrides. Area: about 41 sq. km (16 sq. miles).

colony (ˈkɒlənɪ) *n, pl* **colonies. 1** a body of people who settle in a country distant from their homeland but maintain ties with it. **2** the community formed by such settlers. **3** a subject territory occupied by a settlement from the ruling state. **4a** a community of people who form a national, racial, or cultural minority concentrated in a particular place: *an artists' colony.* **4b** the area itself. **5** Zool. a group of the same type of animal or plant living or growing together. **6** Bacteriol. a group of bacteria, fungi, etc., derived from one or a few spores, esp. when grown on a culture medium. [C16: from L, from *colere* to cultivate, inhabit]

colony-stimulating factor *n* Immunol. any of a number of substances, secreted by the bone marrow, that stimulate the formation of blood cells. Synthetic forms are being tested for their ability to reduce the toxic effects of chemotherapy. Abbrev.: **CSF.**

colophon (ˈkɒləˌfɒn, -fən) *n* **1** a publisher's emblem on a book. **2** (formerly) an inscription at the end of a book showing the title, printer, date, etc. [C17: via LL, from Gk *kolophōn* a finishing stroke]

colophony (kɒˈlɒfənɪ) *n* another name for **rosin** (sense 1). [C14: from L: resin from Colophon, town in Lydia]

color (ˈkʌlə) *n, vb* the US spelling of **colour.**

Colorado ★ (ˌkɒləˈrɑːdəʊ) *n* **1** a state of the central US: consists of the Great Plains in the east and the Rockies in the west; drained chiefly by the Colorado, Arkansas, South Platte, and Rio Grande Rivers. Capital: Denver. Pop.: 3 822 676 (1996 est.). Area: 269 998 sq. km (104 247 sq. miles). Abbrevs.: **Colo.** or (with zip code) **CO 2** a river in SW North America, rising in the Rocky Mountains and flowing southwest to the Gulf of California: famous for the 1600 km (1000 miles) of canyons along its course. Length: about 2320 km (1440 miles). **3** a river in central Texas, flowing southeast to the Gulf of Mexico. Length: about 1450 km (900 miles). **4** a river in central Argentina, flowing southeast to the Atlantic. Length: about 850 km (530 miles). [Sp., lit.: red, from L *colōrātus* coloured, tinted red; see COLOUR]

Colorado beetle *n* a black-and-yellow beetle that is a serious pest of potatoes, feeding on the leaves.

Colorado Desert ★ *n* an arid region of SE California and NW Mexico, West of the Colorado River. Area: over 5000 sq. km (2000 sq. miles).

Colorado Springs ★ *n* a city and resort in central Colorado. Pop.: 316 480 (1994 est.).

colorant (ˈkʌlərənt) *n* any substance that imparts colour, such as a pigment, dye, or ink.

coloration or **colouration** (ˌkʌləˈreɪʃən) *n* **1** arrangement of colour; colouring. **2** the colouring or markings of insects, birds, etc.

coloratura (ˌkɒlərəˈtʊərə) *n* Music. **1** (in 18th- and 19th-century arias) a florid virtuoso passage. **2** Also called: **coloratura soprano.** a soprano who specializes in such music. [C19: from obs. It., lit.: colouring.]

colorific (ˌkʌləˈrɪfɪk) *adj* producing, imparting, or relating to colour.

colorimeter (ˌkʌləˈrɪmɪtə) *n* apparatus for measuring the quality of a colour by comparison with standard colours or combinations of colours.
▶ **colorimetric** (ˌkʌlərɪˈmetrɪk) *adj* ▶ ˌ**color'imetry** *n*

colossal (kəˈlɒsᵊl) *adj* **1** of immense size; huge; gigantic. **2** (in figure sculpture) approximately twice life-size. **3** Archit. of the order of columns that extend more than one storey in a façade.
▶ **co'lossally** *adv*

Colosseum ★ (ˌkɒləˈsɪəm) *n* an amphitheatre in Rome built about 75–80 A.D.

colossus (kəˈlɒsəs) *n, pl* **colossi** (-saɪ) *or* **colossuses.** something very large, esp. a statue. [C14: from L, from Gk *kolossos*]

Colossus of Rhodes *n* a giant bronze statue of Apollo built on Rhodes in about 292–280 B.C.; destroyed by an earthquake in 225 B.C.; one of the Seven Wonders of the World.

colostomy (kəˈlɒstəmɪ) *n, pl* **colostomies.** the surgical formation of an opening from the colon onto the surface of the body, which functions as an anus.

colostrum (kəˈlɒstrəm) *n* the thin milky secretion from the nipples that precedes and follows true lactation. [C16: from L, from ?]

colotomy (kəˈlɒtəmɪ) *n, pl* **colotomies.** a colonic incision. [C19: COLON² + -TOMY]

colour *or US* **color** (ˈkʌlə) *n* **1a** an attribute of things that results from the light they reflect or emit in so far as this causes a visual sensation that depends on its wavelengths. **1b** the aspect of visual perception by which an observer recognizes this attribute. **1c** the quality of the light producing this visual perception. **2** Also called: **chromatic colour. 2a** a colour, such as red or green, that possesses hue, as opposed to achromatic colours such as white or black. **2b** (*as modifier*): *colour television.* **3** a substance, such as a dye or paint, that imparts colour. **4a** the skin complexion of a person, esp. as determined by his race. **4b** (*as modifier*): *colour prejudice.* **5** the use of all the hues in painting as distinct from composition, form, and light and shade. **6** the quantity and quality of ink used in a printing process. **7** the distinctive tone of a musical sound. **8** vividness or authenticity: *period colour.* **9** semblance or pretext: *under colour of.* **10** Physics. one of three characteristics of quarks, designated red, blue, or green, but having only a remote formal relationship with the physical sensation. ◆ *vb* **11** (*tr*) to apply colour to (something). **12** (*tr*) to give a convincing appearance to: *to colour an alibi.* **13** (*tr*) to influence or distort: *anger coloured her judgment.* **14** (*intr*; often foll. by *up*) to become red in the face, esp. when embarrassed or annoyed. ◆ See also **colours.** [C13 from OF *colour* from L *color* tint, hue]

colourable (ˈkʌlərəbºl) *adj* **1** capable of being coloured. **2** appearing to be true; plausible. **3** pretended; feigned.

colour bar *n* discrimination against people of a different race, esp. as practised by Whites against Blacks.

colour-blind *adj* of or relating to any defect in the normal ability to distinguish certain colours.
▸ **colour blindness** *n*

colour code *n* a system of easily distinguishable colours, as for the identification of electrical wires or resistors.

coloured (ˈkʌləd) *adj* **1** possessing colour. **2** having a strong element of fiction or fantasy; distorted (esp. in **highly coloured**).

Coloured (ˈkʌləd) *n* **1** an individual who is not a White person, esp. a Black person. **2** Also called: **Cape Coloured.** (in South Africa) a person of racially mixed parentage or descent. ◆ *adj* **3a** (in South Africa) designating or relating to a person or people of racially mixed descent. **3b** designating or relating to a person or people who are not White.

> USAGE NOTE The use of *Coloured* to refer to people is now generally considered to be offensive.

colourfast (ˈkʌləˌfɑːst) *adj* (of a fabric) having a colour that does not run or change when washed or worn.
▸ **colour fastness** *n*

colourful (ˈkʌləful) *adj* **1** having intense colour or richly varied colours. **2** vivid, rich, or distinctive in character.
▸ **colourfully** *adv*

colour guard *n* a military guard in a parade, ceremony, etc., that carries and escorts the flag.

colouring (ˈkʌlərɪŋ) *n* **1** the process or art of applying

colour. **2** anything used to give colour, such as paint. **3** appearance with regard to shade and colour. **4** arrangements of colours, as in the markings of birds. **5** the colour of a person's complexion. **6** a false or misleading appearance.

colourist (ˈkʌlərɪst) *n* a person who uses colour, esp. an artist.

colourize, colourise, *or US* **colorize** (ˈkʌləˌraɪz) *vb* **colourizes, colourizing, colourized** *or* **colourises, colourising colourised** *or US* **colorizes, colorizing, colorized.** (*tr*) to add colour electronically to (an old black-and-white film).
▸ **colouriʹzation, colouriʹsation** *or US* **coloriʹzation** *n*

colourless (ˈkʌləlɪs) *adj* **1** without colour. **2** lacking in interest: *a colourless individual.* **3** grey or pallid in tone or hue. **4** without prejudice; neutral.
▸ **colourlessly** *adv*

colours (ˈkʌləz) *pl n* **1a** the flag that indicates nationality. **1b** Mil. the ceremony of hoisting or lowering the colours. **2** a pair of silk flags borne by a military unit and showing its crest and battle honours. **3** true nature or character (esp. in **show one's colours**). **4** a distinguishing badge or flag. **5** Sport, Brit. a badge or other symbol denoting membership of a team, esp. at a school or college. **6 nail one's colours to the mast.** **6a** to commit oneself publicly and irrevocably to some party, course of action, etc. **6b** to refuse to admit defeat.

colour sergeant *n* a sergeant who carries the regimental, battalion, or national colours.

colour supplement *n* Brit. an illustrated magazine accompanying a newspaper.

colourway (ˈkʌləˌweɪ) *n* one of several different combinations of colours in which a given pattern is printed or on fabrics or wallpapers, etc.

colposcope (ˈkɒlpəˌskəʊp) *n* an instrument for examining the cervix. [C20: from Gk *kolpos* womb + -SCOPE]

colt (kəʊlt) *n* **1** a male horse or pony under the age of four. **2** Sport. **2a** a young and inexperienced player. **2b** a member of a junior team. [OE *colt* young ass]

colter (ˈkəʊltə) *n* a variant spelling (esp. US) of **coulter.**

coltish (ˈkəʊltɪʃ) *adj* **1** inexperienced; unruly. **2** playful and lively.
▸ **coltishness** *n*

Coltrane ★ (kɒlˈtreɪn) *n* John (William). 1926–67, US jazz saxophonist and composer.

coltsfoot (ˈkəʊltsˌfʊt) *n, pl* **coltsfoots.** a European plant with yellow daisy-like flowers and heart-shaped leaves: a common weed.

colubrine (ˈkɒljʊˌbraɪn) *adj* **1** of or resembling a snake. **2** of or belonging to the Colubrinae, a subfamily of harmless snakes. [C16: from L *colubrīnus*, from *coluber* snake]

Colum ★ (ˈkɒləm) *n* Padraic (ˈpɔːdrɪk). 1881–1972, Irish lyric poet, resident in the US (1914–72).

Columba ★ (kəˈlʌmbə) *n* Saint. ?521–597 A.D., Irish missionary: founded the monastery at Iona (563) from which the Picts were converted to Christianity. Feast day: June 9.

Columbia ★ (kəˈlʌmbɪə) *n* **1** a river in NW North America, rising in the Rocky Mountains and flowing through British Columbia, then west to the Pacific. Length about 1930 km (1200 miles). **2** a city in central South Carolina, on the Congaree River: the state capital. Pop. 104 101 (1994 est.).

columbine (ˈkɒləmˌbaɪn) *n* any plant of the genus *Aquilegia*, having flowers with five spurred petals. Also called **aquilegia.** [C13: from Med. L *columbīna herba* dovelike plant]

Columbine (ˈkɒləmˌbaɪn) *n* the sweetheart of Harlequin in English pantomime.

Columbus¹ ★ (kəˈlʌmbəs) *n* **1** a city in central Ohio: the state capital. Pop.: 635 913 (1994 est.). **2** a city in W Georgia, on the Chattahoochee River. Pop.: 186 470 (1994 est.).

Columbus² ★ (kəˈlʌmbəs) *n* Christopher. Spanish name *Cristóbal Colón*, Italian name *Cristoforo Colombo*. 1451–1506, Italian navigator in the service of Spain, who discovered the New World (1492).

★ people and places

column ('kɒləm) *n* **1** an upright pillar usually having a cylindrical shaft, a base, and a capital. **2a** a form or structure in the shape of a column: *a column of air*. **2b** a monument. **3** a line, as of people in a queue. **4** *Mil.* a narrow formation in which individuals or units follow one behind the other. **5** *Journalism.* **5a** any of two or more vertical sections of type on a printed page, esp. on a newspaper page. **5b** a regular feature in a paper: *the fashion column*. **6** a vertical array of numbers. [C15: from L *columna*, from *columen* top, peak]
▶ **columnar** (kə'lʌmnə) *adj* ▶ **'columned** *adj*

column inch *n* a unit of measurement for advertising space, one inch deep and one column wide.

columnist ('kɒləmnɪst, -əmɪst) *n* a journalist who writes a regular feature in a newspaper.

colure (kə'lʊə, 'kəulʊə) *n* either of two great circles on the celestial sphere, one passing through the poles and the equinoxes, the other through the poles and the solstices. [C16: from LL, from Gk *kolourai*, dock-tailed, from *kolos* docked + *oura* tail (because the lower portion is not visible)]

Colwyn Bay ★ ('kɒlwɪn) *n* a town and resort in N Wales, in Conwy county borough. Pop.: 29 883 (1991).

colza ('kɒlzə) *n* another name for **rape**[2]. [C18: via F (Walloon) from Du., from *kool* cabbage, COLE + *zaad* SEED]

COM (kɒm) *n* direct conversion of computer output to microfiche or film. [C20: C(*omputer*) O(*utput on*) M(*icrofilm*)]

Com. *abbrev. for:* **1** Commander. **2** Committee. **3** Commodore. **4** Communist.

com- or **con-** *prefix* together; with; jointly: *commingle.* [from L *com-*; rel. to *cum* with. In compound words of L origin, *com-* becomes *col-* and *cor-* before *l* and *r*, *co-* before *gn*, *h*, and most vowels, and *con-* before consonants other than *b*, *p*, and *m*]

coma[1] ('kəumə) *n, pl* **comas.** a state of unconsciousness from which a person cannot be aroused, caused by injury, narcotics, poisons, etc. [C17: from medical L, from Gk *kōma* heavy sleep]

coma[2] ('kəumə) *n, pl* **comae** (-miː). **1** *Astron.* the luminous cloud surrounding the nucleus in the head of a comet. **2** *Bot.* **2a** a tuft of hairs attached to the seed coat of some seeds. **2b** the terminal crown of leaves of palms and moss stems. [C17: from L: hair of the head, from Gk *komē*]

comanche (kə'mæntʃɪ) *n* **1** (*pl* **comanches** or **comanche**) a member of a North American Indian people formerly inhabiting the W plains of the US. **2** the language of this people.

Comaneci ★ (,kɒmə'nɛtʃɪ) *n* Nadia. born 1961, Romanian gymnast; gold medal winner in the 1976 Olympic Games; defected to the US in 1989.

comatose ('kəumə,təus) *adj* **1** in a state of coma. **2** torpid; lethargic.

comb (kəum) *n* **1** a toothed device for disentangling or arranging hair. **2** a tool or machine that cleans and straightens wool, cotton, etc. **3** *Austral. & NZ.* the fixed cutter on a sheep-shearing machine. **4** anything resembling a comb in form or function. **5** the fleshy serrated outgrowth on the heads of certain birds, esp. the domestic fowl. **6** a honeycomb. ◆ *vb* **7** (*tr*) to use a comb on. **8** (when *tr*, often foll. by *through*) to search with great care: *the police combed the woods.* ◆ **See also comb out.** [OE *camb*]

combat *n* ('kɒmbæt, -bət, 'kʌm-). **1** a fight, conflict, or struggle. **2a** an action fought between two military forces. **2b** (*as modifier*): *a combat jacket.* **3 single combat.** a duel. ◆ *vb* (kəm'bæt; 'kɒmbæt, 'kʌm-). **-bats, -bating, -bated.** **4** (*tr*) to fight. **5** (*intr*; often foll. by *with* or *against*) to struggle or strive (against): *to combat against disease.* [C16: from F, from OF *combattre*, from Vulgar L *combattere* (unattested), from L *com-* with + *battuere* to beat]

combatant ('kɒmbət³nt, 'kʌm-) *n* **1** a person or group engaged in or prepared for a fight. ◆ *adj* **2** engaged in or ready for combat.

combat fatigue *n* another term for **battle fatigue**.

combative ('kɒmbətɪv, 'kʌm-) *adj* eager or ready to fight, argue, etc.
▶ **'combativeness** *n*

combe or **comb** (kuːm) *n* variant spellings of **coomb**.

comber ('kəumə) *n* **1** a person, tool, or machine that combs wool, flax, etc. **2** a long curling wave; roller.

combination (,kɒmbɪ'neɪʃən) *n* **1** the act of combining or state of being combined. **2** a union of separate parts, qualities, etc. **3** an alliance of people or parties. **4** the set of numbers that opens a combination lock. **5** *Brit.* a motorcycle with a sidecar attached. **6** *Maths.* an arrangement of the numbers, terms, etc., of a set into specified groups without regard to order in the group. **7** the chemical reaction of two or more compounds, usually to form one other compound. **8** *Chess.* a tactical manoeuvre involving a sequence of moves and more than one piece.
▶ **,combi'national** *adj*

combination lock *n* a type of lock that can only be opened when a set of dials is turned to show a specific sequence of numbers.

combinations (,kɒmbɪ'neɪʃənz) *pl n Brit.* a one-piece undergarment with long sleeves and legs. Often shortened to **combs** or **coms.**

combine *vb* (kəm'baɪn), **combines, combining, combined. 1** to join together. **2** to unite or cause to unite to form a chemical compound. ◆ *n* ('kɒmbaɪn). **3** short for **combine harvester.** **4** an association of enterprises, esp. in order to gain a monopoly of a market. **5** an association of related bodies, such as business corporations or sports clubs, for a common purpose. [C15: from LL *combīnāre*, from L *com-* together + *bīnī* two by two]
▶ **com'binable** *adj* ▶ **com,bina'bility** *n* ▶ **combinative** ('kɒmbɪ,neɪtɪv) or **combinatory** (,kɒmbɪ,neɪtərɪ) *adj*

combine harvester ('kɒmbaɪn) *n* a machine that simultaneously cuts, threshes, and cleans a standing crop of grain.

combings ('kəumɪŋz) *pl n* **1** the loose hair removed by combing. **2** the unwanted fibres removed in combing cotton, etc.

combining form *n* a linguistic element that occurs only as part of a compound word, such as *anthropo-* in *anthropology* and *anthropomorph.*

combo ('kɒmbəu) *n, pl* **combos. 1** a small group of jazz musicians. **2** *Inf.* any combination.

comb out *vb* (*tr, adv*) **1** to remove (tangles) from (the hair) with a comb. **2** to remove for a purpose. **3** to examine systematically.

combustible (kəm'bʌstɪb'l) *adj* **1** capable of igniting and burning. **2** easily annoyed; excitable. ◆ *n* **3** a combustible substance.
▶ **com,busti'bility** or **com'bustibleness** *n*

combustion (kəm'bʌstʃən) *n* **1** the process of burning. **2** any process in which a substance reacts to produce a significant rise in temperature and the emission of light. **3** a process in which a compound reacts slowly with oxygen to produce little heat and no light. [C15: from OF, from L *combūrere* to burn up]
▶ **com'bustive** *n, adj*

combustion chamber *n* an enclosed space in which combustion takes place, such as the space above the piston in the cylinder head of an internal-combustion engine.

combustor (kəm'bʌstə) *n* the combustion system of a jet engine or ramjet.

Comdr *Mil. abbrev. for* Commander.

Comdt *Mil. abbrev. for* Commandant.

come (kʌm) *vb* **comes, coming, came, come.** (*mainly intr*) **1** to move towards a specified person or place. **2** to arrive by movement or by making progress. **3** to become perceptible: *light came into the sky.* **4** to occur: *Christmas comes but once a year.* **5** to happen as a result: *no good will come of this.* **6** to be derived: *good may come of evil.* **7** to occur to the mind: *the truth suddenly came to me.* **8** to reach: *she comes up to my shoulder.* **9** to be produced: *that dress comes in red.* **10** to arrive at or be brought into a particular state: *you will soon come to grief.* **11** (foll. by *from*) to be or have been a resident or native (of): *I come from London.* **12** to become: *your wishes will come true.* **13** (*tr; takes an infinitive*) to be given awareness: *I came to realize its value.* **14** *Taboo sl.* to have an orgasm. **15** (*tr*) *Brit. inf.* to play the part of: *don't come the fine gentleman with me.* **16** (*tr*) *Brit. inf.* to cause or produce: *don't come that nonsense.* **17** (*subjunctive use*): *come next August, he will be fifty years old:* when next August arrives. **18 as ... as they come.** the most characteristic example of a type. **19 come again?** *Inf.* what did you say? **20 come good.** to recover and perform well after a setback or poor start. **21 come to light.** to be revealed. **22 come to light with.** *Austral. & NZ inf.* to find or produce. ♦ *interj* **23** an exclamation expressing annoyance, etc.: *come now!* ♦ See also **come about, come across,** etc. [OE *cuman*]

come about *vb* (*intr, adv*) **1** to take place; happen. **2** *Naut.* to change tacks.

come across *vb* (*intr*) **1** (*prep*) to meet or find by accident. **2** (*adv*) to communicate the intended meaning or impression. **3** (often foll. by *with*) to provide what is expected.

come at *vb* (*intr, prep*) **1** to discover (facts, the truth, etc.). **2** to attack: *he came at me with an axe.* **3** (*usually used with a negative*) *Austral. sl.* to agree to do (something).

comeback (ˈkʌmˌbæk) *n Inf.* **1** a return to a former position, status, etc. **2** a response, esp. recriminatory. **3** a quick retort. ♦ *vb* **come back.** (*intr, adv*) **4** to return, esp. to the memory. **5** to become fashionable again. **6 come back to (someone).** (of something forgotten) to return to (someone's) memory.

come between *vb* (*intr, prep*) to cause the estrangement or separation of (two people).

come by *vb* (*intr, prep*) to find or obtain, esp. accidentally: *do you ever come by any old books?*

Comecon (ˈkɒmɪˌkɒn) *n* (formerly) an association of Soviet-oriented Communist nations, founded in 1949 to coordinate economic development, etc.: disbanded in 1991. [C20: *Co*(*uncil for*) *M*(*utual*) *Econ*(*omic Aid*)]

comedian (kəˈmiːdɪən) *n* **1** an entertainer who specializes in jokes, comic skits, etc. **2** an actor in comedy. **3** an amusing person: sometimes used ironically.

comedienne (kəˌmiːdɪˈɛn) *n* a female comedian.

comedo (ˈkɒmɪˌdəʊ) *n*, *pl* **comedos** or **comedones** (ˌkɒmɪˈdəʊniːz). *Pathol.* the technical name for **blackhead.** [C19: from NL, from L: glutton]

comedown (ˈkʌmˌdaʊn) *n* **1** a decline in status or prosperity. **2** *Inf.* a disappointment. ♦ *vb* **come down.** (*intr, adv*) **3** to come to a place regarded as lower. **4** to lose status, etc. (esp. in **come down in the world**). **5** (of prices) to become lower. **6** to reach a decision: *the report came down in favour of a pay increase.* **7** (often foll. by *to*) to be handed down by tradition or inheritance. **8** *Brit.* to leave university. **9** (foll. by *with*) to succumb (to illness). **10** (foll. by *on*) to rebuke harshly. **11** (foll. by *to*) to amount in essence (to): *it comes down to two choices.*

comedy (ˈkɒmɪdɪ) *n*, *pl* **comedies.** **1** a dramatic or other work of light and amusing character. **2** the genre of drama represented by works of this type. **3** (in classical literature) a play in which the main characters triumph over adversity. **4** the humorous aspect of life or of events. **5** an amusing event or sequence of events. **6** humour: *the comedy of Chaplin.* [C14: from OF, from L, from Gk *kōmōidia*, from *kōmos* village festival + *aeidein* to sing]
▶ **comedic** (kəˈmiːdɪk) *adj*

comedy of manners *n* a comedy dealing with the way of life and foibles of a social group.

come forward *vb* (*intr, adv*) **1** to offer one's services; volunteer. **2** to present oneself.

come-hither *adj* (*usually prenominal*) *Inf.* alluring; seductive: *a come-hither look.*

come in *vb* (*intr, mainly adv*) **1** to enter. **2** to prove to be: *it came in useful.* **3** to become fashionable or seasonable. **4** *Cricket.* to begin an innings. **5** to finish a race (in a certain position). **6** to be received: *news is coming in of a big fire in Glasgow.* **7** (of money) to be received as income. **8** to play a role: *where do I come in?* **9** (foll. by *for*) to be the object of: *the Chancellor came in for a lot of criticism.*

come into *vb* (*intr, prep*) **1** to enter. **2** to inherit.

comely (ˈkʌmlɪ) *adj* **comelier, comeliest.** **1** good-looking; attractive. **2** *Arch.* suitable; fitting. [OE *cȳmlīc* beautiful]
▶ **'comeliness** *n*

come of *vb* (*intr, prep*) **1** to be descended from. **2** to result from: *nothing came of it.*

come off *vb* (*intr, mainly adv*) **1** (*also prep*) to fall (from). **2** to become detached. **3** (*prep*) to be removed from (a price, tax, etc.): *will anything come off income tax in the budget?* **4** (*copula*) to emerge from or as if from a contest: *he came off the winner.* **5** *Inf.* to happen. **6** *Inf.* to have the intended effect: *his jokes did not come off.* **7** *Taboo sl.* to have an orgasm.

come on *vb* (*intr, mainly adv*) **1** (of power, water, etc.) to start running or functioning. **2** to progress: *my plants are coming on nicely.* **3** to advance, esp. in battle. **4** to begin: *she felt a cold coming on.* **5** to make an entrance on stage. **6 come on! 6a** hurry up! **6b** cheer up! pull yourself together! **6c** make an effort! **6d** don't exaggerate! stick to the facts! **7** to attempt to give a specified impression: *he came on like a hard man.* **8 come on strong.** to make a forceful or exaggerated impression. **9 come on to.** *Inf.* to make sexual advances to. ♦ *n* **come-on. 10.** anything that serves as a lure or enticement.

come out *vb* (*intr, adv*) **1** to be made public or revealed: *the news of her death came out last week.* **2** to make a debut in society. **3** Also: **come out of the closet. 3a** to declare openly that one is a homosexual. **3b** to reveal or declare any practice or habit formerly concealed. **4** *Chiefly Brit.* to go on strike. **5** to declare oneself: *the government came out in favour of scrapping the project.* **6** to be shown clearly: *you came out very well in the photos.* **7** to yield a satisfactory solution: *these sums just won't come out.* **8** to be published: *the paper comes out on Fridays.* **9** (foll. by *in*) to become covered (with). **10** (foll. by *with*) to declare openly: *you can rely on him to come out with the facts.*

come over *vb* (*intr, adv*) **1** to communicate the intended meaning or impression: *he came over very well.* **2** to change allegiances. **3** *Inf.* to feel a particular sensation: *I came over funny.*

comer (ˈkʌmə) *n* **1** (*in combination*) a person who comes: *all-comers; newcomers.* **2** *Inf.* a potential success.

come round *vb* (*intr, adv*) **1** to be restored to consciousness. **2** to modify one's opinion.

comestible (kəˈmɛstɪbˀl) *n* (*usually pl*) food. [C15: from LL *comestibilis*, from *comedere* to eat up]

comet (ˈkɒmɪt) *n* a celestial body that travels around the sun, usually in a highly elliptical orbit: thought to consist of a frozen nucleus, part of which vaporizes on approaching the sun to form a long luminous tail. [C13: from OF, from L, from Gk *komētēs* long-haired]
▶ **'cometary** or **cometic** (kəˈmɛtɪk) *adj*

come through *vb* (*intr*) **1** (*adv*) to emerge successfully. **2** (*prep*) to survive (an illness, etc.).

come to *vb* (*intr*) **1** (*adv or prep and reflexive*) to regain consciousness. **2** (*adv*) *Naut.* to slow a vessel or bring her to a stop. **3** (*prep*) to amount to (a sum of money). **4** (*prep*) to arrive at: *what is the world coming to?*

come up *vb* (*intr, adv*) **1** to come to a place regarded as higher. **2** (of the sun) to rise. **3** to present itself: *that question will come up again.* **4** *Brit.* to begin a term at a university. **5** to appear from out of the ground: *my beans have come up early.* **6** *Inf.* to win: *have your premium bonds ever come up?* **7 come up against.** to come into conflict with. **8 come up to.** to meet a standard. **9 come up with.** to produce.

come upon *vb* (*intr, prep*) to meet or encounter unexpectedly.

comeuppance (ˌkʌmˈʌpəns) *n Inf.* just retribution. [C19: from *come up* (in the sense): to appear before a court]

comfit (ˈkʌmfɪt, ˈkɒm-) *n* a sugar-coated sweet containing a nut or seed. [C15: from OF, from L *confectum* something prepared]

comfort (ˈkʌmfət) *n* **1** a state of ease or well-being. **2** relief from affliction, grief, etc. **3** a person, thing, or event that brings solace or ease. **4** (*usually pl*) something that affords physical ease and relaxation. ♦ *vb* (*tr*) **5** to soothe; cheer. **6** to bring physical ease to. [C13: from OF

confort, from LL *confortāre* to strengthen, from L *con-* (intensive) + *fortis* strong]
▶ **'comforting** *adj* ▶ **'comfortless** *adj*

comfortable ('kʌmftəbᵊl) *adj* **1** giving comfort. **2** at ease. **3** free from affliction or pain. **4** (of a person or situation) relaxing. **5** *Inf.* having adequate income. **6** *Inf.* (of income, etc.) adequate to provide comfort.
▶ **'comfortably** *adv*

comforter ('kʌmfətə) *n* **1** a person or thing that comforts. **2** *Chiefly Brit.* a woollen scarf. **3** a baby's dummy. **4** *US.* a quilted bed covering.

Comforter ('kʌmfətə) *n Christianity.* an epithet of the Holy Spirit. [C14: translation of L *consolātor,* representing Gk *paraklētos* advocate]

comfrey ('kʌmfrɪ) *n* a hairy Eurasian plant having blue, purplish-pink, or white flowers. [C15: from OF *cunfirie,* from L *conferva* water plant]

comfy ('kʌmfɪ) *adj* **comfier, comfiest.** *Inf.* short for **comfortable.**

comic ('kɒmɪk) *adj* **1** of, characterized by, or characteristic of comedy. **2** *(prenominal)* acting in or composing comedy: *a comic writer.* **3** humorous; funny. ◆ *n* **4** a person who is comic; comedian. **5** a book or magazine containing comic strips. [C16: from L *cōmicus,* from Gk *kōmikos*]

comical ('kɒmɪkᵊl) *adj* **1** causing laughter. **2** ludicrous; laughable.
▶ **'comically** *adv*

comic opera *n* a play largely set to music, employing comic effects or situations.

comic strip *n* a sequence of drawings in a newspaper, magazine, etc., relating a humorous story or an adventure.

coming ('kʌmɪŋ) *adj* **1** *(prenominal)* (of time, events, etc.) approaching or next. **2** promising (esp. in **up and coming**). **3** of future importance: *this is the coming thing.* **4 have it coming to one.** *Inf.* to deserve what one is about to suffer. ◆ *n* **5** arrival or approach.

Comintern or **Komintern** ('kɒmɪn,tɜːn) *n* short for **Communist International;** an international Communist organization founded by Lenin in 1919 and dissolved in 1943; it degenerated under Stalin into an instrument of Soviet politics. Also called: **Third International.**

comity ('kɒmɪtɪ) *n, pl* **comities. 1** mutual civility; courtesy. **2** short for **comity of nations.** [C16: from L *cōmitās,* from *cōmis* affable]

comity of nations *n* the friendly recognition accorded by one nation to the laws and usages of another.

comm. *abbrev. for:* **1** commerce. **2** commercial. **3** committee. **4** commonwealth.

comma ('kɒmə) *n* **1** the punctuation mark , indicating a slight pause and used where there is a listing of items or to separate a nonrestrictive clause from a main clause. **2** *Music.* a minute difference in pitch. [C16: from L, from Gk *komma* clause, from *koptein* to cut]

comma bacillus *n* a comma-shaped bacterium that causes cholera in man.

command (kə'mɑːnd) *vb* **1** (when *tr,* may take a clause as object or an infinitive) to order or compel. **2** to have or be in control or authority over. **3** *(tr)* to receive as due: *his nature commands respect.* **4** to dominate (a view, etc.) as from a height. ◆ *n* **5** an order. **6** the act of commanding. **7** the right to command. **8** the exercise of the power to command. **9** knowledge; control: *a command of French.* **10** *Chiefly mil.* the jurisdiction of a commander. **11** a military unit or units commanding a specific function, as in the RAF. **12** *Brit.* **12a** an invitation from the monarch. **12b** *(as modifier): a command performance.* **13** *Computing.* a word or phrase that can be selected from a menu or typed after a prompt in order to carry out an action. [C13: from OF *commander,* from L *com-* (intensive) + *mandāre* to enjoin]

commandant ('kɒmən,dænt, -,dɑːnt) *n* an officer commanding a group or establishment.

command economy *n* an economy in which business activities and the allocation of resources are determined

by government order rather than market forces. Also called: **planned economy.**

commandeer (,kɒmən'dɪə) *vb (tr)* **1** to seize for public or military use. **2** to seize arbitrarily. [C19: from Afrik. *kommandeer,* from F *commander* to COMMAND]

commander (kə'mɑːndə) *n* **1** an officer in command of a military formation or operation. **2** a naval commissioned rank junior to captain but senior to lieutenant commander. **3** the second in command of larger British warships. **4** someone who holds authority. **5** a high-ranking member of some knightly orders. **6** an officer responsible for a district of the Metropolitan Police in London.
▶ **com'mander,ship** *n*

commander in chief *n, pl* **commanders in chief.** the officer holding supreme command of the forces in an area or operation.

commanding (kə'mɑːndɪŋ) *adj (usually prenominal)* **1** being in command. **2** having the air of authority: *a commanding voice.* **3** (of a situation) exerting control. **4** (of a viewpoint, etc.) overlooking; advantageous.
▶ **com'mandingly** *adv*

commanding officer *n* an officer in command of a military unit.

command language *n Computing.* the language used to access a computer system.

commandment (kə'mɑːndmənt) *n* **1** a divine command, esp. one of the Ten Commandments of the Old Testament. **2** *Literary.* any command.

command module *n* the module used as the living quarters in an Apollo spacecraft and functioning as the splashdown vehicle.

commando (kə'mɑːndəu) *n, pl* **commandos** or **commandoes. 1a** an amphibious military unit trained for raiding. **1b** a member of such a unit. **2** the basic unit of the Royal Marine Corps. **3** (originally) an armed force raised by Boers during the Boer War. **4** *(modifier)* denoting or relating to commandos: *a commando unit.* [C19: from Afrik. *kommando,* from Du. *commando* command]

command paper *n* (in Britain) a government document that is presented to Parliament, in theory by royal command.

command post *n Mil.* the position from which a commander exercises command.

commedia dell'arte (Italian kɔm'me:dia del'larte) *n* a form of popular improvised comedy in Italy during the 16th to 18th centuries, with stock characters such as Punchinello, Harlequin, and Columbine. [It., lit.: comedy of art]

comme il faut *French.* (kɔm il fo) correct or correctly.

commemorate (kə'mɛmə,reɪt) *vb* **commemorates, commemorating, commemorated.** *(tr)* to honour or keep alive the memory of. [C16: from L *commemorāre,* from *com-* (intensive) + *memorāre* to remind]
▶ **com,memo'ration** *n* ▶ **com'memorative** *adj* ▶ **com-'memo,rator** *n*

commence (kə'mɛns) *vb* **commences, commencing, commenced.** to begin; come or cause to come into being, operation, etc. [C14: from OF *comencer,* from Vulgar L *cominitiāre* (unattested), from L *com-* (intensive) + *initiāre* to begin]

commencement (kə'mɛnsmənt) *n* **1** the beginning; start. **2** *US.* a ceremony for the conferment of academic degrees. **3** *US & Canad.* a ceremony for the presentation of awards at secondary schools.

commend (kə'mɛnd) *vb (tr)* **1** to represent as being worthy of regard, confidence, etc.; recommend. **2** to give in charge; entrust. **3** to praise. **4** to give the regards of: *commend me to your aunt.* [C14: from L *commendāre,* from *com-* (intensive) + *mandāre* to entrust]
▶ **com'mendable** *adj* ▶ **com'mendably** *adv* ▶ **com-'mendatory** *adj*

commendation (,kɒmɛn'deɪʃən) *n* **1** the act of commending; praise. **2** *US.* an award.

commensal (kə'mɛnsəl) *adj* **1** (of two different species of plant or animal) living in close association without being interdependent. See also **inquiline** (sense 1). **2** *Rare.*

of or relating to eating together, esp. at the same table. ♦ *n* **3** a commensal plant or animal. **4** *Rare.* a companion at table. [C14: from Med. L *commensālis*, from L *com-* together + *mensa* table]
▸ **com'mensalism** *n* ▸ **commensality** (ˌkɒmɛnˈsælɪtɪ) *n*

commensurable (kəˈmɛnsərəbəl, -ʃə-) *adj* **1** *Maths.* **1a** having a common factor. **1b** having units of the same dimensions and being related by whole numbers. **2** proportionate.
▸ **com,mensura'bility** *n* ▸ **com'mensurably** *adv*

commensurate (kəˈmɛnsərɪt, -ʃə-) *adj* **1** having the same extent or duration. **2** corresponding in degree, amount, or size; proportionate. **3** commensurable. [C17: from LL *commēnsūrātus*, from L *com-* same + *mēnsūrāre* to MEASURE]
▸ **com'mensurately** *adv*

comment (ˈkɒmɛnt) *n* **1** a remark, criticism, or observation. **2** talk or gossip. **3** a note explaining or criticizing a passage in a text. **4** explanatory or critical matter added to a text. ♦ *vb* **5** (when *intr*, often foll. by *on; tr*, takes a clause as object) to remark or express an opinion. **6** (*intr*) to write notes explaining or criticizing a text. [C15: from L *commentum* invention, from *comminiscī* to contrive]
▸ **'commenter** *n*

commentary (ˈkɒməntərɪ) *n, pl* **commentaries.** **1** an explanatory series of notes. **2** a spoken accompaniment to a broadcast, film, etc. **3** an explanatory treatise on a text. **4** (*usually pl*) a personal record of events: *the commentaries of Caesar.*

commentate (ˈkɒmənˌteɪt) *vb* **commentates, commentating, commentated.** **1** (*intr*) to serve as a commentator. **2** (*tr*) *US.* to make a commentary on.

> **USAGE NOTE** The verb *commentate,* derived from *commentator,* is sometimes used as a synonym for *comment on* or *provide a commentary for.* It is not yet fully accepted as standard, though widespread in sports reporting and journalism.

commentator (ˈkɒmənˌteɪtə) *n* **1** a person who provides a spoken commentary for a broadcast, film, etc., esp. of a sporting event. **2** a person who writes notes on a text, etc.

commerce (ˈkɒmɜːs) *n* **1** the activity embracing all forms of the purchase and sale of goods and services. **2** social relations. **3** *Arch.* sexual intercourse. [C16: from L *commercium,* from *commercārī,* from *mercārī* to trade, from *merx* merchandise]

commercial (kəˈmɜːʃəl) *adj* **1** of or engaged in commerce. **2** sponsored or paid for by an advertiser: *commercial television.* **3** having profit as the main aim: *commercial music.* **4** (of chemicals, etc.) unrefined and produced in bulk for use in industry. ♦ *n* **5** a commercially sponsored advertisement on radio or television.
▸ **commerciality** (kəˌmɜːʃɪˈælɪtɪ) *n* ▸ **com'mercially** *adv*

commercial art *n* graphic art for commercial uses such as advertising, packaging, etc.

commercial bank *n* a bank primarily engaged in making short-term loans from funds deposited in current accounts.

commercial break *n* an interruption in a radio or television programme for the broadcasting of advertisements.

commercialism (kəˈmɜːʃəˌlɪzəm) *n* **1** the spirit, principles, or procedure of commerce. **2** exclusive or inappropriate emphasis on profit.

commercialize *or* **commercialise** (kəˈmɜːʃəˌlaɪz) *vb* **commercializes, commercializing, commercialized** *or* **commercialises, commercialising, commercialised.** (*tr*) **1** to make commercial. **2** to exploit for profit, esp. at the expense of quality.
▸ **com,merciali'zation** *or* **com,merciali'sation** *n*

commercial paper *n* a short-term negotiable document, such as a bill of exchange, calling for the transference of a specified sum of money at a designated date.

commercial traveller *n* another name for a **travelling salesman.**

commercial vehicle *n* a vehicle for carrying goods or (less commonly) passengers.

commie *or* **commy** (ˈkɒmɪ) *n, pl* **commies,** *adj Inf. & derog.* short for **communist.**

commination (ˌkɒmɪˈneɪʃən) *n* **1** the act of threatening punishment or vengeance. **2** *Church of England.* a recital of prayers, including a list of God's judgments against sinners, in the office for Ash Wednesday. [C15: from L *comminātiō,* from *com-* (intensive) + *minārī* to threaten]
▸ **comminatory** (ˈkɒmɪnətərɪ) *adj*

commingle (kɒˈmɪŋɡ°l) *vb* **commingles, commingling, commingled.** to mix or be mixed.

comminute (ˈkɒmɪˌnjuːt) *vb* **comminutes, comminuting, comminuted.** **1** to break (a bone) into small fragments. **2** to divide (property) into small lots. [C17: from L *comminuere,* from *com-* (intensive) + *minuere* to reduce]
▸ **,commi'nution** *n*

commis (ˈkɒmɪs, ˈkɒmɪ) *n, pl* **commis.** **1** an agent or deputy. ♦ *adj* **2** (of a waiter or chef) apprentice. [C16 (meaning: deputy): from F, from *committere* to employ]

commiserate (kəˈmɪzəˌreɪt) *vb* **commiserates, commiserating, commiserated.** (when *intr*, usually foll. by *with*) to feel or express sympathy or compassion (for). [C17: from L *commiserārī,* from *com-* together + *miserārī* to bewail]
▸ **com,miser'ation** *n* ▸ **com'miser,ator** *n*

commissar (ˈkɒmɪˌsɑː, ˌkɒmɪˈsɑː) *n* (in the former Soviet Union) **1** an official of the Communist Party responsible for political education. **2** (before 1946) the head of a government department. [C20: from Russian *kommissar*]

commissariat (ˌkɒmɪˈsɛərɪət) *n* **1** (in the former Soviet Union) a government department before 1946. **2** a military department in charge of food supplies, etc. [C17: from NL *commissāriātus,* from Med. L *commissārius* COMMISSARY]

commissary (ˈkɒmɪsərɪ) *n, pl* **commissaries.** **1** *US.* a shop supplying food or equipment, as in a military camp. **2** *US army.* an officer responsible for supplies. **3** *US.* a restaurant in a film studio. **4** a representative or deputy, esp. of a bishop. [C14: from Med. L *commissārius* official in charge, from L *committere* to COMMIT]
▸ **commissarial** (ˌkɒmɪˈsɛərɪəl) *adj*

commission (kəˈmɪʃən) *n* **1** a duty committed to a person or group to perform. **2** authority to perform certain duties. **3** a document granting such authority. **4** *Mil.* **4a** a document conferring a rank on an officer. **4b** the rank granted. **5** a group charged with certain duties: *a commission of inquiry.* **6** a government board empowered to exercise administrative, judicial, or legislative authority. See also **Royal Commission. 7a** the authority given to a person or organization to act as an agent to a principal in commercial transactions. **7b** the fee allotted to an agent for services rendered. **8** the state of being charged with specific responsibilities. **9** the act of committing a sin, crime, etc. **10** good working condition or (esp. of a ship) active service (esp. in **in commission, out of commission**). ♦ *vb* (*mainly tr*) **11** to grant authority to. **12** *Mil.* to confer a rank on. **13** to equip and test (a ship) for active service. **14** to place an order for (something): *to commission a portrait.* **15** to make or become operative or operable: *the plant is due to commission next year.* [C14: from OF, from L *commissiō* a bringing together, from *committere* to COMMIT]

commissionaire (kəˌmɪʃəˈnɛə) *n Chiefly Brit.* a uniformed doorman at a hotel, theatre, etc. [C18: from F, from COMMISSION]

commissioned officer *n* a military officer holding a commission, such as Second Lieutenant in the British Army, Acting Sub-Lieutenant in the Royal Navy, Pilot Officer in the Royal Air Force, and officers of all ranks senior to these.

commissioner (kəˈmɪʃənə) *n* **1** a person endowed with certain powers. **2** any of several types of civil servant. **3** a member of a commission.
▸ **com'missioner,ship** *n*

> ★ people and places

commissioner for oaths *n* a solicitor authorized to authenticate oaths on sworn statements.

commit (kə'mɪt) *vb* **commits, committing, committed.** (*tr*) **1** to hand over, as for safekeeping; entrust. **2 commit to memory.** to memorize. **3** to take into custody: *to commit someone to prison.* **4** (*usually passive*) to pledge or align (oneself), as to a particular cause: *a committed radical.* **5** to order (forces) into action. **6** to perform (a crime, error, etc.). **7** to surrender, esp. for destruction: *she committed the letter to the fire.* **8** to refer (a bill, etc.) to a committee. [C14: from L *committere* to join, from *com-* together + *mittere* to send]
▸ **com'mittable** *adj* ▸ **com'mitter** *n*

commitment (kə'mɪtmənt) *n* **1** the act of committing or pledging. **2** the state of being committed or pledged. **3** an obligation, promise, etc., that restricts freedom of action. **4** Also called (esp. formerly). *Law.* a written order of a court directing that a person be imprisoned. **5** a future financial obligation or contingent liability.
♦ Also called (esp. for sense 4): **committal** (kə'mɪtᵊl).

committee *n* **1** (kə'mɪtɪ). a group of people appointed to perform a specified service or function. **2** (ˌkɒmɪ'tiː). (formerly) a person to whom the care of a mentally incompetent person or his property was entrusted by a court. [C15: from *committen* to entrust + *-EE*]

committeeman (kə'mɪtɪmən, -ˌmæn) *n, pl* **committeemen.** *Chiefly US.* a member of one or more committees.
▸ **com'mittee,woman** *fem n*

Committee of the Whole House *n* (in Britain) an informal sitting of the House of Commons to discuss and amend a bill.

commode (kə'məʊd) *n* **1** a piece of furniture, usually highly ornamented, containing drawers or shelves. **2** a bedside table with a cabinet for a chamber pot or washbasin. **3** a chair with a hinged flap concealing a chamber pot. [C17: from F, from L *commodus* COMMODIOUS]

commodious (kə'məʊdɪəs) *adj* **1** roomy; spacious. **2** *Arch.* convenient. [C15: from Med. L, from L *commodus* convenient, from *com-* with + *modus* measure]
▸ **com'modiousness** *n*

commodity (kə'mɒdɪtɪ) *n, pl* **commodities. 1** an article of commerce. **2** something of use or profit. **3** *Econ.* an exchangeable unit of economic wealth, such as a primary product. [C14: from OF *commodité*, from L *commoditās* suitability; see COMMODIOUS]

commodo (kə'məʊdəʊ) *adv* a variant spelling of **comodo.**

commodore ('kɒməˌdɔː) *n* **1** *Brit.* a naval rank junior to rear admiral and senior to captain. **2** the captain of a shipping line. **3** the officer in command of a merchant convoy. **4** the titular head of a yacht club. [C17: prob. from Du. *commandeur*, from F, from OF *commander* to COMMAND]

Commodus ★ (kə'məʊdəs, 'kɒmədəs) *n* **Lucius Aelius Aurelius** ('luːsɪəs 'iːlɪəs ɔː'riːlɪəs), son of Marcus Aurelius. 161–192 A.D., Roman emperor (180–192), noted for his tyrannical reign.

common ('kɒmən) *adj* **1** belonging to two or more people: *common property.* **2** belonging to members of one or more communities; public: *a common culture.* **3** of ordinary standard; average. **4** prevailing; widespread: *common opinion.* **5** frequently encountered; ordinary: *a common brand of soap.* **6** notorious: *a common nuisance.* **7** *Derog.* considered by the speaker to be low-class, vulgar, or coarse. **8** (*prenominal*) having no special distinction: *the common man.* **9** *Maths.* having a specified relationship with a group of numbers or quantities: *common denominator.* **10** *Prosody.* (of a syllable) able to be long or short. **11** *Grammar.* (in certain languages) denoting or belonging to a gender of nouns that includes both masculine and feminine referents. **12 common or garden.** *Inf.* ordinary; unexceptional. ♦ *n* **13** a tract of open public land. **14** *Law.* the right to go onto someone else's property and remove natural products, as by pasturing cattle (esp. in **right of common**). **15** *Christianity.* **15a** a form of the proper of the Mass used on festivals that have no special proper of their own. **15b** the ordinary of the Mass. **16 in common.** mutually held or used. ♦ See also **commons.** [C13: from OF *commun*, from L *commūnis* general]
▸ **'commonly** *adv* ▸ **'commonness** *n*

commonage ('kɒmənɪdʒ) *n* **1** *Chiefly law.* **1a** the use of something, esp. a pasture, in common with others. **1b** the right to such use. **2** the state of being held in common. **3** another word for **commonalty** (sense 1).

commonality (ˌkɒmə'nælɪtɪ) *n, pl* **commonalities. 1** the fact of being common. **2** another word for **commonalty** (sense 1).

commonalty ('kɒmənəltɪ) *n, pl* **commonalties. 1** the ordinary people as distinct from those with rank or title. **2** the members of an incorporated society. [C13: from OF *comunalte*, from *comunal* communal]

common carrier *n* a person or firm engaged in the business of transporting goods or passengers.

common chord *n Music.* a chord consisting of the keynote, a major or minor third, and a perfect fifth.

common cold *n* a mild viral infection of the upper respiratory tract, characterized by sneezing, coughing, etc.

commoner ('kɒmənə) *n* **1** a person who does not belong to the nobility. **2** a person who has a right in or over common land. **3** *Brit.* a student at a university who is not on a scholarship.

common fraction *n* another name for **simple fraction.**

common knowledge *n* something widely or generally known.

common law *n* **1** the body of law based on judicial decisions and custom, as distinct from statute law. **2** (*modifier*) of or denoting a marriage that is deemed to exist after a man and a woman have cohabited for a number of years: *common-law marriage; common-law wife; common-law husband.*

Common Market *n* **the.** an informal name for the European Economic Community (now the **European Union**) and its policies of greater economic cooperation and free trade between member states. See also **European Community.**

common noun *n Grammar.* a noun that refers to each member of a whole class sharing the features connoted by the noun, as for example *orange* and *drum.* Cf. **proper noun.**

commonplace ('kɒmənˌpleɪs) *adj* **1** ordinary; everyday. **2** trite: *commonplace prose.* ♦ *n* **3** a platitude; truism. **4** a passage in a book marked for inclusion in a commonplace book, etc. **5** an ordinary thing. [C16: translation of L *locus commūnis* argument of wide application]
▸ **'common,placeness** *n*

commonplace book *n* a notebook in which quotations, poems, etc., that catch the owner's attention are entered.

common room *n Chiefly Brit.* a sitting room in schools, colleges, etc.

commons ('kɒmənz) *n* **1** (*functioning as pl*) the lower classes as contrasted with the ruling or noble classes of society. **2** (*functioning as sing*) *Brit.* a hall for dining, recreation, etc., usually attached to a college, etc. **3** (*usually functioning as pl*) *Brit.* food or rations (esp. in **short commons**).

Commons ('kɒmənz) *n* **the.** See **House of Commons.**

common sense *n* **1** sound practical sense. ♦ *adj* **common-sense;** *also* **common-sensical. 2** inspired by or displaying this.

common time *n Music.* a time signature indicating four crotchet beats to the bar; four-four time. Symbol: **C**

commonweal ('kɒmənˌwiːl) *n Arch.* **1** the public good. **2** another name for **commonwealth.**

commonwealth ('kɒmənˌwelθ) *n* **1** the people of a state or nation viewed politically; body politic. **2** a state in which the people possess sovereignty; republic. **3** a group of persons united by some common interest.

Commonwealth ('kɒmənˌwelθ) *n* **the. 1** Official name: **the Commonwealth of Nations.** an association of sovereign states, most of which are or at some time were ruled by Britain. **2** the republic that existed in Britain from 1649 to 1660. **3** the official designation of Australia, four states of the US, and Puerto Rico.

★ people and places

Commonwealth Day *n* the anniversary of Queen Victoria's birth, May 24, celebrated (now on the second Monday in March) in many parts of the Commonwealth. Former name: **Empire Day.**

Commonwealth of Independent States *n* a loose organization of former Soviet republics, excluding the Baltic States, formed in 1991. Abbrev.: **CIS.**

commotion (kə'məʊʃən) *n* **1** violent disturbance; upheaval. **2** political insurrection. **3** a confused noise; din. [C15: from L *commōtiō*, from *commovēre*, from *com-* (intensive) + *movēre* to MOVE]

communal ('kɒmjunᵊl) *adj* **1** belonging to a community as a whole. **2** of a commune or a religious community. ▶ **communality** (ˌkɒmju'nælɪtɪ) *n* ▶ 'communally *adv*

communalism ('kɒmjunəˌlɪzəm) *n* **1** a system or theory of government in which the state is seen as a loose federation of self-governing communities. **2** the practice or advocacy of communal living or ownership. ▶ 'communalist *n* ▶ ˌcommunal'istic *adj*

communalize *or* **communalise** ('kɒmjunəˌlaɪz) *vb* **communalizes, communalizing, communalized** *or* **communalises, communalising, communalised.** (*tr*) to render (something) the property of a commune or community. ▶ ˌcommunali'zation *or* ˌcommunali'sation *n*

communautaire *French.* (kɔmynotɛr) *adj* supporting the principles of the European Union. [lit.: community (as modifier)]

commune¹ *vb* (kə'mju:n), **communes, communing, communed.** (*intr*; usually foll. by *with*) **1** to talk intimately. **2** to experience strong emotion (for): *to commune with nature*. ◆ *n* ('kɒmju:n). **3** intimate conversation; communion. [C13: from OF *comuner* to hold in common, from *comun* COMMON]

commune² ('kɒmju:n) *n* **1** a group of families or individuals living together and sharing possessions and responsibilities. **2** any small group of people having common interests or responsibilities. **3** the smallest administrative unit in Belgium, France, Italy, and Switzerland. **4** a medieval town enjoying a large degree of autonomy. [C18: from F, from Med. L *commūnia*, from L: things held in common]

Commune ('kɒmju:n) *n French history.* **1** See **Paris Commune. 2** a committee that governed Paris during the French Revolution: suppressed 1794.

communicable (kə'mju:nɪkəbᵊl) *adj* **1** capable of being communicated. **2** (of a disease) capable of being passed on readily. ▶ comˌmunica'bility *n* ▶ com'municably *adv*

communicant (kə'mju:nɪkənt) *n* **1** *Christianity.* a person who receives Communion. **2** a person who communicates or informs.

communicate (kə'mju:nɪˌkeɪt) *vb* **communicates, communicating, communicated. 1** to impart (knowledge) or exchange (thoughts) by speech, writing, gestures, etc. **2** (*tr*; usually foll. by *to*) to transmit (to): *the dog communicated his fear to the other animals.* **3** (*intr*) to have a sympathetic mutual understanding. **4** (*intr*; usually foll. by *with*) to make or have a connecting passage: *the kitchen communicates with the dining room.* **5** (*tr*) to transmit (a disease). **6** (*intr*) *Christianity.* to receive Communion. [C16: from L *commūnicāre* to share, from *commūnis* COMMON] ▶ com'muniˌcator *n* ▶ com'municatory *adj*

communication (kəˌmju:nɪ'keɪʃən) *n* **1** the imparting or exchange of information, ideas, or feelings. **2** something communicated, such as a message. **3** (*usually pl; sometimes functioning as sing*) the study of ways in which human beings communicate. **4** a connecting route or link. **5** (*pl*) *Mil.* the system of routes by which forces, supplies, etc., are moved within an area of operations.

communication cord *n Brit.* a cord or chain in a train which may be pulled by a passenger to stop the train in an emergency.

communications satellite *n* an artificial satellite used to relay radio, television, and telephone signals around the earth's surface, usually in geostationary orbit.

communicative (kə'mju:nɪkətɪv) *adj* **1** inclined or able to communicate readily; talkative. **2** of or relating to communication.

communion (kə'mju:njən) *n* **1** an exchange of thoughts, emotions, etc. **2** sharing in common; participation. **3** (foll. by *with*) strong feelings (for): *communion with nature.* **4** a religious group or denomination having common beliefs and practices. **5** spiritual union. [C14: from L *commūniō*, from *commūnis* COMMON]

Communion (kə'mju:njən) *n Christianity.* **1** the act of participating in the Eucharist. **2** the celebration of the Eucharist. **3** the consecrated elements of the Eucharist. ◆ Also called: **Holy Communion.**

communiqué (kə'mju:nɪˌkeɪ) *n* an official communication or announcement, esp. to the press or public. [C19: from F]

communism ('kɒmjuˌnɪzəm) *n* **1** advocacy of a classless society in which private ownership has been abolished and the means of production belong to the community. **2** any movement or doctrine aimed at achieving such a society. **3** (*usually cap.*) a political movement based upon the writings of Marx that considers history in terms of class conflict and revolutionary struggle. **4** (*usually cap.*) a system of government established by a ruling Communist Party, esp. in the former Soviet Union. **5** communal living. [C19: from F *communisme*, from *commun* COMMON]

communist ('kɒmjunɪst) *n* **1** a supporter of communism. **2** (*often cap.*) a supporter of a Communist movement or state. **3** (*often cap.*) a member of a Communist party. **4** (*often cap.*) *Chiefly US.* any person holding left-wing views, esp. when considered subversive. **5** a person who practises communal living. ◆ *adj* **6** of, favouring, or relating to communism. ▶ ˌcommu'nistic *adj*

Communist China ★ *n* another name for (the People's Republic of) **China.**

community (kə'mju:nɪtɪ) *n, pl* **communities. 1a** the people living in one locality. **1b** the locality in which they live. **1c** (*as modifier*): *community spirit.* **2** a group of people having cultural, religious, or other characteristics in common: *the Protestant community.* **3** a group of nations having certain interests in common. **4** the public; society. **5** common ownership. **6** similarity or agreement: *community of interests.* **7** (in Wales and Scotland) the smallest unit of local government. **8** *Ecology.* a group of interdependent plants and animals inhabiting the same region. [C14: from L *commūnitās*, from *commūnis* COMMON]

community centre *n* a building used by a community for social gatherings, etc.

community charge *n* (formerly in Britain) a flat-rate charge paid by each adult in a community to their local authority in place of rates. Also called: **poll tax.**

community chest *n US.* a fund raised by voluntary contribution for local welfare activities.

community council *n* (in Scotland and Wales) an independent voluntary local body set up to attend to local interests and organize community activities.

community education *n* the provision of a wide range of educational and special-interest courses and activities by a local authority.

community home *n* (in Britain) a home provided by a local authority for children who cannot remain with their parents. **2** a boarding school for young offenders.

community medicine *n* the branch of medicine concerned with evaluating and providing for the health needs of populations, esp. through monitoring and preventive measures.

community policing *n* the assigning of the same one or two policemen to a particular area so that they become familiar with the residents and they with them, as a way of reducing crime.

community service *n* work undertaken for the community by an offender without pay, by the order of a court.

communize *or* **communise** ('kɒmjuˌnaɪz) *vb* **communizes, communizing, communized** *or* **communises, communising, communised.** (*tr*) (*sometimes cap.*) **1** to make (property) public; nationalize. **2** to make (a person or country) communist. ▶ ˌcommuni'zation *or* ˌcommuni'sation *n*

★ people and places

commutate ('kɒmjʊˌteɪt) vb **commutates, commutating, commutated.** (tr) **1** to reverse the direction of (an electric current). **2** to convert (an alternating current) into a direct current.

commutation (ˌkɒmjʊ'teɪʃən) n **1** a substitution or exchange. **2** the replacement of one method of payment by another. **3** the reduction in severity of a penalty imposed by law. **4** the process of commutating an electric current.

commutative (kə'mjuːtətɪv, 'kɒmjʊˌteɪtɪv) adj **1** relating to or involving substitution. **2** Maths, logic. **2a** giving the same result irrespective of the order of the arguments; thus addition is commutative but subtraction is not. **2b** relating to this property: the commutative law of addition.

commutator ('kɒmjʊˌteɪtə) n **1** a device used to reverse the direction of flow of an electric current. **2** the segmented metal cylinder or disc of an electric motor, generator, etc., used to make electrical contact with the rotating coils.

commute (kə'mjuːt) vb **commutes, commuting, commuted. 1** (intr) to travel some distance regularly between one's home and one's place of work. **2** (tr) to substitute. **3** (tr) Law. to reduce (a sentence) to one less severe. **4** to pay (an annuity, etc.) at one time, instead of in instalments. **5** to change: to commute base metal into gold. [C17: from L commutāre, from com- mutually + mutāre to change] ▸ **com'mutable** adj ▸ **comˌmuta'bility** n

commuter (kə'mjuːtə) n a person who travels to work over an appreciable distance, usually from the suburbs to the centre of a city.

Como ★ ('kəʊməʊ; Italian 'kɔːmo) n a city in N Italy, in Lombardy at the SW end of **Lake Como:** tourist centre. Pop.: 96 900 (1995 est.). Latin name: **Comum** ('kəʊmʊm).

comodo or **commodo** (kə'məʊdəʊ) adv Music. in a convenient tempo. [It.: comfortable, from L commodus convenient: see COMMODIOUS]

Comoros ★ ('kɒməˌrəʊz, kə'mɔːrəʊz) pl n a republic consisting of three volcanic islands in the Indian Ocean, off the NW coast of Madagascar; a French territory from 1947; became independent in 1976 except for Mayotte, the fourth island in the group, which chose to remain French. Official languages: Comorian, French, and Arabic. Religion: Islam. Currency: franc. Capital: Moroni. Pop.: 514 000 (1997). Area: 1862 sq. km (719 sq. miles). Official name: **Federal Islamic Republic of the Comoros.**

comose ('kəʊməʊs, kəʊ'məʊs) adj Bot. having tufts of hair; hairy. Also: **comate.** [C18: from L comōsus hairy]

comp (kɒmp) Inf. ◆ n **1** a compositor. **2** an accompaniment. **3** a competition. ◆ vb **4** (intr) to work as a compositor in the printing industry. **5** to play an accompaniment (to).

comp. abbrev. for: **1** companion. **2** comparative. **3** compare. **4** compiled. **5** composer. **6** composition. **7** compositor. **8** compound. **9** comprehensive. **10** comprising.

compact[1] adj (kəm'pækt). **1** closely packed together. **2** neatly fitted into a restricted space. **3** concise; brief. **4** well constructed; solid; firm. **5** (foll. by of) composed (of). ◆ vb (kəm'pækt). (tr) **6** to pack closely together; compress. **7** (foll. by of) to form by pressing together: sediment compacted of three types of clay. **8** Metallurgy. to compress (a metal powder) to form a stable product suitable for sintering. ◆ n ('kɒmpækt). **9** a small flat case containing a mirror, face powder, and powder puff, designed to be carried in a woman's handbag. **10** US & Canad. a small and economical car. [C16: from L compactus, from compingere, from com- together + pangere to fasten] ▸ **com'pactly** adv ▸ **com'pactness** n

compact[2] ('kɒmpækt) n an official contract or agreement. [C16: from L compactum, from compaciscī, from com- together + paciscī to contract]

compact disc ('kɒmpækt) n a small digital audio disc on which sound is recorded as a series of metallic pits enclosed in PVC and read by an optical laser system. Also called: **compact audio disc.** Abbrev.: **CD, CAD.**

compact video disc n a compact laser disc that plays both pictures and sound.

compages (kəm'peɪdʒiːz) n (functioning as sing) a structure or framework. [C17: from L: from com- together + pangēre to fasten]

companion[1] (kəm'pænjən) n **1** a person who is an associate of another or others; comrade. **2** (esp. formerly) an employee, usually a woman, who provides company for an employer. **3a** one of a pair. **3b** (as modifier): a companion volume. **4** a guidebook or handbook. **5** a member of the lowest rank of certain orders of knighthood. **6** Astron. the fainter of the two components of a double star. ◆ vb **7** (tr) to accompany. [C13: from LL compāniō, lit.: one who eats bread with another, from L com- with + pānis bread] ▸ **com'panionˌship** n

companion[2] (kəm'pænjən) n Naut. a raised frame on an upper deck with windows to give light to the deck below. [C18: from Du. kompanje quarterdeck, from OF compagne, from OIt. compagna pantry, ? ult. from L pānis bread]

companionable (kəm'pænjənəb°l) adj sociable. ▸ **com'panionableness** n ▸ **com'panionably** adv

companionate (kəm'pænjənɪt) adj **1** resembling, appropriate to, or acting as a companion. **2** harmoniously suited.

companionway (kəm'pænjənˌweɪ) n a ladder from one deck to another in a ship.

company ('kʌmpənɪ) n, pl **companies. 1** a number of people gathered together; assembly. **2** the fact of being with someone; companionship: I enjoy her company. **3** a guest or guests. **4** a business enterprise. **5** the members of an enterprise not specifically mentioned in the enterprise's title. Abbrev.: **Co., co. 6** a group of actors. **7** a small unit of troops. **8** the officers and crew of a ship. **9** a unit of Guides. **10** English history. a medieval guild. **11 keep company. 11a** to accompany (someone). **11b** (esp. of lovers) to spend time together. ◆ vb **companies, companying, companied. 12** Arch. to associate (with someone). [C13: from OF compaignie, from LL compāniō; see COMPANION[1]]

company doctor n **1** a businessman or accountant who specializes in turning ailing companies into profitable enterprises. **2** a physician employed by a company to look after its staff and to advise on health matters.

company sergeant major n Mil. the senior noncommissioned officer in a company.

company town n US & Canad. a town built by a company for its employees.

compar. abbrev. for comparative.

comparable ('kɒmpərəb°l) adj **1** worthy of comparison. **2** able to be compared (with). ▸ **ˌcompara'bility** or **'comparableness** n

comparative (kəm'pærətɪv) adj **1** denoting or involving comparison: comparative literature. **2** relative: a comparative loss of prestige. **3** Grammar. denoting the form of an adjective that indicates that the quality denoted is possessed to a greater extent. In English the comparative is marked by the suffix -er or the word more. ◆ n **4** the comparative form of an adjective. ▸ **com'paratively** adv ▸ **com'parativeness** n

comparative advertising n the usual US term for knocking copy.

compare (kəm'peə) vb **compares, comparing, compared. 1** (tr; foll. by to) to regard as similar; liken: the general has been compared to Napoleon. **2** (tr) to examine in order to observe resemblances or differences: to compare rum and gin. **3** (intr; usually foll. by with) to be the same or similar: gin compares with rum in alcoholic content. **4** (intr) to bear a specified relation when examined: this car compares badly with the other. **5** (tr) Grammar. to give the positive, comparative, and superlative forms of (an adjective). **6 compare notes.** to exchange opinions. ◆ n **7** comparison (esp. in **beyond compare**). [C15: from OF, from L comparāre, from compar, from com- together + par equal]

comparison (kəm'pærɪs°n) n **1** the act of comparing. **2** the state of being compared. **3** likeness: there was no comparison between them. **4** a rhetorical device involving comparison, such as a simile. **5** Also called: **degrees of comparison.** Grammar. the listing of the positive, comparative, and superlative forms of an adjective or adverb. **6**

bear *or* stand **comparison** (**with**). to be sufficiently similar to be compared with (something else), esp. favourably.

compartment (kəm'pɑːtmənt) *n* **1** one of the sections into which an area, esp. an enclosed space, is partitioned. **2** any separate section: *a compartment of the mind*. **3** a small storage space. [C16: from F *compartiment*, ult. from LL *compartīrī* to share]
▸ **compartmental** (ˌkɒmpɑːt'mɛnt°l) *adj* ▸ ˌcompart'mentally *adv*

compartmentalize *or* **compartmentalise** (ˌkɒmpɑːt'mɛnt°ˌlaɪz) *vb* **compartmentalizes, compartmentalizing, compartmentalized** *or* **compartmentalises, compartmentalising, compartmentalised**. (*usually tr*) to put into categories, etc., esp. to an excessive degree.
▸ ˌcompartˌmentali'zation *or* ˌcompartˌmentali'sation *n*

compass ('kʌmpəs) *n* **1** Also called: **magnetic compass**. an instrument for finding direction, having a magnetized needle which points to magnetic north. **2** (*often pl*) Also called: **pair of compasses**. an instrument used for drawing circles, measuring distances, etc., that consists of two arms, joined at one end. **3** limits or range: *within the compass of education*. **4** *Music*. the interval between the lowest and highest note attainable. ◆ *vb* (*tr*) **5** to surround; hem in. **6** to grasp mentally. **7** to achieve; accomplish. **8** *Obs*. to plot. [C13: from OF *compas*, from Vulgar L *compassāre* (unattested) to pace out, ult. from L *passus* step]
▸ 'compassable *adj*

compass card *n* a compass in the form of a card that rotates so that "0°" or "North" points to magnetic north.

compassion (kəm'pæʃən) *n* a feeling of distress and pity for the suffering or misfortune of another. [C14: from OF, from LL *compassiō*, from L *com-* with + *patī* to suffer]

compassionate (kəm'pæʃənɪt) *adj* showing or having compassion.
▸ com'passionately *adv*

compassionate leave *n* leave granted on the grounds of bereavement, family illness, etc.

compassion fatigue *n* the inability to react sympathetically to a crisis, disaster, etc., because of overexposure to previous crises, disasters, etc.

compass rose *n* a circle or decorative device printed on a map or chart showing the points of the compass.

compass saw *n* a hand saw with a narrow tapered blade for making a curved cut.

compatible (kəm'pætɪb°l) *adj* **1** (usually foll. by *with*) able to exist together harmoniously. **2** (usually foll. by *with*) consistent: *her deeds were not compatible with her ideology*. **3** (of pieces of machinery, etc.) capable of being used together without modification or adaptation. [C15: from Med. L *compatibilis*, from LL *compatī*; see COMPASSION]
▸ comˌpati'bility *n* ▸ com'patibly *adv*

compatriot (kəm'pætrɪət) *n* a fellow countryman. [C17: from F *compatriote*, from LL; see PATRIOT]
▸ comˌpatri'otic *adj*

compeer ('kɒmpɪə) *n* **1** a person of equal rank, status, or ability. **2** a comrade. [C13: from OF *comper*, from Med. L *compater* godfather]

compel (kəm'pɛl) *vb* **compels, compelling, compelled**. (*tr*) **1** to cause (someone) by force (to be or do something). **2** to obtain by force; exact: *to compel obedience*. [C14: from L *compellere*, from *com-* together + *pellere* to drive]
▸ com'pellable *adj*

compelling (kəm'pɛlɪŋ) *adj* **1** arousing or denoting strong interest, esp. admiring interest. **2** (of an argument, evidence, etc.) convincing.

compendious (kəm'pɛndɪəs) *adj* stating the essentials of a subject in a concise form.
▸ com'pendiously *adv* ▸ com'pendiousness *n*

compendium (kəm'pɛndɪəm) *n, pl* **compendiums** *or* **compendia** (-dɪə). **1** *Brit*. a book containing a collection of useful hints. **2** *Brit*. a selection, esp. of different games in one container. **3** a summary. [C16: from L: a saving, lit.: something weighed]

compensate ('kɒmpɛnˌseɪt) *vb* **compensates, compensating, compensated**. **1** to make amends to (someone), esp. for loss or injury. **2** (*tr*) to serve as compensation or damages

for (injury, loss, etc.). **3** to counterbalance the effects of (a force, weight, etc.) so as to produce equilibrium. **4** (*intr*) to attempt to conceal one's shortcomings by the exaggerated exhibition of qualities regarded as desirable. [C17: from L *compēnsāre*, from *pendere* to weigh]
▸ **compensatory** ('kɒmpɛnˌseɪtərɪ, kəm'pɛnsətərɪ) *or* **compensative** ('kɒmpɛnˌseɪtɪv, kəm'pɛnsə-) *adj*

compensation (ˌkɒmpɛn'seɪʃən) *n* **1** the act of making amends for something. **2** something given as reparation for loss, injury, etc. **3** the attempt to conceal one's shortcomings by the exaggerated exhibition of qualities regarded as desirable.
▸ ˌcompen'sational *adj*

comper ('kɒmpə) *n Inf*. a person who regularly enters competitions in newspapers, magazines, etc., esp. competitions offering consumer goods as prizes. [C20: COMP(ETITION) + -ER[1]]
▸ 'comping *n*

compere ('kɒmpɛə) *Brit*. ◆ *n* **1** a master of ceremonies who introduces cabaret, television acts, etc. ◆ *vb* **comperes, compering, compered**. **2** to act as a compere (for). [C20: from F, lit.: godfather]

compete (kəm'piːt) *vb* **competes, competing, competed**. (*intr*; often foll. by *with*) to contend (against) for profit, an award, etc. [C17: from LL *competere*, from L, from *com-* together + *petere* to seek]

competence ('kɒmpɪtəns) *or* **competency** *n* **1** the condition of being capable; ability. **2** a sufficient income to live on. **3** the state of being legally competent or qualified.

competent ('kɒmpɪtənt) *adj* **1** having sufficient skill, knowledge, etc.; capable. **2** suitable or sufficient for the purpose: *a competent answer*. **3** *Law*. (of a witness, etc.) qualified to testify, etc. [C14: from L *competēns*, from *competere*; see COMPETE]
▸ 'competently *adv*

competition (ˌkɒmpɪ'tɪʃən) *n* **1** the act of competing. **2** a contest in which a winner is selected from among two or more entrants. **3** a series of games, sports events, etc. **4** the opposition offered by competitors. **5** competitors offering opposition.

competitive (kəm'pɛtɪtɪv) *adj* **1** involving rivalry: *competitive sports*. **2** sufficiently low in price or high in quality to be successful against commercial rivals. **3** characterized by an urge to compete: *a competitive personality*.
▸ com'petitiveness *n*

competitor (kəm'pɛtɪtə) *n* a person, group, team, firm, etc., that vies or competes; rival.

Compiègne ★ (*French* kɔ̃pjɛɲ) *n* a city in N France, on the Oise River: scene of the armistice at the end of World War I (1918) and of the Franco-German armistice of 1940. Pop.: 44 703 (1990).

compile (kəm'paɪl) *vb* **compiles, compiling, compiled**. (*tr*) **1** to make or compose from other sources: *to compile a list of names*. **2** to collect for a book, hobby, etc. **3** *Computing*. to create (a set of machine instructions) from a high-level programming language, using a compiler. [C14: from L *compīlāre*, from *com-* together + *pīlāre* to thrust down, pack]
▸ **compilation** (ˌkɒmpɪ'leɪʃən) *n*

compiler (kəm'paɪlə) *n* **1** a person who compiles something. **2** a computer program by which a high-level programming language is converted into machine language that can be acted upon by a computer. Cf. **assembler**.

complacency (kəm'pleɪsənsɪ) *or* **complacence** *n* extreme self-satisfaction; smugness.

complacent (kəm'pleɪs°nt) *adj* extremely self-satisfied. [C17: from L *complacēns* very pleasing, from *complacēre*, from *com-* (intensive) + *placēre* to please]
▸ com'placently *adv*

complain (kəm'pleɪn) *vb* (*intr*) **1** to express resentment, displeasure, etc.; grumble. **2** (foll. by *of*) to state the presence of pain, illness, etc.: *she complained of a headache*. [C14: from OF *complaindre*, from Vulgar L *complangere* (unattested), from L *com-* (intensive) + *plangere* to bewail]
▸ com'plainer *n* ▸ com'plainingly *adv*

complainant (kəm'pleɪnənt) *n Law*. a plaintiff.

complaint (kəm'pleɪnt) n **1** the act of complaining. **2** a cause for complaining; grievance. **3** a mild ailment.

complaisant (kəm'pleɪz°nt) adj showing a desire to comply or oblige; polite. [C17: from F complaire, from L complacēre to please greatly; cf. COMPLACENT]
▶ com'plaisance n

complement n ('kɒmplɪmənt). **1** a person or thing that completes something. **2** a complete amount, number, etc. (often in **full complement**). **3** the officers and crew needed to man a ship. **4** Grammar. a word, phrase, or clause that completes the meaning of the predicate, as an idiot in He is an idiot or that he would be early in I hoped that he would be early. **5** Maths. the angle that when added to a specified angle produces a right angle. **6** Logic. the class of all the things that are not members of a given class. **7** Immunol. a group of proteins in the blood serum that, when activated by antibodies, destroys alien cells, such as bacteria. ◆ vb ('kɒmplɪˌment). **8** (tr) to complete or form a complement to. [C14: from L complēmentum, from complēre, from com- (intensive) + plēre to fill]
▶ ˌcomplemen'tation n

USAGE NOTE Avoid confusion with **compliment**.

complementary (ˌkɒmplɪ'mentərɪ) adj **1** forming a complement. **2** forming a satisfactory or balanced whole. **3** involving or using the treatments and techniques of alternative (complementary) medicine.
▶ ˌcomple'mentarily adv ▶ ˌcomple'mentariness n

complementary angle n either of two angles whose sum is 90°. Cf. **supplementary angle**.

complementary colour n one of any pair of colours, such as yellow and blue, that give white or grey when mixed in the correct proportions.

complementary DNA n a form of DNA artificially synthesized from a messenger RNA template and used in genetic engineering to produce gene clones. Abbrev.: **cDNA**.

complementary medicine n another name for **alternative medicine**.

complete (kəm'pliːt) adj **1** having every necessary part; entire. **2** finished. **3** (prenominal) thorough: he is a complete rogue. **4** perfect in quality or kind: he is a complete scholar. **5** (of a logical system) constituted such that a contradiction or inconsistency arises on the addition of an axiom that cannot be deduced from the axioms of the system. **6** Arch. skilled; accomplished. ◆ vb **completes, completing, completed.** (tr) **7** to make perfect. **8** to finish. **9** (in land law) to pay any outstanding balance on a contract for the conveyance of land in exchange for the title deeds, so that the ownership of the land changes hands. **10** American football. (of a quarterback) to make a forward pass successfully. [C14: from L complētus, p.p. of complēre to fill up; see COMPLEMENT]
▶ com'pletely adv ▶ com'pleteness n ▶ com'pletion n

completist (kəm'pliːtɪst) n a person who collects objects or memorabilia obsessively.

complex ('kɒmpleks) adj **1** made up of interconnected parts. **2** (of thoughts, writing, etc.) intricate. **3** Maths. **3a** of or involving complex numbers. **3b** consisting of a real and an imaginary part, either of which can be zero. ◆ n **4** a whole made up of related parts: a building complex. **5** Psychoanal. a group of emotional impulses that have been banished from the conscious mind but continue to influence a person's behaviour. **6** Inf. an obsession: he's got a complex about cats. **7** any chemical compound in which one molecule is linked to another by a coordinate bond. [C17: from L complexus, from complectī, from com- together + plectere to braid]
▶ 'complexness n

USAGE NOTE Complex is sometimes wrongly used where complicated is meant. Complex is properly used to say only that something consists of several parts. It should not be used to say that, because something consists of many parts, it is difficult to understand or analyse.

complex fraction n Maths. a fraction in which the numerator or denominator or both contain fractions. Also called: **compound fraction**.

complexion (kəm'plekʃən) n **1** the colour and general appearance of a person's skin, esp. of the face. **2** aspect or nature: the general complexion of a nation's finances. **3** Obs. temperament. [C14: from L complexiō a combination, from complectī to embrace; see COMPLEX]
▶ com'plexional adj

complexioned (kəm'plekʃənd) adj of a specified complexion: light-complexioned.

complexity (kəm'pleksɪtɪ) n, pl **complexities. 1** the state or quality of being intricate or complex. **2** something intricate or complex; complication.

complex number n any number of the form $a + bi$, where a and b are real numbers and $i = \sqrt{-1}$.

complex sentence n Grammar. a sentence containing at least one main clause and one subordinate clause.

compliance (kəm'plaɪəns) or **compliancy** n **1** acquiescence. **2** a disposition to yield to others. **3** a measure of the ability of a mechanical system to respond to an applied vibrating force.

compliance officer or **lawyer** n a specialist, usually a lawyer, employed by a financial group operating in a variety of fields and for multiple clients to ensure that no conflict of interest arises and that all obligations and regulations are complied with.

compliant (kəm'plaɪənt) adj complying, obliging, or yielding.
▶ com'pliantly adv

complicate vb ('kɒmplɪˌkeɪt), **complicates, complicating, complicated. 1** to make or become complex, etc. ◆ adj ('kɒmplɪkɪt). **2** Biol. folded on itself: a complicate leaf. [C17: from L complicāre to fold together]

complicated ('kɒmplɪˌkeɪtɪd) adj made up of intricate parts or aspects that are difficult to understand or analyse.
▶ 'compliˌcatedly adv

complication (ˌkɒmplɪ'keɪʃən) n **1** a condition, event, etc., that is complex or confused. **2** the act of complicating. **3** an event or condition that complicates or frustrates: her coming was a serious complication. **4** a disease arising as a consequence of another.

complicity (kəm'plɪsɪtɪ) n, pl **complicities. 1** the fact of being an accomplice, esp. in a criminal act. **2** a less common word for **complexity**.

compliment n ('kɒmplɪmənt). **1** a remark or act expressing respect, admiration, etc. **2** (usually pl) a greeting of respect or regard. ◆ vb ('kɒmplɪˌment). (tr) **3** to express admiration for; congratulate. **4** to express or show regard for, esp. by a gift. [C17: from F, from It. complimento, from Sp. cumplimiento, from cumplir to complete]

USAGE NOTE Avoid confusion with **complement**.

complimentary (ˌkɒmplɪ'mentərɪ) adj **1** conveying a compliment. **2** flattering. **3** given free, esp. as a courtesy or for publicity purposes.
▶ ˌcompli'mentarily adv

compline ('kɒmplɪn, -plaɪn) or **complin** ('kɒmplɪn) n RC Church. the last of the seven canonical hours of the divine office. [C13: from OF complie, from Med. L hōra complēta, lit.: the completed hour]

comply (kəm'plaɪ) vb **complies, complying, complied.** (intr) (usually foll. by with) to act in accordance with rules, wishes, etc.; to be obedient (to). [C17: from It. complire, from Sp. cumplir to complete]

compo ('kɒmpəʊ) n, pl **compos. 1** a mixture of materials, such as mortar, plaster, etc. **2** Austral. & NZ inf. compensation, esp. for injury or loss of work. ◆ adj **3** Mil. intended to last for several days: a compo pack. [short for composition, compensation, composite]

component (kəm'pəʊnənt) n **1** a constituent part or aspect of something more complex. **2** any electrical device that has distinct electrical characteristics and may be

connected to other devices to form a circuit. **3** *Maths.* one of a set of two or more vectors whose resultant is a given vector. **4** See **phase rule.** ◆ *adj* **5** forming or functioning as a part or aspect; constituent. [C17: from L *compōnere* to put together]
▶ **componential** (ˌkɒmpə'nɛnʃəl) *adj*

comport (kəm'pɔːt) *vb* **1** (*tr*) to conduct or bear (oneself) in a specified way. **2** (*intr*; foll. by *with*) to agree (with). [C16: from L *comportāre* collect, from *com-* together + *portāre* to carry]
▶ **com'portment** *n*

compose (kəm'pəuz) *vb* **composes, composing, composed.** (*mainly tr*) **1** to put together or make up. **2** to be the component elements of. **3** to create (a musical or literary work). **4** (*intr*) to write music. **5** to calm (someone, esp. oneself); make quiet. **6** to adjust or settle (a quarrel, etc.). **7** to order the elements of (a painting, sculpture, etc.); design. **8** *Printing.* to set up (type). [C15: from OF *composer,* from L *compōnere* to put in place]

composed (kəm'pəuzd) *adj* (of people) calm; tranquil.
▶ **composedly** (kəm'pəuzɪdlɪ) *adv*

composer (kəm'pəuzə) *n* **1** a person who composes music. **2** a person or machine that composes anything, esp. type for printing.

composite *adj* (kɒm'pɒzɪt). **1** composed of separate parts; compound. **2** of or belonging to the plant family Compositae. **3** *Maths.* capable of being factorized: *a composite function.* **4** (*sometimes cap.*) denoting one of the five classical orders of architecture: characterized by a combination of the Ionic and Corinthian styles. ◆ *n* ('kɒmpəzɪt). **5** something composed of separate parts; compound. **6** any plant of the family Compositae, having flower heads composed of many small flowers (e.g. dandelion, daisy). **7** a material, such as reinforced concrete, made of two or more distinct materials. **8** a proposal that has been composited. ◆ *vb* ('kɒmpə‚zaɪt), **composites, compositing, composited.** (*tr*) **9** to merge related motions from local branches (of a political party, trade union, etc.) so as to produce a manageable number of proposals for discussion at national level. [C16: from L *compositus* well arranged, from *compōnere* to arrange]
▶ **'compositely** *adv* ▶ **'compositeness** *n*

composite school *n* E. Canad. a secondary school offering both academic and nonacademic courses.

composition (ˌkɒmpə'zɪʃən) *n* **1** the act of putting together or making up by combining parts. **2** something formed in this manner; a mixture. **3** the parts of which something is composed; constitution. **4** a work of music, art, or literature. **5** the harmonious arrangement of the parts of a work of art in relation to each other. **6** a piece of writing undertaken as an academic exercise; an essay. **7** *Printing.* the act or technique of setting up type. **8** a settlement by mutual consent, esp. a legal agreement whereby the creditors agree to accept partial payment of a debt in full settlement. [C14: from OF, from L *compositus*; see COMPOSITE, -ION]

compositor (kəm'pɒzɪtə) *n Printing.* a person who sets and corrects type.

compos mentis *Latin.* ('kɒmpəs 'mɛntɪs) *adj* (*postpositive*) of sound mind; sane.

compost ('kɒmpɒst) *n* **1** a mixture of organic residues such as decomposed vegetation, manure, etc., used as a fertilizer. **2** a mixture, as of sand, peat, and charcoal, in which plants are grown, esp. in pots. **3** *Rare.* a mixture. ◆ *vb* (*tr*) **4** to make (vegetable matter) into compost. **5** to fertilize with compost. [C14: from OF *compost,* from L *compositus* put together]

Compostela ★ (*Spanish* kɒmpɒs'tela) *n* See **Santiago de Compostela.**

composure (kəm'pəuʒə) *n* calmness, esp. of the mind; tranquillity; serenity.

compote ('kɒmpəut) *n* a dish of fruit stewed with sugar or in a syrup. [C17: from F *composte,* from L *compositus* put in place]

compound[1] *n* ('kɒmpaund). **1** a substance that contains atoms of two or more chemical elements held together by chemical bonds. **2** any combination of two or more parts, aspects, etc. **3** a word formed from two existing

words or combining forms. ◆ *vb* (kəm'paund). (*mainly tr*) **4** to combine so as to create a compound. **5** to make by combining parts, aspects, etc.: *to compound a new plastic.* **6** to intensify by an added element: *his anxiety was compounded by her crying.* **7** (*also intr*) to come to an agreement in (a dispute, etc.) or to settle (a debt, etc.) for less than what is owed; compromise. **8** *Law.* to agree not to prosecute in return for a consideration: *to compound a crime.* ◆ *adj* ('kɒmpaund). **9** composed of two or more parts, elements, etc. **10** (of a word) consisting of elements that are also words or combining forms. **11** *Grammar.* (of tense, mood, etc.) formed by using an auxiliary verb in addition to the main verb. **12** *Music.* denoting a time in which the number of beats per bar is a multiple of three: *six-four is an example of compound time.* **12b** (of an interval) greater than an octave. **13** (of a steam engine, etc.) having multiple stages in which the steam or working fluid from one stage is used in a subsequent stage. **14** (of a piston engine) having a supercharger powered by a turbine in the exhaust stream. [C14: from earlier *compounen,* from OF *compondre* to set in order, from L *compōnere*]
▶ **com'poundable** *adj*

compound[2] ('kɒmpaund) *n* **1** (esp. formerly in South Africa) an enclosure, esp. on the mines, containing the living quarters for Black workers. **2** any similar enclosure, such as a camp for prisoners of war. [C17: from Malay *kampong* village]

compound eye *n* the convex eye of insects and some crustaceans, consisting of numerous separate light-sensitive units (ommatidia).

compound fraction *n* another name for **complex fraction.**

compound fracture *n* a fracture in which the broken bone pierces the skin.

compound interest *n* interest calculated on both the principal and its accrued interest.

compound leaf *n* a leaf consisting of two or more leaflets borne on the same leafstalk.

compound number *n* a quantity expressed in two or more different but related units: *3 hours 10 seconds is a compound number.*

compound sentence *n* a sentence containing at least two coordinate clauses.

compound time *n* See **compound**[1] (sense 12).

comprehend (ˌkɒmprɪ'hɛnd) *vb* **1** to understand. **2** (*tr*) to comprise; include. [C14: from L *comprehendere,* from *prehendere* to seize]

comprehensible (ˌkɒmprɪ'hɛnsəb'l) *adj* capable of being comprehended.
▶ **compre‚hensi'bility** *n* ▶ **compre'hensibly** *adv*

comprehension (ˌkɒmprɪ'hɛnʃən) *n* **1** the act or capacity of understanding. **2** the state of including; comprehensiveness.

comprehensive (ˌkɒmprɪ'hɛnsɪv) *adj* **1** of broad scope or content. **2** (of a car insurance policy) providing protection against most risks, including third-party liability, fire, theft, and damage. **3** of or being a comprehensive school. ◆ *n* **4** short for **comprehensive school.**
▶ **compre'hensively** *adv* ▶ **compre'hensiveness** *n*

comprehensive school *n Chiefly Brit.* a secondary school for children of all abilities from the same district.

compress *vb* (kəm'prɛs). **1** (*tr*) to squeeze together; condense. ◆ *n* ('kɒmprɛs). **2** a cloth or gauze pad applied firmly to some part of the body to relieve discomfort, reduce fever, etc. [C14: from LL *compressāre,* from L *comprimere,* from *premere* to press]
▶ **com'pressible** *adj* ▶ **com'pressive** *adj*

compressed air *n* air at a higher pressure than atmospheric pressure: used esp. as a source of power for machines.

compressibility (kəm‚prɛsɪ'bɪlɪtɪ) *n* **1** the ability to be compressed. **2** *Physics.* the reciprocal of the bulk modulus; the ratio of volume strain to stress at constant temperature. Symbol: k

compression (kəm'prɛʃən) *n* **1** the act of compressing or the condition of being compressed. **2** an increase in pressure of the charge in an engine or compressor obtained by reducing its volume.

:ompressor (kəm'presə) *n* **1** any device that compresses a gas. **2** the part of a gas turbine that compresses the air before it enters the combustion chambers. **3** any muscle that causes compression. **4** an electronic device for reducing the variation in signal amplitude in a transmission system.

:omprise (kəm'praız) *vb* **comprises, comprising, comprised.** (*tr*) **1** to be made up of. **2** to constitute the whole of; consist of: *her singing comprised the entertainment.* [C15: from F *compris* included, from *comprendre* to COMPREHEND]
▶ **com'prisable** *adj*

> **USAGE NOTE** The use of *of* after *comprise* should be avoided: *the library comprises* (not *comprises of*) *500,000 books and manuscripts.*

:ompromise ('kɒmprə,maız) *n* **1** settlement of a dispute by concessions on both or all sides. **2** the terms of such a settlement. **3** something midway between different things. ◆ *vb* **compromises, compromising, compromised. 4** to settle (a dispute) by making concessions. **5** (*tr*) to expose (oneself or another) to disrepute. [C15: from OF *compromis*, from L, from *comprōmittere*, from *prōmittere* to promise]
▶ **'compro,miser** *n* ▶ **'compro,misingly** *adv*

compte rendu *French.* (kɔ̃t rãdy) *n, pl* **comptes rendus** (kɔ̃t rãdy). **1** a review or notice. **2** an account. [lit.: account rendered]

Compton ★ *n* **1** ('kɒmptən). **Arthur Holly.** 1892–1962, US physicist, noted for his research on X-rays, gamma rays, and nuclear energy: Nobel prize for physics 1927. **2** ('kʌmptən). **Denis.** 1918–97, English cricketer, who played for Middlesex and England (1937–57).

Compton-Burnett ★ ('kɒmptənbɜː'nɛt, -'bɜːnɪt) *n* Dame **Ivy.** 1884–1969, British novelist. Her novels include *Men and Wives* (1931) and *Mother and Son* (1955).

comptroller (kən'trəulə) *n* a variant spelling of **controller** (sense 2), esp. as a title of any of various financial executives.

compulsion (kəm'pʌlʃən) *n* **1** the act of compelling or the state of being compelled. **2** something that compels. **3** *Psychiatry.* an inner drive that causes a person to perform actions, often repetitive, against his or her will. See also **obsession.** [C15: from OF, from L *compellere* to COMPEL]

compulsive (kəm'pʌlsɪv) *adj* relating to or involving compulsion.
▶ **com'pulsively** *adv*

compulsory (kəm'pʌlsərɪ) *adj* **1** required by regulations or laws; obligatory. **2** involving or employing compulsion; compelling; essential.
▶ **com'pulsorily** *adv* ▶ **com'pulsoriness** *n*

compulsory purchase *n* purchase of a property by a local authority or government department for public use or development, regardless of whether or not the owner wishes to sell.

compunction (kəm'pʌŋkʃən) *n* a feeling of remorse, guilt, or regret. [C14: from Church L *compunctiō*, from L *compungere* to sting]
▶ **com'punctious** *adj* ▶ **com'punctiously** *adv*

computation (,kɒmpju'teɪʃən) *n* a calculation involving numbers or quantities.
▶ **,compu'tational** *adj*

compute (kəm'pju:t) *vb* **computes, computing, computed.** to calculate (an answer, result, etc.), often with the aid of a computer. [C17: from L *computāre*, from *putāre* to think]
▶ **com'putable** *adj* ▶ **com,puta'bility** *n*

computed tomography *n Med.* another name (esp. US) for **computerized tomography.**

computer (kəm'pju:tə) *n* **1a** a device, usually electronic, that processes data according to a set of instructions. The **digital computer** stores data in discrete units and performs operations at very high speed. The **analog computer** has no memory and is slower than the digital computer but has a continuous rather than a discrete input. **1b** (*as modifier*): *computer technology.* **2** a person who computes or calculates.

computer-aided design *n* the use of computer techniques in designing products, esp. involving the use of computer graphics. Abbrev.: **CAD.**

computer-aided engineering *n* the use of computers to automate manufacturing processes. Abbrev.: **CAE.**

computer architecture *n* the structure, behaviour, and design of computing.

computerate (kəm'pju:tərɪt) *adj* able to use computing. [C20: COMPUTER + -ATE[1], by analogy with *literate*]

computer dating *n* the use of computers by dating agencies to match their clients.

computer game *n* any of various games, recorded on cassette or disc for use in a home computer, that are played by manipulating a mouse, joystick or the keys on the keyboard of a computer in response to the graphics on the screen.

computer graphics *n* (*functioning as sing*) the use of a computer to produce and manipulate pictorial images on a video screen, as in animation techniques or the production of audiovisual aids.

computerize *or* **computerise** (kəm'pju:tə,raız) *vb* **computerizes, computerizing, computerized** *or* **computerises, computerising, computerised. 1** (*tr*) to cause (certain operations) to be performed by a computer, esp. as a replacement for human labour. **2** (*intr*) to install a computer. **3** (*tr*) to control or perform (operations) by means of a computer. **4** (*tr*) to process or store (information) by or in a computer.
▶ **com,puteri'zation** *or* **com,puteri'sation** *n*

computerized tomography *n Med.* a radiological technique that produces images of cross sections through a patient's body. Also called (esp. US): **computed tomography.** Abbrev.: **CT.** See also **CT scanner.**

computer language *n* another term for **programming language.**

computer science *n* the study of computers and their application.

comrade ('kɒmreɪd, -rɪd) *n* **1** a companion. **2** a fellow member of a political party, esp. a fellow Communist. [C16: from F *camarade*, from Sp. *camarada* group of soldiers sharing a billet, from *cámara* room, from L]
▶ **'comradely** *adj* ▶ **'comrade,ship** *n*

Comsat ('kɒmsæt) *n Trademark.* short for **communications satellite.**

Comte ★ (*French* kɔ̃t) *n* (**Isidore**) **Auguste (Marie François)** (ogyst). 1798–1857, French mathematician and philosopher; the founder of positivism.
▶ **Comtism** ('kɔːn,tɪzəm) *n* ▶ **'Comtist** *or* **'Comtian** *adj, n*

Comus ★ ('kəuməs) *n* (in late Roman mythology) a god of revelry. [C17: from L, from Gk *kōmos* a revel]

con[1] (kɒn) *Inf.* ◆ *n* **1a** short for **confidence trick. 1b** (*as modifier*): *con man.* ◆ *vb* **cons, conning, conned. 2** (*tr*) to swindle or defraud. [C19: from CONFIDENCE]

con[2] (kɒn) *n* (*usually pl*) an argument or vote against a proposal, motion, etc. See also **pros and cons.** [from L *contrā* against]

con[3] *or esp. US* **conn** (kɒn) *vb* **cons** *or esp. US* **conns, conning, conned.** (*tr*) *Naut.* to direct the steering of (a vessel). [C17 *cun*, from earlier *condien* to guide, from OF *conduire*, from L *condūcere*; see CONDUCT]

con[4] (kɒn) *vb* **cons, conning, conned.** (*tr*) *Arch.* to study attentively or learn. [C15: var. of CAN[1] in the sense: to come to know]

con[5] (kɒn) *prep Music.* with. [It.]

con. *abbrev. for:* **1** concerto. **2** conclusion. **3** connection. **4** consolidated. **5** continued.

con- *prefix* a variant of **com-.**

Conakry *or* **Konakri** ★ (*French* kɔnakri) *n* the capital of Guinea, a port on the island of Tombo. Pop.: 1 508 000 (1995 est.).

con amore (kɒn æ'mɔːrɪ) *adj, adv Music.* (to be performed) lovingly. [C19: from It.: with love]

Conan Doyle ★ ('kəʊnən 'dɔɪl, 'kɒnən) n Sir **Arthur**. 1859–1930, British author of detective stories and creator of *Sherlock Holmes*.

con brio (kɒn 'briːəʊ) *adj, adv Music*. (to be performed) with liveliness or spirit. [It.: with energy]

concatenate (kɒn'kætɪˌneɪt) vb **concatenates, concatenating, concatenated**. (*tr*) to link or join together, esp. in a chain or series. [C16: from LL *concatēnāre*, from L *com*-together + *catēna* CHAIN]
▶ ˌconcate'nation n

concave ('kɒnkeɪv, kɒn'keɪv) *adj* **1** curving inwards; having the shape of a section of the interior of a sphere, paraboloid, etc.: *a concave lens*. ◆ vb **2** (*tr*) to make concave. [C15: from L *concavus* arched, from *cavus* hollow]
▶ 'concavely *adv* ▶ 'concaveness n

concavity (kɒn'kævɪtɪ) n, pl **concavities**. **1** the state of being concave. **2** a concave surface or thing.

concavo-concave (kɒnˌkeɪvəʊkɒn'keɪv) *adj* (esp. of a lens) having both sides concave.

concavo-convex *adj* **1** having one side concave and the other side convex. **2** (of a lens) having a concave face with greater curvature than the convex face.

conceal (kən'siːl) vb (*tr*) **1** to keep from discovery; hide. **2** to keep secret. [C14: from OF *conceler*, from L *concēlāre*, from *com*- (intensive) + *cēlāre* to hide]
▶ con'cealer n ▶ con'cealment n

concede (kən'siːd) vb **concedes, conceding, conceded**. **1** (when *tr, may take a clause as object*) to admit or acknowledge (something) as true or correct. **2** to yield or allow (something, such as a right). **3** (*tr*) to admit as certain in outcome: *to concede an election*. [C17: from L *concēdere*, from *cēdere* to give way]
▶ con'ceder n

conceit (kən'siːt) n **1** a high, often exaggerated, opinion of oneself or one's accomplishments. **2** *Literary*. an elaborate image or far-fetched comparison. **3** *Arch*. **3a** a witty expression. **3b** fancy; imagination. **3c** an idea. ◆ vb (*tr*) **4** *Obs*. to think. [C14: from CONCEIVE]

conceited (kən'siːtɪd) *adj* having an exaggerated opinion of oneself or one's accomplishments.
▶ con'ceitedly *adv* ▶ con'ceitedness n

conceivable (kən'siːvəbᵊl) *adj* capable of being understood, believed, or imagined; possible.
▶ conˌceiva'bility n ▶ con'ceivably *adv*

conceive (kən'siːv) vb **conceives, conceiving, conceived**. **1** (when *intr*, foll. by *of*; when *tr, often takes a clause as object*) to have an idea (of); imagine; think. **2** (*tr; takes a clause as object or an infinitive*) to believe. **3** (*tr*) to develop: *she conceived a passion for music*. **4** to become pregnant with (a child). **5** (*tr*) *Rare*. to express in words. [C13: from OF *conceivre*, from L *concipere* to take in, from *capere* to take]

concelebrate (kən'selɪˌbreɪt) vb **concelebrates, concelebrating, concelebrated**. *Christianity*. to celebrate (the Eucharist or Mass) jointly with one or more other priests. [C16: from L *concelebrāre*]
▶ conˌcele'bration n

concentrate ('kɒnsənˌtreɪt) vb **concentrates, concentrating, concentrated**. **1** to come or cause to come to a single purpose or aim: *to concentrate one's hopes on winning*. **2** to make or become denser or purer by the removal of certain elements. **3** (*intr; often foll. by on*) to think intensely (about). ◆ n **4** a concentrated material or solution. [C17: back formation from CONCENTRATION, ult. from L *com*- same + *centrum* CENTRE]
▶ 'concenˌtrative *adj* ▶ 'concenˌtrator n

concentration (ˌkɒnsən'treɪʃən) n **1** intense mental application. **2** the act of concentrating. **3** something that is concentrated. **4** the strength of a solution, esp. the amount of dissolved substance in a given volume of solvent. **5** *Mil*. **5a** the act of bringing together military forces. **5b** the application of fire from a number of weapons against a target.

concentration camp n a guarded prison camp for nonmilitary prisoners, esp. one in Nazi Germany.

concentre or *US* **concenter** (kən'sentə) vb **concentres, concentring, concentred** or *US* **concenters, concentering,**

concentered. to converge or cause to converge on a common centre; concentrate. [C16: from F *concentrer*]

concentric (kən'sentrɪk) *adj* having a common centre: *concentric circles*. [C14: from Med. L *concentricus*, from L *com*- same + *centrum* CENTRE]
▶ con'centrically *adv*

Concepción ★ (*Spanish* kɒnθep'θjɒn) n an industrial city in S central Chile. Pop.: 350 268 (1995 est.).

concept ('kɒnsept) n **1** an idea, esp. an abstract idea: *the concepts of biology*. **2** *Philosophy*. a general idea that corresponds to some class of entities and consists of the essential features of the class. **3** a new idea; invention. **4** (*modifier*) (of a product, esp. a car) created to demonstrate the technical skills and imagination of the designers, and not for mass production or sale. [C16: from L *conceptum*, from *concipere* to CONCEIVE]

conception (kən'sepʃən) n **1** something conceived; notion, idea, or plan. **2** the description under which someone considers something: *a strange conception of freedom*. **3** the fertilization of an ovum by a sperm in the Fallopian tube followed by implantation in the womb. **4** origin or beginning. [C13: from L *conceptiō*, from *concipere* to CONCEIVE]
▶ con'ceptional or con'ceptive *adj*

conceptual (kən'septjuəl) *adj* of or characterized by concepts.
▶ con'ceptually *adv*

conceptualize or **conceptualise** (kən'septjuəˌlaɪz) vb **conceptualizes, conceptualizing, conceptualized** or **conceptualises, conceptualising, conceptualised**. to form (a concept or concepts) out of observations, experience, data, etc.
▶ conˌceptuali'zation or conˌceptuali'sation n

concern (kən'sɜːn) vb (*tr*) **1** to relate to; affect. **2** (usually foll. by *with* or *in*) to involve or interest (oneself): *he concerns himself with other people's affairs*. ◆ n **3** something that affects a person; affair; business. **4** regard or interest: *he felt a strong concern for her*. **5** anxiety or solicitude. **6** important relation: *his news has great concern for us*. **7** a commercial company. **8** *Inf*. a material thing, esp. one of which one has a low opinion. [C15: from LL *concernere*, from L *com*- together + *cernere* to sift]

concerned (kən'sɜːnd) *adj* **1** (*postpositive*) interested, guilty, or involved: *I shall find the boy concerned and punish him*. **2** worried or solicitous.
▶ **concernedly** (kən'sɜːnɪdlɪ) *adv*

concerning (kən'sɜːnɪŋ) *prep* **1** about; regarding. ◆ *adj* **2** worrying or troublesome.

concernment (kən'sɜːnmənt) n *Rare*. affair or business; concern.

concert n ('kɒnsɜːt). **1a** a performance of music by players or singers that does not involve theatrical staging. **1b** (*as modifier*): *a concert version of an opera*. **2** agreement in design, plan, or action. **3 in concert**. **3a** acting with a common purpose. **3b** (of musicians, etc.) performing live. ◆ vb (kən'sɜːt). **4** to arrange or contrive (a plan) by mutual agreement. [C16: from F *concerter* to bring into agreement, from It., from LL *concertāre* to work together, from L *certāre* to contend]

concertante (ˌkɒntʃə'tæntɪ) *adj Music*. characterized by contrasting alternating tutti and solo passages. [It.: from *concertare* to perform a CONCERT]

concerted (kən'sɜːtɪd) *adj* **1** mutually contrived, planned, or arranged; combined: *a concerted effort*. **2** *Music*. arranged in parts for a group of singers or players.

Concertgebouw ★ (*Dutch* kɒn'sɛrtxəbɔu) n a concert hall in Amsterdam, inaugurated in 1888: the **Concertgebouw Orchestra**, established in 1888, has been independent of the hall since World War II.

concert grand n a grand piano of the largest size.

concertina (ˌkɒnsə'tiːnə) n **1** a hexagonal musical instrument similar to the accordion, in which metallic reeds are vibrated by air from a set of bellows operated by the player's hands. ◆ vb **concertinas, concertinaing, concertinaed**. **2** (*intr*) to collapse or fold up like the bellows of a concertina. [C19: CONCERT + *-ina*]
▶ ˌconcer'tinist n

concertino (ˌkɒntʃə'tiːnəʊ) n, pl **concertini** (-nɪ). *Music*. **1**

the solo group in a concerto grosso. **2** a short concerto. [It.: a little CONCERTO]

oncertmaster ('kɒnsət,mɑːstə) *n* a US and Canad. word for **leader** (of an orchestra).

concerto (kən'tʃeətəu) *n, pl* **concertos** *or* **concerti** (-tɪ). a composition for an orchestra and one or more soloists. [C18: from It.: CONCERT]

concerto grosso ('grɒsəu) *n, pl* **concerti grossi** ('grɒsɪ) *or* **concerto grossos.** a composition for an orchestra and a group of soloists. [It., lit.: big concerto]

concert party *n* **1** a musical entertainment popular in the early 20th century, esp. one at a British seaside resort. **2** *Stock Exchange inf.* a group of individuals or companies who secretly agree together to purchase shares separately in a particular company which they plan to amalgamate later into a single holding: a malpractice which is illegal in some countries.

concert pitch *n* **1** the frequency of 440 hertz assigned to the A above middle C. **2** *Inf.* a state of extreme readiness.

concession (kən'seʃən) *n* **1** the act of yielding or conceding. **2** something conceded. **3** *Brit.* a reduction in the usual price of a ticket granted to a special group of customers: *a student concession*. **4** any grant of rights, land, or property by a government, local authority, corporation, or individual. **5** the right, esp. an exclusive right, to market a particular product in a given area. **6** *Canad.* **6a** a land subdivision in a township survey. **6b** another name for a **concession road.** [C16: from L *concéssiō*, from *concēdere* to CONCEDE]
▶ **con'cessible** *adj* ▶ **con'cessive** *adj*

concessionaire (kən,seʃə'neə), **concessioner** (kən-'seʃənə), *or* **concessionary** *n* someone who holds or operates a concession.

concessionary (kən'seʃənərɪ) *adj* **1** of, granted, or obtained by a concession. ◆ *n, pl* **concessionaries. 2** another word for **concessionaire.**

concession road *n Canad.* one of a series of roads separating concessions in a township.

conch (kɒŋk, kɒntʃ) *n, pl* **conchs** (kɒŋks) *or* **conches** ('kɒntʃɪz). **1** any of various tropical marine gastropod molluscs characterized by a large brightly coloured spiral shell. **2** the shell of such a mollusc, used as a trumpet. [C16: from L *concha*, from Gk *konkhē* shellfish]

conchie *or* **conchy** ('kɒntʃɪ) *n, pl* **conchies.** *Inf.* short for **conscientious objector.**

Conchobar ★ ('kɒŋkəuwə, 'kɒnuə) *n* (in Irish legend) a king of Ulster at about the beginning of the Christian era. See also **Deirdre.**

conchology (kɒŋ'kɒlədʒɪ) *n* the study of mollusc shells.
▶ **con'chologist** *n*

concierge (,kɒnsɪ'ɛəʒ) *n* (esp. in France) a caretaker of a block of flats, hotel, etc., esp. one who lives on the premises. [C17: from F, ult. from L *conservus*, from *servus* slave]

conciliar (kən'sɪlɪə) *adj* of, from, or by means of a council, esp. an ecclesiastical one.

conciliate (kən'sɪlɪ,eɪt) *vb* **conciliates, conciliating, conciliated.** *(tr)* **1** to overcome the hostility of; win over. **2** to gain (favour, regard, etc.), esp. by making friendly overtures. [C16: from L *conciliāre* to bring together, from *concilium* COUNCIL]
▶ **con'ciliable** *adj* ▶ **con'cili,ator** *n*

conciliation (kən,sɪlɪ'eɪʃən) *n* **1** the act or process of conciliating. **2** a method of helping the parties in a dispute to reach agreement, esp. divorcing or separating couples to part amicably.

conciliatory (kən'sɪlɪətərɪ) *or* **conciliative** (kən-'sɪljətɪv) *adj* intended to placate or reconcile.
▶ **con'ciliatorily** *adv*

concise (kən'saɪs) *adj* brief and to the point. [C16: from L *concīsus* cut short, from *concīdere*, from *caedere* to cut, strike down]
▶ **con'cisely** *adv* ▶ **con'ciseness** *or* **concision** (kən'sɪʒən) *n*

conclave ('kɒnkleɪv) *n* **1** a secret meeting. **2** *RC Church.* **2a** the closed apartments where the college of cardinals

elects a new pope. **2b** a meeting of the college of cardinals for this purpose. [C14: from Med. L *conclāve*, from L: place that may be locked, from *clāvis* key]

conclude (kən'kluːd) *vb* **concludes, concluding, concluded.** (*mainly tr*) **1** (*also intr*) to come or cause to come to an end. **2** (*takes a clause as object*) to decide by reasoning; deduce: *the judge concluded that the witness had told the truth.* **3** to settle: *to conclude a treaty.* **4** *Obs.* to confine. [C14: from L *conclūdere*, from *claudere* to close]

conclusion (kən'kluːʒən) *n* **1** end or termination. **2** the last main division of a speech, essay, etc. **3** outcome or result (esp. in **a foregone conclusion**). **4** a final decision or judgment (esp. in **come to a conclusion**). **5** *Logic.* **5a** a statement that purports to follow from another or others (the **premises**) by means of an argument. **5b** a statement that does validly follow from given premises. **6** *Law.* **6a** an admission or statement binding on the party making it; estoppel. **6b** the close of a pleading or of a conveyance. **7** **in conclusion.** lastly; to sum up. **8 jump to conclusions.** to come to a conclusion prematurely, without sufficient thought or on incomplete evidence. [C14: via OF from L; see CONCLUDE, -ION]

conclusive (kən'kluːsɪv) *adj* **1** putting an end to doubt; decisive; final. **2** approaching or involving an end.
▶ **con'clusively** *adv*

concoct (kən'kɒkt) *vb* (*tr*) **1** to make by combining different ingredients. **2** to invent; make up; contrive. [C16: from L *concoctus* cooked together, from *coquere* to cook]
▶ **con'cocter** *or* **con'coctor** *n* ▶ **con'coction** *n*

concomitance (kən'kɒmɪtəns) *n* **1** existence together. **2** *Christianity.* the doctrine that the body and blood of Christ are present in the Eucharist.

concomitant (kən'kɒmɪtənt) *adj* **1** existing or occurring together. ◆ *n* **2** a concomitant act, person, etc. [C17: from LL *concomitārī* to accompany, from *com-* with + *comes* companion]

concord ('kɒnkɔːd) *n* **1** agreement or harmony. **2** a treaty establishing peaceful relations between nations. **3** *Music.* a combination of musical notes, esp. one containing a series of consonant intervals. **4** *Grammar.* another word for **agreement** (sense 6). [C13: from OF *concorde*, from L *concordia*, from *com-* same + *cor* heart]

Concord ★ ('kɒŋkəd) *n* **1** a town in NE Massachusetts: scene of one of the opening military actions (1775) of the War of American Independence. Pop.: 17 080 (1990). **2** a city in New Hampshire, the state capital: printing, publishing. Pop.: 36 364 (1992).

concordance (kən'kɔːdⁿns) *n* **1** a state of harmony. **2** a book that indexes the principal words in a literary work, often with the immediate context and an account of the meaning. **3** an index produced by computer or machine.

concordant (kən'kɔːdⁿnt) *adj* being in agreement; harmonious.
▶ **con'cordantly** *adv*

concordat (kɒn'kɔːdæt) *n* a pact or treaty, esp. one between the Vatican and another state concerning the interests of religion in that state. [C17: via F from Med. L *concordātum*, from L: something agreed; see CONCORD]

concourse ('kɒnkɔːs) *n* **1** a crowd; throng. **2** a coming together; confluence. **3** a large open space for the gathering of people in a public place. [C14: from OF *concours*, ult. from L *concurrere* to run together]

concrete ('kɒnkriːt) *n* **1** a construction material made of cement, sand, stone and water that hardens to a stonelike mass. ◆ *adj* **2** relating to a particular instance; specific as opposed to general. **3** relating to things capable of being perceived by the senses, as opposed to abstractions. **4** formed by the coalescence of particles; condensed; solid. ◆ *vb* **concretes, concreting, concreted. 5** (*tr*) to construct in or cover with concrete. **6** (kən'kriːt). to become or cause to become solid; coalesce. [C14: from L *concrētus*, from *concrēscere* to grow together]
▶ **'concretely** *adv* ▶ **'concreteness** *n*

concrete music *n* music consisting of an electronically modified montage of tape-recorded sounds.

concrete noun *n* a noun that refers to a material object.

concrete poetry n poetry in which the visual form of the poem is used to convey meaning.

concretion (kən'kri:ʃən) n **1** the act of growing together; coalescence. **2** a solidified mass. **3** something made real, tangible, or specific. **4** a rounded or irregular mineral mass different in composition from the sedimentary rock that surrounds it. **5** Pathol. another word for **calculus**.
▶ con'cretionary adj

concretize or **concretise** ('kɒnkrɪˌtaɪz) vb **concretizes, concretizing, concretized** or **concretises, concretising, concretised**. (tr) to render concrete; make real or specific.

concubine ('kɒŋkjuˌbaɪn, 'kɒn-) n **1** (in polygamous societies) a secondary wife. **2** a woman who cohabits with a man, esp. (formerly) the mistress of a king, nobleman, etc. [C13: from OF, from L concubīna, from concumbere to lie together]
▶ **concubinage** (kɒn'kju:bɪnɪdʒ) n ▶ con'cubinary adj

concupiscence (kən'kju:pɪsəns) n strong desire, esp. sexual desire. [C14: from Church L concupiscentia, from L concupiscere to covet]
▶ con'cupiscent adj

concur (kən'kɜ:) vb **concurs, concurring, concurred**. (intr) **1** to agree; be in accord. **2** to combine or cooperate. **3** to occur simultaneously; coincide. [C15: from L concurrere to run together]

concurrence (kən'kʌrəns) n **1** the act of concurring. **2** agreement; accord. **3** cooperation or combination. **4** simultaneous occurrence.

concurrent (kən'kʌrənt) adj **1** taking place at the same time or in the same location. **2** cooperating. **3** meeting at, approaching, or having a common point: concurrent lines. **4** in agreement; harmonious.
▶ con'currently adv

concurrent engineering n a method of designing and marketing new products in which development stages are run in parallel rather than in series, to reduce lead times and costs. Also called: **interactive engineering**.

concuss (kən'kʌs) vb (tr) **1** to injure (the brain) by a violent blow, fall, etc. **2** to shake violently. [C16: from L concussus, from concutere to disturb greatly, from quatere to shake]

concussion (kən'kʌʃən) n **1** a jarring of the brain, caused by a blow or a fall, usually resulting in loss of consciousness. **2** any violent shaking.

Condé ★ (French kɔ̃de) n **Prince de** (prɛs də), title of Louis II de Bourbon, Duc d'Enghien, called the Great Condé. 1621–86, French general, who led Louis XIV's armies against the Fronde (1649) but joined the Fronde in a new revolt (1650–52).

condemn (kən'dɛm) vb (tr) **1** to express strong disapproval of. **2** to pronounce judicial sentence on. **3** to demonstrate the guilt of: his secretive behaviour condemned him. **4** to judge or pronounce unfit for use. **5** to force into a particular state: his disposition condemned him to boredom. [C13: from OF condempner, from L condemnāre, from damnāre to condemn]
▶ **condemnable** (kən'dɛmnəbªl) adj ▶ ˌcondem'nation n ▶ **condemnatory** (kən'dɛmnətərɪ) adj

condensate (kən'dɛnseɪt) n a substance formed by condensation.

condensation (ˌkɒndɛn'seɪʃən) n **1** the act or process of condensing, or the state of being condensed. **2** anything that has condensed from a vapour, esp. on a window. **3** Chem. a type of reaction in which two organic molecules combine to form a larger molecule as well as a simple molecule such as water, etc. **4** an abridged version of a book.
▶ ˌconden'sational adj

condensation trail n another name for **vapour trail**.

condense (kən'dɛns) vb **condenses, condensing, condensed**. **1** (tr) to increase the density of; compress. **2** to reduce or be reduced in volume or size. **3** to change or cause to change from a gaseous to a liquid or solid state. **4** Chem. to undergo or cause to undergo condensation. [C15: from L condēnsāre, from dēnsus DENSE]
▶ con'densable or con'densible adj

condensed matter n Physics. **a** crystalline and amorphous solids and liquids, including liquid crystals, glasses, polymers, and gels. **b** (as modifier): condensed matter physics.

condensed milk n milk reduced by evaporation to a thick concentration, with sugar added.

condenser (kən'dɛnsə) n **1a** an apparatus for reducing gases to their liquid or solid form by the abstraction of heat. **1b** a device for abstracting heat, as in a refrigeration unit. **2** a lens that concentrates light. **3** another name for **capacitor**. **4** a person or device that condenses.

condescend (ˌkɒndɪ'sɛnd) vb (intr) **1** to act graciously towards another or others regarded as being on a lower level; behave patronizingly. **2** to do something that one regards as below one's dignity. [C14: from Church L condēscendere, from L dēscendere to DESCEND]
▶ ˌconde'scending adj ▶ ˌconde'scendingly adv ▶ ˌconde'scension n

condign (kən'daɪn) adj (esp. of a punishment) fitting; deserved. [C15: from OF condigne, from L condignus, from dignus worthy]
▶ con'dignly adv

condiment ('kɒndɪmənt) n any spice or sauce such as salt, pepper, mustard, etc. [C15: from L condīmentum seasoning, from condīre to pickle]

condition (kən'dɪʃən) n **1** a particular state of being or existence: the human condition. **2** something that limits or restricts; a qualification. **3** (pl) circumstances: conditions were right for a takeover. **4** state of physical fitness, esp. good health: out of condition. **5** an ailment: a heart condition. **6** something indispensable: your happiness is a condition of mine. **7** something required as part of an agreement; term: the conditions of the lease are set out. **8** Law. **8a** a provision in a will, contract, etc., that makes some right or liability contingent upon the happening of some event. **8b** the event itself. **9** Logic. a statement whose truth is either required for the truth of a given statement (a **necessary condition**) or sufficient to guarantee the truth of the given statement (a **sufficient condition**). **10** rank, status, or position. **11 on condition that.** (conj) provided that. ◆ vb (mainly tr) **12** Psychol. **12a** to alter the response of (a person or animal) to a particular stimulus or situation. **12b** to establish a conditioned response in. **13** to put into a fit condition. **14** to improve the condition of (one's hair) by use of special cosmetics. **15** to accustom or inure. **16** to subject to a condition. [C14: from L conditiō, from condīcere to discuss, from con- together + dīcere to say]
▶ con'ditioner n ▶ con'ditioning n, adj

conditional (kən'dɪʃənªl) adj **1** depending on other factors. **2** Grammar. expressing a condition on which something else is contingent: "If he comes" is a conditional clause in the sentence "If he comes I shall go". **3** Logic. Also called: **hypothetical**. (of a proposition) consisting of two component propositions associated by the words if...then so that the proposition is false only when the antecedent is true and the consequent false. ◆ n **4** a conditional verb form, clause, sentence, etc.
▶ con,dition'ality n ▶ con'ditionally adv

conditional access n the distortion of television programme transmissions so that only authorized subscribers with suitable decoding apparatus may have access to them.

conditioned response n Psychol. a response that is transferred from the second to the first of a pair of stimuli. A well-known Pavlovian example is salivation by a dog when it hears a bell ring, because food has always been presented when the bell has been rung previously. Also called (esp. formerly): **conditioned reflex**.

condo ('kɒndəʊ) n, pl **condos**. US & Canad. inf. a condominium building or apartment.

condole (kən'dəʊl) vb **condoles, condoling, condoled**. (intr; foll. by with) to express sympathy with someone in grief, pain, etc. [C16: from Church L condolēre, from L com- together + dolēre to grieve]
▶ con'dolence n

condom ('kɒndɒm, 'kɒndəm) n a rubber sheath worn on the penis or in the vagina during sexual intercourse to prevent conception or infection. [C18: from ?]

★ people and places

ondominium (ˌkɒndəˈmɪnɪəm) *n, pl* **condominiums. 1** joint rule or sovereignty. **2** a country ruled by two or more foreign powers. **3** *US & Canad.* **3a** an apartment building in which each apartment is individually owned and the common areas are jointly owned. **3b** an apartment in such a building. Sometimes shortened to **condo.** [C18: from NL, from L *com-* together + *dominium* ownership]

ondone (kənˈdəʊn) *vb* **condones, condoning, condoned.** (*tr*) **1** to overlook or forgive (an offence, etc.). **2** *Law.* (esp. of a spouse) to pardon or overlook (an offence, usually adultery). [C19: from L *condōnāre*, from *com-* (intensive) + *dōnāre* to donate]
▶ **condonation** (ˌkɒndəʊˈneɪʃən) *n* ▶ **conˈdoner** *n*

ondor (ˈkɒndɔː) *n* either of two very large rare New World vultures, the **Andean condor**, which has black plumage with white around the neck, and the **California condor**, which is nearly extinct. [C17: from Sp. *cóndor*, from Quechuan *kuntur*]

ondottiere (ˌkɒndɒˈtjɛərɪ) *n, pl* **condottieri** (-riː). a commander or soldier in a professional mercenary company in Europe from the 13th to the 16th centuries. [C18: from It., from *condotto* leadership, from *condurre* to lead, from L *condūcere*]

onduce (kənˈdjuːs) *vb* **conduces, conducing, conduced.** (*intr*; foll. by *to*) to lead or contribute (to a result). [C15: from L *condūcere*, from *com-* together + *dūcere* to lead]

onducive (kənˈdjuːsɪv) *adj* (when *postpositive*, foll. by *to*) contributing, leading, or tending.

onduct *n* (ˈkɒndʌkt). **1** behaviour. **2** the way of managing a business, affair, etc.; handling. **3** *Rare.* the act of leading. ◆ *vb* (kənˈdʌkt). **4** (*tr*) to accompany and guide (people, a party, etc.) in **conducted tour**). **5** (*tr*) to direct (affairs, business, etc.); control. **6** (*tr*) to carry out; organize: *conduct a survey.* **7** (*tr*) to behave (oneself). **8** to control (an orchestra, etc.) by the movements of the hands or a baton. **9** to transmit (heat, electricity, etc.). [C15: from Med. L *conductus* escorted, from L, from *condūcere* to CONDUCE]
▶ **conˈductible** *adj* ▶ **conˌductiˈbility** *n*

onductance (kənˈdʌktəns) *n* the ability of a system to conduct electricity, measured by the ratio of the current flowing through the system to the potential difference across it. Symbol: G

onducting tissue *n Bot.* another name for **vascular tissue.**

onduction (kənˈdʌkʃən) *n* **1** the transfer of energy by a medium without bulk movement of the medium itself. Cf. **convection** (sense 1). **2** the transmission of an impulse along a nerve fibre. **3** the act of conveying or conducting, as through a pipe. **4** *Physics.* another name for **conductivity** (sense 1).
▶ **conˈductional** *adj*

onductive (kənˈdʌktɪv) *adj* of, denoting, or having the property of conduction.

onductive education *n* an educational system, developed in Hungary, in which teachers (**conductors**) teach children and adults with motor disorders to function independently, by guiding them to attain their own goals in their own way.

onductivity (ˌkɒndʌkˈtɪvɪtɪ) *n, pl* **conductivities. 1** the property of transmitting heat, electricity, or sound. **2** a measure of the ability of a substance to conduct electricity. Symbol: κ

onductivity water *n* water that has a conductivity of less than 0.043×10^{-6} S cm^{-1}.

onductor (kənˈdʌktə) *n* **1** an official on a bus who collects fares. **2** a person who conducts an orchestra, choir, etc. **3** a person who leads or guides. **4** *US & Canad.* a railway official in charge of a train. **5** a substance, body, or system that conducts electricity, heat, etc. **6** See **lightning conductor.**
▶ **conˈductorship** *n* ▶ **conductress** (kənˈdʌktrɪs) *fem n*

onduit (ˈkɒndɪt, -djʊɪt) *n* **1** a pipe or channel for carrying a fluid. **2** a rigid tube for carrying electrical cables. **3** an agency or means of access, communication, etc. [C14: from OF, from Med. L *conductus* channel, from L *condūcere* to lead]

condyle (ˈkɒndɪl) *n* the rounded projection on the articulating end of a bone. [C17: from L *condylus*, from Gk *kondulos*]
▶ **ˈcondylar** *adj*

cone (kəʊn) *n* **1** a geometric solid consisting of a plane base bounded by a closed curve, usually a circle or an ellipse, every point of which is joined to a fixed point lying outside the plane of the base. **2** anything that tapers from a circular section to a point, such as a wafer shell used to contain ice cream. **3a** the reproductive body of conifers and related plants, made up of overlapping scales. **3b** a similar structure in horsetails, club mosses, etc. **4** a small cone used as a temporary traffic marker on roads. **5** any one of the cone-shaped cells in the retina of the eye, sensitive to colour and bright light. ◆ *vb* **cones, coning, coned. 6** (*tr*) to shape like a cone. [C16: from L *cōnus*, from Gk *kōnus* pine cone, geometrical cone]

cone off *vb* (*tr, adv*) *Brit.* to close (one carriageway of a motorway) by placing warning cones across it.

coney (ˈkəʊnɪ) *n* a variant spelling of **cony.**

Coney Island ★ (ˈkəʊnɪ) *n* an island off the S shore of Long Island, New York: site of a large amusement park.

confab (ˈkɒnfæb) *Inf.* ◆ *n* **1** a conversation. ◆ *vb* **confabs, confabbing, confabbed. 2** (*intr*) to converse.

confabulate (kənˈfæbjʊˌleɪt) *vb* **confabulates, confabulating, confabulated.** (*intr*) **1** to talk together; chat. **2** *Psychiatry.* to replace the gaps left by a disorder of the memory with imaginary remembered experiences consistently believed to be true. [C17: from L *confābulārī*, from *fābulārī* to talk, from *fābula* a story]
▶ **conˌfabuˈlation** *n*

confect (kənˈfɛkt) *vb* (*tr*) **1** to prepare by combining ingredients. **2** to make; construct. [C16: from L *confectus* prepared, from *conficere*, from *com-* (intensive) + *facere* to make]

confection (kənˈfɛkʃən) *n* **1** the act of compounding or mixing. **2** any sweet preparation, such as a preserve or a sweet. **3** *Old-fashioned.* an elaborate article of clothing, esp. for women. [C14: from OF, from L *confectiō* a preparing, from *conficere*; see CONFECT]

confectioner (kənˈfɛkʃənə) *n* a person who makes or sells sweets or confections.

confectionery (kənˈfɛkʃənərɪ) *n, pl* **confectioneries. 1** sweets and other confections collectively. **2** the art or business of a confectioner.

confederacy (kənˈfɛdərəsɪ) *n, pl* **confederacies. 1** a union of states, etc.; alliance; league. **2** a combination of groups or individuals for unlawful purposes. [C14: from OF *confederacie*, from LL *confoederātiō* agreement]
▶ **conˈfederal** *adj*

Confederacy ★ (kənˈfɛdərəsɪ, -ˈfɛdrəsɪ) *n* **the.** another name for the **Confederate States of America.**

confederate *n* (kənˈfɛdərɪt). **1** a nation, state, or individual that is part of a confederacy. **2** someone who is part of a conspiracy. ◆ *adj* (kənˈfɛdərɪt). **3** united; allied. ◆ *vb* (kənˈfɛdəˌreɪt), **confederates, confederating, confederated. 4** to form into or become part of a confederacy. [C14: from LL *confoederātus*, from *confoederāre* to unite by a league]

Confederate (kənˈfɛdərɪt) *adj* **1** of or supporting the Confederate States of America. ◆ *n* **2** a supporter of the Confederate States.

Confederate States of America ★ *pl n US history.* the 11 Southern states (Alabama, Arkansas, Florida, Georgia, North Carolina, South Carolina, Texas, Virginia, Tennessee, Louisiana, and Mississippi) that seceded from the Union in 1861, precipitating a civil war with the North. The Confederacy was defeated in 1865 and the South reincorporated into the US.

confederation (kənˌfɛdəˈreɪʃən) *n* **1** the act of confederating or the state of being confederated. **2** a loose alliance of political units. **3** (esp. in Canada) another name for a **federation.**
▶ **conˌfederˈationist** *n*

Confederation ★ (kənˌfɛdəˈreɪʃən) *n* **1** **the.** *US history.* the original 13 states of the United States of America constituted under the Articles of Confederation and superseded by the more formal union established in 1789. **2** the federation of Canada, formed with four original provinces in 1867 and since joined by eight more.

confer (kən'fɜː) *vb* **confers, conferring, conferred. 1** (*tr;* foll. by *on* or *upon*) to grant or bestow (an honour, gift, etc.). **2** (*intr*) to consult together. [C16: from L *conferre,* from *com-* together + *ferre* to bring]
▶ **con'ferment** *or* **con'ferral** *n* ▶ **con'ferrable** *adj*

conferee *or* **conferree** (ˌkɒnfɜː'riː) *n* **1** a person who takes part in a conference. **2** a person on whom an honour or gift is conferred.

conference ('kɒnfərəns) *n* **1** a meeting for consultation or discussion, esp. one with a formal agenda. **2** an assembly of the clergy or of clergy and laity of any of certain Protestant Churches acting as representatives of their denomination. **3** *Sport, US & Canad.* a league or division of clubs or teams. [C16: from Med. L *conferentia,* from L *conferre* to bring together]
▶ **conferential** (ˌkɒnfə'rɛnʃəl) *adj*

conference call *n* a special telephone facility by which three or more people using conventional or cellular phones can be linked up to speak to one another.

conferencing ('kɒnfərənsɪŋ) *n* the practice of holding a conference, esp. by means of a telephone service. See **conference call.**

confess (kən'fɛs) *vb* (when *tr, may take a clause as object*) **1** (when *intr,* often foll. by *to*) to make an admission of faults, crimes, etc.). **2** (*tr*) to admit to be true; concede. **3** *Christianity.* to declare (one's sins) to God or to a priest as his representative, so as to obtain pardon and absolution. [C14: from OF *confesser,* from LL, from L *confessus* confessed, from *confitērī* to admit]

confessedly (kən'fɛsɪdlɪ) *adv* (*sentence modifier*) by admission or confession; avowedly.

confession (kən'fɛʃən) *n* **1** the act of confessing. **2** something confessed. **3** an acknowledgment, esp. of one's faults or crimes. **4** *Christianity.* the act of a penitent accusing himself of his sins. **5 confession of faith.** a formal public avowal of religious beliefs. **6** a religious sect united by common beliefs.
▶ **con'fessionary** *adj*

confessional (kən'fɛʃənˀl) *adj* **1** of or suited to a confession. ◆ *n* **2** *Christianity.* a small stall where a priest hears confessions.

confessor (kən'fɛsə) *n* **1** *Christianity.* a priest who hears confessions and sometimes acts as a spiritual counsellor. **2** *History.* a person who bears witness to his Christian religious faith by the holiness of his life, but does not suffer martyrdom. **3** a person who makes a confession.

confetti (kən'fɛtɪ) *n* small pieces of coloured paper thrown on festive occasions, esp. at weddings. [C19: from It., pl of *confetto,* orig., a bonbon]

confidant *or* (*fem*) **confidante** (ˌkɒnfɪ'dænt, 'kɒnfɪˌdænt) *n* a person to whom private matters are confided. [C17: from F *confident,* from It. *confidente,* n. use of adj: trustworthy]

confide (kən'faɪd) *vb* **confides, confiding, confided. 1** (usually foll. by *in;* when *tr, may take a clause as object*) to disclose (secret or personal matters) in confidence (to). **2** (*intr;* foll. by *in*) to have complete trust. **3** (*tr*) to entrust into another's keeping. [C15: from L *confidere,* from *fidere* to trust]
▶ **con'fider** *n*

confidence ('kɒnfɪdəns) *n* **1** trust in a person or thing. **2** belief in one's own abilities; self-assurance. **3** trust or a trustful relationship: *take me into your confidence.* **4** something confided; secret. **5 in confidence.** as a secret.

confidence trick *or US & Canad.* **confidence game** *n* a swindle involving money in which the victim's trust is won by the swindler.

confident ('kɒnfɪdənt) *adj* **1** (*postpositive;* foll. by *of*) having or showing certainty; sure: *confident of success.* **2** sure of oneself. **3** presumptuous. [C16: from L *confidens,* from *confidere* to have complete trust in]
▶ **'confidently** *adv*

confidential (ˌkɒnfɪ'dɛnʃəl) *adj* **1** spoken or given in

confidence; private. **2** entrusted with another's secret affairs: *a confidential secretary.* **3** suggestive of intimacy: *confidential approach.*
▶ ˌ**confi**ˌ**denti'ality** *n* ▶ ˌ**confi'dentially** *adv*

confiding (kən'faɪdɪŋ) *adj* unsuspicious; trustful.
▶ **con'fidingly** *adv* ▶ **con'fidingness** *n*

configuration (kənˌfɪgjʊ'reɪʃən) *n* **1** the arrangement of the parts of something. **2** the external form or outline achieved by such an arrangement. **3** *Psychol.* the unit or pattern in perception studied by Gestalt psychologists. [C16: from LL *configūrātiō,* from *configūrāre* to model or something, from *figūrāre* to shape, fashion]
▶ **con**ˌ**figu'rational** *or* **con'figurative** *adj*

confine *vb* (kən'faɪn), **confines, confining, confined.** (*tr*) **1** keep within bounds; limit; restrict. **2** to restrict the free movement of: *arthritis confined him to bed.* ◆ *n* ('kɒnfaɪn) **3** (*often pl*) a limit; boundary. [C16: from Med. L *confināre,* from L *confīnis* adjacent, from *fīnis* boundary]
▶ **con'finer** *n*

confined (kən'faɪnd) *adj* **1** enclosed; limited. **2** in childbed; undergoing childbirth.

confinement (kən'faɪnmənt) *n* **1** the act of confining or the state of being confined. **2** the period of the birth of a child.

confirm (kən'fɜːm) *vb* (*tr*) **1** (*may take a clause as object*) to prove to be true or valid; corroborate. **2** (*may take a clause as object*) to assert for a further time, so as to make more definite: *he confirmed that he would appear in court.* **3** to strengthen: *his story confirmed my doubts.* **4** to make valid by a formal act; ratify. **5** to administer the rite of confirmation to. [C13: from OF *confermer,* from L *confirmāre,* from *firmus* FIRM¹]
▶ **con'firmatory** *or* **con'firmative** *adj*

confirmation (ˌkɒnfə'meɪʃən) *n* **1** the act of confirming. **2** something that confirms. **3** a rite in several Christian churches that confirms a baptized person in his faith and admits him to full participation in the church.

confirmed (kən'fɜːmd) *adj* **1** (*prenominal*) long-established in a habit, way of life, etc. **2** having received the rite of confirmation.

confiscate ('kɒnfɪˌskeɪt) *vb* **confiscates, confiscating, confiscated.** (*tr*) **1** to seize (property), esp. for public use and esp. by way of a penalty. ◆ *adj* **2** confiscated; forfeit. [C16: from L *confiscāre* to seize for the public treasury, from *fiscus* treasury]
▶ ˌ**confis'cation** *n* ▶ **'confis**ˌ**cator** *n* ▶ **confiscatory** (kən'fɪskətərɪ) *adj*

Confiteor (kən'fɪtɪˌɔː) *n RC Church.* a prayer consisting of a general confession of sinfulness and an entreaty for forgiveness. [C13: from L: I confess]

conflagration (ˌkɒnflə'greɪʃən) *n* a large destructive fire. [C16: from L *conflagrātiō,* from *conflagrāre,* from *com-* (intensive) + *flagrāre* to burn]

conflate (kən'fleɪt) *vb* **conflates, conflating, conflated.** (*tr*) to combine or blend (two things, esp. two versions of a text) so as to form a whole. [C16: from L *conflāre* to blow together, from *flāre* to blow]
▶ **con'flation** *n*

conflict *n* ('kɒnflɪkt). **1** a struggle between opposing forces; battle. **2** opposition between ideas, interests, etc.; controversy. **3** *Psychol.* opposition between two simultaneous but incompatible wishes or drives, sometimes leading to emotional tension. ◆ *vb* (kən'flɪkt). (*intr*) **4** to come into opposition; clash. **5** to fight. [C15: from L *conflictus,* from *conflīgere* to combat, from *flīgere* to strike]
▶ **con'flicting** *adj* ▶ **con'flictingly** *adv* ▶ **con'fliction** *n*

confluence ('kɒnflʊəns) *or* **conflux** ('kɒnflʌks) *n* **1** a flowing together, esp. of rivers. **2** a gathering.
▶ **'confluent** *adj*

conform (kən'fɔːm) *vb* **1** (*intr;* usually foll. by *to*) to comply in actions, behaviour, etc., with accepted standards. **2** (*intr;* usually foll. by *with*) to be in accordance: *he conforms with my idea of a teacher.* **3** to make or become similar. **4** (*intr*) to comply with the practices of an established church, esp. the Church of England. [C14: from OF *conformer,* from L *conformāre* to strengthen, from *firmāre* to make firm]
▶ **con'former** *n* ▶ **con'formist** *n, adj*

★ people and places

onformable (kənˈfɔːməbᵊl) adj **1** corresponding in character; similar. **2** obedient; submissive. **3** (foll. by to) consistent (with). **4** (of rock strata) lying in a parallel arrangement so that their original relative positions have remained undisturbed.
► con‚formaˈbility n ► conˈformably adv

onformal (kənˈfɔːməl) adj (of a map projection) maintaining true shape and scale in every direction. [C17: from LL conformālis, from L com- same + forma shape]

onformation (‚kɒnfɔːˈmeɪʃən) n **1** the general shape of an object; configuration. **2** the arrangement of the parts of an object. **3** Chem. the three-dimensional arrangement of the atoms in a molecule.

onformity (kənˈfɔːmɪtɪ) or **conformance** n, pl conformities or conformances. **1** compliance in actions, behaviour, etc., with certain accepted standards. **2** likeness; congruity; agreement. **3** compliance with the practices of an established church.

onfound (kənˈfaʊnd) vb (tr) **1** to astound; bewilder. **2** to confuse. **3** to treat mistakenly as similar to or identical with. **4** (kɒnˈfaʊnd). to curse (usually in **confound it!**). **5** to contradict or refute (an argument, etc.). **6** to rout or defeat (an enemy). [C13: from OF confondre, from L confundere to mingle, pour together]
► conˈfounder n

onfounded (kənˈfaʊndɪd) adj **1** bewildered; confused. **2** (prenominal) Inf. execrable; damned.
► conˈfoundedly adv

onfraternity (‚kɒnfrəˈtɜːnɪtɪ) n, pl confraternities. a group of men united for some particular purpose, esp. Christian laymen organized for religious or charitable service; brotherhood. [C15: from Med. L confrāternitās, ult. from L frāter brother]

onfrère (ˈkɒnfreə) n a fellow member of a profession, etc. [C15: from OF, from Med. L confrāter]

onfront (kənˈfrʌnt) vb (tr) **1** (usually foll. by with) to present (with something), esp. in order to accuse or criticize. **2** to face boldly; oppose in hostility. **3** to be face to face with. [C16: from Med. L confrontārī, from frons forehead]
► confrontation (‚kɒnfrʌnˈteɪʃən) n ► ‚confronˈtational adj

Confucian (kənˈfjuːʃən) adj **1** of or relating to the doctrines of Confucius. ◆ n **2** a follower of Confucius.
► Conˈfucianist n

Confucianism (kənˈfjuːʃəˌnɪzəm) n the ethical system of Confucius, emphasizing moral order, the virtue of China's ancient rules, and gentlemanly education.
► Conˈfucianist n

Confucius ★ (kənˈfjuːʃəs) n Chinese name Kong Zi or K'ung Fu-tse. 551–479 B.C., Chinese philosopher and teacher (see **Confucianism**). His doctrines were compiled after his death as The Analects of Confucius.

onfuse (kənˈfjuːz) vb confuses, confusing, confused. (tr) **1** to bewilder; perplex. **2** to mix up (things, ideas, etc.). **3** to make unclear: he confused his talk with irrelevant details. **4** to mistake (one thing) for another. **5** to disconcert; embarrass. **6** to cause to become disordered: the enemy ranks were confused by gas. [C18: back formation from confused, from L confūsus, from confundere to pour together]
► conˈfusable adj ► confusedly (kənˈfjuːzɪdlɪ, -ˈfjuːzd-) adv ► conˈfusing adj ► conˈfusingly adv

onfusion (kənˈfjuːʒən) n **1** the act of confusing or the state of being confused. **2** disorder. **3** bewilderment; perplexity. **4** lack of clarity. **5** embarrassment; abashment.

onfute (kənˈfjuːt) vb confutes, confuting, confuted. (tr) **1** to prove (a person or thing) wrong, invalid, or mistaken; disprove. [C16: from L confūtāre to check, silence]
► conˈfutable adj ► confutation (‚kɒnfjʊˈteɪʃən) n

onga (ˈkɒŋɡə) n **1** a Latin American dance of three steps and a kick to each bar, performed by a number of people in single file. **2** Also called: **conga drum**. a large tubular bass drum played with the hands. ◆ vb congas, congaing, congaed. **3** (intr) to perform this dance. [C20: from American Sp., from fem. of congo belonging to the Congo]

congé (ˈkɒnʒeɪ) n **1** permission to depart or dismissal, esp. when formal. **2** a farewell. [C16: from OF congié, from L commeātus leave of absence, from meāre to go]

congeal (kənˈdʒiːl) vb **1** to change or cause to change from a soft or fluid state to a firm state. **2** to form or cause to form into a coagulated mass; jell. [C14: from OF congeler, from L congelāre, from com- together + gelāre to freeze]
► conˈgealable adj ► conˈgealment n

congelation (‚kɒndʒɪˈleɪʃən) n **1** the process of congealing. **2** something formed by this process.

congener (kənˈdʒiːnə, ˈkɒndʒɪnə) n a member of a class, group, or other category, esp. any animal of a specified genus. [C18: from L, from com- same + genus kind]

congenial (kənˈdʒiːnjəl) adj **1** friendly, pleasant, or agreeable: a congenial atmosphere to work in. **2** having a similar disposition, tastes, etc.; compatible. [C17: from CON- (same) + GENIAL[1]]
► congeniality (kənˌdʒiːnɪˈælɪtɪ) n

congenital (kənˈdʒɛnɪtᵊl) adj **1** denoting any nonhereditary condition, esp. an abnormal condition, existing at birth: congenital blindness. **2** Inf. complete, as if from birth: a congenital idiot. [C18: from L congenitus, from genitus born, from gignere to bear]
► conˈgenitally adv

conger (ˈkɒŋɡə) n a large marine eel occurring in temperate and tropical coastal waters. [C14: from OF congre, from L conger, from Gk gongros]

congeries (kɒnˈdʒɪərɪːz) n (functioning as sing or pl) a collection; mass; heap. [C17: from L, from congerere to pile up, from gerere to carry]

congest (kənˈdʒɛst) vb **1** to crowd or become crowded to excess; overfill. **2** to clog (an organ) with blood or (of an organ) to become clogged with blood. **3** (tr; usually passive) to block (the nose) with mucus. [C16: from L congestus, from congerere; see CONGERIES]
► conˈgestion n

conglomerate n (kənˈglɒmərɪt). **1** a thing composed of heterogeneous elements. **2** any coarse-grained sedimentary rock consisting of rounded fragments of rock embedded in a finer matrix. **3** a large corporation consisting of a group of companies dealing in widely diversified goods, services, etc. ◆ vb (kənˈglɒməˌreɪt), conglomerates, conglomerating, conglomerated. **4** to form into a mass. ◆ adj (kənˈglɒmərɪt). **5** made up of heterogeneous elements. **6** (of sedimentary rocks) consisting of rounded fragments within a finer matrix. [C16: from L conglomerāre to roll up, from glomerāre to wind into a ball, from glomus ball of thread]
► conˌglomerˈation n

Congo ★ (ˈkɒŋɡəʊ) n **1 Republic of the.** a republic in W Central Africa: formerly the French colony of Middle Congo, part of French Equatorial Africa, it became independent in 1960; consists mostly of equatorial forest, with savanna and extensive swamps; drained chiefly by the Rivers Congo and Ubangi. Official language: French. Religion: animist and Christian. Currency: franc. Capital: Brazzaville. Pop.: 2 583 000 (1997). Area: 342 000 sq. km (132 018 sq. miles). Former names: **Middle Congo** (until 1958), **Congo-Brazzaville**. **2 Democratic Republic of the.** a republic in S central Africa, with a narrow strip of land along the Congo estuary leading to the Atlantic in the west: Congo Free State established in 1885, with Leopold II of Belgium as absolute monarch; became the Belgian Congo colony in 1908; gained independence in 1960, followed by civil war and the secession of Katanga (until 1963); President Mobutu Sese Seko seized power in 1965; declared a one-party state in 1978; Sese Seko, accused of corruption on a massive scale, was overthrown by rebels in 1997. The country consists chiefly of the Congo basin, with large areas of dense tropical forest and marshes, and the Mitumba highlands reaching over 5000 m (16 000 ft) in the east. Official language: French. Religion: Christian majority, animist minority. Currency: Congolese franc. Capital: Kinshasa. Pop.: 46 674 000 (1997). Area: 2 344 116 sq. km (905 063 sq. miles). Former names: **Congo Free State** (1885–1908), **Belgian Congo** (1908–60), **Congo-Kinshasa** (1960–71), **Zaïre** (1971–97). **3** the second longest river in Africa, rising as the Lualaba on the Katanga plateau in the Democratic Republic of the Congo and flowing in a wide northerly curve to the Atlantic: forms the border between the

★ people and places

Congo Republic and the Democratic Republic of the Congo. Length: about 4800 km (3000 miles). Area of basin: about 3 000 000 sq. km (1 425 000 sq. miles). Former (Zaïrese) name (1971–97): **Zaïre**.
► **Congolese** (ˌkɒŋgə'liːz) *adj, n*

Congo Free State ★ *n* a former name (1885–1908) of the Democratic Republic of the **Congo** (sense 2).

congrats (kən'græts) *pl n, sentence substitute*. informal shortened form of **congratulations**.

congratulate (kən'grætjʊˌleɪt) *vb* **congratulates, congratulating, congratulated.** (*tr*) **1** (usually foll. by *on*) to communicate pleasure, approval, or praise to; compliment. **2** (often foll. by *on*) to consider (oneself) clever or fortunate (as a result of): *she congratulated herself on her tact.* **3** *Obs.* to greet; salute. [C16: from L *congrātulārī*, from *grātulārī* to rejoice, from *grātus* pleasing]
► **conˌgratuˈlation** *n* ► **conˈgratulatory** *or* **conˈgratulative** *adj*

congratulations (kənˌgrætjʊ'leɪʃənz) *pl n, sentence substitute*. expressions of pleasure or joy on another's success, good fortune, etc.

congregate ('kɒŋgrɪˌgeɪt) *vb* **congregates, congregating, congregated.** to collect together in a body or crowd; assemble. [C15: from L *congregāre* to collect into a flock, from *grex* flock]

congregation (ˌkɒŋgrɪ'geɪʃən) *n* **1** a group of persons gathered for worship, prayer, etc., esp. in a church. **2** the act of congregating together. **3** a group collected together; assemblage. **4** the group of persons habitually attending a given church, chapel, etc. **5** *RC Church.* **5a** a society of persons who follow a common rule of life but who are bound only by simple vows. **5b** an administrative subdivision of the papal curia. **6** *Chiefly Brit.* an assembly of senior members of a university.

congregational (ˌkɒŋgrɪ'geɪʃən°l) *adj* **1** of or relating to a congregation. **2** (*usually cap.*) of or denoting Congregationalism.

Congregationalism (ˌkɒŋgrɪ'geɪʃənəˌlɪzəm) *n* a system of Christian doctrines and ecclesiastical government in which each congregation is self-governing.
► ˌ**Congreˈgationalist** *adj, n*

congress ('kɒŋgrɛs) *n* **1** a meeting or conference, esp. of representatives of sovereign states. **2** a national legislative assembly. **3** a society or association. [C16: from L *congressus*, from *congredī*, from *com-* together + *gradī* to walk]

Congress ('kɒŋgrɛs) *n* **1** the bicameral federal legislature of the US, consisting of the House of Representatives and the Senate. **2** Also called: **Congress Party**. (in India) a major political party.
► **Conˈgressional** *adj*

congressional (kən'grɛʃən°l) *adj* of or relating to a congress.
► **con'gressionalist** *n*

Congressman ('kɒŋgrɛsmən) *or* (*fem*) **Congresswoman** *n, pl* **Congressmen** *or* **Congresswomen.** (in the US) a member of Congress, esp. of the House of Representatives.

Congreve ★ ('kɒŋgriːv) *n* **William.** 1670–1729, English Restoration dramatist, author of *Love for Love* (1695) and *The Way of the World* (1700).

congruence ('kɒŋgrʊəns) *or* **congruency** *n* **1** the quality or state of corresponding, agreeing, or being congruent. **2** *Maths.* the relationship between two integers, *x* and *y*, such that their difference, with respect to another integer called the modulus, *n*, is a multiple of the modulus.

congruent ('kɒŋgrʊənt) *adj* **1** agreeing; corresponding. **2** having identical shapes so that all parts correspond: *congruent triangles.* **3** of or concerning two integers related by a congruence. [C15: from L *congruere* to agree]

congruous ('kɒŋgrʊəs) *adj* **1** corresponding or agreeing. **2** appropriate. [C16: from L *congruus;* see CONGRUENT]
► **congruity** (kən'gruːɪtɪ) *n*

conic ('kɒnɪk) *adj also* **conical.** **1a** having the shape of a cone. **1b** of a cone. ◆ *n* **2** another name for **conic section**.
► **'conically** *adv*

conics ('kɒnɪks) *n* (*functioning as sing*) the geometry o▮ the parabola, ellipse, and hyperbola.

conic section *n* one of a group of curves formed by th▮ intersection of a plane and a right circular cone. It ▮ either a circle, ellipse, parabola, or hyperbola.

conidium (kəʊ'nɪdɪəm) *n, pl* **conidia** (-'nɪdɪə). an asexu▮ spore formed at the tip of a specialized hypha in fung▮ such as *Penicillium*. [C19: from NL, from Gk *konis* dust ▮ -IUM]

conifer ('kəʊnɪfə, 'kɒn-) *n* any tree or shrub of the phy▮ lum *Coniferophyta*, typically bearing cones and evergree▮ leaves. The group includes the pines, spruces, fir▮ larches, etc. [C19: from L, from *cōnus* CONE + *ferre* t▮ bear]
► **co'niferous** *adj*

Coniston Water ★ ('kɒnɪstən) *n* a lake in NW Englan▮ in Cumbria: scene of the establishment of world wate▮ speed records by Sir Malcolm Campbell (1939) and hi▮ son Donald Campbell (1959). Length: 8 km (5 miles).

conj. *abbrev. for:* **1** conjugation. **2** conjunction.

conjectural (kən'dʒɛktʃərəl) *adj* involving or inclined t▮ conjecture.
► **con'jecturally** *adv*

conjecture (kən'dʒɛktʃə) *n* **1** the formation of conclu▮ sions from incomplete evidence; guess. **2** the conclusio▮ so formed. ◆ *vb* **conjectures, conjecturing, conjectured. 3** t▮ infer or arrive at (an opinion, conclusion, etc.) from in▮ complete evidence. [C14: from L *conjectūra*, fron▮ *conicere* to throw together, from *jacere* to throw]
► **con'jecturable** *adj*

conjoin (kən'dʒɔɪn) *vb* to join or become joined. [C14▮ from OF *conjoindre*, from L *conjungere*, from *jungere* t▮ JOIN]
► **con'joiner** *n*

conjoined twins *pl n* the technical name for **Siames**▮ **twins.**

conjoint (kən'dʒɔɪnt) *adj* united, joint, or associated.
► **con'jointly** *adv*

conjugal ('kɒndʒʊg°l) *adj* of or relating to marriage o▮ the relationship between husband and wife: *conjuga*▮ *rights.* [C16: from L *conjugālis*, from *conjunx* wife or hus▮ band]
► **conjugality** (ˌkɒndʒʊ'gælɪtɪ) *n* ► **'conjugally** *adv*

conjugate *vb* ('kɒndʒʊˌgeɪt), **conjugates, conjugating, con**▮ **jugated. 1** (*tr*) *Grammar.* to state or set out the conjugation▮ of (a verb). **2** (*intr*) (of a verb) to undergo inflection ac▮ cording to a specific set of rules. **3** (*intr*) *Biol.* to undergo▮ conjugation. **4** (*tr*) *Obs.* to join together, esp. in marriage▮ ◆ *adj* ('kɒndʒʊgɪt, -ˌgeɪt). **5** joined together in pairs. ◆▮ *Maths.* **6a** (of two angles) having a sum of 360°. **6b** (o▮ two complex numbers) differing only in the sign of the▮ imaginary part as 4 + 3i and 4 − 3i. **7** *Chem.* of the state o▮ equilibrium in which two liquids can exist as separate▮ phases that are both solutions. **8** *Chem.* (of acids and▮ bases) related by loss or gain of a proton. **9** (of a com▮ pound leaf) having one pair of leaflets. **10** (of words▮ cognate; related in origin. ◆ *n* ('kɒndʒʊgɪt). **11** one of ▮ pair or set of conjugate substances, values, quantities▮ words, etc. [C15: from L *conjugāre*, from *com-* together ◆▮ *jugāre* to connect, from *jugum* a yoke]
► **'conjuˌgative** *adj* ► **'conjuˌgator** *n*

conjugation (ˌkɒndʒʊ'geɪʃən) *n* **1** *Grammar.* **1a** inflec▮ tion of a verb for person, number, tense, voice, mood▮ etc. **1b** the complete set of the inflections of a given verb▮ **2** a joining. **3** a type of sexual reproduction in ciliate pro▮ tozoans involving the temporary union of two individu▮ als and the subsequent migration and fusion of the▮ gametic nuclei. **4** the union of gametes, as in some fungi▮ **5** the pairing of chromosomes in the early phase of ▮ meiotic division. **6** *Chem.* the existence of alternating▮ double or triple bonds in a chemical compound, with▮ consequent electron delocalization over part of the mol▮ ecule.
► ˌ**conjuˈgational** *adj*

conjunct ('kɒndʒʌŋkt, kən'dʒʌŋkt) *n* *Logic.* one of the▮ propositions or formulas in a conjunction.

conjunction (kən'dʒʌŋkʃən) *n* **1** the act of joining to▮ gether; union. **2** simultaneous occurrence of events; co▮

incidence. **3** any word or group of words, other than a relative pronoun, that connects words, phrases, or clauses; for example *and* and *while*. **4** *Astron.* **4a** the position of a planet when it is in line with the sun as seen from the earth. **4b** the apparent proximity or coincidence of two celestial bodies on the celestial sphere. **5** *Logic.* **5a** the operator that forms a compound sentence from two given sentences, and corresponds to the English *and*. **5b** a sentence so formed: it is true only when both the component sentences are true. **5c** the relation between such sentences. ► **con'junctional** *adj*

onjunctiva (ˌkɒndʒʌŋkˈtaɪvə) *n, pl* **conjunctivas** or **conjunctivae** (-viː). the delicate mucous membrane that covers the eyeball and the under surface of the eyelid. [C16: from NL *membrāna conjunctīva* the conjunctive membrane] ► ˌ**conjunc'tival** *adj*

onjunctive (kənˈdʒʌŋktɪv) *adj* **1** joining; connective. **2** joined. **3** of or relating to conjunctions. ◆ *n* **4** a less common word for **conjunction** (sense 3). [C15: from LL *conjunctīvus*, from L *conjungere* to CONJOIN]

onjunctivitis (kənˌdʒʌŋktɪˈvaɪtɪs) *n* inflammation of the conjunctiva.

onjuncture (kənˈdʒʌŋktʃə) *n* a combination of events, esp. a critical one.

onjuration (ˌkɒndʒʊˈreɪʃən) *n* **1** a magic spell; incantation. **2** a less common word for **conjuring**. **3** *Arch.* supplication; entreaty.

onjure (ˈkʌndʒə) *vb* **conjures, conjuring, conjured. 1** (*intr*) to practise conjuring. **2** (*intr*) to call upon supposed supernatural forces by spells and incantations. **3** (kənˈdʒʊə). (*tr*) to appeal earnestly to: *I conjure you to help me.* **4** a name to conjure with. **4a** a person thought to have great power or influence. **4b** any name that excites the imagination. [C13: from OF *conjurer* to plot, from L *conjūrāre* to swear together]

conjure up *vb* (*tr, adv*) **1** to present to the mind; evoke or imagine: *he conjured up a picture of his childhood.* **2** to call up or command (a spirit or devil) by an incantation.

onjuring (ˈkʌndʒərɪŋ) *n* **1** the performance of tricks that appear to defy natural laws. ◆ *adj* **2** denoting or of such tricks or entertainment.

onjuror or **conjurer** (ˈkʌndʒərə) *n* **1** a person who practises conjuring, esp. for people's entertainment. **2** a sorcerer.

onk (kɒŋk) *Sl.* ◆ *vb* **1** to strike (someone) a blow, esp. on the head or nose. ◆ *n* **2** a punch or blow, esp. on the head or nose. **3** the head or nose. [C19: prob. changed from CONCH]

onker (ˈkɒŋkə) *n* an informal name for the **horse chestnut** (sense 2).

onkers (ˈkɒŋkəz) *n* (*functioning as sing*) *Brit.* a game in which a player swings a horse chestnut (conker), threaded onto a string, against that of another player to try to break it. [C19: from dialect *conker* snail shell, orig. used in the game]

onk out *vb* (*intr, adv*) *Inf.* **1** (of machines, cars, etc.) to fail suddenly. **2** to tire suddenly or collapse. [C20: from ?]

on man *n Inf.* a person who swindles another by means of a confidence trick. More formal term: **confidence man.**

on moto (kɒn ˈməʊtəʊ) *adj, adv Music.* (to be performed) in a brisk or lively manner. [It., lit.: with movement]

conn (kɒn) *vb, n* a variant spelling (esp. US) of **con**[3].

Conn ★ (kɒn) *n* 2nd century A.D., king of Leinster and high king of Ireland.

Conn. *abbrev.* for Connecticut.

Connacht ★ (ˈkɒnət) *n* a province and ancient kingdom of NW Republic of Ireland: consists of the counties of Galway, Leitrim, Mayo, Roscommon, and Sligo. Pop.: 423 031 (1991). Area: 17 122 sq. km (6611 sq. miles). Former name: **Connaught.**

connate (ˈkɒneɪt) *adj* **1** existing from birth; congenital or innate. **2** allied in nature or origin. **3** *Biol.* (of similar parts or organs) closely joined or united by growth. **4**

Geol. (of fluids) produced at the same time as the rocks surrounding them; *connate water.* [C17: from LL *connātus* born at the same time]

connect (kəˈnɛkt) *vb* **1** to link or be linked. **2** (*tr*) to associate: *I connect him with my childhood.* **3** (*tr*) to establish telephone communications with or between. **4** (*intr*) to be meaningful or meaningfully related. **5** (*intr*) (of two public vehicles, such as trains or buses) to have the arrival of one timed to occur just before the departure of the other, for the convenient transfer of passengers. **6** (*intr*) *Inf.* to hit, punch, kick, etc., solidly. [C17: from L *connectere* to bind together, from *nectere* to tie] ► **con'nectible** or **con'nectable** *adj* ► **con'nector** or **con'necter** *n*

Connecticut ★ (kəˈnɛtɪkət) *n* **1** a state of the northeastern US, in New England. Capital: Hartford. Pop.: 3 274 238 (1996 est.). Area: 12 973 sq. km (5009 sq. miles). Abbrevs.: **Conn.** or (with zip code) **CT 2** a river in the northeastern US, rising in N New Hampshire and flowing south to Long Island Sound. Length: 651 km (407 miles).

connecting rod *n* **1** a rod or bar for transmitting motion, esp. one that connects a rotating part to a reciprocating part. **2** such a rod that connects the piston to the crankshaft in an internal-combustion engine.

connection or **connexion** (kəˈnɛkʃən) *n* **1** the act of connecting; union. **2** something that connects or relates; link or bond. **3** a relationship or association. **4** logical sequence in thought or expression; coherence. **5** the relation of a word or phrase to its context: *in this connection the word has no political significance.* **6** (*often pl*) an acquaintance, esp. one who is influential. **7** a relative, esp. if distant and related by marriage. **8a** an opportunity to transfer from one train, bus, etc., to another. **8b** the vehicle scheduled to provide such an opportunity. **9** a link, usually a wire or metallic strip, between two components in an electric circuit. **10** a communications link, esp. by telephone. **11** *Sl.* a supplier of illegal drugs, such as heroin. **12** *Rare.* sexual intercourse. ► **con'nectional** or **con'nexional** *adj*

connective (kəˈnɛktɪv) *adj* **1** connecting. ◆ *n* **2** a thing that connects. **3** *Grammar, logic.* **3a** any word that connects phrases, clauses, or individual words. **3b** a symbol used in a formal language in the construction of compound sentences, corresponding to terms such as *or, and,* etc., in ordinary speech. **4** *Bot.* the tissue of a stamen that connects the two lobes of the anther.

connective tissue *n* an animal tissue that supports organs, fills the spaces between them, and forms tendons and ligaments.

Connemara ★ (ˌkɒnɪˈmɑːrə) *n* a barren coastal region of W Republic of Ireland, in Co. Galway: consists of quartzite mountains, peat bogs, and many lakes.

Connery ★ (ˈkɒnərɪ) *n* **Sean**, real name *Thomas Connery.* born 1929, Scottish film actor; his films include *Goldfinger* (1964), *The Name of the Rose* (1986), and *The Rock* (1996).

conning tower (ˈkɒnɪŋ) *n* **1** a superstructure of a submarine, used as the bridge when the vessel is on the surface. **2** the armoured pilot house of a warship. [C19: see CON[3]]

connivance (kəˈnaɪvəns) *n* **1** the act or fact of conniving. **2** *Law.* the tacit encouragement of or assent to another's wrongdoing.

connive (kəˈnaɪv) *vb* **connives, conniving, connived.** (*intr*) **1** to plot together; conspire. **2** (foll. by *at*) *Law.* to give assent or encouragement (to the commission of a wrong). [C17: from F *conniver*, from L *connīvēre* to blink, hence, leave uncensured] ► **con'niver** *n*

connoisseur (ˌkɒnɪˈsɜː) *n* a person with special knowledge or appreciation of a field, esp. in the arts. [C18: from F, from OF *conoiseor*, from *conoistre* to know, from L *cognōscere*] ► ˌ**connois'seurship** *n*

Connolly ★ (ˈkɒnəlɪ) *n* **1 Cyril (Vernon).** 1903–74, British writer, founder of *Horizon* (1939–50): his books include *Enemies of Promise* (1938). **2 James.** 1868–1916, Irish labour leader: executed by the British for his part in the Easter Rising (1916).

Connors ★ ('kɒnəz) *n* **Jimmy**. born 1952, US tennis player: Wimbledon champion 1974 and 1982; US champion 1974, 1976, 1978, 1982, and 1983.

connotation (ˌkɒnə'teɪʃən) *n* **1** an association or idea suggested by a word or phrase. **2** the act of connoting. **3** *Logic*. the characteristic or set of characteristics that determines to which object the common name properly applies. In traditional logic synonymous with **intension**.
▸ **connotative** ('kɒnəˌteɪtɪv, kə'nəʊtə-) *or* **con'notive** *adj*

connote (kɒ'nəʊt) *vb* **connotes, connoting, connoted**. (*tr; often takes a clause as object*) **1** (of a word, phrase, etc.) to imply or suggest (associations or ideas) other than the literal meaning: *the word "maiden" connotes modesty*. **2** to involve as a consequence or condition. [C17: from Med. L *connotāre*, from L *notāre* to mark, note, from *nota* sign, note]

connubial (kə'nju:bɪəl) *adj* of or relating to marriage: *connubial bliss*. [C17: from L *cōnūbiālis*, from *cōnūbium* marriage]
▸ **con,nubi'ality** *n*

conoid ('kəʊnɔɪd) *n* **1** a cone-shaped object. ◆ *adj* also **conoidal** (kəʊ'nɔɪdᵊl). **2** cone-shaped. [C17: from Gk *kōnoeidēs*, from *kōnos* CONE]
▸ **co'noidally** *adv*

conquer ('kɒŋkə) *vb* **1** to overcome (an enemy, army, etc.); defeat. **2** to overcome (an obstacle, desire, etc.); surmount. **3** (*tr*) to gain possession or control of as by force or war; win. [C13: from OF *conquere*, from Vulgar L *conquērere* (unattested), from L *conquīrere* to search for, from *quaerere* to seek]
▸ **'conquerable** *adj* ▸ **'conquering** *adj* ▸ **'conqueror** *n*

Conqueror ★ ('kɒŋkərə) *n* **William the**. See **William I**.

conquest ('kɒŋkwɛst) *n* **1** the act of conquering or the state of having been conquered; victory. **2** a person, thing, etc., that has been conquered. **3** a person, whose compliance, love, etc., has been won. [C13: from OF *conqueste*, from Vulgar L *conquēsta* (unattested), from L *conquīsīta*, fem. p.p. of *conquīrere*; see CONQUER]

Conquest ('kɒŋkwɛst) *n* **the**. See **Norman Conquest**.

conquistador (kɒn'kwɪstəˌdɔ:) *n, pl* **conquistadors** *or* **conquistadores** (kɒnˌkwɪstə'dɔːrɛs). an adventurer or conqueror, esp. one of the Spanish conquerors of the New World in the 16th century. [C19: from Sp., from *conquistar* to conquer]

Conrad ★ ('kɒnræd) *n* **Joseph**. real name *Teodor Josef Konrad Korzeniowski*. 1857–1924, British novelist born in Poland, noted for sea stories such as *Lord Jim* (1900) and novels such as *Nostromo* (1904).

cons. *abbrev. for:* **1** consecrated. **2** consigned. **3** consignment. **4** consolidated. **5** consonant. **6** constitutional. **7** construction.

Cons. *abbrev. for* Conservative.

consanguinity (ˌkɒnsæŋ'gwɪnɪtɪ) *n* **1** relationship by blood; kinship. **2** close affinity or connection. [C14: see CON-, SANGUINE]
▸ **,consan'guineous** *or* **con'sanguine** *adj*

conscience ('kɒnʃəns) *n* **1** the sense of right and wrong that governs a person's thoughts and actions. **2** conscientiousness; diligence. **3** a feeling of guilt or anxiety: *he has a conscience about his unkind action*. **4 in (all) conscience**. **4a** with regard to truth and justice. **4b** certainly. **5 on one's conscience**. causing feelings of guilt or remorse. [C13: from OF, from L *conscientia* knowledge, from *conscīre* to know; see CONSCIOUS]

conscience clause *n* a clause in a law or contract exempting persons with moral scruples.

conscience money *n* money paid voluntarily to compensate for dishonesty, esp. for taxes formerly evaded.

conscience-stricken *adj* feeling anxious or guilty. Also: **conscience-smitten**.

conscientious (ˌkɒnʃɪ'ɛnʃəs) *adj* **1** involving or taking great care; painstaking. **2** governed by or done according to conscience.
▸ **,consci'entiously** *adv* ▸ **,consci'entiousness** *n*

conscientious objector *n* a person who refuses to serve in the armed forces on the grounds of conscience.

conscious ('kɒnʃəs) *adj* **1** alert and awake. **2** aware of one's surroundings, one's own motivations and thoughts, etc. **3a** aware (of) and giving value and emphasis (to a particular fact): *I am conscious of your great kindness to me*. **3b** (*in combination*): *clothes-conscious*. **4** deliberate or intended: *a conscious effort; conscious rudeness*. **5a** denoting a part of the human mind that is aware of person's self, environment, and mental activity and that to a certain extent determines his choices of action. **5b** (*as n*): *the conscious is only a small part of the mind*. [C17: from L *conscius* sharing knowledge, from *com-* with + *scīre* to know]
▸ **'consciously** *adv* ▸ **'consciousness** *n*

consciousness raising *n* **a** the process of developing awareness in a person or group of a situation regarded as wrong or unjust, with the aim of producing active participation in changing it. **b** (*as modifier*): *a consciousness-raising group*.

conscript *n* ('kɒnskrɪpt). **1a** a person who is enrolled for compulsory military service. **1b** (*as modifier*): *a conscript army*. ◆ *vb* (kən'skrɪpt). **2** (*tr*) to enrol (youths, civilians, etc.) for compulsory military service. [C15: from L *conscrīptus*, p.p. of *conscrībere* to enrol, from *scrībere* to write]

conscription (kən'skrɪpʃən) *n* compulsory military service.

consecrate ('kɒnsɪˌkreɪt) *vb* **consecrates, consecrating, consecrated**. (*tr*) **1** to make or declare sacred or holy. **2** to dedicate (one's life, time, etc.) to a specific purpose. **3** *Christianity*. to sanctify (bread and wine) for the Eucharist to be received as the body and blood of Christ. **4** to cause to be respected or revered: *time has consecrated this custom*. [C15: from L *consecrāre*, from *com-* (intensive) + *sacrāre* to devote, from *sacer* sacred]
▸ **,conse'cration** *n* ▸ **'conse,crator** *n* ▸ **'conse,cratory** *adj*

Consecration (ˌkɒnsɪ'kreɪʃən) *n* RC Church. the part of the Mass after the sermon during which the bread and wine are believed to change into the Body and Blood of Christ.

consecutive (kən'sɛkjʊtɪv) *adj* **1** (of a narrative, account, etc.) following chronological sequence. **2** following one another without interruption; successive. **3** characterized by logical sequence. **4** *Grammar*. expressing consequence or result: *consecutive clauses*. **5** *Music*. another word for **parallel** (sense 3). [C17: from F *consécutif*, from L *consecūtus*, from *consequī* to pursue]
▸ **con'secutively** *adv* ▸ **con'secutiveness** *n*

consensual (kən'sɛnsjʊəl) *adj* **1** *Law*. (of a contract, etc.) existing by consent. **2** (of reflex actions of the body) responding to stimulation of another part.
▸ **con'sensually** *adv*

consensus (kən'sɛnsəs) *n* general or widespread agreement (esp. in **consensus of opinion**). [C19: from L, from *consentīre*; see CONSENT]

consent (kən'sɛnt) *vb* **1** to give assent or permission; agree. ◆ *n* **2** acquiescence to or acceptance of something done or planned by another. **3** harmony in opinion; agreement (esp. in **with one consent**). [C13: from OF *consentir*, from L *consentīre* to agree, from *sentīre* to feel]
▸ **con'senting** *adj*

consequence ('kɒnsɪkwəns) *n* **1** a result or effect. **2** an unpleasant result (esp. in **take the consequences**). **3** an inference reached by reasoning; conclusion. **4** significance or importance: *it's of no consequence; a man of consequence*. **5 in consequence**. as a result.

consequent ('kɒnsɪkwənt) *adj* **1** following as an effect. **2** following as a logical conclusion. **3** (of a river) flowing in the direction of the original slope of the land. ◆ *n* **4** something that follows something else, esp. as a result. **5** *Logic*. the resultant clause in a conditional sentence.

[C15: from L *consequēns* following closely, from *consequī* to pursue]

> USAGE NOTE   See at **consequential.**

onsequential (ˌkɒnsɪˈkwɛnʃəl) *adj* **1** important or significant. **2** self-important. **3** following as a consequence, esp. indirectly: *consequential loss.*
▶ ˌconseˌquentiˈality *n* ▶ ˌconseˈquentially *adv*

> USAGE NOTE   Although both *consequential* and *consequent* can refer to something which happens as the result of something else, *consequent* is more common in this sense in modern English: *the new measures were put into effect, and the consequent protest led to the dismissal of those responsible.*

onsequently (ˈkɒnsɪkwəntlɪ) *adv, sentence connector.* as a result or effect; therefore; hence.

onservancy (kənˈsɜːvənsɪ) *n, pl* **conservancies.** **1** (in Britain) a court or commission with jurisdiction over a river, port, area of countryside, etc. **2** another word for **conservation** (sense 2).

onservation (ˌkɒnsəˈveɪʃən) *n* **1** the act of conserving or keeping from change, loss, injury, etc. **2a** protection, preservation, and careful management of natural resources. **2b** (*as modifier*): *a conservation area.* **3** *Physics, etc.* the preservation of a specified aspect or value of a system, as in **conservation of charge, conservation of momentum, conservation of parity.**
▶ ˌconserˈvational *adj* ▶ ˌconserˈvationist *n*

onservation of energy *n* the principle that the total energy of any isolated system is constant and independent of any changes occurring within the system.

onservation of mass *n* the principle that the total mass of any isolated system is constant and is independent of any chemical and physical changes taking place within the system.

onservatism (kənˈsɜːvəˌtɪzəm) *n* **1** opposition to change and innovation. **2** a political philosophy advocating the preservation of the best of the established order in society.

onservative (kənˈsɜːvətɪv) *adj* **1** favouring the preservation of established customs, values, etc., and opposing innovation. **2** of conservatism. **3** moderate or cautious: *a conservative estimate.* **4** conventional in style: *a conservative suit.* **5** *Med.* (of treatment) designed to alleviate symptoms. Cf. **radical** (sense 4). ◆ *n* **6** a person who is reluctant to change or consider new ideas; conformist. **7** a supporter of conservatism.
▶ conˈservatively *adv* ▶ conˈservativeness *n*

Conservative (kənˈsɜːvətɪv) ◆ *adj* **1** (in Britain and elsewhere) of, supporting, or relating to a Conservative Party. **2** (in Canada) of, supporting, or relating to the Progressive Conservative Party. **3** of, relating to, or characterizing Conservative Judaism. ◆ *n* **4** a supporter or member of a Conservative Party, or, (in Canada) of the Progressive Conservative Party.

Conservative Judaism *n* a movement rejecting extreme change and advocating moderate relaxations of traditional Jewish law.

Conservative Party *n* **1** (in Britain) the major right-wing party, which developed from the Tories in the 1830s. It encourages property owning and free enterprise. **2** (in Canada) short for Progressive Conservative Party. **3** (in other countries) any of various political parties generally opposing change.

onservatoire (kənˈsɜːˌtwɑː) *n* an institution or school for instruction in music. Also called: **conservatory.** [C18: from F: CONSERVATORY]

onservator (ˈkɒnsəˌveɪtə, kənˈsɜːvə-) *n* a custodian, guardian, or protector.

onservatorium (kənˌsɜːvəˈtɔːrɪəm) *n Austral.* the usual term for **conservatoire.**

conservatory (kənˈsɜːvətrɪ) *n, pl* **conservatories.** **1** a greenhouse, esp. one attached to a house. **2** another word for **conservatoire.**

conserve *vb* (kənˈsɜːv), **conserves, conserving, conserved.** (*tr*) **1** to keep or protect from harm, decay, loss, etc. **2** to preserve (a foodstuff, esp. fruit) with sugar. ◆ *n* (ˈkɒnsɜːv, kənˈsɜːv). **3** a preparation similar to jam but usually containing whole pieces of fruit. [(vb) C14: from L *conservāre* to keep safe, from *servāre* to save; (n) C14: from Med. L *conserva,* from L *conservāre*]

consider (kənˈsɪdə) *vb* (*mainly tr*) **1** (*also intr*) to think carefully about (a problem, decision, etc.). **2** (*may take a clause as object*) to judge; deem: *I consider him a fool.* **3** to have regard for: *consider your mother's feelings.* **4** to look at: *he considered her face.* **5** (*may take a clause as object*) to bear in mind: *when buying a car consider this make.* **6** to describe or discuss. [C14: from L *consīderāre* to inspect closely]

considerable (kənˈsɪdərəbᵊl) *adj* **1** large enough to reckon with: *a considerable quantity.* **2** a lot of; much: *he had considerable courage.* **3** worthy of respect: *a considerable man in the scientific world.*
▶ conˈsiderably *adv*

considerate (kənˈsɪdərɪt) *adj* **1** thoughtful towards other people; kind. **2** *Rare.* carefully thought out; considered.
▶ conˈsiderately *adv*

consideration (kənˌsɪdəˈreɪʃən) *n* **1** deliberation; contemplation. **2 take into consideration.** to bear in mind; consider. **3 under consideration.** being currently discussed. **4** a fact to be taken into account when making a judgment or decision. **5** thoughtfulness for other people; kindness. **6** payment for a service. **7** thought resulting from deliberation; opinion. **8** *Law.* the promise, object, etc., given by one party to persuade another to enter into a contract. **9** esteem. **10 in consideration of. 10a** because of. **10b** in return for.

considered (kənˈsɪdəd) *adj* **1** presented or thought out with care: *a considered opinion.* **2** (*qualified by a preceding adverb*) esteemed: *highly considered.*

considering (kənˈsɪdərɪŋ) *prep* **1** in view of. ◆ *adv* **2** *Inf.* all in all; taking into account the circumstances: *it's not bad considering.* ◆ *conj* **3** (*subordinating*) in view of the fact that.

consign (kənˈsaɪn) *vb* (*mainly tr*) **1** to give into the care or charge of; entrust. **2** to commit irrevocably: *he consigned the papers to the flames.* **3** to commit: *to consign someone to jail.* **4** to address or deliver (goods): *it was consigned to his London address.* [C15: from OF *consigner,* from L *consignāre* to put one's seal to, sign, from *signum* mark]
▶ conˈsignable *adj* ▶ ˌconsignˈee *n* ▶ conˈsignor *or* conˈsigner *n*

consignment (kənˈsaɪnmənt) *n* **1** the act of consigning; commitment. **2** a shipment of goods consigned. **3 on consignment.** for payment by the consignee after sale.

consist (kənˈsɪst) *vb* (*intr*) **1** (foll. by *of* or *in*) to be composed (of). **2** (foll. by *in* or *of*) to have its existence (in): *his religion consists only in going to church.* **3** to be consistent; accord. [C16: from L *consistere* to stand firm, from *sistere* to stand]

consistency (kənˈsɪstənsɪ) *or* **consistence** *n, pl* **consistencies** *or* **consistences. 1** agreement or accordance. **2** degree of viscosity or firmness. **3** the state or quality of holding or sticking together and retaining shape. **4** conformity with previous attitudes, behaviour, practice, etc.

consistent (kənˈsɪstənt) *adj* **1** (usually foll. by *with*) showing consistency or harmony. **2** steady; even: *consistent growth.* **3** *Logic.* (of a logical system) constituted so that the propositions deduced from different axioms of the system do not contradict each other.
▶ conˈsistently *adv*

consistory (kənˈsɪstərɪ) *n, pl* **consistories. 1** *Church of England.* the court of a diocese (other than Canterbury) administering ecclesiastical law. **2** *RC Church.* an assembly of the cardinals and the pope. **3** (in certain Reformed Churches) the governing body of a local congregation. **4** *Arch.* a council. [C14: from OF, from Med. L *consistōrium* ecclesiastical tribunal, ult. from L *consistere* to stand still]
▶ consistorial (ˌkɒnsɪˈstɔːrɪəl) *adj*

consolation (ˌkɒnsəˈleɪʃən) *n* **1** the act of consoling or

state of being consoled. **2** a person or thing that is a comfort in a time of grief, disappointment, etc.
▶ **consolatory** (kən'sɒlətərɪ) *adj*

consolation prize *n* a prize given to console a loser of a game.

console[1] (kən'səʊl) *vb* **consoles, consoling, consoled.** to serve as a comfort to (someone) in disappointment, sadness, etc. [C17: from L *consōlārī*, from *sōlārī* to comfort]
▶ **con'solable** *adj* ▶ **con'soler** *n* ▶ **con'solingly** *adv*

console[2] ('kɒnsəʊl) *n* **1** an ornamental bracket used to support a wall fixture, etc. **2** the part of an organ comprising the manuals, pedals, stops, etc. **3** a unit on which the controls of an electronic system are mounted. **4** a cabinet for a television, etc., designed to stand on the floor. **5** See **console table**. [C18: from F, from OF *consolateur* one that provides support; see CONSOLE[1]]

console table *n* a table with one or more curved legs of bracket-like construction, designed to stand against a wall.

consolidate (kən'sɒlɪˌdeɪt) *vb* **consolidates, consolidating, consolidated. 1** to form or cause to form into a whole. **2** to make or become stronger or more stable. **3** *Mil.* to strengthen one's control over (a situation, area, etc.). [C16: from L *consolidāre* to make firm, from *solidus* strong]
▶ **con,soli'dation** *n* ▶ **con'soli,dator** *n*

consolidated fund *n Brit.* a fund maintained from tax revenue to meet standing charges, esp. national debt interest.

consols ('kɒnsɒlz, kən'sɒlz) *pl n* irredeemable British government securities carrying annual interest. [short for *consolidated stock*]

consommé (kən'sɒmeɪ) *n* a clear soup made from meat stock. [C19: from F, from *consommer* to use up]

consonance ('kɒnsənəns) *n* **1** agreement, harmony, or accord. **2** *Prosody.* similarity between consonants, but not between vowels, as between the *s* and *t* sounds in *sweet silent thought.* **3** *Music.* a combination of notes which can sound together without harshness.

consonant ('kɒnsənənt) *n* **1** a speech sound or letter of the alphabet other than a vowel. ◆ *adj* **2** (postpositive; foll. by *with* or *to*) consistent; in agreement. **3** harmonious. **4** *Music.* characterized by the presence of a consonance. [C14: from L *consonāns*, from *consonāre* to sound at the same time, from *sonāre* to sound]
▶ **'consonantly** *adv*

consonantal (ˌkɒnsə'næntə̩l) *adj* relating to, functioning as, or characterized by consonants.

consort *vb* (kən'sɔːt). (*intr*) **1** (usually foll. by *with*) to keep company (with undesirable people); associate. **2** to harmonize. ◆ *n* ('kɒnsɔːt). **3** (esp. formerly) a small group of instruments, either of the same type (**a whole consort**) or of different types (**a broken consort**). **4** the husband or wife of a reigning monarch. **5** a husband or wife. **6** a ship that escorts another. [C15: from OF, from L *consors* partner, from *sors* lot, portion]

consortium (kən'sɔːtɪəm) *n, pl* **consortia** (-tɪə). **1** an association of financiers, companies, etc., esp. for a particular purpose. **2** *Law.* the right of husband or wife to the company and affection of the other. [C19: from L: partnership; see CONSORT]

conspectus (kən'spɛktəs) *n* **1** an overall view; survey. **2** a summary; résumé. [C19: from L: a viewing, from *conspicere*, from *specere* to look]

conspicuous (kən'spɪkjʊəs) *adj* **1** clearly visible. **2** attracting attention because of a striking feature: *conspicuous stupidity.* [C16: from L *conspicuus*, from *conspicere* to perceive; see CONSPECTUS]
▶ **con'spicuously** *adv* ▶ **con'spicuousness** *n*

conspiracy (kən'spɪrəsɪ) *n, pl* **conspiracies. 1** a secret plan to carry out an illegal or harmful act, esp. with political motivation; plot. **2** the act of making such plans in secret.
▶ **con'spirator** *n* ▶ **con,spira'torial** *adj*

conspiracy theory *n* the belief that the government or a covert organization is responsible for an unusual or unexplained event.

conspire (kən'spaɪə) *vb* **conspires, conspiring, conspired.** (when *intr*, sometimes foll. by *against*) **1** to plan (a crime) together in secret. **2** (*intr*) to act together as if by design: *the elements conspired to spoil our picnic.* [C14: from OF from L *conspīrāre* to plot together, lit.: to breathe together, from *spīrāre* to breathe]

con spirito (kɒn 'spɪrɪtəʊ) *adj, adv Music.* (to be per formed) in a spirited or lively manner. [It.: with spirit]

constable ('kʌnstəb̩l, 'kɒn-) *n* **1** (in Britain, Australia New Zealand, Canada, etc.) a police officer of the lowest rank. **2** any of various officers of the peace, esp. one who arrests offenders, serves writs, etc. **3** the keeper of a roya castle. **4** (in medieval Europe) the chief military officer and functionary of a royal household. **5** an officer of a hundred in medieval England. [C13: from OF, from LL *comes stabulī* officer in charge of the stable]
▶ **'constable,ship** *n*

Constable ★ ('kʌnstəb̩l) *n* **John.** 1776–1837, British landscape painter.

constabulary (kən'stæbjʊlərɪ) *Chiefly Brit.* ◆ *n, pl* **constabularies. 1** the police force of a town or district. ◆ *adj* **2** of or relating to constables.

Constance ★ ('kɒnstəns) *n* **1** a city in S Germany, in Baden-Württemberg on Lake Constance: tourist centre. Pop.: 72 860 (1989 est.). German name: **Konstanz. 2** Lake a lake in W Europe, bounded by S Germany, W Austria, and N Switzerland, through which the Rhine flows. Area: 536 sq. km. (207 sq. miles). German name: **Bodensee.**

constant ('kɒnstənt) *adj* **1** unchanging. **2** incessant: *constant interruptions.* **3** resolute; loyal. ◆ *n* **4** something that is unchanging. **5** a specific quantity that is invariable: *the velocity of light is a constant.* **6a** *Maths.* a symbol representing an unspecified number that remains invariable throughout a particular series of operations. **6b** *Physics.* a quantity or property that is considered invariable throughout a particular series of experiments. [C14: from OF, from L *constāns*, from *constāre* to be steadfast, from *stāre* to stand]
▶ **'constancy** *n* ▶ **'constantly** *adv*

Constanţa ★ (*Romanian* kon'stantsa) *n* a port and resort in SE Romania, on the Black Sea: founded by the Greeks in the 6th century B.C. and rebuilt by Constantine the Great (4th century); exports petroleum. Pop.: 348 985 (1993 est.).

Constantia ★ (kɒn'stænʃə) *n S. African.* **1** a region of the Cape Peninsula. **2** any of several red or white wines produced around Constantia.

Constantine ★ ('kɒnstən,taɪn; *French* kõstātin) *n* a walled city in NE Algeria: built on an isolated rock; military and trading centre. Pop.: 440 842 (1987).

Constantine I ★ ('kɒnstən,taɪn, -,tiːn) *n* **1** known as *Constantine the Great.* Latin name *Flavius Valerius Aurelius Constantinus.* ?280–337 A.D., first Christian Roman emperor (306–337): moved his capital to Byzantium, which he renamed Constantinople (330). **2** 1868–1923, king of Greece (1913–17; 1920–22): deposed (1917), recalled by a plebiscite (1920), but forced to abdicate again (1922) after defeat by the Turks.

Constantine II ★ *n* official title *Constantine XIII.* born 1940, king of Greece (1964–73): exiled in 1967 and deposed in 1973 when Greece became a republic.

Constantine VII ★ *n* known as *Porphyrogenitus.* 905–959 A.D., Byzantine emperor (913–59) and scholar.

Constantine XI ★ *n* 1404–53, last Byzantine emperor (1448–53): killed when Constantinople was captured by the Turks.

Constantinople ★ (ˌkɒnstæntɪ'nəʊp̩l) *n* the former name (330–1926) of **Istanbul.**

constellate ('kɒnstɪˌleɪt) *vb* **constellates, constellating, constellated.** to form into clusters in or as if in constellations.

constellation (ˌkɒnstɪ'leɪʃən) *n* **1** any of the 88 groups of stars as seen from the earth, many of which were named by the ancient Greeks after animals, objects, or mythological persons. **2** a gathering of brilliant people or things. **3** *Psychoanalysis.* a group of ideas felt to be re-

★ people and places

lated. [C14: from LL *constellātiō*, from L *com-* together + *stella* star]
▶ **constellatory** (kən'stɛlətərɪ) *adj*

consternate ('kɒnstəˌneɪt) *vb* **consternates, consternating, consternated.** (*tr; usually passive*) to fill with anxiety, dismay, dread, or confusion. [C17: from L *consternāre*, from *sternere* to lay low]

consternation (ˌkɒnstə'neɪʃən) *n* a feeling of anxiety, dismay, dread, or confusion.

constipate ('kɒnstɪˌpeɪt) *vb* **constipates, constipating, constipated.** (*tr*) to cause constipation in. [C16: from L *constīpāre* to press closely together]
▶ **'constiˌpated** *adj*

constipation (ˌkɒnstɪ'peɪʃən) *n* infrequent or difficult evacuation of the bowels.

constituency (kən'stɪtjʊənsɪ) *n, pl* **constituencies. 1** the whole body of voters who elect one representative to a legislature or all the residents represented by one deputy. **2** a district that sends one representative to a legislature.

constituent (kən'stɪtjʊənt) *adj* (*prenominal*) **1** forming part of a whole; component. **2** having the power to frame a constitution or to constitute a government: *constituent assembly.* ◆ *n* **3** a component part; ingredient. **4** a resident of a constituency. **5** esp. one entitled to vote. **5** *Chiefly law.* a person who appoints another to act for him. [C17: from L *constituēns*, from *constituere* to establish, CONSTITUTE]
▶ **con'stituently** *adv*

constitute ('kɒnstɪˌtjuːt) *vb* **constitutes, constituting, constituted.** (*tr*) **1** to form; compose: *the people who constitute a jury.* **2** to appoint to an office: *a legally constituted officer.* **3** to set up (an institution) formally; found. **4** *Law.* to give legal form to (a court, assembly, etc.). [C15: from L *constituere*, from *com-* (intensive) + *statuere* to place]
▶ **'constiˌtutor** *n*

constitution (ˌkɒnstɪ'tjuːʃən) *n* **1** the act of constituting or state of being constituted. **2** physical make-up; structure. **3** the fundamental principles on which a state is governed, esp. when considered as embodying the rights of the subjects. **4** (*often cap.*) (in certain countries, esp. the US and Australia) a statute embodying such principles. **5** a person's state of health. **6** a person's temperament.

constitutional (ˌkɒnstɪ'tjuːʃənʲl) *adj* **1** of a constitution. **2** authorized by or subject to a constitution: *constitutional monarchy.* **3** inherent in the nature of a person or thing: *a constitutional weakness.* **4** beneficial to one's physical wellbeing. ◆ *n* **5** a regular walk taken for the benefit of one's health.
▶ ˌ**constiˌtution'ality** *n* ▶ ˌ**consti'tutionally** *adv*

constitutionalism (ˌkɒnstɪ'tjuːʃənəˌlɪzəm) *n* **1** the principles or system of government in accord with a constitution. **2** adherence to or advocacy of such a system.
▶ ˌ**consti'tutionalist** *n*

constitutive ('kɒnstɪˌtjuːtɪv) *adj* **1** having power to enact or establish. **2** another word for **constituent** (sense 1).
▶ **'constiˌtutively** *adv*

constrain (kən'streɪn) *vb* (*tr*) **1** to compel, esp. by circumstances, etc. **2** to restrain as by force. [C14: from OF, from L *constringere* to bind together]
▶ **con'strainer** *n*

constrained (kən'streɪnd) *adj* embarrassed, unnatural, or forced: *a constrained smile.*

constraint (kən'streɪnt) *n* **1** compulsion or restraint. **2** repression of natural feelings. **3** a forced unnatural manner. **4** something that serves to constrain; restrictive condition.

constrict (kən'strɪkt) *vb* (*tr*) **1** to make smaller or narrower, esp. by contracting at one place. **2** to hold in or inhibit; limit. [C18: from L *constrictus*, from *constringere* to tie up together]

constriction (kən'strɪkʃən) *n* **1** a feeling of tightness in some part of the body, such as the chest. **2** the act of constricting or condition of being constricted. **3** something that is constricted.
▶ **con'strictive** *adj*

constrictor (kən'strɪktə) *n* **1** any of various nonvenomous snakes, such as the boas, that coil around and squeeze their prey to kill it. **2** any muscle that constricts; sphincter.

construct *vb* (kən'strʌkt). (*tr*) **1** to put together substances or parts systematically; build; assemble. **2** to frame mentally (an argument, sentence, etc.). **3** *Geom.* to draw (a line, angle, or figure) so that certain requirements are satisfied. ◆ *n* ('kɒnstrʌkt). **4** something formulated or built systematically. **5** a complex idea resulting from a synthesis of simpler ideas. [C17: from L *constructus*, from *construere* to build, from *struere* to arrange, erect]
▶ **con'structor** *or* **con'structer** *n*

construction (kən'strʌkʃən) *n* **1** the act of constructing or manner in which a thing is constructed. **2** a structure. **3a** the business or work of building dwellings, offices, etc. **3b** (*as modifier*): *a construction site.* **4** an interpretation: *they put a sympathetic construction on her behaviour.* **5** *Grammar.* a group of words that make up one of the constituents into which a sentence may be analysed; a phrase or clause. **6** an abstract work of art in three dimensions.
▶ **con'structional** *adj* ▶ **con'structionally** *adv*

constructive (kən'strʌktɪv) *adj* **1** serving to improve; positive: *constructive criticism.* **2** *Law.* deduced by inference; not expressed. **3** another word for **structural**.
▶ **con'structively** *adv*

constructivism (kən'strʌktɪˌvɪzəm) *n* a movement in abstract art evolved after World War I, which explored the use of movement and machine-age materials in sculpture.
▶ **con'structivist** *adj, n*

construe (kən'struː) *vb* **construes, construing, construed.** (*mainly tr*) **1** to interpret the meaning of (something): *you can construe that in different ways.* **2** (*may take a clause as object*) to infer; deduce. **3** to analyse the grammatical structure of; parse (esp. a Latin or Greek text as a preliminary to translation). **4** to combine words syntactically. **5** (*also intr*) *Old-fashioned.* to translate literally, esp. aloud. [C14: from L *construere*; see CONSTRUCT]
▶ **con'struable** *adj*

consubstantial (ˌkɒnsəb'stænʃəl) *adj Christian theol.* (esp. of the three persons of the Trinity) regarded as identical in essence though different in aspect. [C15: from Church L, from L *com-* COM- + *substantia* SUBSTANCE]
▶ ˌ**consubˌstanti'ality** *n*

consubstantiation (ˌkɒnsəbˌstænʃɪ'eɪʃən) *n Christian theol.* (in the Lutheran branch of Protestantism) the doctrine that after the consecration of the Eucharist the substance of the body and blood of Christ coexists within the substance of the consecrated bread and wine. Cf. **transubstantiation.**

consuetude ('kɒnswɪˌtjuːd) *n* an established custom or usage, esp. one having legal force. [C14: from L *consuētūdō*, from *consuēscere*, from CON- + *suēscere* to be wont]

consul ('kɒnsʲl) *n* **1** an official appointed by a sovereign state to protect its commercial interests and aid its citizens in a foreign city. **2** (in ancient Rome) either of two annually elected magistrates who jointly exercised the highest authority in the republic. **3** (in France from 1799 to 1804) any of the three chief magistrates of the First Republic. [C14: from L, from *consulere* to CONSULT]
▶ **consular** ('kɒnsjʊlə) *adj* ▶ **'consulˌship** *n*

consulate ('kɒnsjʊlɪt) *n* **1** the premises of a consul. **2** government by consuls. **3** the office or period of office of a consul. **4** (*often cap.*) **4a** the government of France by the three consuls from 1799 to 1804. **4b** this period. **5** (*often cap.*) the consular government of the Roman republic.

consul general *n, pl* **consuls general.** a consul of the highest grade, usually stationed in a city of considerable commercial importance.

consult (kən'sʌlt) *vb* **1** (when *intr*, often foll. by *with*) to ask advice from (someone). **2** (*tr*) to refer to for information: *to consult a map.* **3** (*tr*) to have regard for (a person's feelings, interests, etc.); consider. [C17: from F, from L *consultāre*, from *consulere* to consult]

consultant (kən'sʌltᵊnt) n **1a** a specialist physician who is asked to confirm a diagnosis. **1b** a physician or surgeon holding the highest appointment in a particular branch of medicine or surgery in a hospital. **2** a specialist who gives expert advice or information. **3** a person who asks advice in a consultation.
▶ con'sultancy n

consultation (ˌkɒnsᵊl'teɪʃən) n **1** the act of consulting. **2** a conference for discussion or the seeking of advice.
▶ consultative (kən'sʌltətɪv) adj

consulting (kən'sʌltɪŋ) adj (prenominal) acting in an advisory capacity on professional matters: a consulting engineer.

consulting room n a room in which a doctor sees his patients.

consume (kən'sjuːm) vb **consumes, consuming, consumed. 1** (tr) to eat or drink. **2** (tr; often passive) to obsess. **3** (tr) to use up; expend. **4** to destroy or be destroyed by: fire consumed the forest. **5** (tr) to waste. **6** (passive) to waste away. [C14: from L consumere, from com- (intensive) + sūmere to take up]
▶ con'sumable adj ▶ con'suming adj

consumedly (kən'sjuːmɪdlɪ) adv Old-fashioned. (intensifier): consumedly fascinating.

consumer (kən'sjuːmə) n **1** a person who purchases goods and services for his own personal needs. Cf. **producer** (sense 6). **2** a person or thing that consumes.

consumer durable n a manufactured product that has a relatively long useful life, such as a car or a television.

consumer goods pl n goods that satisfy personal needs rather than those required for the production of other goods or services.

consumerism (kən'sjuːməˌrɪzəm) n **1** protection of the interests of consumers. **2** advocacy of a high rate of consumption as a basis for a sound economy.
▶ con'sumerist n, adj

consumer terrorism n the practice of introducing dangerous substances to foodstuffs or other consumer products, esp. to extort money from the manufacturers.

consummate vb ('kɒnsəˌmeɪt), **consummates, consummating, consummated.** (tr) **1** to bring to completion; fulfil. **2** to complete (a marriage) legally by sexual intercourse. ◆ adj (kən'sʌmɪt, 'kɒnsəmɪt). **3** supremely skilled: a consummate artist. **4** (prenominal) (intensifier): a consummate fool. [C15: from L consummāre to complete, from summus utmost]
▶ con'summately adv ▶ ˌconsum'mation n

consumption (kən'sʌmpʃən) n **1** the act of consuming or the state of being consumed, esp. by eating, burning, etc. **2** Econ. expenditure on goods and services for final personal use. **3** the quantity consumed. **4** a wasting away of the tissues of the body, esp. in tuberculosis of the lungs. [C14: from L consumptiō, from consūmere to CONSUME]

consumptive (kən'sʌmptɪv) adj **1** causing consumption; wasteful; destructive. **2** relating to or affected with tuberculosis of the lungs. ◆ n **3** Pathol. a person who suffers from consumption.
▶ con'sumptively adv ▶ con'sumptiveness n

cont. abbrev. for: **1** contents. **2** continued.

contact n (ˈkɒntækt). **1** the act or state of touching. **2** the state or fact of communication (esp. in **in contact, make contact**). **3a** a junction of electrical conductors. **3b** the part of the conductors that makes the junction. **3c** the part of an electrical device to which such connections are made. **4** an acquaintance, esp. one who might be useful in business, etc. **5** any person who has been exposed to a contagious disease. **6** (modifier) caused by touching the causative agent: contact dermatitis. **7** (modifier) denoting a herbicide or insecticide that kills on contact. **8** (modifier) of or maintaining contact. **9** (modifier) requiring or involving (physical) contact: a contact sport. ◆ vb ('kɒntækt, kən'tækt). **10** (when intr, often foll. by with) to put, come, or be in association, touch, or communication. [C17: from L contactus, from contingere to touch on all sides, from tangere to touch]
▶ contactual (kɒn'tæktjʊəl) adj

contact lens n a thin convex lens, usually of plastic,

which floats on the layer of tears in front of the cornea to correct defects of vision.

contact print n a photographic print made by exposing the printing paper through a negative placed directly on to it.

contagion (kən'teɪdʒən) n **1** the transmission of disease from one person to another by contact. **2** a contagious disease. **3** a corrupting influence that tends to spread. **4** the spreading of an emotional or mental state among a number of people: the contagion of mirth. [C14: from L contāgiō infection, from contingere; see CONTACT]

contagious (kən'teɪdʒəs) adj **1** (of a disease) capable of being passed on by direct contact with a diseased individual or by handling his clothing, etc. **2** (of an organism) harbouring the causative agent of a transmissible disease. **3** causing or likely to cause the same reaction in several people: her laughter was contagious.

contain (kən'teɪn) vb (tr) **1** to hold or be capable of holding: this contains five pints. **2** to restrain (feelings, behaviour, etc.). **3** to consist of: the book contains three sections. **4** Mil. to prevent (enemy forces) from operating beyond a certain area. **5** to be a multiple of, leaving no remainder: 6 contains 2 and 3. [C13: from OF, from L continēre, from com- together + tenēre to hold]
▶ con'tainable adj

container (kən'teɪnə) n **1** an object used for or capable of holding, esp. for transport or storage. **2a** a large cargo-carrying standard-sized container that can be loaded from one mode of transport to another. **2b** (as modifier): a container ship.

containerize or **containerise** (kən'teɪnəˌraɪz) vb **containerizes, containerizing, containerized** or **containerises, containerising, containerised.** (tr) **1** to convey (cargo) in standard-sized containers. **2** to adapt (a port or transportation system) to the use of standard-sized containers.
▶ conˌtaineriˈzation or conˌtaineriˈsation n

containment (kən'teɪnmənt) n the act of containing, esp. of restraining the power of a hostile country or the operations of a hostile military force.

contaminate (kən'tæmɪˌneɪt) vb **contaminates, contaminating, contaminated.** (tr) **1** to make impure; pollute. **2** to make radioactive by the addition of radioactive material. [C15: from L contamināre to defile]
▶ con'taminable adj ▶ con'taminant n ▶ conˌtamiˈnation n
▶ con'tamiˌnator n

contango (kən'tæŋgəʊ) n, pl **contangos. 1** (formerly, on the London Stock Exchange) postponement of payment for and delivery of stock from one account day to the next. **2** the fee paid for such a postponement. ◆ Also called: **carry-over, continuation.** Cf. **backwardation.** [C19: apparently an arbitrary coinage]

conte French. (kɔ̃t) n a tale or short story.

contemn (kən'tem) vb (tr) Formal. to regard with contempt; scorn. [C15: from L contemnere, from temnere to slight]
▶ contemner (kən'temnə, -'temə) n

contemplate ('kɒntemˌpleɪt) vb **contemplates, contemplating, contemplated.** (mainly tr) **1** to think about intently and at length. **2** (intr) to think intently and at length, esp. for spiritual reasons; meditate. **3** to look at thoughtfully. **4** to have in mind as a possibility. [C16: from L contemplāre, from templum TEMPLE¹]
▶ ˌcontemˈplation n ▶ 'contemˌplator n

contemplative ('kɒntemˌpleɪtɪv, -təm-; kən'templə-) adj **1** denoting, concerned with, or inclined to contemplation; meditative. ◆ n **2** a person dedicated to religious contemplation.

contemporaneous (kənˌtempə'reɪnɪəs) adj existing, beginning, or occurring in the same period of time.
▶ **contemporaneity** (kənˌtempərə'niːɪtɪ) or **conˌtempo-'raneousness** n

contemporary (kən'tempˌrərɪ) adj **1** living or occurring in the same period. **2** existing or occurring at the present time. **3** conforming to modern ideas in style, fashion, etc. **4** having approximately the same age as one another. ◆ n, pl **contemporaries. 5** a person living at the same time or of approximately the same age as another. **6** something that is contemporary. [C17: from Med. L

★ people and places

contemporārius, from L *com-* together + *temporārius* relating to time, from *tempus* time]
▶ **con'temporarily** *adv* ▶ **con'temporariness** *n*

> **USAGE NOTE** Since *contemporary* can mean either of the same period or of the present period, it is best to avoid this word where ambiguity might arise, as in *a production of* Othello *in contemporary dress. Modern dress* or *Elizabethan dress* should be used in this example to avoid ambiguity.

:ontemporize *or* **contemporise** (kən'tɛmpə,raɪz) *vb* **contemporizes, contemporizing, contemporized** *or* **contemporises, contemporising, contemporised.** to be or make contemporary.

:ontempt (kən'tɛmpt) *n* **1** the feeling of a person towards a person or thing that he considers despicable; scorn. **2** the state of being scorned; disgrace (esp. in **hold in contempt**). **3** wilful disregard of the authority of a court of law or legislative body: *contempt of court.* [C14: from L *contemptus,* from *contemnere* to CONTEMN]

:ontemptible (kən'tɛmptɪb°l) *adj* deserving or worthy of contempt.
▶ **con,tempti'bility** *or* **con'temptibleness** *n* ▶ **con'temptibly** *adv*

:contemptuous (kən'tɛmptjʊəs) *adj* (when *predicative,* often foll. by *of*) showing or feeling contempt; disdainful.
▶ **con'temptuously** *adv*

:contend (kən'tɛnd) *vb* **1** (*intr;* often foll. by *with*) to struggle in rivalry, battle, etc.; vie. **2** to argue earnestly. **3** (*tr; may take a clause as object*) to assert. [C15: from L *contendere* to strive, from *com-* with + *tendere* to stretch]
▶ **con'tender** *n*

:content[1] ('kɒntɛnt) *n* **1** (*often pl*) everything inside a container. **2** (*usually pl*) **2a** the chapters or divisions of a book. **2b** a list of these printed at the front of a book. **3** the meaning or significance of a work of art, as distinguished from its style or form. **4** all that is contained or dealt with in a piece of writing, etc.; substance. **5** the capacity or size of a thing. **6** the proportion of a substance contained in an alloy, mixture, etc.: *the lead content of petrol.* [C15: from L *contentus* contained, from *continēre* to CONTAIN]

:content[2] (kən'tɛnt) *adj* (*postpositive*) **1** satisfied with things as they are. **2** assenting to or willing to accept circumstances, a proposed course of action, etc. ◆ *vb* **3** (*tr*) to make (oneself or another person) satisfied. ◆ *n* **4** peace of mind. [C14: from OF, from L *contentus* contented, having restrained desires, from *continēre* to restrain]
▶ **con'tentment** *n*

contented (kən'tɛntɪd) *adj* accepting one's situation or life with equanimity and satisfaction.
▶ **con'tentedly** *adv* ▶ **con'tentedness** *n*

contention (kən'tɛnʃən) *n* **1** a struggling between opponents; competition. **2** a point of dispute (esp. in **bone of contention**). **3** a point asserted in argument. [C14: from L *contentiō,* from *contendere* to CONTEND]

contentious (kən'tɛnʃəs) *adj* **1** tending to quarrel. **2** causing or characterized by dispute; controversial.
▶ **con'tentiousness** *n*

conterminous (kən'tɜ:mɪnəs) *or* **coterminous** (kəʊ-'tɜ:mɪnəs) *adj* **1** enclosed within a common boundary. **2** without a break or interruption. [C17: from L *conterminus,* from CON- + *terminus* boundary]

contest *n* ('kɒntɛst). **1** a formal game or match in which people, teams, etc., compete. **2** a struggle for victory between opposing forces. ◆ *vb* (kən'tɛst). **3** (*tr*) to try to disprove; call in question. **4** (when *intr,* foll. by *with* or *against*) to dispute or contend (with): *to contest an election.* [C16: from L *contestārī* to introduce a lawsuit, from *testis* witness]
▶ **con'testable** *adj* ▶ **con'tester** *n*

contestant (kən'tɛstənt) *n* a person who takes part in a contest; competitor.

context ('kɒntɛkst) *n* **1** the parts of a piece of writing, speech, etc., that precede and follow a word or passage and contribute to its full meaning: *it is unfair to quote out of context.* **2** the circumstances that are relevant to an event, fact, etc. [C15: from L *contextus* a putting together, from *contexere,* from *com-* together + *texere* to weave]
▶ **con'textual** *adj*

contiguous (kən'tɪgjʊəs) *adj* **1** touching along the side or boundary; in contact. **2** neighbouring. **3** preceding or following in time. [C17: from L *contiguus,* from *contingere* to touch; see CONTACT]
▶ **con'tiguously** *adv*

continent[1] ('kɒntɪnənt) *n* **1** one of the earth's large land masses (Asia, Australia, Africa, Europe, North and South America, and Antarctica). **2** *Obs.* **2a** mainland. **2b** a continuous extent of land. [C16: from the L phrase *terra continens* continuous land]
▶ **continental** (,kɒntɪ'nɛnt°l) *adj* ▶ **,conti'nentally** *adv*

continent[2] ('kɒntɪnənt) *adj* **1** able to control urination and defecation. **2** exercising self-restraint, esp. from sexual activity; chaste. [C14: from L *continēre;* see CONTAIN]
▶ **'continence** *n*

Continent ★ ('kɒntɪnənt) *n* **the.** the mainland of Europe as distinguished from the British Isles.

Continental (,kɒntɪ'nɛnt°l) *adj* **1** of or characteristic of Europe, excluding the British Isles. **2** of or relating to the 13 original British North American colonies during the War of American Independence. ◆ *n* **3** (*sometimes not cap.*) an inhabitant of Europe, excluding the British Isles. **4** a regular soldier of the rebel army during the War of American Independence.

continental breakfast *n* a light breakfast of coffee and rolls.

continental climate *n* a climate characterized by hot summers, cold winters, and little rainfall, typical of the interior of a continent.

continental drift *n Geol.* the theory that the earth's continents move gradually over the surface of the planet on a substratum of magma.

continental quilt *n Brit.* a quilt, stuffed with down or a synthetic material, used as a bed cover in place of the top sheet and blankets. Also called: **duvet,** (Austral.) **doona.**

continental shelf *n* the sea bed surrounding a continent at depths of up to about 200 metres (100 fathoms), at the edge of which the **continental slope** drops steeply.

contingency (kən'tɪndʒənsɪ) *or* **contingence** (kən-'tɪndʒəns) *n, pl* **contingencies** *or* **contingences. 1a** a possible but not very likely future event or condition. **1b** (*as modifier*): *a contingency plan.* **2** something dependent on a possible future event. **3** a fact, event, etc., incidental to something else. **4** *Logic.* the state of being contingent. **5** uncertainty. **6** *Statistics.* **6a** the degree of association between theoretical and observed common frequencies of two graded or classified variables. **6b** (*as modifier*): *a contingency table.*

contingent (kən'tɪndʒənt) *adj* **1** (when *postpositive,* often foll. by *on* or *upon*) dependent on events, conditions, etc., not yet known; conditional. **2** *Logic.* (of a proposition) true under certain conditions, false under others; not logically necessary. **3** happening by chance; accidental. **4** uncertain. ◆ *n* **5** a part of a military force, parade, etc. **6** a group distinguished by common interests, etc., that is part of a larger group. **7** a chance occurrence. [C14: from L *contingere* to touch; befall]

continual (kən'tɪnjʊəl) *adj* **1** recurring frequently, esp. at regular intervals. **2** occurring without interruption; continuous in time. [C14: from OF *continuel,* from L *continuus* uninterrupted, from *continēre* to CONTAIN]
▶ **con'tinually** *adv.*

> **USAGE NOTE** See at **continuous.**

continuance (kən'tɪnjʊəns) *n* **1** the act of continuing. **2**

the duration of an action, etc. **3** *US.* the adjournment of a legal proceeding.

continuant (kən'tɪnjʊənt) *Phonetics.* ◆ *n* **1** a speech sound, such as (l), (r), (f), or (s), in which the closure of the vocal tract is incomplete, allowing the continuous passage of the breath. ◆ *adj* **2** relating to or denoting a continuant.

continuation (kən,tɪnjʊ'eɪʃən) *n* **1** a part or thing added, esp. to a book or play; sequel. **2** a renewal of an interrupted action, process, etc.; resumption. **3** the act of continuing; prolongation. **4** another word for **contango**.

continue (kən'tɪnjuː) *vb* **continues, continuing, continued.** **1** (when *tr*, may take an infinitive) to remain or cause to remain in a particular condition or place. **2** (when *tr*, may take an infinitive) to carry on uninterruptedly (a course of action): *he continued running.* **3** (when *tr*, may take an infinitive) to resume after an interruption: *we'll continue after lunch.* **4** to prolong or be prolonged: *continue the chord until it meets the tangent.* **5** (*tr*) *Law, chiefly Scots.* to adjourn (legal proceedings).   [C14: from OF *continuer*, from L *continuāre* to join together]

continuity (,kɒntɪ'njuːɪtɪ) *n, pl* **continuities.** **1** logical sequence. **2** a continuous or connected whole. **3** the comprehensive script or scenario of detail in a film or broadcast. **4** the continuous projection of a film.

continuity girl *or* **man** *n* a woman or man whose job is to ensure continuity and consistency in successive shots of a film.

continuo (kən'tɪnjʊəʊ) *n, pl* **continuos.** **1** *Music.* **1a** a shortened form of **basso continuo** (see **thorough bass**). **1b** (*as modifier*): *a continuo accompaniment.* **2** the thorough-bass part as played on a keyboard instrument.   [It., lit.: continuous]

continuous (kən'tɪnjʊəs) *adj* **1** unceasing: *a continuous noise.* **2** in an unbroken series or pattern. **3** *Statistics.* (of a variable) having a continuum of possible values so that its distribution requires integration rather than summation to determine its cumulative probability. **4** *Grammar.* another word for **progressive** (sense 7).   [C17: from L *continuus*, from *continēre* to CONTAIN]
▸ con'tinuously *adv*

> **USAGE NOTE**   Both *continual* and *continuous* can be used to say that something continues without interruption, but only *continual* can correctly be used to say that something keeps happening repeatedly.

continuous assessment *n* the assessment of a pupil's progress throughout a course of study rather than exclusively by examination at the end of it.

continuous creation *n* the theory that matter is created continuously in the universe. See **steady-state theory.**

continuum (kən'tɪnjʊəm) *n, pl* **continua** (-'tɪnjʊə) *or* **continuums.** a continuous series or whole, no part of which is perceptibly different from the adjacent parts.   [C17: from L, neuter of *continuus* CONTINUOUS]

contort (kən'tɔːt) *vb* to twist or bend out of place or shape.   [C15: from L *contortus* intricate, from *contorquēre* to whirl around, from *torquēre* to twist]
▸ con'tortion *n* ▸ con'tortive *adj*

contortionist (kən'tɔːʃənɪst) *n* **1** a performer who contorts his body for the entertainment of others. **2** a person who twists or warps meaning.

contour ('kɒntʊə) *n* **1** the outline of a mass of land, figure, or body; a defining line. **2a** See **contour line.** **2b** (*as modifier*): *a contour map.* **3** (*often pl*) the shape of a curving form: *the contours of her body were full and round.* ◆ *vb* (*tr*) **4** to shape so as to form the contour of something. **5** to mark contour lines on. **6** to construct (a road, railway, etc.) to follow the outline of the land.   [C17: from F, from It. *contorno*, from *contornare* to sketch, from *tornare* to TURN]

contour line *n* a line on a map or chart joining points of equal height or depth.

contour ploughing *n* ploughing along the contour of the land to minimize erosion.

Contra ('kɒntrə) *n* a member of a US-backed guerrill army, founded in 1979, whose aim was to overthrow th Sandinista government in Nicaragua.

contra- *prefix* **1** against; contrary; opposing; contrasting *contraceptive.* **2** (in music) pitched below: *contrabass* [from L, from *contrā* against]

contraband ('kɒntrə,bænd) *n* **1a** goods that are prohibited by law from being exported or imported. **1b** illegall imported or exported goods. **2** illegal traffic in suc goods; smuggling. **3** Also called: **contraband of war.** good that a neutral country may not supply to a belligerent ◆ *adj* **4** (of goods) **4a** forbidden by law from being im ported or exported. **4b** illegally imported or exported [C16: from Sp. *contrabanda*, from It., from Med. L, from CONTRA- + *bannum* ban]
▸ 'contra,bandist *n*

contrabass (,kɒntrə'beɪs) *n* **1** another name for **double bass.** ◆ *adj* **2** denoting the instrument of a family that lower than the bass.

contrabassoon (,kɒntrəbə'suːn) *n* the largest instru ment in the oboe family, pitched an octave below th bassoon; double bassoon.

contraception (,kɒntrə'sepʃən) *n* the intentional pre vention of conception by artificial or natural means [C19: from CONTRA- + CONCEPTION]
▸ contra'ceptive *adj, n*

contract *vb* (kən'trækt). **1** to make or become smaller, narrower, shorter, etc. **2** ('kɒntrækt). (when *intr*, sometimes foll. by *for*; when *tr*, may take an infinitive) to enter into an agreement with (a person, company, etc.) to deliver (goods or services) or to do (something) or mutually agreed terms. **3** to draw or be drawn together. ◆ (*tr*) to incur or become affected by (a disease, debt, etc.). **5** (*tr*) to shorten (a word or phrase) by the omission of letters or syllables, usually indicated in writing by an apostrophe. **6** (*tr*) to wrinkle (the brow or a muscle). **7** (*tr*) to arrange (a marriage) for; betroth. ◆ *n* ('kɒntrækt). **8** a formal agreement between two or more parties. **9** a document that states the terms of such an agreement. **10** the branch of law treating of contracts. **11** marriage considered as a formal agreement. **12** See **contract bridge. 13** *Bridge.* **13a** the highest bid, which determines trumps and the number of tricks one side must make. **13b** the number and suit of these tricks. **14** *Sl.* **14a** a criminal agreement to kill a particular person in return for an agreed sum of money. **14b** (*as modifier*): *a contract killing.* [C16: from L *contractus* agreement, from *contrahere* to draw together, from *trahere* to draw]
▸ con'tractible *adj*

contract bridge ('kɒntrækt) *n* the most common variety of bridge, in which the declarer receives points counting towards game and rubber only for tricks he bids as well as makes. Cf. **auction bridge.**

contractile (kən'træktaɪl) *adj* having the power to contract or to cause contraction.

contraction (kən'trækʃən) *n* **1** an instance of contracting or the state of being contracted. **2** a shortening of a word or group of words, often marked by an apostrophe: *I've come* for *I have come.*
▸ con'tractive *adj*

contractor (kən'træktə) *n* **1** a person or firm that contracts to supply materials or labour, esp. for building. **2** something that contracts.

contract out ('kɒntrækt) *vb* (*intr, adv*) *Brit.* to agree not to participate in something, esp. the state pension scheme.

contractual (kən'træktjʊəl) *adj* of the nature of or assured by a contract.

contradict (,kɒntrə'dɪkt) *vb* **1** (*tr*) to affirm the opposite of (a statement, etc.). **2** (*tr*) to declare (a statement, etc.) to be false or incorrect; deny. **3** (*tr*) to be inconsistent with: *the facts contradicted his theory.* **4** (*intr*) to be at variance; be in contradiction.   [C16: from L *contrādīcere*, from CONTRA- + *dīcere* to speak]
▸ ,contra'dictable *adj* ▸ ,contra'dictor *n*

contradiction (,kɒntrə'dɪkʃən) *n* **1** opposition; denial. **2**

a declaration of the opposite. **3** a statement that is at variance with itself (often in a **contradiction in terms**). **4** conflict or inconsistency, as between events, qualities, etc. **5** a person or thing containing conflicting qualities. **6** *Logic.* a statement that is false under all circumstances; necessary falsehood.

:ontradictory (,kɒntrə'dɪktərɪ) *adj* **1** inconsistent; incompatible. **2** given to argument and contention: *a contradictory person.* **3** *Logic.* (of a pair of statements) unable both to be true or both to be false under the same circumstances.
▸ ,contra'dictorily *adv* ▸ ,contra'dictoriness *n*

:ontradistinction (,kɒntrədɪ'stɪŋkʃən) *n* a distinction made by contrasting different qualities.
▸ ,contradis'tinctive *adj*

:ontraflow ('kɒntrə,fləʊ) *n Brit.* two-way traffic on one carriageway of a motorway.

:ontrail ('kɒntreɪl) *n* another name for **vapour trail.** [C20: from CON(DENSATION) + TRAIL]

:ontralto (kən'træltəʊ) *n, pl* **contraltos** or **contralti** (-tɪ). **1** the lowest female voice: in the context of a choir often shortened to **alto. 2** a singer with such a voice. ◆ *adj* **3** of or denoting a contralto: *the contralto part.* [C18: from It.; see CONTRA-, ALTO]

:ontraposition (,kɒntrəpə'zɪʃən) *n* **1** the act of placing opposite or against. **2** *Logic.* the conclusion drawn from a subject-predicate proposition by negating its terms and changing their order.

:ontraption (kən'træpʃən) *n Inf., often facetious or derog.* a device or contrivance, esp. one considered strange, unnecessarily intricate, or improvised. [C19: ?from CON(TRIVANCE) + TRAP[1] + (INVEN)TION]

:ontrapuntal (,kɒntrə'pʌnt°l) *adj Music.* characterized by counterpoint. [C19: from It. *contrappunto*]
▸ ,contra'puntally *adv* ▸ ,contra'puntist or ,contra-'puntalist *n*

:ontrariety (,kɒntrə'raɪətɪ) *n, pl* **contrarieties. 1** opposition between one thing and another; disagreement. **2** an instance of such opposition; inconsistency; discrepancy.

:ontrariwise ('kɒntrərɪ,waɪz) *adv* **1** from a contrasting point of view. **2** in the reverse way. **3** (kən'treərɪ,waɪz). in a contrary manner.

:ontrary ('kɒntrərɪ) *adj* **1** opposed in nature, position, etc.: *contrary ideas.* **2** (kən'treərɪ). perverse; obstinate. **3** (esp. of wind) adverse; unfavourable. **4** (of plant parts) situated at right angles to each other. **5** *Logic.* (of a pair of propositions) related so they cannot both be true, although they may both be false. ◆ *n, pl* **contraries. 6** the exact opposite (esp. in **to the contrary**). **7 on the contrary.** quite the reverse. **8** either of two exactly opposite objects, facts, or qualities. ◆ *adv* (usually foll. by *to*) **9** in an opposite or unexpected way: *contrary to usual belief.* **10** in conflict (with): *contrary to nature.* [C14: from L *contrārius* opposite, from *contrā* against]
▸ con'trarily *adv* ▸ con'trariness *n*

:ontrast *vb* (kən'trɑːst). **1** (often foll. by *with*) to distinguish or be distinguished by comparison of unlike or opposite qualities. ◆ *n* ('kɒntrɑːst). **2** distinction by comparison of opposite or dissimilar things, qualities, etc. (esp. in **by contrast, in contrast to** or **with**). **3** a person or thing showing differences when compared with another. **4** the effect of the juxtaposition of different colours, tones, etc. **5** the extent to which adjacent areas of an optical image, esp. on a television screen or in a photograph, differ in brightness. [C16: (n): via F from It., from *contrastare* (vb), from L *contra-* against + *stare* to stand]
▸ con'trasting *adj* ▸ con'trastive *adj*

contrast medium *n Med.* a radiopaque substance, such as barium sulphate, used to increase the contrast of an image in radiography.

contravene (,kɒntrə'viːn) *vb* **contravenes, contravening, contravened.** (*tr*) **1** to come into conflict with or infringe (rules, laws, etc.). **2** to dispute or contradict (a statement, proposition, etc.). [C16: from LL *contrāvenīre*, from L CONTRA- + *venīre* to come]
▸ ,contra'vener *n* ▸ **contravention** (,kɒntrə'vɛnʃən) *n*

contretemps ('kɒntrə,tɑːn) *n, pl* **contretemps. 1** an awkward or difficult situation or mishap. **2** a small disagreement that is rather embarrassing. [C17: from F, from *contre* against + *temps* time]

contribute (kən'trɪbjuːt) *vb* **contributes, contributing, contributed.** (often foll. by *to*) **1** to give (support, money, etc.) for a common purpose or fund. **2** to supply (ideas, opinions, etc.). **3** (*intr*) to be partly responsible (for): *drink contributed to the accident.* **4** to write (articles, etc.) for a publication. [C16: from L *contribuere* to collect, from *tribuere* to grant]
▸ con'tributable *adj* ▸ con'tributive *adj* ▸ con'tributor *n*

contribution (,kɒntrɪ'bjuːʃən) *n* **1** the act of contributing. **2** something contributed, such as money. **3** an article, etc., contributed to a newspaper or other publication. **4** *Arch.* a levy.

contributory (kən'trɪbjʊtərɪ, -trɪ) *adj* **1** (often foll. by *to*) being partly responsible: *a contributory factor.* **2** giving to a common purpose or fund. **3** of or designating an insurance or pension scheme in which the premiums are paid partly by the employer and partly by the employees who benefit from it. ◆ *n, pl* **contributories. 4** a person or thing that contributes. **5** *Company law.* a member or former member of a company liable to contribute to the assets on the winding-up of the company.

contrite (kən'traɪt, 'kɒntraɪt) *adj* **1** full of guilt or regret; remorseful. **2** arising from a sense of shame or guilt: *contrite promises.* [C14: from L *contrītus* worn out, from *conterere* to bruise, from *terere* to grind]
▸ con'tritely *adv* ▸ con'triteness or **contrition** (kən'trɪʃən) *n*

contrivance (kən'traɪvəns) *n* **1** something contrived, esp. an ingenious device; contraption. **2** inventive skill or ability. **3** an artificial rather than natural arrangement of details, parts, etc. **4** an elaborate or deceitful plan; stratagem.

contrive (kən'traɪv) *vb* **contrives, contriving, contrived. 1** (*tr*) to manage (something or to do something), esp. by a trick: *he contrived to make them meet.* **2** (*tr*) to think up or adapt ingeniously: *he contrived a new mast for the boat.* **3** to plot or scheme. [C14: from OF *controver*, from LL *contropāre* to represent by figures of speech, compare]
▸ con'triver *n*

contrived (kən'traɪvd) *adj* obviously planned; artificial; forced; unnatural.

control (kən'trəʊl) *vb* **controls, controlling, controlled.** (*tr*) **1** to command, direct, or rule. **2** to check, limit, or restrain: *to control one's emotions.* **3** to regulate or operate (a machine). **4** to verify (a scientific experiment) by conducting a parallel experiment in which the variable being investigated is held constant or is compared with a standard. **5a** to regulate (financial affairs). **5b** to examine (financial accounts). **6** to restrict or regulate the authorized supply of (certain substances, such as drugs). ◆ *n* **7** power to direct: *under control.* **8** a curb; check: *a frontier control.* **9** (*often pl*) a mechanism for operating a car, aircraft, etc. **10a** a standard of comparison used in a statistical analysis, etc. **10b** (*as modifier*): *a control group.* **11a** a device that regulates the operation of a machine. **11b** (*as modifier*): *control room.* [C15: from OF *conteroller* to regulate, from *conterolle* duplicate register, from *contre-* COUNTER- + *rolle* ROLL]
▸ con'trollable *adj* ▸ con,trolla'bility *n* ▸ con'trollably *adv*

control experiment *n* an experiment designed to check or correct the results of another experiment by removing the variable or variables operating in that other experiment.

controller (kən'trəʊlə) *n* **1** a person who directs. **2** Also called: **comptroller.** a business executive or government officer responsible for financial planning, control, etc. **3** the equipment concerned with controlling the operation of an electrical device.
▸ con'troller,ship *n*

controlling interest *n* a quantity of shares in a business that is sufficient to ensure control over its direction.

control tower *n* a tower at an airport from which air traffic is controlled.

controversy ('kɒntrə,vɜːsɪ, kən'trɒvəsɪ) *n, pl* **controversies.** dispute, argument, or debate, esp. one concerning a

matter about which there is strong disagreement and esp. one carried on in public or in the press. [C14: from L *contrōversia*, from *contrōversus*, from CONTRA- + *vertere* to turn]
▶ **controversial** (ˌkɒntrəˈvɜːʃəl) *adj* ▶ ˌ**controˈversialˌism** *n*
▶ ˌ**controˈversialist** *n*

controvert (ˈkɒntrəˌvɜːt, ˌkɒntrəˈvɜːt) *vb* (*tr*) **1** to deny, refute, or oppose (argument or opinion). **2** to argue about. [C17: from L *contrōversus*; see CONTROVERSY]
▶ ˌ**controˈvertible** *adj*

contumacious (ˌkɒntjuˈmeɪʃəs) *adj* stubbornly resistant to authority.
▶ ˌ**contuˈmaciously** *adv*

contumacy (ˈkɒntjuməsɪ) *n*, *pl* **contumacies**. obstinate and wilful resistance to authority, esp. refusal to comply with a court order. [C14: from L *contumācia*, from *contumāx* obstinate]

contumely (ˈkɒntjumɪlɪ) *n*, *pl* **contumelies**. **1** scornful or insulting language or behaviour. **2** a humiliating insult. [C14: from L *contumēlia*, from *tumēre* to swell, as with wrath]
▶ **contumelious** (ˌkɒntjuˈmiːlɪəs) *adj* ▶ ˌ**contuˈmeliously** *adv*

contuse (kənˈtjuːz) *vb* **contuses, contusing, contused**. (*tr*) to injure (the body) without breaking the skin; bruise. [C15: from L *contūsus* bruised, from *contundere* to grind, from *tundere* to beat]
▶ **conˈtusion** *n*

conundrum (kəˈnʌndrəm) *n* **1** a riddle, esp. one whose answer makes a play on words. **2** a puzzling question or problem. [C16: from ?]

conurbation (ˌkɒnɜːˈbeɪʃən) *n* a large densely populated urban sprawl formed by the growth and coalescence of individual towns or cities. [C20: from CON- + -*urbation*, from L *urbs* city]

convalesce (ˌkɒnvəˈlɛs) *vb* **convalesces, convalescing, convalesced**. (*intr*) to recover from illness, injury, or the after-effects of a surgical operation. [C15: from L *convalēscere*, from *com*- (intensive) + *valēscere* to grow strong]

convalescence (ˌkɒnvəˈlɛsəns) *n* **1** gradual return to health after illness, injury, or an operation. **2** the period during which such recovery occurs.
▶ ˌ**convaˈlescent** *n*, *adj*

convection (kənˈvɛkʃən) *n* **1** a process of heat transfer through a gas or liquid by bulk motion of hotter material into a cooler region. Cf. **conduction** (sense 1). **2** *Meteorol.* the process by which masses of relatively warm air are raised into the atmosphere, often cooling and forming clouds, with compensatory downward movements of cooler air. [C19: from LL *convectiō*, from L *convehere* to bring together, from *vehere* to carry]
▶ **conˈvectional** *adj* ▶ **conˈvective** *adj*

convector (kənˈvɛktə) *n* a space-heating device from which heat is transferred to the surrounding air by convection.

convene (kənˈviːn) *vb* **convenes, convening, convened**. **1** to gather, call together or summon, esp. for a formal meeting. **2** (*tr*) to order to appear before a court of law, judge, tribunal, etc. [C15: from L *convenīre* to assemble, from *venīre* to come]
▶ **conˈvenable** *adj*

convener or **convenor** (kənˈviːnə) *n* **1** a person who convenes or chairs a meeting, committee, etc., esp. one who is specifically elected to do so: *a convener of shop stewards*. **2** the chairman and civic head of certain Scottish councils. Cf. **provost** (sense 2).
▶ **conˈvenership** or **conˈvenorship** *n*

convenience (kənˈviːnɪəns) *n* **1** the quality of being suitable or opportune. **2** a convenient time or situation. **3 at your convenience**. at a time suitable to you. **4** usefulness, comfort, or facility. **5** an object that is useful, esp. a labour-saving device. **6** *Euphemistic, chiefly Brit.* a lavatory, esp. a public one. **7 make a convenience of**. to take advantage of; impose upon.

convenience food *n* food that needs little preparation, especially food that has been pre-prepared and preserved for long-term storage.

convenience store *n* a shop that has long opening

hours, caters to local tastes, and is conveniently situ ated.

convenient (kənˈviːnɪənt) *adj* **1** suitable; opportune. easy to use. **3** close by; handy. [C14: from L *conveniēns* from *convenīre* to be in accord with, from *venīre* to come]
▶ **conˈveniently** *adv*

convent (ˈkɒnvənt) *n* **1** a building inhabited by a reli gious community, usually of nuns. **2** the religious com munity inhabiting such a building. **3** Also called: **conver school**. a school in which the teachers are nuns. [C13 from OF, from L *conventus* meeting, from *convenīre*; se CONVENE]

conventicle (kənˈvɛntɪkəl) *n* **1** a secret or unauthorize assembly for worship. **2** a small meeting house or cha pel, esp. of Dissenters. [C14: from L *conventiculum*, fron *conventus*; see CONVENT]

convention (kənˈvɛnʃən) *n* **1** a large formal assembly o a group with common interests, such as a trade union. *US politics*. an assembly of delegates of one party to selec candidates for office. **3** an international agreement sec ond only to a treaty in formality. **4** any agreement o contract. **5** the established view of what is thought to b proper behaviour, good taste, etc. **6** an accepted rule usage, etc.: *a convention used by printers*. **7** *Bridge*. a bid o play not to be taken at its face value, which one's partne can interpret according to a prearranged bidding sys tem. [C15: from L *conventiō* an assembling]

conventional (kənˈvɛnʃənəl) *adj* **1** following the ac cepted customs and proprieties, esp. in a way that lack originality. **2** established by accepted usage or genera agreement. **3** of a convention or assembly. **4** *Visual arts* conventionalized. **5** (of weapons, warfare, etc.) not nu clear.
▶ **conˈventionalism** *n* ▶ **conˈventionally** *adv*

conventionality (kənˌvɛnʃəˈnælɪtɪ) *n*, *pl* **conventionali ties**. **1** the quality of being conventional. **2** (*often pl* something conventional.

conventionalize or **conventionalise** (kən ˈvɛnʃənəˌlaɪz) *vb* **conventionalizes, conventionalizing, conven tionalized** or **conventionalises, conventionalising, conventional ised**. (*tr*) **1** to make conventional. **2** to simplify or styliz (a design, decorative device, etc.).
▶ **conˌventionaliˈzation** or **conˌventionaliˈsation** *n*

conventual (kənˈvɛntjuəl) *adj* **1** of, belonging to, o characteristic of a convent. ◆ *n* **2** a member of a convent.
▶ **conˈventually** *adv*

converge (kənˈvɜːdʒ) *vb* **converges, converging, converged 1** to move or cause to move towards the same point. **2** t meet or join. **3** (*intr*) (of opinions, effects, etc.) to tend to wards a common conclusion or result. **4** (*intr*) *Maths*. (o an infinite series) to approach a finite limit as the num ber of terms increases. **5** (*intr*) (of animals and plants) t undergo convergence. [C17: from LL *convergere*, from L *com*- together + *vergere* to incline]
▶ **conˈvergent** *adj*

convergence (kənˈvɜːdʒəns) *n* **1** Also: **convergency**. the act, degree, or process of converging. **2** Also called: **con vergent evolution**. the evolutionary development of a su perficial resemblance between unrelated animals that occupy a similar environment, as in the evolution of wings in birds and bats.

convergent thinking *n Psychol.* analytical, usually de ductive, thinking in which ideas are examined for their logical validity or in which a set of rules is followed, for example in arithmetic.

conversable (kənˈvɜːsəbəl) *adj* **1** easy or pleasant to talk to. **2** able or inclined to talk.

conversant (kənˈvɜːsənt) *adj* (*usually postpositive* and foll. by *with*) experienced (in), familiar (with), or acquainted (with).
▶ **conˈversance** or **conˈversancy** *n* ▶ **conˈversantly** *adv*

conversation (ˌkɒnvəˈseɪʃən) *n* the interchange through speech of information, ideas, etc.; spoken communication.

conversational (ˌkɒnvəˈseɪʃənəl) *adj* **1** of, using, or in the manner of conversation. **2** inclined to conversation; conversable.
▶ ˌ**converˈsationalist** *n* ▶ ˌ**converˈsationally** *adv*

★ people and places

onversation piece *n* **1** something, esp. an unusual object, that provokes conversation. **2** (esp. in 18th-century Britain) a group portrait in a landscape or domestic setting.

onverse[1] *vb* (kən'vɜːs), **converses, conversing, conversed.** (*intr; often foll. by with*) **1** to engage in conversation (with). **2** to commune spiritually (with). ◆ *n* ('kɒnvɜːs). **3** conversation (often in **hold converse with**). [C16: from OF *converser*, from L *conversārī* to keep company with, from *conversāre* to turn constantly, from *vertere* to turn]
▸ con'verser *n*

onverse[2] ('kɒnvɜːs) *adj* **1** (*prenominal*) reversed; opposite; contrary. ◆ *n* **2** something that is opposite or contrary. **3** *Logic.* a categorial proposition obtained from another by the transposition of the subject and predicate, as *no bad man is bald* from *no bald man is bad.* [C16: from L *conversus* turned around; see CONVERSE[1]]
▸ con'versely *adv*

onversion (kən'vɜːʃən) *n* **1a** a change or adaptation in form, character, or function. **1b** something changed in one of these respects. **2** a change to another belief, as in a change of religion. **3** alteration to the structure or fittings of a building undergoing a change in function or legal status. **4** *Maths.* a change in the units or form of a number or expression: *the conversion of miles to kilometres.* **5** *Rugby.* a score made after a try by kicking the ball over the crossbar from a place kick. **6** *Physics.* a change of fertile material to fissile material in a reactor. **7** an alteration to a car engine to improve its performance. [C14: from L *conversiō* a turning around; see CONVERT]

onversion disorder *n* a psychological disorder in which severe physical symptoms like blindness or paralysis appear with no apparent physical cause.

onvert *vb* (kən'vɜːt). (*mainly tr*) **1** to change or adapt the form, character, or function of. **2** to cause (someone) to change in opinion, belief, etc. **3** (*intr*) to admit of being changed (into): *the table converts into a tray.* **4** (*also intr*) to change or be changed into another state: *to convert water into ice.* **5** *Law.* to assume unlawful proprietary rights over (personal property). **6** (*also intr*) *Rugby.* to make a conversion after (a try). **7** *Logic.* to transpose the subject and predicate of (a proposition). **8** to change (a value or measurement) from one system of units to another. **9** to exchange (a security or bond) for something of equivalent value. ◆ *n* ('kɒnvɜːt). **10** a person who has been converted to another belief, religion, etc. [C13: from OF, from L *convertere* to turn around, alter, from *vertere* to turn]

onverter *or* **convertor** (kən'vɜːtə) *n* **1** a person or thing that converts. **2** *Physics.* **2a** a device for converting alternating current to direct current or vice versa. **2b** a device for converting a signal from one frequency to another. **3** a vessel in which molten metal is refined, using a blast of air or oxygen. **4** *Computing.* a device for converting one form of coded information to another, such as an analogue-to-digital converter.

onverter reactor *n* a nuclear reactor for converting one fuel into another, esp. fertile material into fissionable material.

onvertible (kən'vɜːtɪbᵊl) *adj* **1** capable of being converted. **2** (of a car) having a folding or removable roof. **3** *Finance.* **3a** (of a currency) freely exchangeable into other currencies. **3b** (of a paper currency) exchangeable on demand for precious metal to an equivalent value. **3c** (of a bond, debenture, etc.) able to be exchanged for a share on a specified date at a specified price. ◆ *n* **4** a car with a folding or removable roof. **5** any convertible document or currency.
▸ con,verti'bility *n* ▸ con'vertibly *adv*

onvex ('kɒnvɛks, kɒn'vɛks) *adj* **1** curving outwards. **2** having one or two surfaces curved or ground in the shape of a section of the exterior of a sphere, ellipsoid, etc.: *a convex lens.* [C16: from L *convexus* vaulted, rounded]
▸ con'vexity *n* ▸ 'convexly *adv*

onvexo-concave (kən,vɛksəʊkɒn'keɪv) *adj* **1** having one side convex and the other side concave. **2** (of a lens) having a convex face with greater curvature than the concave face.

convexo-convex *adj* (esp. of a lens) having both sides convex; biconvex.

convey (kən'veɪ) *vb* (*tr*) **1** to take, carry, or transport from one place to another. **2** to communicate (a message, information, etc.). **3** (of a channel, path, etc.) to conduct or transfer. **4** *Law.* to transfer (the title to property). [C13: from OF *conveier*, from Med. L *conviāre* to escort, from L *com-* with + *via* way]
▸ con'veyable *adj*

conveyance (kən'veɪəns) *n* **1** the act of conveying. **2** a means of transport. **3** *Law.* **3a** a transfer of the legal title to property. **3b** the document effecting such a transfer.
▸ con'veyancer *n* ▸ con'veyancing *n*

conveyor *or* **conveyer** (kən'veɪə) *n* **1** a person or thing that conveys. **2** short for **conveyor belt.**

conveyor belt *n* a flexible endless strip of fabric or linked plates driven by rollers and used to transport objects, esp. in a factory.

convict *vb* (kən'vɪkt). (*tr*) **1** to pronounce (someone) guilty of an offence. ◆ *n* ('kɒnvɪkt). **2** a person found guilty of an offence against the law. **3** a person serving a prison sentence. [C14: from L *convictus* convicted, from *convincere* to prove guilty, CONVINCE]

conviction (kən'vɪkʃən) *n* **1** the state of being convinced. **2** a firmly held belief, opinion, etc. **3** the act of convincing. **4** the act of convicting or the state of being convicted. **5 carry conviction.** to be convincing.
▸ con'victional *adj* ▸ con'victive *adj*

convince (kən'vɪns) *vb* **convinces, convincing, convinced.** (*tr*) (*may take a clause as object*) to make (someone) agree, understand, or realize the truth or validity of something; persuade. [C16: from L *convincere* to demonstrate incontrovertibly, from *com-* (intensive) + *vincere* to overcome]
▸ con'vincer *n* ▸ con'vincible *adj* ▸ con'vincing *adj*
▸ con'vincingly *adv*

> **USAGE NOTE**   The use of *convince* to talk about persuading someone to do something is considered by many British speakers to be wrong or unacceptable.

convivial (kən'vɪvɪəl) *adj* sociable; jovial or festive: *a convivial atmosphere.* [C17: from LL *convīviālis*, from L *convīvium*, a living together, banquet, from *vīvere* to live]
▸ con,vivi'ality *n*

convocation (,kɒnvə'keɪʃən) *n* **1** a large formal assembly. **2** the act of convoking or state of being convoked. **3** *Church of England.* either of the synods of the provinces of Canterbury or York. **4** *Episcopal Church.* an assembly of the clergy and part of the laity of a diocese. **5** (*sometimes cap.*) (in some British universities) a legislative assembly. **6** (in Australia and New Zealand) the graduate membership of a university.
▸ ,convo'cational *adj*

convoke (kən'vəʊk) *vb* **convokes, convoking, convoked.** (*tr*) to call (a meeting, assembly, etc.) together; summon. [C16: from L *convocāre*, from *vocāre* to call]
▸ con'voker *n*

convolute ('kɒnvə,luːt) *vb* **convolutes, convoluting, convoluted.** (*tr*) **1** to form into a twisted, coiled, or rolled shape. ◆ *adj* **2** *Bot.* rolled longitudinally upon itself: *a convolute petal.* [C18: from L *convolūtus*, from *convolvere* to roll together, from *volvere* to turn]

convoluted ('kɒnvə,luːtɪd) *adj* **1** (esp. of meaning, style, etc.) difficult to comprehend; involved. **2** coiled.
▸ 'convo,lutedly *adv*

convolution (,kɒnvə'luːʃən) *n* **1** a turn, twist, or coil. **2** an intricate or confused matter or condition. **3** any of the numerous convex folds of the surface of the brain.
▸ ,convo'lutional *or* ,convo'lutionary *adj*

convolve (kən'vɒlv) *vb* **convolves, convolving, convolved.** to wind or roll together; coil; twist. [C16: from L *convolvere*; see CONVOLUTE]

convolvulus (kən'vɒlvjʊləs) *n, pl* **convolvuluses** *or* **convolvuli** (-,laɪ). a twining herbaceous plant having funnel-shaped flowers and triangular leaves. [C16: from L: bindweed; see CONVOLUTE]

convoy ('kɒnvɔɪ) n **1** a group of merchant ships with an escort of warships. **2** a group of land vehicles assembled to travel together. **3** the act of travelling or escorting by convoy (esp. in **in convoy**). ♦ vb **4** (tr) to escort while in transit. [C14: from OF convoier to CONVEY]

convulse (kən'vʌls) vb **convulses, convulsing, convulsed**. **1** (tr) to shake or agitate violently. **2** (tr) to cause (muscles) to undergo violent spasms or contractions. **3** (intr; often foll. by with) Inf. to shake or be overcome (with violent emotion, esp. laughter). **4** (tr) to disrupt the normal running of (a country, etc.): student riots have convulsed India. [C17: from L convulsus, from convellere, from vellere to pluck, pull]
▶ con'vulsive adj ▶ con'vulsively adv

convulsion (kən'vʌlʃən) n **1** a violent involuntary muscular contraction. **2** a violent upheaval, esp. a social one. **3** (usually pl) Inf. uncontrollable laughter: I was in convulsions.

Conwy ★ ('kɒnwɪ) n **1** a market town and resort in N Wales, in Gwynnedd on the estuary of the River Conwy: medieval town walls, 13th-century castle. Pop.: 3627 (1991). Former name: **Conway**. **2** a county borough in N Wales. Pop.: 70 200 (1996 est.). Area: 1130 sq. km (436 sq. miles).

cony or **coney** ('kəʊnɪ) n, pl **conies** or **coneys**. **1** a rabbit or fur made from the skin of a rabbit. **2** (in the Bible) another name for the **hyrax**. [C13: back formation from conies, from OF conis, pl. of conil, from L cunīculus rabbit]

Conybeare ★ ('kɒnɪˌbɪə, 'kʌn-) n **William David**. 1787–1857, British geologist, noted for his Outlines of the Geology of England and Wales (1822).

coo (kuː) vb **coos, cooing, cooed**. **1** (intr) (of doves, pigeons, etc.) to make a characteristic soft throaty call. **2** (tr) to speak in a soft murmur. **3** (intr) to murmur lovingly (esp. in **bill and coo**). ♦ n **4** the sound of cooing. ♦ interj **5** Brit. sl. an exclamation of surprise, awe, etc.
▶ 'cooing adj, n ▶ 'cooingly adv

Cooch Behar or **Kuch Bihar** ★ (kuːtʃ bɪ'hɑː) n **1** a former state of NE India: part of West Bengal since 1950. **2** a city in India, in NE West Bengal: capital of the former state of Cooch Behar. Pop.: 62 500 (latest est.).

cooee or **cooey** ('kuːiː) interj **1** a call used to attract attention, esp. a long loud high-pitched call on two notes. ♦ vb **cooees, cooeeing, cooeed** or **cooeys, cooeying, cooeyed**. **2** (intr) to utter this call. ♦ n **3** Austral. & NZ inf. calling distance (esp. in **within (a) cooee (of)**). [C19: from Abor.]

cook (kʊk) vb **1** to prepare (food) by the action of heat, or (of food) to become ready for eating through such a process. Related adj: **culinary**. **2** to subject or be subjected to intense heat: the town cooked in the sun. **3** (tr) Sl. to alter or falsify (figures, accounts, etc.): to cook the books. **4** (tr) Sl. to spoil (something). **5** (intr) Sl. to happen (esp. in **what's cooking?**). ♦ n **6** a person who prepares food for eating. ♦ See also **cook up**. [OE cōc (n), from L coquus a cook, from coquere to cook]
▶ 'cookable adj

Cook[1] ★ (kʊk) n **Mount**. **1** Official name: **Aorangi-Mount Cook**. a mountain in New Zealand, in the South Island, in the Southern Alps: the highest peak in New Zealand. Height: 3764 m (12 349 ft). **2** a mountain in SE Alaska, in the St Elias Mountains. Height: 4194 m (13 760 ft).

Cook[2] ★ (kʊk) n **1** Captain **James**. 1728–79, British navigator and explorer: claimed the E coast of Australia for Britain, circumnavigated New Zealand, and discovered several Pacific and Atlantic islands (1768–79). **2** Sir **Joseph**. 1860–1947, Australian statesman, born in England: prime minister (1913–14). **3** Peter (**Edward**). 1937–95, British actor and writer, noted esp. for his partnership (1960–73) with Dudley Moore. **4** Robin, full name Robert Finlayson Cook. born 1946, British Labour politician; foreign secretary from 1997. **5** Thomas. 1808–92, British travel agent; innovator of conducted excursions and founder of Thomas Cook and Son.

cook-chill n a method of food preparation used by caterers, in which cooked dishes are chilled rapidly and reheated as required.

cooker ('kʊkə) n **1** an apparatus heated by gas, electri‹ ity, oil, or solid fuel, for cooking food. **2** Brit. anoth‹ name for **cooking apple**.

cookery ('kʊkərɪ) n **1** the art, study, or practice of cool‹ ing. **2** US. a place for cooking.

cookery book or **cookbook** ('kʊkˌbʊk) n a book co‹ taining recipes.

cook-general n, pl **cooks-general**. Brit. (formerly, esp. i‹ the 1920s and 30s) a domestic servant who did cookin‹ and housework.

cookie or **cooky** ('kʊkɪ) n, pl **cookies**. **1** the US an‹ Canad. word for **biscuit**. **2** Inf. a person: smart cookie. that's the way the cookie crumbles. Inf. matters are inevit‹ bly so. [C18: from Du. koekje, dim. of koek cake]

cooking apple n any large sour apple used in cooking.

Cook Islands ★ pl n a group of islands in the SW P‹ cific, an overseas territory of New Zealand: consists ‹ the **Lower Cooks** and the **Northern Cooks**. Capital: Avaru‹ on Rarotonga. Pop.: 18 500 (1994). Area: 234 sq. km (9‹ sq. miles).

cook shop n **1** Brit. a shop that sells cookery equipmen‹ **2** US. a restaurant.

Cookson ★ ('kʊksən) n Dame **Catherine**. 1906–98, Britis‹ novelist, known for her popular novels.

Cook's tour (kʊks) n Inf. a rapid but extensive tour ‹ survey of anything. [C19: after Thomas COOK]

Cookstown ★ ('kʊkstaʊn) n a district of central North‹ ern Ireland, bordering the E shore of Lough Neagh: agr‹ culture. Administrative centre: Cookstown. Pop.: 31 08‹ (1991). Area: 623 sq. km (240 sq. miles).

Cook Strait ★ n the strait between North and South I‹ lands, New Zealand. Width: 26 km (16 miles).

cook up vb (tr, adv) **1** Inf. to concoct or invent (a story‹ alibi, etc.). **2** to prepare (a meal), esp. quickly. **3** Sl. to pre‹ pare (a drug) for use by heating, as by dissolving heroi‹ in a spoon.

cool (kuːl) adj **1** moderately cold: a cool day. **2** comfortabl‹ free of heat: a cool room. **3** calm: a cool head. **4** lacking i‹ enthusiasm, cordiality, etc.: a cool welcome. **5** calmly im‹ pudent. **6** Inf. (of sums of money, etc.) without exaggera‹ tion; actual: a cool ten thousand. **7** (of a colour) havin‹ violet, blue, or green predominating; cold. **8** (of jazz‹ economical and rhythmically relaxed. **9** Inf. sophisti‹ cated or elegant; unruffled. **10** Inf., chiefly US & Canad‹ marvellous. ♦ n **11** coolness: the cool of the evening. **12** S‹ calmness; composure (esp. in **keep** or **lose one's cool**)‹ unruffled elegance or sophistication. ♦ vb **14** (usuall‹ foll. by down or off) to make or become cooler. **15** (usu‹ ally foll. by down or off) to lessen the intensity of (ange‹ or excitement) or (of anger or excitement) to becom‹ less intense; calm down. **16 cool it**. (usually imperative) S‹ to calm down. [OE cōl]
▶ 'coolly adv ▶ 'coolness n

coolant ('kuːlənt) n **1** a fluid used to cool a system or t‹ transfer heat from one part of it to another. **2** a liqui‹ used to lubricate and cool the workpiece and cuttin‹ tool during machining.

cool bag or **box** n an insulated container for keepin‹ food cool.

cool-down n another name for **warm-down**.

cool drink n S. African. a soft drink.

cooler ('kuːlə) n **1** a container, vessel, or apparatus fo‹ cooling, such as a heat exchanger. **2** a slang word fo‹ **prison**. **3** a drink consisting of wine, fruit juice, and ‹ bonated water.

coolibah or **coolabah** ('kuːləˌbɑː) n an Australian euca‹ lyptus that grows along rivers and has smooth bark an‹ long narrow leaves. [from Abor.]

Coolidge ★ ('kuːlɪdʒ) n (**John**) **Calvin**. 1872–1933, 30t‹ president of the US (1923–29).

coolie or **cooly** ('kuːlɪ) n, pl **coolies**. an unskilled Orient‹ labourer. [C17: from Hindi kulī]

cooling-off period n **1** a period during which the con‹ tending sides to a dispute reconsider their options be‹ fore taking further action. **2** Brit. a period, often 14 day‹ that begins when a sale contract or life-assurance polic‹

★ people and places

is received by a member of the public, during which the contract or policy can be cancelled without loss.

ooling tower *n* a tall, hollow structure, designed to permit free passage of air, inside which hot water trickles down, becoming cool as it does so: the water is normally reused as part of an industrial process.

oomaraswamy ★ (kuː,mɑːrəˈswɑːmɪ) *n* **Ananda (Kentish)**. 1877–1947, Ceylonese art historian and interpreter of Indian culture to the West.

oomb, combe, coombe, or **comb** (kuːm) *n* **1** *Chiefly southern English*. a short valley or deep hollow. **2** *Chiefly northern English*. another name for a **cirque**. [OE *cumb*]

oon (kuːn) *n* **1** *Inf*. short for **raccoon**. **2** *Offens. sl*. a Black or a native Australian. **3** *S. African offens*. a person of mixed race.

oonskin (ˈkuːnˌskɪn) *n* **1** the pelt of a raccoon. **2** a raccoon cap with the tail hanging at the back. **3** *US*. an overcoat made of raccoon.

oop[1] (kuːp) *n* **1** a cage or small enclosure for poultry or small animals. **2** a small narrow place of confinement, esp. a prison cell. **3** a wicker basket for catching fish. ◆ *vb* **4** (*tr*; often foll. by *up* or *in*) to confine in a restricted area. [C15: prob. from MLow G *kūpe* basket]

oop[2] or **co-op** (ˈkəʊˌɒp) *n* a cooperative society or a shop run by a cooperative society.

ooper (ˈkuːpə) *n* **1** a person skilled in making and repairing barrels, casks, etc. ◆ *vb* **2** (*tr*) to make or mend (barrels, casks, etc.). [C13: from MDu. *cūper* or MLow G *kūper*; see COOP[1]]

Cooper ★ (ˈkuːpə) *n* **1** **Anthony Ashley**. See (Earl of) **Shaftesbury**. **2** **Gary**, real name *Frank James Cooper*. 1901–61, US film actor; his films include *Sergeant York* (1941) and *High Noon* (1952). **3** **Henry**. born 1934, British boxer; European heavyweight champion (1964; 1968–71). **4** **James Fenimore**. 1789–1851, US novelist, noted for *The Last of the Mohicans* (1826). **5** **Leon Neil**. born 1930, US physicist, noted for his work on superconductivity. He shared the Nobel prize for physics 1972. **6** **Samuel**. 1609–72, English miniaturist.

ooperage (ˈkuːpərɪdʒ) *n* **1** Also called: **coopery**. the craft, place of work, or products of a cooper. **2** the labour fee charged by a cooper.

ooperate or **co-operate** (kəʊˈɒpəˌreɪt) *vb* **cooperates, cooperating, cooperated** or **co-operates, co-operating, co-operated**. (*intr*) **1** to work or act together. **2** to be or be willing to assist. **3** *Econ*. to engage in economic cooperation. [C17: from LL *cooperārī* to combine, from L *operārī* to work]
▸ co'oper,ator or co-'oper,ator *n*

ooperation or **co-operation** (kəʊˌɒpəˈreɪʃən) *n* **1** joint operation or action. **2** assistance or willingness to assist. **3** *Econ*. the combination of consumers, workers, etc., in activities usually embracing production, distribution, or trade.
▸ co,oper'ationist or co-,oper'ationist *n*

ooperative or **co-operative** (kəʊˈɒpərətɪv, -ˈɒprə-) *adj* **1** willing to cooperate; helpful. **2** acting in conjunction with others; cooperating. **3a** (of an enterprise, farm, etc.) owned collectively and managed for joint economic benefit. **3b** (of an economy) based on collective ownership and cooperative use of the means of production and distribution. ◆ *n* **4** a cooperative organization, such as a farm.

ooperative society *n* a commercial enterprise owned and managed by and for the benefit of customers or workers.

Cooper Creek ★ *n* an intermittent river in E central Australia, in the Channel Country: rises in central Queensland and flows generally southwest, reaching Lake Eyre only during wet-year floods; scene of the death of the explorers Burke and Wills in 1861; the surrounding basin provides cattle pastures after the floods subside. Total length: 1420 km (880 miles). Former name: **Cooper's Creek**.

coopt or **co-opt** (kəʊˈɒpt) *vb* (*tr*) to add (someone) to a committee, board, etc., by the agreement of the existing members. [C17: from L *cooptāre*, from *optāre* to choose]
▸ co'option, co-'option or ,coop'tation, ,co-op'tation *n*

coordinate or **co-ordinate** *vb* (kəʊˈɔːdɪˌneɪt), **coordinates, coordinating, coordinated** or **co-ordinates, co-ordinating, co-ordinated**. **1** (*tr*) to integrate (diverse elements) in a harmonious operation. **2** to place (things) in the same class, or (of things) to be placed in the same class, etc. **3** (*intr*) to work together harmoniously. **4** (*intr*) to take or be in the form of a harmonious order. ◆ *n* (kəʊˈɔːdɪnɪt). **5** *Maths*. any of a set of numbers that defines the location of a point with reference to a system of axes. **6** a person or thing equal in rank, type, etc. ◆ *adj* (kəʊˈɔːdɪnɪt). **7** of or involving coordination. **8** of the same rank, type, etc. **9** of or involving the use of coordinates: *coordinate geometry*. **10** *Chem*. denoting a type of covalent bond in which both the shared electrons are provided by one of the atoms.
▸ co'ordinative or co-'ordinative *adj* ▸ co'ordi,nator or co-'ordi,nator *n*

coordinate clause *n* one of two or more clauses in a sentence having the same status and introduced by coordinating conjunctions.

coordinates (kəʊˈɔːdɪnɪts) *pl n* clothes of matching or harmonious colours and design, suitable for wearing together.

coordinating conjunction *n* a conjunction that introduces coordinate clauses, such as *and, but*, and *or*.

coordination or **co-ordination** (kəʊˌɔːdɪˈneɪʃən) *n* **1** balanced and effective interaction of movement, actions, etc. [C17: from LL *coordinātiō*, from L *ordinātiō* an arranging]

coot (kuːt) *n* **1** an aquatic bird of Europe and Asia, having dark plumage, and a white bill with a frontal shield: family Rallidae (rails, etc.). **2** a foolish person, esp. an old man. [C14: prob. from Low G]

cootie (ˈkuːtɪ) *n* *US & NZ*. a slang name for the body louse. [C20: from Maori & ? (for US) Malay *kutu* louse]

cop[1] (kɒp) *Sl*. ◆ *n* **1** another name for **policeman**. **2** *Brit*. an arrest (esp. in **a fair cop**). ◆ *vb* **cops, copping, copped**. (*tr*) **3** to catch. **4** to steal. **5** to suffer (a punishment): *you'll cop a clout if you do that!* **6** **cop it sweet**. *Austral. sl*. **6a** to accept a punishment without complaint. **6b** to have good fortune. **7** **cop this!** just look at this! ◆ See also **cop out**. [C18: (vb) ?from obs. *cap* to arrest, from OF *caper* to seize]

cop[2] (kɒp) *n* **1** a conical roll of thread wound on a spindle. **2** *Now chiefly dialect*. the top or crest, as of a hill. [OE *cop, copp* top, summit]

cop[3] (kɒp) *n Brit. sl*. (*usually used with a negative*) value: *not much cop*. [C19: n use of COP[1]]

copal (ˈkəʊpəl, -pæl) *n* a hard aromatic resin obtained from various tropical trees and used in making varnishes and lacquers. [C16: from Sp., from Nahuatl *copalli*]

copartner (kəʊˈpɑːtnə) *n* a partner or associate, esp. an equal partner in business.
▸ co'partnership *n*

cope[1] (kəʊp) *vb* **copes, coping, coped**. (*intr*) **1** (foll. by *with*) to contend (against). **2** to deal successfully (with); manage: *she coped well with the problem*. [C14: from OF *coper* to strike, cut, from *coup* blow]

cope[2] (kəʊp) *n* **1** a large ceremonial cloak worn at liturgical functions by priests of certain Christian sects. **2** any covering shaped like a cope. ◆ *vb* **copes, coping, coped**. **3** (*tr*) to dress (someone) in a cope. [OE *cāp*, from Med. L *cāpa*, from LL *cappa* hooded cloak]

cope[3] (kəʊp) *vb* **copes, coping, coped**. (*tr*) **1** to provide (a wall, etc.) with a coping. ◆ *n* **2** another name for **coping**. [C17: prob. from F *couper* to cut]

copeck (ˈkəʊpɛk) *n* a variant spelling of **kopeck**.

Copenhagen ★ (ˌkəʊpənˈheɪgən, -ˈhɑː-; ˌkəʊpənˌheɪ-, -ˌhɑː-) *n* the capital of Denmark, a port on Zealand and Amager Islands on a site inhabited for some 6000 years: exports chiefly agricultural products; iron and steel works; university (1479). Pop. (urban area): 1 353 333 (1995 est.). Danish name: **København**.

Copenhagen interpretation *n* an interpretation of quantum mechanics developed by Niels Bohr (1885–1962) and his colleagues at the University of Copenhagen, based on the concept of wave–particle duality and the idea that the observation influences the result of an experiment.

copepod ('kəupɪ,pɒd) n a minute marine or freshwater crustacean, an important constituent of plankton. [C19: from NL *copepoda*, from Gk *kōpē* oar + *pous* foot]

coper ('kəupə) n a horse dealer. [C17 (a dealer): from dialect *cope* to buy, barter, from Low G]

Copernican system n the theory published in 1543 by Copernicus which stated that the earth and the planets rotated round the sun.

Copernicus ★ (kə'pɜːnɪkəs) n **Nicolaus** (,nɪkə'leɪəs). Polish name *Mikolaj Kopernik*. 1473–1543, Polish astronomer, whose theory of the solar system (the **Copernican system**) was published in 1543.
▶ Co'pernican *adj*

copestone ('kəup,stəun) n **1** Also called: **coping stone.** a stone to form a coping. **2** the stone at the top of a building, wall, etc.

copier ('kɒpɪə) n a person or device that copies.

copilot ('kəu,paɪlət) n a second or relief pilot of an aircraft.

coping ('kəupɪŋ) n the sloping top course of a wall, usually made of masonry or brick.

coping saw n a handsaw with a U-shaped frame used for cutting curves in a material too thick for a fret saw.

copious ('kəupɪəs) *adj* **1** abundant; extensive. **2** having an abundant supply. **3** full of words, ideas, etc.; profuse. [C14: from L *cōpiōsus*, from *cōpia* abundance]
▶ 'copiously *adv* ▶ 'copiousness *n*

coplanar (kəu'pleɪnə) *adj* lying in the same plane: *coplanar lines.*
▶ ,copla'narity *n*

Copland ★ ('kəuplənd) n **Aaron.** 1900–90, US composer of orchestral and chamber music, ballets, and film music.

copolymer (kəu'pɒlɪmə) n a chemical compound of high molecular weight formed by uniting the molecules of two or more different compounds (monomers).

cop out *Sl.* ◆ *vb* **1** (*intr, adv*) to fail to assume responsibility or fail to perform. ◆ *n* **cop-out. 2** a way or an instance of avoiding responsibility or commitment. [C20: prob. from COP¹]

copper¹ ('kɒpə) n **1** a malleable reddish metallic element occurring as the free metal, copper glance, and copper pyrites: used in such alloys as brass and bronze. Symbol: Cu; atomic no.: 29; atomic wt.: 63.54. Related adjs.: **cupric, cuprous. 2a** the reddish-brown colour of copper. **2b** (*as adj*) *copper hair.* **3** *Inf.* any copper or bronze coin. **4** *Chiefly Brit.* a large vessel, formerly of copper, used for boiling or washing. **5** any of various small widely distributed butterflies having reddish-brown wings. ◆ *vb* **6** (*tr*) to coat or cover with copper. [OE *coper*, from L *Cyprium aes* Cyprian metal, from Gk *Kupris* Cyprus]

copper² ('kɒpə) n a slang word for **policeman.** Often shortened to **cop.** [C19: from COP¹ (vb)]

copperas ('kɒpərəs) n a less common name for **ferrous sulphate.** [C14 *coperose*, via OF from Med. L *cuperosa*, ? orig. in *aqua cuprosa* copper water]

copper beech n a cultivated variety of European beech that has reddish leaves.

Copper Belt ★ n a region of Central Africa, along the border between Zambia and the Democratic Republic of the Congo: rich in deposits of copper.

copper-bottomed *adj* reliable, esp. financially reliable. [from the practice of coating bottom of ships with copper to prevent the timbers rotting]

copper-fasten *vb* (*tr*) *Irish.* to make (a bargain or agreement) binding.

copperhead ('kɒpə,hɛd) n **1** a venomous pit viper of the US, with a reddish-brown head. **2** a venomous marsh snake of Australia, with a reddish band behind the head.

copperplate ('kɒpə,pleɪt) n **1** a polished copper plate on which a design has been etched or engraved. **2** a print taken from such a plate. **3** a fine handwriting based upon that used on copperplate engravings.

copper pyrites ('paɪraɪts) n (*functioning as sing*) anothe name for **chalcopyrite.**

coppersmith ('kɒpə,smɪθ) n a person who works i copper.

copper sulphate n a copper salt found naturally an made by the action of sulphuric acid on copper oxid used as a mordant, in electroplating, and in plant spray Formula: $CuSO_4$.

coppice ('kɒpɪs) n **1** a dense growth of small trees o bushes, esp. one regularly trimmed back so that a cor tinual supply of small poles and firewood is obtaine ◆ *vb* **coppices, coppicing, coppiced. 2** (*tr*) to trim back (tree or bushes) to form a coppice. [C14: from OF *copeiz*]
▶ 'coppiced *adj*

Coppola ★ ('kɒpələ) n **Francis Ford.** born 1939, US film d rector. His films include *The Godfather* (1972) and *Tuck* (1988).

copra ('kɒprə) n the dried, oil-yielding kernel of the cc conut. [C16: from Port., from Malayalam *koppara* coc nut]

copro- *or before a vowel* **copr-** *combining form.* indicatin dung or obscenity, as in **cop'rology** n preoccupation wit excrement, **cop'rophagous** *adj* feeding on dung. [from G *kopros* dung]

copse (kɒps) n another word for **coppice** (sense 1). [C1 from COPPICE]

Copt (kɒpt) n **1** a member of the Coptic Church. **2** a Egyptian descended from the ancient Egyptians. [C1 from Ar., from Coptic *kyptios* Egyptian, from G *Aiguptios*, from *Aiguptos* Egypt]

Coptic ('kɒptɪk) n **1** an Afro-Asiatic language, written i the Greek alphabet but descended from ancient Egyp tian. Extinct as a spoken language, it survives in th Coptic Church. ◆ *adj* **2** of this language. **3** of the Copts.

Coptic Church n the ancient Christian Church o Egypt.

copula ('kɒpjulə) n, *pl* **copulas** or **copulae** (-,liː). **1** a verl such as *be, seem,* or *taste,* that is used to identify or lin the subject with the complement of a sentence, as in *h became king, sugar tastes sweet.* **2** anything that serves as link. [C17: from L: bond, from *co-* together + *apere* to fas ten]
▶ 'copular *adj*

copulate ('kɒpju,leɪt) *vb* **copulates, copulating, copulate** (*intr*) to perform sexual intercourse. [C17: from *copulāre* to join together; see COPULA]
▶ ,copu'lation n ▶ 'copulatory *adj*

copulative ('kɒpjulətɪv) *adj* **1** serving to join or unite. of copulation. **3** *Grammar.* (of a verb) having the natur of a copula.

copy ('kɒpɪ) n, *pl* **copies. 1** an imitation or reproduction o an original. **2** a single specimen of something that oc curs in a multiple edition, such as a book. **3a** matter to b reproduced in print. **3b** written matter or text as distinc from graphic material in books, etc. **4** the words used t present a promotional message in an advertisement. *Journalism, inf.* suitable material for an article: *disaster are always good copy.* **6** *Arch.* a model to be copied, esp. a example of penmanship. ◆ *vb* **copies, copying, copied.** (when *tr,* often foll. by *out*) to make a copy (of). **8** (*tr*) t imitate as a model. **9** to imitate unfairly. [C14: from Med. L *cōpia* an imitation, from L: abundance]

copybook ('kɒpɪ,buk) n **1** a book of specimens, esp. o penmanship, for imitation. **2** *Chiefly US.* a book for co containing documents. **3** blot one's copybook. *Inf.* to spoi one's reputation by a mistake or indiscretion. **4** (*modifier* trite or unoriginal.

copycat ('kɒpɪ,kæt) n *Inf.* **a** a person, esp. a child, whe imitates or copies another. **b** (*as modifier*): *copycat mur ders.*

copyhold ('kɒpɪ,həuld) n *Law.* (formerly) a tenure les than freehold of land in England evidenced by a copy o the Court roll.

copyist ('kɒpɪɪst) n **1** a person who makes written copies **2** a person who imitates.

copyreader ('kɒpɪ,riːdə) n *US.* a person who edits and prepares newspaper copy for publication; subeditor.

copyright ('kɒpɪˌraɪt) n 1 the exclusive right to produce copies and to control an original literary, musical, or artistic work, granted by law for a specified number of years. ◆ adj 2 (of a work, etc.) subject to copyright. ◆ vb 3 (tr) to take out a copyright on.

copy typist n a typist whose job is to type from written or typed drafts rather than from dictation.

copywriter ('kɒpɪˌraɪtə) n a person employed to write advertising copy.
▸ 'copyˌwriting n

coquet (kəʊˈkɛt, kɒ-) vb coquets, coquetting, coquetted. (intr) 1 to behave flirtatiously. 2 to dally or trifle. [C17: from F: a gallant, lit.: a little cock, from coq cock]
▸ 'coquetry n

coquette (kəʊˈkɛt, kɒ-) n 1 a woman who flirts. 2 any hummingbird of the genus Lophornis. [C17: from F, fem of COQUET]
▸ coˈquettish adj ▸ coˈquettishness n

Cor. Bible. abbrev. for Corinthians.

coracle ('kɒrək³l) n a small roundish boat made of waterproofed hides stretched over a wicker frame. [C16: from Welsh corwgl]

coracoid ('kɒrəˌkɔɪd) n a paired ventral bone of the pectoral girdle in vertebrates. In mammals it is reduced to a peg (the **coracoid process**) on the scapula. [C18: from NL coracoīdēs, from Gk korakoeidēs like a raven, from korax raven]

coral ('kɒrəl) n 1 any of a class of marine colonial coelenterates having a calcareous, horny, or soft skeleton. 2a the calcareous or horny material forming the skeleton of certain of these animals. 2b (as modifier): a coral reef. 3 a rocklike aggregation of certain of these animals or their skeletons, forming an island or reef. 4a something made of coral. 4b (as modifier): a coral necklace. 5a a yellowish-pink colour. 5b (as adj): coral lipstick. 6 the roe of a lobster or crab, which becomes pink when cooked. [C14: from OF, from L corāllium, from Gk korallion, prob. of Semitic origin]

coral reef n a marine reef consisting of coral consolidated into limestone.

coralroot ('kɒrəlˌruːt) n a N temperate leafless orchid with branched roots resembling coral.

Coral Sea ★ n the SW arm of the Pacific, between Australia, New Guinea, and Vanuatu.

coral snake n 1 a venomous snake of tropical and subtropical America, marked with red, black, yellow, and white transverse bands. 2 any of various other brightly coloured snakes of Africa and SE Asia.

cor anglais ('kɔːr 'ɒŋgleɪ) n, pl cors anglais ('kɔːz 'ɒŋgleɪ). Music. a woodwind instrument, the alto of the oboe family. Also called: **English horn**. [C19: from F: English horn]

corbel ('kɔːb³l) Archit. ◆ n 1 a bracket, usually of stone or brick. ◆ vb corbels, corbelling, corbelled or US corbels, corbeling, corbeled. 2 (tr) to lay (a stone) so that it forms a corbel. [C15: from OF, lit.: a little raven, from Med. L corvellus, from L corvus raven]

corbie ('kɔːbɪ) n a Scot. name for raven[1] (sense 1) or crow[1] (sense 1). [C15: from OF corbin, from L corvīnus CORVINE]

corbie-step or **corbel step** n Archit. any of a set of steps on the top of a gable. Also called: **crow step**.

Corbusier ★ (French kɔrbyzje) n Le. See Le Corbusier.

Corcovado ★ n 1 (Spanish korkoˈβaðo). a volcano in S Chile, in the Andes. Height: 2300 m (7546 ft). 2 (Portuguese korkuˈvaːdu). a mountain in SE Brazil, in SW Rio de Janeiro city. Height: 704 m (2310 ft).

Corcyra ★ (kɔːˈsaɪərə) n the ancient name for Corfu.

cord (kɔːd) n 1 string or thin rope made of twisted strands. 2 a length of woven or twisted strands of silk, etc., used as a belt, etc. 3 a ribbed fabric, esp. corduroy. 4 the US and Canad. name for **flex** (sense 1). 5 Anat. any part resembling a rope: the spinal cord. 6 a unit for measuring cut wood, equal to 128 cubic feet. ◆ vb (tr) 7 to bind or furnish with a cord or cords. ◆ See also **cords**. [C13: from OF corde, from L chorda, from Gk khordē]
▸ 'cordˌlike adj

cordage ('kɔːdɪdʒ) n 1 Naut. the lines and rigging of a vessel. 2 an amount of wood measured in cords.

cordate ('kɔːdeɪt) adj heart-shaped.

Corday ★ (French kɔrde) n Charlotte (Jarlɔt), full name Marie Anne Charlotte Corday d'Armont. 1768–93, French Girondist revolutionary, who assassinated Marat.

corded ('kɔːdɪd) adj 1 bound or fastened with cord. 2 (of a fabric) ribbed. 3 (of muscles) standing out like cords.

cordial ('kɔːdɪəl) adj 1 warm and friendly: a cordial greeting. 2 stimulating. ◆ n 3 a drink with a fruit base: lime cordial. 4 another word for **liqueur**. [C14: from Med. L cordiālis, from L cor heart]
▸ 'cordially adv

cordiality (ˌkɔːdɪˈælɪtɪ) n, pl cordialities. warmth of feeling.

cordillera (ˌkɔːdɪlˈjeərə) n a series of parallel ranges of mountains, esp. in the northwestern US. [C18: from Sp., from cordilla, lit.: a little cord]

Cordilleras ★ (ˌkɔːdɪlˈjeərəz; Spanish korðiˈʎeras) pl n the. the complex of mountain ranges on the W side of the Americas, extending from Alaska to Cape Horn and including the Andes and the Rocky Mountains.

cordite ('kɔːdaɪt) n any of various explosive materials containing cellulose nitrate, sometimes mixed with nitroglycerine. [C19: from CORD + -ITE[1], from its stringy appearance]

cordless ('kɔːdlɪs) adj (of an electrical device) operated by an internal battery so that no connection to mains supply is needed.

cordless telephone n a portable battery-powered telephone with a short-range radio link to a fixed base unit.

Córdoba[1] ★ (Spanish ˈkɔrðoβa) n 1 a city in central Argentina: university (1613). Pop.: 1 208 713 (1991). 2 a city in S Spain, on the Guadalquivir River: centre of Moorish Spain (711–1236). Pop.: 315 948 (1994 est.). English name: **Cordova**.

Córdoba[2] or **Córdova** ★ (Spanish ˈkɔrðoβa) n Francisco Fernández de (franˈθisko ferˈnandeθ de). died 1518, Spanish soldier and explorer, who discovered Yucatán.

cordon ('kɔːd³n) n 1 a chain of police, soldiers, ships, etc., stationed around an area. 2 a ribbon worn as insignia of honour. 3 a cord or ribbon worn as an ornament. 4 Archit. another name for **string course**. 5 Horticulture. a fruit tree consisting of a single stem bearing fruiting spurs, produced by cutting back all lateral branches. ◆ vb 6 (tr; often foll. by off) to put or form a cordon (around); close (off). [C16: from OF, lit.: a little cord, from corde CORD]

cordon bleu (French kɔrdõ blø) n 1 French history. the sky-blue ribbon worn by members of the highest order of knighthood under the Bourbon monarchy. 2 any very high distinction. ◆ adj 3 of or denoting food prepared to a very high standard. [F, lit.: blue ribbon]

cordon sanitaire French. (kɔrdõ saniter) n 1 a guarded line isolating an infected area. 2 a line of buffer states shielding a country. [C19: lit.: sanitary line]

Cordova ★ ('kɔːdəvə) n the English name for **Córdoba**[1] (sense 2).

cordovan ('kɔːdəv³n) n a fine leather now made mainly from horsehide. [C16: from Sp. cordobán of CÓRDOBA[1]]

cords (kɔːdz) pl n trousers made of corduroy.

corduroy ('kɔːdəˌrɔɪ, ˌkɔːdəˈrɔɪ) n a heavy cotton pile fabric with lengthways ribs. [C18: ?from the proper name Corderoy]

corduroys (ˌkɔːdəˈrɔɪz, ˈkɔːdəˌrɔɪz) pl n trousers or breeches of corduroy.

cordwainer ('kɔːdˌweɪnə) n Arch. a shoemaker or worker in leather. [C12: cordwaner, from OF, from OSp. cordován CORDOVAN]

cordwood ('kɔːdˌwʊd) n wood that has been cut into lengths of four feet so that it can be stacked in cords.

core (kɔː) n 1 the central part of certain fleshy fruits, such as the apple, consisting of the seeds. 2 the central or essential part of something: the core of the argument. 3 a piece of magnetic material, such as soft iron, inside an electromagnet or transformer. 4 Geol. the central part of the earth. 5 a cylindrical sample of rock, soil, etc., obtained by the use of a hollow drill. **6** *Physics.* the region of a nuclear reactor in which the reaction takes place. **7** *Computing.* **7a** a ferrite ring formerly used in a computer memory to store one bit of information. **7b** (*as modifier*): *core memory.* **8** *Archaeol.* a stone or flint from which flakes have been removed. **9** *Physics.* the nucleus together with all complete electron shells of an atom. ◆ *vb* **cores, coring, cored. 10** (*tr*) to remove the core from (fruit). [C14: from ?]

coreligionist (ˌkəʊrɪˈlɪdʒənɪst) *n* an adherent of the same religion as another.

Corelli ★ *n* **1** (*Italian* koˈrelli). **Arcangelo** (arˈkandʒelo). 1653–1713, Italian violinist and composer of sonatas and concerti grossi. **2** (koˈrelɪ). **Marie**, real name *Mary Mackay.* 1854–1924, British novelist. Her works include *The Murder of Delicia* (1896).

coreopsis (ˌkɒrɪˈɒpsɪs) *n* a plant of America and Africa, with yellow, brown, or yellow-and-red daisy-like flowers. [C18: from NL, from Gk *koris* bedbug + -OPSIS; so called from the appearance of the seed]

co-respondent (ˌkəʊrɪˈspɒndənt) *n Law.* a person cited in divorce proceedings, alleged to have committed adultery with the respondent.

core subjects *pl n Brit. education.* three foundation subjects (English, mathematics, and science) that are compulsory throughout each key stage in the National Curriculum.

core time *n* See **flexitime.**

corf (kɔːf) *n, pl* **corves.** *Brit.* a wagon or basket used formerly in mines. [C14: from MDu. *corf* or MLow G *korf*, prob. from L *corbis* basket]

Corfu ★ (kɔːˈfuː) *n* **1** an island in the Ionian Sea, in the Ionian Islands: forms, with neighbouring islands, a department of Greece. Pop.: 107 592 (1991). Area: 641 sq. km (247 sq. miles). **2** a port on E Corfu island. Pop.: 105 000 (1995 est.). Modern Greek name: **Kérkyra.** ◆ Ancient name: **Corcyra.**

corgi (ˈkɔːgɪ) *n* either of two short-legged sturdy breeds of dog, the Cardigan and the Pembroke. [C20: from Welsh, from *cor* dwarf + *ci* dog]

coriander (ˌkɒrɪˈændə) *n* a European umbelliferous plant, cultivated for its aromatic seeds and leaves, used in flavouring foods. [C14: from OF *coriandre,* from L *coriandrum,* from Gk *koriannon,* from ?]

Corinth ★ (ˈkɒrɪnθ) *n* **1** a port in S Greece, in the NE Peloponnese: the modern town is near the site of the ancient city, the largest and richest of the city-states after Athens. Pop.: 29 600 (1995 est.). Modern Greek name: **Kórinthos. 2** a region of ancient Greece, occupying most of the Isthmus of Corinth and part of the NE Peloponnese. **3 Gulf of.** Also called: **Gulf of Lepanto.** an inlet of the Ionian Sea between the Peloponnese and central Greece. **4 Isthmus of.** a narrow strip of land between the Gulf of Corinth and the Saronic Gulf: crossed by the **Corinth Canal,** making navigation possible between the gulfs.

Corinthian (kəˈrɪnθɪən) *adj* **1** of Corinth. **2** denoting one of the five classical orders of architecture: characterized by a bell-shaped capital having carved ornaments based on acanthus leaves. **3** *Obs.* given to luxury; dissolute. ◆ *n* **4** a native or inhabitant of Corinth.

Coriolanus ★ (ˌkɒrɪəˈleɪnəs) *n* **Gaius Marcius** (ˈgaɪəs ˈmɑːsɪəs). 5th century B.C., a legendary Roman general, who allegedly led an army against Rome but was dissuaded from conquering it by his mother and wife.

Coriolis force (ˌkɒrɪˈəʊlɪs) *n* a hypothetical force postulated to explain a deflection in the path of a body moving relative to the earth: it is due to the earth's rotation and is to the left in the S hemisphere and to the right in the N hemisphere. [C19: after Gaspard G. *Coriolis* (1792–1843), F civil engineer]

corium (ˈkɔːrɪəm) *n, pl* **coria** (-rɪə). the deep inner layer of the skin, beneath the epidermis, containing connective tissue, blood vessels, and fat. Also called: **derma, dermis.** [C19: from L: rind, skin]

cork (kɔːk) *n* **1** the thick light porous outer bark of the cork oak. **2** a piece of cork used as a stopper. **3** an angling float. **4** Also called: **phellem.** *Bot.* a protective layer of dead

impermeable cells on the outside of the stems and roots of woody plants. ◆ *adj* **5** made of cork. Related adj: **suberose.** ◆ *vb* (*tr*) **6** to stop up (a bottle, etc.) with or a with a cork. **7** (often foll. by *up*) to restrain. **8** to blac (the face, hands, etc.) with burnt cork. [C14: prob. from Ar. *qurq,* from L *cortex* bark]
► ˈcorkˌlike *adj*

Cork ★ (kɔːk) *n* **1** a county of SW Republic of Ireland, in Munster province: crossed by ridges of low mountains; scenic coastline. County town: Cork. Pop.: 410 36⁶ (1991). Area: 7459 sq. km (2880 sq. miles). **2** a port in Republic of Ireland, county town of Co. Cork, at the mouth of the River Lee: seat of the University College o Cork (1849). Pop.: 127 253 (1991). Gaelic name: **Corcaigh.**

corkage (ˈkɔːkɪdʒ) *n* a charge made at a restaurant fo serving wine, etc., bought off the premises.

corked (kɔːkt) *adj* tainted through having a cork containing excess tannin.

corker (ˈkɔːkə) *n Old-fashioned sl.* **1** something or some body striking or outstanding. **2** an irrefutable remar that puts an end to discussion.

cork oak *n* an evergreen Mediterranean oak whose po rous bark yields cork.

corkscrew (ˈkɔːkˌskruː) *n* **1** a device for drawing cork from bottles, typically consisting of a pointed metal spi ral attached to a handle or screw mechanism. **2** (*modifier*) resembling a corkscrew in shape. ◆ *vb* **3** to move o cause to move in a spiral or zigzag course.

corm (kɔːm) *n* an organ of vegetative reproduction in plants such as the crocus, consisting of a globular stem base swollen with food and surrounded by papery scale leaves. [C19: from NL *cormus,* from Gk *kormos* tree trunk from which the branches have been lopped]

cormorant (ˈkɔːmərənt) *n* an aquatic bird having a dark plumage, a long neck and body, and a slender hooked beak. [C13: from OF *cormareng,* from *corp* raven + -*mareng* of the sea]

corn[1] (kɔːn) *n* **1** *Brit.* **1a** any of various cereal plants, esp the predominant crop of a region, such as wheat in England and oats in Scotland. **1b** the seeds of such plants esp. after harvesting. **1c** a single seed of such plants; a grain. **2** the usual US, Canad., Austral., and NZ name fo **maize. 3** *Sl.* an idea, song, etc., regarded as banal or sentimental. ◆ *vb* (*tr*) **4a** to preserve in brine. **4b** to salt. [OE *corn*]

corn[2] (kɔːn) *n* **1** a hardening of the skin, esp. of the toes, caused by pressure. **2 tread on (someone's) corns.** *Brit. inf.* to offend or hurt (someone) by touching on a sensitive subject. [C15: from OF *corne* horn, from L *cornū*]

corn borer *n* the larva of a moth native to Europe: in E North America a serious pest of maize.

corn bread *n Chiefly US.* bread made from maize meal. Also called: **Indian bread.**

corn bunting *n* a heavily built European songbird with a streaked brown plumage.

corncob (ˈkɔːnˌkɒb) *n* the core of an ear of maize, to which kernels are attached.

corncob pipe *n* a pipe with a bowl made from a dried corncob.

corncockle (ˈkɔːnˌkɒkᵊl) *n* a European plant that has reddish-purple flowers and grows in cornfields and by roadsides.

corncrake (ˈkɔːnˌkreɪk) *n* a common Eurasian rail with a buff speckled plumage and reddish wings.

corn dolly *n* a decorative figure made by plaiting straw.

cornea (ˈkɔːnɪə) *n, pl* **corneas** *or* **corneae** (-nɪˌiː). the convex transparent membrane that forms the anterior covering of the eyeball. [C14: from Med. L *cornea tēla* horny web, from L *cornū* HORN]
► ˈcorneal *adj*

corned (kɔːnd) *adj* (esp. of beef) cooked and then preserved or pickled in salt or brine.

Corneille ★ (*French* kɔrnɛj) *n* **Pierre** (pjɛr). 1606–84, French dramatist, whose plays include *Médée* (1635), *Le Cid* (1636), and *Polyeucte* (1642).

★ people and places

cornel ('kɔːnᵊl) n any shrub of the genus *Cornus,* such as the dogwood. [C16: prob. from MLow G *kornelle,* ult. from L *cornus*]

cornelian (kɔː'niːliən) n a variant spelling of **carnelian.**

corner ('kɔːnə) n **1** the place or angle formed by the meeting of two converging lines or surfaces. **2** a projecting angle of a solid object. **3** the place where two streets meet. **4** any small, secluded, or private place. **5** a dangerous position from which escape is difficult: *a tight corner.* **6** any region, esp. a remote place. **7** something used to protect or mark a corner, as of the hard cover of a book. **8** *Commerce.* a monopoly over the supply of a commodity so that its market price can be controlled. **9** *Soccer, hockey, etc.* a free kick or shot from the corner of the field, taken against a defending team when the ball goes out of play over their goal line after last touching one of their players. **10** either of two opposite angles of a boxing ring in which the opponents take their rests. **11 cut corners.** to take the shortest or easiest way, esp. at the expense of high standards. **12 turn the corner.** to pass the critical point (in an illness, etc.). **13** (*modifier*) on a corner: *a corner shop.* ♦ vb **14** (*tr*) to manoeuvre (a person or animal) into a position from which escape is difficult or impossible. **15** (*tr*) **15a** to acquire enough of (a commodity) to attain control of the market. **15b** Also: **engross.** to attain control of (a market) in such a manner. **16** (*intr*) (of vehicles, etc.) to turn a corner. **17** (*intr*) (in soccer, etc.) to take a corner. [C13: from OF *corniere,* from L *cornū* point, HORN]

Corner ★ n the. *Inf.* an area in central Australia, at the junction of the borders of Queensland and South Australia.

cornerback ('kɔːnə,bæk) n *American football.* a defensive back.

cornerstone ('kɔːnə,stəun) n **1** a stone at the corner of a wall, uniting two intersecting walls. **2** a stone placed at the corner of a building during a ceremony to mark the start of construction. **3** a person or thing of prime importance: *the cornerstone of the whole argument.*

cornerwise ('kɔːnə,waɪz) or **cornerways** ('kɔːnə,weɪz) *adv, adj* with a corner in front; diagonally.

cornet ('kɔːnɪt) n **1** a three-valved brass instrument of the trumpet family. **2** a person who plays the cornet. **3** a cone-shaped paper container for sweets, etc. **4** *Brit.* a cone-shaped wafer container for ice cream. **5** (*formerly*) the lowest rank of commissioned cavalry officer in the British Army. **6** the large white headdress of some nuns. [C14: from OF, from L *cornū* HORN]
▸ **cor'netist** or **cor'nettist** n

corn exchange n a building where corn is bought and sold.

cornfield ('kɔːn,fiːld) n a field planted with cereal crops.

cornflakes ('kɔːn,fleɪks) *pl* n a breakfast cereal made from toasted maize.

cornflour ('kɔːn,flaʊə) n a fine maize flour, used for thickening sauces. US and Canad. name: **cornstarch.**

cornflower ('kɔːn,flaʊə) n a herbaceous plant, with blue, purple, pink, or white flowers, formerly a common weed in cornfields.

Cornforth ★ ('kɔːn,fɔːθ) n Sir **John Warcup.** born 1917, Australian chemist, who shared the 1975 Nobel prize for chemistry for his work on stereochemistry.

cornice ('kɔːnɪs) n *Archit.* **1a** the top projecting mouldings of an entablature. **1b** a continuous horizontal projecting course or moulding at the top of a wall, building, etc. **2** an overhanging ledge of snow. [C16: from OF, from It., ?from L *cornix* crow, but infl. also by L *corōnis* decorative flourish]

corniche ('kɔːnɪʃ) n a coastal road, esp. one built into the face of a cliff. [C19: from *corniche road;* see CORNICE]

Cornish ('kɔːnɪʃ) *adj* **1** of Cornwall or its inhabitants. ♦ n **2** a former language of Cornwall: extinct by 1800. **3** the. (*functioning as pl*) the natives or inhabitants of Cornwall.
▸ **'Cornishman** n

Cornish pasty ('pæstɪ) n *Cookery.* a pastry case with a filling of meat and vegetables.

corn meal n meal made from maize. Also called: **Indian meal.**

Corno ★ (*Italian* 'kɔrno) n **Monte** ('monte). a mountain in central Italy: the highest peak in the Apennines. Height: 2912 m (9554 ft).

corn salad n a plant which often grows in cornfields and whose leaves are sometimes used in salads. Also called: **lamb's lettuce.**

cornstarch ('kɔːn,stɑːtʃ) n the US and Canad. name for **cornflour.**

cornucopia (,kɔːnju'kəupɪə) n **1** a representation of a horn in painting, sculpture, etc., overflowing with fruit, vegetables, etc.; horn of plenty. **2** a great abundance. **3** a horn-shaped container. [C16: from LL, from L *cornū* *cōpiae* horn of plenty]
▸ ,cornu'copian *adj*

Cornwall ★ ('kɔːn,wɔːl, -wəl) n a county of SW England: hilly, with a deeply indented coastline. Administrative centre: Truro. Pop.: 479 600 (1994 est.). Area: 3564 sq. km (1376 sq. miles).

Cornwallis ★ (kɔːn'wɒlɪs) n **Charles,** 1st Marquis Cornwallis. 1738–1805, British general in the War of American Independence: governor general of Bengal (1786–93, 1805).

corn whisky n whisky made from maize.

corny ('kɔːnɪ) *adj* **cornier, corniest.** *Sl.* **1** trite or banal. **2** sentimental or mawkish. **3** abounding in corn. [C16 (C20 in the sense banal): from CORN¹ + -Y¹]

corolla (kə'rɒlə) n the petals of a flower collectively, forming an inner floral envelope. [C17: dim. of L *corōna* crown]

corollary (kə'rɒlərɪ) n, *pl* **corollaries. 1** a proposition that follows directly from the proof of another proposition. **2** an obvious deduction. **3** a natural consequence. [C14: from L *corollārium* money paid for a garland, from L *corolla* garland]

Coromandel Coast ★ (,kɒrə'mændᵊl) n the SE coast of India, along the Bay of Bengal, extending from Point Calimere to the mouth of the Krishna River.

corona (kə'rəunə) n, *pl* **coronas** or **coronae** (-niː). **1** a circle of light around a luminous body, usually the moon. **2** Also called: **aureole.** the outermost region of the sun's atmosphere, visible as a faint halo during a solar eclipse. **3** *Archit.* the flat vertical face of a cornice. **4** a circular chandelier. **5** *Bot.* **5a** the trumpet-shaped part of the corolla of daffodils and similar plants. **5b** a crown of leafy outgrowths from inside the petals of some flowers. **6** *Anat.* a crownlike structure. **7** a long cigar with blunt ends. **8** *Physics.* an electrical discharge appearing around the surface of a charged conductor. [C16: from L: crown]

coronach ('kɒrənəx) n *Scot. & Irish.* a dirge or lamentation for the dead. [C16: from Scot. Gaelic *corranach*]

coronary ('kɒrənərɪ) *adj* **1** *Anat.* designating blood vessels, nerves, ligaments, etc., that encircle a part or structure. ♦ n, *pl* **coronaries. 2** short for **coronary thrombosis.** [C17: from L *corōnārius* belonging to a wreath or crown]

coronary artery n either of the two arteries branching from the aorta and supplying blood to the heart.

coronary bypass n the surgical bypass of a narrowed or blocked coronary artery by grafting a section of a healthy blood vessel taken from another part of the patient's body.

coronary heart disease n any heart disorder caused by disease of the coronary arteries.

coronary thrombosis n a condition of interrupted blood flow to the heart due to a blood clot in a coronary artery.

coronation (,kɒrə'neɪʃən) n the act or ceremony of crowning a monarch. [C14: from OF, from *coroner* to crown, from L *corōnāre*]

coroner ('kɒrənə) n a public official responsible for the investigation of violent, sudden, or suspicious deaths. [C14: from Anglo-F *corouner,* from OF *corone* CROWN]
▸ **'coroner,ship** n

coronet ('kɒrənɪt) n **1** any small crown, esp. one worn by princes or peers. **2** a woman's jewelled circlet for the head. **3** the margin between the skin of a horse's pastern

★ people and places

and the horn of the hoof. **4** the knob at the base of a deer's antler. [C15: from OF *coronete*]

Corot ★ (*French* kɔro) *n* **Jean Baptiste Camille** (ʒɑ̃ batist kamij). 1796–1875, French landscape and portrait painter.

coroutine ('kəuruːˌtiːn) *n Computing*. a section of a computer program similar to but differing from a subroutine in that it can be left and re-entered at any point.

corp. *abbrev. for*: **1** corporation. **2** corporal.

corporal[1] ('kɔːpərəl, 'kɔːprəl) *adj* of or relating to the body. [C14: from L *corporālis*, from *corpus* body] ► ˌcorpo'rality *n* ► 'corporally *adv*

corporal[2] ('kɔːpərəl) *n* **1** a noncommissioned officer junior to a sergeant in the army, air force, or marines. **2** (in the Royal Navy) a petty officer who assists the master-at-arms. [C16: from OF, via It., from L *caput* head; ? also infl. in OF by *corps* body (of men)]

corporal[3] ('kɔːpərəl) *or* **corporale** (ˌkɔːpə'reɪlɪ) *n* a white linen cloth on which the bread and wine are placed during the Eucharist. [C14: from Med. L *corporāle pallium* eucharistic altar cloth, from L *corporālis*, from *corpus* body (of Christ)]

Corporal of Horse *n* a noncommissioned rank in the British Army, above that of sergeant and below that of staff sergeant.

corporal punishment *n* punishment of a physical nature, such as caning.

corporate ('kɔːpərɪt) *adj* **1** forming a corporation; incorporated. **2** of a corporation or corporations: *corporate finance*. **3** of or belonging to a united group; joint. [C15: from L *corporātus*, from *corpus* body] ► 'corporatism *n*

corporate advertising *n* advertising designed to publicize or create a favourable image of a company rather than a particular product.

corporate anorexia *n* a malaise of a business organization resulting from making too many creative people redundant in a cost-cutting exercise.

corporate culture *n* the distinctive ethos of an organization that influences the level of formality, loyalty, and general behaviour of its employees.

corporate identity *or* **image** *n* the way an organization is presented to or perceived by its members and the public.

corporate raider *n Finance*. a person or organization that acquires a substantial holding of the shares of a company in order to take it over or to force its management to act in a desired way.

corporate venturing *n Finance*. the provision of venture capital by one company for another in order to obtain information about the company requiring capital or as a step towards acquiring it.

corporation (ˌkɔːpə'reɪʃən) *n* **1** a group of people authorized by law to act as an individual and having its own powers, duties, and liabilities. **2** Also called: **municipal corporation**. the municipal authorities of a city or town. **3** a group of people acting as one body. **4** See **public corporation**. **5** *Inf*. a large paunch. ► 'corporative *adj*

corporation tax *n* a British tax on the profits of a company or other incorporated body.

corporeal (kɔː'pɔːrɪəl) *adj* **1** of the nature of the physical body; not spiritual. **2** of a material nature; physical. [C17: from L *corporeus*, from *corpus* body] ► corˌpore'ality *or* **corporeity** (ˌkɔːpɔ'riːɪtɪ) *n* ► cor'poreally *adv*

corps (kɔː) *n, pl* **corps** (kɔːz). **1** a military formation that comprises two or more divisions. **2** a military body with a specific function: *medical corps*. **3** a body of people associated together: *the diplomatic corps*. [C18: from F, from L *corpus* body]

corps de ballet ('kɔː də 'bæleɪ) *n* the members of a ballet company who dance together in a group.

corps diplomatique (ˌdiːpləumæ'tiːk) *n* another name for **diplomatic corps**.

corpse (kɔːps) *n* a dead body, esp. of a human being. [C14: from OF *corps*, from L *corpus*]

corpulent ('kɔːpjulənt) *adj* physically bulky; fat. [C14 from L *corpulentus*] ► 'corpulence *n*

cor pulmonale (ˌkɔː ˌpʌlmə'nɑːlɪ) *n* pulmonary heart disease: a serious heart condition in which there is enlargement and failure of the right ventricle resulting from lung disease. [NL]

corpus ('kɔːpəs) *n, pl* **corpora** (-pərə). **1** a body of writings esp. by a single author or on a specific topic: *the corpus of Dickens' works*. **2** the main body or substance of something. **3** *Anat*. **3a** any distinct mass or body. **3b** the main part of an organ or structure. **4** *Obs*. a corpse. [C14: from L: body]

Corpus Christi[1] ('krɪstɪ) *n Chiefly RC Church*. a festival in honour of the Eucharist, observed on the Thursday after Trinity Sunday. [C14: from L: body of Christ]

Corpus Christi[2] ★ ('krɪstɪ) *n* a port in S Texas, on **Corpus Christi Bay**, an inlet of the Gulf of Mexico. Pop.: 275 419 (1994 est.).

corpuscle ('kɔːpʌsəl) *n* **1** any cell or similar minute body that is suspended in a fluid, esp. any of the **red blood corpuscles** (see **erythrocyte**) or **white blood corpuscles** (see **leucocyte**). **2** Also: **corpuscule** (kɔː'pʌskjuːl). any minute particle. [C17: from L *corpusculum* a little body, from *corpus* body] ► **corpuscular** (kɔː'pʌskjulə) *adj*

corpuscular theory *n* the theory, originally proposed by Newton, that light consists of a stream of particles. Cf. **wave theory**.

corpus delicti (dɪ'lɪktaɪ) *n Law*. the body of facts that constitute an offence. [NL, lit.: the body of the crime]

corpus juris ('dʒuərɪs) *n* a body of law, esp. of a nation or state. [from LL, lit.: a body of law]

corpus luteum ('luːtɪəm) *n, pl* **corpora lutea** ('luːtɪə). a mass of tissue that forms in a Graafian follicle following release of an ovum. [NL, lit.: yellow body]

corral (kɒ'rɑːl) *n* **1** *Chiefly US & Canad*. an enclosure for cattle or horses. **2** *Chiefly US*. (formerly) a defensive enclosure formed by a ring of covered wagons. ◆ *vb* **corrals, corralling, corralled**. (*tr*) *US & Canad*. **3** to drive into a corral. **4** *Inf*. to capture. [C16: from Sp., ult. from L *currere* to run]

corrasion (kə'reɪʒən) *n* erosion of a rock surface by rock fragments transported over it by water, wind, or ice. [C17: from L *corrādere* to scrape together]

correa ('kɒrɪə, kə'riːə) *n* an Australian evergreen shrub with large showy tubular flowers. [C19: after Jose Francesco *Correa* da Serra (1750-1823), Portuguese botanist]

correct (kə'rɛkt) *vb* (*tr*) **1** to make free from errors. **2** to indicate the errors in. **3** to rebuke or punish in order to improve: *to stand corrected*. **4** to rectify (a malfunction, ailment, etc.). **5** to adjust or make conform, esp. to a standard. ◆ *adj* **6** true; accurate: *the correct version*. **7** in conformity with accepted standards: *correct behaviour*. [C14: from L *corrigere* to make straight, from *com-* (intensive) + *regere* to rule] ► cor'rectly *adv* ► cor'rectness *n*

correction (kə'rɛkʃən) *n* **1** the act of correcting. **2** something substituted for an error; an improvement. **3** a reproof. **4** a quantity added to or subtracted from a scientific calculation or observation to increase its accuracy. ► cor'rectional *adj*

corrective (kə'rɛktɪv) *adj* **1** tending or intended to correct. ◆ *n* **2** something that tends or is intended to correct.

Correggio ★ (*Italian* kor'reddʒo) *n* **Antonio Allegri da** (an-'tɔːnjo al'leːgri da). 1494–1534, Italian painter.

Corregidor ★ (kə'rɛgɪˌdɔː) *n* an island at the entrance to Manila Bay, in the Philippines: site of the defeat of American forces by the Japanese (1942) in World War II.

correlate ('kɒrɪˌleɪt) *vb* **correlates, correlating, correlated. 1** to place or be placed in a complementary or reciprocal

★ people and places

relationship. **2** (*tr*) to establish or show a correlation between. ◆ *n* **3** either of two things mutually related.

correlation (ˌkɒrɪˈleɪʃən) *n* **1** a mutual relationship between two or more things. **2** the act of correlating or the state of being correlated. **3** *Statistics*. the extent of correspondence between the ordering of two variables. [C16: from Med. L *correlātiō*, from *com-* together + *relātiō* RELATION]
► ˌcorreˈlational *adj*

correlation coefficient *n Statistics*. a statistic measuring the degree of correlation between two variables.

correlative (kɒˈrɛlətɪv) *adj* **1** in complementary or reciprocal relationship; corresponding. **2** denoting words, usually conjunctions, occurring together though not adjacently in certain grammatical constructions, as *neither* and *nor*. ◆ *n* **3** either of two things that are correlative. **4** a correlative word.
► corˈrelatively *adv* ► corˌrelaˈtivity *n*

correspond (ˌkɒrɪˈspɒnd) *vb* (*intr*) **1** (usually foll. by *with* or *to*) to be consistent or compatible (with); tally (with). **2** (usually foll. by *to*) to be similar in character or function. **3** (usually foll. by *with*) to communicate by letter. [C16: from Med. L *corrēspondēre*, from L *respondēre* to RESPOND]
► ˌcorreˈsponding *adj* ► ˌcorreˈspondingly *adv*

> **USAGE NOTE** See at **similar.**

correspondence (ˌkɒrɪˈspɒndəns) *n* **1** the condition of agreeing or corresponding. **2** similarity. **3** agreement or conformity. **4a** communication by letters. **4b** the letters so exchanged.

correspondence school *n* an educational institution that offers tuition (**correspondence courses**) by post.

correspondent (ˌkɒrɪˈspɒndənt) *n* **1** a person who communicates by letter. **2** a person employed by a newspaper, etc., to report on a special subject or from a foreign country. **3** a person or firm that has regular business relations with another, esp. one abroad. ◆ *adj* **4** similar or analogous.

corrida (koˈrriða) *n* the Spanish word for **bullfight.** [Sp., from *corrida de toros*, lit.: a running of bulls]

corridor (ˈkɒrɪˌdɔː) *n* **1** a passage connecting parts of a building. **2** a strip of land or airspace that affords access, either from a landlocked country to the sea or from a state to an exclave. **3** a passageway connecting the compartments of a railway coach. **4** a flight path that affords safe access for intruding aircraft. **5** the path that a spacecraft must follow when re-entering the atmosphere, above which lift is insufficient and below which heating effects are excessive. **6 corridors of power.** the higher echelons of government, the Civil Service, etc., considered as the location of power and influence. [C16: from OF, from OIt. *corridore*, lit.: place for running]

corrie (ˈkɒrɪ) *n* **1** (in Scotland) a circular hollow on a hillside. **2** *Geol*. another name for **cirque.** [C18: from Gaelic *coire* cauldron]

corrigendum (ˌkɒrɪˈdʒɛndəm) *n, pl* **corrigenda** (-də). **1** an error to be corrected. **2** (*sometimes pl*) Also called: **erratum.** a slip of paper inserted into a book after printing, listing corrections. [C19: from L: that which is to be corrected]

corrigible (ˈkɒrɪdʒɪbʰl) *adj* **1** capable of being corrected. **2** submissive. [C15: from OF, from Med. L *corrigibilis*, from L *corrigere* to CORRECT]

corroborate (kəˈrɒbəˌreɪt) *vb* **corroborates, corroborating, corroborated.** (*tr*) to confirm or support (facts, opinions, etc.), esp. by providing fresh evidence. [C16: from L *corrōborāre*, from *rōborāre* to make strong, from *rōbur* strength]
► corˌroboˈration *n* ► corˈroborative (kəˈrɒbərətɪv) *or* corˈroboratory *adj* ► corˈroboˌrator *n*

corroboree (kəˈrɒbərɪ) *n Austral*. **1** a native assembly of sacred, festive, or warlike character. **2** *Inf*. any noisy gathering. [C19: from Abor.]

corrode (kəˈrəʊd) *vb* **corrodes, corroding, corroded. 1** to eat away or be eaten away, esp. as in the oxidation or rusting

of a metal. **2** (*tr*) to destroy gradually: *his jealousy corroded his happiness*. [C14: from L *corrōdere* to gnaw to pieces, from *rōdere* to gnaw]
► corˈrodible *adj*

corrosion (kəˈrəʊʒən) *n* **1** a process in which a solid, esp. a metal, is eaten away and changed by a chemical action, as in the oxidation of iron. **2** slow deterioration by being eaten or worn away. **3** the product of corrosion.

corrosive (kəˈrəʊsɪv) *adj* **1** tending to eat away or consume. ◆ *n* **2** a corrosive substance, such as a strong acid.
► corˈrosively *adv* ► corˈrosiveness *n*

corrosive sublimate *n* another name for **mercuric chloride.**

corrugate (ˈkɒruˌɡeɪt) *vb* **corrugates, corrugating, corrugated.** (*usually tr*) to fold or be folded into alternate furrows and ridges. [C18: from L *corrūgāre*, from *rūga* a wrinkle]
► ˈcorruˌgated *adj* ► ˌcorruˈgation *n*

corrugated iron *n* a thin sheet of iron or steel, formed with alternating ridges and troughs.

corrupt (kəˈrʌpt) *adj* **1** open to or involving bribery or other dishonest practices: *a corrupt official; corrupt practices*. **2** morally depraved. **3** putrid or rotten. **4** (of a text or manuscript) made meaningless or different in meaning by scribal errors or alterations. **5** (of computer programs or data) containing errors. ◆ *vb* **6** to become or cause to become dishonest or disloyal. **7** (*tr*) to deprave. **8** (*tr*) to infect or contaminate. **9** (*tr*) to cause to become rotten. **10** (*tr*) to alter (a text, etc.) from the original. **11** (*tr*) *Computing*. to introduce errors into (data or a program). [C14: from L *corruptus* spoiled, from *corrumpere* to ruin, from *rumpere* to break]
► corˈrupter *or* corˈruptor *n* ► corˈruptly *adv* ► corˈruptness *n*

corruptible (kəˈrʌptɪbʰl) *adj* capable of being corrupted.
► corˈruptibly *adv*

corruption (kəˈrʌpʃən) *n* **1** the act of corrupting or state of being corrupt. **2** depravity. **3** dishonesty, esp. bribery. **4** decay. **5** alteration, as of a manuscript. **6** an altered form of a word.

corsage (kɔːˈsɑːʒ) *n* **1** a small bunch of flowers worn pinned to the lapel, bosom, etc. **2** the bodice of a dress. [C15: from OF, from *cors* body, from L *corpus*]

corsair (ˈkɔːsɛə) *n* **1** a pirate. **2** a privateer, esp. of the Barbary Coast. [C15: from OF *corsaire*, from Med. L *cursārius*, from L *cursus* a running]

corse (kɔːs) *n* an archaic word for **corpse.**

corselet (ˈkɔːslɪt) *n* Also spelt: **corslet.** a piece of armour for the top part of the body. **2** a one-piece foundation garment. [C15: from OF, from *cors* bodice, from L *corpus* body]

corset (ˈkɔːsɪt) *n* **1a** a stiffened, elasticated, or laced foundation garment, worn esp. by women. **1b** a similar garment worn because of injury, weakness, etc., by either sex. **2** *Inf*. a restriction or limitation, esp. government control of bank lending. ◆ *vb* **3** (*tr*) to dress or enclose in, or as in, a corset. [C14: from OF, lit.: a little bodice]
► corsetière (ˌkɔːsɛtɪˈɛə) *n* ► ˈcorsetry *n*

Corsica ★ (ˈkɔːsɪkə) *n* an island in the Mediterranean, west of N Italy: forms, with 43 islets, a region of France; mountainous; settled by Greeks in about 560 B.C.; sold by Genoa to France in 1768. Capital: Ajaccio. Pop.: 258 879 (1994 est.). Area: 8682 sq. km (3367 sq. miles). French name: **Corse.**
► ˈCorsican *adj, n*

cortege *or* **cortège** (kɔːˈteɪʒ) *n* **1** a formal procession, esp. a funeral procession. **2** a train of attendants; retinue. [C17: from F, from It. *corteggio*, from *corteggiare* to attend]

Cortés (ˈkɔːtɛz; *Spanish* korˈtes) *or* **Cortez** ★ (kɔːˈtɛz) *n* **Hernando** (ɛrˈnando) *or* **Hernán** (ɛrˈnan). 1485–1547, Spanish conquistador: defeated the Aztecs and conquered Mexico (1523).

cortex (ˈkɔːtɛks) *n, pl* **cortices** (-tɪˌsiːz). **1** *Anat*. the outer layer of any organ or part, such as the grey matter in the brain that covers the cerebrum (**cerebral cortex**). **2** *Bot*. **2a** the tissue in plant stems and roots between the vascular bundles and the epidermis. **2b** the outer layer of a part

such as the bark of a stem. [C17: from L: bark, outer layer]
► **cortical** ('kɔ:tɪk°l) *adj*

corticate ('kɔ:tɪkɪt, -ˌkeɪt) *or* **corticated** *adj* (of plants, seeds, etc.) having a bark, husk, or rind. [C19: from L *corticātus*]

cortisone ('kɔ:tɪˌzəun) *n* a steroid hormone, the synthetic form of which has been used in treating rheumatoid arthritis, allergic and skin diseases, leukaemia, etc. [C20: from *corticosterone*, a hormone]

Cortona ★ (kɔ:'təunə; *Italian* kor'tɔ:na) *n* a town in Italy, in Tuscany: Roman and Etruscan remains, 15th-century cathedral. Pop.: 22 700 (1987 est.).

Cortot ★ (*French* kɔrto) *n* **Alfred** (alfrɛd). 1877–1962, French pianist, born in Switzerland.

corundum (kə'rʌndəm) *n* a hard mineral consisting of aluminium oxide: used as an abrasive. Precious varieties include ruby and white sapphire. Formula: Al_2O_3. [C18: from Tamil *kuruntam*; rel. to Sansk. *kuruvinda* ruby]

Corunna ★ (kə'rʌnə) *n* the English name for **La Coruña.**

coruscate ('kɒrəˌskeɪt) *vb* **coruscates, coruscating, coruscated.** (*intr*) to emit flashes of light; sparkle. [C18: from L *coruscāre* to flash]
► **ˌcorusˈcation** *n*

corvée ('kɔ:veɪ) *n* **1** *European history.* a day's unpaid labour owed by a feudal vassal to his lord. **2** the practice or an instance of forced labour. [C14: from OF, from LL *corrogāta* contribution, from L *corrogāre* to collect, from *rogāre* to ask]

corvette (kɔ:'vɛt) *n* a lightly armed escort warship. [C17: from OF, ?from MDu. *corf*]

corvine ('kɔ:vaɪn) *adj* **1** of or resembling a crow. **2** of the passerine bird family Corvidae, which includes the crows, ravens, rooks, jackdaws, magpies, and jays. [C17: from L *corvīnus*, from *corvus* a raven]

Corvo ★ ('kɔ:vəu) *n* **Baron.** See (Frederick William) **Rolfe.**

Corybant ('kɒrɪˌbænt) *n, pl* **Corybants** *or* **Corybantes** (ˌkɒrɪ'bæntiːz). *Classical myth.* a wild attendant of the goddess Cybele. [C14: from L *Corybās*, from Gk *Korubas*]
► **ˌCoryˈbantic** *adj*

corymb ('kɒrɪmb, -rɪm) *n* an inflorescence in the form of a flat-topped flower cluster with the oldest flowers at the periphery. [C18: from L *corymbus*, from Gk *korumbos* cluster]

coryza (kə'raɪzə) *n* acute inflammation of the mucous membrane of the nose, with discharge of mucus; a head cold. [C17: from LL: catarrh, from Gk *koruza*]

cos[1] *or* **cos lettuce** (kɒs) *n* a variety of lettuce with a long slender head and crisp leaves. Usual US and Canad. name: **romaine.** [C17: after *Kos*, the Aegean island of its origin]

cos[2] (kɒz) *abbrev. for* cosine.

Cos ★ (kɒs) *n* a variant spelling of **Kos.**

Cosa Nostra ('kəuzə 'nɒstrə) *n* the branch of the Mafia that operates in the US. [It.: our thing]

cosec ('kəusɛk) *abbrev. for* cosecant.

cosecant (kəu'si:kənt) *n* (of an angle) a trigonometric function that in a right-angled triangle is the ratio of the length of the hypotenuse to that of the opposite side.

coset ('kəuˌsɛt) *n Maths.* a set that produces a specified larger set when added to another set.

Cosgrave ★ ('kɒzˌgreɪv) *n* **1 Liam** ('li:əm). born 1920, Irish politician; prime minister of the Republic of Ireland (1973–77). **2** his father, **W**(illiam) **T**(homas). 1880–1965, Irish statesman; first president of the Irish Free State (1922–32).

cosh[1] (kɒʃ) *Brit.* ◆ *n* **1** a blunt weapon, often made of hard rubber; bludgeon. **2** an attack with such a weapon. ◆ *vb* **3** to hit with such a weapon, esp. on the head. [C19: from Romany *kosh*]

cosh[2] (kɒʃ, kɒs'eɪtʃ) *n* hyperbolic cosine. [C19: from COS(INE) + H(YPERBOLIC)]

cosignatory (kəu'sɪgnətərɪ, -trɪ) *n, pl* **cosignatories. 1** a person, country, etc., that signs a document jointly with others. ◆ *adj* **2** signing jointly.

Cosimo I ★ (*Italian* 'kɔ:zimo) *n* See (Cosimo I) **Medici.**

cosine ('kəuˌsaɪn) *n* (of an angle) a trigonometric function that in a right-angled triangle is the ratio of the length of the adjacent side to that of the hypotenuse. [C17: from NL *cosinus*; see CO-, SINE[1]]

cosmetic (kɒz'mɛtɪk) *n* **1** any preparation applied to the body, esp. the face, with the intention of beautifying it ◆ *adj* **2** serving or designed to beautify the body, esp. the face. **3** having no function than to beautify: *cosmetic illustrations in a book.* [C17: from Gk *kosmētikos* from *kosmein* to arrange, from *kosmos* order]
► **cosˈmetically** *adv*

cosmic ('kɒzmɪk) *adj* **1** of or relating to the whole universe: *cosmic laws.* **2** occurring or originating in outer space, esp. as opposed to the vicinity of the earth: *cosmic rays.* **3** immeasurably extended; vast.
► **ˈcosmically** *adv*

cosmic dust *n* fine particles of solid matter occurring throughout interstellar space and often collecting into clouds of extremely low density.

cosmic rays *pl n* radiation consisting of atomic nuclei esp. protons, of very high energy, that reach the earth from outer space. Also called: **cosmic radiation.**

cosmic string *n* any of a number of linear defects in space-time postulated in certain theories of cosmology to exist in the universe as a consequence of the big bang.

cosmo- *or before a vowel* **cosm-** *combining form.* indicating the world or universe: *cosmology; cosmonaut.* [from Gk: COSMOS]

cosmogony (kɒz'mɒgənɪ) *n, pl* **cosmogonies.** the study of the origin and development of the universe or of a particular system in the universe, such as the solar system. [C17: from Gk *kosmogonia*, from COSMO- + *gonos* creation]
► **cosmogonic** (ˌkɒzmə'gɒnɪk) *or* **ˌcosmoˈgonical** *adj*
► **cosˈmogonist** *n*

cosmography (kɒz'mɒgrəfɪ) *n* **1** a representation of the world or the universe. **2** the science dealing with the whole order of nature.
► **cosˈmographer** *n* ► **cosmographic** (ˌkɒzmə'græfɪk) *or* **ˌcosmoˈgraphical** *adj*

cosmological principle *n Astron.* the theory that the universe is uniform, homogenous, and isotropic, and therefore appears the same from any position.

cosmology (kɒz'mɒlədʒɪ) *n* **1** the study of the origin and nature of the universe. **2** a particular account of the origin or structure of the universe.
► **cosmological** (ˌkɒzmə'lɒdʒɪk°l) *or* **ˌcosmoˈlogic** *adj*
► **cosˈmologist** *n*

cosmonaut ('kɒzməˌnɔ:t) *n* an astronaut, esp. in the former Soviet Union. [C20: from Russian *kosmonavt*, from COSMO- + Gk *nautēs* sailor]

cosmopolitan (ˌkɒzmə'pɒlɪt°n) *n* **1** a person who has lived and travelled in many countries, esp. one who is free of national prejudices. ◆ *adj* **2** familiar with many parts of the world. **3** sophisticated or urbane. **4** composed of people or elements from all parts of the world or from many different spheres. [C17: from F, ult. from Gk *kosmopolitēs*, from *kosmo-* COSMO- + *politēs* citizen]
► **ˌcosmoˈpolitanism** *n*

cosmopolite (kɒz'mɒpəˌlaɪt) *n* **1** a less common word for **cosmopolitan** (sense 1). **2** an animal or plant that occurs in most parts of the world.
► **cosˈmopolitˌism** *n*

cosmos ('kɒzmɒs) *n* **1** the universe considered as an ordered system. **2** any ordered system. **3** (*pl* **cosmos** *or* **cosmoses**) any tropical American plant of the genus *Cosmos* cultivated as garden plants for their brightly coloured flowers. [C17: from Gk *kosmos* order]

Cosmos ('kɒzmɒs) *n Astronautics.* any of various types of Soviet satellite, including Cosmos 1 (launched 1962) and nearly 2000 subsequent satellites.

Cossack ('kɒsæk) *n* **1** (formerly) any of the free warrior-peasants of chiefly East Slavonic descent who served as cavalry under the tsars. ◆ *adj* **2** of, relating to, or characteristic of the Cossacks: *a Cossack dance.* [C16: from Russian *kazak* vagabond, of Turkic origin]

★ people and places

osset ('kɒsɪt) *vb* **cossets, cosseting, cosseted. 1** (*tr*) to pamper; pet. ◆ *n* **2** any pet animal, esp. a lamb. [C16: from ?]

ost (kɒst) *n* **1** the price paid or required for acquiring, producing, or maintaining something, measured in money, time, or energy; outlay. **2** suffering or sacrifice: *I know to my cost.* **3a** the amount paid for a commodity by its seller: *to sell at cost.* **3b** (*as modifier*): *the cost price.* **4** (*pl*) *Law.* the expenses of judicial proceedings. **5 at all costs.** regardless of sacrifice involved. **6 at the cost of.** at the expense of losing. ◆ *vb* **costs, costing, cost. 7** (*tr*) to be obtained or obtainable in exchange for: *the ride cost one pound.* **8** to cause or require the loss or sacrifice (of): *the accident cost him dearly.* **9** (*p.t. & p.p.* **costed**) to estimate the cost of (a product, process, etc.) for the purposes of pricing, budgeting, control, etc. [C13: from OF (n), from *coster* to cost, from L *constāre* to stand at, cost, from *stāre* to stand]

osta ('kɒstə) *n, pl* **costae** (-tiː). **1** the technical name for **rib**[1] (sense 1). **2** a riblike part. [C19: from L: rib, side]
▸ **'costal** *adj*

osta Brava ★ ('kɒstə 'brɑːvə) *n* a coastal region of NE Spain along the Mediterranean, extending from Barcelona to the French border: many resorts.

ost accounting *n* the recording and controlling of all the expenditures of an enterprise in order to facilitate control of separate activities. Also called: **management accounting.**
▸ **cost accountant** *n*

osta Rica ★ ('kɒstə 'riːkə) *n* a republic in Central America: gained independence from Spain in 1821; mostly mountainous and volcanic, with extensive forests. Official language: Spanish. Official religion: Roman Catholic. Currency: colón. Capital: San José. Pop.: 3 468 000 (1997). Area: 50 900 sq. km (19 652 sq. miles).
▸ **Costa Rican** *adj, n*

ost-benefit *adj* denoting or relating to a method of assessing a project that takes into account its costs and its benefits to society as well as the revenue it generates: *a cost-benefit analysis; the project was assessed on a cost-benefit basis.*

ost-effective *adj* providing adequate financial return in relation to outlay.
▸ **,cost-ef'fectiveness** *n*

ostermonger ('kɒstə,mʌŋgə) *or* **coster** *n Brit., rare.* a person who sells fruit, vegetables, etc., from a barrow. [C16: from *costard* a kind of apple + MONGER]

ostive ('kɒstɪv) *adj* **1** constipated. **2** niggardly. [C14: from OF *costivé*, from L *constipātus; see* CONSTIPATE]
▸ **'costiveness** *n*

ostly ('kɒstlɪ) *adj* **costlier, costliest. 1** expensive. **2** entailing great loss or sacrifice: *a costly victory.* **3** splendid; lavish.
▸ **'costliness** *n*

ost of living *n* **a** the basic cost of the food, clothing, shelter, and fuel necessary to maintain life, esp. at a standard of living regarded as basic. **b** (*as modifier*): *the cost-of-living index.*

ost-plus *n* a method of establishing a selling price in which an agreed percentage is added to the cost price to cover profit.

ostume ('kɒstjuːm) *n* **1** a style of dressing, including all the clothes, accessories, etc., worn at one time, as in a particular country or period. **2** *Old-fashioned.* a woman's suit. **3** a set of clothes, esp. unusual or period clothes: *a jester's costume.* **4** short for **swimming costume.** ◆ *vb* **costumes, costuming, costumed.** (*tr*) **5** to furnish the costumes for (a show, film, etc.). **6** to dress (someone) in a costume. [C18: from F, from It.: dress, habit, CUSTOM]

costumier (kɒ'stjuːmɪə) *or* **costumer** *n* a person or firm that makes or supplies theatrical or fancy costumes.

cosy *or US* **cozy** ('kəʊzɪ) *adj* **cosier, cosiest** *or US* **cozier, coziest. 1** warm and snug. **2** intimate; friendly. ◆ *n, pl* **cosies** *or US* **cozies. 3** a cover for keeping things warm: *egg cosy.* [C18: from Scot., from ?]
▸ **'cosily** *or US* **'cozily** *adv* ▸ **'cosiness** *or US* **'coziness** *n*

cot[1] (kɒt) *n* **1** a child's boxlike bed, usually incorporating vertical bars. **2** a portable bed. **3** a light bedstead. **4** *Naut.* a hammock-like bed. [C17: from Hindi *khāt* bedstead]

cot[2] (kɒt) *n* **1** *Literary or arch.* a small cottage. **2** Also called: **cote. 2a** a small shelter, esp. one for pigeons, sheep, etc. **2b** (*in combination*): *dovecot.* [OE *cot*]

cot[3] (kɒt) *abbrev. for* cotangent.

cotangent (kəʊ'tændʒənt) *n* (of an angle) a trigonometric function that in a right-angled triangle is the ratio of the length of the adjacent side to that of the opposite side.

COTC *abbrev. for* Canadian Officers Training Corps.

cot death *n* the unexplained sudden death of an infant during sleep. Technical name: **sudden infant death syndrome.**

cote (kəʊt) *or* **cot** *n* **1** a small shelter for pigeons, sheep, etc. **2** (*in combination*): *dovecote.* [OE *cote*]

Côte d'Azur ★ (*French* kot dazyr) *n* the Mediterranean coast of France, including the French Riviera: forms an administrative region with Provence.

Côte d'Ivoire ★ (*French* kot divwar) *n* a republic in West Africa, on the Gulf of Guinea: Portuguese trading for ivory and slaves began in the 16th century; made a French protectorate in 1842 and became independent in 1960; major producer of coffee and cocoa. Official language: French. Religion: Muslim majority, with animist, atheist, and Roman Catholic minorities. Currency: franc. Capital: Yamoussoukro (administrative); Abidjan (legislative). Pop.: 14 986 000 (1997). Area: 319 820 sq. km (123 483 sq. miles). Former name (until 1986): **the Ivory Coast.**

Côte-d'Or ★ (*French* kotdɔr) *n* a department of E central France, in NE Burgundy. Capital: Dijon. Pop.: 505 896 (1994 est.). Area: 8787 sq. km (3427 sq. miles).

coterie ('kəʊtərɪ) *n* a small exclusive group of people with common interests; clique. [C18: from F, from OF: association of tenants, from *cotier* (unattested) cottager]

coterminous (kəʊ'tɜːmɪnəs) *or* **conterminous** *adj* **1** having a common boundary. **2** coextensive or coincident in range, time, etc.

Côtes-d'Armor ★ (*French* kotdɑːmɔr) *n* a department of W France, on the N coast of Brittany. Capital: St Brieuc. Pop.: 536 320 (1994 est.). Area: 6878 sq. km (2656 sq. miles). Former name: **Côtes-du-Nord.**

coth (kɒθ, 'kɒt'eɪt) *n* hyperbolic cotangent. [C20: from COT(ANGENT) + H(YPERBOLIC)]

cotillion *or* **cotillon** (kə'tɪljən, kəʊ-) *n* **1** a French formation dance of the 18th century. **2** *US.* a quadrille. **3** *US.* a formal ball. [C18: from F *cotillon* dance, from OF: petticoat]

cotinga (kə'tɪŋgə) *n* a tropical American passerine bird having a broad slightly hooked bill.

cotoneaster (kə,təʊnɪ'æstə) *n* any Old World shrub of the rosaceous genus *Cotoneaster:* cultivated for their ornamental flowers and red or black berries. [C18: from NL, from L *cotōneum* QUINCE]

Cotonou ★ (,kəʊtə'nuː) *n* the official capital of Benin, a port on the Bight of Benin. Pop.: 533 212 (1992).

Cotopaxi ★ (*Spanish* koto'paksi) *n* a volcano in central Ecuador, in the Andes: the world's highest active volcano. Height: 5896 m (19 344 ft).

Cotswolds ★ ('kɒts,wəʊldz, -wəldz) *pl n* a range of low hills in SW England, mainly in Gloucestershire: formerly a centre of the wool industry.

cotta ('kɒtə) *n RC Church.* a short form of surplice. [C19: from It.: tunic]

cottage ('kɒtɪdʒ) *n* a small simple house, esp. in a rural area. [C14: from COT[2]]

cottage cheese *n* a mild loose soft white cheese made from skimmed milk curds.

cottage hospital *n Brit.* a small rural hospital.

cottage industry *n* an industry in which employees work in their own homes, often using their own equipment.

cottage pie *n Brit.* another term for **shepherd's pie.**

cottager ('kɒtɪdʒə) *n* **1** a person who lives in a cottage. **2** a rural labourer.

cottaging ('kɒtɪdʒɪŋ) *n Brit. sl.* homosexual activity between men in a public lavatory.

cotter[1] ('kɒtə) *n Machinery.* **1** any part, such as a pin, wedge, key, etc., that is used to secure two other parts so that relative motion between them is prevented. **2** short for **cotter pin**. [C14: shortened from *cotterel*, from ?]

cotter[2] ('kɒtə) *n* **1** *English history.* a villein in late Anglo-Saxon and early Norman times occupying a cottage and land in return for labour. **2** Also called: **cottar**. a peasant occupying a cottage and land in the Scottish Highlands. [C14: from Med. L *cotārius*, from ME *cote* COT[2]]

cotter pin *n Machinery.* a split pin secured, after passing through holes in the parts to be attached, by spreading the ends.

Cottian Alps ★ ('kɒtɪən) *pl n* a mountain range in SW Europe, between NW Italy and SE France: part of the Alps. Highest peak: Monte Viso, 3841 m (12 600 ft).

cotton ('kɒtⁿn) *n* **1** any of various herbaceous plants and shrubs cultivated in warm climates for the fibre surrounding the seeds and the oil within the seeds. **2** the soft white downy fibre of these plants, used to manufacture textiles. **3** cotton plants collectively, as a cultivated crop. **4** a cloth or thread made from cotton fibres. [C14: from OF *coton*, from Ar. *qutn*]
  ► '**cottony** *adj*

Cotton ★ ('kɒtⁿn) *n* Henry. 1907–87, British professional golfer: won the British Open championship (1934; 1937; 1948).

cotton bud *n* a small stick with a cotton-wool tip used for cleaning the ears, applying make-up, etc.

cotton grass *n* any of various N temperate and arctic grasslike bog plants whose clusters of long silky hairs resemble cotton tufts.

cotton on *vb* (*intr, adv;* often foll. by *to*) *Inf.* to perceive the meaning (of).

cotton-picking *adj US & Canad. sl.* (intensifier qualifying something undesirable): *you cotton-picking layabout!*

cottonseed ('kɒtⁿn,si:d) *n, pl* **cottonseeds** *or* **cottonseed.** the seed of the cotton plant: a source of oil and fodder.

cotton wool *n* **1** *Chiefly Brit.* bleached and sterilized cotton from which the impurities, such as the seeds, have been removed. Usual US term: **absorbent cotton. 2** cotton in the natural state. **3** *Brit. inf.* a state of pampered comfort and protection.

cotyledon (,kɒtɪ'li:dⁿn) *n* a simple embryonic leaf in seed-bearing plants, which, in some species, forms the first green leaf after germination. [C16: from L: a plant, navelwort, from Gk *kotulēdōn*, from *kotulē* cup, hollow]
  ► ,**coty'ledonous** *adj* ► ,**coty'ledonal** *adj*

coucal ('ku:kæl) *n* any ground-living bird of the genus *Centropus* of Africa, S Asia, and Australia. [C19: from F, ?from *couc(ou)* cuckoo + *al(ouette)* lark]

couch (kautʃ) *n* **1** a piece of upholstered furniture, usually having a back and armrests, for seating more than one person. **2** a bed, esp. one used in the daytime by the patients of a doctor or a psychoanalyst. ♦ *vb* **3** (*tr*) to express in a particular style of language: *couched in an archaic style.* **4** (when *tr, usually reflexive or passive*) to lie down or cause to lie down for or as for sleep. **5** (*intr*) *Arch.* to crouch. **6** (*intr*) *Arch.* to lie in ambush; lurk. **7** (*tr*) *Surgery.* to remove (a cataract) by downward displacement of the lens of the eye. **8** (*tr*) *Arch.* to lower (a lance) into a horizontal position. [C14: from OF *couche* a bed, lair, from *coucher* to lay down, from L *collocāre* to arrange, from *locāre* to place]

couchant ('kautʃənt) *adj* (*usually postpositive*) *Heraldry.* in a lying position: *a lion couchant.* [C15: from F: lying]

couchette (ku:'ʃɛt) *n* a bed or berth in a railway carriage, esp. one converted from seats. [C20: from F, dim. of *couche* bed]

couch grass (kautʃ, ku:tʃ) *n* a grass with a yellowish-white creeping underground stem by which it spreads quickly: a troublesome weed. Also called: **twitch grass, quitch grass.**

couch potato *n Sl.,* chiefly *US.* a lazy person whose recreation consists chiefly of watching television.

Coué ★ (*French* kue) *n* **Émile** (emil). 1857–1926, French

psychologist: advocated psychotherapy by autosugge
  ► **Couéism** ('ku:eɪ,ɪzəm) *n*

cougar ('ku:gə) *n* another name for **puma.** [C18: from *couguar,* from Port., from Tupi]

cough (kɒf) *vb* **1** (*intr*) to expel air abruptly and explo sively through the partially closed vocal chords. **2** (*int* to make a sound similar to this. **3** (*tr*) to utter or expres with a cough or coughs. ♦ *n* **4** an act or sound of cough ing. **5** a condition of the lungs or throat which cause frequent coughing. [OE *cohhetten*]
  ► '**cougher** *n*

cough drop *n* a lozenge to relieve a cough.

cough mixture *n* any medicine that relieves coughing

cough up *vb* (*adv*) *Inf.* to surrender (money, informa tion, etc.), esp. reluctantly. **2** (*tr*) to bring into the mout or eject (phlegm, food, etc.) by coughing.

could (kud) *vb* (takes an infinitive without *to* or an im plied infinitive) used as an auxiliary: **1** to make the pas tense of **can**[1]. **2** to make the subjunctive mood of **can** esp. used in polite requests or in conditional sentences *could I see you tonight?* **3** to indicate suggestion of a cours of action: *you could take the car if it's raining.* **4** (often foll by *well*) to indicate a possibility: *he could well be a spy* [OE *cūthe*]

couldn't ('kudⁿt) *contraction of* could not.

couldst (kudst) *vb Arch.* the form of **could** used with th pronoun *thou* or its relative form.

coulee ('ku:leɪ, -lɪ) *n* **1a** a flow of molten lava. **1b** suc lava when solidified. **2** *Western US & Canad.* a steep-side ravine. [C19: from Canad. F *coulée* a flow, from F, from *couler* to flow, from L *cōlāre* to sift]

coulis ('ku:li:) *n* a thin purée of vegetables, fruit, etc., usu ally served as a sauce. [C20: F, lit.: purée]

coulomb ('ku:lɒm) *n* the derived SI unit of electri charge; the quantity of electricity transported in one sec ond by a current of 1 ampere. Symbol: C [C19: afte C.A. de COULOMB]

Coulomb ★ ('ku:lɒm; *French* kulɔ̃) *n* **Charles Augustin d** (ʃarl ogystɛ̃ də). 1736–1806, French physicist: made man discoveries in the field of electricity and magnetism.

coulter ('kəultə) *n* a blade or sharp-edged disc attache to a plough so that it cuts through the soil vertically i advance of the ploughshare. Also (esp. US): **colter.** [O *culter,* from L: ploughshare, knife]

coumarin *or* **cumarin** ('ku:mərɪn) *n* a white vanilla scented crystalline ester, used in perfumes and flavour ing. [C19: from F, from *coumarou* tonka-bean tree, from Sp., from Tupi]

council ('kaunsəl) *n* **1** an assembly of people meeting fo discussion, consultation, etc. **2a** a body of people electe or appointed to serve in an administrative, legislative, o advisory capacity: *a student council.* **2b** short for **legislativ council. 3** (*sometimes cap.;* often preceded by *the*) *Brit.* the local governing authority of a town, county, etc. **4** *Austral.* an administrative or legislative assembly, esp the upper house of a state parliament in Australia. **5** a meeting of a council. **6** (*modifier*) of, provided for, o used by a local council: *a council chamber; council offices.* **7** (*modifier*) *Brit.* provided by a local council, esp. (of hous ing) at a subsidized rent: *a council house; a council estate; a council school.* **8** *Christianity.* an assembly of bishops, etc. convened for regulating matters of doctrine or disci pline. [C12: from OF *concile,* from L *concilium* assembly from *com-* together + *calāre* to call]

─────────────────────────────
  USAGE NOTE Avoid confusion with **counsel.**
─────────────────────────────

council area *n* any of the 32 unitary authorities into which Scotland was divided for administrative purposes in 1996.

councillor *or US* **councilor** ('kaunsələ) *n* a member of a council.

─────────────────────────────
  USAGE NOTE Avoid confusion with **counsellor.**
─────────────────────────────

─────────────────────────────
  ★ people and places
─────────────────────────────

ouncilman ('kaʊnsəlmən) *n, pl* **councilmen**. *Chiefly US.* a councillor.

council tax *n* (in Britain) a tax based on the relative value of property levied to fund local council services.

ounsel ('kaʊnsəl) *n* 1 advice or guidance on conduct, behaviour, etc. 2 discussion; consultation: *to take counsel with a friend*. 3 a person whose advice is sought. 4 a barrister or group of barristers engaged in conducting cases in court and advising on legal matters. 5 *Christianity.* any of the **counsels of perfection**, namely poverty, chastity, and obedience. 6 **counsel of perfection**. excellent but unrealizable advice. 7 private opinions (esp. in **keep one's own counsel**). 8 *Arch.* wisdom; prudence. ◆ *vb* **counsels, counselling, counselled** *or US* **counsels, counseling, counseled.** 9 (*tr*) to give advice or guidance to. 10 (*tr; often takes a clause as object*) to recommend; urge. 11 (*intr*) *Arch.* to take counsel; consult. [C13: from OF *counseil*, from L *consilium* deliberating body; rel. to CONSULT]

ounselling *or US* **counseling** ('kaʊnsəlɪŋ) *n* systematic guidance offered by social workers, doctors, etc., in which a person's problems are discussed and advice is given.

ounsellor *or US* **counselor** ('kaʊnsələ) *n* 1 a person who gives counsel; adviser. 2 Also called: **counselor-at-law.** *US.* a lawyer, esp. one who conducts cases in court. 3 a senior diplomatic officer.

ount[1] (kaʊnt) *vb* 1 to add up or check (each unit in a collection) in order to ascertain the sum: *count your change.* 2 (*tr*) to recite numbers in ascending order up to and including. 3 (*tr; often foll. by in*) to take into account or include: *we must count him in.* 4 **not counting**. excluding. 5 (*tr*) to consider; deem: *count yourself lucky.* 6 (*intr*) to have importance: *this picture counts as a rarity.* 7 (*intr*) *Music.* to keep time by counting beats. ◆ *n* 8 the act of counting. 9 the number reached by counting; sum: *a blood count.* 10 *Law.* a paragraph in an indictment containing a separate charge. 11 **keep** *or* **lose count**. to keep or fail to keep an accurate record of items, events, etc. 12 *Boxing, wrestling.* the act of telling off a number of seconds by the referee, as when a boxer has been knocked down by his opponent. 13 **out for the count**. *Boxing.* knocked out and unable to continue after a count of ten by the referee. ◆ See also **count against, countdown**, etc. [C14: from Anglo-F *counter*, from L *computāre* to calculate]
► **'countable** *adj*

ount[2] (kaʊnt) *n* 1 a nobleman in any of various European countries having a rank corresponding to that of a British earl. 2 any of various officials in the late Roman Empire and in the early Middle Ages. [C16: from OF *conte*, from L *comes* associate, from COM- with + *īre* to go]

ount against *vb* (*intr, prep*) to have influence on the disadvantage of.

ountdown ('kaʊnt,daʊn) *n* 1 the act of counting backwards to time a critical operation exactly, such as the launching of a rocket. ◆ *vb* **count down**. (*intr, adv*) 2 to count thus.

ountenance ('kaʊntɪnəns) *n* 1 the face, esp. when considered as expressing a person's character or mood. 2 support or encouragement; sanction. 3 composure; self-control (esp. in **keep** *or* **lose one's countenance**). ◆ *vb* **countenances, countenancing, countenanced.** 4 to support or encourage; sanction. 5 to tolerate; endure. [C13: from OF *contenance* mien, behaviour, from L *continentia* restraint, control; see CONTAIN]

counter[1] ('kaʊntə) *n* 1 a horizontal surface, as in a shop or bank, over which business is transacted. 2 (in some cafeterias) a long table on which food is served. 3a a small flat disc of wood, metal, or plastic, used in various board games. 3b a similar disc or token used as an imitation coin. 4 a person or thing that may be used or ma-

nipulated. 5 **under the counter**. (**under-the-counter** *when prenominal*) (of the sale of goods) clandestine or illegal. 6 **over the counter**. (**over-the-counter** *when prenominal*) (of security transactions) through a broker rather than on a stock exchange. [C14: from OF *comptouer*, ult. from L *computāre* to COMPUTE]

counter[2] ('kaʊntə) *n* 1 a person who counts. 2 an apparatus that records the number of occurrences of events. [C14: from OF *conteor*, from L *computātor*; see COUNT[1]]

counter[3] ('kaʊntə) *adv* 1 in a contrary direction or manner. 2 in a wrong or reverse direction. 3 **run counter to**. to have a contrary effect or action to. ◆ *adj* 4 opposing; opposite; contrary. ◆ *n* 5 something that is contrary or opposite to some other thing. 6 an act, effect, or force that opposes another. 7 a return attack, such as a blow in boxing. 8 *Fencing.* a parry in which the foils move in a circular fashion. 9 the portion of the stern of a boat or ship that overhangs the water aft of the rudder. 10 a piece of leather forming the back of a shoe. ◆ *vb* 11 to say or do (something) in retaliation or response. 12 (*tr*) to move, act, or perform in a manner or direction opposite to (a person or thing). 13 to return the attack of (an opponent). [C15: from OF *contre*, from L *contrā* against]

counter- *prefix* 1 against; opposite; contrary: *counterattack.* 2 complementary; corresponding: *counterfoil.* 3 duplicate or substitute: *counterfeit.* [via OF from L *contrā* against, opposite; see CONTRA-]

counteract (,kaʊntər'ækt) *vb* (*tr*) to oppose or neutralize by contrary action; check.
► **,counter'action** *n* ► **,counter'active** *adj*

counterattack ('kaʊntərə,tæk) *n* 1 an attack in response to an attack. ◆ *vb* 2 to make a counterattack (against).

counterbalance *n* ('kaʊntə,bæləns). 1 a weight or force that balances or offsets another. ◆ *vb* (,kaʊntə'bæləns), **counterbalances, counterbalancing, counterbalanced.** (*tr*) 2 Also: **counterweigh**. to act as a counterbalance to. ◆ Also: **counterpoise.**

counterblast ('kaʊntə,blɑːst) *n* an aggressive response to a verbal attack.

countercheck *n* ('kaʊntə,tʃɛk). 1 a check or restraint, esp. one that acts in opposition to another. 2 a double check, as for accuracy. ◆ *vb* (,kaʊntə'tʃɛk). (*tr*) 3 to oppose by counteraction. 4 to double-check.

counterclaim ('kaʊntə,kleɪm) *Chiefly law.* ◆ *n* 1 a claim set up in opposition to another. ◆ *vb* 2 to set up (a claim) in opposition to another claim.
► **,counter'claimant** *n*

counterclockwise (,kaʊntə'klɒk,waɪz) *adv, adj* the US and Canad. equivalent of **anticlockwise.**

counterculture ('kaʊntə,kʌltʃə) *n* an alternative culture, deliberately at variance with the social norm.

counterespionage (,kaʊntər'ɛspɪə,nɑːʒ) *n* activities to counteract enemy espionage.

counterfeit ('kaʊntəfɪt) *adj* 1 made in imitation of something genuine with the intent to deceive or defraud; forged. 2 simulated; sham: *counterfeit affection.* ◆ *n* 3 an imitation designed to deceive or defraud. ◆ *vb* 4 (*tr*) to make a fraudulent imitation of. 5 (*intr*) to make counterfeits. 6 to feign; simulate. [C13: from OF *contrefait*, from *contrefaire* to copy, from *contre-* COUNTER- + *faire* to make]
► **'counterfeiter** *n*

counterfoil ('kaʊntə,fɔɪl) *n Brit.* the part of a cheque, receipt, etc., retained as a record. Also called (esp. in the US and Canada): **stub.**

counterforce ('kaʊntə,fɔːs) *n* (*modifier*) denoting military strategy based on retaliation against attacking forces.

counterinsurgency (,kaʊntərɪn'sɜːdʒənsɪ) *n* action taken by a government against rebels, guerrillas, etc.

counterintelligence (,kaʊntərɪn'tɛlɪdʒəns) *n* activities designed to frustrate enemy espionage.

counterintuitive *adj Chiefly US.* (of an idea, proposal, etc.) seemingly contrary to common sense.

counterirritant (,kaʊntər'ɪrɪt°nt) *n* 1 an agent that causes a superficial irritation of the skin and thereby re-

lieves inflammation of deep structures. ◆ *adj* **2** producing a counterirritation.
▶ ,counter,irri'tation *n*

countermand *vb* (,kaʊntə'mɑːnd). (*tr*) **1** to revoke or cancel (a command, order, etc.). **2** to order (forces, etc.) to retreat; recall. ◆ *n* ('kaʊntə,mɑːnd). **3** a command revoking another. [C15: from OF *contremander*, from *contre-* COUNTER- + *mander* to command, from L *mandāre*]

countermarch ('kaʊntə,mɑːtʃ) *Chiefly mil.* ◆ *vb* **1** to march or cause to march back or in the opposite direction. ◆ *n* **2** the act or an instance of countermarching.

countermeasure ('kaʊntə,mɛʒə) *n* action taken to oppose, neutralize, or retaliate against some other action.

countermove ('kaʊntə,muːv) *n* **1** an opposing move. ◆ *vb* **countermoves**, **countermoving**, **countermoved**. **2** to make or do (something) as an opposing move.
▶ 'counter,movement *n*

counteroffensive (,kaʊntərə,fɛnsɪv) *n* a series of attacks by a defending force against an attacking enemy.

counteroffer ('kaʊntər,ɒfə) *n* a response to a bid in which a seller amends his original offer, making it more favourable to the buyer.

counterpane ('kaʊntə,peɪn) *n* another word for **bedspread**. [C17: from obs. *counterpoint* (infl. by *pane* coverlet), changed from OF *coutepointe* quilt, from Med. L *culcita puncta* quilted mattress]

counterpart ('kaʊntə,pɑːt) *n* **1** a person or thing identical to or closely resembling another. **2** one of two parts that complement or correspond to each other. **3** a duplicate, esp. of a legal document; copy.

counterparty ('kaʊntə,pɑːtɪ) *n* a person who is a party to a contract.

counterplot ('kaʊntə,plɒt) *n* **1** a plot designed to frustrate another plot. ◆ *vb* **counterplots**, **counterplotting**, **counterplotted**. **2** (*tr*) to oppose with a counterplot.

counterpoint ('kaʊntə,pɔɪnt) *n* **1** the technique involving the simultaneous sounding of two or more parts or melodies. **2** a melody or part combined with another melody or part. **3** the musical texture resulting from the simultaneous sounding of two or more melodies or parts. ◆ *vb* **4** (*tr*) to set in contrast. ◆ Related adj: **contrapuntal**. [C15: from OF *contrepoint*, from *contre-* COUNTER- + *point* dot, note in musical notation, i.e. an accompaniment set against the notes of a melody]

counterpoise ('kaʊntə,pɔɪz) *n* **1** a force, influence, etc., that counterbalances another. **2** a state of balance; equilibrium. **3** a weight that balances another. ◆ *vb* **counterpoises**, **counterpoising**, **counterpoised**. (*tr*) **4** to oppose with something of equal effect, weight, or force; offset. **5** to bring into equilibrium.

counterproductive (,kaʊntəprə'dʌktɪv) *adj* tending to hinder the achievement of an aim; having effects contrary to those intended.

counterproposal ('kaʊntəprə,pəʊzəl) *n* a proposal offered as an alternative to a previous proposal.

Counter-Reformation (,kaʊntə,rɛfə'meɪʃən) *n* the reform movement of the Roman Catholic Church in the 16th and early 17th centuries considered as a reaction to the Reformation.

counter-revolution (,kaʊntə,rɛvə'luːʃən) *n* a revolution opposed to a previous revolution.
▶ ,counter-,revo'lutionist *n* ▶ counter-,revo'lutionary *n*, *adj*

countershaft ('kaʊntə,ʃɑːft) *n* an intermediate shaft driven by a main shaft, esp. in a gear train.

countersign *vb* ('kaʊntə,saɪn, ,kaʊntə'saɪn). **1** (*tr*) to sign (a document already signed by another). ◆ *n* ('kaʊntə,saɪn). **2** Also called: **countersignature**. the signature so written. **3** a secret sign given in response to another sign. **4** *Chiefly mil.* a password.

countersink ('kaʊntə,sɪŋk) *vb* **countersinks**, **countersinking**, **countersank**, **countersunk**. (*tr*) **1** to enlarge the upper part of (a hole) in timber, metal, etc., so that the head of a bolt or screw can be sunk below the surface. **2** to drive (a screw) or sink (a bolt) into such a hole. ◆ *n* **3** Also called: **countersink bit**. a tool for countersinking. **4** a countersunk hole.

countertenor (,kaʊntə'tɛnə) *n* **1** an adult male voice with an alto range. **2** a singer with such a voice.

countervail (,kaʊntə'veɪl, 'kaʊntə,veɪl) *vb* **1** (when *in* usually foll. by *against*) to act or act against with equal power or force. **2** (*tr*) to make up for; compensate; offset. [C14: from OF *contrevaloir*, from L *contrā valēre*, from *contrā* against + *valēre* to be strong]

countervailing duty *n* an extra import duty imposed by a country on certain imports, esp. to prevent dumping or to counteract subsidies in the exporting country

counterweigh (,kaʊntə'weɪ) *vb* another word for **counterbalance** (sense 2).

counterweight ('kaʊntə,weɪt) *n* a counterbalancing weight, influence, or force.

countess ('kaʊntɪs) *n* **1** the wife or widow of a count or earl. **2** a woman of the rank of count or earl.

counting house *n* Rare, chiefly Brit. a room or building used by the accountants of a business.

countless ('kaʊntlɪs) *adj* innumerable; myriad.

count noun *n* a noun that can be qualified by the indefinite article and may be used in the plural, as *telephone* and *thing* but not *airs and graces* or *bravery*. Cf. **mass noun**

count on *vb* (*intr, prep*) to rely on or depend on.

count out *vb* (*tr, adv*) **1** *Inf.* to leave out; exclude. **2** (of boxing referee) to judge (a floored boxer) to have failed to recover within the specified time.

count palatine *n, pl* **counts palatine**. *History.* **1** (in the Holy Roman Empire) a count who exercised royal authority in his own domain. **2** (in England and Ireland) the lord of a county palatine.

countrified *or* **countryfied** ('kʌntrɪ,faɪd) *adj* in the style, manners, etc., of the country; rural.

country ('kʌntrɪ) *n, pl* **countries**. **1** a territory distinguished by its people, culture, geography, etc. **2** an area of land distinguished by its political autonomy; state. **3** the people of a territory or state. **4a** the part of the land that is away from cities or industrial areas; rural districts. **4b** (*as modifier*): *country cottage*. Related adjs: **pastoral**, **rural**. **5** short for **country music**. **6 across country**. not keeping to roads, etc. **7 go** *or* **appeal to the country**. *Chiefly Brit.* to dissolve Parliament and hold an election. **8 up country**. away from the coast or the capital. **9** one's native land or nation of citizenship. [C13: from OF *contrée*, from Med. L *contrāta*, lit.: that which lies opposite, from L *contrā* opposite]

country and western *n* another name for **country music**.

country club *n* a club in the country, having sporting and social facilities.

country dance *n* a type of folk dance in which couples face one another in a line.

country house *n* a large house in the country, esp. belonging to a wealthy family.

countryman ('kʌntrɪmən) *n, pl* **countrymen**. **1** a person who lives in the country. **2** a person from a particular country or from one's own country.
▶ 'country,woman *fem n*

country music *n* a type of 20th-century popular music based on White folk music of the southeastern US.

country park *n* Brit. an area of countryside set aside for public recreation.

country seat *n* a large estate or property in the country

countryside ('kʌntrɪ,saɪd) *n* a rural area or its population.

county ('kaʊntɪ) *n, pl* **counties**. **1a** any of various administrative, political, judicial, or geographic subdivisions of certain English-speaking countries or states. **1b** (*as modifier*): *county cricket*. ◆ *adj* **2** Brit. inf. upper class; of or like the landed gentry. [C14: from OF *conté* land belonging to a count, from LL *comes* COUNT²]

county borough *n* **1** (in England from 1888 to 1974 and in Wales from 1888 to 1974 and from 1996) a borough administered independently of any higher tier of local government. **2** (in the Republic of Ireland) a borough governed by an elected council that constitutes an all-purpose authority.

★ people and places

county palatine *n, pl* **counties palatine. 1** the lands of a count palatine. **2** (in England and Ireland) a county in which the earl (or other lord) exercised many royal powers, esp. judicial authority.

county town *n* the town in which a county's affairs are or were administered.

coup (kuː) *n* **1** a brilliant and successful stroke or action. **2** short for **coup d'état.** [C18: from F: blow, from L *colaphus* blow with the fist, from Gk *kolaphos*]

coup de grâce *French.* (kuː də grɑs) *n, pl* **coups de grâce** (kuː də grɑs). **1** a mortal or finishing blow, esp. one delivered as an act of mercy to a sufferer. **2** a final or decisive stroke. [lit.: blow of mercy]

coup d'état ('kuː deɪ'tɑː) *n, pl* **coups d'état** ('kuːz deɪ'tɑː). a sudden violent or illegal seizure of government. [F, lit.: stroke of state]

coupe (kuːp) *n* **1** a dessert of fruit and ice cream. **2** a dish or stemmed glass bowl designed for this dessert. [C19: from F: goblet, CUP]

coupé ('kuːpeɪ) *n* **1** a four-seater car with a sloping back, and usually two doors. **2** a four-wheeled horse-drawn carriage with two seats inside and one outside for the driver. [C19: from F *carrosse coupé*, lit.: cut-off carriage]

Couperin ★ (*French* kuprɛ̃) *n* **François** (frɑ̃swa). 1668–1733, French composer, noted for his harpsichord suites and organ music.

couple ('kʌpᵊl) *n* **1** two people who regularly associate with each other or live together: *an engaged couple*. **2** (*functioning as sing or pl*) two people considered as a pair, for or as if for dancing, games, etc. **3** a pair of equal and opposite parallel forces that have a tendency to produce rotation. **4** a connector or link between two members, such as a tie connecting a pair of rafters in a roof. **5 a couple of.** (*functioning as sing or pl*) **5a** a combination of two; a pair of: *a couple of men.* **5b** *Inf.* a small number of; a few: *a couple of days.* ◆ *pron* **6** (usually preceded by *a*; *functioning as sing or pl*) two; a pair: *give him a couple.* ◆ *vb* **couples, coupling, coupled. 7** (*tr*) to connect (two things) together or to connect (one thing) to (another): *to couple railway carriages.* **8** to form or be formed into a pair or pairs. **9** to associate, put, or connect together. **10** (*intr*) to have sexual intercourse. [C13: from OF: a pair, from L *cōpula* a bond; see COPULA]

coupledom ('kʌpᵊldəm) *n* the state of living as a couple.

coupler ('kʌplə) *n Music.* a device on an organ or harpsichord connecting two keys, two manuals, etc., so that both may be played at once.

couplet ('kʌplɪt) *n* two successive lines of verse, usually rhymed and of the same metre. [C16: from F, lit.: a little pair; see COUPLE]

coupling ('kʌplɪŋ) *n* **1** a mechanical device that connects two things. **2** a device for connecting railway cars or trucks together.

coupon ('kuːpɒn) *n* **1a** a detachable part of a ticket or advertisement entitling the holder to a discount, free gift, etc. **1b** a detachable slip usable as a commercial order form. **1c** a voucher given away with certain goods, a certain number of which are exchangeable for goods offered by the manufacturers. **2** one of a number of detachable certificates attached to a bond, the surrender of which entitles the bearer to receive interest payments. **3** *Brit.* a detachable entry form for any of certain competitions, esp. football pools. [C19: from F, from OF *colpon* piece cut off, from *colper* to cut, var. of *couper*]

courage ('kʌrɪdʒ) *n* **1** the power or quality of dealing with or facing danger, fear, pain, etc. **2 the courage of one's convictions.** the confidence to act in accordance with one's beliefs. [C13: from OF *corage*, from *cuer* heart, from L *cor*]

courageous (kə'reɪdʒəs) *adj* possessing or expressing courage.
► **cou'rageously** *adv* ► **cou'rageousness** *n*

courante (kʊ'rɑːnt) *n Music.* **1** an old dance in quick triple time. **2** a movement of a (mostly) 16th- to 18th-century suite based on this. [C16: from F, lit.: running, from *courir* to run, from L *currere*]

Courantyne ★ ('kɔːrən,taɪn) *n* a river in N South America, rising in S Guyana and flowing north to the Atlantic, forming the boundary between Guyana and Surinam. Length: 765 km (475 miles). Dutch name: **Corantijn.**

courbaril ('kʊəbərɪl) *n* a tropical American leguminous tree: its wood is a useful timber and its gum is a source of copal. Also called: **West Indian locust.** [C18: from Amerind]

Courbet ★ (*French* kurbɛ) *n* **Gustave** (gystav). 1819–77, French painter, a leader of the realist movement; noted for his depiction of contemporary life.

coureur de bois (*French* kurœr də bwa) *n, pl* **coureurs de bois** (kurœr də bwa). *Canad. history.* a French Canadian woodsman or Métis who traded with Indians for furs. [Canad. F: trapper (lit.: wood-runner)]

courgette (kʊə'ʒɛt) *n* a small variety of vegetable marrow. US, Canad., and Austral. name: **zucchini.** [from F, dim. of *courge* marrow, gourd]

courier ('kʊərɪə) *n* **1** a special messenger, esp. one carrying diplomatic correspondence. **2** a person employed to collect and deliver parcels, packages, etc. **3** a person who makes arrangements for or accompanies a group of travellers on a journey or tour. ◆ *vb* **4** (*tr*) to send (a parcel, letter, etc.) by courier. [C16: from OF *courrier*, from OIt. *correre* to run, from L *currere*]

Cournand ★ ('kʊənənd, -nænd; *French* kurnɑ̃) *n* **André** (**Frederic**). 1895–1988, US physician, born in France: shared the 1956 Nobel prize for physiology or medicine for his work on heart catheterization.

Courrèges ★ (*French* kureʒ) *n* **André** (ɑ̃dre). born 1923, French couturier.

course (kɔːs) *n* **1** a continuous progression in time or space; onward movement. **2** a route or direction followed. **3** the path or channel along which something moves: *the course of a river.* **4** an area or stretch of land or water on which a sport is played or a race is run: *a golf course.* **5** a period of time; duration: *in the course of the next hour.* **6** the usual order of and time required for a sequence of events; regular procedure: *the illness ran its course.* **7** a mode of conduct or action: *if you follow that course, you will fail.* **8** a connected series of events, actions, etc. **9a** a prescribed number of lessons, lectures, etc., in an educational curriculum. **9b** the material covered in such a curriculum. **10** a regimen prescribed for a specific period of time: *a course of treatment.* **11** a part of a meal served at one time. **12** a continuous, usually horizontal, layer of building material, such as a row of bricks, tiles, etc. **13 as a matter of course.** as a natural or normal consequence, mode of action, or event. **14 in course of.** in the process of. **15 in due course.** at some future time, esp. the natural or appropriate time. **16 of course. 16a** (*adv*) as expected; naturally. **16b** (*sentence substitute*) certainly; definitely. **17 the course of nature.** the ordinary course of events. ◆ *vb* **courses, coursing, coursed. 18** (*intr*) to run, race, or flow. **19** to cause (hounds) to hunt by sight rather than scent or (of hounds) to hunt (a quarry) thus. [C13: from OF *cours*, from L *cursus* a running, from *currere* to run]

courser[1] ('kɔːsə) *n* **1** a person who courses hounds or dogs, esp. greyhounds. **2** a hound or dog trained for coursing.

courser[2] ('kɔːsə) *n Literary.* a swift horse; steed. [C13: from OF *coursier*, from *cours* COURSE]

coursework ('kɔːs,wɜːk) *n* written or oral work completed by a student within a given period, which is assessed as part of an educational course.

coursing ('kɔːsɪŋ) *n* **1** hunting with hounds or dogs that follow their quarry by sight. **2** a sport in which hounds are matched against one another in pairs for the hunting of hares by sight.

court (kɔːt) *n* **1** an area of ground wholly or partly surrounded by walls or buildings. **2** *Brit.* **2a** a block of flats. **2b** a mansion or country house. **2c** a short street, sometimes closed at one end. **3a** the residence, retinues, or household of a sovereign or nobleman. **3b** (*as modifier*): *a court ball.* **4** a sovereign or prince and his retinue, advisers, etc. **5** any formal assembly held by a sovereign or nobleman. **6** homage, flattering attention, or amorous approaches (esp. in **pay court to someone**). **7** *Law.* **7a** a tribunal having power to adjudicate in civil, criminal, military, or ecclesiastical matters. **7b** the regular sitting of such a judicial tribunal. **7c** the room or building in which such a tribunal sits. **8a** a marked outdoor or enclosed area used for any of various ball games, such as tennis, squash, etc. **8b** a marked section of such an area. **9 go to court.** to take legal action. **10 hold court.** to preside over admirers, attendants, etc. **11 out of court.** without a trial or legal case. **12 the ball is in your court.** you are obliged to make the next move. ◆ *vb* **13** to attempt to gain the love of; woo. **14** (*tr*) to pay attention to (someone) in order to gain favour. **15** (*tr*) to try to obtain (fame, honour, etc.). **16** (*tr*) to invite, usually foolishly, as by taking risks. [C12: from OF, from L *cohors* COHORT]

Court ★ (kɔːt) *n* **Margaret** (née *Smith*). born 1942, Australian tennis player: Wimbledon champion 1963, 1965, and 1970.

court-bouillon ('kʊət'buːjɒn) *n* a stock made from root vegetables, water, and wine or vinegar, used primarily for poaching fish. [from F, from *court* short, + *bouillon* broth, from *bouillir* to BOIL[1]]

court card *n* (in a pack of playing cards) a king, queen, or jack of any suit. [C17: altered from earlier *coat-card*, from the decorative coats worn by the figures depicted]

court circular *n* a daily report of the activities, engagements, etc., of the sovereign, published in a national newspaper.

Courtelle (kɔː'tɛl) *n* *Trademark*. a synthetic acrylic fibre resembling wool.

courteous ('kɜːtɪəs) *adj* polite and considerate in manner. [C13 *corteis*, lit.: with courtly manners, from OF; see COURT]
▸ **'courteously** *adv* ▸ **'courteousness** *n*

courtesan *or* **courtezan** (,kɔːtɪ'zæn) *n* (esp. formerly) a prostitute, or the mistress of a man of rank. [C16: from OF *courtisane*, from It. *cortigiana* female courtier, from *corte* COURT]

courtesy ('kɜːtɪsɪ) *n*, *pl* **courtesies**. **1** politeness; good manners. **2** a courteous gesture or remark. **3** favour or consent (esp. in (**by**) **courtesy of**). **4** common consent as opposed to right (esp. in **by courtesy**). [C13 *curteisie*, from OF, from *corteis* COURTEOUS]

courtesy light *n* the interior light in a motor vehicle.

courtesy title *n* any of several titles having no legal significance, such as those borne by the children of peers.

courthouse ('kɔːt,haʊs) *n* a public building in which courts of law are held.

courtier ('kɔːtɪə) *n* **1** an attendant at a court. **2** a person who seeks favour in an ingratiating manner. [C13: from Anglo-F *courteour* (unattested), from OF *corteier* to attend at court]

courtly ('kɔːtlɪ) *adj* **courtlier, courtliest**. **1** of or suitable for a royal court. **2** refined in manner. **3** ingratiating.
▸ **'courtliness** *n*

court martial *n*, *pl* **court martials** *or* **courts martial**. **1** a military court that tries persons subject to military law. ◆ *vb* **court-martial, court-martials, court-martialling, court-martialled** *or US* **court-martials, court-martialing, court-martialed**. **2** (*tr*) to try by court martial.

Court of Appeal *n* a court that hears appeals from the High Court and from the county and crown courts.

Court of St James's *n* the official name of the royal court of Britain.

court plaster *n* a plaster, composed of isinglass on silk, formerly used to cover superficial wounds. [C18: so called because formerly used by court ladies for beauty spots]

courtroom ('kɔːt,ruːm, -,rʊm) *n* a room in which the sittings of a law court are held.

courtship ('kɔːtʃɪp) *n* **1** the act, period, or art of seeking the love of someone with intent to marry. **2** the seeking or soliciting of favours.

court shoe *n* a low-cut shoe for women, without any laces or straps.

courtyard ('kɔːt,jɑːd) *n* an open area of ground surrounded by walls or buildings; court.

couscous ('kuːskuːs) *n* a spicy dish, originating in Nort Africa, consisting of steamed semolina served with meat stew. [C17: via F from Ar. *kouskous*, from *kaskasa* t pound until fine]

cousin ('kʌz°n) *n* **1** Also called: **first cousin, cousin-germa full cousin.** the child of one's aunt or uncle. **2** a relative de scended from one of one's common ancestors. **3** a tit used by a sovereign when addressing another sovereig or a nobleman. [C13: from OF *cosin*, from L *consōbrīnu* from *sōbrīnus* cousin on the mother's side]
▸ **'cousin,hood** *or* **'cousin,ship** *n* ▸ **'cousinly** *adj*, *adv*

Cousin ★ (*French* kuzɛ̃) *n* **Victor** (viktɔr). 1792–186ʔ French philosopher and educational reformer.

Cousteau ★ (*French* kusto) *n* **Jacques Yves** (ʒak iv). 1910 97, French underwater explorer.

couture (kuː'tʊə) *n* **a** high-fashion designing and dress making. **b** (*as modifier*): *couture clothes*. [from F: sewing from OF *couture* seam, from L *consuere* to stitch together]

couturier (kuː'tʊərɪ,eɪ) *n* a person who designs, make and sells fashion clothes for women. [from F: dress maker; see COUTURE]
▸ **couturière** (kuː,tʊrɪ'ɛə) *fem n*

couvade (kuː'vɑːd) *n* *Anthropol*. the custom in certai cultures of treating the husband of a woman giving birt as if he were bearing the child. [C19: from F, from *couve* to hatch, from L *cubāre* to lie down]

covalency (kəu'veɪlənsɪ) *or US* **covalence** *n* **1** the for mation and nature of covalent bonds, that is, chemica bonds involving the sharing of electrons between atom in a molecule. **2** the number of covalent bonds that particular atom can make with other atoms in forming molecule.
▸ **co'valent** *adj* ▸ **co'valently** *adv*

cove[1] (kəʊv) *n* **1** a small bay or inlet. **2** a narrow cavern i the side of a cliff, mountain, etc. **3** Also called: **coving** *Archit*. a concave curved surface between the wall an ceiling of a room. [OE *cofa*]

cove[2] (kəʊv) *n* *Sl.*, *Brit*. old-fashioned & *Austral*. a fellow chap. [C16: prob. from Romany *kova* thing, person]

coven ('kʌv°n) *n* a meeting of witches. [C16: prob. from OF *covin* group, ult. from L *convenīre* to come together]

covenant ('kʌvənənt) *n* **1** a binding agreement; con tract. **2** *Law*. an agreement in writing under seal, as t pay a stated annual sum to a charity. **3** *Bible*. God' promise to the Israelites and their commitment to wor ship him alone. ◆ *vb* **4** to agree to a covenant (concern ing). [C13: from OF, from *covenir* to agree, from convenīre* to come together, make an agreement; see CON VENE]
▸ **covenantal** (,kʌvə'næntˀl) *adj* ▸ **'covenantor** *or* **'cov enanter** *n*

Covenanter ('kʌvənəntə, ,kʌvə'næntə) *n* *Scot. history*. person upholding either of two 17th-century covenant to establish and defend Presbyterianism.

Covent Garden ★ ('kʌvənt, 'kɒv-) *n* **1** a district of cen tral London: famous for its former fruit, vegetable, an flower market, now a shopping precinct. **2** the Roya Opera House (built 1858) in Covent Garden.

Coventry ★ ('kɒvəntrɪ) *n* **1** a city in central England, i the West Midlands: devastated in World War II; moder cathedral (1954–62); industrial centre, esp. for motor ve hicles. Pop.: 299 316 (1991). **2** a unitary authority i central England. Pop.: 302 500 (1994 est.). Area: 97 sq km (37 sq. miles). **3 send to Coventry.** to ostracize or ignore

cover ('kʌvə) *vb* (*mainly tr*) **1** to place or spread somethin over so as to protect or conceal. **2** to provide with a cov ering; clothe. **3** to put a garment, esp. a hat, on (the body or head). **4** to extend over or lie thickly on the surface of *snow covered the fields*. **5** to bring upon (oneself); inves (oneself) as if with a covering: *covered with shame*. **6** (sometimes foll. by *up*) to act as a screen or concealmen for; hide from view. **7** *Mil*. to protect (an individual, for mation, or place) by taking up a position from which fir may be returned if those being protected are fired upon **8** (*also sometimes foll. by for*) to assume responsibil ity for (a person or thing). **9** (*intr*; foll. by *for* or *up for*) t provide an alibi (for). **10** to have as one's territory: *thi salesman covers your area*. **11** to travel over. **12** to have o

place in the aim and within the range of (a firearm). **13** to include or deal with. **14** (of an asset or income) to be sufficient to meet (a liability or expense). **15a** to insure against loss, risk, etc. **15b** to provide for (loss, risk, etc.) by insurance. **16** to deposit (an equivalent stake) in a bet. **17** to act as reporter or photographer on (a news event, etc.) for a newspaper or magazine: *to cover sports events*. **18** *Music*. to record a cover version of. **19** *Sport*. to guard or protect (an opponent, team-mate, or area). **20** (of a male animal, esp. a horse) to copulate with (a female animal). ◆ *n* **21** anything that covers, spreads over, protects, or conceals. **22a** a blanket used on a bed for warmth. **22b** another word for **bedspread**. **23** a pretext, disguise, or false identity: *the thief sold brushes as a cover*. **24** an envelope or package for sending through the post: *under plain cover*. **25a** an individual table setting, in a restaurant. **25b** (*as modifier*): *a cover charge*. **26** Also called: **cover version**. a version by a different artist of a previously recorded musical item. **27** *Cricket*. **27a** (*often pl*) the area more or less at right angles to the pitch on the off side and usually about halfway to the boundary. **27b** (*as modifier*): *a cover drive*. **28** *Philately*. an entire envelope that has been postmarked. **29 break cover**. to come out from a shelter or hiding place. **30 take cover**. to make for a place of safety or shelter. **31 under cover**. protected, concealed, or in secret. ◆ See also **cover-up**. [C13: from OF *covrir*, from L *cooperīre* to cover completely, from *operīre* to cover over]
▶ **'coverable** *adj* ▶ **'coverer** *n*

coverage ('kʌvərɪdʒ) *n* **1** the amount or extent to which something is covered. **2** *Journalism*. the amount and quality of reporting or analysis given to a particular subject or event. **3** the extent of the protection provided by insurance.

cover crop *n* a crop planted between main crops to prevent leaching or soil erosion or to provide green manure.

Coverdale ★ ('kʌvə,deɪl) *n* Miles. 1488–1568, the first translator of the complete Bible into English (1535).

covered wagon *n US & Canad*. a large horse-drawn wagon with an arched canvas top, used formerly for prairie travel.

cover girl *n* a glamorous girl whose picture appears on the cover of a magazine.

covering letter *n* an accompanying letter sent as an explanation, introduction, or record.

coverlet ('kʌvəlɪt) *n* another word for **bedspread**.

cover note *n Brit*. a certificate issued by an insurance company stating that a policy is operative: used as a temporary measure between the commencement of cover and the issue of the policy.

cover point *n Cricket*. **a** a fielding position in the covers. **b** a fielder in this position.

cover slip *n* a very thin piece of glass placed over a specimen on a glass slide that is to be examined under a microscope.

covert ('kʌvət) *adj* **1** concealed or secret. ◆ *n* **2** a shelter or disguise. **3** a thicket or woodland providing shelter for game. **4** short for **covert cloth**. **5** *Ornithol*. Also called: **tectrix**. any of the small feathers on the wings and tail of a bird that surround the bases of the larger feathers. [C14: from OF: covered, from *covrir* to COVER]
▶ **'covertly** *adv*

covert cloth *n* a twill-weave cotton or worsted suiting fabric.

coverture ('kʌvətʃə) *n Rare*. shelter, concealment, or disguise. [C13: from OF, from *covert* covered; see COVERT]

cover-up *n* **1** concealment or attempted concealment of a mistake, crime, etc. ◆ *vb* **cover up**. (*adv*) **2** (*tr*) to cover completely. **3** (when *intr*, often foll. by *for*) to attempt to conceal (a mistake or crime).

cover version *n* another name for **cover** (sense 26).

covet ('kʌvɪt) *vb* **covets, coveting, coveted**. (*tr*) to wish, long, or crave for (something), esp. the property of another person). [C13: from OF *coveitier*, from *coveitié* eager desire, ult. from L *cupiditās* CUPIDITY]
▶ **'covetable** *adj*

covetous ('kʌvɪtəs) *adj* (*usually postpositive and foll. by of*) jealously eager for the possession of something (esp. the property of another person).
▶ **'covetously** *adv* ▶ **'covetousness** *n*

covey ('kʌvɪ) *n* **1** a small flock of grouse or partridge. **2** a small group, as of people. [C14: from OF *covee*, from *cover* to sit on, hatch]

cow[1] (kaʊ) *n* **1** the mature female of any species of cattle, esp. domesticated cattle. **2** the mature female of various other mammals, such as the elephant, whale, and seal. **3** (not in technical use) any domestic species of cattle. **4** *Inf*. a disagreeable woman. **5** *Austral. & NZ sl*. something objectionable (esp. in **a fair cow**). [OE *cū*]

cow[2] (kaʊ) *vb* (*tr*) to frighten or overawe, as with threats. [C17: from ON *kūga* to oppress]

coward ('kaʊəd) *n* a person who shrinks from or avoids danger, pain, or difficulty. [C13: from OF *cuard*, from *coue* tail, from L *cauda*; ? suggestive of a frightened animal with its tail between its legs]

Coward ★ ('kaʊəd) *n* Sir Noël (Pierce). 1899–1973, British dramatist and actor, noted for his comedies, which include *Private Lives* (1930) and *Blithe Spirit* (1941).

cowardice ('kaʊədɪs) *n* lack of courage in facing danger, pain, or difficulty.

cowardly ('kaʊədlɪ) *adj* of or characteristic of a coward; lacking courage.
▶ **'cowardliness** *n*

cowbell ('kaʊ,bel) *n* a bell hung around a cow's neck so that the cow can be easily located.

cowberry ('kaʊbərɪ, -brɪ) *n, pl* **cowberries**. **1** a creeping evergreen shrub of N temperate and arctic regions, with pink or red flowers and edible slightly acid berries. **2** the berry of this plant.

cowbird ('kaʊ,bɜːd) *n* any of various American orioles, having dark plumage and a short bill.

cowboy ('kaʊ,bɔɪ) *n* **1** Also called: **cowhand**. a hired man who herds and tends cattle, usually on horseback, esp. in the western US. **2** a conventional character of Wild West folklore, films, etc., esp. one involved in fighting Indians. **3** *Inf*. an irresponsible or unscrupulous operator in business, etc.
▶ **'cow,girl** *fem n*

cowcatcher ('kaʊ,kætʃə) *n* a metal frame on the front of a locomotive to clear the track of animals or other obstructions.

cow-cocky *n, pl* **cow-cockies**. *Austral. & NZ*. a one-man dairy farmer.

Cowdrey ★ ('kaʊdrɪ) *n* (Michael) Colin, Baron. born 1932, English cricketer. He played for Kent and captained England 27 times.

cower ('kaʊə) *vb* (*intr*) to crouch or cringe, as in fear. [C13: from MLow G *kūren* to lie in wait; rel. to Swedish *kura*]

Cowes ★ (kaʊz) *n* a town in S England, on the Isle of Wight: famous for its annual regatta. Pop.: 16 335 (1991).

cowherd ('kaʊ,hɜːd) *n* a person employed to tend cattle.

cowhide ('kaʊ,haɪd) *n* **1** the hide of a cow. **2** the leather made from such a hide.

cowl (kaʊl) *n* **1** a hood, esp. a loose one. **2** the hooded habit of a monk. **3** a cover fitted to a chimney to increase ventilation and prevent draughts. **4** the part of a car body that supports the windscreen and the bonnet. ◆ *vb* (*tr*) **5** to cover or provide with a cowl. [OE *cugele*, from LL *cuculla* cowl, from L *cucullus* hood]

cowlick ('kaʊ,lɪk) *n* a tuft of hair over the forehead.

cowling ('kaʊlɪŋ) *n* a streamlined metal covering, esp. around an aircraft engine.

cowman ('kaʊmən) *n, pl* **cowmen**. **1** *Brit*. another name for **cowherd**. **2** *US & Canad*. a man who owns cattle; rancher.

co-worker *n* a fellow worker; associate.

cow parsley *n* a common Eurasian umbelliferous hedgerow plant having umbrella-shaped clusters of white flowers.

cowpat ('kaʊ,pæt) *n* a single dropping of cow dung.

cowpea ('kau,pi:) *n* **1** a leguminous tropical climbing plant producing pods containing edible pealike seeds. **2** the seed of this plant.

Cowper ★ ('ku:pə, 'kau-) *n* **William**. 1731–1800, British poet, noted for *The Task* (1785) and his hymns.

cowpox ('kau,pɒks) *n* a contagious viral disease of cows characterized by vesicles, esp. on the teats and udder. Inoculation of humans with this virus provides temporary immunity to smallpox.

cowpuncher ('kau,pʌntʃə) *or* **cowpoke** ('kau,pəuk) *n* US & Canad. an informal word for **cowboy**.

cowrie *or* **cowry** ('kauri) *n, pl* **cowries**. **1** any marine gastropod mollusc of a mostly tropical family having a glossy brightly marked shell. **2** the shell of any of these molluscs, esp. the money cowrie, used as money in parts of Africa and S Asia. [C17: from Hindi *kaurī*, from Sansk. *kaparda*]

cowslip ('kau,slip) *n* **1** a primrose native to temperate regions of the Old World, having yellow flowers. **2** US & Canad. another name for **marsh marigold**. [OE *cūslyppe*; see COW[1], SLIP[3]]

cox (kɒks) *n* **1** a coxswain. ◆ *vb* **2** to act as coxswain of (a boat).
▸ **'coxless** *adj*

coxa ('kɒksə) *n, pl* **coxae** ('kɒksi:). **1** a technical name for the hipbone or hip joint. **2** the basal segment of the leg of an insect. [C18: from L: hip]
▸ **'coxal** *adj*

coxalgia (kɒk'sældʒɪə) *n* **1** pain in the hip joint. **2** disease of the hip joint causing pain. [C19: from COXA + -ALGIA]
▸ **cox'algic** *adj*

coxcomb ('kɒks,kəum) *n* **1** a variant spelling of **cockscomb**. **2** *Obs.* the cap, resembling a cock's comb, worn by a jester.
▸ **'cox,combry** *n*

coxswain ('kɒksən, -,swein) *n* **1** (usually shortened to **cox** in competitive rowing) the helmsman of a lifeboat, racing shell, etc. **2** the senior petty officer on a small naval craft. ◆ Also called: **cockswain**. [C15: from *cock* a ship's boat + SWAIN]

coy (kɔɪ) *adj* **1** affectedly demure, esp. in a playful or provocative manner. **2** shy; modest. **3** evasive, esp. in an annoying way. [C14: from OF *coi* reserved, from L *quiētus* QUIET]
▸ **'coyly** *adv* ▸ **'coyness** *n*

Coy. *Mil. abbrev.* for company.

coyote ('kɔɪəut, kɔɪ'əuti; *esp. US.* 'kaɪəut, kaɪ'əuti) *n, pl* **coyotes** *or* **coyote**. a predatory canine mammal of the deserts and prairies of North America. Also called: **prairie wolf**. [C19: from Mexican Sp., from Nahuatl *coyotl*]

coypu ('kɔɪpu:) *n, pl* **coypus** *or* **coypu**. **1** an aquatic South American rodent, naturalized in Europe. It resembles a small beaver and is bred for its fur. **2** the fur of this animal. ◆ Also called: **nutria**. [C18: from American Sp. *coipú*, from Amerind *kóypu*]

coz (kʌz) *n* an archaic word for **cousin**.

cozen ('kʌz³n) *vb* to cheat or trick (someone). [C16: cant term ? rel. to COUSIN]
▸ **'cozenage** *n*

cozy ('kəuzi) *adj, n* the usual US spelling of **cosy**.

CP *abbrev. for:* **1** Canadian Pacific Ltd. **2** Common Prayer. **3** Communist Party.

cp. *abbrev. for* compare.

CPAG *abbrev. for* Child Poverty Action Group.

cpd *abbrev. for* compound.

cpi *abbrev. for* characters per inch.

Cpl *abbrev. for* Corporal.

CPO *abbrev. for* Chief Petty Officer.

CPR *abbrev. for* cardiopulmonary resuscitation.

cps *abbrev. for:* **1** *Physics*. cycles per second. **2** *Computing*. characters per second.

CPS (in England and Wales) *abbrev. for* Crown Prosecution Service.

CPSA *abbrev. for* Civil and Public Services Association.

CPVE (in Britain) *abbrev. for* Certificate of Pre-vocational Education: a certificate awarded for completion of broad-based course of study offered as a less advanced alternative to traditional school-leaving qualifications.

CQ a symbol transmitted by an amateur radio operator requesting communication with any other amateur radio operator.

Cr **1** *abbrev.* for Councillor. **2** *the chemical symbol for* chromium.

cr. *abbrev. for:* **1** credit. **2** creditor.

crab[1] (kræb) *n* **1** any chiefly marine decapod crustacean having a broad flattened carapace covering th cephalothorax, beneath which is folded the abdomen The first pair of limbs are pincers. **2** any of various similar or related arthropods. **3** short for **crab louse**. **4** a mechanical lifting device, esp. the travelling hoist of gantry crane. **5 catch a crab**. *Rowing*. to make a stroke in which the oar either misses the water or digs too deeply causing the rower to fall backwards. ◆ *vb* **crabs**, **crabbing crabbed**. **6** (*intr*) to hunt or catch crabs. [OE *crabba*]

crab[2] (kræb) *Inf.* ◆ *vb* **crabs**, **crabbing**, **crabbed**. **1** (*intr*) to find fault; grumble. ◆ *n* **2** an irritable person. [C16 prob. back formation from CRABBED]

crab[3] (kræb) *n* short for **crab apple**. [C15: ? of Scand. origin; cf. Swedish *skrabbe* crab apple]

Crab (kræb) *n* **the**. the constellation Cancer, the fourth sign of the zodiac.

crab apple *n* **1** any of several rosaceous trees that have white, pink, or red flowers and small sour apple-like fruits. **2** the fruit of any of these trees, used to make jam.

Crabbe ★ (kræb) *n* **George**. 1754–1832, British poet noted for *The Village* (1783) and *The Borough* (1810).

crabbed ('kræbid) *adj* **1** surly; irritable; perverse. **2** of handwriting) cramped and hard to decipher. **3** *Rare* abstruse. [C13: prob. from CRAB[1] (from its wayward gait), infl. by CRAB (APPLE) (from its tartness)]
▸ **'crabbedly** *adv* ▸ **'crabbedness** *n*

crabby ('kræbi) *adj* **crabbier**, **crabbiest**. bad-tempered.

crab louse *n* a parasitic louse that infests the pubic region in man.

crabwise ('kræb,waiz) *adj, adv* (of motion) sideways like a crab.

crack (kræk) *vb* **1** to break or cause to break without complete separation of the parts. **2** to break or cause to break with a sudden sharp sound; snap. **3** to make or cause to make a sudden sharp sound: *to crack a whip*. **4** to cause (the voice) to change tone or become harsh or (of the voice) to change tone, esp. to a higher register; break. **5** *Inf.* to fail or cause to fail. **6** to yield or cause to yield. **7** (*tr*) to hit with a forceful or resounding blow. **8** (*tr*) to break into or force open: *to crack a safe*. **9** (*tr*) to solve or decipher (a code, problem, etc.). **10** (*tr*) *Inf.* to tell (a joke etc.). **11** to break (a molecule) into smaller molecules or radicals by the action of heat, as in the distillation of petroleum. **12** (*tr*) to open (a bottle) for drinking. **13** (*intr*) *Scot. & N English dialect*. to chat; gossip. **14** (*tr*) *Inf.* to achieve (esp. in **crack it**). **15 crack a smile**. *Inf.* to break into a smile. **16 crack hardy** *or* **hearty**. *Austral. & NZ inf.* to disguise one's discomfort, etc.; put on a bold front. ◆ *n* **17** a sudden sharp noise. **18** a break or fracture without complete separation of the two parts. **19** a narrow opening or fissure. **20** *Inf.* a resounding blow. **21** a physical or mental defect; flaw. **22** a moment or specific instant: *the crack of day*. **23** a broken or cracked tone of voice, as a boy's during puberty. **24** (often foll. by *at*) *Inf.* an attempt; opportunity to try. **25** *Sl.* a gibe; wisecrack; joke. **26** *Sl.* a person that excels. **27** *Scot. & N English dialect*. a talk; chat. **28** *Sl.* a concentrated highly addictive form of cocaine made into pellets or powder and smoked. **29** *Inf., chiefly Irish*. fun; informal entertainment. **30 a fair crack of the whip**. *Inf.* a fair chance or opportunity. **31 crack of doom**. doomsday; the end of the world; the Day of Judgment. ◆ *adj* **32** (*prenominal*) *Sl.* first-class; excellent: *a crack shot*. ◆ See also **crack down**, **crack up**. [OE *cracian*]

crackbrained ('kræk,breind) *adj* insane, idiotic, or crazy.

crack down *vb* (*intr, adv*; often foll. by *on*) **1** to take severe measures (against); become stricter (with). ◆ *n* **crackdown**. **2** severe or repressive measures.

cracked (krækt) *adj* **1** damaged by cracking. **2** *Inf.* crazy.

cracked wheat *n* whole wheat cracked between rollers so that it will cook more quickly.

cracker ('krækə) *n* **1** a decorated cardboard tube that emits a bang when pulled apart, releasing a toy, a joke, or a paper hat. **2** short for **firecracker. 3** a thin crisp biscuit, usually unsweetened. **4** a person or thing that cracks. **5** *Brit., Austral., & NZ sl.* a thing or person of notable qualities or abilities. **6** See **catalytic cracker.**

crackerjack ('krækə,dʒæk) *Inf.* ♦ *adj* **1** excellent. ♦ *n* **2** a person or thing of exceptional quality or ability. [C20: changed from CRACK (first-class) + JACK (man)]

crackers ('krækəz) *adj* (*postpositive*) *Brit.* a slang word for **insane.**

crackhead ('kræk,hed) *n Sl.* a person addicted to the drug crack.

cracking ('krækɪŋ) *adj* **1** (*prenominal*) *Inf.* fast; vigorous (esp. in **a cracking pace**). **2 get cracking.** *Inf.* to start doing something quickly or with increased speed. ♦ *adv, adj* **3** *Brit. inf.* first-class; excellent. ♦ *n* **4** the process in which molecules are cracked, esp. the oil-refining process in which heavy oils are broken down into hydrocarbons of lower molecular weight by heat or catalysis.

crackjaw ('kræk,dʒɔː) *Inf.* ♦ *adj* **1** difficult to pronounce. ♦ *n* **2** a word or phrase that is difficult to pronounce.

crackle ('kræk³l) *vb* **crackles, crackling, crackled. 1** to make or cause to make a series of slight sharp noises, as of paper being crushed. **2** (*tr*) to decorate (porcelain or pottery) by causing fine cracks to appear in the glaze. **3** (*intr*) to abound in vivacity or energy. ♦ *n* **4** the act or sound of crackling. **5** intentional crazing in the glaze of porcelain or pottery. **6** Also called: **crackleware.** porcelain or pottery so decorated.
▶ '**crackly** *adj*

crackling ('kræklɪŋ) *n* the crisp browned skin of roast pork.

crackpot ('kræk,pɒt) *Inf.* ♦ *n* **1** an eccentric person; crank. ♦ *adj* **2** eccentric; crazy.

crack up *vb* (*adv*) **1** (*intr*) to break into pieces. **2** (*intr*) *Inf.* to undergo a physical or mental breakdown. **3** (*tr*) *Inf.* to present or report, esp. in glowing terms: *it's not all it's cracked up to be.* **4** *Inf., chiefly US & Canad.* to laugh or cause to laugh uncontrollably. ♦ *n* **crackup. 5** *Inf.* a physical or mental breakdown.

Cracow ★ ('krækau, -əu, -ɒf) *n* an industrial city in S Poland, on the River Vistula: former capital of the country (1320–1609); university (1364). Pop.: 746 000 (1995 est.). Polish name: **Kraków.** German name: **Krakau.**

-cracy *n combining form.* indicating a type of government or rule: *plutocracy; mobocracy.* See also **-crat.** [from Gk *-kratia,* from *kratos* power]

cradle ('kreɪd³l) *n* **1** a baby's bed, often with rockers. **2** a place where something originates. **3** a frame, rest, or trolley made to support a piece of equipment, aircraft, ship, etc. **4** a platform or trolley in which workmen are suspended on the side of a building or ship. **5** *Agriculture.* **5a** a framework of several wooden fingers attached to a scythe to gather the grain into bunches as it is cut. **5b** a scythe with such a cradle. **6** Also called: **rocker.** a boxlike apparatus for washing rocks, sand, etc., containing gold or gemstones. **7 rob the cradle.** *Inf.* to take for a lover, husband, or wife a person much younger than oneself. ♦ *vb* **cradles, cradling, cradled.** (*tr*) **8** to rock or place in or as if in a cradle; hold tenderly. **9** to nurture in or bring up from infancy. **10** to wash (soil bearing gold, etc.) in a cradle. [OE *cradol*]

cradle snatcher *n Inf.* another name for **baby snatcher** (sense 2).

cradlesong ('kreɪd³l,sɒŋ) *n* a lullaby.

craft (krɑːft) *n* **1** skill or ability. **2** skill in deception and trickery. **3** an occupation or trade requiring special skill, esp. manual dexterity. **4a** the members of such a trade, regarded collectively. **4b** (*as modifier*): *a craft union.* **5** a single vessel, aircraft, or spacecraft. **6** (*functioning as pl*) ships, boats, aircraft, or spacecraft collectively. ♦ *vb* **7** (*tr*) to make or fashion with skill, esp. by hand. [OE *cræft* skill, strength]

craftsman ('krɑːftsmən) *n, pl* **craftsmen. 1** a member of a skilled trade; someone who practises a craft; artisan. **2** an artist skilled in an art or craft.
▶ '**craftsman,ship** *n*

crafty ('krɑːftɪ) *adj* **craftier, craftiest. 1** skilled in deception; shrewd; cunning. **2** *Arch.* skilful.
▶ '**craftily** *adv* ▶ '**craftiness** *n*

crag (kræg) *n* a steep rugged rock or peak. [C13: of Celtic origin]

craggy ('krægɪ) *or US* **cragged** ('krægɪd) *adj* **craggier, craggiest. 1** having many crags. **2** (of the face) rugged; rocklike.
▶ '**cragginess** *n*

Craig ★ (kreɪg) *n* **Edward Gordon.** 1872–1966, English theatrical designer, actor, and director. His nonrealistic scenic design greatly influenced theatre in Europe and the US.

Craigavon ★ (kreɪg'eɪvən) *n* a district of S central Northern Ireland, bordering the S shore of Lough Neagh: light industries, agriculture, fruit growing. Administrative centre: Portadown. Pop.: 77 359 (1994). Area: 388 sq. km (150 sq. miles).

Craigie ★ ('kreɪgɪ) *n* **Sir William A(lexander).** 1867–1957, Scottish lexicographer; joint editor of the *Oxford English Dictionary* (1901–33).

crake (kreɪk) *n Zool.* any of several rails of the Old World, such as the corncrake. [C14: from ON *krāka* crow or *krākr* raven, imit.]

cram (kræm) *vb* **crams, cramming, crammed. 1** (*tr*) to force more (people, material, etc.) into (a room, container, etc.) than it can hold; stuff. **2** to eat or cause to eat more than necessary. **3** *Inf.* to study or cause to study (facts, etc.), esp. for an examination, by hastily memorizing. ♦ *n* **4** the act or condition of cramming. **5** a crush. [OE *crammian*]

Cram ★ (kræm) *n* **Steve.** born 1960, British middle-distance runner: European 1500 m champion (1981, 1986); world 1500 m champion (1983).

crambo ('kræmbəu) *n* a word game in which one team says a rhyme or rhyming line for a word or line given by the other team. [C17: from earlier *crambe,* prob. from L *crambē repetīta* cabbage repeated, hence an old story]

crammer ('kræmə) *n* a person or school that prepares pupils for an examination.

cramp[1] (kræmp) *n* **1** a painful involuntary contraction of a muscle, typically caused by overexertion, heat, or chill. **2** temporary partial paralysis of a muscle group: *writer's cramp.* **3** (*usually pl in the US and Canada*) severe abdominal pain. ♦ *vb* **4** (*tr*) to affect with or as if with a cramp. [C14: from OF *crampe,* of Gmc origin]

cramp[2] (kræmp) *n* **1** Also called: **cramp iron.** a strip of metal with its ends bent at right angles, used to bind masonry. **2** a device for holding pieces of wood while they are glued; clamp. **3** something that confines or restricts. ♦ *vb* (*tr*) **4** to hold with a cramp. **5** to confine or restrict. **6 cramp (someone's) style.** *Inf.* to prevent (a person) from using his abilities or acting freely and confidently. [C15: from MDu. *crampe* cramp, hook, of Gmc origin]

cramped (kræmpt) *adj* **1** closed in; restricted. **2** (esp. of handwriting) small and irregular.

crampon ('kræmpən) *or* **crampoon** (kræm'puːn) *n* **1** one of a pair of pivoted steel levers used to lift heavy objects; grappling iron. **2** (*often pl*) one of a pair of frames each with 10 or 12 metal spikes, strapped to boots for climbing or walking on ice or snow. [C15: from F, from MDu. *crampe* hook; see CRAMP[2]]

cran (kræn) *n* a unit of capacity used for fresh herring, equal to 37.5 gallons. [C18: from ?]

Cranach ★ (*German* 'krɑːnax) *n* **Lucas** ('luːkas). 1472–1553, known as *the Elder,* real name *Lucas Müller.* German painter.

cranberry ('krænbərɪ, -brɪ) *n, pl* **cranberries. 1** any of several trailing shrubs that bear sour edible red berries. **2** the berry of this plant. [C17: from Low G *kraanbere,* from *kraan* CRANE + *bere* BERRY]

crane (kreɪn) n **1** a large long-necked long-legged wading bird inhabiting marshes and plains in most parts of the world. **2** (not in ornithological use) any similar bird, such as a heron. **3** a device for lifting and moving heavy objects, typically consisting of a pivoted boom rotating about a vertical axis with lifting gear suspended from the end of the boom. ◆ vb **cranes, craning, craned. 4** (tr) to lift or move (an object) by or as if by a crane. **5** to stretch out (esp. the neck), as to see over other people's heads. [OE cran]

Crane ★ (kreɪn) n **1** (**Harold**) **Hart.** 1899–1932, US poet; author of The Bridge (1930). **2 Stephen.** 1871–1900, US writer, noted for his novel The Red Badge of Courage (1895). **3 Walter.** 1845–1915, British painter.

crane fly n a dipterous fly having long legs, slender wings, and a narrow body. Also called (Brit.): **daddy-longlegs**.

cranesbill ('kreɪnz‚bɪl) n any of various plants of the genus Geranium, having pink or purple flowers and long slender beaked fruits.

cranial ('kreɪnɪəl) adj of or relating to the skull.
▸ 'cranially adv

cranial index n the ratio of the greatest length to the greatest width of the cranium, multiplied by 100.

cranial nerve n any of the 12 paired nerves that have their origin in the brain.

craniate ('kreɪnɪɪt, -‚eɪt) adj **1** having a skull or cranium. ◆ adj, n **2** another word for **vertebrate**.

cranio- or before a vowel **crani-** combining form. indicating the cranium or cranial.

craniology (‚kreɪnɪ'ɒlədʒɪ) n the branch of science concerned with the shape and size of the human skull.
▸ **craniological** (‚kreɪnɪə'lɒdʒɪk'l) adj ▸ ‚cranio'logically adv ▸ ‚crani'ologist n

craniometry (‚kreɪnɪ'ɒmɪtrɪ) n the study and measurement of skulls.
▸ **craniometric** (‚kreɪnɪə'mɛtrɪk) or ‚cranio'metrical adj ▸ ‚cranio'metrically adv ▸ ‚crani'ometrist n

craniotomy (‚kreɪnɪ'ɒtəmɪ) n, pl **craniotomies. 1** surgical incision into the skull. **2** surgical crushing of a fetal skull to extract a dead fetus.

cranium ('kreɪnɪəm) n, pl **craniums** or **crania** (-nɪə). **1** the skull of a vertebrate. **2** the part of the skull that encloses the brain. [C16: from Med. L crānium skull, from Gk kranion]

crank (kræŋk) n **1** a device for communicating or converting motion, consisting of an arm projecting from a shaft, often with a second member attached to it parallel to the shaft. **2** Also called: **crank handle, starting handle.** a handle incorporating a crank, used to start an engine or motor. **3** Inf. **3a** an eccentric or odd person. **3b** US, Canad., Austral., NZ, & Irish. a bad-tempered person. ◆ vb (tr) **4** to rotate (a shaft) by means of a crank. **5** to start (an engine, motor, etc.) by means of a crank handle. [OE cranc]

crankcase ('kræŋk‚keɪs) n the metal housing that encloses the crankshaft, connecting rods, etc., in an internal-combustion engine.

Cranko ★ ('kræŋkəʊ) n **John.** 1927–73, British choreographer, born in South Africa.

crankpin ('kræŋk‚pɪn) n a short cylindrical surface fitted between two arms of a crank parallel to the main shaft of the crankshaft.

crankshaft ('kræŋk‚ʃɑːft) n a shaft having one or more cranks, to which the connecting rods are attached.

crank up vb (adv) Sl. **1** (tr) to increase (loudness, output, etc.): he cranked up his pace. **2** (tr) to set in motion or invigorate: news editors have to crank up tired reporters. **3** (intr) to inject a narcotic drug.

cranky ('kræŋkɪ) adj **crankier, crankiest. 1** Inf. eccentric. **2** Inf. fussy and bad-tempered. **3** shaky; out of order.
▸ 'crankily adv ▸ 'crankiness n

Cranmer ★ ('krænmə) n **Thomas.** 1489–1556, the first Protestant archbishop of Canterbury (1533–56) and principal author of the Book of Common Prayer: burnt as a heretic by Mary I.

crannog ('krænəg) n an ancient Celtic lake or bog dwell-

ing. [C19: from Irish Gaelic crannóg, from OIrish cran tree]

cranny ('krænɪ) n, pl **crannies.** a narrow opening, as in a wall or rock face; chink; crevice (esp. in **every nook and cranny**). [C15: from OF cran notch, fissure; cf. CRENEL]
▸ 'crannied adj

Cranwell ★ ('krænwəl) n a village in E England, in Lincolnshire: Royal Air Force College (1920).

crap[1] (kræp) n **1** a losing throw in the game of craps. **2** another name for **craps**. [C20: back formation from CRAPS]

crap[2] (kræp) Sl. ◆ n **1** nonsense. **2** rubbish. **3** a taboo word for **faeces**. ◆ vb **craps, crapping, crapped. 4** (intr) taboo word for **defecate**. [C15 crappe chaff, from MDu. prob. from crappen to break off]

crape (kreɪp) n **1** a variant spelling of **crepe. 2** crepe, esp when used for mourning clothes. **3** a band of black crepe worn in mourning.

crap out vb (intr, adv) Sl. **1** US. to make a losing throw in craps. **2** US. to fail; withdraw. **3** to fail to attempt something through fear.

craps (kræps) n (usually functioning as sing) **1** a gambling game using two dice. **2 shoot craps.** to play this game [C19: prob. from crabs lowest throw at dice, pl of CRAB[1]]
▸ 'crap‚shooter n

crapulent ('kræpjʊlənt) or **crapulous** ('kræpjʊləs) adj **1** given to or resulting from intemperance. **2** suffering from intemperance; drunken. [C18: from LL crāpulentu drunk, from L crāpula, from Gk kraipalē drunkenness headache resulting therefrom]
▸ 'crapulence n

crash[1] (kræʃ) vb **1** to make or cause to make a loud noise as of solid objects smashing or clattering. **2** to fall o cause to fall with force, breaking in pieces with a loud noise. **3** (intr) to break or smash in pieces with a loud noise. **4** (intr) to collapse or fail suddenly. **5** to cause (an aircraft) to land violently resulting in severe damage o (of an aircraft) to land in this way. **6** to cause (a car, etc. to collide with another car or other object or (of two o more cars) to be involved in a collision. **7** to move o cause to move violently or noisily. **8** (intr) (of a computer system or program) to fail suddenly because of a mal function. **9** Brit. inf. short for **gate-crash**. ◆ n **10** an act o instance of breaking and falling to pieces. **11** a sudden loud noise. **12** a collision, as between vehicles. **13** a sudden descent of an aircraft as a result of which it hits land or water. **14** the sudden collapse of a business, stock ex change, etc. **15** (modifier) requiring or using intensive ef fort and all possible resources in order to accomplish something quickly: a crash course. [C14: prob. from crasen to smash, shatter + dasshen to strike violently DASH[1]; see CRAZE]

crash[2] (kræʃ) n a coarse cotton or linen cloth. [C19: from Russian krashenina coloured linen]

Crashaw ★ ('kræʃɔː) n **Richard.** 1613–49, English religious poet, noted for the Steps to the Temple (1646).

crash barrier n a barrier erected along the centre of a motorway, around a racetrack, etc., for safety purposes.

crash dive n **1** a sudden steep dive from the surface by a submarine. ◆ vb **crash-dive, crash-dives, crash-diving crash-dived. 2** (intr) (usually of an aircraft) to descend steeply and rapidly, before hitting the ground. **3** to per form or cause to perform a crash dive.

crash helmet n a padded helmet worn fo motorcycling, flying, etc., to protect the head.

crashing ('kræʃɪŋ) adj (prenominal) Inf. (intensifier) (esp in **a crashing bore**).

crash-land vb to land (an aircraft) causing some damage to it or (of an aircraft) to land in this way.
▸ 'crash-‚landing n

crash team n a medical team with special equipment able to be mobilized quickly to treat cardiac arrest.

crass (kræs) adj **1** stupid; gross. **2** Rare. thick or coarse [C16: from L crassus thick, dense, gross]
▸ 'crassly adv ▸ 'crassness or 'crassi‚tude n

Crassus ★ ('kræsəs) n **Marcus Licinius** ('mɑːkəs lɪ'sɪnɪəs). ?115–53 B.C., Roman general; member of the first trium virate with Caesar and Pompey.

-crat n combining form. indicating a person who takes part in or is a member of a form of government or class. [from Gk -kratēs, from -kratia -CRACY]
▶ **-cratic** or **-cratical** adj combining form.

crate (kreɪt) n **1** a fairly large container, usually made of wooden slats or wickerwork, used for packing, storing, or transporting goods. **2** Sl. an old car, aeroplane, etc. ◆ vb **crates, crating, crated. 3** (tr) to pack or place in a crate. [C16: from L crātis wickerwork, hurdle]
▶ **'crater** n ▶ **'crateful** n

crater (kreɪtə) n **1** the bowl-shaped opening in a volcano or a geyser. **2** a similar depression formed by the impact of a meteorite or exploding bomb. **3** any of the roughly circular or polygonal walled formations on the moon and some planets. **4** a large open bowl with two handles, used for mixing wines, esp. in ancient Greece. ◆ vb **5** to make or form craters in (a surface, such as the ground). [C17: from L: mixing bowl, crater, from Gk kratēr, from kerannunai to mix]
▶ **'crater-,like** adj ▶ **'craterous** adj

cravat (krə'væt) n a scarf worn round the neck instead of a tie, esp. by men. [C17: from F cravate, from Serbo-Croat Hrvat Croat; so called because worn by Croats in the French army during the Thirty Years' War]

crave (kreɪv) vb **craves, craving, craved. 1** (when intr, foll. by for or after) to desire intensely; long (for). **2** (tr) to need greatly or urgently. **3** (tr) to beg or plead for. [OE crafian]
▶ **'craver** n ▶ **'craving** n

craven ('kreɪvᵊn) adj **1** cowardly. ◆ n **2** a coward. [C13 cravant, prob. from OF crevant bursting, from crever to burst, die, from L crepāre to burst, crack]
▶ **'cravenly** adv ▶ **'cravenness** n

craw (krɔː) n **1** a less common word for **crop** (sense 6). **2** the stomach of an animal. **3 stick in one's craw.** Inf. to be difficult, or against one's conscience, for one to accept, utter, etc. [C14: rel. to MHG krage, MDu. crāghe neck, Icelandic kragi collar]

crawfish ('krɔː,fɪʃ) n, pl **crawfish** or **crawfishes.** a variant of **crayfish** (esp. sense 2).

Crawford ★ ('krɔːfəd) n **1 Joan,** real name Lucille le Sueur. 1908–77, US film actress. **2 Michael,** real name Michael Dumbell Smith. born 1942, British actor.

crawl[1] (krɔːl) vb (intr) **1** to move slowly, either by dragging the body along the ground or on the hands and knees. **2** to proceed very slowly or laboriously. **3** to act in a servile manner; fawn. **4** to be or feel as if overrun by something unpleasant, esp. crawling creatures: the pile of refuse crawled with insects. **5** (of insects, worms, snakes, etc.) to move with the body close to the ground. **6** to swim the crawl. ◆ n **7** a slow creeping pace or motion. **8** Swimming. a stroke in which the feet are kicked like paddles while each arm in turn reaches forward and pulls back through the water. [C14: prob. from ON krafla to creep]
▶ **'crawler** n ▶ **'crawlingly** adv

crawl[2] (krɔːl) n an enclosure in shallow, coastal water for fish, lobsters, etc. [C17: from Du. KRAAL]

crawler lane n a lane on an uphill section of a motorway reserved for slow vehicles.

Crawley ★ ('krɔːlɪ) n a town in S England, in NE West Sussex: designated a new town in 1956. Pop.: 88 203 (1991).

crawling ('krɔːlɪŋ) n a defect in freshly applied paint or varnish characterized by bare patches and ridging.

crawly ('krɔːlɪ) adj **crawlier, crawliest.** Inf. feeling or causing a sensation likes crawling on one's skin.

Craxi ★ ('kræksɪ) n **Bettino** (be'tiːno). born 1934, Italian socialist statesman; prime minister (1983–87).

crayfish ('kreɪ,fɪʃ) or esp. US **crawfish** n, pl **crayfish** or **crayfishes. 1** a freshwater decapod crustacean resembling a small lobster. **2** any of various similar crustaceans, esp. the spiny lobster. [C14: cray, by folk etymology, from OF crevice crab, from OHG krebiz + fish]

crayon ('kreɪən, -ɒn) n **1** a small stick or pencil of charcoal, wax, clay, or chalk mixed with coloured pigment. **2** a drawing made with crayons. ◆ vb **3** to draw or colour with crayons. [C17: from F, from craie, from L crēta chalk]
▶ **'crayonist** n

craze (kreɪz) n **1** a short-lived fashion. **2** a wild or exaggerated enthusiasm. ◆ vb **crazes, crazing, crazed. 3** to make or become mad. **4** Ceramics, metallurgy. to develop or cause to develop fine cracks. [C14 (in the sense: to break, shatter): prob. from ON]

crazy ('kreɪzɪ) adj **crazier, craziest. 1** Inf. insane. **2** fantastic; strange; ridiculous. **3** (postpositive; foll. by about or over) Inf. extremely fond (of).
▶ **'crazily** adv ▶ **'craziness** n

Crazy Horse ★ n Indian name Ta-Sunko-Witko. ?1849–77, Sioux Indian chief, remembered for his attempts to resist White settlement in Sioux territory.

crazy paving n Brit. a form of paving, as for a path, made of irregular slabs of stone.

creak (kriːk) vb **1** to make or cause to make a harsh squeaking sound. **2** (intr) to make such sounds while moving: the old car creaked along. ◆ n **3** a harsh squeaking sound. [C14: var. of CROAK, imit.]
▶ **'creaky** adj ▶ **'creakily** adv ▶ **'creakiness** n ▶ **'creakingly** adv

cream (kriːm) n **1a** the fatty part of milk, which rises to the top. **1b** (as modifier): cream buns. **2** anything resembling cream in consistency. **3** the best one or most essential part of something; pick. **4** a soup containing cream or milk: cream of chicken soup. **5** any of various foods resembling or containing cream. **6a** a yellowish-white colour. **6b** (as adj): cream wallpaper. ◆ vb (tr) **7** to skim or otherwise separate the cream from (milk). **8** to beat (foodstuffs) to a light creamy consistency. **9** to add or apply cream or any creamlike substance to. **10** (sometimes foll. by off) to take away the best part of. **11** to prepare or cook (vegetables, chicken, etc.) with cream or milk. [C14: from OF cresme, from LL crāmum cream, of Celtic origin; infl. by Church L chrisma unction, CHRISM]
▶ **'cream,like** adj

cream cheese n a smooth soft white cheese made from soured cream or milk.

cream cracker n Brit. a crisp unsweetened biscuit, often eaten with cheese.

creamer ('kriːmə) n **1** a vessel or device for separating cream from milk. **2** a powdered substitute for cream, used in coffee. **3** Now chiefly US & Canad. a small jug or pitcher for serving cream.

creamery ('kriːmərɪ) n, pl **creameries. 1** an establishment where milk and cream are made into butter and cheese. **2** a place where dairy products are sold.

cream of tartar n potassium hydrogen tartrate, esp. when used in baking powders.

cream puff n a shell of light pastry with a custard or cream filling.

cream soda n a soft drink flavoured with vanilla.

cream tea n afternoon tea including bread or scones served with clotted cream and jam.

creamy ('kriːmɪ) adj **creamier, creamiest. 1** resembling cream in colour, taste, or consistency. **2** containing cream.
▶ **'creaminess** n

crease (kriːs) n **1** a line or mark produced by folding, pressing, or wrinkling. **2** a wrinkle or furrow, esp. on the face. **3** Cricket. any of four lines near each wicket marking positions for the bowler or batsman. See also **bowling crease, popping crease, return crease.** ◆ vb **creases, creasing, creased. 4** to make or become wrinkled or furrowed. **5** (tr) to graze with a bullet. [C15: from earlier crēst; prob. rel. to OF cresté wrinkled]
▶ **'creaser** n ▶ **'creasy** adj

create (kriː'eɪt) vb **creates, creating, created. 1** (tr) to cause to come into existence. **2** (tr) to invest with a new honour, office, or title; appoint. **3** (tr) to be the cause of. **4** (tr) to act (a role) in the first production of a play. **5** (intr) Brit. sl. to make a fuss or uproar. [C14 creat created, from L creātus, from creāre to produce, make]

creatine ('kriːə,tiːn, -tɪn) n an important compound involved in many biochemical reactions and present in many types of living cells. [C19: from Gk *kreas* flesh + -INE[2]]

creation (kriːˈeɪʃən) *n* 1 the act or process of creating. 2 the fact of being created or produced. 3 something brought into existence or created. 4 the whole universe.

Creation (kriːˈeɪʃən) *n Christianity*. 1 (often preceded by *the*) God's act of bringing the universe into being. 2 the universe as thus brought into being by God.

creative (kriːˈeɪtɪv) *adj* 1 having the ability to create. 2 characterized by originality of thought; having or showing imagination. 3 designed to or tending to stimulate the imagination. 4 characterized by sophisticated bending of the rules or conventions: *creative accounting*.
▶ cre'atively *adv* ▶ cre'ativeness *n* ▶ ˌcrea'tivity *n*

creator (kriːˈeɪtə) *n* a person or thing that creates; originator.
▶ cre'atorship *n*

Creator (kriːˈeɪtə) *n* (usually preceded by *the*) an epithet of God.

creature (ˈkriːtʃə) *n* 1 a living being, esp. an animal. 2 something that has been created, whether animate or inanimate. 3 a human being; person: used as a term of scorn, pity, or endearment. 4 a person who is dependent upon another; tool. [C13: from Church L *creātūra*, from L *creāre* to create]
▶ 'creatural *or* 'creaturely *adj*

crèche (krɛʃ, kreɪʃ) *n* 1 *Chiefly Brit.* 1a a day nursery for very young children. 1b a supervised play area provided for young children for short periods. 2 a tableau of Christ's Nativity. [C19: from OF: manger, crib, ult. of Gmc origin]

Crécy ★ (ˈkrɛsɪ; *French* kresi) *n* a village in N France: scene of the first decisive battle of the Hundred Years' War when the English defeated the French (1346). Official name: **Crécy-en-Ponthieu** (-ɑ̃pɔ̃tjø). English name: **Cressy**.

cred (krɛd) *n Sl.* short for **credibility** (esp. in **street cred**).

credence (ˈkriːdəns) *n* 1 acceptance or belief, esp. with regard to the evidence of others. 2 something supporting a claim to belief; credential (esp. in **letters of credence**). 3 short for **credence table**. [C14: from Med. L *crēdentia* trust, credit, from L *crēdere* to believe]

credence table *n Christianity*. a small table on which the Eucharistic bread and wine are placed.

credenza (krɪˈdɛnzə) *n* another name for **credence table**. [It.: see CREDENCE]

credibility gap *n* a disparity between claims or statements made and the evident facts of the situation or circumstances to which they relate.

credible (ˈkrɛdɪbəl) *adj* 1 capable of being believed. 2 trustworthy or reliable: *the latest claim is the only one to involve a credible witness.* [C14: from L *crēdibilis*, from L *crēdere* to believe]
▶ 'credibleness *or* ˌcredi'bility *n* ▶ 'credibly *adv*

credit (ˈkrɛdɪt) *n* 1 commendation or approval, as for an act or quality. 2 a person or thing serving as a source of good influence, repute, etc. 3 influence or reputation coming from the good opinion of others. 4 belief in the truth, reliability, quality, etc., of someone or something. 5 a sum of money or equivalent purchasing power, available for a person's use. 6a the positive balance in a person's bank account. 6b the sum of money that a bank makes available to a client in excess of any deposit. 7a the practice of permitting a buyer to receive goods or services before payment. 7b the time permitted for paying for such goods or services. 8 reputation for solvency and probity, inducing confidence among creditors. 9 *Accounting*. 9a acknowledgment of an income, liability, or capital item by entry on the right-hand side of an account. 9b the right-hand side of an account. 9c an entry on this side. 9d the total of such entries. 9e (*as modifier*): *credit entries.* 10 *Education*. 10a a distinction awarded to an examination candidate obtaining good marks. 10b a section of an examination syllabus satisfactorily com-

pleted. 11 on credit. with payment to be made at a future date. ◆ *vb* **credits**, **crediting**, **credited**. (*tr*) 12 (foll. by *with*) to ascribe (to); give credit (for). 13 to accept as true; believe. 14 to do credit to. 15 *Accounting*. 15a to enter (an item) as a credit in an account. 15b to acknowledge (a payer) by making such an entry. ◆ See also **credits**. [C16: from OF *crédit*, from It. *credito*, from L *crēditum* loan, from *crēdere* to believe]

creditable (ˈkrɛdɪtəbəl) *adj* deserving credit, honour, etc.; praiseworthy.
▶ 'creditableness *or* ˌcredita'bility *n* ▶ 'creditably *adv*

credit account *n Brit.* a credit system by means of which customers may obtain goods and services before payment.

credit card *n* a card issued by banks, businesses, etc., enabling the holder to obtain goods and services on credit.

Creditiste (ˌkrɛdɪˈtiːst) *Canad.* ◆ *adj* 1 of, supporting, or relating to the Social Credit Rally of Quebec. ◆ *n* 2 a supporter or member of this organization.

creditor (ˈkrɛdɪtə) *n* a person or commercial enterprise to whom money is owed.

credit rating *n* an evaluation of the creditworthiness of an individual or business.

credits (ˈkrɛdɪts) *pl n* a list of those responsible for the production of a film or a television programme.

credit transfer *n* a method of settling a debt by transferring money through a bank or post office, esp. for those who do not have cheque accounts.

creditworthy (ˈkrɛdɪtˌwɜːðɪ) *adj* (of an individual or business) adjudged as meriting credit on the basis of earning power, previous record of debt repayment, etc.
▶ 'credit,worthiness *n*

credo (ˈkriːdəʊ, ˈkreɪ-) *n, pl* **credos**. any formal statement of beliefs, principles, or opinions.

Credo (ˈkriːdəʊ, ˈkreɪ-) *n, pl* **Credos**. 1 the Apostles' or Nicene Creed. 2 a musical setting of the Creed. [C12: from L, lit.: I believe; first word of the Apostles' and Nicene Creeds]

credulity (krɪˈdjuːlɪtɪ) *n* disposition to believe something on little evidence; gullibility.

credulous (ˈkrɛdjʊləs) *adj* 1 tending to believe something on little evidence. 2 arising from or characterized by credulity: *credulous beliefs*. [C16: from L *crēdulus*, from *crēdere* to believe]
▶ 'credulously *adv* ▶ 'credulousness *n*

Cree (kriː) *n* 1 (*pl* **Cree** *or* **Crees**) a member of a N American Indian people living in Ontario, Saskatchewan, and Manitoba. 2 the language of this people.

creed (kriːd) *n* 1 a concise, formal statement of the essential articles of Christian belief, such as the Apostles' Creed or the Nicene Creed. 2 any statement or system of beliefs or principles. [OE *crēda*, from L *crēdo* I believe]
▶ 'creedal *or* 'credal *adj*

creek (kriːk) *n* 1 *Chiefly Brit.* a narrow inlet or bay, esp. of the sea. 2 *US, Canad., Austral., & NZ.* a small stream or tributary. 3 **up the creek**. *Sl.* in trouble; in a difficult position. [C13: from ON *kriki* nook; rel. to MDu. *krēke* creek, inlet]

Creek (kriːk) *n* 1 (*pl* **Creek** *or* **Creeks**) a member of a confederacy of N American Indian tribes formerly living in Georgia and Alabama. 2 any of their languages.

creel (kriːl) *n* 1 a wickerwork basket, esp. one used to hold fish. 2 a wickerwork trap for catching lobsters, etc. [C15: from Scot., from ?]

creep (kriːp) *vb* **creeps**, **creeping**, **crept**. (*intr*) 1 to crawl with the body near to or touching the ground. 2 to move slowly, quietly, or cautiously. 3 to act in a servile way; fawn; cringe. 4 to move or slip out of place, as from pressure or wear. 5 (of plants) to grow along the ground or over rocks. 6 to develop gradually: *creeping unrest*. 7 to have the sensation of something crawling over the skin. ◆ *n* 8 the act of creeping or a creeping movement. 9 *Sl.* a person considered to be obnoxious or servile. 10 *Geol.* the gradual downward movement of loose rock material, soil, etc., on a slope. [OE *crēopan*]

creeper (ˈkriːpə) *n* 1 a person or animal that creeps. 2 a plant, such as the ivy, that grows by creeping. **3** the US and Canad. name for the **tree creeper. 4** a hooked instrument for dragging deep water. **5** *Inf.* a shoe with a soft sole.

creeps (kri:ps) *pl n* (preceded by *the*) *Inf.* a feeling of fear, repulsion, disgust, etc.

creepy ('kri:pɪ) *adj* **creepiest. 1** *Inf.* having or causing a sensation of repulsion or fear, as of creatures crawling on the skin. **2** creeping; slow-moving.
▸ **'creepily** *adv* ▸ **'creepiness** *n*

creepy-crawly *Brit. inf.* ◆ *n, pl* **creepy-crawlies. 1** a small crawling creature. ◆ *adj* **2** feeling or causing a sensation as of creatures crawling on one's skin.

cremate (krɪ'meɪt) *vb* **cremates, cremating, cremated.** (*tr*) to burn up (something, esp. a corpse) and reduce to ash. [C19: from L *cremāre*]
▸ **cre'mation** *n* ▸ **cre'mator** *n* ▸ **crematory** ('krɛmətərɪ, -trɪ) *adj*

crematorium (ˌkrɛmə'tɔːrɪəm) *n, pl* **crematoriums** or **cre-matoria** (-rɪə). a building in which corpses are cremated. Also called (esp. US): **crematory.**

crème (krɛm, kri:m, kreɪm; *French* krɛm) *n* **1** cream. **2** any of various sweet liqueurs: *crème de moka.* ◆ *adj* **3** (of a liqueur) rich and sweet.

crème de la crème *French.* (krɛm də la krɛm) *n* the very best. [lit.: cream of the cream]

crème de menthe ('krɛm də 'mɛnθ, 'mɪnt; 'kri:m, 'kreɪm) *n* a liqueur flavoured with peppermint. [F, lit.: cream of mint]

crème fraîche ('krɛm 'frɛʃ) *n* thickened and slightly fermented cream. [F, lit.: fresh cream]

Cremona ★ (*Italian* kre'mo:na) *n* a city in N Italy, in Lombardy on the River Po: noted for the manufacture of fine violins in the 16th–18th centuries. Pop.: 75 160 (1990).

crenate ('kri:neɪt) or **crenated** *adj* having a scalloped margin, as certain leaves. [C18: from NL *crēnātus*, from Med. L, prob. from LL *crēna* a notch]
▸ **'crenately** *adv* ▸ **crenation** (krɪ'neɪʃən) *n*

crenel ('krɛnʰl) or **crenelle** (krɪ'nɛl) *n* any of a set of openings formed in the top of a wall or parapet and having slanting sides, as in a battlement. [C15: from OF, lit.: a little notch, from *cren* notch, from LL *crēna*]

crenellate or US **crenelate** ('krɛnɪˌleɪt) *vb* **crenellates, crenellating, crenellated** or US **crenelates, crenelating, crenelated.** (*tr*) to supply with battlements. [C19: from OF *creneler*, from CRENEL]
▸ **'crenel,lated** or US **'crenel,ated** *adj* ▸ **ˌcrenel'lation** or US **ˌcrenel'ation** *n*

creole ('kri:əʊl) *n* **1** a language that has its origin in extended contact between two language communities, one of which is European. ◆ *adj* **2** of or relating to creole. **3** (of a sauce or dish) containing or cooked with tomatoes, green peppers, onions, etc. [C17: via F & Sp., prob. from Port. *crioulo* slave born in one's household, prob. from *criar* to bring up, from L *creāre* to CREATE]

Creole ('kri:əʊl) *n* **1** (*sometimes not cap.*) (in the Caribbean and Latin America) **1a** a native-born person of European ancestry. **1b** a native-born person of mixed European and African ancestry who speaks a creole. **2** (in Louisiana and other Gulf States of the US) a native-born person of French ancestry. **3** the French Creole spoken in Louisiana. ◆ *adj* **4** of or relating to any of these peoples.

Creon ★ ('kri:ɒn) *n Greek myth.* the successor to Oedipus as king of Thebes; the brother of Jocasta. See also **Antigone.**

creosol ('kri:əˌsɒl) *n* a colourless or pale yellow insoluble oily liquid with a smoky odour and a burning taste. [C19: from CREOS(OTE) + -OL[1]]

creosote ('krɪəˌsəʊt) *n* **1** a colourless or pale yellow liquid with a burning taste and penetrating odour distilled from wood tar. It is used as an antiseptic. **2** a thick dark liquid mixture prepared from coal tar: used as a preservative for wood. ◆ *vb* **creosotes, creosoting, creosoted. 3** to treat (wood) with creosote. [C19: from Gk *kreas* flesh + *sōtēr* preserver, from *sōzein* to keep safe]
▸ **creosotic** (ˌkrɪə'sɒtɪk) *adj*

crepe or **crape** (kreɪp) *n* **1a** a light cotton, silk, or other fabric with a fine ridged or crinkled surface. **1b** (*as modifier*): *a crepe dress.* **2** a black armband originally made of this, worn as a sign of mourning. **3** a very thin pancake, often folded around a filling. **4** short for **crepe paper** or **crepe rubber.** [C19: from F *crêpe*, from L *crispus* curled, uneven, wrinkled]

crepe de Chine (kreɪp də ʃi:n) *n* a very thin crepe of silk or a similar light fabric. [C19: from F: Chinese crepe]

crepe paper *n* thin crinkled coloured paper, resembling crepe and used for decorations.

creperie ('krɛpərɪ, 'kreɪp-) *n* an eating establishment that specializes in pancakes.

crepe rubber *n* a type of rubber in the form of colourless or pale yellow crinkled sheets: used for the soles of shoes.

crêpe suzette (kreɪp su:'zɛt) *n, pl* **crêpes suzettes.** (*sometimes pl*) an orange-flavoured pancake flambéed in a liqueur or brandy.

crepitate ('krɛpɪˌteɪt) *vb* **crepitates, crepitating, crepitated.** (*intr*) to make a rattling or crackling sound. [C17: from L *crepitāre*]
▸ **'crepitant** *adj* ▸ **ˌcrepi'tation** *n*

crepitus ('krɛpɪtəs) *n* **1** a crackling chest sound heard in pneumonia, etc. **2** the grating sound of two ends of a broken bone rubbing together. ◆ Also called: **crepitation.** [C19: from L, from *crepāre* to crack, creak]

crept (krɛpt) *vb* the past tense and past participle of **creep.**

crepuscular (krɪ'pʌskjʊlə) *adj* **1** of or like twilight; dim. **2** (of certain creatures) active at twilight or just before dawn. [C17: from L *crepusculum* dusk, from *creper* dark]

crepy or **crepey** ('kreɪpɪ) *adj* **crepier, crepiest.** (esp. of the skin) having a dry wrinkled appearance.

Cres. *abbrev.* for Crescent.

crescendo (krɪ'ʃɛndəʊ) *n, pl* **crescendos** or **crescendi** (-dɪ). **1** *Music.* **1a** a gradual increase in loudness or the musical direction or symbol indicating this. Abbrev.: **cresc.** Symbol: < **1b** (*as modifier*): *a crescendo passage.* **2** any similar gradual increase in loudness. **3** a peak of noise or intensity: *the cheers reached a crescendo.* ◆ *vb* **crescendos, crescendoing, crescendoed. 4** (*intr*) to increase in loudness or force. ◆ *adv* **5** with a crescendo. [C18: from It., lit.: increasing, from *crescere* to grow, from L]

crescent ('krɛsʰnt, -zʰnt) *n* **1** the curved shape of the moon in its first or last quarter. **2** any shape or object resembling this. **3** *Chiefly Brit.* a crescent-shaped street. **4** (*often cap.* and preceded by *the*) **4a** the emblem of Islam or Turkey. **4b** Islamic or Turkish power. ◆ *adj* **5** *Arch.* or *poetic.* increasing or growing. [C14: from L *crescēns* increasing, from *crescere* to grow]

cresol ('kri:sɒl) *n* an aromatic compound found in coal tar and creosote and used in making synthetic resins and as an antiseptic and disinfectant. Formula: $C_6H_4(CH_3)OH$. Systematic name: **methylphenol.**

cress (krɛs) *n* any of various plants having pungent-tasting leaves often used in salads and as a garnish. [OE *cressa*]

cresset ('krɛsɪt) *n History.* a metal basket mounted on a pole in which oil or pitch was burned for illumination. [C14: from OF *craisset*, from *craisse* GREASE]

Cressida ('krɛsɪdə), **Criseyde,** or **Cressid** ★ *n* (in medieval adaptations of the story of Troy) a lady who deserts her Trojan lover Troilus for the Greek Diomedes.

Cressy ★ ('krɛsɪ) *n Rare.* the English name for **Crécy.**

crest (krɛst) *n* **1** a tuft or growth of feathers, fur, or skin along the top of the heads of some birds, reptiles, and other animals. **2** something resembling or suggesting this. **3** the top, highest point, or highest stage of something. **4** an ornamental piece, such as a plume, on top of a helmet. **5** *Heraldry.* a symbol of a family or office, borne in addition to a coat of arms and used in medieval times to decorate the helmet. ◆ *vb* **6** (*intr*) to come or rise to a high point. **7** (*tr*) to lie at the top of; cap. **8** (*tr*) to reach the top of (a hill, wave, etc.). [C14: from OF *creste*, from L *crista*]
▸ **'crested** *adj* ▸ **'crestless** *adj*

crestfallen ('krest,fɔːlən) *adj* dejected or disheartened.
▸ 'crest,fallenly *adv*

cretaceous (krɪ'teɪʃəs) *adj* consisting of or resembling chalk. [C17: from L *crētāceus*, from *crēta*, lit.: Cretan earth, that is, chalk]

Cretaceous (krɪ'teɪʃəs) *adj* **1** of, denoting, or formed in the last period of the Mesozoic era, during which chalk deposits were formed. ◆ *n* **2 the.** the Cretaceous period or rock system.

Crete ★ (kriːt) *n* a mountainous island in the E Mediterranean, the largest island of Greece: of archaeological importance for the ruins of Minoan civilization. Capital: Canea (Khaniá). Pop.: 540 054 (1991). Area: 8331 sq. km (3216 sq. miles). Modern Greek name: **Kríti.**
▸ 'Cretan *adj*, *n*

cretin ('kretɪn) *n* **1** a person afflicted with cretinism. **2** a person considered to be extremely stupid. [C18: from F *crétin*, from Swiss F *crestin*, from L *Christiānus* Christian, alluding to the humanity of such people, despite their handicaps]
▸ 'cretinous *adj*

cretinism ('kretɪ,nɪzəm) *n* a condition arising from a deficiency of thyroid hormone, present from birth, characterized by dwarfism and mental retardation. See also **myxoedema.**

cretonne (krɛ'tɒn, 'krɛtɒn) *n* a heavy cotton or linen fabric with a printed design, used for furnishing. [C19: from F, from *Creton* Norman village where it originated]

Creutzfeldt-Jakob disease ('krɔɪtsfɛlt 'jɑːkɒp) *n* a fatal slow-developing disease that affects the central nervous system, characterized by mental deterioration and loss of coordination of the limbs. It is thought to be caused by an abnormal prion protein in the brain. [C20: after Hans G. *Creutzfeldt* (1885–1964) and Alfons *Jakob* (1884–1931), German physicians]

crevasse (krɪ'væs) *n* **1** a deep crack or fissure, esp. in the ice of a glacier. **2** *US.* a break in a river embankment. ◆ *vb* **crevasses, crevassing, crevassed. 3** (*tr*) *US.* to make a break or fissure in (a dyke, wall, etc.). [C19: from F: CREVICE]

crevice ('krevɪs) *n* a narrow fissure or crack; split; cleft. [C14: from OF *crevace*, from *crever* to burst, from L *crepāre* to crack]

crew[1] (kruː) *n* (*sometimes functioning as pl*) **1** the men who man a ship, boat, aircraft, etc. **2** *Naut.* a group of people assigned to a particular job or type of work. **3** *Inf.* a gang, company, or crowd. ◆ *vb* **4** to serve on (a ship) as a member of the crew. [C15 *crue* (military) reinforcement, from OF *creue* augmentation, from OF *creistre* to increase, from L *crescere*]

crew[2] (kruː) *vb Arch.* a past tense of **crow**[2].

crew cut *n* a closely cropped haircut for men. [C20: from the style of haircut worn by the boat crews at Harvard and Yale Universities]

Crewe ★ (kruː) *n* a town in NW England, in Cheshire: major railway junction. Pop.: 63 351 (1991).

crewel ('kruːɪl) *n* a loosely twisted worsted yarn, used in fancy work and embroidery. [C15: from ?]
▸ 'crewelist *n* ▸ 'crewel,work *n*

crew neck *n* a plain round neckline in sweaters.
▸ 'crew-,neck *or* 'crew-,necked *adj*

crib (krɪb) *n* **1** a child's bed with slatted wooden sides; cot. **2** a cattle stall or pen. **3** a fodder rack or manger. **4** a small crude cottage or room. **5** *NZ.* a weekend cottage: term is South Island usage only. **6** any small confined space. **7** a representation of the manger in which the infant Jesus was laid at birth. **8** *Inf.* a theft, esp. of another's writing or thoughts. **9** *Inf., chiefly Brit.* a translation of a foreign text or a list of answers used by students, often illicitly, as an aid in lessons, examinations, etc. **10** short for **cribbage. 11** *Cribbage.* the discard pile. **12** Also called: **cribwork.** a framework of heavy timbers used in the construction of foundations, mines, etc. ◆ *vb* **cribs, cribbing, cribbed. 13** (*tr*) to put or enclose in or as if in a crib; furnish with a crib. **14** (*tr*) *Inf.* to steal (another's writings or thoughts). **15** (*intr*) *Inf.* to copy either from a crib or from someone else during a lesson or examination. **16** (*intr*) *Inf.* to grumble. [OE *cribb*]
▸ 'cribber *n*

cribbage ('krɪbɪdʒ) *n* a game of cards for two to four, in which players try to win a set number of points before their opponents. [C17: from ?]

cribbage board *n* a board, with pegs and holes, used for scoring at cribbage.

crib-biting *n* a harmful habit of horses in which the animal leans on the manger or seizes it with the teeth and swallows a gulp of air.

crick (krɪk) *Inf.* ◆ *n* **1** a painful muscle spasm or cramp, esp. in the neck or back. ◆ *vb* **2** (*tr*) to cause a crick in. [C15: from ?]

Crick ★ (krɪk) *n* Francis Harry Compton. born 1916, British molecular biologist: helped to discover the structure of DNA; shared Nobel prize for physiology or medicine.

cricket[1] ('krɪkɪt) *n* an insect having long antennae and, in the males, the ability to produce a chirping sound by rubbing together the leathery forewings. [C14: from OF *criquet*, from *criquer* to creak, imit.]

cricket[2] ('krɪkɪt) *n* **1a** a game played by two teams of eleven players on a field with a wicket at either end of a 22-yard pitch, the object being for one side to score runs by hitting a hard leather-covered ball with a bat while the other side tries to dismiss them by bowling, catching, running them out, etc. **1b** (*as modifier*): *a cricket bat.* **2 not cricket.** *Inf.* not fair play. ◆ *vb* (*intr*) **3** to play cricket. [C16: from OF *criquet* goalpost, wicket, from ?]
▸ 'cricketer *n*

cricoid ('kraɪkɔɪd) *adj* **1** of or relating to the ring-shaped lowermost cartilage of the larynx. ◆ *n* **2** this cartilage. [C18: from NL *cricoīdes*, from Gk *krikoeidēs* ring-shaped, from *krikos* ring]

cri de coeur (kriː də kɜːr) *n, pl* **cris de coeur.** (kriː də kɜːr). a heartfelt or impassioned appeal. [C20: altered from F *cri du coeur*]

crier ('kraɪə) *n* **1** a person or animal that cries. **2** (formerly) an official who made public announcements, esp. in a town or court.

crime (kraɪm) *n* **1** an act or omission prohibited and punished by law. **2** unlawful acts in general. **3** an evil act. **4** *Inf.* something to be regretted. [C14: from OF, from L *crīmen* verdict, accusation, crime]

Crimea ★ (kraɪ'mɪə) *n* a peninsula and Autonomous Region of the S Ukraine, between the Black Sea and the Sea of Azov: an autonomous republic of the Soviet Union (1921–45). Russian name: **Krym.**
▸ Cri'mean *adj*, *n*

criminal ('krɪmɪnºl) *n* **1** a person charged with and convicted of crime. **2** a person who commits crimes for a living. ◆ *adj* **3** of, involving, or guilty of crime. **4** (*prenominal*) of or relating to crime or its punishment. **5** *Inf.* senseless or deplorable. [C15: from LL *crīminālis*; see CRIME, -AL[1]]
▸ 'criminally *adv* ▸ ,crimi'nality *n*

criminal conversation *n* another term for **adultery.**

criminalize *or* **criminalise** ('krɪmɪnə,laɪz) *vb* **criminalizes, criminalizing, criminalized** *or* **criminalises, criminalising, criminalised.** (*tr*) to declare (an action or activity) criminal.
▸ ,criminali'zation *or* ,criminali'sation *n*

criminal law *n* the body of law dealing with offences and offenders.

criminology (,krɪmɪ'nɒlədʒɪ) *n* the scientific study of crime. [C19: from L *crimin*- CRIME, + -LOGY]
▸ **criminological** (,krɪmɪnə'lɒdʒɪkºl) *or* ,crimino'logic *adj*
▸ ,crimino'logically *adv* ▸ ,crimi'nologist *n*

crimp (krɪmp) *vb* (*tr*) **1** to fold or press into ridges. **2** to fold and pinch together (something, such as two pieces of metal). **3** to curl or wave (the hair) tightly, esp. with curling tongs. **4** *Inf., chiefly US.* to hinder. ◆ *n* **5** the act or result of folding or pressing together or into ridges. **6** a tight wave or curl in the hair. [OE *crympan*; rel. to *crump* bent; see CRAMP]
▸ 'crimper *n* ▸ 'crimpy *adj*

Crimplene ('krɪmpliːn) *n Trademark.* a synthetic material similar to Terylene, characterized by its crease-resistance.

crimson ('krɪmzən) *n* **1a** a deep or vivid red colour. **1b**

(as adj): a crimson rose. ◆ *vb* **2** to make or become crimson. **3** *(intr)* to blush. [C14: from OSp. *cremesin*, from Ar. *qirmizi* red of the kermes, from *qirmiz* KERMES]
► **'crimsonness** *n*

cringe (krɪndʒ) *vb* **cringes, cringing, cringed.** *(intr)* **1** to shrink or flinch, esp. in fear or servility. **2** to behave in a servile or timid way. **3** *Inf.* to experience a sudden feeling of embarrassment or distaste. ◆ *n* **4** the act of cringing. **5** **the cultural cringe.** *Austral.* subservience to overseas cultural standards. [OE *cringan* to yield in battle]
► **'cringer** *n*

cringle ('krɪŋg°l) *n* an eyelet at the edge of a sail. [C17: from Low G *Kringel* small ring]

crinkle ('krɪŋk°l) *vb* **crinkles, crinkling, crinkled. 1** to form or cause to form wrinkles, twists, or folds. **2** to make or cause to make a rustling noise. ◆ *n* **3** a wrinkle, twist, or fold. **4** a rustling noise. [OE *crincan* to bend, give way]

crinkly ('krɪŋklɪ) *adj* **1** wrinkled; crinkled. ◆ *n*, *pl* **crinklies. 2** *Sl.* an old person.

crinoid ('kraɪnɔɪd, 'krɪn-) *n* **1** a primitive echinoderm having delicate feathery arms radiating from a central disc. ◆ *adj* **2** of, relating to, or belonging to the *Crinoidea.* **3** shaped like a lily. [C19: from Gk *krinoeidēs* lily-like]
► **cri'noidal** *adj*

crinoline ('krɪn°lɪn) *n* **1** a stiff fabric, originally of horsehair and linen used in lining garments. **2** a petticoat stiffened with this, worn to distend skirts, esp. in the mid-19th century. **3** a framework of steel hoops worn for the same purpose. [C19: from F, from It. *crinolino*, from *crino* horsehair, from L *crīnis* hair + *lino* flax, from L *līnum*]

Crippen ★ ('krɪp°n) *n* **Hawley Harvey**, known as *Doctor Crippen*. 1862–1910, US doctor living in England: executed for poisoning his wife.

cripple ('krɪp°l) *n* **1** a person who is lame. **2** a person who is or seems disabled or deficient in some way: *a mental cripple.* ◆ *vb* **cripples, crippling, crippled. 3** *(tr)* to make a cripple of; disable. [OE *crypel*; rel. to *crēopan* to creep]
► **'crippler** *n*

Cripple Creek ★ *n* a village in central Colorado: gold-mining centre since 1891, once the richest in the world.

Cripps ★ (krɪps) *n* Sir **(Richard) Stafford.** 1889–1952, British Labour statesman; Chancellor of the Exchequer (1947–50).

Criseyde ★ (krɪ'seɪdə) *n* a variant of **Cressida.**

crisis ('kraɪsɪs) *n*, *pl* **crises** (-siːz). **1** a crucial stage or turning point, esp. in a sequence of events or a disease. **2** an unstable period, esp. one of extreme trouble or danger. **3** *Pathol.* a sudden change in the course of a disease. [C15: from L: decision, from Gk *krisis*, from *krinein* to decide]

crisp (krɪsp) *adj* **1** dry and brittle. **2** fresh and firm. **3** invigorating or bracing: *a crisp breeze.* **4** clear; sharp: *crisp reasoning.* **5** lively or stimulating. **6** clean and orderly. **7** concise and pithy. **8** wrinkled or curly: *crisp hair.* ◆ *vb* **9** to make or become crisp. ◆ *n* **10** *Brit.* a very thin slice of potato fried and eaten cold as a snack. **11** something that is crisp. [OE, from L *crispus* curled, uneven, wrinkled]
► **'crisply** *adv* ► **'crispness** *n*

crispbread ('krɪsp,bred) *n* a thin dry biscuit made of wheat or rye.

crisper ('krɪspə) *n* a compartment in a refrigerator for storing salads, vegetables, etc., in order to keep them fresh.

Crispin ★ ('krɪspɪn) *n* **Saint**, 3rd century A.D., legendary Roman Christian martyr, with his brother **Crispinian** (krɪ'spɪnɪən): they are the patron saints of shoemakers. Feast day: Oct. 25.

crispy ('krɪspɪ) *adj* **crispier, crispiest. 1** crisp. **2** having waves or curls.
► **'crispiness** *n*

crisscross ('krɪs,krɒs) *vb* **1** to move or cause to move in a crosswise pattern. **2** to mark with or consist of a pattern of crossing lines. ◆ *adj* **3** (esp. of lines) crossing one another in different directions. ◆ *n* **4** a pattern made of crossing lines. ◆ *adv* **5** in a crosswise manner or pattern.

crit. *abbrev. for:* **1** *Med.* critical. **2** criticism.

criterion (kraɪ'tɪərɪən) *n*, *pl* **criteria** (-rɪə) *or* **criterions.** a

standard by which something can be judged or decided. [C17: from Gk *kritērion*, from *kritēs* judge, from *krinein* to decide]

> **USAGE NOTE** *Criteria*, the plural of *criterion*, is not acceptable as a singular noun: *this criterion is not valid; these criteria are not valid.*

critic ('krɪtɪk) *n* **1** a person who judges something. **2** a professional judge of art, music, literature, etc. **3** a person who often finds fault and criticizes. [C16: from L *criticus*, from Gk *kritikos* capable of judging, from *kritēs* judge; see CRITERION]

critical ('krɪtɪk°l) *adj* **1** containing or making severe or negative judgments. **2** containing analytical evaluations. **3** of a critic or criticism. **4** of or forming a crisis; crucial. **5** urgently needed. **6** *Inf.* so seriously injured or ill as to be in danger of dying. **7** *Physics.* of, denoting, or concerned with a state in which the properties of a system undergo an abrupt change. **8 go critical.** (of a nuclear power station or reactor) to reach a state in which a nuclear-fission chain reaction becomes self-sustaining.
► **'criti,cality** *n* ► **'critically** *adv* ► **'criticalness** *n*

critical mass *n* the minimum mass of fissionable material that can sustain a nuclear chain reaction.

critical path analysis *n* a technique for planning projects with reference to the critical path, which is the sequence of stages requiring the longest time.

critical temperature *n* the temperature of a substance in its critical state. A gas can only be liquefied at temperatures below this.

criticism ('krɪtɪ,sɪzəm) *n* **1** the act or an instance of making an unfavourable or severe judgment, comment, etc. **2** the analysis or evaluation of a work of art, literature, etc. **3** the occupation of a critic. **4** a work that sets out to evaluate or analyse.

criticize *or* **criticise** ('krɪtɪ,saɪz) *vb* **criticizes, criticizing, criticized** *or* **criticises, criticising, criticised. 1** to judge (something) with disapproval; censure. **2** to evaluate or analyse (something).
► **'criti,cizable** *or* **'criti,cisable** *adj* ► **'criti,cizer** *or* **'criti,ciser** *n*

critique (krɪ'tiːk) *n* **1** a critical essay or commentary. **2** the act or art of criticizing. [C17: from F, from Gk *kritikē*, from *kritikos* able to discern]

croak (krəʊk) *vb* **1** *(intr)* (of frogs, crows, etc.) to make a low, hoarse cry. **2** to utter (something) in this manner. **3** *(intr)* to grumble or be pessimistic. **4** *Sl.* **4a** *(intr)* to die. **4b** *(tr)* to kill. ◆ *n* **5** a low hoarse utterance or sound. [OE *crācettan*]
► **'croaky** *adj* ► **'croakiness** *n*

croaker ('krəʊkə) *n* **1** an animal, bird, etc., that croaks. **2** a grumbling person.

Croat ('krəʊæt) *n* **1a** a native or inhabitant of Croatia. **1b** a speaker of Croatian. ◆ *n*, *adj* **2** another word for **Croatian.**

Croatia ★ (krəʊ'eɪʃə) *n* a republic in SE Europe: settled by Croats in the 7th century; belonged successively to Hungary, Turkey, Austria, and Yugoslavia (1918–91); independence was gained (1991) following armed conflict with Serbia; involved in the civil war in Bosnia-Herzegovina (1991–95). Official language: Croatian. Religion: Roman Catholic majority. Currency: kuna. Capital: Zagreb. Pop.: 4 774 000 (1997). Area: 55 322 sq. km (21 359 sq. miles). Croatian name: **Hrvatska.**

Croatian (krəʊ'eɪʃən) *adj* **1** of or relating to Croatia, its people, or their language. ◆ *n* **2** the official language of Croatia, a dialect of Serbo-Croat. **3a** a native or inhabitant of Croatia. **3b** a speaker of Croatian.

croc (krɒk) *n* short for **crocodile** (senses 1 and 2).

Croce ★ (*Italian* 'krɔːtʃe) *n* **Benedetto** (bene'detto). 1866–1952, Italian philosopher: an opponent of Fascism, he helped re-establish liberalism in postwar Italy.

crochet ('krəʊʃeɪ, -ʃɪ) *vb* **crochets, crocheting** (-ʃeɪɪŋ, -ʃɪɪŋ), **crocheted** (-ʃeɪd, -ʃɪd). **1** to make (a piece of needlework, a garment, etc.) by looping and intertwining thread with a hooked needle (**crochet hook**). ◆ *n* **2** work made by cro-

cheting. [C19: from F *crochet*, dim. of *croc* hook, prob. of Scand. origin]
▶ '**crocheter** *n*

crock[1] (krɒk) *n* **1** an earthen pot, jar, etc. **2** a piece of broken earthenware. [OE *crocc* pot]

crock[2] (krɒk) *Sl.*, *chiefly Brit.* ◆ *n* **1** a person or thing that is old or decrepit (esp. in **old crock**). ◆ *vb* **2** to become or cause to become weak or disabled. [C15: orig. Scot.; rel. to Norwegian *krake* unhealthy animal, Du. *kraak* decrepit person or animal]

crockery ('krɒkərɪ) *n* china dishes, earthen vessels, etc., collectively.

crocket ('krɒkɪt) *n* a carved ornament in the form of a curled leaf or cusp, used in Gothic architecture. [C17: from Anglo-F *croket* a little hook, from *croc* hook, of Scand. origin]

Crockett ★ ('krɒkɪt) *n* **David**, known as *Davy Crockett*. 1786–1836, US frontiersman and soldier.

crocodile ('krɒkə,daɪl) *n* **1** a large tropical reptile having a broad head, tapering snout, massive jaws, and a thick outer covering of bony plates. **2a** leather made from the skin of any of these animals. **2b** (*as modifier*): *crocodile shoes*. **3** *Brit. inf.* a line of people, esp. schoolchildren walking two by two. [C13: via OF, from L *crocodīlus*, from Gk *krokodeilos* lizard, ult. from *krokē* pebble + *drilos* worm; referring to its basking on shingle]

crocodile clip *n* a clasp with serrated interlocking edges used for making electrical connections, etc.

Crocodile River ★ *n* **1** a river in N South Africa; a tributary of the Limpopo. **2** a river that rises in NE South Africa and flows southeastwards into Mozambique.

crocodile tears *pl n* an insincere show of grief; false tears. [from the belief that crocodiles wept over their prey to allure further victims]

crocodilian (,krɒkə'dɪlɪən) *n* **1** any large predatory reptile of the order *Crocodilia*, which includes the crocodiles, alligators, and caymans. ◆ *adj* **2** of, relating to, or belonging to the *Crocodilia*. **3** of, relating to, or resembling a crocodile.

crocus ('krəukəs) *n*, *pl* **crocuses**. any plant of the iridaceous genus *Crocus*, having white, yellow, or purple flowers. [C17: from NL, from L *crocus*, from Gk *krokos* saffron]

Croesus ★ ('kri:səs) *n* **1** died ?546 B.C., the last king of Lydia (560–546), noted for his great wealth. **2** any very rich man.

croft (krɒft) *n Brit.* a small enclosed plot of land, adjoining a house, worked by the occupier and his family, esp. in Scotland. [OE *croft*]
▶ '**crofter** *n* ▶ '**crofting** *adj*, *n*

croissant ('krwʌsɒŋ) *n* a flaky crescent-shaped bread roll. [F, lit.: crescent]

Croix de Guerre *French.* (krwa də gɛr) *n* a French military decoration awarded for gallantry in battle: established 1915. [lit.: cross of war]

Cro-Magnon man ('krəu'mænjɒn, -'mægnɒn) *n* an early type of modern man, *Homo sapiens*, who lived in Europe during late Palaeolithic times. [C19: after the cave (Cro-Magnon), Dordogne, France, where the remains were first found]

Cromer ★ ('krəumə) *n* **1st Earl of**, title of (Evelyn) **Baring**.

cromlech ('krɒmlɛk) *n* **1** a circle of prehistoric standing stones. **2** (no longer in technical usage) a megalithic chamber tomb or dolmen. [C17: from Welsh, from *crom*, fem. of *crwm* bent, arched + *llech* flat stone]

Crompton ★ ('krɒmptən) *n* **1 Richmal**, full name *Richmal Crompton Lamburn*. 1890–1969, British children's author, best known for her *Just William* stories. **2 Samuel**. 1753–1827, British inventor of the spinning mule (1779).

Cromwell ★ ('krɒmwəl, -wɛl) *n* **1 Oliver**. 1599–1658, English general and statesman. A Puritan, he was a leader of the parliamentary army in the Civil War. After the execution of Charles I he quelled the Royalists in Scotland and Ireland, and became Lord Protector of the Commonwealth (1653–58). **2** his son, **Richard**. 1626–1712, Lord Protector of the Commonwealth (1658–59). **3 Thomas**, Earl of Essex. ?1485–1540, English statesman.

He was secretary to Cardinal Wolsey (1514), and later chief adviser to Henry VIII: executed.
▶ **Cromwellian** (krɒm'wɛlɪən) *adj*, *n*

crone (krəun) *n* a witchlike old woman. [C14: from OF *carogne* carrion, ult. from L *caro* flesh]

Cronin ('krəunɪn) *n* **1 A(rchibald) J(oseph)**. 1896–1981, British novelist and physician. His works include *Hatter's Castle* (1931), *The Judas Tree* (1961), and *Dr Finlay's Casebook*, a TV series based on his medical experiences. **2 James Watson**. born 1931, US physicist; shared Nobel prize for physics (1980) for his work on parity conservation.

cronk (krɒŋk) *adj Austral. sl.* **1** unfit; unsound. **2** dishonest. [C19: ?from G *krank* ill]

Cronus ('krəunəs), **Cronos**, *or* **Kronos** ★ ('krəunɒs) *n* *Greek myth.* a Titan, son of Uranus (sky) and Gaea (earth), who ruled the world until his son Zeus dethroned him. Roman counterpart: **Saturn**.

crony ('krəunɪ) *n*, *pl* **cronies**. a friend or companion. [C17: student sl. (Cambridge), from Gk *khronios* of long duration, from *khronos* time]

cronyism ('krəunɪ,ɪzəm) *n* the practice of appointing friends to high-level posts, esp. political posts, regardless of their suitability.

crook (kruk) *n* **1** a curved or hooked thing. **2** a staff with a hooked end, such as a bishop's crosier or shepherd's staff. **3** a turn or curve; bend. **4** *Inf.* a dishonest person, esp. a swindler or thief. ◆ *vb* **5** to bend or curve or cause to bend or curve. ◆ *adj* **6** *Austral. & NZ sl.* **6a** ill. **6b** of poor quality. **6c** unpleasant; bad. **7 go (off) crook**. *Austral. & NZ sl.* to lose one's temper. **8 go crook at** *or* **on**. *Austral. & NZ sl.* to rebuke or upbraid. [C12: from ON *krokr* hook]

crooked ('krukɪd) *adj* **1** bent, angled or winding. **2** set at an angle; not straight. **3** deformed or contorted. **4** *Inf.* dishonest or illegal. **5 crooked on**. (*also* krukt) *Austral. inf.* hostile or averse to.
▶ '**crookedly** *adv* ▶ '**crookedness** *n*

Crookes ★ (kruks) *n* Sir **William**. 1832–1919, British chemist: he investigated cathode rays and invented a type of radiometer and the lens named after him.

croon (kru:n) *vb* **1** to sing or speak in a soft low tone. ◆ *n* **2** a soft low singing or humming. [C14: via MDu. *crōnen* to groan]
▶ '**crooner** *n*

crop (krɒp) *n* **1** the produce of cultivated plants, esp. cereals, vegetables, and fruit. **2a** the amount of such produce in any particular season. **2b** the yield of some other farm produce: *the lamb crop*. **3** a group of products, thoughts, people, etc., appearing at one time or in one season. **4** the stock of a thonged whip. **5** short for **riding crop**. **6** a pouchlike part of the oesophagus of birds, in which food is stored or partially digested before passing on to the gizzard. **7** a short cropped hairstyle. **8** a notch in or a piece cut out of the ear of an animal. **9** the act of cropping. ◆ *vb* **crops**, **cropping**, **cropped**. (*mainly tr*) **10** to cut (hair, grass, etc.) very short. **11** to cut and collect (mature produce) from the land or plant on which it has been grown. **12** to clip part of (the ear or ears) of (an animal), esp. as a means of identification. **13** (of herbivorous animals) to graze on (grass or similar vegetation). ◆ See also **crop out**, **crop up**. [OE *cropp*]

crop-dusting *n* the spreading of fungicide, etc., on crops in the form of dust, often from an aircraft.

crop-eared *adj* having the ears or hair cut short.

crop out *vb* (*intr*, *adv*) (of a formation of rock strata) to appear or be exposed at the surface.

cropper ('krɒpə) *n* **1** a person who cultivates or harvests a crop. **2 come a cropper**. *Inf.* **2a** to fall heavily. **2b** to fail completely.

crop rotation *n* the system of growing a sequence of different crops on the same ground so as to maintain or increase its fertility.

crop up *vb* (*intr*, *adv*) *Inf.* to occur or appear, esp. unexpectedly.

croquet ('krəukeɪ, -kɪ) *n* a game for two to four players who hit a wooden ball through iron hoops with mallets

---

★ people and places

in order to hit a peg. [C19: ?from F dialect, var. of CRO-CHET (little hook)]

croquette ('krəʊ'ket, krɒ-) n a savoury cake of minced meat, fish, etc., fried in breadcrumbs. [C18: from F, from *croquer* to crunch, imit.]

Crosby ★ ('krɒzbɪ) n Bing, real name *Harry Lillis Crosby.* 1904–77, US singer and film actor; noted for the song "White Christmas" from the film *Holiday Inn* (1942).

crosier *or* **crozier** ('krəʊʒə) n a staff surmounted by a crook or cross, carried by bishops as a symbol of pastoral office. [C14: from OF *crossier* staff bearer, from *crosse* pastoral staff]

cross (krɒs) n 1 a structure or symbol consisting of two intersecting lines or pieces at right angles to one another. 2 a wooden structure used as a means of execution, consisting of an upright post with a transverse piece to which people were nailed or tied. 3 a representation of the Cross as an emblem of Christianity or as a reminder of Christ's death. 4 any mark or shape consisting of two intersecting lines, esp. such a symbol (×) used as a signature, error mark, etc. 5 a sign representing the Cross made either by tracing a figure in the air or by touching the forehead, breast, and either shoulder in turn. 6 any variation of the Christian symbol, such as a Maltese or Greek cross. 7 a cruciform emblem awarded to indicate membership of an order or as a decoration for distinguished service. 8 (*sometimes cap.*) Christianity or Christendom, esp. as contrasted with non-Christian religions. 9 the place in a town or village where a cross has been set up. 10 *Biol.* 10a the process of crossing; hybridization. 10b an individual produced as a result of this process. 11 a mixture of two qualities or types. 12 an opposition, hindrance, or misfortune; affliction (esp. in **bear one's cross**). 13 *Boxing.* a straight punch delivered from the side, esp. with the right hand. 14 *Football.* the act or an instance of passing the ball from a wing to the middle of the field. ◆ vb 15 (sometimes foll. by *over*) to move or go across (something); traverse or intersect. 16a to meet and pass. 16b (of each of two letters in the post) to be dispatched before receipt of the other. 17 (tr; usually foll. by *out, off,* or *through*) to cancel with a cross or with lines; delete. 18 (tr) to place or put in a form resembling a cross: *to cross one's legs.* 19 (tr) to mark with a cross or crosses. 20 (tr) *Brit.* to draw two parallel lines across the face of (a cheque) and so make it payable only into a bank account. 21 (tr) 21a to trace the form of the Cross upon (someone or something) in token of blessing. 21b to make the sign of the Cross upon (oneself). 22 (intr) (of telephone lines) to interfere with each other so that several callers are connected together at one time. 23 to cause fertilization between (plants or animals of different breeds, races, varieties, etc.). 24 (tr) to oppose the wishes or plans of; thwart. 25 *Football.* to pass (the ball) from a wing to the middle of the field. 26 **cross one's fingers.** to fold one finger across another in the hope of bringing good luck. 27 **cross one's heart.** to promise or pledge, esp. by making the sign of a cross over one's heart. 28 **cross one's mind.** to occur to one briefly or suddenly. 29 **cross the path (of).** to meet or thwart (someone). 30 **cross swords.** to argue or fight. ◆ adj 31 angry; illhumoured; vexed. 32 lying or placed across; transverse: *a cross timber.* 33 involving interchange; reciprocal. 34 contrary or unfavourable. 35 another word for **crossbred.** [OE *cros*, from OIrish *cross* (unattested), from L *crux*; see CRUX]
▶ '**crossly** adv ▶ '**crossness** n

Cross[1] (krɒs) n the. 1 the cross on which Jesus Christ was crucified. 2 the Crucifixion of Jesus.

Cross[2] ★ (krɒs) n Richard Assheton, 1st Viscount. 1823–1914, British Conservative statesman, home secretary (1874–80).

cross- *combining form.* 1 indicating action from one individual, group, etc., to another: *cross-cultural; cross-fertilize; cross-refer.* 2 indicating movement, position, etc., across something: *crosscurrent; crosstalk.* 3 indicating a crosslike figure or intersection: *crossbones.* [from CROSS (in various senses)]

crossbar ('krɒs,bɑː) n 1 a horizontal bar, line, stripe, etc. 2 a horizontal beam across a pair of goalposts. 3 the horizontal bar on a man's bicycle.

crossbeam ('krɒs,biːm) n a beam that spans from one support to another.

cross-bench n (*usually pl*) Brit. a seat in Parliament occupied by a neutral or independent member.
▶ '**cross-,bencher** n

crossbill ('krɒs,bɪl) n any of various widely distributed finches that occur in coniferous woods and have a bill with crossed tips.

crossbones ('krɒs,bəʊnz) pl n See **skull and crossbones.**

crossbow ('krɒs,bəʊ) n a type of medieval bow fixed transversely on a stock grooved to direct a square-headed arrow.
▶ '**cross,bowman** n

crossbred ('krɒs,bred) adj 1 (of plants or animals) produced as a result of crossbreeding. ◆ n 2 a crossbred plant or animal.

crossbreed ('krɒs,briːd) vb **crossbreeds, crossbreeding, crossbred.** 1 Also: **interbreed.** to breed (animals or plants) using parents of different races, varieties, breeds, etc. ◆ n 2 the offspring produced by such a breeding.

crosscheck (,krɒs'tʃek) vb 1 to verify (a fact, report, etc.) by considering conflicting opinions or consulting other sources. ◆ n 2 the act or an instance of crosschecking.

cross-country adj, adv 1 by way of fields, etc., as opposed to roads. 2 across a country. ◆ n 3 a long race held over open ground.

crosscurrent ('krɒs,kʌrənt) n 1 a current flowing across another current. 2 a conflicting tendency moving counter to the usual trend.

cross-curricular adj Brit. education. denoting or relating to an approach to a topic that includes contributions from several different disciplines and viewpoints.

crosscut ('krɒs,kʌt) adj 1 cut at right angles or obliquely to the major axis. ◆ n 2 a transverse cut or course. 3 *Mining.* a tunnel through a vein of ore or from the shaft to a vein. ◆ vb **crosscuts, crosscutting, crosscut.** 4 to cut across.

crosscut saw n a saw for cutting timber across the grain.

crosse (krɒs) n a light staff with a triangular frame to which a network is attached, used in playing lacrosse. [F, from OF *croce* CROSIER.]

cross-examine vb **cross-examines, cross-examining, cross-examined.** (tr) 1 Law. to examine (a witness for the opposing side), as in attempting to discredit his testimony. 2 to examine closely or relentlessly.
▶ '**cross-ex,ami'nation** n ▶ ,**cross-ex'aminer** n

cross-eye n a turning inwards towards the nose of one or both eyes, caused by abnormal alignment.
▶ '**cross-,eyed** adj

cross-fertilize vb **cross-fertilizes, cross-fertilizing, cross-fertilized.** 1 to fertilize by fusion of male and female gametes from different individuals of the same species. 2 a non-technical term for **cross-pollinate.**
▶ '**cross-,fertili'zation** n

crossfire ('krɒs,faɪə) n 1 Mil., etc. converging fire from one or more positions. 2 a lively exchange of ideas, opinions, etc.

cross-grained adj 1 (of timber) having the fibres arranged irregularly or across the axis of the piece. 2 perverse, cantankerous, or stubborn.

cross hairs pl n two fine mutually perpendicular lines or wires that cross in the focal plane of a theodolite, gunsight, or other optical instrument and are used to define the line of sight. Also called: **cross wires.**

crosshatch ('krɒs,hætʃ) vb Drawing. to shade or hatch with two or more sets of parallel lines that cross one another.

crossing ('krɒsɪŋ) n 1 the place where one thing crosses another. 2 a place where a street, railway, etc., may be crossed. 3 the act or an instance of travelling across something, esp. the sea. 4 the act or process of crossbreeding.

crossing over n Genetics. the interchange of sections between pairing chromosomes during meiosis that produces variations in inherited characteristics by rearranging genes.

cross-legged ('krɒs'lɛgɪd, -'lɛgd) *adj* standing or sitting with one leg crossed over the other.

Crossman ★ ('krɒsmən) *n* **Richard (Howard Stafford).** 1907–74, British Labour politician, noted for his posthumous *Crossman Papers* (1975).

cross-match *vb Immunol.* to test the compatibility of (a donor's and recipient's blood) by checking that the red cells of each do not agglutinate in the other's serum.

crossover ('krɒs,əʊvə) *n* **1** a place at which a crossing is made. **2** *Railways.* a point of transfer between two main lines. **3** short for **crossover network**. **4** *Genetics.* another term for **crossing over**. **5** a recording, book, or other product that becomes popular in a genre other than its own. ◆ *adj* **6** (of music, fashion, art, etc.) combining two distinct styles. **7** (of a performer, writer, recording, book, etc.) having become popular in more than one genre.

crossover network *n Electronics.* an arrangement in a loudspeaker system that separates the signal into two or more frequency bands for feeding into different speakers.

crosspatch ('krɒs,pætʃ) *n Inf.* a bad-tempered person. [C18: from CROSS + obs. *patch* fool]

crosspiece ('krɒs,piːs) *n* a transverse beam, joist, etc.

cross-ply *adj* (of a motor tyre) having the fabric cords in the outer casing running diagonally to stiffen the sidewalls.

cross-pollinate *vb* **cross-pollinates, cross-pollinating, cross-pollinated.** to transfer pollen from the anthers of one flower to the stigma of another.
▶ ,cross-polli'nation *n*

cross-purpose *n* **1** a contrary aim or purpose. **2 at cross-purposes.** conflicting; opposed; disagreeing.

cross-question *vb* **1** to cross-examine. ◆ *n* **2** a question asked in cross-examination.

cross-refer *vb* to refer from one part of something, esp. a book, to another.

cross-reference *n* **1** a reference within a text to another part of the text. ◆ *vb* **cross-references, cross-referencing, cross-referenced.** **2** to cross-refer.

crossroad ('krɒs,rəʊd) *n US & Canad.* **1** a road that crosses another road. **2** Also called: **crossway.** a road that crosses from one main road to another.

crossroads ('krɒs,rəʊdz) *n* (*functioning as sing*) **1** the point at which two or more roads cross each other. **2** the point at which an important choice has to be made (esp. in **at the crossroads**).

crossruff ('krɒs,rʌf) *Bridge, whist.* ◆ *n* **1** the alternate trumping of each other's leads by two partners, or by declarer and dummy. ◆ *vb* **2** (*intr*) to trump alternately in this way.

cross section *n* **1** *Maths.* a plane surface formed by cutting across a solid, esp. perpendicular to its longest axis. **2** a section cut off in this way. **3** the act of cutting anything in this way. **4** a random sample, esp. one regarded as representative.
▶ ,cross-'sectional *adj*

cross-stitch *n* **1** an embroidery stitch made by two stitches forming a cross. **2** embroidery worked with this stitch. ◆ *vb* **3** to embroider (a piece of needlework) with cross-stitch.

crosstalk ('krɒs,tɔːk) *n* **1** unwanted signals in one channel of a communications system as a result of a transfer of energy from other channels. **2** *Brit.* rapid or witty talk.

cross training *n* training in two or more sports to improve performance, esp. in one's main sport.

crosstree ('krɒs,triː) *n Naut.* either of a pair of wooden or metal braces on the head of a mast to support the topmast, etc.

crosswise ('krɒs,waɪz) or **crossways** ('krɒs,weɪz) *adj, adv* **1** across; transversely. **2** in the shape of a cross.

crossword puzzle ('krɒs,wɜːd) *n* a puzzle in which the solver guesses words suggested by numbered clues and writes them into a grid to form a vertical and horizontal pattern.

crotch (krɒtʃ) *n* **1** Also called (Brit.): **crutch. 1a** the angle formed by the legs where they join the human trunk. **1b** the human genital area. **1c** the corresponding part of a pair of trousers, pants, etc. **2** a forked region formed by the junction of two members. **3** a forked pole or stick. [C16: prob. var. of CRUTCH]
▶ **crotched** *adj*

crotchet ('krɒtʃɪt) *n* **1** *Music.* Also called (US and Canad.): **quarter note.** a note having the time value of a quarter of a semibreve. **2** a perverse notion. [C14: from OF *crochet,* lit.: little hook, from *croche* hook; see CROCKET]

crotchety ('krɒtʃɪtɪ) *adj* **1** *Inf.* irritable; contrary. **2** full of crotchets.
▶ 'crotchetiness *n*

croton ('krəʊtⁿn) *n* **1** any shrub or tree of the chiefly tropical genus *Croton,* esp. *C. tiglium,* the seeds of which yield croton oil, formerly used as a purgative. **2** any of various tropical plants of the related genus *Codiaeum.* [C18: from NL, from Gk *krotōn* tick, castor-oil plant (whose berries resemble ticks)]

crouch (kraʊtʃ) *vb* (*intr*) **1** to bend low with the limbs pulled up close together, esp. (of an animal) in readiness to pounce. **2** to cringe, as in humility or fear. ◆ *n* **3** the act of stooping or bending. [C14: ?from OF *crochir* to become bent like a hook, from *croche* hook]

croup[1] (kruːp) *n* a throat condition, occurring usually in children, characterized by a hoarse cough and laboured breathing, resulting from inflammation of the larynx. [C16 *croup* to cry hoarsely, prob. imit.]
▶ 'croupous or 'croupy *adj*

croup[2] (kruːp) *n* the hindquarters, esp. of a horse. [C13: from OF *croupe;* rel. to G *Kruppe*]

croupier ('kruːpɪə) *n* a person who deals cards, collects bets, etc., at a gaming table. [C18: lit.: one who rides behind another, from F *croupe* CROUP[2]]

crouton ('kruːtɒn) *n* a small piece of fried or toasted bread, usually served in soup. [F: dim. of *croûte* CRUST]

crow[1] (krəʊ) *n* **1** any large gregarious songbird of the genus *Corvus* of Europe and Asia, such as the raven, rook, and jackdaw. All have a heavy bill, glossy black plumage, and rounded wings. **2** any of various similar birds. **3** *Sl.* an old or ugly woman. **4 as the crow flies.** as directly as possible. **5 eat crow.** *US & Canad. inf.* to be forced to do something humiliating. **6 stone the crows.** (*interj*) *Brit. & Austral. sl.* an expression of surprise, dismay, etc. [OE *crāwa*]

crow[2] (krəʊ) *vb* (*intr*) **1** (p.t. **crowed** or **crew**) to utter a shrill squawking sound, as a cock. **2** (often foll. by *over*) to boast one's superiority. **3** (esp. of babies) to utter cries of pleasure. ◆ *n* **4** an act or instance of crowing. [OE *crāwan;* rel. to OHG *krāen,* Du. *kraaien*]
▶ 'crowingly *adv*

crowbar ('krəʊ,bɑː) *n* a heavy iron lever with one end forged into a wedge shape.

crowd (kraʊd) *n* **1** a large number of things or people gathered or considered together. **2** a particular group of people, esp. considered as a set: *the crowd from the office.* **3** (preceded by *the*) the common people; the masses. ◆ *vb* **4** (*intr*) to gather together in large numbers; throng. **5** (*tr*) to press together into a confined space. **6** (*tr*) to fill to excess; fill by pushing into. **7** (*tr*) *Inf.* to urge or harass by urging. [OE *crūdan*]
▶ 'crowded *adj* ▶ 'crowdedness *n*

crowfoot ('krəʊ,fʊt) *n, pl* **crowfoots.** any of several plants that have yellow or white flowers and divided leaves resembling the foot of a crow.

crown (kraʊn) *n* **1** an ornamental headdress denoting sovereignty, usually made of gold embedded with precious stones. **2** a wreath or garland for the head, awarded as a sign of victory, success, honour, etc. **3** (*sometimes cap.*) monarchy or kingship. **4** an award, distinction, or title, given as an honour to reward merit, victory, etc. **5** anything resembling or symbolizing a crown. **6a** a coin worth five shillings (25 pence). **6b** a coin worth £5. **6c** any of several continental coins, such as the krona or krone, with a name meaning *crown.* **7** the top or summit of something: *crown of a hill.* **8** the centre part of a road, esp. when it is cambered. **9** the outstanding quality, achievement, state, etc.: *the crown of his achievements*. **10a** the enamel-covered part of a tooth above the gum. **10b** **artificial crown**. a substitute crown, usually of gold, porcelain, or acrylic resin, fitted over a decayed or broken tooth. **11** the part of an anchor where the arms are joined to the shank. ◆ *vb* (*tr*) **12** to put a crown on the head of, symbolically vesting with royal title, powers, etc. **13** to place a crown, wreath, garland, etc., on the head of. **14** to place something on or over the head or top of. **15** to confer a title, dignity, or reward upon. **16** to form the summit or topmost part of. **17** to cap or put the finishing touch to (a series of events): *to crown it all it rained, too*. **18** *Draughts.* to promote (a draught) to a king by placing another draught on top of it. **19** to attach a crown to (a tooth). **20** *Sl.* to hit over the head. [C12: from OF *corone*, from L *corōna* wreath, crown, from Gk *korōnē* crown, something curved]

Crown (kraʊn) *n* (*sometimes not cap.; usually preceded by the*) **1** the sovereignty or realm of a monarch. **2a** the government of a monarchy. **2b** (*as modifier*): *Crown property.*

crown colony *n* a British colony whose administration is controlled by the Crown.

crown court *n English law.* a court of criminal jurisdiction holding sessions in towns throughout England and Wales.

Crown Derby *n* **1** a type of porcelain manufactured at Derby from 1784–1848. **2** *Trademark.* shortened form of Royal Crown Derby.

crown glass *n* **1** another name for **optical crown. 2** an old form of window glass made by blowing a globe and spinning it until it forms a flat disc.

crown green *n* a type of bowling green in which the sides are lower than the middle.

crowning ('kraʊnɪŋ) *n Obstetrics.* the stage of labour at which the infant's head is passing through the vaginal opening.

crown jewels *pl n* the jewellery, including the regalia, used by a sovereign on a state occasion.

Crown Office *n* (in Britain) an administrative office of the Queen's Bench Division of the High Court, where actions are entered for trial.

crown prince *n* the male heir to a sovereign throne.

crown princess *n* **1** the wife of a crown prince. **2** the female heir to a sovereign throne.

Crown Prosecution Service *n* (in England and Wales) an independent prosecuting body, established in 1986, that decides whether cases brought by the police should go to the courts: headed by the Director of Public Prosecutions. Cf. **procurator fiscal**. Abbrev.: **CPS**.

crown wheel *n* **1** *Horology.* a wheel that has one set of teeth at right angles to another. **2** the larger of two wheels in a bevel gear.

crow's-foot *n, pl* **crow's-feet.** (*often pl*) a wrinkle at the outer corner of the eye.

crow's-nest *n* a lookout platform high up on a ship's mast.

crow step *n* another term for **corbie-step.**

Croydon ('krɔɪdᵊn) *n* a borough in S Greater London (since 1965): formerly important for its airport (1915–59). Pop.: 326 800 (1994 est.). Area: 87 sq. km (33 sq. miles).

crozier ('krəʊʒə) *n* a variant spelling of **crosier.**

CRT *abbrev. for:* **1** cathode-ray tube. **2** (in Britain) composite rate tax: a system of paying interest to savers by which a rate of tax for a period is determined in advance and interest is paid net of tax which is deducted at source.

crucial ('kruːʃəl) *adj* **1** involving a final or supremely important decision or event; decisive; critical. **2** *Inf.* very important. **3** *Sl.* very good. [C18: from F, from L *crux* CROSS]
▶ **'crucially** *adv*

crucible ('kruːsɪbᵊl) *n* **1** a vessel in which substances are heated to high temperatures. **2** the hearth at the bottom of a metallurgical furnace in which the metals collects. **3** a severe trial or test. [C15 *corusible*, from Med. L *crūcibulum* night lamp, crucible, from ?]

crucifix ('kruːsɪfɪks) *n* a cross or image of a cross with a figure of Christ upon it. [C13: from Church L *crucifixus* the crucified Christ, from *crucifigere* to CRUCIFY]

crucifixion (ˌkruːsɪ'fɪkʃən) *n* a method of putting to death by nailing or binding to a cross, normally by the hands and feet.

Crucifixion (ˌkruːsɪ'fɪkʃən) *n* **1** (usually preceded by *the*) the crucifying of Christ. **2** a picture or representation of this.

cruciform ('kruːsɪˌfɔːm) *adj* shaped like a cross. [C17: from L *crux* cross + -FORM]
▶ **'cruci,formly** *adv*

crucify ('kruːsɪˌfaɪ) *vb* **crucifies, crucifying, crucified.** (*tr*) **1** to put to death by crucifixion. **2** *Sl.* to defeat, ridicule, etc., totally. **3** to treat very cruelly; torment. [C13: from OF *crucifier*, from LL *crucifigere* to crucify, to fasten to a cross, from L *crux* cross + *figere* to fasten]
▶ **'cruci,fier** *n*

crud (krʌd) *n* **1** *Sl.* a sticky substance, esp. when dirty and encrusted. **2** *Sl.* something or someone that is worthless, disgusting, or contemptible. **3** an undesirable residue, esp. one inside a nuclear reactor. [C14: earlier form of CURD]
▶ **'cruddy** *adj*

crude (kruːd) *adj* **1** lacking taste, tact, or refinement; vulgar. **2** in a natural or unrefined state. **3** lacking care, knowledge, or skill. **4** (*prenominal*) stark; blunt. ◆ *n* **5** short for **crude oil**. [C14: from L *crūdus* bloody, raw; rel. to L *cruor* blood]
▶ **'crudely** *adv* ▶ **'crudity** *or* **'crudeness** *n*

Cruden ★ ('kruːdᵊn) *n* **Alexander.** 1701–70, Scottish bookseller and compiler of a biblical concordance (1737).

crude oil *n* unrefined petroleum.

crudités (ˌkruːdɪ'teɪ) *pl n* a selection of raw vegetables, served as an hors d'oeuvre. [C20: from F, pl of *crudité*, lit.: rawness]

cruel ('kruːəl) *adj* **1** causing or inflicting pain without pity. **2** causing pain or suffering. ◆ *vb* **cruels, cruelling, cruelled** *or US* **cruels, crueling, crueled.** (*tr*) **3** cruel someone's pitch. *Austral. sl.* to ruin someone's chances. [C13: from OF, from L *crūdēlis*, from *crūdus* raw, bloody]
▶ **'cruelly** *adv* ▶ **'cruelness** *n*

cruelty ('kruːəltɪ) *n, pl* **cruelties. 1** deliberate infliction of pain or suffering. **2** the quality or characteristic of being cruel. **3** a cruel action. **4** *Law.* conduct that causes danger to life or limb or a threat to bodily or mental health.

cruelty-free *adj* (of a cosmetic or other product) developed without being tested on animals.

cruet ('kruːɪt) *n* **1** a small container for holding pepper, salt, vinegar, oil, etc., at table. **2** a set of such containers, esp. on a stand. [C13: from Anglo-F, dim. of OF *crue* flask, of Gmc origin]

Cruft ★ (krʌft) *n* **Charles.** 1852–1938, British dog breeder, who organized the first (1886) of the annual dog shows known as Cruft's.

Cruikshank ★ ('krʊkˌʃæŋk) *n* **George.** 1792–1878, British illustrator and caricaturist.

cruise (kruːz) *vb* **cruises, cruising, cruised. 1** (*intr*) to make a trip by sea for pleasure, usually calling at a number of ports. **2** to sail or travel over (a body of water) for pleasure. **3** (*intr*) to search for enemy vessels in a warship. **4** (*intr*) (of a vehicle, aircraft, or vessel) to travel at a moderate and efficient speed. ◆ *n* **5** an act or instance of cruising, esp. a trip by sea. [C17: from Du. *kruisen* to cross, from *cruis* CROSS]

cruise control *n* a system in a road vehicle that automatically maintains a selected speed until cancelled.

cruise missile *n* a low-flying subsonic missile that is guided throughout its flight.

cruiser ('kruːzə) *n* **1** a high-speed, long-range warship armed with medium-calibre weapons. **2** Also called: **cabin cruiser.** a pleasure boat, esp. one that is power-driven and has a cabin. **3** any person or thing that cruises.

cruiserweight ('kruːzəˌweɪt) *n Boxing.* another term (esp. Brit.) for **light heavyweight.**

crumb (krʌm) *n* **1** a small fragment of bread, cake, or other baked foods. **2** a small piece or bit. **3** the soft inner part of bread. **4** *Sl.* a contemptible person. ◆ *vb* **5** (*tr*) to prepare or cover (food) with breadcrumbs. **6** to break into small fragments. [OE *cruma*]

crumble ('krʌmbᵊl) *vb* **crumbles, crumbling, crumbled. 1** to break or be broken into crumbs or fragments. **2** (*intr*) to fall apart or away. ◆ *n* **3** *Brit., Austral., & NZ.* a baked pudding consisting of a crumbly mixture of flour, fat, and sugar over stewed fruit: *apple crumble*. [C16: var. of *crimble*, of Gmc origin]

crumbly ('krʌmblɪ) *adj* **crumblier, crumbliest. 1** easily crumbled or crumbling. ◆ *n, pl* **crumblies. 2** *Brit. sl.* an older person.
► **'crumbliness** *n*

crumby ('krʌmɪ) *adj* **crumbier, crumbiest. 1** full of or littered with crumbs. **2** soft, like the inside of bread. **3** a variant spelling of **crummy.**

crummy ('krʌmɪ) *adj* **crummier, crummiest.** *Sl.* **1** of little value; contemptible. **2** unwell or depressed: *to feel crummy.* [C19: var. spelling of CRUMBY]

crumpet ('krʌmpɪt) *n Chiefly Brit.* **1** a light soft yeast cake, eaten toasted and buttered. **2** *Sl.* women collectively. [C17: from ?]

crumple ('krʌmpᵊl) *vb* **crumples, crumpling, crumpled. 1** (when *intr*, often foll. by *up*) to collapse or cause to collapse. **2** (when *tr*, often foll. by *up*) to crush or cause to be crushed so as to form wrinkles or creases. ◆ *n* **3** a loose crease or wrinkle. [C16: from obs. *crump* to bend]
► **'crumply** *adj*

crumple zones *pl n* parts of a motor vehicle, at the front and the rear, that are designed to crumple in a collision, thereby absorbing part of the energy of the impact.

crunch (krʌntʃ) *vb* **1** to bite or chew with a crushing or crackling sound. **2** to make or cause to make a crisp or brittle sound. ◆ *n* **3** the sound or act of crunching. **4 the crunch.** *Inf.* the critical moment or situation. ◆ *adj* **5** *Inf.* critical; decisive: *crunch time.* [C19: changed (through infl. of MUNCH) from earlier *craunch*, imit.]
► **'crunchy** *adj* ► **'crunchily** *adv* ► **'crunchiness** *n*

crupper ('krʌpə) *n* **1** a strap from the back of a saddle that passes under a horse's tail. **2** the horse's rump. [C13: from OF *crupiere*, from *crupe* CROUP²]

crusade (kru:'seɪd) *n* **1** (*often cap.*) any of the military expeditions undertaken in the 11th, 12th, and 13th centuries by the Christian powers of Europe to recapture the Holy Land from the Muslims. **2** (*formerly*) any holy war. **3** a vigorous and dedicated action or movement in favour of a cause. ◆ *vb* **crusades, crusading, crusaded.** (*intr*) **4** to campaign vigorously for something. **5** to go on a crusade. [C16: from earlier *croisade*, from OF *crois* cross, from L *crux*; infl. also by Sp. *cruzada*, from *cruzar* to take up the cross]
► **cru'sader** *n*

cruse (kru:z) *n* a small earthenware container used, esp. formerly, for liquids. [OE *crūse*]

crush (krʌʃ) *vb* (*mainly tr*) **1** to press, mash, or squeeze so as to injure, break, crease, etc. **2** to break or grind into small particles. **3** to put down or subdue, esp. by force. **4** to extract (juice, water, etc.) by pressing. **5** to oppress harshly. **6** to hug or clasp tightly. **7** to defeat or humiliate utterly, as in argument or by a cruel remark. **8** (*intr*) to crowd; throng. **9** (*intr*) to become injured, broken, or distorted by pressure. ◆ *n* **10** a dense crowd, esp. at a social occasion. **11** the act of crushing; pressure. **12** a drink or pulp prepared by or as if by crushing fruit: *orange crush.* **13** *Inf.* **13a** an infatuation: *she had a crush on him.* **13b** the person with whom one is infatuated. [C14: from OF *croissir*, of Gmc origin]
► **'crushable** *adj* ► **'crusher** *n*

crush barrier *n* a barrier erected to separate sections of large crowds.

Crusoe ★ ('kru:səʊ, -zəʊ) *n* **Robinson.** See **Robinson Crusoe.**

crust (krʌst) *n* **1a** the hard outer part of bread. **1b** a piece of bread consisting mainly of this. **2** the baked shell of a pie, tart, etc. **3** any hard or stiff outer covering or surface: *a crust of ice.* **4** the solid outer shell of the earth. **5** the dry covering of a skin sore or lesion; scab. **6** *Sl.* impertinence.

7 *Brit., Austral., & NZ sl.* a living (esp. in **earn a crust**). ◆ *vb* **8** to cover with or acquire a crust. **9** to form or be formed into a crust. [C14: from L *crūsta* hard surface, rind, shell]

crustacean (krʌ'steɪʃən) *n* **1** any arthropod of the mainly aquatic class *Crustacea*, typically having a carapace and including the lobsters, crabs, woodlice, and water fleas. ◆ *adj also* **crustaceous. 2** of, relating to, or belonging to the *Crustacea.* [C19: from NL *crūstāceus* hard-shelled, from L *crūsta* shell]

crustal ('krʌstᵊl) *adj* of or relating to the earth's crust.

crusty ('krʌstɪ) *adj* **crustier, crustiest. 1** having or characterized by a crust. **2** having a rude or harsh character or exterior.
► **'crustily** *adv* ► **'crustiness** *n*

crutch (krʌtʃ) *n* **1** a long staff having a rest for the armpit, for supporting the weight of the body. **2** something that supports, helps, or sustains. **3** *Brit.* another word for **crotch** (sense 1). ◆ *vb* **4** (*tr*) to support or sustain (a person or thing) as with a crutch. **5** *Austral. & NZ.* to clip (wool) from the hindquarters of a sheep. [OE *crycc*]

crutchings ('krʌtʃɪŋz) *pl n Austral. & NZ.* wool clipped from a sheep's hindquarters.

crux (krʌks) *n, pl* **cruxes** *or* **cruces** ('kru:si:z). **1** a vital or decisive stage, point, etc. (often in **the crux of the matter**). **2** a baffling problem or difficulty. [C18: from L: cross]

Cruyff ★ (krɔɪf; *Dutch* krœjf) *n* **Johan** (jɔ:'hɑn). born 1947, Dutch footballer: captained the Dutch team in the 1974 World Cup.

cruzado (kru:'zeɪdəʊ) *n, pl* **cruzadoes** *or* **cruzados** (-dəʊz). a former standard monetary unit of Brazil. [C16: lit., marked with a cross, from *cruzar* to bear a cross; see CRU-SADE]

cruzeiro (kru:'zɛərəʊ) *n, pl* **cruzeiros** (-rəʊz). a former standard monetary unit of Brazil. [Port.: from *cruz* CROSS]

cry (kraɪ) *vb* **cries, crying, cried. 1** (*intr*) to utter inarticulate sounds, esp. when weeping; sob. **2** (*intr*) to shed tears; weep. **3** (*intr*; usually foll. by *out*) to scream or shout in pain, terror, etc. **4** (*tr*; often foll. by *out*) to utter or shout (words of appeal, exclamation, fear, etc.). **5** (*intr*; often foll. by *out*) (of animals, birds, etc.) to utter loud characteristic sounds. **6** (*tr*) to hawk or sell by public announcement: *to cry newspapers.* **7** to announce (something) publicly or in the streets. **8** (*intr*; foll. by *for*) to clamour or beg. **9 cry for the moon.** to desire the unattainable. **10 cry one's eyes** *or* **heart out.** to weep bitterly. ◆ *n, pl* **cries. 11** the act or sound of crying; a shout, scream, or wail. **12** the characteristic utterance of an animal or bird. **13** a fit of weeping. **14** *Hunting.* the baying of a pack of hounds hunting their quarry by scent. **15 a far cry. 15a** a long way. **15b** something very different. **16 in full cry.** (esp. of a pack of hounds) in hot pursuit of a quarry. ◆ See also **cry down, cry off,** etc. [C13: from OF *crier*, from L *quirītāre* to call for help]

crybaby ('kraɪ,beɪbɪ) *n, pl* **crybabies.** a person, esp. a child, given to frequent crying or complaint.

cry down *vb* (*tr, adv*) to belittle; disparage.

crying ('kraɪɪŋ) *adj* (*prenominal*) notorious; lamentable (esp. in **crying shame**).

cryo- *combining form.* cold or freezing: *cryogenics.* [from Gk *kruos* icy cold, frost]

cryobiology (,kraɪəʊbaɪ'ɒlədʒɪ) *n* the biology of the effects of very low temperatures on organisms.
► **,cryobi'ologist** *n*

cry off *vb* (*intr*) *Inf.* to withdraw from or cancel (an agreement or arrangement).

cryogen ('kraɪədʒən) *n* a substance used to produce low temperatures; a freezing mixture.

cryogenics (,kraɪə'dʒɛnɪks) *n* (*functioning as sing*) the branch of physics concerned with very low temperatures and the phenomena occurring at these temperatures.
► **,cryo'genic** *adj*

cryolite ('kraɪə,laɪt) *n* a white or colourless fluoride of sodium and aluminium: used in the production of aluminium, glass, and enamel. Formula: Na_3AlF_6.

cryonics (kraɪ'ɒnɪks) *n* (*functioning as sing*) the practice of freezing a human corpse in the hope of restoring it to life later.

cryoprecipitate (ˌkraɪəʊprɪˈsɪpɪtɪt) n a precipitate obtained by controlled thawing of a previously frozen substance. Factor VIII, for treating haemophilia, is often obtained as a cryoprecipitate from frozen blood.

cryostat ('kraɪəˌstæt) n an apparatus for maintaining a constant low temperature.

cryosurgery (ˌkraɪəʊˈsɜːdʒərɪ) n surgery involving quick freezing for therapeutic benefit.

cry out vb (intr, adv) 1 to scream or shout aloud, esp. in pain, terror, etc. 2 (often foll. by for) Inf. to demand in an obvious manner.

crypt (krɪpt) n a vault or underground chamber, esp. beneath a church, often used as a chapel, burial place, etc. [C18: from L crypta, from Gk kruptē vault, secret place, ult. from kruptein to hide]

cryptanalysis (ˌkrɪptəˈnælɪsɪs) n the study of codes and ciphers; cryptography. [C20: from CRYPTO- + ANALYSIS]
  ▶ **cryptanalytic** (ˌkrɪptænəˈlɪtɪk) adj ▶ **crypt'analyst** n

cryptic ('krɪptɪk) adj 1 hidden; secret. 2 esoteric or obscure in meaning. 3 (of coloration) effecting camouflage or concealment. [C17: from LL crypticus, from Gk kruptikos, from kruptos concealed; see CRYPT]
  ▶ **'cryptically** adv

crypto- or before a vowel **crypt-** combining form. secret, hidden, or concealed. [NL, from Gk kruptos hidden, from kruptein to hide]

cryptocrystalline (ˌkrɪptəʊˈkrɪstəlaɪn) adj (of rocks) composed of crystals visible only under a polarizing microscope.

cryptogam ('krɪptəʊˌgæm) n (in former plant classification schemes) any organism that does not produce seeds, including algae, fungi, mosses, and ferns. [C19: from NL Cryptogamia, from CRYPTO- + Gk gamos marriage]
  ▶ ˌcrypto'gamic or cryptogamous (krɪp'tɒgəməs) adj

cryptograph ('krɪptəʊˌgrɑːf) n 1 something written in code or cipher. 2 a code using secret symbols (**cryptograms**).

cryptography (krɪp'tɒgrəfɪ) n the science or study of analysing and deciphering codes, ciphers, etc. Also called: **cryptanalysis**.
  ▶ **cryp'tographer** or **cryp'tographist** n ▶ **cryptographic** (ˌkrɪptə'græfɪk) or ˌcrypto'graphical adj ▶ ˌcrypto'graphically adv

crystal ('krɪstᵊl) n 1 a solid, such as quartz, with a regular shape in which plane faces intersect at definite angles. 2 a single grain of a crystalline substance. 3 anything resembling a crystal, such as a piece of cut glass. 4a a highly transparent and brilliant type of glass. 4b (as modifier): a crystal chandelier. 5 something made of or resembling crystal. 6 crystal glass articles collectively. 7 Electronics. 7a a crystalline element used in certain electronic devices as a detector, oscillator, etc. 7b (as modifier): crystal pick-up. 8 a transparent cover for the face of a watch. 9 (modifier) of or relating to a crystal or the regular atomic arrangement of crystals: crystal structure. ◆ adj 10 resembling crystal; transparent: crystal water. [OE cristalla, from L crystallum, from Gk krustallos ice, crystal, from krustainein to freeze]

crystal ball n the glass globe used in crystal gazing.

crystal class n Crystallography. any of 32 possible types of crystals, classified according to their rotational symmetry about axes through a point. Also called: **point group**.

crystal detector n Electronics. a demodulator, used esp. in early radio receivers, incorporating a semiconductor crystal.

crystal gazing n 1 the act of staring into a crystal ball supposedly in order to arouse visual perceptions of the future, etc. 2 the act of trying to foresee or predict.
  ▶ **crystal gazer** n

crystal healing n (in alternative therapy) the use of the supposed power of crystals to affect the human energy field.

crystal lattice n the regular array of points about which the atoms, ions, or molecules composing a crystal are centred.

crystalline ('krɪstəˌlaɪn) adj 1 having the characteristics or structure of crystals. 2 consisting of or containing crystals. 3 made of or like crystal; transparent; clear.

crystalline lens n a biconvex transparent elastic lens in the eye.

crystallize or **crystallise** ('krɪstəˌlaɪz) vb **crystallizes**, **crystallizing**, **crystallized** or **crystallises**, **crystallising**, **crystallised**. 1 to form or cause to form crystals; assume or cause to assume a crystalline form or structure. 2 to coat or become coated with sugar. 3 to give a definite form or expression to (an idea, argument, etc.) or (of an idea, argument, etc.) to assume a definite form.
  ▶ **'crystal,lizable** or **'crystal,lisable** adj ▶ ˌcrystalli'zation or ˌcrystalli'sation n

crystallo- or before a vowel **crystall-** combining form. crystal: crystallography.

crystallography (ˌkrɪstə'lɒgrəfɪ) n the science of crystal structure.
  ▶ **crystal'lographer** n ▶ **crystallographic** (ˌkrɪstələʊ-'græfɪk) adj

crystalloid ('krɪstəˌlɔɪd) adj 1 resembling or having the properties of a crystal. ◆ n 2 a substance that in solution can pass through a semipermeable membrane.

Crystal Palace ★ n a building of glass and iron designed by Joseph Paxton to house the Great Exhibition of 1851. Erected in Hyde Park, London, it was moved to Sydenham (1852–53): destroyed by fire in 1936.

crystal set n an early form of radio receiver having a crystal detector.

cry up vb (tr, adv) to praise highly; extol.

Cs the chemical symbol for caesium.

CS abbrev. for: 1 Also: **cs**. capital stock. 2 chartered surveyor. 3 Christian Science. 4 Civil Service. 5 Also: **cs**. Court of Session.

CSA (in Britain) abbrev. for Child Support Agency.

csc abbrev. for cosecant.

CSC abbrev. for Civil Service Commission.

CSE (in Britain) abbrev. for Certificate of Secondary Education; a former examination the first grade pass of which was an equivalent to a GCE O level.

CSEU abbrev. for Confederation of Shipbuilding and Engineering Unions.

CSF abbrev. for: 1 cerebrospinal fluid. 2 Immunol. colony-stimulating factor.

CS gas n a gas causing tears, salivation, and painful breathing, used in civil disturbances. [C20: from the surname initials of its US inventors, Ben Carson and Roger Staughton]

CSIRO (in Australia) abbrev. for Commonwealth Scientific and Industrial Research Organization.

CSM (in Britain) abbrev. for Company Sergeant-Major.

C-spanner n a sickle-shaped spanner having a projection at the end of the curve, used for turning large narrow nuts that have an indentation into which the projection on the spanner fits.

CST (in the US and Canada) abbrev. for Central Standard Time.

CSU abbrev. for Civil Service Union.

ct abbrev. for: 1 carat. 2 cent. 3 court.

CTC (in Britain) abbrev. for city technology college.

ctenophore ('tenəˌfɔː, 'tiːnə-) n any marine invertebrate of the phylum Ctenophora, whose body bears eight rows of fused cilia, for locomotion. [C19: from NL ctenophorus, from Gk kteno-, kteis comb + -PHORE]

ctn abbrev. for cotangent.

CT scanner n computerized tomography scanner: an X-ray machine that can produce multiple cross-sectional images of the soft tissues (**CT scans**). Former name: **CAT scanner**.

CTT abbrev. for Capital Transfer Tax.

CTV abbrev. for Canadian Television (Network Limited).

Cu the chemical symbol for copper. [from LL cuprum]

★ people and places

cu. *abbrev. for* cubic.

cub (kʌb) *n* **1** the young of certain animals, such as the lion, bear, etc. **2** a young or inexperienced person. ◆ *vb* **cubs, cubbing, cubbed. 3** to give birth to (cubs). [C16: ?from ON *kubbi* young seal]
▶ **'cubbish** *adj*

Cub (kʌb) *n* short for **Cub Scout.**

Cuba ★ ('kju:bə) *n* a republic and the largest island in the Caribbean, at the entrance to the Gulf of Mexico: became a Spanish colony after its discovery by Columbus in 1492; gained independence after the Spanish-American War of 1898 but remained subject to US influence until declared a people's republic under Castro in 1960; subject of an international crisis in 1962, when the US blockaded the island in order to compel the Soviet Union to dismantle its nuclear missile base. Sugar comprises about 80 per cent of total exports, but the economy was devastated by loss of trade following the collapse of the Soviet Union. Language: Spanish. Religion: nonreligious majority. Currency: peso. Capital: Havana. Pop.: 11 190 000 (1997). Area: 110 922 sq. km (42 827 sq. miles).
▶ **'Cuban** *adj, n*

cubby ('kʌbɪ) *n, pl* **cubbies.** *Austral.* a small room or enclosed area, esp. one used as a child's play area. Also: **cubbyhole, cubby-house.**

cubbyhole ('kʌbɪ,həʊl) *n* a small enclosed space or room. [C19: from dialect *cub* cattle pen]

cube (kju:b) *n* **1** a solid having six plane square faces in which the angle between two adjacent sides is a right angle. **2** the product of three equal factors. **3** something in the form of a cube. ◆ *vb* **cubes, cubing, cubed. 4** to raise (a number or quantity) to the third power. **5** (*tr*) to make, shape, or cut (something) into cubes. [C16: from L *cubus* die, cube, from Gk *kubos*]
▶ **'cuber** *n*

cubeb ('kju:bɛb) *n* **1** a SE Asian treelike climbing plant. **2** its spicy fruit, dried and used as a stimulant and diuretic and sometimes smoked in cigarettes. [C14: from OF *cubebe*, from Med. L *cubēba*, from Ar. *kubābah*]

cube root *n* the number or quantity whose cube is a given number or quantity: 2 is the cube root of 8 (usually written $^3\sqrt{8}$ or $8^{1/3}$).

cubic ('kju:bɪk) *adj* **1** having the shape of a cube. **2a** having three dimensions. **2b** denoting or relating to a linear measure that is raised to the third power: *a cubic metre.* **3** *Maths.* of, relating to, or containing a variable to the third power or a term in which the sum of the exponents of the variables is three.
▶ **'cubical** *adj*

cubicle ('kju:bɪk°l) *n* an enclosed compartment, screened for privacy, as in a dormitory, shower, etc. [C15: from L *cubiculum,* from *cubāre* to lie down]

cubic measure *n* a system of units for the measurement of volumes.

cubiform ('kju:bɪ,fɔ:m) *adj* having the shape of a cube.

cubism ('kju:bɪzəm) *n* (*often cap.*) a French school of art, initiated in 1907 by Picasso and Braque, which amalgamated viewpoints of natural forms into a multifaceted surface of geometrical planes.
▶ **'cubist** *adj, n* ▶ **cu'bistic** *adj*

cubit ('kju:bɪt) *n* an ancient measure of length based on the length of the forearm. [C14: from L *cubitum* elbow, cubit]

cuboid ('kju:bɔɪd) *adj also* **cuboidal** (kju:'bɔɪd°l). **1** shaped like a cube; cubic. **2** of or denoting the cuboid bone. ◆ *n* **3** the cubelike bone of the foot. **4** *Maths.* a geometric solid whose six faces are rectangles.

Cub Scout *or* **Cub** *n* a member of the junior branch of the Scout Association.

Cuchulain, Cuchulainn, *or* **Cuchullain** ★ (ku:'kʌlɪn, kʊ'xʊlɪn) *n Celtic myth.* a legendary hero of Ulster.

cucking stool ('kʌkɪŋ) *n History.* a stool to which suspected witches, scolds, etc., were tied and pelted or ducked into water. [C13 *cucking stol,* lit.: defecating chair, from *cukken* to defecate]

cuckold ('kʌkəld) *n* **1** a man whose wife has committed adultery. ◆ *vb* **2** (*tr*) to make a cuckold of. [C1. *cukeweld,* from OF *cucuault,* from *cucu* CUCKOO; ? an allusion to cuckoos that lay eggs in the nests of other birds]
▶ **'cuckoldry** *n*

cuckoo ('kʊku:) *n, pl* **cuckoos. 1** any bird of the family Cuculidae, having pointed wings and a long tail. Many species, including the **European cuckoo,** lay their eggs in the nests of other birds and have a two-note call. **2** *Inf.* an insane or foolish person. ◆ *adj* **3** *Inf.* insane or foolish ◆ *interj* **4** an imitation or representation of the call of a cuckoo. ◆ *vb* **cuckoos, cuckooing, cuckooed. 5** (*intr*) to make the sound imitated by the word *cuckoo.* [C13. from OF *cucu,* imit.]

cuckoo clock *n* a clock in which a mechanical cuckoo pops out with a sound like a cuckoo's call when the clock strikes.

cuckoopint ('kʊku:,paɪnt, -,pɪnt) *n* a European plant with arrow-shaped leaves, a spathe marked with purple a pale purple spadix, and scarlet berries. Also called **lords-and-ladies.**

cuckoo spit *n* a white frothy mass on the stems and leaves of many plants, produced by froghopper larvae.

cucumber ('kju:,kʌmbə) *n* **1** a creeping plant cultivated in many forms for its edible fruit. **2** the cylindrical fruit of this plant, which has hard thin green rind and white crisp flesh. [C14: from L *cucumis,* from ?]

cucurbit (kju:'kɜ:bɪt) *n* any of a family of creeping flowering plants that includes the pumpkin, cucumber, and gourds. [C14: from OF, from L *cucurbita* gourd, cup]
▶ **cu,curbi'taceous** *adj*

cud (kʌd) *n* **1** partially digested food regurgitated from the first stomach of ruminants to the mouth for a second chewing. **2 chew the cud.** to reflect or think over something. [OE *cudu,* from *cwidu* what has been chewed]

cuddle ('kʌd°l) *vb* **cuddles, cuddling, cuddled. 1** to hold close or (of two people, etc.) to hold each other close, as for affection or warmth; hug. **2** (*intr;* foll. by *up*) to curl o snuggle up into a comfortable or warm position. ◆ *n* **3** a close embrace, esp. when prolonged. [C18: from ?]
▶ **'cuddlesome** *adj* ▶ **'cuddly** *adj*

cuddy ('kʌdɪ) *n, pl* **cuddies.** a small cabin in a boat. [C17 ?from Du. *kajute*]

cudgel ('kʌdʒəl) *n* **1** a short stout stick used as a weapon **2 take up the cudgels.** (often foll. by *for* or *on behalf of*) to join in a dispute, esp. to defend oneself or another. ◆ *vb* **cudgels, cudgelling, cudgelled** *or US* **cudgels, cudgeling, cud geled. 3** (*tr*) to strike with a cudgel. **4 cudgel one's brains.** to think hard. [OE *cycgel*]

cudgerie ('kʌdʒərɪ) *n Austral.* any of various large rain forest trees, such as the pink poplar or blush cudgerie with pink wood. [from Abor.]

Cudlipp ★ ('kʌdlɪp) *n* **Hugh,** Baron. 1913–98, British newspaper editor, a pioneer of tabloid journalism.

cudweed ('kʌd,wi:d) *n* any of various temperate woolly plants having clusters of whitish or yellow button-like flowers.

cue[1] (kju:) *n* **1a** (in the theatre, films, music, etc.) anything that serves as a signal to an actor, musician, etc., to follow with specific lines or action. **1b on cue.** at the right moment. **2** a signal or reminder to do something. ◆ *vb* **cues, cueing, cued. 3** (*tr*) to give a cue or cues to (an actor) **4** (usually foll. by *in* or *into*) to signal (to something o somebody) at a specific moment in a musical or dramatic performance. [C16: prob. from name of the lette *q,* used in an actor's script to represent L *quando* when]

cue[2] (kju:) *n* **1** *Billiards, etc.* a long tapered shaft used to drive the balls. **2** hair caught at the back forming a tail o braid. ◆ *vb* **cues, cueing, cued. 3** to drive (a ball) with a cue. [C18: var. of QUEUE]

cue ball *n* *Billiards, etc.* the ball struck by the cue, as distinguished from the object balls.

Cuernavaca ★ (*Spanish* kwɛrna'βaka) *n* a city in S central Mexico, capital of Morelos state: resort with nearby Cacahuamilpa Caverns. Pop.: 279 187 (1990).

cuesta ('kwɛstə) *n* a long low ridge with a steep scarp slope and a gentle back slope. [Sp.: shoulder, from L *costa* side, rib]

cuff[1] (kʌf) *n* **1** the end of a sleeve, sometimes turned back. **2** the part of a glove that extends past the wrist. **3** the US, Canad., and Austral. name for **turn-up** (sense 4). **4 off the cuff.** *Inf.* improvised; extemporary. [C14 *cuffe* glove, from ?]

cuff[2] (kʌf) *vb* **1** (*tr*) to strike with an open hand. ♦ *n* **2** a blow of this kind. [C16: from ?]

cuff link *n* one of a pair of linked buttons, used to join the buttonholes on the cuffs of a shirt.

Cuiabá *or* **Cuyabá** ★ (*Portuguese* kuia'ba) *n* **1** a port in W Brazil, capital of Mato Grosso state, on the Cuibá River. Pop.: 167 894 (1980). **2** a river in SW Brazil, rising on the Mato Grosso plateau and flowing southwest into the São Lourenço River. Length: 483 km (300 miles).

cui bono *Latin*. (kwi: 'bəʊnəʊ) for whose benefit? for what purpose?

cuirass (kwɪ'ræs) *n* **1** a piece of armour covering the chest and back. ♦ *vb* **2** (*tr*) to equip with a cuirass. [C15: from F *cuirasse*, from LL *coriacea*, from *coriaceus* made of leather]

cuirassier (ˌkwɪərə'sɪə) *n* a mounted soldier, esp. of the 16th century, who wore a cuirass.

Cuisenaire rod (ˌkwɪzə'neə) *n Trademark*. one of a set of rods of various colours and lengths representing different numbers, used to teach arithmetic to young children. [C20: after Emil-Georges *Cuisenaire* (?1891–1976), Belgian educationalist]

cuisine (kwɪ'zi:n) *n* **1** a style or manner of cooking: *French cuisine*. **2** the food prepared by a restaurant, household, etc. [C18: from F, lit.: kitchen, from LL *coquīna*, from L *coquere* to cook]

cuisse (kwɪs) *or* **cuish** (kwɪʃ) *n* a piece of armour for the thigh. [C15: back formation from *cuisses* (pl), from OF *cuisseaux*, from *cuisse* thigh]

Culbertson ★ ('kʌlbəts°n) *n* Ely ('i:laɪ). 1891–1955, US authority on contract bridge.

cul-de-sac ('kʌldəˌsæk, 'kʊl-) *n, pl* **culs-de-sac** *or* **cul-de-sacs. 1** a road with one end blocked off; dead end. **2** an inescapable position. [C18: from F, lit.: bottom of the bag]

-cule *suffix forming nouns*. indicating smallness. [from L *-culus*, dim. suffix]

Culebra Cut ★ (ku:'lebrə) *n* the former name of the **Gaillard Cut.**

culex ('kju:leks) *n, pl* **culices** (-lɪˌsi:z). any mosquito of the genus *Culex*, such as *C. pipiens*, the common mosquito. [C15: from L: midge, gnat]

Culham ★ ('kʌləm) *n* a village in S central England, in Oxfordshire: site of the UK centre for thermonuclear reactor research and of the Joint European Torus (JET).

Culiacán ★ (*Spanish* kulja'kan) *n* a city in NW Mexico, capital of Sinaloa state. Pop.: 415 046 (1990).

culinary ('kʌlɪnərɪ) *adj* of, relating to, or used in the kitchen or in cookery. [C17: from L *culīnārius*, from *culīna* kitchen]
▶ **'culinarily** *adv*

cull (kʌl) *vb* (*tr*) **1** to choose or gather the best or required examples of. **2** to take out (an animal, esp. an inferior one) from a herd or group. **3** to reduce the size of (a herd, etc.) by killing a proportion of its members. **4** to gather (flowers, fruit, etc.). ♦ *n* **5** the act or product of culling. **6** an inferior animal taken from a herd or group. [C15: from OF *coillir* to pick, from L *colligere*; see COLLECT[1]]
▶ **'culler** *n*

Culloden ★ (kə'lɒd°n) *n* a moor near Inverness in N Scotland: site of a battle in 1746 in which government troops under the Duke of Cumberland defeated the Jacobites under Prince Charles Edward Stuart.

culm[1] (kʌlm) *n Mining*. **1** coal-mine waste. **2** inferior anthracite. [C14: prob. rel. to COAL]

culm[2] (kʌlm) *n* the hollow jointed stem of a grass or sedge. [C17: from L *culmus* stalk; see HAULM]

culminate ('kʌlmɪˌneɪt) *vb* **culminates, culminating, culminated. 1** (when *intr*, usually foll. by *in*) to reach or bring to

a final or climactic stage. **2** (*intr*) (of a celestial body) to cross the meridian. [C17: from LL *culmināre* to reach the highest point, from L *culmen* top]
▶ **'culminant** *adj*

culmination (ˌkʌlmɪ'neɪʃən) *n* **1** the final or highest point. **2** the act of culminating. **3** *Astron*. the highest or lowest altitude attained by a heavenly body as it crosses the meridian.

culottes (kju:'lɒts) *pl n* women's flared trousers cut to look like a skirt. [C20: from F, lit.: breeches, from *cul* bottom]

culpable ('kʌlpəb°l) *adj* deserving censure; blameworthy. [C14: from OF *coupable*, from L *culpābilis*, from *culpāre* to blame, from *culpa* fault]
▶ ˌculpa'bility *n* ▶ 'culpably *adv*

culpable homicide *n Scots Law*. manslaughter.

Culpeper ★ ('kʌlˌpepə) *n* Nicholas. 1616–54, English herbalist and astrologer.

culprit ('kʌlprɪt) *n* **1** *Law*. a person awaiting trial. **2** the person responsible for a particular offence, misdeed, etc. [C17: from Anglo-F *cul-*, short for *culpable* guilty + *prit* ready, indicating that the prosecution was ready to prove the guilt of the one charged]

cult (kʌlt) *n* **1** a specific system of religious worship. **2** a sect devoted to such a system. **3** a quasi-religious organization using devious psychological techniques to gain and control adherents. **4** intense interest in and devotion to a person, idea, or activity. **5** the person, idea, etc., arousing such devotion. **6** something regarded as fashionable or originated by a particular group; craze. **7** (*modifier*) of, relating to, or characteristic of a cult or cults: *a cult figure; a cult show*. [C17: from L *cultus* cultivation, refinement, from *colere* to till]
▶ **'cultism** *n* ▶ **'cultist** *n*

cultic ('kʌltɪk) *adj* of or relating to a religious cult.

cultish ('kʌltɪʃ) *or* **culty** ('kʌltɪ) *adj* intended to appeal to a small group of fashionable people.

cultivable ('kʌltɪvəb°l) *or* **cultivatable** ('kʌltɪˌveɪtəb°l) *adj* (of land) capable of being cultivated. [C17: from F, from OF *cultiver* to CULTIVATE]
▶ ˌcultiva'bility *n*

cultivar ('kʌltɪˌvɑː) *n* a variety of a plant produced from a natural species and maintained by cultivation. [C20: from CULTI(VATED) + VAR(IETY)]

cultivate ('kʌltɪˌveɪt) *vb* **cultivates, cultivating, cultivated.** (*tr*) **1** to prepare (land or soil) for the growth of crops. **2** to plant, tend, harvest, or improve (plants). **3** to break up (land or soil) with a cultivator or hoe. **4** to improve the mind, body, etc.) as by study, education, or labour. **5** to give special attention to: *to cultivate a friendship*. [C17: from Med. L *cultivāre* to till, from *cultīvus* cultivable, from L *cultus* cultivated, from *colere* to till, toil over]
▶ **'culti,vated** *adj*

cultivation (ˌkʌltɪ'veɪʃən) *n* **1** *Agriculture*. **1a** the cultivating of crops or plants. **1b** the preparation of ground to promote their growth. **2** development, esp. through education, training, etc. **3** culture or sophistication.

cultivator ('kʌltɪˌveɪtə) *n* **1** a farm implement used to break up soil and remove weeds. **2** a person or thing that cultivates.

cultural ('kʌltʃərəl) *adj* **1** of or relating to artistic or social pursuits or events considered valuable or enlightened. **2** of or relating to a culture. **3** obtained by specialized breeding.

culture ('kʌltʃə) *n* **1** the total of the inherited ideas, beliefs, values, and knowledge, which constitute the shared bases of social action. **2** the total range of activities and ideas of a people. **3** a particular civilization at a particular period. **4** the artistic and social pursuits, expression, and tastes valued by a society or class. **5** the enlightenment or refinement resulting from these pursuits. **6** the cultivation of plants to improve stock or to produce new ones. **7** the rearing and breeding of animals, esp. with a view to improving the strain. **8** the act or practice of tilling or cultivating the soil. **9** *Biol*. **9a** the experimental growth of microorganisms in a nutrient substance. **9b** a group of microorganisms grown in this way. ♦ *vb* **cultures, culturing, cultured.** (*tr*) **10** to cultivate

(plants or animals). **11** to grow (microorganisms) in a culture medium. [C15: from OF, from L *cultūra* a cultivating, from *colere* to till; see CULT]
▶ **'culturist** *n*

cultured ('kʌltʃəd) *adj* **1** showing or having good taste, manners, and education. **2** artificially grown or synthesized: *cultured pearls.* **3** treated by a culture of microorganisms.

cultured pearl *n* a pearl induced to grow in the shell of an oyster or clam, by the insertion of a small object.

culture shock *n Sociol.* the feelings of isolation, rejection, etc., experienced when one culture is brought into sudden contact with another.

culture vulture *n Inf.* a person considered to be excessively, and often pretentiously, interested in the arts.

cultus ('kʌltəs) *n, pl* **cultuses** or **culti** (-taɪ). another word for **cult** (sense 1). [C17: from L: a toiling over something, refinement, CULT]

culverin ('kʌlvərɪn) *n* **1** a medium-to-heavy cannon used during the 15th, 16th, and 17th centuries. **2** a medieval musket. [C15: from OF *coulevrine*, from *couleuvre*, from L *coluber* serpent]

culvert ('kʌlvət) *n* **1** a drain or covered channel that crosses under a road, railway, etc. **2** a channel for an electric cable. [C18: from ?]

cum (kʌm) *prep* used between nouns to designate a combined nature: *a kitchen-cum-dining room.* [L: with, together with]

Cumae ★ ('kjuːmiː) *n* the oldest Greek colony in Italy, founded about 750 B.C. near Naples.
▶ **Cu'maean** *adj*

cumber ('kʌmbə) *vb* (*tr*) **1** to obstruct or hinder. **2** *Obs.* to inconvenience. [C13: prob. from OF *combrer* to impede, prevent, from *combre* barrier; see ENCUMBER]

Cumberland[1] ★ ('kʌmbələnd) *n* (until 1974) a county of NW England, now part of Cumbria.

Cumberland[2] ★ ('kʌmbələnd) *n* **William Augustus**, Duke of Cumberland, known as *Butcher Cumberland.* 1721–65, British soldier, younger son of George II, noted for his defeat of Charles Edward Stuart at Culloden (1746) and his subsequent ruthless destruction of Jacobite rebels.

cumbersome ('kʌmbəsəm) or **cumbrous** ('kʌmbrəs) *adj* **1** awkward because of size, weight, or shape. **2** difficult because of extent or complexity: *cumbersome accounts.* [C14: *cumber*, short for ENCUMBER + -SOME[1]]
▶ **'cumbersomeness** or **'cumbrousness** *n*

Cumbria ★ ('kʌmbrɪə) *n* (since 1974) a county of NW England comprising the former counties of Westmorland and Cumberland together with N Lancashire: includes the Lake District mountain area and surrounding coastal lowlands with the Pennine uplands in the extreme east. Administrative centre: Carlisle. Pop.: 490 200 (1994 est.). Area: 6810 sq. km (2629 sq. miles).
▶ **'Cumbrian** *adj, n*

Cumbrian Mountains ★ ('kʌmbrɪən) *pl n* a mountain range in NW England, in Cumbria. Highest peak: Scafell Pike, 978 m (3210 ft).

cumin or **cummin** ('kʌmɪn) *n* **1** an umbelliferous Mediterranean plant with small white or pink flowers. **2** the aromatic seeds (collectively) of this plant, used as a condiment and a flavouring. [C12: from OF, from L *cumīnum*, from Gk *kuminon*, of Semitic origin]

cummerbund ('kʌmə,bʌnd) *n* a wide sash worn round the waist, esp. with a dinner jacket. [C17: from Hindi *kamarband*, from Persian, from *kamar* loins, waist + *band* band]

Cummings ★ ('kʌmɪŋz) *n* **Edward Estlin**, (preferred typographical representation of name *e. e. cummings*). 1894–1962, US poet.

cum new *adv, adj* (of shares, etc.) with the right to take up any scrip issue or rights issue. Cf. **ex new.**

cumquat ('kʌmkwɒt) *n* a variant spelling of **kumquat.**

cumulate *vb* ('kjuːmju,leɪt), **cumulates, cumulating, cumulated. 1** to accumulate. **2** (*tr*) to combine (two or more sequences) into one. ♦ *adj* ('kjuːmjulɪt). **3** heaped up. [C16: from L *cumulāre* from *cumulus* heap]
▶ **,cumu'lation** *n*

cumulative ('kjuːmjulətɪv) *adj* **1** growing in quantity strength, or effect by successive additions. **2** (of dividends or interest) intended to be accumulated. **3** *Statistics.* **3a** (of a frequency) including all values of a variable either below or above a specified value. **3b** (of error) tending to increase as the sample size is increased.
▶ **'cumulatively** *adv* ▶ **'cumulativeness** *n*

cumulonimbus (,kjuːmjuləu'nɪmbəs) *n, pl* **cumulonimbi** (-baɪ) or **cumulonimbuses.** *Meteorol.* a cumulus cloud of great vertical extent, the bottom being dark-coloured indicating rain or hail.

cumulus ('kjuːmjuləs) *n, pl* **cumuli** (-,laɪ). a bulbous or billowing white or dark grey cloud. [C17: from L: mass]
▶ **'cumulous** *adj*

Cunaxa ★ (kjuː'næksə) *n* the site near the lower Euphrates where Artaxerxes II defeated Cyrus the Younger in 401 B.C.

cuneate ('kjuːnɪɪt, -,eɪt) *adj* wedge-shaped. [C19: from L *cuneāre* to make wedge-shaped, from *cuneus* a wedge]
▶ **'cuneately** *adv* ▶ **'cuneal** *adj*

cuneiform ('kjuːnɪ,fɔːm) *adj* **1** Also: **cuneal.** wedge-shaped. **2** of, relating to, or denoting the wedge-shaped characters in several ancient languages of Mesopotamia and Persia. **3** of or relating to a tablet in which this script is employed. ♦ *n* **4** cuneiform characters. [C17: prob. from OF *cunéiforme*, from L *cuneus* wedge]

cunjevoi ('kʌndʒɪ,vɔɪ) *n Austral.* **1** an arum of tropical Asia and Australia, cultivated for its edible rhizome. **2** a sea squirt. Often shortened to **cunjie, cunjy.** [C19: from Abor.]

cunnilingus (,kʌnɪ'lɪŋgəs) or **cunnilinctus** (,kʌnɪ'lɪŋktəs) *n* a sexual activity in which the female genitalia are stimulated by the partner's lips and tongue. Cf. **fellatio.** [C19: from NL, from L *cunnus* vulva + *lingere* to lick]

cunning ('kʌnɪŋ) *adj* **1** crafty and shrewd, esp. in deception. **2** made with or showing skill; ingenious. ♦ *n* **3** craftiness, esp. in deceiving. **4** skill or ingenuity. [OF *cunninde*; rel. to *cunnan* to know (see CAN[1])]
▶ **'cunningly** *adv* ▶ **'cunningness** *n*

Cunningham ★ ('kʌnɪŋhæm) *n* **Merce** (mɜːs). born 1919, US dancer and choreographer. His experimental ballets include *Suit for Five* (1956) and *Travelogue* (1977).

Cunninghame Graham ★ ('kʌnɪŋhəm 'greɪəm) *n* **R(obert) B(ontine).** 1852–1936, Scottish writer and politician: first president (1928) of the Scottish Nationalist Party.

Cunobelinus ★ (,kjuːnəubə'laɪnəs) *n* died ?42 A.D., British ruler of the Catuvellauni tribe (?10–?42); founder of Colchester (?10). Also called: **Cymbeline.**

cunt (kʌnt) *n Taboo.* **1** the female genitals. **2** *Offens. sl.* a woman considered sexually. **3** *Offens. sl.* a mean or obnoxious person. [C13: of Gmc origin; rel. to ON *kunta,* MLow G *kunte*]

cup (kʌp) *n* **1** a small open container, usually having one handle, used for drinking from. **2** the contents of such a container. **3** Also called: **teacup, cupful.** a unit of capacity used in cooking. **4** something resembling a cup. **5** either of two cup-shaped parts of a brassiere. **6** a cup-shaped trophy awarded as a prize. **7** *Brit.* **7a** a sporting contest in which a cup is awarded to the winner. **7b** (*as modifier*): *a cup competition.* **8** a mixed drink with one ingredient as a base: *claret cup.* **9** *Golf.* the hole or metal container in the hole on a green. **10** the chalice or the consecrated wine used in the Eucharist. **11** one's lot in life. **12** in **one's cups.** drunk. **13** one's cup of tea. *Inf.* one's chosen or preferred thing, task, company, etc. ♦ *vb* **cups, cupping, cupped.** (*tr*) **14** to form (something, such as the hands) into the shape of a cup. **15** to put into or as if into a cup. **16** to draw blood to the surface of the body of (a person) by cupping. [OE *cuppe,* from LL *cuppa* cup, alteration of L *cūpa* cask]

cupbearer ('kʌp,beərə) *n* an attendant who fills and serves wine cups, as in a royal household.

cupboard ('kʌbəd) *n* a piece of furniture or a recessed area of a room, with a door concealing storage space.

cupboard love *n* a show of love inspired only by some selfish or greedy motive.

★ people and places

cupcake ('kʌp,keɪk) *n* a small cake baked in a cup-shaped foil or paper case.

cupel ('kju:pᵊl, kju'pɛl) *n* **1** a refractory pot in which gold or silver is refined. **2** a small bowl in which gold and silver are recovered during assaying. ◆ *vb* **cupels, cupelling, cupelled** *or US* **cupels, cupeling, cupeled**. **3** (*tr*) to refine (gold or silver) using a cupel. [C17: from F *coupelle*, dim. of *coupe* CUP]
▷ ,cupel'lation *n*

Cup Final *n* **1** (often preceded by *the*) the annual final of the FA or Scottish Cup soccer competition. **2** (*often not cap.*) the final of any cup competition.

Cupid ★ ('kju:pɪd) *n* **1** the Roman god of love, represented as a winged boy with a bow and arrow. Greek counterpart: **Eros**. **2** (*not cap.*) any similar figure. [C14: from L *Cupīdō*, from *cupīdō* desire, from *cupidus* desirous; see CUPIDITY]

cupidity (kju:'pɪdɪtɪ) *n* strong desire, esp. for wealth; greed. [C15: from L *cupiditās*, from *cupidus* eagerly desiring, from *cupere* to long for]

cupola ('kju:pələ) *n* **1** a roof or ceiling in the form of a dome. **2** a small structure, usually domed, on the top of a roof or dome. **3** a protective dome for a gun on a warship. **4** a furnace in which iron is remelted. [C16: from It., from LL *cūpula* a small cask, from L *cūpa* tub]
▷ 'cupo,lated *adj*

cuppa *or* **cupper** ('kʌpə) *n Brit. inf.* a cup of tea.

cupping ('kʌpɪŋ) *n Med.* formerly, the use of an evacuated glass cup to draw blood to the surface of the skin for blood-letting.

cupreous ('kju:prɪəs) *adj* **1** of, containing, or resembling copper. **2** of the colour of copper. [C17: from LL *cupreus*, from *cuprum* COPPER¹]

cupressus (kə'presəs) *n* any evergreen tree of the genus *Cupressus*.

cupric ('kju:prɪk) *adj* of or containing copper in the divalent state. [C18: from LL *cuprum* copper]

cupriferous (kju:'prɪfərəs) *adj* (of a substance such as an ore) containing or yielding copper.

cupro-, cupri-, *or before a vowel* **cupr-** *combining form.* indicating copper. [from L *cuprum*]

cupronickel (,kju:prəʊ'nɪkᵊl) *n* any copper alloy containing up to 40 per cent nickel: used in coins, condenser tubes, etc.

cuprous ('kju:prəs) *adj* of or containing copper in the monovalent state.

cup tie *n Sport.* an eliminating match or round between two teams in a cup competition.

cupule ('kju:pju:l) *n Biol.* a cup-shaped part or structure. [C19: from LL *cūpula*; see CUPOLA]

cur (kɜ:) *n* **1** any vicious dog, esp. a mongrel. **2** a despicable or cowardly person. [C13: from *kurdogge*; prob. rel. to ON *kurra* to growl]

curable ('kjʊərəbᵊl) *adj* capable of being cured.
▷ ,cura'bility *or* 'curableness *n*

Curaçao ★ (,kjʊərə'səʊ) *n* **1** an island in the Caribbean, the largest in the Netherlands Antilles. Capital: Willemstad. Pop.: 149 376 (1994 est.). Area: 444 sq. km (171 sq. miles). **2** an orange-flavoured liqueur originally made there.

curacy ('kjʊərəsɪ) *n, pl* **curacies.** the office or position of a curate.

curare *or* **curari** (kju'rɑ:rɪ) *n* **1** black resin obtained from certain tropical South American trees, which causes muscular paralysis: used medicinally as a muscle relaxant and by South American Indians as an arrow poison. **2** any of various trees from which this resin is obtained. [C18: from Port. & Sp., from Carib *kurari*]

curassow ('kjʊərə,səʊ) *n* any of various ground-nesting birds of S North, Central, and South America, having long legs and tail and a crest of curled feathers. [C17: anglicized from CURAÇAO (island)]

curate ('kjʊərɪt) *n* **1** a clergyman appointed to assist a parish priest. **2** *Irish.* an assistant barman. [C14: from Med. L *cūrātus*, from *cūra* spiritual oversight, CURE]

curate's egg *n* something that has good and bad parts.

[C20: derived from a cartoon in *Punch* (Nov., 1895) in which a timid curate, who has been served a bad egg while breakfasting with his bishop, says that parts of the egg are excellent]

curative ('kjʊərətɪv) *adj* **1** able or tending to cure. ◆ *n* **2** anything able to heal or cure.
▷ 'curatively *adv* ▷ 'curativeness *n*

curator (kjʊə'reɪtə) *n* the administrative head of a museum, art gallery, etc. [C14: from L: one who cares, from *cūrāre* to care for, from *cūra* care]
▷ curatorial (,kjʊərə'tɔ:rɪəl) *adj* ▷ cu'rator,ship *n*

curb (kɜ:b) *n* **1** something that restrains or holds back. **2** any enclosing framework, such as a wall around the top of a well. **3** *Also called:* **curb bit.** a horse's bit with an attached chain or strap, which checks the horse. ◆ *vb* (*tr*) **4** to control with or as if with a curb; restrain. ◆ *See also* **kerb.** [C15: from OF *courbe* curved piece of wood or metal, from L *curvus* curved]

curcuma ('kɜ:kjumə) *n* any tropical Asian tuberous plant of the genus *Curcuma*, such as *C. longa*, which is the source of turmeric. [C17: from NL, from Ar. *kurkum* turmeric]

curd (kɜ:d) *n* **1** (*often pl*) a substance formed from the coagulation of milk, used in making cheese or eaten as a food. **2** something similar in consistency. ◆ *vb* **3** to turn into or become curd. [C15: from earlier *crud*, from ?]
▷ 'curdy *adj*

curdle ('kɜ:dᵊl) *vb* **curdles, curdling, curdled.** **1** to turn or cause to turn into curd. **2 curdle someone's blood.** to fill someone with fear. [C16 (*crudled*, p.p.): from CURD]

cure (kjʊə) *vb* **cures, curing, cured.** **1** (*tr*) to get rid of (an ailment or problem); heal. **2** (*tr*) to restore to health or good condition. **3** (*intr*) to bring about a cure. **4** (*tr*) to preserve (meat, fish, etc.) by salting, smoking, etc. **5** (*tr*) **5a** to treat or finish (a substance) by chemical or physical means. **5b** to vulcanize (rubber). **6** (*tr*) to assist the hardening of (concrete, mortar, etc.) by keeping it moist. ◆ *n* **7** a return to health. **8** any course of medical therapy, esp. one proved effective. **9** a means of restoring health or improving a situation, etc. **10** the spiritual and pastoral charge of a parish. **11** a process or method of preserving meat, fish, etc. [(n) C13: from OF, from L *cūra* care; in ecclesiastical sense, from Med. L *cūra* spiritual charge; (vb) C14: from OF *curer*, from L *cūrāre* to attend to, heal, from *cūra* care]
▷ 'cureless *adj* ▷ 'curer *n*

curé ('kjʊəreɪ) *n* a parish priest in France. [F, from Med. L *cūrātus*; see CURATE]

cure-all *n* something reputed to cure all ailments.

curettage (,kjʊəri'tɑ:ʒ, kjʊə'retɪdʒ) *or* **curettement** (kjʊə'retmənt) *n* the process of using a curette. See also **D** and **C.**

curette *or* **curet** (kjʊə'ret) *n* **1** a surgical instrument for removing dead tissue, growths, etc., from the walls of body cavities. ◆ *vb* **curettes** *or* **curets, curetting, curetted.** **2** (*tr*) to scrape or clean with such an instrument. [C18: from F *curette*, from *curer* to heal, make clean; see CURE]

curfew ('kɜ:fju:) *n* **1** an official regulation setting restrictions on movement, esp. after a specific time at night. **2** the time set as a deadline by such a regulation. **3** (in medieval Europe) **3a** the ringing of a bell to prompt people to extinguish fires and lights. **3b** the time at which the curfew bell was rung. **3c** the bell itself. [C13: from OF *cuevrefeu*, lit.: cover the fire]

curia ('kjʊərɪə) *n, pl* **curiae** (-rɪ,iː). **1** (*sometimes cap.*) the papal court and government of the Roman Catholic Church. **2** (in the Middle Ages) a court held in the king's name. [C16: from L, from OL *coviria* (unattested), from co- + *vir* man]
▷ 'curial *adj*

curie ('kjʊərɪ, -riː) *n* a unit of radioactivity equal to 3.7×10^{10} disintegrations per second. [C20: after Pierre CURIE]

Curie ★ ('kjʊərɪ, -riː; *French* kyri) *n* **1 Marie** (mari). 1867–1934, French physicist, born in Poland: discovered and isolated radium and polonium. She shared a Nobel prize for physics (1903) with her husband and Henri Becquerel, and was awarded a Nobel prize for chemistry

(1911). **2** her husband, **Pierre** (pjɛr). 1859–1906, French physicist.

curio ('kjʊərɪˌəʊ) *n, pl* **curios**. a small article valued as a collector's item, esp. something unusual. **[C19**: shortened from CURIOSITY]

curiosity (ˌkjʊərɪ'ɒsɪtɪ) *n, pl* **curiosities**. **1** an eager desire to know; inquisitiveness. **2** the quality of being curious; strangeness. **3** something strange or fascinating.

curious ('kjʊərɪəs) *adj* **1** eager to learn; inquisitive. **2** overinquisitive; prying. **3** interesting because of oddness or novelty. **[C14**: from L *cūriōsus* taking pains over something, from *cūra* care]
▶ **'curiously** *adv* ▶ **'curiousness** *n*

Curitiba ★ (ˌkʊərɪ'tiːbə) *n* a city in SE Brazil, capital of Paraná state: seat of the University of Paraná (1946). Pop.: 841 882 (1991).

curium ('kjʊərɪəm) *n* a silvery-white metallic transuranic element artificially produced from plutonium. Symbol: Cm; at. no.: 96; half-life of most stable isotope, ^{247}Cm: 1.6×10^7 years. **[C20**: NL, after Pierre and Marie CURIE]

curl (kɜːl) *vb* **1** (*intr*) (esp. of hair) to grow into curves or ringlets. **2** (*tr*; sometimes foll. by *up*) to twist or roll (esp. hair) into coils or ringlets. **3** (often foll. by *up*) to become or cause to become spiral-shaped or curved. **4** (*intr*) to move in a curving or twisting manner. **5** (*intr*) to play the game of curling. **6 curl one's lip**. to show contempt, as by raising a corner of the lip. ◆ *n* **7** a curve or coil of hair. **8** a curved or spiral shape or mark. **9** the act of curling or state of being curled. ◆ See also **curl up**. **[C14**: prob. from MDu. *crullen* to curl]

curler ('kɜːlə) *n* **1** any of various pins, clasps, or rollers used to curl or wave hair. **2** a person or thing that curls. **3** a person who plays curling.

curlew ('kɜːljuː) *n* any of certain large shore birds of Europe and Asia. They have a long downward-curving bill and occur in northern and arctic regions. **[C14**: from OF *corlieu*, ? imit.]

curlicue ('kɜːlɪˌkjuː) *n* an intricate ornamental curl or twist. **[C19**: from CURLY + CUE^2]

curling ('kɜːlɪŋ) *n* a game played on ice, esp. in Scotland, in which heavy stones with handles (**curling stones**) are slid towards a target (**tee**).

curling tongs *pl n* a metal scissor-like device that is heated, so that strands of hair may be twined around it in order to form curls. Also called: **curling iron, curling irons, curling pins**.

curl up *vb* (*adv*) **1** (*intr*) to adopt a reclining position with the legs close to the body and the back rounded. **2** to become or cause to become spiral-shaped or curved. **3** (*intr*) to retire to a quiet cosy setting: *to curl up with a good novel*. **4** *Brit. inf.* to be or cause to be embarrassed or disgusted (esp. in **curl up and die**).

curly ('kɜːlɪ) *adj* **curlier, curliest**. **1** tending to curl; curling. **2** having curls. **3** (of timber) having waves in the grain.
▶ **'curliness** *n*

curmudgeon (kɜː'mʌdʒən) *n* a surly or miserly person. **[C16**: from ?]
▶ **cur'mudgeonly** *adj*

Curnow ★ (kɜː'naʊ) *n* **T.A.M.** born 1911, New Zealand poet and anthologist.

currach *or* **curragh** *Gaelic.* ('kʌrəx, 'kʌrə) *n* a Scottish or Irish name for **coracle**. **[C15**: from Irish Gaelic *currach*; Cf. CORACLE]

currajong ('kʌrəˌdʒɒŋ) *n* a variant spelling of **kurrajong**.

currant ('kʌrənt) *n* **1** a small dried seedless grape of the Mediterranean region. **2** any of several mainly N temperate shrubs, esp. redcurrant and blackcurrant. **3** the small acid fruit of any of these plants. **[C16**: shortened from *rayson of Corantte* raisin of Corinth]

currawong ('kʌrəˌwɒŋ) *n* any Australian crowlike songbird of the genus *Strepera*, having black, grey, and white plumage. Also called: **bell-magpie**. **[from Abor.]**

currency ('kʌrənsɪ) *n, pl* **currencies**. **1** a metal or paper medium of exchange in current use in a particular country. **2** general acceptance or circulation; prevalence. **3** the period of time during which something is valid, accepted, or in force. ◆ *adj* **4** *Austral. inf.* native-born as

distinct from immigrant: *a currency lad*. **[C17**: from Med L *currentia*, lit.: a flowing, from L *currere* to run, flow]

current ('kʌrənt) *adj* **1** of the immediate present; in progress. **2** most recent; up-to-date. **3** commonly known, practised, or accepted. **4** circulating and valid at present: *current coins*. ◆ *n* **5** (esp. of water or air) a steady, usually natural, flow. **6** a mass of air, body of water, etc., that has a steady flow in a particular direction. **7** the rate of flow of such a mass. **8** *Physics*. **8a** a flow of electric charge through a conductor. **8b** the rate of flow of this charge. **9** a general trend or drift: *currents of opinion*. **[C13**: from OF *corant*, lit.: running, from *corre* to run, from L *currere*]
▶ **'currently** *adv* ▶ **'currentness** *n*

current account *n* an account at a bank or building society against which cheques may be drawn at any time.

current-cost accounting *n* a method of accounting that values assets at their current replacement cost rather than their original cost. It is often used in times of high inflation. Cf. **historical-cost accounting**.

curricle ('kʌrɪk°l) *n* a two-wheeled open carriage drawn by two horses side by side. **[C18**: from L *curriculum* from *currus* chariot, from *currere* to run]

curriculum (kə'rɪkjʊləm) *n, pl* **curricula** (-lə) *or* **curriculums**. **1** a course of study in one subject at a school or college. **2** a list of all the courses of study offered by a school or college. **3** any programme or plan of activities. **[C19**: from L: course, from *currere* to run]
▶ **cur'ricular** *adj*

curriculum vitae (kə'rɪkjʊləm 'viːtaɪ, 'vaɪtiː) *n, pl* **curricula vitae** (kə'rɪkjʊlə). an outline of a person's educational and professional history, usually prepared for job applications. **[L, lit.: the course of one's life]**

currish ('kɜːrɪʃ) *adj* of or like a cur; rude or bad-tempered.
▶ **'currishly** *adv* ▶ **'currishness** *n*

curry^1 ('kʌrɪ) *n, pl* **curries**. **1** a spicy dish of oriental, esp. Indian, origin that usually consists of meat or fish prepared in a hot piquant sauce. **2** curry seasoning or sauce. **3 give someone curry**. *Austral. sl.* to assault (a person) verbally or physically. ◆ *vb* **curries, currying, curried**. **4** (*tr*) to prepare (food) with curry powder or sauce. **[C16**: from Tamil *kari* sauce, relish]

curry^2 ('kʌrɪ) *vb* **curries, currying, curried**. **1** to beat vigorously, as in order to clean. **2** to dress and finish (leather) after it has been tanned. **3** to groom (a horse). **4 curry favour**. to ingratiate oneself, esp. with superiors. **[C13**: from OF *correer* to make ready]

currycomb ('kʌrɪˌkəʊm) *n* a square comb used for grooming horses.

curry powder *n* a mixture of finely ground pungent spices, such as turmeric, cumin, coriander, ginger, etc., used in making curries.

curse (kɜːs) *n* **1** a profane or obscene expression of anger, disgust, surprise, etc.; oath. **2** an appeal to a supernatural power for harm to come to a specific person, group, etc. **3** harm resulting from an appeal to a supernatural power. **4** something that brings or causes great trouble or harm. **5** (preceded by *the*) *Inf.* menstruation or a menstrual period. ◆ *vb* **curses, cursing, cursed** *or* (*Arch.*) **curst. 6** (*intr*) to utter obscenities or oaths. **7** (*tr*) to abuse (someone) with obscenities or oaths. **8** (*tr*) to invoke supernatural powers to bring harm to (someone or something). **9** (*tr*) to bring harm upon. **[OE *cursian* to curse, from *curs* curse]**
▶ **'curser** *n*

cursed ('kɜːsɪd, kɜːst) *or* **curst** *adj* **1** under a curse. **2** deserving to be cursed; detestable; hateful.
▶ **'cursedly** *adv* ▶ **'cursedness** *n*

cursive ('kɜːsɪv) *adj* **1** of or relating to handwriting in which letters are joined in a flowing style. **2** *Printing*. of or relating to typefaces that resemble handwriting. ◆ *n* **3** a cursive letter or printing type. **[C18**: from Med. L *cursīvus* running, ult. from L *currere* to run]
▶ **'cursively** *adv*

cursor ('kɜːsə) *n* **1** the sliding part of a measuring instrument, esp. on a slide rule. **2** any of various means, typically a flashing bar or underline, of identifying a particular position on a computer screen.

★ people and places

cursorial (kɜːˈsɔːrɪəl) *adj Zool.* adapted for running: *a cursorial skeleton; cursorial birds.*

cursory (ˈkɜːsərɪ) *adj* hasty and usually superficial; quick. [C17: from LL *cursōrius* of running, from L *cursus* a course, from *currere* to run]
▸ **'cursorily** *adv* ▸ **'cursoriness** *n*

curst (kɜːst) *vb* **1** *Arch.* a past tense and past participle of **curse.** ◆ *adj* **2** a variant of **cursed.**

curt (kɜːt) *adj* **1** rudely blunt and brief. **2** short or concise. [C17: from L *curtus* cut short, mutilated]
▸ **'curtly** *adv* ▸ **'curtness** *n*

curtail (kɜːˈteɪl) *vb* (*tr*) to cut short; abridge. [C16: changed (through infl. of TAIL[1]) from obs. *curtal* to dock]
▸ **cur'tailer** *n* ▸ **cur'tailment** *n*

curtain (ˈkɜːt²n) *n* **1** a piece of material that can be drawn across an opening or window, to shut out light or to provide privacy. **2** a barrier to vision, access, or communication. **3** a hanging cloth or similar barrier for concealing all or part of a theatre stage from the audience. **4** (often preceded by *the*) the end of a scene of a play, opera, etc., marked by the fall or closing of the curtain. **5** the rise or opening of the curtain at the start of a performance. ◆ *vb* **6** (*tr*; sometimes foll. by *off*) to shut off or conceal as with a curtain. **7** (*tr*) to provide (a window, etc.) with curtains. [C13: from OF *courtine*, from LL *cortīna* enclosed place, curtain, prob. from L *cohors* courtyard]

curtain call *n* the appearance of performers at the end of a theatrical performance to acknowledge applause.

curtain lecture *n* a scolding or rebuke given in private, esp. by a wife to her husband. [alluding to the curtained beds where such rebukes were once given]

curtain-raiser *n* **1** *Theatre.* a short dramatic piece presented before the main play. **2** any preliminary event.

curtains (ˈkɜːt²nz) *pl n Inf.* death or ruin: the end.

curtain wall *n* a non-load-bearing external wall attached to a framed structure.

Curtin ★ (ˈkɜːtɪn) *n* **John Joseph.** 1885–1945, Australian statesman; prime minister (1941–45).

curtsy *or* **curtsey** (ˈkɜːtsɪ) *n, pl* **curtsies** *or* **curtseys. 1** a formal gesture of greeting and respect made by women, in which the knees are bent and the head slightly bowed. ◆ *vb* **curtsies, curtsying, curtsied** *or* **curtseys, curtseying, curtseyed. 2** (*intr*) to make a curtsy. [C16: var. of COURTESY]

curvaceous (kɜːˈveɪʃəs) *adj Inf.* (of a woman) having a well-rounded body.

curvature (ˈkɜːvətʃə) *n* **1** something curved or a curved part of a thing. **2** any curving of a bodily part. **3** the act of curving or the state or degree of being curved or bent.

curve (kɜːv) *n* **1** a continuously bending line that has no straight parts. **2** something that curves or is curved. **3** the act or extent of curving; curvature. **4** *Maths.* a system of points whose coordinates satisfy a given equation. **5** a line representing data on a graph. ◆ *vb* **curves, curving, curved. 6** to take or cause to take the shape or path of a curve; bend. [C15: from L *curvāre* to bend, from *curvus* crooked]
▸ **'curvedness** *n* ▸ **'curvy** *adj*

curvet (kɜːˈvet) *n* **1** *Dressage.* a low leap with all four feet off the ground. ◆ *vb* **curvets, curvetting, curvetted** *or* **curvets, curveting, curveted. 2** *Dressage.* to make or cause to make such a leap. **3** (*intr*) to prance or frisk about. [C16: from OIt. *corvetta*, from OF *courbette*, from *courber* to bend, from L *curvāre*]

curvilinear (ˌkɜːvɪˈlɪnɪə) *or* **curvilineal** *adj* consisting of, bounded by, or characterized by a curved line.

Curzon ★ (ˈkɜːz²n) *n* **1** Sir **Clifford.** 1907–82, British pianist. **2 George Nathaniel,** 1st Marquis Curzon of Kedleston. 1859–1925, British Conservative statesman; viceroy of India (1898–1905).

Cusack ★ (ˈkjuːsæk) *n* **Cyril (James).** 1910–93, Irish actor.

Cusanus ★ (kjuːˈseɪnəs) *n* **Nicholas.** See **Nicholas of Cusa.**

Cusco ★ (*Spanish* ˈkusko) *n* a variant of **Cuzco.**

cuscus (ˈkʌskʌs) *n, pl* **cuscuses.** any of several large nocturnal phalangers of N Australia, New Guinea, and adjacent islands, having dense fur, prehensile tails, large

eyes, and a yellow nose. [C17: NL, prob. from a native name in New Guinea]

cusec (ˈkjuːsɛk) *n* a unit of flow equal to 1 cubic foot per second. [C20: from *cu(bic foot per) sec(ond)*]

Cush *or* **Kush** ★ (kʌʃ, kuʃ) *n Old Testament.* **1** the son of Ham and brother of Canaan (Genesis 10:6). **2** the country of the supposed descendants of Cush (ancient Ethiopia), comprising approximately Nubia and the modern Sudan, and the territory of southern (or Upper) Egypt.

cushat (ˈkʌʃət) *n* another name for **wood pigeon.** [OE *cūscote;* ? rel. to *scēotan* to shoot]

Cushing ★ (ˈkuʃɪŋ) *n* **Harvey Williams.** 1869–1939, US neurosurgeon: identified a pituitary tumour as a cause of the disease named after him.

cushion (ˈkuʃən) *n* **1** a bag filled with a yielding substance, used for sitting on, leaning against, etc. **2** something resembling a cushion in function or appearance, esp. one to support or pad or to absorb shock. **3** the resilient felt-covered rim of a billiard table. ◆ *vb* (*tr*) **4** to place on or as on a cushion. **5** to provide with cushions. **6** to protect. **7** to lessen or suppress the effects of. **8** to provide with a means of absorbing shock. [C14: from OF *coussin,* from L *culcita* mattress]
▸ **'cushiony** *adj*

cushion plant *n* a type of low-growing plant having many closely spaced short upright shoots, typical of alpine and arctic habitats.

Cushitic (kuˈʃɪtɪk) *n* **1** a group of languages of Somalia, Ethiopia, and adjacent regions. ◆ *adj* **2** of or relating to this group of languages.

cushy (ˈkuʃɪ) *adj* **cushier, cushiest.** *Inf.* easy; comfortable. [C20: from Hindi *khush* pleasant, from Persian *khōsh*]

CUSO (ˈkjuːsəu) *n acronym for* Canadian University Services Overseas; an organization that sends students to work as volunteers in developing countries.

cusp (kʌsp) *n* **1** any of the small elevations on the grinding or chewing surface of a tooth. **2** any of the triangular flaps of a heart valve. **3** a point or pointed end. **4** *Geom.* a point at which two arcs of a curve intersect and at which the two tangents are coincident. **5** *Archit.* a carving at the meeting place of two arcs. **6** *Astron.* either of the points of a crescent moon. **7** *Astrol.* any division between houses or signs of the zodiac. [C16: from L *cuspis* point, pointed end]
▸ **'cuspate** *adj*

cuspid (ˈkʌspɪd) *n* a tooth having one point; canine tooth.

cuspidate (ˈkʌspɪˌdeɪt), **cuspidated,** *or* **cuspidal** (ˈkʌspɪd²l) *adj* **1** having a cusp or cusps. **2** (esp. of leaves) narrowing to a point. [C17: from L *cuspidāre* to make pointed, from *cuspis* a point]

cuspidor (ˈkʌspɪˌdɔː) *n* another name (esp. US) for **spittoon.** [C18: from Port., from *cuspir* to spit, from L *conspuere,* from *spuere* to spit]

cuss (kʌs) *Inf.* ◆ *n* **1** a curse; an oath. **2** a person or animal, esp. an annoying one. ◆ *vb* **3** another word for **curse** (senses 6, 7).

cussed (ˈkʌsɪd) *adj Inf.* **1** another word for **cursed. 2** obstinate. **3** annoying: *a cussed nuisance.*
▸ **'cussedly** *adv* ▸ **'cussedness** *n*

custard (ˈkʌstəd) *n* **1** a baked sweetened mixture of eggs and milk. **2** a sauce made of milk and sugar and thickened with cornflour. [C15: alteration of ME *crustade* kind of pie]

custard apple *n* **1** a West Indian tree. **2** its large heart-shaped fruit, which has a fleshy edible pulp.

custard pie *n* **a** a flat, open pie filled with real or artificial custard, as thrown in slapstick comedy. **b** (*as modifier*): *custard-pie humour.*

Custer ★ (ˈkʌstə) *n* **George Armstrong.** 1839–76, US cavalry general: Civil War hero, killed fighting the Sioux Indians at Little Bighorn, Montana.

custodian (kʌˈstəudɪən) *n* **1** a person who has custody, as of a prisoner, ward, etc. **2** a keeper of an art collection, etc.
▸ **cus'todian,ship** *n*

custody (ˈkʌstədɪ) *n, pl* **custodies. 1** the act of keeping safe

or guarding. **2** the state of being held by the police; arrest. [C15: from L *custōdia*, from *custōs* guard, defender]
▶ **custodial** (kʌ'stəʊdɪəl) *adj*

custom ('kʌstəm) *n* **1** a usual or habitual practice; typical mode of behaviour. **2** the long-established habits or traditions of a society collectively; convention. **3a** a practice which by long-established usage has come to have the force of law. **3b** such practices collectively (esp. in **custom and practice**). **4** habitual patronage, esp. of a shop or business. **5** the customers of a shop or business collectively. ◆ *adj* **6** made to the specifications of an individual customer. ◆ See also **customs**. [C12: from OF *costume*, from L *consuētūdō*, from *consuēscere* to grow accustomed to]

customary ('kʌstəmərɪ, -təmrɪ) *adj* **1** in accordance with custom or habitual practice; usual. **2** *Law*. **2a** founded upon long-continued practices and usage. **2b** (of land) held by custom. ◆ *n, pl* **customaries**. **3** a statement in writing of customary laws and practices.
▶ **'customarily** *adv* ▶ **'customariness** *n*

custom-built *adj* (of cars, houses, etc.) made according to the specifications of an individual buyer.

customer ('kʌstəmə) *n* **1** a person who buys. **2** *Inf*. a person with whom one has dealings.

custom house *n* a government office, esp. at a port, where customs are collected and ships cleared for entry.

customize *or* **customise** ('kʌstə,maɪz) *vb* **customizes, customizing, customized** *or* **customises, customising, customised**. (*tr*) to make (something) according to a customer's individual requirements.

custom-made *adj* (of suits, dresses, etc.) made according to the specifications of an individual buyer.

customs ('kʌstəmz) *n* (*functioning as sing or pl*) **1** duty on imports or exports. **2** the government department responsible for the collection of these duties. **3** the part of a port, airport, etc., where baggage and freight are examined for dutiable goods and contraband.

cut (kʌt) *vb* **cuts, cutting, cut**. **1** to open up or incise (a person or thing) with a sharp edge or instrument. **2** (of a sharp instrument) to penetrate or incise (a person or thing). **3** to divide or be divided with or as if with a sharp instrument. **4** (*intr*) to use an instrument that cuts. **5** (*tr*) to trim or prune by or as if by clipping. **6** (*tr*) to reap or mow (a crop, grass, etc.). **7** (*tr*; sometimes foll. by *out*) to make, form, or shape by cutting. **8** (*tr*) to hollow or dig out; excavate. **9** to strike (an object) sharply. **10** *Cricket*. to hit (the ball) to the off side with a roughly horizontal bat. **11** to hurt the feelings of (a person). **12** (*tr*) *Inf*. to refuse to recognize; snub. **13** (*tr*) *Inf*. to absent oneself from, esp. without permission or in haste: *to cut a class*. **14** (*tr*) to abridge or shorten. **15** (*tr*; often foll. by *down*) to lower, reduce, or curtail. **16** (*tr*) to dilute or weaken: *to cut whisky with water*. **17** (*tr*) to dissolve or break up: *to cut fat*. **18** (when *intr*, foll. by *across* or *through*) to cross or traverse. **19** (*intr*) to make a sharp or sudden change in direction; veer. **20** to grow (teeth) through the gums or (of teeth) to appear through the gums. **21** (*intr*) *Films*. **21a** to call a halt to a shooting sequence. **21b** (foll. by *to*) to move quickly to another scene. **22** *Films*. to edit (film). **23** to switch off (a light, car engine, etc.). **24** (*tr*) to make (a record or tape of a song, performance, etc.). **25** *Cards*. **25a** to divide (the pack) at random into two parts after shuffling. **25b** (*intr*) to pick cards from a spread pack to decide dealer, partners, etc. **26** (*tr*) (of a tool) to bite into (an object). **27 cut a dash**. to make a stylish impression. **28 cut (a person) dead**. *Inf*. to ignore (a person) completely. **29 cut a (good, poor**, etc.) **figure**. to appear or behave in a specified manner. **30 cut and run**. *Inf*. to make a rapid escape. **31 cut both ways**. **31a** to have both good and bad effects. **31b** to affect both sides, as two parties in an argument, etc. **32 cut it fine**. *Inf*. to allow little margin of time, space etc. **33 cut loose**. to free or become freed from restraint, custody, anchorage, etc. **34 cut no ice**. *Inf*. to fail to make an impression. **35 cut one's teeth on**. *Inf*. **35a** to use at an early age or stage. **35b** to practise on. ◆ *adj* **36** detached, divided, or separated by cutting. **37** made, shaped, or fashioned by cutting. **38** reduced or diminished as by cutting: *cut prices*. **39** weakened or diluted. **40** *Brit*. a slang word for **drunk**: *half cut*. **41 cut and dried**. *Inf*. settled or arranged in advance. ◆ *n* **42** the act of cutting. **43** a stroke or incision made by cutting; gash. **44** a piece or part cut off: *a cut of meat*. **45** the edge of anything cut or sliced. **46** a passage, channel, path, etc., cut or hollowed out. **47** an omission or deletion, esp. in a text, film, or play. **48** a reduction in price, salary, etc. **49** a decrease in government finance in a particular department or area. **50** *Inf*. a portion or share. **51** *Inf*. a straw, slip of paper, etc., used in drawing lots. **52** the manner or style in which a thing, esp. a garment, is cut. **53a** *Irish inf*. a person's general appearance: *I didn't like the cut of him*. **53b** *Irish derog*. a dirty or untidy condition: *look at the cut of your shoes*. **54** a direct route; short cut. **55** the US name for **block** (sense 13) **56** *Cricket*. a stroke made with the bat in a roughly horizontal position. **57** *Films*. an immediate transition from one shot to the next. **58** words or an action that hurt another person's feelings. **59** a refusal to recognize an acquaintance; snub. **60** *Brit*. a stretch of water, esp. a canal. **61 a cut above**. *Inf*. superior to; better than. ◆ See also **cut across, cutback**, etc. [C13: prob. from ON]

cut across *vb* (*intr, prep*) **1** to be contrary to ordinary procedure or limitations. **2** to cross or traverse, making a shorter route.

cut and paste *n* a technique used in word processing by which a section of text can be moved within a document.

cutaneous (kju:'teɪnɪəs) *adj* of or relating to the skin [C16: from NL *cutāneus*, from L *cutis* skin]

cutaway ('kʌtə,weɪ) *n* **1** a man's coat cut diagonally from the front waist to the back of the knees. **2a** a drawing or model of a machine, engine, etc., in which part of the casing is omitted to reveal the workings. **2b** (*as modifier*): *a cutaway model*. **3** *Films, television*. a shot separate from the main action of a scene.

cutback ('kʌt,bæk) *n* **1** a decrease or reduction. ◆ *vb* **cut back** (*adv*) **2** (*tr*) to shorten by cutting off the end. **3** (when *intr*, foll. by *on*) to reduce or make a reduction (in).

Cutch ★ (kʌtʃ) *n* a variant spelling of **Kutch**.

cut down *vb* (*adv*) **1** (*tr*) to fell. **2** (when *intr*, often foll. by *on*) to reduce or make a reduction (in). **3** (*tr*) to remake (an old garment) in order to make a smaller one. **4** (*tr*) to kill. **5 cut (a person) down to size**. to reduce in importance or decrease the conceit of (a person).

cute (kju:t) *adj* **1** appealing or attractive, esp. in a pretty way. **2** *Inf*. affecting cleverness or prettiness. **3** clever; shrewd. [C18 (in the sense: clever): shortened from ACUTE]
▶ **'cutely** *adv* ▶ **'cuteness** *n*

cut glass *n* **1a** glass, esp. bowls, vases, etc., decorated by facet-cutting or grinding. **1b** (*as modifier*): *a cut-glass vase*. **2** (*modifier*) (of an accent) upper-class; refined.

Cuthbert ★ ('kʌθbət) *n* **Saint**. ?635–87A.D., English monk; bishop of Lindisfarne. Feast day: March 20.

cuticle ('kju:tɪk°l) *n* **1** dead skin, esp. round the base of a fingernail or toenail. **2** another name for **epidermis**. **3** the protective layer that covers the epidermis in higher plants. **4** the protective layer covering the epidermis of many invertebrates. [C17: from L *cutīcula* dim. of *cutis* skin]
▶ **cuticular** (kju:'tɪkjulə) *adj*

cut in *vb* (*adv*) **1** (*intr*; often foll. by *on*) Also: **cut into**. to break in or interrupt. **2** (*intr*) to interrupt a dancing couple to dance with one of them. **3** (*intr*) (of a driver, motor vehicle, etc.) to draw in front of another vehicle leaving too little space. **4** (*tr*) *Inf*. to allow to have a share. **5** (*intr*) to take the place of a person in a card game.

cutis ('kju:tɪs) *n, pl* **cutes** (-ti:z) *or* **cutises**. *Anat*. a technical name for the **skin**. [C17: from L: skin]

cutlass ('kʌtləs) *n* a curved, one-edged sword formerly used by sailors. [C16: from F *coutelas*, from *coutel* knife, ult. from L *culter* knife]

cutler ('kʌtlə) *n* a person who makes or sells cutlery [C14: from F *coutelier*, ult. from L *culter* knife]

cutlery ('kʌtlərɪ) *n* **1** implements used for eating, such as knives, forks, and spoons. **2** instruments used for cutting. **3** the art or business of a cutler.

★ people and places

cutlet ('kʌtlɪt) *n* **1** a piece of meat taken esp. from the best end of neck of lamb, pork, etc. **2** a flat croquette of minced chicken, lobster, etc. [C18: from OF *costelette*, lit.: a little rib, from *coste* rib, from L *costa*]

cut off *vb* (*tr, adv*) **1** to remove by cutting. **2** to intercept or interrupt something, esp. a telephone conversation. **3** to discontinue the supply of. **4** to bring to an end. **5** to deprive of rights; disinherit: *cut off without a penny*. **6** to sever or separate. **7** to occupy a position so as to prevent or obstruct (a retreat or escape). ◆ *n* **cutoff**. **8a** the act of cutting off; limit or termination. **8b** (*as modifier*): *the cut-off point*. **9** *Chiefly US*. a short cut. **10** a device to terminate the flow of a fluid in a pipe or duct.

cut out *vb* (*adv*) **1** (*tr*) to delete or remove. **2** (*tr*) to shape or form by cutting. **3** (*tr; usually passive*) to suit or equip for: *you're not cut out for this job*. **4** (*intr*) (of an engine, etc.) to cease to operate suddenly. **5** (*intr*) (of an electrical device) to switch off, usually automatically. **6** (*tr*) *Inf.* to oust and supplant (a rival). **7** (*intr*) (of a person) to be excluded from a card game. **8** (*tr*) *Inf.* to cease doing something, esp. something undesirable (esp. in **cut it out**). **9** (*tr*) *Soccer.* to intercept (a pass). **10** (*tr*) to separate (cattle) from a herd. **11** (*tr*) *Austral.* to end or finish: *the road cuts out at the creek*. **12 have one's work cut out**. to have as much work as one can manage. ◆ *n* **cutout**. **13** something that has been or is intended to be cut out from something else. **14** a device that switches off or interrupts an electric circuit, esp. as a safety device. **15** *Austral. sl.* the end of shearing.

cut-price *or esp. US* **cut-rate** *adj* **1** available at prices or rates below the standard price or rate. **2** (*prenominal*) offering goods or services at prices below the standard price.

cutpurse ('kʌt,pɜːs) *n* an archaic word for **pickpocket**.

cutter ('kʌtə) *n* **1** a person or thing that cuts, esp. a person who cuts cloth for clothing. **2** a sailing boat with its mast stepped further aft than that of a sloop. **3** a ship's boat, powered by oars or sail, for carrying passengers or light cargo. **4** a small lightly armed boat, as used in the enforcement of customs regulations.

cut-throat ('kʌt,θrəʊt) *n* **1** a person who cuts throats; murderer. **2** Also called: **cut-throat razor, straight razor**. *Brit.* a razor with a long blade that usually folds into the handle. ◆ *adj* **3** bloodthirsty or murderous; cruel. **4** fierce or relentless in competition: *cut-throat prices*. **5** (of some games) played by three people: *cut-throat poker*.

cutting ('kʌtɪŋ) *n* **1** a piece cut off from something. **2** *Horticulture*. **2a** a method of propagation in which a part of a plant is induced to form its own roots. **2b** a part separated for this purpose. **3** Also called (esp. in US and Canad.): **clipping**. an article, photograph, etc., cut from a publication. **4** the editing process of a film. **5** an excavation in a piece of high land for a road, railway, etc. **6** *Irish inf.* sharp-wittedness: *there is no cutting in him*. ◆ *adj* **7** designed for or adapted to cutting; sharp. **8** keen; piercing. **9** tending to hurt the feelings: *a cutting remark*.
▶ **'cuttingly** *adv*

cutting compound *n Engineering*. a mixture, such as oil, water, and soap, used for cooling drills and other cutting tools.

cutting edge *n* the leading position in any field; forefront: *on the cutting edge of space technology*.

cuttlebone ('kʌt³l,bəʊn) *n* the internal calcareous shell of the cuttlefish, used as a mineral supplement to the diet of cagebirds and as a polishing agent. [C16: OE *cudele* + BONE]

cuttlefish ('kʌt³l,fɪʃ) *n, pl* **cuttlefish** *or* **cuttlefishes**. a cephalopod mollusc which occurs near the bottom of inshore waters and has a broad flattened body. Sometimes shortened to **cuttle**.

cut up *vb* (*tr, adv*) **1** to cut into pieces. **2** to inflict injuries on. **3** (*usually passive*) *Inf.* to affect the feelings of deeply. **4** *Inf.* to subject to severe criticism. **5** *Inf.* (of a driver) to overtake or pull in front of (another driver) in a dangerous manner. **6 cut up rough**. *Brit. inf.* to become angry or bad-tempered. ◆ *n* **cut-up**. **7** *Inf., chiefly US*. a joker or prankster.

cutwater ('kʌt,wɔːtə) *n* the forward part of the stem of a vessel, which cuts through the water.

cutworm ('kʌt,wɜːm) *n* the caterpillar of various noctuid moths, which is a pest of young crop plants in North America.

cuvée (kuːˈveɪ) *n* an individual batch or blend of wine. [C19: from F, lit.: put in a cask, from *cuve* cask]

Cuxhaven ★ ('kʊks,haːvᵊn; *German* kʊksˈhaːfən) *n* a port in NW Germany, at the mouth of the River Elbe. Pop.: 55 250 (1989 est.).

Cuyabá ★ (*Portuguese* kuja'ba) *n* a variant spelling of **Cuiabá**.

Cuyp *or* **Kuyp** ★ (kaɪp; *Dutch* kœip) *n* **Aelbert** ('aːlbert). 1620–91, Dutch painter of landscapes and animals.

Cuzco (*Spanish* 'kuθko) *or* **Cusco** ★ *n* a city in S central Peru: former capital of the Inca Empire, with extensive Inca remains; university (1692). Pop.: 255 568 (1993).

CV *abbrev. for* curriculum vitae.

CVS *abbrev. for* chorionic villus sampling.

Cwlth *abbrev. for* Commonwealth.

cwm (kuːm) *n* **1** (in Wales) a valley. **2** *Geol.* another name for **cirque**.

c.w.o. *or* **CWO** *abbrev. for* cash with order.

CWS *abbrev. for* Cooperative Wholesale Society.

cwt *abbrev. for* hundredweight. [*c*, from the L numeral *C* one hundred (*centum*)]

CWU (in Britain) *abbrev. for* Communication Workers' Union.

-cy *suffix*. **1** indicating state, quality, or condition: *plutocracy; lunacy*. **2** rank or office: *captaincy*. [via OF from L *-cia, -tia*, Gk *-kia, -tia*, abstract noun suffixes]

cyan ('saɪæn, 'saɪən) *n* **1** a green-blue colour. ◆ *adj* **2** of this colour. [C19: from Gk *kuanos* dark blue]

cyanate ('saɪə,neɪt) *n* any salt or ester of cyanic acid.

cyanic (saɪˈænɪk) *adj* **1** of or containing cyanogen. **2** blue.

cyanic acid *n* a colourless poisonous volatile liquid acid. Formula: HOCN.

cyanide ('saɪə,naɪd) *or* **cyanid** ('saɪənɪd) *n* any salt of hydrocyanic acid. Cyanides are extremely poisonous.
▶ ,cyani'dation *n*

cyanite ('saɪə,naɪt) *n* a grey, green, or blue mineral consisting of aluminium silicate in crystalline form.
▶ cyanitic (,saɪə'nɪtɪk) *adj*

cyano- *or before a vowel* **cyan-** *combining form*. **1** blue or dark blue. **2** indicating cyanogen. **3** indicating cyanide. [from Gk *kuanos* (adj) dark blue, (n) dark blue enamel, lapis lazuli]

cyanobacteria (,saɪənəʊbæk'tɪərɪə) *pl n, sing* **cyanobacterium** (-ɪəm). a group of bacteria (phylum *Cyanobacteria*) containing a blue photosynthetic pigment and formerly regarded as algae. Former name: **blue-green algae**.

cyanocobalamin (,saɪənəʊkəʊ'bæləmɪn) *n* vitamin B₁₂, a complex crystalline compound of cobalt and cyanide, lack of which leads to pernicious anaemia. [C20: from CYANO- + COBALT(T) + (VIT)AMIN]

cyanogen (saɪˈænədʒɪn) *n* an extremely poisonous colourless flammable gas. Formula: $(CN)_2$. [C19: from F *cyanogène*; see CYANO-, -GEN; so named because it is one of the constituents of Prussian blue]

cyanosis (,saɪə'nəʊsɪs) *n Pathol.* a bluish-purple discoloration of skin and mucous membranes usually resulting from a deficiency of oxygen in the blood.
▶ cyanotic (,saɪə'nɒtɪk) *adj*

Cybele ★ ('sɪbɪlɪ) *n Classical myth.* the Phrygian goddess of nature, mother of all living things and consort of Attis; identified with the Greek Rhea or Demeter.

cyber- *combining form*. indicating computers: *cyberphobia*. [C20: back formation from CYBERNETICS]

cybercafé ('saɪbə,kæfɪ, -,kæfeɪ) *n* a café with computer equipment that gives public access to the Internet.

cybernate ('saɪbə,neɪt) *vb* **cybernates, cybernating, cybernated**. to control with a servomechanism or to be con-

trolled by a servomechanism. [C20: from CYBER(NETICS) + -ATE[1]]
▶ ˌcyberˈnation n

cybernetics (ˌsaɪbəˈnetɪks) n (functioning as sing) the branch of science concerned with control systems and comparisons between man-made and biological systems. [C20: from Gk kubernētēs steersman, from kubernan to steer]
▶ ˌcyberˈnetic adj ▶ ˌcyberˈneticist n

cyberpet ('saɪbəˌpet) n an electronic toy that simulates the activities of a pet, requiring the owner to feed, discipline, and entertain it.

cyberphobia (ˌsaɪbəˈfəʊbɪə) n an irrational fear of computing.
▶ ˌcyberˈphobic adj

cyberpunk ('saɪbəˌpʌŋk) n 1 a genre of science fiction that features rebellious computer hackers and is set in a society integrated by computer networks. 2 a writer of cyberpunk.

cyberspace ('saɪbəˌspeɪs) n all of the data stored in a large computer or network represented as a three-dimensional model through which a virtual-reality user can move.

cycad ('saɪkæd) n a tropical or subtropical plant, having an unbranched stem with fernlike leaves crowded at the top. [C19: from NL Cycas name of genus, from Gk kukas, scribe's error for koïkas, from koïx a kind of palm]
▶ ˌcycaˈdaceous adj

Cyclades ★ ('sɪkləˌdiːz) pl n a group of over 200 islands in the S Aegean Sea, forming a department of Greece. Capital: Hermoupolis (Siros). Pop.: 94 005 (1991). Area: 2572 sq. km (993 sq. miles). Modern Greek name: **Kikládhes.**
▶ **Cycladic** (sɪˈklædɪk) adj

cyclamate ('saɪkləˌmeɪt, 'sɪkləmeɪt) n any of certain compounds formerly used as food additives and sugar substitutes. [C20: from cycl(ohexyl-sulph)amate]

cyclamen ('sɪkləmən, -ˌmen) n 1 any Old World plant of the genus Cyclamen, having white, pink, or red flowers, with reflexed petals. ◆ adj 2 of a dark reddish-purple colour. [C16: from Med. L, from L cyclamīnos, from Gk kuklaminos, prob. from kuklos circle, referring to the bulblike roots]

cycle ('saɪkᵊl) n 1 a recurring period of time in which certain events or phenomena occur and reach completion. 2 a completed series of events that follows or is followed by another series of similar events occurring in the same sequence. 3 the time taken or needed for one such series. 4 a vast period of time; age; aeon. 5 a group of poems or prose narratives about a central figure or event: the Arthurian cycle. 6 short for **bicycle, motorcycle,** etc. 7 a recurrent series of events or processes in plants and animals: a life cycle. 8 one of a series of repeated changes in the magnitude of a periodically varying quantity, such as current or voltage. ◆ vb cycles, cycling, cycled. 9 (tr) to process through a cycle or system. 10 (intr) to move in or pass through cycles. 11 to travel by or ride a bicycle or tricycle. [C14: from LL cyclus, from Gk kuklos cycle, circle, ring, wheel]

cyclic ('saɪklɪk, 'sɪklɪk) or **cyclical** adj 1 recurring or revolving in cycles. 2 (of an organic compound) containing a closed saturated or unsaturated ring of atoms. 3 Bot. 3a arranged in whorls: cyclic petals. 3b having parts arranged in this way: cyclic flowers.
▶ 'cyclically adv

cycling shorts pl n tight-fitting shorts reaching partway to the knee for cycling, sport, etc.

cyclist ('saɪklɪst) or US **cycler** n a person who rides or travels by bicycle, motorcycle, etc.

cyclo- or before a vowel **cycl-** combining form. 1 indicating a circle or ring: cyclotron. 2 denoting a cyclic compound: cyclopropane. [from Gk kuklos CYCLE]

cyclogiro ('saɪkləˌdʒaɪrəʊ) n, pl **cyclogiros.** Aeronautics. an aircraft lifted and propelled by pivoted blades rotating parallel to roughly horizontal transverse axes.

cyclohexanone (ˌsaɪkləʊˈheksəˌnəʊn) n a colourless liquid used as a solvent for cellulose lacquers. Formula: $C_6H_{10}O$.

cycloid ('saɪklɔɪd) adj 1 resembling a circle. ◆ n 2 Geom. the curve described by a point on the circumference of a circle as the circle rolls along a straight line.
▶ cyˈcloidal adj

cyclometer (saɪˈklɒmɪtə) n a device that records the number of revolutions made by a wheel and hence the distance travelled.

cyclone ('saɪkləʊn) n 1 another name for **depression** (sense 6). 2 a violent tropical storm; hurricane. ◆ adj 3 Austral. & NZ trademark. (of fencing) made of interlaced wire and metal. [C19: from Gk kuklōn a turning around, from kuklos wheel]
▶ **cyclonic** (saɪˈklɒnɪk) adj ▶ cyˈclonically adv

Cyclopean (ˌsaɪkləʊˈpiːən, saɪˈkləʊpɪən) adj 1 of, relating to, or resembling the Cyclops. 2 denoting or having the kind of masonry used in preclassical Greek architecture, characterized by large undressed blocks of stone.

cyclopedia or **cyclopaedia** (ˌsaɪkləʊˈpiːdɪə) n a less common word for **encyclopedia.**

cyclopentadiene (ˌsaɪkləʊˌpentəˈdaɪiːn) n a colourless liquid unsaturated cyclic hydrocarbon obtained in the cracking of petroleum hydrocarbons and the distillation of coal tar: used in the manufacture of plastics and insecticides. Formula: C_5H_6.

cyclophosphamide (ˌsaɪkləʊˈfɒsfəˌmaɪd) n a cytotoxic drug used in the treatment of leukaemia and lymphoma. [C20: from CYCLO- + PHOSPH(ORUS) + AMIDE]

cyclopropane (ˌsaɪkləʊˈprəʊpeɪn) n a colourless gaseous hydrocarbon, used as an anaesthetic. Formula: C_3H_6.

Cyclops ('saɪklɒps) n, pl **Cyclopes** (saɪˈkləʊpiːz) or **Cyclopses.** Classical myth. one of a race of giants having a single eye in the middle of the forehead. [C15: from L Cyclōps, from Gk Kuklōps, lit.: round eye, from kuklos circle + ōps eye]

cyclorama (ˌsaɪkləʊˈrɑːmə) n 1 a large picture on the interior wall of a cylindrical room, designed to appear in natural perspective to a spectator. 2 Theatre. a curtain or wall curving along the back of a stage, usually painted to represent the sky. [C19: CYCLO- + Gk horama view, sight, on the model of panorama]
▶ **cycloramic** (ˌsaɪkləʊˈræmɪk) adj

cyclosporin-A (ˌsaɪkləʊˈspɔːrɪn-) n a drug extracted from a fungus and used in transplant surgery to suppress the body's immune mechanisms, and so prevent rejection of an organ.

cyclostome ('saɪkləˌstəʊm, 'sɪk-) n any primitive aquatic jawless vertebrate, such as the lamprey, having a round sucking mouth.
▶ **cyclostomate** (saɪˈklɒstəmɪt, -ˌmeɪt) or **cyclostomatous** (ˌsaɪkləʊˈstɒmətəs, -ˈstəʊmə-, ˌsɪk-) adj

cyclostyle ('saɪkləˌstaɪl) n 1 a kind of pen with a small toothed wheel, used for cutting holes in a specially prepared stencil. 2 an office duplicator using such a stencil. ◆ vb cyclostyles, cyclostyling, cyclostyled. 3 (tr) to print using such a stencil.
▶ 'cycloˌstyled adj

cyclothymia (ˌsaɪkləʊˈθaɪmɪə) n Psychiatry. a condition characterized by alternating periods of excitement and depression. [from CYCLO- + Gk thumos, cast of mind + -IA]
▶ ˌcycloˈthymic adj

cyclotron ('saɪkləˌtrɒn) n a type of particle accelerator in which the particles spiral under the effect of a strong vertical magnetic field.

cyder ('saɪdə) n a variant spelling of **cider.**

cygnet ('sɪgnɪt) n a young swan. [C15 sygnett, from OF cygne swan, from L cygnus, from Gk kuknos]

cylinder ('sɪlɪndə) n 1 a solid consisting of two parallel planes bounded by identical closed curves, usually circles, that are interconnected at every point by a set of parallel lines, usually perpendicular to the planes. 2 a surface formed by a line moving round a closed plane curve at a fixed angle to it. 3 any object shaped like a cylinder. 4 the chamber in a reciprocating internal-combustion engine, pump, or compressor within which the piston moves. The cylinders are housed in the metal **cylinder block,** which is topped by the **cylinder head. 5** the

rotating mechanism of a revolver, containing cartridge chambers. **6** *Printing*. any of the rotating drums on a printing press. **7** Also called: **cylinder seal**. an ancient cylindrical seal found in the Middle East and Balkans. [C16: from L *cylindrus*, from Gk *kulindros* a roller, from *kulindein* to roll]
▶ **'cylinder-,like** *adj*

cylindrical (sɪ'lɪndrɪk°l) *or* **cylindric** *adj* of, shaped like, or characteristic of a cylinder.
▶ **cy,lindri'cality** *n* ▶ **cy'lindrically** *adv*

cymbal ('sɪmb°l) *n* a percussion instrument consisting of a thin circular piece of brass, which vibrates when clashed together with another cymbal or struck with a stick. [OE *cymbala*, from L *cymbalum*, from Gk *kumbalon*, from *kumbē* something hollow]
▶ **'cymbalist** *n*

Cymbeline ★ ('sɪmbə,liːn) *n* See **Cunobelinus**.

cyme (saɪm) *n* an inflorescence in which the first flower is the terminal bud of the main stem and subsequent flowers develop as terminal buds of lateral stems. [C18: from L *cȳma* cabbage sprout, from Gk *kuma* anything swollen]
▶ **cymiferous** (saɪ'mɪfərəs) *adj* ▶ **cymose** ('saɪməus, -məuz, saɪ'məus) *adj*

Cymric *or* **Kymric** ('kɪmrɪk) *n* **1** the Welsh language. **2** the Brythonic group of Celtic languages. ◆ *adj* **3** of or relating to the Cymry, any of their languages, Wales, or the Welsh.

Cymru ★ (*Welsh* kum'ri) *n* the Welsh name for **Wales**.

Cymry *or* **Kymry** ('kɪmrɪ) *n* **the.** (*functioning as pl*) **1** the Brythonic Celts, comprising the present-day Welsh, Cornish, and Bretons. **2** the Welsh people. [Welsh: the Welsh]

Cynewulf, Kynewulf, *or* **Cynwulf** ★ ('kɪn,wulf) *n* ?8th century A.D., Anglo-Saxon poet; author of *Juliana*, *The Ascension*, and *The Fates of the Apostles*.

cynic ('sɪnɪk) *n* **1** a person who believes the worst about people or the outcome of events. ◆ *adj* **2** a less common word for **cynical**. [C16: via L from Gk *Kunikos*, from *kuōn* dog]

Cynic ('sɪnɪk) *n* a member of an ancient Greek sect that scorned worldly things.

cynical ('sɪnɪk°l) *adj* **1** believing the worst of others, esp. that all acts are selfish. **2** sarcastic; mocking. **3** showing contempt for accepted standards, esp. of honesty or morality.
▶ **'cynically** *adv* ▶ **'cynicalness** *n*

cynicism ('sɪnɪ,sɪzəm) *n* **1** the attitude or beliefs of a cynic. **2** cynical action, idea, etc.

Cynicism ('sɪnɪ,sɪzəm) *n* the doctrines of the Cynics.

cynosure ('sɪnə,zjuə, -juə) *n* **1** a person or thing that attracts notice. **2** something that serves as a guide. [C16: from L *Cynosūra* the constellation of Ursa Minor, from Gk *Kunosoura*, from *kuōn* dog + *oura* tail]

Cynthia ★ ('sɪnθɪə) *n* another name for **Artemis** (Diana).

cypher ('saɪfə) *n, vb* a variant spelling of **cipher**.

cypress ('saɪprəs) *n* **1** any coniferous tree of a N temperate genus having dark green scalelike leaves and rounded cones. **2** any of several similar and related trees. **3** the wood of any of these trees. **4** cypress branches used as a symbol of mourning. [OE *cypresse*, from L *cyparissus*, from Gk *kuparissos*; rel. to L *cupressus*]

cypress pine *n* any coniferous tree of an Australian genus yielding valuable timber.

Cyprian ★ ('sɪprɪən) *n* **Saint**. ?200–258 A.D., bishop of Carthage and martyr. Feast day: Sept. 26 or 16.

cyprinid (sɪ'praɪnɪd, 'sɪprɪnɪd) *n* **1** any teleost fish of the mainly freshwater family Cyprinidae, typically having toothless jaws and including the carp, tench, and dace. ◆ *adj* **2** of, relating to, or belonging to the Cyprinidae. **3** resembling a carp; cyprinoid. [C19: from NL *Cyprīnidae*, from L *cyprīnus* carp, from Gk *kuprinos*]

cyprinoid ('sɪprɪ,nɔɪd, sɪ'praɪnɔɪd) *adj* **1** of or relating to the Cyprinoidea, a large suborder of teleost fishes including the cyprinids, electric eels, and loaches. **2** of, relating to, or resembling the carp. ◆ *n* **3** any fish belonging to the Cyprinoidea. [C19: from L *cyprīnus* carp]

Cypriot ('sɪprɪət) *or* **Cypriote** ('sɪprɪ,əut) *n* **1** a native or inhabitant of Cyprus. **2** the dialect of Greek spoken in Cyprus. ◆ *adj* **3** denoting or relating to Cyprus, its inhabitants, or dialects.

cypripedium (,sɪprɪ'piːdɪəm) *n* any orchid of a genus having large flowers with an inflated pouchlike lip. See also **lady's-slipper**. [C18: from NL, from L *Cypria* the Cyprian, that is, Venus + *pēs* foot (that is, Venus' slipper)]

Cyprus ★ ('saɪprəs) *n* an island in the E Mediterranean: ceded to Britain by Turkey in 1878 and made a colony in 1925; became an independent republic and member of the Commonwealth in 1960; invaded by Turkey in 1974 following a Greek-supported military coup, leading to the virtual partition of the island. In 1983 the Turkish-controlled northern sector declared itself to be an independent state as the Turkish Republic of Northern Cyprus but failed to receive international recognition. Attempts by the UN to negotiate a reunification agreement have failed. Languages: Greek and Turkish. Religions: Greek Orthodox and Muslim. Currency: pound and Turkish lira. Capital: Nicosia. Pop. (Greek): 662 000 (1997); (Turkish): 198 000 (1997). Area: 9251 sq. km (3571 sq. miles).

Cyrano de Bergerac ★ (*French* sirano də bɛrʒərak) *n* **Savinien** (savinjē). 1619–55, French writer and soldier, famous as a duellist and for his large nose.

Cyrenaic (,saɪrə'neɪɪk, ,sɪrə-) *adj* **1** of or relating to the ancient Greek city of Cyrene. **2** of or relating to the philosophical school founded by Aristippus in Cyrene that held pleasure to be the highest good. ◆ *n* **3** a follower of the Cyrenaica school of philosophy.

Cyrene ★ (saɪ'riːnɪ) *n* an ancient Greek city of N Africa: famous for its medical school.

Cyril ★ ('sɪrəl) *n* **Saint**. ?827–869 A.D., Greek Christian theologian, missionary to the Moravians and said to be the inventor of the Cyrillic alphabet; he and his brother Saint Methodius were called *the Apostles of the Slavs*. Feast day: Feb. 14 or May 11.

Cyrillic (sɪ'rɪlɪk) *adj* **1** denoting or relating to the alphabet said to have been devised by Saint Cyril, for Slavonic languages: now used primarily for Russian and Bulgarian. ◆ *n* **2** this alphabet.

Cyril of Alexandria ★ *n* **Saint**. ?375–444 A.D., Christian theologian and patriarch of Alexandria. Feast day: June 27 or June 9.

Cyrus ★ ('saɪrəs) *n* **1** known as *Cyrus the Great* or *Cyrus the Elder*. died ?529 B.C., king of Persia and founder of the Persian empire. **2** called *the Younger*. died 401 B.C., Persian satrap of Lydia: revolted against his brother Artaxerxes II, but was killed at the battle of Cunaxa. See also **anabasis**.

cyst (sɪst) *n* **1** *Pathol*. any abnormal membranous sac or blister-like pouch containing fluid or semisolid material. **2** *Anat*. any normal sac in the body. **3** a protective membrane enclosing a cell, larva, or organism. [C18: from NL *cystis*, from Gk *kustis* pouch, bag, bladder]

-cyst *n combining form*. indicating a bladder or sac: *otocyst*. [from Gk *kustis* bladder]

cystectomy (sɪ'stɛktəmɪ) *n, pl* **cystectomies**. **1** surgical removal of the gall bladder or part of the urinary bladder. **2** surgical removal of a cyst.

cystic ('sɪstɪk) *adj* **1** of, relating to, or resembling a cyst. **2** having or containing within a cyst; encysted. **3** of the gall bladder or urinary bladder.

cysticercus (,sɪstɪ'sɜːkəs) *n, pl* **cysticerci** (-saɪ). an encysted larval form of many tapeworms, consisting of a head inverted in a fluid-filled bladder. [C19: from NL, from Gk *kustis* pouch, bladder + *kerkos* tail]

cystic fibrosis *n* an inheritable disease of the exocrine glands, controlled by a recessive gene: affected children inherit defective alleles from both parents. It is characterized by chronic infection of the respiratory tract and by pancreatic insufficiency.

cystitis (sɪ'staɪtɪs) *n* inflammation of the urinary bladder.

★ people and places

cysto- *or before a vowel* **cyst-** *combining form.* indicating a cyst or bladder: *cystoscope.*

cystoid ('sɪstɔɪd) *adj* **1** resembling a cyst or bladder. ◆ *n* **2** a tissue mass that resembles a cyst but lacks an outer membrane.

cystoscope ('sɪstə,skəʊp) *n* a slender tubular medical instrument for examining the interior of the urethra and urinary bladder.
▸ **cystoscopic** (,sɪstə'skɒpɪk) *adj* ▸ **cystoscopy** (sɪs-'tɒskəpɪ) *n*

-cyte *n combining form.* indicating a cell. [from NL *-cyta,* from Gk *kutos* vessel]

Cythera ★ (sɪ'θɪərə) *n* **1** a Greek island off the SE coast of the Peloponnese: in ancient times a centre of the worship of Aphrodite. Pop.: 3500 (latest est.). Area: about 285 sq. km (110 sq. miles). **2** the chief town of this island, on the S coast. Pop.: 300 (latest est.). ◆ Modern Greek name: **Kíthira.**

Cytherea ★ (,sɪθə'riːə) *n* another name for **Aphrodite** (Venus).
▸ **,Cyther'ean** *adj*

cyto- *combining form.* indicating a cell: *cytoplasm.* [from Gk *kutos* vessel]

cytogenetics (,saɪtəʊdʒɪ'nɛtɪks) *n* (*functioning as sing*) the branch of genetics that correlates the structure of chromosomes with heredity and variation.
▸ **,cytoge'netic** *adj*

cytokine ('saɪtəʊ,kaɪn) *n* any of various proteins, secreted by cells, that carry signals to neighbouring cells. Cytokines include interferon.

cytokinin (,saɪtəʊ'kaɪnɪn) *n* any of a group of plant hormones that promote cell division and retard ageing. Also called: **kinin.**

cytology (saɪ'tɒlədʒɪ) *n* **1** the study of plant and animal cells. **2** the detailed structure of a tissue as revealed by microscopic examination.
▸ **cytological** (,saɪtə'lɒdʒɪk°l) *adj* ▸ **,cyto'logically** *adv* ▸ **cy'tologist** *n*

cytomegalovirus (,saɪtəʊ,mɛgələʊ'vaɪrəs) *n* a virus that may cause serious disease in patients whose immune systems are compromised and the birth of handicapped children to pregnant women infected with it. Abbrev.: **CMV.**

cytoplasm ('saɪtəʊ,plæzəm) *n* the protoplasm of a cell excluding the nucleus.
▸ **,cyto'plasmic** *adj*

cytosine ('saɪtəsɪn) *n* a white crystalline base occurring in nucleic acids. [C19: from CYTO- + -OSE^2 + -INE^2]

cytotoxic (,saɪtəʊ'tɒksɪk) *adj* destructive to cells, esp. to cancer cells: *cytotoxic drugs.*
▸ **cytotoxicity** (,saɪtəʊtɒk'sɪsɪtɪ) *n*

cytotoxin (,saɪtəʊ'tɒksɪn) *n* any substance that is poisonous to living cells.

Cyzicus ★ ('sɪzɪkəs) *n* an ancient Greek colony in NW Asia Minor on the S shore of the Sea of Marmara: site of Alcibiades' victory over the Peloponnesians (410 B.C.).

czar (zɑː) *n* a variant spelling (esp. US) of **tsar.**
▸ **'czardom** *n* ▸ **'Czarevitch, cza'revna, cza'rina, 'czarism, 'czarist:** see **ts-** spellings.

czardas ('tʃɑːdæʃ) *n* **1** a Hungarian national dance of alternating slow and fast sections. **2** music for this dance [from Hungarian *csárdás*]

Czech (tʃɛk) *adj* **1a** of, relating to, or characteristic of the Czech Republic, its people, or their language. **1b** of, relating to, or characteristic of Bohemia and Moravia, their people, or their language. **1c** (loosely) of, relating to, or characteristic of the former Czechoslovakia or its people. ◆ *n* **2** the official languages of the Czech Republic, belonging to the West Slavonic branch of the Indo-European family. Czech is closely related to Slovak; they are mutually intelligible. **3a** a native or inhabitant of the Czech Republic. **3b** a native or inhabitant of Bohemia or Moravia. **3c** (loosely) a native, inhabitant, or citizen of the former Czechoslovakia. [C19: from Polish, from Czech *Čech*]

Czechoslovak (,tʃɛkəʊ'sləʊvæk) *or* **Czechoslovakian** (,tʃɛkəʊsləʊ'vækɪən) *adj* **1** of or relating to the former Czechoslovakia, its peoples, or languages. ◆ *n* **2** (loosely) either of the two languages of the former Czechoslovakia: Czech or Slovak.

Czechoslovakia ★ (,tʃɛkəʊsləʊ'vækɪə) *n* a former republic in central Europe: formed after the defeat of Austria-Hungary (1918) as a nation of Czechs in Bohemia and Moravia and Slovaks in Slovakia; occupied by Germany from 1939 until its liberation by the Soviet Union in 1945; became a people's republic under the Communists in 1948; invaded by Warsaw Pact troops in 1968, ending Dubček's attempt to liberalize communism; in 1989 popular unrest led to the resignation of the Politburo and the formation of a non-Communist government. It consisted of two federal republics, the **Czech Republic** and the **Slovak Republic,** which became independent countries in 1993. Czech name: **Československo.**
▸ **,Czechoslo'vakian** *adj, n*

Czech Republic ★ *n* a country in central Europe formed part of Czechoslovakia until 1993; mostly wooded, with lowlands surrounding the River Morava rising to the Bohemian plateau in the W and to highlands in the N. Language: Czech. Religion: Christian majority Currency: koruna. Capital: Prague. Pop. 10 307 000 (1997). Area: 78 864 sq. km (30 450 sq miles).

Czernowitz ★ ('tʃɜːnovɪts) *n* the German name for **Chernovtsy.**

Czerny ★ (*German* 'tʃɛrni) *n* **Karl** (karl). 1791–1857, Austrian pianist, composer, and teacher, noted for his studies.

Częstochowa ★ (*Polish* tʃɛ̃stɔ'xɔva) *n* an industrial city in S Poland, on the River Warta: pilgrimage centre. Pop. 259 800 (1995 est.).

Dd

d or **D** (diː) *n, pl* **d's, D's,** or **Ds. 1** the fourth letter of the modern English alphabet. **2** a speech sound represented by this letter.

d *symbol for Physics.* density.

D *symbol for:* **1** *Music.* **1a** the second note of the scale of C major. **1b** the major or minor key having this note as its tonic. **2** *Chem.* deuterium. **3a** a semiskilled or unskilled manual worker, or a trainee or apprentice to a skilled worker. **3b** *(as modifier):* D worker. ◆ See also **occupation groupings.** ◆ **4** *the Roman numeral for* 500.

2,4-D *n* a synthetic auxin widely used as a weedkiller; 2,4-dichlorophenoxyacetic acid.

d. *abbrev. for:* **1** date. **2** daughter. **3** degree. **4** delete. **5** *Brit.* currency before decimalization. penny or pennies. [L *denarius* or *denarii*] **6** depart(s). **7** diameter. **8** died. **9** dose.

D. *abbrev. for:* **1** *US.* Democrat(ic). **2** Department. **3** Deus. [L: God] **4** *Optics.* dioptre. **5** Director. **6** Dominus. [L: Lord] **7** Dutch.

'd *contraction for* would *or* had: *I'd; you'd.*

DA *abbrev. for:* **1** (in the US) District Attorney. **2** Diploma of Art. **3** duck's arse (hairstyle). **4** drug addict.

dab[1] (dæb) *vb* **dabs, dabbing, dabbed. 1** to touch or pat lightly and quickly. **2** *(tr)* to daub with short tapping strokes: *to dab the wall with paint.* **3** *(tr)* to apply (paint, cream, etc.) with short tapping strokes. ◆ *n* **4** a small amount, esp. of something soft or moist. **5** a light stroke or tap, as with the hand. **6** *(often pl) Chiefly Brit.* a slang word for **fingerprint.** [C14: imit.]
▶ **'dabber** *n*

dab[2] (dæb) *n* **1** a small common European flatfish covered with rough toothed scales. **2** any of various other small flatfish. [C15: from Anglo-F *dabbe*, from ?]

dabble (ˈdæbəl) *vb* **dabbles, dabbling, dabbled. 1** to dip, move, or splash (the fingers, feet, etc.) in a liquid. **2** *(intr; usually foll. by in, with,* or *at)* to deal (with) or work (at) frivolously or superficially. **3** *(tr)* to splash or smear. [C16: prob. from Du. *dabbelen*]
▶ **'dabbler** *n*

dabchick (ˈdæbˌtʃɪk) *n* any of several small grebes. [C16: prob. from OE *dop* to dive + CHICK]

dab hand *n Brit. inf.* a person who is particularly skilled at something: *a dab hand at chess.* [?from DAB[1]]

da capo (dɑː ˈkɑːpəʊ) *adj, adv Music.* to be repeated from the beginning. [C18: from It., lit.: from the head]

Dacca ★ (ˈdækə) *n* the former name (until 1982) of **Dhaka.**

dace (deɪs) *n, pl* **dace** or **daces. 1** a European freshwater fish of the carp family. **2** any of various similar fishes. [C15: from OF *dars* DART]

dacha or **datcha** (ˈdætʃə) *n* a country house or cottage in Russia. [from Russian: a giving, gift]

Dachau ★ (German ˈdaxau) *n* a town in S Germany, in Bavaria: site of a Nazi concentration camp. Pop.: 34 183 (1989 est.).

dachshund (ˈdæksˌhʊnd, ˈdæʃənd) *n* a long-bodied short-legged breed of dog. [C19: from G, from *Dachs* badger + *Hund* dog]

Dacia ★ (ˈdeɪsɪə) *n* an ancient region bounded by the Carpathians, the Tisza, and the Danube, roughly corresponding to modern Romania. United under kings from about 60 B.C., it later contained the Roman province of the same name (about 105 to 270 A.D.).
▶ **'Dacian** *adj, n*

dacoit (dəˈkɔɪt) *n* (in India and Myanmar) a member of a gang of armed robbers. [C19: from Hindi *dakait*, from *dākā* robbery]

Dacron (ˈdeɪkrɒn, ˈdæk-) *n* the US name (trademark) for **Terylene.**

dactyl (ˈdæktɪl) *n Prosody.* a metrical foot of three sylla-

bles, one long followed by two short (–◡◡) [C14: via L from Gk *daktulos* finger, comparing the finger's three joints to the three syllables]

dactylic (dækˈtɪlɪk) *adj* **1** of, relating to, or having a dactyl: *dactylic verse.* ◆ *n* **2** a variant of **dactyl.**
▶ **dac'tylically** *adv*

dad (dæd) *n* an informal word for **father.** [C16: childish word]

Dada (ˈdɑːdɑː) or **Dadaism** (ˈdɑːdɑːˌɪzəm) *n* a nihilistic artistic movement of the early 20th century, founded on principles of irrationality, incongruity, and irreverence towards accepted aesthetic criteria. [C20: from F, from children's word for hobbyhorse]
▶ **'Dadaist** *n, adj* ▶ **Dada'istic** *adj*

daddy (ˈdædɪ) *n, pl* **daddies. 1** an informal word for **father. 2 the daddy.** *Sl., chiefly US, Canad., & Austral.* the supreme or finest example.

daddy-longlegs *n* **1** *Brit., Austral., & NZ.* an informal name for **crane fly. 2** *US, Canad., Austral., & NZ.* an informal name for **harvestman** (sense 2).

dado (ˈdeɪdəʊ) *n, pl* **dadoes** or **dados. 1** the lower part of an interior wall that is decorated differently from the upper part. **2** *Archit.* the part of a pedestal between the base and the cornice. ◆ *vb* **3** *(tr)* to provide with a dado. [C17: from It.: die, die-shaped pedestal]

Dadra and Nagar Haveli ★ (dəˈdrɑː; ˈnʌgə əˈvelɪ) *n* a union territory of W India, on the Gulf of Cambay: until 1961 administratively part of Portuguese Damão. Capital: Silvassa. Pop.: 153 000 (1994 est.). Area: 489 sq. km (191 sq. miles).

Daedalus ★ (ˈdiːdələs) *n Greek myth.* an Athenian architect and inventor who built the labyrinth for Minos on Crete and fashioned wings for himself and his son Icarus to flee their imprisonment on the island.
▶ **Daedalian, Daedalean** (dɪˈdeɪlɪən) or **Daedalic** (dɪˈdælɪk) *adj*

daemon (ˈdiːmən) or **daimon** *n* **1** a demigod. **2** the guardian spirit of a place or person. **3** a variant spelling of **demon** (sense 3).
▶ **daemonic** (diːˈmɒnɪk) *adj*

daff (dæf) *n Inf.* short for **daffodil.**

daffodil (ˈdæfədɪl) *n* **1** Also called: **Lent lily.** a widely cultivated Eurasian plant, *Narcissus pseudonarcissus*, having spring-blooming yellow nodding flowers. **2** any other plant of the genus *Narcissus*. **3a** a brilliant yellow colour. **3b** *(as adj):* daffodil paint. **4** a daffodil as a national emblem of Wales. [C14: from Med. L *affodillus*, var. of L *asphodelus* ASPHODEL]

daffy (ˈdæfɪ) *adj* **daffier, daffiest.** *Inf.* another word for **daft** (senses 1, 2). [C19: from obs. *daff* fool]

daft (dɑːft) *adj* *Chiefly Brit.* **1** *Inf.* foolish, simple, or stupid. **2** a slang word for **insane. 3** *(postpositive; foll. by about) Inf.* extremely fond (of). **4** *Sl.* frivolous; giddy. [OE *gedæfte* gentle, foolish]
▶ **'daftness** *n*

daftie (ˈdɑːftɪ) *n Inf.* a daft person.

Dafydd ap Gruffudd ★ (Welsh ˈdaviδ æp ˈgrɪfɪθ) *n* died 1283, Welsh leader. Claiming the title Prince of Wales (1282), he led an unsuccessful revolt against Edward I: executed.

Dafydd ap Gwilym ★ (Welsh ˈgwɪlɪm) *n* ?1320–?1380, Welsh poet.

dag[1] (dæg) *n* **1** short for **daglock.** ◆ *vb* **dags, dagging, dagged. 2** to cut the daglock away from (a sheep). [C18: from ?]
▶ **'dagger** *n*

dag[2] (dæg) *n Austral. & NZ inf.* **1** a character; eccentric. **2** a person who is untidily dressed. **3** a person with a good sense of humour. [back formation from DAGGY]

Da Gama ★ (də ˈgɑːmə) *n* See (Vasco da) **Gama.**

Dagan ★ ('dɑːgən) *n* an earth god of the Babylonians and Assyrians.

Dagenham ★ ('dægənəm) *n* part of the Greater London borough of Barking and Dagenham: motor-vehicle manufacturing.

Dagestan Republic ★ (,dɑːgɪ'stɑːn) *n* a constituent republic of S Russia, on the Caspian Sea: annexed from Persia in 1813; rich mineral resources. Capital: Makhachkala. Pop.: 2 009 000 (1995 est.). Area: 50 278 sq. km (19 416 sq. miles). Also called: **Dagestan** or **Daghestan**.

dagga ('daxə, 'dɑːgə) *n* S. *African inf.* a local name for marijuana. [C19: from Afrik., from Khoikhoi *dagab*]

dagger ('dægə) *n* **1** a short stabbing weapon with a pointed blade. **2** Also called: **obelisk.** a character (†) used in printing to indicate a cross reference. **3 at daggers drawn.** in a state of open hostility. **4 look daggers.** to glare with hostility; scowl. [C14: from ?]

daggy ('dægɪ) *adj* **daggier, daggiest.** *Austral. & NZ inf.* untidy; dishevelled. [from DAG¹]

daglock ('dæg,lɒk) *n* a dung-caked lock of wool around the hindquarters of a sheep. [C17: see DAG¹, LOCK²]

dago ('deɪgəʊ) *n, pl* **dagos** *or* **dagoes.** *Derog.* a foreigner, esp. a Spaniard or Portuguese. [C19: from *Diego,* a common Sp. name]

Dagon ★ ('deɪgɒn) *n Bible.* a god worshipped by the Philistines, represented as half man and half fish. [C14: via L and Gk from Heb. *Dāgōn,* lit.: little fish]

Daguerre ★ (*French* dager) *n* **Louis Jacques Mandé** (lwi ʒɑk mãde). 1789–1851, French inventor, who devised one of the first practical photographic processes (1838).

daguerreotype (də'gerəʊ,taɪp) *n* **1** one of the earliest photographic processes, in which the image was produced on iodine-sensitized silver and developed in mercury vapour. **2** a photograph formed by this process.
▸ **da'guerreo,typy** *n*

Dahl ★ (dɑːl) *n* **Roald** ('rəʊəld). 1916–90, British writer with Norwegian parents, noted for such children's books as *Charlie and the Chocolate Factory* (1964).

dahlia ('deɪljə) *n* **1** any herbaceous perennial plant of the Mexican genus *Dahlia,* having showy flowers and tuberous roots. **2** the flower or root of any of these plants. [C19: after Anders *Dahl,* 18th-cent. Swedish botanist]

Dahna ★ ('dɑːxnɑː) *n* another name for **Rub' al Khali.**

Dahomey ★ (də'həʊmɪ) *n* the former name (until 1975) of **Benin.**

Dáil Éireann ('dɑːl 'eːrɪn) *or* **Dáil** *n* (in the Republic of Ireland) the lower chamber of parliament. [from Irish *dáil* assembly + *Éireann* of Eire]

daily ('deɪlɪ) *adj* **1** of or occurring every day or every weekday. ◆ *n, pl* **dailies. 2** a daily newspaper. **3** *Brit.* a charwoman. ◆ *adv* **4** every day. **5** constantly; often. [OE *dæglīc*]

Daimler ★ ('deɪmlə) *n* **Gottlieb (Wilhelm)** (*German* 'gɔtliːp). 1834–1900, German engineer and car manufacturer, who collaborated with Nikolaus Otto in inventing the first internal-combustion engine (1876).

daimon ('daɪmɒn) *n* a variant spelling of **daemon** or **demon** (sense 3).
▸ **dai'monic** *adj*

daimyo bond ('daɪmjəʊ) *n* a bearer bond issued in Japan and the eurobond market by the World Bank. [from Japanese, from Ancient Chinese]

dainty ('deɪntɪ) *adj* **daintier, daintiest. 1** delicate or elegant. **2** choice; delicious: *a dainty morsel.* **3** excessively genteel; fastidious. ◆ *n, pl* **dainties. 4** a choice piece of food; delicacy. [C13: from OF *deintié,* from L *dignitās* DIGNITY]
▸ **'daintily** *adv*

daiquiri ('daɪkɪrɪ, 'dæk-) *n, pl* **daiquiris.** an iced drink containing rum, lime juice, and sugar. [C20: after *Daiquiri,* town in Cuba]

dairy ('deərɪ) *n, pl* **dairies. 1** a company that supplies milk and milk products. **2** a room or building where milk and cream are stored or made into butter and cheese. **3a** (*modifier*) of, relating to, or containing milk and milk products. **3b** (*in combination*): *a dairymaid.* **4a** a general shop, selling provisions, esp. milk and milk products. **4b** *NZ.* a shop that remains open outside normal trading hours. [C13 *daierie,* from OE *dæge* servant girl, one who kneads bread]

dairying ('deərɪɪŋ) *n* the business of producing, processing, and selling dairy products.

dairyman ('deərɪmən) *n, pl* **dairymen.** a man who works in a dairy.

dais ('deɪɪs, deɪs) *n* a raised platform, usually at one end of a hall, used by speakers, etc. [C13: from OF *deis,* from L *discus* DISCUS]

daisy ('deɪzɪ) *n, pl* **daisies. 1** a small low-growing European plant having flower heads with a yellow centre and pinkish-white outer rays. **2** any of various other composite plants having conspicuous ray flowers. **3** *Sl.* an excellent person or thing. **4 pushing up the daisies.** dead and buried. [OE *dægeseġe* day's eye]
▸ **'daisied** *adj*

daisy chain *n* a garland made, esp. by children, by threading daisies together.

daisycutter ('deɪzɪ,kʌtə) *n Cricket.* a ball bowled so that it rolls along the ground.

daisywheel ('deɪzɪ,wiːl) *n Computing.* a component of a computer printer shaped like a wheel with many spokes that prints using a disk with characters around the circumference. Also called: **printwheel.**

Dak. *abbrev. for* Dakota.

Dakar ★ ('dækə) *n* the capital and chief port of Senegal, on the SE side of Cape Verde peninsula. Pop.: 785 071 (1994 est.).

Dakota ★ (də'kəʊtə) *n* a former territory of the US: divided into the states of North Dakota and South Dakota in 1889.
▸ **Da'kotan** *adj, n*

daks (dæks) *pl n Austral. inf.* trousers. [C20: from trade name *Daks*]

dal (dɑːl) *n* **1** split grain, a common foodstuff in India; pulse. **2** a variant spelling of **dhal.**

Daladier ★ (*French* daladje) *n* **Édouard** (edwar). 1884–1970, French socialist statesman; premier (1933; 1934; 1938–40).

Dalai Lama ★ ('dælaɪ 'lɑːmə) *n* **1** (until 1959) the chief lama and ruler of Tibet. **2** born 1935, the 14th holder of this office (from 1940), who fled to India (1959); Nobel peace prize 1989. [from Mongolian *dalai* ocean; see LAMA]

dale (deɪl) *n* an open valley. [OE *dæl*]

Dale ★ (deɪl) *n* **Sir Henry Hallet.** 1875–1968, British physiologist: shared a Nobel prize for physiology or medicine in 1936 for work on the transmission of nerve impulses.

Dalek ('dɑːlɛk) *n* a fictional robot-like creation that is aggressive, mobile, and produces rasping staccato speech. [C20: from a children's television series, *Dr Who*]

d'Alembert ★ (*French* dalãber) *n* See (Jean le Rond d') **Alembert.**

Dales ★ (deɪlz) *pl n* (*sometimes not cap.*) **the.** short for the **Yorkshire Dales.**

dalesman ('deɪlzmən) *n, pl* **dalesmen.** a person living in a dale, esp. in the dales of N England.

Dalglish ★ (dæl'gliːʃ, dəl-) *n* **Kenny,** born 1951, Scottish footballer: Scotland's most-capped footballer.

Dalhousie ★ (dæl'haʊzɪ) *n* **1 9th Earl of,** title of *George Ramsay.* 1770–1838, British general; governor of British Canada (1819–28). **2** his son, **1st Marquis and 10th Earl of,** title of *James Andrew Broun Ramsay.* 1812–60, British statesman: governor general of India (1848–56).

Dali ★ ('dɑːlɪ; *Spanish* da'li:) *n* **Salvador** ('sælvədɔː). 1904–89, Spanish surrealist painter.

Dalian (dɑː'ljɛn) *or* **Talien** ★ (tɑː'ljɛn) *n* a city in NE China; with the adjoining city of Lü-shun comprises the port complex of Lüda. Pop.: 2 330 000 (1993). Former name: **Dairen.**

Dallapiccola ★ (*Italian* dalla'pikkola) *n* **Luigi** (lu'iːdʒi). 1904–75, Italian composer; his works include the opera *Il Prigioniero* (1944–48) and the ballet *Marsia* (1948).

Dallas ★ ('dæləs) *n* a city in NE Texas, on the Trinity River: scene of the assassination of President John F. Kennedy (1963). Pop.: 1 022 830 (1994 est.).

dalles ('dælɪz, dælz) *pl n Canad.* a stretch of river between high rock walls, with rapids and dangerous currents. [from Canad. F.: sink; see DALE]

dalliance ('dælɪəns) *n* waste of time in frivolous action or in dawdling.

dally ('dælɪ) *vb* **dallies, dallying, dallied.** (*intr*) **1** to waste time idly; dawdle. **2** (usually foll. by *with*) to deal frivolously; trifle: *to dally with someone's affections.* [C14: from Anglo-F *dalier* to gossip, from ?]

Dalmatia ★ (dæl'meɪʃə) *n* a region of W Croatia along the Adriatic: mountainous, with many offshore islands; formerly part of Yugoslavia (1947–91).

Dalmatian (dæl'meɪʃən) *n* **1** a large breed of dog having a short smooth white coat with black or brown spots. **2** a native or inhabitant of Dalmatia. ◆ *adj* **3** of Dalmatia or its inhabitants.

dalmatic (dæl'mætɪk) *n* a wide-sleeved tunic-like vestment open at the sides, worn by deacons and bishops, and by a king at his coronation. [C15: from LL *dalmatica* (*vestis*) Dalmatian (robe) (orig. made of Dalmatian wool)]

dal segno ('dæl 'senjəʊ) *adj, adv Music.* to be repeated from the point marked with a sign to the word *fine*. [It., lit.: from the sign]

dalton ('dɔːltən) *n* another name for **atomic mass unit.** [C20: after J. DALTON]

Dalton ★ ('dɔːltən) *n* **John.** 1766–1844, British chemist, who formulated the modern form of the atomic theory and the law of partial pressures for gases.

daltonism ('dɔːltə,nɪzəm) *n* colour blindness, esp. the confusion of red and green. [C19: from F *daltonisme*, after J. DALTON]

Dalton's atomic theory *n Chem.* the theory that matter consists of indivisible particles called atoms and that atoms of a given element are all identical and can neither be created nor destroyed. [C19: after J. DALTON]

dam[1] (dæm) *n* **1** a barrier of concrete, earth, etc., built across a river to create a body of water. **2** a reservoir of water created by such a barrier. **3** something that resembles or functions as a dam. ◆ *vb* **dams, damming, dammed. 4** (*tr*; often foll. by *up*) to restrict by a dam. [C12: prob. from MLow G]

dam[2] (dæm) *n* the female parent of an animal, esp. of domestic livestock. [C13: var. of DAME]

damage ('dæmɪdʒ) *n* **1** injury or harm impairing the function or condition of a person or thing. **2** loss of something desirable. **3** *Inf.* cost; expense. ◆ *vb* **damages, damaging, damaged. 4** (*tr*) to cause damage to. **5** (*intr*) to suffer damage. [C14: from OF, from L *damnum* injury, loss]
▸ **'damaging** *adj*

damages ('dæmɪdʒɪz) *pl n Law.* money to be paid as compensation for injury, loss, etc.

Daman ★ (dɑː'mɑːn) *n* the chief town of Daman and Diu, on the coast. Pop.: 26 895 (1991 est.). Portuguese name: **Damão.**

Daman and Diu ★ ('diːuː) *n* a Union Territory in W India: formerly part of Portuguese India (1559–1961) then part of the Union Territory of Goa, Daman, and Diu (1961–87). Area: 112 sq. km (43 sq. miles). Pop.: 111 000 (1994 est.).

damascene ('dæmə,siːn) *vb* **damascenes, damascening, damascened. 1** (*tr*) to ornament (metal, esp. steel) by etching or by inlaying other metals, usually gold or silver. ◆ *n* **2** a design or article produced by this process. ◆ *adj* **3** of or relating to this process. [C14: from L *damascēnus* of Damascus]

Damascene ('dæmə,siːn) *adj* **1** of Damascus. ◆ *n* **2** a native or inhabitant of Damascus.

Damascus ★ (də'mɑːskəs, -'mæs-) *n* the capital of Syria, in the southwest: reputedly the oldest city in the world, having been inhabited continuously since before 2000 B.C. Pop.: 1 549 932 (1994 est.). Arabic names: **Dimashq, Esh Sham** (ɛʃ ʃæm).

Damascus steel *or* **damask steel** *n History.* a hard flexible steel with wavy markings, used for sword blades.

damask ('dæməsk) *n* **1a** a reversible fabric, usually silk or linen, with a pattern woven into it. It is used for table linen, curtains, etc. **1b** table linen made from this. **1c** (*as modifier*): *a damask tablecloth.* **2** short for **Damascus steel. 3** the wavy markings on such steel. **4a** the greyish-pink colour of the damask rose. **4b** (*as adj*): *damask wallpaper.* ◆ *vb* **5** (*tr*) another word for **damascene.** [C14: from Med. L *damascus*, from Damascus, where fabric orig. made]

damask rose *n* a rose with fragrant flowers, which are used to make the perfume attar. [C16: from Med. L *rosa damascēna* rose of Damascus]

dame (deɪm) *n* **1** (formerly) a woman of rank or dignity; lady. **2** *Arch., chiefly Brit.* an elderly woman. **3** *Sl., chiefly US & Canad.* a woman. **4** *Brit.* the role of a comic old woman in a pantomime, usually played by a man. [C13: from OF, from L *domina* lady, mistress of household]

Dame (deɪm) *n* (in Britain) **1** the title of a woman who has been awarded the Order of the British Empire or any of certain other orders of chivalry. **2** the title of the wife of a knight or baronet.

dame school *n* (formerly) a small school, offering basic education, usually run by an elderly woman in her own home.

Damien ★ (*French* damjɛ̃) *n* **Joseph** (ʒozɛf), known as *Father Damien.* 1840–89, Belgian Roman Catholic missionary to the leper colony at Molokai, Hawaii.

damn (dæm) *interj* **1** *Sl.* an exclamation of annoyance. **2** *Inf.* an exclamation of surprise or pleasure. ◆ *adj* **3** (*prenominal*) *Sl.* deserving damnation. ◆ *adv, adj* **4** (*prenominal*) *Sl.* (intensifier): *a damn good pianist.* ◆ *adv* **5 damn all.** *Sl.* absolutely nothing. ◆ *vb* (*mainly tr*) **6** to condemn as bad, worthless, etc. **7** to curse. **8** to condemn to eternal damnation. **9** (*often passive*) to doom to ruin. **10** (*also intr*) to prove (someone) guilty: *damning evidence.* **11 damn with faint praise.** to praise so unenthusiastically that the effect is condemnation. ◆ *n* **12** *Sl.* something of negligible value (esp. in **not worth a damn**). **13 not give a damn.** *Inf.* not care. [C13: from OF *dampner*, from L *damnāre*, from *damnum* loss, injury]

damnable ('dæmnəb'l) *adj* **1** execrable; detestable. **2** liable to or deserving damnation.
▸ **'damnableness** *or* ,**damna'bility** *n*

damnably ('dæmnəblɪ) *adv* **1** in a detestable manner. **2** (intensifier): *it was damnably unfair.*

damnation (dæm'neɪʃən) *n* **1** the act of damning or state of being damned. ◆ *interj* **2** an exclamation of anger, disappointment, etc.

damnatory ('dæmnətərɪ) *adj* threatening or occasioning condemnation.

damned (dæmd) *adj* **1a** condemned to hell. **1b** (*as collective n*; preceded by *the*): *the damned.* ◆ *adv, adj Sl.* **2** (intensifier): *a damned good try.* **3** used to indicate amazement, disavowal, or refusal (as in **damned if I care**).

damnedest ('dæmdɪst) *n Inf.* utmost; best (esp. in the phrases **do** or **try one's damnedest**).

damnify ('dæmnɪ,faɪ) *vb* **damnifies, damnifying, damnified.** (*tr*) *Law.* to cause loss or damage to (a person); injure. [C16: from OF *damnifier*, ult. from L *damnum* harm, + *facere* to make]
▸ ,**damnifi'cation** *n*

Damocles ★ ('dæmə,kliːz) *n Classical legend.* a sycophant forced by Dionysius, tyrant of Syracuse, to sit under a sword suspended by a hair to demonstrate that being a king was not the happy state Damocles had said it was. See also **Sword of Damocles.**
▸ ,**Damo'clean** *adj*

Damodar ★ ('dæmə,dɑː) *n* a river in NE India, rising in Bihar and flowing east through West Bengal to the Hooghly River: the **Damodar Valley** is an important centre of heavy industry.

damoiselle, damosel, *or* **damozel** (,dæmə'zɛl) *n* archaic variants of **damsel.**

damp (dæmp) *adj* **1** slightly wet. ◆ *n* **2** slight wetness; moisture. **3** rank air or poisonous gas, esp. in a mine. **4** a

discouragement; damper. ◆ vb (tr) **5** to make slightly wet. **6** (often foll. by *down*) to stifle or deaden: *to damp one's ardour*. **7** (often foll. by *down*) to reduce the flow of air to (a fire) to make it burn more slowly. **8** *Physics*. to reduce the amplitude of (an oscillation or wave). **9** *Music*. to muffle (the sound of an instrument).   [C14: from MLow G *damp* steam]
▶ **'dampness** *n*

dampcourse ('dæmp,kɔːs) *n* a layer of impervious material in a wall, to stop moisture rising. Also called: **damp-proof course.**

dampen ('dæmpən) *vb* **1** to make or become damp. **2** (*tr*) to stifle; deaden.
▶ **'dampener** *n*

damper ('dæmpə) *n* **1** a person, event, or circumstance that depresses or discourages. **2 put a damper on.** to produce a depressing or stultifying effect on. **3** a movable plate to regulate the draught in a stove or furnace flue. **4** a device to reduce electronic, mechanical, acoustic, or aerodynamic oscillations in a system. **5** the pad in a piano or harpsichord that deadens the vibration of each string as its key is released. **6** *Chiefly Austral. & NZ.* any of various unleavened loaves and scones, typically cooked on an open fire.

damping off *n* any of various diseases of plants caused by fungi in conditions of excessive moisture.

damp-proof *Building trades.* ◆ *vb* **1** to protect against the incursion of damp by adding a dampcourse or by coating with a moisture-resistant preparation. ◆ *adj* **2** protected against damp or causing protection against damp: *a damp-proof course.*

damsel ('dæmzᵊl) *n Arch. or poetic.* a young unmarried woman; maiden.   [C13: from OF *damoisele*, from Vulgar L *domnicella* (unattested) young lady, from L *domina* mistress]

damselfly ('dæmzᵊl,flaɪ) *n, pl* **damselflies.** any of various insects similar to dragonflies but usually resting with the wings closed over the back.

damson ('dæmzən) *n* **1** a small tree cultivated for its blue-black edible plumlike fruit. **2** the fruit of this tree. [C14: from L *prūnum damascēnum* Damascus plum]

dan (dæn) *n Judo, karate, etc.* **1** any one of the 10 black-belt grades of proficiency. **2** a competitor entitled to dan grading.   [Japanese]

Dan ★ (dæn) *n Old Testament.* **1a** the fourth son of Jacob (Genesis 30:1–6). **1b** the tribe descended from him. **2** a city in the northern territory of Canaan.

Dan. *abbrev. for:* **1** *Bible.* Daniel. **2** Danish.

Dana ★ ('deɪnə) *n* James Dwight (dwaɪt). 1813–95, US geologist; noted for *The System of Mineralogy* (1837).

Danaë ★ ('dæneɪ,iː) *n Greek myth.* the mother of Perseus by Zeus, who came to her in prison as a shower of gold.

Danaides ★ (də'neɪɪ,diːz) *pl n, sing* **Danaid**. *Greek myth.* the fifty daughters of Danaüs. All but Hypermnestra murdered their bridegrooms and were punished in Hades by having to pour water perpetually into a jar with a hole in the bottom.
▶ **Danaidean** (,dænɪ'ɪdɪən, ,dænɪə'diːən) *adj*

Da Nang ★ (dɑː 'næŋ) *n* a port in central Vietnam, on the South China Sea. Pop.: 382 674 (1992 est.). Former name: **Tourane.**

Danaüs ★ ('dænɪəs) *n Greek myth.* a king of Argos who told his fifty daughters, the Danaides, to kill their bridegrooms on their wedding night.

dance (dɑːns) *vb* **dances, dancing, danced.** **1** (*intr*) to move the feet and body rhythmically, esp. in time to music. **2** (*tr*) to perform (a particular dance). **3** (*intr*) to skip or leap. **4** to move or cause to move in a rhythmic way. **5 dance attendance on (someone).** to attend (someone) solicitously or obsequiously. ◆ *n* **6** a series of rhythmic steps and movements, usually in time to music. **7** an act of dancing. **8a** a social meeting arranged for dancing. **8b** (*as modifier*): *a dance hall.* **9** a piece of music in the rhythm of a particular dance form. **10** dancelike movements. **11 lead (someone) a dance.** *Brit. inf.* to cause (someone) continued worry and exasperation.   [C13: from OF *dancier*]
▶ **'danceable** *adj* ▶ **'dancer** *n* ▶ **'dancing** *n, adj*

dance floor *n* **a** an area of floor in a disco, etc., where patrons may dance. **b** (*as modifier*): *dancefloor music.*

dancehall ('dɑːns,hɔːl) *n* a style of dance-oriented reggae, originating in the late 1980s.

dance of death *n* a medieval representation of a dance in which people are led off to their graves, by a personification of death. Also called (French): **danse macabre.**

D and C *n Med.* dilation (of the cervix) and curettage (of the uterus).

dandelion ('dændɪ,laɪən) *n* **1** a plant native to Europe and Asia and naturalized as a weed in North America, having yellow rayed flowers and deeply notched leaves. **2** any of several similar plants.   [C15: from OF *dent de lion*, lit.: tooth of a lion, referring to its leaves]

dander ('dændə) *n* **1** small particles of hair or feathers. **2 get one's (or someone's) dander up.** *Inf.* to become (or cause to become) annoyed or angry.   [C19: from DANDRUFF]

dandify ('dændɪ,faɪ) *vb* **dandifies, dandifying, dandified.** (*tr*) to dress like or cause to resemble a dandy.

dandle ('dændᵊl) *vb* **dandles, dandling, dandled.** (*tr*) **1** to move (a young child) up and down (on the knee or in the arms). **2** to pet; fondle.   [C16: from ?]
▶ **'dandler** *n*

dandruff ('dændrəf) *n* loose scales of dry dead skin shed from the scalp.   [C16: *dand-* from ? + *-ruff*, prob. from ME *roufe* scab, from ON *hrúfa*]

dandy ('dændɪ) *n, pl* **dandies. 1** a man greatly concerned with smartness of dress. ◆ *adj* **dandier, dandiest. 2** *Inf.* good or fine.   [C18: ? short for *jack-a-dandy*]
▶ **'dandyish** *adj*

dandy-brush *n* a stiff brush used for grooming a horse.

dandy roll or **roller** *n* a roller used in the manufacture of paper to produce watermarks.

Dane (deɪn) *n* **1** a native, citizen, or inhabitant of Denmark. **2** any of the Vikings who invaded England from the late 8th to the 11th century A.D.

Danegeld ('deɪn,geld) or **Danegelt** ('deɪn,gelt) *n* the tax levied in Anglo-Saxon England to provide protection money for or to finance forces to oppose Viking invaders.   [C11: from *Dan* Dane + *geld* tribute; see YIELD]

Danelaw ('deɪn,lɔː) *n* the parts of Anglo-Saxon England in which Danish law and custom were observed.   [OE *Dena lagu* Danes' law]

danger ('deɪndʒə) *n* **1** the state of being vulnerable to injury, loss, or evil; risk. **2** a person or thing that may cause injury, pain, etc. **3 in danger of.** liable to. **4 on the danger list.** critically ill in hospital.   [C13 *daunger* power, hence power to inflict injury, from OF *dongier* from L *dominium* ownership]
▶ **'dangerless** *adj*

danger money *n* extra money paid to compensate for the risks involved in certain dangerous jobs.

dangerous ('deɪndʒərəs) *adj* causing danger; perilous.
▶ **'dangerously** *adv*

dangle ('dæŋɡᵊl) *vb* **dangles, dangling, dangled. 1** to hang or cause to hang freely: *his legs dangled over the wall.* **2** (*tr*) to display as an enticement.   [C16: ?from Danish *dangle*, prob. imit.]
▶ **'dangler** *n*

Daniel ★ ('dænjəl) *n* **1** *Old Testament.* **1a** a youth who was taken into the household of Nebuchadnezzar, received guidance and apocalyptic visions from God, and given divine protection when thrown into the lions' den. **1b** the book that recounts these experiences and visions (in full **The Book of the Prophet Daniel**). **2** (often preceded by *a*) a wise upright person.   [sense 2: referring to Daniel in the Apocryphal *Book of Susanna*]

Danish ('deɪnɪʃ) *adj* **1** of Denmark, its people, or their language. ◆ *n* **2** the official language of Denmark.

Danish blue *n* a strong-tasting white cheese with blue veins.

Danish pastry *n* a rich puff pastry filled with apple, almond paste, icing, etc.

Danish West Indies ★ *pl n* the former possession of Denmark in the W Lesser Antilles, sold to the US in 1917

───────────────
★ people and places

and since then named the **Virgin Islands of the United States.**

dank (dæŋk) *adj* (esp. of cellars, caves, etc.) unpleasantly damp and chilly. [C14: prob. from ON]
▶ **'dankly** *adv* ▶ **'dankness** *n*

Dankworth ★ ('dæŋkwɜːθ) *n* **John (Philip William)**. born 1927, British jazz composer and saxophonist: married to Cleo Laine.

Danmark ★ ('danmarg) *n* the Danish name for **Denmark.**

D'Annunzio ★ (*Italian* dan'nuntsjo) *n* **Gabriele** (ga-'brjeːle). 1863–1938, Italian writer and Fascist. His works include the poems in *Alcione* (1904) and the drama *La Figlia di Iorio* (1904).

danseur *French.* (dɑ̃sœr) *or* (*fem*) **danseuse** (dɑ̃søz) *n* a ballet dancer.

Dante ★ ('dæntɪ, 'dɑːnteɪ; *Italian* 'dante) *n* full name **Dante Alighieri** (*Italian* aliˈgjeːri). 1265–1321, Italian poet. His works include *La Divina Commedia* (?1309–?1320) and *La Vita Nuova* (?1292).
▶ **Dantean** ('dæntɪən, dænˈtiːən) *or* **Dantesque** (dænˈtɛsk) *adj*

Danton ★ ('dæntən; *French* dɑ̃tɔ̃) *n* **Georges Jacques** (ʒɔrʒ ʒak). 1759–94, French revolutionary leader: a founder member of the Committee of Public Safety (1793) and minister of justice (1792–94): guillotined.

Danube ★ ('dænjuːb) *n* a river in central and SE Europe, rising in the Black Forest in Germany and flowing to the Black Sea. Length: 2859 km (1776 miles). German name: **Donau.** Czech name: **Dunaj.** Hungarian name: **Duna.** Serbo-Croat name: **Dunav** (dunaf). Romanian name: **Dunărea.**
▶ **Danubian** (dænˈjuːbɪən) *adj*

Danzig ★ ('dænsɪg; *German* 'dantsɪç) *n* the German name for **Gdańsk.**

dap (dæp) *vb* **daps, dapping, dapped. 1** *Angling.* to fly-fish so that the fly bobs on and off the water. **2** (*intr*) to dip lightly into water. **3** to bounce or cause to bounce. [C17: imit.]

daphne ('dæfnɪ) *n* any of various Eurasian ornamental shrubs with shiny evergreen leaves and clusters of small bell-shaped flowers. [via L from Gk: laurel]

Daphne ('dæfnɪ) *n Greek myth.* a nymph who was saved from the amorous attentions of Apollo by being changed into a laurel tree.

daphnia ('dæfnɪə) *n* any of several waterfleas having a rounded body enclosed in a transparent shell. [C19: prob. from DAPHNE]

Daphnis ★ ('dæfnɪs) *n Greek myth.* a Sicilian shepherd, the son of Hermes and a nymph, who was regarded as the inventor of pastoral poetry.

Da Ponte ★ (*Italian* da ˈpɔnte) *n* **Lorenzo** (loˈrɛntso), real name *Emmanuele Conegliano.* 1749–1838, Italian writer; Mozart's librettist for *The Marriage of Figaro* (1786), *Don Giovanni* (1787), and *Così fan tutte* (1790).

dapper ('dæpə) *adj* **1** neat in dress and bearing. **2** small and nimble. [C15: from MDu.: active, nimble]
▶ **'dapperly** *adv* ▶ **'dapperness** *n*

dapple ('dæp³l) *vb* **dapples, dappling, dappled. 1** to mark or become marked with spots of a different colour; mottle. ◆ *n* **2** mottled or spotted markings. **3** a dappled horse, etc. ◆ *adj* **4** marked with dapples or spots. [C14: from ?]

dapple-grey *n* a horse with a grey coat having spots of darker colour.

Dapsang ★ (dʌpˈsʌŋ) *n* another name for **K2.**

darbies ('dɑːbɪz) *pl n Brit.* a slang term for **handcuffs.** [C16: ?from *Father Derby's* (or *Darby's*) *bonds,* a rigid agreement between a usurer and his client]

Darby and Joan ('dɑːbɪ) *n* **1** an ideal elderly married couple living in domestic harmony. **2 Darby and Joan Club.** a club for elderly people. [C18: couple in 18th-cent. English ballad]

Darcy ★ ('dɑːsɪ) *n* (**James**) **Les**(lie). 1895–1917, Australian boxer and folk hero.

Dardanelles ★ (ˌdɑːdəˈnɛlz) *n* the strait between the Aegean and the Sea of Marmara, separating European from Asian Turkey. Ancient name: **Hellespont.**

dare (dɛə) *vb* **dares, daring, dared. 1** (*tr*) to challenge (a person to do something) as proof of courage. **2** (can take an infinitive with or without *to*) to be courageous enough to try (to do something). **3** (*tr*) *Rare.* to oppose without fear; defy. **4 I dare say. 4a** (it is) quite possible (that). **4b** probably. ◆ *n* **5** a challenge to do something as proof of courage. **6** something done in response to such a challenge. [OE *durran*]
▶ **'darer** *n*

daredevil ('dɛəˌdɛvᵊl) *n* **1** a recklessly bold person. ◆ *adj* **2** reckless; daring; bold.
▶ **'dare,devilry** *or* **'dare,deviltry** *n*

Dar es Salaam ★ ('dɑːr ɛs səˈlɑːm) *n* the chief port of Tanzania, on the Indian Ocean: capital of German East Africa (1891–1916); capital of Tanzania until 1983 when it was replaced by Dodoma; university (1963). Pop.: 1 360 850 (1988).

Darfur ★ (dɑːˈfʊə) *n* a region of W Sudan; an independent kingdom until conquered by Egypt in 1874.

Darien ★ ('dɛərɪən, 'dæ-) *n* **1** the E part of the Isthmus of Panama, between the **Gulf of Darien** on the Caribbean coast and the Gulf of San Miguel on the Pacific coast; chiefly within the republic of Panama but extending also into Colombia: site of a disastrous attempt to establish a Scottish colony in 1698. **2 Isthmus of.** the former name of the Isthmus of **Panama.** ◆ Spanish name: **Darién** (daˈrjen).

daring ('dɛərɪŋ) *adj* **1** bold or adventurous. ◆ *n* **2** courage in taking risks; boldness.

Dario ★ (*Spanish* da'rio) *n* **Rubén** (ruˈβen), real name *Félix Rubén Garcia Sarmiento.* 1867–1916, Nicaraguan poet whose work includes *Prosas Profanas* (1896).

Darius I ★ (da'raɪəs) *n* known as *Darius the Great,* surname *Hystaspis.* ?550–486 B.C., king of Persia (521–486). He led two expeditions against Greece but was defeated at Marathon (490).

Darjeeling ★ (dɑːˈdʒiːlɪŋ) *n* **1** a town in NE India, in West Bengal in the Himalayas, at an altitude of about 2250 m (7500 ft). Pop.: 73 090 (1991). **2** a high-quality black tea grown in the mountains around Darjeeling.

dark (dɑːk) *adj* **1** having little or no light. **2** (of a colour) reflecting or transmitting little light: *dark brown.* **3** (of complexion, hair colour, etc.) not fair; swarthy; brunette. **4** gloomy or dismal. **5** sinister; evil: *a dark purpose.* **6** sullen or angry. **7** ignorant or unenlightened: *a dark period in our history.* **8** secret or mysterious. ◆ *n* **9** absence of light; darkness. **10** night or nightfall. **11** a dark place. **12** a state of ignorance (esp. in **in the dark**). [OE *deorc*]
▶ **'darkish** *adj* ▶ **'darkly** *adv* ▶ **'darkness** *n*

Dark Ages *pl n European history.* the period from about the late 5th century A.D. to about 1000 A.D., once considered an unenlightened period.

Dark Continent ★ *n the.* a term for Africa when it was relatively unexplored by Europeans.

darken ('dɑːkən) *vb* **1** to make or become dark or darker. **2** to make or become gloomy, angry, or sad. **3 darken (someone's) door.** (*usually used with a negative*) to visit someone: *never darken my door again!*
▶ **'darkener** *n*

dark horse *n* **1** a competitor in a race or contest about whom little is known. **2** a person who reveals little about himself, esp. one who has unexpected talents. **3** *US politics.* a candidate who is unexpectedly nominated or elected.

dark lantern *n* a lantern having a sliding shutter or panel to dim or hide the light.

darkling ('dɑːklɪŋ) *adv*, *adj Poetic.* in the dark or night. [C15: from DARK + -LING²]

dark matter *n Astron.* matter known to make up a substantial part of the mass of the universe, but not detectable by its absorption or emission of electromagnetic radiation.

darkroom ('dɑːk,ruːm, -,rʊm) *n* a room in which photographs are processed in darkness or safe light.

darksome ('dɑːksəm) *adj Literary.* dark or darkish.

dark star *n* an invisible star known to exist only from observation of its radio, infrared, or other spectrum or of its gravitational effect.

Darlan ★ (*French* darlɑ̃) *n* **Jean Louis Xavier François** (ʒɑ̃ lwi gzavje frɑ̃swa). 1881–1942, French admiral and member of the Vichy government. He cooperated with the Allies after their invasion of North Africa; assassinated.

darling ('dɑːlɪŋ) *n* **1** a person very much loved. **2** a favourite. ◆ *adj* (*prenominal*) **3** beloved. **4** much admired; pleasing: *a darling hat.* [OE *dēorling*; see DEAR, -LING[1]]

Darling ★ ('dɑːlɪŋ) *n* **Grace.** 1815–42, British national heroine, famous for her rescue (1838) of some shipwrecked sailors with her father, a lighthouse keeper.

Darling Downs ★ *pl n* a plateau in NE Australia, in SE Queensland: a vast agricultural and stock-raising area.

Darling Range ★ *n* a ridge in SW Western Australia, parallel to the coast. Highest point: about 582 m (1669 ft).

Darling River ★ *n* a river in SE Australia, rising in the Eastern Highlands and flowing southwest to the Murray River. Length: 2740 km (1702 miles).

Darlington ★ ('dɑːlɪŋtən) *n* **1** an industrial town in NE England in S Durham: developed mainly with the opening of the Stockton-Darlington railway (1825). Pop.: 86 767 (1991). **2** a unitary authority in NE England, in Durham. Pop.: 101 106 (1997 est.). Area: 198 sq. km (77 sq. miles).

Darmstadt ★ ('dɑːmstæt; *German* 'darmʃtat) *n* an industrial city in central Germany, in Hesse: former capital of the grand duchy of Hesse-Darmstadt (1567–1945). Pop.: 139 063 (1995 est.).

darn[1] (dɑːn) *vb* **1** to mend (a hole or a garment) with a series of crossing or interwoven stitches. ◆ *n* **2** a patch of darned work on a garment. [C16: prob. from F (dialect) *darner*]
▶ 'darner *n*

darn[2] (dɑːn) *interj, adj, adv, n* a euphemistic word for **damn** (senses 1–5, 12, 13).

darnel ('dɑːn°l) *n* any of several grasses that grow as weeds in grain fields in Europe and Asia. [C14: prob. rel. to F (dialect) *darnelle*, from ?]

darning ('dɑːnɪŋ) *n* **1** the act of mending a hole using interwoven stitches. **2** garments needing to be darned.

darning needle *n* a long needle with a large eye used for darning.

Darnley ★ ('dɑːnlɪ) *n* **Lord.** title of *Henry Stuart* (or *Stewart*). 1545–67, Scottish nobleman; second husband of Mary, Queen of Scots and father of James I of England. After murdering his wife's secretary, Rizzio (1566), he was assassinated.

dart (dɑːt) *n* **1** a small narrow pointed missile that is thrown or shot, as in the game of darts. **2** a sudden quick movement. **3** *Zool.* a slender pointed structure, as in snails for aiding copulation. **4** a tapered tuck made in dressmaking. ◆ *vb* **5** to move or throw swiftly and suddenly; shoot. [C14: from OF, of Gmc origin]
▶ 'darting *adj*

dartboard ('dɑːt,bɔːd) *n* a circular piece of wood, cork, etc., used as the target in the game of darts.

darter ('dɑːtə) *n* **1** Also called: **anhinga, snakebird.** any of various aquatic birds of tropical and subtropical inland waters, having a long slender neck and bill. **2** any of various small brightly coloured North American freshwater fish.

Dartford ★ ('dɑːtfəd) *n* a town in SE England, in NW Kent. Pop.: 59 411 (1991).

Dartmoor ★ ('dɑːt,mʊə) *n* **1** a moorland plateau in SW England, in SW Devon: a national park since 1951. Area: 945 sq. km (365 sq. miles). **2** a prison in SW England, on Dartmoor: England's main prison for long-term convicts. **3** a small strong breed of pony, originally from

Dartmoor. **4** a hardy coarse-woolled breed of sheep originally from Dartmoor.

Dartmouth ★ ('dɑːtməθ) *n* **1** a port in SW England, in S Devon: Royal Naval College (1905). Pop.: 5676 (1991). **2** a city in SE Canada, in S Nova Scotia, on Halifax Harbour: oil refineries and shipyards. Pop.: 67 798 (1991).

darts (dɑːts) *n* (*functioning as sing*) any of various competitive games in which darts are thrown at a dartboard.

Darwin[1] ★ ('dɑːwɪn) *n* a port in N Australia, capital of the Northern Territory: destroyed by a cyclone in 1974 but rebuilt on the same site. Pop.: 78 100 (1994). Former name (1869–1911): **Palmerston.**

Darwin[2] ★ ('dɑːwɪn) *n* **1 Charles** (**Robert**). 1809–82, British naturalist who formulated the theory of evolution, expounded in *On the Origin of Species* (1859) and applied to man in *The Descent of Man* (1871). **2** his grandfather, **Erasmus.** 1731–1802, British physician and poet; author of *Zoonomia* (1794–96), anticipating Lamarck's views on evolution. **3** Sir **George Howard,** son of Charles Darwin. 1845–1912, British astronomer.

Darwinian (dɑːˈwɪnɪən) *adj* **1** of or relating to Charles Darwin or his theory of evolution. ◆ *n* **2** a person who accepts, supports, or uses this theory.

Darwinism ('dɑːwɪ,nɪzəm) *or* **Darwinian theory** *n* the theory of the origin of animal and plant species by evolution through a process of natural selection.
▶ 'Darwinist *n, adj*

dash[1] (dæʃ) *vb* (*mainly tr*) **1** to hurl; crash: *he dashed the cup to the floor.* **2** to mix: *white paint dashed with blue.* **3** (*intr*) to move hastily or recklessly; rush. **4** (usually foll. by *off* or *down*) to write (down) or finish (off) hastily. **5** to frustrate: *his hopes were dashed.* **6** to daunt (someone); discourage. ◆ *n* **7** a sudden quick movement. **8** a small admixture: *coffee with a dash of cream.* **9** a violent stroke or blow. **10** the sound of splashing or smashing. **11** panache; style: *he rides with dash.* **12** Also called: **rule.** the punctuation mark —, used to indicate a sudden change of subject or to enclose a parenthetical remark. **13** the symbol (–) used, in combination with the symbol *dot* (·), in the written representation of Morse and other telegraphic codes. **14** *Athletics.* another word for **sprint.** [ME *daschen, dassen,* ?from ON]

dash[2] (dæʃ) *interj Inf.* a euphemistic word for **damn** (senses 1, 2).

dashboard ('dæʃ,bɔːd) *n* **1** Also called (Brit.): **fascia.** the instrument panel in a car, boat, or aircraft. **2** *Obs.* a board at the side of a carriage or boat to protect against splashing.

dasher ('dæʃə) *n* **1** one that dashes. **2** *Canad.* the ledge along the top of the boards of an ice hockey rink.

dashiki (dɑːˈʃiːkɪ) *n* a large loose-fitting upper garment worn esp. by Blacks in the US, Africa, and the Caribbean. [C20: of W African origin]

dashing ('dæʃɪŋ) *adj* **1** spirited; lively: *a dashing young man.* **2** stylish; showy.

dashlight ('dæʃ,laɪt) *n* a light that illuminates the dashboard of a car, esp. at night.

Dasht-i-Kavir *or* **Dasht-e-Kavir** ★ (,dæʃtiːkæˈvɪə) *n* a salt waste on the central plateau of Iran: a treacherous marsh beneath a salt crust. Also called: **Kavir Desert.**

Dasht-i-Lut *or* **Dasht-e-Lut** ★ (,dæʃtiːˈlʊt) *n* a desert plateau in central and E central Iran.

Dassehra ('dæsəəræ) *n* an annual Hindu festival celebrated on the 10th lunar day of Navaratri; images of the goddess Durga are immersed in water.

dassie ('dæsɪ) *n* another name for a **hyrax,** esp. the rock hyrax. [C19: from Afrik.]

dastardly ('dæstədlɪ) *adj* mean and cowardly. [C15 *dastard* (in the sense: dullard): prob. from ON *dæstr* exhausted, out of breath]
▶ 'dastardliness *n*

dasyure ('dæsɪ,jʊə) *n* **1** any of several small carnivorous marsupials of Australia, New Guinea, and adjacent islands. **2** the ursine dasyure. See **Tasmanian devil.** [C19: from NL, from Gk *dasus* shaggy + *oura* tail]

DAT *abbrev. for* digital audio tape.

dat. *abbrev. for* dative.

data ('deɪtə, 'dɑːtə) *pl n* **1** a series of observations, measurements, or facts; information. **2** Also called: **information.** *Computing.* the information operated on by a computer program. [C17: from L, lit.: (things) given, from *dare* to give]

> **USAGE NOTE** Although now often used as a singular noun, *data* is properly a plural.

database ('deɪtə,beɪs) *n* **1** Also called: **data bank.** a store of a large amount of information, esp. in a form that can be handled by a computer. **2** *Inf.* any large store of information: *a database of knowledge.*

data capture *n* any process for converting information into a form that can be handled by a computer.

data pen *n* a device for reading or scanning magnetically coded data on labels, packets, etc.

data processing *n* **a** a sequence of operations performed on data, esp. by a computer, in order to extract information, reorder files, etc. **b** (*as modifier*): *a data-processing centre.*

data protection *n* (in Britain) safeguards for individuals relating to personal data stored on a computer.

data set *n Computing.* another name for **file**[1] (sense 6).

date[1] (deɪt) *n* **1** a specified day of the month. **2** the particular day or year of an event. **3** an inscription on a coin, letter, etc., stating when it was made or written. **4a** an appointment for a particular time, esp. with a person of the opposite sex. **4b** the person with whom the appointment is made. **5** the present moment; now (esp. in **to date, up to date**). ◆ *vb* **dates, dating, dated**. **6** (*tr*) to mark (a letter, coin, etc.) with the day, month, or year. **7** (*tr*) to assign a date of occurrence or creation to. **8** (*intr*; foll. by *from* or *back to*) to have originated (at a specified time). **9** (*tr*) to reveal the age of: *that dress dates her.* **10** to make or become old-fashioned: *some good films hardly date at all.* **11** *Inf., chiefly US & Canad.* **11a** to be a boyfriend or girlfriend of (someone of the opposite sex). **11b** to accompany (a member of the opposite sex) on a date. [C14: from OF, from L *dare* to give, as in *epistula data Romae* letter handed over at Rome]

> ▸ 'datable *or* 'dateable *adj*

> **USAGE NOTE** See at **year.**

date[2] (deɪt) *n* **1** the fruit of the date palm, having sweet edible flesh and a single large woody seed. **2** short for **date palm**. [C13: from OF, from L, from Gk *daktulos* finger]

dated ('deɪtɪd) *adj* **1** unfashionable; outmoded. **2** (of a security) having a fixed date for redemption.

dateless ('deɪtlɪs) *adj* likely to remain fashionable, good, or interesting regardless of age.

dateline ('deɪt,laɪn) *n Journalism.* the date and location of a story, placed at the top of an article.

date line *n* (*often caps.*) short for **International Date Line.**

date palm *n* a tall feather palm grown in tropical regions for its sweet edible fruit.

date rape *n* **1** the act or an instance of a man raping a woman while they are on a date together. **2** an act of sexual intercourse regarded as tantamount to rape, esp. if the woman was encouraged to drink excessively or was subjected to undue pressure.

date stamp *n* **1** an adjustable rubber stamp for recording the date. **2** an inked impression made by this.

dating ('deɪtɪŋ) *n* any of several techniques, such as radiocarbon dating, dendrochronology, or varve dating, for establishing the age of rocks, palaeontological or archaeological specimens, etc.

dating agency *n* an agency that provides introductions to people seeking a companion with similar interests.

dative ('deɪtɪv) *Grammar.* ◆ *adj* **1** denoting a case of nouns, pronouns, and adjectives used to express the indirect object, to identify the recipients, and for other purposes. ◆ *n* **2a** the dative case. **2b** a word or speech element in this case. [C15: from L *datīvus*, from *dare* to give]

> ▸ **datival** (deɪ'taɪvəl) *adj* ▸ **'datively** *adv*

datum ('deɪtəm, 'dɑːtəm) *n, pl* **data. 1** a single piece of information; fact. **2** a proposition taken as unquestionable, often in order to construct some theoretical framework upon it. See also **sense datum.** [C17: from L: something given; see DATA]

datura (də'tjʊərə) *n* any of various chiefly Indian plants and shrubs with large trumpet-shaped flowers. [C16: from NL, from Hindi]

daub (dɔːb) *vb* **1** (*tr*) to smear or spread (paint, mud, etc.), esp. carelessly. **2** (*tr*) to cover or coat (with paint, plaster, etc.) carelessly. **3** to paint (a picture) clumsily or badly. ◆ *n* **4** an unskilful or crude painting. **5** something daubed on, esp. as a wall covering. **6** a smear of (paint, mud, etc.). [C14: from OF *dauber* to paint, whitewash, from L *dealbāre*, from *albāre* to whiten]

> ▸ 'dauber *n*

Daubigny ★ (*French* dobiɲi) *n* **Charles François** (ʃarl frɑ̃swa). 1817–78, French landscape painter associated with the Barbizon School.

Daudet ★ (*French* dodɛ) *n* **Alphonse** (alfɔ̃s). 1840–97, French novelist, short-story writer, and dramatist: noted particularly for his humorous sketches of Provençal life, as in *Lettres de mon moulin* (1866).

Daugava ★ ('daugaˌva) *n* the Latvian name for the Western **Dvina.**

Daugavpils ★ (*Latvian* 'daugafˌpils) *n* a city in SE Latvia on the Western Dvina River: founded in 1274 by Teutonic Knights; ruled by Poland (1559–1772) and Russia (1772–1915; 1940–91). Pop.: 120 152 (1995 est.). German name (until 1893): **Dünaburg.** Former Russian name (1893–1920): **Dvinsk.**

daughter ('dɔːtə) *n* **1** a female offspring; a girl or woman in relation to her parents. **2** a female descendant. **3** a female from a certain country, etc., or one closely connected with a certain environment, etc.: *a daughter of the church.* ◆ (*modifier*) **4** *Biol.* denoting a cell or unicellular organism produced by the division of one of its own kind. **5** *Physics.* (of a nuclide) formed from another nuclide by radioactive decay. [OE *dohtor*]

> ▸ 'daughterhood *n* ▸ 'daughterless *adj* ▸ 'daughterly *adj*

daughter-in-law *n, pl* **daughters-in-law.** the wife of one's son.

Daumier ★ (*French* domje) *n* **Honoré** (ɔnɔre). 1808–79, French painter and lithographer, noted particularly for his political and social caricatures.

daunt (dɔːnt) *vb* (*tr; often passive*) **1** to intimidate. **2** to dishearten. [C13: from OF *danter*, changed from *donter* to conquer, from L *domitāre* to tame]

> ▸ 'daunting *adj* ▸ 'dauntingly *adv*

dauntless ('dɔːntlɪs) *adj* bold; fearless; intrepid.

> ▸ 'dauntlessly *adv* ▸ 'dauntlessness *n*

dauphin ('dɔːfɪn; *French* dofɛ̃) *n* (1349–1830) the title of the eldest son of the king of France. [C15: from OF: orig. a family name]

dauphine ('dɔːfiːn; *French* dofin) *or* **dauphiness** ('dɔːfɪnɪs) *n French history.* the wife of a dauphin.

davenport ('dævən,pɔːt) *n* **1** *Chiefly Brit.* a tall narrow writing desk with drawers. **2** *US & Canad.* a large sofa, esp. one convertible into a bed. [C19: sense 1 supposedly after Captain *Davenport*, who commissioned the first ones]

Daventry ★ ('dævəntrɪ) *n* a town in central England, in Northamptonshire: light industries, site of an important international radio transmitter. Pop.: 18 099 (1991).

David ★ ('deɪvɪd) *n* **1** the second king of the Hebrews (about 1000–962 B.C.), who united Israel as a kingdom with Jerusalem as its capital. **2 Elizabeth.** 1914–92, British cookery writer. Her books include *Mediterranean Food* (1950). **3** (*French* david). **Jacques Louis** (ʒak lwi). 1748–1825, French neoclassical painter. **4 Saint.** 6th century A.D., Welsh bishop; patron saint of Wales. Feast day: March 1.

David I ★ *n* 1084–1153, king of Scotland (1124–53) who supported his niece Matilda's claim to the English throne and unsuccessfully invaded England on her behalf.

David II ★ *n* 1324–71, king of Scotland (1329–71): he was forced into exile in France (1334–41) by Edward de Baliol; captured following the battle of Neville's Cross (1346), and imprisoned by the English (1346–57).

Davies ★ ('deɪvɪs) *n* **1** Sir **John**. 1569–1626, English poet, author of *Orchestra or a Poem of Dancing* (1596). **2** Sir **Peter Maxwell**. born 1934, British composer whose works include the opera *Taverner* (1967), four symphonies, and a violin concerto (1985). **3** (**William**) **Robertson**. 1913–95, Canadian novelist and dramatist. His novels include *Murther and Walking Spirits* (1991). **4** W(illiam) H(enry). 1871–1940, Welsh poet, noted also for his *Autobiography of a Super-tramp* (1908).

da Vinci ★ (də 'vɪntʃɪ) *n* See **Leonardo da Vinci**.

Davis ★ ('deɪvɪs) *n* **1** Bette ('bɛtɪ), real name *Ruth Elizabeth Davis* 1908–89, US film actress, whose films include *Jezebel* (1938) and *Now Voyager* (1942). **2** Sir **Colin** (**Rex**). born 1927, British conductor. **3 Jefferson**. 1808–89, president of the Confederate States of America during the Civil War (1861–65). **4 Joe**. 1901–78, British billiards and snooker player: world champion from 1927 to 1946. **5 John**. Also called: **John Davys**. ?1550–1605, English navigator: discovered the Falkland Islands (1592). **6 Miles** (**Dewey**). 1926–91, US jazz trumpeter and composer. **7 Steve**. born 1957, British snooker player: world champion 1981, 1983–84, 1987–89.

Davisson ★ ('deɪvɪsⁿn) *n* Clinton Joseph. 1881–1958, US physicist, noted for his discovery of electron diffraction; shared the Nobel prize for physics 1937.

Davis Strait ★ *n* a strait between Baffin Island, in Canada, and Greenland. [after John Davis]

davit ('dævɪt, 'deɪ-) *n* a cranelike device, usually one of a pair, fitted with a tackle for suspending or lowering equipment, esp. a lifeboat. [C14: from Anglo-F *daviot*, dim. of *Davi* David]

Davos ★ ('dɑːvɒs) *n* a mountain resort in Switzerland: winter sports, site of the Parsenn ski run. Pop.: 10 500 (1990). Height: about 1560 m (5118 ft). Romansh name: **Tarau**.

Davy ★ ('deɪvɪ) *n* Sir **Humphry**. 1778–1829, British chemist who isolated sodium, chlorine, and other elements. He invented the **Davy lamp**.

Davy Jones *n* **1** Also called: **Davy Jones's locker**. the ocean's bottom, esp. when regarded as the grave of those lost or buried at sea. **2** the spirit of the sea. [C18: from ?]

Davy lamp *n* See **safety lamp**. [C19: after Sir H. Davy, who invented it]

daw (dɔ:) *n* an archaic, dialect, or poetic name for a **jackdaw**. [C15: rel. to OHG *taha*]

dawdle ('dɔːdˁl) *vb* **dawdles, dawdling, dawdled. 1** (*intr*) to be slow or lag behind. **2** (when *tr*, often foll. by *away*) to waste (time); trifle. [C17: from ?]
▸ '**dawdler** *n*

Dawes ★ (dɔːz) *n* **Charles Gates**. 1865–1951, US financier and statesman, who devised the Dawes Plan for German reparations after World War I; Nobel peace prize 1925.

Dawkins ★ ('dɔːkɪnz) *n* Richard. born 1941, British zoologist and author of *The Selfish Gene* (1976) and *River Out of Eden* (1995).

dawn (dɔ:n) *n* **1** daybreak. Related adj: **auroral. 2** the sky when light first appears in the morning. **3** the beginning of something. ◆ *vb* (*intr*) **4** to begin to grow light after the night. **5** to begin to develop or appear. **6** (usually foll. by *on* or *upon*) to begin to become apparent (to). [OE *dagian* to dawn]
▸ '**dawn,like** *adj*

dawn chorus *n* the singing of large numbers of birds at dawn.

dawn raid *n Stock Exchange*. an unexpected attempt to acquire a substantial proportion of a company's shares at the start of a day's trading as a preliminary to a take-over bid.

Dawson Creek ★ ('dɔːsⁿn) *n* a town in W Canada, in NE British Columbia: SE terminus of the Alaska Highway. Pop.: 10 981 (1991).

day (deɪ) *n* **1** Also called: **civil day**. the period of time, or **calendar day**, of 24 hours' duration reckoned from one midnight to the next. **2a** the period of light between sunrise and sunset. **2b** (*as modifier*): *the day shift*. **3** the part of a day occupied with regular activity, esp. work. **4** (*sometimes pl*) a period or point in time: *in days gone by; any day now*. **5** the period of time, the **sidereal day**, during which the earth makes one complete revolution on its axis relative to a particular star. **6** the period of time, the **solar day**, during which the earth makes one complete revolution on its axis relative to the sun. **7** the period of time taken by a specified planet to make one complete rotation on its axis: *the Martian day*. **8** (*often cap.*) a day designated for a special observance: *Christmas Day*. **9** a time of success, recognition, etc.: *his day will come*. **10** a struggle or issue at hand: *the day is lost*. **11** all in a day's work. part of one's normal activity. **12 at the end of the day**. in the final reckoning. **13 call it a day**. to stop work or other activity. **14 day after day**. without respite; relentlessly. **15 day by day**. gradually or progressively. **16 day in, day out**. every day and all day long. **17 day of rest**. the Sabbath; Sunday. **18 every dog has his day**. one's luck will come. **19 in this day and age**. nowadays. **20 that will be the day**. **20a** that is most unlikely to happen. **20b** I look forward to that. ◆ Related adj: **diurnal**. ◆ See also **days**. [OE *dæg*]

Dayak ('daɪæk) *n, pl* **Dayaks** or **Dayak**. a variant spelling of **Dyak**.

Dayan ★ (daɪ'jɑːn) *n* Moshe ('mɒʃe). 1915–81, Israeli soldier and statesman; minister of defence (1967; 1969–74) and foreign minister (1977–79).

day bed *n* a narrow bed intended for use as a seat and as a bed.

daybook ('deɪ,bʊk) *n Book-keeping*. a book in which the transactions of each day are recorded as they occur.

dayboy ('deɪ,bɔɪ) *n Brit*. a boy who attends a boarding school daily, but returns home each evening.
▸ '**daygirl** *fem n*

daybreak ('deɪ,breɪk) *n* the time in the morning when light first appears; dawn; sunrise.

daycare ('deɪ,keə) *n Brit. social welfare*. **1** occupation, treatment, or supervision during the working day for people who might be at risk if left on their own. **2** welfare services provided by a local authority, health service, etc., during the day.

daycentre ('deɪ,sɛntə) or **day centre** *n Social welfare*. (in Britain) **1** a building used for daycare or other welfare services. **2** the enterprise itself, including staff, users, and organization.

daydream ('deɪ,driːm) *n* **1** a pleasant dreamlike fantasy indulged in while awake. **2** a pleasant scheme or wish that is unlikely to be fulfilled. ◆ *vb* **3** (*intr*) to indulge in idle fantasy.
▸ '**day,dreamer** *n* ▸ '**day,dreamy** *adj*

Day-Glo *n Trademark*. **a** a brand of fluorescent colouring materials, as of paint. **b** (*as modifier*): *Day-Glo colours*.

day labourer *n* an unskilled worker hired and paid by the day.

Day-Lewis ('deɪ'luːɪs) or **Day Lewis** ★ *n* Cecil. 1904–72, British poet and (under the pen name *Nicholas Blake*) author of detective stories; poet laureate (1968–72).

daylight ('deɪ,laɪt) *n* **1** light from the sun. **2** daytime. **3** daybreak. **4** see **daylights**. **4a** to understand something previously obscure. **4b** to realize that the end of a difficult task is approaching.

daylight robbery *n Inf*. blatant overcharging.

daylights ('deɪ,laɪts) *pl n* consciousness or wits (esp. in **scare, knock,** or **beat the (living) daylights out of someone**).

daylight-saving time *n* time set usually one hour ahead of the local standard time, widely adopted in the summer to provide extra daylight in the evening.

daylong ('deɪ,lɒŋ) *adj, adv* lasting the entire day; all day.

day release *n Brit*. a system whereby workers are released for part-time education without loss of pay.

★ people and places

day return *n* a reduced fare for a journey (by train, etc.) travelling both ways in one day.

day room *n* a communal living room in a residential institution such as a hospital.

days (deɪz) *adv Inf.* during the day, esp. regularly: *he works days.*

day school *n* **1** a private school taking day students only. **2** a school giving instruction during the daytime.

daytime ('deɪˌtaɪm) *n* the time between dawn and dusk.

day-to-day *adj* routine; everyday.

day trip *n* a journey made to and from a place within one day.
▶ **'day-ˌtripper** *n*

Da Yunhe ★ ('dæ ˈjuːnhə) *n* Pinyin transliteration of the Chinese name for the **Grand Canal** (sense 1).

daze (deɪz) *vb* **dazes, dazing, dazed.** (*tr*) **1** to stun, esp. by a blow or shock. **2** to bewilder or amaze. ◆ *n* **3** a state of stunned confusion or shock (esp. in **in a daze**). [C14: from ON *dasa-*, as in *dasast* to grow weary]

dazzle ('dæzᵊl) *vb* **dazzles, dazzling, dazzled. 1** (*usually tr*) to blind or be blinded partially and temporarily by sudden excessive light. **2** (*tr*) to amaze, as with brilliance. ◆ *n* **3** bright light that dazzles. **4** bewilderment caused by glamour, brilliance, etc.: *the dazzle of fame.* [C15: from DAZE]
▶ **'dazzler** *n* ▶ **'dazzling** *adj* ▶ **'dazzlingly** *adv*

dazzle gun *n* a weapon consisting of a laser gun used to dazzle enemy pilots.

dB *or* **db** *symbol for* decibel *or* decibels.

OBE *abbrev. for* Dame (Commander of the Order) of the British Empire (a Brit. title).

OBMS *abbrev. for* database management system.

OBS *abbrev. for* direct broadcasting by satellite.

dbx *or* **DBX** *n Trademark. Electronics.* a noise-reduction system that works across the full frequency spectrum.

OC *abbrev. for:* **1** *Music.* da capo. **2** direct current. Cf. **AC. 3** Also: **D.C.** District of Columbia.

OCB *abbrev. for* Dame Commander of the Order of the Bath (a Brit. title).

OCC *abbrev. for* digital compact cassette.

OCM *Brit. mil. abbrev. for* Distinguished Conduct Medal.

OD *abbrev. for:* **1** Doctor of Divinity. **2** Also: **dd.** direct debit.

O-day *n* the day selected for the start of some operation, esp. of the Allied invasion of Europe on June 6, 1944. [C20: from *D(ay)-day*]

ODR *abbrev. for* Deutsche Demokratische Republik (the former East Germany; GDR).

ODS *or* **DDSc** *abbrev. for* Doctor of Dental Surgery *or* Science.

ODT *n* dichlorodiphenyltrichloroethane; a colourless odourless substance used as an insecticide. It is now banned in the UK.

de- *prefix forming verbs and verbal derivatives.* **1** removal of or from something: *deforest; dethrone.* **2** reversal of something: *decode; desegregate.* **3** departure from: *decamp.* [from L, from *dē* (prep) from, away from, out of, etc. In compound words of Latin origin, *de-* also means away, away from (*decease*); down (*degrade*); reversal (*detect*); removal (*defoliate*); and is used intensively (*devote*) and pejoratively (*detest*)]

deacon ('diːkən) *n Christianity.* **1** (in the Roman Catholic and other episcopal churches) an ordained minister ranking immediately below a priest. **2** (in some other churches) a lay official who assists the minister, esp. in secular affairs. [OE, ult. from Gk *diakonos* servant]
▶ **'deaconate** *n* ▶ **'deaconˌship** *n*

deaconess ('diːkənɪs) *n Christianity.* (in the early church and in some modern Churches) a female member of the laity with duties similar to those of a deacon.

deactivate (diːˈæktɪˌveɪt) *vb* **deactivates, deactivating, deactivated. 1** (*tr*) to make (a bomb, etc.) harmless or inoperative. **2** (*intr*) to become less radioactive.
▶ **deˈactiˌvator** *n*

dead (dɛd) *adj* **1a** no longer alive. **1b** (*as collective n*; pre-

ceded by *the*): *the dead.* **2** not endowed with life; inanimate. **3** no longer in use, effective, or relevant: *a dead issue; a dead language.* **4** unresponsive or unaware. **5** lacking in freshness or vitality. **6** devoid of physical sensation; numb. **7** resembling death: *a dead sleep.* **8** no longer burning or hot: *dead coals.* **9** (of flowers or foliage) withered; faded. **10** (prenominal) (intensifier): *a dead stop.* **11** *Inf.* very tired. **12** *Electronics.* **12a** drained of electric charge. **12b** not connected to a source of potential difference or electric charge. **13** lacking acoustic reverberation: *a dead sound.* **14** *Sport.* (of a ball, etc.) out of play. **15** accurate; precise (esp. in **a dead shot**). **16** lacking resilience or bounce: *a dead ball.* **17** not yielding a return: *dead capital.* **18** (of colours) not glossy or bright. **19** stagnant: *dead air.* **20** *Mil.* shielded from view, as by a geographic feature. **21 dead from the neck up.** *Inf.* stupid. **22 dead to the world.** *Inf.* unaware of one's surroundings, esp. asleep or drunk. ◆ *n* **23** a period during which coldness, darkness, etc. is at its most intense: *the dead of winter.* ◆ *adv* **24** (intensifier): *dead easy; stop dead.* **25 dead on.** exactly right. [OE *dēad*]
▶ **'deadness** *n*

dead-and-alive *adj Brit.* (of a place, activity, or person) dull; uninteresting.

dead-ball line *n Rugby.* a line behind the goal line beyond which the ball is out of play.

deadbeat ('dɛdˌbiːt) *n* **1** *Inf.* a lazy or socially undesirable person. **2** a high grade escapement used in pendulum clocks. **3** (*modifier*) without recoil.

dead beat *adj Inf.* very tired; exhausted.

dead-cat bounce *n Stock Exchange inf.* a temporary recovery in prices following a substantial fall as a result of speculators buying stocks they have already sold rather than as a result of a genuine reversal of the downward trend.

dead centre *n* **1** the exact top or bottom of the piston stroke in a reciprocating engine or pump. **2** a rod mounted in the tailstock of a lathe to support a workpiece. ◆ Also called: **dead point.**

dead duck *n Sl.* a person or thing doomed to death, failure, etc., esp. because of a mistake.

deaden ('dɛdᵊn) *vb* **1** to make or become less sensitive, intense, lively, etc. **2** (*tr*) to make acoustically less resonant.
▶ **'deadening** *adj*

dead end *n* **1** a cul-de-sac. **2** a situation in which further progress is impossible.

deadeye ('dɛdˌaɪ) *n* **1** *Naut.* either of a pair of dislike wooden blocks, supported by straps in grooves around them, between which a line is rove so as to draw them together to tighten a shroud. **2** *Inf., chiefly US.* an expert marksman.

deadfall ('dɛdˌfɔːl) *n* a trap in which a heavy weight falls to crush the prey.

deadhead ('dɛdˌhɛd) *n* **1** a person who uses a free ticket, as for the theatre, etc. **2** a train, etc., travelling empty. **3** *US & Canad.* a dull person. **4** *US & Canad.* a totally or partially submerged log floating in a lake, etc. ◆ *vb* **5** (*intr*) *US & Canad.* to drive an empty bus, train, etc. **6** (*tr*) to remove dead flower heads.

Dead Heart ★ *n* (usually preceded by *the*) *Austral.* the remote interior of Australia. [C20: from *The Dead Heart of Australia* (1906) by J. W. Gregory (1864–1932), British geologist]

dead heat *n* **a** a race or contest in which two or more participants tie for first place. **b** a tie between two or more contestants in any position.

dead leg *n Inf.* temporary loss of sensation in the leg, caused by a blow to a muscle.

dead letter *n* **1** a law or ordinance that is no longer enforced. **2** a letter that cannot be delivered or returned because it lacks adequate directions.

deadlight ('dɛdˌlaɪt) *n* **1** *Naut.* **1a** a bull's-eye to admit light to a cabin. **1b** a shutter for sealing off a porthole or cabin window. **2** a skylight designed not to be opened.

deadline ('dɛdˌlaɪn) *n* a time limit for any activity.

deadlock ('dɛdˌlɒk) *n* **1** a state of affairs in which further

★ people and places

action between two opposing forces is impossible. **2** a tie between opponents. **3** a lock having a bolt that can be opened only with a key. ◆ *vb* **4** to bring or come to a deadlock.

dead loss *n* **1** a complete loss for which no compensation is paid. **2** *Inf.* a useless person or thing.

deadly ('dɛdlɪ) *adj* **deadlier, deadliest. 1** likely to cause death. **2** *Inf.* extremely boring. ◆ *adv, adj* **3** like death in appearance or certainty.

deadly nightshade *n* a poisonous Eurasian plant having purple bell-shaped flowers and black berries. Also called: **belladonna, dwale.**

deadly sins *pl n* the sins of pride, covetousness, lust, envy, gluttony, anger, and sloth.

dead man's handle *or* **pedal** *n* a safety switch on a piece of machinery that allows operation only while depressed by the operator.

dead march *n* a piece of solemn funeral music played to accompany a procession.

dead-nettle *n* any of several Eurasian plants having leaves resembling nettles but lacking stinging hairs.

deadpan ('dɛd,pæn) *adj, adv* with a deliberately emotionless face or manner.

dead reckoning *n* a method of establishing one's position using the distance and direction travelled rather than astronomical observations.

Dead Sea ★ *n* a lake between Israel and Jordan, 397 m (1302 ft) below sea level: the lowest lake in the world, with no outlet and very high salinity. Area: 1020 sq. km (394 sq. miles).

dead set *adv* **1** absolutely: *he is dead set against going to Spain.* ◆ *n* **2** the motionless position of a dog when pointing towards game. ◆ *adj* **3** (of a hunting dog) in this position.

dead soldier *or* **marine** *n Inf.* an empty beer or spirit bottle.

dead time *n Electronics.* the time immediately following a stimulus, during which an electrical device, component, etc. is insensitive to a further stimulus.

dead weight *n* **1** a heavy weight or load. **2** an oppressive burden. **3** the difference between the loaded and the unloaded weights of a ship. **4** the intrinsic invariable weight of a structure, such as a bridge.

deadwood ('dɛd,wʊd) *n* **1** dead trees or branches. **2** *Inf.* a useless person; encumbrance.

deaf (dɛf) *adj* **1a** partially or totally unable to hear. **1b** (*as collective n*; preceded by *the*): *the deaf.* **2** refusing to heed. [OE *dēaf*]
▶ '**deafness** *n*

┌───┐
│ **USAGE NOTE**   See at **disabled.**   │
└───┘

deaf aid *n* another name for **hearing aid.**

deaf-and-dumb *Offens.* ◆ *adj* **1** unable to hear or speak. ◆ *n* **2** a deaf-mute person.

deafblind ('dɛf,blaɪnd) *adj* **a** unable to hear or see. **b** (*as collective n*; preceded by *the*): *the deafblind.*

┌───┐
│ **USAGE NOTE**   See at **disabled.**   │
└───┘

deafen ('dɛf°n) *vb* (*tr*) to make deaf, esp. momentarily, as by a loud noise.
▶ '**deafening** *adj* ▶ '**deafeningly** *adv*

deaf-mute *n* **1** a person who is unable to hear or speak. See also **mute** (sense 7). ◆ *adj* **2** unable to hear or speak. [C19: translation of F *sourd-muet*]

Deakin ★ ('di:kɪn) *n* Alfred. 1856–1919, Australian statesman: prime minister (1903–04; 1905–08; 1909–10).

deal[1] (di:l) *vb* **deals, dealing, dealt. 1** (*intr*; foll. by *in*) to engage in commercially: *to deal in upholstery.* **2** (often foll. by *out*) to apportion or distribute. **3** (*tr*) to give (a blow, etc.) to (someone); inflict. **4** (*intr*) *Sl.* to sell any illegal drug. ◆ *n* **5** *Inf.* a bargain, transaction, or agreement. **6** a

particular type of treatment received, esp. as the result of an agreement: *a fair deal.* **7** an indefinite amount (esp. in **good** *or* **great deal**). **8** *Cards.* **8a** the process of distributing the cards. **8b** a player's turn to do this. **8c** a single round in a card game. **9** big deal. *Sl.* an important person, event, or matter: often used sarcastically. ◆ See also **deal with.** [OE *dǣlan*, from *dǣl* a part; cf. OHG *teil* a part, ON *deild* a share]

deal[2] (di:l) *n* **1** a plank of softwood timber, such as fir or pine, or such planks collectively. **2** the sawn wood of various coniferous trees. ◆ *adj* **3** of fir or pine. [C14: from MLow G *dele* plank]

Deal ★ (di:l) *n* a town in SE England, in Kent, on the English Channel: two 16th-century castles: tourism, light industries. Pop.: 28 504 (1991).

dealer ('di:lə) *n* **1** a person or firm engaged in commercial purchase and sale; trader: *a car dealer.* **2** *Cards.* the person who distributes the cards. **3** *Sl.* a person who sells illegal drugs.

dealings ('di:lɪŋz) *pl n* (*sometimes sing*) transactions or business relations.

dealt (dɛlt) *vb* the past tense and past participle of **deal**[1].

deal with *vb* (*tr, adv*) **1** to take action on: *to deal with each problem in turn.* **2** to punish: *the headmaster will deal with the culprit.* **3** to treat or be concerned with: *the book deals with architecture.* **4** to conduct oneself (towards others), esp. with regard to fairness. **5** to do business with.

dean (di:n) *n* **1** the chief administrative official of a college or university faculty. **2** (at Oxford and Cambridge universities) a college fellow with responsibility for undergraduate discipline. **3** *Chiefly Church of England.* the head of a chapter of canons and administrator of a cathedral or collegiate church. **4** *RC Church.* the cardinal bishop senior by consecration and head of the college of cardinals. Related adj: **decanal.** See also **rural dean.** [C14: from OF *deien*, from LL *decānus* one set over ten persons, from L *decem* ten]

Dean[1] (di:n) ★ *n* **Forest of.** a forest in W England, in Gloucestershire, between the Rivers Severn and Wye: formerly a royal hunting ground.

Dean[2] ★ (di:n) *n* **James** (**Byron**). 1931–55, US film actor and cult figure; his films include *East of Eden* and *Rebel Without a Cause* (both 1955). He died in a car crash.

deanery ('di:nərɪ) *n, pl* **deaneries. 1** the office or residence of a dean. **2** the group of parishes presided over by a rural dean.

dear (dɪə) *adj* **1** beloved; precious. **2** used in conventional forms of address, as in *Dear Sir.* **3** (*postpositive*; foll. by *to*) important; close. **4a** highly priced. **4b** charging high prices. **5** appealing. **6 for dear life.** with extreme vigour or desperation. ◆ *interj* **7** used in exclamations of surprise or dismay, such as *Oh dear!* ◆ *n* **8** Also: **dearest.** (*often used in direct address*) someone regarded with affection and tenderness. ◆ *adv* **9** dearly. [OE *dēore*]
▶ '**dearness** *n*

dearly ('dɪəlɪ) *adv* **1** very much. **2** affectionately. **3** at a great cost.

dearth (dɜːθ) *n* an inadequate amount, esp. of food; scarcity. [C13 *derthe*, from *dēr* DEAR]

deary *or* **dearie** ('dɪərɪ) *n* **1** (*pl* **dearies**) *Inf.* a term of affection: now often sarcastic or facetious. **2 deary** *or* **dearie me!** an exclamation of surprise or dismay.

death (dɛθ) *n* **1** the permanent end of all functions of life in an organism. **2** an instance of this: *his death ended an era.* **3** a murder or killing. **4** termination or destruction. **5** a state of affairs or an experience considered as terrible as death. **6** a cause or source of death. **7** (*usually cap.*) a personification of death, usually a skeleton or an old man holding a scythe. **8 at death's door.** likely to die soon. **9 catch one's death (of cold).** *Inf.* to contract a severe cold. **10 do to death. 10a** to kill. **10b** to overuse. **11 in at the death. 11a** present when a hunted animal is killed. **11b** present at the finish or climax. **12 like death warmed up.** *Inf.* very ill. **13 like grim death.** as if afraid of one's life. **14 put to death.** to kill deliberately or execute. **15 to death. 15a** until dead. **15b** very much. ◆ Related adjs.: **fatal, lethal, mortal.** [OE *dēath*]

┌───┐
│ ★ people and places   │
└───┘

death adder *n* a venomous thick-bodied Australian snake.

deathbed ('dɛθ,bɛd) *n* the bed in which a person is about to die.

deathblow ('dɛθ,bləʊ) *n* a thing or event that destroys life or hope, esp. suddenly.

death camp *n* a concentration camp in which the conditions are so brutal that few prisoners survive, or one to which prisoners are sent for execution.

death cap *or* **angel** *n* a poisonous woodland fungus with white gills and a cuplike structure at the base of the stalk.

death certificate *n* a legal document issued by a qualified medical practitioner certifying the death of a person and stating the cause if known.

death duty *n* a tax on property inheritances, in Britain replaced by capital transfer tax in 1975 and since 1986 by inheritance tax. Also called: **estate duty**.

death futures *pl n* life insurance policies of terminally ill people that are bought speculatively for a lump sum by a company, enabling it to collect the proceeds of the policies when the ill people die.

death knell *or* **bell** *n* **1** something that heralds death or destruction. **2** a bell rung to announce a death.

deathless ('dɛθlɪs) *adj* immortal, esp. because of greatness; everlasting. ▸ **'deathlessness** *n*

deathly ('dɛθlɪ) *adj* **1** deadly. **2** resembling death: *a deathly quiet*.

death mask *n* a cast of a dead person's face.

death rate *n* the ratio of deaths in a specified area, group, etc., to the population of that area, group, etc. Also called: **mortality rate**.

death rattle *n* a low-pitched gurgling sound sometimes made by a dying person.

death's-head *n* a human skull or a representation of one.

death's-head moth *n* a European hawk moth having markings resembling a human skull on its upper thorax.

death star *n* a weapon consisting of a flat star-shaped piece of metal with sharpened points that is thrown at an opponent. Also called: **throwing star**.

deathtrap ('dɛθ,træp) *n* a building, vehicle, etc., that is considered very unsafe.

Death Valley ★ *n* a desert valley in E California and W Nevada: the lowest, hottest, and driest area of the US. Lowest point: 86 m (282 ft) below sea level. Area: about 3885 sq. km (1500 sq. miles).

death warrant *n* **1** the official authorization for carrying out a sentence of death. **2 sign one's (own) death warrant**. to cause one's own destruction.

deathwatch ('dɛθ,wɒtʃ) *n* **1** a vigil held beside a dying or dead person. **2 deathwatch beetle**. a beetle whose woodboring larvae are a serious pest. The adult produces a tapping sound that was once supposed to presage death.

death wish *n* (in Freudian psychology) the desire for self-annihilation.

Deauville ★ ('dəʊviːl; *French* dovil) *n* a town and resort in NW France: casino. Pop.: 4770 (latest est.).

deb (dɛb) *n Inf.* short for **debutante**.

debacle (deɪˈbɑːkˈl, dɪ-) *n* **1** a sudden disastrous collapse or defeat; rout. **2** the breaking up of ice in a river, often causing flooding. **3** a violent rush of water carrying along debris. [C19: from F, from OF *desbacler* to unbolt]

debag (diːˈbæg) *vb* **debags, debagging, debagged**. (*tr*) *Brit. sl.* to remove the trousers from (someone) by force.

debar (dɪˈbɑː) *vb* **debars, debarring, debarred**. (*tr;* usually foll. by *from*) to exclude from a place, a right, etc.; bar. ▸ **deˈbarment** *n*

USAGE NOTE See at **disbar**.

debark¹ (dɪˈbɑːk) *vb* another word for **disembark**. [C17: from F *débarquer*, from *dé-* DIS-¹ + *barque* BARQUE] ▸ **debarkation** (,diːbɑːˈkeɪʃən) *n*

debark² (diːˈbɑːk) *vb* (*tr*) to remove the bark from (a tree). [C18: from DE-+ BARK²]

debase (dɪˈbeɪs) *vb* **debases, debasing, debased**. (*tr*) to lower in quality, character, or value; adulterate. [C16: see DE-, BASE²] ▸ **deˈbasement** *n* ▸ **deˈbaser** *n*

debate (dɪˈbeɪt) *n* **1** a formal discussion, as in a legislative body, in which opposing arguments are put forward. **2** discussion or dispute. **3** the formal presentation and opposition of a specific motion, followed by a vote. ◆ *vb* **debates, debating, debated**. **4** to discuss (a motion, etc.), esp. in a formal assembly. **5** to deliberate upon (something). [C13: from OF *debatre* to discuss, argue, from L *battuere*] ▸ **deˈbatable** *adj* ▸ **deˈbater** *n*

debauch (dɪˈbɔːtʃ) *vb* **1** (when *tr, usually passive*) to lead into a life of depraved self-indulgence. **2** (*tr*) to seduce (a woman). ◆ *n* **3** an instance or period of extreme dissipation. [C16: from OF *desbaucher* to corrupt, lit.: to shape (timber) roughly, from *bauch* beam, of Gmc origin] ▸ **deˈbaucher** *n* ▸ **deˈbauchery** *n*

debauchee (,dɛbɔːˈtʃiː) *n* a man who leads a life of promiscuity and self-indulgence.

debenture (dɪˈbɛntʃə) *n* **1** a long-term bond, bearing fixed interest and usually unsecured, issued by a company or governmental agency. **2** a certificate acknowledging a debt. **3** a customs certificate providing for a refund of excise or import duty. [C15: from L *dēbentur mihi* there are owed to me, from *dēbēre*] ▸ **deˈbentured** *adj*

debenture stock *n* shares issued by a company, which guarantee a fixed return at regular intervals.

debilitate (dɪˈbɪlɪ,teɪt) *vb* **debilitates, debilitating, debilitated**. (*tr*) to make feeble; weaken. [C16: from L, from *dēbilis* weak] ▸ **de,biliˈtation** *n* ▸ **deˈbilitative** *adj*

debility (dɪˈbɪlɪtɪ) *n, pl* **debilities**. weakness or infirmity.

debit ('dɛbɪt) *n* **1a** acknowledgment of a sum owing by entry on the left side of an account. **1b** the left side of an account. **1c** an entry on this side. **1d** the total of such entries. **1e** (*as modifier*): *a debit balance*. ◆ *vb* **debits, debiting, debited**. **2** (*tr*) **2a** to record (an item) as a debit in an account. **2b** to charge (a person or his account) with a debt. [C15: from L *dēbitum* DEBT]

debit card *n* a card issued by a bank or building society enabling customers to pay for goods or services by inserting it into a computer-controlled device at the place of sale, which is connected through the telephone network to the bank or building society.

debonair *or* **debonnaire** (,dɛbəˈnɛə) *adj* **1** suave and refined. **2** carefree; light-hearted. **3** courteous and cheerful. [C13: from OF, from *de bon aire* having a good disposition] ▸ **,deboˈnairly** *adv* ▸ **,deboˈnairness** *n*

Deborah ★ ('dɛbərə, -brə) *n Old Testament*. **1** a prophetess and judge of Israel who fought the Canaanites (Judges 4, 5). **2** Rebecca's nurse (Genesis 35:8).

debouch (dɪˈbaʊtʃ) *vb* (*intr*) **1** (esp. of troops) to move into a more open space. **2** (of a river, glacier, etc.) to flow into a larger area or body. [C18: from F *déboucher*, from *dé-* DIS-¹ + *bouche* mouth] ▸ **deˈbouchment** *n*

Debrett (dəˈbrɛt) *n* a list, considered exclusive, of the British aristocracy. In full: **Debrett's Peerage**. [C19: after J. Debrett (c 1750-1822), London publisher who first issued it]

debrief (diːˈbriːf) *vb* (*tr*) to elicit a report from (a soldier, diplomat, etc.) after a mission or event. ▸ **deˈbriefing** *n*

debris *or* **débris** ('deɪbriː, 'dɛbrɪ) *n* **1** fragments of something destroyed or broken; rubble. **2** a collection of loose material derived from rocks, or an accumulation of animal or vegetable matter. [C18: from F, from obs. *debrisier* to break into pieces, of Celtic origin]

de Broglie ★ (*French* də brɔj) *n* See (Louis Victor de) Broglie.

debt (dɛt) n **1** something owed, such as money, goods, or services. **2 bad debt.** a debt that has little prospect of being paid. **3** an obligation to pay or perform something. **4** the state of owing something, or of being under an obligation (esp. **in debt, in (someone's) debt**). [C13: from OF *dette*, from L *dēbitum*, from *dēbēre* to owe, from DE- + *habēre* to have]

debt collector n a person employed to collect debts for creditors.

debt of honour n a debt that is morally but not legally binding.

debtor ('dɛtə) n a person or commercial enterprise that owes a financial obligation.

debt swap n See **swap** (sense 4).

debud (diː'bʌd) vb **debuds, debudding, debudded.** another word for **disbud.**

debug (diː'bʌg) vb **debugs, debugging, debugged.** (tr) Inf. **1** to locate and remove concealed microphones from (a room, etc.). **2** to locate and remove defects in (a device, system, plan, etc.). **3** to remove insects from. [C20: from DE- + BUG]

debunk (diː'bʌŋk) vb (tr) Inf. to expose the pretensions or falseness of, esp. by ridicule. [C20: from DE- + BUNK²]
▸ de'**bunker** n

debus (diː'bʌs) vb **debuses, debusing, debused** or **debusses, debussing, debussed.** to unload (goods, etc.) or (esp. of troops) to alight from a bus.

Debussy ★ (də'bjuːsɪ, ˌdeɪbjuː'sɪ; French dəbysi) n (Achille) **Claude** (klod). 1862–1918, French impressionist composer. His works include *Prélude à l'après-midi d'un faune* (1894) and *La Mer* (1905) for orchestra and the opera *Pelléas et Mélisande* (1902).

debut ('deɪbjuː, 'dɛbjuː) n **1a** the first public appearance of an actor, musician, etc. **1b** (as modifier): *debut album.* **2** the presentation of a debutante. [C18: from F, from OF *desbuter* to play first, from *des-* DE- + *but* goal, target]

debutante ('dɛbjuˌtɑːnt, -ˌtænt) n **1** a young upper-class woman who is formally presented to society. **2** a young woman regarded as being upper-class, wealthy, and frivolous. [C19: from F, from *débuter* to lead off in a game, make one's first appearance; see DEBUT]

Debye ★ (Dutch de'bɛiə) n Peter Joseph Wilhelm. 1884–1966, Dutch chemist, working in the US: Nobel prize for chemistry (1936) for work on dipole moments.

dec. abbrev. for: **1** deceased. **2** decimal. **3** decimetre. **4** declaration. **5** declension. **6** declination. **7** decrease. **8** Music. decrescendo.

Dec. abbrev. for December.

deca-, deka- or before a vowel **dec-, dek-** prefix denoting ten: *decagon.* In conjunction with scientific units the symbol da is used. [from Gk *deka*]

decade ('dɛkeɪd, dɪ'keɪd) n **1** a period of ten years. **2** a group of ten. [C15: from OF, from LL, from Gk, from *deka* ten]
▸ de'**cadal** adj

decadence ('dɛkədəns) or **decadency** n **1** deterioration, esp. of morality or culture. **2** the state reached through such a process. **3** (often cap.) the period or style associated with the 19th-century decadents. [C16: from F, from Med. L *dēcadentia*, lit.: a falling away; see DECAY]

decadent ('dɛkədənt) adj **1** characterized by decline, as in being self-indulgent or morally corrupt. **2** belonging to a period of decline in artistic standards. ◆ n **3** a decadent person. **4** (often cap.) one of a group of French and English writers of the late 19th century whose works were characterized by refinement of style and a tendency toward the artificial and abnormal.

decaf ('diːkæf) Inf. ◆ n **1** decaffeinated coffee. ◆ adj **2** decaffeinated.

decaffeinate (dɪ'kæfɪˌneɪt) vb **decaffeinates, decaffeinating, decaffeinated.** (tr) to remove all or part of the caffeine from (coffee, tea, etc.).

decagon ('dɛkəˌgɒn) n a polygon having ten sides.
▸ **decagonal** (dɪ'kægən°l) adj

decahedron (ˌdɛkə'hiːdrən) n a solid figure having ten plane faces.
▸ ˌdeca'**hedral** adj

decal (dɪ'kæl, 'diːkæl) n **1** short for **decalcomania.** ◆ vb **decals, decalling, decalled** or US **decals, decaling, decaled.** **2** to transfer (a design, etc.) by decalcomania.

decalcify (diː'kælsɪˌfaɪ) vb **decalcifies, decalcifying, decalcified.** (tr) to remove calcium or lime from (bones, etc.).
▸ de'**calci,fier** n

decalcomania (dɪˌkælkə'meɪnɪə) n **1** the process of transferring a design from prepared paper onto another surface, such as glass or paper. **2** a design so transferred. [C19: from F, from *décalquer*, from *de-* DE- + *calquer* to trace + *-manie* -MANIA]

decalitre or US **decaliter** ('dɛkəˌliːtə) n a metric measure of volume equivalent to 10 litres.

Decalogue ('dɛkəˌlɒg) n another name for the **Ten Commandments.** [C14: from Church L *decalogus*, from Gk, from *deka* ten + *logos* word]

decametre or US **decameter** ('dɛkəˌmiːtə) n a metric measure of length equivalent to 10 metres.

decamp (dɪ'kæmp) vb (intr) **1** to leave a camp; break camp. **2** to depart secretly or suddenly; abscond.
▸ de'**campment** n

decanal (dɪ'keɪn°l) adj **1** of a dean or deanery. **2** on the same side of a cathedral, etc., as the dean; on the S side of the choir. [C18: from Med. L *decānālis, decānus* DEAN]

decani (dɪ'keɪnaɪ) adj, adv Music. to be sung by the decanal side of a choir. Cf. **cantoris.** [L: genitive of *decānus*]

decant (dɪ'kænt) vb **1** to pour (a liquid, such as wine) from one container to another, esp. without disturbing any sediment. **2** (tr) to rehouse (people) while their homes are being rebuilt or refurbished. [C17: from Med. L *dēcanthāre*, from *canthus* spout, rim]

decanter (dɪ'kæntə) n a stoppered bottle, into which a drink is poured for serving.

decapitate (dɪ'kæpɪˌteɪt) vb **decapitates, decapitating, decapitated.** (tr) to behead. [C17: from LL *dēcapitāre*, from L DE- + *caput* head]
▸ de,**capi'tation** n ▸ de'**capi,tator** n

decapod ('dɛkəˌpɒd) n **1** any crustacean having five pairs of walking limbs, as a crab, lobster, shrimp, etc. **2** any cephalopod mollusc having eight short tentacles and two longer ones, as a squid or cuttlefish.
▸ **decapodal** (dɪ'kæpəd°l), de'**capodan,** or de'**capodous** adj

decarbonate (diː'kɑːbəˌneɪt) vb **decarbonates, decarbonating, decarbonated.** (tr) to remove carbon dioxide from.
▸ de,**carbon'ation** n ▸ de'**carbon,ator** n

decarbonize or **decarbonise** (diː'kɑːbəˌnaɪz) vb **decarbonizes, decarbonizing, decarbonized** or **decarbonises, decarbonising, decarbonised.** (tr) to remove carbon from (an internal-combustion engine, etc.). Also: **decoke, decarburize.**
▸ de,**carboni'zation** or de,**carboni'sation** n ▸ de'**carbon,izer** or de'**carbon,iser** n

decarboxylase (ˌdiːkɑː'bɒksɪˌleɪz) n an enzyme that catalyses the removal of carbon dioxide from a compound.

decastyle ('dɛkəˌstaɪl) n Archit. a portico consisting of ten columns.

decasyllable ('dɛkəˌsɪləb°l) n a word or line of verse consisting of ten syllables.
▸ **decasyllabic** (ˌdɛkəsɪ'læbɪk) adj

decathlon (dɪ'kæθlɒn) n an athletic contest in which each athlete competes in ten different events. [C20: from DECA- + Gk *athlon* contest, prize; see ATHLETE]
▸ de'**cathlete** n

decay (dɪ'keɪ) vb **1** to decline or cause to decline gradually in health, prosperity, excellence, etc.; deteriorate. **2** to rot or cause to rot; decompose. **3** (intr) Also: **disintegrate.** Physics. **3a** (of an atomic nucleus) to undergo radioactive disintegration. **3b** (of an elementary particle) to transform into two or more different elementary particles. **4** (intr) Physics. (of a stored charge, magnetic flux, etc.) to decrease gradually when the source of energy has

been removed. ◆ *n* **5** the process of decline, as in health, mentality, etc. **6** the state brought about by this process. **7** decomposition. **8** rotten or decayed matter. **9** *Physics.* **9a** See **radioactive decay**. **9b** a spontaneous transformation of an elementary particle into two or more different particles. **10** *Physics.* a gradual decrease of a stored charge, current, etc., when the source of energy has been removed. [C15: from OF *decair*, from LL *dēcadere*, lit.: to fall away, from L *cadere* to fall]
▸ **de'cayable** *adj*

Deccan ★ ('dɛkən) *n* **the. 1** a plateau in S India, between the Eastern Ghats, the Western Ghats, and the Narmada River. **2** the whole Indian peninsula south of the Narmada River.

decease (dɪ'siːs) *n* **1** a more formal word for **death**. ◆ *vb* **deceases, deceasing, deceased. 2** (*intr*) a more formal word for **die**[1]. [C14 (n): from OF, from L *dēcēdere* to depart]

deceased (dɪ'siːst) *adj* **a** a more formal word for **dead** (sense 1). **b** (*as n*; preceded by *the*): *the deceased.*

deceit (dɪ'siːt) *n* **1** the act or practice of deceiving. **2** a statement, act, or device intended to mislead; fraud; trick. **3** a tendency to deceive. [C13: from OF, from *deceivre* to DECEIVE]

deceitful (dɪ'siːtful) *adj* full of deceit.

deceive (dɪ'siːv) *vb* **deceives, deceiving, deceived.** (*tr*) **1** to mislead by deliberate misrepresentation or lies. **2** to delude (oneself). **3** to be unfaithful to (one's sexual partner). **4** *Arch.* to disappoint. [C13: from OF *deceivre*, from L *dēcipere* to ensnare, cheat, from *capere* to take]
▸ **de'ceivable** *adj* ▸ **de'ceiver** *n*

decelerate (diː'sɛləˌreɪt) *vb* **decelerates, decelerating, decelerated.** to slow down or cause to slow down. [C19: from DE- + (AC)CELERATE]
▸ **de,celer'ation** *n* ▸ **de'celer,ator** *n*

December (dɪ'sɛmbə) *n* the twelfth month of the year, consisting of 31 days. [C13: from OF, from L: the tenth month (the Roman year orig. began with March), from *decem* ten]

decencies ('diːsʰnsɪz) *pl n* **1** **the.** those things that are considered necessary for a decent life. **2** another word for **proprieties**, see **propriety** (sense 3).

decency ('diːsʰnsɪ) *n, pl* **decencies. 1** conformity to the prevailing standards of propriety, morality, modesty, etc. **2** the quality of being decent.

decennial (dɪ'sɛnɪəl) *adj* **1** lasting for ten years. **2** occurring every ten years. ◆ *n* **3** a tenth anniversary.
▸ **de'cennially** *adv*

decent ('diːsʰnt) *adj* **1** polite or respectable. **2** proper and suitable; fitting. **3** conforming to conventions of sexual behaviour; not indecent. **4** free of oaths, blasphemy, etc. **5** good or adequate: *a decent wage.* **6** *Inf.* kind; generous. **7** *Inf.* sufficiently clothed to be seen by other people: *are you decent?* [C16: from L *decēns* suitable, from *decēre* to be fitting]
▸ **'decently** *adv*

decentralize *or* **decentralise** (diː'sɛntrəˌlaɪz) *vb* **decentralizes, decentralizing, decentralized** *or* **decentralises, decentralising, decentralised. 1** to reorganize into smaller more autonomous units. **2** to disperse (a concentration, as of industry or population).
▸ **de'centralist** *n, adj* ▸ **de,centrali'zation** *or* **de,centrali-'sation** *n*

deception (dɪ'sɛpʃən) *n* **1** the act of deceiving or the state of being deceived. **2** something that deceives; trick.

deceptive (dɪ'sɛptɪv) *adj* likely or designed to deceive; misleading.
▸ **de'ceptively** *adv* ▸ **de'ceptiveness** *n*

deci- *prefix* denoting one tenth: *decimetre.* Symbol: d [from F *déci-*, from L *decimus* tenth]

decibel ('dɛsɪˌbɛl) *n* **1** a unit for comparing two currents, voltages, or power levels, equal to one tenth of a bel. **2** a similar unit for measuring the intensity of a sound. Abbrev.: **dB.**

decide (dɪ'saɪd) *vb* **decides, deciding, decided. 1** (*may take a clause or an infinitive as object; when intr, sometimes foll. by on or about*) to reach a decision: *decide what you want; he decided to go.* **2** (*tr*) to cause to reach a decision. **3** (*tr*) to

determine or settle (a contest or question). **4** (*tr*) to influence decisively the outcome of (a contest or question). **5** (*intr;* foll. by *for* or *against*) to pronounce a formal verdict. [C14: from OF, from L *dēcīdere*, lit.: to cut off, from *caedere* to cut]
▸ **de'cidable** *adj*

decided (dɪ'saɪdɪd) *adj* (*prenominal*) **1** unmistakable. **2** determined; resolute: *a girl of decided character.*
▸ **de'cidedly** *adv*

decider (dɪ'saɪdə) *n* the point, goal, game, etc., that determines who wins a match or championship.

deciduous (dɪ'sɪdjʊəs) *adj* **1** (of trees and shrubs) shedding all leaves annually at the end of the growing season. Cf. **evergreen. 2** (of antlers, teeth, etc.) being shed at the end of a period of growth. [C17: from L: falling off, from *dēcidere* to fall down, from *cadere* to fall]
▸ **de'ciduousness** *n*

decilitre *or US* **deciliter** ('dɛsɪˌliːtə) *n* a metric measure of volume equivalent to one tenth of a litre.

decillion (dɪ'sɪljən) *n* **1** (in Britain, France, and Germany) the number represented as one followed by 60 zeros (10^{60}). **2** (in the US and Canada) the number represented as one followed by 33 zeros (10^{33}). [C19: from L *decem* ten + *-illion* as in *million*]
▸ **de'cillionth** *adj*

decimal ('dɛsɪməl) *n* **1** Also called: **decimal fraction.** a fraction that has an unwritten denominator of a power of ten. It is indicated by a decimal point to the left of the numerator: *.2=2/10.* **2** any number used in the decimal system. ◆ *adj* **3a** relating to or using powers of ten. **3b** of the base ten. **4** (*prenominal*) expressed as a decimal. [C17: from Med. L *decimālis* of tithes, from L *decima* a tenth]
▸ **'decimally** *adv*

decimal classification *n* another term for **Dewey Decimal System.**

decimal currency *n* a system of currency in which the monetary units are parts or powers of ten.

decimalize *or* **decimalise** ('dɛsɪməˌlaɪz) *vb* **decimalizes, decimalizing, decimalized** *or* **decimalises, decimalising, decimalised.** to change (a system, number, etc.) to the decimal system.
▸ **,decimali'zation** *or* **,decimali'sation** *n*

decimal place *n* **1** the position of a digit after the decimal point. **2** the number of digits to the right of the decimal point.

decimal point *n* a full stop or a raised full stop placed between the integral and fractional parts of a number in the decimal system.

USAGE NOTE Conventions relating to the use of the decimal point are confused. The IX General Conference on Weights and Measures resolved in 1948 that the decimal point should be a point on the line or a comma, but not a centre dot. It also resolved that figures could be grouped in threes about the decimal point, but that no point or comma should be used for this purpose. These conventions are adopted in this dictionary. However, the Decimal Currency Board recommended that for sums of money the centre dot should be used as the decimal point and that the comma should be used as the thousand marker. Moreover, in some countries the position is reversed, the comma being used as the decimal point and the dot as the thousand marker.

decimal system *n* **1** the number system in general use, having a base of ten, in which numbers are expressed by combinations of the ten digits 0 to 9. **2** a system of measurement in which the multiple and submultiple units are related to a basic unit by powers of ten.

decimate ('dɛsɪˌmeɪt) *vb* **decimates, decimating, decimated.** (*tr*) **1** to destroy or kill a large proportion of. **2** (esp. in the ancient Roman army) to kill every tenth man of (a

mutinous section). [C17: from L *decimāre*, from *decem* ten]
► ˌdeci'mation *n* ► 'deci,mator *n*

decimetre *or US* **decimeter** ('dɛsɪˌmiːtə) *n* one tenth of a metre. Symbol: **dm.**

decipher (dɪ'saɪfə) *vb* (*tr*) **1** to determine the meaning of (something obscure or illegible). **2** to convert from code into plain text; decode.
► de'cipherable *adj* ► de'cipherment *n*

decision (dɪ'sɪʒən) *n* **1** a judgment, conclusion, or resolution reached or given; verdict. **2** the act of making up one's mind. **3** firmness of purpose or character; determination. [C15: from OF, from L *dēcīsiō*, lit.: a cutting off; see DECIDE]

decision tree *n* a treelike diagram illustrating the choices available to a decision maker, each possible decision and its estimated outcome being shown as a separate branch of the tree.

decisive (dɪ'saɪsɪv) *adj* **1** influential; conclusive. **2** characterized by the ability to make decisions, esp. quickly; resolute.
► de'cisively *adv* ► de'cisiveness *n*

deck (dek) *n* **1** *Naut.* any of various platforms built into a vessel. **2** a similar platform, as in a bus. **3a** the horizontal platform that supports the turntable and pick-up of a record player. **3b** See **tape deck. 4** *Chiefly US.* a pack of playing cards. **5** *Computing.* a collection of punched cards relevant to a particular program. **6 clear the decks.** *Inf.* to prepare for action, as by removing obstacles. **7 hit the deck.** *Inf.* **7a** to fall to the ground, esp. to avoid injury. **7b** to prepare for action. **7c** to get out of bed. ♦ *vb* (*tr*) **8** (often foll. by *out*) to dress or decorate. **9** to build a deck on (a vessel). **10** *Sl.* to knock (someone) to the floor or ground. [C15: from MDu. *dec* a covering]

deck-access *adj* (of a block of flats) having a continuous balcony at each level onto which the front door of each flat opens.

deck chair *n* a folding chair consisting of a wooden frame suspending a length of canvas.

Decker ★ ('dɛkə) *n* a variant spelling of (Thomas) **Dekker.**

-decker *adj* (*in combination*) having a certain specified number of levels or layers: *a double-decker bus.*

deck hand *n* **1** a seaman assigned duties on the deck of a ship. **2** (in Britain) a seaman who has seen sea duty for at least one year. **3** a helper aboard a yacht.

deckle *or* **deckel** ('dɛkᵊl) *n* **1** a frame used to contain pulp on the mould in the making of handmade paper. **2** a strap on a paper-making machine that fixes the width of the paper. [C19: from G *Deckel* lid, from *decken* to cover]

deckle edge *n* **1** the rough edge of paper made using a deckle, often left as ornamentation. **2** an imitation of this.
► 'deckle-'edged *adj*

declaim (dɪ'kleɪm) *vb* **1** to make (a speech, etc.) loudly and in a rhetorical manner. **2** to speak lines from (a play, poem, etc.) with studied eloquence. **3** (*intr*; foll. by *against*) to protest (against) loudly and publicly. [C14: from L *dēclāmāre*, from *clāmāre* to call out]
► de'claimer *n* ► declamatory (dɪ'klæmətərɪ) *adj*

declamation (ˌdɛklə'meɪʃən) *n* **1** a rhetorical or emotional speech, made esp. in order to protest; tirade. **2** a speech, verse, etc., that is or can be spoken. **3** the act or art of declaiming.

declaration (ˌdɛklə'reɪʃən) *n* **1** an explicit or emphatic statement. **2** a formal statement or announcement. **3** the act of declaring. **4** the ruling of a judge or court on a question of law. **5** *Law.* an unsworn statement of a witness admissible in evidence under certain conditions. **6** *Cricket.* the voluntary closure of an innings before all ten wickets have fallen. **7** *Contract bridge.* the final contract. **8** a statement or inventory of goods, etc., submitted for tax assessment.

declarative (dɪ'klærətɪv) *or* **declaratory** (dɪ'klærətərɪ, -trɪ) *adj* making or having the nature of a declaration.
► de'claratively *or* de'claratorily *adv*

declare (dɪ'klɛə) *vb* **declares, declaring, declared.** (*mainly tr*) **1** (*may take a clause as object*) to make clearly known or announce officially: *war was declared.* **2** to state officially that (a person, fact, etc.) is as specified: *he declared him fit.* **3** (*may take a clause as object*) to state emphatically; assert. **4** to show, reveal, or manifest. **5** (*intr*; often foll. by *for* or *against*) to make known one's choice or opinion. **6** to make a statement of (dutiable goods, etc.). **7** (*also intr*) *Cards.* **7a** to display (cards) on the table so as to add to one's score. **7b** to decide (the trump suit) by making the winning bid. **8** (*intr*) *Cricket.* to close an innings voluntarily before all ten wickets have fallen. **9** to authorize payment of (a dividend). [C14: from L *dēclārāre* to make clear, from *clārus* clear]
► de'clarable *adj* ► de'clarer *n*

declassify (diː'klæsɪˌfaɪ) *vb* **declassifies, declassifying, declassified.** (*tr*) to release (a document or information) from the security list.
► deˌclassifi'cation *n*

declension (dɪ'klɛnʃən) *n* **1** *Grammar.* **1a** inflection of nouns, pronouns, or adjectives for case, number, and gender. **1b** the complete set of the inflections of such a word. **2** a decline or deviation. **3** a downward slope. [C15: from L *dēclīnātiō*, lit.: a bending aside, hence variation; see DECLINE]
► de'clensional *adj*

declination (ˌdɛklɪ'neɪʃən) *n* **1** *Astron.* the angular distance of a star, planet, etc., north or south from the celestial equator. Symbol: δ. **2** the angle made by a compass needle with the direction of the geographical north pole. **3** a refusal, esp. a courteous or formal one.
► ˌdecli'national *adj*

decline (dɪ'klaɪn) *vb* **declines, declining, declined. 1** to refuse to do or accept (something), esp. politely. **2** (*intr*) to grow smaller; diminish. **3** to slope or cause to slope downwards. **4** (*intr*) to deteriorate gradually. **5** *Grammar.* to list the inflections of (a noun, adjective, or pronoun), or (of a noun, adjective, or pronoun) to be inflected for number, case, or gender. ♦ *n* **6** gradual deterioration or loss. **7** a movement downward; diminution. **8** a downward slope. **9** *Arch.* any slowly progressive disease, such as tuberculosis. [C14: from OF *decliner*, from L *dēclīnāre* to bend away, inflect grammatically]
► de'clinable *adj* ► de'cliner *n*

declivity (dɪ'klɪvɪtɪ) *n, pl* **declivities.** a downward slope, esp. of the ground. [C17: from L *dēclīvitās*, from DE- + *clīvus* a slope, hill]
► de'clivitous *adj*

declutch (dɪ'klʌtʃ) *vb* (*intr*) to disengage the clutch of a motor vehicle.

decoct (dɪ'kɒkt) *vb* to extract the essence or active principle from (a medicinal or similar substance) by boiling. [C15: see DECOCTION]

decoction (dɪ'kɒkʃən) *n* **1** *Pharmacol.* the extraction of the water-soluble substances of a drug or medicinal plants by boiling. **2** the liquor resulting from this. [C14: from OF, from LL, from *dēcoquere* to boil down, from *coquere* to cook]

decode (diː'kəʊd) *vb* **decodes, decoding, decoded.** to convert from code into ordinary language.
► de'coder *n*

decoke (diː'kəʊk) *vb* **decokes, decoking, decoked.** (*tr*) another word for **decarbonize.**

décolletage (ˌdeɪkɒl'tɑːʒ) *n* a low-cut dress or neckline. [C19: from F; see DÉCOLLETÉ]

décolleté (deɪ'kɒlteɪ) *adj* **1** (of a woman's garment) low-cut. **2** wearing a low-cut garment. ♦ *n* **3** a low-cut neckline. [C19: from F *décolleter* to cut out the neck (of a dress), from *collet* collar]

decolonize *or* **decolonise** (diː'kɒləˌnaɪz) *vb* **decolo-**

nizes, decolonizing, decolonized *or* **decolonises, decolonising, decolonised.** (*tr*) to grant independence to (a colony).
▶ de,coloni'zation *or* ▶ de,coloni'sation *n*

decolour (diːˈkʌlə), **decolorize,** *or* **decolorise** *vb* **decolorizes, decolorizing, decolorized** *or* **decolorises, decolorising, decolorised.** (*tr*) to deprive of colour.
▶ de,colori'zation *or* de,colori'sation *n*

decommission (ˌdiːkəˈmɪʃən) *vb* (*tr*) to dismantle or remove from service (a nuclear reactor, weapon, ship, etc. which is no longer required).

decompose (ˌdiːkəmˈpəʊz) *vb* **decomposes, decomposing, decomposed.** **1** to break down or be broken down into constituent elements by bacterial or fungal action; rot. **2** *Chem.* to break down or cause to break down into simpler chemical compounds. **3** to break up or separate into constituent parts.
▶ decomposition (ˌdiːkɒmpəˈzɪʃən) *n*

decomposer (ˌdiːkəmˈpəʊzə) *n* a person or thing that causes decomposition, esp. any of the organisms, such as bacteria, that do so in an ecosystem.

decompress (ˌdiːkəmˈprɛs) *vb* **1** to relieve or be relieved of pressure. **2** to return (a diver, etc.) to a condition of normal atmospheric pressure or to be returned to such a condition.
▶ ,decom'pression *n*

decompression chamber *n* a chamber in which the pressure of air can be varied slowly for returning people safely from abnormal pressures to atmospheric pressure.

decompression sickness *or* **illness** *n* a disorder characterized by severe pain, cramp, and difficulty in breathing, caused by a sudden and sustained decrease in atmospheric pressure.

decongestant (ˌdiːkənˈdʒɛstənt) *adj* **1** relieving congestion, esp. nasal congestion. ◆ *n* **2** a decongestant drug.

deconsecrate (diːˈkɒnsɪˌkreɪt) *vb* **deconsecrates, deconsecrating, deconsecrated.** (*tr*) to transfer (a church, etc.) to secular use.
▶ de,conse'cration *n*

deconstruct (ˌdiːkənˈstrʌkt) *vb* (*tr*) **1** to apply the theories of deconstruction to (a text, film, etc.). **2** to expose or dismantle the existing structure in (a system, organization, etc.).

deconstruction (ˌdiːkənˈstrʌkʃən) *n* a technique of literary analysis that regards meaning as resulting from the differences between words rather than their reference to the things they stand for.

decontaminate (ˌdiːkənˈtæmɪˌneɪt) *vb* **decontaminates, decontaminating, decontaminated.** (*tr*) to render harmless by the removal or neutralization of poisons, radioactivity, etc.
▶ ,decon,tami'nation *n*

decontrol (ˌdiːkənˈtrəʊl) *vb* **decontrols, decontrolling, decontrolled.** (*tr*) to free of restraints or controls, esp. government controls: *to decontrol prices.*

décor *or* **decor** (ˈdeɪkɔː) *n* **1** a style or scheme of interior decoration, furnishings, etc., as in a room or house. **2** stage decoration; scenery. [C19: from F, from *décorer* to DECORATE]

decorate (ˈdɛkəˌreɪt) *vb* **decorates, decorating, decorated.** **1** (*tr*) to ornament; adorn. **2** to paint or wallpaper. **3** (*tr*) to confer a mark of distinction, esp. a medal, upon. [C16: from L *decorāre*, from *decus* adornment]
▶ 'decorative *adj*

Decorated style *n* a 14th-century style of English architecture characterized by geometrical tracery and floral decoration.

decoration (ˌdɛkəˈreɪʃən) *n* **1** an addition that renders something more attractive or ornate. **2** the act or art of decorating. **3** a medal, etc., conferred as a mark of honour.

decorator (ˈdɛkəˌreɪtə) *n* **1** *Brit.* a person whose profession is the painting and wallpapering of buildings or their interiors. **2** a person who decorates.

decorous (ˈdɛkərəs) *adj* characterized by propriety in manners, conduct, etc. [C17: from L, from *decor* elegance]
▶ 'decorously *adv* ▶ 'decorousness *n*

decorum (dɪˈkɔːrəm) *n* **1** propriety, esp. in behaviour or conduct. **2** a requirement of correct behaviour in polite society. [C16: from L: propriety]

decoupage (ˌdeɪkuːˈpɑːʒ) *n* the decoration of a surface with cutout shapes or illustrations. [C20: from F, from *découper*, from DE- + *couper* to cut]

decoy *n* (ˈdiːkɔɪ, dɪˈkɔɪ). **1** a person or thing used to lure someone into danger. **2** *Mil.* something designed to deceive an enemy. **3** a bird or animal, or an image of one, used to lure game into a trap or within shooting range. **4** a place into which game can be lured for capture. **5** *Canad.* another word for **deke** (sense 2). ◆ *vb* (dɪˈkɔɪ). **6** to lure or be lured by or as if by means of a decoy. **7** (*tr*) *Canad.* another word for **deke** (sense 1). [C17: prob. from Du. *de kooi*, lit.: the cage, from L *cavea* CAGE]

decrease *vb* (dɪˈkriːs). **decreases, decreasing, decreased.** **1** to diminish or cause to diminish in size, strength, etc. ◆ *n* (ˈdiːkriːs, dɪˈkriːs). **2** a diminution; reduction. **3** the amount by which something has been diminished. [C14: from OF, from L *dēcrescere* to grow less, from DE- + *crescere* to grow]
▶ de'creasing *adj* ▶ de'creasingly *adv*

decree (dɪˈkriː) *n* **1** an edict, law, etc., made by someone in authority. **2** an order or judgment of a court. ◆ *vb* **decrees, decreeing, decreed.** **3** to order, adjudge, or ordain by decree. [C14: from OF, from L *dēcrētum* ordinance, from *dēcrētus* decided, p.p. of *dēcernere*]

decree absolute *n* the final decree in divorce proceedings, which leaves the parties free to remarry.

decree nisi (ˈnaɪsaɪ) *n* a provisional decree, esp. in divorce proceedings, which will later be made absolute unless cause is shown why it should not.

decrement (ˈdɛkrɪmənt) *n* **1** the act of decreasing; diminution. **2** *Maths.* a negative increment. **3** *Physics.* a measure of the damping of an oscillator or oscillation, expressed by the ratio of amplitudes in successive cycles. [C17: from L *dēcrēmentum*, from *dēcrescere* to DECREASE]

decrepit (dɪˈkrɛpɪt) *adj* **1** enfeebled by old age; infirm. **2** broken down or worn out by hard or long use; dilapidated. [C15: from L *dēcrepitus*, from *crepāre* to creak]
▶ de'crepi,tude *n*

decrescendo (ˌdiːkrɪˈʃɛndəʊ) *n, adj* another word for **diminuendo.** [It., from *decrescere* to DECREASE]

decrescent (dɪˈkrɛsənt) *adj* (esp. of the moon) decreasing; waning. [C17: from L *dēcrēscēns* growing less; see DECREASE]
▶ de'crescence *n*

decretal (dɪˈkriːtəl) *n* **1** *RC Church.* a papal decree; edict on doctrine or church law. ◆ *adj* **2** of or relating to a decree. [C15: from OF, from LL *dēcrētālis;* see DECREE]

decriminalize *or* **decriminalise** (diːˈkrɪmɪnəˌlaɪz) *vb* **decriminalizes, decriminalizing, decriminalized** *or* **decriminalises, decriminalising, decriminalised.** (*tr*) to remove (an action) from the legal category of criminal offence: *to decriminalize the possession of marijuana.*

decry (dɪˈkraɪ) *vb* **decries, decrying, decried.** (*tr*) **1** to express open disapproval of; disparage. **2** to depreciate by proclamation: *to decry obsolete coinage.* [C17: from OF *descrier*, from *des-* DIS-[1] + *crier* to CRY]

decumbent (dɪˈkʌmbənt) *adj* **1** lying down. **2** *Bot.* (of stems) lying flat with the tip growing upwards. [C17: from L, present participle of *dēcumbere* to lie down]
▶ de'cumbency *n*

Dedéagach, Dedeagatch, *or* **Dedeağaç** ★ (ˈdedeɑːˈgɑːtʃ) *n* a former name (until the end of World War I) of **Alexandroúpolis.**

Dedekind ★ (German ˈdedəˌkɪnt) *n* (**Julius Wilhelm**) **Richard** (ˈrɪxaːt). 1831–1916, German mathematician, who devised a way (the **Dedekind cut**) of according irrational and rational numbers the same status.

dedicate (ˈdɛdɪˌkeɪt) *vb* **dedicates, dedicating, dedicated.** (*tr*) **1** (often foll. by *to*) to devote (oneself, one's time, etc.) wholly to a special purpose or cause. **2** (foll. by *to*) to address a book, performance, etc., to a person, cause, etc., as a token of affection or respect. **3** (foll. by *to*) to request or play (a record) on radio for another person as a greeting. **4** to assign or allocate to a particular project, func-

tion, etc. **5** to set apart for a deity or for sacred uses. [C15: from L *dēdicāre* to announce, from *dicāre* to make known]
▸ **'dedi,cator** *n* ▸ **dedicatory** ('dɛdɪ,keɪtərɪ, 'dɛdɪkətərɪ) *or* **'dedi,cative** *adj*

dedicated ('dɛdɪ,keɪtɪd) *adj* **1** devoted to a particular purpose or cause. **2** assigned or allocated to a particular project, function, etc.: *a dedicated transmission line.* **3** *Computing.* designed to fulfil one function.

dedication (,dɛdɪ'keɪʃən) *n* **1** the act of dedicating or being dedicated. **2** an inscription prefixed to a book, etc., dedicating it to a person or thing. **3** wholehearted devotion, esp. to a career, ideal, etc.
▸ **,dedi'cational** *adj*

deduce (dɪ'djuːs) *vb* **deduces, deducing, deduced.** (*tr*) **1** (*may take a clause as object*) to reach (a conclusion) by reasoning; conclude (that); infer. **2** *Arch.* to trace the origin or derivation of. [C15: from L *dēdūcere* to lead away, derive, from DE- + *dūcere* to lead]
▸ **de'ducible** *adj*

deduct (dɪ'dʌkt) *vb* (*tr*) to take away or subtract (a number, quantity, part, etc.). [C15: from L *dēductus*, p.p. of *dēdūcere* to DEDUCE]

deductible (dɪ'dʌktɪbᵊl) *adj* **1** capable of being deducted. **2** *US.* short for **tax-deductible.** ◆ *n* **3** *Insurance.* the US name for **excess** (sense 5).

deduction (dɪ'dʌkʃən) *n* **1** the act or process of deducting or subtracting. **2** something that is or may be deducted. **3** *Logic.* **3a** a process of reasoning by which a specific conclusion necessarily follows from a set of general premises. **3b** a logical conclusion reached by this process.
▸ **de'ductive** *adj*

Dee ★ (diː) *n* **1** a river in N Wales and NW England, rising in S Gwynedd and flowing east and north to the Irish Sea. Length: about 112 km (70 miles). **2** a river in NE Scotland, rising in the Cairngorms and flowing east to the North Sea. Length: about 140 km (87 miles). **3** a river in S Scotland, flowing south to the Solway Firth. Length: about 80 km (50 miles).

deed (diːd) *n* **1** something that is done or performed; act. **2** a notable achievement. **3** action as opposed to words. **4** *Law.* a legal document signed, witnessed, and delivered to effect a conveyance or transfer of property or to create a legal contract. ◆ *vb* **5** (*tr*) *US.* to convey or transfer (property) by deed. [OE *dēd*]

deed box *n* a strong box in which deeds and other documents are kept.

deed poll *n Law.* a deed made by one party only, esp. one by which a person changes his name.

deejay ('diː,dʒeɪ) *n* an informal name for **disc jockey.** [C20: from the initials DJ (disc jockey)]

deem (diːm) *vb* (*tr*) to judge or consider. [OE *dēman*]

de-emphasize *or* **de-emphasise** (diː'ɛmfə,saɪz) *vb* **de-emphasizes, de-emphasizing, de-emphasized** *or* **de-emphasises, de-emphasising, de-emphasised.** (*tr*) to remove emphasis from.

deemster ('diːmstə) *n* the title of one of the two justices in the Isle of Man. Also called: **dempster.**

de-energize *or* **de-energise** (diː'ɛnədʒaɪz) *vb* **de-energizes, de-energizing, de-energized** *or* **de-energises, de-energising, de-energised.** (*tr*) *Electrical engineering.* to disconnect (an electrical circuit) from its source.
▸ **de-,energi'zation** *or* **de-,energi'sation** *n*

deep (diːp) *adj* **1** extending or situated far down from a surface: *a deep pool.* **2** extending or situated far inwards, backwards, or sideways. **3** *Cricket.* far from the pitch: *the deep field.* **4** (*postpositive*) of a specified dimension downwards, inwards, or backwards: *six feet deep.* **5** coming from or penetrating to a great depth. **6** difficult to understand; abstruse. **7** intellectually demanding: *a deep discussion.* **8** of great intensity: *deep trouble.* **9** (*postpositive*; foll. by *in*) absorbed (by); immersed (in): *deep in study.* **10** very cunning; devious. **11** mysterious: *a deep secret.* **12** (of a colour) having an intense or dark hue. **13** low in pitch: *a deep voice.* **14 go off the deep end.** *Inf.* **14a** to lose one's temper; react angrily. **14b** *Chiefly US.* to act rashly. **15 in deep water.** *Inf.* in a tricky position or in trouble. ◆ *n* **16**

any deep place on land or under water. **17 the deep. 17a** a poetic term for the **ocean. 17b** *Cricket.* the area of the field relatively far from the pitch. **18** the most profound, intense, or central part: *the deep of winter.* **19** a vast extent, as of space or time. ◆ *adv* **20** far on in time; late: *they worked deep into the night.* **21** profoundly or intensely. **22 deep down.** *Inf.* in reality, esp. as opposed to appearance. [OE *dēop*]
▸ **'deeply** *adv* ▸ **'deepness** *n*

deep-discount bond *n* a fixed-interest security that pays little or no interest but is issued at a substantial discount to its redemption value, thus largely substituting capital gain for income.

deepen ('diːpᵊn) *vb* to make or become deep, deeper, or more intense.
▸ **'deepener** *n*

deepfreeze (,diːp'friːz) *n* **1** another name for **freezer. 2** storage in a freezer. **3** *Inf.* a state of suspended activity. ◆ *vb* **deep-freeze, deep-freezes, deep-freezing, deep-froze, deep-frozen. 4** (*tr*) to freeze (food) or keep (food) in a freezer.

deep-fry *vb* **deep-fries, deep-frying, deep-fried.** to cook (fish, etc.) in sufficient hot fat to cover the food.

deep-laid *adj* (of a plot or plan) carefully worked out and kept secret.

deep-rooted *or* **deep-seated** *adj* (of ideas, beliefs, etc.) firmly fixed or held; ingrained.

deep-sea *n* (*modifier*) of, found in, or characteristic of the deep parts of the sea.

deep-set *adj* (esp. of eyes) deeply set.

Deep South ★ *n* the SE part of the US, esp. South Carolina, Georgia, Alabama, Mississippi, and Louisiana.

deep space *n* any region of outer space beyond the system of the earth and moon.

deep structure *n Generative grammar.* a representation of a sentence at a level where logical or grammatical relations are made explicit. Cf. **surface structure.**

deer (dɪə) *n, pl* **deer** *or* **deers.** any of a family of hoofed, ruminant mammals including reindeer, elk, and roe deer, typically having antlers in the male. Related adj: **cervine.** [OE *dēor* beast]

deer lick *n* a naturally or artificially salty area of ground where deer come to lick the salt.

deerskin ('dɪə,skɪn) *n* **a** the hide of a deer. **b** (*as modifier*): *a deerskin jacket.*

deerstalker ('dɪə,stɔːkə) *n* **1** a person who stalks deer, esp. in order to shoot them. **2** a hat, peaked in front and behind, with earflaps usually tied together on the top.
▸ **'deer,stalking** *adj, n*

de-escalate (diː'ɛskə,leɪt) *vb* **de-escalates, de-escalating, de-escalated.** to reduce the level or intensity of (a crisis, etc.) or (of a crisis, etc.) to decrease in level or intensity.
▸ **de-,esca'lation** *n*

def (dɛf) *adj Sl.* very good. [C20: ?from *definitive*]

def. *abbrev. for:* **1** defective. **2** defence. **3** defendant. **4** deferred. **5** definite. **6** definition.

deface (dɪ'feɪs) *vb* **defaces, defacing, defaced.** (*tr*) to spoil or mar the surface or appearance of; disfigure.
▸ **de'faceable** *adj* ▸ **de'facement** *n* ▸ **de'facer** *n*

de facto (deɪ 'fæktəʊ) *adv* **1** in fact. ◆ *adj* **2** existing in fact, whether legally recognized or not: *a de facto regime.* Cf. **de jure.** ◆ *n, pl* **de factos. 3** *Austral. & NZ.* a de facto wife or husband. [C17: L]

defalcate ('diːfæl,keɪt) *vb* **defalcates, defalcating, defalcated.** (*intr*) *Law.* to misuse or misappropriate property or funds entrusted to one. [C15: from Med. L *dēfalcāre* to cut off, from L DE- + *falx* sickle]
▸ **'defal,cator** *n*

defame (dɪ'feɪm) *vb* **defames, defaming, defamed.** (*tr*) to attack the good name or reputation of; slander; libel. [C14: from OF, from L, from *diffāmāre* to spread by unfavourable report, from *fāma* FAME]
▸ **defamation** (,dɛfə'meɪʃən) *n* ▸ **defamatory** (dɪ'fæmətərɪ) *adj*

default (dɪ'fɔːlt) *n* **1** a failure to act, esp. a failure to meet a financial obligation or to appear in a court of law at a time specified. **2** absence or lack. **3 by default.** in the absence of opposition or a better alternative: *he became prime minister by default.* **4 in default of.** through or in the lack or absence of. **5 judgment by** *or* **in default.** *Law.* a judgment in the plaintiff's favour when the defendant fails to plead or to appear. **6** (*also* 'di:fɔ:lt). *Computing.* **6a** the preset selection of an option offered by a system, which will always be followed except when explicitly altered. **6b** (*as modifier*): *default setting.* ♦ *vb* **7** (*intr*; often foll. by *on* or *in*) to fail to make payment when due. **8** (*intr*) to fail to fulfil an obligation. **9** *Law.* to lose (a case) by failure to appear in court. [C13: from OF *defaute*, from *defaillir* to fail, from Vulgar L *dēfallīre* (unattested) to be lacking]

defaulter (dɪ'fɔ:ltə) *n* **1** a person who defaults. **2** *Chiefly Brit.* a person, esp. a soldier, who has broken the disciplinary code of his service.

defeat (dɪ'fi:t) *vb* (*tr*) **1** to overcome; win a victory over. **2** to thwart or frustrate. **3** *Law.* to render null and void. ♦ *n* **4** a defeating or being defeated. [C14: from OF, from *desfaire* to undo, ruin, from *des-* DIS-[1] + *faire* to do, from *facere*]

defeatism (dɪ'fi:tɪzəm) *n* a ready acceptance or expectation of defeat.
  ▸ de'featist *n, adj*

defecate ('defɪ,keɪt) *vb* **defecates, defecating, defecated. 1** (*intr*) to discharge waste from the body through the anus. **2** (*tr*) to remove impurities from. [C16: from L *dēfaecāre* to cleanse from dregs, from DE- + *faex* dregs]
  ▸ ,defe'cation *n* ▸ 'defe,cator *n*

defect *n* ('di:fɛkt). **1** a lack of something necessary for completeness; deficiency. **2** an imperfection or blemish. ♦ *vb* (dɪ'fɛkt). **3** (*intr*) to desert one's country, cause, etc., esp. in order to join the opposing forces. [C15: from L, from *dēficere* to forsake, fail]
  ▸ de'fector *n*

defection (dɪ'fɛkʃən) *n* **1** abandonment of duty, allegiance, principles, etc. **2** a shortcoming.

defective (dɪ'fɛktɪv) *adj* **1** having a defect or flaw; imperfect. **2** (of a person) below the usual standard or level, esp. in intelligence. **3** *Grammar.* lacking the full range of inflections characteristic of its form class.
  ▸ de'fectiveness *n*

defence *or US* **defense** (dɪ'fɛns) *n* **1** resistance against danger or attack. **2** a person or thing that provides such resistance. **3** a plea, essay, etc., in support of something. **4** a country's military measures or resources. **5** *Law.* a defendant's denial of the truth of the allegations or charge against him. **6** *Law.* the defendant and his legal advisers collectively. **7** *Sport.* **7a** the action of protecting oneself or part of the playing area against an opponent's attacks. **7b** (usually preceded by *the*) the players in a team whose function is to do this. **8** *American football.* (usually preceded by *the*) **8a** the team that does not have possession of the ball. **8b** the members of a team that play in such circumstances. **9** (*pl*) fortifications. [C13: from OF, from LL *dēfensum*, p.p. of *dēfendere* to DEFEND]
  ▸ de'fenceless *or US* de'fenseless *adj*

defence mechanism *n* **1** *Psychoanalysis.* an unconscious mental process designed to reduce anxiety or shame. **2** *Physiol.* the protective response of the body against disease.

defend (dɪ'fɛnd) *vb* **1** (*tr*) to protect from harm or danger. **2** (*tr*) to support in the face of criticism, esp. by argument. **3** to represent (a defendant) in court. **4** *Sport.* to guard (one's goal, etc.) against attack. **5** (*tr*) to protect (a title, etc.) against a challenge. [C13: from OF, from L *dēfendere* to ward off, from DE- + *-fendere* to strike]
  ▸ de'fender *n*

defendant (dɪ'fɛndənt) *n* **1** a person against whom an action or claim is brought in a court of law. Cf. **plaintiff.** ♦ *adj* **2** defending.

defenestration (di:,fɛnɪ'streɪʃən) *n* the act of throwing someone out of a window. [C17: from NL *dēfenestrātiō*, from L DE- + *fenestra* window]

defensible (dɪ'fɛnsɪbʰl) *adj* capable of being defended, as in war, an argument, etc.
  ▸ de,fensi'bility *or* de'fensibleness *n*

defensive (dɪ'fɛnsɪv) *adj* **1** intended for defence. **2** rejecting criticisms of oneself. ♦ *n* **3** a position of defence. **4 on the defensive.** in a position of defence, as in being ready to reject criticism.
  ▸ de'fensively *adv*

defer[1] (dɪ'fɜ:) *vb* **defers, deferring, deferred.** (*tr*) to delay until a future time; postpone. [C14: from OF *differer* to be different, postpone; see DIFFER]
  ▸ de'ferment *or* de'ferral *n* ▸ de'ferrer *n*

defer[2] (dɪ'fɜ:) *vb* **defers, deferring, deferred.** (*intr*; foll. by *to*) to yield to or comply with the wishes or judgments (of). [C15: from L *dēferre*, lit.: to bear down, from DE- + *ferre* to bear]

deference ('defərəns) *n* **1** compliance with the wishes of another. **2** courteous regard; respect. [C17: from F *déférence*; see DEFER[2]]

deferent[1] ('defərənt) *adj* another word for **deferential.**

deferent[2] ('defərənt) *adj* (esp. of a nerve or duct) conveying an impulse, fluid, etc., down or away; efferent. [C17: from L *dēferre*; see DEFER[2]]

deferential (,defə'rɛnʃəl) *adj* showing deference; respectful.
  ▸ ,defer'entially *adv*

defiance (dɪ'faɪəns) *n* **1** open or bold resistance to authority, opposition, or power. **2** a challenge.
  ▸ de'fiant *adj*

defibrillation (dɪ,faɪbrɪ'leɪʃən) *n Med.* the application of an electric current to the heart to restore normal contractions after a heart attack caused by fibrillation.

defibrillator (dɪ'faɪbrɪ,leɪtə) *n Med.* an apparatus for stopping fibrillation of the heart by application of an electric current.

deficiency (dɪ'fɪʃənsɪ) *n, pl* **deficiencies. 1** the state or quality of being deficient. **2** a lack or insufficiency; shortage. **3** a deficit. **4** *Biol.* the absence of a gene or a region of a chromosome normally present.

deficiency disease *n* **1** *Med.* any condition, such as pellagra, beriberi, or scurvy, produced by a lack of vitamins or other essential substances. **2** *Bot.* any disease caused by lack of essential minerals.

deficient (dɪ'fɪʃənt) *adj* **1** lacking some essential; incomplete; defective. **2** inadequate in quantity or supply; insufficient. [C16: from L *dēficiēns* lacking, from *dēficere* to fall short]
  ▸ de'ficiently *adv*

deficit ('defɪsɪt, dɪ'fɪsɪt) *n* **1** the amount by which an actual sum is lower than that expected or required. **2a** an excess of liabilities over assets. **2b** an excess of expenditures over revenues. [C18: from L, lit.: there is lacking, from *dēficere*]

deficit financing *n* government spending in excess of revenues so that a budget deficit is incurred, which is financed by borrowing.

defile[1] (dɪ'faɪl) *vb* **defiles, defiling, defiled.** (*tr*) **1** to make foul or dirty; pollute. **2** to taint; corrupt. **3** to damage or sully (someone's reputation, etc.). **4** to make unfit for ceremonial use. **5** to violate the chastity of. [C14: from earlier *defoilen*, from OF *defouler* to trample underfoot, abuse, from DE- + *fouler* to tread upon; see FULL[2]]
  ▸ de'filement *n*

defile[2] ('di:faɪl, dɪ'faɪl) *n* **1** a narrow pass or gorge. **2** a single file of soldiers, etc. ♦ *vb* **defiles, defiling, defiled. 3** (*intr*) to march in single file. [C17: from F, from *défiler* to file off, from *filer* to march in a column, from OF, from L *filum* thread]

define (dɪ'faɪn) *vb* **defines, defining, defined.** (*tr*) **1** to state precisely the meaning of (words, terms, etc.). **2** to describe the nature, properties, or essential qualities of. **3** to determine the boundary or extent of. **4** (*often passive*) to delineate the form or outline of: *the shape of the tree was clearly defined by the light behind it.* **5** to fix with precision; specify. [C14: from OF: to determine, from L *dēfinīre* to set bounds to, from *finīre* to FINISH]
  ▸ de'finable *adj* ▸ de'finer *n*

definite ('defɪnɪt) *adj* **1** clearly defined; exact. **2** having

precise limits or boundaries. **3** known for certain. [C15: from L *dēfīnītus* limited, distinct; see DEFINE]
▶ **'definiteness** *n*

> **USAGE NOTE** *Definite* and *definitive* should be carefully distinguished. *Definite* indicates precision and firmness, as in *a definite decision*. *Definitive* includes these senses but also indicates conclusiveness. *A definite answer* indicates a clear and firm answer to a particular question; *a definitive answer* implies an authoritative resolution of a complex question.

definite article *n Grammar.* a determiner that expresses specificity of reference, such as *the* in English. Cf. **indefinite article.**

definite integral *n* See **integral.**

definitely ('dɛfɪnɪtlɪ) *adv* **1** in a definite manner. **2** (*sentence modifier*) certainly: *he said he was coming, definitely.* ◆ *sentence substitute.* **3** unquestionably.

definition (ˌdɛfɪ'nɪʃən) *n* **1** a formal and concise statement of the meaning of a word, phrase, etc. **2** the act of defining. **3** specification of the essential properties of something. **4** the act of making clear or definite. **5** the state of being clearly defined. **6** a measure of the clarity of an optical, photographic, or television image as characterized by its sharpness and contrast.

definitive (dɪ'fɪnɪtɪv) *adj* **1** serving to decide or settle finally. **2** most reliable or authoritative. **3** serving to define or outline. **4** *Zool.* fully developed. **5** (of postage stamps) permanently on sale. ◆ *n* **6** *Grammar.* a word indicating specificity of reference.
▶ **de'finitively** *adv*

deflate (diː'fleɪt) *vb* **deflates, deflating, deflated. 1** to collapse through the release of gas. **2** (*tr*) to take away the self-esteem or conceit from. **3** (*tr*) to take away the enthusiasm or excitement from. **4** *Econ.* to cause deflation of (an economy, the money supply, etc.). [C19: from DE- + (IN)FLATE]
▶ **de'flator** *n*

deflation (diː'fleɪʃən) *n* **1** the act of deflating or the state of being deflated. **2** *Econ.* a reduction in spending and economic activity resulting in lower levels of output, employment, investment, trade, profits, and prices. **3** the removal of loose rock material, etc., by wind.
▶ **de'flationary** *adj* ▶ **de'flationist** *n, adj*

deflect (dɪ'flɛkt) *vb* to turn or cause to turn aside from a course. [C17: from L *dēflectere*, from *flectere* to bend]
▶ **de'flector** *n*

deflection *or* **deflexion** (dɪ'flɛkʃən) *n* **1** a deflecting or being deflected. **2** the amount of deviation. **3** the change in direction of a light beam as it crosses a boundary between two media with different refractive indexes. **4** a deviation of the indicator of a measuring instrument from its zero position.
▶ **de'flective** *adj*

deflocculate (diː'flɒkjʊˌleɪt) *vb* **deflocculates, deflocculating, deflocculated.** (*tr*) to cause (an aggregate) to separate into particles.
▶ **deˌfloccu'lation** *n* ▶ **de'flocculant** *n*

deflower (diː'flaʊə) *vb* (*tr*) **1** to deprive (esp. a woman) of virginity. **2** to despoil of beauty, innocence, etc. **3** to rob or despoil of flowers.
▶ **ˌdeflo'ration** *n*

Defoe ★ (dɪ'fəʊ) *n* Daniel. ?1660–1731, English novelist and pamphleteer, noted for his novels *Robinson Crusoe* (1719) and *Moll Flanders* (1722).

defoliant (diː'fəʊlɪənt) *n* a chemical sprayed or dusted onto trees to cause their leaves to fall, esp. to remove cover from an enemy in warfare.

defoliate (diː'fəʊlɪˌeɪt) *vb* **defoliates, defoliating, defoliated.** to deprive (a plant) of its leaves. [C18: from Med. L *dēfoliāre*, from L DE- + *folium* leaf]
▶ **deˌfoli'ation** *n*

deforest (diː'fɒrɪst) *vb* (*tr*) to clear of trees. Also: **disforest.**
▶ **deˌfores'tation** *n*

De Forest ★ (də 'fɒrɪst) *n* Lee. 1873–1961, US inventor of telegraphic, telephonic, and radio equipment: patented the first triode valve (1907).

deform (dɪ'fɔːm) *vb* **1** to make or become misshapen or distorted. **2** (*tr*) to mar the beauty of; disfigure. **3** (*tr*) to subject or be subjected to a stress that causes a change of dimensions. [C15: from L *dēformāre*, from DE- + *forma* shape, beauty]
▶ **de'formable** *adj* ▶ **ˌdefor'mation** *n*

deformed (dɪ'fɔːmd) *adj* **1** disfigured or misshapen. **2** morally perverted; warped.

deformity (dɪ'fɔːmɪtɪ) *n, pl* **deformities. 1** a deformed condition. **2** *Pathol.* a distortion of an organ or part. **3** a deformed person or thing. **4** a defect, esp. of the mind or morals; depravity.

defraud (dɪ'frɔːd) *vb* (*tr*) to take away or withhold money, rights, property, etc., from (a person) by fraud; swindle.
▶ **de'frauder** *n*

defray (dɪ'freɪ) *vb* (*tr*) to provide money for (costs, expenses, etc.); pay. [C16: from OF *deffroier* to pay expenses, from *de-* DIS- + *frai* expenditure]
▶ **de'frayable** *adj* ▶ **de'frayal** *or* **de'frayment** *n*

defrock (diː'frɒk) *vb* (*tr*) to deprive (a person in holy orders) of ecclesiastical status; unfrock.

defrost (diː'frɒst) *vb* **1** to make or become free of frost or ice. **2** to thaw, esp. through removal from a deepfreeze.

defroster (diː'frɒstə) *n* a device by which a de-icing process, as of a refrigerator, is accelerated.

deft (dɛft) *adj* quick and neat in movement; nimble; dexterous. [C13 (in the sense: gentle): see DAFT]
▶ **'deftly** *adv* ▶ **'deftness** *n*

defunct (dɪ'fʌŋkt) *adj* **1** no longer living; dead or extinct. **2** no longer operative or valid. [C16: from L *dēfungī* to discharge (one's obligations), die; see DE-, FUNCTION]
▶ **de'functness** *n*

defuse *or US (sometimes)* **defuze** (diː'fjuːz) *vb* **defuses, defusing, defused** *or US (sometimes)* **defuzes, defuzing, defuzed** (*tr*) **1** to remove the triggering device of (a bomb, etc.). **2** to remove the cause of tension from (a crisis, etc.).

> **USAGE NOTE** Avoid confusion with **diffuse.**

defy (dɪ'faɪ) *vb* **defies, defying, defied.** (*tr*) **1** to resist openly and boldly. **2** to elude, esp. in a baffling way. **3** *Formal.* to challenge (someone to do something); dare. **4** *Arch.* to invite to do battle or combat. [C14: from OF *desfier*, from *des-* DE- + *fier* to trust, from L *fīdere*]
▶ **de'fier** *n*

deg. *abbrev. for* degree.

Degas ★ ('deɪgɑː; *French* dəgɑ) *n* Hilaire Germain Edgar (ilɛr ʒɛrmɛ̃ ɛdgar). 1834–1917, French impressionist painter and sculptor, noted for his studies of ballet dancers.

De Gasperi ★ (*Italian* de 'gasperi) *n* Alcide (al'tʃiːde). 1881–1954, Italian statesman; prime minister (1945–53).

de Gaulle ★ (*French* də gol) *n* Charles (**André Joseph Marie**) (ʃarl). 1890–1970, French general and statesman. During World War II, he founded the Free French movement in England (1940). He was head of the provisional governments (1944–46) and became first president of the Fifth Republic (1959–69).

degauss (diː'gaʊs) *vb* (*tr*) to neutralize by producing an opposing magnetic field.
▶ **de'gausser** *n*

degeneracy (dɪ'dʒɛnərəsɪ) *n, pl* **degeneracies. 1** the act or state of being degenerate. **2** the process of becoming degenerate.

degenerate *vb* (dɪ'dʒɛnəˌreɪt). **degenerates, degenerating, degenerated.** (*intr*) **1** to become degenerate. **2** *Biol.* (of organisms or their parts) to become less specialized or functionally useless. ◆ *adj* (dɪ'dʒɛnərɪt). **3** having declined or deteriorated to a lower mental, moral, or physical level; degraded; corrupt. ◆ *n* (dɪ'dʒɛnərɪt). **4** a degenerate person. [C15: from L, from *dēgener* departing from its kind, ignoble, from DE- + *genus* race]
▶ **de'generately** *adv* ▶ **de'generateness** *n* ▶ **de'generative** *adj*

★ **people and places**

degenerate matter n Astrophysics. the highly compressed state of a star's matter when its atoms virtually touch in the final stage of its evolution into a white dwarf.

degeneration (dɪˌdʒɛnəˈreɪʃən) n 1 the process of degenerating. 2 the state of being degenerate. 3 Biol. the loss of specialization, function, or structure by organisms and their parts. 4 impairment or loss of the function and structure of cells or tissues, as by disease or injury. 5 Electronics. negative feedback of a signal.

degradable (dɪˈɡreɪdəb°l) adj 1 capable of being decomposed chemically or biologically. 2 capable of being degraded.

degradation (ˌdɛɡrəˈdeɪʃən) n 1 a degrading or being degraded. 2 a state of degeneration or squalor. 3 some act, constraint, etc., that is degrading. 4 the wearing down of the surface of rocks, cliffs, etc., by erosion. 5 Chem. a breakdown of a molecule into atoms or smaller molecules. 6 Physics. an irreversible process in which the energy available to do work is decreased. 7 RC Church. the permanent unfrocking of a priest.

degrade (dɪˈɡreɪd) vb degrades, degrading, degraded. 1 (tr) to reduce in worth, character, etc.; disgrace. 2 (dɪˈɡreɪd) (tr) to reduce in rank or status; demote. 3 (tr) to reduce in strength, quality, etc. 4 to reduce or be reduced by erosion or down-cutting, as a land surface or bed of a river. 5 Chem. to decompose into atoms or smaller molecules. [C14: from LL dēgradāre, from L DE- + gradus rank, degree] ▶ deˈgrader n

degrading (dɪˈɡreɪdɪŋ) adj causing humiliation; debasing. ▶ deˈgradingly adv

degree (dɪˈɡriː) n 1 a stage in a scale of relative amount or intensity: a high degree of competence. 2 an academic award conferred by a university or college on successful completion of a course or as an honorary distinction (**honorary degree**). 3 any of three categories of seriousness of a burn. 4 (in the US) any of the categories into which a crime is divided according to its seriousness. 5 Genealogy. a step in a line of descent. 6 Grammar. any of the forms of an adjective used to indicate relative amount or intensity: in English they are positive, comparative, and superlative. 7 Music. any note of a diatonic scale relative to the other notes in that scale. 8 a unit of temperature on a specified scale. Symbol: °. See also **Celsius scale, Fahrenheit scale.** 9 a measure of angle equal to one three-hundred-and-sixtieth of the angle traced by one complete revolution of a line about one of its ends. Symbol: °. 10 a unit of latitude or longitude used to define points on the earth's surface. Symbol: °. 11 a unit on any of several scales of measurement, as for specific gravity. Symbol: °. 12 Maths. 12a the highest power or the sum of the powers of any term in a polynomial or by itself: $x^4 + x + 3$ and xyz^2 are of the fourth degree. 12b the greatest power of the highest order derivative in a differential equation. 13 Obs. a step; rung. 14 Arch. a stage in social status or rank. 15 **by degrees.** little by little; gradually. 16 **one degree under.** Inf. off colour; ill. 17 **to a degree.** somewhat; rather. [C13: from OF degre, from L DE- + gradus step]

degree of freedom n 1 Chem. the least number of independently variable properties needed to determine the state of a system. See also **phase rule.** 2 one of the independent components of motion (translation, vibration, and rotation) of an atom or molecule.

De Havilland ★ (də ˈhævɪlənd) n Sir Geoffrey. 1882–1965, British aircraft designer.

dehisce (dɪˈhɪs) vb dehisces, dehiscing, dehisced. (intr) (of fruits, anthers, etc.) to burst open spontaneously, releasing seeds, pollen, etc. [C17: from L dēhiscere to split open, from DE- + hiscere to yawn, gape] ▶ deˈhiscent adj

dehorn (diːˈhɔːn) vb (tr) to remove the horns of (cattle, sheep, or goats).

dehumanize or **dehumanise** (diːˈhjuːməˌnaɪz) vb dehumanizes, dehumanizing, dehumanized or dehumanises, dehumanising, dehumanised. (tr) 1 to deprive of human qualities. 2 to render mechanical, artificial, or routine. ▶ deˌhumaniˈzation or deˌhumaniˈsation n

dehumidify (ˌdiːhjuːˈmɪdɪˌfaɪ) vb dehumidifies, dehumidifying, dehumidified. (tr) to remove water from (the air, etc.) ▶ ˌdehuˌmidifiˈcation n ▶ ˌdehuˈmidiˌfier n

dehydrate (diːˈhaɪdreɪt, ˌdiːhaɪˈdreɪt) vb dehydrates, dehydrating, dehydrated. 1 to lose or cause to lose water. 2 to lose or deprive of water, as the body or tissues. ▶ ˌdehyˈdration n ▶ deˈhydrator n

dehydrogenate (diːˈhaɪdrədʒəˌneɪt), **dehydrogenize**, or **dehydrogenise** (diːˈhaɪdrədʒəˌnaɪz) vb dehydrogenates, dehydrogenating, dehydrogenated, dehydrogenizing, dehydrogenized or dehydrogenises, dehydrogenising, dehydrogenised. (tr) to remove hydrogen from. ▶ deˌhydrogeˈnation, deˌhydrogeniˈzation, or deˌhydrogeniˈsation n

de-ice (diːˈaɪs) vb de-ices, de-icing, de-iced. to free or be freed of ice.

de-icer (diːˈaɪsə) n 1 a mechanical or thermal device designed to melt or stop the formation of ice on an aircraft. 2 a substance used for this purpose, esp. an aerosol that can be sprayed on car windscreens to remove ice or frost.

deictic (ˈdaɪktɪk) adj 1 Logic. proving by direct argument. Cf. **elenctic** (see **elenchus**). ♦ n 2 another word for **indexical** (sense 2). [C17: from Gk deiktikos concerning proof, from deiknunai to show]

deify (ˈdiːɪˌfaɪ, ˈdeɪɪ-) vb deifies, deifying, deified. (tr) 1 to exalt to the position of a god or personify as a god. 2 to accord divine honour or worship to. [C14: from OF, from LL deificāre, from L deus god + facere to make] ▶ ˌdeifiˈcation n ▶ ˈdeiˌfier n

Deighton ★ (ˈdeɪtʰn) n Len. born 1929, British writer. His books include The Ipcress File (1962) and the trilogy Berlin Game, Mexico Set, and London Match (1983–85).

deign (deɪn) vb 1 (intr) to think it fit or worthy of oneself (to do something); condescend. 2 (tr) Arch. to vouchsafe. [C13: from OF, from L dignārī to consider worthy, from dignus]

deindividuation (diːˌɪndɪˌvɪdjuˈeɪʃən) n Psychol. the loss of a person's sense of individuality and responsibility.

de-industrialization or **de-industrialisation** (diːˌɪndʌstrɪəlaɪˈzeɪʃən) n a decline in importance of a country's manufacturing industry.

de-ionize or **de-ionise** (diːˈaɪəˌnaɪz) vb de-ionizes, de-ionizing, de-ionized or de-ionises, de-ionising, de-ionised. (tr) to remove ions from (water, etc.), esp. by ion exchange. ▶ deˌioniˈzation or deˌioniˈsation n

Deirdre ★ (ˈdɪədrɪ) n Irish myth. a beautiful girl who was raised by Conchobar to be his wife but eloped with Naoise. When Conchobar treacherously killed Naoise she took her own life: often used to symbolize Ireland. See also **Naoise.**

deism (ˈdiːɪzəm, ˈdeɪ-) n belief in the existence of God based on natural reason, without revelation. Cf. **theism.** [C17: from F déisme, from L deus god] ▶ ˈdeist n, adj ▶ deˈistic or deˈistical adj ▶ deˈistically adv

deity (ˈdiːɪtɪ, ˈdeɪ-) n, pl deities. 1 a god or goddess. 2 the state of being divine; godhead. 3 the rank of a god. 4 the nature or character of God. [C14: from OF, from LL deitās, from L deus god]

Deity (ˈdiːɪtɪ, ˈdeɪ-) n the. God.

déjà vu (ˈdeɪʒæ ˈvuː) n the experience of perceiving a new situation as if it had occurred before. [from F, lit.: already seen]

deject (dɪˈdʒɛkt) vb (tr) to have a depressing effect on; dispirit; dishearten. [C15: from L dēicere to cast down, from DE- + iacere to throw]

dejected (dɪˈdʒɛktɪd) adj miserable; despondent; downhearted. ▶ deˈjectedly adv

dejection (dɪˈdʒɛkʃən) n 1 lowness of spirits; depression. 2a faecal matter. 2b defecation.

de jure (deɪ ˈdʒʊərɪ) adv according to law; by right; legally. Cf. **de facto.** [L]

deka- or **dek-** combining form. variants of **deca-.**

deke (diːk) Canad. sl. ♦ vb dekes, deking, deked. 1 (tr) (in ice hockey or box lacrosse) to draw a defending player out of position by faking a shot or movement. ◆ *n* **2** such a shot or movement. ◆ Also: **decoy**. [C20: from DECOY]

Dekker *or* **Decker** ★ ('dɛkə) *n* Thomas. ?1572–?1632, English dramatist and pamphleteer, noted particularly for his comedy *The Shoemaker's Holiday* (1600).

dekko ('dɛkəʊ) *n, pl* **dekkos**. *Brit. sl.* a look; glance. [C19: from Hindi *dekho!* look! from *dekhnā* to see]

de Klerk ★ (də 'klɜːk) *n* F(rederik) W(illem). born 1936, South African statesman; president (1989–94); second executive deputy president (1994–97). In 1990 he began to dismantle the apartheid system; shared Nobel peace prize with Nelson Mandela 1993.

de Kooning ★ (də 'kuːnɪŋ) *n* Willem. See (Willem de) Kooning.

del (dɛl) *n Maths.* the differential operator $i(\partial/\partial x) + j(\partial/\partial y) + k(\partial/\partial z)$, where *i, j,* and *k* are unit vectors in the *x, y,* and *z* directions. Symbol: ∇ Also called: **nabla**.

del. *abbrev. for* delegate.

Del. *abbrev. for* Delaware.

Delacroix ★ (*French* dəlakrwa) *n* (Ferdinand Victor) Eugène (øʒɛn). 1798–1863, French romantic painter.

Delagoa Bay ★ (ˌdɛlə'gəʊə) *n* an inlet of the Indian Ocean, in S Mozambique. Official name: **Baía de Lourenço Marques**.

de la Mare ★ (də lɑː mɛə) *n* Walter (John). 1873–1956, British poet and novelist, noted for *The Listeners and Other Poems* (1912) and *Memoirs of a Midget* (1921).

Delaroche ★ (*French* dəlarɔʃ) *n* (Hippolyte) Paul (pɔl). 1797–1859, French painter.

Delaunay ★ (*French* dəlonɛ) *n* Robert (rɔbɛr). 1885–1941, French painter.

Delaware[1] ('dɛləˌwɛə) *n* **1** (*pl* **Delawares** *or* **Delaware**) a member of a North American Indian people formerly living near the Delaware River **2** the language of this people.

Delaware[2] ★ ('dɛləˌwɛə) *n* **1** a state of the northeastern US, on the Delmarva Peninsula: mostly flat and low-lying, with hills in the extreme north and cypress swamps in the extreme south. Capital: Dover. Pop.: 724 842 (1996 est.). Area: 5004 sq. km (1932 sq. miles). Abbrevs.: **Del.** or (with zip code) **DE** **2** a river in the northeastern US, rising in the Catskill Mountains and flowing south into **Delaware Bay**, an inlet of the Atlantic. Length 660 km (410 miles).
▶ ˌDela'warean *adj*

De La Warr ★ ('dɛləˌwɛə) *n* Baron, title of *Thomas West*, known as *Lord Delaware*. 1577–1618, English administrator in America; first governor of Virginia (1610).

delay (dɪ'leɪ) *vb* **1** (*tr*) to put off to a later time; defer. **2** (*tr*) to slow up or cause to be late. **3** (*intr*) to be irresolute or put off doing something. **4** (*intr*) to linger; dawdle. ◆ *n* **5** a delaying or being delayed. **6** the interval between one event and another. [C13: from OF, from *des-* off + *laier* to leave, from L *laxāre* to loosen]
▶ de'layer *n*

delayed action *or* **delay action** *n* a device for operating a mechanism, such as a camera shutter, a short time after setting.

delayed drop *n Aeronautics.* a parachute descent in which the opening of the parachute is delayed for a pre-determined time.

delayering (diː'leɪərɪŋ) *n* the process of pruning the administrative structure of a large organization by reducing the number of tiers in its hierarchy.

dele ('diːlɪ) *n, pl* **deles. 1** a sign (δ) indicating that typeset matter is to be deleted. ◆ *vb* **deles, deleing, deled. 2** (*tr*) to mark (matter to be deleted) with a dele. [C18: from L: delete (imperative), from *dēlēre* to destroy, obliterate]

delectable (dɪ'lɛktəbºl) *adj* highly enjoyable, esp. pleasing to the taste; delightful. [C14: from L *dēlectābilis*, from *dēlectāre* to DELIGHT]
▶ de'lectableness *or* deˌlecta'bility *n*

delectation (ˌdiːlɛk'teɪʃən) *n* pleasure; enjoyment.

delegate *n* ('dɛlɪˌgeɪt, -gɪt). **1** a person chosen to act for another or others, esp. at a conference or meeting. ◆ *vb*

('dɛlɪˌgeɪt), **delegates, delegating, delegated. 2** to give (duties, powers, etc.) to another as representative; depute. **3** (*tr*) to authorize (a person) as representative. [C14: from L *dēlēgāre* to send on a mission, from *lēgāre* to send, depute]
▶ 'delegable *adj*

delegation (ˌdɛlɪ'geɪʃən) *n* **1** a person or group chosen to represent another or others. **2** a delegating or being delegated.

de Lesseps ★ (*French* də lɛsɛps) *n* Vicomte. title of (Ferdinand Marie) Lesseps.

delete (dɪ'liːt) *vb* **deletes, deleting, deleted.** (*tr*) to remove (something printed or written); erase; strike out. [C17: from L *dēlēre* to destroy, obliterate]
▶ de'letion *n*

deleterious (ˌdɛlɪ'tɪərɪəs) *adj* harmful; injurious; hurtful. [C17: from NL, from Gk *dēlētērios*, from *dēleisthai* to hurt]
▶ ˌdele'teriousness *n*

Delft ★ (dɛlft) *n* **1** a town in the SW Netherlands, in South Holland province. Pop.: 91 941 (1994). **2** Also called: 'delftware. tin-glazed earthenware made in Delft since the 17th century, typically having blue decoration on a white ground. **3** a similar earthenware made in England.

Delhi ★ ('dɛlɪ) *n* **1** the capital of India, in the N central part, on the Jumna river: consists of **Old Delhi** (a walled city reconstructed in 1639 on the site of former cities of Delhi, which date from the 15th century B.C.) and **New Delhi** to the south, chosen as the capital in 1912, replacing Calcutta; university (1922). Pop. (urban area) 8 419 084 (1991). **2** a Union Territory of N India. Capital: Delhi. Area: 1418 sq. km (553 sq. miles). Pop. 10 865 000 (1994 est.).

deli ('dɛlɪ) *n, pl* **delis.** an informal word for **delicatessen**.

deliberate *adj* (dɪ'lɪbərɪt). **1** carefully thought out in advance; intentional. **2** careful or unhurried: *a deliberate pace*. ◆ *vb* (dɪ'lɪbəˌreɪt). **deliberates, deliberating, deliberated. 3** to consider (something) deeply; think over. [C15: from L *dēlīberāre*, from *lībrāre* to weigh, from *lībra* scales]
▶ de'liberately *adv* ▶ de'liberateness *n* ▶ de'liberˌator *n*

deliberation (dɪˌlɪbə'reɪʃən) *n* **1** careful consideration. **2** (*often pl*) formal discussion, as of a committee. **3** care or absence of hurry.

deliberative (dɪ'lɪbərətɪv) *adj* **1** of or for deliberating: *a deliberative assembly*. **2** characterized by deliberation.
▶ de'liberatively *adv* ▶ de'liberativeness *n*

Delibes ★ (*French* dəlib) *n* (Clément Philibert) Léo (leo). 1836–91, French composer, noted for his ballets *Coppélia* (1870) and *Sylvia* (1876), and the opera *Lakmé* (1883).

delicacy ('dɛlɪkəsɪ) *n, pl* **delicacies. 1** fine or subtle quality, character, construction, etc. **2** fragile or graceful beauty. **3** something that is considered choice to eat, such as caviar. **4** fragile construction or constitution. **5** refinement of feeling, manner, or appreciation. **6** fussy or squeamish refinement, esp. in matters of taste; propriety, etc. **7** need for tactful or sensitive handling. **8** sensitivity of response, as of an instrument.

delicate ('dɛlɪkɪt) *adj* **1** fine or subtle in quality, character, construction, etc. **2** having a soft or fragile beauty. **3** (of colour, tone, taste, etc.) pleasantly subtle. **4** easily damaged or injured; fragile. **5** precise or sensitive in action: *a delicate mechanism*. **6** requiring tact. **7** showing regard for the feelings of others. **8** excessively refined; squeamish. [C14: from L *dēlicātus* affording pleasure, from *dēliciae* (pl) delight, pleasure]
▶ 'delicately *adv* ▶ 'delicateness *n*

delicatessen (ˌdɛlɪkə'tɛsºn) *n* **1** a shop selling various foods, esp. unusual or imported foods, already cooked or prepared. **2** such foods. [C19: from G *Delikatessen*, lit.: delicacies, from F *délicatesse*]

delicious (dɪ'lɪʃəs) *adj* **1** very appealing, esp. to taste or smell. **2** extremely enjoyable. [C13: from OF, from L *dēliciōsus*, from L *dēliciae* delights, from *dēlicere* to entice; see DELIGHT]
▶ de'liciously *adv* ▶ de'liciousness *n*

delight (dɪ'laɪt) *vb* **1** (*tr*) to please greatly. **2** (*intr*; foll. by

in) to take great pleasure (in). ◆ *n* **3** extreme pleasure. **4** something that causes this. [C13: from OF, from *deleitier* to please, from L *dēlectāre*, from *dēlicere* to allure, from DE- + *lacere* to entice]
► de'lighted *adj* ► de'lightedly *adv*

delightful (dɪ'laɪtfʊl) *adj* giving great delight; very pleasing, beautiful, charming, etc.
► de'lightfully *adv* ► de'lightfulness *n*

Delilah ★ (dɪ'laɪlə) *n* **1** Samson's Philistine mistress, who betrayed him (Judges 16). **2** a voluptuous and treacherous woman; temptress.

delimit (diː'lɪmɪt) *or* **delimitate** *vb* delimits, delimiting, delimited *or* delimitates, delimitating, delimitated. *(tr)* to mark or prescribe the limits or boundaries of.
► de,limi'tation *n* ► de'limitative *adj*

delineate (dɪ'lɪnɪ,eɪt) *vb* delineates, delineating, delineated. *(tr)* **1** to trace the outline of. **2** to represent pictorially; depict. **3** to portray in words; describe. [C16: from L *dēlīneāre* to sketch out, from *līnea* LINE¹]
► de,line'ation *n* ► de'lineative *adj*

delinquency (dɪ'lɪŋkwənsɪ) *n, pl* delinquencies. **1** an offence or misdeed, esp. one committed by a young person. See **juvenile delinquency**. **2** failure or negligence in duty or obligation. **3** a delinquent nature or delinquent behaviour. [C17: from LL *dēlinquentia* fault, offence, from L *dēlinquere* to transgress, from DE- + *linquere* to forsake]

delinquent (dɪ'lɪŋkwənt) *n* **1** someone, esp. a young person, guilty of delinquency. ◆ *adj* **2** guilty of an offence or misdeed. **3** failing in or neglectful of duty or obligation. [C17: from L *dēlinquēns* offending; see DELINQUENCY]

deliquesce (,dɛlɪ'kwɛs) *vb* deliquesces, deliquescing, deliquesced. *(intr)* (esp. of certain salts) to dissolve gradually in water absorbed from the air. [C18: from L *dēliquēscere*, from DE- + *liquēscere* to melt, from *liquēre* to be liquid]
► ,deli'quescence *n* ► ,deli'quescent *adj*

delirious (dɪ'lɪrɪəs) *adj* **1** affected with delirium. **2** wildly excited, esp. with joy or enthusiasm.
► de'liriously *adv*

delirium (dɪ'lɪrɪəm) *n, pl* deliriums *or* deliria (-'lɪrɪə). **1** a state of excitement and mental confusion, often accompanied by hallucinations, caused by high fever, poisoning, brain injury, etc. **2** violent excitement or emotion; frenzy. [C16: from L: madness, from *dēlīrāre*, lit.: to swerve from a furrow, hence be crazy, from DE- + *līra* furrow]

delirium tremens ('trɛmɛnz, 'triː-) *n* a severe psychotic condition occurring in some persons with chronic alcoholism, characterized by delirium, tremor, anxiety, and vivid hallucinations. Abbrevs.: **DT's** (informal), **dt**. [C19: NL, lit.: trembling delirium]

Delius ★ ('diːlɪəs) *n* **Frederick.** 1862–1934, British composer. His works include the opera *A Village Romeo and Juliet* (1901), *A Mass of Life* (1905), and the orchestral variations *Brigg Fair* (1907).

deliver (dɪ'lɪvə) *vb* (mainly tr) **1** to carry to a destination, esp. to distribute (goods, mail, etc.) to several places. **2** (often foll. by *over* or *up*) to hand over or transfer. **3** (often foll. by *from*) to release or rescue (from captivity, harm, etc.). **4** (also intr) **4a** to aid in the birth of (offspring). **4b** to give birth to (offspring). **4c** (usually foll. by *of*) to aid (a female) in the birth (of offspring). **4d** (passive; foll. by *of*) to give birth (to offspring). **5** to present (a speech, idea, etc.). **6** to utter: *to deliver a cry of exultation.* **7** to discharge or release (something, such as a blow or shot) suddenly. **8** (intr) *Inf.* Also: **deliver the goods.** to produce something promised or expected. **9** *Chiefly US.* to cause (voters, etc.) to support a given candidate, cause, etc. **10 deliver oneself of.** to speak with deliberation or at length. [C13: from OF, from LL *dēlīberāre* to set free, from L DE- + *līberāre* to free]
► de'liverable *adj* ► de'liverer *n*

deliverance (dɪ'lɪvərəns) *n* **1** a formal expression of opinion. **2** rescue from moral corruption or evil; salvation.

delivery (dɪ'lɪvərɪ) *n, pl* deliveries. **1a** the act of delivering or distributing goods, mail, etc. **1b** something that is de-

livered. **2** the act of giving birth to a child. **3** manner or style of utterance, esp. in public speaking: *the chairman had a clear delivery.* **4** the act of giving or transferring or the state of being given or transferred. **5** a rescuing or being rescued; liberation. **6** *Sport.* the act or manner of bowling or throwing a ball. **7** the handing over of property, a deed, etc.

dell (dɛl) *n* a small, esp. wooded hollow. [OE]

della Robbia ★ (*Italian* 'della 'robbja) *n* See (Luca della) **Robbia.**

Deller ★ ('dɛlə) *n* **Alfred (George).** 1912–79, British countertenor.

Del Mar ★ (dɛl 'mɑː) *n* **Norman.** 1919–94, British conductor.

Delmarva Peninsula ★ (dɛl'mɑːvə) *n* a peninsula of the northeast US, between Chesapeake Bay and the Atlantic.

Delors ★ (*French* dəlɔr) *n* **Jacques (Lucien Jean)** (ʒɑk). born 1925, French politician and economist, President of the European Commission (1985–94): originator of the **Delors plan** for closer European union.

Delos ★ ('diːlɒs) *n* a Greek island in the SW Aegean Sea, in the Cyclades: a commercial centre in ancient times; the legendary birthplace of Apollo and Artemis. Area: about 5 sq. km (2 sq. miles). Modern Greek name: **Dhílos.**

de los Angeles ★ (*Spanish* de los 'aŋxeles) *n* **Victoria** (bik'torja). born 1923, Spanish soprano.

delouse (diː'laʊs, -'laʊz) *vb* delouses, delousing, deloused. *(tr)* to rid (a person or animal) of lice as a sanitary measure.

Delphi ★ ('dɛlfɪ) *n* an ancient Greek city on the S slopes of Mount Parnassus: site of the most famous oracle of Apollo.

Delphic ('dɛlfɪk) *or* **Delphian** *adj* **1** of or relating to the ancient Greek city of Delphi or its oracle or temple. **2** obscure or ambiguous.

Delphic oracle ★ *n* the oracle of Apollo at Delphi that gave answers held by the ancient Greeks to be of great authority but also noted for their ambiguity.

delphinium (dɛl'fɪnɪəm) *n, pl* delphiniums *or* delphinia (-ɪə). a plant with spikes of blue, pink, or white spurred flowers. See also **larkspur.** [C17: NL, from Gk *delphinion* larkspur, from *delphis* dolphin, referring to the shape of the nectary]

del Sarto ★ (*Italian* del 'sarto) *n* See (Andrea del) **Sarto.**

delta ('dɛltə) *n* **1** the fourth letter in the Greek alphabet (Δ or δ). **2** (*cap. when part of name*) the flat alluvial area at the mouth of some rivers where the mainstream splits up into several distributaries. **3** *Maths.* a finite increment in a variable. [C16: via L from Gk, of Semitic origin]
► deltaic (dɛl'teɪɪk) *or* 'deltic *adj*

delta connection *n* a connection used in a three-phase electrical system in which three elements in series form a triangle, the supply being input and output at the three junctions.

delta particle *n* *Physics* a very short-lived type of hyperon.

delta ray *n* a particle, esp. an electron, ejected from matter by ionizing radiation.

delta rhythm *or* **wave** *n* *Physiol.* the normal electrical activity of the cerebral cortex during deep sleep. See also **brain wave.**

delta stock *n* any of the fourth rank of active securities on the London stock exchange. Market makers need not display prices of these securities continuously.

delta wing *n* a triangular swept-back aircraft wing.

deltiology (,dɛltɪ'ɒlədʒɪ) *n* the collection and study of postcards. [C20: from Gk *deltion*, dim. of *deltos* a writing tablet + -LOGY]
► ,delti'ologist *n*

deltoid ('dɛltɔɪd) *n* a thick muscle of the shoulder that acts to raise the arm. [C18: from Gk *deltoeidēs* triangular, from DELTA]

delude (dɪ'luːd) *vb* deludes, deluding, deluded. *(tr)* to deceive; mislead; beguile. [C15: from L *dēlūdere* to mock, play false, from DE- + *lūdere* to play]
► de'ludable *adj* ► de'luder *n*

---

deluge ('dɛljuːdʒ) n **1** a great flood of water. **2** torrential rain. **3** an overwhelming rush or number. ◆ vb **deluges, deluging, deluged.** (tr) **4** to flood. **5** to overwhelm; inundate. [C14: from OF, from L dīluvium, from dīluere to wash away, drench, from di- DIS-¹ + -luere, from lavere to wash]

Deluge ('dɛljuːdʒ) n **the.** another name for the **Flood.**

delusion (dɪ'luːʒən) n **1** a mistaken idea, belief, etc. **2** Psychiatry. a belief held in the face of evidence to the contrary, that is resistant to all reason. **3** a deluding or being deluded.
▸ de'**lusional** adj ▸ de'**lusive** adj ▸ **delusory** (dɪ'luːsərɪ) adj

de luxe (də 'lʌks, 'luks) adj **1** rich or sumptuous; superior in quality: the de luxe model of a car. ◆ adv **2** Chiefly US. in a luxurious manner. [C19: from F, lit.: of luxury]

delve (dɛlv) vb **delves, delving, delved.** (mainly intr; often foll. by in or into) **1** to research deeply or intensively (for information, etc.). **2** to search or rummage. **3** to dig or burrow deeply. **4** (also tr) Arch. or Brit. dialect. to dig. [OE delfan]
▸ '**delver** n

Dem. (in the US) abbrev. for Democrat(ic).

demagnetize or **demagnetise** (diː'mægnɪ,taɪz) vb **demagnetizes, demagnetizing, demagnetized** or **demagnetises, demagnetising, demagnetised.** to remove or lose magnetic properties. Also: **degauss.**
▸ de,magneti'**zation** or de,magneti'**sation** n ▸ de'**magnet,izer** or de'**magnet,iser** n

demagogue or US (sometimes) **demagog** ('dɛmə,gɒg) n **1** a political agitator who appeals with crude oratory to the prejudice and passions of the mob. **2** (esp. in the ancient world) any popular political leader or orator. [C17: from Gk dēmagōgos people's leader, from dēmos people + agein to lead]
▸ ,dema'**gogic** adj ▸ ,dema'**goguery** n

demagogy ('dɛmə,gɒgɪ) n, pl **demagogies. 1** demagoguery. **2** rule by a demagogue or by demagogues. **3** a group of demagogues.

demand (dɪ'mɑːnd) vb (tr; may take a clause as object or an infinitive) **1** to request peremptorily or urgently. **2** to require as just, urgent, etc.: the situation demands attention. **3** to claim as a right; exact. **4** Law. to make a formal legal claim to (property). ◆ n **5** an urgent or peremptory requirement or request. **6** something that requires special effort or sacrifice. **7** the act of demanding something or the thing demanded. **8** an insistent question. **9** Econ. **9a** willingness and ability to purchase goods and services. **9b** the amount of a commodity that consumers are willing and able to purchase at a specified price. Cf. **supply**¹ (sense 9). **10** Law. a formal legal claim, esp. to real property. **11 in demand.** sought after. **12 on demand.** as soon as requested. [C13: from Anglo-F, from Med. L dēmandāre, from L: to commit to, from DE- + mandāre to command, entrust]
▸ de'**mandable** adj ▸ de'**mander** n

demand feeding n the practice of feeding a baby whenever it is hungry, rather than at set intervals.

demanding (dɪ'mɑːndɪŋ) adj requiring great patience, skill, etc.: a demanding job.

demarcate ('diːmɑː,keɪt) vb **demarcates, demarcating, demarcated.** (tr) **1** to mark the boundaries, limits, etc., of. **2** to separate; distinguish.
▸ '**demar,cator** n

demarcation or **demarkation** (,diːmɑː'keɪʃən) n **1** the act of establishing limits or boundaries. **2** a limit or boundary. **3a** a strict separation of the kinds of work performed by members of different trade unions. **3b** (as modifier): demarcation dispute. **4** separation or distinction (as in **line of demarcation**). [C18: from Sp. demarcar to appoint the boundaries of, from marcar to mark, from It., of Gmc origin]

démarche French. (demarʃ) n a move, step, or manoeuvre, esp. in diplomatic affairs. [C17: lit.: walk, gait, from OF demarcher to tread, trample]

dematerialize or **dematerialise** (diːmə'tɪərɪə,laɪz) vb **dematerializes, dematerializing, dematerialized** or **dematerialises, dematerialising, dematerialised.** (intr) **1** to

cease to have material existence, as in science fiction c spiritualism. **2** to vanish.
▸ dema,teriali'**zation** or dema,teriali'**sation** n

deme (diːm) n **1** (in ancient Attica) a geographical unit c local government. **2** Biol. a group of individuals within species that possess particular characteristics of cyto ogy, genetics, etc. [C19: from Gk dēmos district in loca government, the populace]

demean¹ (dɪ'miːn) vb (tr) to lower (oneself) in dignity status, or character; humble; debase. [C17: see DE MEAN²]

demean² (dɪ'miːn) vb (tr) Rare. to behave or conduc (oneself). [C13: from OF, from DE- + mener to lead, fron L mināre to drive (animals), from minārī to use threats]

demeanour or US **demeanor** (dɪ'miːnə) n **1** the way person behaves towards others. **2** bearing or mier [C15: see DEMEAN²]

dement (dɪ'mɛnt) vb **1** (intr) to deteriorate mentally, esp because of old age. **2** (tr) Rare. to drive mad; make insane [C16: from LL dēmentāre to drive mad, from L DE- + men mind]

demented (dɪ'mɛntɪd) adj mad; insane.
▸ de'**mentedly** adv ▸ de'**mentedness** n

dementia (dɪ'mɛnʃə, -ʃɪə) n a state of serious menta deterioration, of organic or functional origin. [C1¢ from L: madness; see DEMENT]

dementia praecox ('priːkɒks) n a former name fo schizophrenia. [C19: NL, lit.: premature dementia]

demerara (,dɛmə'rɛərə, -'rɑːrə) n brown crystallized can sugar from the Caribbean. [C19: after Demerara, a re gion of Guyana]

Demerara ★ (,dɛmə'rɛərə, -'rɑːrə) n **the.** a river in Guy ana, rising in the central forest area and flowing nort to the Atlantic at Georgetown. Length: 346 km (21 miles).

demerit (diː'mɛrɪt) n **1** something that deserves censure **2** US & Canad. a mark given against a student, etc., fo failure or misconduct. **3** a fault. [C14 (orig.: worth desert, ult.: something worthy of blame): from L dēmerē to deserve]
▸ de,meri'**torious** adj

demersal (dɪ'mɜːsᵊl) adj living or occurring in dee water or on the bottom of a sea or lake. [C19: from dēmersus submerged (from mergere to dip) + -AL¹]

demesne (dɪ'meɪn, -'miːn) n **1** land surrounding a hous or manor. **2** Property law. the possession and use of one own property or land; domain. **4** a region or dis trict. [C14: from OF demeine; see DOMAIN]

Demeter ★ (dɪ'miːtə) n Greek myth. the goddess of agri cultural fertility and protector of marriage and women Roman counterpart: **Ceres.**

demi- prefix **1** half: demirelief. **2** of less than full size, sta tus, or rank: demigod. [via F from Med. L, from dīmīdius half, from dis- apart + medius middle]

demigod ('dɛmɪ,gɒd) n **1a** a being who is part mortal part god. **1b** a lesser deity. **2** a person with godlike attrib utes. [C16: translation of L sēmideus]
▸ '**demi,goddess** fem n

demijohn ('dɛmɪ,dʒɒn) n a large bottle with a short nar row neck, often encased in wickerwork. [C18: prob from F dame-jeanne, from dame lady + Jeanne Jane]

demilitarize or **demilitarise** (diː'mɪlɪtə,raɪz) vb **demil itarizes, demilitarizing, demilitarized** or **demilitarises, demilita rising, demilitarised.** (tr) **1** to remove and prohibit an military presence or function in (an area): demilitarize zone. **2** to free of military character, purpose, etc.
▸ de,militari'**zation** or de,militari'**sation** n

De Mille ★ (də 'mɪl) n Cecil B(lount). 1881–1959, US film producer and director.

demimondaine (,dɛmɪ'mɒndeɪn) n a woman of the demimonde. [C19: from F]

demimonde (,dɛmɪ'mɒnd) n **1** (esp. in the 19th cen tury) those women considered to be outside respectable society, esp. on account of sexual promiscuity. **2** any group considered to be not wholly respectable. [C19 from F, lit.: half-world]

emise (dɪˈmaɪz) *n* **1** failure or termination. **2** a euphemistic or formal word for **death**. **3** *Property law.* a transfer of an estate by lease or on the death of the owner. **4** the transfer of sovereignty to a successor upon the death, abdication, etc., of a ruler (esp. in **demise of the crown**). ◆ *vb* **demises, demising, demised. 5** to transfer or be transferred by inheritance, will, or succession. **6** (*tr*) *Property law.* to transfer for a limited period; lease. **7** (*tr*) to transfer (sovereignty, a title, etc.) [C16: from OF, fem of *demis* dismissed, from *demettre* to send away, from L *dīmittere*] ▸ de'**misable** *adj*

emi-sec (ˌdɛmɪˈsɛk) *adj* (of wine) medium-dry. [C20: from F, from *demi* half + *sec* dry]

emisemiquaver (ˈdɛmɪˌsɛmɪˌkweɪvə) *n Music.* a note having the time value of one thirty-second of a semibreve. Usual US and Canad. name: **thirty-second note.**

emist (diˈmɪst) *vb* to free or become free of condensation. ▸ de'**mister** *n*

emitasse (ˈdɛmɪˌtæs) *n* **1** a small cup used to serve coffee, esp. after a meal. **2** the coffee itself. [C19: F, lit.: half-cup]

emiurge (ˈdɛmɪˌɜːdʒ) *n* **1** (in the philosophy of Plato) the creator of the universe. **2** (in Gnostic philosophy) the creator of the universe, supernatural but subordinate to the Supreme Being. [C17: from Church L, from Gk *dēmiourgos* skilled workman, lit.: one who works for the people, from *dēmos* people + *ergon* work] ▸ ˌdemi'**urgic** *or* ˌdemi'**urgical** *adj*

emiveg (ˈdɛmɪˌvɛdʒ) *Inf.* ◆ *n* **1** a person who eats poultry and fish, but no red meat. ◆ *adj* **2** denoting a person who eats poultry and fish, but no red meat. [C20: from DEMI- + VEG(ETARIAN)]

emo (ˈdɛməʊ) *n, pl* **demos.** *Inf.* **1** short for **demonstration** (sense 4). **2** a demonstration record or tape.

emo- *or before a vowel* **dem-** *combining form.* indicating people or population: *demography.* [from Gk *dēmos*]

emob *Brit. inf.* ◆ *vb* (diːˈmɒb), **demobs, demobbing, demobbed. 1** to demobilize. ◆ *n* (ˈdiːmɒb). **2** demobilization.

emobilize *or* **demobilise** (diːˈməʊbɪˌlaɪz) *vb* **demobilizes, demobilizing, demobilized** *or* **demobilises, demobilising, demobilised.** to disband, as troops, etc. ▸ de,**mobili'zation** *or* de,**mobili'sation** *n*

Demochristian (ˌdɛməʊˈkrɪstjən) *n* an informal name for a **Christian Democrat.**

emocracy (dɪˈmɒkrəsɪ) *n, pl* **democracies. 1** government by the people or their elected representatives. **2** a political or social unit governed ultimately by all its members. **3** the practice or spirit of social equality. **4** a social condition of classlessness and equality. [C16: from F, from LL, from Gk *dēmokratia* government by the people]

emocrat (ˈdɛməˌkræt) *n* **1** an advocate of democracy. **2** a member or supporter of a democratic party or movement.

Democrat (ˈdɛməˌkræt) *n* (in the US) a member or supporter of the Democratic Party. ▸ ˌDemo'**cratic** *adj*

emocratic (ˌdɛməˈkrætɪk) *adj* **1** of or relating to the principles of democracy. **2** upholding democracy or the interests of the common people. **3** popular with or for the benefit of all. ▸ ˌdemo'**cratically** *adv*

emocratic centralism *n* the Leninist principle that policy should be decided centrally by officials, who are nominally democratically elected.

Democratic Republic of the Congo ★ *n* **the.** See **Congo** (sense 2).

emocratize *or* **democratise** (dɪˈmɒkrəˌtaɪz) *vb* **democratizes, democratizing, democratized** *or* **democratises, democratising, democratised.** (*tr*) to make democratic. ▸ de,**mocrati'zation** *or* de,**mocrati'sation** *n*

Democritus ★ (dɪˈmɒkrɪtəs) *n* ?460–?370 B.C., Greek philosopher who developed the atomic theory of matter of his teacher, Leucippus.

démodé *French.* (demɔde) *adj* outmoded. [F, from *dé-* out of + *mode* fashion]

---

demodulate (diːˈmɒdjʊˌleɪt) *vb* **demodulates, demodulating, demodulated.** to carry out demodulation on. ▸ de'**modu,lator** *n*

demodulation (ˌdiːmɒdjʊˈleɪʃən) *n Electronics.* the act or process by which an output wave or signal is obtained having the characteristics of the original modulating wave or signal; the reverse of modulation.

demographic timebomb *n Chiefly Brit.* a predicted shortage of school-leavers and consequently of available workers, caused by an earlier drop in the birth rate.

demography (dɪˈmɒgrəfɪ) *n* the scientific study of human populations, esp. of their size, distribution, etc. [C19: from F, from Gk *dēmos* the populace; see -GRAPHY] ▸ de'**mographer** *n* ▸ **demographic** (ˌdiːməˈgræfɪk, ˌdɛmə-) *adj*

demoiselle (dəmwɑːˈzɛl) *n* **1** a small crane of central Asia, N Africa, and SE Europe, having a grey plumage with black breast feathers and white ear tufts. **2** a less common name for a **damselfly. 3** a literary word for **damsel.** [C16: from F: young woman; see DAMSEL]

demolish (dɪˈmɒlɪʃ) *vb* (*tr*) **1** to tear down or break up (buildings, etc.). **2** to put an end to (an argument, etc.). **3** *Facetious.* to eat up. [C16: from F, from L *dēmōlīrī* to throw down, from DE- + *mōlīrī* to construct, from *mōles* mass] ▸ de'**molisher** *n*

demolition (ˌdɛməˈlɪʃən, ˌdiː-) *n* **1** a demolishing or being demolished. **2** *Chiefly mil.* destruction by explosives. ▸ ˌdemo'**litionist** *n, adj*

demon (ˈdiːmən) *n* **1** an evil spirit or devil. **2** a person, obsession, etc., thought of as evil or cruel. **3** Also called: **daemon, daimon.** an attendant or ministering spirit; genius: *the demon of inspiration.* **4a** a person extremely skilful in or devoted to a given activity, esp. a sport: *a demon at cycling.* **4b** (*as modifier*): *a demon cyclist.* **5** a variant spelling of **daemon** (senses 1, 2). **6** *Austral. & NZ sl.* a detective or policeman, esp. one in plain clothes. [C15: from L *daemōn* (evil) spirit, from Gk *daimōn* spirit, deity, fate] ▸ **demonic** (dɪˈmɒnɪk) *adj*

demonetize *or* **demonetise** (diːˈmʌnɪˌtaɪz) *vb* **demonetizes, demonetizing, demonetized** *or* **demonetises, demonetising, demonetised.** (*tr*) **1** to deprive (a metal) of its capacity as a monetary standard. **2** to withdraw from use as currency. ▸ de,**moneti'zation** *or* de,**moneti'sation** *n*

demoniac (dɪˈməʊnɪˌæk) *adj also* **demoniacal** (ˌdiːmə'naɪək°l). **1** of or like a demon. **2** suggesting inner possession or inspiration. **3** frantic; frenzied. ◆ *n* **4** a person possessed by a demon. ▸ ˌdemo'**niacally** *adv*

demonism (ˈdiːməˌnɪzəm) *n* **1** belief in the existence and power of demons. **2** another name for **demonology** (sense 1). ▸ **'demonist** *n*

demonize *or* **demonise** (ˌdiːməˌnaɪz) *vb* (*tr*) **1** to make into or like a demon. **2** to subject to demonic influence. **3** to mark out or describe as evil or culpable: *they demonized the enemy in the run-up to war.*

demonolatry (ˌdiːmə'nɒlətrɪ) *n* the worship of demons. [C17: see DEMON, -LATRY]

demonology (ˌdiːmə'nɒlədʒɪ) *n* **1** Also called: **demonism.** the study of demons or demonic beliefs. **2** a set of people or things that are disliked or feared: *Adolf Hitler's place in contemporary demonology.* ▸ ˌdemon'**ologist** *n*

demonstrable (ˈdɛmənstrəb°l, dɪˈmɒn-) *adj* able to be demonstrated or proved. ▸ ˌdemonstra'**bility** *n* ▸ '**demonstrably** *adv*

demonstrate (ˈdɛmənˌstreɪt) *vb* **demonstrates, demonstrating, demonstrated. 1** (*tr*) to show or prove, esp. by reasoning, evidence, etc. **2** (*tr*) to evince; reveal the existence of. **3** (*tr*) to explain by experiment, example, etc. **4** (*tr*) to display and explain the workings of (a machine, product, etc.). **5** (*intr*) to manifest support, protest, etc., by public parades or rallies. **6** (*intr*) to be employed as a demonstrator of machinery, etc. **7** (*intr*)

Mil. to make a show of force. [C16: from L *dēmonstrāre* to point out, from *monstrāre* to show]

demonstration (,dɛmən'streɪʃən) *n* **1** the act of demonstrating. **2** proof or evidence leading to proof. **3** an explanation, illustration, or experiment showing how something works. **4** Also: **demo.** a manifestation of support or protest by public rallies, parades, etc. **5** a manifestation of emotion. **6** a show of military force. ▸ ,demon'strational *adj* ▸ ,demon'strationist *n*

demonstration model *n* a nearly new product, such as a car, that has been used to demonstrate its performance by a dealer and is offered at a discount.

demonstrative (dɪ'mɒnstrətɪv) *adj* **1** tending to express one's feelings easily or unreservedly. **2** (*postpositive*; foll. by *of*) serving as proof; indicative. **3** involving or characterized by demonstration. **4** conclusive. **5** *Grammar.* denoting or belonging to a class of determiners used to point out the individual referent or referents intended, such as *this* and *those*. Cf. **interrogative, relative.** ◆ *n* **6** *Grammar.* a demonstrative word. ▸ de'monstratively *adv* ▸ de'monstrativeness *n*

demonstrator ('dɛmən,streɪtə) *n* **1** a person who demonstrates equipment, machines, products, etc. **2** a person who takes part in a public demonstration.

demoralize *or* **demoralise** (dɪ'mɒrə,laɪz) *vb* **demoralizes, demoralizing, demoralized** *or* **demoralises, demoralising, demoralised.** (*tr*) **1** to undermine the morale of; dishearten. **2** to corrupt. **3** to throw into confusion. ▸ de,morali'zation *or* de,morali'sation *n*

Demosthenes ★ (dɪ'mɒsθə,niːz) *n* 384–322 B.C., Athenian statesman, orator, and lifelong opponent of the power of Macedonia over Greece.

demote (dɪ'məʊt) *vb* **demotes, demoting, demoted.** (*tr*) to lower in rank or position; relegate. [C19: from DE- + (PRO)MOTE] ▸ de'motion *n*

demotic (dɪ'mɒtɪk) *adj* **1** of or relating to the common people; popular. **2** of or relating to a simplified form of hieroglyphics used in ancient Egypt. Cf. **hieratic.** ◆ *n* **3** the demotic script of ancient Egypt. [C19: from Gk *dēmotikos* of the people, from *dēmotēs* a man of the people, commoner] ▸ de'motist *n*

Dempsey ★ ('dɛmpsɪ) *n* **Jack.** real name *William Harrison Dempsey*. 1895–1983, US boxer; world heavyweight champion (1919–26).

dempster ('dɛmpstə) *n* a variant spelling of **deemster.**

demulcent (dɪ'mʌlsᵊnt) *adj* **1** soothing. ◆ *n* **2** a drug or agent that soothes irritation. [C18: from L *dēmulcēre*, from DE- + *mulcēre* to stroke]

demur (dɪ'mɜː) *vb* **demurs, demurring, demurred.** (*intr*) **1** to show reluctance. **2** *Law.* to raise an objection by entering a demurrer. ◆ *n also* **demurral** (dɪ'mʌrəl). **3** the act of demurring. **4** an objection raised. [C13: from OF, from L *dēmorārī*, from *morārī* to delay] ▸ de'murrable *adj*

demure (dɪ'mjʊə) *adj* **1** sedate; decorous; reserved. **2** affectedly modest or prim; coy. [C14: ?from OF *demorer* to delay, linger; ? infl. by *meur* ripe, MATURE] ▸ de'murely *adv* ▸ de'mureness *n*

demurrage (dɪ'mʌrɪdʒ) *n* **1** the delaying of a ship, etc., caused by the charterer's failure to load, unload, etc., before the time of scheduled departure. **2** the extra charge required for such delay. [C14: from OF *demorage, demourage*; see DEMUR]

demurrer (dɪ'mʌrə) *n* **1** *Law.* a pleading that admits an opponent's point but denies that it is relevant or valid. **2** any objection raised.

demutualize *or* **demutualise** (diː'mjuːtjʊə,laɪz) *vb* **demutualizes, demutualizing, demutualized** *or* **demutualises, demutualising, demutualised.** (*intr*) (of a mutual savings or life-assurance organization) to convert to a public limited company. ▸ ,demutuali'zation *or* ,demutuali'sation *n*

demy (dɪ'maɪ) *n, pl* **demies. 1** a size of printing paper, 17½ by 22½ inches (444.5 × 571.5 mm). **2** a size of writing

paper, 15½ by 20 inches (Brit.) (393.7 × 508 mm) or 16 by 21 inches (US) (406.4 × 533.4 mm). [C16: see DEMI-]

demystify (diː'mɪstɪ,faɪ) *vb* **demystifies, demystifying, demystified.** (*tr*) to remove the mystery from. ▸ de,mystifi'cation *n*

demythologize *or* **demythologise** (,diːmɪ'θɒlə,dʒaɪz) *vb* **demythologizes, demythologizing, demythologized** *or* **demythologises, demythologising, demythologised.** (*tr*) **1** to eliminate mythical elements from (a piece of writing, esp. the Bible). **2** to restate (a religious message) in rational terms.

den (dɛn) *n* **1** the habitat or retreat of a wild animal; lair. **2** a small or secluded room in a home, often used for carrying on a hobby. **3** a squalid room or retreat. **4** a site or haunt: *a den of vice*. **5** *Scot.* a small wooded valley. ◆ *vb* **dens, denning, denned. 6** (*intr*) to live in or as if in a den [OE *denn*]

Den. *abbrev. for* Denmark.

denar (dɪ'nɑː) *n* the standard monetary unit of (the Former Yugoslav Republic of) Macedonia.

denarius (dɪ'nɛərɪəs) *n, pl* **denarii** (-'nɛərɪ,aɪ). **1** a silver coin of ancient Rome, often called a penny in translation. **2** a gold coin worth 25 silver denarii. [C16: from L coin orig. equal to ten asses, from *dēnārius* (adj) containing ten, from *decem* ten]

denary ('diːnərɪ) *adj* **1** calculated by tens; decimal. **2** containing ten parts; tenfold. [C16: from L *dēnārius*; see DENARIUS]

denationalize *or* **denationalise** (diː'næʃənᵊ,laɪz) *vb* **denationalizes, denationalizing, denationalized** *or* **denationalises, denationalising, denationalised. 1** to transfer (an industry, etc.) from public to private ownership. **2** to deprive of national character or nationality. ▸ de,nationali'zation *or* de,nationali'sation *n*

denaturalize *or* **denaturalise** (diː'nætʃrə,laɪz) *vb* **denaturalizes, denaturalizing, denaturalized** *or* **denaturalises, denaturalising, denaturalised.** (*tr*) **1** to deprive of nationality. **2** to make unnatural. ▸ de,naturali'zation *or* de,naturali'sation *n*

denature (diː'neɪtʃə) *or* **denaturize, denaturise** (diː'neɪtʃə,raɪz) *vb* **denatures, denaturing, denatured** *or* **denaturizes, denaturizing, denaturized; denaturises, denaturising, denaturised.** (*tr*) **1** to change the nature of. **2** to change the properties of (a protein), as by the action of acid or heat. **3** to render (something, such as alcohol) unfit for consumption by adding nauseous substances. **4** to render (fissile material) unfit for use in nuclear weapons by addition of an isotope. ▸ de'naturant *n* ▸ de,natur'ation *n*

Denbighshire ★ ('dɛnbɪ,ʃɪə, -ʃə) *n* a county of N Wales, part of Clwyd and Gwynedd (1974–96). Administrative centre: Ruthin. Pop.: 91 585 (1996 est.). Area: 844 sq. km (327 sq. miles).

Den Bosch ★ (dən bɒs) *n* another name for 's Hertogenbosch.

Dench ★ (dɛntʃ) *n* Dame **Judi** (**Olivia**). born 1934, British actress and theatre director.

dendrite ('dɛndraɪt) *n* **1** Also called: **dendron.** any of the branched extensions of a nerve cell, which conduct impulses towards the cell body. **2** a branching mosslike crystalline structure in some rocks and minerals. **3** a crystal that has branched during growth. [C18: from Gk *dendritēs* relating to a tree] ▸ dendritic (dɛn'drɪtɪk) *adj*

dendro-, dendri-, *or before a vowel* **dendr-** *combining form.* tree: *dendrochronology.* [NL, from Gk, from *dendron* tree]

dendrochronology (,dɛndrəʊkrə'nɒlədʒɪ) *n* the study of the annual rings of trees, used esp. to date past events.

dendrology (dɛn'drɒlədʒɪ) *n* the branch of botany that is concerned with the natural history of trees. ▸ dendrological (,dɛndrə'lɒdʒɪkᵊl) *or* ,dendro'logic *adj* ▸ den'drologist *n*

dene[1] *or* **dean** (diːn) *n Brit.* a narrow wooded valley. [OE *denu* valley]

dene[2] *or* **dean** (diːn) *n Dialect, chiefly southern English.* a sandy stretch of land or dune near the sea. [C13: prob. rel. to OE *dūn* hill]

denervate ('dɛnə,veɪt) *vb* **denervates, denervating, denervated.** (*tr*) to deprive (a tissue or organ) of its nerve supply.
▶ ,dener'vation *n*

Deneuve ★ (*French* dənœv) *n* **Catherine** (katrin), original name *Catherine Dorléac*. born 1943, French film actress: her films include *Belle de Jour* (1967) and *Indochine* (1992).

dengue ('dɛŋgɪ) *or* **dandy** ('dændɪ) *n* an acute viral disease transmitted by mosquitoes, characterized by headache, fever, pains in the joints, and skin rash. [C19: from Sp., prob. of African origin]

Deng Xiaoping ('dʌŋ 'sjaupɪŋ) *or* **Teng Hsiao-ping** ★ *n* 1904–97, Chinese Communist statesman; deputy prime minister of China (1973–76; 1977–80) and dominant figure in the Chinese government from 1977 until his death.

Den Haag ★ (dɛn 'ha:x) *n* the Dutch name for (The) Hague.

deniable (dɪ'naɪəb³l) *adj* able to be denied; questionable.
▶ de'niably *adv*

denial (dɪ'naɪəl) *n* **1** a refusal to agree or comply with a statement. **2** the rejection of the truth of a proposition, doctrine, etc. **3** a rejection of a request. **4** a refusal to acknowledge; disavowal. **5** a psychological process by which painful truths are not admitted into an individual's consciousness. **6** abstinence; self-denial.

denier[1] *n* **1** ('dɛnɪ,eɪ, 'dɛnjə). a unit of weight used to measure the fineness of silk and man-made fibres, esp. when woven into women's tights, etc. **2** (də'njeɪ, -'nɪə). any of several former European coins of various denominations. [C15: from OF: coin, from L *dēnārius* DENARIUS]

denier[2] (dɪ'naɪə) *n* a person who denies.

denigrate ('dɛnɪ,greɪt) *vb* **denigrates, denigrating, denigrated.** (*tr*) to belittle or disparage the character of; defame. [C16: from L *dēnigrāre* to make very black, from *nigrāre*, from *niger* black]
▶ ,deni'gration *n* ▶ 'deni,grator *n*

denim ('dɛnɪm) *n* **1** a hard-wearing twill-weave cotton fabric used for trousers, work clothes, etc. **2** a similar lighter fabric used in upholstery. [C17: from F (*serge*) *de Nîmes* (serge) of Nîmes, in S France]

denims ('dɛnɪmz) *pl n* jeans or overalls made of denim.

De Niro ★ (də 'nɪərəʊ) *n* **Robert.** born 1943, US film actor. His films include *The Deer Hunter* (1978), *Raging Bull* (1980), *Awakenings* (1991), and *Analyze This* (1999).

Denis ★ ('dɛnɪs; *French* dəni) *n* **Saint**. Also: **Denys**. 3rd century A.D., first bishop of Paris; patron saint of France. Feast day: Oct. 9.

denizen ('dɛnɪzən) *n* **1** an inhabitant; resident. **2** *Brit*. an individual permanently resident in a foreign country where he enjoys certain rights of citizenship. **3** a plant or animal established in a place to which it is not native. **4** a naturalized foreign word. [C15: from Anglo-F *denisein*, from OF *denzein*, from *denz* within, from L *de intus* from within]

Denmark ★ ('dɛnmɑːk) *n* a kingdom in N Europe, between the Baltic and the North Sea: consists of the mainland of Jutland and about 100 inhabited islands (chiefly Zealand, Lolland, Funen, Falster, Langeland, and Bornholm); extended its territory throughout the Middle Ages, ruling Sweden until 1523 and Norway until 1814; it was occupied (1940–45) by Germany. It incorporated Greenland as a province from 1953 to 1979; a member of the European Union; an important exporter of dairy produce. Language: Danish. Religion: chiefly Lutheran. Currency: krone. Capital: Copenhagen. Pop.: 5 284 000 (1997). Area: 43 031 sq. km (16 614 sq. miles). Danish name: **Danmark**.

Denmark Strait ★ *n* a channel between SE Greenland and Iceland, linking the Arctic Ocean with the Atlantic.

Denning ★ ('dɛnɪŋ) *n* Baron **Alfred Thompson**. 1899–1999, British judge; Master of the Rolls 1962–82.

Dennis ★ ('dɛnɪs) *n* **C(larence) J(ames)**. 1876–1938, the poet of the Australian larrikin, esp. in *The Songs of a Sentimental Bloke* (1915) and *The Moods of Ginger Mick* (1916).

denominate *vb* (dɪ'nɒmɪ,neɪt). **denominates, denominating, denominated.** **1** (*tr*) to give a specific name to; designate. ◆ *adj* (dɪ'nɒmɪnɪt, -,neɪt). **2** *Maths*. (of a number) representing a multiple of a unit of measurement: *4 is the denominate number in 4 miles*. [C16: from L *denōminare* from DE- (intensive) + *nōminare* to name]

denomination (dɪ,nɒmɪ'neɪʃən) *n* **1** a group having a distinctive interpretation of a religious faith and usually its own organization. **2** a grade or unit in a series of designations of value, weight, measure, etc. **3** a name given to a class or group; classification. **4** the act of giving a name. **5** a name; designation.
▶ de,nomi'national *adj*

denominative (dɪ'nɒmɪnətɪv) *adj* **1** giving or constituting a name. **2** *Grammar*. **2a** formed from or having the same form as a noun. **2b** (*as n*): *the verb "to mushroom" is a denominative*.

denominator (dɪ'nɒmɪ,neɪtə) *n* the divisor of a fraction, as in ⅞. Cf. **numerator**.

denotation (,diːnəʊ'teɪʃən) *n* **1** a denoting; indication. **2** a particular meaning given by a sign or symbol. **3** specific meaning as distinguished from suggestive meaning and associations. **4** *Logic*. another word for **extension** (sense 10).

denote (dɪ'nəʊt) *vb* **denotes, denoting, denoted.** (*tr; may take a clause as object*) **1** to be a sign of; designate. **2** (of words, phrases, etc.) to have as a literal or obvious meaning. [C16: from L *dēnotāre* to mark, from *notāre* to mark, NOTE]
▶ de'notative *adj*

denouement (deɪ'nuːmɒn) *or* **dénouement** (*French* denumɑ̃) *n* **1** the clarification or resolution of a plot in a play or other work. **2** final outcome; solution. [C18: from F, lit.: an untying, from OF *desnoer*, from *des-* DE- + *noer* to tie, from L *nōdus* a knot]

denounce (dɪ'naʊns) *vb* **denounces, denouncing, denounced.** (*tr*) **1** to condemn openly or vehemently. **2** to give information against; accuse. **3** to announce formally the termination of (a treaty, etc.). [C13: from OF *denoncier*, from L *dēnuntiāre* to make an official proclamation, threaten, from DE- + *nuntiāre* to announce]
▶ de'nouncement *n* ▶ de'nouncer *n*

de novo *Latin*. (diː 'nəʊvəʊ) *adv* from the beginning; anew.

dense (dɛns) *adj* **1** thickly crowded or closely set. **2** thick; impenetrable. **3** *Physics*. having a high density. **4** stupid; dull. **5** (of a photographic negative) having many dark or exposed areas. [C15: from L *densus* thick]
▶ 'densely *adv* ▶ 'denseness *n*

densimeter (dɛn'sɪmɪtə) *n Physics*. any instrument for measuring density.
▶ **densimetric** (,dɛnsɪ'mɛtrɪk) *adj* ▶ den'simetry *n*

density ('dɛnsɪtɪ) *n, pl* **densities.** **1** the degree to which something is filled or occupied: *high density of building in towns*. **2** stupidity. **3** a measure of the compactness of a substance, expressed as its mass per unit volume. Symbol: ρ. See also **relative density**. **4** a measure of a physical quantity per unit of length, area, or volume. **5** *Physics, photog*. a measure of the extent to which a substance or surface transmits or reflects light.

dent (dɛnt) *n* **1** a hollow in a surface, as one made by pressure or a blow. **2** an appreciable effect, esp. of lessening: *a dent in our resources*. ◆ *vb* (*tr*) to make a dent in. [C13 (in the sense: a stroke, blow): var. of DINT]

dental ('dɛnt³l) *adj* **1** of or relating to the teeth or dentistry. **2** *Phonetics*. pronounced with the tip of the tongue touching the backs of the upper teeth, as for *t* in French *tout*. ◆ *n* **3** *Phonetics*. a dental consonant. [C16: from Med. L *dentālis*, from L *dens* tooth]

dental floss *n* a waxed thread used to remove food particles from between the teeth.

dental plaque *n* a filmy deposit on the surface of a tooth consisting of a mixture of mucus, bacteria, food, etc.

dental surgeon *n* another name for **dentist**.

dentate ('dɛnteɪt) *adj* **1** having teeth or toothlike pro-

cesses. **2** (of leaves) having a toothed margin. [C19: from L *dentātus*]
▶ '**dentately** *adv*

denti- *or before a vowel* **dent-** *combining form.* indicating a tooth: *dentine.* [from L *dens, dent-*]

denticulate (dɛnˈtɪkjʊlɪt, -ˌleɪt) *adj* **1** *Biol.* very finely toothed: *denticulate leaves.* **2** *Arch.* having dentils. [C17: from L *denticulātus* having small teeth]

dentifrice ('dɛntɪfrɪs) *n* any substance, esp. paste or powder, for use in cleaning the teeth. [C16: from L *dentifricium*, from *dent-, dens* tooth + *fricāre* to rub]

dentil ('dɛntɪl) *n* one of a set of small square or rectangular blocks evenly spaced to form an ornamental row. [C17: from F, from obs. *dentille* a little tooth, from *dent* tooth]

dentine ('dɛntiːn) *or* **dentin** ('dɛntɪn) *n* the calcified tissue comprising the bulk of a tooth. [C19: from DENTI- + -IN]
▶ '**dentinal** *adj*

dentist ('dɛntɪst) *n* a person qualified to practise dentistry. [C18: from F *dentiste*, from *dent* tooth]

dentistry ('dɛntɪstrɪ) *n* the branch of medical science concerned with the diagnosis and treatment of disorders of the teeth and gums.

dentition (dɛnˈtɪʃən) *n* **1** the arrangement, type, and number of the teeth in a particular species. **2** the time or process of teething. [C17: from L *dentītiō* a teething]

D'Entrecasteaux Islands ★ (*French* dãtrəkasto) *pl n* a group of volcanic islands in the Pacific, off the SE coast of New Guinea: part of Papua New Guinea. Pop.: 49 167 (1990 est.). Area: 3141 sq. km (1213 sq. miles).

denture ('dɛntʃə) *n* (*usually pl*) **1** a partial or full set of artificial teeth. **2** *Rare.* a set of natural teeth. [C19: from F, from *dent* tooth + -URE]

denuclearize *or* **denuclearise** (diːˈnjuːklɪəˌraɪz) *vb* **denuclearizes, denuclearizing, denuclearized** *or* **denuclearises, denuclearising, denuclearised.** (*tr*) to deprive (a state, etc.) of nuclear weapons.
▶ de,nucleari'zation *or* de,nucleari'sation *n*

denudate ('dɛnjuˌdeɪt, dɪˈnjuːdeɪt) *vb* **denudates, denudating, denudated.** **1** a less common word for **denude.** ♦ *adj* **2** denuded.

denude (dɪˈnjuːd) *vb* **denudes, denuding, denuded.** (*tr*) **1** to make bare; strip. **2** to expose (rock) by the erosion of the layers above.
▶ **denudation** (ˌdɛnjuˈdeɪʃən) *n*

denumerable (dɪˈnjuːmərəbˀl) *adj Maths.* capable of being put into a one-to-one correspondence with the positive integers; countable.
▶ de'numerably *adv*

denunciate (dɪˈnʌnsɪˌeɪt) *vb* **denunciates, denunciating, denunciated.** (*tr*) to condemn; denounce. [C16: from L *dēnuntiāre*; see DENOUNCE]
▶ de'nunci,ator *n* ▶ de'nunciatory *adj*

denunciation (dɪˌnʌnsɪˈeɪʃən) *n* **1** open condemnation; denouncing. **2** *Law, obsolete.* a charge or accusation of crime made before a public prosecutor or tribunal. **3** a formal announcement of the termination of a treaty.

Denver ★ ('dɛnvə) *n* a city in central Colorado: the state capital. Pop.: 493 559 (1994 est.).

Denver boot *n* a slang name for **wheel clamp.** [C20: from DENVER, where the device was first used]

deny (dɪˈnaɪ) *vb* **denies, denying, denied.** (*tr*) **1** to declare (a statement, etc.) to be untrue. **2** to reject as false. **3** to withhold. **4** to refuse to fulfil the expectations of: *it is hard to deny a child.* **5** to refuse to acknowledge; disown. **6** to refuse (oneself) things desired. [C13: from OF *denier*, from L *dēnegāre*, from *negāre*]

Denys ★ ('dɛnɪs; *French* dəni) *n* **Saint.** a variant spelling of (Saint) **Denis.**

deodar ('diːəʊˌdɑː) *n* **1** a Himalayan cedar with drooping branches. **2** the durable fragrant highly valued wood of this tree. [C19: from Hindi, from Sansk. *devadāru*, lit.: wood of the gods]

deodorant (diːˈəʊdərənt) *n* **1** a substance applied to the body to suppress or mask the odour of perspiration. **2** any substance for destroying or masking odours.

deodorize *or* **deodorise** (diːˈəʊdəˌraɪz) *vb* **deodorizes, deodorizing, deodorized** *or* **deodorises, deodorising, deodorised.** (*tr*) to remove, disguise, or absorb the odour of, esp. when unpleasant.
▶ de,odori'zation *or* de,odori'sation *n* ▶ de'odor,izer *or* de'odor,iser *n*

deontic (diːˈɒntɪk) *adj Logic.* **a** of such ethical concepts as obligation and permissibility. **b** designating the branch of logic that deals with the formalization of these concepts. [C19: from Gk *deon* duty, from impersonal *dei* it behoves, it is binding]
▶ ,deon'tology *n*

deoxidize *or* **deoxidise** (diːˈɒksɪˌdaɪz) *vb* **deoxidizes, deoxidizing, deoxidized** *or* **deoxidises, deoxidising, deoxidised.** **1** (*tr*) to remove oxygen atoms from (a compound, molecule, etc.). **2** another word for **reduce** (sense 12).
▶ de,oxidi'zation *or* de,oxidi'sation *n* ▶ de'oxi,dizer *or* de'oxi,diser *n*

deoxygenate (diːˈɒksɪdʒɪˌneɪt) *or* **deoxygenize, deoxygenise** (diːˈɒksɪdʒɪˌnaɪz) *vb* **deoxygenates, deoxygenating, deoxygenated** *or* **deoxygenizes, deoxygenizing, deoxygenized; deoxygenises, deoxygenising, deoxygenised.** (*tr*) to remove oxygen from.
▶ de,oxygen'ation *n*

deoxyribonuclease (diːˌɒksɪˌraɪbəʊˈnjuːklɪeɪz) *n* the full name for **DNAase.**

deoxyribonucleic acid (diːˌɒksɪˌraɪbəʊnjuːˈkleɪɪk) *or* **desoxyribonucleic acid** *n* the full name for **DNA.**

dep. *abbrev. for:* **1** department. **2** departure. **3** deposed. **4** deposit. **5** depot. **6** deputy.

Depardieu ★ (*French* dəpardjø) *n* **Gérard** (ʒerar). born 1948, French film actor. His films include *Jean de Florette* (1986), *Cyrano de Bergerac* (1990), and *Green Card* (1991).

depart (dɪˈpɑːt) *vb* (*mainly intr*) **1** to leave. **2** to set forth. **3** (*usually foll. by from*) to differ; vary: *to depart from normal procedure.* **4** (*tr*) to quit (archaic, except in **depart this life**). [C13: from OF *departir*, from DE- + *partir* to go away, divide, from L *partīrī* to divide, distribute, from *pars* a part]

departed (dɪˈpɑːtɪd) *adj Euphemistic.* **a** dead. **b** (*as sing or collective n; preceded by the*): *the departed.*

department (dɪˈpɑːtmənt) *n* **1** a specialized division of a large concern, such as a business, store, or university. **2** a major subdivision of the administration of a government. **3** a branch of learning. **4** an administrative division in several countries, such as France. **5** *Inf.* a specialized sphere of skill or activity: *wine-making is my wife's department.* [C18: from F *département*, from *départir* to divide; see DEPART]
▶ departmental (ˌdiːpɑːtˈmɛntˀl) *adj*

departmentalize *or* **departmentalise** (ˌdiːpɑːtˈmɛntˀˌlaɪz) *vb* **departmentalizes, departmentalizing, departmentalized** *or* **departmentalises, departmentalising, departmentalised.** (*tr*) to organize into departments, esp. excessively.
▶ ,depart,mentali'zation *or* ,depart,mentali'sation *n*

department store *n* a large shop divided into departments selling a great many kinds of goods.

departure (dɪˈpɑːtʃə) *n* **1** the act or an instance of departing. **2** a variation from previous custom. **3** a course of action, venture, etc.: *selling is a new departure for him.* **4** *Naut.* the net distance travelled due east or west by a vessel. **5** a euphemistic word for **death.**

depend (dɪˈpɛnd) *vb* (*intr*) **1** (foll. by *on* or *upon*) to put trust (in); rely (on). **2** (usually foll. by *on* or *upon*) to be influenced or determined (by): *it all depends on you.* **3** (foll. by *on* or *upon*) to rely (on) for income, support, etc. **4** (foll. by *from*) *Rare.* to hang down. **5** to be undecided. [C15: from OF, from L *dēpendēre* to hang from, from DE- + *pendēre*]

dependable (dɪˈpɛndəbˀl) *adj* able to be depended on; reliable.
▶ de,penda'bility *or* de'pendableness *n* ▶ de'pendably *adv*

dependant (dɪˈpɛndənt) *n* a person who depends on another person, organization, etc., for support, aid, or sustenance, esp. financial support.

> USAGE NOTE Avoid confusion with **dependent**.

dependence or US (sometimes) **dependance** (dɪˈpɛndəns) n **1** the state or fact of being dependent, esp. for support or help. **2** reliance; trust; confidence.

dependency or US (sometimes) **dependancy** (dɪˈpɛndənsɪ) n, pl **dependencies** or US (sometimes) **dependancies**. **1** a territory subject to a state on which it does not border. **2** a dependent or subordinate person or thing. **3** Psychol. overreliance on another person or on a drug, etc. **4** another word for **dependence**.

dependent or US (sometimes) **dependant** (dɪˈpɛndənt) adj **1** depending on a person or thing for aid, support, etc. **2** (postpositive; foll. by on or upon) influenced or conditioned (by); contingent (on). **3** subordinate; subject. **4** Obs. hanging down. ◆ n **5** a variant spelling (esp. US) of **dependant**.
> **deˈpendently** adv

> USAGE NOTE Avoid confusion with **dependant**.

dependent clause n Grammar. another term for **subordinate clause**.

dependent variable n a variable in a mathematical equation or statement whose value depends on that taken on by the independent variable.

depersonalize or **depersonalise** (diːˈpɜːsnəˌlaɪz) vb **depersonalizes, depersonalizing, depersonalized** or **depersonalises, depersonalising, depersonalised**. (tr) **1** to deprive (a person, organization, etc.) of individual or personal qualities. **2** to cause (someone) to lose his sense of identity.
> **deˌpersonaliˈzation** or **deˌpersonaliˈsation** n

depict (dɪˈpɪkt) vb (tr) **1** to represent by drawing, sculpture, painting, etc.; delineate; portray. **2** to represent in words; describe. [C17: from L dēpingere, from pingere to paint]
> **deˈpicter** or **deˈpictor** n > **deˈpiction** n > **deˈpictive** adj

depilate (ˈdɛpɪˌleɪt) vb **depilates, depilating, depilated**. (tr) to remove the hair from. [C16: from L dēpilāre, from pilāre to make bald, from pilus hair]
> **ˌdepiˈlation** n > **ˈdepiˌlator** n

depilatory (dɪˈpɪlətərɪ, -trɪ) adj **1** able or serving to remove hair. ◆ n, pl **depilatories**. **2** a chemical used to remove hair from the body.

deplane (diːˈpleɪn) vb **deplanes, deplaning, deplaned**. (intr) Chiefly US. & Canad. to disembark from an aeroplane. [C20: from DE- + PLANE[1]]

deplete (dɪˈpliːt) vb **depletes, depleting, depleted**. (tr) **1** to use up (supplies, money, etc.); exhaust. **2** to empty entirely or partially. [C19: from L dēplēre to empty out, from DE- + plēre to fill]
> **deˈpletion** n

depletion layer n a region at the interface between dissimilar zones of conductivity in a semiconductor, in which there are few charge carriers.

deplorable (dɪˈplɔːrəbˀl) adj **1** lamentable. **2** worthy of censure or reproach; very bad.
> **deˈplorably** adv

deplore (dɪˈplɔː) vb **deplores, deploring, deplored**. (tr) **1** to express or feel sorrow about. **2** to express or feel strong disapproval of; censure. [C16: from OF, from L dēplōrāre to weep bitterly, from plōrāre to weep]
> **deˈploringly** adv

deploy (dɪˈplɔɪ) vb Chiefly mil. **1** to adopt or cause to adopt a battle formation. **2** (tr) to redistribute (forces) to or within a given area. [C18: from F, from L displicāre to unfold; see DISPLAY]
> **deˈployment** n

depolarize or **depolarise** (diːˈpəʊləˌraɪz) vb **depolarizes, depolarizing, depolarized** or **depolarises, depolarising, depola-**

rised. to undergo or cause to undergo a loss of polarity or polarization.
> **deˌpolariˈzation** or **deˌpolariˈsation** n

deponent (dɪˈpəʊnənt) adj **1** Grammar. (of a verb, esp. in Latin) having the inflectional endings of a passive verb but the meaning of an active verb. ◆ n **2** Grammar. a deponent verb. **3** Law. a person who makes an affidavit or a deposition. [C16: from L dēpōnēns putting aside, putting down, from dēpōnere]

depopulate (dɪˈpɒpjuˌleɪt) vb **depopulates, depopulating, depopulated**. to be or cause to be reduced in population.
> **deˌpopuˈlation** n

deport (dɪˈpɔːt) vb (tr) **1** to remove forcibly from a country; expel. **2** to conduct, hold, or behave (oneself) in a specified manner. [C15: from F, from L dēportāre to carry away, banish, from DE- + portāre to carry]
> **deˈportable** adj

deportation (ˌdiːpɔːˈteɪʃən) n the act of expelling someone from a country.

deportee (ˌdiːpɔːˈtiː) n a person deported or awaiting deportation.

deportment (dɪˈpɔːtmənt) n the manner in which a person behaves, esp. in physical bearing: military deportment. [C17: from F, from OF deporter to conduct (oneself); see DEPORT]

depose (dɪˈpəʊz) vb **deposes, deposing, deposed**. **1** (tr) to remove from an office or position of power. **2** Law. to testify or give (evidence, etc.) on oath. [C13: from OF: to put away, put down, from LL dēpōnere to depose from office, from L: to put aside]

deposit (dɪˈpɒzɪt) vb (tr) **1** to put or set down, esp. carefully; place. **2** to entrust for safekeeping. **3** to place (money) in a bank or similar institution to earn interest or for safekeeping. **4** to give (money) in part payment or as security. **5** to lay down naturally: the river deposits silt. ◆ n **6a** an instance of entrusting money or valuables to a bank or similar institution. **6b** the money or valuables so entrusted. **7** money given in part payment or as security. **8** an accumulation of sediments, minerals, coal, etc. **9** any deposited material, such as a sediment. **10** a depository or storehouse. **11 on deposit**. payable as the first instalment, as when buying on hire-purchase. [C17: from Med. L dēpositāre, from L dēpositus put down]

deposit account n Brit. a bank account that earns interest and usually requires notice of withdrawal.

depositary (dɪˈpɒzɪtərɪ, -trɪ) n, pl **depositaries**. **1** a person or group to whom something is entrusted for safety. **2** a variant spelling of **depository**.

deposition (ˌdɛpəˈzɪʃən) n **1** Law. **1a** the giving of testimony on oath. **1b** the testimony given. **1c** the sworn statement of a witness used in court in his absence. **2** the act or an instance of deposing. **3** the act or an instance of depositing. **4** something deposited. [C14: from LL dēpositiō a laying down, disposal, burying, testimony]

depositor (dɪˈpɒzɪtə) n a person who places or has money on deposit, esp. in a bank.

depository (dɪˈpɒzɪtərɪ, -trɪ) n, pl **depositories**. **1** a store for furniture, valuables, etc.; repository. **2** a variant spelling of **depositary**. [C17 (in the sense: place of a deposit): from Med. L dēpositōrium; C18 (in the sense: depositary): see DEPOSIT, -ORY[1]]

depot (ˈdɛpəʊ; US & Canad. ˈdiːpəʊ) n **1** a storehouse or warehouse. **2** Mil. **2a** a store for supplies. **2b** a training and holding centre for recruits and replacements. **3** Chiefly Brit. a building used for the storage and servicing of buses or railway engines. **4** US & Canad. a bus or railway station. [C18: from F dépôt, from L dēpositum a deposit, trust]

deprave (dɪˈpreɪv) vb **depraves, depraving, depraved**. (tr) to make morally bad; corrupt. [C14: from L dēprāvāre to distort, corrupt, from DE- + prāvus crooked]
> **depravation** (ˌdɛprəˈveɪʃən) n > **deˈpraved** adj

depravity (dɪˈprævɪtɪ) n, pl **depravities**. the state or an instance of moral corruption.

deprecate (ˈdɛprɪˌkeɪt) vb **deprecates, deprecating, deprecated**. (tr) **1** to express disapproval of; protest against. **2** to depreciate; belittle. [C17: from L dēprecārī to avert, ward

off by entreaty, from DE- + *precārī* to PRAY]
▶ 'depre,cating *adj* ▶ 'depre,catingly *adv* ▶ ,depre'cation
n ▶ 'deprecative *adj* ▶ 'depre,cator *n*

> **USAGE NOTE** Avoid confusion with **depreciate.**

deprecatory ('dɛprɪkətərɪ) *adj* **1** expressing disapproval;
protesting. **2** expressing apology; apologetic.
▶ 'deprecatorily *adv*

depreciate (dɪ'priːʃɪˌeɪt) *vb* **depreciates, depreciating, de-**
preciated. 1 to reduce or decline in value or price. **2** (*tr*) to
lessen the value of by derision, criticism, etc. [C15:
from LL *dēpretiāre* to lower the price of, from L DE- +
pretium PRICE]
▶ de'preci,atingly *adv* ▶ depreciatory (dɪ'priːʃɪətərɪ) *or* de-
'preciative *adj*

> **USAGE NOTE** Avoid confusion with **deprecate.**

depreciation (dɪˌpriːʃɪ'eɪʃən) *n* **1** *Accounting.* **1a** the reduction in value of a fixed asset due to use, obsoles-
cence, etc. **1b** the amount deducted from gross profit to
allow for this. **2** the act or an instance of depreciating or
belittling. **3** a decrease in the exchange value of a currency brought about by excess supply of that currency
under conditions of fluctuating exchange rates.

depredation (ˌdɛprɪ'deɪʃən) *n* the act or an instance of
plundering; pillage. [C15: from LL *dēpraedārī* to ravage]

depress (dɪ'prɛs) *vb* (*tr*) **1** to lower in spirits; make
gloomy. **2** to weaken the force, or energy of. **3** to lower
prices of. **4** to press or push down. [C14: from OF
depresser, from L *dēprimere* from DE- + *premere* to PRESS[1]]
▶ de'pressing *adj* ▶ de'pressingly *adv*

depressant (dɪ'prɛsᵊnt) *adj* **1** *Med.* able to reduce nervous or functional activity. **2** causing gloom; depressing.
◆ *n* **3** a depressant drug.

depressed (dɪ'prɛst) *adj* **1** low in spirits; downcast. **2**
lower than the surrounding surface. **3** pressed down or
flattened. **4** Also: **distressed.** characterized by economic
hardship, such as unemployment: *a depressed area.* **5** lowered in force, intensity, or amount. **6** *Bot., zool.* flattened.

depression (dɪ'prɛʃən) *n* **1** a depressing or being depressed. **2** a sunken place. **3** a mental disorder characterized by feelings of gloom and inadequacy. **4** *Pathol.* an
abnormal lowering of the rate of any physiological activity or function. **5** an economic condition characterized by unemployment, low investment, etc.; slump. **6**
Also called: **cyclone, low.** *Meteorol.* a body of moving air
below normal atmospheric pressure, which often brings
rain. **7** (esp. in surveying and astronomy) the angular
distance of an object below the horizontal plane.

Depression (dɪ'prɛʃən) *n* (usually preceded by *the*) the
worldwide economic depression of the early 1930s,
when there was mass unemployment.

depressive (dɪ'prɛsɪv) *adj* **1** tending to depress. **2**
Psychol. tending to be subject to periods of depression.
▶ de'pressively *adv*

depressor (dɪ'prɛsə) *n* **1** a person or thing that depresses. **2** any muscle that draws down a part. **3** *Med.* an
instrument used to press down or aside an organ or part.

depressurize *or* **depressurise** (diː'prɛʃəˌraɪz) *vb*
depressurizes, depressurizing, depressurized *or* **depressurises,**
depressurising, depressurised. (*tr*) to reduce the pressure of
a gas inside (an enclosed space), as in an aircraft cabin.
▶ de,pressuri'zation *or* de,pressuri'sation *n*

deprive (dɪ'praɪv) *vb* **deprives, depriving, deprived.** (*tr*) **1**
(foll. by *of*) to prevent from possessing or enjoying; dispossess (of). **2** *Arch.* to depose; demote. [C14: from OF,
from Med. L *dēprīvāre*, from L DE- + *prīvāre* to deprive of]
▶ de'prival *n* ▶ deprivation (ˌdɛprɪ'veɪʃən) *n*

deprived (dɪ'praɪvd) *adj* lacking adequate food, shelter,
education, etc.: *deprived inner-city areas.*

deprogramme *or esp. US* **deprogram** (diː'prəʊɡræm)
vb **deprogrammes, deprogramming, deprogrammed** *or esp. US*
deprograms, deprogramming, deprogrammed. to attempt to
reverse the brainwashing of (a person).

dept *abbrev. for* department.

depth (dɛpθ) *n* **1** the distance downwards, backwards, o
inwards. **2** the quality of being deep; deepness. **3** inten
sity of emotion. **4** profundity of moral character; sagac
ity; integrity. **5** complexity or abstruseness, as o
thought. **6** intensity, as of silence, colour, etc. **7** lownes
of pitch. **8** (*often pl*) a deep, inner, or remote part, such a
an inaccessible region of a country. **9** (*often pl*) the mos
intense or severe part: *the depths of winter.* **10** (*usually pl*) a
low moral state. **11** (*often pl*) a vast space or abyss. **12** be
yond *or* **out of one's depth. 12a** in water deeper than one i
tall. **12b** beyond the range of one's competence or un
derstanding. [C14: from *dep* DEEP + -TH[1]]

depth charge *or* **bomb** *n* a bomb used to attack sub
marines that explodes at a preset depth of water.

depth gauge *n* a device attached to a drill bit to preven
the hole from exceeding a predetermined depth.

depth of field *n* the range of distance in front of anc
behind an object focused by an optical instrument, such
as a camera or microscope, within which other object:
will also appear sharply defined in the resulting image.

depth psychology *n Psychol.* the study of unconsciou:
motives and attitudes.

depuration (ˌdɛpjʊ'reɪʃən) *n* the act or process of elimi
nating impurities; self-purification. [C17: from F o
Med. L, ult. from L *pūrus* pure]

deputation (ˌdɛpjʊ'teɪʃən) *n* **1** the act of appointing a
person or body of people to represent others. **2** a person
or body of people so appointed; delegation.

depute *vb* (dɪ'pjuːt), **deputes, deputing, deputed.** (*tr*) **1** to appoint as an agent. **2** to assign (authority, duties, etc.) to a
deputy. ◆ *n* ('dɛpjuːt). **3** *Scot.* **3a** a deputy. **3b** (*as modifier,
usually postpositive*): *a sheriff-depute.* [C15: from OF, from
LL *dēputāre* to assign, allot, from L DE- + *putāre* to think,
consider]

deputize *or* **deputise** ('dɛpjʊˌtaɪz) *vb* **deputizes, deputiz-**
ing, deputized *or* **deputises, deputising, deputised.** to appoint
or act as deputy.

deputy ('dɛpjʊtɪ) *n, pl* **deputies. 1a** a person appointed to
act on behalf of or represent another. **1b** (*as modifier*): *the
deputy chairman.* **2** a member of a legislative assembly in
various countries, such as France. [C16: from OF, from
deputer to appoint; see DEPUTE]

De Quincey ★ (də 'kwɪnsɪ) *n* **Thomas.** 1785–1859, British
critic and essayist, noted particularly for his *Confessions
of an English Opium Eater* (1821).

der. *abbrev. for:* **1** derivation. **2** derivative.

deracinate (dɪ'ræsɪˌneɪt) *vb* **deracinates, deracinating,**
deracinated. (*tr*) to pull up by or as if by the roots; uproot.
[C16: from OF *desraciner*, from *des-* DIS-[1] + *racine* root,
from LL, from L *rādīx* a root]
▶ de,raci'nation *n*

derail (dɪ'reɪl) *vb* to go or cause to go off the rails, as a
train, tram, etc.
▶ de'railment *n*

Derain ★ (*French* dərɛ̃) *n* **André** (ɑ̃dre). 1880–1954, French
Fauvist painter.

derange (dɪ'reɪndʒ) *vb* **deranges, deranging, deranged.** (*tr*) **1**
to throw into disorder; disarrange. **2** to disturb the action of. **3** to make insane. [C18: from OF *desrengier*, from
des- DIS-[1] + *reng* row, order]
▶ de'rangement *n*

derby ('dɜːrbɪ) *n, pl* **derbies.** the US and Canad. name for
bowler[2].

Derby[1] ('dɑːbɪ; *US* 'dɜːrbɪ) *n, pl* **Derbies. 1** the. an annual
horse race run at Epsom Downs, Surrey, since 1780. **2**
(*usually not cap.*) any of various other horse races. **3** local
derby. a football match between two teams from the
same area. [C18: after the twelfth Earl of *Derby* (died
1834), who founded the race in 1780]

Derby[2] ★ ('dɑːbɪ) *n* **1** a city in central England, in
Derbyshire. Pop.: 223 836 (1991). **2** a unitary authority
in central England, in Derbyshire. Pop.: 230 500 (1994
est.). Area: 78 sq. km (30 sq. miles). **3** a firm pale-
coloured cheese. **4 sage Derby.** a green-and-white Derby
cheese flavoured with sage.

Derby[3] ★ ('dɑːbɪ) *n* **Earl of.** title of *Edward George Geoffrey*

> ★ people and places

Smith Stanley. 1799–1869, British statesman; Conservative prime minister (1852; 1858–59; 1866–68).

Derbyshire ★ ('dɑːbɪˌʃɪə, -ʃə) *n* a county of N central England: contains the Peak District and several resorts with mineral springs. Administrative centre: Matlock. Pop. (including Derby unitary authority): 954 100 (1991). Area (including Derby unitary authority): 2631 sq. km (1016 sq. miles).

derecognize *or* **derecognise** (diːˈrɛkəgˌnaɪz) *vb* **derecognizes, derecognizing, derecognized** *or* **derecognises, derecognising, derecognised.** (*tr*) to cease to recognize (a trade union) as having special negotiating rights within a company or industry.
▸ ˌderecogˈnition *n*

deregulate (diːˈrɛgjuˌleɪt) *vb* **deregulates, deregulating, deregulated.** (*tr*) to remove regulations from.
▸ deˌreguˈlation *n*

derelict ('dɛrɪlɪkt) *adj* **1** deserted or abandoned, as by an owner, occupant, etc. **2** falling into ruins. **3** neglectful of duty; remiss. ◆ *n* **4** a social outcast or vagrant. **5** property deserted or abandoned by an owner, occupant, etc. **6** a vessel abandoned at sea. **7** a person who is neglectful of duty. [C17: from L, from *dērelinquere* to abandon, from DE- + *relinquere* to leave]

dereliction (ˌdɛrɪˈlɪkʃən) *n* **1** conscious or wilful neglect (esp. in **dereliction of duty**). **2** an abandoning or being abandoned. **3** *Law.* accretion of dry land gained by the gradual receding of the sea.

derestrict (ˌdiːrɪˈstrɪkt) *vb* (*tr*) to render or leave free from restriction, esp. a road from speed limits.
▸ ˌdereˈstriction *n*

deride (dɪˈraɪd) *vb* **derides, deriding, derided.** (*tr*) to speak of or treat with contempt or ridicule; scoff at. [C16: from L *dērīdēre* to laugh to scorn, from DE- + *rīdēre* to laugh, smile]
▸ deˈrider *n* ▸ deˈridingly *adv*

de rigueur *French.* (də rigœr) *adj* required by etiquette or fashion. [lit.: of strictness]

derision (dɪˈrɪʒən) *n* the act of deriding; mockery; scorn. [C15: from LL *dērīsiō*, from L *dērīsus*; see DERIDE]
▸ deˈrisible *adj*

derisive (dɪˈraɪsɪv) *adj* characterized by derision; mocking; scornful.
▸ deˈrisively *adv* ▸ deˈrisiveness *n*

derisory (dɪˈraɪsərɪ) *adj* **1** subject to or worthy of derision. **2** another word for **derisive**.

deriv. *abbrev. for:* **1** derivation. **2** derivative. **3** derived.

derivation (ˌdɛrɪˈveɪʃən) *n* **1** a deriving or being derived. **2** the origin or descent of something, such as a word. **3** something derived; a derivative. **4a** the process of deducing a mathematical theorem, formula, etc., as a necessary consequence of a set of accepted statements. **4b** this sequence of statements.
▸ ˌderiˈvational *adj*

derivative (dɪˈrɪvətɪv) *adj* **1** derived. **2** based on other sources; not original. ◆ *n* **3** a term, idea, etc., that is based on or derived from another in the same class. **4** a word derived from another word. **5** *Chem.* a compound that is formed from, or can be regarded as formed from, a structurally related compound. **6** *Maths.* Also called: **differential coefficient, first derivative.** the change of a function, f(x), with respect to an infinitesimally small change in the independent variable, x. **6b** the rate of change of one quantity with respect to another. **7** *Finance.* a financial instrument, such as a futures contract or option, the price of which is largely determined by the commodity, currency, share price, interest rate, etc., to which it is linked.
▸ deˈrivatively *adv*

derive (dɪˈraɪv) *vb* **derives, deriving, derived. 1** (usually foll. by *from*) to draw or be drawn (from) in source or origin. **2** (*tr*) to obtain by reasoning; deduce; infer. **3** (*tr*) to trace the source or development of. **4** (usually foll. by *from*) to produce or be produced (from) by a chemical reaction. [C14: from OF: to spring from, from L *dērīvāre* to draw off, from DE- + *rīvus* a stream]
▸ deˈrivable *adj* ▸ deˈriver *n*

derived unit *n* a unit of measurement obtained by mul-

tiplication or division of the base units of a system without the introduction of numerical factors.

-derm *n combining form.* indicating skin: *endoderm.* [via F from Gk *derma* skin]

derma ('dɜːmə) *n* another name for **corium.** Also: **derm.** [C18: NL, from Gk: skin]

dermal ('dɜːməl) *adj* of or relating to the skin.

dermatitis (ˌdɜːməˈtaɪtɪs) *n* inflammation of the skin.

dermato-, derma- *or before a vowel* **dermat-, derm-** *combining form.* indicating skin: *dermatitis.* [from Gk *derma* skin]

dermatology (ˌdɜːməˈtɒlədʒɪ) *n* the branch of medicine concerned with the skin and its diseases.
▸ **dermatological** (ˌdɜːmətəˈlɒdʒɪkºl) *adj* ▸ ˌdermaˈtologist *n*

dermis ('dɜːmɪs) *n* another name for **corium.** [C19: NL, from EPIDERMIS]
▸ 'dermic *adj*

dernier cri *French.* (dɛrnje kri) *n* le (lə). the latest fashion; the last word. [lit.: last cry]

derogate ('dɛrəˌgeɪt) *vb* **derogates, derogating, derogated. 1** (*intr*; foll. by *from*) to cause to seem inferior; detract. **2** (*intr.* foll. by *from*) to deviate in standard or quality. **3** (*tr*) to cause to seem inferior, etc.; disparage. **4** (*tr*) to curtail the application of (a law or regulation). [C15: from L *dērogāre* to repeal some part of a law, modify it, from DE- + *rogāre* to ask, propose a law]
▸ ˌderoˈgation *n* ▸ **derogative** (dɪˈrɒgətɪv) *adj*

derogatory (dɪˈrɒgətərɪ) *adj* tending or intended to detract, disparage, or belittle; intentionally offensive.
▸ deˈrogatorily *adv*

derrick ('dɛrɪk) *n* **1** a simple crane having lifting tackle slung from a boom. **2** the framework erected over an oil well to enable drill tubes to be raised and lowered. [C17 (in the sense: gallows): from *Derrick*, celebrated hangman at Tyburn, London]

Derrida ★ (*French* derɪdɑ) *n* **Jacques** (ʒɑk). born 1930, French philosopher and literary critic, regarded as the founder of deconstruction: author of *L'Écriture et la différence* (1967).

derrière (ˌdɛrɪˈɛə) *n* a euphemistic word for **buttocks.** [C18: lit.: behind (prep), from OF *deriere*, from L *dē retrō* from the back]

derring-do ('dɛrɪŋ'duː) *n Arch. or literary.* boldness or bold action. [C16: from ME *during don* daring to do, from *durren* to dare + *don* to do]

derringer *or* **deringer** ('dɛrɪndʒə) *n* a short-barrelled pocket pistol of large calibre. [C19: after Henry *Deringer*, US gunsmith, who invented it]

derris ('dɛrɪs) *n* **1** an East Indian woody climbing plant. **2** an insecticide made from its powdered roots. [C19: NL, from Gk: covering, leather, from *deros* skin, hide, from *derein* to skin]

Derry ★ ('dɛrɪ) *n* **1** Also called: **Londonderry.** a district in NW Northern Ireland, bordering the Irish Republic: textiles, light industry, agriculture. Administrative centre: Londonderry. Pop.: 95 371 (1991). Area: 384 sq. km (148 sq. miles). **2** another name for **Londonderry** (senses 1 and 2).

derv (dɜːv) *n* a Brit. name for **diesel oil** when used for road transport. [C20: from d(*iesel*) e(*ngine*) r(*oad*) v(*ehicle*)]

dervish ('dɜːvɪʃ) *n* a member of any of various Muslim orders of ascetics, some of which (**whirling dervishes**) are noted for a frenzied, ecstatic, whirling dance. [C16: from Turkish, from Persian *darvīsh* mendicant monk]

Derwent ★ ('dɜːwənt) *n* **1** a river in S Australia, in S Tasmania, flowing southeast to the Tasman Sea. Length: 172 km (107 miles). **2** a river in N central England, in N Derbyshire, flowing southeast to the River Trent. Length: 96 km (60 miles). **3** a river in N England, in Yorkshire, rising on the North York Moors and flowing south to the River Ouse. Length: 92 km (57 miles). **4** a river in NW England, in Cumbria, rising on the Borrowdale Fells and flowing north and west to the Irish Sea. Length: 54 km (34 miles).

Derwentwater ★ ('dɜːwəntˌwɔːtə) *n* a lake in NW England, in Cumbria in the Lake District. Area: about 8 sq. km (3 sq. miles).

DES (in Britain) *abbrev. for* (the former) Department of Education and Science.

Desai ★ (deˈsaɪ) *n* **Morarji (Ranchhodji)** (məˈrɑːdʒɪ). 1896–1995, Indian statesman. He founded the Janata party in opposition to Indira Gandhi, whom he defeated in the 1977 election; prime minister of India (1977–79).

desalination (diːˌsælɪˈneɪʃən) *or* **desalinization**, **desalinisation** *n* the process of removing salt, esp. from sea water.

descale (ˌdiːˈskeɪl) *vb* **descales, descaling, descaled.** (*tr*) to remove the hard deposit formed by chemicals in water from (a kettle, pipe, etc.).

descant (ˈdɛskænt) *n* **1** Also called: **discant.** a decorative counterpoint added above a basic melody. **2** a comment or discourse. ◆ *adj* **3** Also: **discant.** of the highest member in common use in a family of musical instruments: *a descant recorder.* ◆ *vb* (*intr*) **4** Also: **discant.** (often foll. by *on* or *upon*) to perform a descant. **5** (often foll. by *on* or *upon*) to discourse or make comments. **6** *Arch.* to sing sweetly. [C14: from OF, from Med. L *discanthus*, from L DIS-[1] + *cantus* song]
▸ **des'canter** *n*

Descartes ★ (ˈdeɪˌkɑːt; *French* dekart) *n* **René** (rəne). 1596–1650, French philosopher and mathematician. He is regarded as the founder of modern philosophy and of analytic geometry. His works include *Meditationes de Prima Philosophia* (1641) and *Principia Philosophiae* (1644). Related adj: **Cartesian.**

descend (dɪˈsɛnd) *vb* (*mainly intr*) **1** (*also tr*) to move down (a slope, staircase, etc.). **2** to lead or extend down; slope. **3** to move to a lower level, pitch, etc.; fall. **4** (often foll. by *from*) to be connected by a blood relationship (to a dead or extinct individual, species, etc.). **5** to be inherited. **6** to sink or come down in morals or behaviour. **7** (often foll. by *on* or *upon*) to arrive or attack in a sudden or overwhelming way. **8** (of the sun, moon, etc.) to move towards the horizon. [C13: from OF, from L *descendere*, from DE- + *scandere* to climb]
▸ **des'cendable** *or* **des'cendible** *adj*

descendant (dɪˈsɛndənt) *n* **1** a person, animal, or plant when described as descended from an individual, race, species, etc. **2** something that derives from an earlier form. ◆ *adj* **3** a variant spelling of **descendent.**

descendent (dɪˈsɛndənt) *adj* descending.

descender (dɪˈsɛndə) *n* **1** *Printing.* the part of certain lower-case letters, such as j, p, or y, that extends below the body of the letter. **2** a person or thing that descends.

descent (dɪˈsɛnt) *n* **1** the act of descending. **2** a downward slope. **3** a path or way leading downwards. **4** derivation from an ancestor; lineage. **5** a generation in a particular lineage. **6** a decline or degeneration. **7** a movement or passage in degree or state from higher to lower. **8** (often foll. by *on*) a sudden and overwhelming arrival or attack. **9** *Property law.* (formerly) the transmission of real property to the heir.

deschool (ˌdiːˈskuːl) *vb* (*tr*) to separate education from the institution of school and operate through the pupil's life experience as opposed to a set curriculum.

describe (dɪˈskraɪb) *vb* **describes, describing, described.** (*tr*) **1** to give an account or representation of in words. **2** to pronounce or label. **3** to draw a line or figure, such as a circle. [C15: from L *dēscrībere* to copy off, write out, from DE- + *scrībere* to write]
▸ **de'scribable** *adj* ▸ **de'scriber** *n*

description (dɪˈskrɪpʃən) *n* **1** a statement or account that describes. **2** the act, process, or technique of describing. **3** sort or variety: *reptiles of every description.*

descriptive (dɪˈskrɪptɪv) *adj* **1** characterized by or containing description. **2** *Grammar.* (of an adjective) serving to describe the referent of the noun modified, as for example the adjective *brown* as contrasted with *my.* **3** relating to description or classification rather than explanation or prescription.
▸ **de'scriptively** *adv* ▸ **de'scriptiveness** *n*

descry (dɪˈskraɪ) *vb* **descries, descrying, descried.** (*tr*) **1** to catch sight of. **2** to discover by looking carefully. [C14: from OF *descrier* to proclaim, DECRY]

desecrate (ˈdɛsɪˌkreɪt) *vb* **desecrates, desecrating, desecrated.** (*tr*) **1** to violate the sacred character of (an objec or place) by destructive, blasphemous, or sacrilegious ac tion. **2** to deconsecrate. [C17: from DE- + CONSECRATE]
▸ **'dese,crator** *or* **'dese,crater** *n* ▸ **,dese'cration** *n*

desegregate (diːˈsɛɡrɪˌɡeɪt) *vb* **desegregates, desegregat ing, desegregated.** to end racial segregation in (a school o other public institution).
▸ **,desegre'gation** *n*

deselect (ˌdiːsɪˈlɛkt) *vb* (*tr*) *Brit. politics.* (of a constituency organization) to refuse to select (an existing MP) for re election.
▸ **,dese'lection** *n*

desensitize *or* **desensitise** (diːˈsɛnsɪˌtaɪz) *vb* **desensi tizes, desensitizing, desensitized** *or* **desensitises, desensitising desensitised.** (*tr*) to render less sensitive or insensitive: *the patient was desensitized to the allergen.*
▸ **de,sensiti'zation** *or* **de,sensiti'sation** *n* ▸ **de'sensi,tize** *or* **de'sensi,tiser** *n*

desert[1] (ˈdɛzət) *n* **1** a region that is devoid or almost de void of vegetation, esp. because of low rainfall. **2** an un cultivated uninhabited region. **3** a place which lack some desirable feature or quality: *a cultural desert.* **4** (*mod ifier*) of, relating to, or like a desert. [C13: from OF, from Church L *dēsertum*, from L *dēserere* to abandon, lit.: to sever one's links with, from DE- + *serere* to bind together]

desert[2] (dɪˈzɜːt) *vb* **1** (*tr*) to abandon (a person, place, etc. without intending to return, esp. in violation of a prom ise or obligation. **2** *Mil.* to abscond from (a post or duty) with no intention of returning. **3** (*tr*) to fail (someone) in time of need. [C15: from F *déserter*, from LL *dēsertāre*, from L *dēserere* to forsake; see DESERT[1]]
▸ **de'serted** *adj* ▸ **de'serter** *n*

desert[3] (dɪˈzɜːt) *n* **1** (*often pl*) just reward or punishment. **2** the state of deserving a reward or punishment. [C13: from OF *deserte*, from *deservir* to DESERVE]

desert boots *pl n* ankle-high boots, often of suede, with laces and soft soles.

desertification (dɪˌzɜːtɪfɪˈkeɪʃən) *n* the transformation of fertile land into an arid or semiarid region as a result of intensive farming, soil erosion, etc.

desertion (dɪˈzɜːʃən) *n* **1** a deserting or being deserted. **2** *Law.* wilful abandonment, esp. of one's spouse or chil dren.

desert island *n* a small remote tropical island.

desert pea *n* an Australian trailing leguminous plant with scarlet flowers.

desert rat *n* **1** a jerboa inhabiting the deserts of N Africa. **2** *Brit. inf.* a soldier who served in North Africa with the British 7th Armoured Division in 1941–42.

deserve (dɪˈzɜːv) *vb* **deserves, deserving, deserved. 1** (*tr*) to be entitled to or worthy of; merit. **2** (*intr;* foll. by *of*) *Obs.* to be worthy. [C13: from OF *deservir*, from L *dēservīre* to serve devotedly, from DE- + *servīre* to SERVE]

deserved (dɪˈzɜːvd) *adj* rightfully earned; justified; war ranted.
▸ **deservedly** (dɪˈzɜːvɪdlɪ) *adv* ▸ **deservedness** (dɪ- ˈzɜːvɪdnɪs) *n*

deserving (dɪˈzɜːvɪŋ) *adj* (often *postpositive* and foll. by *of*) worthy, esp. of praise or reward.
▸ **de'servingly** *adv* ▸ **de'servingness** *n*

deshabille (ˌdeɪzæˈbiːl) *or* **dishabille** *n* the state of being partly or carelessly dressed. [C17: from F *déshabillé*, from *dés* DIS-[1] + *habiller* to dress]

de Sica ★ (*Italian* de ˈsiːka) *n* **Vittorio** (vitˈtɔːrjo). 1902–74, Italian film actor and director. His films, in the realist tradition, include *Shoeshine* (1946) and *Bicycle Thieves* (1948).

desiccant (ˈdɛsɪkənt) *adj* **1** drying. ◆ *n* **2** a substance that absorbs water and is used to remove moisture. [C17: from L *dēsiccāns* drying up; see DESICCATE]

desiccate (ˈdɛsɪˌkeɪt) *vb* **desiccates, desiccating, desic cated. 1** (*tr*) to remove most of the water from; dehydrate. **2** (*tr*) to preserve (food) by removing moisture; dry. **3**

desiccate (*intr*) to become dried up. [C16: from L *dēsiccāre* to dry up, from DE- + *siccāre*, from *siccus* dry]
▶ 'desic‚cated *adj* ▶ ‚desic'cation *n*

desiderate (dɪ'zɪdə‚reɪt) *vb* **desiderates, desiderating, desiderated.** (*tr*) to feel the lack of or need for; miss. [C17: from L *dēsīderāre*, from DE- + *sīdus* star; see DESIRE]
▶ de‚sider'ation *n*

desideratum (dɪ‚zɪdə'rɑːtəm) *n, pl* **desiderata** (-tə). something lacked and wanted. [C17: from L; see DESIDERATE]

design (dɪ'zaɪn) *vb* **1** to work out the structure or form of (something), as by making a sketch or plans. **2** to plan and make (something) artistically or skilfully. **3** (*tr*) to invent. **4** (*tr*) to intend, as for a specific purpose; plan. ♦ *n* **5** a plan or preliminary drawing. **6** the arrangement, elements, or features of an artistic or decorative work: *the design of the desk is Chippendale.* **7** a finished artistic or decorative creation. **8** the art of designing. **9** a plan or project. **10** an intention; purpose. **11** (*often pl*; often foll. by *on* or *against*) a plot, often to gain possession of (something) by illegitimate means. [C16: from L *dēsignāre* to mark out, describe, from DE- + *signāre*, from *signum* a mark]
▶ de'signer *n*

designate *vb* ('dezɪg‚neɪt). **designates, designating, designated.** (*tr*) **1** to indicate or specify. **2** to give a name to; style; entitle. **3** to select or name for an office or duty; appoint. ♦ *adj* ('dezɪgnɪt, -‚neɪt). **4** (*immediately postpositive*) appointed, but not yet in office: *a minister designate.* [C15: from L *dēsignātus* marked out, defined; see DESIGN]
▶ 'desig‚nator *n*

designation (‚dezɪg'neɪʃən) *n* **1** something that designates, such as a name. **2** the act of designating or the fact of being designated.

designedly (dɪ'zaɪnɪdlɪ) *adv* by intention or design; on purpose.

designer (dɪ'zaɪnə) *n* **1** a person who devises and executes designs, as for clothes, machines, etc. **2** (*modifier*) designed by and bearing the label of a well-known fashion designer: *designer jeans.* **3** (*modifier*) (of things, ideas, etc.) fashionably trendy: *designer stubble.* **4** (*modifier*) (of cells, chemicals, etc.) designed or produced to perform a specific function or combat a specific problem: *designer insecticide.* **5** a person who devises plots; intriguer.

designer drug *n* **1** *Med.* a synthetic antibiotic designed to be effective against a particular bacterium. **2** a synthetic drug that has the same properties as an illegal narcotic or hallucinogen but can be manufactured legally.

designing (dɪ'zaɪnɪŋ) *adj* artful and scheming.

desirable (dɪ'zaɪərəb°l) *adj* **1** worthy of desire: *a desirable residence.* **2** arousing desire, esp. sexual desire; attractive.
▶ de‚sira'bility *or* de'sirableness *n* ▶ de'sirably *adv*

desire (dɪ'zaɪə) *vb* **desires, desiring, desired.** (*tr*) **1** to wish or long for; crave. **2** to request; ask for. ♦ *n* **3** a wish or longing. **4** an expressed wish; request. **5** sexual appetite. **6** a person or thing that is desired. [C13: from OF, from L *dēsīderāre* to desire earnestly; see DESIDERATE]
▶ de'sirer *n*

desirous (dɪ'zaɪərəs) *adj* (usually *postpositive* and foll. by *of*) having or expressing desire (for).

desist (dɪ'zɪst) *vb* (*intr*; often foll. by *from*) to cease, as from an action; stop or abstain. [C15: from OF, from L *dēsistere* to leave off, stand apart, from DE- + *sistere* to stand, halt]

desk (desk) *n* **1** a piece of furniture with a writing surface and usually drawers or other compartments. **2** a service counter or table in a public building, such as a hotel. **3** a support for the book from which services are read in a church. **4** the editorial section of a newspaper, etc., responsible for a particular subject: *the news desk.* **5** a music stand shared by two orchestral players. [C14: from Med. L *desca* table, from L *discus* disc, dish]

desk-bound *adj* obliged by one's occupation to work sitting at a desk.

desk editor *n* (in a publishing house) an editor responsible for the preparation and checking of manuscripts for printing.

deskill (diː'skɪl) *vb* (*tr*) **1** to mechanize or computerize (a job) so that little skill is required to do it. **2** to deprive (employees) of the opportunity for skilled work.

desktop ('desk‚top) *n* (*modifier*) denoting a computer system, esp. for word processing, that is small enough to use at a desk.

desktop publishing *n* a means of publishing reports, advertising material, etc., to near-typeset quality using a desktop computer and a laser printer. Abbrev.: **DTP.**

desman ('desmən) *n, pl* **desmans.** either of two molelike amphibious mammals, the Russian desman or the Pyrenean desman, with dense fur and webbed feet. [C18: from Swedish *desmansrätta*, from *desman* musk + *rätta* rat]

Des Moines ★ (də 'mɔɪn, 'mɔɪnz) *n* **1** a city in S central Iowa: state capital. Pop.: 193 965 (1994 est.). **2** a river in the N central US, rising in SW Minnesota and flowing southeast to join the Mississippi. Length: 861 km (535 miles).

Desmoulins ★ (*French* dɛmulɛ̃) *n* (**Lucie Simplice**) **Camille** (**Benoît**) (kamij). 1760–94, French revolutionary leader, pamphleteer, and orator.

desolate *adj* ('desəlɪt). **1** uninhabited; deserted. **2** made uninhabitable; laid waste; devastated. **3** without friends, hope, or encouragement. **4** dismal; depressing. ♦ *vb* ('desə‚leɪt), **desolates, desolating, desolated.** (*tr*) **5** to deprive of inhabitants; depopulate. **6** to lay waste; devastate. **7** to make wretched or forlorn. **8** to forsake or abandon. [C14: from L *dēsōlāre* to leave alone, from DE- + *sōlāre* to make lonely, lay waste, from *sōlus* alone]
▶ 'deso‚later *or* 'deso‚lator *n* ▶ 'desolately *adv* ▶ 'desolateness *n*

desolation (‚desə'leɪʃən) *n* **1** a desolating or being desolated; ruin or devastation. **2** solitary misery; wretchedness. **3** a desolate region.

De Soto ★ (də 'səʊtəʊ; *Spanish* de 'soto) *n* **Hernando** (ɛr'nando). ?1500–42, Spanish explorer, who discovered the Mississippi River (1541). Also called: **Fernando De Soto** (fer'nando).

despair (dɪ'speə) *vb* **1** (*intr*; often foll. by *of*) to lose or give up hope: *I despair of his coming.* ♦ *n* **2** total loss of hope. **3** a person or thing that causes hopelessness or for which there is no hope. [C14: from OF *despoir* hopelessness, from *desperer* to despair, from L *dēspērāre*, from DE- + *spērāre* to hope]

despairing (dɪ'speərɪŋ) *adj* hopeless, despondent; feeling or showing despair.
▶ de'spairingly *adv*

despatch (dɪ'spætʃ) *vb* (*tr*), *n* a less common spelling of **dispatch.**
▶ des'patcher *n*

Despenser ★ (dɪs'pensə) *n* **Hugh le,** Earl of Winchester. 1262–1326, English statesman, a favourite of Edward II. Together with his son **Hugh,** *the Younger* (?1290–1326), he was executed by the king's enemies.

desperado (‚despə'rɑːdəʊ) *n, pl* **desperadoes** *or* **desperados.** a reckless or desperate person, esp. one ready to commit any violent illegal act. [C17: prob. pseudo-Spanish var. of obs. *desperate* (n)]

desperate ('despərɪt, -prɪt) *adj* **1** careless of danger, as from despair. **2** (of an act) reckless; risky. **3** used or undertaken as a last resort. **4** critical; very grave: *in desperate need.* **5** (often *postpositive* and foll. by *for*) in distress and having a great need or desire. **6** moved by or showing despair. [C15: from L *dēspērāre* to have no hope; see DESPAIR]
▶ 'desperately *adv* ▶ 'desperateness *n*

desperation (‚despə'reɪʃən) *n* **1** desperate recklessness. **2** the state of being desperate.

despicable ('despɪkəb°l, dɪ'spɪk-) *adj* worthy of being despised; contemptible; mean. [C16: from LL *dēspicābilis*, from *dēspicārī* to disdain; cf. DESPISE]
▶ 'despicably *adv*

despise (dɪ'spaɪz) *vb* **despises, despising, despised.** (*tr*) to look down on with contempt; scorn: *he despises flattery.* [C13: from OF *despire*, from L *dēspicere* to look down, from DE- + *specere* to look]
▶ de'spiser *n*

despite (dɪ'spaɪt) *prep* **1** in spite of; undeterred by. ♦ *n* **2** *Arch.* contempt; insult. **3 in despite of.** (*prep*) *Rare.* in spite of. [C13: from OF *despit*, from L *dēspectus* contempt; see DESPISE]

despoil (dɪ'spɔɪl) *vb* (*tr*) to deprive by force; plunder; loot. [C13: from OF, from L *dēspoliāre*, from DE- + *spoliāre* to rob (esp. of clothing)]
▸ de'spoiler *n* ▸ de'spoilment *n*

despoliation (dɪ,spəʊlɪ'eɪʃən) *n* **1** plunder or pillage. **2** the state of being despoiled.

despond (dɪ'spɒnd) *vb* (*intr*) **1** to become disheartened; despair. ♦ *n* **2** *Arch.* despondency. [C17: from L *dēspondēre* to promise, make over to, yield, lose heart, from DE- + *spondēre* to promise]
▸ de'spondingly *adv*

despondent (dɪ'spɒndənt) *adj* downcast or disheartened; dejected.
▸ de'spondence *or* de'spondency *n* ▸ de'spondently *adv*

despot ('dɛspɒt) *n* **1** an absolute or tyrannical ruler. **2** any person in power who acts tyrannically. [C16: from Med. L *despota*, from Gk *despotēs* lord, master]
▸ de'spotic (dɛs'pɒtɪk) *or* des'potical *adj* ▸ des'potically *adv*

despotism ('dɛspə,tɪzəm) *n* **1** the rule of a despot; absolute or tyrannical government. **2** arbitrary or tyrannical authority or behaviour.

des Prés *or* **Desprez** ★ (*French* de pre) *n* Josquin (ʒɔskē). ?1450–1521, Flemish Renaissance composer of masses, motets, and chansons.

des res ('dɛz 'rɛz) *n* (in estate agents' jargon) a desirable residence.

Dessau ★ (*German* 'dɛsaʊ) *n* an industrial city in central Germany, in Saxony-Anhalt: capital of Anhalt state from 1340 to 1918. Pop.: 95 100 (1991).

dessert (dɪ'zɜːt) *n* **1** the sweet, usually last course of a meal. **2** *Chiefly Brit.* (esp. formerly) fruit, dates, nuts, etc., served at the end of a meal. [C17: from F, from *desservir* to clear a table, from *des-* DIS-¹ + *servir* to SERVE]

dessertspoon (dɪ'zɜːt,spuːn) *n* a spoon intermediate in size between a tablespoon and a teaspoon.

destination (,dɛstɪ'neɪʃən) *n* **1** the predetermined end of a journey. **2** the end or purpose for which something is created or a person is destined.

destine ('dɛstɪn) *vb* **destines, destining, destined.** (*tr*) to set apart (for a certain purpose or person); intend; design. [C14: from OF, from L *dēstināre* to appoint, from DE- + *-stināre*, from *stāre* to stand]

destined ('dɛstɪnd) *adj* (*postpositive*) **1** foreordained; meant. **2** (usually foll. by *for*) heading (towards a specific destination).

destiny ('dɛstɪnɪ) *n, pl* **destinies. 1** the future destined for a person or thing. **2** the predetermined or inevitable course of events. **3** the power that predetermines the course of events. [C14: from OF, from *destiner* to DESTINE]

destitute ('dɛstɪ,tjuːt) *adj* **1** lacking the means of subsistence; totally impoverished. **2** (*postpositive*; foll. by *of*) completely lacking: *destitute of words*. [C14: from L, from *dēstituere* to leave alone, from *statuere* to place]

destitution (,dɛstɪ'tjuːʃən) *n* the state of being destitute; utter poverty.

destrier ('dɛstrɪə) *n Arch.* a warhorse. [C13: from OF, from *destre* right hand, from L *dextra;* from the fact that a squire led a knight's horse with his right hand]

destroy (dɪ'strɔɪ) *vb* (*mainly tr*) **1** to ruin; spoil. **2** to tear down or demolish. **3** to put an end to. **4** to kill or annihilate. **5** to crush or defeat. **6** (*intr*) to be destructive or cause destruction. [C13: from OF, from L *dēstruere* to pull down, from DE- + *struere* to pile up, build]

destroyer (dɪ'strɔɪə) *n* **1** a small fast lightly armoured but heavily armed warship. **2** a person or thing that destroys.

destruct (dɪ'strʌkt) *vb* **1** to destroy (one's own missile, etc.) for safety. **2** (*intr*) (of a missile, etc.) to be destroyed, for safety, by those controlling it. ♦ *n* **3** the act of destructing. ♦ *adj* **4** designed to be capable of destroying itself or the object containing it: *destruct mechanism*.

destructible (dɪ'strʌktɪbᵊl) *adj* capable of being or liable to be destroyed.

destruction (dɪ'strʌkʃən) *n* **1** the act of destroying o state of being destroyed; demolition. **2** a cause of ruin o means of destroying. [C14: from L *dēstructiō* a pulling down; see DESTROY]

destructive (dɪ'strʌktɪv) *adj* **1** (often *postpositive* and foll. by *of* or *to*) causing or tending to cause the destruction (of). **2** intended to discredit, esp. without positive suggestions or help; negative: *destructive criticism*.
▸ de'structively *adv* ▸ de'structiveness *n*

destructive distillation *n* the decomposition of a complex substance, such as wood or coal, by heating i in the absence of air and collecting the volatile products.

destructor (dɪ'strʌktə) *n* **1** a furnace or incinerator fo the disposal of refuse. **2** a device used to blow up a defective missile.

desuetude (dɪ'sjuːɪ,tjuːd, 'dɛswɪ,tjuːd) *n Formal.* the condition of not being in use or practice; disuse. [C15: from L, from *dēsuescere* to lay aside a habit, from DE- + *suescere* to grow accustomed]

desulphurize *or* **desulphurise** (diː'sʌlfjʊ,raɪz) *vb* **desulphurizes, desulphurizing, desulphurized** *or* **desulphurises, desulphurising, desulphurised.** to free or become free from sulphur.

desultory ('dɛsəltərɪ, -trɪ) *adj* **1** passing from one thing to another, esp. in a fitful way; unmethodical; disconnected. **2** random or incidental: *a desultory thought.* [C16: from L: relating to one who vaults or jumps, hence superficial, from *dēsilīre* to jump down, from DE- + *salīre* to jump]
▸ 'desultorily *adv* ▸ 'desultoriness *n*

Det. *abbrev. for* Detective.

detach (dɪ'tætʃ) *vb* (*tr*) **1** to disengage and separate or remove; unfasten; disconnect. **2** *Mil.* to separate (a small unit) from a larger, for a special assignment. [C17: from OF *destachier*, from *des-* DIS-¹ + *atachier* to ATTACH]
▸ de'tachable *adj* ▸ de,tacha'bility *n*

detached (dɪ'tætʃt) *adj* **1** disconnected or standing apart; not attached: *a detached house.* **2** showing no bias or emotional involvement. **3** *Ophthalmol.* (of the retina) separated from the choroid layer of the eyeball to which it is normally attached, resulting in loss of vision in the affected part.

detachment (dɪ'tætʃmənt) *n* **1** indifference; aloofness. **2** freedom from self-interest or bias; disinterest. **3** the act of detaching something. **4** the condition of being detached; disconnection. **5** *Mil.* **5a** the separation of a small unit from its main body. **5b** the unit so detached.

detail ('diːteɪl) *n* **1** an item that is considered separately; particular. **2** an item that is unimportant: *passengers' comfort was regarded as a detail.* **3** treatment of particulars: *this essay includes too much detail.* **4** items collectively; particulars. **5** a small section or element in a painting, building, statue, etc., esp. when considered in isolation. **6** *Mil.* **6a** the act of assigning personnel for a specific duty. **6b** the personnel selected. **6c** the duty. **7 in detail.** including all or most particulars or items thoroughly. ♦ *vb* (*tr*) **8** to list or relate fully. **9** *Mil.* to select (personnel) for a specific duty. [C17: from F, from OF *detailler* to cut in pieces, from *de-* DIS-¹ + *tailler* to cut]

detailed ('diːteɪld) *adj* having many details or giving careful attention to details.

detain (dɪ'teɪn) *vb* (*tr*) **1** to delay; hold back. **2** to confine or hold in custody. [C15: from OF, from L *dētinēre* to hold off, keep back, from DE- + *tenēre* to hold]
▸ de'tainable *adj* ▸ detainee (,diːteɪ'niː) *n* ▸ de'tainment *n*

detect (dɪ'tɛkt) *vb* (*tr*) **1** to perceive or notice. **2** to discover the existence or presence of (esp. something likely to elude observation). **3** *Obs.* to discover, or reveal (a crime, criminal, etc.). **4** to extract information from (an electromagnetic wave). [C15: from L *dētectus*, from *dētegere* to uncover, from DE- + *tegere* to cover]
▸ de'tectable *or* de'tectible *adj*

detection (dɪ'tɛkʃən) *n* **1** the act of discovering or the fact of being discovered. **2** the act or process of extracting information, esp. at audio or video frequencies, from an electromagnetic wave; demodulation.

★ people and places

detective (dɪˈtɛktɪv) *n* **1a** a police officer who investigates crimes. **1b** See **private detective**. **1c** (*as modifier*): *a detective story*. ◆ *adj* **2** of or for detection.

detector (dɪˈtɛktə) *n* **1** a person or thing that detects. **2** any mechanical sensing device. **3** *Electronics*. a device used in the detection of radio signals.

detent (dɪˈtɛnt) *n* the locking piece of a mechanism, often spring-loaded to check the movement of a wheel in only one direction. [C17: from OF *destente* a loosening, trigger; see DÉTENTE]

détente (deɪˈtɑːnt; *French* detɑ̃t) *n* the relaxing or easing of tension, esp. between nations. [F, lit.: a loosening, from OF *destendre* to release, from *tendre* to stretch]

detention (dɪˈtɛnʃən) *n* **1** a detaining or being detained. **2a** custody or confinement, esp. of a suspect awaiting trial. **2b** (*as modifier*): *a detention order*. **3** a form of punishment in which a pupil is detained after school. [C16: from L *dētentiō* a keeping back; see DETAIN]

detention centre *n* (formerly) a place in which young persons could be detained for short periods by order of a court.

deter (dɪˈtɜː) *vb* **deters, deterring, deterred.** (*tr*) to discourage (from acting) or prevent (from occurring), usually by instilling fear, doubt, or anxiety. [C16: from L *dēterrēre*, from DE- + *terrēre* to frighten]
▸ de'terment *n*

deterge (dɪˈtɜːdʒ) *vb* **deterges, deterging, deterged.** (*tr*) to cleanse: *to deterge a wound*. [C17: from L *dētergēre* to wipe away, from DE- + *tergēre* to wipe]

detergent (dɪˈtɜːdʒənt) *n* **1** a cleansing agent, esp. a chemical such as an alkyl sulphonate, widely used in industry, laundering, etc. ◆ *adj* **2** having cleansing power. [C17: from L *dētergēns* wiping off; see DETERGE]

deteriorate (dɪˈtɪərɪəˌreɪt) *vb* **deteriorates, deteriorating, deteriorated. 1** to make or become worse; depreciate. **2** (*intr*) to wear away or disintegrate. [C16: from LL *dēteriōrāre*, from *dēterior* worse]
▸ de,terioˈration *n* ▸ deˈteriorative *adj*

determinacy (dɪˈtɜːmɪnəsɪ) *n* **1** the quality of being defined or fixed. **2** the condition of being predicted or deduced.

determinant (dɪˈtɜːmɪnənt) *adj* **1** serving to determine. ◆ *n* **2** a factor that influences or determines. **3** *Maths*. a square array of elements that represents the sum of certain products of these elements, used to solve simultaneous equations, in vector studies, etc.

determinate (dɪˈtɜːmɪnɪt) *adj* **1** definitely limited, defined, or fixed. **2** determined. **3** able to be predicted or deduced. **4** *Bot*. having the main and branch stems ending in flowers.
▸ deˈterminateness *n*

determination (dɪˌtɜːmɪˈneɪʃən) *n* **1** the act of making a decision. **2** the condition of being determined; resoluteness. **3** an ending of an argument by the decision of an authority. **4** the act of fixing the quality, limit, position, etc., of something. **5** a decision or opinion reached. **6** a resolute movement towards some object or end. **7** *Law*. the termination of an estate or interest. **8** *Law*. the decision reached by a court of justice on a disputed matter.

determinative (dɪˈtɜːmɪnətɪv) *adj* **1** serving to settle or determine; deciding. ◆ *n* **2** a factor, circumstance, etc., that settles or determines.
▸ deˈterminatively *adv* ▸ deˈterminativeness *n*

determine (dɪˈtɜːmɪn) *vb* **determines, determining, determined. 1** to settle or decide (an argument, question, etc.) conclusively. **2** (*tr*) to conclude, esp. after observation or consideration. **3** (*tr*) to influence; give direction to. **4** (*tr*) to fix in scope, variety, etc.: *the river determined the edge of the property*. **5** to make or cause to make a decision. **6** (*tr*) *Logic*. to define or limit (a notion) by adding or requiring certain features or characteristics. **7** (*tr*) *Geom*. to fix or specify the position or form of. **8** *Chiefly law*. to come or bring to an end, as an estate. [C14: from OF, from L *dētermināre* to set boundaries to, from DE- + *termināre* to limit]
▸ deˈterminable *adj*

determined (dɪˈtɜːmɪnd) *adj* of unwavering mind; resolute; firm.
▸ deˈterminedly *adv*

determiner (dɪˈtɜːmɪnə) *n* **1** a word, such as a number, article, or personal pronoun, that determines (limits) the meaning of a noun phrase, e.g. *their* in 'their black cat'. **2** a person or thing that determines.

determinism (dɪˈtɜːmɪˌnɪzəm) *n* the philosophical doctrine that all events, including human actions, are fully determined by preceding events, and so freedom of choice is illusory. Also called: **necessitarianism.** Cf. **free will.**
▸ deˈterminist *n, adj* ▸ de,terminˈistic *adj*

deterrent (dɪˈtɛrənt) *n* **1** something that deters. **2** a weapon, esp. nuclear, held by one state, etc., to deter attack by another. ◆ *adj* **3** tending or used to deter. [C19: from L *dēterrēns* hindering; see DETER]
▸ deˈterrence *n*

detest (dɪˈtɛst) *vb* (*tr*) to dislike intensely; loathe. [C16: from L *dētestārī* to curse (while invoking a god as witness), from DE- + *testārī*, from *testis* a witness]
▸ deˈtester *n*

detestable (dɪˈtɛstəb°l) *adj* being or deserving to be abhorred or detested.
▸ de,testaˈbility *or* deˈtestableness *n* ▸ deˈtestably *adv*

detestation (ˌdiːtɛsˈteɪʃən) *n* **1** intense hatred; abhorrence. **2** a person or thing that is detested.

dethrone (dɪˈθrəʊn) *vb* **dethrones, dethroning, dethroned.** (*tr*) to remove from a throne or deprive of any high position or title.
▸ deˈthronement *n* ▸ deˈthroner *n*

detonate (ˈdɛtəˌneɪt) *vb* **detonates, detonating, detonated.** to cause (a bomb, mine, etc.) to explode or (of a bomb, mine, etc.) to explode. [C18: from L *dētonāre* to thunder down, from DE- + *tonāre* to THUNDER]
▸ ˌdetoˈnation *n*

detonator (ˈdɛtəˌneɪtə) *n* **1** a small amount of explosive, as in a percussion cap, used to initiate a larger explosion. **2** a device, such as an electrical generator, used to set off an explosion from a distance. **3** an explosive.

detour (ˈdiːtʊə) *n* **1** a deviation from a direct route or course of action. ◆ *vb* **2** to deviate or cause to deviate from a direct route or course of action. [C18: from F, from OF *destorner* to divert, turn away, from *des-* DE- + *torner* to TURN]

detox (ˈdiːˌtɒks) *Inf.* ◆ *n* **1** treatment designed to rid the body of poisonous substances, esp. alcohol and drugs. ◆ *vb* (*intr*) **2** to undergo treatment to rid the body of poisonous substances, esp. alcohol and drugs.

detoxification centre *n* a place that specializes in the treatment of alcoholism or drug addiction.

detoxify (diːˈtɒksɪˌfaɪ) *vb* **detoxifies, detoxifying, detoxified.** (*tr*) **1** to remove poison from. **2** to treat (a person) for alcoholism or drug dependency.
▸ de,toxifiˈcation *n*

detract (dɪˈtrækt) *vb* **1** (when *intr*, usually foll. by *from*) to take away a part (of); diminish: *her anger detracts from her beauty*. **2** (*tr*) to distract or divert. **3** (*tr*) *Obs*. to belittle or disparage. [C15: from L *dētractus*, from *dētrahere* to pull away, disparage, from DE- + *trahere* to drag]
▸ deˈtractive *adj* ▸ deˈtractor *n* ▸ deˈtraction *n*

> **USAGE NOTE** *Detract* is sometimes wrongly used where *distract* is meant: *a noise distracted* (not *detracted*) *my attention*.

detrain (diːˈtreɪn) *vb* to leave or cause to leave a railway train.
▸ deˈtrainment *n*

detriment (ˈdɛtrɪmənt) *n* **1** disadvantage or damage. **2** a cause of disadvantage or damage. [C15: from L *dētrīmentum*, a rubbing off, hence damage, from *dēterere*, from DE- + *terere* to rub]

detrimental (ˌdetrɪˈment°l) *adj* (when *postpositive*, foll. by *to*) harmful; injurious.

detritus (dɪˈtraɪtəs) *n* **1** a loose mass of stones, silt, etc.,

worn away from rocks. **2** the organic debris formed from the decay of organisms. [C18: from F, from L: a rubbing away; see DETRIMENT]
▸ **de'trital** adj

Detroit ★ (dɪ'trɔɪt) n **1** a city in SE Michigan, on the Detroit River: a major Great Lakes port; largest car-manufacturing centre in the world. Pop.: 992 038 (1994 est.). **2** a river in central North America, flowing along the US-Canadian border from Lake St Clair to Lake Erie.

de trop French. (də tro) adj (postpositive) not wanted; in the way. [lit.: of too much]

detumescence (ˌdiːtjuˈmɛsəns) n the subsidence of a swelling. [C17: from L dētumescere to cease swelling, from DE- + tumescere, from tumēre to swell]

deuce[1] (djuːs) n **1a** a playing card or dice with two spots. **1b** a throw of two in dice. **2** Tennis, etc. a tied score that requires one player to gain two successive points to win the game. [C15: from OF deus two, from L duos, from duo two]

deuce[2] (djuːs) Inf. ◆ interj **1** an expression of annoyance or frustration. ◆ n **2 the deuce.** (intensifier) used in such phrases as **what the deuce**, **where the deuce**, etc. [C17: prob. special use of DEUCE[1] (in the sense: lowest throw at dice)]

deuced ('djuːsɪd, djuːst) Brit. inf. ◆ adj **1** (intensifier) confounded: he's a deuced idiot. ◆ adv **2** (intensifier): deuced good luck.

Deus Latin. ('deɪʊs) n God. [rel. to Gk Zeus]

deus ex machina Latin. ('deɪʊs ɛks 'mækɪnə) n **1** (in ancient Greek and Roman drama) a god introduced into a play to resolve the plot. **2** any unlikely device serving this purpose. [lit.: god out of a machine]

Deut. Bible. abbrev. for Deuteronomy.

deuteride ('djuːtəˌraɪd) n a compound of deuterium and another element.

deuterium (djuːˈtɪərɪəm) n a stable isotope of hydrogen, occurring in natural hydrogen and in heavy water. Symbol: D or ^{2}H; atomic no.: 1; atomic wt.: 2.014. [C20: NL; see DEUTERO-, -IUM; from the fact that it is the second heaviest hydrogen isotope]

deuterium oxide n the compound D_2O; water in which the normal hydrogen atoms are replaced by deuterium atoms. See also **heavy water.**

deutero-, deuto- or before a vowel **deuter-, deut-** combining form. second or secondary: deuterium. [from Gk deuteros second]

deuteron ('djuːtəˌrɒn) n the nucleus of a deuterium atom.

Deutsch ★ (dɔɪtʃ; German dɔytʃ) n **Otto Erich** ('ɔto 'eːrɪç). 1883–1967, Austrian music historian, noted for his catalogue of Schubert's works (1951).

Deutschland ★ ('dɔytʃlant) n the German name for **Germany.**

Deutschmark ('dɔɪtʃˌmɑːk) or **Deutsche Mark** ('dɔɪtʃə) n the standard monetary unit of Germany.

deutzia ('djuːtsɪə, 'dɔɪtsɪə) n any of various shrubs with white, pink, or purplish flowers in early summer. [C19: NL, after J. Deutz, 18th-cent. Du. patron of botany]

Deux-Sèvres ★ (French døsɛvrə) n a department of W France, in Poitou-Charentes region. Capital: Niort. Pop.: 346 612 (1994 est.). Area: 6054 sq. km (2337 sq. miles).

de Valera ★ (də vəˈlɛərə, -ˈlɪə-) n **Eamon** ('eɪmən). 1882–1975, Irish statesman; president of Sinn Fein (1917) and of the Dáil (1918–22); formed the Fianna Fáil party (1927); prime minister (1937–48; 1951–54; 1957–59) and president (1959–73) of the Irish Republic.

de Valois ★ (də 'vælwɑː) n See (Ninette de) **Valois**[3].

devalue (diːˈvæljuː) or **devaluate** (diːˈvæljuːˌeɪt) vb **devalues, devaluing, devalued** or **devaluates, devaluating, devaluated. 1** to reduce (a currency) or (of a currency) be reduced in exchange value. **2** (tr) to reduce the value of.
▸ **deˌvaluˈation** n

Devanagari (ˌdeɪvəˈnɑːɡərɪ) n a syllabic script in which Sanskrit, Hindi, and other modern languages of India are written. [C18: from Sansk.: alphabet of the gods]

devastate ('dɛvəˌsteɪt) vb **devastates, devastating, devas-**

tated. (tr) **1** to lay waste or make desolate; ravage; destroy. **2** to confound or overwhelm. [C17: from L dēvastāre from DE- + vastāre to ravage; rel. to vastus waste, empty]
▸ **devasˈtation** n ▸ **'devasˌtator** n

develop (dɪ'vɛləp) vb **1** to come to or bring to a later or more advanced or expanded stage; grow or cause to grow gradually. **2** (tr) to work out in detail. **3** to disclose or unfold (thoughts, a plot, etc.) gradually or (of thoughts, etc.) to be gradually disclosed or unfolded. **4** to come or bring into existence: he developed a new faith in God. **5** (intr) to follow as a result of something; ensue: row developed after her remarks. **6** (tr) to contract (a disease or illness). **7** (tr) to improve the value or change the use of (land). **8** to exploit or make available the natural resources of (a country or region). **9** (tr) Photog. to treat (exposed film, plate, or paper) with chemical solutions in order to produce a visible image. **10** Biol. to progress or cause to progress from simple to complex stages in the growth of an individual or the evolution of a species. **11** (tr) to elaborate upon (a musical theme) by varying the melody, key, etc. **12** (tr) Maths. to expand (a function or expression) in the form of a series. **13** (tr) Geom. to project or roll out (a surface) onto a plane without stretching or shrinking any element. **14** Chess. to bring (a piece) into play from its initial position on the back rank. [C19: from OF desvoloper to unwrap, from des- DIS-[1] + voloper to wrap; see ENVELOP]
▸ **de'velopable** adj

developer (dɪ'vɛləpə) n **1** a person or thing that develops something, esp. a person who develops property. Also called: **developing agent.** Photog. a chemical used to convert the latent image recorded in the emulsion of film or paper into a visible image.

developing country n a poor or non-industrial country that is seeking to develop its resources by industrialization.

development (dɪ'vɛləpmənt) n **1** the act or process of growing or developing. **2** the product of developing. **3** a fact or event, esp. one that changes a situation. **4** an area of land that has been developed. **5** the section of a movement, usually in sonata form, in which the basic musical themes are developed. **6** Chess. the process of developing pieces.
▸ **deˌvelopˈmental** adj

developmental disorder n Psychiatry. any condition such as autism or dyslexia, that appears in childhood and is characterized by delay in the development of one or more psychological functions, such as language skill.

development area n (in Britain) an area which has experienced economic depression because of the decline of its main industry or industries, and which is given government assistance to establish new industry.

Devereux ★ ('dɛvərə) n **Robert.** See (2nd Earl of) **Essex.**

Devi ★ ('deɪviː) n a Hindu goddess and embodiment of the female energy of Siva. [Sansk.: goddess]

deviance ('diːvɪəns) n **1** Also called: **deviancy.** the act or state of being deviant. **2** Statistics. a measure of the degree of fit of a statistical model compared to that of a more complete model.

deviant ('diːvɪənt) adj **1** deviating, as from what is considered acceptable behaviour. ◆ n **2** a person whose behaviour, esp. sexual behaviour, deviates from what is considered to be acceptable.

deviate vb ('diːvɪˌeɪt), **deviates, deviating, deviated. 1** (usually intr) to differ or cause to differ, as in belief or thought. **2** (usually intr) to turn aside or cause to turn aside. **3** (intr) Psychol. to depart from an accepted standard. **4** another word for **deviant.** [C17: from LL dēviāre to turn aside from the direct road, from DE- + via road]
▸ **'deviˌator** n ▸ **'deviatory** adj

deviation (ˌdiːvɪ'eɪʃən) n **1** an act or result of deviating. **2** Statistics. the difference between an observed value in a series of such values and their arithmetic mean. **3** the error of a compass due to local magnetic disturbances.

device (dɪ'vaɪs) n **1** a machine or tool used for a specific task. **2** Euphemistic. a bomb. **3** a plan, esp. a clever or evil one; trick. **4** any ornamental pattern or picture, as in embroidery. **5** computer hardware designed for a specific function. **6** a design or figure, used as a heraldic sign, emblem, etc. **7** a particular pattern of words, figures of speech, etc., used in literature to produce an effect on the reader. **8 leave (someone) to his own devices.** to leave (someone) alone to do as he wishes. [C13: from OF *devis* purpose, contrivance & *devise* difference, intention, from *deviser* to divide, control; see DEVISE]

devil ('dɛv°l) *n* **1** (*often cap.*) *Theol.* the chief spirit of evil and enemy of God, often depicted as a human figure with horns, cloven hoofs, and tail. **2** any subordinate evil spirit. **3** a person or animal regarded as wicked or ill-natured. **4** a person or animal regarded as unfortunate or wretched. **5** a person or animal regarded as daring, mischievous, or energetic. **6** *Inf.* something difficult or annoying. **7** *Christian Science.* an error, lie, or false belief. **8** (in Malaysia) a ghost. **9** a portable furnace or brazier. **10** any of various mechanical devices, such as a machine for making wooden screws or a rag-tearing machine. **11** See **printer's devil**. **12** *Law.* (in England) a junior barrister who does work for another in order to gain experience, usually for a half fee. **13** *Meteorol.* a small whirlwind in arid areas that raises dust or sand in a column. **14 between the devil and the deep blue sea.** between equally undesirable alternatives. **15 devil of a** *Inf.* (intensifier): *a devil of a fine horse.* **16 give the devil his due.** to acknowledge the talent or success of an unpleasant person. **17 go to the devil. 17a** to fail or become dissipated. **17b** (*interj*) used to express annoyance with the person causing it. **18 (let) the devil take the hindmost.** look after oneself and leave others to their fate. **19 talk** (*or* **speak**) **of the devil!** used when an absent person who has been the subject of conversation appears. **20 the devil!** (intensifier): **20a** used in **what the devil, where the devil,** etc. **20b** an exclamation of anger, surprise, disgust, etc. **21 the devil to pay.** trouble to be faced as a consequence of an action. ◆ *vb* **devils, devilling, devilled** *or US* **devils, deviling, deviled. 22** (*tr*) to prepare (food) by coating with a highly flavoured spiced paste or mixture of condiments before cooking. **23** (*tr*) to tear (rags) with a devil. **24** (*intr*) to serve as a printer's devil. **25** (*intr*) *Chiefly Brit.* to do hackwork, esp. for a lawyer or author. **26** (*tr*) *US inf.* to harass, vex, etc. [OE *dēofol*, from L *diabolus*, from Gk *diabolos* enemy, accuser, slanderer]

devilfish ('dɛv°l,fɪʃ) *n, pl* **devilfish** *or* **devilfishes. 1** Also called: **devil ray**. another name for **manta** (the fish). **2** another name for **octopus**.

devilish ('dɛvəlɪʃ) *adj* **1** of, resembling, or befitting a devil; diabolic; fiendish. ◆ *adv, adj* **2** *Inf.* (intensifier): *devilish good food.*
▶ **'devilishly** *adv* ▶ **'devilishness** *n*

devil-may-care *adj* careless or reckless; happy-go-lucky: *a devil-may-care attitude.*

devilment ('dɛv°lmənt) *n* devilish or mischievous conduct.

devilry ('dɛv°lrɪ) *or* **deviltry** *n, pl* **devilries** *or* **deviltries. 1** reckless or malicious fun or mischief. **2** wickedness. **3** black magic or other forms of diabolism. [C18: from F *diablerie*, from *diable* DEVIL]

devil's advocate *n* **1** a person who advocates an opposing or unpopular view, often for the sake of argument. **2** *RC Church.* the official appointed to put the case against the beatification or canonization of a candidate. [translation of NL *advocātus diabolī*]

devil's coach-horse *n* a large black beetle with large jaws and ferocious habits.

devil's food cake *n* *Chiefly US & Canad.* a rich chocolate cake.

Devil's Island ★ *n* one of the three Safety Islands, off the coast of French Guiana: formerly a leper colony, then a French penal colony from 1895 until 1938. Area: less than 2 sq. km (1 sq. mile). French name: **Île du Diable.**

Devine ★ (də'vi:n) *n* **George (Alexander Cassady). 1910–65,** British stage director and actor: founded (1956) the English Stage Company.

devious ('di:vɪəs) *adj* **1** not sincere or candid; deceitful. **2** (of a route or course of action) rambling; indirect. **3** going astray; erring. [C16: from L *dēvius* lying to one side of the road, from DE- + *via* road]
▶ **'deviously** *adv* ▶ **'deviousness** *n*

devise (dɪ'vaɪz) *vb* **devises, devising, devised. 1** to work out or plan (something) in one's mind. **2** (*tr*) *Law.* to dispose of (real property) by will. ◆ *n Law.* **3** a disposition of property by will. **4** a will or clause in a will disposing of real property. [C15: from OF *deviser* to divide, apportion, intend, from L *dīvidere* to DIVIDE]
▶ **de'viser** *n*

devitalize *or* **devitalise** (di:'vaɪtə,laɪz) *vb* **devitalizes, devitalizing, devitalized** *or* **devitalises, devitalising, devitalised.** (*tr*) to lower or destroy the vitality of; make weak or lifeless.
▶ **de,vitali'zation** *or* **de,vitali'sation** *n*

Devizes ★ (də'vaɪzəz) *n* a market town in S England, in Wiltshire: agricultural products. Pop.: 13 205 (1991).

devoid (dɪ'vɔɪd) *adj* (*postpositive; foll. by of*) destitute or void (of); free (from). [C15: orig. p.p. of *devoid* (*vb*) to remove, from OF *devoider* from DE- + *voider* to void]

devoirs (də'vwɑ:) *pl n* (*sometimes sing*) compliments or respects. [C13: from OF: duty, from *devoir* to be obliged to, owe, from L *dēbēre*]

devolution (,di:və'lu:ʃən) *n* **1** a devolving. **2** a passing onwards or downwards from one stage to another. **3** a transfer of authority from a central government to regional governments. [C16: from Med. L *dēvolūtiō* a rolling down, from L *dēvolvere*; see DEVOLVE]
▶ **,devo'lutionary** *adj* ▶ **,devo'lutionist** *n, adj*

devolve (dɪ'vɒlv) *vb* **devolves, devolving, devolved. 1** (foll. by *on, upon, to*, etc.) to pass or cause to pass to a successor or substitute, as duties, power, etc. **2** (*intr*; foll. by *on* or *upon*) *Law.* (of an estate, etc.) to pass to another by operation of law. [C15: from L *dēvolvere* to roll down, fall into, from DE- + *volvere* to roll]
▶ **de'volvement** *n*

Devon ★ ('dɛv°n) *n* **1** Also called: **Devonshire.** a county of SW England, between the Bristol Channel and the English Channel, including the island of Lundy: hilly, rising to the uplands of Exmoor and Dartmoor, with wooded river valleys and a rugged coastline. Administrative centre: Exeter. Pop.: 1 053 400 (1994 est.). Area: 6712 sq. km (2591 sq. miles). **2** a breed of large red cattle originally from Devon.

Devonian (də'vəʊnɪən) *adj* **1** of, denoting, or formed in the fourth period of the Palaeozoic era, between the Silurian and Carboniferous periods. **2** of or relating to Devon. ◆ *n* **3 the.** the Devonian period or rock system.

Devonshire ★ ('dɛv°nʃɪə, -ʃə) *n* **8th Duke of,** title of *Spencer Compton Cavendish.* 1833–1908, British politician, also known (1858–91) as Lord Hartington. He led the Liberal Party (1874–80) and left it to found the Liberal Unionist Party (1886).

Devonshire split *n* a kind of yeast bun split open and served with cream or jam.

devoré (dəvɒ'reɪ) *n* a velvet fabric with a raised pattern created by disintegrating some of the pile with chemicals. [from F, p.p. of *dévorer* to devour]

devote (dɪ'vəʊt) *vb* **devotes, devoting, devoted.** (*tr*) to apply or dedicate (oneself, money, etc.) to some pursuit, cause, etc. [C16: from L *dēvōtus* solemnly promised, from *dēvovēre* to vow; see DE-, VOW]

devoted (dɪ'vəʊtɪd) *adj* **1** feeling or demonstrating loyalty or devotion; devout. **2** (*postpositive; foll. by to*) dedicated or consecrated.
▶ **de'votedly** *adv* ▶ **de'votedness** *n*

devotee (,dɛvə'ti:) *n* **1** a person ardently enthusiastic about something, such as a sport or pastime. **2** a zealous follower of a religion.

devotion (dɪ'vəʊʃən) *n* **1** (often foll. by *to*) strong attachment (to) or affection (for a cause, person, etc.) marked by dedicated loyalty. **2** religious zeal; piety. **3** (*often pl*) religious observance or prayers.
▶ **de'votional** *adj*

devour (dɪ'vaʊə) *vb* (*tr*) **1** to eat up greedily or voraciously. **2** to waste or destroy; consume. **3** to consume greedily or avidly with the senses or mind. **4** to engulf or absorb. [C14: from OF, from L *dēvorāre* to gulp down, from DE- + *vorāre*; see VORACIOUS]
▶ **de'vourer** *n* ▶ **de'vouring** *adj*

★ people and places

devout (dɪ'vaʊt) *adj* **1** deeply religious; reverent. **2** sincere; earnest; heartfelt. [C13: from OF *devot*, from LL *dēvōtus*, from L: faithful; see DEVOTE]
▶ de'voutly *adv* ▶ de'voutness *n*

De Vries ★ (*Dutch* də vri:s) *n* Hugo ('hy:xo:). 1848–1935, Dutch botanist, who rediscovered Mendel's laws and developed the mutation theory of evolution.

dew (dju:) *n* **1** drops of water condensed on a cool surface, esp. at night, from vapour in the air. **2** something like this, esp. in freshness: *the dew of youth*. **3** small drops of moisture, such as tears. ◆ *vb* **4** (*tr*) to moisten with or as with dew. [OE *dēaw*]

Dewar ★ ('dju:ə) *n* **1** Donald. born 1937, Scottish Labour politician; secretary of state for Scotland from 1997. **2** Sir James. 1842–1923, Scottish chemist and physicist: invented the vacuum flask.

dewberry ('dju:bərɪ, -brɪ) *n, pl* dewberries. **1** any trailing bramble having blue-black fruits. **2** the fruit of any such plant.

dewclaw ('dju:ˌklɔ:) *n* **1** a nonfunctional claw in dogs. **2** an analogous rudimentary hoof in deer, goats, etc.
▶ 'dew,clawed *adj*

dewdrop ('dju:ˌdrɒp) *n* a drop of dew.

de Wet ★ (də 'vet) *n* Christian Rudolf. 1854–1922, Afrikaner military commander and politician, who led the Orange Free State army in the second Boer War (1899–1902). He was imprisoned for treason (1914) after organizing an Afrikaner nationalist rebellion.

Dewey ★ ('dju:ɪ) *n* John. 1859–1952, US pragmatist philosopher and educator. His works include *Democracy and Education* (1916).

Dewey Decimal System ('dju:ɪ) *n* a system of library book classification with ten main subject classes. Also called: **decimal classification.** [C19: after Melvil *Dewey* (1851–1931), US educator]

dewlap ('dju:ˌlæp) *n* **1** a loose fold of skin hanging from beneath the throat in cattle, dogs, etc. **2** loose skin on an elderly person's throat. [C14 *dewlappe*, from DEW (prob. from an earlier form of different meaning) + LAP¹ (from OE *læppa* hanging flap), ?from ON]

DEW line (dju:) *n acronym for* distant early warning line, a network of radar stations situated mainly in Arctic regions of North America.

dew point *n* the temperature at which dew begins to form.

dew pond *n* a shallow pond, usually man-made, that is kept full by dew and mist.

dewy ('dju:ɪ) *adj* dewier, dewiest. **1** moist with or as with dew. **2** of or resembling dew. **3** *Poetic.* suggesting, falling, or refreshing like dew: *dewy sleep*.
▶ 'dewily *adv* ▶ 'dewiness *n*

dexter ('dɛkstə) *adj* **1** *Arch.* of or located on the right side. **2** (*usually postpositive*) *Heraldry.* of, on, or starting from the right side of a shield from the bearer's point of view and therefore on the spectator's left. ◆ Cf. **sinister.** [C16: from L; cf. Gk *dexios* on the right hand]

dexterity (dɛk'stɛrɪtɪ) *n* **1** physical, esp. manual, skill or nimbleness. **2** mental skill or adroitness. [C16: from L *dexteritās* aptness, readiness; see DEXTER]

dexterous ('dɛkstrəs) *adj* possessing or done with dexterity.
▶ 'dexterously *adv* ▶ 'dexterousness *n*

dextral ('dɛkstrəl) *adj* **1** of or located on the right side, esp. of the body. **2** of a person who prefers to use his right foot, hand, or eye; right-handed. **3** (of shells) coiling in an anticlockwise direction from the apex.
▶ dextrality (dɛk'strælɪtɪ) *n* ▶ 'dextrally *adv*

dextran ('dɛkstrən) *n Biochem.* a chainlike polymer of glucose produced by the action of bacteria on sucrose: used as a substitute for plasma in blood transfusions. [C19: from DEXTRO- + -AN]

dextrin ('dɛkstrɪn) *or* **dextrine** ('dɛkstrɪn, -tri:n) *n* any of a group of sticky substances obtained from starch: used as thickening agents in foods and as gums. [C19: from F *dextrine*; see DEXTRO-, -IN]

dextro- *or before a vowel* **dextr-** *combining form.* on or to-

wards the right: *dextrorotation*. [from L, from *dexter* or the right side]

dextrorotation (ˌdɛkstrəʊrəʊ'teɪʃən) *n* a rotation to the right; clockwise rotation, esp. of the plane of polarization of plane-polarized light. Cf. **laevorotation.**
▶ **dextrorotatory** (ˌdɛkstrəʊ'rəʊtətərɪ, -trɪ) *or* ˌdextro'rotary *adj*

dextrorse ('dɛkstrɔ:s) *or* **dextrorsal** (dɛk'strɔ:s°l) *adj* (of some climbing plants) growing upwards in a spiral from left to right or anticlockwise. [C19: from L *dextrorsum* towards the right, from DEXTRO- + *vorsus*, var of *versus*, from *vertere* to turn]
▶ 'dextrorsely *adv*

dextrose ('dɛkstrəʊz, -trəʊs) *n* a glucose occurring widely in fruit, honey, and in the blood and tissue of animals Formula: $C_6H_{12}O_6$. Also called: **grape sugar, dextroglucose.**

dextrous ('dɛkstrəs) *adj* a variant spelling of **dexterous.**
▶ 'dextrously *adv* ▶ 'dextrousness *n*

Dezhnev ★ (*Russian* dɪʒ'njɔf) *n* Cape. a cape in NE Russia, at the E end of Chukotski Peninsula: the northeastern-most point of Asia. Former name: **East Cape.**

DF *abbrev. for* Defender of the Faith.

D/F *or* **DF** *Telecomm.* ◆ *abbrev. for:* **1** direction finder. **2** direction finding.

DFC *abbrev. for* Distinguished Flying Cross.

DfEE (in Britain) *abbrev. for* Department for Education and Employment.

DFM *abbrev. for* Distinguished Flying Medal.

dg *symbol for* decigram.

DH (in Britain) *abbrev. for* Department of Health.

Dhahran ★ (dɑː'rɑːn) *n* a town in E Saudi Arabia: site of the original discovery of oil in the country (1938).

Dhaka *or* **Dacca** ★ ('dækə) *n* the capital of Bangladesh, in the E central part: capital of Bengal (1608–39; 1660–1704) and of East Pakistan (1949–71); jute and cotton mills; university (1921). Pop.: 3 839 000 (1991).

dhal, dal, *or* **dholl** (dɑːl) *n* **1** a tropical African and Asian shrub cultivated for its nutritious pealike seeds. **2** the seed of this shrub. **3** a curry made from lentils or other pulses. [C17: from Hindi, from Sansk. *dal* to split]

dharma ('dɑːmə) *n* **1** *Hinduism.* social custom regarded as a religious and moral duty. **2** *Hinduism.* **2a** the essential principle of the cosmos; natural law. **2b** conduct that conforms with this. **3** *Buddhism.* ideal truth. [Sansk.: habit, usage, law]

Dhílos ★ ('ðilos) *n* transliteration of the Modern Greek name for **Delos.**

dhobi ('dəʊbɪ) *n, pl* dhobis. (in India, E Africa, etc.) a washerman. [C19: from Hindi, from *dhōb* washing]

Dhodhekánisos ★ (ðɔðe'kanisɔs) *n* a transliteration of the modern Greek name for the **Dodecanese.**

dhoti ('dəʊtɪ), **dhooti, dhootie,** *or* **dhuti** ('du:tɪ) *n, pl* dhotis. a long loincloth worn by men in India. [C17: from Hindi]

dhow (daʊ) *n* a lateen-rigged coastal Arab sailing vessel. [C19: from Ar.]

DHSS (formerly, in Britain) *abbrev. for* Department of Health and Social Security.

DI *abbrev. for* donor insemination.

di. *or* **dia.** *abbrev. for* diameter.

di-¹ *prefix* **1** twice; two; double: *dicotyledon*. **2a** containing two specified atoms or groups of atoms: *carbon dioxide*. **2b** a nontechnical equivalent of **bi-** (sense 5). [via L from Gk, from *dis* twice, double, rel. to *duo* two. Cf. BI-]

di-² *combining form.* a variant of **dia-** before a vowel: *dioptre*.

dia- *or* **di-** *prefix* **1** through or during: *diachronic*. **2** across: *diactinic*. **3** apart: *diacritic*. [from Gk *dia* through, between, across, by]

diabetes (ˌdaɪə'bi:tɪs, -ti:z) *n* any of various disorders, esp. diabetes mellitus, characterized by excessive thirst and excretion of an abnormally large amount of urine. [C16: from L: siphon, from Gk, lit.: a passing through]

diabetes mellitus (mə'laɪtəs) *n* a form of diabetes, caused by a deficiency of insulin, in which the body is

★ people and places

unable to metabolize sugars. [C18: NL, lit.: honey-sweet betes]

diabetic (ˌdaɪəˈbɛtɪk) *adj* **1** of, relating to, or having diabetes. **2** for the use of diabetics. ◆ *n* **3** a person who has diabetes.

diablerie (dɪˈɑːblərɪ) *n* **1** magic or witchcraft connected with devils. **2** esoteric knowledge of devils. **3** devilry; mischief. [C18: from OF, from *diable* devil, from L *diabolus*; see DEVIL]

diabolic (ˌdaɪəˈbɒlɪk) *adj* **1** of the devil; satanic. **2** extremely cruel or wicked; fiendish. **3** very difficult or unpleasant. [C14: from LL, from Gk *diabolikos*, from *diabolos* DEVIL]
▶ ˌdiaˈbolically *adv* ▶ ˌdiaˈbolicalness *n*

diabolical (ˌdaɪəˈbɒlɪkˀl) *adj Inf.* **1** excruciatingly bad. **2** (intensifier): *a diabolical liberty.*
▶ ˌdiaˈbolically *adv* ▶ ˌdiaˈbolicalness *n*

diabolism (daɪˈæbəˌlɪzəm) *n* **1a** witchcraft or sorcery. **1b** worship of devils or beliefs concerning them. **2** character or conduct that is devilish.
▶ diˈabolist *n*

diabolo (dɪˈæbəˌləʊ) *n, pl* **diabolos.** **1** a game in which one throws and catches a top on a cord fastened to two sticks. **2** the top used in this. [C20: from It., lit.: devil]

diachronic (ˌdaɪəˈkrɒnɪk) *adj* of, relating to, or studying the development of a phenomenon through time; historical. Cf. **synchronic.** [C19: from DIA- + Gk *khronos* time]

diacidic (ˌdaɪəˈsɪdɪk) *adj* (of a base) capable of neutralizing two protons with one of its molecules. Also: **diacid.**

diaconal (daɪˈækənˀl) *adj* of or associated with a deacon or the diaconate. [C17: from LL *diāconālis*, from *diāconus* DEACON]

diaconate (daɪˈækənɪt, -ˌneɪt) *n* the office, sacramental status, or period of office of a deacon. [C17: from LL *diāconātus*; see DEACON]

diacritic (ˌdaɪəˈkrɪtɪk) *n* **1** a sign placed above or below a character or letter to indicate that it has a different phonetic value, is stressed, or for some other reason. ◆ *adj* **2** another word for **diacritical.** [C17: from Gk *diakritikos* serving to distinguish, from *diakrinein*, from DIA- + *krinein* to separate]

diacritical (ˌdaɪəˈkrɪtɪkˀl) *adj* **1** of or relating to a diacritic. **2** showing up a distinction.

diadem (ˈdaɪəˌdɛm) *n* **1** a royal crown, esp. a light jewelled circlet. **2** royal dignity or power. [C13: from L, from Gk: fillet, royal headdress, from *diadein*, from DIA- + *dein* to bind]

diaeresis or **dieresis** (daɪˈɛrɪsɪs) *n, pl* **diaereses** or **diereses** (-ˌsiːz). **1** the mark ¨ placed over the second of two adjacent vowels to indicate that it is to be pronounced separately, as in some spellings of *coöperate, naïve,* etc. **2** this mark used for any other purpose, such as to indicate a special pronunciation for a particular vowel. **3** a pause in a line of verse when the end of a foot coincides with the end of a word. [C17: from L, from Gk: a division, from *diairein*, from DIA- + *hairein* to take; cf. HERESY]
▶ **diaeretic** or **dieretic** (ˌdaɪəˈrɛtɪk) *adj*

diag. *abbrev. for* diagram.

Diaghilev ★ (*Russian* ˈdjagɪlif) *n* **Sergei Pavlovich** (sɪrˈgjej ˈpavləvɪtʃ). 1872–1929, Russian ballet impresario. He founded (1909) the *Ballet Russe.*

diagnose (ˈdaɪəɡˌnəʊz) *vb* **diagnoses, diagnosing, diagnosed.** **1** to determine by diagnosis. **2** (*tr*) to examine (a person or thing), as for a disease.
▶ ˌdiagˈnosable *adj*

diagnosis (ˌdaɪəɡˈnəʊsɪs) *n, pl* **diagnoses** (-siːz). **1a** the identification of diseases from the examination of symptoms. **1b** an opinion so reached. **2a** a thorough analysis of facts or problems in order to gain understanding. **2b** an opinion reached through such analysis. [C17: NL, from Gk: a distinguishing, from *diagignōskein,* from *gignōskein* to perceive, KNOW]
▶ **diagnostic** (ˌdaɪəɡˈnɒstɪk) *adj*

diagonal (daɪˈæɡənˀl) *adj* **1** *Maths.* connecting any two vertices that are not adjacent and in a polyhedron are not in the same face. **2** slanting; oblique. **3** marked with slanting lines or patterns. ◆ *n* **4** a diagonal

line, plane, or pattern. **5** something put, set, or drawn obliquely. [C16: from L, from Gk *diagōnios,* from DIA- + *gōnia* angle]
▶ diˈagonally *adv*

diagram (ˈdaɪəˌɡræm) *n* **1** a sketch or plan demonstrating the form or workings of something. **2** *Maths.* a pictorial representation of a quantity or of a relationship. ◆ *vb* **diagrams, diagramming, diagrammed** or *US* **diagrams, diagraming, diagramed.** **3** to show in or as if in a diagram. [C17: from L, from Gk, from *diagraphein,* from *graphein* to write]
▶ **diagrammatic** (ˌdaɪəɡrəˈmætɪk) *adj*

dial (ˈdaɪəl) *n* **1** the face of a watch, clock, etc., marked with divisions representing units of time. **2** the graduated disc of various measuring instruments. **3a** the control on a radio or television set used to change the station or channel. **3b** the panel on a radio on which the frequency, wavelength, or station is indicated. **4** a numbered disc on a telephone that is rotated a set distance for each digit of a number being called. **5** *Brit.* a slang word for **face.** ◆ *vb* **dials, dialling, dialled** or *US* **dials, dialing, dialed.** **6** to try to establish a telephone connection with (a subscriber) by operating the dial or buttons on a telephone. **7** (*tr*) to indicate, measure, or operate with a dial. [C14: from Med. L *diālis* daily, from L *diēs* day]
▶ **'dialler** or *US* **'dialer** *n*

dial. *abbrev. for* dialect(al).

dialect (ˈdaɪəˌlɛkt) *n* **a** a form of a language spoken in a particular geographical area or by members of a particular social class or occupational group, distinguished by its vocabulary, grammar, and pronunciation. **b** a form of a language that is considered inferior. [C16: from L, from Gk *dialektos* speech, dialect, discourse, from *dialegesthai* to converse, from *legein* to talk, speak]
▶ ˌdiaˈlectal *adj*

dialectic (ˌdaɪəˈlɛktɪk) *n* **1** disputation or debate, esp. when intended to resolve differences between two views. **2** logical argumentation. **3** a variant of **dialectics** (sense 1). **4** *Philosophy.* an interpretive method used by Hegel in which contradictions are resolved at a higher level of truth (synthesis). ◆ *adj* **5** of or relating to logical disputation. [C17: from L, from Gk *dialektikē (tekhnē)* (the art) of argument; see DIALECT]
▶ ˌdialecˈtician *n*

dialectical (ˌdaɪəˈlɛktɪkˀl) *adj* of or relating to dialectic or dialectics.
▶ ˌdiaˈlectically *adv*

dialectical materialism *n* the economic, political, and philosophical system of Marx and Engels that combines traditional materialism and Hegelian dialectic.

dialectics (ˌdaɪəˈlɛktɪks) *n* (*functioning as pl or* (*sometimes*) *sing*) **1** the study of reasoning. **2** a particular methodology or system. **3** the application of the Hegelian dialectic or the rationale of dialectical materialism.

dialling code *n* a sequence of numbers which is dialled for connection with another exchange before an individual subscriber's telephone number is dialled.

dialling tone or *US & Canad.* **dial tone** *n* a continuous sound, either purring or high-pitched, heard over a telephone indicating that a number can be dialled.

dialogue or *US* (*often*) **dialog** (ˈdaɪəˌlɒg) *n* **1** conversation between two or more people. **2** an exchange of opinions; discussion. **3** the lines spoken by characters in drama or fiction. **4** a passage of conversation in a literary or dramatic work. **5** a literary composition in the form of a dialogue. **6** a political discussion between representatives of two nations or groups. [C13: from OF, from L, from Gk, from *dialegesthai*; see DIALECT]

dialyse or *US* **dialyze** (ˈdaɪəˌlaɪz) *vb* **dialyses, dialysing, dialysed** or *US* **dialyzes, dialyzing, dialyzed.** (*tr*) to separate by dialysis.
▶ ˌdialyˈsation or *US* ˌdialyˈzation *n*

dialyser or *US* **dialyzer** (ˈdaɪəˌlaɪzə) *n* a machine that performs dialysis, esp. one that removes impurities from the blood of patients with malfunctioning kidneys; kidney machine.

dialysis (daɪˈælɪsɪs) *n, pl* **dialyses** (-ˌsiːz). **1** the separation of small molecules from large molecules and colloids in

a solution by the selective diffusion of the small molecules through a semipermeable membrane. **2** *Med.* the filtering of blood through a semipermeable membrane to remove waste products. [C16: from LL: a separation, from Gk *dialusis*, from *dialuein* to tear apart, dissolve, from *luein* to loosen]
▶ **dialytic** (ˌdaɪə'lɪtɪk) *adj*

diam. *abbrev. for* diameter.

diamagnetic (ˌdaɪəmæg'nɛtɪk) *adj* of, exhibiting, or concerned with diamagnetism.

diamagnetism (ˌdaɪə'mægnɪˌtɪzəm) *n* the phenomenon exhibited by substances that have a relative permeability less than unity and a negative susceptibility; caused by the orbital motion of electrons in the atoms of the material.

diamanté (ˌdaɪə'mæntɪ) *adj* **1** decorated with glittering ornaments, such as sequins. ◆ *n* **2** a fabric so covered. [C20: from F, from *diamanter* to adorn with diamonds]

diameter (daɪ'æmɪtə) *n* **1a** a straight line connecting the centre of a circle, sphere, etc. with two points on the perimeter or surface. **1b** the length of such a line. **2** the thickness of something, esp. with circular cross section. [C14: from Med. L, from Gk: diameter, diagonal, from DIA- + *metron* measure]

diametric (ˌdaɪə'mɛtrɪk) *or* **diametrical** *adj* **1** Also: **diametral**. of, related to, or along a diameter. **2** completely opposed.

diametrically (ˌdaɪə'mɛtrɪkəlɪ) *adv* completely; utterly (esp. in **diametrically opposed**).

diamond ('daɪəmənd) *n* **1a** a usually colourless exceptionally hard form of carbon in cubic crystalline form. It is used as a precious stone and for industrial cutting or abrading. **1b** (*as modifier*): *a diamond ring.* **2** *Geom.* a figure having four sides of equal length forming two acute angles and two obtuse angles; rhombus. **3a** a red lozenge-shaped symbol on a playing card. **3b** a card with one or more of these symbols or (*when pl*) the suit of cards so marked. **4** *Baseball.* **4a** the whole playing field. **4b** the square formed by the four bases. ◆ *vb* **5** (*tr*) to decorate with or as with diamonds. [C13: from OF *diamant*, from Med. L *diamas*, from L *adamas* the hardest iron or steel, diamond; see ADAMANT]
▶ **diamantine** (ˌdaɪə'mæntaɪn) *adj*

diamond anniversary *n* a 60th, or occasionally 75th, anniversary.

diamondback ('daɪəmənd,bæk) *n* **1** Also called: **diamondback terrapin** *or* **turtle**. any edible North American terrapin having diamond-shaped markings on the shell. **2** a large North American rattlesnake having diamond-shaped markings.

diamond wedding *n* the 60th, or occasionally 75th, anniversary of a marriage.

diamorphine (ˌdaɪə'mɔːfiːn) *n* a technical name for **heroin**.

Diana ★ (daɪ'ænə) *n* **1** the virginal Roman goddess of the hunt and the moon. Greek counterpart: **Artemis**. **2** title *Diana, Princess of Wales*, original name *Lady Diana Frances Spencer*. 1961–97, she married Charles, Prince of Wales, in 1981; they were divorced in 1996.

dianthus (daɪ'ænθəs) *n, pl* **dianthuses**. any Eurasian plant of the widely cultivated genus *Dianthus*, such as the carnation, pink, and sweet william. [C19: NL, from Gk DI-[1] + *anthos* flower]

diapason (ˌdaɪə'peɪzˀn) *n Music.* **1** either of two stops (**open** and **stopped diapason**) found throughout the compass of a pipe organ that give it its characteristic tone colour. **2** the compass of an instrument or voice. **3a** a standard pitch used for tuning. **3b** a tuning fork or pitch pipe. **4** (in classical Greece) an octave. [C14: from L: the whole octave, from Gk: (*hē*) *dia pasōn* (*khordōn sumphōnia*) (concord) through all (the notes)]

diapause ('daɪə,pɔːz) *n* a period of suspended development, growth and growth accompanied by decreased metabolism in insects and some other animals. [C19: from Gk *diapausis* pause, from *diapauein* to pause, bring to an end, from DIA- + *pauein* to stop]

diaper ('daɪəpə) *n* **1** the US and Canad. word for **nappy**[1].

2a a fabric having a pattern of a small repeating design, esp. diamonds. **2b** such a pattern, used as decoration. ◆ *vb* **3** (*tr*) to decorate with such a pattern. [C14: from OF *diaspre*, from Med. L *diasprus* made of diaper, from Med. Gk *diaspros* pure white, from DIA- + *aspros* white, shining]

diaphanous (daɪ'æfənəs) *adj* (usually of fabrics) fine and translucent. [C17: from Med. L, from Gk *diaphanēs* transparent, from DIA- + *phainein* to show]
▶ **di'aphanously** *adv*

diaphoresis (ˌdaɪəfə'riːsɪs) *n* perspiration, esp. when perceptible and excessive. [C17: via LL from Gk, from *diaphorein* to disperse by perspiration, from DIA- + *phorein* to carry]

diaphoretic (ˌdaɪəfə'rɛtɪk) *adj* **1** relating to or causing perspiration. ◆ *n* **2** a diaphoretic drug.

diaphragm ('daɪə,fræm) *n* **1** *Anat.* any separating membrane, esp. the muscular partition that separates the abdominal and thoracic cavities in mammals. **2** another name for **cap** (sense 11). **3** any thin dividing membrane. **4** Also called: **stop**. a device to control the amount of light entering an optical instrument, such as a camera. **5** a thin vibrating disc used to convert sound signals to electrical signals or vice versa in telephones, etc. [C17: from LL, from Gk, from DIA- + *phragma* fence]
▶ **diaphragmatic** (ˌdaɪəfræg'mætɪk) *adj*

diapositive (ˌdaɪə'pɒzɪtɪv) *n* a positive transparency; slide.

diarist ('daɪərɪst) *n* a person who writes a diary, esp. one that is subsequently published.

diarrhoea *or esp. US* **diarrhea** (ˌdaɪə'rɪə) *n* frequent and copious discharge of abnormally liquid faeces. [C16: from LL, from Gk, from *diarrhein*, from DIA- + *rhein* to flow]
▶ ,**diar'rhoeal**, ,**diar'rhoeic** *or esp. US* ,**diar'rheal**, ,**diar'rheic** *adj*

diary ('daɪərɪ) *n, pl* **diaries**. **1** a personal record of daily events, appointments, observations, etc. **2** a book for this. [C16: from L *diārium* daily allocation of food or money, journal, from *diēs* day]

Dias *or* **Diaz** ★ ('diːəs; *Portuguese* 'diəʃ) *n* **Bartholomeu** (ˌbərtuluː'meu). ?1450–1500, Portuguese navigator.

Diaspora (daɪ'æspərə) *n* **1a** the dispersion of the Jews after the Babylonian and Roman conquests of Palestine. **1b** the Jewish people and communities outside Israel. **2** (*often not cap.*) a dispersion, as of people originally belonging to one nation. [C19: from Gk: a scattering, from *diaspeirein*, from DIA- + *speirein* to scatter, sow]

diastalsis (ˌdaɪə'stælsɪs) *n, pl* **diastalses** (-siːz). *Physiol.* a downward wave of contraction occurring in the intestine during digestion. [C20: NL, from DIA- + (PERI)-STALSIS]
▶ ,**dia'staltic** *adj*

diastase ('daɪə,steɪs, -,steɪz) *n* any of a group of enzymes that hydrolyse starch to maltose. They are present in germinated barley and in the pancreas. [C19: from F, from Gk *diastasis* a separation]
▶ ,**dia'stasic** *adj*

diastole (daɪ'æstəlɪ) *n* the dilation of the chambers of the heart that follows each contraction, during which they refill with blood. Cf. **systole**. [C16: via LL from Gk, from *diastellein* to expand, from DIA- + *stellein* to place, bring together, make ready]
▶ **diastolic** (ˌdaɪə'stɒlɪk) *adj*

diastrophism (daɪ'æstrə,fɪzəm) *n* the process of movement of the earth's crust that gives rise to mountains, continents, and other large-scale features. [C19: from Gk *diastrophē* a twisting; see DIA-, STROPHE]
▶ **diastrophic** (ˌdaɪə'strɒfɪk) *adj*

diathermancy (ˌdaɪə'θɜːmənsɪ) *n, pl* **diathermancies**. the property of transmitting infrared radiation. [C19: from F, from DIA- + Gk *thermansis* heating, from *thermos* hot]
▶ ,**dia'thermanous** *adj*

diathermy ('daɪə,θɜːmɪ) *or* **diathermia** (ˌdaɪə'θɜːmɪə) *n* local heating of the body tissues with an electric current for medical purposes. [C20: from NL, from DIA- + *thermē* heat]

diatom ('daɪətəm) *n* a microscopic unicellular alga having a cell wall impregnated with silica. [C19: from NL, from Gk *diatomos* cut in two, from DIA- + *temnein* to cut]

diatomaceous (ˌdaɪətə'meɪʃəs) *adj* of or containing diatoms or their fossil remains.

diatomic (ˌdaɪə'tɒmɪk) *adj* (of a compound or molecule) containing two atoms.

diatomite (daɪ'ætəˌmaɪt) *n* a soft whitish rock consisting of the siliceous remains of diatoms.

diatonic (ˌdaɪə'tɒnɪk) *adj* **1** of, relating to, or based upon any scale of five tones and two semitones produced by playing the white keys of a keyboard instrument. **2** not involving the sharpening or flattening of the notes of the major or minor scale nor the use of such notes as modified by accidentals. [C16: from LL, from Gk, from *diatonos* extending, from DIA- + *teinein* to stretch]

diatonic scale *n Music.* the major and minor scales, made up of both tones and semitones.

diatribe ('daɪəˌtraɪb) *n* a bitter or violent criticism or attack. [C16: from L *diatriba* learned debate, from Gk *diatribē* discourse, pastime, from *diatribein* to while away, from DIA- + *tribein* to rub]

Díaz de Vivar ★ (*Spanish* 'diaθ dɛ bi'βar) *n* **Rodrigo** (rɔ'ðriɣo). the original name of (El) **Cid.**

diazepam (daɪ'æzəˌpæm) *n* a chemical compound used as a tranquillizer and muscle relaxant. [C20: from DI-[1] + *azo- + ep(oxide) + -am*]

diazo (daɪ'eɪzəʊ) *adj* **1** of, consisting of, or containing the divalent group, =N:N, or the divalent group, -N:N-. **2** of the reproduction of documents using the bleaching action of ultraviolet radiation on diazonium salts. ♦ *n, pl* **diazos** *or* **diazoes**. **3** a document produced by this method.

diazonium (ˌdaɪə'zəʊnɪəm) *n* (modifier) of, consisting of, or containing the group ArN:N–, where Ar is an aryl group: *a diazonium salt.*

dibasic (daɪ'beɪsɪk) *adj* **1** (of an acid) containing two acidic hydrogen atoms. **2** (of a salt) derived by replacing two acidic hydrogen atoms.
▸ **dibasicity** (ˌdaɪbeɪ'sɪsɪtɪ) *n*

dibble ('dɪb°l) *n* **1** Also: **dibber.** a small hand tool used to make holes in the ground for bulbs, seeds, or roots. ♦ *vb* **dibbles, dibbling, dibbled. 2** to make a hole in (the ground) with a dibble. **3** to plant (seeds, etc.) with a dibble. [C15: from ?]

dibs (dɪbz) *pl n* **1** another word for **jacks. 2** *Sl.* money. **3** (foll. by *on*) *Inf.* rights (to) or claims (on): used mainly by children. [C18: from *dibstones* game played with knucklebones or pebbles, prob. from *dib* to tap]

dice (daɪs) *pl n* **1** cubes of wood, plastic, etc., each of whose sides has a different number of spots (1 to 6), used in games of chance. **2** (*functioning as sing*) Also called: **die.** one of these cubes. **3** small cubes as of vegetables, meat, etc. **4 no dice.** *Sl., chiefly US & Canad.* an expression of refusal. ♦ *vb* **dices, dicing, diced. 5** to cut (food, etc.) into small cubes. **6** (*intr*) to gamble or play with dice. **7** (*intr*) to take a chance or risk (esp. in **dice with death**). **8** (*tr*) *Austral. inf.* to abandon or reject. [C14: pl of DIE[2]]
▸ **'dicer** *n*

dicey ('daɪsɪ) *adj* **dicier, diciest.** *Inf., chiefly Brit.* difficult or dangerous; risky; tricky.

dichloride (daɪ'klɔːraɪd) *n* a compound in which two atoms of chlorine are combined with another atom or group. Also called: **bichloride.**

dichlorodiphenyltrichloroethane (daɪˌklɔːrəʊˌdaɪˌfiːˌnaɪltraɪˌklɔːrəʊ'iːθeɪn) *n* the full name for **DDT.**

dichloromethane (daɪˌklɔːrəʊ'miːθeɪn) *n* a noxious colourless liquid widely used as a solvent, e.g. in paint strippers. Formula: CH_2Cl_2. Traditional name: **methylene dichloride.**

dichotomy (daɪ'kɒtəmɪ) *n, pl* **dichotomies. 1** division into two parts or classifications, esp. when they are sharply distinguished or opposed. **2** *Bot.* a simple method of branching by repeated division into two equal parts.
▸ **di'chotomous** *adj*

USAGE NOTE *Dichotomy* should always refer to a division of some kind into two groups. It is sometimes used to refer to a puzzling situation which seems to involve a contradiction, but this use is generally thought to be incorrect.

dichroism ('daɪkrəʊˌɪzəm) *n* a property of a uniaxial crystal of showing a difference in colour when viewed along two different axes (in transmitted white light). Also called: **dichromaticism.** See also **pleochroism.**
▸ **di'chroic** *adj*

dichromate (daɪ'krəʊmeɪt) *n* any salt or ester of dichromic acid. Also called: **bichromate.**

dichromatic (ˌdaɪkrəʊ'mætɪk) *adj* **1** Also: **dichroic.** having two colours. **2** (of animal species) having two different colour varieties. **3** able to perceive only two colours (and mixes of them).
▸ **dichromatism** (daɪ'krəʊməˌtɪzəm) *n*

dichromic (daɪ'krəʊmɪk) *adj* of or involving only two colours; dichromatic.

dick (dɪk) *n Sl.* **1** *Brit.* a fellow or person. **2 clever dick.** *Brit.* an opinionated person; know-all. **3** a taboo word for **penis.** [C16 (meaning: fellow): from *Dick*, familiar form of *Richard*, applied to any fellow, lad, etc.; hence, C19: penis]

dickens ('dɪkɪnz) *n Inf.* a euphemistic word for **devil** (used as intensifier in **what the dickens**). [C16: from the name *Dickens*]

Dickens ★ ('dɪkɪnz) *n* **Charles** (**John Huffam**), pen name *Boz.* 1812–70, British novelist. His works include *Pickwick Papers* (1837), *Oliver Twist* (1839), *Nicholas Nickleby* (1839), *Old Curiosity Shop* (1840–41), *Martin Chuzzlewit* (1844), *David Copperfield* (1850), *Bleak House* (1853), *Little Dorrit* (1857), and *Great Expectations* (1861).

Dickensian (dɪ'kɛnzɪən) *adj* **1** of Charles Dickens or his novels. **2a** denoting poverty, distress, and exploitation as depicted in the novels of Dickens. **2b** grotesquely comic, as some of the characters of Dickens.

dicker ('dɪkə) *vb* **1** to trade (goods) by bargaining; barter. ♦ *n* **2** a petty bargain or barter. [C12: ult. from L *decuria* company of ten, from *decem* ten]

dickhead ('dɪkˌhɛd) *n Sl.* a stupid or despicable man or boy. [C20: from DICK (in the sense: penis) + HEAD]

Dickinson ★ ('dɪkɪns°n) *n* **Emily.** 1830–86, US poet.

dicky[1] *or* **dickey** ('dɪkɪ) *n, pl* **dickies** *or* **dickeys. 1** a false blouse or shirt front. **2** Also called: **dicky bow.** *Brit.* a bow tie. **3** Also called: **dicky-bird, dickeybird.** a child's word for a bird. **4** a folding outside seat at the rear of some early cars. [C18 (in the sense: shirt front): from *Dickey*, dim. of *Dick* (name)]

dicky[2] *or* **dickey** ('dɪkɪ) *adj* **dickier, dickiest.** *Brit. inf.* shaky, unsteady, or unreliable: *I feel a bit dicky today.* [C18: ?from *as queer as Dick's hatband* feeling ill]

diclinous ('daɪklɪnəs) *adj* (of flowering plants) unisexual. Cf. **monoclinous.**
▸ **'diclinism** *n*

dicotyledon (ˌdaɪkɒtɪ'liːd°n) *n* a flowering plant having two embryonic seed leaves.
▸ **ˌdicoty'ledonous** *adj*

dict. *abbrev. for:* **1** dictation. **2** dictator. **3** dictionary.

dicta ('dɪktə) *n* a plural of **dictum.**

Dictaphone ('dɪktəˌfəʊn) *n Trademark.* a tape recorder designed for recording dictation for subsequent typing.

dictate *vb* (dɪk'teɪt), **dictates, dictating, dictated. 1** to say (letters, speeches, etc.) aloud for mechanical recording or verbatim transcription by another person. **2** (*tr*) to prescribe (commands, etc.) authoritatively. **3** (*intr*) to seek to impose one's will on others. ♦ *n* ('dɪkteɪt). **4** an authoritative command. **5** a guiding principle: *the dictates of reason.* [C17: from L *dictāre* to say repeatedly, order, from *dīcere* to say]

dictation (dɪk'teɪʃən) *n* **1** the act of dictating material to be recorded or taken down in writing. **2** the material dictated. **3** authoritative commands or the act of giving them.

dictator (dɪk'teɪtə) n **1a** a ruler who is not effectively restricted by a constitution, laws, etc. **1b** an absolute, esp. tyrannical, ruler. **2** (in ancient Rome) a person appointed during a crisis to exercise supreme authority. **3** a person who makes pronouncements, which are regarded as authoritative. **4** a person who behaves in an authoritarian or tyrannical manner.

dictatorial (ˌdɪktə'tɔːrɪəl) adj **1** of or characteristic of a dictator. **2** tending to dictate; tyrannical; overbearing.
▶ ˌdicta'torially adv

dictatorship (dɪk'teɪtəˌʃɪp) n **1** the rank, office, or period of rule of a dictator. **2** government by a dictator. **3** a country ruled by a dictator. **4** absolute power or authority.

diction ('dɪkʃən) n **1** the choice of words in writing or speech. **2** the manner of enunciating words and sounds. [C15: from L dictiō a saying, mode of expression, from dīcere to speak, say]

dictionary ('dɪkʃənərɪ) n, pl **dictionaries. 1a** a book that consists of an alphabetical list of words with their meanings, parts of speech, pronunciations, etymologies, etc. **1b** a similar book giving equivalent words in two or more languages. **2** a reference book listing words or terms and giving information about a particular subject or activity. **3** a collection of information or examples with the entries alphabetically arranged: a dictionary of quotations. [C16: from Med. L dictiōnārium collection of words, from LL dictiō word; see DICTION]

dictum ('dɪktəm) n, pl **dictums** or **dicta. 1** a formal or authoritative statement; pronouncement. **2** a popular saying or maxim. **3** Law. See **obiter dictum.** [C16: from L, from dīcere to say]

did (dɪd) vb the past tense of **do**[1].

didactic (dɪ'dæktɪk) adj **1** intended to instruct, esp. excessively. **2** morally instructive. **3** (of works of art or literature) containing a political or moral message to which aesthetic considerations are subordinated. [C17: from Gk didaktikos skilled in teaching, from didaskein]
▶ di'dactically adv ▶ di'dacticism n

didactics (dɪ'dæktɪks) n (functioning as sing) the art or science of teaching.

diddle ('dɪdᵊl) vb **diddles, diddling, diddled.** (tr) Inf. to cheat or swindle. [C19: back formation from Jeremy Diddler, a scrounger in J. Kenney's farce Raising the Wind (1803)]
▶ 'diddler n

Diderot ★ ('diːdərəʊ; French didro) n **Denis** (dəni). 1713–84, French philosopher, noted for the Encyclopédie.

didgeridoo (ˌdɪdʒərɪ'duː) n Music. a native deep-toned Australian wind instrument. [C20: imit.]

didn't ('dɪdᵊnt) contraction of did not.

dido ('daɪdəʊ) n, pl **didos** or **didoes.** (usually pl) Inf. an antic; prank; trick. [C19: from ?]

Dido ★ ('daɪdəʊ) n Classical myth. a princess of Tyre who founded Carthage and became its queen. Virgil tells of her suicide when abandoned by her lover Aeneas.

didst (dɪdst) vb Arch. (used with thou) a form of the past tense of **do**[1].

didymium (daɪ'dɪmɪəm) n a mixture of the metallic rare earths neodymium and praseodymium, once thought to be an element. [C19: from NL, from Gk didumos twin + -IUM]

die[1] (daɪ) vb **dies, dying, died.** (mainly intr) **1** (of an organism, organs, etc.) to cease all biological activity permanently. **2** (of something inanimate) to cease to exist. **3** (often foll. by away, down, or out) to lose strength, power, or energy, esp. by degrees. **4** (often foll. by away or down) to become calm; subside. **5** to stop functioning: the engine died. **6** to languish, as with love, longing, etc. **7** (usually foll. by of) Inf. to be nearly overcome (with laughter, boredom, etc.). **8** Christianity. to lack spiritual life within the soul. **9** (tr) to suffer (a death of a specified kind): he died a saintly death. **10 be dying.** (foll. by for or an infinitive) to be eager or desperate (for something or to do something). **11 die hard.** to cease to exist after a struggle: old habits die hard. **12 die in harness.** to die while still working or active. **13 never say die.** Inf. never give up. ◆ See also **die down, die out.** [OE dīegan, prob. of Scand. origin]

die[2] (daɪ) n **1a** a shaped block used to cut or form metal in a drop forge, press, etc. **1b** a tool with a conical hole through which wires, etc. are drawn to reduce their diameter. **2** an internally-threaded tool for cutting external threads. **3** a casting mould. **4** Archit. the dado of a pedestal, usually cubic. **5** another name for **dice** (sense 2). **6 the die is cast.** the irrevocable decision has been taken. [C13 dee, from OF de, ?from Vulgar L datum (unattested) a piece in games, from L dare to give, play]

die-cast vb **die-casts, die-casting, die-cast.** (tr) to shape or form (an object) by introducing molten metal or plastic into a reusable mould, esp. under pressure.
▶ 'die-ˌcasting n

die down vb (intr, adv) **1** (of plants) to wither above ground, leaving only the root alive during the winter. **2** to lose strength or power, esp. by degrees. **3** to become calm.

Diefenbaker ★ ('diːfᵊnˌbeɪkə) n **John George.** 1895–1979, Canadian Conservative statesman; prime minister (1957–63).

die-hard n **1** a person who resists change or who holds onto an untenable position. **2** (modifier) obstinately resistant to change.

dieldrin ('diːldrɪn) n a crystalline substance, consisting of a chlorinated derivative of naphthalene: a contact insecticide the use of which is now restricted. [C20: from Diel(s-Al)d(e)r (reaction) + -IN; Diels & Alder were G chemists]

dielectric (ˌdaɪɪ'lɛktrɪk) n **1** a substance that can sustain an electric field. **2** a substance of very low electrical conductivity; insulator. ◆ adj **3** concerned with or having the properties of a dielectric. [from DIA- + ELECTRIC]
▶ ˌdie'lectrically adv

Dien Bien Phu ★ (ˌdjɛn bjɛn 'fuː) n a village in NW Vietnam: French military post during the Indochina War; scene of a major defeat of French forces by the Vietminh (1954).

diene ('daɪiːn) n Chem. a hydrocarbon that contains two carbon-to-carbon double bonds in its molecules. [from DI-[1] + -ENE]

die out or **off** vb (intr, adv) **1** to die one after another until few or none are left. **2** to become extinct, esp. after a period of gradual decline.

Dieppe ★ (dɪ'ɛp; French djɛp) n a port and resort in N France, on the English Channel. Pop.: 36 600 (1990).

dieresis (daɪ'ɛrɪsɪs) n, pl **diereses** (-ˌsiːz). a variant spelling of **diaeresis.**

diesel ('diːzᵊl) n **1** See **diesel engine. 2** a ship, locomotive, lorry, etc., driven by a diesel engine. **3** Inf. short for **diesel oil** (or **fuel**).

Diesel ★ ('diːzᵊl) n **Rudolf** ('ruːdɔlf). 1858–1913, German engineer, who invented the diesel engine (1892).

diesel-electric n **1** a locomotive fitted with a diesel engine driving an electric generator that feeds electric traction motors. ◆ adj **2** of or relating to such a locomotive or system.

diesel engine or **motor** n a type of internal-combustion engine in which atomized fuel oil is ignited by compression alone.

diesel oil or **fuel** n a fuel obtained from petroleum distillation that is used in diesel engines. Also called (Brit.): **derv.**

Dies Irae Latin. ('diːeɪz 'ɪraɪ) n **1** a Latin hymn of the 13th century, describing the Last Judgment. It is used in the Mass for the dead. **2** a musical setting of this. [lit.: day of wrath]

diesis ('daɪɪsɪs) n, pl **dieses** (-ˌsiːz). Printing. another name for **double dagger.** [C16: via L from Gk: a quarter tone, lit.: a sending through, from diienai; the double dagger was orig. used in musical notation]

diestock ('daɪ,stɒk) *n* the device holding the dies used to cut an external screw thread.

diet[1] ('daɪət) *n* **1** a specific allowance or selection of food, esp. prescribed to control weight or for health reasons: *a salt-free diet*. **2** the food and drink that a person or animal regularly consumes. **3** regular activities or occupations. ◆ *vb* **4** (*usually intr*) to follow or cause to follow a dietary regimen. [C13: from OF *diete*, from L *diaeta*, from Gk *diaita* mode of living, from *diaitan* to direct one's own life]
▶ **'dieter** *n*

diet[2] ('daɪət) *n* **1** (*sometimes cap.*) a legislative assembly in various countries. **2** (*sometimes cap.*) the assembly of the estates of the Holy Roman Empire. **3** *Scots Law*. a single session of a court. [C15: from Med. L *diēta* public meeting, prob. from L *diaeta* DIET[1] but associated with L *diēs* day]

dietary ('daɪətərɪ, -trɪ) *adj* **1** of or relating to a diet. ◆ *n, pl* **dietaries**. **2** a regulated diet. **3** a system of dieting.

dietary fibre *n* fibrous substances in fruits and vegetables, such as the structural polymers of cell walls, which aid digestion. Also called: **roughage**.

dietetic (,daɪɪ'tɛtɪk) *or* **dietetical** *adj* **1** denoting or relating to diet. **2** prepared for special dietary requirements.
▶ ,**die'tetically** *adv*

dietetics (,daɪɪ'tɛtɪks) *n* (*functioning as sing*) the scientific study and regulation of food intake and preparation.

diethylene glycol *n* a colourless soluble liquid used as an antifreeze and solvent.

dietitian *or* **dietician** (,daɪɪ'tɪʃən) *n* a person who specializes in dietetics.

Dietrich ★ (*German* 'diːtrɪç) *n* **Marlene** (marˈleːnə), real name *Maria Magdalene von Losch*. 1901–92, US actress, born in Germany.

differ ('dɪfə) *vb* (*intr*) **1** (often foll. by *from*) to be dissimilar in quality, nature, or degree (to); vary (from). **2** (often foll. by *from* or *with*) to disagree (with). **3** *Dialect*. to quarrel or dispute. [C14: from L *differre*, to scatter, put off, be different, from *dis-* apart + *ferre* to bear]

difference ('dɪfərəns) *n* **1** the state or quality of being unlike. **2** a specific instance of being unlike. **3** a distinguishing mark or feature. **4** a significant change. **5** a disagreement or argument. **6** a degree of distinctness, as between two people or things. **7** Also called: **remainder**. the result of the subtraction of one number, quantity, etc., from another. **8** *Maths*. (of two sets) the set of members of the first that are not members of the second. **9** *Heraldry*. an addition to the arms of a family to represent a younger branch. **10 make a difference**. **10a** to have an effect. **10b** to treat differently. **11 split the difference**. **11a** to compromise. **11b** to divide a remainder equally. **12 with a difference**. with some distinguishing quality, good or bad.

different ('dɪfərənt) *adj* **1** partly or completely unlike. **2** not identical or the same; other. **3** unusual.
▶ **'differently** *adv* ▶ **'differentness** *n*

differentia (,dɪfə'rɛnʃɪə) *n, pl* **differentiae** (-ʃɪ,iː). *Logic*. a feature by which two subclasses of the same class or named objects can be distinguished. [C19: from L: difversity]

differential (,dɪfə'rɛnʃəl) *adj* **1** of, relating to, or using a difference. **2** constituting a difference; distinguishing. **3** *Maths*. involving one or more derivatives or differentials. **4** *Physics, engineering*. relating to, operating on, or based on the difference between two opposing effects, motions, forces, etc. ◆ *n* **5** a factor that differentiates between two comparable things. **6** *Maths*. **6a** an increment in a given function, expressed as the product of the derivative of that function and the corresponding increment in the independent variable. **6b** an increment in a given function of two or more variables, $f(x_1, x_2, ... x_n)$, expressed as the sum of the products of each partial derivative and the increment in the corresponding variable. **7** See **differential gear**. **8** *Chiefly Brit.* the difference between rates of pay for different types of labour, esp. when forming a pay structure within an industry. **9** (in commerce) a difference in rates, esp. between comparable services.
▶ ,**differ'entially** *adv*

differential calculus *n* the branch of calculus concerned with the study, evaluation, and use of derivatives and differentials.

differential equation *n* an equation containing differentials or derivatives of a function of one independent variable.

differential gear *n* the epicyclic gear mounted in the driving axle of a road vehicle that permits one driving wheel to rotate faster than the other, as when cornering.

differential operator *n* the mathematical operator del, ∇, used in vector analysis.

differentiate (,dɪfə'rɛnʃɪ,eɪt) *vb* **differentiates, differentiating, differentiated**. **1** (*tr*) to serve to distinguish between. **2** (when *intr*, often foll. by *between*) to perceive, show, or make a difference (in or between); discriminate. **3** (*intr*) to become dissimilar or distinct. **4** *Maths*. to perform a differentiation on (a quantity, expression, etc.). **5** (*intr*) (of unspecialized cells, etc.) to change during development to more specialized forms.
▶ ,**differ'enti,ator** *n*

differentiation (,dɪfə,rɛnʃɪ'eɪʃən) *n* **1** the act, process, or result of differentiating. **2** *Maths*. an operation used in calculus in which the derivative of a function or variable is determined.

difficult ('dɪfɪkˀlt) *adj* **1** not easy to do; requiring effort. **2** not easy to understand or solve. **3** troublesome: *a difficult child*. **4** not easily convinced, pleased, or satisfied. **5** full of hardships or trials. [C14: back formation from DIFFICULTY]
▶ **'difficultly** *adv*

difficulty ('dɪfɪkˀltɪ) *n, pl* **difficulties**. **1** the state or quality of being difficult. **2** a task, problem, etc., that is hard to deal with. **3** (*often pl*) a troublesome or embarrassing situation, esp. a financial one. **4** a disagreement. **5** (*often pl*) an objection or obstacle. **6** a trouble or source of trouble; worry. **7** lack of ease; awkwardness. [C14: from L *difficultās*, from *difficilis*, from *dis-* not + *facilis* easy]

diffident ('dɪfɪdənt) *adj* lacking self-confidence; shy. [C15: from L *diffīdere*, from *dis-* not + *fīdere* to trust]
▶ **'diffidence** *n* ▶ **'diffidently** *adv*

diffract (dɪ'frækt) *vb* to undergo or cause to undergo diffraction.
▶ **dif'fractive** *adj* ▶ **dif'fractively** *adv* ▶ **dif'fractiveness** *n*

diffraction (dɪ'frækʃən) *n* **1** *Physics*. a deviation in the direction of a wave at the edge of an obstacle in its path. **2** any phenomenon caused by diffraction, such as the formation of light and dark fringes by the passage of light through a small aperture. [C17: from NL *diffractiō* a breaking to pieces, from L *diffringere* to shatter, from *dis-* apart + *frangere* to break]

diffuse *vb* (dɪ'fjuːz), **diffuses, diffusing, diffused**. **1** to spread in all directions. **2** to undergo or cause to undergo diffusion. **3** to scatter; disperse. ◆ *adj* (dɪ'fjuːs). **4** spread out over a wide area. **5** lacking conciseness. **6** characterized by diffusion. [C15: from L *diffūsus* spread abroad,

from *diffundere* to pour forth, from *dis-* away + *fundere* to pour]
▸ **diffusely** (dɪˈfjuːslɪ) *adv* ▸ **dif'fuseness** *n* ▸ **diffusible** (dɪˈfjuːzɪbʰl) *adj*

diffuser *or* **diffusor** (dɪˈfjuːzə) *n* **1** a person or thing that diffuses. **2** a part of a lighting fixture, as a translucent covering, used to scatter the light and prevent glare. **3** a cone, wedge, or baffle placed in front of the diaphragm of a loudspeaker to diffuse the sound waves. **4** a duct, esp. in a wind tunnel or jet engine, that reduces the speed and increases the pressure of the air or fluid. **5** *Photog.* a light-scattering medium, such as a screen of fine fabric, used to reduce the sharpness of shadows and thus soften the lighting. **6** a device attached to a hair dryer that diffuses the warm air as it comes out.

diffusion (dɪˈfjuːʒən) *n* **1** a diffusing or being diffused; dispersion. **2** verbosity. **3** *Physics.* **3a** the random thermal motion of atoms, molecules, etc., in gases, liquids, and some solids. **3b** the transfer of atoms or molecules by their random motion from one part of a medium to another. **4** *Physics.* the transmission or reflection of electromagnetic radiation, esp. light, in which the radiation is scattered in many directions. **5** *Anthropol.* the transmission of social institutions, skills, and myths from one culture to another.

diffusionism (dɪˈfjuːʒənˌɪzəm) *n Anthropol.* the theory that diffusion is responsible for the similarities between different cultures.
▸ **dif'fusionist** *n, adj*

diffusive (dɪˈfjuːsɪv) *adj* characterized by diffusion.
▸ **dif'fusively** *adv* ▸ **dif'fusiveness** *n*

dig (dɪg) *vb* **digs, digging, dug.** **1** (when *tr*, often foll. by *up*) to cut into, break up, and turn over or remove (earth, etc.), esp. with a spade. **2** to excavate (a hole, tunnel, etc.) by digging, usually with an implement or (of animals) with claws, etc. **3** (often foll. by *through*) to make or force (one's way): *he dug his way through the crowd.* **4** (*tr*; often foll. by *out* or *up*) to obtain by digging. **5** (*tr*; often foll. by *out* or *up*) to find by effort or searching: *to dig out facts.* **6** (*tr*; foll. by *in* or *into*) to thrust or jab. **7** (*tr*; foll. by *in* or *into*) to mix (compost, etc.) with soil by digging. **8** (*intr*; foll. by *in* or *into*) *Inf.* to begin vigorously to do something. **9** (*tr*) *Inf.* to like, understand, or appreciate. **10** (*intr*) *US sl.* to work hard, esp. for an examination. ◆ *n* **11** the act of digging. **12** a thrust or poke. **13** a cutting remark. **14** *Inf.* an archaeological excavation. **15** *Austral. & NZ inf.* short for **digger** (sense 4). ◆ See also **dig in.** [C13 *diggen*, from ?]

digest *vb* (dɪˈdʒɛst, daɪ-). **1** to subject (food) to a process of digestion. **2** (*tr*) to assimilate mentally. **3** *Chem.* to soften or disintegrate by the action of heat, moisture, or chemicals. **4** (*tr*) to arrange in a methodical order; classify. **5** (*tr*) to reduce to a summary. ◆ *n* (ˈdaɪdʒɛst). **6** a comprehensive and systematic compilation of information or material, often condensed. **7** a magazine, periodical, etc., that summarizes news. **8** a compilation of rules of law. [C14: from LL *dīgesta* writings grouped under various heads, from L *dīgerere* to divide, from *di-* apart + *gerere* to bear]

Digest (ˈdaɪdʒɛst) *n Roman law.* the books of law compiled by order of Justinian in the sixth century A.D.

digestible (dɪˈdʒɛstɪbʰl, daɪ-) *adj* capable of being digested.
▸ **di,gesti'bility** *n*

digestion (dɪˈdʒɛstʃən, daɪ-) *n* **1** the act or process in living organisms of breaking down food into easily absorbed substances by the action of enzymes, etc. **2** mental assimilation, esp. of ideas. **3** the decomposition of sewage by bacteria. **4** *Chem.* the treatment of material with heat, solvents, etc., to cause decomposition. [C14: from OF, from L *digestiō* a dissolving, digestion]
▸ **di'gestional** *adj*

digestive (dɪˈdʒɛstɪv, daɪ-) *or* **digestant** (daɪˈdʒɛstənt) *adj* **1** relating to, aiding, or subjecting to digestion. ◆ *n* **2** any substance that aids digestion.
▸ **di'gestively** *adv*

digestive biscuit *n* a round semisweet biscuit made from wholemeal flour.

digger (ˈdɪgə) *n* **1** a person, animal, or machine that digs. **2** a miner. **3** a tool or machine used for excavation. **4** (*sometimes cap.*) *Austral. & NZ inf.* an Australian or New Zealander, esp. a soldier: often used as a friendly term of address.

diggings (ˈdɪgɪŋz) *pl n* **1** (*functioning as pl*) material that has been dug out. **2** (*functioning as sing or pl*) a place where mining has taken place. **3** (*functioning as pl*) *Brit inf.* a less common name for **digs.**

dight (daɪt) *vb* **dights, dighting, dight** *or* **dighted.** (*tr*) *Arch.* to adorn or equip, as for battle. [OE *dihtan* to compose, from L *dictāre* to DICTATE]

dig in *vb* (*adv*) **1** *Mil.* to dig foxholes, trenches, etc. **2** *Inf.* to entrench (oneself). **3** (*intr*) *Inf.* to defend a position firmly, as in an argument. **4** (*intr*) *Inf.* to begin to eat vigorously: *don't wait, just dig in.* **5 dig one's heels in.** *Inf.* to refuse to move or be persuaded.

digit (ˈdɪdʒɪt) *n* **1** a finger or toe. **2** any of the ten Arabic numerals from 0 to 9. [C15: from L *digitus* toe, finger]

digital (ˈdɪdʒɪtʰl) *adj* **1** of, resembling, or possessing a digit or digits. **2** performed with the fingers. **3** representing data as a series of numerical values. **4** displaying information as numbers rather than by a pointer moving over a dial. ◆ *n* **5** *Music.* a key on a piano, harpsichord, etc.
▸ **'digitally** *adv*

digital audio tape *n* magnetic tape on which sound is recorded digitally, giving high-fidelity reproduction. Abbrev.: **DAT.**

digital camera *n* a camera that produces digital images, which can be stored on a computer, displayed on a screen, and printed.

digital clock *or* **watch** *n* a clock or watch in which the time is indicated by digits rather than by hands on a dial.

digital compact cassette *n* a magnetic tape cassette on which sound can be recorded in digital format. Abbrev.: **DCC.**

digital computer *n* an electronic computer in which the input is discrete, consisting of numbers, letters, etc. that are represented internally in binary notation.

digitalin (ˌdɪdʒɪˈteɪlɪn) *n* a poisonous glycoside extracted from digitalis and used in treating heart disease. [C19: from DIGITAL(IS) + -IN]

digitalis (ˌdɪdʒɪˈteɪlɪs) *n* **1** any of a genus of Eurasian plants such as the foxglove, having long spikes of bell-shaped flowers. **2** a drug prepared from the dried leaves of the foxglove: used medicinally as a heart stimulant. [C17: from NL, from L: relating to a finger; based on G *Fingerhut* foxglove, lit.: finger-hat]

digitalize *or* **digitalise** (ˈdɪdʒɪtəˌlaɪz) *vb* **digitalizes, digitalizing, digitalized** *or* **digitalises, digitalising, digitalised.** (*tr*) another word for **digitize.**

digital mapping *n* a method of preparing maps in which the data is stored in a computer for ease of access and updating.
▸ **digital map** *n*

digital recording *n* a sound recording process that converts audio or analogue signals into a series of pulses that correspond to the voltage level.

digital television *n* television in which the picture information is transmitted in digital form and decoded at the receiver.

digital video *n* video output based on digital rather than analogue signals.

digitate (ˈdɪdʒɪˌteɪt) *or* **digitated** *adj* **1** (of leaves) having the leaflets in the form of a spread hand. **2** (of animals) having digits.
▸ **'digi,tately** *adv* ▸ **,digi'tation** *n*

digitigrade (ˈdɪdʒɪtɪˌgreɪd) *adj* **1** (of dogs, cats, horses, etc.) walking so that only the toes touch the ground. ◆ *n* **2** a digitigrade animal.

digitize *or* **digitise** (ˈdɪdʒɪˌtaɪz) *vb* **digitizes, digitizing, dig-**

itized *or* **digitises, digitising, digitised**. (*tr*) to transcribe (data) into a digital form for processing by a computer.
▶ ˌdigiti'zation *or* ˌdigiti'sation *n* ▶ 'digiˌtizer *or* 'digiˌtiser *n*

dignified ('dɪgnɪˌfaɪd) *adj* characterized by dignity of manner or appearance; stately; noble.
▶ 'digniˌfiedly *adv* ▶ 'digniˌfiedness *n*

dignify ('dɪgnɪˌfaɪ) *vb* **dignifies, dignifying, dignified**. (*tr*) **1** to invest with honour or dignity. **2** to add distinction to. **3** to add a semblance of dignity to, esp. by the use of a pretentious name or title. [C15: from OF *dignifier*, from LL *dignificāre*, from L *dignus* worthy + *facere* to make]

dignitary ('dɪgnɪtərɪ) *n, pl* **dignitaries**. a person of high official position or rank.

dignity ('dɪgnɪtɪ) *n, pl* **dignities**. **1** a formal, stately, or grave bearing. **2** the state or quality of being worthy of honour. **3** relative importance; rank. **4** sense of self-importance (often in **stand** (*or* **be**) **on one's dignity, beneath one's dignity**). **5** high rank, esp. in government or the church. [C13: from OF *dignite*, from L *dignitās* merit, from *dignus* worthy]

digoxin (daɪ'dʒɒksɪn) *n* a glycoside extracted from digitalis leaves and used in the treatment of heart failure.

digraph ('daɪgrɑːf) *n* a combination of two letters used to represent a single sound such as *gh* in *tough*.
▶ **digraphic** (daɪ'græfɪk) *adj*

digress (daɪ'grɛs) *vb* (*intr*) **1** to depart from the main subject in speech or writing. **2** to wander from one's path. [C16: from L *dīgressus* turned aside, from *dīgredī*, from *dis-* apart + *gradī* to go]
▶ **di'gresser** *n* ▶ **di'gression** *n*

digressive (daɪ'grɛsɪv) *adj* characterized by digression or tending to digress.
▶ **di'gressively** *adv* ▶ **di'gressiveness** *n*

digs (dɪgz) *pl n Brit. inf.* lodgings. [C19: from DIGGINGS, ? referring to where one *digs* or works, but see also DIG IN]

dihedral (daɪ'hiːdrəl) *adj* **1** having or formed by two intersecting planes. ◆ *n* **2** Also called: **dihedron, dihedral angle**. the figure formed by two intersecting planes. **3** the upward inclination of an aircraft wing in relation to the lateral axis.

Dijon ★ (*French* diʒɔ̃) *n* a city in E France: capital of the former duchy of Burgundy. Pop.: 151 636 (1990).

dik-dik ('dɪkˌdɪk) *n* any of several small antelopes inhabiting semiarid regions of Africa. [C19: E African, prob. imit.]

dike (daɪk) *n, vb* **dikes, diking, diked**. a variant spelling of **dyke**¹.

diktat ('dɪktɑːt) *n* **1** a decree or settlement imposed, esp. by a ruler or a victorious nation. **2** a dogmatic statement. [from G: dictation, from L *dictātum*, from *dictāre* to DICTATE]

dilapidate (dɪ'læpɪˌdeɪt) *vb* **dilapidates, dilapidating, dilapidated**. to fall or cause to fall into ruin. [C16: from L *dīlapidāre* to waste, from *dis-* apart + *lapidāre* to stone, from *lapis* stone]
▶ **diˌlapi'dation** *n*

dilapidated (dɪ'læpɪˌdeɪtɪd) *adj* falling to pieces or in a state of disrepair; shabby.

dilate (daɪ'leɪt, dɪ-) *vb* **dilates, dilating, dilated**. **1** to make or become wider or larger. **2** (*intr*; often foll. by *on* or *upon*) to speak or write at length. [C14: from L *dīlātāre* to spread out, from *dis-* apart + *lātus* wide]
▶ **di'latable** *adj* ▶ **diˌlata'bility** *n* ▶ **di'lation** *or* **dilatation** (ˌdaɪlə'teɪʃən) *n* ▶ **dilative** (daɪ'leɪtɪv) *adj*

dilatory ('dɪlətərɪ, -trɪ) *adj* **1** tending to delay or waste time. **2** intended to waste time or defer action. [C15: from LL *dīlātōrius* inclined to delay, from *differre* to postpone; see DIFFER]
▶ **'dilatorily** *adv* ▶ **'dilatoriness** *n*

dildo *or* **dildoe** ('dɪldəʊ) *n, pl* **dildos** *or* **dildoes**. an object used as a substitute for an erect penis. [C16: from ?]

dilemma (dɪ'lɛmə, daɪ-) *n* **1** a situation necessitating a choice between two equally undesirable alternatives. **2** a problem that seems incapable of a solution. **3** *Logic*. a type of argument which forces the maintainer of a proposition to accept one of two conclusions each of which

contradicts the original assertion. **4 on the horns of a dilemma**. **4a** faced with the choice between two equally unpalatable alternatives. **4b** in an awkward situation. [C16: via L from Gk, from DI-¹ + *lēmma* proposition, from *lambanein* to grasp]
▶ **dilemmatic** (ˌdɪlɪ'mætɪk) *adj*

USAGE NOTE The use of *dilemma* to refer to a problem that seems incapable of a solution is considered by some people to be incorrect.

dilettante (ˌdɪlɪ'tæntɪ) *n, pl* **dilettantes** *or* **dilettanti** (-'tæntɪ). **1** a person whose interest in a subject is superficial rather than professional. **2** a person who loves the arts. ◆ *adj* **3** of or characteristic of a dilettante. [C18: from It., from *dilettare* to delight, from L *dēlectāre*]
▶ ˌdilet'tantish *or* ˌdilet'tanteish *adj* ▶ ˌdilet'tantism *or* ˌdilet'tanteism *n*

diligence¹ ('dɪlɪdʒəns) *n* **1** steady and careful application. **2** proper attention or care. [C14: from L *dīligentia* care]

diligence² ('dɪlɪdʒəns) *n History*. a stagecoach. [C18: from F, shortened from *carosse de diligence*, lit.: coach of speed]

diligent ('dɪlɪdʒənt) *adj* **1** careful and persevering in carrying out tasks or duties. **2** carried out with care and perseverance: *diligent work*. [C14: from OF, from L *dīligere* to value, from *dis-* apart + *legere* to read]
▶ **'diligently** *adv*

dill¹ (dɪl) *n* **1** an aromatic Eurasian plant with umbrella-shaped clusters of yellow flowers. **2** the leaves or fruits of this plant, used for flavouring and in medicine. [OE *dile*]

dill² (dɪl) *n Austral. & NZ sl.* a fool. [C20: from DILLY²]

dill pickle *n* a pickled cucumber flavoured with dill.

dilly¹ ('dɪlɪ) *n, pl* **dillies**. *Sl.*, chiefly US & Canad. a person or thing that is remarkable. [C20: ?from girl's name *Dilly*]

dilly² ('dɪlɪ) *adj* **dillier, dilliest**. *Austral. sl.* silly. [C20: from E dialect, ?from SILLY]

dilly bag *n Austral.* a small bag, esp., formerly, one made of plaited grass, etc., often used for carrying food. [from Abor. *dilly* small bag or basket]

dilly-dally (ˌdɪlɪ'dælɪ) *vb* **dilly-dallies, dilly-dallying, dilly-dallied**. (*intr*) *Inf.* to loiter or vacillate. [C17: by reduplication from DALLY]

dilute (daɪ'luːt) *vb* **dilutes, diluting, diluted**. **1** to make or become less concentrated, esp. by adding water or a thinner. **2** to make or become weaker in force, effect, etc. ◆ *adj* **3** *Chem*. **3a** (of a solution, etc.) having a low concentration. **3b** (of a substance) present in solution, esp. a weak solution in water: *dilute acetic acid*. [C16: from L *dīluere*, from *dis-* apart + *-luere*, from *lavāre* to wash]
▶ **di'luter** *n*

dilution (daɪ'luːʃən) *n* **1** the act of diluting or state of being diluted. **2** a diluted solution.

diluvial (daɪ'luːvɪəl, dɪ-) *or* **diluvian** *adj* of or connected with a deluge, esp. with the great Flood described in Genesis. [C17: from LL *dīluviālis*, from L *dīluere* to wash away; see DILUTE]

dim (dɪm) *adj* **dimmer, dimmest**. **1** badly illuminated. **2** not clearly seen; faint. **3** having weak or indistinct vision. **4** mentally dull. **5** not clear in the mind; obscure: *a dim memory*. **6** lacking in brightness or lustre. **7** unfavourable, gloomy or disapproving (esp. in **take a dim view**). ◆ *vb* **dims, dimming, dimmed**. **8** to become or cause to become dim. **9** (*tr*) to cause to seem less bright. **10** the US and Canad. word for **dip** (sense 5). [OE *dimm*]
▶ **'dimly** *adv* ▶ **'dimness** *n*

dim. *abbrev. for*: **1** dimension. **2** Also: **dimin.** *Music*. diminuendo. **3** Also: **dimin.** diminutive.

Dimashq ★ (dɪ'mæʃk) *n* an Arabic name for **Damascus**.

Dimbleby ★ ('dɪmb°lbɪ) *n* **Richard**. 1913–65, British broadcaster.

dime (daɪm) *n* **1** a coin of the US and Canada, worth one tenth of a dollar or ten cents. **2 a dime a dozen**. very cheap or common. [C14: from OF *disme*, from L *decimus* tenth, from *decem* ten]

dimenhydrinate (,daɪmɛn'haɪdrɪ,neɪt) *n* a crystalline substance, used as an antihistamine and for the prevention of nausea, esp. in travel sickness. [from DI-' + ME(THYL) + (AMI)N(E) + (*diphen*)*hydr*(*am*)*in*(*e*) + -ATE¹]

dime novel *n US.* (formerly) a cheap melodramatic novel, usually in paperback.

dimension (dɪ'mɛnʃən) *n* **1** (*often pl*) a measurement of the size of something in a particular direction, such as the length, width, height, or diameter. **2** (*often pl*) scope; size; extent. **3** aspect: *a new dimension to politics.* **4** *Maths.* the number of coordinates required to locate a point in space. ♦ *vb* **5** (*tr*) Chiefly US. to cut to or mark with specified dimensions. [C14: from OF, from L *dīmēnsiō* an extent, from *dīmētīrī* to measure out, from *mētīrī*] ► di'**mensional** *adj* ► di'**mensionless** *adj*

dimer ('daɪmə) *n Chem.* a compound the molecule of which is formed by the linking of two identical molecules. [C20: from DI-¹ + -MER] ► **dimeric** (daɪ'mɛrɪk) *adj*

dimerize *or* **dimerise** ('daɪmə,raɪz) *vb* **dimerizes, dimerizing, dimerized** *or* **dimerises, dimerising, dimerised.** to react or cause to react to form a dimer. ► ,dimeri'**zation** *or* ,dimeri'**sation** *n*

dimeter ('dɪmɪtə) *n Prosody.* a line of verse consisting of two metrical feet or a verse written in this metre.

dimethylformamide (daɪ,mi:θaɪl'fɔːmə,maɪd) *n* a colourless liquid widely used as a solvent and sometimes as a catalyst. Formula: $(CH_3)_2NCHO$. Abbrev.: **DMF.**

dimethylsulphoxide (daɪ,mi:θaɪlsʌl'fɒksaɪd) *n* a liquid used as a solvent and in medicine to improve the penetration of drugs applied to the skin. Abbrev.: **DMSO.**

diminish (dɪ'mɪnɪʃ) *vb* **1** to make or become smaller, fewer, or less. **2** (*tr*) Archit. to cause to taper. **3** (*tr*) Music. to decrease (a minor or perfect interval) by a semitone. **4** to reduce in authority, status, etc. [C15: blend of *diminuen* to lessen (from L *dēminuere*, from *minuere*) + archaic *minish* to lessen] ► di'**minishable** *adj*

diminished (dɪ'mɪnɪʃt) *adj* **1** reduced or lessened; made smaller. **2** *Music.* denoting any minor or perfect interval reduced by a semitone.

diminished responsibility *n Law.* a plea under which mental derangement is submitted as demonstrating lack of criminal responsibility.

diminishing returns *pl n Econ.* progressively smaller increases in output resulting from equal increases in production.

diminuendo (dɪ,mɪnju'ɛndəʊ) *Music.* ♦ *n, pl* **diminuendos. 1a** a gradual decrease in loudness. Symbol: > **1b** a musical passage affected by a diminuendo. ♦ *adj* **2** gradually decreasing in loudness. **3** with a diminuendo. [C18: from It., from *diminuire* to DIMINISH]

diminution (,dɪmɪ'njuːʃən) *n* **1** reduction; decrease. **2** *Music.* the presentation of the subject of a fugue, etc., in which the note values are reduced in length. [C14: from L *dēminūtiō*; see DIMINISH]

diminutive (dɪ'mɪnjʊtɪv) *adj* **1** very small; tiny. **2** *Grammar.* **2a** denoting an affix added to a word to convey the meaning *small* or *unimportant* or to express affection. **2b** denoting a word formed by the addition of a diminutive affix. ♦ *n* **3** *Grammar.* a diminutive word or affix. **4** a tiny person or thing. ► di'**minutively** *adv* ► di'**minutiveness** *n*

dimissory (dɪ'mɪsərɪ) *adj* **1** granting permission to be ordained: *a bishop's dimissory letter.* **2** granting permission to depart.

Dimitrovo ★ (di'mitrovo) *n* the former name (1949–62) of **Pernik.**

dimity ('dɪmɪtɪ) *n, pl* **dimities.** a light strong cotton fabric with woven stripes or squares. [C15: from Med. L *dimitum*, from Gk *dimiton*, from DI-¹ + *mitos* thread of the warp]

dimmer ('dɪmə) *n* **1** a device for dimming an electric light. **2** (*often pl*) US. **2a** a dipped headlight on a road vehicle. **2b** a parking light on a car.

dimorphism (daɪ'mɔːfɪzəm) *n* **1** the occurrence within a plant of two distinct forms of any part. **2** the occurrence in an animal species of two distinct types of individual. **3** a property of certain substances that enables them to exist in two distinct crystalline forms. ► di'**morphic** *or* di'**morphous** *adj*

dimple ('dɪmpəl) *n* **1** a small natural dent, esp. on the cheeks or chin. **2** any slight depression in a surface. ♦ *vb* **dimples, dimpling, dimpled. 3** to make or become dimpled. **4** (*intr*) to produce dimples by smiling. [C13 *dympull*] ► '**dimply** *adj*

dim sum (,dɪm 'sʌm) *n* a Chinese appetizer of steamed dumplings containing various fillings. [Cantonese]

dimwit ('dɪm,wɪt) *n Inf.* a stupid or silly person. ► ,dim-'**witted** *adj* ► ,dim-'**wittedness** *n*

din (dɪn) *n* **1** a loud discordant confused noise. ♦ *vb* **dins, dinning, dinned. 2** (*tr*; usually foll. by *into*) to instil by constant repetition. **3** (*tr*) to subject to a din. **4** (*intr*) to make a din. [OE *dynn*]

DIN *n* **1** a formerly used logarithmic expression of the speed of a photographic film, plate, etc.; high-speed films have high numbers. **2** a system of standard plugs, sockets, etc. formerly used for interconnecting domestic audio and video equipment. [C20: from G *D(eutsche) I(ndustrie) N(ormen)* German Industry Standards]

dinar ('diːnɑː) *n* the standard monetary unit of Algeria, Bahrain, Bosnia-Herzegovina, Iraq, Jordan, Kuwait, Libya, Sudan, Tunisia, and Yugoslavia. [C17: from Ar. from LGk *dēnarion*, from L *dēnārius* DENARIUS]

d'Indy ★ (French dɛ̃di) *n* (**Paul Marie Theodore**) **Vincent** 1851–1931, French composer.

dine (daɪn) *vb* **dines, dining, dined. 1** (*intr*) to eat dinner. **2** (*intr*; often foll. by *on, off,* or *upon*) to make one's meal (of): *the guests dined upon roast beef.* **3** (*tr*) Inf. to entertain to dinner (esp. in **wine and dine someone**). [C13: from OF *disner*, from Vulgar L *disjējūnāre* (unattested), from *dis*-not + LL *jējūnāre* to fast]

dine out *vb* (*intr, adv*) **1** to dine away from home. **2** (foll. by *on*) to have dinner at the expense of someone else mainly for the sake of one's conversation about (a subject or story).

diner ('daɪnə) *n* **1** a person eating a meal, esp. in a restaurant. **2** Chiefly US & Canad. a small cheap restaurant. **3** a fashionable bar, or a section of one, where food is served.

Dinesen ★ ('dɪnɪsᵊn) *n Isak* ('aɪzək), pen name of *Baroness Karen Blixen.* 1885–1962, Danish author of short stories. Her life story was told in the film *Out of Africa* (1986).

dinette (daɪ'nɛt) *n* an alcove or small area for use as a dining room.

ding (dɪŋ) *vb* **1** to ring, esp. with tedious repetition. **2** (*tr*) another word for **din** (sense 2). ♦ *n* **3** an imitation of the sound of a bell. [C13: prob. imit., but infl. by DIN + RING²]

dingbat ('dɪŋ,bæt) *n Austral. sl.* a crazy or stupid person.

dingbats ('dɪŋ,bæts) *pl n Austral. & NZ sl.* an attack of nervousness, irritation, or loathing: *he had the dingbats.*

ding-dong *n* **1** the sound of a bell or bells. **2** an imitation of the sound of a bell. **3a** a violent exchange of blows or words. **3b** (*as modifier*): *a ding-dong battle.* ♦ *adj* **4** sounding or ringing repeatedly. [C16: imit.; see DING]

dinges ('dɪŋəs) *n S. African inf.* a jocular word for something whose name is unknown or forgotten; thingumabob. [from Afrik., from Du. *dinges* thing]

dinghy ('dɪŋɪ, 'dɪŋgɪ) *n, pl* **dinghies.** any small boat, powered by sail, oars, or outboard motor. Also (esp. formerly): **dingy, dingey.** [C19: from Hindi or Bengali *dingī*]

dingle ('dɪŋgəl) *n* a small wooded dell. [C13: from ?]

dingo ('dɪŋgəʊ) *n, pl* **dingoes.** a wild dog of Australia, having a yellowish-brown coat and resembling a wolf. [C18: from Abor.]

dingy ('dɪndʒɪ) *adj* **dingier, dingiest. 1** lacking light or brightness; drab. **2** dirty; discoloured. [C18: perhaps from an earlier dialect word rel. to OE *dynge* dung] ► '**dingily** *adv* ► '**dinginess** *n*

dining car n a railway coach in which meals are served at tables. Also called: **restaurant car**.

dining room n a room where meals are eaten.

dinitrogen oxide (daɪˈnaɪtrədʒən) n the systematic name for **nitrous oxide**.

dinkie (ˈdɪŋkɪ) n **1** an affluent married childless person. ◆ adj **2** designed for or appealing to dinkies. [C20: from d(ouble) i(ncome) n(o) k(ids) + -IE]

dinkum (ˈdɪŋkəm) adj Austral. & NZ inf. **1** genuine or right: a fair dinkum offer. **2 dinkum oil.** the truth. [C19: from E dialect: work, from ?]

dinky (ˈdɪŋkɪ) adj **dinkier, dinkiest.** Inf. **1** Brit. small and neat; dainty. **2** US. inconsequential; insignificant. [C18: from Scot. & N English dialect dink neat, neatly dressed]

dinky-di (ˈdɪŋkɪˈdaɪ) adj Austral. inf. typical: dinky-di Pom idleness. [C20: var. of DINKUM]

dinner (ˈdɪnə) n **1** a meal taken in the evening. **2** a meal taken at midday, esp. when it is the main meal of the day; lunch. **3** a formal meal or banquet in honour of someone or something. **4** (as modifier): dinner table; dinner hour. [C13: from OF disner; see DINE]

dinner dance n a formal dinner followed by dancing.

dinner jacket n a man's semiformal evening jacket without tails, usually black. US and Canad. name: **tuxedo**.

dinner service n a set of matching plates, dishes, etc., suitable for serving a meal.

dinosaur (ˈdaɪnəˌsɔː) n **1** any of a large order of extinct reptiles many of which were of gigantic size and abundant in the Mesozoic era. **2** a person or thing that is considered to be out of date. [C19: from NL dinosaurus, from Gk deinos fearful + sauros lizard]
► ˌdinoˈsaurian adj

dint (dɪnt) n **1 by dint of.** by means or use of: by dint of hard work. **2** Arch. a blow or a mark made by a blow. ◆ vb **3** (tr) to mark with dints. [OE dynt]

dioc. abbrev. for: **1** diocesan. **2** diocese.

Dio Cassius ★ (ˈdaɪəʊ ˈkæsɪəs) n ?155–?230 A.D., Roman historian. His History of Rome covers the period of Rome's transition from Republic to Empire.

diocesan (daɪˈɒsɪsᵊn) adj **1** of or relating to a diocese. ◆ n **2** the bishop of a diocese.

diocese (ˈdaɪəsɪs) n the district under the jurisdiction of a bishop. [C14: from OF, from LL diocēsis, from Gk dioikēsis administration, from dioikein to manage a household, from oikos house]

Dio Chrysostom ★ (ˈdaɪəʊ ˈkrɪsəstəm) n 2nd century A.D., Greek orator and philosopher.

Diocletian ★ (ˌdaɪəˈkliːʃən) n full name Gaius Aurelius Valerius Diocletianus. 245–313 A.D., Roman emperor (284–305), who divided the empire into East and West (293).

diode (ˈdaɪəʊd) n **1** a semiconductor device used in circuits for converting alternating current to direct current. **2** the earliest type of electronic valve having two electrodes between which a current can flow only in one direction. [C20: from DI-¹ + -ODE²]

dioecious (daɪˈiːʃəs) adj (of plants) having the male and female reproductive organs on separate plants. [C18: from NL Dioecia name of class, from DI-¹ + Gk oikia house]

Diogenes ★ (daɪˈɒdʒɪˌniːz) n ?412–?323 B.C., Greek Cynic philosopher.

Diomede Islands ★ (ˈdaɪəˌmiːd) pl n two small islands in the Bering Strait, separated by the international date line and by the boundary line between the US and Russia.

Diomedes (ˌdaɪəˈmiːdiːz), **Diomede,** or **Diomed** ★ (ˈdaɪəˌmɛd) n Greek myth. a king of Argos, and suitor of Helen, who fought with the Greeks at Troy.

Dionysian (ˌdaɪəˈnɪzɪən) adj **1** of or relating to Dionysus. **2** (often not cap.) wild or orgiastic.

Dionysius ★ (ˌdaɪəˈnɪsɪəs) n called the Elder. ?430–367 B.C., tyrant of Syracuse (405–367).

Dionysus or **Dionysos** ★ (ˌdaɪəˈnaɪsəs) n the Greek god of wine, fruitfulness, and vegetation, worshipped in orgiastic rites. He was also known as the bestower of ecstasy and god of the drama, and identified with Bacchus.

Diophantine equation (ˌdaɪəʊˈfæntaɪn) n (in number theory) an equation in more than one variable, for which integral solutions are sought. [from DIOPHANTUS]

Diophantus ★ (ˌdaɪəʊˈfæntəs) n 3rd century A.D., Greek mathematician, noted for his treatise on the theory of numbers, Arithmetica.

dioptre or US **diopter** (daɪˈɒptə) n a unit for measuring the refractive power of a lens: the reciprocal of the focal length of the lens expressed in metres. [C16: from L dioptra optical instrument, from Gk, from dia- through + opsesthai to see]
► diˈoptral adj

dioptrics (daɪˈɒptrɪks) n (functioning as sing) the branch of geometrical optics concerned with the formation of images by lenses. [C20: from DIOPTRE + -ICS]

Dior ★ (diːˈɔː; French djɔr) n **Christian** (ˈkrɪstʃən; French kristjɑ̃). 1905–57, French couturier.

diorama (ˌdaɪəˈrɑːmə) n **1** a miniature three-dimensional scene, in which models of figures are seen against a background. **2** a picture made up of illuminated translucent curtains, viewed through an aperture. **3** a museum display, as of an animal, of a specimen in its natural setting. [C19: from F, from Gk dia- through + horama view, from horan to see]
► dioramic (ˌdaɪəˈræmɪk) adj

dioxide (daɪˈɒksaɪd) n any oxide containing two oxygen atoms per molecule, both of which are bonded to an atom of another element.

dioxin (daɪˈɒksɪn) n any of various chemical by-products of the manufacture of certain herbicides and bactericides, esp. the extremely toxic tetrachlorodibenzoparadioxin (TCDD).

dip (dɪp) vb **dips, dipping, dipped. 1** to plunge or be plunged quickly or briefly into a liquid, esp. to wet or coat. **2** (intr) to undergo a slight decline, esp. temporarily: sales dipped in November. **3** (intr) to slope downwards. **4** (intr) to sink quickly. **5** (tr) to switch (car headlights) from the main to the lower beam. US and Canad. word: **dim. 6** (tr) **6a** to immerse (sheep, etc.) briefly in a chemical to rid them of or prevent infestation by insects, etc. **6b** to immerse (grain, vegetables, or wood) in a preservative liquid. **7** (tr) to dye by immersing in a liquid. **8** (tr) to baptize (someone) by immersion. **9** (tr) to plate or galvanize (a metal, etc.) by immersion in an electrolyte or electrolytic cell. **10** (tr) to scoop up a liquid or something from a liquid in the hands or in a container. **11** to lower or be lowered briefly. **12** (tr) to make (a candle) by plunging the wick into melted wax. **13** (intr) to plunge a container, the hands, etc., into something, esp. to obtain an object. **14** (intr) (of an aircraft) to drop suddenly and then regain height. ◆ n **15** the act of dipping or state of being dipped. **16** a brief swim in water. **17a** any liquid chemical in which sheep, etc. are dipped. **17b** any liquid preservative into which objects are dipped. **18** a dye into which fabric is immersed. **19** a depression, esp. in a landscape. **20** something taken up by dipping. **21** a container used for dipping; dipper. **22** a momentary sinking down. **23** the angle of slope of rock strata, etc., from the horizontal plane. **24** the angle between the direction of the earth's magnetic field and the plane of the horizon; the angle that a magnetic needle free to swing in a vertical plane makes with the horizontal. **25** a creamy savoury mixture into which pieces of food are dipped before being eaten. **26** Surveying. the angular distance of the horizon below the plane of observation. **27** a candle made by plunging a wick into wax. **28** a momentary loss of altitude when flying. ◆ See also **dip into**. [OE dyppan]

dip. or **Dip.** abbrev. for diploma.

DipAD abbrev. for Diploma in Art and Design.

DipEd (in Britain) abbrev. for Diploma in Education.

diphtheria (dɪpˈθɪərɪə) n an acute contagious disease caused by a bacillus, producing fever, severe prostration, and difficulty in breathing and swallowing as the result of swelling of the throat and the formation of a false

membrane. [C19: NL, from F *diphthérie*, from Gk *diphthera* leather; from the nature of the membrane]
▶ **diph'therial, diphtheritic** (ˌdɪpθəˈrɪtɪk), *or* **diphtheric** (dɪpˈθɛrɪk) *adj*

diphthong ('dɪfθɒŋ) *n* 1 a vowel sound, occupying a single syllable, during the articulation of which the tongue moves continuously from one position to another, as in the pronunciation of *a* in *late*. 2 a digraph or ligature representing a composite vowel such as this, as *ae* in *Caesar*. [C15: from LL *diphthongus*, from Gk *diphthongos*, from DI-[1] + *phthongos* sound]
▶ **diph'thongal** *adj*

diphthongize *or* **diphthongise** ('dɪfθɒŋˌaɪz) *vb* **diphthongizes, diphthongizing, diphthongized** *or* **diphthongises, diphthongising, diphthongised**. (*often passive*) to make (a simple vowel) into a diphthong.
▶ ˌ**diphthongi'zation** *or* ˌ**diphthongi'sation** *n*

dip into *vb* (*intr, prep*) 1 to draw upon: *he dipped into his savings*. 2 to dabble (in); play at. 3 to read passages at random from (a book, newspaper, etc.).

diplodocus (ˌdɪpləʊ'dəʊkəs, dɪ'plɒdəkəs) *n, pl* **diplodocuses**. a herbivorous dinosaur characterized by a very long neck and tail and a total body length of 27 metres. [C19: from NL, from Gk *diplo-*, (from *diploos*, from DI-[1] + *-ploos* -fold)+ *dokos* beam]

diploid ('dɪplɔɪd) *adj* 1 *Biol*. (of cells or organisms) having paired homologous chromosomes so that twice the haploid number is present. 2 double or twofold. ◆ *n* 3 a diploid cell or organism.
▶ **dip'loidic** *adj*

diploma (dɪ'pləʊmə) *n* 1 a document conferring a qualification, recording success in examinations or successful completion of a course of study. 2 an official document that confers an honour or privilege. [C17: from L: official letter or document, lit.: letter folded double, from Gk]

diplomacy (dɪ'pləʊməsɪ) *n, pl* **diplomacies**. 1 the conduct of the relations of one state with another by peaceful means. 2 skill in the management of international relations. 3 tact, skill, or cunning in dealing with people. [C18: from F *diplomatie*, from *diplomatique* DIPLOMATIC]

diplomat ('dɪpləˌmæt) *n* 1 an official such as an ambassador, engaged in diplomacy. 2 a person who deals with people tactfully or skilfully. ◆ Also called: **diplomatist** (dɪ'pləʊmətɪst).

diplomatic (ˌdɪplə'mætɪk) *adj* 1 of or relating to diplomacy or diplomats. 2 skilled in negotiating, esp. between states or people. 3 tactful in dealing with people. [C18: from F *diplomatique* concerning the documents of diplomacy, from NL *diplōmaticus*; see DIPLOMA]
▶ ˌ**diplo'matically** *adv*

diplomatic bag *n* a container or bag in which official mail is sent, free from customs inspection, to and from an embassy or consulate.

diplomatic corps *or* **body** *n* the entire body of diplomats accredited to a given state.

diplomatic immunity *n* the immunity from local jurisdiction and exemption from taxation in the country to which they are accredited afforded to diplomats.

Diplomatic Service *n* 1 (in Britain) the division of the Civil Service which provides diplomats to represent the UK abroad. 2 (*not caps.*) the equivalent institution of any other country.

dipole ('daɪˌpəʊl) *n* 1 two equal but opposite electric charges or magnetic poles separated by a small distance. 2 a molecule in which the centre of positive charge does not coincide with the centre of negative charge. 3 a directional aerial consisting of two metal rods with a connecting wire fixed between them in the form of a T.
▶ **di'polar** *adj*

dipole moment *n Chem*. a measure of the polarity in a chemical bond or molecule, equal to the product of one charge and the distance between the charges. Symbol: μ

dipper ('dɪpə) *n* 1 a ladle used for dipping. 2 Also called: **water ouzel**. any of a genus of aquatic songbirds that inhabit fast-flowing streams. 3 a person or thing that dips. 4 *Arch*. an Anabaptist. ◆ See also **big dipper**.

dippy ('dɪpɪ) *adj* **dippier, dippiest.** *Sl.* odd, eccentric, or crazy. [C20: from ?]

dipsomania (ˌdɪpsəʊ'meɪnɪə) *n* a compulsive desire to drink alcoholic beverages. [C19: NL, from Gk *dips* thirst + -MANIA]
▶ ˌ**dipso'maniac** *n, adj*

dipstick ('dɪpˌstɪk) *n* 1 a graduated rod or strip dipped into a container to indicate the fluid level. 2 *Brit. sl.* fool.

dip switch *n* a device for dipping car headlights.

dipteran ('dɪptərən) *or* **dipteron** ('dɪptəˌrɒn) *n* 1 a dipterous insect. ◆ *adj* 2 another word for **dipterous** (sense 1).

dipterous ('dɪptərəs) *adj* 1 Also: **dipteran**. of a large order of insects having a single pair of wings and sucking or piercing mouthparts. The group includes flies, mosquitoes, and midges. 2 *Bot*. having two winglike parts. [C18: from Gk *dipteros* two-winged]

diptych ('dɪptɪk) *n* 1 a pair of hinged wooden tablets with waxed surfaces for writing. 2 a painting or carving on two hinged panels. [C17: from Gk *diptukhos* folded together, from DI-[1] + *ptukhos* fold]

Dirac ★ (dɪ'ræk) *n* **Paul Adrien Maurice**. 1902–84, British physicist, noted for his work on the quantum theory: shared the Nobel prize for physics 1933.

dire ('daɪə) *adj* (*usually prenominal*) 1 Also: **direful**. disastrous; fearful. 2 desperate; urgent: *a dire need*. 3 foreboding disaster; ominous. [C16: from L *dīrus* ominous]
▶ '**direly** *adv* ▶ '**direness** *n*

direct (dɪ'rekt, daɪ-) *vb* (*mainly tr*) 1 to conduct or control the affairs of. 2 (*also intr*) to give commands or orders with authority to (a person or group). 3 to tell or show (someone) the way to a place. 4 to aim, point, or cause to move towards a goal. 5 to address (a letter, etc.). 6 to address (remarks, etc.). 7 (*also intr*) 7a to provide guidance to (actors, cameramen, etc.) in a play or film. 7b to supervise the making or staging of (a film or play). 8 (*also intr*) to conduct (a piece of music or musicians), usually while performing oneself. ◆ *adj* 9 without delay or evasion; straightforward. 10 without turning aside; shortest; straight: *a direct route*. 11 without intervening persons or agencies: *a direct link*. 12 honest; frank. 13 (*usually prenominal*) precise; exact: *a direct quotation*. 14 diametrical: *the direct opposite*. 15 in an unbroken line of descent: *a direct descendant*. 16 (of government, decisions, etc.) by or from the electorate rather than through representatives. 17 *Logic, maths.* (of a proof) progressing from the premises to the conclusion, rather than eliminating the possibility of the falsehood of the conclusion. Cf. **indirect proof.** 18 *Astron*. moving from west to east. Cf. **retrograde.** 19 of or relating to direct current. 20 *Music*. (of an interval or chord) in root position; not inverted. ◆ *adv* 21 directly; straight. [C14: from L *dīrectus*, from *dīrigere* to guide, from *dis-* apart + *regere* to rule]
▶ **di'rectness** *n*

direct access *n* a method of reading data from a computer file without reading through the file from the beginning.

direct action *n* action such as strikes or civil disobedience employed to obtain demands from an employer, government, etc.

direct current *n* a continuous electric current that flows in one direction only.

direct debit *n* an order given to a bank or building society by a holder of an account, instructing it to pay to a specified person or organization any sum demanded by that person or organization. Cf. **standing order.**

direct-grant school *n* (in Britain, formerly) a school financed by endowment, fees, and a state grant conditional upon admittance of a percentage of nonpaying pupils.

direction (dɪ'rekʃən, daɪ-) *n* 1 the act of directing or the state of being directed. 2 management, control, or guidance. 3 the work of a stage or film director. 4 the course or line along which a person or thing moves, points, or lies. 5 the place towards which a person or thing is directed. 6 a line of action; course. 7 the name and address on a letter, parcel, etc. 8 *Music*. the process of conducting an orchestra, choir, etc. **9** *Music.* an instruction to indicate tempo, dynamics, mood, etc.

directional (dɪˈrɛkʃənəl, daɪ-) *adj* **1** of or relating to a spatial direction. **2** *Electronics.* **2a** having or relating to an increased sensitivity to radio waves, nuclear particles, etc., coming from a particular direction. **2b** (of an aerial) transmitting or receiving radio waves more effectively in some directions than in others. **3** *Physics, electronics.* concentrated in, following, or producing motion in a particular direction. ▸ di,rection'ality *n*

directional drilling *n* a method of drilling for oil in which the well is not drilled vertically, as when a number of wells are to be drilled from a single platform. Also called: **deviated drilling.**

direction finder *n* a device to determine the direction of incoming radio signals, used esp. as a navigation aid.

directions (dɪˈrɛkʃənz, daɪ-) *pl n* (*sometimes sing*) instructions for doing something or for reaching a place.

directive (dɪˈrɛktɪv, daɪ-) *n* **1** an instruction; order. ◆ *adj* **2** tending to direct; directing. **3** indicating direction.

directly (dɪˈrɛktlɪ, daɪ-) *adv* **1** in a direct manner. **2** at once; without delay. **3** (foll. by *before* or *after*) immediately; just. ◆ *conj* **4** (*subordinating*) as soon as.

direct marketing *n* selling goods directly to consumers rather than through retailers, as by mail order, telephone selling, etc. Also called: **direct selling.**

direct object *n Grammar.* a noun, pronoun, or noun phrase whose referent receives the direct action of a verb. For example, *a book* in *They bought Anne a book.*

directoire (dɪˈrɛktwɑː) *adj* (of ladies' knickers) knee-length, with elastic at waist and knees. [C19: after fashions of the period of the French *Directoire* Directorate (1795–99)]

director (dɪˈrɛktə, daɪ-) *n* **1** a person or thing that directs, controls, or regulates. **2** a member of the governing board of a business concern. **3** a person who directs the affairs of an institution, trust, etc. **4** the person responsible for the artistic and technical aspects of the making of a film or television programme or the staging of a play. Cf. **producer** (sense 3). **5** *Music.* another word (esp. US) for **conductor.**
▸ ,direc'torial *adj* ▸ ,di'rector,ship *n* ▸ di'rectress *fem n*

directorate (dɪˈrɛktərɪt, daɪ-) *n* **1** a board of directors. **2** Also: **directorship.** the position of director.

director-general *n, pl* **directors-general.** the head of a large organization such as the CBI or BBC.

Director of Public Prosecutions *n* (in Britain) an official who, as head of the Crown Prosecution Service, is responsible for conducting all criminal prosecutions initiated by the police. Abbrev.: **DPP.**

director's chair *n* a light wooden folding chair with arm rests and a canvas seat and back, as used by film directors.

directory (dɪˈrɛktərɪ, -trɪ; daɪ-) *n, pl* **directories.** **1** a book listing names, addresses, telephone numbers, etc., of individuals or firms. **2** a book giving directions. **3** a book containing the rules to be observed in the forms of worship used in churches. **4** a directorate. **5** *Computing.* an area of a disk, Winchester disk, or floppy disk that contains the names and locations of files currently held on that disk. ◆ *adj* **6** directing.

Directory (dɪˈrɛktərɪ, -trɪ; daɪ-) *n* the. *History.* the body of five directors in power in France from 1795 until their overthrow by Napoleon in 1799. Also called: **French Directory.**

direct primary *n US government.* a primary in which voters directly select the candidates who will run for office.

direct selling *n* another name for **direct marketing.**

direct speech *or esp. US* **direct discourse** *n* the reporting of what someone has said or written by quoting his exact words.

direct tax *n* a tax paid by the person or organization on which it is levied.

dirge (dɜːdʒ) *n* **1** a chant of lamentation for the dead. **2** the funeral service in its solemn or sung forms. **3** any

mourning song or melody. [C13: from L *dīrigē* direct (imperative), opening word of antiphon used in the office of the dead]
▸ 'dirgeful *adj*

dirham ('dɪəræm) *n* **1** the standard monetary unit of Morocco and the United Arab Emirates. **2** a monetary unit of Kuwait, Libya, Qatar, and Tunisia. **3** any of various N African coins. [C18: from Ar., from L: DRACHMA]

dirigible ('dɪrɪdʒɪbəl) *adj* **1** able to be steered or directed.
◆ *n* **2** another name for **airship.** [C16: from L *dīrigere* to DIRECT]
▸ ,dirigi'bility *n*

dirigisme (diːriːˈʒiːzəm) *n* control by the state of economic and social matters. [C20: from F]
▸ diri'giste *adj*

dirk (dɜːk) *n* **1** a dagger, esp. as formerly worn by Scottish Highlanders. ◆ *vb* **2** (*tr*) to stab with a dirk. [C16: from Scot. *durk*, ?from G *Dolch* dagger]

dirndl ('dɜːndəl) *n* **1** a woman's dress with a full gathered skirt and fitted bodice; originating from Tyrolean peasant wear. **2** a gathered skirt of this kind. [G (Bavarian and Austrian): from *Dirndlkleid*, from *Dirndl* little girl + *Kleid* dress]

dirt (dɜːt) *n* **1** any unclean substance, such as mud, etc.; filth. **2** loose earth; soil. **3a** packed earth, gravel, cinders, etc., used to make a racetrack. **3b** (*as modifier*): *a dirt track.* **4** *Mining.* the gravel or soil from which minerals are extracted. **5** a person or thing regarded as worthless. **6** obscene or indecent speech or writing. **7** *Sl.* gossip; scandalous information. **8** moral corruption. **9 do (someone) dirt.** *Sl.* to do something vicious to (someone). **10 eat dirt.** *Sl.* to accept insult without complaining. [C13: from ON *drit* excrement]

dirt-cheap *adj, adv Inf.* at an extremely low price.

dirty ('dɜːtɪ) *adj* **dirtier, dirtiest. 1** covered or marked with dirt; filthy. **2a** obscene: *dirty books.* **2b** sexually clandestine: *a dirty weekend.* **3** causing one to become grimy: *a dirty job.* **4** (of a colour) not clear and bright. **5** unfair; dishonest. **6** mean; nasty: *a dirty cheat.* **7** scandalous; unkind. **8** revealing dislike or anger. **9** (of weather) rainy or squally; stormy. **10** (of a nuclear weapon) producing a large quantity of radioactive fallout. **11 dirty linen.** *Inf.* intimate secrets, esp. those that might give rise to gossip. **12 dirty work.** unpleasant or illicit activity. ◆ *n* **13 do the dirty on.** *Inf.* to behave meanly towards. ◆ *vb* **dirties, dirtying, dirtied. 14** to make or become dirty; stain; soil.
▸ 'dirtily *adv* ▸ 'dirtiness *n*

dis (dɪs) *vb* a variant spelling of **diss.**

Dis ★ (dɪs) *n* **1** Also called: **Orcus, Pluto.** the Roman god of the underworld. **2** the abode of the dead; underworld.
◆ Greek equivalent: **Hades.**

dis-[1] *prefix* **1** indicating reversal: *disconnect.* **2** indicating negation, lack, or deprivation: *dissimilar; disgrace.* **3** indicating removal or release: *disembowel.* **4** expressing intensive force: *dissever.* [from L *dis-* apart; in some cases, via OF *des-*. In compound words of L origin, *dis-* becomes *dif-* before *f*, and *di-* before some consonants]

dis-[2] *combining form.* a variant of **di-**[1] before *s*: *dissyllable.*

disability (,dɪsəˈbɪlɪtɪ) *n, pl* **disabilities. 1** the condition of being physically or mentally impaired. **2** something that disables; handicap. **3** lack of necessary intelligence, strength, etc. **4** an incapacity in the eyes of the law to enter into certain transactions.

disable (dɪsˈeɪbəl) *vb* **disables, disabling, disabled.** (*tr*) **1** to make ineffective, unfit, or incapable, as by crippling. **2** to make or pronounce legally incapable. **3** to switch off (an electronic device).
▸ dis'ablement *n*

disabled (dɪsˈeɪbəld) *adj* **a** lacking one or more physical powers, such as the ability to walk or to coordinate one's movements. **b** (*as collective n*; preceded by *the*): *the disabled.* See usage note below.

> **USAGE NOTE** The use of *the disabled, the blind,* etc. can be offensive and should be avoided. Instead one should talk about *disabled people, blind people,* etc.

disabuse (ˌdɪsəˈbjuːz) *vb* **disabuses, disabusing, disabused.** (*tr; usually foll. by of*) to rid of a mistaken idea; set right.

disadvantage (ˌdɪsədˈvɑːntɪdʒ) *n* **1** an unfavourable circumstance, thing, person, etc. **2** injury, loss, or detriment. **3** an unfavourable situation (esp. in **at a disadvantage**). ♦ *vb* **disadvantages, disadvantaging, disadvantaged. 4** (*tr*) to put at a disadvantage; handicap.

disadvantaged (ˌdɪsədˈvɑːntɪdʒd) *adj* socially or economically deprived or discriminated against.

disadvantageous (ˌdɪsædvɑːnˈteɪdʒəs, dɪsˌædvən-ˈteɪdʒəs) *adj* unfavourable; detrimental.
  ▶ ˌdisadvanˈtageously *adv* ▶ ˌdisadvanˈtageousness *n*

disaffect (ˌdɪsəˈfɛkt) *vb* (*tr; often passive*) to cause to lose loyalty or affection; alienate.
  ▶ ˌdisafˈfectedly *adv* ▶ ˌdisafˈfection *n*

disaffiliate (ˌdɪsəˈfɪlɪˌeɪt) *vb* **disaffiliates, disaffiliating, disaffiliated.** to sever an affiliation (with).
  ▶ ˌdisafˌfiliˈation *n*

disafforest (ˌdɪsəˈfɒrɪst) *vb* (*tr*) *Law.* to reduce (land) from the status of a forest to the state of ordinary ground.
  ▶ ˌdisafˌforesˈtation *n*

disaggregate (dɪsˈægrɪˌgeɪt) *vb* **disaggregates, disaggregating, disaggregated. 1** to separate from a group or mass. **2** to divide into parts.
  ▶ ˌdisaggreˈgation *n*

disagree (ˌdɪsəˈgriː) *vb* **disagrees, disagreeing, disagreed.** (*intr; often foll. by with*) **1** to dissent in opinion or dispute (about an idea, fact, etc.). **2** to fail to correspond; conflict. **3** to be unacceptable (to) or unfavourable (for): *curry disagrees with me.* **4** to be opposed (to).

disagreeable (ˌdɪsəˈgriːəbəl) *adj* **1** not likable; badtempered, esp. disobliging, etc. **2** not to one's liking; unpleasant.
  ▶ ˌdisaˈgreeableness *n* ▶ ˌdisaˈgreeably *adv*

disagreement (ˌdɪsəˈgriːmənt) *n* **1** refusal or failure to agree. **2** a failure to correspond. **3** an argument or dispute.

disallow (ˌdɪsəˈlaʊ) *vb* (*tr*) **1** to reject as untrue or invalid. **2** to cancel.
  ▶ ˌdisalˈlowable *adj* ▶ ˌdisalˈlowance *n*

disappear (ˌdɪsəˈpɪə) *vb* **1** (*intr*) to cease to be visible; vanish. **2** (*intr*) to go away or become lost, esp. without explanation. **3** (*intr*) to cease to exist; become extinct or lost. **4** (*tr*) (esp. in South and Central America) to arrest secretly and presumably imprison or kill (a member of an opposing political group).
  ▶ ˌdisapˈpearance *n*

disapplication (ˌdɪsæplɪˈkeɪʃən) *n Brit. education.* a provision for exempting schools or individuals from the requirements of the National Curriculum in special circumstances.

disappoint (ˌdɪsəˈpɔɪnt) *vb* (*tr*) **1** to fail to meet the expectations, hopes, etc. of; let down. **2** to prevent the fulfilment of (a plan, etc.); frustrate. [C15 (orig. meaning: to remove from office): from OF *desapointier*; see DIS-[1], APPOINT]
  ▶ ˌdisapˈpointed *adj* ▶ ˌdisapˈpointing *adj* ▶ ˌdisapˈpointingly *adv*

disappointment (ˌdɪsəˈpɔɪntmənt) *n* **1** a disappointing or being disappointed. **2** a person or thing that disappoints.

disapprobation (ˌdɪsæprəʊˈbeɪʃən) *n* moral or social disapproval.

disapproval (ˌdɪsəˈpruːvəl) *n* the act or a state or feeling of disapproving; censure.

disapprove (ˌdɪsəˈpruːv) *vb* **disapproves, disapproving, disapproved. 1** (*intr; often foll. by of*) to consider wrong, bad, etc. **2** (*tr*) to withhold approval from.
  ▶ ˌdisapˈproving *adj* ▶ ˌdisapˈprovingly *adv*

disarm (dɪsˈɑːm) *vb* **1** (*tr*) to remove defensive or offensive capability from (a country, army, etc.). **2** (*tr*) to deprive of weapons. **3** (*tr*) to win the confidence or affection of. **4** (*intr*) (of a nation, etc.) to decrease the size and capability of one's armed forces. **5** (*intr*) to lay down weapons.
  ▶ disˈarmer *n*

disarmament (dɪsˈɑːməmənt) *n* **1** the reduction of fighting capability, as by a nation. **2** a disarming or being disarmed.

disarming (dɪsˈɑːmɪŋ) *adj* tending to neutralize hostility, suspicion, etc.
  ▶ disˈarmingly *adv*

disarrange (ˌdɪsəˈreɪndʒ) *vb* **disarranges, disarranging, disarranged.** (*tr*) to throw into disorder.
  ▶ ˌdisarˈrangement *n*

disarray (ˌdɪsəˈreɪ) *n* **1** confusion, dismay, and lack of discipline. **2** (esp. of clothing) disorderliness; untidiness. ♦ *vb* (*tr*) **3** to throw into confusion. **4** *Arch.* to undress.

disassemble (ˌdɪsəˈsɛmbəl) *vb* **disassembles, disassembling, disassembled.** (*tr*) to take apart (a piece of machinery, etc.); dismantle.

disassembler (ˌdɪsəˈsɛmblə) *n Computing.* a computer program that translates machine code into assembly language.

disassociate (ˌdɪsəˈsəʊʃɪˌeɪt, -sɪ-) *vb* **disassociates, disassociating, disassociated.** a less common word for **dissociate.**
  ▶ ˌdisasˌsociˈation *n*

disaster (dɪˈzɑːstə) *n* **1** an occurrence that causes great distress or destruction. **2** a thing, project, etc., that fails or has been ruined. [C16 (orig. in the sense: malevolent astral influence): from It. *disastro*, from *dis-* (pejorative) + *astro* star, ult. from Gk *astron*]
  ▶ disˈastrous *adj*

disavow (ˌdɪsəˈvaʊ) *vb* (*tr*) to deny knowledge of, connection with, or responsibility for.
  ▶ ˌdisaˈvowal *n* ▶ **disavowedly** (ˌdɪsəˈvaʊɪdlɪ) *adv*

disband (dɪsˈbænd) *vb* to cease to function or cause to stop functioning, as a unit, group, etc.
  ▶ disˈbandment *n*

disbar (dɪsˈbɑː) *vb* **disbars, disbarring, disbarred.** (*tr*) *Law.* to deprive of the status of barrister; expel from the Bar.
  ▶ disˈbarment *n*

USAGE NOTE *Disbar* is sometimes wrongly used where *debar* is meant: *he was debarred* (not *disbarred*) *from attending meetings.*

disbelief (ˌdɪsbɪˈliːf) *n* refusal or reluctance to believe.

disbelieve (ˌdɪsbɪˈliːv) *vb* **disbelieves, disbelieving, disbelieved. 1** (*tr*) to reject as false or lying. **2** (*intr; usually foll. by in*) to have no faith (in).
  ▶ ˌdisbeˈliever *n* ▶ ˌdisbeˈlieving *adj*

disbud (dɪsˈbʌd) *or* **debud** (diːˈbʌd) *vb* **disbuds, disbudding, disbudded** *or* **debuds, debudding, debudded. 1** to remove superfluous buds from (a plant). **2** *Vet. science.* to remove the horn buds of (calves, lambs, and kids).

disburden (dɪsˈbɜːdən) *vb* **1** to remove a load from. **2** (*tr*) to relieve (one's mind, etc.) of a distressing worry.

disburse (dɪsˈbɜːs) *vb* **disburses, disbursing, disbursed.** (*tr*) to pay out. [C16: from OF *desborser*, from *des-* DIS-[1] + *borser* to obtain money, from *borse* bag, from LL *bursa*]
  ▶ disˈbursable *adj* ▶ disˈbursement *n* ▶ disˈburser *n*

USAGE NOTE *Disburse* is sometimes wrongly used where *disperse* is meant: *the police used a water cannon to disperse* (not *disburse*) *the crowd.*

disc (dɪsk) *n* **1** a flat circular plate. **2** something resembling this. **3** a gramophone record. **4** *Anat.* any approximately circular flat structure in the body, esp. an intervertebral disc. **5** the flat receptacle of composite flowers, such as the daisy. **6a** Also called: **parking disc.** a marker or device for display in a parked vehicle showing the time of arrival or the latest permitted time of departure or both. **6b** (*as modifier*): *disc parking.* **7** *Computing.* a variant spelling of **disk.** [C18: from L *discus* DISCUS]
  ▶ ˈdiscal *adj*

disc. *abbrev. for:* **1** discount. **2** discovered.

discard *vb* (dɪsˈkɑːd). **1** (*tr*) to get rid of as useless or undesirable. **2** *Cards.* to throw out (a card or cards) from one's hand. **3** *Cards.* to play (a card not of the suit led nor a trump) when unable to follow suit. ◆ *n* ('dɪskɑːd). **4** a person or thing that has been cast aside. **5** *Cards.* a discarded card. **6** the act of discarding.

disc brake *n* a type of brake in which two pads rub against a flat disc attached to the wheel hub when the brake is applied.

discern (dɪˈsɜːn) *vb* **1** (*tr*) to recognize or perceive clearly. **2** to recognize or perceive (differences). [C14: from OF *discerner,* from L *discernere* to divide, from DIS-[1] apart + *cernere* to separate]
▶ **disˈcernible** *adj* ▶ **disˈcernibly** *adv*

discerning (dɪˈsɜːnɪŋ) *adj* having or showing good taste or judgment; discriminating.

discernment (dɪˈsɜːnmənt) *n* keen perception or judgment.

disc flower *or* **floret** *n* any of the small tubular flowers at the centre of the flower head of certain composite plants, such as the daisy.

discharge *vb* (dɪsˈtʃɑːdʒ). **discharges, discharging, discharged. 1** (*tr*) to release or allow to go. **2** (*tr*) to dismiss from or relieve of duty, employment, etc. **3** to fire or be fired, as a gun. **4** to pour forth or cause to pour forth: *the boil discharges pus.* **5** (*tr*) to remove (the cargo) from (a boat, etc.); unload. **6** (*tr*) to perform the duties of or meet the demands of (an office, obligation, etc.). **7** (*tr*) to relieve (oneself) of (a responsibility, debt, etc.). **8** (*intr*) *Physics.* **8a** to lose or remove electric charge. **8b** to form an arc, spark, or corona in a gas. **8c** to take or supply electrical current from a cell or battery. **9** (*tr*) *Law.* to release (a prisoner from custody, etc.). ◆ *n* ('dɪstʃɑːdʒ, dɪsˈtʃɑːdʒ). **10** a person or thing that is discharged. **11a** dismissal or release from an office, job, institution, etc. **11b** the document certifying such release. **12** the fulfilment of an obligation or release from a responsibility or liability. **13** the act of removing a load, as of cargo. **14** a pouring forth of a fluid; emission. **15a** the act of firing a projectile. **15b** the volley, bullet, etc., fired. **16** *Law.* **16a** a release, as of a person held under legal restraint. **16b** an annulment, as of a court order. **17** *Physics.* **17a** the act or process of removing or losing charge. **17b** a conduction of electricity through a gas by the formation and movement of electrons and ions in an applied electric field.
▶ **disˈchargeable** *adj* ▶ **disˈcharger** *n*

discharge tube *n Electronics.* an electrical device in which current flow is by electrons and ions in an ionized gas, as in a fluorescent light or neon tube.

disc harrow *n* a harrow with sharp-edged discs used to cut clods on the surface of the soil or to cover seed after planting.

disciple (dɪˈsaɪpᵊl) *n* **1** a follower of the doctrines of a teacher or a school of thought. **2** one of the personal followers of Christ (including his 12 apostles) during his earthly life. [OE *discipul,* from L *discipulus* pupil, from *discere* to learn]
▶ **disˈcipleˌship** *n* ▶ **discipular** (dɪˈsɪpjʊlə) *adj*

disciplinarian (ˌdɪsɪplɪˈnɛərɪən) *n* a person who imposes or advocates strict discipline.

disciplinary ('dɪsɪˌplɪnərɪ) *adj* **1** of, promoting, or used for discipline; corrective. **2** relating to a branch of learning.

discipline ('dɪsɪplɪn) *n* **1** training or conditions imposed for the improvement of physical powers, self-control, etc. **2** systematic training in obedience. **3** the state of improved behaviour, etc., resulting from such training. **4** punishment or chastisement. **5** a system of rules for behaviour, etc. **6** a branch of learning or instruction. **7** the laws governing members of a Church. ◆ *vb* **disciplines, disciplining, disciplined.** (*tr*) **8** to improve or attempt to improve the behaviour, orderliness, etc., of by training, conditions, or rules. **9** to punish or penalize. [C13: from L *disciplīna* teaching, from *discipulus* DISCIPLE]
▶ **'disciˌplinable** *adj* ▶ **disciplinal** (ˌdɪsɪˈplaɪnᵊl) *adj*
▶ **'disciˌpliner** *n*

disc jockey *n* a person who announces and plays recorded music, esp. pop music, on a radio programme, etc.

disclaim (dɪsˈkleɪm) *vb* **1** (*tr*) to deny or renounce (any claim, connection, etc.). **2** (*tr*) to deny the validity or authority of. **3** *Law.* to renounce or repudiate (a legal claim or right).

disclaimer (dɪsˈkleɪmə) *n* a repudiation or denial.

disclose (dɪsˈkləʊz) *vb* **discloses, disclosing, disclosed.** (*tr*) **1** to make known. **2** to allow to be seen.
▶ **disˈcloser** *n*

disclosure (dɪsˈkləʊʒə) *n* **1** something that is disclosed. **2** the act of disclosing; revelation.

disco ('dɪskəʊ) *n, pl* **discos. 1a** an occasion at which people dance to pop records. **1b** (*as modifier*): *disco music.* **2** a nightclub or other public place where such dances are held. **3** mobile equipment for providing music for a disco. [C20: from DISCOTHEQUE]

discobolus (dɪsˈkɒbələs) *n, pl* **discoboli** (-ˌlaɪ). a discus thrower. [C18: from L, from Gk, from *diskos* DISCUS + *-bolos,* from *ballein* to throw]

discography (dɪsˈkɒɡrəfɪ) *n* a classified list of gramophone records.
▶ **disˈcographer** *n*

discoid ('dɪskɔɪd) *adj also* **discoidal. 1** like a disc. ◆ *n* **2** a disclike object.

discolour *or US* **discolor** (dɪsˈkʌlə) *vb* to change in colour; fade or stain.
▶ **disˌcolorˈation** *or* **disˌcolourˈation** *n*

discombobulate (ˌdɪskəmˈbɒbjʊˌleɪt) *vb* **discombobulates, discombobulating, discombobulated.** (*tr*) *Inf., chiefly US & Canad.* to throw into confusion. [C20: prob. a whimsical alteration of DISCOMPOSE or DISCOMFIT]

discomfit (dɪsˈkʌmfɪt) *vb* (*tr*) **1** to make uneasy or confused. **2** to frustrate the plans or purpose of. **3** *Arch.* to defeat. [C14: from OF *desconfire* to destroy, from *des-* (indicating reversal) + *confire* to make, from L *conficere* to produce]
▶ **disˈcomfiture** *n*

discomfort (dɪsˈkʌmfət) *n* **1** an inconvenience, distress, or mild pain. **2** something that disturbs or deprives of ease. ◆ *vb* **3** (*tr*) to make uncomfortable or uneasy.

discommode (ˌdɪskəˈməʊd) *vb* **discommodes, discommoding, discommoded.** (*tr*) to cause inconvenience to; disturb.
▶ **ˌdiscomˈmodious** *adj*

discompose (ˌdɪskəmˈpəʊz) *vb* **discomposes, discomposing, discomposed.** (*tr*) **1** to disturb the composure of; disconcert. **2** *Now rare.* to disarrange.
▶ **ˌdiscomˈposure** *n*

disconcert (ˌdɪskənˈsɜːt) *vb* (*tr*) **1** to disturb the composure of. **2** to frustrate or upset.
▶ **ˌdisconˈcerted** *adj* ▶ **ˌdisconˈcerting** *adj* ▶ **ˌdisconˈcertion** *n*

disconformity (ˌdɪskənˈfɔːmɪtɪ) *n, pl* **disconformities. 1** lack of conformity; discrepancy. **2** the junction between two parallel series of stratified rocks.

disconnect (ˌdɪskəˈnɛkt) *vb* (*tr*) to undo or break the connection of or between (something, as a plug and a socket).
▶ **ˌdisconˈnection** *n*

disconnected (ˌdɪskəˈnɛktɪd) *adj* **1** not rationally connected; confused or incoherent. **2** not connected or joined.

disconsolate (dɪsˈkɒnsəlɪt) *adj* **1** sad beyond comfort; inconsolable. **2** disappointed; dejected. [C14: from Med. L *disconsōlātus,* from DIS-[1] + *consōlātus* comforted]
▶ **disˈconsolately** *adv* ▶ **disˈconsolateness** *or* **disˌconsoˈlation** *n*

discontent (ˌdɪskənˈtɛnt) *n* **1** *Also called:* **discontentment.** lack of contentment, as with one's condition or lot in life. ◆ *vb* **2** (*tr*) to make dissatisfied.
▶ **ˌdisconˈtented** *adj* ▶ **ˌdisconˈtentedness** *n*

discontinue (ˌdɪskənˈtɪnjuː) *vb* **discontinues, discontinuing, discontinued. 1** to come or bring to an end; interrupt or be interrupted; stop. **2** (*tr*) *Law.* to terminate or abandon (an action, suit, etc.).
▶ **ˌdisconˈtinuance** *n* ▶ **ˌdisconˌtinuˈation** *n*

discontinuity (ˌdɪskɒntɪˈnjuːɪtɪ, dɪsˌkɒntɪ-) *n, pl* **discontinuities. 1** lack of rational connection or cohesion. **2** a break or interruption.

discontinuous (ˌdɪskən'tɪnjʊəs) *adj* characterized by interruptions or breaks; intermittent.
► ˌdiscon'tinuously *adv* ► ˌdiscon'tinuousness *n*

discord *n* ('dɪskɔːd). **1** lack of agreement or harmony. **2** harsh confused mingling of sounds. **3** a combination of musical notes, esp. one containing one or more dissonant intervals. ◆ *vb* (dɪs'kɔːd). **4** (*intr*) to disagree; clash. [C13: from OF *descort*, from *descorder* to disagree, from L *discordāre*, from *discors* at variance, from DIS-¹ + *cor* heart]

discordant (dɪs'kɔːdᵊnt) *adj* **1** at variance; disagreeing. **2** harsh in sound; inharmonious.
► dis'cordance *n* ► dis'cordantly *adv*

discotheque ('dɪskəˌtɛk) *n* the full term for **disco**. [C20: from F *discothèque*, from Gk *diskos* disc + -o- + Gk *thēkē* case]

discount *vb* (dɪs'kaʊnt, 'dɪskaʊnt). (*mainly tr*) **1** to leave out of account as being unreliable, prejudiced, or irrelevant. **2** to anticipate and make allowance for. **3a** to deduct (an amount or percentage) from the price, cost, etc. **3b** to reduce (the regular price, etc.) by a percentage or amount. **4** to sell or offer for sale at a reduced price. **5** to buy or sell (a bill of exchange, etc.) before maturity, with a deduction for interest. **6** (*also intr*) to loan money on (a negotiable instrument) with a deduction for interest. ◆ *n* ('dɪskaʊnt). **7** a deduction from the full amount of a price or debt. See also **cash discount, trade discount. 8** Also called: **discount rate. 8a** the amount of interest deducted in the purchase or sale of or the loan of money on unmatured negotiable instruments. **8b** the rate of interest deducted. **9** (in the issue of shares) a percentage deducted from the par value to give a reduced amount payable by subscribers. **10** a discounting. **11 at a discount. 11a** below the regular price. **11b** held in low regard. **12** (*modifier*) offering or selling at reduced prices: *a discount shop*.
► dis'countable *adj* ► 'discounter *n*

discounted cash flow *n* the cash flow of an organization taking into account the future values of benefits and assets in addition to their present values.

discountenance (dɪs'kaʊntɪnəns) *vb* discountenances, discountenancing, discountenanced. (*tr*) **1** to make ashamed or confused. **2** to disapprove of. ◆ *n* **3** disapproval.

discount house *n* **1** *Chiefly Brit.* a financial organization engaged in discounting bills of exchange, etc., on a large scale. **2** Also called: **discount store.** *Chiefly US.* a shop offering for sale most of its merchandise at prices below the recommended prices.

discount market *n* the part of the money market consisting of banks, discount houses, and brokers on which bills are discounted.

discourage (dɪs'kʌrɪdʒ) *vb* discourages, discouraging, discouraged. (*tr*) **1** to deprive of the will to persist in something. **2** to inhibit; prevent: *this solution discourages rust*. **3** to oppose by expressing disapproval.
► dis'couragement *n* ► dis'couragingly *adv*

discourse *n* ('dɪskɔːs, dɪs'kɔːs). **1** verbal communication; talk; conversation. **2** a formal treatment of a subject in speech or writing. **3** a unit of text used by linguists for the analysis of linguistic phenomena that range over more than one sentence. **4** *Arch.* the ability to reason. ◆ *vb* (dɪs'kɔːs). **5** (*intr*; often foll. by *on* or *upon*) to speak or write (about) formally. **6** (*intr*) to hold a discussion. **7** (*tr*) *Arch.* to give forth (music). [C14: from Med. L *discursus* argument, from L: a running to and fro, from *discurrere*, from DIS-¹ + *currere* to run]

discourteous (dɪs'kɜːtɪəs) *adj* showing bad manners; impolite; rude.
► dis'courteously *adv* ► dis'courteousness *n*

discourtesy (dɪs'kɜːtɪsɪ) *n, pl* discourtesies. **1** bad manners; rudeness. **2** a rude remark or act.

discover (dɪs'kʌvə) *vb* (*tr; may take a clause as object*) **1** to be the first to find or find out about. **2** to learn about for the first time; realize. **3** to find after study or search. **4** to reveal or make known.
► dis'coverable *adj* ► dis'coverer *n*

discovery (dɪs'kʌvərɪ) *n, pl* discoveries. **1** the act, process, or an instance of discovering. **2** a person, place, or thing

that has been discovered. **3** *Law.* the compulsory disclosure by a party to an action of relevant documents in his possession.

discredit (dɪs'krɛdɪt) *vb* (*tr*) **1** to damage the reputation of. **2** to cause to be disbelieved or distrusted. **3** to reject as untrue. ◆ *n* **4** something that causes disgrace. **5** damage to a reputation. **6** lack of belief or confidence.

discreditable (dɪs'krɛdɪtəbᵊl) *adj* tending to bring discredit; shameful or unworthy.

discreet (dɪ'skriːt) *adj* **1** careful to avoid embarrassment, esp. by keeping confidences secret; tactful. **2** unobtrusive. [C14: from OF *discret*, from Med. L *discrētus*, from L *discernere* to DISCERN]
► dis'creetly *adv* ► dis'creetness *n*

> **USAGE NOTE** Avoid confusion with **discrete.**

---

discrepancy (dɪ'skrɛpənsɪ) *n, pl* discrepancies. a conflict or variation, as between facts, figures, or claims. [C15: from L *discrepāns*, from *discrepāre* to differ in sound, from DIS-¹ + *crepāre* to be noisy]
► dis'crepant *adj*

> **USAGE NOTE** *Discrepancy* is sometimes wrongly used where *disparity* is meant. A *discrepancy* exists between things which ought to be the same; it can be small but is usually significant. A *disparity* is a large difference between measurable things such as age, rank, or wages

---

discrete (dɪ'skriːt) *adj* **1** separate or distinct. **2** consisting of distinct or separate parts. [C14: from L *discrētus* separated; see DISCREET]
► dis'cretely *adv* ► dis'creteness *n*

> **USAGE NOTE** Avoid confusion with **discreet.**

---

discretion (dɪ'skrɛʃən) *n* **1** the quality of behaving so as to avoid social embarrassment or distress. **2** freedom or authority to make judgments and to act as one sees fit (esp. in **at one's own discretion, at the discretion of**). **3 age of years of discretion.** the age at which a person is thought able to manage his own affairs.

discretionary (dɪ'skrɛʃənərɪ, -ənrɪ) *or* **discretional** *adj* having or using the ability to decide at one's own discretion: *discretionary powers*.

discretionary trust *n* a trust in which the beneficiaries' shares are not fixed in the trust deed but are left to the discretion of other persons, often the trustees.

discriminate *vb* (dɪ'skrɪmɪˌneɪt). discriminates, discriminating, discriminated. **1** (*intr*; usually foll. by *in favour of* or *against*) to single out a particular person, group, etc., for special favour or, esp., disfavour. **2** (when *intr*, foll. by *between* or *among*) to recognize or understand the difference (between); distinguish. **3** (*intr*) to constitute or mark a difference. **4** (*intr*) to be discerning in matters of taste. ◆ *adj* (dɪ'skrɪmɪnɪt). **5** showing or marked by discrimination. [C17: from L *discrīmināre* to divide, from *discrīmen* a separation, from *discernere* to DISCERN]
► dis'criminately *adv*

discriminating (dɪ'skrɪmɪˌneɪtɪŋ) *adj* **1** able to see fine distinctions and differences. **2** discerning in matters of taste. **3** (of a tariff, import duty, etc.) levied at differential rates.

discrimination (dɪˌskrɪmɪ'neɪʃən) *n* **1** unfair treatment of a person, racial group, minority, etc.; action based on prejudice. **2** subtle appreciation in matters of taste. **3** the ability to see fine distinctions and differences.

discriminatory (dɪ'skrɪmɪnətərɪ, -trɪ) *or* **discriminative** (dɪ'skrɪmɪnətɪv) *adj* **1** based on or showing prejudice; biased. **2** capable of making fine distinctions.

discursive (dɪ'skɜːsɪv) *adj* **1** passing from one topic to another; digressive. **2** *Philosophy.* of or relating to knowledge obtained by reason and argument rather than intu-

---

ition. [C16: from Med. L *discursīvus,* from LL *discursus* DISCOURSE]
▸ **dis'cursively** *adv* ▸ **dis'cursiveness** *n*

discus ('dɪskəs) *n, pl* **discuses** or **disci** ('dɪskaɪ). **1** (originally) a circular stone or plate used in throwing competitions by the ancient Greeks. **2** *Field sports.* a similar disc-shaped object with a heavy middle, thrown by athletes. **3** (preceded by *the*) the event or sport of throwing the discus. [C17: from L, from Gk *diskos,* from *dikein* to throw]

discuss (dɪ'skʌs) *vb* (*tr*) **1** to have a conversation about; consider by talking over. **2** to treat (a subject) in speech or writing. [C14: from LL *discussus* examined, from *discutere,* from L: to dash to pieces, from DIS-^{1} + *quatere* to shake]
▸ **dis'cussant** or **dis'cusser** *n* ▸ **dis'cussible** or **dis-'cussable** *adj*

discussion (dɪ'skʌʃən) *n* the examination or consideration of a matter in speech or writing.

disdain (dɪs'deɪn) *n* **1** a feeling or show of superiority and dislike; contempt; scorn. ◆ *vb* **2** (*tr; may take an infinitive*) to refuse or reject with disdain. [C13 *dedeyne,* from OF *desdeign,* from *desdeigner* to reject as unworthy, from L *dēdignārī;* see DIS-^{1}, DEIGN]
▸ **dis'dainful** *adj*

disease (dɪ'zi:z) *n* **1** any impairment of normal physiological function affecting an organism, esp. a change caused by infection, stress, etc., producing characteristic symptoms; illness or sickness in general. **2** a corresponding condition in plants. **3** any condition likened to this. [C14: from OF *desaise;* see DIS-^{1}, EASE]
▸ **dis'eased** *adj*

diseconomy (ˌdɪsɪ'kɒnəmɪ) *n Econ.* disadvantage, such as lower efficiency or higher costs, resulting from the scale on which an enterprise operates.

disembark (ˌdɪsɪm'ba:k) *vb* to land or cause to land from a ship, aircraft, etc.
▸ **disembarkation** (dɪsˌembɑ:'keɪʃən) *n*

disembarrass (ˌdɪsɪm'bærəs) *vb* (*tr*) **1** to free from embarrassment, entanglement, etc. **2** to relieve or rid of something burdensome.

disembodied (ˌdɪsɪm'bɒdɪd) *adj* **1** lacking a body or freed from the body. **2** lacking in substance or any firm relation to reality.

disembody (ˌdɪsɪm'bɒdɪ) *vb* **disembodies, disembodying, disembodied.** (*tr*) to free from the body or from physical form.
▸ **disem'bodiment** *n*

disembogue (ˌdɪsɪm'bəʊg) *vb* **disembogues, disemboguing, disembogued. 1** (of a river, stream, etc.) to discharge (water) at the mouth. **2** (*intr*) to flow out. [C16: from Sp. *desembocar,* from *des-* DIS-^{1} + *embocar* to put into the mouth]
▸ **disem'boguement** *n*

disembowel (ˌdɪsɪm'baʊəl) *vb* **disembowels, disembowelling, disembowelled** or *US* **disembowels, disemboweling, disemboweled.** (*tr*) to remove the entrails of.
▸ **disem'bowelment** *n*

disempower (ˌdɪsɪm'paʊə) *vb* (*tr*) to deprive (a person) of power or authority.
▸ **disem'powerment** *n*

disenchant (ˌdɪsɪn'tʃɑ:nt) *vb* (*tr*) to free from or as if from an enchantment; disillusion.
▸ **ˌdisen'chantingly** *adv* ▸ **ˌdisen'chantment** *n*

disencumber (ˌdɪsɪn'kʌmbə) *vb* (*tr*) to free from encumbrances.
▸ **ˌdisen'cumberment** *n*

disenfranchise (ˌdɪsɪn'fræntʃaɪz) or **disfranchise** *vb* **disenfranchises, disenfranchising, disenfranchised** or **disfranchises, disfranchising, disfranchised.** (*tr*) **1** to deprive (a person) of the right to vote or other rights of citizenship. **2** to deprive (a place) of the right to send representatives to an elected body. **3** to deprive (a person, place, etc.) of any franchise or right.
▸ **disenfranchisement** (ˌdɪsɪn'fræntʃɪzmənt) or **dis-'franchisement** *n*

disengage (ˌdɪsɪn'geɪdʒ) *vb* **disengages, disengaging, dis-**

engaged. **1** to release or become released from a connection, obligation, etc. **2** *Mil.* to withdraw (forces) from close action. **3** *Fencing.* to move (one's blade) from one side of an opponent's blade to another in a circular motion.
▸ **ˌdisen'gaged** *adj* ▸ **ˌdisen'gagement** *n*

disentangle (ˌdɪsɪn'tæŋgəl) *vb* **disentangles, disentangling, disentangled. 1** to release or become free from entanglement or confusion. **2** (*tr*) to unravel or work out.
▸ **ˌdisen'tanglement** *n*

disequilibrium (ˌdɪsi:kwɪ'lɪbrɪəm) *n* a loss or absence of equilibrium, esp. in an economy.

disestablish (ˌdɪsɪ'stæblɪʃ) *vb* (*tr*) to deprive (a church, custom, institution, etc.) of established status.
▸ **ˌdises'tablishment** *n*

disesteem (ˌdɪsɪ'sti:m) *vb* **1** (*tr*) to think little of. ◆ *n* **2** lack of esteem.

disfavour or *US* **disfavor** (dɪs'feɪvə) *n* **1** disapproval or dislike. **2** the state of being disapproved of or disliked. **3** an unkind act. ◆ *vb* **4** (*tr*) to treat with disapproval or dislike.

disfigure (dɪs'fɪgə) *vb* **disfigures, disfiguring, disfigured.** (*tr*) **1** to spoil the appearance or shape of; deface. **2** to mar the effect or quality of.
▸ **dis'figurement** *n*

disforest (dɪs'fɒrɪst) *vb* (*tr*) **1** another word for **deforest. 2** *English law.* a less common word for **disafforest.**
▸ **dis,fores'tation** *n*

disfranchise (dɪs'fræntʃaɪz) *vb* another word for **disenfranchise.**

disgorge (dɪs'gɔ:dʒ) *vb* **disgorges, disgorging, disgorged. 1** to throw out (food, etc.) from the throat or stomach; vomit. **2** to discharge or empty of (contents). **3** (*tr*) to yield up unwillingly.
▸ **dis'gorgement** *n*

disgrace (dɪs'greɪs) *n* **1** a condition of shame, loss of reputation, or dishonour. **2** a shameful person or thing. **3** exclusion from confidence or trust: *he is in disgrace with his father.* ◆ *vb* **disgraces, disgracing, disgraced.** (*tr*) **4** to bring shame upon. **5** to treat or cause to be treated with disfavour.

disgraceful (dɪs'greɪsfʊl) *adj* shameful; scandalous.
▸ **dis'gracefully** *adv*

disgruntle (dɪs'grʌntəl) *vb* **disgruntles, disgruntling, disgruntled.** (*tr*) to make sulky or discontented. [C17: DIS-^{1} + obs. *gruntle* to complain]
▸ **dis'gruntled** *adj* ▸ **dis'gruntlement** *n*

disguise (dɪs'gaɪz) *vb* **disguises, disguising, disguised. 1** to modify the appearance or manner in order to conceal the identity of (someone or something). **2** (*tr*) to misrepresent in order to obscure the actual nature or meaning. ◆ *n* **3** a mask, costume, or manner that disguises. **4** a disguising or being disguised. [C14: from OF *desguisier,* from *des-* DIS-^{1} + *guise* manner]
▸ **dis'guised** *adj*

disgust (dɪs'gʌst) *vb* (*tr*) **1** to sicken or fill with loathing. **2** to offend the moral sense of. ◆ *n* **3** a great loathing or distaste. **4** in disgust, as a result of disgust. [C16: from OF *desgouster,* from *des-* DIS-^{1} + *gouster* to taste, from L *gustus* taste]
▸ **dis'gustedly** *adv* ▸ **dis'gustedness** *n*

dish (dɪʃ) *n* **1** a container used for holding or serving food, esp. an open shallow container. **2** the food in a dish. **3** a particular kind of food. **4** Also called: **dishful.** the amount contained in a dish. **5** something resembling a dish. **6** a concavity. **7** short for **dish aerial. 8** *Inf.* an attractive person. ◆ *vb* (*tr*) **9** to put into a dish. **10** to make concave. **11** *Brit. inf.* to ruin or spoil. ◆ See also **dish out, dish up.** [OE *disc,* from L *discus* quoit]
▸ **'dish,like** *adj*

dishabille (ˌdɪsæ'bi:l) *n* a variant of **deshabille.**

dish aerial *n* a microwave aerial, used esp. in radar, radio telescopes, and satellite broadcasting (**satellite dish aerial**), consisting of a parabolic reflector. Formal name: **parabolic aerial.** ◆ Also called: **dish antenna.** Often shortened to **dish.**

disharmony (dɪs'hɑ:mənɪ) *n, pl* **disharmonies. 1** lack of

accord or harmony. **2** a situation, circumstance, etc., that is inharmonious.
▶ **disharmonious** (ˌdɪshɑːˈməʊnɪəs) *adj*

dishcloth (ˈdɪʃˌklɒθ) *n* a cloth or rag for washing or drying dishes.

dishearten (dɪsˈhɑːtᵊn) *vb* (*tr*) to weaken or destroy the hope, courage, enthusiasm, etc., of.
▶ **disˈhearteningly** *adv* ▶ **disˈheartenment** *n*

dished (dɪʃt) *adj* **1** shaped like a dish. **2** (of wheels) closer to one another at the bottom than at the top. **3** *Inf.* exhausted or defeated.

dishevel (dɪˈʃevᵊl) *vb* **dishevels, dishevelling, dishevelled** or *US* **dishevels, disheveling, disheveled.** to disarrange (the hair or clothes) of (someone).   [C15: back formation from DI-SHEVELLED]
▶ **diˈshevelment** *n*

dishevelled or *US* **disheveled** (dɪˈʃevᵊld) *adj* **1** (esp. of hair) hanging loosely. **2** unkempt; untidy.   [C15 *dischevelee*, from OF *deschevelé*, from *des-* DIS-ᵉ + *chevel* hair, from L *capillus*]

dishonest (dɪsˈɒnɪst) *adj* not honest or fair; deceiving or fraudulent.
▶ **disˈhonestly** *adv*

dishonesty (dɪsˈɒnɪstɪ) *n, pl* **dishonesties. 1** lack of honesty. **2** a deceiving act or statement.

dishonour or *US* **dishonor** (dɪsˈɒnə) *vb* (*tr*) **1** to treat with disrespect. **2** to fail or refuse to pay (a cheque, etc.). **3** to cause the disgrace of (a woman) by seduction or rape. ◆ *n* **4** a lack of honour or respect. **5** a state of shame or disgrace. **6** a person or thing that causes a loss of honour. **7** an insult; affront. **8** refusal or failure to accept or pay a commercial paper.

dishonourable or *US* **dishonorable** (dɪsˈɒnərəbᵊl) *adj* **1** characterized by or causing dishonour or discredit. **2** having little or no integrity; unprincipled.
▶ **disˈhonourableness** or *US* **disˈhonorableness** *n* ▶ **disˈhonourably** or *US* **disˈhonorably** *adv*

dish out *vb* (*tr, adv*) **1** *Inf.* to distribute. **2 dish it out.** to inflict punishment.

dishtowel (ˈdɪʃˌtaʊəl) *n* another name (esp. Scot., US and Canad.) for a **tea towel.**

dish up *vb* (*adv*) **1** to serve (a meal, food, etc.). **2** (*tr*) *Inf.* to prepare or present, esp. in an attractive manner.

dishwasher (ˈdɪʃˌwɒʃə) *n* **1** a machine for washing dishes, etc. **2** a person who washes dishes, etc.

dishwater (ˈdɪʃˌwɔːtə) *n* **1** water in which dishes have been washed. **2** something resembling this.

dishy (ˈdɪʃɪ) *adj* **dishier, dishiest.** *Inf., chiefly Brit.* good-looking or attractive.

disillusion (ˌdɪsɪˈluːʒən) *vb* **1** (*tr*) to destroy the ideals, illusions, or false ideas of. ◆ *n also* **disillusionment. 2** the act of disillusioning or the state of being disillusioned.

disincentive (ˌdɪsɪnˈsentɪv) *n* **1** something that acts as a deterrent. ◆ *adj* **2** acting as a deterrent: *a disincentive effect on productivity.*

disincline (ˌdɪsɪnˈklaɪn) *vb* **disinclines, disinclining, disinclined.** to make or be unwilling, reluctant, or averse.
▶ **disinclination** (ˌdɪsɪnklɪˈneɪʃən) *n*

disinfect (ˌdɪsɪnˈfekt) *vb* (*tr*) to rid of microorganisms potentially harmful to man, esp. by chemical means.
▶ **ˌdisinˈfection** *n*

disinfectant (ˌdɪsɪnˈfektənt) *n* an agent that destroys or inhibits the activity of microorganisms that cause disease.

disinfest (ˌdɪsɪnˈfest) *vb* (*tr*) to rid of vermin.
▶ **disinfesˈtation** *n*

disinflation (ˌdɪsɪnˈfleɪʃən) *n Econ.* a reduction or stabilization of the general price level intended to improve the balance of payments without incurring reductions in output, employment, etc.

disinformation (ˌdɪsɪnfəˈmeɪʃən) *n* false information intended to deceive or mislead.

disingenuous (ˌdɪsɪnˈdʒenjʊəs) *adj* not sincere; lacking candour.
▶ **ˌdisinˈgenuously** *adv* ▶ **ˌdisinˈgenuousness** *n*

disinherit (ˌdɪsɪnˈherɪt) *vb* (*tr*) **1** *Law.* to deprive (an heir

or next of kin) of inheritance or right to inherit. **2** to deprive of a right or heritage.
▶ **ˌdisinˈheritance** *n*

disintegrate (dɪsˈɪntɪˌɡreɪt) *vb* **disintegrates, disintegrating, disintegrated. 1** to break or be broken into fragments or parts; shatter. **2** to lose or cause to lose cohesion. **3** (*intr*) to lose judgment or control. **4** *Physics.* **4a** to induce or undergo nuclear fission. **4b** another word for **decay** (sense 3).
▶ **disˌinteˈgration** *n* ▶ **disˈinteˌgrator** *n*

disinter (ˌdɪsɪnˈtɜː) *vb* **disinters, disinterring, disinterred.** (*tr*) **1** to remove or dig up; exhume. **2** to bring to light; expose.
▶ **ˌdisinˈterment** *n*

disinterest (dɪsˈɪntrɪst, -tərɪst) *n* **1** freedom from bias or involvement. **2** lack of interest.

disinterested (dɪsˈɪntrɪstɪd, -tərɪs-) *adj* **1** free from bias or partiality; objective. **2** not interested.
▶ **disˈinterestedly** *adv* ▶ **disˈinterestedness** *n*

> **USAGE NOTE**   Many people consider that the use of *disinterested* to mean not interested is incorrect and *uninterested* should be used.

disintermediation (ˌdɪsˌɪntəˌmiːdɪˈeɪʃən) *n Finance.* the elimination of such financial intermediaries as banks and brokers in transactions between principals, often as a result of deregulation and the use of computing.

disinvest (ˌdɪsɪnˈvest) *vb Econ.* **1** (usually foll. by *in*) to remove investment (from). **2** (*intr*) to reduce the capital stock of an economy or enterprise, as by not replacing obsolete machinery.
▶ **ˌdisinˈvestment** *n*

disjoin (dɪsˈdʒɔɪn) *vb* to disconnect or become disconnected; separate.
▶ **disˈjoinable** *adj*

disjoint (dɪsˈdʒɔɪnt) *vb* **1** to take apart or come apart at the joints. **2** (*tr*) to disunite or disjoin. **3** to dislocate or become dislocated. **4** (*tr; usually passive*) to end the unity, sequence, or coherence of.

disjointed (dɪsˈdʒɔɪntɪd) *adj* **1** having no coherence; disconnected. **2** separated at the joint. **3** dislocated.
▶ **disˈjointedly** *adv*

disjunct (ˈdɪsdʒʌŋkt) *n Logic.* one of the propositions in a disjunction.

disjunction (dɪsˈdʒʌŋkʃən) *n* **1** Also called: **disjuncture.** a disconnecting or being disconnected; separation. **2** *Logic.* **2a** the operator that forms a compound sentence from two given sentences and corresponds to the English *or.* **2b** the relation between such sentences.

disjunctive (dɪsˈdʒʌŋktɪv) *adj* **1** serving to disconnect or separate. **2** *Grammar.* denoting a word, esp. a conjunction, that serves to express opposition or contrast: *but* in *She was poor but she was honest.* **3** *Logic.* relating to, characterized by, or containing disjunction. ◆ *n* **4** *Grammar.* a disjunctive word, esp. a conjunction. **5** *Logic.* a disjunctive proposition.
▶ **disˈjunctively** *adv*

disk (dɪsk) *n* **1** a variant spelling (esp. US and Canad.) of **disc. 2** Also called: **magnetic disk, hard disk.** *Computing.* a direct-access storage device consisting of a stack of plates coated with a magnetic layer, the whole assembly rotating rapidly as a single unit.

disk drive *n Computing.* the controller and mechanism for reading and writing data on computer disks.

diskette (dɪsˈket) *n* another name for **floppy disk.**

disk operating system *n* an operating system used on a computer system with one or more disk drives. Often shortened to: **DOS.**

dislike (dɪsˈlaɪk) *vb* **dislikes, disliking, disliked. 1** (*tr*) to consider unpleasant or disagreeable. ◆ *n* **2** a feeling of aversion or antipathy.
▶ **disˈlikable** or **disˈlikeable** *adj*

dislocate (ˈdɪsləˌkeɪt) *vb* **dislocates, dislocating, dislocated.** (*tr*) **1** to disrupt or shift out of place. **2** to displace from its normal position, esp. a bone from its joint.

★ people and places

dislocation (ˌdɪslə'keɪʃən) n 1 a displacing or being displaced. 2 the state or condition of being dislocated.

dislodge (dɪs'lɒdʒ) vb dislodges, dislodging, dislodged. to remove from or leave a lodging place, hiding place, or previously fixed position.
▶ dis'lodgment or dis'lodgement n

disloyal (dɪs'lɔɪəl) adj not loyal or faithful; deserting one's allegiance.
▶ dis'loyally adv

disloyalty (dɪs'lɔɪəltɪ) n, pl disloyalties. the condition or an instance of being unfaithful or disloyal.

dismal ('dɪzməl) adj 1 causing gloom or depression. 2 causing dismay or terror. 3 of poor quality or a low standard; feeble. [C13: from dismal (n) list of 24 unlucky days in the year, from Med. L diēs malī, from L diēs day + malus bad]
▶ 'dismally adv ▶ 'dismalness n

dismantle (dɪs'mæntˀl) vb dismantles, dismantling, dismantled. (tr) 1 to take apart. 2 to demolish or raze. 3 to strip of covering. [C17: from OF desmanteler to remove a cloak from]
▶ dis'mantlement n

dismast (dɪs'mɑːst) vb (tr) to break off the mast or masts of (a sailing vessel).

dismay (dɪs'meɪ) vb (tr) 1 to fill with apprehension or alarm. 2 to fill with depression or discouragement. ◆ n 3 consternation or agitation. [C13: from OF desmaier (unattested), from des- DIS-[1] + esmayer to frighten, ult. of Gmc origin]
▶ dis'maying adj

dismember (dɪs'membə) vb (tr) 1 to remove the limbs or members of. 2 to cut to pieces. 3 to divide or partition (something, such as an empire).
▶ dis'memberment n

dismiss (dɪs'mɪs) vb (tr) 1 to remove or discharge from employment or service. 2 to send away or allow to go. 3 to dispel from one's mind; discard. 4 to cease to consider (a subject). 5 to decline further hearing to (a claim or action). 6 Cricket. to bowl out a side for a particular number of runs. [C15: from Med. L dimissus sent away, from dīmittere, from dī- DIS-[1] + mittere to send]
▶ dis'missal n ▶ dis'missible adj ▶ dis'missive adj

dismount (dɪs'maʊnt) vb 1 to get off a horse, bicycle, etc. 2 (tr) to disassemble or remove from a mounting. ◆ n 3 the act of dismounting.

Disney ★ ('dɪznɪ) n Walt(er Elias). 1901–66, US film producer, who pioneered animated cartoons: noted esp. for his creations Mickey Mouse and Donald Duck and films such as Fantasia (1940).
▶ ˌDisney'esque adj

Disneyfication (ˌdɪznɪfɪ'keɪʃən) n Derog. the process by which historical places, local customs, etc. are transformed into trivial entertainment for tourists: the Disneyfication of Britain's heritage. [C20: from the Disneyland amusement park in California]
▶ ˌDisney'fy vb (tr).

disobedience (ˌdɪsə'biːdɪəns) n lack of obedience.

disobedient (ˌdɪsə'biːdɪənt) adj not obedient; neglecting or refusing to obey.
▶ ˌdiso'bediently adv

disobey (ˌdɪsə'beɪ) vb to neglect or refuse to obey (someone, an order, etc.).
▶ ˌdiso'beyer n

disoblige (ˌdɪsə'blaɪdʒ) vb disobliges, disobliging, disobliged. (tr) 1 to disregard the desires of. 2 to slight; insult. 3 Inf. to cause trouble or inconvenience to.
▶ ˌdiso'bliging adj

disorder (dɪs'ɔːdə) n 1 a lack of order; confusion. 2 a disturbance of public order. 3 an upset of health; ailment. 4 a deviation from the normal system or order. ◆ vb (tr) 5 to upset the order of. 6 to disturb the health or mind of.

disorderly (dɪs'ɔːdəlɪ) adj 1 untidy; irregular. 2 uncontrolled; unruly. 3 Law. violating public peace or order.
▶ dis'orderliness n

disorderly house n Law. an establishment in which unruly behaviour habitually occurs, esp. a brothel or a gaming house.

disorganize or **disorganise** (dɪs'ɔːgəˌnaɪz) vb disorganizes, disorganizing, disorganized or disorganises, disorganising, disorganised. (tr) to disrupt the arrangement, system, or unity of.
▶ disˌorgani'zation or disˌorgani'sation n

disorientate (dɪs'ɔːrɪenˌteɪt) or **disorient** vb disorientates, disorientating, disorientated or disorients, disorienting, disoriented. (tr) 1 to cause (someone) to lose his bearings. 2 to perplex; confuse.
▶ disˌorien'tation n

disown (dɪs'əʊn) vb (tr) to deny any connection with; refuse to acknowledge.
▶ dis'owner n

disparage (dɪ'spærɪdʒ) vb disparages, disparaging, disparaged. (tr) 1 to speak contemptuously of; belittle. 2 to damage the reputation of. [C14: from OF desparagier, from des- DIS-[1] + parage equality, from L par equal]
▶ dis'paragement n ▶ dis'paraging adj

disparate ('dɪspərɪt) adj 1 utterly different or distinct in kind. ◆ n 2 (pl) unlike things or people. [C16: from L disparāre to divide, from DIS-[1] + parāre to prepare; also infl. by L dispar unequal]
▶ 'disparately adv ▶ 'disparateness n

disparity (dɪ'spærɪtɪ) n, pl disparities. 1 inequality or difference, as in age, rank, wages, etc. 2 dissimilarity.

> **USAGE NOTE** See at **discrepancy**.

dispassionate (dɪs'pæʃənɪt) adj devoid of or uninfluenced by emotion or prejudice; objective; impartial.
▶ dis'passionately adv

dispatch or **despatch** (dɪ'spætʃ) vb (tr) 1 to send off promptly, as to a destination or to perform a task. 2 to discharge or complete (a duty, etc.) promptly. 3 Inf. to eat up quickly. 4 to murder or execute. ◆ n 5 the act of sending off a letter, messenger, etc. 6 prompt action or speed (often in with dispatch). 7 an official communication or report, sent in haste. 8 a report sent to a newspaper, etc., by a correspondent. 9 murder or execution. [C16: from It. dispacciare, from Provençal despachar, from OF despeechier to set free, from des- DIS-[1] + -peechier, ult. from L pedica a fetter]
▶ dis'patcher n

dispatch box n a case or box used to hold valuables or documents, esp. official state documents.

dispatch case n a case used for carrying papers, documents, books, etc.

dispatch rider n a horseman or motorcyclist who carries dispatches.

dispel (dɪ'spel) vb dispels, dispelling, dispelled. (tr) to disperse or drive away. [C17: from L dispellere, from DIS-[1] + pellere to drive]
▶ dis'peller n

dispensable (dɪ'spensəbˀl) adj 1 not essential; expendable. 2 (of a law, vow, etc.) able to be relaxed.
▶ disˌpensa'bility n

dispensary (dɪ'spensərɪ) n, pl dispensaries. a place where medicine, etc., is dispensed.

dispensation (ˌdɪspen'seɪʃən) n 1 the act of distributing or dispensing. 2 something distributed or dispensed. 3 a system or plan of administering or dispensing. 4 Chiefly RC Church. permission to dispense with an obligation of church law. 5 any exemption from an obligation. 6a the ordering of life and events by God. 6b a religious system or code of prescriptions for life and conduct regarded as of divine origin.
▶ dispen'sational adj

dispensatory (dɪ'spensətərɪ, -trɪ) n, pl dispensatories. a book listing the composition, preparation, and application of various drugs.

dispense (dɪ'spens) vb dispenses, dispensing, dispensed. 1 (tr) to give out or distribute in portions. 2 (tr) to prepare and distribute (medicine), esp. on prescription. 3 (tr) to administer (the law, etc.). 4 (intr; foll. by with) to do away (with) or manage (without). 5 to grant a dispensation to. 6 to exempt or excuse from a rule or obligation. [C14:

from Med. L *dispensāre* to pardon, from L *dispendere* to weigh out, from DIS-¹ + *pendere*]

> **USAGE NOTE** *Dispense with* is sometimes wrongly used where *dispose of* is meant: *the task can be disposed of* (not *dispensed with*) *quickly and easily.*

dispenser (dɪ'spensə) *n* **1** a device that automatically dispenses a single item or a measured quantity. **2** a person or thing that dispenses.

dispensing optician *n* See optician.

dispersal (dɪ'spɜːsᵊl) *n* **1** a dispersing or being dispersed. **2** the spread of animals, plants, or seeds to new areas.

dispersant (dɪs'pɜːsənt) *n* a liquid or gas used to disperse small particles or droplets, as in an aerosol.

disperse (dɪ'spɜːs) *vb* disperses, dispersing, dispersed. **1** to scatter; distribute over a wide area. **2** to dissipate. **3** to leave or cause to leave a gathering. **4** to separate or be separated by dispersion. **5** (*tr*) to spread (news, etc.). **6** to separate (particles) throughout a solid, liquid, or gas. ◆ *adj* **7** of or consisting of the particles in a colloid or suspension: *disperse phase.* [C14: from L *dispersus*, from *dispergere* to scatter widely, from DI-² + *spargere* to strew]
> **dis'perser** *n*

> **USAGE NOTE** See at disburse.

dispersion (dɪ'spɜːʃən) *n* **1** another word for dispersal. **2** *Physics.* **2a** the separation of electromagnetic radiation into constituents of different wavelengths. **2b** a measure of the ability of a substance to separate by refraction. **3** *Statistics.* the degree to which values of a frequency distribution are scattered around some central point, usually the arithmetic mean or median. **4** *Chem.* a system containing particles dispersed in a solid, liquid, or gas. **5** *Ecology.* the distribution pattern of a population of animals or plants.

dispirit (dɪ'spɪrɪt) *vb* (*tr*) to lower the spirit of; make downhearted; discourage.
> **dis'pirited** *adj* > **dis'piritedness** *n* > **dis'piriting** *adj*

displace (dɪs'pleɪs) *vb* displaces, displacing, displaced. (*tr*) **1** to move from the usual or correct location. **2** to remove from office or employment. **3** to occupy the place of; replace; supplant.

displaced person *n* a person forced from his or her home or country, esp. by war or revolution.

displacement (dɪs'pleɪsmənt) *n* **1** a displacing or being displaced. **2** the weight or volume displaced by a body in a fluid. **3** *Psychoanal.* the transferring of emotional feelings from their original object to one that disguises their real nature. **4** *Maths.* the distance measured in a particular direction from a reference point. Symbol: *s*

displacement activity *n* *Psychol.* behaviour that occurs typically when there is a conflict of motives and that has no relevance to either motive: e.g. head scratching.

display (dɪ'spleɪ) *vb* **1** (*tr*) to show or make visible. **2** (*tr*) to put out to be seen; exhibit. **3** (*tr*) to disclose; reveal. **4** (*tr*) to flaunt in an ostentatious way. **5** (*tr*) to spread out; unfold. **6** (*tr*) to give prominence to. **7** (*intr*) *Zool.* to engage in a display. ◆ *n* **8** an exhibiting or displaying; show. **9** something exhibited or displayed. **10** an ostentatious exhibition. **11** an arrangement of certain typefaces to give prominence to headings, etc. **12** *Electronics.* **12a** a device capable of representing information visually, as on a cathode-ray tube screen. **12b** the information so presented. **13** *Zool.* a pattern of behaviour by which the animal attracts attention while it is courting the female, defending its territory, etc. **14** (*modifier*) designating typefaces that give prominence to the words they are used to set. [C14: from Anglo-F *despleier* to unfold, from LL *displicāre* to scatter, from DIS-¹ + *plicāre* to fold]
> **dis'player** *n*

displease (dɪs'pliːz) *vb* displeases, displeasing, displeased. to annoy, offend, or cause displeasure to (someone).
> **dis'pleasing** *adj* > **dis'pleasingly** *adv*

displeasure (dɪs'plɛʒə) *n* **1** the condition of being displeased. **2** *Arch.* a pain. **2a** Arch. act or cause of offence.

disport (dɪ'spɔːt) *vb* **1** (*tr*) to indulge (oneself) in pleasure. **2** (*intr*) to frolic or gambol. ◆ *n* **3** *Arch.* amusement. [C14: from Anglo-F *desporter*, from *des-* DIS-¹ + *porter* to carry]

disposable (dɪ'spəuzəbᵊl) *adj* **1** designed for disposal after use: *disposable cups.* **2** available for use if needed: *disposable assets.* ◆ *n* **3** something, such as a baby's nappy, that is designed for disposal. **4** (*pl*) short for disposable goods.
> **dis,posa'bility** *or* **dis'posableness** *n*

disposable goods *pl n* consumer goods that are used up a short time after purchase, including perishables, newspapers, clothes, etc. Also called: **disposables.**

disposable income *n* **1** the money a person has available to spend after paying taxes, pension contributions, etc. **2** the total amount of money that the individuals in a community, country, etc., have available to buy consumer goods.

disposal (dɪ'spəuzᵊl) *n* **1** the act or means of getting rid of something. **2** arrangement in a particular order. **3** a specific method of tending to matters, as in business. **4** the act or process of transferring something to or providing something for another. **5** the power or opportunity to make use of someone or something (esp. in **at one's disposal**).

dispose (dɪ'spəuz) *vb* disposes, disposing, disposed. **1** (*intr*; foll. by *of*) **1a** to deal with or settle. **1b** to give, sell, or transfer to another. **1c** to throw out or away. **1d** to consume, esp. hurriedly. **1e** to kill. **2** to arrange or settle (matters). **3** (*tr*) to make willing or receptive. **4** (*tr*) to place in a certain order. **5** (*tr*; often foll. by *to*) to accustom or condition. [C14: from OF *disposer*, from L *dispōnere* to set in different places, from DIS-¹ + *pōnere* to place]
> **dis'poser** *n*

disposed (dɪ'spəuzd) *adj* **a** having an inclination as specified (towards something). **b** (*in combination*): *well-disposed.*

disposition (,dɪspə'zɪʃən) *n* **1** a person's usual temperament or frame of mind. **2** a tendency, inclination, or habit. **3** another word for disposal (senses 2–5). **4** *Arch.* manner of placing or arranging.

dispossess (,dɪspə'zɛs) *vb* (*tr*) to take away possession of something, esp. property; expel.
> **,dispos'session** *n* > **,dispos'sessor** *n*

dispraise (dɪs'preɪz) *vb* dispraises, dispraising, dispraised. **1** (*tr*) to express disapproval or condemnation of. ◆ *n* **2** the disapproval, etc., expressed.
> **dis'praiser** *n*

disproof (dɪs'pruːf) *n* **1** facts that disprove something. **2** the act of disproving.

disproportion (,dɪsprə'pɔːʃən) *n* **1** lack of proportion or equality. **2** an instance of disparity or inequality. ◆ *vb* **3** (*tr*) to cause to become exaggerated or unequal.
> **,dispro'portional** *adj*

disproportionate (,dɪsprə'pɔːʃənɪt) *adj* out of proportion; unequal.
> **,dispro'portionately** *adv* > **,dispro'portionateness** *n*

disprove (dɪs'pruːv) *vb* disproves, disproving, disproved. (*tr*) to show (an assertion, claim, etc.) to be incorrect.
> **dis'provable** *adj* > **dis'proval** *n*

disputable (dɪ'spjuːtəbᵊl, 'dɪspjutə-) *adj* capable of being argued; debatable.
> **dis,puta'bility** *or* **dis'putableness** *n* > **dis'putably** *adv*

disputant (dɪ'spjuːtᵊnt, 'dɪspjutənt) *n* **1** a person who argues; contestant. ◆ *adj* **2** engaged in argument.

disputation (,dɪspjuː'teɪʃən) *n* **1** the act or an instance of arguing. **2** a formal academic debate on a thesis. **3** an obsolete word for **conversation.**

disputatious (,dɪspjuː'teɪʃəs) *or* **disputative** (dɪ'spjuːtətɪv) *adj* inclined to argument.
> **,dispu'tatiousness** *or* **dis'putativeness** *n*

★ people and places

dispute vb (dɪ'spjuːt) **disputes, disputing, disputed. 1** to argue, debate, or quarrel about (something). **2** (tr; may take a clause as object) to doubt the validity, etc., of. **3** (tr) to seek to win; contest for. **4** (tr) to struggle against; resist. ◆ n (dɪ'spjuːt, 'dɪspjuːt). **5** an argument or quarrel. **6** Rare. a fight. [C13: from LL disputāre to contend verbally, from L: to discuss, from DIS-[1] + putāre to think]
▶ **dis'puter** n

disqualify (dɪs'kwɒlɪ,faɪ) vb **disqualifies, disqualifying, disqualified.** (tr) **1** to make unfit or unqualified. **2** to make ineligible, as for entry to an examination. **3** to debar from a contest. **4** to deprive of rights, powers, or privileges.
▶ **dis,qualifi'cation** n

disquiet (dɪs'kwaɪət) n **1** a feeling or condition of anxiety or uneasiness. ◆ vb **2** (tr) to make anxious or upset.
▶ **dis'quieting** adj

disquietude (dɪs'kwaɪɪ,tjuːd) n a feeling or state of anxiety or uneasiness.

disquisition (,dɪskwɪ'zɪʃən) n a formal examination of a subject. [C17: from L disquīsītiō, from disquīrere to make an investigation, from DIS-[1] + quaerere to seek]
▶ ,**disqui'sitional** adj

Disraeli ★ (dɪz'reɪlɪ) n **Benjamin, 1st Earl of Beaconsfield.** 1804–81, British Tory statesman and novelist; prime minister (1868; 1874–80). He gave coherence to the Tory principles of protectionism and imperialism, was responsible for the Reform Bill (1867) and, as prime minister, bought a controlling interest in the Suez Canal. His novels include Coningsby (1844) and Sybil (1845).

disregard (,dɪsrɪ'gɑːd) vb (tr) **1** to give little or no attention to; ignore. **2** to treat as unworthy of consideration or respect. ◆ n **3** lack of attention or respect.
▶ ,**disre'gardful** adj

disremember (,dɪsrɪ'membə) vb Inf., chiefly US. to fail to recall.

disrepair (,dɪsrɪ'pɛə) n the condition of being worn out or in poor working order; a condition requiring repairs.

disreputable (dɪs'rɛpjʊtəb°l) adj **1** having or causing a lack of repute. **2** disordered in appearance.
▶ **dis'reputably** adv

disrepute (,dɪsrɪ'pjuːt) n a loss or lack of credit or repute.

disrespect (,dɪsrɪ'spɛkt) n contempt; rudeness; lack of respect.
▶ ,**disre'spectful** adj

disrobe (dɪs'rəʊb) vb **disrobes, disrobing, disrobed. 1** to undress. **2** (tr) to divest of authority, etc.
▶ **dis'robement** n

disrupt (dɪs'rʌpt) vb **1** (tr) to throw into turmoil or disorder. **2** (tr) to interrupt the progress of. **3** to break or split apart. [C17: from L disruptus burst asunder, from dīrumpere to dash to pieces, from DIS-[1] + rumpere to burst]
▶ **dis'rupter** or **dis'ruptor** n ▶ **dis'ruption** n

disruptive (dɪs'rʌptɪv) adj involving, causing, or tending to cause disruption.

diss or **dis** (dɪs) vb **disses, dissing, dissed.** Sl., chiefly US. to treat (someone) with contempt. [C20: orig. US Black rap slang, short for DISRESPECT]

dissatisfy (dɪs'sætɪs,faɪ) vb **dissatisfies, dissatisfying, dissatisfied.** (tr) to fail to satisfy; disappoint.
▶ ,**dissatis'faction** n ▶ ,**dissatis'factory** adj

dissect (dɪ'sɛkt, daɪ-) vb **1** to cut open and examine the structure of (a dead animal or plant). **2** (tr) to examine critically and minutely. [C17: from L dissecāre, from DIS-[1] + secāre to cut]
▶ **dis'section** n ▶ **dis'sector** n

dissected (dɪ'sɛktɪd, daɪ-) adj **1** Bot. in the form of narrow lobes or segments. **2** Geol. cut by erosion into hills and valleys.

disselboom ('dɪs°l,buːm) n S. African. the single shaft of a wagon, esp. an ox wagon. [from Du. dissel shaft + boom beam]

dissemble (dɪ'sɛmb°l) vb **dissembles, dissembling, dissembled. 1** to conceal (one's real motives, emotions, etc.) by pretence. **2** (tr) to pretend; simulate. [C15: from earlier dissimulen, from L dissimulāre; prob. infl. by obs. semble to resemble]
▶ **dis'semblance** n ▶ **dis'sembler** n

disseminate (dɪ'sɛmɪ,neɪt) vb **disseminates, disseminating, disseminated.** (tr) to distribute or scatter about; diffuse. [C17: from L dissēmināre, from DIS-[1] + sēmināre to sow, from sēmen seed]
▶ **dis,semi'nation** n ▶ **dis'semi,nator** n

disseminated sclerosis n another name for **multiple sclerosis.**

dissension (dɪ'sɛnʃən) n disagreement, esp. when leading to a quarrel. [C13: from L dissēnsiō, from dissentīre to DISSENT]

dissent (dɪ'sɛnt) vb (intr) **1** to have a disagreement or withhold assent. **2** Christianity. to reject the doctrines, beliefs, or practices of an established church, and to adhere to a different system of beliefs. ◆ n **3** a difference of opinion. **4** Christianity. separation from an established church; Nonconformism. **5** the voicing of a minority opinion in the decision on a case at law. [C16: from L dissentīre to disagree, from DIS-[1] + sentīre to feel]
▶ **dis'senter** n ▶ **dis'senting** adj

Dissenter (dɪ'sɛntə) n Christianity, chiefly Brit. a Nonconformist or a person who refuses to conform to the established church.

dissentient (dɪ'sɛnʃənt) adj **1** dissenting, esp. from the opinion of the majority. ◆ n **2** a dissenter.
▶ **dis'sentience** or **dis'sentiency** n

dissertation (,dɪsə'teɪʃən) n **1** a written thesis, often based on original research, usually required for a higher degree. **2** a formal discourse. [C17: from L dissertāre to debate, from disserere to examine, from DIS-[1] + serere to arrange]
▶ ,**disser'tational** adj

disserve (dɪs'sɜːv) vb **disserves, disserving, disserved.** (tr) Arch. to do a disservice to.

disservice (dɪs'sɜːvɪs) n an ill turn; wrong; injury, esp. when trying to help.

dissever (dɪ'sɛvə) vb **1** to break off or become broken off. **2** (tr) to divide up into parts. [C13: from OF dessevrer, from LL DIS-[1] + sēparāre to SEPARATE]
▶ **dis'severance** or **dis'severment** n

dissident ('dɪsɪdənt) adj **1** disagreeing; dissenting. ◆ n **2** a person who disagrees, esp. one who disagrees with the government. [C16: from L dissidēre to be remote from, from DIS-[1] + sedēre to sit]
▶ '**dissidence** n ▶ '**dissidently** adv

dissimilar (dɪ'sɪmɪlə) adj not alike; not similar; different.
▶ **dis'similarly** adv ▶ ,**dissimi'larity** n

dissimilate (dɪ'sɪmɪ,leɪt) vb **dissimilates, dissimilating, dissimilated. 1** to make or become dissimilar. **2** (usually foll. by to) Phonetics. to change or displace (a consonant) or (of a consonant) to be changed to or displaced by (another consonant) so that its manner of articulation becomes less similar to a speech sound in the same word. Thus (r) in the final syllable of French marbre is dissimilated to (l) in its English form marble. [C19: from DIS-[1] + ASSIMILATE]

dissimilation (,dɪsɪmɪ'leɪʃən) n **1** the act or an instance of making dissimilar. **2** Phonetics. the alteration or omission of a consonant as a result of being dissimilated.

dissimilitude (,dɪsɪ'mɪlɪ,tjuːd) n **1** dissimilarity; difference. **2** a point of difference.

dissimulate (dɪ'sɪmjʊ,leɪt) vb **dissimulates, dissimulating, dissimulated.** to conceal (one's real feelings) by pretence.
▶ **dis,simu'lation** n ▶ **dis'simu,lator** n

dissipate ('dɪsɪ,peɪt) vb **dissipates, dissipating, dissipated. 1** to exhaust or be exhausted by dispersion. **2** (tr) to scatter or break up. **3** (intr) to indulge in the pursuit of pleasure. [C15: from L dissipāre to disperse, from DIS-[1] + supāre to throw]
▶ '**dissi,pater** or '**dissi,pator** n ▶ '**dissi,pative** adj

dissipated ('dɪsɪ,peɪtɪd) adj **1** indulging without restraint in the pursuit of pleasure; debauched. **2** wasted, scattered, or exhausted.

dissipation (,dɪsɪ'peɪʃən) n **1** a dissipating or being dissipated. **2** unrestrained indulgence in physical pleasures. **3** excessive expenditure; wastefulness.

dissociate (dɪ'səʊʃɪ,eɪt, -sɪ-) vb **dissociates, dissociating,**

dissociated. 1 to break or cause to break the association between (people, organizations, etc.). **2** (*tr*) to regard or treat as separate or unconnected. **3** to undergo or subject to dissociation.
▸ **dis'sociative** *adj*

dissociation (dɪˌsəʊsɪ'eɪʃən, -ʃɪ-) *n* **1** a dissociating or being dissociated. **2** *Chem.* the decomposition of the molecules of a single compound into two or more other compounds, atoms, ions, or radicals. **3** *Psychiatry.* the separation of a group of mental processes or ideas from the rest of the personality, so that they lead an independent existence, as in cases of multiple personality.

dissoluble (dɪ'sɒljʊbəl) *adj* a less common word for **soluble**. [C16: from L *dissolūbilis*, from *dissolvere* to DISSOLVE]
▸ **dis,solu'bility** *n*

dissolute ('dɪsəˌluːt) *adj* given to dissipation; debauched. [C14: from L *dissolūtus* loose, from *dissolvere* to DISSOLVE]
▸ **'disso,lutely** *adv* ▸ **'disso,luteness** *n*

dissolution (ˌdɪsə'luːʃən) *n* **1** separation into component parts; disintegration. **2** destruction by breaking up and dispersing. **3** the termination of a meeting or assembly, such as Parliament. **4** the termination of a formal or legal relationship, such as a business, marriage, etc. **5** the act or process of dissolving.

dissolve (dɪ'zɒlv) *vb* **dissolves, dissolving, dissolved. 1** to go or cause to go into solution. **2** to become or cause to become liquid; melt. **3** to disintegrate or disperse. **4** to come or bring to an end. **5** to dismiss (a meeting, Parliament, etc.) or (of a meeting, etc.) to be dismissed. **6** to collapse or cause to collapse emotionally: *to dissolve into tears.* **7** to lose or cause to lose distinctness. **8** (*tr*) to terminate legally, as a marriage, etc. **9** (*intr*) *Films, television.* to fade out one scene and replace with another to make two scenes merge imperceptibly or slowly overlap. ♦ *n* **10** *Films, television.* a scene filmed or televised by dissolving. [C14: from L *dissolvere* to make loose, from DIS-[1] + *solvere* to release]
▸ **dis'solvable** *adj*

dissonance ('dɪsənəns) *or* **dissonancy** *n* **1** a discordant combination of sounds. **2** lack of agreement or consistency. **3** *Music.* **3a** a sensation of harshness and incompleteness associated with certain intervals and chords. **3b** an interval or chord of this kind.

dissonant ('dɪsənənt) *adj* **1** discordant. **2** incongruous or discrepant. **3** *Music.* characterized by dissonance. [C15: from L *dissonāre* to be discordant, from DIS-[1] + *sonāre* to sound]

dissuade (dɪ'sweɪd) *vb* **dissuades, dissuading, dissuaded.** (*tr*) **1** (often foll. by *from*) to deter (someone) by persuasion from a course of action, policy, etc. **2** to advise against (an action, etc.). [C15: from L *dissuādēre*, from DIS-[1] + *suādēre* to persuade]
▸ **dis'suader** *n* ▸ **dis'suasion** *n* ▸ **dis'suasive** *adj*

dissyllable (dɪ'sɪləbəl) *or* **disyllable** *n* a word of two syllables.
▸ **dissyllabic** (ˌdɪsɪ'læbɪk) *or* **disyllabic** (ˌdaɪsɪ'læbɪk) *adj*

dissymmetry (dɪ'sɪmɪtrɪ, dɪs'sɪm-) *n, pl* **dissymmetries. 1** lack of symmetry. **2** the relationship between two objects when one is the mirror image of the other.
▸ **dissymmetric** (ˌdɪsɪ'mɛtrɪk, ˌdɪssɪ-) *or* **,dissym'metrical** *adj*

dist. *abbrev. for:* **1** distant. **2** distinguish(ed). **3** district.

distaff ('dɪstɑːf) *n* **1** the rod on which flax is wound preparatory to spinning. **2** *Figurative.* women's work. [OE *distæf*, from *dis-* bunch of flax + *stæf* STAFF[1]]

distaff side the female side of a family.

distal ('dɪstəl) *adj Anat.* situated farthest from the centre or point of attachment or origin. [C19: from DISTANT + -AL[1]]
▸ **'distally** *adv*

distance ('dɪstəns) *n* **1** the space between two points. **2** the length of this gap. **3** the state of being apart in space; remoteness. **4** an interval between two points in time. **5** the extent of progress. **6** a distant place or time. **7** a separation or remoteness in relationship. **8** (preceded by *the*) the most distant or a faraway part of the visible scene. **9** *Horse racing.* **9a** *Brit.* a point on a racecourse 240 yards

from the winning post. **9b** *US.* the part of a racecourse that a horse must reach before the winner passes the finishing line in order to qualify for later heats. **10 go the distance. 10a** *Boxing.* to complete a bout without being knocked out. **10b** to be able to complete an assigned task or responsibility. **11 keep one's distance.** to maintain a reserve in respect of another person. **12 middle distance.** halfway between the foreground or the observer and the horizon. ♦ *vb* **distances, distancing, distanced.** (*tr*) **13** to hold or place at a distance. **14** to separate (oneself) mentally from something. **15** to outdo; outstrip.

distance learning *n* a teaching system consisting of video, audio, and written material designed for a person to use in studying a subject at home.

distant ('dɪstənt) *adj* **1** far apart in space or time. **2** (*postpositive*) separated in space or time by a specified distance. **3** apart in relationship: *a distant cousin.* **4** coming from or going to a faraway place. **5** remote in manner; aloof. **6** abstracted; absent: *a distant look.* [C14: from L *distāre* to be distant, from DIS-[1] + *stāre* to stand]
▸ **'distantly** *adv* ▸ **'distantness** *n*

distaste (dɪs'teɪst) *n* (often foll. by *for*) a dislike (of); aversion (to).

distasteful (dɪs'teɪstfʊl) *adj* unpleasant or offensive.
▸ **dis'tastefulness** *n*

distemper[1] (dɪs'tɛmpə) *n* **1** any of various infectious diseases of animals, esp. **canine distemper,** a highly contagious viral disease of dogs. **2** *Arch.* **2a** a disorder. **2b** disturbance. **2c** discontent. [C14: from LL *distemperāre* to derange the health of, from L DIS-[1] + *temperāre* to mix in correct proportions]

distemper[2] (dɪs'tɛmpə) *n* **1** a technique of painting in which the pigments are mixed with water, glue, size, etc.: used for poster, mural, and scene painting. **2** the paint used in this technique or any of various waterbased paints. ♦ *vb* **3** to paint (something) with distemper. [C14: from Med. L *distemperāre* to soak, from L DIS-[1] + *temperāre* to mingle]

distend (dɪ'stɛnd) *vb* **1** to expand by or as if by pressure from within; swell; inflate. **2** (*tr*) to stretch out or extend. [C14: from L *distendere*, from DIS-[1] + *tendere* to stretch]
▸ **dis'tensible** *adj* ▸ **dis'tension** *or* **dis'tention** *n*

distich ('dɪstɪk) *n Prosody.* a unit of two verse lines, usually a couplet. [C16: from Gk *distikhos* having two lines, from DI-[1] + *stikhos* row, line]

distil *or US* **distill** (dɪs'tɪl) *vb* **distils, distilling, distilled** *or US* **distills, distilling, distilled. 1** to subject to or undergo distillation. **2** (sometimes foll. by *out* or *off*) to purify, separate, or concentrate, or be purified, separated, or concentrated by distillation. **3** to obtain or be obtained by distillation. **4** to exude or give off (a substance) in drops. **5** (*tr*) to extract the essence of. [C14: from L *dēstillāre* to drip, from DE- + *stillāre* to drip]

distillate ('dɪstɪlɪt) *n* **1** the product of distillation. **2** a concentrated essence.

distillation (ˌdɪstɪ'leɪʃən) *n* **1** a distilling. **2** the process of evaporating or boiling a liquid and condensing its vapour. **3** purification or separation of mixtures by using different evaporation rates or boiling points of their components. **4** the process of obtaining the essence or an extract of a substance, usually by heating it in a solvent. **5** a distillate. **6** a concentrated essence.
▸ **dis'tillatory** *adj*

distiller (dɪ'stɪlə) *n* a person or organization that distils, esp. a company that makes spirits.

distillery (dɪ'stɪlərɪ) *n, pl* **distilleries.** a place where alcoholic drinks, etc., are made by distillation.

distinct (dɪ'stɪŋkt) *adj* **1** easily sensed or understood; clear. **2** (when *postpositive,* foll. by *from*) not the same (as); separate (from). **3** not alike; different. **4** sharp; clear. **5** recognizable; definite. **6** explicit; unequivocal. **7** *Bot.* (of parts of a plant) not joined together; separate. [C14: from L *distinctus,* from *distinguere* to DISTINGUISH]
▸ **dis'tinctly** *adv* ▸ **dis'tinctness** *n*

distinction (dɪ'stɪŋkʃən) *n* **1** the act or an instance of distinguishing or differentiating. **2** a distinguishing feature. **3** the state of being different or distinguishable. **4** special honour, recognition, or fame. **5** excellence of character; distinctive qualities. **6** distinguished appearance. **7** a symbol of honour or rank.

distinctive (dɪ'stɪŋktɪv) *adj* serving or tending to distinguish; characteristic.
► **dis'tinctively** *adv* ► **dis'tinctiveness** *n*

distingué *French.* (distɛ̃ge) *adj* distinguished or noble.

distinguish (dɪ'stɪŋgwɪʃ) *vb* (*mainly tr*) **1** (when *intr*, foll. by *between* or *among*) to make, show, or recognize a difference (between or among); differentiate (between). **2** to be a distinctive feature of; characterize. **3** to make out; perceive. **4** to mark for a special honour. **5** to make (oneself) noteworthy. **6** to classify. [C16: from L *distinguere* to separate]
► **dis'tinguishable** *adj* ► **dis'tinguishing** *adj*

distinguished (dɪ'stɪŋgwɪʃt) *adj* **1** noble or dignified in appearance or behaviour. **2** eminent; famous; celebrated.

distort (dɪ'stɔːt) *vb* (*tr*) **1** (*often passive*) to twist or pull out of shape; contort; deform. **2** to alter or misrepresent (facts, etc.). **3** *Electronics.* to reproduce or amplify (a signal) inaccurately. [C16: from L *distortus*, from *distorquēre* to turn different ways, from DIS-[1] + *torquēre* to twist]
► **dis'torted** *adj*

distortion (dɪ'stɔːʃən) *n* **1** a distorting or being distorted. **2** something that is distorted. **3** *Electronics.* an undesired change in the shape of an electrical wave or signal resulting in a loss of clarity in radio reception or sound reproduction.
► **dis'tortional** *adj*

distract (dɪ'strækt) *vb* (*tr*) **1** (*often passive*) to draw the attention of (a person) away from something. **2** to divide or confuse the attention of (a person). **3** to amuse or entertain. **4** to trouble greatly. **5** to make mad. [C14: from L *distractus* perplexed, from *distrahere* to pull in different directions, from DIS-[1] + *trahere* to drag]

distracted (dɪ'stræktɪd) *adj* **1** bewildered; confused. **2** mad.
► **dis'tractedly** *adv*

distraction (dɪ'strækʃən) *n* **1** a distracting or being distracted. **2** something that serves as a diversion or entertainment. **3** an interruption; obstacle to concentration. **4** mental turmoil or madness.

distrain (dɪ'streɪn) *vb Law.* to seize (personal property) as security or indemnity for a debt. [C13: from OF *destreindre*, from L *distringere* to impede, from DIS-[1] + *stringere* to draw tight]
► **dis'trainment** *n* ► **dis'trainor** or **dis'trainer** *n*

distraint (dɪ'streɪnt) *n Law.* the act or process of distraining; distress.

distrait (dɪ'streɪ; *French* distrɛ) *adj* absent-minded; abstracted. [C18: from F, from *distraire* to DISTRACT]

distraught (dɪ'strɔːt) *adj* **1** distracted or agitated. **2** *Rare.* mad. [C14: changed from obs. *distract* through influence of obs. *straught*, p.p. of STRETCH]

distress (dɪ'strɛs) *vb* (*tr*) **1** to cause mental pain to; upset badly. **2** (*usually passive*) to subject to financial or other trouble. **3** to treat (something, esp. furniture or fabric) in order to make it appear older than it is. **4** *Law.* a less common word for **distrain.** ◆ *n* **5** mental pain; anguish. **6** a distressing or being distressed. **7** physical or financial trouble. **8 in distress.** (of a ship, etc.) in dire need of help. **9** *Law.* **9a** the seizure of property as security for or in satisfaction of a debt, claim, etc.; distraint. **9b** the property thus seized. **9c** (*as modifier*) *US: distress merchandise.* [C13: from OF *destresse*, via Vulgar L, from L *districtus* divided in mind]
► **dis'tressful** *adj* ► **dis'tressing** *adj* ► **dis'tressingly** *adv*

distressed (dɪ'strɛst) *adj* **1** much troubled; upset; afflicted. **2** in financial straits; poor. **3** (of furniture, fabric, etc.) having signs of ageing artificially applied. **4** *Econ.* another word for **depressed.**

distress signal *n* a signal by radio, Very light, etc., from a ship in need of immediate assistance.

distribute (dɪ'strɪbjuːt) *vb* distributes, distributing, distributed. (*tr*) **1** to give out in shares; dispense. **2** to hand out or deliver. **3** (*often passive*) to spread throughout an area. **4** (*often passive*) to divide into classes or categories. **5** *Printing.* to return (used type) to the correct positions in

the typecase. **6** *Logic.* to incorporate in a distributed term of a categorical proposition. **7** *Maths.* to expand an expression containing two operators so as to change the order, as in expressing $a(b + c)$ as $ab + ac$. [C15: from L *distribuere*, from DIS-[1] + *tribuere* to give]
► **dis'tributable** *adj*

distributed logic *n* a computer system in which remote terminals and electronic devices supplement the main computer by doing some of the computing or decision making.

distributed term *n Logic.* a term applying equally to every member of the class it designates, as *men* in *all men are mortal.*

distribution (ˌdɪstrɪ'bjuːʃən) *n* **1** the act of distributing or the state or manner of being distributed. **2** a thing or portion distributed. **3** arrangement or location. **4** the process of physically satisfying the demand for goods and services. **5** *Econ.* the division of the total income of a community among its members. **6** *Statistics.* the set of possible values of a random variable, considered in terms of theoretical or observed frequency. **7** *Law.* the apportioning of the estate of a deceased intestate. **8** *Law.* the lawful division of the assets of a bankrupt among his creditors. **9** *Finance.* **9a** the division of part of a company's profit as a dividend to its shareholders. **9b** the amount paid by dividend in a particular distribution. **10** *Engineering.* the way in which the fuel-air mixture is supplied to each cylinder of a multicylinder internal-combustion engine.
► ˌ**distri'butional** *adj*

distributive (dɪ'strɪbjʊtɪv) *adj* **1** characterized by or relating to distribution. **2** *Grammar.* referring separately to the individual people or items in a group, as the words *each* and *every.* ◆ *n* **3** *Grammar.* a distributive word.
► **dis'tributively** *adv* ► **dis'tributiveness** *n*

distributive law *n Maths, logic.* a theorem asserting that one operator can validly be distributed over another. See **distribute** (sense 7).

distributor (dɪ'strɪbjʊtə) *n* **1** a person or thing that distributes. **2** a wholesaler or middleman engaged in the distribution of a category of goods, esp. to retailers in a specific area. **3** the device in a petrol engine that distributes the high-tension voltage to the sparking plugs.

district ('dɪstrɪkt) *n* **1a** an area of land marked off for administrative or other purposes. **1b** (*as modifier*): *district nurse.* **2** a locality separated by geographical attributes; region. **3** any subdivision of a territory, region, etc. **4** a political subdivision of a county, region, etc., that elects a council responsible for certain local services. ◆ *vb* **5** (*tr*) to divide into districts. [C17: from Med. L *districtus* area of jurisdiction, from L *distringere* to stretch out]

district attorney *n* (in the US) the state prosecuting officer in a specified judicial district.

District Court *n* **1** (in Scotland) a court of summary jurisdiction which deals with minor criminal offences. **2** (in the US) **2a** a Federal trial court in each US district. **2b** in some states, a court of general jurisdiction. **3** (in New Zealand) a court lower than a High Court. Formerly called: **magistrates' court.**

district high school *n* (in New Zealand) a school in a rural area providing both primary and secondary education.

district nurse *n* (in Britain) a nurse appointed to attend patients within a particular district, usually in the patients' homes.

District of Columbia ★ *n* a federal district of the eastern US, coextensive with the federal capital, Washington. Pop.: 543 213 (1996 est.). Area: 178 sq. km (69 sq. miles). Abbrevs.: **D.C.** or (with zip code) **DC**

distrust (dɪs'trʌst) *vb* **1** to regard as untrustworthy or dishonest. ◆ *n* **2** suspicion; doubt.
► **dis'truster** *n* ► **dis'trustful** *adj*

disturb (dɪ'stɜːb) *vb* (*tr*) **1** to intrude on; interrupt. **2** to destroy the quietness or peace of. **3** to disarrange; muddle. **4** (*often passive*) to upset; trouble. **5** to inconvenience; put out. [C13: from L *disturbāre*, from DIS-[1] + *turbāre* to confuse]
► **dis'turber** *n* ► **dis'turbing** *adj* ► **dis'turbingly** *adv*

disturbance (dɪ'stɜːbəns) n **1** a disturbing or being disturbed. **2** an interruption or intrusion. **3** an unruly outburst or tumult. **4** *Law.* an interference with another's rights. **5** *Geol.* a minor movement of the earth causing a small earthquake. **6** *Meteorol.* a small depression. **7** *Psychiatry.* a mental or emotional disorder.

disturbed (dɪ'stɜːbd) adj *Psychiatry.* emotionally upset, troubled, or maladjusted.

disulphide (daɪ'sʌlfaɪd) n any chemical compound containing two sulphur atoms per molecule.

disunite (ˌdɪsjuː'naɪt) vb disunites, disuniting, disunited. **1** to separate; disrupt. **2** (tr) to set at variance; estrange.
▸ **dis'union** n ▸ **dis'unity** n

disuse (dɪs'juːs) n the condition of being unused; neglect (often in **in** or **into disuse**).

disutility (ˌdɪsjuː'tɪlɪtɪ) n, pl **disutilities.** *Econ.* the shortcomings of a commodity or activity in satisfying human wants. Cf. **utility** (sense 4).

disyllable ('daɪˌsɪləbᵊl) n a variant of **dissyllable.**

ditch (dɪtʃ) n **1** a narrow channel dug in the earth, usually used for drainage, irrigation, or as a boundary marker. ◆ vb **2** to make a ditch in. **3** (intr) to edge with a ditch. **4** *Sl.* to crash, esp. deliberately, as to avoid more unpleasant circumstances: *he had to ditch the car.* **5** (tr) *Sl.* to abandon. **6** *Sl.* to land (an aircraft) on water in an emergency. **7** (tr) *US sl.* to evade. [OE dīc]
▸ **'ditcher** n

ditchwater ('dɪtʃˌwɔːtə) n **1** stagnant water, esp. found in ditches. **2 as dull as ditchwater.** very dull; very uninteresting.

dither ('dɪðə) vb (intr) **1** *Chiefly Brit.* to be uncertain or indecisive. **2** *Chiefly US.* to be in an agitated state. **3** to tremble, as with cold. ◆ n **4** *Chiefly Brit.* a state of indecision. **5** a state of agitation. [C17: var. of C14 (N English dialect) *didder*, from ?]
▸ **'ditherer** n ▸ **'dithery** adj

dithyramb ('dɪθɪˌræm, -ˌræmb) n **1** (in ancient Greece) a passionate choral hymn in honour of Dionysus. **2** any utterance or a piece of writing that resembles this. [C17: from L *dīthyrambus*, from Gk *dithurambos*]
▸ ˌdithy'rambic adj

dittany ('dɪtənɪ) n, pl **dittanies. 1** an aromatic Cretan plant with pink flowers: formerly credited with medicinal properties. **2** a North American plant with purplish flowers. [C14: from OF *ditan*, from L *dictamnus*, from Gk *diktamnon*, ?from *Diktē*, mountain in Crete]

ditto ('dɪtəʊ) n, pl **dittos. 1** the aforementioned; the above; the same. Used in accounts, lists, etc., to avoid repetition, and symbolized by two small marks (ˌˌ) known as **ditto marks**, placed under the thing repeated. **2** *Inf.* a duplicate. ◆ adv **3** in the same way. ◆ sentence substitute. **4** *Inf.* used to avoid repeating or to confirm agreement with an immediately preceding sentence. ◆ vb **dittos, dittoing,** dittoed. **5** (tr) to copy; repeat. [C17: from It. (dialect): var. of *detto* said, from *dicere* to say, from L]

ditty ('dɪtɪ) n, pl **ditties.** a short simple song or poem. [C13: from OF *ditie* poem, from *ditier* to compose, from L *dictāre* to DICTATE]

ditty bag or **box** n a sailor's bag or box for personal belongings or tools. [C19: ?from obs. *dutty* calico, from Hindi *dhōtī* loincloth]

ditzy or **ditsy** ('dɪtzɪ, 'dɪtsɪ) adj **ditzier, ditziest** or **ditsier, ditsiest.** *Sl.* silly and scatterbrained. [C20: perhaps from DOTTY + DIZZY]

Diu ★ ('diːuː) n a small island off the NW coast of India: together with a mainland area, it formed a district of Portuguese India (1535–1961); formerly part of the Indian Union Territory of Goa, Daman, and Diu (1962–87).

diuretic (ˌdaɪjʊ'rɛtɪk) adj **1** acting to increase the flow of urine. ◆ n **2** a drug or agent that increases the flow of urine. [ME, from LL, from Gk, from *dia-* through + *ourein* to urinate]
▸ **diuresis** (ˌdaɪjʊ'riːsɪs) n

diurnal (daɪ'ɜːnᵊl) adj **1** happening during the day or daily. **2** (of flowers) open during the day and closed at night. **3** (of animals) active during the day. ◆ Cf. **noctur-**

nal. [C15: from LL *diurnālis*, from L *diurnus*, from *diēs* day]
▸ **di'urnally** adv

div (dɪv) n *Sl.* a shortened form of **divvy**[1].

div. abbrev. for: **1** divide(d). **2** dividend. **3** division. **4** divorce(d).

diva ('diːvə) n, pl **divas** or **dive** (-vɪ). a highly distinguished female singer; prima donna. [C19: via It. from L: a goddess, from *dīvus* DIVINE]

divagate ('daɪvəˌgeɪt) vb divagates, divagating, divagated. (intr) *Rare.* to digress or wander. [C16: from L DI-[2] + *vagārī* to wander]
▸ ˌdiva'gation n

divalent (daɪ'veɪlənt, 'daɪˌveɪ-) adj *Chem.* **1** having a valency of two. **2** having two valencies. ◆ Also: **bivalent.**
▸ **di'valency** n

divan (dɪ'væn) n **1a** a backless sofa or couch. **1b** a bed resembling such a couch. **2** (esp. formerly) a smoking room. **3a** a Muslim law court, council chamber, or counting house. **3b** a Muslim council of state. [C16: from Turkish *dīvān*, from Persian *dīwān*]

dive (daɪv) vb dives, diving, dived or US dove (dəʊv), dived. (mainly intr) **1** to plunge headfirst into water. **2** (of a submarine, etc.) to submerge under water. **3** (also tr) to fly in a steep nose-down descending path. **4** to rush, go, or reach quickly, as in a headlong plunge: *he dived for the ball.* **5** (also tr; foll. by *in* or *into*) to dip or put (one's hand) quickly or forcefully (into). **6** (usually foll. by *in* or *into*) to involve oneself (in something), as in eating food. ◆ n **7** a headlong plunge into water. **8** an act or instance of diving. **9** a steep nose-down descent of an aircraft. **10** *Sl.* a disreputable bar or club. **11** *Boxing sl.* the act of a boxer pretending to be knocked down or out. [OE *dȳfan*]

dive bomber n a military aircraft designed to release its bombs on a target during a steep dive.
▸ **'dive-bomb** vb (tr)

diver ('daɪvə) n **1** a person or thing that dives. **2** a person who works or explores underwater. **3** any of various aquatic birds of northern oceans: noted for skill in diving. *US and Canad.* name: **loon. 4** any of various other diving birds.

diverge (daɪ'vɜːdʒ) vb diverges, diverging, diverged. **1** to separate or cause to separate and go in different directions from a point. **2** (intr) to be at variance; differ. **3** (intr) to deviate from a prescribed course. **4** (intr) *Maths.* (of a series) to have no limit. [C17: from Med. L *dīvergere*, from L DI-[2] + *vergere* to turn]

divergence (daɪ'vɜːdʒəns) or **divergency** n **1** the act or result of diverging or the amount by which something diverges. **2** the condition of being divergent.

divergent (daɪ'vɜːdʒənt) adj **1** diverging or causing divergence. **2** *Maths.* (of a series) having no limit.
▸ **di'vergently** adv

USAGE NOTE The use of *divergent* to mean different as in *they hold widely divergent views* is considered by some people to be incorrect.

divergent thinking n *Psychol.* thinking in an unusual and unstereotyped way, for instance to generate several possible solutions to a problem.

divers ('daɪvəz) determiner *Arch.* or *literary.* various; sundry; some. [C13: from OF, from L *dīversus* turned in different directions]

diverse (daɪ'vɜːs, 'daɪvɜːs) adj **1** having variety; assorted. **2** distinct in kind. [C13: from L *dīversus*; see DIVERS]
▸ **di'versely** adv

diversify (daɪ'vɜːsɪˌfaɪ) vb diversifies, diversifying, diversified. **1** (tr) to create different forms of; variegate; vary. **2** (of an enterprise) to vary (products, operations, etc.) in order to spread risk, expand, etc. **3** to distribute (investments) among several securities in order to spread risk. [C15: from OF *diversifier*, from Med. L *dīversificāre*, from L *dīversus* DIVERSE + *facere* to make]
▸ diˌversifi'cation n

diversion (daɪ'vɜːʃən) n **1** the act of diverting from a

specified course. **2** *Chiefly Brit.* an official detour used by traffic when a main route is closed. **3** something that distracts from business, etc.; amusement. **4** *Mil.* a feint attack designed to draw an enemy away from the main attack.
▶ di'**versional** *or* di'**versionary** *adj*

diversity (daɪˈvɜːsɪtɪ) *n* **1** the state or quality of being different or varied. **2** a point of difference.

divert (daɪˈvɜːt) *vb* **1** to turn aside; deflect. **2** (*tr*) to entertain; amuse. **3** (*tr*) to distract the attention of. [C15: from F *divertir*, from L *dīvertere* to turn aside, from DI-² + *vertere* to turn]
▶ di'**verting** *adj* ▶ di'**vertingly** *adv*

diverticulitis (ˌdaɪvəˌtɪkjʊˈlaɪtɪs) *n* inflammation of one or more diverticula, esp. of the colon.

diverticulum (ˌdaɪvəˈtɪkjʊləm) *n, pl* **diverticula** (-lə). any sac or pouch formed by herniation of the wall of a tubular organ or part, esp. the intestines. [C16: from NL, from L *dēverticulum* by-path, from *dēvertere* to turn aside, from *vertere* to turn]

divertimento (dɪˌvɜːtɪˈmɛntəʊ) *n, pl* **divertimenti** (-tɪ). **1** a piece of entertaining music, often scored for a mixed ensemble and having no fixed form. **2** an episode in a fugue. [C18: from It.]

divertissement (dɪˈvɜːtɪsmənt) *n* a brief entertainment or diversion, usually between the acts of a play. [C18: from F: entertainment]

Dives ★ (ˈdaɪviːz) *n* **1** a rich man in the parable in Luke 16:19–31. **2** a very rich man.

divest (daɪˈvɛst) *vb* (*tr*; usually foll. by *of*) **1** to strip (of clothes). **2** to deprive or dispossess. [C17: changed from earlier *devest*]
▶ di'**vestiture** (daɪˈvɛstɪtʃə), **divesture** (daɪˈvɛstʃə), *or* di'**vestment** *n*

divi (ˈdɪvɪ) *n* an alternative spelling of **divvy**¹.

divide (dɪˈvaɪd) *vb* **divides, dividing, divided. 1** to separate into parts; split up. **2** to share or be shared out in parts; distribute. **3** to diverge or cause to diverge in opinion or aim. **4** (*tr*) to keep apart or be a boundary between. **5** (*intr*) to vote by separating into two groups. **6** to categorize; classify. **7** to calculate the quotient of (one number or quantity) and (another number or quantity) by division. **8** (*intr*) to diverge: *the roads divide.* **9** (*tr*) to mark increments of (length, angle, etc.). ◆ *n* **10** *Chiefly US & Canad.* an area of relatively high ground separating drainage basins; watershed. **11** a division; split. [C14: from L *dīvidere* to force apart, from DIS-¹ + *vid-* separate, from the source of *viduus* bereaved]

divided (dɪˈvaɪdɪd) *adj* **1** *Bot.* another word for **dissected** (sense 1). **2** split; not united.

dividend (ˈdɪvɪˌdɛnd) *n* **1a** a distribution from the net profits of a company to its shareholders. **1b** a portion of this distribution received by a shareholder. **2** the share of a cooperative society's surplus allocated to members. **3** *Insurance.* a sum of money distributed from a company's net profits to the holders of certain policies. **4** something extra; a bonus. **5** a number or quantity to be divided by another number or quantity. **6** *Law.* the proportion of an insolvent estate payable to the creditors. [C15: from L *dīvidendum* what is to be divided]

divider (dɪˈvaɪdə) *n* **1** Also called: **room divider.** a screen or piece of furniture placed so as to divide a room into separate areas. **2** a person or thing that divides. **3** *Electronics.* an electrical circuit with an output that is a well-defined fraction of a given input: *a voltage divider.*

dividers (dɪˈvaɪdəz) *pl n* a type of compass with two pointed arms, used for measuring lines or dividing them.

divination (ˌdɪvɪˈneɪʃən) *n* **1** the art or practice of discovering future events or unknown things, as though by supernatural powers. **2** a prophecy. **3** a guess.
▶ di'**vinatory** (dɪˈvɪnətərɪ, -trɪ) *adj*

divine (dɪˈvaɪn) *adj* **1** of God or a deity. **2** godlike. **3** of or associated with religion or worship. **4** of supreme excellence or worth. **5** *Inf.* splendid; perfect. ◆ *n* **6** (*often cap.*; preceded by *the*) another word for **God. 7** a priest, esp. one learned in theology. ◆ *vb* **divines, divining, divined. 8** to perceive (something) by intuition. **9** to conjecture

(something); guess. **10** to discern (a hidden or future reality) as though by supernatural power. **11** (*tr*) to search for (water, metal, etc.) using a divining rod. [C14: from L *dīvīnus*, from *dīvus* a god]
▶ di'**vinely** *adv* ▶ di'**viner** *n*

divine office *n* (*sometimes cap.*) the canonical prayers recited daily by priests, etc. Also called: **Liturgy of the Hours.**

divine right of kings *n History.* the concept that the right to rule derives from God and that kings are answerable for their actions to God alone.

diving bell *n* an early diving submersible having an open bottom and being supplied with compressed air.

diving board *n* a platform or springboard from which swimmers may dive.

diving suit *or* **dress** *n* a waterproof suit used by divers, having a heavy detachable helmet and an air supply.

divining rod *n* a forked twig said to move when held over ground in which water, metal, etc., is to be found. Also called: **dowsing rod.**

divinity (dɪˈvɪnɪtɪ) *n, pl* **divinities. 1** the nature of a deity or the state of being divine. **2** a god. **3** (*often cap.*; preceded by *the*) another term for **God. 4** another word for **theology.**

divisible (dɪˈvɪzɪbəl) *adj* capable of being divided, usually with no remainder.
▶ di,visi'**bility** *or* di'**visibleness** *n* ▶ di'**visibly** *adv*

division (dɪˈvɪʒən) *n* **1** a dividing or being divided. **2** the act of sharing out; distribution. **3** something that divides; boundary. **4** one of the parts, groups, etc., into which something is divided. **5** a part of a government, business, etc., that has been made into a unit for administrative or other reasons. **6** a formal vote in Parliament or a similar legislative body. **7** a difference of opinion. **8** (in sports) a section or class organized according to age, weight, skill, etc. **9** a mathematical operation in which the quotient of two numbers or quantities is calculated. Usually written: $a \div b$, a/b, $\frac{a}{b}$. **10** *Army.* a major formation, larger than a brigade but smaller than a corps, containing the necessary arms to sustain independent combat. **11** *Biol.* (in traditional classification systems) a major category of the plant kingdom that contains one or more related classes. Cf. **phylum** (sense 1). [C14: from L *dīvīsiō*, from *dīvidere* to DIVIDE]
▶ di'**visional** *or* di'**visionary** *adj* ▶ di'**visionally** *adv*

division sign *n* the symbol ÷, placed between the dividend and the divisor to indicate division, as in $12 \div 6 = 2$.

divisive (dɪˈvaɪsɪv) *adj* tending to cause disagreement or dissension.
▶ di'**visively** *adv* ▶ di'**visiveness** *n*

divisor (dɪˈvaɪzə) *n* **1** a number or quantity to be divided into another number or quantity (the dividend). **2** a number that is a factor of another number.

divorce (dɪˈvɔːs) *n* **1** the legal dissolution of a marriage. **2** a judicial decree declaring a marriage to be dissolved. **3** a separation, esp. one that is total or complete. ◆ *vb* **divorces, divorcing, divorced. 4** to separate or be separated by divorce; give or obtain a divorce. **5** (*tr*) to remove or separate, esp. completely. [C14: from OF, from L *dīvortium*, from *dīvertere* to separate]
▶ di'**vorceable** *adj*

divorcée (dɪvɔːˈsiː) *or* (*masc*) **divorcé** (dɪˈvɔːseɪ) *n* a person who has been divorced.

divot (ˈdɪvət) *n* a piece of turf dug out of a grass surface, esp. by a golf club or by horses' hooves. [C16: from Scot., from ?]

divulge (daɪˈvʌldʒ) *vb* **divulges, divulging, divulged.** (*tr; may take a clause as object*) to make known; disclose. [C15: from L *dīvulgāre*, from DI-² + *vulgāre* to spread among people, from *vulgus* the common people]
▶ di'**vulgence** *or* di'**vulgement** *n* ▶ di'**vulger** *n*

divvy¹ (ˈdɪvɪ) *Inf.* ◆ *n, pl* **divvies. 1** *Brit.* short for **dividend,** esp. (formerly) one paid by a cooperative society. **2** *US & Canad.* a share; portion. ◆ *vb* **divvies, divvying, divvied. 3** (*tr*; usually foll. by *up*) to divide and share.

divvy² (ˈdɪvɪ) *n, pl* **divvies.** *Sl.* a stupid or odd person; misfit. [C20: ? from DEVIANT]

Diwali (dɪ'wɑːlɪ) *n* a major Hindu religious festival, honouring Lakshmi, the goddess of wealth. Held over the New Year according to the Vikrama calendar, it is marked by feasting, gifts, and the lighting of lamps.

dixie ('dɪksɪ) *n* **1** *Chiefly mil.* a large metal pot for cooking, brewing tea, etc. **2** a mess tin. [C19: from Hindi *degcī*, dim. of *degcā* pot]

Dixie ('dɪksɪ) *n* **1** Also called: **Dixieland**. the southern states of the US. ◆ *adj* **2** of the southern states of the US. [C19: ?from the nickname of New Orleans, from *dixie* a ten-dollar bill printed there, from F *dix* ten]

Dixieland ('dɪksɪˌlænd) *n* **1** a form of jazz that originated in New Orleans in the 1920s. **2** a revival of this style in the 1950s. **3** See **Dixie** (sense 1).

DIY *or* **d.i.y.** *Brit., Austral., & NZ abbrev. for* do-it-yourself.

dizzy ('dɪzɪ) *adj* **dizzier, dizziest. 1** affected with a whirling or reeling sensation; giddy. **2** mentally confused or bewildered. **3** causing or tending to cause vertigo or bewilderment. **4** *Inf.* foolish or flighty. ◆ *vb* **dizzies, dizzying, dizzied. 5** (*tr*) to make dizzy. [OE *dysig* silly]
▶ '**dizzily** *adv* ▶ '**dizziness** *n*

DJ *or* **dj** ('diː,dʒeɪ) *n* **1** a variant of **deejay**. **2** an informal term for **dinner jacket**.

Djailolo *or* **Jilolo** ★ (dʒaɪ'ləʊləʊ) *n* the Dutch name for **Halmahera**.

Djaja ★ ('dʒɑː dʒə) *n* a variant spelling of (Mount) **Jaya**.

Djajapura ★ (ˌdʒɑːdʒɑː'pʊərə) *n* a variant spelling of **Jayapura**.

Djakarta ★ (dʒə'kɑːtə) *n* a variant spelling of **Jakarta**.

Djambi ★ ('dʒæmbɪ) *n* a variant spelling of **Jambi**.

djellaba, djellabah *or* **jellaba, jellabah** ('dʒɛləbə) *n* a kind of loose cloak with a hood, worn by men esp. in N Africa and the Middle East. [from Ar. *jallabah*]

Djibouti *or* **Jibouti** ★ (dʒɪ'buːtɪ) *n* **1** a republic in E Africa, on the Gulf of Aden: a French overseas territory (1946–77); became independent in 1977; mainly desert. Official languages: Arabic and French. Currency: Djibouti franc. Capital: Djibouti. Pop.: 622 000 (1997). Area: 23 200 sq. km (8950 sq. miles). **2** the capital of Djibouti, a port on the Gulf of Aden: an outlet for Ethiopian merchandise. Pop.: 383 000 (1995 est).

djinni *or* **djinny** (dʒɪ'niː, 'dʒɪnɪ) *n, pl* **djinn** (dʒɪn). variant spellings of **jinni**.

dl *symbol for* decilitre.

DLitt *or* **DLit** *abbrev. for:* **1** Doctor of Letters. **2** Doctor of Literature. [L *Doctor Litterarum*]

dm *symbol for* decimetre.

DM *abbrev. for* Deutschmark.

DMA *Computing. abbrev. for* direct memory access.

D-mark *or* **D-Mark** *n* short for **Deutschmark**.

DMF *abbrev. for* dimethylformamide.

DMs *Inf. abbrev. for* Doc Martens.

DMus *abbrev. for* Doctor of Music.

DNA *n* deoxyribonucleic acid, the main constituent of the chromosomes of all organisms (except some viruses) in the form of a double helix. DNA is self-replicating and is responsible for the transmission of hereditary characteristics.

DNAase (ˌdiːɛn'eɪeɪz) *or* **DNase** (ˌdiːɛn'eɪz) *n* deoxyribonuclease; any of a number of enzymes that hydrolyse DNA.

DNA fingerprinting *or* **profiling** *n* another name for **genetic fingerprinting**.

Dnepropetrovsk ★ (*Russian* dnɪprəpɪ'trɔfsk) *n* a major industrial city in the E central Ukraine, on the Dnieper River. Pop.: 1 147 000 (1996 est.). Former name (1787–1796, 1802–1926): **Yekaterinoslav**.

Dnieper ★ ('dniːpə) *n* a river in E Europe, rising in Russia, in the Valdai Hills NE of Smolensk and flowing south to the Black Sea: the third longest river in Europe; a major navigable waterway. Length: 2200 km (1370 miles). Russian name: **Dnepr** ('dnjepə).

Dniester ★ ('dniːstə) *n* a river in E Europe, rising in the Ukraine, in the Carpathian Mountains, and flowing generally southeast to the Black Sea. Length: 1411 km (877 miles). Russian name: **Dnestr** ('dnjestə).

D-notice *n Brit.* an official notice sent to newspapers prohibiting the publication of certain security information. [C20: from their administrative classification letter]

do[1] (duː; *unstressed* dʊ, də) *vb* **does, doing, did, done. 1** to perform or complete (a deed or action): *to do a portrait.* **2** (often *intr.* foll. by *for*) to serve the needs of; be suitable for; suffice. **3** (*tr*) to arrange or fix. **4** (*tr*) to prepare or provide; serve: *this restaurant doesn't do lunch on Sundays.* **5** (*tr*) to make tidy, elegant, ready, etc.: *to do one's hair.* **6** (*tr*) to improve (esp. in **do something to** *or* **for**). **7** (*tr*) to find an answer to (a problem or puzzle). **8** (*tr*) to translate or adapt the form or language of: *the book was done into a play.* **9** (*intr*) to conduct oneself: *do as you please.* **10** (*intr*) to fare or manage. **11** (*tr*) to cause or produce: *complaints do nothing to help.* **12** (*tr*) to give or render: *do me a favour.* **13** (*tr*) to work at, esp. as a course of study or a profession. **14** (*tr*) to perform (a play, etc.); act. **15** (*tr*) to mimic or play the part of: *she does a wonderful elderly aunt.* **16** (*tr*) to travel at a specified speed, esp. as a maximum. **17** (*tr*) to travel or traverse (a distance). **18** (takes an infinitive without *to*) used as an auxiliary **18a** before the subject of an interrogative sentence as a way of forming a question: *do you agree?* **18b** to intensify positive statements and commands: *I do like your new house; do hurry!* **18c** before a negative adverb to form negative statements or commands: *do not leave me here alone!* **18d** in inverted constructions: *little did he realize that.* **19** used as an auxiliary to replace an earlier verb or verb phrase: *he likes you as much as I do.* **20** (*tr*) *Inf.* to visit as a sightseer or tourist. **21** (*tr*) to wear out; exhaust. **22** (*intr*) to happen (esp. in **nothing doing**). **23** (*tr*) *Sl.* to serve (a period of time) as a prison sentence. **24** (*tr*) *Inf.* to cheat or swindle. **25** (*tr*) *Sl.* to rob. **26** (*tr*) *Sl.* **26a** to arrest. **26b** to convict of a crime. **27** (*tr*) *Austral. sl.* to spend (money). **28** (*tr*) *Sl., chiefly Brit.* to treat violently; assault. **29** *Sl.* to take or use (a drug). **30** (*tr*) *Taboo sl.* (of a male) to have sexual intercourse with. **31 do or die.** to make a final or supreme effort. **32 make do.** to manage with whatever is available. ◆ *n, pl* **dos** *or* **do's. 33** *Sl.* an act or instance of cheating or swindling. **34** *Inf., chiefly Brit. & NZ.* a formal or festive gathering; party. **35 do's and don'ts.** *Inf.* rules. ◆ See also **do away with, do by, do in** etc. [OE *dōn*]

do[2] (dəʊ) *n, pl* **dos.** a variant spelling of **doh**.

do. *abbrev. for* ditto.

DOA *abbrev. for* dead on arrival.

doable ('duːəbəl) *adj* capable of being done.

do away with *vb* (*intr, adv + prep*) **1** to kill or destroy. **2** to discard or abolish.

dobbin ('dɒbɪn) *n* a name for a horse, esp. a workhorse. [C16: from *Robin*, pet form of *Robert*]

Dobell ★ (dəʊ'bɛl) *n* Sir **William**. 1899–1970, Australian portrait and landscape painter.

Doberman pinscher ('dəʊbəmən 'pɪnʃə) *or* **Doberman** *n* a breed of large dog with a glossy black-and-tan coat. Also: **Dobermann**. [C19: after L. *Dobermann* (19th-cent. G dog breeder) who bred it + *Pinscher*, ? after *Pinzgau*, district in Austria]

dob in *vb* **dobs, dobbing, dobbed.** (*adv*) *Austral. & NZ sl.* **1** (*tr*) to inform against, esp. to the police. **2** to contribute to a fund.

dobra ('dəʊbrə) *n* the standard monetary unit of São Tomé e Principe.

Dobruja ★ (*Bulgarian* 'dɔbrudʒə) *n* a region of E Europe, between the River Danube and the Black Sea: the north passed to Romania and the south to Bulgaria after the Berlin Congress (1878). Romanian name: **Dobrogea** (do-'brodʒea).

do by *vb* (*intr, prep*) to treat in the manner specified.

doc (dɒk) *n Inf.* short for **doctor**.

DOC *abbrev. for* Denominazione di Origine Controllata: used of wines. [It., lit.: name of origin controlled]

docent ('dəʊsᵊnt) *n* a voluntary worker acting as a guide in a museum, art gallery, etc. [C19: from G *Dozent*, from L *docēns* from *docēre* to teach]

DOCG *abbrev. for* Denominazione di Origine Controllata Garantita: used of wines. [It., lit: name of origin guaranteed controlled]

docile ('dəʊsaɪl) *adj* **1** easy to manage or discipline; submissive. **2** *Rare.* easy to teach. [C15: from L *docilis* easily taught, from *docēre* to teach]
▸ **'docilely** *adv* ▸ **docility** (dɒ'sɪlɪtɪ) *n*

dock¹ (dɒk) *n* **1** a wharf or pier. **2** a space between two wharves or piers for the mooring of ships. **3** an area of water that can accommodate a ship and can be closed off to allow regulation of the water level. **4** short for **dry dock. 5** *in* or *into* **dock.** *Brit. inf.* **5a** (of people) in hospital. **5b** (of cars, etc.) in a repair shop. **6** *Chiefly US & Canad.* a platform from which lorries, goods trains, etc., are loaded and unloaded. ◆ *vb* **7** to moor or be moored at a dock. **8** to put (a vessel) into, or (of a vessel) to come into a dry dock. **9** (of two spacecraft) to link together in space or link together (two spacecraft) in space. [C14: from MDu. *docke*; ? rel. to L *ducere* to lead]

dock² (dɒk) *n* **1** the bony part of the tail of an animal. **2** the part of an animal's tail left after the major part of it has been cut off. ◆ *vb* (*tr*) **3** to remove (the tail or part of the tail) of (an animal) by cutting through the bone. **4** to deduct (an amount) from (a person's wages, pension, etc.). [C14: *dok* from ?]

dock³ (dɒk) *n* an enclosed space in a court of law where the accused sits or stands during his trial. [C16: from Flemish *dok* sty]

dock⁴ (dɒk) *n* any of various weedy plants having greenish or reddish flowers and broad leaves. [OE *docce*]

dockage ('dɒkɪdʒ) *n* **1** a charge levied upon a vessel for using a dock. **2** facilities for docking vessels. **3** the practice of docking vessels.

docker ('dɒkə) *n Brit.* a man employed in the loading or unloading of ships. US and Canad. equivalent: **longshoreman.** Austral. and NZ equivalent: **watersider, wharfie.** See also **stevedore.**

docket ('dɒkɪt) *n* **1** *Chiefly Brit.* a piece of paper accompanying or referring to a package or other delivery, stating contents, delivery instructions, etc., sometimes serving as a receipt. **2** *Law.* **2a** a summary of the proceedings in a court. **2b** a register containing this. **3** *Brit.* **3a** a customs certificate declaring that duty has been paid. **3b** a certificate giving particulars of a shipment. **4** a summary of contents, as in a document. **5** *US.* a list of things to be done. **6** *US law.* a list of cases awaiting trial. ◆ *vb* **dockets, docketing, docketed.** (*tr*) **7** to fix a docket to (a package, etc.). **8** *Law.* **8a** to make a summary of (a judgment, etc.). **8b** to abstract and enter in a register. **9** to endorse (a document, etc.) with a summary. [C15: from ?]

dockland ('dɒk,lænd) *n* the area around the docks.

dockside ('dɒk,saɪd) *n* an area beside a dock.

dockyard ('dɒk,jɑːd) *n* a naval establishment with docks, workshops, etc., for the building, fitting out, and repair of vessels.

Doc Martens (dɒk 'mɑːtənz) *pl n Trademark.* a brand of lace-up boots with thick lightweight resistant soles. In full: **Doctor Martens.** Abbrev.: **DMs.**

doctor ('dɒktə) *n* **1** a person licensed to practise medicine. **2** a person who has been awarded a higher academic degree in any field of knowledge. **3** *Chiefly US & Canad.* a person licensed to practise dentistry or veterinary medicine. **4** (*often cap.*) Also called: **Doctor of the Church.** a title given to any of several of the early Fathers of the Christian Church. **5** *Angling.* any of various artificial flies. **6** *Inf.* a person who mends or repairs things. **7** *Sl.* a cook on a ship or at a camp. **8** *Arch.* a man, esp. a teacher, of learning. **9 go for the doctor.** *Austral. sl.* to make a great effort or move very fast. **10 what the doctor ordered.** something needed or desired. ◆ *vb* **11** (*tr*) to give medical treatment to. **12** (*intr*) *Inf.* to practise medicine. **13** (*tr*) to repair or mend. **14** (*tr*) to make different in order to deceive. **15** (*tr*) to adapt. **16** (*tr*) *Inf.* to castrate (a cat, dog, etc.). [C14: from L: teacher, from *docēre* to teach]
▸ **'doctoral** or **doctorial** (dɒk'tɔːrɪəl) *adj*

doctorate ('dɒktərɪt, -trɪt) *n* the highest academic degree in any field of knowledge.

Doctor of Philosophy *n* a doctorate awarded for orig-

inal research in any subject except law, medicine, or theology.

doctrinaire (,dɒktrɪ'nɛə) *adj* **1** stubbornly insistent on the observation of the niceties of a theory, esp. without regard to practicality, suitability, etc. **2** theoretical; impractical. ◆ *n* **3** a person who stubbornly attempts to apply a theory without regard to practical difficulties.
▸ **,doctri'nairism** *n* ▸ **,doctri'narian** *n*

doctrine ('dɒktrɪn) *n* **1** a creed or body of teachings of a religious, political, or philosophical group presented for acceptance or belief; dogma. **2** a principle or body of principles that is taught or advocated. [C14: from OF, from L *doctrīna* teaching, from *doctor*; see DOCTOR]
▸ **doctrinal** (dɒk'traɪn'l) *adj* ▸ **doc'trinally** *adv*

docudrama ('dɒkjʊ,drɑːmə) *n* a film or television programme based on true events, presented in a dramatized form.

document *n* ('dɒkjʊmənt). **1** a piece of paper, booklet, etc., providing information, esp. of an official nature. **2** a piece of text or graphics, such as a letter or article, stored in a computer as a file for manipulation by document processing software. **3** *Arch.* proof. ◆ *vb* ('dɒkjʊ,mɛnt). (*tr*) **4** to record or report in detail, as in the press, on television, etc. **5** to support (statements in a book) with references, etc. **6** to support (a claim, etc.) with evidence. **7** to furnish (a vessel) with documents specifying its registration, dimensions, etc. [C15: from L *documentum* a lesson, from *docēre* to teach]

documentary (,dɒkjʊ'mɛntərɪ) *adj* **1** Also: **documental.** consisting of or relating to documents. **2** presenting factual material with few or no fictional additions. ◆ *n, pl* **documentaries. 3** a factual film or television programme about an event, person, etc., presenting the facts with little or no fiction.
▸ **,docu'mentarily** *adv*

documentation (,dɒkjʊmɛn'teɪʃən) *n* **1** the act of supplying with or using documents or references. **2** the documents or references supplied.

document reader *n Computing.* a device that reads and inputs into a computer marks and characters on a special form, as by optical or magnetic character recognition.

docu-soap or **docusoap** ('dɒkjʊ,səʊp) *n* a television documentary series in which the lives of the people filmed are presented as entertainment or drama. [C20: from DOCU(MENTARY) + SOAP (OPERA)]

dodder¹ ('dɒdə) *vb* (*intr*) **1** to move unsteadily; totter. **2** to shake or tremble, as from age. [C17: var. of earlier *dadder*]
▸ **'dodderer** *n* ▸ **'doddery** *adj*

dodder² ('dɒdə) *n* any of a genus of rootless parasitic plants lacking chlorophyll and having suckers for drawing nourishment from the host plant. [C13: of Gmc origin]

doddle ('dɒd'l) *n Brit. inf.* something easily accomplished. [C20: ?from *doddle* (vb) to totter]

dodeca- *combining form.* indicating twelve: *dodecaphonic.* [from Gk *dōdeka* twelve]

dodecagon (dəʊ'dɛkə,gɒn) *n* a polygon having twelve sides.

dodecahedron (,dəʊdɛkə'hiːdrən) *n* a solid figure having twelve plane faces.
▸ **,dodeca'hedral** *adj*

Dodecanese ★ (,dəʊdɪkə'niːz) *pl n* a group of islands in the SE Aegean Sea, forming a department of Greece: part of the Southern Sporades. Capital: Rhodes. Pop.: 162 439 (1991). Area: 2663 sq. km (1028 sq. miles). Modern Greek name: **Dhodhekánisos.**

dodecaphonic (,dəʊdɛkə'fɒnɪk) *adj* of or relating to the twelve-tone system of serial music.

dodge (dɒdʒ) *vb* **dodges, dodging, dodged. 1** to avoid or attempt to avoid (a blow, discovery, etc.), as by moving suddenly. **2** to evade by cleverness or trickery. **3** (*intr*) *Change-ringing.* to make a bell change places with its neighbour when sounding in successive changes. **4** (*tr*) *Photog.* to lighten or darken (selected areas on a print). ◆ *n* **5** a plan contrived to deceive. **6** a sudden evasive movement. **7** a clever contrivance. **8** *Change-ringing.* the act of dodging. [C16: from ?]

Dodge City ★ *n* a city in SW Kansas, on the Arkansas River: famous as a frontier town on the Santa Fe Trail. Pop.: 21 130 (1990).

Dodgem ('dɒdʒəm) *n Trademark.* an electrically-propelled vehicle driven and bumped against similar cars in a rink at a funfair.

dodger ('dɒdʒə) *n* **1** a person who evades or shirks. **2** a shifty dishonest person. **3** a canvas shelter on a ship's bridge, etc., to protect the helmsman from bad weather. **4** *Dialect & Austral.* food, esp. bread.

dodgy ('dɒdʒɪ) *adj* **dodgier, dodgiest.** *Brit., Austral. & NZ inf.* **1** risky, difficult, or dangerous. **2** uncertain or unreliable; tricky.

dodo ('dəʊdəʊ) *n, pl* **dodos** *or* **dodoes. 1** any of a now extinct family of flightless birds formerly found on Mauritius. They had a hooked bill and short stout legs. **2** *Inf.* an intensely conservative person who is unaware of changing fashions, ideas, etc. **3** (**as**) **dead as a dodo.** irretrievably defunct or out of date. [C17: from Port. *doudo,* from *duodo* stupid]

Dodoma ★ ('dəʊdəmə) *n* a city in central Tanzania, the legislative capital of the country. Pop.: 203 833 (1988).

do down *vb* (*tr, adv*) **1** to belittle or humiliate. **2** to deceive or cheat.

doe (dəʊ) *n, pl* **does** *or* **doe.** the female of the deer, hare, rabbit, and certain other animals. [OE *dā*]

Doe (dəʊ) *n* **John.** *Law.* **1** (formerly) the plaintiff in a fictitious action, Doe versus Roe, to test a point of law. See also **Roe. 2** Also: **Jane Doe.** *US.* an unknown or unidentified person.

DOE (in Britain) *abbrev. for* Department of the Environment.

doek (dʊk) *n S. African inf.* a square of cloth worn mainly by African women to cover the head. [C18: from Afrik.: cloth]

Doenitz ★ (*German* 'dø:nɪts) *n* a variant spelling of (Karl) **Dönitz.**

doer ('du:ə) *n* **1** a person or thing that does something. **2** an active or energetic person. **3** a thriving animal, esp. a horse.

does (dʌz) *vb* (used with a singular noun or the pronouns *he, she,* or *it*) a form of the present tense (indicative mood) of **do**[1].

doeskin ('dəʊ,skɪn) *n* **1** the skin of a deer, lamb, or sheep. **2** a very supple leather made from this. **3** a heavy smooth cloth.

doff (dɒf) *vb* (*tr*) **1** to take off or lift (one's hat) in salutation. **2** to remove (clothing). [OE *dōn of;* see DO[1], OFF; cf. DON[1]]
▸ **'doffer** *n*

do for *vb* (*prep*) *Inf.* **1** (*tr*) to convict of a crime or offence. **2** (*intr*) to cause the ruin, death, or defeat of. **3** (*intr*) to do housework for. **4 do well for oneself.** to thrive or succeed.

dog (dɒg) *n* **1** a domesticated canine mammal occurring in many breeds that show a great variety in size and form. **2** any other carnivore of the dog family, such as the dingo and coyote. **3** the male of animals of the dog family. **4** (*modifier*) spurious, inferior, or useless. **5** a mechanical device for gripping or holding. **6** *Inf.* a fellow; chap. **7** *Inf.* a man or boy regarded as unpleasant or wretched. **8** *Sl.* an unattractive girl or woman. **9** *US & Canad. inf.* something unsatisfactory or inferior. **10** short for **firedog. 11 a dog's chance.** no chance at all. **12 a dog's dinner** *or* **breakfast.** *Inf.* something messy or bungled. **13 a dog's life.** a wretched existence. **14 dog eat dog.** ruthless competition. **15 like a dog's dinner.** dressed smartly or ostentatiously. **16 put on the dog.** *US & Canad. inf.* to behave or dress in an ostentatious manner. ◆ *vb* **dogs, dogging, dogged.** (*tr*) **17** to pursue or follow after with determination. **18** to trouble; plague. **19** to chase with a dog. **20** to grip or secure by a mechanical device. ◆ *adv* **21** (*usually in combination*) thoroughly; utterly: *dog-tired.* ◆ See also **dogs.** [OE *docga,* from ?]

dog biscuit *n* a hard biscuit for dogs.

dog box *n NZ inf.* disgrace; disfavour: *in the dog box.*

dogcart ('dɒg,kɑ:t) *n* a light horse-drawn two-wheeled vehicle.

dog-catcher *n Now chiefly US & Canad.* a local official whose job is to impound and dispose of stray dogs.

dog collar *n* **1** a collar for a dog. **2** *Inf.* a clerical collar. **3** *Inf.* a tight-fitting necklace.

dog days *pl n* the hot period of the summer reckoned in ancient times from the heliacal rising of Sirius (the Dog Star). [C16: translation of LL *diēs caniculārēs,* translation of Gk *hēmerai kunades*]

doge (dəʊdʒ) *n* (formerly) the chief magistrate in the republics of Venice and Genoa. [C16: via F from It. (Venetian dialect), from L *dux* leader]

dog-ear *vb* **1** (*tr*) to fold down the corner of (a page). ◆ *n* also **dog's-ear. 2** a folded-down corner of a page.

dog-eared *adj* **1** having dog-ears. **2** shabby or worn.

dog-end *n Inf.* a cigarette end.

dogfight ('dɒg,faɪt) *n* **1** close-quarters combat between fighter aircraft. **2** any rough fight.

dogfish ('dɒg,fɪʃ) *n, pl* **dogfish** *or* **dogfishes. 1** any of several small sharks. **2** a less common name for the **bowfin.**

dogged ('dɒgɪd) *adj* obstinately determined; wilful or tenacious.
▸ **'doggedly** *adv* ▸ **'doggedness** *n*

Dogger Bank ★ ('dɒgə) *n* an extensive submerged sandbank in the North Sea between N England and Denmark: fishing ground.

doggerel ('dɒgərəl) *or* **dogrel** ('dɒgrəl) *n* **1a** comic verse, usually irregular in measure. **1b** (*as modifier*): *a doggerel rhythm.* **2** nonsense. [C14 *dogerel* worthless, ?from *dogge* DOG]

doggish ('dɒgɪʃ) *adj* **1** of or like a dog. **2** surly; snappish.

doggo ('dɒgəʊ) *adv Brit. inf.* in hiding and keeping quiet (esp. in **lie doggo**). [C19: prob. from DOG]

doggone ('dɒgɒn) *US & Canad.* ◆ *interj* **1** an exclamation of annoyance, etc. ◆ *adj* (*prenominal*), *adv* **2** Also **doggoned.** another word for **damn.** [C19: euphemism for *God damn*]

doggy *or* **doggie** ('dɒgɪ) *n, pl* **doggies. 1** a child's word for a **dog.** ◆ *adj* **doggier, doggiest. 2** of, like, or relating to a dog. **3** fond of dogs.

doggy bag *n* a bag in which leftovers from a meal may be taken away, supposedly for the diner's dog.

doggy paddle *or* **doggie paddle** *n, vb* another word for **dog paddle.**

doghouse ('dɒg,haʊs) *n* **1** the US and Canad. name for **kennel. 2** *Inf.* disfavour (in **in the doghouse**).

dogie, dogy, or dogey ('dəʊgɪ) *n, pl* **dogies** *or* **dogeys.** *US & Canad.* a motherless calf. [C19: from *dough-guts,* because they were fed on flour-and-water paste]

dog in the manger *n* a person who prevents others from using something he has no use for.

dog Latin *n* spurious or incorrect Latin.

dogleg ('dɒg,lɛg) *n* **1** a sharp bend or angle. ◆ *vb* **doglegs, doglegging, doglegged. 2** (*intr*) to go off at an angle. ◆ *adj* **3** of or with the shape of a dogleg.
▸ **doglegged** (,dɒg'lɛgɪd, 'dɒg,lɛgd) *adj*

dogma ('dɒgmə) *n, pl* **dogmas** *or* **dogmata** (-mətə). **1** a religious doctrine or system of doctrines proclaimed by ecclesiastical authority as true. **2** a belief, principle, or doctrine or a code of beliefs, principles, or doctrines. [C17: via L from Gk: opinion, from *dokein* to seem good]

dogman ('dɒgmən) *n, pl* **dogmen.** *Austral.* a person who directs the operation of a crane whilst riding on an object being lifted by it.

dogmatic (dɒg'mætɪk) *or* **dogmatical** *adj* **1a** (of a statement, opinion, etc.) forcibly asserted as if authoritative and unchallengeable. **1b** (of a person) prone to making such statements. **2** of or constituting dogma. **3** based on assumption rather than observation.
▸ **dog'matically** *adv*

dogmatics (dɒg'mætɪks) *n* (*functioning as sing*) the study of religious dogmas and dogmas. Also called: **dogmatic** (*or* **doctrinal**) **theology.**

dogmatize *or* **dogmatise** ('dɒgmə,taɪz) *vb* **dogmatizes,**

★ people and places

dogmatizing, dogmatized *or* **dogmatises, dogmatising, dogmatised.** to say or state (something) in a dogmatic manner.
▸ 'dogmatism *n* ▸ 'dogmatist *n*

do-gooder *n Inf.* a well-intentioned person, esp. a naive or impractical one.
▸ ,do-'gooding *n, adj*

dog paddle *n* 1 a swimming stroke in which the swimmer paddles his hands in imitation of a swimming dog. ◆ *vb* **dog-paddle, dog-paddles, dog-paddling, dog-paddled.** 2 (*intr*) to swim using the dog paddle. ◆ Also: **doggy paddle** *or* **doggie paddle.**

dog rose *n* a prickly wild European rose that has pink or white scentless flowers. [from belief that its root was effective against the bite of a mad dog]

dogs (dɒgz) *pl n* 1 *Sl.* the feet. 2 *Marketing inf.* goods with a low market share, which are unlikely to yield substantial profits. 3 **go to the dogs.** *Inf.* to go to ruin physically or morally. 4 **let sleeping dogs lie.** to leave things undisturbed. 5 **the dogs.** *Brit. inf.* greyhound racing.

Dogs ★ (dɒgz) *n* **Isle of.** a district in the East End of London, bounded on three sides by the River Thames.

dogsbody ('dɒgz,bɒdɪ) *Inf.* ◆ *n, pl* **dogsbodies.** 1 a person who carries out menial tasks for others. ◆ *vb* **dogsbodies, dogsbodying, dogsbodied.** (*intr*) 2 to act as a dogsbody.

dog's disease *n Austral. inf.* influenza.

dogsled ('dɒg,slɛd) *n Chiefly US & Canad.* a sleigh drawn by dogs. Also called (Brit.): **dog sledge.**

Dog Star *n* **the.** another name for **Sirius.**

dog-tired *adj* (*usually postpositive*) *Inf.* exhausted.

dogtooth ('dɒg,tuːθ) *n, pl* **dogteeth.** *Archit.* a carved ornament in the form of a series of four-cornered pyramids set diagonally and often decorated with leaf shapes along each edge, used in England in the 13th century.

dogtooth violet *n* any of a genus of plants, esp. a European plant with purple flowers.

dogtrot ('dɒg,trɒt) *n* a gently paced trot.

dog violet *n* any of three wild violets found in Britain and northern Europe.

dogwatch ('dɒg,wɒtʃ) *n* either of two two-hour watches aboard ship, from four to six p.m. or from six to eight p.m.

dogwood ('dɒg,wʊd) *n* any of various trees or shrubs, esp. a European shrub with small white flowers and black berries.

dogy ('dəʊgɪ) *n, pl* **dogies.** a variant of **dogie.**

doh (dəʊ) *n Music.* (in tonic sol-fa) the first degree of any major scale. [C18: from It., replacing *ut*; see GAMUT]

Doha ★ ('dəʊhɑː, 'dəʊə) *n* the capital and chief port of Qatar, on the E coast of the peninsula. Pop.: 339 471 (1993 est.). See also: **Bida, El Beda.**

Dohnányi ★ (dɒk'nɑːnjɪ, dɒx-; *Hungarian* 'dohnɑːnji) *n* **Ernö** ('ɛrnøː) *or* **Ernst von** (ɛrnst fɒn). 1877–1960, Hungarian composer.

doily *or* **doyley** ('dɔɪlɪ) *n, pl* **doilies** *or* **doyleys.** a decorative mat of lace or lacelike paper, etc., laid on plates. [C18: after *Doily*, a London draper]

do in *vb* (*tr, adv*) *Sl.* 1 to kill. 2 to exhaust.

doing ('duːɪŋ) *n* 1 an action or the performance of an action: *whose doing is this?* 2 *Inf.* a beating or castigation.

doings ('duːɪŋz) *n* 1 (*functioning as pl*) deeds, actions, or events. 2 (*functioning as sing*) *Inf.* anything of which the name is not known, or euphemistically left unsaid, etc.

do-it-yourself *n* **a** the hobby or process of constructing and repairing things oneself. **b** (*as modifier*): *a do-it-yourself kit.*

dol. *abbrev. for:* 1 *Music.* dolce. 2 (*pl* **dols.**) dollar.

Dolby ('dɒlbɪ) *n Trademark.* any of various specialized electronic circuits, esp. those used in tape recorders for noise reduction in high-frequency signals. [after R. Dolby (born 1933), US inventor]

dolce ('dɒltʃɪ) *adj, adv Music.* (to be performed) gently and sweetly. [It.]

Dolcelatte (,dɒltʃɪ'lɑːtɪ) *n* a soft creamy blue-veined Italian cheese. [It., lit: sweet milk]

dolce vita ('dɒltʃɪ 'viːtə) *n* a life of luxury. [It., lit.: sweet life]

doldrums ('dɒldrəmz) *n* **the.** 1 a depressed or bored state of mind. 2 a state of inactivity or stagnation. 3 a belt of light winds or calms along the equator. [C19: prob. from OE *dol* DULL, infl. by TANTRUM]

dole¹ (dəʊl) *n* 1 (*usually preceded by the*) *Brit. & Austral. inf.* money received from the state while out of work. 2 **on the dole.** *Brit. & Austral. inf.* receiving such money. 3 a small portion of money or food given to a poor person. 4 the act of distributing such portions. 5 *Arch.* fate. ◆ *vb* **doles, doling, doled.** 6 (*tr;* usually foll. by *out*) to distribute, esp. in small portions. [OE *dāl* share]

dole² (dəʊl) *n Arch.* grief or mourning. [C13: from OF, from LL *dolus,* from L *dolēre* to lament]

dole-bludger *n Austral. sl.* a person who draws unemployment benefit without making any attempt to get work.

doleful ('dəʊlfʊl) *adj* dreary; mournful.
▸ 'dolefully *adv* ▸ 'dolefulness *n*

dolerite ('dɒlə,raɪt) *n* 1 a dark basic igneous rock; a coarse-grained basalt. 2 any dark igneous rock whose composition cannot be determined with the naked eye. [C19: from F *dolérite,* from Gk *doleros* deceitful; from the difficulty in determining its composition]

Dolgellau ★ (dɒl'gɛθlaɪ, *Welsh* dol'gɛhla) *n* a market town and tourist centre in NW Wales, in Gwynedd. Pop.: 2396 (1991).

dolichocephalic (,dɒlɪkəʊsɪ'fælɪk) *or* **dolichocephalous** (,dɒlɪkəʊ'sɛfələs) *adj* having a head much longer than it is broad. [C19: from Gk *dolichos* long + -CEPHALIC]

Dolin ★ ('dəʊlɪn) *n* **Sir Anton,** real name *Sydney Healey-Kay.* 1904–83, British ballet dancer and choreographer: cofounder (1949) of the London Festival Ballet.

doll (dɒl) *n* 1 a small model or dummy of a human being, used as a toy. 2 *Sl.* a pretty girl or woman of little intelligence. [C16: prob. from *Doll,* pet name for *Dorothy*]

dollar ('dɒlə) *n* 1 the standard monetary unit of the US, divided into 100 cents. 2 the standard monetary unit, comprising 100 cents, of various other countries including: Australia, the Bahamas, Canada, Jamaica, Malaysia, New Zealand, Singapore, Taiwan, and Zimbabwe. [C16: from Low G *daler,* from G *Taler, Thaler,* short for *Joachimsthaler,* coin made from metal mined in *Joachimsthal* Jachymov, town in the Czech Republic]

dollarbird ('dɒlə,bɜːd) *n* a bird of S and SE Asia and Australia with a round white spot on each wing.

dollar diplomacy *n Chiefly US.* 1 a foreign policy that encourages and protects commercial and financial involvement abroad. 2 use of financial power as a diplomatic weapon.

Dollfuss ★ (*German* 'dɒlfuːs) *n* **Engelbert** ('ɛŋəlbɛrt). 1892–1934, Austrian chancellor (1932–34); assassinated by Austrian Nazis.

dollop ('dɒləp) *Inf.* ◆ *n* 1 a semisolid lump. 2 a measure or serving. ◆ *vb* 3 (*tr;* foll. by *out*) to serve out (food). [C16: from ?]

doll up *vb* (*tr, adv*) *Sl.* to dress in a stylish or showy manner.

dolly ('dɒlɪ) *n, pl* **dollies.** 1 a child's word for a **doll.** 2 *Films, etc.* a wheeled support on which a camera may be mounted. 3 a cup-shaped anvil used to hold a rivet. 4 *Cricket.* **4a** a simple catch. **4b** a full toss bowled in a slow high arc. Also called: **dolly bird.** *Sl., chiefly Brit.* an attractive and fashionable girl. ◆ *vb* **dollies, dollying, dollied.** 6 *Films, etc.* to wheel (a camera) backwards or forwards on a dolly.

dolly mixture *n* 1 a mixture of tiny coloured sweets. 2 one such sweet.

dolma ('dɒlmə) *n, pl* **dolmas** *or* **dolmades** (dɒl'mɑːdɪz). a vine leaf stuffed with a filling of meat and rice. [C19: Turkish *dolma* lit. something filled]

dolman sleeve ('dɒlmən) *n* a sleeve that is very wide at the armhole and tapers to a tight wrist. [C19: from *dolman,* a type of Turkish robe, ult. from Turkish *dolamak* to wind]

dolmen ('dɒlmɛn) *n* a Neolithic stone formation, consisting of a horizontal stone supported by several vertical stones, and thought to be a tomb. [C19: from F, prob. from OBreton *tol* table, from L *tabula* board + Breton *mēn* stone, of Celtic origin]

Dolmetsch ★ ('dɒlmɛtʃ) *n* **Arnold**. 1858–1940, British musician, born in France. He contributed greatly to the revival of interest in early music and instruments.

dolomite ('dɒlə,maɪt) *n* **1** a mineral consisting of calcium magnesium carbonate. **2** a rock resembling limestone but consisting principally of the mineral dolomite. [C18: after Déodat de *Dolomieu* (1750–1801), F mineralogist]
▶ **dolomitic** (,dɒlə'mɪtɪk) *adj*

Dolomites ★ ('dɒlə,maɪts) *pl n* a mountain range in NE Italy: part of the Alps; formed of dolomitic limestone. Highest peak: Marmolada, 3342 m (10 965 ft).

doloroso (,dɒlə'rəusəu) *adj, adv Music.* (to be performed) in a sorrowful manner. [It.]

dolorous ('dɒlərəs) *adj* causing or involving pain or sorrow.
▶ **'dolorously** *adv*

dolos ('dɒlɒs) *n, pl* **dolosse**. *S. African*. a knucklebone of a sheep, buck, etc., used esp. by diviners. [from ?]

dolour *or US* **dolor** ('dɒlə) *n Poetic.* grief or sorrow. [C14: from L, from *dolēre* to grieve]

dolphin ('dɒlfɪn) *n* **1** any of various marine mammals that are typically smaller than whales and larger than porpoises and have a beaklike snout. **2 river dolphin.** any of various freshwater mammals inhabiting rivers of North and South America and S Asia. **3** Also called: **dorado.** either of two large marine fishes that have an iridescent coloration. **4** *Naut.* a post or buoy for mooring a vessel. [C13: from OF *dauphin*, via L, from Gk *delphin-, delphis*]

dolphinarium (,dɒlfɪ'nɛərɪəm) *n, pl* **dolphinariums** *or* **dolphinaria** (-ɪə). a pool or aquarium for dolphins, esp. one in which they give public displays.

dolt (dəult) *n* a slow-witted or stupid person. [C16: prob. rel. to OE *dol* stupid]
▶ **'doltish** *adj* ▶ **'doltishness** *n*

dom. *abbrev. for:* **1** domain. **2** domestic.

-dom *suffix forming nouns.* **1** state or condition: *freedom.* **2** rank, office, or domain of: *earldom.* **3** a collection of persons: *officialdom.* [OE *-dōm*]

Domagk ★ (*German* 'do:mak) *n* **Gerhard** ('ge:rhart). 1895–1964, German biochemist: Nobel prize for medicine (1939) for isolating sulphanilamide.

domain (də'meɪn) *n* **1** land governed by a ruler or government. **2** land owned by one person or family. **3** a field or scope of knowledge or activity. **4** a region having specific characteristics. **5** *Austral. & NZ.* a park or recreation reserve maintained by a public authority, often the government. **6** *Law.* the absolute ownership and right to dispose of land. **7** *Maths.* the set of values of the independent variable of a function for which the functional value exists. **8** *Logic.* another term for **universe of discourse. 9** *Philosophy.* range of significance. **10** *Physics.* one of the regions in a ferromagnetic solid in which all the atoms have the same magnetic moments aligned in the same direction. **11** *Computing.* a group of computers that have the same suffix (**domain name**) in their names on the Internet, specifying the country, type of institution, etc. where they are located. [C17: from F *domaine*, from L *dominium* property, from *dominus* lord]

dome (dəum) *n* **1** a hemispherical roof or vault. **2** something shaped like this. **3** a slang word for the **head.** ◆ *vb* **domes, doming, domed.** (*tr*) **4** to cover with or as if with a dome. **5** to shape like a dome. [C16: from F, from It. *duomo* cathedral, from L *domus* house]
▶ **'dome,like** ▶ **domical** ('dəumɪk'l, 'dɒm-) *adj*

Dome of the Rock ★ *n* a mosque in Jerusalem, Israel, on the Temple Mount: the third most holy place of Islam.

Domesday Book *or* **Doomsday Book** ('du:mz,deɪ) *n History.* the record of a survey of the land of England carried out by the commissioners of William I in 1086.

domestic (də'mɛstɪk) *adj* **1** of the home or family. **2** enjoying or accustomed to home or family life. **3** (of an animal) bred or kept by man as a pet or for purposes such as the supply of food. **4** of one's own country or a specific country: *domestic and foreign affairs.* ◆ *n* **5** a household servant. [C16: from OF *domestique*, from L *domesticus* belonging to the house, from *domus* house]
▶ **do'mestically** *adv*

domesticate (də'mɛstɪ,keɪt) *or US* (*sometimes*) **domesticize** (də'mɛstɪ,saɪz) *vb* **domesticates, domesticating, domesticated** *or US* **domesticizes, domesticizing, domesticized.** (*tr*) **1** to bring or keep (wild animals or plants) under control or cultivation. **2** to accustom to home life. **3** to adapt to an environment.
▶ **do'mesticable** *adj* ▶ **do,mesti'cation** *n*

domesticity (,dəume'stɪsɪtɪ) *n, pl* **domesticities. 1** home life. **2** devotion to or familiarity with home life. **3** (*usually pl*) a domestic duty or matter.

domestic science *n* the study of cooking, needlework, and other subjects concerned with household skills.

domicile ('dɒmɪ,saɪl) *or* **domicil** ('dɒmɪsɪl) *Formal.* ◆ *n* **1** a dwelling place. **2** a permanent legal residence. **3** *Commerce, Brit.* the place where a bill of exchange is to be paid. ◆ *vb also* **domiciliate** (,dɒmɪ'sɪlɪ,eɪt), **domiciles, domiciling, domiciled** *or* **domiciliates, domiciliating, domiciliated. 4** to establish or be established in a dwelling place. [C15: from L *domicilium*, from *domus* house]
▶ **domiciliary** (,dɒmɪ'sɪlɪərɪ) *adj*

dominance ('dɒmɪnəns) *n* control; ascendancy.

dominant ('dɒmɪnənt) *adj* **1** having primary authority or influence; governing; ruling. **2** predominant or primary: *the dominant topic of the day.* **3** occupying a commanding position. **4** *Genetics.* (of a gene) producing the same phenotype in the organism whether its allele is identical or dissimilar. Cf. **recessive. 5** *Music.* of or relating to the fifth degree of a scale. **6** *Ecology.* (of a plant or animal species) more prevalent than any other species and determining the appearance and composition of the community. ◆ *n* **7** *Genetics.* a dominant gene. **8** *Music.* **8a** the fifth degree of a scale. **8b** a key or chord based on this. **9** *Ecology.* a dominant plant or animal in a community.
▶ **'dominantly** *adv*

dominant seventh chord *n Music.* a chord consisting of the dominant and the major third, perfect fifth, and minor seventh above it.

dominate ('dɒmɪ,neɪt) *vb* **dominates, dominating, dominated. 1** to control, rule, or govern. **2** to tower above (surroundings, etc.). **3** (*tr; usually passive*) to predominate in. [C17: from L *dominārī* to be lord over, from *dominus* lord]
▶ **'domi,nating** *adj* ▶ **,domi'nation** *n*

dominatrix (,dɒmɪ'neɪtrɪks) *n, pl* **dominatrices** (,dɒmɪnə'traɪsi:z). **1** a woman who is the dominant sexual partner in a sadomasochistic relationship. **2** a dominant woman. [C16: from L., fem of *dominātor*, from *dominārī* to be lord over]

dominee ('du:mɪnɪ, 'duə-) *n* (in South Africa) a minister in any of the Afrikaner Churches. [from Afrik., from Du.; cf. DOMINIE]

domineer (,dɒmɪ'nɪə) *vb* (*intr; often foll. by over*) to act with arrogance or tyranny; behave imperiously. [C16: from Du. *domineren*, from F *dominer* to DOMINATE]
▶ **,domi'neering** *adj*

Domingo ★ (də'mɪŋgəu; *Spanish* do'miŋgo) *n* **Placido** ('plæsɪdəu; *Spanish* 'plaθiðo). born 1941, Spanish operatic tenor.

Dominic ★ ('dɒmɪnɪk) *n* **Saint**. original name *Domingo de Guzman*. ?1170–1221, Spanish priest; founder of the Dominican order. Feast day: Aug. 7.

Dominica ★ (,dɒmɪ'ni:kə, də'mɪnɪkə) *n* a republic in the E Caribbean, comprising a volcanic island in the Windward Islands group; a former British colony; became independent as a member of the Commonwealth in 1978. Official language: English. Religion: mostly Roman Catholic. Currency: East Caribbean dollar. Capital: Roseau. Pop.: 74 400 (1997). Area: 751 sq. km (290 sq. miles). Official name: **Commonwealth of Dominica.**

★ people and places

dominical (də'mɪnɪkªl) *adj* **1** of Jesus Christ as Lord. **2** of Sunday as the Lord's Day. [C15: from LL *dominicālis*, from L *dominus* lord]

Dominican[1] (də'mɪnɪkən) *n* **1a** a member of an order of preaching friars founded by Saint Dominic in 1215; a Blackfriar. **1b** a nun of one of the orders founded under his patronage. ◆ *adj* **2** of Saint Dominic or the Dominican order.

Dominican[2] (də'mɪnɪkən) *adj* **1** of or relating to the Dominican Republic or Dominica. ◆ *n* **2** a native or inhabitant of the Dominican Republic or Dominica.

Dominican Republic ★ *n* a republic in the Caribbean, occupying the eastern half of the island of Hispaniola: colonized by the Spanish after its discovery by Columbus in 1492; gained independence from Spain in 1821. It is generally mountainous, dominated by the Cordillera Central, which rises over 3000 m (10 000 ft), with fertile lowlands. Language: Spanish. Religion: mostly Roman Catholic. Currency: peso. Capital: Santo Domingo. Pop.: 7 802 000 (1997). Area: 48 441 sq. km (18 703 sq. miles). Former name (until 1844): **Santo Domingo.**

dominie ('dɒmɪnɪ) *n* **1** a Scots word for **schoolmaster**. **2** a minister or clergyman. [C17: from L *dominē*, vocative case of *dominus* lord]

dominion (də'mɪnjən) *n* **1** rule; authority. **2** the land governed by one ruler or government. **3** sphere of influence; area of control. **4** a name formerly applied to self-governing divisions of the British Empire. **5 the Dominion.** New Zealand. [C15: from OF, from L *dominium* ownership, from *dominus* master]

Dominion Day *n* the former name for **Canada Day.**

domino[1] ('dɒmɪ,nəʊ) *n, pl* **dominoes.** a small rectangular block marked with dots, used in dominoes. [C19: from F, from It., ?from *domino!* master!, said by the winner]

domino[2] ('dɒmɪ,nəʊ) *n, pl* **dominoes** or **dominos. 1** a large hooded cloak worn with an eye mask at a masquerade. **2** the eye mask worn with such a cloak. [C18: from F or It., prob. from L *dominus* lord, master]

Domino ★ ('dɒmɪnəʊ) *n* **Fats.** real name *Antoine Domino.* born 1928, US rhythm-and-blues and rock-and-roll pianist, singer, and songwriter. His singles include "Ain't that a Shame" (1955) and "Blueberry Hill" (1956).

domino effect *n* a series of similar or related events occurring as a direct and inevitable result of one initial event. [C20: alluding to a row of dominoes, each standing on end, all of which fall when one is pushed]

dominoes ('dɒmɪ,nəʊz) *n* (*functioning as sing*) any of several games in which dominoes with matching halves are laid together.

Dominus *Latin.* ('dɒmɪnʊs) *n* God or Christ.

Domitian ★ (də'mɪʃən) *n* full name *Titus Flavius Domitianus.* 51–96 A.D., Roman emperor (81–96): instigated a reign of terror (93); assassinated.

Domrémy-la-Pucelle (*French* dɔ̃remilapysɛl) *or* **Domrémy** ★ *n* a village in NE France, in the Vosges: birthplace of Joan of Arc.

don[1] (dɒn) *vb* **dons, donning, donned.** (*tr*) to put on (clothing). [C14: from DO[1] + ON; cf. DOFF]

don[2] (dɒn) *n* **1** *Brit.* a member of the teaching staff at a university or college, esp. at Oxford or Cambridge. **2** the head of a student dormitory at certain Canadian universities and colleges. **3** a Spanish gentleman or nobleman. **4** (in the Mafia) the head of the family. **5** *Arch.* a person of rank. [C17: ult. from L *dominus* lord]

Don[1] (dɒn) *n* a Spanish title equivalent to *Mr.* [C16: via Sp., from L *dominus* lord]

Don[2] ★ (dɒn) *n* **1** a river rising in W Russia, southeast of Tula and flowing generally south to the Sea of Azov: linked by canal to the River Volga. Length: 1870 km (1162 miles). **2** a river in NE Scotland, rising in the Cairngorm Mountains and flowing east to the North Sea. Length: 100 km (62 miles). **3** a river in N central England, rising in S Yorkshire and flowing northeast to the Humber. Length: about 96 km (60 miles).

Doña ('dɒnjə) *n* a Spanish title of address equivalent to *Mrs* or *Madam.* [C17: via Sp., from L *domina*]

Donar ★ ('dəʊnɑ:; *German* 'do:nar) *n* the Germanic god of thunder, corresponding to Thor in Norse mythology.

donate (dəʊ'neɪt) *vb* **donates, donating, donated.** to give (money, time, etc.), esp. to a charity.
► **do'nator** *n*

Donatello ★ (*Italian* dona'tɛllo) *n* real name *Donato di Betto Bardi.* 1386–1466, Florentine Renaissance sculptor, whose work includes the classic bronze *David.*

donation (dəʊ'neɪʃən) *n* **1** the act of donating. **2** a contribution. [C15: from L *dōnātiō* a presenting, from *dōnāre* to give, from *dōnum* gift]

donative ('dəʊnətɪv) *n* **1** a gift or donation. **2** a benefice capable of being conferred as a gift. ◆ *adj* **3** of or like a donation. **4** being or relating to a benefice. [C15: from L *dōnātīvum* a donation made to soldiers by a Roman emperor, from *dōnāre* to present]

Donatus ★ (dəʊ'nɑ:təs) *n* **1 Aelius** ('i:lɪəs). 4th century A.D., Latin grammarian, who taught Saint Jerome; his textbook *Ars Grammatica* was used throughout the Middle Ages. **2** 4th century A.D., bishop of Carthage; leader of the Donatists, a heretical Christian sect originating in N Africa in 311 A.D.

Donau ★ ('do:nau) *n* the German name for the **Danube.**

Donbass *or* **Donbas** ★ (dɒn'bɑ:s) *n* an industrial region of the E Ukraine, in the plain of the Rivers Donets and lower Dnieper: the site of a major coalfield. Also called: **Donets Basin.**

Doncaster ★ ('dɒŋkəstə) *n* **1** an industrial town in N England, on the River Don. Pop.: 71 595 (1991). **2** a unitary authority in N England. Pop.: 292 500 (1994 est.). Area: 582 sq. km (225 sq. miles).

donder ('dɒndə) *S. African sl.* ◆ *vb* **1** (*tr*) to beat (someone) up. ◆ *n* **2** a wretch; swine. [from Afrik., from Du. *donderen* to swear, bully]

done (dʌn) *vb* **1** the past participle of **do**[1]. **2** be or have done with. to end relations with. **3** have done. to be completely finished: *have you done?* ◆ *interj* **4** an expression of agreement, as on the settlement of a bargain. ◆ *adj* **5** completed. **6** cooked enough. **7** used up. **8** socially acceptable. **9** *Inf.* cheated; tricked. **10** done for. *Inf.* **10a** dead or almost dead. **10b** in serious difficulty. **11** done in *or* up. *Inf.* exhausted.

donee (dəʊ'ni:) *n* a person who receives a gift. [C16: from DON(OR) + -EE]

Donegal ★ ('dɒnɪ,gɔ:l, ,dɒnɪ'gɔ:l) *n* a county in NW Republic of Ireland, on the Atlantic: mountainous, with a rugged coastline and many offshore islands. County town: Lifford. Pop.: 128 117 (1991). Area: 4830 sq. km (1865 sq. miles).

doner kebab ('dɒnə) *n* a fast-food dish comprising grilled meat and salad served in pitta bread with chilli sauce. [from Turkish *döner* rotating + KEBAB]

Donets ★ (*Russian* da'njets) *n* a river in E Europe, rising in Russia, in the Kursk steppe, and flowing southeast, through the Ukraine, to the Don River. Length: about 1078 km (670 miles).

Donets Basin ★ (də'nɛts) *n* another name for the **Donbass.**

Donetsk ★ (*Russian* da'njetsk) *n* a city in the E Ukraine: the chief industrial centre of the Donbass; first ironworks founded by a Welshman, John Hughes (1872), after whom the town was named **Yuzovka** (Hughesovka). Pop.: 1 088 000 (1996 est.). Former names (from 1924 until 1961): **Stalin** or **Stalino.**

dong (dɒŋ) *n* **1** an imitation of the sound of a bell. **2** *Austral. & NZ inf.* a heavy blow. ◆ *vb* **3** (*intr*) to make such a sound. **4** *Austral. & NZ inf.* to strike or punch. [C19: imit.]

donga ('dɒŋgə) *n* *S. African, Austral., & NZ.* a steep-sided gully created by soil erosion. [C19: from Afrik., from Zulu]

Dongola ★ ('dɒŋgələ) *n* a small town in the N Sudan, on the Nile: built on the site of Old Dongola, the capital of the Christian Kingdom of Nubia (6th to 14th centuries). Pop.: 5937 (latest est.).

Dongting ('dʊŋ'tɪŋ), **Tungting,** *or* **Tung-t'ing** ★ *n* a lake in S China, in NE Hunan province: main outlet flows to the Yangtze; rice-growing in winter. Area: (in winter) 3900 sq. km (1500 sq. miles).

Dönitz *or* **Doenitz** ★ (*German* 'dø:nɪts) *n* **Karl** (karl). 1891–1980, German admiral; commander of the German navy (1943–45); after Hitler's death he surrendered to the Allies.

Donizetti ★ (ˌdɒnɪ'zetɪ; *Italian* donid'dzetti) *n* **Gaetano** (gae'ta:no). 1797–1848, Italian operatic composer: his works include *Lucia di Lammermoor* (1835), *La Fille du régiment* (1840), and *Don Pasquale* (1843).

donjon ('dʌndʒən, 'dɒn-) *n* the heavily fortified central tower or keep of a medieval castle. Also: **dungeon**. [C14: arch. var. of *dungeon*]

Don Juan ★ ('dɒn 'dʒu:ən) *n* **1** a legendary Spanish nobleman and philanderer: hero of many poems, plays, and operas. **2** a successful seducer of women.

donkey ('dɒŋkɪ) *n* **1** a long-eared member of the horse family. **2** a stupid or stubborn person. **3 talk the hind leg(s) off a donkey.** to talk endlessly. [C18: ?from *dun* dark + -*key*, as in *monkey*]

donkey jacket *n* a thick hip-length jacket, usually navy blue, with a waterproof panel across the shoulders.

donkey's years *pl n Inf.* a long time.

donkey vote *n Austral.* a vote in which the voter's order of preference follows the order in which the candidates are listed.

donkey-work *n* **1** groundwork. **2** drudgery.

Donleavy ★ (dɒn'li:vɪ) *n* **J**(ames) **P**(atrick). born 1926, Irish novelist, born in the US. His books include *The Ginger Man* (1956), *The Onion Eaters* (1971), and *The Lady who Liked Clean Rest Rooms* (1995).

Donna ('dɒnə) *n* an Italian title of address equivalent to *Madam*. [C17: from It., from L *domina* lady]

Donne ★ (dʌn) *n* **John**. 1573–1631, English metaphysical poet and preacher.

donnish ('dɒnɪʃ) *adj* of or resembling a university don, esp. denoting pedantry or fussiness.
► '**donnishness** *n*

donnybrook ('dɒnɪˌbrʊk) *n* a rowdy brawl. [C19: after *Donnybrook Fair*, an annual event until 1855 near Dublin]

donor ('dəʊnə) *n* **1** a person who makes a donation. **2** *Med.* any person who gives blood, organs, etc., for use in the treatment of another person. **3** the atom supplying both electrons in a coordinate bond. [C15: from OF *doneur*, from L *dōnātor*, from *dōnāre* to give]

donor card *n* a card carried to show that the bodily organs specified on it may be used for transplants after the carrier's death.

Don Quixote ('dɒn ki:'həʊtiː, 'kwɪksət) *n* an impractical idealist. [after the hero of Cervantes' *Don Quixote de la Mancha* (1605)]

don't (dəʊnt) *contraction of* do not.

don't know *n* a person who has no definite opinion, esp. as a response to a questionnaire.

doodah ('du:dɑ:) *or US & Canad.* **doodad** ('du:dæd) *n Inf.* an unnamed thing, esp. an object the name of which is unknown or forgotten. [C20: from ?]

doodle ('du:d°l) *Inf.* ◆ *vb* **doodles, doodling, doodled. 1** to scribble or draw aimlessly. **2** to play or improvise idly. **3** (*intr;* often foll. by *away*) *US.* to dawdle or waste time. ◆ *n* **4** a shape, picture, etc., drawn aimlessly. [C20: ?from C17: a foolish person, but infl. in meaning by DAWDLE]
► '**doodler** *n*

doodlebug ('du:d°l,bʌg) *n* **1** another name for the **V-1. 2** a diviner's rod. **3** a US name for an **antlion** (the larva). [C20: prob. from DOODLE + BUG]

doo-doo ('du:ˌdu:) *n US & Canad. inf.* a child's word for **excrement.**

doohickey ('du:ˌhɪkɪ) *n US & Canad. inf.* another name for **doodah.**

Doolittle ★ ('du:lɪt°l) *n* **Hilda**. known as *H.D.* 1886–1961, US imagist poet and novelist, lived in Europe.

doom (du:m) *n* **1** death or a terrible fate. **2** a judgment. **3**

(*sometimes cap.*) another term for the **Last Judgment.** ◆ *vb* **4** (*tr*) to destine or condemn to death or a terrible fate. [OE *dōm*]

doomsday *or* **domesday** ('du:mzˌdeɪ) *n* **1** (*sometimes cap.*) the day on which the Last Judgment will occur. **2** any day of reckoning. **3** (*modifier*) characterized by predictions of disaster: *doomsday scenario*. [OE *dōmes dæg* Judgment Day]

doona ('du:nə) *n* the Austral. name for **continental quilt.** [from a trademark]

door (dɔ:) *n* **1** a hinged or sliding panel for closing the entrance to a room, cupboard, etc. **2** a doorway or entrance. **3** a means of access or escape: *a door to success*. **4 lay at someone's door.** to lay (the blame or responsibility) on someone. **5 out of doors.** in or into the open air. **6 show someone the door.** to order someone to leave. [OE *duru*]

do-or-die *adj* (*prenominal*) of a determined and sometimes reckless effort to succeed.

door furniture *n* locks, handles, etc., designed for use on doors.

doorjamb ('dɔ:ˌdʒæm) *n* one of the two vertical members forming the sides of a doorframe. Also called: **doorpost.**

doorkeeper ('dɔ:ˌki:pə) *n* a person attending or guarding a door or gateway.

doorman ('dɔ:ˌmæn, -mən) *n, pl* **doormen.** a man employed to attend the doors of certain buildings.

doormat ('dɔ:ˌmæt) *n* **1** a mat, placed at an entrance, for wiping dirt from shoes. **2** *Inf.* a person who offers little resistance to ill-treatment.

Doorn ★ (*Dutch* do:rn) *n* a town in the central Netherlands, in Utrecht province: residence of Kaiser William II of Germany from his abdication (1919) until his death (1941).

doornail ('dɔ:ˌneɪl) *n* (as) **dead as a doornail.** dead beyond any doubt.

Dornik ★ ('dɔ:rnɪk) *n* the Flemish name for **Tournai.**

doorsill ('dɔ:ˌsɪl) *n* a horizontal member of wood, stone, etc., forming the bottom of a doorframe.

doorstep ('dɔ:ˌstep) *n* **1** a step in front of a door. **2** *Inf.* a thick slice of bread. ◆ *vb* **doorsteps, doorstepping, doorstepped.** (*tr*) **3** to canvass (a district or member of the public) by or in the course of door-to-door visiting. **4** (of journalists) to wait outside the house of (someone) in order to obtain an interview or photograph when he or she emerges.

doorstop ('dɔ:ˌstɒp) *n* **1** any device which prevents an open door from moving. **2** a piece of rubber, etc., fixed to the floor to stop a door striking a wall.

door to door *adj* (**door-to-door** *when prenominal*), *adv* **1** (of selling, etc.) from one house to the next. **2** (of journeys, etc.) direct.

doorway ('dɔ:ˌweɪ) *n* **1** an opening into a building, room, etc., esp. one that has a door. **2** a means of access or escape: *a doorway to freedom*.

do over *vb* (*tr, adv*) **1** *Inf.* to redecorate. **2** *Brit., Austral. & NZ sl.* to beat up; thrash.

doo-wop ('du:ˌwɒp) *n* vocalizing based on rhythm-and-blues harmony. [C20: imit.]

dop (dɒp) *n S. African sl.* **1** Cape brandy. **2** a tot of this. [from Afrik., from ?]

dope (dəʊp) *n* **1** any of a number of preparations applied to fabric in order to improve strength, tautness, etc. **2** an additive, such as an antiknock compound added to petrol. **3** a thick liquid, such as a lubricant, applied to a surface. **4** a combustible absorbent material used to hold the nitroglycerine in dynamite. **5** *Sl.* an illegal drug, usually cannabis. **6** a drug administered to a racehorse or greyhound to affect its performance. **7** *Inf.* a stupid or slow-witted person. **8** *Inf.* news or facts, esp. confidential information. ◆ *vb* **dopes, doping, doped.** (*tr*) **9** *Electronics.* to add impurities to (a semiconductor) in order to produce or modify its properties. **10** to apply or add dope to. **11** to administer a drug to (oneself or another). [C19: from Du. *doop* sauce, from *doopen* to dip]

dopey *or* **dopy** ('dəʊpɪ) *adj* **dopier, dopiest. 1** *Sl.* silly. **2** *Inf.*

half-asleep or semiconscious, as when under the influence of a drug.

doppelgänger ('dɒpˀl,gɛŋə) n Legend. a ghostly duplicate of a living person. [from G Doppelgänger, lit.: double-goer]

Doppler effect ('dɒplə) n a change in the apparent frequency of a sound or light wave, etc., as a result of relative motion between the observer and the source. Also called: **Doppler shift**. [C19: after C. J. Doppler (1803–53), Austrian physicist]

Doráti ★ (də'rɑːtɪ) n Antal ('æntæl). 1906–88, US conductor and composer.

Dorcas ★ ('dɔːkəs) n a charitable woman of Joppa (Acts 9:36–42).

Dorchester ★ ('dɔːtʃɪstə) n a town in S England, administrative centre of Dorset: associated with Thomas Hardy, esp. as the Casterbridge of his novels. Pop.: 15 037 (1991). Latin name: **Durnovaria** (,djuːrnəʊ'vɛːrɪə).

Dordogne ★ (French dɔrdɔɲ) n 1 a river in SW France, rising in the Auvergne Mountains and flowing southwest and west to join the Garonne river and form the Gironde estuary. Length: 472 km (293 miles). 2 a department of SW France, in Aquitaine region. Capital: Périgueux. Pop.: 388 521 (1994 est.). Area: 9224 sq. km (3597 sq. miles).

Dordrecht ★ (Dutch 'dɔrdrɛxt) n a port in the SW Netherlands, in South Holland province: chief port of the Netherlands until the 17th century. Pop.: 114 152 (1995 est.). Also called: **Dort**.

Doré ★ (French dɔre) n (Paul) Gustave (gystav). 1832–83, French illustrator; he illustrated the Bible, Dante's Inferno, and works by Rabelais.

Doric ('dɒrɪk) adj 1 of the inhabitants of Doris in ancient Greece or their dialect. 2 of or denoting one of the five classical orders of architecture: characterized by a heavy fluted column and a simple capital. 3 (sometimes not cap.) rustic. ♦ n 4 one of four chief dialects of Ancient Greek. 5 any rural dialect of English, esp. a Scots one.

Doris[1] ★ ('dɒrɪs) n (in ancient Greece) 1 a small landlocked area north of the Gulf of Corinth. Traditionally regarded as the home of the Dorians, it was perhaps settled by some of them during their southward migration. 2 the coastal area of Caria in SW Asia Minor, settled by Dorians.

Doris[2] ★ ('dɒrɪs) n Greek myth. a sea nymph.

dorm (dɔːm) n Inf. short for **dormitory**.

dormant ('dɔːmənt) adj 1 quiet and inactive, as during sleep. 2 latent or inoperative. 3 (of a volcano) neither extinct nor erupting. 4 Biol. alive but in a resting condition with reduced metabolism. 5 (usually postpositive) Heraldry. (of a beast) in a sleeping position. [C14: from OF dormant, from dormir to sleep, from L dormīre]
► **'dormancy** n

dormer ('dɔːmə) n a construction with a gable roof and a window that projects from a sloping roof. Also called: **dormer window**. [C16: from OF dormoir, from L dormītōrium DORMITORY]

dormie or **dormy** ('dɔːmɪ) adj Golf. as many holes ahead of an opponent as there are still to play: dormie three. [C19: from ?]

dormitory ('dɔːmɪtərɪ, -trɪ) n, pl **dormitories**. 1 a large room, esp. at a school, containing several beds. 2 US. a building, esp. at a college or camp, providing living and sleeping accommodation. 3 (modifier) Brit. denoting or relating to an area from which most of the residents commute to work (esp. in **dormitory suburb**). [C15: from L dormītōrium, from dormīre to sleep]

Dormobile ('dɔːməʊ,biːl) n Trademark. a vanlike vehicle specially equipped for living in while travelling.

dormouse ('dɔː,maʊs) n, pl **dormice**. a small Eurasian rodent resembling a mouse with a furry tail. [C15: dor-, ?from OF dormir to sleep, (from L dormīre) + MOUSE]

dorp (dɔːp) n S. African. a small town or village. [C16: from Du.]

Dorpat ★ ('dɔːpat) n the German name for **Tartu**.

dorsal ('dɔːsˀl) adj Anat., zool. relating to the back or spi-

nal part of the body. [C15: from Med. L dorsālis, from L dorsum back]
► **'dorsally** adv

dorsal fin n an unpaired fin on the back of a fish that maintains balance during locomotion.

Dorset ★ ('dɔːsɪt) n a county in SW England, on the English Channel: mainly hilly but low-lying in the east: Bournemouth and Poole are administered by separate unitary authorities. Administrative centre: Dorchester. Pop. (including Bournemouth and Poole): 673 000 (1994 est.). Area (including Bournemouth and Poole): 2654 sq. km (1024 sq. miles).

Dort ★ (Dutch dɔrt) n another name for **Dordrecht**.

Dortmund ★ ('dɔːtmənd; German 'dɔrtmunt) n an industrial city in W Germany, in North Rhine-Westphalia at the head of the **Dortmund–Ems Canal**: university 1966. Pop.: 600 918 (1995 est.).

dory[1] ('dɔːrɪ) n, pl **dories**. any of various spiny-finned food fishes, esp. the John Dory. [C14: from F dorée gilded, from LL deaurāre to gild, ult. from L aurum gold]

dory[2] ('dɔːrɪ) n, pl **dories**. US & Canad. a flat-bottomed rowing boat with a high bow, stern, and sides. [C18: from Amerind dóri dugout]

DOS (dɒs) n Computers, trademark. acronym for disk-operating system, often prefixed, as in MS-DOS and PC-DOS; a computer operating system.

dosage ('dəʊsɪdʒ) n 1 the administration of a drug or agent in prescribed amounts. 2 the optimum therapeutic dose and interval between doses. 3 another name for **dose** (senses 3, 4).

dose (dəʊs) n 1 Med. a specific quantity of a therapeutic drug or agent taken at any one time or at specified intervals. 2 Inf. something unpleasant to experience: a dose of influenza. 3 Also called: **dosage**. the total energy of ionizing radiation absorbed by unit mass of material, esp. of living tissue; usually measured in grays (SI unit) or rads. 4 Also called: **dosage**. a small amount of syrup added to wine during bottling. 5 Sl. a sexually transmitted infection. ♦ vb **doses, dosing, dosed**. (tr) 6 to administer a dose to (someone). 7 Med. to prescribe (a drug) in appropriate quantities. 8 to add syrup to (wine) during bottling. [C15: from F, from LL dosis, from Gk: a giving, from didonai to give]

dosh (dɒʃ) n Brit. a slang word for **money**. [C20: of unknown origin]

dosimeter (dəʊ'sɪmɪtə) n an instrument for measuring the dose of radiation absorbed by matter or the intensity of a source of radiation.
► **dosimetric** (,dəʊsɪ'mɛtrɪk) adj

dosing strip n (in New Zealand) an area set aside for treating dogs suspected of having hydatid disease.

Dos Passos ★ ('dɒs 'pæsɒs) n John (Roderigo). 1896–1970, US novelist, best known for the trilogy USA (1930–36).

doss (dɒs) Brit. sl. ♦ vb 1 (intr; often foll. by down) to sleep, esp. in a dosshouse. 2 (intr; often foll. by around) to pass time aimlessly. ♦ n 3 a bed, esp. in a dosshouse. 4 another word for **sleep**. 5 short for **dosshouse**. 6 a task or pastime requiring little effort: making a film is a bit of a doss. [C18: from ?]

dosser ('dɒsə) n 1 Brit. sl. a person who sleeps in dosshouses. 2 Brit. sl. another word for **dosshouse**. 3 Sl. a lazy person.

dosshouse ('dɒs,haʊs) n Brit. sl. a cheap lodging house, esp. one used by tramps. US name: **flophouse**.

dossier ('dɒsɪ,eɪ) n a collection of papers about a subject or person. [C19: from F: a file with a label on the back, from dos back, from L dorsum]

dost (dʌst) vb Arch. or dialect. (used with thou) a singular form of the present tense (indicative mood) of **do**[1].

Dostoevsky, Dostoyevsky, Dostoevski, or **Dostoyevski** ★ (,dɒstɔɪ'ɛfskɪ; Russian dəstʌ'jefskij) n Fyodor Mikhailovich ('fjɔdər mi'xajləvitʃ). 1821–81, Russian novelist. His works include Crime and Punishment (1866), The Idiot (1868), and The Brothers Karamazov (1879–80).

dot[1] (dɒt) n 1 a small round mark; spot; point. 2 anything

resembling a dot; a small amount. **3** the mark (˙) above the letters *i*, *j*. **4** *Music.* **4a** the symbol (·) placed after a note or rest to increase its time value by half. **4b** this symbol written above or below a note indicating staccato. **5** *Maths, logic.* **5a** the symbol (.) indicating multiplication or logical conjunction. **5b** a decimal point. **6** the symbol (·) used, in combination with the symbol for *dash* (—), in Morse and other codes. **7 on the dot.** at exactly the arranged time. ◆ *vb* **dots, dotting, dotted. 8** (*tr*) to mark or form with a dot. **9** (*tr*) to scatter or intersperse (as with dots): *bushes dotting the plain.* **10** (*intr*) to make a dot or dots. **11 dot one's i's and cross one's t's.** *Inf.* to pay meticulous attention to detail. [OE *dott* head of a boil]
▶ 'dotter *n*

dot² (dɒt) *n* a woman's dowry. [C19: from F from L *dōs*; rel. to *dōtāre* to endow, *dāre* to give]

dotage ('dəʊtɪdʒ) *n* **1** feebleness of mind, esp. as a result of old age. **2** foolish infatuation. [C14: from DOTE + -AGE]

dotard ('dəʊtəd) *n* a person who is weak-minded, esp. through senility. [C14: from DOTE + -ARD]
▶ 'dotardly *adj*

dote (dəʊt) *vb* **dotes, doting, doted.** (*intr*) **1** (foll. by *on* or *upon*) to love to an excessive or foolish degree. **2** to be foolish or weak-minded, esp. as a result of old age. [C13: rel. to MDu. *doten* to be silly]
▶ 'doter *n*

doth (dʌθ) *vb Arch. or dialect.* (used with *he, she,* or *it*) a singular form of the present tense of **do¹**.

dot-matrix printer *n Computing.* a printer in which each character is produced by a subset of an array of needles.

dotterel *or* **dottrel** ('dɒtrəl) *n* **1** a rare Eurasian plover with white bands around the head and neck. **2** *Dialect.* a person who is foolish or easily duped. [C15 *dotrelle;* see DOTE]

dottle ('dɒt²l) *n* the plug of tobacco left in a pipe after smoking. [C15: dim. of *dot* lump]

dotty ('dɒtɪ) *adj* **dottier, dottiest. 1** *Sl.,* chiefly Brit. feeble-minded; slightly crazy. **2** *Brit. sl.* (foll. by *about*) extremely fond (of). **3** marked with dots. [C19: from DOT¹]
▶ 'dottily *adv* ▶ 'dottiness *n*

Douai ★ ('duːeɪ; *French* dwɛ) *n* an industrial city in N France: a centre for exiled English Catholics in the 16th and 17th centuries. Pop.: 199 562 (1990).

Douala *or* **Duala ★** (duˈɑːlə) *n* the chief port and largest city in W Cameroon, on the Bight of Bonny. Pop.: 1 200 000 (1992 est.).

Douay Bible *or* **Version** ('duːeɪ) *n* an English translation of the Bible from the Vulgate by Catholic scholars at Douai in 1610.

double ('dʌb²l) *adj* (usually prenominal) **1** as much again in size, strength, number, etc.: *a double portion.* **2** composed of two equal or similar parts. **3** designed for two users: *a double room.* **4** folded in two; composed of two layers. **5** stooping; bent over. **6** having two aspects; ambiguous: *a double meaning.* **7** false, deceitful, or hypocritical: *a double life.* **8** (of flowers) having more than the normal number of petals. **9** *Music.* **9a** (of an instrument) sounding an octave lower: *a double bass.* **9b** (of time) duple. ◆ *adv* **10** twice over; twofold. **11** two together; two at a time (esp. in **see double**). ◆ *n* **12** twice the number, amount, size, etc. **13** a double measure of spirits. **14** a duplicate or counterpart, esp. a person who closely resembles another; understudy. **15** a ghostly apparition of a living person; doppelgänger. **16** a sharp turn, esp. a return on one's own tracks. **17** *Bridge.* a call that increases certain scoring points if the last preceding bid becomes the contract. **18** *Billiards, etc.* a strike in which the object ball is struck so as to make it rebound against the cushion to an opposite pocket. **19** a bet on two horses in different races in which any winnings from the first race are placed on the horse in the later race. **20a** the narrow outermost ring on a dartboard. **20b** a hit on this ring. **21** **at** *or* **on the double.** at twice normal marching speed. **21b** quickly or immediately. ◆ *vb* **doubles, doubling, doubled. 22** to make or become twice as much. **23** to bend or fold (material, etc.). **24** (*tr;* sometimes foll. by *up*) to clench (a fist). **25** (*tr;* often foll. by *together* or *up*) to join

or couple. **26** (*tr*) to repeat exactly; copy. **27** (*intr*) to play two parts or serve two roles. **28** (*intr*) to turn sharply; follow a winding course. **29** *Naut.* to sail around (a headland or other point). **30** *Music.* **30a** to duplicate (a part) either in unison or at the octave above or below it. **30b** (*intr;* usually foll. by *on*) to be capable of performing (upon an additional instrument). **31** *Bridge.* to make a call that will double certain scoring points if the preceding bid becomes the contract. **32** *Billiards, etc.* to cause (a ball) to rebound or (of a ball) to rebound from a cushion. **33** (*intr;* foll. by *for*) to act as substitute. **34** (*intr*) to go or march at twice the normal speed. ◆ See also **double back, doubles, double up.** [C13: from OF, from L *duplus* twofold, from *duo* two + -*plus* -FOLD]
▶ 'doubler *n*

double agent *n* a spy employed by two mutually antagonistic countries, companies, etc.

double back *vb* (*intr, adv*) to go back in the opposite direction (esp. in **double back on one's tracks**).

double-bank *vb Austral. & NZ inf.* to carry (a second person) on (a horse, bicycle, etc.). Also: **dub.**

double bar *n Music.* a symbol, consisting of two ordinary bar lines or a single heavy one, that marks the end of a composition or section.

double-barrelled *or US* **double-barreled** *adj* **1** (of a gun) having two barrels. **2** extremely forceful. **3** *Brit.* (of a surname) having hyphenated parts. **4** serving two purposes; ambiguous: *a double-barrelled remark.*

double bass (beɪs) *n* **1** Also called (US): **bass viol.** a stringed instrument, the largest and lowest member of the violin family with a range of almost three octaves. *Inf.* name: **bass fiddle.** ◆ *adj* **double-bass. 2** of an instrument whose pitch lies below the bass; contrabass.

double bassoon *n Music.* the lowest and largest instrument in the oboe class; contrabassoon.

double-blind *adj* of or denoting an experimental study of a new drug in which neither the experimenters nor the patients know which are the test subjects and which are the controls.

double boiler *n* the US and Canad. name for **double saucepan.**

double-breasted *adj* (of a garment) having overlapping fronts.

double-check *vb* **1** to check again; verify. ◆ *n* **double check. 2** a second examination or verification. **3** *Chess.* a simultaneous check from two pieces.

double chin *n* a fold of fat under the chin.
▶ ˌdouble-'chinned *adj*

double concerto *n* a concerto for two solo instruments and orchestra.

double cream *n Brit.* thick cream with a high fat content.

double-cross *vb* **1** (*tr*) to cheat or betray. ◆ *n* **2** the act or an instance of double-crossing; betrayal.
▶ ˌdouble-'crosser *n*

double dagger *n* a character (‡) used in printing to indicate a cross-reference. Also called: **diesis, double obelisk.**

double-dealing *n* **a** action characterized by treachery or deceit. **b** (*as modifier*): *double-dealing treachery.*
▶ ˌdouble-'dealer *n*

double-decker *n* **1** *Chiefly Brit.* a bus with two passenger decks. **2** *Inf.* **2a** a thing or structure having two decks, layers, etc. **2b** (*as modifier*): *a double-decker sandwich.*

double-declutch *vb* (*intr*) *Brit., Austral., & NZ.* to change to a lower gear in a motor vehicle by first placing the gear lever into neutral before engaging the desired gear. US term: **double-clutch.**

double Dutch *n Brit. inf.* incomprehensible talk; gibberish.

double-edged *adj* **1** acting in two ways. **2** (of a remark, etc.) having two possible interpretations, esp. applicable both for and against, or being malicious though apparently innocuous. **3** (of a knife, etc.) having a cutting edge on either side of the blade.

double entendre (ɑːnˈtɑːndrə) *n* **1** a word, phrase, etc., that can be interpreted in two ways, esp. one having one meaning that is indelicate. **2** the type of humour that depends upon this. [C17: from obs. F: double meaning]

double entry *n* **a** a book-keeping system in which any commercial transaction is entered as a debit in one account and as a credit in another. **b** (*as modifier*): *double-entry book-keeping.*

double exposure *n* **1** the act or process of recording two superimposed images on a photographic medium. **2** the photograph resulting from such an act.

double-faced *adj* **1** (of textiles) having a finished nap on each side; reversible. **2** insincere or deceitful.

double feature *n Films.* a programme showing two full-length films. Inf. name (US): **twin bill.**

double first *n Brit.* a first-class honours degree in two subjects.

double glazing *n* **1** two panes of glass in a window, fitted to reduce heat loss, etc. **2** the fitting of glass in such a manner.

double-header *n* **1** a train drawn by two locomotives coupled together. **2** Also called: **twin bill.** *Sport, US & Canad.* two games played consecutively. **3** *Austral. & NZ inf.* a coin with the impression of a head on each side. **4** *Austral. inf.* a double ice-cream cone.

double helix *n* the form of the molecular structure of DNA, consisting of two helical chains coiled around the same axis.

double-jointed *adj* having unusually flexible joints permitting an abnormal degree of motion.

double knitting *n* a widely used medium thickness of knitting wool.

double negative *n* a construction, often considered ungrammatical, in which two negatives are used where one is needed, as in *I wouldn't never have believed it.*

> **USAGE NOTE** There are two contexts where double negatives are found. An adjective with negative force is often used with a negative in order to express a nuance of meaning somewhere between the positive and the negative: *he was a not infrequent visitor; it is not an uncommon sight.* Two negatives are also found together where they reinforce each other rather than conflict: *he never went back, not even to collect his belongings.* These two uses of what is technically a double negative are acceptable. A third case, illustrated by *I shouldn't wonder if it didn't rain today*, has the force of a weak positive statement (*I expect it to rain today*) and is common in informal English.

double-park *vb* to park (a vehicle) alongside or opposite another already parked by the roadside, thereby causing an obstruction.

double pneumonia *n* pneumonia affecting both lungs.

double-quick *adj* **1** very quick; rapid. ◆ *adv* **2** in a very quick or rapid manner.

double-reed *adj* relating to or denoting a wind instrument having two reeds that vibrate against each other.

double refraction *n* the splitting of a ray of unpolarized light into two unequally refracted rays polarized in mutually perpendicular planes. Also called: **birefringence.**

doubles ('dʌbᵊlz) *n* (*functioning as sing or pl*) **a** a game between two pairs of players. **b** (*as modifier*): *a doubles match.*

double saucepan *n Brit.* a cooking utensil consisting of two saucepans: the lower pan is used to boil water to heat food in the upper pan. US and Canad. name: **double boiler.**

double-space *vb* **double-spaces, double-spacing, double-spaced.** to type (copy) with a full space between lines.

double spread *n Printing.* two facing pages of a publication treated as a single unit.

double standard *n* a set of principles that allows greater freedom to one person or group than to another.

double-stop *vb* **double-stops, double-stopping, double-stopped.** to play (two notes or parts) simultaneously on a violin or related instrument.

doublet ('dʌblɪt) *n* **1** (formerly) a man's close-fitting jacket, with or without sleeves (esp. in **doublet and hose**). **2a** a pair of similar things, esp. two words deriving ultimately from the same source. **2b** one of such a pair. **3** *Jewellery.* a false gem made by welding or fusing stones together. **4** *Physics.* a closely spaced pair of related spectral lines. **5** (*pl*) two dice each showing the same number of spots on one throw. [C14: from OF, from DOUBLE]

double take *n* (esp. in comedy) a delayed reaction by a person to a remark, situation, etc.

double talk *n* **1** rapid speech with a mixture of nonsense syllables and real words; gibberish. **2** empty, deceptive, or ambiguous talk.

doublethink ('dʌbᵊl,θɪŋk) *n* deliberate, perverse, or unconscious acceptance or promulgation of conflicting facts, principles, etc.

double time *n* **1** a doubled wage rate, paid for working on public holidays, etc. **2** *Music.* two beats per bar. **3** a slow running pace, keeping in step. **4** *US Army.* a fast march.

double up *vb* (*adv*) **1** to bend or cause to bend in two. **2** (*intr*) to share a room or bed designed for one person, family, etc. **3** (*intr*) *Brit.* to use the winnings from one bet as the stake for another. US and Canad. term: **parlay.**

double whammy *n Inf., chiefly US.* a devastating setback made up of two elements.

doubloon (dʌ'bluːn) *n* **1** a former Spanish gold coin. **2** (*pl*) *Sl.* money. [C17: from Sp. *doblón*, from *dobla*, from L *dupla*, fem. of *duplus* twofold]

doubly ('dʌblɪ) *adv* **1** to or in a double degree, quantity, or measure. **2** in two ways.

Doubs ★ (French du) *n* **1** a department of E France, in Franche-Comté region. Capital: Besançon. Pop.: 493 133 (1994 est.). Area: 5258 sq. km (2030 sq. miles). **2** a river in E France, rising in the Jura Mountains, becoming part of the border between France and Switzerland and flowing generally southwest to the Saône River. Length: 430 km (267 miles).

doubt (daʊt) *n* **1** uncertainty about the truth, fact, or existence of something (esp. in **in doubt, without doubt,** etc.). **2** (*often pl*) lack of belief in or conviction about something. **3** an unresolved difficulty, point, etc. **4** *Obs.* fear. **5** **give (someone) the benefit of the doubt.** to presume (someone suspected of guilt) innocent. **6 no doubt.** almost certainly. ◆ *vb* **7** (*tr; may take a clause as object*) to be inclined to disbelieve. **8** (*tr*) to distrust or be suspicious of. **9** (*intr*) to feel uncertainty or be undecided. **10** (*tr*) *Arch.* to fear. [C13: from OF *douter*, from L *dubitāre*]
► **'doubtable** *adj* ► **'doubter** *n* ► **'doubtingly** *adv*

> **USAGE NOTE** Where a clause follows *doubt* in a positive sentence, it was formerly considered correct to use *whether*: (*I doubt whether he will come*), but now *if* and *that* are also acceptable. In negative statements, *doubt* is followed by *that*: *I do not doubt that he is telling the truth.* In such sentences, *but* (*I do not doubt but that he is telling the truth*) is redundant.

doubtful ('daʊtful) *adj* **1** unlikely; improbable. **2** uncertain: *a doubtful answer.* **3** unsettled; unresolved. **4** of questionable reputation or morality. **5** having reservations or misgivings.
► **'doubtfully** *adv* ► **'doubtfulness** *n*

> **USAGE NOTE** It was formerly considered correct to use *whether* after *doubtful* (*it is doubtful whether he will come*), but now *if* and *that* are also acceptable.

doubting Thomas *n* a person who insists on proof before he will believe anything. [after THOMAS (the apostle), who did not believe that Jesus had been resurrected]

★ people and places

doubtless ('daʊtlɪs) *adv also* **doubtlessly** (*sentence modifier*), *sentence substitute.* **1** certainly. **2** probably. ◆ *adj* **3** certain; assured.
▶ **'doubtlessness** *n*

douche (duːʃ) *n* **1** a stream of water directed onto or into the body for cleansing or medical purposes. **2** the application of such a stream of water. **3** an instrument for applying a douche. ◆ *vb* **douches, douching, douched.** **4** to cleanse or treat or be cleansed or treated by means of a douche. [C18: from F, from It. *doccia* pipe]

dough (dəʊ) *n* **1** a thick mixture of flour or meal and water or milk, used for making bread, pastry, etc. **2** any similar pasty mass. **3** a slang word for **money**. [OE *dāg*]

doughboy ('dəʊ,bɔɪ) *n* **1** *US inf.* an infantryman, esp. in World War I. **2** dough that is boiled or steamed as a dumpling.

doughnut ('dəʊnʌt) *n* **1** a small cake of sweetened dough, often ring-shaped, cooked in hot fat. **2** anything shaped like a ring, such as the reaction vessel of a thermonuclear reactor. ◆ *vb* **doughnuts, doughnutting, doughnutted. 3** (*tr*) *Inf.* (of Members of Parliament) to surround (a speaker) during the televising of Parliament to give the impression that the chamber is crowded or the speaker is well supported.

doughty ('daʊtɪ) *adj* **doughtier, doughtiest.** hardy; resolute. [OE *dohtig*]
▶ **'doughtily** *adv* ▶ **'doughtiness** *n*

doughy ('dəʊɪ) *adj* **doughier, doughiest.** resembling dough; soft, pallid, or flabby.

Douglas[1] ★ ('dʌgləs) *n* the capital of the Isle of Man, a resort on the E coast. Pop.: 22 214 (1991).

Douglas[2] ★ ('dʌgləs) *n* **1 C(lifford) H(ugh).** 1879–1952, British economist, who originated the theory of social credit. **2 Gavin.** ?1474–1522, Scottish poet, the first British translator of the *Aeneid.* **3 Keith (Castellain).** 1920–44, British poet noted for his poems in World War II: killed in action. **4 (George) Norman.** 1868–1952, British writer, noted for the novel *South Wind* (1917).

Douglas fir, spruce, *or* **hemlock** *n* a North American pyramidal coniferous tree, widely planted for ornament and for timber. [C19: after David *Douglas* (1798–1834), Scot. botanist]

Douglas-Home ★ ('dʌgləs'hjuːm) *n* Sir **Alexander.** See (Baron Alexander) **Home of the Hirsel.**

Doukhobor *or* **Dukhobor** ('duːkəʊ,bɔː) *n* a member of a Russian sect of Christians that originated in the 18th century. In the late 19th century a large number emigrated to W Canada, where most Doukhobors now live. [C19: from Russian *dukhoborets* spirit wrestlers]

Dounreay ★ (,duːn'reɪ) *n* the site in N Scotland of a nuclear power station, which contained the world's first fast-breeder reactor (1962–77).

do up *vb* (*adv; mainly tr*) **1** to wrap and make into a bundle: *to do up a parcel.* **2** to beautify or adorn. **3** (*also intr*) to fasten or be fastened. **4** *Inf.* to renovate or redecorate. **5** *Sl.* to assault. **6** *Inf.* to cause the downfall of (a person).

dour (dʊə, 'daʊə) *adj* **1** sullen. **2** hard or obstinate. [C14: prob. from L *dūrus* hard]
▶ **'dourly** *adv* ▶ **'dourness** *n*

douroucouli (,duːruː'kuːlɪ) *n* a nocturnal New World monkey of Central and South America with thick fur and large eyes. [from Amerind]

douse *or* **dowse** (daʊs) *vb* **douses, dousing, doused** *or* **dowses, dowsing, dowsed. 1** to plunge or be plunged into liquid; duck. **2** (*tr*) to drench with water. **3** (*tr*) to put out (a light, candle, etc.). ◆ *n* **4** an immersion. [C16: ? rel. to obs. *douse* to strike, from ?]

dove (dʌv) *n* **1** any of a family of birds having a heavy body, small head, short legs, and long pointed wings. **2** *Politics.* a person opposed to war. **3** a gentle or innocent person: used as a term of endearment. **4a** a greyish-brown colour. **4b** (*as adj*): *dove walls.* [OE *dūfe* (untested except as a fem proper name)]
▶ **'dove,like** *adj*

Dove (dʌv) *n* **the.** *Christianity.* a manifestation of the Holy Spirit (John 1:32).

dovecote ('dʌv,kəʊt) *or* **dovecot** ('dʌv,kɒt) *n* a structure for housing pigeons.

Dover ★ ('dəʊvə) *n* **1** a port in SE England, in E Kent on the Strait of Dover: the only one of the Cinque Ports that is still important; a stronghold since ancient times and Caesar's first point of attack in the invasion of Britain (55 B.C.). Pop.: 34 179 (1991). **2 Strait of.** a strait between SE England and N France, linking the English Channel with the North Sea. Width: about 32 km (20 miles). French name: **Pas de Calais. 3** a city in the US, the capital of Delaware, founded in 1683: 18th-century buildings. Pop.: 27 630 (1990).

dovetail ('dʌv,teɪl) *n* **1** a wedge-shaped tenon. **2** Also called: **dovetail joint.** a joint containing such tenons. ◆ **3** (*tr*) to join by means of dovetails. **4** to fit or cause to fit together closely or neatly.

dowager ('daʊədʒə) *n* **1a** a widow possessing property or a title obtained from her husband. **1b** (*as modifier*): *the dowager duchess.* **2** a wealthy or dignified elderly woman. [C16: from OF *douagiere*, from *douage* DOWER]

Dowding ★ ('daʊdɪŋ) *n* Baron **Hugh Caswall Tremenheere,** nicknamed *Stuffy.* 1882–1970, British air chief marshal in charge of Fighter Command (1936–40) during the Battle of Britain (1940).

dowdy ('daʊdɪ) *adj* **dowdier, dowdiest. 1** (esp. of a woman or a woman's dress) shabby or old-fashioned. ◆ *n, pl* **dowdies. 2** a dowdy woman. [C14: *dowd* slut, from ?]
▶ **'dowdily** *adv* ▶ **'dowdiness** *n* ▶ **'dowdyish** *adj*

dowel ('daʊəl) *n* a wooden or metal peg that fits into two corresponding holes to join two adjacent parts. [C14: from MLow G *dövel* plug, from OHG *tubili*]

Dowell ★ ('daʊəl) *n* **Anthony.** born 1943, British ballet dancer. He became director of the Royal Ballet in 1986.

dower ('daʊə) *n* **1** the life interest in a part of her husband's estate allotted to a widow by law. **2** an archaic word for **dowry** (sense 1). **3** a natural gift. ◆ *vb* **4** (*tr*) to endow. [C14: from OF *douaire*, from Med. L *dōtārium*, from L *dōs* gift]

dower house *n* a house for the use of a widow, often on her deceased husband's estate.

do with *vb* **1 could** *or* **can do with.** to find useful; benefit from. **2 have to do with.** to be involved in or connected with. **3 to do with.** concerning; related to. **4 what...do with. 4a** to put or place: *what did you do with my coat?* **4b** to handle or treat. **4c** to fill one's time usefully: *she didn't know what to do with herself when the project was finished.*

do without *vb* (*intr*) **1** to forgo; manage without. **2** (*prep*) not to require (uncalled-for comments): *we can do without your criticisms.*

Dow-Jones average ('daʊ'dʒəʊnz) *n US.* a daily index of average stock-exchange prices. [C20: after Charles H. *Dow* (died 1902) & Edward D. *Jones* (died 1920), American financial statisticians]

Dowland ★ ('daʊlənd) *n* **John.** ?1563–1626, English lutenist and composer of songs and lute music.

down[1] (daʊn) *prep* **1** used to indicate movement from a higher to a lower position. **2** at a lower or further level or position on, in, or along: *he ran down the street.* ◆ *adv* **3** downwards; at or to a lower level or position. **4** (*particle*) used with many verbs when the result of the verb's action is to lower or destroy its object: *knock down.* **5** (*particle*) used with several verbs to indicate intensity or completion: *calm down.* **6** immediately: *cash down.* **7** on paper: *write this down.* **8** arranged; scheduled. **9** in a helpless position. **10a** away from a more important place. **10b** away from a more northerly place. **10c** (of a member of some British universities) away from the university. **10d** in a particular part of a country: *down south.* **11** *Naut.* (of a helm) having the rudder to windward. **12** reduced to a state of lack or want: *down to the last pound.* **13** lacking a specified amount. **14** lower in price. **15** including all intermediate grades. **16** from an earlier to a later time. **17** to a finer or more concentrated state: *to grind down.* **18** *Sport.* being a specified number of points, goals, etc., behind another competitor, team, etc. **19** (of a person) being inactive, owing to illness: *down with flu.* **20** (*functioning as imperative*) (to dogs): *down, Rover!* **21** (*functioning as imperative*) **down with.** wanting the end of somebody or something: *down with the king!* **22 get down on something.** *Austral. & NZ.* to procure something, esp. in advance of needs or in anticipation of someone else. ◆ *adj* **23** (*postpositive*) depressed. **24** (*prenominal*) of or relating to a train or trains from a more important place or one regarded as higher: *the down line.* **25** (*postpositive*) (of a device, machine, etc., esp. a computer) temporarily out of action. **26** made in cash: *a down payment.* **27 down to.** the responsibility or fault of: *this defeat was down to me.* ◆ *vb* (*tr*) **28** to knock, push, or pull down. **29** to cause to go or come down. **30** *Inf.* to drink, esp. quickly. **31** to bring (someone) down, esp. by tackling. ◆ *n* **32** a descent; downward movement. **33** a lowering or a poor period (esp. in **ups and downs**). **34** (in American football) any of a series of four attempts to advance the ball ten yards. **35 have a down on.** *Inf.* to bear ill will towards. [OE *dūne*, short for *adūne*, var. of *of dūne*, lit.: from the hill]

down² (daʊn) *n* **1** soft fine feathers. **2** another name for **eiderdown** (sense 1). **3** *Bot.* a fine coating of soft hairs, as on certain leaves, fruits, and seeds. **4** any growth or coating of soft fine hair. [C14: from ON]

down³ (daʊn) *n Arch.* a hill, esp. a sand dune. See also **downs**. [OE *dūn*]

Down ★ (daʊn) *n* **1** a historic county of SE Northern Ireland, on the Irish Sea: hilly, rising to the Mountains of Mourne. Area: 2 446 sq. km (952 sq. miles). **2** a district of SE Northern Ireland, bordering the Irish Sea E of Strangford Lough. Administrative centre: Downpatrick. Pop.: 58 008 (1991). Area: 646 sq. km (249 sq. miles).

down-and-out *adj* **1** without any means of livelihood; poor and, often, socially outcast. ◆ *n* **2** a person who is destitute and, often, homeless.

downbeat (ˈdaʊnˌbiːt) *n* **1** *Music.* the first beat of a bar or the downward gesture of a conductor's baton indicating this. ◆ *adj Inf.* **2** depressed; gloomy. **3** relaxed.

downcast (ˈdaʊnˌkɑːst) *adj* **1** dejected. **2** (of the eyes) directed downwards. ◆ *n* **3** *Mining.* a ventilation shaft.

downer (ˈdaʊnə) *n Sl.* **1** a barbiturate, tranquillizer, or narcotic. **2** a depressing experience. **3** a state of depression.

downfall (ˈdaʊnˌfɔːl) *n* **1** a sudden loss of position, health, or reputation. **2** a fall of rain, snow, etc., esp. a sudden heavy one.

downgrade (ˈdaʊnˌɡreɪd) *vb* **downgrades, downgrading, downgraded.** (*tr*) **1** to reduce in importance or value, esp. to demote (a person) to a poorer job. **2** to speak of disparagingly. ◆ *n* **3** *Chiefly US & Canad.* a downward slope. **4 on the downgrade.** waning in importance, health, etc.

downhearted (ˌdaʊnˈhɑːtɪd) *adj* discouraged; dejected.
▸ ˌdown'heartedly *adv*

downhill (ˈdaʊnˈhɪl) *adj* **1** going or sloping down. ◆ *adv* **2** towards the bottom of a hill; downwards. **3 go downhill.** *Inf.* to decline; deteriorate. ◆ *n* **4** the downward slope of a hill; a descent. **5** a skiing race downhill.

downhole (ˈdaʊnˌhəʊl) *adj* (in the oil industry) denoting any piece of equipment used in the well itself.

downhome (ˌdaʊnˈhəʊm) *adj Sl., chiefly US.* of, relating to, or reminiscent of rural life, esp. in the southern US; unsophisticated; homely.

Downing Street ★ (ˈdaʊnɪŋ) *n* **1** a street in W central London: official residences of the prime minister of Great Britain and the Chancellor of the Exchequer. **2** the office of the prime minister. [after Sir George *Downing* (1623–84), E statesman]

download (ˈdaʊnˌləʊd) *vb* (*tr*) to copy or transfer (data or a program) from one computer's memory to that of another, esp. in a network of computing.

down-market *adj* relating to commercial products, services, etc., that are cheap, unfashionable, or poor quality.

Downpatrick ★ (ˌdaʊnˈpætrɪk) *n* a market town in Northern Ireland: Saint Patrick is said to be buried here. Pop.: 10 257 (1991).

down payment *n* the deposit paid on an item purchased on hire-purchase, mortgage, etc.

downpipe (ˈdaʊnˌpaɪp) *n Brit. and NZ.* a pipe for carrying rainwater from a roof gutter to ground level. Usual US & Canad. name: **downspout**.

downpour (ˈdaʊnˌpɔː) *n* a heavy continuous fall of rain.

downrange (ˈdaʊnˈreɪndʒ) *adj, adv* in the direction of the intended flight path of a rocket or missile.

downright (ˈdaʊnˌraɪt) *adj* **1** frank or straightforward; blunt. ◆ *adv, adj* (*prenominal*) **2** (intensifier): *downright rude.*
▸ ˈdownˌrightly *adv* ▸ ˈdownˌrightness *n*

downs (daʊnz) *pl n* **1** rolling upland, esp. in the chalk areas of S Britain, characterized by lack of trees and used mainly as pasture. **2** *Austral. & NZ.* a flat grassy area, not necessarily of uplands.

Downs ★ (daʊnz) *n the.* **1** any of various ranges of low chalk hills in S England, esp. the **South Downs** in Sussex. **2** a roadstead off the SE coast of Kent, protected by the Goodwin Sands.

downshifting (ˈdaʊnˌʃɪftɪŋ) *n* the practice of simplifying one's lifestyle and becoming less materialistic.

downside (ˈdaʊnˌsaɪd) *n* the disadvantageous aspect of a situation: *the downside of twentieth-century living.*

downsize (ˈdaʊnˌsaɪz) *vb* **downsizes, downsizing, downsized.** (*tr*) **1** to reduce the number of people employed by (a company). **2** to upgrade (a computer system) by replacing a mainframe or minicomputer with a network of microcomputing. Cf. **rightsize**.

Down's syndrome (daʊnz) *n a Pathol.* a chromosomal abnormality resulting in a flat face and nose, a vertical fold of skin at the inner edge of the eye, and mental retardation. Former name: **mongolism. b** (*as modifier*): *a Down's syndrome baby.* [C19: after John *Langdon-Down* (1828–96), Brit. physician]

downstage (ˈdaʊnˈsteɪdʒ) *Theatre.* ◆ *adv* **1** at or towards the front of the stage. ◆ *adj* **2** of or relating to the front of the stage.

downstairs (ˈdaʊnˈstɛəz) *adv* **1** down the stairs; to or on a lower floor. ◆ *n* **2a** a lower or ground floor. **2b** (*as modifier*): *a downstairs room.* **3** *Brit. inf., old-fashioned.* the servants of a household collectively.

downstream (ˈdaʊnˈstriːm) *adv, adj* in or towards the lower part of a stream; with the current. Cf. **upstream** (sense 1).

downswing (ˈdaʊnˌswɪŋ) *n* a statistical downward trend in business activity, the death rate, etc.

downtime (ˈdaʊnˌtaɪm) *n Commerce.* time during which a computer or machine is not working, as when under repair.

down-to-earth *adj* sensible; practical; realistic.

downtown (ˈdaʊnˈtaʊn) *Chiefly US, Canad., & NZ.* ◆ *n* **1** the central or lower part of a city, esp. the main commercial area. ◆ *adv* **2** towards, to, or into this area. ◆ *adj* **3** of, relating to, or situated in the downtown area: *a downtown cinema.*

downtrodden (ˈdaʊnˌtrɒdᵊn) *adj* **1** subjugated; oppressed. **2** trodden down.

downturn (ˈdaʊnˌtɜːn) *n* a drop or reduction in the success of a business or economy.

down under *Inf.* ◆ *n* **1** Australia or New Zealand. ◆ *adv* **2** in or to Australia or New Zealand.

downward (ˈdaʊnwəd) *adj* **1** descending from a higher to a lower level, condition, position, etc. **2** descending from a beginning. ◆ *adv* **3** a variant of **downwards**.
▸ ˈdownwardly *adv*

downwards (ˈdaʊnwədz) *or* **downward** *adv* **1** from a higher to a lower place, level, etc. **2** from an earlier time or source to a later.

downwind (ˈdaʊnˈwɪnd) *adv, adj* in the same direction towards which the wind is blowing; with the wind from behind.

downy (ˈdaʊnɪ) *adj* **downier, downiest. 1** covered with soft fine hair or feathers. **2** light, soft, and fluffy. **3** made from or filled with down. **4** *Brit. sl.* sharp-witted.
▸ ˈdowniness *n*

dowry (ˈdaʊərɪ) *n, pl* **dowries. 1** the property brought by a woman to her husband at marriage. **2** a natural talent or gift. [C14: from Anglo-F *douarie*, from Med. L *dōtārium*; see DOWER]

dowse (daʊz) *vb* **dowses, dowsing, dowsed.** (*intr*) to search

for underground water, minerals, etc., using a divining rod; divine. [C17: from ?]
▸ **'dowser** n

Dowson ★ ('daʊs°n) n Ernest (**Christopher**). 1867–1900, British Decadent poet noted for his lyric *Cynara*.

doxology (dɒk'sɒlədʒɪ) n, pl **doxologies**. a hymn, verse, or form of words in Christian liturgy glorifying God. [C17: from Med. L *doxologia*, from Gk, from *doxologos* uttering praise, from *doxa* praise; see -LOGY]
▸ **doxological** (ˌdɒksə'lɒdʒɪk°l) adj

doxy ('dɒksɪ) n, pl **doxies**. Arch. sl. a prostitute or mistress. [C16: prob. from MFlemish *docke* doll]

doyen ('dɔɪən) n the senior member of a group, profession, or society. [C17: from F, from LL *decānus* leader of a group of ten]
▸ **doyenne** (dɔɪ'en) fem n

doyley ('dɔɪlɪ) n a variant spelling of **doily**.

D'Oyly Carte ★ (ˌdɔɪlɪ 'kɑːt) n Richard. 1844–1901, British impresario noted for his productions of the operettas of Gilbert and Sullivan.

doz. abbrev. for dozen.

doze (dəʊz) vb **dozes, dozing, dozed**. (intr) 1 to sleep lightly or intermittently. 2 (often foll. by off) to fall into a light sleep. ◆ n 3 a short sleep. [C17: prob. from ON *dūs* lull]
▸ **'dozer** n

dozen ('dʌz°n) determiner 1 (preceded by a or a numeral) twelve or a group of twelve. ◆ n, pl **dozens** or **dozen**. 2 by **the dozen**. in large quantities. 3 **daily dozen**. Brit. regular physical exercises. 4 **talk nineteen to the dozen**. to talk without stopping. [C13: from OF *douzaine*, from *douze* twelve, from L *duodecim*, from *duo* two + *decem* ten]
▸ **'dozenth** adj

dozy ('dəʊzɪ) adj **dozier, doziest**. 1 drowsy. 2 Brit. inf. stupid.
▸ **'dozily** adv ▸ **'doziness** n

DP abbrev. for: 1 data processing. 2 displaced person.

DPB (in New Zealand) abbrev. for domestic purposes benefit: an allowance paid to single parents.

DPhil or **DPh** abbrev. for Doctor of Philosophy. Also: **PhD**.

dpi abbrev. for dots per inch: a measure of the resolution of a typesetting machine, computer screen, etc.

DPP (in Britain) abbrev. for Director of Public Prosecutions.

dpt abbrev. for: 1 department. 2 depot.

dr abbrev. for: 1 Also: **dr**. dram. 2 debtor.

Dr abbrev. for: 1 Doctor. 2 Drive.

DR abbrev. for dry riser.

dr. abbrev. for: 1 debit. 2 drachma.

drab[1] (dræb) adj **drabber, drabbest**. 1 dull; dingy. 2 cheerless; dreary. 3 of the colour drab. ◆ n 4 a light olive-brown colour. [C16: from OF *drap* cloth, from LL *drappus*, ? of Celtic origin]
▸ **'drably** adv ▸ **'drabness** n

drab[2] (dræb) Arch. ◆ n 1 a slatternly woman. 2 a whore. ◆ vb **drabs, drabbing, drabbed**. 3 (intr) to consort with prostitutes. [C16: of Celtic origin]

Drabble ★ ('dræb°l) n Margaret. born 1939, British novelist and editor. Her novels include *The Needle's Eye* (1972) and *The Gates of Ivory* (1991).

drachm (dræm) n 1 Also called: **fluid dram**. Brit. one eighth of a fluid ounce. 2 US. another name for **dram** (sense 2). 3 another name for **drachma**. [C14: learned var. of DRAM]

drachma ('drækmə) n, pl **drachmas** or **drachmae** (-miː). 1 the standard monetary unit of Greece. 2 US. another name for **dram** (sense 2). 3 a silver coin of ancient Greece. [C16: from L, from Gk *drakhmē* a handful, from *drassesthai* to seize]

drack or **drac** (dræk) adj Austral. sl. (of a woman) unattractive. [C20: ?from *Dracula's* daughter]

Draco ★ ('dreɪkəʊ) n 7th century B.C., Athenian statesman, whose code of laws (621) prescribed death for most offences.

Draconian (dreɪ'kəʊnɪən) or **Draconic** (dreɪ'kɒnɪk) adj (sometimes not cap.) 1 of or relating to Draco or his code of laws. 2 harsh.
▸ **Dra'conianism** n ▸ **Dra'conically** adv

Dracula ('drækjʊlə) n 1 a cruel or bloodthirsty person. 2 a person who preys ruthlessly on others. [C20: from the vampire in Bram Stoker's Gothic novel *Dracula* (1897)]

draff (dræf) n the residue of husks after fermentation of the grain in brewing, used as cattle fodder. [C13: from ON *draf*]

draft (drɑːft) n 1 a plan, sketch, or drawing of something. 2 a preliminary outline of a book, speech, etc. 3 another word for **bill of exchange**. 4 a demand or drain on something. 5 US & Austral. selection for compulsory military service. 6 detachment of military personnel from one unit to another. 7 Austral. & NZ. a group of livestock separated from the rest of the herd or flock. ◆ vb (tr) 8 to draw up an outline or sketch for. 9 to prepare a plan or design of. 10 to detach (military personnel) from one unit to another. 11 US & Austral. to select for compulsory military service. 12 Austral. & NZ. 12a to select (cattle or sheep) from a herd or flock. 12b to select (farm stock) for sale. ◆ n, vb 13 the usual US spelling of **draught**. [C16: var. of DRAUGHT]
▸ **'drafter** n

draftee (drɑːf'tiː) n US. a conscript.

drafty ('drɑːftɪ) adj **draftier, draftiest**. the usual US spelling of **draughty**.

drag (dræg) vb **drags, dragging, dragged**. 1 to pull or be pulled with force, esp. along the ground. 2 (tr; often foll. by away or from) to persuade to come away. 3 to trail or cause to trail on the ground. 4 (tr) to move with effort or difficulty. 5 to linger behind. 6 (often foll. by on or out) to prolong or be prolonged unnecessarily or tediously: *his talk dragged on for hours*. 7 (when intr, usually foll. by for) to search (the bed of a river, etc.) with a dragnet or hook. 8 (tr; foll. by out or from) to crush (clods) or level (a soil surface) by use of a drag. 9 (of hounds) to follow (a fox or its trail). 10 (intr) Sl. to draw (on a cigarette, etc.). 11 Computing. to move (a graphics image) from one place to another on the screen using a mouse. 12 **drag anchor**. (of a vessel) to move away from its mooring because the anchor has failed to hold. 13 **drag one's feet** or **heels**. Inf. to act with deliberate slowness. ◆ n 14 the act of dragging or the state of being dragged. 15 an implement, such as a dragnet, dredge, etc., used for dragging. 16 a type of harrow used to crush clods, level soil, etc. 17 a coach with seats inside and out, usually drawn by four horses. 18 a braking device. 19 a person or thing that slows up progress. 20 slow progress or movement. 21 Aeronautics. the resistance to the motion of a body passing through a fluid, esp. through air. 22 the trail of scent left by a fox, etc. 23 an artificial trail of scent drawn over the ground for hounds to follow. 24 See **drag hunt**. 25 Inf. a person or thing that is very tedious. 26 Sl. a car. 27 short for **drag race**. 28 Sl. 28a women's clothes worn by a man (esp. in in **drag**). 28b (as modifier): *a drag show*. 28c clothes collectively. 29 Inf. a draw on a cigarette, etc. 30 US sl. influence. 31 Chiefly US sl. a street (esp. in **main drag**). ◆ See also **drag out of, drag up**. [OE *dragan* to DRAW]

dragée (dræ'ʒeɪ) n 1 a sweet coated with a hard sugar icing. 2 a tiny beadlike sweet used for decorating cakes, etc. 3 a medicinal pill coated with sugar. [C19: from F; see DREDGE[2]]

draggle ('dræg°l) vb **draggles, draggling, draggled**. 1 to make or become wet or dirty by trailing on the ground; bedraggle. 2 (intr) to lag; dawdle. [ME, prob. frequentative of DRAG]

drag hunt n 1 a hunt in which hounds follow an artificial trail of scent. 2 a club that organizes such hunts.
▸ **'drag-ˌhunt** vb

dragnet ('dræg,nɛt) n 1 a net used to scour the bottom of a pond, river, etc., as when searching for something. 2 any system of coordinated efforts to track down wanted persons.

dragoman ('drægəʊmən) n, pl **dragomans** or **dragomen**. (in some Middle Eastern countries, esp. formerly) a professional interpreter or guide. [C14: from F, from It., from Med. Gk *dragoumanos*, from Ar. *targumān*, ult. from Akkadian]

dragon ('drægən) n 1 a mythical monster usually represented as breathing fire and having a scaly reptilian body, wings, claws, and a long tail. 2 Inf. a fierce person,

---

★ people and places

esp. a woman. **3** any of various very large lizards, esp. the Komodo dragon. **4** *Commerce.* a newly industrialized country, esp. one in SE Asia. **5 chase the dragon.** *Sl.* to smoke opium or heroin.   [C13: from OF, from L *draco*, from Gk *drakōn*]

dragonet ('drægǝnɪt) *n* a small fish with spiny fins, a flat head, and a tapering brighty coloured body.   [C14 (meaning: small dragon): from F; applied to fish C18]

dragonfly ('drægǝn,flaɪ) *n, pl* **dragonflies.** a predatory insect having a long slender body and two pairs of iridescent wings that are outspread at rest.

dragon light *n* an extremely powerful light used by police to dazzle and immobilize criminal suspects.

dragonnade (,drægǝ'neɪd) *n* **1** *History.* the persecution of French Huguenots during the reign of Louis XIV by dragoons quartered in their villages and homes. **2** subjection by military force.   ◆ *vb* **dragonnades, dragonnading, dragonnaded. 3** (*tr*) to subject to persecution by military troops.   [C18: from F, from *dragon* DRAGOON]

dragoon (drǝ'guːn) *n* **1** (originally) a mounted infantryman armed with a carbine. **2** (*sometimes cap.*) a domestic fancy pigeon. **3a** a type of cavalryman. **3b** (*pl; cap. when part of a name*): *the Royal Dragoons.*   ◆ *vb* **4** to coerce; force. **5** to persecute by military force.   [C17: from F *dragon* (special use of DRAGON), soldier armed with a carbine]

drag out of *vb* (*tr, adv + prep*) to obtain or extract (a confession, statement, etc.), esp. by force. Also: **drag from.**

drag race *n* a type of motor race in which specially built or modified cars or motorcycles are timed over a measured course.
 ▸ **drag racing** *n*

dragster ('drægstǝ) *n* a car specially built or modified for drag racing.

drag up *vb* (*tr, adv*) *Inf.* **1** to rear (a child) poorly and in an undisciplined manner. **2** to introduce or revive (an unpleasant fact or story).

drain (dreɪn) *n* **1** a pipe or channel that carries off water, sewage, etc. **2** an instance or cause of continuous diminution in resources or energy; depletion. **3** *Surgery.* a device, such as a tube, to drain off pus, etc. **4 down the drain.** wasted.   ◆ *vb* **5** (*tr*; often foll. by *off*) to draw off or remove (liquid) from. **6** (*intr*; often foll. by *away*) to flow (away) or filter (off). **7** (*intr*) to dry or be emptied as a result of liquid running off or flowing away. **8** (*tr*) to drink the entire contents of (a glass, etc.). **9** (*tr*) to consume or make constant demands on (resources, energy, etc.); exhaust. **10** (*intr*) to disappear or leave, esp. gradually. **11** (of a river, etc.) to carry off the surface water from (an area). **12** (*intr*) (of an area) to discharge its surface water into rivers, streams, etc.   [OE *drēahnian*]
 ▸ **'drainer** *n*

drainage ('dreɪnɪdʒ) *n* **1** the process or a method of draining. **2** a system of watercourses or drains. **3** liquid, sewage, etc., that is drained away.

drainage basin *or* **area** *n* another name for **catchment area.**

draining board *n* a sloping grooved surface at the side of a sink, used for draining washed dishes, etc. Also called: **drainer.**

drainpipe ('dreɪn,paɪp) *n* a pipe for carrying off rainwater, sewage, etc.; downpipe.

drainpipes ('dreɪn,paɪps) *pl n* trousers with very narrow legs, worn esp. by teddy boys in the 1950s.

drake (dreɪk) *n* the male of any duck.   [C13: ?from Low G]

Drake ★ (dreɪk) *n* Sir **Francis.** ?1540–96, English buccaneer, who sailed round the world (1577–80). He commanded a fleet against the Spanish Armada (1588).

Drakensberg ★ ('drɑːkǝnz,bɜːg) *n* a mountain range in southern Africa, extending through Lesotho, E South Africa, and Swaziland. Highest peak: Thabana Ntlenyana, 3482 m (11 425 ft). Sotho name: **Quathlamba.**

Dralon ('dreɪlɒn) *n Trademark.* an acrylic fibre fabric used esp. for upholstery.

dram (dræm) *n* **1** one sixteenth of an ounce (avoirdupois). 1 dram is equivalent to 0.0018 kilogram. **2** *US.* one eighth of an apothecaries' ounce; 60 grains. 1 dram is

equivalent to 0.0039 kilogram. **3** a small amount of an alcoholic drink, esp. a spirit; tot. **4** the standard monetary unit of Armenia.   [C15: from OF *dragme*, from LL *dragma*, from Gk *drakhmē*; see DRACHMA]

DRAM *or* **D-RAM** ('diːræm) *n acronym for* dynamic random access memory: **a** a widely used type of random access memory. See **RAM**[1]. **b** a chip containing such a memory.

drama ('drɑːmǝ) *n* **1** a work to be performed by actors; play. **2** the genre of literature represented by works intended for the stage. **3** the art of the writing and production of plays. **4** a situation that is highly emotional, tragic, or turbulent.   [C17: from LL: a play, from Gk: something performed, from *drān* to do]

dramatic (drǝ'mætɪk) *adj* **1** of drama. **2** like a drama in suddenness, emotional impact, etc. **3** striking; effective. **4** acting or performed in a flamboyant way.
 ▸ **dra'matically** *adv*

dramatic irony *n Theatre.* the irony occurring when the implications of a situation, speech, etc., are understood by the audience but not by the characters in the play.

dramatics (drǝ'mætɪks) *n* **1** (*functioning as sing or pl*) **1a** the art of acting or producing plays. **1b** dramatic productions. **2** (*usually functioning as pl*) histrionic behaviour.

dramatis personae ('drɑːmǝtɪs pǝ'sǝʊnaɪ) *pl n* (*often functioning as sing*) the characters in a play.   [C18: from NL]

dramatist ('dræmǝtɪst) *n* a playwright.

dramatize *or* **dramatise** ('dræmǝ,taɪz) *vb* **dramatizes, dramatizing, dramatized** *or* **dramatises, dramatising, dramatised. 1** (*tr*) to put into dramatic form. **2** to express (something) in a dramatic or exaggerated way.
 ▸ **,dramati'zation** *or* **,dramati'sation** *n*

dramaturge ('dræmǝ,tɜːdʒ) *n* **1** Also called: **dramaturgist.** a dramatist. **2** Also called: **dramaturg.** a literary adviser on the staff of a theatre, film company, etc.   [C19: prob. from F, from Gk *dramatourgos* playwright, from DRAMA + *ergon* work]

dramaturgy ('dræmǝ,tɜːdʒɪ) *n* the art and technique of the theatre; dramatics.
 ▸ **,drama'turgic** *or* **,drama'turgical** *adj*

drank (dræŋk) *vb* the past tense of **drink.**

drape (dreɪp) *vb* **drapes, draping, draped. 1** (*tr*) to hang or cover with material or fabric, usually in folds. **2** to hang or arrange or be hung or arranged, esp. in folds. **3** (*tr*) to place casually and loosely.   ◆ *n* **4** (*often pl*) a cloth or hanging that covers something in folds. **5** the way in which fabric hangs.   [C15: from OF *draper*, from *drap* piece of cloth; see DRAB[1]]

draper ('dreɪpǝ) *n* **1** *Brit.* a dealer in fabrics and sewing materials. **2** *Arch.* a maker of cloth.

drapery ('dreɪpǝrɪ) *n, pl* **draperies. 1** fabric or clothing arranged and draped. **2** (*often pl*) curtains or hangings that drape. **3** *Brit.* the occupation or shop of a draper. **4** fabrics and cloth collectively.
 ▸ **'draperied** *adj*

drapes (dreɪps) *or* **draperies** ('dreɪpǝrɪz) *pl n Chiefly US & Canad.* curtains, esp. ones of heavy fabric.

drastic ('dræstɪk) *adj* extreme or forceful; severe.   [C17: from Gk *drastikos*, from *drān* to do, act]
 ▸ **'drastically** *adv*

drat (dræt) *interj Sl.* an exclamation of annoyance.   [C19: prob. alteration of *God rot*]

draught *or US* **draft** (drɑːft) *n* **1** a current of air, esp. in an enclosed space. **2a** the act of pulling a load, as by a vehicle or animal. **2b** (*as modifier*): *a draught horse.* **3** the load or quantity drawn. **4** a portion of liquid to be drunk, esp. a dose of medicine. **5** the act or an instance of drinking; a gulp or swallow. **6** the act or process of drawing air, etc., into the lungs. **7** the amount of air, etc., inhaled. **8a** beer, wine, etc., stored in bulk, esp. in a cask. **8b** (*as modifier*): *draught beer.* **8c on draught.** drawn from a cask or keg. **9** any one of the flat discs used in the game of draughts. US and Canad. equivalent: **checker. 10** the depth of a loaded vessel in the water. **11 feel the**

draught. to be short of money. [C14: prob. from ON *drahtr*, of Gmc origin]

draughtboard ('drɑːft,bɔːd) *n* a square board divided into 64 squares of alternating colours, used for playing draughts or chess.

draughts (drɑːfts) *n* (*functioning as sing*) a game for two players using a draughtboard and 12 draughtsmen each. US and Canad. name: **checkers.** [C14: pl of DRAUGHT (in obs. sense: a chess move)]

draughtsman *or US* **draftsman** ('drɑːftsmən) *n*, *pl* **draughtsmen** *or US* **draftsmen.** 1 a person employed to prepare detailed scale drawings of machinery, buildings, etc. 2 a person skilled in drawing. 3 *Brit.* any of the flat discs used in the game of draughts. US and Canad. equivalent: **checker.**
▷ **'draughtsman,ship** *or US* **'draftsman,ship** *n*

draughty *or US* **drafty** ('drɑːftɪ) *adj* **draughtier, draughtiest** *or US* **draftier, draftiest.** characterized by or exposed to draughts of air.
▷ **'draughtily** *or US* **'draftily** *adv* ▷ **'draughtiness** *or US* **'draftiness** *n*

Dravidian (drə'vɪdɪən) *n* 1 a family of languages spoken in S and central India and Sri Lanka, including Tamil, Malayalam, etc. 2 a member of one of the aboriginal races of India, pushed south by the Indo-Europeans and now mixed with them. ◆ *adj* 3 of or denoting this family of languages or these peoples.

draw (drɔː) *vb* **draws, drawing, drew, drawn.** 1 to cause (a person or thing) to move towards or away by pulling. 2 to bring, take, or pull (something) out, as from a drawer, holster, etc. 3 (*tr*) to extract or pull or take out: *to draw teeth.* 4 (*tr*; often foll. by *off*) to take (liquid) out of a cask, etc., by means of a tap. 5 (*intr*) to move, esp. in a specified direction: *to draw alongside.* 6 (*tr*) to attract: *to draw attention.* 7 (*tr*) to cause to flow: *to draw blood.* 8 to depict or sketch (a figure, picture, etc.) in lines, as with a pencil or pen. 9 (*tr*) to make, formulate, or derive: *to draw conclusions.* 10 (*tr*) to write (a legal document) in proper form. 11 (*tr*; sometimes foll. by *in*) to suck or take in (air, etc.). 12 (*intr*) to induce or allow a draught to carry off air, smoke, etc. 13 (*tr*) to take or receive from a source: *to draw money from the bank.* 14 (*tr*) to earn: *draw interest.* 15 (*tr*) to write out (a bill of exchange, etc.). 16 (*tr*) to choose at random. 17 (*tr*) to reduce the diameter of (a wire) by pulling it through a die. 18 (*tr*) to shape (metal or glass) by rolling, by pulling through a die, or by stretching. 19 *Archery.* to bend (a bow) by pulling the string. 20 to steep (tea) or (of tea) to steep in boiling water. 21 (*tr*) to disembowel. 22 (*tr*) to cause (pus, etc.) to discharge from an abscess or wound. 23 (*intr*) (of two teams, etc.) to finish a game with an equal number of points, goals, etc.; tie. 24 (*tr*) *Bridge, whist.* to keep leading a suit in order to force out (all outstanding cards). 25 **draw trumps.** *Bridge, whist.* to play the trump suit until the opponents have none left. 26 (*tr*) *Billiards.* to cause (the cue ball) to spin back after a direct impact with another ball. 27 (*tr*) to search (a place) in order to find wild animals, etc., for hunting. 28 *Golf.* to cause (a golf ball) to move with a controlled right-to-left trajectory or (of a golf ball) to veer gradually from right to left. 29 (*tr*) *Naut.* (of a vessel) to require (a certain depth) in which to float. 30 **draw and quarter.** to disembowel and dismember (a person) after hanging. 31 **draw stumps.** *Cricket.* to close play. 32 **draw the shot.** *Bowls.* to deliver the bowl in such a way that it approaches the jack. ◆ *n* 33 the act of drawing. 34 *US.* a sum of money advanced to finance anticipated expenses. 35 *Inf.* an event, act, etc., that attracts a large audience. 36 a raffle or lottery. 37 something taken at random, as a ticket in a lottery. 38 a contest or game ending in a tie. 39 *US &* *Canad.* a small natural drainage way or gully. ◆ See also **drawback, draw in,** etc. [OE *dragan*]

drawback ('drɔː,bæk) *n* 1 a disadvantage or hindrance. 2 a refund of customs or excise paid on goods that are being exported or used in making goods for export. ◆ *vb* **draw back.** (*intr, adv*; often foll. by *from*) 3 to retreat; move backwards. 4 to turn aside from an undertaking.

drawbridge ('drɔː,brɪdʒ) *n* a bridge that may be raised to prevent access or to enable vessels to pass.

drawee (drɔː'iː) *n* the person or organization on which an order for payment is drawn.

drawer ('drɔːə) *n* 1 a person or thing that draws, esp. a draughtsman. 2 a person who draws a cheque. See **draw** (sense 15). 3 a person who draws up a commercial paper. 4 *Arch.* a person who draws beer, etc., in a bar. 5 (drɔː). a boxlike container in a chest, table, etc., made for sliding in and out.

drawers (drɔːz) *pl n* a legged undergarment for either sex, worn below the waist.

draw in *vb* (*intr, adv*) 1 (of hours of daylight) to become shorter. 2 (of a train) to arrive at a station.

drawing ('drɔːɪŋ) *n* 1 a picture or plan made by means of lines on a surface, esp. one made with a pencil or pen. 2 a sketch or outline. 3 the art of making drawings; draughtsmanship.

drawing pin *n Brit.* a short tack with a broad smooth head for fastening papers to a drawing board, etc. US and Canad. name: **thumbtack.**

drawing room *n* 1 a room where visitors are received and entertained; living room; sitting room. 2 *Arch.* a formal reception.

drawknife ('drɔː,naɪf) *or* **drawshave** *n*, *pl* **drawknives** *or* **drawshaves.** a tool with two handles, used to shave wood. US name: **spokeshave.**

drawl (drɔːl) *vb* 1 to speak or utter (words) slowly, esp. prolonging the vowel sounds. ◆ *n* 2 the way of speech of someone who drawls. [C16: prob. frequentative of DRAW]
▷ **'drawling** *adj*

drawn (drɔːn) *vb* 1 the past participle of **draw.** ◆ *adj* 2 haggard, tired, or tense in appearance.

drawn work *n* ornamental needlework done by drawing threads out of the fabric and using the remaining threads to form lacelike patterns. Also called: **drawn-thread work.**

draw off *vb* (*adv*) 1 (*tr*) to cause (a liquid) to flow from something. 2 to withdraw (troops).

draw on *vb* 1 (*intr, prep*) to use or exploit (a source, fund, etc.). 2 (*intr, adv*) to come near. 3 (*tr, prep*) to withdraw (money) from (an account). 4 (*tr, adv*) to put on (clothes). 5 (*tr, adv*) to lead further; entice.

draw out *vb* (*adv*) 1 to extend. 2 (*tr*) to cause (a person) to talk freely. 3 (*tr*; foll. by *of*) to elicit (information) (from). 4 (*tr*) to withdraw (money) as from a bank account. 5 (*intr*) (of hours of daylight) to become longer. 6 (*intr*) (of a train) to leave a station. 7 (*tr*) to extend (troops) in line. 8 (*intr*) (of troops) to proceed from camp.

drawstring ('drɔː,strɪŋ) *n* a cord, etc., run through a hem around an opening, so that when it is pulled tighter, the opening closes.

draw up *vb* (*adv*) 1 to come or cause to come to a halt. 2 (*tr*) 2a to prepare a draft of (a document, etc.). 2b to formulate and write out: *to draw up a contract.* 3 (*used reflexively*) to straighten oneself. 4 to form or arrange (a body of soldiers, etc.) in order or formation.

dray[1] (dreɪ) *n* a a low cart used for carrying heavy loads. b (*in combination*): *a drayman.* [OE *dræge* dragnet]

dray[2] (dreɪ) *n* a variant spelling of **drey.**

Drayton ★ ('dreɪt°n) *n* **Michael.** 1563–1631, English poet. His work includes odes and pastorals, and *Poly-Olbion* (1613–22), on the topography of England.

dread (drɛd) *vb* (*tr*) 1 to anticipate with apprehension or terror. 2 to fear greatly. 3 *Arch.* to be in awe of. ◆ *n* 4 great fear. 5 an object of terror. 6 *Sl.* a Rastafarian. 7 *Arch.* deep reverence. [OE *drǣdan*]

dreadful ('drɛdfʊl) *adj* 1 extremely disagreeable, shocking, or bad. 2 (intensifier): *a dreadful waste of time.* 3 causing dread; terrifying. 4 *Arch.* inspiring awe.

dreadfully ('drɛdfʊlɪ) *adv* 1 in a shocking or disagreeable manner. 2 (intensifier): *you're dreadfully kind.*

dreadlocks ('drɛd,lɒks) *pl n Inf.* hair worn in the Rastafarian style of long tightly-curled strands.

dreadnought ('drɛd,nɔːt) *n* 1 a battleship armed with heavy guns of uniform calibre. 2 an overcoat made of heavy cloth.

dream (driːm) *n* 1a mental activity, usually an imagined

series of events, occurring during sleep. **1b** (*as modifier*): *a dream sequence*. **1c** (*in combination*): *dreamland*. **2a** a sequence of imaginative thoughts indulged in while awake; daydream; fantasy. **2b** (*as modifier*): *a dream world*. **3** a person or thing seen or occurring in a dream. **4** a cherished that is as pleasant or seemingly unreal as a dream. **5** a vain hope. **6** a person or thing that is as pleasant or seemingly unreal as a dream. **7 go like a dream**. to move, develop, or work very well. ◆ *vb* **dreams, dreaming, dreamed** *or* **dreamt**. **8** (*may take a clause as object*) to undergo or experience (a dream or dreams). **9** (*intr*) to indulge in daydreams. **10** (*intr*) to suffer delusions; be unrealistic. **11** (when *intr*, foll. by *of* or *about*) to have an image (of) or fantasy (about) in or as if in a dream. **12** (*intr*; foll. by *of*) to consider the possibility (of). ◆ *adj* **13** too good to be true; ideal: *dream kitchen*. [OE *drēam* song]
▷ **'dreamer** *n*

dreamboat ('driːmˌbəʊt) *n Sl*. an ideal or desirable person, esp. one of the opposite sex.

dreamt (drɛmt) *vb* a past tense and past participle of **dream**.

dream ticket *n* a combination of two people, usually candidates in an election, that is considered to be ideal.

Dreamtime ('driːmˌtaɪm) *n* **1** Also called: **alcheringa**. (in the mythology of Australian Aboriginal peoples) a mythical golden age of the past, when the first men were created. **2** *Austral. inf*. any remote period, out of touch with the realities of the present.

dream up *vb* (*tr, adv*) to invent by ingenuity and imagination: *to dream up an excuse*.

dreamy ('driːmɪ) *adj* **dreamier, dreamiest**. **1** vague or impractical. **2** resembling a dream. **3** relaxing; gentle. **4** *Inf*. wonderful. **5** having dreams, esp. daydreams.
▷ **'dreamily** *adv* ▷ **'dreaminess** *n*

dreary ('drɪərɪ) *adj* **drearier, dreariest**. **1** sad or dull. **2** wearying; boring. ◆ Also (literary): **drear**. [OE *drēorig* gory]
▷ **'drearily** *adv* ▷ **'dreariness** *n*

dredge[1] (drɛdʒ) *n* **1** a machine used to scoop or suck up material from a riverbed, channel, etc. **2** another name for **dredger**. ◆ *vb* **dredges, dredging, dredged**. **3** to remove (material) from a riverbed, etc., by means of a dredge. **4** (*tr*) to search for (a submerged object) with or as if with a dredge; drag. [C16: ? ult. from OE *dragan* to DRAW]

dredge[2] (drɛdʒ) *vb* **dredges, dredging, dredged**. to sprinkle or coat (food) with flour, etc. [C16: from OF *dragie*, ?from L *tragēmata* spices, from Gk]
▷ **'dredger** *n*

dredger ('drɛdʒə) *n* **1** a vessel used for dredging. **2** another name for **dredge**[1] (sense 1).

dredge up *vb* (*tr, adv*) **1** *Inf*. to bring to notice, esp. with effort and from an obscure source. **2** to raise, as with a dredge.

dree (driː) *Scot., literary*. ◆ *vb* **drees, dreeing, dreed**. **1** (*tr*) to endure. ◆ *adj* **2** dreary. [OE *drēogan*]

D region *or* **layer** *n* the lowest region of the ionosphere, extending from a height of about 60 km to about 90 km.

dregs (drɛgz) *pl n* **1** solid particles that settle at the bottom of some liquids. **2** residue or remains. **3 the dregs**. *Brit. sl.* a despicable person or people. [C14 *dreg*, from ON *dregg*]

dreich *or* **dreigh** (driːx) *adj Scot. dialect*. dreary. [ME *dreig, drih* enduring, from OE *drēog* (unattested)]

drench (drɛntʃ) *vb* (*tr*) **1** to make completely wet; soak. **2** to give liquid medicine to (an animal). ◆ *n* **3** a drenching. **4** a dose of liquid medicine given to an animal. [OE *drencan* to cause to drink]
▷ **'drenching** *n, adj*

Drenthe ★ (*Dutch* 'drɛntə) *n* a province of the NE Netherlands: a low plateau, with many raised bogs, partially reclaimed; agricultural, with oil deposits. Capital: Assen. Pop.: 454 864 (1995). Area: 2647 sq. km (1032 sq. miles).

Dresden ★ ('drɛzdᵊn) *n* **1** an industrial city in SE Germany, on the River Elbe: capital of Saxony from the 16th century until 1952 and from 1990; it was severely damaged in the Seven Years' War (1760); the baroque city was almost totally destroyed in World War II by Allied bombing (1945). Pop.: 474 443 (1995 est.). ◆ *adj* **2** relating to, designating, or made of Dresden china.

Dresden china *n* porcelain ware, esp. delicate and elegantly decorative objects and figures of high quality, made at Meissen, near Dresden, since 1710.

dress (drɛs) *vb* **1** to put clothes on; attire. **2** (*intr*) to put on more formal attire. **3** (*tr*) to provide (someone) with clothing; clothe. **4** (*tr*) to arrange merchandise in (a shop window). **5** (*tr*) to arrange (the hair). **6** (*tr*) to apply protective or therapeutic covering to (a wound, sore, etc.). **7** (*tr*) to prepare (food, esp. fowl and fish) by cleaning, gutting, etc. **8** (*tr*) to put a finish on (stone, metal, etc.). **9** (*tr*) to cultivate (land), esp. by applying fertilizer. **10** (*tr*) to trim (trees, etc.). **11** (*tr*) to groom (a horse). **12** (*tr*) to convert (tanned hides) into leather. **13** *Angling*. to tie (a fly). **14** *Mil*. to bring (troops) into line or (of troops) to come into line (esp. in **dress ranks**). **15 dress ship**. *Naut*. to decorate a vessel by displaying signal flags on lines. ◆ *n* **16** a one-piece garment for a woman, consisting of a skirt and bodice. **17** complete style of clothing; costume: *military dress*. **18** (*modifier*) suitable for a formal occasion: *a dress shirt*. **19** outer covering or appearance. ◆ See also **dress down, dress up**. [C14: from OF *drecier*, ult. from L *dīrigere* to DIRECT]

dressage ('drɛsɑːʒ) *n* **a** the training of a horse to perform manoeuvres in response to the rider's body signals. **b** the manoeuvres performed. [F: preparation, from OF *dresser* to prepare; see DRESS]

dress circle *n* a tier of seats in a theatre or other auditorium, usually the first gallery, in which evening dress formerly had to be worn.

dress code *n* a set of rules or guidelines regarding the manner of dress acceptable in an office, restaurant, etc.

dress down *vb* (*adv*) **1** (*tr*) *Inf*. to reprimand severely or scold (a person). **2** (*intr*) to dress in casual clothes.

dresser[1] ('drɛsə) *n* **1** a set of shelves, usually also with cupboards, for storing or displaying dishes, etc. **2** *US*. a chest of drawers for storing clothing, often having a mirror on top. [C14 *dressour*, from OF *dreceore*, from *drecier* to arrange; see DRESS]

dresser[2] ('drɛsə) *n* **1** a person who dresses in a specified way: *a fashionable dresser*. **2** *Theatre*. a person employed to assist actors with their costumes. **3** a tool used for dressing stone, etc. **4** *Brit*. a person who assists a surgeon during operations. **5** *Brit*. See **window-dresser**.

dressing ('drɛsɪŋ) *n* **1** a sauce for food, esp. for salad. **2** the US and Canad. name for **stuffing** (sense 2). **3** a covering for a wound, etc. **4** fertilizer spread on land. **5** size used for stiffening textiles. **6** the processes in the conversion of hides into leather.

dressing-down *n Inf*. a severe scolding.

dressing gown *n* a full robe worn before dressing or for lounging.

dressing room *n* **1** *Theatre*. a room backstage for an actor to change clothing and to make up. **2** any room used for changing clothes.

dressing station *n Mil*. a first-aid post close to a combat area.

dressing table *n* a piece of bedroom furniture with a mirror and a set of drawers for clothes, cosmetics, etc.

dressmaker ('drɛsˌmeɪkə) *n* a person whose occupation is making clothes, esp. for women.
▷ **'dress,making** *n*

dress parade *n Mil*. a formal parade in dress uniform.

dress rehearsal *n* **1** the last rehearsal of a play, etc., using costumes, lighting, etc., as for the first night. **2** any full-scale practice.

dress shirt *n* a man's evening shirt, worn as part of formal evening dress.

dress suit *n* a man's evening suit, esp. tails.

dress uniform *n Mil*. formal ceremonial uniform.

dress up *vb* (*adv*) **1** to attire (oneself or another) very smartly or elaborately. **2** to put fancy dress, etc., on. **3** (*tr*) to improve the appearance or impression of: *to dress up the facts*.

dressy ('drɛsɪ) *adj* **dressier, dressiest. 1** (of clothes) elegant. **2** (of persons) dressing stylishly. **3** overelegant.
▶ **'dressiness** *n*

drew (druː) *vb* the past tense of **draw**.

drey *or* **dray** (dreɪ) *n* a squirrel's nest. [C17: from ?]

Dreyfus ★ ('dreɪfəs; *French* drefys) *n* **Alfred** (alfred). 1859–1935, French army officer, a Jew whose false imprisonment for treason (1894) raised issues of anti-semitism and militarism that dominated French politics until his release (1906).

dribble ('drɪb⁰l) *vb* **dribbles, dribbling, dribbled. 1** (*usually intr*) to flow or allow to flow in a thin stream or drops; trickle. **2** (*intr*) to allow saliva to trickle from the mouth. **3** (in soccer, basketball, hockey, etc.) to propel (the ball) by repeatedly tapping it with the hand, foot, or a stick. ◆ *n* **4** a small quantity of liquid falling in drops or flowing in a thin stream. **5** a small quantity or supply. **6** an act or instance of dribbling. [C16: frequentative of *drib*, var. of DRIP]
▶ **'dribbler** *n* ▶ **'dribbly** *adj*

driblet *or* **dribblet** ('drɪblɪt) *n* a small amount. [C17: from obs. *drib* to fall bit by bit + -LET]

dribs and drabs (drɪbz) *pl n Inf.* small sporadic amounts.

dried (draɪd) *vb* the past tense and past participle of **dry**.

drier¹ ('draɪə) *adj* a comparative of **dry**.

drier² ('draɪə) *n* a variant spelling of **dryer¹**.

driest ('draɪɪst) *adj* a superlative of **dry**.

drift (drɪft) *vb* (*mainly intr*) **1** (*also tr*) to be carried along as by currents of air or water or (of a current) to carry (a vessel, etc.) along. **2** to move aimlessly from one place or activity to another. **3** to wander away from a fixed course or point; stray. **4** (*also tr*) (of snow, etc.) to accumulate in heaps or to drive (snow, etc.) into heaps. ◆ *n* **5** something piled up by the wind or current, as a snowdrift. **6** tendency or meaning: *the drift of the argument*. **7** a state of indecision or inaction. **8** the extent to which a vessel, aircraft, etc., is driven off course by winds, etc. **9** a general tendency of surface ocean water to flow in the direction of the prevailing winds. **10** a driving movement, force, or influence; impulse. **11** a controlled four-wheel skid used to take bends at high speed. **12** a deposit of sand, gravel, etc., esp. one transported and deposited by a glacier. **13** a horizontal passage in a mine that follows the mineral vein. **14** something, esp. a group of animals, driven along. **15** a steel tool driven into holes to enlarge or align them. **16** an uncontrolled slow change in some operating characteristic of a piece of equipment. **17** *S. African.* a ford. [C13: from ON: snowdrift]

driftage ('drɪftɪdʒ) *n* **1** the act of drifting. **2** matter carried along by drifting. **3** the amount by which an aircraft or vessel has drifted.

drifter ('drɪftə) *n* **1** a person or thing that drifts. **2** a person who moves aimlessly from place to place. **3** a boat used for drift-net fishing.

drift ice *n* masses of ice floating in the sea.

drift net *n* a large fishing net that is allowed to drift with the tide or current.

driftwood ('drɪft,wʊd) *n* wood floating on or washed ashore by the sea or other body of water.

drill¹ (drɪl) *n* **1** a machine or tool for boring holes. **2** *Mil.* **2a** training in procedures or movements, as for parades or the use of weapons. **2b** (*as modifier*): *drill hall*. **3** strict and often repetitious training or exercises used in teaching. **4** *Inf.* correct procedure. **5** a marine mollusc that preys on oysters. ◆ *vb* **6** to pierce, bore, or cut (a hole) in (material) with or as if with a drill. **7** to instruct or be instructed in military procedures or movements. **8** (*tr*) to teach by rigorous exercises or training. **9** (*tr*) *Inf.* to riddle with bullets. [C17: from MDu. *drillen*]
▶ **'driller** *n*

drill² (drɪl) *n* **1** a machine for planting seeds in rows. **2** a furrow in which seeds are sown. **3** a row of seeds planted by means of a drill. ◆ *vb* **4** to plant (seeds) by means of a drill. [C18: from ?; cf. G *Rille* furrow]
▶ **'driller** *n*

drill³ (drɪl) *n* a hard-wearing twill-weave cotton cloth,

used for uniforms, etc. [C18: var. of G *Drillich*, from L *trilīx*, from TRI- + *līcium* thread]

drill⁴ (drɪl) *n* an Old World monkey of W Africa, related to the mandrill. [C17: from a West African word]

drilling fluid *n* a fluid, usually consisting of a suspension of clay in water, pumped down when an oil well is being drilled. Also called: **mud**.

drilling platform *n* a structure, either fixed to the sea bed or mobile, which supports the drilling rig, stores, etc., required for drilling an offshore oil well.

drilling rig *n* **1** the complete machinery, equipment, and structures needed to drill an oil well. **2** a mobile drilling platform used for exploratory offshore drilling.

drillmaster ('drɪl,mɑːstə) *n* **1** Also called: **drill sergeant.** a military drill instructor. **2** a person who instructs in a strict manner.

drill press *n* a machine tool for boring holes.

drily *or* **dryly** ('draɪlɪ) *adv* in a dry manner.

drink (drɪŋk) *vb* **drinks, drinking, drank, drunk. 1** to swallow (a liquid). **2** (*tr*) to soak up (liquid); absorb. **3** (*tr*; usually foll. by *in*) to pay close attention to. **4** (*tr*) to bring (oneself) into a certain condition by consuming alcohol. **5** (*tr*; often foll. by *away*) to dispose of or ruin by excessive expenditure on alcohol. **6** (*intr*) to consume alcohol, esp. to excess. **7** (when *intr*, foll. by *to*) to drink (a toast). **8** **drink the health of.** to salute or celebrate with a toast. **9** **drink with the flies.** *Austral. inf.* to drink alone. ◆ *n* **10** liquid suitable for drinking. **11** alcohol or its habitual or excessive consumption. **12** a portion of liquid for drinking; draught. **13** **the drink.** *Inf.* the sea. [OE *drincan*]
▶ **'drinkable** *adj* ▶ **'drinker** *n*

drink-driving *n* (*modifier*) of or relating to driving a car after drinking alcohol: *drink-driving offences*.

drinking fountain *n* a device for providing a flow or jet of drinking water, esp. in public places.

drinking-up time *n* (in Britain) a short time for finishing drinks after last orders in a public house.

drinking water *n* water reserved or suitable for drinking.

Drinkwater ★ ('drɪŋk,wɔːtə) *n* **John.** 1882–1937, British writer; author of such plays as *Abraham Lincoln* (1918).

drip (drɪp) *vb* **drips, dripping, dripped. 1** to fall or let fall in drops. ◆ *n* **2** the formation and falling of drops of liquid. **3** the sound made by falling drops. **4** a projection at the edge of a sill or cornice designed to throw water clear of the wall. **5** *Inf.* an inane, insipid person. **6** *Med.* **6a** the apparatus used for the intravenous drop-by-drop administration of a solution. **6b** the solution so administered. [OE *dryppan*, from *dropa* DROP]

drip-dry *adj* **1** designating clothing or a fabric that will dry relatively free of creases if hung up when wet. ◆ *vb* **drip-dries, drip-drying, drip-dried. 2** to dry or become dry thus.

drip-feed *vb* **drip-feeds, drip-feeding, drip-fed.** (*tr*) **1** to feed (someone) a liquid drop by drop, esp. intravenously. **2** *Inf.* to fund (a new company) in stages rather than by injecting a large sum at its inception. ◆ *n* **drip feed. 3** another term for **drip** (sense 6).

dripping ('drɪpɪŋ) *n* **1** the fat exuded by roasting meat. **2** (*often pl*) liquid that falls in drops. ◆ *adv* **3** (intensifier): *dripping wet*.

drippy ('drɪpɪ) *adj* **drippier, drippiest. 1** *Inf.* mawkish, insipid, or inane. **2** tending to drip.

drive (draɪv) *vb* **drives, driving, drove, driven. 1** to push, propel, or be pushed or propelled. **2** to guide the movement of (a vehicle, animal, etc.). **3** (*tr*) to compel or urge to work or act, esp. excessively. **4** (*tr*) to goad into a specified attitude or state: *work drove him mad*. **5** (*tr*) to cause (an object) to make (a hole, crack, etc.). **6** to move rapidly by striking or throwing with force. **7** *Sport.* to hit (a ball) very hard and straight. **8** *Golf.* to strike (the ball) with a driver. **9** (*tr*) to chase (game) from cover. **10** to transport or be transported in a vehicle. **11** (*intr*) to rush or dash violently, esp. against an obstacle. **12** (*tr*) to transact with vigour (esp. in **drive a hard bargain**). **13** (*tr*) to force (a component) into or out of its location by means of blows or a press. **14** (*tr*) *Mining.* to excavate horizontally. **15** **drive home. 15a** to cause to penetrate to the full-

est extent. **15b** to make clear by special emphasis. ◆ *n* **16** the act of driving. **17** a journey in a driven vehicle. **18** a road for vehicles, esp. a private road leading to a house. **19** vigorous pressure, as in business. **20** a united effort, esp. towards a common goal. **21** *Brit.* a large gathering of persons to play cards, etc. **22** energy, ambition, or initiative. **23** *Psychol.* a motive or interest, such as sex or ambition. **24** a sustained and powerful military offensive. **25a** the means by which force, motion, etc., is transmitted in a mechanism. **25b** (*as modifier*): *a drive shaft.* **26** *Sport.* a hard straight shot or stroke. **27** a search for and chasing of game towards waiting guns. **28** *Electronics.* the signal applied to the input of an amplifier. [OE *drīfan*]
▶ 'drivable *or* 'driveable *adj*

drive at *vb* (*intr, prep*) *Inf.* to intend or mean: *what are you driving at?*

drive-by shooting *n* an incident in which a person, building, or vehicle is shot at by someone in a moving vehicle. Sometimes shortened to **drive-by.**

drive-in *adj* **1** denoting a public facility or service designed to be used by patrons seated in their cars: *a drive-in bank.* ◆ *n.* **2** *Chiefly US & Canad.* a cinema designed to be used in such a manner.

drivel ('drɪv°l) *vb* **drivels, drivelling, drivelled** *or US* **drivels, driveling, driveled. 1** to allow (saliva) to flow from the mouth; dribble. **2** (*intr*) to speak foolishly. ◆ *n* **3** foolish or senseless talk. **4** saliva flowing from the mouth; slaver. [OE *dreflian* to slaver]
▶ 'driveller *or US* 'driveler *n*

driven ('drɪv°n) *vb* the past participle of **drive.**

driver ('draɪvə) *n* **1** a person who drives a vehicle. **2 in the driver's seat.** in a position of control. **3** a person who drives animals. **4** a mechanical component that exerts a force on another to produce motion. **5** *Golf.* a club, a No. 1 wood, used for tee shots. **6** *Electronics.* a circuit whose output provides the input of another circuit. **7** *Computing.* a computer program that controls a device.
▶ 'driverless *adj*

drive-thru *n* **a** a takeaway restaurant, bank, etc., designed so that customers can use it without leaving their cars. **b** (*as modifier*): *a drive-thru restaurant.*

drive-time *n* **a** the time of day when many people are driving to or from work, considered as a broadcasting slot. **b** (*as modifier*): *the daily drive-time show.*

driveway ('draɪv,weɪ) *n* a path for vehicles, often connecting a house with a public road.

driving chain *n* *Engineering.* a roller chain that transmits power from one toothed wheel to another. Also called: **drive chain.**

driving licence *n* an official document authorizing a person to drive a motor vehicle.

drizzle ('drɪz°l) *n* **1** very light rain. ◆ *vb* **drizzles, drizzling, drizzled. 2** (*intr*) to rain lightly. [OE *drēosan* to fall]
▶ 'drizzly *adj*

Drogheda ★ ('drɔɪɪdə) *n* a port in NE Republic of Ireland, in Co. Louth near the mouth of the River Boyne: captured by Cromwell in 1649 and its inhabitants massacred. Pop.: 23 800 (1991).

drogue (drəug) *n* **1** any funnel-like device used as a sea anchor. **2a** a small parachute released behind an aircraft to reduce its landing speed. **2b** a small parachute released during the landing of a spacecraft. **3** a device towed behind an aircraft as a target for firing practice. **4** a device on the end of the hose of a tanker aircraft, to assist location of the probe of the receiving aircraft. **5** a windsock. [C18: prob. based ult. on OE *dragan* to DRAW]

droll (drəul) *adj* amusing in a quaint or odd manner; comical. [C17: from F *drôle* scamp, from MDu.: imp]
▶ 'drollness *n* ▶ 'drolly *adv*

drollery ('drəulərɪ) *n, pl* **drolleries. 1** humour; comedy. **2** *Rare.* a droll act, story, or remark.

Drôme ★ (*French* drom) *n* a department of SE France, in Rhône-Alpes region. Capital: Valence. Pop.: 425 476 (1994 est.). Area: 6561 sq. km (2559 sq. miles).

-drome *n combining form.* **1** a course or race-course: *hippodrome.* **2** a large place for a special purpose: *aerodrome.* [via L from Gk *dromos* race, course]

dromedary ('drʌmədərɪ) *n, pl* **dromedaries.** a type of Arabian camel bred for racing and riding, having a single hump. [C14: from LL *dromedārius* (*camēlus*), from Gk *dromas* running]

-dromous *adj combining form.* moving or running: *anadromous; catadromous.* [via NL from Gk *-dromos,* from *dromos* a running]

drone¹ (drəun) *n* **1** a male honeybee whose sole function is to mate with the queen. **2** a person who lives off the work of others. **3** a pilotless radio-controlled aircraft. [OE *drān*; see DRONE²]

drone² (drəun) *vb* **drones, droning, droned. 1** (*intr*) to make a monotonous low dull sound. **2** (when *intr*, often foll. by *on*) to utter (words) in a monotonous tone, esp. to talk without stopping. ◆ *n* **3** a monotonous low dull sound. **4** *Music.* a sustained bass note or chord. **5** one of the single-reed pipes in a set of bagpipes. **6** a person who speaks in a low monotonous tone. [C16: rel. to DRONE¹ & MDu. *drōnen,* G *dröhnen*]
▶ 'droning *adj*

drongo ('drɒŋgəu) *n, pl* **drongos. 1** any of various songbirds of the Old World tropics, having a glossy black plumage. **2** *Austral. & NZ sl.* a slow-witted person. [C19: from Malagasy]

drool (dru:l) *vb* **1** (*intr*; often foll. by *over*) to show excessive enthusiasm (for) or pleasure (in); gloat (over). ◆ *vb, n* **2** another word for **drivel** (senses 1, 2, 4). [C19: prob. alteration of DRIVEL]

droop (dru:p) *vb* **1** to sag or allow to sag, as from weakness. **2** (*intr*) to be overcome by weariness. **3** (*intr*) to lose courage. ◆ *n* **4** the act or state of drooping. [C13: from ON *drūpa*]
▶ 'drooping *adj* ▶ 'droopy *adj*

drop (drɒp) *n* **1** a small quantity of liquid that forms or falls in a spherical mass. **2** a very small quantity of liquid. **3** a very small quantity of anything. **4** something resembling a drop in shape or size. **5** the act or an instance of falling; descent. **6** a decrease in amount or value. **7** the vertical distance that anything may fall. **8** a steep incline or slope. **9** short for **fruit drop. 10** the act of unloading troops, etc., by parachute. **11** (in cable television) a short spur from a trunk cable that feeds signals to an individual house. **12** *Theatre.* See **drop curtain. 13** another word for **trap door** or **gallows. 14** *Chiefly US & Canad.* a slot through which an object can be dropped into a receptacle. **15** *Austral. cricket sl.* a fall of the wicket. **16** See **drop shot. 17** **at the drop of a hat.** without hesitation or delay. **18** **have the drop on (someone).** *US & NZ.* to have the advantage over (someone). ◆ *vb* **drops, dropping, dropped. 19** (of liquids) to fall or allow to fall in globules. **20** to fall or allow to fall vertically. **21** (*tr*) to allow to fall by letting go of. **22** to sink or fall or cause to sink to the ground, as from a blow, weariness, etc. **23** (*intr*; foll. by *back, behind,* etc.) to move in a specified manner, direction, etc. **24** (*intr*; foll. by *in, by,* etc.) *Inf.* to pay a casual visit (to). **25** to decrease in amount or value. **26** to sink or cause to sink to a lower position. **27** to make or become less in strength, volume, etc. **28** (*intr*) to decline in health or condition. **29** (*intr*; sometimes foll. by *into*) to pass easily into a condition: *to drop into a habit.* **30** (*intr*) to move gently as with a current of air. **31** (*tr*) to mention casually: *to drop a hint.* **32** (*tr*) to leave out (a word or letter). **33** (*tr*) to set down (passengers or goods). **34** (*tr*) to send or post: *drop me a line.* **35** (*tr*) to discontinue: *let's drop the matter.* **36** (*tr*) to cease to associate with. **37** (*tr*) *Sl., chiefly US.* to cease to employ. **38** (*tr*; sometimes foll. by *in, off,* etc.) *Inf.* to leave or deposit. **39** (of animals) to give birth to (offspring). **40** *Sl., chiefly US & Canad.* to lose (money). **41** (*tr*) to lengthen (a hem, etc.). **42** (*tr*) to unload (troops, etc.) by parachute. **43** (*tr*) *Naut.* to sail out of sight of. **44** (*tr*) *Sport.* to omit (a player) from a team. **45** (*tr*) to lose (a game, etc.). **46** (*tr*) *Golf, basketball, etc.* to hit or throw (a ball) into a goal. **47** (*tr*) to hit (a ball) with a drop shot. ◆ *n, vb* **48** *Rugby.* short for **drop kick** or **drop-kick.** ◆ See also **drop off, dropout, drops.** [OE *dropian*]

drop curtain *n* *Theatre.* a curtain that can be raised and lowered onto the stage.

drop-dead *adv Sl.* outstandingly or exceptionally: *drop-dead gorgeous.*

drop forge n a device for forging metal between two dies, one of which is fixed, the other acting by gravity or by pressure.
▸ '**drop-,forge** vb (tr)

drop goal n Rugby. a goal scored with a drop kick during the run of play.

drop hammer n another name for **drop forge.**

drop-in centre n (in Britain) a daycentre run by the social services or a charity that clients may attend on an informal basis.

drop kick n 1 a kick in which the ball is dropped and kicked as it bounces from the ground. 2 a wrestling attack in which a wrestler leaps in the air and kicks his opponent. ◆ vb **drop-kick.** 3 to kick (a ball, a wrestling opponent, etc.) by the use of a drop kick.

drop leaf n **a** a hinged flap on a table that can be raised to extend the surface. **b** (as modifier): a drop-leaf table.

droplet ('dropltt) n a tiny drop.

drop lock n Finance. a variable-rate bank loan that is automatically replaced by a fixed-rate long-term bond if the long-term interest rates fall to a specified level.

drop off vb (adv) 1 (intr) to grow smaller or less. 2 (tr) to set down. 3 (intr) Inf. to fall asleep. ◆ n **drop-off.** 4 a steep descent. 5 a sharp decrease.

dropout ('drop,aut) n 1 a student who fails to complete a course. 2 a person who rejects conventional society. 3 **drop-out.** Rugby. a drop kick taken to restart play. ◆ vb **drop out.** (intr, adv; often foll. by of) 4 to abandon or withdraw from (a school, job, etc.).

dropper ('dropə) n 1 a small tube having a rubber bulb at one end for dispensing drops of liquid. 2 a person or thing that drops.

droppings ('droprŋz) pl n the dung of certain animals, such as rabbits, sheep, and birds.

drops (drops) pl n any liquid medication applied by means of a dropper.

drop scone n a flat spongy cake made by dropping a spoonful of batter on a hot griddle.

drop shot n **a** Tennis. a softly played return that drops abruptly after clearing the net. **b** Squash. a shot that stops abruptly after hitting the front wall of the court.

dropsy ('dropsɪ) n 1 Pathol. a condition characterized by an accumulation of watery fluid in the tissues or in a body cavity. 2 Sl. a tip or bribe. [C13: from ydropesie, from L hydrōpisis, from Gk hudrōps, from hudōr water]
▸ **dropsical** ('dropsɪk'l) adj

droshky ('drofkɪ) or **drosky** ('droskɪ) n, pl **droshkies** or **droskies.** an open four-wheeled carriage, formerly used in Russia. [C19: from Russian, dim. of drogi wagon]

drosophila (drɒ'sɒfɪlə) n, pl **drosophilas** or **drosophilae** (-,liː). any of a genus of small flies that are widely used in laboratory genetics studies. Also called: **fruit fly.** [C19: NL, from Gk drosos dew + -phila -PHILE]

dross (drɒs) n 1 the scum formed on the surfaces of molten metals. 2 worthless matter; waste. [OE drōs dregs]
▸ '**drossy** adj ▸ '**drossiness** n

drought (draut) n 1 a prolonged period of scanty rainfall. 2 a prolonged shortage. [OE drūgoth]
▸ '**droughty** adj

drove[1] (drəuv) vb the past tense of **drive.**

drove[2] (drəuv) n 1 a herd of livestock being driven together. 2 (often pl) a moving crowd of people. ◆ vb **droves, droving, droved.** (tr) 3 to drive (livestock), usually for a considerable distance. [OE drāf herd]

drover ('drəuvə) n a person who drives sheep or cattle, esp. to and from market.

drown (draun) vb 1 to die or kill by immersion in liquid. 2 (tr) to get rid of: he drowned his sorrows in drink. 3 (tr) to drench thoroughly. 4 (tr; sometimes foll. by out) to render (a sound) inaudible by making a loud noise. [C13: prob. from OE druncnian]

drowse (drauz) vb **drowses, drowsing, drowsed.** 1 to be or cause to be sleepy, dull, or sluggish. ◆ n 2 the state of being drowsy. [C16: prob. from OE drūsian to sink]

drowsy ('drauzɪ) adj **drowsier, drowsiest.** 1 heavy with sleepiness; sleepy. 2 inducing sleep; soporific. 3 sluggish or lethargic; dull.
▸ '**drowsily** adv ▸ '**drowsiness** n

drub (drʌb) vb **drubs, drubbing, drubbed.** (tr) 1 to beat with a stick. 2 to defeat utterly, as in a contest. 3 to drum or stamp (the feet). 4 to instil with force or repetition. ◆ n 5 a blow, as from a stick. [C17: prob. from Ar. dáraba to beat]

drubbing ('drʌbɪŋ) n 1 a beating. 2 a total defeat.

drudge (drʌdʒ) n 1 a person who works hard at wearisome menial tasks. ◆ vb **drudges, drudging, drudged.** 2 (intr) to toil at such tasks. [C16: ?from druggen to toil]
▸ '**drudger** n ▸ '**drudgingly** adv

drudgery ('drʌdʒərɪ) n, pl **drudgeries.** hard, menial, and monotonous work.

drug (drʌg) n 1 any substance used in the treatment, prevention, or diagnosis of disease. Related adj: **pharmaceutical.** 2 a chemical substance, esp. a narcotic, taken for the effects it produces. 3 **drug on the market.** a commodity available in excess of demand. ◆ vb **drugs, drugging, drugged.** (tr) 4 to mix a drug with (food, etc.). 5 to administer a drug to. 6 to stupefy or poison with or as if with a drug. [C14: from OF drogue, prob. of Gmc origin]

drug addict n any person who is abnormally dependent on narcotic drugs.

drugget ('drʌgɪt) n a coarse fabric used as a protective floor covering, etc. [C16: from F droguet useless fabric, from drogue trash]

druggie ('drʌgɪ) n Inf. a drug addict.

druggist ('drʌgɪst) n a US and Canad. term for **pharmacist.**

drugstore ('drʌg,stɔː) n US & Canad. a shop where medical prescriptions are made up and a wide variety of goods and sometimes light meals are sold.

druid ('druːɪd) n (sometimes cap.) 1 a member of an ancient order of priests in Gaul, Britain, and Ireland in the pre-Christian era. 2 a member of any of several modern movements attempting to revive druidism. [C16: from L druides, of Gaulish origin]
▸ '**druidess** fem n ▸ **dru'idic** or **dru'idical** adj ▸ '**druid,ism** n

drum (drʌm) n 1 a percussion instrument sounded by striking a membrane stretched across the opening of a hollow cylinder or hemisphere. 2 the sound produced by a drum or any similar sound. 3 an object that resembles a drum in shape, such as a large spool or a cylindrical container. 4 Archit. a cylindrical block of stone used to construct the shaft of a column. 5 short for **eardrum.** 6 any of various North American fishes that utter a drumming sound. 7 a type of hollow rotor for steam turbines or axial compressors. 8 Arch. a drummer. 9 **beat the drum for.** Inf. to attempt to arouse interest in. 10 **the drum.** Austral. inf. the necessary information (esp. in **give (someone) the drum).** ◆ vb **drums, drumming, drummed.** 11 to play (music) on or as if on a drum. 12 to tap rhythmically or regularly. 13 (tr; sometimes foll. by up) to summon or call by drumming. 14 (tr) to instil by constant repetition. ◆ See also **drum up.** [C16: prob. from MDu. tromme, imit.]

drumbeat ('drʌm,biːt) n the sound made by beating a drum.

drum brake n a type of brake used on the wheels of vehicles, consisting of two shoes that rub against the brake drum when the brake is applied.

drumhead ('drʌm,hed) n 1 the part of a drum that is actually struck. 2 the head of a capstan. 3 another name for **eardrum.**

drumlin ('drʌmlɪn) n a streamlined mound of glacial drift. [C19: from Irish Gaelic druim ridge + -lin -LING]

drum machine n a synthesizer specially programmed to reproduce the sound of drums and other percussion instruments in variable rhythms and combinations selected by the musician; the resulting beat is produced continually until stopped or changed.

drum major n the noncommissioned officer, usually of warrant officer's rank, who commands the corps of drums of a military band and who is in command of both the drums and the band when paraded together.

drum majorette n a girl who marches at the head of a procession, twirling a baton.

★ people and places

drummer ('drʌmə) *n* **1** a drum player. **2** *Chiefly US.* a travelling salesman.

drumstick ('drʌmˌstɪk) *n* **1** a stick used for playing a drum. **2** the lower joint of the leg of a cooked fowl.

drum up *vb* (*tr, adv*) to obtain (support, business, etc.) by solicitation or canvassing.

drunk (drʌŋk) *adj* **1** intoxicated with alcohol to the extent of losing control over normal functions. **2** overwhelmed by strong influence or emotion. ♦ *n* **3** a person who is drunk. **4** *Inf.* a drinking bout. [OE *druncen*, p.p. of *drincan* to drink]

drunkard ('drʌŋkəd) *n* a person who is frequently or habitually drunk.

drunken ('drʌŋkən) *adj* **1** intoxicated. **2** habitually drunk. **3** (*prenominal*) caused by or relating to alcoholic intoxication: *a drunken brawl.*
▶ **'drunkenly** *adv* ▶ **'drunkenness** *n*

drupe (druːp) *n* any fruit that has a fleshy or fibrous part around a stone that encloses a seed, as the peach, plum, and cherry. [C18: from L *druppa* wrinkled overripe olive, from Gk: olive]
▶ **drupaceous** (druːˈpeɪʃəs) *adj*

drupelet ('druːplɪt) *or* **drupel** ('druːpʰl) *n* a small drupe, usually one of a number forming a compound fruit.

Druse *or* **Druze** (druːz) *n, pl* **Druse** *or* **Druze. a** a member of a religious sect, mainly living in Syria, Lebanon, and Israel, having certain characteristics in common with Muslims. **b** (*as modifier*): *Druse customs.* [C18: from Arabic *Durūz*, after Ismail al-*Darazi*, 11th-century founder of the sect]

dry (draɪ) *adj* **drier, driest** *or* **dryer, dryest. 1** lacking moisture; not damp or wet. **2** having little or no rainfall. **3** not in or under water. **4** having the water drained away or evaporated: *a dry river.* **5** not providing milk: *a dry cow.* **6** (of the eyes) free from tears. **7a** *Inf.* thirsty. **7b** causing thirst. **8** eaten without butter, jam, etc.: *dry toast.* **9** *Electronics* (of a soldered joint) imperfect because the solder has not adhered to the metal. **10** (of wine, etc.) not sweet. **11** not producing a mucous or watery discharge: *a dry cough.* **12** consisting of solid as opposed to liquid substances. **13** without adornment; plain: *dry facts.* **14** lacking interest: *a dry book.* **15** lacking warmth: *a dry greeting.* **16** (of humour) shrewd and keen in an impersonal, sarcastic, or laconic way. **17** *Inf.* opposed to or prohibiting the sale of alcoholic liquor: *a dry country.* ♦ *vb* **dries, drying, dried. 18** (when *intr*, often foll. by *off*) to make or become dry. **19** (*tr*) to preserve (fruit, etc.) by removing the moisture. ♦ *n, pl* **drys** *or* **dries. 20** *Brit. inf.* a Conservative politician who is a hardliner. **21 the dry.** (*sometimes cap.*) *Austral. inf.* the dry season. ♦ See also **dry out, dry up.** [OE *drȳge*]
▶ **'dryness** *n*

dryad ('draɪəd, -æd) *n, pl* **dryads** *or* **dryades** (-əˌdiːz). *Greek myth.* a nymph or divinity of the woods. [C14: from L *Dryas*, from Gk *Druas*, from *drus* tree]

dry battery *n* an electric battery consisting of two or more dry cells.

dry cell *n* a primary cell in which the electrolyte is in the form of a paste or is treated in some way to prevent it from spilling.

dry-clean *vb* (*tr*) to clean (fabrics, etc.) with a solvent other than water.
▶ **ˌdry-'cleaner** *n* ▶ **ˌdry-'cleaning** *n*

Dryden ★ ('draɪdʰn) *n* **John.** 1631–1700, English poet and dramatist. His works include *All for Love* (1678) and *Absalom and Achitophel* (1681).

dry dock *n* a dock that can be pumped dry for work on a ship's bottom.

dryer[1] ('draɪə) *n* **1** a person or thing that dries. **2** an apparatus for removing moisture by forced draught, heating, or centrifuging. **3** any of certain chemicals added to oils to accelerate their drying when used in paints, etc.

dryer[2] ('draɪə) *adj* a variant spelling of **drier**[1].

dry fly *n Angling.* **a** an artificial fly designed to be floated on the surface of the water. **b** (*as modifier*): *dry-fly fishing.*

dry hole *n* (in the oil industry) a well which proves unsuccessful.

dry ice *n* solid carbon dioxide used as a refrigerant, and

to create billows of smoke in stage shows. Also called: **carbon dioxide snow.**

drying ('draɪɪŋ) *n* the processing of timber until it has a moisture content suitable for the purposes for which it is to be used.

dryly ('draɪlɪ) *adv* a variant spelling of **drily.**

dry measure *n* a unit or system of units for measuring dry goods, such as fruit, grains, etc.

dry out *vb* (*adv*) **1** to make or become dry. **2** to undergo or cause to undergo treatment for alcoholism or drug addiction.

dry point *n* **1** a technique of intaglio engraving with a hard steel needle, without acid, on a copper plate. **2** the sharp steel needle used. **3** the engraving or print produced.

dry riser *n* a vertical pipe, not containing water, having connections on different floors of a building for a fireman's hose to be attached. A fire tender can be connected at the lowest level to make water rise under pressure within the pipe. Abbrev.: **DR.**

dry rot *n* **1** crumbling and drying of timber, bulbs, potatoes, or fruit, caused by certain fungi. **2** any fungus causing this decay. **3** moral degeneration or corruption.

dry run *n* **1** *Mil.* practice in firing without live ammunition. **2** *Inf.* a rehearsal.

drysalter ('draɪˌsɔːltə) *n Obs.* a dealer in dyestuffs and gums, and in dried, tinned, or salted foods and edible oils.

Drysdale ★ ('draɪzdeɪl) *n* Sir **George Russell.** 1912–81, Australian painter, esp. of landscapes.

dry-stone *adj* (of a wall) made without mortar.

dry up *vb* (*adv*) **1** (*intr*) to become barren or unproductive; fail. **2** to dry (dishes, cutlery, etc.) with a tea towel after they have been washed. **3** (*intr*) *Inf.* to stop talking or speaking.

DS *or* **ds** *Music. abbrev. for* dal segno.

DSc *abbrev. for* Doctor of Science.

DSC *Mil. abbrev. for* Distinguished Service Cross.

DSM *Mil. abbrev. for* Distinguished Service Medal.

DSO *Brit. mil. abbrev. for* Distinguished Service Order.

DSS *Brit. abbrev. for:* **1** Department of Social Security. **2** Director of Social Services.

DST *abbrev. for* Daylight Saving Time.

DSW (in New Zealand) *abbrev. for* Department of Social Welfare.

DTI (in Britain) *abbrev. for* Department of Trade and Industry.

DTP *abbrev for* desktop publishing.

DT's *Inf. abbrev. for* delirium tremens.

Du. *abbrev. for* Dutch.

dual ('djuːəl) *adj* **1** relating to or denoting two. **2** twofold; double. **3** (in the grammar of some languages) denoting a form of a word indicating that exactly two referents are being referred to. **4** *Maths, logic.* (of a pair of operators) convertible into one another by the distribution of negation over either. ♦ *n* **5** *Grammar.* **5a** the dual number. **5b** a dual form of a word. [C17: from L *duālis* concerning two, from *duo* two]
▶ **'dually** *adv* ▶ **duality** (djuːˈælɪtɪ) *n*

dual carriageway *n Brit.* a road on which traffic travelling in opposite directions is separated by a central strip of turf, etc. US and Canad. name: **divided highway.**

dualism ('djuːəˌlɪzəm) *n* **1** the state of being twofold or double. **2** *Philosophy.* the doctrine that reality consists of two basic types of substance, usually taken to be mind and matter or mental and physical entities. Cf. **monism** (sense 1). **3a** the theory that the universe has been ruled from its origins by two conflicting powers, one good and one evil. **3b** the theory that there are two personalities, one human and one divine, in Christ.
▶ **'dualist** *n* ▶ **dual'istic** *adj*

dub[1] (dʌb) *vb* **dubs, dubbing, dubbed. 1** (*tr*) to invest (a person) with knighthood by tapping on the shoulder with a sword. **2** (*tr*) to invest with a title, name, or nickname. **3**

(*tr*) to dress (leather) by rubbing. **4** *Angling.* to dress (a fly). [OE *dubbian*]

dub² (dʌb) *vb* **dubs, dubbing, dubbed. 1** to alter the soundtrack of (a film, etc.). **2** (*tr*) to provide (a film) with a new soundtrack, esp. in a different language. **3** (*tr*) to provide (a film or tape) with a soundtrack. ◆ *n* **4** the new sounds added. **5** *Music.* a style of record production associated with reggae, involving the use of echo, delay, etc. [C20: shortened from DOUBLE]

dub³ (dʌb) *vb* **dubs, dubbing, dubbed.** *Austral. & NZ inf.* short for **double-bank.**

Dubai ★ (duːˈbaɪ) *n* a sheikhdom in the NE United Arab Emirates, consisting principally of the port of Dubai, on the Persian Gulf: oilfields. Pop.: 548 000 (1993).

du Barry ★ (dju: ˈbærɪ; *French* dy bari) *n* **Comtesse** (kɔ̃tɛs), original name *Marie Jeanne Bécu.* ?1743–93, mistress of Louis XV, guillotined in the French Revolution.

dubbin (ˈdʌbɪn) *n Brit.* a greasy preparation applied to leather to soften it and make it waterproof. [C18: from *dub* to dress leather]

dubbing¹ (ˈdʌbɪŋ) *n Films.* **1** the replacement of a soundtrack, esp. by one in another language. **2** the combination of several soundtracks. **3** the addition of a soundtrack to a film, etc.

dubbing² (ˈdʌbɪŋ) *n* **1** *Angling.* fibrous material used for the body of an artificial fly. **2** a variant of **dubbin.**

Dubček ★ (*Czech* ˈduptʃɛk) *n* **Alexander** (ˈaleksandʳr). 1921–92, Czechoslovak statesman. His reforms as first secretary of the Czechoslovak Communist Party (1968–69) prompted the Soviet occupation (1968) and his enforced resignation. Following the uprising of 1989 he was elected chairman of the new Czech parliament.

du Bellay ★ (*French* dy bele) *n* See (Joachim du) **Bellay.**

dubiety (djuːˈbaɪɪtɪ) *n, pl* **dubieties. 1** the state of being doubtful. **2** a doubtful matter. [C18: from LL *dubietās*, from L *dubius* DUBIOUS]

dub in *or* **up** *vb* (*adv*) *Sl.* to contribute to the cost of something: *we'll all dub in a fiver for the trip.*

dubious (ˈdjuːbɪəs) *adj* **1** marked by or causing doubt. **2** uncertain; doubtful. **3** of doubtful quality; untrustworthy. **4** not certain in outcome. [C16: from L *dubius* wavering]
► **'dubiously** *adv* ► **'dubiousness** *n*

Dublin ★ (ˈdʌblɪn) *n* **1** the capital of the Republic of Ireland, on **Dublin Bay**: under English rule from 1171 until 1922; commercial and cultural centre; contains one of the world's largest breweries and exports whiskey, stout, and agricultural produce. Pop.: 478 389 (1991). Gaelic name: **Baile Átha Cliath. 2** a county, comprising four county boroughs, in E Republic of Ireland, in Leinster on the Irish Sea: mountainous in the south but low-lying in the north and centre. County seat: Dublin. Pop.: 1 025 324 (1991). Area: 922 sq. km (356 sq. miles).
► **'Dubliner** *n*

Dublin Bay prawn (ˈdʌblɪn) *n* a large prawn usually used in a dish of scampi.

dubnium (ˈdʌb,nɪəm) *n* a synthetic transactinide element produced in minute quantities by bombarding plutonium with high-energy neon ions. Symbol: Du; atomic no. 105. [C20: from *Dubna*, city in Russia where it was first reported]

Dubrovnik ★ (duˈbrɒvnɪk) *n* a port in W Croatia, on the Dalmatian coast: an important commercial centre in the Middle Ages; tourist centre. Pop.: 49 730 (1991). Former Italian name (until 1918): **Ragusa.**

Dubuffet ★ (*French* dybyfɛ) *n* **Jean** (ʒɑ̃). 1901–85, French painter.

ducal (ˈdjuːkˀl) *adj* of a duke or duchy. [C16: from F, from LL *ducālis* of a leader, from L *dux* leader]

ducat (ˈdʌkət) *n* **1** any of various former European gold or silver coins. **2** (*often pl*) money. [C14: from OF, from OIt. *ducato* coin stamped with the doge's image]

Duccio di Buoninsegna ★ (*Italian* ˈduttʃo di buonin-ˈseɲɲa) *n* ?1255–?1318, Italian painter; founder of the Sienese school.

duce (ˈduːtʃɪ) *n* leader. [C20: from It., from L *dux*]

Duce (*Italian* ˈduːtʃe) *n* **Il** (il). the title assumed by Mussolini as leader of Fascist Italy (1922–43).

Duchamp ★ (*French* dyʃɑ̃) *n* **Marcel** (marsɛl). 1887–1968, US painter and sculptor, born in France.

Duchenne dystrophy (duˈʃɛn) *or* **Duchenne muscular dystrophy** *n* the most common form of muscular dystrophy, usually affecting only boys. [after Guillaume *Duchenne* (1806–75), F neurologist]

duchess (ˈdʌtʃɪs) *n* **1** the wife or widow of a duke. **2** a woman who holds the rank of duke in her own right. ◆ *vb* **3** (*tr*) *Austral. inf.* to overwhelm with flattering attention. [C14: from OF *duchesse*]

duchy (ˈdʌtʃɪ) *n, pl* **duchies.** the territory of a duke or duchess; dukedom. [C14: from OF *duche*, from *duc* DUKE]

duck¹ (dʌk) *n, pl* **ducks** *or* **duck. 1** any of a family of aquatic birds, esp. those having short legs, webbed feet, and a broad blunt bill. **2** the flesh of this bird, used as food. **3** the female of such a bird, as opposed to the male (drake). **4** Also: **ducks.** *Brit. inf.* dear or darling: used as a term of address. See also **ducky. 5** *Cricket.* a score of nothing by a batsman. **6** **like water off a duck's back.** *Inf.* without effect. [OE *dūce* duck, diver; rel. to DUCK²]

duck² (dʌk) *vb* **1** to move (the head or body) quickly downwards or away, esp. to escape observation or evade a blow. **2** to plunge suddenly under water. **3** (when *intr*, often foll. by *out*) *Inf.* to dodge or escape (a person, duty, etc.). **4** (*intr*) *Bridge.* to play a low card rather than try to win a trick. ◆ *n* **5** the act or an instance of ducking. [C14: rel. to OHG *tūhhan* to dive, MDu. *dūken*]
► **'ducker** *n*

duck³ (dʌk) *n* a heavy cotton fabric of plain weave, used for clothing, tents, etc. [C17: from MDu. *doek*]

duck⁴ (dʌk) *n* an amphibious vehicle used in World War II. [C20: from code name DUKW]

duck-billed platypus *n* an amphibious egg-laying mammal of E Australia having dense fur, a broad bill and tail, and webbed feet.

duckboard (ˈdʌk,bɔːd) *n* a board or boards laid so as to form a path over wet or muddy ground.

ducking stool *n History.* a chair used for punishing offenders by plunging them into water.

duckling (ˈdʌklɪŋ) *n* a young duck.

ducks and drakes *n* (*functioning as sing*) **1** a game in which a flat stone is bounced across the surface of water. **2** **make ducks and drakes of** *or* **play (at) ducks and drakes with.** *Inf.* to use recklessly; squander.

duck's arse *n* a hairstyle in which the hair is swept back to a point at the nape of the neck, resembling a duck's tail. Abbrev.: **DA.**

duck soup *n US sl.* something that is easy to do.

duckweed (ˈdʌk,wiːd) *n* any of various small stemless aquatic plants that occur floating on still water in temperate regions.

ducky *or* **duckie** (ˈdʌkɪ) *Inf.* ◆ *n, pl* **duckies. 1** *Brit.* darling or dear: a term of endearment. ◆ *adj* **duckier, duckiest. 2** delightful; fine.

duct (dʌkt) *n* **1** a tube, pipe, or canal by means of which a substance, esp. a fluid or gas, is conveyed. **2** any bodily passage, esp. one conveying secretions or excretions. **3** a narrow tubular cavity in plants. **4** a channel or pipe carrying electric wires. **5** a passage through which air can flow, as in air conditioning. [C17: from L *ductus* a leading (in Med. L: aqueduct), from *dūcere* to lead]
► **'ductless** *adj*

ductile (ˈdʌktaɪl) *adj* **1** (of a metal) able to sustain large deformations without fracture and able to be hammered into sheets or drawn out into wires. **2** able to be moulded. **3** easily led or influenced. [C14: from OF, from L *ductilis*, from *dūcere* to lead]
► **ductility** (dʌkˈtɪlɪtɪ) *n*

ductless gland *n Anat.* See **endocrine gland.**

dud (dʌd) *Inf.* ◆ *n* **1** a person or thing that proves ineffectual. **2** a shell, etc., that fails to explode. **3** (*pl*) Old-fashioned. clothes or other belongings. ◆ *adj* **4** failing in its purpose or function. [C15 (in the sense: an article of clothing, a thing, used disparagingly): from ?]

dude (duːd, djuːd) *n Inf.* **1** *Western US & Canad.* a city dweller, esp. one holidaying on a ranch. **2** *US & Canad.* a dandy. **3** *US & Canad.* any person: often used to any male in direct address. [C19: from ?]
▶ **'dudish** *adj* ▶ **'dudishly** *adv*
dude ranch *n US & Canad.* a ranch used as a holiday resort.
dudgeon ('dʌdʒən) *n* anger or resentment (arch., except in **in high dudgeon**). [C16: from ?]
Dudley[1] ★ ('dʌdlɪ) *n* **1** a town in W central England, in the West Midlands: clothing and light-engineering industries. Pop.: 192 171 (1991). **2** a unitary authority in W central England. Pop.: 312 200 (1994 est.). Area: 98 sq. km (38 sq. miles).
Dudley[2] ★ ('dʌdlɪ) *n* **Robert**. See (Earl of) **Leicester**.
due (djuː) *adj* **1** (*postpositive*) immediately payable. **2** (*postpositive*) owed as a debt. **3** fitting; proper. **4** (*prenominal*) adequate or sufficient. **5** (*postpositive*) expected or appointed to be present or arrive. **6 due to.** attributable to or caused by. ◆ *n* **7** something that is owed, required, or due. **8 give (a person) his due.** to give or allow what is deserved or right. ◆ *adv* **9** directly or exactly. [C13: from OF *deu*, from *devoir* to owe, from L *debēre*]

> **USAGE NOTE** The use of *due to* as a compound preposition (*the performance has been cancelled due to bad weather*) was formerly considered incorrect, but is now acceptable.

duel ('djuːəl) *n* **1** a formal prearranged combat with deadly weapons between two people in the presence of seconds, usually to settle a quarrel. **2** a contest or conflict between two persons or parties. ◆ *vb* **duels, duelling, duelled** *or US* **duels, dueling, dueled.** (*intr*) **3** to fight in a duel. **4** to contest closely. [C15: from Med. L *duellum*, from L, poetical var. of *bellum* war; associated with L *duo* two]
▶ **'dueller, 'duellist** *or US* **'dueler, 'duelist** *n*
duenna (djuːˈɛnə) *n* (in Spain and Portugal, etc.) an elderly woman retained by a family to act as governess and chaperon to girls. [C17: from Sp. *dueña*, from L *domina* lady]
due process of law *n* the administration of justice in accordance with established rules and principles.
dues (djuːz) *pl n* (*sometimes sing*) charges, as for membership of a club or organization; fees.
duet (djuːˈɛt) *n* **1** a musical composition for two performers or voices. **2** a pair of closely connected individuals; duo. [C18: from It. *duetto* a little duet, from *duo* duet, from L: two]
▶ **du'ettist** *n*
duff[1] (dʌf) *n* **1** a thick flour pudding boiled in a cloth bag. **2 up the duff.** *Sl.* pregnant. [C19: N English var. of DOUGH]
duff[2] (dʌf) *vb* (*tr*) **1** *Sl.* to give a false appearance to (old or stolen goods); fake. **2** (foll. by *up*) *Brit. sl.* to beat (a person) severely. **3** *Austral. sl.* to steal (cattle), altering the brand. **4** *Golf. inf.* to bungle a shot by hitting the ground behind the ball. ◆ *adj* **5** *Brit., Austral., & NZ inf.* bad or useless. [C19: prob. back formation from DUFFER]
duffel *or* **duffle** ('dʌfᵊl) *n* **1** a heavy woollen cloth. **2** *Chiefly US & Canad.* equipment or supplies. [C17: after *Duffel*, Belgian town]
duffel bag *n* a cylindrical drawstring canvas bag, originally used esp. by sailors for carrying personal articles.
duffel coat *n* a usually knee-length wool coat, usually with a hood and fastened with toggles.
duffer ('dʌfə) *n* **1** *Inf.* a dull or incompetent person. **2** *Sl.* something worthless. **3** *Austral. sl.* **3a** a mine that proves unproductive. **3b** a person who steals cattle. [C19: from ?]
Dufy ★ (*French* dyfi) *n* **Raoul** (raul). 1877–1953, French painter.
dug[1] (dʌg) *vb* the past tense and past participle of **dig**.
dug[2] (dʌg) *n* a nipple, teat, udder, or breast. [C16: of Scand. origin]

dugong ('duːgɒŋ) *n* a whalelike mammal occurring in shallow tropical waters from E Africa to Australia. [C19: from Malay *duyong*]
dugout ('dʌg,aʊt) *n* **1** a canoe made by hollowing out a log. **2** *Mil.* a covered excavation dug to provide shelter. **3** (at a sports ground) the covered bench where managers, substitutes, etc., sit. **4** (in the Canadian prairies) a reservoir dug on a farm in which water from rain and snow is collected for use in irrigation, watering livestock, etc.
duiker *or* **duyker** ('daɪkə) *n, pl* **duikers, duiker** *or* **duykers, duyker. 1** Also: **duikerbok.** any of various small African antelopes. **2** *S. African.* any of several cormorants, esp. the long-tailed shag. [C18: via Afrik., from Du. *duiker* diver, from *duiken* to dive]
Duisburg ★ (*German* 'dyːsburk) *n* an industrial city in NW Germany, in North Rhine-Westphalia at the confluence of the Rivers Rhine and Ruhr: the largest European inland port. Pop.: 536 106 (1995 est.).
Dukas ★ (*French* dykɑ) *n* **Paul** (pɔl). 1865–1935, French composer noted for the orchestral scherzo *The Sorcerer's Apprentice* (1897).
duke (djuːk) *n* **1** a nobleman of high rank: in the British Isles standing above the other grades of the nobility. **2** the prince or ruler of a small principality or duchy. [C12: from OF *duc*, from L *dux* leader]
▶ **'dukedom** *n*
dukes (djuːks) *pl n Sl.* the fists. [C19: from *Duke of Yorks* rhyming sl. for *forks* (fingers)]
dulcet ('dʌlsɪt) *adj* (of a sound) soothing or pleasant; sweet. [C14: from L *dulcis* sweet]
dulcimer ('dʌlsɪmə) *n* **1** a tuned percussion instrument consisting of a set of strings stretched over a sounding board and struck with hammers. **2** an instrument used in US folk music, with an elliptical body and usually three strings plucked with a goose quill. [C15: from OF *doulcemer*, from OIt. *dolcimelo*, from *dolce* (from L *dulcis* sweet) + -*melo*, ?from Gk *melos* song]
dull (dʌl) *adj* **1** slow to think or understand; stupid. **2** lacking in interest. **3** lacking in perception; insensitive. **4** lacking sharpness. **5** not acute, intense, or piercing. **6** (of weather) not bright or clear. **7** not active, busy, or brisk. **8** lacking in spirit; listless. **9** (of colour) lacking brilliance; sombre. **10** not loud or clear; muffled. ◆ *vb* **11** to make or become dull. [OE *dol*]
▶ **'dullish** *adj* ▶ **'dullness** *or* **'dulness** *n* ▶ **'dully** *adv*
dullard ('dʌləd) *n* a dull or stupid person.
dulse (dʌls) *n* any of several seaweeds that occur on rocks and have large red edible fronds. [C17: from OIrish *duilesc* seaweed]
Dulwich ★ ('dʌlɪtʃ) *n* a residential district in the Greater London borough of Southwark: site of Dulwich College.
duly ('djuːlɪ) *adv* **1** in a proper manner. **2** at the proper time. [C14: see DUE, -LY[2]]
duma *Russian.* ('duːmə) *n Russian history.* **1** (*usually cap.*) the elective legislative assembly established by Tsar Nicholas II in 1905: overthrown in 1917. **2** (before 1917) any official assembly or council. **3** short for **State Duma**, the lower chamber of the Russian parliament. [C20: from *duma* thought, of Gmc origin]
Dumas ★ (*French* dymɑ) *n* **1 Alexandre** (alɛksɑ̃drə), known as *Dumas père.* 1802–70, French writer, noted for his novels *The Count of Monte Cristo* (1844) and *The Three Musketeers* (1844). **2** his son, **Alexandre**, known as *Dumas fils.* 1824–95, French writer, noted esp. for *La Dame aux camélias* (1852). **3** **Jean-Baptiste André** (ʒɑ̃batist ɑ̃dre). 1800–84, French chemist.
Du Maurier ★ (du ˈmɒrɪ,eɪ) *n* **1** Dame **Daphne**. 1907–89, British novelist; author of *Rebecca* (1938) and *My Cousin Rachel* (1951). **2** her grandfather, **George Louis Palmella Busson** ('pælmelə 'bjuːsᵊn). 1834–96, British novelist and illustrator; author of *Trilby* (1894). **3** his son, Sir **Gerald (Hubert Edward)**. 1873–1934, British actor-manager: father of Daphne Du Maurier.
dumb (dʌm) *adj* **1** lacking the power to speak; mute. **2** lacking the power of human speech: *dumb animals.* **3** temporarily bereft of the power to speak: *struck dumb.* **4** refraining from speech; uncommunicative. **5** producing

no sound: *a dumb piano.* **6** made, done, or performed without speech. **7** *Inf.* **7a** dim-witted. **7b** foolish. ♦ See also **dumb down.** [OE]
► **'dumbly** *adv* ► **'dumbness** *n*

Dumbarton ★ (dʌmˈbɑːt⁹n) *n* a town in W Scotland, in West Dunbartonshire near the confluence of the Rivers Leven and Clyde: centred around the **Rock of Dumbarton,** an important stronghold since ancient times; engineering and distilling. Pop.: 21 962 (1991).

Dumbarton Oaks ★ (ˈdʌmˌbɑːt⁹n) *n* an estate in the District of Columbia in the US: scene of conferences in 1944 concerned with creating the United Nations.

dumbbell (ˈdʌmˌbel) *n* **1** an exercising weight consisting of a short bar with a heavy ball or disc at either end, used for single-arm movements. **2** a small wooden or rubber object of a similar shape used to train dogs in retrieval. **3** *Sl., chiefly US & Canad.* a fool.

dumb down *vb* (tr) to make less intellectually demanding or sophisticated: *the alleged dumbing down of BBC radio.*

dumbfound *or* **dumfound** (dʌmˈfaʊnd) *vb* (tr) to strike dumb with astonishment; amaze. [C17: from DUMB + (CON)FOUND]

dumb show *n* **1** formerly, a part of a play acted in pantomime. **2** meaningful gestures.

dumbstruck (ˈdʌmˌstrʌk) *adj* temporarily deprived of speech through shock or surprise.

dumbwaiter (ˈdʌmˌweɪtə) *n* **1** *Brit.* **1a** a stand placed near a dining table to hold food. **1b** a revolving circular tray placed on a table to hold food. US and Canad. name: **lazy Susan. 2** a lift for carrying food, rubbish, etc., between floors.

dumdum (ˈdʌmˌdʌm) *n* a soft-nosed bullet that expands on impact and inflicts extensive laceration. [C19: after *Dum-Dum,* town near Calcutta where orig. made]

Dumfries ★ (dʌmˈfriːs) *n* a town in S Scotland on the River Nith, administrative centre of Dumfries and Galloway. Pop.: 32 136 (1991).

Dumfries and Galloway ★ *n* a council area in SW Scotland. Administrative centre: Dumfries. Pop.: 147 900 (1993 est.). Area: 6439 sq. km (2486 sq. miles).

Dumfriesshire ★ (dʌmˈfriːsˌʃɪə, -ʃə) *n* (until 1975) a county in S Scotland, on the Solway Firth, now part of Dumfries and Galloway.

dummy (ˈdʌmɪ) *n, pl* **dummies. 1** a figure representing the human form, used for displaying clothes, as a target, etc. **2a** a copy of an object, often lacking some essential feature of the original. **2b** (*as modifier*): *a dummy drawer.* **3** *Sl.* a stupid person. **4** *Derog., sl.* a person without the power of speech. **5** *Inf.* a person who says or does nothing. **6a** a person who appears to act for himself while acting on behalf of another. **6b** (*as modifier*): *a dummy buyer.* **7** *Mil.* a weighted round without explosives. **8** *Bridge.* **8a** the hand exposed on the table by the declarer's partner and played by the declarer. **8b** the declarer's partner. **9a** a prototype of a book, indicating the appearance of the finished product. **9b** a designer's layout of a page. **10** *Sport.* a feigned pass or move. **11** *Brit.* a rubber teat for babies to suck or bite on. US and Canad. equivalent: **pacifier. 12** (*modifier*) counterfeit; sham. **13** (*modifier*) (of a card game) played with one hand exposed or unplayed. **14 sell (someone) a dummy.** *Sport.* to trick (an opponent) with a dummy pass. [C16: see DUMB, -Y³]

dummy run *n* an experimental run; practice; rehearsal.

Du Mont ★ (ˈdjuːˌmɒnt) *n* **Allen Balcom.** 1901–65, US engineer, who developed the cathode-ray tube.

dump (dʌmp) *vb* **1** to drop, fall, or let fall heavily or in a mass. **2** (tr) to empty (objects or material) out of a container. **3** to unload or empty (a container), as by overturning. **4** (tr) *Inf.* to dispose of without subtlety or proper care. **4b** to dispose of (nuclear waste). **5** *Commerce.* to market (goods) in bulk and at low prices, esp. abroad, in order to maintain a high price in the home market and obtain a share of the foreign markets. **6** (tr) to store (supplies, etc.) temporarily. **7** (intr) *Sl., chiefly US.* to defecate. **8** (tr) *Surfing.* (of a wave) to hurl a swimmer or surfer down. **9** (tr) *Austral. & NZ.* to compact (bales of wool) by hydraulic pressure. **10** (tr) *Computing.* to record (the con-

tents of the memory) on a storage device at a series of points during a computer run. ♦ *n* **11** a place or area where waste materials are dumped. **12** a pile or accumulation of rubbish. **13** the act of dumping. **14** *Inf.* a dirty or unkempt place. **15** *Mil.* a place where weapons, supplies, etc., are stored. **16** *Sl., chiefly US.* an act of defecation. [C14: prob. from ON]

dumper (ˈdʌmpə) *n* **1** a person or thing that dumps. **2** *Surfing.* a wave that hurls a swimmer or surfer down.

dumpling (ˈdʌmplɪŋ) *n* **1** a small ball of dough cooked and served with stew. **2** a pudding consisting of a round pastry case filled with fruit: *apple dumpling.* **3** *Inf.* a short plump person. [C16: dump-, ? var. of LUMP¹ + -LING¹]

dumps (dʌmps) *pl n Inf.* a state of melancholy or depression (esp. in **down in the dumps**). [C16: prob. from MDu. *domp* haze]

dump truck *or* **dumper-truck** *n* a small truck used on building sites, having a load-bearing container at the front that can be tipped up to dump the contents.

dumpy (ˈdʌmpɪ) *adj* **dumpier, dumpiest.** short and plump; squat. [C18: ? rel. to DUMPLING]
► **'dumpily** *adv* ► **'dumpiness** *n*

dun¹ (dʌn) *vb* **duns, dunning, dunned. 1** (tr) to press (a debtor) for payment. ♦ *n* **2** a person, esp. a hired agent, who importunes another for the payment of a debt. **3** a demand for payment. [C17: from ?]

dun² (dʌn) *n* **1** a brownish-grey colour. **2** a horse of this colour. **3** *Angling.* **3a** an immature adult mayfly. **3b** an artificial fly resembling this. ♦ *adj* **dunner, dunnest. 4** of a dun colour. **5** dark and gloomy. [OE *dunn*]

Duna ★ (ˈdunɒ) *n* the Hungarian name for the **Danube.**

Dünaburg ★ (ˈdyːnaburk) *n* the German name (until 1893) for **Daugavpils.**

Dunaj ★ (ˈdunaj) *n* the Czech name for the **Danube.**

Dunant ★ (*French* dynɑ̃) *n* **Jean Henri** (ʒɑ̃ ɑ̃ri). 1828–1910, Swiss humanitarian, founder of the International Red Cross (1864): shared the Nobel peace prize 1901.

Dunărea ★ (ˈdunərja) *n* the Romanian name for the **Danube.**

Dunbar¹ ★ (dʌnˈbɑː) *n* a port and resort in SE Scotland, in East Lothian: scene of Cromwell's defeat of the Scots (1650). Pop.: 6518 (1991).

Dunbar² ★ (dʌnˈbɑː) *n* **William.** ?1460–?1520, Scottish poet, noted for his satirical, allegorical, and elegiac works.

Dunbartonshire ★ (dʌnˈbɑːt⁹nʃɪə, -ʃə) *n* a historic county of W Scotland, now part of East Dunbartonshire and West Dunbartonshire.

Duncan ★ (ˈdʌŋkən) *n* **Isadora** (ˌɪzəˈdɔːrə). 1878–1927, US dancer and choreographer.

Duncan I ★ (ˈdʌŋkən) *n* died 1040, king of Scotland (1034–40); killed by Macbeth.

dunce (dʌns) *n* a person who is stupid or slow to learn. [C16: from *Dunses* or *Dunsmen,* term of ridicule applied to the followers of John *Duns* Scotus (?1265–1308), Scot. scholastic theologian, esp. by 16th-cent. humanists]

dunce cap *or* **dunce's cap** *n* a conical paper hat, formerly placed on the head of a dull child at school.

Dundalk ★ (dʌnˈdɔːk) *n* a town in NE Republic of Ireland, on **Dundalk Bay:** county town of Co. Louth. Pop.: 25 800 (1991).

Dundee¹ ★ (dʌnˈdiː) *n* **1** a port in E Scotland on the Firth of Tay: centre of the former British jute industry. Pop.: 158 981 (1991). **2 City of.** a council area in E Scotland. Pop.: 167 500 (1996 est.). Area: 65 sq. km (25 sq. miles).
► **Dundonian** (dʌnˈdəʊnɪən) *n, adj*

Dundee² ★ (dʌnˈdiː) *n* **1st Viscount,** title of *John Graham of Claverhouse.* ?1649–89, Scottish Jacobite leader, who died after winning the battle of Killiecrankie.

Dundee cake (dʌnˈdiː) *n Chiefly Brit.* a fairly rich fruit cake decorated with almonds.

dunderhead (ˈdʌndəˌhɛd) *n* a slow-witted person. [C17: prob. from Du. *donder* thunder + HEAD]
► **'dunder,headed** *adj*

dune (djuːn) *n* a mound or ridge of drifted sand. [C18: via OF from MDu. *dūne*]

★ people and places

Dunedin ★ (dʌnˈiːdɪn) *n* a port in New Zealand, on SE South Island: founded (1848) by Scottish settlers. Pop. (urban area): 113 500 (1995 est.).

Dunfermline ★ (dʌnˈfɜːmlɪn) *n* a city in E Scotland, in SW Fife: ruined palace, a former residence of Scottish kings. Pop.: 55 083 (1991).

dung (dʌŋ) *n* **1** excrement, esp. of animals; manure. **2** something filthy. ◆ *vb* **3** (*tr*) to cover with manure. [OE: prison; rel. to OHG *tunc* cellar roofed with dung, ON *dyngja* manure heap]

Dungannon ★ (dʌnˈgænən) *n* a district of central Northern Ireland, bordering the W shore of Lough Neagh and the Irish Republic: agriculture. Administrative centre: Dungannon. Pop.: 45 428 (1991). Area: 783 sq. km (302 sq. miles)

dungaree (ˌdʌŋgəˈriː) *n* **1** a coarse cotton fabric used chiefly for work clothes, etc. **2** (*pl*) **2a** a suit of workman's overalls made of this material, consisting of trousers with a bib attached. **2b** a casual garment resembling this, usually worn by women or children. **3** (*pl*) *US*. jeans. [C17: from Hindi, after *Dungrī*, district of Bombay, where this fabric originated]

Dungeness ★ (ˌdʌndʒəˈnɛs) *n* a low shingle headland on the S coast of England, in Kent: two nuclear power stations: automatic lighthouse.

dungeon (ˈdʌndʒən) *n* **1** a prison cell, often underground. **2** a variant spelling of donjon. [C14: from OF *donjon*]

dunghill (ˈdʌŋˌhɪl) *n* **1** a heap of dung. **2** a foul place, condition, or person.

dunk (dʌŋk) *vb* **1** to dip (bread, etc.) in tea, soup, etc., before eating. **2** to submerge or be submerged. [C20: from Pennsylvania Du., from MHG *dunken*, from OHG *dunkōn*]
▸ **'dunker** *n*

Dunkerque ★ (French dœ̃kɛrk) *n* a port in N France, on the Strait of Dover: scene of the evacuation of British and other Allied troops after the fall of France in 1940; industrial centre. Pop.: 190 879 (1990). English name: **Dunkirk** (dʌnˈkɜːk).

Dún Laoghaire ★ (duːn ˈlɪərɪ) *n* a port in E Republic of Ireland, on Dublin Bay. Pop.: 185 400 (1991). Former names: **Dunleary** (until 1821), **Kingstown** (1821–1921).

dunlin (ˈdʌnlɪn) *n* a small sandpiper of northern and arctic regions, having a brown back and black belly in summer. [C16: DUN² + -LING¹]

Dunlop ★ (ˈdʌnlɒp) *n* **John Boyd**. 1840–1921, Scottish veterinary surgeon, who devised the first successful pneumatic tyre.

dunnage (ˈdʌnɪdʒ) *n* loose material used for packing cargo. [C14: from ?]

dunno (dʌˈnəʊ, də-) *Sl.* contraction of (I) do not know.

dunnock (ˈdʌnək) *n* another name for a hedge sparrow. [C15: from DUN² + -OCK]

dunny (ˈdʌnɪ) *n, pl* **dunnies**. **1** *Scot. dialect*. a cellar or basement. **2** *Austral. & NZ inf.* a lavatory, esp. one which is outside. [C20: from ?]

Dunsinane ★ (dʌnˈsɪnən) *n* a hill in central Scotland, in the Sidlaw Hills: the ruined fort at its summit is regarded as Macbeth's castle. Height: 308 m (1012 ft).

> **USAGE NOTE** The pronunciation ˈdʌnsɪˌneɪn is used in Shakespeare's *Macbeth* for the purposes of rhyme.

Duns Scotus ★ (ˈdʌnz ˈskɒtəs) *n* **John**. ?1265–1308, Scottish scholastic theologian and Franciscan priest: opposed the teachings of St Thomas Aquinas.

Dunstable ★ (ˈdʌnstəbəl) *n* an industrial town in SE central England, in Bedfordshire. Pop.: 49 666 (1991).

Dunstan ★ (ˈdʌnstən) *n* **Saint**. ?909–988 A.D., English prelate; archbishop of Canterbury (959–988). Feast day: May 19.

duo (ˈdjuːəʊ) *n, pl* **duos** or **dui** (ˈdjuːiː). **1** *Music*. **1a** a pair of performers. **1b** a duet. **2** a pair of actors, etc. **3** *Inf.* a pair of closely connected individuals. [C16: via It. from L: two]

duo- *combining form.* indicating two. [from L]

duodecimal (ˌdjuːəʊˈdɛsɪməl) *adj* **1** relating to twelve or twelfths. ◆ *n* **2** a twelfth. **3** one of the numbers used in a duodecimal number system.
▸ ˌduo'decimally *adv*

duodecimo (ˌdjuːəʊˈdɛsɪˌməʊ) *n, pl* **duodecimos**. **1** Also called: **twelvemo**. a book size resulting from folding a sheet of paper into twelve leaves. **2** a book of this size. [C17: from L *in duodecimō* in twelfth]

duodenum (ˌdjuːəʊˈdiːnəm) *n, pl* **duodena** (-nə) *or* **duodenums**. the first part of the small intestine, between the stomach and the jejunum. [C14: from Med. L, from *intestinum duodenum digitorum* intestine of twelve fingers' length]
▸ ˌduo'denal *adj*

duologue *or US* (*sometimes*) **duolog** (ˈdjuːəˌlɒg) *n* **1** a part or all of a play in which the speaking roles are limited to two actors. **2** a less common word for **dialogue**.

duopoly (djuːˈɒpəlɪ) *n, pl* **duopolies**. a situation in which control of a commodity or service in a particular market is vested in two producers or suppliers.
▸ du,opo'listic *adj*

dup. *abbrev. for* duplicate.

dupe (djuːp) *n* **1** a person who is easily deceived. ◆ *vb* **dupes, duping, duped**. **2** (*tr*) to deceive; cheat; fool. [C17: from F, from OF *duppe*, contraction of *de huppe* (a) hoopoe; from the bird's reputation for stupidity]
▸ **'dupable** *adj* ▸ **'duper** *n*

duple (ˈdjuːpəl) *adj* **1** a less common word for **double**. **2** *Music*. (of time or music) having two beats in a bar. [C16: from L *duplus* twofold, double]

duplex (ˈdjuːplɛks) *n* **1** *US & Canad.* a duplex apartment or house. **2** *Biochem.* a double-stranded region in a nucleic acid molecule. ◆ *adj* **3** having two parts. **4** having pairs of components of independent but identical function. **5** permitting the transmission of simultaneous signals in both directions. [C19: from L: twofold, from *duo* two + *-plex* -FOLD]
▸ du'plexity *n*

duplex apartment *n US & Canad.* an apartment on two floors.

duplex house *n US & Canad.* a house divided into two separate dwellings. Also called (US): **semidetached**.

duplicate *adj* (ˈdjuːplɪkɪt). **1** copied exactly from an original. **2** identical. **3** existing as a pair or in pairs. ◆ *n* (ˈdjuːplɪkɪt). **4** an exact copy. **5** something additional of the same kind. **6** two exact copies (esp. in **in duplicate**). ◆ *vb* (ˈdjuːplɪˌkeɪt), **duplicates, duplicating, duplicated**. (*tr*) **7** to make a replica of. **8** to do or make again. **9** to make in a pair; make double. [C15: from L *duplicāre* to double, from *duo* two + *plicāre* to fold]
▸ **'duplicable** *adj*

duplication (ˌdjuːplɪˈkeɪʃən) *n* **1** the act of duplicating or the state of being duplicated. **2** a copy; duplicate. **3** *Genetics*. a mutation in which there are two or more copies of a gene or of a segment of a chromosome.

duplicator (ˈdjuːplɪˌkeɪtə) *n* an apparatus for making replicas of an original, such as a machine using a stencil wrapped on an ink-loaded drum.

duplicity (djuːˈplɪsɪtɪ) *n, pl* **duplicities**. deception; double-dealing. [C15: from OF *duplicite*, from LL *duplicitās* a being double, from L DUPLEX]

du Pré ★ (dʊ ˈpreɪ) *n* **Jacqueline**. 1945–87, British cellist. Multiple sclerosis ended her performing career (1973).

Dupré ★ (French dypre) *n* **Marcel**. 1886–1971, French organist and composer, noted as an improviser.

Duque de Caxias ★ (Portuguese ˈduːke də kəˈʃiəʃ) *n* a city in SE Brazil. Pop.: 325 903 (1991).

Dur. *abbrev. for* Durham.

durable (ˈdjʊərəbəl) *adj* long-lasting; enduring. [C14: from OF, from L *dūrābilis*, from *dūrāre* to last]
▸ ˌdura'bility *n* ▸ **'durably** *adv*

durable goods *pl n* goods that require infrequent replacement. Also called: **durables**.

dural (ˈdjʊərəl) *adj* relating to or affecting the dura mater.

Duralumin (djuˈræljumɪn) *n Trademark*. a light strong

aluminium alloy containing copper, silicon, magnesium, and manganese.

dura mater ('djʊərə 'meɪtə) *n* the outermost and toughest of the three membranes covering the brain and spinal cord. Often shortened to **dura**. [C15: from Med. L: hard mother]

duramen (djʊ'reɪmɛn) *n* another name for **heartwood**. [C19: from L: hardness, from *dūrāre* to harden]

Durán ★ (dju'ræn) *n* **Roberto**. born 1951, Panamanian boxer.

durance ('djʊərəns) *n Arch. or literary.* **1** imprisonment. **2** duration. [C15: from OF, from *durer* to last, from L *dūrāre*]

Durango ★ (dju'ræŋɡəʊ; *Spanish* du'raŋɡo) *n* **1** a state in N central Mexico: high plateau, with the Sierra Madre Occidental in the west; irrigated agriculture (esp. cotton) and rich mineral resources. Capital: Durango. Pop.: 1 430 964 (1995 est.). Area: 119 648 sq. km (46 662 sq. miles). **2** a city in NW central Mexico, capital of Durango state: mining centre. Pop.: 348 036 (1990). Official name: **Victoria de Durango**.

Durante ★ (də'ræntɪ) *n* **Jimmy**, known as *Schnozzle*. 1893–1980, US comedian.

Duras ★ (*French* dyra) *n* **Marguerite** (margərit), real name *Marguerite Donnadieu*. 1914–96, French novelist born in Indochina. Her works include the script for the film *Hiroshima mon amour* (1960).

duration (dju'reɪʃən) *n* the length of time that something lasts or continues. [C14: from Med. L *dūrātiō*, from L *dūrāre* to last]
▸ **du'rational** *adj*

durative ('djʊərətɪv) *Grammar.* ◆ *adj* **1** denoting an aspect of verbs that includes the imperfective and the progressive. ◆ *n* **2a** the durative aspect of a verb. **2b** a verb in this aspect.

Durban ★ ('dɜːbᵊn) *n* a port in E South Africa, in E Natal on the Indian Ocean: University of Natal (1909); resort and industrial centre, with oil refineries, shipbuilding yards, etc. Pop.: 715 669 (1991).

durbar ('dɜːbɑː, ˌdɜː'bɑː) *n* a (formerly) the court of a native ruler or a governor in India. **b** a levee at such a court. [C17: from Hindi *darbār*, from Persian, from *dar* door + *bār* entry, audience]

Dürer ★ (*German* 'dyːrər) *n* **Albrecht** ('albrɛçt). 1471–1528, German Renaissance painter and engraver.

duress (dju'rɛs, djuə-) *n* **1** compulsion by use of force or threat; coercion (often in **under duress**). **2** imprisonment. [C14: from OF *duresse*, from L *dūritia* hardness, from *dūrus* hard]

Durga Puja (ˌdʊəɡə 'puːdʒə) *n* another name for **Navaratri**. [from Sanskr. *Durga* (Hindu goddess) and *puja* worship]

Durham ★ ('dʌrəm) *n* **1** a county of NE England, on the North Sea: rises to the N Pennines in the west: contains three unitary authorities. Administrative centre: Durham. Pop. (including unitary authorities): 874 809 (1994 est.). Area (including unitary authorities): 2722 sq. km (1051 sq. miles). Abbrev.: **Dur. 2** a city in NE England, administrative centre of Co. Durham, on the River Wear: Norman cathedral; 11th-century castle (founded by William the Conqueror), now occupied by the University of Durham (1832). Pop.: 36 937 (1991). **3** a variety of shorthorn cattle.

during ('djʊərɪŋ) *prep* **1** concurrently with (some other activity). **2** within the limit of (a period of time). [C14: from *duren* to last, ult. from L *dūrāre* to last]

Durkheim ★ ('dɜːkhaɪm; *French* dyrkɛm) *n* **Émile** (emil). 1858–1917, French sociologist, whose pioneering works include *De la Division du travail social* (1893).

durmast *or* **durmast oak** ('dɜːˌmɑːst) *n* a large Eurasian oak tree with lobed leaves and sessile acorns. Also called: **sessile oak**. [C18: prob. from DUN² + MAST²]

durra ('dʌrə) *n* an Old World variety of sorghum, cultivated for grain and fodder. [C18: from Ar. *dhurah* grain]

Durrell ★ ('dʌrəl) *n* **1 Gerald (Malcolm)**, 1925–95, British zoologist and writer: his books include *My Family and Other Animals* (1956). **2** his brother, **Lawrence (George)**. 1912–90, British poet and novelist; author of *The Alexan-*

dria Quartet of novels, consisting of *Justine* (1957), *Balthazar* (1958), *Mountolive* (1958), and *Clea* (1960).

Dürrenmatt ★ (*German* 'dyrənmat) *n* **Friedrich** ('friːdrɪç). 1921–90, Swiss dramatist and novelist, whose works include the plays *The Visit* (1956) and *The Physicists* (1962).

durry ('dʌrɪ) *n, pl* **durries**. *Austral. sl.* a cigarette. [from *durrie* a type of Indian carpet]

durst (dɜːst) *vb* an archaic past tense of **dare**.

durum *or* **durum wheat** ('djʊərəm) *n* a variety of wheat with a high gluten content, used chiefly to make pastas. [C20: from NL *trīticum dūrum*, lit.: hard wheat]

Duse ★ (*Italian* 'duːze) *n* **Eleonora** (ˌɛliə'nɔːrə). 1858–1924, Italian actress, noted as a tragedienne.

Dushanbe ★ (duːˈʃɑːnbɪ) *n* the capital of Tajikistan; a cultural centre. Pop.: 524 000 (1994 est.). Former name (1929–61): **Stalinabad**.

dusk (dʌsk) *n* **1** the darker part of twilight. **2** *Poetic.* gloom; shade. ◆ *adj* **3** *Poetic.* shady; gloomy. ◆ *vb* **4** *Poetic.* to make or become dark. [OE *dox*]

dusky ('dʌskɪ) *adj* **duskier, duskiest. 1** dark in colour; swarthy or dark-skinned. **2** dim.
▸ **'duskily** *adv* ▸ **'duskiness** *n*

Düsseldorf ★ ('dʊsəlˌdɔːf; *German* 'dʏsəldɔrf) *n* an industrial city in W Germany, capital of North Rhine-Westphalia, on the Rhine: commercial centre of the Rhine-Ruhr industrial area. Pop.: 572 638 (1995 est.).

dust (dʌst) *n* **1** dry fine powdery material, such as particles of dirt, earth, or pollen. **2** a cloud of such fine particles. **3a** the mortal body of man. **3b** the corpse of a dead person. **4** the earth; ground. **5** *Inf.* a disturbance; fuss (esp. in **kick up a dust, raise a dust**). **6** something of little worth. **7** short for **gold dust. 8** ashes or household refuse. **9** **dust and ashes**. something that is very disappointing. **10** **shake the dust off** (*or* **from**) **one's feet**. to depart angrily or contemptuously. **11** **throw dust in the eyes of**. to confuse or mislead. ◆ *vb* **12** (*tr*) to sprinkle or cover (something) with (dust or some other powdery substance). **13** to remove dust (from) by wiping, sweeping, or brushing. **14** *Arch.* to make or become dirty with dust. ◆ See also **dust down, dust-up**. [OE *dūst*]
▸ **'dustless** *adj*

dustbin ('dʌstˌbɪn) *n* a large, usually cylindrical container for rubbish, esp. one used by a household. US and Canad. names: **garbage can, trash can**.

dust bowl *n* a semiarid area in which the surface soil is exposed to wind erosion.

Dust Bowl ★ *n* **the**. the area of the south central US that became denuded of topsoil by wind erosion during the droughts of the mid-1930s.

dustcart ('dʌstˌkɑːt) *n* a road vehicle for collecting refuse. US and Canad. name: **garbage truck**.

dust cover *n* **1** another name for **dustsheet. 2** another name for **dust jacket. 3** a Perspex cover for the turntable of a record player.

dust devil *n* a strong miniature whirlwind that whips up dust, litter, leaves, etc., into the air.

dust down *vb* (*tr, adv*). **1** to remove dust from by brushing or wiping. **2** to reprimand severely.
▸ **dusting down** *n*

duster ('dʌstə) *n* **1** a cloth used for dusting. US name: **dust cloth. 2** a machine for blowing out dust. **3** a person or thing that dusts.

dusting-powder *n* fine powder (such as talcum powder) used to absorb moisture, etc.

dust jacket *or* **cover** *n* a removable paper cover used to protect a bound book.

dustman ('dʌstmən) *n, pl* **dustmen**. *Brit.* a man whose job is to collect domestic refuse.

dustpan ('dʌstˌpæn) *n* a short-handled hooded shovel into which dust is swept from floors, etc.

dustsheet ('dʌstˌʃiːt) *n Brit.* a large cloth used to protect furniture from dust.

dust storm *n* a windstorm that whips up clouds of dust.

dust-up *Inf.* ◆ *n* **1** a fight or argument. ◆ *vb* **dust up. 2** (*tr, adv*) to attack (someone).

★ people and places

dusty ('dʌstɪ) *adj* **dustier, dustiest. 1** covered with or involving dust. **2** like dust. **3** (of a colour) tinged with grey; pale. **4 give** (*or* **get**) **a dusty answer.** to give (*or* get) an unhelpful or bad-tempered reply.
► '**dustily** *adv* ► '**dustiness** *n*

Dutch (dʌtʃ) *n* **1** the language of the Netherlands. **2 the Dutch.** (*functioning as pl*) the natives, citizens, or inhabitants of the Netherlands. **3** See **double Dutch. 4 in Dutch.** *Sl.* in trouble. ♦ *adj* **5** of the Netherlands, its inhabitants, or their language. ♦ *adv* **6 go Dutch.** *Inf.* to share expenses equally.

Dutch auction *n* an auction in which the price is lowered by stages until a buyer is found.

Dutch barn *n Brit.* a farm building consisting of a steel frame and a curved roof.

Dutch courage *n* **1** false courage gained from drinking alcohol. **2** alcoholic drink.

Dutch door *n* the US and Canad. name for **stable door.**

Dutch East Indies ★ *n* **the.** a former name (1798–1945) of **Indonesia.** Also called: **Netherlands East Indies.**

Dutch elm disease *n* a fungal disease of elm trees characterized by withering of the foliage and stems and eventual death of the tree.

Dutch Guiana *or* **Netherlands Guiana** ★ *n* the former name of **Surinam.**

Dutchman ('dʌtʃmən) *n, pl* **Dutchmen. 1** a native, citizen, or inhabitant of the Netherlands. **2** *S. African derog.* an Afrikaner.

Dutch medicine *n S. African.* patent medicine, esp. made of herbs.

Dutch New Guinea ★ *n* a former name (until 1963) of **Irian Jaya.**

Dutch oven *n* **1** an iron or earthenware container with a cover, used for stews, etc. **2** a metal box, open in front, for cooking in front of an open fire.

Dutch treat *n Inf.* an entertainment, meal, etc., where each person pays for himself.

Dutch uncle *n Inf.* a person who criticizes or reproves frankly and severely.

Dutch West Indies ★ *pl n* **the.** a former name of the **Netherlands Antilles.**

duteous ('djuːtɪəs) *adj Formal or arch.* dutiful; obedient.
► '**duteously** *adv*

dutiable ('djuːtɪəbəl) *adj* (of goods) liable to duty.
► ,**dutia'bility** *n*

dutiful ('djuːtɪful) *adj* **1** exhibiting or having a sense of duty. **2** characterized by or resulting from a sense of duty: *a dutiful answer.*

duty ('djuːtɪ) *n, pl* **duties. 1** a task or action that a person is bound to perform for moral or legal reasons. **2** respect or obedience due to a superior, older persons, etc. **3** the force that binds one morally or legally to one's obligations. **4** a government tax, esp. on imports. **5** *Brit.* **5a** the quantity of work for which a machine is designed. **5b** a measure of the efficiency of a machine. **6a** a job or service allocated. **6b** (*as modifier*): *duty rota.* **7 do duty for.** to act as a substitute for. **8 on** (*or* **off**) **duty.** at (*or* not at) work. [C13: from Anglo-F *dueté*, from OF *deu* DUE]

duty-bound *adj* morally obliged.

duty-free *adj, adv* **1** with exemption from customs or excise duties. ♦ *n* **2** goods sold in a duty-free shop.

duty-free shop *n* a shop, esp. one at an airport or on board a ship, that sells perfume, tobacco, etc., at duty-free prices.

duumvir (dju:'ʌmvə) *n, pl* **duumvirs** *or* **duumviri** (-vɪˌriː). **1** *Roman history.* one of two coequal magistrates. **2** either of two men who exercise a joint authority. [C16: from L, from *duo* two + *vir* man]
► **duumvirate** (dju:'ʌmvɪrɪt) *n*

Duvalier ★ (*French* dyvalje) *n* **1 François** (frɑ̃swa), known as *Papa Doc.* 1907–71, president of Haiti (1957–71). **2** his son, **Jean-Claude** (ʒɑ̃klod), known as *Baby Doc.* born 1951, Haitian statesman; president of Haiti 1971–86; deposed and exiled.

duvet ('duːveɪ) *n* **1** another name for **continental quilt. 2** Also called: **duvet jacket.** a down-filled jacket. [C18: from F, from earlier *dumet,* from OF *dum* DOWN²]

dux (dʌks) *n* (esp. in Scottish schools) the top pupil in a class or school. [L: leader]

DV *abbrev. for:* **1** Deo volente. [L: God willing] **2** Douay Version (of the Bible).

DVD *abbrev. for* Digital Versatile Disk or (formerly) Digital Video Disk.

Dvina ★ (*Russian* dvi'na) *n* **1 Northern.** a river in NW Russia, formed by the confluence of the Sukhona and Yug Rivers and flowing northwest to Dvina Bay in the White Sea. Length: 750 km (466 miles). Russian name: **Severnaya Dvina. 2 Western.** a river in E Europe, rising in the Valdai Hills in W Russia, and flowing south and southwest then northwest to the Gulf of Riga in Latvia. Length: 1021 km (634 miles). Russian name: **Zapadnaya Dvina** ('zapədnəjə). Latvian name: **Daugava.**

Dvina Bay *or* **Dvina Gulf** ★ *n* an inlet of the White Sea, off the coast of NW Russia.

Dvinsk ★ (dvinsk) *n* transliteration of the former Russian name for **Daugavpils.**

DVLA *abbrev. for* Driver and Vehicle Licensing Agency.

Dvořák ★ ('dvɔːʒæk; *Czech* 'dvɔrʒaːk) *n* **Antonín** ('antɔnjiːn), known as *Anton Dvořák.* 1841–1904, Czech composer; noted for the *Symphony No. 9 From the New World* (1893).

dwaal (dwɑːl) *n S. African.* a state of befuddlement; daze. [from Afrik. *dwaal* wander]

dwale (dweɪl) *n* another name for **deadly nightshade.** [C14: ?from ON]

dwarf (dwɔːf) *n, pl* **dwarfs** *or* **dwarves** (dwɔːvz). **1** an abnormally undersized person. **2a** an animal or plant much below the average height for the species. **2b** (*as modifier*): *a dwarf tree.* **3** (in folklore) a small ugly manlike creature, often possessing magical powers. **4** *Astron.* short for **dwarf star.** ♦ *vb* **5** to become or cause to become comparatively small in size, importance, etc. **6** (*tr*) to stunt the growth of. [OE *dweorg*]
► '**dwarfish** *adj*

dwarf star *n* any unevolved star, such as the sun, lying in the main sequence of the Hertzsprung-Russell diagram. Also called: **main sequence star.** See also **red dwarf, white dwarf.**

dwell (dwel) *vb* **dwells, dwelling, dwelt** *or* **dwelled.** (*intr*) **1** *Formal, literary.* to live as a permanent resident. **2** to live (in a specified state): *to dwell in poverty.* ♦ *n* **3** a regular pause in the operation of a machine. [OE *dwellan* to seduce, get lost]
► '**dweller** *n*

dwelling ('dwelɪŋ) *n Formal, literary.* a place of residence.

dwell on *or* **upon** *vb* (*intr, prep*) to think, speak, or write at length about.

dwelt (dwelt) *vb* a past tense and past participle of **dwell.**

dwindle ('dwɪndəl) *vb* **dwindles, dwindling, dwindled.** to grow or cause to grow less in size, intensity, or number. [C16: from OE *dwīnan* to waste away]

Dy *the chemical symbol for* dysprosium.

dyad ('daɪæd) *n* **1** *Maths.* an operator that is the unspecified product of two vectors. **2** an atom or group that has a valency of two. **3** a group of two; couple. [C17: from LL *dyas,* from Gk *duas* two]
► **dy'adic** *adj*

Dyak *or* **Dayak** ('daɪæk) *n, pl* **Dyaks, Dyak** *or* **Dayaks, Dayak.** a member of a Malaysian people of Borneo. [from Malay: upcountry, from *darat* land]

dybbuk ('dɪbək) *n, pl* **dybbuks** *or* **dybbukkim.** *Judaism.* (in folklore) the soul of a dead sinner that has transmigrated into the body of a living person. [from Yiddish: devil, from Heb.]

dye (daɪ) *n* **1** a staining or colouring substance. **2** a liquid that contains a colouring material and can be used to stain fabrics, skins, etc. **3** the colour produced by dyeing. ♦ *vb* **dyes, dyeing, dyed. 4** (*tr*) to impart a colour or stain to (fabric, hair, etc.) by or as if by the application of a dye. [OE *dēagian,* from *dēag* a dye]
► '**dyable** *or* '**dyeable** *adj* ► '**dyer** *n*

★ people and places

dyed-in-the-wool *adj* **1** uncompromising or unchanging in attitude, opinion, etc. **2** (of a fabric) made of dyed yarn.

dyeing ('daɪɪŋ) *n* the process or industry of colouring yarns, fabric, etc.

dyestuff ('daɪ,stʌf) *n* a substance that can be used as a dye or which yields a dye.

Dyfed ★ ('dʌved) *n* a former county in SW Wales, formed in 1974 from Cardiganshire, Pembrokeshire, and Carmarthenshire, replaced in 1996 by Pembrokeshire, Carmarthenshire, and Ceredigion.

dying ('daɪɪŋ) *vb* **1** the present participle of **die**[1]. ◆ *adj* **2** relating to or occurring at the moment of death: *a dying wish.*

dyke[1] *or* **dike** (daɪk) *n* **1** an embankment constructed to prevent flooding, keep out the sea, or confine a river to a particular course. **2** a ditch or watercourse. **3** a bank made of earth alongside a ditch. **4** *Scot.* a wall, esp. a drystone wall. **5** a barrier or obstruction. **6** a wall-like mass of igneous rock in older sedimentary rock. **7** *Austral. & NZ inf.* a lavatory. ◆ *vb* **dykes, dyking, dyked. 8** (*tr*) to protect, enclose, or drain (land) with a dyke. [C13: from OE *dic* ditch]

dyke[2] *or* **dike** (daɪk) *n Sl.* a lesbian. [C20: from ?]

Dylan ★ ('dɪlən) *n* **Bob.** real name *Robert Allen Zimmerman.* born 1941, US rock singer and songwriter. His albums include *Blonde on Blonde* (1966), *Blood on the Tracks* (1974), and *Time Out of Mind* (1997).

dynamic (daɪ'næmɪk) *adj* **1** of or concerned with energy or forces that produce motion, as opposed to *static.* **2** of or concerned with dynamics. **3** Also: **dynamical.** characterized by force of personality, ambition, energy, etc. **4** *Computing.* (of a memory) needing its contents refreshed periodically. [C19: from F *dynamique*, from Gk *dunamikos* powerful, from *dunamis* power, from *dunasthai* to be able]
▸ **dy'namically** *adv*

dynamics (daɪ'næmɪks) *n* **1** (*functioning as sing*) the branch of mechanics concerned with the forces that change or produce the motions of bodies. **2** (*functioning as sing*) the branch of mechanics that includes statics and kinetics. **3** (*functioning as sing*) the branch of any science concerned with forces. **4** (*functioning as pl*) those forces that produce change in any field or system. **5** (*functioning as pl*) *Music.* **5a** the various degrees of loudness called for in performance. **5b** directions and symbols used to indicate degrees of loudness.

dynamism ('daɪnə,mɪzəm) *n* **1** *Philosophy.* any of several theories that attempt to explain phenomena in terms of an immanent force or energy. **2** the forcefulness of an energetic personality.
▸ **'dynamist** *n* ▸ **,dyna'mistic** *adj*

dynamite ('daɪnə,maɪt) *n* **1** an explosive consisting of nitroglycerine mixed with an absorbent. **2** *Inf.* a spectacular or potentially dangerous person or thing. ◆ *vb* **dynamites, dynamiting, dynamited. 3** (*tr*) to mine or blow up with dynamite. [C19 (coined by Alfred Nobel): from DYNAMO- + -ITE[1]]
▸ **'dyna,miter** *n*

dynamo ('daɪnə,məʊ) *n, pl* **dynamos. 1** a device for converting mechanical energy into electrical energy. **2** *Inf.* an energetic hard-working person. [C19: short for *dynamoelectric machine*]

dynamo- *or sometimes before a vowel* **dynam-** *combining form.* indicating power: *dynamite.* [from Gk, from *dunamis* power]

dynamoelectric (,daɪnəməʊɪ'lektrɪk) *or* **dynamo-electrical** *adj* of or concerned with the interconversion of mechanical and electrical energy.

dynamometer (,daɪnə'mɒmɪtə) *n* an instrument for measuring power or force.

dynamotor ('daɪnə,məʊtə) *n* an electrical machine having two independent armature windings of which one acts as a motor and the other a generator: used to convert direct current into alternating current.

dynast ('dɪnəst, -æst) *n* a ruler, esp. a hereditary one.

[C17: from L *dynastēs*, from Gk, from *dunasthai* to be powerful]

dynasty ('dɪnəstɪ) *n, pl* **dynasties. 1** a sequence of hereditary rulers. **2** any sequence of powerful leaders of the same family. [C15: via LL from Gk, from *dunastēs* DYNAST]
▸ **dynastic** (dɪ'næstɪk) *adj*

dyne (daɪn) *n* the cgs unit of force; the force that imparts an acceleration of 1 centimetre per second per second to a mass of 1 gram. 1 dyne is equivalent to 10^{-5} newton or 7.233×10^{-5} poundal. [C19: from F, from Gk *dunamis* power, force]

dys- *prefix* **1** diseased, abnormal, or faulty. **2** difficult or painful. [via L from Gk *dus-*]

dysentery ('dɪs°ntrɪ) *n* infection of the intestine marked by severe diarrhoea with the passage of mucus and blood. [C14: via L from Gk, from *dusentera*, lit.: bad bowels, from DYS- + *enteron* intestine]
▸ **dysenteric** (,dɪs°n'terɪk) *adj*

dysfunction (dɪs'fʌŋkʃən) *n* **1** *Med.* any disturbance or abnormality in the function of an organ or part. **2** (esp. of a family) failure to show the characteristics or fulfil the purposes accepted as normal or beneficial.

dysfunctional (dɪs'fʌŋkʃən°l) *adj* **1** *Med.* (of an organ or part) not functioning normally. **2** (esp. of a family) characterized by a breakdown of normal or beneficial relationships between the members of a group.

dysgraphia (dɪs'græfɪə) *n* inability to write correctly, caused by disease of part of the brain.

dyslexia (dɪs'leksɪə) *n* a developmental disorder which can cause learning difficulty in one or more of the areas of reading, writing, and numeracy. [C19: NL, from DYS- + -lexia, from Gk *lexis* word]
▸ **dyslectic** (dɪs'lektɪk) *adj* ▸ **dys'lexic** *adj, n*

dysmenorrhoea *or esp. US* **dysmenorrhea** (,dɪsmenə'rɪə) *n* abnormally difficult or painful menstruation. [C19: from DYS- + Gk *mēn* month + *rhoia* a flowing]

dyspepsia (dɪs'pepsɪə) *n* indigestion or upset stomach. [C18: from L, from Gk *duspepsia*, from DYS- + *pepsis* digestion]

dyspeptic (dɪs'peptɪk) *adj* **1** relating to or suffering from dyspepsia. **2** irritable. ◆ *n* **3** a person suffering from dyspepsia.

dysphasia (dɪs'feɪzɪə) *n* a disorder of language caused by a brain lesion.
▸ **dys'phasic** *adj, n*

dysphoria (dɪs'fɔːrɪə) *n* a feeling of being ill at ease. [C20: NL, from Gk DYS- + -phoria, from *pherein* to bear]

dyspnoea *or US* **dyspnea** (dɪsp'niːə) *n* difficulty in breathing or in catching the breath. [C17: via L from Gk *duspnoia*, from DYS- + *pnoē* breath, from *pnein* to breathe]
▸ **dysp'noeal, dysp'noeic** *or US* **dysp'neal, dysp'neic** *adj*

dysprosium (dɪs'prəʊsɪəm) *n* a metallic element of the lanthanide series: used in laser materials and as a neutron absorber in nuclear control rods. Symbol: Dy; atomic no.: 66; atomic wt.: 162.50. [C20: NL, from Gk *dusprositos* difficult to get near + -IUM]

dysthymia (dɪs'θaɪmɪə) *n Psychiatry.* the characteristics of the neurotic and introverted, including anxiety, depression, and compulsive behaviour. [C19: NL, from Gk *dusthumia*, from DYS- + *thumos* mind]
▸ **dys'thymic** *adj*

dysthymic disorder *n* a psychiatric disorder characterized by generalized depression that lasts for at least a year.

dystrophy ('dɪstrəfɪ) *n* any of various bodily disorders, characterized by wasting of tissues. See also **muscular dystrophy.** [C19: NL *dystrophia*, from DYS- + Gk *trophē* food]
▸ **dystrophic** (dɪs'trɒfɪk) *adj*

dz. *abbrev.* for dozen.

Dzaudzhikau ★ (dzaʊdʒi'kaʊ) *n* the former name (1944–54) of **Ordzhonikidze.**

dzo (zəʊ) *n, pl* **dzos** *or* **dzo.** a variant spelling of **zo.**

Dzungaria ★ (dzʊŋ'gɑːrɪə, zʊŋ-) *n* a variant transliteration of the Chinese name for **Junggar Pendi.**

★ people and places

Ee

e or **E** (iː) *n, pl* **e's, E's,** or **Es. 1** the fifth letter and second vowel of the English alphabet. **2** any of several speech sounds represented by this letter, as in *he, bet,* or *below*.

e *symbol for:* **1** *Maths.* a transcendental number used as the base of natural logarithms. Approximate value: 2.718 282... **2** electron.

E *symbol for:* **1** *Music.* **1a** the third note of the scale of C major. **1b** the major or minor key having this note as its tonic. **2** earth. **3** East. **4** English. **5** Egypt(ian). **6** *Physics.* **6a** energy. **6b** electromotive force. **7** exa-. **8a** a person without a regular income, or who is dependent on the state on a long-term basis because of unemployment, sickness, old age, etc. **8b** (*as modifier*): *E worker.* ◆ See also **occupation groupings. 9** the drug ecstasy.

e. *abbrev. for* engineer(ing).

E. *abbrev. for* Earl.

e- *prefix* electronic: *e-mail; e-money*.

E- *prefix* used with numbers indicating a standardized system within the European Union, as of food additives. See also **E number.**

ea. *abbrev. for* each.

each (iːtʃ) *determiner* **1a** every (one) of two or more considered individually: *each day; each person*. **1b** (*as pron*): *each gave according to his ability.* ◆ *adv* **2** for, to, or from each one; apiece: *four apples each.* [OE *ǣlc*]

> **USAGE NOTE** *Each* is a singular pronoun and should be used with a singular form of a verb: *each of the candidates was* (not *were*) *interviewed separately*. See also at **either.**

Eadred ★ ('ɛdrɪd) *n* died 955 A.D., king of England (946–55): regained Northumbria (954) from the Norwegian king Eric Bloodaxe.

eager ('iːgə) *adj* **1** (*postpositive;* often foll. by *to* or *for*) impatiently desirous (of); anxious or avid (for). **2** characterized by or feeling expectancy or great desire: *an eager look*. **3** *Arch.* biting; sharp. [C13: from OF *egre,* from L *acer* sharp, keen]
> ▸ **'eagerly** *adv* ▸ **'eagerness** *n*

eager beaver *n Inf.* a person who displays conspicuous diligence.

eagle ('iːg°l) *n* **1** any of various birds of prey having large broad wings and strong soaring flight. Related adj: **aquiline. 2** a representation of an eagle used as an emblem, etc., esp. representing power: *the Roman eagle.* **3** a standard, seal, etc., bearing the figure of an eagle. **4** *Golf.* a score of two strokes under par for a hole. **5** a former US gold coin worth ten dollars. ◆ *vb* **6** *Golf.* to score two strokes under par for a hole. [C14: from OF *aigle,* from OProvençal *aigla,* from L *aquila*]

eagle-eyed *adj* having keen or piercing eyesight.

eagle-hawk *n* a large brown Australian eagle. Also called: **wedge-tailed eagle.**

eagle owl *n* a large Eurasian owl with brownish speckled plumage and large ear tufts.

eaglet ('iːglɪt) *n* a young eagle.

Eakins ★ ('iːkɪnz) *n* **Thomas.** 1844–1916, US painter of portraits and sporting life: a noted realist.

ealdorman ('ɔːldəmən) *n, pl* **ealdormen.** an official of Anglo-Saxon England, appointed by the king, and responsible for law and order in his shire and for leading local militia. [OE *ealdor* lord + MAN]

Ealing ★ ('iːlɪŋ) *n* a borough of W Greater London, formed in 1965 from Acton, Ealing, and Southall. Pop.: 289 800 (1994 est.). Area: 55 sq. km (21 sq. miles).

-ean *suffix forming adjectives and nouns.* a variant of **-an:** *Caesarean.*

ear[1] (ɪə) *n* **1** the organ of hearing and balance in higher vertebrates (see **middle ear**). Related adj: **aural. 2** the outermost cartilaginous part of the ear in mammals, esp. man. **3** the sense of hearing. **4** sensitivity to musical sounds, poetic diction, etc.: *he has an ear for music.* **5** attention; consideration (esp. in **give ear to, lend an ear**). **6** an object resembling the external ear. **7 all ears.** very attentive; listening carefully. **8 a thick ear.** *Inf.* a blow on the ear. **9 fall on deaf ears.** to be ignored or pass unnoticed. **10 in one ear and out the other.** heard but unheeded. **11 keep** (*or* **have**) **one's ear to the ground.** to be or try to be well informed about current trends and opinions. **12 out on one's ear.** *Inf.* dismissed unceremoniously. **13 play by ear. 13a** *Inf.* to act according to the demands of a situation; improvise. **13b** to perform a musical piece on an instrument without written music. **14 turn a deaf ear.** to be deliberately unresponsive. **15 up to one's ears.** *Inf.* deeply involved, as in work or debt. [OE *ēare*]
> ▸ **eared** *adj* ▸ **'earless** *adj*

ear[2] (ɪə) *n* **1** the part of a cereal plant, such as wheat or barley, that contains the seeds, grains, or kernels. ◆ *vb* **2** (*intr*) (of cereal plants) to develop such parts. [OE *ēar*]

earache ('ɪəˌeɪk) *n* pain in the ear.

eardrum ('ɪəˌdrʌm) *n* the nontechnical name for **tympanic membrane.**

earful ('ɪəful) *n Inf.* **1** something heard or overheard. **2** a rebuke or scolding.

Earhart ★ ('ɛəˌhɑːt) *n* **Amelia.** 1898–1937, US aviator: the first woman to fly the Atlantic (1928). She disappeared on a Pacific flight (1937).

earl (ɜːl) *n* (in Britain) a nobleman ranking below a marquess and above a viscount. Female equivalent: **countess.** [OE *eorl*]
> ▸ **'earldom** *n*

Earl Grey *n* a variety of China tea flavoured with oil of bergamot.

Earl Marshal *n* an officer of the English peerage who presides over the College of Heralds and organizes royal processions and other important ceremonies.

early ('ɜːlɪ) *adj, adv* **earlier, earliest. 1** before the expected or usual time. **2** occurring in or characteristic of the first part of a period or sequence. **3** occurring in or characteristic of a period far back in time. **4** occurring in the near future. **5 in the early days.** during the first years of any enterprise, such as marriage. [OE *ǣrlīce,* from *ǣr* ERE + *-līce* -LY[2]]
> ▸ **'earliness** *n*

early closing *n Brit.* the shutting of shops in a town one afternoon each week.

Early English *n* a style of architecture used in England in the 12th and 13th centuries, characterized by lancet arches and plate tracery.

early music *n* **1** music of the Middle Ages and Renaissance, sometimes also including music of the baroque and early classical periods. ◆ (*modifier*) **early-music. 2** of or denoting an approach to musical performance emphasizing the use of period instruments and historically researched scores and playing techniques: *the early-music movement.*

early warning *n* advance notice of some impending event.

earmark ('ɪəˌmɑːk) *vb* (*tr*) **1** to set aside or mark out for a specific purpose. **2** to make an identification mark on the ear of (a domestic animal). ◆ *n* **3** such a mark of identification. **4** any distinguishing mark or characteristic.

earmuff ('ɪəˌmʌf) *n* one of a joined pair of pads of fur or cloth for keeping the ears warm.

earn (ɜːn) *vb* **1** to gain or be paid (money or other payment) in return for work or service. **2** (*tr*) to acquire or deserve through behaviour or action. **3** (*tr*) (of securities, investments, etc.) to gain (interest, profit, etc.). [OE *earnian*]

earned income *n* income derived from paid employment.

earner ('ɜːnə) *n* **1** a person who earns money. **2** *Sl.* an activity or thing that produces income, esp. illicitly: *a nice little earner.*

earnest[1] (ɜːnɪst) *adj* **1** serious in mind or intention. **2** characterized by sincerity of intention. **3** demanding or receiving serious attention. ♦ *n* **4 in earnest**. with serious or sincere intentions. [OE *eornost*]
▶ 'earnestly *adv* ▶ 'earnestness *n*

earnest[2] ('ɜːnɪst) *n* **1** a part of something given in advance as a guarantee of the remainder. **2** Also called: **earnest money**. *Contract law.* something given, usually a nominal sum of money, to confirm a contract. **3** any token of something to follow. [C13: from OF *erres* pledges, pl of *erre* earnest money, from L *arrha*, from *arrabō* pledge, from Gk *arrabon*, from Heb. *'ērābhōn* pledge]

earnings ('ɜːnɪŋz) *pl n* **1** money or other payment earned. **2** the profits of an enterprise.

EAROM ('ɪərɒm) *n Computing. acronym for* electrically alterable read only memory.

earphone ('ɪə,fəʊn) *n* a device for converting electric currents into sound waves, held close to or inserted into the ear.

ear piercing *n* **1** the making of a hole in the lobe of an ear, using a sterilized needle, so that earrings may be worn fastened in the hole. ♦ *adj* **ear-piercing. 2** so loud or shrill as to hurt the ears.

earplug (ɪə,plʌg) *n* a piece of soft material placed in the ear to keep out noise or water.

earring ('ɪə,rɪŋ) *n* an ornament for the ear, usually clipped onto the lobe or fastened through a hole pierced in the lobe.

earshot ('ɪə,ʃɒt) *n* the range or distance within which sound may be heard (esp. in **out of earshot**, etc.)

ear-splitting *adj* so loud or shrill as to hurt the ears.

earth (ɜːθ) *n* **1** (*sometimes cap.*) the third planet from the sun, the only planet on which life is known to exist. Related adjs.: **terrestrial, telluric. 2** the inhabitants of this planet: *the whole earth rejoiced.* **3** the dry surface of this planet; land; ground. **4** the loose soft material on the surface of the ground that consists of disintegrated rock particles, mould, clay, etc.; soil. **5** worldly or temporal matters as opposed to the concerns of the spirit. **6** the hole in which a burrowing animal, esp. a fox, lives. **7** *Chem.* See **rare earth, alkaline earth. 8** Also (US and Canad.): **ground. 8a** a connection between an electric circuit or device and the earth, which is at zero potential. **8b** a terminal to which this connection is made. **9** (*modifier*) *Astrol.* of or relating to a group of three signs of the zodiac: Taurus, Virgo, and Capricorn. **10 come back** *or* **down to earth**. to return to reality from a fantasy or daydream. **11 on earth**. used as an intensifier in **what on earth, who on earth**, etc. **12 run to earth. 12a** to hunt (an animal, esp. a fox) to its earth and trap it there. **12b** to find (someone) after hunting. ♦ *vb* **13** Also (US and Canad.): **ground**. (*tr*) to connect (a circuit, device, etc.) to earth. ♦ See also **earth up**. [OE *eorthe*]

earthbound ('ɜːθ,baʊnd) *adj* **1** confined to the earth. **2** heading towards the earth.

earth closet *n* a type of lavatory in which earth is used to cover excreta.

earthen ('ɜːθən) *adj* (*prenominal*) **1** made of baked clay: *an earthen pot.* **2** made of earth.

earthenware ('ɜːθən,wɛə) *n* **a** vessels, etc., made of baked clay. **b** (*as adj*): *an earthenware pot.*

earth-grazer *n* an asteroid in an orbit that takes it close to the earth. Also called: **near-earth asteroid.**

earthly ('ɜːθlɪ) *adj* **earthlier, earthliest. 1** of or characteristic of the earth as opposed to heaven; materialistic; worldly. **2** (*usually with a negative*) *Inf.* conceivable or possible (in **not an earthly** (**chance**), etc.).
▶ 'earthliness *n*

earthman ('ɜːθ,mæn) *n, pl* **earthmen.** (esp. in science fiction) an inhabitant or native of the earth. Also called **earthling.**

earthnut ('ɜːθ,nʌt) *n* **1** a perennial umbelliferous plant of Europe and Asia, having edible dark brown tubers. **2** any of various plants having an edible root, tuber, or underground pod, such as the peanut or truffle.

earthquake ('ɜːθ,kweɪk) *n* a series of vibrations at the earth's surface caused by movement along a fault plane volcanic activity, etc. Related adj: **seismic.**

earth science *n* any of various sciences, such as geology and geography, that are concerned with the structure, age, etc., of the earth.

earth up *vb* (*tr, adv*) to cover (part of a plant) with soil to protect from frost, light, etc.

earthward ('ɜːθwəd) *adj* **1** directed towards the earth ♦ *adv* **2** a variant of **earthwards.**

earthwards ('ɜːθwədz) *or* **earthward** *adv* towards the earth.

earthwork ('ɜːθ,wɜːk) *n* **1** excavation of earth, as in engineering construction. **2** a fortification made of earth.

earthworm ('ɜːθ,wɜːm) *n* any of numerous worms which burrow in the soil and help aerate and break up the ground.

earthy ('ɜːθɪ) *adj* **earthier, earthiest. 1** of, composed of, or characteristic of earth. **2** unrefined, coarse, or crude.
▶ 'earthily *adv* ▶ 'earthiness *n*

ear trumpet *n* a trumpet-shaped instrument held to the ear: an old form of hearing aid.

earwax ('ɪə,wæks) *n* the nontechnical name for **cerumen.**

earwig ('ɪə,wɪg) *n* **1** any of various insects that typically have an elongated body with small leathery forewings, semicircular membranous hindwings, and curved forceps at the tip of the abdomen. ♦ *vb* **earwigs, earwigging earwigged. 2** (*intr*) *Inf.* to eavesdrop. **3** (*tr*) *Arch.* to attempt to influence (a person) by private insinuation. [OE *ēarwicga*, from *ēare* ear + *wicga* beetle, insect; prob. from superstition that the insect crept into human ears]

earwigging ('ɪə,wɪgɪŋ) *n Inf.* a scolding or harangue: *I'll give him an earwigging about that.*

ease (iːz) *n* **1** freedom from discomfort, worry, or anxiety. **2** lack of difficulty, labour, or awkwardness. **3** rest, leisure, or relaxation. **4** freedom from poverty; affluence: *a life of ease.* **5** lack of restraint, embarrassment, or stiffness: *ease of manner.* **6 at ease. 6a** *Mil.* (of a standing soldier, etc.) in a relaxed position with the feet apart, rather than at attention. **6b** a command to adopt such a position. **6c** in a relaxed attitude or frame of mind. ♦ *vb* **eases, easing, eased. 7** to make or become less burdensome. **8** (*tr*) to relieve (a person) of worry or care; comfort. **9** (*tr*) to make comfortable or give rest to. **10** (*tr*) to make less difficult; facilitate. **11** to move or cause to move into, out of, etc., with careful manipulation. **12** (when *intr*, often foll. by *off* or *up*) to lessen or cause to lessen in severity, pressure, tension, or strain. **13 ease oneself** *or* **ease nature**. *Arch., euphemistic.* to urinate or defecate. [C13: from OF *aise* ease, opportunity, from L *adjacēns* neighbouring (area); see ADJACENT]
▶ 'easeful *adj*

easel ('iːzᵊl) *n* a frame, usually an upright tripod, for supporting or displaying an artist's canvas, a blackboard, etc. [C17: from Du. *ezel*; ult. from L *asinus* ass]

easement ('iːzmənt) *n* **1** *Property law.* the right enjoyed by a landowner of making limited use of his neighbour's land, as by crossing it to reach his own property. **2** the act of easing or something that brings ease.

easily ('iːzɪlɪ) *adv* **1** with ease; without difficulty or exertion. **2** by far; undoubtedly: *easily the best.* **3** probably; almost certainly.

> **USAGE NOTE** See at **easy.**

easiness ('iːzɪnɪs) *n* **1** the quality or condition of being easy to accomplish, do, obtain, etc. **2** ease or relaxation of manner; nonchalance.

east (iːst) *n* **1** the direction along a parallel towards the sunrise, at 90° to north; the direction of the earth's rotation. **2 the east.** (*often cap.*) any area lying in or towards the east. Related adj: **oriental. 3** (*usually cap.*) *Cards.* the player or position at the table corresponding to east on the compass. ◆ *adj* **4** situated in, moving towards, or facing the east. **5** (esp. of the wind) from the east. ◆ *adv* **6** in, to, or towards the east. **7 back East.** *Canad.* in or to E Canada, esp. east of Quebec. ◆ Symbol: E [OE *ēast*]

ast (iːst) *n* **the. 1** the continent of Asia regarded as culturally distinct from Europe and the West; the Orient. **2** the countries under Communist rule and those under Communist rule until *c.* 1991, lying mainly in the E hemisphere. ◆ *adj* **3** of or denoting the eastern part of a specified country, area, etc.

ast Africa ★ *n* a region of Africa comprising Kenya, Uganda, and Tanzania.
▶ **East African** adj, n

ast Anglia ★ *n* **1** a region of E England south of the Wash: consists of Norfolk and Suffolk, and parts of Essex and Cambridgeshire. **2** an Anglo-Saxon kingdom that consisted of Norfolk and Suffolk in the 6th century A.D.; became a dependency of Mercia in the 8th century.
▶ **East Anglian** adj, n

ast Ayrshire ★ *n* a council area of SE Scotland. Administrative centre: Kilmarnock. Pop.: 123 820 (1996 est.). Area: 1252 sq. km (483 sq. miles).

ast Bengal ★ *n* the part of the former Indian province of Bengal assigned to Pakistan in 1947 (now Bangladesh).
▶ **East Bengali** adj, n

ast Berlin ★ *n* (formerly) the part of Berlin under East German control.
▶ **East Berliner** n

astbound ('iːst,baund) *adj* going or leading towards the east.

astbourne ★ ('iːst,bɔːn) *n* a resort in SE England, in East Sussex on the English Channel. Pop.: 83 200 (1991 est.).

ast by north *n* one point on the compass north of east.

ast by south *n* one point on the compass south of east.

East Cape ★ *n* **1** the easternmost point of New Guinea, on Milne Bay. **2** the easternmost point of New Zealand, on North Island. **3** the former name for Cape **Dezhnev.**

East China Sea ★ *n* part of the N Pacific, between the E coast of China and the Ryukyu Islands.

East Dunbartonshire ★ *n* a council area of central Scotland. Administrative centre: Kirkintilloch. Pop.: 110 220 (1996 est.). Area: 172 sq. km (66 sq. miles).

East End ★ *n* **the.** a densely populated part of E London containing former industrial and dock areas.
▶ **East Ender** n

Easter ('iːstə) *n* **1** a festival of the Christian Church commemorating the Resurrection of Christ: falls on the Sunday following the first full moon after the vernal equinox. **2** Also called: **Easter Sunday, Easter Day.** the day on which this festival is celebrated. **3** the period between Good Friday and Easter Monday. ◆ Related adj: **Paschal.** [OE *ēastre*]

Easter cactus *n* a Brazilian cactus, *Rhipsalidopsis gaertneri*, widely cultivated as an ornamental for its showy red flowers.

Easter egg *n* an egg given to children at Easter, usually a chocolate egg or a hen's egg with its shell painted.

Easter Island ★ *n* an isolated volcanic island in the Pacific, 3700 km (2300 miles) west of Chile, of which it is a dependency: discovered on Easter Sunday, 1722; annexed by Chile in 1888; noted for the remains of an aboriginal culture, which includes gigantic stone figures. Pop.: 2095 (1989). Area: 166 sq. km (64 sq. miles). Also called: **Rapa Nui.**
▶ **Easter Islander** n

easterly ('iːstəlɪ) *adj* **1** of or in the east. ◆ *adv, adj* **2** towards the east. **3** from the east: *an easterly wind.* ◆ *n, pl* **easterlies. 4** a wind from the east.

eastern ('iːstən) *adj* **1** situated in or towards the east. **2** facing or moving towards the east.

Eastern Cape ★ *n* a province of S South Africa; formed in 1994 from part of the former Cape Province. Capital: Bisho. Pop.: 6 481 300 (1995 est.). Area: 169 000 sq. km (65 483 sq. miles).

Eastern Church *n* **1** any of the Christian Churches of the former Byzantine Empire. **2** any Church owing allegiance to the Orthodox Church. **3** any Church having Eastern forms of liturgy and institutions.

Easterner ('iːstənə) *n* (*sometimes not cap.*) a native or inhabitant of the east of any specified region.

Eastern Ghats ★ *pl n* a mountain range in S India, parallel to the Bay of Bengal: united with the Western Ghats by the Nilgiri Hills; forms the E margin of the Deccan plateau.

eastern hemisphere *n* (*often caps.*) **1** that half of the globe containing Europe, Asia, Africa, and Australia, lying east of the Greenwich meridian. **2** the lands in this, esp. Asia.

Eastern Orthodox Church *n* another name for the **Orthodox Church.**

Eastern Townships ★ *n* an area of central Canada, in S Quebec: consists of 11 townships south of the St Lawrence.

Eastertide ('iːstə,taɪd) *n* the Easter season.

East Flanders ★ *n* a province of W Belgium: low-lying, with reclaimed land in the northeast: textile industries. Capital: Ghent. Pop.: 1 349 382 (1995 est.). Area: 2979 sq. km (1150 sq. miles).

East Germany ★ *n* a former republic in N central Europe: established in 1949 and declared a sovereign state by the Soviet Union in 1954; Communist regime replaced by a multiparty democracy in 1989; reunited with West Germany in 1990. Official name: **German Democratic Republic.** Abbrevs.: **DDR, GDR.** See also **Germany.**
▶ **East German** adj, n

East Indies ★ *pl n* **the. 1** the Malay Archipelago, including or excluding the Philippines. **2** SE Asia in general.

easting ('iːstɪŋ) *n* **1** *Naut.* the net distance eastwards made by a vessel moving towards the east. **2** *Cartography.* the distance eastwards of a point from a given meridian indicated by the first half of a map grid reference.

East Kilbride ★ (kɪl'braɪd) *n* a town in W Scotland, in South Lanarkshire near Glasgow: designated a new town in 1947. Pop.: 70 422 (1991).

Eastleigh ★ ('iːst,liː) *n* a town in S England, in S Hampshire: railway engineering industry. Pop.: 49 934 (1991).

East London ★ *n* a port in S South Africa, on the Indian Ocean. Pop.: 102 325 (1991).

East Lothian ★ *n* a council area and historic county of E central Scotland, formerly part of Lothian region (1975–96). Administrative centre: Haddington. Pop.: 85 640 (1996 est.). Area: 678 sq. km (262 sq. miles).

Eastman ★ ('iːstmən) *n* George. 1854–1932, US manufacturer of photographic equipment: noted for the introduction of roll film and developments in colour photography.

east-northeast *n* **1** the point on the compass or the direction midway between northeast and east. ◆ *adj, adv* **2** in, from, or towards this direction.

East Pakistan ★ *n* the former name (until 1971) of **Bangladesh.**
▶ **East Pakistani** adj, n

East Prussia ★ *n* a former province of NE Germany on the Baltic Sea: separated in 1919 from the rest of Germany by the Polish Corridor and Danzig: in 1945 Poland received the south part, the Soviet Union the north. German name: **Ostpreussen** (ost'prɔysən).
▶ **East Prussian** adj, n

East Renfrewshire ★ *n* a council area of W central Scotland, formerly part of Strathclyde region (1975–96). Administrative centre: Giffnock. Pop.: 86 780 (1996 est.). Area: 173 sq. km (67 sq. miles).

East Riding of Yorkshire ★ *n* a county of NE England, a historical division of Yorkshire, formerly part of

---

★ people and places

Humberside (1974–96); includes Hull unitary authority. Administrative centre: Beverley. Pop.: 595 400 (1996 est.). Area: 1819 sq. km (704 sq. miles).

east-southeast n **1** the point on the compass or the direction midway between east and southeast. ◆ adj, adv **2** in, from, or towards this direction.

East Sussex ★ n a county of SE England; includes Brighton and Hove unitary authority: mainly undulating agricultural land, with the South Downs and seaside resorts in the south. Administrative centre: Lewes. Pop.: 726 500 (1994 est.). Area: 1795 sq. km (693 sq. miles).

eastward ('i:stwəd) adj **1** situated or directed towards the east. ◆ adv **2** a variant of **eastwards**. ◆ n **3** the eastward part, direction, etc.
▶ **'eastwardly** adv, adj

eastwards ('i:stwədz) or **eastward** adv towards the east.

Eastwood ★ ('i:stwʊd) n Clint. born 1930, US film actor and director. His films include The Good The Bad and The Ugly (1966) and as actor and director Unforgiven (1993) and Absolute Power (1997).

easy ('i:zɪ) adj easier, easiest. **1** not requiring much labour or effort; not difficult. **2** free from pain, care, or anxiety. **3** not restricting; lenient: easy laws. **4** tolerant and undemanding; easy-going: an easy disposition. **5** readily influenced; pliant: an easy victim. **6** not constricting; loose: an easy fit. **7** not strained or extreme; moderate: an easy pace. **8** Inf. ready to fall in with any suggestion made; not predisposed: he is easy about what to do. **9** Sl. sexually available. ◆ adv **10** Inf. in an easy or relaxed manner. **11 easy does it.** Inf. go slowly and carefully; be careful. **12 go easy.** (usually imperative; often foll. by on) to exercise moderation. **13 stand easy.** Mil. a command to soldiers standing at ease that they may relax further. **14 take it easy. 14a** to avoid stress or undue hurry. **14b** to remain calm. [C12: from OF aisié, p.p. of aisier to relieve, EASE]

> **USAGE NOTE** Easy is not used as an adverb by careful speakers and writers except in certain set phrases: to take it easy; easy does it. Where a fixed expression is not involved, the usual adverbial form of easily is preferred: this polish goes on more easily (not easier) than the other.

easy-care adj (esp. of a fabric or garment) hard-wearing and requiring no special treatment during washing, etc.

easy chair n a comfortable upholstered armchair.

easy-going ('i:zɪ'gəʊɪŋ) adj **1** relaxed in manner or attitude; excessively tolerant. **2** moving at a comfortable pace: an easy-going horse.

easy meat n Inf. **1** someone easily seduced or deceived. **2** something easy.

easy money n **1** money made with little effort, sometimes dishonestly. **2** Commerce. money that can be borrowed at a low interest rate.

Easy Street n (sometimes not caps.) Inf. a state of financial security.

eat (i:t) vb eats, eating, ate, eaten. **1** to take into the mouth and swallow (food, etc.), esp. after biting and chewing. **2** (tr; often foll. by away or up) to destroy as if by eating: the damp had eaten away the woodwork. **3** (often foll. by into) to use up or waste: taxes ate into his inheritance. **4** (often foll. by into or through) to make (a hole, passage, etc.) by eating or gnawing: rats ate through the floor. **5** to take or have (a meal or meals): we eat at six. **6** (tr) to include as part of one's diet: he doesn't eat fish. **7** (tr) Inf. to cause to worry: what's eating you? ◆ See also **eat out, eats, eat up**. [OE etan]
▶ **'eater** n

eatable ('i:təb°l) adj fit or suitable for eating; edible.

eatables ('i:təb°lz) pl n food.

eating ('i:tɪŋ) n **1** food, esp. in relation to quality or taste: this fruit makes excellent eating. ◆ adj **2** suitable for eating uncooked: eating apples. **3** relating to or for eating: an eating house.

eat out vb (intr, adv) to eat away from home, esp. in a restaurant.

eats (i:ts) pl n Inf. articles of food; provisions.

eat up vb (adv, mainly tr) **1** (also intr) to eat or consume entirely. **2** Inf. to listen to with enthusiasm or appreciation: the audience ate up his every word. **3** (often passive) Inf. to affect grossly: she was eaten up by jealousy. **4** Inf. to travel (a distance) quickly: we just ate up the miles.

eau de Cologne (ˌəʊ də kəˈləʊn) n See **cologne**. [F, lit. water of Cologne]

eau de nil (ˌəʊ də ˈniːl) n, adj (of) a pale yellowish-green colour. [F, lit.: water of (the) Nile]

eau de vie (ˌəʊ də ˈviː) n brandy or other spirits. [F, lit. water of life]

eaves (i:vz) pl n the edge of a roof that projects beyond the wall. [OE efes]

eavesdrop ('i:vzˌdrɒp) vb eavesdrops, eavesdropping, eavesdropped. (intr) to listen secretly to the private conversation of others. [C17: back formation from evesdropper, from OE yfesdrype water dripping from the eaves]
▶ **'eaves,dropper** n

ebb (ɛb) vb (intr) **1** (of tide water) to flow back or recede. Cf. **flow** (sense 8). **2** to fall away or decline. ◆ n **3a** the flowing back of the tide from high to low water or the period in which this takes place. **3b** (as modifier): the ebb tide. Cf. **flood** (sense 3). **4 at a low ebb.** in a state of weakness or decline. [OE ebba]

Ebbinghaus ★ ('ɛbɪŋhaʊs) n Hermann ('hɛrman). 1850–1909, German experimental psychologist who under took the first systematic large-scale studies of memory.

Ebbw Vale ★ ('ɛbu: 'veɪl) n a town in S Wales, in Blaenau Gwent: a former coal-mining centre. Pop. 19 484 (1991).

EBCDIC ('ɛpsɪˌdɪk) n acronym for extended binary-coded decimal-interchange code: a computer code for representing alphanumeric characters.

Ebert ★ (German 'e:bərt) n Friedrich ('fri:drɪç). 1871–1925, German Social Democratic statesman; first president of the German Republic (1919–25).

ebon ('ɛb°n) adj, n a poetic word for **ebony**. [C14: from hebenus; see EBONY]

ebonite ('ɛbəˌnaɪt) n another name for **vulcanite**.

ebonize or **ebonise** ('ɛbəˌnaɪz) vb ebonizes, ebonizing, ebonized or ebonises, ebonising, ebonised. (tr) to stain or otherwise finish in imitation of ebony.

ebony ('ɛbənɪ) n, pl ebonies. **1** any of various tropical and subtropical trees that have hard dark wood. **2** the wood of such a tree. **3a** a black colour. **3b** (as adj): an ebony skin. [C16 hebeny, from LL, from Gk, from ebenos ebony, from Egyptian]

Ebor. ('i:bɔ:) abbrev. for Eboracensis. [L.: (Archbishop) of York]

Eboracum ★ (i:'bɒrəkəm, ˌi:bɔ:'rɑ:kəm) n the Roman name for **York**[1] (sense 1).

EBRD abbrev. for European Bank for Reconstruction and Development.

Ebro ★ ('i:brəʊ; Spanish 'eβro) n the second largest river in Spain, rising in the Cantabrian Mountains and flowing southeast to the Mediterranean. Length: 910 km (565 miles).

ebullient (ɪ'bʌljənt, ɪ'bʊl-) adj **1** overflowing with enthusiasm or excitement. **2** boiling. [C16: from L ēbullīre to bubble forth, be boisterous, from bullīre to BOIL[1]]
▶ e'**bullience** or e'**bulliency** n

ebulliometer (ɪˌbʌlɪ'ɒmɪtə) n Physics. a device used to determine the boiling point of a solution.

ebullition (ˌɛbə'lɪʃən) n **1** the process of boiling. **2** a sudden outburst, as of intense emotion. [C16: from LL ēbullītiō; see EBULLIENT]

EC abbrev. for: **1** European Community (now called European Union). **2** (in London postal codes) East Central.

ec- combining form. out from; away from: eccentric; ecdysis. [from Gk ek (before a vowel ex) out of, away from; see EX-[1]]

ECB abbrev. for European Central Bank.

Ecbatana ★ (ɛk'bætənə) n an ancient city in Iran, on the site of modern Hamadān; capital of Media and royal residence of the Persians and Parthians.

ccentric (ɪk'sɛntrɪk) *adj* **1** deviating or departing from convention; irregular or odd. **2** situated away from the centre or the axis. **3** not having a common centre: *eccentric circles*. **4** not precisely circular. ◆ *n* **5** a person who deviates from normal forms of behaviour. **6** a device for converting rotary motion to reciprocating motion. [C16: from Med. L *eccentricus*, from Gk *ekkentros*, from *ek*-EX-¹ + *kentron* centre]
▶ ec'centrically *adv*

ccentricity (ˌɛksɛn'trɪsɪtɪ) *n*, *pl* **eccentricities**. **1** unconventional or irregular behaviour. **2** the state of being eccentric. **3** deviation from a circular path or orbit. **4** *Geom.* a number that expresses the shape of a conic section. **5** the degree of displacement of the geometric centre of a part from the true centre, esp. of the axis of rotation of a wheel.

ccl. *or* **eccles.** *abbrev. for* ecclesiastic(al).

ccles¹ ('ɛk²lz) ★ *n* a town in NW England, in Salford unitary authority, in Greater Manchester. Pop.: 36 000 (1991).

ccles² ('ɛk²lz) ★ *n* Sir **John Carew.** 1903–97, Australian physiologist: shared the Nobel prize for physiology (1963) with A. L. Hodgkin and A. F. Huxley for their work on conduction of nervous impulses.

ccles. *or* **Eccl.** *Bible. abbrev. for* Ecclesiastes.

cclesiastic (ɪˌkliːzɪ'æstɪk) *n* **1** a clergyman or other person in holy orders. ◆ *adj* **2** of or associated with the Christian Church or clergy.

cclesiastical (ɪˌkliːzɪ'æstɪk²l) *adj* of or relating to the Christian Church.
▶ ec,clesi'astically *adv*

cclesiasticism (ɪˌkliːzɪ'æstɪˌsɪzəm) *n* exaggerated attachment to the practices or principles of the Christian Church.

cclesiology (ɪˌkliːzɪ'ɒlədʒɪ) *n* **1** the study of the Christian Church. **2** the study of Church architecture and decoration.
▶ ecclesio'logical (ɪˌkliːzɪə'lɒdʒɪk²l) *adj*

ccrine ('ɛkrɪn) *adj* of or denoting glands that secrete externally, esp. the sweat glands. Cf. **apocrine**. [from Gk *ekkrinein*, from *ek*- EC- + *krinein* to separate]
▶ ec'crinology (ˌɛkrɪ'nɒlədʒɪ) *n*

cdemic (ɛk'dɛmɪk) *adj* not indigenous or endemic; foreign: *an ecdemic disease.*

cdysis ('ɛkdɪsɪs) *n*, *pl* **ecdyses** (-ˌsiːz). the periodic shedding of the cuticle in insects and other arthropods or the outer epidermal layer in reptiles. [C19: NL, from Gk *ekdusis*, from *ekduein* to strip, from *ek*- EX-¹ + *duein* to put on]

CG *abbrev. for:* **1** electrocardiogram. **2** electrocardiograph.

chelon ('ɛʃəˌlɒn) *n* **1** a level of command, responsibility, etc. (esp. in **the upper echelons**). **2** *Mil.* **2a** a formation in which units follow one another but are offset sufficiently to allow each unit a line of fire ahead. **2b** a group formed in this way. ◆ *vb* **3** to assemble in echelon. [C18: from F *échelon*, lit.: rung of a ladder, from OF *eschiele* ladder, from L *scāla*]

chidna (ɪk'ɪdnə) *n*, *pl* **echidnas** *or* **echidnae** (-niː). a spine-covered monotreme mammal of Australia and New Guinea, having a long snout and claws. Also called: **spiny anteater.** [C19: from NL, from L: viper, from Gk *ekhidna*]

chinoderm (ɪ'kaɪnəʊˌdɜːm) *n* any of various marine invertebrates characterized by tube feet, a calcite body-covering, and a five-part symmetrical body. The group includes the starfish, sea urchins, and sea cucumbers.

chinus (ɪ'kaɪnəs) *n*, *pl* **echini** (-naɪ). **1** *Archit.* a moulding between the shaft and the abacus of a Doric column. **2** any sea urchin of the genus *Echinus*, such as the Mediterranean edible sea urchin. [C14: from L, from Gk *ekhinos*]

cho ('ɛkəʊ) *n*, *pl* **echoes**. **1a** the reflection of sound or other radiation by a reflecting medium, esp. a solid object. **1b** the sound so reflected. **2** a repetition or imitation, esp. an unoriginal reproduction of another's

opinions. **3** something that evokes memories. **4** (*sometimes pl*) an effect that continues after the original cause has disappeared: *echoes of the French Revolution.* **5** a person who copies another, esp. one who obsequiously agrees with another's opinions. **6a** the signal reflected by a radar target. **6b** the trace produced by such a signal on a radar screen. ◆ *vb* **echoes, echoing, echoed.** **7** to resound or cause to resound with an echo. **8** (*intr*) (of sounds) to repeat or resound by echoes; reverberate. **9** (*tr*) (of persons) to repeat (words, opinions, etc.) in imitation, agreement, or flattery. **10** (*tr*) (of things) to resemble or imitate (another style, an earlier model, etc.). [C14: via L from Gk *ēkhō*; rel. to Gk *ēkhē* sound]
▶ 'echoing *adj* ▶ 'echoless *adj* ▶ 'echo-ˌlike *adj*

Echo ★ ('ɛkəʊ) *n Greek myth.* a nymph who, spurned by Narcissus, pined away until only her voice remained.

echocardiography (ˌɛkəʊˌkɑːdɪ'ɒɡrəfɪ) *n* examination of the heart using ultrasound techniques.

echo chamber *n* a room with walls that reflect sound. It is used to make acoustic measurements and as a recording studio when echo effects are required. Also called: **reverberation chamber.**

echography (ɛ'kɒɡrəfɪ) *n* medical examination of the internal structures of the body by means of ultrasound.

echoic (ɛ'kəʊɪk) *adj* **1** characteristic of or resembling an echo. **2** onomatopoeic; imitative.

echolalia (ˌɛkəʊ'leɪlɪə) *n Psychiatry.* the tendency to repeat mechanically words just spoken by another person. [C19: from NL, from ECHO + Gk *lalia* talk, chatter]

echolocation (ˌɛkəʊləʊ'keɪʃən) *n* determination of the position of an object by measuring the time taken for an echo to return from it and its direction.

echo sounder *n* a navigation device that determines depth by measuring the time taken for a pulse of sound to reach the sea bed or a submerged object and for the echo to return.
▶ **echo sounding** *n*

echovirus *or* **ECHO virus** ('ɛkəʊˌvaɪrəs) *n* any of a group of viruses that can cause symptoms of mild meningitis, the common cold, or infections of the intestinal and respiratory tracts. [C20: from initials of *Enteric Cytopathic Human Orphan* ("orphan" because orig. believed to be unrelated to any disease) + VIRUS]

Eck ★ (ɛk) *n* **Johann** (jo'han), original name *Johann Mayer*. 1486–1543, German Roman Catholic theologian; opponent of Luther and the Reformation.

Eckert ★ ('ɛkət) *n* **John Presper.** 1919–95, US electronics engineer: built the first electronic computer with John W. Mauchly in 1946.

éclair (eɪ'klɛə, ɪ'klɛə) *n* a finger-shaped cake of choux pastry, usually filled with cream and covered with chocolate. [C19: from F, lit.: lightning (prob. because it does not last long)]

eclampsia (ɪ'klæmpsɪə) *n Pathol.* a toxic condition that sometimes develops in the last three months of pregnancy, characterized by high blood pressure, weight gain, and convulsions. [C19: from NL, from Gk *eklampsis* a shining forth]

éclat (eɪ'klɑː) *n* **1** brilliant or conspicuous success, effect, etc. **2** showy display; ostentation. **3** social distinction. **4** approval; acclaim; applause. [C17: from F, from *éclater* to burst]

eclectic (ɪ'klɛktɪk, ɛ'klɛk-) *adj* **1** selecting from various styles, ideas, methods, etc. **2** composed of elements drawn from a variety of sources, styles, etc. ◆ *n* **3** a person who favours an eclectic approach. [C17: from Gk *eklektikos*, from *eklegein* to select, from *legein* to gather]
▶ e'clectically *adv* ▶ e'clecticism *n*

eclipse (ɪ'klɪps) *n* **1** the total or partial obscuring of one celestial body by another (**total eclipse** *or* **partial eclipse**). A **solar eclipse** occurs when the moon passes between the sun and the earth; a **lunar eclipse** when the earth passes between the sun and the moon. **2** the period of time during which such a phenomenon occurs. **3** any dimming or obstruction of light. **4** a loss of importance, power, fame, etc., esp. through overshadowing by another. ◆ *vb* **eclipses, eclipsing, eclipsed.** (*tr*) **5** to cause an eclipse of. **6** to cast a shadow upon; obscure. **7** to overshadow or

surpass. [C13: back formation from OE *eclypsis*, from L, from Gk *ekleipsis* a forsaking, from *ekleipein* to abandon]
▸ e'**clipser** n

eclipsing binary n a binary star whose orbital plane lies in or near the line of sight so that one component is regularly eclipsed by its companion.

ecliptic (ɪ'klɪptɪk) n 1 *Astron.* **1a** the great circle on the celestial sphere representing the apparent annual path of the sun relative to the stars. **1b** (*as modifier*): *the ecliptic plane.* **2** an equivalent great circle on the terrestrial globe. ◆ *adj* **3** of or relating to an eclipse.
▸ e'**cliptically** *adv*

eclogue ('ɛklɒg) n a pastoral or idyllic poem, usually in the form of a conversation. [C15: from L *ecloga* short poem, collection of extracts, from Gk *eklogē* selection]

eclosion (ɪ'kləʊʒən) n the emergence of an insect larva from the egg or an adult from the pupal case. [C19: from F, from *éclore* to hatch, ult. from L *exclūdere* to shut out]

Eco ★ ('ɛkəʊ) n Umberto. born 1932, Italian writer. His novels include *The Name of the Rose* (1981) and *The Island of the Day Before* (1995).

eco- *combining form.* denoting ecology or ecological: *ecocide; ecosphere.*

ecocentric (ˌiːkəʊ'sɛntrɪk) *adj* having a serious concern for environmental issues: *ecocentric management.*

ecofriendly ('iːkəʊˌfrɛndlɪ) *adj* having a beneficial effect on the environment or at least not causing environmental damage.

ecol. *abbrev. for:* **1** ecological. **2** ecology.

E. coli (iː'kəʊlaɪ) n short for *Escherichia coli*, see **Escherichia**.

ecological (ˌiːkə'lɒdʒɪk°l) *adj* **1** of or relating to ecology. **2** (of a practice, policy, product, etc.) tending to benefit or cause minimal damage to the environment.
▸ ˌeco'**logically** *adv*

ecology (ɪ'kɒlədʒɪ) n **1** the study of the relationships between living organisms and their environment. **2** the set of relationships of a particular organism with its environment. [C19: from G *Ökologie*, from Gk *oikos* house (hence, environment)]
▸ e'**cologist** n

econ. *abbrev. for:* **1** economical. **2** economics. **3** economy.

econometrics (ɪˌkɒnə'mɛtrɪks) n (*functioning as sing*) the application of mathematical and statistical techniques to economic theories.
▸ eˌcono'**metric** or eˌcono'**metrical** *adj* ▸ **econometrician** (ɪˌkɒnəmə'trɪʃən) or **econometrist** (ˌiːkə'nɒmətrɪst, -ˌɛkə-) n

economic (ˌiːkə'nɒmɪk, ˌɛkə-) *adj* **1** of or relating to an economy, economics, or finance. **2** *Brit.* capable of being produced, operated, etc., for profit; profitable. **3** concerning or affecting material resources or welfare: *economic pests.* **4** concerned with or relating to the necessities of life; utilitarian. **5** a variant of **economical. 6** *Inf.* inexpensive; cheap.

economical (ˌiːkə'nɒmɪk°l, ˌɛkə-) *adj* **1** using the minimum required; not wasteful. **2** frugal; thrifty. **3** a variant of **economic** (senses 1–4). **4** *Euphemistic.* deliberately withholding information (esp. in **economical with the truth**).
▸ ˌeco'**nomically** *adv*

economic indicator n a statistical measure representing an economic variable: *the retail price index is an economic indicator of the actual level of prices.*

economic migrant or **refugee** n a person who emigrates from a poor country to a developed one in the hope of improving his or her standard of living.

economics (ˌiːkə'nɒmɪks, ˌɛkə-) n **1** (*functioning as sing*) the social science concerned with the production and consumption of goods and services and the analysis of the commercial activities of a society. **2** (*functioning as pl*) financial aspects.

economic sanctions *pl* n any actions taken by one nation or group of nations to harm the economy of another nation or group, often to force a political change.

economist (ɪ'kɒnəmɪst) n a specialist in economics.

economize or **economise** (ɪ'kɒnəˌmaɪz) *vb* econo-

mizes, economizing, economized or economises, economisin economised. (often foll. by *on*) to limit or reduce (expens waste, etc.).
▸ eˌconomi'**zation** or eˌconomi'**sation** n

economy (ɪ'kɒnəmɪ) n, *pl* **economies. 1** careful manage ment of resources to avoid unnecessary expenditure c waste; thrift. **2** a means or instance of this; saving. **3** spa ing, restrained, or efficient use. **4a** the complex of acti ities concerned with the production, distribution, an consumption of goods and services. **4b** a particular typ or branch of this: *a socialist economy.* **5** the managemen of the resources, finances, income, and expenditure of community, business enterprise, etc. **6a** a class of trave in aircraft, cheaper and less luxurious than first class. **6** (*as modifier*): *economy class.* **7** (*modifier*) purporting t offer a larger quantity for a lower price: *economy pack.* the orderly interplay between the parts of a system c structure. [C16: via L from Gk *oikonomia* domestic mar agement, from *oikos* house + *-nomia*, from *nemein* to manage]

ecosphere ('iːkəʊˌsfɪə, 'ɛkəʊ-) n the parts of the universe esp. on earth, where life can exist.

écossaise (ˌeɪkɒ'seɪz) n **1** a lively dance in two-fou time. **2** the tune for such a dance. [C19: F, lit.: Scottis (dance)]

ecosystem ('iːkəʊˌsɪstəm, 'ɛkəʊ-) n *Ecology.* a system ir volving the interactions between a community and it nonliving environment. [C20: from ECO- + SYSTEM]

ecoterrorist ('iːkəʊˌtɛrərɪst) n a person who uses vic lence in order to achieve environmentalist aims.

ecotourism ('iːkəʊˌtʊərɪzəm) n tourism which is de signed to contribute to the protection of the enviror ment or at least minimize damage to it, often involvin travel to areas of natural interest in developing countrie or participation in environmental projects.
▸ 'eco,**tourist** n

ecru ('ɛkruː, 'eɪkruː) n, *adj* (of) a greyish-yellow to a ligh greyish colour. [C19: from F, from *é-* (intensive) + *cr* raw, from L *crūdus*; see CRUDE]

ecstasy ('ɛkstəsɪ) n, *pl* **ecstasies. 1** (*often pl*) a state of ex alted delight, joy, etc.; rapture. **2** intense emotion of an kind: *an ecstasy of rage.* **3** *Psychol.* overpowering emotio sometimes involving temporary loss of consciousnes often associated with mysticism. **4** *Sl.* 3,4-methylened oxymethamphetamine: a powerful drug that acts as stimulant and can produce hallucinations. [C14: fror OF via Med. L from Gk *ekstasis* displacement, trance from *ex-* out + *histanai* to cause to stand]

ecstatic (ɛk'stætɪk) *adj* **1** in a trancelike state of raptur or delight. **2** showing or feeling great enthusiasm. ◆ *n* a person who has periods of intense trancelike joy.
▸ ec'**statically** *adv*

ECT *abbrev. for* electroconvulsive therapy.

ecto- *combining form.* indicating outer, outside. [fror Gk *ektos* outside, from *ek, ex* out]

ectoblast ('ɛktəʊˌblæst) n another name for **ectoderm**.
▸ ˌecto'**blastic** *adj*

ectoderm ('ɛktəʊˌdɜːm) or **exoderm** n the outer gern layer of an animal embryo, which gives rise to epidermi and nervous tissue.
▸ ˌecto'**dermal** or ˌecto'**dermic** *adj*

ectomorph ('ɛktəʊˌmɔːf) n a type of person having body build characterized by thinness, weakness, and lack of weight.
▸ ˌecto'**morphic** *adj* ▸ 'ecto,**morphy** n

-ectomy n *combining form.* indicating surgical excision o a part: *appendectomy.* [from NL *-ectomia*, from Gk *ek-* ou + -TOMY]

ectopic pregnancy (ɛk'tɒpɪk) n *Pathol.* the abnorma development of a fertilized egg outside the uterus, usu ally within a Fallopian tube.

ectoplasm ('ɛktəʊˌplæzəm) n **1** *Cytology.* the outer laye of cytoplasm. **2** *Spiritualism.* the substance supposedl emanating from the body of a medium during trances.
▸ ˌecto'**plasmic** *adj*

ECU (also 'eɪkjuː, 'ɛkjuː) *abbrev. for* European Currency Unit.

★ people and places

:cua. *abbrev. for* Ecuador.

:cuador ★ ('ɛkwə,dɔ:) *n* a republic in South America, on the Pacific: under the Incas when Spanish colonization began in 1532; gained independence in 1822; declared a republic in 1830. It consists chiefly of a coastal plain in the west, separated from the densely forested upper Amazon basin (Oriente) by ranges and plateaus of the Andes. Official language: Spanish; Quechua is also widely spoken. Religion: Roman Catholic. Currency: sucre. Capital: Quito. Pop.: 11 937 000 (1997). Area: 283 560 sq. km (109 483 sq. miles).
 ▸ ,Ecua'dorian *or* ,Ecua'doran *adj, n*

•cumenical, oecumenical (,i:kju'mɛnɪk°l, ,ɛk-) *or* **ecumenic, oecumenic** *adj* **1** of or relating to the Christian Church throughout the world, esp. with regard to its unity. **2** tending to promote unity among Churches. [C16: via LL from Gk *oikoumenikos*, from *oikein* to inhabit, from *oikos* house]
 ▸ ,ecu'menically *or* ,oecu'menically *adv*

•cumenism (ɪ'kju:mə,nɪzəm, 'ɛkjʊm-), **ecumenicism** (,i:kju'mɛnɪ,sɪzəm, ,ɛk-) *or* **ecumenicalism** (,i:kju'mɛnɪkə,lɪzəm, ,ɛk-) *n* the aim of unity among all Christian churches throughout the world.

•czema ('ɛksɪmə) *n Pathol.* a skin inflammation with lesions that scale, crust, or ooze a serous fluid, often accompanied by intense itching. [C18: from NL, from Gk *ekzema*, from *ek-* out + *zein* to boil]
 ▸ **eczematous** (ɛk'sɛmətəs) *adj*

:d. *abbrev. for:* **1** edited. **2** (*pl* **eds.**) edition. **3** (*pl* **eds.**) editor. **4** education.

ed[1] *suffix.* forming the past tense of most English verbs. [OE *-de, -ede, -ode, -ade*]

ed[2] *suffix.* forming the past participle of most English verbs. [OE *-ed, -od, -ad*]

ed[3] *suffix forming adjectives from nouns.* possessing or having the characteristics of: *salaried; red-blooded.* [OE *-ede*]

:dam ★ ('i:dæm) *n* **1** a town in the NW Netherlands, in North Holland province, on the IJsselmeer: cheese, light manufacturing. Pop.: 24 572 (1989). **2** a hard round mild-tasting Dutch cheese with a red outside covering.

:dberg ★ ('ɛdbɜ:g) *n* **Stefan.** born 1966, Swedish tennis player: Wimbledon champion 1988, 1990.

:DC *abbrev. for* European Defence Community.

:dda ('ɛdə) *n* **1** Also called: **Elder Edda, Poetic Edda.** a 12th-century collection of mythological Old Norse poems. **2** Also called: **Younger Edda, Prose Edda.** a treatise on versification together with a collection of Scandinavian myths, legends, and poems (?1222). [C18: ON]
 ▸ **Eddaic** (ɛ'deɪɪk) *adj*

:ddery ★ ('ɛdərɪ) *n* **Patrick,** known as *Pat.* born 1952, Irish jockey.

:ddington ★ ('ɛdɪŋtən) *n* Sir **Arthur Stanley.** 1882–1944, British astronomer, noted for his research on stars.

•ddo ('ɛdəʊ) *n, pl* **eddoes.** another name for **taro.**

•ddy ('ɛdɪ) *n, pl* **eddies. 1** a movement in air, water, or other fluid in which the current doubles back on itself causing a miniature whirlwind or whirlpool. **2** a deviation or disturbance in the main trend of thought, life, etc. ◆ *vb* **eddies, eddying, eddied. 3** to move or cause to move against the main current. [C15: prob. from ON]

:ddy ★ ('ɛdɪ) *n* **Mary Baker.** 1821–1910, US religious leader; founder of the Christian Science movement (1866).

•ddy current *n* an electric current induced in a massive conductor by an alternating magnetic field.

:ddystone Rocks ★ ('ɛdɪstən) *n* a dangerous group of rocks at the W end of the English Channel, southwest of Plymouth: lighthouse.

:de ★ ('eɪdə) *n* a city in the central Netherlands, in Gelderland province. Pop.: 98 220 (1994).

:delman ★ ('ed°lmən) *n* **Gerald Maurice.** born 1929, US biochemist: he shared the Nobel prize for physiology or medicine (1972) with Rodney Porter for determining the structure of antibodies.

•delweiss ('eɪd°l,vaɪs) *n* a small alpine flowering plant having white woolly oblong leaves and a tuft of floral leaves surrounding the flowers. [C19: G, lit.: noble white]

edema (ɪ'di:mə) *n, pl* **edemata** (-mətə). the usual US spelling of **oedema.**

Eden[1] ★ ('i:d°n) *n* **1** Also called: **Garden of Eden.** *Bible.* the garden in which Adam and Eve were placed at the Creation. **2** a place or state of great delight or contentment. [C14: from LL, from Heb. *'ēdhen* place of pleasure]
 ▸ **Edenic** (i:'dɛnɪk) *adj*

Eden[2] ★ ('i:d°n) *n* Sir (**Robert) Anthony,** Earl of Avon. 1897–1977, British Conservative statesman; foreign secretary (1935–38; 1940–45; 1951–55) and prime minister (1955–57). He resigned after the controversy caused by the occupation of the Suez Canal zone by British and French forces (1956).

edentate (i:'dɛntert) *n* **1** any mammal of the order *Edentata,* of tropical Central and South America, which have few or no teeth. The order includes anteaters, sloths, and armadillos. ◆ *adj* **2** of or relating to the order *Edentata.* [C19: from L *ēdentātus* lacking teeth, from *ēdentāre* to render toothless, from *e-* out + *dēns* tooth]

Edessa ★ (ɪ'dɛsə) *n* **1** an ancient city on the N edge of the Syrian plateau, founded as a Macedonian colony by Seleucus I: a centre of early Christianity. Modern name: **Urfa. 2** a market town in Greece: ancient capital of Macedonia. Pop.: 15 980 (1981). Ancient name: **Aegae** ('i:gi:). Modern Greek name: **Edhessa.**

Edgar ★ ('ɛdgə) *n* **1** 944–975 A.D., king of Mercia and Northumbria (957–975) and of England (959–975). **2** ?1074–1107, king of Scotland (1097–1107), fourth son of Malcolm III. He overthrew his uncle Donald to gain the throne. **3** David. born 1948, British dramatist, noted for political plays such as *Destiny* (1976) and *Maydays* (1983).

Edgar Atheling ★ ('æθɪlɪŋ) *n* ?1050–?1125, grandson of Edmund II; Anglo-Saxon pretender to the English throne in 1066.

edge (ɛdʒ) *n* **1** a border, brim, or margin. **2** a brink or verge. **3** a line along which two faces or surfaces of a solid meet. **4** the sharp cutting side of a blade. **5** keenness, sharpness, or urgency. **6** force, effectiveness, or incisiveness: *the performance lacked edge.* **7** a ridge. **8** **have the edge on** *or* **over.** to have a slight advantage or superiority over. **9** **on edge. 9a** nervously irritable; tense. **9b** nervously excited or eager. **10 set (someone's) teeth on edge.** to make (someone) acutely irritated or uncomfortable. ◆ *vb* **edges, edging, edged. 11** (*tr*) to provide an edge or border for. **12** (*tr*) to shape or trim the edge or border of (something). **13** to push (one's way, someone, something, etc.) gradually, esp. edgeways. **14** (*tr*) *Cricket.* to hit (a bowled ball) with the edge of the bat. **15** (*tr*) to sharpen (a knife, etc.). [OE *ecg*]
 ▸ **'edger** *n*

Edgehill ★ (,ɛdʒ'hɪl) *n* a ridge in S Warwickshire: site of the indecisive first battle between Charles I and the Parliamentarians (1642) in the Civil War.

edgeways ('ɛdʒ,weɪz) *or esp. US & Canad.* **edgewise** ('ɛdʒ,waɪz) *adv* **1** with the edge forwards or uppermost. **2** on, by, with, or towards the edge. **3 get a word in edgeways.** (*usually with a negative*) to interrupt a conversation in which someone else is talking incessantly.

Edgeworth ★ ('ɛdʒwɜːθ) *n* **Maria.** 1767–1849, Anglo-Irish novelist: her works include *Castle Rackrent* (1800).

edging ('ɛdʒɪŋ) *n* **1** anything placed along an edge to finish it, esp. as an ornament. **2** the act of making an edge. ◆ *adj* **3** used for making an edge: *edging shears.*

edgy ('ɛdʒɪ) *adj* **edgier, edgiest.** (*usually postpositive*) nervous, irritable, tense, or anxious.
 ▸ **'edgily** *adv* ▸ **'edginess** *n*

edh (ɛð) *or* **eth** (ɛθ, ɛð) *n* a character of the runic alphabet (ð) used to represent the voiced dental fricative as in *then, mother, bathe.*

Edhessa ★ (*Greek* 'ɛðɛsa) *n* transliteration of the Modern Greek name for **Edessa.**

edible ('ɛdɪb°l) *adj* fit to be eaten; eatable. [C17: from LL *edibilis,* from L *edere* to eat]
 ▸ ,edi'bility *n*

edibles ('ɛdɪbᵊlz) *pl n* articles fit to eat; food.

edict ('iːdɪkt) *n* **1** a decree or order issued by any authority. **2** any formal or authoritative command, proclamation, etc. [C15: from L *ēdictum*, from *ēdīcere* to declare] ► e'**dictal** *adj*

edifice ('ɛdɪfɪs) *n* **1** a building, esp. a large or imposing one. **2** a complex or elaborate institution or organization. [C14: from OF, from L *aedificium*, from *aedificāre* to build; see EDIFY]

edify ('ɛdɪ,faɪ) *vb* **edifies, edifying, edified.** (*tr*) to improve the morality, intellect, etc., of, esp. by instruction. [C14: from OF, from L *aedificāre* to construct, from *aedēs* a dwelling, temple + *facere* to make] ► ,edifi'**cation** *n* ► 'edi,**fying** *adj*

Edinburgh[1] ★ ('ɛdɪnbərə, -brə) *n* **1** the capital of Scotland, in Lothian region on the S side of the Firth of Forth: became the capital in the 15th century; castle; universities (1583, 1966); commercial and cultural centre, noted for its annual festival. Pop.: 401 910 (1991). **2 City of.** a council area in central Scotland. Pop.: 447 550 (1996 est.). Area: 262 sq. km (101 sq. miles).

Edinburgh[2] ★ ('ɛdɪnbərə, -brə) *n* **Duke of,** title of Prince *Philip Mountbatten.* born 1921, husband of Elizabeth II of Great Britain and Northern Ireland.

Edirne ★ (ɛ'dɪrnɛ) *n* a city in NW Turkey: a Thracian town, rebuilt and renamed by the Roman emperor Hadrian. Pop.: 115 500 (1994 est.). Former name: **Adrianople.**

Edison ★ ('ɛdɪsᵊn) *n* **Thomas Alva.** 1847–1931, US inventor. His inventions include the phonograph and the incandescent electric lamp.

edit ('ɛdɪt) *vb* **edits, editing, edited.** (*tr*) **1** to prepare (text) for publication by checking and improving its accuracy, clarity, etc. **2** to be in charge of (a publication, esp. a periodical). **3** to prepare (a film, tape, etc.) by rearrangement or selection of material. **4** (*tr*) to modify (a computer file). **5** (often foll. by *out*) to remove, as from a manuscript or film. [C18: back formation from EDITOR]

edit. *abbrev. for:* **1** edited. **2** edition. **3** editor.

edition (ɪ'dɪʃən) *n* **1** *Printing.* **1a** the entire number of copies of a book or other publication printed at one time. **1b** a copy from this number: *a first edition.* **2** one of a number of printings of a book or other publication, issued at separate times with alterations, amendments, etc. **3a** an issue of a work identified by its format: *a leather-bound edition.* **3b** an issue of a work identified by its editor or publisher: *the Oxford edition.* [C16: from L *ēditiō* a bringing forth, publishing, from *ēdere* to give out; see EDITOR]

editor ('ɛdɪtə) *n* **1** a person who edits written material for publication. **2** a person in overall charge of a newspaper or periodical. **3** a person in charge of one section of a newspaper or periodical: *the sports editor.* **4** *Films.* a person who makes a selection and arrangement of shots. **5** a person in overall control of a television or radio programme that consists of various items. [C17: from LL: producer, exhibitor, from *ēdere* to give out, publish, from + *dāre* to give] ► 'editor,**ship** *n*

editorial (,ɛdɪ'tɔːrɪəl) *adj* **1** of or relating to editing or editors. **2** of, relating to, or expressed in an editorial. **3** of or relating to the content of a publication. ◆ *n* **4** an article in a newspaper, etc., expressing the opinion of the editor or the publishers. ► ,edi'**torially** *adv*

editorialize *or* **editorialise** (,ɛdɪ'tɔːrɪə,laɪz) *vb* **editorializes, editorializing, editorialized** *or* **editorialises, editorialising, editorialised.** (*intr*) to express an opinion as in an editorial. ► ,edi,toriali'**zation** *or* ,edi,toriali'**sation** *n*

Edmonton ★ ('ɛdməntən) *n* a city in W Canada, capital of Alberta: oil industry. Pop.: 616 741 (1991).

Edmund ★ ('ɛdmənd) *n* **Saint,** also called *Saint Edmund Rich.* 1175–1240, English churchman: archbishop of Canterbury (1234–40). Feast day: Nov. 16.

Edmund I ★ *n* ?922–946 A.D., king of England (940–946).

Edmund II ★ *n* called *Edmund Ironside.* ?980–1016, king

of England in 1016. His succession was contested b Canute and they divided the kingdom between them.

EDT (in the US and Canada) *abbrev. for* Eastern Daylig Time.

educate ('ɛdju,keɪt) *vb* **educates, educating, educate** (*mainly tr*) **1** (*also intr*) to impart knowledge by formal ir struction to (a pupil); teach. **2** to provide schooling for. to improve or develop (a person, taste, skills, etc.). **4** t train for some particular purpose or occupation. [C1 from L *ēducāre* to rear, educate, from *dūcere* to lead] ► 'educable *or* 'edu,catable *adj* ► ,educa'bility *or* ,edu ,cata'bility *n* ► 'educative *adj*

educated ('ɛdju,keɪtɪd) *adj* **1** having an education, esp. good one. **2** displaying culture, taste, and knowledge cultivated. **3** (*prenominal*) based on experience or info mation (esp. in **an educated guess**).

education (,ɛdju'keɪʃən) *n* **1** the act or process of acqui ing knowledge. **2** the knowledge or training acquired b this process. **3** the act or process of imparting know edge, esp. at a school, college, or university. **4** the theor of teaching and learning. **5** a particular kind of instruc tion or training: *a university education.* ► ,edu'**cational** *adj* ► ,edu'**cationalist** *or* ,edu'**cationist** *n*

educator ('ɛdju,keɪtə) *n* **1** a person who educate teacher. **2** a specialist in education.

educe (ɪ'djuːs) *vb* **educes, educing, educed.** (*tr*) *Rare.* **1** t evolve or develop. **2** to draw out or elicit (information solutions, etc.). [C15: from L *ēdūcere*, from *ē-* out + *dūcer* to lead] ► e'**ducible** *adj* ► **eductive** (ɪ'dʌktɪv) *adj*

Edward[1] ★ ('ɛdwəd) *n* **Lake.** a lake in central Africa, be tween Uganda and the Democratic Republic of th Congo in the Great Rift Valley: empties through th Semliki River into Lake Albert. Area: about 2150 sq. kr (830 sq. miles). Former official name: **Lake Amin.**

Edward[2] ★ ('ɛdwəd) *n* **1** known as the *Black Prince.* 1330 76, Prince of Wales, the son of Edward III of England. H won victories over the French at Crécy (1346) an Poitiers (1356) in the Hundred Years' War. **2 Prince.** bor 1964, third son of Elizabeth II of Great Britain an Northern Ireland.

Edward I ★ *n* 1239–1307, king of England (1272–1307 son of Henry III. He conquered Wales (1284).

Edward II ★ *n* 1284–1327, king of England (1307–27 son of Edward I. He invaded Scotland but was defeate by Robert Bruce at Bannockburn (1314). He was depose by his wife Isabella and Roger Mortimer; died in prison.

Edward III ★ *n* 1312–77, king of England (1327–77 son of Edward II. His claim to the French throne in righ of his mother Isabella provoked the Hundred Years' Wa (1337).

Edward IV ★ *n* 1442–83, king of England (1461–7C 1471–83); son of Richard, duke of York. He defeate Henry VI in the Wars of the Roses and became kin (1461). In 1470 Henry was restored to the throne, bu Edward recovered the crown by his victory at Tewkes bury.

Edward V ★ *n* 1470–?83, king of England in 1483; so of Edward IV. He was deposed by his uncle, Richard Duke of Gloucester (Richard III), and is thought to hav been murdered with his brother in the Tower of Lon don.

Edward VI ★ *n* 1537–53, king of England (1547–53 son of Henry VIII and Jane Seymour. His uncle the Duk of Somerset was regent until 1552, when he was exe cuted. Edward then came under the control of Dudley Duke of Northumberland.

Edward VII ★ *n* 1841–1910, king of Great Britain an Ireland (1901–10); son of Queen Victoria.

Edward VIII ★ *n* 1894–1972, king of Great Britain an Northern Ireland in 1936; son of George V. He abdicate to marry Mrs Wallis Simpson (1896–1986); created Duk of Windsor (1937).

Edwardian (ɛd'wɔːdɪən) *adj* of or characteristic of th reign of Edward VII. ► Ed'**wardian,ism** *n*

Edward the Confessor ★ *n* **Saint.** ?1002–66, king o

★ people and places

England (1042–66); son of Ethelred II; founder of Westminster Abbey. Feast day: Oct. 13.

Edward the Elder ★ *n* died 924 A.D., king of England (899–924), son of Alfred the Great.

Edward the Martyr ★ *n* Saint. ?963–978 A.D., king of England (975–78), son of Edgar: murdered. Feast day: March 18.

Edwin ★ ('ɛdwɪn) *n* ?585–633 A.D., king of Northumbria (617–633) and overlord of all England except Kent.

-ee *suffix forming nouns.* **1** indicating a recipient of an action (as opposed, esp. in legal terminology, to the agent): *assignee; lessee.* **2** indicating a person in a specified state or condition: *absentee.* **3** indicating a diminutive form of something: *bootee.* [via OF *-é, -ée*, p.p. endings, from L *-ātus, -āta* -ATE¹]

EEC *abbrev. for* (the former) European Economic Community.

EEG *abbrev. for:* **1** electroencephalogram. **2** electroencephalograph.

eel (iːl) *n* **1** any teleost fish such as the European freshwater eel, having a long snakelike body, a smooth slimy skin, and reduced fins. **2** any of various similar animals, such as the mud eel and the electric eel. **3** an evasive or untrustworthy person. [OE *ǣl*]
➤ **'eel-, like** *adj* ➤ **'eely** *adj*

eelgrass ('iːl,grɑːs) *n* any of several perennial submerged marine plants having grasslike leaves.

eelpout ('iːl,paʊt) *n* **1** a marine eel-like fish. **2** another name for **burbot.** [OE *ǣlepūte*]

eelworm ('iːl,wɜːm) *n* any of various nematode worms, esp. the wheatworm and the vinegar eel.

e'en (iːn) *adv, n Poetic or arch.* contraction of **even**² or **evening.**

e'er (ɛə) *adv Poetic or arch.* contraction of **ever.**

-eer *or* **-ier** *suffix.* **1** (*forming nouns*) indicating a person who is concerned with or who does something specified: *auctioneer; engineer; profiteer; mutineer.* **2** (*forming verbs*) to be concerned with something specified: *electioneer.* [from OF *-ier*, from L *-arius* -ARY]

eerie ('ɪərɪ) *adj* **eerier, eeriest.** uncannily frightening or disturbing; weird. [C13: orig. Scot. & N English, prob. from OE *earg* cowardly]
➤ **'eerily** *adv* ➤ **'eeriness** *n*

EETPU (in Britain) *abbrev. for* Electrical, Electronic, Telecommunications, and Plumbing Union.

eff (ɛf) *vb* **1** euphemism for **fuck** (esp. in **eff off**). **2 eff and blind.** *Sl.* to use obscene language.
➤ **'effing** *n, adj, adv*

efface (ɪ'feɪs) *vb* **effaces, effacing, effaced.** (*tr*) **1** to obliterate or make dim. **2** to make (oneself) inconspicuous or humble. **3** to rub out; erase. [C15: from F *effacer*, lit.: to obliterate the face; see FACE]
➤ **ef'faceable** *adj* ➤ **ef'facement** *n* ➤ **ef'facer** *n*

effect (ɪ'fɛkt) *n* **1** something produced by a cause or agent; result. **2** power to influence or produce a result. **3** the condition of being operative (esp. in **in** or **into effect**). **4 take effect.** to become operative or begin to produce results. **5** basic meaning or purpose (esp. in **to that effect**). **6** an impression, usually contrived (esp. in **for effect**). **7** a scientific phenomenon: *the Doppler effect.* **8 in effect. 8a** in fact; actually. **8b** for all practical purposes. **9** the overall impression or result. ◆ *vb* **10** (*tr*) to cause to occur; accomplish. [C14: from L *effectus* a performing, tendency, from *efficere* to accomplish, from *facere* to do]
➤ **ef'fecter** *n* ➤ **ef'fectible** *adj*

effective (ɪ'fɛktɪv) *adj* **1** productive of or capable of producing a result. **2** in effect; operative. **3** impressive: *an effective entrance.* **4** (*prenominal*) actual rather than theoretical. **5** (of a military force, etc.) equipped and prepared for action. ◆ *n* **6** a serviceman equipped and prepared for action.
➤ **ef'fectively** *adv* ➤ **ef'fectiveness** *n*

effects (ɪ'fɛkts) *pl n* **1** Also called: **personal effects.** personal belongings. **2** lighting, sounds, etc., to accompany a stage, film, or broadcast production.

effectual (ɪ'fɛktjʊəl) *adj* **1** capable of or successful in pro-

ducing an intended result; effective. **2** (of documents, etc.) having legal force.
➤ **ef,fectu'ality** *or* **ef'fectualness** *n*

effectually (ɪ'fɛktjʊəlɪ) *adv* **1** with the intended effect. **2** in effect.

effectuate (ɪ'fɛktjʊ,eɪt) *vb* **effectuates, effectuating, effectuated.** (*tr*) to cause to happen; effect; accomplish.
➤ **ef,fectu'ation** *n*

effeminate (ɪ'fɛmɪnɪt) *adj* (of a man or boy) displaying characteristics regarded as typical of a woman; not manly. [C14: from L *effēmināre* to make into a woman, from *fēmina* woman]
➤ **ef'feminacy** *or* **ef'feminateness** *n*

effendi (e'fɛndɪ) *n, pl* **effendis. 1** (in the Ottoman Empire) a title of respect. **2** (in Turkey since 1934) the oral title of address equivalent to *Mr.* [C17: from Turkish *efendi* master, from Mod. Gk *aphentēs*, from Gk *authentēs* lord, doer]

efferent ('ɛfərənt) *adj Physiol.* carrying or conducting outwards, esp. from the brain or spinal cord. Cf. **afferent.** [C19: from L *efferre* to bear off, from *ferre* to bear]
➤ **'efference** *n*

effervesce (,ɛfə'vɛs) *vb* **effervesces, effervescing, effervesced.** (*intr*) **1** (of a liquid) to give off bubbles of gas. **2** (of a gas) to issue in bubbles from a liquid. **3** to exhibit great excitement, vivacity, etc. [C18: from L *effervescere* to foam up, ult. from *fervēre* to boil, ferment]
➤ **,effer'vescingly** *adv*

effervescent (,ɛfə'vɛs²nt) *adj* **1** (of a liquid) giving off bubbles of gas. **2** high-spirited; vivacious.
➤ **,effer'vescence** *n*

effete (ɪ'fiːt) *adj* **1** weak or decadent. **2** exhausted; spent. **3** (of animals or plants) no longer capable of reproduction. [C17: from L *effētus* exhausted by bearing, from *fētus* having brought forth; see FETUS]
➤ **ef'feteness** *n*

efficacious (,ɛfɪ'keɪʃəs) *adj* capable of or successful in producing an intended result; effective. [C16: from L *efficāx* powerful, efficient, from *efficere* to achieve]
➤ **efficacy** ('ɛfɪkəsɪ) *or* **effi'caciousness** *n*

efficiency (ɪ'fɪʃənsɪ) *n, pl* **efficiencies. 1** the quality or state of being efficient. **2** the ratio of the useful work done by a machine, etc., to the energy input, often expressed as a percentage.

efficient (ɪ'fɪʃənt) *adj* **1** functioning or producing effectively and with the least waste of effort; competent. **2** *Philosophy.* producing a direct effect. [C14: from L *efficiēns* effecting]

effigy ('ɛfɪdʒɪ) *n, pl* **effigies. 1** a portrait, esp. as a monument. **2** a crude representation of someone, used as a focus for contempt or ridicule (often in **burn** or **hang in effigy**). [C18: from L *effigiēs*, from *effingere* to form, portray, from *fingere* to shape]

effleurage (,ɛflɜː'rɑːʒ) *n Med.* a light stroking movement used in massage. [C19: from F]

effloresce (,ɛflɔː'rɛs) *vb* **effloresces, efflorescing, effloresced.** (*intr*) **1** to burst forth as into flower; bloom. **2** to become powdery by loss of water or crystallization. **3** to become encrusted with powder or crystals as a result of chemical change or evaporation. [C18: from L *efflōrēscere* to blossom, from *flōrēscere*, from *flōs* flower]

efflorescence (,ɛflɔː'rɛs²ns) *n* **1** a bursting forth or flowering. **2** *Chem., geol.* **2a** the process of efflorescing. **2b** the powdery substance formed as a result of this process. **3** any skin rash or eruption.
➤ **,efflo'rescent** *adj*

effluence ('ɛflʊəns) *or* **efflux** ('ɛflʌks) *n* **1** the act or process of flowing out. **2** something that flows out.

effluent ('ɛflʊənt) *n* **1** liquid discharged as waste, as from an industrial plant or sewage works. **2** radioactive waste released from a nuclear power station. **3** a stream that flows out of another body of water. **4** something that flows out or forth. ◆ *adj* **5** flowing out or forth. [C18: from L *effluere* to run forth, from *fluere* to flow]

effluvium (ɛ'fluːvɪəm) *n, pl* **effluvia** (-vɪə) *or* **effluviums.** an unpleasant smell or exhalation, as of gaseous waste or

decaying matter. [C17: from L: a flowing out; see EFFLU-ENT]
▶ ef'fluvial *adj*

effort ('ɛfət) *n* **1** physical or mental exertion. **2** a determined attempt. **3** achievement; creation. [C15: from OF *esfort*, from *esforcier* to force, ult. from L *fortis* strong]
▶ 'effortful *adj* ▶ 'effortless *adj*

effrontery (ɪ'frʌntərɪ) *n, pl* **effronteries.** shameless or insolent boldness. [C18: from F, from OF *esfront* barefaced, shameless, from LL *effrons*, lit.: putting forth one's forehead]

effulgent (ɪ'fʌldʒənt) *adj* radiant; brilliant. [C18: from L *effulgēre* to shine forth, from *fulgēre* to shine]
▶ ef'fulgence *n* ▶ ef'fulgently *adv*

effuse *vb* (ɪ'fju:z), **effuses, effusing, effused. 1** to pour or flow out. **2** to spread out; diffuse. ◆ *adj* (ɪ'fju:s). **3** *Bot.* (esp. of an inflorescence) spreading out loosely. [C16: from L *effūsus* poured out, from *effundere* to shed]

effusion (ɪ'fju:ʒən) *n* **1** an unrestrained outpouring in speech or words. **2** the act or process of being poured out. **3** something that is poured out. **4** *Med.* **4a** the escape of blood or other fluid into a body cavity or tissue. **4b** the fluid that has escaped.

effusive (ɪ'fju:sɪv) *adj* **1** extravagantly demonstrative of emotion; gushing. **2** (of rock) formed by the solidification of magma.
▶ ef'fusively *adv* ▶ ef'fusiveness *n*

EFL *abbrev. for* English as a Foreign Language.

eft (ɛft) *n* a dialect or archaic name for a **newt.** [OE *efeta*]

EFTA ('ɛftə) *n acronym for* European Free Trade Association; established in 1960 to eliminate trade tariffs on industrial products; the current members are Austria, Iceland, Norway, Sweden, and Switzerland.

EFTPOS ('ɛftpɒs) *n acronym for* electronic funds transfer at point of sale.

EFTS *abbrev. for* electronic funds transfer system.

Eg. *abbrev. for:* **1** Egypt(ian). **2** Egyptology.

e.g., eg, *or* **eg.** *abbrev. for* exempli gratia. [L: for example]

egad (ɪ'gæd, i:'gæd) *interj Arch.* a mild oath. [C17: prob. var. of *Ah God!*]

egalitarian (ɪ,gælɪ'tɛərɪən) *adj* **1** of or upholding the doctrine of the equality of mankind. ◆ *n* **2** an adherent of egalitarian principles. [C19: alteration of *equalitarian*, through infl. of F *égal* equal]
▶ e,gali'tarian,ism *n*

Egbert ★ ('ɛgbɜːt) *n* ?775–839 A.D., king of Wessex (802–839); first overlord of all England (829–830).

Eger ★ *n* **1** (*Hungarian* 'ɛgɛr). a city in N central Hungary. Pop.: 60 000 (1995 est.). **2** ('e:gər). the German name for **Cheb.**

egg[1] (ɛg) *n* **1** the oval or round reproductive body laid by the females of birds, reptiles, fishes, insects, and some other animals, consisting of a developing embryo, its food store, and sometimes jelly or albumen, all surrounded by an outer shell or membrane. **2** Also called: **egg cell.** any female gamete; ovum. **3** the egg of the domestic hen used as food. **4** something resembling an egg, esp. in shape. **5 good** (*or* **bad**) **egg.** *Old-fashioned inf.* a good (or bad) person. **6 put** *or* **have all one's eggs in one basket.** to stake everything on a single venture. **7 teach one's grandmother to suck eggs.** *Inf.* to presume to teach someone something that he knows already. **8 with egg on one's face.** *Inf.* made to look ridiculous. [C14: from ON *egg;* rel. to OE *æg*]

egg[2] (ɛg) *vb* (*tr;* usually foll. by *on*) to urge or incite, esp. to daring or foolish acts. [OE *eggian*]

egg-and-spoon race *n* a race in which runners carry an egg balanced in a spoon.

eggbeater ('ɛg,bi:tə) *n* **1** Also called: **eggwhisk.** a utensil for beating eggs; whisk. **2** *Chiefly US & Canad.* an informal name for **helicopter.**

egger *or* **eggar** ('ɛgə) *n* any of various European moths having brown bodies and wings. [C18: from EGG[1], from the egg-shaped cocoon]

egghead ('ɛg,hɛd) *n Inf.* an intellectual.

eggnog (,ɛg'nɒg) *n* a drink made of eggs, milk, sugar, spice, and brandy, rum, or other spirit. Also called: **egg flip.** [C19: from EGG[1] + NOG]

eggplant ('ɛg,plɑ:nt) *n* another name (esp. US, Canad., & Austral.) for **aubergine.**

eggshell ('ɛg,ʃɛl) *n* **1** the hard porous outer layer of a bird's egg. **2** (*modifier*) (of paint) having a very slight sheen.

eggshell porcelain *or* **china** *n* a very thin translucent porcelain originally from China.

egg tooth *n* (in embryo reptiles) a temporary tooth or (in birds) projection of the beak used for piercing the eggshell.

Egham ★ ('ɛgəm) *n* a town in S England, in N Surrey on the River Thames. Pop.: 23 816 (1991).

eglantine ('ɛglən,taɪn) *n* another name for **sweetbrier.** [C14: from OF *aiglent*, ult. from L *acus* needle, from *acer* sharp, keen]

EGM *abbrev. for* extraordinary general meeting.

Egmont[1] ★ ('ɛgmɒnt) *n* **Mount.** a mountain in New Zealand, in W central North Island in the **Egmont National Park:** an almost perfect volcanic cone. Height: 2518 m (8261 ft). Maori name: **Taranaki.**

Egmont[2] ★ ('ɛgmɒnt) *n* **Lamoral** (lamo'ral), Count of Egmont, Prince of Gavre. 1522–68, Flemish statesman. He tried to reform the Spanish government of the Netherlands, refused to join William the Silent's rebellion, but was executed for treason.

ego ('i:gəʊ, 'ɛgəʊ) *n, pl* **egos. 1** the self of an individual person; the conscious subject. **2** *Psychoanalysis.* the conscious mind based on perception of the environment: modifies the antisocial instincts of the id and is itself modified by the conscience (superego). **3** one's image of oneself; morale. **4** egotism; conceit. [C19: from L: I]

egocentric (,i:gəʊ'sɛntrɪk, ,ɛg-) *adj* **1** regarding everything only in relation to oneself; self-centred. ◆ *n* **2** a self-centred person; egotist.
▶ ,egocen'tricity *n* ▶ ,ego'centrism *n*

egoism ('i:gəʊ,ɪzəm, 'ɛg-) *n* **1** concern for one's own interests and welfare. **2** *Ethics.* the theory that the pursuit of one's own interests is the highest good. **3** self-centredness; egotism.
▶ 'egoist *n* ▶ ,ego'istic *or* ,ego'istical *adj*

egomania (,i:gəʊ'meɪnɪə, ,ɛg-) *n Psychiatry.* obsessive love for oneself.
▶ ,ego'mani,ac *n* ▶ **egomaniacal** (,i:gəʊmə'naɪk[ə]l, ,ɛg-) *adj*

egotism ('i:gə,tɪzəm, 'ɛgə-) *n* **1** an inflated sense of self-importance or superiority; self-centredness. **2** excessive reference to oneself. [C18: from L *ego* I + -ISM]
▶ 'egotist *n* ▶ ,ego'tistic *or* ,ego'tistical *adj*

ego trip *n Inf.* something undertaken to boost or draw attention to a person's own image or appraisal of himself.

egregious (ɪ'gri:dʒəs, -dʒɪəs) *adj* **1** outstandingly bad; flagrant. **2** *Arch.* distinguished; eminent. [C16: from L *ēgregius* outstanding (lit.: standing out from the herd), from *ē-* out + *grex* flock, herd]
▶ e'gregiousness *n*

egress ('i:grɛs) *n* **1** Also: **egression.** the act of going or coming out; emergence. **2** a way out; exit. **3** the right to go out or depart. [C16: from L *ēgredī* to come forth, depart, from *gradī* to move, step]

egret ('i:grɪt) *n* any of various wading birds similar to herons but usually having white plumage and, in the breeding season, long feathery plumes. [C15: from OF *aigrette*, of Gmc origin]

Egypt ★ ('i:dʒɪpt) *n* a republic in NE Africa, on the Mediterranean and Red Sea: its history dates back about 5000 years. Occupied by the British from 1882, it became an independent kingdom in 1922 and a republic in 1953. Over 96 per cent of the total area is desert, with the chief areas of habitation and cultivation in the Nile delta and valley. Cotton is the main export. Official language: Arabic. Official religion: Muslim (Sunni majority). Currency: pound. Capital: Cairo. Pop.: 62 110 000 (1997). Area: 997 739 sq. km (385 229 sq. miles). Official name:

★ people and places

Arab Republic of Egypt. Former official name (1958–71): United Arab Republic.

Egyptian (ɪˈdʒɪpjən) *adj* **1** of or relating to Egypt, its inhabitants, or their dialect of Arabic. **2** of or characteristic of the ancient Egyptians, their language, or culture. ◆ *n* **3** a native or inhabitant of Egypt. **4** a member of a people who established an advanced civilization in Egypt that flourished from the late fourth millennium B.C. **5** the extinct language of the ancient Egyptians.

Egyptology (ˌiːdʒɪpˈtɒlədʒɪ) *n* the study of the archaeology and language of ancient Egypt.
▸ ˌEgypˈtologist *n*

eh (eɪ) *interj* an exclamation used to express questioning surprise or to seek the repetition or confirmation of a statement or question.

EHF *abbrev. for* extremely high frequency.

Ehrenburg *or* **Erenburg** ★ (ˈɛərənˌbɜːg; *Russian* erɪnˈburk) *n* **Ilya Grigorievich** (ilʲˈja griˈɡɔrjɪvitʃ). 1891–1967, Soviet novelist and journalist. His novel *The Thaw* (1954) was the first published in the Soviet Union to deal with repression under Stalin.

Ehrlich ★ (*German* ˈeːrlɪç) *n* **Paul** (paul). 1854–1915, German bacteriologist, noted for his pioneering work in immunology and chemotherapy: Nobel prize for physiology or medicine 1908.

EI *abbrev. for:* **1** East Indian. **2** East Indies.

Eichler ★ (*German* ˈaɪçlər) *n* **August Wilhelm** (ˈaugust ˈvɪlhɛlm). 1839–87, German botanist: devised the system on which modern plant classification is based.

Eichmann ★ (*German* ˈaɪçman) *n* (**Karl**) **Adolf** (ˈaːdɔlf). 1902–62, Austrian Nazi, who organized the extermination of European Jews; executed in Israel.

eider *or* **eider duck** (ˈaɪdə) *n* any of several sea ducks of the N hemisphere. See **eiderdown.** [C18: from ON *æthr*]

eiderdown (ˈaɪdəˌdaun) *n* **1** the breast down of the female eider duck, used for stuffing pillows, quilts, etc. **2** a thick, warm cover for a bed, enclosing a soft filling.

eidetic (aɪˈdɛtɪk) *adj Psychol.* **1** (of visual, or sometimes auditory, images) very vivid and allowing detailed recall of something previously perceived: thought to be common in children. **2** relating to or subject to such imagery. [C20: from Gk *eidētikos*, from *eidos* shape, form]
▸ eiˈdetically *adv*

Eid-ul-Adha (ˈiːdʊlˌɑːdə) *n* an annual Muslim festival marking the end of the pilgrimage to Mecca. Animals are sacrificed and their meat shared among the poor. [from Ar. *id ul adha* festival of sacrifice]

Eid-ul-Fitr (ˈiːdʊlˌfiːtə) *n* an annual Muslim festival marking the end of Ramadan, involving the exchange of gifts and a festive meal. [from Ar. *id ul fitr* festival of fast-breaking]

Eifel ★ (ˈaɪf²l; *German* ˈaɪfəl) *n* a plateau region in W Germany, between the River Moselle and the Belgian frontier: quarrying.

Eiffel ★ (ˈaɪf²l; *French* ɛfɛl) *n* **Alexandre Gustave** (alɛksɑ̃drə gystav). 1832–1923, French engineer.

Eiffel Tower ★ (ˈaɪf²l) *n* a tower in Paris: designed by A. G. Eiffel; erected for the 1889 Paris Exposition. Height: 300 m (984 ft), raised in 1959 to 321 m (1052 ft).

Eigen ★ (*German* ˈaɪɡən) *n* **Manfred.** born 1927, German chemist: shared the Nobel prize for chemistry (1967) for his relaxation technique for studying fast reactions.

Eiger (*German* ˈaɪɡər) *n* a mountain in central Switzerland, in the Bernese Alps. Height: 3970 m (13 025 ft).

eight (eɪt) *n* **1** the cardinal number that is the sum of one and seven and the product of two and four. **2** a numeral, 8, VIII, etc., representing this number. **3** the amount or quantity that is one greater than seven. **4** something representing, represented by, or consisting of eight units. **5** *Rowing.* **5a** a racing shell propelled by eight oarsmen. **5b** the crew of such a shell. **6** Also called: **eight o'clock.** eight hours after noon or midnight. **7** **have one over the eight.** *Sl.* to be drunk. ◆ *determiner* **8a** amounting to eight. **8b** (*as pron*): *I could only find eight.* [OE *eahta*]

eighteen (ˈeɪˈtiːn) *n* **1** the cardinal number that is the sum of ten and eight and the product of two and nine. **2** a numeral, 18, XVIII, etc., representing this number. **3**

the amount or quantity that is eight more than ten. **4** something represented by, representing, or consisting of 18 units. ◆ *determiner* **5a** amounting to eighteen: *eighteen weeks.* **5b** (*as pron*): *eighteen of them knew.* [OE *eahtatēne*]
▸ ˈeighˈteenth *adj, n*

eightfold (ˈeɪtˌfəuld) *adj* **1** equal to or having eight times as many or as much. **2** composed of eight parts. ◆ *adv* **3** by eight times as much.

eighth (eɪtθ) *adj* **1** (*usually prenominal*) **1a** coming after the seventh and before the ninth in numbering, position, etc.; being the ordinal number of *eight:* often written 8th. **1b** (*as n*): *the eighth in line.* ◆ *n* **2a** one of eight equal parts of something. **2b** (*as modifier*): *an eighth part.* **3** the fraction one divided by eight (1/8). **4** another word for **octave.** ◆ *adv* **5** Also: **eighthly.** after the seventh person, position, event, etc.

eighth note *n Music.* the usual US and Canad. name for **quaver.**

eightsome reel (ˈeɪtsəm) *n* a Scottish dance for eight people.

eighty (ˈeɪtɪ) *n, pl* **eighties. 1** the cardinal number that is the product of ten and eight. **2** a numeral, 80, LXXX, etc., representing this number. **3** (*pl*) the numbers 80-89, esp. the 80th to the 89th year of a person's life or of a century. **4** the amount or quantity that is eight times ten. **5** something represented by, representing, or consisting of 80 units. ◆ *determiner* **6a** amounting to eighty: *eighty pages of nonsense.* **6b** (*as pron*): *eighty are expected.* [OE *eahtatig*]
▸ ˈeightieth *adj, n*

Eilat, Elat, *or* **Elath** ★ (eɪˈlɑːt) *n* a port in S Israel, on the Gulf of Aqaba: Israel's only outlet to the Red Sea. Pop.: 26 010 (1989 est.).

Eindhoven ★ (ˈaɪntˌhəuv°n, *Dutch* ˈɛinthoːvə) *n* a city in the SE Netherlands, in North Brabant province: radio and electrical industry. Pop.: 197 055 (1995 est.).

Einstein ★ (ˈaɪnstaɪn) *n* **Albert.** 1879–1955, US physicist and mathematician, born in Germany. He formulated the special theory of relativity (1905) and the general theory of relativity (1916), and made major contributions to the quantum theory, for which he was awarded the Nobel prize for physics in 1921. He was noted also for his work for world peace.
▸ Einˈsteinian *adj*

einsteinium (aɪnˈstaɪnɪəm) *n* a radioactive metallic transuranic element artificially produced from plutonium. Symbol: Es; atomic no.: 99; half-life of most stable isotope, ^{252}Es: 276 days. [C20: NL, after Albert EINSTEIN]

Einthoven ★ (*Dutch* ˈɛinthoːvə) *n* **Willem** (ˈwɪləm). 1860–1927, Dutch physiologist. A pioneer of electrocardiography, he was awarded the Nobel prize for physiology or medicine in 1924.

Eire ★ (ˈɛərə) *n* **1** the Irish Gaelic name for **Ireland**[1]: often used to mean the **Republic of Ireland. 2** a former name for the **Republic of Ireland** (1937–49).

EIS *abbrev. for* Educational Institute of Scotland.

Eisenach ★ (*German* ˈaɪzənax) *n* a city in central Germany, in Thuringia. Pop.: 48 361 (1989 est.).

Eisenhower ★ (ˈaɪzənˌhauə) *n* **Dwight D(avid)**, known as *Ike.* 1890–1969, US general and Republican statesman; Supreme Commander of the Allied Expeditionary Force (1943–45) and 34th president of the US (1953–61). He was also Supreme Commander of the combined land forces of NATO (1950–52).

Eisenstadt ★ (*German* ˈaɪzənʃtat) *n* a town in E Austria, capital of Burgenland province: Hungarian until 1921. Pop.: 10 506 (1991).

Eisenstein ★ (ˈaɪz°nˌstaɪn; *Russian* ejzɪnˈʃtjejn) *n* **Sergei Mikhailovich** (sɪrˈgjej miˈxajləvitʃ). 1898–1948, Soviet film director. His films include *Battleship Potemkin* (1925), *Alexander Nevsky* (1938), and *Ivan the Terrible* (1944).

Eisk *or* **Eysk** ★ (*Russian* jejsk) *n* variant transliterations of the Russian name for **Yeisk.**

eisteddfod (aɪˈstɛdfəd) *n, pl* **eisteddfods** *or* **eisteddfodau** (*Welsh* aɪˌstɛðˈvodaɪ). any of a number of annual festivals in Wales in which competitions are held in music, poetry, drama, and the fine arts. [C19: from Welsh, lit.: session, from *eisteddd* to sit + -*fod,* from *bod* to be]

either ('aɪðə, 'iːðə) *determiner* **1a** one or the other (of two). **1b** (*as pron*): *either is acceptable.* **2** both one and the other: *at either end of the table.* ◆ *conj* **3** (*coordinating*) used preceding two or more possibilities joined by "*or*". ◆ *adv* (*sentence modifier*) **4** (*with a negative*) used to indicate that the clause immediately preceding is a partial reiteration of a previous clause: *John isn't a liar, but he isn't exactly honest either.* [OE *ǣgther,* short for *ǣghwǣther* each of two; see WHETHER]

> USAGE NOTE *Either* is followed by a singular verb in good usage: *either is good; either of these books is useful.* Care should be taken to avoid ambiguity when using *either* to mean *both* or *each,* as in the following sentence: *a ship could be moored on either side of the channel.* Agreement between verb and subject in *either...or...* constructions follows the pattern for *neither...nor...* See at **neither.**

ejaculate *vb* (ɪ'dʒækjuˌleɪt), **ejaculates, ejaculating, ejaculated.** **1** to eject or discharge (semen) in orgasm. **2** (*tr*) to utter abruptly; blurt out. ◆ *n* (ɪ'dʒækjulɪt). **3** another word for **semen.** [C16: from L *ējaculārī* to hurl out, from *jaculum* javelin, from *jacere* to throw]
▸ e‚jacu'lation *n* ▸ e'jaculatory *or* e'jaculative *adj*
▸ e'jacu‚lator *n*

eject (ɪ'dʒɛkt) *vb* **1** (*tr*) to force out; expel or emit. **2** (*tr*) to compel (a person) to leave; evict. **3** (*tr*) to dismiss, as from office. **4** (*intr*) to leave an aircraft rapidly, using an ejection seat or capsule. [C15: from L *ējicere,* from *jacere* to throw]
▸ e'jection *n* ▸ e'jective *adj* ▸ e'jector *n*

ejection seat *or* **ejector seat** *n* a seat, esp. in military aircraft, fired by a cartridge or rocket to eject the occupant in an emergency.

Ekaterinburg ★ (*Russian* jɪkətɪrim'burk) *n* a variant of **Yekaterinburg.**

Ekaterinodar ★ (*Russian* jɪkətɪrina'dar) *n* the former name (until 1920) of **Krasnodar.**

eke (iːk) *sentence connector. Arch.* also; moreover. [OE *eac*]

eke out (iːk) *vb* (*tr, adv*) **1** to make (a supply) last, esp. by frugal use. **2** to support (existence) with difficulty and effort. **3** to add to (something insufficient), esp. with effort. [from obs. *eke* to enlarge]

Ekman ★ (*Swedish* 'ɛkman) *n* **Vagn Walfrid** (vaɡⁿ waːlfriːd). 1874–1954, Swedish oceanographer: discoverer of the **Ekman Spiral** (a complex interaction on the surface of the sea between wind, rotation of the earth, and friction forces) and the **Ekman layer** (the thin top layer of the sea that flows at 90° to the wind direction).

El Aaiún ★ (ɛl aɪ'juːn) *n* a city in Morocco, in Western Sahara: the capital of the former Spanish Sahara; port facilities at **Playa de El Aaiún,** 20 km (12 miles) away. Pop.: 136 950 (1994).

elaborate *adj* (ɪ'læbərɪt). **1** planned with care and exactness. **2** marked by complexity or detail. ◆ *vb* (ɪ'læbəˌreɪt), **elaborates, elaborating, elaborated. 3** (*intr;* usually foll. by *on* or *upon*) to add detail (to an account); expand (upon). **4** (*tr*) to work out in detail; develop. **5** (*tr*) to produce by careful labour. **6** (*tr*) *Physiol.* to change (food or simple substances) into more complex substances for use in the body. [C16: from L *ēlabōrāre* to take pains, from *labōrāre* to toil]
▸ e'laborateness *n* ▸ e‚labo'ration *n* ▸ **elaborative** (ɪ'læbərətɪv) *adj* ▸ e'labo‚rator *n*

Elagabalus ★ (ˌɛlə'gæbələs, ˌiːlə-) *n* a variant of **Heliogabalus.**

El Alamein *or* **Alamein** ★ (ɛl 'æləˌmeɪn) *n* a village on the N coast of Egypt, about 112 km (70 miles) west of Alexandria: scene of a decisive Allied victory over the Axis forces (1942).

Elam ★ ('iːləm) *n* an ancient kingdom east of the River Tigris: established before 4000 B.C.; probably inhabited by a non-Semitic people.

élan (eɪ'lɑːn) *n* a combination of style and vigour. [C19 from F, from *élancer* to throw forth, ult. from L *lancea* LANCE]

eland ('iːlənd) *n* **1** a large spiral-horned antelope inhabiting bushland in eastern and southern Africa. **2 giant eland.** a similar but larger animal of central and W Africa [C18: via Afrik., from Du. *eland* elk]

elapse (ɪ'læps) *vb* **elapses, elapsing, elapsed.** (*intr*) (of time) to pass by. [C17: from L *ēlābī* to slip away]

elasmobranch (ɪ'læsməˌbræŋk) *n* **1** any cartilaginous fish of the subclass *Elasmobranchii,* which includes sharks, rays, and skates. ◆ *adj* **2** of or relating to the *Elasmobranchii.* [C19: from NL *elasmobranchii,* from Gk *elasmos* metal plate + *brankhia* gills]

elastane (ɪ'læsteɪn) *n* a synthetic fibre characterized by its ability to revert to its original shape after being stretched.

elastic (ɪ'læstɪk) *adj* **1** (of a body or material) capable of returning to its original shape after compression, stretching, or other deformation. **2** capable of adapting to change. **3** quick to recover from fatigue, dejection, etc. **4** springy or resilient. **5** made of elastic. ◆ *n* **6** tape, cord, or fabric containing flexible rubber or similar substance allowing it to stretch and return to its original shape. [C17: from NL *elasticus* impulsive, from Gk *elastikos,* from *elaunein* to beat, drive]
▸ e'lastically *adv* ▸ **elas'ticity** *n*

elasticate (ɪ'læstɪˌkeɪt) *vb* **elasticates, elasticating, elasticated.** (*tr*) to insert elastic into (a fabric or garment).
▸ e‚lasti'cation *n*

elastic band *n* another name for **rubber band.**

elasticize *or* **elasticise** (ɪ'læstɪˌsaɪz) *vb* **elasticizes, elasticizing, elasticized** *or* **elasticises, elasticising, elasticised. 1** to make elastic. **2** another word for **elasticate.**

elastomer (ɪ'læstəmə) *n* any material, such as rubber, able to resume its original shape when a deforming force is removed. [C20: from ELASTIC + -MER]
▸ **elastomeric** (ɪˌlæstə'mɛrɪk) *adj*

Elastoplast (ɪ'læstəˌplɑːst) *n Trademark.* a gauze surgical dressing backed by adhesive tape.

Elat *or* **Elath** ★ (eɪ'lɑːt) *n* variant spellings of **Eilat.**

elate (ɪ'leɪt) *vb* **elates, elating, elated.** (*tr*) to fill with high spirits, exhilaration, pride, or optimism. [C16: from p.p. of L *efferre* to bear away, from *ferre* to carry]
▸ e'lated *adj* ▸ e'latedly *adv* ▸ e'latedness *n*

elation (ɪ'leɪʃən) *n* joyfulness or exaltation of spirit, as from success, pleasure, or relief.

E layer *n* another name for **E region.**

Elba ★ ('ɛlbə) *n* a mountainous island off the W coast of Italy, in the Mediterranean: Napoleon Bonaparte's first place of exile (1814–15). Pop.: 27 722 (1991 est.). Area: 223 sq. km (86 sq. miles).

Elbe ★ (ɛlb; *German* 'ɛlbə) *n* a river in central Europe, rising in the N Czech Republic and flowing generally northwest through Germany to the North Sea at Hamburg. Length: 1165 km (724 miles). Czech name: **Labe.**

Elbert ★ ('ɛlbət) *n* **Mount.** a mountain in central Colorado, in the Sawatch range. Height: 4399 m (14 431 ft).

Elbląg ★ (*Polish* 'ɛlblɔŋk) *n* a port in N Poland: metallurgical industries. Pop.: 128 500 (1995 est.). German name: **Elbing** ('ɛlbɪŋ).

elbow ('ɛlbəu) *n* **1** the joint between the upper arm and the forearm. **2** the corresponding joint of birds or mammals. **3** the part of a garment that covers the elbow. **4** something resembling an elbow, such as a sharp bend in a road. **5 at one's elbow.** within easy reach. **6 out at elbow(s).** ragged or impoverished. ◆ *vb* **7** to make (one's way) by shoving, jostling, etc. **8** (*tr*) to knock or shove as with the elbow. **9** (*tr*) to reject; dismiss (esp. in **give** *or* **get the elbow**). [OE *elnboga*]

elbow grease *n Facetious.* vigorous physical labour, esp. hard rubbing.

elbowroom ('ɛlbəuˌruːm, -ˌrum) *n* sufficient scope to move or function.

Elbrus ★ (ɪl'bruːs) *n* a mountain in S W Russia, on the border with Georgia, with two extinct volcanic peaks:

★ people and places

the highest mountain in Europe. Height: 5642 m (18 510 ft).

Iburz Mountains ★ (ɛlˈbʊəz) *pl n* a mountain range in N Iran, parallel to the SW and S shores of the Caspian Sea. Highest peak: Mount Demavend, 5601 m (18 376 ft).

El Capitan ★ (ɛl ˌkɑpɪˈtæn) *n* a mountain in E central California, in the Sierra Nevada: a monolith with a precipice rising over 1100 m (3600 ft) above the floor of the Yosemite Valley. Height: 2306 m (7564 ft).

Iche ★ (*Spanish* ˈɛltʃe) *n* a town in S Spain, in Valencia: noted for Iberian and Roman archaeological finds and the medieval religious drama performed there annually: fruit growing, esp. dates, pomegranates, figs. Pop.: 191 305 (1994 est.).

El Cid Campeador ★ (*Spanish* ɛl ˈθið kampeaˈðɔr) *n* See (El) **Cid.**

Ider[1] (ˈɛldə) *adj* **1** born earlier; senior. Cf. **older. 2** (in certain card games) denoting or relating to the nondealer (the **elder hand**), who has certain advantages in the play. **3** *Arch.* prior in rank or office. **3b** of a previous time. ◆ *n* **4** an older person; one's senior. **5** *Anthropol.* a senior member of a tribe who has authority. **6** (in certain Protestant Churches) a lay office. **7** another word for **presbyter.** [OE *eldra,* comp. of *eald* OLD]
▶ **'elder,ship** *n*

Ider[2] (ˈɛldə) *n* any of various shrubs or small trees having clusters of small white flowers and red, purple, or black berry-like fruits. Also called: **elderberry.** [OE *ellern*]

Iderberry (ˈɛldəˌbɛrɪ) *n, pl* **elderberries. 1** the fruit of the elder. **2** another name for **elder**[2].

Ider brother *n* one of the senior members of Trinity House.

Iderly (ˈɛldəlɪ) *adj* (of people) quite old; past middle age.
▶ **'elderliness** *n*

Idest (ˈɛldɪst) *adj* being the oldest, esp. the oldest surviving child of the same parents. [OE *eldesta,* sup. of *eald* OLD]

El Dorado (ɛl dɒˈrɑːdəʊ) *n* **1** a fabled city in South America, rich in treasure. **2** Also: **eldorado.** any place of great riches or fabulous opportunity. [C16: from Sp., lit.: the gilded (place)]

Idritch *or* **eldrich** (ˈɛldrɪtʃ) *adj Poetic, Scot.* unearthly; weird. [C16: ?from OE *ælf* elf + *rīce* realm]

Ilea ★ (ˈiːlɪə) *n* (in ancient Italy) a Greek colony on the Tyrrhenian coast of Lucana.

Ileanor of Aquitaine ★ (ˈɛlɪnə, -ˌnɔː) *n* ?1122–1204, queen of France (1137–52) by her marriage to Louis VII and queen of England (1154–89) by her marriage to Henry II; mother of the English kings Richard I and John.

Ileanor of Castile ★ (ˈɛlɪnə, -ˌnɔː) *n* 1246–90, Spanish wife of Edward I of England. **Eleanor Crosses** were erected at each place at which her body rested between Nottingham, where she died, and London, where she is buried.

Ilect (ɪˈlɛkt) *vb* **1** (*tr*) to choose (someone) to be (a representative or official) by voting. **2** to select; choose. **3** (*tr*) (of God) to predestine for the grace of salvation. ◆ *adj* **4** (*immediately postpositive*) voted into office but not yet installed: *president elect.* **5a** chosen; elite. **5b** (*as collective n; preceded by the*): *the elect.* **6** *Christian theol.* **6a** predestined by God to receive salvation. **6b** (*as collective n; preceded by the*): *the elect.* [C15: from L *ēligere* to select, from *legere* to choose]
▶ **e'lectable** *adj*

elect. *or* **elec.** *abbrev. for:* **1** electric(al). **2** electricity.

election (ɪˈlɛkʃən) *n* **1** the selection by vote of a person or persons for a position, esp. a political office. **2** a public vote. **3** the act or an instance of choosing. **4** *Christian theol.* **4a** the doctrine that God chooses individuals for salvation without reference to faith or works. **4b** the doctrine that God chooses for salvation those who, by grace, persevere in faith and works.

electioneer (ɪˌlɛkʃəˈnɪə) *vb* (*intr*) **1** to be active in a political election or campaign. ◆ *n* **2** a person who engages in this activity.
▶ **e,lection'eering** *n, adj*

elective (ɪˈlɛktɪv) *adj* **1** of or based on selection by vote. **2** selected by vote. **3** having the power to elect. **4** open to choice; optional. ◆ *n* **5** an optional course or hospital placement undertaken by a medical student.
▶ **electivity** (ˌɛlɛkˈtɪvɪtɪ) *or* **e'lectiveness** *n*

elector (ɪˈlɛktə) *n* **1** someone who is eligible to vote in the election of a government. **2** (*often cap.*) a member of the US electoral college. **3** (*often cap.*) (in the Holy Roman Empire) any of the German princes entitled to take part in the election of a new emperor.
▶ **e'lectoral** *adj* ▶ **e'lector,ship** *n* ▶ **e'lectress** *fem n*

electoral college *n* (*often cap.*) **1** *US.* a body of electors chosen by the voters who formally elect the president and vice president. **2** any body of electors with similar functions.

electorate (ɪˈlɛktərɪt) *n* **1** the body of all qualified voters. **2** the rank, position, or territory of an elector of the Holy Roman Empire. **3** *Austral. & NZ.* the area represented by a Member of Parliament. **4** *Austral. & NZ.* the voters in a constituency.

Electra ★ (ɪˈlɛktrə) *n Greek myth.* the daughter of Agamemnon and Clytemnestra. She persuaded her brother Orestes to avenge their father by killing his murderess Clytemnestra and her lover Aegisthus.

electret (ɪˈlɛktrət) *n* a permanently polarized dielectric material; its field is similar to that of a permanent magnet. [C20: from *electr(icity* + *magn)et*]

electric (ɪˈlɛktrɪk) *adj* **1** of, derived from, produced by, producing, transmitting, or powered by electricity. **2** (of a musical instrument) amplified electronically. **3** very tense or exciting; emotionally charged. ◆ *n* **4** *Inf.* an electric train, car, etc. **5** (*pl*) an electric circuit or electric appliances. [C17: from NL *electricus* amber-like (because friction causes amber to become charged), from L *ēlectrum* amber, from Gk *ēlektron,* from ?]

USAGE NOTE See at **electronic.**

electrical (ɪˈlɛktrɪk°l) *adj* of, relating to, or concerned with electricity.
▶ **e'lectrically** *adv*

USAGE NOTE See at **electronic.**

electrical engineering *n* the branch of engineering concerned with practical applications of electricity.
▶ **electrical engineer** *n*

electric blanket *n* a blanket that contains an electric heating element, used to warm a bed.

electric chair *n* (in the US) **a** an electrified chair for executing criminals. **b** (usually preceded by *the*) execution by this method.

electric circuit *n Physics.* another name for **circuit** (sense 3a).

electric constant *n* the permittivity of free space, which has the value $8.854\,185 \times 10^{-12}$ farad per metre.

electric discharge *n Physics.* another name for **discharge** (sense 17b).

electric displacement *n Physics.* the charge per unit area displaced across a layer of conductor in an electric field. Symbol: *D* Also called: **electric flux density.**

electric eel *n* an eel-like freshwater fish of N South America, having electric organs in the body.

electric eye *n* another name for **photocell.**

electric field *n* a field of force surrounding a charged particle within which another charged particle experiences a force.

electric flux *n* the amount of electricity displaced across a given area in a dielectric. Symbol: Ψ

electric flux density *n* another name for **electric displacement.**

electric guitar *n* an electrically amplified guitar, used mainly in pop music.

electrician (ɪlɛkˈtrɪʃən, ˌiːlɛk-) *n* a person whose occupation is the installation, maintenance, and repair of electrical devices.

electricity (ɪlɛk'trɪsɪtɪ, ˌiːlɛk-) n **1** any phenomenon associated with stationary or moving electrons, ions, or other charged particles. **2** the science of electricity. **3** an electric current or charge. **4** emotional tension or excitement.

electric motor n a device that converts electrical energy to mechanical torque.

electric organ n **1** Music. **1a** a pipe organ operated by electrical means. **1b** another name for **electronic organ. 2** a group of cells on certain fishes, such as the electric eel, that gives an electric shock to any animal touching them.

electric potential n **a** the work required to transfer a unit positive electric charge from an infinite distance to a given point. **b** the potential difference between the point and some other point. Sometimes shortened to **potential**.

electric ray n any ray of tropical and temperate seas, having a flat rounded body and an organ for producing electricity in each fin.

electric shock n the physiological reaction, characterized by pain and muscular spasm, to the passage of an electric current through the body. It can affect the respiratory system and heart rhythm. Sometimes shortened to **shock**.

electric susceptibility n another name for **susceptibility** (sense 4a).

electrify (ɪ'lɛktrɪˌfaɪ) vb **electrifies, electrifying, electrified.** (tr) **1** to adapt or equip (a system, device, etc.) for operation by electrical power. **2** to charge with or subject to electricity. **3** to startle or excite intensely.
► **e'lectri,fiable** adj ► **e,lectrifi'cation** n ► **e'lectri,fier** n

electro (ɪ'lɛktrəʊ) n, pl **electros.** short for **electroplate** or **electrotype.**

electro- or sometimes before a vowel **electr-** combining form. **1** electric or electrically: electrodynamic. **2** electrolytic: electrodialysis. [from NL, from L ēlectrum amber, from Gk ēlektron]

electroacoustic (ɪˌlɛktrəʊəˈkuːstɪk) adj (of music) combining both computer-generated and acoustic sounds.

electrocardiograph (ɪˌlɛktrəʊˈkɑːdɪəʊˌɡrɑːf) n an instrument for making tracings (**electrocardiograms**) recording the electrical activity of the heart.
► **e,lectro,cardio'graphic** or **e,lectro,cardio'graphical** adj ► **electrocardiography** (ɪˌlɛktrəʊˌkɑːdɪˈɒɡrəfɪ) n

electrochemistry (ɪˌlɛktrəʊˈkɛmɪstrɪ) n the branch of chemistry concerned with electric cells and electrolysis.
► ˌelectro'chemical adj ► **e,lectro'chemist** n

electroconvulsive therapy (ɪˌlɛktrəʊkənˈvʌlsɪv) n Med. the treatment of certain psychotic conditions by passing an electric current through the brain to induce coma or convulsions. See also **shock therapy**.

electrocute (ɪ'lɛktrəˌkjuːt) vb **electrocutes, electrocuting, electrocuted.** (tr) **1** to kill as a result of an electric shock. **2** US. to execute in the electric chair. [C19: from ELECTRO- + (EXE)CUTE]
► **e,lectro'cution** n

electrode (ɪ'lɛktrəʊd) n **1** a conductor through which an electric current enters or leaves an electrolyte, an electric arc, or an electronic valve or tube. **2** an element in a semiconducting device that emits, collects, or controls the movement of electrons or holes.

electrodeposit (ɪˌlɛktrəʊdɪ'pɒzɪt) vb **1** (tr) to deposit (a metal) by electrolysis. ♦ n **2** the deposit so formed.
► **electrodeposition** (ɪˌlɛktrəʊˌdɛpəˈzɪʃən) n

electrodynamics (ɪˌlɛktrəʊdaɪˈnæmɪks) n (functioning as sing) the branch of physics concerned with the interactions between electrical and mechanical forces.

electroencephalograph (ɪˌlɛktrəʊɛnˈsɛfələˌɡrɑːf) n an instrument for making tracings (**electroencephalograms**) recording the electrical activity of the brain, usually by means of electrodes placed on the scalp. See also **brain wave**.
► **e,lectroen,cephalo'graphic** adj ► **electroencephalography** (ɪˌlɛktrəʊɛnˌsɛfəˈlɒɡrəfɪ) n

electrolyse or US **electrolyze** (ɪ'lɛktrəʊˌlaɪz) vb **electrolyses, electrolysing, electrolysed** or US **electrolyzes, electrolyzing, electrolyzed.** (tr) **1** to decompose (a chemical compound) by electrolysis. **2** to destroy (living tissue, such as hair roots) by electrolysis.
► **e'lectro,lyser** or US **e'lectro,lyzer** n

electrolysis (ɪlɛk'trɒlɪsɪs) n **1** the conduction of electricity by an electrolyte, esp. the use of this process to induce chemical changes. **2** the destruction of living tissue, such as hair roots, by an electric current, usually for cosmetic reasons.

electrolyte (ɪ'lɛktrəʊˌlaɪt) n **1** a solution or molten substance that conducts electricity. **2a** a chemical compound that dissociates in solution into ions. **2b** any of the ions themselves.

electrolytic (ɪˌlɛktrəʊ'lɪtɪk) adj **1** Physics. **1a** of, concerned with, or produced by electrolysis or electrodeposition. **1b** of, relating to, or containing an electrolyte. ♦ n **2** Electronics. Also called: **electrolytic capacitor.** a small capacitor consisting of two electrodes separated by an electrolyte.
► **e,lectro'lytically** adv

electromagnet (ɪˌlɛktrəʊ'mæɡnɪt) n a magnet consisting of an iron or steel core wound with a coil of wire through which a current is passed.

electromagnetic (ɪˌlɛktrəʊmæɡ'nɛtɪk) adj **1** of, containing, or operated by an electromagnet. **2** of, relating to, or consisting of electromagnetism. **3** of or relating to electromagnetic radiation.
► **e,lectromag'netically** adv

electromagnetic radiation n radiation consisting of an electric and magnetic field at right angles to each other and to the direction of propagation.

electromagnetics (ɪˌlɛktrəʊmæɡ'nɛtɪks) n (functioning as sing) Physics. another name for **electromagnetism** (sense 2).

electromagnetic spectrum n the complete range of electromagnetic radiation from the longest radio wave to the shortest gamma radiation.

electromagnetic unit n any unit of a system of electrical cgs units in which the magnetic constant is given the value of unity.

electromagnetic wave n a wave of energy propagated in an electromagnetic field.

electromagnetism (ɪˌlɛktrəʊ'mæɡnɪˌtɪzəm) n **1** magnetism produced by electric current. **2** Also called **electromagnetics.** the branch of physics concerned with this magnetism and with the interaction of electric and magnetic fields.

electrometer (ɪlɛk'trɒmɪtə, ˌiːlɛk-) n an instrument for detecting or measuring a potential difference or charge by the electrostatic forces between charged bodies.
► **electrometric** (ɪˌlɛktrəʊ'mɛtrɪk) or **e,lectro'metrical** adj ► **elec'trometry** n

electromotive (ɪˌlɛktrəʊ'məʊtɪv) adj of, concerned with, or producing an electric current.

electromotive force n Physics. **a** a source of energy that can cause current to flow in an electrical circuit. **b** the rate at which energy is drawn from this source when unit current flows through the circuit, measured in volts.

electromyography (ɪˌlɛktrəʊmaɪ'ɒɡrəfɪ) n Med. a technique for recording the electrical activity of muscles, used in the diagnosis of nerve and muscle disorders.

electron (ɪ'lɛktrɒn) n an elementary particle in all atoms, orbiting the nucleus in numbers equal to the atomic number of the element. [C19: from ELECTRO- + -ON]

electronegative (ɪˌlɛktrəʊ'nɛɡətɪv) adj **1** having a negative electric charge. **2** (of an atom, molecule, etc.) tending to attract electrons and form negative ions or polarized bonds.

electron gun n a heated cathode for producing and focusing a beam of electrons, used esp. in cathode-ray tubes.

electronic (ɪlɛk'trɒnɪk, ˌiːlɛk-) adj **1** of, concerned with, using, or operated by devices, such as transistors, in

which electrons are conducted through a semiconductor, free space, or gas. **2** of or concerned with electronics. **3** of or concerned with electrons. **4** involving or concerned with the representation, storage, or transmission of information by electronic systems: *electronic mail; electronic shopping.*
► elec'tronically *adv*

> **USAGE NOTE** *Electronic* is used to refer to equipment, such as television sets, computers, etc., in which current is controlled by transistors, valves, and similar components and also to the components themselves. *Electrical* is used in a more general sense, often to refer to the use of electricity as opposed to other forms of energy: *electrical engineering; an electrical appliance. Electric,* in many cases used interchangeably with *electrical,* is often restricted to the description of devices or to concepts relating to the flow of current: *electric fire; electric charge.*

:lectronic flash *n Photog.* an electronic device for producing a very bright flash of light by means of an electric discharge in a gas-filled tube.

:lectronic funds transfer at point of sale *n* a system for debiting a retail sale direct to the customer's bank, building-society, or credit-card account by means of a computer link using the telephone network. The customer inserts his debit card or credit card into the computer at the point of sale. Acronym: **EFTPOS**.

:lectronic ignition *n* any system that uses an electronic circuit to supply the voltage to the sparking plugs of an internal-combustion engine.

:lectronic keyboard *n* a typewriter keyboard used to operate an electronic device such as a computer.

:lectronic mail *n* the transmission of information, messages, facsimiles, etc., from one computer terminal to another. Often shortened to **E-mail, e-mail, email**.

:lectronic music *n* music consisting of sounds produced by electric currents either controlled from an instrument panel or keyboard or prerecorded on magnetic tape.

:lectronic organ *n Music.* an instrument played by means of a keyboard, in which sounds are produced by electronic or electrical means.

:lectronic organizer *n* a computerized personal organizer.

:lectronic point of sale *n* a computerized system for recording sales in retail shops, using a laser scanner at the cash till to read bar codes on the packages of the items sold. The retailer's stock record is automatically adjusted and the customer receives an itemized bill. Acronym: **EPOS**.

:lectronic publishing *n* the publication of information on magnetic tape, discs, etc., so that it can be accessed by a computer.

:lectronics (ɪlɛk'trɒnɪks, ˌiːlɛk-) *n* **1** (*functioning as sing*) the science and technology concerned with the development, behaviour, and applications of electronic devices and circuits. **2** (*functioning as pl*) the circuits and devices of a piece of electronic equipment.

:lectronic surveillance *n* **1** the use of such electronic devices as television monitors, video cameras, etc., to prevent burglary, shop lifting, break-ins, etc. **2** monitoring events, conversations, etc. at a distance by electronic means, esp. by such covert means as wire tapping or bugging.

:lectronic tag *n* another name for **tag**[1] (sense 2).

:lectronic transfer of funds *n* the transfer of money from one bank or building-society account to another by means of a computer link using the telephone network. Abbrev.: **ETF**.

:lectron lens *n* a system, such as an arrangement of electrodes or magnets, that produces a field for focusing a beam of electrons.

electron micrograph *n* a photograph of a specimen taken through an electron microscope.

electron microscope *n* a powerful microscope that uses electrons, rather than light, and electron lenses to produce a magnified image.

electron tube *n* an electrical device, such as a valve, in which a flow of electrons between electrodes takes place.

electronvolt (ɪˌlɛktrɒn'vəʊlt) *n* a unit of energy equal to the work done on an electron accelerated through a potential difference of 1 volt.

electrophoresis (ɪˌlɛktrəʊfə'riːsɪs) *n* the motion of charged particles in a colloid under the influence of an applied electric field.
► **electrophoretic** (ɪˌlɛktrəʊfə'rɛtɪk) *adj*

electrophorus (ɪlɛk'trɒfərəs, ˌiːlɛk-) *n* an apparatus for generating static electricity by induction. [C18: from ELECTRO- + -*phorus*, from Gk, from *pherein* to bear]

electroplate (ɪ'lɛktrəʊˌpleɪt) *vb* **electroplates, electroplating, electroplated. 1** (*tr*) to plate (an object) by electrolysis. ♦ *n* **2** electroplated articles collectively, esp. when plated with silver.
► e'lectro,plater *n*

electropositive (ɪˌlɛktrəʊ'pɒzɪtɪv) *adj* **1** having a positive electric charge. **2** (of an atom, molecule, etc.) tending to release electrons and form positive ions or polarized bonds.

electrorheology (ɪˌlɛktrəʊrɪ'ɒlədʒɪ) *n* **1** the study of the flow of fluids under the influence of electric fields. **2** the way in which fluid flow is influenced by an electric field.
► e,lectro,rheo'logical *adj*

electroscope (ɪ'lɛktrəˌskəʊp) *n* an apparatus for detecting an electric charge, typically consisting of a rod holding two gold foils that separate when a charge is applied.
► **electroscopic** (ɪˌlɛktrəʊ'skɒpɪk) *adj*

electroshock therapy (ɪ'lɛktrəʊˌʃɒk) *n* another name for **electroconvulsive therapy**.

electrostatics (ɪˌlɛktrəʊ'stætɪks) *n* (*functioning as sing*) the branch of physics concerned with static electricity.
► e,lectro'static *adj*

electrostatic unit *n* any unit of a system of electrical cgs units in which the electric constant is given the value of unity.

electrotherapeutics (ɪˌlɛktrəʊˌθɛrə'pjuːtɪks) *n* (*functioning as sing*) the branch of medical science concerned with the use of electrotherapy.
► e,lectro,thera'peutic *or* e,lectro,thera'peutical *adj*

electrotherapy (ɪˌlɛktrəʊ'θɛrəpɪ) *n* treatment in which electric currents are passed through the tissues to stimulate muscle function in paralysed patients.
► e,lectro'therapist *n*

electrotype (ɪ'lɛktrəʊˌtaɪp) *n* **1** a duplicate printing plate made by electrolytically depositing a layer of copper or nickel onto a mould of the original. ♦ *vb* **electrotypes, electrotyping, electrotyped. 2** (*tr*) to make an electrotype of (printed matter, etc.).
► e'lectro,typer *n*

electrovalent bond (ɪˌlɛktrəʊ'veɪlənt) *n* a type of chemical bond in which one atom loses an electron to form a positive ion and the other atom gains the electron to form a negative ion. The resulting ions are held together by electrostatic attraction.
► e,lectro'valency *n*

electroweak (ɪˌlɛktrəʊ'wiːk) *adj Physics.* involving both electromagnetic interaction and weak interaction.

electrum (ɪ'lɛktrəm) *n* an alloy of gold and silver. [C14: from L, from Gk *ēlektron* amber]

electuary (ɪ'lɛktjʊərɪ) *n, pl* **electuaries.** *Med.* a paste taken orally, containing a drug mixed with syrup or honey. [C14: from LL *ēlēctuārium,* prob. from Gk *ēkleikton,* from *leikhein* to lick]

eleemosynary (ˌɛliː'mɒsɪnərɪ) *adj* **1** of or dependent on charity. **2** given as an act of charity. [C17: from Church L *eleēmosyna* ALMS]

elegance ('ɛlɪgəns) *or* **elegancy** *n, pl* **elegances** *or*

elegancies. 1 dignified grace. **2** good taste in design, style, arrangement, etc. **3** something elegant; a refinement.

elegant ('ɛlɪɡənt) *adj* **1** tasteful in dress, style, or design. **2** dignified and graceful. **3** cleverly simple; ingenious: *an elegant solution*. [C16: from L *ēlegāns* tasteful; see ELECT]

elegiac (,ɛlɪ'dʒaɪək) *adj* **1** resembling, characteristic of, relating to, or appropriate to an elegy. **2** lamenting; mournful. **3** denoting or written in elegiac couplets (which consist of a dactylic hexameter followed by a dactylic pentameter) or elegiac stanzas (which consist of a quatrain in iambic pentameters with alternate lines rhyming). ◆ *n* **4** (*often pl*) an elegiac couplet or stanza.
► ,ele'giacally *adv*

elegize *or* **elegise** ('ɛlɪ,dʒaɪz) *vb* **elegizes, elegizing, elegized** *or* **elegises, elegising, elegised. 1** to compose an elegy (in memory of). **2** (*intr*) to write elegiacally.
► 'elegist *n*

elegy ('ɛlɪdʒɪ) *n, pl* **elegies. 1** a mournful poem or song, esp. a lament for the dead. **2** poetry written in elegiac couplets or stanzas. [C16: via F & L from Gk, from *elegos* lament sung to flute accompaniment]

USAGE NOTE Avoid confusion with **eulogy**.

Eleia ★ ('iːlɪə) *n* a variant spelling of **Elia**[1].

elem. *abbrev. for:* **1** element(s). **2** elementary.

element ('ɛlɪmənt) *n* **1** any of the 109 known substances that consist of atoms with the same number of protons in their nuclei. **2** one of the fundamental or irreducible components making up a whole. **3** a cause that contributes to a result; factor. **4** any group that is part of a larger unit, such as a military formation. **5** a small amount; hint. **6** a distinguishable section of a social group. **7** the most favourable environment for an animal or plant. **8** the situation in which a person is happiest or most effective (esp. in **in** *or* **out of one's element**). **9** the resistance wire that constitutes the electrical heater in a cooker, heater, etc. **10** one of the four substances thought in ancient and medieval cosmology to constitute the universe (earth, air, water, or fire). **11** (*pl*) atmospheric conditions, esp. wind, rain, and cold. **12** (*pl*) the basic principles. **13** *Christianity*. the bread or wine consecrated in the Eucharist. [C13: from L *elementum* a first principle, element]

elemental (,ɛlɪ'mɛntəl) *adj* **1** fundamental; basic. **2** motivated by or symbolic of primitive powerful natural forces or passions. **3** of or relating to earth, air, water, and fire considered as elements. **4** of or relating to atmospheric forces, esp. wind, rain, and cold. **5** of or relating to a chemical element. ◆ *n* **6** *Rare*. a spirit or force that is said to appear in physical form.
► ,ele'mental,ism *n*

elementary (,ɛlɪ'mɛntərɪ) *adj* **1** not difficult; rudimentary. **2** of or concerned with the first principles of a subject; introductory or fundamental. **3** *Chem*. another word for **elemental** (sense 5).
► ,ele'mentariness *n*

elementary particle *n* any of several entities, such as electrons, neutrons, or protons, that are less complex than atoms.

elementary school *n* **1** *Brit*. a former name for **primary school**. **2** *US & Canad*. a state school for the first six to eight years of a child's education.

elenchus (ɪ'lɛŋkəs) *n, pl* **elenchi** (-kaɪ). *Logic*. refutation of an argument by proving the contrary of its conclusion, esp. syllogistically. [C17: from L, from Gk, from *elenkhein* to refute]
► e'lenctic *adj*

elephant ('ɛlɪfənt) *n, pl* **elephants** *or* **elephant**. either of two proboscidean mammals. The **African elephant** is the larger species, with large flapping ears and a less humped back than the **Indian elephant**, of S and SE Asia. [C13: from L, from Gk *elephas* elephant, ivory]

elephantiasis (,ɛlɪfən'taɪəsɪs) *n Pathol*. a complication of chronic filariasis, in which nematode worms block the lymphatic vessels, usually in the legs or scrotum, causing extreme enlargement of the affected area. [C1... via L from Gk, from *elephas* ELEPHANT + -IASIS]

elephantine (,ɛlɪ'fæntaɪn) *adj* **1** denoting, relating to, c characteristic of an elephant or elephants. **2** huge clumsy, or ponderous.

elephant seal *n* either of two large earless seals, c southern oceans or of the N Atlantic, the males of whic have a trunklike snout.

Eleusinian mysteries *pl n* a mystical religious fest val, held at Eleusis in classical times, to celebrate th gods Persephone, Demeter, and Dionysus.

Eleusis ★ (ɪ'luːsɪs) *n* a town in Greece, in Attica about 2 km (14 miles) west of Athens, of which it is now an in dustrial suburb. Modern Greek name: **Elevsís**.
► **Eleusinian** (,ɛlju'sɪnɪən) *n, adj*

elev. *or* **el.** *abbrev. for* elevation.

elevate ('ɛlɪ,veɪt) *vb* **elevates, elevating, elevated.** (*tr*) **1** t move to a higher place. **2** to raise in rank or status. **3** t put in a cheerful mood; elate. **4** to put on a higher cul tural plane; uplift. **5** to raise the axis of a gun. **6** to rais the intensity or pitch of (the voice). [C15: from *ēlevāre*, from *levāre* to raise, from *levis* (adj) light]
► 'ele,vatory *adj*

elevated ('ɛlɪ,veɪtɪd) *adj* **1** raised to or being at a highe level. **2** inflated or lofty; exalted. **3** in a cheerful mood. *Inf*. slightly drunk.

elevation (,ɛlɪ'veɪʃən) *n* **1** the act of elevating or the stat of being elevated. **2** the height of something above given place, esp. above sea level. **3** a raised area; height. nobleness or grandeur. **5** a drawing to scale of the exter nal face of a building or structure. **6** a ballet dancer' ability to leap high. **7** *Astron*. another name for **altitud** (sense 3). **8** the angle formed between the muzzle of gun and the horizontal.
► ,ele'vational *adj*

elevator ('ɛlɪ,veɪtə) *n* **1** a person or thing that elevates. a mechanical hoist, often consisting of a chain of scoop linked together on a conveyor belt. **3** the US and Canad name for **lift** (sense 14a). **4** *Chiefly US & Canad*. a granar equipped with an elevator and, usually, facilities fo cleaning and grading the grain. **5** a control surface o the tailplane of an aircraft, for making it climb or de scend. **6** any muscle that raises a part of the body.

eleven (ɪ'lɛvən) *n* **1** the cardinal number that is the sun of ten and one. **2** a numeral, 11, XI, etc., representin this number. **3** something representing, represented by or consisting of 11 units. **4** (*functioning as sing or pl*) team of 11 players in football, cricket, etc. **5** Also called **eleven o'clock**. eleven hours after noon or midnight ◆ *determiner* **6a** amounting to eleven. **6b** (*as pron*): anothe *eleven*. [OE *endleofan*]
► e'leventh *adj, n*

eleven-plus *n* (in Britain, esp. formerly) an examina tion taken by children aged 10 or 11 that determines th type of secondary education a child will be given.

elevenses (ɪ'lɛvənzɪz) *pl n* (*sometimes functioning as sing Brit. inf.* a light snack taken in mid-morning.

eleventh hour *n* the latest possible time; last minute.

Elevsís ★ (,ɛlɛf'sɪs) *n* transliteration of the Modern Greek name for **Eleusis**.

elf (elf) *n, pl* **elves. 1** (in folklore) one of a kind of legendary beings, usually characterized as small, manlike, and mis chievous. **2** a mischievous or whimsical child. [OE *ælf*]
► 'elfish *or* 'elvish *adj*

El Faiyûm (el faɪ'juːm) *or* **Al Faiyûm** ★ (æl faɪ'juːm) *n* city in N Egypt: a site of towns going back at least to the 12th dynasty. Pop.: 250 000 (1992 est.).

El Ferrol ★ (*Spanish* ɛl fe'rrɔl) *n* a port in NW Spain, or the Atlantic: fortified naval base, with a deep natura harbour. Pop.: 82 371 (1991). Official name (since 1939): **El Ferrol del Caudillo** (del kau'ðiʎo).

elfin ('ɛlfɪn) *adj* **1** of or like an elf or elves. **2** small, deli cate, and charming.

elflock ('elf,lɒk) *n* a lock of hair, fancifully regarded a having been tangled by the elves.

Elgar ★ ('elgaː) *n* Sir **Edward (William)**. 1857–1934, British composer, whose works include the *Enigma Variations*

★ people and places

(1899), the oratorio *The Dream of Gerontius* (1900), two symphonies, a cello concerto, and a violin concerto.

lgin ★ (ˈɛlɡɪn) *n* a market town in NE Scotland, the administrative centre of Moray, on the River Lossie: ruined 13th-century cathedral: distilling, engineering. Pop.: 19 027 (1994).

l Gîza ★ (ɛl ˈɡiːzə) *n* a city in NE Egypt, on the W bank of the Nile opposite Cairo: nearby are the Great Pyramid of Cheops (Khufu) and the Sphinx. Pop.: 2 144 000 (1992 est.).

lgon ★ (ˈɛlɡɒn) *n* **Mount.** an extinct volcano in E Africa, on the Kenya-Uganda border. Height: 4321 m (14 178 ft).

l Greco ★ (ɛl ˈɡrɛkəu) *n* real name *Domenikos Theotocopoulos*. 1541–1614, Spanish painter, born in Crete.

li ★ (ˈiːlaɪ) *n Old Testament*. the highest priest at Shiloh and teacher of Samuel (I Samuel 1–3).

lia[1] *or* **Eleia** ★ (ˈiːlɪə) *n* a department of SW Greece, in the W Peloponnese: in ancient times most of the region formed the state of Elis. Pop.: 179 429 (1991). Area: 2681 sq. km (1035 sq. miles). Modern Greek name: **Ilía.**

lia[2] ★ (ˈiːlɪə) *n* the pen name of (Charles) **Lamb.**

lias ★ (ɪˈlaɪəs) *n Bible*. the Douay spelling of **Elijah.**

licit (ɪˈlɪsɪt) *vb* (*tr*) **1** to give rise to; evoke. **2** to bring to light. [C17: from L *ēlicere*, from *licere* to entice]
▸ e'licitable *adj* ▸ e,lici'tation *n* ▸ e'licitor *n*

lide (ɪˈlaɪd) *vb* elides, eliding, elided. to undergo or cause to undergo elision. [C16: from L *ēlīdere* to knock, from *laedere* to hit, wound]
▸ e'lidible *adj*

ligible (ˈɛlɪdʒəb³l) *adj* **1** fit, worthy, or qualified, as for office. **2** desirable, esp. as a spouse. [C15: from LL *ēligere* to ELECT]
▸ ,eligi'bility *n* ▸ 'eligibly *adv*

lijah ★ (ɪˈlaɪdʒə) *n Old Testament*. a Hebrew prophet of the 9th century B.C., who was persecuted for denouncing Ahab and Jezebel. (I Kings 17–21: 21; II Kings 1–2:18).

likón ★ (ɛliˈkɒn) *n* transliteration of the Modern Greek name for **Helicon.**

liminate (ɪˈlɪmɪˌneɪt) *vb* eliminates, eliminating, eliminated. (*tr*) **1** to remove or take out. **2** to reject; omit from consideration. **3** to remove (a competitor, team, etc.) from a contest, usually by defeat. **4** *Sl.* to murder in cold blood. **5** *Physiol.* to expel (waste) from the body. **6** *Maths.* to remove (an unknown variable) from simultaneous equations. [C16: from L *ēlīmināre* to turn out of the house, from *e-* out + *līmen* threshold]
▸ e'liminable *adj* ▸ e,limi'nation *n* ▸ e'liminative *adj*
▸ e'limi,nator *n*

> **USAGE NOTE** *Eliminate* is sometimes wrongly used to talk about avoiding the repetition of something undesirable: *we must prevent* (not *eliminate*) *further mistakes of this kind.*

liot ★ (ˈɛlɪət) *n* **1 George,** real name *Mary Ann Evans*. 1819–80, British novelist, noted for *The Mill on the Floss* (1860), *Silas Marner* (1861), and *Middlemarch* (1872). **2** Sir **John.** 1592–1632, English statesman, a leader of parliamentary opposition to Charles I. **3 T(homas) S(tearns).** 1888–1965, British poet, dramatist, and critic, born in the US. His poetry includes *The Waste Land* (1922) and *Four Quartets* (1943). Among his verse plays are *Murder in the Cathedral* (1935) and *The Confidential Clerk* (1954): Nobel prize for literature 1948.

lis ★ (ˈiːlɪs) *n* an ancient city-state of SW Greece, in the NW Peloponnese: site of the ancient Olympic games.

LISA (ɪˈlaɪzə) *n acronym for* enzyme-linked immunosorbent assay: an immunological technique for accurately measuring the amount of a substance, for example in a blood sample.

lisabeth ★ (ɪˈlɪzəbəθ) *n* a variant spelling of **Elizabeth**[2] (sense 1).

lisabethville ★ (ɪˈlɪzəbəθˌvɪl) *n* the former name (until 1966) of **Lubumbashi.**

Elisavetgrad ★ (*Russian* jɪlizaˈvjɛtɡrət) *n* a former name (until 1924) of **Kirovograd.**

Elisavetpol ★ (*Russian* jɪlizaˈvjɛtpəlj) *n* a former name (until 1920) of **Kirovabad.**

Elisha ★ (ɪˈlaɪʃə) *n Old Testament*. a Hebrew prophet of the 9th century B.C.: successor of Elijah (II Kings 3–9).

elision (ɪˈlɪʒən) *n* **1** omission of a syllable or vowel from a word. **2** omission of parts of a book, etc. [C16: from L *ēlidere* to ELIDE]

elite *or* **élite** (ɪˈliːt, eɪ-) *n* **1** (*sometimes functioning as pl*) the most powerful, rich, or gifted members of a group, community, etc. **2** a typewriter type size having 12 characters to the inch. ◆ *adj* **3** of or suitable for an elite. [C18: from F, from OF *eslit* chosen, from L *ēligere* to ELECT]

elitism (ɪˈliːtɪzəm, eɪ-) *n* **1a** the belief that society should be governed by an elite. **1b** such government. **2** pride in or awareness of being one of an elite group.
▸ e'litist *adj, n*

elixir (ɪˈlɪksə) *n* **1** an alchemical preparation supposed to be capable of prolonging life (**elixir of life**) or of transmuting base metals into gold. **2** anything that purports to be a sovereign remedy. **3** a quintessence. **4** a liquid containing a medicine with syrup, glycerine, or alcohol added to mask its unpleasant taste. [C14: from Med. L, from Ar., prob. from Gk *xērion* powder used for drying wounds]

Elizabeth[1] ★ (ɪˈlɪzəbəθ) *n* **1** a city in NE New Jersey, on Newark Bay. Pop.: 106 298 (1994 est.). **2** a town in SE South Australia, near Adelaide. Pop.: 34 000 (latest est.).

Elizabeth[2] ★ (ɪˈlɪzəbəθ) *n* **1** Also: **Elisabeth. Saint.** *New Testament*. the wife of Zacharias, mother of John the Baptist, and kinswoman of the Virgin Mary. Feast day: Nov. 5 or 8. **2** pen name *Carmen Sylva*. 1843–1916, queen of Romania (1881–1914) and author. **3** Russian name *Yelizaveta Petrovna*. 1709–62, empress of Russia (1741–62); daughter of Peter the Great. **4** title *the Queen Mother*; original name Lady *Elizabeth Bowes-Lyon*. born 1900, queen of Great Britain and Northern Ireland (1936–52) as the wife of George VI; mother of Elizabeth II.

Elizabeth I ★ *n* 1533–1603, queen of England (1558–1603); daughter of Henry VIII and Anne Boleyn. She established the Church of England (1559), executed Mary Queen of Scots (1587), and defeated the Spanish Armada (1588).

Elizabeth II ★ *n* born 1926, queen of Great Britain and Northern Ireland from 1952; daughter of George VI.

Elizabethan (ɪˌlɪzəˈbiːθən) *adj* **1** of, characteristic of, or relating to the reigns of Elizabeth I or Elizabeth II. **2** of, relating to, or designating a style of architecture used in England during the reign of Elizabeth I. ◆ *n* **3** a person who lived in England during the reign of Elizabeth I.

Elizabethan sonnet *n* another term for **Shakespearean sonnet.**

Elizabeth of Hungary ★ *n* **Saint.** 1207–31, Hungarian princess who devoted herself to charity and asceticism. Feast day: Nov. 17 and 19.

elk (ɛlk) *n, pl* elks *or* elk. **1** a large deer of N Europe and Asia: also occurs in N America, where it is called a moose. **2 American elk.** another name for **wapiti.** [OE *eolh*]

El Khalil ★ (æl xɒˈliːl) *n* transliteration of the Arabic name for **Hebron.**

ell (ɛl) *n* an obsolete unit of length, approximately 45 inches. [OE *eln* forearm (the measure orig. being from elbow to fingertips)]

Ellás ★ (ɛˈlas) *n* transliteration of the Modern Greek name for **Greece.**

Ellesmere Island ★ (ˈɛlzmɪə) *n* a Canadian island in the Arctic Ocean: part of the Northwest Territories; mountainous, with many glaciers. Area: 212 688 sq. km (82 119 sq. miles).

Ellesmere Port ★ *n* a port in NW England, in NW Cheshire on the Mersey estuary and Manchester Ship Canal. Pop.: 64 504 (1991).

Ellice Islands ★ (ˈɛlɪs) *pl n* the former name (until 1975) of **Tuvalu.**

Ellington ★ (ˈɛlɪŋtən) *n* **Duke,** nickname of *Edward*

★ people and places

Kennedy Ellington. 1899–1974, US jazz composer and pianist.

ellipse (ɪ'lɪps) *n* a closed conic section shaped like a flattened circle and formed by an inclined plane that does not cut the base of the cone. [C18: back formation from ELLIPSIS]

ellipsis (ɪ'lɪpsɪs) *n, pl* **ellipses** (-si:z). **1** omission of parts of a word or sentence. **2** *Printing.* a sequence of three dots (…) indicating an omission in text. [C16: from L, from Gk, from *en* in + *leipein* to leave]

ellipsoid (ɪ'lɪpsɔɪd) *n* **a** a geometric surface, symmetrical about the three coordinate axes, whose plane sections are ellipses or circles. **b** a solid having this shape.
▶ **ellipsoidal** (ɪlɪp'sɔɪd°l, ˌɛl-) *adj*

ellipsoid of revolution *n* a geometric surface produced by rotating an ellipse about one of its two axes and having circular plane sections perpendicular to the axis of revolution.

elliptical (ɪ'lɪptɪk°l) *adj* **1** relating to or having the shape of an ellipse. **2** relating to or resulting from ellipsis. **3** (of speech, literary style, etc.) **3a** very concise, often so as to be obscure or ambiguous. **3b** circumlocutory. ◆ Also (for senses 1 and 2): **elliptic.**
▶ **el'lipticalness** *n*

> **USAGE NOTE** The use of *elliptical* to mean *circumlocutory* should be avoided as it may be interpreted wrongly as meaning *condensed* or *concise.*

Ellis ★ ('ɛlɪs) *n* (**Henry**) **Havelock** ('hævlɒk). 1859–1939, British essayist: author of works on the psychology of sex.

elm (ɛlm) *n* **1** any tree of the genus *Ulmus,* occurring in the N hemisphere, having serrated leaves and winged fruits (samaras). **2** the hard heavy wood of this tree. [OE *elm*]

El Mansûra (ɛl mæn'suərə) *or* **Al Mansûrah** ★ *n* a city in NE Egypt: scene of a battle (1250) in which the Crusaders were defeated by the Mamelukes and Louis IX of France was captured; cotton-manufacturing centre. Pop.: 371 000 (1992 est.).

El Minya ★ (ɛl 'mɪnjə) *n* a river port in central Egypt on the Nile. Pop.: 208 000 (1992 est.).

El Misti ★ (ɛl 'mi:sti:) *n* a volcano in S Peru, in the Andes. Height: 5852 m (19 199 ft).

El Niño (ɛl 'ni:njəu) *n Meteorol.* a warming of the eastern tropical Pacific occurring every few years, which disrupts the weather pattern of the region. [from Sp.: The Child, i.e. Christ, referring to its original occurrence at Christmas time]

El Obeid ★ (ɛl əu'beɪd) *n* a city in the central Sudan, in Kordofan province: scene of the defeat of a British and Egyptian army by the Mahdi (1883). Pop.: 228 096 (1993).

elocution (ˌɛlə'kju:ʃən) *n* the art of public speaking. [C15: from L *ēloquī,* from *loquī* to speak]
▶ ˌelo'cutionary *adj* ▶ ˌelo'cutionist *n*

Elohim ★ (ɛ'ləuhɪm, ˌɛlɒ'hi:m) *n Old Testament.* a Hebrew word for God or gods. [C17: from Heb. *'Elōhīm,* pl (to indicate uniqueness) of *'Elōah* God]

Elohist ★ (ɛ'ləuhɪst) *n Bible.* the supposed author or authors of the Pentateuch, identified chiefly by the use of the word *Elohim* for God.

elongate ('i:lɒŋgeɪt) *vb* **elongates, elongating, elongated. 1** to make or become longer; stretch. ◆ *adj* **2** long and narrow. **3** lengthened or tapered. [C16: from LL *ēlongāre* to keep at a distance, from *ē-* away + L *longē* (adv) far]
▶ ˌelon'gation *n*

elope (ɪ'ləup) *vb* **elopes, eloping, eloped.** (*intr*) to run away secretly with a lover, esp. in order to marry. [C16: from Anglo-F *aloper,* ?from MDu. *lōpen* to run; see LOPE]
▶ **e'lopement** *n* ▶ **e'loper** *n*

eloquence ('ɛləkwəns) *n* **1** ease in using language. **2** powerful and effective language. **3** the quality of being persuasive or moving.

eloquent ('ɛləkwənt) *adj* **1** (of speech, writing, etc.) fluent and persuasive. **2** visibly or vividly expressive: *an eloquent yawn.* [C14: from L *ēloquēns,* from *loquī* to speak]
▶ **'eloquentness** *n*

El Paso ★ (ɛl 'pæsəu) *n* a city in W Texas, on the Rio Grande opposite Ciudad Juárez, Mexico. Pop.: 579 307 (1994 est.).

El Salvador ★ (ɛl 'sælvəˌdɔ:) *n* a republic in Central America, on the Pacific: colonized by the Spanish from 1524; declared independence in 1841, becoming a republic in 1856. It consists of coastal lowlands rising to a central plateau. Coffee constitutes about half of the total exports. Official language: Spanish. Religion: Roman Catholic. Currency: colón. Capital: San Salvador. Pop.: 5 662 000 (1997). Area: 21 393 sq. km (8236 sq. miles)
▶ ˌSalva'doran, ˌSalva'dorean, *or* ˌSalva'dorian *adj, n*

Elsan ('ɛlsæn) *n Trademark.* a type of portable chemical lavatory. [C20: from initials of *E. L.* Jackson, manufacturer + SAN(ITATION)]

Elsass ★ ('ɛlzas) *n* the German name for **Alsace.**

Elsass-Lothringen ★ ('ɛlzas'lo:trɪŋən) *n* the German name for **Alsace-Lorraine.**

else (ɛls) *determiner* (*postpositive; used after an indefinite pronoun or an interrogative*) **1** in addition; more: *there is nobody else here.* **2** different: *where else could he be?* ◆ *adv* **3 or else. 3a** if not, then: *go away or else I won't finish my work today.* **3b** or something terrible will result: *used as a threat: sit down, or else!* [OE *elles,* genitive of *el* strange, foreign]

elsewhere (ˌɛls'wɛə) *adv* in or to another place; somewhere else. [OE *elles hwǣr;* see ELSE, WHERE]

Elsinore ★ (ˌɛlsɪˌnɔ:, ˌɛlsɪ'nɔ:) *n* the English name for **Helsingør.**

ELT *abbrev. for* English Language Teaching.

Elton ★ ('ɛlt°n) *n* **Charles Sutherland.** 1900–91, British zoologist: initiated the study of animal ecology.

eluate ('ɛljuːˌeɪt) *n* a solution of adsorbed material in the eluant obtained during the process of elution.

elucidate (ɪ'lu:sɪˌdeɪt) *vb* **elucidates, elucidating, elucidated.** to make clear (something obscure or difficult); clarify. [C16: from LL *ēlūcidāre* to enlighten; see LUCID]
▶ eˌluci'dation *n* ▶ e'luciˌdative *or* e'luciˌdatory *adj*
▶ e'luciˌdator *n*

elude (ɪ'lu:d) *vb* **eludes, eluding, eluded.** (*tr*) **1** to escape from or avoid, esp. by cunning. **2** to avoid fulfilment of (a responsibility, obligation, etc.); evade. **3** to escape discovery or understanding by; baffle. [C16: from L *ēlūdere* to deceive, from *lūdere* to play]
▶ e'luder *n* ▶ e'lusion *n*

> **USAGE NOTE** *Elude* is sometimes wrongly used where *allude* is meant: *he was alluding* (not *eluding*) *to his previous visit to the city.*

eluent *or* **eluant** ('ɛljuənt) *n* a solvent used for eluting

elusive (ɪ'lu:sɪv) *adj* **1** difficult to catch. **2** preferring or living in solitude and anonymity. **3** difficult to remember.
▶ e'lusiveness *n*

> **USAGE NOTE** See at **illusory.**

elute (i:'lu:t, ɪ'lu:t) *vb* **elutes, eluting, eluted.** (*tr*) to wash out (a substance) by the action of a solvent, as in chromatography. [C18: from L *ēlūtus* rinsed out, from *luere* to wash, LAVE]
▶ e'lution *n*

elutriate (ɪ'lu:trɪˌeɪt) *vb* **elutriates, elutriating, elutriated.** (*tr*) to purify or separate (a substance or mixture) by washing and straining or decanting. [C18: from L *ēluere* from *ē-* out + *lavere* to wash]
▶ eˌlutri'ation *n*

elver ('ɛlvə) *n* a young eel, esp. one migrating up a river. [C17: var. of *eelfare,* lit.: eel-journey; see EEL, FARE]

★ people and places

lves (ɛlvz) *n* the plural of **elf.**

lvish ('ɛlvɪʃ) *adj* a variant of **elfish**: see **elf.**

ly ★ ('iːlɪ) *n* **1** a cathedral city in E England, in E Cambridgeshire on the River Ouse. Pop.: 10 329 (1991). **2 Isle of.** a former county of E England, part of Cambridgeshire since 1965.

lysée ★ (eɪ'liːzeɪ) *n* a palace in Paris, in the Champs Elysées: official residence of the president of France.

lysium ★ (ɪ'lɪzɪəm) *n* **1** Also called: **Elysian fields.** *Greek myth.* the dwelling place of the blessed after death. **2** a state or place of perfect bliss. [C16: from L, from Gk *Elusion pedion* Elysian (that is, blessed) fields]

lytron ('ɛlɪˌtrɒn) *or* **elytrum** ('ɛlɪtrəm) *n, pl* **elytra** (-trə). either of the horny front wings of beetles and some other insects. [C18: from Gk *elutron* sheath]

m (ɛm) *n Printing.* **1** the square of a body of any size of type, used as a unit of measurement. **2** Also called: **pica em, pica.** a unit of measurement in printing, equal to twelve points or one sixth of an inch. [C19: from the name of the letter *M*]

m- *prefix* a variant of **en-¹** and **en-²** before *b*, *m*, and *p*.

em (əm) *pron* an informal variant of **them.**

maciate (ɪ'meɪsɪˌeɪt) *vb* **emaciates, emaciating, emaciated.** (*usually tr*) to become or cause to become abnormally thin. [C17: from L, from *macer* thin]
▶ **e'maci.ated** *adj* ▶ **e.maci'ation** *n*

-mail, e-mail, *or* **email** ('iːmeɪl) *n* **1** short for **electronic mail.** ◆ *vb* (*tr*) **2** to contact (a person) by electronic mail. **3** to send (a message, document, etc.) by electronic mail.

manate ('ɛməˌneɪt) *vb* **emanates, emanating, emanated. 1** (*intr*; often foll. by *from*) to issue or proceed from or as from a source. **2** (*tr*) to send forth; emit. [C18: from L *ēmānāre* to flow out, from *mānāre* to flow]
▶ **emanative** ('ɛmənətɪv) *adj* ▶ **'ema.nator** *n* ▶ **'ema- .natory** *adj*

manation (ˌɛmə'neɪʃən) *n* **1** an act or instance of emanating. **2** something that emanates or is produced. **3** a gaseous product of radioactive decay.
▶ **ema'national** *adj*

mancipate (ɪ'mænsɪˌpeɪt) *vb* **emancipates, emancipating, emancipated.** (*tr*) **1** to free from restriction or restraint, esp. social or legal restraint. **2** (*often passive*) to free from the inhibitions of conventional morality. **3** to liberate (a slave) from bondage. [C17: from L *ēmancipāre* to give independence (to a son), from *mancipāre* to transfer property; see MANCIPLE]
▶ **e'manci.pated** *adj* ▶ **e.manci'pation** *n* ▶ **e'manci.pator** *n* ▶ **emancipatory** (ɪ'mænsɪpətərɪ, -trɪ) *adj*

masculate *vb* (ɪ'mæskjuˌleɪt), **emasculates, emasculating, emasculated.** (*tr*) **1** to remove the testicles or; castrate; geld. **2** to deprive of vigour, effectiveness, etc. **3** *Bot.* to remove the stamens from (a flower) to prevent self-pollination for the purposes of plant breeding. ◆ *adj* (ɪ'mæskjʊlɪt, -ˌleɪt). **4** castrated; gelded. **5** Also: **emasculated.** deprived of strength, effectiveness, etc. [C17: from L *ēmasculāre*, from *masculus* male; see MASCULINE]
▶ **e.mascu'lation** *n* ▶ **e'mascu.lator** *n* ▶ **e'masculatory** *adj*

mbalm (ɪm'bɑːm) *vb* (*tr*) **1** to treat (a dead body) with preservatives to retard putrefaction. **2** to preserve or cherish the memory of. **3** *Poetic.* to give a sweet fragrance to. [C13: from OF *embaumer*; see BALM]
▶ **em'balmer** *n* ▶ **em'balmment** *n*

mbank (ɪm'bæŋk) *vb* (*tr*) to protect, enclose, or confine with an embankment.

mbankment (ɪm'bæŋkmənt) *n* a man-made ridge of earth or stone that carries a road or railway or confines a waterway.

mbargo (ɛm'bɑːgəʊ) *n, pl* **embargoes. 1** a government order prohibiting the departure or arrival of merchant ships in its ports. **2** any legal stoppage of commerce. **3** a restraint or prohibition. ◆ *vb* **embargoes, embargoing, embargoed.** (*tr*) **4** to lay an embargo upon. **5** to seize for use by the state. [C16: from Sp., from *embargar*, from L IM- + *barra* BAR¹]

mbark (ɛm'bɑːk) *vb* **1** to board (a ship or aircraft). **2** (*intr*; usually foll. by *on* or *upon*) to commence or engage (in) a

new project, venture, etc. [C16: via F from OF, from EM- + *barca* boat, BARQUE]
▶ **.embar'kation** *n*

embarrass (ɪm'bærəs) *vb* (*mainly tr*) **1** to cause to feel confusion or self-consciousness; disconcert. **2** (*usually passive*) to involve in financial difficulties. **3** *Arch.* to complicate. **4** *Arch.* to impede or hamper. [C17 (in the sense: to impede): via F & Sp. from It., from *imbarrare* to confine within bars]
▶ **em'barrassed** *adj* ▶ **em'barrassing** *adj* ▶ **em- 'barrassment** *n*

embassy ('ɛmbəsɪ) *n, pl* **embassies. 1** the residence or place of business of an ambassador. **2** an ambassador and his entourage collectively. **3** the position, business, or mission of an ambassador. **4** any important or official mission. [C16: from OF *ambaisada*; see AMBASSADOR]

embattle (ɪm'bætəl) *vb* **embattles, embattling, embattled.** (*tr*) **1** to deploy (troops) for battle. **2** to fortify (a position, town, etc.). **3** to provide with battlements. [C14: from OF *embataillier*; see EN-¹ BATTLE]

embay (ɪm'beɪ) *vb* (*tr*) (*usually passive*) **1** to form into a bay. **2** to enclose in or as if in a bay.

embed (ɪm'bɛd) *vb* **embeds, embedding, embedded. 1** (*usually foll. by in*) to fix or become fixed firmly and deeply in a surrounding solid mass. **2** (*tr*) to surround closely. **3** (*tr*) to fix or retain (a thought, idea, etc.) in the mind.
◆ Also: **imbed.**
▶ **em'bedment** *n*

embellish (ɪm'bɛlɪʃ) *vb* (*tr*) **1** to beautify; adorn. **2** to make (a story, etc.) more interesting by adding detail. [C14: from OF *embelir*, from *bel* beautiful, from L *bellus*]
▶ **em'bellisher** *n* ▶ **em'bellishment** *n*

ember ('ɛmbə) *n* **1** a glowing or smouldering piece of coal or wood, as in a dying fire. **2** the remains of a past emotion. [OE *ǣmyrge*]

Ember days *pl n RC & Anglican Church.* any of four groups in the year of three days (always Wednesday, Friday, and Saturday) of prayer and fasting. [OE *ymbrendæg*, from *ymb* around + *ryne* a course + *dæg* day]

embezzle (ɪm'bɛzəl) *vb* **embezzles, embezzling, embezzled.** to convert (money or property entrusted to one) fraudulently to one's own use. [C15: from Anglo-F *embeseiller* to destroy, from OF *beseiller* to make away with, from ?]
▶ **em'bezzlement** *n* ▶ **em'bezzler** *n*

embitter (ɪm'bɪtə) *vb* (*tr*) **1** to make (a person) bitter. **2** to aggravate (a hostile feeling, difficult situation, etc.).
▶ **em'bittered** *adj* ▶ **em'bitterment** *n*

emblazon (ɪm'bleɪzən) *vb* (*tr*) **1** to portray heraldic arms on (a shield, one's notepaper, etc.). **2** to make bright or splendid, as with colours, flowers, etc. **3** to glorify, praise, or extol.
▶ **em'blazonment** *n*

emblem ('ɛmbləm) *n* a visible object or representation that symbolizes a quality, type, group, etc. [C15: from L *emblēma*, from Gk, from *emballein* to insert, from *en* in + *ballein* to throw]
▶ **.emblem'atic** *or* **.emblem'atical** *adj* ▶ **.emblem'atically** *adv*

embody (ɪm'bɒdɪ) *vb* **embodies, embodying, embodied.** (*tr*) **1** to give a tangible, bodily, or concrete form to (an abstract concept). **2** to be an example of or express (an idea, principle, etc.). **3** (*often foll. by in*) to collect or unite in a comprehensive whole. **4** to invest (a spiritual entity) with bodily form.
▶ **em'bodiment** *n*

embolden (ɪm'bəʊldən) *vb* (*tr*) to encourage; make bold.

embolism ('ɛmbəˌlɪzəm) *n* the occlusion of a blood vessel by an embolus. [C14: from Med. L, from LGk *embolismos*; see EMBOLUS]
▶ **embolic** (ɛm'bɒlɪk) *adj*

embolus ('ɛmbələs) *n, pl* **emboli** (-ˌlaɪ). material, such as part of a blood clot or an air bubble, that becomes lodged within a small blood vessel and impedes the circulation. [C17: via L from Gk *embolos* stopper; see EMBLEM]

embonpoint *French.* (ãbɔ̃pwɛ̃) *n* **1** plumpness or stoutness. ◆ *adj* **2** plump; stout. [C18: from *en bon point* in good condition]

embosom (ɪmˈbʊzəm) *vb* (*tr*) *Arch.* **1** to enclose or envelop, esp. protectively. **2** to clasp to the bosom; hug. **3** to cherish.

emboss (ɪmˈbɒs) *vb* **1** to mould or carve (a decoration) on (a surface) so that it is raised above the surface in low relief. **2** to cause to bulge; make protrude. [C14: from OF *embocer*, from EM- + *boce* BOSS²]
▶ em'bossed *adj* ▶ em'bosser *n* ▶ em'bossment *n*

embouchure (ˌɒmbʊˈʃʊə) *n* **1** the mouth of a river or valley. **2** *Music.* **2a** the correct application of the lips and tongue in playing a wind instrument. **2b** the mouthpiece of a wind instrument. [C18: from F, from OF, from *bouche* mouth, from L *bucca* cheek]

embower (ɪmˈbaʊə) *vb* (*tr*) *Arch.* to enclose in or as in a bower.

embrace (ɪmˈbreɪs) *vb* **embraces, embracing, embraced.** (*mainly tr*) **1** (*also intr*) (of a person) to take or clasp (another person) in the arms, or (of two people) to clasp each other, as in affection, greeting, etc.; hug. **2** to accept willingly or eagerly. **3** to take up (a new idea, faith, etc.); adopt. **4** to comprise or include as an integral part. **5** to encircle or enclose. **6** *Rare.* to perceive or understand. ◆ *n* **7** the act of embracing. [C14: from OF, from EM- + *brace* a pair of arms, from L *bracchia* arms]
▶ em'braceable *adj* ▶ em'bracement *n* ▶ em'bracer *n*

embrasure (ɪmˈbreɪʒə) *n* **1** *Fortifications.* an opening or indentation, as in a battlement, for shooting through. **2** a door or window having splayed sides that increase the width of the opening in the interior. [C18: from F, from obs. *embraser* to widen]
▶ em'brasured *adj*

embrocate (ˈɛmbrəʊˌkeɪt) *vb* **embrocates, embrocating, embrocated.** (*tr*) to apply a liniment or lotion to (a part of the body). [C17: from Med. L *embrocha* poultice, from Gk, from *brokhē* a moistening]

embrocation (ˌɛmbrəʊˈkeɪʃən) *n* a drug or agent for rubbing into the skin; liniment.

embroider (ɪmˈbrɔɪdə) *vb* **1** to do decorative needlework (upon). **2** to add fictitious or exaggerated detail to (a story, etc.). [C15: from OF *embroder*]
▶ em'broiderer *n*

embroidery (ɪmˈbrɔɪdərɪ) *n, pl* **embroideries.** **1** decorative needlework done usually on loosely woven cloth or canvas, often being a picture or pattern. **2** elaboration or exaggeration, esp. in writing or reporting; embellishment.

embroil (ɪmˈbrɔɪl) *vb* (*tr*) **1** to involve (a person, oneself, etc.) in trouble, conflict, or argument. **2** to throw (affairs, etc.) into a state of confusion or disorder; complicate; entangle. [C17: from F *embrouiller*, from *brouiller* to mingle, confuse]
▶ em'broiler *n* ▶ em'broilment *n*

embryo (ˈɛmbrɪˌəʊ) *n, pl* **embryos.** **1** an animal in the early stages of development up to birth or hatching. **2** the human product of conception up to approximately the end of the second month of pregnancy. Cf. **fetus. 3** a plant in the early stages of development. **4** an undeveloped or rudimentary state (esp. in **in embryo**). **5** something in an early stage of development. [C16: from LL, from Gk *embruon*, from *bruein* to swell]

embryology (ˌɛmbrɪˈɒlədʒɪ) *n* **1** the scientific study of embryos. **2** the structure and development of the embryo of a particular organism.
▶ **embryological** (ˌɛmbrɪəˈlɒdʒɪkᵊl) *or* ˌembryo'logic *adj*
▶ ˌembry'ologist *n*

embryonic (ˌɛmbrɪˈɒnɪk) *or* **embryonal** (ˈɛmbrɪənᵊl) *adj* **1** of or relating to an embryo. **2** in an early stage; rudimentary; undeveloped.
▶ ˌembry'onically *adv*

emcee (ˌɛmˈsiː) *Inf.* ◆ *n* **1** a master of ceremonies. ◆ *vb* **emcees, emceeing, emceed. 2** to act as master of ceremonies (for or at). [C20: from MC]

Emden ★ (*German* ˈɛmdən) *n* a port in NW Germany, in Lower Saxony at the mouth of the River Ems. Pop.: 51 100 (1991).

-eme *suffix forming nouns. Linguistics.* indicating a mini-

mal distinctive unit of a specified type in a languag *morpheme; phoneme.* [C20: via F, abstracted from PH NEME]

emend (ɪˈmɛnd) *vb* (*tr*) to make corrections or improv ments in (a text) by critical editing. [C15: from L, fro *ē-* out + *mendum* a mistake]
▶ e'mendable *adj*

emendation (ˌiːmɛnˈdeɪʃən) *n* **1** a correction or im provement in a text. **2** the act or process of emendin;
▶ 'emenˌdator *n* ▶ **emendatory** (ɪˈmɛndətərɪ, -trɪ) *adj*

emerald (ˈɛmərəld, ˈɛmrəld) *n* **1** a green transparent var ety of beryl; highly valued as a gem. **2a** its clear gree colour. **2b** (*as adj*): *an emerald carpet.* [C13: from C *esmeraude*, from L *smaragdus*, from Gk *smaragdos*]

Emerald Isle ★ *n* a poetic name for **Ireland**[1].

emerge (ɪˈmɜːdʒ) *vb* **emerges, emerging, emerged.** (*int* often foll. by *from*) **1** to come up to the surface of or ris from water or other liquid. **2** to come into view, as fron concealment or obscurity. **3** (foll. by *from*) to come ou (of) or live (through (a difficult experience, etc.)). **4** t become apparent. [C17: from L *ēmergere* to rise up fron from *mergere* to dip]
▶ e'mergence *n* ▶ e'merging *adj*

emergency (ɪˈmɜːdʒənsɪ) *n, pl* **emergencies. 1a** an unfore seen or sudden occurrence, esp. of danger demandin; immediate action. **1b** (*as modifier*): *an emergency exit.* **2a** patient requiring urgent treatment. **2b** (*as modifier*): *a emergency ward.* **3** *NZ.* a player selected to stand by to r place an injured member of a team; reserve. **4 state emergency.** a condition, declared by a government, i which martial law applies, usually because of civil unre or natural disaster.

emergent (ɪˈmɜːdʒənt) *adj* **1** coming into being or n tice. **2** (of a nation) recently independent.
▶ e'mergently *adv*

emeritus (ɪˈmɛrɪtəs) *adj* (*usually postpositive*) retired c honourably discharged from full-time work, but retair ing one's title on an honorary basis: *a professor emeritu.* [C19: from L, from *merēre* to deserve; see MERIT]

emersion (ɪˈmɜːʃən) *n* **1** the act or an instance of emerg ing. **2** *Astron.* the reappearance of a celestial body afte an eclipse or occultation. [C17: from L *ēmersus;* se EMERGE]

Emerson ★ (ˈɛməsᵊn) *n* **Ralph Waldo** (rælf ˈwɔːldəʊ). 1803 82, US poet, essayist, and transcendentalist.

emery (ˈɛmərɪ) *n* **a** a hard greyish-black mineral consist ing of corundum with either magnetite or haematite used as an abrasive and polishing agent. **b** (*as modifier emery paper.* [C15: from OF *esmeril*, ult. from Gk *smur* powder for rubbing]

emery board *n* a strip of cardboard or wood witl a rough surface of crushed emery, for filing one' nails.

emetic (ɪˈmɛtɪk) *adj* **1** causing vomiting. ◆ *n* **2** an emeti agent or drug. [C17: from LL, from Gk *emetikos*, fron *emein* to vomit]

emf *or* **EMF** *abbrev. for* electromotive force.

-emia *n combining form.* a US variant of *-aemia.*

emigrant (ˈɛmɪgrənt) *n* **a** a person who leaves one place esp. his native country, to settle in another. **b** (*as mod fier*): *an emigrant worker.*

emigrate (ˈɛmɪˌgreɪt) *vb* **emigrates, emigrating, emigratec** (*intr*) to leave one place, esp. one's native country, to set tle in another. [C18: from L *ēmigrāre*, from *mīgrāre* to de part, MIGRATE]
▶ ˌemi'gration *n* ▶ 'emiˌgratory *adj*

émigré (ˈɛmɪˌgreɪ) *n* an emigrant, esp. one forced t leave his native country for political reasons. [C18 from F, from *émigrer* to EMIGRATE]

Emilia-Romagna ★ (ɪˈmiːlɪərəʊˈmænjə; *Italia* eˈmiːljaroˈmaɲɲa) *n* a region of N central Italy, on the Adriatic: rises from the plains of the Po valley in the north to the Apennines in the south. Capital: Bologna Pop.: 3 924 348 (1994 est.). Area: 22 123 sq. km (862 sq. miles).

eminence (ˈɛmɪnəns) *n* **1** a position of superiority o fame. **2** a high or raised piece of ground. ◆ *Also* eminency. [C17: from F, from L *ēminentia* a standing out; see EMINENT]

Eminence ('ɛmɪnəns) *or* **Eminency** *n, pl* **Eminences** *or* **Eminencies.** (preceded by *Your* or *His*) a title used to address or refer to a cardinal.

éminence grise *French.* (eminãs griz) *n, pl* **éminences grises** (eminãs griz). a person who wields power and influence unofficially or behind the scenes. [lit.: grey eminence, orig. applied to Père Joseph (François Le Clerc du Tramblay; died 1638), F monk, secretary of Cardinal RICHELIEU]

eminent ('ɛmɪnənt) *adj* **1** above others in rank, merit, or reputation; distinguished. **2** (*prenominal*) noteworthy or outstanding. **3** projecting or protruding; prominent. [C15: from L *ēminēre* to project, stand out, from *minēre* to stand]

eminent domain *n Law.* the right of a state to confiscate private property for public use, payment usually being made in compensation.

emir (ɛ'mɪə) *n* (in the Islamic world) **1** an independent ruler or chieftain. **2** a military commander or governor. **3** a descendant of Mohammed. [C17: via F from Sp., from Ar. *'amīr* commander]
▶ e'**mirate** *n*

emissary ('ɛmɪsərɪ, -ɪsrɪ) *n, pl* **emissaries. 1a** an agent sent on a mission, esp. one who represents a government or head of state. **1b** (*as modifier*): *an emissary delegation.* **2** an agent sent on a secret mission, as a spy. ♦ *adj* **3** (of veins) draining blood from sinuses in the dura mater to veins outside the skull. [C17: from L *ēmissārius*, from *ēmittere* to send out; see EMIT]

emission (ɪ'mɪʃən) *n* **1** the act of emitting or sending forth. **2** energy, in the form of heat, light, radio waves, etc., emitted from a source. **3** a substance, fluid, etc., that is emitted; discharge. **4** *Physiol.* any bodily discharge, esp. of semen. [C17: from L *ēmissiō*, from *ēmittere* to send forth, EMIT]
▶ e'**missive** *adj*

emission spectrum *n* the spectrum or pattern of bright lines or bands seen when the electromagnetic radiation emitted by a substance is passed into a spectrometer.

emissivity (ˌiːmɪ'sɪvɪtɪ, ˌɛm-) *n* a measure of the ability of a surface to radiate energy; the ratio of the radiant flux emitted per unit area to that emitted by a black body at the same temperature.

emit (ɪ'mɪt) *vb* **emits, emitting, emitted.** (*tr*) **1** to give or send forth; discharge. **2** to give voice to; utter. **3** *Physics.* to give off (radiation or particles). [C17: from L *ēmittere* to send out, from *mittere* to send]

emitter (ɪ'mɪtə) *n* **1** a person or thing that emits. **2** a substance that emits radiation. **3** the region in a transistor in which the charge-carrying holes or electrons originate.

Emmanuel ★ (ɪ'mænjʊəl) *n* a variant spelling of **Immanuel.**

Emmen ★ ('ɛmən; *Dutch* 'ɛmə) *n* a city in the NE Netherlands, in Drenthe province: a new town developed since World War II. Pop.: 93 476 (1994).

Emmenthal, Emmental ('ɛmən,tɑːl), *or* **Emmenthaler** *n* a hard Swiss cheese with holes in it. [C20: after *Emmenthal,* valley in Switzerland]

Emmet ★ ('ɛmɪt) *n Robert.* 1778–1803, Irish nationalist, executed for leading an uprising for Irish independence.

Emmy ('ɛmɪ) *n, pl* **Emmys** *or* **Emmies.** (in the US) one of the statuettes awarded for outstanding television performances and productions. [C20: from *Immy,* short for *image orthicon tube*]

emollient (ɪ'mɒljənt) *adj* **1** softening or soothing, esp. to the skin. **2** helping to avoid confrontation; calming. ♦ *n* **3** any preparation or substance that has this effect. [C17: from L *ēmollīre* to soften, from *mollis* soft]
▶ e'**mollience** *n*

emolument (ɪ'mɒljʊmənt) *n* the profit arising from an office or employment; fees or wages. [C15: from L *ēmolumentum* benefit; orig., fee paid to a miller, from *molere* to grind]

emote (ɪ'məʊt) *vb* **emotes, emoting, emoted.** (*intr*) to display exaggerated emotion, as in acting. [C20: back formation from EMOTION]
▶ e'**moter** *n*

emotion (ɪ'məʊʃən) *n* any strong feeling, as of joy, sorrow, or fear. [C16: from F, from OF, from L *ēmovēre* to disturb, from *movēre* to MOVE]

emotional (ɪ'məʊʃənəl) *adj* **1** of, characteristic of, or expressive of emotion. **2** readily or excessively affected by emotion. **3** appealing to or arousing emotion. **4** caused or determined by emotion rather than reason: *an emotional argument.*
▶ e,**motion'ality** *n*

emotionalism (ɪ'məʊʃənə,lɪzəm) *n* **1** emotional nature or quality. **2** a tendency to yield readily to the emotions. **3** an appeal to the emotions, esp. as to an audience.
▶ e'**motionalist** *n* ▶ e,**motional'istic** *adj*

emotionalize *or* **emotionalise** (ɪ'məʊʃənə,laɪz) *vb* **emotionalizes, emotionalizing, emotionalized** *or* **emotionalises, emotionalising, emotionalised.** (*tr*) to make emotional; subject to emotional treatment.

emotive (ɪ'məʊtɪv) *adj* **1** tending or designed to arouse emotion. **2** of or characterized by emotion.
▶ e'**motiveness** *or* ,emo'**tivity** *n*

> **USAGE NOTE** *Emotional* is preferred to *emotive* when describing a display of emotion: *he was given an emotional* (not *emotive*) *welcome.*

Emp. *abbrev. for:* **1** Emperor. **2** Empire. **3** Empress.

empanel *or* **impanel** (ɪm'pænəl) *vb* **empanels, empanelling, empanelled** *or* **US empanels, empaneling, empaneled** *or* **impanels, impanelling, impanelled** *or* **US impanels, impaneling, impaneled.** (*tr*) *Law.* **1** to enter on a list (names of persons to be summoned for jury service). **2** to select (a jury) from such a list.
▶ em'**panelment** *or* im'**panelment** *n*

empathize *or* **empathise** ('ɛmpə,θaɪz) *vb* **empathizes, empathizing, empathized** *or* **empathises, empathising, empathised.** (*intr*) to engage in or feel empathy.

empathy ('ɛmpəθɪ) *n* **1** the power of understanding and imaginatively entering into another person's feelings. **2** the attribution to an object, such as a work of art, of one's own feelings about it. [C20: from Gk *empatheia* affection, passion]
▶ em'**pathic** *or* ,empa'**thetic** *adj*

Empedocles ★ (ɛm'pɛdə,kliːz) *n* ?490–430 B.C., Greek philosopher and scientist, who held that the world is composed of four elements, air, fire, earth, and water, which are governed by the opposing forces of love and discord.

emperor ('ɛmpərə) *n* a monarch who rules or reigns over an empire. [C13: from OF, from L *imperāre* to command, from IM- + *parāre* to make ready]
▶ '**emperor,ship** *n*

emperor penguin *n* an Antarctic penguin with orange-yellow patches on the neck: the largest penguin, reaching a height of 1.3 m (4 ft).

emphasis ('ɛmfəsɪs) *n, pl* **emphases** (-siːz). **1** special importance or significance. **2** an object, idea, etc., that is given special importance or significance. **3** stress on a particular syllable, word, or phrase in speaking. **4** force or intensity of expression. **5** sharpness or clarity of form or outline. [C16: via L from Gk: meaning, (in rhetoric) significant stress; see EMPHATIC]

emphasize *or* **emphasise** ('ɛmfə,saɪz) *vb* **emphasizes, emphasizing, emphasized** *or* **emphasises, emphasising, emphasised.** (*tr*) to give emphasis or prominence to; stress.

emphatic (ɪm'fætɪk) *adj* **1** expressed, spoken, or done with emphasis. **2** forceful and positive; definite; direct. **3** sharp or clear in form, contour, or outline. **4** important or significant; stressed. [C18: from Gk, from *emphainein* to display, from *phainein* to show]
▶ em'**phatically** *adv*

emphysema (ˌɛmfɪ'siːmə) *n Pathol.* **1** a condition in which the air sacs of the lungs are grossly enlarged, causing breathlessness and wheezing. **2** the abnormal presence of air in a tissue or part. [C17: from NL, from Gk *emphusēma* a swelling up, from *phusan* to blow]

empire ('empaɪə) *n* **1** an aggregate of peoples and territories under the rule of a single person, oligarchy, or sovereign state. **2** any monarchy that has an emperor as head of state. **3** the period during which a particular empire exists. **4** supreme power; sovereignty. **5** a large industrial organization with many ramifications. [C13: from OF, from L, from *imperāre* to command, from *parāre* to prepare]

Empire ('empaɪə) *n* **the. 1** See **British Empire. 2** *French history.* **2a** the period of imperial rule in France from 1804 to 1815 under Napoleon Bonaparte. **2b** Also called: **Second Empire.** the period from 1852 to 1870 when Napoleon III ruled as emperor. ♦ *adj* **3** denoting, characteristic of, or relating to the British Empire. **4** denoting, characteristic of, or relating to either French Empire, esp. the first.

empire-builder *n Inf.* a person who seeks extra power, esp. by increasing the number of his staff.
▶ '**empire-,building** *n, adj*

Empire Day *n* the former name of **Commonwealth Day.**

Empire State ★ *n* nickname of **New York** (state).

empiric (em'pɪrɪk) *n* **1** a person who relies on empirical methods. **2** a medical quack. ♦ *adj* **3** a variant of **empirical.** [C16: from L, from Gk *empeirikos* practised, from *peiran* to attempt]

empirical (em'pɪrɪkəl) *adj* **1** derived from or relating to experiment and observation rather than theory. **2** (of medical treatment) based on practical experience rather than scientific proof. **3** *Philosophy.* (of knowledge) derived from experience rather than by logic from first principles. **4** of or relating to medical quackery.
▶ em'pirica**lness** *n*

empiricism (em'pɪrɪ,sɪzəm) *n* **1** *Philosophy.* the doctrine that all knowledge derives from experience. **2** the use of empirical methods. **3** medical quackery.
▶ em'piricist *n, adj*

emplace (ɪm'pleɪs) *vb* **emplaces, emplacing, emplaced.** (*tr*) to put in position.

emplacement (ɪm'pleɪsmənt) *n* **1** a prepared position for a gun or other weapon. **2** the act of putting or state of being put in place. [C19: from F, from obs. *emplacer* to put in position, from PLACE]

emplane (ɪm'pleɪn) *vb* **emplanes, emplaning, emplaned.** to board or put on board an aeroplane.

employ (ɪm'plɔɪ) *vb* (*tr*) **1** to engage or make use of the services of (a person) in return for money; hire. **2** to provide work or occupation for; keep busy. **3** to use as a means. ♦ *n* **4** the state of being employed (esp. in **in someone's employ**). [C15: from OF *emploier*, from L *implicāre* to entangle, engage, from *plicāre* to fold]
▶ em'ployable *adj* ▶ em,ploya'bility *n*

employee *or US* **employe** (em'plɔɪiː, ,emplɔɪ'iː) *n* a person who is hired to work for another or for a business, firm, etc., in return for payment.

employer (ɪm'plɔɪə) *n* **1** a person, firm, etc., that employs workers. **2** a person who employs.

employment (ɪm'plɔɪmənt) *n* **1** the act of employing or state of being employed. **2** a person's work or occupation.

employment exchange *n Brit.* a former name for **employment office.**

employment office *n Brit.* any government office established to collect and supply to the unemployed information about job vacancies and to employers information about availability of prospective workers. See also **Jobcentre.**

emporium (em'pɔːrɪəm) *n, pl* **emporiums** *or* **emporia** (-rɪə). a large retail shop offering for sale a wide variety of merchandise. [C16: from L, from Gk, from *emporos* merchant, from *poros* a journey]

empower (ɪm'paʊə) *vb* (*tr*) **1** to give power or authority to; authorize. **2** to give ability to; enable or permit.
▶ em'powerment *n*

empress ('empris) *n* **1** the wife or widow of an emperor.

2 a woman who holds the rank of emperor in her own right. [C12: from OF *empereriz*, from L *imperātrix*; see EMPEROR]

Empson ★ ('emps°n) *n* Sir **William.** 1906–84, English poet and critic; author of *Seven Types of Ambiguity* (1930).

empty ('empti) *adj* **emptier, emptiest. 1** containing nothing. **2** without inhabitants; vacant or unoccupied. **3** carrying no load, passengers, etc. **4** without purpose, substance, or value: *an empty life.* **5** insincere or trivial: *empty words.* **6** not expressive or vital; vacant: *an empty look.* **7** *Inf.* hungry. **8** (*postpositive;* foll. by *of*) devoid; destitute. **9** *Inf.* drained of energy or emotion. **10** *Maths, logic.* (of a set or class) containing no members. ♦ *vb* **empties, emptying, emptied. 11** to make or become empty. **12** (when *intr,* foll. by *into*) to discharge (contents). **13** (*tr;* often foll. by *of*) to unburden or rid (oneself). ♦ *n, pl* **empties. 14** an empty container, esp. a bottle. [OE *ǣmtig*]
▶ 'emptiable *adj* ▶ 'emptier *n* ▶ 'emptily *adv* ▶ 'emptiness *n*

empty-handed *adj* **1** carrying nothing in the hands. **2** having gained nothing.

empty-headed *adj* lacking sense; frivolous.

empty-nester (-'nestə) *n Inf.* a married person whose children have grown up and left home.

Empty Quarter ★ *n* another name for **Rub' al Khali.**

empyema (,empaɪ'iːmə) *n, pl* **empyemata** (-'iːmətə) *or* **empyemas.** a collection of pus in a body cavity, esp. in the chest. [C17: from Med. L, from Gk *empuēma* abscess, from *empuein* to suppurate, from *puon* pus]
▶ ,empy'emic *adj*

empyrean (,empaɪ'riːən) *n* **1** *Arch.* the highest part of the heavens, thought in ancient times to contain the pure element of fire and by early Christians to be the abode of God. **2** *Poetic.* the heavens or sky. ♦ *adj also* **empyreal. 3** of or relating to the sky. **4** heavenly or sublime. [C17: from LL, from Gk *empurios* fiery]

empyreuma (,empɪ'ruːmə) *n, pl* **empyreumata** (-mətə). the smell and taste associated with burning vegetable and animal matter. [C17: from Gk, from *empureuein* to set on fire]

Ems ★ (emz) *n* **1** a town in W Germany, in the Rhineland-Palatinate: famous for the **Ems Telegram** (1870), Bismarck's dispatch that led to the outbreak of the Franco-Prussian War. Pop.: 10 250 (latest est.). **2** a river in West Germany, rising in the Teutoburger Wald and flowing generally north to the North Sea. Length: about 370 km (230 miles).

EMS *abbrev. for* European Monetary System.

emu ('iːmjuː) *n* a large Australian flightless bird, similar to the ostrich. [C17: changed from Port. *ema* ostrich, from Arab. *Na-'amah* ostrich]

EMU 1 *abbrev. for* European monetary union. **2** See **e.m.u.**

e.m.u. *or* **EMU** *abbrev. for* electromagnetic unit.

emu-bob *Austral. inf.* ♦ *vb* **emu-bobs, emu-bobbing, emu-bobbed. 1** (*intr*) to bend over to collect litter or small pieces of wood. ♦ *n* **2** Also called: **emu parade.** a parade of soldiers or schoolchildren for litter collection.
▶ 'emu-,bobbing *n*

emulate ('emju,leɪt) *vb* **emulates, emulating, emulated.** (*tr*) **1** to attempt to equal or surpass, esp. by imitation. **2** to rival or compete with. [C16: from L *aemulus* competing with]
▶ 'emulative *adj* ▶ ,emu'lation *n* ▶ 'emu,lator *n*

emulous ('emjuləs) *adj* **1** desiring or aiming to equal or surpass another. **2** characterized by or arising from emulation. [C14: from L; see EMULATE]
▶ 'emulousness *n*

emulsifier (ɪ'mʌlsɪ,faɪə) *n* an agent that forms an emulsion, esp. a food additive that prevents separation of processed foods.

emulsify (ɪ'mʌlsɪ,faɪ) *vb* **emulsifies, emulsifying, emulsified.** to make or form into an emulsion.
▶ e,mulsi'fiable *or* e'mulsible *adj* ▶ e,mulsifi'cation *n*

emulsion (ɪ'mʌlʃən) *n* **1** *Photog.* a light-sensitive coating on a base, such as paper or film, consisting of silver bromide suspended in gelatine. **2** *Chem.* a colloid in which both phases are liquids. **3** a type of paint in which the

pigment is suspended in a vehicle that is dispersed in water as an emulsion. **4** *Pharmacol.* a mixture in which an oily medicine is dispersed in another liquid. **5** any liquid resembling milk. [C17: from NL *ēmulsiō*, from L, from *ēmulgēre* to milk out, from *mulgēre* to milk]
► e**'mulsive** *adj*

emu-wren *n* an Australian wren having long plumy tail feathers.

en (ɛn) *n Printing.* a unit of measurement, half the width of an em.

EN (in Britain) *abbrev. for:* **1** enrolled nurse. **2** English Nature.

en-[1] *or* **em-** *prefix forming verbs.* **1** (*from nouns*) **1a** put in or on: *entomb; enthrone.* **1b** go on or into: *enplane.* **1c** surround or cover with: *enmesh.* **1d** furnish with: *empower.* **2** (*from adjectives and nouns*) cause to be in a certain condition: *enable; enslave.* [via OF from L in- IN-[2]]

en-[2] *or* **em-** *prefix forming nouns and adjectives.* in; into; inside: *endemic.* [from Gk (often via L); cf. IN-[1], IN-[2]]

-en[1] *suffix forming verbs from adjectives and nouns.* cause to be; become; cause to have: *blacken; heighten.* [OE *-n-*, as in *fæst-n-ian* to fasten, of Gmc origin]

-en[2] *suffix forming adjectives from nouns.* of; made of; resembling: *ashen; wooden.* [OE *-en*]

enable (ɪn'eɪbᵊl) *vb* **enables, enabling, enabled.** (*tr*) **1** to provide (someone) with adequate power, means, opportunity, or authority (to do something). **2** to make possible.
► en**'ablement** *n* ► en**'abler** *n*

enabling act *n* a legislative act conferring certain specified powers on a person or organization.

enact (ɪn'ækt) *vb* (*tr*) **1** to make into an act or statute. **2** to establish by law; decree. **3** to represent or perform as in a play.
► en**'actable** *adj* ► en**'active** *or* en**'actory** *adj* ► en**'actment** *or* en**'action** *n* ► en**'actor** *n*

enamel (ɪ'næməl) *n* **1** a coloured glassy substance, translucent or opaque, fused to the surface of articles made of metal, glass, etc., for ornament or protection. **2** an article or articles ornamented with enamel. **3** an enamel-like paint or varnish. **4** any coating resembling enamel. **5** the hard white substance that covers the crown of each tooth. **6** (*modifier*) decorated or covered with enamel. ◆ *vb* **enamels, enamelling, enamelled** *or US* **enamels, enameling, enameled.** (*tr*) **7** to decorate with enamel. **8** to ornament with glossy variegated colours, as if with enamel. **9** to portray in enamel. [C15: from OF *esmail*, of Gmc origin]
► e**'nameller, e'namellist** *or US* e**'nameler, e'namelist** *n* ► e**'namel,work** *n*

enamour *or US* **enamor** (ɪn'æmə) *vb* (*tr; usually passive* and foll. by *of*) to inspire with love; captivate. [C14: from OF, from *amour* love, from L *amor*]
► en**'amoured** *or US* en**'amored** *adj*

en bloc *French.* (ã blɔk) *adv* in a lump or block; as a body or whole; all together.

en brosse *French.* (ã brɔs) *adj, adv* (of the hair) cut very short so that the hair stands up stiffly. [lit.: in the style of a brush]

enc. *abbrev. for:* **1** enclosed. **2** enclosure.

encamp (ɪn'kæmp) *vb* to lodge or cause to lodge in a camp.

encampment (ɪn'kæmpmənt) *n* **1** the act of setting up a camp. **2** the place where a camp, esp. a military camp, is set up.

encapsulate *or* **incapsulate** (ɪn'kæpsjʊ,leɪt) *vb* **encapsulates, encapsulating, encapsulated** *or* **incapsulates, incapsulating, incapsulated.** **1** to enclose or be enclosed as in a capsule. **2** (*tr*) to sum up in a short or concise form.
► en,capsu**'lation** *or* in,capsu**'lation** *n*

encase *or* **incase** (ɪn'keɪs) *vb* **encases, encasing, encased.** (*tr*) to place or enclose as in a case.
► en**'casement** *or* in**'casement** *n*

encash (ɪn'kæʃ) *vb* (*tr*) *Brit., formal.* to exchange (a cheque) for cash.
► en**'cashable** *adj* ► en**'cashment** *n*

encaustic (ɪn'kɔstɪk) *Ceramics, etc.* ◆ *adj* **1** decorated by any process involving burning in colours, esp. by inlay-ing coloured clays and baking or by fusing wax colours to the surface. ◆ *n* **2** the process of burning in colours. **3** a product of such a process. [C17: from L *encausticus*, from Gk, from *enkaiein* to burn in, from *kaiein* to burn]
► en**'caustically** *adv*

-ence *or* **-ency** *suffix forming nouns.* indicating an action, state, condition, or quality: *benevolence; residence; patience.* [via OF from L *-entia*, from *-ēns,* present participial ending]

enceinte (ɒn'sænt) *adj* another word for **pregnant.** [C17: from F, from L *inciēns* pregnant]

Enceladus ★ (ɛn'sɛlədəs) *n Greek myth.* a giant who was punished for his rebellion against the gods by a fatal blow from a stone cast by Athena. He was believed to be buried under Mount Etna in Sicily.

encephalic (,ɛnsɪ'fælɪk) *adj* of or relating to the brain.

encephalin (ɛn'sɛfəlɪn) *n* a variant of **enkephalin.**

encephalitis (,ɛnsɛfə'laɪtɪs) *n* inflammation of the brain.
► **encephalitic** (,ɛnsɛfə'lɪtɪk) *adj*

encephalitis lethargica (lɪ'θɑːdʒɪkə) *n* a technical name for **sleeping sickness** (sense 2).

encephalo- *or before a vowel* **encephal-** *combining form.* indicating the brain: *encephalogram; encephalitis.* [from NL, from Gk *enkephalos,* from *en-* in + *kephalē* head]

encephalogram (ɛn'sɛfələ,græm) *n* **1** an X-ray photograph of the brain, esp. one (a **pneumoencephalogram**) taken after replacing some of the cerebrospinal fluid with air or oxygen. **2** short for **electroencephalogram;** see **electroencephalograph.**

encephalon (ɛn'sɛfə,lɒn) *n, pl* **encephala** (-lə). a technical name for **brain.** [C18: from NL, from Gk *enkephalos* brain, from EN-[2] + *kephalē* head]
► en**'cephalous** *adj*

encephalopathy (,ɛnsɛfə'lɒpəθɪ) *n* any degenerative disease of the brain, often associated with toxic conditions. See also **BSE.**

enchain (ɪn'tʃeɪn) *vb* (*tr*) **1** to bind with chains. **2** to hold fast or captivate (the attention, etc.).
► en**'chainment** *n*

enchant (ɪn'tʃɑːnt) *vb* (*tr*) **1** to cast a spell on; bewitch. **2** to delight or captivate utterly. [C14: from OF, from L *incantāre,* from *cantāre* to chant]
► en**'chanted** *adj* ► en**'chanter** *n* ► en**'chantress** *fem n*

enchanting (ɪn'tʃɑːntɪŋ) *adj* pleasant; delightful.
► en**'chantingly** *adv*

enchantment (ɪn'tʃɑːntmənt) *n* **1** the act of enchanting or state of being enchanted. **2** a magic spell. **3** great charm or fascination.

enchase (ɪn'tʃeɪs) *vb* **enchases, enchasing, enchased.** (*tr*) a less common word for **chase**[3]. [C15: from OF *enchasser* to enclose, set, from EN-[1] + *casse* CASE[2]]
► en**'chaser** *n*

enchilada (,ɛntʃɪ'lɑːdə) *n* a Mexican dish of a tortilla filled with meat, served with a chilli sauce. [American Sp., from *enchilado,* from *enchilar* to spice with chilli]

-enchyma *n combining form.* denoting cellular tissue. [C20: abstracted from PARENCHYMA]

encipher (ɪn'saɪfə) *vb* (*tr*) to convert (a message, etc.) into code or cipher.
► en**'cipherer** *n* ► en**'cipherment** *n*

encircle (ɪn'sɜːkᵊl) *vb* **encircles, encircling, encircled.** (*tr*) to form a circle around; enclose within a circle; surround.
► en**'circlement** *n*

enclave ('ɛnkleɪv) *n* a part of a country entirely surrounded by foreign territory: viewed from the position of the surrounding territories. [C19: from F, from OF *enclaver* to enclose, from Vulgar L *inclāvāre* (unattested) to lock up, from L IN-[2] + *clavis* key]

enclitic (ɪn'klɪtɪk) *adj* **1** denoting or relating to a monosyllabic word or form that is treated as a suffix of the preceding word. ◆ *n* **2** an enclitic word or form. [C17: from LL, from Gk, from *enklinein* to cause to lean, from EN-[2] + *klinein* to lean]
► en**'clitically** *adv*

enclose *or* **inclose** (ɪn'kləʊz) *vb* **encloses, enclosing, en-**

closed *or* **incloses, inclosing, inclosed.** (*tr*) **1** to close; hem in; surround. **2** to surround (land) with or as if with a fence. **3** to put in an envelope or wrapper, esp. together with a letter. **4** to contain or hold.
▶ **en'closable** *or* **in'closable** *adj* ▶ **en'closer** *or* **in'closer** *n*

enclosed order *n* a Christian religious order that does not permit its members to go into the outside world.

enclosure *or* **inclosure** (ɪnˈkləʊʒə) *n* **1** the act of enclosing or state of being enclosed. **2** an area enclosed as by a fence. **3** the act of appropriating land by setting up a fence, hedge, etc., around it. **4** a fence, wall, etc., that encloses. **5** something enclosed within an envelope or wrapper, esp. together with a letter. **6** *Brit.* a section of a sports ground, racecourse, etc., allotted to certain spectators.

encode (ɪnˈkəʊd) *vb* **encodes, encoding, encoded.** (*tr*) to convert (a message) into code.
▶ **en'codement** *n* ▶ **en'coder** *n*

encomiast (enˈkəʊmɪˌæst) *n* a person who speaks or writes an encomium. [C17: from Gk, from *enkōmiazein* to utter an ENCOMIUM]
▶ **en,comi'astic** *or* **en,comi'astical** *adj*

encomium (enˈkəʊmɪəm) *n, pl* **encomiums** *or* **encomia** (-mɪə). a formal expression of praise; eulogy. [C16: from L, from Gk, from EN-² + *kōmos* festivity]

encompass (ɪnˈkʌmpəs) *vb* (*tr*) **1** to enclose within a circle; surround. **2** to bring about: *he encompassed the enemy's ruin.* **3** to include entirely or comprehensively.
▶ **en'compassment** *n*

encore (ˈɒŋkɔː) *sentence substitute.* **1** again: used by an audience to demand an extra or repeated performance. ◆ *n* **2** an extra or repeated performance given in response to enthusiastic demand. ◆ *vb* **encores, encoring, encored.** **3** (*tr*) to demand an extra or repeated performance of (a work, piece of music, etc.) by (a performer). [C18: from F: still, again, ?from L *in hanc hōram* until this hour]

encounter (ɪnˈkaʊntə) *vb* **1** to come upon or meet casually or unexpectedly. **2** to meet (an enemy, army, etc.) in battle or contest. **3** (*tr*) to be faced with; contend with. ◆ *n* **4** a casual or unexpected meeting. **5** a hostile meeting; contest. [C13: from OF, from Vulgar L *incontrāre* (unattested), from L IN-² + *contrā* against, opposite]

encounter group *n* a group of people who meet in order to develop self-awareness and mutual understanding by openly expressing their feelings, by confrontation, etc.

encourage (ɪnˈkʌrɪdʒ) *vb* **encourages, encouraging, encouraged.** (*tr*) **1** to inspire (someone) with the courage or confidence (to do something). **2** to stimulate (something or someone) by approval or help.
▶ **en'couragement** *n* ▶ **en'courager** *n* ▶ **en'couraging** *adj* ▶ **en'couragingly** *adv*

encroach (ɪnˈkrəʊtʃ) *vb* (*intr*) **1** (often foll. by *on* or *upon*) to intrude gradually or stealthily upon the rights, property, etc., of another. **2** to advance beyond certain limits. [C14: from OF *encrochier* to seize, lit.: fasten upon with hooks, of Gmc origin]
▶ **en'croacher** *n* ▶ **en'croachment** *n*

encrust *or* **incrust** (ɪnˈkrʌst) *vb* **1** (*tr*) to cover or overlay with or as with a crust or hard coating. **2** to form or cause to form a crust or hard coating. **3** (*tr*) to decorate lavishly, as with jewels.
▶ **ˌencrus'tation** *or* **ˌincrus'tation** *n*

encumber *or* **incumber** (ɪnˈkʌmbə) *vb* (*tr*) **1** to hinder or impede; hamper. **2** to fill with superfluous or useless matter. **3** to burden with debts, obligations, etc. [C14: from OF, from EN-¹ + *combre* a barrier, from LL *combrus*]

encumbrance *or* **incumbrance** (ɪnˈkʌmbrəns) *n* **1** a thing that impedes or is burdensome; hindrance. **2** *Law.* a burden or charge upon property, such as a mortgage or lien.

ency., encyc., *or* **encycl.** *abbrev. for* encyclopedia.

-ency *suffix forming nouns.* a variant of **-ence:** *fluency; permanency.*

encyclical (enˈsɪklɪkᵊl) *n* **1** a letter sent by the pope to all Roman Catholic bishops. ◆ *adj also* **encyclic. 2** (of let-

ters) intended for general circulation. [C17: from LL, from Gk, from *kuklos* circle]

encyclopedia *or* **encyclopaedia** (enˌsaɪkləʊˈpiːdɪə) *n* a book, often in many volumes, containing articles, often arranged in alphabetical order, dealing either with the whole range of human knowledge or with one particular subject. [C16: from NL, erroneously for Gk *enkuklios paideia* general education]
▶ **en,cyclo'pedic** *or* **en,cyclo'paedic** *adj*

encyclopedist *or* **encyclopaedist** (enˌsaɪkləʊˈpiːdɪst) *n* a person who compiles or contributes to an encyclopedia.
▶ **en,cyclo'pedism** *or* **en,cyclo'paedism** *n*

encyst (enˈsɪst) *vb Biol.* to enclose or become enclosed by a cyst, thick membrane, or shell.
▶ **en'cystment** *or* **ˌencys'tation** *n*

end (end) *n* **1** the extremity of the length of something, such as a road, line, etc. **2** the surface at either extremity of an object. **3** the extreme extent, limit, or degree of something. **4** the most distant place or time that can be imagined: *the ends of the earth.* **5** the time at which something is concluded. **6** the last section or part. **7** a share or part. **8** (*often pl*) a remnant or fragment (esp. in **odds and ends**). **9** a final state, esp. death; destruction. **10** the purpose of an action or existence. **11** *Sport.* either of the two defended areas of a playing field, rink, etc. **12** *Bowls, etc.* a section of play from one side of the rink to the other. **13 at an end.** exhausted or completed. **14 come to an end.** to become completed or exhausted. **15 have one's end away.** *sl.* to have sexual intercourse. **16 in the end.** finally. **17 keep one's end up.** **17a** to sustain one's part in a joint undertaking. **17b** to hold one's own in an argument, contest, etc. **18 make (both) ends meet.** to spend no more than the money one has. **19 no end (of).** *Inf.* (intensifier): *I had no end of work.* **20 on end.** *Inf.* without pause or interruption. **21 the end.** *Sl.* the worst, esp. something that goes beyond the limits of endurance. ◆ *vb* **22** to bring or come to a finish; conclude. **23** to die or cause to die. **24** (*tr*) to surpass or outdo: *a novel to end all novels.* **25 end it all.** *Inf.* to commit suicide. ◆ See also **end up.** [OE *ende*]
▶ **'ender** *n*

end- *combining form.* a variant of **endo-** before a vowel.

-end *suffix forming nouns.* See **-and.**

endamoeba *or US* **endameba** (ˌendəˈmiːbə) *n* variant spellings of **entamoeba.**

endanger (ɪnˈdeɪndʒə) *vb* (*tr*) to put in danger or peril; imperil.
▶ **en'dangerment** *n*

endangered (ɪnˈdeɪndʒəd) *adj* in danger, esp. of extinction: *an endangered species.*

endear (ɪnˈdɪə) *vb* (*tr*) to cause to be beloved or esteemed.
▶ **en'dearing** *adj*

endearment (ɪnˈdɪəmənt) *n* something that endears, such as an affectionate utterance.

endeavour *or US* **endeavor** (ɪnˈdevə) *vb* **1** to try (to do something). ◆ *n* **2** an effort to do or attain something. [C14 *endeveren*, from EN-¹ + *-deveren* from *dever* duty, from OF *deveir*; see DEVOIRS]
▶ **en'deavourer** *or US* **en'deavorer** *n*

endemic (enˈdemɪk) *adj also* **endemial** (enˈdemɪəl) *or* **endemical. 1** present within a localized area or peculiar to persons in such an area. ◆ *n* **2** an endemic disease or plant. [C18: from NL *endēmicus*, from Gk *endēmos* native, from EN-² + *dēmos* the people]
▶ **en'demically** *adv* ▶ **'endemism** *or* **ˌende'micity** *n*

Enderby Land ★ (ˈendəbɪ) *n* part of the coastal region of Antarctica, between Kempland and Queen Maud Land: the westernmost part of the Australian Antarctic Territory; discovered in 1831.

endermic (enˈdɜːmɪk) *adj* (of a medicine, etc.) acting by absorption through the skin. [C19: from EN-² + Gk *derma* skin]

endgame (ˈendˌgeɪm) *n* the closing stage of any of certain games, esp. chess, when there are only a few pieces left in play.

ending (ˈendɪŋ) *n* **1** the act of bringing to or reaching an

---

★ people and places

end. **2** the last part of something. **3** the final part of a word, esp. a suffix.

ndive ('endaɪv) *n* a plant cultivated for its crisp curly leaves, which are used in salads. Cf. **chicory**. [C15: from OF, from Med. L, from var. of L *intubus, entubus*]

ndless ('endlɪs) *adj* **1** having or seeming to have no end; eternal or infinite. **2** continuing too long or continually recurring. **3** formed with the ends joined.
▶ **'endlessness** *n*

ndmost ('end,məʊst) *adj* nearest the end; most distant.

ndo- *or before a vowel* **end-** *combining form.* inside; within: *endocrine*. [from Gk, from *endon* within]

ndoblast ('endəʊ,blæst) *n* **1** *Embryol.* a less common name for **endoderm**. **2** another name for **hypoblast**.
▶ ,endo'blastic *adj*

ndocarditis (,endəʊkɑː'daɪtɪs) *n* inflammation of the lining of the heart. [C19: from NL, from ENDO- + Gk *kardia* heart + -ITIS]
▶ **endocarditic** (,endəʊkɑː'dɪtɪk) *adj*

ndocarp ('endə,kɑːp) *n* the inner layer of the pericarp of a fruit, such as the stone of a peach.
▶ ,endo'carpal *or* ,endo'carpic *adj*

ndocrine ('endəʊ,kraɪn) *adj also* ,endo'crinal, endocrinic (,endəʊ'krɪnɪk). **1** of or denoting endocrine glands or their secretions. ◆ *n* **2** an endocrine gland. [C20: from ENDO- + -*crine*, from Gk *krinein* to separate]

ndocrine gland *n* any of the glands that secrete hormones directly into the bloodstream, e.g. the pituitary, pineal, and thyroid.

ndocrinology (,endəʊkraɪ'nɒlədʒɪ, -krɪ-) *n* the branch of medical science concerned with the endocrine glands and their secretions.
▶ ,endocri'nologist *n*

ndoderm ('endəʊ,dɜːm) *or* **entoderm** *n* the inner germ layer of an animal embryo, which gives rise to the lining of the digestive and respiratory tracts.
▶ ,endo'dermal, ,endo'dermic *or* ,ento'dermal, ,ento'dermic *adj*

end of steel *n Canad.* **1** a point up to which railway tracks have been laid. **2** a town located at such a point.

ndogamy (en'dɒgəmɪ) *n* **1** *Anthropol.* marriage within one's own tribe or similar unit. **2** pollination between two flowers on the same plant.
▶ en'dogamous *or* endogamic (,endəʊ'gæmɪk) *adj*

ndogenous (en'dɒdʒɪnəs) *adj* **1** *Biol.* developing or originating within an organism or part of an organism. **2** having no apparent external cause: *endogenous depression*.
▶ en'dogeny *n*

ndometritis (,endəʊmɪ'traɪtɪs) *n* inflammation of the endometrium, which is caused by infection, as by bacteria, foreign bodies, etc.

ndometrium (,endəʊ'miːtrɪəm) *n, pl* **endometria** (-trɪə). the mucous membrane that lines the uterus. [C19: NL, from ENDO- + Greek *mētra* uterus]
▶ ,endo'metrial *adj*

ndomorph ('endəʊ,mɔːf) *n* **1** a type of person having a body build characterized by fatness and heaviness. **2** a mineral that naturally occurs enclosed within another mineral.
▶ ,endo'morphic *adj* ▶ 'endo,morphy *n*

ndomorphism (,endəʊ'mɔː,fɪzəm) *n Geol.* metamorphism in which changes are induced in cooling molten rock by contact with older rocks.

ndophyte ('endəʊ,faɪt) *n* any plant, parasitic fungus, or alga that lives within a plant.
▶ endophytic (,endəʊ'fɪtɪk) *adj*

ndoplasm ('endəʊ,plæzəm) *n Cytology.* the inner cytoplasm of a cell.
▶ ,endo'plasmic *adj*

end organ *n Anat.* the expanded end of a peripheral motor or sensory nerve.

ndorphin (en'dɔːfɪn) *n* any of a class of chemicals occurring in the brain, including enkephalin, which have a similar effect to morphine.

endorsation (,endɔː'seɪʃən) *n Canad.* approval or support.

endorse *or* **indorse** (ɪn'dɔːs) *vb* **endorses, endorsing, endorsed** *or* **indorses, indorsing, indorsed**. (*tr*) **1** to give approval or sanction to. **2** to sign (one's name) on the back of (a cheque, etc.) to specify oneself as payee. **3** *Commerce.* **3a** to sign the back of (a document) to transfer ownership of the rights to a specified payee. **3b** to specify (a sum) as transferable to another as payee. **4** to write (a qualifying comment, etc.) on the back of a document. **5** to sign a document, as when confirming receipt of payment. **6** *Chiefly Brit.* to record a conviction on (a driving licence). [C16: from OF *endosser* to put on the back, from EN-[1] + *dos* back]
▶ en'dorsable *or* in'dorsable *adj* ▶ en'dorser, en'dorsor *or* in'dorser, in'dorsor *n* ▶ en,dor'see *or* in,dor'see *n*

endorsement *or* **indorsement** (ɪn'dɔːsmənt) *n* **1** the act or an instance of endorsing. **2** something that endorses, such as a signature. **3** approval or support. **4** a record of a motoring offence on a driving licence.

endoscope ('endəʊ,skəʊp) *n* a medical instrument for examining the interior of hollow organs such as the stomach or bowel.
▶ endoscopic (,endəʊ'skɒpɪk) *adj*

endoskeleton (,endəʊ'skelɪt°n) *n* an internal skeleton, esp. the bony or cartilaginous skeleton of vertebrates.
▶ ,endo'skeletal *adj*

endosperm ('endəʊ,spɜːm) *n* the tissue within the seed of a flowering plant that surrounds and nourishes the embryo.
▶ ,endo'spermic *adj*

endothermic (,endəʊ'θɜːmɪk) *or* **endothermal** *adj* (of a chemical reaction or compound) occurring or formed with the absorption of heat.
▶ ,endo'thermically *adv* ▶ ,endo'thermism *n*

endow (ɪn'daʊ) *vb* (*tr*) **1** to provide with or bequeath a source of permanent income. **2** (*usually foll. by with*) to provide (with qualities, characteristics, etc.). [C14: from OF, from EN-[1] + *douer*, from L *dōtāre*, from *dōs* dowry]

endowment (ɪn'daʊmənt) *n* **1** the income with which an institution, etc., is endowed. **2** the act or process of endowing. **3** (*usually pl*) natural talents or qualities.

endowment assurance *or* **insurance** *n* a form of life insurance that provides for the payment of a specified sum directly to the policyholder at a designated date or to his beneficiary should he die before this date.

endpaper ('end,peɪpə) *n* either of two leaves at the front and back of a book pasted to the inside of the board covers and the first leaf of the book.

end point *n* **1** *Chem.* the point at which a titration is complete. **2** the point at which anything is complete.

end product *n* the final result of a process, series, etc., esp. in manufacturing.

endue *or* **indue** (ɪn'djuː) *vb* **endues, enduing, endued** *or* **indues, induing, indued**. (*tr*) (usually foll. by *with*) to invest or provide, as with some quality or trait. [C15: from OF, from L *indūcere*, from *dūcere* to lead]

end up *vb* (*adv*) **1** (*copula*) to become eventually; turn out to be. **2** (*intr*) to arrive, esp. by a circuitous or lengthy route or process.

endurance (ɪn'djʊərəns) *n* **1** the capacity, state, or an instance of enduring. **2** something endured; a hardship, strain, or privation.

endure (ɪn'djʊə) *vb* **endures, enduring, endured**. **1** to undergo (hardship, strain, etc.) without yielding; bear. **2** (*tr*) to permit or tolerate. **3** (*intr*) to last or continue to exist. [C14: from OF, from L *indūrāre* to harden, from *dūrus* hard]
▶ en'durable *adj*

enduring (ɪn'djʊərɪŋ) *adj* **1** permanent; lasting. **2** having forbearance; long-suffering.
▶ en'duringly *adv* ▶ en'duringness *n*

end user *n* **1** (in international trading) the person, organization, or nation that will be the ultimate user of goods such as arms. **2** *Computing.* the ultimate destination of information that is being transferred within a system.

★ people and places

endways ('ɛnd،weɪz) *or esp. US & Canad.* **endwise** ('ɛnd،waɪz) *adv* **1** having the end forwards or upwards. ◆ *adj* **2** vertical or upright. **3** lengthways. **4** standing or lying end to end.

Endymion ★ (ɛn'dɪmɪən) *n Greek myth.* a handsome youth who was visited every night by the moon goddess Selene, who loved him.

end zone *n American football.* the area behind the goals at each end of the field that the ball must cross for a touchdown to be awarded.

ENE *symbol for* east-northeast.

-ene *n combining form.* (in chemistry) indicating an unsaturated compound containing double bonds: *benzene; ethylene.* [from Gk -*ēnē*, fem. patronymic suffix]

enema ('ɛnɪmə) *n, pl* **enemas** *or* **enemata** (-mətə) *Med.* **1** the introduction of liquid into the rectum to evacuate the bowels, medicate, or nourish. **2** the liquid so introduced. [C15: from NL, from Gk: injection, from *enienai* to send in]

enemy ('ɛnəmɪ) *n, pl* **enemies. 1** a person hostile or opposed to a policy, cause, person, or group. **2a** an armed adversary; opposing military force. **2b** (*as modifier*): *enemy aircraft.* **3a** a hostile nation or people. **3b** (*as modifier): an enemy alien.* **4** something that harms or opposes. ◆ Related adj: **inimical.** [C13: from OF, from L *inimīcus* hostile, from IN-^{1} + *amīcus* friend]

energetic (،ɛnə'dʒɛtɪk) *adj* having or showing energy; vigorous.
▸ ،ener'getically *adv*

energize *or* **energise** ('ɛnə،dʒaɪz) *vb* **energizes, energizing, energized** *or* **energises, energising, energised. 1** to have or cause to have energy; invigorate. **2** (*tr*) to apply electric current or electromotive force to (a circuit, etc.).
▸ 'ener،gizer *or* 'ener،giser *n*

energy ('ɛnədʒɪ) *n, pl* **energies. 1** intensity or vitality of action or expression; forcefulness. **2** capacity or tendency for intense activity; vigour. **3** *Physics.* **3a** the capacity of a body or system to do work. **3b** a measure of this capacity, measured in joules (SI units). [C16: from LL, from Gk *energeia* activity, from EN-^{2} + *ergon* work]

energy band *n Physics.* a range of energies associated with the quantum states of electrons in a crystalline solid.

energy conversion *n* the process of changing one form of energy into another, such as nuclear energy into heat or solar energy into electrical energy.

enervate *vb* ('ɛnə،veɪt), **enervates, enervating, enervated. 1** (*tr*) to deprive of strength or vitality. ◆ *adj* (ɪ'nɜːvɪt). **2** deprived of strength or vitality. [C17: from L *ēnervāre* to remove the nerves from, from *nervus* nerve]
▸ 'ener،vating *adj* ▸ ،ener'vation *n*

Enesco ★ (ɛ'nɛskəʊ) *n* **Georges** (ʒɔrʒ), original name *George Enescu.* 1881–1955, Romanian violinist and composer.

en famille *French.* (ã famij) *adv* **1** with one's family; at home. **2** in a casual way; informally.

enfant terrible *French.* (ãfã tɛriblə) *n, pl* **enfants terribles** (ãfã tɛriblə). a person given to unconventional conduct or indiscreet remarks. [C19: lit.: terrible child]

enfeeble (ɪn'fiːb°l) *vb* **enfeebles, enfeebling, enfeebled.** (*tr*) to make weak.
▸ en'feeblement *n* ▸ en'feebler *n*

en fête *French.* (ã fɛt) *adv* dressed for or engaged in a festivity. [C19: lit.: in festival]

Enfield ★ ('ɛnfiːld) *n* a borough of N Greater London: a residential suburb. Pop.: 259 800 (1994 est.). Area: 55 sq. km (31 sq. miles).

enfilade (،ɛnfɪ'leɪd) *Mil.* ◆ *n* **1** gunfire directed along the length of a position or formation. **2** a position or formation subject to such fire. ◆ *vb* **enfilades, enfilading, enfiladed.** (*tr*) **3** to attack (a position or formation) with enfilade. [C18: from F: suite, from *enfiler* to thread on string, from *fil* thread]

enfold *or* **infold** (ɪn'fəʊld) *vb* (*tr*) **1** to cover by enclosing. **2** to embrace.
▸ en'folder *or* in'folder *n* ▸ en'foldment *or* in'foldment *n*

enforce (ɪn'fɔːs) *vb* **enforces, enforcing, enforced.** (*tr*) **1** to

ensure obedience to (a law, decision, etc.). **2** to impos◖ (obedience, etc.) as by force. **3** to emphasize or reinforc◖ (an argument, etc.).
▸ en'forceable *adj* ▸ en،forcea'bility *n* ▸ enforcedl◖ (ɪn'fɔːsɪdlɪ) *adv* ▸ en'forcement *n* ▸ en'forcer *n*

enfranchise (ɪn'fræntʃaɪz) *vb* **enfranchises, enfranchising◖ enfranchised.** (*tr*) **1** to grant the power of voting to. **2** t◖ liberate, as from servitude. **3** (in England) to invest (◖ town, city, etc.) with the right to be represented in Par◖ liament.
▸ en'franchisement *n* ▸ en'franchiser *n*

ENG *abbrev. for* electronic news gathering: TV news ob◖ tained at the point of action by means of modern vide◖ equipment.

Eng. *abbrev. for:* **1** England. **2** English.

Engadine ★ ('ɛngə،diːn) *n* the upper part of the valley o◖ the River Inn in Switzerland, in Graubünden canton◖ tourist and winter sports centre.

engage (ɪn'geɪdʒ) *vb* **engages, engaging, engaged.** (*mainl◖ tr*) **1** to secure the services of. **2** to secure for use; reserve◖ **3** to involve (a person or his attention) intensely. **4** to at◖ tract (the affection) of (a person). **5** to draw (somebody◖ into conversation. **6** (*intr*) to take part; participate. **7** t◖ promise (to do something). **8** (*also intr*) *Mil.* to begin a◖ action with (an enemy). **9** to bring (a mechanism) int◖ operation. **10** (*also intr*) to undergo or cause to underg◖ interlocking, as of the components of a driving mecha◖ nism. **11** *Machinery.* to locate (a locking device) in its op◖ erative position or to advance (a tool) into a workpiec◖ to commence cutting. [C15: from OF, from EN-^{1} + *gage* ◖ pledge; see GAGE^1]
▸ en'gager *n*

engagé *or* (*fem*) **engagée** *French.* (ãgaʒe) *adj* (of an art◖ ist) committed to some ideology.

engaged (ɪn'geɪdʒd) *adj* **1** pledged to be married; be◖ trothed. **2** occupied or busy. **3** *Archit.* built against or at◖ tached to a wall or similar structure. **4** (of a telephone◖ line) in use.

engaged tone *n Brit.* a repeated single note heard on ◖ telephone when the number called is already in use.

engagement (ɪn'geɪdʒmənt) *n* **1** a pledge of marriage◖ betrothal. **2** an appointment or arrangement, esp. fo◖ business or social purposes. **3** the act of engaging or con◖ dition of being engaged. **4** a promise, obligation, o◖ other condition that binds. **5** a period of employment◖ esp. a limited period. **6** an action; battle.

engagement ring *n* a ring given by a man to a woma◖ as a token of their betrothal.

engaging (ɪn'geɪdʒɪŋ) *adj* pleasing, charming, or win◖ ning.
▸ en'gagingness *n*

en garde *French.* (ã gard) *sentence substitute.* **1** on guard; ◖ call to a fencer to adopt a defensive stance in readines◖ for an attack or bout. ◆ *adj* **2** (of a fencer) in such ◖ stance.

Engels ★ (*German* 'ɛŋ°ls) *n* **Friedrich** ('friːdrɪç). 1820–95◖ German socialist leader and political philosopher, in◖ England from 1849. He collaborated with Marx on *Th◖ Communist Manifesto* (1848) and his own works includ◖ *Condition of the Working Classes in England* (1844).

engender (ɪn'dʒɛndə) *vb* (*tr*) **1** to bring about or give ris◖ to; cause to be born. [C14: from OF, from L *ingenerāre◖ from *generāre* to beget]

engin. *abbrev. for* engineering.

engine ('ɛndʒɪn) *n* **1** any machine designed to conver◖ energy into mechanical work. **2** a railway locomotive. **3◖ *Mil.* any piece of equipment formerly used in warfare◖ such as a battering ram. **4** *Obs.* any instrument or device◖ [C13: from OF, from L *ingenium* nature, talent, ingeniou◖ contrivance, from IN-^{2} + -*genium,* rel. to *gignere* to beget◖ produce]

engine driver *n Chiefly Brit.* a man who drives a railwa◖ locomotive; train driver.

engineer (،ɛndʒɪ'nɪə) *n* **1** a person trained in any branc◖ of engineering. **2** the originator or manager of a situa◖ tion, system, etc. **3** *US & Canad.* the driver of a railwa◖ comotive. **4** an officer responsible for a ship's engines. **5**

★ people and places

a member of the armed forces trained in engineering and construction work. ◆ *vb* (*tr*) **6** to originate, cause, or plan in a clever or devious manner. **7** to design, plan, or construct as a professional engineer. [C14 *enginer*, from OF, from *enginier* to contrive, ult. from L *ingenium* skill, talent; see ENGINE]

engineering (ˌɛndʒɪˈnɪərɪŋ) *n* the profession of applying scientific principles to the design, construction, and maintenance of engines, cars, machines, etc. (**mechanical engineering**), buildings, bridges, roads, etc. (**civil engineering**), electrical machines and communication systems (**electrical engineering**), chemical plant and machinery (**chemical engineering**), or aircraft (**aeronautical engineering**).

England ★ (ˈɪŋɡlənd) *n* the largest division of Great Britain, bordering on Scotland and Wales: unified in the mid-tenth century and conquered by the Normans in 1066; united with Wales in 1536 and Scotland in 1707; monarchy overthrown in 1649 but restored in 1660. Capital: London. Pop.: 47 058 200 (1991). Area: 130 439 sq. km (50 352 sq. miles). See **United Kingdom**, **Great Britain**.

English (ˈɪŋɡlɪʃ) *n* **1** the official language of Britain, the US, most of the Commonwealth, and certain other countries. **2 the English**. (*functioning as pl*) the natives or inhabitants of England collectively. **3** (*often not cap.*) the usual US & Canad. term for **side** (in billiards). ◆ *adj* **4** of or relating to the English language. **5** relating to or characteristic of England or the English. ◆ *vb* (*tr*) **6** *Arch.* to translate or adapt into English.
▸ ˈEnglishness *n*

English Channel ★ *n* an arm of the Atlantic Ocean between S England and N France, linked with the North Sea by the Strait of Dover. Length: about 560 km (350 miles). Width: between 32 km (20 miles) and 161 km (100 miles).

English horn *n Music.* another name for **cor anglais**.

Englishman (ˈɪŋɡlɪʃmən) *or* (*fem*) **Englishwoman** *n*, *pl* **Englishmen** *or* **Englishwomen**. a native or inhabitant of England.

engorge (ɪnˈɡɔːdʒ) *vb* **engorges**, **engorging**, **engorged**. (*tr*) **1** *Pathol.* to congest with blood. **2** to eat (food) greedily. **3** to gorge (oneself); glut.
▸ enˈgorgement *n*

engr *abbrev. for:* **1** engineer. **2** engraver.

engraft *or* **ingraft** (ɪnˈɡrɑːft) *vb* (*tr*) **1** to graft (a shoot, bud, etc.) onto a stock. **2** to incorporate in a firm or permanent way; implant.
▸ ˌengrafˈtation, ˌingrafˈtation *or* enˈgraftment, inˈgraftment *n*

engrain (ɪnˈɡreɪn) *vb* a variant spelling of **ingrain**.

engrave (ɪnˈɡreɪv) *vb* **engraves**, **engraving**, **engraved**. (*tr*) **1** to inscribe (a design, writing, etc.) onto (a block, plate, or other printing surface) by carving, etching, or other process. **2** to print (designs or characters) from a plate so made. **3** to fix deeply or permanently in the mind. [C16: from EN-[1] + GRAVE[3], on the model of F *engraver*]
▸ enˈgraver *n*

engraving (ɪnˈɡreɪvɪŋ) *n* **1** the art of a person who engraves. **2** a printing surface that has been engraved. **3** a print made from this.

engross (ɪnˈɡrəʊs) *vb* (*tr*) **1** to occupy one's attention completely; absorb. **2** to write or copy (manuscript) in large legible handwriting. **3** *Law.* to write or type out formally (a document) preparatory to execution. [C14 (in the sense: to buy up wholesale); C15 (in the sense: to write in large letters): from L *grossus* thick, GROSS]
▸ enˈgrossed *adj* ▸ enˈgrossing *adj* ▸ enˈgrossment *n*

engulf *or* **ingulf** (ɪnˈɡʌlf) *vb* (*tr*) **1** to immerse, plunge, bury, or swallow up. **2** (*often passive*) to overwhelm.
▸ enˈgulfment *n*

enhance (ɪnˈhɑːns) *vb* **enhances**, **enhancing**, **enhanced**. (*tr*) to intensify or increase in quality, value, power, etc.; improve; augment. [C14: from OF, from EN-[1] + *haucier* to raise, from Vulgar L *altiāre* (unattested), from L *altus* high]
▸ enˈhancement *n* ▸ enˈhancer *n*

enharmonic (ˌɛnhɑːˈmɒnɪk) *adj Music.* **1** denoting or relating to a small difference in pitch between two notes,

such as A flat and G sharp: not present in instruments of equal temperament, but significant in the intonation of stringed instruments. **2** denoting or relating to enharmonic modulation. [C17: from L, from Gk, from EN-[2] + *harmonia*; see HARMONY]
▸ ˌenharˈmonically *adv*

Enid ★ (ˈiːnɪd) *n* (in Arthurian legend) the faithful wife of Geraint.

enigma (ɪˈnɪɡmə) *n* a person, thing, or situation that is mysterious, puzzling, or ambiguous. [C16: from L, from Gk, from *ainissesthai* to speak in riddles, from *ainos* fable, story]
▸ enigmatic (ˌɛnɪɡˈmætɪk) *or* ˌenigˈmatical *adj* ▸ ˌenigˈmatically *adv*

Eniwetok ★ (ˌɛnəˈwiːtɒk, əˈniːwɪˌtɒk) *n* an atoll in the W Pacific Ocean, in the NW Marshall Islands: taken by the US from Japan in 1944; became a naval base and later a testing ground for atomic weapons. Pop.: 715 (1988).

enjambment *or* **enjambement** (ɪnˈdʒæmmənt) *n Prosody.* the running over of a sentence from one line of verse into the next. [C19: from F, lit.: a straddling, from EN-[1] + *jambe* leg; see JAMB]
▸ enˈjambed *adj*

enjoin (ɪnˈdʒɔɪn) *vb* (*tr*) **1** to order (someone) to do something. **2** to impose or prescribe (a mode of behaviour, etc.). **3** *Law.* to require (a person) to do or refrain from some act, esp. by an injunction. [C13: from OF *enjoindre*, from L *injungere* to fasten to, from IN-[2] + *jungere* to JOIN]
▸ enˈjoiner *n* ▸ enˈjoinment *n*

enjoy (ɪnˈdʒɔɪ) *vb* (*tr*) **1** to receive pleasure from; take joy in. **2** to have the benefit of; use. **3** to have as a condition; experience. **4 enjoy oneself**. to have a good time. [C14: from OF, from EN-[1] + *joir* to find pleasure in, from L *gaudēre* to rejoice]
▸ enˈjoyable *adj* ▸ enˈjoyableness *n* ▸ enˈjoyably *adv*
▸ enˈjoyer *n*

enjoyment (ɪnˈdʒɔɪmənt) *n* **1** the act or condition of receiving pleasure from something. **2** the use or possession of something that is satisfying. **3** something that provides joy or satisfaction.

enkephalin (ɛnˈkɛfəlɪn) *or* **encephalin** (ɛnˈsɛfəlɪn) *n* a chemical occurring in the brain, having effects similar to those of morphine.

enkindle (ɪnˈkɪndəl) *vb* **enkindles**, **enkindling**, **enkindled**. (*tr*) **1** to set on fire; kindle. **2** to excite to activity or ardour; arouse.

enlace (ɪnˈleɪs) *vb* **enlaces**, **enlacing**, **enlaced**. (*tr*) **1** to bind or encircle with or as with laces. **2** to entangle; intertwine.
▸ enˈlacement *n*

enlarge (ɪnˈlɑːdʒ) *vb* **enlarges**, **enlarging**, **enlarged**. **1** to make or grow larger; increase or expand. **2** (*tr*) to make (a photographic print) of a larger size than the negative. **3** (*intr*; foll. by *on* or *upon*) to speak or write (about) in greater detail.
▸ enˈlargeable *adj* ▸ enˈlargement *n* ▸ enˈlarger *n*

enlighten (ɪnˈlaɪtən) *vb* (*tr*) **1** to give information or understanding to; instruct. **2** to free from prejudice, superstition, etc. **3** to give spiritual or religious revelation to. **4** *Poetic.* to shed light on.
▸ enˈlightening *adj*

enlightened (ɪnˈlaɪtənd) *adj* **1** well-informed, tolerant, and guided by rational thought: *an enlightened administration.* **2** claiming a spiritual revelation of truth.

enlightenment (ɪnˈlaɪtənmənt) *n* the act or means of enlightening or the state of being enlightened.

Enlightenment (ɪnˈlaɪtənmənt) *n* **the**. an 18th-century philosophical movement stressing the importance of reason.

enlist (ɪnˈlɪst) *vb* **1** to enter or persuade to enter the armed forces. **2** (*tr*) to engage or secure (a person or his support) for a venture, cause, etc. **3** (*intr*; foll. by *in*) to enter into or join an enterprise, cause, etc.
▸ enˈlister *n* ▸ enˈlistment *n*

enlisted man *n US.* a serviceman who holds neither a commission nor a warrant.

★ people and places

enliven (ɪn'laɪvᵊn) vb (tr) **1** to make active, vivacious, or spirited. **2** to make cheerful or bright; gladden.
▶ en'livening adj ▶ en'livenment n

en masse (French ã mas) adv in a group or mass; as a whole; all together. [C19: from F]

enmesh (ɪn'mɛʃ) vb (tr) to catch or involve in or as if in a net or snare; entangle.
▶ en'meshment n

enmity ('ɛnmɪtɪ) n, pl enmities. a feeling of hostility or ill will, as between enemies. [C13: from OF; see ENEMY]

Ennerdale Water ★ ('ɛnə,deɪl) n a lake in NW England, in Cumbria in the Lake District. Length: 4 km (2.5 miles).

Ennis ★ ('ɛnɪs) n a town in the W Republic of Ireland, county town of Co. Clare. Pop.: 13 750 (1991).

Enniskillen (,ɛnɪs'kɪlɪn) or (formerly) **Inniskilling** ★ n a town in SW Northern Ireland, in Fermanagh, on an island in the River Erne: scene of the defeat of James II's forces in 1689. Pop.: 11 436 (1991).

Ennius ('ɛnɪəs) n **Quintus** ('kwɪntəs). 239–169 B.C., Roman epic poet and dramatist.

ennoble (ɪ'nəʊbᵊl) vb ennobles, ennobling, ennobled. (tr) **1** to make noble, honourable, or excellent; dignify; exalt. **2** to raise to a noble rank.
▶ en'noblement n ▶ en'nobler n ▶ en'nobling adj

ennui ('ɒnwiː) n a feeling of listlessness and general dissatisfaction resulting from lack of activity or excitement. [C18: from F: apathy, from OF enui annoyance, vexation; see ANNOY]

Enoch ★ ('iːnɒk) n Old Testament. **1** the eldest son of Cain after whom the first city was named (Genesis 4:17). **2** the father of Methuselah: said to have walked with God and to have been taken by God at the end of his earthly life (Genesis 5:24).

enology (iː'nɒlədʒɪ) n the usual US spelling of oenology.

enormity (ɪ'nɔːmɪtɪ) n, pl enormities. **1** the quality or character of extreme wickedness. **2** an act of great wickedness; atrocity. **3** Inf. vastness of size or extent. [C15: from OF, from LL ēnormitās hugeness; see ENORMOUS]

> **USAGE NOTE** In modern English, it is common to talk about the *enormity* of something such as a task or a problem, but one should not talk about the *enormity* of an object or area: *distribution is a problem because of India's enormous size* (not *India's enormity*).

enormous (ɪ'nɔːməs) adj **1** unusually large in size, extent, or degree; immense; vast. **2** Arch. extremely wicked; heinous. [C16: from L, from ē- out of, away from + norma rule, pattern]
▶ e'normously adv ▶ e'normousness n

Enos ★ ('iːnɒs) n Old Testament. a son of Seth (Genesis 4:26; 5:6).

enosis ('ɛnəʊsɪs) n the union of Greece and Cyprus: the aim of a group of Greek Cypriots. [C20: Mod. Gk: from Gk henoun to unite, from heis one]

enough (ɪ'nʌf) determiner **1a** sufficient to answer a need, demand or supposition. **1b** (as pron): enough is now known. **2** that's enough! that will do: used to put an end to an action, speech, performance, etc. ◆ adv **3** so as to be sufficient; as much as necessary. **4** (not used with a negative) very or quite; rather. **5** (intensifier): oddly enough. **6** just adequately; tolerably. [OE genōh]

en passant (ɒn pæ'sɑːnt) adv in passing: in chess, said of capturing a pawn that has made an initial move of two squares. The capture is made as if the captured pawn had moved one square instead of two. [C17: from F]

enprint ('ɛnprɪnt) n a standard photographic print (5 × 3·5 in.) produced from a negative.

enquire (ɪn'kwaɪə) vb enquires, enquiring, enquired. a variant of inquire.
▶ en'quirer n ▶ en'quiry n

enrage (ɪn'reɪdʒ) vb enrages, enraging, enraged. (tr) to provoke to fury; put into a rage.
▶ en'raged adj ▶ en'ragement n

en rapport French. (ã rapɔr) adj (postpositive), adv in sympathy, harmony, or accord.

enrapture (ɪn'ræptʃə) vb enraptures, enrapturing, enraptured. (tr) to fill with delight; enchant.

enrich (ɪn'rɪtʃ) vb (tr) **1** to increase the wealth of. **2** to endow with fine or desirable qualities. **3** to make more beautiful; adorn; decorate. **4** to improve in quality, colour, flavour, etc. **5** to increase the food value of by adding nutrients. **6** to fertilize (soil). **7** Physics. to increase the concentration or abundance of one component of an isotope in (a solution or mixture).
▶ en'riched adj ▶ en'richment n

Enright ★ ('ɛnraɪt) n D(ennis) J(oseph). born 1920, British poet, essayist, and editor.

enrol or US **enroll** (ɪn'rəʊl) vb enrols or US enrolls, enrolling, enrolled. (mainly tr) **1** to record or note in a roll or list. **2** (also intr) to become or cause to become a member; enlist; register. **3** to put on record.
▶ ,enrol'lee n ▶ en'roller n

enrolment or US **enrollment** (ɪn'rəʊlmənt) n **1** the act of enrolling or state of being enrolled. **2** a list of people enrolled. **3** the total number of people enrolled.

en route (ɒn 'ruːt) adv on or along the way. [C18: from F]

Ens. abbrev. for Ensign.

ENSA ('ɛnsə) n acronym for Entertainments National Service Association.

Enschede ★ (Dutch 'ɛnsxədeː) n a city in the E Netherlands, in Overijssel province: a major centre of the Dutch cotton industry. Pop.: 147 924 (1995 est.).

ensconce (ɪn'skɒns) vb ensconces, ensconcing, ensconced. (tr; often passive) **1** to establish or settle firmly or comfortably. **2** to place in safety; hide. [C16: see EN-¹, SCONCE²]

ensemble (ɒn'sɒmbᵊl) n **1** all the parts of something considered together. **2** a person's complete costume outfit. **3** the cast of a play other than the principals. **4** Music. a group of soloists singing or playing together. **5** Music. the degree of precision and unity exhibited by a group of instrumentalists or singers performing together. **6** the general effect of something made up of individual parts. ◆ adv **7** all together or at once. [C15: from F: together, from L, from IN-² + simul at the same time]

enshrine or **inshrine** (ɪn'ʃraɪn) vb enshrines, enshrining, enshrined. (tr) **1** to place or enclose as in a shrine. **2** to hold as sacred; cherish; treasure.
▶ en'shrinement n

enshroud (ɪn'ʃraʊd) vb (tr) to cover or hide as with a shroud.

ensign ('ɛnsaɪn) n **1** (also 'ɛnsən). a flag flown by a ship, branch of the armed forces, etc., to indicate nationality, allegiance, etc. See also Red Ensign, White Ensign. **2** any flag, standard, or banner. **3** a standard-bearer. **4** a symbol or emblem; sign. **5** (in the US Navy) a commissioned officer of the lowest rank. **6** (in the British infantry) a colours bearer. **7** (formerly in the British infantry) a commissioned officer of the lowest rank. [C14: from OF enseigne, from L INSIGNIA]
▶ 'ensign,ship or 'ensigncy n

ensilage ('ɛnsɪlɪdʒ) n **1** the process of ensiling green fodder. **2** a less common name for silage.

ensile (ɛn'saɪl, 'ɛnsaɪl) vb ensiles, ensiling, ensiled. (tr) **1** to store and preserve (green fodder) in a silo. **2** to turn (green fodder) into silage by causing it to ferment in a silo. [C19: from F, from Sp., from EN-¹ + silo SILO]

enslave (ɪn'sleɪv) vb enslaves, enslaving, enslaved. (tr) to make a slave of; subjugate.
▶ en'slavement n ▶ en'slaver n

ensnare or **insnare** (ɪn'snɛə) vb ensnares, ensnaring, ensnared or insnares, insnaring, insnared. (tr) **1** to catch or trap as in a snare. **2** to trap or gain power over (someone) by dishonest or underhand means.
▶ en'snarement n ▶ en'snarer n

ensue (ɪn'sjuː) vb ensues, ensuing, ensued. **1** (intr) to come next or afterwards. **2** (intr) to occur as a consequence; result. **3** (tr) Obs. to pursue. [C14: from Anglo-F, from OF, from EN-¹ + suivre to follow, from L sequī]
▶ en'suing adj

en suite *French.* (ã sɥit) *adv* forming a unit: *a room with bathroom en suite.* [lit.: in sequence]

insure (ɛn'ʃʊə, -'ʃɔː) *or esp. US* **insure** *vb* ensures, ensuring, ensured *or US* insures, insuring, insured. (*tr*) **1** (*may take a clause as object*) to make certain or sure; guarantee. **2** to make safe or secure; protect.
▶ en'surer *n*

ENT *Med. abbrev. for* ear, nose, and throat.

ent *suffix forming adjectives and nouns.* causing or performing an action or existing in a certain condition; the agent that performs an action: *astringent; dependent.* [from L *-ent-, -ens,* present participial ending]

entablature (ɛn'tæblətʃə) *n Archit.* **1** the part of a classical temple above the columns, having an architrave, a frieze, and a cornice. **2** any similar construction. [C17: from F, from It. *intavolatura* something put on a table, hence, something laid flat, from *tavola* table]

entablement (ɪn'teɪbˀlmənt) *n* the platform of a pedestal, above the dado, that supports a statue. [C17: from OF]

entail (ɪn'teɪl) *vb* (*tr*) **1** to bring about or impose inevitably: *this task entails careful thought.* **2** *Property law.* to restrict (the descent of an estate) to designated heirs. **3** *Logic.* to have as a necessary consequence. ◆ *n* **4** *Property law.* **4a** the restriction imposed by entailing an estate. **4b** an entailed estate. [C14 *entaillen,* from EN-¹ + *taille* limitation, TAIL²]
▶ en'tailer *n* ▶ en'tailment *n*

entamoeba (ˌɛntə'miːbə), **endamoeba** *or US* **entameba, endameba** *n, pl* **entamoebae** (-biː), **entamoebas, endamoebae, endamoebas** *or US* **entamebae, entamebas, endamebae, endamebas.** any parasitic amoeba of the genus *Entamoeba* (or *Endamoeba*) which lives in the intestines of man and causes amoebic dysentery.

entangle (ɪn'tæŋgˀl) *vb* entangles, entangling, entangled. (*tr*) **1** to catch or involve in or as if in a tangle; ensnare or enmesh. **2** to make tangled or twisted; snarl. **3** to make complicated; confuse. **4** to involve in difficulties.
▶ en'tanglement *n* ▶ en'tangler *n*

entasis ('ɛntəsɪs) *n, pl* **entasises** (-siːz). a slightly convex curve given to the shaft of a column, or similar structure, to correct the illusion of concavity produced by a straight shaft. [C18: from Gk, from *enteinein* to stretch tight, from *teinein* to stretch]

Entebbe ★ (ɛn'tɛbɪ) *n* a town in S Uganda, on Lake Victoria: British administrative centre of Uganda (1893–1958); international airport. Pop.: 41 638 (1991).

entellus (ɛn'tɛləs) *n* an Old World monkey of S Asia. [C19: NL, apparently after a character in Virgil's *Aeneid*]

entente (*French* ãtãt) *n* **1** short for **entente cordiale**. **2** the parties to an entente cordiale collectively. [C19: F: understanding]

entente cordiale (*French* ãtãt kɔrdjal) *n* **1** a friendly understanding between political powers. **2** (*often caps.*) the understanding reached by France and Britain in 1904, over colonial disputes. [C19: F: cordial understanding]

enter ('ɛntə) *vb* **1** to come or go into (a place, house, etc.). **2** to penetrate or pierce. **3** (*tr*) to introduce or insert. **4** to join (a party, organization, etc.). **5** (when *intr,* foll. by *into*) to become involved or take part (in). **6** (*tr*) to record (an item) in a journal, account, etc. **7** (*tr*) to record (a name, etc.) on a list. **8** (*tr*) to present or submit: *to enter a proposal.* **9** (*intr*) *Theatre.* to come on stage: used as a stage direction: *enter Juliet.* **10** (when *intr,* often foll. by *into, on,* or *upon*) to begin; start: *to enter upon a new career.* **11** (*intr;* often foll. by *upon*) to come into possession (of). **12** (*tr*) to place (evidence, etc.) before a court of law. [C13: from OF, from L *intrāre,* from *intrā* within]
▶ 'enterable *adj* ▶ 'enterer *n*

enteric (ɛn'tɛrɪk) *or* **enteral** ('ɛntərəl) *adj* intestinal. [C19: from Gk, from *enteron* intestine]

enter into *vb* (*intr, prep*) **1** to be considered as a necessary part of (one's plans, calculations, etc.). **2** to be in sympathy with.

enteritis (ˌɛntə'raɪtɪs) *n* inflammation of the intestine.

entero- *or before a vowel* **enter-** *combining form.* indicat-

ing an intestine: *enterovirus; enteritis.* [from NL, from Gk *enteron* intestine]

enterobiasis (ˌɛntərəʊ'baɪəsɪs) *n* a disease, common in children, caused by infestation of the large intestine with pinworms. [C20: NL, from *enterobius* (generic name of worm) + -IASIS]

enterprise ('ɛntə,praɪz) *n* **1** a project or undertaking, esp. one that requires boldness or effort. **2** participation in such projects. **3** readiness to embark on new ventures; boldness and energy. **4a** initiative in business. **4b** (*as modifier*): *the enterprise culture.* **5** a company or firm. [C15: from OF *entreprise* (n), from *entreprendre* from *entre-* between (from L: INTER-) + *prendre* to take, from L *prehendere* to grasp]
▶ 'enter,priser *n*

Enterprise Allowance Scheme *n* (in Britain) a scheme to provide a weekly allowance to an unemployed person who wishes to set up a business and is willing to invest a specified amount in it during its first year.

enterprise zone *n* one of several areas in the UK in which industrial development is encouraged by tax and other concessions.

enterprising ('ɛntə,praɪzɪŋ) *adj* ready to embark on new ventures; full of boldness and initiative.
▶ 'enter,prisingly *adv*

entertain (ˌɛntə'teɪn) *vb* **1** to provide amusement for (a person or audience). **2** to show hospitality to (guests). **3** (*tr*) to hold in the mind. [C15: from OF, from *entre-* mutually + *tenir* to hold]

entertainer (ˌɛntə'teɪnə) *n* **1** a professional performer in public entertainments. **2** any person who entertains.

entertaining (ˌɛntə'teɪnɪŋ) *adj* serving to entertain or give pleasure; diverting; amusing.

entertainment (ˌɛntə'teɪnmənt) *n* **1** the act or art of entertaining or state of being entertained. **2** an act, production, etc., that entertains; diversion; amusement.

enthral *or US* **enthrall** (ɪn'θrɔːl) *vb* enthrals *or US* enthralls, enthralling, enthralled. (*tr*) **1** to hold spellbound; enchant; captivate. **2** *Obs.* to hold as thrall; enslave.
▶ en'thraller *n* ▶ en'thralling *adj* ▶ en'thralment *or US* en'thrallment *n*

enthrone (ɛn'θrəʊn) *vb* enthrones, enthroning, enthroned. (*tr*) **1** to place on a throne. **2** to honour or exalt. **3** to assign authority to.
▶ en'thronement *n*

enthuse (ɪn'θjuːz) *vb* enthuses, enthusing, enthused. to feel or show or cause to feel or show enthusiasm.

enthusiasm (ɪn'θjuːzɪˌæzəm) *n* **1** ardent and lively interest or eagerness. **2** an object of keen interest. **3** *Arch.* extravagant religious fervour. [C17: from LL, from Gk, from *enthousiazein* to be possessed by a god, from EN-² + *theos* god]

enthusiast (ɪn'θjuːzɪˌæst) *n* **1** a person motivated by enthusiasm; fanatic. **2** *Arch.* one whose zeal for religion is extravagant.
▶ en,thusi'astic *adj* ▶ en,thusi'astically *adv*

enthymeme ('ɛnθɪˌmiːm) *n Logic.* a syllogism in which one or more premises are unexpressed. [C16: via L from Gk *enthumeisthai* to infer, from EN-² + *thumos* mind]

entice (ɪn'taɪs) *vb* entices, enticing, enticed. (*tr*) to attract by exciting hope or desire; tempt; allure. [C13: from OF, from Vulgar L *intitiāre* (unattested) to incite]
▶ en'ticement *n* ▶ en'ticer *n* ▶ en'ticing *adj* ▶ en'ticingly *adv*

entire (ɪn'taɪə) *adj* **1** (*prenominal*) whole; complete. **2** (*prenominal*) without reservation or exception. **3** not broken or damaged. **4** undivided; continuous. **5** (of leaves, petals, etc.) having a smooth margin not broken up into teeth or lobes. **6** not castrated: *an entire horse.* **7** *Obs.* unmixed; pure. ◆ *n* **8** an uncastrated horse. [C14: from OF, from L *integer* whole, from IN-¹ + *tangere* to touch]
▶ en'tireness *n*

entirely (ɪn'taɪəlɪ) *adv* **1** wholly; completely. **2** solely or exclusively.

entirety (ɪn'taɪərɪtɪ) *n, pl* **entireties. 1** the state of being entire or whole; completeness. **2** a thing, sum, amount, etc., that is entire; whole; total.

entitle (ɪnˈtaɪt⁰l) *vb* **entitles, entitling, entitled.** (*tr*) **1** to give (a person) the right to do or have something; qualify; allow. **2** to give a name or title to. **3** to confer a title of rank or honour upon. [C14: from OF *entituler*, from LL, from L *titulus* TITLE]
▶ en'titlement *n*

entity (ˈɛntɪtɪ) *n, pl* **entities. 1** something having real or distinct existence. **2** existence or being. [C16: from Med. L, from *ēns* being, from L *esse* to be]
▶ 'entitative *adj*

ento- *combining form.* inside; within: *entoderm.* [NL, from Gk *entos* within]

entomb (ɪnˈtuːm) *vb* (*tr*) **1** to place in or as if in a tomb; bury; inter. **2** to serve as a tomb for.
▶ en'tombment *n*

entomo- *combining form.* indicating an insect: *entomology.* [from Gk *entomon* insect]

entomol. *or* **entom.** *abbrev. for* entomology.

entomology (ˌɛntəˈmɒlədʒɪ) *n* the branch of science concerned with the study of insects.
▶ ˌento'mological *adj* ▶ ˌento'mologist *n*

entophyte (ˈɛntəʊˌfaɪt) *n Bot.* a variant spelling of **endophyte.**
▶ entophytic (ˌɛntəʊˈfɪtɪk) *adj*

entourage (ˌɒntʊˈrɑːʒ) *n* **1** a group of attendants or retainers; retinue. **2** surroundings. [C19: from F, from *entourer* to surround, from *tour* circuit; see TOUR, TURN]

entr'acte (ɒnˈtrækt) *n* **1** an interval between two acts of a play or opera. **2** (esp. formerly) an entertainment during such an interval. [C19: F, lit.: between-act]

entrails (ˈɛntreɪlz) *pl n* **1** the internal organs of a person or animal; intestines; guts. **2** the innermost parts of anything. [C13: from OF, from Med. L *intrālia*, changed from L *interānea* intestines]

entrain (ɪnˈtreɪn) *vb* to board or put aboard a train.
▶ en'trainment *n*

entrance[1] (ˈɛntrəns) *n* **1** the act or an instance of entering; entry. **2** a place for entering, such as a door. **3a** the power, liberty, or right of entering. **3b** (*as modifier*): *an entrance fee.* **4** the coming of an actor or other performer onto a stage. [C16: from F, from *entrer* to ENTER]

entrance[2] (ɪnˈtrɑːns) *vb* **entrances, entrancing, entranced.** (*tr*) **1** to fill with wonder and delight; enchant. **2** to put into a trance; hypnotize.
▶ en'trancement *n* ▶ en'trancing *adj*

entrant (ˈɛntrənt) *n* a person who enters. [C17: from F, lit.: entering, from *entrer* to ENTER]

entrap (ɪnˈtræp) *vb* **entraps, entrapping, entrapped.** (*tr*) **1** to catch or snare as in a trap. **2** to trick into danger, difficulty, or embarrassment.
▶ en'trapment *n* ▶ en'trapper *n*

entreat *or* **intreat** (ɪnˈtriːt) *vb* **1** to ask (a person) earnestly; beg or plead with; implore. **2** to make an earnest request or petition for (something). **3** an archaic word for **treat** (sense 4). [C15: from OF, from EN-[1] + *traiter* to TREAT]
▶ en'treatment *or* in'treatment *n*

entreaty (ɪnˈtriːtɪ) *n, pl* **entreaties.** an earnest request or petition; supplication; plea.

entrechat (*French* ɑ̃trəʃa) *n* a leap in ballet during which the dancer repeatedly crosses his feet or beats them together. [C18: from F *entrechase,* changed by folk etymology from It. (*capriola*) *intrecciata,* lit.: entwined (caper)]

entrecôte (*French* ɑ̃trəkot) *n* a beefsteak cut from between the ribs. [F, from *entre-* INTER- + *côte* rib]

entrée (ˈɒntreɪ) *n* **1** a dish served before a main course. **2** *Chiefly US.* the main course of a meal. **3** the power or right of entry. [C18: from F, from *entrer* to ENTER; in cookery, so called because formerly the course was served after an intermediate course called the *relevé* (remove)]

entremets (*French* ɑ̃trəme) *n, pl* **entremets** (*French* -mɛ). **1** a dessert. **2** a light dish formerly served between the main course and the dessert. [C18: from F, from O] from *entre-* between + *mes* dish]

entrench *or* **intrench** (ɪnˈtrentʃ) *vb* **1** (*tr*) to construct defensive position by digging trenches around it. **2** (*t* to fix or establish firmly. **3** (*intr;* foll. by *on* or *upon*) t trespass or encroach.
▶ en'trenched *or* in'trenched *adj* ▶ en'trenchment *or* ir 'trenchment *n*

entrepôt (*French* ɑ̃trəpo) *n* **1** a warehouse for commercia goods. **2a** a trading centre or port at which goods are in ported and re-exported without incurring duty. **2b** (*a modifier*): *an entrepôt trade.* [C18: F, from *entreposer,* fror *entre* between + *poser* to place; formed on the model c DEPOT]

entrepreneur (ˌɒntrəprəˈnɜː) *n* **1** the owner or manage of a business enterprise who, by risk and initiative, a tempts to make profits. **2** a middleman or commercia intermediary. [C19: from F, from *entreprendre* to under take; see ENTERPRISE]
▶ ˌentrepre'neurial *adj* ▶ ˌentrepre'neurship *n*

entropy (ˈɛntrəpɪ) *n, pl* **entropies. 1** a thermodynami quantity that changes in a reversible process by a amount equal to the heat absorbed or emitted divide by the thermodynamic temperature. It is measured i joules per kelvin. **2** lack of pattern or organization; diso der. [C19: from EN-[2] + -TROPE]

entrust *or* **intrust** (ɪnˈtrʌst) *vb* (*tr*) **1** (usually foll. b *with*) to invest or charge (with a duty, responsibility etc.). **2** (often foll. by *to*) to put into the care or protec tion of someone.
▶ en'trustment *or* in'trustment *n*

USAGE NOTE It is usually considered incorrect to talk about *entrusting* someone *to do* something: *the army cannot be trusted* (not *entrusted*) *to carry out orders.*

---

entry (ˈɛntrɪ) *n, pl* **entries. 1** the act or an instance of enter ing; entrance. **2** a point or place for entering, such as door, etc. **3a** the right or liberty of entering. **3b** (*as mod fier*): *an entry permit.* **4** the act of recording an item in journal, account, etc. **5** an item recorded, as in a diary dictionary, or account. **6** a person, horse, car, etc., enter ing a competition or contest. **7** the competitors enterin a contest considered collectively. **8** the action of an acto in going on stage. **9** *Property law.* the act of going upo land with the intention of asserting the right to posses sion. **10** any point in a piece of music at which a per former commences or resumes singing or playing. **1** *Bridge, etc.* a card that enables one to transfer the lea from one's own hand to that of one's partner or to th dummy hand. **12** *Dialect.* a passage between the backs o two rows of houses. [C13: from OF *entree,* p.p. of *entre* to ENTER]

entryism (ˈɛntrɪɪzəm) *n* the policy or practice of joinin an existing political party with the intention of chang ing it instead of forming a new party.
▶ 'entryist *n, adj*

entry-level *adj* **1** (of a job or worker) at the most ele mentary level in a career structure. **2** (of a product) char acterized by being at the most appropriate level for use by a beginner: *an entry-level camera.*

entwine *or* **intwine** (ɪnˈtwaɪn) *vb* **entwines, entwining entwined** *or* **intwines, intwining, intwined.** (of two or mor things) to twine together or (of one or more things) t twine around (something else).
▶ en'twinement *or* in'twinement *n*

Enugu ★ (ɛˈnuːguː) *n* **1** a city in S Nigeria, capital o Enugu state: capital of the former Eastern region and o the breakaway state of Biafra during the Civil Wa (1967–70): coal-mining. Pop.: 308 200 (1995 est.). **2** a state in S Nigeria. Capital: Enugu. Pop.: 3 256 134 (1992 est.). Area: 12 831 sq. km (4954 sq. miles).

E number *n* any of a series of numbers with the prefix I indicating a specific food additive recognized by the Eu ropean Union.

enumerate (ɪˈnjuːməˌreɪt) *vb* **enumerates, enumerating**

★ people and places

enumerated. (tr) **1** to name one by one; list. **2** to determine the number of; count. [C17: from L, from *numerāre* to count, reckon; see NUMBER]
► e'numerate adj ► e,numer'ation n ► e'numerative adj

enumerator (ɪ'njuːmə,reɪtə) n **1** a person or thing that enumerates. **2** Brit. a person who issues and retrieves census forms.

enunciable (ɪ'nʌnsɪəbʰl) adj capable of being enunciated.

enunciate (ɪ'nʌnsɪ,eɪt) vb **enunciates, enunciating, enunciated. 1** to articulate or pronounce (words), esp. clearly and distinctly. **2** (tr) to state precisely or formally. [C17: from L *ēnuntiāre* to declare, from *nuntiāre* to announce]
► e,nunci'ation n ► e'nunciative or e'nunciatory adj ► e'nunci,ator n

enuresis (,ɛnju'riːsɪs) n involuntary discharge of urine, esp. during sleep. [C19: from NL, from Gk EN-² + *ouron* urine]
► enuretic (,ɛnju'rɛtɪk) adj

envelop (ɪn'vɛləp) vb **envelops, enveloping, enveloped.** (tr) **1.** to wrap or enclose as in a covering. **2** to conceal or obscure. **3** to surround (an enemy force). [C14: from OF *envoluper*, from EN-¹ + *voluper, voloper*, from ?]
► en'velopment n

envelope ('ɛnvə,ləʊp, 'ɒn-) n **1** a flat covering of paper, usually rectangular and with a flap that can be sealed, used to enclose a letter, etc. **2** any covering or wrapper. **3** Biol. any enclosing structure, such as a membrane, shell, or skin. **4** the bag enclosing gas in a balloon. **5** Maths. a curve or surface that is tangential to each one of a group of curves or surfaces. [C18: from F, from *envelopper* to wrap around; see ENVELOP]

envenom (ɪn'vɛnəm) vb (tr) **1** to fill or impregnate with venom; make poisonous. **2** to fill with bitterness or malice.

Enver Pasha ★ ('ɛnvə 'pɑːʃə) n 1881–1922, Turkish soldier and leader of the Young Turks: minister of war (1914–18).

enviable ('ɛnvɪəbʰl) adj exciting envy; fortunate or privileged.
► 'enviableness n

envious ('ɛnvɪəs) adj feeling, showing, or resulting from envy. [C13: from Anglo-Norman, ult. from L *invidiōsus* full of envy, INVIDIOUS; see ENVY]
► 'enviously adv ► 'enviousness n

environ (ɪn'vaɪrən) vb (tr) to encircle or surround. [C14: from OF *environner* to surround, from EN-¹ + *viron* a circle, from *virer* to turn, VEER]

environment (ɪn'vaɪrənmənt) n **1** external conditions or surroundings. **2** Ecology. the external surroundings in which a plant or animal lives, which influence its development and behaviour. **3** Computing. an operating system, program, or integrated suite of programs that provides all the facilities necessary for a particular application: *a word-processing environment*.
► en,viron'mental adj

environmentalist (ɪn,vaɪrən'mɛntəlɪst) n **1** a specialist in the maintenance of ecological balance and the conservation of the environment. **2** a person concerned with issues that affect the environment, such as pollution.

environs (ɪn'vaɪrənz) pl n a surrounding area or region, esp. the suburbs or outskirts of a city.

envisage (ɪn'vɪzɪdʒ) vb **envisages, envisaging, envisaged.** (tr) **1** to form a mental image of; visualize. **2** to conceive of as a possibility in the future. [C19: from F, from EN-¹ + *visage* face, VISAGE]
► en'visagement n

> **USAGE NOTE** It was formerly considered incorrect to use a clause after *envisage* as in *it is envisaged that the new centre will cost £40 million*, but this use is now acceptable.

envision (ɪn'vɪʒən) vb (tr) to conceive of as a possibility, esp. in the future; foresee.

envoy¹ ('ɛnvɔɪ) n **1** Also called: **minister, minister plenipotentiary.** a diplomat ranking between an ambassador and a minister resident. **2** an accredited agent or representative. [C17: from F, from *envoyer* to send, from Vulgar L *inviāre* (unattested) to send on a journey, from IN-² + *via* road]
► 'envoyship n

envoy² or **envoi** ('ɛnvɔɪ) n **1** a brief concluding stanza, notably in ballades. **2** a postscript in other forms of verse or prose. [C14: from OF, from *envoyer* to send; see ENVOY¹]

envy ('ɛnvɪ) n, pl **envies. 1** a feeling of grudging or somewhat admiring discontent aroused by the possessions, achievements, or qualities of another. **2** the desire to have something possessed by another; covetousness. **3** an object of envy. ◆ vb **envies, envying, envied. 4** to be envious of (a person or thing). [C13: via OF from L *invidia*, from *invidēre* to eye maliciously, from IN-² + *vidēre* to see]
► 'envier n ► 'envyingly adv

enwrap or **inwrap** (ɪn'ræp) vb **enwraps, enwrapping, enwrapped.** (tr) **1** to wrap or cover up; envelop. **2** (usually passive) to engross or absorb.

enwreath (ɪn'riːð) vb (tr) to surround or encircle with or as with a wreath or wreaths.

Enzed ★ ('ɛn'zɛd) n Austral & NZ inf. **1** New Zealand. **2** Also called: **En'zedder.** a New Zealander.

enzootic (,ɛnzəʊ'ɒtɪk) adj **1** (of diseases) affecting animals within a limited region. ◆ n **2** an enzootic disease. [C19: from EN-² + Gk *zōion* animal + -OTIC]
► ,enzo'otically adv

enzyme ('ɛnzaɪm) n any of a group of complex proteins produced by living cells, that act as catalysts in specific biochemical reactions. [C19: from Med. Gk *enzumos* leavened, from Gk EN-² + *zumē* leaven]
► enzymatic (,ɛnzaɪ'mætɪk, -zɪ-) or enzymic (ɛn'zaɪmɪk, -'zɪm-) adj

enzyme-linked immunosorbent assay (,ɪmjʊnəʊ'sɔːbənt) n the full name for ELISA.

eo- combining form. early or primeval: *Eocene; eohippus*. [from Gk, from *ēōs* dawn]

EOC abbrev. for Equal Opportunities Commission.

Eocene ('iːəʊ,siːn) adj **1** of or denoting the second epoch of the Tertiary period, during which hooved mammals appeared. ◆ n **2** the. the Eocene epoch or rock series. [C19: from EO- + -CENE]

eohippus (,iːəʊ'hɪpəs) n, pl **eohippuses.** the earliest horse: an extinct Eocene dog-sized animal. [C19: NL, from EO- + Gk *hippos* horse]

Eolithic (,iːəʊ'lɪθɪk) adj denoting or relating to the early part of the Stone Age, characterized by the use of crude stone tools (**eoliths**).

eon ('iːən, 'iːɒn) n **1** the usual US spelling of **aeon. 2** Geol. the longest division of geological time, comprising two or more eras.

Eos ★ ('iːɒs) n Greek myth. the winged goddess of the dawn, the daughter of Hyperion. Roman counterpart: **Aurora.**

eosin ('iːəʊsɪn) or **eosine** ('iːəʊsɪn, -,siːn) n **1** a red fluorescent crystalline water-insoluble compound. Its soluble salts are used as dyes. **2** any of several similar dyes. [C19: from Gk *ēōs* dawn + -IN; referring to colour it gives to silk]

Eötvös ★ (Hungarian 'øtvøʃ) n Baron **Roland von.** 1848–1919, Hungarian physicist noted for his studies of gravity.

-eous suffix forming adjectives. relating to or having the nature of: *gaseous*. [from L *-eus*]

EP n an extended-play gramophone record, usually 7 inches (18 cm) in diameter: a longer recording than a single.

EPA abbrev. for eicosapentaenoic acid: a fatty acid, found in certain fish oils, that can reduce blood cholesterol.

epact ('iːpækt) n **1** the difference in time, about 11 days, between the solar year and the lunar year. **2** the number of days between the beginning of the calendar year and the new moon immediately preceding this. [C16: via LL from Gk *epaktē*, from *epagein* to bring in, intercalate]

Epaminondas ★ (ɛ,pæmɪ'nɒndæs) *n* ?418–362 B.C., Greek Theban statesman and general: defeated the Spartans at Leuctra (371) and Mantinea (362) and restored power in Greece to Thebes.

eparch ('epɑːk) *n* **1** a bishop or metropolitan in the Orthodox Church. **2** a governor of a subdivision of a province of modern Greece. [C17: from Gk *eparkhos*, from *epi-* over, on + -ARCH]
▶ '**eparchy** *n*

epaulette *or US* **epaulet** ('epəˌlet, -lɪt) *n* a piece of ornamental material on the shoulder of a garment, esp. a military uniform. [C18: from F, from L *spatula* shoulder blade]

épée ('epeɪ) *n* a sword similar to the foil but with a heavier blade. [C19: from F: sword, from L *spatha*, from Gk *spathē* blade; see SPADE[1]]
▶ '**épéeist** *n*

epeirogeny (ˌepaɪ'rɒdʒɪnɪ) *or* **epeirogenesis** (ɪ,paɪrəʊ'dʒenɪsɪs) *n* the formation of continents by relatively slow displacements of the earth's crust. [C19: from Gk *ēpeiros* continent + -GENY]
▶ **epeirogenic** (ɪ,paɪrəʊ'dʒenɪk) *or* **epeirogenetic** (ɪ,paɪrəʊdʒɪ'netɪk) *adj*

epergne (ɪ'pɜːn) *n* an ornamental centrepiece for a table, holding fruit, flowers, etc. [C18: prob. from F *épargne* a saving, from *épargner* to economize, of Gmc origin]

epexegesis (ɛ,peksɪ'dʒiːsɪs) *n, pl* **epexegesises** (-,siːz). *Rhetoric.* **1** the addition of a phrase, clause, or sentence to a text to provide further explanation. **2** the phrase, clause, or sentence added for this purpose. [C17: from Gk; see EPI-, EXEGESIS]
▶ **epexegetic** (ɛ,peksɪ'dʒetɪk) *or* **ep,exe'getical** *adj*

Eph. *or* **Ephes.** *Bible. abbrev. for* Ephesians.

ephah *or* **epha** ('iːfə) *n* a Hebrew unit of measure equal to approximately one bushel or about 33 litres. [C16: from Heb., from Egyptian]

ephedrine *or* **ephedrin** (ɪ'fedrɪn, 'efɪ,driːn, -drɪn) *n* a white crystalline alkaloid used for the treatment of asthma and hay fever. [C19: from NL from L from Gk, from EPI- + *hedra* seat + -INE[1]]

ephemera (ɪ'femərə) *n, pl* **ephemeras** *or* **ephemerae** (-ə,riː). **1** a mayfly, esp. one of the genus *Ephemera*. **2** something transitory or short-lived. **3** (*functioning as pl*) collectable items not originally intended to be long-lasting, such as tickets, posters, etc. **4** a plural of **ephemeron**. [C16: see EPHEMERAL]

ephemeral (ɪ'femərəl) *adj* **1** transitory; short-lived: *ephemeral pleasure.* ◆ *n* **2** a short-lived organism, such as the mayfly. [C16: from Gk *ephēmeros* lasting only a day, from *hēmera* day]
▶ **e,phemer'ality** *or* **e'phemeralness** *n*

ephemerid (ɪ'femərɪd) *n* any insect of the order *Ephemeroptera* (or *Ephemerida*), which comprises the mayflies. Also: **ephemeropteran.** [C19: from NL, from Gk *ephēmeros* short-lived + -ID[1]]

ephemeris (ɪ'femərɪs) *n, pl* **ephemerides** (,efɪ'merɪ,diːz). a table giving the future positions of a planet, comet, or satellite during a specified period. [C16: from L, from Gk: diary, journal; see EPHEMERAL]

ephemeron (ɪ'femə,rɒn) *n, pl* **ephemera** (-ərə) *or* **ephemerons.** (*usually pl*). something transitory or short-lived. [C16: see EPHEMERAL]

Ephesus ★ ('efɪsəs) *n* (in ancient Greece) a major trading city on the W coast of Asia Minor: famous for its temple of Artemis (Diana); sacked by the Goths (262 A.D.).

ephod ('iːfɒd) *n Bible.* an embroidered vestment worn by priests in ancient Israel. [C14: from Heb.]

ephor ('efɔː) *n, pl* **ephors** *or* **ephori** (-ə,raɪ) (in ancient Greece) a senior magistrate, esp. one of the five Spartan ephors, who wielded effective power. [C16: from Gk, from *ephoran* to supervise, from EPI- + *horan* to look]
▶ '**ephoral** *adj* ▶ '**ephorate** *n*

Ephraim ★ ('iːfreɪɪm) *n Old Testament.* **1a** the younger son of Joseph, who received the principal blessing of his grandfather Jacob (Genesis 48:8–22). **1b** the tribe descended from him. **1c** the territory of this tribe, west of the River Jordan. **2** the northern kingdom of Israel afte the kingdom of Solomon had been divided into two.

Ephraimite ('iːfreɪ,maɪt) *n* a member of the tribe o Ephraim.

epi-, eph-, *or before a vowel* **ep-** *prefix* **1** upon; above over: *epidermis; epicentre.* **2** in addition to: *epiphenomenon* **3** after: *epilogue.* **4** near; close to: *epicalyx.* [from Gk, from *epi* (prep)]

epic ('epɪk) *n* **1** a long narrative poem recounting in elevated style the deeds of a legendary hero. **2** the genre o epic poetry. **3** any work of literature, film, etc., having qualities associated with the epic. **4** an episode in th lives of men in which heroic deeds are performed. ◆ *ac* **5** denoting, relating to, or characteristic of an epic o epics. **6** of heroic or impressive proportions. [C16: from L, from Gk *epikos*, from *epos* speech, word, song]

epicalyx (,epɪ'keɪlɪks, -'kæl-) *n, pl* **epicalyxes** *or* **epicalyce** (-lɪ,siːz). *Bot.* a series of small sepal-like bracts forming a outer calyx beneath the true calyx in some flowers.

epicanthus (,epɪ'kænθəs) *n, pl* **epicanthi** (-θaɪ). a fold o skin extending vertically over the inner angle of the eye characteristic of Mongolian peoples. [C19: NL, from EP + L *canthus* corner of the eye, from Gk *kanthos*]
▶ '**epi'canthic** *adj*

epicardium (,epɪ'kɑːdɪəm) *n, pl* **epicardia** (-dɪə). *Anat.* the innermost layer of the pericardium. [C19: NL, from EP + Gk *kardia* heart]
▶ '**epi'cardiac** *or* '**epi'cardial** *adj*

epicarp ('epɪ,kɑːp) *or* **exocarp** *n* the outermost layer o the pericarp of fruits. [C19: from F, from EPI- + Gk *karpo* fruit]

epicene ('epɪ,siːn) *adj* **1** having the characteristics o both sexes. **2** of neither sex; sexless. **3** effeminate. *Grammar.* **4a** denoting a noun that may refer to a male o a female. **4b** (in Latin, Greek, etc.) denoting a noun tha retains the same gender regardless of the sex of the refer ent. [C15: from L *epicoenus* of both genders, from G *epikoinos* common to many, from *koinos* common]
▶ '**epi'cenism** *n*

epicentre *or US* **epicenter** ('epɪ,sentə) *n* the point or the earth's surface immediately above the origin of a earthquake. [C19: from NL, from Gk *epikentros* over th centre, from EPI- + CENTRE]
▶ '**epi'central** *adj*

Epictetus ★ (,epɪk'tiːtəs) *n* ?50–?120 A.D., Greek Stoi philosopher, who stressed self-renunciation and the brotherhood of man.

epicure ('epɪ,kjʊə) *n* **1** a person who cultivates a discrimi nating palate for good food and drink. **2** a person de voted to sensual pleasures. [C16: from Med. L *epicūrus* after EPICURUS]
▶ '**epicur,ism** *n*

epicurean (,epɪkjʊ'riːən) *adj* **1** devoted to sensual plea sures, esp. food and drink. **2** suitable for an epicure. ◆ *r* **3** an epicure; gourmet.
▶ '**epicu'rean,ism** *n*

Epicurean (,epɪkjʊ'riːən) *adj* **1** of or relating to the philosophy of Epicurus. ◆ *n* **2** a follower of the philosophy of Epicurus.
▶ '**Epicu'rean,ism** *n*

Epicurus ★ (,epɪ'kjʊərəs) *n* 341–270 B.C., Greek philoso pher, who held that the highest good is pleasure an that the world is a series of fortuitous combinations o atoms.

epicycle ('epɪ,saɪkⁿl) *n* a circle that rolls around the in side or outside of another circle. [C14: from LL, from Gk; see EPI-, CYCLE]
▶ '**epicyclic** (,epɪ'saɪklɪk, -'sɪklɪk) *or* '**epi'cyclical** *adj*

epicyclic train *n* a cluster of gears consisting of a cen tral gearwheel, a coaxial gearwheel of greater diameter and one or more planetary gears engaging with both o them.

epicycloid (,epɪ'saɪklɔɪd) *n* the curve described by a point on the circumference of a circle as this circle roll around the outside of another fixed circle.
▶ '**epicy'cloidal** *adj*

Epidaurus ★ (,epɪ'dɔːrəs; *Greek* ɛ'piðavrɔs) *n* an ancien port in Greece, in the NE Peloponnese, in Argolis on the Saronic Gulf.

epideictic (ˌɛpɪ'daɪktɪk) *adj* designed to display something, esp. the skill of the speaker in rhetoric. Also: **epidictic** (ˌɛpɪ'dɪktɪk). [C18: from Gk, from *epideiknunai* to display, from *deiknunai* to show]

epidemic (ˌɛpɪ'dɛmɪk) *adj* 1 (esp. of a disease) attacking or affecting many persons simultaneously in a community or area. ◆ *n* 2 a widespread occurrence of a disease. 3 a rapid development, spread, or growth of something. [C17: from F, via LL Gk *epidēmia*, lit.: among the people, from EPI- + *dēmos* people]
▸ ˌepi'demically *adv*

epidemiology (ˌɛpɪˌdiːmɪ'ɒlədʒɪ) *n* the branch of medical science concerned with the occurrence, distribution, and control of diseases in populations.
▸ epidemiological (ˌɛpɪˌdiːmɪə'lɒdʒɪkᵊl) *adj* ▸ ˌepiˌdemi'ologist *n*

epidermis (ˌɛpɪ'dɜːmɪs) *n* 1 the thin protective outer layer of the skin. 2 the outer layer of cells of an invertebrate. 3 the outer protective layer of cells of a plant. [C17: via LL from Gk, from EPI- + *derma* skin]
▸ ˌepi'dermal, ˌepi'dermic, *or* ˌepi'dermoid *adj*

epidiascope (ˌɛpɪ'daɪəˌskəʊp) *n* an optical device for projecting a magnified image onto a screen.

epididymis (ˌɛpɪ'dɪdɪmɪs) *n, pl* **epididymides** (-dɪ'dɪmɪˌdiːz). *Anat.* a convoluted tube behind each testis, in which spermatozoa are stored and conveyed to the vas deferens. [C17: from Gk *epididumis*, from EPI- + *didumos* twin, testicle]

epidural (ˌɛpɪ'djʊərəl) *adj* 1 Also: **extradural**. upon or outside the dura mater. ◆ *n* 2 Also: **epidural anaesthesia, spinal anaesthesia. 2a** injection of anaesthetic into the space outside the dura mater enveloping the spinal cord. **2b** anaesthesia induced by this method. [C19: from EPI- + DUR(A MATER) + -AL¹]

epigamic (ˌɛpɪ'gæmɪk) *adj Zool.* attractive to the opposite sex: *epigamic coloration*.

epigeal (ˌɛpɪ'dʒiːəl), **epigean**, *or* **epigeous** *adj* 1 of or relating to seed germination in which the cotyledons appear above the ground. 2 living or growing on or close to the surface of the ground. [C19: from Gk *epigeios* of the earth, from EPI- + *gē* earth]

epiglottis (ˌɛpɪ'glɒtɪs) *n, pl* **epiglottises** *or* **epiglottides** (-tɪˌdiːz). a thin cartilaginous flap that covers the entrance to the larynx during swallowing, preventing food from entering the trachea.
▸ ˌepi'glottal *or* ˌepi'glottic *adj*

Epigoni ★ (ɪ'pɪgəˌnaɪ) *pl n, sing* **-onus** (-ənəs). *Greek myth.* the descendants of the Seven against Thebes, who undertook a second expedition against the city and eventually captured and destroyed it. [C20: from Gk *epigonoi* those born after]

epigram ('ɛpɪˌgræm) *n* 1 a witty, often paradoxical remark, concisely expressed. 2 a short poem, esp. one having a witty and ingenious ending. [C15: from L *epigramma*, from Gk: inscription, from *graphein* to write]
▸ ˌepigram'matic *adj* ▸ ˌepigram'matically *adv*

epigrammatize *or* **epigrammatise** (ˌɛpɪ'græməˌtaɪz) *vb* **epigrammatizes, epigrammatizing, epigrammatized** *or* **epigrammatises, epigrammatising, epigrammatised.** to make an epigram (about).
▸ ˌepigram'matism *n* ▸ ˌepigram'matist *n*

epigraph ('ɛpɪˌgrɑːf) *n* 1 a quotation at the beginning of a book, chapter, etc. 2 an inscription on a monument or building. [C17: from Gk; see EPIGRAM]
▸ epigraphic (ˌɛpɪ'græfɪk) *or* ˌepi'graphical *adj*

epigraphy (ɪ'pɪgrəfɪ) *n* 1 the study of ancient inscriptions. 2 epigraphs collectively.
▸ e'pigraphist *or* e'pigrapher *n*

epilator ('ɛpɪˌleɪtə) *n* an electrical appliance consisting of a metal spiral head that rotates at high speed, plucking unwanted hair.

epilepsy ('ɛpɪˌlɛpsɪ) *n* a disorder of the central nervous system characterized by periodic loss of consciousness with or without convulsions. [C16: from LL *epilēpsia*, from Gk, from *epilambanein* to attack, seize]

epileptic (ˌɛpɪ'lɛptɪk) *adj* 1 of, relating to, or having epilepsy. ◆ *n* 2 a person who has epilepsy.
▸ ˌepi'leptically *adv*

epilogue ('ɛpɪˌlɒg) *n* 1a a speech addressed to the audience by an actor at the end of a play. 1b the actor speaking this. 2 a short postscript to any literary work. 3 *Brit.* the concluding programme of the day on a radio or television station. [C15: from L, from Gk *epilogos*, from *logos* word, speech]
▸ epilogist (ɪ'pɪlədʒɪst) *n*

epinephrine (ˌɛpɪ'nɛfrɪn, -riːn) *or* **epinephrin** *n* a US name for **adrenaline**. [C19: from EPI- + *nephro-* + -INE²]

epiphany (ɪ'pɪfənɪ) *n, pl* **epiphanies. 1** the manifestation of a supernatural or divine reality. 2 any moment of great or sudden revelation.
▸ epiphanic (ˌɛpɪ'fænɪk) *adj*

Epiphany (ɪ'pɪfənɪ) *n, pl* **Epiphanies.** a Christian festival held on Jan. 6, commemorating, in the Western Church, the manifestation of Christ to the Magi. [C17: via Church L from Gk *epiphaneia* an appearing, from EPI- + *phainein* to show]

epiphenomenon (ˌɛpɪfɪ'nɒmɪnən) *n, pl* **epiphenomena** (-nə). 1 a secondary or additional phenomenon. 2 *Philosophy.* mind or consciousness regarded as a by-product of the biological activity of the human brain. 3 *Pathol.* an unexpected symptom or occurrence during the course of a disease.
▸ ˌepiphe'nomenal *adj*

epiphyte ('ɛpɪˌfaɪt) *n* a plant that grows on another plant but is not parasitic on it. [C19: via NL from Gk, from EPI- + *phusis* growth]
▸ epiphytic (ˌɛpɪ'fɪtɪk), ˌepi'phytal, *or* ˌepi'phytical *adj*

Epirus ★ (ɪ'paɪərəs) *n* 1 a region of NW Greece, part of ancient Epirus ceded to Greece after independence in 1830. 2 (in ancient Greece) a region between the Pindus mountains and the Ionian Sea, straddling the modern border with Albania.

Epis. *abbrev. for:* 1 Also: **Episc.** Episcopal *or* Episcopalian. 2 *Bible.* Also: **Epist.** Epistle.

episcopacy (ɪ'pɪskəpəsɪ) *n, pl* **episcopacies. 1** government of a Church by bishops. 2 another word for **episcopate.**

episcopal (ɪ'pɪskəpᵊl) *adj* of, denoting, governed by, or relating to a bishop or bishops. [C15: from Church L, from *episcopus* BISHOP]

Episcopal (ɪ'pɪskəpᵊl) *adj* of or denoting the Episcopal Church, an autonomous church of Scotland and the US which is in full communion with the Church of England.

episcopalian (ɪˌpɪskə'peɪlɪən) *adj also* **episcopal. 1** practising or advocating the principle of Church government by bishops. ◆ *n* 2 an advocate of such Church government.
▸ eˌpisco'palianism *n*

Episcopalian (ɪˌpɪskə'peɪlɪən) *adj* 1 belonging to or denoting the Episcopal Church. ◆ *n* 2 a member or adherent of this Church.

episcopate (ɪ'pɪskəpɪt, -ˌpeɪt) *n* 1 the office, status, or term of office of a bishop. 2 bishops collectively.

episiotomy (ɪˌpiːzɪ'ɒtəmɪ) *n, pl* **episiotomies.** surgical incision into the perineum during labour to prevent its laceration during childbirth. [C20: from Gk *epision* pubic region + -TOMY]

episode ('ɛpɪˌsəʊd) *n* 1 an event or series of events. 2 any of the sections into which a serialized novel or radio or television programme is divided. 3 an incident or sequence that forms part of a narrative but may be a digression from the main story. 4 (in ancient Greek tragedy) a section between two choric songs. 5 *Music.* a contrasting section between statements of the subject, as in a fugue. [C17: from Gk *epeisodion* something added, from *epi-* (in addition) + *eisodios* coming in, from *eis-* in + *hodos* road]

episodic (ˌɛpɪ'sɒdɪk) *or* **episodical** *adj* 1 resembling or relating to an episode. 2 divided into episodes. 3 irregular or sporadic.
▸ ˌepi'sodically *adv*

★ people and places

epistaxis (ˌɛpɪˈstæksɪs) n the technical name for **nose-bleed**. [C18: from Gk: a dropping, from *epistazein* to drop on, from *stazein* to drip]

epistemology (ɪ,pɪstɪˈmɒlədʒɪ) n the theory of knowledge, esp. the critical study of its validity, methods, and scope. [C19: from Gk *epistēmē* knowledge]
▶ **epistemological** (ɪ,pɪstɪməˈlɒdʒɪkˀl) adj ▶ e,pis-te'mologist n

epistle (ɪˈpɪsˀl) n 1 a letter, esp. one that is long, formal, or didactic. 2 a literary work in letter form, esp. a verse letter. [OE *epistol*, via L from Gk *epistolē*]

Epistle (ɪˈpɪsˀl) n 1 *Bible.* any of the letters of the apostles. 2 a reading from one of the Epistles, part of the Eucharistic service in many Christian Churches.

epistolary (ɪˈpɪstələrɪ) or (*arch.*) **epistolatory** adj 1 relating to, denoting, conducted by, or contained in letters. 2 (of a novel, etc.) in the form of a series of letters.

epistyle (ˈɛpɪ,staɪl) n another name for **architrave** (sense 1). [C17: via L from Gk, from EPI- + *stulos* column, STYLE]

epitaph (ˈɛpɪ,tɑːf) n 1 a commemorative inscription on a tombstone or monument. 2 a commemorative speech or written passage. 3 a final judgment on a person or thing. [C14: via L from Gk, from EPI- + *taphos* tomb]
▶ **epitaphic** (ˌɛpɪˈtæfɪk) adj ▶ 'epi,taphist n

epitaxy (ˈɛpɪ,tæksɪ) n the growth of a layer of one substance on the surface of a crystal so that the layer has the same structure as the underlying crystal.
▶ **epitaxial** (ˌɛpɪˈtæksɪəl) adj

epithalamium (ˌɛpɪθəˈleɪmɪəm) or **epithalamion** n, pl **epithalamiumia** (-mɪə). a poem or song written to celebrate a marriage. [C17: from L, from Gk *epithalamion* marriage song, from *thalamos* bridal chamber]
▶ **epithalamic** (ˌɛpɪθəˈlæmɪk) adj

epithelium (ˌɛpɪˈθiːlɪəm) n, pl **epitheliums** or **epithelia** (-lɪə). an animal cellular tissue covering the external and internal surfaces of the body. [C18: NL, from EPI- + Gk *thēlē* nipple]
▶ ,epi'thelial adj

epithet (ˈɛpɪ,θɛt) n a descriptive word or phrase added to or substituted for a person's name. [C16: from L, from Gk, from *epitithenai* to add, from *tithenai* to put]
▶ ,epi'thetic or ,epi'thetical adj

epitome (ɪˈpɪtəmɪ) n 1 a typical example of a characteristic or class; embodiment; personification. 2 a summary of a written work; abstract. [C16: via L from Gk, from *epitemnein* to abridge, from EPI- + *temnein* to cut]
▶ **epitomical** (ˌɛpɪˈtɒmɪkˀl) or ,epi'tomic adj

epitomize or **epitomise** (ɪˈpɪtə,maɪz) vb **epitomizes, epitomizing, epitomized** or **epitomises, epitomising, epitomised**. (*tr*) 1 to be a personification of; typify. 2 to make an epitome of.
▶ e'pitomist n ▶ e,pitomi'zation or e,pitomi'sation n

epizootic (ˌɛpɪzəʊˈɒtɪk) adj 1 (of a disease) suddenly and temporarily affecting a large number of animals. ◆ n 2 an epizootic disease.

EPNS *abbrev. for* electroplated nickel silver.

epoch (ˈiːpɒk) n 1 a point in time beginning a new or distinctive period. 2 a long period of time marked by some predominant characteristic; era. 3 *Astron.* a precise date to which information relating to a celestial body is referred. 4 a unit of geological time within a period during which a series of rocks is formed. [C17: from NL, from Gk *epokhē* cessation]
▶ **epochal** (ˈɛp,ɒkˀl) adj

epode (ˈɛpəʊd) n *Greek prosody.* 1 the part of a lyric ode that follows the strophe and the antistrophe. 2 a type of lyric poem composed of couplets in which a long line is followed by a shorter one. [C16: via L from Gk, from *epaidein* to sing after, from *aidein* to sing]

eponym (ˈɛpənɪm) n 1 a name, esp. a place name, derived from the name of a real or mythical person. 2 the name of the person from which such a name is derived. [C19: from Gk *epōnumos* giving a significant name]
▶ e'ponymy n

eponymous (ɪˈpɒnɪməs) adj 1 (of a person) being the person after whom a literary work, film, etc., is named:

the eponymous heroine in the film of Jane Eyre. 2 (of a literary work, film, etc.) named after its central character or creator: *The Stooges' eponymous debut album.*
▶ e'ponymously adv

EPOS (ˈiːpɒs) n *acronym for* electronic point of sale.

epoxidize or **epoxidise** vb **epoxidizes, epoxidizing, epoxidized** or **epoxidises, epoxidising, epoxidised**. (*tr*) to convert into or treat with an epoxy resin.

epoxy (ɪˈpɒksɪ) adj *Chem.* 1 of, consisting of, or containing an oxygen atom joined to two different groups that are themselves joined to other groups: *epoxy group.* 2 of, relating to, or consisting of an epoxy resin. ◆ n, pl **epoxies.** 3 short for **epoxy resin.** [C20: from EPI- + OXY-²]

epoxy or **epoxide resin** (ɪˈpɒksaɪd) n any of various tough resistant thermosetting synthetic resins containing epoxy groups: used in surface coatings, laminates, and adhesives.

Epping ★ (ˈɛpɪŋ) n a town in E England, in Essex, on the edge of Epping Forest: a residential centre for London. Pop.: 9922 (1991).

Epping Forest ★ n a forest in E England, northeast of London: formerly a royal hunting ground.

eps *abbrev. for* earnings per share.

epsilon (ˈɛpsɪ,lɒn) n the fifth letter of the Greek alphabet (E, ε). [Gk *e psilon*, lit.: simple *e*]

Epsom ★ (ˈɛpsəm) n a town in SE England, in Surrey: famous for its mineral springs and for horse racing. Pop. (with Ewell): 64 405 (1991).

Epsom salts n (*functioning as sing or pl*) a medicinal preparation of hydrated magnesium sulphate, used as a purgative, etc. [C18: after EPSOM, where they occur in the water]

Epstein ★ (ˈɛpstaɪn) n Sir Jacob. 1880–1959, British sculptor, born in the US of Russo-Polish parents.

equable (ˈɛkwəbˀl) adj 1 even-tempered; placid. 2 unvarying; uniform: *an equable climate.* [C17: from L *aequābilis*, from *aequāre* to make equal]
▶ ,equa'bility or 'equableness n

equal (ˈiːkwəl) adj 1 (often foll. by *to* or *with*) identical in size, quantity, degree, intensity, etc. 2 having identical privileges, rights, status, etc. 3 having uniform effect or application: *equal opportunities.* 4 evenly balanced or proportioned. 5 (usually foll. by *to*) having the necessary or adequate strength, ability, means, etc. (for). ◆ n 6 a person or thing equal to another, esp. in merit, ability, etc. ◆ vb **equals, equalling, equalled** or *US* **equals, equaling, equaled.** 7 (*tr*) to be equal to; match. 8 (*intr*; usually foll. by *out*) to become equal. 9 (*tr*) to make or do something equal to. [C14: from L *aequālis*, from *aequus* level]
▶ 'equally adv

USAGE NOTE The use of *more equal* as in *from now on their relationship will be a more equal one* is acceptable in modern English usage. *Equally* is preferred to *equally as* in sentences such as *reassuring the victims is equally important. Just as* is preferred to *equally as* in sentences such as *their surprise was just as great as his.*

---

equalitarian (ɪ,kwɒlɪˈtɛərɪən) adj, n a less common word for **egalitarian**.
▶ e,quali'tarianism n

equality (ɪˈkwɒlɪtɪ) n, pl **equalities.** the state of being equal.

equalize or **equalise** (ˈiːkwə,laɪz) vb **equalizes, equalizing, equalized** or **equalises, equalising, equalised.** 1 (*tr*) to make equal or uniform. 2 (*intr*) (in sports) to reach the same score as one's opponent or opponents.
▶ ,equali'zation or ,equali'sation n

equal opportunity n a the offering of employment, pay, or promotion without discrimination as to sex, race, etc. b (*as modifier*): *an equal-opportunities employer.*

equal sign or **equals sign** n the symbol =, used to indicate a mathematical equality.

equanimity (ˌiːkwəˈnɪmɪtɪ, ˌɛkwə-) n calmness of mind

★ people and places

or temper; composure. [C17: from L, from *aequus* even, EQUAL + *animus* mind, spirit]
▸ **equanimous** (ɪ'kwænɪməs) *adj*

equate (ɪ'kweɪt) *vb* **equates, equating, equated.** (*mainly tr*) **1** to make or regard as equivalent or similar. **2** *Maths.* to indicate the equality of; form an equation from. **3** (*intr*) to be equal. [C15: from L *aequāre* to make EQUAL]
▸ **e'quatable** *adj* ▸ **e,quata'bility** *n*

equation (ɪ'kweɪʒən, -ʃən) *n* **1** a mathematical statement that two expressions are equal. **2** the act of equating. **3** the state of being equal, equivalent, or equally balanced. **4** a representation of a chemical reaction using symbols of the elements. **5** a situation or problem in which a number of factors need to be considered.
▸ **e'quational** *adj* ▸ **e'quationally** *adv*

equator (ɪ'kweɪtə) *n* **1** the great circle of the earth, equidistant from the poles, dividing the N and S hemispheres. **2** a circle dividing a sphere into two equal parts. **3** *Astron.* See **celestial equator.** [C14: from Med. L (*circulus*) *aequātor* (*diei et noctis*) (circle) that equalizes (the day and night), from L *aequāre* to make EQUAL]

equatorial (,ɛkwə'tɔ:rɪəl) *adj* **1** of, like, or existing at or near the equator. **2** *Astron.* of or referring to the celestial equator. **3** (of a telescope) mounted on perpendicular axes, one of which is parallel to the earth's axis. ◆ *n* **4** an equatorial mounting for a telescope.

Equatorial Guinea ★ *n* a republic of W Africa, consisting of Río Muni on the mainland and the island of Bioko in the Gulf of Guinea, with four smaller islands: ceded by Portugal to Spain in 1778; gained independence in 1968. Official languages: Spanish and French. Religion: Roman Catholic majority. Currency: franc. Capital: Malabo. Pop.: 443 000 (1997). Area: 28 049 sq. km (10 830 sq. miles). Former name (until 1964): **Spanish Guinea.**

equerry ('ɛkwərɪ; *at the British court* ɪ'kwɛrɪ) *n, pl* **equerries.** **1** an officer attendant upon the British sovereign. **2** (formerly) an officer in a royal household responsible for the horses. [C16: alteration (through infl. of L *equus* horse) of earlier *escuirie*, from OF: stable]

equestrian (ɪ'kwɛstrɪən) *adj* **1** of or relating to horses and riding. **2** on horseback; mounted. **3** of, relating to, or composed of knights. ◆ *n* **4** a person skilled in riding and horsemanship. [C17: from L *equestris*, from *equus* horse]
▸ **e'questrian,ism** *n*

equi- *combining form.* equal or equally: *equidistant; equilateral.*

equiangular (,i:kwɪ'æŋgjʊlə) *adj* having all angles equal.

equidistant (,i:kwɪ'dɪstənt) *adj* equally distant.
▸ **,equi'distance** *n* ▸ **,equi'distantly** *adv*

equilateral (,i:kwɪ'lætərəl) *adj* **1** having all sides of equal length. ◆ *n* **2** a geometric figure having all sides of equal length. **3** a side that is equal in length to other sides.

equilibrant (ɪ'kwɪlɪbrənt) *n* a force capable of balancing another force.

equilibrate (,i:kwɪ'laɪbreɪt, ɪ'kwɪlɪ,breɪt) *vb* **equilibrates, equilibrating, equilibrated.** to bring to or be in equilibrium; balance. [C17: from LL, from *aequilībris* in balance; see EQUILIBRIUM]
▸ **,equili'bration** *n*

equilibrist (ɪ'kwɪlɪbrɪst) *n* a person who performs balancing feats, esp. on a high wire.
▸ **e,quili'bristic** *adj*

equilibrium (,i:kwɪ'lɪbrɪəm) *n, pl* **equilibriums** or **equilibria** (-rɪə). **1** a stable condition in which forces cancel one another. **2** a state or feeling of mental balance; composure. **3** any unchanging state of a body, system, etc., resulting from the balance of the influences to which it is subjected. **4** *Physiol.* a state of bodily balance, maintained primarily by receptors in the inner ear. [C17: from L, from *aequi-* EQUI- + *lībra* pound, balance]

equine ('ɛkwaɪn) *adj* of, relating to, or resembling a horse. [C18: from L, from *equus* horse]

equinoctial (,i:kwɪ'nɒkʃəl) *adj* **1** relating to or occurring at either or both equinoxes. **2** *Astron.* of or relating to the celestial equator. ◆ *n* **3** a storm or gale at or near an

equinox. **4** another name for **celestial equator.** [C14: from L: see EQUINOX]

equinoctial circle or **line** *n* another name for **celestial equator.**

equinoctial point *n* either of two points at which the celestial equator intersects the ecliptic.

equinox ('i:kwɪ,nɒks) *n* **1** either of the two occasions, six months apart, when day and night are of equal length. In the N hemisphere the **vernal equinox** occurs around March 21 (Sept. 23 in the S hemisphere). The **autumnal equinox** occurs around Sept. 23 in the N hemisphere (March 21 in the S hemisphere). **2** another name for **equinoctial point.** [C14: from Med. L *equinoxium,* changed from L *aequinoctium,* from *aequi-* EQUI- + *nox* night]

equip (ɪ'kwɪp) *vb* **equips, equipping, equipped.** (*tr*) **1** to furnish (with necessary supplies, etc.). **2** (*usually passive*) to provide with abilities, understanding, etc. **3** to dress out; attire. [C16: from OF *eschiper* to embark, fit out (a ship), of Gmc origin]
▸ **e'quipper** *n*

equipage ('ɛkwɪpɪdʒ) *n* **1** a horse-drawn carriage, esp. one attended by liveried footmen. **2** the stores and equipment of a military unit. **3** *Arch.* a set of useful articles.

equipment (ɪ'kwɪpmənt) *n* **1** an act or instance of equipping. **2** the items provided. **3** a set of tools, kit, etc., assembled for a specific purpose.

equipoise ('ɛkwɪ,pɔɪz) *n* **1** even balance of weight; equilibrium. **2** a counterbalance; counterpoise. ◆ *vb* **equipoises, equipoising, equipoised.** **3** (*tr*) to offset or balance.

equipollent (,i:kwɪ'pɒlənt) *adj* **1** equal or equivalent in significance, power, or effect. ◆ *n* **2** something that is equipollent. [C15: from L *aequipollēns* of equal importance, from EQUI- + *pollēre* to be able, be strong]
▸ **,equi'pollence** or **,equi'pollency** *n*

equisetum (,ɛkwɪ'si:təm) *n, pl* **equisetums** or **equiseta** (-tə). any plant of the horsetail genus. [C19: NL, from L, from *equus* horse + *saeta* bristle]

equitable ('ɛkwɪtəb°l) *adj* **1** fair; just. **2** *Law.* relating to or valid in equity, as distinct from common law or statute law. [C17: from F, from *équité* EQUITY]
▸ **'equitableness** *n*

equitation (,ɛkwɪ'teɪʃən) *n* the study and practice of riding and horsemanship. [C16: from L *equitātiō,* from *equitāre* to ride, from *equus* horse]

equities ('ɛkwɪtɪz) *pl n* another name for **ordinary shares.**

equity ('ɛkwɪtɪ) *n, pl* **equities.** **1** the quality of being impartial; fairness. **2** an impartial or fair act, decision, etc. **3** *Law.* a system of jurisprudence founded on principles of natural justice and fair conduct. It supplements common law, as by providing a remedy where none exists at law. **4** *Law.* an equitable right or claim. **5** the interest of ordinary shareholders in a company. **6** the value of a debtor's property in excess of debts to which it is liable. [C14: from OF, from L *aequitās,* from *aequus* level, EQUAL]

Equity ('ɛkwɪtɪ) *n* the actors' trade union.

equity capital *n* the part of the share capital of a company owned by ordinary shareholders or in certain circumstances by other classes of shareholder.

equity-linked policy *n* an insurance or assurance policy in which premiums are invested partially or wholly in ordinary shares for the eventual benefit of the beneficiaries of the policy.

equivalence (ɪ'kwɪvələns) or **equivalency** *n* **1** the state of being equivalent. **2** *Logic, maths.* another term for **biconditional.**

equivalent (ɪ'kwɪvələnt) *adj* **1** equal in value, quantity, significance, etc. **2** having the same or a similar effect or meaning. **3** *Logic, maths.* (of two propositions) having a biconditional between them. ◆ *n* **4** something that is equivalent. **5** Also called: **equivalent weight.** the weight of a substance that will combine with or displace 8 grams of oxygen or 1.007 97 grams of hydrogen. [C15: from LL, from L *aequi-* EQUI- + *valēre* to be worth]
▸ **e'quivalently** *adv*

equivocal (ɪ'kwɪvək°l) *adj* **1** capable of varying interpretations; ambiguous. **2** deliberately misleading or vague.

3 of doubtful character or sincerity. [C17: from LL, from L EQUI- + *vōx* voice]
▸ e,quivo'cality *or* e'quivocalness *n*

equivocate (ɪ'kwɪvə,keɪt) *vb* **equivocates, equivocating, equivocated.** (*intr*) to use equivocal language, esp. to avoid speaking directly or honestly. [C15: from Med. L, from LL *aequivocus* ambiguous, EQUIVOCAL]
▸ e'quivo,catingly *adv* ▸ e,quivo'cation *n* ▸ e'quivo,cator *n* ▸ e'quivocatory *adj*

er (ə, ɜː) *interj* a sound made when hesitating in speech.

Er *the chemical symbol for* erbium.

ER *abbrev. for:* **1** Elizabeth Regina. [L: Queen Elizabeth] **2** Eduardus Rex. [L: King Edward]

-er[1] *suffix forming nouns.* **1** a person or thing that performs a specified action: *reader; lighter.* **2** a person engaged in a profession, occupation, etc.: *writer; baker.* **3** a native or inhabitant of: *Londoner; villager.* **4** a person or thing having a certain characteristic: *newcomer; fiver.* [OE *-ere*]

-er[2] *suffix.* forming the comparative degree of adjectives (*deeper, freer,* etc.) and adverbs (*faster, slower,* etc.). [OE *-rd, -re* (adj), *-or* (advy]

era ('ɪərə) *n* **1** a period of time considered as being of a distinctive character; epoch. **2** an extended period of time the years of which are numbered from a fixed point: *the Christian era.* **3** a point in time beginning a new or distinctive period. **4** a major division of geological time, divided into periods. [C17: from L *aera* counters, pl of *aes* brass, pieces of brass money]

ERA ('ɪərə) *n* (in Britain) *acronym for* Education Reform Act: the 1988 act which established the key elements of the National Curriculum and the Basic Curriculum.

eradicate (ɪ'rædɪ,keɪt) *vb* **eradicates, eradicating, eradicated.** (*tr*) **1** to obliterate. **2** to pull up by the roots. [C16: from L *ērādīcāre* to uproot, from EX-[1] + *rādīx* root]
▸ e'radicable *adj* ▸ e,radi'cation *n* ▸ e'radicative *adj*

erase (ɪ'reɪz) *vb* **erases, erasing, erased. 1** to obliterate or rub out (something written, typed, etc.). **2** (*tr*) to destroy all traces of. **3** to remove (a recording) from (magnetic tape). [C17: from L, from EX-[1] + *rādere* to scratch, scrape]
▸ e'rasable *adj*

eraser (ɪ'reɪzə) *n* an object, such as a piece of rubber, for erasing something written, typed, etc.

Erasmus ★ (ɪ'ræzməs) *or* **Desiderius** (,dɛzɪ'dɪərɪəs), real name *Gerhard Gerhards.* ?1466–1536, Dutch Renaissance humanist.

erasure (ɪ'reɪʒə) *n* **1** the act or an instance of erasing. **2** the place or mark, as on a piece of paper, where something has been erased.

Erato ★ ('ɛrə,təʊ) *n Greek myth.* the Muse of love poetry.

Eratosthenes ★ (,ɛrə'tɒsθɪ,niːz) *n* ?276–?194 B.C., Greek mathematician and astronomer, who calculated the circumference of the earth by observing the angle of the sun's rays at different places.

Erbil, Irbil ('ɜːbɪl), *or* **Arbil** ★ *n* a city in N Iraq: important in Assyrian times. Pop.: 485 968 (1987). Ancient name: **Arbela.**

erbium ('ɜːbɪəm) *n* a soft malleable silvery-white element of the lanthanide series of metals. Symbol: Er; atomic no.: 68; atomic wt.: 167.26. [C19: from NL, from (*Ytt*)*erb*(*y*), Sweden, where it was first found + -IUM]

Erciyas Daği ★ (*Turkish* 'ɛrdʒijas dɑː'i) *n* an extinct volcano in central Turkey. Height 3916 m (12 848 ft).

ERDF *abbrev. for* European Regional Development Fund: a fund to provide money for specific projects for work on the infrastructure in countries of the European Union.

ere (ɛə) *conj, prep* a poetic word for **before.** [OE *ǣr*]

Erebus[1] ★ ('ɛrɪbəs) *n Greek myth.* **1** the god of darkness, son of Chaos and brother of Night. **2** the darkness below the earth, thought to be the abode of the dead or the region that souls pass through on their way to Hades.

Erebus[2] ★ ('ɛrɪbəs) *n* **Mount.** a volcano in Antarctica, on Ross Island: discovered by Sir James Ross in 1841 and named after his ship. Height: 3794 m (12 448 ft).

Erechtheum (ɪ'rɛkθɪəm, ,ɛrək'θiːəm) *or* **Erechtheion** ★

(ɪ'rɛkθɪən, ,ɛrək'θiːən) *n* a temple on the Acropolis at Athens, which has a porch of caryatids.

Erechtheus ★ (e'rɛkθjuːs, -θɪəs) *n Greek myth.* a king of Athens who sacrificed one of his daughters because the oracle at Delphi said this was the only way to win the war against the Eleusinians.

erect (ɪ'rɛkt) *adj* **1** upright in posture or position. **2** *Physiol.* (of the penis, clitoris, or nipples) firm or rigid after swelling with blood, esp. as a result of sexual excitement. **3** (of plant parts) growing vertically or at right angles to the parts from which they arise. ◆ *vb* (mainly tr) **4** to put up; build. **5** to raise to an upright position. **6** to found or form; set up. **7** (*also intr*) *Physiol.* to become or cause to become firm or rigid by filling with blood. **8** to exalt. **9** to draw or construct (a line, figure, etc.) on a given line or figure. [C14: from L *ērigere* to set up, from *regere* to control, govern]
▸ e'rectable *adj* ▸ e'recter *or* e'rector *n* ▸ e'rectness *n*

erectile (ɪ'rɛktaɪl) *adj* **1** *Physiol.* (of tissues or organs, such as the penis or clitoris) capable of becoming erect. **2** capable of being erected.
▸ erectility (ɪrɛk'tɪlɪtɪ, ,iːrɛk-) *n*

erection (ɪ'rɛkʃən) *n* **1** the act of erecting or the state of being erected. **2** a building or construction. **3** *Physiol.* the enlarged state of erectile tissues or organs, esp. the penis, when filled with blood. **4** an erect penis.

E region *or* **layer** *n* a region of the ionosphere, extending from a height of 90 to about 150 kilometres. It reflects radio waves of medium wavelength.

eremite ('ɛrɪ,maɪt) *n* a Christian hermit or recluse. [C13: see HERMIT]
▸ eremitic (,ɛrɪ'mɪtɪk) or ,ere'mitical *adj* ▸ 'eremit,ism *n*

Erenburg ★ ('ɛərən,bɜːg; *Russian* ɛrɪn'burk) *n* a variant spelling of (Ilya Grigorievich) **Ehrenburg.**

erepsin (ɪ'rɛpsɪn) *n* a mixture of proteolytic enzymes secreted by the small intestine. [C20: er-, from L *ēripere* to snatch + (P)EPSIN]

erethism ('ɛrɪ,θɪzəm) *n* **1** *Physiol.* an abnormal irritability or sensitivity in any part of the body. **2** *Psychiatry.* **2a** a personality disorder resulting from mercury poisoning. **2b** an abnormal tendency to become aroused quickly, esp. sexually, as the result of a verbal or psychic stimulus. [C18: from F, from Gk, from *erethizein* to excite, irritate]

Eretria ★ (ɪ'rɛtrɪə) *n* an ancient city in Greece, on the S coast of Euboea: founded as an Ionian colony; destroyed by the Persians in 490 B.C. following which it never regained its former significance.

Erevan ★ (*Russian* jɪrɪ'van) *n* a variant spelling of **Yerevan.**

erf (ɜːf) *n, pl* **erven** ('ɜːvən). *S. African.* a plot of land, usually urban. [from Afrik., from Du.: inheritance]

Erf (ɜːf) *n acronym for* electrorheological fluid: a man-made liquid that thickens or solidifies when an electric current passes through it and returns to a liquid when the current ceases.

Erfurt ★ (*German* 'ɛrfurt) *n* an industrial city in central Germany, the capital of Thuringia: university (1392). Pop.: 213 472 (1995 est.).

erg[1] (ɜːg) *n* the cgs unit of work or energy. [C19: from Gk *ergon* work]

erg[2] (ɜːg) *n, pl* **ergs** *or* **areg** (ə'rɛg). an area of shifting sand dunes, esp. in the Sahara Desert in N Africa. [C19: from Ar. *'irj*]

ergo ('ɜːgəʊ) *sentence connector.* therefore; hence. [C14: from L: therefore]

ergonomic (,ɜːgə'nɒmɪk) *adj* **1** of or relating to ergonomics. **2** designed to minimize physical effort and discomfort, and hence maximize efficiency.

ergonomics (,ɜːgə'nɒmɪks) *n* (*functioning as sing*) the study of the relationship between workers and their environment, esp. the equipment they use. [C20: from Gk *ergon* work + (ECO)NOMICS]
▸ ergonomist (ɜː'gɒnəmɪst) *n*

ergosterol (ɜː'gɒstə,rɒl) *n* a plant sterol that is converted into vitamin D by the action of ultraviolet radiation.

ergot ('ɜːgət, -gɒt) *n* **1** a disease of cereals and other grasses caused by fungi of the genus *Claviceps.* **2** any fun-

---

★ people and places

gus causing this disease. **3** the dried fungus, used as the source of certain alkaloids used in medicine. [C17: from F: spur (of a cock), from ?]

ergotism ('ɜːgəˌtɪzəm) *n* ergot poisoning, producing either burning pains and eventually gangrene or itching skin and convulsions.

Erhard ★ (*German* 'eːrhart) *n* **Ludwig** ('luːtvɪç). 1897–1977, German statesman: chief architect of the *Wirtschaftswunder* ("economic miracle") of West Germany's recovery after World War II; chancellor (1963–66).

erica ('ɛrɪkə) *n* any shrub of the ericaceous genus *Erica*, including the heaths and some heathers. [C19: via NL from Gk *ereikē* heath]

ericaceous (ˌɛrɪ'keɪʃəs) *adj* of or relating to the Ericaceae, a family of trees and shrubs with typically bell-shaped flowers: includes heather, rhododendron, azalea, and arbutus.

Ericson *or* **Ericsson** ★ ('ɛrɪksən) *n* **Leif** (liːf). 10th–11th centuries A.D., Norse navigator, who discovered Vinland (?1000), variously identified as the coast of New England, Labrador, or Newfoundland; son of Eric the Red.

Eric the Red ★ ('ɛrɪk) *n* ?940–?1010 A.D., Norse navigator: discovered and colonized Greenland; father of Leif Ericson.

Erie ★ ('ɪərɪ) *n* **1 Lake.** a lake between the US and Canada: the southernmost and the shallowest of the Great Lakes; empties by the Niagara River into Lake Ontario. Area: 25 718 sq. km (9930 sq. miles). **2** a port in NW Pennsylvania, on Lake Erie. Pop.: 108 398 (1994 est.).

Erie Canal ★ *n* a canal in New York State between Albany and Buffalo, linking the Hudson River with Lake Erie. Length: 579 km (360 miles).

erigeron (ɪ'rɪdʒərən, -'rɪg-) *n* any plant of the genus *Erigeron*, whose flowers resemble asters. [C17: via L from Gk, from *ēri* early + *gerōn* old man; from the white down of some species]

Erin ★ ('ɪərɪn, 'ɛrɪn) *n* an archaic or poetic name for **Ireland**[1]. [from Irish Gaelic *Éirinn*, dative of Ireland]

Erinyes ★ (ɪ'rɪnɪˌiːz) *pl n, sing* **Erinys** (ɪ'rɪnɪs, ɪ'raɪ-). *Myth.* another name for the **Furies**. [Gk]

Eris ★ ('ɛrɪs) *n Greek myth.* the goddess of discord, sister of Ares.

Eritrea ★ (ˌɛrɪ'treɪə) *n* a country in NE Africa, on the Red Sea: became an Italian colony in 1890; federated with Ethiopia (1952–93); after civil war with the Ethiopian government for independence (1961–91), a provisional Eritrean government was established (1991); full independence was gained in 1993. It consists of hot and arid coastal lowlands, rising to the foothills of the Ethiopian highlands. Languages: Arabic, English, Afar, and others. Religions: Muslim and Christian. Currency: nakfa. Capital: Asmara. Pop.: 3 590 000 (1997). Area: 117 400 sq. km (45 300 sq. miles).
► ˌEri'trean *n*

Erivan ★ (*Russian* jɪrɪ'van) *n* a variant spelling of **Yerevan**.

erk (ɜːk) *n Brit. sl.* an aircraftman or naval rating. [C20: ? a corruption of *AC* (aircraftman)]

Erlangen ★ (*German* 'ɛrlaŋən) *n* a town in central Germany, in Bavaria: university (1743). Pop.: 101 450 (1995 est.).

Erlanger ★ ('ɜːˌlæŋə) *n* **Joseph.** 1874–1965, US physiologist. He shared a Nobel prize for physiology or medicine (1944) for work on the electrical signs of nervous activity.

ERM *abbrev. for* Exchange Rate Mechanism.

ermine ('ɜːmɪn) *n, pl* **ermines** *or* **ermine. 1** the stoat in northern regions, where it has a white winter coat with a black-tipped tail. **2** the fur of this animal. **3** the dignity or office of a judge, noble, etc., whose state robes are trimmed with ermine. [C12: from OF, from Med. L *Armenius* (*mūs*) Armenian (mouse)]

erne *or* **ern** (ɜːn) *n* a fish-eating sea eagle. [OE *earn*]

Erne ★ (ɜːn) *n* a river in N central Republic of Ireland, rising in County Cavan and flowing north across the border, through **Upper Lough Erne** and **Lower Lough Erne**, and

then west to Donegal Bay. Length: about 96 km (60 miles).

Ernie ('ɜːnɪ) *n* (in Britain) a machine that randomly selects winning numbers of Premium Bonds. [C20: acronym of *Electronic Random Number Indicator Equipment*]

Ernst ★ (*German* ɛrnst) *n* **Max** (maks). 1891–1976, German painter, resident in France and the US: developed the technique of collage.

erode (ɪ'rəud) *vb* **erodes, eroding, eroded. 1** to grind or wear down or away or become ground or worn down or away. **2** to deteriorate or cause to deteriorate. [C17: from L, from EX-[1] + *rōdere* to gnaw]
► e'rodible *adj*

erogenous (ɪ'rɒdʒɪnəs) *or* **erogenic** (ˌɛrə'dʒɛnɪk) *adj* **1** sensitive to sexual stimulation. **2** arousing sexual desire or giving sexual pleasure. [C19: from Gk *erōs* love, desire + -GENOUS]
► **erogeneity** (ˌɛrədʒɪ'niːɪtɪ) *n*

Eros ★ ('ɪərɒs, 'ɛrɒs) *n Greek myth.* the god of love, son of Aphrodite. Roman counterpart: **Cupid.**

erosion (ɪ'rəuʒən) *n* **1** the wearing away of rocks, soil, etc., by the action of water, ice, wind, etc. **2** the act or process of eroding or the state of being eroded.
► e'rosive *or* e'rosional *adj*

erotic (ɪ'rɒtɪk) *adj* **1** of, concerning, or arousing sexual desire or giving sexual pleasure. **2** marked by strong sexual desire or being especially sensitive to sexual stimulation. Also: **erotical.** [C17: from Gk *erōtikos*, from *erōs* love]
► e'rotically *adv*

erotica (ɪ'rɒtɪkə) *pl n* explicitly sexual literature or art. [C19: from Gk: see EROTIC]

eroticism (ɪ'rɒtɪˌsɪzəm) *or* **erotism** ('ɛrəˌtɪzəm) *n* **1** erotic quality or nature. **2** the use of sexually arousing or pleasing symbolism in literature or art. **3** sexual excitement or desire.

erotogenic (ɪˌrɒtə'dʒɛnɪk) *adj* originating from or causing sexual stimulation; erogenous.

err (ɜː) *vb* (*intr*) **1** to make a mistake; be incorrect. **2** to deviate from a moral standard. **3** to act with bias, esp. favourable bias: *to err on the right side.* [C14 *erren* to wander, stray, from OF, from L *errāre*]
► 'errancy *n*

errand ('ɛrənd) *n* **1** a short trip undertaken to perform a task or commission (esp. in **run errands**). **2** the purpose or object of such a trip. [OE *ǣrende*]

errant ('ɛrənt) *adj* (*often postpositive*) **1** *Arch. or literary.* wandering in search of adventure. **2** erring or straying from the right course or accepted standards. [C14: from OF: journeying, from Vulgar L *iterāre* (unattested), from L *iter* journey; infl. by L *errāre* to err]
► 'errantry *n*

erratic (ɪ'rætɪk) *adj* **1** irregular in performance, behaviour, or attitude; unpredictable. **2** having no fixed or regular course. ♦ *n* **3** a piece of rock that has been transported from its place of origin, esp. by glacial action. [C14: from L, from *errāre* to wander, err]
► er'ratically *adv*

erratum (ɪ'rɑːtəm) *n, pl* **errata** (-tə). **1** an error in writing or printing. **2** another name for **corrigendum.** [C16: from L: mistake, from *errāre* to err]

Er Rif ★ (ɛə 'rɪf) *n* a mountainous region of N Morocco, near the Mediterranean coast.

erroneous (ɪ'rəunɪəs) *adj* based on or containing error; incorrect. [C14 (in the sense: deviating from what is right), from L, from *errāre* to wander]
► er'roneousness *n*

error ('ɛrə) *n* **1** a mistake or inaccuracy. **2** an incorrect belief or wrong judgment. **3** the condition of deviating from accuracy or correctness. **4** deviation from a moral standard; wrongdoing. **5** *Maths, statistics.* a measure of the difference between some quantity and an approximation of it, often expressed as a percentage. [C13: from L, from *errāre* to err]
► 'error-ˌfree *adj*

ersatz ('ɛəzæts, 'ɜː-) *adj* **1** made in imitation; artificial.

◆ *n* **2** an ersatz substance or article. [C20: G, from *ersetzen* to substitute]

Erse (ɜːs) *n* **1** another name for Irish **Gaelic**. ◆ *adj* **2** of or relating to the Irish Gaelic language. [C14: from Lowland Scots *Erisch* Irish]

erst (ɜːst) *adv Arch.* **1** long ago; formerly. **2** at first. [OE *ǣrest* earliest, sup. of *ǣr* early]

erstwhile ('ɜːst,waɪl) *adj* **1** former; one-time. ◆ *adv* **2** *Arch.* long ago; formerly.

Erté ★ (*French* ɛrte) *n* real name *Romain de Tirtoff*. 1892–1990, French fashion illustrator and designer, born in Russia.

eruct (ɪ'rʌkt) *or* **eructate** *vb* **eructs, eructing, eructed** *or* **eructates, eructating, eructated.** **1** to belch. **2** (of a volcano) to pour out (fumes or volcanic matter). [C17: from L, from *ructāre* to belch]
  ▸ **eructation** (ˌɪ,rʌk'teɪʃən, ˌiːrʌk-) *n*

erudite ('ɛrʊ,daɪt) *adj* having or showing extensive scholarship; learned. [C15: from L, from *ērudīre* to polish]
  ▸ **erudition** (ˌɛrʊ'dɪʃən) *or* **'eru,diteness** *n*

erupt (ɪ'rʌpt) *vb* **1** to eject (steam, water, and volcanic material) violently or (of volcanic material, etc.) to be so ejected. **2** (*intr*) (of a blemish) to appear on the skin. **3** (*intr*) (of a tooth) to emerge through the gum during normal tooth development. **4** (*intr*) to burst forth suddenly and violently. [C17: from L *ēruptus* having burst forth, from *ērumpere*, from *rumpere* to burst]
  ▸ **e'ruptive** *adj* ▸ **e'ruption** *n*

-ery *or* **-ry** *suffix forming nouns.* **1** indicating a place of business or activity: *bakery; refinery.* **2** indicating a class or collection of things: *cutlery.* **3** indicating qualities or actions: *snobbery; trickery.* **4** indicating a practice or occupation: *husbandry.* **5** indicating a state or condition: *slavery.* [from OF *-erie*; see -ER[1], -Y[3]]

Erymanthus ★ (ˌɛrɪ'mænθəs) *n* **Mount.** a mountain in SW Greece, in the NW Peloponnese. Height: 2224 m (7297 ft). Modern Greek name: **Erímanthos** (e'rimanθos).

erysipelas (ˌɛrɪ'sɪpɪləs) *n* an acute streptococcal infectious disease of the skin, characterized by fever and purplish lesions. [C16: from L, from Gk, from *erusi-* red + *-pelas* skin]

erythro- *or before a vowel* **erythr-** *combining form.* red: *erythrocyte.* [from Gk *eruthros* red]

erythrocyte (ɪ'rɪθrəʊ,saɪt) *n* a blood cell of vertebrates that transports oxygen and carbon dioxide, combined with haemoglobin.
  ▸ **erythrocytic** (ɪ,rɪθrəʊ'sɪtɪk) *adj*

erythromycin (ɪ,rɪθrəʊ'maɪsɪn) *n* an antibiotic used in treating bacterial infections. [C20: from ERYTHRO- + Gk *mukēs* fungus + -IN]

erythropoiesis (ɪ,rɪθrəʊpɔɪ'iːsɪs) *n Physiol.* the formation of red blood cells. [C19: from ERYTHRO- + Gk *poiēs* a making, from *poiein* to make]
  ▸ **erythropoietic** (ɪ,rɪθrəʊpɔɪ'etɪk) *adj*

Erzgebirge ★ (*German* 'eːrtsgəbɪrgə) *pl n* a mountain range on the border between Germany and the Czech Republic: formerly rich in mineral resources. Highest peak: Mount Klínovec (Keilberg), 1244 m (4081 ft). Czech name: **Krušné Hory.** Also called: **Ore Mountains.**

Erzurum ★ ('ɛəzurum) *n* a city in E Turkey: a strategic centre; scene of two major battles against Russian forces (1877 and 1916); important military base and a closed city to unofficial visitors. Pop.: 250 100 (1994 est.).

Es *the chemical symbol for* einsteinium.

-es *suffix.* **1** a variant of **-s**[1] for nouns ending in *ch, s, sh, z,* postconsonantal *y,* for some nouns ending in a vowel, and nouns in *f* with *v* in the plural: *ashes; heroes; calves.* **2** a variant of **-s**[2] for verbs ending in *ch, s, sh, z,* postconsonantal *y,* or a vowel: *preaches; steadies; echoes.*

Esau ★ ('iːsɔː) *n Bible.* son of Isaac and Rebecca and twin brother of Jacob, to whom he sold his birthright (Genesis 25).

Esbjerg ★ (*Danish* 'ɛsbjɛr) *n* a port in SW Denmark, in Jutland on the North Sea: Denmark's chief fishing port. Pop.: 82 579 (1995 est.).

escadrille (ˌɛskə'drɪl) *n* a French squadron of aircraft,

esp. in World War I. [from F: flotilla, from Sp., from *escuadra* SQUADRON]

escalade (ˌɛskə'leɪd) *n* **1** an assault using ladders, esp. on a fortification. ◆ *vb* **escalades, escalading, escaladed.** **2** to gain access to (a place) by ladders. [C16: from F, from It., from *scalare* to mount, SCALE[3]]

escalate ('ɛskə,leɪt) *vb* **escalates, escalating, escalated.** to increase or be increased in extent, intensity, or magnitude. [C20: back formation from ESCALATOR]
  ▸ **,esca'lation** *n*

escalator ('ɛskə,leɪtə) *n* **1** a moving staircase consisting of stair treads fixed to a conveyor belt. **2** short for **escalator clause.** [C20: orig. a trademark]

escalator clause *n* a clause in a contract stipulating an adjustment in wages, prices, etc., in the event of specified changes in conditions, such as a large rise in the cost of living.

escallop (ɛ'skɒləp, ɛ'skæl-) *n, vb* another word for **scallop.**

escalope ('ɛskə,lɒp) *n* a thin slice of meat, usually veal. [C19: from OF: shell]

escapade ('ɛskə,peɪd, ,ɛskə'peɪd) *n* **1** an adventure, esp. one that is mischievous or unlawful. **2** a prank; romp. [C17: from F, from OIt., from Vulgar L *excappāre* (unattested) to ESCAPE]

escape (ɪ'skeɪp) *vb* **escapes, escaping, escaped.** **1** to get away or break free from confinement, etc.). **2** to manage to avoid (danger, etc.). **3** (*intr*; usually foll. by *from*) (of gases, liquids, etc.) to issue gradually, as from a crack; seep; leak. **4** (*tr*) to elude; be forgotten by: *the figure escapes me.* **5** (*tr*) to be articulated inadvertently or involuntarily from: *a roar escaped his lips.* ◆ *n* **6** the act of escaping or state of having escaped. **7** avoidance of injury, harm, etc. **8a** a means or way of escape. **8b** (*as modifier*): *an escape route.* **9** a means of distraction or relief. **10** a gradual outflow; leakage; seepage. **11** Also called: **escape valve, escape cock.** a valve that releases air, steam, etc., above a certain pressure. **12** a plant originally cultivated but now growing wild. [C14: from OF, from Vulgar L *excappāre* (unattested) to escape (lit.: to slip out of one's cloak, hence free oneself), from EX-[1] + LL *cappa* cloak]
  ▸ **es'capable** *adj* ▸ **es'caper** *n*

escapee (ɪ,skeɪ'piː) *n* a person who has escaped, esp. an escaped prisoner.

escapement (ɪ'skeɪpmənt) *n* **1** a mechanism consisting of a toothed wheel (**escape wheel**) and anchor, used in timepieces to provide periodic impulses to the pendulum or balance. **2** any similar mechanism that regulates movement. **3** in pianos, the mechanism which allows the hammer to clear the string after striking, so the string can vibrate. **4** *Rare.* an act or means of escaping.

escape road *n* a road provided on a hill for a driver to drive into if his brakes fail or on a bend if he loses control of the turn.

escape velocity *n* the minimum velocity necessary for a body to escape from the gravitational field of the earth or other celestial body.

escapism (ɪ'skeɪpɪzəm) *n* an inclination to retreat from unpleasant reality, as through diversion or fantasy.
  ▸ **es'capist** *n, adj*

escapologist (ˌɛskə'pɒlədʒɪst) *n* an entertainer who specializes in freeing himself from confinement.
  ▸ **,esca'pology** *n*

escargot *French.* (ɛskargo) *n* a variety of edible snail.

escarpment (ɪ'skɑːpmənt) *n* **1** the long continuous steep face of a ridge or plateau formed by erosion or faulting; scarp. **2** a steep artificial slope made immediately in front of a fortified place. [C19: from F *escarpe*; see SCARP]

Escaut ★ (ɛsko) *n* the French name for the **Scheldt.**

-escent *suffix forming adjectives.* beginning to be, do, show, etc.: *convalescent; luminescent.* [via OF from L *-ēscent-*, stem of present participial suffix of *-ēscere*, ending of inceptive verbs]
  ▸ **-escence** *suffix forming nouns.*

eschatology (ˌɛskə'tɒlədʒɪ) *n* the branch of theology

concerned with the end of the world. [C19: from Gk *eskhatos* last]

▸ **eschatological** (ˌɛskətəˈlɒdʒɪkᵉl) *adj* ▸ ˌescha'tologist *n*

escheat (ɪs'tʃiːt) *Law.* ✦ *n* **1** (in England before 1926) the reversion of property to the Crown in the absence of legal heirs. **2** *Feudalism.* the reversion of property to the feudal lord in the absence of legal heirs. **3** the property so reverting. ✦ *vb* **4** to take (land) by escheat or (of land) to revert by escheat. [C14: from OF, from *escheoir* to fall to the lot of, from LL *excadere* (unattested), from L *cadere* to fall]

▸ es'cheatable *adj* ▸ es'cheatage *n*

Escherichia (ˌɛʃəˈrɪkɪə) *n* a genus of bacteria that form acid and gas in the presence of carbohydrates and are found in the intestines of humans and many animals, esp. *E. coli*, which is sometimes pathogenic and is widely used in genetic research. [C19: after Theodor *Escherich* (1857–1911), G paediatrician]

eschew (ɪs'tʃuː) *vb* (*tr*) to keep clear of or abstain from (something disliked, injurious, etc.); shun; avoid. [C14: from OF *eschiver*, of Gmc origin; see SHY¹, SKEW]

▸ es'chewal *n* ▸ es'chewer *n*

eschscholzia or **eschscholtzia** (ɪs'kɒlʃə) *n* another name for California poppy. [C19: after J. F. von *Eschscholtz* (1793–1831), G botanist]

Escoffier ★ (French ɛskɔfje) *n* (**Georges**) **Auguste** (ogyst). 1846–1935, French chef.

Escorial (ˌɛskɒrɪˈɑːl, ɛˈskɔːrɪəl) or **Escurial** ★ *n* a village in central Spain, northwest of Madrid: site of an architectural complex containing a monastery, palace, and college, built by Philip II between 1563 and 1584.

escort *n* ('ɛskɔːt). **1** one or more persons, soldiers, vehicles, etc., accompanying another or others for protection, as a mark of honour, etc. **2** a man or youth who accompanies a woman or girl on a social occasion. ✦ *vb* (ɪs'kɔːt). **3** (*tr*) to accompany or attend as an escort. [C16: from F, from It., from *scorgere* to guide, from L *corrigere* to straighten; see CORRECT]

escritoire (ˌɛskrɪˈtwɑː) *n* a writing desk with compartments and drawers. [C18: from F, from Med. L *scriptōrium* writing room in a monastery, from L *scrībere* to write]

escrow ('ɛskrəʊ, ɛ'skrəʊ) *Law.* ✦ *n* **1** money, goods, or a written document, held by a third party pending fulfilment of some condition. **2** the state or condition of being an escrow (esp. in **in escrow**). ✦ *vb* (*tr*) **3** to place (money, a document, etc.) in escrow. [C16: from OF *escroe*, of Gmc origin; see SCREED, SHRED, SCROLL]

escudo (ɛ'skuːdəʊ) *n*, *pl* **escudos**. **1** the standard monetary unit of Cape Verde and Portugal. **2** a former standard monetary unit of Chile. **3** an old Spanish silver coin. [C19: Sp., lit.: shield, from L *scūtum*]

esculent ('ɛskjʊlənt) *n* **1** any edible substance. ✦ *adj* **2** edible. [C17: from L *ēsculentus* good to eat, from *ēsca* food, from *edere* to eat]

Escurial ★ (ɛˌskjʊərɪˈɑːl, ɛˈskjʊərɪəl) *n* a variant of **Escorial**.

escutcheon (ɪ'skʌtʃən) *n* **1** a shield, esp. a heraldic one that displays a coat of arms. **2** a plate or shield around a keyhole, door handle, etc. **3** the place on the stern of a vessel where the name is shown. **4 blot on one's escutcheon.** a stain on one's honour. [C15: from OF *escuchon*, ult. from L *scūtum* shield]

▸ es'cutcheoned *adj*

Esdraelon ★ (ˌɛsdreɪˈiːlɒn) *n* a plain in N Israel, east of Mount Carmel. Also called: (Plain of) **Jezreel**.

SE *symbol for* east-southeast.

-ese *suffix forming adjectives and nouns.* indicating place of origin, language, or style: *Cantonese; Japanese; journalese.*

Esfahan ★ (ˌɛsfəˈhɑːn) *n* a variant of **Isfahan**.

SG (in Britain) *abbrev. for* Educational Support Grant: a government grant given to a Local Education Authority to fund educational schemes dealing with social issues, such as drug abuse.

Esher ★ ('iːʃə) *n* a town in SE England, in NE Surrey near London: racecourse. Pop.: 46 599 (1991).

esker ('ɛskə) or **eskar** ('ɛskɑː, -kə) *n* a long winding ridge of gravel, sand, etc., originally deposited by a meltwater

stream running under a glacier. [C19: from OIrish *escir* ridge]

Eskilstuna ★ (Swedish 'ɛskilstuːna) *n* an industrial city in SE Sweden. Pop.: 89 761 (1994).

Eskimo ('ɛskɪˌməʊ) *n* **1** (*pl* **Eskimos** or **Eskimo**) a member of a group of peoples inhabiting N Canada, Greenland, Alaska, and E Siberia. The Eskimos are more properly referred to as the **Inuit**. **2** the language of these peoples. ✦ *adj* **3** of or relating to the Eskimos. [C18 *Esquimawes*: rel. to *esquimantsic* (from a native language) eaters of raw flesh]

> **USAGE NOTE** *Eskimo* is considered by many people to be offensive, and in North America the term *Inuit* is often used.

Eskimo dog *n* a large powerful breed of dog with a long thick coat and curled tail, developed for hauling sledges.

Eskişehir ★ (Turkish es'kiʃeˌhir) *n* an industrial city in NW Turkey: founded around hot springs in Byzantine times. Pop.: 451 000 (1994 est.).

Esky ('ɛskɪ) *n*, *pl* **Eskies**. (*sometimes not cap.*) *Austral. trademark.* a portable insulated container for keeping food and drink cool. [C20: from ESKIMO, alluding to the Eskimos' cold habitat]

ESN *abbrev. for* educationally subnormal.

esophagus (iː'sɒfəgəs) *n* the US spelling of **oesophagus**.

esoteric (ˌɛsəʊˈtɛrɪk) *adj* **1** restricted to or intended for an enlightened or initiated minority. **2** difficult to understand; abstruse. **3** not openly admitted; private. [C17: from Gk, from *esōterō* inner]

▸ ˌeso'terically *adv* ▸ ˌeso'teriˌcism *n*

ESP *abbrev. for* extrasensory perception.

esp. *abbrev. for* especially.

espadrille (ˌɛspə'drɪl) *n* a light shoe with a canvas upper, esp. with a braided cord sole. [C19: from F, from Provençal *espardilho*, dim. of *espart* ESPARTO; from use of esparto for the soles]

espalier (ɪ'spæljə) *n* **1** an ornamental shrub or fruit tree trained to grow flat, as against a wall. **2** the trellis or framework on which such plants are trained. ✦ *vb* **3** (*tr*) to train (a plant) on an espalier. [C17: from F: trellis, from OIt.: shoulder supports, from *spalla* shoulder]

España ★ (es'paɲa) *n* the Spanish name for **Spain**.

esparto or **esparto grass** (e'spɑːtəʊ) *n*, *pl* **espartos**. any of various grasses of S Europe and N Africa, used to make ropes, mats, etc. [C18: from Sp., via L from Gk *spartos* a kind of rush]

especial (ɪ'spɛʃəl) *adj* (*prenominal*) **1** unusual; notable. **2** applying to one person or thing in particular; specific; peculiar: *he had an especial dislike of relatives.* [C14: from OF, from L *speciālis* individual; see SPECIAL]

▸ es'pecially *adv*

> **USAGE NOTE** *Especial* and *especially* have a more limited use than *special* and *specially*. *Special* is always used in preference to *especial* when the sense is one of being out of the ordinary: *a special lesson; he has been specially trained.* *Special* is also used when something is referred to as being for a particular purpose: *the word was specially underlined for you.* Where an idea of pre-eminence or individuality is involved, either *especial* or *special* may be used: *he is my especial* (or *special*) *friend; he is especially* (or *specially*) *good at his job.* In informal English, however, *special* is usually preferred in all contexts.

Esperanto (ˌɛspə'ræntəʊ) *n* an international artificial language based on words common to the chief European languages. [C19: lit.: the one who hopes, pseudonym of Dr L. L. Zamenhof (1859–1917), its Polish inventor]

▸ ˌEspe'rantist *n*, *adj*

espial (ɪ'spaɪəl) *n Arch.* **1** the act or fact of being seen or discovered. **2** the act of noticing. **3** the act of spying upon; secret observation.

espionage ('ɛspɪəˌnɑːʒ) n **1** the use of spies to obtain secret information, esp. by governments. **2** the act of spying. [C18: from F, from *espion* spy]

Espírito Santo ★ (*Portuguese* ɪʃ'piritu 'sɐntu) n a state of E Brazil, on the Atlantic: swampy coastal plain with mountains in the west; heavily forested. Capital: Vitória. Pop.: 2 786 700 (1995 est.). Area: 45 597 sq. km (17 601 sq. miles).

Espíritu Santo ★ (es'piritu: 'sæntəu) n an island in the SW Pacific: the largest and westernmost of the Vanuatu islands. Pop.: 25 581 (1989). Area: 4856 sq. km (1875 sq. miles).

esplanade (ˌɛsplə'neɪd) n **1** a long open level stretch of ground for walking along, esp. beside the seashore. Cf. **promenade** (sense 1). **2** an open area in front of a fortified place. [C17: from F, from *spianata*, from *spianare* to make level, from L *explānāre*; see EXPLAIN]

Espoo ★ (*Finnish* 'espoː) n a city in S Finland. Pop.: 196 260 (1997 est.).

espousal (ɪ'spauzˈl) n **1** adoption or support: *an espousal of new beliefs.* **2** (*sometimes pl*) *Arch.* a marriage or betrothal ceremony.

espouse (ɪ'spauz) vb **espouses, espousing, espoused.** (*tr*) **1** to adopt or give support to (a cause, ideal, etc.): *to espouse socialism.* **2** *Arch.* (esp. of a man) to take as spouse; marry. [C15: from OF *espouser*, from L *spōnsāre* to affiance, espouse]
▸ **es'pouser** n

espressivo (ˌɛsprɛ'siːvəu) adv *Music.* in an expressive manner. [It.]

espresso (ɛ'sprɛsəu) n, pl **espressos.** **1** coffee made by forcing steam or boiling water through ground coffee beans. **2** an apparatus for making coffee in this way. [C20: It., lit.: pressed]

esprit (ɛ'spriː) n spirit and liveliness, esp. in wit. [C16: from F, from L *spīritus* a breathing, SPIRIT[1]]

esprit de corps (ɛ'spriː də 'kɔː) n consciousness of and pride in belonging to a particular group; the sense of shared purpose and fellowship.

espy (ɪ'spaɪ) vb **espies, espying, espied.** (*tr*) to catch sight of or perceive; detect. [C14: from OF *espier* to SPY, of Gmc origin]
▸ **es'pier** n

Esq. *abbrev. for* esquire.

-esque *suffix forming adjectives.* indicating a specified character, manner, style, or resemblance: *picturesque; Romanesque; statuesque.* [via F from It. *-esco*]

Esquiline ★ ('ɛskwəˌlaɪn) n one of the seven hills on which ancient Rome was built.

Esquimau ('ɛskɪˌməu) n, pl **Esquimaus** or **Esquimau,** adj a former spelling of **Eskimo.**

esquire (ɪ'skwaɪə) n **1** *Chiefly Brit.* a title of respect, usually abbreviated *Esq.,* placed after a man's name. **2** (in medieval times) the attendant of a knight, subsequently often knighted himself. [C15: from OF *escuier,* from LL *scūtārius* shield bearer, from L *scūtum* shield]

ESRC (in Britain) *abbrev. for* Economic and Social Research Council.

ESRO ('ɛzrəu) n *acronym for* European Space Research Organization.

-ess *suffix forming nouns.* indicating a female: *waitress; lioness.* [via OF from LL *-issa,* from Gk]

USAGE NOTE The suffix *-ess* in such words as *poetess, authoress* is now often regarded as disparaging; a sexually neutral term *poet, author* is preferred.

Essaouira ★ (ˌɛsə'wɪərə) n a port in SW Morocco on the Atlantic. Pop.: 42 000 (1982). Former name (until 1956): **Mogador.**

essay n ('ɛseɪ; *senses 2, 3 also* ɛ'seɪ). **1** a short literary composition. **2** an attempt; effort. **3** a test or trial. ◆ vb (ɛ'seɪ). (*tr*) **4** to attempt or try. **5** to test or try out. [C15: from OF *essai* an attempt, from LL *exagium* a weighing, from L *agere* to do, infl. by *exigere* to investigate]

essayist ('ɛseɪɪst) n a person who writes essays.

Essen ★ (*German* 'ɛsən) n a city in W Germany, in North Rhine-Westphalia: the leading industrial centre of the Ruhr, with extensive iron and steel factories. Pop.: 617 955 (1995 est.).

essence ('ɛsˈns) n **1** the characteristic or intrinsic feature of a thing, which determines its identity; fundamental nature. **2** a perfect or complete form of something. **3** *Philosophy.* the unchanging and unchangeable inward nature of something. **4a** the constituent of a plant, usually an oil, alkaloid, or glycoside, that determines its chemical properties. **4b** an alcoholic solution of such a substance. **5** a substance containing the properties of a plant or foodstuff in concentrated form: *vanilla essence.* **6** a rare word for **perfume. 7 in essence.** essentially; fundamentally. **8 of the essence.** indispensable; vitally important. [C14: from Med. L *essentia,* from L: the being (of something), from *esse* to be]

Essene ('ɛsiːn, ɛ'siːn) n *Judaism.* a member of an ascetic sect that flourished in Palestine from the second century B.C. to the second century A.D.
▸ **Essenian** (ɛ'siːnɪən) or **Essenic** (ɛ'sɛnɪk) adj

essential (ɪ'sɛnʃəl) adj **1** vitally important; absolutely necessary. **2** basic; fundamental. **3** absolutely perfect. **4** derived from or relating to an extract of plant, drug, etc.: *an essential oil.* **5** *Biochem.* (of an amino acid or a fatty acid) necessary for the normal growth of an organism but not synthesized by the organism and therefore required in the diet. **6** *Pathol.* (of disease) having no obvious external cause: *essential hypertension.* ◆ n **7** something fundamental or indispensable.
▸ **essentiality** (ɪˌsɛnʃɪ'ælɪtɪ) or **es'sentialness** n ▸ **es'sentially** adv

essential element n *Biochem.* any chemical element required by an organism for healthy growth. It may be required in large amounts (**macronutrient**) or in very small amounts (**trace element**).

essentialism (ɪ'sɛnʃəˌlɪzəm) n *Philosophy.* any doctrine that material objects have an essence distinguishable from their attributes and existence.
▸ **es'sentialist** n

essential oil n any of various volatile oils in plants having the odour or flavour of the plant from which they are extracted.

Essequibo ★ (ˌɛsɪ'kwiːbəu) n a river in Guyana, rising near the Brazilian border and flowing north to the Atlantic: drains over half of Guyana. Length: 1014 km (630 miles).

Essex[1] ★ ('ɛsɪks) n **1** a county of SE England, on the North Sea and the Thames estuary. Administrative centre: Chelmsford. Pop.: 1 569 900 (1994 est.). Area: 367 sq. km (1417 sq. miles). **2** an Anglo-Saxon kingdom that in the early 7th century A.D. comprised the modern county of Essex and much of Hertfordshire and Surrey. By the late 8th century, Essex had become a dependency of the kingdom of Mercia.

Essex[2] ★ ('ɛsɪks) n **2nd Earl of,** title of *Robert Devereux.* ?1566–1601, English soldier and favourite of Elizabeth I: executed for treason.

Essex Man n *Inf., derog.* a self-made man, esp. of working-class origins, characterized by philistinism and bigoted right-wing views. [C20: from the supposed prevalence of such people in ESSEX[1] (sense 1)]

Esslingen ★ ('ɛslɪŋən) n a town in SW Germany, on the River Neckar: Gothic church, medieval buildings: wine, light industry. Pop.: 91 685 (1991 est.).

Essonne ★ (*French* ɛsɔn) n a department of N France south of Paris in Île-de-France region: formed in 1964. Capital: Évry. Pop.: 1 141 679 (1994 est.). Area: 1811 sq. km (706 sq. miles).

EST *abbrev. for:* **1** (in the US and Canada) Eastern Standard Time. **2** electric-shock treatment.

est. *abbrev. for:* **1** established. **2** estimate(d).

★ people and places

-est[1] *suffix.* forming the superlative degree of adjectives and adverbs: *fastest.* [OE *-est, -ost*]

-est[2] *or* **-st** *suffix.* forming the archaic second person singular present and past indicative tense of verbs: *thou goest; thou hadst.* [OE *-est, -ast*]

establish (ɪ'stæblɪʃ) *vb* (tr) **1** to make secure or permanent in a certain place, condition, job, etc. **2** to create or set up (an organization, etc.) as on a permanent basis. **3** to prove correct; validate: *establish a fact.* **4** to cause (a principle, theory, etc.) to be accepted: *establish a precedent.* **5** to give (a Church) the status of a national institution. **6** to cause (a person) to become recognized and accepted. **7** (in works of imagination) to cause (a character, place, etc.) to be credible and recognized. [C14: from OF, from L *stabilis* STABLE[2]]
▶ **es'tablisher** *n*

Established Church *n* a Church that is officially recognized as a national institution, esp. the Church of England.

establishment (ɪ'stæblɪʃmənt) *n* **1** the act of establishing or state of being established. **2a** a business organization or other large institution. **2b** a place of business. **3** the staff and equipment of an organization. **4** any large organization or system. **5** a household; residence. **6** a body of employees or servants. **7** (*modifier*) belonging to or characteristic of the Establishment.

Establishment (ɪ'stæblɪʃmənt) *n* **the.** a group or class having institutional authority within a society: usually seen as conservative.

estate (ɪ'steɪt) *n* **1** a large piece of landed property, esp. in the country. **2** *Chiefly Brit.* a large area of property development, esp. of new houses or (**trading estate**) of factories. **3** *Law.* **3a** property or possessions. **3b** the nature of interest that a person has in land or other property. **3c** the total extent of the property of a deceased person or bankrupt. **4** Also called: **estate of the realm.** an order or class in a political community, regarded as a part of the body politic: the lords spiritual (**first estate**), lords temporal or peers (**second estate**), and commons (**third estate**). See also **fourth estate. 5** state, period, or position in life: *youth's estate; a poor man's estate.* [C13: from OF *estat,* from L *status* condition, STATE]

estate agent *n* **1** *Brit.* an agent concerned with the valuation, management, lease, and sale of property. **2** the administrator of a large landed property; estate manager.

estate car *n* *Brit.* a car containing a large carrying space, reached through a rear door: usually the back seats fold forward to increase the carrying space.

estate duty *n* another name for **death duty.**

Este ★ ('este) *n* a noble family of Italy founded by Alberto Azzo II (996–1097), who was invested with the town of Este in NE Italy as a fief of the Holy Roman Empire. The family governed Ferrara (13th–16th centuries), Modena, and Reggio (13th–18th centuries).

esteem (ɪ'stiːm) *vb* (tr) **1** to have great respect or high regard for. **2** *Formal.* to judge or consider; deem. ◆ *n* **3** high regard or respect; good opinion. **4** *Arch.* judgment; opinion. [C15: from OF *estimer,* from L *aestimāre* ESTIMATE]
▶ **es'teemed** *adj*

ester ('estə) *n* *Chem.* any of a class of compounds produced by reaction between acids and alcohols with the elimination of water. [C19: from G, prob. a contraction of *Essigäther* acetic ether, from *Essig* vinegar (ult. from L *acētum*) + *Äther* ETHER]

Esterházy ★ ('estə,hɑːzɪ) *n* a noble Hungarian family that produced many soldiers, diplomats, and patrons of the arts.

Esth. *Bible. abbrev.for* Esther.

Esther ★ ('estə) *n* *Old Testament.* **1** a beautiful Jewess who became queen of Persia and saved her people from massacre. **2** the book in which this episode is recounted.

esthesia (iːs'θiːzɪə) *n* a US spelling of **aesthesia.**

esthete ('iːsθiːt) *n* a US spelling of **aesthete.**

Esthonia ★ (ε'stəʊnɪə, ε'sθəʊ-) *n* See **Estonia.**

estimable ('estɪməb°l) *adj* worthy of respect; deserving of admiration.
▶ **'estimableness** *n* ▶ **'estimably** *adv*

estimate *vb* ('estɪ,meɪt), **estimates, estimating, estimated. 1** to form an approximate idea of (size, cost, etc.); calculate roughly. **2** (tr; *may take a clause as object*) to form an opinion about; judge. **3** to submit (an approximate price) for (a job) to a prospective client. ◆ *n* ('estɪmɪt). **4** an approximate calculation. **5** a statement of the likely charge for certain work. **6** a judgment; appraisal. [C16: from L *aestimāre* to assess the worth of, from ?]
▶ **'esti,mator** *n* ▶ **'estimative** *adj*

estimation (,estɪ'meɪʃən) *n* **1** a considered opinion; judgment. **2** esteem; respect. **3** the act of estimating.

estival (iː'staɪv°l, 'estɪ-) *adj* the usual US spelling of **aestival.**

estivate ('iːstɪ,veɪt, 'es-) *vb* **estivates, estivating, estivated.** (*intr*) the usual US spelling of **aestivate.**

Estonia *or* **Esthonia** ★ (ε'stəʊnɪə, ε'sθəʊ-) *n* a republic on the Gulf of Finland and the Baltic: low-lying with many lakes and forests. It was under Scandinavian and Teutonic rule from the 13th century to 1721, when it passed to Russia: became an independent republic from 1920 to 1940, when it was annexed by the Soviet Union as the Estonian Soviet Socialist Republic: regained independence in 1991. Official language: Estonian. Currency: kroon. Religion: believers are mostly Lutheran. Capital: Tallinn. Pop.: 1 463 000 (1997). Area: 45 227 sq. km (17 462 sq. miles).

Estonian *or* **Esthonian** (ε'stəʊnɪən, ε'sθəʊ-) *adj* **1** of, relating to, or characteristic of Estonia, its people, or their language. ◆ *n* **2** the official language of Estonia. **3** a native or inhabitant of Estonia.

estop (ɪ'stɒp) *vb* **estops, estopping, estopped.** (tr) **1** *Law.* to preclude by estoppel. **2** *Arch.* to stop. [C15: from OF *estoper* to plug, ult. from L *stuppa* tow; see STOP]
▶ **es'toppage** *n*

estoppel (ɪ'stɒp°l) *n* *Law.* a rule of evidence whereby a person is precluded from denying the truth of a statement he has previously asserted. [C16: from OF *estoupail* plug; see ESTOP]

Estoril ★ (,eʃtu'riːl) *n* a resort in W Portugal, near Lisbon, on the Atlantic Ocean: noted esp. for a famous avenue of palm trees leading to the seafront. Pop.: 24 850 (1991).

estovers (ε'stəʊvəz) *pl n* *Law.* necessaries allowed to tenants of land, esp. wood for fuel and repairs. [C15: from Anglo-F., pl of *estover,* from OF *estovoir* to be necessary, from L *est opus* there is need]

estradiol (,estrə'daɪɒl, ,iːstrə-) *n* the usual US spelling of **oestradiol.**

estrange (ɪ'streɪndʒ) *vb* **estranges, estranging, estranged.** (tr) to antagonize or lose the affection of (someone previously friendly); alienate. [C15: from OF *estranger,* from LL *extrāneāre* to treat as a stranger, from L *extrāneus* foreign]
▶ **es'tranged** *adj* ▶ **es'trangement** *n*

Estremadura ★ (*Portuguese* ɪʃtrəmə'ðurə) *n* **1** a region of W Spain: arid and sparsely populated except in the valleys of the Tagus and Guadiana Rivers. Area: 41 593 sq. km (16 059 sq. miles). Spanish name: **Extremadura. 2** a region, formerly a province, in Portugal around Lisbon.

estrogen ('estrədʒən, 'iːstrə-) *n* the usual US spelling of **oestrogen.**

estrus ('estrəs, 'iːstrəs) *n* the usual US spelling of **oestrus.**

estuary ('estjʊərɪ) *n, pl* **estuaries.** the widening channel of a river where it nears the sea. [C16: from L *aestuārium* marsh, from *aestus* tide]
▶ **estuarial** (,estjʊ'eərɪəl) *adj* ▶ **'estuarine** *adj*

e.s.u. *or* **ESU** *abbrev. for* electrostatic unit.

E. Sussex *abbrev. for* East Sussex.

ET (in Britain) *abbrev. for* Employment Training: a government scheme offering training in technological and business skills to unemployed people.

-et *suffix of nouns.* small or lesser: *islet; baronet.* [from OF *-et, -ete*]

eta ('iːtə) *n* the seventh letter in the Greek alphabet (H, η). [Gk, from Phoenician]

ETA *abbrev. for* estimated time of arrival.

et al. *abbrev. for:* **1** et alibi. [L: and elsewhere] **2** et alii. [L: and others]

etalon ('etə,lɒn) *n Physics.* a device used in spectroscopy to measure wavelengths by interference effects produced by multiple reflections between parallel half-silvered glass plates. [C20: F *étalon* a standard of weights & measures]

etc. *abbrev. for* et cetera.

et cetera *or* **etcetera** (ɪt 'setrə) *n and vb substitute.* **1** and the rest; and others; and so forth. **2** or the like; or something similar. [from L *et* and + *cetera* the other (things)]

> **USAGE NOTE** It is unnecessary to use *and* before *etc.* as *etc.* (*et cetera*) already means *and other things*. The repetition of *etc.*, as in *he brought paper, ink, notebooks, etc., etc.*, is avoided except in informal contexts.

etceteras (ɪt'setrəz) *pl n* miscellaneous extra things or persons.

etch (etʃ) *vb* **1** (*tr*) to wear away the surface of (a metal, glass, etc.) by the action of an acid. **2** to cut or corrode (a design, etc.) on (a metal or other printing plate) by the action of acid on parts not covered by an acid-resistant coating. **3** (*tr*) to cut as with a sharp implement. **4** (*tr; usually passive*) to imprint vividly. [C17: from Du. *etsen*, from OHG *azzen* to feed, bite]
> ▸ **'etcher** *n*

etching ('etʃɪŋ) *n* **1** the art, act, or process of preparing etched surfaces or of printing designs from them. **2** an etched plate. **3** an impression made from an etched plate.

ETD *abbrev. for* estimated time of departure.

Eteocles ★ (ɪ'tiːə,kliːz, 'etɪə-) *n Greek myth.* a son of Oedipus and Jocasta. He and his brother, Polynices, were to share the kingdom of Thebes but Eteocles expelled Polynices from Thebes; they killed each other in single combat when Polynices returned as leader of the Seven against Thebes.

eternal (ɪ'tɜːn°l) *adj* **1a** without beginning or end; lasting forever. **1b** (*as n*): *the eternal.* **2** (*often cap.*) a name applied to God. **3** unchanged by time; immutable: *eternal truths.* **4** seemingly unceasing. [C14: from LL, from L *aeternus*; rel. to L *aevum* age]
> ▸ ,eter'nality *or* e'ternalness *n* ▸ e'ternally *adv*

Eternal City ★ *n* the. Rome.

eternalize (ɪ'tɜːnə,laɪz) *or* **eternize** (ɪ'tɜːnaɪz), **eternalise** *vb* eternalizes, eternalizing, eternalized *or* eternalises, eternalising, eternalised. (*tr*) **1** to make eternal. **2** to make famous forever; immortalize.
> ▸ e,ternali'zation *or* e,terni'zation, e,ternali'sation *n*

eternal triangle *n* an emotional relationship usually involving three people, two of whom are rival lovers of the third person.

eternity (ɪ'tɜːnɪtɪ) *n, pl* **eternities.** **1** endless or infinite time. **2** the quality, state, or condition of being eternal. **3** (*usually pl*) any aspect of life and thought considered timeless. **4** the timeless existence, believed by some to characterize the afterlife. **5** a seemingly endless period of time.

eternity ring *n* a ring given as a token of lasting affection, esp. one set all around with stones to symbolize continuity.

etesian (ɪ'tiːʒɪən) *adj* (of NW winds) recurring annually in the summer in the E Mediterranean. [C17: from L *etēsius* yearly, from Gk *etos* year]

ETF *abbrev. for* electronic transfer of funds.

Eth. *abbrev. for:* **1** Ethiopia(n). **2** Ethiopic.

-eth[1] *suffix.* forming the archaic third person singular present indicative tense of verbs: *goeth; taketh.* [OE *-eth, -th*]

-eth[2] *suffix forming ordinal numbers.* a variant of **-th**[2]: *twentieth.*

ethanal ('eθə,næl) *n* the systematic name for **acetaldehyde.**

ethane ('iːθeɪn, 'eθ-) *n* a colourless odourless flammable gaseous alkane obtained from natural gas and petroleum: used as a fuel. Formula: C_2H_6. [C19: from ETH(YL)+ -ANE]

ethanediol ('iːθeɪn,daɪɒl, 'eθ-) *n* a colourless soluble liquid used as an antifreeze and solvent. Formula: $C_2H_4(OH)_2$. [C20: from ETHANE + DI-[1] + -OL[1]]

ethanoic acid (,eθə'nəʊɪk, ,iːθə-) *n* the systematic name for **acetic acid.**

ethanol ('eθə,nɒl, 'iːθ-) *n* the systematic name for **alcohol** (sense 1).

Ethelbert ('eθəl,bɜːt) *or* **Æthelbert** ★ ('æθəl,bɜːt) *n* Saint. ?552–616 A.D., king of Kent (560–616): converted to Christianity by St Augustine; issued the earliest known code of English laws. Feast day: Feb. 24 or 25.

Ethelred I ('eθəl,red) *or* **Æthelred** ★ ('æθəl,red) *n* died 871, king of Wessex (866–71). He led resistance to the Danish invasion of England; died following his victory at Ashdown.

Ethelred II *or* **Æthelred** ★ *n* known as *Ethelred the Unready.* ?968–1016 A.D., king of England (978–1016). He was temporarily deposed by the Danish king Sweyn (1013) but was recalled on Sweyn's death (1014).

Ethelwulf ('eθəl,wulf) *or* **Æthelwulf** ★ ('æθəl,wulf) *n* died 858 A.D., king of Wessex (839–858).

ethene ('eθiːn) *n* the systematic name for **ethylene.**

ether ('iːθə) *n* **1** Also called: **diethyl ether, ethyl ether, ethoxyethane.** a colourless volatile highly flammable liquid: used as a solvent and anaesthetic. Formula: $C_2H_5OC_2H_5$. **2** any of a class of organic compounds with the general formula ROR′, as in methyl ethyl ether, $CH_3OC_2H_5$. **3** the medium formerly believed to fill all space and to support the propagation of electromagnetic waves. **4** *Greek myth.* the upper atmosphere; clear sky or heaven. ◆ Also (for senses 3 and 4): **aether.** [C17: from L, from Gk *aithein* to burn]
> ▸ e'theric *adj*

ethereal (ɪ'θɪərɪəl) *adj* **1** extremely delicate or refined. **2** almost as light as air; airy. **3** celestial or spiritual. **4** of, containing, or dissolved in an ether, esp. diethyl ether. **5** of or relating to the ether. [C16: from L, from Gk *aithēr* ETHER]
> ▸ e,there'ality *or* e'therealness *n*

etherealize *or* **etherealise** (ɪ'θɪərɪə,laɪz) *vb* etherealizes, etherealizing, etherealized *or* etherealises, etherealising, etherealised. (*tr*) **1** to make or regard as being ethereal. **2** to add ether to or make into ether.
> ▸ e,thereali'zation *or* e,thereali'sation *n*

etherize *or* **etherise** ('iːθə,raɪz) *vb* etherizes, etherizing, etherized *or* etherises, etherising, etherised. (*tr*) *Obs.* to subject (a person) to the anaesthetic influence of ether fumes; anaesthetize.
> ▸ ,etheri'zation *or* ,etheri'sation *n* ▸ 'ether,izer *or* 'ether,iser *n*

Ethernet ('iːθə,net) *n Trademark, computing.* a widely used type of local area network.

ethic ('eθɪk) *n* **1** a moral principle or set of moral values held by an individual or group. ◆ *adj* **2** another word for **ethical.** [C15: from L, from Gk *ēthos* custom]

ethical ('eθɪk°l) *adj* **1** in accordance with principles of conduct that are considered correct, esp. those of a given profession or group. **2** of or relating to ethics. **3** (of a medicinal agent) available legally only with a doctor's prescription.
> ▸ 'ethically *adv* ▸ 'ethicalness *or* ,ethi'cality *n*

ethical investment *n* an investment in a company whose activities or products are not considered by the investor to be unethical.

ethics ('eθɪks) *n* **1** (*functioning as sing*) the philosophical study of the moral value of human conduct and of the rules and principles that ought to govern it. **2** (*functioning as pl*) a code of behaviour considered correct, esp. that of a particular group, profession, or individual. **3** (*functioning as pl*) the moral fitness of a decision, course of action, etc.
> ▸ **ethicist** ('eθɪsɪst) *n*

Ethiopia ★ (,iːθɪ'əʊpɪə) *n* a state in NE Africa, on the Red Sea: consolidated as an empire under Menelik II (1889–1913); federated with Eritrea (1952–93); Emperor Haile

★ people and places

Selassie was deposed by the military in 1974 and the monarchy was abolished in 1975. It lies along the Great Rift Valley and consists of deserts in the southeast and northeast and a high central plateau with many rivers (including the Blue Nile) and mountains rising over 4500 m (15 000 ft); the main export is coffee. Language: Amharic. Religion: Christian majority. Currency: birr. Capital: Addis Ababa. Pop.: 58 733 000 (1997). Area: 1 128 215 sq. km (435 614 sq. miles). Former name: **Abyssinia**. See also **Eritrea**.

Ethiopian (ˌiːθɪˈəʊpɪən) *adj* **1** of or relating to Ethiopia, its people, or any of their languages. ◆ *n* **2** a native or inhabitant of Ethiopia. **3** any of the languages of Ethiopia, esp. Amharic. ◆ *n, adj* **4** an archaic word for **Black**[1].

Ethiopic (ˌiːθɪˈɒpɪk, -ˈəʊpɪk) *n* **1** the ancient Semitic language of Ethiopia: a Christian liturgical language. **2** the group of languages developed from this language, including Amharic. ◆ *adj* **3** denoting or relating to this language or group of languages. **4** a less common word for **Ethiopian**.

ethnic (ˈɛθnɪk) *or* **ethnical** *adj* **1** of or relating to a human group having racial, religious, linguistic, and other traits in common. **2** relating to the classification of mankind into groups, esp. on the basis of racial characteristics. **3** denoting or deriving from the cultural traditions of a group of people. **4** characteristic of another culture, esp. a peasant one. ◆ *n* **5** *Chiefly US.* a member of an ethnic group, esp. a minority one. [C14 (in the senses: heathen, Gentile): from LL *ethnicus*, from Gk *ethnos* race]
▸ **'ethnically** *adv* ▸ **ethnicity** (ɛθˈnɪsɪtɪ) *n*

ethnic cleansing *n Euphemistic.* the violent removal by one ethnic group of other ethnic groups from the population of a particular area: used esp. of the activities of Serbs against Croats and Muslims in the former Yugoslavia.

ethno- *combining form.* indicating race, people, or culture. [via F from Gk *ethnos* race]

ethnocentrism (ˌɛθnəʊˈsɛnˌtrɪzəm) *n* belief in the intrinsic superiority of the nation, culture, or group to which one belongs.
▸ ˌ**ethno'centric** *adj* ▸ ˌ**ethno'centrically** *adv* ▸ ˌ**ethnocen'tricity** *n*

ethnography (ɛθˈnɒɡrəfɪ) *n* the branch of anthropology that deals with the scientific description of individual human societies.
▸ ˌ**eth'nographer** *n* ▸ **ethnographic** (ˌɛθnəʊˈɡræfɪk) *or* ˌ**ethno'graphical** *adj*

ethnology (ɛθˈnɒlədʒɪ) *n* the branch of anthropology that deals with races and peoples, their origins, characteristics, etc.
▸ ▸ **ethnologic** (ˌɛθnəˈlɒdʒɪk) *or* ˌ**ethno'logical** *adj* ▸ **eth'nologist** *n*

ethnomusicology (ˌɛθnəʊˌmjuːzɪˈkɒlədʒɪ) *n* the study of the origins of music, esp. from non-European cultures.

ethology (ɪˈθɒlədʒɪ) *n* the study of the behaviour of animals in their normal environment. [C17 (in the obs. sense: mimicry): via L from Gk *ēthos* character; current sense, C19]
▸ **ethological** (ˌɛθəˈlɒdʒɪkˀl) *adj* ▸ **e'thologist** *n*

ethos (ˈiːθɒs) *n* the distinctive character, spirit, and attitudes of a people, culture, era, etc.: *the revolutionary ethos.* [C19: from LL: habit, from Gk]

ethyl (ˈiːθaɪl, ˈɛθɪl) *n* (*modifier*) of, consisting of, or containing the monovalent group C_2H_5-. [C19: from ETH(ER) + -YL]
▸ **ethylic** (ɪˈθɪlɪk) *adj*

ethyl acetate *n* a colourless volatile flammable liquid ester: used in perfumes and flavourings and as a solvent. Formula: $CH_3COOC_2H_5$.

ethyl alcohol *n* another name for **alcohol** (sense 1).

ethylene (ˈɛθɪˌliːn) *or* **ethene** (ˈɛθiːn) *n* a colourless flammable gaseous alkene used in the manufacture of polythene and other chemicals. Formula: $CH_2:CH_2$.
▸ **ethylenic** (ˌɛθɪˈliːnɪk) *adj*

ethylene glycol *n* another name for **ethanediol**.

ethylene group *or* **radical** *n Chem.* the divalent group, $-CH_2CH_2-$, derived from ethylene.

ethylene series *n Chem.* another name for **alkene series**.

ethyne (ˈɛθaɪn) *n Chem.* the systematic name for **acetylene**.

ethyne series *n Chem.* another name for **acetylene series**.

etiolate (ˈiːtɪəʊˌleɪt) *vb* **etiolates, etiolating, etiolated.** **1** *Bot.* to whiten (a green plant) through lack of sunlight. **2** to become or cause to become pale and weak. [C18: from F *étioler* to make pale, prob. from OF *estuble* straw, from L *stipula*]
▸ ˌ**etio'lation** *n*

etiology (ˌiːtɪˈɒlədʒɪ) *n, pl* **etiologies.** a variant spelling of **aetiology**.

etiquette (ˈɛtɪˌkɛt, ˌɛtɪˈkɛt) *n* **1** the customs or rules governing behaviour regarded as correct in social life. **2** a conventional code of practice followed in certain professions or groups. [C18: from F, from OF *estiquette* label, from *estiquier* to attach; see STICK[2]]

Etna ★ (ˈɛtnə) *n Mount.* an active volcano in E Sicily: the highest volcano in Europe and the highest peak in Italy south of the Alps. Height: 3323 m (10 902 ft).

Eton ★ (ˈiːtˀn) *n* **1** a town in S England, in Berkshire near the River Thames: site of **Eton College**, a public school for boys founded in 1440. Pop.: 1974 (1991). **2** this college.
▸ **Etonian** (iːˈtəʊnɪən) *adj, n*

Eton collar *n* (formerly) a broad stiff white collar worn outside a boy's jacket.

Eton crop *n* a very short mannish hairstyle worn by women in the 1920s.

Eton jacket *n* (formerly) a boy's waist-length jacket with a V-shaped back, open in front.

Etruria ★ (ɪˈtrʊərɪə) *n* **1** an ancient country of central Italy, between the Rivers Arno and Tiber, roughly corresponding to present-day Tuscany and part of Umbria. **2** a factory established in Staffordshire by Josiah Wedgwood in 1769.

Etruscan (ɪˈtrʌskən) *or* **Etrurian** (ɪˈtrʊərɪən) *n* **1** a member of an ancient people of Etruria whose civilization greatly influenced the Romans. **2** the language of the ancient Etruscans. ◆ *adj* **3** of or relating to Etruria, the Etruscans, their culture, or their language.

et seq. *abbrev. for:* **1** et sequens [L: and the following] **2** Also: **et seqq.** et sequentia [L: and those that follow]

-ette *suffix of nouns.* **1** small: *cigarette.* **2** female: *majorette.* **3** (esp. in trade names) imitation: *Leatherette.* [from F, fem of -ET]

étude (ˈeɪtjuːd) *n* a short musical composition for a solo instrument, esp. one designed as an exercise or exploiting virtuosity. [C19: from F: STUDY]

étui (ɛˈtwiː) *n, pl* **étuis.** a small usually ornamented case for holding needles, cosmetics, or other small articles. [C17: F, from OF *estuier* to enclose; see TWEEZERS]

etymology (ˌɛtɪˈmɒlədʒɪ) *n, pl* **etymologies.** **1** the study of the sources and development of words. **2** an account of the source and development of a word. [C14: via L from Gk; see ETYMON, -LOGY]
▸ **etymological** (ˌɛtɪməˈlɒdʒɪkˀl) *adj* ▸ ˌ**ety'mologist** *n*
▸ ˌ**ety'molo,gize** *or* ˌ**ety'molo,gise** *vb*

etymon (ˈɛtɪˌmɒn) *n, pl* **etymons** *or* **etyma** (-mə). a form of a word, usually the earliest recorded form or a reconstructed form, from which another word is derived. [C16: via L from Gk *etumon* basic meaning, from *etumos* true, actual]

Etzel ★ (ˈɛtsˀl) *n German legend.* a great king who, according to the *Nibelungenlied*, was the second husband of Kriemhild after the death of Siegfried: identified with Attila the Hun. Cf. **Atli**.

Eu the chemical symbol for europium.

EU *abbrev. for* European Union.

eu- *combining form.* well, pleasant, or good: *eupeptic; euphony.* [via L from Gk, from *eus* good]

Euboea ★ (juːˈbiːə) *n* an island in the W Aegean Sea: the largest island after Crete in the Greek archipelago; linked with the mainland by a bridge across the Euripus channel. Capital: Chalcis. Pop.: 188 410 (1981). Area:

★ people and places

3908 sq. km (1509 sq. miles). Modern Greek name: Évvoia. Former English name: **Negropont**.
▶ **Eu'boean** *adj, n*

eucalyptus (ˌjuːkəˈlɪptəs) *or* **eucalypt** (ˈjuːkəˌlɪpt) *n, pl* **eucalyptuses, eucalypti** (-ˈlɪptaɪ), *or* **eucalypts**. any tree of the mostly Australian genus *Eucalyptus*, widely cultivated for timber and gum, as ornament, and for the medicinal oil in their leaves (**eucalyptus oil**). [C19: NL, from EU- + Gk *kaluptos* covered, from *kaluptein* to cover, hide]

Eucharist (ˈjuːkərɪst) *n* **1** the Christian sacrament in which Christ's Last Supper is commemorated by the consecration of bread and wine. **2** the consecrated elements of bread and wine offered in the sacrament. [C14: via Church L from Gk *eukharistos* thankful, from EU- + *kharis* favour]
▶ ˌEuchaˈristic *or* ˌEuchaˈristical *adj*

euchre (ˈjuːkə) *n* **1** a US and Canad. card game for two, three, or four players, using a poker pack. **2** an instance of euchring another player. ◆ *vb* **euchres, euchring, euchred**. (*tr*) **3** to prevent (a player) from making his contracted tricks. **4** (usually foll. by *out*) *US, Canad., Austral., & NZ inf.* to outwit or cheat. [C19: from ?]

Euclid ★ (ˈjuːklɪd) *n* **1** 3rd century B.C., Greek mathematician of Alexandria; author of *Elements*, setting out the principles of geometry. **2** the works of Euclid, esp. his system of geometry.
▶ **Euclidean** *or* **Euclidian** (juːˈklɪdɪən) *adj*

eucryphia (juːˈkrɪfɪə) *n* any of various mostly evergreen trees and shrubs of S America and Australia. [NL, from EU- + Gk *kryphios* covered]

eudiometer (ˌjuːdɪˈɒmɪtə) *n* a graduated glass tube used in the study and volumetric analysis of gas reactions. [C18: from Gk *eudios*, lit.: clear-skied + -METER]

Eugène ★ (French øʒɛn) *n* **Prince**, title of *François Eugène de Savoie-Carignan*. 1663–1736, Austrian general, born in France: with Marlborough defeated the French at Blenheim (1704) and Malplaquet (1709).

eugenics (juːˈdʒɛnɪks) *n* (*functioning as sing*) the study of methods of improving the quality of the human race, esp. by selective breeding. [C19: from Gk *eugenēs* well-born, from EU- + *-genēs* born; see -GEN]
▶ **euˈgenic** *adj* ▶ **euˈgenically** *adv* ▶ **euˈgenicist** *n* ▶ **eugenist** (ˈjuːdʒənɪst) *n*

Eugénie ★ (French øʒeni) *n* original name *Eugénia Maria de Montijo de Guzman, Comtesse de Téba*. 1826–1920, Empress of France (1853–71) as wife of Napoleon III.

eukaryote *or* **eucaryote** (juːˈkærɪəʊt) *n* an organism having cells each with a nucleus within which the genetic material is contained. Cf. **prokaryote**. [from EU- + KARYO- + *-ote* as in *zygote*]
▶ **eukaryotic** *or* **eucaryotic** (juˌkærɪˈɒtɪk) *adj*

Euler ★ (German ˈɔɪlər) *n* **1 Leonhard** (ˈleːɔnhart). 1707–83, Swiss mathematician, noted esp. for his work on the calculus of variation: considered the founder of modern mathematical analysis. **2 Ulf (Svante) von** (ʊlf fɔn). 1905–83, Swedish physiologist: shared the Nobel prize (1970) for physiology or medicine.

Euler-Chelpin ★ (German ˈɔɪlərˈkɛlpiːn) *n* **Hans (Karl August) von**. 1873–1964, Swedish biochemist, born in Germany: shared the Nobel prize for chemistry (1929) for work on enzymes: father of Ulf von Euler.

eulogize *or* **eulogise** (ˈjuːləˌdʒaɪz) *vb* **eulogizing, eulogized** *or* **eulogises, eulogising, eulogised**. to praise (a person or thing) highly in speech or writing.
▶ **'eulogist, 'euloˌgizer,** *or* **'euloˌgiser** *n* ▶ ˌeuloˈgistic *or* ˌeuloˈgistical *adj*

eulogy (ˈjuːlədʒɪ) *n, pl* **eulogies. 1** a speech or piece of writing praising a person or thing, esp. a person who has recently died. **2** high praise or commendation. ◆ Also called (archaic): **eulogium** (juːˈləʊdʒɪəm). [C16: from LL, from Gk: praise, from EU- + -LOGY]

USAGE NOTE Avoid confusion with **elegy**.

Eumenides (juːˈmɛnɪˌdiːz) *pl n* another name for the **Furies**, used by the Greeks as a euphemism. [from Gk, lit: the benevolent ones]

eunuch (ˈjuːnək) *n* **1** a man who has been castrated, esp. (formerly) for some office such as a guard in a harem. **2** *Inf.* an ineffective man. [C15: via L from Gk *eunoukhos* bedchamber attendant]

euonymus (juːˈɒnɪməs) *or* **evonymus** (ɛˈvɒnɪməs) *n* any tree or shrub of the N temperate genus *Euonymus*, such as the spindle tree. [C18: from L: spindle tree, from Gk *euōnumos* fortunately named, from EU- + *onoma* NAME]

Eupen and Malmédy ★ (French øpɛn; malmedi) *n* a region of Belgium in Liège province: ceded by Germany in 1919. Pop.: 27 675 (1995 est.).

eupepsia (juːˈpɛpsɪə) *or* **eupepsy** (juːˈpɛpsɪ) *n Physiol.* good digestion. [C18: from NL, from Gk, from EU- + *pepsis* digestion]
▶ **eupeptic** (juːˈpɛptɪk) *adj*

euphemism (ˈjuːfɪˌmɪzəm) *n* **1** an inoffensive word or phrase substituted for one considered offensive or hurtful. **2** the use of such inoffensive words or phrases. [C17: from Gk, from EU- + *phēmē* speech]
▶ ˌeupheˈmistic *adj* ▶ ˌeupheˈmistically *adv*

euphemize *or* **euphemise** (ˈjuːfɪˌmaɪz) *vb* **euphemizes, euphemizing, euphemized** *or* **euphemises, euphemising, euphemised**. to speak in euphemisms or refer to by means of a euphemism.
▶ **'eupheˌmizer** *or* **'eupheˌmiser** *n*

euphonic (juːˈfɒnɪk) *or* **euphonious** (juːˈfəʊnɪəs) *adj* **1** denoting or relating to euphony. **2** (of speech sounds) altered for ease of pronunciation.
▶ **euˈphonically** *or* **euˈphoniously** *adv* ▶ **euˈphoniousness** *n*

euphonium (juːˈfəʊnɪəm) *n* a brass musical instrument with four valves. [C19: NL, from EUPH(ONY + HARM)ONIUM]

euphonize *or* **euphonise** (ˈjuːfəˌnaɪz) *vb* **euphonizes, euphonizing, euphonized** *or* **euphonises, euphonising, euphonised**. **1** to make pleasant to hear. **2** to change (speech sounds) so as to facilitate pronunciation.

euphony (ˈjuːfənɪ) *n, pl* **euphonies. 1** the alteration of speech sounds, esp. by assimilation, so as to make them easier to pronounce. **2** a pleasing sound, esp. in speech. [C17: from LL, from Gk, from EU- + *phōnē* voice]

euphorbia (juːˈfɔːbɪə) *n* any plant of the genus *Euphorbia*, such as the spurges. [C14 *euforbia*, from L *euphorbea* African plant, after *Euphorbus*, first-cent. A.D. Gk physician]

euphoria (juːˈfɔːrɪə) *n* a feeling of great elation, esp. when exaggerated. [C19: from Gk: good ability to endure, from EU- + *pherein* to bear]
▶ **euphoric** (juːˈfɒrɪk) *adj*

euphoriant (juːˈfɔːrɪənt) *adj* **1** able to produce euphoria. ◆ *n* **2** a euphoriant drug or agent.

euphotic (juːˈfəʊtɪk, -ˈfɒt-) *adj* denoting or relating to the uppermost part of a sea or lake, which receives enough light for photosynthesis to take place. [C20: from EU- + PHOTIC]

euphrasy (ˈjuːfrəsɪ) *n, pl* **euphrasies**. another name for **eyebright**. [C15: *eufrasie*, from Med. L, from Gk *euphrasia* gladness, from EU- + *phrēn* mind]

Euphrates ★ (juːˈfreɪtiːz) *n* a river in SW Asia, rising in E Turkey and flowing south across Syria and Iraq to join the Tigris, forming the Shatt-al-Arab, which flows to the head of the Persian Gulf: important in ancient times for the extensive irrigation of its valley (in Mesopotamia). Length: 3598 km (2235 miles).

Euphrosyne ★ (juːˈfrɒzɪˌniː) *n Greek myth.* one of the three Graces. [from Gk: mirth, merriment]

euphuism (ˈjuːfjuːˌɪzəm) *n* **1** an artificial prose style of the Elizabethan period, marked by extreme use of antithesis, alliteration, and extended similes and allusions. **2** any stylish affectation in speech or writing. [C16: after *Euphues*, prose romance by John LYLY]
▶ **'euphuist** *n* ▶ ˌeuphuˈistic *or* ˌeuphuˈistical *adj*

eur. *or* **Eur.** *abbrev. for* Europe(an).

eur- *combining form.* (*sometimes cap.*) a variant of **euro-** before a vowel.

Eurasia ★ (jʊəˈreɪʒə, -ʃə) *n* the continents of Europe and Asia considered as a whole.

Eurasian (jʊəˈreɪʃən, -ʒən) *adj* **1** of or relating to Eurasia.

★ people and places

2 of mixed European and Asian descent. ♦ *n* **3** a person of mixed European and Asian descent.

Euratom (jʊəˈrætəm) *n* short for **European Atomic Energy Community**; an authority established by the EEC (now the EU) to develop peaceful uses of nuclear energy.

Eure ★ (*French* œr) *n* a department of N France, in Haute-Normandie region. Capital: Évreux. Pop.: 533 731 (1994 est.). Area: 6037 sq. km (2354 sq. miles).

Eure-et-Loir ★ (*French* œrelwar) *n* a department of N central France, in Centre region. Capital: Chartres. Pop.: 409 420 (1994 est.). Area: 5940 sq. km (2317 sq. miles).

eureka (juˈriːkə) *interj* an exclamation of triumph on discovering or solving something. [C17: from Gk *heurēka* I have found (it), from *heuriskein* to find; traditionally the exclamation of Archimedes when he realized, during bathing, that the volume of an irregular solid could be calculated by measuring the water displaced when it was immersed]

eurhythmic (juːˈrɪðmɪk), **eurhythmical**, *or esp. US* **eurythmic, eurythmical** *adj* **1** having a pleasing and harmonious rhythm, order, or structure. **2** of or relating to eurhythmics. [C19: from L, from Gk, from EU- + *rhuthmos* proportion, RHYTHM]

eurhythmics *or esp. US* **eurythmics** (juːˈrɪðmɪks) *n* (*functioning as sing*) **1** a system of training through physical movement to music. **2** dancing of this style. [C20: from EURHYTHMIC]
▸ eu'rhythmy *or* eu'rythmy *n*

Euripides ★ (juˈrɪpɪˌdiːz) *n* ?480–406 B.C., Greek tragic dramatist. His plays, 18 of which are extant, include *Alcestis, Medea, Hippolytus, Hecuba, Trojan Women, Electra, Iphigeneia in Tauris, Iphigeneia in Aulis*, and *Bacchae*.

euro (ˈjʊərəʊ) *n* the currency unit of the member countries of the European Union who have adopted European Monetary Union.

euro- (ˈjʊərəʊ) *or before a vowel* **eur-** *combining form.* (*sometimes cap.*) Europe or European.

eurobond (ˈjʊərəʊˌbɒnd) *n* (*sometimes cap.*) a bond issued in a eurocurrency.

Eurocentric (ˌjʊərəʊˈsɛntrɪk) *adj* chiefly concerned with or concentrating on Europe and European culture: *the Eurocentric curriculum.*

eurocheque (ˈjʊərəʊˌtʃɛk) *n* (*sometimes cap.*) a cheque drawn on a European bank that can be cashed at any bank or bureau de change displaying the EU sign or that can be used to pay for goods or services at any outlet displaying this sign.

Eurocommunism (ˌjʊərəʊˈkɒmjʊˌnɪzəm) *n* the policies, doctrines, and practices of Communist Parties in Western Europe in the 1970s and 1980s, esp. those rejecting democratic centralism and favouring non-alignment with the Soviet Union and China.
▸ ˌEuro'communist *n, adj*

eurocrat (ˈjʊərəˌkræt) *n* (*sometimes cap.*) a member of the administration of the European Union.

eurocurrency (ˈjʊərəʊˌkʌrənsɪ) *n* (*sometimes cap.*) the currency of any country held on deposit in Europe outside its home market: used as a source of short- or medium-term finance because of easy convertibility.

eurodollar (ˈjʊərəʊˌdɒlə) *n* (*sometimes cap.*) a US dollar as part of a European holding. See **eurocurrency.**

euromarket (ˈjʊərəʊˌmɑːkɪt) *n* **1** a market for financing international trade backed by the central banks and commercial banks of the European Union. **2** the European Union treated as one large market for the sale of goods and services.

Euro MP *n Inf.* a member of the European Parliament.

euronote (ˈjʊərəʊˌnəʊt) *n* a form of euro-commercial paper consisting of short-term negotiable bearer notes.

Europa ★ (jʊˈrəʊpə) *n Greek myth.* a Phoenician princess who had three children by Zeus in Crete, where he had taken her after assuming the guise of a white bull. Their offspring were Rhadamanthys, Minos, and Sarpedon.

Europe ★ (ˈjʊərəp) *n* **1** the second smallest continent, forming the W extension of Eurasia: the border with Asia runs from the Urals to the Caspian and the Black Sea. The coastline is generally extremely indented and

there are several peninsulas (notably Scandinavia, Italy, and Iberia) and offshore islands (including the British Isles and Iceland). It contains a series of great mountain systems in the south (Pyrenees, Alps, Apennines, Carpathians, Caucasus), a large central plain, and a N region of lakes and mountains in Scandinavia. Pop.: 729 370 000 (1996 est.). Area: about 10 400 000 sq. km (4 000 000 sq. miles). **2** *Brit.* the continent of Europe except for the British Isles: *we're going to Europe for our holiday.* **3** *Brit.* the European Union: *when did Britain go into Europe?*

European (ˌjʊərəˈpɪən) *adj* **1** of or relating to Europe or its inhabitants. **2** native to or derived from Europe. ♦ *n* **3** a native or inhabitant of Europe. **4** a person of European descent. **5** *S. African.* any White person.
▸ ˌEuro'pean,ism *n*

European Commission *n* the executive body of the European Union, formed in 1967 to initiate action in the union and mediate between member governments.

European Community *or* **Communities** *n* the former name (until 1993) of the **European Union.**

European Council *n* an executive body of the European Union, made up of the President of the European Commission and representatives of the member states, including foreign and other ministers. The Council acts at the request of the Commission.

European Currency Unit *n* See **ECU.**

European Economic Community *n* the former W European economic association created by the Treaty of Rome (1957); in 1967 it merged with the European Coal and Steel Community and the European Atomic Energy Community to form the European Community, which was replaced in 1993 by the European Union. Informal name: **Common Market.** Abbrev.: **EEC.**

Europeanize *or* **Europeanise** (ˌjʊərəˈpɪəˌnaɪz) *vb* **Europeanizes, Europeanizing, Europeanized** *or* **Europeanises, Europeanising, Europeanised.** (*tr*) **1** to make European. **2** to integrate (a country, economy, etc.) into the European Union.
▸ ˌEuro,peani'zation *or* ˌEuro,peani'sation *n*

European Monetary System *n* the system used in the European Union for stabilizing exchange rates between the currencies of member states. It relies on the Exchange Rate Mechanism and the balance-of-payments support mechanism. Abbrev.: **EMS.**

European Parliament *n* the assembly of the European Union in Strasbourg.

European Union *n* the economic and political organization of European states created in 1967 (as the European Community) by the merger of the European Economic Community with the European Coal and Steel Community and the European Atomic Energy Community. The current members are Belgium, Denmark, France, Germany, Greece, Ireland, Italy, Luxembourg, the Netherlands, Portugal, Spain, and the UK; Austria, Finland, and Sweden joined in 1995. Abbrev.: **EU.**

Europhile (ˈjʊərəʊˌfaɪl) (*sometimes not cap.*) ♦ *n* **1** a person who admires Europe, Europeans, or the European Union. ♦ *adj* **2** marked by admiration for Europe, Europeans, or the European Union.

europium (juˈrəʊpɪəm) *n* a silvery-white element of the lanthanide series of metals. Symbol: Eu; atomic no.: 63; atomic wt.: 151.96. [C20: after EUROPE + -IUM]

Europoort ★ (*Dutch* ˈøːroːpoːrt) *n* a port in the Netherlands near Rotterdam: developed in the 1960s; handles oil.

Euro-sceptic (ˈjʊərəʊˌskɛptɪk) (in Britain) ♦ *n* **1** a person who is opposed to closer links with the European Union. ♦ *adj* **2** opposing closer links with the European Union: *Euro-sceptic MPs.*

Eurotunnel (ˈjʊərəʊˌtʌnᵊl) *n* another name for **Channel Tunnel.**

Eurus ★ (ˈjʊərəs) *n Greek myth.* the east or southeast wind personified. [L, from Gk *euros*]

Euryale ★ (juˈraɪəlɪ) *n Greek myth.* one of the three Gorgons.

★ people and places

Eurydice ★ (juˈrɪdɪsɪ) *n Greek myth.* a dryad married to Orpheus, who sought her in Hades after she died. She would have been able to leave Hades with him had he not broken his pact and looked back at her.

Eurystheus ★ (juˈrɪsθjuːs, -θɪəs) *n Greek myth.* a grandson of Perseus, who, through the favour of Hera, inherited the kingship of Mycenae, which Zeus had intended for Hercules.

eurythmics (juːˈrɪðmɪks) *n* a variant spelling (esp. US) of **eurhythmics.**

Eusebio ★ (juːˈseɪbɪəu) *n* Silva Ferreira da (*Portuguese* ˈsɪlvə fəˈrrəɪrə da). born 1942, Portuguese footballer.

Eusebius ★ (juːˈsiːbɪəs) *n* ?265–?340 A.D., bishop of Caesarea: author of a history of the Christian Church to 324 A.D.

Eustachian tube (juːˈsteɪʃən) *n* a tube that connects the middle ear with the pharynx and equalizes the pressure between the two sides of the eardrum. [C18: after Bartolomeo *Eustachio,* 16th-cent. It. anatomist]

eustatic (juːˈstætɪk) *adj* denoting or relating to worldwide changes in sea level, caused by the melting of ice sheets, sedimentation, etc. [C20: from Gk, from EU- + STATIC]

eutectic (juːˈtɛktɪk) *adj* **1** (of a mixture of substances) having the lowest freezing point of all possible mixtures of the substances. **2** concerned with or suitable for the formation of eutectic mixtures. ◆ *n* **3** a eutectic mixture. **4** the temperature at which a eutectic mixture forms. [C19: from Gk *eutēktos* melting readily, from EU- + *tēkein* to melt]

Euterpe ★ (juːˈtɜːpɪ) *n Greek myth.* the Muse of lyric poetry and music.
  ▸ **Eu'terpean** *adj*

euthanasia (ˌjuːθəˈneɪzɪə) *n* the act of killing someone painlessly, esp. to relieve suffering from an incurable illness. [C17: via NL from Gk: easy death]

euthenics (juːˈθɛnɪks) *n* (*functioning as sing*) the study of the control of the environment, esp. with a view to improving the health and living standards of the human race. [C20: from Gk *euthēnein* to thrive]
  ▸ **eu'thenist** *n*

eutrophic (juːˈtrɒfɪk, -ˈtrəu-) *adj* (of lakes, etc.) rich in organic and mineral nutrients and supporting an abundant plant life. [C18: prob. from *eutrophy,* from Gk, from *eutrophos* well-fed]
  ▸ **'eutrophy** *n*

Euxine Sea ★ (ˈjuːksaɪn) *n* another name for the **Black Sea.**

eV *abbrev.* for electronvolt.

EVA *Astronautics. abbrev.* for extravehicular activity.

evacuate (ɪˈvækjuˌeɪt) *vb* **evacuates, evacuating, evacuated.** (*mainly tr*) **1** (*also intr*) to withdraw or cause to withdraw (from a place of danger) to a place of safety. **2** to make empty. **3** (*also intr*) *Physiol.* **3a** to eliminate or excrete (faeces). **3b** to discharge (any waste) from (the body). **4** (*tr*) to create a vacuum in (a bulb, flask, etc.). [C16: from L *ēvacuāre* to void, from *vacuus* empty]
  ▸ **e,vacu'ation** *n* ▸ **e'vacuative** *adj* ▸ **e'vacu,ator** *n*
  ▸ **e,vacu'ee** *n*

evade (ɪˈveɪd) *vb* **evades, evading, evaded.** (*mainly tr*) **1** to get away from or avoid (imprisonment, captors, etc.). **2** to get around, shirk, or dodge (the law, a duty, etc.). **3** (*also intr*) to avoid answering (a question). [C16: from F, from L *ēvādere* to go forth]
  ▸ **e'vadable** *adj* ▸ **e'vader** *n*

evaginate (ɪˈvædʒɪˌneɪt) *vb* **evaginates, evaginating, evaginated.** (*tr*) *Med.* to turn (an organ or part) inside out. [C17: from LL *ēvāgīnāre* to unsheathe, from L *vāgīna* sheath]

evaluate (ɪˈvæljuˌeɪt) *vb* **evaluates, evaluating, evaluated.** (*tr*) **1** to ascertain or set the amount or value of. **2** to judge or assess the worth of. [C19: back formation from *evaluation,* from F, from *évaluer;* see VALUE]
  ▸ **e,valu'ation** *n* ▸ **e'valuative** *adj* ▸ **e'valu,ator** *n*

evanesce (ˌevəˈnes) *vb* **evanesces, evanescing, evanesced.** (*intr*) (of smoke, mist, etc.) to fade gradually from sight; vanish. [C19: from L *ēvānēscere* to disappear; see VANISH]

evanescent (ˌevəˈnesᵊnt) *adj* **1** passing out of sight; fading away; vanishing. **2** ephemeral or transitory.
  ▸ **,eva'nescence** *n*

evangel (ɪˈvændʒəl) *n* **1** *Arch.* the gospel of Christianity. **2** (*often cap.*) any of the four Gospels of the New Testament. **3** any body of teachings regarded as basic. **4** *US.* an evangelist. [C14: from Church L, from Gk *evangelion* good news, from EU- + *angelos* messenger; see ANGEL]

evangelical (ˌiːvænˈdʒelɪkᵊl) *Christianity.* ◆ *adj* **1** of or following from the Gospels. **2** denoting or relating to any of certain Protestant sects, which emphasize personal conversion and faith in atonement through the death of Christ as a means of salvation. **3** denoting or relating to an evangelist. ◆ *n* **4** a member of an evangelical sect.
  ▸ **,evan'gelicalism** *n* ▸ **,evan'gelically** *adv*

evangelism (ɪˈvændʒɪˌlɪzəm) *n* **1** the practice of spreading the Christian gospel. **2** ardent or missionary zeal for a cause.

evangelist (ɪˈvændʒɪlɪst) *n* **1** an occasional preacher, sometimes itinerant. **2** a preacher of the Christian gospel.
  ▸ **e,vange'listic** *adj*

Evangelist (ɪˈvændʒɪlɪst) *n* any of the writers of the New Testament Gospels: Matthew, Mark, Luke, or John.

evangelize *or* **evangelise** (ɪˈvændʒɪˌlaɪz) *vb* **evangelizes, evangelizing, evangelized** *or* **evangelises, evangelising, evangelised.** **1** to preach the Christian gospel (to). **2** (*intr*) to advocate a cause with the object of making converts.
  ▸ **e,vangeli'zation** *or* **e,vangeli'sation** *n* ▸ **e'vange,lizer** *or* **e'vange,liser** *n*

Evans (ˈevənz) *n* **1** Sir **Arthur John.** 1851–1941, British archaeologist, whose excavations of the palace of Knossos in Crete provided evidence for the existence of the Minoan civilization. **2** Dame **Edith.** 1888–1976, British actress. **3** Sir **Geraint** (**Llewellyn**) (ˈgɛraɪnt). 1922–92, Welsh operatic baritone. **4** **Herbert McLean.** 1882–1971, US anatomist and embryologist; discoverer of vitamin E (1922).

Evanston ★ (ˈevənstən) *n* a city in NE Illinois, on Lake Michigan north of Chicago: Northwestern University (1851). Pop.: 73 233 (1990).

Evansville ★ (ˈevənzˌvɪl) *n* a city in SW Indiana, on the Ohio River. Pop.: 129 452 (1994 est.).

evaporate (ɪˈvæpəˌreɪt) *vb* **evaporates, evaporating, evaporated.** **1** to change or cause to change from a liquid or solid state to a vapour. **2** to lose or cause to lose liquid by vaporization leaving a more concentrated residue. **3** to disappear or cause to disappear. [C16: from LL, from L *vapor* steam; see VAPOUR]
  ▸ **e'vaporable** *adj* ▸ **e,vapo'ration** *n* ▸ **e'vaporative** *adj*
  ▸ **e'vapo,rator** *n*

evaporated milk *n* thick unsweetened tinned milk from which some of the water has been evaporated.

evasion (ɪˈveɪʒən) *n* **1** the act of evading, esp. a distasteful duty, responsibility, etc., by cunning or by illegal means: *tax evasion.* **2** cunning or deception used to dodge a question, duty, etc.; means of evading. [C15: from LL *ēvāsio;* see EVADE]

evasive (ɪˈveɪsɪv) *adj* **1** tending or seeking to evade; not straightforward. **2** avoiding or seeking to avoid trouble or difficulties. **3** hard to catch or obtain; elusive.
  ▸ **e'vasively** *adv* ▸ **e'vasiveness** *n*

eve (iːv) *n* **1** the evening or day before some special event. **2** the period immediately before an event: *the eve of war.* **3** an archaic word for **evening.** [C13: var. of EVEN²]

Eve ★ (iːv) *n Old Testament.* the first woman; mother of the human race, fashioned by God from the rib of Adam (Genesis 2:18-25).

Evelyn ★ (ˈiːvlɪn, ˈev-) *n* **John.** 1620–1706, English author, noted chiefly for his diary (1640–1706).

even¹ (ˈiːvᵊn) *adj* **1** level and regular; flat. **2** (*postpositive;* foll. by *with*) on the same level or in the same plane (as). **3** without variation or fluctuation; regular; constant. **4** not readily moved or excited; calm: *an even temper.* **5** equally balanced between two sides: *an even game.* **6** equal or identical in number, quantity, etc. **7a** (of a

number) divisible by two. **7b** characterized or indicated by such a number: *the even pages.* Cf. **odd** (sense 4). **8** relating to or denoting two or either of two alternatives, events, etc., that have an equal probability: *an even chance of missing or catching a train.* **9** having no balance of debt; neither owing nor being owed. **10** just and impartial; fair. **11** exact in number, amount, or extent: *an even pound.* **12** equal, as in score; level. **13 even money. 13a** a bet in which the winnings are the same as the amount staked. **13b** (*as modifier*): *the even-money favourite.* **14 get even** (**with**). *Inf.* to exact revenge (on); settle accounts (with). ◆ *adv* **15** (intensifier; used to suggest that the content of a statement is unexpected or paradoxical): *even an idiot can do that.* **16** (intensifier; used with comparative forms): *even better.* **17** notwithstanding; in spite of. **18** used to introduce a more precise version of a word, phrase, or statement: *he is base, even depraved.* **19** used preceding a clause of supposition or hypothesis to emphasize that whether or not the condition in it is fulfilled, the statement in the main clause remains valid: *even if she died he wouldn't care.* **20** *Arch.* all the way; fully: *I love thee even unto death.* **21 even as.** (*conj*) at the very same moment or in the very same way that. **22 even so.** in spite of any assertion to the contrary: nevertheless. ◆ See also **even out, evens, even up.** [OE *efen*]
▸ **'evener** *n* ▸ **'evenly** *adv* ▸ **'evenness** *n*

even² ('iːvᵊn) *n* an archaic word for **eve** or **evening.** [OE *æfen*]

even-handed *adj* fair; impartial.
▸ ,even-'handedly *adv* ▸ ,even-'handedness *n*

evening ('iːvnɪŋ) *n* **1** the latter part of the day, esp. from late afternoon until nightfall. **2** the latter or concluding period: *the evening of one's life.* **3** the early part of the night spent in a specified way: *an evening at the theatre.* **4** (*modifier*) of, used in, or occurring in the evening: *the evening papers.* [OE *æfnung*]

evening dress *n* attire for a formal occasion during the evening.

evening primrose *n* any plant of the genus *Oenothera,* typically having yellow flowers that open in the evening.

evening primrose oil *n* an oil, obtained from the seeds of the evening primrose, that is claimed to stimulate the production of prostaglandins.

evenings ('iːvnɪŋz) *adv Inf.* in the evening, esp. regularly.

evening star *n* a planet, usually Venus, seen just after sunset during the time that the planet is east of the sun.

even out *vb* (*adv*) to make or become even, as by the removal of bumps, inequalities, etc.

evens ('iːvənz) *adj, adv* **1** (of a bet) winning the same as the amount staked if successful. **2** (of a runner) offered at such odds.

evensong ('iːvᵊn,sɒŋ) *n* **1** Also called: **Evening Prayer, vespers.** *Church of England.* the daily evening service. **2** *RC Church, arch.* another name for **vespers.**

event (ɪ'vɛnt) *n* **1** anything that takes place, esp. something important; an incident. **2** the actual or final outcome (esp. in **in the event, after the event**). **3** any one contest in a programme of sporting or other contests. **4 in any event** *or* **at all events.** regardless of circumstances; in any case. **5 in the event of.** in case of; if (such a thing) happens. **6 in the event that.** if it should happen that. [C16: from L *ēvenīre* to come forth, happen]

even-tempered *adj* not easily angered or excited; calm.

eventful (ɪ'vɛntfʊl) *adj* full of events.
▸ e'ventfully *adv* ▸ e'ventfulness *n*

event horizon *n Astron.* the spherical boundary of a black hole: objects passing through it would disappear completely and for ever, as no information can escape across the event horizon from the interior.

eventide ('iːvᵊn,taɪd) *n Arch. or poetic.* another word for **evening.**

eventide home *n Euphemistic.* an old people's home.

eventing (ɪ'vɛntɪŋ) *n Chiefly Brit.* taking part in equestrian competitions (esp. **three-day events**), usually involving cross-country riding, jumping, and dressage.

eventual (ɪ'vɛntʃʊəl) *adj* **1** (*prenominal*) happening in due course of time; ultimate. **2** *Arch.* contingent or possible.

eventuality (ɪ,vɛntʃʊ'ælɪtɪ) *n, pl* **eventualities.** a possible event, occurrence, or result; contingency.

eventually (ɪ'vɛntʃʊəlɪ) *adv* **1** at the very end; finally. **2** (*sentence modifier*) after a long time or long delay: *eventually, he arrived.*

eventuate (ɪ'vɛntʃʊ,eɪt) *vb* **eventuates, eventuating, eventuated.** (*intr*) **1** (often foll. by *in*) to result ultimately (in). **2** to come about as a result.
▸ e,ventu'ation *n*

even up *vb* (*adv*) to make or become equal, esp. in respect of claims or debts.

ever ('ɛvə) *adv* **1** at any time. **2** by any chance; in any case: *how did you ever find out?* **3** at all times; always. **4** in any possible way or manner: *come as fast as ever you can.* **5** *Inf., chiefly Brit.* (intensifier, in **ever so, ever such, ever such a**). **6 is he** *or* **she ever!** *US & Canad. sl.* he *or* she displays the quality concerned in abundance. ◆ See also **forever.** [OE *æfre,* from ?]

Everest ★ ('ɛvərɪst) *n* **1 Mount.** a mountain in S Asia on the border between Nepal and Tibet, in the Himalayas: the highest mountain in the world; first climbed by a British expedition (1953). Height: 8848 m (29 028 ft). **2** any high point of ambition or achievement. [C19: after Sir G. *Everest* (1790–1866), Surveyor-General of India]

Everglades ★ ('ɛvə,gleɪdz) *pl n* **the.** a subtropical marshy region of Florida, south of Lake Okeechobee: contains the **Everglades National Park,** established to preserve the flora and fauna of the swamps. Area: over 13 000 sq. km (5000 sq. miles).

evergreen ('ɛvə,griːn) *adj* **1** (of certain trees and shrubs) bearing foliage throughout the year. Cf. **deciduous.** **2** remaining fresh and vital. ◆ *n* **3** an evergreen tree or shrub.

evergreen fund *n* a fund that provides capital for new companies and makes regular injections of capital to support their development.

everlasting (,ɛvə'lɑːstɪŋ) *adj* **1** never coming to an end; eternal. **2** lasting for an indefinitely long period. **3** lasting so long or occurring so often as to become tedious. ◆ *n* **4** eternity. **5** Also called: **everlasting flower.** another name for **immortelle.**
▸ ,ever'lastingly *adv*

evermore (,ɛvə'mɔː) *adv* (often preceded by *for*) all time to come.

evert (ɪ'vɜːt) *vb* (*tr*) to turn (an eyelid or other bodily part) outwards or inside out. [C16: from L *ēvertere* to overthrow, from *vertere* to turn]
▸ e'versible *adj* ▸ e'version *n*

Evert ★ ('ɛvət) *n* **Chris(tine).** born 1954, US tennis player: Wimbledon champion 1974, 1976, and 1981; US champion 1975–78, 1980, and 1982.

every ('ɛvrɪ) *determiner* **1** each one (of the class specified), without exception. **2** (*not used with a negative*) the greatest or best possible: *every hope.* **3** each: used before a noun phrase to indicate the recurrent, intermittent, or serial nature of a thing: *every third day.* **4 every bit.** (used in comparisons with *as*) quite; just; equally. **5 every second.** each alternate; every second. **6 every which way.** *US & Canad.* **6a** in all directions; everywhere. **6b** from all sides. [C15 *everich,* from OE *æfre ælc,* from *æfre* EVER + *ælc* EACH]

everybody ('ɛvrɪ,bɒdɪ) *pron* every person; everyone.

USAGE NOTE See at **everyone.**

everyday ('ɛvrɪ,deɪ) *adj* **1** happening each day. **2** commonplace or usual. **3** suitable for or used on ordinary days.

Everyman ('ɛvrɪ,mæn) *n* **1** a medieval English morality play in which the central figure represents mankind. **2** (*often not cap.*) the ordinary person; common man.

everyone ('ɛvrɪ,wʌn, -wən) *pron* every person; everybody.

USAGE NOTE *Everyone* and *everybody* are interchangeable, as are *no one* and *nobody,* and some-

one and *somebody*. Care should be taken to distinguish between *everyone* and *someone* as single words and *every one* and *some one* as two words, the latter form correctly being used to refer to each individual person or thing in a particular group: *every one of them is wrong*.

every one *pron* each person or thing in a group, without exception.

everything ('εντιˌθɪŋ) *pron* **1** the entirety of a specified or implied class. **2** a great deal, esp. of something very important.

everywhere ('εντιˌwεə) *adv* to or in all parts or places.

Evesham ★ ('iːvʃəm) *n* a town in W central England, in E Hereford and Worcester, on the River Avon: scene of the Battle of Evesham in 1265 (Lord Edward's defeat of Simon de Montfort and the barons); centre of the **Vale of Evesham**, famous for market gardens and orchards. Pop.: 17 823 (1991).

evict (ɪ'vɪkt) *vb* (*tr*) **1** to expel (a tenant) from property by process of law; turn out. **2** to recover (property or the title to property) by judicial process or by virtue of a superior title. [C15: from LL *ēvincere*, from L: to vanquish utterly]
  ▶ e'viction *n* ▶ e'victor *n*

evidence ('εvɪdəns) *n* **1** ground for belief or disbelief; data on which to base proof or to establish truth or falsehood. **2** a mark or sign that makes evident. **3** *Law.* matter produced before a court of law in an attempt to prove or disprove a point in issue. **4 in evidence.** on display; apparent. ◆ *vb* **evidences, evidencing, evidenced.** (*tr*) **5** to make evident; show clearly. **6** to give proof of or evidence for.

evident ('εvɪdənt) *adj* easy to see or understand; apparent. [C14: from L *ēvidēns*, from *vidēre* to see]

evidential (ˌεvɪ'dεnʃəl) *adj* relating to, serving as, or based on evidence.
  ▶ ˌevi'dentially *adv*

evidently ('εvɪdəntlɪ) *adv* **1** without question; clearly. **2** to all appearances; apparently.

evil ('iːvªl) *adj* **1** morally wrong or bad; wicked. **2** causing harm or injury. **3** marked or accompanied by misfortune: *an evil fate*. **4** (of temper, disposition, etc.) characterized by anger or spite. **5** infamous: *an evil reputation*. **6** offensive or unpleasant: *an evil smell*. **7** *Sl.*, *chiefly US.* excellent or outstanding. ◆ *n* **8** the quality or an instance of being morally wrong; wickedness. **9** (*sometimes cap.*) a force or power that brings about wickedness or harm. ◆ *adv* **10** (*now usually in combination*) in an evil manner; badly: *evil-smelling*. [OE *yfel*]
  ▶ 'evilly *adv* ▶ 'evilness *n*

evildoer ('iːvªlˌduːə) *n* a person who does evil.
  ▶ 'evilˌdoing *n*

evil eye *n* **the. 1** a look or glance superstitiously supposed to have the power of inflicting harm or injury. **2** the power to inflict harm, etc., by such a look.
  ▶ ˌevil-'eyed *adj*

evil-minded *adj* inclined to evil thoughts; malicious or spiteful.
  ▶ ˌevil-'mindedly *adv* ▶ ˌevil-'mindedness *n*

evince (ɪ'vɪns) *vb* **evinces, evincing, evinced.** (*tr*) to make evident; show (something) clearly. [C17: from L *ēvincere* to overcome; see EVICT]
  ▶ e'vincible *adj*.

> **USAGE NOTE**   *Evince* is sometimes wrongly used where *evoke* is meant: *the proposal evoked* (not *evinced*) *a storm of protest*.

eviscerate (ɪ'vɪsəˌreɪt) *vb* **eviscerates, eviscerating, eviscerated.** (*tr*) **1** to remove the internal organs of; disembowel. **2** to deprive of meaning or significance. [C17: from L *ēviscerāre*, from *viscera* entrails]
  ▶ eˌviscer'ation *n* ▶ e'vis|cerˌator *n*

evocation (ˌεvə'keɪʃən) *n* the act or an instance of evoking. [C17: from L: see EVOKE]
  ▶ **evocative** (ɪ'vɒkətɪv) *adj*

evoke (ɪ'vəuk) *vb* **evokes, evoking, evoked.** (*tr*) **1** to call or summon up (a memory, feeling, etc.), esp. from the past. **2** to provoke; elicit. **3** to cause (spirits) to appear; conjure up. [C17: from L *ēvocāre* to call forth, from *vocāre* to call]
  ▶ **evocable** ('εvəkəbªl) *adj* ▶ e'voker *n*

> **USAGE NOTE**   See at **evince** and **invoke**.

evolute ('εvəˌluːt) *n* **1** a geometric curve that describes the locus of the centres of curvature of another curve (the **involute**). ◆ *adj* **2** *Biol.* having the margins rolled outwards. [C19: from L *ēvolūtus* unrolled, from *ēvolvere* to roll out, EVOLVE]

evolution (ˌiːvə'luːʃən) *n* **1** *Biol.* a gradual change in the characteristics of a population of animals or plants over successive generations. **2** a gradual development, esp. to a more complex form: *the evolution of modern art*. **3** the act of throwing off, as heat, gas, vapour, etc. **4** a pattern formed by a series of movements or something similar. **5** an algebraic operation in which the root of a number, expression, etc., is extracted. **6** *Mil.* an exercise carried out in accordance with a set procedure or plan. [C17: from L *ēvolūtiō* unrolling, from *ēvolvere* to EVOLVE]
  ▶ ˌevo'lutionary *or* ˌevo'lutional *adj*

evolutionist (ˌiːvə'luːʃənɪst) *n* **1** a person who believes in a theory of evolution. ◆ *adj* **2** of or relating to a theory of evolution.
  ▶ ˌevo'lutionism *n* ▶ ˌevolution'istic *adj*

evolve (ɪ'vɒlv) *vb* **evolves, evolving, evolved. 1** to develop or cause to develop gradually. **2** (of animal or plant species) to undergo evolution of (organs or parts). **3** (*tr*) to yield, emit, or give off (heat, gas, vapour, etc.). [C17: from L *ēvolvere* to unfold, from *volvere* to roll]
  ▶ e'volvable *adj* ▶ e'volvement *n*

Évora ★ (*Portuguese* 'εvura) *n* a city in S central Portugal: ancient Roman settlement; occupied by the Moors from 712 to 1166; residence of the Portuguese court in 15th and 16th centuries. Pop.: 34 100 (latest est.). Ancient name: **Ebora** ('iːbərə).

Évreux ★ (*French* evrø) *n* an industrial town in NW France: severely damaged in World War II; cathedral (12th–16th centuries). Pop.: 51 450 (1990).

Évros ★ ('εvrɒs) *n* transliteration of the Modern Greek name for the **Maritsa**.

Évvoia ★ ('εvia) *n* transliteration of the Modern Greek name for **Euboea**.

evzone ('εvzəun) *n* a soldier in an elite Greek infantry regiment. [C19: from Mod. Gk, from Gk *euzōnos*, lit.: well-girt, from EU- + *zōne* girdle]

ewe (juː) *n* **a** a female sheep. **b** (*as modifier*): *a ewe lamb*. [OE *ēowu*]

ewer ('juːə) *n* a large jug or pitcher with a wide mouth. [C14: from OF *evier*, from L *aquārius* water carrier, from *aqua* water]

ex[1] (εks) *prep* **1** *Finance.* excluding; without: *ex dividend*. **2** *Commerce.* without charge to the buyer until removed from: *ex warehouse*. [C19: from L: out of, from]

ex[2] (εks) *n* *Inf.* (a person's) former wife, husband, etc.

Ex. *Bible. abbrev.* for Exodus.

ex-[1] *prefix* **1** out of; outside of; from: *exclosure*; *exurbia*. **2** former: *ex-wife*. [from L, from *ex* (prep), identical with Gk *ex, ek*; see EC-]

ex-[2] *combining form.* a variant of **exo-** before a vowel: *exergonic*.

exa- *prefix* denoting 10^{18}: *exametres*. Symbol: E

exacerbate (ɪg'zæsəˌbeɪt, ɪk'sæs-) *vb* **exacerbates, exacerbating, exacerbated.** (*tr*) **1** to make (pain, disease, etc.) more intense; aggravate. **2** to irritate (a person). [C17: from L *exacerbāre* to irritate, from *acerbus* bitter]
  ▶ exˌacer'bation *n*

exact (ɪg'zækt) *adj* **1** correct in every detail; strictly accurate. **2** precise, as opposed to approximate. **3** (*prenominal*

specific; particular. **4** operating with very great precision. **5** allowing no deviation from a standard; rigorous; strict. **6** based on measurement and the formulation of laws, as opposed to description and classification: *an exact science.* ◆ *vb* (*tr*) **7** to force or compel (payment, etc.); extort: *to exact tribute.* **8** to demand as a right; insist upon. **9** to call for or require. [C16: from L *exactus* driven out, from *exigere* to drive forth, from *agere* to drive]
▶ ex'actable *adj* ▶ ex'actness *n* ▶ ex'actor *or* ex'acter *n*

exacting (ɪɡ'zæktɪŋ) *adj* making rigorous or excessive demands.
▶ ex'actingness *n*

exaction (ɪɡ'zækʃən) *n* **1** the act or an instance of exacting. **2** an excessive or harsh demand, esp. for money. **3** a sum or payment exacted.

exactitude (ɪɡ'zæktɪˌtjuːd) *n* the quality of being exact; precision; accuracy.

exactly (ɪɡ'zæktlɪ) *adv* **1** in an exact manner; accurately or precisely. **2** in every respect; just. ◆ *sentence substitute.* **3** just so!, precisely! **4 not exactly.** *Ironical.* not at all; by no means.

exacum ('ɛksəkəm) *n* any of various Asian flowering herbs. [NL, from EX-[1] + Gk *ago* to arrive]

exaggerate (ɪɡ'zædʒəˌreɪt) *vb* **exaggerates, exaggerating, exaggerated. 1** to regard or represent as larger or greater, more important or more successful, etc., than is true. **2** (*tr*) to make greater, more noticeable, etc. [C16: from L *exaggerāre* to magnify, from *aggerāre* to heap, from *agger* heap]
▶ ex'agger,ated *adj* ▶ ex,agger'ation *n* ▶ ex'agger,ator *n*

ex all *adv, adj Finance.* without the right to any benefits: *shares quoted ex all.*

exalt (ɪɡ'zɔːlt) *vb* (*tr*) **1** to elevate in rank, dignity, etc. **2** to praise highly; extol. **3** to stimulate; excite. **4** to fill with joy or delight; elate. [C15: from L *exaltāre* to raise, from *altus* high]
▶ ex'alted *adj* ▶ ex'alter *n*

> **USAGE NOTE** *Exalt* is sometimes wrongly used where *exult* is meant: *he was exulting* (not *exalting*) *in his win earlier that day.*

exaltation (ˌɛɡzɔːl'teɪʃən) *n* **1** the act of exalting or state of being exalted. **2** exhilaration; elation; rapture.

exam (ɪɡ'zæm) *n* short for **examination.**

examination (ɪɡˌzæmɪ'neɪʃən) *n* **1** the act of examining or state of being examined. **2** *Education.* **2a** written exercises, oral questions, etc., set to test a candidate's knowledge and skill. **2b** (*as modifier*): *an examination paper.* **3** *Med.* **3a** physical inspection of a patient. **3b** laboratory study of secretory or excretory products, tissue samples, etc. **4** *Law.* the formal interrogation of a person on oath.
▶ ex,ami'national *adj*

examine (ɪɡ'zæmɪn) *vb* **examines, examining, examined.** (*tr*) **1** to inspect or scrutinize carefully or in detail; investigate. **2** *Education.* to test the knowledge or skill of (a candidate) in (a subject or activity) by written or oral questions, etc. **3** *Law.* to interrogate (a person) formally on oath. **4** *Med.* to investigate the state of health of (a patient). [C14: from OF, from L *exāmināre* to weigh, from *exāmen* means of weighing]
▶ ex'aminable *adj* ▶ ex,ami'nee *n* ▶ ex'aminer *n* ▶ ex-'amining *adj*

example (ɪɡ'zɑːmpᵊl) *n* **1** a specimen or instance that is typical of its group or set; sample. **2** a person, action, thing, etc., that is worthy of imitation; pattern. **3** a precedent, illustration of a principle, or model. **4** a punishment or the recipient of a punishment intended to serve as a warning. **5 for example.** as an illustration; for instance. ◆ *vb* examples, exampling, exampled. **6** (*tr; now usually passive*) to present an example of; exemplify. [C14: from OF, from L *exemplum* pattern, from *eximere* to take out]

exanthema (ˌɛksæn'θiːmə) *n, pl* **exanthemata** (-'θiːmətə) *or* **exanthemas.** a skin rash occurring in a disease such as

measles. [C17: via LL from Gk, from *exanthein* to burst forth, from *anthein* to blossom]

exasperate (ɪɡ'zɑːspəˌreɪt) *vb* **exasperates, exasperating, exasperated.** (*tr*) **1** to cause great irritation or anger to. **2** to cause (something unpleasant) to worsen; aggravate. [C16: from L *exasperāre* to make rough, from *asper* rough]
▶ ex'asper,atedly *adv* ▶ ex'asper,atingly *adv* ▶ ex,asper-'ation *n*

ex cathedra (ɛks kə'θiːdrə) *adj, adv* **1** with authority. **2** *RC Church.* (of doctrines of faith or morals) defined by the pope as infallibly true, to be accepted by all Catholics. [L, lit.: from the chair]

excavate ('ɛkskəˌveɪt) *vb* **excavates, excavating, excavated. 1** to remove (soil, earth, etc.) by digging; dig out. **2** to make (a hole or tunnel) in (solid matter) by hollowing. **3** to unearth (buried objects) methodically to discover information about the past. [C16: from L *cavāre* to make hollow, from *cavus* hollow]
▶ ,exca'vation *n* ▶ 'exca,vator *n*

exceed (ɪk'siːd) *vb* **1** to be superior (to); excel. **2** (*tr*) to go beyond the limit or bounds of. **3** (*tr*) to be greater in degree or quantity than. [C14: from L *excēdere* to go beyond]
▶ ex'ceedable *adj* ▶ ex'ceeder *n*

exceeding (ɪk'siːdɪŋ) *adj* **1** very great; exceptional or excessive. ◆ *adv* **2** *Arch.* to a great or unusual degree.
▶ ex'ceedingly *adv*

excel (ɪk'sɛl) *vb* **excels, excelling, excelled. 1** to be superior to (another or others); surpass. **2** (*intr;* foll. by *in* or *at*) to be outstandingly good or proficient. [C15: from L *excellere* to rise up]

excellence ('ɛksələns) *n* **1** the state or quality of excelling or being exceptionally good; extreme merit. **2** an action, feature, etc., in which a person excels.
▶ 'excellent *adj* ▶ 'excellently *adv*

Excellency ('ɛksələnsɪ) *or* **Excellence** *n, pl* **Excellencies** *or* **Excellences. 1** (usually preceded by *Your, His,* or *Her*) a title used to address or refer to a high-ranking official, such as an ambassador. **2** *RC Church.* a title of bishops and archbishops in many non-English-speaking countries.

excelsior (ɪk'sɛlsɪˌɔː) *interj, n* **1** excellent: used as a motto and as a trademark for various products. **2** upward. [C19: from L: higher]

except (ɪk'sɛpt) *prep* **1** Also: **except for.** other than; apart from. **2 except that.** (*conj*) but for the fact that; were it not true that. ◆ *conj* **3** an archaic word for **unless. 4** *Inf.* (*not standard in the US*) except that; but for the fact that. ◆ *vb* **5** (*tr*) to leave out; omit; exclude. **6** (*intr;* often foll. by *to*) *Rare.* to take exception; object. [C14: from OF *excepter* to leave out, from L *excipere* to take out]

excepting (ɪk'sɛptɪŋ) *prep* **1** except; except for (esp. in **not excepting**). ◆ *conj* **2** an archaic word for **unless.**

> **USAGE NOTE** The use of *excepting* is considered by many people to be acceptable only after *not, only, always,* or *without.* Elsewhere *except* is preferred: *every country agreed to the proposal except* (not *excepting*) *Spain; he was well again except for* (not *excepting*) *a slight pain in his chest.*

exception (ɪk'sɛpʃən) *n* **1** the act of excepting or fact of being excepted; omission. **2** anything excluded from or not in conformance with a general rule, principle, class, etc. **3** criticism, esp. adverse; objection. **4** *Law.* (formerly) a formal objection in legal proceedings. **5 take exception. 5a** (usually foll. by *to*) to make objections (to); demur (at). **5b** (often foll. by *at*) to be offended (by); be resentful (at).

exceptionable (ɪk'sɛpʃənəbᵊl) *adj* open to or subject to objection; objectionable.
▶ ex'ceptionableness *n* ▶ ex'ceptionably *adv*

exceptional (ɪk'sɛpʃənᵊl) *adj* **1** forming an exception; not ordinary. **2** having much more than average intelligence, ability, or skill.

excerpt *n* ('ɛksɜːpt). **1** a part or passage taken from a

book, speech, etc.; extract. ◆ vb (εk'sɜːpt). **2** (tr) to take (a part or passage) from a book, speech, etc. [C17: from L *excerptum*, lit.: (something) picked out, from *excerpere* to select, from *carpere* to pluck]
► **ex'cerptible** adj ► **ex'cerption** n ► **ex'cerptor** n

excess n (ık'sɛs, 'ɛksɛs). **1** the state or act of going beyond normal, sufficient, or permitted limits. **2** an immoderate or abnormal amount. **3** the amount, number, etc., by which one thing exceeds another. **4** overindulgence or intemperance. **5** *Insurance, chiefly Brit.* a specified contribution towards the cost of a claim, payable by the policyholder. US name: **deductible. 6 in excess of.** of more than; over. **7 to excess.** to an inordinate extent; immoderately. ◆ adj ('ɛksɛs, ık'sɛs). (*usually prenominal*) **8** more than normal, necessary, or permitted; surplus: *excess weight.* **9** payable as a result of previous underpayment: *excess postage.* [C14: from L *excēdere* to go beyond; see EX-CEED]

excessive (ık'sɛsıv) adj exceeding the normal or permitted limits; immoderate; inordinate.
► **ex'cessively** adv ► **ex'cessiveness** n

excess luggage *or* **baggage** n luggage that is more in weight or number of pieces than an airline, etc., will carry free.

exchange (ıks'tʃeındʒ) vb **exchanges, exchanging, exchanged. 1** (tr) to give up or transfer (one thing) for an equivalent. **2** (tr) to give and receive (information, ideas, etc.); interchange. **3** (tr) to replace (one thing) with another, esp. to replace unsatisfactory goods. **4** to hand over (goods) in return for the equivalent value in kind; barter; trade. ◆ n **5** the act or process of exchanging. **6a** anything given or received as an equivalent or substitute for something else. **6b** (*as modifier*): *an exchange student.* **7** an argument or quarrel. **8** Also called: **telephone exchange.** a switching centre in which telephone lines are interconnected. **9** a place where securities or commodities are sold, bought, or traded, esp. by brokers or merchants. **10a** the system by which commercial debts are settled by commercial documents, esp. bills of exchange, instead of by direct payment of money. **10b** the percentage or fee charged for accepting payment in this manner. **11** a transfer or interchange of sums of money of equivalent value, as between different currencies. **12 win** (*or* **lose**) **the exchange.** *Chess.* to win (or lose) a rook in return for a bishop or knight. ◆ See also **bill of exchange, exchange rate, labour exchange.** [C14: from Anglo-French *eschaungier*, from Vulgar L *excambiāre* (unattested), from L *cambīre* to barter]
► **ex'changeable** adj ► **ex,changea'bility** n ► **ex'changeably** adv ► **ex'changer** n

exchange rate n the rate at which the currency unit of one country may be exchanged for that of another.

Exchange Rate Mechanism n the mechanism used in the European Monetary System in which participating governments commit themselves to maintain the values of their currencies in relation to the ECU. Abbrev.: **ERM.**

exchequer (ıks'tʃɛkə) n **1** (*often cap.*) *Government.* (in Britain and certain other countries) the accounting department of the Treasury. **2** *Inf.* personal funds; finances. [C13 (in the sense: chessboard, counting table): from OF *eschequier*, from *eschec* CHECK]

excisable (ık'saızəbᵊl) adj **1** liable to an excise tax. **2** suitable for deletion.

excise[1] n ('ɛksaız, ɛk'saız). **1** Also called: **excise tax.** a tax on goods, such as spirits, produced for the home market. **2** a tax paid for a licence to carry out various trades, sports, etc. **3** *Brit.* that section of the government service responsible for the collection of excise, now the Board of Customs and Excise. ◆ vb (ık'saız), **excises, excising, excised. 4** (tr) *Rare.* to compel (a person) to pay excise. [C15: prob. from MDu. *excijs*, prob. from OF *assise* a sitting, assessment, from L *assidēre* to sit beside, assist in judging]
► **ex'cisable** adj

excise[2] (ık'saız) vb **excises, excising, excised.** (tr) **1** to delete (a passage, sentence, etc.). **2** to remove (an organ or part) surgically. [C16: from L *excīdere* to cut down]
► **excision** (ık'sıʒən) n

exciseman ('ɛksaız,mæn) n, pl **excisemen.** *Brit.* (formerly) a government agent whose function was to collect excise and prevent smuggling.

excitable (ık'saıtəbᵊl) adj **1** easily excited; volatile. **2** (esp. of a nerve) ready to respond to a stimulus.
► **ex,cita'bility** *or* **ex'citableness** n

excitation (,ɛksı'teıʃən) n **1** the act or process of exciting or state of being excited. **2** a means of exciting or cause of excitement. **3** the current in a field coil of a generator, motor, etc., or the magnetizing current in a transformer. **4** the action of a stimulus on an animal or plant organ, inducing it to respond.

excite (ık'saıt) vb **excites, exciting, excited.** (tr) **1** to arouse (a person), esp. to pleasurable anticipation or nervous agitation. **2** to arouse or elicit (an emotion, response, etc.); evoke. **3** to cause or bring about; stir up. **4** to arouse sexually. **5** *Physiol.* to cause a response in or increase the activity of (an organ, tissue, or part); stimulate. **6** to raise (an atom, molecule, etc.) from the ground state to a higher energy level. **7** to supply electricity to (the coils of a generator or motor) in order to create a magnetic field. [C14: from L *excière* to stimulate, from *ciēre* to set in motion, rouse]
► **ex'citant** n ► **ex'citative** *or* **ex'citatory** adj ► **ex'citer** n ► **ex'citor** n

excited (ık'saıtıd) adj **1** emotionally aroused, esp. to pleasure or agitation. **2** characterized by excitement. **3** sexually aroused. **4** (of an atom, molecule, etc.) having an energy level above the ground state.
► **ex'citedness** n

excitement (ık'saıtmənt) n **1** the state of being excited. **2** a person or thing that excites.

exciting (ık'saıtıŋ) adj causing excitement; stirring; stimulating.
► **ex'citingly** adv

exclaim (ık'skleım) vb to cry out or speak suddenly or excitedly, as from surprise, delight, horror, etc. [C16: from L *exclāmāre*, from *clāmāre* to shout]
► **ex'claimer** n

exclamation (,ɛksklə'meıʃən) n **1** an abrupt or excited cry or utterance; ejaculation. **2** the act of exclaiming.
► **,excla'mational** adj ► **ex'clamatory** adj

exclamation mark *or US* **point** n **1** the punctuation mark ! used after exclamations and vehement commands. **2** this mark used for any other purpose, as to draw attention to an obvious mistake, in road warning signs, etc.

exclave ('ɛkskleıv) n a part of a country entirely surrounded by foreign territory: viewed from the position of the home country. [C20: from EX-[1] + *-clave*, on the model of ENCLAVE]

exclosure (ık'skləuʒə) n an area of land fenced round to keep out unwanted animals.

exclude (ık'sklu:d) vb **excludes, excluding, excluded.** (tr) **1** to keep out; prevent from entering. **2** to reject or not consider; leave out. **3** to expel forcibly; eject. [C14: from L *exclūdere*, from *claudere* to shut]
► **ex'cludable** *or* **ex'cludible** adj ► **ex'cluder** n

exclusion (ık'sklu:ʒən) n the act or an instance of excluding or the state of being excluded.
► **ex'clusionary** adj

exclusion principle n See **Pauli exclusion principle.**

exclusive (ık'sklu:sıv) adj **1** excluding all else; rejecting other considerations, events, etc. **2** belonging to a particular individual or group and to no other; not shared. **3** belonging to or catering for a privileged minority, esp. a fashionable clique. **4** (*postpositive;* foll. by *to*) limited (to); found only (in). **5** single; unique; only. **6** separate and incompatible. **7** (*immediately postpositive*) not including the numbers, dates, letters, etc., mentioned. **8** (*postpositive;* foll. by *of*) except (for); not taking account (of). **9** *Logic.* (of a disjunction) true if only one rather than both of its component propositions is true. ◆ n **10** an exclusive story: a story reported in only one newspaper.
► **ex'clusively** adv ► **exclusivity** (,ɛksklu:'sıvıtı) *or* **ex'clusiveness** n

exclusive OR circuit *or* **gate** n *Electronics.* a computer logic circuit having two or more input wires and one output wire and giving a high-voltage output signal if a low-voltage signal is fed to one or more, but not all, of the input wires. Cf. **OR circuit**.

xcommunicate *RC Church.* ◆ *vb* (ˌɛkskəˈmjuːnɪˌkeɪt), **excommunicates, excommunicating, excommunicated. 1** (*tr*) to sentence (a member of the Church) to exclusion from the communion of believers and from the privileges and public prayers of the Church. ◆ *adj* (ˌɛkskəˈmjuːnɪkɪt, -ˌkeɪt). **2** having incurred such a sentence. ◆ *n* (ˌɛkskəˈmjuːnɪkɪt, -ˌkeɪt). **3** an excommunicated person. [C15: from LL *excommūnicāre*, lit.: to exclude from the community, from L *commūnis* COMMON]
▸ ˌexcomˌmuniˈcation *n* ▸ ˌexcomˈmuniˌcator *n*

xcoriate (ɪkˈskɔːrɪˌeɪt) *vb* **excoriates, excoriating, excoriated.** (*tr*) **1** to strip the skin from (a person or animal). **2** to denounce vehemently. [C15: from LL *excoriāre* to strip, flay, from L *corium* skin, hide]
▸ exˌcoriˈation *n*

xcrement (ˈɛkskrɪmənt) *n* waste matter discharged from the body, esp. faeces; excreta. [C16: from L *excernere* to sift, EXCRETE]
▸ **excremental** (ˌɛkskrɪˈmɛntᵊl) *or* **excrementitious** (ˌɛkskrɪmɛnˈtɪʃəs) *adj*

xcrescence (ɪkˈskrɛsᵊns) *n* a projection or protuberance, esp. an outgrowth from an organ or part of the body.
▸ exˈcrescent *adj* ▸ excrescential (ˌɛkskrɪˈsɛnʃəl) *adj*

xcreta (ɪkˈskriːtə) *pl n* waste matter, such as urine, faeces, or sweat, discharged from the body. [C19: NL, from L: see EXCRETE]
▸ exˈcretal *adj*

xcrete (ɪkˈskriːt) *vb* **excretes, excreting, excreted. 1** to discharge (waste matter, such as urine, sweat, or faeces) from the body. **2** (of plants) to eliminate (waste matter) through the leaves, roots, etc. [C17: from L *excernere* to separate, discharge, from *cernere* to sift]
▸ exˈcreter *n* ▸ exˈcretion *n* ▸ exˈcretive *or* exˈcretory *adj*

xcruciate (ɪkˈskruːʃɪˌeɪt) *vb* **excruciates, excruciating, excruciated.** (*tr*) to inflict mental suffering on; torment. [C16: from L *excruciāre*, from *cruciāre* to crucify, from *crux* cross]

xcruciating (ɪkˈskruːʃɪˌeɪtɪŋ) *adj* **1** unbearably painful; agonizing. **2** intense; extreme. **3** *Inf.* irritating; trying. **4** *Humorous.* very bad: *an excruciating pun.*
▸ exˈcruciatingly *adv*

xculpate (ˈɛkskʌlˌpeɪt, ɪkˈskʌlpeɪt) *vb* **exculpates, exculpating, exculpated.** (*tr*) to free from blame or guilt; vindicate or exonerate. [C17: from Med. L, from L EX-¹ + *culpa* fault, blame]
▸ ˌexculˈpation *n* ▸ exˈculpatory *adj*

xcursion (ɪkˈskɜːʃən, -ʒən) *n* **1** a short outward and return journey, esp. for sightseeing, etc.; outing. **2** a group going on such a journey. **3** (*modifier*) of or relating to reduced rates offered on certain journeys by rail: *an excursion ticket.* **4** a digression or deviation; diversion. **5** (formerly) a raid or attack. [C16: from L *excursiō* an attack, from *excurrere* to run out, from *currere* to run]
▸ exˈcursionist *n*

xcursive (ɪkˈskɜːsɪv) *adj* **1** tending to digress. **2** involving detours; rambling. [C17: from L *excursus*, from *excurrere* to run forth]
▸ exˈcursively *adv* ▸ exˈcursiveness *n*

xcuse *vb* (ɪkˈskjuːz), **excuses, excusing, excused.** (*tr*) **1** to pardon or forgive. **2** to seek pardon or exemption for (a person, esp. oneself). **3** to make allowances for: *to excuse someone's ignorance.* **4** to serve as an apology or explanation for; justify: *her age excuses her.* **5** to exempt from a task, obligation, etc. **6** to dismiss or allow to leave. **7** to seek permission for (someone, esp. oneself) to leave. **8 be excused.** *Euphemistic.* to go to the lavatory. **9 excuse me!** an expression used to catch someone's attention or to apologize for an interruption, disagreement, etc. ◆ *n* (ɪkˈskjuːs). **10** an explanation offered in defence of some fault or as a reason for not fulfilling an obligation, etc. **11** *Inf.* an inferior example of something; makeshift substitute: *she is a poor excuse for a hostess.* **12** the act of excusing. [C13: from L, from EX-¹ + *causa* cause, accusation]
▸ exˈcusable *adj* ▸ exˈcusableness *n* ▸ exˈcusably *adv*

excuse-me *n* a dance in which a person may take another's partner.

ex-directory *adj Chiefly Brit.* not listed in a telephone directory, by request, and not disclosed to inquirers.

ex dividend *adj, adv* without the right to the current dividend: *to quote shares ex dividend.*

exeat (ˈɛksɪˌat) *n Brit.* **1** leave of absence from school or some other institution. **2** a bishop's permission for a priest to leave his diocese in order to take up an appointment elsewhere. [C18: L, lit.: he may go out, from *exīre*]

exec. *abbrev. for:* **1** executive. **2** executor.

execrable (ˈɛksɪkrəbᵊl) *adj* **1** deserving to be execrated; abhorrent. **2** of very poor quality. [C14: from L: see EXECRATE]
▸ ˈexecrableness *n* ▸ ˈexecrably *adv*

execrate (ˈɛksɪˌkreɪt) *vb* **execrates, execrating, execrated. 1** (*tr*) to loathe; detest; abhor. **2** (*tr*) to denounce; deplore. **3** to curse (a person or thing); damn. [C16: from L *exsecrārī* to curse, from EX-¹ + *-secrārī* from *sacer* SACRED]
▸ ˌexeˈcration *n* ▸ ˈexeˌcrative *or* ˈexeˌcratory *adj*

execute (ˈɛksɪˌkjuːt) *vb* **executes, executing, executed.** (*tr*) **1** to put (a condemned person) to death; inflict capital punishment upon. **2** to carry out; complete. **3** to perform; accomplish; effect. **4** to make or produce: *to execute a drawing.* **5** to carry into effect (a judicial sentence, the law, etc.). **6** *Law.* to render (a deed, etc.) effective, as by signing, sealing, and delivering. **7** to carry out the terms of (a contract, will, etc.). [C14: from OF *executer*, back formation from *executeur* EXECUTOR]
▸ ˈexeˌcutable *adj* ▸ **executant** (ɪgˈzɛkjʊtənt) *n* ▸ ˈexeˌcuter *n*

execution (ˌɛksɪˈkjuːʃən) *n* **1** the act or process of executing. **2** the carrying out or undergoing of a sentence of death. **3** the style or manner in which something is accomplished or performed; technique. **4a** the enforcement of the judgment of a court of law. **4b** the writ ordering such enforcement.

executioner (ˌɛksɪˈkjuːʃənə) *n* an official charged with carrying out the death sentence passed upon a condemned person.

executive (ɪgˈzɛkjʊtɪv) *n* **1** a person or group responsible for the administration of a project, activity, or business. **2a** the branch of government responsible for carrying out laws, decrees, etc. **2b** any administration. ◆ *adj* **3** having the function of carrying plans, orders, laws, etc., into effect. **4** of or relating to an executive. **5** *Inf.* very expensive or exclusive: *executive housing.*
▸ exˈecutively *adv*

Executive Council *n* (in Australia and New Zealand) a body of ministers of the Crown presided over by the governor or governor-general that formally approves cabinet decisions, etc.

executive director *n* a member of the board of directors of a company who is also an employee (usually full-time) and who often has a specified area of responsibility, such as finance or production. Cf. **nonexecutive director.**

executive officer *n* the second-in-command of any of certain military units.

executor (ɪgˈzɛkjʊtə) *n* **1** *Law.* a person appointed by a testator to carry out his will. **2** a person who executes. [C14: from Anglo-F *executour*, from L *execūtor*]
▸ exˌecuˈtorial *adj* ▸ exˈecutory *adj* ▸ exˈecutorˌship *n*

executrix (ɪgˈzɛkjʊtrɪks) *n, pl* **executrices** (ɪgˌzɛkjuˈtraɪsiːz) *or* **executrixes.** *Law.* a female executor.

exegesis (ˌɛksɪˈdʒiːsɪs) *n, pl* **exegeses** (-siːz). explanation or critical interpretation of a text, esp. of the Bible. [C17: from Gk, from *exēgeisthai* to interpret, from EX-¹ + *hēgeisthai* to guide]
▸ **exegetic** (ˌɛksɪˈdʒɛtɪk) *adj*

exegete (ˈɛksɪˌdʒiːt) *or* **exegetist** (ˌɛksɪˈdʒiːtɪst, -ˈdʒɛt-) *n* a person who practises exegesis.

exemplar (ɪgˈzɛmplə, -plɑː) *n* **1** a person or thing to be copied or imitated; model. **2** a typical specimen or instance; example. [C14: from L, from *exemplum* EXAMPLE]

exemplary (ɪgˈzɛmplərɪ) *adj* **1** fit for imitation; model. **2**

serving as a warning; admonitory. **3** representative; typical.
 ▸ ex'emplarily *adv* ▸ ex'emplariness *n*

exemplary damages *pl n Law.* damages awarded to a plaintiff above the value of actual loss sustained so that they serve also as a punishment to the defendant.

exemplify (ɪgˈzɛmplɪˌfaɪ) *vb* **exemplifies, exemplifying, exemplified.** (*tr*) **1** to show by example. **2** to serve as an example of. **3** *Law.* to make an official copy of (a document) under seal. [C15: via OF from Med. L *exemplificāre*, from L *exemplum* EXAMPLE + *facere* to make]
 ▸ exˈempliˌfiable *adj* ▸ exˌemplifiˈcation *n* ▸ exˈemplifiˌcative *adj* ▸ exˈempliˌfier *n*

exempt (ɪgˈzɛmpt) *vb* **1** (*tr*) to release from an obligation, tax, etc.; excuse. ◆ *adj* **2a** freed from or not subject to an obligation, tax, etc.; excused. **2b** (*in combination*): *tax-exempt*. ◆ *n* **3** a person who is exempt. [C14: from L *exemptus* removed, from *eximere* to take out, from *emere* to buy, obtain]
 ▸ exˈemption *n*

exequies (ˈɛksɪkwɪz) *pl n, sing* **exequy.** the rites and ceremonies used at funerals. [C14: from L *exequiae* (pl) funeral procession, rites, from *exequī* to follow to the end]

exercise (ˈɛksəˌsaɪz) *vb* **exercises, exercising, exercised.** (*mainly tr*) **1** to put into use; employ. **2** (*intr*) to take exercise or perform exercises. **3** to practise using in order to develop or train. **4** to perform or make use of: *to exercise one's rights*. **5** to bring to bear: *to exercise one's influence*. **6** (*often passive*) to occupy the attentions of, esp. so as to worry or vex: *to be exercised about a decision*. **7** *Mil.* to carry out or cause to carry out simulated combat, manoeuvres, etc. ◆ *n* **8** physical exertion, esp. for development, training, or keeping fit. **9** mental or other activity or practice, esp. to develop a skill. **10** a set of movements, tasks, etc., designed to train, improve, or test one's ability: *piano exercises*. **11** a performance or work of art done as practice or to demonstrate a technique. **12** the performance of a function: *the exercise of one's rights*. **13** (*usually pl*) *Mil.* a manoeuvre or simulated combat operation. **14** *Gymnastics.* a particular event, such as the horizontal bar. [C14: from OF, from L, from *exercēre* to drill, from EX-¹ + *arcēre* to ward off]
 ▸ ˈexerˌcisable *adj* ▸ ˈexerˌciser *n*

exercise bike *or* **cycle** *n* a stationary exercise machine that is pedalled like a bicycle as a method of increasing cardiovascular fitness.

exercise book *n* a notebook used by pupils and students.

exercise price *n Stock Exchange.* the price at which the holder of a traded option may exercise his right to buy (or sell) a security.

exert (ɪgˈzɜːt) *vb* (*tr*) **1** to use (influence, authority, etc.) forcefully or effectively. **2** to apply (oneself) diligently; make a strenuous effort. [C17 (in the sense: push forth, emit): from L *exserere* to thrust out, from EX-¹ + *serere* to bind together, entwine]
 ▸ exˈertion *n* ▸ exˈertive *adj*

Exeter ★ (ˈɛksɪtə) *n* a city in SW England, administrative centre of Devon; university (1955). Pop.: 94 717 (1991).

exeunt (ˈɛksɪˌʌnt) *Latin.* they go out: used as a stage direction.

exeunt omnes (ˈɒmneɪz) *Latin.* they all go out: used as a stage direction.

exfoliate (ɛksˈfəʊlɪˌeɪt) *vb* **exfoliates, exfoliating, exfoliated.** (of bark, skin, minerals, etc.) to peel off in layers, flakes, or scales. [C17: from LL *exfoliāre* to strip off leaves, from L *folium* leaf]
 ▸ exˌfoliˈation *n* ▸ exˈfoliative *adj*

ex gratia (ˈgreɪʃə) *adj* given as a favour or gratuitously where no legal obligation exists: *an ex gratia payment*. [NL, lit.: out of kindness]

exhale (ɛksˈheɪl, ɪgˈzeɪl) *vb* **exhales, exhaling, exhaled.** **1** to expel (breath, smoke, etc.) from the lungs; breathe out. **2** to give off (air, fumes, etc.) or (of air, etc.) to be given off. [C14: from L *exhālāre*, from *hālāre* to breathe]
 ▸ exˈhalable *adj* ▸ ˌexhaˈlation *n*

exhaust (ɪgˈzɔːst) *vb* (*mainly tr*) **1** to drain the energy of; tire out. **2** to deprive of resources, etc. **3** to deplete to-

tally; consume. **4** to empty (a container) by drawing off or pumping out (the contents). **5** to develop or discuss thoroughly so that no further interest remains. **6** to remove gas from (a vessel, etc.) in order to reduce pressure or create a vacuum. **7** (*intr*) (of steam or other gases) to be emitted or to escape from an engine after being expanded. ◆ *n* **8** gases ejected from an engine as waste products. **9** the expulsion of expanded gas or steam from an engine. **10a** the parts of an engine through which exhausted gases or steam pass. **10b** (*as modifier*): *exhaust pipe*. [C16: from L *exhaustus* made empty, from *exhaurīre* to draw out, from *haurīre* to draw, drain]
 ▸ exˈhausted *adj* ▸ exˈhaustible *adj* ▸ exˈhausting *adj*

exhaustion (ɪgˈzɔːstʃən) *n* **1** extreme tiredness. **2** the condition of being used up. **3** the act of exhausting or the state of being exhausted.

exhaustive (ɪgˈzɔːstɪv) *adj* **1** comprehensive; thorough. **2** tending to exhaust.
 ▸ exˈhaustively *adv* ▸ exˈhaustiveness *n*

exhibit (ɪgˈzɪbɪt) *vb* (*mainly tr*) **1** (*also intr*) to display (something) to the public. **2** to manifest; display; show. **3** *Law.* to produce (a document or object) in court as evidence. ◆ *n* **4** an object or collection exhibited to the public. **5** *Law.* a document or object produced in court as evidence. [C15: from L *exhibēre* to hold forth, from *habēre* to have]
 ▸ exˈhibitor *n* ▸ exˈhibitory *adj*

exhibition (ˌɛksɪˈbɪʃən) *n* **1** a public display of art, skill, etc. **2** the act of exhibiting or the state of being exhibited. **3 make an exhibition of oneself.** to behave so foolishly that one excites notice or ridicule. **4** *Brit.* an allowance or scholarship awarded to a student at a university or school.

exhibitioner (ˌɛksɪˈbɪʃənə) *n Brit.* a student who has been awarded an exhibition.

exhibitionism (ˌɛksɪˈbɪʃəˌnɪzəm) *n* **1** a compulsive desire to attract attention to oneself, esp. by exaggerated behaviour. **2** a compulsive desire to expose one's genital organs publicly.
 ▸ ˌexhiˈbitionist *n* ▸ ˌexhiˌbitionˈistic *adj*

exhibitive (ɪgˈzɪbɪtɪv) *adj* (*usually postpositive and foll. by of*) illustrative or demonstrative.

exhilarate (ɪgˈzɪləˌreɪt) *vb* **exhilarates, exhilarating, exhilarated.** (*tr*) to make lively and cheerful; elate. [C16: from L *exhilārāre*, from *hilārāre* to cheer]
 ▸ exˈhilaˌrating *adj* ▸ exˌhilaˈration *n* ▸ exˈhilarative *adj*

exhort (ɪgˈzɔːt) *vb* to urge or persuade (someone) earnestly; advise strongly. [C14: from L *exhortārī*, from *hortārī* to urge]
 ▸ exˈhortative *or* exˈhortatory *adj* ▸ ˌexhorˈtation *n* ▸ exˈhorter *n*

exhume (ɛksˈhjuːm) *vb* **exhumes, exhuming, exhumed.** (*tr*) to dig up (something buried, esp. a corpse); disinter. **2** to reveal; disclose. [C18: from Med. L, from L EX-¹ + *humāre* to bury, from *humus* the ground]
 ▸ exhumation (ˌɛkshjuˈmeɪʃən) *n* ▸ exˈhumer *n*

ex hypothesi (ɛks haɪˈpɒθəsɪ) *adv* in accordance with the hypothesis stated. [C17: NL]

exigency (ˈɛksɪdʒənsɪ, ɪgˈzɪdʒənsɪ) *or* **exigence** (ˈɛksɪdʒəns) *n, pl* **exigencies** *or* **exigences. 1** urgency. **2** (*often pl*) an urgent demand; pressing requirement. **3** an emergency.

exigent (ˈɛksɪdʒənt) *adj* **1** urgent; pressing. **2** exacting; demanding. [C15: from L *exigere* to drive out, weigh out, from *agere* to drive, compel]

exiguous (ɪgˈzɪgjʊəs, ɪkˈsɪg-) *adj* scanty or slender; meagre. [C17: from L *exiguus*, from *exigere* to weigh out; see EXIGENT]
 ▸ exiguity (ˌɛksɪˈgjuːɪtɪ) *or* exˈiguousness *n*

exile (ˈɛgzaɪl, ˈɛksaɪl) *n* **1** a prolonged, usually enforced absence from one's home or country. **2** the official expulsion of a person from his native land. **3** a person banished or living away from his home or country; expatriate. ◆ *vb* **exiles, exiling, exiled. 4** (*tr*) to expel from home or country, esp. by official decree; banish. [C13: from L *exsilium* banishment, from *exsul* banished person]
 ▸ exilic (ɛgˈzɪlɪk, ɛkˈsɪlɪk) *adj*

exist (ɪgˈzɪst) vb (intr) **1** to have being or reality; be. **2** to eke out a living; stay alive. **3** to be living; live. **4** to be present under specified conditions or in a specified place. [C17: from L *exsistere* to step forth, from EX-[1] + *sistere* to stand]
▸ exˈistent adj ▸ exˈisting adj

existence (ɪgˈzɪstəns) n **1** the fact or state of existing; being. **2** the continuance or maintenance of life; living, esp. in adverse circumstances. **3** something that exists; a being or entity. **4** everything that exists.

existential (ˌɛgzɪˈstɛnʃəl) adj **1** of or relating to existence, esp. human existence. **2** Philosophy. known by experience rather than reason. **3** of a formula or proposition asserting the existence of at least one object fulfilling a given condition. **4** of or relating to existentialism.

existentialism (ˌɛgzɪˈstɛnʃəˌlɪzəm) n a modern philosophical movement stressing personal experience and responsibility and their demands on the individual, who is seen as a free agent in a deterministic and seemingly meaningless universe.
▸ ˌexisˈtentialist adj, n

exit (ˈɛgzɪt, ˈɛksɪt) n **1** a way out. **2** the act or an instance of going out. **3a** the act of leaving or right to leave a particular place. **3b** (as modifier): an exit visa. **4** departure from life; death. **5** Theatre. the act of going offstage. **6** Brit. a point at which vehicles may leave or join a motorway. ◆ vb **exits, exiting, exited. 7** (intr) to go away or out; depart. **8** (intr) Theatre. to go offstage: used as a stage direction: *exit Hamlet.* **9** Computing. to leave (a computer program or system). [C17: from L *exitus* a departure, from *exīre* to go out, from EX-[1] + *īre* to go]

exitance (ˈɛksɪtəns) n a measure of the ability of a surface to emit radiation. [C20: from EXIT + -ANCE]

exit poll n a poll taken by asking people how they voted in an election as they leave a polling station.

ex libris (ɛks ˈliːbrɪs) prep **1** from the collection or library of. ◆ n **ex-libris**, pl **ex-libris. 2** a bookplate bearing the owner's name, coat of arms, etc. [C19: from L, lit.: from the books (of)]

Exmoor ★ (ˈɛksˌmʊə, -ˌmɔː) n a high moorland in SW England, in W Somerset and N Devon: largely forested until the 19th century, now chiefly grazing ground for Exmoor ponies, sheep, and red deer.

Exmouth ★ (ˈɛksməθ) n a town in SW England, in Devon, at the mouth of the River Exe: tourism, fishing. Pop.: 28 414 (1991).

ex new adv, adj (of shares, etc.) without the right to take up any scrip issue or rights issue. Cf. **cum new.**

exo- combining form. external, outside, or beyond: *exothermal.* [from Gk *exō* outside]

exobiology (ˌɛksəʊbaɪˈɒlədʒɪ) n another name for **astrobiology.**
▸ ˌexobiˈologist n

exocarp (ˈɛksəʊˌkɑːp) n another name for **epicarp.**

exocrine (ˈɛksəʊˌkraɪn, -krɪn) adj **1** of or relating to exocrine glands or their secretions. ◆ n **2** an exocrine gland. [C20: EXO- + -crine from Gk *krinein* to separate]

exocrine gland n any gland, such as a salivary or sweat gland, that secretes its products through a duct onto an epithelial surface.

Exod. Bible. abbrev. for Exodus.

exodus (ˈɛksədəs) n the act or an instance of going out. [C17: via L from Gk *exodos*, from EX-[1] + *hodos* way]

Exodus (ˈɛksədəs) n **1** the. the departure of the Israelites from Egypt. **2** the second book of the Old Testament, recounting the events connected with this.

ex officio (ˈɛks əˈfɪʃɪəʊ, əˈfɪsɪəʊ) adv, adj by right of position or office. [L]

exogamy (ɛkˈsɒgəmɪ) n Anthropol., sociol. marriage outside one's own tribe or similar unit.
▸ exˈogamous or exogamic (ˌɛksəʊˈgæmɪk) adj

exogenous (ɛkˈsɒdʒɪnəs) adj **1** having an external origin. **2** Biol. **2a** originating outside an organism. **2b** of or relating to external factors, such as light, that influence an organism. **3** Psychiatry (of a mental illness) caused by external factors.

exon (ˈɛksɒn) n Brit. one of the four officers who command the Yeomen of the Guard. [C17: a pronunciation spelling of F *exempt* EXEMPT]

exonerate (ɪgˈzɒnəˌreɪt) vb **exonerates, exonerating, exonerated.** (tr) **1** to absolve from blame or a criminal charge. **2** to relieve from an obligation. [C16: from L *exonerāre* to free from a burden, from *onus* a burden]
▸ exˌonerˈation n ▸ exˈonerative adj ▸ exˈonerˌator n

exophthalmos (ˌɛksɒfˈθælmɒs), **exophthalmus** (ˌɛksɒfˈθælməs), or **exophthalmia** (ˌɛksɒfˈθælmɪə) n abnormal protrusion of the eyeball, as caused by hyperthyroidism. [C19: via NL from Gk, from EX-[1] + *ophthalmos* eye]
▸ ˌexophˈthalmic adj

exorbitant (ɪgˈzɔːbɪt³nt) adj (of prices, demands, etc.) excessive; extravagant; immoderate. [C15: from LL *exorbitāre* to deviate, from L *orbita* track]
▸ exˈorbitance n ▸ exˈorbitantly adv

exorcize or **exorcise** (ˈɛksɔːˌsaɪz) vb **exorcizes, exorcizing, exorcized** or **exorcises, exorcising, exorcised.** (tr) to expel (evil spirits) from (a person or place), by adjurations and religious rites. [C15: from LL, from Gk, from EX-[1] + *horkizein* to adjure]
▸ ˈexorcism n ▸ ˈexorcist n ▸ ˈexorˌcizer or ˈexorˌciser n

exordium (ɛkˈsɔːdɪəm) n, pl **exordiums** or **exordia** (-dɪə). an introductory part or beginning, esp. of an oration or discourse. [C16: from L, from *exōrdīrī* to begin, from *ōrdīrī* to begin]
▸ exˈordial adj

exoskeleton (ˌɛksəʊˈskɛlɪt³n) n the protective or supporting structure covering the outside of the body of many animals, such as the thick cuticle of arthropods.
▸ ˌexoˈskeletal adj

exosphere (ˈɛksəʊˌsfɪə) n the outermost layer of the earth's atmosphere. It extends from about 400 kilometres above the earth's surface.

exothermic (ˌɛksəʊˈθɜːmɪk) or **exothermal** adj (of a chemical reaction or compound) occurring or formed with the evolution of heat.
▸ ˌexoˈthermically or ˌexoˈthermally adv

exotic (ɪgˈzɒtɪk) adj **1** originating in a foreign country, esp. one in the tropics; not native: *an exotic plant.* **2** having a strange or bizarre allure, beauty, or quality. ◆ n **3** an exotic person or thing. [C16: from L, from Gk *exōtikos* foreign, from *exō* outside]
▸ exˈotically adv ▸ exˈotiˌcism n ▸ exˈoticness n

exotica (ɪgˈzɒtɪkə) pl n exotic objects, esp. when forming a collection. [C19: L, neut pl of *exōticus*; see EXOTIC]

exotic dancer n a striptease or belly dancer.

expand (ɪkˈspænd) vb **1** to make or become greater in extent, volume, size, or scope. **2** to spread out; unfold; stretch out. **3** (intr; foll. by on) to enlarge or expatiate (on a story, topic, etc.). **4** (intr) to become increasingly relaxed, friendly, or talkative. **5** Maths. to express (a function or expression) as the sum or product of terms. [C15: from L *expandere* to spread out]
▸ exˈpandable adj

expanded (ɪkˈspændɪd) adj (of a plastic) having been foamed during manufacture by a gas to make a light packaging material or heat insulator: *expanded polystyrene.*

expanded metal n an open mesh of metal used for reinforcing brittle or friable materials and in fencing.

expander (ɪkˈspændə) n **1** a device for exercising and developing the muscles of the body. **2** an electronic device for increasing the variations in signal amplitude in a transmission system according to a specified law.

expanse (ɪkˈspæns) n **1** an uninterrupted surface of something that extends, esp. over a wide area; stretch. **2** expansion or extension. [C17: from NL *expansum* the heavens, from L *expansus* spread out, from *expandere* to expand]

expansible (ɪkˈspænsəb³l) adj able to expand or be expanded.
▸ exˌpansiˈbility n

expansion (ɪkˈspænʃən) n **1** the act of expanding or the state of being expanded. **2** something expanded. **3** the

degree or amount by which something expands. **4** an increase or development, esp. in the activities of a company. **5** the increase in the dimensions of a body or substance when subjected to an increase in temperature, internal pressure, etc.
▸ **ex'pansionary** *adj*

expansionism (ɪkˈspænʃəˌnɪzəm) *n* the doctrine or practice of expanding the economy or territory of a country.
▸ **ex'pansionist** *n, adj* ▸ **ex,pansion'istic** *adj*

expansive (ɪkˈspænsɪv) *adj* **1** able or tending to expand or characterized by expansion. **2** wide; extensive. **3** friendly, open, or talkative. **4** grand or extravagant.
▸ **ex'pansiveness** *n*

expansivity (ˌekspænˈsɪvɪtɪ) *n* the fractional increase in length or volume of a substance or body on being heated through a one degree rise in temperature; coefficient of expansion.

ex parte (ɛks ˈpɑːtɪ) *adj Law.* (of an application in a judicial proceeding) on behalf of one side or party only: *an ex parte injunction.*

expat (ˌeksˈpæt) *n, adj Inf.* short for **expatriate**.

expatiate (ɪkˈspeɪʃɪˌeɪt) *vb* **expatiates, expatiating, expatiated.** (*intr*) **1** (foll. by *on* or *upon*) to enlarge (on a theme, topic, etc.); elaborate (on). **2** *Rare.* to wander about. [C16: from L *exspatiārī* to digress, from *spatiārī* to walk about]
▸ **ex,pati'ation** *n* ▸ **ex'pati,ator** *n*

expatriate *adj* (eksˈpætrɪɪt, -ˌeɪt). **1** resident outside one's native country. **2** exiled or banished from one's native country. ◆ *n* (eksˈpætrɪɪt, -ˌeɪt). **3** a person living outside his native country **4** an exile; expatriate person. ◆ *vb* (eksˈpætrɪˌeɪt), **expatriates, expatriating, expatriated.** (*tr*) **5** to exile (oneself) from one's native country or cause (another) to go into exile. [C18: from Med. L, from L EX-[1] + *patria* native land]
▸ **ex,patri'ation** *n*

expect (ɪkˈspekt) *vb* (*tr; may take a clause as object or an infinitive*) **1** to regard as likely; anticipate. **2** to look forward to or be waiting for. **3** to decide that (something) is necessary; require: *the teacher expects us to work late.* ◆ See also **expecting**. [C16: from L *exspectāre* to watch for, from *spectāre* to look at]
▸ **ex'pectable** *adj*

expectancy (ɪkˈspektənsɪ) *or* **expectance** *n* **1** something expected, esp. on the basis of a norm or average: *his life expectancy was 30 years.* **2** anticipation; expectation. **3** the prospect of a future interest or possession.

expectant (ɪkˈspektənt) *adj* **1** expecting, anticipating, or hopeful. **2** having expectations, esp. of possession of something. **3** pregnant. ◆ *n* **4** a person who expects something.
▸ **ex'pectantly** *adv*

expectation (ˌekspekˈteɪʃən) *n* **1** the act or state of expecting or the state of being expected. **2** (*usually pl*) something looked forward to, whether feared or hoped for. **3** an attitude of expectancy or hope. **4** *Statistics.* **4a** the numerical probability that an event will occur. **4b** another term for **expected value.**

expected frequency *n Statistics.* the number of occasions on which an event may be presumed to occur on average in a given number of trials.

expected value *n Statistics.* the sum or integral of all possible values of a random variable, or any given function of it, multiplied by the respective probabilities of the values of the variable.

expecting (ɪkˈspektɪŋ) *adj Inf.* pregnant.

expectorant (ɪkˈspektərənt) *Med.* ◆ *adj* **1** promoting the secretion, liquefaction, or expulsion of sputum from the respiratory passages. ◆ *n* **2** an expectorant drug or agent.

expectorate (ɪkˈspektəˌreɪt) *vb* **expectorates, expectorating, expectorated.** to cough up and spit out (sputum from the respiratory passages). [C17: from L *expectorāre,* lit.: to drive from the breast, expel, from *pectus* breast]
▸ **ex,pecto'ration** *n* ▸ **ex'pecto,rator** *n*

expediency (ɪkˈspiːdɪənsɪ) *or* **expedience** *n, pl* expedi-

encies *or* expediences. **1** appropriateness; suitability. **2** the use of or inclination towards methods that are advantageous rather than fair or just. **3** another word for **expedient** (sense 3).

expedient (ɪkˈspiːdɪənt) *adj* **1** suitable to the circumstances; appropriate. **2** inclined towards methods that are advantageous rather than fair or just. ◆ *n also* **expediency. 3** something suitable or appropriate, esp. during an urgent situation. [C14: from L *expediēns* setting free; see EXPEDITE]

expedite (ˈekspɪˌdaɪt) *vb* **expedites, expediting, expedited.** (*tr*) **1** to hasten or assist the progress of. **2** to do or process with speed and efficiency. [C17: from L *expedīre,* lit.: to free the feet (as from a snare), hence, liberate, from EX-[1] + *pēs* foot]
▸ **'expe,diter** *or* **'expe,ditor** *n*

expedition (ˌekspɪˈdɪʃən) *n* **1** an organized journey or voyage, esp. for exploration or for a scientific or military purpose. **2** the people and equipment comprising an expedition. **3** promptness; dispatch. [C15: from L *expedīre* to prepare, EXPEDITE]
▸ **,expe'ditionary** *adj*

expeditious (ˌekspɪˈdɪʃəs) *adj* characterized by or done with speed and efficiency; prompt; quick.
▸ **,expe'ditiously** *adv* ▸ **,expe'ditiousness** *n*

expel (ɪkˈspel) *vb* **expels, expelling, expelled.** (*tr*) **1** to eject or drive out with force. **2** to deprive of participation in or membership of a school, club, etc. [C14: from L *expellere* to drive out, from *pellere* to thrust, drive]
▸ **ex'pellable** *adj* ▸ **expellee** (ˌekspeˈliː) *n* ▸ **ex'peller** *n*

expellant *or* **expellent** (ɪkˈspelənt) *adj* **1** forcing out or able to force out. ◆ *n* **2** a medicine used to expel undesirable substances or organisms from the body.

expend (ɪkˈspend) *vb* (*tr*) **1** to spend; disburse. **2** to consume or use up. [C15: from L *expendere,* from *pendere* to weigh]
▸ **ex'pender** *n*

expendable (ɪkˈspendəb³l) *adj* **1** that may be expended or used up. **2** able to be sacrificed to achieve an objective, esp. a military one. ◆ *n* **3** something expendable.
▸ **ex,penda'bility** *n*

expenditure (ɪkˈspendɪtʃə) *n* **1** something expended, esp. money. **2** the act of expending.

expense (ɪkˈspens) *n* **1** a particular payment of money; expenditure. **2** money needed for individual purchases; cost; charge. **3** (*pl*) money spent in the performance of a job, etc., usually reimbursed by an employer or allowable against tax. **4** something requiring money for its purchase or upkeep. **5 at the expense of.** to the detriment of. [C14: from LL, from L *expēnsus* weighed out; see EXPEND]

expense account *n* **1** an arrangement by which an employee's expenses are refunded by his employer or deducted from his income for tax purposes. **2** a record of such expenses.

expensive (ɪkˈspensɪv) *adj* high-priced; costly; dear.
▸ **ex'pensiveness** *n*

experience (ɪkˈspɪərɪəns) *n* **1** direct personal participation or observation. **2** a particular incident, feeling, etc., that a person has undergone. **3** accumulated knowledge, esp. of practical matters. ◆ *vb* **experiences, experiencing, experienced.** (*tr*) **4** to participate in or undergo. **5** to be moved by; feel. [C14: from L *experīrī* to prove; rel. to L *perīculum* PERIL]
▸ **ex'perienceable** *adj*

experienced (ɪkˈspɪərɪənst) *adj* having become skilful or knowledgeable from extensive participation or observation.

experiential (ɪkˌspɪərɪˈenʃəl) *adj Philosophy.* relating to or derived from experience; empirical.

experiment *n* (ɪkˈsperɪmənt). **1** a test or investigation, esp. one planned to provide evidence for or against a hypothesis. **2** the act of conducting such an investigation or test; research. **3** an attempt at something new or original. ◆ *vb* (ɪkˈsperɪˌment). **4** (*intr*) to make an experiment or experiments. [C14: from L *experīmentum* proof, trial, from *experīrī* to test; see EXPERIENCE]
▸ **ex'peri,menter** *n*

★ **people and places**

experimental (ɪkˌspɛrɪ'mɛntªl) *adj* **1** relating to, based on, or having the nature of experiment. **2** based on or derived from experience; empirical. **3** tending to experiment. **4** tentative or provisional.
► ex‚peri'mentalism *n*

experimentation (ɪkˌspɛrɪmɛn'teɪʃən) *n* the act, process, or practice of experimenting.

expert ('ɛkspɜːt) *n* **1** a person who has extensive skill or knowledge in a particular field. ♦ *adj* **2** skilful or knowledgeable. **3** of, involving, or done by an expert: *an expert job.* [C14: from L *expertus* known by experience; see EXPERIENCE]
► 'expertly *adv* ► 'expertness *n*

expertise (ˌɛkspɜː'tiːz) *n* special skill, knowledge, or judgment; expertness. [C19: from F: expert skill, from EXPERT]

expiate ('ɛkspɪˌeɪt) *vb* **expiates, expiating, expiated.** (*tr*) to atone for (sin or wrongdoing); make amends for. [C16: from L *expiāre*, from *pius* dutiful; see PIOUS]
► 'expiable *adj* ► ‚expi'ation *n* ► 'expiˌator *n*

expiatory ('ɛkspɪətərɪ, -trɪ) *adj* **1** capable of making expiation. **2** offered in expiation.

expiration (ˌɛkspɪ'reɪʃən) *n* **1** the finish of something; expiry. **2** the act, process, or sound of breathing out.

expire (ɪk'spaɪə) *vb* **expires, expiring, expired. 1** (*intr*) to finish or run out; come to an end. **2** to breathe out (air). **3** (*intr*) to die. [C15: from OF, from L *exspīrāre* to breathe out, from *spīrāre* to breathe]
► ex'pirer *n*

expiry (ɪk'spaɪərɪ) *n, pl* **expiries. 1a** a coming to an end, esp. of a contract period; termination. **1b** (*as modifier*): *the expiry date.* **2** death.

explain (ɪk'spleɪn) *vb* **1** (when *tr, may take a clause as object*) to make (something) comprehensible, esp. by giving a clear and detailed account of it. **2** (*tr*) to justify or attempt to justify (oneself) by reasons for one's actions. [C15: from L *explānāre* to flatten, from *plānus* level]
► ex'plainable *adj* ► ex'plainer *n*

explain away *vb* (*tr, adv*) to offer excuses or reasons for (bad conduct, mistakes, etc.).

explanation (ˌɛksplə'neɪʃən) *n* **1** the act or process of explaining. **2** something that explains. **3** a clarification of disputed points.

explanatory (ɪk'splænətərɪ, -trɪ) *or* **explanative** *adj* serving or intended to serve as an explanation.
► ex'planatorily *adv*

expletive (ɪk'spliːtɪv) *n* **1** an exclamation or swearword; an oath or sound expressing emotion rather than meaning. **2** any syllable, word, or phrase conveying no independent meaning, esp. one inserted in verse for the sake of metre. ♦ *adj also* **expletory** (ɪk'spliːtərɪ, -trɪ). **3** without particular meaning, esp. when filling out a line of verse. [C17: from LL *explētīvus* for filling out, from *explēre*, from *plēre* to fill]

explicable ('ɛksplɪkəbªl, ɪk'splɪk-) *adj* capable of being explained.

explicate ('ɛksplɪˌkeɪt) *vb* **explicates, explicating, explicated.** (*tr*) *Formal.* **1** to make clear or explicit; explain. **2** to formulate or develop (a theory, hypothesis, etc.). [C16: from L *explicāre* to unfold]
► ‚expli'cation *n*

explicit (ɪk'splɪsɪt) *adj* **1** precisely and clearly expressed, leaving nothing to implication; fully stated. **2** leaving little to the imagination; graphically detailed. **3** openly expressed without reservations; unreserved. [C17: from L *explicitus* unfolded]
► ex'plicitly *adv* ► ex'plicitness *n*

explode (ɪk'spləʊd) *vb* **explodes, exploding, exploded. 1** to burst or cause to burst with great violence, esp. through detonation of an explosive; blow up. **2** to destroy or be destroyed in this manner. **3** (of a gas) to undergo or cause (a gas) to undergo a sudden violent expansion, as a result of a fast exothermic chemical or nuclear reaction. **4** (*intr*) to react suddenly or violently with emotion, etc. **5** (*intr*) (esp. of a population) to increase rapidly. **6** (*tr*) to

show (a theory, etc.) to be baseless. [C16: from L *explōdere* to drive off by clapping]
► ex'ploder *n*

exploded view *n* a drawing or photograph of a mechanism that shows its parts separately, usually indicating their relative positions.

exploit *n* ('ɛksplɔɪt). **1** a notable deed or feat, esp. one that is heroic. ♦ *vb* (ɪk'splɔɪt). (*tr*) **2** to take advantage of (a person, situation, etc.) for one's own ends. **3** to make the best use of. [C14: from OF: accomplishment, from L *explicitum* (something) unfolded, from *explicāre* to EXPLICATE]
► ex'ploitable *adj* ► ‚exploi'tation *n* ► ex'ploitive *or* ex'ploitative *adj*

exploration (ˌɛksplə'reɪʃən) *n* **1** the act or process of exploring. **2** an organized trip into unfamiliar regions, esp. for scientific purposes.
► **exploratory** (ɪk'splɒrətərɪ, -trɪ) *or* ex'plorative *adj*

explore (ɪk'splɔː) *vb* **explores, exploring, explored. 1** (*tr*) to examine or investigate, esp. systematically. **2** to travel into (unfamiliar regions), esp. for scientific purposes. **3** (*tr*) *Med.* to examine (an organ or part) for diagnostic purposes. [C16: from L, from EX-[1] + *plōrāre* to cry aloud; prob. from the shouts of hunters sighting prey]
► ex'plorer *n*

explosion (ɪk'spləʊʒən) *n* **1** the act or an instance of exploding. **2** a violent release of energy resulting from a rapid chemical or nuclear reaction. **3** a sudden or violent outburst of activity, noise, emotion, etc. **4** a rapid increase, esp. in a population. [C17: from L *explōsiō*, from *explōdere* to EXPLODE]

explosive (ɪk'spləʊsɪv) *adj* **1** of, involving, or characterized by explosion. **2** capable of exploding or tending to explode. **3** potentially violent or hazardous: *an explosive situation.* ♦ *n* **4** a substance capable of exploding or tending to explode.
► ex'plosiveness *n*

expo ('ɛkspəʊ) *n, pl* **expos.** short for **exposition** (sense 3).

exponent (ɪk'spəʊnənt) *n* **1** (usually foll. *by of*) a person or thing that acts as an advocate (of an idea, cause, etc.). **2** a person or thing that explains or interprets. **3** a performer or artist. **4** Also called: **power, index.** *Maths.* a number or variable placed as a superscript to another number or quantity to indicate the number of times the designated number or quantity should appear in a repeated multiplication, as in $x^3 = x \times x \times x$, where 3 is the exponent. ♦ *adj* **5** offering a declaration, explanation, or interpretation. [C16: from L *expōnere* to set out, expound]

exponential (ˌɛkspəʊ'nɛnʃəl) *adj* **1** *Maths.* (of a function, curve, etc.) of or involving numbers or quantities raised to an exponent, esp. e^x. **2** *Maths.* raised to the power of e, the base of natural logarithms. **3** of or involving an exponent or exponents. **4** *Inf.* very rapid. ♦ *n* **5** *Maths.* an exponential function, etc.

exponential distribution *n* *Statistics.* a continuous single-parameter distribution used esp. when making statements about the length of life of materials or times between random events.

export *n* ('ɛkspɔːt). **1** (*often pl*) **1a** goods (**visible exports**) or services (**invisible exports**) sold to a foreign country or countries. **1b** (*as modifier*): *an export licence.* ♦ *vb* (ɪk'spɔːt, 'ɛkspɔːt). **2** to sell (goods or services) or ship (goods) to a foreign country. **3** (*tr*) to transmit or spread (an idea, institution, etc.) abroad. [C15: from L *exportāre* to carry away]
► ex'portable *adj* ► ex‚porta'bility *n* ► ‚expor'tation *n* ► ex'porter *n*

export reject *n* an article that fails to meet a standard of quality required for export and that is sold on the home market.

expose (ɪk'spəʊz) *vb* **exposes, exposing, exposed.** (*tr*) **1** to display for viewing; exhibit. **2** to bring to public notice; disclose. **3** to divulge the identity of; unmask. **4** (foll. by *to*) to make subject or susceptible (to attack, criticism, etc.). **5** to abandon (a child, etc.) in the open to die. **6** (foll. by *to*) to introduce (to) or acquaint (with). **7** *Photog.* to subject (a film or plate) to light, X-rays, etc. **8 expose**

oneself. to display one's sexual organs in public. [C15: from OF *exposer*, from L *expōnere* to set out]
▶ ex'posable *adj* ▶ ex'posal *n* ▶ ex'poser *n*

exposé (ɛks'pəʊzeɪ) *n* the act or an instance of bringing a scandal, crime, etc., to public notice.

exposed (ɪk'spəʊzd) *adj* 1 not concealed; displayed for viewing. 2 without shelter from the elements. 3 susceptible to attack or criticism; vulnerable.

exposition (,ɛkspə'zɪʃən) *n* 1 a systematic, usually written statement about or explanation of a subject. 2 the act of expounding or setting forth information or a viewpoint. 3 a large public exhibition, esp. of industrial products or arts and crafts. 4 the act of exposing or the state of being exposed. 5 *Music.* the first statement of the subjects or themes of a movement in sonata form or a fugue. 6 *RC Church.* the exhibiting of the consecrated Eucharistic Host or a relic for public veneration. [C14: from L *expositiō* a setting forth, from *expōnere* to display]
▶ ,expo'sitional *adj*

expositor (ɪk'spɒzɪtə) *n* a person who expounds.

expository (ɪk'spɒzɪtərɪ, -trɪ) or **expositive** *adj* of or involving exposition; explanatory.

ex post facto (ɛks pəʊst 'fæktəʊ) *adj* having retrospective effect. [C17: from L *ex* from + *post* afterwards + *factus* done, from *facere* to do]

expostulate (ɪk'spɒstjʊ,leɪt) *vb* **expostulates, expostulating, expostulated.** (*intr*; usually foll. by *with*) to argue or reason (with), esp. in order to dissuade. [C16: from L *expostulāre* to require, from *postulāre* to demand; see POSTULATE]
▶ ex,postu'lation *n* ▶ ex'postu,lator *n*

exposure (ɪk'spəʊʒə) *n* 1 the act of exposing or the condition of being exposed. 2 the position or outlook of a house, building, etc.: *a southern exposure.* 3 lack of shelter from the weather, esp. the cold. 4 a surface that is exposed. 5 *Photog.* 5a the act of exposing a film or plate to light, X-rays, etc. 5b an area on a film or plate that has been exposed. 6 *Photog.* 6a the intensity of light falling on a film or plate multiplied by the time for which it is exposed. 6b a combination of lens aperture and shutter speed used in taking a photograph. 7 appearance before the public, as in a theatre, on television, etc.

exposure meter *n Photog.* an instrument for measuring the intensity of light so that suitable camera settings can be determined. Also called: **light meter.**

expound (ɪk'spaʊnd) *vb* (when *intr*, foll. by *on* or *about*) to explain or set forth (an argument, theory, etc.) in detail. [C13: from OF, from L *expōnere* to set forth, from *pōnere* to put]
▶ ex'pounder *n*

express (ɪk'sprɛs) *vb* (*tr*) 1 to transform (ideas) into words; utter; verbalize. 2 to show or reveal. 3 to communicate (emotion, etc.) without words, as through music, painting, etc. 4 to indicate through a symbol, formula, etc. 5 to squeeze out: *to express the juice from an orange.* 6 **express oneself.** to communicate one's thoughts or ideas. ◆ *adj* (*prenominal*) 7 clearly indicated; explicitly stated. 8 done or planned for a definite reason; particular. 9 of or designed for rapid transportation of people, mail, etc.: *express delivery.* ◆ *n* 10a a system for sending mail, money, etc., rapidly. 10b mail, etc., conveyed by such a system. 10c *Chiefly US & Canad.* an enterprise operating such a system. 11 Also: **express train.** a fast train stopping at no or only a few stations between its termini. ◆ *adv* 12 by means of express delivery. [C14: from L *expressus*, lit.: squeezed out, hence, prominent, from *exprimere* to force out, from EX-[1] + *premere* to press]
▶ ex'presser *n* ▶ ex'pressible *adj*

expression (ɪk'sprɛʃən) *n* 1 the act or an instance of transforming ideas into words. 2 a manifestation of an emotion, feeling, etc., without words. 3 communication of emotion through music, painting, etc. 4 a look on the face that indicates mood or emotion. 5 the choice of words, intonation, etc., in communicating. 6 a particular phrase used conventionally to express something. 7 the act or process of squeezing out a liquid. 8 *Maths.* a variable, function, or some combination of these.
▶ ex'pressional *adj* ▶ ex'pressionless *adj*

expressionism (ɪk'sprɛʃə,nɪzəm) *n* (*sometimes cap.*) an artistic and literary movement originating in the early 20th century, which sought to express emotions rather than to represent external reality: characterized by symbolism and distortion.
▶ ex'pressionist *n, adj* ▶ ex,pression'istic *adj*

expression mark *n* one of a set of musical directions, usually in Italian, indicating how a piece or passage is to be performed.

expressive (ɪk'sprɛsɪv) *adj* 1 of, involving, or full of expression. 2 (*postpositive;* foll. by *of*) indicative or suggestive (of). 3 having a particular meaning or force; significant.
▶ ex'pressiveness *n*

expressly (ɪk'sprɛslɪ) *adv* 1 for an express purpose. 2 plainly, exactly, or unmistakably.

expresso (ɪk'sprɛsəʊ) *n, pl* **expressos.** a variant of **espresso.**

expressway (ɪk'sprɛs,weɪ) *n* a motorway.

expropriate (ɛks'prəʊprɪ,eɪt) *vb* **expropriates, expropriating, expropriated.** (*tr*) to deprive (an owner) of (property), esp. by taking it for public use. [C17: from Med. L *expropriāre* to deprive of possessions, from *proprius* own]
▶ ex,propri'ation *n* ▶ ex'propri,ator *n*

expulsion (ɪk'spʌlʃən) *n* the act of expelling or the fact or condition of being expelled. [C14: from L *expulsiō* a driving out, from *expellere* to EXPEL]
▶ ex'pulsive *adj*

expunge (ɪk'spʌndʒ) *vb* **expunges, expunging, expunged.** (*tr*) to delete or erase; blot out; obliterate. [C17: from L *expungere* to blot out, from *pungere* to prick]
▶ expunction (ɪk'spʌŋkʃən) *n* ▶ ex'punger *n*

expurgate ('ɛkspə,geɪt) *vb* **expurgates, expurgating, expurgated.** (*tr*) to amend (a book, text, etc.) by removing (offensive sections). [C17: from L *expurgāre* to clean out, from *purgāre* to purify; see PURGE]
▶ ,expur'gation *n* ▶ 'expur,gator *n*

exquisite (ɪk'skwɪzɪt, 'ɛkskwɪzɪt) *adj* 1 possessing qualities of unusual delicacy and craftsmanship. 2 extremely beautiful. 3 outstanding or excellent. 4 sensitive; discriminating. 5 fastidious and refined. 6 intense or sharp in feeling. ◆ *n* 7 *Obs.* a dandy. [C15: from L *exquīsītus* excellent, from *exquīrere* to search out, from *quaerere* to seek]
▶ ex'quisitely *adv* ▶ ex'quisiteness *n*

ex-serviceman or (*fem*) **ex-servicewoman** *n, pl* ex-servicemen or ex-servicewomen. a person who has served in the armed forces.

extant (ɛk'stænt, 'ɛkstənt) *adj* still in existence; surviving. [C16: from L *exstāns* standing out, from *exstāre*, from *stāre* to stand]

USAGE NOTE *Extant* is sometimes wrongly used to say that something exists, without any connotation of survival: *plutonium is perhaps the deadliest element in existence* (not *the deadliest element extant*).

extemporaneous (ɪk,stɛmpə'reɪnɪəs) or **extemporary** (ɪk'stɛmpərərɪ) *adj* 1 spoken, performed, etc., without preparation; extempore. 2 done in a temporary manner; improvised.
▶ ex,tempo'raneously or ex'temporarily *adv* ▶ ex,tempo'raneousness or ex'temporariness *n*

extempore (ɪk'stɛmpərɪ) *adv, adj* without planning or preparation. [C16: from L *ex tempore* instantaneously, from EX-[1] out of + *tempus* time]

extemporize or **extemporise** (ɪk'stɛmpə,raɪz) *vb* **temporizes, extemporizing, extemporized** or **extemporises, extemporising, extemporised.** 1 to perform, speak, or compose (an act, speech, music, etc.) without preparation. 2 to use a temporary solution; improvise.
▶ ex,tempori'zation or ex,tempori'sation *n* ▶ ex'tempo,rizer or ex'tempo,riser *n*

extend (ɪk'stɛnd) *vb* 1 to draw out or be drawn out; stretch. 2 to last or cause to last for a certain time. 3 (*intr*,

★ people and places

to reach a certain point in time or distance. **4** (*intr*) to exist or occur. **5** (*tr*) to increase (a building, etc.) in size; add to or enlarge. **6** (*tr*) to broaden the meaning or scope of: *the law was extended*. **7** (*tr*) to present or offer. **8** to stretch forth (an arm, etc.). **9** (*tr*) to lay out (a body) at full length. **10** (*tr*) to strain or exert (a person or animal) to the maximum. **11** (*tr*) to prolong (the time) for payment of (a debt or loan), completion of (a task), etc. [C14: from L *extendere* to stretch out, from *tendere* to stretch]
 ▶ ex'tendible *or* ex'tendable *adj* ▶ ex,tendi'bility *or* ex,tenda'bility *n*

extended family *n Sociol., anthropol.* the nuclear family together with relatives, often spanning three or more generations.

extended-play *adj* denoting an EP record.

extender (ɪk'stɛndə) *n* **1** a person or thing that extends. **2** a substance added to paints to give body and decrease their rate of settlement. **3** a substance added to glues and resins to dilute them or to modify their viscosity.

extensible (ɪk'stɛnsɪb°l) *or* **extensile** (ɪk'stɛnsaɪl) *adj* capable of being extended.
 ▶ ex,tensi'bility *or* ex'tensibleness *n*

extension (ɪk'stɛnʃən) *n* **1** the act of extending or the condition of being extended. **2** something that can be extended or that extends another object. **3** the length, range, etc., over which something is extended. **4** an additional telephone set connected to the same telephone line as another set. **5** a room or rooms added to an existing building. **6** a delay in the date originally set for payment of a debt or completion of a contract. **7** the property of matter by which it occupies space. **8a** the act of straightening or extending an arm or leg. **8b** its position after being straightened or extended. **9a** a service by which the facilities of an educational establishment, library, etc., are offered to outsiders. **9b** (*as modifier*): *a university extension course*. **10** *Logic*. the class of entities to which a given word correctly applies. [C14: from LL *extensiō* a stretching out; see EXTEND]
 ▶ ex'tensional *adj* ▶ ex,tension'ality *or* ex'tensional,ism *n*

extensive (ɪk'stɛnsɪv) *adj* **1** having a large extent, area, degree, etc. **2** widespread. **3** *Agriculture*. involving or farmed with minimum expenditure of capital or labour, esp. depending on a large extent of land. Cf. **intensive** (sense 3). **4** of or relating to logical extension.
 ▶ ex'tensiveness *n*

extensor (ɪk'stɛnsə, -sɔː) *n* any muscle that stretches or extends an arm, leg, or other bodily part. Cf. **flexor**. [C18: from NL, from L *extensus* stretched out]

extent (ɪk'stɛnt) *n* **1** the range over which something extends; scope. **2** an area or volume. [C14: from OF, from L *extentus* extensive, from *extendere* to EXTEND]

extenuate (ɪk'stɛnjʊˌeɪt) *vb* **extenuates, extenuating, extenuated.** (*tr*) **1** to represent (an offence, fault, etc.) as being less serious than it appears, as by showing mitigating circumstances. **2** to cause to be or appear less serious; mitigate. **3** *Arch.* **3a** to emaciate or weaken. **3b** to dilute or thin out. [C16: from L *extenuāre* to make thin, from *tenuis* thin, frail]
 ▶ ex'tenu,ating *adj* ▶ ex,tenu'ation *n* ▶ ex'tenu,ator *n*

exterior (ɪk'stɪərɪə) *n* **1** a part, surface, or region that is on the outside. **2** the outward behaviour or appearance of a person. **3** a film or scene shot outside a studio. ◆ *adj* **4** of, situated on, or suitable for the outside. **5** coming or acting from without. [C16: from L, comp. of *exterus* on the outside, from *ex* out of]
 ▶ ex'teriorly *adv*

exterior angle *n* **1** an angle of a polygon contained between one side extended and the adjacent side. **2** any of the four angles made by a transversal that are outside the region between the two intersected lines.

exteriorize *or* **exteriorise** (ɪk'stɪərɪəˌraɪz) *vb* **exteriorizes, exteriorizing, exteriorized** *or* **exteriorises, exteriorising, exteriorised.** (*tr*) **1** *Surgery*. to expose (an attached organ or part) outside the body. **2** another word for **externalize**.
 ▶ ex,teriori'zation *or* ex,teriori'sation *n*

exterminate (ɪk'stɜːmɪˌneɪt) *vb* **exterminates, exterminat-**

ing, **exterminated**. (*tr*) to destroy (living things, esp. pests or vermin) completely; annihilate; eliminate. [C16: from L *extermināre* to drive away, from *terminus* boundary]
 ▶ ex'terminable *adj* ▶ ex,termi'nation *n* ▶ ex'termi,nator *n*

external (ɪk'stɜːn°l) *adj* **1** of, situated on, or suitable for the outside; outer. **2** coming or acting from without. **3** of or involving foreign nations. **4** of, relating to, or designating a medicine that is applied to the outside of the body. **5** *Anat.* situated on or near the outside of the body. **6** (of a student) studying a university subject extramurally. **7** *Philosophy*. (of objects, etc.) taken to exist independently of a perceiving mind. ◆ *n* **8** (*often pl*) an external circumstance or aspect, esp. one that is superficial. **9** *Austral. & NZ.* an extramural student. [C15: from L *externus* outward, from *exterus* on the outside, from *ex* out of]
 ▶ ex'ternally *adv* ▶ ,exter'nality *n*

externalize *or* **externalise** (ɪk'stɜːnəˌlaɪz) *vb* **externalizes, externalizing, externalized** *or* **externalises, externalising, externalised.** (*tr*) **1** to make external; give outward shape to. **2** *Psychol.* to attribute (one's feelings) to one's surroundings.
 ▶ ex,ternali'zation *or* ex,ternali'sation *n*

extinct (ɪk'stɪŋkt) *adj* **1** (of an animal or plant species) having died out. **2** quenched or extinguished. **3** (of a volcano) no longer liable to erupt; inactive. [C15: from L *exstinctus* quenched, from *exstinguere* to EXTINGUISH]

extinction (ɪk'stɪŋkʃən) *n* **1** the act of making extinct or the state of being extinct. **2** the act of extinguishing or the state of being extinguished. **3** complete destruction; annihilation. **4** *Physics*. reduction of the intensity of radiation as a result of absorption or scattering by matter.

extinguish (ɪk'stɪŋgwɪʃ) *vb* (*tr*) **1** to put out or quench (a light, flames, etc.). **2** to remove or destroy entirely; annihilate. **3** *Arch.* to eclipse or obscure. [C16: from L *exstinguere*, from *stinguere* to quench]
 ▶ ex'tinguishable *adj* ▶ ex'tinguisher *n* ▶ ex'tinguishment *n*

extirpate ('ɛkstəˌpeɪt) *vb* **extirpates, extirpating, extirpated.** (*tr*) **1** to remove or destroy completely. **2** to pull up or out; uproot. [C16: from L *exstirpāre* to root out, from *stirps* root, stock]
 ▶ ,extir'pation *n* ▶ 'extir,pator *n*

extol *or US* **extoll** (ɪk'stəʊl) *vb* **extols** *or US* **extolls, extolling, extolled.** (*tr*) to praise lavishly; exalt. [C15: from L *extollere* to elevate, from *tollere* to raise]
 ▶ ex'toller *n* ▶ ex'tolment *n*

extort (ɪk'stɔːt) *vb* (*tr*) **1** to secure (money, favours, etc.) by intimidation, violence, or the misuse of authority. **2** to obtain by importunate demands. [C16: from L *extortus* wrenched out, from *extorquēre* to wrest away, from *torquēre* to twist, wrench]
 ▶ ex'tortion *n* ▶ ex'tortioner, ex'tortionist, *or* ex'torter *n* ▶ ex'tortive *adj*

extortionate (ɪk'stɔːʃənɪt) *adj* **1** (of prices, etc.) excessive; exorbitant. **2** (of persons) using extortion.
 ▶ ex'tortionately *adv*

extra ('ɛkstrə) *adj* **1** being more than what is usual or expected; additional. ◆ *n* **2** a person or thing that is additional. **3** something for which an additional charge is made. **4** an additional edition of a newspaper, esp. to report a new development. **5** *Films*. a person temporarily engaged, usually for crowd scenes. **6** *Cricket*. a run not scored from the bat, such as a wide, no-ball, or bye. ◆ *adv* **7** unusually; exceptionally: *an extra fast car*. [C18: ? shortened from EXTRAORDINARY]

extra- *prefix* outside or beyond an area or scope: *extrasensory; extraterritorial*. [from L *extrā* outside, beyond, from *extera*, from *exterus* outward]

extra cover *n Cricket*. a fielding position between cover and mid-off.

extract *vb* (ɪk'strækt). (*tr*) **1** to pull out or uproot by force. **2** to remove or separate. **3** to derive (pleasure, information, etc.) from some source. **4** to deduce or develop (a doctrine, policy, etc.). **5** *Inf.* to extort (money, etc.). **6** to obtain (a substance) from a mixture or material by a pro-

cess, such as digestion, distillation, mechanical separation, etc. **7** to cut out or copy out (an article, passage, etc.) from a publication. **8** to determine the value of (the root of a number). ◆ *n* ('ɛkstrækt). **9** something extracted, such as a passage from a book, etc. **10** a preparation containing the active principle or concentrated essence of a material. [C15: from L *extractus* drawn forth, from *extrahere*, from *trahere* to drag]
▶ ex'tractable *adj* ▶ ex,tracta'bility *n* ▶ ex'tractive *adj*

> **USAGE NOTE** *Extract* is sometimes wrongly used where *extricate* would be better: *he will find it difficult extricating* (not *extracting*) *himself from this situation.*

extraction (ɪk'strækʃən) *n* **1** the act of extracting or the condition of being extracted. **2** something extracted. **3** the act or an instance of extracting a tooth. **4** origin or ancestry.

extractor (ɪk'stræktə) *n* **1** a person or thing that extracts. **2** an instrument for pulling something out or removing tight-fitting components. **3** short for **extractor fan**.

extractor fan *or* **extraction fan** *n* a fan used in kitchens, bathrooms, workshops, etc., to remove stale air or fumes.

extracurricular (,ɛkstrəkə'rɪkjulə) *adj* **1** taking place outside the normal school timetable. **2** beyond the regular duties, schedule, etc.

extradite (‘ɛkstrə,daɪt) *vb* **extradites, extraditing, extradited.** (*tr*) **1** to surrender (an alleged offender) for trial to a foreign state. **2** to procure the extradition of. [C19: back formation from EXTRADITION]
▶ 'extra,ditable *adj*

extradition (,ɛkstrə'dɪʃən) *n* the surrender of an alleged offender to the state where the alleged offence was committed. [C19: from F, from L *trāditiō* a handing over]

extrados (ɛk'streɪdɒs) *n, pl* **extrados** (-dəuz) *or* **extradoses.** *Archit.* the outer curve of an arch or vault. [C18: from F, from EXTRA- + *dos* back]

extradural (,ɛkstrə'djuərəl) *adj* another word for **epidural** (sense 1).

extragalactic (,ɛkstrəgə'læktɪk) *adj* occurring or existing beyond the Galaxy.

extramarital (,ɛkstrə'mærɪt°l) *adj* (esp. of sexual relations) occurring outside marriage.

extramural (,ɛkstrə'mjuərəl) *adj* **1** connected with but outside the normal courses of a university, college, etc. **2** beyond the boundaries or walls of a city, castle, etc.

extraneous (ɪk'streɪnɪəs) *adj* **1** not essential. **2** not pertinent; irrelevant. **3** coming from without. **4** not belonging. [C17: from L *extrāneus* external, from *extrā* outside]
▶ ex'traneousness *n*

extraordinary (ɪk'strɔ:d°nrɪ) *adj* **1** very unusual or surprising. **2** not in an established manner or order. **3** employed for particular purposes. **4** (*usually postpositive*) (of an official, etc.) additional or subordinate. [C15: from L *extraordinārius* beyond what is usual; see ORDINARY]
▶ ex'traordinarily *adv* ▶ ex'traordinariness *n*

extraordinary general meeting *n* a meeting specially called to discuss an important item of a company's business. It may be called by a group of shareholders or by the directors. Abbrev.: **EGM**.

extrapolate (ɪk'stræpə,leɪt) *vb* **extrapolates, extrapolating, extrapolated. 1** *Maths.* to estimate (a value of a function etc.) beyond the known values, by the extension of a curve. Cf. **interpolate** (sense 4). **2** to infer (something) by using but not strictly deducing from known facts. [C19: EXTRA- + *-polate*, as in INTERPOLATE]
▶ ex,trapo'lation *n* ▶ ex'trapolative *or* ex'trapolatory *adj*
▶ ex'trapo,lator *n*

extrasensory (,ɛkstrə'sɛnsərɪ) *adj* of or relating to extrasensory perception.

extrasensory perception *n* the supposed ability of certain individuals to obtain information about the environment without the use of normal sensory channels.

extraterritorial (,ɛkstrə,tɛrɪ'tɔ:rɪəl) *or* **exterritorial** *adj* **1** beyond the limits of a country's territory. **2** of, relating to, or possessing extraterritoriality.

extraterritoriality (,ɛkstrə,tɛrɪ,tɔ:rɪ'ælɪtɪ) *n* **1** the privilege granted to some aliens, esp. diplomats, of being exempt from the jurisdiction of the state in which they reside. **2** the right of a state to exercise authority in certain circumstances beyond the limits of its territory.

extra time *n* *Sport.* an additional period played at the end of a match, to compensate for time lost through injury or (in certain circumstances) to allow the teams to achieve a conclusive result.

extravagance (ɪk'strævɪgəns) *n* **1** excessive outlay of money; wasteful spending. **2** immoderate or absurd speech or behaviour.

extravagant (ɪk'strævɪgənt) *adj* **1** spending money excessively or immoderately. **2** going beyond usual bounds; unrestrained. **3** ostentatious; showy. **4** exorbitant in price; overpriced. [C14: from Med. L *extravagāns*, from L EXTRA- + *vagārī* to wander]

extravaganza (ɪk,strævə'gænzə) *n* **1** an elaborately staged light entertainment. **2** any lavish or fanciful display, literary composition, etc. [C18: from It.: extravagance]

extravasate (ɪk'strævə,seɪt) *vb* **extravasates, extravasating, extravasated.** *Pathol.* to cause (blood or lymph) to escape or (of blood or lymph) to escape into the surrounding tissues from their proper vessels. [C17: from L EXTRA- + *vās* vessel]
▶ ex,trava'sation *n*

extravehicular (,ɛkstrəvɪ'hɪkjulə) *adj* occurring or used outside a spacecraft, either in space or on the surface of a planet.

extraversion (,ɛkstrə'vɜ:ʃən) *n* a variant spelling of **extroversion.**
▶ 'extra,vert *n, adj*

extra virgin *adj* (of olive oil) of the highest quality, extracted by cold pressing rather than chemical treatment.

Extremadura ★ (estrema'ðura) *n* the Spanish name for **Estremadura.**

extreme (ɪk'stri:m) *adj* **1** being of a high or of the highest degree or intensity. **2** exceeding what is usual or reasonable; immoderate. **3** very strict or severe; drastic. **4** (*prenominal*) farthest or outermost. ◆ *n* **5** the highest or furthest degree (often in **in the extreme, go to extremes**). **6** (*often pl*) either of the two limits or ends of a scale or range. **7** *Maths.* the first or last term of a series or a proportion. [C15: from L *extrēmus* outermost, from *exterus* on the outside; see EXTERIOR]
▶ ex'tremely *adv* ▶ ex'tremeness *n*

> **USAGE NOTE** See at **very.**

extreme unction *n* *RC Church.* the former name for anointing of the sick.

extremist (ɪk'stri:mɪst) *n* **1** a person who favours immoderate or fanatical methods, esp. in being politically radical. ◆ *adj* **2** of or characterized by immoderate or excessive actions, opinions, etc.
▶ ex'tremism *n*

extremity (ɪk'strɛmɪtɪ) *n, pl* **extremities. 1** the farthest or outermost point or section. **2** the greatest degree. **3** an extreme condition or state, as of adversity. **4** a limb, such as a leg or wing, or the end of such a limb. **5** (*usually pl*) *Arch.* a drastic or severe measure.

extricate ('ɛkstrɪ,keɪt) *vb* **extricates, extricating, extricated.** (*tr*) to remove or free from complication, hindrance, or difficulty; disentangle. [C17: from L *extrīcāre* to disentangle]
▶ 'extricable *adj* ▶ ,extri'cation *n*

> **USAGE NOTE** See at **extract.**

extrinsic (ɛk'strɪnsɪk) *adj* **1** not contained or included within; extraneous. **2** originating or acting from outside

---

★ people and places

[C16: from LL *extrinsecus* (adj) outward, from L (adv), ult. from *exter* outward + *secus* alongside]
▶ ex'trinsically *adv*

extroversion *or* **extraversion** (ˌɛkstrə'vɜːʃən) *n Psychol.* the directing of one's interest outwards, esp. towards social contacts. [C17: from *extro*- (var. of EXTRA-, contrasting with *intro*-) + *-version*, from L *vertere* to turn]
▶ ˌextro'versive *or* ˌextra'versive *adj*

extrovert *or* **extravert** ('ɛkstrəˌvɜːt) *Psychol.* ◆ *n* **1** a person concerned more with external reality than inner feelings. ◆ *adj* **2** of or characterized by extroversion. [C20: from *extro*- (var. of EXTRA-, contrasting with *intro*-) + *-vert*, from L *vertere* to turn]
▶ 'extroˌverted *or* 'extraˌverted *adj*

extrude (ɪk'struːd) *vb* **extrudes, extruding, extruded.** (tr) **1** to squeeze or force out. **2** to produce (moulded sections of plastic, metal, etc.) by ejection from a shaped nozzle or die. **3** to chop up or pulverize (an item of food) and re-form it to look like a whole. [C16: from L *extrūdere* to thrust out, from *trūdere* to push, thrust]
▶ ex'truded *adj*

extrusion (ɪk'struːʒən) *n* **1** the act or process of extruding. **2a** the movement of magma through volcano craters and cracks in the earth's crust, forming igneous rock. **2b** any igneous rock formed in this way. **3** anything formed by the process of extruding.
▶ ex'trusive *adj*

exuberant (ɪg'zjuːbərənt) *adj* **1** abounding in vigour and high spirits. **2** lavish or effusive; excessively elaborate. **3** growing luxuriantly or in profusion. [C15: from L *exūberāns*, from *ūberāre* to be fruitful]
▶ ex'uberance *n*

exuberate (ɪg'zjuːbəˌreɪt) *vb* **exuberates, exuberating, exuberated.** (intr) *Rare.* **1** to be exuberant. **2** to abound. [C15: from L *exūberāre* to be abundant; see EXUBERANT]

exude (ɪg'zjuːd) *vb* **exudes, exuding, exuded. 1** to release or be released through pores, incisions, etc., as sweat or sap. **2** (tr) to make apparent by mood or behaviour. [C16: from L *exsūdāre*, from *sūdāre* to sweat]
▶ **exudation** (ˌɛksjuː'deɪʃən) *n*

exult (ɪg'zʌlt) *vb* (intr) **1** to be joyful or jubilant, esp. because of triumph or success. **2** (often by *over*) to triumph (over). [C16: from L *exsultāre* to jump or leap for joy, from *saltāre* to leap]
▶ **exultation** (ˌɛgzʌl'teɪʃən) *n* ▶ ex'ultingly *adv*

USAGE NOTE See at **exalt.**

---

exultant (ɪg'zʌltənt) *adj* elated or jubilant, esp. because of triumph or success.
▶ ex'ultantly *adv*

exurbia (ɛks'ɜːbɪə) *n Chiefly US.* the region outside the suburbs of a city, consisting of residential areas (**exurbs**) occupied predominantly by rich commuters (**ex-urbanites**). [C20: from EX-¹ + L *urbs* city]
▶ ex'urban *adj*

exuviate (ɪg'zjuːvɪˌeɪt) *vb* **exuviates, exuviating, exuviated.** to shed (a skin or similar outer covering). [C17: from L *exuere* to strip off]
▶ exˌuvi'ation *n*

-ey *suffix.* a variant of -y¹ and -y².

Eyam ★ ('iːəm) *n* a village in N central England, in Derbyshire. When plague reached the village in 1665 the inhabitants isolated themselves to prevent it spreading further: as a result, most of them died.

eyas ('aɪəs) *n* a nestling hawk or falcon, esp. one reared for falconry. [C15: mistaken division of earlier *a nyas*, from OF *niais* nestling, from L *nīdus* nest]

eye¹ (aɪ) *n* **1** the organ of sight of animals. Related adjs: **ocular, ophthalmic. 2** (often pl) the ability to see; sense of vision. **3** the external part of an eye, often including the area around it. **4** a look, glance, expression, or gaze. **5** a sexually inviting or provocative look (esp. in **give (some-one) the (glad) eye, make eyes at**). **6** attention or observation (often in **catch someone's eye, keep an eye on, cast an eye over**). **7** ability to recognize, judge, or appreciate. **8**

(often *pl*) opinion, judgment, point of view, or authority: *in the eyes of the law.* **9** a structure or marking resembling an eye, such as the bud on a potato tuber or a spot on a butterfly wing. **10** a small loop or hole, as at one end of a needle. **11** a small area of low pressure and calm in the centre of a storm, hurricane, or tornado. **12 electric eye.** another name for **photocell. 13 all eyes.** *Inf.* acutely vigilant or observant. **14 (all) my eye.** *Inf.* rubbish; nonsense. **15 an eye for an eye.** retributive or vengeful justice; retaliation. **16 get one's eye in.** *Chiefly sport.* to become accustomed to the conditions, light, etc., with a consequent improvement in one's performance. **17 go eyes out.** *Austral. & NZ.* to make every possible effort. **18 half an eye.** a modicum of perceptiveness. **19 have eyes for.** to be interested in. **20 in one's mind's eye.** pictured within the mind; imagined or remembered vividly. **21 in the public eye.** exposed to public curiosity or publicity. **22 keep an eye open** *or* **out (for).** to watch with special attention (for). **23 keep one's eyes peeled** (*or* **skinned**). to watch vigilantly (for). **24 lay, clap,** *or* **set eyes on.** (*usually with a negative*) to see. **25 look (someone) in the eye.** to look openly and without shame or embarrassment at (someone). **26 make sheep's eyes (at).** *Old-fashioned.* to ogle amorously. **27 more than meets the eye.** hidden motives, meaning, or facts. **28 see eye to eye (with).** to agree (with). **29 turn a blind eye to** *or* **close one's eyes to.** to pretend not to notice or to ignore deliberately. **30 up to one's eyes (in).** extremely busy (with). **31 with** *or* **having an eye to.** (prep) **31a** regarding; with reference to. **31b** with the intention or purpose of. **32 with one's eyes open.** in the full knowledge of all relevant facts. **33 with one's eyes shut. 33a** with great ease, esp. as a result of thorough familiarity. **33b** without being aware of all the facts. ◆ *vb* **eyes, eyeing** *or* **eying, eyed.** (tr) **34** to look at carefully or warily. **35** Also: **eye up.** to look at in a manner indicating sexual interest; ogle. [OE *ēage*]
▶ 'eyeless *adj* ▶ 'eyeˌlike *adj*

eye² (aɪ) *n* another word for **nye.**

eyeball ('aɪˌbɔːl) *n* **1** the entire ball-shaped part of the eye. **2 eyeball to eyeball.** in close confrontation. ◆ *vb* **3** (tr) *Sl.* to stare at.

eyebank ('aɪˌbæŋk) *n* a place in which corneas are stored for use in corneal grafts.

eyebath ('aɪˌbɑːθ) *n* a small vessel for applying medicated or cleansing solutions to the eye. Also called (US and Canad.): **eyecup.**

eyeblack ('aɪˌblæk) *n* another name for **mascara.**

eyebright ('aɪˌbraɪt) *n* an annual plant having small white-and-purple flowers: formerly used in the treatment of eye disorders.

eyebrow ('aɪˌbraʊ) *n* **1** the transverse bony ridge over each eye. **2** the arch of hair that covers this ridge. **3 raise an eyebrow.** to give rise to doubt or disapproval.

eyebrow pencil *n* a cosmetic in pencil form for applying colour and shape to the eyebrows.

eye-catching *adj* tending to attract attention; striking.

eye contact *n* a direct look between two people; meeting of eyes.

eyed (aɪd) *adj* **a** having an eye or eyes (as specified). **b** (in combination): *brown-eyed.*

eye dog *n NZ.* a dog trained to control sheep by staring fixedly at them. Also called: **strong-eye dog.**

eyeful ('aɪful) *n Inf.* **1** a view, glance, or gaze. **2** a beautiful or attractive sight, esp. a woman.

eyeglass ('aɪˌɡlɑːs) *n* **1** a lens for aiding or correcting defective vision, esp. a monocle. **2** another word for **eyepiece** or **eyebath.**

eyeglasses ('aɪˌɡlɑːsɪz) *pl n Now chiefly US.* another word for **spectacles.**

eyehole ('aɪˌhəʊl) *n* **1** a hole through which a rope, hook, etc., is passed. **2** the cavity that contains the eyeball. **3** another word for **peephole.**

eyelash ('aɪˌlæʃ) *n* **1** any one of the short curved hairs that grow from the edge of the eyelids. **2** a row or fringe of these hairs.

eyelet ('aɪlɪt) *n* **1** a small hole for a lace, cord, or hook to be passed through. **2** a small metal ring or tube reinforcing an eyehole in fabric. **3** a small opening, such as a peephole. **4** *Embroidery.* a small hole with finely stitched edges. **5** a small eye or eyelike marking. ♦ *vb* **6** (*tr*) to supply with an eyelet or eyelets. [C14: from OF *oillet*, lit.: a little eye, from *oill* eye, from L *oculus* eye]

eyelevel ('aɪ,levᵊl) *adj* level with a person's eyes when looking straight ahead: *an eyelevel grill.*

eyelid ('aɪ,lɪd) *n* either of the two muscular folds of skin that can be moved to cover the exposed portion of the eyeball.

eyeliner (aɪ,laɪnə) *n* a cosmetic used to outline the eyes.

eye-opener *n Inf.* **1** something startling or revealing. **2** *US & Canad.* an alcoholic drink taken early in the morning.

eyepiece ('aɪ,piːs) *n* the lens or lenses in an optical instrument nearest the eye of the observer.

eye rhyme *n* a rhyme involving words that are similar in spelling but not in sound, such as *stone* and *none.*

eye shadow *n* a coloured cosmetic put around the eyes.

eyeshot ('aɪ,ʃɒt) *n* range of vision; view.

eyesight ('aɪ,saɪt) *n* the ability to see; faculty of sight.

eyesore ('aɪ,sɔː) *n* something very ugly.

eyespot ('aɪ,spɒt) *n* **1** a small area of light-sensitive pigment in some simple organisms. **2** an eyelike marking, as on a butterfly wing.

eyestrain ('aɪ,streɪn) *n* fatigue or irritation of the eyes, resulting from excessive use or uncorrected defects of vision.

Eyetie ('aɪtaɪ) *n, adj Brit. sl., offensive.* Italian. [C20: from jocular mispronunciation of *Italian*]

eyetooth (,aɪ'tuːθ) *n, pl* **eyeteeth. 1** either of the two canine teeth in the upper jaw. **2 give one's eyeteeth for.** to go to any lengths to achieve or obtain (something).

eyewash ('aɪ,wɒʃ) *n* **1** a lotion for the eyes. **2** *Inf.* nonsense; rubbish.

eyewitness ('aɪ,wɪtnɪs) *n* a person present at an event who can describe what happened.

eyot (aɪt) *n Brit., obs. except in place names.* island. [var. of AIT]

Eyre¹ (εə) ★ *n* **Lake.** a shallow salt lake in NE central South Australia, about 11 m (35 ft) below sea level. Area: 9600 sq. km (3700 sq. miles). [C19: after E. J. EYRE]

Eyre² (εə) ★ *n* **1 Edward John.** 1815–1901, British explorer and colonial administrator. He was governor of Jamaica (1864–66); his authorization of 400 executions led to his recall. **2 Richard.** born 1943, British theatre director: director of the Royal National Theatre (1988–97).

Eyre Peninsula ★ *n* a peninsula of South Australia, between the Great Australian Bight and Spencer Gulf.

eyrie ('ɪərɪ, 'εərɪ, 'aɪərɪ) *or* **aerie** *n* **1** the nest of an eagle or other bird of prey, built in a high inaccessible place. **2** any high isolated position or place. [C16: from Med. L *airea*, from L *ārea* open field, hence, nest]

eyrir ('eɪrɪə) *n, pl* **aurar** ('ɔɪrɑː). an Icelandic monetary unit worth one hundredth of a krona. [ON: ounce (of silver), money; rel. to L *aureus* golden]

Eysenck ★ ('aɪzεŋk) *n* **Hans Jürgen** (hænz 'jɜːgən). 1916–97, British psychologist, born in Germany, who developed a theory of personality based on heredity.

Ez. *or* **Ezr.** *Bible. abbrev. for* Ezra.

Ezek. *Bible. abbrev. for* Ezekiel.

Ezekiel ★ (ɪ'ziːkɪəl) *n Old Testament.* **1** a Hebrew prophet of the 6th century B.C., exiled to Babylon in 597 B.C. **2** the book containing his oracles, which describe the downfall of Judah and Jerusalem and their subsequent restoration. Douay spelling: **Ezechiel.**

Ezra ★ ('εzrə) *n Old Testament.* **1** a Jewish priest of the 5th century B.C., who was sent from Babylon by the Persian king Artaxerxes I to reconstitute observance of the Jewish law and worship in Jerusalem after the captivity. **2** the book recounting his efforts to perform this task.

★ people and places

Ff

f *or* **F** (ɛf) *n, pl* **f's, F's,** *or* **Fs. 1** the sixth letter of the English alphabet. **2** a speech sound represented by this letter, as in *fat*.

f *symbol for:* **1** *Music.* forte: an instruction to play loudly. **2** *Physics.* frequency. **3** *Maths.* function (of). **4** *Physics.* femto-.

f, f/, *or* **f:** *symbol for* f-number.

F *symbol for:* **1** *Music.* **1a** the fourth note of the scale of C major. **1b** the major or minor key having this note as its tonic. **2** Fahrenheit. **3** farad(s). **4** *Chem.* fluorine. **5** *Physics.* force. **6** franc(s). **7** *Genetics.* a generation of filial offspring, F_1 being the first generation of offspring.

f. *or* **F.** *abbrev. for:* **1** fathom(s). **2** female. **3** *Grammar.* feminine. **4** (*pl* **ff.** *or* **FF.**) folio. **5** (*pl* **ff.**) following (page).

F- (of US military aircraft) *abbrev. for* fighter.

fa (fɑː) *n Music.* the syllable used in the fixed system of solmization for the note F. **[C14:** see GAMUT]

FA (in Britain) *abbrev. for* Football Association.

f.a. *or* **FA** *abbrev. for* fanny adams.

FAB *abbrev. for* fuel air bomb.

Fabergé ★ ('fæbəˌʒeɪ) *n* **Peter Carl.** 1846–1920, Russian goldsmith and jeweller, known for the golden Easter eggs he created for the Russian and other royal families.

Fabian ('feɪbɪən) *adj* **1** of or resembling the delaying tactics of Q. Fabius Maximus; cautious. **2** a member of or sympathizer with the Fabian Society. **[C19:** from L *Fabiānus* of Fabius]
▶ **'Fabiaˌnism** *n*

Fabian Society *n* an association of British socialists advocating the establishment of socialism by gradual reforms.

Fabius Maximus ★ ('feɪbɪəs 'mæksɪməs) *n* full name *Quintus Fabius Maximus Verrucosus*, called *Cunctator* (the delayer). died 203 B.C., Roman general and statesman. As commander of the Roman army during the Second Punic War, he withstood Hannibal by his strategy of harassing the Carthaginians while avoiding a pitched battle.

fable ('feɪbʰl) *n* **1** a short moral story, esp. one with animals as characters. **2** a false, fictitious, or improbable account. **3** a story or legend about supernatural or mythical characters or events. **4** legends or myths collectively. ◆ *vb* **fables, fabling, fabled.** **5** to relate or tell (fables). **6** (*intr*) to tell lies. **7** (*tr*) to talk about or describe in the manner of a fable. **[C13:** from L *fābula* story, narrative, from *fārī* to speak, say]
▶ **'fabler** *n*

fabled ('feɪbʰld) *adj* **1** made famous in fable. **2** fictitious.

fabliau ('fæblɪˌəʊ) *n, pl* **fabliaux** ('fæblɪˌəʊz). a comic usually ribald verse tale, popular in France in the 12th and 13th centuries. **[C19:** from F: a little tale, from *fable* tale]

Fablon ('fæblən, -lɒn) *n Trademark.* a brand of adhesive-backed plastic material used to cover and decorate shelves, worktops, etc.

Fabre ★ (*French* fabrə) *n* **Jean Henri** (ʒɑ̃ ɑ̃ri). 1823–1915, French entomologist; author of many works on insect life, esp. *Souvenirs Entomologiques* (1879–1907). Nobel prize for literature 1910.

fabric ('fæbrɪk) *n* **1** any cloth made from yarn or fibres by weaving, knitting, felting, etc. **2** the texture of a cloth. **3** a structure or framework: *the fabric of society.* **4** a style or method of construction. **5** *Rare.* a building. **[C15:** from L *fabrica* workshop, from *faber* craftsman]

fabricate ('fæbrɪˌkeɪt) *vb* **fabricates, fabricating, fabricated.** (*tr*) **1** to make, build, or construct. **2** to devise or concoct (a story, etc.). **3** to fake or forge. **[C15:** from L, from *fabrica* workshop; see FABRIC]
▶ **ˌfabriˈcation** *n* ▶ **'fabriˌcator** *n*

Fabry ★ (*French* fabri) *n* **Charles** (ʃarl). 1867–1945, French physicist: discovered ozone in the upper atmosphere.

fabulist ('fæbjʊlɪst) *n* **1** a person who invents or recounts fables. **2** a person who lies.

fabulous ('fæbjʊləs) *adj* **1** almost unbelievable; astounding; legendary: *fabulous wealth.* **2** *Inf.* extremely good: *a fabulous time at the party.* **3** of, relating to, or based upon fable: *a fabulous beast.* **[C15:** from L *fābulōsus* celebrated in fable, from *fābula* FABLE]
▶ **'fabulously** *adv* ▶ **'fabulousness** *n*

Fac. *abbrev. for* Faculty.

façade *or* **facade** (fə'sɑːd, fæ-) *n* **1** the face of a building, esp. the main front. **2** a front or outer appearance, esp. a deceptive one. **[C17:** from F, from It., from *faccia* FACE]

face (feɪs) *n* **1a** the front of the head from the forehead to the lower jaw. **1b** (*as modifier*): *face flannel.* **2a** the expression of the countenance: *a sad face.* **2b** a distorted expression, esp. to indicate disgust. **3** *Inf.* make-up (esp. in **put one's face on**). **4** outward appearance: *the face of the countryside is changing.* **5** appearance or pretence (esp. in **put a bold, good, bad,** etc., **face on**). **6** dignity (esp. in **lose** *or* **save face**). **7** *Inf.* impudence or effrontery. **8** the main side of an object, building, etc., or the front: *a cliff face.* **9** the marked surface of an instrument, esp. the dial of a timepiece. **10** the functional or working side of an object, as of a tool or playing card. **11a** the exposed area of a mine from which coal, ore, etc., may be mined. **11b** (*as modifier*): *face worker.* **12** the uppermost part or surface: *the face of the earth.* **13** Also called: **side.** any one of the plane surfaces of a crystal or other solid figure. **14** Also called: **typeface.** *Printing.* **14a** the printing surface of any type character. **14b** the style or design of the character on the type. **15** *NZ.* the exposed slope of a hill. **16** *Brit. sl.* a well-known or important person. **17 in (the) face of.** despite. **18 on the face of it.** to all appearances. **19 set one's face against.** to oppose with determination. **20 show one's face.** to make an appearance. **21 to someone's** presence: *I told him the truth to his face.* ◆ *vb* **faces, facing, faced. 22** (when *intr,* often foll. by *to, towards,* or *on*) to look at or be situated or placed (in a specified direction): *the house faces onto the square.* **23** to be opposite: *facing page 9.* **24** (*tr*) to be confronted by: *he faces many problems.* **25** (*tr*) to provide with a surface of a different material. **26** to dress the surface of (stone or other material). **27** (*tr*) to expose (a card) with the face uppermost. **28** *Mil.* to order (a formation) to turn in a certain direction or (of a formation) to turn as required: *right face!* ◆ See also **face down, face up to. [C13:** from OF, from Vulgar L *facia* (unattested), from L *faciēs* form]

face card *n* the usual US and Canad. term for **court card.**

face cloth *or* **face flannel** *n Brit.* a small piece of cloth used to wash the face and hands. US equivalent: **washcloth.**

facedown ('feɪsdaʊn) *n Inf.* another word for **face-off** (sense 2).

face down *vb* (*tr, adv*) to confront and force (someone or something) to back down.

faceless ('feɪslɪs) *adj* **1** without a face. **2** without identity; anonymous.
▶ **'facelessness** *n*

face-lift *n* **1** a cosmetic surgical operation for tightening sagging skin and smoothing wrinkles on the face. **2** any improvement or renovation. ◆ *vb* (*tr*) **3** to improve the appearance of, as by a face-lift.

face-off *n* **1** *Ice hockey.* the method of starting a game, in which the referee drops the puck, etc. between two opposing players. **2** Also called: **facedown.** a confrontation, esp. one in which each party attempts to make the other back down. ◆ *vb* **face off.** (*intr, adv*) **3** to start play by a face-off.

face powder *n* a cosmetic powder worn to make the face look less shiny, softer, etc.

facer ('feɪsə) *n* 1 a person or thing that faces. 2 *Brit. inf.* a difficulty or problem.

face-saving *adj* maintaining dignity or prestige.
▶ 'face-,saver *n*

facet ('fæsɪt) *n* 1 any of the surfaces of a cut gemstone. 2 an aspect or phase, as of a subject or personality. ♦ *vb* **facets, faceting** *or* **facetting, faceted** *or* **facetted. 3** (*tr*) to cut facets in (a gemstone). [C17: from F *facette* a little FACE]

facetiae (fə'siːʃɪˌiː) *pl n* 1 humorous or witty sayings. 2 obscene or coarsely witty books. [C17: from L: jests, pl of *facētia* witticism, from *facētus* elegant]

facetious (fə'siːʃəs) *adj* 1 characterized by love of joking. 2 jocular or amusing, esp. at inappropriate times: *facetious remarks*. [C16: from OF *facetieux*, from *facetie* witticism; see FACETIAE]
▶ fa'cetiously *adv* ▶ fa'cetiousness *n*

face to face *adv, adj* (**face-to-face** *as adj*) 1 opposite one another. 2 in confrontation.

face up to *vb* (*intr, adv + prep*) to accept (an unpleasant fact, reality, etc.).

face value *n* 1 the value written or stamped on the face of a commercial paper or coin. 2 apparent worth or value.

facia ('feɪʃɪə) *n* a variant spelling of **fascia**.

facial ('feɪʃəl) *adj* 1 of or relating to the face. ♦ *n* 2 a beauty treatment for the face involving massage and cosmetic packs.
▶ 'facially *adv*

-facient *suffix forming adjectives and nouns.* indicating a state or quality: *absorbefacient*. [from L *facient-, faciēns*, present participle of *facere* to do]

facies ('feɪʃɪˌiːz) *n, pl* **facies. 1** the general form and appearance of an individual or a group. 2 the characteristics of a rock or rocks reflecting their appearance and conditions of formation. 3 *Med.* the general facial expression of a patient. [C17: from L: appearance, FACE]

facile ('fæsaɪl) *adj* 1 easy to perform or achieve. 2 working or moving easily or smoothly. 3 superficial: *a facile solution*. [C15: from L *facilis* easy, from *facere* to do]
▶ 'facilely *adv* ▶ 'facileness *n*

facilitate (fə'sɪlɪˌteɪt) *vb* **facilitates, facilitating, facilitated.** (*tr*) to assist the progress of.
▶ fa,cili'tation *n*

facility (fə'sɪlɪtɪ) *n, pl* **facilities. 1** ease of action or performance. 2 ready skill or ease deriving from practice or familiarity. 3 (*often pl*) the means or equipment facilitating the performance of an action. 4 *Rare.* easy-going disposition. 5 (*usually pl*) a euphemistic word for **lavatory**. [C15: from L *facilitās*, from *facilis* easy; see FACILE]

facing ('feɪsɪŋ) *n* 1 a piece of material used esp. to conceal the seam of a garment and prevent fraying. 2 (*usually pl*) the collar, cuffs, etc., of the jacket of a military uniform. 3 an outer layer or coat of material applied to the surface of a wall.

facsimile (fæk'sɪmɪlɪ) *n* 1 an exact copy or reproduction. 2 an image produced by facsimile transmission; fax. ♦ *vb* **facsimiles, facsimileing, facsimiled. 3** (*tr*) to make an exact copy of. [C17: from L *fac simile!* make something like it!, from *facere* to make + *similis* similar, like]

facsimile transmission *n* an international system of transmitting a written, printed, or pictorial document over the telephone system by scanning it photoelectrically and reproducing the image xerographically after transmission. Often shortened to **fax**.

fact (fækt) *n* 1 an event or thing known to have happened or existed. 2 a truth verifiable from experience or observation. 3 a piece of information: *get me all the facts of this case*. 4 (*often pl*) *Law.* an actual event, happening, etc., as distinguished from its legal consequences. 5 **after** (*or* **before**) **the fact.** *Criminal law.* after (or before) the commission of the offence. 6 **as a matter of fact, in fact, in point of fact.** in reality or actuality. 7 **fact of life.** an inescapable truth, esp. an unpleasant one. See also **facts of life.** [C16: from L *factum* something done, from *factus* made, from *facere* to do, make]

faction[1] ('fækʃən) *n* 1 a group of people forming a minority within a larger body, esp. a dissentious group. 2 strife or dissension within a group. [C16: from L *factiō* a making, from *facere* to do, make]
▶ 'factional *adj*

faction[2] ('fækʃən) *n* a television programme, film, or literary work comprising a dramatized presentation of actual events. [C20: a blend of FACT & FICTION]

faction fight *n* conflict between different groups within a larger body, esp. in S Africa a fight between Blacks of different tribes.

factious ('fækʃəs) *adj* given to, producing, or characterized by faction.
▶ 'factiously *adv*

> **USAGE NOTE**   See at **fractious.**

factitious (fæk'tɪʃəs) *adj* 1 artificial rather than natural. 2 not genuine; sham: *factitious enthusiasm*. [C17: from L *factīcius*, from *facere* to do, make]
▶ fac'titiously *adv* ▶ fac'titiousness *n*

factitive ('fæktɪtɪv) *adj Grammar.* denoting a verb taking a direct object as well as a noun in apposition, as for example *elect* in *They elected John president*, where *John* is the direct object and *president* is the complement. [C19: from NL, from L *factitāre* to do frequently, from *facere* to do, make]

factoid ('fæktɔɪd) *n* a piece of unreliable information believed to be true because of the way it is presented or repeated in print. [C20: coined by Norman MAILER, from FACT + -OID]

factor ('fæktə) *n* 1 an element or cause that contributes to a result. 2 *Maths.* one of two or more integers or polynomials whose product is a given integer or polynomial: *2 and 3 are factors of 6*. 3 (foll. by identifying numeral) *Med.* any of several substances that participate in the clotting of blood: *factor VIII*. 4 a person who acts on another's behalf, esp. one who transacts business for another. 5 former name for a **gene**. 6 *Commercial law.* a person to whom goods are consigned for sale and who is paid a commission. 7 (in Scotland) the manager of an estate. ♦ *vb* 8 (*intr*) to engage in the business of a factor. [C15: from L: one who acts, from *facere* to do, make]
▶ 'factorable *adj* ▶ 'factorship *n*

> **USAGE NOTE**   *Factor* (sense 1) should only be used to refer to something which contributes to a result. It should not be used to refer to a part of something such as a plan or arrangement; instead a word such as *component* or *element* should be used.

factor VIII *n* a protein that participates in the clotting of blood. It is extracted from donated serum and used in the treatment of haemophilia.

factorial (fæk'tɔːrɪəl) *Maths.* ♦ *n* 1 the product of all the positive integers from one up to and including a given integer: *factorial four is $1 \times 2 \times 3 \times 4$.* ♦ *adj* 2 of or involving factorials or factors.
▶ fac'torially *adv*

factorize *or* **factorise** ('fæktəˌraɪz) *vb* **factorizes, factorizing, factorized** *or* **factorises, factorising, factorised.** (*tr*) *Maths.* to resolve (an integer or polynomial) into factors.
▶ ,factori'zation *or* ,factori'sation *n*

factory ('fæktərɪ) *n, pl* **factories. a** a building or group of buildings containing a plant assembly for the manufacture of goods. **b** (*as modifier*): *a factory worker*. [C16: from LL *factorium*; see FACTOR]
▶ 'factory-,like *adj*

factory farm *n* a farm in which animals are intensively reared using modern industrial methods.
▶ factory farming *n*

factory ship *n* a vessel that processes fish supplied by a fleet.

factotum (fæk'təʊtəm) *n* a person employed to do all

★ people and places

kinds of work. [C16: from Med. L, from L *fac! do!* + *tōtum*, from *tōtus* (adj) all]

acts and figures *pl n* details.

actsheet ('fækt,ʃiːt) *n* a printed sheet containing information relating to items covered in a television or radio programme.

acts of life *pl n* **the.** the details of sexual behaviour and reproduction.

actual ('æktʃʊəl) *adj* **1** of, relating to, or characterized by facts. **2** real; actual.
► **'factually** *adv* ► **'factualness** or **,factu'ality** *n*

acula ('fækjʊlə) *n, pl* **faculae** (-,liː). any of the bright areas on the sun's surface, usually appearing just before a sunspot. [C18: from L: little torch, from *fax* torch]
► **'facular** *adj*

acultative ('fæk°ltətɪv) *adj* **1** empowering but not compelling the doing of an act. **2** that may or may not occur. **3** *Biol.* able to exist under more than one set of environmental conditions. **4** of or relating to a faculty.
► **'facultatively** *adv*

aculty ('fæk°ltɪ) *n, pl* **faculties. 1** one of the inherent powers of the mind or body, such as memory, sight, or hearing. **2** any ability or power, whether acquired or inherent. **3** a conferred power or right. **4a** a department within a university or college devoted to a particular branch of knowledge. **4b** the staff of such a department. **4c** *Chiefly US & Canad.* all the teaching staff at a university, school, etc. **5** all members of a learned profession. [C14 (in the sense: department of learning): from L *facultās* capability; rel. to L *facilis* easy]

A Cup *n Soccer.* (in England and Wales) **1** an annual knockout competition among member teams of the Football Association. **2** the trophy itself.

ad (fæd) *n Inf.* **1** an intense but short-lived fashion. **2** a personal idiosyncrasy. [C19: from ?]
► **'faddish** or **'faddy** *adj*

adden ★ ('fæd°n) *n* Sir **Arthur William**. 1895–1973, Australian statesman; prime minister of Australia (1941).

ade (feɪd) *vb* **fades, fading, faded. 1** to lose or cause to lose brightness, colour, or clarity. **2** (*intr*) to lose vigour or youth. **3** (*intr;* usually foll. by *away* or *out*) to vanish slowly. **4a** to decrease the brightness or volume of (a television or radio programme) or (of a television or radio programme, etc.) to decrease in this way. **4b** to decrease the volume of (a sound) in a recording system or (of a sound) to be so reduced in volume. **5** (*intr*) (of the brakes of a vehicle) to lose power. **6** to cause (a golf ball) to veer from a straight line or (of a golf ball) to veer from a straight flight. ♦ *n* **7** the act or an instance of fading. [C14: from *fade* (adj) dull, from OF, from Vulgar L *fatidus* (unattested), prob. blend of L *vapidus* VAPID + L *fatuus* FATUOUS]
► **'fadeless** *adj* ► **'fadedness** *n* ► **'fader** *n*

ade-in *n* **1** *Films.* an optical effect in which a shot appears gradually out of darkness. ♦ *vb* **fade in.** (*adv*) **2** to increase or cause to increase gradually, as vision or sound in a film or broadcast.

ade-out *n* **1** *Films.* an optical effect in which a shot slowly disappears into darkness. **2** a gradual and temporary loss of a radio or television signal. **3** a slow or gradual disappearance. ♦ *vb* **fade out.** (*adv*) **4** to decrease or cause to decrease gradually, as vision or sound in a film or broadcast.

aeces or *esp. US* **feces** ('fiːsiːz) *pl n* bodily waste matter discharged through the anus. [C15: from L *faecēs*, pl. of *faex* sediment, dregs]
► **faecal** or *esp. US* **fecal** ('fiːk°l) *adj*

aenza ★ (*Italian* fa'entsa) *n* a city in N Italy, in Emilia-Romagna: famous in the 15th and 16th centuries for its majolica earthenware, esp. faïence. Pop.: 54 050 (1990).

aerie or **faery** ('feɪərɪ, 'fɛərɪ) *n, pl* **faeries.** *Arch.* or *poetic.* **1** the land of fairies. ♦ *adj,* *n* **2** a variant spelling of **fairy.**

aeroes or **Faroes** ★ ('feərəʊz) *pl n* a group of 21 basalt islands in the North Atlantic between Iceland and the Shetland Islands: a self-governing community within the kingdom of Denmark; fishing. Capital: Thorshavn.

Pop.: 43 719 (1994). Area: 1400 sq. km (540 sq. miles). Also called: **Faeroe Islands** or **Faroe Islands.**

Faeroese or **Faroese** (,feərəʊ'iːz) *adj* **1** of or characteristic of the Faeroes, their inhabitants, or their language. ♦ *n* **2** the language of the Faeroes, closely related to Icelandic. **3** (*pl* **Faeroese** or **Faroese**) a native or inhabitant of the Faeroes.

faff (fæf) *vb* (*intr;* often foll. by *about*) *Brit. inf.* to dither or fuss. [C19: from ?]

Fafnir ★ ('fæfnɪə, 'fæv-) *n Norse myth.* the son of Hreidmar, whom he killed to gain the cursed treasure of Andvari. He became a dragon and was slain by Sigurd while guarding the treasure.

fag[1] (fæg) *n* **1** *Inf.* a boring or wearisome task. **2** *Brit.* (esp. formerly) a young public school boy who performs menial chores for an older boy or prefect. ♦ *vb* **fags, fagging, fagged. 3** (when *tr,* often foll. by *out*) *Inf.* to become or cause to become exhausted by hard work **4** (*usually intr*) *Brit.* to do or cause to do menial chores in a public school. [C18: from ?]

fag[2] (fæg) *n Brit. sl.* a cigarette. [C16 (in the sense: something hanging loose, flap): from ?]

fag[3] (fæg) *n Sl., chiefly US & Canad.* short for **faggot**[2].

fag end *n* **1** the last and worst part. **2** *Brit. inf.* the stub of a cigarette. [C17: see FAG[2]]

faggot[1] or *esp. US* **fagot** ('fægət) *n* **1** a bundle of sticks or twigs, esp. when used as fuel. **2** a bundle of iron bars, esp. to be forged into wrought iron. **3** a ball of chopped meat bound with herbs and bread and eaten fried. ♦ *vb* (*tr*) **4** to collect into a bundle or bundles. **5** *Needlework.* to do faggoting on (a garment, etc.). [C14: from OF, ?from Gk *phakelos* bundle]

faggot[2] ('fægət) *n Sl., chiefly US & Canad.* a male homosexual. [C20: special use of FAGGOT[1]]

faggoting or *esp. US* **fagoting** ('fægətɪŋ) *n* **1** decorative needlework done by tying vertical threads together in bundles. **2** a decorative way of joining two hems by crisscross stitches.

fag hag *n US sl., usually derog.* a heterosexual woman who prefers the company of homosexual men.

fah *n Music.* (in tonic sol-fa) the fourth degree of any major scale. [C14: later variant of *fa;* see GAMUT]

Fah. or **Fahr.** *abbrev. for* Fahrenheit.

Fahd ibn Abdul Aziz ★ (fɑːd 'ɪb°n ˈæbdʊl ə'ziːz) *n* born 1923, king of Saudi Arabia from 1982.

Fahrenheit[1] ('færən,haɪt) *adj* of or measured according to the Fahrenheit scale of temperature. Symbol: F

Fahrenheit[2] ★ (*German* 'faːrənhaɪt) *n* **Gabriel Daniel** ('gaːbrieːl 'daːnieːl). 1686–1736, German physicist, who invented the mercury thermometer and devised the temperature scale that bears his name.

Fahrenheit scale *n* a scale of temperatures in which 32° represents the melting point of ice and 212° represents the boiling point of pure water under standard atmospheric pressure. Cf. **Celsius scale.**

Faial or **Fayal** ★ (*Portuguese* fə'jal) *n* an island in the central Azores archipelago. Chief town: Horta. Area: 171 sq. km (66 sq. miles).

faïence (faɪ'ɑːns, feɪ-) *n* tin-glazed earthenware, usually that of French, German, Italian, or Scandinavian origin. [C18: from F, strictly: pottery from FAENZA]

fail (feɪl) *vb* **1** to be unsuccessful in an attempt (at something or to do something). **2** (*intr*) to stop operating or working properly: *the steering failed suddenly.* **3** to judge or be judged as being below the officially accepted standard required in (a course, examination, etc.). **4** (*tr*) to prove disappointing or useless to (someone). **5** (*tr*) to neglect or be unable to (do something). **6** (*intr*) to prove insufficient in quantity or extent. **7** (*intr*) to weaken. **8** (*intr*) to go bankrupt. ♦ *n* **9** a failure to attain the required standard. **10** without fail. definitely. [C13: from OF *faillir,* ult. from L *fallere* to disappoint]

failing ('feɪlɪŋ) *n* **1** a weak point. ♦ *prep* **2** (*used to express a condition*) in default of: *failing a solution, the problem will have to wait until Monday.*

fail-safe *adj* **1** designed to return to a safe condition in the event of a failure or malfunction. **2** safe from failure; foolproof.

failure ('feɪljə) *n* **1** the act or an instance of failing. **2** a person or thing that is unsuccessful or disappointing. **3** nonperformance of something required or expected: *failure to attend will be punished.* **4** cessation of normal operation: *a power failure.* **5** an insufficiency: *a crop failure.* **6** a decline or loss, as in health. **7** the fact of not reaching the required standard in an examination, test, etc. **8** bankruptcy.

fain (feɪn) *adv* **1** (usually with *would*) *Arch.* gladly: *she would fain be dead.* ◆ *adj* **2** *Obs.* **2a** willing. **2b** compelled. [OE *fægen;* see FAWN²]

faint (feɪnt) *adj* **1** lacking clarity, brightness, volume, etc. **2** lacking conviction or force: *faint praise.* **3** feeling dizzy or weak as if about to lose consciousness. **4** timid (esp. in **faint-hearted**). **5 not the faintest** (idea *or* notion). no idea whatsoever: *I haven't the faintest.* ◆ *vb* (*intr*) **6** to lose consciousness, as through weakness. **7** *Arch. or poetic.* to become weak, esp. in courage. ◆ *n* **8** a sudden spontaneous loss of consciousness caused by an insufficient supply of blood to the brain. [C13: from OF, from *faindre* to be idle]
▶ 'faintish *adj* ▶ 'faintly *adv* ▶ 'faintness *n*

fair¹ (feə) *adj* **1** free from discrimination, dishonesty, etc. **2** in conformity with rules or standards: *a fair fight.* **3** (of the hair or complexion) light in colour. **4** beautiful to look at. **5** quite good: *a fair piece of work.* **6** unblemished; untainted. **7** (of the tide or wind) favourable to the passage of a vessel. **8** fine or cloudless. **9** pleasant or courteous. **10** apparently good or valuable: *fair words.* **11 fair and square.** in a correct or just way. ◆ *adv* **12** in a fair way: *act fair, now!* **13** absolutely or squarely; quite. ◆ *vb* **14** (*intr*) *Dialect.* (of the weather) to become fine. ◆ *n* **15** *Arch.* a person or thing that is beautiful or valuable. [OE *fæger*]
▶ 'fairish *adj* ▶ 'fairness *n*

fair² (feə) *n* **1** a travelling entertainment with sideshows, rides, etc. **2** a gathering of producers and dealers in a given class of products to facilitate business: *a world fair.* **3** a regular assembly at a specific place for the sale of goods, esp. livestock. [C13: from OF *feire*, from LL *fēria* holiday, from L *fēriae* days of rest]

Fairbanks¹ ★ ('feə,bæŋks) *n* a city in central Alaska, at the terminus of the Alaska Highway. Pop.: 30 800 (1990).

Fairbanks² ★ ('feə,bæŋks) *n* **1 Douglas (Elton)**, real name *Julius Ullman.* 1883–1939, US film actor and producer. **2** his son, **Douglas, Jnr.** born 1909, US film actor.

Fairfax ★ ('feəfæks) *n* **Thomas**, 3rd Baron Fairfax. 1612–71, English general and statesman: commanded the Parliamentary army (1645–50), defeating Charles I at Naseby (1645). He was instrumental in restoring Charles II to the throne (1660).

fair game *n* a legitimate object for ridicule or attack.

fairground ('feə,graʊnd) *n* an open space used for a fair or exhibition.

fairing¹ ('feərɪŋ) *n* an external metal structure fitted around parts of an aircraft, car, etc., to reduce drag. [C20: from *fair* to streamline + -ING¹]

fairing² ('feərɪŋ) *n Arch.* a present, esp. from a fair.

Fair Isle *n* an intricate multicoloured pattern knitted with Shetland wool into various garments, such as sweaters. [C19: after one of the Shetland Islands where this type of pattern originated]

fairly ('feəlɪ) *adv* **1** (*not used with a negative*) moderately. **2** as deserved; justly. **3** (*not used with a negative*) positively: *the hall fairly rang with applause.*

fair-minded *adj* just or impartial.
▶ ,fair-'mindedness *n*

fair play *n* **1** an established standard of decency, etc. **2** abidance by this standard.

fair sex *n* **the.** women collectively.

fair-spoken *adj* civil, courteous, or elegant in speech.
▶ ,fair-'spokenness *n*

fairway ('feə,weɪ) *n* **1** (on a golf course) the avenue approaching a green bordered by rough. **2** *Naut.* the navigable part of a river, harbour, etc.

fair-weather *adj* **1** suitable for use in fair weather only. **2** not reliable in situations of difficulty: *fair-weather friend.*

fairy ('feərɪ) *n, pl* **fairies. 1** an imaginary supernatural being, usually represented in diminutive human form and characterized as having magical powers. **2** *Sl.* a male homosexual. ◆ *adj* (*prenominal*) **3** of a fairy or fairies. resembling a fairy or fairies. [C14: from OF *faerie* fairy land, from *feie* fairy, from L *Fāta* the Fates; see FATE, FAY]
▶ 'fairy-,like *adj*

fairy cycle *n* a child's bicycle.

fairyfloss ('feərɪ,flɒs) *n* the Australian word for **candyfloss.**

fairy godmother *n* a benefactress, esp. an unknown one.

fairyland ('feərɪ,lænd) *n* **1** the imaginary domain of the fairies. **2** a fantasy world, esp. one resulting from a person's wild imaginings.

fairy lights *pl n* small coloured electric bulbs strung together and used as decoration, esp. on a Christmas tree.

fairy penguin *n* a small penguin with a bluish head and back, found on the Australian coast. Also called: **little** *or* **blue penguin.**

fairy ring *n* a ring of dark luxuriant vegetation in grassy ground corresponding to the outer edge of an underground fungal mycelium.

fairy tale *or* **story** *n* **1** a story about fairies or other mythical or magical beings. **2** a highly improbable account.

fairy-tale *adj* **1** of or relating to a fairy tale. **2** resembling a fairy tale, esp. in being extremely happy or fortunate: *fairy-tale ending.* **3** highly improbable: *a fairy-tale account.*

Faisal I *or* **Feisal I** ★ ('faɪsⁿl) *n* 1885–1933, king of Syria (1920) and first king of Iraq (1921–33): a leader of the Arab revolt against the Turks.

Faisal II *or* **Feisal II** ★ *n* 1935–58, last king of Iraq (1939–58).

Faisalabad ★ (faɪˈʒɑːlə,bɑːd) *n* a city in NE Pakistan: commercial and manufacturing centre of a cotton- and wheat-growing region; university (1961). Pop.: 1 875 000 (1995 est.). Former name (until 1979) **Lyallpur.**

Faisal Ibn Abdul Aziz ★ ('ɪbⁿn ˈæbdʊl əˈziːz) *n* 1905–75, king of Saudi Arabia (1964–75).

fait accompli *French.* (fɛt akɔ̃pli) *n, pl* **faits accomplis** (fɛ akɔ̃pli). something already done and beyond alteration. [lit.: accomplished fact]

faith (feɪθ) *n* **1** strong or unshakeable belief in something, esp. without proof. **2** a specific system of religious beliefs: *the Jewish faith.* **3** *Christianity.* trust in God and in his actions and promises. **4** a conviction of the truth of certain doctrines of religion. **5** complete confidence or trust in a person, remedy, etc. **6** loyalty, as to a person or cause (esp. in **keep faith**, **break faith**). **7 bad faith.** dishonesty. **8 good faith.** honesty. **9** (*modifier*) using or relating to the supposed ability to cure bodily ailments by means of religious faith: *a faith healer.* ◆ *interj* **10** *Arch.* indeed. [C12: from Anglo-F *feid*, from L *fidēs* trust, confidence]

faithful ('feɪθfʊl) *adj* **1** remaining true or loyal. **2** maintaining sexual loyalty to one's lover or spouse. **3** consistently reliable: *a faithful worker.* **4** reliable or truthful. **5** accurate in detail: *a faithful translation.* ◆ *n* **6 the faithful. 6a** the believers in a religious faith, esp. Christianity. **6b** any group of loyal and steadfast followers.
▶ 'faithfully *adv* ▶ 'faithfulness *n*

faithless ('feɪθlɪs) *adj* **1** unreliable or treacherous. **2** dishonest or disloyal. **3** lacking religious faith.
▶ 'faithlessness *n*

Faiyûm *or* **Fayum** ★ (faɪˈjuːm) *n* See **El Faiyûm.**

fajitas (fəˈhiːtəz) *pl n* a Mexican dish of soft tortillas wrapped round fried strips of meat, vegetables, etc. [Mexican Sp.]

fake (feɪk) *vb* **fakes, faking, faked. 1** (*tr*) to cause (something inferior or not genuine) to appear more valuable or real by fraud or pretence. **2** to pretend to have (an illness, emotion, etc.). ◆ *n* **3** an object, person, or act that is not

genuine; sham. ◆ *adj* **4** not genuine. [C18: prob. ult. from It. *facciare* to make or do]
▶ 'faker *n* ▶ 'fakery *n*

fakir ('feɪkɪə, fə'kɪə) *n* **1** a member of any religious order of Islam. **2** a Hindu ascetic mendicant. [C17: from Ar. *faqīr* poor]

falafel *or* **felafel** (fə'lɑːfəl) *n* a ball or cake of ground spiced chickpeas, deep-fried and often served with pitta bread. [C20: from Arabic *felāfil*]

Falange ('fælændʒ) *n* the Fascist movement founded in Spain in 1933. [Sp.: PHALANX]
▶ Fa'langist *n, adj*

falcate ('fælkeɪt) *or* **falciform** ('fælsɪ,fɔːm) *adj Biol.* shaped like a sickle. [C19: from L *falcātus*, from *falx* sickle]

falchion ('fɔːltʃən, 'fɔːlʃən) *n* **1** a short and slightly curved medieval sword. **2** an archaic word for **sword**. [C14: from It., from *falce*, from L *falx* sickle]

falcon ('fɔːlkən, 'fɔːlkən) *n* **1** a diurnal bird of prey such as the gyrfalcon, peregrine falcon, etc., having pointed wings and a long tail. **2a** any of these or related birds, trained to hunt small game. **2b** the female of such a bird (cf. **tercel**). [C13: from OF, from LL *falcō* hawk, prob. of Gmc origin; ? rel. to L *falx* sickle]

falconet ('fɔːlkə,nɛt, 'fɔːlkə-) *n* **1** any of various small falcons. **2** a small light cannon used from the 15th to 17th centuries.

falconry ('fɔːlkənrɪ, 'fɔːlkən-) *n* the art of keeping falcons and training them to return from flight to a lure or to hunt quarry.
▶ 'falconer *n*

falderal ('fældə,ræl) *or* **folderol** ('fɒldə,rɒl) *n* **1** a showy but worthless trifle. **2** foolish nonsense. **3** a nonsensical refrain in old songs.

Faldo ★ ('fældəʊ) *n* **Nick.** born 1957, British golfer: won the British Open Championship (1987, 1990, 1992) and the US Masters (1989, 1990, 1996).

faldstool ('fɔːld,stuːl) *n* a backless seat, sometimes capable of being folded, used by bishops and certain other prelates. [C11 *fyldestol*, prob. a translation of Med. L *faldistolium* folding stool, of Gmc origin; cf. OHG *faldstuol*]

Falerii ★ (fə'lɪərɪ,aɪ) *n* an ancient city of S Italy, in Latium: important in pre-Roman times.

Falkirk ★ ('fɔːlkɜːk) *n* **1** a town in Scotland, the administrative centre of Falkirk council area: scene of Edward I's defeat of Wallace (1298) and Prince Charles Edward's defeat of General Hawley (1746); iron works. Pop.: 35 610 (1991). **2** a council area in central Scotland: created in 1996 from part of Central Region. Administrative centre: Falkirk. Pop.: 142 610 (1996 est.). Area: 299 sq. km (115 sq. miles).

Falkland Islands ★ ('fɔːlkländ) *pl n* a group of over 100 islands in the S Atlantic: a United Kingdom overseas territory; invaded by Argentina, who had long laid claim to the islands, on 2 April 1982; recaptured by a British expeditionary force on 14 June 1982. Chief town: Stanley. Pop.: 2121 (1991). Area: about 12 200 sq. km (4700 sq. miles). Spanish name: **Islas Malvinas.**

Falkland Islands Dependencies ★ *pl n* a group of almost uninhabited islands south of the Falkland Islands: consisting of the South Sandwich Islands and South Georgia: part of the United Kingdom overseas territory of the Falkland Islands. Area: 4090 sq. km (1580 sq. miles).

Falkner ★ ('fɔːknə) *n* a variant spelling of (William) **Faulkner.**

fall (fɔːl) *vb* **falls, falling, fell, fallen.** (*mainly intr*) **1** to descend by the force of gravity from a higher to a lower place. **2** to drop suddenly from an erect position. **3** to collapse to the ground, esp. in pieces. **4** to become less or lower in number, quality, etc.: *prices fell.* **5** to become lower in pitch. **6** to extend downwards: *her hair fell to her waist.* **7** to be badly wounded or killed. **8** to slope in a downward direction. **9** to yield to temptation or sin. **10** to diminish in status, estimation, etc. **11** to yield to attack: *the city fell under the assault.* **12** to lose power: *the government fell after*

the riots. **13** to pass into or take on a specified condition: *to fall asleep.* **14** to adopt a despondent expression: *her face fell.* **15** to be averted: *her gaze fell.* **16** to come by chance or presumption: *suspicion fell on the butler.* **17** to occur; take place: *night fell.* **18** (foll. by *back, behind,* etc.) to move in a specified direction. **19** to occur at a specified place: *the accent falls on the last syllable.* **20** (foll. by *to*) to be inherited (by): *the estate falls to the eldest son.* **21** (often foll. by *into, under,* etc.) to be classified: *the subject falls into two main areas.* **22** to issue forth: *a curse fell from her lips.* **23** (*tr*) *Dialect, Austral. & NZ.* to fell (trees). **24** *Cricket.* (of a batsman's wicket) to be taken by the bowling side: *the sixth wicket fell for 96.* **25 fall short. 25a** to prove inadequate. **25b** (often foll. by *of*) to fail to reach or measure up to (a standard). ◆ *n* **26** an act or instance of falling. **27** something that falls: *a fall of snow.* **28** *Chiefly US.* autumn. **29** the distance that something falls: *a hundred-foot fall.* **30** a sudden drop from an upright position. **31** (*often pl*) **31a** a waterfall or cataract. **31b** (*cap. when part of a name*): *Niagara Falls.* **32** a downward slope or decline. **33** a decrease in value, number, etc. **34** a decline in status or importance. **35** a capture or overthrow: *the fall of the city.* **36** *Machinery, naut.* the end of a tackle to which power is applied to hoist it. **37** Also called: **pinfall.** *Wrestling.* a scoring move, pinning both shoulders of one's opponent to the floor for a specified period. **38a** the birth of an animal. **38b** the animals produced at a single birth. ◆ See also **fall about, fall away,** etc. [OE *feallan*: cf. FELL[2]]

Fall (fɔːl) *n* **the.** *Theol.* Adam's sin of disobedience and the state of innate sinfulness ensuing from this for himself and all mankind.

Falla ★ (*Spanish* 'faʎa) *n* **Manuel de** (ma'nwel de). 1876–1946, Spanish composer and pianist, composer of the opera *La Vida Breve* (1905), the ballet *The Three-Cornered Hat* (1919), guitar and piano music, and songs.

fall about *vb* (*intr, adv*) to laugh in an uncontrolled manner: *we fell about at the sight.*

fallacious (fə'leɪʃəs) *adj* **1** containing or involving a fallacy. **2** tending to mislead. **3** delusive or disappointing.
▶ fal'laciously *adv*

fallacy ('fæləsɪ) *n, pl* **fallacies. 1** an incorrect or misleading notion or opinion based on inaccurate facts or invalid reasoning. **2** unsound reasoning. **3** the tendency to mislead. **4** *Logic.* an error in reasoning that renders an argument logically invalid. [C15: from L, from *fallax* deceitful, from *fallere* to deceive]

fall apart *vb* (*intr adv*) **1** to break owing to long use or poor construction: *the chassis is falling apart.* **2** to become disorganized and ineffective: *since you resigned, the office has fallen apart.*

fall away *vb* (*intr, adv*) **1** (of friendship, etc.) to be withdrawn. **2** to slope down.

fall back *vb* (*intr, adv*) **1** to recede or retreat. **2** (foll. by *on* or *upon*) to have recourse (to). ◆ *n* **fall-back. 3** a retreat. **4** a reserve, esp. money, that can be called upon in need. **5a** anything to which one can have recourse as a second choice. **5b** (*as modifier*): *a fall-back position.*

fall behind *vb* (*intr, adv*) **1** to drop back; fail to keep up. **2** to be in arrears, as with a payment.

fall down *vb* (*intr, adv*) **1** to drop suddenly or collapse. **2** (often foll. by *on*) *Inf.* to fail.

fallen ('fɔːlən) *vb* **1** the past participle of **fall.** ◆ *adj* **2** having sunk in reputation or honour: *a fallen woman.* **3** killed in battle with glory.

fallen arch *n* collapse of the arch formed by the instep of the foot, resulting in flat feet.

fall for *vb* (*intr, prep*) **1** to become infatuated with (a person). **2** to allow oneself to be deceived by (a lie, trick, etc.).

fall guy *n Inf.* **1** a person who is the victim of a confidence trick. **2** a scapegoat.

fallible ('fælɪbªl) *adj* **1** capable of being mistaken. **2** liable to mislead. [C15: from Med. L *fallibilis*, from *fallere* to deceive]
▶ ,falli'bility *n*

fall in *vb* (*intr, adv*) **1** to collapse. **2** to adopt a military formation, esp. as a soldier taking his place in a line. **3** (of a lease) to expire. **4** (often foll. by *with*) **4a** to meet and join. **4b** to agree with or support a person, suggestion, etc.

falling sickness *or* **evil** *n* a former name (nontechnical) for **epilepsy**.

falling star *n* an informal name for **meteor**.

Fall Line ★ *n* a natural junction, running parallel to the E coast of the US, between the hard rocks of the Appalachians and the softer coastal plain, along which rivers form falls and rapids.

fall off *vb (intr)* **1** to drop unintentionally to the ground from (a high object, bicycle, etc.), esp. after losing one's balance. **2** (*adv*) to diminish in size, intensity, etc. ◆ *n* **fall-off. 3** a decline or drop.

fall on *vb (intr, prep)* **1** Also: **fall upon**. to attack or snatch (an army, booty, etc.). **2 fall on one's feet**. to emerge unexpectedly well from a difficult situation.

Fallopian tube (fə'ləʊpɪən) *n* either of a pair of slender tubes through which ova pass from the ovaries to the uterus in female mammals. [C18: after Gabriello *Fallopio* (1523–62), It. anatomist who first described the tubes]

fallout ('fɔːlˌaʊt) *n* **1** the descent of radioactive material following a nuclear explosion. **2** any particles that so descend. **3** secondary consequences. ◆ *vb* **fall out**. (*intr, adv*) **4** *Inf.* to disagree. **5** (*intr*) to occur. **6** *Mil.* to leave a disciplinary formation.

fallow[1] ('fæləʊ) *adj* **1** (of land) left unseeded after being ploughed to regain fertility for a crop. **2** (of an idea, etc.) undeveloped, but potentially useful. ◆ *n* **3** land treated in this way. ◆ *vb* **4** (*tr*) to leave (land) unseeded after ploughing it. [OE *fealga*]
▶ **'fallowness** *n*

fallow[2] ('fæləʊ) *n, adj* (of) a light yellowish-brown colour. [OE *fealu*]

fallow deer *n* either of two species of deer, one of which is native to the Mediterranean region and the other to Persia. The summer coat is reddish with white spots.

fall through *vb (intr, adv)* to fail.

fall to *vb (intr)* **1** (*adv*) to begin some activity, as eating, working, or fighting. **2** (*prep*) to devolve on (a person): *the task fell to me*.

Falmouth ★ ('fælməθ) *n* a port and resort in SW England, in S Cornwall. Pop.: 20 297 (1991).

false (fɔːls) *adj* **1** not in accordance with the truth or facts. **2** irregular or invalid: *a false start*. **3** untruthful or lying: *a false account*. **4** artificial; fake: *false teeth*. **5** being or intended to be misleading or deceptive: *a false rumour*. **6** treacherous: *a false friend*. **7** based on mistaken or irrelevant ideas or facts: *a false argument*. **8** (*prenominal*) (esp. of plants) superficially resembling the species specified: *false hellebore*. **9** serving to supplement or replace, often temporarily: *a false keel*. **10** *Music*. (of a note, interval, etc.) out of tune. ◆ *adv* **11** in a false or dishonest manner (esp. in **play (someone) false**). [OE *fals*]
▶ **'falsely** *adv* ▶ **'falseness** *n*

false colour *n* colour used in a computer or photographic display to help in interpreting the image, as in the use of red to show high temperatures and blue to show low temperatures in an infrared image converter.

false dawn *n* light appearing just before sunrise.

false diamond *n* any of a number of semiprecious stones that resemble diamond, such as zircon and white topaz.

falsehood ('fɔːlsˌhʊd) *n* **1** the quality of being untrue. **2** an untrue statement; lie. **3** the act of deceiving or lying.

false imprisonment *n Law*. the restraint of a person's liberty without lawful authority.

false pretences *pl n* a misrepresentation used to obtain anything, such as trust or affection (esp. in **under false pretences**).

false ribs *pl n* any of the lower five pairs of ribs in man, not attached directly to the breastbone.

false step *n* **1** an unwise action. **2** a stumble; slip.

falsetto (fɔːl'sɛtəʊ) *n, pl* **falsettos**. a form of vocal production used by male singers to extend their range upwards

by limiting the vibration of the vocal cords. [C18: from It., from *falso* false]

falsies ('fɔːlsɪz) *pl n Inf*. pads of soft material, such as foam rubber, worn to exaggerate the size of a woman's breasts.

falsify ('fɔːlsɪˌfaɪ) *vb* **falsifies, falsifying, falsified.** (*tr*) **1** to make (a report, evidence, etc.) false or inaccurate by alteration, esp. in order to deceive. **2** to prove false. [C15: from OF, from LL, from L *falsus* FALSE+ *facere* to do, make]
▶ **'falsiˌfiable** *adj* ▶ **falsification** (ˌfɔːlsɪfɪ'keɪʃən) *n*

falsity ('fɔːlsɪtɪ) *n, pl* **falsities**. **1** the state of being false or untrue. **2** a lie or deception.

Falstaffian (fɔːl'stɑːfɪən) *adj* jovial, plump, and dissolute. [C19: after Sir John *Falstaff*, a character in Shakespeare's play *Henry IV*]

Falster ★ ('fɑːlstə) *n* an island in the Baltic Sea, part of SE Denmark. Chief town: Nykøbing. Pop.: 42 846 (1990). Area: 513 sq. km (198 sq. miles).

falter ('fɔːltə) *vb* **1** (*intr*) to be hesitant, weak, or unsure. **2** (*intr*) to move unsteadily or hesitantly. **3** to utter haltingly or hesitantly. ◆ *n* **4** hesitancy in speech or action. **5** a quavering sound. [C14: prob. from ON]
▶ **'falterer** *n* ▶ **'falteringly** *adv*

Falun ★ (ˌfɑː'lʌn) *n* a city in central Sweden: iron and pyrites mines. Pop.: 55 014 (1994).

Famagusta ★ (ˌfæmə'ɡʊstə) *n* a port in E Cyprus, on **Famagusta Bay**: became one of the richest cities in Christendom in the 14th century. Pop.: 67 167 (1994).

fame (feɪm) *n* **1** the state of being widely known or recognized. **2** *Arch.* rumour or public report. ◆ *vb* **fame, faming, famed. 3** (*tr; now usually passive*) to make famous: *he was famed for his ruthlessness*. [C13: from L *fāma* report; rel. to *fārī* to say]

familial (fə'mɪlɪəl) *adj* **1** of or relating to the family. **2** occurring in the members of a family: *a familial disease*.

familiar (fə'mɪlɪə) *adj* **1** well-known: *a familiar figure*. **2** frequent or customary: *a familiar excuse*. **3** (*postpositive; foll. by* **with**) acquainted. **4** friendly; informal. **5** close; intimate. **6** more intimate than is acceptable; presumptuous. ◆ *n* **7** Also called: **familiar spirit**. a supernatural spirit supposed to attend and aid a witch, wizard, etc. **8** a person attached to the household of the pope or a bishop, who renders service in return for support. **9** a friend. [C14: from L *familiāris* domestic, from *familia* FAMILY]
▶ **fa'miliarly** *adv* ▶ **fa'miliarness** *n*

familiarity (fəˌmɪlɪ'ærɪtɪ) *n, pl* **familiarities**. **1** knowledge, as of a subject or place. **2** close acquaintanceship. **3** undue intimacy. **4** (*sometimes pl*) an instance of unwarranted intimacy.

familiarize *or* **familiarise** (fə'mɪljəˌraɪz) *vb* **familiarizes, familiarizing, familiarized** *or* **familiarises, familiarising, familiarised.** (*tr*) **1** to make (oneself or someone else) familiar, as with a particular subject. **2** to make (something) generally known.
▶ **faˌmiliari'zation** *or* **faˌmiliari'zati'sation** *n*

famille *French*. (famij) *n* a type of Chinese porcelain characterized either by a design on a background of yellow (**famille jaune**) or black (**famille noire**) or by a design in which the predominant colour is pink (**famille rose**) or green (**famille verte**). [C19: lit.: family]

family ('fæmɪlɪ, 'fæmlɪ) *n, pl* **families**. **1a** a primary social group consisting of parents and their offspring. **1b** (*as modifier*): *a family unit*. **2** one's wife or husband and one's children. **3** one's children, as distinguished from one's husband or wife. **4** a group descended from a common ancestor. **5** all the persons living together in one household. **6** any group of related things or beings, esp. when scientifically categorized. **7** *Biol.* any of the taxonomic groups into which an order is divided and which contains one or more genera. **8** a group of historically related languages assumed to derive from one original language. **9** *Maths.* a group of curves or surfaces whose equations differ from a given equation only in the values assigned to one or more constants. **10** **in the family way**. *Inf.* pregnant. [C15: from L *familia* a household, servants of the house, from *famulus* servant]

family allowance *n* **1** (in Britain) a former name for child benefit. **2** (*caps.*) the Canadian equivalent of **child benefit.**

family Bible *n* a large Bible in which births, marriages, and deaths of the members of a family are recorded.

Family Compact *n Canad.* **1 the.** the ruling oligarchy in Upper Canada in the early 19th century. **2** (*often not cap.*) any influential clique.

family credit *n* (in Britain) a means-tested allowance paid to families who have at least one dependent child and whose earnings from full-time work are low. It replaced **family income supplement.**

family man *n* a man who is married and has children, esp. one who is devoted to his family.

family name *n* a surname, esp. when regarded as representing the family honour.

family planning *n* the control of the number of children in a family and of the intervals between them, esp. by the use of contraceptives.

family support *n NZ.* a means-tested allowance for families in need.

family therapy *n* a form of psychotherapy in which the members of a family participate, with the aim of improving communications between them and the ways in which they relate to each other.

family tree *n* a chart showing the genealogical relationships and lines of descent of a family. Also called: **genealogical tree.**

famine ('fæmɪn) *n* **1** a severe shortage of food, as through crop failure or overpopulation. **2** acute shortage of anything. **3** violent hunger. [C14: from OF, via Vulgar L, from L *famēs* hunger]

famish ('fæmɪʃ) *vb* (*now usually passive*) to be or make very hungry or weak. [C14: from OF, from L *famēs* FAMINE]

famous ('feɪməs) *adj* **1** known to or recognized by many people. **2** *Inf.* excellent; splendid. [C14: from L *famōsus*; see FAME]
► **'famously** *adv* ► **'famousness** *n*

fan[1] (fæn) *n* **1** any device for creating a current of air by movement of a surface or number of surfaces, esp. a rotating device consisting of a number of blades attached to a central hub. **2** any of various hand-agitated devices for cooling oneself, esp. a collapsible semicircular series of flat segments of paper, ivory, etc. **3** something shaped like such a fan, such as the tail of certain birds. **4** *Agriculture.* a kind of basket formerly used for winnowing grain.
♦ *vb* **fans, fanning, fanned.** (*mainly tr*) **5** to cause a current of air to blow upon, as by means of a fan: *to fan one's face.* **6** to agitate or move (air, etc.) with or as if with a fan. **7** to make fiercer, more ardent, etc.: *fan one's passion.* **8** (*also intr*; often foll. by *out*) to spread out or cause to spread out in the shape of a fan. **9** to winnow (grain) by blowing the chaff away from it. [OE *fann*, from L *vannus*]
► **'fanlike** *adj* ► **'fanner** *n*

fan[2] (fæn) *n* **1** an ardent admirer of a pop star, football team, etc. **2** a devotee of a sport, hobby, etc. [C17, reformed C19: from FAN(ATIC)]

Fanagalo ('fænəgələu) *or* **Fanakalo** *n* (in South Africa) a Zulu-based pidgin with English and Afrikaans components. [C20: from Fanagalo *fana ga lo*, lit.: to be like this]

fanatic (fə'nætɪk) *n* **1** a person whose enthusiasm or zeal for something is extreme or beyond normal limits. **2** *Inf.* a person devoted to a particular hobby or pastime. ♦ *adj* **3** a variant of **fanatical.** [C16: from L *fānāticus* belonging to a temple, hence, inspired by a god, frenzied, from *fānum* temple]

fanatical (fə'nætɪkˀl) *adj* surpassing what is normal or accepted in enthusiasm for or belief in something.
► **fa'natically** *adv*

fanaticism (fə'nætɪˌsɪzəm) *n* wildly excessive or irrational devotion, dedication, or enthusiasm.

fan belt *n* the belt that drives a cooling fan in a car engine.

fancied ('fænsɪd) *adj* **1** imaginary; unreal. **2** thought likely to win or succeed: *a fancied runner.*

fancier ('fænsɪə) *n* **1** a person with a special interest in

something. **2** a person who breeds special varieties of plants or animals: *a pigeon fancier.*

fanciful ('fænsɪful) *adj* **1** not based on fact: *fanciful notions.* **2** made or designed in a curious, intricate, or imaginative way. **3** indulging in or influenced by fancy.
► **'fancifully** *adv* ► **'fancifulness** *n*

fan club *n* **1** an organized group of admirers of a particular pop singer, film star, etc. **2 be a member of someone's fan club.** *Inf.* to approve of someone strongly.

fancy ('fænsɪ) *adj* **fancier, fanciest. 1** ornamented or decorative: *fancy clothes.* **2** requiring skill to perform: *a fancy dance routine.* **3** capricious or illusory. **4** (often used ironically) superior in quality. **5** higher than expected: *fancy prices.* **6** (of a domestic animal) bred for particular qualities. ♦ *n, pl* **fancies. 7** a sudden capricious idea. **8** a sudden or irrational liking for a person or thing. **9** the power to conceive and represent decorative and novel imagery, esp. in poetry. **10** an idea or thing produced by this. **11** a mental image. **12** *Music.* a composition for solo lute, keyboard, etc., current during the 16th and 17th centuries. **13 the fancy.** *Arch.* those who follow a particular sport, esp. prize fighting. ♦ *vb* **fancies, fancying, fancied.** (*tr*) **14** to picture in the imagination. **15** to imagine: *I fancy it will rain.* **16** (often used with a negative) to like: *I don't fancy your chances!* **17** (*reflexive*) to have a high or ill-founded opinion of oneself. **18** *Inf.* to have a wish for: *she fancied some chocolate.* **19** *Brit. inf.* to be physically attracted to (another person). **20** to breed (animals) for particular characteristics. ♦ *interj* **21** Also: **fancy that!** an exclamation of surprise. [C15 *fantsy*, shortened from *fantasie*; see FANTASY]
► **'fancily** *adv* ► **'fanciness** *n*

fancy dress *n* a costume worn at masquerades, etc., representing an historical figure, etc. **b** (*as modifier*): *a fancy-dress ball.*

fancy-free *adj* having no commitments.

fancy goods *pl n* small decorative gifts.

fancy man *n Sl.* **1** a woman's lover. **2** a pimp.

fancy woman *n Sl.* a mistress or prostitute.

fancywork ('fænsɪˌwɜːk) *n* any ornamental needlework, such as embroidery or crochet.

fan dance *n* a dance in which large fans are manipulated in front of the body, partially revealing or suggesting nakedness.

fandangle (fæn'dæŋgˀl) *n Inf.* **1** elaborate ornament. **2** nonsense. [C19: ?from FANDANGO]

fandango (fæn'dæŋgəu) *n, pl* **fandangos. 1** an old Spanish courtship dance in triple time. **2** a piece of music composed for or in the rhythm of this dance. [C18: from Sp., from ?]

fane (feɪn) *n Arch. or poetic.* a temple or shrine. [C14: from L *fānum*]

fanfare ('fænfeə) *n* **1** a flourish or short tune played on brass instruments. **2** an ostentatious flourish or display. [C17: from F, back formation from *fanfarer*, from Sp, from *fanfarron* boaster, from Ar. *farfār* garrulous]

fang (fæŋ) *n* **1** the long pointed hollow or grooved tooth of a venomous snake through which venom is injected. **2** any large pointed tooth, esp. the canine tooth of a carnivorous mammal. **3** the root of a tooth. **4** (*usually pl*) *Brit. inf.* a tooth. [OE *fang* what is caught, prey]
► **fanged** *adj* ► **'fangless** *adj*

Fangio ★ (*Spanish* 'faŋxjo) *n* **Juan Manuel** (xwan ma'nwɛl). 1911–95, Argentinian racing driver who won the World Championship five times between 1951 and 1957.

fan heater *n* a space heater consisting of an electrically heated element with an electrically driven fan to disperse the heat.

fanjet ('fænˌdʒɛt) *n* another name for **turbofan.**

fanlight ('fænˌlaɪt) *n* **1** a semicircular window over a door or window, often having sash bars like the ribs of a fan. **2** a small rectangular window over a door. US name: **transom.**

fan mail *n* mail sent to a famous person, such as a pop musician or film star, by admirers.

fanny ('fænɪ) *n, pl* **fannies.** *Sl.* **1** *Taboo, Brit.* the female genitals. **2** *Chiefly US & Canad.* the buttocks. [C20: ?from *Fanny*, pet name from *Frances*]

fanny adams *n Brit. sl.* **1** (usually preceded by *sweet*) absolutely nothing at all. **2** *Chiefly naut.* (formerly) tinned meat. [C19: from the name of a young murder victim whose body was cut up into small pieces. For sense 1: a euphemism for *fuck all*]

fantail ('fæn,teɪl) *n* **1** a breed of domestic pigeon having a large tail that can be opened like a fan. **2** an Old World flycatcher of Australia, New Zealand, and SE Asia, having a broad fan-shaped tail. **3** a tail shaped like an outspread fan. **4** an auxiliary sail on the upper portion of a windmill. **5** *US.* a part of the deck projecting aft of the sternpost of a ship.
▶ 'fan-,tailed *adj*

fan-tan *n* **1** a Chinese gambling game. **2** a card game played in sequence, the winner being the first to use up all his cards. [C19: from Chinese (Cantonese) *fan t'an* repeated divisions, from *fan* times + *t'an* division]

fantasia (fæn'teɪzɪə) *n* **1** any musical composition of a free or improvisatory nature. **2** a potpourri of popular tunes woven loosely together. [C18: from It.: fancy; see FANTASY]

fantasize *or* **fantasise** ('fæntə,saɪz) *vb* **fantasizes, fantasizing, fantasized** *or* **fantasises, fantasising, fantasised. 1** (when *tr*, takes a clause as object) to conceive extravagant or whimsical ideas, images, etc. **2** (*intr*) to conceive pleasant mental images.

fantastic (fæn'tæstɪk) *adj also* **fantastical. 1** strange or fanciful in appearance, conception, etc. **2** created in the mind; illusory. **3** unrealistic: *fantastic plans.* **4** incredible or preposterous: *a fantastic verdict.* **5** *Inf.* very large or extreme: *a fantastic fortune.* **6** *Inf.* very good; excellent. **7** of or characterized by fantasy. **8** capricious; fitful. [C14 *fantastik* imaginary, via LL from Gk *phantastikos* capable of imagining, from *phantazein* to make visible]
▶ fan,tasti'cality *or* fan'tasticalness *n* ▶ fan'tastically *adv*

fantasy *or* **phantasy** ('fæntəsɪ) *n, pl* **fantasies** *or* **phantasies. 1a** imagination unrestricted by reality. **1b** (*as modifier*): *a fantasy world.* **2** a creation of the imagination, esp. a weird or bizarre one. **3** *Psychol.* a series of pleasing mental images, usually serving to fulfil a need not gratified in reality. **4** a whimsical or far-fetched notion. **5** an illusion or phantom. **6** a highly elaborate imaginative design or creation. **7** *Music.* another word for **fantasia**. **8** literature, etc., having a large fantasy content. ◆ *vb* **fantasies, fantasying, fantasied** *or* **phantasies, phantasying, phantasied. 9** a less common word for **fantasize**. [C14 *fantasie*, from L, from Gk *phantazein* to make visible]

Fantin-Latour ★ (*French* fɑ̃tɛ̃latur) *n* (**Ignace**) **Henri** (**Joseph Théodore**) (ɑ̃ri). 1836–1904, French painter, noted for his still lifes and portrait groups.

fan vaulting *n Archit.* vaulting having ribs that radiate like those of a fan and spring from the top of a capital. Also called: **palm vaulting**.

fanzine ('fæn,ziːn) *n* a magazine produced by amateurs for fans of a specific interest, pop group, etc. [C20: from FAN² + (MAGA)ZINE]

FAO *abbrev. for:* **1** Food and Agriculture Organization (of the United Nations). **2** for the attention of.

f.a.q. *abbrev. for:* **1** *Commerce.* fair average quality. **2** free alongside quay.

far (fɑː) *adv* **farther** *or* **further, farthest** *or* **furthest. 1** at, to, or from a great distance. **2** at or to a remote time: *far in the future.* **3** to a considerable degree: *a far better plan.* **4 as far as. 4a** to the degree or extent that. **4b** to the distance or place of. **4c** *Inf.* with reference to; as for. **5 by far.** by a considerable margin. **6 far and away.** by a very great margin. **7 far and wide.** everywhere. **8 far be it from me.** on no account: *far be it from me to tell you what to do.* **9 go far. 9a** to be successful: *your son will go far.* **9b** to be sufficient or last long: *the wine didn't go far.* **10 go too far.** to exceed reasonable limits. **11 so far. 11a** up to the present moment. **11b** up to a certain point, extent, degree, etc. ◆ *adj* (*prenominal*) **12** remote in space or time: *in the far past.* **13** extending a great distance. **14** more distant: *the far end of the room.* **15**

far from. in a degree, state, etc. remote from: *he is far from happy.* [OE *feorr*]
▶ 'farness *n*

farad ('færəd) *n Physics.* the derived SI unit of electric capacitance; the capacitance of a capacitor between the plates of which a potential of 1 volt is created by a charge of 1 coulomb. Symbol: F [C19: see FARADAY]

faraday ('færə,deɪ) *n* a quantity of electricity, used in electrochemical calculations, equivalent to unit amount of substance of electrons. Symbol: *F* [C20: after Michael FARADAY]

Faraday ★ ('færə,deɪ) *n* **Michael.** 1791–1867, English physicist and chemist who discovered electromagnetic induction, leading to the invention of the dynamo. He also carried out research into the principles of electrolysis.

faradic (fə'rædɪk) *adj* of or concerned with an intermittent alternating current such as that induced in the secondary winding of an induction coil. [C19: from F *faradique*; from Michael FARADAY]

farandole ('færən,dəʊl) *n* **1** a lively dance from Provence. **2** a piece of music composed for or in the rhythm of this dance. [C19: from F, from Provençal *farandoulo*, from ?]

faraway ('fɑːrə,weɪ) *adj* (**far away** *when postpositive*). **1** very distant. **2** absent-minded.

farce (fɑːs) *n* **1** a broadly humorous play based on the exploitation of improbable situations. **2** the genre of comedy represented by works of this kind. **3** a ludicrous situation or action. **4** another name for **forcemeat**. [C14 (in the sense: stuffing): from OF, from L *farcīre* to stuff, interpolate passages (in the mass, in religious plays, etc.)]

farcical ('fɑːsɪkᵊl) *adj* **1** absurd. **2** of or relating to farce.
▶ ,farci'cality *n* ▶ 'farcically *adv*

fardel ('fɑːdᵊl) *n Arch.* a bundle or burden. [C13: from OF *farde*, ult. from Ar. *fardah*]

fare (fɛə) *n* **1** the sum charged or paid for conveyance in a bus, train, etc. **2** a paying passenger, esp. when carried by taxi. **3** a range of food and drink. ◆ *vb* **fares, faring, fared.** (*intr*) **4** to get on (as specified): *he fared well.* **5** (with *it* as a subject) to happen as specified: *it fared badly with him.* **6** *Arch.* to eat: *we fared sumptuously.* **7** (often foll. by *forth*) *Arch.* to travel. [OE *faran*]
▶ 'farer *n*

Far East *n* the. the countries of E Asia, including China, Japan, North and South Korea, E Siberia, Indonesia, Malaysia, and the Philippines: sometimes extended to include all territories east of Afghanistan.
▶ Far Eastern *adj*

fare stage *n* **1** a section of a bus journey for which a set charge is made. **2** the bus stop marking the end of such a section.

farewell (,fɛə'wɛl) *sentence substitute.* **1** goodbye; adieu. ◆ *n* **2** a parting salutation. **3** an act of departure. **4** (*modifier*) expressing leave-taking: *a farewell speech.*

far-fetched *adj* unlikely.

far-flung *adj* **1** widely distributed. **2** far distant; remote.

Fargo ★ ('fɑːgəʊ) *n* **William.** 1818–81, US businessman: founded (1852) with Henry Wells the express mail service Wells, Fargo and Company.

farina (fə'riːnə) *n* **1** flour or meal made from any kind of cereal grain. **2** *Chiefly Brit.* starch. [C18: from L *fār* spelt, coarse meal]

farinaceous (,færɪ'neɪʃəs) *adj* **1** consisting or made of starch. **2** having a mealy texture or appearance. **3** containing starch: *farinaceous seeds.*

farm (fɑːm) *n* **1a** a tract of land, usually with house and buildings, cultivated as a unit or used to rear livestock. **1b** (*as modifier*): *farm produce.* **1c** (*in combination*): *farmland.* **2** a unit of land or water devoted to the growing or rearing of some particular type of vegetable, fruit, animal, or fish: *a fish farm.* **3** an installation for storage or disposal: *a sewage farm.* ◆ *vb* **4** (*tr*) **4a** to cultivate (land). **4b** to rear (stock, etc.) on a farm. **5** (*intr*) to engage in agricultural work, esp. as a way of life. **6** (*tr*) to look after a child for a fixed sum. **7** to collect the moneys due and re-

tain the profits from (a tax district, business, etc.) for a specified period. ◆ See also **farm out**. [C13: from OF *ferme* rented land, ult. from L *firmāre* to settle]
▸ **'farmable** *adj*

farmed (fɑ:md) *adj* (of fish and game) reared on a farm rather than caught in the wild.

farmer ('fɑ:mə) *n* **1** a person who operates or manages a farm. **2** a person who obtains the right to collect and retain a tax, rent, etc., on payment of a fee. **3** a person who looks after a child for a fixed sum.

Farmer ★ ('fɑ:mə) *n* **John**. ?1565–1605, English madrigal composer and organist.

farmer's lung *n* inflammation of the alveoli of the lungs caused by an allergic response to fungal spores in hay.

farm hand *n* a person who is hired to work on a farm.

farmhouse ('fɑ:m,haʊs) *n* a house attached to a farm, esp. the dwelling from which the farm is managed.

farming ('fɑ:mɪŋ) *n* **a** the business or skill of agriculture. **b** (*as modifier*): *farming methods*.

farm out *vb* (*tr, adv*) **1** to send (work) to be done by another person, firm, etc. **2** to put (a child, etc.) into the care of a private individual. **3** to lease to another for a fee the right to collect (taxes).

farmstead ('fɑ:m,sted) *n* a farm or the part of a farm comprising its main buildings together with adjacent grounds.

farmyard ('fɑ:m,jɑ:d) *n* an area surrounded by or adjacent to farm buildings.

Farnborough ★ ('fɑ:nbərə, -brə) *n* a town in S England, in NE Hampshire: military base, with an aeronautical research centre. Pop.: 52 535 (1991).

Farnese ★ (*Italian* far'ne:se) *n* **1 Alessandro** (ales'sandro). original name of (Pope) **Paul III. 2 Alessandro**, duke of Parma and Piacenza. 1545–92, Italian general, statesman, and diplomat in the service of Philip II of Spain. As governor of the Netherlands (1578–92), he successfully suppressed revolts against Spanish rule.

Far North *n* the. the Arctic and sub-Arctic regions of the world.

faro ('fɛərəʊ) *n* a gambling game in which players bet against the dealer on what cards he will turn up. [C18: prob. spelling var. of *Pharoah*]

Faroes ★ ('fɛərəʊz) *n* a variant spelling of **Faeroes**.
▸ **Faroese** (,fɛərəʊ'i:z) *adj, n*

far-off *adj* (**far off** when postpositive). remote in space or time; distant.

farouche *French*. (faruʃ) *adj* sullen or shy. [C18: from F, from OF, from LL *forasticus* from without, from L *foras* out of doors]

Farouk I *or* **Faruk I** ★ (fə'ru:k) *n* 1920–65, last king of Egypt (1936–52). He was forced to abdicate (1952).

far-out *Sl.* ◆ *adj* (**far out** when postpositive) **1** bizarre or avant-garde. **2** wonderful. ◆ *interj* **far out. 3** an expression of amazement or delight.

Farquhar ★ ('fɑ:kwə, -kə) *n* **George**. 1678–1707, Irish-born dramatist; author of comedies such as *The Recruiting Officer* (1706) and *The Beaux' Stratagem* (1707).

Farquhar Islands ★ *pl n* an island group in the Indian Ocean: administratively part of the Seychelles.

farrago (fə'rɑ:gəʊ) *n, pl* **farragos** *or* **farragoes**. a hotchpotch. [C17: from L: mash for cattle (hence, a mixture), from *fār* spelt]
▸ **farraginous** (fə'rædʒɪnəs) *adj*

far-reaching *adj* extensive in influence, effect, or range.

Farrell ★ ('færəl) *n* **1 J**(ames) **G**(ordon). 1935–79, British novelist; author of *The Siege of Krishnapur* (1973) and *The Singapore Grip* (1978). **2 James T**(homas). 1904–79, US writer. His works include the trilogy *Young Lonigan* (1932), *The Young Manhood of Studs Lonigan* (1934), and *Judgment Day* (1935).

farrier ('færɪə) *n Chiefly Brit.* **1** a person who shoes horses. **2** another name for **veterinary surgeon**. [C16: from OF, from L *ferrārius* smith, from *ferrum* iron]
▸ **'farriery** *n*

farrow ('færəʊ) *n* **1** a litter of piglets. ◆ *vb* **2** (of a sow) to give birth to (a litter). [OE *fearh*]

far-seeing *adj* having shrewd judgment.

Farsi ('fɑ:sɪ) *n* a language spoken in Iran.

far-sighted *adj* **1** possessing prudence and foresight. **2** another word for **long-sighted**.
▸ **,far-'sightedly** *adv* ▸ **,far-'sightedness** *n*

fart (fɑ:t) *Taboo*. ◆ *n* **1** an emission of intestinal gas from the anus. **2** *Sl.* a contemptible person. ◆ *vb* (*intr*) **3** to break wind. **4 fart about** *or* **around**. *Sl.* **4a** to behave foolishly. **4b** to waste time. [ME *farten*]

farther ('fɑ:ðə) *adv* **1** to or at a greater distance in space or time. **2** in addition. ◆ *adj* **3** more distant or remote in space or time. **4** additional. [C13: see FAR, FURTHER]

> **USAGE NOTE** *Farther, farthest, further,* and *furthest* can all be used to refer to literal distance, but *further* and *furthest* are regarded as more correct for figurative senses denoting greater or additional amount, time, etc.: *further to my letter*. *Further* and *furthest* are also preferred for figurative distance.

farthermost ('fɑ:ðə,məʊst) *adj* most distant or remote.

farthest ('fɑ:ðɪst) *adv* **1** to or at the greatest distance in space or time. ◆ *adj* **2** most distant in space or time. **3** most extended. [C14 *ferthest*, from *ferther* FURTHER]

farthing ('fɑ:ðɪŋ) *n* **1** a former British bronze coin worth a quarter of an old penny: withdrawn in 1961. **2** something of negligible value; jot. [OE *fēorthing* from *fēortha* FOURTH + -ING¹]

farthingale ('fɑ:ðɪŋ,geɪl) *n* a hoop or framework worn under skirts, esp. in the Elizabethan period, to shape and spread them. [C16: from F *verdugale*, from OSp. *verdugado*, from *verdugo* rod]

Faruk I ★ (fə'ru:k) *n* a variant spelling of **Farouk I**.

fasces ('fæsi:z) *pl n, sing* **fascis** (-sɪs). **1** (in ancient Rome) one or more bundles of rods containing an axe with its blade protruding; a symbol of a magistrate's power. **2** (in modern Italy) such an object used as the symbol of Fascism. [C16: from L, pl of *fascis* bundle]

fascia *or* **facia** ('feɪʃɪə) *n, pl* **fasciae** *or* **faciae** (-ʃɪ,i:). **1** the flat surface above a shop window. **2** *Archit.* a flat band or surface, esp. a part of an architrave. **3** ('fæʃɪə). fibrous connective tissue occurring in sheets between muscles. **4** *Biol.* a distinctive band of colour, as on an insect or plant. **5** *Brit.* the outer panel which covers the dashboard of a motor vehicle. [C16: from L: band; rel. to *fascis* bundle]
▸ **'fascial** *or* **'facial** *adj*

fasciate ('fæʃɪ,eɪt) *or* **fasciated** *adj* **1** *Bot.* (of stems and branches) abnormally flattened due to coalescence. **2** (of birds, insects, etc.) marked by bands of colour. [C17: prob. from NL *fasciātus* (unattested) having bands; see FASCIA]

fascicle ('fæsɪk°l) *n* **1** a bundle of branches, leaves, etc. **2** Also called: **fasciculus**. *Anat.* a small bundle of fibres, esp. nerve fibres. [C15: from L *fasciculus* a small bundle, from *fascis* a bundle]
▸ **'fascicled** *adj* ▸ **fascicular** (fə'sɪkjʊlə) *or* **fasciculate** (fə'sɪkjʊ,leɪt) *adj* ▸ **fas,cicu'lation** *n*

fascicule ('fæsɪ,kju:l) *n* one part of a printed work that is published in instalments. Also called: **fascicle, fasciculus**.

fascinate ('fæsɪ,neɪt) *vb* **fascinates, fascinating, fascinated**. (*mainly tr*) **1** to attract and delight by arousing interest: *his stories fascinated me for hours*. **2** to render motionless, as by arousing terror or awe. **3** *Arch.* to put under a spell. [C16: from L, from *fascinum* a bewitching]
▸ **,fasci'nation** *n*

> **USAGE NOTE** A person can be fascinated *by* or *with* another person or thing. It is correct to speak of someone's fascination *with* a person or thing; one can also say a person or thing has a fascination *for* someone.

fascinating ('fæsɪ,neɪtɪŋ) *adj* **1** arousing great interest. **2** enchanting or alluring.

fascinator ('fæsɪ,neɪtə) *n Rare.* a lace or crocheted head covering for women.

Fascism ('fæʃɪzəm) *n* **1** the political movement, doctrine, system, or regime of Benito Mussolini in Italy. Fascism encouraged militarism and nationalism, organizing the country along hierarchical authoritarian lines. **2** (*sometimes not cap.*) any ideology or movement modelled on or inspired by this. **3** *Inf.* (*often not cap.*) any doctrine, system, or practice, regarded as authoritarian, militaristic, or extremely right-wing. [C20: from It. *fascismo*, from *fascio* political group, from L *fascis* bundle; see FASCES]

Fascist ('fæʃɪst) *n* **1** a supporter or member of a Fascist movement. **2** (*sometimes not cap.*) any person regarded as having right-wing authoritarian views. ◆ *adj* **3** characteristic of or relating to Fascism.

fashion ('fæʃən) *n* **1a** style in clothes, behaviour, etc., esp. the latest style. **1b** (*as modifier*): *a fashion magazine.* **2** (*modifier*) designed to be in the current fashion. **3a** manner of performance: *in a striking fashion.* **3b** (*in combination*): *crab-fashion.* **4** a way of life that revolves around the activities, dress, interests, etc., that are most fashionable. **5** shape or form. **6** sort; kind. **7 after** *or* **in a fashion.** in some manner, but not very well: *I mended it, after a fashion.* **8 of fashion.** of high social standing. ◆ *vb* (*tr*) **9** to give a particular form to. **10** to make suitable or fitting. **11** *Obs.* to contrive. [C13 *facioun* form, manner, from OF *faceon*, from L, from *facere* to make] ▸ **'fashioner** *n*

fashionable ('fæʃənəb³l) *adj* **1** conforming to fashion; in vogue. **2** of or patronized by people of fashion: *a fashionable café.* **3** (*usually foll. by with*) patronized (by). ▸ **'fashionableness** *n* ▸ **'fashionably** *adv*

fashion plate *n* **1** an illustration of the latest fashion in dress. **2** a fashionably dressed person.

fashion victim *n Inf.* a person who slavishly follows fashion.

Fassbinder ★ (*German* 'fasbɪndər) *n* **Rainer Werner** ('raɪnər 'vernər). 1946–82, German film director. His films include *Fear Eats the Soul* (1974) and *The Marriage of Maria Braun* (1978).

fast[1] (fɑːst) *adj* **1** acting or moving or capable of acting or moving quickly. **2** accomplished in or lasting a short time: *a fast visit.* **3** (*prenominal*) adapted to or facilitating rapid movement: *the fast lane of a motorway.* **4** (of a clock, etc.) indicating a time in advance of the correct time. **5** given to an active dissipated life. **6** of or characteristic of such activity: *a fast life.* **7** not easily moved; firmly fixed; secure. **8** firmly fastened or shut. **9** steadfast; constant (esp. in **fast friends**). **10** *Sport.* (of a playing surface, running track, etc.) conducive to rapid speed, as of a ball used on it or of competitors racing on it. **11** that will not fade or change colour readily. **12** proof against fading. **13** *Photog.* **13a** requiring a relatively short time of exposure to produce a given density: *a fast film.* **13b** permitting a short exposure time: *a fast shutter.* **14 a fast one.** *Inf.* a deceptive or unscrupulous trick (esp. in **pull a fast one**). **15 fast worker.** a person who achieves results quickly, esp. in seductions. ◆ *adv* **16** quickly; rapidly. **17** soundly; deeply: *fast asleep.* **18** firmly; tightly. **19** in quick succession. **20** in advance of the correct time: *my watch is running fast.* **21** in a reckless or dissipated way. **22 fast by** *or* **beside.** *Arch.* close by. **23 play fast and loose.** *Inf.* to behave in an insincere or unreliable manner. [OE *fæst* strong, tight]

fast[2] (fɑːst) *vb* **1** (*intr*) to abstain from eating all or certain foods or meals, esp. as a religious observance. ◆ *n* **2a** an act or period of fasting. **2b** (*as modifier*): *a fast day.* [OE *fæstan*] ▸ **'faster** *n*

fastback ('fɑːst,bæk) *n* a car having a back that forms one continuous slope from roof to rear.

fast-breeder reactor *n* a nuclear reactor that uses little or no moderator and produces more fissionable material than it consumes.

fasten ('fɑːs³n) *vb* **1** to make or become fast or secure. **2** to

make or become attached or joined. **3** to close or become closed by fixing firmly in place, locking, etc. **4** (*tr;* foll. by *in* or *up*) to enclose or imprison. **5** (*tr;* usually foll. by *on*) to cause (blame, a nickname, etc.) to be attached (to). **6** (usually foll. by *on* or *upon*) to direct or be directed in a concentrated way. **7** (*intr;* usually foll. by *on*) to take a firm hold (of). [OE *fæstnian;* see FAST[1]] ▸ **'fastener** *n*

fastening ('fɑːs³nɪŋ) *n* something that fastens, such as a clasp or lock.

fast food *n* **a** food, esp. hamburgers, fried chicken, etc., that is prepared and served very quickly. **b** (*as modifier*): *a fast-food restaurant.*

fast-forward *n* **1** (*sometimes not hyphenated*) the control on a tape deck or video recorder used to wind the tape or video forwards at speed. **2** *Inf.* a state of urgency or rapid progress: *put the deal into fast-forward.* ◆ *vb* (*tr*) **3** to wind (a tape, etc.) forward using the fast-forward control. *Inf.* **4a** to deal with or dispatch (something) rapidly: *fast-forward this to the press.* **4b** to skip (something): *fast-forward the small talk and get down to business.*

fastidious (fæ'stɪdɪəs) *adj* **1** hard to please. **2** excessively particular about details. **3** exceedingly delicate. [C15: from L *fastidiōsus* scornful, from *fastidium* loathing, from *fastus* pride + *taedium* weariness] ▸ **fas'tidiously** *adv* ▸ **fas'tidiousness** *n*

fastigiate (fæ'stɪdʒɪɪt) *or* **fastigiated** *adj Biol.* (of parts or organs) united in a tapering group. [C17: from Med. L *fastigiātus* lofty, from L *fastigium* height]

fast lane *n* **1** the outside lane on a motorway for vehicles overtaking or travelling at high speed. **2** *Inf.* the quickest but most competitive route to success.

fastness ('fɑːstnɪs) *n* **1** a stronghold; fortress. **2** the state or quality of being firm or secure. [OE *fæstnes;* see FAST[1]]

fast-track *adj* taking the quickest but most competitive route to success or personal advancement: *fast-track executives.* ▸ **,fast-'tracker** *n*

fat (fæt) *n* **1** any of a class of naturally occurring soft greasy solids that are present in some plants and animals, and are used in making soap and paint and in the food industry. **2** vegetable or animal tissue containing fat. **3** corpulence, obesity, or plumpness. **4** the best or richest part of something. **5 the fat is in the fire.** an irrevocable action has been taken from which dire consequences are expected. **6 the fat of the land.** the best that is obtainable. ◆ *adj* **fatter, fattest. 7** having much or too much flesh or fat. **8** consisting of or containing fat; greasy. **9** profitable; lucrative. **10** affording great opportunities: *a fat part in the play.* **11** fertile or productive: *a fat land.* **12** thick, broad, or extended: *a fat log of wood.* **13** *Sl.* very little or none (in **a fat chance, a fat lot of good,** etc.). ◆ *vb* **fats, fatting, fatted. 14** to make or become fat; fatten. [OE *fætt,* p.p. of *fætan* to cram] ▸ **'fatless** *adj* ▸ **'fatly** *adv* ▸ **'fatness** *n* ▸ **'fattish** *adj*

fatal ('feɪt³l) *adj* **1** resulting in death: *a fatal accident.* **2** bringing ruin. **3** decisively important. **4** inevitable. [C14: from OF or L from L *fātum;* see FATE] ▸ **'fatally** *adv*

fatalism ('feɪtə,lɪzəm) *n* **1** the philosophical doctrine that all events are predetermined so that man is powerless to alter his destiny. **2** the acceptance of and submission to this doctrine. ▸ **'fatalist** *n* ▸ **,fatal'istic** *adj*

fatality (fə'tælɪtɪ) *n, pl* **fatalities. 1** an accident or disaster resulting in death. **2** a person killed in an accident or disaster. **3** the power of causing death or disaster. **4** the quality or condition of being fated. **5** something caused by fate.

fate (feɪt) *n* **1** the ultimate agency that predetermines the course of events. **2** the inevitable fortune that befalls a person or thing. **3** the end or final result. **4** death, destruction, or downfall. ◆ *vb* **fates, fating, fated. 5** (*tr; usually passive*) to predetermine: *he was fated to lose.* [C14: from L *fātum* oracular utterance, from *fārī* to speak]

fated ('feɪtɪd) *adj* **1** destined. **2** doomed to death or destruction.

fateful ('feɪtful) *adj* **1** having important consequences. **2**

bringing death or disaster. **3** controlled by or as if by fate. **4** prophetic.
▸ 'fatefully *adv* ▸ 'fatefulness *n*

Fates ★ (feɪts) *pl n* **1** *Greek myth.* the three goddesses who control the destinies of the lives of man, which are likened to skeins of thread that they spin, measure out, and at last cut. See **Atropos, Clotho, Lachesis. 2** *Norse myth.* another name for the **Norns** (see **Norn**[1]).

fat farm *n Sl.* a health farm or similar establishment to which people go to lose weight.

fathead ('fæt,hed) *n Inf.* a stupid person; fool.
▸ 'fat,headed *adj*

father ('fɑːðə) *n* **1** a male parent. **2** a person who founds a line or family; forefather. **3** any male acting in a paternal capacity. **4** (*often cap.*) a respectful term of address for an old man. **5** a male who originates something: *the father of modern psychology.* **6** a leader of an association, council, etc.: *a city father.* **7** *Brit.* the eldest or most senior member in a union, profession, etc. **8** (*often pl*) a senator in ancient Rome. ◆ *vb* (*tr*) **9** to procreate or generate (offspring). **10** to create, found, etc. **11** to act as a father to. **12** to acknowledge oneself as father or originator of. **13** (foll. by *on* or *upon*) to impose or foist upon. [OE *fæder*]
▸ 'fatherhood *n* ▸ 'fatherless *adj* ▸ 'father-,like *adj*

Father ('fɑːðə) *n* **1** God, esp. when considered as the first person of the Christian Trinity. **2** any of the early writers on Christian doctrine. **3** a title used for Christian priests.

father confessor *n* **1** *Christianity.* a priest who hears confessions. **2** any person to whom one tells private matters.

father-in-law *n, pl* **fathers-in-law.** the father of one's wife or husband.

fatherland ('fɑːðə,lænd) *n* **1** a person's native country. **2** the country of a person's ancestors.

fatherly ('fɑːðəlɪ) *adj* of, resembling, or suitable to a father, esp. in kindliness, encouragement, etc.
▸ 'fatherliness *n*

Father's Day *n* a day observed in honour of fathers; in Britain the third Sunday in June.

fathom ('fæðəm) *n* **1** a unit of length equal to six feet (1.829 metres), used to measure depths of water. ◆ *vb* (*tr*) **2** to measure the depth of, esp. with a sounding line. **3** to penetrate (a mystery, problem, etc.). [OE *fæthm*]
▸ 'fathomable *adj*

Fathometer (fə'ðɒmɪtə) *n Trademark.* a type of echo sounder used for measuring the depth of water.

fathomless ('fæðəmlɪs) *adj* another word for **unfathomable.**
▸ 'fathomlessness *n*

fatigue (fə'tiːg) *n* **1** physical or mental exhaustion due to exertion. **2** a tiring activity or effort. **3** *Physiol.* the temporary inability of an organ or part to respond to a stimulus because of overactivity. **4** the weakening of a material subjected to alternating stresses, esp. vibrations. **5** the temporary inability to respond to a situation resulting from overexposure to it: *compassion fatigue.* **6** any of the mainly domestic duties performed by military personnel, esp. as a punishment. **7** (*pl*) special clothing worn by military personnel to carry out such duties. ◆ *vb* **fatigues, fatiguing, fatigued. 8** to make or become weary or exhausted. [C17: from F, from *fatiguer* to tire, from L *fatigāre*]
▸ 'fatigable *or* 'fatiguable ('fætɪgəb'l) *adj*

Fatima ★ ('fætɪmə) *n* ?606–632 A.D., daughter of Mohammed; wife of Ali.

Fátima ★ (*Portuguese* 'fatimə) *n* a village in central Portugal: Roman Catholic shrine and pilgrimage centre.

Fatshan ★ (faːt'ʃɑːn) *n* a variant transliteration of the Chinese name for **Foshan.**

fatshedera (fæts'hedərə) *n* a hybrid plant with five-lobed leaves. [from NL, from *Fatsia japonica* + *Hedera hibernica*]

fatsia ('fætsɪə) *n* an evergreen hardy shrub. Also known as the **false castor-oil plant.** [from NL]

fatso ('fætsəu) *n Sl.* a fat person.

fat-soluble *adj* soluble in substances, such as ether,

chloroform, and oils. Fat-soluble compounds are often insoluble in water.

fat stock *n* livestock fattened and ready for market.

fatten ('fæt'n) *vb* **1** to grow or cause to grow fat or fatter. **2** (*tr*) to cause (an animal or fowl) to become fat by feeding it. **3** (*tr*) to make fuller or richer. **4** (*tr*) to enrich (soil).
▸ 'fattening *adj*

fatty ('fætɪ) *adj* **fattier, fattiest. 1** containing or derived from fat. **2** greasy; oily. **3** (esp. of tissues, organs, etc.) characterized by the excessive accumulation of fat. ◆ *n*, *pl* **fatties. 4** *Inf.* a fat person.
▸ 'fattily *adv* ▸ 'fattiness *n*

fatty acid *n* an aliphatic carboxylic acid, esp. one found in lipids, such as palmitic acid, stearic acid, and oleic acid.

fatty degeneration *n Pathol.* the abnormal formation of tiny globules of fat within the cytoplasm of a cell.

fatuity (fə'tjuːɪtɪ) *n, pl* **fatuities. 1** inanity. **2** a fatuous remark, act, sentiment, etc.
▸ fa'tuitous *adj*

fatuous ('fætjuəs) *adj* complacently or inanely foolish. [C17: from L *fatuus*; rel. to *fatiscere* to gape]
▸ 'fatuously *adv* ▸ 'fatuousness *n*

fatwa *or* **fatwah** ('fætwə) *n* a religious decree issued by a Muslim leader. [Ar.]

fauces ('fɔːsiːz) *pl n, sing* **fauces.** *Anat.* the area between the cavity of the mouth and the pharynx. [C16: from L: throat]
▸ 'faucal ('fɔːk'l) *or* 'faucial ('fɔːʃəl) *adj*

faucet ('fɔːsɪt) *n* **1** a tap fitted to a barrel. **2** the US and Canad. name for **tap**[2] (sense 1). [C14: from OF from Provençal *falsar* to bore]

Faulkner *or* **Falkner** ★ ('fɔːknə) *n* **William.** 1897–1962, US writer. His novels include *The Sound and the Fury* (1929), *Light in August* (1932), and *The Reivers* (1962). Nobel prize for literature 1949.

fault (fɔːlt) *n* **1** a failing or defect; flaw. **2** a mistake or error. **3** a misdeed. **4** responsibility for a mistake or misdeed. **5** *Electronics.* a defect in a circuit, component, or line, such as a short circuit. **6** *Geol.* a fracture in the earth's crust resulting in the relative displacement of the rocks on either side of it. **7** *Tennis, squash, etc.* an invalid serve. **8** (in showjumping) a penalty mark given for failing to clear, or refusing, a fence, etc. **9 at fault.** guilty of error; culpable. **10 find fault** (with). to seek out minor imperfections or errors (in). **11 to a fault.** excessively. ◆ *vb* **12** *Geol.* to undergo or cause to undergo a fault. **13** (*tr*) to criticize or blame. **14** (*intr*) to commit a fault. [C13: from OF *faute* ult. from L *fallere* to fail]

fault-finding *n* **1** continual criticism. ◆ *adj* **2** given to finding fault.
▸ 'fault-,finder *n*

faultless ('fɔːltlɪs) *adj* perfect or blameless.
▸ 'faultlessly *adv* ▸ 'faultlessness *n*

faulty ('fɔːltɪ) *adj* **faultier, faultiest.** defective or imperfect.
▸ 'faultily *adv* ▸ 'faultiness *n*

faun (fɔːn) *n* (in Roman legend) a rural deity represented as a man with a goat's ears, horns, tail, and hind legs. [C14: back formation from *Faunes* (pl), from L *Faunus* deity of forests]
▸ 'faun,like *adj*

fauna ('fɔːnə) *n, pl* **faunas** *or* **faunae** (-niː). **1** all the animal life of a given place or time. **2** a descriptive list of such animals. [C18: from NL, from LL *Fauna* a goddess of living things]
▸ 'faunal *adj*

Faunus ★ ('fɔːnəs) *n* an ancient Italian deity of pastures and forests, later identified with the Greek Pan.

Fauré ★ ('fɔːreɪ; *French* fore) *n* **Gabriel** (**Urbain**) (gabriɛl). 1845–1924, French composer, noted for his song settings, piano music, and *Messe de Requiem* (1887).

Faust (faust) *or* **Faustus** ★ ('faustəs) *n German legend.* a magician and alchemist who sells his soul to the devil in exchange for knowledge and power.
▸ 'Faustian *adj*

Fauvism ('fəuvɪzəm) *n* a form of expressionist painting

characterized by the use of bright colours and simplified forms. [C20: from F, from *fauve* wild beast]
▶ **Fauve** *n, adj* ▶ **'Fauvist** *n, adj*

faux pas (fəʊ pɑː) *n, pl* **faux pas** (fəʊ pɑːz). a social blunder. [C17: from F: false step]

favour *or US* **favor** ('feɪvə) *n* **1** an approving attitude; goodwill. **2** an act performed out of goodwill or mercy. **3** prejudice and partiality. **4** a condition of being regarded with approval (esp. in **in favour, out of favour**). **5** a token of love, goodwill, etc. **6** a small gift or toy given to a guest at a party. **7** *History.* a badge or ribbon worn or given to indicate loyalty. **8 find favour with.** to be approved of by someone. **9 in favour of. 9a** approving. **9b** to the benefit of. **9c** (of a cheque, etc.) made out to. **9d** in order to show preference for. ◆ *vb* (*tr*) **10** to regard with especial kindness. **11** to treat with partiality. **12** to support; advocate. **13** to oblige. **14** to help; facilitate. **15** *Inf.* to resemble: *he favours his father.* **16** to wear habitually: *she favours red.* **17** to treat gingerly: *a footballer favouring an injured leg.* [C14: from L, from *favēre* to protect]
▶ **'favourer** *or US* **'favorer** *n*

favourable *or US* **favorable** ('feɪvərəbʰl) *adj* **1** advantageous, encouraging or promising. **2** giving consent.
▶ **'favourably** *or US* **'favorably** *adv*

-favoured *adj* (*in combination*) having an appearance (as specified): *ill-favoured.*

favourite *or US* **favorite** ('feɪvərɪt) *adj* **1** (*prenominal*) most liked. ◆ *n* **2** a person or thing regarded with especial preference or liking. **3** *Sport.* a competitor thought likely to win. [C16: from It., from *favorire* to favour, from L *favēre*]

favouritism *or US* **favoritism** ('feɪvərɪˌtɪzəm) *n* the practice of giving special treatment to a person or group.

Fawcett ★ ('fɔːsɪt) *n* Dame **Millicent Garrett.** 1847–1929, British suffragette.

Fawkes ★ (fɔːks) *n* **Guy.** 1570–1606, English conspirator, executed for his part in the Gunpowder Plot to blow up King James I and the Houses of Parliament (1605). Effigies of him (guys) are burnt in Britain on Guy Fawkes Day (Nov. 5).

fawn[1] (fɔːn) *n* **1** a young deer of either sex aged under one year. **2a** a light greyish-brown colour. **2b** (*as adj*): *a fawn raincoat.* ◆ *vb* **3** (of deer) to bear (young). [C14: from OF, from L *fētus* offspring; see FETUS]
▶ **'fawn,like** *adj*

fawn[2] (fɔːn) *vb* (*intr;* often foll. by *on* or *upon*) **1** to seek attention and admiration (from) by cringing and flattering. **2** (of animals, esp. dogs) to try to please by a show of extreme friendliness. [OE *fægnian* to be glad, from *fægen* glad; see FAIN]
▶ **'fawner** *n* ▶ **'fawning** *adj*

fax (fæks) *n* **1** short for **facsimile transmission. 2** a message or document sent by facsimile transmission. **3** Also called: **fax machine, facsimile machine.** a machine which transmits and receives exact copies of documents. ◆ *vb* **4** (*tr*) to send (a message or document) by facsimile transmission.

fay (feɪ) *n* a fairy or sprite. [C14: from OF *feie*, ult. from L *fātum* FATE]

Fayal ★ (*Portuguese* fə'ial) *n* a variant spelling of **Faial.**

Fayum ★ (faɪ'juːm) *n* See **El Faiyûm.**

faze (feɪz) *vb* **fazes, fazing, fazed.** (*tr*) *Inf.* to disconcert; worry; disturb. [C19: var. of arch. *feeze* to beat off]

FBA *abbrev. for* Fellow of the British Academy.

FBI (in the US) *abbrev. for* Federal Bureau of Investigation; an agency responsible for investigating violations of Federal laws.

FC (in Britain) *abbrev. for:* **1** Football Club. **2** Free Church.

fcap *abbrev. for* foolscap.

F clef *n* another name for **bass clef.**

FD *abbrev. for* Fidei Defensor. [L: Defender of the Faith]

FDR *abbrev. for* Franklin Delano Roosevelt.

Fe *the chemical symbol for* iron. [from NL *ferrum*]

fealty ('fiːəltɪ) *n, pl* **fealties.** (in feudal society) the loyalty sworn to one's lord on becoming his vassal. [C14: from OF, from L *fidēlitās* FIDELITY]

fear (fɪə) *n* **1** a feeling of distress, apprehension, or alarm caused by impending danger, pain, etc. **2** a cause of this feeling. **3** awe; reverence: *fear of God.* **4** concern; anxiety. **5** possibility; chance. **6 for fear of, that** *or* **lest.** to forestall or avoid. **7 no fear.** certainly not. ◆ *vb* **8** to be afraid (to do something) or of (a person or thing). **9** (*tr*) to revere; respect. **10** (*tr; takes a clause as object*) to be sorry: *I fear that you have not won.* **11** (*intr;* foll. by *for*) to feel anxiety about something. [OE *fǣr*]
▶ **'fearless** *adj* ▶ **'fearlessly** *adv* ▶ **'fearlessness** *n*

fearful ('fɪəful) *adj* **1** afraid. **2** causing fear. **3** *Inf.* very unpleasant: *a fearful cold.*
▶ **'fearfully** *adv* ▶ **'fearfulness** *n*

fearsome ('fɪəsəm) *adj* **1** frightening. **2** timorous; afraid.
▶ **'fearsomely** *adv*

feasibility study *n* a study designed to determine the practicality of a system or plan.

feasible ('fiːzəbʰl) *adj* **1** able to be done or put into effect; possible. **2** likely; probable. [C15: from Anglo-F *faisable*, from *faire* to do, from L *facere*]
▶ **,feasi'bility** *n* ▶ **'feasibly** *adv*

feast (fiːst) *n* **1** a large and sumptuous meal. **2** a periodic religious celebration. **3** something extremely pleasing: *a feast for the eyes.* **4 movable feast.** a festival of variable date. ◆ *vb* **5** (*intr*) **5a** to eat a feast. **5b** (usually foll. by *on*) to enjoy the eating (of): *to feast on cakes.* **6** (*tr*) to give a feast to. **7** (*intr;* foll. by *on*) to take great delight (in): *to feast on beautiful paintings.* **8** (*tr*) to regale or delight: *to feast one's eyes.* [C13: from OF, from L *festa*, neuter pl (later assumed to be fem sing) of *festus* joyful; rel. to L *fānum* temple, *fēriae* festivals]
▶ **'feaster** *n*

Feast of Dedication *n* a literal translation of **Chanukah.**

Feast of Lights *n* an English name for **Chanukah.**

Feast of Tabernacles *n* a literal translation of **Sukkoth.**

Feast of Weeks *n* a literal translation of **Shavuot.**

feat (fiːt) *n* a remarkable, skilful, or daring action. [C14: from Anglo-F *fait*, from L *factum* deed; see FACT]

feather ('feðə) *n* **1** any of the flat light waterproof structures forming the plumage of birds, each consisting of a hollow shaft having a vane of barbs on either side. **2** something resembling a feather, such as a tuft of hair or grass. **3** *Archery.* **3a** a bird's feather or artificial substitute fitted to an arrow to direct its flight. **3b** the feathered end of an arrow. **4** *Rowing.* the position of an oar turned parallel to the water between strokes. **5** condition of spirits; fettle: *in fine feather.* **6** something of negligible value: *I don't care a feather.* **7 feather in one's cap.** a cause for pleasure at one's achievements. ◆ *vb* **8** (*tr*) to fit, cover, or supply with feathers. **9** *Rowing.* to turn (an oar) parallel to the water during recovery between strokes, in order to lessen wind resistance. **10** to change the pitch of (an aircraft propeller) so that the chord lines of the blades are in line with the airflow. **11** (*intr*) (of a bird) to grow feathers. **12 feather one's nest.** to provide oneself with comforts. [OE *fether*]
▶ **'feathering** *n* ▶ **'feather-,like** *adj* ▶ **'feathery** *adj*

feather bed *n* **1** a mattress filled with feathers or down. ◆ *vb* **featherbed, featherbeds, featherbedding, featherbedded. 2** (*tr*) to pamper; spoil.

featherbedding ('feðəˌbedɪŋ) *n* the practice of limiting production or of overmanning in order to prevent redundancies or create jobs.

featherbrain ('feðəˌbreɪn) *or* **featherhead** *n* a frivolous or forgetful person.
▶ **'feather,brained** *or* **'feather,headed** *adj*

featheredge ('feðərˌedʒ) *n* a board or plank that tapers to a thin edge at one side.

featherstitch ('feðəˌstɪtʃ) *n* **1** a zigzag embroidery stitch. ◆ *vb* **2** to decorate (cloth) with featherstitch.

featherweight ('feðəˌweɪt) *n* **1a** something very light or of little importance. **1b** (*as modifier*): *featherweight considerations.* **2a** a professional boxer weighing 118–126 pounds (53.5–57 kg). **2b** an amateur boxer weighing 54–

57 kg (119–126 pounds). **3** an amateur wrestler weighing usually 127–137 pounds (58–62 kg).

feature ('fiːtʃə) n **1** any one of the parts of the face, such as the nose, chin, or mouth. **2** a prominent or distinctive part, as of a landscape, book, etc. **3** the principal film in a programme at a cinema. **4** an item or article appearing regularly in a newspaper, magazine, etc.: *a gardening feature.* **5** Also called: **feature story.** a prominent story in a newspaper, etc.: *a feature on prison reform.* **6** a programme given special prominence on radio or television. **7** Arch. general form. ◆ vb **features, featuring, featured. 8** (tr) to have as a feature or make a feature of. **9** to give prominence to (an actor, famous event, etc.) in a film or (of an actor, etc.) to have prominence in a film. **10** (tr) Arch. to draw the main features or parts of. [C14: from Anglo-F *feture*, from L *factūra* a making, from *facere* to make]
▶ **'featureless** adj

-featured adj (in combination) having features as specified: *heavy-featured.*

Feb. abbrev. for February.

febri- combining form. indicating fever: *febrifuge.* [from L *febris* fever]

febrifuge ('fɛbrɪˌfjuːdʒ) n **1** any drug or agent for reducing fever. ◆ adj **2** serving to reduce fever. [C17: from Med. L *febrifugia* feverfew; see FEBRI-, -FUGE]
▶ **febrifugal** (fɪˈbrɪfjʊg⁰l) adj

febrile ('fiːbraɪl) adj of or relating to fever; feverish. [C17: from Medical L *febrīlis*, from L *febris* fever]
▶ **febrility** (fɪˈbrɪlɪtɪ) n

February ('fɛbrʊərɪ) n, pl **Februaries.** the second month of the year, consisting of 28 or (in a leap year) 29 days. [C13: from L *Februārius mēnsis* month of expiation, from *februa* Roman festival of purification held on February 15, from pl of *februum* a purgation]

feces ('fiːsiːz) pl n the usual US spelling of **faeces.**
▶ **fecal** ('fiːk⁰l) adj

Fechner ★ (German 'fɛçnər) n **Gustav Theodor** ('gustaf 'teːodoːər). 1801–87, German physicist, philosopher, and psychologist, noted particularly for his work on psychophysics, *Elemente der Psychophysik* (1860).

feckless ('fɛklɪs) adj feeble; weak; ineffectual. [C16: from obs. *feck* value, effect + -LESS]
▶ **'fecklessly** adv ▶ **'fecklessness** n

feculent ('fɛkjʊlənt) adj **1** filthy or foul. **2** of or containing waste matter. [C15: from L *faeculentus;* see FAECES]
▶ **'feculence** n

fecund ('fiːkənd, 'fɛk-) adj **1** fertile. **2** intellectually productive. [C14: from L *fēcundus*]
▶ **fecundity** (fɪˈkʌndɪtɪ) n

fecundate ('fiːkənˌdeɪt, 'fɛk-) vb **fecundates, fecundating, fecundated.** (tr) **1** to make fruitful. **2** to fertilize. [C17: from L *fēcundāre* to fertilize]
▶ **ˌfecun'dation** n

fed¹ (fɛd) vb **1** the past tense and past participle of **feed. 2 fed to death** or **fed (up) to the (back) teeth.** Inf. bored or annoyed.

fed² (fɛd) n US sl. an agent of the FBI.

Fed (fɛd) n short for **Federal Reserve System.**

Fed. or **fed.** abbrev. for: **1** Federal. **2** Federation. **3** Federated.

fedayee (fəˈdɑːjiː) n, pl **fedayeen** (-jiːn). **a** (sometimes cap.) (in Arab states) a commando, esp. one fighting against Israel. **b** (esp. in Iran and Afghanistan) a member of a guerrilla organization. [from Ar. *fidā'i* one who risks his life in a cause, from *fidā'* redemption]

federal ('fɛdərəl) adj **1** of or relating to a form of government or a country in which power is divided between one central and several regional governments. **2** of or relating to the central government of a federation. [C17: from L *foedus* league]
▶ **'federaˌlism** n ▶ **'federalist** n, adj ▶ **'federally** adv

Federal ('fɛdərəl) adj **1** characteristic of or supporting the Union government during the American Civil War. ◆ n **2** a supporter of the Union government during the American Civil War.

Federal Government n the national government of a

federated state, such as the Canadian national government located in Ottawa.

federalize or **federalise** ('fɛdərəˌlaɪz) vb **federalizes, federalizing, federalized** or **federalises, federalising, federalised.** (tr) **1** to unite in a federal union. **2** to subject to federal control.
▶ ˌfederaliˈzation or ˌfederaliˈsation n

Federal Republic of Germany ★ n the official name of **Germany,** formerly of West Germany.

Federal Reserve System n (in the US) a banking system consisting of twelve **Federal Reserve Banks** and their member banks. It performs functions similar to those of the Bank of England.

federate vb ('fɛdəˌreɪt), **federates, federating, federated. 1** to unite or cause to unite in a federal union. ◆ adj ('fɛdərɪt). **2** federal; federated.
▶ **'federative** adj

Federated Malay States ★ pl n See **Malay States.**

federation (ˌfɛdəˈreɪʃən) n **1** the act of federating. **2** the union of several provinces, states, etc., to form a federal union. **3** a political unit formed in such a way. **4** any league, alliance, or confederacy.

Federation of Rhodesia and Nyasaland ★ n a federation (1953–63) of Northern Rhodesia, Southern Rhodesia, and Nyasaland.

fedora (fɪˈdɔːrə) n a soft felt brimmed hat, usually with a band. [C19: allegedly after *Fédora* (1882), play by Victorien Sardou (1831–1908)]

fed up adj (usually postpositive) Inf. annoyed or bored: *I'm fed up with your conduct.*

fee (fiː) n **1** a payment asked by professional people or public servants for their services: *school fees.* **2** a charge made for a privilege: *an entrance fee.* **3** Property law. an interest in land capable of being inherited. The interest can be with unrestricted rights of disposal (**fee simple**) or with restricted rights to one class of heirs (**fee tail**). **4** (in feudal Europe) the land granted by a lord to his vassal. **5 in fee.** Law. (of land) in absolute ownership. ◆ vb **fees, feeing, feed. 6** Rare. to give a fee to. **7** Chiefly Scot. to hire for a fee. [C14: from OF *fie*, of Gmc origin; see FIEF]

feeble ('fiːb⁰l) adj **1** lacking in physical or mental strength. **2** unconvincing: *feeble excuses.* **3** easily influenced. [C12: from OF *feble, fleible*, from L *flēbilis* to be lamented, from *flēre* to weep]
▶ **'feebleness** n ▶ **'feebly** adv

feeble-minded adj **1** lacking in intelligence. **2** mentally defective.

feed (fiːd) vb **feeds, feeding, fed.** (mainly tr) **1** to give food to: *to feed the cat.* **2** to give as food: *to feed meat to the cat.* **3** (intr) to eat food: *the horses feed at noon.* **4** to provide food for. **5** to gratify; satisfy. **6** (also intr) to supply (a machine, furnace, etc.) with (the necessary materials or fuel) for its operation, or (of such materials) to flow or move forwards into a machine, etc. **7** Theatre, inf. to cue (an actor, esp. a comedian) with lines. **8** Sport. to pass a ball to (a team-mate). **9** (also intr; foll. by on or upon) to eat or cause to eat. ◆ n **10** the act or an instance of feeding. **11** food, esp. that of animals or babies. **12** the process of supplying a machine or furnace with a material or fuel. **13** the quantity of material or fuel so supplied. **14** Theatre, inf. a performer, esp. a straight man, who provides cues. **15** Inf. a meal. [OE *fēdan*]
▶ **'feedable** adj

feedback ('fiːdˌbæk) n **1** information or an opinion in response to an inquiry, proposal, etc. **2a** the return of part of the output of an electronic circuit, device, or mechanical system to its input. In **negative feedback** a rise in output energy reduces the input energy; in **positive feedback** an increase in output energy reinforces the input energy. **2b** that part of the output signal fed back into the input. **3** the return of part of the sound output of a loudspeaker to the microphone or pick-up, so that a high-pitched whistle is produced. **4** the whistling noise so produced. **5** the effect of a product or action in a cyclic biological reaction on another stage in the same reaction.

feeder ('fiːdə) n **1** a person or thing that feeds or is fed. **2** a child's feeding bottle or bib. **3** a person or device that feeds the working material into a system or machine. **4** a tributary channel. **5** a road, service, etc., that links secondary areas to the main traffic network. **6** a power line for transmitting electrical power from a generating station to a distribution network.

feeding bottle *n* a bottle fitted with a rubber teat from which infants suck liquids.

feel (fiːl) *vb* **feels, feeling, felt. 1** to perceive (something) by touching. **2** to have a physical or emotional sensation of (something): *to feel anger.* **3** (*tr*) to examine (something) by touch. **4** (*tr*) to find (one's way) by testing or cautious exploration. **5** (*copula*) to seem in respect of the sensation given: *it feels warm.* **6** to sense (esp. in **feel (it) in one's bones**). **7** to consider; believe; think. **8** (*intr*; foll. by *for*) to show sympathy or compassion (towards): *I feel for you in your sorrow.* **9** (*tr*; often foll. by *up*) *Sl.* to pass one's hands over the sexual organs of. **10 feel like.** to have an inclination (for something or doing something): *I don't feel like going to the pictures.* **11 feel up to.** (*usually used with a negative or in a question*) to be fit enough for (something or doing something): *I don't feel up to going out.* ◆ *n* **12** the act or an instance of feeling. **13** the quality of or an impression from something perceived through feeling: *a homely feel.* **14** the sense of touch. **15** an instinctive aptitude; knack: *she's got a feel for this sort of work.* [OE *fēlan*]

feeler ('fiːlə) *n* **1** a person or thing that feels. **2** an organ in certain animals, such as an antenna, that is sensitive to touch. **3** a remark designed to probe the reactions or intentions of others.

feeler gauge *n* a thin metal strip of known thickness used to measure a narrow gap or to set a gap between two parts.

feel-good *adj* causing or characterized by a feeling of self-satisfaction: *feel-good factor.*

feeling ('fiːlɪŋ) *n* **1** the sense of touch. **2a** the ability to experience physical sensations, such as heat, etc. **2b** the sensation so experienced. **3** a state of mind. **4** a physical or mental impression: *a feeling of warmth.* **5** fondness; sympathy: *to have a great deal of feeling for someone.* **6** a sentiment: *a feeling that the project is feasible.* **7** an emotional disturbance, esp. anger or dislike: *a lot of bad feeling.* **8** intuitive appreciation and understanding: *a feeling for words.* **9** sensibility in the performance of something. **10** (*pl*) emotional or moral sensitivity (esp. in **hurt** or **injure the feelings of**). ◆ *adj* **11** sentient; sensitive. **12** expressing or containing emotion.
▸ 'feelingly *adv*

feet (fiːt) *n* **1** the plural of **foot. 2 at (someone's) feet.** as someone's disciple. **3 be run** or **rushed off one's feet.** to be very busy. **4 carry** or **sweep off one's feet.** to fill with enthusiasm. **5 feet of clay.** a weakness that is not widely known. **6 have** (or **keep) one's feet on the ground.** to be practical and reliable. **7 on one's** or **its feet. 7a** standing up. **7b** in good health. **8 stand on one's own feet.** to be independent.

feign (feɪn) *vb* **1** to pretend: *to feign innocence.* **2** (*tr*) to invent: *to feign an excuse.* **3** (*tr*) to copy; imitate. [C13: from OF, from L *fingere* to form, shape, invent]
▸ 'feigningly *adv*

feijoa (fiːˈdʒəʊə) *n* **1** an evergreen shrub of South America. **2** the fruit of this shrub. [C19: NL, after J. da Silva *Feijo*, 19th-cent. Sp. botanist]

Feininger ★ ('faɪnɪŋə) *n* **Lyonel.** 1871–1956, US artist, who worked at the Bauhaus, noted for his use of superimposed translucent planes of colour.

feint[1] (feɪnt) *n* **1** a mock attack or movement designed to distract an adversary, as in boxing, fencing, etc. **2** a misleading action or appearance. ◆ *vb* **3** (*intr*) to make a feint. [C17: from F, from OF *feindre* to FEIGN]

feint[2] (feɪnt) *n Printing.* a narrow rule used in the production of ruled paper. [C19: var. of FAINT]

Feisal ★ ('faɪsˀl) *n* a variant spelling of **Faisal.**

feisty ('faɪstɪ) *adj* **feistier, feistiest.** *Inf.* **1** lively, resilient, and self-reliant. **2** *US & Canad.* frisky. **3** *US & Canad.* irritable. [C19: dialect *feist, fist* small dog]

felafel (fəˈlɑːfəl) *n* a variant spelling of **falafel.**

feldspar ('fɛldˌspɑː, 'fɛlˌspɑː) or **felspar** *n* any of a group of hard rock-forming minerals consisting of aluminium silicates of potassium, sodium, calcium, or barium: the

principal constituents of igneous rocks. [C18: from G, from *Feld* field + *Spat(h)* SPAR[3]]
▸ **feldspathic** (fɛldˈspæθɪk, fɛlˈspæθ-) or **fel'spathic** *adj*

felicitate (fɪˈlɪsɪˌteɪt) *vb* **felicitates, felicitating, felicitated.** to congratulate.
▸ fe,lici'tation *n* ▸ fe'lici,tator *n*

felicitous (fɪˈlɪsɪtəs) *adj* **1** well-chosen; apt. **2** possessing an agreeable style. **3** marked by happiness.
▸ fe'licitously *adv*

felicity (fɪˈlɪsɪtɪ) *n, pl* **felicities. 1** happiness. **2** a cause of happiness. **3** an appropriate expression or style. **4** the display of such expressions or style. [C14: from L *fēlicitās* happiness, from *fēlix* happy]

feline ('fiːlaɪn) *adj* **1** of, relating to, or belonging to a family of predatory mammals, including cats, lions, leopards, and cheetahs, having a round head and retractile claws. **2** resembling or suggestive of a cat, esp. in stealth or grace. ◆ *n* **3** any member of the cat family; a cat. [C17: from L, from *fēlēs* cat]
▸ 'felinely *adv* ▸ felinity (fɪˈlɪnɪtɪ) *n*

Felixstowe ★ ('fiːlɪkˌstəʊ) *n* a port and resort in E England, in Suffolk: ferry connections to Rotterdam and Zeebrugge. Pop.: 28 606 (1991).

fell[1] (fɛl) *vb* the past tense of **fall.**

fell[2] (fɛl) *vb* (*tr*) **1** to cut or knock down: *to fell a tree.* **2** *Needlework.* to fold under and sew flat (the edges of a seam). ◆ *n* **3** *US & Canad.* the timber felled in one season. **4** a seam finished by felling. [OE *fellan*; cf. FALL]
▸ 'feller *n*

fell[3] (fɛl) *adj* **1** *Arch.* cruel or fierce. **2** *Arch.* destructive or deadly. **3 one fell swoop.** a single hasty action or occurrence. [C13 *fel*, from OF: cruel, from Med. L *fellō* villain; see FELON[1]]

fell[4] (fɛl) *n* an animal skin or hide. [OE]

fell[5] (fɛl) *n* (*often pl*) *Scot. & N English.* **a** a mountain, hill, or moor. **b** (*in combination*): *fell-walking.* [C13: from ON *fjall*; rel. to OHG *felis* rock]

fellah ('fɛlə) *n, pl* **fellahs, fellahin,** or **fellaheen** (ˌfɛləˈhiːn). a peasant in Arab countries. [C18: from Ar., dialect var. of *fallāh*, from *falaha* to cultivate]

fellatio (fɪˈleɪʃɪəʊ) *n* a sexual activity in which the penis is stimulated by the mouth. [C19: NL, from L *fellāre* to suck]

Felling ★ ('fɛlɪŋ) *n* a town in NE England, in Gateshead unitary authority, Tyne and Wear; formerly noted for coal mining. Pop.: 35 053 (1991).

Fellini ★ (fəˈliːnɪ; *Italian* felˈliːni) *n* **Federico** (fedeˈriːko). 1920–93, Italian film director. His films include *La Dolce Vita* (1959), *Satyricon* (1969), and *Intervista* (1987).

felloe ('fɛləʊ) or **felly** ('fɛlɪ) *n, pl* **felloes** or **fellies.** a segment or the whole rim of a wooden wheel to which the spokes are attached. [OE *felge*]

fellow ('fɛləʊ) *n* **1** a man or boy. **2** an informal word for **boyfriend. 3** *Inf.* one or oneself: *a fellow has to eat.* **4** a person considered to be of little worth. **5a** (*often pl*) a companion; associate. **5b** (*as modifier*): *fellow travellers.* **6** a member of the governing body at any of various universities or colleges. **7** a postgraduate student employed, esp. for a fixed period, to undertake research. **8a** a person in the same group, class, or condition: *the surgeon asked his fellows.* **8b** (*as modifier*): *a fellow sufferer.* **9** one of a pair; counterpart; mate. [OE *fēolaga*]

Fellow ('fɛləʊ) *n* a member of any of various learned societies: *Fellow of the British Academy.*

fellow feeling *n* **1** mutual sympathy or friendship. **2** an opinion held in common.

fellowship ('fɛləʊˌʃɪp) *n* **1** the state of sharing mutual interests, activities, etc. **2** a society of people sharing mutual interests, activities, etc. **3** companionship; friendship. **4** the state or relationship of being a fellow. **5** *Education.* **5a** a financed research post providing study facilities, privileges, etc., often in return for teaching services. **5b** an honorary title carrying certain privileges awarded to a postgraduate student.

fellow traveller *n* **1** a companion on a journey. **2** a non-Communist who sympathizes with Communism.

felon[1] ('fɛlən) *n* **1** *Criminal law.* (formerly) a person who

★ people and places

has committed a felony. ◆ *adj* **2** *Arch.* evil. [C13: from OF: villain, from Med. L *fellō*, from ?]

felon² ('fɛlən) *n* a purulent inflammation of the end joint of a finger. [C12: from Med. L *fellō*, ?from L *fel* poison]

felonious (fɪ'ləʊnɪəs) *adj* **1** *Criminal law.* of, involving, or constituting a felony. **2** *Obs.* wicked.
▸ fe'loniously *adv* ▸ fe'loniousness *n*

felony ('fɛlənɪ) *n, pl* **felonies**. *Criminal law.* (formerly) a serious crime, such as murder or arson.

felspar ('fɛl,spɑː) *n* a variant spelling (esp. Brit.) of **feldspar**.
▸ felspathic (fɛl'spæθɪk) *adj*

felt¹ (fɛlt) *vb* the past tense and past participle of **feel**.

felt² (fɛlt) *n* **1** a matted fabric of wool, hair, etc., made by working the fibres together under pressure or by heat or chemical action. **2** any material, such as asbestos, made by a similar process of matting. ◆ *vb* **3** (*tr*) to make into or cover with felt. **4** (*intr*) to become matted. [OE]

felt-tip pen *n* a pen whose writing point is made from pressed fibres. Also called: **fibre-tip pen**.

felucca (fɛ'lʌkə) *n* a narrow lateen-rigged vessel of the Mediterranean. [C17: from It., prob. from obs. Sp. *faluca*, prob. from Ar. *fulūk* ships, from Gk, from *ephelkein* to tow]

fem. *abbrev. for:* **1** female. **2** feminine.

female ('fiːmeɪl) *adj* **1** of, relating to, or designating the sex producing gametes (ova) that can be fertilized by male gametes (spermatozoa). **2** of or characteristic of a woman. **3** for or composed of women or girls: *a female choir*. **4** (of reproductive organs such as the ovary and carpel) capable of producing female gametes. **5** (of flowers) lacking, or having nonfunctional, stamens. **6** having an internal cavity into which a projecting male counterpart can be fitted: *a female thread*. ◆ *n* **7** a female animal or plant. [C14: from earlier *femelle* (infl. by *male*), from L *fēmella* a young woman, from *fēmina* a woman]
▸ 'femaleness *n*

female impersonator *n* a male theatrical performer who acts as a woman.

feminine ('fɛmɪnɪn) *adj* **1** suitable to or characteristic of a woman. **2** possessing qualities or characteristics considered typical of or appropriate to a woman. **3** effeminate; womanish. **4** *Grammar.* **4a** denoting or belonging to a gender of nouns that includes all kinds of referents as well as some female animate referents. **4b** (*as n*): *German Zeit "time" and Ehe "marriage" are feminines.* [C14: from L, from *fēmina* woman]
▸ 'femininely *adv* ▸ femi'ninity *or* 'feminineness *n*

feminism ('fɛmɪ,nɪzəm) *n* a doctrine or movement that advocates equal rights for women.
▸ 'feminist *n, adj*

feminize *or* **feminise** ('fɛmɪ,naɪz) *vb* **feminizes, feminizing, feminized** *or* **feminises, feminising, feminised**. **1** to make or become feminine. **2** to cause (a male animal) to develop female characteristics.
▸ femini'zation *or* femini'sation *n*

femme fatale *French.* (fam fatal) *n, pl* **femmes fatales** (fam fatal). an alluring or seductive woman, esp. one who causes men to love her to their own distress. [fatal woman]

femto- *prefix* denoting 10⁻¹⁵: *femtometer*. Symbol: f [from Danish or Norwegian *femten* fifteen]

femur ('fiːmə) *n, pl* **femurs** *or* **femora** ('fɛmərə). **1** the longest thickest bone of the human skeleton, with the pelvis above and the knee below. Nontechnical name: **thighbone**. **2** the corresponding bone in other vertebrates or the corresponding segment of an insect's leg. [C18: from L: thigh]
▸ 'femoral *adj*

fen (fɛn) *n* low-lying flat land that is marshy or artificially drained. [OE *fenn*]
▸ 'fenny *adj*

fence (fɛns) *n* **1** a structure that serves to enclose an area such as a garden or field, usually made of posts of timber, concrete, or metal connected by wire netting, rails, or boards. **2** *Sl.* a dealer in stolen property. **3** an obstacle

for a horse to jump in steeplechasing or showjumping. **4** *Machinery.* a guard or guide, esp. in a circular saw or plane. **5** (**sit**) **on the fence**. (to be) unable or unwilling to commit oneself. ◆ *vb* **fences, fencing, fenced**. **6** (*tr*) to construct a fence on or around (a piece of land, etc.). **7** (*tr;* foll. by *in* or *off*) to close (in) or separate (off) with or as if with a fence: *he fenced in the livestock.* **8** (*intr*) to fight using swords or foils. **9** (*intr*) to evade a question or argument. **10** (*intr*) *Sl.* to receive stolen property. [C14 *fens*, shortened from *defens* DEFENCE]
▸ 'fenceless *adj* ▸ 'fencer *n*

fencible ('fɛnsəbʰl) *n* (formerly) a person who undertook military service in immediate defence of his homeland only.

fencing ('fɛnsɪŋ) *n* **1** the practice, art, or sport of fighting with foils, épées, sabres, etc. **2a** wire, stakes, etc., used as fences. **2b** fences collectively.

fend (fɛnd) *vb* **1** (*intr;* foll. by *for*) to give support (to someone, esp. oneself). **2** (*tr;* usually foll. by *off*) to ward off or turn aside (blows, questions, etc.). ◆ *n* **3** *Scot. & N English dialect.* a shift or effort. [C13 *fenden,* shortened from *defenden* to DEFEND]

fender ('fɛndə) *n* **1** a low metal frame which confines falling coals to the hearth. **2** *Chiefly US.* a metal frame fitted to the front of locomotives to absorb shock, etc. **3** a cushion-like device, such as a car tyre hung over the side of a vessel to reduce damage resulting from collision. **4** the US and Canad. name for the wing of a car.

Fénelon ★ (*French* fenlɔ̃) *n* **François de Salignac de La Mothe** (frãswa də salijnak də la mɔt). 1651–1715, French theologian, author of *Maximes des saints* (1697) and *Les aventures de Télémaque* (1699), criticizing the government of Louis XIV.

fenestra (fɪ'nɛstrə) *n, pl* **fenestrae** (-triː). **1** *Biol.* a small opening, esp. either of two openings between the middle and inner ears. **2** *Zool.* a transparent marking or spot, as on the wings of moths. **3** *Archit.* a window or window-like opening in the outside wall of a building. [C19: via NL from L: wall opening, window]

fenestrated (fɪ'nɛstreɪtɪd, 'fɛnɪ,streɪtɪd) *or* **fenestrate** *adj* **1** *Archit.* having windows. **2** *Biol.* perforated or having fenestrae.

fenestration (,fɛnɪ'streɪʃən) *n* **1** the arrangement of windows in a building. **2** an operation to restore hearing by making an artificial opening into the labyrinth of the ear.

feng shui ('fʌŋ 'ʃweɪ) *n* the Chinese art of determining the most propitious design and placement of a grave, building, room, etc., so that the maximum harmony is achieved between the flow of chi of the environment and that of the user, believed to bring good fortune. [C20: from Chinese *feng* wind + *shui* water]

Fenian ('fiːnɪən, 'fiːnjən) *n* **1** (formerly) a member of an Irish revolutionary organization founded in the US in the 19th century to fight for an independent Ireland. ◆ *adj* **2** of or relating to the Fenians. [C19: from Irish Gaelic *fēinne,* after *Fiann* Irish folk hero]
▸ 'Fenianism *n*

fennec ('fɛnɛk) *n* a very small nocturnal fox inhabiting deserts of N Africa and Arabia, having enormous ears. [C18: from Ar. *fenek* fox]

fennel ('fɛnʰl) *n* a strong-smelling yellow-flowered umbelliferous plant whose seeds, feathery leaves, and bulbous aniseed-flavoured root are used in cookery. [OE *fenol*]

Fenrir ('fɛnrɪə), **Fenris** ('fɛnrɪs), *or* **Fenriswolf** ★ ('fɛnrɪs,wulf) *n Norse myth.* an enormous wolf, fathered by Loki, which killed Odin.

Fens ★ (fɛnz) *pl n* **the**. a flat low-lying area of E England, west and south of the Wash: consisted of marshes until reclaimed in the 17th to 19th centuries.

Fenton ★ ('fɛntʰn) *n* **James** (**Martin**). born 1949, British poet and journalist. His poetry includes the collections *A German Requiem* (1980) and *Out of Danger* (1993).

fenugreek ('fɛnju,griːk) *n* an annual heavily scented Mediterranean leguminous plant with hairy stems and white flowers. [OE *fēnogrēcum*]

feoff (fi:f) *History.* ◆ *n* **1** a variant spelling of **fief.** ◆ *vb* **2** (*tr*) to invest with a benefice or fief. [C13: from Anglo-F: a FIEF]
▶ **'feoffee** *n* ▶ **'feoffment** *n* ▶ **'feoffor** *or* **'feoffer** *n*

-fer *n combining form.* indicating a person or thing that bears something specified: *crucifer; conifer.* [from L, from *ferre* to bear]

feral ('fɪərəl) *adj* **1** (of animals and plants) existing in a wild or uncultivated state. **2** savage; brutal. [C17: from Med. L, from L, from *ferus* savage]

fer-de-lance (ˌfɛədə'lɑ:ns) *n* a large highly venomous tropical American snake with a greyish-brown mottled coloration. [C19: from F, lit.: iron (head) of a lance]

Ferdinand ★ ('fɜ:dɪˌnænd; German 'fɛrdinant) *n* See **Franz Ferdinand.**

Ferdinand I ★ ('fɜ:dɪˌnænd) *n* **1** known as *Ferdinand the Great.* ?1016–65, king of Castile (1035–65) and León (1037–65): achieved control of the Moorish kings of Saragossa, Seville, and Toledo. **2** 1503–64, king of Hungary and Bohemia (1526–64); Holy Roman Emperor (1558–64), bringing years of religious warfare to an end. **3** 1751–1825, king of the Two Sicilies (1816–25); king of Naples (1759–1806; 1815–25), as Ferdinand IV, being dispossessed by Napoleon (1806–15). **4** 1793–1875, king of Hungary (1830–48) and emperor of Austria (1835–48); abdicated after the Revolution of 1848 in favour of his nephew, Franz Josef I. **5** 1861–1948, ruling prince of Bulgaria (1887–1908) and tsar from 1908 until his abdication in 1918. **6** 1865–1927, king of Romania (1914–27); sided with the Allies in World War I.

Ferdinand II ★ *n* **1** 1578–1637, Holy Roman Emperor (1619–37); king of Bohemia (1617–19; 1620–37) and of Hungary (1617–37). His anti-Protestant policies led to the Thirty Years' War. **2** title as king of Aragon and Sicily of **Ferdinand V.**

Ferdinand III ★ *n* **1** 1608–57, Holy Roman Emperor (1637–57) and king of Hungary (1625–57); son of Ferdinand II. **2** title as king of Naples of **Ferdinand V.**

Ferdinand V ★ *n* known as *Ferdinand the Catholic.* 1452–1516, king of Castile (1474–1504); as Ferdinand II, king of Aragon (1479–1516) and Sicily (1468–1516); as Ferdinand III, king of Naples (1504–16). His marriage to Isabella I of Castile (1469) led to the union of Aragon and Castile and his reconquest of Granada from the Moors (1492) completed the unification of Spain. He introduced the Inquisition (1478), expelled the Jews from Spain (1492), and financed Columbus' voyage to the New World.

Ferdinand VII ★ *n* 1784–1833, king of Spain (1808; 1814–33). He precipitated the Carlist Wars by excluding his brother Don Carlos as his successor.

feretory ('fɛrɪtərɪ, -trɪ) *n, pl* **feretories.** *Chiefly RC Church.* **1** a shrine, usually portable, for a saint's relics. **2** the chapel in which a shrine is kept. [C14: from MF *fiertre*, from L *feretrum* a bier, from Gk, from *pherein* to bear]

Fergana *or* **Ferghana** ★ (fə'gɑːnə) *n* **1** a region of W central Asia, surrounded by high mountains and accessible only from the west; mainly in Uzbekistan and partly in Tajikistan and Kyrgyzstan. **2** the chief city of this region, in E Uzbekistan. Pop.: 191 000 (1993 est.).

Fergus ★ ('fɜːgəs) *n* (in Irish legend) a warrior king of Ulster, who was supplanted by Conchobar.

feria ('fɪərɪə) *n, pl* **ferias** *or* **feriae** (-rɪ,iː). *RC Church.* a weekday, other than Saturday, on which no feast occurs. [C19: from LL: day of the week (as in *prīma fēria* Sunday), sing of L *fēriae* festivals]
▶ **'ferial** *adj*

Ferlinghetti ★ (ˌfɜːlɪŋ'gɛtɪ) *n* **Lawrence.** born 1920, US poet of the Beat Generation. His poetry includes the collection *Pictures of the Gone World* (1955).

Fermanagh ★ (fə'mænə) *n* a district and historic county of SW Northern Ireland, bordering the Irish Republic: contains the Upper and Lower Lough Erne. Administrative centre: Enniskillen. Pop.: 54 033 (1991). Area (excluding water): 1700 sq. km (656 sq. miles).

Fermat ★ (fɜː'mæt; French fɛrma) *n* **Pierre de** (pjɛr də). 1601–65, French mathematician, regarded as the founder of the modern theory of numbers.

fermata (fə'mɑːtə) *n, pl* **fermatas** *or* **fermate** (-tɪ). *Music.* another word for **pause** (sense 5). [from It., from *fermare* to stop, from L *firmāre* to establish]

ferment *n* ('fɜːmɛnt). **1** any agent or substance, such as a bacterium, mould, yeast, or enzyme, that causes fermentation. **2** another word for **fermentation.** **3** commotion; unrest. ◆ *vb* (fə'mɛnt). **4** to undergo or cause to undergo fermentation. **5** to stir up or seethe with excitement. [C15: from L *fermentum* yeast, from *fervēre* to seethe]
▶ **fer'mentable** *adj*

USAGE NOTE   See at **foment.**

fermentation (ˌfɜːmɛn'teɪʃən) *n* a chemical reaction in which an organic molecule splits into simpler substances, esp. the conversion of sugar to ethyl alcohol by yeast.
▶ **fer'mentative** *adj*

fermentation lock *n* a valve placed on the top of bottles of fermenting wine to allow bubbles to escape.

fermi ('fɜːmɪ) *n* a unit of length used in nuclear physics equal to 10^{-15} metre. [C20: after Enrico FERMI]

Fermi ★ ('fɜːmɪ; Italian 'fermi) *n* **Enrico** (en'riːko). 1901–54, Italian nuclear physicist, in the US from 1939. He was awarded a Nobel prize for physics (1938) for his work on nuclear bombardment; headed the group that produced the first controlled nuclear reaction (1942).

fermion ('fɜːmɪˌɒn) *n* any of a group of elementary particles, such as a nucleon, that has half-integral spin and obeys the Pauli exclusion principle. Cf. **boson.** [C20: after Enrico FERMI; see -ON]

fermium ('fɜːmɪəm) *n* a transuranic element artificially produced by neutron bombardment of plutonium. Symbol: Fm; atomic no.: 100; half-life of most stable isotope, ^{257}Fm: 80 days (approx.). [C20: after Enrico FERMI]

Fermor ★ ('fɜːmɔː) *n* **Patrick (Michael) Leigh.** born 1915, British author, noted for the travel books *A Time of Gifts* (1977) and *Between the Woods and the Water* (1986).

fern (fɜːn) *n* **1** a plant having roots, stems, and fronds and reproducing by spores formed in structures (sori) on the fronds. **2** any of certain similar but unrelated plants, such as the sweet fern. [OE *fearn*]
▶ **'ferny** *adj*

Fernandel ★ (French fɛrnɑdɛl) *n* real name *Fernand Joseph Désiré Contandin.* 1903–71, French comic film actor.

Fernando de Noronha ★ (Portuguese fer'nɐndu di no-'roɲɐ) *n* a volcanic island in the S Atlantic northeast of Cape São Roque: constitutes a federal territory of Brazil; a penal colony since the 18th century and inhabited by military personnel. Area: 26 sq. km (10 sq. miles).

Fernando Po ★ (fə'nændəʊ pəʊ) *n* a former name (until 1973) of **Bioko.**

fernbird ('fɜːnˌbɜːd) *n* a New Zealand swamp bird with a fernlike tail.

ferocious (fə'rəʊʃəs) *adj* savagely fierce or cruel: *a ferocious tiger.* [C17: from L *ferox* fierce, warlike]
▶ **ferocity** (fə'rɒsɪtɪ) *n*

-ferous *adj combining form.* bearing or producing: *coniferous.* [from -FER + -OUS]

Ferrara ★ (fə'rɑːrə; Italian fer'rara) *n* a city in N Italy, in Emilia–Romagna: a centre of the Renaissance under the House of Este; university (1391). Pop.: 137 384 (1994 est.).

Ferrari ★ (fə'rɑːrɪ; Italian fer'raːri) *n* **Enzo** ('entso). 1898–1988, Italian designer and manufacturer of racing cars.

ferrate ('fɛreɪt) *n* a salt containing the divalent ion, FeO_4^{2-}. [C19: from L *ferrum* iron]

ferret ('fɛrɪt) *n* **1** a domesticated albino variety of the polecat bred for hunting rats, rabbits, etc. **2** an assiduous searcher. ◆ *vb* **ferrets, ferreting, ferreted. 3** to hunt (rabbits, rats, etc.) with ferrets. **4** (*tr*; usually foll. by *out*) to drive from hiding: *to ferret out snipers.* **5** (*tr*; usually foll. by *out*) to find by persistent investigation. **6** (*intr*) to search around. [C14: from OF *furet*, from L *fur* thief]
▶ **'ferreter** *n* ▶ **'ferrety** *adj*

ferri- *combining form.* indicating the presence of iron, esp. in the trivalent state: *ferricyanide; ferriferous.* Cf. **ferro-**. [from L *ferrum* iron]

ferriage ('fɛrɪdʒ) *n* **1** transportation by ferry. **2** the fee charged for passage on a ferry.

ferric ('fɛrɪk) *adj* of or containing iron in the trivalent state; designating an iron(III) compound. [C18: from L *ferrum* iron]

ferric oxide *n* a red crystalline insoluble oxide of iron that occurs as haematite and rust, used as a pigment and metal polish (**jeweller's rouge**), and as a sensitive coating on magnetic tape. Formula: Fe_2O_3. Systematic name: **iron(III) oxide.**

Ferrier ★ ('fɛrɪə) *n* **Kathleen.** 1912–53, British contralto.

ferrimagnetism (,fɛrɪ'mægnɪ,tɪzəm) *n* a phenomenon exhibited by certain substances, such as ferrites, in which the magnetic moments of neighbouring ions are nonparallel and unequal in magnitude.
► **ferrimagnetic** (,fɛrɪmæg'nɛtɪk) *adj*

Ferris wheel ('fɛrɪs) *n* a fairground wheel having seats freely suspended from its rim. [C19: after G.W.G. *Ferris* (1859–96), American engineer]

ferrite ('fɛraɪt) *n* any of a class of nonconducting magnetic mixed-oxide ceramics.

ferrite-rod aerial *n* a type of aerial, normally used in radio reception, consisting of a small coil of wire mounted on a ferromagnetic ceramic core, the coil serving as a tuning inductance.

ferro- *combining form.* **1** indicating a property of iron or the presence of iron: *ferromagnetism.* **2** indicating the presence of iron in the divalent state: *ferrocyanide.* Cf. **ferri-**. [from L *ferrum* iron]

ferrocene ('fɛrəʊ,siːn) *n* a reddish-orange compound in which the molecules have an iron atom sandwiched between two cyclopentadiene rings. Formula: $Fe(C_5H_5)_2$. [C20: from FERRO- + C(YCLOPENTADI)ENE]

ferroconcrete (,fɛrəʊ'kɒnkriːt) *n* another name for **reinforced concrete.**

Ferrol ★ (*Spanish* fɛ'rrɔl) *n* See **El Ferrol.**

ferromagnetism (,fɛrəʊ'mægnɪ,tɪzəm) *n* the phenomenon exhibited by substances, such as iron, that have relative permeabilities much greater than unity and increasing magnetization with applied magnetizing field. Certain of these substances retain their magnetization in the absence of the applied field.
► **ferromagnetic** (,fɛrəʊmæg'nɛtɪk) *adj*

ferromanganese (,fɛrəʊ'mæŋgə,niːz) *n* an alloy of iron and manganese, used in making additions of manganese to cast iron and steel.

ferrous ('fɛrəs) *adj* of or containing iron in the divalent state; designating an iron(II) compound. [C19: from FERRI- + -OUS]

ferrous sulphate *n* an iron salt usually obtained as greenish crystals: used in inks, tanning, etc. Formula: $FeSO_4$. Systematic name: **iron(II) sulphate.** Also called: **copperas.**

ferruginous (fɛ'ruːdʒɪnəs) *adj* **1** (of minerals, rocks, etc.) containing iron: *a ferruginous clay.* **2** rust-coloured. [C17: from L *ferrūgineus* of a rusty colour, from *ferrum* iron]

ferrule ('fɛruːl) *n* **1** a metal ring, tube, or cap placed over the end of a stick or post for added strength or to increase wear. **2** a small length of tube, etc., esp. one used for making a joint. [C17: from ME *virole*, from OF, from L, from *viria* bracelet; infl. by L *ferrum* iron]

ferry ('fɛrɪ) *n, pl* **ferries. 1** Also called: **ferryboat.** a vessel for transporting passengers and usually vehicles across a body of water, esp. as a regular service. **2a** such a service. **2b** (*in combination*): *a ferryman.* **3** the delivering of aircraft by flying them to their destination. ◆ *vb* **ferries, ferrying, ferried. 4** to transport or go by ferry. **5** to deliver (an aircraft) by flying it to its destination. **6** (*tr*) to convey (passengers, goods, etc.). [OE *ferian* to carry, bring]

fertile ('fɜːtaɪl) *adj* **1** capable of producing offspring. **2a** (of land) capable of sustaining an abundant growth of plants. **2b** (of farm animals) capable of breeding stock. **3** *Biol.* capable of undergoing growth and development: *fertile seeds; fertile eggs.* **4** producing many offspring; pro-

lific. **5** highly productive: *a fertile brain.* **6** *Physics.* (of a substance) able to be transformed into fissile or fissionable material. [C15: from L *fertilis*, from *ferre* to bear]
► **'fertilely** *adv* ► **'fertileness** *n*

Fertile Crescent *n* an area of fertile land in the Middle East, extending around the Rivers Tigris and Euphrates in a semicircle from Israel to the Persian Gulf.

fertility (fɜː'tɪlɪtɪ) *n* **1** the ability to produce offspring. **2** the state or quality of being fertile.

fertility drug *n* any of a group of preparations used to stimulate ovulation in women hitherto infertile.

fertilize *or* **fertilise** ('fɜːtɪ,laɪz) *vb* **fertilizes, fertilizing, fertilized** *or* **fertilises, fertilising, fertilised.** (*tr*) **1** to provide (an animal, plant, etc.) with sperm or pollen to bring about fertilization. **2** to supply (soil or water) with nutrients to aid the growth of plants. **3** to make fertile.
► **,fertili'zation** *or* **,fertili'sation** *n*

fertilizer *or* **fertiliser** ('fɜːtɪ,laɪzə) *n* **1** any substance, such as manure, added to soil or water to increase its productivity. **2** an object or organism that fertilizes an animal or plant.

ferula ('fɛrʊlə) *n, pl* **ferulas** *or* **ferulae** (-,liː). a large umbelliferous plant having thick stems and dissected leaves. [C14: from L: giant fennel]

ferule ('fɛruːl) *n* **1** a flat piece of wood, such as a ruler, used in some schools to cane children on the hand. ◆ *vb* **ferules, feruling, feruled. 2** (*tr*) *Rare.* to punish with a ferule. [C16: from L *ferula* giant fennel]

fervent ('fɜːvənt) *or* **fervid** ('fɜːvɪd) *adj* **1** intensely passionate; ardent. **2** *Arch. or poetic.* burning or glowing. [C14: from L *fervēre* to boil, glow]
► **'fervency** *n* ► **'fervently** *or* **'fervidly** *adv*

fervour *or US* **fervor** ('fɜːvə) *n* **1** great intensity of feeling or belief. **2** *Rare.* intense heat. [C14: from L *fervor* heat, from *fervēre* to glow, boil]

Fès (fɛs) *or* **Fez** ★ *n* a city in N central Morocco, traditional capital of the north: became an independent kingdom in the 11th century, at its height in the 14th century; religious centre; university (850). Pop.: 564 000 (1993 est.).

fescue ('fɛskjuː) *or* **fescue grass** *n* a widely cultivated pasture and lawn grass, having stiff narrow leaves. [C14: from OF *festu*, ult. from L *festūca* stem, straw]

fesse *or* **fess** (fɛs) *n Heraldry.* an ordinary consisting of a horizontal band across a shield. [C15: from Anglo-F, from L *fascia* band, fillet]

fest (fɛst) *n* **a** a meeting or event at which the emphasis is on a particular activity: *a fashion fest.* **b** (*in combination*): *schmaltz-fest; lovefest.* [C19: from G *Fest* festival]

festal ('fɛst³l) *adj* another word for **festive.** [C15: from L *festum* holiday]
► **'festally** *adv*

fester ('fɛstə) *vb* **1** to form or cause to form pus. **2** (*intr*) to become rotten; decay. **3** to become or cause to become bitter, irritated, etc., esp. over a long period of time. ◆ *n* **4** a small ulcer or sore containing pus. [C13: from OF *festre* suppurating sore, from L: FISTULA]

festival ('fɛstɪv³l) *n* **1** a day or period set aside for celebration or feasting, esp. one of religious significance. **2** any occasion for celebration. **3** an organized series of special events and performances: *a festival of drama.* **4** *Arch.* a time of revelry. **5** (*modifier*) relating to or characteristic of a festival. [C14: from Church L *fēstivālis* of a feast, from L *festīvus* FESTIVE]

Festival Hall ★ *n* a concert hall in London, on the South Bank of the Thames: built for the 1951 Festival of Britain; completed 1964–65. Official name: **Royal Festival Hall.**

festive ('fɛstɪv) *adj* appropriate to or characteristic of a holiday, etc. [C17: from L *festīvus* joyful, from *festus* of a FEAST]
► **'festively** *adv*

festivity (fɛs'tɪvɪtɪ) *n, pl* **festivities. 1** merriment characteristic of a festival, etc. **2** any festival or other celebration. **3** (*pl*) celebrations.

festoon (fɛ'stuːn) *n* **1** a decorative chain of flowers, ribbons, etc., suspended in loops. **2** a carved or painted representation of this, as in architecture, furniture, or pottery. ◆ *vb* (*tr*) **3** to decorate or join together with festoons. **4** to form into festoons. [C17: from F, from It. *festone* ornament for a feast, from *festa* FEAST]

festoon blind *n* a window blind consisting of vertical rows of horizontally gathered fabric that may be drawn up to form a series of ruches.

feta ('fɛtə) *n* a white sheep or goat cheese popular in Greece. [Mod. Gk, from the phrase *turi pheta*, from *turi* cheese + *pheta*, from It. *fetta* a slice]

fetal *or* **foetal** ('fi:t°l) *adj* of, relating to, or resembling a fetus.

fetal alcohol syndrome *n* a condition in newborn babies caused by excessive intake of alcohol by the mother during pregnancy: characterized by various defects including mental retardation.

fetch[1] (fɛtʃ) *vb* (*mainly tr*) **1** to go after and bring back: *to fetch help.* **2** to cause to come; bring or draw forth. **3** (*also intr*) to cost or sell for (a certain price): *the table fetched six hundred pounds.* **4** to utter (a sigh, groan, etc.). **5** *Inf.* to deal (a blow, slap, etc.). **6** (used esp. as a command to dogs) to retrieve (an object thrown, etc.). **7 fetch and carry.** to perform menial tasks or run errands. ◆ *n* **8** the reach, stretch, etc., of a mechanism. **9** a trick or stratagem. [OE *feccan*]
▶ 'fetcher *n*

fetch[2] (fɛtʃ) *n* the ghost or apparition of a living person. [C18: from ?]

fetching ('fɛtʃɪŋ) *adj Inf.* **1** attractively befitting. **2** charming.

fetch up *vb* (*adv*) **1** (*intr*; usually foll. by *at* or *in*) *Inf.* to arrive (at) or end up (in): *to fetch up in New York.* **2** *Sl.* to vomit (food, etc.).

fête *or* **fete** (feɪt) *n* **1** a gala, bazaar, or similar entertainment, esp. one held outdoors in aid of charity. **2** a feast day or holiday, esp. one of religious significance. ◆ *vb* **fêtes, fêting, fêted** *or* **fetes, feting, feted.** **3** (*tr*) to honour or entertain with or as if with a fête. [C18: from F: FEAST]

fetid *or* **foetid** ('fɛtɪd, 'fi:-) *adj* having a stale nauseating smell, as of decay. [C16: from L, from *fētēre* to stink; rel. to *fūmus* smoke]
▶ 'fetidly *or* 'foetidly *adv* ▶ 'fetidness *or* 'foetidness *n*

fetish ('fɛtɪʃ, 'fi:tɪʃ) *n* **1** something, esp. an inanimate object, that is believed to have magical powers. **2a** a form of behaviour involving fetishism. **2b** any object that is involved in fetishism. **3** any object, activity, etc., to which one is excessively devoted. [C17: from F, from Port. *feitiço* (n) sorcery, from adj: artificial, from L *factīcius* made by art, FACTITIOUS]

fetishism ('fɛtɪˌʃɪzəm, 'fi:-) *n* **1** a condition in which the handling of an inanimate object or a part of the body other than the sexual organs is a source of sexual satisfaction. **2** belief in or recourse to a fetish for magical purposes.
▶ 'fetishist *n* ▶ ˌfetish'istic *adj*

fetlock ('fɛt,lɒk) *n* **1** a projection behind and above a horse's hoof. **2** Also called: **fetlock joint.** the joint at this part of the leg. **3** the tuft of hair growing from this part. [C14 *fetlak*]

fetor *or* **foetor** ('fi:tə) *n* an offensive stale or putrid odour. [C15: from L, from *fētēre* to stink]

fetter ('fɛtə) *n* **1** (*often pl*) a chain or bond fastened round the ankle. **2** (*usually pl*) a check or restraint. ◆ *vb* (*tr*) **3** to restrict or confine. **4** to bind in fetters. [OE *fetor*]

fettle ('fɛt°l) *vb* **fettles, fettling, fettled.** (*tr*) **1** to line or repair (the walls of a furnace). **2** *Brit. dialect.* **2a** to prepare or arrange (a thing, oneself, etc.). **2b** to repair or mend (something). ◆ *n* **3** state of health, spirits, etc. (esp. in **in fine fettle**). [C14 (in the sense: to put in order): back formation from *fetled* girded up, from OE *fetel* belt]

fettler ('fɛtlə) *n Austral.* a person employed to maintain railway tracks.

fetus *or* **foetus** ('fi:təs) *n, pl* **fetuses** *or* **foetuses.** the embryo of a mammal in the later stages of development, esp. a human embryo from the end of the second month of pregnancy until birth. [C14: from L: offspring]

feu (fju:) *n* **1** *Scot. legal history.* **1a** a feudal tenure of land for which rent was paid in money or grain instead of by the performance of military service. **1b** the land so held. **2** *Scots Law.* a right to the use of land in return for a fixed annual payment **(feu duty).** [C15: from OF; see FEE]

Feuchtwanger ★ (*German* 'fɔɪçtvaŋər) *n* **Lion** ('li:ɒn). 1884–1958, German novelist and dramatist, lived in the US (1940–58): noted for his novel *Jew Süss* (1925).

feud[1] (fju:d) *n* **1** long and bitter hostility between two families, clans, or individuals. **2** a quarrel or dispute. ◆ *vb* **3** (*intr*) to carry on a feud. [C13 *fede*, from OF, from OHG *fēhida*; rel. to OE *fæhth* hostility; see FOE]
▶ 'feudist *n*

feud[2] *or* **feod** (fju:d) *n Feudal law.* land held in return for service. [C17: from Med. L *feodum*, of Gmc origin; see FEE]

feudal ('fju:d°l) *adj* **1** of or characteristic of feudalism or its institutions. **2** of or relating to a fief. **3** *Disparaging.* old-fashioned. [C17: from Med. L, from *feudum* FEUD[2]]

feudalism ('fju:dəˌlɪzəm) *n* the legal and social system that evolved in W Europe in the 8th and 9th centuries, in which vassals were protected and maintained by their lords, usually through the granting of fiefs, and were required to serve under them in war. Also called: **feudal system.**
▶ 'feudalist *n* ▶ ˌfeudal'istic *adj*

feudality (fju:'dælɪtɪ) *n, pl* **feudalities.** **1** the state or quality of being feudal. **2** a fief or fee.

feudalize *or* **feudalise** ('fju:dəˌlaɪz) *vb* **feudalizes, feudalizing, feudalized** *or* **feudalises, feudalising, feudalised.** (*tr*) to create feudal institutions in (a society, etc.).
▶ ˌfeudali'zation *or* ˌfeudali'sation *n*

feudatory ('fju:dətərɪ) (in feudal Europe) ◆ *n, pl* **feudatories.** **1** a person holding a fief; vassal. ◆ *adj* **2** relating to or characteristic of the relationship between lord and vassal. [C16: from Med. L *feudātor*]

Feuerbach ★ (*German* 'fɔɪərbax) *n* **Ludwig Andreas** ('lu:tvɪç an'dre:as). 1804–72, German materialist philosopher: in *The Essence of Christianity* (1841), translated into English by George Eliot (1853), he maintained that God is merely an outward projection of man's inner self.

feuilleton (*French* fœjtɔ̃) *n* **1** the part of a European newspaper carrying reviews, serialized fiction, etc. **2** such a review or article. [C19: from F, from *feuillet* sheet of paper, dim. of *feuille* leaf, from L *folium*]

fever ('fi:və) *n* **1** an abnormally high body temperature, accompanied by a fast pulse rate, dry skin, etc. Related adj: **febrile. 2** any of various diseases, such as yellow fever or scarlet fever, characterized by a high temperature. **3** intense nervous excitement. ◆ *vb* **4** (*tr*) to affect with or as if with fever. [OE *fēfor*, from L *febris*]
▶ 'fevered *adj*

feverfew ('fi:vəˌfju:) *n* a bushy European strong-scented perennial plant with white flower heads, formerly used medicinally. [OE *feferfuge*, from LL, from L *febris* fever + *fugāre* to put to flight]

feverish ('fi:vərɪʃ) *or* **feverous** *adj* **1** suffering from fever. **2** in a state of restless excitement. **3** of, caused by, or causing fever.
▶ 'feverishly *or* 'feverously *adv*

fever pitch *n* a state of intense excitement.

fever therapy *n* a former method of treating disease by raising the body temperature.

few (fju:) *determiner* **1a** hardly any: *few men are so cruel.* **1b** (*as pronoun; functioning as pl*): *many are called but few are chosen.* **2** (preceded by *a*) **2a** a small number of: *a few drinks.* **2b** (*as pronoun; functioning as pl*): *a few of you.* **3 a good few.** *Inf.* several. **4 few and far between. 4a** widely spaced. **4b** scarce. **5 not** *or* **quite a few.** *Inf.* several. ◆ *n* **6 the few.** a small number of people considered as a class: *the few who fell at Thermopylae.* [OE *fēawa*]
▶ 'fewness *n*

USAGE NOTE See at **less.**

---

fey (feɪ) *adj* **1** interested in or believing in the supernatural. **2** clairvoyant; visionary. **3** *Chiefly Scot.* fated to die;

★ people and places

doomed. **4** *Chiefly Scot.* in a state of high spirits. [OE *fæge* marked out for death]
▸ **'feyness** *n*

Feydeau ★ (*French* fɛdo) *n* **Georges** (ʒɔrʒ). 1862–1921, French dramatist, noted for his farces, esp. *La Dame de chez Maxim* (1899) and *Occupe-toi d'Amélie* (1908).

Feynman ★ ('faɪnmən) *n* **Richard**. 1918–88, US physicist, noted for his research on quantum electrodynamics; shared the Nobel prize for physics in 1965.

fez (fɛz) *n, pl* **fezzes**. an originally Turkish brimless felt or wool cap, shaped like a truncated cone. [C19: via F from Turkish, from **Fès**]

Fez ★ (fɛz) *n* a variant of **Fès**.

Fezzan ★ (fɛ'zɑːn) *n* a region of SW Libya, in the Sahara: a former province (until 1963).

ff *Music. symbol for* fortissimo.

ff. **1** *abbrev. for* folios. **2** *symbol for* and the following (pages, lines, etc.).

Ffestiniog ★ (fɛs'tɪnɪɒg) *n* a town in N Wales, in Gwynedd: tourist attractions include former slate quarries and a narrow-gauge railway at nearby Blaenau Ffestiniog. Pop.: 800 (latest est.).

FI *abbrev. for* Falkland Islands.

fiacre (fɪ'ɑːkrə) *n* a small four-wheeled horse-drawn carriage. [C17: after the Hotel de St *Fiacre*, Paris, where these vehicles were first hired out]

fiancé *or (fem)* **fiancée** (fɪ'ɒnseɪ) *n* a person who is engaged to be married. [C19: from F, from OF *fiancier* to promise, betroth, from *fiance* a vow, from *fier* to trust, from L *fidere*]

Fianna ('fiːənə) *pl n* a legendary band of Irish warriors noted for their heroic exploits, attributed to the 2nd and 3rd centuries A.D. Also called: **Fenians**.

fiasco (fɪ'æskəʊ) *n, pl* **fiascos** *or* **fiascoes**. a complete failure, esp. one that is ignominious or humiliating. [C19: from It., lit.: FLASK; sense development obscure]

fiat ('faɪət) *n* **1** official sanction. **2** an arbitrary order or decree. [C17: from L, lit.: let it be done]

fib (fɪb) *n* **1** a trivial and harmless lie. ◆ *vb* **fibs, fibbing, fibbed. 2** (*intr*) to tell such a lie. [C17: ?from *fibble-fable* an unlikely story; see FABLE]
▸ **'fibber** *n*

Fibonacci ★ (*Italian* fibo'nattʃi) *n* **Leonardo** (leo'nardo), also called *Leonardo of Pisa*. ?1170–?1250, Italian mathematician: popularized the decimal system in Europe.

Fibonacci sequence *or* **series** (ˌfɪbə'nɑːtʃɪ) *n* the infinite sequence of numbers, 0, 1, 1, 2, 3, 5, 8, etc., in which each member (**Fibonacci number**) is the sum of the previous two. [after Leonardo FIBONACCI]

fibre *or US* **fiber** ('faɪbə) *n* **1** a natural or synthetic filament that may be spun into yarn, such as cotton or nylon. **2** cloth or other material made from such yarn. **3** a long fine continuous thread or filament. **4** the texture of any material or substance. **5** essential substance or nature. **6** strength of character (esp. in **moral fibre**). **7** *Bot.* **7a** a narrow elongated thick-walled cell. **7b** a very small root or twig. **8** a fibrous substance, such as bran, as part of someone's diet: *dietary fibre.* [C14: from L *fibra* filament, entrails]
▸ **'fibred** *or US* **'fibered** *adj*

fibreboard *or US* **fiberboard** ('faɪbəˌbɔːd) *n* a building material made of compressed wood or other plant fibres.

fibreglass *or US* **fiberglass** ('faɪbəˌglɑːs) *n* **1** material consisting of matted fine glass fibres, used as insulation in buildings, etc. **2** a light strong material made by bonding fibreglass with a synthetic resin; used for car bodies, etc.

fibre optics *or US* **fiber optics** *n* (*functioning as sing*) the transmission of information modulated on light down very thin flexible fibres of glass. See also **optical fibre**.
▸ ˌfibre-'optic *or US* ˌfiber-'optic *adj*

fibrescope *or US* **fiberscope** ('faɪbəˌskəʊp) *n* a medical instrument using fibre optics used to examine internal organs, such as the stomach.

fibril ('faɪbrɪl) *or* **fibrilla** (faɪ'brɪlə) *n, pl* **fibrils** *or* **fibrillae**

(-'brɪliː). **1** a small fibre or part of a fibre. **2** *Biol.* a root hair. [C17: from NL *fibrilla* a little FIBRE]
▸ **fi'brillar** *or* **fi'brillose** *adj*

fibrillation (ˌfaɪbrɪ'leɪʃən, ˌfɪb-) *n* **1** a local and uncontrollable twitching of muscle fibres. **2** irregular twitchings of the muscular wall of the heart.

fibrin ('fɪbrɪn) *n* a white insoluble elastic protein formed from fibrinogen when blood clots: forms a network that traps red cells and platelets.

fibrinogen (fɪ'brɪnədʒən) *n* a soluble protein in blood plasma, converted to fibrin by the action of the enzyme thrombin when blood clots.

fibro ('faɪbrəʊ) *n Austral. inf.* **a** short for **fibrocement**. **b** (*as modifier*): *a fibro shack.*

fibro- *combining form.* **1** indicating fibrous tissue: *fibrosis.* **2** indicating fibre: *fibrocement.* [from L *fibra* FIBRE]

fibrocement (ˌfaɪbrəʊsɪ'mɛnt) *n* cement combined with asbestos fibre, used esp. in sheets for building.

fibroid ('faɪbrɔɪd) *adj* **1** *Anat.* (of structures or tissues) containing or resembling fibres. ◆ *n* **2** a benign tumour, composed of fibrous and muscular tissue, occurring in the wall of the uterus and often causing heavy menstruation.

fibroin ('faɪbrəʊɪn) *n* a tough elastic protein that is the principal component of spiders' webs and raw silk.

fibroma (faɪ'brəʊmə) *n, pl* **fibromata** (-mətə) *or* **fibromas.** a benign tumour derived from fibrous connective tissue.

fibrosis (faɪ'brəʊsɪs) *n* the formation of an abnormal amount of fibrous tissue in an organ or part.

fibrositis (ˌfaɪbrə'saɪtɪs) *n* inflammation of white fibrous tissue, esp. that of muscle sheaths.

fibrous ('faɪbrəs) *adj* consisting of or resembling fibres: *fibrous tissue.*
▸ **'fibrously** *adv*

fibula ('fɪbjʊlə) *n, pl* **fibulae** (-ˌliː) *or* **fibulas. 1** the outer and thinner of the two bones between the knee and ankle of the human leg. Cf. **tibia**. **2** the corresponding bone in other vertebrates. **3** a metal brooch resembling a safety pin. [C17: from L: clasp, prob. from *figere* to fasten]
▸ **'fibular** *adj*

-fic *suffix forming adjectives.* making or producing: *honorific.* [from L *-ficus,* from *facere* to do, make]

fiche (fiːʃ) *n* See **microfiche, ultrafiche**.

fichu ('fiːʃuː) *n* a woman's shawl worn esp. in the 18th century. [C19: from F: small shawl, from *ficher* to fix with a pin, from L *figere* to fasten, FIX]

fickle ('fɪk'l) *adj* changeable in purpose, affections, etc. [OE *ficol* deceitful]
▸ **'fickleness** *n*

fictile ('fɪktaɪl) *adj* **1** moulded or capable of being moulded from clay. **2** made of clay by a potter. [C17: from L *fictilis* that can be moulded, from *fingere* to shape]

fiction ('fɪkʃən) *n* **1** literary works invented by the imagination, such as novels or short stories. **2** an invented story or explanation. **3** the act of inventing a story. **4** *Law.* something assumed to be true for the sake of convenience, though probably false. [C14: from L *fictiō* a fashioning, hence something imaginary, from *fingere* to shape]
▸ **'fictional** *adj* ▸ **'fictionally** *adv* ▸ **'fictive** *adj*

fictionalize *or* **fictionalise** ('fɪkʃənəˌlaɪz) *vb* **fictionalizes, fictionalizing, fictionalized** *or* **fictionalises, fictionalising, fictionalised.** (*tr*) to make into fiction.
▸ ˌfictionali'zation *or* ˌfictionali'sation *n*

fictitious (fɪk'tɪʃəs) *adj* **1** not genuine or authentic: *to give a fictitious address.* **2** of, related to, or characteristic of fiction.
▸ **fic'titiously** *adv* ▸ **fic'titiousness** *n*

fid (fɪd) *n Naut.* **1** a spike for separating strands of rope in splicing. **2** a wooden or metal bar for supporting the topmast. [C17: from ?]

-fid *adj combining form.* divided into parts or lobes: *bifid.* [from L *-fidus,* from *findere* to split]

fiddle ('fɪd'l) *n* **1** *Inf. or disparaging.* the violin. **2** a violin played as a folk instrument. **3** *Naut.* a small railing around the top of a table to prevent objects from falling off it. **4** *Brit. inf.* an illegal transaction or arrangement. **5** *Brit. inf.* a manually delicate or tricky operation. **6 at** *or* **on the fiddle.** *Inf.* engaged in an illegal or fraudulent undertaking. **7 fit as a fiddle.** *Inf.* in very good health. **8 play second fiddle.** *Inf.* to play a minor part. ◆ *vb* **fiddles, fiddling, fiddled. 9** to play (a tune) on the fiddle. **10** (*intr*; often foll. by *with*) to make aimless movements with the hands. **11** (when *intr*, often foll. by *about* or *around*) *Inf.* to waste (time). **12** (often foll. by *with*) *Inf.* to interfere (with). **13** *Inf.* to contrive to do (something) by illicit means or deception. **14** (*tr*) *Inf.* to falsify (accounts, etc.). [OE *fithele*; see VIOLA¹]

fiddle-faddle ('fɪdᵊl,fædᵊl) *n, interj* **1** trivial matter; nonsense. ◆ *vb* **fiddle-faddles, fiddle-faddling, fiddle-faddled. 2** (*intr*) to fuss or waste time. [C16: reduplication of FID-DLE]
▸ **'fiddle-,faddler** *n*

fiddler ('fɪdlə) *n* **1** a person who plays the fiddle. **2** See **fiddler crab. 3** *Inf.* a petty rogue.

fiddler crab *n* any of various burrowing crabs of American coastal regions, the males of which have one of their pincer-like claws enlarged. [C19: referring to the rapid fiddling movement of the enlarged anterior claw of the males, used to attract females]

fiddlestick ('fɪdᵊl,stɪk) *n* **1** *Inf.* a violin bow. **2** any trifle. **3 fiddlesticks!** an expression of annoyance or disagreement.

fiddling ('fɪdlɪŋ) *adj* **1** trifling or insignificant. **2** another word for **fiddly.**

fiddly ('fɪdlɪ) *adj* **fiddlier, fiddliest.** small and awkward to do or handle.

Fidei Defensor *Latin.* ('faɪdɪ,aɪ dɪ'fɛnsɔː) *n* defender of the faith; a title given to Henry VIII by Pope Leo X, and appearing on British coins as FID DEF (before decimalization) or FD (after decimalization).

fidelity (fɪ'dɛlɪtɪ) *n, pl* **fidelities. 1** devotion to duties, obligations, etc. **2** loyalty or devotion, as to a person or cause. **3** faithfulness to one's spouse, lover, etc. **4** accuracy in reporting detail. **5** *Electronics.* the degree to which an amplifier or radio accurately reproduces the characteristics of the input signal. [C15: from L, from *fidēs* faith, loyalty]

fidget ('fɪdʒɪt) *vb* **1** (*intr*) to move about restlessly. **2** (*intr*; often foll. by *with*) to make restless or uneasy movements (with something). **3** (*tr*) to cause to fidget. ◆ *n* **4** (*often pl*) a state of restlessness or unease: *he's got the fidgets.* **5** a person who fidgets. [C17: from earlier *fidge*, prob. from ON *fikjast* to desire eagerly]
▸ **'fidgety** *adj*

fiducial (fɪ'djuːʃɪəl) *adj* **1** *Physics, etc.* used as a standard of reference or measurement: *a fiducial point.* **2** of or based on trust or faith. [C17: from LL *fidūciālis*, from L *fidūcia* confidence, from *fīdere* to trust]

fiduciary (fɪ'duːʃɪərɪ) *Law.* ◆ *n, pl* **fiduciaries. 1** a person bound to act for another's benefit, as a trustee. ◆ *adj* **2a** of or relating to a trust or trustee. **2b** of or relating to a trust or trustee. [C17: from L *fidūciārius* relating to something held in trust, from *fidūcia* trust]

fiduciary issue *n* an issue of banknotes not backed by gold.

fie (faɪ) *interj Obs. or facetious.* an exclamation of distaste or mock dismay. [C13: from OF *fi*, from L *fī*, exclamation of disgust]

fief *or* **feoff** (fiːf) *n* (in feudal Europe) the property or fee granted to a vassal for his maintenance by his lord in return for service. [C17: from OF *fie*, of Gmc origin; cf. OE *fēo* cattle, money, L *pecus* cattle, *pecūnia* money, Gk *pokos* fleece]

fiefdom ('fiːfdəm) *n* **1** (in feudal Europe) the property owned by a lord. **2** an area over which a person or organization exerts authority or influence.

field (fiːld) *n* **1** an open tract of uncultivated grassland; meadow. **2** a piece of land cleared of trees and undergrowth used for pasture or growing crops: *a field of barley.* **3** a limited or marked off area on which any of various sports, athletic competitions, etc., are held: *a soccer field.* **4** an area that is rich in minerals or other natural resources: *a coalfield.* **5** short for **battlefield** or **airfield. 6** the

mounted followers that hunt with a pack of hounds. **7a** all the runners in a race or competitors in a competition. **7b** the runners in a race or competitors in a competition excluding the favourite. **8** *Cricket.* the fielders collectively, esp. with regard to their positions. **9** a wide or open expanse: *a field of snow.* **10a** an area of human activity: *the field of human knowledge.* **10b** a sphere or division of knowledge, etc.: *his field is physics.* **11** a place away from the laboratory, office, library, etc., where practical work is done. **12** the surface or background, as of a flag, coin, or heraldic shield, on which a design is displayed. **13** Also called: **field of view.** the area within which an object may be observed with a telescope, etc. **14** *Physics.* See **field of force. 15** *Maths.* a set of entities, such as numbers, subject to two binary operations, addition and multiplication, such that the set is a commutative group under addition and the set, minus the zero, is a commutative group under multiplication. **16** *Computing.* a set of one or more characters comprising a unit of information. **17 play the field.** *Inf.* to disperse one's interests or attentions among a number of activities, people, or objects. **18 take the field.** to begin or carry on activity, esp. in sport or military operations. **19** (*modifier*) *Mil.* of or relating to equipment, personnel, etc., specifically trained for operations in the field: *a field gun.* ◆ *vb* **20** (*tr*) *Sport.* to stop, catch, or return (the ball) as a fielder. **21** (*tr*) *Sport.* to send (a player or team) onto the field to play. **22** (*intr*) *Sport.* (of a player or team) to act or take turn as a fielder or fielders. **23** (*tr*) to enter (a person) in a competition: *each party fielded a candidate.* **24** (*tr*) *Inf.* to deal with or handle: *to field a question.* [OE *feld*]

Field ★ (fiːld) *n* **John.** 1782–1837, Irish composer and pianist, lived in Russia from 1803: invented the nocturne.

field artillery *n* artillery capable of deployment in support of front-line troops, due mainly to its mobility.

field day *n* **1** a day spent in some special outdoor activity, such as nature study. **2** *Mil.* a day devoted to manoeuvres or exercises, esp. before an audience. **3** *Inf.* a day or time of exciting activity: *the children had a field day with their new toys.*

field effect transistor *n* a unipolar transistor in which the transverse application of an electric field produces amplification.

fielder ('fiːldə) *n Cricket, etc.* **a** a player in the field. **b** a member of the fielding side.

field event *n* a competition, such as the discus, etc., that takes place on a field or similar area as opposed to those on the running track.

fieldfare ('fiːld,fɛə) *n* a large Old World thrush having a pale grey head, brown wings and back, and a blackish tail. [OE *feldefare*; see FIELD, FARE]

field glasses *pl n* another name for **binoculars.**

field goal *n* **1** *Basketball.* a goal scored while the ball is in normal play rather than from a free throw. **2** *American & Canadian football.* a score of three points made by kicking the ball through the opponent's goalposts above the crossbar.

field hockey *n US & Canad.* hockey played on a field, as distinguished from ice hockey.

field hospital *n* a temporary hospital set up near a battlefield for emergency treatment.

Fielding ★ ('fiːldɪŋ) *n* **Henry.** 1707–54, English novelist and dramatist, noted particularly for his picaresque novel *Tom Jones* (1749) and for *Joseph Andrews* (1742), which starts as a parody of Richardson's *Pamela*: also noted as an enlightened magistrate and a founder of the Bow Street runners (1749).

field magnet *n* a permanent magnet or an electromagnet that produces the magnetic field in a generator, electric motor, or similar device.

field marshal *n* an officer holding the highest rank in certain armies.

fieldmouse ('fiːld,maʊs) *n, pl* **fieldmice.** a nocturnal mouse inhabiting woods, fields, and gardens of the Old World that has yellowish-brown fur.

field officer *n* an officer holding the rank of major, lieutenant colonel, or colonel.

field of force *n* the region of space surrounding a body,

★ people and places

such as a charged particle or a magnet, within which it can exert a force on another similar body not in contact with it.

Fields ★ (fiːldz) *n* **1** Dame **Gracie**. real name *Grace Stansfield*. 1898–1979, British singer and entertainer. **2 W. C.** real name *William Claude Dukenfield*. 1880–1946, US film actor.

fieldsman ('fiːldzmən) *n, pl* **fieldsmen**. *Cricket*. another name for **fielder**.

field sports *pl n* sports carried on in the countryside, such as hunting or fishing.

field tile *n Brit. & NZ.* an earthenware drain used in farm drainage.

field trial *n* (*often pl*) a test to display performance, efficiency, or durability, as of a vehicle or invention.

field trip *n* an expedition, as by a group of students, to study something at first hand.

field winding ('waɪndɪŋ) *n* the current-carrying coils on a field magnet that produce the magnetic field intensity required to set up the electrical excitation in a generator or motor.

fieldwork ('fiːld,wɜːk) *n Mil.* a temporary structure used in fortifying a place or position.

field work *n* an investigation or search for material, data, etc., made in the field as opposed to the classroom or laboratory.
▸ **field worker** *n*

fiend (fiːnd) *n* **1** an evil spirit. **2** a cruel, brutal, or spiteful person. **3** *Inf.* **3a** a person who is intensely interested in or fond of something: *a fresh-air fiend*. **3b** an addict: *a drug fiend*. [OE *fēond*]

fiendish ('fiːndɪʃ) *adj* **1** of or like a fiend. **2** diabolically wicked or cruel. **3** *Inf.* extremely difficult or unpleasant: *a fiendish problem*.

fierce (fɪəs) *adj* **1** having a violent and unrestrained nature: *a fierce dog*. **2** wild or turbulent in force, action, or intensity: *a fierce storm*. **3** intense or strong: *fierce competition*. **4** *Inf.* very unpleasant. [C13: from OF *fiers*, from L *ferus*]
▸ **'fiercely** *adv* ▸ **'fierceness** *n*

fiery ('faɪərɪ) *adj* **fierier, fieriest**. **1** of, containing, or composed of fire. **2** resembling fire in heat, colour, ardour, etc.: *a fiery speaker*. **3** easily angered or aroused: *a fiery temper*. **4** (of food) producing a burning sensation: *a fiery curry*. **5** (of the skin or a sore) inflamed. **6** flammable.
▸ **'fierily** *adv* ▸ **'fieriness** *n*

Fiesole[1] ★ (*Italian* 'fiɛːzole) *n* a town in central Italy, in Tuscany near Florence: Etruscan and Roman remains. Pop.: 4000 (1987 est.). Ancient name: **Faesulae** ('fiːsuliː).

Fiesole[2] ★ (*Italian* 'fiɛːzole) *n* **Giovanni da** (dʒoˈvanni da). the monastic name of (Fra) **Angelico**.

fiesta (fɪˈɛstə) *n* (esp. in Spain and Latin America) **1** a religious festival or celebration. **2** a holiday or carnival. [Sp., from L *festa*; see FEAST]

FIFA ('fiːfə) *n acronym for* Fédération Internationale de Football Association. [from F]

fife (faɪf) *n* **1** a small high-pitched flute similar to the piccolo, used esp. in military bands. ◆ *vb* **fifes, fifing, fifed. 2** to play (music) on a fife. [C16: from OHG *pfifa*; see PIPE[1]]
▸ **'fifer** *n*

Fife[1] (faɪf) ★ *n* a council area and historic county of E central Scotland, bordering on the North Sea between the Firths of Tay and Forth: coastal lowlands in the north and east, with several ranges of hills; mainly agricultural. Administrative centre: Glenrothes. Pop.: 352 100 (1994 est.). Area: 1305 sq. km (504 sq. miles).

Fife[2] ★ (faɪf) *n* **Duncan**. See (Duncan) **Phyfe**.

FIFO ('faɪfəʊ) *n acronym for* first in, first out (as an accounting principle in costing stock). Cf. **LIFO**.

fifteen ('fɪf'tiːn) *n* **1** the cardinal number that is the sum of ten and five. **2** a numeral, 15, XV, etc., representing this number. **3** something represented by, representing, or consisting of 15 units. **4** a Rugby Union (football) team. ◆ *determiner* **5a** amounting to fifteen: *fifteen jokes*. **5b** (*as pronoun*): *fifteen of us danced*. [OE *fīftēne*]
▸ **'fif'teenth** *adj, n*

fifth (fɪfθ) *adj* (*usually prenominal*) **1a** coming after the fourth in order, position, etc. Often written 5th. **1b** (*as n*): *he came on the fifth*. ◆ *n* **2a** one of five equal parts of an object, quantity, etc. **2b** (*as modifier*): *a fifth part*. **3** the fraction equal to one divided by five (1/5). **4** *Music*. **4a** the interval between one note and another five notes away from it in a diatonic scale. **4b** one of two notes constituting such an interval in relation to the other. ◆ *adv* **5** Also: **fifthly**. after the fourth person, position, event, etc. ◆ *sentence connector*. **6** Also: **fifthly**. as the fifth point. [OE *fifta*]

fifth column *n* **1** (originally) a group of Falangist sympathizers in Madrid during the Spanish Civil War who were prepared to join the insurgents marching on the city. **2** any group of hostile infiltrators.
▸ **fifth columnist** *n*

fifth wheel *n* **1** a spare wheel for a four-wheeled vehicle. **2** a superfluous or unnecessary person or thing.

fifty ('fɪftɪ) *n, pl* **fifties**. **1** the cardinal number that is the product of ten and five. **2** a numeral, 50, L, etc., representing this number. **3** something represented by, representing, or consisting of 50 units. ◆ *determiner* **4a** amounting to fifty: *fifty people*. **4b** (*as pronoun*): *fifty should be sufficient*. [OE *fiftig*]
▸ **'fiftieth** *adj, n*

fifty-fifty *adj, adv Inf.* in equal parts.

fig (fɪg) *n* **1** a tree or shrub in which the flowers are borne inside a pear-shaped receptacle. **2** the fruit of any of these trees, which develops from the receptacle and has sweet flesh containing numerous seedlike structures. **3** (*used with a negative*) something of negligible value: *I don't care a fig for your opinion*. [C13: from OF, from *figa*, from L *ficus* fig tree]

fig. *abbrev. for:* **1** figurative(ly). **2** figure.

fight (faɪt) *vb* **fights, fighting, fought. 1** to oppose or struggle against (an enemy) in battle. **2** to oppose or struggle against (a person, cause, etc.) in any manner. **3** (*tr*) to engage in or carry on (a battle, contest, etc.). **4** (when *intr*, often foll. by *for*) to uphold or maintain (a cause, etc.) by fighting or struggling: *to fight for freedom*. **5** (*tr*) to make or achieve (a way) by fighting. **6** to engage (another or others) in combat. **7 fight it out**. to contend until a decisive result is obtained. **8 fight shy**. to keep aloof from. ◆ *n* **9** a battle, struggle, or physical combat. **10** a quarrel, dispute, or contest. **11** resistance (esp. in **to put up a fight**). **12** a boxing match. ◆ See also **fight off**. [OE *feohtan*]

fighter ('faɪtə) *n* **1** a person who fights, esp. a professional boxer. **2** a person who has determination. **3** *Mil.* an armed aircraft designed for destroying other aircraft.

fighter-bomber *n* an aircraft that combines the roles of fighter and bomber.

fighting chance *n* a slight chance of success dependent on a struggle.

fighting cock *n* **1** a gamecock. **2** a pugnacious person.

fighting fish *n* any of various tropical fishes of the genus *Betta*, esp. the Siamese fighting fish.

fight off *vb* (*tr, adv*) **1** to repulse; repel. **2** to struggle to avoid or repress: *to fight off a cold*.

fight-or-flight *n* (*modifier*) involving or relating to an involuntary response to stress in which the hormone adrenaline is secreted into the blood in readiness for physical action, such as fighting or running away.

fig leaf *n* **1** a leaf from a fig tree. **2** a representation of a fig leaf used in sculpture, etc. to cover the genitals of nude figures. **3** a device to conceal something regarded as shameful.

figment ('fɪgmənt) *n* a fantastic notion or fabrication: *a figment of the imagination*. [C15: from LL *figmentum* a fiction, from L *fingere* to shape]

figurant ('fɪgjʊrənt) *n* a ballet dancer who does group work but no solo roles. [C18: from F, from *figurer* to represent, appear, FIGURE]
▸ **figurante** (ˌfɪgjuˈrɒnt) *fem n*

figuration (ˌfɪgəˈreɪʃən) *n* **1** *Music*. **1a** the employment of characteristic patterns of notes, esp. in variations on a theme. **1b** florid ornamentation. **2** the act or an instance of representing figuratively, as by means of allegory. **3** a figurative representation. **4** the act of decorating with a design.

figurative ('fɪɡərətɪv) *adj* **1** involving a figure of speech; not literal; metaphorical. **2** using or filled with figures of speech. **3** representing by means of an emblem, likeness, etc.
▶ **'figuratively** *adv* ▶ **'figurativeness** *n*

figure ('fɪɡə) *n* **1** any written symbol other than a letter, esp. a whole number. **2** another name for **digit** (sense 2). **3** an amount expressed numerically: *a figure of £1800 was suggested.* **4** (*pl*) calculations with numbers: *he's good at figures.* **5** visible shape or form; outline. **6** the human form: *a girl with a slender figure.* **7** a slim bodily shape (esp. in **keep** or **lose one's figure**). **8** a character or personage: *a figure in politics.* **9** the impression created by a person through behaviour (esp. in **to cut a fine, bold,** etc., **figure**). **10a** a person as impressed on the mind. **10b** (*in combination*): *father-figure.* **11** a representation in painting or sculpture, esp. of the human form. **12** an illustration or diagram in a text. **13** a representative object or symbol. **14** a pattern or design, as in wood. **15** a predetermined set of movements in dancing or skating. **16** *Geom.* any combination of points, lines, curves, or planes. **17** *Logic.* one of four possible arrangements of the terms in the major and minor premises of a syllogism that give the same conclusion. **18** *Music.* **18a** a numeral written above or below a note in a part. **18b** a characteristic short pattern of notes. ◆ *vb* **figures, figuring, figured. 19** (when *tr,* often foll. by *up*) to calculate or compute (sums, amounts, etc.). **20** (*tr; usually takes a clause as object*) *Inf., US, Canad., & NZ.* to consider. **21** (*tr*) to represent by a diagram or illustration. **22** (*tr*) to pattern or mark with a design. **23** (*tr*) to depict or portray in a painting, etc. **24** (*tr*) to imagine. **25** (*tr*) *Music.* to decorate (a melody line or part) with ornamentation. **26** (*intr;* usually foll. by *in*) to be included: *his name figures in the article.* **27** (*intr*) *Inf.* to accord with expectation: *it figures that he wouldn't come.* ◆ See also **figure out.** [C13: from L *figūra* a shape, from *fingere* to mould]
▶ **'figurer** *n*

figured ('fɪɡəd) *adj* **1** depicted as a figure in painting or sculpture. **2** decorated with a design. **3** having a form. **4** *Music.* **4a** ornamental. **4b** (of a bass part) provided with numerals indicating accompanying harmonies.

figured bass (beɪs) *n* a shorthand method of indicating a thorough-bass part in which each bass note is accompanied by figures indicating the intervals to be played in the chord above it.

figurehead ('fɪɡə,hɛd) *n* **1** a person nominally having a prominent position, but no real authority. **2** a carved bust on the bow of some sailing vessels.

figure of speech *n* an expression of language, such as metaphor, by which the literal meaning of a word is not employed.

figure out *vb* (*tr, adv; may take a clause as object*) *Inf.* **1** to calculate. **2** to understand.

figure skating *n* **1** ice skating in which the skater traces outlines of selected patterns. **2** the whole art of skating, as distinct from skating at speed.
▶ **figure skater** *n*

figurine (,fɪɡə'riːn) *n* a small carved or moulded figure; statuette. [C19: from F, from It. *figurina* a little FIGURE]

figwort ('fɪɡ,wɜːt) *n* a plant related to the foxglove having square stems and small greenish flowers.

Fiji ★ ('fiːdʒiː, fiː'dʒiː) *n* **1** an independent republic (within the British Commonwealth 1970–87 and from 1997), consisting of 844 islands (chiefly Viti Levu and Vanua Levu) in the SW Pacific: a British colony (1874–1970); the large islands are of volcanic origin, surrounded by coral reefs; smaller ones are of coral. Official language: English. Religion: Christian and Hindu. Currency: dollar. Capital: Suva. Pop.: 778 000 (1997). Area: 18 272 sq. km (7055 sq. miles). ◆ *n, adj* **2** another word for **Fijian.**

Fijian (fiː'dʒiːən) *n* **1** a member of the indigenous people inhabiting Fiji. **2** the language of this people, belonging to the Malayo-Polynesian family. ◆ *adj* **3** of or characteristic of Fiji or its inhabitants. ◆ Also: **Fiji.**

filagree ('fɪlə,griː) *n, adj* a less common spelling of **filigree.**

filament ('fɪləmənt) *n* **1** the thin wire, usually tungsten, inside a light bulb that emits light when heated to incandescence by an electric current. **2** *Electronics.* a high-resistance wire forming the cathode in some valves. **3** a single strand of a natural or synthetic fibre. **4** *Bot.* the stalk of a stamen. **5** any slender structure or part. [C16: from NL, from Med. L *filāre* to spin, from L *filum* thread]
▶ **filamentary** (,fɪlə'mɛntərɪ) *or* ,fila'mentous *adj*

filaria (fɪ'lɛərɪə) *n, pl* **filariae** (-ɪ,iː). a parasitic nematode worm that lives in the blood of vertebrates and is transmitted by insects: the cause of filariasis. [C19: NL (former name of genus), from L *filum* thread]
▶ **fi'larial** *adj*

filariasis (,fɪlə'raɪəsɪs, fɪ,lɛərɪ'eɪsɪs) *n* a disease common in tropical and subtropical countries resulting from infestation of the lymphatic system with nematode worms transmitted by mosquitoes: characterized by inflammation. See also **elephantiasis.** [C19: from NL; see FILARIA]

filbert ('fɪlbət) *n* **1** any of several N temperate shrubs that have edible rounded brown nuts. **2** Also called: **hazelnut, cobnut.** the nut of any of these shrubs. [C14: after St *Philbert,* 7th-century Frankish abbot, because the nuts are ripe around his feast day, Aug. 22]

filch (fɪltʃ) *vb* (*tr*) to steal or take in small amounts. [C16 *filchen* to steal, attack, ?from OE *gefylce* band of men]
▶ **'filcher** *n*

file[1] (faɪl) *n* **1** a folder, box, etc., used to keep documents or other items in order. **2** the documents, etc., kept in this way. **3** documents or information about a specific subject, person, etc. **4** a line of people in marching formation, one behind another. **5** any of the eight vertical rows of squares on a chessboard. **6** *Computing.* a named collection of information, in the form of text, programs, graphics, etc., held on a permanent storage device, such as a magnetic disk. **7** **on file.** recorded or catalogued for reference, as in a file. ◆ *vb* **files, filing, filed. 8** to place (a document, etc.) in a file. **9** (*tr*) to place (a legal document) on public or official record. **10** (*tr*) to bring (a suit, esp. a divorce suit) in a court of law. **11** (*tr*) to submit (copy) to a newspaper. **12** (*intr*) to march or walk in a file or files: *the ants filed down the hill.* [C16 (in the sense: string on which documents are hung): from OF, from Med. L *filāre; see* FILAMENT]
▶ **'filer** *n*

file[2] (faɪl) *n* **1** a hand tool consisting of a steel blade with small cutting teeth on some or all of its faces. It is used for shaping or smoothing. ◆ *vb* **files, filing, filed. 2** (*tr*) to shape or smooth (a surface) with a file. [OE *fil*]
▶ **'filer** *n*

filefish ('faɪl,fɪʃ) *n, pl* **filefish** *or* **filefishes.** any tropical triggerfish having a narrow compressed body and a very long dorsal spine. [C18: referring to its file-like scales]

filename ('faɪl,neɪm) *n* an arrangement of characters that enables a computer system to permit the user to have access to a particular file.

file server *n* *Computing.* the central unit of a local area network that controls its operation and provides access to separately stored data files.

filet ('fɪlɪt, 'fɪleɪ) *n* a variant spelling of **fillet** (senses 1–3). [C20: from F: net, from OF, from *fil* thread, from L *filum*]

filet mignon ('fɪleɪ 'miːnjɒn) *n* a small tender boneless cut of beef. [from F, lit.: dainty fillet]

filial ('fɪlɪəl) *adj* **1** of, resembling, or suitable to a son or daughter: *filial affection.* **2** *Genetics.* designating any of the generations following the parental generation. [C15: from LL *filiālis,* from L *filius* son]
▶ **'filially** *adv*

filibeg *or* **philibeg** ('fɪlɪ,bɛg) *n* the kilt worn by Scottish Highlanders. [C18: from Scot. Gaelic *fèileadhbeag,* from *fèileadh* kilt + *beag* small]

filibuster ('fɪlɪ,bʌstə) *n* **1** the process of obstructing legislation by means of delaying tactics. **2** Also called: **filibusterer.** a legislator who engages in such obstruction. **3** a freebooter or military adventurer, esp. in a foreign country. ◆ *vb* **4** to obstruct (legislation) with delaying tactics.

★ people and places

5 (*intr*) to engage in unlawful military action. [C16: from Sp., from F *flibustier*, prob. from Du. *vrijbuiter* pirate, lit.: one plundering freely; see FREEBOOTER]
▶ '**fili,busterer** *n*

filigree ('fɪlɪˌgriː) *or* **filagree** *n* **1** delicate ornamental work of twisted gold, silver, or other wire. **2** any fanciful delicate ornamentation. ◆ *adj* **3** made of or as if with filigree. [C17: from earlier *filigreen*, from F *filigrane*, from L *filum* thread + *grānum* GRAIN]
▶ '**fili,greed** *adj*

filings ('faɪlɪŋz) *pl n* shavings or particles removed by a file: *iron filings*.

Filipino (ˌfɪlɪ'piːnəʊ) *n* **1** (*pl* **Filipinos**) Also (*fem*): **Filipina**. a native or inhabitant of the Philippines. **2** another name for **Tagalog**. ◆ *adj* **3** of or relating to the Philippines or their inhabitants.

fill (fɪl) *vb* (*mainly tr*; often foll. by *up*) **1** (*also intr*) to make or become full: *to fill up a bottle*. **2** to occupy the whole of: *the party filled the house*. **3** to plug (a gap, crevice, etc.). **4** to meet (a requirement or need) satisfactorily. **5** to cover (a page or blank space) with writing, drawing, etc. **6** to hold and perform the duties of (an office or position). **7** to appoint or elect an occupant to (an office or position). **8** (*also intr*) to swell or cause to swell with wind, as in manoeuvring the sails of a sailing vessel. **9** *Chiefly US & Canad.* to put together the necessary materials for (a prescription or order). **10 fill the bill**. *Inf.* to serve or perform adequately. ◆ *n* **11** material such as gravel, stones, etc., used to bring an area of ground up to a required level. **12 one's fill**. the quantity needed to satisfy one. ◆ See also **fill in**, **fill out**. [OE *fyllan*]

filler ('fɪlə) *n* **1** a person or thing that fills. **2** an object or substance used to add weight or size to something or to fill in a gap. **3** a paste, used for filling in cracks, holes, etc., in a surface before painting. **4** the inner portion of a cigar. **5** *Journalism*. articles, photographs, etc., to fill space between more important articles in a newspaper or magazine.

fillet ('fɪlɪt) *n* **1a** Also called: **fillet steak**. a strip of boneless meat. **1b** the boned side of a fish. **2** a narrow strip of any material. **3** a thin strip of ribbon, lace, etc., worn in the hair or around the neck. **4** a narrow flat moulding, esp. one between other mouldings. **5** a narrow band between flutings on the shaft of a column. **6** *Heraldry*. a horizontal division of a shield. **7** a narrow decorative line, impressed on the cover of a book. ◆ *vb* **fillets, filleting, filleted**. (*tr*) **8** to cut or prepare (meat or fish) as a fillet. **9** to cut fillets from (meat or fish). **10** to bind or decorate with or as if with a fillet. ◆ Also (for senses 1–3): **filet**. [C14: from OF *filet*, from *fil* thread, from L *filum*]

fill in *vb* (*adv*) **1** (*tr*) to complete (a form, drawing, etc.). **2** (*intr*) to act as a substitute. **3** (*tr*) to put material into (a hole or cavity), esp. so as to make it level with a surface. **4** (*tr*) *Inf.* to inform with facts or news. ◆ *n* **fill-in. 5** a substitute.

filling ('fɪlɪŋ) *n* **1** the substance or thing used to fill a space or container: *pie filling*. **2** *Dentistry*. any of various substances (metal, plastic, etc.) for inserting into the prepared cavity of a tooth. **3** *Chiefly US*. the weft in weaving. ◆ *adj* **4** (of food or a meal) substantial and satisfying.

filling station *n* a place where petrol and other supplies for motorists are sold.

fillip ('fɪlɪp) *n* **1** something that adds stimulation or enjoyment. **2** the action of holding a finger towards the palm with the thumb and suddenly releasing it outwards to produce a snapping sound. **3** a quick blow or tap made by this. ◆ *vb* **4** (*tr*) to stimulate or excite. **5** (*tr*) to strike or project sharply with a fillip. **6** (*intr*) to make a fillip. [C15 *philippe*, imit.]

Fillmore ★ ('fɪlmɔː) *n* Millard. 1800–74, 13th president of the US (1850-53); a leader of the Whig Party.

fill out *vb* (*adv*) **1** to make or become fuller, thicker, or rounder. **2** to make more substantial. **3** (*tr*) *Chiefly US & Canad.* to fill in (a form, etc.).

fill up *vb* (*adv*) **1** (*tr*) to complete (a form, application, etc.). **2** to make or become full. ◆ *n* **fill-up. 3** the act of

filling something completely, esp. the petrol tank of a car.

filly ('fɪlɪ) *n, pl* **fillies**. a female horse or pony under the age of four. [C15: from ON *fylja*; see FOAL]

film (fɪlm) *n* **1a** a sequence of images of moving objects photographed by a camera and providing the optical illusion of continuous movement when projected onto a screen. **1b** a form of entertainment, etc., composed of such a sequence of images. **1c** (*as modifier*): *film techniques*. **2** a thin flexible strip of cellulose coated with a photographic emulsion, used to make negatives and transparencies. **3** a thin coating or layer. **4** a thin sheet of any material, as of plastic for packaging. **5** a fine haze, mist, or blur. **6** a gauzy web of filaments or fine threads. ◆ *vb* **7a** to photograph with a cine camera. **7b** to make a film of (a screenplay, event, etc.). **8** (often foll. by *over*) to cover or become covered or coated with a film. [OE *filmen* membrane]

filmic ('fɪlmɪk) *adj* **1** of or relating to films or the cinema. **2** suggestive of films or the cinema.
▶ '**filmically** *adv*

film noir (nwɑː) *n* a type of gangster thriller, made esp. in the 1940s in Hollywood, characterized by stark lighting, an involved plot, and an atmosphere of cynicism and corruption. [C20: F, lit.: black film]

filmography (fɪl'mɒgrəfɪ) *n* **1** a list of the films made by a particular director, actor, etc. **2** any writing that deals with films or the cinema. .

filmset ('fɪlmˌsɛt) *vb* **filmsets, filmsetting, filmset**. (*tr*) *Brit.* to set (type matter) by filmsetting.
▶ '**film,setter** *n*

filmsetting ('fɪlmˌsɛtɪŋ) *n Brit., printing.* typesetting by exposing type characters onto photographic film from which printing plates are made.

film speed *n* **1** the sensitivity to light of a photographic film, specified in terms of the film's ISO rating. **2** the rate at which the film passes through a motion picture camera or projector.

film strip *n* a strip of film composed of different images projected separately as slides.

filmy ('fɪlmɪ) *adj* **filmier, filmiest. 1** transparent or gauzy. **2** hazy; blurred.
▶ '**filmily** *adv* ▶ '**filminess** *n*

filo ('fiːləʊ) *n* a type of Greek flaky pastry in very thin sheets. [C20: Mod. Gk *phullon* leaf]

Filofax ('faɪləʊˌfæks) *n Trademark*. a type of loose-leaf ring binder with sets of different-coloured paper, used as a portable personal filing system, including appointments, addresses, etc.

filter ('fɪltə) *n* **1** a porous substance, such as paper or sand, that allows fluid to pass but retains suspended solid particles. **2** any device containing such a porous substance for separating suspensions from fluids. **3** any of various porous substances built into the mouth end of a cigarette or cigar for absorbing impurities such as tar. **4** any electronic, optical, or acoustic device that blocks signals or radiations of certain frequencies while allowing others to pass. **5** any transparent disc of gelatine or glass used to eliminate or reduce the intensity of given frequencies from the light leaving a lamp, entering a camera, etc. **6** *Brit.* a traffic signal at a road junction which permits vehicles to turn either left or right when the main signals are red. ◆ *vb* **7** (often foll. by *out*) to remove or separate (suspended particles, etc.) from (a liquid, gas, etc.) by the action of a filter. **8** (*tr*) to obtain by filtering. **9** (*intr*; foll. by *through*) to pass (through a filter or something like a filter). **10** (*intr*) to flow slowly; trickle. [C16 *filtre*, from Med. L *filtrum* piece of felt used as a filter, of Gmc origin]

filterable ('fɪltərəbᵊl) *or* **filtrable** ('fɪltrəbᵊl) *adj* **1** capable of being filtered. **2** (of most viruses and certain bacteria) capable of passing through the pores of a fine filter.

filter bed *n* a layer of sand or gravel in a tank or reservoir through which a liquid is passed so as to purify it.

filter feeding *n Zool.* a method of feeding in some aquatic animals, such as whalebone whales, in which

minute food particles are filtered from the surrounding water.
▶ **filter feeder** *n*

filter out *or* **through** *vb* (*intr, adv*) to become known gradually; leak.

filter paper *n* a porous paper used for filtering liquids.

filter tip *n* **1** an attachment to the mouth end of a cigarette for trapping impurities such as tar during smoking. **2** a cigarette having such an attachment.
▶ **'filter-,tipped** *adj*

filth (fɪlθ) *n* **1** foul or disgusting dirt; refuse. **2** extreme physical or moral uncleanliness. **3** vulgarity or obscenity. **4 the filth.** *Sl.* the police. [OE *fÿlth*]

filthy ('fɪlθɪ) *adj* **filthier, filthiest. 1** very dirty or obscene. **2** offensive or vicious: *that was a filthy trick to play.* **3** *Inf., chiefly Brit.* extremely unpleasant: *filthy weather.* ◆ *adv* **4** extremely; disgustingly (esp. in **filthy rich**).
▶ **'filthily** *adv* ▶ **'filthiness** *n*

filtrate ('fɪltreɪt) *n* **1** a liquid or gas that has been filtered. ◆ *vb* **filtrates, filtrating, filtrated. 2** to filter. [C17: from Med. L *filtrāre* to FILTER]
▶ **fil'tration** *n*

fin (fɪn) *n* **1** any of the firm appendages that are the organs of locomotion and balance in fishes and some other aquatic animals. **2** a part or appendage that resembles a fin. **3a** *Brit.* a vertical surface to which the rudder is attached at the rear of an aeroplane. **3b** a tail surface fixed to a rocket or missile to give stability. **4** *Naut.* a fixed or adjustable blade projecting under water from the hull of a vessel to give it stability or control. **5** a projecting rib to dissipate heat from the surface of an engine cylinder or radiator. ◆ *vb* **fins, finning, finned. 6** (*tr*) to provide with fins. [OE *finn*]
▶ **'finless** *adj* ▶ **finned** *adj*

fin. *abbrev. for:* **1** finance. **2** financial.

Fin. *abbrev. for:* **1** Finland. **2** Finnish.

finable *or* **fineable** ('faɪnəb³l) *adj* liable to a fine.
▶ **'finableness** *or* **'fineableness** *n*

finagle (fɪ'neɪg³l) *vb* **finagles, finagling, finagled.** *Inf.* **1** (*tr*) to get or achieve by craftiness or persuasion. **2** to use trickery on (a person). [C20: ?from dialect *fainaigue* cheat]
▶ **fi'nagler** *n*

final ('faɪn³l) *adj* **1** of or occurring at the end; last. **2** having no possibility of further discussion, action, or change: *a final decree of judgment.* **3** relating to or constituting an end or purpose: *a final clause may be introduced by "in order to".* **4** *Music.* another word for **perfect** (sense 9b.). ◆ *n* **5** a last thing; end. **6** a deciding contest between the winners of previous rounds in a competition. ◆ See also **finals.** [C14: from L *fīnālis*, from *fīnis* limit, boundary]

finale (fɪ'nɑːlɪ) *n* **1** the concluding part of any performance or presentation. **2** the closing section or movement of a musical composition. [C18: from It., n use of adj *finale*, from L *fīnālis* FINAL]

finalist ('faɪnəlɪst) *n* a contestant who has reached the last stage of a competition.

finality (faɪ'nælɪtɪ) *n, pl* **finalities. 1** the condition or quality of being final or settled: *the finality of death.* **2** a final or conclusive act.

finalize *or* **finalise** ('faɪnə,laɪz) *vb* **finalizes, finalizing, finalized** *or* **finalises, finalising, finalised. 1** (*tr*) to put into final form; settle: *to finalize plans for the merger.* **2** to reach agreement on a transaction.
▶ **,finali'zation** *or* **,finali'sation** *n*

USAGE NOTE Although *finalize* has been in widespread use for some time, many speakers and writers still prefer to use *complete, conclude,* or *make final,* esp. in formal contexts.

---

finally ('faɪnəlɪ) *adv* **1** at last; eventually. **2** at the end or final point; lastly. **3** completely; conclusively. ◆ *sentence connector.* **4** in the end; lastly: *finally, he put his tie on.* **5** as the last or final point.

finals ('faɪn³lz) *pl n* **1** the deciding part of a competition.

2 *Education.* the last examinations in an academic or professional course.

finance (fɪ'næns, 'faɪnæns) *n* **1** the system of money, credit, etc., esp. with respect to government revenues and expenditures. **2** funds or the provision of funds. **3** (*pl*) financial condition. ◆ *vb* **finances, financing, financed. 4** (*tr*) to provide or obtain funds or credit for. [C14: from OF, from *finer* to end, settle by payment]

finance company *or* **house** *n* an enterprise engaged in the loan of money against collateral, esp. one specializing in the financing of hire-purchase contracts.

financial (fɪ'nænʃəl, faɪ-) *adj* **1** of or relating to finance or finances. **2** of or relating to persons who manage money, capital, or credit. **3** *Austral. & NZ inf.* having money; in funds. **4** *Austral. & NZ.* (of a club member) fully paid-up.
▶ **fi'nancially** *adv*

financial futures *pl n* futures in a stock-exchange index, currency exchange rate, or interest rate enabling banks, building societies, brokers, and speculators to hedge their involvement in these markets.

Financial Ombudsman *n* any of five British ombudsmen: the **Banking Ombudsman,** set up in 1986 to investigate complaints from banking customers; the **Building Society Ombudsman,** set up in 1987 to investigate complaints from building society customers; the **Insurance Ombudsman,** set up in 1981 to investigate complaints by policyholders (since 1988 this ombudsman has also operated a **Unit Trust Ombudsman** scheme); the **Investment Ombudsman,** set up in 1989 to investigate complaints by investors (the **Personal Investment Authority Ombudsman** is responsible for investigating complaints by personal investors); and the **Pensions Ombudsman,** set up in 1993 to investigate complaints regarding pension schemes.

financial year *n Brit.* **1** any annual period at the end of which a firm's accounts are made up. **2** the annual period ending April 5, over which Budget estimates are made by the British Government. ◆ *US and Canad.* equivalent: **fiscal year.**

financier (fɪ'nænsɪə, faɪ-) *n* a person who is engaged in large-scale financial operations.

financing gap *n* the difference between a country's requirements for foreign exchange to finance its debts and imports and its income from overseas.

finback ('fɪn,bæk) *n* another name for **rorqual.**

finch (fɪntʃ) *n* any of various songbirds having a short stout bill for feeding on seeds, such as the bullfinch, chaffinch, siskin, and canary. [OE *finc*]

Finchley ★ ('fɪntʃlɪ) *n* a residential district of N London, part of the Greater London borough of Barnet from 1965.

find (faɪnd) *vb* **finds, finding, found.** (*mainly tr*) **1** to meet with or discover by chance. **2** to discover or obtain, esp. by search or effort: *to find happiness.* **3** (*may take a clause as object*) to realize: *he found that nobody knew.* **4** (*may take a clause as object*) to consider: *I find this wine a little sour.* **5** to look for and point out (something to be criticized). **6** (*also intr*) *Law.* to determine an issue and pronounce a verdict (upon): *the court found the accused guilty.* **7** to regain (something lost or not functioning): *to find one's tongue.* **8** to reach (a target): *the bullet found its mark.* **9** to provide, esp. with difficulty: *we'll find room for you too.* **10** to be able to pay: *I can't find that amount of money.* **11 find oneself.** to realize and accept one's true character; discover one's vocation. **12 find one's feet.** to become capable or confident. ◆ *n* **13** a person, thing, etc., that is found, esp. a valuable discovery. [OE *findan*]

finder ('faɪndə) *n* **1** a person or thing that finds. **2** *Physics.* a small telescope fitted to a more powerful larger telescope. **3** *Photog.* short for **viewfinder. 4 finders keepers.** *Inf.* whoever finds something has the right to keep it.

fin de siècle *French.* (fɛ̃ də sjɛklə) *n* **1** the end of the 19th century. ◆ *adj* **fin-de-siècle. 2** of or relating to the close of the 19th century. **3** decadent, esp. in artistic tastes.

finding ('faɪndɪŋ) *n* **1** a thing that is found or discovered. **2** *Law.* the conclusion reached after a judicial inquiry; verdict.

find out *vb* (*adv*) **1** to gain knowledge of (something);

learn. **2** to detect the crime, deception, etc., of (someone).

fine[1] (faɪn) *adj* **1** very good of its kind: *a fine speech.* **2** superior in skill or accomplishment: *a fine violinist.* **3** (of weather) clear and dry. **4** enjoyable or satisfying: *a fine time.* **5** (*postpositive*) *Inf.* quite well: *I feel fine.* **6** satisfactory; acceptable: *that's fine by me.* **7** of delicate composition or careful workmanship: *fine crystal.* **8** (of precious metals) pure or having a high degree of purity: *fine silver.* **9** discriminating: *a fine eye for antique brasses.* **10** abstruse or subtle: *a fine point.* **11** very thin or slender: *fine hair.* **12** very small: *fine print.* **13** (of edges, blades, etc.) sharp; keen. **14** ornate, showy, or smart. **15** good-looking: *a fine young woman.* **16** polished, elegant, or refined: *a fine gentleman.* **17** *Cricket.* (of a fielding position) oblique to and behind the wicket: *fine leg.* **18** (*prenominal*) *Inf.* disappointing or terrible: *a fine mess.* ◆ *adv* **19** *Inf.* all right: *that suits me fine.* **20** finely. ◆ *vb* **fines, fining, fined.** **21** to make or become finer; refine. **22** (often foll. by *down* or *away*) to make or become smaller. [C13: from OF *fin,* from L *finis* end, boundary, as in *finis honōrum* the highest degree of honour]
▶ 'finely *adv* ▶ 'fineness *n*

fine[2] (faɪn) *n* **1** a certain amount of money exacted as a penalty: *a parking fine.* **2** a payment made by a tenant at the start of his tenancy to reduce his subsequent rent; premium. **3 in fine. 3a** in short. **3b** in conclusion. ◆ *vb* **fines, fining, fined.** **4** (*tr*) to impose a fine on. [C12 (in the sense: conclusion, settlement): from OF *fin;* see FINE[1]]

fine[3] ('fiːneɪ) *n Music.* the point at which a piece is to end. [It., from L *finis* end]

fine art *n* **1** art produced chiefly for its aesthetic value. **2** (*often pl*) any of the fields in which such art is produced, such as painting, sculpture, and engraving.

fine-draw *vb* **fine-draws, fine-drawing, fine-drew, fine-drawn.** (*tr*) to sew together so finely that the join is scarcely noticeable.

fine-drawn *adj* **1** (of arguments, distinctions, etc.) precise or subtle. **2** (of wire, etc.) drawn out until very fine.

fine-grained *adj* (of wood, leather, etc.) having a fine smooth even grain.

finery[1] ('faɪnərɪ) *n* elaborate or showy decoration, esp. clothing and jewellery.

finery[2] ('faɪnərɪ) *n, pl* **fineries.** a hearth for converting cast iron into wrought iron. [C17: from OF *finerie,* from *finer* to refine; see FINE[1]]

fines herbes (*French* finz ɛrb) *pl n* a mixture of finely chopped herbs, used to flavour omelettes, salads, etc.

finespun ('faɪn'spʌn) *adj* **1** spun or drawn out to a fine thread. **2** excessively subtle or refined.

finesse (fɪ'nɛs) *n* **1** elegant skill in style or performance. **2** subtlety and tact in handling difficult situations. **3** *Bridge, whist.* an attempt to win a trick when opponents hold a high card in the suit led by playing a lower card. **4** a trick, artifice, or strategy. ◆ *vb* **finesses, finessing, finessed.** **5** to bring about with finesse. **6** to play (a card) as a finesse. [C15: from OF, from *fin* fine, delicate; see FINE[1]]

fine-tooth comb *or* **fine-toothed comb** *n* **1** a comb with fine teeth set closely together. **2 go over** (*or* **through**) **with a fine-tooth(ed) comb.** to examine very thoroughly.

fine-tune *vb* **fine-tunes, fine-tuning, fine-tuned.** (*tr*) to make fine adjustments to (something) in order to obtain optimum performance.

Fingal's Cave ★ ('fɪŋɡ°lz) *n* a cave in W Scotland, on Staffa Island in the Inner Hebrides: basaltic pillars. Length: 69 m (227 ft). Height: 36 m (117 ft).

finger ('fɪŋɡə) *n* **1a** any of the digits of the hand, often excluding the thumb. **1b** (*as modifier*): *a finger bowl.* **1c** (*in combination*): *a fingernail.* Related adj: **digital.** **2** the part of a glove made to cover a finger. **3** something that resembles a finger in shape or function: *a finger of land.* **4** the length or width of a finger used as a unit of measurement. **5** a quantity of liquid in a glass, etc., as deep as a finger is wide. **6 get** *or* **pull one's finger out.** *Brit. inf.* to begin or speed up activity, esp. after initial delay. **7 have a** (*or* **one's**) **finger in the pie.** **7a** to have an interest in or take part in some activity. **7b** to meddle or interfere. **8 lay** *or* **put one's finger on.** to indicate or locate accurately. **9 not lift** (*or* **raise**) **a finger.** (*foll. by an infinitive*) not to make any effort (to do something). **10 twist** *or* **wrap around one's little finger.** to have easy and complete control or influence over. **11 put the finger on.** *Inf.* to inform on or identify, esp. for the police. ◆ *vb* **12** (*tr*) to touch or manipulate with the fingers; handle. **13** (*tr*) *Inf., chiefly US.* to identify as a criminal or suspect. **14** to use one's fingers in playing (an instrument, such as a piano or clarinet). **15** to indicate on (a composition or part) the fingering required by a pianist, etc. [OE]
▶ 'fingerless *adj*

fingerboard ('fɪŋɡə,bɔːd) *n* the long strip of hard wood on a violin, guitar, etc. upon which the strings are stopped by the fingers.

finger bowl *n* a small bowl filled with water for rinsing the fingers at the table after a meal.

finger buffet ('bufeɪ) *n* a buffet meal at which food that may be picked up in the fingers (**finger food**), such as canapés or vol-au-vents, is served.

fingered ('fɪŋɡəd) *adj* **1** marked or dirtied by handling. **2a** having a finger or fingers. **2b** (*in combination*): *red-fingered.* **3** (of a musical part) having numerals indicating the fingering.

fingering ('fɪŋɡərɪŋ) *n* **1** the technique or art of using one's fingers in playing a musical instrument, esp. the piano. **2** the numerals in a musical part indicating this.

fingerling ('fɪŋɡəlɪŋ) *n* a very young fish, esp. the parr of salmon or trout.

fingermark ('fɪŋɡə,mɑːk) *n* a mark left by dirty or greasy fingers on paintwork, walls, etc.

fingernail ('fɪŋɡə,neɪl) *n* a thin horny translucent plate covering part of the dorsal surface of the end joint of each finger.

finger painting *n* the process or art of painting with **finger paints** of starch, glycerine, and pigments, using the fingers, hand, or arm.

finger post *n* a signpost showing a pointing finger or hand.

fingerprint ('fɪŋɡə,prɪnt) *n* **1** an impression of the pattern of ridges on the surface of the end joint of each finger and thumb. **2** any unique identifying characteristic. ◆ *vb* (*tr*) **3** to take an inked impression of the fingerprints of (a person). **4** to take a sample of (a person's) DNA.

fingerstall ('fɪŋɡə,stɔːl) *n* a protective covering for a finger. Also called: **cot.**

fingertip ('fɪŋɡə,tɪp) *n* **1** the end joint or tip of a finger. **2 at one's fingertips.** readily available.

finial ('faɪnɪəl) *n* **1** an ornament on top of a spire, etc., esp. in the form of a fleur-de-lys. **2** an ornament at the top of a piece of furniture, etc. [C14: from *finial* (adj), var. of FINAL]

finicky ('fɪnɪkɪ) *or* **finicking** *adj* **1** excessively particular; fussy. **2** overelaborate. [C19: from *finical,* from FINE[1]]

finis ('fɪnɪs) *n* the end; finish: used at the end of books, films, etc. [C15: from L]

finish ('fɪnɪʃ) *vb* (*mainly tr*) **1** to bring to an end; conclude or stop. **2** (*intr*; sometimes foll. by *up*) to be at or come to the end; use up. **3** to bring to a desired or complete condition. **4** to put a particular surface texture on (wood, cloth, etc.). **5** (often foll. by *off*) to destroy or defeat completely. **6** to train (a person) in social graces and talents. **7** (*intr*; foll. by *with*) to end a relationship or association. ◆ *n* **8** the final or last stage or part; end. **9** the death or absolute defeat of a person or one side in a contest: *a fight to the finish.* **10** the surface texture or appearance of wood, cloth, etc.: *a rough finish.* **11** a thing, event, etc., that completes. **12** completeness and high quality of workmanship. **13** *Sport.* ability to sprint at the end of a race. [C14: from OF, from L *finīre*; see FINE[1]]
▶ 'finished *adj* ▶ 'finisher *n*

finishing school *n* a private school for girls that teaches social graces.

Finistère ★ (,fɪnɪ'stɛə; *French* finistɛr) *n* a department of NW France, at the tip of the Breton peninsula. Capital:

Quimper. Pop.: 840 103 (1994 est.). Area: 7029 sq. km (2741 sq. miles).

Finisterre ★ (ˌfɪnɪˈstɛə) n **1 Cape.** a headland in NW Spain: the westernmost point of the Spanish mainland. **2** an English name for **Finistère.**

finite (ˈfaɪnaɪt) adj **1** bounded in magnitude or spatial or temporal extent. **2** Maths, logic. having a countable number of elements. **3** limited or restricted in nature: human existence is finite. **4** denoting any form of a verb inflected for grammatical features such as person, number, and tense. [C15: from L finītus limited, from finīre to limit, end]
▸ **ˈfinitely** adv ▸ **ˈfiniteness** or **finitude** (ˈfaɪnɪˌtjuːd) n

fink (fɪŋk) n Sl., chiefly US & Canad. **1** a strikebreaker. **2** an unpleasant or contemptible person. [C20: from ?]

Finland ★ (ˈfɪnlənd) n **1** a republic in N Europe, on the Baltic Sea: ceded to Russia by Sweden in 1809; gained independence in 1917; Soviet invasion successfully withstood in 1939–40, with the loss of Karelia; a member of the European Union. It is generally low-lying, with about 50 000 lakes, extensive forests, and peat bogs. Official languages: Finnish and Swedish. Religion: Christian (Lutheran) majority. Currency: markka and euro. Capital: Helsinki. Pop.: 5 145 000 (1997). Area: 337 000 sq. km (130 120 sq. miles). Finnish name: **Suomi. 2 Gulf of.** an arm of the Baltic Sea between Finland, Estonia, and Russia.

Finlandization or **Finlandisation** (ˌfɪnləndaɪˈzeɪʃən) n neutralization of a small country by a superpower, using conciliation rather than confrontation, as the former Soviet Union did in relation to Finland.

Finlay ★ (ˈfɪnlɪ) n **Carlos Juan** (Spanish ˈkarlɔs xwan). 1833–1915, Cuban physician: discovered that the mosquito was the vector of yellow fever.

Finn[1] (fɪn) n a native, inhabitant, or citizen of Finland. [OE Finnas (pl)]

Finn[2] ★ (fɪn) n known as **Finn MacCool.** (in Irish legend) chief of the Fianna, father of the heroic poet Ossian.

finnan haddock (ˈfɪnən) or **haddie** (ˈhædɪ) n smoked haddock. [C18: finnan after Findon, a village in NE Scotland]

Finney ★ (ˈfɪnɪ) n **1 Albert.** born 1936, British actor. **2 Tom.** born 1922, British footballer: won 76 international caps.

Finnic (ˈfɪnɪk) n **1** one of the two branches of the Finno-Ugric family of languages, including Finnish and several languages of NE Europe. ◆ adj **2** of or relating to this group of languages or to the Finns.

Finnish (ˈfɪnɪʃ) adj **1** of or characteristic of Finland, the Finns, or their language. ◆ n **2** the official language of Finland, belonging to the Finno-Ugric family.

Finnmark ★ (ˈfɪnˌmɑːk) n a county of N Norway: the largest, northernmost, and least populated county; mostly a barren plateau. Capital: Vadsø. Pop.: 76 502 (1996 est.). Area: 48 649 sq. km (18 779 sq. miles).

Finno-Ugric (ˈfɪnəʊˈuːgrɪk, -ˈjuː-) or **Finno-Ugrian** n **1** a family of languages spoken in Scandinavia, E Europe, and W Asia, including Finnish, Estonian, and Hungarian. ◆ adj **2** of, relating to, speaking, or belonging to this family of languages.

finny (ˈfɪnɪ) adj **finnier, finniest. 1** Poetic. relating to or containing many fishes. **2** having or resembling a fin or fins.

fino (ˈfiːnəʊ) n a very dry sherry. [Sp.: FINE[1]]

Finsen ★ (Danish ˈfensən) n **Niels Ryberg** (neːls ˈryber). 1860–1904, Danish physician; founder of phototherapy: Nobel prize for physiology or medicine 1903.

Finsteraarhorn ★ (German ˌfɪnstərˈaːrhɔrn) n a mountain in S central Switzerland: highest peak in the Bernese Alps. Height: 4274 m (14 022 ft).

fiord (fjɔːd) n a variant spelling of **fjord.**

fioriture (ˌfjɔːrɪˈtuəreɪ) pl n Music. flourishes; embellishments. [C19: It, from fiorire to flower]

fipple (ˈfɪpˀl) n a wooden plug forming a flue in the end of a pipe, as the mouthpiece of a recorder. [C17: from ?]

fipple flute n an end-blown flute provided with a fipple, such as the recorder or flageolet.

fir (fɜː) n **1** any of a genus of pyramidal coniferous trees having single needle-like leaves and erect cones. **2** any of various other related trees, such as the Douglas fir. **3** the wood of any of these trees. [OE furh]

Firbank ★ (ˈfɜːbæŋk) n (**Arthur Annesley**) Ronald. 1886–1926, British novelist, whose works include Valmouth (1919), The Flower beneath the Foot (1923), and Concerning the Eccentricities of Cardinal Pirelli (1926).

Firdausi (fɪəˈdaʊsɪ) or **Firdusi** ★ (fɪəˈduːsɪ) n pen name of Abul Qasim Mansur. ?935–1020 A.D., Persian poet; author of Shah Nama (The Book of Kings).

fire (ˈfaɪə) n **1** the state of combustion in which inflammable material burns, producing heat, flames, and often smoke. **2a** a mass of burning coal, wood, etc., used esp. in a hearth to heat a room. **2b** (in combination): firelighter. **3** a destructive conflagration, as of a forest, building, etc. **4** a device for heating a room, etc. **5** something resembling a fire in light or brilliance: a diamond's fire. **6** the act of discharging weapons, artillery, etc. **7** a burst or rapid volley: a fire of questions. **8** intense passion; ardour. **9** liveliness, as of imagination, etc. **10** fever and inflammation. **11** a severe trial or torment (esp. in **go through fire and water**). **12** between two fires. under attack from two sides. **13 catch fire.** to ignite. **14 on fire. 14a** in a state of ignition. **14b** ardent or eager. **15 open fire.** to start firing a gun, artillery, etc. **16 play with fire.** to be involved in something risky. **17 set fire to** or **set on fire. 17a** to ignite. **17b** to arouse or excite. **18 under fire.** being attacked, as by weapons or by harsh criticism. **19** (modifier) Astrol. of or relating to a group of three signs of the zodiac, Aries, Leo, and Sagittarius. ◆ vb **fires, firing, fired. 20** to discharge (a firearm or projectile), or (of a firearm, etc.) to be discharged. **21** to detonate (an explosive charge or device), or (of such a charge or device) to be detonated. **22** (intr) (of an engine) to start working; ignite. **23** (tr) Inf. to dismiss from employment. **24** (tr) Ceramics. to bake in a kiln to harden the clay, etc. **25** to kindle or be kindled. **26** (tr) to provide with fuel: oil fires the heating system. **27** (tr) to subject to heat. **28** (tr) to heat slowly so as to dry. **29** (tr) to arouse to strong emotion. **30** to glow or cause to glow. ◆ sentence substitute. **31** a cry to warn others of a fire. **32** the order to begin firing a gun, artillery, etc. [OE fȳr]
▸ **ˈfirer** n

fire alarm n a device to give warning of fire, esp. a bell, siren, or hooter.

fire appliance n another name for fire engine.

firearm (ˈfaɪərˌɑːm) n a weapon from which a projectile can be discharged by an explosion caused by igniting gunpowder, etc.

fireback (ˈfaɪəˌbæk) n an ornamental iron slab against the back wall of a hearth.

fireball (ˈfaɪəˌbɔːl) n **1** a ball-shaped discharge of lightning. **2** the region of hot ionized gas at the centre of a nuclear explosion. **3** Astron. a large bright meteor. **4** Sl. an energetic person.

fire blight n a disease of apples, pears, and similar fruit trees, caused by a bacterium and characterized by blackening of the blossoms and leaves.

fireboat (ˈfaɪəˌbəʊt) n a motor vessel equipped with fire-fighting apparatus.

firebomb (ˈfaɪəˌbɒm) n another name for **incendiary** (sense 6).

firebox (ˈfaɪəˌbɒks) n the furnace chamber of a boiler in a steam locomotive.

firebrand (ˈfaɪəˌbrænd) n **1** a piece of burning wood. **2** a person who causes unrest.

firebreak (ˈfaɪəˌbreɪk) n a strip of open land in forest or prairie, serving to arrest the advance of a fire.

firebrick (ˈfaɪəˌbrɪk) n a refractory brick made of fire clay, used for lining furnaces, flues, etc.

fire brigade n Chiefly Brit. an organized body of firefighters.

firebug (ˈfaɪəˌbʌg) n Inf. a person who deliberately sets fire to property.

fire clay n a heat-resistant clay used in the making of firebricks, furnace linings, etc.

fire company n **1** an insurance company selling policies relating to fire risk. **2** US. an organized body of fire-men.

fire control n Mil. the procedures by which weapons are brought to engage a target.

firecracker ('faɪə,krækə) n a small cardboard container filled with explosive powder.

firecrest ('faɪə,krɛst) n a small European warbler having a crown striped with yellow, black, and white.

firedamp ('faɪə,dæmp) n an explosive mixture of hydro-carbons, chiefly methane, formed in coal mines. See also **afterdamp**.

firedog ('faɪə,dɒg) n either of a pair of metal stands used to support logs in an open fire.

fire door n **1** a door made of noncombustible material that prevents a fire spreading within a building. **2** a simi-lar door leading to the outside of a building that can be easily opened from inside; emergency exit.

fire-eater n **1** a performer who simulates the swallowing of fire. **2** a belligerent person.

fire engine n a vehicle that carries firemen and fire-fighting equipment to a fire.

fire escape n a means of evacuating persons from a building in the event of fire.

fire-extinguisher n a portable device for extinguish-ing fires, usually consisting of a canister with a direc-tional nozzle used to direct a spray of water, etc., onto the fire.

firefighter ('faɪə,faɪtə) n a person who assists in extin-guishing fires and rescuing those endangered by them, usually a public employee or trained volunteer.
▶ 'fire-,fighting n, adj

firefly ('faɪə,flaɪ) n, pl **fireflies**. a nocturnal beetle com-mon in warm and tropical regions, having luminescent abdominal organs.

fireguard ('faɪə,gɑːd) n a meshed frame put before an open fire to protect against falling logs, sparks, etc.

fire hall n Canad. a fire station.

fire hydrant n a hydrant for use as an emergency supply for fighting fires.

fire insurance n insurance covering damage or loss caused by fire or lightning.

fire irons pl n metal fireside implements, such as poker, shovel, and tongs.

firelock ('faɪə,lɒk) n **1** an obsolete type of gunlock with a priming mechanism ignited by sparks. **2** a gun or mus-ket having such a lock.

fireman ('faɪəmən) n, pl **firemen**. **1** a man who fights fires; firefighter. **2a** (on steam locomotives) the man who stokes the fire. **2b** (on diesel and electric locomotives) the driver's assistant. **3** a man who tends furnaces; stoker.

Firenze ★ (fi'rɛntse) n the Italian name for **Florence**.

fire opal n an orange-red translucent variety of opal, val-ued as a gemstone.

fireplace ('faɪə,pleɪs) n **1** an open recess at the base of a chimney, etc., for a fire; hearth. **2** Austral. an authorized place or installation for outside cooking, esp. by a road-side.

fireplug ('faɪə,plʌg) n another name (esp. US and NZ) for **fire hydrant**.

fire power n Mil. **1** the amount of fire that can be deliv-ered by a unit or weapon. **2** the capability of delivering fire.

fireproof ('faɪə,pruːf) adj **1** capable of resisting damage by fire. ◆ vb **2** (tr) to make resistant to fire.

fire raiser n a person who deliberately sets fire to prop-erty, etc.
▶ 'fire ,raising n

fire screen n **1** a decorative screen placed in the hearth when there is no fire. **2** a screen placed before a fire to protect the face.

fire ship n a vessel loaded with explosives and used, esp. formerly, as a bomb by igniting it and directing it to drift among an enemy's warships.

fireside ('faɪə,saɪd) n **1** the hearth. **2** family life; the home.

fire station n a building where fire-fighting vehicles and equipment are stationed and where firefighters on duty wait. Also called (US): **firehouse, station house**.

firestorm ('faɪə,stɔːm) n an uncontrollable blaze sus-tained by violent winds that are drawn into the column of rising hot air over the burning area: often the result of heavy bombing.

fire trail n Austral. a permanent track cleared through the bush to provide access for fire-fighting.

firetrap ('faɪə,træp) n a building that would burn easily or one without fire escapes.

firewall ('faɪə,wɔːl) n **1** a fireproof wall or partition used to impede the progress of a fire. **2** Computing. a computer system that isolates another computer from the Internet in order to prevent unauthorized access.

firewater ('faɪə,wɔːtə) n any strong spirit, esp. whisky.

fireweed ('faɪə,wiːd) n any of various plants that appear as first vegetation in burnt-over areas.

firework ('faɪə,wɜːk) n a device, such as a Catherine wheel or rocket, in which combustible materials are ig-nited and produce coloured flames, sparks, and smoke.

fireworks ('faɪə,wɜːks) pl n **1** a show in which large num-bers of fireworks are let off. **2** Inf. an exciting exhibition, as of musical virtuosity or wit. **3** Inf. a burst of temper.

firing ('faɪərɪŋ) n **1** the process of baking ceramics, etc., in a kiln. **2** the act of stoking a fire or furnace. **3** a discharge of a firearm. **4** something used as fuel, such as coal or wood.

firing line n **1** Mil. the positions from which fire is deliv-ered. **2** the leading or most advanced position in an ac-tivity.

firkin ('fɜːkɪn) n **1** a small wooden barrel. **2** Brit. a unit of capacity equal to nine gallons. [C14 fir, from MDu. vierde FOURTH + -KIN]

firm¹ (fɜːm) adj **1** not soft or yielding to a touch or pres-sure. **2** securely in position; stable or stationary. **3** de-cided; settled. **4** enduring or steady. **5** having determination or strength. **6** (of prices, markets, etc.) tending to rise. ◆ adv **7** in a secure or unyielding man-ner: he stood firm. ◆ vb **8** (sometimes foll. by up) to make or become firm. [C14: from L firmus]
▶ 'firmly adv ▶ 'firmness n

firm² (fɜːm) n **1** a business partnership. **2** any commercial enterprise. **3** a team of doctors and their assistants. **4 the**. (often cap.) Sl. any organized group of people, such as in-telligence agents, criminals, or football hooligans. [C16 (in the sense: signature): from Sp. firma signature, from firmar to sign, from L firmāre to confirm, from firmus firm]

firmament ('fɜːməmənt) n the expanse of the sky; heav-ens. [C13: from LL firmāmentum sky (considered as fixed above the earth), from L: prop, support, from firmāre to make FIRM¹]

firmware ('fɜːm,wɛə) n Computing. a series of fixed in-structions built into the hardware of a computer that can be changed only if the hardware itself is modified in some way.

first (fɜːst) adj (usually prenominal) **1a** coming before all others. **1b** (as n): I was the first to arrive. **2** preceding all others in numbering or counting order; the ordinal number of one. Often written: 1st. **3** rated, graded, or ranked above all other levels. **4** denoting the lowest for-ward ratio of a gearbox in a motor vehicle. **5** Music. **5a** denoting the highest part assigned to one of the voice parts in a chorus or one of the sections of an orchestra: the first violins. **5b** denoting the principal player in a spe-cific orchestral section: he plays first horn. **6 first thing**. as the first action of the day: I'll see you first thing tomorrow. ◆ n **7** the beginning; outset: I couldn't see at first because of the mist. **8** Education, chiefly Brit. an honours degree of the highest class. Full term: **first-class honours degree**. **9** the lowest forward ratio of a gearbox in a motor vehicle. ◆ adv **10** Also: **firstly**. before anything else in order, time, importance, etc.: do this first. **11 first and last**. on the whole. **12 from first to last**. throughout. **13 for the first time: *I've loved you since I first saw you.* **14** (*sentence modifier*) in the first place or beginning of a series of actions. [OE *fyrest*]

first aid *n* a immediate medical assistance given in an emergency. **b** (*as modifier*): *first-aid box.*

first-born *adj* **1** eldest of the children in a family. ◆ *n* **2** the eldest child in a family.

first class *n* **1** the class or grade of the best or highest value, quality, etc. ◆ *adj* (**first-class** *when prenominal*) **2** of the best or highest class or grade: *a first-class citizen.* **3** excellent. **4** of or denoting the most comfortable class of accommodation in a hotel, aircraft, train, etc. **5** (in Britain) of mail that is processed most quickly. ◆ *adv* **first-class. 6** by first-class mail, means of transportation, etc.

first-day cover *n Philately.* an envelope postmarked on the first day of the issue of its stamps.

first-degree burn *n Pathol.* the least severe type of burn, in which the skin surface is red and painful.

first-foot *Chiefly Scot.* ◆ *n also* **first-footer. 1** the first person to enter a household in the New Year. ◆ *vb* **2** to enter (a house) as first-foot.
▸ **'first-'footing** *n*

first fruits *pl n* **1** the first results or profits of an undertaking. **2** fruit that ripens first.

first-hand *adj, adv* **1** from the original source: *he got the news first-hand.* **2 at first hand.** directly.

first lady *n* (*often caps.*) (in the US) the wife or official hostess of a state governor or a president.

firstling ('fɜːstlɪŋ) *n* the first, esp. the first offspring.

first-loss policy *n* an insurance policy for goods in which a total loss is extremely unlikely and the insurer agrees to provide cover for a sum less than the total value of the property.

firstly ('fɜːstlɪ) *adv* another word for **first.**

first mate *n* an officer second in command to the captain of a merchant ship.

First Minister *n* **1** the chief minister of the Northern Ireland Assembly. **2** (from 2000) the chief minister of the Scottish Parliament.

first mortgage *n* a mortgage that has priority over other mortgages on the same property.

first name *n* a name given to a person at birth, as opposed to a surname. Also called: **Christian name, forename, given name.**

First Nation *n Canad.* a formally recognized group of Indians on a reserve.

first night *n* **a** the first public performance of a play, etc. **b** (*as modifier*): *first-night nerves.*

first offender *n* a person convicted of a criminal offence for the first time.

first officer *n* **1** another name for **first mate. 2** the member of an aircraft crew who is second in command to the captain.

first-past-the-post *n* (*modifier*) of a voting system in which a candidate may be elected by a simple majority.

first person *n* a grammatical category of pronouns and verbs used by the speaker to refer to or talk about himself.

first-rate *adj* **1** of the best or highest rated class or quality. **2** *Inf.* very good; excellent.

first reading *n* the introduction of a bill into a legislative assembly.

first refusal *n* the right to buy something before it is offered to others.

first-strike *adj* (of a nuclear missile) intended for use in an opening attack calculated to destroy the enemy's nuclear weapons.

first water *n* **1** the finest quality of diamond or other precious stone. **2** the highest grade or best quality.

firth (fɜːθ) *or* **frith** *n* a narrow inlet of the sea, esp. in Scotland. [C15: from ON *fjörthr* FJORD]

fiscal ('fɪsk*ə*l) *adj* **1** of or relating to government finances, esp. tax revenues. **2** of or involving financial matters. ◆ *n* **3a** (in some countries) a public prosecutor. **3b** *Scot.*

short for **procurator fiscal.** [C16: from L *fiscālis* concerning the state treasury, from *fiscus* public money]
▸ **'fiscally** *adv*

fiscal year *n* the US and Canad. term for **financial year.**

Fischer ★ (*German* 'fɪʃər) *n* **1 Emil Hermann** ('eːmiːl 'herman). 1852–1919, German chemist, noted for his work on synthetic sugars: Nobel prize for chemistry 1902. **2 Ernst Otto** (ɛrnst 'oto). 1918–94, German chemist: shared the Nobel prize for chemistry (1973) for work on inorganic complexes. **3 Hans** (hans). 1881–1945, German chemist, noted for his work on chlorophyll, haemin, and the porphyrins: Nobel prize for chemistry 1930. **4** ('fɪʃə). **Robert James,** known as *Bobby.* born 1943, US chess player; world champion 1972–75.

Fischer-Dieskau ★ (*German* -'diːskau) *n* **Dietrich** ('diːtrɪç). born 1925, German baritone.

fish (fɪʃ) *n, pl* **fish** *or* **fishes. 1a** any of a large group of cold-blooded aquatic vertebrates having jaws, gills, and usually fins and a skin covered in scales: includes the sharks, rays, teleosts, lungfish, etc. **1b** (*in combination*): *fishpond.* Related adj: **piscine. 2** any of various similar but jawless vertebrates, such as the hagfish and lamprey. **3** (*not in technical use*) any of various aquatic invertebrates, such as the cuttlefish and crayfish. **4** the flesh of fish used as food. **5** *Inf.* a person of little emotion or intelligence: *a poor fish.* **6 drink like a fish.** to drink (esp. alcohol) to excess. **7 have other fish to fry.** to have other activities to do, esp. more important ones. **8 like a fish out of water.** out of one's usual place. **9 make fish of one and flesh of another.** *Irish.* to discriminate unfairly between people. **10 neither fish, flesh, nor fowl.** neither this nor that. ◆ *vb* **11** (*intr*) to attempt to catch fish, as with a line and hook or with nets, traps, etc. **12** (*tr*) to fish in (a particular area of water). **13** to search (a body of water) for something or to search for something, esp. in a body of water. **14** (*intr*; foll. by *for*) to seek something indirectly: *to fish for compliments.* ◆ See also **fish out.** [OE *fisc*]
▸ **'fish,like** *adj*

fish and chips *n* fish fillets coated with batter and deep-fried, eaten with potato chips.

fish cake *n* a fried flattened ball of flaked fish mixed with mashed potatoes.

fisher ('fɪʃə) *n* **1** a fisherman. **2** Also called: **pekan. 2a** a large North American marten having dark brown fur. **2b** the fur of this animal.

Fisher ★ ('fɪʃə) *n* **1 Andrew.** 1862–1928, Australian statesman, born in Scotland: prime minister (1908–09; 1910–13; 1914–15). **2 Saint John.** ?1469–1535, English prelate and scholar: executed for refusing to acknowledge Henry VIII as supreme head of the church. Feast day: June 22. **3 John Arbuthnot,** 1st Baron Fisher of Kilverstone. 1841–1920, British admiral; First Sea Lord (1904–10; 1914–15); introduced the dreadnought.

fisherman ('fɪʃəmən) *n, pl* **fishermen. 1** a person who fishes as a profession or for sport. **2** a vessel used for fishing.

fishery ('fɪʃərɪ) *n, pl* **fisheries. 1a** the industry of catching, processing, and selling fish. **1b** a place where this is carried on. **2** a place where fish are reared. **3** a fishing ground.

Fishes ('fɪʃɪz) *n* **the.** the constellation Pisces, the twelfth sign of the zodiac.

fisheye lens ('fɪʃ,aɪ) *n Photog.* a lens of small focal length, having a highly curved protruding front element that covers an angle of view of almost 180°.

fishfinger ('fɪʃ'fɪŋgə) *or US & Canad.* **fish stick** *n* an oblong piece of filleted or minced fish coated in breadcrumbs.

Fishguard ★ ('fɪʃ,gɑːd) *n* a port and resort in SW Wales, in Pembrokeshire: ferry connections to Cork and Rosslare. Pop.: 2679 (1991).

fish hawk *n* another name for the **osprey.**

fish-hook *n* a sharp hook used in angling, esp. one with a barb.

fishing ('fɪʃɪŋ) *n* **a** the occupation of catching fish. **b** (*as modifier*): *a fishing match.*

★ people and places

fishing ground *n* an area of water that is good for fishing.

fishing rod *n* a long tapered flexible pole for use with a fishing line and, usually, a reel.

fish joint *n* a connection formed by fishplates at the meeting point of two rails, beams, etc.

fishmeal ('fɪʃ,miːl) *n* ground dried fish used as feed for farm animals, as a fertilizer, etc.

fishmonger ('fɪʃ,mʌŋɡə) *n Chiefly Brit.* a retailer of fish.

fishnet ('fɪʃ,nɛt) *n* **a** an open mesh fabric resembling netting. **b** (*as modifier*): *fishnet tights*.

fish out *vb* (*tr, adv*) to find or extract (something): *to fish keys out of a pocket.*

fishplate ('fɪʃ,pleɪt) *n* a flat piece of metal joining one rail or beam to the next, esp. on railway tracks.

fishtail ('fɪʃ,teɪl) *n* **1** an aeroplane manoeuvre in which the tail is moved from side to side to reduce speed. **2** a nozzle having a long narrow slot at the top, placed over a Bunsen burner to produce a thin fanlike flame.

fishwife ('fɪʃ,waɪf) *n, pl* **fishwives. 1** a woman who sells fish. **2** a coarse scolding woman.

fishy ('fɪʃɪ) *adj* **fishier, fishiest. 1** of, involving, or suggestive of fish. **2** abounding in fish. **3** *Inf.* suspicious, doubtful, or questionable. **4** dull and lifeless: *a fishy look.*
▸ **'fishily** *adv*

fissile ('fɪsaɪl) *adj* **1** *Brit.* capable of undergoing nuclear fission. **2** fissionable. **3** tending to split or capable of being split. [C17: from L, from *fissus* split]

fission ('fɪʃən) *n* **1** the act or process of splitting or breaking into parts. **2** *Biol.* a form of asexual reproduction involving a division into two or more equal parts. **3** short for **nuclear fission.** [C19: from L *fissiō* a cleaving]
▸ **'fissionable** *adj*

fission-track dating *n* the dating of samples of minerals by comparing the tracks in them made by fission fragments of the uranium nuclei they contain, before and after irradiation by neutrons.

fissiparous (fɪ'sɪpərəs) *adj Biol.* reproducing by fission.
▸ **fis'siparously** *adv*

fissure ('fɪʃə) *n* **1** any long narrow cleft or crack, esp. in a rock. **2** a weakness or flaw. **3** *Anat.* a narrow split or groove that divides an organ such as the brain, lung, or liver into lobes. ◆ *vb* **fissures, fissuring, fissured. 4** to crack or split apart. [C14: from Medical L *fissūra*, from L *fissus* split]

fist (fɪst) *n* **1** a hand with the fingers clenched into the palm, as for hitting. **2** Also called: **fistful.** the quantity that can be held in a fist or hand. **3** *Inf.* handwriting. **4** an informal word for **index** (sense 9). ◆ *vb* **5** (*tr*) to hit with the fist. [OE *fyst*]

fisticuffs ('fɪstɪ,kʌfs) *pl n* combat with the fists. [C17: prob. from *fisty* with the fist + CUFF²]

fistula ('fɪstjʊlə) *n, pl* **fistulas** *or* **fistulae** (-,liː). *Pathol.* an abnormal opening between one hollow organ and another or between a hollow organ and the surface of the skin, caused by ulceration, malformation, etc. [C14: from L: pipe, tube, hollow reed, ulcer]
▸ **'fistulous** *or* **'fistular** *adj*

fit¹ (fɪt) *vb* **fits, fitting, fitted** *or US* **fit. 1** to be appropriate or suitable for (a situation, etc.). **2** to be of the correct size or shape for (a container, etc.). **3** (*tr*) to adjust in order to render appropriate. **4** (*tr*) to supply with that which is needed. **5** (*tr*) to try clothes on (someone) in order to make adjustments if necessary. **6** (*tr*) to make competent or ready. **7** (*tr*) to locate with care. **8** (*intr*) to correspond with the facts or circumstances. ◆ *adj* **fitter, fittest. 9** appropriate. **10** having the right qualifications; qualifying. **11** in good health. **12** worthy or deserving. **13** (foll. by an infinitive) *Inf.* ready (to); strongly disposed (to): *she was fit to scream.* ◆ *n* **14** the manner in which something fits. **15** the act or process of fitting. **16** *Statistics.* the correspondence between observed and predicted characteristics of a distribution or model. ◆ See also **fit in, fit out.** [C14: prob. from MDu. *vitten*; rel. to ON *fitja* to knit]
▸ **'fitly** *adv* ▸ **'fittable** *adj*

fit² (fɪt) *n* **1** *Pathol.* a sudden attack or convulsion, such as an epileptic seizure. **2** a sudden spell of emotion: *a fit of* anger. **3** an impulsive period of activity or lack of activity. **4** **have** *or* **throw a fit.** *Inf.* to become very angry. **5 in** *or* **by fits and starts.** in spasmodic spells. [OE *fitt* conflict]

fitch (fɪtʃ) *n* **1** a polecat. **2** the fur of the polecat. [C16: prob. from *ficheux*, from OF, from ?]

fitful ('fɪtfʊl) *adj* characterized by or occurring in irregular spells.
▸ **'fitfully** *adv*

fit in *vb* **1** (*tr*) to give a place or time to. **2** (*intr, adv*) to belong or conform, esp. after adjustment: *he didn't fit in with their plans.*

fitment ('fɪtmənt) *n* **1** *Machinery.* an accessory attached to an assembly of parts. **2** *Chiefly Brit.* a detachable part of the furnishings of a room.

fitness ('fɪtnɪs) *n* **1** the state of being fit. **2** *Biol.* **2a** the degree of adaptation of an organism to its environment, determined by its genetic constitution. **2b** the ability of an organism to produce viable offspring capable of surviving to the next generation.

fit out *vb* (*tr, adv*) to equip.

fitted ('fɪtɪd) *adj* **1** designed for excellent fit: *a fitted suit.* **2** (of a garment) cut or sewn to cover a floor completely. **3a** (of furniture) built to fit a particular space: *a fitted cupboard.* **3b** (of a room) equipped with fitted furniture: *a fitted kitchen.* **4** (of sheets) having ends that are elasticated and shaped to fit tightly over a mattress.

fitter ('fɪtə) *n* **1** a person who fits a garment, esp. when it is made for a particular person. **2** a person who is skilled in the assembly and adjustment of machinery, esp. of a specified sort.

fitting ('fɪtɪŋ) *adj* **1** appropriate or proper. ◆ *n* **2** an accessory or part: *an electrical fitting.* **3** (*pl*) furnishings or accessories in a building. **4** work carried out by a fitter. **5** the act of trying on clothes so that they can be adjusted to fit.
▸ **'fittingly** *adv*

Fittipaldi ★ (,fɪtɪ'pældɪ) *n* **Emerson.** born 1946, Brazilian motor-racing driver: world champion in 1972 and 1974.

Fitzgerald ★ (fɪts'dʒɛrəld) *n* **1 Edward.** 1809–83, British poet, noted for his translation of the *Rubáiyát of Omar Khayyám* (1859). **2 Ella.** 1918–96, US jazz singer. **3 F(rancis) Scott (Key).** 1896–1940, US writer, noted for his novels *The Great Gatsby* (1925) and *Tender is the Night* (1934). **4 Garret.** born 1926, Irish politician; leader of Fine Gael Party (1977–87); prime minister of the Republic of Ireland (1981–82; and 1982–87).

Fitzgerald-Lorentz contraction *n Physics.* the contraction that a moving body exhibits when its velocity approaches that of light. [C19: after G. F. *Fitzgerald* (1851–1901), Irish physicist, and H. A. LORENTZ]

Fitzrovia ★ (fɪts'rəʊvɪə) *n Inf.* the district north of Oxford Street, London, around Fitzroy Square and its pubs, noted in the 1930s and 40s as a haunt of poets.

Fitzsimmons ★ (,fɪt'sɪmənz) *n* **Bob.** 1862–1917, New Zealand boxer, born in England: world middleweight (1891–97), heavyweight (1897–99), and light-heavyweight (1903–05) champion.

Fiume ★ ('fjuːme) *n* the Italian name for **Rijeka.**

five (faɪv) *n* **1** the cardinal number that is the sum of four and one. **2** a numeral, 5, V, etc., representing this number. **3** the amount or quantity that is one greater than four. **4** something representing, represented by, or consisting of five units, such as a playing card with five symbols on it. **5 five o'clock.** five hours after noon or midnight. ◆ *determiner* **6a** amounting to five: *five nights.* **6b** (*as pronoun*): *choose any five you like.* ◆ See also **fives.** [OE *fīf*]

five-a-side *n* a version of soccer with five players on each side.

five-eighth *n Austral. & NZ.* a rugby player positioned between the halfbacks and three-quarters.

five-finger *n* any of various plants having five-petalled flowers or five lobed leaves, such as cinquefoil and Virginia creeper.

fivefold ('faɪv,fəʊld) *adj* **1** equal to or having five times as many or as much. **2** composed of five parts. ◆ *adv* **3** by or up to five times as many or as much.

★ people and places

five-o'clock shadow *n* beard growth visible late in the day on a man's shaven face.

fivepins ('faɪvˌpɪnz) *n* (*functioning as sing*) a bowling game using five pins, played esp. in Canada.
► **'five,pin** *adj*

fiver ('faɪvə) *n Brit. inf.* a five-pound note.

fives (faɪvz) *n* (*functioning as sing*) a ball game similar to squash but played with bats or the hands.

Five Towns ★ *n* **the.** the name given in his fiction by Arnold Bennett to the Potteries towns (actually six in number) of Burslem, Fenton, Hanley, Longton, Stoke-upon-Trent, and Tunstall, now part of the city of Stoke-on-Trent.

Five-Year Plan *n* (in socialist economies) a government plan for economic development over a period of five years.

fix (fɪks) *vb* (*mainly tr*) **1** (*also intr*) to make or become firm, stable, or secure. **2** to attach or place permanently. **3** (often foll. by *up*) to settle definitely; decide. **4** to hold or direct (eyes, etc.) steadily: *he fixed his gaze on the woman.* **5** to call to attention or rivet. **6** to make rigid: *to fix one's jaw.* **7** to place or ascribe: *to fix the blame.* **8** to mend or repair. **9** *Inf.* to provide or be provided with: *how are you fixed for supplies?* **10** *Inf.* to influence (a person, etc.) unfairly, as by bribery. **11** *Sl.* to take revenge on. **12** *Inf.* to give (someone) his just deserts: *that'll fix him.* **13** *Inf., chiefly US & Canad.* to prepare: *to fix a meal.* **14** *Dialect or inf.* to spay or castrate (an animal). **15** *Photog.* to treat (a film, plate, or paper) with fixer to make permanent the image rendered visible by developer. **16** to convert (atmospheric nitrogen) into nitrogen compounds, as in the manufacture of fertilizers or the action of bacteria in the soil. **17** to reduce (a substance) to a solid state or a less volatile state. **18** (*intr*) *Sl.* to inject a narcotic drug. ♦ *n* **19** *Inf.* a predicament; dilemma. **20** the ascertaining of the navigational position, as of a ship, by radar, etc. **21** *Sl.* an intravenous injection of a narcotic such as heroin. ♦ See also **fix up.** [C15: from Med. L *fixāre*, from L *fixus* fixed, from L *figere*]
► **'fixable** *adj*

fixate (fɪk'seɪt) *vb* **fixates, fixating, fixated. 1** to become or cause to become fixed. **2** *Psychol.* to engage in fixation. **3** (*tr; usually passive*) *Inf.* to obsess. [C19: from L *fixus* fixed + -ATE¹]

fixation (fɪk'seɪʃən) *n* **1** the act of fixing or the state of being fixed. **2** a preoccupation or obsession. **3** *Psychol.* **3a** the situation of being set in a certain way of thinking or acting. **3b** a strong attachment of a person to another person or an object in early life. **4** *Chem.* the conversion of nitrogen in the air into a compound, esp. a fertilizer. **5** the reduction of a substance to a nonvolatile or solid form.

fixative ('fɪksətɪv) *adj* **1** serving or tending to fix. ♦ *n* **2** a fluid sprayed over drawings to prevent smudging or one that fixes tissues and cells for microscopic study. **3** a substance added to a liquid, such as a perfume, to make it less volatile.

fixed (fɪkst) *adj* **1** attached or placed so as to be immovable. **2** stable: *fixed prices.* **3** steadily directed: *a fixed expression.* **4** established as to relative position: *a fixed point.* **5** always at the same time: *a fixed holiday.* **6** (of ideas, etc.) firmly maintained. **7** (of an element) held in chemical combination: *fixed nitrogen.* **8** (of a substance) nonvolatile. **9** arranged. **10** *Inf.* equipped or provided for, as with money, possessions, etc. **11** *Inf.* illegally arranged: *a fixed trial.*
► **fixedly** ('fɪksɪdlɪ) *adv* ► **'fixedness** *n*

fixed assets *pl n* nontrading business assets of a relatively permanent nature, such as plant, fixtures, or goodwill. Also called: **capital assets.**

fixed oil *n* a natural animal or vegetable oil that is not volatile: a mixture of esters of fatty acids.

fixed-point representation *n Computing.* the representation of numbers by a single set of digits such that the radix point has a predetermined location. Cf. **floating-point representation.**

fixed satellite *n* a satellite revolving in a stationary orbit so that it appears to remain over a fixed point on the earth's surface.

fixed star *n* an extremely distant star whose position appears to be almost stationary over a long period of time.

fixer ('fɪksə) *n* **1** a person or thing that fixes. **2** *Photog.* a solution used to dissolve unexposed silver halides after developing. **3** *Sl.* a person who makes arrangements, esp. by underhand or illegal means.

fixing ('fɪksɪŋ) *n* a means of attaching one thing to another, as a pipe to a wall, a slate to a roof, etc.

fixity ('fɪksɪtɪ) *n, pl* **fixities. 1** the state or quality of being fixed. **2** a fixture.

fixture ('fɪkstʃə) *n* **1** an object firmly fixed in place, esp. a household appliance. **2** a person or thing regarded as fixed in a particular place or position. **3** *Property law.* an article attached to land and regarded as part of it. **4** *Chiefly Brit.* **4a** a sports match or social occasion. **4b** the date of such an event. [C17: from LL *fixūra* a fastening (with *-t-* by analogy with *mixture*)]

fix up *vb* (*tr, adv*) **1** to arrange: *let's fix up a date.* **2** (often foll. by *with*) to provide: *I'm sure we can fix you up with a room.*

fizgig ('fɪzˌgɪg) *n* **1** a frivolous or flirtatious girl. **2** a firework that fizzes as it moves. [C16: prob. from obs. *fise* a breaking of wind + *gig* girl]

fizz (fɪz) *vb* (*intr*) **1** to make a hissing or bubbling sound. **2** (of a drink) to produce bubbles of carbon dioxide. ♦ *n* **3** a hissing or bubbling sound. **4** the bubbly quality of a drink; effervescence. **5** any effervescent drink. [C17: imit.]
► **'fizzy** *adj* ► **'fizziness** *n*

fizzle ('fɪz³l) *vb* **fizzles, fizzling, fizzled.** (*intr*) **1** to make a hissing or bubbling sound. **2** (often foll. by *out*) *Inf.* to fail or die out, esp. after a promising start. ♦ *n* **3** a hissing or bubbling sound. **4** *Inf.* a failure. [C16: prob. from obs. *fist* to break wind]

fjord *or* **fiord** (fjɔːd) *n* a long narrow inlet of the sea between high steep cliffs, common in Norway. [C17: from Norwegian, from ON *fjörthr;* see FIRTH, FORD]

FL *abbrev. for:* **1** Flight Lieutenant. **2** Florida.

fl. *abbrev. for:* **1** floor. **2** floruit. **3** fluid.

Fl. *abbrev. for:* **1** Flanders. **2** Flemish.

Fla. *abbrev. for* Florida.

flab (flæb) *n* unsightly or unwanted fat on the body. [C20: back formation from FLABBY]

flabbergast ('flæbəˌgɑːst) *vb* (*tr; usually passive*) *Inf.* to amaze utterly; astound. [C18: from ?]

flabby ('flæbɪ) *adj* **flabbier, flabbiest. 1** loose or yielding: *flabby muscles.* **2** having flabby flesh, esp. through being overweight. **3** lacking vitality; weak. [C17: alteration of *flappy* from FLAP + -Y¹; cf. Du. *flabbe* drooping lip]
► **'flabbiness** *n*

flaccid ('flæksɪd) *adj* lacking firmness; soft and limp. [C17: from L *flaccidus,* from *flaccus*]
► **flac'cidity** *n*

flacon (French flakɔ̃) *n* a small stoppered bottle, esp. used for perfume. [C19: from F; see FLAGON]

flag¹ (flæg) *n* **1** a piece of cloth, esp. bunting, often attached to a pole or staff, decorated with a design and used as an emblem, symbol, or standard or as a means of signalling. **2** a small piece of paper, etc., sold on flag days. **3** the conspicuously marked or shaped tail of a deer or of certain dogs. **4** anything used like a flag to attract attention, esp. a code inserted into a computer file to distinguish certain information. **5** *Brit., Austral., & NZ.* the part of a taximeter that is raised when a taxi is for hire. **6 show the flag. 6a** to assert a claim by military presence. **6b** *Inf.* to make an appearance. ♦ *vb* **flags, flagging, flagged.** (*tr*) **7** to decorate or mark with a flag or flags. **8** (often foll. by *down*) to warn or signal (a vehicle) to stop. **9** to send or communicate (messages, information, etc.) by flag. [C16: from ?]
► **'flagger** *n*

flag² (flæg) *n* **1** any of various plants that have long swordlike leaves, esp. an iris (**yellow flag**). **2** the leaf of any such plant. [C14: prob. from ON]

flag³ (flæg) vb **flags, flagging, flagged.** (intr) **1** to hang down; droop. **2** to become weak or tired. [C16: from ?]

flag⁴ (flæg) n **1** short for **flagstone.** ◆ vb **flags, flagging, flagged. 2** (tr) to furnish (a floor, etc.) with flagstones.

flag day n Brit. a day on which money is collected by a charity and small flags or emblems are given to contributors.

flagellant ('flædʒɪlənt, flə'dʒɛlənt) or **flagellator** ('flædʒɪˌleɪtə) n a person who whips himself or others either as part of a religious penance or for sexual gratification. [C16: from L flagellāre to whip, from FLAGELLUM]

flagellate vb ('flædʒɪˌleɪt), **flagellates, flagellating, flagellated. 1** (tr) to whip; flog. ◆ adj ('flædʒɪlɪt), also **flagellated. 2** possessing one or more flagella. **3** whiplike. ◆ n ('flædʒɪlɪt). **4** a flagellate organism.
▸ ˌflagel'lation n

flagellum (flə'dʒɛləm) n, pl **flagella** (-lə) or **flagellums. 1** Biol. a long whiplike outgrowth from a cell that acts as an organ of locomotion: occurs in some protozoans, gametes, etc. **2** Bot. a long thin shoot or runner. [C19: from L: a little whip, from flagrum a whip, lash]
▸ fla'gellar adj

flageolet¹ (ˌflædʒə'lɛt) n a high-pitched musical instrument of the recorder family. [C17: from F, modification of OF flajolet a little flute, from Vulgar L flabeolum (unattested), from L flāre to blow]

flageolet² (ˌflædʒə'lɛt) n a type of kidney bean. [C19: from F, corruption of fageolet, dim. of fageol, from L faseolus]

flag fall n Austral. the minimum charge for hiring a taxi, to which the rate per kilometre is added.

flag of convenience n a national flag flown by a ship registered in that country to gain financial or legal advantage.

flag of truce n a white flag indicating an invitation to an enemy to negotiate.

flagon ('flægən) n **1** a large bottle of wine, cider, etc. **2** a vessel having a handle, spout, and narrow neck. [C15: from OF flascon, from LL flascō, prob. of Gmc origin; see FLASK]

flagpole ('flæg,pəʊl) or **flagstaff** ('flæg,stɑːf) n, pl **flagpoles, flagstaffs** or **flagstaves** (-,steɪvz). a pole or staff on which a flag is hoisted and displayed.

flagrant ('fleɪgrənt) adj openly outrageous. [C15: from L flagrāre to blaze, burn]
▸ 'flagrancy n ▸ 'flagrantly adv

flagrante delicto (flə'græntɪ dɪ'lɪktəʊ) adv See **in flagrante delicto.**

flagship ('flæg,ʃɪp) n **1** a ship, esp. in a fleet, aboard which the commander of the fleet is quartered. **2** the most important ship belonging to a shipping company. **3** the item in a group considered most important esp. in establishing a public image: costume drama is the flagship of the BBC.

Flagstad ★ ('flægstæd; Norwegian 'flaksta) n **Kirsten** ('çɪrstən). 1895–1962, Norwegian operatic soprano, noted particularly for her interpretations of Wagner.

flagstone ('flæg,stəʊn) n **1** a hard fine-textured rock that can be split up into slabs for paving. **2** a slab of such a rock. [C15 flag (in the sense: sod, turf), from ON flaga slab; cf. OE flæcg plaster, poultice]

flag-waving n Inf. an emotional appeal intended to arouse patriotic feeling.
▸ 'flag,waver n

Flaherty ★ ('flɑːhətɪ) n **Robert (Joseph).** 1884–1951, US film director, his work includes Nanook of the North (1922) and Elephant Boy (1935).

flail (fleɪl) n **1** an implement used for threshing grain, consisting of a wooden handle with a free-swinging metal or wooden bar attached to it. ◆ vb **2** (tr) to beat with or as if with a flail. **3** to thresh about: with arms flailing. [C12 fleil, ult. from LL flagellum flail, from L: whip]

flair (fleə) n **1** natural ability; talent. **2** perceptiveness. **3** Inf. stylishness or elegance: to dress with flair. [C19: from F, lit.: sense of smell, from OF: scent, ult. from L frāgrāre to smell sweet; see FRAGRANT]

flak (flæk) n **1** anti-aircraft fire or artillery. **2** Inf. adverse criticism. [C20: from G Fl(ieger)a(bwehr)k(anone), lit.: aircraft defence gun]

flake¹ (fleɪk) n **1** a small thin piece or layer chipped off or detached from an object or substance. **2** a small piece or particle: a flake of snow. **3** Archaeol. a fragment removed by chipping from a larger stone used as a tool or weapon. **4** Chiefly US sl. an eccentric, crazy, or unreliable person. ◆ vb **flakes, flaking, flaked. 5** to peel or cause to peel off in flakes. **6** to cover or become covered with or as with flakes. **7** (tr) to form into flakes. [C14: from ON]

flake² (fleɪk) n a rack or platform for drying fish. [C14: from ON flaki; rel. to Du. vlaak hurdle]

flake out vb (intr, adv) Inf. to collapse or fall asleep as through extreme exhaustion.

flake white n a pigment made from flakes of white lead.

flak jacket n a reinforced jacket for protection against gunfire or shrapnel worn by soldiers, policemen, etc.

flaky ('fleɪkɪ) adj **flakier, flakiest. 1** like or made of flakes. **2** tending to break easily into flakes. **3** Also spelt: **flakey.** US sl. eccentric; crazy.
▸ 'flakily adv ▸ 'flakiness n

flambé ('flɒːmbeɪ) adj **1** (of food, such as steak or pancakes) served in flaming brandy ◆ vb **flambés, flambéing, flambéed. 2** (tr) to serve (food) in such a manner. [F, p.p. of flamber to FLAME]

flambeau ('flæmbəʊ) n, pl **flambeaux** (-bəʊ, -bəʊz) or **flambeaus.** a burning torch, as used in night processions, etc. [C17: from OF: torch, lit.: a little flame, from flambe FLAME]

Flamborough Head ★ ('flæmbərə, -brə) n a chalk promontory in NE England, on the coast of the East Riding of Yorkshire.

flamboyant (flæm'bɔɪənt) adj **1** elaborate or extravagant; showy. **2** rich or brilliant in colour. **3** exuberant or ostentatious. **4** of the French Gothic style of architecture characterized by flamelike tracery and elaborate carving. [C19: from F: flaming, from flamboyer to FLAME]
▸ flam'boyance or flam'boyancy n ▸ flam'boyantly adv

flame (fleɪm) n **1** a hot usually luminous body of burning gas emanating in flickering streams from burning material or produced by a jet of ignited gas. **2** (often pl) the state or condition of burning with flames: to burst into flames. **3** a brilliant light. **4a** a strong reddish-orange colour. **4b** (as adj): a flame carpet. **5** intense passion or ardour. **6** Inf. a lover or sweetheart (esp. in **an old flame**). **7** Inf. an abusive message sent by electronic mail. ◆ vb **flames, flaming, flamed. 8** to burn or cause to burn brightly. **9** (intr) to become red or fiery: his face flamed with anger. **10** (intr) to become angry or excited. **11** (tr) to apply a flame to (something). **12** Inf. to send an abusive message by electronic mail. [C14: from Anglo-F, from OF flambe, from L flammula a little flame, from flamma flame]
▸ 'flame,like adj ▸ 'flamy adj

flame gun n a type of flame-thrower for destroying garden weeds, etc.

flamen ('fleɪmɛn) n, pl **flamens** or **flamines** ('flæmɪˌniːz). (in ancient Rome) any of 15 priests who each served a particular deity. [C14: from L; prob. rel. to OE blōtan to sacrifice, Gothic blotan to worship]

flamenco (flə'mɛŋkəʊ) n, pl **flamencos. 1** a type of dance music for vocal soloist and guitar, characterized by sad mood. **2** the dance performed to such music. [from Sp.: like a Gipsy, lit.: Fleming, from MDu. Vlaminc Fleming]

flameout ('fleɪm,aʊt) n the failure of an aircraft jet engine in flight due to extinction of the flame.

flame-thrower n a weapon that ejects a stream or spray of burning fluid.

flame tree n any of various tropical trees with red or orange flowers.

flaming ('fleɪmɪŋ) adj **1** burning with or emitting flames. **2** glowing brightly. **3** intense or ardent: a flaming temper. **4** Inf. (intensifier): you flaming idiot.

flamingo (flə'mɪŋgəʊ) n, pl **flamingos** or **flamingoes.** a large wading bird having a pink-and-red plumage and downward-bent bill and inhabiting brackish lakes. [C16:

from Port., from Provençal, from L *flamma* flame + Gmc suffix *-ing* denoting descent from; cf. *-ING*[3]]

Flaminian Way ★ (fləˈmɪnɪən) *n* an ancient road in Italy, extending north from Rome to Rimini: constructed in 220 B.C. by Gaius Flaminius. Length: over 322 km (200 miles). Latin name: **Via Flaminia**.

Flamininus ★ (ˌflæmɪˈnaɪnəs) *n* **Titus Quinctius** (ˈtaɪtəs ˈkwɪŋktɪəs). ?230-?174 B.C., Roman general and statesman: defeated Macedonia (197) and proclaimed the independence of the Greek states (196).

Flaminius ★ (fləˈmɪnɪəs) *n* **Gaius** (ˈgaɪəs). died 217 B.C., Roman statesman and general: built the Flaminian Way; defeated by Hannibal at Trasimene (217).

flammable (ˈflæməbəl) *adj* readily combustible; inflammable.
▸ ˌflammaˈbility *n*

> **USAGE NOTE** *Flammable* and *inflammable* are interchangeable when used of the properties of materials. *Flammable* is, however, often preferred for warning labels as there is less likelihood of misunderstanding (*inflammable* being sometimes taken to mean *not flammable*). *Inflammable* is preferred in figurative contexts: *this could prove to be an inflammable situation.*

Flamsteed ★ (ˈflæmˌstiːd) *n* **John**. 1646–1719, English astronomer: the first Astronomer Royal and first director of the Royal Observatory, Greenwich (1675).

flan (flæn) *n* **1** an open pastry or sponge tart filled with fruit or a savoury mixture. **2** a piece of metal ready to receive the die or stamp in the production of coins. [C19: from F, from OF *flaon*, from LL *fladō* flat cake, of Gmc origin]

Flanders ★ (ˈflɑːndəz) *n* a powerful medieval principality in the SW part of the Low Countries, now in the Belgian provinces of East and West Flanders, the Netherlands province of Zeeland, and the French department of the Nord; scene of battles in many wars.

flange (flændʒ) *n* **1** a radially projecting collar or rim on an object for strengthening it or for attaching it to another object. **2** a flat outer face of a rolled-steel joist. ◆ *vb* **flanges, flanging, flanged.** **3** (*tr*) to provide (a component) with a flange. [C17: prob. changed from earlier *flaunche* curved segment at side of a heraldic field, from F *flanc* FLANK]
▸ **flanged** *adj* ▸ ˈflangeless *adj*

flank (flæŋk) *n* **1** the side of a man or animal between the ribs and the hip. **2** a cut of beef from the flank. **3** the side of anything, such as a mountain or building. **4** the side of a naval or military formation. ◆ *vb* **5** (when *intr*, often foll. by *on* or *upon*) to be located at the side of (an object, etc.). **6** *Mil.* to position or guard on or beside the flank of (a formation, etc.). [C12: from OF *flanc*, of Gmc origin]

flanker (ˈflæŋkə) *n* **1** one of a detachment of soldiers detailed to guard the flanks. **2** a fortification used to protect a flank. **3** Also called: **flank forward.** *Rugby.* another name for **winger**.

flannel (ˈflænᵊl) *n* **1** a soft light woollen fabric with a slight nap, used for clothing, etc. **2** (*pl*) trousers or other garments made of flannel. **3** *Brit.* a small piece of cloth used to wash the face and hands; face flannel. US and Canad. equivalent: **washcloth.** **4** *Brit. inf.* indirect or evasive talk. ◆ *vb* **flannels, flannelling, flannelled** *or US* **flannels, flanneling, flanneled.** (*tr*) **5** to cover or wrap with flannel. **6** to rub or polish with flannel. **7** *Brit. inf.* to flatter. [C14: prob. var. of *flanen* sackcloth, from Welsh, from *gwlân* wool]
▸ ˈflannelly *adj*

flannelette (ˌflænᵊˈlɛt) *n* a cotton imitation of flannel.

flap (flæp) *vb* **flaps, flapping, flapped.** **1** to move (wings or arms) up and down, esp. in or as if in flying, or (of wings or arms) to move in this way. **2** to move or cause to move noisily back and forth or up and down: *the curtains flapped in the breeze.* **3** (*intr*) *Inf.* to become agitated or flustered. **4** to deal (a person or thing) a blow with a broad flexible object. ◆ *n* **5** the action, motion, or noise made

by flapping: *with one flap of its wings the bird was off.* **6** a piece of material, etc., attached at one edge and usually used to cover an opening, as on a tent, envelope, or pocket. **7** a blow dealt with a flat object. **8** a movable surface fixed to an aircraft wing that increases lift during takeoff and drag during landing. **9** *Inf.* a state of panic or agitation. [C14: prob. imit.]

flapdoodle (ˈflæpˌduːdᵊl) *n Sl.* foolish talk; nonsense. [C19: from ?]

flapjack (ˈflæpˌdʒæk) *n* **1** a chewy biscuit made with rolled oats. **2** *Chiefly US & Canad.* another word for **pancake**.

flapper (ˈflæpə) *n* (in the 1920s) a young woman, esp. one flaunting her unconventional behaviour.

flare (fleə) *vb* **flares, flaring, flared.** **1** to burn or cause to burn with an unsteady or sudden bright flame. **2** to burn off excess gas or oil. **3** to spread or cause to spread outwards from a narrow to a wider shape. ◆ *n* **4** an unsteady flame. **5** a sudden burst of flame. **6a** a blaze of light or fire used to illuminate, signal distress, alert, etc. **6b** the device producing such a blaze. **7** a spreading shape or anything with a spreading shape: *a skirt with a flare.* **8** an open flame used to burn off unwanted gas at an oil well. **9** *Astron.* short for **solar flare.** [C16: (to spread out): from ?]

flares (fleəz) *pl n Inf.* trousers with legs that widen below the knee.

flare-up *n* **1** a sudden burst of fire or light. **2** *Inf.* a sudden burst of emotion or violence. ◆ *vb* **flare up.** (*intr, adv*). **3** to burst suddenly into fire or light. **4** *Inf.* to burst into anger.

flash (flæʃ) *n* **1** a sudden short blaze of intense light or flame: *a flash of sunlight.* **2** a sudden occurrence or display, esp. one suggestive of brilliance: *a flash of understanding.* **3** a very brief space of time: *over in a flash.* **4** Also called: **newsflash.** a short news announcement concerning a new event. **5** Also called: **patch.** *Chiefly Brit.* an insignia or emblem worn on a uniform, vehicle, etc., to identify its military formation. **6** a sudden rush of water down a river or watercourse. **7** *Photog., inf.* short for **flashlight** (sense 2). **8** (*modifier*) involving, using, or produced by a flash of heat, light, etc.: *flash distillation.* **9** **flash in the pan.** a project, person, etc., that enjoys only short-lived success. ◆ *adj* **10** *Inf.* ostentatious or vulgar. **11** sham or counterfeit. **12** *Inf.* relating to or characteristic of the criminal underworld. **13** brief and rapid: *flash freezing.* ◆ *vb* **14** to burst or cause to burst suddenly or intermittently into flame. **15** to emit or reflect or cause to emit or reflect light suddenly or intermittently. **16** (*intr*) to move very fast: *he flashed by on his bicycle.* **17** (*intr*) to come rapidly (into the mind or vision). **18** (*intr*; foll. by *out* or *up*) to appear like a sudden light. **19a** to signal or communicate very fast: *to flash a message.* **19b** to signal by use of a light, such as car headlights. **20** (*tr*) *Inf.* to display ostentatiously: *to flash money around.* **21** (*tr*) *Inf.* to show suddenly and briefly. **22** (*intr*) *Brit. sl.* to expose oneself indecently. **23** to send a sudden rush of water down (a river, etc.), or to carry (a vessel) down by this method. [C14 (in the sense: to rush, as of water): from ?]
▸ ˈflasher *n*

flashback (ˈflæʃˌbæk) *n* a transition in a novel, film, etc., to an earlier scene or event.

flashboard (ˈflæʃˌbɔːd) *n* a board or boarding that is placed along the top of a dam to increase its height and capacity.

flashbulb (ˈflæʃˌbʌlb) *n Photog.* a small expendable glass light bulb formerly used to produce a bright flash of light.

flashbulb memory *n Psychol.* the clear recollections that a person may have of the circumstances associated with a dramatic event.

flash burn *n Pathol.* a burn caused by momentary exposure to intense radiant heat.

flash card *n* a card on which are written or printed words for children to look at briefly, used as an aid to learning.

flashcube (ˈflæʃˌkjuːb) *n* a boxlike camera attachment, holding four flashbulbs, that turns so that each flashbulb can be used.

flash flood *n* a sudden short-lived torrent, usually caused by a heavy storm, esp. in desert regions.

flashgun ('flæʃ,gʌn) *n* a type of electronic flash, attachable to or sometimes incorporated in a camera, that emits a very brief flash of light when the shutter is open.

flashing ('flæʃɪŋ) *n* a weatherproof material, esp. thin sheet metal, used to cover the valleys between the slopes of a roof, the junction between a chimney and a roof, etc.

flashlight ('flæʃ,laɪt) *n* **1** another word (esp. US and Canad.) for **torch**. **2** *Photog.* the brief bright light emitted by an electronic flash unit. Often shortened to **flash**.

flash point *n* **1** the lowest temperature at which the vapour above a liquid can be ignited in air. **2** a critical time or place beyond which a situation will inevitably erupt into violence.

flashy ('flæʃɪ) *adj* **flashier, flashiest. 1** brilliant and dazzling, esp. for a short time or in a superficial way. **2** cheap and ostentatious.
▶ 'flashily *adv* ▶ 'flashiness *n*

flask (flɑːsk) *n* **1** a bottle with a narrow neck, esp. used in a laboratory or for wine, oil, etc. **2** Also called: **hip flask.** a small flattened container of glass or metal designed to be carried in a pocket, esp. for liquor. **3** See **vacuum flask.** [C14: from OF, from Med. L *flasca, flasco,* ? of Gmc origin; cf. OE *flasce, flaxe*]

flat[1] (flæt) *adj* **flatter, flattest. 1** horizontal; level: *a flat roof.* **2** even or smooth, without projections or depressions: *a flat surface.* **3** lying stretched out at full length: *he lay flat on the ground.* **4** having little depth or thickness: *a flat dish.* **5** (*postpositive; often foll. by* *against*) having a surface or side in complete contact with another surface: *flat against the wall.* **6** (of a tyre) deflated. **7** (of shoes) having an unraised heel. **8** *Chiefly Brit.* **8a** (of races, racetracks, or racecourses) not having obstacles to be jumped. **8b** of, relating to, or connected with flat racing as opposed to steeplechasing and hurdling. **9** without qualification; total: *a flat denial.* **10** fixed: *a flat rate.* **11** (*prenominal or immediately postpositive*) neither more nor less; exact: *he did the journey in thirty minutes flat.* **12** unexciting: *a flat joke.* **13** without variation or resonance; monotonous: *a flat voice.* **14** (of beer, sparkling wines, etc.) having lost effervescence, as by exposure to air. **15** (of trade, business, etc.) commercially inactive. **16** (of a battery) fully discharged. **17** (of a print, photograph, or painting) lacking contrast. **18** (of paint) without gloss or lustre. **19** (of lighting) diffuse. **20** *Music.* **20a** (*immediately postpositive*) denoting a note of a given letter name (or the sound it represents) that has been lowered in pitch by one chromatic semitone: *B flat.* **20b** (of an instrument, voice, etc.) out of tune by being too low in pitch. Cf. **sharp** (sense 12). **21** *Phonetics.* **flat 21a** the vowel sound of *a* as in the usual US or S Brit. pronunciation of *hand, cat.* ◆ *adv* **22** in or into a prostrate, level, or flat state or position: *he held his hand out flat.* **23** completely or utterly; absolutely. **24** exactly; precisely: *in three minutes flat.* **25** *Music.* **25a** lower than a standard pitch. **25b** too low in pitch: *she sings flat.* Cf. **sharp** (sense 17). **26 fall flat (on one's face).** to fail to achieve a desired effect. **27 flat out.** *Inf.* **27a** with the maximum speed or effort. **27b** totally exhausted. ◆ *n* **28** a flat object, surface, or part. **29** (*often pl*) a low-lying tract of land, esp. a marsh or swamp. **30** (*often pl*) a mud bank exposed at low tide. **31** *Music.* **31a** an accidental that lowers the pitch of a note by one chromatic semitone. Usual symbol: ♭ **31b** a note affected by this accidental. Cf. **sharp** (sense 18). **32** *Theatre.* a wooden frame covered with painted canvas, etc., used to form part of a stage setting. **33** a punctured car tyre. **34** (*often cap.; preceded by the*) *Chiefly Brit.* **34a** flat racing, esp. as opposed to steeplechasing and hurdling. **34b** the season of flat racing. **35** *US & Canad.* a shallow box used for holding plants, etc. ◆ *vb* **flats, flatting, flatted. 36** to make or become flat. [C14: from ON *flatr*]
▶ 'flatly *adv* ▶ 'flatness *n* ▶ 'flattish *adj*

flat[2] (flæt) *n* a set of rooms comprising a residence entirely on one floor of a building. Usual US and Canad. name: **apartment.** [OE *flett* floor, hall, house]

flatbed lorry ('flæt,bɛd) *n* a lorry with a flat platform for its body.

flatbed scanner *n Computing.* a computer-controlled device that electronically scans images placed on its flat glass, to produce digitized images for use in desktop publishing, etc.

flatboat ('flæt,bəʊt) *n* any boat with a flat bottom, usually for transporting goods on a canal.

flatette (,flæt'ɛt) *n Austral.* a very small flat.

flatfish ('flæt,fɪʃ) *n, pl* **flatfish** *or* **flatfishes.** any of an order of marine spiny-finned fish including the halibut, plaice, turbot, and sole, all of which have a flat body which has both eyes on the uppermost side.

flatfoot ('flæt,fʊt) *n* **1** Also called: **splayfoot.** a condition in which the instep arch of the foot is flattened. **2** (*pl* **flatfoots** *or* **flatfeet**) a slang word (usually derogatory) for a policeman.

flat-footed (,flæt'fʊtɪd) *adj* **1** having flatfoot. **2** *Inf.* **2a** awkward. **2b** downright. **3** *Inf.* off guard (often in **catch flat-footed**).
▶ ,flat-'footedly *adv* ▶ ,flat-'footedness *n*

flathead ('flæt,hɛd) *n, pl* **flathead** *or* **flatheads.** a Pacific food fish which resembles the gurnard.

flatiron ('flæt,aɪən) *n* (formerly) an iron for pressing clothes that was heated by being placed on a stove, etc.

flatlet ('flætlɪt) *n* a flat having only a few rooms.

flatmate ('flæt,meɪt) *n* a person with whom one shares a flat.

flat racing *n* **a** the racing of horses on racecourses without jumps. **b** (*as modifier*): *the flat-racing season.*

flat spin *n* **1** an aircraft spin in which the longitudinal axis is more nearly horizontal than vertical. **2** *Inf.* a state of confusion; dither.

flat spot *n* **1** *Engineering.* a region of poor acceleration over a narrow range of throttle openings, caused by a weak mixture in the carburettor. **2** any narrow region of poor performance in a mechanical device.

flatten ('flæt²n) *vb* **1** (sometimes foll. by *out*) to make or become flat or flatter. **2** (*tr*) *Inf.* **2a** to knock down or injure. **2b** to crush or subdue. **3** (*tr*) *Music.* to lower the pitch of (a note) by one chromatic semitone.
▶ 'flattener *n*

flatter ('flætə) *vb* **1** to praise insincerely, esp. in order to win favour or reward. **2** to show to advantage: *that dress flatters her.* **3** (*tr*) to make to appear more attractive, etc., than in reality. **4** to gratify the vanity of (a person). **5** (*tr*) to encourage, esp. falsely. **6** (*tr*) to deceive (oneself): *I flatter myself that I am the best.* [C13: prob. from OF *flater* to lick, fawn upon, of Frankish origin]
▶ 'flatterable *adj* ▶ 'flatterer *n*

flattery ('flætərɪ) *n, pl* **flatteries. 1** the act of flattering. **2** excessive or insincere praise.

flattie ('flætɪ) *n NZ inf.* a flounder or other flatfish.

flatties ('flætɪz) *pl n* shoes with flat heels.

flat top *n* a style of haircut in which the hair is cut shortest on the top of the head so that it stands up from the scalp and appears flat from the crown to the forehead.

flatulent ('flætjʊlənt) *adj* **1** suffering from or caused by an excessive amount of gas in the alimentary canal. **2** generating excessive gas in the alimentary canal. **3** pretentious. [C16: from NL *flātulentus,* from L *flatus,* from *flāre* to breathe, blow]
▶ 'flatulence *or* 'flatulency *n* ▶ 'flatulently *adv*

flatus ('fleɪtəs) *n, pl* **flatuses.** gas generated in the alimentary canal. [C17: from L: a blowing, from *flāre* to breathe, blow]

flatworm ('flæt,wɜːm) *n* any parasitic or free-living invertebrate of the phylum *Platyhelminthes,* including flukes and tapeworms, having a flattened body.

Flaubert ★ ('fləʊbɛə; *French* floˈbɛr) *n* **Gustave** (gystav). 1821–80, French writer. His works include *Madame Bovary* (1857), for which he was prosecuted (and acquitted) on charges of immorality, *L'Éducation sentimentale* (1869), *La Tentation de Saint Antoine* (1874), and *Trois contes* (1877).

★ people and places

flaunt (flɔːnt) vb **1** to display (possessions, oneself, etc.) ostentatiously. **2** to wave or cause to wave freely. ◆ n **3** the act of flaunting. [C16: ? of Scand. origin]

> **USAGE NOTE** *Flaunt* is sometimes wrongly used where *flout* is meant: *they must be prevented from flouting* (not *flaunting*) *the law.*

flautist ('flɔːtɪst) or US & Canad. **flutist** ('fluːtɪst) n a player of the flute. [C19: from It. *flautista*, from *flauto* FLUTE]

flavescent (flə'vesənt) adj turning yellow; yellowish. [C19: from L *flāvēscere* to become yellow]

flavin or **flavine** ('fleɪvɪn) n **1** a heterocyclic ketone that forms the nucleus of certain natural yellow pigments, such as riboflavin. **2** any yellow pigment based on flavin. [C19: from L *flāvus* yellow]

flavine ('fleɪvɪn) n another name for **acriflavine hydrochloride.**

flavone ('fleɪvəʊn) n **1** a crystalline compound occurring in plants. **2** any of a class of yellow plant pigments derived from flavone. [C19: from G, from L *flāvus* yellow + -ONE]

flavoprotein (ˌfleɪvəʊ'prəʊtiːn) n any of a group of enzymes that contain a derivative of riboflavin linked to a protein and catalyse oxidation in cells.

flavour or US **flavor** ('fleɪvə) n **1** taste perceived in food or liquid in the mouth. **2** a substance added to food, etc., to impart a specific taste. **3** a distinctive quality or atmosphere. **4** *Physics.* a property of quarks that distinguishes different types. ◆ vb **5** (tr) to impart a flavour or quality to. [C14: from OF *flaour*, from LL *flātor* (unattested) bad smell, breath, from L *flāre* to blow]
▸ **'flavourless** or US **'flavorless** adj ▸ **'flavourful** or US **'flavorful** adj

flavour enhancer n another term for **monosodium glutamate.**

flavouring or US **flavoring** ('fleɪvərɪŋ) n a substance used to impart a particular flavour to food.

flaw[1] (flɔː) n **1** an imperfection or blemish. **2** a crack or rift. **3** *Law.* an invalidating defect in a document or proceeding. ◆ vb **4** to make or become blemished or imperfect. [C14: prob. from ON *flaga* stone slab]
▸ **'flawless** adj

flaw[2] (flɔː) n a sudden short gust of wind; squall. [C16: of Scand. origin]

flax (flæks) n **1** a herbaceous plant or shrub that has blue flowers and is cultivated for its seeds (flaxseed) and for the fibres of its stems. **2** the fibre of this plant, made into thread and woven into linen fabrics. **3** any of various similar plants. **4** *NZ.* a swamp plant producing a fibre that is used by Maoris for clothing, baskets, etc. [OE *fleax*]

flaxen ('flæksən) adj **1** of or resembling flax. **2** of a soft yellow colour: *flaxen hair.*

Flaxman ★ ('flæksmən) n **John.** 1755–1826, British neoclassical sculptor and draughtsman, noted for his monuments and his illustrations for the *Iliad* and the *Odyssey.*

flaxseed ('flæksˌsiːd) n the seed of the flax plant, which yields linseed oil. Also called: **linseed.**

flay (fleɪ) vb (tr) **1** to strip off the skin or covering of, esp. by whipping. **2** to attack with savage criticism. [OE *flēan*]
▸ **'flayer** n

flea (fliː) n **1** a small wingless parasitic blood-sucking jumping insect living on the skin of mammals and birds. **2 flea in one's ear.** *Inf.* a sharp rebuke. [OE *flēah*]

fleabane ('fliːˌbeɪn) n any of several plants, including one having purplish tubular flower heads with orange centres and one having yellow daisy-like flower heads, that are reputed to ward off fleas.

fleabite ('fliːˌbaɪt) n **1** the bite of a flea. **2** a slight or trifling annoyance or discomfort.

flea-bitten adj **1** bitten by or infested with fleas. **2** *Inf.* shabby or decrepit.

flea market n an open-air market selling cheap and often second-hand goods.

fleapit ('fliːˌpɪt) n *Inf.* a shabby cinema or theatre.

fleawort ('fliːˌwɜːt) n **1** any of various plants with yellow daisy-like flowers and rosettes of downy leaves. **2** a Eurasian plantain whose seeds were formerly used as a flea repellent.

flèche (fleɪʃ, fleʃ) n a slender spire, esp. over the intersection of the nave and transept ridges of a church roof. Also called: **spirelet.** [C18: from F: spire (lit.: arrow), prob. of Gmc origin]

fleck (flek) n **1** a small marking or streak. **2** a speck: *a fleck of dust.* ◆ vb **3** (tr) Also: **flecker.** to speckle. [C16: prob. from ON *flekkr* stain, spot]

Flecker ★ ('flekə) n **James Elroy.** 1884–1915, British poet and dramatist; author of *Hassan* (1922).

fled (fled) vb the past tense and past participle of **flee.**

fledge (fledʒ) vb **fledges, fledging, fledged.** (tr) **1** to feed and care for (a young bird) until it is able to fly. **2** Also called: **fletch.** to fit (something, esp. an arrow) with a feather or feathers. **3** to cover or adorn with or as if with feathers. [OE -*flycge*, as in *unflycge* unfledged; see FLY[1]]

fledgling or **fledgeling** ('fledʒlɪŋ) n **1** a young bird that has grown feathers. **2** a young and inexperienced person.

flee (fliː) vb **flees, fleeing, fled. 1** to run away from (a place, danger, etc.). **2** (intr) to run or move quickly. [OE *flēon*]
▸ **'fleer** n

fleece (fliːs) n **1** the coat of wool that covers the body of a sheep or similar animal. **2** the wool removed from a single sheep. **3** something resembling a fleece. **4** sheepskin or a fabric with soft pile, used as a lining for coats, etc. ◆ vb **fleeces, fleecing, fleeced.** (tr) **5** to defraud or charge exorbitantly. **6** another term for **shear** (sense 1). [OE *flēos*]

fleecie ('fliːsɪ) n *NZ.* a person who collects fleeces after shearing and prepares them for baling. Also called: **fleece-oh.**

fleecy ('fliːsɪ) adj **fleecier, fleeciest.** of or resembling fleece.
▸ **'fleecily** adv

fleer (flɪə) *Arch.* ◆ vb **1** to scoff; sneer. ◆ n **2** a derisory glance. [C14: from ON; cf. Norwegian *flire* to snigger]

fleet[1] (fliːt) n **1** a number of warships organized as a tactical unit. **2** all the warships of a nation. **3** a number of aircraft, ships, buses, etc., operating together or under the same ownership. [OE *flēot*]

fleet[2] (fliːt) adj **1** rapid in movement; swift. **2** *Poetic.* fleeting. ◆ vb **3** (intr) to move rapidly. **4** (tr) *Obs.* to cause (time) to pass rapidly. [prob. OE *flēotan* to float, glide rapidly]
▸ **'fleetly** adv ▸ **'fleetness** n

Fleet ★ (fliːt) n **the. 1** a stream that formerly ran into the Thames between Ludgate Hill and Fleet Street and is now a covered sewer. **2** Also called: **Fleet Prison.** a former London prison, used esp. for holding debtors.

Fleet Air Arm n the aviation branch of the Royal Navy.

fleet chief petty officer n a noncommissioned officer in the Royal Navy comparable in rank to a warrant officer in the army or the Royal Air Force.

fleeting ('fliːtɪŋ) adj rapid and transient: *a fleeting glimpse of the sea.*
▸ **'fleetingly** adv

fleet rate or **rating** n a reduced rate quoted by an insurance company to underwrite the risks to a fleet of vehicles, aircraft, etc.

Fleet Street ★ n **1** a street in central London in which many newspaper offices were formerly situated. **2** British journalism or journalists collectively.

Fleetwood ★ ('fliːtˌwʊd) n a fishing port in NW England, in Lancashire. Pop.: 27 227 (1991).

Flémalle ★ (French flemal) n **Master of.** See (Robert) **Campin.**

Fleming[1] ('flemɪŋ) n a native or inhabitant of Flanders or of Flemish-speaking Belgium.

Fleming[2] ★ ('flemɪŋ) n **1** Sir **Alexander.** 1881–1955, Scottish bacteriologist: discovered lysozyme (1922) and penicillin (1928): shared the Nobel prize for physiology or medicine in 1945. **2 Ian (Lancaster).** 1908–64, British au-

★ people and places

thor of spy novels; creator of the agent James Bond. **3 Sir John Ambrose.** 1849–1945, British electrical engineer: invented the thermionic valve (1904).

Flemish ('flɛmɪʃ) *n* **1** one of the two official languages of Belgium. **2 the Flemish.** (*functioning as pl*) the Flemings collectively. ◆ *adj* **3** of or characteristic of Flanders, the Flemings, or their language.

Flemish Brabant ★ *n* a province of central Belgium, formed in 1995 from the N part of Brabant province. Pop.: 995 266 (1995 est.). Area: 2106 sq. km (813 sq. miles).

Flensburg ★ (*German* 'flɛnsburk) *n* a port in N Germany, in Schleswig-Holstein: taken from Denmark by Prussia in 1864; voted to remain German in 1920. Pop.: 87 240 (1991).

flense (flɛns), **flench** (flɛntʃ), *or* **flinch** (flɪntʃ) *vb* **flenses, flensing, flensed** *or* **flenches, flenching, flenched** *or* **flinches, flinching, flinched.** (*tr*) to strip (a whale, seal, etc.) of (its blubber or skin). [C19: from Danish *flense*; rel. to Du. *flensen*]

flesh (flɛʃ) *n* **1** the soft part of the body of an animal or human, esp. muscular tissue, as distinct from bone and viscera. **2** *Inf.* excess weight; fat. **3** *Arch.* the edible tissue of animals as opposed to that of fish or, sometimes, fowl. **4** the thick soft part of a fruit or vegetable. **5** the human body and its physical or sensual nature as opposed to the soul or spirit. Related adj: **carnal. 6** mankind in general. **7** animate creatures in general. **8** one's own family; kin (esp. in **one's own flesh and blood**). **9a** a yellowish-pink colour. **9b** (*as adj*): *flesh tights.* **10 in the flesh.** in person; actually present. **11 press the flesh.** *Inf.* to shake hands, usually with large numbers of people, esp. as a political campaigning ploy. ◆ *vb* **12** (*tr*) *Hunting.* to stimulate the hunting instinct of (hounds or falcons) by giving them small quantities of raw flesh. **13** *Arch. or poetic.* to accustom or incite to bloodshed or battle by initial experience. **14** to fatten; fill out. [OE *flǣsc*]

fleshings ('flɛʃɪŋz) *pl n* flesh-coloured tights.

fleshly ('flɛʃlɪ) *adj* **fleshlier, fleshliest. 1** relating to the body; carnal: *fleshly desire.* **2** worldly as opposed to spiritual. **3** fat.
▶ **'fleshliness** *n*

flesh out *vb* (*adv*) **1** (*tr*) to give substance to (an argument, description, etc.). **2** (*intr*) to expand or become more substantial.

fleshpots ('flɛʃ,pɒts) *pl n Often facetious.* **1** luxurious living. **2** places where bodily desires are gratified. [C16: from the Biblical use as applied to Egypt (Exodus 16:3)]

flesh wound (wuːnd) *n* a wound affecting superficial tissues.

fleshy ('flɛʃɪ) *adj* **fleshier, fleshiest. 1** plump. **2** related to or resembling flesh. **3** *Bot.* (of some fruits, etc.) thick and pulpy.
▶ **'fleshiness** *n*

fletcher ('flɛtʃə) *n* a person who makes arrows. [C14: from OF *flechier*, from *fleche* arrow; see FLÈCHE]

Fletcher ★ ('flɛtʃə) *n* **John.** 1579–1625, English Jacobean dramatist, noted for his romantic tragicomedies written in collaboration with Francis Beaumont, esp. *Philaster* (1610) and *The Maid's Tragedy* (1611).

fleur-de-lys *or* **fleur-de-lis** (,flɜːdə'liː) *n, pl* **fleurs-de-lys** *or* **fleurs-de-lis** (,flɜːdə'liːz). **1** *Heraldry.* a charge representing a lily with three distinct petals. **2** another name for **iris** (sense 2). [C19: from OF *flor de lis*, lit.: lily flower]

fleurette *or* **fleuret** (fluə'rɛt) *n* an ornament or motif resembling a flower. [C19: F, lit.: a small flower, from *fleur* flower]

Fleury ★ (*French* flœri) *n* **André Hercule de** (ɑ̃dre ɛrkyl də). 1653–1743, French cardinal and statesman: Louis XV's chief adviser and virtual ruler of France (1726–43).

flew (fluː) *vb* the past tense of **fly**[1].

flews (fluːz) *pl n* the fleshy hanging upper lip of a bloodhound or similar dog. [C16: from ?]

flex (flɛks) *n* **1** *Brit.* a flexible insulated electric cable, used esp. to connect appliances to mains. US and Canad. name: **cord.** ◆ *vb* **2** to bend or be bent: *he flexed his arm.* **3** to contract (a muscle) or (of a muscle) to contract. **4** (*intr*)

to work flexitime. [C16: from L *flexus* bent, winding, from *flectere* to bend, bow]

flexible ('flɛksɪbˀl) *adj* **1** Also **flexile** ('flɛksaɪl). able to be bent easily without breaking. **2** adaptable or variable: *flexible working hours.* **3** able to be persuaded easily.
▶ ,flexi'bility *n* ▶ 'flexibly *adv*

flexion ('flɛkʃən) *or* **flection** *n* **1** the act of bending a joint or limb. **2** the condition of the joint or limb so bent.
▶ 'flexional *adj*

flexitime ('flɛksɪ,taɪm) *n* a system permitting flexibility of working hours at the beginning or end of the day, provided an agreed period (**core time**) is spent at work. Also called: **flextime.**

flexor ('flɛksə) *n* any muscle whose contraction serves to bend a joint or limb. Cf. **extensor.** [C17: NL; see FLEX]

flexuous ('flɛksjuəs) *adj* full of bends or curves; winding. [C17: from L *flexuōsus* full of bends, tortuous, from *flexus* a bending; see FLEX]
▶ 'flexuously *adv*

flexure ('flɛksə) *n* **1** the act of flexing or the state of being flexed. **2** a bend, turn, or fold.

flex-wing *n Aeronautics.* a collapsible fabric delta wing, as used with hang-gliders.

flibbertigibbet ('flɪbətɪ,dʒɪbɪt) *n* an irresponsible, silly, or gossipy person. [C15: from ?]

flick[1] (flɪk) *vb* **1** (*tr*) to touch with or as if with the finger or hand in a quick jerky movement. **2** (*tr*) to propel or remove by a quick jerky movement, usually of the fingers or hand. **3** to move or cause to move quickly or jerkily. **4** (*intr*; foll. by *through*) to read or look at (a book, etc.) quickly or idly. ◆ *n* **5** a tap or quick stroke with the fingers, a whip, etc. **6** the sound made by such a stroke. **7** a flick or particle. **8 give** (**someone**) **the flick.** to dismiss (someone) from consideration. [C15: imit.; cf. F *flicflac*]

flick[2] (flɪk) *n Sl.* **1** a cinema film. **2 the flicks.** the cinema: *what's on at the flicks tonight?*

flicker[1] ('flɪkə) *vb* **1** (*intr*) to shine with an unsteady or intermittent light. **2** (*intr*) to move quickly to and fro. **3** (*tr*) to cause to flicker. ◆ *n* **4** an unsteady or brief light or flame. **5** a swift quivering or fluttering movement. [OE *flicorian*]

flicker[2] ('flɪkə) *n* a North American woodpecker which has a yellow undersurface to the wings and tail. [C19: ? imit. of the bird's call]

flick knife *n* a knife with a retractable blade that springs out when a button is pressed.

flier ('flaɪə) *n* a variant spelling of **flyer.**

flight[1] (flaɪt) *n* **1** the act, skill, or manner of flying. **2** a journey made by a flying animal or object. **3** a group of flying birds or aircraft: *a flight of swallows.* **4** the basic tactical unit of a military air force. **5** a journey through space, esp. of a spacecraft. **6** an aircraft flying on a scheduled journey. **7** a soaring mental journey above or beyond the normal everyday world: *a flight of fancy.* **8** a single line of hurdles across a track in a race. **9** a feather or plastic attachment fitted to an arrow or dart to give it stability in flight. **10** a set of steps or stairs between one landing or floor and the next. ◆ *vb* (*tr*) **11** *Sport.* to cause (a ball, dart, etc.) to float slowly towards its target. **12** to shoot (a bird) in flight. **13** to fledge (an arrow or dart). [OE *flyht*]

flight[2] (flaɪt) *n* **1** the act of fleeing or running away, as from danger. **2 put to flight.** to cause to run away. **3 take** (**to**) **flight.** to run away; flee. [OE *flyht* (unattested)]

flight attendant *n* a person who attends to the needs of passengers on a commercial flight.

flight deck *n* **1** the crew compartment in an airliner. **2** the upper deck of an aircraft carrier from which aircraft take off.

flightless ('flaɪtlɪs) *adj* (of certain birds and insects) unable to fly. See also **ratite.**

flight lieutenant *n* an officer holding a commissioned rank senior to a flying officer and junior to a squadron leader in the Royal Air Force.

flight path *n* the course through the air of an aircraft, rocket, or projectile.

flight recorder *n* an electronic device fitted to an aircraft for collecting and storing information concerning its performance in flight. It is often used to determine the cause of a crash. Also called: **black box.**

flight sergeant *n* a noncommissioned officer in the Royal Air Force, junior in rank to that of master aircrew.

flight simulator *n* a ground-training device that reproduces exactly the conditions experienced on the flight deck of an aircraft.

flighty ('flaɪtɪ) *adj* **flightier, flightiest. 1** frivolous and irresponsible. **2** mentally erratic or wandering.
▶ 'flightiness *n*

flimflam ('flɪm,flæm) *Inf.* ◆ *n* **1a** nonsense; rubbish; foolishness. **1b** (*as modifier*): *flimflam arguments.* **2** a deception; trick; swindle. ◆ *vb* **flimflams, flimflamming, flimflammed. 3** (*tr*) to deceive; trick; swindle; cheat. [C16: prob. of Scand. origin]
▶ 'flim,flammer *n*

flimsy ('flɪmzɪ) *adj* **flimsier, flimsiest. 1** not strong or substantial: *a flimsy building.* **2** light and thin: *a flimsy dress.* **3** unconvincing; weak: *a flimsy excuse.* ◆ *n* **4** thin paper used for making carbon copies of a letter, etc. **5** a copy made on such paper. [C17: from ?]
▶ 'flimsiness *n*

flinch (flɪntʃ) *vb* (*intr*) **1** to draw back suddenly, as from pain, shock, etc.; wince. **2** (often foll. by *from*) to avoid contact (with): *he never flinched from his duty.* [C16: from OF *flenchir*; rel. to MHG *lenken* to bend, direct]
▶ 'flinchingly *adv*

flinders ('flɪndəz) *pl n Rare.* small fragments or splinters (esp. in **fly into flinders**). [C15: prob. from ON; cf. Norwegian *flindra* thin piece of stone]

Flinders Island ★ ('flɪndəz) *n* an island off the coast of NE Tasmania: the largest of the Furneaux Islands. Pop.: 1100 (latest est.). Area: 2077 sq. km (802 sq. miles).

Flinders Range ★ *n* a mountain range in E South Australia, between Lake Torrens and Lake Frome. Highest peak: 1188 m (3898 ft).

fling (flɪŋ) *vb* **flings, flinging, flung.** (*mainly tr*) **1** to throw, esp. with force or abandon. **2** to put or send without warning or preparation: *to fling someone into jail.* **3** (*also intr*) to move (oneself or a part of the body) with abandon or speed. **4** (usually foll. by *into*) to apply (oneself) diligently and with vigour (to). **5** to cast aside: *she flung away her scruples.* ◆ *n* **6** the act or an instance of flinging. **7** a period or occasion of unrestrained or extravagant behaviour. **8** any of various vigorous Scottish reels full of leaps and turns, such as the Highland fling. **9** a trial; try: *to have a fling at something different.* [C13: from ON]
▶ 'flinger *n*

flint (flɪnt) *n* **1** an impure greyish-black form of quartz that occurs in chalk. It produces sparks when struck with steel and is used in the manufacture of pottery and road-construction materials. Formula: SiO_2. **2** any piece of flint, esp. one used as a primitive tool or for striking fire. **3** a small cylindrical piece of an iron alloy, used in cigarette lighters. **4** Also called: **flint glass.** colourless glass other than plate glass. [OE]

Flint ★ (flɪnt) *n* **1** a town in NE Wales, in Flintshire, on the Dee estuary. Pop.: 11 737 (1991). **2** a city in SE Michigan. Pop.: 138 164 (1994 est.).

flintlock ('flɪnt,lɒk) *n* **1** an obsolete gunlock in which the charge is ignited by a spark produced by a flint in the hammer. **2** a firearm having such a lock.

Flintshire ★ ('flɪnt,ʃɪə, -ʃə) *n* a county of NE Wales: became part of Clwyd in 1974, reinstated with new borders in 1996. Administrative centre: Mold. Pop.: 145 000 (1996 est.). Area: 437 sq. km (169 sq. miles).

flinty ('flɪntɪ) *adj* **flintier, flintiest. 1** of or resembling flint. **2** hard or cruel; unyielding.
▶ 'flintily *adv* ▶ 'flintiness *n*

flip (flɪp) *vb* **flips, flipping, flipped. 1** to throw (something light or small) carelessly or briskly. **2** to throw or flick (an object such as a coin) so that it turns or spins in the air. **3** to flick: *to flip a crumb across the room.* **4** (foll. by *through*) to read or look at (a book, etc.) quickly, idly, or incompletely. **5** (*intr*) to make a snapping movement or noise with the finger and thumb. **6** (*intr*) *Sl.* to fly into a rage or

an emotional outburst (also in **flip one's lid, flip one's top, flip out**). ◆ *n* **7** a snap or tap, usually with the fingers. **8** a rapid jerk. **9** any alcoholic drink containing beaten egg. ◆ *adj* **10** *Inf.* flippant or pert. [C16: prob. imit.; see FILLIP]

flip chart *n* a pad, containing large sheets of paper that can be easily turned over, mounted on a stand and used to present reports, data, etc.

flip-flop *n* **1** a backward handspring. **2** Also called: **bistable.** an electronic device or circuit that can assume either of two states by the application of a suitable pulse. **3** a complete change of opinion, policy, etc. **4** a repeated flapping noise. **5** Also called (esp. US, Austral., NZ, and Canad.): **thong** or (S. Afr.) **slip-slop.** a rubber-soled sandal attached to the foot by a thong between the big toe and the next toe. ◆ *vb* **flip-flops, flip-flopping, flip-flopped. 6** (*intr*) to move with repeated flaps. [C16: reduplication of FLIP]

flippant ('flɪpənt) *adj* **1** marked by inappropriate levity; frivolous. **2** impertinent; saucy. [C17: ?from FLIP]
▶ 'flippancy *n* ▶ 'flippantly *adv*

flipper ('flɪpə) *n* **1** the flat broad limb of seals, whales, etc., specialized for swimming. **2** (*often pl*) either of a pair of rubber paddle-like devices worn on the feet as an aid in swimming.

flip side *n* **1** another term for **B-side. 2** another, less familiar, aspect of a person or thing.

flirt (flɜːt) *vb* **1** (*intr*) to behave or act amorously without emotional commitment. **2** (*intr*; usually foll. by *with*) to deal playfully or carelessly (with something dangerous or serious): *the motorcyclist flirted with death.* **3** (*intr*; usually foll. by *with*) to toy (with): *to flirt with the idea of leaving.* **4** (*intr*) to dart; flit. **5** (*tr*) to flick or toss. ◆ *n* **6** a person who acts flirtatiously. [C16: from ?]
▶ 'flirter *n* ▶ 'flirty *adj*

flirtation (flɜː'teɪʃən) *n* **1** behaviour intended to arouse sexual feelings or advances without emotional commitment. **2** any casual involvement.

flirtatious (flɜː'teɪʃəs) *adj* **1** given to flirtation. **2** expressive of playful sexual invitation: *a flirtatious glance.*
▶ flir'tatiously *adv*

flit (flɪt) *vb* **flits, flitting, flitted.** (*intr*) **1** to move along rapidly and lightly. **2** to fly rapidly and lightly. **3** to pass quickly: *a memory flitted into his mind.* **4** *Scot. & N English dialect.* to move house. **5** *Brit. inf.* to depart hurriedly and stealthily in order to avoid obligations. ◆ *n* **6** the act or an instance of flitting. **7** *Brit. inf.* a hurried and stealthy departure in order to avoid obligations. [C12: from ON *flytja* to carry]
▶ 'flitter *n*

flitch (flɪtʃ) *n* **1** a side of pork salted and cured. **2** a piece of timber cut lengthways from a tree trunk. [OE *flicce*; cf. FLESH]

flitter ('flɪtə) *vb* a less common word for **flutter.**

flittermouse ('flɪtə,maʊs) *n, pl* **flittermice.** a dialect name for **bat²** (sense 1). [C16: translation of G *Fledermaus*]

float (fləʊt) *vb* **1** to rest or cause to rest on the surface of a fluid or in a fluid or space without sinking: *oil floats on water.* **2** to move or cause to move buoyantly, lightly, or freely across a surface or through air, water, etc. **3** to move about aimlessly, esp. in the mind: *thoughts floated before him.* **4** (*tr*) **4a** to launch or establish (a commercial enterprise, etc.). **4b** to offer for sale (stock or bond issues, etc.) on the stock market. **5** (*tr*) *Finance.* to allow (a currency) to fluctuate against other currencies in accordance with market forces. **6** (*tr*) to flood, inundate, or irrigate (land). ◆ *n* **7** something that floats. **8** *Angling.* an indicator attached to a baited line that sits on the water and moves when a fish bites. **9** a small hand tool with a rectangular blade used for smoothing plaster, etc. **10** Also called: **paddle.** a blade of a paddle wheel. **11** *Brit.* a buoyant garment or device to aid a person in staying afloat. **12** a structure fitted to the underside of an aircraft to allow it to land on water. **13** a motor vehicle used to carry a tableau or exhibit in a parade, esp. a civic parade. **14** a small delivery vehicle, esp. one powered by batteries: *a milk float.* **15** *Austral. & NZ.* a vehicle for transporting horses. **16** a sum of money used by shopkeepers to

provide change at the start of the day's business. **17** the hollow floating ball of a ballcock. [OE *flotian;* see FLEET[2]]
▶ **'floatable** *adj* ▶ **floata'bility** *n* ▶ **'floaty** *adj*

floatage ('fləʊtɪdʒ) *n* a variant spelling of **flotage**.

floatation (fləʊ'teɪʃən) *n* a variant spelling of **flotation**.

floatel (fləʊ'tɛl) *n* a variant spelling of **flotel**.

floater ('fləʊtə) *n* **1** a person or thing that floats. **2** a dark spot that appears in one's vision as a result of dead cells or cell fragments in the eye. **3** *US & Canad.* a person of no fixed political opinion. **4** *US inf.* a person who often changes employment, residence, etc.

float glass *n* polished glass made by floating molten glass on liquid metal in a reservoir.

floating ('fləʊtɪŋ) *adj* **1** having little or no attachment. **2** (of an organ or part) displaced from the normal position or abnormally movable: *a floating kidney.* **3** uncommitted or unfixed: *floating voters.* **4a** *Finance.* **4a** (of capital) available for current use. **4b** (of debt) short-term and unfunded, usually raised to meet current expenses. **4c** (of a currency) free to fluctuate against other currencies in accordance with market forces.
▶ **'floatingly** *adv*

floating-point representation *n Computing.* the representation of numbers by two sets of digits (*a, b*), the set *a* indicating the significant digits, the set *b* giving the position of the radix point. Also called: **floating decimal point representation.** Cf. **fixed-point representation.**

floating rib *n* any rib of the lower two pairs of ribs in man, which are not attached to the breastbone.

floats (fləʊts) *pl n Theatre.* another word for **footlights**.

flob (flɒb) *vb* **flobs, flobbing, flobbed.** (*intr*) *Brit. sl.* to spit. [C20: from?]

flocculate ('flɒkjʊˌleɪt) *vb* **flocculates, flocculating, flocculated.** to form or be formed into an aggregated flocculent mass.
▶ **floccu'lation** *n*

flocculent ('flɒkjʊlənt) *adj* **1** like wool; fleecy. **2** *Chem.* aggregated in woolly cloudlike masses: *a flocculent precipitate.* **3** *Biol.* covered with tufts or flakes. [C19: from L *floccus* FLOCK[2] +-ULENT]
▶ **'flocculence** *n*

flocculus ('flɒkjʊləs) *n, pl* **flocculi** (-ˌlaɪ). **1** Also called: **plage.** a cloudy marking on the sun's surface. It consists of calcium when lighter than the surroundings and of hydrogen when darker. **2** *Anat.* a tiny prominence on each side of the cerebellum.

flock[1] (flɒk) *n* (*sometimes functioning as pl*) **1** a group of animals of one kind, esp. sheep or birds. **2** a large number of people. **3** a body of Christians regarded as the pastoral charge of a priest, bishop, etc. ◆ *vb* (*intr*) **4** to gather together or move in a flock. **5** to go in large numbers: *people flocked to the church.* [OE *flocc*]

flock[2] (flɒk) *n* **1** a tuft, as of wool, hair, cotton, etc. **2** waste from fabrics such as cotton or wool used for stuffing mattresses, etc. **3** Also called: **flocking.** very small tufts of wool applied to fabrics, wallpaper, etc., to give a raised pattern. [C13: from OF *floc,* from L *floccus*]
▶ **'flocky** *adj*

Flodden ★ ('flɒdən) *n* a hill in Northumberland where invading Scots were defeated by the English in 1513 and James IV of Scotland was killed. Also called: **Flodden Field.**

floe (fləʊ) *n* See **ice floe**. [C19: prob. from Norwegian *flo* slab, layer, from ON; see FLAW[1]]

flog (flɒg) *vb* **flogs, flogging, flogged. 1** (*tr*) to beat harshly, esp. with a whip, strap, etc. **2** *Brit. sl.* to sell. **3** (*intr*) to make progress by painful work. **4 flog a dead horse.** *Chiefly Brit.* **4a** to harp on some long discarded subject. **4b** to pursue the solution of a problem long realized to be insoluble. [C17: prob. from L *flagellāre;* see FLAGELLANT]
▶ **'flogger** *n*

flong (flɒŋ) *n Printing.* a material used for making moulds in stereotyping. [C20: var. of FLAN]

flood (flʌd) *n* **1a** the inundation of land that is normally dry through the overflowing of a body of water, esp. a river. **1b** the state of a river that is at an abnormally high level. Related adj: **diluvial. 2** a great outpouring or flow: *a flood of words.* **3a** the rising of the tide from low to high

water. **3b** (*as modifier*): *the flood tide.* Cf. **ebb** (sense 3). **4** *Theatre.* short for **floodlight.** ◆ *vb* **5** (of water) to inundate or submerge (land) or (of land) to be inundated or submerged. **6** to fill or be filled to overflowing, as with a flood. **7** (*intr*) to flow; surge: *relief flooded through him.* **8** to supply an excessive quantity of petrol to (a carburettor or petrol engine) or (of a carburettor, etc.) to be supplied with such an excess. **9** (*intr*) to overflow. **10** (*intr*) to bleed profusely from the uterus, as following childbirth. [OE *flōd;* see FLOW, FLOAT]

Flood (flʌd) *n Old Testament.* **the.** the flood from which Noah and his family and livestock were saved in the ark (Genesis 7–8).

floodgate ('flʌdˌgeɪt) *n* **1** Also called: **head gate, water gate.** a gate in a sluice that is used to control the flow of water. **2** (*often pl*) a control or barrier against an outpouring or flow.

flooding ('flʌdɪŋ) *n* **1** *Psychol.* a method of eliminating anxiety in a given situation, by exposing a person to the situation until the anxiety subsides. **2** *Pathol.* excessive bleeding from the uterus.

floodlight ('flʌdˌlaɪt) *n* **1** a broad intense beam of artificial light, many of which are used in the theatre or to illuminate the exterior of buildings. **2** the lamp producing such light. ◆ *vb* **floodlights, floodlighting, floodlit. 3** (*tr*) to illuminate as by floodlight.

flood plain *n* the flat area bordering a river, composed of sediment deposited during flooding.

floor (flɔː) *n* **1** Also called: **flooring.** the inner lower surface of a room. **2** a storey of a building: *the second floor.* **3** a flat bottom surface in or on any structure: *a dance floor.* **4** the bottom surface of a tunnel, cave, sea, etc. **5** that part of a legislative hall in which debate and other business is conducted. **6** the right to speak in a legislative body (esp. in **get, have,** or **be given the floor**). **7** the room in a stock exchange where trading takes place. **8** the earth; ground. **9** a minimum price charged or paid. **10 take the floor.** to begin dancing on a dance floor. ◆ *vb* **11** to cover with or construct a floor. **12** (*tr*) to knock to the floor or ground. **13** (*tr*) *Inf.* to disconcert, confound, or defeat. [OE *flōr*]

floorboard ('flɔːˌbɔːd) *n* one of the boards forming a floor.

flooring ('flɔːrɪŋ) *n* **1** the material used in making a floor. **2** another word for **floor** (sense 1).

floor manager *n* **1** the stage manager of a television programme. **2** a person in overall charge of one floor of a large shop.

floor plan *n* a drawing to scale of the arrangement of rooms on one floor of a building.

floor show *n* a series of entertainments, such as singing and dancing, performed in a nightclub.

floozy, floozie, *or* **floosie** ('fluːzɪ) *n, pl* **floozies** *or* **floosies.** *Sl.* a disreputable woman. [C20: from ?]

flop (flɒp) *vb* **flops, flopping, flopped. 1** (*intr*) to bend, fall, or collapse loosely or carelessly: *his head flopped backwards.* **2** (when *intr,* often foll. by *into, onto,* etc.) to fall, cause to fall, or move with a sudden noise. **3** (*intr*) *Inf.* to fail: *the scheme flopped.* **4** (*intr*) to fall flat onto the surface of water. **5** (*intr;* often foll. by *out*) *Sl.* to go to sleep. ◆ *n* **6** the act of flopping. **7** *Inf.* a complete failure. [C17: var. of FLAP]

floppy ('flɒpɪ) *adj* **floppier, floppiest. 1** limp or hanging loosely. ◆ *n, pl* **floppies. 2** short for **floppy disk.**
▶ **'floppily** *adv* ▶ **'floppiness** *n*

floppy disk *n* a flexible magnetic disk that stores information and can be used to store data in the memory of a digital computer.

flops *abbrev.* (*sometimes caps.*) for floating-point operations per second: a measure of computer processing power.

flora ('flɔːrə) *n, pl* **floras** *or* **florae** (-riː). **1** all the plant life of a given place or time. **2** a descriptive list of such plants, often including a key for identification. [C18: from NL, from FLORA]

Flora ★ ('flɔːrə) *n* the Roman goddess of flowers. [C16: from L, from *flōs* flower]

floral ('flɔːrəl) *adj* **1** decorated with or consisting of flowers or patterns of flowers. **2** of or associated with flowers.
▶ **'florally** *adv*

Florence ★ ('florəns) *n* a city in central Italy, on the River Arno in Tuscany: became an independent republic in the 14th century; under Austrian and other rule intermittently from 1737 to 1859; capital of Italy 1865–70. It was the major cultural and artistic centre of the Renaissance and is still one of the world's chief art centres. Pop.: 392 800 (1994 est.). Ancient name: **Florentia** (flɒˈrɛntsɪə, -ˈrɛntɪə). Italian name: **Firenze.**

Florentine ('florən,taɪn) *adj* **1** of or relating to Florence, in Italy. ◆ *n* **2** a native or inhabitant of Florence.

Flores ★ ('flɔːres) *n* **1** an island in Indonesia, one of the Lesser Sunda Islands, between the Flores Sea and the Savu Sea: mountainous, with active volcanoes and unexplored forests. Chief town: Ende. Area: 17 150 sq. km (6622 sq. miles). **2** (*also Portuguese* 'florɪʃ). an island in the Atlantic, the westernmost of the Azores. Chief town: Santa Cruz. Area: 142 sq. km (55 sq. miles).

florescence (flɔːˈrɛsəns) *n* the process, state, or period of flowering. [C18: from NL, from L *flōrēscere* to come into flower]

Flores Sea ★ *n* a part of the Pacific Ocean in Indonesia between Celebes and the Lesser Sunda Islands.

floret ('flɔːrɪt) *n* a small flower, esp. one of many making up the head of a composite flower. [C17: from OF, from *flor* FLOWER]

Florey ★ ('flɔːrɪ) *n* **Howard Walter,** Baron Florey. 1898–1968, British pathologist: shared the Nobel prize for physiology or medicine (1945) for work on penicillin.

Florianópolis ★ (*Portuguese* florɪəˈnɔpulis) *n* a port in S Brazil, capital of Santa Caterina state, on the W coast of Santa Caterina Island. Pop.: 191 664 (1991).

floriated *or* **floreated** ('flɔːrɪ,eɪtɪd) *adj* Archit. having ornamentation based on flowers and leaves. [C19: from L *flōs* FLOWER]

floribunda (,flɔːrɪˈbʌndə) *n* any of several varieties of cultivated hybrid roses whose flowers grow in large sprays. [C19: from NL, fem of *flōribundus* flowering freely]

floriculture ('flɔːrɪ,kʌltʃə) *n* the cultivation of flowering plants.
▶ ,**flori'cultural** *adj* ▶ ,**flori'culturist** *n*

florid ('florɪd) *adj* **1** having a red or flushed complexion. **2** excessively ornate; flowery: *florid architecture.* [C17: from L *flōridus* blooming]
▶ **flo'ridity** *n* ▶ **'floridly** *adv*

Florida ★ ('florɪdə) *n* **1** a state of the southeastern US, between the Atlantic and the Gulf of Mexico: consists mostly of a low-lying peninsula ending in the Florida **Keys,** a chain of small islands off the coast of S Florida, extending southwest for over 160 km (100 miles). Capital: Tallahassee. Pop.: 14 399 985 (1996 est.). Area: 143 900 sq. km (55 560 sq. miles). Abbrevs.: **Fla.** or (with zip code) **FL 2 Straits of.** a sea passage between the Florida Keys and Cuba, linking the Atlantic with the Gulf of Mexico.
▶ **Flo'ridian** *adj*

floriferous (flɔːˈrɪfərəs) *adj* bearing or capable of bearing many flowers.

florin ('florɪn) *n* **1** a former British coin, originally silver, equivalent to ten (new) pence. **2** (formerly) another name for **guilder** (sense 1). [C14: from F, from OIt. *fiorino* Florentine coin, from *fiore* flower, from L *flōs*]

florist ('florɪst) *n* a person who grows or deals in flowers.

floristic (flɒˈrɪstɪk) *adj* of or relating to flowers or a flora.
▶ **flo'ristically** *adv*

-florous *adj combining form.* indicating number or type of flowers: *tubuliflorous.*

floruit *Latin.* ('flɔːruːɪt) *vb* (he or she) flourished: used to indicate the period when a figure, whose birth and death dates are unknown, was most active.

floss (flɒs) *n* **1** the mass of fine silky fibres obtained from cotton and similar plants. **2** any fine similar silky material. **3** untwisted silk thread used in embroidery, etc. **4** See **dental floss.** ◆ *vb* **5** (*tr*) to clean (between one's teeth) with dental floss. [C18: ?from OF *flosche* down]

flossy ('flɒsɪ) *adj* **flossier, flossiest.** consisting of or resembling floss.

flotage *or* **floatage** ('fləʊtɪdʒ) *n* **1** the act or state of floating. **2** power or ability to float. **3** flotsam.

flotation *or* **floatation** (fləʊˈteɪʃən) *n* **1a** the launching or financing of a commercial enterprise by bond or share issues. **1b** the raising of a loan or new capital by bond or share issues. **2** power or ability to float. **3** Also called: **froth flotation.** a process to concentrate the valuable ore in low-grade ores by using induced differences in surface tension to carry the valuable fraction to the surface.

flotel *or* **floatel** ('fləʊtɛl) *n* a rig used for accommodation of workers in off-shore oil fields. [C20: FLO(ATING) + (HO)TEL]

flotilla (flə'tɪlə) *n* a small fleet or a fleet of small vessels. [C18: from Sp., from F *flotte*, ult. from ON *floti*]

flotsam ('flɒtsəm) *n* **1** wreckage from a ship found floating. Cf. **jetsam. 2** odds and ends (esp. in **flotsam and jetsam**). **3** vagrants. [C16: from Anglo-F *floteson*, from *floter* to FLOAT]

flounce[1] (flaʊns) *vb* **flounces, flouncing, flounced. 1** (*intr*, often foll. by *about, away, out,* etc.) to move or go with emphatic movements. ◆ *n* **2** the act of flouncing. [C16: of Scand. origin]

flounce[2] (flaʊns) *n* an ornamental gathered ruffle sewn to a garment by its top edge. [C18: from OF, from *froncir* to wrinkle, of Gmc origin]

flounder[1] ('flaʊndə) *vb* (*intr*) **1** to move with difficulty, in mud. **2** to make mistakes. ◆ *n* **3** the act of floundering. [C16: prob. a blend of FOUNDER[2] + BLUNDER; ? infl. by FLOUNDER[2]]

> **USAGE NOTE** *Flounder* is sometimes wrongly used where *founder* is meant: *the project foundered (not floundered) because of lack of funds.*

flounder[2] ('flaʊndə) *n, pl* **flounder** *or* **flounders.** a European flatfish having a greyish-brown body covered with prickly scales: an important food fish. [C14: from ON]

flour ('flaʊə) *n* **1** a powder, which may be either fine or coarse, prepared by grinding the meal of a grass, esp. wheat. **2** any finely powdered substance. ◆ *vb* (*tr*) **3** to make (grain, etc.) into flour. **4** to dredge or sprinkle (food or utensils) with flour. [C13 *flur* finer portion of meal, FLOWER]
▶ **'floury** *adj*

flourish ('flʌrɪʃ) *vb* **1** (*intr*) to thrive; prosper. **2** (*intr*) to be at the peak of condition. **3** (*intr*) to be healthy: *plants flourish in the light.* **4** to wave or cause to wave in the air with sweeping strokes. **5** to display or make a display. **6** to play (a fanfare, etc.) on a musical instrument. ◆ *n* **7** the act of waving or brandishing. **8** a showy gesture: *he entered with a flourish.* **9** an ornamental embellishment in writing. **10** a display of ornamental language or speech. **11** a grandiose passage of music. [C13: from OF, ult. from L *flōrēre* to flower, from *flōs* a flower]
▶ **'flourisher** *n*

flout (flaʊt) *vb* (when *intr*, usually foll. by *at*) to show contempt (for). [C16: ?from ME *flouten* to play the flute, from OF *flauter*]
▶ **'floutingly** *adv*

> **USAGE NOTE** See at **flaunt.**

flow (fləʊ) *vb* (*mainly intr*) **1** (of liquids) to move or be conveyed as in a stream. **2** (of blood) to circulate around the body. **3** to move or progress freely as if in a stream: *the crowd flowed into the building.* **4** to be produced continuously and effortlessly: *ideas flowed from her pen.* **5** to be marked by smooth or easy movement. **6** to hang freely or loosely: *her hair flowed down her back.* **7** to be present in abundance: *wine flows at their parties.* **8** (of tide water) to advance or rise. Cf. **ebb** (sense 1). **9** (of rocks such as slate) to yield to pressure so that the structure and arrangement of the constituent minerals are altered. ◆ *n* **10** the act, rate, or manner of flowing: *a fast flow.* **11** a continuous stream or discharge. **12** continuous progression. **13** the advancing of the tide. **14** *Scot.* **14a** a marsh or swamp. **14b** an inlet or basin of the sea. **14c** (*cap. when part of a name*): *Scapa Flow.* [OE *flōwan*]

flow chart *or* **sheet** *n* a diagrammatic representation of the sequence of operations in an industrial process, computer program, etc.

Flow Country ★ *n* an area of moorland and peat bogs in northern Scotland known for its wildlife, now partly afforested.

flower ('flaʊə) *n* **1a** a bloom or blossom on a plant. **1b** a plant that bears blooms or blossoms. **2** the reproductive structure of angiosperm plants, consisting of stamens and carpels surrounded by petals and sepals. In some plants it is brightly coloured and attracts insects for pollination. Related adj: **floral. 3** any similar reproductive structure in other plants. **4** the prime; peak: *in the flower of his youth.* **5** the choice or finest product, part, or representative. **6** a decoration or embellishment. **7** (*pl*) fine powder, usually produced by sublimation: *flowers of sulphur.* ◆ *vb* **8** (*intr*) to produce flowers; bloom. **9** (*intr*) to reach full growth or maturity. **10** (*tr*) to deck or decorate with flowers or floral designs. [C13: from OF *flor*, from L *flōs*]
▸ **'flowerless** *adj* ▸ **'flower-,like** *adj*

flowered ('flaʊəd) *adj* **1** having flowers. **2** decorated with flowers or a floral design.

floweret ('flaʊərɪt) *n* another name for **floret.**

flower girl *n* a girl or woman who sells flowers in the street.

flowering ('flaʊərɪŋ) *adj* (of certain species of plants) capable of producing conspicuous flowers.

flowerpot ('flaʊə,pɒt) *n* a pot in which plants are grown.

flower power *n Inf.* a youth cult of the late 1960s advocating peace and love; associated with drug-taking. Its adherents were known as **flower children** or **flower people.**

flowery ('flaʊərɪ) *adj* **1** abounding in flowers. **2** decorated with flowers or floral patterns. **3** like or suggestive of flowers. **4** (of language or style) elaborate.
▸ **'floweriness** *n*

flown (fləʊn) *vb* the past participle of **fly**[1].

flow-on *n Austral. & NZ.* **a** a wage or salary increase granted to one group of workers as a consequence of a similar increase granted to another group. **b** (*as modifier*): *a flow-on effect.*

fl. oz. *abbrev. for* fluid ounce.

flu (fluː) *n Inf.* **1** (often preceded by *the*) short for **influenza. 2** any of various viral infections, esp. a respiratory or intestinal infection.

fluctuate ('flʌktjʊ,eɪt) *vb* fluctuates, fluctuating, fluctuated. **1** to change or cause to change position constantly. **2** (*intr*) to rise and fall like a wave. [C17: from L, from *fluctus* a wave, from *fluere* to flow]
▸ **'fluctuant** *adj* ▸ **,fluctu'ation** *n*

flue (fluː) *n* a shaft, tube, or pipe, esp. as used in a chimney, to carry off smoke, gas, etc. [C16: from ?]

fluent ('fluːənt) *adj* **1** able to speak or write a specified foreign language with facility. **2** spoken or written with facility. **3** graceful in motion or shape. **4** flowing or able to flow freely. [C16: from L: flowing, from *fluere* to flow]
▸ **'fluency** *n* ▸ **'fluently** *adv*

flue pipe *or* **flue** *n* an organ pipe whose sound is produced by the passage of air across a fissure in the side, as distinguished from a **reed pipe.**

fluff (flʌf) *n* **1** soft light particles, such as the down or nap of cotton or wool. **2** any light downy substance. **3** *Inf.* a mistake, esp. in speaking or reading lines or performing music. **4** *Inf.* a young woman (esp. in **a bit of fluff**). ◆ *vb* **5** to make or become soft and puffy. **6** *Inf.* to make a mistake in performing (an action, music, etc.). [C18: ?from *flue* downy matter]

fluffy ('flʌfɪ) *adj* fluffier, fluffiest. **1** of, resembling, or covered with fluff. **2** soft and light.
▸ **'fluffily** *adv* ▸ **'fluffiness** *n*

flugelhorn ('fluːg⁰l,hɔːn) *n* a type of valved brass instrument consisting of a tube of conical bore with a cup-shaped mouthpiece, used esp. in brass bands. [G, from *Flügel* wing + *Horn* HORN]

fluid ('fluːɪd) *n* **1** a substance, such as a liquid or gas, that can flow, has no fixed shape, and offers little resistance to an external stress. ◆ *adj* **2** capable of flowing and easily changing shape. **3** of or using a fluid or fluids. **4** constantly changing or apt to change. **5** flowing. [C15: from L, from *fluere* to flow]
▸ **'fluidal** *adj* ▸ **flu'idity** *or* **'fluidness** *n*

fluidics (fluː'ɪdɪks) *n* (*functioning as sing*) the study and use of systems in which the flow of fluids in tubes simulates the flow of electricity in conductors.
▸ **flu'idic** *adj*

fluidize *or* **fluidise** ('fluːɪ,daɪz) *vb* fluidizes, fluidizing, fluidized *or* fluidises, fluidising, fluidised. (*tr*) to make fluid, esp. to make (solids) fluid by pulverizing them so that they can be transported in gas as if they were liquids.
▸ **,fluidi'zation** *or* **,fluidi'sation** *n*

fluid mechanics *n* (*functioning as sing*) the study of the mechanical and flow properties of fluids, esp. as they apply to practical engineering. Also called: **hydraulics.**

fluid ounce *n* **1** *Brit.* a unit of capacity equal to one twentieth of an Imperial pint. **2** *US.* a unit of capacity equal to one sixteenth of a US pint.

fluke[1] (fluːk) *n* **1** a flat bladelike projection at the end of the arm of an anchor. **2** either of the two lobes of the tail of a whale. **3** the barb of a harpoon, arrow, etc. [C16: ? a special use of FLUKE[3] (in the sense: a flounder)]

fluke[2] (fluːk) *n* **1** an accidental stroke of luck. **2** any chance happening. ◆ *vb* flukes, fluking, fluked. **3** (*tr*) to gain, make, or hit by a fluke. [C19: from ?]

fluke[3] (fluːk) *n* any parasitic flatworm, such as the blood fluke and liver fluke. [OE *flōc*; rel. to ON *flōki* flounder]

fluky *or* **flukey** ('fluːkɪ) *adj* flukier, flukiest. *Inf.* **1** done or gained by an accident, esp. a lucky one. **2** variable; uncertain.
▸ **'flukiness** *n*

flume (fluːm) *n* **1** a ravine through which a stream flows. **2** a narrow artificial channel made for providing water for power, floating logs, etc. **3** a slide in the form of a long and winding tube with a stream of water running through it that descends into a purpose-built pool. ◆ *vb* flumes, fluming, flumed. **4** (*tr*) to transport (logs) in a flume. [C12: from OF, ult. from L *flūmen* stream, from *fluere* to flow]

flummery ('flʌmərɪ) *n, pl* flummeries. **1** *Inf.* meaningless flattery. **2** *Chiefly Brit.* a cold pudding of oatmeal, etc. [C17: from Welsh *llymru*]

flummox ('flʌməks) *vb* (*tr*) to perplex or bewilder. [C19: from ?]

flung (flʌŋ) *vb* the past tense and past participle of **fling.**

flunk (flʌŋk) *vb Inf., US, Canad., & NZ.* **1** to fail or cause to fail to reach the required standard in (an examination, course, etc.). **2** (*intr*; foll. by *out*) to be dismissed from a school. [C19: ?from FLINCH + FUNK[1]]

flunky *or* **flunkey** ('flʌŋkɪ) *n, pl* flunkies *or* flunkeys. **1** a servile person. **2** a person who performs menial tasks. **3** *Usually derog.* a manservant in livery. [C18: from ?]

fluor ('fluːɔː) *n* another name for **fluorspar.** [C17: from L: a flowing; so called from its use as a metallurgical flux]

fluor- *combining form.* a variant of **fluoro-** before a vowel: *fluorine.*

fluoresce (,flʊə'rɛs) *vb* fluoresces, fluorescing, fluoresced. (*intr*) to exhibit fluorescence. [C19: back formation from FLUORESCENCE]

fluorescence (,flʊə'rɛsəns) *n* **1** *Physics.* **1a** the emission of light or other radiation from atoms or molecules that are bombarded by particles, such as electrons, or by radiation from a separate source. **1b** such an emission of photons that ceases as soon as the bombarding radiation is discontinued. **2** the radiation emitted as a result

of fluorescence. Cf. **phosphorescence**. [C19: FLUOR + -*escence* (as in *opalescence*)]
▸ ˌfluoˈrescent *adj*

fluorescent lamp *n* a type of lamp in which ultraviolet radiation from an electrical gas discharge causes a thin layer of phosphor on a tube's inside surface to fluoresce.

fluoridate ('fluərɪˌdeɪt) *vb* **fluoridates, fluoridating, fluoridated.** to subject (water) to fluoridation.

fluoridation (ˌfluərɪ'deɪʃən) *n* the addition of fluorides to the public water supply as a protection against tooth decay.

fluoride ('fluəˌraɪd) *n* **1** any salt of hydrofluoric acid, containing the fluoride ion, F⁻. **2** any compound containing fluorine, such as methyl fluoride.

fluorinate ('fluərɪˌneɪt) *vb* **fluorinates, fluorinating, fluorinated.** to treat or combine with fluorine.
▸ ˌfluoriˈnation *n*

fluorine ('fluəriːn) *n* a toxic pungent pale yellow gas of the halogen group that is the most electronegative and reactive of all the elements: used in the production of uranium, fluorocarbons, and other chemicals. Symbol: F; atomic no.: 9; atomic wt.: 18.998.

fluorite ('fluəraɪt) *n* the US and Canad. name for **fluorspar**.

fluoro- *or before a vowel* **fluor-** *combining form.* **1** indicating the presence of fluorine: *fluorocarbon.* **2** indicating fluorescence: *fluoroscope.*

fluorocarbon (ˌfluərəʊ'kɑːbˀn) *n* any compound derived by replacing all or some of the hydrogen atoms in hydrocarbons by fluorine atoms. Many of these are used as lubricants, solvents, coatings, and aerosol propellants. See also **Freon, CFC**.

fluorometer (ˌfluə'rɒmɪtə) *or* **fluorimeter** (ˌfluə-'rɪmɪtə) *n* a device for detecting and measuring ultraviolet radiation by determining the amount of fluorescence that it produces from a phosphor.

fluoroscope ('fluərəˌskəʊp) *n* a device consisting of a fluorescent screen and an X-ray source that enables an X-ray image of an object, person, or part to be observed directly.

fluoroscopy (fluə'rɒskəpɪ) *n* examination of a person or object by means of a fluoroscope.

fluorosis (fluə'rəʊsɪs) *n* fluoride poisoning, due to ingestion of too much fluoride.

fluorspar ('fluəˌspɑː), **fluor,** *or US & Canad.* **fluorite** *n* a white or colourless soft mineral, sometimes fluorescent or tinted by impurities, consisting of calcium fluoride (CaF) in crystalline form: the chief ore of fluorine.

flurry ('flʌrɪ) *n, pl* **flurries. 1** a sudden commotion. **2** a light gust of wind or rain or fall of snow. ◆ *vb* **flurries, flurrying, flurried. 3** to confuse or bewilder or be confused or bewildered. [C17: from obs. *flurr* to scatter, ? formed on analogy with HURRY]

flush¹ (flʌʃ) *vb* **1** to blush or cause to blush. **2** to flow or flood or cause to flow or flood with or as if with water. **3** to glow or shine or cause to glow or shine with a rosy colour. **4** to send a volume of water quickly through (a pipe, etc.) or into (a toilet) for the purpose of cleansing, etc. **5** (*tr; usually passive*) to excite or elate. ◆ *n* **6** a rosy colour, esp. in the cheeks. **7** a sudden flow or gush, as of water. **8** a feeling of excitement or elation: *the flush of success.* **9** freshness: *the flush of youth.* **10** redness of the skin, as from the effects of a fever, alcohol, etc. [C16: (in the sense: to gush forth): ?from FLUSH³]
▸ 'flusher *n*

flush² (flʌʃ) *adj* (*usually postpositive*) **1** level or even with another surface. **2** directly adjacent; continuous. **3** *Inf.* having plenty of money. **4** *Inf.* abundant or plentiful, as money. **5** full to the brim. ◆ *adv* **6** so as to be level or even. **7** directly or squarely. ◆ *vb* (*tr*) **8** to cause (surfaces) to be on the same level or in the same plane. ◆ *n* **9** a period of fresh growth of leaves, shoots, etc. [C18: prob. from FLUSH¹ (in the sense: spring out)]
▸ 'flushness *n*

flush³ (flʌʃ) *vb* (*tr*) to rouse (game, etc.) and put to flight. [C13 *flusshen,* ? imit.]

flush⁴ (flʌʃ) *n* (in poker and similar games) a hand containing only one suit. [C16: from OF, from L *fluxus* FLUX]

Flushing ★ ('flʌʃɪŋ) *n* a port in the SW Netherlands, in Zeeland province, on Walcheren Island, at the mouth of the West Scheldt river: the first Dutch city to throw off Spanish rule (1572). Pop.: 43 947 (1989). Dutch name **Vlissingen.**

fluster ('flʌstə) *vb* **1** to make or become nervous or upset. ◆ *n* **2** a state of confusion or agitation. [C15: from ON]

flute (fluːt) *n* **1** a wind instrument consisting of an open cylindrical tube of wood or metal having holes in the side stopped either by the fingers or by pads controlled by keys. The breath is directed across a mouth hole cut in the side. **2** *Archit.* a rounded shallow concave groove on the shaft of a column, pilaster, etc. **3** a tall narrow wineglass. ◆ *vb* **flutes, fluting, fluted. 4** to produce or utter (sounds) in the manner or tone of a flute. **5** (*tr*) to make grooves or furrows in. [C14: from OF *flahute,* from Vulgar L *flabeolum* (unattested); ? also infl. by OF *laut* lute]
▸ 'flute,like *adj* ▸ 'fluty *adj*

fluting ('fluːtɪŋ) *n* a design or decoration of flutes on a column, pilaster, etc.

flutist ('fluːtɪst) *n Now chiefly US & Canad.* a variant spelling of **flautist**.

flutter ('flʌtə) *vb* **1** to wave or cause to wave rapidly. **2** (*intr*) (of birds, butterflies, etc.) to flap the wings. **3** (*intr*) to move, esp. downwards, with an irregular motion. **4** (*intr*) *Pathol.* (of the heart) to beat abnormally rapidly, esp. in a regular rhythm. **5** to be or make nervous or restless. **6** (*intr*) to move about restlessly. ◆ *n* **7** a quick flapping or vibrating motion. **8** a state of nervous excitement or confusion. **9** excited interest; stir. **10** *Brit. inf.* a modest bet or wager. **11** *Pathol.* an abnormally rapid beating of the heart, esp. in a regular rhythm. **12** *Electronics.* a slow variation in pitch in a sound-reproducing system, similar to wow but occurring at higher frequencies. **13** a potentially dangerous oscillation of an aircraft, or part of an aircraft. **14** Also called: **flutter tonguing.** *Music.* a method of sounding a wind instrument, esp. the flute, with a rolling movement of the tongue. [OE *floterian* to float to and fro]
▸ 'flutterer *n* ▸ 'fluttery *adj*

fluvial ('fluːvɪəl) *adj* of or occurring in a river: *fluvial deposits.* [C14: from L, from *fluvius* river, from *fluere* to flow]

flux (flʌks) *n* **1** a flow or discharge. **2** continuous change; instability. **3** a substance, such as borax or salt, that gives a low melting-point mixture with a metal oxide to assist in fusion. **4** *Metallurgy.* a chemical used to increase the fluidity of refining slags. **5** *Physics.* **5a** the rate of flow of particles, energy, or a fluid, such as that of neutrons (**neutron flux**) or of light energy (**luminous flux**). **5b** the strength of a field in a given area: *magnetic flux.* **6** *Pathol.* an excessive discharge of fluid from the body, such as watery faeces in diarrhoea. ◆ *vb* **7** to make or become fluid. **8** (*tr*) to apply flux to (a metal, soldered joint, etc.). [C14: from L *fluxus* a flow, from *fluere* to flow]

flux density *n Physics.* the amount of flux per unit of cross-sectional area.

fluxion ('flʌkʃən) *n Maths., obs.* the rate of change of a function, especially the instantaneous velocity of a moving body; derivative. [C16: from LL *fluxiō* a flowing]

fly¹ (flaɪ) *vb* **flies, flying, flew, flown. 1** (*intr*) (of birds, aircraft, etc.) to move through the air in a controlled manner using aerodynamic forces. **2** to travel over (an area of land or sea) in an aircraft. **3** to operate (an aircraft or spacecraft). **4** to float, flutter, or be displayed in the air or cause to float, etc., in this way: *they flew the flag.* **5** to transport or be transported by or through the air by aircraft, wind, etc. **6** (*intr*) to move or be moved very quickly, or suddenly: *the door flew open.* **7** (*intr*) to pass swiftly: *time flies.* **8** to escape from (an enemy, place, etc.); flee. **9** (*intr*; may be foll. by *at* or *upon*) to attack a person. **10 fly a kite. 10a** to procure money by an accommodation bill. **10b** to release information or take a step in order to test public opinion. **11 fly high.** *Inf.* **11a** to have a high aim. **11b** to prosper or flourish. **12 let fly.** *Inf.* **12a** to lose one's temper (with a person): *she really let fly at him.* **12b** to shoot or throw (an object). ◆ *n, pl* **flies. 13** (*often*

★ people and places

pl) Also called: **fly front**. a closure that conceals a zip, buttons, or other fastening, by having one side overlapping, as on trousers. **14** Also called: **fly sheet**. **14a** a flap forming the entrance to a tent. **14b** a piece of canvas drawn over the ridgepole of a tent to form an outer roof. **15** short for **flywheel**. **16a** the outer edge of a flag. **16b** the distance from the outer edge of a flag to the staff. **17** *Brit.* a light one-horse covered carriage formerly let out on hire. **18** (*pl*) *Theatre*. the space above the stage out of view of the audience, used for storing scenery, etc. **19** *Rare*. the act of flying. [OE *flēogan*]
▶ **ˈflyable** *adj*

fly² (flaɪ) *n, pl* **flies**. **1** any dipterous insect, esp. the housefly, characterized by active flight. **2** any of various similar but unrelated insects, such as the caddis fly, firefly, and dragonfly. **3** *Angling*. a lure made from a fish-hook dressed with feathers, tinsel, etc., to resemble any of various flies or nymphs: used in fly-fishing. **4 fly in the ointment**. *Inf.* a slight flaw that detracts from value or enjoyment. **5 fly on the wall**. **5a** a person who watches others, while not being noticed himself. **5b** (*as modifier*): *a fly-on-the-wall documentary*. **6 there are no flies on him, her**, etc. *Inf.* he, she, etc., is no fool. [OE *flēoge*]
▶ **ˈflyless** *adj*

fly³ (flaɪ) *adj Sl., chiefly Brit.* knowing and sharp; smart. [C19: from ?]

fly agaric *n* a woodland fungus having a scarlet cap with white warts and white gills: poisonous but rarely fatal. [so named from its use as a poison on flypaper]

fly ash *n* fine solid particles of ash carried into the air during combustion.

flyaway (ˈflaɪəˌweɪ) *adj* **1** (of hair or clothing) loose and fluttering. **2** frivolous or flighty; giddy.

flyblow (ˈflaɪˌbləʊ) *vb* **flyblows, flyblowing, flyblew, flyblown**. **1** (*tr*) to contaminate, esp. with the eggs or larvae of the blowfly; taint. ◆ *n* **2** (*usually pl*) the eggs or young larva of a blowfly.

flyblown (ˈflaɪˌbləʊn) *adj* **1** covered with flyblows. **2** contaminated; tainted.

flybook (ˈflaɪˌbʊk) *n* a small case or wallet used by anglers for storing artificial flies.

flyby (ˈflaɪˌbaɪ) *n, pl* **flybys**. a flight past a particular position or target, esp. the close approach of a spacecraft to a planet or satellite.

fly-by-night *Inf.* ◆ *adj* **1** unreliable or untrustworthy, esp. in finance. ◆ *n* **2** an untrustworthy person, esp. one who departs secretly or by night to avoid paying debts.

flycatcher (ˈflaɪˌkætʃə) *n* **1** a small insectivorous songbird of the Old World having a small slender bill fringed with bristles. **2** an American passerine bird.

fly-drive *adj, adv* describing a type of package-deal holiday in which the price includes outward and return flights and car hire while away.

flyer *or* **flier** (ˈflaɪə) *n* **1** a person or thing that flies or moves very fast. **2** an aviator or pilot. **3** *Inf.* a large flying leap. **4** a rectangular stair in a straight flight of stairs. Cf. **winder** (sense 5). **5** *Athletics inf.* a flying start. **6** *Chiefly US.* a speculative business transaction. **7** a small handbill.

fly-fish *vb* (*intr*) *Angling*. to fish using artificial flies as lures.
▶ **ˈfly-ˌfishing** *n*

fly half *n Rugby*. another name for **stand-off half**.

flying (ˈflaɪɪŋ) *adj* **1** (*prenominal*) hurried; fleeting: *a flying visit*. **2** (*prenominal*) designed for fast action. **3** (*prenominal*) moving or passing quickly on or as if on wings: *flying hours*. **4** hanging, waving, or floating freely: *flying hair*. ◆ *n* **5** the act of piloting, navigating, or travelling in an aircraft. **6** (*modifier*) relating to, accustomed to, or adapted for flight: *a flying machine*.

flying boat *n* a seaplane in which the fuselage consists of a hull that provides buoyancy.

flying bridge *n* an auxiliary bridge of a vessel.

flying buttress *n* a buttress supporting a wall or other structure by an arch that transmits the thrust outwards and downwards.

flying colours *pl n* conspicuous success; triumph: *he passed his test with flying colours*.

flying doctor *n* (in areas of sparse or scattered population) a doctor who visits patients by aircraft.

flying fish *n* a fish common in warm and tropical seas, having enlarged winglike pectoral fins used for gliding above the surface of the water.

flying fox *n* **1** any large fruit bat of tropical Africa and Asia. **2** *Austral. & NZ.* a cable mechanism used for transportation across a river, gorge, etc.

flying gurnard *n* a marine spiny-finned gurnard-like fish having enlarged fan-shaped pectoral fins used to glide above the surface of the sea.

flying jib *n* the jib set furthest forward or outboard on a vessel with two or more jibs.

flying lemur *n* either of the two arboreal mammals of S and SE Asia that resemble lemurs but have a fold of skin between the limbs enabling movement by gliding leaps.

flying officer *n* an officer holding commissioned rank senior to a pilot officer but junior to a flight lieutenant in the British and certain other air forces.

flying phalanger *n* a nocturnal arboreal phalanger of E Australia and New Guinea, moving with gliding leaps using folds of skin between the hind limbs and forelimbs.

flying picket *n* (in industrial disputes) a member of a group of pickets organized to be able to move quickly from place to place.

flying saucer *n* any unidentified disc-shaped flying object alleged to come from outer space.

flying squad *n* a small group of police, soldiers, etc., ready to move into action quickly.

flying squirrel *n* a nocturnal rodent of Asia and North America, related to the squirrel. Furry folds of skin between the forelegs and hind legs enable these animals to move by gliding leaps.

flying start *n* **1** (in sprinting) a start by a competitor anticipating the starting signal. **2** a start to a race in which the competitor is already travelling at speed as he passes the starting line. **3** any promising beginning. **4** an initial advantage.

flying wing *n* **1** an aircraft consisting mainly of one large wing or tailplane and no fuselage. **2** (in Canadian football) the twelfth player, who has a variable position behind the scrimmage line.

flyleaf (ˈflaɪˌliːf) *n, pl* **flyleaves**. the inner leaf of the endpaper of a book, pasted to the first leaf.

Flynn ★ (flɪn) *n* **1** Errol. 1909–59, Australian actor, who was noted for his swashbuckling roles; his films included *Captain Blood* (1935), *The Adventures of Robin Hood* (1938), and *Too Much Too Soon* (1958). **2** Rev. **John.** 1880–1951, founder of the Australian flying doctor service.

flyover (ˈflaɪˌəʊvə) *n* **1** *Brit.* an intersection of two roads at which one is carried over the other by a bridge. **2** the US name for **fly-past**.

flypaper (ˈflaɪˌpeɪpə) *n* paper with a sticky and poisonous coating, usually hung from the ceiling to trap flies.

fly-past *n* a ceremonial flight of aircraft over a given area.

flyposting (ˈflaɪˌpəʊstɪŋ) *n* the posting of advertising or political posters, etc., in unauthorized places.

flyscreen (ˈflaɪˌskriːn) *n* a wire-mesh screen over a window to prevent flies entering a room.

fly sheet *n* **1** another term for **fly¹** (sense 14). **2** a short handbill.

flyspeck (ˈflaɪˌspɛk) *n* **1** the small speck of the excrement of a fly. **2** a small spot or speck. ◆ *vb* **3** (*tr*) to mark with flyspecks.

fly spray *n* a liquid used to destroy flies and other insects, sprayed from an aerosol.

fly-tipping *n* the deliberate dumping of rubbish in an unauthorized place.

flytrap (ˈflaɪˌtræp) *n* **1** any of various insectivorous plants. **2** a device for catching flies.

fly way *n* the usual route used by birds when migrating.

flyweight (ˈflaɪˌweɪt) *n* **1a** a professional boxer weighing not more than 112 pounds (51 kg). **1b** an amateur boxer weighing 48–51 kg (106–112 pounds). **2** an amateur wrestler weighing 107–115 pounds (49–52 kg).

flywheel ('flaɪˌwiːl) *n* a heavy wheel that stores kinetic energy and smooths the operation of a reciprocating engine by maintaining a constant speed of rotation over the whole cycle.

fm *abbrev. for:* **1** fathom. **2** from.

Fm *the chemical symbol for* fermium.

FM *abbrev. for:* **1** frequency modulation. **2** Field Marshal.

f-number, f number, f-stop, *or* **f stop** *n Photog.* the numerical value of the relative aperture. If the relative aperture is f8, 8 is the f-number.

Fo ★ (fəʊ) *n* Dario ('dærɪəʊ). born 1926, Italian playwright and actor. His plays include *The Accidental Death of an Anarchist* (1970) and *The Tricks of the Trade* (1991): Nobel prize for literature 1997.

FO *abbrev. for:* **1** *Army.* Field Officer. **2** *Air Force.* Flying Officer. **3** Foreign Office.

fo. *abbrev. for* folio.

foal (fəʊl) *n* **1** the young of a horse or related animal. ◆ *vb* **2** to give birth to (a foal). [OE *fola*]

foam (fəʊm) *n* **1** a mass of small bubbles of gas formed on the surface of a liquid, such as the froth produced by a solution of soap or detergent in water. **2** frothy saliva sometimes formed in and expelled from the mouth, as in rabies. **3** the frothy sweat of a horse or similar animal. **4a** any of a number of light cellular solids made by creating bubbles of gas in the liquid material: used as insulation and packaging. **4b** (*as modifier*): *foam rubber; foam plastic.* ◆ *vb* **5** to produce or cause to produce foam; froth. **6** (*intr*) to be very angry (esp. in **foam at the mouth**). [OE *fām*]
▸ 'foamless *adj*

foamy ('fəʊmɪ) *adj* **foamier, foamiest.** of, resembling, consisting of, or covered with foam.

fob[1] (fɒb) *n* **1** a chain or ribbon by which a pocket watch is attached to a waistcoat. **2** any ornament hung on such a chain. **3** a small pocket in a man's waistcoat, etc., for holding a watch. [C17: prob. of Gmc origin]

fob[2] (fɒb) *vb* **fobs, fobbing, fobbed.** (*tr*) *Arch.* to cheat. [C15: prob. from G *foppen* to trick]

f.o.b. *or* **FOB** *Commerce. abbrev. for* free on board.

fob off *vb* (*tr, adv*) **1** to trick (a person) with lies or excuses. **2** to dispose of (goods) by trickery.

focal ('fəʊkᵊl) *adj* **1** of or relating to a focus. **2** situated at or measured from the focus.

focalize *or* **focalise** ('fəʊkəˌlaɪz) *vb* **focalizes, focalizing, focalized** *or* **focalises, focalising, focalised.** a less common word for **focus.**
▸ ˌfocali'zation *or* ˌfocali'sation *n*

focal length *or* **distance** *n* the distance from the focal point of a lens or mirror to the reflecting surface of the mirror or the centre point of the lens.

focal plane *n* the plane that is perpendicular to the axis of a lens or mirror and passes through the focal point.

focal point *n* the point on the axis of a lens or mirror to which parallel rays of light converge or from which they appear to diverge after refraction or reflection. Also called: **focus.**

Foch ★ (*French* fɔʃ) *n* Ferdinand (fɛrdinã). 1851–1929, marshal of France; commander in chief of Allied armies on the Western front in World War I (1918).

fo'c's'le *or* **fo'c'sle** ('fəʊksᵊl) *n* a variant spelling of **forecastle.**

focus ('fəʊkəs) *n, pl* **focuses** *or* **foci** (-saɪ). **1** a point of convergence of light or sound waves, etc., or a point from which they appear to diverge. **2** another name for **focal point** *or* **focal length.** **3** *Optics.* the state of an optical image when it is distinct and clearly defined or the state of an instrument producing this image: *the telescope is out of focus.* **4** a point upon which attention, activity, etc., is concentrated. **5** *Geom.* a fixed reference point on the concave side of a conic section, used when defining its eccentricity. **6** the point beneath the earth's surface at which an earthquake originates. **7** *Pathol.* the main site of an infection. ◆ *vb* **focuses, focusing, focused** *or* **focusses,**

focussing, focussed. 8 to bring or come to a focus or into focus. **9** (*tr*; often foll. by *on*) to concentrate. [C17: via NL from L: hearth, fireplace]
▸ 'focuser *n*

focus group *n* a group of people gathered by a market research company to discuss and assess a product or service.

focus puller *n Films.* the member of a camera crew who adjusts the focus of the lens as the camera is tracked in or out.

fodder ('fɒdə) *n* **1** bulk feed for livestock, esp. hay, straw, etc. ◆ *vb* **2** (*tr*) to supply (livestock) with fodder. [OE *fōdor*]

foe (fəʊ) *n Formal or literary.* another word for **enemy.** [OE *fāh* hostile]

FoE *or* **FOE** *abbrev. for* Friends of the Earth.

foehn (fɜːn; *German* føːn) *n Meteorol.* a variant spelling of **föhn.**

foeman ('fəʊmən) *n, pl* **foemen.** *Arch. & poetic.* an enemy in war; foe.

foetal ('fiːtᵊl) *adj* a variant spelling of **fetal.**

foetid ('fɛtɪd, 'fiː-) *adj* a variant spelling of **fetid.**
▸ 'foetidly *adv* ▸ 'foetidness *n*

foetus ('fiːtəs) *n, pl* **foetuses.** a variant spelling of **fetus.**

fog[1] (fɒg) *n* **1** a mass of droplets of condensed water vapour suspended in the air, often greatly reducing visibility. **2** a cloud of any substance in the atmosphere reducing visibility. **3** a state of mental uncertainty. **4** *Photog.* a blurred area on a developed negative, print, or transparency. ◆ *vb* **fogs, fogging, fogged. 5** to envelop or become enveloped with or as if with fog. **6** to confuse or become confused. **7** *Photog.* to produce fog on (a negative, print, or transparency) or (of a negative, print, or transparency) to be affected by fog. [C16: ? back formation from *foggy* damp, boggy, from FOG[2]]

fog[2] (fɒg) *n* a second growth of grass after the first mowing. [C14: prob. from ON]

fog bank *n* a distinct mass of fog, esp. at sea.

fogbound ('fɒgˌbaʊnd) *adj* prevented from operation by fog: *the airport was fogbound.*

fogbow ('fɒgˌbəʊ) *n* a faint arc of light sometimes seen in a fog bank.

fogey *or* **fogy** ('fəʊgɪ) *n, pl* **fogeys** *or* **fogies.** an extremely fussy or conservative person (esp. in **old fogey**). [C18: from ?]
▸ 'fogeyish *or* 'fogyish *adj*

Foggia (*Italian* 'fɔddʒa) *n* a city in SE Italy, in Apulia: seat of Emperor Frederick II; centre for Carbonari revolutionary societies in the revolts of 1820, 1848, and 1860. Pop.: 155 892 (1994 est.).

foggy ('fɒgɪ) *adj* **foggier, foggiest. 1** thick with fog. **2** obscure or confused. **3 not the foggiest** (*idea or notion*). no idea whatsoever: *I haven't the foggiest.*
▸ 'fogginess *n*

foghorn ('fɒgˌhɔːn) *n* **1** a mechanical instrument sounded at intervals to serve as a warning to vessels in fog. **2** *Inf.* a loud deep resounding voice.

fog signal *n* a signal used to warn railway engine drivers in fog, consisting of a detonator placed on the line.

föhn *or* **foehn** (fɜːn; *German* føːn) *n* a warm dry wind blowing down the northern slopes of the Alps. [G, from OHG, from L *favōnius*; rel. to *fovēre* to warm]

foible ('fɔɪbᵊl) *n* **1** a slight peculiarity or minor weakness; idiosyncrasy. **2** the most vulnerable part of a sword's blade, from the middle to the tip. [C17: from obs. F, from obs. adj: FEEBLE]

foie gras (*French* fwa grɑ) *n See* pâté de foie gras.

foil[1] (fɔɪl) *vb* (*tr*) **1** to baffle or frustrate (a person, attempt, etc.). **2** *Hunting.* (of hounds, hunters, etc.) to obliterate the scent left by a hunted animal or (of a hunted animal) to run back over its own trail. ◆ *n* **3** *Arch.* a setback or defeat. [C13 *foilen* to trample, from OF, *fuler* tread down]
▸ 'foilable *adj*

foil[2] (fɔɪl) *n* **1** metal in the form of very thin sheets: *tin foil.* **2** the thin metallic sheet forming the backing of a mirror. **3** a thin leaf of shiny metal set under a gemstone to

★ people and places

add brightness or colour. **4** a person or thing that gives contrast to another. **5** *Archit.* a small arc between cusps. **6** short for **hydrofoil.** ◆ *vb* (*tr*) **7** Also: **foliate.** *Archit.* to ornament (windows, etc.) with foils. [C14: from OF, from L *folia* leaves]

foil³ (fɔɪl) *n* a light slender flexible sword tipped by a button. [C16: from ?]

foist (fɔɪst) *vb* (*tr*) **1** (often foll. by *off* or *on*) to sell or pass off (something, esp. an inferior article) as genuine, valuable, etc. **2** (usually foll. by *in* or *into*) to insert surreptitiously or wrongly. [C16: prob. from obs. Du. *vuisten* to enclose in one's hand, from MDu. *vuist* fist]

Fokine ★ (*Russian* 'fɔkin; *French* fɔkin) *n* **Michel** (miʃɛl). 1880–1942, US choreographer, born in Russia; worked with Diaghilev as director of the Ballet Russe (1909–15).

Fokker ★ ('fɔkə; *Dutch* 'fɔkər) *n* **Anthony Herman Gerard** (ɑn'tɔːni: 'herman 'xeːrɑrt). 1890–1939, Dutch aircraft manufacturer, born in Java; had German factories to make World War I aircraft. Moved to US (1922).

FOL (in New Zealand) *abbrev. for* Federation of Labour.

fol. *abbrev. for:* **1** folio. **2** following.

fold¹ (fəʊld) *vb* **1** to bend or be bent double so that one part covers another. **2** (*tr*) to bring together and intertwine (the arms, legs, etc.). **3** (*tr*) of birds, insects, etc.) to close (the wings) together from an extended position. **4** (*tr*; often foll. by *up* or *in*) to enclose in or as if in a surrounding material. **5** (*tr*; foll. by *in*) to clasp (a person) in the arms. **6** (*tr*; usually foll. by *round, about,* etc.) to wind (around); entwine. **7** Also: **fold in.** (*tr*) to mix (a whisked mixture) with other ingredients by gently turning one part over the other with a spoon. **8** (*intr*; often foll. by *up*) *Inf.* to collapse; fail: *the business folded.* ◆ *n* **9** a piece or section that has been folded: *a fold of cloth.* **10** a mark, crease, or hollow made by folding. **11** a hollow in undulating terrain. **12** a bend in stratified rocks that results from movements within the earth's crust. **13** a coil, as in a rope, etc. [OE *fealdan*]
▶ 'foldable *adj*

fold² (fəʊld) *n* **1a** a small enclosure or pen for sheep or other livestock, where they can be gathered. **1b** a flock of sheep. **2** a church or the members of it. ◆ *vb* **3** (*tr*) to gather or confine (sheep, etc.) in a fold. [OE *falod*]

-fold *suffix forming adjectives and adverbs.* having so many parts or being so many times as much or as many: *threehundredfold.* [OE -*fald,* -*feald*]

foldaway ('fəʊldə,weɪ) *adj* (*prenominal*) (of a bed, etc.) able to be folded away when not in use.

folded dipole *n* a type of aerial consisting of two parallel dipoles connected together at their outer ends and fed at the centre of one of them. The length is usually half the operating wavelength.

folder ('fəʊldə) *n* **1** a binder or file for holding loose papers, etc. **2** a folded circular. **3** a person or thing that folds.

folderol ('fɔldə,rɒl) *n* a variant spelling of **falderal.**

folding door *n* a door in the form of two or more vertical hinged leaves that can be folded one against another.

folding money *n Inf.* paper money.

foley *or* **foley artist** ('fəʊlɪ) *n Films.* the US name for footsteps editor. [C20: after the inventor of the technique]

foliaceous (,fəʊlɪ'eɪʃəs) *adj* **1** having the appearance of the leaf of a plant. **2** bearing leaves or leaflike structures. **3** *Geol.* consisting of thin layers. [C17: from L *foliāceus*]

foliage ('fəʊlɪɪdʒ) *n* **1** the green leaves of a plant. **2** sprays of leaves used for decoration. **3** an ornamental leaflike design. [C15: from OF *fuellage,* from *fuelle* leaf; infl. in form by L *folium*]

foliar ('fəʊlɪə) *adj* of or relating to a leaf or leaves. [C19: from F, from L *folium* leaf]

foliate *adj* ('fəʊlɪt, -,eɪt). **1a** relating to, possessing, or resembling leaves. **1b** (*in combination*): *trifoliate.* ◆ *vb* ('fəʊlɪ,eɪt), **foliates, foliating, foliated. 2** (*tr*) to ornament with foliage or with leaf forms such as foils. **3** to hammer or cut (metal) into thin plates or foil. **4** (*tr*) to number the leaves of (a book, etc.). Cf. **paginate. 5** (*intr*) (of plants) to grow leaves. [C17: from L *foliātus* leaved, leafy]

foliation (,fəʊlɪ'eɪʃən) *n* **1** *Bot.* **1a** the process of produc-

ing leaves. **1b** the state of being in leaf. **1c** the arrangement of leaves in a leaf bud. **2** *Archit.* ornamentation consisting of cusps and foils. **3** the consecutive numbering of the leaves of a book. **4** *Geol.* the arrangement of the constituents of a rock in leaflike layers, as in schists.

folic acid ('fəʊlɪk) *n* any of a group of vitamins of the B complex, used in the treatment of anaemia. Also called: **folacin.** [C20: from L *folium* leaf; so called because it may be obtained from green leaves]

folio ('fəʊlɪəʊ) *n, pl* **folios. 1** a sheet of paper folded in half to make two leaves for a book. **2** a book of the largest common size made up of such sheets. **3a** a leaf of paper numbered on the front side only. **3b** the page number of a book. **4** *Law.* a unit of measurement of the length of legal documents, determined by the number of words, generally 72 or 90 in Britain and 100 in the US. ◆ *adj* **5** relating to or having the format of a folio: *a folio edition.* [C16: from L phrase *in foliō* in a leaf, from *folium* leaf]

folk (fəʊk) *n, pl* **folk** *or* **folks. 1** (*functioning as pl; often pl in form*) people in general, esp. those of a particular group or class: *country folk.* **2** (*functioning as pl; usually pl in form*) *Inf.* members of a family. **3** (*functioning as sing*) *Inf.* short for **folk music. 4** a people or tribe. **5** (*modifier*) originating from or traditional to the common people of a country: *a folk song.* [OE *folc*]
▶ 'folkish *adj*

folk dance *n* **1** any of various traditional rustic dances. **2** a piece of music composed for or in the rhythm of such a dance.
▶ folk dancing *n*

Folkestone ★ ('fəʊkstən) *n* a port and resort in SE England, in E Kent. Pop.: 45 587 (1991).

folk etymology *n* the gradual change in the form of a word through the influence of a more familiar word or phrase with which it becomes associated, as for example *sparrow-grass* for *asparagus.*

folkie *or* **folky** ('fəʊkɪ) *n, pl* **folkies.** *Inf.* a devotee of folk music.

folklore ('fəʊk,lɔ:) *n* **1** the unwritten literature of a people as expressed in folk tales, songs, etc. **2** the body of stories and legends attached to a particular place, group, etc.: *rugby folklore.* **3** study of folkloric materials.
▶ 'folk,loric *adj* ▶ 'folk,lorist *n, adj*

folk medicine *n* medicine as practised among rustic communities and primitive peoples, consisting typically of the use of herbal remedies.

folk music *n* **1** music that is passed on from generation to generation. **2** any music composed in this idiom.

folk-rock *n* a style of rock music influenced by folk.

folk song *n* **1** a song which has been handed down among the common people. **2** a modern song which reflects the folk idiom.

folksy ('fəʊksɪ) *adj* **folksier, folksiest. 1** of or like ordinary people; sometimes used derogatorily to describe affected simplicity. **2** *Inf., chiefly US.* friendly; affable.

folk tale *or* **story** *n* a tale or legend originating among a people and becoming part of an oral tradition.

folk weave *n* a type of fabric with a loose weave.

follicle ('fɒlɪk²l) *n* **1** any small sac or cavity in the body having an excretory, secretory, or protective function: *a hair follicle.* **2** *Bot.* a dry fruit that splits along one side only to release its seeds. [C17: from L *folliculus* small bag, from *follis* pair of bellows, leather money-bag]
▶ **follicular** (fɒ'lɪkjʊlə), **folliculate** (fɒ'lɪkjʊ,leɪt), *or* **fol'licu,lated** *adj*

follow ('fɒləʊ) *vb* **1** to go or come after in the same direction. **2** (*tr*) to accompany: *she followed her sister everywhere.* **3** to come after as a logical or natural consequence. **4** (*tr*) to keep to the course or track of: *she followed the towpath.* **5** (*tr*) to act in accordance with: *to follow instructions.* **6** (*tr*) to accept the ideas or beliefs of (a previous authority, etc.): *he followed Donne in most of his teachings.* **7** to understand (an explanation, etc.): *the lesson was difficult to follow.* **8** to watch closely or continuously: *she followed his progress.* **9** (*tr*) to have a keen interest in: *to follow athletics.* **10** (*tr*) to help in the cause of: *the men who followed Napoleon.* [OE *folgian*]

follower ('folǝuǝ) *n* **1** a person who accepts the teachings of another: *a follower of Marx.* **2** an attendant. **3** a supporter, as of a sport or team. **4** (esp. formerly) a male admirer.

following ('folǝuɪŋ) *adj* **1a** (*prenominal*) about to be mentioned, specified, etc.: *the following items.* **1b** (*as n*): *will the following please raise their hands?* **2** (of winds, currents, etc.) moving in the same direction as a vessel. ◆ *n* **3** a group of supporters or enthusiasts: *he attracted a large following.* ◆ *prep* **4** as a result of: *he was arrested following a tip-off.*

> **USAGE NOTE** The use of *following* to mean *as a result of* is very common in journalism, but should be avoided in other kinds of writing.

follow-on *Cricket.* ◆ *n* **1** an immediate second innings forced on a team scoring a prescribed number of runs fewer than its opponents in the first innings. ◆ *vb* **follow on. 2** (*intr, adv*) (of a team) to play a follow-on.

follow out *vb* (*tr, adv*) to implement (an idea or action) to a conclusion.

follow through *vb* (*adv*) **1** *Sport.* to complete (a stroke or shot) by continuing the movement to the end of its arc. **2** (*tr*) to pursue (an aim) to a conclusion. ◆ *n* **follow-through. 3** the act of following through.

follow up *vb* (*tr, adv*) **1** to pursue or investigate (a person, etc.) closely. **2** to continue (action) after a beginning, esp. to increase its effect. ◆ *n* **follow-up. 3a** something done to reinforce an initial action. **3b** (*as modifier*): *a follow-up letter.* **4** *Med.* an examination of a patient at intervals after treatment.

folly ('folɪ) *n, pl* **follies. 1** the state or quality of being foolish. **2** a foolish action, idea, etc. **3** a building in the form of a castle, temple, etc., built to satisfy a fancy or conceit. **4** (*pl*) *Theatre.* an elaborately costumed revue. [C13: from OF *folie* madness, from *fou* mad; see FOOL[1]]

foment (fǝ'mɛnt) *vb* (*tr*) **1** to encourage or instigate (trouble, discord, etc.). **2** *Med.* to apply heat and moisture to (a part of the body) to relieve pain. [C15: from LL, from L *fōmentum* a poultice, ult. from *fovēre* to foster]
▶ **fomentation** (ˌfǝumɛn'teɪʃǝn) *n* ▶ **fo'menter** *n*

> **USAGE NOTE** Both *foment* and *ferment* can be used to talk about stirring up trouble: *he was accused of fomenting/fermenting unrest.* Only *ferment* can be used intransitively or as a noun: *his anger continued to ferment* (not *foment*); *rural areas were unaffected by the ferment in the cities.*

fond (fond) *adj* **1** (*postpositive; foll. by of*) having a liking (for). **2** loving; tender. **3** indulgent: *a fond mother.* **4** (of hopes, wishes, etc.) cherished but unlikely to be realized: *he had fond hopes of starting his own firm.* **5** *Arch. or dialect.* **5a** foolish. **5b** credulous. [C14 *fonned,* from *fonne* a fool]
▶ **'fondly** *adv* ▶ **'fondness** *n*

Fonda ★ ('fondǝ) *n* **1** Henry. 1905–82, US film actor. His films include *The Grapes of Wrath* (1940), *Twelve Angry Men* (1957), and *On Golden Pond* (1981). **2** his daughter **Jane.** born 1937, US film actress. Her films include *Klute* (1971), *Julia* (1977), and *The China Syndrome* (1979). **3** her brother, **Peter.** born 1939, US film actor, noted for his part in *Easy Rider* (1969).

fondant ('fondǝnt) *n* **1** a thick flavoured paste of sugar and water, used in sweets and icings. **2** a sweet made of this mixture. ◆ *adj* **3** (of a colour) soft, pastel. [C19: from F, lit.: melting, from *fondre* to melt, from L *fundere*; see FOUND[3]]

fondle ('fond°l) *vb* **fondles, fondling, fondled.** (*tr*) to touch or stroke tenderly. [C17: from (obs.) vb *fond* to fondle; see FOND]
▶ **'fondler** *n*

fondue ('fondju:; *French* fɔ̃dy) *n* a Swiss dish, consisting of melted cheese into which small pieces of bread are dipped. [C19: from F, fem of *fondu* melted; see FONDANT]

Fonseca ★ (*Spanish* fɔn'seka) *n* **Gulf of.** an inlet of the Pacific Ocean in W Central America.

font[1] (font) *n* **1a** a large bowl for baptismal water. **1b** a receptacle for holy water. **2** the reservoir for oil in an oil lamp. **3** *Arch. or poetic.* a fountain or well. [OE, from Church L *fons,* from L: fountain]

font[2] (font) *n Printing.* another name (esp. US and Canad.) for **fount**[2].

Fontainebleau ★ ('fontɪnˌblǝu; *French* fɔ̃tɛnblo) *n* a town in N France, in the **Forest of Fontainebleau:** famous for its palace (now a museum), one of the largest royal residences in France, built largely by Francis I (16th century). Pop.: 18 753 (1982).

fontanelle *or chiefly US* **fontanel** (ˌfontǝ'nɛl) *n Anat.* any of the soft connective gaps between the bones of the skull in a fetus or infant. [C16 (in the sense: hollow between muscles): from OF *fontanele,* lit.: a little spring, from *fontaine* FOUNTAIN]

Fonteyn ★ (fon'teɪn) *n* Dame **Margot.** real name *Margaret Hookham.* 1919–91, British ballerina.

Foochow ★ ('fu:'tʃau) *n* a variant transliteration of the Chinese name for **Fuzhou.**

food (fu:d) *n* **1** any substance that can be ingested by a living organism and metabolized into energy and body tissue. Related adj: **alimentary. 2** nourishment in more or less solid form: *food and drink.* **3** anything that provides mental nourishment or stimulus. [OE *fōda*]

food additive *n* any of various natural or synthetic substances, such as salt or citric acid, used in the commercial processing of food as preservatives, antioxidants, emulsifiers, etc.

food chain *n Ecology.* a series of organisms in a community, each member of which feeds on another in the chain and is in turn eaten.

foodie *or* **foody** ('fu:dɪ) *n, pl* **foodies.** a person having an enthusiastic interest in the preparation and consumption of good food.

food poisoning *n* an acute illness caused by food that is either naturally poisonous or contaminated by bacteria.

food processor *n Cookery.* an electric domestic appliance for automatic chopping, grating, blending, etc.

foodstuff ('fu:dˌstʌf) *n* any material, substance, etc., that can be used as food.

food value *n* the relative degree of nourishment obtained from different foods.

fool[1] (fu:l) *n* **1** a person who lacks sense or judgement. **2** a person who is made to appear ridiculous. **3** (formerly) a professional jester living in a royal or noble household. **4** *Obs.* an idiot or imbecile: *the village fool.* **5 play** *or* **act the fool.** to deliberately act foolishly. ◆ *vb* **6** (*tr*) to deceive (someone), esp. in order to make him look ridiculous. **7** (*intr*; foll. by *with, around with,* or *about with*) *Inf.* to act or play (with) irresponsibly or aimlessly. **8** (*intr*) to speak or act in a playful or jesting manner. **9** (*tr*; foll. by *away*) to squander; fritter. ◆ *adj* **10** *US inf.* short for **foolish.** [C13: from OF *fol* mad person, from LL *follis* empty-headed fellow, from L: bellows]

fool[2] (fu:l) *n Chiefly Brit.* a dessert made from a purée of fruit with cream. [C16: ?from FOOL[1]]

foolery ('fu:lǝrɪ) *n, pl* **fooleries. 1** foolish behaviour. **2** an instance of this.

foolhardy ('fu:lˌhɑ:dɪ) *adj* **foolhardier, foolhardiest.** heedlessly rash or adventurous. [C13: from OF, from *fol* foolish + *hardi* bold]
▶ **'foolˌhardily** *adv* ▶ **'foolˌhardiness** *n*

foolish ('fu:lɪʃ) *adj* **1** unwise; silly. **2** resulting from folly or stupidity. **3** ridiculous or absurd. **4** weak-minded; simple.
▶ **'foolishly** *adv* ▶ **'foolishness** *n*

foolproof ('fu:lˌpru:f) *adj Inf.* **1** proof against failure. **2** (esp. of machines, etc.) proof against human misuse, error, etc.

foolscap ('fu:lzˌkæp) *n Chiefly Brit.* a size of writing or printing paper, 13½ by 17 inches. [C17: see FOOL[1], CAP; so called from the watermark formerly used on this kind of paper]

★ people and places

fool's cap n 1 a hood or cap with bells or tassels, worn by court jesters. 2 a dunce's cap.

fool's errand n a fruitless undertaking.

fool's gold n any of various yellow minerals, esp. pyrite, that can be mistaken for gold.

fool's paradise n illusory happiness.

fool's-parsley n an evil-smelling Eurasian umbelliferous plant with small white flowers.

foot (fut) n, pl **feet**. 1 the part of the vertebrate leg below the ankle joint that is in contact with the ground during standing and walking. Related adj: **pedal**. 2 the part of a garment covering an attachment to a foot. 3 any of various organs of locomotion or attachment in invertebrates, including molluscs. 4 Bot. the lower part of some plants or plant structures. 5 a unit of length equal to one third of a yard or 12 inches. 1 foot is equivalent to 0.3048 metre. 6 any part resembling a foot in form or function: *the foot of a chair*. 7 the lower part of something; bottom: *the foot of a hill*. 8 the end of a series or group: *the foot of the list*. 9 manner of walking or moving: *a heavy foot*. 10a infantry, esp. in the British army. 10b (*as modifier*): *a foot soldier*. 11 any of various attachments on a sewing machine that hold the fabric in position. 12 Prosody. a group of two or more syllables in which one syllable has the major stress, forming the basic unit of poetic rhythm. 13 **my foot!** an expression of disbelief, often of the speaker's own preceding statement. 14 **of foot**. Arch. in manner of movement: *fleet of foot*. 15 **one foot in the grave**. Inf. near to death. 16 **on foot**. 16a walking or running. 16b astir; afoot. 17 **put a foot wrong**. to make a mistake. 18 **put one's best foot forward**. 18a to try to do one's best. 18b to hurry. 19 **put one's foot down**. Inf. to act firmly. 20 **put one's foot in it**. Inf. to blunder. 21 **under foot**. on the ground; beneath one's feet. ◆ vb 22 to dance to music (esp. in **foot it**). 23 (tr) to walk over or set foot on (esp. in **foot it**). 24 (tr) to pay the entire cost of (esp. in **foot the bill**). [OE *fōt*] ◆ See also **feet**.
▸ **'footless** adj

> **USAGE NOTE** In front of another noun, the plural for the unit of length is *foot: a 20-foot putt; his 70-foot ketch. Foot* can also be used instead of *feet* when mentioning a quantity and in front of words like *tall: four foot of snow; he is at least six foot tall.*

Foot ★ (fut) n **Michael** (**Mackintosh**). born 1913, British Labour politician; secretary of state for employment (1974–76); leader of the House of Commons (1976–79); leader of the Labour Party (1980–83).

footage ('futɪdʒ) n 1 a length or distance measured in feet. 2 the extent of film material shot and exposed.

foot-and-mouth disease n an acute highly infectious viral disease of cattle, pigs, sheep, and goats, characterized by the formation of vesicular eruptions in the mouth and on the feet.

football ('fut,bɔːl) n 1a any of various games played with a round or oval ball and usually based on two teams competing to kick, head, carry, or otherwise propel the ball into each other's goal, territory, etc. 1b (*as modifier*): *a football supporter*. 2 the ball used in any of these games or their variants. 3 a problem, issue, etc., that is continually passed from one group or person to another as a pretext for argument.
▸ **'foot,baller** n

footboard ('fut,bɔːd) n 1 a board for a person to stand or rest his feet on. 2 a treadle or foot-operated lever on a machine. 3 a vertical board at the foot of a bed.

footbridge ('fut,brɪdʒ) n a narrow bridge for the use of pedestrians.

-footed adj 1 having a foot or feet as specified: *four-footed*. 2 having a tread as specified: *heavy-footed*.

footer[1] ('futə) n (*in combination*) a person or thing of a specified length or height in feet: *a six-footer*.

footer[2] ('futə) n Brit. inf. short for **football** (the game).

footfall ('fut,fɔːl) n the sound of a footstep.

foot fault n Tennis. a fault that occurs when the server

fails to keep both feet behind the baseline until he has served.

foothill ('fut,hɪl) n (*often pl*) a relatively low hill at the foot of a mountain.

foothold ('fut,həʊld) n 1 a ledge or other place affording a secure grip, as during climbing. 2 a secure position from which further progress may be made.

footing ('futɪŋ) n 1 the basis or foundation on which something is established: *the business was on a secure footing*. 2 the relationship or status existing between two persons, groups, etc. 3 a secure grip by or for the feet. 4 the lower part of a foundation of a column, wall, building, etc.

footle ('fuːt[l]) vb **footles, footling, footled**. (*intr*; often foll. by *around* or *about*) Inf. to loiter aimlessly. [C19: prob. from F *foutre* to copulate with, from L *futuere*]
▸ **'footling** adj

footlights ('fut,laɪts) pl n Theatre. lights set in a row along the front of the stage floor.

footloose ('fut,luːs) adj 1 free to go or do as one wishes. 2 restless: *to feel footloose*.

footman ('futmən) n, pl **footmen**. 1 a male servant, esp. one in livery. 2 (formerly) a foot soldier.

footnote ('fut,nəʊt) n 1 a note printed at the bottom of a page, to which attention is drawn by means of a mark in the text. ◆ vb **footnotes, footnoting, footnoted**. 2 (tr) to supply (a page, etc.) with footnotes.

footpad ('fut,pæd) n Arch. a robber or highwayman, on foot rather than horseback.

footpath ('fut,pɑːθ) n 1 a narrow path for walkers only. 2 Chiefly Austral. & NZ. another word for **pavement**.

footplate ('fut,pleɪt) n Chiefly Brit. a platform in the cab of a locomotive on which the crew stand to operate the controls.

foot-pound-second n See **fps units**.

footprint ('fut,prɪnt) n an indentation or outline of the foot of a person or animal on a surface.

footrest ('fut,rest) n something that provides a support for the feet, such as a low stool, rail, etc.

foot rot n Vet. science. See **rot** (sense 10).

footsie ('futsɪ) n Inf. flirtation involving the touching together of feet, etc.

Footsie ('futsɪ) n Brit. inf. the Financial Times Stock Exchange 100 index. See **FT Index** (sense 2).

foot soldier n an infantryman.

footsore ('fut,sɔː) adj having sore or tired feet, esp. from much walking.
▸ **'foot,soreness** n

footstep ('fut,step) n 1 the action of taking a step in walking. 2 the sound made by walking. 3 the distance covered with a step. 4 a footmark. 5 a single stair. 6 **follow in someone's footsteps**. to continue the example of another.

footsteps editor n Brit. films. the technician who adds sound effects, such as doors closing, rain falling, etc., during the postproduction sound-dubbing process. US name: **foley** or **foley artist**.

footstool ('fut,stuːl) n a low stool used for supporting or resting the feet of a seated person.

footwear ('fut,weə) n anything worn to cover the feet.

footwork ('fut,wɜːk) n the use of the feet, esp. in sports, dancing, etc.

footy or **footie** ('futɪ) n Inf. **a** football. **b** (*as modifier*): *footy boots*.

fop (fop) n a man who is excessively concerned with fashion and elegance. [C15: rel. to G *foppen* to trick]
▸ **'foppery** n ▸ **'foppish** adj

for (fɔː; *unstressed* fə) prep 1 directed or belonging to: *there's a phone call for you*. 2 to the advantage of: *I only did it for you*. 3 in the direction of: *heading for the border*. 4 over a span of (time or distance): *working for six days*. 5 in favour of: *vote for me*. 6 in order to get or achieve: *I do it for money*. 7 designed to meet the needs of: *these kennels are for puppies*. 8 at a cost of: *I got it for hardly any money*. 9 such as explains or results in: *his reason for changing his job* was not given. **10** in place of: *a substitute for the injured player.* **11** because of: *she wept for pure relief.* **12** with regard or consideration to the usual characteristics of: *it's cool for this time of year.* **13** concerning: *desire for money.* **14** as being: *I know that for a fact.* **15** at a specified time: *a date for the next evening.* **16** to do or partake of: *an appointment for supper.* **17** in the duty or task of: *that's for him to say.* **18** to allow of: *too big a job for us to handle.* **19** despite: *she's a good wife, for all her nagging.* **20** in order to preserve, retain, etc.: *to fight for survival.* **21** as a direct equivalent to: *word for word.* **22** in order to become or enter: *to train for the priesthood.* **23** in recompense for: *I paid for it last week.* **24 for it.** *Brit. inf.* liable for punishment or blame: *you'll be for it if she catches you.* ◆ *conj* **25** (*coordinating*) because; seeing that: *I couldn't stay, for the area was violent.* [OE]

for- *prefix* **1** indicating rejection or prohibition: *forbid.* **2** indicating falsity: *forswear.* **3** used to give intensive force: *forlorn.* [OE *for-*]

forage ('forɪdʒ) *n* **1** food for horses or cattle, esp. hay or straw. **2** the act of searching for food or provisions. ◆ *vb* **forages, foraging, foraged. 3** to search (the countryside or a town) for food, etc. **4** (*intr*) *Mil.* to carry out a raid. **5** (*tr*) to obtain by searching about. **6** (*tr*) to give food or other provisions to. **7** (*tr*) to feed (cattle or horses) with such food. [C14: from OF *fourrage*, prob. of Gmc origin]
▸ **'forager** *n*

forage cap *n* a soldier's undress cap.

foramen (fɒ'reɪmɛn) *n, pl* **foramina** (-'ræmɪnə) or **foramens.** a natural hole, esp. one in a bone. [C17: from L, from *forāre* to bore, pierce]

foraminifer (ˌfɒrə'mɪnɪfə) *n* a protozoan of the phylum *Foraminifera,* having a shell with numerous openings through which the cytoplasmic processes protrude. [C19: from NL, from FORAMEN + -FER]

forasmuch as (fərəz'mʌtʃ) *conj* (*subordinating*) *Arch.* or *legal.* seeing that.

foray ('fɒreɪ) *n* **1** a short raid or incursion. ◆ *vb* **2** to raid or ravage (a town, district, etc.). [C14: from *forrayen* to pillage, from OF, from *fuerre* fodder]

forbade (fə'bæd, -'beɪd) or **forbad** (fə'bæd) *vb* the past tense of **forbid.**

forbear[1] (fɔː'bɛə) *vb* **forbears, forbearing, forbore, forborne. 1** (when *intr*, often foll. by *from* or an infinitive) to cease or refrain (from doing something). **2** *Arch.* to tolerate (misbehaviour, etc.). [OE *forberan*]

forbear[2] ('fɔːˌbɛə) *n* a variant spelling of **forebear.**

forbearance (fɔː'bɛərəns) *n* **1** the act of forbearing. **2** self-control; patience.

Forbes ★ (fɔːbz) *n* George William. 1869–1947, New Zealand statesman; prime minister (1930–35).

forbid (fə'bɪd) *vb* **forbids, forbidding, forbade** or **forbad, forbidden** or **forbid.** (*tr*) **1** to prohibit (a person) in a forceful or authoritative manner (from doing or having something). **2** to make impossible. **3** to shut out or exclude. [OE *forbēodan*; see FOR-, BID]
▸ **for'bidder** *n*

> **USAGE NOTE** It was formerly considered incorrect to talk of *forbidding* someone *from* doing something, but in modern usage either *from* or *to* can be used: *he was forbidden from entering/to enter the building.*

forbidden (fə'bɪdⁿn) *adj* **1** not permitted by order or law. **2** *Physics.* involving a change in quantum numbers that is not permitted by certain rules derived from quantum mechanics.

Forbidden City ★ *n* **the. 1** Lhasa, Tibet: once famed for its inaccessibility and hostility to strangers. **2** a walled section of Beijing, China, enclosing the Imperial Palace and associated buildings of the former Chinese Empire.

forbidden fruit *n* any pleasure or enjoyment regarded as illicit, esp. sexual indulgence.

forbidding (fə'bɪdɪŋ) *adj* **1** hostile or unfriendly. **2** dangerous or ominous.

forbore (fɔː'bɔː) *vb* the past tense of **forbear**[1].

forborne (fɔː'bɔːn) *vb* the past participle of **forbear**[1].

force[1] (fɔːs) *n* **1** strength or energy; power: *the force of the blow.* **2** exertion or the use of exertion against a person or thing that resists. **3** *Physics.* **3a** a dynamic influence that changes a body from a state of rest to one of motion or changes its rate of motion. **3b** a static influence that produces a strain in a body or system. Symbol: *F* **4a** intellectual, political, or moral influence or strength: *the force of his argument.* **4b** a person or thing with such influence: *he was a force in the land.* **5** vehemence or intensity: *she spoke with great force.* **6** a group of persons organized for military or police functions: *armed forces.* **7** (*sometimes cap.;* preceded by *the*) *Inf.* the police force. **8** a group of persons organized for particular duties or tasks: *a workforce.* **9** *Criminal law.* violence unlawfully committed or threatened. **10 in force. 10a** (of a law) having legal validity. **10b** in great strength or numbers. ◆ *vb* **forces, forcing, forced.** (*tr*) **11** to compel or cause (a person, group, etc.) to do something through effort, superior strength, etc. **12** to acquire or produce through effort, superior strength, etc.: *to force a confession.* **13** to propel or drive despite resistance. **14** to break down or open (a lock, door, etc.). **15** to impose or inflict: *he forced his views on them.* **16** to cause (plants or farm animals) to grow or fatten artificially at an increased rate. **17** to strain to the utmost: *to force the voice.* **18** to rape. **19** *Cards.* **19a** to compel a player by the lead of a particular suit to play (a certain card). **19b** (in bridge) to induce (a bid) from one's partner. [C13: from OF, from Vulgar L *fortia* (unattested), from L *fortis* strong]
▸ **'forceable** *adj* ▸ **'forceless** *adj* ▸ **'forcer** *n*

force[2] (fɔːs) *n* (in N England) a waterfall. [C17: from ON *fors*]

forced (fɔːst) *adj* **1** done because of force: *forced labour.* **2** false or unnatural: *a forced smile.* **3** due to an emergency or necessity: *a forced landing.*

force de frappe (*French* fɔrs də frap) *n* a military strike force, esp. the independent nuclear strike force of France. [C20: F, lit.: striking force]

force-feed *vb* **force-feeds, force-feeding, force-fed.** (*tr*) to force (a person or animal) to eat or swallow food.

forceful ('fɔːsful) *adj* **1** powerful. **2** persuasive or effective.
▸ **'forcefully** *adv* ▸ **'forcefulness** *n*

forcemeat ('fɔːsˌmiːt) *n* a mixture of chopped ingredients used for stuffing. Also called: **farce.** [C17: from *force* (see FARCE) + MEAT]

forceps ('fɔːsɪps) *n, pl* **forceps. 1a** a surgical instrument in the form of a pair of pincers, used esp. in the delivery of babies. **1b** (*as modifier*): *a forceps baby.* **2** any part of an organism shaped like a forceps. [C17: from L, from *formus* hot + *capere* to seize]

force pump *n* a pump that ejects fluid under pressure. Cf. **lift pump.**

Forces ('fɔːsɪz) *pl n* (usually preceded by *the*) the armed services of a nation.

forcible ('fɔːsəbᵊl) *adj* **1** done by, involving, or having force. **2** convincing or effective: *a forcible argument.*
▸ **'forcibly** *adv*

ford (fɔːd) *n* **1** a shallow area in a river that can be crossed by car, on horseback, etc. ◆ *vb* **2** (*tr*) to cross (a river, brook, etc.) over a shallow area. [OE]
▸ **'fordable** *adj*

Ford ★ (fɔːd) *n* **1 Ford Madox** ('mædəks), real name *Ford Madox Hueffer.* 1873–1939, British writer; works include *The Good Soldier* (1915) and the war tetralogy *Parade's End* (1924–28). **2 Gerald R(udolph).** born 1913, US politician; 38th president of the US (1974–77). **3 Harrison.** born 1942, US film actor. His films include *Star Wars* (1977), *Raiders of the Lost Ark* (1981), *Bladerunner* (1982), and *Air Force One* (1997). **4 Henry.** 1863–1947, US car manufacturer, who pioneered mass production. **5 John.** 1586–?1639, English dramatist; author of such tragedies as *'Tis Pity She's a Whore* (1633). **6 John,** real name *Sean O'Feeney.* 1895–1973, US film director, esp. of Westerns such as *Stagecoach* (1939).

fore[1] (fɔː) *adj* **1** (*usually in combination*) located at, in, or towards the front: *the forelegs of a horse.* ◆ *n* **2** the front

★ **people and places**

part. **3** something located at, or towards the front. **4 fore and aft.** located at both ends of a vessel: *a fore-and-aft rig.* **5 to the fore.** to the front or conspicuous position. ◆ *adv* **6** at or towards a ship's bow. **7** *Obs.* before. ◆ *prep, conj* **8** a less common word for **before.** [OE]

fore² (fɔː) *sentence substitute.* (in golf) a warning shout made by a player about to make a shot. [C19: prob. short for BEFORE]

fore- *prefix* **1** before in time or rank: *forefather.* **2** at or near the front: *forecourt.* [OE, from *fore* (adv)]

fore-and-after *n Naut.* **1** any vessel with a fore-and-aft rig. **2** a double-ended vessel.

forearm¹ ('fɔːrˌɑːm) *n* the part of the arm from the elbow to the wrist. [C18: from FORE- + ARM¹]

forearm² (fɔːrˈɑːm) *vb* (*tr*) to prepare or arm (someone) in advance. [C16: from FORE- + ARM²]

forebear *or* **forbear** ('fɔːˌbɛə) *n* an ancestor.

forebode (fɔːˈbəʊd) *vb* **forebodes, foreboding, foreboded.** **1** to warn of or indicate (an event, result, etc.) in advance. **2** to have a premonition of (an event).

foreboding (fɔːˈbəʊdɪŋ) *n* **1** a feeling of impending evil, disaster, etc. **2** an omen or portent. ◆ *adj* **3** presaging something.

forebrain ('fɔːˌbreɪn) *n* the nontechnical name for **prosencephalon.**

forecast ('fɔːˌkɑːst) *vb* **forecasts, forecasting, forecast** *or* **forecasted.** **1** to predict or calculate (weather, events, etc.), in advance. **2** (*tr*) to serve as an early indication of. ◆ *n* **3** a statement of probable future weather calculated from meteorological data. **4** a prediction. **5** the practice or power of forecasting. ▶ 'fore,caster *n*

forecastle, fo'c's'le, *or* **fo'c'sle** ('fəʊksᵊl) *n* the part of a vessel at the bow where the crew is quartered.

foreclose (fɔːˈkləʊz) *vb* **forecloses, foreclosing, foreclosed.** **1** *Law.* to deprive (a mortgagor, etc.) of the right to redeem (a mortgage or pledge). **2** (*tr*) to shut out; bar. **3** (*tr*) to prevent or hinder. [C15: from OF, from *for-* out + *clore* to close, from L *claudere*] ▶ **fore'closable** *adj* ▶ **foreclosure** (fɔːˈkləʊʒə) *n*

forecourt ('fɔːˌkɔːt) *n* **1** a courtyard in front of a building, as one in a filling station. **2** the section of the court in tennis, badminton, etc., between the service line and the net.

foredoom (fɔːˈduːm) *vb* (*tr*) to doom or condemn beforehand.

forefather ('fɔːˌfɑːðə) *n* an ancestor, esp. a male. ▶ 'fore,fatherly *adj*

forefinger ('fɔːˌfɪŋɡə) *n* the finger next to the thumb. Also called: **index finger.**

forefoot ('fɔːˌfʊt) *n, pl* **forefeet.** either of the front feet of a quadruped.

forefront ('fɔːˌfrʌnt) *n* **1** the extreme front. **2** the position of most prominence or action.

foregather *or* **forgather** (fɔːˈɡæðə) *vb* (*intr*) **1** to gather together. **2** (foll. by *with*) to socialize.

forego¹ (fɔːˈɡəʊ) *vb* **foregoes, foregoing, forewent, foregone.** to precede in time, place, etc. [OE *foregān*]

forego² (fɔːˈɡəʊ) *vb* **foregoes, foregoing, forewent, foregone.** (*tr*) a variant spelling of **forgo.**

foregoing (fɔːˈɡəʊɪŋ) *adj* (*prenominal*) (esp. of writing or speech) going before; preceding.

foregone (fɔːˈɡɒn, 'fɔːˌɡɒn) *adj* gone or completed; past. ▶ **fore'goneness** *n*

foregone conclusion *n* an inevitable result or conclusion.

foreground ('fɔːˌɡraʊnd) *n* **1** the part of a scene situated towards the front or nearest to the viewer. **2** a conspicuous position.

forehand ('fɔːˌhænd) *adj* (*prenominal*) **1** *Tennis, squash, etc.* (of a stroke) made with the palm of the hand facing the direction of the stroke. ◆ *n* **2** *Tennis, squash, etc.* **2a** a forehand stroke. **2b** the side on which such strokes are made. **3** the part of a horse in front of the saddle.

forehead ('fɒrɪd, 'fɔːˌhɛd) *n* the part of the face between the natural hairline and the eyes. Related adj: **frontal.** [OE *forhēafod*]

foreign ('fɒrɪn) *adj* **1** of, located in, or coming from another country, area, people, etc.: *a foreign resident.* **2** dealing or concerned with another country, area, people, etc.: *a foreign office.* **3** not pertinent or related: *a matter foreign to the discussion.* **4** not familiar; strange. **5** in an abnormal place or position: *foreign matter.* [C13: from OF, from Vulgar L *forānus* (unattested) on the outside, from L *foris* outside] ▶ 'foreignness *n*

foreign affairs *pl n* matters abroad that involve the homeland, such as relations with another country.

foreigner ('fɒrɪnə) *n* **1** a person from a foreign country. **2** an outsider. **3** something from a foreign country, such as a ship or product.

foreign minister *or* **secretary** *n* (*often caps.*) a cabinet minister who is responsible for a country's dealings with other countries. US equivalent: **secretary of state.**

foreign office *n* the ministry of a country or state that is concerned with dealings with other states. US equivalent: **State Department.**

foreknowledge (fɔːˈnɒlɪdʒ) *n* knowledge of a thing before it exists or occurs; prescience. ▶ **fore'know** *vb* ▶ **fore'knowable** *adj*

foreland ('fɔːlənd) *n* **1** a headland, cape, or promontory. **2** land lying in front of something, such as water.

foreleg ('fɔːˌlɛɡ) *n* either of the front legs of a horse, sheep, or other quadruped.

forelimb ('fɔːˌlɪm) *n* either of the front or anterior limbs of a four-limbed vertebrate.

forelock ('fɔːˌlɒk) *n* a lock of hair growing or falling over the forehead.

foreman ('fɔːmən) *n, pl* **foremen. 1** a person, often experienced, who supervises other workmen. **2** *Law.* the principal juror, who presides at the deliberations of a jury.

Foreman ★ ('fɔːmən) *n* George. born 1949, US boxer: WBA world heavyweight champion (1973–74); he regained the title in 1994 but had it withdrawn in 1995 when he refused to fight a challenger; remained WBU champion until 1997.

foremast ('fɔːˌmɑːst; *Naut.* 'fɔːməst) *n* the mast nearest the bow on vessels with two or more masts.

foremost ('fɔːˌməʊst) *adj, adv* first in time, place, rank, etc. [OE, from *forma* first]

forename ('fɔːˌneɪm) *n* another term for **first name.**

forenamed ('fɔːˌneɪmd) *adj* (*prenominal*) named or mentioned previously; aforesaid.

forenoon ('fɔːˌnuːn) *n* the daylight hours before or just before noon.

forensic (fəˈrɛnsɪk) *adj* used in, or connected with a court of law: *forensic science.* [C17: from L *forēnsis* public, from FORUM] ▶ **fo'rensically** *adv*

forensic medicine *n* the use of medical knowledge, esp. pathology, for the purposes of the law, as in determining the cause of death. Also called: **medical jurisprudence.**

foreordain (ˌfɔːrɔːˈdeɪn) *vb* (*tr; may take a clause as object*) to determine (events, etc.) in the future. ▶ **foreordination** (ˌfɔːrɔːdɪˈneɪʃən) *n*

forepaw ('fɔːˌpɔː) *n* either of the front feet of most land mammals that do not have hoofs.

foreplay ('fɔːˌpleɪ) *n* mutual sexual stimulation preceding sexual intercourse.

forequarter ('fɔːˌkwɔːtə) *n* the front portion, including the leg, or half of a carcass, as of beef.

forequarters ('fɔːˌkwɔːtəz) *pl n* the part of the body of a horse, etc. that consists of the forelegs, shoulders, and adjoining parts.

forerun (fɔːˈrʌn) *vb* **foreruns, forerunning, foreran, forerun.** (*tr*) **1** to serve as a herald for. **2** to precede. **3** to forestall.

forerunner ('fɔːˌrʌnə) *n* **1** a person or thing that precedes another. **2** a person or thing coming in advance to herald the arrival of someone or something. **3** an omen; portent.

foresail ('fɔː,seɪl; *Naut.* 'fɔːsᵊl) *n Naut.* **1** the aftermost headsail of a fore-and-aft rigged vessel. **2** the lowest sail set on the foremast of a square-rigged vessel.

foresee (fɔː'siː) *vb* **foresees, foreseeing, foresaw, foreseen**. (*tr; may take a clause as object*) to see or know beforehand: *he did not foresee that*.
▶ **fore'seeable** *adj* ▶ **fore'seer** *n*

foreshadow (fɔː'ʃædəʊ) *vb* (*tr*) to show, indicate, or suggest in advance; presage.

foreshank ('fɔː,ʃæŋk) *n* **1** the top of the front leg of an animal. **2** a cut of meat from this part.

foresheet ('fɔː,ʃiːt) *n* **1** the sheet of a foresail. **2** (*pl*) the part forward of the foremost thwart of a boat.

foreshock ('fɔː,ʃɒk) *n Chiefly US.* a relatively small earthquake heralding the arrival of a much larger one.

foreshore ('fɔː,ʃɔː) *n* **1** the part of the shore that lies between the limits for high and low tides. **2** the part of the shore that lies just above the high water mark.

foreshorten (fɔː'ʃɔːtᵊn) *vb* (*tr*) to represent (a line, form, object, etc.) as shorter than actual length in order to give an illusion of recession or projection.

foreshow (fɔː'ʃəʊ) *vb* **foreshows, foreshowing, foreshowed; foreshown** or **foreshowed**. (*tr*) *Arch.* to indicate in advance.

foresight ('fɔː,saɪt) *n* **1** provision for or insight into future problems, needs, etc. **2** the act or ability of foreseeing. **3** the act of looking forward. **4** *Surveying.* a reading taken looking forwards. **5** the front sight on a firearm.
▶ ,**fore'sighted** *adj* ▶ ,**fore'sightedly** *adv* ▶ ,**fore'sightedness** *n*

foreskin ('fɔː,skɪn) *n Anat.* the nontechnical name for **prepuce**.

forest ('fɒrɪst) *n* **1** a large wooded area having a thick growth of trees and plants. **2** the trees of such an area. **3** *NZ.* an area planted with pines or similar trees, not native trees. Cf. **bush**¹ (sense 4). **4** something resembling a large wooded area, esp. in density: *a forest of telegraph poles*. **5** *Law.* (formerly) an area of woodland, esp. one owned by the sovereign and set apart as a hunting ground. **6** (*modifier*) of, involving, or living in a forest or forests: *a forest glade*. ◆ *vb* **7** (*tr*) to create a forest. [C13: from OF, from Med. L *forestis* unfenced woodland, from L *foris* outside]
▶ '**forested** *adj*

forestall (fɔː'stɔːl) *vb* (*tr*) **1** to delay, stop, or guard against beforehand. **2** to anticipate. **3** to buy up merchandise for profitable resale. [C14 *forestallen* to waylay, from OE, from *fore-* in front of + *steall* place]
▶ **fore'staller** *n* ▶ **fore'stalment** *n*

forestation (,fɒrɪ'steɪʃən) *n* the planting of trees over a wide area.

forestay ('fɔː,steɪ) *n Naut.* an adjustable stay leading from the truck of the foremast to the deck, for controlling the bending of the mast.

forester ('fɒrɪstə) *n* **1** a person skilled in forestry or in charge of a forest. **2** a person or animal that lives in a forest. **3** (*cap.*) a member of the Ancient Order of Foresters, a friendly society.

Forester ★ ('fɒrɪstə) *n* **C(ecil) S(cott)**. 1899–1966, English novelist; creator of Captain Horatio Hornblower in a series of novels on the Napoleonic Wars.

forest park *n NZ.* a recreational reserve which may include bush and exotic trees.

forestry ('fɒrɪstrɪ) *n* **1** the science of planting and caring for trees. **2** the planting and management of forests. **3** *Rare.* forest land.

foretaste ('fɔː,teɪst) *n* an early but limited experience of something to come.

foretell (fɔː'tɛl) *vb* **foretells, foretelling, foretold**. (*tr; may take a clause as object*) to tell or indicate (an event, a result, etc.) beforehand.

forethought ('fɔː,θɔːt) *n* **1** advance consideration or deliberation. **2** thoughtful anticipation of future events.

foretoken *n* ('fɔː,təʊkən). **1** a sign of a future event. ◆ *vb* (fɔː'təʊkən). **2** (*tr*) to foreshadow.

foretop ('fɔː,tɒp; *Naut.* 'fɔːtəp) *n Naut.* a platform at the top of the foremast.

fore-topgallant (,fɔːtɒp'gælənt, ,fɔːtə'gælənt) *adj Naut.* of, relating to, or being the topmost portion of a foremast.

fore-topmast (fɔː'tɒp,mɑːst; *Naut.* fɔː'tɒpməst) *n Naut.* a mast stepped above a foremast.

fore-topsail (fɔː'tɒp,seɪl; *Naut.* fɔː'tɒpsᵊl) *n Naut.* a sail set on a fore-topmast.

forever (fɔː'rɛvə, fə-) *adv* **1** Also: **for ever**. without end; everlastingly. **2** at all times. **3** *Inf.* for a very long time: *he went on speaking forever*. ◆ *n* **forever**. **4** (*as object*) *Inf.* a very long time: *it took him forever to reply*.

> **USAGE NOTE** *Forever* and *for ever* can both be used to say that something is without end. For all other meanings, *forever* is the preferred form.

for evermore or **forevermore** (fɔː,rɛvə'mɔː, fə-) *adv* a more emphatic or emotive term for **forever**.

forewarn (fɔː'wɔːn) *vb* (*tr*) to warn beforehand.
▶ **fore'warner** *n*

forewent (fɔː'wɛnt) *vb* the past tense of **forego**.

forewing ('fɔː,wɪŋ) *n* either wing of the anterior pair of an insect's two pairs of wings.

foreword ('fɔː,wɜːd) *n* an introductory statement to a book. [C19: literal translation of G *Vorwort*]

forfaiting ('fɔː,feɪtɪŋ) *n* the financial service of discounting, without recourse, a promissory note, bill of exchange, letter of credit, etc., received from an overseas buyer by an exporter; a form of debt discounting. [C20: from F *forfaire* to forfeit or surrender]

Forfar ★ ('fɔːfər, -fɑː) *n* a market town in E Scotland, the administrative centre of Angus council area: site of a castle, residence of Scottish kings between the 11th and 14th centuries. Pop.: 12 961 (1991).

forfeit ('fɔːfɪt) *n* **1** something lost or given up as a penalty for a fault, mistake, etc. **2** the act of losing or surrendering something in this manner. **3** *Law.* something confiscated as a penalty for an offence, etc. **4** (*sometimes pl*) **4a** a game in which a player has to give up an object, perform a specified action, etc., if he commits a fault. **4b** an object so given up. ◆ *vb* (*tr*) **5** to lose or be liable to lose in consequence of a mistake, fault, etc. **6** *Law.* to confiscate as punishment. ◆ *adj* **7** surrendered or liable to be surrendered as a penalty. [C13: from OF *forfet* offence, from *forfaire* to commit a crime, from Med. L, from L *foris* outside + *facere* to do]
▶ '**forfeiter** *n*

forfeiture ('fɔːfɪtʃə) *n* **1** something forfeited. **2** the act of forfeiting or paying a penalty.

forfend or **forefend** (fɔː'fɛnd) *vb* (*tr*) **1** *US.* to protect or secure. **2** *Obs.* to prevent.

forgather (fɔː'gæðə) *vb* a variant spelling of **foregather**.

forgave (fə'geɪv) *vb* the past tense of **forgive**.

forge¹ (fɔːdʒ) *n* **1** a place in which metal is worked by heating and hammering; smithy. **2** a hearth or furnace used for heating metal. ◆ *vb* **forges, forging, forged**. **3** (*tr*) to shape (metal) by heating and hammering. **4** (*tr*) to form, make, or fashion (objects, etc.). **5** (*tr*) to invent or devise (an agreement, etc.). **6** to make a fraudulent imitation of (a signature, etc.) or to commit forgery. [C14: from OF *forgier* to construct, from L *fabricāre*, from *faber* craftsman]
▶ '**forger** *n*

forge² (fɔːdʒ) *vb* **forges, forging, forged**. (*intr*) **1** to move at a steady pace. **2 forge ahead**. to increase speed. [C17: from ?]

forgery ('fɔːdʒərɪ) *n, pl* **forgeries**. **1** the act of reproducing something for a fraudulent purpose. **2** something forged, such as an antique. **3** *Criminal law.* **3a** the false making or altering of a document, such as a cheque, etc., or any tape or disc storing information, with intent to defraud. **3b** something forged.

forget (fə'gɛt) *vb* **forgets, forgetting, forgot, forgotten** or (*Arch.*

or dialect) **forgot. 1** (when *tr, may take a clause as object or an infinitive*) to fail to recall (someone or something once known). **2** (*tr; may take a clause as object or an infinitive*) to neglect, either as the result of an unintentional error or intentionally. **3** (*tr*) to leave behind by mistake. **4 forget oneself. 4a** to act in an improper manner. **4b** to be unselfish. **4c** to be deep in thought.   [OE *forgietan*]
▶ **for'gettable** *adj* ▶ **for'getter** *n*

forgetful (fə'gɛtfʊl) *adj* **1** tending to forget. **2** (*often postpositive; foll. by of*) inattentive (to) or neglectful (of).
▶ **for'getfully** *adv* ▶ **for'getfulness** *n*

forget-me-not *n* a temperate low-growing plant having clusters of small blue flowers.

forgive (fə'gɪv) *vb* **forgives, forgiving, forgave, forgiven. 1** to cease to blame (someone or something). **2** to grant pardon for (a mistake, etc.). **3** (*tr*) to free (someone) from penalty. **4** (*tr*) to free from the obligation of (a debt, etc.).   [OE *forgiefan*]
▶ **for'givable** *adj* ▶ **for'giver** *n*

forgiveness (fə'gɪvnɪs) *n* **1** the act of forgiving or the state of being forgiven. **2** willingness to forgive.

forgiving (fə'gɪvɪŋ) *adj* willing to forgive.

forgo *or* **forego** (fɔː'gəʊ) *vb* **forgoes, forgoing, forwent, forgone.** (*tr*) to give up or do without.   [OE *forgān*]

forgot (fə'gɒt) *vb* **1** the past tense of **forget. 2** *Arch. or dialect.* a past participle of **forget**.

forgotten (fə'gɒt³n) *vb* a past participle of **forget**.

forint (*Hungarian* 'forint) *n* the standard monetary unit of Hungary.   [from Hungarian, from It. *fiorino* FLORIN]

fork (fɔːk) *n* **1** a small usually metal implement consisting of two, three, or four long thin prongs on the end of a handle, used for lifting food to the mouth, etc. **2** a similar-shaped agricultural tool, used for lifting, digging, etc. **3** a pronged part of any machine, device, etc. **4** (of a road, river, etc.) **4a** a division into two or more branches. **4b** the point where the division begins. **4c** such a branch. ◆ *vb* **5** (*tr*) to pick up, dig, etc., with a fork. **6** (*tr*) *Chess.* to place (two enemy pieces) under attack with one of one's own pieces. **7** (*intr*) to be divided into two or more branches. **8** to take one or other branch at a fork in a road, etc.   [OE *forca*, from L *furca*]

forked (fɔːkt) *adj* **1a** having a fork or forklike parts. **1b** (*in combination*): *two-forked.* **2** zigzag: *forked lightning.*
▶ **forkedly** ('fɔːkɪdlɪ) *adv*

fork-lift truck *n* a vehicle having two power-operated horizontal prongs that can be raised and lowered for transporting and unloading goods. Sometimes shortened to **fork-lift.**

fork out, over, *or* **up** *vb* (*adv*) *Sl.* to pay (money, goods, etc.), esp. with reluctance.

forlorn (fə'lɔːn) *adj* **1** miserable or cheerless. **2** forsaken. **3** (*postpositive; foll. by of*) bereft: *forlorn of hope.* **4** desperate: *the last forlorn attempt.*   [OE *forloren* lost, from *forlēosan* to lose]
▶ **for'lornness** *n*

forlorn hope *n* **1** a hopeless enterprise. **2** a faint hope. **3** *Obs.* a group of soldiers assigned to an extremely dangerous duty.   [C16 (in the obs. sense): changed (by folk etymology) from Du. *verloren hoop* lost troop, from *verloren,* p.p. of *verliezen* to lose + *hoop* troop (lit.: heap)]

form (fɔːm) *n* **1** the shape or configuration of something as distinct from its colour, texture, etc. **2** the particular mode, appearance, etc., in which a thing or person manifests itself: *water in the form of ice.* **3** a type or kind: *imprisonment is a form of punishment.* **4** a printed document, esp. one with spaces in which to insert facts or answers: *an application form.* **5** physical or mental condition, esp. good condition, with reference to ability to perform: *off form.* **6** the previous record of a horse, athlete, etc., esp. with regard to fitness. **7** *Brit. sl.* a criminal record. **8** a fixed mode of artistic expression or representation in literary, musical, or other artistic works: *sonata form.* **9** a mould, frame, etc., that gives shape to something. **10** *Education, chiefly Brit.* a group of children who are taught together. **11** behaviour or procedure, esp. as governed by custom or etiquette: *good form.* **12** formality or ceremony. **13** a prescribed set or order of words, terms, etc., as in a religious ceremony or legal document. **14** *Philoso-*

phy. **14a** the structure of anything as opposed to its content. **14b** essence as opposed to matter. **15** See **logical form. 16** *Brit., Austral., & NZ.* a bench, esp. one that is long, low, and backless. **17** a hare's nest. **18** any of the various ways in which a word may be spelt or inflected. ◆ *vb* **19** to give shape or form to or to take shape or form, esp. a particular shape. **20** to come or bring into existence: *a scum formed.* **21** to make or construct or be made or constructed. **22** to construct or develop in the mind: *to form an opinion.* **23** (*tr*) to train or mould by instruction or example. **24** (*tr*) to acquire or develop: *to form a habit.* **25** (*tr*) to be an element of or constitute: *this plank will form a bridge.* **26** (*tr*) to organize: *to form a club.*   [C13: from OF, from L *forma* shape, model]

-form *adj combining form.* having the shape or form of or resembling: *cruciform; vermiform.*   [from NL *-formis,* from L, from *fōrma* FORM]

formal ('fɔːməl) *adj* **1** of or following established forms, conventions, etc.: *a formal document.* **2** characterized by observation of conventional forms of ceremony, behaviour, etc.: *a formal dinner.* **3** methodical or stiff. **4** suitable for occasions organized according to conventional ceremony: *formal dress.* **5** denoting idiom, vocabulary, etc., used by educated speakers and writers of a language. **6** acquired by study in academic institutions. **7** symmetrical in form: *a formal garden.* **8** of or relating to the appearance, form, etc., of something as distinguished from its substance. **9** logically deductive: *formal proof.* **10** denoting a second-person pronoun in some languages: *in French the pronoun "vous" is formal, while "tu" is informal.*   [C14: from L *formālis*]
▶ **'formally** *adv* ▶ **'formalness** *n*

formaldehyde (fɔː'mældɪˌhaɪd) *n* a colourless poisonous irritating gas with a pungent characteristic odour, used as formalin and in the manufacture of synthetic resins. Formula: HCHO. Systematic name: **methanal.**   [C19: FORM(IC) + ALDEHYDE; on the model of G *Formaldehyd*]

formalin ('fɔːməlɪn) *n* a solution of formaldehyde in water, used as a disinfectant, preservative for biological specimens, etc.

formalism ('fɔːməˌlɪzəm) *n* **1** scrupulous or excessive adherence to outward form at the expense of content. **2** the mathematical or logical structure of a scientific argument as distinguished from its subject matter. **3** *Theatre.* a stylized mode of production. **4** (in Marxist criticism, etc.) excessive concern with artistic technique at the expense of social values, etc.
▶ **'formalist** *n* ▶ ˌ**formal'istic** *adj*

formality (fɔː'mælɪtɪ) *n, pl* **formalities. 1** a requirement of custom, etiquette, etc. **2** the quality of being formal or conventional. **3** strict or excessive observance of ceremony, etc.

formalize *or* **formalise** ('fɔːməˌlaɪz) *vb* **formalizes, formalizing, formalized** *or* **formalises, formalising, formalised. 1** to be or make formal. **2** (*tr*) to make official or valid. **3** (*tr*) to give a definite shape or form to.
▶ ˌ**formali'zation** *or* ˌ**formali'sation** *n*

formal language *n* any of various languages designed for use in fields such as mathematics, logic, or computer programming, the symbols and formulas of which stand in precisely specified syntactic and semantic relations to one another.

formal logic *n* the study of systems of deductive argument in which symbols are used to represent precisely defined categories of expressions.

Forman ★ ('fɔːmən) *n* **Miloš** ('miːlɒʃ). born 1932, Czech film director working in the USA since 1968. His films include *One Flew over the Cuckoo's Nest* (1976), *Amadeus* (1985), and *The People vs Larry Flynt* (1996).

formant ('fɔːmənt) *n Acoustics, phonetics.* any of the constituents of a sound, esp. a vowel sound, that impart to the sound its own special quality, tone colour, or timbre.

format ('fɔːmæt) *n* **1** the general appearance of a publication, including type style, paper, binding, etc. **2** style, plan, or arrangement, as of a television programme. **3** *Computing.* **3a** the defined arrangement of data encoded in a file or, for example, on magnetic disk or CD-ROM, that is essential for the correct recording and recovery of data on different devices. **3b** the arrangement of text on printed output or on a display screen. ◆ *vb* **formats, formatting, formatted.** (*tr*) **4** to arrange (a book, page, etc.) into a specified format. [C19: via F from G, from L *liber formātus* volume formed]

formation (fɔː'meɪʃən) *n* **1** the act of giving or taking form or existence. **2** something that is formed. **3** the manner in which something is arranged. **4a** a formal arrangement of a number of persons or things acting as a unit, such as a troop of soldiers or a football team. **4b** (*as modifier*): *formation dancing.* **5** a series of rocks with certain characteristics in common.

formative ('fɔːmətɪv) *adj* **1** of or relating to formation, development, or growth: *formative years.* **2** shaping; moulding: *a formative experience.* **3** functioning in the formation of derived, inflected, or compound words. ◆ *n* **4** an inflectional or derivational affix.
▸ **'formatively** *adv* ▸ **'formativeness** *n*

Formby ★ ('fɔːmbɪ) *n* **George.** Real name *George Booth.* 1904–61, British comedian. He made many musical films in the 1930s, accompanying his songs on the ukulele.

form class *n* **1** another term for **part of speech. 2** a group of words distinguished by common inflections, such as the weak verbs of English.

forme *or US* **form** (fɔːm) *n Printing.* type matter, blocks, etc., assembled in a chase and ready for printing. [C15: from F: FORM]

former[1] ('fɔːmə) *adj* (*prenominal*) **1** belonging to or occurring in an earlier time: *former glory.* **2** having been at a previous time: *a former colleague.* **3** denoting the first or first mentioned of two. ◆ *n* **4 the former.** the first or first mentioned of two: distinguished from *latter.*

former[2] ('fɔːmə) *n* **1** a person or thing that forms or shapes. **2** *Electrical engineering.* a tool for giving a coil or winding the required shape.

formerly ('fɔːməlɪ) *adv* at or in a former time; in the past.

formic ('fɔːmɪk) *adj* **1** of, relating to, or derived from ants. **2** of, containing, or derived from formic acid. [C18: from L *formīca* ant; the acid occurs naturally in ants]

Formica (fɔː'maɪkə) *n Trademark.* any of various laminated plastic sheets used esp. for heat-resistant surfaces.

formic acid *n* a colourless corrosive liquid carboxylic acid found in some insects, esp. ants, and many plants: used in the manufacture of insecticides. Formula: HCOOH. Systematic name: **methanoic acid.**

formidable ('fɔːmɪdəbᵊl) *adj* **1** arousing or likely to inspire fear or dread. **2** extremely difficult to defeat, overcome, manage, etc. **3** tending to inspire awe or admiration because of great size, excellence, etc. [C15: from L, from *formīdāre* to dread, from *formīdō* fear]
▸ **'formidably** *adv*

formless ('fɔːmlɪs) *adj* without a definite shape or form; amorphous.
▸ **'formlessly** *adv*

form letter *n* a single copy of a letter that has been mechanically reproduced in large numbers for circulation.

Formosa ★ (fɔː'məʊsə) *n* the former name of **Taiwan.**

Formosa Strait ★ *n* an arm of the Pacific between Taiwan and mainland China, linking the East and South China Seas. Also called: **Taiwan Strait.**

formula ('fɔːmjʊlə) *n, pl* **formulas** *or* **formulae** (-ˌliː). **1** an established form or set of words, as used in religious ceremonies, legal proceedings, etc. **2** *Maths., physics.* a general relationship, principle, or rule stated, often as an equation, in the form of symbols. **3** *Chem.* a representation of molecules, radicals, ions, etc., expressed in the symbols of the atoms of their constituent elements. **4a** a method, pattern, or rule for doing or producing something, often one proved to be successful. **4b** (*as modifier*): *formula fiction.* **5** *US & Canad.* a prescription for making up a medicine, baby's food, etc. **6** *Motor racing.* the category in which a type of car competes, judged according to engine size, weight, and fuel capacity. [C17: from L: dim. of *forma* FORM]
▸ **formulaic** (ˌfɔːmjʊ'leɪɪk) *adj*

Formula One *n* **1** the top class of professional motor racing. **2** the most important world championship in motor racing.

formularize *or* **formularise** ('fɔːmjʊləˌraɪz) *vb* **formularizes, formularizing, formularized** *or* **formularises, formularising, formularised.** a less common word for **formulate** (sense 1).

formulary ('fɔːmjʊlərɪ) *n, pl* **formularies. 1** a book of prescribed formulas, esp. relating to religious procedure or doctrine. **2** a formula. **3** *Pharmacol.* a book containing a list of pharmaceutical products with their formulas. ◆ *adj* **4** of or relating to a formula.

formulate ('fɔːmjʊˌleɪt) *vb* **formulates, formulating, formulated.** (*tr*) **1** to put into or express in systematic terms; express in or as if in a formula. **2** to devise.
▸ **ˌformu'lation** *n*

formwork ('fɔːmˌwɜːk) *n* an arrangement of wooden boards, etc., used to shape concrete while it is setting.

fornicate ('fɔːnɪˌkeɪt) *vb* **fornicates, fornicating, fornicated.** (*intr*) to commit fornication. [C16: from LL *fornicārī*, from L *fornix* vault, brothel situated therein]
▸ **'forni,cator** *n*

fornication (ˌfɔːnɪ'keɪʃən) *n* **1** voluntary sexual intercourse outside marriage. **2** *Bible.* sexual immorality in general, esp. adultery.

Forrest ★ ('fɒrɪst) *n* **John,** 1st Baron Forrest. 1847–1918, Australian statesman and explorer; first premier of Western Australia (1890–1901).

forsake (fə'seɪk) *vb* **forsakes, forsaking, forsook, forsaken.** (*tr*) **1** to abandon. **2** to give up (something valued or enjoyed). [OE *forsacan*]
▸ **for'saker** *n*

forsaken (fə'seɪkən) *vb* **1** the past participle of **forsake.** ◆ *adj* **2** completely deserted or helpless.
▸ **for'sakenly** *adv* ▸ **for'sakenness** *n*

forsook (fə'sʊk) *vb* the past tense of **forsake.**

forsooth (fə'suːθ) *adv Arch.* in truth; indeed. [OE *forsōth*]

Forster ★ ('fɔːstə) *n* **E(dward) M(organ).** 1879–1970, English novelist, short-story writer, and essayist. His best-known novels are *A Room with a View* (1908), *Howard's End* (1910), and *A Passage to India* (1924), in all of which he stresses the need for sincerity and sensitivity in human relationships and criticizes English middle-class values.

forswear (fɔː'sweə) *vb* **forswears, forswearing, forswore, forsworn. 1** (*tr*) to reject or renounce with determination or as upon oath. **2** (*tr*) to deny or disavow absolutely or upon oath. **3** to perjure (oneself). [OE *forswearian*]
▸ **for'swearer** *n*

forsworn (fɔː'swɔːn) *vb* the past participle of **forswear.**
▸ **for'swornness** *n*

Forsyth ★ (fɔː'saɪθ) *n* **1 Bill.** born 1947, Scottish screenwriter and film director. His films include *Gregory's Girl* (1981), *Local Hero* (1983), and *Rebecca's Daughters* (1992). **2 Frederick.** born 1938, British thriller writer. His books include *The Day of the Jackal* (1970), *The Odessa File* (1972), and *The Fourth Protocol* (1984).

forsythia (fɔː'saɪθɪə) *n* a shrub native to China, Japan, and SE Europe but widely cultivated for its showy yellow bell-shaped flowers, which appear in spring before the foliage. [C19: NL, after William *Forsyth* (1737–1804), E botanist]

fort (fɔːt) *n* **1** a fortified enclosure, building, or position able to be defended against an enemy. **2 hold the fort.** *Inf.* to guard something temporarily. [C15: from OF, from *fort* (adj) strong, from L *fortis*]

fort. *abbrev. for:* **1** fortification. **2** fortified.

Fortaleza ★ (*Portuguese* fortaˈleza) *n* a port in NE Brazil, capital of Ceará state. Pop.: 2 660 000 (1995). Also called: **Ceará.**

Fort-de-France ★ (*French* fɔrdəfrãs) *n* the capital of Martinique, a port on the W coast: commercial centre of the French Antilles. Pop.: 101 540 (1990).

forte[1] (fɔːt, 'fɔːteɪ) *n* **1** something at which a person excels: *cooking is my forte.* **2** *Fencing.* the stronger section of a sword, between the hilt and the middle. [C17: from F, from *fort* (adj) strong, from L *fortis*]

★ people and places

forte[2] ('fɔːtɪ) *Music.* ◆ *adj, adv* **1** loud or loudly. Symbol: f ◆ *n* **2** a loud passage in music. [C18: from It., from L *fortis* strong]

forte-piano (ˌfɔːtɪ'pjɑːnəʊ) *Music.* ◆ *adj, adv* **1** loud and then immediately soft. Symbol: fp ◆ *n* **2** a note played in this way.

forth (fɔːθ) *adv* **1** forward in place, time, order, or degree. **2** out, as from concealment or inaction. **3** away, as from a place or country. **4 and so forth.** and so on. ◆ *prep* **5** *Arch.* out of. [OE]

Forth ★ (fɔːθ) *n* **1 Firth of.** an inlet of the North Sea in SE Scotland: spanned by a cantilever railway bridge 1600 m (almost exactly 1 mile) long (1889), and by a road bridge (1964). **2** a river in central Scotland, flowing generally SE to the Firth of Forth. Length: about 104 km (65 miles).

forthcoming (ˌfɔːθ'kʌmɪŋ) *adj* **1** approaching in time: *the forthcoming debate.* **2** about to appear: *his forthcoming book.* **3** available or ready. **4** open or sociable.

forthright *adj* ('fɔːθ,raɪt). **1** direct and outspoken. ◆ *adv* (ˌfɔːθ'raɪt, 'fɔːθ,raɪt), *also* **forthrightly. 2** in a direct manner; frankly. **3** at once. ▸ **'forth,rightness** *n*

forthwith (ˌfɔːθ'wɪθ) *adv* at once.

fortification (ˌfɔːtɪfɪ'keɪʃən) *n* **1** the act, art, or science of fortifying or strengthening. **2a** a wall, mound, etc., used to fortify a place. **2b** such works collectively.

fortify ('fɔːtɪ,faɪ) *vb* **fortifies, fortifying, fortified.** (*mainly tr*) **1** (*also intr*) to make (a place) defensible, as by building walls, etc. **2** to strengthen physically, mentally, or morally. **3** to add alcohol to (wine), in order to produce sherry, port, etc. **4** to increase the nutritious value of (a food), as by adding vitamins. **5** to confirm: *to fortify an argument.* [C15: from OF, from LL, from L *fortis* strong + *facere* to make] ▸ **'forti,fiable** *adj* ▸ **'forti,fier** *n*

fortissimo (fɔː'tɪsɪ,məʊ) *Music.* ◆ *adj, adv* **1** very loud. Symbol: ff ◆ *n* **2** a very loud passage in music. [C18: from It., from L, from *fortis* strong]

fortitude ('fɔːtɪ,tjuːd) *n* strength and firmness of mind. [C15: from L *fortitūdō* courage]

Fort Knox ★ (nɒks) *n* a military reservation in N Kentucky: site of the US Gold Bullion Depository. Pop.: 38 277 (1989 est.).

Fort Lamy ★ ('fɔːt 'lɑːmɪ; *French* fɔr lami) *n* the former name (until 1973) of **Ndjamena.**

fortnight ('fɔːt,naɪt) *n* a period of 14 consecutive days; two weeks. [OE *fēowertīene niht* fourteen nights]

fortnightly ('fɔːt,naɪtlɪ) *Chiefly Brit.* ◆ *adj* **1** occurring or appearing once each fortnight. ◆ *adv* **2** once a fortnight. ◆ *n, pl* **fortnightlies. 3** a publication issued at intervals of two weeks.

Fortran ('fɔːtræn) *n* a high-level computer programming language for mathematical and scientific purposes. [C20: from *for(mula) tran(slation)*]

fortress ('fɔːtrɪs) *n* **1** a large fort or fortified town. **2** a place or source of refuge or support. ◆ *vb* **3** (*tr*) to protect. [C13: from OF, from Med. L *fortalitia*, from L *fortis* strong]

Fort Sumter ★ ('sʌmtə) *n* a fort in SE South Carolina, guarding Charleston Harbour. Its capture by Confederate forces (1861) was the first action of the Civil War.

fortuitous (fɔː'tjuːɪtəs) *adj* happening by chance, esp. by a lucky chance. [C17: from L *fortuitus* happening by chance, from *fors* chance, luck] ▸ **for'tuitously** *adv*

fortuity (fɔː'tjuːɪtɪ) *n, pl* **fortuities. 1** a chance or accidental occurrence. **2** chance or accident.

Fortuna ★ (fɔː'tjuːnə) *n* the Roman goddess of fortune and good luck. Greek counterpart: **Tyche.**

fortunate ('fɔːtʃənɪt) *adj* **1** having good luck. **2** occurring by or bringing good fortune or luck. ▸ **'fortunately** *adv*

fortune ('fɔːtʃən) *n* **1** an amount of wealth or material prosperity, esp. a great amount. **2 small fortune.** a large sum of money. **3** a power or force, often personalized, regarded as being responsible for human affairs. **4** luck,

esp. when favourable. **5** (*often pl*) a person's destiny. ◆ *vb* **fortunes, fortuning, fortuned. 6** (*intr*) *Arch.* to happen by chance. [C13: from OF, from L, from *fors* chance]

fortune-hunter *n* a person who seeks to secure a fortune, esp. through marriage.

fortune-teller *n* a person who makes predictions about the future as by looking into a crystal ball, etc. ▸ **'fortune-,telling** *adj, n*

Fort William ★ *n* a town in W Scotland, in Highland council area at the head of Loch Linnhe: tourist centre; the fort itself, built in 1655 and renamed after William III in 1690, was demolished in 1866. Pop.: 10 391 (1991).

Fort Worth ★ (wɜːθ) *n* a city in N Texas, at the junction of the Clear and West forks of the Trinity River: aircraft works, electronics. Pop.: 451 814 (1994 est.).

forty ('fɔːtɪ) *n, pl* **forties. 1** the cardinal number that is the product of ten and four. **2** a numeral, 40, XL, etc., representing this number. **3** something representing, represented by, or consisting of 40 units. ◆ *determiner* **4a** amounting to forty: *forty thieves.* **4b** (*as pronoun*): *there were forty in the herd.* [OE *fēowertig*] ▸ **'fortieth** *adj, n*

forty-five *n* a gramophone record played at 45 revolutions per minute.

Forty-Five *n* **the.** *British history.* another name for the **Jacobite Rebellion** of 1745–46. See **Young Pretender.**

forty-niner *n* (*sometimes cap.*) *US history.* a prospector who took part in the California gold rush of 1849.

forty winks *n* (*functioning as sing or pl*) *Inf.* a short light sleep; nap.

forum ('fɔːrəm) *n, pl* **forums** *or* **fora** (-rə). **1** a meeting for the open discussion of subjects of public interest. **2** a medium for open discussion, such as a magazine. **3** a public meeting place for open discussion. **4** a court; tribunal. **5** (in ancient Italy) an open space serving as a city's marketplace and centre of public business. [C15: from L: public place]

Forum *or* **Forum Romanum** ★ (rəʊ'mɑːnəm) *n* **the.** the main forum of ancient Rome.

forward ('fɔːwəd) *adj* **1** directed or moving ahead. **2** lying or situated at or near the front part of something. **3** presumptuous, pert, or impudent. **4** well developed or advanced, esp. in physical or intellectual development. **5a** of or relating to the future or favouring change. **5b** (*in combination*): *forward-looking.* **6** (*often postpositive*) *Arch.* ready, eager, or willing. **7** *Commerce.* relating to fulfilment at a future date. ◆ *n* **8** an attacking player in any of various sports, such as soccer. ◆ *adv* **9** a variant of **forwards. 10** ('fɔːwəd; *Naut.* 'fɒrəd). towards the front or bow of an aircraft or ship. **11** into a position of being subject to public scrutiny: *the witness came forward.* ◆ *vb* (*tr*) **12** to send forward or pass on to an ultimate destination: *the letter was forwarded.* **13** to advance or promote: *to forward one's career.* [OE *foreweard*] ▸ **'forwarder** *n* ▸ **'forwardly** *adv* ▸ **'forwardness** *n*

forwards ('fɔːwədz) *or* **forward** *adv* **1** towards or at a place ahead or in advance, esp. in space but also in time. **2** towards the front.

forwent (fɔː'wɛnt) *vb* the past tense of **forgo.**

forza ('fɔːtsə) *n Music.* force. [C19: It., lit.: force]

Foshan ('fɔː'ʃɑːn) *or* **Fatshan** ★ *n* a city in SE China, in W Guangdong province. Pop.: 303 160 (1990 est). Also called: **Namhoi.**

fossa ('fɒsə) *n, pl* **fossae** (-siː). an anatomical depression or hollow area. [C19: from L: ditch, from *fossus* dug up, from *fodere* to dig up]

fosse *or* **foss** (fɒs) *n* a ditch or moat, esp. one dug as a fortification. [C14: from OF, from L *fossa*; see FOSSA]

Fosse Way ★ (fɒs) *n* a Roman road in Britain between Lincoln and Exeter, with a fosse on each side.

fossick ('fɒsɪk) *vb Austral. & NZ.* **1** (*intr*) to search for gold or precious stones in abandoned workings, rivers, etc. **2** to rummage or search for (something): *to fossick around for.* [C19: Austral., prob. from E dialect *fussock* to bustle about, from FUSS] ▸ **'fossicker** *n*

fossil ('fɒsᵊl) n **1a** a relic or representation of a plant or animal that existed in a past geological age, occurring in the form of mineralized bones, shells, etc. **1b** (as modifier): fossil insects. **2** Inf., derog. a person, idea, thing, etc., that is outdated or incapable of change. **3** Linguistics. a form once current but now appearing only in one or two special contexts. [C17: from L fossilis dug up, from fodere to dig]

fossil fuel n any naturally occurring fuel, such as coal, and natural gas, formed by the decomposition of prehistoric organisms.

fossiliferous (ˌfɒsɪˈlɪfərəs) adj (of sedimentary rocks) containing fossils.

fossilize or **fossilise** ('fɒsɪˌlaɪz) vb **fossilizes, fossilizing, fossilized** or **fossilises, fossilising, fossilised**. **1** to convert or be converted into a fossil. **2** to become or cause to become antiquated or inflexible.
▸ ˌfossiliˈzation or ˌfossiliˈsation n

fossorial (fɒˈsɔːrɪəl) adj (of the forelimbs and skeleton of burrowing animals) adapted for digging. [C19: from Med. L, from L fossor digger, from fodere to dig]

foster ('fɒstə) vb (tr) **1** to promote the growth or development of. **2** to bring up (a child, etc.). **3** to cherish (a plan, hope, etc.) in one's mind. **4** Chiefly Brit. **4a** to place (a child) in the care of foster parents. **4b** to bring up under fosterage. ◆ adj **5** indicating relationship through fostering and not through birth: foster child, foster mother. **6** of or involved in the rearing of a child by persons other than his natural parents: foster home. [OE fōstrian to feed, from fōstor FOOD]
▸ 'fosterer n ▸ 'fostering n

Foster ★ ('fɒstə) n **1** Sir **Norman**. born 1935, British architect. His works include the Willis Faber building (1978) in Ipswich, Stansted Airport, Essex (1991), and Hong Kong airport, China (1998). **2** Jodie. born 1962, US film actress and director: her films include Taxi Driver (1976), Little Man Tate (1991; also directed), and Contact (1997). **3** Stephen Collins. 1826–64, US composer of songs such as The Old Folks at Home and Oh Susanna.

fosterage ('fɒstərɪdʒ) n **1** the act of caring for a foster child. **2** the state of being a foster child. **3** the act of encouraging.

Fotheringhay ★ ('fɒðərɪŋˌgeɪ) n a village in E England, in NE Northamptonshire: ruined castle, scene of the imprisonment and execution of Mary Queen of Scots (1587).

Foucault ★ (French fuko) n **1** Jean Bernard Léon (ʒɑ̃ bɛrnar leɔ̃). 1819–68, French physicist. He determined the speed of light, devised a pendulum to demonstrate the rotation of the earth, and invented the gyroscope. **2** Michel (miʃɛl). 1926–84, French philosopher. His publications include Histoire de la folie (1961) and Les Mots et les choses (1966).

Foucquet ★ (French fukɛ) n a variant spelling of (Nicolas) **Fouquet**.

fought (fɔːt) vb the past tense and past participle of **fight**.

foul (faʊl) adj **1** offensive to the senses; revolting. **2** stinking. **3** charged with or full of dirt or offensive matter. **4** (of food) putrid; rotten. **5** morally or spiritually offensive. **6** obscene; vulgar: foul language. **7** unfair: to resort to foul means. **8** (esp. of weather) unpleasant or adverse. **9** blocked or obstructed with dirt or foreign matter: a foul drain. **10** (of the bottom of a vessel) covered with barnacles that slow forward motion. **11** Inf. unsatisfactory; bad: a foul book. ◆ n **12** Sport. **12a** a violation of the rules. **12b** (as modifier): a foul blow. **13** an entanglement or collision, esp. in sailing or fishing. ◆ vb **14** to make or become polluted. **15** to become or cause to become entangled. **16** (tr) to disgrace. **17** to become or cause to become clogged. **18** (tr) Naut. (of underwater growth) to cling to (the bottom of a vessel) so as to slow its motion. **19** (tr) Sport. to commit a foul against (an opponent). **20** (intr) Sport. to infringe the rules. **21** to collide (with a boat, etc.). ◆ adv **22** in a foul manner. **23 fall foul of. 23a** come into conflict with. **23b** Naut. to come into collision with. [OE fūl]
▸ 'foully adv ▸ 'foulness n

foulard (fuːˈlɑːd) n a soft light fabric of plain-weave or twill-weave silk or rayon, usually with a printed design. [C19: from F, from ?]

Foulness ★ (faʊlˈnɛs) n a flat marshy island in SE England, in Essex north of the Thames estuary.

foul play n **1** violent or treacherous conduct, esp. murder. **2** a violation of the rules in a game or sport.

foul up vb (adv) **1** (tr) to bungle. **2** (tr) to contaminate. **3** to be or cause to be blocked, choked, or entangled. ◆ n **foul-up**. **4** a state of confusion or muddle caused by bungling.

found[1] (faʊnd) vb **1** the past tense and past participle of **find**. ◆ adj **2** furnished or fitted out. **3** Brit. with meals, heating, etc., provided without extra charge.

found[2] (faʊnd) vb **1** (tr) to bring into being or establish (something, such as an institution, etc.). **2** (tr) to build or establish the foundation of. **3** (also intr; foll. by on or upon) to have a basis (in). [C13: from OF, from L, from fundus bottom]

found[3] (faʊnd) vb (tr) **1** to cast (a material, such as metal or glass) by melting and pouring into a mould. **2** to make (articles) in this way. [C14: from OF, from L fundere to melt]

foundation (faʊnˈdeɪʃən) n **1** that on which something is founded. **2** (often pl) a construction below the ground that distributes the load of a building, wall, etc. **3** the base on which something stands. **4** the act of founding or establishing or the state of being founded or established. **5** an endowment for the support of an institution such as a school. **6** an institution supported by an endowment, often one that provides funds for charities, research, etc. **7** a cosmetic used as a base for make-up.
▸ founˈdational adj

foundation garment n a woman's undergarment worn to shape and support the figure. Also called: **foundation.**

foundation stone n a stone laid at a ceremony to mark the foundation of a new building.

foundation subjects pl n Brit. education. the subjects studied as part of the National Curriculum, including the compulsory core subjects.

founder[1] ('faʊndə) n a person who establishes an institution, society, etc. [C14: see FOUND[2]]

founder[2] ('faʊndə) vb (intr) **1** (of a ship, etc.) to sink. **2** to break down or fail: the project foundered. **3** to sink into or become stuck in soft ground. **4** to collapse. **5** (of a horse) to stumble or go lame. [C13: from OF fondrer to submerge, from L fundus bottom]

> **USAGE NOTE** Founder is sometimes wrongly used where flounder is meant: this unexpected turn of events left him floundering (not foundering).

founder[3] ('faʊndə) n **a** a person who makes metal castings. **b** (in combination): an iron founder. [C15: see FOUND[3]]

foundling ('faʊndlɪŋ) n an abandoned infant whose parents are not known. [C13 foundeling; see FIND]

foundry ('faʊndrɪ) n, pl **foundries**. a place in which metal castings are produced. [C17: from OF, from fondre; see FOUND[3]]

fount[1] (faʊnt) n **1** Poetic. a spring or fountain. **2** source. [C16: back formation from FOUNTAIN]

fount[2] (faʊnt, fɒnt) n Printing. a complete set of type of one style and size. Also called (esp. US and Canad.): **font**. [C16: from OF fonte a founding, casting, from Vulgar L funditus (unattested) a casting, from L fundere to melt]

fountain ('faʊntɪn) n **1** a jet or spray of water or some other liquid. **2** a structure from which such a jet or a number of such jets spurt. **3** a natural spring of water, esp. the source of a stream. **4** a stream, jet, or cascade of sparks, lava, etc. **5** a principal source. **6** a reservoir, as for oil in a lamp. [C15: from OF, from LL, from L fons spring, source]
▸ 'fountained adj

fountainhead ('faʊntɪnˌhɛd) n **1** a spring that is the source of a stream. **2** a principal or original source.

★ people and places

fountain pen *n* a pen the nib of which is supplied with ink from a cartridge or a reservoir in its barrel.

Fouqué ★ (*German* fuˈkeː) *n* **Friedrich Heinrich Karl** (ˈfriːdrɪç ˈhainrɪç karl), Baron de la Motte. 1777–1843, German romantic writer; author of *Undine* (1811).

Fouquet ★ (*French* fukɛ) *n* **1 Jean** (ʒɑ̃). ?1420–?80, French painter and miniaturist. **2** Also: **Foucquet. Nicolas** (nikɔla), *Marquis de Belle-Isle*. 1615–80, French statesman; superintendent of finance (1653–61) under Louis XIV; imprisoned for embezzlement.

Fouquier-Tinville ★ (*French* fukjetɛ̃vil) *n* **Antoine Quentin** (ɑ̃twan kɑ̃tɛ̃). 1746–95, French revolutionary; as public prosecutor (1793–94) during the Reign of Terror, he sanctioned the guillotining of Robespierre and many others.

four (fɔː) *n* **1** the cardinal number that is the sum of three and one. **2** a numeral, 4, IV, etc., representing this number. **3** something representing, represented by, or consisting of four units, such as a playing card with four symbols on it. **4** Also called: **four o'clock.** four hours after noon or midnight. **5** *Cricket.* **5a** a shot that crosses the boundary after hitting the ground. **5b** the four runs scored for such a shot. **6** *Rowing.* **6a** a racing shell propelled by four oarsmen. **6b** the crew of such a shell. ◆ *determiner* **7a** amounting to four: *four times.* **7b** (*as pronoun*): *four are ready.* [OE *fēower*]

four-by-four *n* a vehicle equipped with four-wheel drive.

four flush *n* a useless poker hand, containing four of a suit and one odd card.

fourfold (ˈfɔːˌfəʊld) *adj* **1** equal to or having four times as many or as much. **2** composed of four parts. ◆ *adv* **3** by or up to four times as many or as much.

Fourier (ˈfʊərɪˌeɪ; *French* furje) *n* **1** (**François Marie**) **Charles** (ʃarl). 1772–1837, French social reformer; propounded a system of cooperatives in *Le Nouveau monde industriel* (1829–30). **2 Jean Baptiste Joseph** (ʒɑ̃ batist ʒozɛf). 1768–1830, French mathematician and Egyptologist, noted for the method of analysis named after him.

four-in-hand *n* **1** a road vehicle drawn by four horses and driven by one driver. **2** a four-horse team. **3** *US.* a long narrow tie tied in a flat slipknot with the ends dangling.

four-leaf clover or **four-leaved clover** *n* a clover with four leaves rather than three, supposed to bring good luck.

four-letter word *n* any of several short English words referring to sex or excrement: regarded generally as offensive or obscene.

Fournier ★ (*French* furnje) *n* See **Alain-Fournier.**

four-o'clock *n* a tropical American plant, cultivated for its tubular yellow, red, or white flowers that open in late afternoon. Also called: **marvel-of-Peru.**

four-poster *n* a bed with posts at each corner supporting a canopy and curtains.

fourscore (ˌfɔːˈskɔː) *determiner* an archaic word for **eighty.**

foursome (ˈfɔːsəm) *n* **1** a set or company of four. **2** Also called: **four-ball.** *Golf.* a game between two pairs of players.

foursquare (ˌfɔːˈskwɛə) *adv* **1** squarely; firmly. ◆ *adj* **2** solid and strong. **3** forthright. **4** a rare word for **square.**

four-stroke *adj* designating an internal-combustion engine in which the piston makes four strokes for every explosion.

fourteen (ˈfɔːˈtiːn) *n* **1** the cardinal number that is the sum of ten and four. **2** a numeral, 14, XIV, etc., representing this number. **3** something represented by or consisting of 14 units. ◆ *determiner* **4a** amounting to fourteen: *fourteen cats.* **4b** (*as pronoun*): *the fourteen who remained.* [OE *fēowertīene*]
▶ **'four'teenth** *adj, n*

fourth (fɔːθ) *adj* (*usually prenominal*) **1a** coming after the third in order, position, time, etc. Often written: 4th. **1b** (*as n*): *the fourth in succession.* **2** denoting the highest forward ratio of a gearbox in most motor vehicles. ◆ *n* **3** *Music.* **3a** the interval between one note and another

four notes away from it in a diatonic scale. **3b** one of two notes constituting such an interval in relation to the other. **4** the fourth forward ratio of a gearbox in a motor vehicle, usually the highest gear in cars. **5** a less common word for **quarter** (sense 2). ◆ *adv* also: **fourthly. 6** after the third person, position, event, etc. ◆ *sentence connector. also:* **fourthly. 7** as the fourth point.

fourth dimension *n* **1** the dimension of time, which in addition to three spatial dimensions specifies the position of a point or particle. **2** the concept in science fiction of a dimension in addition to three spatial dimensions.
▶ **ˌfourth-diˈmensional** *adj*

fourth estate *n* (*sometimes caps.*) journalists or their profession; the press.

four-wheel drive *n* a system used in motor vehicles in which all four wheels are connected to the source of power.

fovea (ˈfəʊvɪə) *n, pl* **foveae** (-vɪˌiː). *Anat.* any small pit or depression in the surface of a bodily organ or part. [C19: from L: a small pit]

Fowey ★ (fɔɪ) *n* a resort and fishing village in SW England, in Cornwall, linked administratively with St Austell in 1968. Pop.: 1939 (1991).

fowl (faʊl) *n* **1** Also called: **domestic fowl.** a domesticated gallinaceous bird occurring in many varieties. **2** any other bird that is used as food or hunted as game. **3** the flesh or meat of fowl, esp. of chicken. **4** an archaic word for any **bird.** ◆ *vb* **5** (*intr*) to hunt or snare wildfowl. [OE *fugol*]
▶ **'fowler** *n* ▶ **'fowling** *n, adj*

Fowler ★ (ˈfaʊlə) *n* **Henry Watson.** 1858–1933, English lexicographer and grammarian; compiler of *Modern English Usage* (1926).

Fowles ★ (faʊlz) *n* **John.** born 1926, British novelist. His books include *The Collector* (1963), *The French Lieutenant's Woman* (1969), and *The Tree* (1991).

Fowliang or **Fou-liang** ★ (ˈfuːˈljæŋ) *n* a variant transliteration of the Chinese name for **Jingdezhen.**

fowl pest *n* an acute and usually fatal viral disease of domestic fowl, characterized by discoloration of the comb and wattles.

fox (fɒks) *n, pl* **foxes** or **fox. 1** any canine mammal of the genus *Vulpes* and related genera. They are mostly predators and have a pointed muzzle and a bushy tail. **2** the fur of any of these animals, usually reddish-brown or grey in colour. **3** a person who is cunning and sly. ◆ *vb* **4** (*tr*) *Inf.* to perplex: *to fox a person with a problem.* **5** to cause (paper, wood, etc.) to become discoloured with spots, or (of paper, etc.) to become discoloured. **6** (*tr*) to trick; deceive. **7** (*intr*) to act deceitfully or craftily. [OE]
▶ **'fox,like** *adj*

Fox ★ (fɒks) *n* **1 Charles James.** 1749–1806, British Whig statesman. He advocated abolition of the slave trade. **2 George.** 1624–91, English religious leader; founder (1647) of the Society of Friends (Quakers). **3 Sir William.** 1812–93, New Zealand statesman, born in England: prime minister (1856; 1861–62; 1869–72; 1873).

Foxe ★ (fɒks) *n* **John.** 1516–87, English Protestant clergyman; author of *History of the Acts and Monuments of the Church* (1563), popularly known as the *Book of Martyrs.*

Foxe Basin ★ *n* an arm of the Atlantic in NE Canada, between Melville Peninsula and Baffin Island.

foxfire (ˈfɒksˌfaɪə) *n* a luminescent glow emitted by certain fungi on rotting wood.

foxglove (ˈfɒksˌglʌv) *n* a plant having spikes of purple or white thimble-like flowers. The soft wrinkled leaves are a source of digitalis. [OE]

foxhole (ˈfɒksˌhəʊl) *n Mil.* a small pit dug to provide shelter against hostile fire.

foxhound (ˈfɒksˌhaʊnd) *n* a breed of short-haired hound, usually kept for hunting foxes.

fox hunt *n* **1a** the hunting of foxes with hounds. **1b** an instance of this. **2** an organization for fox hunting within a particular area.
▶ **'fox-,hunter** *n* ▶ **'fox-,hunting** *n*

foxtail (ˈfɒksˌteɪl) *n* any grass of Europe, Asia, and South

America, having soft cylindrical spikes of flowers: cultivated as a pasture grass.

Fox Talbot ★ ('tɔːlbət) *n* **William Henry.** 1800–77, British physicist; a pioneer of photography.

fox terrier *n* either of two breeds of small tan-black-and-white terrier, the wire-haired and the smooth.

foxtrot ('fɒks,trɒt) *n* **1** a ballroom dance in quadruple time, combining short and long steps in various sequences. ◆ *vb* **foxtrots, foxtrotting, foxtrotted. 2** (*intr*) to perform this dance.

foxy ('fɒksɪ) *adj* **foxier, foxiest. 1** of or resembling a fox, esp. in craftiness. **2** of a reddish-brown colour. **3** (of paper, etc.) spotted, esp. by mildew. **4** *Sl.* sexy; sexually attractive.
▸ 'foxily *adv* ▸ 'foxiness *n*

foyer ('fɔɪeɪ, 'fɔɪə) *n* a hall, lobby, or anteroom, as in a hotel, theatre, cinema, etc. [C19: from F: fireplace, from Med. L, from L *focus* fire]

fp *Music. abbrev. for* forte-piano.

FP *abbrev. for:* **1** fire plug. **2** former pupil. **3** Also: **fp.** freezing point.

FPA *abbrev. for* Family Planning Association.

fps *abbrev. for:* **1** feet per second. **2** foot-pound-second. **3** *Photog.* frames per second.

fps units *pl, n* an Imperial system of units based on the foot, pound, and second as the units of length, mass, and time.

Fr *abbrev. for:* **1** *Christianity:* **1a** Father. **1b** Frater. [L: brother] **2** *the chemical symbol for* francium.

fr. *abbrev. for:* **1** fragment. **2** franc. **3** from.

Fr. *abbrev. for:* **1** France. **2** French.

Fra (frɑː) *n* brother: a title given to an Italian monk or friar. [It., short for *frate* brother, from L *frāter* BROTHER]

fracas ('frækɑː) *n* a noisy quarrel; brawl. [C18: from F, from *fracasser* to shatter, from L *frangere* to break, infl. by *quassāre* to shatter]

fractal ('fræktəl) *n* any of various irregular and fragmented shapes or surfaces that are generated by a series of successive subdivisions. [C20: from L *frāctus*, p.p. of *frangere* to break]

fraction ('frækʃən) *n* **1** *Maths.* a ratio of two expressions or numbers other than zero. **2** any part or subdivision. **3** a small piece; fragment. **4** *Chem.* a component of a mixture separated by fractional distillation. **5** *Christianity.* the formal breaking of the bread in Communion. [C14: from LL, from L *fractus* broken, from *frangere* to break]
▸ 'fractional *adj* ▸ 'fraction,ize *or* 'fraction,ise *vb*

fractional crystallization *n Chem.* the process of separating the components of a solution on the basis of their different solubilities, by means of evaporating the solution until the least soluble component crystallizes out.

fractional distillation *n* the process of separating the constituents of a liquid mixture by heating it and condensing separately the components according to their different boiling points. Sometimes shortened to **distillation.**

fractionate ('frækʃə,neɪt) *vb* **fractionates, fractionating, fractionated. 1** to separate or cause to separate into constituents. **2** (*tr*) *Chem.* to obtain (a constituent of a mixture) by a fractional process.
▸ ,fraction'ation *n*

fractious ('frækʃəs) *adj* **1** irritable. **2** unruly. [C18: from (obs.) *fraction* discord + -OUS]
▸ 'fractiously *adv* ▸ 'fractiousness *n*

> **USAGE NOTE** *Fractious* is sometimes wrongly used where *factious* is meant: *this factious* (not *fractious*) *dispute has split the party still further.*

fracture ('fræktʃə) *n* **1** the act of breaking or the state of being broken. **2a** the breaking or cracking of a bone or the tearing of a cartilage. **2b** the resulting condition. **3** a division, split, or breach. **4** *Mineralogy.* **4a** the characteristic appearance of the surface of a freshly broken mineral

or rock. **4b** the way in which a mineral or rock naturally breaks. ◆ *vb* **fractures, fracturing, fractured. 5** to break or cause to break. **6** to break or crack (a bone) or (of a bone) to become broken or cracked. [C15: from OF, from L, from *frangere* to break]
▸ 'fractural *adj*

fraenum *or* **frenum** ('friːnəm) *n, pl* **fraena** *or* **frena** (-nə). a fold of membrane or skin, such as the fold beneath the tongue. [C18: from L: bridle]

fragile ('frædʒaɪl) *adj* **1** able to be broken easily. **2** in a weakened physical state. **3** delicate; light: *a fragile touch.* **4** slight; tenuous. [C17: from L *fragilis*, from *frangere* to break]
▸ 'fragilely *adv* ▸ fragility (frə'dʒɪlɪtɪ) *n*

fragment *n* ('frægmənt). **1** a piece broken off or detached. **2** an incomplete piece: *fragments of a novel.* **3** a scrap; bit. ◆ *vb* (fræg'mɛnt). **4** to break or cause to break into fragments. [C15: from L *fragmentum*, from *frangere* to break]
▸ ,fragmen'tation *n*

fragmentary ('frægməntərɪ) *adj* made up of fragments; disconnected. Also: **fragmental.**

Fragonard ★ (*French* fragɔnar) *n* **Jean-Honoré** (ʒɑ̃ ɔnɔre). 1732–1806, French painter of French court life.

fragrance ('freɪgrəns) *or* **fragrancy** *n, pl* **fragrances** *or* **fragrancies. 1** a pleasant or sweet odour. **2** the state of being fragrant.

fragrant ('freɪgrənt) *adj* having a pleasant or sweet smell. [C15: from L, from *frāgrāre* to emit a smell]
▸ 'fragrantly *adv*

frail[1] (freɪl) *adj* **1** physically weak and delicate. **2** fragile: *a frail craft.* **3** easily corrupted or tempted. [C13: from OF *frele*, from L *fragilis*, FRAGILE]

frail[2] (freɪl) *n* **1** a rush basket for figs or raisins. **2** a quantity of raisins or figs equal to between 50 and 75 pounds. [C13: from OF *fraiel*, from ?]

frailty ('freɪltɪ) *n, pl* **frailties. 1** physical or moral weakness. **2** (*often pl*) a fault symptomatic of moral weakness.

framboesia *or US* **frambesia** (fræm'biːzɪə) *n Pathol.* another name for **yaws.** [C19: from NL, from F *framboise* raspberry; from its raspberry-like excrescences]

frame (freɪm) *n* **1** an open structure that gives shape and support to something, such as the ribs of a ship's hull or an aircraft's fuselage or the beams of a building. **2** an enclosing case or border into which something is fitted: *the frame of a picture.* **3** the system around which something is built up: *the frame of government.* **4** the structure of the human body. **5** a condition; state (esp. in **frame of mind**). **6a** one of a series of exposures on film used in making motion pictures. **6b** an exposure on a film used in still photography. **7** a television picture scanned by one or more electron beams at a particular frequency. **8** *Snooker, etc.* **8a** the wooden triangle used to set up the balls. **8b** the balls when set up. **8c** a single game finished when all the balls have been potted. **9** short for **cold frame. 10** one of the sections of which a beehive is composed, esp. one designed to hold a honeycomb. **11** *Statistics.* an enumeration of a population for the purposes of sampling. **12** *Sl.* another word for **frame-up. 13** *Obs.* shape; form. ◆ *vb* **frames, framing, framed.** (*mainly tr*) **14** to construct by fitting parts together. **15** to draw up the plans or basic details for: *to frame a policy.* **16** to compose or conceive: *to frame a reply.* **17** to provide, support, or enclose with a frame: *to frame a picture.* **18** to form (words) with the lips, esp. silently. **19** *Sl.* to conspire to incriminate (someone) on a false charge. [OE *framian* to avail]
▸ 'frameless *adj* ▸ 'framer *n*

Frame ★ (freɪm) *n* **Janet.** born 1924, New Zealand writer: author of the novels *Owls Do Cry* (1957) and *Faces in the Water* (1961), the collection of verse *The Pocket Mirror* (1967), and volumes of autobiography including *An Angel at My Table* (1984).

frame house *n* a house that has a timber framework and cladding.

frame of reference *n* **1** *Sociol.* a set of standards that determines and sanctions behaviour. **2** any set of planes or curves, such as the three coordinate axes, used to locate a point in space.

frame-up *n Sl.* **1** a conspiracy to incriminate someone on a false charge. **2** a plot to bring about a dishonest result, as in a contest.

framework ('freɪm‚wɜːk) *n* **1** a structural plan or basis of a project. **2** a structure or frame supporting or containing something.

franc (fræŋk; *French* frā) *n* **1** the standard monetary unit of France, French dependencies, and Monaco, divided into 100 centimes. Also called: **French franc. 2** the standard monetary and currency unit, comprising 100 centimes, of various countries including Belgium, the Central African Republic, Gabon, Guinea, Liechtenstein, Luxembourg, Mauritania, Niger, the Republic of Congo, Senegal, Switzerland, Togo, etc. **3** a Moroccan monetary unit worth one hundredth of a dirham. [C14: from OF; from L *Rex Francōrum* King of the Franks, inscribed on 14th-century francs]

France[1] ★ *n* (frɑːns) *n* a republic in W Europe, between the English Channel, the Mediterranean, and the Atlantic: the largest country wholly in Europe; became a republic in 1793 after the French Revolution and an empire in 1804 under Napoleon; reverted to a monarchy (1815–48), followed by the Second Republic (1848–52); the Second Empire (1852–70), the Third Republic (1870–1940), and the Fourth and Fifth Republics (1946 and 1958); a member of the European Union. It is generally flat and undulating in the north and west and mountainous in the south and east. Official language: French. Religion: mostly Roman Catholic. Currency: franc and euro. Capital: Paris. Pop.: 58 616 000 (1997). Area: (including Corsica) 551 600 sq. km (212 973 sq. miles). Related adj: **Gallic.**

France[2] ★ (*French* frɑs) *n* **Anatole** (anatɔl), real name *Anatole François Thibault*. 1844–1924, French writer. His works include *Le Crime de Sylvestre Bonnard* (1881) and *La Révolte des anges* (1914): Nobel prize for literature 1921.

Francesca ★ (*Italian* fran'tʃeska) *n* See **Piero della Francesca.**

Franche-Comté ★ (*French* frāʃkɔ̃te) *n* a region of E France, covering the Jura and the low country east of the Saône: part of the Kingdom of Burgundy (6th cent. A.D.– 1137); autonomous as the Free County of Burgundy (1137–1384); under Burgundian rule again (1384–1477) and Hapsburg rule (1493–1674); annexed by France (1678).

franchise ('fræntʃaɪz) *n* **1** (usually preceded by *the*) the right to vote, esp. for representatives in a legislative body. **2** any exemption, privilege, or right granted to an individual or group by a public authority. **3** *Commerce.* authorization granted by a manufacturing enterprise to a distributor to market the manufacturer's products. **4** the full rights of citizenship. ◆ *vb* **franchises, franchising, franchised. 5** (*tr*) *Commerce, chiefly US & Canad.* to grant (a person, firm, etc.) a franchise. [C13: from OF, from *franchir* to set free, from *franc* free]
▸ ‚franchi'see *n* ▸ **franchisement** ('fræntʃɪzmənt) *n*
▸ 'franchiser *n*

Francis ★ ('frɑːnsɪs) *n* **1 Dick**, full name *Richard Stanley Francis.* born 1920, British thriller writer, formerly a jockey. His books include *Dead Cert* (1962), *The Edge* (1988), and *Come to Grief* (1995). **2** Sir **Philip**. 1740–1818, British politician; probable author of the *Letters of Junius* (1769–72).

Francis I ★ *n* **1** 1494–1547, king of France (1515–47). His reign was dominated by his rivalry with Emperor Charles V for the control of Italy. He was a noted patron of the arts and learning. **2** 1708–65, duke of Lorraine (1729–37), grand duke of Tuscany (1737–65), and Holy Roman Emperor (1745–65). His marriage (1736) to Maria Theresa led to the War of the Austrian Succession (1740–48). **3** title as emperor of Austria of **Francis II.**

Francis II ★ *n* **1** 1544–60, king of France (1559–60); son of Henry II and Catherine de' Medici; first husband of Mary, Queen of Scots. **2** 1768–1835, last Holy Roman Emperor (1792–1806) and, as Francis I, first emperor of Austria (1804–35). The Holy Roman Empire was dissolved (1806) following his defeat by Napoleon at Austerlitz.

Franciscan (fræn'sɪskən) *n* **a** a member of a Christian religious order of friars or nuns tracing their origins back to Saint Francis of Assisi. **b** (*as modifier*): *a Franciscan friary.*

Francis of Assisi ★ *n* **Saint.** original name *Giovanni di Bernardone.* ?1181–1226, Italian monk; founder of the Franciscan order. According to tradition, he was the first person to exhibit the stigmata (1224). Feast day: Oct. 4.

Francis of Sales ★ (seɪlz; *French* sal) *n* **Saint.** 1567–1622, French ecclesiastic and theologian; bishop of Geneva (1602–22) and an opponent of Calvinism; author of *Introduction to a Devout Life* (1609) and founder of the Order of the Visitation (1610). Feast day: Jan. 24.

Francis Xavier ★ ('zeɪvɪə) *n* **Saint.** See (Saint Francis) **Xavier.**

francium ('frænsɪəm) *n* an unstable radioactive element of the alkali-metal group, occurring in minute amounts in uranium ores. Symbol: Fr; atomic no.: 87; half-life of most stable isotope, ^{223}Fr: 22 minutes. [C20: from NL, from FRANCE + -IUM; because first found in France]

Franck ★ *n* **1** (*French* frāk). **César** (**Auguste**) (sezar). 1822–90, French composer, born in Belgium. His works include a violin sonata, a string quartet, the *Symphony in D Minor* (1888), and much organ music. **2** (fræŋk). **James.** 1882–1964, US physicist, born in Germany: shared a Nobel prize for physics (1925) for work on the quantum theory.

Franco ★ ('fræŋkəʊ; *Spanish* 'franko) *n* **Francisco** (fran'θisko), called *el Caudillo.* 1892–1975, Spanish general and statesman; head of state (1939–1975). He was commander-in-chief of the Falangists in the Spanish Civil War (1936–39), defeating the republican government and establishing a dictatorship (1939).

Franco- ('fræŋkəʊ-) *combining form.* indicating France or French: *Franco-Prussian.* [from Med. L *Francus,* from LL: FRANK[1]]

francolin ('fræŋkəʊlɪn) *n* an African or Asian partridge. [C17: from F, from OIt. *francolino,* from ?]

Franconia (fræŋ'kəʊnɪə) *n* a medieval duchy of Germany, inhabited by the Franks from the 7th century, now chiefly in Bavaria, Hesse, and Baden-Württemberg.

Francophobe ('fræŋkəʊ‚fəʊb) *n* **1** a person who hates or fears France or its people. **2** *Canad.* a person who hates or fears Canadian Francophones.

Francophone ('fræŋkəʊ‚fəʊn) (*often not cap.*) ◆ *n* **1** a person who speaks French, esp. a native speaker. ◆ *adj* **2** speaking French as a native language. **3** using French as a lingua franca.

frangible ('frændʒɪb⁰l) *adj* breakable or fragile. [C15: from OF, ult. from L *frangere* to break]
▸ ‚frangi'bility *or* 'frangibleness *n*

frangipane ('frændʒɪ‚peɪn) *n* **1** a pastry filled with cream and flavoured with almonds. **2** a variant of **frangipani** (the perfume).

frangipani (‚frændʒɪ'pɑːnɪ) *n, pl* **frangipanis** *or* **frangipani. 1** a tropical American shrub cultivated for its waxy white or pink flowers, which have a sweet overpowering scent. **2** a perfume prepared from this plant or resembling the odour of its flowers. **3** native **frangipani.** *Austral.* an Australian evergreen tree with large fragrant yellow flowers. [C17: via F from It.: perfume for scenting gloves, after the Marquis Muzio *Frangipani,* 16th-century Roman nobleman who invented it]

Franglais (*French* frāglɛ) *n* informal French containing a high proportion of English. [C20: from F *français* French + *anglais* English]

frank (fræŋk) *adj* **1** honest and straightforward in speech or attitude: *a frank person.* **2** outspoken or blunt. **3** open and avowed: *frank interest.* ◆ *vb* (*tr*) **4** *Chiefly Brit.* to put a mark on (a letter, etc.), either cancelling the postage stamp or in place of a stamp, ensuring free carriage. **5** to mark (a letter, etc.) with an official mark or signature, indicating the right of free delivery. **6** to facilitate or assist (a person) to enter easily. **7** to obtain immunity for (a person). ◆ *n* **8** an official mark or signature affixed to a letter, etc., ensuring free delivery or delivery without stamps. [C13: from OF, from Med. L *francus* free; identical with FRANK[1] (in Frankish Gaul only members of this people enjoyed full freedom)]
▸ 'frankable *adj* ▸ 'franker *n* ▸ 'frankness *n*

Frank[1] (fræŋk) *n* a member of a group of West Germanic peoples who spread from the east in the late 4th century A.D., gradually conquering most of Gaul and Germany. [OE *Franca; ?*from the name of a Frankish weapon (cf. OE *franca* javelin)]

Frank[2] ★ (*Dutch* fraŋk) *n* **Anne.** 1929–45, Dutch Jewess, whose *Diary* (1947) recorded the experiences of her family while in hiding from the Nazis in Amsterdam (1942–44). They were betrayed and she died in a concentration camp.

franked investment income *n* dividends from one UK company received by another on which the paying company has paid corporation tax.

Frankenstein ('fræŋkɪn,staɪn) *n* **1** a person who creates something that brings about his ruin. **2** Also called: **Frankenstein's monster.** a thing that destroys its creator. [C19: after Baron *Frankenstein*, who created a destructive monster from parts of corpses in the novel by Mary Shelley (1818)]
▶ ,Franken'steinian *adj*

Frankfort ★ ('fræŋkfət) *n* **1** a city in N Kentucky: the state capital. Pop.: 25 535 (1990). **2** *Now rare.* an English spelling of **Frankfurt.**

Frankfurt (am Main) ★ (*German* 'fraŋkfurt (am 'main)) *n* a city in central Germany, in Hesse on the Main River: a Roman settlement in the 1st century; a free imperial city (1372–1806); seat of the federal assembly (1815–66); university (1914); trade fairs since the 13th century. Pop.: 652 412 (1995 est.).

Frankfurt (an der Oder) ★ (*German* 'fraŋkfurt (an der 'o:dər)) *n* a city in E Germany on the Polish border: member of the Hanseatic League (1368–1450). Pop.: 85 360 (1991).

frankfurter ('fræŋk,fɜːtə) *n* a smoked sausage, made of finely minced pork or beef. [C20: short for G *Frankfurter Wurst* sausage from FRANKFURT AM MAIN]

Frankfurter ('fræŋk,fɜːtə) *n* an inhabitant or native of Frankfurt.

frankincense ('fræŋkɪn,sɛns) *n* an aromatic gum resin obtained from trees of the genus *Boswellia,* which occur in Asia and Africa. [C14: from OF *franc* free, pure + *encens* INCENSE[1]; see FRANK]

Frankish ('fræŋkɪʃ) *n* **1** the ancient West Germanic language of the Franks. ◆ *adj* **2** of or relating to the Franks or their language.

franklin ('fræŋklɪn) *n* (in 14th- and 15th-century England) a substantial landholder of free but not noble birth. [C13: from Anglo-F, from OF *franc* free, on the model of CHAMBERLAIN]

Franklin ★ ('fræŋklɪn) *n* **1 Benjamin.** 1706–90, American statesman, scientist, and author. He helped draw up the Declaration of Independence (1776) and, as ambassador to France (1776–85), he negotiated an alliance with France. As a scientist, he is noted for his invention of the lightning conductor. **2 Sir John.** 1786–1847, British explorer of the Arctic: lieutenant-governor of Van Diemen's Land (now Tasmania) (1836–43). **3 Rosalind.** 1920–58, British x-ray crystallographer. She contributed to the discovery of the structure of DNA.

frankly ('fræŋklɪ) *adv* **1** (*sentence modifier*) to be honest. **2** in a frank manner.

frantic ('fræntɪk) *adj* **1** distracted with fear, pain, joy, etc. **2** marked by or showing frenzy: *frantic efforts.* [C14: from OF, from L *phreneticus* mad]
▶ 'frantically *or* 'franticly *adv*

Franz Ferdinand ★ (*German* frants 'ferdinant) *n* English name *Francis Ferdinand.* 1863–1914, archduke of Austria; heir apparent of Franz Josef I. His assassination contributed to the outbreak of World War I.

Franz Josef I ★ (*German* frants 'joːzɛf) *n* English name *Francis Joseph I.* 1830–1916, emperor of Austria (1848–1916) and king of Hungary (1867–1916).

Franz Josef Land ★ *n* an archipelago of over 100 islands in the Arctic Ocean, administratively part of Russia. Area: about 21 000 sq. km (8000 sq. miles). Russian name: **Zemlya Frantsa Iosifa** (zji'mlja 'frantsə 'josifə).

frappé ('fræpeɪ) *n* **1** a drink consisting of a liqueur, etc.,

poured over crushed ice. ◆ *adj* **2** (*postpositive*) (esp. of drinks) chilled. [C19: from F, from *frapper* to strike, hence, chill]

Fraser[1] ★ ('freɪzə) *n* a river in SW Canada, in S central British Columbia, flowing northwest, south, and west through spectacular canyons in the Coast Mountains to the Strait of Georgia. Length: 1370 km (850 miles).

Fraser[2] ★ ('freɪzə) *n* **1 (John) Malcolm.** born 1930, Australian statesman; prime minister (1975–83). **2 Peter.** 1884–1950, New Zealand statesman, born in Scotland; prime minister (1940–49).

frater ('freɪtə) *n Arch.* a refectory. [C13: from OF *fraiteur,* from *refreitor,* from LL *refectōrium* REFECTORY]

fraternal (frə'tɜːnⁿl) *adj* **1** of or suitable to a brother; brotherly. **2** of a fraternity. **3** designating twins of the same or opposite sex that developed from two separate fertilized ova. Cf. **identical** (sense 3). [C15: from L, from *fráter* brother]
▶ fra'ternalism *n*

fraternity (frə'tɜːnɪtɪ) *n, pl* **fraternities. 1** a body of people united in interests, aims, etc.: *the teaching fraternity.* **2** brotherhood. **3** *US & Canad.* a secret society joined by male students, functioning as a social club.

fraternize *or* **fraternise** ('frætə,naɪz) *vb* **fraternizes, fraternizing, fraternized** *or* **fraternises, fraternising, fraternised.** (*intr*; often foll. by *with*) to associate on friendly terms.
▶ ,fraterni'zation *or* ,fraterni'sation *n* ▶ 'frater,nizer *or* 'frater,niser *n*

fratricide ('frætrɪ,saɪd, 'freɪ-) *n* **1** the act of killing one's brother. **2** a person who kills his brother. [C15: from L, from *fráter* brother + -CIDE]
▶ ,fratri'cidal *adj*

Frau (frau) *n, pl* **Frauen** ('frauən) *or* **Fraus.** a married German woman: usually used as a title equivalent to *Mrs.* [from OHG *frouwa*]

fraud (frɔːd) *n* **1** deliberate deception, trickery, or cheating intended to gain an advantage. **2** an act or instance of such deception. **3** *Inf.* a person who acts in a false or deceitful way. [C14: from OF, from L *fraus* deception]

fraudster ('frɔːdstə) *n* a swindler.

fraudulent ('frɔːdjʊlənt) *adj* **1** acting with or having the intent to deceive. **2** relating to or proceeding from fraud. [C15: from L *fraudulentus* deceitful]
▶ 'fraudulence *n* ▶ 'fraudulently *adv*

Frauenfeld ★ (*German* 'frauənfɛlt) *n* a town in NE Switzerland, capital of Thurgau canton. Pop.: 19 402 (1990).

fraught (frɔːt) *adj* (*usually postpositive* and foll. by *with*) filled or charged: *a venture fraught with peril.* **2** *Inf.* showing or producing tension or anxiety. [C14: from MDu. *vrachten,* from *vracht* FREIGHT]

Fräulein (*German* 'frɔylaɪn) *n, pl* **Fräulein** *or English* **Fräuleins.** an unmarried German woman: often used as a title equivalent to *Miss.* [from MHG *vrouwelín,* dim. of *vrouwe* lady]

Fraunhofer ★ ('fraunhəʊfə; *German* 'fraunhoːfər) *n* **Joseph von** ('joːzɛf fɔn). 1787–1826, German physicist who investigated spectra of the sun, planets, and stars, and improved telescopes and other optical instruments.

Fraunhofer lines *pl n* a set of dark lines appearing in the continuous emission spectrum of the sun.

fraxinella (,fræksɪ'nɛlə) *n* another name for **gas plant.** [C17: from NL: a little ash tree, from L *fráxinus* ash]

fray[1] (freɪ) *n* **1** a noisy quarrel. **2** a fight or brawl. [C14: short for AFFRAY]

fray[2] (freɪ) *vb* **1** to wear or cause to wear away into loose threads, esp. at an edge or end. **2** to make or become strained or irritated. **3** to rub or chafe (another object). [C14: from F *frayer* to rub, from L *fricáre* to rub]

Fray Bentos ★ (,freɪ 'bɛntɒs) *n* a port in W Uruguay, on the River Uruguay: noted for meat-packing. Pop.: 21 400 (1995 est.).

Frazer ★ ('freɪzə) *n* **Sir James George.** 1854–1941, Scottish anthropologist; author of many works on religion and magic, esp. *The Golden Bough* (1890).

Frazier ★ ('freɪʒə) *n* **Joe.** born 1944, US boxer: won the world heavyweight title in 1970.

frazil ('freɪzɪl) *n* small pieces of ice that form in water moving turbulently enough to prevent the formation of a sheet of ice. [C19: from Canad. F, from F *fraisil* cinders, ult. from L *fax* torch]

frazzle ('fræz°l) *Inf.* ◆ *vb* **frazzles, frazzling, frazzled. 1** to make or become exhausted or weary. ◆ *n* **2** the state of being frazzled or exhausted. **3 to a frazzle.** completely (esp. in **burnt to a frazzle**). [C19: prob. from ME *faselen* to fray, from *fasel* fringe; infl. by FRAY²]

freak (friːk) *n* **1** a person, animal, or plant that is abnormal or deformed. **2a** an object, event, etc., that is abnormal. **2b** (*as modifier*): *a freak storm.* **3** a personal whim or caprice. **4** *Inf.* a person who acts or dresses in a markedly unconventional way. **5** *Inf.* a person who is ardently fond of something specified: *a jazz freak.* ◆ *vb* **6** See **freak out.** [C16: from ?]
▸ **'freakish** *adj* ▸ **'freaky** *adj*

freak out *vb* (*adv*) *Inf.* to be or cause to be in a heightened emotional state.

freckle ('frek°l) *n* **1** a small brownish spot on the skin developed by exposure to sunlight. Technical name: **lentigo. 2** any small area of discoloration. ◆ *vb* **freckles, freckling, freckled. 3** to mark or become marked with freckles or spots. [C14: from ON *freknur*]
▸ **'freckled** *or* **'freckly** *adj*

Fredericia ★ (*Danish* freðə'redsja) *n* a port in Denmark, in E Jutland at the N end of the Little Belt. Pop.: 28 000 (1990).

Frederick I ★ ('fredrɪk) *n* **1** See **Frederick Barbarossa. 2** 1657–1713, first king of Prussia (1701–13); son of Frederick William.

Frederick II ★ *n* **1** 1194–1250, Holy Roman Emperor (1220–50), king of Germany (1212–50), and king of Sicily (1198–1250). **2** See **Frederick the Great.**

Frederick III ★ *n* **1** 1415–93, Holy Roman Emperor (1452–93) and, as Frederick IV, king of Germany (1440–93). **2** called *the Wise.* 1463–1525, elector of Saxony (1486–1525). He protected Martin Luther in Wartburg Castle after the Diet of Worms (1521).

Frederick IV ★ *n* See **Frederick III** (sense 1).

Frederick V ★ *n* called *the Winter King.* 1596–1632, elector of the Palatinate (1610–23) and king of Bohemia (1619–20). He led the revolt of Bohemian Protestants at the beginning of the Thirty Years' War.

Frederick IX ★ *n* 1899–1972, king of Denmark (1947–72).

Frederick Barbarossa ★ (ˌbɑːbə'rɒsə) *n* official title *Frederick I.* ?1123–90, Holy Roman Emperor (1155–90), king of Germany (1152–90). His attempt to assert imperial rights in Italy ended in his defeat at Legnano (1176) and the independence of the Lombard cities (1183).

Frederick the Great ★ *n* official title *Frederick II.* 1712–86, king of Prussia (1740–86); son of Frederick William I. He gained Silesia during the War of Austrian Succession (1740–48) and established Prussia as a European power.

Frederick William ★ *n* called *the Great Elector.* 1620–88, elector of Brandenburg (1640–88).

Frederick William I ★ *n* 1688–1740, king of Prussia (1713–40); son of Frederick I: reformed the Prussian army.

Frederick William III ★ *n* 1770–1840, king of Prussia (1797–1840).

Frederick William IV ★ *n* 1795–1861, king of Prussia (1840–61). He submitted to the 1848 Revolution but refused the imperial crown offered by the Frankfurt Parliament (1849). In 1857 he became insane and his brother, William I, became regent (1858–61).

Fredericton ★ ('fredrɪktən) *n* a city in SE Canada, capital of New Brunswick, on the St John River. Pop.: 45 364 (1991).

Frederiksberg ★ (*Danish* freðregs'ber) *n* a city in E Denmark, within the area of greater Copenhagen: founded in 1651 by King Frederick III. Pop.: 88 002 (1995 est.).

Fredrikstad ★ (*Norwegian* 'fredrikstad) *n* a port in SE Norway at the entrance to Oslo Fjord. Pop.: 26 546 (1990).

free (friː) *adj* **freer, freest. 1** able to act at will; not under compulsion or restraint. **2a** not enslaved or confined. **2b** (*as n*): *land of the free.* **3** (*often postpositive* and foll. by *from*) not subject (to) or restricted (by some regulation, constraint, etc.): *free from pain.* **4** (of a country, etc.) autonomous or independent. **5** exempt from external direction: *free will.* **6** not subject to conventional constraints: *free verse.* **7** not exact or literal: *a free translation.* **8** provided without charge: *free entertainment.* **9** *Law.* (of property) **9a** not subject to payment of rent or performance of services; freehold. **9b** not subject to any burden or charge; unencumbered. **10** (*postpositive*; often foll. by *of* or *with*) ready or generous in using or giving: *free with advice.* **11** not occupied or in use; available: *a free cubicle.* **12** (of a person) not busy. **13** open or available to all. **14** without charge to the subscriber or user: *freepost; freephone.* **15** not fixed or joined; loose: *the free end of a chain.* **16** without obstruction or impediment: *free passage.* **17** *Chem.* chemically uncombined: *free nitrogen.* **18** *Logic.* denoting an occurrence of a variable not bound by a quantifier. Cf. **bound¹** (sense 8). **19** (of routines in figure skating competitions) chosen by the competitor. **20** (of jazz) totally improvised. **21 for free.** *Nonstandard.* without charge or cost. **22 free and easy.** casual or tolerant; easygoing. **23 make free with.** to behave too familiarly towards. ◆ *adv* **24** in a free manner; freely. **25** without charge or cost. **26** *Naut.* with the wind blowing from the quarter. ◆ *vb* **frees, freeing, freed.** (*tr*) **27** to set at liberty; release. **28** to remove obstructions or impediments from. **29** (often foll. by *of* or *from*) to relieve or rid (of obstacles, pain, etc.). [OE *frēo*]
▸ **'freely** *adv* ▸ **'freeness** *n*

-free *adj combining form.* free from: *trouble-free; lead-free petrol.*

free alongside ship *adj* (of a shipment of goods) delivered to the dock without charge to the buyer, but excluding the cost of loading onto the vessel. Cf. **free on board.**

free association *n Psychoanal.* a method of exploring a person's unconscious by eliciting words and thoughts that are associated with key words provided by a psychoanalyst.

freebase ('friːˌbeɪs) *Sl.* ◆ *n* **1** cocaine that has been refined by heating it in ether or some other solvent. ◆ *vb* **freebases, freebasing, freebased. 2** to refine (cocaine) in this way. **3** to smoke or inhale the fumes from (refined cocaine).

freebie ('friːbɪ) *n Sl.* something provided without charge.

freeboard ('friːˌbɔːd) *n* the space or distance between the deck of a vessel and the waterline.

freebooter ('friːˌbuːtə) *n* a person, such as a pirate, living from plunder. [C16: from Du., from *vrijbuit* booty; see FILIBUSTER]
▸ **'freeboot** *vb* (*intr*)

freeborn ('friːˌbɔːn) *adj* **1** not born in slavery. **2** of or suitable for people not born in slavery.

Free Church *n Chiefly Brit.* any Protestant Church, esp. the Presbyterian, other than the Established Church.

free city *n* a sovereign or autonomous city.

freedman ('friːdˌmæn) *n, pl* **freedmen.** a man who has been freed from slavery.

freedom ('friːdəm) *n* **1** personal liberty, as from slavery, serfdom, etc. **2** liberation, as from confinement or bondage. **3** the quality or state of being free, esp. to enjoy political and civil liberties. **4** (usually foll. by *from*) exemption or immunity: *freedom from taxation.* **5** the right or privilege of unrestricted use or access: *the freedom of a city.* **6** autonomy, self-government, or independence. **7** the power or liberty to order one's own actions. **8** *Philosophy.* the quality, esp. of the will or the individual, of not being totally constrained. **9** ease or frankness of manner: *she talked with complete freedom.* **10** excessive familiarity of manner. **11** ease and grace, as of movement. [OE *frēodōm*]

freedom fighter *n* a militant revolutionary.

free energy *n* a thermodynamic property that expresses the capacity of a system to perform work under certain conditions.

free enterprise *n* an economic system in which commercial organizations compete for profit with little state control.

free fall *n* **1** free descent of a body in which the gravitational force is the only force acting on it. **2** the part of a parachute descent before the parachute opens.

free flight *n* the flight of a rocket, missile, etc., when its engine has ceased to produce thrust.

free-for-all *n Inf.* **1** a disorganized brawl or argument, usually involving all those present. **2a** a contest, discussion, etc., that is open to everyone. **2b** (*as modifier*): *a free-for-all contest.*

free-form *adj Arts.* freely flowing, spontaneous.

free hand *n* **1** unrestricted freedom to act (esp. in **give** (someone) **a free hand**). ♦ *adj, adv* **freehand. 2** (done) by hand without the use of guiding instruments: *a freehand drawing.*

free-handed *adj* generous or liberal; unstinting.
▶ ˌfree-ˈhandedly *adv*

freehold (ˈfriːˌhəʊld) *Property law.* ♦ *n* **1a** tenure by which land is held in fee simple, fee tail, or for life. **1b** an estate held by such tenure. ♦ *adj* **2** relating to or having the nature of freehold.
▶ ˈfreeholder *n*

free house *n Brit.* a public house not bound to sell only one brewer's products.

free kick *n Soccer.* a place kick awarded for a foul or infringement.

freelance (ˈfriːˌlɑːns) *n* **1a** Also called: **freelancer.** a self-employed person, esp. a writer or artist, who is hired to do specific assignments. **1b** (*as modifier*): *a freelance journalist.* **2** (in medieval Europe) a mercenary soldier or adventurer. ♦ *vb* **freelances, freelancing, freelanced. 3** to work as a freelance on (an assignment, etc.). ♦ *adv* **4** as a freelance. [C19 (in sense 2): later applied to politicians, writers, etc.]

free-living *adj* **1** given to ready indulgence of the appetites. **2** (of animals and plants) not parasitic.
▶ ˌfree-ˈliver *n*

freeloader (ˈfriːˌləʊdə) *n Sl.* a person who habitually depends on others for food, shelter, etc.

free love *n* the practice of sexual relationships without fidelity to a single partner.

freeman (ˈfriːmən) *n, pl* **freemen. 1** a person who is not a slave. **2** a person who enjoys political and civil liberties. **3** a person who enjoys a privilege, such as the freedom of a city.

free market *n* **a** an economic system that allows supply and demand to regulate prices, wages, etc., rather than government policy. **b** (*as modifier*): *a free-market economy.*

freemartin (ˈfriːˌmɑːtɪn) *n* the female of a pair of twin calves of unlike sex that is imperfectly developed and sterile. [C17: from ?]

Freemason (ˈfriːˌmeɪsᵊn) *n* a member of the widespread secret order, constituted in London in 1717, of **Free and Accepted Masons,** pledged to brotherly love, faith, and charity. Sometimes shortened to **Mason.**

freemasonry (ˈfriːˌmeɪsᵊnrɪ) *n* natural or tacit sympathy and understanding.

Freemasonry (ˈfriːˌmeɪsᵊnrɪ) *n* **1** the institutions, rites, practices, etc., of Freemasons. **2** Freemasons collectively.

free on board *adj* (of a shipment of goods) delivered on board ship or other carrier without charge to the buyer. Cf. **free alongside ship.**

free port *n* **1** a port open to all commercial vessels on equal terms. **2** a port that permits the duty-free entry of foreign goods intended for re-export.

free radical *n* an atom or group of atoms containing at least one unpaired electron and existing for a brief period of time before reacting to produce a stable molecule.

free-range *adj Chiefly Brit.* kept or produced in natural conditions: *free-range eggs.*

free-select *vb* (*tr*) *Austral. history.* to select (areas of crown land) and acquire the freehold by a series of annual payments.
▶ ˈfree-seˈlection *n* ▶ ˈfree-seˈlector *n*

freesia (ˈfriːzɪə) *n* a plant of Southern Africa, cultivated for its white, yellow, or pink tubular fragrant flowers. [C19: NL, after F. H. T. *Freese* (died 1876), G physician]

free skating *n* either of two parts in a figure-skating competition in which the skater chooses the sequence of figures and the music and which are judged on technique and artistic presentation. The short programme consists of specified movements and the long programme is entirely the skater's own choice.

free space *n* a region that has no gravitational and electromagnetic fields. It is used as an absolute standard and was formerly referred to as a vacuum.

free-spoken *adj* speaking frankly or without restraint.
▶ ˌfree-ˈspokenly *adv*

freestanding (ˌfriːˈstændɪŋ) *adj* not attached to or supported by another object.

Free State *n* a province of central South Africa; replaced Orange Free State in 1994. Capital: Bloemfontein. Pop.: 2 782 500 (1995 est.). Area: 129 480 sq. km (49 992 sq. miles).

freestone (ˈfriːˌstəʊn) *n* **1** any fine-grained stone, esp. sandstone or limestone, that can be worked in any direction without breaking. **2** *Bot.* a fruit, such as a peach, in which the flesh separates readily from the stone.

freestyle (ˈfriːˌstaɪl) *n* **1** a competition or race, as in swimming, in which each participant may use a style of his or her choice instead of a specified style. **2a International freestyle.** an amateur style of wrestling with an agreed set of rules. **2b** Also called: **all-in wrestling.** a style of professional wrestling with no internationally agreed set of rules.

freethinker (ˌfriːˈθɪŋkə) *n* a person who forms his ideas and opinions independently of authority or accepted views, esp. in matters of religion.
▶ **free thought** *n*

Freetown ★ (ˈfriːˌtaʊn) *n* the capital and chief port of Sierra Leone: founded in 1787 for slaves freed and destitute in England. Pop.: 669 000 (1990 est.).

free trade *n* **1** international trade that is free of such government interference as protective tariffs. **2** *Arch.* smuggling.

free verse *n* unrhymed verse without a metrical pattern.

freeware (ˈfriːˌwɛə) *n* computer software that may be distributed and used without payment.

freeway (ˈfriːˌweɪ) *n US.* **1** an expressway. **2** a major road that can be used without paying a toll.

freewheel (ˌfriːˈwiːl) *n* **1** a ratchet device in the rear hub of a bicycle wheel that permits the wheel to rotate freely while the pedals are stationary. ♦ *vb* **2** (*intr*) to coast on a bicycle using the freewheel.

free will *n* **1a** the apparent human ability to make choices that are not externally determined. **1b** the doctrine that such human freedom of choice is not illusory. Cf. **determinism. 2** the ability to make a choice without outside coercion: *he left of his own free will.*

Free World *n the.* the non-Communist countries collectively.

freeze (friːz) *vb* **freezes, freezing, froze, frozen. 1** to change (a liquid) into a solid as a result of a reduction in temperature, or (of a liquid) to solidify in this way. **2** (when *intr*, sometimes foll. by *over* or *up*) to cover, clog, or harden with ice, or become so covered, clogged, or hardened. **3** to fix fast or become fixed (to something) because of the action of frost. **4** (*tr*) to preserve (food) by subjection to extreme cold, as in a freezer. **5** to feel or cause to feel the sensation or effects of extreme cold. **6** to die or cause to die of extreme cold. **7** to become or cause to become paralysed, fixed, or motionless, esp. through fear, shock, etc. **8** (*tr*) to cause (moving film) to stop at a particular frame. **9** to make or become formal, haughty, etc., in manner. **10** (*tr*) to fix (prices, incomes, etc.) at a particular level. **11** (*tr*) to forbid by law the exchange, liquidation, or collection of (loans, assets, etc.). **12** (*tr*) to stop (a process) at a particular stage of development. **13** (*intr*, foll. by *onto*) *Inf., chiefly US.* to cling. ♦ *n* **14** the act of freezing or state of being frozen. **15** *Meteorol.* a spell of

★ people and places

temperatures below freezing point, usually over a wide area. **16** the fixing of incomes, prices, etc., by legislation. ◆ *sentence substitute*. **17** *Chiefly US*. a command to stop instantly or risk being shot. [OE *frēosan*]
▶ 'freezable *adj*

freeze-dry *vb* **freeze-dries, freeze-drying, freeze-dried**. (*tr*) to preserve (a substance) by rapid freezing and subsequently drying in a vacuum.

freeze-frame *n* **1** *Films, television*. a single frame of a film repeated to give an effect like a still photograph. **2** *Video*. a single frame of a video recording viewed as a still by stopping the tape.

freeze out *vb* (*tr, adv*) *Inf*. to exclude, as by unfriendly behaviour, etc.

freezer ('fri:zə) *n* an insulated cold-storage cabinet for long-term storage of perishable foodstuffs. Also called: **deepfreeze**.

freezing ('fri:zɪŋ) *adj Inf*. extremely cold.

freezing point *n* the temperature below which a liquid turns into a solid.

freezing works *n* *Austral. & NZ*. a slaughterhouse at which animal carcasses are frozen for export.

Frege ★ (*German* 'fre:gə) *n* **Gottlob**. 1848–1925, German logician and philosopher, who laid the foundations of modern formal logic and semantics in his *Begriffsschrift* (1879).

Freiburg ★ (*German* 'fraɪburk) *n* **1** a city in SW Germany, in SW Baden-Württemberg: under Austrian rule (1368–1805); university (1457). Pop.: 198 496 (1995 est.). Official name: **Freiburg im Breisgau** (ɪm 'braɪsgaʊ). **2** the German name for **Fribourg**.

freight (freɪt) *n* **1a** commercial transport that is slower and cheaper than express. **1b** the price charged for such transport. **1c** goods transported by this means. **1d** (*as modifier*): *freight transport*. **2** *Chiefly Brit*. a ship's cargo or part of it. ◆ *vb* (*tr*) **3** to load with goods for transport. [C16: from MDu *vrecht*, var. of *vracht*]

freightage ('freɪtɪdʒ) *n* **1** the commercial conveyance of goods. **2** the goods so transported. **3** the price charged for such conveyance.

freighter ('freɪtə) *n* **1** a ship or aircraft designed for transporting cargo. **2** a person concerned with the loading of a ship.

freightliner ('freɪt,laɪnə) *n* *Trademark*. a type of goods train carrying containers that can be transferred onto lorries or ships.

Fremantle ★ ('fri:,mænt²l) *n* a port in SW Western Australia, on the Indian Ocean. Pop.: 24 010 (1986).

French[1] (frɛntʃ) *n* **1** the official language of France: also an official language of Switzerland, Belgium, Canada, and certain other countries. Historically, French is an Indo-European language belonging to the Romance group. **2 the French**. (*functioning as pl*) the natives, citizens, or inhabitants of France collectively. ◆ *adj* **3** relating to, denoting, or characteristic of France, the French, or their language. **4** (in Canada) of French Canadians. [OE *Frencisc* French, Frankish]
▶ 'Frenchness *n*

French[2] ★ (frɛntʃ) *n* Sir **John Denton Pinkstone**, 1st Earl of Ypres. 1852–1925, British field marshal in World War I: commanded the British Expeditionary Force in France and Belgium (1914–15); Lord Lieutenant of Ireland (1918–21).

French bread *n* white bread in a long slender loaf that has a crisp brown crust.

French Cameroons ★ *pl n* the part of Cameroon formerly administered by France (1919–60).

French Canada ★ *n* the areas of Canada, esp. in the province of Quebec, where French Canadians predominate.

French Canadian *n* **1** a Canadian citizen whose native language is French. ◆ *adj* **French-Canadian**. **2** of or relating to French Canadians or their language.

French chalk *n* a variety of talc used to mark cloth, remove grease stains, or as a dry lubricant.

French doors *pl n* the US and Canad. name for **French windows**.

French dressing *n* a salad dressing made from oil and vinegar with seasonings; vinaigrette.

French Equatorial Africa ★ *n* the former French overseas territories of Chad, Gabon, Middle Congo, and Ubangi-Shari (1910–58).

French fried potatoes *pl n* a more formal name for chips. Often shortened to **French fries, fries**.

French Guiana ★ *n* a French overseas region in NE South America, on the Atlantic: colonized by the French in about 1637; tropical forests. Capital: Cayenne. Pop.: 90 500 (1988 est.). Area: about 91 000 sq. km (23 000 sq. miles).
▶ **French Guianese** *or* **Guianan** *adj, n*

French Guinea ★ *n* a former French territory of French West Africa: became independent as Guinea in 1958.

French horn *n* *Music*. a valved brass instrument with a funnel-shaped mouthpiece and a tube of conical bore coiled into a spiral.

Frenchify ('frɛntʃɪ,faɪ) *vb* **Frenchifies, Frenchifying, Frenchified**. *Inf*. to make or become French in appearance, etc.

French India ★ *n* a former French overseas territory in India, including Chandernagore and Pondicherry: restored to India between 1949 and 1954.

French Indochina ★ *n* the territories of SE Asia that were colonized by France and held mostly until 1954: included Cochin China, Annam, and Tonkin (now largely Vietnam), Cambodia, Laos, and Kuang-Chou Wan (returned to China in 1945, now Zhanjiang).

French kiss *n* a kiss involving insertion of the tongue into the partner's mouth.

French knickers *pl n* women's wide-legged underpants.

French leave *n* an unauthorized or unannounced absence or departure. [C18: alluding to a custom in France of leaving without saying goodbye to one's host or hostess]

French letter *n* *Brit*. a slang term for **condom**.

Frenchman ('frɛntʃmən) *n*, *pl* **Frenchmen**. a native, citizen, or inhabitant of France.
▶ 'French,woman *fem n*

French Morocco ★ *n* a former French protectorate in NW Africa, united in 1956 with Spanish Morocco and Tangier to form the kingdom of Morocco.

French mustard *n* a mild mustard paste made with vinegar rather than water.

French North Africa ★ *n* the former French possessions of Algeria, French Morocco, and Tunisia.

French Oceania ★ *n* a former name (until 1958) of **French Polynesia**.

French polish *n* **1** a varnish for wood consisting of shellac dissolved in alcohol. **2** the gloss finish produced by this polish.

French-polish *vb* to treat with French polish or give a French polish to.

French Polynesia ★ *n* a French Overseas Territory in the S Pacific Ocean, including the Society Islands, the Tuamotu group, the Gambier group, the Tubuai Islands, and the Marquesas Islands. Capital: Papeete, on Tahiti. Pop.: 191 400 (1988 est.). Area: about 4000 sq. km (1500 sq. miles). Former name (until 1958): **French Oceania**.

French seam *n* a seam in which the edges are not visible.

French Somaliland ★ *n* a former name (until 1967) of **Djibouti**.

French Southern and Antarctic Territories ★ *pl n* a French overseas territory, comprising Adélie Land in Antarctica and the islands of Amsterdam and St Paul and the Kerguelen and Crozet archipelagos in the S Indian Ocean.

French Sudan ★ *n* a former name (1898–1959) of **Mali**.

French toast *n* **1** *Brit*. toast cooked on one side only. **2** bread dipped in beaten egg and lightly fried.

French Togoland ★ *n* a former United Nations Trust Territory in W Africa, administered by France (1946–60), now the independent republic of Togo.

French West Africa ★ *n* a former group (1895–1958) of French Overseas Territories: consisted of Senegal, Mauritania, French Sudan, Burkina-Faso, Niger, French Guinea, the Ivory Coast, and Dahomey.

French windows *pl n* (*sometimes sing*) *Brit.* a pair of casement windows extending to floor level and opening onto a balcony, garden, etc.

frenetic (frɪ'nɛtɪk) *adj* distracted or frantic. [C14: via OF, from L, from Gk, from *phrenitis* insanity, from *phrēn* mind]
▶ fre'netically *adv*

frenum ('friːnəm) *n, pl* **frena** (-nə). a variant spelling (esp. US) of **fraenum.**

frenzy ('frɛnzɪ) *n, pl* **frenzies. 1** violent mental derangement. **2** wild excitement or agitation. **3** a bout of wild or agitated activity: *a frenzy of preparations.* ◆ *vb* **frenzies, frenzying, frenzied. 4** (*tr*) to drive into a frenzy. [C14: from OF, from LL *phrenēsis* madness, from LGk, ult. from Gk *phrēn* mind]
▶ 'frenzied *adj*

Freon ('friːɒn) *n Trademark.* any of a group of chemically unreactive gaseous or liquid derivatives of methane in which hydrogen atoms have been replaced by chlorine and fluorine atoms: used as aerosol propellants, refrigerants, and solvents.

freq. *abbrev. for:* **1** frequent(ly). **2** frequentative.

frequency ('friːkwənsɪ) *n, pl* **frequencies. 1** the state of being frequent. **2** the number of times that an event occurs within a given period. **3** *Physics.* the number of times that a periodic function or vibration repeats itself in a specified time, often 1 second. It is usually measured in hertz. **4** *Statistics.* **4a** the number of individuals in a class (**absolute frequency**). **4b** the ratio of this number to the total number of individuals under survey (**relative frequency**). **5** *Ecology.* the number of individuals of a species within a given area. [C16: from L, from *frequēns* crowded]

frequency distribution *n Statistics.* the function of the distribution of a sample corresponding to the probability density function of the underlying population and tending to it as the sample size increases.

frequency modulation *n* a method of transmitting information using a radio-frequency carrier wave. The frequency of the carrier wave is varied in accordance with the amplitude of the input signal, the amplitude of the carrier remaining unchanged. Cf. **amplitude modulation.**

frequent *adj* ('friːkwənt). **1** recurring at short intervals. **2** habitual. ◆ *vb* (frɪ'kwɛnt). **3** (*tr*) to visit repeatedly or habitually. [C16: from L *frequēns* numerous]
▶ ,frequen'tation *n* ▶ fre'quenter *n* ▶ 'frequently *adv*

frequentative (frɪ'kwɛntətɪv) *Grammar.* ◆ *adj* **1** denoting an aspect of verbs in some languages used to express repeated or habitual action. **2** (in English) denoting a verb or an affix meaning repeated action, such as the verb *wrestle*, from *wrest.* ◆ *n* **3** a frequentative verb or affix.

fresco ('frɛskəʊ) *n, pl* **frescoes** or **frescos. 1** a very durable method of wall-painting using watercolours on wet plaster. **2** a painting done in this way. [C16: from It.: fresh plaster, from *fresco* (adj) fresh, cool, of Gmc origin]

Frescobaldi ★ (*Italian* fresko'baldi) *n* **Girolamo** (dʒi'rɔːlamo). 1583–1643, Italian composer, noted esp. for his organ and harpsichord music.

fresh (frɛʃ) *adj* **1** newly made, harvested, etc.: *fresh bread; fresh strawberries.* **2** newly acquired, found, etc.: *fresh publications.* **3** novel; original: *a fresh outlook.* **4** most recent: *fresh developments.* **5** further; additional: *fresh supplies.* **6** not canned, frozen, or otherwise preserved: *fresh fruit.* **7** (of water) not salt. **8** bright or clear: *a fresh morning.* **9** chilly or invigorating: *a fresh breeze.* **10** not tired; alert. **11** not worn or faded: *fresh colours.* **12** having a healthy or ruddy appearance. **13** newly or just arrived: *fresh from the presses.* **14** youthful or inexperienced. **15** *Inf.* presumptuous or disrespectful; forward. ◆ *n* **16** the fresh part or

time of something. **17** another name for **freshet.** ◆ *adv* **18** in a fresh manner. [OE *fersc* fresh, unsalted]
▶ 'freshly *adv* ▶ 'freshness *n*

fresh breeze *n* a wind of force 5 on the Beaufort scale, blowing at speeds between 19 and 24 mph.

freshen ('frɛʃən) *vb* **1** to make or become fresh or fresher. **2** (often foll. by *up*) to refresh (oneself), esp. by washing. **3** (*intr*) (of the wind) to increase.

fresher ('frɛʃə) or **freshman** ('frɛʃmən) *n, pl* **freshers** or **freshmen.** a first-year student at college or university.

freshet ('frɛʃɪt) *n* **1** the sudden overflowing of a river caused by heavy rain or melting snow. **2** a stream of fresh water emptying into the sea.

freshwater ('frɛʃ,wɔːtə) *n (modifier)* **1** of or living in fresh water. **2** (esp. of a sailor who has not sailed on the sea) inexperienced. **3** *US.* little known: *a freshwater school.*

fresnel ('freɪnɛl) *n* a unit of frequency equivalent to 10^{12} hertz. [C20: after A. J. Fresnel]

Fresnel ★ (*French* frɛnɛl) *n* **Augustin Jean** (ogystɛ̃ ʒɑ̃). 1788–1827, French physicist: worked on the interference of light, contributing to the wave theory of light.

Fresno ★ (ˈfrɛznəʊ) *n* a city in central California, in the San Joaquin Valley. Pop.: 386 551 (1994 est.).

fret[1] (frɛt) *vb* **frets, fretting, fretted. 1** to distress or be distressed. **2** to rub or wear away. **3** to feel or give annoyance or vexation. **4** to eat away or be eaten away, as by chemical action. **5** (*tr*) to make by wearing away; erode. ◆ *n* **6** a state of irritation or anxiety. [OE *fretan* to eat]

fret[2] (frɛt) *n* **1** a repetitive geometrical figure, esp. one used as an ornamental border. **2** such a pattern made in relief; fretwork. ◆ *vb* **frets, fretting, fretted. 3** (*tr*) to ornament with fret or fretwork. [C14: from OF *frete* interlaced design used on a shield, prob. of Gmc origin]
▶ 'fretless *adj*

fret[3] (frɛt) *n* any of several small metal bars set across the fingerboard of a musical instrument of the lute, guitar, or viol family at various points along its length so as to produce the desired notes. [C16: from ?]
▶ 'fretless *adj*

fretboard ('frɛtbɔːd) *n* a fingerboard with frets on a stringed instrument.

fretful ('frɛtfʊl) *adj* peevish, irritable, or upset.
▶ 'fretfully *adv* ▶ 'fretfulness *n*

fret saw *n* a fine-toothed saw with a long thin narrow blade, used for cutting designs in thin wood or metal.

fretwork ('frɛt,wɜːk) *n* decorative geometrical carving or openwork.

Freud ★ (frɔɪd) *n* **1 Anna.** 1895–1982, Austrian psychiatrist: daughter of Sigmund Freud and pioneer of child psychoanalysis. **2 Lucian.** born 1922, British painter; grandson of Sigmund Freud. **3 Sigmund** ('sɪgmənd; *German* 'ziːkmʊnt). 1856–1939, Austrian psychiatrist; originator of psychoanalysis. His works include *The Interpretation of Dreams* (1900) and *The Ego and the Id* (1923).

Freudian ('frɔɪdɪən) *adj* **1** of or relating to Sigmund Freud or his ideas. ◆ *n* **2** a person who follows or believes in the basic ideas of Sigmund Freud.
▶ 'Freudian,ism *n*

Freudian slip *n* any action, such as a slip of the tongue, that may reveal an unconscious thought.

Frey (freɪ) or **Freyr** ★ (freɪə) *n Norse myth.* the god of earth's fertility and dispenser of prosperity.

Freya or **Freyja** ★ ('freɪə) *n Norse myth.* the goddess of love and fecundity; sister of Frey.

Freytag ★ (*German* 'fraitaːk) *n* **Gustav** ('gustaf). 1816–95, German novelist and dramatist; author of the comedy *Die Journalisten* (1853) and *Soll und Haben* (1855).

Fri. *abbrev. for* Friday.

friable ('fraɪəbəl) *adj* easily broken up; crumbly. [C16: from L, from *friāre* to crumble]
▶ ,fria'bility or 'friableness *n*

friar ('fraɪə) *n* a member of any of various chiefly mendicant religious orders of the Roman Catholic Church. [C13 *frere*, from OF: brother, from L *frāter* BROTHER]

friar's balsam *n* a compound containing benzoin,

mixed with hot water and used as an inhalant to relieve colds and sore throats.

friary ('fraɪərɪ) *n, pl* **friaries.** *Christianity.* a convent or house of friars.

Fribourg ★ (*French* fribur) *n* **1** a canton in W Switzerland. Capital: Fribourg. Pop.: 222 227 (1995 est.). Area: 1676 sq. km (645 sq. miles). **2** a town in W Switzerland, capital of Fribourg canton: university (1889). Pop.: 35 000 (1989). ◆ German name: **Freiburg.**

fricandeau ('frɪkən,dəʊ) *n, pl* **fricandeaus** *or* **fricandeaux** (-,dəʊz). a larded and braised veal fillet. [C18: from OF, prob. based on FRICASSEE]

fricassee (,frɪkə'siː, 'frɪkəsɪ) *n* **1** stewed meat, esp. chicken or veal, served in a thick white sauce. ◆ *vb* **fricassees, fricasseeing, fricasseed.** **2** (*tr*) to prepare (meat, etc.) as a fricassee. [C16: from OF, from *fricasser* to fricassee]

fricative ('frɪkətɪv) *n* **1** a consonant produced by partial occlusion of the airstream, such as (f) or (z). ◆ *adj* **2** relating to or denoting a fricative. [C19: from NL, from L *fricāre* to rub]

friction ('frɪkʃən) *n* **1** a resistance encountered when one body moves relative to another body with which it is in contact. **2** the act, effect, or an instance of rubbing one object against another. **3** disagreement or conflict. [C16: from F, from L *frictiō* a rubbing, from *fricāre* to rub]
▶ **'frictional** *adj* ▶ **'frictionless** *adj*

Friday ('fraɪdɪ) *n* **1** the sixth day of the week; fifth day of the working week. **2** See **man Friday.** [OE *Frīgedæg*]

fridge (frɪdʒ) *n* short for **refrigerator.**

fried (fraɪd) *vb* the past tense and past participle of **fry**[1].

Friedan ★ ('friːdən) *n* **Betty.** born 1921, US feminist, founder and first president (1966–70) of the National Organization for Women. Her books include *The Feminine Mystique* (1963) and *The Fountain of Life* (1993).

Friedman ★ ('friːdmən) *n* **Milton.** born 1912. US economist, particularly associated with monetarism and an advocate of free market capitalism.
▶ **'Friedman,ite** *n, adj*

Friedrich ★ (*German* 'friːdrɪç) *n* **Caspar David** ('kaspar 'daːfrɪt). 1774–1840, German landscape painter.

friend (frɛnd) *n* **1** a person known well to another and regarded with liking, affection, and loyalty. **2** an acquaintance or associate. **3** an ally in a fight or cause. **4** a fellow member of a party, society, etc. **5** a patron or supporter. **6 be friends (with).** to be friendly (with). **7 make friends (with).** to become friendly (with). ◆ *vb* **8** (*tr*) an archaic word for **befriend.** [OE *frēond*]
▶ **'friendless** *adj* ▶ **'friendship** *n*

Friend (frɛnd) *n* a member of the Religious Society of Friends; Quaker.

friend at court *n* an influential acquaintance who can promote one's interests.

friendly ('frɛndlɪ) *adj* **friendlier, friendliest.** **1** showing or expressing liking, goodwill, or trust. **2** on the same side; not hostile. **3** tending or disposed to help or support: *a friendly breeze helped them escape.* ◆ *n, pl* **friendlies.** **4** Also: **friendly match.** *Sport.* a match played for its own sake.
▶ **'friendlily** *adv* ▶ **'friendliness** *n*

-friendly *adj combining form.* helpful, easy, or good for the person or thing specified: *ozone-friendly.*

friendly fire *n Mil.* firing by one's own side, esp. when it harms one's own personnel.

Friendly Islands ★ *pl n* another name for **Tonga.**

friendly society *n Brit.* an association of people who pay regular dues or other sums in return for old-age pensions, sickness benefits, etc.

Friends of the Earth *n* an organization of environmentalists and conservationists.

frier ('fraɪə) *n* a variant spelling of **fryer.** See **fry**[1].

fries (fraɪz) *pl n* short for **French fried potatoes**; chips.

Friese-Greene ★ (,friːz'griːn) *n* **William.** 1855–1921, British photographer. He invented (with Mortimer Evans) the first practicable motion-picture camera.

Friesian ('friːʒən) *n* **1** *Brit.* any of several breeds of black-and-white dairy cattle having a high milk yield. **2** see **Frisian.**

Friesland ★ ('friːzlənd; *Dutch* 'friːslɑnt) *n* **1** a province of the N Netherlands, on the IJsselmeer and the North Sea: includes four of the West Frisian Islands. Capital: Leeuwarden. Pop.: 609 579 (1995). Area: 3319 sq. km (1294 sq. miles). Official name: **Fryslân. 2** an area comprising the province of Friesland in the Netherlands along with the regions of East Friesland and North Friesland in Germany.

frieze[1] (friːz) *n* **1** *Archit.* **1a** the horizontal band between the architrave and cornice of a classical entablature. **1b** the upper part of the wall of a room, below the cornice. **2** any ornamental band on a wall. [C16: from F *frise,* ?from Med. L *frisium,* changed from L *Phrygium* Phrygian (work), from Phrygia, famous for embroidery in gold]

frieze[2] (friːz) *n* a heavy woollen fabric used for coats, etc. [C15: from OF, from MDu. ?from *Vriese* Frisian]

frigate ('frɪgɪt) *n* **1** a medium-sized square-rigged warship of the 18th and 19th centuries. **2a** *Brit.* a warship smaller than a destroyer. **2b** *US.* (formerly) a warship larger than a destroyer. **2c** *US.* a small escort vessel. [C16: from F *frégate,* from It. *fregata,* from ?]

frigate bird *n* a bird of tropical and subtropical seas, having a large wingspan, and a forked tail.

Frigg (frɪg) *or* **Frigga** ★ ('frɪgə) *n Norse myth.* the wife of Odin; goddess of the heavens and married love.

fright (fraɪt) *n* **1** sudden fear or alarm. **2** a sudden alarming shock. **3** *Inf.* a horrifying or ludicrous person or thing: *she looks a fright.* **4 take fright.** to become frightened. ◆ *vb* **5** a poetic word for **frighten.** [OE *fryhto*]

frighten ('fraɪt²n) *vb* (*tr*) **1** to terrify; scare. **2** to drive or force to go (away, off, out, in, etc.) by making afraid.
▶ **'frightener** *n* ▶ **'frighteningly** *adv*

frightful ('fraɪtful) *adj* **1** very alarming or horrifying. **2** unpleasant, annoying, or extreme: *a frightful hurry.*
▶ **'frightfully** *adv* ▶ **'frightfulness** *n*

frigid ('frɪdʒɪd) *adj* **1** formal or stiff in behaviour or temperament. **2** (esp. of women) lacking sexual responsiveness. **3** characterized by physical coldness: *a frigid zone.* [C15: from L *frigidus* cold, from *frigēre* to be cold]
▶ **fri'gidity** *or* **'frigidness** *n* ▶ **'frigidly** *adv*

Frigid Zone *n* the cold region inside the Arctic or Antarctic Circle where the sun's rays are very oblique.

frijol (*Spanish* fri'xol) *n, pl* **frijoles** (*Spanish* -'xoles). a variety of bean extensively cultivated for food in Mexico. [C16: from Sp., ult. from L *phaseolus,* from Gk *phasēlos* bean with edible pod]

frill (frɪl) *n* **1** a gathered, ruched, or pleated strip of cloth sewn on at one edge only, as on garments, as ornament, or to give extra body. **2** a ruff of hair or feathers around the neck of a dog or bird or a fold of skin around the neck of a reptile or amphibian. **3** (*often pl*) *Inf.* a superfluous or pretentious thing or manner; affectation: *he made a plain speech with no frills.* ◆ *vb* **4** (*tr*) to adorn or fit with a frill or frills. **5** to form into a frill or frills. [C14: ? of Flemish origin]
▶ **'frilliness** *n* ▶ **'frilly** *adj*

frilled lizard *n* a large arboreal insectivorous Australian lizard having an erectile fold of skin around the neck.

fringe (frɪndʒ) *n* **1** an edging consisting of hanging threads, tassels, etc. **2a** an outer edge; periphery. **2b** (*as modifier*): *a fringe area.* **3** (*modifier*) unofficial; not conventional in form: *fringe theatre.* **4** *Chiefly Brit.* a section of the front hair cut short over the forehead. **5** an ornamental border. **6** *Physics.* any of the light and dark bands produced by diffraction or interference of light. ◆ *vb* **fringes, fringing, fringed.** (*tr*) **7** to adorn with a fringe or fringes. **8** to be a fringe for. [C14: from OF *frenge,* ult. from L *fimbria* fringe, border]
▶ **'fringeless** *adj*

fringe benefit *n* an additional advantage, esp. a benefit provided by an employer to supplement an employee's regular pay.

fringing reef *n* a coral reef close to the shore to which it is attached, having a steep seaward edge.

Frink ★ (frɪŋk) *n* Dame **Elisabeth.** 1930–93, British sculptor.

frippery ('frɪpərɪ) *n, pl* **fripperies.** **1** ornate or showy clothing or adornment. **2** ostentation. **3** trifles; trivia. [C16: from OF, from *frepe* frill, rag, from Med. L *faluppa* a straw, splinter, from ?]

Frisbee ('frɪzbɪ) *n Trademark.* a light plastic disc thrown with a spinning motion for recreation or in competition.

Frisch ★ (frɪʃ) *n* **1 Karl von** (*German* karl fɒn). 1886–1982, Austrian zoologist; studied animal behaviour, esp. of bees; shared the Nobel prize for physiology or medicine 1973. **2 Max** (*German* maks). 1911–91, Swiss dramatist and novelist. His works include the play *Biedermann und die Brandstifter* (1953) and the novel *Stiller* (1954). **3 Otto.** 1904–79, British nuclear physicist, born in Austria, who contributed to the development of the first atomic bomb. **4 Ragnar** (**Anton Kittil**) (*Norwegian* 'rɑːŋnɑːr). 1895–1973, Norwegian economist, who pioneered the study of econometrics: shared the first Nobel prize for economics (1969).

Frisches Haff ★ ('frɪʃəs haf) *n* the German name for **Vistula** (sense 2).

Frisian ('frɪʒən) *or* **Friesian** *n* **1** a language spoken in the NW Netherlands, parts of N Germany, and some of the adjacent islands. **2** a speaker of this language or a native or inhabitant of Friesland. ◆ *adj* **3** of or relating to this language, its speakers, or the peoples and culture of Friesland. [C16: from L *Frīsiī* people of northern Germany]

Frisian Islands ★ *pl n* a chain of islands in the North Sea along the coasts of the Netherlands, Germany, and Denmark: separated from the mainland by shallows.

frisk (frɪsk) *vb* **1** (*intr*) to leap, move about, or act in a playful manner. **2** (*tr*) (esp. of animals) to whisk or wave briskly: *the dog frisked its tail.* **3** (*tr*) *Inf.* to search (someone) by feeling for concealed weapons. ◆ *n* **4** a playful antic or movement. **5** *Inf.* an instance of frisking a person. [C16: from OF *frisque*, of Gmc origin]
▶ 'frisker *n*

frisky ('frɪskɪ) *adj* **friskier, friskiest.** lively, high-spirited, or playful.
▶ 'friskily *adv*

frisson *French.* (frisɔ̃) *n* a shiver; thrill. [C18 (but in common use only from C20): lit.: shiver]

frit (frɪt) *n* **1a** the basic materials, partially or wholly fused, for making glass, glazes for pottery, enamel, etc. **1b** a glassy substance used in some soft-paste porcelain. ◆ *vb* **frits, fritting, fritted. 2** (*tr*) to fuse (materials) in making frit. [C17: from It. *fritta*, lit.: fried, from *friggere* to fry, from L *frīgere*]

fritillary (frɪ'tɪlərɪ) *n, pl* **fritillaries. 1** a liliaceous plant having purple or white drooping bell-shaped flowers, typically marked in a chequered pattern. **2** any of various butterflies having brownish wings chequered with black and silver. [C17: from NL *fritillāria*, from L *fritillus* dice box; prob. with reference to the markings]

fritter[1] ('frɪtə) *vb* (*tr*) **1** (usually foll. by *away*) to waste: *to fritter away time.* **2** to break into small pieces. [C18: prob. from obs. *fitter* to break into small pieces, ult. from OE *fitt* a piece]

fritter[2] ('frɪtə) *n* a piece of food, such as apple, that is dipped in batter and fried in deep fat. [C14: from OF, from L *frictus* fried, from *frīgere* to fry]

Friuli ★ (*Italian* fri'uːli) *n* a historic region of SW Europe, between the Carnic Alps and the Gulf of Venice: the W part (**Venetian Friuli**) was ceded by Austria to Italy in 1866 and **Eastern Friuli** in 1919; in 1947 Eastern Friuli (except Gorizia) was ceded to Yugoslavia.

Friuli-Venezia Giulia ★ (*Italian* 'dʒuːlja) *n* a region of NE Italy, formed in 1947 from **Venetian Friuli** and part of **Eastern Friuli.** Capital: Trieste. Pop.: 1 193 217 (1994 est.). Area: 7851 sq. km (3031 sq. miles).

frivolous ('frɪvələs) *adj* **1** not serious or sensible in content, attitude, or behaviour. **2** unworthy of serious or sensible treatment: *frivolous details.* [C15: from L *frīvolus*]
▶ 'frivolously *adv* ▶ 'frivolousness *or* frivolity (frɪ'vɒlɪtɪ) *n*

frizz (frɪz) *vb* **1** (of the hair, nap, etc.) to form or cause (the hair, etc.) to form tight curls or crisp tufts. ◆ *n* **2** hair

that has been frizzed. **3** the state of being frizzed. [C19: from F *friser* to curl]

frizzle[1] ('frɪz³l) *vb* **frizzles, frizzling, frizzled. 1** to form (the hair) into tight crisp curls. ◆ *n* **2** a tight curl. [C16: prob. rel. to OE *frīs* curly]

frizzle[2] ('frɪz³l) *vb* **frizzles, frizzling, frizzled. 1** to scorch or be scorched, esp. with a sizzling noise. **2** (*tr*) to fry (bacon, etc.) until crisp. [C16: prob. blend of FRY[1] + SIZZLE]

frizzy ('frɪzɪ) *or* **frizzly** ('frɪzlɪ) *adj* **frizzier, frizziest** *or* **frizzlier, frizzliest.** (of the hair) in tight crisp wiry curls.
▶ 'frizziness *or* 'frizzliness *n*

fro (frəʊ) *adv* back or from. [C12: from ON *frā*]

Frobisher ★ ('frəʊbɪʃə) *n* Sir **Martin.** ?1535–94, English navigator and explorer: made three unsuccessful voyages in search of the Northwest Passage (1576; 1577; 1578), visiting Labrador and Baffin Island.

Frobisher Bay ★ *n* **1** an inlet of the Atlantic in NE Canada, on the SE coast of Baffin Island. **2** the former name of **Iqaluit.**

frock (frɒk) *n* **1** a girl's or woman's dress. **2** a loose garment of several types, such as a peasant's smock. **3** a wide-sleeved outer garment worn by members of some religious orders. ◆ *vb* **4** (*tr*) to invest (a person) with the office of a cleric. [C14: from OF *froc*]

frock coat *n* a man's single- or double-breasted skirted coat, as worn in the 19th century.

Fröding ★ (*Swedish* 'frœːdɪŋ) *n* **Gustaf** ('gustav). 1860–1911, Swedish poet. His popular lyric verse includes the collections *Guitar and Concertina* (1891), *New Poems* (1894), and *Splashes and Rags* (1896).

Froebel *or* **Fröbel** ★ *n* (*German* 'frøːbəl). **1 Friedrich** (**Wilhelm August**) ('friːdrɪç). 1782–1852, German educator: founded the first kindergarten (1840). ◆ *adj* ('frəʊb³l). **2** of, denoting, or relating to a system of kindergarten education developed by him or to the training and qualification of teachers to use this system.

frog[1] (frɒg) *n* **1** an insectivorous amphibian, having a short squat tailless body with a moist smooth skin and very long hind legs specialized for hopping. **2** any of various similar amphibians, such as the tree frog. **3** any spiked object that is used to support plant stems in a flower arrangement. **4 a frog in one's throat.** phlegm on the vocal cords that affects one's speech. [OE *frogga*]
▶ 'froggy *adj*

frog[2] (frɒg) *n* **1** (*often pl*) a decorative fastening of looped braid or cord, as on a military uniform. **2** an attachment on a belt to hold the scabbard of a sword, etc. [C18: ? ult. from L *floccus* tuft of hair]
▶ 'frogged *adj* ▶ 'frogging *n*

frog[3] (frɒg) *n* a tough elastic horny material in the centre of the sole of a horse's foot. [C17: from ?]

frog[4] (frɒg) *n* a plate of iron or steel to guide train wheels over an intersection of railway lines. [C19: from ?; a special use of FROG[1]]

Frog (frɒg) *or* **Froggy** ('frɒgɪ) *n, pl* **Frogs** *or* **Froggies.** *Brit. sl.* a derogatory word for a French person.

froghopper ('frɒg,hɒpə) *n* any small leaping insect whose larvae secrete a protective spittle-like substance around themselves.

frogman ('frɒgmən) *n, pl* **frogmen.** a swimmer equipped with a rubber suit, flippers, and breathing equipment for working underwater.

frogmarch ('frɒg,mɑːtʃ) *Chiefly Brit.* ◆ *n* **1** a method of carrying a resisting person in which each limb is held and the victim is carried horizontally and face downwards. **2** any method of making a person move against his will. ◆ *vb* **3** (*tr*) to carry in a frogmarch or cause to move forward unwillingly.

frogmouth ('frɒg,maʊθ) *n* a nocturnal insectivorous bird of SE Asia and Australia, similar to the nightjars.

frogspawn ('frɒg,spɔːn) *n* a mass of fertilized frogs' eggs surrounded by a protective nutrient jelly.

frog spit *or* **spittle** *n* **1** another name for **cuckoo spit.** **2** a foamy mass of threadlike green algae floating on ponds.

Froissart ★ (*French* frwasar) *n* **Jean** (ʒɑ̃). ?1333–?1400, French chronicler and poet, noted for his *Chronique*.

★ people and places

frolic ('frɒlɪk) n **1** a light-hearted entertainment or occasion. **2** light-hearted activity; gaiety. ◆ vb **frolics, frolicking, frolicked. 3** (intr) to caper about. ◆ adj **4** Arch. full of fun; gay. [C16: from Du. vrolijk, from MDu. vro happy]
▸ **'frolicker** n

frolicsome ('frɒlɪksəm) adj merry and playful.
▸ **'frolicsomely** adv

from (frɒm; unstressed frəm) prep **1** used to indicate the original location, situation, etc.: from behind the bushes. **2** in a period of time starting at: he lived from 1910 to 1970. **3** used to indicate the distance between two things or places: a hundred miles from here. **4** used to indicate a lower amount: from five to fifty pounds. **5** showing the model of: painted from life. **6** used with the gerund to mark prohibition, etc.: nothing prevents him from leaving. **7** because of: exhausted from his walk. [OE fram]

fromage frais ('frɒmɑːʒ 'freɪ; French frɔmaʒ frɛ) n a low-fat soft cheese with a smooth light texture. [F, lit.: fresh cheese]

Frome ★ (frəum) n Lake. a shallow salt lake in NE South Australia: intermittently filled with water. Length: 100 km (60 miles). Width: 48 km (30 miles).

Fromm ★ (from) n **Erich** ('ɛrɪk). 1900–80, US psychologist and philosopher, born in Germany. His works include The Art of Loving (1956) and To Have and To Be (1976).

frond (frɒnd) n **1** the compound leaf of a fern. **2** the leaf of a palm. [C18: from L frōns]

front (frʌnt) n **1** that part or side that is forward, or most often seen or used. **2** a position or place directly before or ahead: a fountain stood at the front of the building. **3** the beginning, opening, or first part. **4** the position of leadership: in the front of scientific knowledge. **5** land bordering a lake, street, etc. **6** land along a seashore or large lake, esp. a promenade. **7** Mil. **7a** the total area in which opposing armies face each other. **7b** the space in which a military unit is operating: to advance on a broad front. **8** Meteorol. the dividing line or plane between two air masses of different origins. **9** outward aspect or bearing, as when dealing with a situation: a bold front. **10** Inf. a business or other activity serving as a respectable cover for another, usually criminal, organization. **11** Also called: **front man**. a nominal leader of an organization etc.; figurehead. **12** Inf. outward appearance of rank or wealth. **13** a particular field of activity: on the wages front. **14** a group of people with a common goal: a national liberation front. **15** a false shirt front; a dicky. **16** Arch. the forehead or the face. ◆ adj (prenominal) **17** of, at, or in the front: a front seat. **18** Phonetics. of or denoting a vowel articulated with the tongue brought forward, as for the sound of ee in English see or a in English hat. ◆ vb **19** (when intr, foll. by on or onto) to face (onto): this house fronts the river. **20** (tr) to be a front of or for. **21** (tr) to appear as a presenter in a television show. **22** (tr) to be the lead singer or player in a band. **23** (tr) to confront. **24** to supply a front for. **25** (intr; often foll. by up) Austral. inf. to appear (at): to front up at the police station. [C13 (in the sense: forehead, face): from L frōns forehead, foremost part]
▸ **'frontless** adj

frontage ('frʌntɪdʒ) n **1** the façade of a building or the front of a plot of ground. **2** the extent of the front of a shop, plot of land, etc. **3** the direction in which a building faces.

frontal ('frʌntəl) adj **1** of, at, or in the front. **2** of or relating to the forehead: frontal artery. ◆ n **3** a decorative hanging for the front of an altar. [C14 (in the sense: adornment for forehead, altarcloth): via OF frontel, from L frōns forehead]
▸ **'frontally** adv

frontal lobe n Anat. the anterior portion of each cerebral hemisphere.

front bench n **1** Brit. **1a** the foremost bench of either the Government or Opposition in the House of Commons. **1b** the leadership (**frontbenchers**) of either group, who occupy this bench. **2** the leadership of the government or opposition in various legislative assemblies.

front-end adj (of money, costs, etc.) required or incurred in advance of a project in order to get it under way.

frontier ('frʌntɪə, frʌn'tɪə) n **1a** the region of a country bordering on another or a line, barrier, etc., marking such a boundary. **1b** (as modifier): a frontier post. **2** US. the edge of the settled area of a country. **3** (often pl) the limit of knowledge in a particular field: the frontiers of physics have been pushed back. [C14: from OF, from front (in the sense: part which is opposite)]

frontiersman ('frʌntɪəzmən, frʌn'tɪəz-) or (fem) **frontierswoman** (-,wumən) n, pl **frontiersmen** or **frontierswomen**. (formerly) a person living on a frontier, esp. in a newly pioneered territory of the US.

frontispiece ('frʌntɪs,piːs) n **1** an illustration facing the title page of a book. **2** the principal façade of a building. **3** a pediment over a door, window, etc. [C16 frontispice, from F, from LL frontispicium façade, from L frōns forehead + specere to look at; infl. by PIECE]

frontlet ('frʌntlɪt) n Judaism. a phylactery attached to the forehead. [C15: from OF frontelet a little FRONTAL]

front line n **1** Military. **1a** the most advanced military units in a battle. **1b** (modifier): of, relating to, or suitable for the military front line: frontline troops. **2** (modifier) close to a hostile country or scene of armed conflict: the frontline states.

front loader n a washing machine with a door at the front which opens one side of the drum into which washing is placed.

front-page n (modifier) important enough to be put on the front page of a newspaper.

frontrunner ('frʌnt,rʌnə) n Inf. the leader or a favoured contestant in a race, election, etc.

frontrunning ('frʌnt,rʌnɪŋ) n Stock Exchange. the practice by market makers of using advance information provided by their own investment analysts before it has been given to their clients.

frost (frɒst) n **1** a white deposit of ice particles, esp. one formed on objects out of doors at night. **2** an atmospheric temperature of below freezing point, characterized by the production of this deposit. **3 degrees of frost**. degrees below freezing point. **4** Inf. something given a cold reception; failure. **5** Inf. coolness of manner. **6** the act of freezing. ◆ vb **7** to cover or be covered with frost. **8** (tr) to give a frostlike appearance to (glass, etc.), as by means of a fine-grained surface. **9** (tr) Chiefly US & Canad. to decorate (cakes, etc.) with icing or frosting. **10** (tr) to kill or damage (crops, etc.) with frost. [OE frost]

Frost ★ (frɒst) n **Robert** (**Lee**). 1874–1963, US poet, noted for his lyrical verse on country life in New England. His books include A Boy's Will (1913), North of Boston (1914), and New Hampshire (1923).

frostbite ('frɒst,baɪt) n destruction of tissues, esp. those of the fingers, ears, toes, and nose, by freezing.
▸ **'frost,bitten** adj

frosted ('frɒstɪd) adj **1** covered or injured by frost. **2** covered with icing, as a cake. **3** (of glass, etc.) having a surface roughened to prevent clear vision through it.

frost hollow n a depression in a hilly area in which cold air collects, becoming very cold at night.

frosting ('frɒstɪŋ) n **1** another word (esp. US and Canad.) for **icing**. **2** a rough or matt finish on glass, silver, etc.

frosty ('frɒstɪ) adj **frostier, frostiest**. **1** characterized by frost: a frosty night. **2** covered by or decorated with frost. **3** lacking warmth or enthusiasm: the new plan had a frosty reception.
▸ **'frostily** adv ▸ **'frostiness** n

froth (frɒθ) n **1** a mass of small bubbles of air or a gas in a liquid, produced by fermentation, etc. **2** a mixture of saliva and air bubbles formed at the lips in certain diseases, such as rabies. **3** trivial ideas or entertainment. ◆ vb **4** to produce or cause to produce froth. **5** (tr) to give out in the form of froth. [C14: from ON frotha or frauth]
▸ **'frothy** adj ▸ **'frothily** adv

Froude ★ (fruːd) n **1 James Anthony**. 1818–94, British historian; author of a controversial biography (1882–84) of Carlyle. **2** his brother **William**. 1810–79, British civil engineer.

froufrou ('fruː,fruː) n a swishing sound, as made by a long silk dress. [C19: from F, imit.]

★ people and places

froward ('frəʊəd) *adj Arch.* obstinate; contrary. [C14: see FRO, -WARD]
▶ 'frowardly *adv* ▶ 'frowardness *n*

frown (fraʊn) *vb* **1** (*intr*) to draw the brows together and wrinkle the forehead, esp. in worry, anger, or concentration. **2** (*intr*; foll. by *on* or *upon*) to look disapprovingly (upon). **3** (*tr*) to express (worry, etc.) by frowning. ◆ *n* **4** the act of frowning. **5** a show of dislike or displeasure. [C14: from OF *froigner*, of Celtic origin]
▶ 'frowner *n* ▶ 'frowningly *adv*

frowst (fraʊst) *n Brit. inf.* a hot and stale atmosphere; fug. [C19: back formation from *frowsty* musty, stuffy, var. of FROWZY]

frowsty ('fraʊstɪ) *adj* **frowstier, frowstiest.** ill-smelling; stale; musty.
▶ 'frowstiness *n*

frowzy *or* **frowsy** ('fraʊzɪ) *adj* **frowzier, frowziest,** *or* **frowsier, frowsiest. 1** untidy or unkempt in appearance. **2** ill-smelling; frowsty. [C17: from ?]
▶ 'frowziness *or* 'frowsiness *n*

froze (frəʊz) *vb* the past tense of **freeze.**

frozen ('frəʊz³n) *vb* **1** the past participle of **freeze.** ◆ *adj* **2** turned into or covered with ice. **3** killed or stiffened by extreme cold. **4** (of a region or climate) icy or snowy. **5** (of food) preserved by a freezing process. **6a** (of prices, wages, etc.) arbitrarily pegged at a certain level. **6b** (of business assets) not convertible into cash. **7** frigid or disdainful in manner. **8** motionless or unyielding: *he was frozen with horror.*
▶ 'frozenly *adv*

frozen shoulder *n Pathol.* painful stiffness in a shoulder joint.

FRS (in Britain) *abbrev. for* Fellow of the Royal Society.

FRSNZ *abbrev. for* Fellow of the Royal Society of New Zealand.

fructify ('frʌktɪˌfaɪ) *vb* **fructifies, fructifying, fructified. 1** to bear or cause to bear fruit. **2** to make or become fruitful. [C14: from OF, from LL *frūctificāre,* from L *frūctus* fruit + *facere* to produce]
▶ ˌfructifiˈcation *n* ▶ frucˈtiferous *adj* ▶ 'fructiˌfier *n*

fructose ('frʌktəʊs) *n* a white crystalline sugar occurring in many fruits. Formula: $C_6H_{12}O_6$. [C19: from L *frūctus* fruit + -OSE²]

frugal ('fruːgªl) *adj* **1** practising economy; thrifty. **2** not costly; meagre. [C16: from L, from *frūgī* useful, temperate, from *frux* fruit]
▶ fruˈgality *n* ▶ 'frugally *adv*

frugivorous (fruːˈdʒɪvərəs) *adj* fruit-eating. [C18: from *frugi-* (as in FRUGAL) + -VOROUS]

fruit (fruːt) *n* **1** *Bot.* the ripened ovary of a flowering plant, containing one or more seeds. It may be dry, as in the poppy, or fleshy, as in the peach. **2** any fleshy part of a plant that supports the seeds and is edible, such as the strawberry. **3** any plant product useful to man, including grain, vegetables, etc. **4** (*often pl*) the result or consequence of an action or effort. **5** *Arch.* offspring of man or animals. **6** *Inf., chiefly US & Canad.* a male homosexual. ◆ *vb* **7** to bear or cause to bear fruit. [C12: from OF, from L *frūctus* enjoyment, fruit, from *fruī* to enjoy]
▶ 'fruit,like *adj*

fruit bat *n* a large Old World bat occurring in tropical and subtropical regions and feeding on fruit.

fruitcake ('fruːtˌkeɪk) *n* a rich cake containing mixed dried fruit, lemon peel, etc.

fruit drop *n* **1** the premature shedding of fruit from a tree before fully ripe. **2** a boiled sweet with a fruity flavour.

fruiterer ('fruːtərə) *n Chiefly Brit.* a fruit dealer or seller.

fruit fly *n* **1** a small dipterous fly which feeds on and lays its eggs in plant tissues. **2** any dipterous fly of the genus Drosophila. See **drosophila.**

fruitful ('fruːtful) *adj* **1** bearing fruit in abundance. **2** productive or prolific. **3** producing results or profits: *a fruitful discussion.*
▶ 'fruitfully *adv* ▶ 'fruitfulness *n*

fruition (fruːˈɪʃən) *n* **1** the attainment of something

worked for or desired. **2** enjoyment of this. **3** the act or condition of bearing fruit. [C15: from LL, from L *fruī* to enjoy]

fruitless ('fruːtlɪs) *adj* **1** yielding nothing or nothing of value; unproductive. **2** without fruit.
▶ 'fruitlessly *adv* ▶ 'fruitlessness *n*

fruit machine *n Brit.* a gambling machine that pays out when certain combinations of diagrams, usually of fruit, appear on a dial.

fruit salad *n* a dessert consisting of sweet fruits cut up and served in a syrup.

fruit sugar *n* another name for **fructose.**

fruit tree *n* any tree that bears edible fruit.

fruity ('fruːtɪ) *adj* **fruitier, fruitiest. 1** of or resembling fruit. **2** (of a voice) mellow or rich. **3** *Inf., chiefly Brit.* erotically stimulating; salacious. **4** *Inf., chiefly US & Canad.* homosexual.
▶ 'fruitily *adv* ▶ 'fruitiness *n*

frumenty ('fruːməntɪ) *or* **furmenty** *n Brit.* a kind of porridge made from hulled wheat boiled with milk, sweetened, and spiced. [C14: from OF, from *frument* grain, from L *frūmentum*]

frump (frʌmp) *n* a woman who is dowdy, drab, or unattractive. [C16 (in the sense: to be sullen; C19: dowdy woman): from MDu. *verrompelen* to wrinkle]
▶ 'frumpy *or* 'frumpish *adj*

Frunze ★ (*Russian* 'frunzɪ) *n* the former name (until 1991) of **Bishkek.**

frustrate (frʌˈstreɪt) *vb* **frustrates, frustrating, frustrated.** (*tr*) **1** to hinder or prevent (the efforts, plans, or desires) of. **2** to upset, agitate, or tire. ◆ *adj* **3** *Arch.* frustrated or thwarted. [C15: from L *frustrāre* to cheat, from *frustrā* in error]
▶ frusˈtration *n*

frustrated (frʌˈstreɪtɪd) *adj* having feelings of dissatisfaction or lack of fulfilment.

frustum ('frʌstəm) *n, pl* **frustums** *or* **frusta** (-tə). *Geom.* **a** the part of a solid, such as a cone or pyramid, contained between the base and a plane parallel to the base that intersects the solid. **b** the part of such a solid contained between two parallel planes intersecting the solid. [C17: from L: piece]

fry¹ (fraɪ) *vb* **fries, frying, fried. 1** (when *tr*, sometimes foll. by *up*) to cook or be cooked in fat, oil, etc., usually over direct heat. **2** *Sl., chiefly US.* to kill or be killed by electrocution. ◆ *n, pl* **fries. 3** a dish of something fried, esp. the offal of a specified animal: *pig's fry.* **4** fry-up. *Brit. inf.* the act of preparing a mixed fried dish or the dish itself. [C13: from OF *frire,* from L *frīgere* to fry]
▶ 'fryer *or* 'frier *n*

fry² (fraɪ) *pl n* **1** the young of various species of fish. **2** the young of certain other animals, such as frogs. [C14 (in the sense: young, offspring): from OF *freier* to spawn, from L *fricāre* to rub]

Fry ★ (fraɪ) *n* **1 Christopher.** born 1907, English dramatist; author of the verse dramas *A Phoenix Too Frequent* (1946), *The Lady's Not For Burning* (1948), *Venus Observed* (1950), and *One Thing More* (1986). **2 Elizabeth.** 1780–1845, English prison reformer and Quaker. **3 Roger Eliot.** 1866–1934, English art critic and painter who helped to introduce the postimpressionists to Britain. His books include *Vision and Design* (1920) and *Cézanne* (1927).

frying pan *n* **1** a long-handled shallow pan used for frying. **2 out of the frying pan into the fire.** from a bad situation to a worse one.

f-stop ('ɛfˌstɒp) *n* any of the settings for the f-number of a camera.

ft. *abbrev. for* foot *or* feet.

fth. *or* **fthm.** *abbrev. for* fathom.

FT Index *abbrev. for:* **1** Financial Times Industrial Ordinary Share Index: an index designed to show the general trend in share prices, produced daily by the *Financial Times* newspaper. **2** Financial Times Stock Exchange 100 Index: an index produced by the *Financial Times* based on an average of 100 securities and giving the best indication of daily movements. Also: **FTSE Index.** Informal name: **Footsie.**

FTP *abbrev.* (*sometimes not caps.*) *for* file transfer protocol: the standard mechanism used to transfer files between computer systems or across the Internet.

Fuad I ★ (fuːˈɑːd) *n* original name *Ahmed Fuad Pasha*. 1868–1936, sultan of Egypt (1917–22) and king (1922–36).

Fu-chou ★ (ˈfuːˈtʃəu) *n* a variant transliteration of the Chinese name for **Fuzhou**.

Fuchs ★ (fuks, fuːks) *n* **1 Klaus Emil** (*German* klaus ˈeːmiːl). 1911–88, German physicist, who became a British citizen (1942) and was imprisoned (1950–59) for giving secret atomic information to the Soviet Union. **2 Sir Vivian Ernest.** born 1908, British explorer and geologist: led the Commonwealth Trans-Antarctic Expedition (1955–58).

fuchsia (ˈfjuːʃə) *n* **1** a shrub widely cultivated for its showy drooping purple, red, or white flowers. **2a** a reddish-purple to purplish-pink colour. **2b** (*as adj*): *a fuchsia dress*. [C18: from NL, after Leonhard *Fuchs* (1501–66), G botanist]

fuchsin (ˈfuːksɪn) *or* **fuchsine** (ˈfuːksiːn, -sɪn) *n* an aniline dye forming a red solution in water: used as a textile dye and a biological stain. [C19: from FUCHS(IA) + -IN; from its similarity in colour to the flower]

fuck (fʌk) *Taboo.* ◆ *vb* **1** to have sexual intercourse with (someone). ◆ *n* **2** an act of sexual intercourse. **3** *Sl.* a partner in sexual intercourse. **4 not care** *or* **give a fuck.** not to care at all. ◆ *interj* **5** *Offens.* an expression of strong disgust or anger. [C16: of Gmc origin]

fucus (ˈfjuːkəs) *n, pl* **fuci** (-saɪ) *or* **fucuses**. a seaweed of the genus *Fucus*, having greenish-brown slimy fronds. [C16: from L: rock lichen, from Gk *phukos* seaweed, of Semitic origin]

fuddle (ˈfʌdˀl) *vb* **fuddles, fuddling, fuddled. 1** (*tr; often passive*) to cause to be confused or intoxicated. ◆ *n* **2** a muddled or confused state. [C16: from ?]

fuddy-duddy (ˈfʌdɪˌdʌdɪ) *n, pl* **fuddy-duddies.** *Inf.* a person, esp. an elderly one, who is extremely conservative or dull. [C20: from ?]

fudge[1] (fʌdʒ) *n* a soft variously flavoured sweet made from sugar, butter, etc. [C19: from ?]

fudge[2] (fʌdʒ) *n* **1** foolishness; nonsense. ◆ *interj* **2** a mild exclamation of annoyance. [C18: from ?]

fudge[3] (fʌdʒ) *n* **1** a small section of type matter in a box in a newspaper allowing late news to be included without the whole page having to be remade. **2** the late news so inserted. **3** an unsatisfactory compromise reached to evade a difficult problem or controversial issue. ◆ *vb* **fudges, fudging, fudged. 4** (*tr*) to make or adjust in a false or clumsy way. **5** (*tr*) to misrepresent; falsify. **6** to evade (a problem, issue, etc.). [C19: ? rel. to arch. *fadge* to agree, succeed]

fuel (fjuəl) *n* **1** any substance burned as a source of heat or power, such as coal or petrol. **2** the material, containing a fissile substance such as uranium-235, that produces energy in a nuclear reactor. **3** something that nourishes or builds up emotion, action, etc. ◆ *vb* **fuels, fuelling, fuelled** *or US* **fuels, fueling, fueled. 4** to supply with or receive fuel. [C14: from OF, from *feu* fire, ult. from L *focus* hearth]

fuel air bomb *n* a type of bomb that spreads a cloud of gas, which is then detonated, over the target area, causing extensive destruction.

fuel cell *n* a cell in which chemical energy is converted directly into electrical energy.

fuel injection *n* a system for introducing fuel directly into the combustion chambers of an internal-combustion engine without the use of a carburettor.

fuel oil *n* a liquid petroleum product used as a substitute for coal in industrial furnaces, ships, and locomotives.

Fuentes ★ (*Spanish* ˈfwentes) *n* **Carlos** (ˈkarlɔs). born 1928, Mexican writer. His novels include *The Death of Artemio Cruz* (1962), *Terra Nostra* (1975), *The Old Gringo* (1985), and *Cristóbal Nonato* (1987).

fug (fʌg) *n Chiefly Brit.* a hot, stale, or suffocating atmosphere. [C19: ? var. of FOG[1]]
▶ **'fuggy** *adj*

fugacity (fjuːˈɡæsɪtɪ) *n Thermodynamics.* a property of a gas that expresses its tendency to escape or expand.

Fugard ★ (ˈfjuːɡɑːd) *n* **Athol** (ˈæθəl). born 1932, South African dramatist and director. His plays include *The Blood-Knot* (1961), *Sizwe Banzi is Dead* (1972), and *Sign of Hope* (1992).

-fuge *n combining form.* indicating an agent or substance that expels or drives away: *vermifuge*. [from L *fugāre* to expel]

fugitive (ˈfjuːdʒɪtɪv) *n* **1** a person who flees. **2** a thing that is elusive or fleeting. ◆ *adj* **3** fleeing, esp. from arrest or pursuit. **4** not permanent; fleeting. [C14: from L, from *fugere* to take flight]
▶ **'fugitively** *adv*

fugleman (ˈfjuːɡˀlmən) *n, pl* **fuglemen. 1** (formerly) a soldier used as an example for those learning drill. **2** a leader or example. [C19: from G *Flügelmann*, from *Flügel* wing + *Mann* MAN]

fugue (fjuːɡ) *n* **1** a musical form consisting of a theme repeated a fifth above or a fourth below the continuing first statement. **2** *Psychiatry.* a dreamlike altered state of consciousness, during which a person may lose his memory and wander away. [C16: from F, from It. *fuga*, from L: a running away]
▶ **'fugal** *adj*

Führer *or* **Fuehrer** *German.* (ˈfyːrər) *n* a leader: applied esp. to Adolf Hitler while he was Chancellor. [G, from *führen* to lead]

Fuji ★ (ˈfuːdʒɪ) *n* **Mount.** an extinct volcano in central Japan, in S central Honshu: the highest mountain in Japan, famous for its symmetrical snow-capped cone. Height: 3776 m (12 388 ft). Also called: **Fujiyama, Fuji-san.**

Fujian *or* **Fukien** ★ (ˈfuːˈkjen) *n* **1** a province of SE China: mountainous and forested, drained chiefly by the Min River; noted for the production of flower-scented teas. Capital: Fuzhou. Pop.: 31 830 000 (1995 est.). Area: 123 000 sq. km (47 470 sq. miles). **2** any of the Chinese dialects of this province.

Fukuoka ★ (ˌfuːkuːˈəukə) *n* an industrial city and port in SW Japan, in N Kyushu: an important port in ancient times; site of Kyushu university. Pop.: 1 284 741 (1995).

-ful *suffix.* **1** (*forming adjectives*) full of or characterized by: *painful; restful.* **2** (*forming adjectives*) able or tending to: *useful.* **3** (*forming nouns*) indicating as much as will fill the thing specified: *mouthful.* [OE *-ful, -full*, from FULL[1]]

> **USAGE NOTE** Where the amount held by a spoon, etc., is used as a rough unit of measurement, the correct form is *spoonful*, as in *take a spoonful of this medicine every day*. *Spoon full* is used in a sentence such as *he held out a spoon full of dark liquid*, where *full* of describes the spoon. A plural form such as *spoonfuls* is preferred by many speakers and writers to *spoonsful*.

fulcrum (ˈfulkrəm, ˈfʌl-) *n, pl* **fulcrums** *or* **fulcra** (-krə). **1** the pivot about which a lever turns. **2** something that supports or sustains; prop. [C17: from L: foot of a couch, from *fulcire* to prop up]

fulfil *or US* **fulfill** (fulˈfɪl) *vb* **fulfils, fulfilling, fulfilled** *or US* **fulfills, fulfilling, fulfilled.** (*tr*) **1** to bring about the completion or achievement of (a desire, promise, etc.). **2** to carry out or execute (a request, etc.). **3** to conform with or satisfy (regulations, etc.). **4** to finish or reach the end of. **5 fulfil oneself.** to achieve one's potential or desires. [OE *fulfyllan*]
▶ **ful'filment** *or US* **ful'fillment** *n*

fulgent (ˈfʌldʒənt) *adj Poetic.* shining brilliantly; gleaming. [C15: from L *fulgēre* to shine]

fulgurate (ˈfʌlɡjuˌreɪt) *vb* **fulgurates, fulgurating, fulgurated.** (*intr*) *Rare.* to flash like lightning. [C17: from L, from *fulgur* lightning]

fulgurite (ˈfʌlɡjuˌraɪt) *n* glassy mineral matter found in sand and rock, formed by the action of lightning. [C19: from L *fulgur* lightning]

Fulham ★ (ˈfuləm) *n* a district of the Greater London borough of Hammersmith and Fulham (since 1965): contains **Fulham Palace** (16th century), residence of the Bishop of London.

fuliginous (fjuːˈlɪdʒɪnəs) *adj* **1** sooty or smoky. **2** of the colour of soot. [C16: from LL *fūlīginōsus* full of soot, from L *fūlīgō* soot]

full[1] (ful) *adj* **1** holding or containing as much as possible. **2** abundant in supply, quantity, number, etc.: *full of energy*. **3** having consumed enough food or drink. **4** (esp. of the face or figure) rounded or plump. **5** (*prenominal*) complete: *a full dozen*. **6** (*prenominal*) with all privileges, rights, etc.: *a full member*. **7** (*prenominal*) having the same parents: *a full brother*. **8** filled with emotion or sentiment: *a full heart*. **9** (*postpositive*; foll. by *of*) occupied or engrossed (with): *full of his own projects*. **10** *Music*. **10a** powerful or rich in volume and sound. **10b** completing a piece or section; concluding: *a full close*. **11** (of a garment, esp. a skirt) containing a large amount of fabric. **12** (of sails, etc.) distended by wind. **13** (of wine, such as a burgundy) having a heavy body. **14** (of a colour) rich; saturated. **15** *Inf*. drunk. **16 full of oneself**. full of pride or conceit. **17 full up**. filled to capacity. **18 in full swing**. at the height of activity: *the party was in full swing*. ◆ *adv* **19a** completely; entirely. **19b** (*in combination*): *full-fledged*. **20** directly; right: *he hit him full in the stomach*. **21** very; extremely (esp. in **full well**). ◆ *n* **22** the greatest degree, extent, etc. **23 in full**. without omitting or shortening: *we paid in full for our mistake*. **24 to the full**. thoroughly; fully. ◆ *vb* **25** (*tr*) *Needlework*. to gather or tuck. **26** (*intr*) (of the moon) to be fully illuminated. [OE]
▸ ˈfullness *or esp. US* ˈfulness *n*

full[2] (ful) *vb* (of cloth, yarn, etc.) to become or to make (cloth, yarn, etc.) more compact during manufacture through shrinking and pressing. [C14: from OF *fouler*, ult. from L *fullō* a FULLER]

fullback (ˈfulˌbæk) *n Soccer, hockey, rugby*. **a** a defensive player. **b** the position held by this player.

full-blooded *adj* **1** (esp. of horses) of unmixed ancestry. **2** having great vigour or health; hearty.
▸ ˌfull-ˈbloodedness *n*

full-blown *adj* **1** characterized by the fullest, strongest, or best development. **2** in full bloom.

full board *n* accommodation at a hotel, etc., that includes all meals.

full-bodied *adj* having a full rich flavour or quality.

full-court press *n Basketball*. the tactic of harrying the opposing team in all areas of the court, as opposed to the more usual practice of trying to defend one's own basket.

full dress *n* **a** a formal style of dress, such as white tie and tails for a man. **b** (*as modifier*): *full-dress uniform*.

full employment *n* a state in which the labour force and other economic resources of a country are utilized to their maximum extent.

fuller (ˈfulə) *n* a person who fulls cloth for his living. [OE *fullere*]

Fuller ★ (ˈfulə) *n* **1** (**Richard**) **Buckminster**. 1895–1983, US architect and engineer: developed the geodesic dome. **2 Roy** (**Broadbent**). 1912–91, British poet, whose collections of poetry include *The Middle of a War* (1942), *A Lost Season* (1944), and *Epitaphs and Occasions* (1949). **3 Thomas**. 1608–61, English clergyman and antiquarian: author of *The Worthies of England* (1662).

fullerene (ˈfuləˌriːn) *n* short for **buckminsterfullerene**.

fuller's earth *n* a natural absorbent clay used, after heating, for clarifying oils and fats, fulling cloth, etc.

full face *adj* facing towards the viewer, with the entire face visible.

full-fledged *adj* See **fully fledged**.

full-frontal *Inf*. ◆ *adj* **1** (of a nude person or a photograph of a nude person) exposing the genitals to full view. **2** all-out; unrestrained. ◆ *n* **full frontal**. **3** a full-frontal photograph.

full house *n* **1** *Poker*. a hand with three cards of the same value and another pair. **2** a theatre, etc., filled to capacity. **3** (in bingo, etc.) the set of numbers needed to win.

full-length *n* (*modifier*) **1** showing the complete length. **2** not abridged.

full moon *n* one of the four phases of the moon when the moon is visible as a fully illuminated disc.

full monty (ˈmɒntɪ) *n* **the**. *Inf*. something in its entirety. [from ?]

full nelson *n* a wrestling hold in which a wrestler places both arms under his opponent's arms from behind and exerts pressure on the back of the neck.

full-on *adj Inf*. complete; unrestrained: *full-on military intervention; full-on hard rock*.

full sail *adv* **1** at top speed. ◆ *adj* (*postpositive*), *adv* **2** with all sails set.

full-scale *n* (*modifier*) **1** (of a plan, etc.) of actual size. **2** using all resources; all-out.

full stop *or* **full point** *n* the punctuation mark (.) used at the end of a sentence that is not a question or exclamation, after abbreviations, etc. Also called (esp. US and Canad.): **period**.

full time *n* the end of a football or other match.

full-time *adj* **1** for the entire time appropriate to an activity: *a full-time job*. ◆ *adv* **full time**. **2** on a full-time basis: *he works full time*. ◆ Cf. **part-time**.
▸ ˌfull-ˈtimer *n*

full toss *or* **full pitch** *n Cricket*. a bowled ball that reaches the batsman without bouncing.

fully (ˈfulɪ) *adv* **1** to the greatest degree or extent. **2** amply; adequately: *they were fully fed*. **3** at least: *it was fully an hour before she came*.

fully fashioned *adj* (of stockings, knitwear, etc.) shaped and seamed so as to fit closely.

fully fledged *or* **full-fledged** *adj* **1** (of a young bird) having acquired adult feathers, enabling it to fly. **2** developed to the fullest degree. **3** of full rank or status.

fulmar (ˈfulmə) *n* a heavily built short-tailed oceanic bird of polar regions. [C17: of Scand. origin]

fulminate (ˈfʌlmɪˌneɪt) *vb* **fulminates, fulminating, fulminated**. **1** (*intr*; often foll. by *against*) to make severe criticisms or denunciations; rail. **2** to explode with noise and violence. ◆ *n* **3** any salt or ester of **fulminic acid**, an isomer of cyanic acid, which is used as a detonator. [C15: from Med. L, from L, from *fulmen* lightning that strikes]
▸ ˈfulminant *adj* ▸ ˌfulmiˈnation *n* ▸ ˈfulmiˌnatory *adj*

fulsome (ˈfulsəm) *adj* **1** excessive or insincere, esp. in an offensive or distasteful way: *fulsome compliments*. **2** *Not standard*. extremely complimentary.
▸ ˈfulsomely *adv* ▸ ˈfulsomeness *n*

Fulton ★ (ˈfultᵊn) *n* **Robert**. 1765–1815, US engineer and inventor: designed the first commercially successful steamboat (1807) and the first steam warship (1814).

fulvous (ˈfʌlvəs) *adj* of a dull brownish-yellow colour. [C17: from L *fulvus* reddish yellow]

fumarole (ˈfjuːməˌrəʊl) *n* a vent in or near a volcano from which hot gases, esp. steam, are emitted. [C19: from F, from LL *fūmāriolum* smoke hole, from L *fūmus* smoke]

fumble (ˈfʌmbᵊl) *vb* **fumbles, fumbling, fumbled**. **1** (*intr*; often foll. by *for* or *with*) to grope about clumsily or blindly, esp. in searching. **2** (*intr*; foll. by *at* or *with*) to finger or play with, esp. in an absent-minded way. **3** to say or do awkwardly: *he fumbled the introduction badly*. **4** to fail to catch or grasp (a ball, etc.) cleanly. ◆ *n* **5** the act of fumbling. [C16: prob. of Scand. origin]
▸ ˈfumbler *n* ▸ ˈfumblingly *adv*

fume (fjuːm) *vb* **fumes, fuming, fumed**. **1** (*intr*) to be overcome with anger or fury. **2** to give off (fumes) or (of fumes) to be given off, esp. during a chemical reaction. **3** (*tr*) to fumigate. ◆ *n* **4** (*often pl*) a pungent or toxic vapour, gas, or smoke. **5** a sharp or pungent odour. [C14: from OF *fum*, from L *fūmus* smoke, vapour]
▸ ˈfumeless *adj* ▸ ˈfumingly *adv* ˈfumy *adj*

fumed (fjuːmd) *adj* (of wood, esp. oak) having a dark colour and distinctive grain from exposure to ammonia fumes.

fumigant (ˈfjuːmɪgənt) *n* a substance used for fumigating.

★ people and places

fumigate ('fjuːmɪˌɡeɪt) *vb* **fumigates, fumigating, fumigated.** to treat (something contaminated or infected) with fumes or smoke. [C16: from L, from *fūmus* smoke + *agere* to drive]
► ˌfumiˈgation *n* ► ˈfumiˌgator *n*

fuming sulphuric acid *n* a mixture of acids, made by dissolving sulphur trioxide in concentrated sulphuric acid. Also called: **oleum.**

fumitory ('fjuːmɪtərɪ) *n, pl* **fumitories.** any plant of the genus *Fumaria* having spurred flowers and formerly used medicinally. [C14: from OF, from Med. L *fūmus terrae*, lit.: smoke of the earth]

fun (fʌn) *n* **1** a source of enjoyment, amusement, diversion, etc. **2** pleasure, gaiety, or merriment. **3** jest or sport (esp. in **in** *or* **for fun**). **4 fun and games.** *Ironic or facetious.* frivolous or hetic activity. **5 make fun of** *or* **poke fun at.** to ridicule or deride. **6** (*modifier*) full of amusement, diversion, gaiety, etc.: *a fun sport.* [C17: ?from obs. *fon* to make a fool of; see FOND]

funambulist (fjuːˈnæmbjʊlɪst) *n* a tightrope walker. [C18: from L, from *fūnis* rope + *ambulāre* to walk]
► fuˈnambulism *n*

Funchal ★ (Portuguese fũˈʃal) *n* the capital and chief port of the Madeira Islands, on the S coast of Madeira. Pop.: 44 111 (1987).

function ('fʌŋkʃən) *n* **1** the natural action of a person or thing: *the function of the kidneys is to filter waste products from the blood.* **2** the intended purpose of a person or thing in a specific role: *the function of a hammer is to hit nails into wood.* **3** an official or formal social gathering or ceremony. **4** a factor dependent upon another or other factors. **5** Also called: **map, mapping.** *Maths, logic.* a relation between two sets that associates a unique element (the value) of the second (the range) with each element (the argument) of the first (the domain). Symbol: f(x). The value of f(x) for x=2 is f(2). ◆ *vb* (*intr*) **6** to operate or perform as specified. **7** (foll. by *as*) to perform the action or role (of something or someone else): *a coin may function as a screwdriver.* [C16: from L *functiō*, from *fungī* to perform]

functional ('fʌŋkʃənºl) *adj* **1** of, involving, or containing a function or functions. **2** practical rather than decorative; utilitarian. **3** capable of functioning; working. **4** *Med.* affecting a function of an organ without structural change.
► ˈfunctionally *adv*

functionalism ('fʌŋkʃənəˌlɪzəm) *n* **1** the theory of design that the form of a thing should be determined by its use. **2** any doctrine that stresses purpose.
► ˈfunctionalist *n, adj*

functionary ('fʌŋkʃənərɪ) *n, pl* **functionaries.** a person acting in an official capacity, as for a government; an official.

fund (fʌnd) *n* **1** a reserve of money, etc., set aside for a certain purpose. **2** a supply or store of something; stock: *it exhausted his fund of wisdom.* ◆ *vb* (*tr*) **3** to furnish money to in the form of a fund. **4** to place or store up in a fund. **5** to convert (short-term floating debt) into long-term debt bearing fixed interest and represented by bonds. **6** to accumulate a fund for the discharge of (a recurrent liability): *to fund a pension plan.* ◆ See also **funds.** [C17: from L *fundus* the bottom, piece of land]
► ˈfunder *n*

fundament ('fʌndəmənt) *n* *Euphemistic or facetious.* the buttocks. [C13: from L, from *fundāre* to FOUND²]

fundamental (ˌfʌndəˈmentºl) *adj* **1** of, involving, or comprising a foundation; basic. **2** of, involving, or comprising a source; primary. **3** *Music.* denoting or relating to the principal or lowest note of a harmonic series. ◆ *n* **4** a principle, law, etc., that serves as the basis of an idea or system. **5a** the principal or lowest note of a harmonic series. **5b** the bass note of a chord in root position.
► ˌfundamenˈtality *n* ► ˌfundaˈmentally *adv*

fundamental interaction *n* any of the four basic interactions that occur in nature: the gravitational, electromagnetic, strong, and weak interactions.

fundamentalism (ˌfʌndəˈmentəˌlɪzəm) *n* **1** *Christianity.* the view that the Bible is divinely inspired and is there-

fore literally true. **2** *Islam.* a movement favouring strict observance of the teachings of the Koran and Islamic law.
► ˌfundaˈmentalist *n, adj*

fundamental particle *n* another name for **elementary particle.**

fundamental unit *n* one of a set of unrelated units that form the basis of a system of units. For example, the metre, kilogram, and second are fundamental SI units.

funded debt *n* that part of the British national debt that the government is not obliged to repay by a fixed date.

fundholding ('fʌndˌhəʊldɪŋ) *n* (formerly, in the National Health Service in Britain) the system enabling general practitioners to receive a fixed budget from which to pay for primary care, drugs, and non-urgent hospital treatment for patients; abolished in 1999.
► ˈfundˌholder *n*

fundraiser ('fʌndˌreɪzə) *n* **1** a person engaged in fundraising. **2** an event held to raise money for a cause.

fundraising ('fʌndˌreɪzɪŋ) *n* **1** the activity involved in raising money for a cause. ◆ *adj* **2** of, for, or related to fundraising.

funds (fʌndz) *pl n* **1** money that is readily available. **2** British government securities representing national debt.

fundus ('fʌndəs) *n, pl* **fundi** (-daɪ). *Anat.* the base of an organ or the part farthest away from its opening. [C18: from L, lit.: the bottom]

Fundy ★ ('fʌndɪ) *n* **Bay of.** an inlet of the Atlantic in SE Canada, between S New Brunswick and W Nova Scotia: remarkable for its swift tides of up to 21 m (70 ft).

Funen ★ ('fuːnən) *n* the second largest island of Denmark, between the Jutland peninsula and the island of Sjælland. Pop.: 605 868 (1995 est.). Area: 3481 sq. km (1344 sq. miles). Danish name: **Fyn.** German name: **Fünen.**

funeral ('fjuːnərəl) *n* **1a** a ceremony at which a dead person is buried or cremated. **1b** (*as modifier*): *funeral service.* **2** a procession of people escorting a corpse to burial. **3** *Inf.* concern; affair: *it's your funeral.* [C14: from Med. L, from LL, from L *fūnus* funeral]
► ˈfunerary *adj*

funeral director *n* an undertaker.

funeral parlour *n* a place where the dead are prepared for burial or cremation. Usual US name: **funeral home.**

funereal (fjuːˈnɪərɪəl) *adj* suggestive of a funeral; gloomy or mournful. Also: **funebrial.** [C18: from L *fūnereus*]
► fuˈnereally *adv*

funfair ('fʌnˌfeə) *n* *Brit.* an amusement park or fairground.

fungible ('fʌndʒɪbºl) *n* *Law.* (*often pl*) moveable perishable goods of a sort that may be estimated by number or weight, such as grain, wine, etc. [C18: from Med. L *fungibilis*, from L *fungī* to perform]
► ˌfungiˈbility *n*

fungicide ('fʌndʒɪˌsaɪd) *n* a substance or agent that destroys or is capable of destroying fungi.
► ˌfungiˈcidal *adj*

fungoid ('fʌŋɡɔɪd) *adj* resembling a fungus or fungi.

fungous ('fʌŋɡəs) *adj* appearing suddenly and spreading quickly like a fungus.

fungus ('fʌŋɡəs) *n, pl* **fungi** ('fʌŋɡaɪ, 'fʌndʒaɪ, 'fʌndʒɪ) or **funguses. 1** any member of a kingdom of organisms, formerly classified as plants, that lack chlorophyll, leaves, true stems, and roots, reproduce by spores, and live as saprotrophs or parasites. **2** something resembling a fungus, esp. in suddenly growing. **3** *Pathol.* any soft tumorous growth. [C16: from L: mushroom, fungus]
► ˈfungal *adj*

funicular (fjuːˈnɪkjʊlə) *n* **1** Also called: **funicular railway.** a railway up the side of a mountain, consisting of two cars at either end of a cable passing round a driving wheel at the summit. ◆ *adj* **2** relating to or operated by a rope, etc. [C17: from L, from *fūnis* rope]

funk[1] (fʌŋk) *Inf., chiefly Brit.* ◆ *n* **1** Also called: **blue funk.** a state of nervousness, fear, or depression. **2** a coward. ◆ *vb* **3** to flinch from (responsibility, etc.) through fear. **4** (*tr; usually passive*) to make afraid. [C18: university sl., ? rel. to *funk* to smoke]

funk² (fʌŋk) *n* a type of polyrhythmic Black dance music with heavy syncopation. [C20: back formation from FUNKY]

Funk ★ (fʌŋk) *n* Casimir ('kæzɪˌmɪə). 1884–1967, US biochemist, born in Poland: studied and named vitamins.

funky ('fʌŋkɪ) *adj* **funkier, funkiest.** *Inf.* (of jazz, pop, etc.) passionate; soulful. [C20: from *funk* to smoke (tobacco), ? alluding to music that was smelly, that is, earthy]

funnel ('fʌnªl) *n* **1** a hollow utensil with a wide mouth tapering to a small hole, used for pouring liquids, etc., into a narrow-necked vessel. **2** something resembling this in shape or function. **3** a smokestack for smoke and exhaust gases, as on a steam locomotive. ◆ *vb* **funnels, funnelling, funnelled** *or US* **funnels, funneling, funneled. 4** to move or cause to move or pour through or as if through a funnel. [C15: from OProvençal *fonilh*, ult. from L *infundibulum*, from *infundere* to pour in]
► '**funnel-ˌlike** *adj*

funnel-web *n Austral.* a large poisonous black spider that constructs funnel-shaped webs.

funny ('fʌnɪ) *adj* **funnier, funniest. 1** causing amusement or laughter; humorous. **2** peculiar; odd. **3** suspicious or dubious (esp. in **funny business**). **4** *Inf.* faint or ill. ◆ *n, pl* **funnies. 5** *Inf.* a joke or witticism.
► '**funnily** *adv* ► '**funniness** *n*

funny bone *n* the area near the elbow where the ulnar nerve is close to the surface of the skin: when it is struck, a sharp tingling sensation is experienced.

fun run *n* a long run or part-marathon run for exercise and pleasure, often by large numbers of people.

fuoco (fuːˈəʊkəʊ) *Music.* ◆ *n* **1** fire. ◆ *adv, adj* **2 con fuoco.** in a fiery manner. [C19: It., lit.: fire]

fur (fɜː) *n* **1** the dense coat of fine silky hairs on such mammals as the cat and mink. **2a** the dressed skin of certain fur-bearing animals, with the hair left on. **2b** (*as modifier*): *a fur coat.* **3** a garment made of fur, such as a stole. **4** a pile fabric made in imitation of animal fur. **5** *Heraldry.* any of various stylized representations of animal pelts used in coats of arms. **6 make the fur fly.** to cause a scene or disturbance. **7** *Inf.* a whitish coating on the tongue, caused by excessive smoking, illness, etc. **8** *Brit.* a whitish-grey deposit precipitated from hard water onto the insides of pipes, kettles, etc. ◆ *vb* **furs, furring, furred. 9** (*tr*) to line or trim a garment, etc., with fur. **10** (often foll. by *up*) to cover or become covered with a furlike lining or deposit. [C14: from OF *forrer* to line a garment, from *fuerre* sheath, of Gmc origin]
► '**furless** *adj*

fur. *abbrev. for* furlong.

furbelow ('fɜːbɪˌləʊ) *n* **1** a flounce, ruffle, or other ornamental trim. **2** (*often pl*) showy ornamentation. ◆ *vb* **3** (*tr*) to put a furbelow on (a garment, etc.). [C18: by folk etymology from F dialect *farbella* a frill]

furbish ('fɜːbɪʃ) *vb* (*tr*) **1** to make bright by polishing. **2** (often foll. by *up*) to renovate; restore. [C14: from OF *fourbir* to polish, of Gmc origin]
► '**furbisher** *n*

furcate ('fɜːkeɪt) *vb* **furcates, furcating, furcated. 1** to divide into two parts. ◆ *adj* **2** forked: *furcate branches.* [C19: from LL, from L *furca* a fork]
► fur'**cation** *n*

furfuraceous (ˌfɜːfjʊˈreɪʃəs) *adj* **1** relating to or resembling bran. **2** *Med.* resembling dandruff. [C17: from L *furfur* bran, scurf + -ACEOUS]

Furies ('fjʊərɪz) *pl n, sing* **Fury.** *Classical myth.* the snake-haired goddesses of vengeance, usually three in number, who pursued unpunished criminals. Also called: **Erinyes, Eumenides.**

furioso (ˌfjʊərɪˈəʊsəʊ) *Music.* ◆ *adj, adv* **1** in a frantically rushing manner. ◆ *n* **2** a passage or piece to be performed in this way. [C19: It., lit.: furious]

furious ('fjʊərɪəs) *adj* **1** extremely angry or annoyed. **2** violent or unrestrained, as in speed, energy, etc.
► '**furiously** *adv* ► '**furiousness** *n*

furl (fɜːl) *vb* **1** to roll up (an umbrella, flag, etc.) neatly and securely or (of an umbrella, flag, etc.) to be rolled up in this way. ◆ *n* **2** the act or an instance of furling. **3** a single rolled-up section. [C16: from OF, from *ferm* tight (from L *firmus* FIRM¹) + *lier* to bind, from L *ligāre*]
► '**furlable** *adj*

furlong ('fɜːˌlɒŋ) *n* a unit of length equal to 220 yards (201.168 metres). [OE *furlang*, from *furh* furrow + *lang* long]

furlough ('fɜːləʊ) *n* **1** leave of absence from military duty. ◆ *vb* (*tr*) **2** to grant a furlough to. [C17: from Du. *verlof*, from *ver*- FOR- + *lof* leave, permission]

furnace ('fɜːnɪs) *n* **1** an enclosed chamber in which heat is produced to destroy refuse, smelt or refine ores, etc. **2** a very hot place. [C13: from OF, from L *fornax* oven, furnace]

Furness ★ ('fɜːnɪs) *n* a region in NW England in Cumbria, forming a peninsula between the Irish Sea and Morecambe Bay.

furnish ('fɜːnɪʃ) *vb* (*tr*) **1** to provide (a house, room, etc.) with furniture, etc. **2** to equip with what is necessary. **3** to supply: *the records furnished the information.* [C15: from OF *fournir*, of Gmc origin]
► '**furnisher** *n*

furnishings ('fɜːnɪʃɪŋz) *pl n* furniture, carpets, etc., with which a room or house is furnished.

furniture ('fɜːnɪtʃə) *n* **1** the movable articles that equip a room, house, etc. **2** the equipment necessary for a ship, factory, etc. **3** *Printing.* lengths of wood, plastic, or metal, used in assembling formes to surround the type. ◆ See also **door furniture, street furniture.** [C16: from F, from *fournir* to equip]

Furnivall ★ ('fɜːnɪvªl) *n* Frederick James. 1825–1910, British philologist: founder of the Early English Text Society and one of the founders of the *Oxford English Dictionary.*

furore (fjʊˈrɔːrɪ) *or esp. US* **furor** ('fjʊərɔː) *n* **1** a public outburst; uproar. **2** a sudden widespread enthusiasm; craze. **3** frenzy; rage. [C15: from L: frenzy, from *furere* to rave]

furphy ('fɜːfɪ) *n, pl* **furphies.** *Austral. sl.* a rumour or fictitious story. [C20: from *Furphy* carts (used for water or sewage in World War I), made at a foundry established by the Furphy family]

Furphy ★ ('fɜːfɪ) *n* Joseph, pen name *Tom Collins.* 1843–1912, Australian author. His works include the novels *Such is Life* (1903) and *The Buln-Buln and the Brolga* (1948).

furred (fɜːd) *adj* **1** made of, lined with, or covered in fur. **2** wearing fur. **3** (of animals) having fur. **4** another word for **furry** (sense 3). **5** provided with furring strips. **6** (of a pipe, kettle, etc.) lined with hard lime.

furrier ('fʌrɪə) *n* a person whose occupation is selling, making, or repairing fur garments. [C14: *furour*, from OF *fourrer* to trim with FUR]
► '**furriery** *n*

furring ('fɜːrɪŋ) *n* **1** short for **furring strip. 2** the formation of fur on the tongue. **3** trimming of animal fur, as on a coat.

furring strip *n* a strip of wood or metal fixed to a wall, floor, or ceiling to provide a surface for the fixing of plasterboard, floorboards, etc.

furrow ('fʌrəʊ) *n* **1** a long narrow trench made in the ground by a plough. **2** any long deep groove, esp. a deep wrinkle on the forehead. ◆ *vb* **3** to develop or cause to develop furrows or wrinkles. **4** to make a furrow or furrows in (land). [OE *furh*]
► '**furrower** *n* ► '**furrowless** *adj* ► '**furrowy** *adj*

furry ('fɜːrɪ) *adj* **furrier, furriest. 1** covered with fur or something furlike. **2** of, relating to, or resembling fur. **3** Also: **furred.** (of the tongue) coated with whitish cellular debris.
► '**furrily** *adv* ► '**furriness** *n*

Fur Seal Islands ★ *pl n* another name for the **Pribilof Islands.**

further ('fɜːðə) *adv* **1** in addition; furthermore. **2** to a greater degree or extent. **3** to or at a more advanced

---

point. **4** to or at a greater distance in time or space. ◆ *adj* **5** additional; more. **6** more distant or remote in time or space. ◆ *vb* **7** (*tr*) to assist the progress of. ◆ See also **far, furthest**. [OE *furthor*]

furtherance ('fɜːðərəns) *n* **1** the act of furthering. **2** something that furthers.

further education *n* (in Britain) formal education beyond school other than at a university or polytechnic.

furthermore ('fɜːðə,mɔː) *adv* in addition; moreover.

furthermost ('fɜːðə,məust) *adj* most distant; furthest.

furthest ('fɜːðɪst) *adv* **1** to the greatest degree or extent. **2** to or at the greatest distance in time or space; farthest. ◆ *adj* **3** most distant or remote in time or space; farthest.

furtive ('fɜːtɪv) *adj* characterized by stealth; sly and secretive. [C15: from L *furtīvus* stolen, from *furtum* a theft, from *fūr* a thief]
▸ **'furtively** *adv* ▸ **'furtiveness** *n*

Furtwängler ★ (*German* 'furtvɛŋlər) *n* **Wilhelm** ('vɪlhɛlm). 1886–1954, German conductor.

furuncle ('fjuər,ʌŋkᵊl) *n Pathol.* the technical name for **boil**². [C17: from L *fūrunculus* pilferer, sore, from *fūr* thief]
▸ **furuncular** (fju'rʌŋkjulə) *or* **fu'runculous** *adj*

furunculosis (fju,rʌŋkju'ləusɪs) *n* **1** a skin condition characterized by the presence of multiple boils. **2** a disease of salmon and trout caused by a bacterium.

fury ('fjuərɪ) *n, pl* **furies. 1** violent or uncontrolled anger. **2** an outburst of such anger. **3** uncontrolled violence: *the fury of the storm.* **4** a person, esp. a woman, with a violent temper. **5** See **Furies. 6** like **fury**. *Inf.* violently; furiously. [C14: from L, from *furere* to be furious]

furze (fɜːz) *n* another name for **gorse**. [OE *fyrs*]
▸ **'furzy** *adj*

fuscous ('fʌskəs) *adj* of a brownish-grey colour. [C17: from L *fuscus* dark, swarthy, tawny]

fuse¹ *or chiefly US* **fuze** (fjuːz) *n* **1** a lead of combustible black powder (**safety fuse**), or a lead containing an explosive (**detonating fuse**), used to fire an explosive charge. **2** any device by which an explosive charge is ignited. ◆ *vb* **fuses, fusing, fused** *or chiefly US* **fuzes, fuzing, fuzed. 3** (*tr*) to equip with such a fuse. [C17: from It. *fuso* spindle, from L *fūsus*]
▸ **'fuseless** *adj*

fuse² (fjuːz) *vb* **fuses, fusing, fused. 1** to unite or become united by melting, esp. by the action of heat. **2** to become or cause to become liquid, esp. by the action of heat. **3** to join or become combined. **4** (*tr*) to equip (a plug, etc.) with a fuse. **5** *Brit.* to fail or cause to fail as a result of the blowing of a fuse: *the lights fused.* ◆ *n* **6** a protective device for safeguarding electric circuits, etc., containing a wire that melts and breaks the circuit when the current exceeds a certain value. [C17: from L *fūsus* melted, cast, from *fundere* to pour out; sense 5 infl. by FUSE¹]

fusee *or* **fuzee** (fjuː'ziː) *n* **1** (in early clocks and watches) a spirally grooved spindle, functioning as an equalizing force on the unwinding of the mainspring. **2** a friction match with a large head. [C16: from F *fusée* spindleful of thread, from OF *fus* spindle, from L *fūsus*]

fuselage ('fjuːzɪ,lɑːʒ) *n* the main body of an aircraft. [C20: from F, from *fuseler* to shape like a spindle, from OF *fusel* spindle]

fusel oil *or* **fusel** ('fjuːzᵊl) *n* a poisonous by-product formed in the distillation of fermented liquors and used as a source of amyl alcohols. [C19: from G *Fusel* bad spirits]

Fushih *or* **Fu-shih** ★ ('fuː'ʃiː) *n* another name for **Yanan**.

Fushun ★ ('fuː'ʃʌn) *n* a city in NE China, in central Liaoning province near Shenyang: situated on one of the richest coalfields in the world; site of the largest thermal power plant in NE Asia. Pop.: 1 350 000 (1991 est.).

fusible ('fjuːzəᵊl) *adj* capable of being fused or melted.
▸ ,**fusi'bility** *n* ▸ **'fusibly** *adv*

fusiform ('fjuːzɪ,fɔːm) *adj* elongated and tapering at both ends. [C18: from L *fūsus* spindle]

fusil ('fjuːzɪl) *n* a light flintlock musket. [C16 (in the sense: steel for a tinderbox): from OF, from Vulgar L *focīlis* (unattested), from L *focus* fire]

fusilier (,fjuːzɪ'lɪə) *n* **1** (formerly) an infantryman armed with a light musket. **2** Also: **fusileer. 2a** a soldier, esp. a private, serving in any of certain British or other infantry regiments. **2b** (*pl; cap. when part of a name): the Royal Welch Fusiliers.* [C17: from F; see FUSIL]

fusillade (,fjuːzɪ'leɪd) *n* **1** a rapid continual discharge of firearms. **2** a sudden outburst, as of criticism. ◆ *vb* **fusillades, fusillading, fusilladed. 3** (*tr*) to attack with a fusillade. [C19: from F, from *fusiller* to shoot; see FUSIL]

fusion ('fjuːʒən) *n* **1** the act or process of fusing or melting together. **2** the state of being fused. **3** something produced by fusing. **4** a kind of popular music that is a blend of two or more styles, such as jazz and funk. **5** See **nuclear fusion. 6** a coalition of political parties. [C16: from L *fūsiō* a pouring out, melting, from *fundere* to pour out, FOUND³]

fusion bomb *n* a type of bomb in which most of the energy is provided by nuclear fusion. Also called: **thermonuclear bomb, fission-fusion bomb.**

fuss (fʌs) *n* **1** nervous activity or agitation, esp. when unnecessary. **2** complaint or objection: *he made a fuss over the bill.* **3** an exhibition of affection or admiration: *they made a great fuss over the new baby.* **4** a quarrel. ◆ *vb* **5** (*intr*) to worry unnecessarily. **6** (*intr*) to be excessively concerned over trifles. **7** (when *intr*, usually foll. by *over*) to show great or excessive concern, affection, etc. (for). **8** (*tr*) to bother (a person). [C18: from ?]
▸ **'fusser** *n*

fusspot ('fʌs,pɒt) *n Brit. inf.* a person who fusses unnecessarily.

fussy ('fʌsɪ) *adj* **fussier, fussiest. 1** inclined to fuss over minor points. **2** very particular about detail. **3** characterized by overelaborate detail.
▸ **'fussily** *adv* ▸ **'fussiness** *n*

fustanella (,fʌstə'nɛlə) *n* a white knee-length pleated skirt worn by men in Greece and Albania. [C19: from It., from Mod. Gk *phoustani*, prob. from It. *fustagno* FUSTIAN]

fustian ('fʌstɪən) *n* **1a** a hard-wearing fabric of cotton mixed with flax or wool. **1b** (*as modifier): a fustian jacket.* **2** pompous talk or writing. ◆ *adj* **3** cheap; worthless. **4** bombastic. [C12: from OF, from Med. L *fūstāneum*, from L *fustis* cudgel]

fustic ('fʌstɪk) *n* **1** Also called: **old fustic.** a large tropical American tree. **2** the yellow dye obtained from the wood of this tree. **3** any of various trees or shrubs that yield a similar dye, esp. a European sumach (**young fustic**). [C15: from F *fustoc*, from Sp., from Ar. *fustuq*, from Gk *pistake* pistachio tree]

fusty ('fʌstɪ) *adj* **fustier, fustiest. 1** smelling of damp or mould. **2** old-fashioned in attitude. [C14: from *fust* wine cask, from OF: cask, from L *fustis* cudgel]
▸ **'fustily** *adv* ▸ **'fustiness** *n*

fut. *abbrev. for* future.

futhark ('fuːθɑːk) *or* **futhorc, futhork** ('fuːθɔːk) *n* a phonetic alphabet consisting of runes. [C19: from the first six letters: *f, u, th, a, r, k*]

futile ('fjuːtaɪl) *adj* **1** having no effective result; unsuccessful. **2** pointless; trifling. **3** inane or foolish. [C16: from L *futtilis* pouring out easily, from *fundere* to pour out]
▸ **'futilely** *adv* ▸ **futility** (fjuː'tɪlɪtɪ) *n*

futon ('fuː,tɒn) *n* a Japanese padded quilt, laid on the floor as a bed. [C19: from Japanese]

futtock ('fʌtək) *n Naut.* one of the ribs in the frame of a wooden vessel. [C13: ? var. of *foothook*]

future ('fjuːtʃə) *n* **1** the time yet to come. **2** undetermined events that will occur in that time. **3** the condition of a person or thing at a later date: *the future of the school is undecided.* **4** likelihood of later improvement: *he has a future*

as a singer. **5** *Grammar.* **5a** a tense of verbs used when the action or event described is to occur after the time of utterance. **5b** a verb in this tense. **6 in future.** from now on. ◆ *adj* **7** that is yet to come or be. **8** of or expressing time yet to come. **9** (*prenominal*) destined to become. **10** *Grammar.* in or denoting the future as a tense of verbs. ◆ See also **futures.** [C14: from L *fūtūrus* about to be, from *esse* to be]
▸ **'futureless** *adj*

future perfect *Grammar.* ◆ *adj* **1** denoting a tense of verbs describing an action that will have been performed by a certain time. ◆ *n* **2a** the future perfect tense. **2b** a verb in this tense.

futures ('fjuːtʃəz) *pl n* **a** commodities or other financial products bought or sold at an agreed price for delivery at a specified future date. See also **financial futures. b** (*as modifier*): *futures contract; futures market.*

future value *n* the value that a sum of money invested at compound interest will have after a specified period.

futurism ('fjuːtʃə‚rɪzəm) *n* an artistic movement that arose in Italy in 1909 to replace traditional aesthetic values with the characteristics of the machine age.
▸ **'futurist** *n, adj*

futuristic (‚fjuːtʃə'rɪstɪk) *adj* **1** denoting or relating to design, etc., that is thought likely to be fashionable at some future time. **2** of or relating to futurism.
▸ **‚futur'istically** *adv*

futurity (fjuː'tjʊərɪtɪ) *n, pl* **futurities. 1** a less common word for **future. 2** the quality of being in the future. **3** a future event.

futurology (‚fjuːtʃə'rɒlədʒɪ) *n* the study or prediction of the future of mankind.
▸ **‚futur'ologist** *n*

fuze (fjuːz) *n, vb* **fuzes, fuzing, fuzed.** *Chiefly US.* a variant spelling of **fuse**[1].

fuzee (fjuː'ziː) *n* a variant spelling of **fusee.**

Fuzhou ('fuː'dʒəʊ), **Foochow,** *or* **Fuchou** ★ *n* a port in SE China, capital of Fujian province on the Min Jiang: one of the original five treaty ports (1842). Pop.: 874 809 (1990 est.).

fuzz[1] (fʌz) *n* **1** a mass or covering of fine or curly hairs, fibres, etc. **2** a blur. ◆ *vb* **3** to make or become fuzzy. **4** to make or become indistinct. [C17: ?from Low G *fussig* loose]

fuzz[2] (fʌz) *n* a slang word for **police** or **policeman.** [C20 from ?]

fuzzy ('fʌzɪ) *adj* **fuzzier, fuzziest. 1** of, resembling, or covered with fuzz. **2** unclear or distorted. **3** (of the hair) tightly curled or very wavy.
▸ **'fuzzily** *adv* ▸ **'fuzziness** *n*

fuzzy logic *n* a branch of logic that allows degrees of imprecision in reasoning and knowledge to be represented in such a way that the information can be processed by computer.

fuzzy-wuzzy ('fʌzɪ‚wʌzɪ) *n, pl* **fuzzy-wuzzies.** *Offens. arch. sl.* a Black fuzzy-haired native of any of various countries.

fwd *abbrev. for* forward.

f-word *n* the. (*sometimes cap.*) a euphemistic way of referring to the word **fuck.** [from F(UCK) + WORD]

FX *n Films, inf.* short for **special effects.** [C20: a phonetic respelling of EFFECTS]

-fy *suffix forming verbs.* to make or become: *beautify.* [from OF *-fier*, from L *-ficāre*, from *-ficus* -FIC]

Fylde ★ (faɪld) *n* a region in NW England in Lancashire between the Wyre and Ribble estuaries.

fylfot ('faɪlfɒt) *n* a rare word for **swastika.** [C16 (apparently meaning: a sign or device for the lower part or foot of a painted window): from *fillen* to fill + *fot* foot]

Fyn ★ (*Danish* fyːn) *n* the Danish name for **Funen.**

FYROM *abbrev. for* Former Yugoslav Republic of Macedonia.

Gg

g or **G** (dʒiː) n, pl **g's, G's,** or **Gs. 1** the seventh letter of the English alphabet. **2** a speech sound represented by this letter, usually either as in *grass,* or as in *page.*

g *symbol for:* **1** gallon(s). **2** gram(s). **3** grav. **4** acceleration of free fall (due to gravity).

G *symbol for:* **1** *Music.* **1a** the fifth note of the scale of C major. **1b** the major or minor key having this note as its tonic. **2** gauss. **3** gravitational constant. **4** *Physics.* conductance. **5** *Biochem.* guanine. **6** German. **7** giga. **8** good. **9** *Sl., chiefly US.* grand (a thousand dollars or pounds). **10** (in Australia) **10a** general exhibition (used to describe a category of film certified as suitable for viewing by anyone). **10b** (*as modifier*): *a G film.*

G. or **g.** *abbrev. for:* **1** a G gauge. **2** gelding. **3** guilder(s). **4** guinea(s). **5** Gulf.

G3 *abbrev. for* Group of Three.

G5 *abbrev. for* Group of Five.

G7 *abbrev. for* Group of Seven.

G10 *abbrev. for* Group of Ten.

G24 *abbrev. for* Group of Twenty-Four.

G77 *abbrev. for* Group of Seventy-Seven.

Ga *the chemical symbol for* gallium.

GA *abbrev. for:* **1** General Assembly (of the United Nations). **2** general average. **3** Georgia.

Ga. *abbrev. for* Georgia.

gab (gæb) *Inf.* ◆ *vb* **gabs, gabbing, gabbed. 1** (*intr*) to talk excessively or idly; gossip. ◆ *n* **2** idle or trivial talk. **3 gift of the gab.** ability to speak glibly or persuasively. [C18: prob. from Irish Gaelic *gob* mouth]
▸ **'gabber** n

gabardine or **gaberdine** (ˈgæbəˌdiːn, ˌgæbəˈdiːn) n **1** a twill-weave worsted, cotton, or spun-rayon fabric. **2** an ankle-length loose coat or frock worn by men, esp. by Jews, in the Middle Ages. **3** any of various other garments made of gabardine, esp. a child's raincoat. [C16: from OF *gauvardine* pilgrim's garment, from MHG *wallewart* pilgrimage]

gabble (ˈgæbəl) *vb* **gabbles, gabbling, gabbled. 1** to utter (words, etc.) rapidly and indistinctly; jabber. **2** (*intr*) (of geese, etc.) to utter rapid cackling noises. ◆ *n* **3** rapid and indistinct speech or noises. [C17: from MDu. *gabbelen,* imit.]
▸ **'gabbler** n

gabbro (ˈgæbrəʊ) n, pl **gabbros.** a dark coarse-grained igneous rock consisting of feldspar, pyroxene, and often olivine. [C19: from It., prob. from L *glaber* smooth, bald]

gabby (ˈgæbɪ) adj **gabbier, gabbiest.** *Inf.* inclined to chatter; talkative.

Gaberones ★ (ˌgæbəˈrəʊnɛs) n the former name for Gaborone.

Gabès ★ (ˈgɑːbɛs; *French* gabɛs) n **1** a port in E Tunisia. Pop.: 98 800 (1994). **2 Gulf of.** an inlet of the Mediterranean on the E coast of Tunisia. Ancient name: **Syrtis Minor.** Arabic name: **Qabis.**

gabfest (ˈgæbˌfɛst) n *Inf., chiefly US & Canad.* **1** prolonged gossiping or conversation. **2** an informal gathering for conversation. [C19: from GAB + FEST]

gabion (ˈgeɪbɪən) n **1** a cylindrical metal container filled with stones, used in the construction of underwater foundations. **2** a wickerwork basket filled with stones or earth, used (esp. formerly) as part of a fortification. [C16: from F: basket, from It., from *gabbia* cage, from L *cavea;* see CAGE]

gable (ˈgeɪbəl) n **1** the triangular upper part of a wall between the sloping ends of a pitched roof (**gable roof**). **2** a triangular ornamental feature, esp. as used over a door or window. [C14: OF, prob. from ON *gafl*]
▸ **'gabled** adj

Gable ★ (ˈgeɪbəl) n (**William**) **Clark.** 1901–60, US film actor. His films include *It Happened One Night* (1934), *San Francisco* (1936), *Gone with the Wind* (1939), and *The Misfits* (1960).

gable end n the end wall of a building on the side which is topped by a gable.

Gabo ★ (ˈgɑːbəʊ, -bə) n **Naum** (naʊm), original name *Naum Neemia Pevsner.* 1890–1977, US sculptor, born in Russia: a leading constructivist.

Gabon ★ (gæˈbɒn; *French* gabɔ̃) n a republic in W central Africa, on the Atlantic: settled by the French in 1839; made part of the French Congo in 1888; became independent in 1960; almost wholly forested. Official language: French. Religion: Christian and animist. Currency: franc. Capital: Libreville. Pop.: 1 190 000 (1997). Area: 267 675 sq. km (103 350 sq. miles).
▸ **Gabonese** (ˌgæbəˈniːz) adj, n

gaboon (gəˈbuːn) n a dark mahogany-like wood from an African tree, used in plywood, for furniture, and as a veneer. [C20: altered from GABON]

gaboon viper n a large venomous viper of African rainforests. It has brown and purple markings and hornlike projections on its snout.

Gabor ★ (gəˈbɔː) n **Dennis.** 1900–79, British electrical engineer, born in Hungary. He invented holography: Nobel prize for physics 1971.

Gaborone ★ (ˌgæbəˈrəʊnɪ) n the capital of Botswana (since 1964), in the extreme southeast. Pop.: 156 803 (1993 est.). Former name: **Gaberones.**

Gabriel¹ ★ (ˈgeɪbrɪəl) n *Bible.* one of the archangels, the messenger of good news (Daniel 8:16–26; Luke 1:11–20, 26–38).

Gabriel² ★ (*French* gabriɛl) n **Jacques-Ange** (ʒɑkɑ̃ʒ). 1698–1782, French architect: designed the Petit Trianon at Versailles.

Gabrieli (*Italian* gaˈbrjɛːle) or **Gabrielli** ★ (gaˈbrjɛlli) n **1 Andrea** (anˈdrɛːa). 1520–86, Italian organist and composer; chief organist of St Mark's, Venice. **2** his nephew **Giovanni** (dʒoˈvanni). 1558–1612, Italian organist and composer.

gaby (ˈgeɪbɪ) n, pl **gabies.** *Arch.* or *dialect.* a simpleton. [C18: from ?]

gad (gæd) *vb* **gads, gadding, gadded. 1** (*intr; often foll. by* **about** or **around**) to go out in search of pleasure; gallivant. ◆ *n* **2** carefree adventure (esp. in **on the gad**). [C15: back formation from obs. *gadling* companion, from OE, from *gæd* fellowship]
▸ **'gadder** n

Gad ★ (gæd) n *Old Testament.* **1a** Jacob's sixth son, whose mother was Zilpah, Leah's maid. **1b** the Israelite tribe descended from him. **1c** the territory of this tribe, lying to the east of the Jordan and extending southwards from the Sea of Galilee. **2** a prophet and admonisher of David (I Samuel 22; II Samuel 24).

gadabout (ˈgædəˌbaʊt) n *Inf.* a person who restlessly seeks amusement, etc.

Gadarene (ˈgædəˌriːn) adj relating to or engaged in a headlong rush. [C19: via LL from Gk *Gadarēnos,* of Gadara (Palestine), alluding to the Gadarene swine (Matthew 8:28ff.)]

Gaddafi or **Qaddafi** ★ (gəˈdɑːfɪ) n **Moamar al** (ˈməʊəˌmɑːˈæl). born 1942, Libyan army officer and statesman; head of state from 1969.

gadfly (ˈgædˌflaɪ) n, pl **gadflies. 1** any of various large dipterous flies, esp. the horsefly, that annoy livestock by sucking their blood. **2** a constantly irritating person. [C16: from *gad* sting + FLY²]

gadget (ˈgædʒɪt) n **1** a small mechanical device or appliance. **2** any object that is interesting for its ingenuity. [C19: ?from F *gâchette* lock catch, dim. of *gâche* staple]

gadgetry ('gædʒɪtrɪ) *n* **1** gadgets collectively. **2** use of or preoccupation with gadgets.

gadoid ('geɪdɔɪd) *adj* **1** of or belonging to an order of marine soft-finned fishes typically having the pectoral and pelvic fins close together and small cycloid scales. The group includes cod and hake. ◆ *n* **2** any gadoid fish. [C19: from NL *Gadidae*, from *gadus* cod; see -OID]

gadolinium (,gædə'lɪnɪəm) *n* a ductile malleable silvery-white ferromagnetic element of the lanthanide series of metals. Symbol: Gd; atomic no.: 64; atomic wt.: 157.25. [C19: NL, after Johan *Gadolin* (1760–1852), Finnish mineralogist]

gadroon *or* **godroon** (gə'druːn) *n* a decorative moulding composed of a series of convex flutes and curves, used esp. as an edge to silver articles. [C18: from F *godron*, ?from OF *godet* cup, goblet]

Gadsden Purchase ★ ('gædzdən) *n* an area of about 77 000 sq. km (30 000 sq. miles) in present-day Arizona and New Mexico, bought by the US from Mexico for 10 million dollars in 1853. The purchase was negotiated by James Gadsden (1788–1858), US diplomat.

gadwall ('gæd,wɔːl) *n, pl* **gadwalls** *or* **gadwall**. a duck related to the mallard. The male has a grey body and black tail. [C17: from ?]

gadzooks (gæd'zuːks) *interj Arch.* a mild oath. [C17: ?from *God's hooks* (the nails of the cross) from *Gad* arch. euphemism for God]

Gaea ('dʒiːə), **Gaia**, *or* **Ge** ★ *n Greek myth.* the goddess of the earth, who bore Uranus and by him Oceanus, Cronus and the Titans. [from Gk *gaia* earth]

Gael (geɪl) *n* a person who speaks a Gaelic language, esp. a Highland Scot or an Irishman. [C19: from Gaelic *Gaidheal*]
  ▶ **'Gaeldom** *n*

Gaelic ('geɪlɪk, 'gæ-) *n* **1** any of the closely related languages of the Celts in Ireland, Scotland, or the Isle of Man. ◆ *adj* **2** of, denoting, or relating to the Celtic people of Ireland, Scotland, or the Isle of Man or their language or customs.

Gaelic coffee *n* another name for **Irish coffee**.

Gaeltacht ('geːltəxt) *n* any of the regions in Ireland in which Irish Gaelic is the vernacular speech. [C20: from Irish Gaelic]

gaff¹ (gæf) *n* **1** *Angling*. a stiff pole with a stout prong or hook attached for landing large fish. **2** *Naut.* a boom hoisted aft of a mast to support a fore-and-aft sail. **3** a metal spur fixed to the leg of a gamecock. ◆ *vb* **4** (*tr*) *Angling*. to hook or land (a fish) with a gaff. [C13: from F *gaffe*, from Provençal *gaf* boat hook]

gaff² (gæf) *n* **1** *Sl.* nonsense. **2 blow the gaff**. *Brit. sl.* to divulge a secret. [C19: from ?]

gaffe (gæf) *n* a social blunder, esp. a tactless remark. [C19: from F]

gaffer ('gæfə) *n* **1** an old man: often used affectionately or patronizingly. **2** *Inf., chiefly Brit.* a boss, foreman, or owner of a factory, etc. **3** *Inf.* the senior electrician on a television or film set. [C16: from GODFATHER]

gag¹ (gæg) *vb* **gags, gagging, gagged**. **1** (*tr*) to stop up (a person's mouth), esp. with a piece of cloth, etc., to prevent him from speaking or crying out. **2** (*tr*) to suppress or censor (free expression, information, etc.). **3** to retch or cause to retch. **4** (*intr*) to struggle for breath; choke. ◆ *n* **5** a piece of cloth, rope, etc., stuffed into or tied across the mouth. **6** any restraint on or suppression of information, free speech, etc. **7** *Parliamentary procedure*. another word for **closure** (sense 4). [C15 *gaggen*; ? imit. of a gasping sound]

gag² (gæg) *Inf.* ◆ *n* **1** a joke or humorous story, esp. one told by a professional comedian. **2** a hoax, practical joke, etc. ◆ *vb* **gags, gagging, gagged**. **3** (*intr*) to tell jokes or funny stories, as comedians in nightclubs, etc. [C19: ? special use of GAG¹]

gaga ('gɑːgɑː) *adj Inf.* **1** senile; doting. **2** slightly crazy. [C20: from F, imit.]

Gagarin ★ (*Russian* ga'garin) *n* Yuri ('juːrɪ). 1934–68, Soviet cosmonaut: made the first manned space flight (1961).

gage¹ (geɪdʒ) *n* **1** something deposited as security against the fulfilment of an obligation; pledge. **2** (formerly) a glove or other object thrown down to indicate a challenge to combat. ◆ *vb* **gages, gaging, gaged**. **3** (*tr*) *Arch.* to stake, pledge, or wager. [C14: from OF, of Gmc origin]

gage² (geɪdʒ) *n* short for **greengage**.

gage³ (geɪdʒ) *n, vb* **gages, gaging, gaged**. *US.* a variant spelling of **gauge**.

Gage ★ (geɪdʒ) *n* **Thomas**. 1721–87, British general and governor in America; commander in chief of British forces at Bunker Hill (1775).

gaggle ('gæg'l) *vb* **gaggles, gaggling, gaggled**. **1** (*intr*) (of geese) to cackle. ◆ *n* **2** a flock of geese. **3** *Inf.* a disorderly group of people. [C14: of Gmc origin; imit.]

Gaia ★ ('gaɪə) *n* a variant of **Gaea**.

Gaia hypothesis *or* **theory** *n* the theory that the earth and everything on it constitutes a single self-regulating living entity.

gaiety ('geɪətɪ) *n, pl* **gaieties**. **1** the state or condition of being merry, bright, or lively. **2** festivity; merrymaking. **3** bright appearance.

> **USAGE NOTE**   See at **gay.**

Gaillard Cut ★ (gɪl'jɑːd, 'geɪlɑːd) *n* the SE section of the Panama Canal, cut through Culebra Mountain. Length: about 13 km (8 miles). Former name: **Culebra Cut**. [C19: after David Du Bose *Gaillard* (1859–1913), US army engineer in charge of the work]

gaillardia (geɪ'lɑːdɪə) *n* a plant of the composite family having ornamental flower heads with yellow or red rays and purple discs. [C19: from NL, after *Gaillard* de Marentonneau, 18th-cent. F amateur botanist]

gaily ('geɪlɪ) *adv* **1** in a gay manner; merrily. **2** with bright colours; showily.

gain (geɪn) *vb* **1** (*tr*) to acquire (something desirable); obtain. **2** (*tr*) to win in competition: *to gain the victory*. **3** to increase, improve, or advance: *the car gained speed*. **4** (*tr*) to earn (a wage, living, etc.). **5** (*intr*; usually foll. by *on* or *upon*) **5a** to get nearer (to) or catch up (on). **5b** to get farther away (from). **6** (*tr*) (esp. of ships) to get to; reach: *the steamer gained port*. **7** (of a timepiece) to operate too fast, so as to indicate a time ahead of the true time. ◆ *n* **8** something won, acquired, earned, etc.; profit; advantage. **9** an increase in size, amount, etc. **10** the act of gaining; attainment; acquisition. **11** Also called: **amplification**. *Electronics*. the ratio of the output signal of an amplifier to the input signal, usually measured in decibels. [C15: from OF *gaaignier*, of Gmc origin]

gainer ('geɪnə) *n* **1** a person or thing that gains. **2** a type of dive in which the diver leaves the board facing forward and completes a full backward somersault to enter the water feet first with his back to the diving board.

gainful ('geɪnful) *adj* profitable; lucrative.
  ▶ **'gainfully** *adv* ▶ **'gainfulness** *n*

gainsay (geɪn'seɪ) *vb* **gainsays, gainsaying, gainsaid**. (*tr*) *Arch. or literary*. to deny (an allegation, statement, etc.); contradict. [C13 *gainsaien*, from *gain-* AGAINST + *saien* to SAY]
  ▶ **gain'sayer** *n*

Gainsborough ★ ('geɪnzbərə, -brə) *n* **Thomas**. 1727–88, British landscape and portrait painter.

'gainst *or* **gainst** (genst, geɪnst) *prep Poetic*. short for **against**.

Gaiseric ★ ('gaɪzərɪk) *n* a variant of **Genseric**.

gait (geɪt) *n* **1** manner of walking or running. **2** (used esp. of horses and dogs) the pattern of footsteps at a particular speed, as the walk, canter, etc. ◆ *vb* **3** (*tr*) to teach (a horse) a particular gait. [C16: var. of GATE]

gaiter ('geɪtə) *n* (*often pl*) **1** a cloth or leather covering for the leg or ankle. **2** Also called: **spat**. a similar covering extending from the ankle to the instep. [C18: from F *guêtre*, prob. of Gmc origin]

Gaitskell ★ ('geɪtskɪl) *n* **Hugh** (**Todd Naylor**). 1906–63, British politician; leader of the Labour Party (1955–63).

> ★ people and places

Gaius ('gaɪəs) *or* **Caius** ★ *n* 1 ?110–?180 A.D., Roman jurist. His *Institutes* were later used as the basis for those of Justinian. **2 Gaius Caesar.** See **Caligula.**

gal (gæl) *n Sl.* a girl.

gal. *or* **gall.** *abbrev. for* gallon.

Gal. *Bible. abbrev. for* Galatians.

gala ('gɑːlə, 'geɪlə) *n* **1a** a celebration; festive occasion. **1b** (*as modifier*): *a gala occasion.* **2** *Chiefly Brit.* a sporting occasion involving competitions in several events: *a swimming gala.* [C17: from F or It., from OF *gale*, from *galer* to make merry, prob. of Gmc origin]

galactic (ɡə'læktɪk) *adj* **1** *Astron.* of or relating to a galaxy, esp. the Galaxy. **2 galactic plane.** the plane passing through the spiral arms of the Galaxy, contained by the great circle of the celestial sphere (**galactic equator**) and perpendicular to an imaginary line joining opposite points (**galactic poles**) on the celestial sphere. **3** *Med.* of or relating to milk. [C19: from Gk *galaktikos*; see GALAXY]

galactic halo *n Astron.* a spheroidal aggregation of globular clusters, individual stars, dust, and gas that surrounds the Galaxy.

galago (ɡə'lɑːɡəʊ) *n, pl* **galagos.** another name for **bushbaby.** [C19: from NL, ?from Wolof *golokh* monkey]

galah (ɡə'lɑː) *n* **1** an Australian cockatoo, having grey wings, back, and crest, and a pink body. **2** *Austral. sl.* a fool or simpleton. [C19: from Abor.]

Galahad ★ ('ɡæləˌhæd) *n* **1** *Sir.* (in Arthurian legend) the most virtuous knight of the Round Table. **2** a pure or noble man.

galantine ('ɡælənˌtiːn) *n* a cold dish of meat or poultry, which is boned, cooked, then pressed and glazed. [C14: from OF, from Med. L *galatina*, prob. from L *gelātus* frozen, set]

Galápagos Islands ★ (ɡə'læpəɡəs; *Spanish* ɡa'lapaɣɔs) *pl n* a group of 15 islands in the Pacific west of Ecuador, of which they form a province: discovered (1535) by the Spanish; main settlement on San Cristóbal. Pop.: 13 976 (1996 est.). Area: 7844 sq. km (3028 sq. miles). Official Spanish name: **Archipiélago de Colón.**

Galashiels ★ (ˌɡælə'ʃiːlz) *n* a town in SE Scotland, in central Scottish Borders. Pop.: 13 753 (1997).

Galata ★ ('ɡælətə) *n* a port in NW Turkey, a suburb and the chief business section of Istanbul.

Galatea ★ (ˌɡælə'tɪə) *n Greek myth.* a statue of a maiden brought to life by Aphrodite in response to the prayers of the sculptor Pygmalion, who had fallen in love with his creation.

Galaţi ★ (*Romanian* ɡa'latsj) *n* an inland port in SE Romania, on the River Danube. Pop.: 324 234 (1993 est.).

Galatia ★ (ɡə'leɪʃə, -ʃɪə) *n* an ancient region in central Asia Minor, conquered by Gauls 278–277 B.C.: later a Roman province.
▸ **Ga'latian** *adj, n*

galaxy ('ɡæləksɪ) *n, pl* **galaxies. 1** any of a vast number of star systems held together by gravitational attraction. **2** a splendid gathering, esp. one of famous or distinguished people. [C14 (in the sense: the Milky Way): from Med. L *galaxia*, from L, from Gk, from *gala* milk]

Galaxy ('ɡæləksɪ) *n* **the.** the spiral galaxy that contains the solar system about three fifths of the distance from its centre. Also called: the **Milky Way System.**

galbanum ('ɡælbənəm) *n* a bitter aromatic gum resin extracted from any of several Asian umbelliferous plants. [C14: from L, from Gk, from Heb. *helbenāh*]

Galbraith ★ (ɡæl'breɪθ) *n* **John Kenneth.** born 1908, US economist and diplomat born in Canada; author of *The Affluent Society* (1958).
▸ **Gal'braithian** *adj*

gale (ɡeɪl) *n* **1** a strong wind, specifically one of force 8 on the Beaufort scale or from 39–46 mph. **2** (*often pl*) a loud outburst, esp. of laughter. **3** *Arch. & poetic.* a gentle breeze. [C16: from ?]

galea ('ɡeɪlɪə) *n, pl* **galeae** (-lɪˌiː). a part shaped like a helmet, such as the petals of certain flowers. [C18: from L: helmet]
▸ **'gale,ate** *or* **'gale,ated** *adj*

Galen ★ ('ɡeɪlən) *n* Latin name *Claudius Galenus.* ?130–?200 A.D., Greek physician, anatomist, and physiologist. He codified existing medical knowledge and his authority continued until the Renaissance.

galena (ɡə'liːnə) *or* **galenite** (ɡə'liːnaɪt) *n* a soft heavy bluish-grey or black mineral consisting of lead sulphide: the chief source of lead. Formula: PbS. [C17: from L: lead ore]

Galenic (ɡeɪ'lɛnɪk, ɡə-) *adj* of or relating to Galen or his teachings or methods.

Galicia ★ *n* **1** (ɡə'lɪʃɪə, -'lɪʃə). a region of E central Europe on the N side of the Carpathians, now in SE Poland and the Ukraine. **2** (*Spanish* ɡa'liθja). an autonomous region and former kingdom of NW Spain, on the Bay of Biscay and the Atlantic. Pop.: 2 720 761 (1994 est.).
▸ **Galician** (ɡə'lɪʃɪən, -ʃən) *adj, n*

Galilean[1] (ˌɡælɪ'liːən) *n* **1** a native or inhabitant of Galilee. **2 the.** an epithet of Jesus Christ. ◆ *adj* **3** of Galilee.

Galilean[2] (ˌɡælɪ'leɪən) *adj* of or relating to Galileo.

Galilee ★ ('ɡælɪˌliː) *n* **1 Sea of.** Also called: Lake **Tiberias,** Lake **Kinneret.** a lake in NE Israel, 209 m (686 ft) below sea level, through which the River Jordan flows. Area: 165 sq. km (64 sq. miles). **2** a northern region of Israel: scene of Christ's early ministry.

Galileo ★ (ˌɡælɪ'leɪəʊ) *n* full name *Galileo Galilei.* 1564–1642, Italian mathematician, astronomer, and physicist. He perfected the refracting telescope, which led to his discovery of Jupiter's satellites. He was forced by the Inquisition to recant his support of the Copernican system.

galingale ('ɡælɪŋˌɡeɪl) *or* **galangal** (ɡə'læŋɡ³l) *n* a European plant with rough-edged leaves, reddish spikelets of flowers, and aromatic roots. [C13: from OF, from Ar., from Chinese]

galiot *or* **galliot** ('ɡælɪət) *n* **1** a small swift galley formerly sailed on the Mediterranean. **2** a ketch formerly used along the coasts of Germany and the Netherlands. [C14: from OF, from It., from Med. L *galea* GALLEY]

galipot ('ɡælɪˌpɒt) *n* a resin obtained from several species of pine. [C18: from F, from ?]

gall[1] (ɡɔːl) *n* **1** *Inf.* impudence. **2** bitterness; rancour. **3** something bitter or disagreeable. **4** *Physiol.* an obsolete term for **bile.** See also **gall bladder.** [from ON, replacing OE *gealla*]

gall[2] (ɡɔːl) *n* **1** a sore on the skin caused by chafing. **2** something that causes vexation or annoyance. **3** irritation; exasperation. ◆ *vb* **4** to abrade (the skin, etc.) as by rubbing. **5** (*tr*) to irritate or annoy; vex. [C14: of Gmc origin; rel. to OE *gealla* sore on a horse, & ? to GALL[1]]

gall[3] (ɡɔːl) *n* an abnormal outgrowth in plant tissue caused by certain parasitic insects, fungi, or bacteria. [C14: from OF, from L *galla*]

gall. *or* **gal.** *abbrev. for* gallon.

gallant *adj* ('ɡælənt). **1** brave and high-spirited; courageous and honourable: *a gallant warrior.* **2** (ɡə'lænt, 'ɡælənt). (of a man) attentive to women; chivalrous. **3** imposing; dignified; stately: *a gallant ship.* **4** *Arch.* showy in dress. ◆ *n* ('ɡælənt, ɡə'lænt). *Arch.* **5** a woman's lover or suitor. **6** a dashing or fashionable young man, esp. one who pursues women. **7** a brave, high-spirited, or adventurous man. ◆ *vb* (ɡə'lænt, 'ɡælənt). *Rare.* **8** (when *intr*, usually foll. by *with*) to court or flirt (with). [C15: from OF, from *galer* to make merry, from *gale* enjoyment, of Gmc origin]
▸ **'gallantly** *adv*

gallantry ('ɡæləntrɪ) *n, pl* **gallantries. 1** conspicuous courage, esp. in war. **2** polite attentiveness to women. **3** a gallant action, speech, etc.

gall bladder *n* a muscular sac, attached to the right lobe of the liver, that stores bile.

Galle ★ ('ɡɑːlə) *n* a port in SW Sri Lanka. Pop.: 84 000 (1990). Former name: **Point de Galle.**

galleass ('ɡælɪˌæs) *n* a three-masted galley used as a warship in the Mediterranean from the 15th to the 18th centuries. [C16: from F, from It., from Med. L *galea* GALLEY]

galleon ('ɡælɪən) *n* a large sailing ship having three or more masts, used as a warship or trader from the 15th to the 18th centuries. [C16: from Sp. *galeón*, from F, from OF *galie* GALLEY]

gallery ('gælərɪ) *n, pl* **galleries. 1** a room or building for exhibiting works of art. **2** a covered passageway open on one side or on both sides. **3** a balcony running along or around the inside wall of a church, hall, etc. **4** *Theatre.* **4a** an upper floor that projects from the rear and contains the cheapest seats. **4b** the seats there. **4c** the audience seated there. **5** a long narrow room, esp. one used for a specific purpose: *a shooting gallery.* **6** an underground passage, as in a mine, etc. **7** a small ornamental railing, esp. one surrounding the top of a desk, table, etc. **8** any group of spectators, as at a golf match. **9** a glass-fronted soundproof room overlooking a television studio, used for lighting, etc. **10 play to the gallery.** to try to gain popular favour, esp. by crude appeals. [C15: from OF, from Med. L, prob. from *galilea* galilee, porch or chapel at entrance to medieval church]
▸ 'galleried *adj*

galley ('gælɪ) *n* **1** any of various kinds of ship propelled by oars or sails used in ancient or medieval times. **2** the kitchen of a ship, boat, or aircraft. **3** any of various long rowing boats. **4** *Printing.* **4a** a tray for holding composed type. **4b** short for **galley proof**. [C13: from OF *galie*, from Med. L *galea*, from Gk *galaia*, from ?]

galley proof *n* a printer's proof, esp. one taken from type in a galley, used to make corrections before the matter has been split into pages. Often shortened to **galley.**

galley slave *n* **1** a criminal or slave condemned to row in a galley. **2** *Inf.* a drudge.

gallfly ('gɔːlˌflaɪ) *n, pl* **gallflies.** any of several small insects that produce galls in plant tissues.

Gallia ★ ('gælɪə) *n* the Latin name of **Gaul.**

galliard ('gæljəd) *n* **1** a spirited dance in triple time for two persons, popular in the 16th and 17th centuries. **2** a piece of music composed for or in the rhythm of this dance. [C14: from OF *gaillard* valiant, ? of Celtic origin]

Gallic ('gælɪk) *adj* **1** of or relating to France. **2** of or relating to ancient Gaul or the Gauls.

gallic acid *n* a colourless crystalline compound obtained from tannin: used as a tanning agent and in making inks and paper. [C18: from F *galligue*; see GALL³]

Gallicism ('gælɪˌsɪzəm) *n* a word or idiom borrowed from French.

Gallicize *or* **Gallicise** ('gælɪˌsaɪz) *vb* **Gallicizes, Gallicizing, Gallicized** *or* **Gallicises, Gallicising, Gallicised.** to make or become French in attitude, language, etc.

galligaskins (ˌgælɪ'gæskɪnz) *pl n* **1** loose wide breeches or hose, esp. as worn by men in the 17th century. **2** leather leggings, as worn in the 19th century. [C16: from obs. F, from It. *grechesco* Greek, from L *Graecus*]

gallimaufry (ˌgælɪ'mɔːfrɪ) *n, pl* **gallimaufries.** a jumble; hotchpotch. [C16: from F *galimafrée* ragout, hash, from ?]

gallinacean (ˌgælɪ'neɪʃən) *n* any gallinaceous bird.

gallinaceous (ˌgælɪ'neɪʃəs) *adj* of, relating to, or belonging to an order of birds, including domestic fowl, pheasants, grouse, etc., having a heavy rounded body, short bill, and strong legs. [C18: from L *gallīna* hen]

Gallinas Point ★ (gɑː'jiːnəs) *n* a cape in NE Colombia: the northernmost point of South America. Spanish name: **Punta Gallinas** ('punta ga'ʎinas).

galling ('gɔːlɪŋ) *adj* irritating, exasperating, or bitterly humiliating.
▸ 'gallingly *adv*

gallinule ('gælɪˌnjuːl) *n* any of various aquatic birds, typically having a dark plumage, red bill, and a red shield above the bill. [C18: from NL *Gallīnula*, from L *gallīna* hen]

galliot ('gælɪət) *n* a variant spelling of **galiot.**

Gallipoli ★ (gə'lɪpəlɪ) *n* **1** a peninsula in NW Turkey, between the Dardanelles and the Gulf of Saros: scene of a costly and unsuccessful Allied campaign in 1915. **2** a port in NW Turkey, at the entrance to the Sea of Marmara:

historically important for its strategic position. Pop.: 16 751 (1985 est.). Turkish name: **Gelibolu.**

gallipot ('gælɪˌpɒt) *n* a small earthenware pot used by pharmacists as a container for ointments, etc. [C16: prob. from GALLEY + POT¹; because imported in galleys]

gallium ('gælɪəm) *n* a silvery metallic element that is liquid for a wide temperature range. It is used in high-temperature thermometers and low-melting alloys. **Gallium arsenide** is a semiconductor. Symbol: Ga; atomic no.: 31; atomic wt.: 69.72. [C19: from NL, from L *gallus* cock, translation of F *coq* in the name of its discoverer, *Lecoq* de Boisbaudran, 19th-cent. F chemist]

gallivant ('gælɪˌvænt) *vb* (*intr*) to go about in search of pleasure, etc.; gad about. [C19: ? whimsical from GALLANT]

Gällivare ★ (*Swedish* 'jelivɑːrə) *n* a town in N Sweden, within the Arctic Circle: iron mines. Pop.: 22 400 (1990).

galliwasp ('gælɪˌwɒsp) *n* a lizard of the Caribbean. [C18: from ?]

gallnut ('gɔːlˌnʌt) *or* **gall-apple** *n* a type of plant gall that resembles a nut.

Gallo- ('gæləʊ) *combining form.* denoting Gaul or France: *Gallo-Roman.* [from L *Gallus* Gaul]

gallon ('gælən) *n* **1** Also called: **imperial gallon.** *Brit.* a unit of capacity equal to 277.42 cubic inches. 1 Brit. gallon is equivalent to 1.20 US gallons or 4.55 litres. **2** *US.* a unit of capacity equal to 231 cubic inches. 1 US gallon is equivalent to 0.83 imperial gallon or 3.79 litres. **3** (*pl*) *Inf.* great quantities. [C13: from ONorthern F *galon* (OF *jalon*), ? of Celtic origin]

gallonage ('gælənɪdʒ) *n* a capacity measured in gallons.

galloon (gə'luːn) *n* a narrow band of cord, embroidery, silver or gold braid, etc., used on clothes and furniture. [C17: from F, from OF *galonner* to trim with braid, from ?]

gallop ('gæləp) *vb* **gallops, galloping, galloped. 1** (*intr*) (of a horse or other quadruped) to run fast with a two-beat stride in which all four legs are off the ground at once. **2** to ride (a horse, etc.) at a gallop. **3** (*intr*) to move, read, progress, etc., rapidly. ◆ *n* **4** the fast two-beat gait of horses. **5** an instance of galloping. [C16: from OF *galoper*, from ?]
▸ 'galloper *n*

Galloway ★ ('gæləˌweɪ) *n* **1** an area of SW Scotland, on the Solway Firth: consists of the former counties of Kirkcudbright and Wigtown, now part of Dumfries and Galloway; in the west is a large peninsula, the **Rhinns of Galloway**, with the **Mull of Galloway**, a promontory, at the south end of it (the southernmost point of Scotland). Related adj: **Galwegian. 2** a breed of hardy cattle, usually black, originally bred in Galloway.

gallows ('gæləʊz) *n, pl* **gallowses** *or* **gallows. 1** a wooden structure usually consisting of two upright posts with a crossbeam, used for hanging criminals. **2** any timber structure resembling this. **3 the gallows.** execution by hanging. [C13: from ON *galgi*, replacing OE *gealga*]

gallows bird *n Inf.* a person considered deserving of hanging.

gallows humour *n* sinister and ironic humour.

gallows tree *or* **gallow tree** *n* another name for **gallows** (sense 1).

gallsickness ('gɔːlˌsɪknɪs) *n* a disease of cattle and sheep, caused by infection with rickettsiae, resulting in anaemia and jaundice. Also called: **anaplasmosis.**

gallstone ('gɔːlˌstəʊn) *n* a small hard concretion formed in the gall bladder or its ducts.

Gallup ★ ('gæləp) *n* **George Horace.** 1901–84, US statistician: devised the Gallup Poll.

Gallup Poll *n* a sampling of the views of a representative cross section of the population, used esp. as a means of forecasting voting.

gall wasp *n* any small solitary wasp that produces galls in plant tissue.

galoot *or* **galloot** (gə'luːt) *n Sl., chiefly US.* a clumsy or uncouth person. [C19: from ?]

galop ('gæləp) *n* **1** a 19th-century dance in quick duple

★ people and places

time. **2** a piece of music for this dance. [C19: from F; see GALLOP]

galore (gə'lɔː) *determiner* (*immediately postpositive*) in great numbers or quantity: *there were daffodils galore in the park.* [C17: from Irish Gaelic *go leór* to sufficiency]

galoshes *or* **goloshes** (gə'lɒʃɪz) *pl n* (*sometimes sing*) a pair of waterproof overshoes. [C14 (in the sense: wooden shoe): from OF, from LL *gallicula* Gallic shoe]

Galsworthy ★ ('gɔːlz,wɜːðɪ) *n* **John**. 1867–1933, British novelist and dramatist, noted for *The Forsyte Saga* (1906–28): Nobel prize for literature 1932.

Galton ★ ('gɔːltən) *n* Sir **Francis**. 1822–1911, British explorer and scientist noted for his researches in heredity, meteorology, and statistics.

galumph (gə'lʌmpf, -'lʌmf) *vb* (*intr*) *Inf.* to leap or move about clumsily or joyfully. [C19 (coined by Lewis Carroll): prob. a blend of GALLOP + TRIUMPH]

Galvani ★ (*Italian* gal'vaːni) *n* **Luigi** (lu'iːdʒi). 1737–98, Italian physiologist: observed that muscles contracted on contact with dissimilar metals. This led to the galvanic cell and the electrical theory of muscle control.

galvanic (gæl'vænɪk) *adj* **1** of, producing, or concerned with an electric current, esp. a direct current produced chemically. **2** *Inf.* resembling the effect of an electric shock; convulsive, startling, or energetic.
▸ **gal'vanically** *adv*

galvanism ('gælvə,nɪzəm) *n* **1** *Obs.* electricity, esp. when produced by chemical means as in a cell or battery. **2** *Med.* treatment involving the application of electric currents to tissues. [C18: via F from It. *galvanismo*, after GALVANI]

galvanize *or* **galvanise** ('gælvə,naɪz) *vb* **galvanizes, galvanizing, galvanized** *or* **galvanises, galvanising, galvanised**. (*tr*) **1** to stimulate to action; excite; startle. **2** to cover (iron, steel, etc.) with a protective zinc coating. **3** to stimulate by application of an electric current.
▸ **,galvani'zation** *or* **,galvani'sation** *n*

galvanized iron *or* **galvanised iron** *n Building trades*. iron, esp. a sheet of corrugated iron, covered with a protective coating of zinc.

galvano- *combining form*. indicating a galvanic current: *galvanometer.*

galvanometer (,gælvə'nɒmɪtə) *n* any sensitive instrument for detecting or measuring small electric currents.
▸ **galvanometric** (,gælvənəʊ'metrɪk, gæl,vænəʊ-) *adj* ▸ **,galva'nometry** *n*

Galway ★ ('gɔːlweɪ) *n* **1** a county of W Republic of Ireland, in S Connacht, on **Galway Bay** and the Atlantic: it has a deeply indented coastline and many offshore islands, including the Aran Islands. County town: Galway. Pop.: 180 364 (1991). Area: 5939 sq. km (2293 sq. miles). **2** a port in W Ireland, county town of Co. Galway, on Galway Bay: important fisheries (esp. for salmon). Pop.: 50 853 (1991).

gam (gæm) *n Sl.* a leg. [C18: from F *jambe* leg]

Gama ★ ('gɑːmə) *n* **Vasco da** ('væskəʊ də). ?1469–1524, Portuguese navigator, who discovered the sea route from Portugal to India around the Cape of Good Hope (1498).

Gambetta ★ (gæm'betə; *French* gãbeta) *n* **Léon** (leõ). 1838–82, French statesman; prime minister (1881–82). He organized resistance during the Franco-Prussian War (1870–71) and was a founder of the Third Republic (1871).

Gambia ★ ('gæmbɪə) *n* **The**. a republic in W Africa, entirely surrounded by Senegal except for an outlet to the Atlantic: sold to English merchants by the Portuguese in 1588; became a British colony in 1843; gained independence and joined the Commonwealth in 1965; joined with Senegal in 1982 to form the Confederation of Senegambia; consists of a strip of land about 16 km (10 miles) wide, on both banks of the **Gambia River**, extending inland for about 480 km (300 miles). Official language: English. Religion: Muslim majority. Currency: dalasi. Capital: Banjul. Pop.: 1 248 000 (1997). Area: 11 295 sq. km (4361 sq. miles).
▸ **'Gambian** *adj, n*

gambier *or* **gambir** ('gæmbɪə) *n* an astringent resinous substance obtained from a tropical Asian plant: used as an astringent and tonic and in tanning. [C19: from Malay]

Gambier Islands ★ ('gæmbɪə) *pl n* a group of islands in the S Pacific Ocean, in French Polynesia. Chief settlement: Rikitéa. Pop.: 582 (1988). Area: 30 sq. km (11 sq. miles).

gambit ('gæmbɪt) *n* **1** *Chess*. an opening move in which a chessman, usually a pawn, is sacrificed to secure an advantageous position. **2** an opening comment, manoeuvre, etc., intended to secure an advantage. [C17: from F, from It. *gambetto* a tripping up, from *gamba* leg]

gamble ('gæmb°l) *vb* **gambles, gambling, gambled**. **1** (*intr*) to play games of chance to win money, etc. **2** to risk or bet (money, etc.) on the outcome of an event, sport, etc. **3** (*intr; often foll. by on*) to act with the expectation of: *to gamble on its being a sunny day.* **4** (often foll. by *away*) to lose by or as if by betting; squander. ◆ *n* **5** a risky act or venture. **6** a bet or wager. [C18: prob. var. of GAME¹]
▸ **'gambler** *n* ▸ **'gambling** *n*

gamboge (gæm'bəʊdʒ, -'buːʒ) *n* **1a** a gum resin used as the source of a yellow pigment and as a purgative. **1b** the pigment made from this resin. **2 gamboge tree**. any of several tropical Asian trees that yield this resin. [C18: from NL *gambaugium*, from CAMBODIA, where first found]

gambol ('gæmb°l) *vb* **gambols, gambolling, gambolled** *or US* **gambols, gamboling, gamboled**. **1** (*intr*) to skip or jump about in a playful manner; frolic. ◆ *n* **2** a playful antic; frolic. [C16: from F *gambade*; see JAMB]

gambrel ('gæmbrəl) *n* **1** the hock of a horse or similar animal. **2** short for **gambrel roof**. [C16: from OF, from *gambe* leg]

gambrel roof *n* **1** *Chiefly Brit.* a hipped roof having a small gable at both ends. **2** *Chiefly US & Canad.* a roof having two slopes on both sides, the lower slopes being steeper than the upper.

game¹ (geɪm) *n* **1** an amusement or pastime; diversion. **2** a contest with rules, the result being determined by skill, strength, or chance. **3** a single period of play in such a contest, sport, etc. **4** the score needed to win a contest. **5** a single contest in a series; match. **6** (*pl; often cap.*) an event consisting of various sporting contests, esp. in athletics: *Olympic Games.* **7** equipment needed for playing certain games. **8** short for **computer game**. **9** style or ability in playing a game. **10** a scheme, proceeding, etc., practised like a game: *the game of politics.* **11** an activity undertaken in a spirit of levity; joke: *marriage is just a game to him.* **12a** wild animals, including birds and fish, hunted for sport, food, or profit. **12b** (*as modifier*): *game laws.* **13** the flesh of such animals, used as food. **14** an object of pursuit; quarry; prey (esp. in **fair game**). **15** *Inf.* work or occupation. **16** *Inf.* a trick, strategy, or device: *I can see through your little game.* **17** *Sl., chiefly Brit.* prostitution (esp. in **on the game**). **18** give the game away. to reveal one's intentions or a secret. **19** make (a) game of. to make fun of; ridicule; mock. **20 play the game.** to behave fairly or in accordance with the rules. **21 the game is up.** there is no longer a chance of success. ◆ *adj* **22** *Inf.* full of fighting spirit; plucky; brave. **23** (usually foll. by *for*) *Inf.* prepared or ready; willing: *I'm game for a try.* ◆ *vb* **games, gaming, gamed**. **24** (*intr*) to play games of chance for money, stakes, etc.; gamble. [OE *gamen*]
▸ **'gamely** *adv* ▸ **'gameness** *n*

game² (geɪm) *adj* a less common word for **lame** (esp. in **game leg**). [C18: prob. from Irish *cam* crooked]

gamecock ('geɪm,kɒk) *n* a cock bred and trained for fighting. Also called: **fighting cock**.

game fish *n* any fish providing sport for the angler.

gamekeeper ('geɪm,kiːpə) *n* a person employed to take care of game, as on an estate.

gamelan ('gæmɪ,læn) *n* a type of percussion orchestra common in the East Indies. [from Javanese]

game laws *pl n* laws governing the hunting and preservation of game.

game plan *n* **1** a strategy. **2** a plan of campaign, esp. in politics.

game point *n Tennis, etc.* a stage at which winning one further point would enable one player or side to win a game.

gamesmanship ('geɪmzmən,ʃɪp) *n Inf.* the art of winning games or defeating opponents by cunning practices without actually cheating.

gamesome ('geɪmsəm) *adj* full of merriment; sportive.
▸ '**gamesomeness** *n*

gamester ('geɪmstə) *n* a person who habitually plays games for money; gambler.

gametangium (,gæmɪ'tændʒɪəm) *n, pl* **gametangia** (-dʒɪə). *Biol.* an organ or cell in which gametes are produced, esp. in algae and fungi. [C19: NL, from GAMETO- + Gk *angeion* vessel]

gamete ('gæmiːt, gə'miːt) *n* a haploid germ cell that fuses with another during fertilization. [C19: from NL, from Gk *gametē* wife, from *gamos* marriage]
▸ **gametic** (gə'mɛtɪk) *adj*

gamete intrafallopian transfer (,ɪntrəfə'ləʊpɪən) *n* See GIFT.

game theory *n* mathematical theory concerned with the optimum choice of strategy in situations involving a conflict of interest.

gameto- *or sometimes before a vowel* **gamet-** *combining form.* gamete: *gametophyte.*

gametophyte (gə'miːtəʊ,faɪt) *n* the plant body, in species showing alternation of generations, that produces the gametes.
▸ **gametophytic** (,gæmɪtəʊ'fɪtɪk) *adj*

gamey *or* **gamy** ('geɪmɪ) *adj* **gamier, gamiest. 1** having the smell or flavour of game, esp. high game. **2** *Inf.* spirited; plucky; brave.
▸ '**gamily** *adv* ▸ '**gaminess** *n*

gamin ('gæmɪn) *n* a street urchin. [from F]

gamine ('gæmiːn) *n* a slim and boyish girl or young woman; an elfish tomboy. [from F]

gaming ('geɪmɪŋ) *n* a gambling on games of chance. **b** (*as modifier*): *gaming house.*

gamma ('gæmə) *n* **1** the third letter in the Greek alphabet (Γ, γ). **2** the third in a group or series. [C14: from Gk]

gamma distribution *n Statistics.* a continuous two-parameter distribution from which the chi-square and exponential distributions are derived.

gamma globulin *n* any of a group of proteins in blood plasma that includes most known antibodies.

gamma radiation *n* electromagnetic radiation of shorter wavelength and higher energy than X-rays.

gamma-ray astronomy *n* the investigation of cosmic gamma rays, such as those from quasars.

gamma rays *pl n* streams of gamma radiation.

gamma stock *n* any of the third rank of active securities on the London stock exchange. Prices displayed by market makers are given as an indication rather than an offer to buy or sell.

gammer ('gæmə) *n Rare, chiefly Brit.* a dialect word for an old woman: now chiefly humorous or contemptuous. [C16: prob. from GODMOTHER or GRANDMOTHER]

gammon[1] ('gæmən) *n* **1** a cured or smoked ham. **2** the hindquarter of a side of bacon, cooked either whole or in rashers. [C15: from OF *gambon*, from *gambe* leg]

gammon[2] ('gæmən) *n* **1** a double victory in backgammon in which one player throws off all his pieces before his opponent throws any. ◆ *vb* **2** (*tr*) to score such a victory over. [C18: prob. special use of ME *gamen* GAME[1]]

gammon[3] ('gæmən) *Brit. inf.* ◆ *n* **1** deceitful nonsense; humbug. ◆ *vb* **2** to deceive (a person). [C18: ? special use of GAMMON[1]]

gammy ('gæmɪ) *adj* **gammier, gammiest.** *Brit. sl.* (esp. of the leg) malfunctioning, injured, or lame; game. [C19: dialect var. of GAME[2]]

gamo- *or before a vowel* **gam-** *combining form.* **1** indicating sexual union or reproduction: *gamogenesis.* **2** united or fused: *gamopetalous.* [from Gk *gamos* marriage]

gamopetalous (,gæməʊ'pɛtələs) *adj* (of flowers) having petals that are united or partly united, as the primrose.

gamp (gæmp) *n Brit. inf.* an umbrella. [C19: after Mrs

Sarah *Gamp*, a nurse in Dickens' *Martin Chuzzlewit*, who carried a faded cotton umbrella]

gamut ('gæmət) *n* **1** entire range or scale, as of emotions. **2** *Music.* **2a** a scale, esp. (in medieval theory) one starting on the G on the bottom line of the bass staff. **2b** the whole range of notes. **3** *Physics.* the range of chromaticities that can be obtained by mixing three colours. [C14: from Med. L, from *gamma*, the lowest note of the hexachord as established by Guido d'Arezzo + *ut* (now, *doh*), the first of the notes of the scale *ut, re, mi, fa, sol, la, si*]

-gamy *n combining form.* denoting marriage or sexual union: *bigamy.* [from Gk, from *gamos* marriage]
▸ **-gamous** *adj combining form.*

Gance ★ (*French* gɑ̃s) *n* **Abel** (abel). 1889–1981, French film director, whose works include *J'accuse* (1919, 1937) and *Napoléon* (1927).

Gand ★ (gɑ̃) *n* the French name for **Ghent**.

gander ('gændə) *n* **1** a male goose. **2** *Inf.* a quick look (esp. in **take** (*or* **have**) **a gander**). **3** *Inf.* a simpleton. [OE *gandra, ganra*]

Gandhi ★ ('gændɪ) *n* **1 Mrs Indira (Priyadarshini)** (ɪn'dɪərə, 'ɪndərə), daughter of Jawaharlal Nehru. 1917–84, Indian stateswoman; prime minister of India (1966–77; 1980–84); assassinated. **2 Mohandas Karamchand** (,məʊhən'dʌs ,kʌrəm'tʃʌnd), known as *Mahatma Gandhi.* 1869–1948, Indian political and spiritual leader. He played a major part in India's struggle for home rule and was frequently imprisoned by the British for civil disobedience. He advocated passive resistance and attempted to unite Muslims and Hindus; assassinated. **3 Rajiv** (rə'dʒiːv), son of Indira Gandhi. 1944–91, Indian statesman; prime minister of India (1984–89); assassinated.

Gandhian ('gændɪən) *adj* **1** of or relating to Mahatma Gandhi or his ideas. ◆ *n* **2** a follower of Gandhi or his ideas.

G & S *abbrev. for* Gilbert and Sullivan.

Gandzha ★ (*Russian* gan'dʒa) *n* a city in NW Azerbaijan: annexed by the Russians in 1804; centre of a cotton-growing region. Pop.: 282 200 (1991 est.). Former names: **Yelisavetpol** (1813–1920), **Kirovabad** (1935–91).

Ganesa ★ (gæ'niːsə) *n* the Hindu god of prophecy, represented as having an elephant's head.

gang[1] (gæŋ) *n* **1** a group of people who associate together or act as an organized body, esp. for criminal or illegal purposes. **2** an organized group of workmen. **3** a series of similar tools arranged to work simultaneously in parallel. ◆ *vb* **4** to form into, become part of, or act as a gang. ◆ See also **gang up**. [OE: journey]

gang[2] (gæŋ) *n* a variant spelling of **gangue**.

gang[3] (gæŋ) *vb* (*intr*) *Scot.* to go or walk. [OE *gangan*]

gangbang ('gæŋ,bæŋ) *n Sl.* an instance of sexual intercourse between one woman and several men one after the other, esp. against her will.

gang-banger *n US sl.* a member of a street gang.
▸ '**gang-,banging** *n*

ganger ('gæŋə) *n Chiefly Brit.* the foreman of a gang of labourers.

Ganges ★ ('gændʒiːz) *n* the great river of N India and central Bangladesh: rises in two headstreams in the Himalayas and flows southeast to Allahabad, where it is joined by the Jumna; continues southeast into Bangladesh, where it enters the Bay of Bengal in a great delta; the most sacred river to Hindus, with many places of pilgrimage, esp. Varanasi. Length: 2507 km (1557 miles). Hindi name: **Ganga** ('gʌŋgə, 'gɑːŋ-).
▸ **Gangetic** (gæn'dʒɛtɪk) *adj*

gangland ('gæŋ,lænd, -lənd) *n* the criminal underworld.

gangling ('gæŋglɪŋ) *or* **gangly** *adj* tall, lanky, and awkward in movement. [see GANG[3]]

ganglion ('gæŋglɪən) *n, pl* **ganglia** (-glɪə) *or* **ganglions. 1** an encapsulated collection of nerve-cell bodies, usually located outside the brain and spinal cord. **2** any concentration or centre of energy, activity, or strength. **3** a cystic tumour on a tendon sheath. [C17: from LL: swelling, from Gk: cystic tumour]
▸ '**gangliar** *adj* ▸ ,**gangli'onic** *or* '**gangli,ated** *adj*

gangplank ('gæŋˌplæŋk) or **gangway** n Naut. a portable bridge for boarding and leaving a vessel at dockside.

gangrene ('gæŋgriːn) n **1** death and decay of tissue due to an interrupted blood supply, disease, or injury. ◆ vb **gangrenes, gangrening, gangrened. 2** to become or cause to become affected with gangrene. [C16: from L, from Gk *gangraina* an eating sore]
▸ **gangrenous** ('gæŋgrɪnəs) adj

gang-saw n a multiple saw used in a timber mill to cut planks from logs.

gangsta rap ('gæŋstə) n a style of rap music, usually characterized by songs about Black street gangs in the US, with nihilistic and misogynistic lyrics. [C20: phonetic rendering of GANGSTER]
▸ **gangsta rapper** n

gangster ('gæŋstə) n a member of an organized gang of criminals.

Gangtok ★ ('gʌŋtɒk) n a city in NE India: capital of Sikkim state. Pop.: 24 970 (1991).

gangue or **gang** (gæŋ) n valueless and undesirable material in an ore. [C19: from F, from G *Gang* vein of metal, course]

gang up vb (intr, adv; often foll. by on or against) Inf. to combine in a group (against).

gangway ('gæŋˌweɪ) n **1** another word for **gangplank. 2** an opening in a ship's side to take a gangplank. **3** Brit. an aisle between rows of seats. **4** temporary planks over mud, as on a building site. ◆ sentence substitute. **5** clear a path!

ganister or **gannister** ('gænɪstə) n a refractory siliceous sedimentary rock occurring beneath coal seams: used for lining furnaces. [C20: from ?]

gannet ('gænɪt) n **1** any of several heavily built marine birds having a long stout bill and typically white plumage with dark markings. **2** Sl. a greedy person. [OE *ganot*]

ganoid ('gænɔɪd) adj **1** (of the scales of certain fishes) consisting of an inner bony layer and an outer layer of an enamel-like substance (**ganoin**). **2** denoting fishes, including the sturgeon, having such scales. ◆ n **3** a ganoid fish. [C19: from F, from Gk *ganos* brightness + -OID]

Gansu ('gæn'suː) or **Kansu** ★ n a province of NW China, between Tibet and Inner Mongolia: mountainous, with desert regions; forms a corridor, the Old Silk Road, much used in early and medieval times for trade with Turkestan, India, and Persia. Capital: Lanzhou. Pop.: 23 780 000 (1995 est.). Area: 366 500 sq. km (141 500 sq. miles).

gantry ('gæntrɪ) n, pl **gantries. 1** a bridgelike framework used to support a travelling crane, signals over a railway track, etc. **2** Also called: **gantry scaffold.** the framework tower used to attend to a large rocket on its launch pad. **3** a supporting framework for a barrel. **4a** the area behind a bar where bottles, esp. spirit bottles mounted in optics, are kept. **4b** the range or quality of the spirits on display there. [C16 (in the sense: wooden platform for barrels): from OF *chantier*, from Med. L, from L *canthērius* supporting frame, pack ass]

Gantt chart (gænt) n a chart showing, in horizontal lines, activity planned to take place during specified periods, which are indicated in vertical bands. [C20: named after Henry L. *Gantt* (1861–1919), US management consultant]

Ganymede ★ ('gænɪˌmiːd) n Classical myth. a beautiful Trojan youth who was abducted by Zeus to Olympus and made the cupbearer of the gods.

Gao ★ ('gɑːəʊ, gaʊ) n a town in E Mali, on the River Niger: a small river port. Pop.: 54 874 (1987).

gaol (dʒeɪl) n, vb (tr) Brit. a variant spelling of **jail.**
▸ **'gaoler** n

Gaoxiong ('gaʊ'ljɒŋ) or **Kaohsiung** ★ n a city in SW Taiwan, on the South China Sea: the chief port of the island. Pop.: 1 426 518 (1996 est.). Japanese name: **Takao.**

gap (gæp) n **1** a break or opening in a wall, fence, etc. **2** a break in continuity; interruption; hiatus. **3** a break in a line of hills or mountains affording a route through. **4** Chiefly US. a gorge or ravine. **5** a divergence or difference;

disparity: the generation gap. **6** Electronics. **6a** a break in a magnetic circuit that increases the inductance and saturation point of the circuit. **6b** See spark gap. **7** bridge, close, fill, or stop a gap. to remedy a deficiency. ◆ vb **gaps, gapping, gapped. 8** (tr) to make a breach or opening in. [C14: from ON *gap* chasm]
▸ **'gappy** adj

gape (geɪp) vb **gapes, gaping, gaped.** (intr) **1** to stare in wonder, esp. with the mouth open. **2** to open the mouth wide, esp. involuntarily, as in yawning. **3** to be or become wide open: the crater gaped under his feet. ◆ n **4** the act of gaping. **5** a wide opening. **6** the width of the widely opened mouth of a vertebrate. **7** a stare of astonishment. [C13: from ON *gapa*]
▸ **'gaper** n ▸ **'gaping** adj

gapes (geɪps) n (functioning as sing) **1** a disease of young domestic fowl, characterized by gaping and caused by parasitic worms (**gapeworms**). **2** Inf. a fit of yawning.

gap year n a year's break taken by a student between leaving school and starting further education.

gar (gɑː) n, pl **gar** or **gars.** short for **garpike.**

garage ('gærɑːʒ, -rɪdʒ) n **1** a building used to house a motor vehicle. **2** a commercial establishment in which motor vehicles are repaired, serviced, bought, and sold, and which usually also sells motor fuels. ◆ vb **garages, garaging, garaged. 3** (tr) to put into or keep in a garage. [C20: from F, from OF: to protect, from OHG *warōn*]

garage band n a rough-and-ready amateurish rock group. [?from the practice of such bands rehearsing in a garage]

garage sale n a sale of personal belongings or household effects held at a person's home, usually in the garage.

garb (gɑːb) n **1** clothes, esp. the distinctive attire of an occupation: clerical garb. **2** style of dress; fashion. **3** external appearance, covering, or attire. ◆ vb **4** (tr) to clothe; attire. [C16: from OF: graceful contour, from OIt. *garbo* grace, prob. of Gmc origin]

garbage ('gɑːbɪdʒ) n **1** worthless, useless, or unwanted matter. **2** another word (esp. US and Canad.) for **rubbish. 3** Computing. invalid data. **4** Inf. nonsense. [C15: prob. from Anglo-F *garbelage* removal of discarded matter, from ?]

garble ('gɑːbəl) vb **garbles, garbling, garbled.** (tr) **1** to jumble (a story, quotation, etc.), esp. unintentionally. **2** to distort the meaning of (an account, text, etc.), as by making misleading omissions; corrupt. ◆ n **3a** the act of garbling. **3b** garbled matter. [C15: from OIt. *garbellare* to strain, sift, from Ar., from LL *crībellum* small sieve]
▸ **'garbler** n

Garbo ★ ('gɑːbəʊ) n Greta ('grɛtə), real name *Greta Lovisa Gustafson.* 1905–90, US film actress, born in Sweden. Her films include *Anna Karenina* (1935) and *Camille* (1936).

garboard ('gɑːˌbɔːd) n Naut. the bottommost plank of a vessel's hull. Also called: **garboard strake.** [C17: from Du. *gaarboord*, prob. from MDu. *gaderen* to GATHER + *boord* BOARD]

garbology (gɑː'bɒlədʒɪ) n Chiefly US. **1** analysis of refuse as a means of investigating the lifestyle of the person or people who produced it. **2** the study of waste disposal. [C20: from GARBAGE + -OLOGY]
▸ **gar'bologist** n

García Lorca ★ (Spanish gar'θia 'lɔrka) n See (Federico García) **Lorca.**

García Márquez ★ (Spanish gar'sia mar'kes) n **Gabriel** (ga'βrjel). born 1928, Colombian writer. His works include the novel *One Hundred Years of Solitude* (1967) and the factual *News of a Kidnapping* (1996). Nobel prize for literature 1982.

garçon (French garsɔ̃) n a waiter or male servant, esp. if French. [C19: from OF *gars* lad, prob. of Gmc origin]

Gard ★ (French gar) n a department of S France, in Languedoc-Roussillon region. Capital: Nîmes. Pop.: 605 847 (1994 est.). Area: 5881 sq. km (2294 sq. miles).

garda ('gɑːrdə) n, pl **gardaí** ('gɑːrdɪ). a member of the **Garda Síochána,** the police force of the Republic of Ireland.

Garda ★ ('gɑːdə) n **Lake.** a lake in N Italy: the largest lake in the country. Area: 370 sq. km (143 sq. miles).

garden ('gɑːdᵊn) n **1** *Brit.* **1a** an area of land, usually planted with grass, trees, flowerbeds, etc., adjoining a house. US and Canad. word: **yard. 1b** (*as modifier*): *a garden chair.* **2a** an area of land used for the cultivation of ornamental plants, herbs, fruit, vegetables, trees, etc. **2b** (*as modifier*): *garden tools.* Related adj: **horticultural. 3** (*often pl*) such an area of land that is open to the public, sometimes part of a park: *botanical gardens.* **4** a fertile and beautiful region. **5 lead (a person) up the garden path.** *Inf.* to mislead or deceive. ◆ *vb* **6** to work in, cultivate, or take care of (a garden, plot of land, etc.). [C14: from OF *gardin*, of Gmc origin]
▸ '**gardener** n ▸ '**gardening** n

garden centre n a place where gardening tools and equipment, plants, seeds, etc., are sold.

garden city n *Brit.* a planned town of limited size surrounded by a rural belt.

gardenia (gɑːˈdiːnɪə) n **1** any evergreen shrub or tree of the Old World tropical genus *Gardenia*, cultivated for their large fragrant waxlike typically white flowers. **2** the flower of any of these shrubs. [C18: NL, after Dr Alexander *Garden* (1730–91), American botanist]

Garden of Eden ★ n the full name for **Eden**[1].

garderobe ('gɑːdˌrəʊb) n *Arch.* **1** a wardrobe or its contents. **2** a private room. **3** a privy. [C14: from F, from *garder* to keep + *robe* dress, clothing; see WARDROBE]

Gardiner ★ ('gɑːdnə) n **Stephen.** ?1483–1555, English bishop and statesman; lord chancellor (1553–55). He opposed Protestantism, supporting the anti-Reformation policies of Mary I.

Gardner ★ ('gɑːdnə) n **Ava.** 1922–90, US film actress. Her films include *The Killers* (1946), *The Sun also Rises* (1957), and *The Night of the Iguana* (1964).

Garfield ★ ('gɑːˌfiːld) n **James Abram.** 1831–81, 20th president of the US (1881); assassinated in office.

garfish ('gɑːfɪʃ) n, pl **garfish** or **garfishes. 1** another name for **garpike** (sense 1). **2** an elongated marine teleost fish with long toothed jaws: related to the flying fishes. [OE *gār* spear + FISH]

garganey ('gɑːgənɪ) n a small Eurasian duck closely related to the mallard. The male has a white stripe over each eye. [C17: from It. dialect *garganei*, imit.]

gargantuan (gɑːˈgæntjʊən) adj (*sometimes cap.*) huge; enormous. [after *Gargantua*, a giant in Rabelais' satire *Gargantua and Pantagruel* (1534)]

USAGE NOTE Some people think that *gargantuan* should only be used to describe things connected with food: *a gargantuan meal; his gargantuan appetite.*

gargle ('gɑːgᵊl) vb **gargles, gargling, gargled. 1** to rinse the mouth and throat with (a liquid, esp. a medicinal fluid) by slowly breathing out through the liquid. ◆ n **2** the liquid used for gargling. **3** the sound produced by gargling. [C16: from OF, from *gargouille* throat, ? imit.]

gargoyle ('gɑːgɔɪl) n **1** a waterspout carved in the form of a grotesque face or creature and projecting from a roof gutter. **2** a person with a grotesque appearance. [C15: from OF *gargouille* gargoyle, throat; see GARGLE]

garibaldi (ˌgærɪˈbɔːldɪ) n *Brit.* a type of biscuit having a layer of currants in the centre.

Garibaldi ★ (ˌgærɪˈbɔːldɪ) n **Giuseppe** (*Italian* dʒuˈzɛppe). 1807–82, Italian patriot; a leader of the Risorgimento. He conquered Sicily and Naples for the emerging kingdom of Italy (1860).

garish ('gɛərɪʃ) adj gay or colourful in a crude manner; gaudy. [C16: from earlier *gaure* to stare + -ISH]
▸ '**garishly** adv ▸ '**garishness** n

garland ('gɑːlənd) n **1** a wreath of flowers, leaves, etc., worn round the head or neck or hung up. **2** a collection of short literary pieces, such as poems; anthology. ◆ vb **3** (*tr*) to adorn with a garland or garlands. [C14: from OF *garlande*, ? of Gmc origin]

Garland ★ ('gɑːlənd) n **Judy,** real name *Frances Gumm.* 1922–69, US singer and film actress. Her films include *The Wizard of Oz* (1939) and *A Star is Born* (1954).

garlic ('gɑːlɪk) n **1** a hardy widely cultivated Asian alliaceous plant having whitish flowers. **2** the bulb of this plant, made up of small segments (cloves) that have a strong odour and pungent taste and are used in cooking. [OE *gārlēac*, from *gār* spear + *lēac* LEEK]
▸ '**garlicky** adj

garment ('gɑːmənt) n **1** (*often pl*) an article of clothing. **2** outer covering. ◆ vb **3** (*tr; usually passive*) to cover or clothe. [C14: from OF *garniment*, from *garnir* to equip; see GARNISH]

garner ('gɑːnə) vb (*tr*) **1** to gather or store as in a granary. ◆ n **2** an archaic word for **granary. 3** *Arch.* a place for storage. [C12: from OF: granary, from L *grānārium*, from *grānum* grain]

Garner ★ ('gɑːnə) n **Erroll.** 1921–77, US jazz pianist and composer.

garnet ('gɑːnɪt) n any of a group of hard glassy red, yellow, or green minerals consisting of silicates in cubic crystalline form: used as a gemstone and abrasive. [C13: from OF, from *grenat* (adj) red, from *pome grenate* POMEGRANATE]

garnish ('gɑːnɪʃ) vb (*tr*) **1** to decorate; trim. **2** to add something to (food) in order to improve its appearance or flavour. **3** *Law.* **3a** to serve with notice of proceedings; warn. **3b** to attach (a debt). ◆ n **4** a decoration; trimming. **5** something, such as parsley, added to a dish for its flavour or decorative effect. [C14: from OF *garnir* to adorn, equip, of Gmc origin]
▸ '**garnisher** n

garnishee (ˌgɑːnɪˈʃiː) *Law.* ◆ n **1** a person upon whom a garnishment has been served. ◆ vb **garnishees, garnisheeing, garnisheed.** (*tr*) **2** to attach (a debt or other property) by garnishment. **3** to serve (a person) with a garnishment.

garnishment ('gɑːnɪʃmənt) n **1** decoration or embellishment. **2** *Law.* **2a** a notice or warning. **2b** *Obs.* a summons to court proceedings already in progress. **2c** a notice warning a person holding money or property belonging to a debtor whose debt has been attached to hold such property until directed by the court to apply it.

garniture ('gɑːnɪtʃə) n decoration or embellishment. [C16: from F, from *garnir* to GARNISH]

Garonne ★ (*French* garɔn) n a river in SW France, rising in the central Pyrenees in Spain and flowing northeast then northwest into the Gironde estuary. Length: 580 km (360 miles).

garpike ('gɑːˌpaɪk) n **1** Also called: **garfish, gar.** any primitive freshwater elongated bony fish of North and Central America, having very long toothed jaws and a body covering of thick scales. **2** another name for **garfish** (sense 2).

garret ('gærɪt) n another word for **attic** (sense 1). [C14: from OF: watchtower, from *garir* to protect, of Gmc origin]

garret window n a skylight that lies along the slope of the roof.

Garrick ★ ('gærɪk) n **David.** 1717–79, British actor and theatre manager.

garrison ('gærɪsᵊn) n **1** the troops who maintain and guard a base or fortified place. **2** the place itself. ◆ vb **3** (*tr*) to station (troops) in (a fort, etc.). [C13: from OF, from *garir* to defend, of Gmc origin]

garron ('gærən) n a small sturdy pony bred and used chiefly in Scotland and Ireland. [C16: from Gaelic *gearran*]

garrotte or **garotte** (gəˈrɒt) n **1** a Spanish method of execution by strangulation. **2** the device, usually an iron collar, used in such executions. **3** *Obs.* strangulation of one's victim while committing robbery. ◆ vb **garrottes, garrotting, garrotted** or **garottes, garotting, garotted.** (*tr*) **4** to execute by means of the garrotte. **5** to strangle, esp. in order to commit robbery. [C17: from Sp. *garrote*, ?from OF *garrot* cudgel; from ?]
▸ **gar'rotter** or **ga'rotter** n

★ people and places

garrulous ('gærʊləs) adj 1 given to constant chatter; talkative. 2 wordy or diffuse. [C17: from L, from garrīre to chatter]
▶ 'garrulously adv ▶ 'garrulousness or garrulity (gæ'ruːlɪtɪ) n

garryowen (ˌgærɪ'əʊɪn) n (in rugby union) another term for up-and-under. [from Garryowen RFC, Ireland]

garter ('gɑːtə) n 1 a band, usually of elastic, worn round the leg to hold up a sock or stocking. 2 the US and Canad. word for suspender. ◆ vb 3 (tr) to fasten or secure as with a garter. [C14: from OF gartier, from garet bend of the knee, prob. of Celtic origin]

Garter ('gɑːtə) n the. 1 Order of the Garter. the highest order of British knighthood, open to women since 1987. 2 (sometimes not cap.) 2a the badge of this Order. 2b membership of this Order.

garter snake n a nonvenomous North American snake, typically marked with longitudinal stripes.

garter stitch n knitting in which all the rows are knitted in plain stitch.

garth (gɑːθ) n 1 a courtyard surrounded by a cloister. 2 Arch. a yard or garden. [C14: from ON garthr]

Gary ★ ('gærɪ) n a port in NW Indiana, on Lake Michigan: a major world steel producer. Pop.: 114 256 (1994 est.).

gas (gæs) n, pl gases or gasses. 1 a substance in a physical state in which it does not resist change of shape and will expand indefinitely to fill any container. Cf. liquid (sense 1), solid (sense 1). 2 any substance that is gaseous at room temperature and atmospheric pressure. 3 any gaseous substance that is above its critical temperature and therefore not liquefiable by pressure alone. Cf. vapour (sense 2). 4a a fossil fuel in the form of a gas, used as a source of domestic and industrial heat. 4b (as modifier): a gas cooker; gas fire. 5 a gaseous anaesthetic, such as nitrous oxide. 6 Mining. firedamp or the explosive mixture of firedamp and air. 7 the usual US, Canad., Austral., and NZ word for petrol, a shortened form of gasoline. 8 step on the gas. Inf. 8a to accelerate a motor vehicle. 8b to hurry. 9 a toxic, etc., substance in suspension in air used against an enemy, etc. 10 Inf. idle talk or boasting. 11 Sl. a delightful or successful person or thing: his latest record is a gas. 12 US. an informal name for flatus. ◆ vb gases or gasses, gassing, gassed. 13 (tr) to provide or fill with gas. 14 (tr) to subject to gas fumes, esp. so as to asphyxiate or render unconscious. 15 (intr; foll. by to) Inf. to talk in an idle or boastful way (to a person). [C17 (coined by J. B. van Helmont (1577–1644), Flemish chemist): from Gk khaos atmosphere]

gasbag ('gæsˌbæg) n Inf. a person who talks in a voluble way, esp. about unimportant matters.

gas chamber or **oven** n an airtight room into which poison gas is introduced to kill people or animals.

gas chromatography n a technique for analysing a mixture of volatile substances in which the mixture is carried by an inert gas through a column packed with a selective adsorbent or absorbent and a detector records on a moving strip the conductivity of the gas leaving the tube.

Gascoigne ★ ('gæskɔɪn) n Paul, known as Gazza. born 1967, British footballer.

Gascon ('gæskən) n 1 a native or inhabitant of Gascony. 2 the dialect of French spoken in Gascony. ◆ adj 3 of or relating to Gascony, its inhabitants, or their dialect of French.

gasconade (ˌgæskə'neɪd) Rare. ◆ n 1 boastful talk or bluster. ◆ vb gasconades, gasconading, gasconaded. 2 (intr) to boast, brag, or bluster. [C18: from F, from gasconner to chatter, boast like a GASCON]

gas constant n the constant in the gas equation, having the value 8.3143 joules per kelvin per mole. Symbol R Also called: universal gas constant.

Gascony ★ ('gæskənɪ) n a former province of SW France. French name: Gascogne (gaskɔɲ).

gas-cooled reactor n a nuclear reactor using a gas as the coolant.

gas-discharge tube n Electronics. any tube in which an electric discharge takes place through a gas.

gaseous ('gæsɪəs, -ʃəs, -ʃɪəs, 'geɪ-) adj of, concerned with, or having the characteristics of a gas.
▶ 'gaseousness n

gas equation n an equation relating the product of the pressure and the volume of an ideal gas to the product of its thermodynamic temperature and the gas constant.

gas gangrene n gangrene resulting from infection of a wound by anaerobic bacteria that cause gas bubbles in the surrounding tissues.

gas guzzler n Sl., chiefly US. a car that consumes large quantities of petrol.

gash (gæʃ) vb 1 (tr) to make a long deep cut in; slash. ◆ n 2 a long deep cut. [C16: from OF garser to scratch, from Vulgar L, from Gk kharassein]

gasholder ('gæsˌhəʊldə) n 1 Also called: gasometer. a large tank for storing coal gas or natural gas prior to distribution to users. 2 any vessel for storing or measuring a gas.

gasify ('gæsɪˌfaɪ) vb gasifies, gasifying, gasified. to make into or become a gas.
▶ ˌgasifi'cation n

Gaskell ★ ('gæskəl) n Mrs. married name of Elizabeth Cleghorn Stevenson. 1810–65, British novelist, whose books include Mary Barton (1848) and Cranford (1853).

gasket ('gæskɪt) n 1 a compressible packing piece of paper, rubber, asbestos, etc., sandwiched between the faces of a metal joint to provide a seal. 2 Naut. a piece of line used as a sail stop. [C17 (in the sense: rope lashing a furled sail): prob. from F garcette rope's end, lit.: little girl, from OF]

gaslight ('gæsˌlaɪt) n 1 a type of lamp in which the illumination is produced by an incandescent mantle heated by a jet of gas. 2 the light produced by such a lamp.

gasman ('gæsˌmæn) n, pl gasmen. a man employed to read household gas meters, supervise gas fittings, etc.

gas mantle n a mantle for use in a gaslight. See mantle (sense 4).

gas mask n a mask fitted with a chemical filter to enable the wearer to breathe air free of poisonous or corrosive gases.

gas meter n an apparatus for measuring and recording the amount of gas passed through it.

gasoline or **gasolene** ('gæsəˌliːn) n a US and Canad. name for petrol.

gasometer (gæs'ɒmɪtə) n a nontechnical name for gasholder.

gasp (gɑːsp) vb 1 (intr) to draw in the breath sharply or with effort, esp. in expressing awe, horror, etc. 2 (intr; foll. by after or for) to crave. 3 (tr; often foll. by out) to utter breathlessly. ◆ n 4 a short convulsive intake of breath. 5 at the last gasp. 5a at the point of death. 5b at the last moment. [C14: from ON geispa to yawn]

Gaspar ★ ('gæspə, 'gæspɑː) n a variant of Caspar.

Gaspé Peninsula ★ (gæ'speɪ; French gaspe) n a peninsula in E Canada, in SE Quebec between the St Lawrence River and New Brunswick: mountainous and wooded with many lakes and rivers. Area: about 29 500 sq. km (11 400 sq. miles). Also called: the Gaspé.

gasper ('gɑːspə) n 1 a person who gasps. 2 Brit. dated sl. a cheap cigarette.

gas plant n an aromatic white-flowered Eurasian plant that emits vapour capable of being ignited. Also called: burning bush, dittany, fraxinella.

gas ring n a circular assembly of gas jets, used esp. for cooking.

Gasser ★ ('gæsə) n Herbert Spencer. 1888–1963, US physiologist: shared a Nobel prize for physiology or medicine (1944) for work on electrical signs of nervous activity.

gassy ('gæsɪ) adj gassier, gassiest. 1 filled with, containing, or resembling gas. 2 Inf. full of idle or vapid talk.
▶ 'gassiness n

gasteropod ('gæstərəˌpɒd) n, adj a variant spelling of gastropod.

gas thermometer *n* a device for measuring temperature by observing the pressure of gas at a constant volume or the volume of a gas kept at a constant pressure.

gastric ('gæstrɪk) *adj* of, relating to, near, or involving the stomach.

gastric juice *n* a digestive fluid secreted by the stomach, containing hydrochloric acid, pepsin, rennin, etc.

gastric ulcer *n* an ulcer of the mucous membrane lining the stomach.

gastritis (gæs'traɪtɪs) *n* inflammation of the stomach.

gastro- *or often before a vowel* **gastr-** *combining form.* stomach: *gastroenteritis; gastritis.* [from Gk *gastēr*]

gastrocolic (ˌgæstrəʊ'kɒlɪk) *adj* of or relating to the stomach and colon: *gastrocolic reflex.*

gastroenteritis (ˌgæstrəʊˌentə'raɪtɪs) *n* inflammation of the stomach and intestines.

gastrointestinal (ˌgæstrəʊɪn'testɪn°l) *adj* of or relating to the stomach and intestinal tract.

gastronome ('gæstrəˌnəʊm), **gastronomer** (gæs-'trɒnəmə), *or* **gastronomist** *n* less common words for **gourmet**.

gastronomy (gæs'trɒnəmɪ) *n* the art of good eating. [C19: from F, from Gk, from *gastēr* stomach; see -NOMY]
▸ **gastronomic** (ˌgæstrə'nɒmɪk) *or* ˌgastro'nomical *adj*
▸ ˌgastro'nomically *adv*

gastropod ('gæstrəˌpɒd) *or* **gasteropod** *n* any of a class of molluscs typically having a flattened muscular foot for locomotion and a head that bears stalked eyes. The class includes the snails, whelks, and slugs.
▸ **gastropodan** (gæs'trɒpəd'n) *adj, n*

gastroscope ('gæstrəˌskəʊp) *n* a medical instrument for examining the interior of the stomach.

gastrula ('gæstrʊlə) *n, pl* **gastrulas** *or* **gastrulae** (-ˌliː). a saclike animal embryo consisting of three layers of cells surrounding a central cavity with a small opening to the exterior. [C19: NL: little stomach, from Gk *gastēr* belly]

gas turbine *n* an internal-combustion engine in which the expanding gases emerging from one or more combustion chambers drive a turbine.

gasworks ('gæsˌwɜːks) *n* (*functioning as sing*) a plant in which gas, esp. coal gas, is made.

gat (gæt) *vb Arch.* a past tense of **get**.

gate (geɪt) *n* **1** a movable barrier, usually hinged, for closing an opening in a wall, fence, etc. **2** an opening to allow passage into or out of an enclosed place. **3** any means of entrance or access. **4** a mountain pass or gap, esp. one providing entry into another country or region. **5a** the number of people admitted to a sporting event or entertainment. **5b** the total entrance money received from them. **6** *Electronics.* a logic circuit having one or more input terminals and one output terminal, the output being switched between two voltage levels determined by the combination of input signals. **7** a component in a motion-picture camera or projector that holds each frame flat and momentarily stationary behind the lens. **8** a slotted metal frame that controls the positions of the gear lever in a motor vehicle. ♦ *vb* **gates**, **gating**, **gated**. **9** (*tr*) *Brit.* to restrict (a student) to the school or college grounds as a punishment. [OE *geat*]

gâteau ('gætəʊ) *n, pl* **gâteaux** (-təʊz). a rich cake usually layered with cream and elaborately decorated. [F: cake]

gate-crash *vb Inf.* to gain entry to (a party, concert, etc.) without invitation or payment.
▸ 'gate-ˌcrasher *n*

gatefold ('geɪtˌfəʊld) *n* an oversize page in a book or magazine that is folded in. Also called: **foldout**.

gatehouse ('geɪtˌhaʊs) *n* **1** a building at or above a gateway, used by a porter or guard, or, formerly, as a fortification. **2** a small house at the entrance to the grounds of a country mansion.

gatekeeper ('geɪtˌkiːpə) *n* **1** a person who has charge of a gate and controls who may pass through it. **2** a manager in a large organization who controls the flow of information, esp. to parent and subsidiary companies. **3** any of several Eurasian butterflies having brown-bordered orange wings.

gate-leg table *or* **gate-legged table** *n* a table with one or two leaves supported by a hinged leg swung out from the frame.

gatepost ('geɪtˌpəʊst) *n* **1a** the post on which a gate is hung. **1b** the post to which a gate is fastened when closed. **2 between you, me, and the gatepost.** confidentially.

Gates ★ (geɪts) *n* **1** Bill, full name *William Henry Gates.* born 1955, US computer-software executive; founder (1976) of Microsoft Corporation. **2** Horatio. ?1728–1806, American Revolutionary general: defeated the British at Saratoga (1777).

Gateshead ★ ('geɪtsˌhed) *n* **1** a port in NE England, in Tyne and Wear: engineering works. Pop.: 83 159 (1991). **2** a unitary authority in NE England. Pop.: 202 400 (1994 est.). Area: 142 sq. km (55 sq. miles).

gateway ('geɪtˌweɪ) *n* **1** an entrance that may be closed by or as by a gate. **2** a means of entry or access: *Bombay, gateway to India.* **3** *Computing.* hardware and software that connect incompatible computer networks.

Gath ★ (gæθ) *n Old Testament.* one of the five cities of the Philistines, from which Goliath came (I Samuel 17:4) and near which Saul fell in battle (II Samuel 1:20). Douay spelling: **Geth** (geθ).

gather ('gæðə) *vb* **1** to assemble or cause to assemble. **2** to collect or be collected gradually; muster. **3** (*tr*) to learn from information given; conclude or assume. **4** (*tr*) to pick or harvest (flowers, fruit, etc.). **5** (*tr*) to bring close (to). **6** to increase or cause to increase gradually, as in force, speed, intensity, etc. **7** to contract (the brow) or (of the brow) to become contracted into wrinkles; knit. **8** (*tr*) to assemble (sections of a book) in the correct sequence for binding. **9** (*tr*) to prepare or make ready: *to gather one's wits.* **10** to draw (material) into a series of small tucks or folds. **11** (*intr*) (of a boil or other sore) to come to a head; form pus. ♦ *n* **12a** the act of gathering. **12b** the amount gathered. **13** a small fold in material, as made by a tightly pulled stitch; tuck. [OE *gadrian*]
▸ 'gatherer *n*

gathering ('gæðərɪŋ) *n* **1** a group of people, things, etc., that are gathered together; assembly. **2** *Sewing.* a series of gathers in material. **3** *Inf.* 3a the formation of pus in a boil. **3b** the pus so formed. **4** *Printing.* an informal name for **section** (sense 16).

Gatling gun ('gætlɪŋ) *n* a machine gun equipped with a rotating cluster of barrels that are fired in succession. [C19: after R. J. *Gatling* (1818–1903), its US inventor]

GATT (gæt) *n acronym for* General Agreement on Tariffs and Trade: a multilateral international treaty signed in 1947 to promote trade; replaced in 1995 by the World Trade Organization.

Gatún Lake ★ (*Spanish* ga'tun) *n* a lake in Panama, part of the Panama Canal: formed in 1912 on the completion of the **Gatún Dam** across the Chagres River. Area: 424 sq. km (164 sq. miles).

gauche (gəʊʃ) *adj* lacking ease of manner; tactless. [C18: F: awkward, left, from OF *gauchir* to swerve, ult. of Gmc origin]
▸ 'gauchely *adv* ▸ 'gaucheness *n*

gaucherie (ˌgəʊʃə'riː, 'gəʊʃərɪ) *n* **1** the quality of being gauche. **2** a gauche act.

gaucho ('gaʊtʃəʊ) *n, pl* **gauchos.** a cowboy of the South American pampas, usually of mixed Spanish and Indian descent. [C19: from American Sp., prob. from Quechuan *wáhcha* orphan, vagabond]

gaud (gɔːd) *n* an article of cheap finery. [C14: prob. from OF *gaudir* to be joyful, from L *gaudēre*]

Gaudí ★ ('gaʊdɪ; *Spanish* gau'ði) *n* **Antonio** (an'tonjo). 1852–1926, Spanish architect, an exponent of Art Nouveau in Europe.

Gaudier-Brzeska ★ (*French* godjebʒeska) *n* **Henri** (ãri), original name *Henri Gaudier.* 1891–1915, French vorticist sculptor.

gaudy[1] ('gɔːdɪ) *adj* **gaudier, gaudiest.** bright or colourful in a crude or vulgar manner. [C16: from GAUD]
▸ 'gaudily *adv* ▸ 'gaudiness *n*

gaudy[2] ('gɔːdɪ) *n, pl* **gaudies.** *Brit.* a celebratory feast held

---

★ people and places

at some schools and colleges. [C16: from L *gaudium* joy, from *gaudēre* to rejoice]

auge *or* **gage** (geɪdʒ) *vb* **gauges, gauging, gauged** *or* **gages, gaging, gaged.** (*tr*) **1** to measure or determine the amount, quantity, size, condition, etc., of. **2** to estimate or appraise; judge. **3** to check for conformity or bring into conformity with a standard measurement, etc. ◆ *n* **4** a standard measurement, dimension, capacity, or quantity. **5** any of various instruments for measuring a quantity: *a pressure gauge.* **6** any of various devices used to check for conformity with a standard measurement. **7** a standard or means for assessing; test; criterion. **8** scope, capacity, or extent. **9** the diameter of the barrel of a gun, esp. a shotgun. **10** the thickness of sheet metal or the diameter of wire. **11** the distance between the rails of a railway track. **12** the distance between two wheels on the same axle of a vehicle, truck, etc. **13** *Naut.* the position of a vessel in relation to the wind and another vessel. **14** a measure of the fineness of woven or knitted fabric. **15** the width of motion-picture film or magnetic tape. ◆ *adj* **16** (of a pressure measurement) measured on a pressure gauge that registers zero at atmospheric pressure. [C15: from OF, prob. of Gmc origin] ▷ **'gaugeable** *or* **'gageable** *adj*

auge boson *n Physics.* a boson that mediates the interaction between elementary particles. There are four types: photons for electromagnetic interactions, gluons for strong interactions, intermediate vector bosons for weak interactions, and gravitons for gravitational interactions.

auge theory *n Physics.* a type of theory of elementary particles designed to explain the strong, weak, and electromagnetic interactions in terms of exchange of virtual particles.

iauguin ★ (*French* gogɛ̃) *n* **Paul** (pɔl). 1848–1903, French postimpressionist painter who worked in the South Pacific from 1891.

iauhati ★ (gaʊ'hɑːtɪ) *n* a city in NE India, in Assam on the River Brahmaputra: centre of British administration in Assam (1826–74). Pop.: 584 342 (1991).

aul ★ (gɔːl) *n* **1** an ancient region of W Europe corresponding to N Italy, France, Belgium, part of Germany, and the S Netherlands: divided into Cisalpine Gaul, which became a Roman province before 100 B.C., and Transalpine Gaul, which was conquered by Julius Caesar (58–51 B.C.). Latin name: **Gallia. 2** a native of ancient Gaul. **3** a Frenchman.

iauleiter ('gaʊ,laɪtə) *n* **1** a provincial governor in Germany under Hitler. **2** (*sometimes not cap.*) a person in a position of petty authority who behaves in an overbearing manner. [G, from *Gau* district + *Leiter* leader]

iaulish ('gɔːlɪʃ) *n* **1** the extinct Celtic language of the pre-Roman Gauls. ◆ *adj* **2** of ancient Gaul, the Gauls, or their language.

iaulle ★ (gəʊl, gɔːl; *French* gol) *n* **Charles de.** See (Charles) **de Gaulle.**

aunt (gɔːnt) *adj* **1** bony and emaciated in appearance. **2** (of places) bleak or desolate. [C15: ?from ON] ▷ **'gauntly** *adv* ▷ **'gauntness** *n*

auntlet[1] ('gɔːntlɪt) *n* **1** a medieval armoured leather glove. **2** a heavy glove with a long cuff. **3 take up** (*or* **throw down**) **the gauntlet.** to accept (or offer) a challenge. [C15: from OF *gantelet*, dim. of *gant* glove, of Gmc origin]

auntlet[2] ('gɔːntlɪt) *n* **1** a punishment in which the victim is forced to run between two rows of men who strike at him as he passes: formerly a military punishment. **2 run the gauntlet. 2a** to suffer this punishment. **2b** to endure an onslaught, as of criticism. **3** a testing ordeal. [C15: changed (through infl. of GAUNTLET[1]) from earlier *gantlope*, from Swedish *gatlopp* passageway]

aur ('gaʊə) *n* a large wild ox of mountainous regions of S Asia. [C19: from Hindi, from Sansk. *gāura*]

auss (gaʊs) *n, pl* **gauss.** the cgs unit of magnetic flux density. 1 gauss is equivalent to 10^{-4} tesla. [after K. F. GAUSS]

iauss ★ (*German* gaus) *n* **Karl Friedrich** (karl 'friːdrɪç). 1777–1855, German mathematician: developed the

theory of numbers and applied mathematics to astronomy, electricity and magnetism, and geodesy. ▷ **Gaussian** ('gaʊsɪən) *adj*

Gaussian distribution *n* another name for **normal distribution.**

Gauteng ★ (xaʊ'tɛŋ) *n* a province of N South Africa; formed in 1994 from part of the former Transvaal. Capital: Johannesburg. Pop.: 7 048 300 (1995 est.). Area: 18 810 sq. km (7262 sq. miles).

Gautier ★ (*French* gotje) *n* **Théophile** (teɔfil). 1811–72, French poet, novelist, and critic.

gauze (gɔːz) *n* **1** a transparent cloth of loose weave. **2** a surgical dressing of muslin or similar material. **3** any thin openwork material, such as wire. **4** a fine mist or haze. [C16: from F *gaze*, ?from GAZA, where it was believed to originate]

gauzy ('gɔːzɪ) *adj* **gauzier, gauziest.** resembling gauze; thin and transparent. ▷ **'gauzily** *adv* ▷ **'gauziness** *n*

Gavaskar ★ (gæ'væska:) *n* **Sunil Manohar** ('sʊnɪl 'mænəʊhaː). born 1949, Indian cricketer. He captained India 1978–83 and 1984–85.

gave (geɪv) *vb* the past tense of **give.**

gavel ('gævᵊl) *n* a small hammer used by a chairman, auctioneer, etc., to call for order or attention. [C19: from ?]

gavial ('geɪvɪəl), **gharial,** *or* **garial** ('gærɪəl) *n* a large fish-eating Indian crocodile with a very long slender snout. [C19: from F, from Hindi]

Gävle ★ (*Swedish* 'jɛːvlə) *n* a port in E Sweden, on an inlet of the Gulf of Bothnia. Pop.: 90 270 (1994).

gavotte *or* **gavot** (gə'vɒt) *n* **1** an old formal dance in quadruple time. **2** a piece of music composed for or in the rhythm of this dance. [C17: from F, from Provençal, from *gavot* mountaineer, dweller in the Alps (where the dance originated)]

gawk (gɔːk) *n* **1** a clumsy stupid person; lout. ◆ *vb* **2** (*intr*) to stare in a stupid way; gape. [C18: from ODanish *gaukr*; prob. rel. to GAPE]

gawky ('gɔːkɪ) *adj* **gawkier, gawkiest.** clumsy or ungainly; awkward. Also: **gawkish.** ▷ **'gawkily** *adv* ▷ **'gawkiness** *n*

gawp *or* **gaup** (gɔːp) *vb* (*intr; often foll. by at*) *Brit. sl.* to stare stupidly; gape. [C14 *galpen*; prob. rel. to OE *gielpan* to boast, YELP] ▷ **'gawper** *n*

gay (geɪ) *adj* **1a** homosexual. **1b** of or for homosexuals: *a gay club.* **2** carefree and merry: *a gay temperament.* **3** brightly coloured; brilliant: *a gay hat.* **4** given to pleasure, esp. in social entertainment: *a gay life.* ◆ *n* **5** a homosexual. [C13: from OF *gai*, from OProvençal, of Gmc origin] ▷ **'gayness** *n*

USAGE NOTE *Gayness* is the state of being homosexual. The noun which refers to the state of being carefree and merry is *gaiety.*

Gay ★ (geɪ) *n* **John.** 1685–1732, English poet and dramatist; author of *The Beggar's Opera* (1728).

Gaya ★ ('gɑːjə, 'gaɪə) *n* a city in NE India, in central Bihar: Hindu place of pilgrimage and one of the holiest sites of Buddhism. Pop.: 291 675 (1991).

Gay-Lussac ★ ('geɪ'luːsæk; *French* gɛlysak) *n* **Joseph Louis** (ʒozɛf lwi). 1778–1850, French physicist and chemist: discovered the law of combining gases named after him (1808).

Gaza ★ ('gɑːzə) *n* a city in the Gaza Strip: a Philistine city in biblical times. It was under Egyptian administration from 1949 until occupied by Israel (1967). Pop.: 293 000 (1990 est.). Arabic name: **Ghazzah.**

gazania (gæ'zeɪnɪə) *n* any of a genus of S. African plants of the composite family having large showy flowers. [? after Theodore of *Gaza* (1398–1478), who translated the botanical works of Theophrastus into Latin]

Gazankulu ★ (,gazaŋ'kuːluː) *n* (formerly) a Bantu homeland in South Africa, consisting of four exclaves in Transvaal; reintegrated into South Africa in 1994. Capital: Giyani.

Gaza Strip ★ *n* a coastal region on the SE corner of the Mediterranean, formerly part of Palestine: administered by Egypt (1949–56, 1957–67); occupied by Israel since 1967; granted autonomy in 1993 and administered by the Palestinian National Authority from 1994. Pop.: 748 400 (1993).

gaze (geɪz) *vb* **gazes, gazing, gazed. 1** (*intr*) to look long and fixedly, esp. in wonder. ♦ *n* **2** a fixed look. [C14: from Swedish dialect *gasa* to gape at]
▶ **ˈgazer** *n*

gazebo (gəˈziːbəʊ) *n, pl* **gazebos** *or* **gazeboes.** a summerhouse, garden pavilion, or belvedere, sited to command a view. [C18: ? a pseudo-Latin coinage based on GAZE]

gazelle (gəˈzɛl) *n, pl* **gazelles** *or* **gazelle.** any small graceful usually fawn-coloured antelope of Africa and Asia. [C17: from OF, from Ar. *ghazāl*]

gazette (gəˈzɛt) *n* **1** a newspaper or official journal. **2** *Brit.* an official document containing public notices, appointments, etc. ♦ *vb* **gazettes, gazetting, gazetted. 3** (*tr*) *Brit.* to announce or report (facts or an event) in a gazette. [C17: from F, from It., from Venetian dialect *gazeta* news-sheet costing one *gazet*, small copper coin]

gazetteer (ˌgæzɪˈtɪə) *n* **1** a book or section of a book that lists and describes places. **2** *Arch.* a writer for a gazette.

Gaziantep ★ (ˌɡɑːziɑːnˈtɛp) *n* a city in S Turkey: base for Ibrahim Pasha's campaign against the Turks (1839) and centre of Turkish resistance to French forces (1921). Pop.: 716 000 (1994 est.). Former name (until 1921): **Aintab.**

gazpacho (gəzˈpɑːtʃəʊ, gæs-) *n* a Spanish soup made from tomatoes, peppers, etc., and served cold. [from Sp.]

gazump (gəˈzʌmp) *Brit.* ♦ *vb* **1** to raise the price of something, esp. a house, after agreeing a price verbally with (an intending buyer). **2** (*tr*) to swindle or overcharge. ♦ *n* **3** an instance of gazumping. [C20: from ?]
▶ **gaˈzumper** *n*

gazunder (gəˈzʌndə) *Brit.* ♦ *vb* **1** to reduce an offer on a property immediately before exchanging contracts, having previously agreed to a higher price with (the seller). ♦ *n* **2** an act or instance of gazundering. [C20: modelled on GAZUMP]
▶ **gaˈzunderer** *n*

GB *abbrev. for* Great Britain.

GBE *abbrev. for* (Knight or Dame) Grand Cross of the British Empire (a Brit. title).

GBH *abbrev. for* grievous bodily harm.

GC *abbrev. for* George Cross (a Brit. award for bravery).

GCB *abbrev. for* (Knight) Grand Cross of the Bath (a Brit. title).

gcd *or* **GCD** *abbrev. for* greatest common divisor.

GCE (in Britain) *abbrev. for* General Certificate of Education: a public examination in specified subjects taken as qualifying examinations for entry into a university, college, etc. The GCSE has replaced it at O level. See also **A level, S level.**

GCHQ (in Britain) *abbrev. for* Government Communications Headquarters.

G clef *n* another name for **treble clef.**

GCMG *abbrev. for* (Knight or Dame) Grand Cross of the Order of St Michael and St George (a Brit. title).

GCSE (in Britain) *abbrev. for* General Certificate of Secondary Education: a public examination in specified subjects for 16-year-old schoolchildren. It replaced GCE O level and CSE.

GCVO *abbrev. for* (Knight or Dame) Grand Cross of the Royal Victorian Order (a Brit. title).

Gd *the chemical symbol for* gadolinium.

Gdańsk ★ (*Polish* gdajinsk) *n* **1** the chief port of Poland, on the Baltic: a member of the Hanseatic league; under Prussian rule (1793–1807 and 1814–1919); a free city under the League of Nations from 1919 until annexed by Germany in 1939; returned to Poland in 1945. Pop.:

463 100 (1995 est.). German name: **Danzig. 2 Bay of.** a wide inlet of the Baltic Sea on the N coast of Poland.

g'day *or* **gidday** (gəˈdaɪ) *sentence substitute.* an Australian and NZ informal variant of **good day.**

Gdns *abbrev. for* Gardens.

GDR *abbrev. for* German Democratic Republic (East Germany; DDR).

Gdynia ★ (*Polish* ˈgdɪnja) *n* a port in N Poland, near Gdańsk: developed 1924–39 as the outlet for trade through the Polish Corridor; naval base. Pop.: 251 400 (1995 est.).

Ge[1] ★ (dʒiː) *n* another name for **Gaea.**

Ge[2] *the chemical symbol for* germanium.

gean (giːn) *n* a white-flowered tree of the rose family of Europe, W Asia, and N Africa; the ancestor of the cultivated sweet cherries.

gear (gɪə) *n* **1** a toothed wheel that engages with another toothed wheel or with a rack in order to change the speed or direction of transmitted motion. **2** a mechanism for transmitting motion by gears. **3** the engagement or specific ratio of a system of gears: *in gear; high gear.* **4** personal belongings. **5** equipment and supplies for a particular operation, sport, etc. **6** *Naut.* all equipment or appurtenances belonging to a certain vessel or sailor, etc. **7** short for **landing gear. 8** *Inf.* up-to-date clothes and accessories. **9** *Sl.* drugs of any type. **10** a less common word for **harness** (sense 1). **11 out of gear.** out of order; not functioning properly. ♦ *vb* **12** (*tr*) to adjust or adapt (one thing) so as to fit in or work with another: *to gear our output to current demand.* **13** (*tr*) to equip with or connect by gears. **14** (*intr*) to be in or come into gear. **15** (*tr*) to equip with a harness. [C13: from ON *gervi*]

gearbox (ˈgɪəˌbɒks) *n* **1** the metal casing within which a train of gears is sealed. **2** this metal casing and its contents, esp. in a motor vehicle.

gearing (ˈgɪərɪŋ) *n* **1** an assembly of gears designed to transmit motion. **2** the act or technique of providing gears to transmit motion. **3** Also called: **capital gearing.** *Accounting, Brit.* the ratio of a company's debt capital to its equity capital. US word: **leverage.**

gear lever *or US & Canad.* **gearshift** (ˈgɪəˌʃɪft) *n* a lever used to move gearwheels relative to each other, esp. in a motor vehicle.

gear train *n Engineering.* a system of gears that transmit power from one shaft to another.

gearwheel (ˈgɪəˌwiːl) *n* another name for **gear** (sense 1).

Geber ★ (ˈdʒiːbə) *n* Latinized form of Jabir, assumed in honour of Jabir ibn Hayyan by a 14th-century alchemist, probably Spanish: he described the preparation of nitric and sulphuric acids.

gecko (ˈgɛkəʊ) *n, pl* **geckos** *or* **geckoes.** a small insectivorous terrestrial lizard of warm regions. [C18: from Malay *ge'kok,* imit.]

gee[1] (dʒiː) *interj* **1** Also: **gee up!** an exclamation, as to a horse or draught animal, to encourage it to turn to the right, go on, or go faster. ♦ *vb* **gees, geeing, geed. 2** (usually foll. by *up*) to move (an animal, esp. a horse) ahead or urge on. [C17: from ?]

gee[2] (dʒiː) *interj US & Canad. inf.* a mild exclamation of surprise, admiration, etc. Also: **gee whizz.** [C20: euphemism for JESUS]

Gee ★ (dʒiː) *n* **Maurice.** born 1931, New Zealand novelist.

geebung (ˈdʒiːbʌŋ) *n* **1** any of several Australian trees or shrubs with edible but tasteless fruit. **2** the fruit of these trees. [from Abor.]

geek (giːk) *n Sl.* **1** a boring or unattractive social misfit. **2** a degenerate. [C19: prob. from Scot. *geck* fool]
▶ **ˈgeeky** *adj*

geelbek (ˈxiːlˌbɛk) *n S. African.* an edible marine fish with yellow jaws. Also called: **Cape salmon.** [from Afrik. *geel* yellow + *bek* mouth]

Geelong ★ (dʒəˈlɒŋ) *n* a port in SE Australia, in S Victoria on Port Phillip Bay. Pop.: 152 600 (1995 est.).

geese (giːs) *n* the plural of **goose**[1].

geezer (ˈɡiːzə) *n Inf.* a man. [C19: prob. from dialect pronunciation of GUISER]

★ people and places

Gehenna ★ (gɪ'hɛnə) n 1 Old Testament. the valley below Jerusalem, where children were sacrificed and, later, unclean things were burnt. 2 New Testament, Judaism. a place where the wicked are punished after death. 3 a place or state of pain and torment. [C16: from LL, from Gk, from Heb. Gê' Hinnōm, lit.: valley of Hinnom, symbolic of hell]

Geiger counter or **Geiger-Müller counter** ('gaɪgə 'mulə) n an instrument for detecting and measuring the intensity of ionizing radiation. [C20: after Hans Geiger and W. Müller (20th-cent.), G physicists]

geisha ('geɪʃə) n, pl geisha or geishas. a professional female companion for men in Japan, trained in music, dancing, and the art of conversation. [C19: from Japanese, from Ancient Chinese]

Geissler tube ('gaɪslə) n a glass or quartz vessel for maintaining an electric discharge in a low-pressure gas as a source of visible or ultraviolet light for spectroscopy, etc. [C19: after Heinrich Geissler (1814–79), G mechanic]

gel (dʒɛl) n 1 a semirigid jelly-like colloid in which a liquid is dispersed in a solid: nondrip paint is a gel. 2 a jelly-like substance applied to the hair before styling in order to retain the style. ♦ vb gels, gelling, gelled. 3 to become or cause to become a gel. 4 a variant spelling of jell. [C19: from GELATINE]

gelatine ('dʒɛlə,tiːn) or **gelatin** ('dʒɛlətɪn) n 1 a colourless or yellowish water-soluble protein prepared by boiling animal hides and bones: used in foods, glue, photographic emulsions, etc. 2 an edible jelly made of this substance. [C19: from F gélatine, from Med. L, from L gelāre to freeze]

gelatinize or **gelatinise** (dʒɪ'lætɪ,naɪz) vb gelatinizes, gelatinizing, gelatinized or gelatinises, gelatinising, gelatinised. 1 to make or become gelatinous. 2 (tr) Photog. to coat (glass, paper, etc.) with gelatine.
  ▶ ge,latini'zation or ge,latini'sation n

gelatinous (dʒɪ'lætɪnəs) adj 1 consisting of or resembling jelly; viscous. 2 of, containing, or resembling gelatine.
  ▶ ge'latinously adv ▶ ge'latinousness n

gelation[1] (dʒɪ'leɪʃən) n the act or process of freezing a liquid. [C17: from L gelātiō a freezing; see GELATINE]

gelation[2] (dʒɪ'leɪʃən) n the act or process of forming into a gel. [C20: from GEL]

geld (gɛld) vb gelds, gelding, gelded or gelt (gɛlt). (tr) 1 to castrate (a horse or other animal). 2 to deprive of virility or vitality; emasculate; weaken. [C13: from ON, from geldr barren]

Gelderland or **Guelderland** ★ ('gɛldə,lænd; Dutch 'xɛldərlɑnt) n a province of the E Netherlands: formerly a duchy, belonging successively to several different European powers. Capital: Arnhem. Pop.: 1 864 732 (1995). Area: 5014 sq. km (1955 sq. miles). Also called: Guelders.

gelding ('gɛldɪŋ) n a castrated male horse. [C14: from ON geldingr; see GELD, -ING[1]]

Geldof ★ ('gɛldɒf) n Bob, full name Robert Frederick Zenon Geldof. born 1954, Irish rock singer: lead vocalist with the Boomtown Rats (1977–86): organizer of the Band Aid charity for famine relief in Africa. He received an honorary knighthood in 1986.

Gelée ★ (French ʒəle) n Claude (klod). the original name of Claude Lorrain.

Gelibolu ★ (ge'libolu) n the Turkish name for Gallipoli.

gelid ('dʒɛlɪd) adj very cold, icy, or frosty. [C17: from L gelidus, from gelu frost]
  ▶ ge'lidity n

gelignite ('dʒɛlɪg,naɪt) n a type of dynamite in which the nitrogelatine is absorbed in a base of wood pulp and potassium or sodium nitrate. Also called (informal): gelly. [C19: from GEL(ATINE) + L ignis fire + -ITE[1]]

Gelligaer ★ (Welsh ,gɛhliː'gaɪr) n a town in S Wales, in Caerphilly county borough. Pop.: 15 906 (1991).

Gell-Mann ★ (,gɛl'mæn) n Murray. born 1929, US physicist, noted for his research on elementary particles: Nobel prize for physics in 1969.

Gelsenkirchen ★ (German gɛlzən'kɪrçən) n an industrial city in W Germany, in North Rhine-Westphalia. Pop.: 293 542 (1995 est.).

gem (dʒɛm) n 1 a precious or semiprecious stone used in jewellery as a decoration; jewel. 2 a person or thing held to be a perfect example; treasure. ♦ vb gems, gemming, gemmed. 3 (tr) to set or ornament with gems. [C14: from OF, from L gemma bud, precious stone]
  ▶ 'gem,like adj ▶ 'gemmy adj

Gemara (gə'mɑːrə; Hebrew gɛma'ra) n Judaism. the later main part of the Talmud, being a commentary on the Mishnah: the primary source of Jewish religious law. [C17: from Aramaic gemārā completion]

geminate adj ('dʒɛmɪnɪt, -,neɪt) also geminated. 1 combined in pairs; doubled: a geminate leaf. ♦ vb ('dʒɛmɪ,neɪt), geminates, geminating, geminated. 2 to arrange or be arranged in pairs: the "t"s in "fitted" are geminated. [C17: from L gemināre to double, from geminus twin]
  ▶ 'geminately adv ▶ ,gemi'nation n

Gemini ('dʒɛmɪ,naɪ, -,niː) n 1 Astron. a zodiacal constellation in the N hemisphere containing the stars Castor and Pollux. 2 Classical myth. another name for Castor and Pollux. 3 Astrol. Also called: the Twins. the third sign of the zodiac. The sun is in this sign between about May 21 and June 20.

gemma ('dʒɛmə) n, pl gemmae (-miː). 1 a small asexual reproductive structure in mosses, etc., that becomes detached from the parent and develops into a new individual. 2 Zool. another name for gemmule. [C18: from L: bud, GEM]

gemmate ('dʒɛmeɪt) adj 1 (of some plants and animals) having or reproducing by gemmae. ♦ vb gemmates, gemmating, gemmated. 2 (intr) to produce or reproduce by gemmae.
  ▶ gem'mation n

gemmiparous (dʒɛ'mɪpərəs) adj (of plants and animals) reproducing by gemmae or buds. Also: gemmiferous.

gemmule ('dʒɛmjuːl) n 1 Zool. a cell or mass of cells produced asexually by sponges and developing into a new individual; bud. 2 Bot. a small gemma. [C19: from F, from L gemmula a little bud; see GEM]

gemology or **gemmology** (dʒɛ'mɒlədʒɪ) n the branch of mineralogy concerned with gems and gemstones.
  ▶ gemological or gemmological (,dʒɛmə'lɒdʒɪk'l) adj
  ▶ gem'ologist or gem'mologist n

gemsbok or **gemsbuck** ('gɛmz,bʌk) n, pl gemsbok, gemsboks or gemsbuck, gemsbucks. an oryx of southern Africa, marked with a broad black band along its flanks. [C18: from Afrik., from G Gemsbock, from Gemse chamois + Bock BUCK[1]]

gemstone ('dʒɛm,stəʊn) n a precious or semiprecious stone, esp. one cut and polished.

gen (dʒɛn) n Brit., Austral., & NZ inf. information: give me the gen on your latest project. See also gen up. [C20: from gen(eral information)]

gen. abbrev. for: 1 gender. 2 general(ly). 3 generic. 4 genitive. 5 genus.

Gen. abbrev. for: 1 General. 2 Bible. Genesis.

-gen suffix forming nouns. 1 producing or that which produces: hydrogen. 2 something produced: carcinogen. [via F -gène, from Gk -genēs born]

Genck ★ (Flemish xɛŋk) n a variant spelling of Genk.

gendarme ('ʒɒndɑːm) n 1 a member of the police force in France or in countries influenced or controlled by France. 2 a sharp pinnacle of rock on a mountain ridge. [C16: from French gens d'armes people of arms]

gendarmerie or **gendarmery** (ʒɒn'dɑːmərɪ) n 1 the whole corps of gendarmes. 2 the headquarters of a body of gendarmes.

gender ('dʒɛndə) n 1 a set of two or more grammatical categories into which the nouns of certain languages are divided. 2 any of the categories, such as masculine, feminine, neuter, or common, within such a set. 3 Inf. the state of being male, female, or neuter. 4 Inf. all the mem-

---

★ people and places

bers of one sex: *the female gender*. [C14: from OF, from L *genus* kind]

gender-bender *n Inf.* a person who adopts an androgynous style of dress, hair, etc.

gene (dʒiːn) *n* a unit of heredity composed of DNA occupying a fixed position on a chromosome and transmitted from parent to offspring during reproduction. [C20: from G *Gen*, shortened from *Pangen*; see PAN-, -GEN]

-gene *suffix forming nouns.* a variant of **-gen**.

genealogy (ˌdʒiːnɪˈælədʒɪ) *n, pl* **genealogies. 1** the direct descent of an individual or group from an ancestor. **2** the study of the evolutionary development of animals and plants from earlier forms. **3** a chart showing the relationships and descent of an individual, group, etc. [C13: from OF, from LL, from Gk, from *genea* race] ▶ **genealogical** (ˌdʒiːnɪəˈlɒdʒɪkˀl) *adj* ▶ ˌ**geneaˈlogically** *adv* ▶ ˌ**geneˈalogist** *n*

gene bank *n Bot.* a collection of seeds, plants, tissue cultures, etc., of potentially useful species, esp. species containing genes of significance to the breeding of crops.

gene clone *n* See **clone** (sense 2).

genecology (ˌdʒiːnɪˈkɒlədʒɪ) *n* the study of the gene frequency of a species in relation to its population distribution within a particular environment.

gene library *n* a collection of gene clones that represents the genetic material of an organism: used in genetic engineering.

gene pool *n* the total of all the genes and their alleles in a population of a plant or animal species.

genera (ˈdʒɛnərə) *n* a plural of **genus.**

general (ˈdʒɛnərəl, ˈdʒɛnrəl) *adj* **1** common; widespread. **2** of, applying to, or participated in by all or most of the members of a group, category, or community. **3** relating to various branches of an activity, profession, etc.; not specialized: *general office work.* **4** including various or miscellaneous items: *general knowledge; a general store.* **5** not specific as to detail; overall: *a general description.* **6** not definite; vague: *the general idea.* **7** applicable or true in most cases; usual. **8** (*prenominal or immediately postpositive*) having superior or extended authority or rank: *general manager; consul general.* ♦ *n* **9** an officer of a rank senior to lieutenant general, esp. one who commands a large military formation. **10** any person acting as a leader and applying strategy or tactics. **11** a general condition or principle: opposed to *particular.* **12** a title for the head of a religious order, congregation, etc. **13** *Arch.* the people; public. **14 in general.** generally; mostly or usually. [C13: from L *generālis* of a particular kind, from *genus* kind]

general anaesthetic *n* See **anaesthesia.**

General Assembly *n* **1** the deliberative assembly of the United Nations. Abbrev.: **GA. 2** *NZ.* an older name for **parliament. 3** the supreme governing body of certain religious denominations, esp. of the Presbyterian Church.

general average *n Insurance.* loss or damage to a ship or its cargo that is shared among the shipowners and all the cargo owners. Abbrev.: **GA.** Cf. **particular average.**

General Certificate of Education *n* See **GCE.**

General Certificate of Secondary Education *n* See **GCSE.**

general election *n* **1** an election in which representatives are chosen in all constituencies of a state. **2** *US.* a final election from which successful candidates are sent to a legislative body. **3** *US & Canad.* a national, state, or provincial election.

generalissimo (ˌdʒɛnərəˈlɪsɪˌməʊ, ˌdʒɛnrə-) *n, pl* **generalissimos.** a supreme commander of combined military, naval, and air forces. [C17: from It., sup. of *generale* GENERAL]

generality (ˌdʒɛnəˈrælɪtɪ) *n, pl* **generalities. 1** a principle or observation having general application. **2** the state or quality of being general. **3** *Arch.* the majority.

generalization *or* **generalisation** (ˌdʒɛnrəlaɪˈzeɪʃən) *n* **1** a principle, theory, etc., with general application. **2** the act or an instance of generalizing. **3** *Logic.* the derivation of a general statement from a particular one, formally by prefixing a quantifier and replacing a subject

term by a bound variable. If the quantifier is universal (**universal generalization**) the argument is not in general valid; if it is existential (**existential generalization**) it is valid.

generalize *or* **generalise** (ˈdʒɛnrəˌlaɪz) *vb* **generalizes, generalizing, generalized** *or* **generalises, generalising, generalised. 1** to form (general principles or conclusions) from (detailed facts, experience, etc.); create. **2** (*intr*) to think or speak in generalities, esp. in a prejudiced way. **3** (*tr; usually passive*) to cause to become widely used or known.

generally (ˈdʒɛnrəlɪ) *adv* **1** usually; as a rule. **2** commonly or widely. **3** without reference to specific details or facts; broadly.

general practitioner *n* a physician who does not specialize but has a medical practice (**general practice**) in which he treats all illnesses. Informal name: **family doctor.** Abbrev.: **GP.**

general-purpose *adj* having a range of uses; not restricted to one function.

generalship (ˈdʒɛnrəlˌʃɪp) *n* **1** the art or duties of exercising command of a major military formation or formations. **2** tactical or administrative skill.

general staff *n* officers assigned to advise commanders in the planning and execution of military operations.

general strike *n* a strike by all or most of the workers of a country, province, city, etc.

General Synod *n* the governing body, under Parliament, of the Church of England, made up of the bishops and elected clerical and lay representatives.

generate (ˈdʒɛnəˌreɪt) *vb* **generates, generating, generated.** (*mainly tr*) **1** to produce or bring into being; create. **2** (*also intr*) to produce (electricity). **3** to produce (a substance) by a chemical process. **4** *Maths, linguistics.* to provide a precise criterion for membership in (a set). **5** *Geom.* to trace or form by moving a point, line, or plane in a specific way: *circular motion of a line generates a cylinder.* [C16: from L *generāre* to beget, from *genus* kind] ▶ ˈ**generable** *adj*

generation (ˌdʒɛnəˈreɪʃən) *n* **1** the act or process of bringing into being; production or reproduction, esp. of offspring. **2** a successive stage in natural descent of people or animals or the individuals produced at each stage. **3** the average time between two such generations of a species: about 35 years for humans. **4** all the people of approximately the same age, esp. when considered as sharing certain attitudes, etc. **5** production of electricity, heat, etc. **6** (*modifier, in combination*) **6a** belonging to a generation specified as having been born in or as having parents, grandparents, etc., born in a given country: *a third-generation American.* **6b** belonging to a specified stage of development in manufacture: *a second-generation computer.*

generation gap *n* the years separating one generation from the next, esp. when regarded as representing the difference in outlook and the lack of understanding between them.

Generation X *n* members of the generation of people born between the mid-1960s and the mid-1970s who are highly educated and underemployed, reject consumer culture, and have little hope for the future. [C20: from the novel *Generation X: Tales for an Accelerated Culture* by Douglas Coupland]

generative (ˈdʒɛnərətɪv) *adj* **1** of or relating to the production of offspring, parts, etc. **2** capable of producing or originating.

generative grammar *n* a description of a language in terms of explicit rules that ideally generate all and only the grammatical sentences of the language.

generator (ˈdʒɛnəˌreɪtə) *n* **1** *Physics.* **1a** any device for converting mechanical energy into electrical energy. **1b** a device for producing a voltage electrostatically. **2** an apparatus for producing a gas. **3** a person or thing that generates.

generatrix (ˈdʒɛnəˌreɪtrɪks) *n, pl* **generatrices** (ˈdʒɛnəˌreɪtrɪˌsiːz). a point, line, or plane moved in a specific way to produce a geometric figure.

generic (dʒɪˈnɛrɪk) *adj* **1** applicable or referring to a whole class or group; general. **2** *Biol.* of, relating to, or be-

longing to a genus: *the generic name*. **3** (of a drug, food product, etc.) not having a trademark. [C17: from F; see GENUS]
▸ ge'nerically *adv*

generic advertising *n* advertising designed to promote a class of product rather than a particular brand.

generosity (ˌdʒenə'rɒsɪtɪ) *n, pl* **generosities**. **1** willingness and liberality in giving away one's money, time, etc.; magnanimity. **2** freedom from pettiness in character and mind. **3** a generous act. **4** abundance; plenty.

generous ('dʒenərəs, 'dʒenrəs) *adj* **1** willing and liberal in giving away one's money, time, etc.; munificent. **2** free from pettiness in character and mind. **3** full or plentiful: *a generous portion.* **4** (of wine) rich in alcohol. [C16: via OF from L *generōsus* nobly born, from *genus* race]
▸ 'generously *adv* ▸ 'generousness *n*

genesis ('dʒenɪsɪs) *n, pl* **geneses** (-ˌsiːz). a beginning or origin of anything. [OE: via L from Gk; rel. to Gk *gignesthai* to be born]

Genesis ('dʒenɪsɪs) *n* the first book of the Old Testament recounting the Creation of the world.

-genesis *n combining form*. indicating genesis, development, or generation: *parthenogenesis*. [NL, from L: GENESIS]
▸ **-genetic** or **-genic** *adj combining form*.

genet[1] ('dʒenɪt) or **genette** (dʒɪ'net) *n* **1** an agile catlike mammal of Africa and S Europe, having thick spotted fur and a very long tail. **2** the fur of such an animal. [C15: from OF, from Ar. *jarnayt*]

genet[2] ('dʒenɪt) *n* an obsolete spelling of **jennet**.

Genet ★ (*French* ʒəne) *n* **Jean** (ʒɑ̃). 1910–86, French writer; his novels include *Notre-Dame des Fleurs* (1944) and his plays *Le Balcon* (1956).

gene therapy *n* the replacement or alteration of defective genes in order to prevent the occurrence of such inherited diseases as haemophilia. Effected by genetic engineering techniques, it is still at an early stage of development.

genetic (dʒɪ'netɪk) or **genetical** *adj* of or relating to genetics, genes, or the origin of something. [C19: from GENESIS]
▸ ge'netically *adv*

genetic code *n Biochem.* the order in which the four nitrogenous bases of DNA are arranged in the molecule, which determines the type and amount of protein synthesized in the cell.

genetic counselling *n* the provision of advice for couples with a history of inherited disorders who wish to have children, including the likelihood of having affected children, the course and management of the disorder, etc.

genetic engineering *n* alteration of the DNA of a cell as a means of manufacturing animal proteins, making improvements to plants and animals bred by man, etc.

genetic fingerprint *n* the pattern of DNA unique to each individual, that can be analysed in a sample of blood, saliva, or tissue: used as a means of identification.
▸ **genetic fingerprinting** *n*

genetic map *n* a graphic representation of the order of genes within chromosomes by means of detailed analysis of the DNA. See also **chromosome map**.
▸ **genetic mapping** *n*

genetics (dʒɪ'netɪks) *n* **1** (*functioning as sing*) the study of heredity and variation in organisms. **2** (*functioning as pl*) the genetic features and constitution of a single organism, species, or group.
▸ ge'neticist *n*

Geneva ★ (dʒɪ'niːvə) *n* **1** a city in SW Switzerland, in the Rhône valley on Lake Geneva: centre of Calvinism; headquarters of the International Red Cross (1864), the International Labour Office (1925), the League of Nations (1929–46), the World Health Organization, and the European office of the United Nations; banking centre. Pop.: 172 737 (1995 est.). **2** a canton in SW Switzerland. Capital: Geneva. Pop.: 380 000 (1988 est.). Area: 282 sq. km (109 sq. miles). **3 Lake.** a lake between SW Switzerland and E France: fed and drained by the River

Rhône, it is the largest of the Alpine lakes; the surface is subject to changes of level. Area: 580 sq. km (224 sq. miles). French name: **Lac Léman**. German name: **Genfersee**. ◆ (for senses 1 and 2) French name: **Genève**; German name: **Genf**.

Geneva bands *pl n* a pair of white lawn or linen strips hanging from the front of the neck or collar of some ecclesiastical and academic robes. [C19: after GENEVA, where orig. worn by Swiss Calvinist clergy]

Geneva Convention *n* the international agreement, first formulated in 1864 at Geneva, establishing a code for wartime treatment of the sick or wounded: revised and extended to cover maritime warfare and prisoners of war.

Geneva gown *n* a black gown with wide sleeves worn by Protestant clerics. [C19: after GENEVA; see GENEVA BANDS]

Genevan (dʒɪ'niːvⁿn) or **Genevese** (ˌdʒenə'viːz) *adj* **1** of, relating to, or characteristic of Geneva. **2** of, adhering to, or relating to the teachings of Calvin or the Calvinists. ◆ *n, pl* **Genevans** or **Genevese**. **3** a native or inhabitant of Geneva. **4** a less common name for a **Calvinist**.

Geneva protocol *n* the agreement in 1925 to ban the use of asphyxiating, poisonous, or other gases in war. It does not ban the development or manufacture of such gases.

Genève ★ (ʒənɛv) *n* the French name for **Geneva**.

Geneviève ★ ('dʒenɪˌviːv; *French* ʒənvjev) *n* **Saint**. ?422–?512 A.D., French nun; patron saint of Paris. Feast day: Jan. 3.

Genf ★ (genf) *n* the German name for **Geneva** (senses 1, 2).

Genfersee ★ ('genfərzeː) *n* the German name for (Lake) **Geneva**.

Genghis Khan ★ ('dʒeŋgɪs kɑːn) *n* original name *Temuchin* or *Temujin*. ?1162–1227, Mongol ruler, whose empire stretched from the Black Sea to the Pacific. Also called: **Jinghis Khan, Jenghis Khan**.

genial[1] ('dʒiːnjəl, -nɪəl) *adj* **1** cheerful, easy-going, and warm in manner. **2** pleasantly warm, so as to give life, growth, or health. [C16: from L *geniālis* relating to birth or marriage, from *genius* tutelary deity; see GENIUS]
▸ **geniality** (ˌdʒiːnɪ'ælɪtɪ) *n* ▸ 'genially *adv*

genial[2] (dʒɪ'niːəl) *adj Anat.* of or relating to the chin. [C19: from Gk, from *genus* jaw]

genic ('dʒenɪk) *adj* of or relating to a gene or genes.

-genic *adj combining form*. **1** relating to production or generation: *carcinogenic*. **2** suited to or suitable for: *photogenic*. [from -GEN + -IC]

genie ('dʒiːnɪ) *n* **1** (in fairy tales and stories) a servant who appears by magic and fulfils a person's wishes. **2** another word for **jinni**. [C18: from F, from Ar. *jinni* demon, infl. by L *genius* attendant spirit; see GENIUS]

genista (dʒɪ'nɪstə) *n* any of a genus of leguminous deciduous shrubs, usually having yellow, often fragrant, flowers; broom. [C17: from L]

genital ('dʒenɪtⁿl) *adj* **1** of or relating to the sexual organs or to reproduction. **2** *Psychoanal*. relating to the mature stage of psychosexual development. [C14: from L *genitālis* concerning birth, from *gignere* to beget]

genital herpes *n* a sexually transmitted disease caused by the herpes simplex virus, in which painful blisters occur in the genital region.

genitals ('dʒenɪtⁿlz) or **genitalia** (ˌdʒenɪ'teɪlɪə, -'teɪljə) *pl n* the external sexual organs.

genitive ('dʒenɪtɪv) *Grammar*. ◆ *adj* **1** denoting a case of nouns, pronouns, and adjectives in inflected languages used to indicate a relation of ownership or association. ◆ *n* **2a** the genitive case. **2b** a word or speech element in this case. [C14: from L *genetīvus* relating to birth, from *gignere* to produce]
▸ **genitival** (ˌdʒenɪ'taɪvⁿl) *adj*

genitourinary (ˌdʒenɪtəʊ'jʊərɪnərɪ) *adj* of or relating to both the reproductive and excretory organs; urogenital: *genitourinary medicine*.

genius ('dʒiːnɪəs, -njəs) *n, pl* **geniuses** or (for senses 5, 6)

genii ('dʒiːnɪ,aɪ). **1** a person with exceptional ability, esp. of a highly original kind. **2** such ability. **3** the distinctive spirit of a nation, era, language, etc. **4** a person considered as exerting influence of a certain sort: *an evil genius.* **5** *Roman myth.* **5a** the guiding spirit who attends a person from birth to death. **5b** the guardian spirit of a place. **6** (*usually pl*) *Arabic myth.* a demon; jinn. [C16: from L, from *gignere* to beget]

genizah (gəˈniːzə) *n, pl* **genizahs** *or* **genizoth** (gəˈniːzəθ). *Judaism.* a repository for sacred objects which can no longer be used but which may not be destroyed. [C19: from Heb., lit.: a hiding place]

Genk *or* **Genck** ★ (*Flemish* xɛŋk) *n* a town in NE Belgium, in Limburg province: coal-mining. Pop.: 61 996 (1995 est.).

genoa ('dʒɛnəʊə) *n Yachting.* a large jib sail.

Genoa ★ ('dʒɛnəʊə) *n* a port in NW Italy, capital of Liguria, on the **Gulf of Genoa**: Italy's main port; an independent commercial city with many colonies in the Middle Ages; university (1243); heavy industries. Pop.: 659 754 (1994 est.). Italian name: **Genova.**

genocide ('dʒɛnəʊˌsaɪd) *n* the policy of deliberately killing a nationality or ethnic group. [C20: from Gk *genos* race + -CIDE]
▸ ˌgenoˈcidal *adj*

Genoese (ˌdʒɛnəʊˈiːz) *or* **Genovese** (ˌdʒɛnəˈviːz) *n, pl* **Genoese** *or* **Genovese.** **1** a native or inhabitant of Genoa.
♦ *adj* **2** of or relating to Genoa or its inhabitants.

genome ('dʒɛˌnəʊm) *n* the complete set of heploid chromosomes that an organism passes on to its offspring in its reproductive cells. [C20: from GEN(E) + (CHROMOS)OME]

genotype ('dʒɛnəʊˌtaɪp) *n* **1** the genetic constitution of an organism. **2** a group of organisms with the same genetic constitution.
▸ **genotypic** (ˌdʒɛnəʊˈtɪpɪk) *adj*

-genous *adj combining form.* **1** yielding or generating: *erogenous.* **2** generated by or issuing from: *endogenous.* [from -GEN + -OUS]

Genova ★ ('dʒɛːnova) *n* the Italian name for **Genoa.**

genre ('ʒɒːnrə) *n* **1a** kind, category, or sort, esp. of literary or artistic work. **1b** (*as modifier*): *genre fiction.* **2** a category of painting in which incidents from everyday life are depicted. [C19: from F, from OF *gendre*; see GENDER]

gens (dʒɛnz) *n, pl* **gentes** ('dʒɛntiːz). **1** (in ancient Rome) any of a group of families, having a common name and claiming descent from a common ancestor in the male line. **2** *Anthropol.* a group based on descent in the male line. [C19: from L: race]

Genseric ('gɛnsərɪk, 'dʒɛn-) *or* **Gaiseric** ★ *n* ?390–477 A.D., king of the Vandals (428–77). He seized Roman lands, esp. extensive parts of N Africa, and sacked Rome (455).

gent (dʒɛnt) *n Inf.* short for **gentleman.**

Gent ★ (xɛnt) *n* the Flemish name for **Ghent.**

genteel (dʒɛnˈtiːl) *adj* **1** affectedly proper or refined; excessively polite. **2** respectable, polite, and well-bred. **3** appropriate to polite or fashionable society. [C16: from F *gentil* well-born; see GENTLE]
▸ genˈteelly *adv* ▸ genˈteelness *n*

gentian ('dʒɛnʃən) *n* **1** any plant of the genus *Gentiana*, having blue, yellow, white, or red showy flowers. **2** the bitter-tasting roots of the yellow gentian, which can be used as a tonic. [C14: from L *gentiāna*; ? after *Gentius*, a second-century B.C. Illyrian king, reputedly the first to use it medicinally]

gentian violet *n* a greenish crystalline substance that forms a violet solution in water, used as an indicator, antiseptic, and in the treatment of burns.

Gentile[1] ('dʒɛntaɪl) *n* **1** a person, esp. a Christian, who is not a Jew. **2** a Christian, as contrasted with a Jew. **3** a person who is not a member of one's own church: used esp. by Mormons. **4** a heathen or pagan. ♦ *adj* **5** of or relating to a race or religion that is not Jewish. **6** Christian, as contrasted with Jewish. **7** not being a member of one's own church: used esp. by Mormons. **8** pagan or hea-

then. [C15 *gentil*, from LL *gentīlis*, from L: one belonging to the same tribe]

Gentile[2] ★ (*Italian* dʒenˈtiːle) *n* **Giovanni** (dʒoˈvanni). 1875–1944, Italian Idealist philosopher and Fascist politician: minister of education (1922–24).

Gentile da Fabriano ★ (*Italian* da faˈbrjaːno) *n* original name *Niccolo di Giovanni di Massio*. ?1370–1427, Italian painter. His works include the *Adoration of the Magi* (1423).

gentility (dʒɛnˈtɪlɪtɪ) *n, pl* **gentilities.** **1** respectability and polite good breeding. **2** affected politeness. **3** noble birth or ancestry. **4** people of noble birth. [C14: from OF, from L *gentīlitās* relationship of those belonging to the same tribe or family; see GENS]

gentle ('dʒɛntəl) *adj* **1** having a mild or kindly nature or character. **2** soft or temperate; mild; moderate. **3** gradual: *a gentle slope.* **4** easily controlled; tame. **5** *Arch.* of good breeding; noble: *gentle blood.* **6** *Arch.* gallant; chivalrous. ♦ *vb* **gentles, gentling, gentled.** (*tr*) **7** to tame or subdue (a horse, etc.). **8** to appease or mollify. ♦ *n* **9** a maggot, esp. when used as bait in fishing. [C13: from OF *gentil* noble, from L *gentīlis* belonging to the same family; see GENS]
▸ 'gentleness *n* ▸ 'gently *adv*

gentle breeze *n* a wind of force 3 on the Beaufort scale, blowing at 8-12 mph.

gentlefolk ('dʒɛntəlˌfəʊk) *or* **gentlefolks** *pl n* persons regarded as being of good breeding.

gentleman ('dʒɛntəlmən) *n, pl* **gentlemen.** **1** a man regarded as having qualities of refinement associated with a good family. **2** a man who is cultured, courteous, and well-educated. **3** a polite name for a man. **4** the personal servant of a gentleman (esp. in **gentleman's gentleman**).
▸ 'gentlemanly *adj* ▸ 'gentlemanliness *n*

gentleman-farmer *n, pl* **gentlemen-farmers.** **1** a person who engages in farming but does not depend on it for his living. **2** a person who owns farmland but does not farm it personally.

gentleman's agreement *or* **gentleman's agreement** *n* an understanding or arrangement based on honour and not legally binding.

gentlewoman ('dʒɛntəlˌwʊmən) *n, pl* **gentlewomen.** **1** *Arch.* a woman regarded as being of good family or breeding; lady. **2** (formerly) a woman in personal attendance on a high-ranking lady.

gentrification (ˌdʒɛntrɪfɪˈkeɪʃən) *n Brit.* a process by which middle-class people take up residence in a traditionally working-class area, changing its character. [C20: from *gentrify* (to become GENTRY)]
▸ 'gentriˌfier *n*

gentry ('dʒɛntrɪ) *n* **1** *Brit.* persons just below the nobility in social rank. **2** people of a particular class, esp. one considered to be inferior. [C14: from OF *genterie*, from *gentil* GENTLE]

gents (dʒɛnts) *n* (*functioning as sing*) *Brit. inf.* a men's public lavatory.

genuflect ('dʒɛnjuːˌflɛkt) *vb* (*intr*) **1** to act in a servile or deferential manner. **2** *RC Church.* to bend one or both knees as a sign of reverence. [C17: from Med. L, from L *genu* knee + *flectere* to bend]
▸ ˌgenuˈflection *or* (*esp. Brit.*) ˌgenuˈflexion *n* ▸ 'genuˌflector *n*

genuine ('dʒɛnjuːɪn) *adj* **1** not fake or counterfeit; original; real; authentic. **2** not pretending; frank; sincere. **3** being of authentic or original stock. [C16: from L *genuīnus* inborn, hence (in LL) authentic]
▸ 'genuinely *adv* ▸ 'genuineness *n*

gen up *vb* **gens, genning, genned.** (*adv; often passive;* when *intr,* usually foll. by *on*) *Brit. inf.* to make or become fully conversant (with).

genus ('dʒiːnəs) *n, pl* **genera** *or* **genuses.** **1** *Biol.* any of the taxonomic groups into which a family is divided and which contains one or more species. **2** *Logic.* a class of objects or individuals that can be divided into two or more groups or species. **3** a class, group, etc., with common characteristics. [C16: from L: race]

★ people and places

-geny *n combining form.* origin or manner of development: *phylogeny.* [from Gk, from *-genēs* born]
▶ **-genic** *adj combining form.*

geo- *combining form.* indicating earth: *geomorphology.* [from Gk, from *gē* earth]

geocentric (ˌdʒiːəʊˈsɛntrɪk) *adj* **1** having the earth at its centre. **2** measured as from the centre of the earth.
▶ ˌ**geoˈcentrically** *adv*

geochronology (ˌdʒiːəʊkrəˈnɒlədʒɪ) *n* the branch of geology concerned with ordering and dating events in the earth's history.
▶ **geochronological** (ˌdʒiːəʊˌkrɒnəˈlɒdʒɪkᵊl) *adj*

geode ('dʒiːəʊd) *n* a cavity, usually lined with crystals, within a rock mass or nodule. [C17: from L *geōdēs* a precious stone, from Gk: earthlike; see GEO-, -ODE[1]]
▶ **geodic** (dʒɪˈɒdɪk) *adj*

geodesic (ˌdʒiːəʊˈdɛsɪk, -ˈdiː-) *adj* **1** Also: **geodetic.** relating to the geometry of curved surfaces. ◆ *n* **2** Also called: **geodesic line.** the shortest line between two points on a curved surface.

geodesic dome *n* a light structural framework arranged as a set of polygons in the form of a shell.

geodesy (dʒɪˈɒdɪsɪ) *n* the branch of science concerned with determining the exact position of geographical points and the shape and size of the earth. [C16: from F, from Gk *geōdaisia,* from GEO- + *daiein* to divide]
▶ **geˈodesist** *n*

geodetic (ˌdʒiːəʊˈdɛtɪk) *adj* **1** of or relating to geodesy. **2** another word for **geodesic.**
▶ ˌ**geoˈdetically** *adv*

Geoffrey of Monmouth ★ ('dʒɛfrɪ) *n* ?1100–54, Welsh bishop and chronicler; author of *Historia Regum Britanniae,* the chief source of Arthurian legends.

geog. *abbrev. for:* **1** geographer. **2** geographic(al). **3** geography.

geographical mile *n* a former name for **nautical mile.**

geography (dʒɪˈɒɡrəfɪ) *n, pl* **geographies. 1** the study of the natural features of the earth's surface, including topography, climate, soil, vegetation, etc., and man's response to them. **2** the natural features of a region.
▶ **geˈographer** *n* ▶ **geographical** (ˌdʒɪəˈɡræfɪkᵊl) *or* ˌ**geoˈgraphic** *adj* ▶ ˌ**geoˈgraphically** *adv*

geoid ('dʒiːɔɪd) *n* **1** a hypothetical surface that corresponds to mean sea level and extends under the continents. **2** the shape of the earth.

geol. *abbrev. for:* **1** geologic(al). **2** geologist. **3** geology.

geology (dʒɪˈɒlədʒɪ) *n* **1** the scientific study of the origin, structure, and composition of the earth. **2** the geological features of a district or country.
▶ **geological** (ˌdʒɪəˈlɒdʒɪkᵊl) *or* ˌ**geoˈlogic** *adj* ▶ ˌ**geoˈlogically** *adv* ▶ **geˈologist** *n*

geom. *abbrev. for:* **1** geometric(al). **2** geometry.

geomagnetism (ˌdʒiːəʊˈmæɡnɪˌtɪzəm) *n* **1** the magnetic field of the earth. **2** the branch of physics concerned with this.
▶ **geomagnetic** (ˌdʒiːəʊmæɡˈnɛtɪk) *adj*

geometric (ˌdʒɪəˈmɛtrɪk) *or* **geometrical** *adj* **1** of, relating to, or following the methods and principles of geometry. **2** consisting of, formed by, or characterized by points, lines, curves, or surfaces. **3** (of design or ornamentation) composed predominantly of simple geometric forms, such as circles, triangles, etc.
▶ ˌ**geoˈmetrically** *adv*

geometric mean *n* the average value of a set of *n* integers, terms, or quantities, expressed as the *n*th root of their product.

geometric progression *n* **1** a sequence of numbers, each of which differs from the succeeding one by a constant ratio, as 1, 2, 4, 8, … Cf. **arithmetic progression. 2** geometric series. such numbers written as a sum.

geometrid (dʒɪˈɒmɪtrɪd) *n* any of a family of moths, the larvae of which are called measuring worms, inchworms, or loopers. [C19: from NL, from L, from Gk *geometrēs* land measurer, from the looping gait of the larvae]

geometry (dʒɪˈɒmɪtrɪ) *n* **1** the branch of mathematics

concerned with the properties, relationships, and measurement of points, lines, curves, and surfaces. **2** a shape, configuration, or arrangement. [C14: from L, from Gk, from *geōmetrein* to measure the land]
▶ **geˌomeˈtrician** *n*

geomorphology (ˌdʒiːəʊmɔːˈfɒlədʒɪ) *n* the branch of geology that is concerned with the structure, origin, and development of the topographical features of the earth's crust.
▶ **geomorphological** (ˌdʒiːəʊˌmɔːfəˈlɒdʒɪkᵊl) *or* ˌ**geoˌmorphoˈlogic** *adj*

geophysics (ˌdʒiːəʊˈfɪzɪks) *n* (*functioning as sing*) the study of the earth's physical properties and of the physical processes acting upon, above, and within the earth. It includes seismology, meteorology, and oceanography.
▶ ˌ**geoˈphysical** *adj* ▶ ˌ**geoˈphysicist** *n*

geopolitics (ˌdʒiːəʊˈpɒlɪtɪks) *n* **1** (*functioning as sing*) the study of the effect of geographical factors on politics. **2** (*functioning as pl*) the combination of geographical and political factors affecting a country or area. **3** (*functioning as pl*) politics as they affect the whole world; global politics.
▶ **geopolitical** (ˌdʒiːəʊpəˈlɪtɪkᵊl) *adj*

Geordie ('dʒɔːdɪ) *Brit.* ◆ *n* **1** a person who comes from or lives in Tyneside. **2** the dialect spoken by these people. ◆ *adj* **3** of or relating to these people or their dialect. [C19: a dim. of *George*]

George ★ (dʒɔːdʒ) *n* **1** David Lloyd. See **Lloyd George. 2** Henry. 1839–97, US economist: advocated a single tax on land values. **3** Saint. died ?303 A.D., Christian martyr, the patron saint of England; the hero of a legend in which he slew a dragon. Feast day: April 23.

George I ★ *n* 1660–1727, first Hanoverian king of Great Britain and Ireland (1714–27) and elector of Hanover (1698–1727).

George II ★ *n* **1** 1683–1760, king of Great Britain and Ireland and elector of Hanover (1727–60); son of George I. His victory over the French at Dettingen (1743) in the War of the Austrian Succession was the last appearance on a battlefield by a British king. **2** 1890–1947, king of Greece (1922–24; 1935–47). He was overthrown by the republicans (1924) and exiled during the German occupation of Greece (1941–45).

George III ★ *n* 1738–1820, king of Great Britain and Ireland (1760–1820) and of Hanover (1814–20). During his reign the American colonies were lost. He became insane in 1811, and his son acted as regent for the rest of the reign.

George IV ★ *n* 1762–1830, king of Great Britain and Ireland and also of Hanover (1820–30); regent (1811–20).

George V ★ *n* 1865–1936, king of Great Britain and Northern Ireland and emperor of India (1910–36).

George VI ★ *n* 1895–1952, king of Great Britain and Northern Ireland (1936–52) and emperor of India (1936–47). The second son of George V, he succeeded to the throne after the abdication of his brother, Edward VIII.

George Cross *n* a British award for bravery, esp. of civilians. Abbrev.: **GC.**

Georgetown ★ (ˈdʒɔːdʒˌtaʊn) *n* **1** the capital and chief port of Guyana, at the mouth of the Demerara River: became capital of the Dutch colonies of Essequibo and Demerara in 1784; seat of the University of Guyana. Pop.: 248 500 (1992 est.). Former name (until 1812): **Stabroek. 2** the capital of the Cayman Islands: a port on Grand Cayman Island. Pop.: 16 600 (1995 est.).

George Town ★ *n* a port in NW Malaysia, capital of Penang state, in NE Penang Island: the first chartered city of the Malayan federation. Pop.: 219 376 (1991). Also called: **Penang.**

georgette *or* **georgette crepe** (dʒɔːˈdʒɛt) *n* a thin silk or cotton crepe fabric. [C20: from Mme *Georgette,* a F modiste]

Georgia ★ ('dʒɔːdʒə) *n* **1** a republic in NW Asia, on the Black Sea: an independent kingdom during the middle ages, it was divided by Turkey and Persia in 1555; became part of Russia in 1918 and a separate Soviet

---

★ people and places

republic in 1936; its independence was recognized internationally in 1992. It is rich in minerals and has hydroelectric resources. Official language: Georgian. Religion: believers are mainly Christian or Muslim. Currency: lari. Capital: Tbilisi. Pop.: 5 377 000 (1997). Area: 69 493 sq. km (26 831 sq. miles). **2** a state of the southeastern US, on the Atlantic: consists of coastal plains with forests and swamps, rising to the Cumberland Plateau and the Appalachians in the northwest. Capital: Atlanta. Pop.: 7 353 225 (1996 est.). Area: 152 489 sq. km (58 876 sq. miles). Abbrevs.: **Ga.** or (with zip code) **GA**.

Georgian ('dʒɔːdʒjən) *adj* **1** of or relating to any or all of the four kings who ruled Great Britain from 1714 to 1830, or to their reigns. **2** of or relating to George V of Great Britain or his reign (1910–36): *the Georgian poets*. **3** of or relating to Georgia, its people, or their language. **4** of or relating to the American State of Georgia or its inhabitants. **5** (of furniture, architecture, etc.) in or imitative of the style prevalent in Britain during the 18th century. ♦ *n* **6** the official language of Georgia, belonging to the South Caucasian family. **7** a native or inhabitant of Georgia. **8** a native or inhabitant of the American State of Georgia.

Georgian Bay ★ *n* a bay in S central Canada, in Ontario, containing many small islands: the NE part of Lake Huron. Area: 15 000 sq. km (5800 sq. miles).

geostatics (ˌdʒiːəʊˈstætɪks) *n* (*functioning as sing*) the branch of physics concerned with the statics of rigid bodies, esp. the balance of forces within the earth.

geostationary (ˌdʒiːəʊˈsteɪʃənərɪ) *adj* (of a satellite, etc.) in a circular equatorial orbit in which it circles the earth once in 24 hours so that it appears stationary in relation to the earth's surface.

geostrophic (ˌdʒiːəʊˈstrɒfɪk) *adj* of, relating to, or caused by the force produced by the rotation of the earth: *geostrophic wind*.

geosynchronous (ˌdʒiːəʊˈsɪŋkrənəs) *n* (of a satellite) in an orbit in which it circles the earth once in 24 hours.

geosyncline (ˌdʒiːəʊˈsɪŋklaɪn) *n* a broad elongated depression in the earth's crust.

geotextile (ˌdʒiːəʊˈtɛkstaɪl) *n* any strong synthetic fabric used in civil engineering, as to retain an embankment.

geothermal (ˌdʒiːəʊˈθɜːməl) *or* **geothermic** *adj* of or relating to the heat in the interior of the earth.

geotropism (dʒɪˈɒtrəˌpɪzəm) *n* the response of a plant part to the stimulus of gravity. Plant stems, which grow upwards irrespective of the position in which they are placed, show **negative geotropism**.
  ▶ **geotropic** (ˌdʒiːəʊˈtrɒpɪk) *adj*

Ger. *abbrev. for:* **1** German. **2** Germany.

Gera ★ (*German* 'geːra) *n* an industrial city in S Germany, in Thuringia. Pop.: 126 035 (1995 est.).

geranium (dʒɪˈreɪnɪəm) *n* **1** a cultivated plant of the genus *Pelargonium* having scarlet, pink, or white showy flowers. See also **pelargonium.** **2** any plant such as cranesbill and herb Robert, having divided leaves and pink or purplish flowers. [C16: from L: cranesbill, from Gk, from *geranos* CRANE]

Gérard ★ (*French* ʒerar) *n* François (**Pascal Simon**) (frāswa), Baron. 1770–1837, French painter, court painter to Napoleon I and Louis XVIII.

gerbera ('dʒɜːbərə) *n* a genus of African or Asian plants belonging to the composite family, esp. the Transvaal daisy. [C19: from NL, after T. *Gerber* (died 1743), G naturalist]

gerbil *or* **gerbille** ('dʒɜːbɪl) *n* a burrowing rodent inhabiting hot dry regions of Asia and Africa. [C19: from F, from NL *gerbillus* a little JERBOA]

gerfalcon ('dʒɜːˌfɔːlkən, -ˌfɔːkən) *n* a variant spelling of **gyrfalcon.**

geriatric (ˌdʒɛrɪˈætrɪk) *adj* **1** of or relating to geriatrics or to elderly people. **2** *Inf.* old, decrepit, or useless. ♦ *n* **3** an elderly person. [C20: from Gk *gēras* old age + IATRIC]

geriatrics (ˌdʒɛrɪˈætrɪks) *n* (*functioning as sing*) the branch of medical science concerned with the diagnosis and treatment of diseases affecting elderly people.
  ▶ ˌgeriaˈtrician *n*

Géricault ★ (*French* ʒeriko) *n* (**Jean Louis André**) **Théodore** (teɔdɔr). 1791–1824, French romantic painter.

Gerlachovka ★ (*Czech* 'gɛrlaxɔfka) *n* a mountain in N Slovakia, in the Tatra Mountains: the highest peak of the Carpathian Mountains. Height: 2663 m (8737 ft).

germ (dʒɜːm) *n* **1** a microorganism, esp. one that produces disease. **2** (*often pl*) the rudimentary or initial form of something: *the germs of revolution.* **3** a simple structure that is capable of developing into a complete organism. [C17: from F, from L *germen* sprout, seed]

german ('dʒɜːmən) *adj* **1** (used in combination) **1a** having the same parents as oneself: *a brother-german.* **1b** having a parent that is a brother or sister of either of one's own parents: *cousin-german.* **2** a less common word for **germane.** [C14: via OF, from L *germānus* of the same race, from *germen* sprout, offshoot]

German ('dʒɜːmən) *n* **1** the official language of Germany and Austria and one of the official languages of Switzerland. **2** a native, inhabitant, or citizen of Germany. **3** a person whose native language is German. ♦ *adj* **4** denoting, relating to, or using the German language. **5** relating to, denoting, or characteristic of any German state or its people.

German Democratic Republic ★ *n* (formerly) the official name of **East Germany.** Abbrevs.: **GDR, DDR.**

germander (dʒɜːˈmændə) *n* any of several plants of Europe, having two-lipped flowers with a very small upper lip. [C15: from Med. L, ult. from Gk *khamai* on the ground + *drus* oak tree]

germane (dʒɜːˈmeɪn) *adj* (*postpositive;* usually foll. by *to*) related (to the topic being considered); akin; relevant. [var. of GERMAN]
  ▶ **ger'manely** *adv* ▶ **ger'maneness** *n*

German East Africa ★ *n* a former German territory in E Africa, consisting of Tanganyika and Ruanda-Urundi: divided in 1919 between Great Britain and Belgium; now in Tanzania, Rwanda, and Burundi.

Germanic (dʒɜːˈmænɪk) *n* **1** a branch of the Indo-European family of languages that includes English, Dutch, German, the Scandinavian languages, and Gothic. Abbrev.: **Gmc. 2** Also called: **Proto-Germanic.** the unrecorded language from which all of these languages developed. ♦ *adj* **3** of, denoting, or relating to this group of languages. **4** of, relating to, or characteristic of the German language or any people that speaks a Germanic language. **5** (formerly) of the German people.

Germanicus Caesar ★ (dʒɜːˈmænɪkəs) *n* 15 B.C.–19 A.D., Roman general; nephew of the emperor Tiberius; waged decisive campaigns against the Germans (14–16).

germanium (dʒɜːˈmeɪnɪəm) *n* a brittle crystalline grey element that is a semiconducting metalloid: used in transistors, and to strengthen alloys. Symbol: Ge; atomic no.: 32; atomic wt.: 72.59. [C19: NL, after GERMANY]

German measles *n* (*functioning as sing*) a nontechnical name for **rubella.**

German Ocean ★ *n* a former name for the **North Sea.**

German shepherd dog *n* another name for **Alsatian.**

German silver *n* another name for **nickel silver.**

Germany ★ ('dʒɜːmənɪ) *n* a country in central Europe: in the Middle Ages the centre of the Holy Roman Empire; dissolved into numerous principalities; united under the leadership of Prussia in 1871 after the Franco-Prussian War; became a republic with reduced size in 1919 after being defeated in World War I; under the dictatorship of Hitler from 1933 to 1945; defeated in World War II and divided by the Allied Powers into four zones, which became established as East and West Germany in the late 1940s; reunified in 1990: a member of the European Union. It is flat and low-lying in the north with plateaus and uplands (including the Black Forest and Bavarian Alps) in the centre and south. Official language: German. Religion: Christian with a Protestant majority. Currency: Deutschmark and euro. Capital: Berlin, some government offices have not yet been transferred from Bonn. Pop.: 82 143 000 (1997). Area: 357 041 sq. km (137 825 sq. miles). German name: **Deutschland.** Official name: **Federal Republic of Germany.** Related adj: **Teutonic.**

★ people and places

germ cell *n* a sexual reproductive cell.

germicide ('dʒɜːmɪ,saɪd) *n* any substance that kills germs.
▸ ,germi'cidal *adj*

germinal ('dʒɜːmɪn°l) *adj* **1** of, relating to, or like germs or a germ cell. **2** of or in the earliest stage of development. [C19: from NL, from L *germen* bud; see GERM]
▸ 'germinally *adv*

germinate ('dʒɜːmɪ,neɪt) *vb* **germinates, germinating, germinated. 1** to cause (seeds or spores) to sprout or (of seeds or spores) to sprout. **2** to grow or cause to grow; develop. **3** to come or bring into existence; originate: *the idea germinated with me.* [C17: from L *germināre* to sprout; see GERM]
▸ 'germinative *adj* ▸ ,germi'nation *n* ▸ 'germi,nator *n*

Germiston ★ ('dʒɜːmɪstən) *n* a city in South Africa, southeast of Johannesburg: industrial centre, with the world's largest gold refinery, serving the Witwatersrand mines. Pop.: 134 005 (1991).

germ plasm *n* **a** the part of a germ cell that contains hereditary material. **b** the germ cells collectively.

germ warfare *n* the military use of disease-spreading bacteria against an enemy.

Gerona ★ (*Spanish* xe'rona) *n* a city in NE Spain: city walls and 14th-century cathedral; often besieged, in particular by the French (1809). Pop.: 67 578 (1986). Ancient name: **Gerunda** (dʒə'ruːndə).

Geronimo ★ (dʒə'rɒnɪ,məu) *n* **1** 1829–1909, Apache Indian chieftain: led a campaign against the White settlers until his capture in 1886. **2** *US.* a shout given by paratroopers as they jump into battle.

gerontology (,dʒɛrɒn'tɒlədʒɪ) *n* the scientific study of ageing and the problems associated with elderly people.
▸ **gerontological** (,dʒɛrɒntə'lɒdʒɪk°l) *adj* ▸ ,geron'tologist *n*

gerous *adj combining form.* bearing or producing: *armigerous.* [from L *-ger* bearing + -OUS]

gerrymander ('dʒɛrɪ,mændə) *vb* **1** to divide the constituencies of (a voting area) so as to give one party an unfair advantage. **2** to manipulate or adapt to one's advantage. ◆ *n* **3** an act or result of gerrymandering. [C19: from Elbridge *Gerry*, US politician + (SALA)MANDER; from the salamander-like outline of an electoral district reshaped (1812) for political purposes while Gerry was governor of Massachusetts]

Gers ★ (*French* ʒɛr) *n* a department of SW France, in Midi-Pyrénées region. Capital: Auch. Pop.: 172 622 (1994 est.). Area: 6291 sq. km (2453 sq. miles).

Gershwin ★ ('gɜːʃwɪn) *n* **1** **George,** original name *Jacob Gershvin.* 1898–1937, US composer: incorporated jazz into such works as *Rhapsody in Blue* (1924) and the opera *Porgy and Bess* (1935). **2** his brother, **Ira,** original name *Israel Gershwin.* 1896–1983, US song lyricist.

gerund ('dʒɛrənd) *n* a noun formed from a verb, ending in *-ing,* denoting an action or state: *the living is easy.* [C16: from LL, from L *gerundum* something to be carried on, from *gerere* to wage]
▸ **gerundial** (dʒɪ'rʌndɪəl) *adj*

gerundive (dʒɪ'rʌndɪv) *n* **1** (in Latin grammar) an adjective formed from a verb, expressing the desirability, etc., of the activity denoted by the verb. ◆ *adj* **2** of or relating to the gerund or gerundive. [C17: from LL, from *gerundium* GERUND]
▸ **gerundival** (,dʒɛrən'daɪv°l) *adj*

Geryon ★ ('gɛrɪən) *n Greek myth.* a winged monster with three bodies joined at the waist, killed by Hercules, who stole the monster's cattle as his tenth labour.

gesso ('dʒɛsəu) *n* **1** a white ground of plaster and size, used to prepare panels or canvas for painting or gilding. **2** any white substance, esp. plaster of Paris, that forms a ground when mixed with water. [C16: from It.: chalk, GYPSUM]

gest or **geste** (dʒɛst) *n Arch.* **1** a notable deed or exploit. **2** a tale of adventure or romance, esp. in verse. [C14: from OF, from L *gesta* deeds, from *gerere* to carry out]

Gestalt psychology (gə'ʃtælt) *n* a system of thought that regards all mental phenomena as being arranged in patterns or structures (**gestalts**) perceived as a whole and not merely as the sum of their parts. [C20: from G *Gestalt* form]

Gestapo (gɛ'stɑːpəʊ) *n* the secret state police in Nazi Germany. [from G *Ge(heime) Sta(ats)po(lizei),* lit.: secret state police]

gestate ('dʒɛsteɪt) *vb* **gestates, gestating, gestated. 1** (*tr*) to carry (developing young) in the uterus during pregnancy. **2** (*tr*) to develop (a plan or idea) in the mind. **3** (*intr*) to be in the process of gestating. [C19: from L p.p. of *gestare,* from *gerere* to bear]
▸ **ges'tation** *n*

gesticulate (dʒɛ'stɪkjʊ,leɪt) *vb* **gesticulates, gesticulating, gesticulated.** to express by or make gestures. [C17: from L, from *gesticulus* (unattested except in LL) gesture, from *gerere* to bear, conduct]
▸ **ge,sticu'lation** *n* ▸ **ge'sticulative** *adj* ▸ **ges'ticu,lator** *n* ▸ **ges'ticulatory** *adj*

gesture ('dʒɛstʃə) *n* **1** a motion of the hands, head, or body to express or emphasize an idea or emotion. **2** something said or done as a formality or as an indication of intention. ◆ *vb* **gestures, gesturing, gestured. 3** to express by or make gestures; gesticulate. [C15: from Med. L *gestūra* bearing, from L *gestus,* p.p. of *gerere* to bear]
▸ 'gestural *adj*

get (gɛt) *vb* **gets, getting, got; got** or *esp. US* **gotten.** (*mainly tr*) **1** to come into possession of; receive or earn. **2** to bring or fetch. **3** to contract or be affected by: *he got a chill.* **4** to capture or seize: *the police got him.* **5** (*also intr*) to become or cause to become or act as specified: *to get one's hair cut; get wet.* **6** (*intr;* foll. by a preposition or adverbial particle) to succeed in going, coming, leaving, etc.: *get off the bus.* **7** (takes an infinitive) to manage or contrive: *how did you get to be captain?* **8** to make ready or prepare: *to get a meal.* **9** to hear, notice, or understand: *I didn't get your meaning.* **10** to learn or master by study. **11** (*intr;* often foll. by *to*) to come (to) or arrive (at): *we got home safely; to get to London.* **12** to catch or enter: *to get a train.* **13** to induce or persuade: *get him to leave.* **14** to reach by calculation: *add 2 and 2 and you will get 4.* **15** to receive (a broadcast signal). **16** to communicate with (a person or place), as by telephone. **17** (*also intr;* foll. by *to*) *Inf.* to have an emotional effect (on): *that music really gets me.* **18** *Inf.* to annoy or irritate: *her voice gets me.* **19** *Inf.* to bring a person into a difficult position from which he cannot escape. **20** *Inf.* to puzzle; baffle. **21** *Inf.* to hit: *the blow got him in the back.* **22** *Inf.* to be revenged on, esp. by killing. **23** *Inf.* to have the better of: *your extravagant habits will get you in the end.* **24** (*intr;* foll. by present participle) *Inf.* to begin: *get moving.* **25** (used as a command) *Inf.* go! leave now! **26** *Arch.* to beget or conceive. **27 get with child.** *Arch.* to make pregnant. ◆ *n* **28** *Rare.* the act of begetting. **29** *Rare.* something begotten; offspring. **30** *Brit. sl.* a variant of **git.** ◆ See also **get about, get across,** etc. [OE *gietan*]
▸ 'getable or 'gettable *adj* ▸ 'getter *n*

> **USAGE NOTE** The use of *off* after *get* as in *I got this chair off an antique dealer* is acceptable in conversation, but should not be used in formal writing.

get about or **around** *vb* (*intr, adv*) **1** to move around, as when recovering from an illness. **2** to be socially active. **3** (of news, rumour, etc.) to become known; spread.

get across *vb* **1** to cross or cause to cross. **2** (*adv*) to be or cause to be understood.

get at *vb* (*intr, prep*) **1** to gain access to. **2** to mean or intend: *what are you getting at?* **3** to irritate or annoy persistently; criticize: *she is always getting at him.* **4** to influence or seek to influence, esp. illegally by bribery, intimidation, etc.: *someone had got at the witness before the trial.*

get away *vb* (*adv, mainly intr*) **1** to make an escape; leave. **2** to make a start. **3 get away with.** **3a** to steal and escape with (money, goods, etc.). **3b** to do (something wrong, illegal, etc.) without being discovered or punished. ◆ *interj* **4** an exclamation indicating mild disbelief. ◆ *n* **getaway. 5** the act of escaping, esp. by criminals. **6** a start or acceleration. **7** a short holiday away from home. **8** (*modifier*) used for escaping: *a getaway car.*

get back *vb* (*adv*) **1** (*tr*) to recover or retrieve. **2** (*intr*; often foll. by *to*) to return, esp. to a former position or activity. **3** (*intr*; foll. by *at*) to retaliate (against); wreak vengeance (on). **4 get one's own back.** *Inf.* to obtain one's revenge.

get by *vb* **1** to pass; go past or overtake. **2** (*intr, adv*) *Inf.* to manage, esp. in spite of difficulties. **3** (*intr*) to be accepted or permitted: *that book will never get by the authorities.*

Gethsemane ★ (gεθ'sεmənɪ) *n New Testament.* the garden in Jerusalem where Christ was betrayed on the night before his Crucifixion (Matthew 26:36–56).

get in *vb* (*mainly adv*) **1** (*intr*) to enter a car, train, etc. **2** (*intr*) to arrive, esp. at one's home or place of work. **3** (*tr*) to bring in or inside: *get the milk in.* **4** (*tr*) to insert or slip in: *he got his suggestion in before anyone else.* **5** (*tr*) to gather or collect (crops, debts, etc.). **6** to be elected or cause to be elected. **7** (*intr*) to obtain a place at university, college, etc. **8** (foll. by *on*) to join or cause to join (an activity or organization).

get off *vb* **1** (*intr, adv*) to escape the consequences of an action: *he got off very lightly.* **2** (*adv*) to be or cause to be acquitted: *a good lawyer got him off.* **3** (*adv*) to depart or cause to depart: *to get the children off to school.* **4** (*intr*) to descend (from a bus, train, etc.); dismount: *she got off at the terminus.* **5** to move or cause to move to a distance (from): *get off the field.* **6** (*tr, adv*) to remove; take off: *get your coat off.* **7** (*adv*) to go or send to sleep. **8** (*adv*) to send (letters) or (of letters) to be sent. **9 get off with.** *Brit. inf.* to establish an amorous or sexual relationship (with).

get on *vb* (*mainly adv*) **1** Also (*when prep*): **get onto.** to board or cause or help to board (a bus, train, etc.). **2** (*tr*) to dress in (clothes as specified). **3** (*intr*) to grow late or (of time) to elapse: *it's getting on and I must go.* **4** (*intr*) (of a person) to grow old. **5** (*intr*; foll. by *for*) to approach (a time, age, amount, etc.): *she is getting on for seventy.* **6** (*intr*) to make progress, manage, or fare: *how did you get on in your exam?* **7** (*intr*; foll. by *with*) to establish a friendly relationship: *he gets on well with other people.* **8** (*intr*; foll. by *with*) to continue to do: *get on with your homework!*

get out *vb* (*adv*) **1** to leave or escape or cause to leave or escape: used in the imperative when dismissing a person. **2** to make or become known; publish or be published. **3** (*tr*) to express with difficulty. **4** (*tr*; often foll. by *of*) to extract (information or money) (from a person): *to get a confession out of a criminal.* **5** (*tr*) to gain or receive something, esp. something of significance or value. **6** (foll. by *of*) to avoid or cause to avoid: *she always gets out of swimming.* **7** *Cricket.* to dismiss or be dismissed.

get over *vb* **1** to cross or surmount (something). **2** (*intr, prep*) to recover from (an illness, shock, etc.). **3** (*intr, prep*) to overcome or master (a problem). **4** (*intr, prep*) to appreciate fully: *I just can't get over seeing you again.* **5** (*tr, adv*) to communicate effectively. **6** (*tr, adv*; sometimes foll. by *with*) to bring (something necessary but unpleasant) to an end: *let's get this job over with quickly.*

get round *or* **around** *vb* (*intr*) **1** (*prep*) to circumvent or overcome. **2** (*prep*) *Inf.* to have one's way with; cajole: *that girl can get round anyone.* **3** (*prep*) to evade (a law or rules). **4** (*adv*; foll. by *to*) to reach or come to at length: *I'll get round to that job in an hour.*

get through *vb* **1** to succeed or cause or help to succeed in an examination, test, etc. **2** to bring or come to a destination, esp. after overcoming problems: *we got through the blizzards to the survivors.* **3** (*intr, adv*) to contact, as by telephone. **4** (*intr, prep*) to use, spend, or consume (money, supplies, etc.). **5** to complete or cause to complete (a task, process, etc.): *to get a bill through Parliament.* **6** (*adv*; foll. by *to*) to reach the awareness and understanding (of a person): *I just can't get the message through to him.*

get-together *n* **1** *Inf.* a small informal meeting or social gathering. ◆ *vb* **get together.** (*adv*) **2** (*tr*) to gather or collect. **3** (*intr*) (of people) to meet socially. **4** (*intr*) to discuss, esp. in order to reach an agreement.

Getty ★ ('gεtɪ) *n* **J(ean) Paul.** 1892–1976, US oil executive, millionaire, and art collector.

Gettysburg ★ ('gεtɪz,bɜːg) *n* a small town in S Pennsylvania, southwest of Harrisburg: scene of a crucial battle (1863) during the American Civil War, in which Meade's Union forces defeated Lee's Confederate army; site of the national cemetery dedicated by President Lincoln. Pop.: 7194 (1980).

get up *vb* (*mainly adv*) **1** to wake and rise from one's bed or cause to wake and rise from bed. **2** (*intr*) to rise to one's feet; stand up. **3** (*also prep*) to ascend or cause to ascend. **4** to increase or cause to increase in strength: *the wind got up at noon.* **5** (*tr*) *Inf.* to dress (oneself) in a particular way, esp. elaborately. **6** (*tr*) *Inf.* to devise or create: *to get up an entertainment for Christmas.* **7** (*tr*) *Inf.* to study or improve one's knowledge of: *I must get up my history.* **8** (*intr*; foll. by *to*) *Inf.* to be involved in: *he's always getting up to mischief.* ◆ *n* **get-up.** *Inf.* **9** a costume or outfit. **10** the arrangement or production of a book, etc.

get-up-and-go *n Inf.* energy or drive.

Getz ★ (gets) *n* **Stanley,** known as **Stan.** 1927–91, US jazz saxophonist.

geum ('dʒiːəm) *n* any herbaceous plant of the rose type, having compound leaves and red, orange, yellow, or white flowers. [C19: NL, from L: herb bennet, avens]

gewgaw ('gjuːgɔː, 'guː-) *n* a showy but valueless trinket. [C15: from ?]

geyser ('giːzə; *US* 'gaɪzər) *n* **1** a spring that discharges steam and hot water. **2** *Brit.* a domestic gas water heater. [C18: from Icelandic *Geysir,* from ON *geysa* to gush]

Gezira ★ (dʒə'zɪərə) *n* a region of the E central Sudan between the Blue and White Niles: site of a large-scale irrigation system.

G-force *n* the force of gravity.

Ghana ★ ('gɑːnə) *n* a republic in W Africa, on the Gulf of Guinea: a powerful empire from the 4th to the 13th centuries; a major source of gold and slaves for Europeans after 1471; British colony of the Gold Coast established in 1874; united with British Togoland in 1957 and became a republic and a member of the Commonwealth in 1960. Official language: English. Religions: Christian, Muslim, and animist. Currency: cedi. Capital: Accra. Pop.: 18 101 000 (1997). Area: 238 539 sq. km (92 100 sq. miles).
▸ **Ghanaian** (gɑː'neɪən) *or* **Ghanian** *adj, n*

gharry *or* **gharri** ('gærɪ) *n, pl* **gharries.** a horse-drawn vehicle used in India. [C19: from Hindi *gārī*]

ghastly ('gɑːstlɪ) *adj* **ghastlier, ghastliest. 1** *Inf.* very bad or unpleasant. **2** deathly pale; wan. **3** *Inf.* extremely unwell; ill. **4** terrifying; horrible. ◆ *adv* **5** unhealthily; sickly: *ghastly pale.* [OE *gāstlīc* spiritual]
▸ **ghastliness** *n*

ghat (gɔːt) *n* (in India) **1** stairs or a passage leading down to a river. **2** a mountain pass. **3** a place of cremation. [C17: from Hindi, from Sansk.]

Ghats ★ (gɔːts) *pl n* See **Eastern Ghats** and **Western Ghats.**

Ghazali ★ ('gɑːz,ɑːlɪ) *n* **al-.** 1058–1111, Muslim theologian and mystic.

ghazi ('gɑːzɪ) *n, pl* **ghazis. 1** a Muslim fighter against infidels. **2** (*often cap.*) a Turkish warrior of high rank. [C18: from Ar., from *ghazā* he made war]

Ghazzah ★ ('gɑːzə, 'gʌzə) *n* transliteration of the Arabic name for **Gaza.**

ghee (giː) *n* a clarified butter used in Indian cookery. [C17: from Hindi *ghī,* from Sansk. *ghri* sprinkle]

Ghent ★ (gεnt) *n* an industrial city and port in NW Belgium, capital of East Flanders province, at the confluence of the Rivers Lys and Scheldt: formerly famous for its cloth industry; university (1816). Pop.: 227 483 (1995 est.). Flemish name: **Gent.** French name: **Gand.**

gherkin ('gɜːkɪn) *n* **1** the small immature fruit of any of various cucumbers, used for pickling. **2a** a tropical American climbing plant. **2b** its small spiny edible fruit. [C17: from Du., dim. of *gurk,* ult. from Gk *angourion*]

ghetto ('gεtəʊ) *n, pl* **ghettos** *or* **ghettoes. 1** a densely populated slum area of a city inhabited by a socially and economically deprived minority. **2** an area or community that is segregated or isolated. **3** an area in a European city in which Jews were formerly required to live. [C17:

★ people and places

from It., ?from *borghetto*, dim. of *borgo* settlement outside a walled city, or from *ghetto* foundry, because one occupied the site of the later Venetian ghetto]

ghettoblaster ('gɛtəʊˌblɑːstə) *n Inf.* a large portable cassette recorder with built-in speakers.

ghettoize *or* **ghettoise** ('gɛtəʊˌaɪz) *vb* **ghettoizes, ghettoizing, ghettoized** *or* **ghettoises, ghettoising, ghettoised.** (*tr*) to confine or restrict to a particular area, activity, or category: *to ghettoize women as housewives.*
► ˌghettoi'zation *or* ˌghetto'sation *n*

Ghiberti ★ (*Italian* gi'bɛrti) *n* **Lorenzo** (lo'rɛntso). 1378–1455, Italian sculptor, painter, and goldsmith: noted for the baptistry doors of Florence Cathedral.

ghillie ('gɪlɪ) *n* a variant spelling of **gillie.**

Ghirlandaio *or* **Ghirlandajo** ★ (*Italian* girlan'daːjo) *n* **Domenico** (do'meːniko). original name *Domenico Bigordi.* 1449–94, Italian painter of frescoes.

ghost (gəʊst) *n* **1** the disembodied spirit of a dead person, supposed to haunt the living as a pale or shadowy vision; phantom. Related adj: **spectral. 2** a haunting memory: *the ghost of his former life rose up before him.* **3** a faint trace or possibility of something; glimmer: *a ghost of a smile.* **4** the spirit; soul (archaic, except in **the Holy Ghost**). **5** *Physics.* **5a** a faint secondary image produced by an optical system. **5b** a similar image on a television screen. **6** (*modifier*) falsely recorded as doing a particular job or fulfilling a particular function in order that some benefit, esp. money, may be obtained: *a ghost worker.* **7 give up the ghost.** to die. ◆ *vb* **8** See **ghostwrite. 9** (*tr*) to haunt. [OE *gāst*]
► 'ghost,like *adj* ► 'ghostly *adj*

ghost town *n* a deserted town, esp. one in the western US that was formerly a boom town.

ghost word *n* a word that has entered the language through the perpetuation, in dictionaries, etc., of an error.

ghostwrite ('gəʊstˌraɪt) *vb* **ghostwrites, ghostwriting, ghostwrote, ghostwritten.** to write (an article, etc.) on behalf of a person who is then credited as the author. Often shortened to **ghost.**
► 'ghost,writer *n*

ghoul (guːl) *n* **1** a malevolent spirit or ghost. **2** a person interested in morbid or disgusting things. **3** a person who robs graves. **4** (in Muslim legend) an evil demon thought to eat corpses. [C18: from Ar. *ghūl*, from *ghāla* he seized]
► 'ghoulish *adj* ► 'ghoulishly *adv* ► 'ghoulishness *n*

GHQ *Mil. abbrev.* for General Headquarters.

ghyll (gɪl) *n* a variant spelling of **gill³.**

GI *US inf.* ◆ *n* **1** (*pl* **GIs** *or* **GI's**) a soldier in the US Army, esp. an enlisted man. ◆ *adj* **2** conforming to US Army regulations. [C20: abbrev. of *government issue*]

gi. *abbrev.* for gill (unit of measure).

Giacometti ★ (*Italian* dʒako'metti) *n* **Alberto** (al'bɛrto). 1901–66, Swiss sculptor and painter, noted for his long skeletal statues.

Giambologna ★ (*Italian* dʒambo'loɲɲa) *n*, original name *Giovanni da Bologna* or *Jean de Boulogne.* 1529–1608, Italian mannerist sculptor, born in Flanders.

giant ('dʒaɪənt) *n* **1** Also (fem): **giantess** ('dʒaɪəntɪs). a mythical figure of superhuman size and strength, esp. in folklore or fairy tales. **2** a person or thing of exceptional size, reputation, etc. ◆ *adj* **3** remarkably or supernaturally large. [C13: from OF *geant*, from L *gigant-, gigās,* from Gk]

giant hogweed *n* a species of cow parsley that grows up to 3½ metres (10 ft) and whose irritant hairs and sap can cause a severe reaction.

giantism ('dʒaɪənˌtɪzəm) *n* another term for **gigantism** (sense 1).

giant panda *n* See **panda** (sense 1).

Giant's Causeway ★ *n* a promontory of columnar basalt on the N coast of Northern Ireland, in Antrim: consists of several thousand pillars, mostly hexagonal, that were formed by the rapid cooling of lava and the inward contraction of the lava flow.

giant slalom *n Skiing.* a type of slalom in which the course is longer and the obstacles are further apart than in a standard slalom.

giant star *n* any of a class of stars that have swelled and brightened as they approach the end of their life, their energy supply having changed.

giaour ('dʒaʊə) *n* a derogatory term for a non-Muslim, esp. a Christian. [C16: from Turkish: unbeliever, from Persian *gaur*]

gib (gɪb) *n* **1** a metal wedge, pad, or thrust bearing, esp. a brass plate let into a steam engine crosshead. ◆ *vb* **gibs, gibbing, gibbed. 2** (*tr*) to fasten or supply with a gib. [C18: from ?]

Gib (dʒɪb) *n* an informal name for **Gibraltar.**

gibber¹ ('dʒɪbə) *vb* **1** to utter rapidly and unintelligibly; prattle. **2** (*intr*) (of monkeys and related animals) to make characteristic chattering sounds. [C17: imit.]

gibber² ('gɪbə) *n Austral.* **1** a stone or boulder. **2** (*modifier*) of or relating to a dry flat area of land covered with wind-polished stones: *gibber plains.* [C19: from Abor.]

Gibberd ★ ('gɪbəd) *n* **Sir Frederick.** 1908–84, British architect and town planner. His buildings include the Liverpool Roman Catholic cathedral (1960–67).

gibberellin (ˌdʒɪbə'rɛlɪn) *n* any of several plant hormones whose main action is to cause elongation of the stem. [C20: from NL *Gibberella*, lit.: a little hump, from L *gibber* hump + -IN]

gibberish ('dʒɪbərɪʃ) *n* **1** rapid chatter. **2** incomprehensible talk; nonsense.

gibbet ('dʒɪbɪt) *n* **1a** a wooden structure resembling a gallows, from which the bodies of executed criminals were formerly hung to public view. **1b** a gallows. ◆ *vb* (*tr*) **2** to put to death by hanging on a gibbet. **3** to hang (a corpse) on a gibbet. **4** to expose to public ridicule. [C13: from OF: gallows, lit.: little cudgel, from *gibe* cudgel; from ?]

gibbon ('gɪbᵊn) *n* a small agile arboreal anthropoid ape inhabiting forests in S Asia. [C18: from F, prob. from an Indian dialect word]

Gibbon ★ ('gɪbᵊn) *n* **1 Edward.** 1737–94, British historian; author of *The History of the Decline and Fall of the Roman Empire* (1776–88). **2 Lewis Grassic** ('græsɪk), real name *James Leslie Mitchell.* 1901–35, Scottish writer: best known for his trilogy of novels *A Scots Quair* (1932–34).

Gibbons ★ ('gɪbᵊnz) *n* **1 Grinling.** 1648–1721, English sculptor and woodcarver. **2 Orlando.** 1583–1625, English organist and composer, esp. of anthems, motets, and madrigals.

gibbous ('gɪbəs) *or* **gibbose** ('gɪbəʊs) *adj* **1** (of the moon or a planet) more than half but less than fully illuminated. **2** hunchbacked. **3** bulging. [C17: from LL *gibbōsus* humpbacked, from L *gibba* hump]
► 'gibbously *adv* ► 'gibbousness *or* gibbosity (gɪ'bɒsɪtɪ) *n*

Gibbs ★ (gɪbz) *n* **1 James.** 1682–1754, British architect; his buildings include St Martin's-in-the-Fields, London (1722–26), and the Radcliffe Camera, Oxford (1737–49). **2 Josiah Willard.** 1839–1903, US physicist and mathematician: founder of chemical thermodynamics.

gibe¹ *or* **jibe** (dʒaɪb) *vb* **gibes, gibing, gibed** *or* **jibes, jibing, jibed. 1** to make jeering or scoffing remarks (at); taunt. ◆ *n* **2** a derisive or provoking remark. [C16: ?from OF *giber* to treat roughly, from ?]
► 'giber *or* 'jiber *n*

gibe² (dʒaɪb) *vb* **gibes, gibing, gibed**, *n Naut.* a variant spelling of **gybe.**

Gibeon ★ ('gɪbɪən) *n* an ancient town of Palestine: the excavated site of what are thought to be its remains lies about 9 kilometres (6 miles) northwest of Jerusalem.

giblets ('dʒɪblɪts) *pl n* (*sometimes sing*) the gizzard, liver, heart, and neck of a fowl. [C14: from OF *gibelet* stew of game birds, prob. from *gibier* game, of Gmc origin]

Gibraltar ★ (dʒɪ'brɔːltə) *n* **1 City of.** a city on the **Rock of Gibraltar**, a limestone promontory at the tip of S Spain: settled by Moors in 711 and taken by Spain in 1462; ceded to Britain in 1713; a British crown colony (1830–1969), now a United Kingdom overseas territory; a naval and air base of strategic importance. Pop.: 27 100 (1996 est.).

★ people and places

Area: 6.5 sq. km (2.5 sq. miles). Ancient name: **Calpe. 2 Strait of.** a narrow strait between the S tip of Spain and the NW tip of Africa, linking the Mediterranean with the Atlantic.
▸ **Gibraltarian** (,dʒɪbrɔːl'tɛərɪən) *adj, n*

Gibran ★ (dʒɪ'brɑːn) *n* Kahlil ('kɑːliːl). 1883–1931, Syro-Lebanese poet and painter, resident in the US after 1910; author of *The Prophet* (1923).

Gibson ★ ('gɪbsən) *n* Mel. born 1956, Australian film actor, born in the US; his films include *Mad Max* (1979) and *Braveheart* (1996; also directed).

Gibson Desert ★ ('gɪbsən) *n* a desert in W central Australia, between the Great Sandy Desert and the Victoria Desert: salt marshes, salt lakes, and scrub. Area: about 220 000 sq. km (85 000 sq. miles).

gidday (gə'daɪ) *sentence substitute.* a variant spelling of **g'day.**

giddy ('gɪdɪ) *adj* **giddier, giddiest. 1** affected with a reeling sensation and feeling as if about to fall; dizzy. **2** causing or tending to cause vertigo. **3** impulsive; scatterbrained. ♦ *vb* **giddies, giddying, giddied. 4** to make or become giddy. [OE *gydig* mad, frenzied, possessed by God; rel. to GOD]
▸ **'giddily** *adv* ▸ **'giddiness** *n*

Gide ★ (*French* ʒid) *n* André (ādre). 1869–1951, French writer. His novels include *L'Immoraliste* (1902) and *Les Faux-Monnayeurs* (1926): Nobel prize for literature 1947.

Gideon ★ ('gɪdɪən) *n Old Testament.* a Hebrew judge who led the Israelites to victory over their Midianite oppressors (Judges 6:11–8:35).

gidgee *or* **gidjee** ('gɪdʒiː) *n Austral.* **1** a small acacia tree yielding useful timber. **2** a spear made of this. [C19: from Abor.]

gie (giː) *vb* **gies, gi'ing, gi'ed.** a Scot. word for **give.**

Gielgud ★ ('giːlgud) *n* Sir John. born 1904, leading British actor and director.

Giessen ★ (*German* 'giːsən) *n* a city in central Germany, in Hesse: university (1607). Pop.: 71 750 (1989 est.).

gift (gɪft) *n* **1** something given; a present. **2** a special aptitude, ability, or power; talent. **3** the power or right to give or bestow (esp. **in the gift of, in (someone's) gift). 4** the act or process of giving. **5 look a gift-horse in the mouth.** (*usually negative*) to find fault with a free gift or chance benefit. ♦ *vb* (*tr*) **6** to present (something) as a gift to (a person). [OE *gift* payment for a wife, dowry; see GIVE]

GIFT (gɪft) *n acronym for* gamete intrafallopian transfer: a technique, similar to IVF, that enables some women who cannot conceive to bear children.

gifted ('gɪftɪd) *adj* having or showing natural talent or aptitude: *a gifted musician.*
▸ **'giftedly** *adv* ▸ **'giftedness** *n*

gift of tongues *n* an utterance, partly or wholly unintelligible, produced under the influence of ecstatic religious emotion. Also called: **glossolalia.**

giftwrap ('gɪft,ræp) *vb* **giftwraps, giftwrapping, giftwrapped.** to wrap (a gift) attractively.

Gifu ★ ('giːfuː) *n* a city in Japan, on central Honshu: hot springs. Pop.: 407 145 (1995).

gig[1] (gɪg) *n* **1** a light two-wheeled one-horse carriage without a hood. **2** *Naut.* a light tender for a vessel. **3** a long light rowing boat, used esp. for racing. ♦ *vb* **gigs, gigging, gigged. 4** (*intr*) to travel in a gig. [C13 (in the sense: flighty girl, spinning top): ?from ON]

gig[2] (gɪg) *n* **1** a cluster of barbless hooks drawn through a shoal of fish to try to impale them. ♦ *vb* **gigs, gigging, gigged. 2** to catch (fish) with a gig. [C18: ? shortened from obs. *fishgig* or *fizgig* kind of harpoon]

gig[3] (gɪg) *n* **1** a job, esp. a single booking for jazz or pop musicians. **2** the performance itself. ♦ *vb* **gigs, gigging, gigged. 3** (*intr*) to perform at a gig or gigs. [C20: from ?]

giga- ('gɪgə, 'gaɪgə) *combining form.* **1** denoting 10[9]: *giga-hertz.* **2** *Computing.* denoting 2[30]: *gigabyte.* Symbol: G [from Gk *gigas* GIANT]

gigaflop ('gaɪgə,flɒp) *n Computing.* a measure of processing speed, consisting of a thousand million floating-point operations a second. [C20: from GIGA- + flo(*ating*) p(*oint*)]

gigantic (dʒaɪ'gæntɪk) *adj* **1** very large; enormous. **2** Also: **gigantesque** (,dʒaɪgæn'tɛsk). of or suitable for giants. [C17: from Gk *gigantikos,* from *gigas* GIANT]
▸ **gi'gantically** *adv*

gigantism ('dʒaɪgæn,tɪzəm, dʒaɪ'gæntɪzəm) *n* **1** Also called: **giantism.** excessive growth of the entire body, caused by overproduction of growth hormone by the pituitary gland. **2** the state or quality of being gigantic.

giggle ('gɪg³l) *vb* **giggles, giggling, giggled. 1** (*intr*) to laugh nervously or foolishly. ♦ *n* **2** such a laugh. **3** *Inf.* something or someone that causes amusement. [C16: imit.]
▸ **'giggler** *n* ▸ **'giggling** *adj, n* ▸ **'giggly** *adj*

Gigli ★ (*Italian* 'dʒiʎʎi) *n* Beniamino (benja'miːno). 1890–1957, Italian operatic tenor.

gigolo ('ʒɪgə,ləʊ) *n, pl* **gigolos. 1** a man who is kept by a woman, esp. an older woman. **2** a man who is paid to dance with or escort women. [C20: from F, back formation from *gigolette* girl for hire as a dancing partner, prostitute, ult. from *gigue* a fiddle]

gigot ('dʒɪgət) *n* **1** a leg of lamb or mutton. **2** a leg-of-mutton sleeve. [C16: from OF: leg, a small fiddle, from *gigue* a fiddle, of Gmc origin]

gigue (ʒiːg) *n* a piece of music, usually in six-eight time, incorporated into the classical suite. [C17: from F, from It. *giga,* lit.: a fiddle; see GIGOT]

Gijón ★ (giː'hɔːn; *Spanish* xi'xɔn) *n* a port in NW Spain, on the Bay of Biscay: capital of the kingdom of Asturias until 791. Pop.: 269 644 (1994 est.). Ancient name: **Gigia.**

Gila monster ('hiːlə) *n* a large venomous brightly coloured lizard inhabiting deserts of the southwestern US and Mexico. [C19: after the *Gila,* a river in New Mexico and Arizona]

gilbert ('gɪlbət) *n* the cgs unit of magnetomotive force. Symbol: Gb, Gi [C19: after William GILBERT]

Gilbert ★ ('gɪlbət) *n* **1** Grove Karl. 1843–1918, US geologist who pioneered the study of river development. **2** Sir Humphrey. ?1539–83, English navigator: founded the colony at St John's, Newfoundland (1583). **3** William. 1540–1603, English physician and physicist, noted for his study of terrestrial magnetism in *De Magnete* (1600). **4** Sir W(illiam) S(chwenck). 1836–1911, British dramatist, humorist, and librettist. He collaborated (1871–96) with Arthur Sullivan on such comic operettas as *The Pirates of Penzance* (1879) and *The Mikado* (1885).

Gilbert Islands ★ *pl n* a group of islands in the W Pacific: with Banaba, the Phoenix Islands, and three of the Line Islands they constitute the independent state of Kiribati; until 1975 they formed part of the British colony of **Gilbert and Ellice Islands;** achieved full independence in 1979. Pop.: 67 508 (1990). Area: 295 sq. km (114 sq. miles).

gild[1] (gɪld) *vb* **gilds, gilding, gilded** *or* **gilt.** (*tr*) **1** to cover with or as if with gold. **2 gild the lily. 2a** to adorn unnecessarily something already beautiful. **2b** to praise someone inordinately. **3** to give a falsely attractive or valuable appearance to. [OE *gyldan,* from *gold* GOLD]
▸ **'gilder** *n*

gild[2] (gɪld) *n* a variant spelling of **guild.**

gilding ('gɪldɪŋ) *n* **1** the act or art of applying gilt to a surface. **2** the surface so produced. **3** another word for **gilt**[1] (sense 2).

Gilead[1] ★ ('gɪlɪ,æd) *n* a historic mountainous region east of the River Jordan, rising over 1200 m (4000 ft).

Gilead[2] ★ ('gɪlɪ,æd) *n Old Testament.* a grandson of Manasseh; ancestor of the Coileadites (Numbers 26: 29–30).

Giles ★ (dʒaɪlz) *n* **1** Saint. 7th century A.D., Greek hermit in France; patron saint of cripples, beggars, and lepers. Feast day: Sept. 1. **2** William Ernest Powell. 1835–97, Australian explorer, born in England. He was noted for his exploration of the western desert (1875–76).

gilet (dʒɪ'leɪ) *n* a garment resembling a waistcoat. [C20: F, lit.: waistcoat]

gill[1] (gɪl) *n* **1** the respiratory organ in many aquatic animals. **2** any of the radiating leaflike spore-producing structures on the undersurface of the cap of a mushroom. [C14: from ON]
▸ **gilled** *adj*

gill[2] (dʒɪl) *n* a unit of liquid measure equal to one quarter of a pint. [C14: from OF *gille* vat, tub, from LL *gillō*, from ?]

gill[3] *or* **ghyll** (gɪl) *n Dialect.* **1** a narrow stream; rivulet. **2** a wooded ravine. [C11: from ON *gil* steep-sided valley]

Gill ★ (gɪl) *n* (**Arthur**) **Eric** (**Rowton**). 1882–1940, British sculptor and typographer: his sculptures include the *Stations of the Cross* in Westminster Cathedral, London.

Gillespie ★ (gɪ'lɛspɪ) *n* **Dizzy**, nickname of *John Birks Gillespie*. 1917–93, US jazz trumpeter.

gillie, ghillie, *or* **gilly** ('gɪlɪ) *n, pl* **gillies** *or* **ghillies.** *Scot.* **1** an attendant or guide for hunting or fishing. **2** (formerly) a Highland chieftain's male attendant. [C17: from Scot. Gaelic *gille* boy, servant]

Gillingham ★ ('dʒɪlɪŋəm) *n* a town in SE England, in N Kent on the Medway estuary: former dockyards. Pop.: 94 923 (1991).

Gillray ★ ('gɪlreɪ) *n* **James.** 1757–1815, British caricaturist.

gills (gɪlz) *pl n* **1** (*sometimes sing*) the wattle of birds such as domestic fowl. **2** the cheeks and jowls of a person. **3** **green about the gills.** *Inf.* looking or feeling nauseated.

gillyflower *or* **gilliflower** ('dʒɪlɪˌflaʊə) *n* **1** any of several plants having fragrant flowers, such as the stock and wallflower. **2** an archaic name for **carnation.** [C14: from *gilofre,* from OF *girofle,* from Med. L, from Gk: clove tree, from *karuon* nut + *phullon* leaf]

Gilolo ★ (dʒaɪ'ləʊləʊ, dʒɪ-) *n* See **Halmahera.**

gilt[1] (gɪlt) *vb* **1** a past tense and past participle of **gild**[1]. ◆ *n* **2** gold or a substance simulating it, applied in gilding. **3** another word for **gilding** (senses 1, 2). **4** superficial or false appearance of excellence. **5** a gilt-edged security. **6** **take the gilt off the gingerbread.** to destroy the part of something that gives it its appeal. ◆ *adj* **7** covered with or as if with gold or gilt; gilded.

gilt[2] (gɪlt) *n* a young female pig, esp. one that has not had a litter. [C15: from ON *gyltr*]

gilt-edged *adj* **1** denoting government securities on which interest payments will certainly be met and that will certainly be repaid at par on the due date. **2** of the highest quality: *the last track on the album is a gilt-edged classic.* **3** (of books, papers, etc.) having gilded edges.

gimbals ('dʒɪmbᵊlz, 'gɪm-) *pl n* a device, consisting of two or three pivoted rings at right angles to each other, that provides free suspension in all planes for a compass, chronometer, etc. Also called: **gimbal ring.** [C16: var. of earlier *gimmal,* from OF *gemel* double finger ring, from L *gemellus,* dim. of *geminus* twin]

gimcrack ('dʒɪmˌkræk) *adj* **1** cheap; shoddy. ◆ *n* **2** a cheap showy trifle or gadget. [C18: from C14 *gibecrake* little ornament, from ?]
▸ **'gimˌcrackery** *n*

gimlet ('gɪmlɪt) *n* **1** a small hand tool consisting of a pointed spiral tip attached at right angles to a handle, used for boring small holes in wood. **2** *US.* a cocktail consisting of half gin or vodka and half lime juice. ◆ *vb* **3** (*tr*) to make holes in (wood) using a gimlet. ◆ *adj* **4** penetrating; piercing (esp. in **gimlet-eyed**). [C15: from OF *guimbelet,* of Gmc origin, see WIMBLE]

gimmick ('gɪmɪk) *n Inf.* **1** something designed to attract extra attention, interest, or publicity. **2** any clever device, gadget, or stratagem, esp. one used to deceive. [C20: orig. US sl., from ?]
▸ **'gimmickry** *n* ▸ **'gimmicky** *adj*

gimp *or* **guimpe** (gɪmp) *n* a tapelike trimming. [C17: prob. from Du. *gimp,* from ?]

gin[1] (dʒɪn) *n* an alcoholic drink obtained by distillation of the grain of malted barley, rye, or maize, flavoured with juniper berries. [C18: from Du. *genever,* via OF from L *jūniperus* JUNIPER]

gin[2] (dʒɪn) *n* **1** a primitive engine in which a vertical shaft is turned by horses driving a horizontal beam in a circle. **2** Also called: **cotton gin.** a machine of this type used for separating seeds from raw cotton. **3** a trap for catching small mammals, consisting of a noose of thin strong wire. ◆ *vb* **gins, ginning, ginned.** (*tr*) **4** to free (cotton) of

seeds with a gin. **5** to trap or snare (game) with a gin. [C13 *gyn,* from ENGINE]

gin[3] (gɪn) *vb* **gins, ginning, gan** (gæn), **gun** (gʌn). an archaic word for **begin.**

gin[4] (dʒɪn) *n Austral. offens. sl.* an Aboriginal woman. [C19: from Abor.]

ginger ('dʒɪndʒə) *n* **1** any of several plants of the East Indies, cultivated throughout the tropics for their spicy hot-tasting underground stems. **2** the underground stem of this plant, which is used fresh or powdered as a flavouring or crystallized as a sweetmeat. **3a** a reddish-brown or yellowish-brown colour. **3b** (*as adj*): *ginger hair.* **4** *Inf.* liveliness; vigour. [C13: from OF *gingivre,* ult. from Sansk. *śṛṅgaveram,* from *śṛṅga-* horn + *vera-* body, referring to its shape]
▸ **'gingery** *adj*

ginger ale *n* a sweetened effervescent nonalcoholic drink flavoured with ginger extract.

ginger beer *n* a slightly alcoholic drink made by fermenting a mixture of syrup and root ginger.

gingerbread ('dʒɪndʒəˌbred) *n* **1** a moist brown cake, flavoured with ginger and treacle. **2a** a biscuit, similarly flavoured, cut into various shapes. **2b** (*as modifier*): *gingerbread man.* **3** an elaborate but unsubstantial ornamentation.

ginger group *n Chiefly Brit.* a group within a party, association, etc., that enlivens or radicalizes its parent body.

gingerly ('dʒɪndʒəlɪ) *adv* **1** in a cautious, reluctant, or timid manner. ◆ *adj* **2** cautious, reluctant, or timid. [C16: ?from OF *gensor* dainty, from *gent* of noble birth; see GENTLE]

ginger nut *or* **snap** *n* a crisp biscuit flavoured with ginger.

gingham ('gɪŋəm) *n* a cotton fabric, usually woven of two coloured yarns in a checked or striped design. [C17: from F, from Malay *ginggang* striped cloth]

gingili ('dʒɪndʒɪlɪ) *n* **1** the oil obtained from sesame seeds. **2** another name for **sesame.** [C18: from Hindi *jingalī*]

gingiva ('dʒɪndʒɪvə, dʒɪn'dʒaɪvə) *n, pl* **gingivae** (-dʒɪˌviː, -dʒaɪviː). *Anat.* the technical name for the **gum**[2]. [from L]
▸ **'gingival** *adj*

gingivitis (ˌdʒɪndʒɪ'vaɪtɪs) *n* inflammation of the gums.

ginglymus ('dʒɪŋɡlɪməs, 'gɪŋ-) *n, pl* **ginglymi** (-ˌmaɪ). *Anat.* a hinge joint. [C17: NL, from Gk *ginglumos* hinge]

gink (gɪŋk) *n Sl.* a man or boy, esp. one considered to be odd. [C20: from ?]

ginkgo ('gɪŋkgəʊ) *or* **gingko** ('gɪŋkəʊ) *n, pl* **ginkgoes** *or* **gingkoes.** a widely planted ornamental Chinese tree with fan-shaped deciduous leaves and fleshy yellow fruit. Also called: **maidenhair tree.** [C18: from Japanese, from Ancient Chinese: silver + apricot]

ginormous (dʒaɪ'nɔːməs) *adj Inf.* very large. [C20: blend of *giant* or *gigantic* & *enormous*]

gin palace (dʒɪn) *n* (formerly) a gaudy drinking house.

gin rummy (dʒɪn) *n* a version of rummy in which a player may go out if the odd cards outside his sequences total less than ten points. [C20: from GIN[1] + RUMMY]

Ginsberg ★ ('gɪnzbɜːɡ) *n* **Allen.** 1926–97, US poet of the Beat Generation. His poetry includes *Howl* (1956).

ginseng ('dʒɪnsɛŋ) *n* **1** either of two plants of China or of North America, whose forked aromatic roots are used medicinally. **2** the root of either of these plants or a substance obtained from the roots, believed to possess tonic and energy-giving properties. [C17: from Mandarin Chinese *jen shen*]

Ginzburg ★ (*Italian* 'gindzburg) *n* **Natalia** (nata'liːa). 1916–91, Italian writer. Her books include *The Road to the City* (1942) and *Family Sayings* (1963).

Gioconda (*Italian* dʒo'konda) *n* **1** **La.** Also called: **Mona Lisa.** the portrait by Leonardo da Vinci of a young woman with an enigmatic smile. ◆ *adj* **2** mysterious or enigmatic. [It.: the smiling (lady)]

giocoso (dʒə'kəʊzəʊ) *adj Music.* jocose. [It.]

Giorgione ★ (*Italian* dʒor'dʒoːne) *n* **Il.** original name

Giorgio Barbarelli. ?1478–1511, Italian painter of the Venetian school.

Giotto ★ (*Italian* 'dʒɔtto) *n* also known as *Giotto di Bondone.* ?1267–1337, Florentine painter of the early Renaissance.

gip (dʒɪp) *vb* **gips, gipping, gipped. 1** a variant spelling of **gyp**[1]. ♦ *n* **2** a variant spelling of **gyp**[2].

Gippsland ★ ('gɪps,lænd) *n* a fertile region of SE Australia, in SE Victoria, extending east along the coast from Melbourne to the New South Wales border. Area: 35 200 sq. km (13 600 sq. miles).

Gipsy ('dʒɪpsɪ) *n, pl* **Gipsies.** (*sometimes not cap.*) a variant spelling of **Gypsy.**

gipsy moth *n* a variant spelling of **gypsy moth.**

giraffe (dʒɪ'rɑːf, -'ræf) *n, pl* **giraffes** *or* **giraffe.** a large ruminant mammal inhabiting savannas of tropical Africa: the tallest mammal, with very long legs and neck. [C17: from It. *giraffa*, from Ar. *zarāfah*, prob. of African origin]

Giraldus Cambrensis ★ (dʒɪ'rældəs kæm'brɛnsɪs) *n* literary name of *Gerald de Barri.* ?1146–?1223, Welsh chronicler and churchman.

girandole ('dʒɪrən,dəʊl) *n* **1** a branched wall candleholder. **2** an earring or pendant having a central gem surrounded by smaller ones. **3** a revolving firework. **4** *Artillery.* a group of connected mines. [C17: from F, from It. *girandola*, from L *gȳrāre* to GYRATE]

girasol *or* **girasole** ('dʒɪrə,sɒl, -,səʊl) *n* a type of opal that has a red or pink glow; fire opal. [C16: from It., from *girare* to revolve (see GYRATE) + *sole* the sun]

Giraud ★ (*French* ʒiro) *n* Henri Honoré (ɑ̃ri ɔnɔre). 1879–1949, French general, who commanded French forces in North Africa (1942–43).

Giraudoux ★ (*French* ʒirodu) *n* (**Hyppolyte**) **Jean** (ʒɑ̃). 1882–1944, French dramatist. His works include the novel *Suzanne et le Pacifique* (1921) and the play *Amphitryon 38* (1929).

gird[1] (gɜːd) *vb* **girds, girding, girded** *or* **girt.** (*tr*) **1** to put a belt, girdle, etc., around (the waist or hips). **2** to bind or secure with or as if with a belt: *to gird on one's armour.* **3** to surround; encircle. **4** to prepare (oneself) for action (esp. in **gird (up) one's loins**). [OE *gyrdan*, of Gmc origin]

gird[2] (gɜːd) *N English dialect.* ♦ *vb* **1** (when *intr*, foll. by *at*) to jeer (at someone); mock. ♦ *n* **2** a taunt; gibe. [C13 *girden* to strike, cut, from ?]

girder ('gɜːdə) *n* a large beam, esp. one made of steel, used in the construction of bridges, buildings, etc.

girdle[1] ('gɜːd°l) *n* **1** a woman's elastic corset covering the waist to the thigh. **2** anything that surrounds or encircles. **3** a belt or sash. **4** *Jewellery.* the outer edge of a gem. **5** *Anat.* any encircling structure or part. **6** the mark left on a tree trunk after the removal of a ring of bark. ♦ *vb* **girdles, girdling, girdled.** (*tr*) **7** to put a girdle on or around. **8** to surround or encircle. **9** to remove a ring of bark from (a tree). [OE *gyrdel*, of Gmc origin; see GIRD[1]]

girdle[2] ('gɜːd°l) *n Scot. & N English dialect.* another word for **griddle.**

Girgenti ★ (*Italian* dʒir'dʒɛnti) *n* a former name (until 1927) of **Agrigento.**

girl (gɜːl) *n* **1** a female child from birth to young womanhood. **2** a young unmarried woman; lass; maid. **3** *Inf.* a sweetheart or girlfriend. **4** *Inf.* a woman of any age. **5** a female employee, esp. a female servant. **6** *S. African derog.* a Black female servant. [C13: from ?; ? rel. to Low G *Göre* boy, girl]
▸ **'girlish** *adj*

girlfriend ('gɜːl,frɛnd) *n* **1** a female friend with whom a person is romantically or sexually involved. **2** any female friend.

Girl Guide *n* See **Guide.**

girlhood ('gɜːl,hʊd) *n* the state or time of being a girl.

girlie ('gɜːlɪ) *adj* **1** *Inf.* featuring nude or scantily dressed women: *a girlie magazine.* **2** suited to or designed to appeal to young women: *a real girlie night out.*

giro ('dʒaɪrəʊ) *n, pl* **giros. 1** a system of transferring money within a financial organization, such as a bank or post office, directly from the account of one person into that

of another. **2** *Brit. inf.* an unemployment benefit or income support payment by giro cheque. [C20: ult. from Gk *guros* circuit]

Gironde ★ (*French* ʒirɔ̃d) *n* **1** a department of SW France, in Aquitaine region. Capital: Bordeaux. Pop.: 1 259 579 (1994 est.). Area: 10 726 sq. km (4183 sq. miles). **2** an estuary in SW France, formed by the confluence of the Rivers Garonne and Dordogne. Length: 72 km (45 miles).

girt[1] (gɜːt) *vb* a past tense and past participle of **gird**[1].

girt[2] (gɜːt) *vb* **1** (*tr*) to bind or encircle; gird. **2** to measure the girth of (something).

girth (gɜːθ) *n* **1** the distance around something; circumference. **2** a band around a horse's belly to keep the saddle in position. ♦ *vb* **3** (usually foll. by *up*) to fasten a girth on (a horse). **4** (*tr*) to encircle or surround. [C14: from ON *gjörth* belt; see GIRD[1]]

Gisborne ★ ('gɪzbən) *n* a port in N New Zealand, on E North Island on Poverty Bay. Pop.: 31 700 (1994).

Giscard d'Estaing ★ (*French* ʒiskardɛstɛ̃) *n* **Valéry** (valeri). born 1926, French politician; minister of finance and economic affairs (1962–66; 1969–74); president (1974–81).

Gish ★ (gɪʃ) *n* **1 Dorothy.** 1898–1968, US actress, chiefly in silent films. **2** her sister, **Lillian.** 1896–1993, US actress, noted for her roles in such silent films as *The Birth of a Nation* (1915) and *Intolerance* (1916).

Gissing ★ ('gɪsɪŋ) *n* **George** (**Robert**). 1857–1903, British novelist. His works include *New Grub Street* (1891).

gist (dʒɪst) *n* the point or substance of an argument, speech, etc. [C18: from Anglo-F, as in *cest action gist en* this action consists in, lit.: lies in, from OF *gésir*, from L *jacēre*]

git (gɪt) *n Brit. sl.* **1** a contemptible person, often a fool. **2** a bastard. [C20: from GET (in the sense: *to beget*, hence a bastard, fool)]

gîte (ʒiːt) *n* a self-catering holiday cottage for let in France. [C20: F]

gittern ('gɪtɜːn) *n* an obsolete medieval stringed instrument resembling the guitar. [C14: from OF, ult. from OSp. *guitarra* GUITAR; see CITTERN]

Giulini ★ (*Italian* dʒuˈliːni) *n* **Carlo Maria** ('karlo ma'riːa). born 1914, Italian orchestral conductor, esp. of opera.

Giulio Romano ★ (*Italian* 'dʒuːljo roˈmaːno) *n* ?1499–1546, Italian architect and painter; a founder of mannerism.

giusto ('dʒuːstəʊ) *adj Music.* (of tempo) exact; strict. [It.]

give (gɪv) *vb* **gives, giving, gave, given.** (*mainly tr*) **1** (*also intr*) to present or deliver voluntarily (something that is one's own) to another. **2** (often foll. by *for*) to transfer (something that is one's own, esp. money) to the possession of another as part of an exchange: *to give fifty pounds for a painting.* **3** to place in the temporary possession of another: *I gave him my watch while I went swimming.* **4** (when *intr*, foll. by *of*) to grant, provide, or bestow: *give me some advice.* **5** to administer: *to give a reprimand.* **6** to award or attribute: *to give blame, praise, etc.* **7** to be a source of: *he gives no trouble.* **8** to impart or communicate: *to give news.* **9** to utter or emit: *to give a shout.* **10** to perform, make, or do: *the car gave a jolt.* **11** to sacrifice or devote: *he gave his life for his country.* **12** to surrender: *to give place to others.* **13** to concede or yield: *I will give you this game.* **14** (*intr*) *Inf.* to happen: *what gives?* **15** (often foll. by *to*) to cause; lead: *she gave me to believe that she would come.* **16** to perform or present as an entertainment: *to give a play.* **17** to act as a host of (a party, etc.). **18** (*intr*) to yield or break under force or pressure: *this surface will give if you sit on it.* **19 give as good as one gets.** to respond to verbal or bodily blows to at least an equal extent as those received. **20 give or take.** plus or minus: *three thousand people came, give or take a few hundred.* ♦ *n* **21** tendency to yield under pressure; resilience. ♦ See also **give away, give in,** etc. [OE *giefan*]
▸ **'givable** *or* **'giveable** *adj* ▸ **'giver** *n*

give-and-take *n* **1** mutual concessions, shared benefits, and cooperation. **2** a smoothly flowing exchange of ideas and talk. ♦ *vb* **give and take.** (*intr*) **3** to make mutual concessions.

give away vb (tr, adv) **1** to donate or bestow as a gift, prize, etc. **2** to sell very cheaply. **3** to reveal or betray. **4** to fail to use (an opportunity) through folly or neglect. **5** to present (a bride) formally to her husband in a marriage ceremony. ◆ n **giveaway**. **6** a betrayal or disclosure esp. when unintentional. **7** (modifier) **7a** very cheap (esp. in **giveaway prices**). **7b** free of charge: a giveaway property magazine.

give in vb (adv) **1** (intr) to yield; admit defeat. **2** (tr) to submit or deliver (a document).

given ('gɪvⁿn) vb **1** the past participle of **give**. ◆ adj **2** (postpositive; foll. by to) tending (to); inclined or addicted (to). **3** specific or previously stated. **4** assumed as a premise. **5** Maths. known or determined independently: a given volume. **6** (on official documents) issued or executed, as on a stated date.

given name n another term (esp. US) for **first name**.

give off vb (tr, adv) to emit or discharge: the mothballs gave off an acrid odour.

give out vb (adv) **1** (tr) to emit or discharge. **2** (tr) to publish or make known: the chairman gave out that he would resign. **3** (tr) to hand out or distribute: they gave out free chewing gum. **4** (intr) to become exhausted; fail: the supply of candles gave out.

give over vb (adv) **1** (tr) to transfer, esp. to the care or custody of another. **2** (tr) to assign or resign to a specific purpose or function: the day was given over to pleasure. **3** Inf. to cease (an activity): give over fighting, will you!

give up vb (adv) **1** to abandon hope (for). **2** (tr) to renounce (an activity, belief, etc.): I have given up smoking. **3** (tr) to relinquish or resign from: he gave up the presidency. **4** (tr; usually reflexive) to surrender: the escaped convict gave himself up. **5** (intr) to admit one's defeat or inability to do something. **6** (tr; often passive or reflexive) to devote completely (to): she gave herself up to caring for the sick.

Gîza ★ ('giːzə) n See **El Gîza**.

gizmo or **gismo** ('gɪzməʊ) n, pl **gizmos**, **gismos**. Sl. a device; gadget. [C20: from ?]

gizzard ('gɪzəd) n **1** the thick-walled part of a bird's stomach, in which hard food is broken up. **2** Inf. the stomach and entrails generally. [C14: from OF guisier fowl's liver, from L gigēria entrails of poultry when cooked, from ?]

Gk abbrev. for Greek.

glabella (glə'bɛlə) n, pl **glabellae** (-liː). Anat. a smooth elevation of the frontal bone just above the bridge of the nose. [C19: NL, from L, from glaber bald, smooth]
▸ **gla'bellar** adj

glabrous ('gleɪbrəs) adj Biol. without hair or a similar growth; smooth. [C17 glabrous, from L glaber]

glacé ('glæsɪ) adj **1** crystallized or candied: glacé cherries. **2** covered in icing. **3** (of leather, silk, etc.) having a glossy finish. ◆ vb **glacés**, **glacéing**, **glacéed**. **4** (tr) to ice or candy (cakes, fruits, etc.). [C19: from F glacé, lit.: iced, from glacer to freeze, from L glaciēs ice]

glacial ('gleɪsɪəl, -ʃəl) adj **1** characterized by the presence of masses of ice. **2** relating to, caused by, or deposited by a glacier. **3** extremely cold; icy. **4** cold or hostile in manner. **5** (of a chemical compound) of or tending to form crystals that resemble ice.
▸ **'glacially** adv

glacial acetic acid n pure acetic acid.

glacial period n **1** any period of time during which a large part of the earth's surface was covered with ice, due to the advance of glaciers. **2** (often caps.) the Pleistocene epoch. ◆ Also called: **glacial epoch**, **ice age**.

glaciate ('gleɪsɪ,eɪt) vb **glaciates**, **glaciating**, **glaciated**. **1** to cover or become covered with glaciers or masses of ice. **2** (tr) to subject to the effects of glaciers, such as denudation and erosion.
▸ **glaci'ation** n

glacier ('glæsɪə, 'gleɪs-) n a slowly moving mass of ice originating from an accumulation of snow. [C18: from F (dialect), from OF glace ice, from LL, from L glaciēs ice]

glaciology (,glæsɪ'ɒlədʒɪ, ,gleɪ-) n the study of the distribution, character, and effects of glaciers.
▸ **glaciological** (,glæsɪə'lɒdʒɪkⁿl, ,gleɪ-) adj ▸ **glaci'ologist** n

glacis ('glæsɪs, 'glæsɪ, 'gleɪ-) n, pl **glacises** or **glacis** (-iːz, -ɪz). **1** a slight incline; slope. **2** an open slope in front of a fortified place. [C17: from F, from OF glacier to freeze, slip, from L, from glaciēs ice]

glad[1] (glæd) adj **gladder**, **gladdest**. **1** happy and pleased; contented. **2** causing happiness or contentment. **3** (postpositive; foll. by to) very willing: he was glad to help. **4** (postpositive; foll. by of) happy or pleased to have: glad of her help. ◆ vb **glads**, **gladding**, **gladded**. **5** (tr) an archaic word for **gladden**. [OE glæd]
▸ **'gladly** adv ▸ **'gladness** n

glad[2] (glæd) n Inf. short for **gladiolus**.

Gladbeck ★ (German 'glatbɛk) n a city in NW Germany, in North Rhine-Westphalia. Pop.: 79 190 (1989 est.).

gladden ('glædⁿn) vb to make or become glad and joyful.
▸ **'gladdener** n

glade (gleɪd) n an open place in a forest; clearing. [C16: from ?; ? rel. to GLAD[1] (in obs. sense: bright); see GLEAM]

glad eye n Inf. an inviting or seductive glance (esp. in **give (someone) the glad eye**).

gladiator ('glædɪ,eɪtə) n **1** (in ancient Rome) a man trained to fight in arenas to provide entertainment. **2** a person who supports and fights publicly for a cause. [C16: from L: swordsman, from gladius sword]
▸ **gladiatorial** (,glædɪə'tɔːrɪəl) adj

gladiolus (,glædɪ'əʊləs) n, pl **gladiolus**, **gladioli** (-laɪ), or **gladioluses**. any plant of a widely cultivated genus having sword-shaped leaves and spikes of funnel-shaped brightly coloured flowers. Also called: **gladiola**. [C16: from L: a small sword, sword lily, from gladius a sword]

glad rags pl n Inf. best clothes or clothes used on special occasions.

gladsome ('glædsəm) adj an archaic word for **glad**[1].
▸ **'gladsomely** adv ▸ **'gladsomeness** n

Gladstone ★ ('glædstən) n William Ewart. 1809–98, British statesman. He became leader of the Liberal Party in 1867 and was prime minister (1868–74; 1880–85; 1886; 1892–94).

Gladstone bag n a piece of hand luggage consisting of two equal-sized hinged compartments. [C19: after W. E. GLADSTONE]

Glagolitic (,glægə'lɪtɪk) adj of, relating to, or denoting a Slavic alphabet whose invention is attributed to Saint Cyril. [C19: from NL, from Serbo-Croat glagolica the Glagolitic alphabet]

glair (glɛə) n **1** white of egg, esp. when used as a size or adhesive. **2** any substance resembling this. ◆ vb **3** (tr) to apply glair to (something). [C14: from OF glaire, from Vulgar L clāria (unattested) CLEAR, from L clārus]
▸ **'glairy** or **'glaireous** adj

glam (glæm) adj Inf. short for **glamorous**.

Glamorgan (glə'mɔːgən) or **Glamorganshire** ★ (glə-'mɔːgən,ʃɪə, -ʃə) n a former county of SE Wales, now administered by Swansea county and six county boroughs.

glamorize, **glamorise**, or US (sometimes) **glamourize** ('glæmə,raɪz) vb **glamorizes**, **glamorizing**, **glamorized**; **glamorises**, **glamorising**, **glamorised** or US (sometimes) **glamourizes**, **glamourizing**, **glamourized**. (tr) to cause to be or seem glamorous; romanticize or beautify.
▸ **,glamori'zation** or **,glamori'sation** n

glamorous ('glæmərəs) adj **1** possessing glamour; alluring and fascinating. **2** beautiful and smart, esp. in a showy way: a glamorous woman.
▸ **'glamorously** adv

glamour or US (sometimes) **glamor** ('glæmə) n **1** charm and allure; fascination. **2a** fascinating or voluptuous beauty. **2b** (as modifier): a glamour girl. **3** Arch. a magic spell; charm. [C18: Scot. var. of GRAMMAR (hence a magic spell, because occult practices were popularly associated with learning)]

glance[1] (glɑːns) vb **glances**, **glancing**, **glanced**. **1** (intr) to look hastily or briefly. **2** (intr; foll. by over, through, etc.) to look over briefly: to glance through a report. **3** (intr) to reflect, glint, or gleam: the sun glanced on the water. **4** (intr; usually foll. by off) to depart (from an object struck) at an oblique angle: the arrow glanced off the tree. ◆ n **5** a hasty or brief look; peep. **6** a flash or glint of light;

gleam. **7** the act or an instance of an object glancing off another. **8** a brief allusion. [C15: from *glacen* to strike obliquely, from OF *glacier* to slide (see GLACIS)]
▶ 'glancing *adj* ▶ 'glancingly *adv*

> **USAGE NOTE** *Glance* is sometimes wrongly used where *glimpse* is meant: *he caught a glimpse* (not *glance*) *of her making her way through the crowd.*

glance[2] (glɑːns) *n* any mineral having a metallic lustre. [C19: from G *Glanz* brightness, lustre]

gland[1] (glænd) *n* **1** a cell or organ in man and other animals that synthesizes chemical substances and secretes them for the body to use or eliminate, either through a duct (exocrine gland) or directly into the bloodstream (endocrine gland). **2** a structure, such as a lymph node, that resembles a gland in form. **3** a cell or organ in plants that synthesizes and secretes a particular substance. [C17: from L *glāns* acorn]

gland[2] (glænd) *n* a device that prevents leakage of fluid along a rotating shaft or reciprocating rod passing between areas of high and low pressure. It often consists of a flanged metal sleeve bedding into a stuffing box. [C19: from ?]

glanders ('glændəz) *n* (*functioning as sing*) a highly infectious bacterial disease of horses, sometimes communicated to man, characterized by inflammation and ulceration of the mucous membranes of the air passages, skin and lymph glands. [C16: from OF *glandres*, from L *glandulae*, lit.: little acorns, from *glāns* acorn; see GLAND[2]]

glandular ('glændjʊlə) *or* **glandulous** ('glændjʊləs) *adj* of, relating to, containing, functioning as, or affecting a gland. [C18: from L *glandula*, lit.: a little acorn; see GLANDERS]
▶ 'glandularly *or* 'glandulously *adv*

glandular fever *n* another name for **infectious mononucleosis.**

glandule ('glændjuːl) *n* a small gland.

glans (glænz) *n*, *pl* **glandes** ('glændiːz). *Anat.* any small rounded body or glandlike mass, such as the head of the penis (**glans penis**). [C17: from L: acorn; see GLAND[1]]

glare (gleə) *vb* **glares, glaring, glared. 1** (*intr*) to stare angrily; glower. **2** (*tr*) to express by glowering. **3** (*intr*) (of light, colour, etc.) to be very bright and intense. **4** (*intr*) to be dazzlingly ornamented or garish. ◆ *n* **5** an angry stare. **6** a dazzling light or brilliance. **7** garish ornamentation or appearance. [C13: prob. from MLow G, MDu. *glaren* to gleam]

glaring ('gleərɪŋ) *adj* **1** conspicuous: *a glaring omission.* **2** dazzling or garish.
▶ 'glaringly *adv* ▶ 'glaringness *n*

Glarus ★ (*German* 'glaːrʊs) *n* **1** an Alpine canton of E central Switzerland. Capital: Glarus. Pop.: 39 388 (1995 est.). Area 684 sq. km (264 sq. miles). **2** a town in E central Switzerland, the capital of Glarus canton. Pop.: 5541 (1990). ◆ French name: **Glaris** (glari).

Glaser ★ ('gleɪzə) *n* Donald Arthur. born 1926, US physicist: invented the bubble chamber; Nobel prize for physics 1960.

Glasgow ★ ('glɑːzgəʊ, 'glæz-) *n* **1** a city in W central Scotland, in City of Glasgow council area on the River Clyde: the largest city in Scotland; centre of a major industrial region, formerly an important port; universities (1451, 1964). Pop.: 662 954 (1991). Related adj: **Glaswegian. 2 City of.** a council area in W Scotland. Pop.: 623 850 (1996 est.). Area: 175 sq. km (68 sq. miles).

glasnost ('glæs,nɒst) *n* the policy of public frankness and accountability developed in the former Soviet Union under the leadership of Mikhail Gorbachov. [C20: Russian, lit.: publicity, openness]

glass (glɑːs) *n* **1a** a hard brittle transparent or translucent noncrystalline solid, consisting of metal silicates or similar compounds. It is made from a fused mixture of oxides, such as lime, silicon dioxide, phosphorus pentoxide, etc. **1b** (*as modifier*): *a glass bottle.* Related adj: **vitreous. 2** something made of glass, esp. a drinking vessel, a barometer, or a mirror. **3** Also called: **glassful.** the amount or volume contained in a drinking glass: *he drank a glass of wine.* **4** glassware collectively. **5** See **fibreglass.** ◆ *vb* **6** (*tr*) to cover with, enclose in, or fit with glass. [OE *glæs*]
▶ 'glassless *adj* ▶ 'glass,like *adj*

Glass ★ (glɑːs) *n* Philip. born 1937, US avant-garde composer: his works include *Music in Fifths* (1970) and *Monsters of Grace* (1998).

glass-blowing *n* the process of shaping a mass of molten glass by blowing air into it through a tube.
▶ 'glass-,blower *n*

glass ceiling *n* a situation in which progress, esp. promotion, appears to be possible but restrictions or discrimination create a barrier that prevents it.

glasses ('glɑːsɪz) *pl n* a pair of lenses for correcting faulty vision, in a frame that rests on the bridge of the nose and hooks behind the ears. Also called: **spectacles, eyeglasses.**

glass fibre *n* another name for **fibreglass.**

glass harmonica *n* a musical instrument of the 18th century consisting of a set of glass bowls of graduated pitches, played by rubbing the fingers over the moistened rims or by a keyboard mechanism. Sometimes shortened to **harmonica.** Also called: **musical glasses.**

glasshouse ('glɑːs,haʊs) *n* **1** Brit. a glass building, esp. a greenhouse, used for growing plants in protected or controlled conditions. **2** Inf., chiefly Brit. a military detention centre.

glassine (glæ'siːn) *n* a glazed translucent paper.

glass snake *n* any snakelike lizard of Europe, Asia, or North America, with vestigial hind limbs and a tail that breaks off easily.

glassware ('glɑːs,weə) *n* articles made of glass, esp. drinking glasses.

glass wool *n* fine spun glass massed into a wool-like bulk, used in insulation, filtering, etc.

glasswort ('glɑːs,wɜːt) *n* **1** any plant of salt marshes having fleshy stems and scalelike leaves: formerly used as a source of soda for glass-making. **2** another name for **saltwort.**

glassy ('glɑːsɪ) *adj* **glassier, glassiest. 1** resembling glass, esp. in smoothness or transparency. **2** void of expression, life, or warmth: *a glassy stare.*
▶ 'glassily *adv* ▶ 'glassiness *n*

Glastonbury ★ ('glæstənbərɪ, -brɪ) *n* a town in SW England, in Somerset: remains of prehistoric lake villages; the reputed burial place of King Arthur; site of a ruined Benedictine abbey, probably the oldest in England. Pop.: 7747 (1991).

Glaswegian (glæz'wiːdʒən) *adj* **1** of or relating to Glasgow or its inhabitants. ◆ *n* **2** a native or inhabitant of Glasgow. [C19: infl. by NORWEGIAN]

Glauber's salt ('glaʊbəz) *or* **Glauber salt** *n* the crystalline decahydrate of sodium sulphate: used in making glass, detergents, and pulp. [C18: after J. R. *Glauber* (1604–68), G chemist]

Glauce ★ ('glɔːsɪ) *n* Greek myth. **1** the second bride of Jason, murdered on her wedding day by Medea, whom Jason had deserted. **2** a sea nymph, one of the Nereids.

glaucoma (glɔː'kəʊmə) *n* a disease of the eye in which increased pressure within the eyeball causes impaired vision, sometimes progressing to blindness. [C17: from L, from Gk, from *glaukos*; see GLAUCOUS]
▶ glau'comatous *adj*

glaucous ('glɔːkəs) *adj* **1** Bot. covered with a waxy or powdery bloom. **2** bluish-green. [C17: from L *glaucus* silvery, bluish-green, from Gk *glaukos*]

glaze (gleɪz) *vb* **glazes, glazing, glazed. 1** (*tr*) to fit or cover with glass. **2** (*tr*) Ceramics. to cover with a vitreous solution, rendering impervious to liquid. **3** (*tr*) to cover (foods) with a shiny coating by applying beaten egg, sugar, etc. **4** (*tr*) to make glossy or shiny. **5** (when *intr*, often foll. by *over*) to become or cause to become glassy: *his eyes were glazing over.* ◆ *n* **6** Ceramics. **6a** a vitreous coating. **6b** the substance used to produce such a coating. **7** a smooth lustrous finish on a fabric produced by applying various chemicals. **8** something used to give a

★ people and places

glossy surface to foods: *a syrup glaze.* [C14 *glasen,* from *glas* GLASS]
▶ **glazed** *adj* ▶ **'glazer** *n*

glaze ice *n Brit.* a thin clear layer of ice caused by the freezing of rain in the air or by refreezing after a thaw.

glazier ('gleɪzɪə) *n* a person who fits windows, doors, etc., with glass.
▶ **'glaziery** *n*

glazing ('gleɪzɪŋ) *n* 1 the surface of a glazed object. 2 glass fitted, or to be fitted, in a door, frame, etc.

Glazunov ★ ('glæzʊnɒf; *Russian* gləzu'nɔf) *n* **Aleksandr Konstantinovich** (alɪk'sandr kənstan'tinəvitʃ). 1865–1936, Russian composer, in France from 1928. A pupil of Rimsky-Korsakov, his works include eight symphonies and concertos for piano and for violin.

GLC *abbrev. for* Greater London Council; abolished 1986.

gleam (gliːm) *n* 1 a small beam or glow of light, esp. reflected light. 2 a brief or dim indication: *a gleam of hope.*
♦ *vb* (*intr*) 3 to send forth or reflect a beam of light. 4 to appear, esp. briefly. [OE *glǣm*]
▶ **'gleaming** *adj* ▶ **'gleamingly** *adv* ▶ **'gleamy** *adj*

glean (gliːn) *vb* 1 to gather (something) slowly and carefully in small pieces: *to glean information.* 2 to gather (the useful remnants of a crop) from the field after harvesting. [C14: from OF *glener,* from LL *glennāre,* prob. of Celtic origin]
▶ **'gleaner** *n*

gleanings ('gliːnɪŋz) *pl n* the useful remnants of a crop that can be gathered from the field after harvesting.

glebe (gliːb) *n* 1 *Brit.* land granted to a clergyman as part of his benefice. 2 *Poetic.* land, esp. for growing things. [C14: from L *glaeba*]

glee (gliː) *n* 1 great merriment or delight, often caused by someone else's misfortune. 2 a type of song originating in 18th-century England, sung by three or more unaccompanied voices. [OE *glēo*]

glee club *n Now chiefly US & Canad.* a society organized for the singing of choral music.

gleeful ('gliːfʊl) *adj* full of glee; merry.
▶ **'gleefully** *adv* ▶ **'gleefulness** *n*

gleeman ('gliːmən) *n, pl* **gleemen.** *Obs.* a minstrel.

Gleiwitz ★ ('glaɪvɪts) *n* the German name for **Gliwice**.

glen (glɛn) *n* a narrow and deep mountain valley, esp. in Scotland or Ireland. [C15: from Scot. Gaelic *gleann,* from OIrish *glend*]

Glen Albyn ★ ('ælbɪn, 'ɔːl-) *n* another name for the **Great Glen**.

Glencoe ★ (glɛn'kəʊ) *n* a glen in W Scotland, in S Highland: site of a massacre of Macdonalds by Campbells and English troops (1692).

Glendower ★ (glɛn'daʊə) *n* **Owen,** Welsh name *Owain Glyndŵr.* ?1350–?1416, Welsh chieftain, who led a revolt against Henry IV's rule in Wales (1400–15).

glengarry (glɛn'gærɪ) *n, pl* **glengarries.** a brimless Scottish cap with a crease down the crown, often with ribbons at the back. Also called: **glengarry bonnet.** [C19: after *Glengarry,* Scotland]

Glen More ★ (mɔː) *n* another name for the **Great Glen**.

Glenn ★ (glɛn) *n* **John.** born 1921, US astronaut and politician. The first American to orbit the earth (Feb., 1962), he later became a senator. In 1998, as a passenger aboard the space shuttle, he became the oldest person to have gone into space.

Glenrothes ★ (glɛn'rɒθɪs) *n* a new town in E central Scotland, the administrative centre of Fife: founded in 1948. Pop.: 38 650 (1991).

glia ('gliːə) *n* the delicate web of connective tissue that surrounds and supports nerve cells. Also called: **neuroglia.**
▶ **'glial** *adj*

glib (glɪb) *adj* **glibber, glibbest.** fluent and easy, often in an insincere or deceptive way. [C16: prob. from MLow G *glibberich* slippery]
▶ **'glibly** *adv* ▶ **'glibness** *n*

glide (glaɪd) *vb* **glides, gliding, glided.** 1 to move or cause to move easily without jerks or hesitations. 2 (*intr*) to pass

slowly or without perceptible change: *to glide into sleep.* 3 to cause (an aircraft) to come into land without engine power, or (of an aircraft) to land in this way. 4 (*intr*) to fly a glider. 5 (*intr*) *Music.* to execute a portamento from one note to another. 6 (*intr*) *Phonetics.* to produce a glide. ♦ *n* 7 a smooth easy movement. 8a any of various dances featuring gliding steps. 8b a step in such a dance. 9 a manoeuvre in which an aircraft makes a gentle descent without engine power. 10 the act or process of gliding. 11 *Music.* a portamento or slur. 12 *Phonetics.* a transitional sound as the speech organs pass from the articulatory position of one speech sound to that of the next. [OE *glīdan*]
▶ **'glidingly** *adv*

glide path *n* the path of an aircraft as it descends to land.

glider ('glaɪdə) *n* 1 an aircraft capable of gliding and soaring in air currents without the use of an engine. 2 a person or thing that glides.

glide time *n* the NZ term for **flexitime.**

glimmer ('glɪmə) *vb* (*intr*) 1 (of a light) to glow faintly or flickeringly. 2 to be indicated faintly: *hope glimmered in his face.* ♦ *n* 3 a glow or twinkle of light. 4 a faint indication. [C14: cf. MHG *glimmern*]
▶ **'glimmeringly** *adv*

glimpse (glɪmps) *n* 1 a brief or incomplete view: *to catch a glimpse of the sea.* 2 a vague indication. 3 *Arch.* a glimmer of light. ♦ *vb* **glimpses, glimpsing, glimpsed.** 4 (*tr*) to catch sight of momentarily. [C14: of Gmc origin; cf. MHG *glimsen* to glimmer]
▶ **'glimpser** *n*

> **USAGE NOTE** *Glimpse* is sometimes wrongly used where *glance* is meant: *he gave a quick glance* (not *glimpse*) *at his watch.*

Glinka ★ (*Russian* 'glinkə) *n* **Mikhail Ivanovich** (mixa'il i'vanəvitʃ). 1803–57, Russian composer. His operas include *Russlan and Ludmilla* (1842).

glint (glɪnt) *vb* 1 to gleam or cause to gleam brightly. ♦ *n* 2 a bright gleam or flash. 3 brightness or gloss. 4 a brief indication. [C15: prob. from ON]

glioma (glaɪ'əʊmə) *n, pl* **gliomata** (-mətə) *or* **gliomas.** a tumour of the brain and spinal cord, composed of glia cells and fibres. [C19: from NL, from Gk *glia* glue + -OMA]

glissade (glɪ'sɑːd, -'seɪd) *n* 1 a gliding step in ballet. 2 a controlled slide down a snow slope. ♦ *vb* **glissades, glissading, glissaded.** 3 (*intr*) to perform a glissade. [C19: from F, from *glisser* to slip, from OF *glicier,* of Frankish origin]

glissando (glɪ'sændəʊ) *n, pl* **glissandi** (-diː) *or* **glissandos.** a rapidly executed series of notes, each of which is discretely audible. [C19: prob. It. var. of GLISSADE]

glisten ('glɪsᵊn) *vb* (*intr*) 1 (of a wet or glossy surface) to gleam by reflecting light. 2 (of light) to reflect with brightness: *the sunlight glistens on wet leaves.* ♦ *n* 3 *Rare.* a gleam or gloss. [OE *glisnian*]

glister ('glɪstə) *vb, n* an archaic word for **glitter.** [C14: prob. from MDu. *glisteren*]

glitch (glɪtʃ) *n* 1 a sudden instance of malfunctioning in an electronic system. 2 a change in the rotation rate of a pulsar. [C20: from ?]

glitter ('glɪtə) *vb* (*intr*) 1 (of a hard, wet, or polished surface) to reflect light in bright flashes. 2 (of light) to be reflected in bright flashes. 3 (usually foll. by *with*) to be decorated or enhanced by the glamour (of): *the show glitters with famous actors.* ♦ *n* 4 sparkle or brilliance. 5 show and glamour. 6 tiny pieces of shiny decorative material. 7 *Canad.* Also called: **silver thaw.** ice formed from freezing rain. [C14: from ON *glitra*]
▶ **'glitteringly** *adv* ▶ **'glittery** *adj*

glitterati (ˌglɪtə'rɑːtiː) *pl n Inf.* the leaders of society, esp. the rich and beautiful. [C20: from GLITTER + *-ati* as in LITERATI]

glitzy ('glɪtsɪ) *adj* **glitzier, glitziest.** *Sl.* showily attractive;

flashy or glittery. [C20: prob. via Yiddish from G *glitzern* to glitter]

Gliwice ★ (*Polish* gli'vitsɛ) *n* an industrial city in S Poland. Pop.: 214 200 (1995 est.). German name: **Gleiwitz**.

gloaming ('gləʊmɪŋ) *n Scot. or poetic.* twilight or dusk. [OE *glōmung*, from *glōm*]

gloat (gləʊt) *vb* **1** (*intr;* often foll. by *over*) to dwell (on) with malevolent smugness or exultation. ◆ *n* **2** the act of gloating. [C16: prob. of Scand. origin; cf. ON *glotta* to grin, MHG *glotzen* to stare]
▶ 'gloater *n*

glob (glɒb) *n Inf.* a rounded mass of some thick fluid substance. [C20: prob. from GLOBE, infl. by BLOB]

global ('gləʊbᵊl) *adj* **1** covering or relating to the whole world. **2** comprehensive; total.
▶ 'globally *adv*

globalization *or* **globalisation** (ˌgləʊbᵊlaɪ'zeɪʃən) *n* **1** the process enabling financial and investment markets to operate internationally, largely as a result of deregulation and improved communications. **2** the process by which a company, etc., expands to operate internationally.

globalize *or* **globalise** ('gləʊbᵊˌlaɪz) *vb* **globalizes, globalizing, globalized** *or* **globalises, globalising, globalised.** (*tr*) to put into effect or spread worldwide.

global product *n* a commercial product, such as Coca Cola, that is marketed throughout the world under the same brand name.

global warming *n* an increase in the average temperature worldwide believed to be caused by the greenhouse effect.

globe (gləʊb) *n* **1** a sphere on which a map of the world is drawn. **2** **the globe.** the world; the earth. **3** a planet or some other astronomical body. **4** an object shaped like a sphere, such as a glass lampshade or fishbowl. **5** an orb, usually of gold, symbolic of sovereignty. ◆ *vb* **globes, globing, globed. 6** to form or cause to form into a globe. [C16: from OF, from L *globus*]
▶ 'globe,like *adj*

globefish ('gləʊbˌfɪʃ) *n, pl* **globefish** *or* **globefishes.** another name for **puffer.**

globeflower ('gləʊbˌflaʊə) *n* a plant having pale yellow, white, or orange globe-shaped flowers.

globetrotter ('gləʊbˌtrɒtə) *n* a habitual worldwide traveller, esp. a tourist.
▶ 'globe,trotting *n, adj*

globigerina (gləʊˌbɪdʒə'raɪnə) *n, pl* **globigerinas** *or* **globigerinae** (-niː). **1** a marine protozoan having a rounded shell with spiny processes. **2** **globigerina ooze.** a deposit on the ocean floor consisting of the shells of these protozoans. [C19: from NL, from L *globus* GLOBE + *gerere* to bear]

globoid ('gləʊbɔɪd) *adj* **1** shaped like a globe. ◆ *n* **2** a globoid body.

globose ('gləʊbəʊs, gləʊ'bəʊs) *or* **globous** ('gləʊbəs) *adj* spherical or approximately spherical. [C15: from L *globōsus;* see GLOBE]
▶ 'globosely *adv*

globular ('glɒbjʊlə) *or* **globulous** *adj* **1** shaped like a globe or globule. **2** having or consisting of globules.

globule ('glɒbjuːl) *n* a small globe, esp. a drop of liquid. [C17: from L *globulus*, dim. of *globus* GLOBE]

globulin ('glɒbjʊlɪn) *n* any of a group of simple proteins that are generally insoluble in water but soluble in salt solutions.

glockenspiel ('glɒkənˌspiːl, -ˌʃpiːl) *n* a percussion instrument consisting of a set of tuned metal plates played with a pair of small hammers. [C19: G, from *Glocken* bells + *Spiel* play]

glomerate ('glɒmərɪt) *adj* **1** gathered into a compact rounded mass. **2** *Anat.* (esp. of glands) conglomerate in structure. [C18: from L *glomerāre*, from *glomus* ball]
▶ ,glome'ration *n*

glomerule ('glɒməˌruːl) *n Bot.* an inflorescence in the form of a ball-like cluster of flowers. [C18: from NL *glomerulus*]

Glomma ★ (*Norwegian* 'glɔma) *n* a river in SE Norway, rising near the border with Sweden and flowing generally south to the Skagerrak: the largest river in Scandinavia; important for hydroelectric power and floating timber. Length: 588 km (365 miles).

gloom (gluːm) *n* **1** partial or total darkness. **2** a state of depression or melancholy. **3** an appearance or expression of despondency or melancholy. **4** *Poetic.* a dim or dark place. ◆ *vb* **5** (*intr*) to look sullen or depressed. **6** to make or become dark or gloomy. [C14 *gloumben* to look sullen]

gloomy ('gluːmɪ) *adj* **gloomier, gloomiest. 1** dark or dismal. **2** causing depression or gloom: *gloomy news.* **3** despairing; sad.
▶ 'gloomily *adv* ▶ 'gloominess *n*

gloop (gluːp) *or esp.* US **glop** (glɒp) *n Inf.* any messy sticky fluid or substance. [C20: from ?]
▶ 'gloopy *or esp.* US 'gloppy *adj*

gloria ('glɔːrɪə) *n* a halo or nimbus, esp. as represented in art. [C16: from L: GLORY]

Gloria ('glɔːrɪə, -ˌɑː) *n* **1** any of several doxologies beginning with the word *Gloria.* **2** a musical setting of one of these.

glorify ('glɔːrɪˌfaɪ) *vb* **glorifies, glorifying, glorified.** (*tr*) **1** to make glorious. **2** to make more splendid; adorn. **3** to worship, exalt, or adore. **4** to extol. **5** to cause to seem more splendid or imposing than reality.
▶ ,glorifi'cation *n*

gloriole ('glɔːrɪˌəʊl) *n* another name for a **halo.** [C19: from L *glōriola*, lit.: a small GLORY]

glorious ('glɔːrɪəs) *adj* **1** having or full of glory; illustrious. **2** conferring glory or renown: *a glorious victory.* **3** brilliantly beautiful. **4** delightful or enjoyable.
▶ 'gloriously *adv* ▶ 'gloriousness *n*

glory ('glɔːrɪ) *n, pl* **glories. 1** exaltation, praise, or honour. **2** something that brings or is worthy of praise (esp. in **crowning glory**). **3** thanksgiving, adoration, or worship: *glory be to God.* **4** pomp; splendour: *the glory of the king's reign.* **5** radiant beauty; resplendence: *the glory of the sunset.* **6** the beauty and bliss of heaven. **7** a state of extreme happiness or prosperity. **8** another word for **halo** or **nimbus.** ◆ *vb* **glories, glorying, gloried. 9** (*intr;* often foll. by *in*) to triumph or exult. ◆ *interj* **10** *Inf.* a mild interjection to express pleasure or surprise (often **glory be!**). [C13: from OF *glorie*, from L *glōria*, from ?]

glory box *n Austral. & NZ.* (esp. formerly) a box in which a young woman stores clothes, etc., in preparation for marriage.

glory hole *n* **1** a cupboard or storeroom, esp. one which is very untidy. **2** *Naut.* another term for **lazaretto** (sense 1).

Glos *abbrev.* for Gloucestershire.

gloss¹ (glɒs) *n* **1a** lustre or sheen, as of a smooth surface. **1b** (*as modifier*): *gloss paint.* **2** a superficially attractive appearance. **3** a cosmetic used to give a sheen. ◆ *vb* **4** to give a gloss to or obtain a gloss. **5** (*tr;* often foll. by *over*) to hide under a deceptively attractive surface or appearance. [C16: prob. of Scand. origin]
▶ 'glosser *n*

gloss² (glɒs) *n* **1** a short or expanded explanation or interpretation of a word, expression, or foreign phrase in the margin or text of a manuscript, etc. **2** an intentionally misleading explanation. **3** short for **glossary.** ◆ *vb* (*tr*) **4** to add glosses to. **5** (often foll. by *over*) to give a false or misleading interpretation of. [C16: from L *glōssa* unusual word requiring explanatory note, from Ionic Gk]

glossary ('glɒsərɪ) *n, pl* **glossaries.** an alphabetical list of terms peculiar to a field of knowledge with explanations. [C14: from LL *glossārium;* see GLOSS²]
▶ 'glossarial (glɒ'sɛərɪəl) *adj* ▶ 'glossarist *n*

glosseme ('glɒsiːm) *n* the smallest meaningful unit of a language, such as stress, form, etc. [C20: from Gk; see GLOSS², -EME]

glossitis (glɒ'saɪtɪs) *n* inflammation of the tongue.
▶ 'glossitic (glɒ'sɪtɪk) *adj*

glosso- *or before a vowel* **gloss-** *combining form.* indicat-

★ people and places

ing a tongue or language: *glossolaryngeal*. [from Gk *glossa* tongue]

glossolalia (ˌglɒsəˈleɪlɪə) *n* another term for **gift of tongues**. [C19: NL, from GLOSSO- + Gk *lalein* to babble]

glossy ('glɒsɪ) *adj* **glossier, glossiest. 1** smooth and shiny; lustrous. **2** superficially attractive; plausible. **3** (of a magazine) lavishly produced on shiny paper. ♦ *n, pl* **glossies. 4** Also called (US): **slick.** an expensively produced magazine, printed on shiny paper and containing high-quality colour photography. **5** a photograph printed on paper that has a smooth shiny surface.
▶ **'glossily** *adv* ▶ **'glossiness** *n*

glottal ('glɒtᵊl) *adj* **1** of or relating to the glottis. **2** *Phonetics*. articulated or pronounced at or with the glottis.

glottal stop *n* a plosive speech sound produced by tightly closing the glottis and allowing the air pressure to build up before opening the glottis, causing the air to escape with force.

glottis ('glɒtɪs) *n, pl* **glottises** *or* **glottides** (-tɪˌdiːz). the vocal apparatus of the larynx, consisting of the two true vocal cords and the opening between them. [C16: from NL, from Gk, from Attic form of Ionic *glōssa* tongue; see GLOSS²]

Gloucester[1] ★ ('glɒstə) *n* a city in SW England, administrative centre of Gloucestershire, on the River Severn; cathedral (founded 1100). Pop.: 104 800 (1993 est.). Latin name: **Glevum** ('gliːvʊm).

Gloucester[2] ★ ('glɒstə) *n* **1 Humphrey,** Duke of. 1391–1447, English soldier and statesman; son of Henry IV. He acted as protector during Henry VI's minority (1422–29) and was noted for his patronage of humanists. **2 Duke of.** See **Richard III. 3 Duke of.** See **Thomas of Woodstock.**

Gloucestershire ★ ('glɒstəˌʃɪə, -ʃə) *n* a county of SW England, situated around the lower Severn valley: contains the Forest of Dean and the main part of the Cotswold Hills; includes the unitary authority of South Gloucestershire. Administrative centre: Gloucester. Pop.: 769 500 (1996 est.). Area: 3153 sq. km (1217 sq. miles). Abbrev.: **Glos.**

glove (glʌv) *n* **1** (*often pl*) a shaped covering for the hand with individual sheaths for the fingers and thumb, made of leather, fabric, etc. **2** any of various large protective hand covers worn in sports, such as a boxing glove. ♦ *vb* **gloves, gloving, gloved. 3** (*tr*) to cover or provide with or as if with gloves. [OE *glōfe*]

glove box *n* a closed box in which toxic or radioactive substances can be handled by an operator who places his hands through protective gloves sealed to the box.

glove compartment *n* a small compartment in a car dashboard for the storage of miscellaneous articles.

glover ('glʌvə) *n* a person who makes or sells gloves.

glow (gləʊ) *n* **1** light emitted by a substance or object at a high temperature. **2** a steady even light without flames. **3** brilliance of colour. **4** brightness of complexion. **5** a feeling of wellbeing or satisfaction. **6** intensity of emotion. ♦ *vb* (*intr*) **7** to emit a steady even light without flames. **8** to shine intensely, as if from great heat. **9** to be exuberant, as from excellent health or intense emotion. **10** to experience a feeling of wellbeing or satisfaction: *to glow with pride*. **11** (esp. of the complexion) to show a strong bright colour, esp. red. **12** to be very hot. [OE *glōwan*]

glow discharge *n* a silent luminous discharge of electricity through a low-pressure gas.

glower ('glaʊə) *vb* **1** (*intr*) to stare hard and angrily. ♦ *n* **2** a sullen or angry stare. [C16: prob. of Scand. origin]
▶ **'gloweringly** *adv*

glowing ('gləʊɪŋ) *adj* **1** emitting light without flames: *glowing embers*. **2** warm and rich in colour: *glowing shades of gold and orange*. **3** flushed and rosy: *glowing cheeks*. **4** displaying or indicative of extreme pride or emotion: *a glowing account of his son's achievements*.

glow-worm *n* a European beetle, the females and larvae of which bear luminescent organs producing a soft greenish light.

gloxinia (glɒkˈsɪnɪə) *n* any of several tropical plants cultivated for their large white, red, or purple bell-shaped flowers. [C19: after Benjamin P. *Gloxin*, 18th-cent. G physician & botanist]

gloze (gləʊz) *vb* **glozes, glozing, glozed.** *Arch.* **1** (*tr*; often foll. by *over*) to explain away; minimize the effect or importance of. **2** to make explanatory notes or glosses on (a text). **3** to use flattery (on). [C13: from OF *glosser* to comment; see GLOSS²]

Gluck ★ (*German* glʊk) *n* **Christoph Willibald von** ('krɪstɔf 'vɪlɪbalt fɔn). 1714–87, German composer, esp. of operas, including *Orfeo ed Euridice* (1762) and *Alceste* (1767).

glucose ('gluːkəʊz, -kəʊs) *n* **1** a white crystalline sugar, the most abundant form being dextrose. Formula: $C_6H_{12}O_6$. **2** a yellowish syrup obtained by incomplete hydrolysis of starch: used in confectionery, fermentation, etc. [C19: from F, from Gk *gleukos* sweet wine; rel. to Gk *glukus* sweet]

glucoside ('gluːkəʊˌsaɪd) *n Biochem.* any of a large group of glycosides that yield glucose on hydrolysis.
▶ **glucosidic** (ˌgluːkəʊˈsɪdɪk) *adj*

glue (gluː) *n* **1** any natural or synthetic adhesive, esp. a sticky gelatinous substance prepared by boiling animal products such as bones, skin, and horns. **2** any other sticky or adhesive substance. ♦ *vb* **glues, gluing** *or* **glueing, glued.** (*tr*) to join or stick together as with glue. [C14: from OF *glu*, from LL *glūs*]
▶ **'glue‿like** *adj* ▶ **'gluer** *n* ▶ **'gluey** *adj*

glue ear *n* accumulation of fluid in the middle ear in children, caused by infection and resulting in deafness.

glue-sniffing *n* the practice of inhaling the fumes of certain types of glue to produce intoxicating or hallucinatory effects.
▶ **'glue‿sniffer** *n*

gluhwein ('gluːˌvaɪn) *n* mulled wine. [G]

glum (glʌm) *adj* **glummer, glummest.** silent or sullen, as from gloom. [C16: var. of GLOOM]
▶ **'glumly** *adv* ▶ **'glumness** *n*

glume (gluːm) *n Bot.* one of a pair of dry membranous bracts at the base of the spikelet of grasses. [C18: from L *glūma* husk of corn]
▶ **glu'maceous** *adj*

gluon ('gluːɒn) *n* a hypothetical particle believed to be exchanged between quarks in order to bind them together to form particles. [C20: coined from GLUE + -ON]

glut (glʌt) *n* **1** an excessive amount, as in the production of a crop. **2** the act of glutting or state of being glutted. ♦ *vb* **gluts, glutting, glutted.** (*tr*) **3** to feed or supply beyond capacity. **4** to supply (a market, etc.) with a commodity in excess of the demand for it. [C14: prob. from OF *gloutir*, from L *gluttīre*; see GLUTTON¹]

glutamic acid (gluːˈtæmɪk) *n* an amino acid, occurring in proteins.

gluten ('gluːtᵊn) *n* a protein present in cereal grains, esp. wheat. [C16: from L: GLUE]
▶ **'glutenous** *adj*

gluteus (gluːˈtiːəs) *n, pl* **glutei** (-ˈtiːaɪ). any one of the three large muscles that form the human buttock. [C17: from NL, from Gk *gloutos* buttock, rump]
▶ **glu'teal** *adj*

glutinous ('gluːtɪnəs) *adj* resembling glue in texture; sticky.
▶ **'glutinously** *adv*

glutton[1] ('glʌtᵊn) *n* **1** a person devoted to eating and drinking to excess; greedy person. **2** a person who has or appears to have a voracious appetite for something: *a glutton for punishment*. [C13: from OF *glouton*, from L from *gluttīre* to swallow]
▶ **'gluttonous** *adj* ▶ **'gluttonously** *adv*

glutton[2] ('glʌtᵊn) *n* another name for **wolverine.** [C17: from GLUTTON¹, apparently translating G *Vielfrass* great eater]

gluttony ('glʌtᵊnɪ) *n* the act or practice of eating to excess.

glyceride ('glɪsəˌraɪd) *n* any fatty-acid ester of glycerol.

glycerine ('glɪsəriːn, ˌglɪsəˈriːn) *or* **glycerin** ('glɪsərɪn) *n* another name (not in technical usage) for **glycerol.** [C19:

from F, from Gk *glukeros* sweet + *-ine* -IN; rel. to Gk *glukus* sweet]

glycerol ('glɪsə,rɒl) *n* a colourless odourless syrupy liquid: a by-product of soap manufacture, used as a solvent, antifreeze, plasticizer, and sweetener (**E422**). Formula: $CH_2OHCHOHCH_2OH$. [C19: from GLYCER(IN) + -OL[1]]

glycine ('glaɪsiːn, glaɪ'siːn) *n* a white sweet crystalline amino acid occurring in most proteins. [C19: GLYCO- + -INE[2]]

glyco- *or before a vowel* **glyc-** *combining form.* sugar: *glycogen.* [from Gk *glukus* sweet]

glycogen ('glaɪkəʊdʒən) *n* a polysaccharide consisting of glucose units: the form in which carbohydrate is stored in animals.
▸ **glycogenic** (,glaɪkəʊ'dʒɛnɪk) *adj* ▸ ,**glyco**'**genesis** *n*

glycol ('glaɪkɒl) *n* another name (not in technical usage) for **ethanediol.**

glycolic acid (glaɪ'kɒlɪk) *n* a colourless crystalline compound found in sugar cane and sugar beet: used in the manufacture of pharmaceuticals, pesticides, and plasticizers.

glycolysis (glaɪ'kɒlɪsɪs) *n Biochem.* the breakdown of glucose by enzymes with the liberation of energy.

glycoside ('glaɪkəʊ,saɪd) *n* any of a group of substances derived from simple sugars by replacing the hydroxyl group by another group.
▸ **glycosidic** (,glaɪkəʊ'sɪdɪk) *adj*

glycosuria (,glaɪkəʊ'sjʊərɪə) *n* the presence of excess sugar in the urine, as in diabetes. [C19: from NL, from F *glycose* GLUCOSE + -URIA]

Glyndebourne ★ ('glaɪnd,bɔːn) *n* an estate in SE England, in East Sussex: site of an annual festival of opera, founded in 1934 by John Christie (1882–1962).

glyph (glɪf) *n* **1** a carved channel or groove, esp. a vertical one. **2** *Now rare.* another word for **hieroglyphic.** [C18: from F, from Gk, from *gluphein* to carve]
▸ '**glyphic** *adj*

glyptic ('glɪptɪk) *adj* of or relating to engraving or carving, esp. on precious stones. [C19: from F, from Gk, from *gluphein* to carve]

glyptodont ('glɪptə,dɒnt) *n* an extinct mammal of South America which resembled the giant armadillo. [C19: from Gk *gluptos* carved + -ODONT]

GM *abbrev. for:* **1** general manager. **2** genetically modified. **3** (in Britain) George Medal. **4** Grand Master. **5** grant-maintained.

G-man *n, pl* **G-men. 1** *US sl.* an FBI agent. **2** *Irish.* a political detective.

Gmc *abbrev. for* Germanic.

GMT *abbrev. for* Greenwich Mean Time.

GMWU (in Britain) *abbrev. for* National Union of General and Municipal Workers.

gnarl (nɑːl) *n* **1** any knotty swelling on a tree. ◆ *vb* **2** (*tr*) to knot or cause to knot. [C19: back formation from *gnarled*]

gnarled (nɑːld) *or* **gnarly** *adj* **1** having gnarls: *the gnarled trunk of the old tree.* **2** (esp. of hands) rough, twisted, and weather-beaten.

gnash (næʃ) *vb* **1** to grind (the teeth) together, as in pain or anger. **2** (*tr*) to bite or chew as by grinding the teeth. ◆ *n* **3** the act of gnashing the teeth. [C15: prob. from ON; cf. *gnastan* gnashing of teeth]

gnat (næt) *n* any of various small fragile biting two-winged insects. [OE *gnætt*]

gnathic ('næθɪk) *adj Anat.* of or relating to the jaw. [C19: from Gk *gnathos* jaw]

-gnathous *adj combining form.* indicating or having a jaw of a specified kind: *prognathous.* [from NL, from Gk *gnathos* jaw]

gnaw (nɔː) *vb* **gnaws, gnawing, gnawed; gnawed** *or* **gnawn. 1** (when *intr*, often foll. by *at* or *upon*) to bite (at) or chew (upon) constantly so as to wear away little by little. **2** (*tr*) to form by gnawing: *to gnaw a hole.* **3** to cause erosion of (something). **4** (when *intr*, often foll. by *at*) to cause constant distress or anxiety (to). ◆ *n* **5** the act or an instance of gnawing. [OE *gnagan*]

gnawing ('nɔːɪŋ) *n* a dull persistent pang or pain, esp. of hunger.

gneiss (naɪs) *n* any coarse-grained metamorphic rock that is banded or foliated. [C18: from G *Gneis*, prob. from MHG *ganeist* spark]
▸ '**gneissic,** '**gneissoid,** *or* '**gneissose** *adj*

gnocchi ('nɒkɪ) *pl n* dumplings made of pieces of semolina pasta, or sometimes potato, served with sauce. [It., pl of *gnocco* lump, prob. of Gmc origin]

gnome (nəʊm) *n* **1** one of a species of legendary creatures, usually resembling small misshapen old men, said to live in the depths of the earth and guard buried treasure. **2** the statue of a gnome, esp. in a garden. **3** a very small or ugly person. **4** *Facetious or derog.* an international banker or financier (esp. in **gnomes of Zürich**). [C18: from F, from NL *gnomus*, coined by Paracelsus (1493-1541), Swiss alchemist, from ?]
▸ '**gnomish** *adj*

gnomic ('nəʊmɪk, 'nɒm-) *adj* of or relating to aphorisms; pithy.
▸ '**gnomically** *adv*

gnomon ('nəʊmɒn) *n* **1** the stationary arm that projects the shadow on a sundial. **2** a geometric figure remaining after a parallelogram has been removed from one corner of a larger parallelogram. [C16: from L, from Gk: interpreter, from *gignōskein* to know]
▸ **gno'monic** *adj*

-gnosis *n combining form.* (esp. in medicine) recognition or knowledge: *diagnosis.* [via L from Gk: knowledge]
▸ **-gnostic** *adj combining form.*

gnostic ('nɒstɪk) *adj* of, relating to, or possessing knowledge, esp. spiritual knowledge.

Gnostic ('nɒstɪk) *n* **1** an adherent of Gnosticism. ◆ *adj* **2** of or relating to Gnostics or to Gnosticism. [C16: from LL, from Gk *gnōstikos* relating to knowledge]

Gnosticism ('nɒstɪ,sɪzəm) *n* a religious movement characterized by a belief in intuitive spiritual knowledge: regarded as a heresy by the Christian Church.

gnotobiotic (,nəʊtəʊbaɪ'ɒtɪk) *adj* of or pertaining to germ-free conditions, esp. in a laboratory in which animals are injected with known strains of organisms. [C20: from Gk *gnōtos*, from *gignōskein* to know + BIOTIC]

GNP *abbrev. for* gross national product.

gnu (nuː) *n, pl* **gnus** *or* **gnu.** either of two sturdy antelopes inhabiting the savannas of Africa, having an oxlike head and a long tufted tail. Also called: **wildebeest.** [C18: from Xhosa *nqu*]

GNVQ (in Britain) *abbrev. for* general national vocational qualification: a qualification which rewards the development of skills likely to be of use to employers.

go (gəʊ) *vb* **goes, going, went, gone.** (*mainly intr*) **1** to move or proceed, esp. to or from a point or in a certain direction: *go home.* **2** (*tr; takes an infinitive, often with* to *omitted or replaced by* and) to proceed towards a particular point or place with some specified purpose: *I must go and get that book.* **3** to depart: *we'll have to go at eleven.* **4** to start, as in a race: *often used in commands.* **5** to make regular journeys: *this train service goes to the east coast.* **6** to operate or function effectively: *the radio won't go.* **7** (*copula*) to become: *his face went red.* **8** to make a noise as specified: *the gun went bang.* **9** to enter into a specified state or condition: *to go into hysterics.* **10** to be or continue to be in a specified state or condition: *to go in rags; to go in poverty.* **11** to lead, extend, or afford access: *this route goes to the north.* **12** to proceed towards an activity: *to go to sleep.* **13** (*tr; takes an infinitive*) to serve or contribute: *this letter goes to prove my point.* **14** to follow a course as specified; fare: *the lecture went badly.* **15** to be applied or allotted to a particular purpose or recipient: *his money went on drink.* **16** to be sold: *the necklace went for three thousand pounds.* **17** to be ranked; compare: *this meal is good as my meals go.* **18** to blend or harmonize: *these chairs won't go with the rest of your furniture.* **19** (foll. by *by* or *under*) to be known (by a name or disguise). **20** to have a usual or proper place: *those books go on this shelf.* **21** (of music, poetry, etc.) to be sounded; expressed, etc.: *how does that song go?* **22** to fail or give way: *my eyesight is going.* **23** to break down or collapse abruptly: *the ladder went at the critical moment.* **24** to die: *the old man went at 2 a.m.* **25** (often foll. by *by*) **25a** (of time, etc.) to elapse: *the hours go by so slowly.* **25b** to travel past: *the train goes by her house.* **25c** to be guided (by). **26** to occur: *happiness does not always go with riches.* **27** to be eliminated, abolished, or given up: *this entry must go to save space.* **28** to be spent or finished: *all his money has gone.* **29** to attend: *go to school.* **30** to join a stated profession: *go on the stage.* **31** (foll. by *to*) to have recourse to; turn: *to go to arbitration.* **32** (foll. by *to*) to subject or put oneself (to): *she goes to great pains to please him.* **33** to proceed, go up to or beyond certain limits: *you will go too far one day and then you will be punished.* **34** to be acceptable or tolerated: *anything goes.* **35** to carry the weight of final authority: *what the boss says goes.* **36** (*tr*) Nonstandard. to say: *Then she goes, "Give it to me!" and she just snatched it.* **37** (foll. by *into*) to be contained in: *four goes into twelve three times.* **38** (often foll. by *for*) to endure or last out: *we can't go for much longer without water.* **39** (*tr*) Cards. to bet or bid: *I go two hearts.* **40 be going.** to intend or be about to start (to do or be doing something): often used as an alternative future construction: *what's going to happen to us?* **41 go and.** Inf. to be so foolish or unlucky as to: *then she had to go and lose her hat.* **42 go it.** Sl. to do something or move energetically. **43 go it alone.** Inf. to act or proceed without allies or help. **44 go one better.** Inf. to surpass or outdo (someone). **45 let go.** 45a to relax one's hold (on); release. **45b** to discuss or consider no further. **46 let oneself go.** 46a to act in an uninhibited manner. **46b** to lose interest in one's appearance, manners, etc. **47 to go.** 47a remaining. **47b** US & Canad. inf. (of food served by a restaurant) for taking away. ◆ *n, pl* **goes.** **48** the act of going. **49a** an attempt or try: *he had a go at the stamp business.* **49b** an attempt at stopping a person suspected of a crime: *the police are not always in favour of the public having a go.* **49c** an attack, esp. verbal: *she had a real go at them.* **50** a turn: *it's my go next.* **51** Inf. the quality of being active and energetic: *she has much more go than I have.* **52** Inf. hard or energetic work: *it's all go.* **53** Inf. a successful venture or achievement: *he made a go of it.* **54** Inf. a bargain or agreement. **55 from the word go.** Inf. from the very beginning. **56 no go.** Inf. impossible; abortive or futile: *it's no go, I'm afraid.* **57 on the go.** Inf. active and energetic. ◆ *adj* **58** (*postpositive*) Inf. functioning properly and ready for action: esp. used in astronautics: *all systems are go.* ◆ See also **go about, go against**, etc. [OE *gān*]

Goa ★ ('gəʊə) *n* a state on the W coast of India: a Portuguese overseas territory from 1510 until annexed by India in 1961. Pop.: 1 235 000 (1994 est.). Area: 3702 sq. km (1430 sq. miles).

go about *vb* (intr) **1** (*prep*) to busy oneself with: *to go about one's duties.* **2** (*prep*) to tackle (a problem or task). **3** to circulate (in): *there's a lot of flu going about.* **4** (*adv*) (of a sailing ship) to change from one tack to another.

goad (gəʊd) *n* **1** a sharp pointed stick for urging on cattle, etc. **2** anything that acts as a spur or incitement. ◆ *vb* **3** (*tr*) to drive as if with a goad; spur; incite. [OE *gād*, of Gmc origin]

Goa, Daman, and Diu ★ *n* a former Union Territory of India consisting of the widely separated districts of Goa and Daman and the island of Diu. Capital: Panaji. Area: 3814 sq. km (1472 sq. miles).

go against *vb* (intr, prep) **1** to be contrary to (principles or beliefs). **2** to be unfavourable to (a person): *the case went against him.*

go-ahead *n* **1** (usually preceded by *the*) Inf. permission to proceed. ◆ *adj* **2** enterprising or ambitious.

goal (gəʊl) *n* **1** the aim or object towards which an endeavour is directed. **2** the terminal point of a journey or race. **3** (in various sports) the net, basket, etc., into or over which players try to propel the ball, puck, etc., to score. **4** Sport. **4a** a successful attempt at scoring. **4b** the score so made. **5** (in soccer, hockey, etc.) the position of goalkeeper. [C16: ? rel. to ME *gol* boundary, OE *gǣlan* to hinder]
▶ **'goalless** *adj*

goalball ('gəʊl,bɔːl) *n* **1** a game played by two teams who compete to score goals by throwing a ball that emits sound when in motion. Players are blindfolded during play. **2** the ball used in this game.

goalie ('gəʊlɪ) *n Inf.* short for **goalkeeper**.

goalkeeper ('gəʊl,kiːpə) *n Sport.* a player in the goal whose duty is to prevent the ball, puck, etc., from entering or crossing it.

goal kick *n Soccer.* a kick taken from the six-yard line by the defending team after the ball has been put out of play by an opposing player.

goal line *n Sport.* the line marking each end of the pitch, on which the goals stand.

go along *vb* (intr, adv; often foll. by *with*) to refrain from disagreement; assent.

goalpost ('gəʊl,pəʊst) *n* **1** either of two upright posts supporting the crossbar of a goal. **2 move the goalposts.** to change the target required during negotiations, etc.

goanna (gəʊ'ænə) *n* any of various Australian monitor lizards. [C19: from IGUANA]

goat (gəʊt) *n* **1** any sure-footed agile ruminant mammal with hollow horns, naturally inhabiting rough stony ground in Europe, Asia, and N Africa. **2** Inf. a lecherous man. **3** a foolish person. **4 get (someone's) goat.** Sl. to cause annoyance to (someone). [OE *gāt*]
▶ **'goatish** *adj*

Goat (gəʊt) *n* **the.** the constellation Capricorn, the tenth sign of the zodiac.

go at *vb* (intr, prep) **1** to make an energetic attempt at (something). **2** to attack vehemently.

goatee (gəʊ'tiː) *n* a pointed tuftlike beard on the chin. [C19: from GOAT + *-ee* (see -Y²)]

goatherd ('gəʊt,hɜːd) *n* a person employed to tend or herd goats.

goatsbeard or **goat's-beard** ('gəʊts,bɪəd) *n* **1** Also called: **Jack-go-to-bed-at-noon**. a Eurasian plant of the composite family, with woolly stems and large heads of yellow rayed flowers. **2** an American plant with long spikes of small white flowers.

goatskin ('gəʊt,skɪn) *n* **1** the hide of a goat. **2** something made from the hide of a goat, such as leather or a container for wine.

goatsucker ('gəʊt,sʌkə) *n* the US and Canad. name for **nightjar**.

gob[1] (gɒb) *n* **1** a lump or chunk, esp. of a soft substance. **2** (*often pl*) Inf. a great quantity or amount. **3** Inf. a globule of spittle or saliva. **4** a lump of molten glass used to make a piece of glassware. ◆ *vb* **gobs, gobbing, gobbed.** **5** (intr) Brit. inf. to spit. [C14: from OF *gobe* lump, from *gober*; see GOBBET]

gob[2] (gɒb) *n* a slang word (esp. Brit.) for the **mouth**. [C16: ?from Gaelic *gob*]

go back *vb* (intr, adv) **1** to return. **2** (often foll. by *to*) to originate (in): *the links with France go back to the Norman Conquest.* **3** (foll. by *on*) to change one's mind about; repudiate (esp. in **go back on one's word**).

gobbet ('gɒbɪt) *n* a chunk, lump, or fragment, esp. of raw meat. [C14: from OF *gobet*, from *gober* to gulp down]

Gobbi ★ (Italian 'gɔbbi) *n* **Tito** ('tiːto). 1915–84, Italian operatic baritone.

gobble[1] ('gɒbªl) *vb* **gobbles, gobbling, gobbled.** **1** (when *tr*, often foll. by *up*) to eat or swallow (food) hastily and in large mouthfuls. **2** (*tr*; often foll. by *up*) Inf. to snatch. [C17: prob. from GOB¹]

gobble[2] ('gɒbªl) *n* **1** the loud rapid gurgling sound made by male turkeys. ◆ *vb* **gobbles, gobbling, gobbled.** **2** (intr) (of a turkey) to make this sound. [C17: prob. imit.]

gobbledegook or **gobbledygook** ('gɒbªl dɪ,guːk) *n* pretentious or unintelligible jargon, such as that used by officials. [C20: whimsical formation from GOBBLE²]

gobbler ('gɒblə) *n Inf.* a male turkey.

Gobelin ('gəʊbəlɪn; French gɔblɛ̃) *adj* **1** of or resembling tapestry made at the Gobelins' factory in Paris, having vivid pictorial scenes. ◆ *n* **2** a tapestry of this kind. [C19: from the *Gobelin* family, who founded the factory]

go-between *n* a person who acts as agent or intermediary for two people or groups in a transaction or dealing.

Gobi ★ ('gəʊbɪ) *n* a desert in E Asia, mostly in Mongolia and the Inner Mongolian Autonomous Region of

China: sometimes considered to include all the arid regions east of the Pamirs and north of the plateau of Tibet and the Great Wall of China: one of the largest deserts in the world. Length: about 1600 km (1000 miles). Width: about 1000 km (625 miles). Average height: 900 m (3000 ft). Chinese name: **Shamo.**
▶ **'Gobian** adj

Gobind Singh ('gəʊbɪnd 'sɪŋ) or **Govind Singh** ★ ('gəʊvɪnd 'sɪŋ) n 1666–1708, tenth and last guru of the Sikhs (1675–1708): assassinated.

goblet ('gɒblɪt) n 1 a vessel for drinking, with a base and stem but without handles. 2 *Arch.* a large drinking cup. [C14: from OF *gobelet* a little cup, ult. of Celtic origin]

goblin ('gɒblɪn) n (in folklore) a small grotesque supernatural creature, regarded as malevolent towards human beings. [C14: from OF, from MHG *kobolt*; cf. CO-BALT]

gobo ('gəʊbəʊ) n, pl **gobos** or **goboes**. a shield placed round a microphone to exclude unwanted sounds, or round a camera lens, etc., to reduce the incident light. [C20: from ?]

gobshite ('gɒb,ʃaɪt) n Irish taboo sl. a stupid person. [C20: from GOB² + *shite* excrement; see SHIT]

gobsmacked ('gɒb,smækt) adj Brit. sl. astounded; astonished. [C20: from GOB² + SMACK]

goby ('gəʊbɪ) n, pl **goby** or **gobies**. a small spiny-finned fish of coastal or brackish waters, having a large head, an elongated tapering body, and the ventral fins modified as a sucker. [C18: from L *gōbius* gudgeon from Gk *kōbios*]

go-by n Sl. a deliberate snub or slight (esp. in **give (a person) the go-by).**

go by vb (intr) 1 to pass: *as the years go by.* 2 (prep) to be guided by: *in the darkness we could only go by the stars.* 3 (prep) to use as a basis for forming an opinion or judgment: *it's wise not to go only by appearances.*

go-cart n See **kart.**

god (gɒd) n 1 a supernatural being, who is worshipped as the controller of some part of the universe or some aspect of life in the world or is the personification of some force. 2 an image, idol, or symbolic representation of such a deity. 3 any person or thing to which excessive attention is given: *money was his god.* 4 a man who has qualities regarded as making him superior to other men. 5 (pl) the gallery of a theatre. [OE *god*]

God ★ (gɒd) n 1 the sole Supreme Being, eternal, spiritual, and transcendent, who is the Creator and ruler of all and is infinite in all attributes; the object of worship in monotheistic religions. ◆ interj 2 an oath or exclamation used to indicate surprise, annoyance, etc. (and in such expressions as **My God!** or **God Almighty!).**

Godard ★ (French gɔdar) n **Jean-Luc** (ʒɑ̃lyk). born 1930, French film director and writer. His works include *À bout de souffle* (1960) and *Hélas pour moi* (1993).

Godavari ★ (gəʊ'dɑːvərɪ) n a river in central India, rising in the Western Ghats and flowing southeast to the Bay of Bengal: extensive delta, linked by canal with the Krishna delta; a sacred river to Hindus. Length: about 1500 km (900 miles).

godchild ('gɒd,tʃaɪld) n, pl **godchildren.** a person who is sponsored by adults at baptism.

Goddard ★ ('gɒdɑːd) n **Robert Hutchings.** 1882–1945, US physicist. He made the first workable liquid-fuelled rocket.

goddaughter ('gɒd,dɔːtə) n a female godchild.

goddess ('gɒdɪs) n 1 a female divinity. 2 a woman who is adored or idealized, esp. by a man.

Gödel ★ ('gɜːdʰl) n **Kurt** (kʊrt). 1906–78, US logician and mathematician, born in Austria-Hungary. He showed (**Gödel's proof**) that in a formal axiomatic system, such as logic or mathematics, it is impossible to prove consistency without using methods from outside the system.

Goderich ★ ('gəʊdrɪtʃ) n **Viscount,** title of *Frederick John Robinson,* 1st Earl of Ripon. 1782–1859, British statesman; prime minister (1827–28).

Godesberg ★ (German 'goːdəsbɛrk) n a town and spa in W Germany, in North Rhine-Westphalia on the Rhine: a SE suburb of Bonn. Official name: **Bad Godesberg.**

godetia (gə'diːʃə) n any plant of the American genus *Godetia,* esp. one grown as a showy-flowered annual garden plant. [C19: after C. H. *Godet* (died 1879), Swiss botanist]

godfather ('gɒd,fɑːðə) n 1 a male godparent. 2 the head of a Mafia family or other criminal ring. 3 an originator or leading exponent: *the godfather of South African pop.*

godfather offer n Inf. a takeover bid pitched so high that the management of the target company is unable to dissuade shareholders from accepting it. [from the 1972 film *The Godfather,* in which a character was made an offer he could not refuse]

God-fearing adj pious; devout.

godforsaken ('gɒdfə,seɪkən) adj (sometimes cap.) 1 (usually prenominal) desolate; dreary; forlorn. 2 wicked.

Godhead ('gɒd,hed) n (sometimes not cap.) 1 the essential nature and condition of being God. 2 **the Godhead.** God.

godhood ('gɒd,hʊd) n the state of being divine.

Godiva ★ (gə'daɪvə) n **Lady.** ?1040–1080, wife of Leofric, Earl of Mercia. According to legend, she rode naked through Coventry to obtain remission for the townspeople from the heavy taxes imposed by her husband.

godless ('gɒdlɪs) adj 1 wicked or unprincipled. 2 lacking a god. 3 refusing to acknowledge God.
▶ **'godlessly** adv ▶ **'godlessness** n

godlike ('gɒd,laɪk) adj resembling or befitting a god or God; divine.

godly ('gɒdlɪ) adj **godlier, godliest.** having a religious character; pious; devout.
▶ **'godliness** n

godmother ('gɒd,mʌðə) n a female godparent.

Godolphin ★ (gə'dɒlfɪn) n **Sidney.** 1st Earl of Godolphin. 1645–1712, English statesman; as Lord Treasurer, he managed the financing of Marlborough's campaigns in the War of the Spanish Succession.

godown ('gəʊ,daʊn) n (in the East, esp. in India) a warehouse. [C16: from Malay *godong*]

go down vb (intr, mainly adv) 1 (also prep) to move or lead to or as if to a lower place or level; sink, decline, decrease, etc. 2 to be defeated; lose. 3 to be remembered or recorded (esp. in **go down in history**). 4 to be received: *his speech went down well.* 5 (of food) to be swallowed. 6 Brit. to leave a college or university at the end of a term. 7 (usually foll. by with) to fall ill; be infected. 8 (of a celestial body) to sink or set. 9 **go down on.** Taboo sl. to perform cunnilingus or fellatio on.

godparent ('gɒd,peərənt) n a person who stands sponsor to another at baptism.

God's acre n Literary. a churchyard or burial ground. [C17: translation of G *Gottesacker*]

godsend ('gɒd,send) n a person or thing that comes unexpectedly but is particularly welcome. [C19: from C17 *God's send,* alteration of *goddes sand* God's message, from OE *sand*; see SEND]

godslot ('gɒd,slɒt) n Inf. a time in a television or radio schedule traditionally reserved for religious broadcasts.

godson ('gɒd,sʌn) n a male godchild.

Godspeed ('gɒd'spiːd) sentence substitute, n an expression of good wishes for a person's success and safety. [C15: from *God spede* may God prosper (you)]

godsquad ('gɒd,skwɒd) n Inf., derog. any group of evangelical Christians, members of which are regarded as intrusive and exuberantly pious.

Godthaab ★ (Danish 'gɔdhɔːb) n the former name for **Nuuk.**

Godunov ★ ('gɒdə,nɒf, 'gʊd-; Russian gədu'nɔf) n **Boris Fyodorovich** (ba'ris 'fjɔdərəvitʃ). ?1551–1605, Russian regent (1584–98) and tsar (1598–1605).

Godwin ★ ('gɒdwɪn) n 1 died 1053, Earl of Wessex. He was chief adviser to Canute and Edward the Confessor. His son succeeded Edward to the throne as Harold II. 2 **Mary.** See (Mary) **Wollstonecraft. 3 William.** 1756–1836, British political philosopher and novelist, noted for his *An Enquiry concerning Political Justice* (1793).

Godwin Austen ★ n another name for **K2.**

★ people and places

godwit ('gɒdwɪt) *n* a large shore bird of the sandpiper family having long legs and a long upturned bill. [C16: from ?]

Goebbels ★ (*German* 'gœbəls) *n* **Paul Joseph** (paul 'joːzɛf). 1897–1945, German Nazi politician; minister of propaganda (1933–45).

goer ('gəʊə) *n* **1a** a person who attends something regularly. **1b** (*in combination*): *filmgoer.* **2** a person or thing that goes, esp. one that goes very fast. **3** an energetic person. **4** *Austral. inf.* an acceptable or feasible idea, proposal, etc.

Goering ★ (*German* 'gøːrɪŋ) *n* See (Hermann Wilhelm) **Göring.**

Goethe ★ (*German* 'gøːtə) *n* **Johann Wolfgang von** (joˈhan 'vɔlfgaŋ fɔn). 1749–1832, German writer, who settled in Weimar in 1775. His early works of the *Sturm und Drang* period include the play *Götz von Berlichingen* (1773) and the novel *The Sorrows of Young Werther* (1774). Later works include the *Wilhelm Meister* novels (1796–1829) and the drama *Faust* (1808; 1832).

go-faster stripe *n Inf.* a decorative line, often suggestive of high speed, on the bodywork of a car.

gofer ('gəʊfə) *n Sl.* a person who runs errands. [C20: from GO + FOR]

goffer ('gəʊfə) *vb* (*tr*) **1** to press pleats into (a frill). **2** to decorate (the edges of a book). ◆ *n* **3** an ornamental frill made by pressing pleats. **4** the decoration formed by goffering books. **5** the iron or tool used in making goffers. [C18: from F *gaufrer* to impress a pattern, from *gaufre,* from MLow G *wāfel*; see WAFFLE¹, WAFER]

go for *vb* (*intr, prep*) **1** to go somewhere in order to have or fetch: *he went for a drink.* **2** to seek to obtain: *I'd go for that job if I were you.* **3** to prefer or choose; like: *I really go for that new idea of yours.* **4** to make a physical or verbal attack on. **5** to be considered to be of a stated importance or value: *his twenty years went for nothing when he was made redundant.* **6 go for it.** *Inf.* to make the maximum effort to achieve a particular goal.

Gog and Magog ★ (gɒg; 'meɪgɒg) *n* **1** *Old Testament.* a hostile prince and the land from which he comes to attack Israel (Ezekiel 38). **2** *New Testament.* two kings, who are to attack the Church in a climactic battle, but are then to be destroyed by God (Revelation 20:8–10). **3** *Brit. folklore.* two giants, the only survivors of a race of giants destroyed by Brutus, the legendary founder of Britain.

go-getter *n Inf.* an ambitious enterprising person.
▶ ˌgo-ˈgetting *adj*

gogga ('xɔxa) *n S. African inf.* any small animal that crawls or flies, esp. an insect. [C20: from Khoikhoi *xoxon* insects collectively]

goggle ('gɒgˀl) *vb* **goggles, goggling, goggled. 1** (*intr*) to stare fixedly, as in astonishment. **2** to cause (the eyes) to roll or bulge or (of the eyes) to roll or bulge. ◆ *n* **3** a bulging stare. **4** (*pl*) spectacles, often of coloured glass or covered with gauze: used to protect the eyes. [C14: from *gogelen* to look aside, from ?; see AGOG]
▶ ˈgoggle-ˌeyed *adj*

gogglebox ('gɒgˀl,bɒks) *n Brit. sl.* a television set.

Gogh ★ (gɒx; *Dutch* xɔx) *n* See (Vincent) **van Gogh.**

Go-Go *n* a form of soul music originating in Washington, DC, characterized by the use of funk rhythms and a brass section.

go-go dancer *n* a dancer, usually scantily dressed, who performs rhythmic and often erotic modern dance routines, esp. in a nightclub.

Gogol ★ ('gəʊgɒl; *Russian* 'gɔgəlj) *n* **Nikolai Vasilievich** (nika'laj va'siljɪvitʃ). 1809–52, Russian writer. His works include the play *The Government Inspector* (1836).

Gogra ★ ('gɒgrə) *n* a river in N India, rising in Tibet, in the Himalayas, and flowing southeast through Nepal as the Karnali, then through Uttar Pradesh to join the Ganges. Length: about 1000 km (600 miles).

Goiânia ★ (gɔɪˈɑːnɪə; *Portuguese* goˈjənjə) *n* a city in central Brazil, capital of Goiás state: planned in 1933 to replace the old capital, Goiás; two universities. Pop.: 1 033 000 (1995).

Goiás ★ (*Portuguese* gɔˈjas) *n* a state of central Brazil, in

the Brazilian Highlands: contains Brasília, the capital of Brazil. Capital: Goiânia. Pop.: 4 308 400 (1995 est.). Area: 341 289 sq. km (131 772 sq. miles).

Goidelic (gɔɪˈdɛlɪk) *n* **1** the N group of Celtic languages, consisting of Irish Gaelic, Scottish Gaelic, and Manx. ◆ *adj* **2** of, relating to, or characteristic of this group of languages. [C19: from OIrish *Goidel* a Celt, from OWelsh, from *gwydd* savage]

go in *vb* (*intr, adv*) **1** to enter. **2** (*prep*) See **go into. 3** (of the sun) to become hidden behind a cloud. **4 go in for. 4a** to enter as a competitor or contestant. **4b** to adopt as an activity, interest, or guiding principle: *she went in for nursing.*

going ('gəʊɪŋ) *n* **1** a departure or farewell. **2** the condition of a surface such as a road or field with regard to walking, riding, etc.: *muddy going.* **3** *Inf.* speed, progress, etc.: *we made good going on the trip.* ◆ *adj* **4** thriving (esp. in a **going concern**). **5** current or accepted: *the going rate.* **6** (*postpositive*) available: *the best going.*

going-over *n, pl* **goings-over.** *Inf.* **1** a check, examination, or investigation. **2** a castigation or thrashing.

goings-on *pl n Inf.* **1** actions or conduct, esp. when regarded with disapproval. **2** happenings or events, esp. when mysterious or suspicious.

go into *vb* (*intr, prep*) **1** to enter. **2** to start a career in: *to go into publishing.* **3** to investigate or examine. **4** to discuss: *we won't go into that now.* **5** to be admitted to, esp. temporarily: *she went into hospital.* **6** to enter a specified state: *she went into fits of laughter.*

goitre *or US* **goiter** ('gɔɪtə) *n Pathol.* a swelling of the thyroid gland, in some cases nearly doubling the size of the neck. [C17: from F, from OF *goitron* ult. from L *guttur* throat]
▶ ˈgoitred *or US* ˈgoitered *adj* ▶ ˈgoitrous *adj*

go-kart *or* **go-cart** *n* See **kart.**

Golan Heights ★ ('gəʊ,læn) *pl n* a range of hills in the Middle East, possession of which is disputed between Israel and Syria: under Syrian control until 1967 when they were stormed by Israeli forces; Jewish settlements have since been established. Highest peak: 2224 m (7297 ft).

Golconda ★ (gɒlˈkɒndə) *n* **1** a ruined town and fortress in S central India, in W Andhra Pradesh near Hyderabad city: capital of one of the five Muslim kingdoms of the Deccan from 1512 to 1687, then annexed to the Mogul empire; renowned for its diamonds. **2** (*sometimes not cap.*) a source of wealth or riches, esp. a mine.

gold (gəʊld) *n* **1a** a dense inert bright yellow element that is the most malleable and ductile metal, occurring in rocks and alluvial deposits: used as a monetary standard and in jewellery, dentistry, and plating. Symbol: Au; atomic no.: 79; atomic wt.: 196.97. Related adj: **auric. 1b** (*as modifier*): *a gold mine.* **2** a coin or coins made of this metal. **3** money; wealth. **4** something precious, beautiful, etc., such as a noble nature (esp. in **heart of gold**). **5a** a deep yellow colour, sometimes with a brownish tinge. **5b** (*as adj*): *a gold carpet.* **6** short for **gold medal.** [OE *gold*]

Gold ★ (gəʊld) *n* **Thomas.** born 1920, Austrian-born astronomer, working in England and the US: with Bondi and Hoyle he proposed the steady-state theory of the universe.

gold card *n* a credit card issued by credit-card companies to favoured clients, entitling them to high unsecured overdrafts, some insurance cover, etc.

Gold Coast ★ *n* **1** the former name (until 1957) of **Ghana. 2** a line of resort towns and beaches in E Australia, extending for over 30 km (20 miles) along the S coast of Queensland.

goldcrest ('gəʊld,krɛst) *n* a small Old World warbler having a greenish plumage and a bright yellow-and-black crown.

gold-digger *n* **1** a person who prospects or digs for gold. **2** *Inf.* a woman who uses her sexual attractions to accumulate gifts and wealth.

gold disc *n* **1** (in Britain) an LP record certified to have sold 100 000 copies or a single certified to have sold 400 000 copies. **2** (in the US) an LP record or single certified to have sold 500 000 copies.

gold dust *n* gold in the form of small particles or powder.

golden ('gəʊldən) *adj* **1** of the yellowish colour of gold: *golden hair*. **2** made from or largely consisting of gold: *a golden statue*. **3** happy or prosperous: *golden days*. **4** (*sometimes cap.*) (of anniversaries) the 50th in a series: *Golden Jubilee; golden wedding*. **5** *Inf.* very successful or destined for success: *the golden girl of tennis*. **6** extremely valuable or advantageous: *a golden opportunity*.
▶ **'goldenly** *adv* ▶ **'goldenness** *n*

golden age *n* **1** *Classical myth.* the first and best age of mankind, when existence was happy, prosperous, and innocent. **2** the most flourishing and outstanding period, esp. in the history of an art or nation: *the golden age of poetry*.

golden eagle *n* a large eagle of mountainous regions of the N hemisphere, having a plumage that is golden brown on the back.

goldeneye ('gəʊldən,aɪ) *n, pl* **goldeneyes** *or* **goldeneye**. either of two black-and-white diving ducks of northern regions.

Golden Fleece *n Greek myth.* the fleece of a winged ram stolen by Jason and the Argonauts.

Golden Gate ★ *n* a strait between the Pacific and San Francisco Bay: crossed by the **Golden Gate Bridge**, with a central span of 1280 m (4200 ft).

golden goose *n* a goose in folklore that laid a golden egg every day until its greedy owner killed it in an attempt to get all the gold at once.

golden handcuffs *pl n* payments deferred over a number of years that induce a person to stay with a particular company or in a particular job.

golden handshake *n Inf.* a sum of money given to an employee, either on retirement or as compensation for loss of employment.

golden hello *n* a payment made to a sought-after recruit on signing a contract of employment with a company.

Golden Horn ★ *n* an inlet of the Bosporus in NW Turkey, forming the harbour of Istanbul. Turkish name: **Haliç**.

golden hour *n* the first hour after a serious accident, when it is crucial that the victim receives medical treatment in order to have a chance of surviving.

golden mean *n* **1** the middle course between extremes. **2** another term for **golden section**.

golden number *n* a number between 1 and 19, used to indicate the position of any year in the Metonic cycle: so called from its importance in fixing the date of Easter.

golden parachute *n Inf.* a clause in the employment contract of a senior executive providing for special benefits if the executive's employment is terminated as a result of a takeover.

golden retriever *n* a breed of retriever with a silky wavy coat of a golden colour.

goldenrod (,gəʊldən'rɒd) *n* a plant of the composite family of North America, Europe, and Asia, having spikes of small yellow flowers.

golden rule *n* **1** any of a number of rules of fair conduct, such as *Whatsoever ye would that men should do to you, do ye even so to them* (Matthew 7:12). **2** any important principle: *a golden rule of sailing is to wear a life jacket*. **3** another name for **rule of three**.

golden section *or* **mean** *n* the proportion of the two divisions of a straight line such that the smaller is to the larger as the larger is to the sum of the two.

golden share *n* a share in a company that controls at least 51% of the voting rights, esp. one retained by the UK government in some privatization issues.

Golden Starfish *n* an award given to a bathing beach that meets EU standards of cleanliness but that does not provide facilities.

golden syrup *n Brit.* a light golden-coloured treacle produced by the evaporation of cane sugar juice, used to flavour cakes, puddings, etc.

Golden Triangle ★ *n the.* an opium-producing area of SE Asia, comprising parts of Myanmar, Laos, and Thailand.

golden wattle *n* **1** an Australian yellow-flowered plant that yields a useful gum and bark. **2** any of several similar and related Australian plants.

goldfinch ('gəʊld,fɪntʃ) *n* a common European finch, the adult of which has a red-and-white face and yellow-and-black wings.

goldfish ('gəʊld,fɪʃ) *n, pl* **goldfish** *or* **goldfishes**. a freshwater fish of E Europe and Asia, esp. China, widely introduced as a pond or aquarium fish. It resembles the carp and has a typically golden or orange-red coloration.

gold foil *n* thin gold sheet that is thicker than gold leaf.

Golding ★ ('gəʊldɪŋ) *n* Sir **William (Gerald)**. 1911–93, British writer, his novels include *Lord of the Flies* (1954), *Rites of Passage* (1980), and *Fire Down Below* (1989). Nobel prize for literature 1983.

gold leaf *n* very thin gold sheet produced by rolling or hammering gold and used for gilding woodwork, etc.

gold medal *n* a medal of gold, awarded to the winner of a competition or race.

Goldoni ★ (*Italian* gol'doːni) *n* **Carlo** ('karlo). 1707–93, Italian dramatist; author of over 250 plays in Italian or French, including *La Locandiera* (1753).

gold plate *n* **1** a thin coating of gold, usually produced by electroplating. **2** vessels or utensils made of gold.
▶ **,gold-'plate** *vb* (*tr*)

gold reserve *n* the gold reserved by a central bank to support domestic credit expansion, to cover balance of payments deficits, and to protect currency.

gold rush *n* a large-scale migration of people to a territory where gold has been found.

Goldschmidt ★ ('gəʊld,ʃmɪt) *n* **Richard Benedikt**. 1878–1958, US geneticist, born in Germany.

goldsmith ('gəʊld,smɪθ) *n* **1** a dealer in articles made of gold. **2** an artisan who makes such articles.

Goldsmith ★ ('gəʊld,smɪθ) *n* **Oliver**. ?1730–74, Irish writer. His works include the novel *The Vicar of Wakefield* (1766), the poem *The Deserted Village* (1770), and the comedy *She Stoops to Conquer* (1773).

gold standard *n* a monetary system in which the unit of currency is defined with reference to gold.

Goldwyn ★ ('gəʊldwɪn) *n* **Samuel**, original name *Samuel Goldfish*. 1882–1974, US film producer, born in Poland.

golf (gɒlf) *n* **1** a game played on a large open course, the object of which is to hit a ball using clubs, with as few strokes as possible, into each of usually 18 holes. ◆ *vb* **2** (*intr*) to play golf. [C15: ?from MDu. *colf* CLUB]
▶ **'golfer** *n*

golf ball *n* **1** a small resilient, usually white, ball of either two-piece or three-piece construction, the former consisting of a solid inner core with a thick covering of toughened material, the latter consisting of a liquid centre, rubber-wound core, and a thin layer of balata. **2** (in some electric typewriters) a small detachable metal sphere, around the surface of which type characters are arranged.

golf club *n* **1** any of various long-shafted clubs with wood or metal heads used to strike a golf ball. **2a** an association of golf players, usually having its own course and facilities. **2b** the premises of such an association.

golf course *or* **links** *n* an area of ground laid out for the playing of golf.

Golgi ★ (*Italian* 'gɔldʒi) *n* **Camillo** (ka'millo). 1844–1926, Italian neurologist and histologist, noted for his discovery in animal cells of the bodies known by his name: shared the Nobel prize for physiology or medicine 1906.

Golgotha ★ ('gɒlgəθə) *n* **1** another name for **Calvary**. **2** (*sometimes not cap.*) *Now rare.* a place of burial. [C17: from LL, from Gk, from Aramaic, based on Heb. *gulgōleth* skull]

Goliath ★ (gə'laɪəθ) *n Bible.* a Philistine giant who was killed by David with a stone from his sling (I Samuel 17).

golliwog ('gɒlɪ,wɒg) *n* a soft doll with a black face, usually made of cloth or rags. [C19: from a doll in a series of American children's books]

gollop ('gɒləp) *vb* **gollops, golloping, golloped.** to eat or drink (something) quickly or greedily. [dialect var. of GULP]

golly ('gɒlɪ) *interj* an exclamation of mild surprise. [C19: orig. a euphemism for GOD]

goloshes (gə'lɒʃɪz) *pl n* a less common spelling of **galoshes.**

Gomel ★ (*Russian* 'gɒmɪlj) *n* an industrial city in SE Belarus: belonged to Lithuania until 1772. Pop.: 512 000 (1996 est.).

Gomorrah or **Gomorrha** ★ (gə'mɒrə) *n* **1** *Old Testament.* one of two ancient cities near the Dead Sea, the other being Sodom, that were destroyed by God as a punishment for the wickedness of their inhabitants (Genesis 19:24). **2** any place notorious for vice and depravity.
▸ **Go'morrean** or **Go'morrhean** *adj*

Gomulka ★ (*Polish* gɔ'muwka) *n* **Władysław** (vwa'diswaf). 1905–82, Polish statesman; first secretary of the Polish Communist Party (1956–70).

gon *n combining form.* indicating a figure having a specified number of angles: *pentagon.* [from Gk *-gōnon*, from *gōnia* angle]

gonad ('gɒnæd) *n* an animal organ in which gametes are produced, such as a testis or an ovary. [C19: from NL *gonas*, from Gk *gonos* seed]
▸ **'gonadal** or **gonadial** (gɒ'neɪdɪəl) *adj*

gonadotrophin (ˌgɒnədəu'trəufɪn) or **gonadotropin** (-'trəupɪn) *n* any of several hormones that stimulate the gonads. See also **HCG.**
▸ **gonadotrophic** (ˌgɒnədəu'trɒfɪk) or **gonado'tropic** *adj*

Gonaïves ★ (*French* gɔnaiv) *n* a port in W Haiti, on the **Gulf of Gonaïves;** scene of the proclamation of Haiti's independence (1804). Pop.: 63 291 (1992).

Goncharov ★ (*Russian* gəntʃɪ'rɔf) *n* **Ivan Aleksandrovich** (i'van alɪk'sandrəvitʃ). 1812–91, Russian novelist: his best-known work is *Oblomov* (1859).

Goncourt ★ (*French* gɔkur) *n* **Edmond Louis Antoine Huot de** (edmɔ̃ lwi ɑ̃twan yo da), 1822–96, and his brother, **Jules Alfred Huot de** (ʒyl alfrɛd), 1830–70, French writers, noted for their collaboration, esp. on their *Journal,* and for the Académie Goncourt founded by Edmond's will.

Gondar ★ ('gɒndɑ:) *n* a city in NW Ethiopia: capital of Ethiopia from the 17th century until 1868. Pop.: 166 593 (1994 est.).

gondola ('gɒndələ) *n* **1** a long narrow flat-bottomed boat with a high ornamented stem: traditionally used on the canals of Venice. **2a** a car or cabin suspended from an airship or balloon. **2b** a moving cabin suspended from a cable across a valley, etc. **3** a flat-bottomed barge used on canals and rivers of the US. **4** *US & Canad.* a low open flat-bottomed railway goods wagon. **5** a set of island shelves in a self-service shop: used for displaying goods. **6** *Canad.* a broadcasting booth built close to the roof of an ice-hockey stadium. [C16: from It. (dialect), from Med. L, ? ult. from Gk *kondu* drinking vessel]

gondolier (ˌgɒndə'lɪə) *n* a man who propels a gondola.

Gondwanaland ★ (gɒnd'wɑ:nəˌlænd) *n* one of the two ancient supercontinents comprising chiefly what are now Africa, South America, Australia, Antarctica, and the Indian subcontinent. [C19: from *Gondwana,* region in central north India, where the rock series was orig. found]

gone (gɒn) *vb* **1** the past participle of **go.** ◆ *adj* (*usually postpositive*) **2** ended; past. **3** lost; ruined. **4** dead. **5** spent; consumed; used up. **6** *Inf.* faint or weak. **7** *Inf.* having been pregnant (for a specified time): *six months gone.* **8** (usually foll. by *on*) *Sl.* in love (with).

goner ('gɒnə) *n Sl.* a person or thing beyond help or recovery, esp. a person who is about to die.

gonfalon ('gɒnfələn) *n* **1** a banner hanging from a crossbar, used esp. by certain medieval Italian republics. **2** a battle flag suspended crosswise on a staff, usually having a serrated edge. [C16: from OIt., from OF, of Gmc origin]

gong (gɒŋ) *n* **1** a percussion instrument consisting of a metal platelike disc struck with a soft-headed drumstick.

2 a rimmed metal disc, hollow metal hemisphere, or metal strip, tube, or wire that produces a note when struck. **3** a fixed saucer-shaped bell, as on an alarm clock, struck by a mechanically operated hammer. **4** *Brit. sl.* a medal, esp. a military one. ◆ *vb* **5** (*intr*) to sound a gong. **6** (*tr*) (of traffic police) to summon (a driver) to stop by sounding a gong. [C17: from Malay, imit.]

goniometer (ˌgəunɪ'ɒmɪtə) *n* **1** an instrument for measuring the angles between the faces of a crystal. **2** an instrument used to determine the bearing of a distant radio station. [C18: via F from Gk *gōnia* angle]
▸ **goniometric** (ˌgəunɪə'metrɪk) *adj* ˌ**goni'ometry** *n*

-gonium *n combining form.* indicating a seed or reproductive cell: *archegonium.* [from NL, from Gk *gonos* seed]

gonococcus (ˌgɒnəu'kɒkəs) *n, pl* **gonococci** (-'kɒksaɪ). a spherical bacterium that causes gonorrhoea.

gonorrhoea or *esp. US* **gonorrhea** (ˌgɒnə'rɪə) *n* an infectious venereal disease characterized by a discharge of mucus and pus from the urethra or vagina. [C16: from L, from Gk *gonos* semen + *rhoia* flux]
▸ ˌ**gonor'rhoeal** or *esp. US* ˌ**gonor'rheal** *adj*

-gony *n combining form.* genesis, origin, or production: *cosmogony.* [from L, from Gk, from *gonos* seed, procreation]

González Márquez ★ (*Spanish* gɒn'θaleθ 'markeθ) *n* **Felipe** (fe'lipe). born 1942, Spanish statesman; prime minister of Spain (1982–96).

gonzo ('gɒnzəu) *Sl.* ◆ *adj* **1** wild or crazy. **2** (of journalism) focusing on the eccentric personality or lifestyle of the reporter as much as on the events reported. ◆ *n, pl* **gonzos. 3** a wild or crazy person. [C20: coined by Hunter S. Thompson, US journalist, ? from It., lit.: fool, or Sp. *ganso* idiot (lit.: goose)]

goo (gu:) *n Inf.* **1** a sticky substance. **2** coy or sentimental language or ideas. [C20: from ?]

Gooch ★ (gu:tʃ) *n* **Graham (Alan).** born 1953, English cricketer; captain of England (1988, 1989–93).

good (gud) *adj* **better, best. 1** having admirable, pleasing, superior, or positive qualities; not negative, bad, or mediocre: *a good teacher.* **2a** morally excellent or admirable; virtuous; righteous: *a good man.* **2b** (*as collective n; preceded by the*): *the good.* **3** suitable or efficient for a purpose: *a good winter coat.* **4** beneficial or advantageous: *vegetables are good for you.* **5** not ruined or decayed: *the meat is still good.* **6** kindly or generous: *you are good to him.* **7** valid or genuine: *I would not do this without good reason.* **8** honourable or held in high esteem: *a good family.* **9** financially secure, sound, or safe: *a good investment.* **10** (of a draft, etc.) drawn for a stated sum. **11** (of debts) expected to be fully paid. **12** clever, competent, or talented: *he's good at science.* **13** obedient or well-behaved: *a good dog.* **14** reliable, safe, or recommended: *a good make of clothes.* **15** affording material pleasure: *the good life.* **16** having a well-proportioned or generally fine appearance: *a good figure.* **17** complete; full: *I took a good look round the house.* **18** propitious; opportune: *a good time to ask for a rise.* **19** satisfying or gratifying: *a good rest.* **20** comfortable: *did you have a good night?* **21** newest or of the best quality: *keep the good plates for guests.* **22** fairly large, extensive, or long: *a good distance away.* **23** ample: *we have a good supply of food.* **24 a good one. 24a** an unbelievable assertion. **24b** a very funny joke. **25 as good as.** virtually; practically: *it's as good as finished.* **26 good and.** *Inf.* (intensifier): *good and mad.* ◆ *interj* **27** an exclamation of approval, agreement, pleasure, etc. ◆ *n* **28** moral or material advantage or use; benefit or profit: *for the good of our workers; what is the good of worrying?* **29** positive moral qualities; goodness; virtue; righteousness; piety. **30** (*sometimes cap.*) moral qualities seen as an abstract entity: *we must pursue the Good.* **31** a good thing. **32 for good (and all).** forever; permanently: *I have left them for good.* **33 good for** or **on you.** well done, well said, etc.: a term of congratulation. **34 make good. 34a** to recompense or repair damage or injury. **34b** to be successful. **34c** to prove the truth of (a statement or accusation). **34d** to secure and retain (a position). **34e** to effect or fulfil (something intended or promised). ◆ See also **goods.** [OE *gōd*]
▸ **'goodish** *adj*

Good Book *n* a name for the **Bible.**

goodbye (ˌgʊdˈbaɪ) *sentence substitute.* **1** farewell: a conventional expression used at leave-taking or parting with people. ◆ *n* **2** a leave-taking; parting: *they prolonged their goodbyes.* **3** a farewell: *they said goodbyes to each other.* [C16: from *God be with ye*]

good day *sentence substitute.* a conventional expression of greeting or farewell used during the day.

good-for-nothing *n* **1** an irresponsible or worthless person. ◆ *adj* **2** irresponsible; worthless.

Good Friday *n* the Friday before Easter, observed as a commemoration of the Crucifixion of Jesus.

Good Hope ★ *n* Cape of. See Cape of Good Hope.

good-humoured *adj* being in or expressing a pleasant, tolerant, and kindly state of mind.
▸ ˌgood-ˈhumouredly *adv*

goodies (ˈgʊdɪz) *pl n* any objects, rewards, etc., considered particularly desirable.

good-looking *adj* handsome or pretty.

goodly (ˈgʊdlɪ) *adj* **goodlier, goodliest.** **1** considerable: *a goodly amount of money.* **2** *Obs.* attractive, pleasing, or fine.
▸ ˈgoodliness *n*

goodman (ˈgʊdmən) *n, pl* **goodmen.** *Arch.* **1** a husband. **2** a man not of gentle birth: used as a title. **3** a master of a household.

Goodman ★ (ˈgʊdmən) *n* Benny, full name *Benjamin David Goodman.* 1909–86, US jazz clarinettist and bandleader, who helped to create swing.

good morning *sentence substitute.* a conventional expression of greeting or farewell used in the morning.

good-natured *adj* of a tolerant and kindly disposition.
▸ ˌgood-ˈnaturedly *adv*

goodness (ˈgʊdnɪs) *n* **1** the state or quality of being good. **2** generosity; kindness. **3** moral excellence; piety; virtue. **4** what is good in something; essence. ◆ *interj* **5** a euphemism for **God:** used as an exclamation of surprise.

goodness of fit *n Statistics.* the extent to which observed sample values of a variable approximate to values derived from a theoretical density.

good night *sentence substitute.* a conventional expression of farewell, used in the evening or at night, esp. when departing to bed.

good-oh *or* **good-o** (ˈgʊdˈəʊ) *interj Brit. & Austral. inf.* an exclamation of pleasure, agreement, etc.

good oil *n* (usually preceded by *the*) *Austral. sl.* true or reliable facts, information, etc.

goods (gʊdz) *pl n* **1** possessions and personal property. **2** (*sometimes sing*) *Econ.* commodities that are tangible, usually movable, and generally not consumed at the same time as they are produced. **3** articles of commerce; merchandise. **4** *Chiefly Brit.* **4a** merchandise when transported, esp. by rail; freight. **4b** (*as modifier*): *a goods train.* **5 the goods. 5a** *Inf.* that which is expected or promised: *to deliver the goods.* **5b** *Sl.* the real thing. **5c** *US & Canad. sl.* incriminating evidence (esp. in **have the goods on someone**).

Good Samaritan ★ *n* **1** *New Testament.* a figure in one of Christ's parables (Luke 10:30–37) who is an example of compassion towards those in distress. **2** a kindly person who helps another in difficulty or distress.

Good Shepherd *n New Testament.* a title given to Jesus Christ in John 10:11–12.

good-sized *adj* quite large.

good-tempered *adj* of a kindly and generous disposition.

good turn *n* a helpful and friendly act; favour.

goodwife (ˈgʊdˌwaɪf) *n, pl* **goodwives.** *Arch.* **1** the mistress of a household. **2** a woman not of gentle birth: used as a title.

goodwill (ˌgʊdˈwɪl) *n* **1** benevolence, approval, and kindly interest. **2** willingness or acquiescence. **3** an intangible asset of an enterprise reflecting its commercial reputation, customer connections, etc.

Goodwin Sands ★ (ˈgʊdwɪn) *pl n* a dangerous stretch of shoals at the entrance to the Strait of Dover: separated from the E coast of Kent by the Downs roadstead.

Goodwood ★ (ˈgʊdˌwʊd) *n* an area in SE England, in Sussex: site of a famous racecourse and of **Goodwood House,** built 1780–1800.

goody[1] (ˈgʊdɪ) *interj* **1** a child's exclamation of pleasure. ◆ *n, pl* **goodies. 2** short for **goody-goody. 3** *Inf.* the hero in a film, book, etc. **4** See **goodies.**

goody[2] (ˈgʊdɪ) *n, pl* **goodies.** *Arch.* or *literary.* a married woman of low rank: used as a title: *Goody Two-Shoes.* [C16: from GOODWIFE]

Goodyear ★ (ˈgʊdˌjɪə) *n* Charles. 1800–60, US inventor of vulcanized rubber.

goody-goody *n, pl* **goody-goodies. 1** *Inf.* a smugly virtuous or sanctimonious person. ◆ *adj* **2** smug and sanctimonious.

gooey (ˈguːɪ) *adj* **gooier, gooiest.** *Inf.* **1** sticky, soft, and often sweet. **2** oversweet and sentimental.
▸ ˈgooily *adv*

goof (guːf) *Inf.* ◆ *n* **1** a foolish error. **2** a stupid person. ◆ *vb* **3** to bungle (something); botch. **4** (*intr; often foll. by about* or *around*) to fool (around); mess (about). [C20: prob. from (dialect) *goff* simpleton, from OF *goffe* clumsy, from It. *goffo,* from ?]

go off *vb* (*intr*) **1** (*adv*) (of power, a water supply, etc.) to cease to be available or functioning: *the lights suddenly went off.* **2** (*adv*) to explode. **3** (*adv*) to occur as specified: *the meeting went off well.* **4** to leave (a place): *the actors went off stage.* **5** (*adv*) (of a sensation) to gradually cease to be felt. **6** (*adv*) to fall asleep. **7** (*adv*) (of concrete, mortar, etc.) to harden. **8** (*adv*) *Brit. inf.* (of food, etc.) to become stale or rotten. **9** (*prep*) *Brit. inf.* to cease to like.

goofy (ˈguːfɪ) *adj* **goofier, goofiest.** *Inf.* foolish; silly.
▸ ˈgoofily *adv* ▸ ˈgoofiness *n*

goog (gʊg) *n Austral. sl.* an egg. [?from Du. *oog*]

googly (ˈguːglɪ) *n, pl* **googlies.** *Cricket.* an off break bowled with a leg break action. [C20: Austral. from ?]

Goolagong ★ (ˈguːləˌgɒŋ) *n* Evonne. See (Evonne) **Cawley.**

Goole ★ (guːl) *n* an inland port in NE England, in the East Riding of Yorkshire at the confluence of the Ouse and Don Rivers, 75 km (47 miles) from the North Sea. Pop.: 19 410 (1991).

goolie *or* **gooly** (ˈguːlɪ) *n, pl* **goolies. 1** (*usually pl*) *Taboo sl.* a testicle. **2** *Austral. sl.* a stone or pebble. [from Hindi *goli* ball]

goon (guːn) *n* **1** a stupid or deliberately foolish person. **2** *US inf.* a thug hired to commit acts of violence or intimidation, esp. in an industrial dispute. [C20: partly from dialect *gooney* fool, partly after the character Alice the Goon, created by E. C. Segar (1894–1938), American cartoonist]

go on *vb* (*intr, mostly adv*) **1** to continue or proceed. **2** to happen: *there's something peculiar going on here.* **3** (*prep*) to ride on, esp. as a treat: *children love to go on donkeys at the seaside.* **4** *Theatre.* to make an entrance on stage. **5** to talk excessively; chatter. **6** to continue talking, esp. after a short pause. **7** to criticize or nag: *stop going on at me all the time!* ◆ *sentence substitute.* **8** I don't believe what you're saying.

gooney bird (ˈguːnɪ) *n* an informal name for **albatross,** esp. the black-footed albatross. [C19 *gony* (orig. sailors' sl.), prob. from dialect *gooney* fool, from ?]

goop (guːp) *n US & Canad. sl.* **1** a rude or ill-mannered person. **2** any sticky or semiliquid substance. [C20: coined by G. Burgess (1866–1951), American humorist]
▸ ˈgoopy *adj*

goorie *or* **goory** (ˈguːrɪ) *n, pl* **goories.** *NZ inf.* a mongrel dog. [from Maori *kuri*]

goosander (guːˈsændə) *n* a common merganser (a duck) of Europe and North America, having a dark head and white body in the male. [C17: prob. from GOOSE[1] + ON *önd* (genitive *andar*) duck]

goose[1] (guːs) *n, pl* **geese. 1** any of various web-footed long-necked birds typically larger and less aquatic than ducks. They are gregarious and migratory. **2** the female of such a bird, as opposed to the male (gander). **3** *Inf.* a silly person. **4** (*pl* **gooses**) a pressing iron with a long curving handle, used esp. by tailors. **5** the flesh of the goose, used as food. **6 cook someone's goose.** *Inf.* **6a** to spoil someone's chances or plans completely. **6b** to bring about someone's downfall. **7 kill the goose that lays the golden eggs.** See **golden goose.** [OE *gōs*]

goose[2] (guːs) *Sl.* ◆ *vb* **gooses, goosing, goosed. 1** (*tr*) to prod (a person) playfully in the bottom. ◆ *n, pl* **gooses. 2** such a prod. [C19: from GOOSE[1], prob. from a comparison with the jabbing of a goose's bill]

gooseberry ('guzbərɪ, -brɪ) *n, pl* **gooseberries. 1** a Eurasian shrub having ovoid yellow-green or red-purple berries. **2a** the berry of this plant. **2b** (*as modifier*): *gooseberry jam*. **3** *Brit. inf.* an unwanted single person, esp. a third person with a couple (often in **play gooseberry**).

goose flesh *n* the bumpy condition of the skin induced by cold, fear, etc., caused by contraction of the muscles at the base of the hair follicles with consequent erection of papillae. Also called: **goose bumps, goose pimples, goose skin.**

goosefoot ('guːs,fʊt) *n, pl* **goosefoots.** any typically weedy plant having small greenish flowers and leaves shaped like a goose's foot.

goosegog ('guzgɒg) *n Brit.* a dialect or informal word for **gooseberry.** [from *goose* in GOOSEBERRY + *gog*, var. of GOB[1]]

goosegrass ('guːs,grɑːs) *n* another name for **cleavers.**

gooseneck ('guːs,nek) *n* something, such as a jointed pipe, in the form of the neck of a goose.

goose step *n* **1** a military march step in which the leg is swung rigidly to an exaggerated height. ◆ *vb* **goose-step, goose-steps, goose-stepping, goose-stepped. 2** (*intr*) to march in goose step.

Goossens ★ ('guːsənz) *n* **1** Sir **Eugene.** 1893–1962, British composer and conductor, born in Belgium. **2** his brother, **Leon.** 1896–1988, British oboist.

go out *vb* (*intr, adv*) **1** to depart from a room, house, country, etc. **2** to cease to illuminate, burn, or function: *the fire has gone out.* **3** to cease to be fashionable or popular: *that style went out ages ago!* **4** (of a broadcast) to be transmitted. **5** to go to entertainments, social functions, etc. **6** (usually foll. by *with* or *together*) to associate (with a person of the opposite sex) regularly. **7** (of workers) to begin to strike. **8** *Card games, etc.* to get rid of the last card, token, etc., in one's hand.

go over *vb* (*intr*) **1** to be received in a specified manner: *the concert went over very well.* **2** (*prep*) Also: **go through.** to examine and revise as necessary: *he went over the accounts.* **3** (*prep*) to check and repair: *can you go over my car, please?* **4** (*prep*) Also: **go through.** to rehearse: *I'll go over my lines before the play.*

gopak ('gəʊ,pæk) *n* a spectacular high-leaping Russian peasant dance for men. [from Russian]

gopher ('gəʊfə) *n* **1** Also called: **pocket gopher.** a burrowing rodent of North and Central America, having a thickset body, short legs, and cheek pouches. **2** another name for **ground squirrel. 3** a burrowing tortoise of SE North America. [C19: from earlier *megopher* or *magopher*, from ?]

Gorakhpur ★ ('gɔːrək,pʊə) *n* a city in N India, in SE Uttar Pradesh: formerly an important Muslim garrison. Pop.: 505 566 (1991).

goral ('gɔːrəl) *n* a small goat antelope inhabiting mountainous regions of S Asia. [C19: from Hindi, prob. from Sansk.]

Gorbachov *or* **Gorbachev** ★ ('gɔːbə,tʃɒf; *Russian* gərbaˈtʃɔf) *n* **Mikhail Sergeevich** (mixaˈil sɪrˈgjejɪvitʃ). born 1931, Soviet statesman; general secretary of the Soviet Communist Party (1985–91): president (1988–91): resigned as president on dissolution of Soviet Union. Nobel peace prize 1990.

Gorbals ★ ('gɔːbˀlz) *n* **the.** a district of Glasgow, formerly known for its slums.

Gordian knot ('gɔːdɪən) *n* **1** (in Greek legend) a complicated knot, tied by King Gordius of Phrygia, that Alexander the Great cut with a sword. **2** a complicated and intricate problem (esp. in **cut the Gordian knot**).

Gordimer ★ ('gɔːdɪmə) *n* **Nadine.** born 1923, South African novelist. Her books include *The Lying Days* (1952), *The Conservationist* (1974), *July's People* (1981), and *The House Gun* (1998): Nobel prize for literature 1991.

Gordon ★ ('gɔːdˀn) *n* **1** Adam **Lindsay.** 1833–70, Australian

poet and horseman, born in the Azores, who developed the bush ballad, esp. in *Bush Ballads and Galloping Rhymes* (1870). **2** Charles **George,** known as *Chinese Gordon*. 1833–85, British general and administrator. He helped to crush the Taiping rebellion (1863–64), and was governor of the Sudan (1877–80), returning in 1884 to aid Egyptian forces against the Mahdi. He was killed in the siege of Khartoum. **3** Lord **George.** 1751–93, British religious agitator, who led the Protestant opposition to legislation relieving Roman Catholics of certain disabilities, which culminated in the Gordon riots (1780). **4** George **Hamilton.** See (4th Earl of) **Aberdeen.**

gore[1] (gɔː) *n* **1** blood shed from a wound, esp. when coagulated. **2** *Inf.* killing, fighting, etc. [OE *gor* dirt]

gore[2] (gɔː) *vb* **gores, goring, gored.** (*tr*) (of an animal, such as a bull) to pierce or stab (a person or another animal) with a horn or tusk. [C16: prob. from OE *gār* spear]

gore[3] (gɔː) *n* **1** a tapering or triangular piece of material used in making a shaped skirt, umbrella, etc. ◆ *vb* **gores, goring, gored. 2** (*tr*) to make into or with a gore or gores. [OE *gāra*]
▸ **gored** *adj*

Gore ★ (gɔː) *n* **Al**(bert) Jr. born 1948, US Democrat politician; vice president of the US from 1993.

gorge (gɔːdʒ) *n* **1** a deep ravine, esp. one through which a river runs. **2** the contents of the stomach. **3** feelings of disgust or resentment (esp. in **one's gorge rises**). **4** an obstructing mass: *an ice gorge.* **5** *Fortifications.* a narrow rear entrance to a work. **6** *Arch.* the throat or gullet. ◆ *vb* **gorges, gorging, gorged. 7** to swallow (food) ravenously. **8** (*tr*) to stuff (oneself) with food. [C14: from OF *gorger*, from *gorge* throat, from LL *gurga*, from L *gurges* whirlpool]

gorgeous ('gɔːdʒəs) *adj* **1** strikingly beautiful or magnificent: *a gorgeous array; a gorgeous girl.* **2** *Inf.* extremely pleasing, fine, or good: *gorgeous weather.* [C15: from OF *gorgias* elegant, from *gorge*; see GORGE]
▸ **'gorgeously** *adv* ▸ **'gorgeousness** *n*

gorget ('gɔːdʒɪt) *n* **1** a collar-like piece of armour worn to protect the throat. **2** a part of a wimple worn by women to cover the throat and chest, esp. in the 14th century. **3** a band of distinctive colour on the throat of an animal, esp. a bird. [C15: from OF, from *gorge*; see GORGE]

Gorgio ('gɔːdʒɪəʊ) *n, pl* **Gorgios.** the Gypsy name for a non-Gypsy. [C19: from Romany]

Gorgon ('gɔːgən) *n* **1** *Greek myth.* any of three winged monstrous sisters who had live snakes for hair, huge teeth, and brazen claws. **2** (*often not cap.*) *Inf.* a fierce or unpleasant woman. [via L *Gorgō* from Gk *gorgos* terrible]

gorgonian (gɔːˈgəʊnɪən) *n* any of various corals having a horny or calcareous branching skeleton, such as the sea fans and red corals.

Gorgonzola (ˌgɔːgənˈzəʊlə) *n* a semihard blue-veined cheese of sharp flavour, made from pressed milk. [C19: after *Gorgonzola*, It. town where it originated]

Gorica ★ ('gɒrɪtsa) *n* the Serbo-Croat name for **Gorizia.**

gorilla (gəˈrɪlə) *n* **1** the largest anthropoid ape, inhabiting the forests of central W Africa. It is stocky with a short muzzle and coarse dark hair. **2** *Inf.* a large, strong, and brutal-looking man. [C19: NL, from Gk *Gorillai*, an African tribe renowned for their hirsute appearance]

Göring *or* **Goering** ★ (*German* 'gøːrɪŋ) *n* **Hermann Wilhelm** ('herman 'vɪlhelm). 1893–1946, German Nazi leader and field marshal. He founded the Gestapo and mobilized Germany for war. Sentenced to death at Nuremberg, he committed suicide.

Gorizia ★ (*Italian* goˈrittsja) *n* a city in NE Italy, in Friuli-Venezia Giulia, on the Isonzo River: cultural centre under the Hapsburgs. Pop.: 39 230 (1990). German name: **Görz.** Serbo-Croat name: **Gorica.**

Gorki[1] *or* **Gorky** ★ (*Russian* 'gɔrjkij) *n* the former name (1932–91) of Nizhni Novgorod.

Gorki[2] *or* **Gorky** ★ (*Russian* 'gɔrjkij) *n* **Maxim** (makˈsim), pen name of *Aleksey Maximovich Peshkov*. 1868–1936, Russian writer. His works include the play *The Lower Depths* (1902) and the novel *Mother* (1907).

Gorky ★ ('gɔːkɪ) *n* **Arshile** ('ɑːʃiːl). 1904–48, US abstract expressionist painter, born in Armenia.

Görlitz ★ (*German* 'gœrlɪts) *n* a city in E Germany, in Saxony, on the Neisse River; formerly in East Germany: divided in 1945, the area on the E bank of the river becoming the Polish town of **Zgorzelec**. Pop.: 70 450 (1991).

Gorlovka ★ (*Russian* 'gɔrləfkə) *n* a city in the SE Ukraine, in the centre of the Donets Basin: a major coal-mining centre. Pop.: 322 000 (1996 est.).

gormand ('gɔːmənd) *n* a less common spelling of **gourmand**.

gormandize *or* **gormandise** ('gɔːmənˌdaɪz) *vb* **gormandizes, gormandizing, gormandized** *or* **gormandises, gormandising, gormandised.** to eat (food) greedily and voraciously.
▶ **'gormandˌizer** *or* **'gormandˌiser** *n*

gormless ('gɔːmlɪs) *adj Brit. inf.* stupid; dull. [C19: var. of C18 *gaumless*, from dialect *gome*, from OE *gom, gome*, from ON *gaumr* heed]

Gorno-Altai Republic ★ ('gɔːnəʊælˈtaɪ, -'æltaɪ) *n* a constituent republic of S Russia: mountainous, rising over 4350 m (14 500 ft) in the Altai Mountains of the south. Capital: Gorno-Altaisk. Pop.: 200 000 (1995 est.). Area: 92 600 sq. km (35 740 sq. miles). Also called: **Altai Republic.**

Gorno-Badakhshan Autonomous Republic ★ (-bə'dækʃɑːn) *n* an administrative division of Tajikistan: the region is generally mountainous and inaccessible. Capital: Khorog. Pop.: 167 100 (1991 est.). Area: 63 700 sq. km (24 590 sq. miles). Also called: **Badakhshan.**

go round *vb* (*intr*) **1** (*adv*) to be sufficient: *are there enough sweets to go round?* **2** to circulate (in): *measles is going round the school.* **3** to be long enough to encircle: *will that belt go round you?*

gorse (gɔːs) *n* an evergreen shrub which has yellow flowers and thick green spines instead of leaves. Also called: **furze, whin.** [OE *gors*]
▶ **'gorsy** *adj*

Gorton ★ ('gɔːt°n) *n* Sir **John Grey.** born 1911, Australian statesman; prime minister (1968–71).

gory ('gɔːrɪ) *adj* **gorier, goriest. 1** horrific or bloodthirsty: *a gory story.* **2** involving bloodshed and killing: *a gory battle.* **3** covered in gore.
▶ **'gorily** *adv* ▶ **'goriness** *n*

Görz ★ (gœrts) *n* the German name for **Gorizia**.

gosh (gɒʃ) *interj* an exclamation of mild surprise or wonder. [C18: euphemistic for GOD]

goshawk ('gɒsˌhɔːk) *n* a large hawk of Europe, Asia, and North America, having a bluish-grey back and wings and paler underparts: used in falconry. [OE *gōshafoc;* see GOOSE[1], HAWK[1]]

Goshen ★ ('gəʊʃən) *n* **1** a region of ancient Egypt, east of the Nile delta: granted to Jacob and his descendants by the king of Egypt and inhabited by them until the Exodus (Genesis 45:10). **2** a place of comfort and plenty.

gosling ('gɒzlɪŋ) *n* **1** a young goose. **2** an inexperienced or youthful person. [C15: from ON *gæslingr;* rel. to Danish *gäsling;* see GOOSE[1], -LING[1]]

go-slow *n* **1** *Brit.* a deliberate slackening of the rate of production by organized labour as a tactic in industrial conflict. US and Canad. equivalent: **slowdown.** ◆ *vb* **go slow. 2** (*intr*) to work deliberately slowly as a tactic in industrial conflict.

gospel ('gɒsp°l) *n* **1** Also called: **gospel truth.** an unquestionable truth: *to take someone's word as gospel.* **2** a doctrine maintained to be of great importance. **3** Black religious music originating in the churches of the Southern states of the United States. **4** the message or doctrine of a religious teacher. **5a** the story of Christ's life and teachings as narrated in the Gospels. **5b** the good news of salvation in Jesus Christ. **5c** (*as modifier*): *the gospel story.* [OE *gōdspell*, from *gōd* GOOD + *spell* message; see SPELL[2]]

Gospel ('gɒsp°l) *n* **1** any of the first four books of the New Testament, namely Matthew, Mark, Luke, and John. **2** a reading from one of these in a religious service.

Gosport ★ ('gɒsˌpɔːt) *n* a town in S England, in Hampshire on Portsmouth harbour: naval base since the 16th century. Pop.: 67 802 (1991).

gossamer ('gɒsəmə) *n* **1** a gauze or silk fabric of the very finest texture. **2** a filmy cobweb often seen on foliage or floating in the air. **3** anything resembling gossamer in fineness or filminess. [C14 (in sense 2): prob. from *gos* GOOSE[1] + *somer* SUMMER; the phrase refers to *St Martin's summer*, a period in November when goose was traditionally eaten; from the prevalence of the cobweb in the autumn]
▶ **'gossamery** *adj*

Gosse ★ (gɒs) *n* Sir **Edmund William.** 1849–1928, British writer, noted for his autobiographical *Father and Son* (1907).

gossip ('gɒsɪp) *n* **1** casual and idle chat. **2** a conversation involving malicious chatter or rumours about other people. **3** Also called: **gossipmonger.** a person who habitually talks about others, esp. maliciously. **4** light easy communication: *to write a letter full of gossip.* **5** *Arch.* a close woman friend. ◆ *vb* **gossips, gossiping, gossiped. 6** (*intr;* often foll. by *about*) to talk casually or maliciously (about other people). [OE *godsibb* godparent, from GOD + SIB; came to be applied esp. to a woman's female friends at the birth of a child, hence a woman fond of light talk]
▶ **'gossiper** *n* ▶ **'gossipy** *adj*

gossypol ('gɒsɪˌpɒl) *n* a toxic crystalline pigment that is a constituent of cottonseed oil. [C19: from Mod. L *gossypium* cotton plant + -OL[1]]

got (gɒt) *vb* **1** the past tense and past participle of **get. 2 have got. 2a** to possess. **2b** (*takes an infinitive*) used as an auxiliary to express compulsion: *I've got to get a new coat.*

Göta ★ (*Swedish* 'jøːta) *n* a river in S Sweden, draining Lake Vänern and flowing south-southwest to the Kattegat: forms part of the **Göta Canal,** which links Göteborg in the west with Stockholm in the east. Length: 93 km (58 miles).

Göteborg (*Swedish* jœtə'bɔrj) *or* **Gothenburg** ★ *n* a port in SW Sweden, at the mouth of the Göta River: the largest port and second largest city in the country; developed through the Swedish East India Company and grew through Napoleon's continental blockade and with the opening of the Göta Canal (1832); university (1891). Pop.: 454 016 (1997 est.).

Goth (gɒθ) *n* **1** a member of an East Germanic people from Scandinavia who settled south of the Baltic early in the first millennium A.D. They moved on to the Ukrainian steppes and raided and later invaded many parts of the Roman Empire from the 3rd to the 5th century. **2** a rude or barbaric person. [C14: from LL (pl) *Gothī* from Gk *Gothoi*]

Gotha ★ ('gəʊθə; *German* 'goːta) *n* a town in central Germany, in Thuringia on the N edge of the Thuringian forest: capital of Saxe-Coburg-Gotha (1826–1918); noted for the *Almanach de Gotha* (a record of the royal and noble houses of Europe, first published in 1764). Pop.: 57 360 (1989 est.).

Gotham ★ ('gəʊtəm, 'gɒtəm) *n* a village in N central England, in Nottinghamshire near Nottingham: renowned for the legend of its early inhabitants, the Wise Men of Gotham, who feigned stupidity in order to dissuade King John from residing in their neighbourhood.

Gothenburg ★ ('gɒθən,bɜːg) *n* the English name for **Göteborg.**

Gothic ('gɒθɪk) *adj* **1** denoting, relating to, or resembling the style of architecture that was used in W Europe from the 12th to the 16th centuries, characterized by the lancet arch, the ribbed vault, and the flying buttress. See also **Gothic Revival. 2** of or relating to the style of sculpture, painting, or other arts as practised in W Europe from the 12th to the 16th centuries. **3** (*sometimes not cap.*) of or relating to a literary style characterized by gloom, the grotesque, and the supernatural, popular esp. in the late 18th century: when used of modern literature, films, etc., sometimes spelt: **Gothick. 4** of, relating to, or characteristic of the Goths or their language. **5** (*sometimes not cap.*) primitive and barbarous in style, behaviour, etc. **6** of or relating to the Middle Ages. ◆ *n* **7** Gothic architecture or art. **8** the extinct language of the

ancient Goths, known mainly from fragments of a translation of the Bible made in the 4th century by Bishop Wulfila. **9** Also called (esp. Brit): **black letter.** a family of heavy script typefaces.
▶ **'Gothically** adv

Gothic Revival n a Gothic style of architecture popular between the late 18th and late 19th centuries, exemplified by the Houses of Parliament in London (1840). Also called: **neogothic.**

go through vb (intr) **1** (adv) to be approved or accepted: the amendment went through. **2** (prep) to consume; exhaust: we went through our supplies in a day. **3** (prep) Also: **go over.** to examine: he went through the figures. **4** (prep) to suffer: she went through tremendous pain. **5** (prep) Also: **go over.** to rehearse: let's just go through the details again. **6** (prep) to search: she went through the cupboards. **7** (adv; foll. by with) to come or bring to a successful conclusion, often by persistence.

Gotland ('gɒtlənd; Swedish 'gɒtlant), **Gothland** ('gɒθlənd) or **Gottland** ★ ('gɒtlənd) n an island in the Baltic Sea, off the SE coast of Sweden: important trading centre since the Bronze Age; long disputed between Sweden and Denmark, finally becoming Swedish in 1645; tourism and agriculture now important. Capital: Visby. Pop. (including associated islands): 58 237 (1994 est.). Area: 3140 sq. km (1212 sq. miles).

go together vb (intr, adv) **1** to be mutually suited; harmonize: the colours go well together. **2** Inf. (of two people) to have a romantic or sexual relationship: they had been going together for two years.

gotten ('gɒt°n) vb Chiefly US. a past participle of **get.**

Götterdämmerung (,gɒtə'dɛmə,rʊŋ) n German myth. the twilight of the gods; their ultimate destruction in a battle with the forces of evil.

Gottfried von Strassburg ★ (German 'gɒtfri:t fɔn 'ʃtra:sbʊrk) n early 13th-century German poet; author of the incomplete epic Tristan and Isolde, the basis of Wagner's opera.

Göttingen ★ (German 'gœtɪŋən) n a city in central Germany, in Lower Saxony: important member of the Hanseatic League (14th century); university, founded in 1734 by George II of England. Pop.: 127 519 (1995 est.).

gouache (gʊ'ɑːʃ) n **1** Also called: **body colour.** a painting technique using opaque watercolour in which the pigments are bound with glue and lighter tones contain white. **2** the paint used in this technique. **3** a painting done by this method. [C19: from F, from It. guazzo puddle, from L, from aqua water]

Gouda ★ ('gaʊdə; Dutch 'xɔudaː) n **1** a town in the W Netherlands, in South Holland province: important medieval cloth trade; famous for its cheese. Pop.: 69 917 (1994). **2** a large round Dutch cheese, mild and similar in taste to Edam.

gouge (gaʊdʒ) vb gouges, gouging, gouged. (mainly tr) **1** (usually foll. by out) to scoop or force (something) out of its position. **2** (sometimes foll. by out) to cut (a hole or groove) in (something) with a sharp instrument or tool. **3** US & Canad. inf. to extort from. **4** (also intr) Austral. to dig for (opal). ◆ n **5** a type of chisel with a blade that has a concavo-convex section. **6** a mark or groove made as with a gouge. **7** US & Canad. inf. extortion; swindling. [C15: from F, from LL gulbia a chisel, of Celtic origin]
▶ **'gouger** n

goujon ('guːʒɒn) n a small strip of fish or chicken, coated in breadcrumbs and deep-fried. [F, lit.: gudgeon]

goulash ('guːlæʃ) n **1** Also called: **Hungarian goulash.** a rich stew, originating in Hungary, made of beef, lamb, or veal thickly seasoned with paprika. **2** Bridge. a method of dealing in threes and fours without first shuffling the cards, to produce freak hands. [C19: from Hungarian gulyás hus herdsman's meat]

Gould ★ (guːld) n **1** Benjamin Apthorp. 1824–96, US astronomer: the first to use the telegraph to determine longitudes; founded the Astronomical Journal (1849). **2** Glenn. 1932–82, Canadian pianist.

go under vb (intr, mainly adv) **1** (also prep) to sink below (a surface). **2** to be overwhelmed: the firm went under in the economic crisis.

Gounod ★ ('guːnəʊ; French guno) n Charles François (ʃarl frɑ̃swa). 1818–93, French composer of the operas Faust (1859) and Romeo and Juliet (1867).

go up vb (intr, mainly adv) **1** (also prep) to move or lead as to a higher place or level; rise; increase: prices are always going up. **2** to be destroyed: the house went up in flames. **3** Brit. to go or return (to college or university) at the beginning of a term or academic year.

gourami ('gʊərəmɪ) n, pl **gourami** or **gouramis. 1** a large SE Asian labyrinth fish used for food. **2** any of various other labyrinth fishes, many of which are brightly coloured and popular aquarium fishes. [from Malay gurami]

gourd (gʊəd) n **1** the fruit of any of various plants of the cucumber family, esp. the bottle gourd and some squashes, whose dried shells are used for ornament, drinking cups, etc. **2** any plant that bears this fruit. **3** a bottle or flask made from the dried shell of the bottle gourd. [C14: from OF gourde, ult. from L cucurbita]

gourmand ('gʊəmənd) or **gormand** n a person devoted to eating and drinking, esp. to excess. [C15: from OF gourmant, from ?]
▶ **'gourmand,ism** n

gourmet ('gʊəmeɪ) n a person who cultivates a discriminating palate for the enjoyment of good food and drink. [C19: from F, from OF gromet serving boy]

gout (gaʊt) n **1** a metabolic disease characterized by painful inflammation of certain joints, esp. of the big toe, caused by deposits of sodium urate. **2** Arch. a drop or splash, esp. of blood. [C13: from OF, from L gutta drop]
▶ **'gouty** adj ▶ **'goutily** adv ▶ **'goutiness** n

Gov. or **gov.** abbrev. for: **1** government. **2** governor.

govern ('gʌv°n) vb (mainly tr) **1** (also intr) to direct and control the actions, affairs, policies, functions, etc., of (an organization, nation, etc.); rule. **2** to exercise restraint over; regulate or direct: to govern one's temper. **3** to decide or determine (something): his injury governed his decision to avoid sports. **4** to control the speed of (an engine, machine, etc.) using a governor. **5** (of a word) to determine the inflection of (another word): Latin nouns govern adjectives that modify them. [C13: from OF, from L gubernāre to steer, from Gk kubernan]
▶ **'governable** adj

governance ('gʌvənəns) n **1** government, control, or authority. **2** the action, manner, or system of governing.

governess ('gʌvənɪs) n a woman teacher employed in a private household to teach and train the children.

government ('gʌvnmənt, 'gʌvənmənt) n **1** the exercise of political authority over the actions, affairs, etc., of a political unit, people, etc.; the action of governing; political rule and administration. **2** the system or form by which a community, etc., is ruled: tyrannical government. **3a** the executive policy-making body of a political unit, community, etc.; ministry or administration. **3b** (cap. when of a specific country): the British Government. **4a** the state and its administration: blame it on the government. **4b** (as modifier): a government agency. **5** regulation; direction. **6** Grammar. the determination of the form of one word by another word.
▶ **governmental** (,gʌvən'mɛnt°l, ,gʌvə'mɛnt°l) adj ▶ **,gov-ern'mentally** adv

governor ('gʌvənə) n **1** a person who governs. **2** the ruler or chief magistrate of a colony, province, etc. **3** the representative of the Crown in a British colony. **4** Brit. the senior administrator of a society, prison, etc. **5** the chief executive of any state in the US. **6** a device that controls the speed of an engine, esp. by regulating the supply of fuel. **7** Brit. inf. a name or title of respect for a father, employer, etc.
▶ **'governor,ship** n

governor general n, pl **governors general** or **governor generals. 1** the representative of the Crown in a dominion of the Commonwealth or a British colony; vicegerent. **2** Brit. a governor with jurisdiction or precedence over other governors.
▶ **,governor-'general,ship** n

Govt or **govt** abbrev. for government.

Gower[1] ★ ('gaʊə) n **the.** a peninsula in S Wales, in

Swansea county in the Bristol Channel: mainly agricultural with several resorts.

Gower[2] ★ ('gaʊə) n **1 David (Ivon).** born 1957, English cricketer: captained England (1984–86; 1989). **2 John.** ?1330–1408, English poet, noted particularly for his tales of love, the *Confessio Amantis*.

go with vb (intr, prep) **1** to accompany. **2** to blend or harmonize: *that new wallpaper goes well with the furniture.* **3** to be a normal part of: *three acres of land go with the house.* **4** (of two people of the opposite sex) to associate frequently with each other.

go without vb (intr) *Chiefly Brit.* to be denied or deprived of (something, esp. food): *if you don't like your tea you can go without.*

gowk (gauk) n *Scot. & N English dialect.* **1** a fool. **2** a cuckoo. [from ON *gaukr* cuckoo]

gown (gaʊn) n **1** any of various outer garments, such as a woman's elegant or formal dress, a dressing robe, or a protective garment, esp. one worn by surgeons during operations. **2** a loose wide garment indicating status, such as worn by academics. **3** the members of a university as opposed to the other residents of the university town. ◆ vb **4** (tr) to supply with or dress in a gown. [C14: from OF, from LL *gunna* garment made of leather or fur, of Celtic origin]

goy (gɔɪ) n, pl **goyim** ('gɔɪɪm) or **goys.** a Jewish word for a Gentile. [from Yiddish, from Heb. *goi* people]
▸ **'goyish** adj

Goya ★ ('gɔɪə; Spanish 'goja) n **Francisco de** (fran'θisko de), full name *Francisco José de Goya y Lucientes.* 1746–1828, Spanish painter and etcher; court painter to Charles IV of Spain (1799).

GP abbrev. for: **1** Gallup Poll. **2** *Music.* general pause. **3** general practitioner. **4** (in Britain) graduated pension. **5** Grand Prix.

GPMU (in Britain) abbrev. for Graphical, Paper and Media Union.

GPO abbrev. for general post office.

Gr. abbrev. for: **1** Grecian. **2** Greece. **3** Greek.

Graafian follicle ('grɑːfɪən) n a fluid-filled vesicle in the mammalian ovary containing a developing egg cell. [C17: after R. de *Graaf* (1641–73), Du. anatomist]

grab (græb) vb **grabs, grabbing, grabbed. 1** to seize hold of (something). **2** (tr) to seize illegally or unscrupulously. **3** (tr) to arrest; catch. **4** (tr) *Inf.* to catch the attention or interest of; impress. ◆ n **5** the act or an instance of grabbing. **6** a mechanical device for gripping objects, esp. the hinged jaws of a mechanical excavator. **7** something that is grabbed. [C16: prob. from MLow G or MDu. *grabben*]
▸ **'grabber** n

grab bag n **1** a collection of miscellaneous things. **2** *US, Canad., & Austral.* a bag or other container from which gifts are drawn at random.

grabby ('græbɪ) adj **grabbier, grabbiest. 1** grasping or avaricious. **2** seizing the attention: *a grabby headline; a grabby performance.*

Gracchus ★ ('grækəs) n **Tiberius Sempronius** (taɪ'bɪərɪəs sem'prəʊnɪəs). ?163–133 B.C., and his younger brother, **Gaius Sempronius** ('gaɪəs), 153–121 B.C., known as *the Gracchi.* Roman tribunes and reformers. Tiberius attempted to redistribute public land among the poor but was murdered in the ensuing riot. Violence again occurred when the reform was revived by Gaius, and he too was killed.

grace (greɪs) n **1** elegance and beauty of movement, form, expression, or proportion. **2** a pleasing or charming quality. **3** goodwill or favour. **4** a delay granted for the completion of a task or payment of a debt. **5** a sense of propriety and consideration for others. **6** (pl) **6a** affectation of manner (esp. in **airs and graces**). **6b in (someone's) good graces.** regarded favourably and with kindness by (someone). **7** mercy; clemency. **8** *Christian theol.* **8a** the free and unmerited favour of God shown towards man. **8b** the divine assistance given to man in spiritual rebirth. **8c** the condition of being favoured or sanctified by God. **8d** an unmerited gift, favour, etc., granted by

God. **9** a short prayer recited before or after a meal to give thanks for it. **10** *Music.* a melodic ornament or decoration. **11 with (a) bad grace.** unwillingly or grudgingly. **12 with (a) good grace.** willingly or cheerfully. ◆ vb **graces, gracing, graced. 13** (tr) to add elegance and beauty to: *flowers graced the room.* **14** (tr) to honour or favour: *to grace a party with one's presence.* **15** to ornament or decorate (a melody, part, etc.) with nonessential notes. [C12: from OF, from L *grātia*, from *grātus* pleasing]

Grace[1] (greɪs) n (preceded by *your, his,* or *her*) a title used to address or refer to a duke, duchess, or archbishop.

Grace[2] ★ (greɪs) n **W(illiam) G(ilbert).** 1848–1915, English cricketer.

grace-and-favour n (modifier) *Brit.* (of a house, flat, etc.) owned by the sovereign and granted free of rent to a person to whom the sovereign wishes to express gratitude.

graceful ('greɪsful) adj characterized by beauty of movement, style, form, etc.
▸ **'gracefully** adv ▸ **'gracefulness** n

graceless ('greɪslɪs) adj **1** lacking manners. **2** lacking elegance.
▸ **'gracelessly** adv ▸ **'gracelessness** n

grace note n *Music.* a note printed in small type to indicate that it is melodically and harmonically nonessential.

Graces ★ ('greɪsɪz) pl n *Greek myth.* three sister goddesses, givers of charm and beauty.

gracious ('greɪʃəs) adj **1** characterized by or showing kindness and courtesy. **2** condescendingly courteous, benevolent, or indulgent. **3** characterized by or suitable for a life of elegance, ease, and indulgence: *gracious living.* **4** merciful or compassionate. ◆ interj **5** an expression of mild surprise or wonder.
▸ **'graciously** adv ▸ **'graciousness** n

grackle ('græk'l) n **1** an American songbird of the oriole family, having a dark iridescent plumage. **2** any of various starlings, such as the Indian grackle or hill myna. [C18: from NL, from L *grāculus* jackdaw]

grad. abbrev. for: **1** *Maths.* gradient. **2** *Education.* graduate(d).

gradate (grə'deɪt) vb **gradates, gradating, gradated. 1** to change or cause to change imperceptibly, as from one colour, tone, or degree to another. **2** (tr) to arrange in grades or ranks.

gradation (grə'deɪʃən) n **1** a series of systematic stages; gradual progression. **2** (often pl) a stage or degree in such a series or progression. **3** the act or process of arranging or forming in stages, grades, etc., or of progressing evenly. **4** (in painting, drawing, or sculpture) transition from one colour, tone, or surface to another through a series of very slight changes. **5** *Linguistics.* any change in the quality or length of a vowel within a word indicating certain distinctions, such as inflectional or tense differentiations. See **ablaut.**
▸ **gra'dational** adj

grade (greɪd) n **1** a position or degree in a scale, as of quality, rank, size, or progression: *high-grade timber.* **2** a group of people or things of the same category. **3** *Chiefly US.* a military or other rank. **4** a stage in a course of progression. **5** a mark or rating indicating achievement or the worth of work done, as at school. **6** *US & Canad.* a unit of pupils of similar age or ability taught together at school. **7 make the grade.** *Inf.* **7a** to reach the required standard. **7b** to succeed. ◆ vb **grades, grading, graded. 8** (tr) to arrange according to quality, rank, etc. **9** (tr) to determine the grade of or assign a grade to. **10** (intr) to achieve or deserve a grade or rank. **11** to change or blend (something) gradually; merge. **12** (tr) to level (ground, a road, etc.) to a suitable gradient. [C16: from F, from L *gradus* step, from *gradī* to step]

-grade adj combining form. indicating a kind or manner of movement or progression: *plantigrade; retrograde.* [via F from L *-gradus*, from *gradus* a step, from *gradī* to walk]

gradely ('greɪdlɪ) adj **gradelier, gradeliest.** *Midland English dialect.* fine; excellent. [C13: from ON *greidhligr*, from *greidhr* ready]

grader ('greɪdə) n **1** a person or thing that grades. **2** a machine that levels earth, rubble, etc., as in road construction.

gradient ('greɪdɪənt) n **1** Also called (esp. US): **grade**. a part of a railway, road, etc., that slopes upwards or downwards; inclination. **2** Also called (esp. US and Canad.): **grade**. a measure of such a slope, esp. the ratio of the vertical distance between two points on the slope to the horizontal distance between them. **3** Physics. a measure of the change of some physical quantity, such as temperature or electric potential, over a specified distance. **4** Maths. (of a curve) the slope of the tangent at any point on a curve with respect to the horizontal axis. ◆ adj **5** sloping uniformly. [C19: from L gradiēns stepping, from gradī to go]

gradin ('greɪdɪn) or **gradine** (grə'diːn) n **1** a ledge above or behind an altar for candles, etc., to stand on. **2** one of a set of steps or seats arranged on a slope, as in an amphitheatre. [C19: from F, from It. gradino, dim. of grado a step]

gradual ('grædjʊəl) adj **1** occurring, developing, moving, etc., in small stages: a gradual improvement in health. **2** not steep or abrupt: a gradual slope. ◆ n **3** (often cap.) Christianity. **3a** an antiphon usually from the Psalms, sung or recited immediately after the epistle at Mass. **3b** a book of plainsong containing the words and music of the parts of the Mass that are sung by the cantors and choir. [C16: from Med. L: relating to steps, from L gradus a step] ▶ 'gradually adv ▶ 'gradualness n

gradualism ('grædjʊə,lɪzəm) n **1** the policy of seeking to change something gradually, esp. in politics. **2** the theory that explains major changes in fossils, rock strata, etc., in terms of gradual evolutionary processes rather than sudden violent catastrophes. ▶ 'gradualist n, adj ▶ ˌgradual'istic adj

graduand ('grædjʊ,ænd) n Chiefly Brit. a person who is about to graduate. [C19: from Med. L gerundive of graduārī to GRADUATE]

graduate n ('grædjʊɪt). **1** a person who has been awarded a first degree from a university or college. **2** US & Canad. a student who has completed a course of studies at a high school and received a diploma. ◆ vb ('grædjʊ,eɪt), **graduates, graduating, graduated. 3** to receive or cause to receive a degree or diploma. **4** Chiefly US & Canad. to confer a degree, diploma, etc., upon. **5** (tr) to mark (a thermometer, flask, etc.) with units of measurement; calibrate. **6** (tr) to arrange or sort into groups according to type, quality, etc. **7** (intr; often foll. by to) to change by degrees (from something to something else). [C15: from Med. L graduārī to take a degree, from L gradus a step] ▶ 'gradu,ator n

graduated pension n (in Britain) a national pension scheme in which employees' contributions are scaled in accordance with their wage rate.

graduation (ˌgrædjʊ'eɪʃən) n **1** the act of graduating or the state of being graduated. **2** the ceremony at which school or college degrees and diplomas are conferred. **3** a mark or division or all the marks or divisions that indicate measure on an instrument or vessel.

Graeae ('griːi) or **Graiae** ★ pl n Greek myth. three aged sea deities, having only one eye and one tooth among them, guardians of their sisters, the Gorgons.

Graecism or esp. US **Grecism** ('griːsɪzəm) n **1** Greek characteristics or style. **2** admiration for or imitation of these, as in sculpture or architecture. **3** a form of words characteristic of the idiom of the Greek language.

Graeco- or esp. US **Greco-** ('griːkəʊ, 'grɛkəʊ) combining form. Greek: Graeco-Roman.

Graeco-Roman or esp. US **Greco-Roman** adj of, characteristic of, or relating to Greek and Roman influences.

Graf ★ (græf) n Steffi. born 1969, German tennis player: Wimbledon champion 1988, 1989, 1991, 1992, 1993, 1995, and 1996.

graffiti (græ'fiːtɪ) pl n (sometimes functioning as sing) drawings, messages, etc., often obscene, scribbled on the walls of public lavatories, advertising posters, etc. [C19: see GRAFFITO]

graffito (græ'fiːtəʊ) n, pl **graffiti** (-tɪ). **1** Archaeol. any inscription or drawing scratched onto a surface, esp. rock or pottery. **2** See **graffiti**. [C19: from It.: a little scratch, from L graphium stylus, from Gk grapheion; see GRAFT¹]

graft¹ (grɑːft) n **1** Horticulture. **1a** a small piece of plant tissue (the scion) that is made to unite with an established plant (the stock), which supports and nourishes it. **1b** the plant resulting from the union of scion and stock. **1c** the point of union between the scion and stock. **2** Surgery. a piece of tissue transplanted from a donor or from the patient's own body to an area of the body in need of the tissue. **3** the act of joining one thing to another as by grafting. ◆ vb **4** Horticulture. **4a** to induce (a plant or part of a plant) to unite with another part or (of a plant or part of a plant) to unite in this way. **4b** to produce (fruit, flowers, etc.) by this means or (of fruit, etc.) to grow by this means. **5** to transplant (tissue) or (of tissue) to be transplanted. **6** to attach or incorporate or become attached or incorporated: to graft a happy ending onto a sad tale. [C15: from OF graffe, from Med. L graphium, from L: stylus, from Gk grapheion, from graphein to write] ▶ 'grafting n

graft² (grɑːft) n **1** Inf. work (esp. in **hard graft**). **2a** the acquisition of money, power, etc., by dishonest or unfair means, esp. by taking advantage of a position of trust. **2b** something gained in this way. **2c** a payment made to a person profiting by such a practice. ◆ vb **3** (intr) Inf. to work, esp. hard. **4** to acquire by or practise graft. [C19: from ?] ▶ 'grafter n

Graham ★ ('greɪəm) n **1** Martha. 1893–1991, US dancer and choreographer. **2** Thomas. 1805–69, British physicist: proposed **Graham's law** (1831) of diffusion and coined the terms osmosis, crystalloids, and colloids. **3** William Franklin, known as Billy. born 1918, US evangelist.

Grahame ★ ('greɪəm) n Kenneth. 1859–1932, British author, noted for the children's classic The Wind in the Willows (1908).

Graham Land ★ n the N part of the Antarctic Peninsula: became part of the British Antarctic Territory in 1962 (formerly part of the Falkland Islands Dependencies).

Graiae ★ ('greɪiː, 'graɪiː) pl n a variant of **Graeae**.

Graian Alps ★ ('greɪən, 'graɪ-) pl n the N part of the Western Alps, in France and NW Piedmont, Italy. Highest peak: Gran Paradiso, 4061 m (13 323 ft).

Grail (greɪl) n See **Holy Grail**.

grain (greɪn) n **1** the small hard seedlike fruit of a grass, esp. a cereal plant. **2** a mass of such fruits, esp. when gathered for food. **3** the plants, collectively, from which such fruits are harvested. **4** a small hard particle: a grain of sand. **5a** the general direction or arrangement of the fibres, layers, or particles in wood, leather, stone, etc. **5b** the pattern or texture resulting from such an arrangement. **6** the relative size of the particles of a substance: sugar of fine grain. **7** the granular texture of a rock, mineral, etc. **8** the outer layer of a hide or skin from which the hair or wool has been removed. **9** the smallest unit of weight in the avoirdupois, Troy, and apothecaries' systems: equal to 0.0648 gram. **10** the threads or direction of threads in a woven fabric. **11** Photog. any of a large number of particles in a photographic emulsion. **12** cleavage lines in crystalline material. **13** Chem. any of a large number of small crystals forming a solid. **14** a very small amount: a grain of truth. **15** natural disposition, inclination, or character (esp. in **go against the grain**). **16** Astronautics. a homogenous mass of solid propellant in a form designed to give the required combustion characteristics for a particular rocket. **17** (not in technical usage) kermes or a red dye made from this insect. ◆ vb (mainly tr) **18** (also intr) to form into grains or cause to form into grains; granulate; crystallize. **19** to give a granular or roughened appearance or texture to. **20** to paint, stain, etc., in imitation of the grain of wood or leather. **21a** to remove the hair or wool from (a hide or skin) before tanning. **21b** to raise the grain pattern on (leather). [C13: from OF, from L grānum]

grain alcohol *n* ethanol containing about 10 per cent of water, made by the fermentation of grain.

grain elevator *n* a machine for raising grain to a higher level, esp. one having an endless belt fitted with scoops.

Grainger ★ ('greɪndʒə) *n* **Percy Aldridge**. 1882–1961, Australian pianist, composer, and collector of folk music.

graining ('greɪnɪŋ) *n* **1** the pattern or texture of the grain of wood, leather, etc. **2** the process of painting, printing, staining, etc., a surface in imitation of a grain. **3** a surface produced by such a process.

grainy ('greɪnɪ) *adj* **grainier, grainiest. 1** resembling, full of, or composed of grain; granular. **2** resembling the grain of wood, leather, etc. **3** *Photog.* having poor definition because of a large grain size.
▶ '**graininess** *n*

grallatorial (,græləˈtɔːrɪəl) *adj* of or relating to long-legged wading birds. [C19: from NL, from L *grallātor* one who walks on stilts, from *grallae* stilts]

gram[1] (græm) *n* a metric unit of mass equal to one thousandth of a kilogram. Symbol: g [C18: from F *gramme*, from LL *gramma*, from Gk: small weight, from *graphein* to write]

gram[2] (græm) *n* **1** any of several leguminous plants whose seeds are used as food in India. **2** the seed of any of these plants. [C18: from Port. *gram* (modern spelling: *grão*), from L *grānum* GRAIN]

gram. *abbrev. for:* **1** grammar. **2** grammatical.

-gram *n combining form.* indicating a drawing or something written or recorded: *hexagram; telegram.* [from L *-gramma*, from Gk, from *gramma* letter & *grammē* line]

gram atom *or* **gram-atomic weight** *n* an amount of an element equal to its atomic weight expressed in grams: now replaced by the mole.

gramineous (grəˈmɪnɪəs) *adj* **1** of, relating to, or belonging to the grass family. **2** resembling a grass; grasslike.
◆ Also: **graminaceous** (,græmɪˈneɪʃəs). [C17: from L, from *grāmen* grass]

graminivorous (,græmɪˈnɪvərəs) *adj* (of animals) feeding on grass. [C18: from L *grāmen* grass + -VOROUS]

grammar ('græmə) *n* **1** the branch of linguistics that deals with syntax and morphology, sometimes also phonology and semantics. **2** the abstract system of rules in terms of which a person's mastery of his native language can be explained. **3** a systematic description of the grammatical facts of a language. **4** a book containing an account of the grammatical facts of a language or recommendations as to rules for the proper use of a language. **5** the use of language with regard to its correctness or social propriety, esp. in syntax: *the teacher told him to watch his grammar.* [C14: from OF, from L, from Gk *grammatikē* (*tekhnē*) the grammatical (art), from *grammatikos* concerning letters, from *gramma* letter]

grammarian (grəˈmɛərɪən) *n* **1** a person whose occupation is the study of grammar. **2** the author of a grammar.

grammar school *n* **1** *Brit.* (esp. formerly) a state-maintained secondary school providing an education with an academic bias. **2** *US.* another term for **elementary school. 3** *Austral.* a private school, esp. one controlled by a church. **4** *NZ.* a secondary school forming part of the public education system.

grammatical (grəˈmætɪkᵊl) *adj* **1** of or relating to grammar. **2** (of a sentence) well formed; regarded as correct.
▶ **gram'matically** *adv* ▶ **gram'maticalness** *n*

gram molecule *or* **gram-molecular weight** *n* an amount of a compound equal to its molecular weight expressed in grams: now replaced by the mole. See **mole**[3].

Grammy ('græmɪ) *n, pl* **Grammys** *or* **Grammies.** (in the US) one of the gold-plated discs awarded annually for outstanding achievement in the record industry. [C20: from GRAM(OPHONE) + -*my* as in EMMY]

gramophone ('græmə,fəʊn) *n* **1a** Also called: **record player.** a device for reproducing the sounds stored on a record: now usually applied to the early type that uses an acoustic horn. US and Canad. word: **phonograph. 1b** (*as modifier*): *a gramophone record.* **2** the technique of recording sound on disc: *the gramophone has made music*

widely available. [C19: orig. a trademark, ? based on an inversion of *phonogram;* see PHONO-, -GRAM]

Grampian Mountains ★ ('græmpɪən) *pl n* **1** a mountain system of central Scotland, extending from the southwest to the northeast and separating the Highlands from the Lowlands. Highest peak: Ben Nevis, 1343 m (4406 ft). **2** a mountain range in SE Australia, in W Victoria. ◆ Also called: **the Grampians.**

Grampian Region ★ *n* a former (1975–96) local government region in NE Scotland.

grampus ('græmpəs) *n, pl* **grampuses. 1** a widely distributed slaty-grey dolphin with a blunt snout. **2** another name for **killer whale.** [C16: from OF *graspois*, from *gras* fat (from L *crassus*) + *pois* fish (from L *piscis*)]

Gram's method (græmz) *n Bacteriol.* **1** a technique used to classify bacteria by staining them with a violet iodine solution. **2 Gram-positive** (*or* **Gram-negative**). *adj* denoting bacteria that do (*or* do not) retain this stain. [C19: after H. C. J. *Gram* (1853–1938), Danish physician]

gran (græn) *n* an informal word for **grandmother.**

Granada ★ (grəˈnɑːdə) *n* **1** a former kingdom of S Spain, in Andalusia: founded in the 13th century and divided in 1833 into the present-day provinces of Granada, Almería, and Málaga. **2** a city in S Spain, in Andalusia: capital of the Moorish kingdom of Granada from 1238 to 1492 and a great commercial and cultural centre, containing the Alhambra palace (13th and 14th centuries); university (1531). Pop.: 271 180 (1994 est.). **3** a city in SW Nicaragua, on the NW shore of Lake Nicaragua: the oldest city in the country, founded in 1523 by Córdoba; attacked frequently by pirates in the 17th century. Pop.: 74 396 (1995 est.).

granadilla (,grænəˈdɪlə) *n* **1** any of various passionflowers that have edible egg-shaped fleshy fruit. **2** Also called: **passion fruit.** the fruit of such a plant. [C18: from Sp., dim. of *granada* pomegranate, from LL *grānātum*]

Granados ★ (*Spanish* graˈnaðɒs) *n* **Enrique** (enˈrrike), full name *Enrique Granados y Campina.* 1867–1916, Spanish composer.

granary ('grænərɪ; *US* 'greɪnərɪ) *n, pl* **granaries. 1** a building for storing threshed grain. **2** a region that produces a large amount of grain. ◆ *adj* **3** (*cap.*) *Trademark.* (of bread, flour, etc.) containing malted wheat grain. [C16: from L *grānārium*, from *grānum* GRAIN]

Gran Canaria ★ (gran kaˈnarja) *n* the Spanish name for **Grand Canary.**

Gran Chaco ★ (*Spanish* gran ˈtʃako) *n* a plain of S central South America, between the Andes and the Paraguay River in SE Bolivia, E Paraguay, and N Argentina: huge swamps and scrub forest. Area: about 780 000 sq. km (300 000 sq. miles). Often shortened to: **Chaco.**

grand (grænd) *adj* **1** large or impressive in size, extent, or consequence: *grand mountain scenery.* **2** characterized by or attended with magnificence or display; sumptuous: *a grand feast.* **3** of great distinction or pretension; dignified or haughty. **4** designed to impress: *grand gestures.* **5** very good; wonderful. **6** comprehensive; complete: *a grand total.* **7** worthy of respect; fine: *a grand old man.* **8** large or impressive in conception or execution: *grand ideas.* **9** most important; chief: *the grand arena.* ◆ *n* **10** See **grand piano. 11** (*pl* **grand**) *Sl.* a thousand pounds or dollars. [C16: from OF, from L *grandis*]
▶ '**grandly** *adv* ▶ '**grandness** *n*

grand- *prefix* (in designations of kinship) one generation removed in ascent or descent: *grandson; grandfather.* [from F *grand-*, on the model of L *magnus* in such phrases as *avunculus magnus* great-uncle]

grandad, granddad ('græn,dæd) *or* **grandaddy, granddaddy** ('græn,dædɪ) *n, pl* **grandads, granddads** *or* **grandaddies, granddaddies.** informal words for **grandfather.**

grandam ('grændəm, -dæm) *or* **grandame** ('grændeɪm, -dəm) *n* an archaic word for **grandmother.** [C13: from Anglo-F *grandame*, from OF GRAND- + *dame* lady, mother]

grandaunt ('grænd,ɑːnt) *n* another name for **great-aunt.**

Grand Bahama ★ *n* an island in the Atlantic, in the W

Bahamas. Pop.: 40 898 (1990). Area: 1114 sq. km (430 sq. miles).

Grand Banks ★ *pl n* a part of the continental shelf in the Atlantic, extending for about 560 km (350 miles) off the SE coast of Newfoundland: meeting place of the cold Labrador Current and the warm Gulf Stream, producing frequent fogs and rich fishing grounds.

Grand Canal ★ *n* **1** a canal in E China, extending north from Hangzhou to Tianjin: the longest canal in China, now partly silted up; central section, linking the Yangtze and Yellow Rivers, finished in 486 B.C.; north section finished by Kublai Khan between 1282 and 1292. Length: about 1600 km (1000 miles). Chinese name: **Da Yunhe.** **2** a canal in Venice, forming the main water thoroughfare: noted for its bridges, the Rialto, and the fine palaces along its banks.

Grand Canary ★ *n* an island in the Atlantic, in the Canary Islands: part of the Spanish province of Las Palmas. Capital: Las Palmas. Pop.: 631 000 (latest est.). Area: 1533 sq. km (592 sq. miles). Spanish name: **Gran Canaria.**

Grand Canyon ★ *n* a gorge of the Colorado River in N Arizona, extending from its junction with the Little Colorado River to Lake Mead; cut by vertical river erosion through the multicoloured strata of a high plateau; partly contained in the **Grand Canyon National Park,** covering 2610 sq. km (1008 sq. miles). Length: 451 km (280 miles). Width: 6 km (4 miles) to 29 km (18 miles). Greatest depth: over 1.5 km (1 mile).

grandchild ('græn,tʃaɪld) *n, pl* **grandchildren.** the son or daughter of one's child.

Grand Coulee ★ ('ku:lɪ) *n* a canyon in central Washington State, over 120 m (400 ft) deep, at the N end of which is situated the **Grand Coulee Dam,** on the Columbia River. Height of dam: 168 m (550 ft). Length of dam: 1310 km (4300 ft).

granddaughter ('græn,dɔ:tə) *n* a daughter of one's son or daughter.

grand duchess *n* **1** the wife or widow of a grand duke. **2** a woman who holds the rank of grand duke in her own right.

grand duchy *n* the territory, state, or principality of a grand duke or grand duchess.

grand duke *n* **1** a prince or nobleman who rules a territory, state, or principality. **2** a son or a male descendant in the male line of a Russian tsar. **3** a medieval Russian prince who ruled over other princes.

grande dame *French.* (grãd dam) *n* a woman regarded as the most experienced, prominent, or venerable member of her profession, etc.

grandee (græn'di:) *n* **1** a Spanish or Portuguese prince or nobleman of the highest rank. **2** a person of high station. [C16: from Sp. *grande*]

Grande-Terre ★ (*French* grãdter) *n* a French island in the Caribbean, in the Lesser Antilles: one of the two main islands which constitute Guadeloupe. Chief town: Pointe-à-Pitre.

grandeur ('grændʒə) *n* **1** personal greatness, esp. when based on dignity, character, or accomplishments. **2** magnificence; splendour. **3** pretentious or bombastic behaviour.

Grand Falls ★ *pl n* the former name (until 1965) of **Churchill Falls.**

grandfather ('græn,fɑ:ðə, 'grænd-) *n* **1** the father of one's father or mother. **2** (*often pl*) a male ancestor. **3** (*often cap.*) a familiar term of address for an old man.
▶ **'grand,fatherly** *adj*

grandfather clock *n* a long-pendulum clock in a tall standing wooden case.

Grand Guignol *French.* (grã giɲɔl) *n* **a** a brief sensational play intended to horrify. **b** (*modifier*) of or like plays of this kind. [C20: after *Le Grand Guignol,* a small theatre in Montmartre, Paris]

grandiloquent (græn'dɪləkwənt) *adj* inflated, pompous, or bombastic in style or expression. [C16: from L *grandiloquus,* from *grandis* great + *loquī* to speak]
▶ **gran'diloquence** ▶ **gran'diloquently** *adv*

grandiose ('grændɪ,əʊs) *adj* **1** pretentiously grand or

stately. **2** imposing in conception or execution. [C19: from F, from It., from *grande* great; see GRAND]
▶ **'grandi,osely** *adv* ▶ **grandiosity** (,grændɪ'ɒsɪtɪ) *n*

grand jury *n Law.* (esp. in the US and, now rarely, in Canada) a jury summoned to inquire into accusations of crime and ascertain whether the evidence is adequate to found an indictment. Abolished in Britain in 1948.

grand larceny *n* **1** (formerly, in England) the theft of property valued at over 12 pence. Abolished in 1827. **2** (in some states of the US) the theft of property of which the value is above a specified figure.

grandma ('græn,mɑ:), **grandmama,** *or* **grand-mamma** ('grænmə,mɑ:) *n* informal words for **grandmother.**

grand mal (grɒn mæl) *n* a form of epilepsy characterized by loss of consciousness for up to five minutes and violent convulsions. Cf. **petit mal.** [F: great illness]

Grandma Moses ★ *n* the nickname of (Anna Mary Robertson) **Moses.**

Grand Manan ★ (mə'næn) *n* a Canadian island, off the SW coast of New Brunswick: separated from the coast of Maine by the **Grand Manan Channel.** Area: 147 sq. km (57 sq. miles).

grandmaster ('grænd,mɑ:stə) *n* **1** *Chess.* one of the top chess players of a particular country. **2** a leading exponent of any of various arts.

Grand Master *n* the title borne by the head of any of various societies, orders, and other organizations, such as the Templars, Freemasons, or the various martial arts.

grandmother ('græn,mʌðə, 'grænd-) *n* **1** the mother of one's father or mother. **2** (*often pl*) a female ancestor.
▶ **'grand,motherly** *adj*

Grand National *n* **the.** an annual steeplechase run at Aintree, Liverpool, since 1839.

grandnephew ('græn,nɛvju:, -,nɛfju:, 'grænd-) *n* another name for **great-nephew.**

grandniece ('græn,ni:s, 'grænd-) *n* another name for **great-niece.**

grand opera *n* an opera that has a serious plot and is entirely in musical form, with no spoken dialogue.

grandpa ('græn,pɑ:) *or* **grandpapa** ('grænpə,pɑ:) *n* informal words for **grandfather.**

grandparent ('græn,pɛərənt, 'grænd-) *n* the father or mother of either of one's parents.

grand piano *n* a form of piano in which the strings are arranged horizontally.

Grand Pré ★ (grɒn preɪ; *French* grã pre) *n* a village in SE Canada, in W Nova Scotia: setting of Longfellow's *Evangeline.*

Grand Prix (*French* grã pri) *n* **1** any of a series of formula motor races to determine the annual Driver's World Championship. **2** a very important competitive event in various other sports, such as athletics, snooker, or powerboating. [F: great prize]

Grand Rapids ★ *n* (*functioning as sing*) a city in SW Michigan: electronics, car parts. Pop.: 190 395 (1995 est.).

grandsire ('græn,saɪə, 'grænd-) *n* an archaic word for **grandfather.**

grand slam *n* **1** *Bridge, etc.* the winning of 13 tricks by one player or side or the contract to do so. Cf. **little slam. 2** the winning of all major competitions in a season, esp. in tennis and golf. **3** (*often caps.*) *Rugby union.* the winning of all four games in the annual Five Nations Championship involving Scotland, England, Wales, Ireland, and France.

grandson ('grænsʌn, 'grænd-) *n* a son of one's son or daughter.

grandstand ('græn,stænd, 'grænd-) *n* **1** a terraced block of seats commanding the best view at racecourses, football pitches, etc. **2** the spectators in a grandstand.

grand tour *n* **1** (formerly) an extended tour through the major cities of Europe, esp. one undertaken by a rich or aristocratic Englishman to complete his education. **2** *Inf.* an extended sightseeing trip, tour of inspection, etc.

granduncle ('grænd,ʌŋkᵊl) n another name for **great-uncle**.

grand unified theory n Physics. any of a number of theories of elementary particles and fundamental interactions designed to explain the electromagnetic, strong, and weak interactions in terms of a single mathematical formalism. Abbrev.: **GUT**.

Grand Union Canal ★ n a canal in S England linking London and the Midlands: opened in 1801.

grange (greɪndʒ) n **1** Chiefly Brit. a farm, esp. a farmhouse or country house with its various outbuildings. **2** Arch. a granary or barn. [C13: from Anglo-F graunge, from Med. L grānica, from L grānum GRAIN]

Grangemouth ★ ('greɪndʒmaʊθ, -məθ) n a port in Scotland, in Falkirk council area: now Scotland's second port, with oil refineries, shipyards, and chemical industries. Pop.: 18 739 (1991).

Granicus ★ (grə'naɪkəs) n an ancient river in NW Asia Minor where Alexander the Great won his first major battle against the Persians (334 B.C.).

granite ('grænɪt) n **1** a light-coloured coarse-grained acid plutonic igneous rock consisting of quartz and feldspars: widely used for building. **2** great hardness, endurance, or resolution. [C17: from It. granito grained, from grano grain, from L grānum]
▸ **granitic** (grə'nɪtɪk) adj

graniteware ('grænɪt,weə) n **1** iron vessels coated with enamel of a granite-like appearance. **2** a type of pottery with a speckled glaze.

granivorous (græ'nɪvərəs) adj (of animals) feeding on seeds and grain.
▸ **granivore** ('grænɪ,vɔː) n

granny or **grannie** ('grænɪ) n, pl **grannies**. **1** informal words for **grandmother**. **2** Inf. an irritatingly fussy person. **3** See **granny knot**.

granny bond n Brit. inf. a savings scheme available originally only to people over retirement age.

granny farm n Derog. sl. an old people's home, esp. one that charges high fees and offers poor care.

granny flat n self-contained accommodation within or built onto a house, suitable for an elderly parent.

granny knot or **granny's knot** n a reef knot with the ends crossed the wrong way, making it liable to slip or jam.

Gran Paradiso ★ (Italian gram para'diːzo) n a mountain in NW Italy, in NW Piedmont: the highest peak of the Graian Alps. Height: 4061 m (13 323 ft).

grant (grɑːnt) vb (tr) **1** to consent to perform or fulfil: to grant a wish. **2** (may take a clause as object) to permit as a favour, indulgence, etc.: to grant an interview. **3** (may take a clause as object) to acknowledge the validity of; concede: I grant what you say is true. **4** to bestow, esp. in a formal manner. **5** to transfer (property) to another, esp. by deed; convey. **6 take for granted**. **6a** to accept or assume without question: one takes certain amenities for granted. **6b** to fail to appreciate the value, merit, etc., of (a person). ◆ n **7** a sum of money provided by a government, local authority, or public fund to finance educational study, building repairs, overseas aid, etc. **8** a privilege, right, etc., that has been granted. **9** the act of granting. **10** a transfer of property by deed; conveyance. [C13: from OF graunter, from Vulgar L credentāre (unattested), from L crēdere to believe]
▸ **'grantable** adj ▸ **'granter** or (Law) **'grantor** n

Grant ★ (grɑːnt) n **1 Cary**, real name Alexander Archibald Leach. 1904–86, US film actor, born in England. His films include The Philadelphia Story (1940) and Arsenic and Old Lace (1944). **2 Duncan (James Corrowr)**. 1885–1978, British painter. **3 Ulysses S(impson)**, real name Hiram Ulysses Grant. 1822–85, 18th president of the US (1869–77); commander in chief of Union forces in the American Civil War (1864–65).

Granta ★ ('græntə, 'grɑːntə) n the original name, still in use locally, for the River Cam.

grantee (grɑːn'tiː) n Law. a person to whom a grant is made.

Granth (grʌnt) n the sacred scripture of the Sikhs. [from Hindi, from Sansk. grantha a book]

Grantham ★ ('grænθəm) n a town in E England, in Lincolnshire: birthplace of Sir Isaac Newton and Margaret Thatcher. Pop.: 33 243 (1991).

grant-in-aid n, pl **grants-in-aid**. a sum of money granted by one government to a lower level of government for a programme, etc.

grant-maintained adj (**grant maintained** when postpositive) (of schools or educational institutions) funded directly by central government.

gran turismo ('græn tʊə'rɪzməʊ) n, pl **gran turismos**. See **GT**. [C20: from It.]

granular ('grænjʊlə) adj **1** of, like, or containing granules. **2** having a grainy surface.
▸ **granularity** (,grænjʊ'lærɪtɪ) n ▸ **'granularly** adv

granulate ('grænjʊ,leɪt) vb **granulates, granulating, granulated**. **1** (tr) to make into grains: granulated sugar. **2** to make or become roughened in surface texture.
▸ **,granu'lation** n ▸ **'granulative** adj ▸ **'granu,lator** or **'granu,later** n

granule ('grænjuːl) n a small grain. [C17: from LL grānulum a small GRAIN]

granulocyte ('grænjʊlə,saɪt) n any of a group of unpigmented blood cells having cytoplasmic granules that take up various dyes.

Granville ★ ('grænvɪl) n **1st Earl**, title of John Carteret. 1690–1763, British statesman: secretary of state (1742–44); a leading opponent of Walpole.

Granville-Barker ★ (-'bɑːkə) n **Harley**. 1877–1946, British dramatist, theatre director, and critic, noted particularly for his Prefaces to Shakespeare (1927–47).

grape (greɪp) n **1** the fruit of the grapevine, which has a purple or green skin and sweet flesh: eaten raw, dried to make raisins, currants, or sultanas, or used for making wine. **2** See **grapevine** (sense 1). **3 the grape**. Inf. wine. **4** See **grapeshot**. [C13: from OF grape bunch of grapes, of Gmc origin; rel. to CRAMP², GRAPPLE]
▸ **'grapey** or **'grapy** adj

grapefruit ('greɪp,fruːt) n, pl **grapefruit** or **grapefruits**. **1** a tropical or subtropical evergreen tree. **2** the large round edible fruit of this tree, which has yellow rind and juicy slightly bitter pulp.

grape hyacinth n any of various Eurasian bulbous plants of the lily family with clusters of rounded blue flowers resembling tiny grapes.

grapeshot ('greɪp,ʃɒt) n ammunition for cannons consisting of a cluster of iron balls that scatter after firing.

grape sugar n another name for **dextrose**.

grapevine ('greɪp,vaɪn) n **1** any of several vines of E Asia, widely cultivated for its fruit (grapes). **2** Inf. an unofficial means of relaying information, esp. from person to person.

graph (grɑːf) n **1** Also called: **chart**. a drawing depicting the relation between certain sets of numbers or quantities by means of a series of dots, lines, etc., plotted with reference to a set of axes. **2** Maths. a drawing depicting a functional relation between two or three variables by means of a curve or surface containing only those points whose coordinates satisfy the relation. **3** Linguistics. a symbol in a writing system not further subdivisible into other such symbols. ◆ vb **4** (tr) to draw or represent in a graph. [C19: short for graphic formula]

-graph n combining form. **1** an instrument that writes or records: telegraph. **2** a writing, record, or drawing: autograph; lithograph. [via L from Gk, from graphein to write]
▸ **-graphic** or **-graphical** adj combining form. ▸ **-graphically** adv combining form.

grapheme ('græfiːm) n Linguistics. the complete class of letters or combinations of letters that represent one speech sound: for instance, the f in full, the gh in cough, and the ph in photo are members of the same grapheme. [C20: from Gk graphēma a letter]
▸ **gra'phemically** adv

-grapher n combining form. **1** indicating a person skilled in a subject: geographer; photographer. **2** indicating a person who writes or draws in a specified way: *stenographer; lithographer*.

graphic ('græfɪk) *or* **graphical** *adj* **1** vividly or clearly described: *a graphic account of the disaster*. **2** of or relating to writing: *graphic symbols*. **3** *Maths*. using, relating to, or determined by a graph: *a graphic representation of the figures*. **4** of or relating to the graphic arts. **5** *Geol*. having or denoting a texture resembling writing: *graphic granite*. [C17: from L *graphicus*, from Gk *graphikos*, from *graphein* to write]
▸ 'graphically *adv* ▸ 'graphicness *n*

graphicacy ('græfɪkəsɪ) *n* the ability to understand and use maps, symbols, etc. [C20: formed on the model of *literacy*]

graphical user interface *n* an interface between a user and a computer system that allows the user to operate the system by means of pictorial devices, such as menus and icons.

graphic arts *pl n* any of the fine or applied visual arts based on drawing or the use of line, esp. illustration and printmaking of all kinds.

graphic equalizer *n* a tone control that enables the output signal of an audio amplifier to be adjusted in each of a series of frequency bands by means of sliding contacts.

graphic novel *n* a novel in the form of a comic strip.

graphics ('græfɪks) *n* **1** (*functioning as sing*) the process or art of drawing in accordance with mathematical principles. **2** (*functioning as sing*) the study of writing systems. **3** (*functioning as pl*) the drawings, photographs, etc., in a magazine or book, or in a television or film production. **4** (*functioning as pl*) *Computing*. information displayed in the form of diagrams, graphs, etc.

graphite ('græfaɪt) *n* a blackish soft form of carbon used in pencils, electrodes, as a lubricant, as a moderator in nuclear reactors, and, in carbon fibre form, for tough lightweight sports equipment. [C18: from G *Graphit*, from Gk *graphein* to write + -ITE¹]
▸ **graphitic** (grə'fɪtɪk) *adj*

graphology (græ'fɒlədʒɪ) *n* **1** the study of handwriting, esp. to analyse the writer's character. **2** *Linguistics*. the study of writing systems.
▸ ,grapho'logical *adj* ▸ gra'phologist *n*

graph paper *n* paper printed with intersecting lines for drawing graphs, diagrams, etc.

-graphy *n combining form*. **1** indicating a form of writing, representing, etc.: *calligraphy; photography*. **2** indicating an art or descriptive science: *choreography; oceanography*. [via L from Gk, from *graphein* to write]

grapnel ('græpn°l) *n* **1** a device with a multiple hook at one end and attached to a rope, which is thrown or hooked over a firm mooring to secure an object attached to the other end of the rope. **2** a light anchor for small boats. [C14: from OF *grapin*, from *grape* a hook; see GRAPE]

grappa ('græpə) *n* a spirit distilled from the fermented remains of grapes after pressing. [It.: grape stalk, of Gmc origin; see GRAPE]

Grappelli *or* **Grappelly ★** (grə'pelɪ) *n* Stéphane ('stefᵊn). 1908–97, French jazz violinist: with Django Reinhardt, he led the Quintet of the Hot Club of France (1934–39).

grapple ('græp°l) *vb* **grapples, grappling, grappled**. **1** to come to grips with (one or more persons), esp. to struggle in hand-to-hand combat. **2** (*intr*; foll. by *with*) to cope or contend: *to grapple with a financial problem*. **3** (*tr*) to secure with a grapple. ◆ *n* **4** any form of hook or metal instrument by which something is secured, such as a grapnel. **5a** the act of gripping or seizing, as in wrestling. **5b** a grip or hold. [C16: from OF *grappelle* a little hook, from *grape* hook; see GRAPNEL]
▸ 'grappler *n*

grappling iron *or* **hook** *n* a grapnel, esp. one used for securing ships.

graptolite ('græptə,laɪt) *n* an extinct Palaeozoic colonial animal: a common fossil. [C19: from Gk *graptos* written, from *graphein* to write + -LITE]

Grasmere ★ ('grɑːs,mɪə) *n* a village in NW England, in

Cumbria at the head of **Lake Grasmere**: home of William Wordsworth and of Thomas de Quincey.

grasp (grɑːsp) *vb* **1** to grip (something) firmly as with the hands. **2** (when *intr*, often foll. by *at*) to struggle, snatch, or grope (for). **3** (*tr*) to understand, esp. with effort. ◆ *n* **4** the act of grasping. **5** a grip or clasp, as of a hand. **6** total rule or possession. **7** understanding; comprehension. [C14: from Low G *grapsen*; rel. to OE *græppian* to seize]
▸ 'graspable *adj* ▸ 'grasper *n*

grasping ('grɑːspɪŋ) *adj* greedy; avaricious.
▸ 'graspingly *adv* ▸ 'graspingness *n*

grass (grɑːs) *n* **1** any of a family of plants having jointed stems sheathed by long narrow leaves, flowers in spikes, and seedlike fruits. The family includes cereals, bamboo, etc. **2** such plants collectively, in a lawn, meadow, etc. Related adj: **verdant**. **3** ground on which such plants grow; a lawn, field, etc. **4** ground on which animals are grazed; pasture. **5** a slang word for **marijuana**. **6** *Brit. sl.* a person who informs, esp. on criminals. **7** **let the grass grow under one's feet**. to squander time or opportunity. ◆ *vb* **8** to cover or become covered with grass. **9** to feed or be fed with grass. **10** (*tr*) to spread (cloth, etc.) out on grass for drying or bleaching in the sun. **11** (*intr*; usually foll. by *on*) *Brit. sl.* to inform, esp. to the police. ◆ See also **grass up**. [OE *græs*]
▸ 'grass,like *adj*

Grass ★ (German gras) *n* Günter (Wilhelm) ('gyntər). born 1927, German writer, noted particularly for his novels *The Tin Drum* (1959) and *The Rat* (1986), his other books include *Toad Croaks* (1992).

grass hockey *n* in W Canada, field hockey, as contrasted with ice hockey.

grasshopper ('grɑːs,hɒpə) *n* an insect having hind legs adapted for leaping: typically terrestrial, feeding on plants, and producing a ticking sound by rubbing the hind legs against the leathery forewings.

grassland ('grɑːs,lænd) *n* **1** land, such as a prairie, on which grass predominates. **2** land reserved for natural grass pasture.

grass roots *pl n* **1** ordinary people as distinct from the active leadership of a group or organization, esp. a political party. **2** the essentials.

grass snake *n* **1** a harmless nonvenomous European snake having a brownish-green body with variable markings. **2** any of several similar related European snakes.

grass tree *n* **1** Also called: **blackboy**. an Australian plant of the lily family, having a woody stem, stiff grasslike leaves, and a spike of small white flowers. **2** any of several similar Australasian plants.

grass up *vb* (*tr, adv*) *Sl*. to inform on (someone), esp. to the police.

grass widow *or* (*masc*) **grass widower** *n* a person whose spouse is regularly away for a short period. [C16: ? an allusion to a grass bed as representing an illicit relationship]

grassy ('grɑːsɪ) *adj* **grassier, grassiest**. covered with, containing, or resembling grass.
▸ 'grassiness *n*

grate¹ (greɪt) *vb* **grates, grating, grated**. **1** (*tr*) to reduce to small shreds by rubbing against a rough or sharp perforated surface: *to grate carrots*. **2** to scrape (an object) against something or (objects) together, producing a harsh rasping sound, or (of objects) to scrape with such a sound. **3** (*intr*; foll. by *on* or *upon*) to annoy. [C15: from OF *grater* to scrape, of Gmc origin]
▸ 'grater *n*

grate² (greɪt) *n* **1** a framework of metal bars for holding fuel in a fireplace, stove, or furnace. **2** a less common word for **fireplace**. **3** another name for **grating¹**. ◆ *vb* **4** (*tr*) to provide with a grate or grates. [C14: from OF, from L *crātis* hurdle]

grateful ('greɪtfʊl) *adj* **1** thankful for gifts, favours, etc.; appreciative. **2** showing gratitude: *a grateful letter*. **3** favourable or pleasant: *a grateful rest*. [C16: from obs. *grate*, from L *grātus* + -FUL]
▸ 'gratefully *adv* ▸ 'gratefulness *n*

Gratian ★ ('greɪʃɪən) n Latin name *Flavius Gratianus*. 359–383 A.D., Roman emperor (367–383): ruled with his father Valentinian I (367–375); ruled the Western Roman Empire with his brother Valentinian II (375-83); appointed Theodosius I emperor of the Eastern Roman Empire (379).

graticule ('grætɪ,kjuːl) n **1** the grid of intersecting lines of latitude and longitude on which a map is drawn. **2** another name for **reticle**. [C19: from F, from L *crāticula*, from *crātis* wickerwork]

gratify ('grætɪ,faɪ) vb **gratifies, gratifying, gratified.** (*tr*) **1** to satisfy or please. **2** to yield to or indulge (a desire, whim, etc.). [C16: from L *grātificārī*, from *grātus* grateful + *facere* to make]
▸ ˌgratifiˈcation n ▸ ˈgratiˌfier n ▸ ˈgratiˌfying adj ▸ ˈgratiˌfyingly adv

gratin (*French* gratɛ̃) See **au gratin**.

grating[1] ('greɪtɪŋ) n a framework of metal bars in the form of a grille set into a wall, pavement, etc., serving as a cover or guard but admitting air and sometimes light. Also called: **grate**.

grating[2] ('greɪtɪŋ) adj **1** (of sounds) harsh and rasping. **2** annoying; irritating. ◆ n **3** (*often pl*) something produced by grating.
▸ ˈgratingly adv

gratis ('greɪtɪs, 'grætɪs, 'grɑːtɪs) adv, adj (*postpositive*) without payment; free of charge. [C15: from L: out of kindness, from *grātiīs*, ablative pl of *grātia* favour]

gratitude ('grætɪ,tjuːd) n a feeling of thankfulness, as for gifts or favours. [C16: from Med. L *grātitūdō*, from L *grātus* GRATEFUL]

gratuitous (grə'tjuːɪtəs) adj **1** given or received without payment or obligation. **2** without cause; unjustified. [C17: from L *grātuītus* from *grātia* favour]
▸ graˈtuitously adv ▸ graˈtuitousness n

gratuity (grə'tjuːɪtɪ) n, pl **gratuities. 1** a gift or reward, usually of money, for services rendered; tip. **2** *Mil.* a financial award granted for long or meritorious service.

gratulatory ('grætjʊlətərɪ) adj expressing congratulation. [C16: from L *grātulārī* to congratulate]

Graubünden ★ (*German* grau'byndən) n an Alpine canton of E Switzerland: the largest of the cantons, but sparsely populated. Capital: Chur. Pop.: 184 300 (1994 est.). Area: 7109 sq. km (2773 sq. miles). Italian name: **Grigioni**. Romansch name: **Grischun**. French name: **Grisons**.

grav (græv) n a unit of acceleration equal to the standard acceleration of free fall. 1 grav is equivalent to 9.806 65 metres per second per second. Symbol: g

gravadlax ('grævəd,læks) n another name for **gravlax**.

gravamen (grə'veɪmen) n, pl **gravamina** (-'væmɪnə). **1** *Law.* that part of an accusation weighing most heavily against an accused. **2** *Law.* the substance or material grounds of a complaint. **3** a rare word for **grievance**. [C17: from LL: trouble, from L *gravis* heavy]

grave[1] (greɪv) n **1** a place for the burial of a corpse, esp. beneath the ground and usually marked by a tombstone. Related adj: **sepulchral. 2** something resembling a grave or resting place: *the ship went to its grave*. **3** (*often preceded by the*) a poetic term for **death. 4 make (someone) turn in his grave.** to do something that would have shocked or distressed a person now dead. [OE *græf*]

grave[2] (greɪv) adj **1** serious and solemn: *a grave look*. **2** full of or suggesting danger: *a grave situation*. **3** important; crucial: *grave matters of state*. **4** (of colours) sober or dull. **5** (grɑːv). *Phonetics.* of or relating to an accent (`) over vowels, denoting a pronunciation with lower or falling musical pitch (as in ancient Greek), with certain special quality (as in French), or in a manner that gives the vowel status as a syllable (as in English *agèd*). ◆ n **6** (*also* grɑːv). a grave accent. [C16: from OF, from L *gravis*]
▸ ˈgravely adv ▸ ˈgraveness n

grave[3] (greɪv) vb **graves, graving, graved; graved** or **graven.** (*tr*) *Arch.* **1** to carve or engrave. **2** to fix firmly in the mind. [OE *grafan*]

grave[4] ('grɑːveɪ) adj *Music.* solemn. [It.]

grave clothes (greɪv) pl n the wrappings in which a dead body is interred.

gravel ('grævᵊl) n **1** a mixture of rock fragments and pebbles that is coarser than sand. **2** *Pathol.* small rough calculi in the kidneys or bladder. ◆ vb **gravels, gravelling, gravelled** or *US* **gravels, graveling, graveled.** (*tr*) **3** to cover with gravel. **4** to confound or confuse. **5** *US inf.* to annoy or disturb. [C13: from OF *gravele*, dim. of *grave*, ? of Celtic origin]

gravel-blind adj *Literary.* almost completely blind. [C16: from GRAVEL + BLIND]

gravelly ('grævəlɪ) adj **1** consisting of or abounding in gravel. **2** of or like gravel. **3** (esp. of a voice) harsh and grating.

graven ('greɪvᵊn) vb **1** a past participle of **grave**[3]. ◆ adj **2** strongly fixed.

Gravenhage ★ (xraːvən'haːxə) n 's. a Dutch name for (The) **Hague.**

graven image n *Chiefly Bible.* a carved image used as an idol.

graver ('greɪvə) n any of various engraving or sculpting tools, such as a burin.

Graves[1] (grɑːv) n (*sometimes not cap.*) a white or red wine from the district around Bordeaux, France.

Graves[2] ★ (greɪvz) n **Robert (Ranke).** 1895–1985, British writer, whose works include his autobiography, *Goodbye to All That* (1929), and the historical novels *I, Claudius* (1934) and *Claudius the God* (1934).

Gravesend ★ (ˌgreɪvz'ɛnd) n a river port in SE England, in NW Kent on the Thames. Pop.: 51 435 (1991).

gravestone ('greɪv,stəʊn) n a stone marking a grave.

graveyard ('greɪv,jɑːd) n a place for graves; a burial ground, esp. a small one or one in a churchyard.

graveyard shift n *US.* the working shift between midnight and morning.

graveyard slot n *Television.* the hours from late night until early morning when the number of people watching television is at its lowest.

gravid ('grævɪd) adj the technical word for **pregnant.** [C16: from L *gravidus*, from *gravis* heavy]

gravimeter (grə'vɪmɪtə) n **1** an instrument for measuring the earth's gravitational field at points on its surface. **2** an instrument for measuring relative density. [C18: from F *gravimètre*, from L *gravis* heavy]
▸ graˈvimetry n

gravimetric (ˌgrævɪ'mɛtrɪk) adj **1** of, concerned with, or using measurement by weight. **2** *Chem.* of analysis of quantities by weight.

graving dock n another term for **dry dock.**

gravitas ('grævɪ,tæs) n seriousness or solemnity, esp. of conduct or demeanour; weight or authority. [C20: from L *gravitās* weight, from *gravis* heavy]

gravitate ('grævɪ,teɪt) vb **gravitates, gravitating, gravitated.** (*intr*) **1** *Physics.* to move under the influence of gravity. **2** (usually foll. by *to* or *towards*) to be influenced or drawn, as by strong impulses. **3** to sink or settle.
▸ ˈgraviˌtater n ▸ ˈgraviˌtative adj

gravitation (ˌgrævɪ'teɪʃən) n **1** the force of attraction that bodies exert on one another as a result of their mass. **2** any process or result caused by this interaction. ◆ Also called: **gravity.**
▸ ˌgraviˈtational adj ▸ ˌgraviˈtationally adv

gravitational constant n the factor relating force to mass and distance in Newton's law of gravitation. Symbol: G

gravitational field n the field of force surrounding a body of finite mass in which another body would experience an attractive force that is proportional to the product of the masses and inversely proportional to the square of the distance between them.

gravitational mass n the mass of a body expressed in terms of the gravitational force between it and the earth. Cf. **inertial mass.**

graviton ('grævɪ,tɒn) n a postulated quantum of gravitational energy, usually considered to be a particle with zero charge and rest mass and a spin of 2.

gravity ('grævɪtɪ) n, pl **gravities. 1** the force of attraction that moves or tends to move bodies towards the centre of a celestial body, such as the earth or moon. **2** the property of being heavy or having weight. **3** another name for **gravitation**. **4** seriousness or importance, esp. as a consequence of an action or opinion. **5** manner or conduct that is solemn or dignified. **6** lowness in pitch. **7** (*modifier*) of or relating to gravity or gravitation or their effects: *gravity feed*. [C16: from L *gravitās* weight, from *gravis* heavy]

gravity wave *n Physics*. **1** a wave propagated in a gravitational field, predicted to occur as a result of an accelerating mass. **2** a surface wave on water or other liquid propagated because of the weight of liquid in the crests. ♦ Also called: **gravitational wave**.

gravlax ('græv,læks) *or* **gravadlax** *n* dry-cured salmon, marinated in salt, sugar, and spices, as served in Scandinavia. [C20: from Norwegian, from *grav* grave (because the salmon is left to ferment) + *laks* or Swedish *lax* salmon]

gravure (grə'vjʊə) *n* **1** a method of intaglio printing using a plate with many small etched recesses. See also **rotogravure**. **2** See **photogravure**. **3** matter printed by this process. [C19: from F, from *graver* to engrave]

gravy ('greɪvɪ) *n*, *pl* **gravies**. **1a** the juices that exude from meat during cooking. **1b** the sauce made by thickening and flavouring such juices. **2** *Sl.* money or gain acquired with little effort, esp. above that needed for ordinary living. [C14: from OF *gravé*, from ?]

gravy boat *n* a small often boat-shaped vessel for serving gravy or other sauces.

gray[1] (greɪ) *adj, n, vb* a variant spelling (now esp. US) of **grey**.

gray[2] (greɪ) *n* the derived SI unit of the absorbed dose of ionizing radiation: equal to 1 joule per kilogram. Symbol: Gy [C20: after L. H. *Gray*, Brit. radiobiologist]

Gray ★ (greɪ) *n* **1 Simon** (**James Holiday**). born 1936, British writer: his plays include *Butley* (1971), *The Common Pursuit* (1988), and *Hidden Laughter* (1990). **2 Thomas**. 1716–71, British poet, best known for his *Elegy written in a Country Churchyard* (1751).

grayling ('greɪlɪŋ) *n, pl* **grayling** *or* **graylings**. **1** a freshwater food fish of the salmon family of the N hemisphere, having a long spiny dorsal fin, a silvery back, and greyish-green sides. **2** any of various European butterflies having grey or greyish-brown wings.

Graz ★ (*German* gra:ts) *n* an industrial city in SE Austria, capital of Styria province: the second largest city in the country. Pop.: 237 810 (1991).

graze[1] (greɪz) *vb* **grazes, grazing, grazed**. **1** to allow (animals) to consume the vegetation on (an area of land), or (of animals) to feed thus. **2** (*tr*) to tend (livestock) while at pasture. **3** (*intr*) *Inf.* to eat snacks throughout the day rather than formal meals. **4** (*intr*) *US.* to pilfer and eat sweets, vegetables, etc., from supermarket shelves while shopping. [OE *grasian*, from *græs* GRASS]

graze[2] (greɪz) *vb* **grazes, grazing, grazed**. **1** (when *intr*, often foll. by *against* or *along*) to brush or scrape (against) gently, esp. in passing. **2** (*tr*) to break the skin of (a part of the body) by scraping. ♦ *n* **3** the act of grazing. **4** a scrape or abrasion made by grazing. [C17: prob. special use of GRAZE[1]]

grazier ('greɪzɪə) *n* a rancher or farmer who rears or fattens cattle or sheep on grazing land.

grazing ('greɪzɪŋ) *n* **1** the vegetation on pastures that is available for livestock to feed upon. **2** the land on which this is growing.

grazioso (,grɑːtsɪ'əʊsəʊ) *adj Music*. graceful. [It.]

grease (griːs, griːz) *n* **1** animal fat in a soft or melted condition. **2** any thick fatty oil, esp. one used as a lubricant for machinery, etc. ♦ *vb* **greases, greasing, greased**. (*tr*) **3** to soil, coat, or lubricate with grease. **4 grease the palm** (*or* **hand**) **of**. *Sl.* to bribe; influence by giving money to. [C13: from OF *craisse*, from L *crassus* thick]
▸ **'greaser** *n*

grease gun *n* a device for forcing grease through nipples into bearings.

grease monkey *n Inf.* a mechanic, esp. one who works on cars or aircraft.

grease nipple *n* a metal nipple designed to engage with a grease gun for injecting grease into a bearing, etc.

greasepaint ('griːs,peɪnt) *n* **1** a waxy or greasy substance used as make-up by actors. **2** theatrical make-up.

greaseproof paper ('griːs,pruːf) *n* any paper that is resistant to penetration by greases and oils.

greasy ('griːsɪ, -zɪ) *adj* **greasier, greasiest**. **1** coated or soiled with or as if with grease. **2** composed of or full of grease. **3** resembling grease. **4** unctuous or oily in manner.
▸ **'greasily** *adv* ▸ **'greasiness** *n*

greasy wool *n* untreated wool still retaining the lanolin; used for waterproof clothing.

great (greɪt) *adj* **1** relatively large in size or extent; big. **2** relatively large in number; having many parts or members: *a great assembly*. **3** of relatively long duration: *a great wait*. **4** of larger size or more importance than others of its kind: *the great auk*. **5** extreme or more than usual: *great worry*. **6** of significant importance or consequence: *a great decision*. **7a** of exceptional talents or achievements; remarkable: *a great writer*. **7b** (*as n*): *the great; one of the greats*. **8** doing or exemplifying (something) on a large scale: *she's a great reader*. **9** arising from or possessing idealism in thought, action, etc.; heroic: *great deeds*. **10** illustrious or eminent: *a great history*. **11** impressive or striking: *a great show of wealth*. **12** active or enthusiastic: *a great walker*. **13** (often foll. by *at*) skilful or adroit: *a great carpenter; you are great at singing*. **14** *Inf.* excellent; fantastic. ♦ *n* **15** Also called: **great organ**. the principal manual on an organ. [OE *grēat*]
▸ **'greatly** *adv* ▸ **'greatness** *n*

great- *prefix* **1** being the parent of a person's grandparent (in the combinations **great-grandfather, great-grandmother, great-grandparent**). **2** being the child of a person's grandchild (in the combinations **great-grandson, great-granddaughter, great-grandchild**).

great auk *n* a large flightless auk, extinct since the middle of the 19th century.

great-aunt *or* **grandaunt** *n* an aunt of one's father or mother; sister of one's grandfather or grandmother.

Great Australian Bight ★ *n* a wide bay of the Indian Ocean, in S Australia, extending from Cape Pasley to the Eyre Peninsula: notorious for storms.

Great Barrier Reef ★ *n* a coral reef in the Coral Sea, off the NE coast of Australia, extending for about 2000 km (1250 miles) from the Torres Strait along the coast of Queensland; the largest coral reef in the world.

Great Basin ★ *n* a semiarid region of the western US, between the Wasatch and the Sierra Nevada Mountains, having no drainage to the ocean: includes Nevada, W Utah, and parts of E California, S Oregon, and Idaho. Area: about 490 000 sq. km (189 000 sq. miles).

Great Bear *n* the. the English name for **Ursa Major.**

Great Bear Lake ★ *n* a lake in NW Canada, in the Northwest Territories: the largest freshwater lake entirely in Canada; drained by the **Great Bear River,** which flows to the Mackenzie River. Area: 31 792 sq. km (12 275 sq. miles).

Great Belt ★ *n* a strait in Denmark, between Zealand and Funen islands, linking the Kattegat with the Baltic. Danish name: **Store Bælt.**

Great Britain ★ *n* England, Wales, and Scotland including those adjacent islands governed from the mainland (i.e. excluding the Isle of Man and the Channel Islands). The United Kingdom of Great Britain was formed by the Act of Union (1707), although the term Great Britain had been in use since 1603, when James VI of Scotland became James I of England (including Wales). Later unions created the United Kingdom of Great Britain and Ireland (1801) and the United Kingdom of Great Britain and Northern Ireland (1922). Pop.: 56 388 200 (1992 est.). Area: 229 523 sq. km (88 619 sq. miles). See also **United Kingdom.**

great circle *n* a circular section of a sphere that has a radius equal to that of the sphere.

greatcoat ('greɪt,kəʊt) *n* a heavy overcoat.

Great Dane *n* one of a very large breed of dog with a short smooth coat.

Great Dividing Range ★ *pl n* a series of mountain ranges and plateaus roughly parallel to the E coast of Australia, in Queensland, New South Wales, and Victoria; the highest range is the Australian Alps, in the south.

Greater Antilles ★ *pl n* the. a group of islands in the Caribbean, including Cuba, Jamaica, Hispaniola, and Puerto Rico.

Greater London ★ *n* See **London**[1] (sense 2).

Greater Manchester ★ *n* a metropolitan county of NW England, administered since 1986 by the unitary authorities of Wigan, Bolton, Bury, Rochdale, Salford, Manchester, Oldham, Trafford, Stockport, and Tameside. Area: 1286 sq. km (496 sq. miles).

Greater Sunda Islands ★ *pl n* a group of islands in the W Malay Archipelago, forming the larger part of the Sunda Islands: consists of Borneo, Sumatra, Java, and Sulawesi.

Great Glen ★ *n* the. a fault valley across the whole of Scotland, extending southwest from the Moray Firth in the east to Loch Linnhe and containing Loch Ness and Loch Lochy. Also called: **Glen More, Glen Albyn**.

great gross *n* a unit of quantity equal to one dozen gross (or 1728).

great-hearted *adj* benevolent or noble; magnanimous.
▸ ˌgreat-ˈheartedness *n*

Great Indian Desert ★ *n* another name for the **Thar Desert**.

Great Lakes ★ *pl n* a group of five lakes in central North America with connecting waterways: the largest group of lakes in the world: consists of Lakes Superior, Huron, Erie, and Ontario, which are divided by the border between the US and Canada and Lake Michigan, which is wholly in the US; constitutes the most important system of inland waterways in the world, discharging through the St Lawrence into the Atlantic. Total length: 3767 km (2340 miles). Area: 246 490 sq. km (95 170 sq. miles).

great-nephew *or* **grandnephew** *n* a son of one's nephew or niece; grandson of one's brother or sister.

great-niece *or* **grandniece** *n* a daughter of one's nephew or niece; grand-daughter of one's brother or sister.

Great Ouse ★ *n* See **Ouse** (sense 1).

Great Plains ★ *pl n* a vast region of North America east of the Rocky Mountains, extending from the lowlands of the Mackenzie River (Canada), south to the Big Bend of the Rio Grande.

Great Red Spot *n* a large long-lived oval feature, south of Jupiter's equator, that is an anticyclonic disturbance in the atmosphere.

Great Rift Valley ★ *n* the most extensive rift in the earth's surface, extending from the Jordan valley in Syria to Mozambique; marked by a chain of steep-sided lakes, volcanoes, and escarpments.

Great Russian *n* **1** *Linguistics.* the technical name for **Russian. 2** a member of the chief East Slavonic people of Russia. ◆ *adj* **3** of or relating to this people or their language.

Greats (greɪts) *pl n* (at Oxford University) **1** the Honour School of Literae Humaniores, involving the study of Greek and Roman history and literature and philosophy. **2** the final examinations at the end of this course.

Great Saint Bernard Pass ★ *n, usually abbreviated to* **Great St Bernard Pass.** a pass over the W Alps, between SW central Switzerland and N Italy: noted for the hospice at the summit, founded in the 11th century. Height: 2469 m (8100 ft).

Great Salt Lake ★ *n* a shallow salt lake in NW Utah, in the Great Basin at an altitude of 1260 m (4200 ft): the area has fluctuated from less than 2500 sq. km (1000 sq. miles) to over 5000 sq. km (2000 sq. miles).

Great Sandy Desert ★ *n* **1** a desert in NW Australia. Area: about 415 000 sq. km (160 000 sq. miles). **2** the English name for the **Rub' al Khali**.

great seal *n* (*often caps.*) the principal seal of a nation, sovereign, etc., used to authenticate documents of the highest importance.

Great Slave Lake ★ *n* a lake in NW Canada, in the Northwest Territories: drained by the Mackenzie River into the Arctic Ocean. Area: 28 440 sq. km (10 980 sq. miles).

Great Slave River ★ *n* another name for the **Slave River.**

Great Smoky Mountains *or* **Great Smokies** ★ *pl n* the W part of the Appalachians, in W North Carolina and E Tennessee. Highest peak: Clingman's Dome, 2024 m (6642 ft).

Great Stour ★ *n* See **Stour.**

great tit *n* a Eurasian tit with yellow-and-black underparts and a black-and-white head.

great-uncle *or* **granduncle** *n* an uncle of one's father or mother; brother of one's grandfather or grandmother.

Great Victoria Desert ★ *n* a desert in S Australia, in SE Western Australia and W South Australia. Area: 323 750 sq. km (125 000 sq. miles).

Great Wall of China ★ *n* a defensive wall in N China, extending from W Gansu to the Gulf of Liaodong: constructed in the 3rd century B.C. as a defence against the Mongols; substantially rebuilt in the 15th century. Length: over 2400 km (1500 miles). Average height: 6 m (20 ft). Average width: 6 m (20 ft).

Great War *n* another name for **World War I.**

Great Yarmouth ★ (ˈjɑːməθ) *n* a port and resort in E England, in E Norfolk. Pop.: 56 190 (1991).

greave (griːv) *n* (*often pl*) a piece of armour worn to protect the shin. [C14: from OF *greve*, ?from *graver* to part the hair, of Gmc origin]

grebe (griːb) *n* an aquatic bird, such as the great crested grebe and little grebe, similar to the divers but with lobate rather than webbed toes and a vestigial tail. [C18: from F *grèbe*, from ?]

Grecian (ˈgriːʃən) *adj* **1** (esp. of beauty or architecture) conforming to Greek ideals. ◆ *n* **2** a scholar of Greek. ◆ *adj, n* **3** another word for **Greek.**

Grecism (ˈgriːˌsɪzəm) *n* a variant spelling (esp. US) of **Graecism.**

Greco ★ (ˈgrekəʊ) *n* El. See **El Greco.**

Greco- (ˈgriːkəʊ, ˈgrekəʊ) *combining form.* a variant (esp. US) of **Graeco-.**

Greece ★ (griːs) *n* a republic in SE Europe, occupying the S part of the Balkan Peninsula and many islands in the Ionian and Aegean Seas; site of two of Europe's earliest civilizations (the Minoan and Mycenaean); in the classical era divided into many small independent city-states, the most important being Athens and Sparta; part of the Roman and Byzantine Empires; passed under Turkish rule in the late Middle Ages; became an independent kingdom in 1827; taken over by a military junta (1967–74); the monarchy was abolished in 1973; became a republic in 1975; a member of the European Union. Official language: Greek. Official religion: Eastern (Greek) Orthodox. Currency: drachma. Capital: Athens. Pop.: 10 541 000 (1997). Area: 131 944 sq. km (50 944 sq. miles). Modern Greek name: **Ellás.** Related adj: **Hellenic.**

greed (griːd) *n* **1** excessive consumption of or desire for food. **2** excessive desire, as for wealth or power. [C17: back formation from GREEDY]

greedy (ˈgriːdɪ) *adj* **greedier, greediest. 1** excessively desirous of food or wealth, esp. in large amounts; voracious. **2** (*postpositive*; foll. by *for*) eager (for): *a man greedy for success.* [OE *grǣdig*]
▸ ˈgreedily *adv* ▸ ˈgreediness *n*

greegree (ˈgriːgriː) *n* a variant spelling of **grigri.**

Greek (griːk) *n* **1** the official language of Greece, constituting the Hellenic branch of the Indo-European family of languages. **2** a native or inhabitant of Greece or a descendant of such a native. **3** a member of the Greek Orthodox Church. **4** *Inf.* anything incomprehensible (esp. in **it's (all) Greek to me**). ◆ *adj* **5** denoting, relating to, or characteristic of Greece, the Greeks, or the Greek language; Hellenic. **6** of, relating to, or designating the Greek Orthodox Church.
▸ ˈGreekness *n*

★ people and places

Greek cross *n* a cross with each of the four arms of the same length.

Greek fire *n* a Byzantine weapon consisting of an unknown mixture that caught fire when wetted.

Greek gift *n* a gift given with the intention of tricking and causing harm to the recipient. [C19: in allusion to Virgil's *Aeneid* ii 49; see also TROJAN HORSE]

Greek Orthodox Church *n* **1** Also called: **Greek Church.** the established Church of Greece, governed by the holy synod of Greece, in which the Metropolitan of Athens has primacy of honour. **2** another name for **Orthodox Church.**

green (griːn) *n* **1** any of a group of colours, such as that of fresh grass, that lie between yellow and blue in the visible spectrum. Related adj: **verdant.** **2** a dye or pigment of or producing these colours. **3** something of the colour green. **4** a small area of grassland, esp. in the centre of a village. **5** an area of smooth turf kept for a special purpose: *a putting green.* **6** (*pl*) **6a** the edible leaves and stems of certain plants, eaten as a vegetable. **6b** freshly cut branches of ornamental trees, shrubs, etc., used as a decoration. **7** (*sometimes cap.*) a person, esp. a politician, who supports environmentalist issues. ◆ *adj* **8** of the colour green. **9** greenish in colour or having parts or marks that are greenish. **10** (*sometimes cap.*) of or concerned with conservation of natural resources and improvement of the environment: used esp. in a political context. **11** vigorous; not faded: *a green old age.* **12** envious or jealous. **13** immature, unsophisticated, or gullible. **14** characterized by foliage or green plants: *a green wood; a green salad.* **15** denoting a unit of account that is adjusted in accordance with fluctuations between the currencies of the EU nations and is used to make payments to agricultural producers within the EU: *green pound.* **16** fresh, raw, or unripe: *green bananas.* **17** unhealthily pale in appearance: *he was green after his boat trip.* **18** (of meat) not smoked or cured: *green bacon.* **19** (of timber) freshly felled; not dried or seasoned. ◆ *vb* **20** to make or become green. [OE *grēne*]
▸ 'greenish *or* 'greeny *adj* ▸ 'greenly *adv* ▸ 'greenness *n*

Green ★ (griːn) *n* **1 Henry,** real name *Henry Vincent Yorke.* 1905–73, British novelist; author of *Living* (1929), *Loving* (1945), and *Back* (1946). **2 John Richard.** 1837–83, British historian; author of *A Short History of the English People* (1874). **3 T(homas) H(ill).** 1836–82, British idealist philosopher. His chief work, *Prolegomena to Ethics,* was unfinished at his death.

Greenaway ★ ('griːnə,weɪ) *n* **1 Kate.** 1846–1901, British painter, noted as an illustrator of children's books. **2 Peter.** born 1942, British film director, his films include *The Draughtsman's Contract* (1982) and *The Pillow Book* (1995).

greenback ('griːn,bæk) *n US.* **1** *Inf.* a legal-tender US currency note. **2** *Sl.* a dollar bill.

green ban *n Austral.* a trade-union ban on any development that might be considered harmful to the environment.

green bean *n* any bean plant, such as the French bean, having narrow green edible pods.

green belt *n* a zone of farmland, parks, and open country surrounding a town or city.

Green Cross Code *n Brit.* a code for children giving rules for road safety.

Greene ★ (griːn) *n* **Graham.** 1904–91, British writer; his works include the novels *Brighton Rock* (1938), *The Power and the Glory* (1940), and *The Captain and the Enemy* (1988), and the film script *The Third Man* (1949).

greenery ('griːnərɪ) *n, pl* **greeneries.** green foliage, esp. when used for decoration.

green-eyed *adj* **1** jealous or envious. **2 the green-eyed monster.** jealousy or envy.

greenfield ('griːn,fiːld) *n* (*modifier*). denoting or located in a rural area which has not previously been built on.

greenfinch ('griːn,fɪntʃ) *n* a European finch the male of which has a dull green plumage with yellow patches on the wings and tail.

green fingers *pl n* considerable talent or ability to grow plants.

greenfly ('griːn,flaɪ) *n, pl* **greenflies.** a greenish aphid commonly occurring as a pest on garden and crop plants.

greengage ('griːn,geɪdʒ) *n* **1** a cultivated variety of plum tree with edible green plumlike fruits. **2** the fruit of this tree. [C18: GREEN + -*gage,* after Sir W. *Gage* (1777–1864), E botanist who brought it from France]

greengrocer ('griːn,grəʊsə) *n Chiefly Brit.* a retail trader in fruit and vegetables.
▸ 'green,grocery *n*

Greenham Common ★ ('griːnəm) *n* a village in Berkshire, near Newbury; site of a US missile base and, since 1981, a camp of women protesters against nuclear weapons: the base had been closed by 1991 but a small number of women still live at the site.

greenheart ('griːn,hɑːt) *n* **1** Also called: **bebeeru.** a tropical American tree that has dark green durable wood. **2** any of various similar trees. **3** the wood of any of these trees.

greenhorn ('griːn,hɔːn) *n* **1** an inexperienced person, esp. one who is extremely gullible. **2** *Chiefly US.* a newcomer. [C17: orig. an animal with *green* (that is, young) horns]

greenhouse ('griːn,haʊs) *n* **1** a building with glass walls and roof for the cultivation of plants under controlled conditions. ◆ *adj* **2** relating to or contributing to the greenhouse effect: *greenhouse gases, such as carbon dioxide.*

greenhouse effect *n* **1** an effect occurring in greenhouses, etc., in which ultraviolet radiation from the sun passes through the glass warming the contents, the infrared radiation from inside being trapped by the glass. **2** the application of this effect to a planet's atmosphere, esp. the warming up of the earth as man-made carbon dioxide in the atmosphere traps the infrared radiation emitted by the earth's surface. The greenhouse effect is made more serious by damage to the ozone layer, which permits more ultraviolet radiation to reach the earth.

greenie ('griːnɪ) *n Austral. inf.* a conservationist.

greenkeeper ('griːn,kiːpə) *n* a person responsible for maintaining a golf course or bowling green.

Greenland ★ ('griːnlənd) *n* a large island, lying mostly within the Arctic Circle off the NE coast of North America: first settled by Icelanders in 986; resettled by Danes from 1721 onwards; integral part of Denmark (1953–79); granted internal autonomy 1979; mostly covered by an icecap up to 3300 m (11 000 ft) thick, with ice-free coastal strips and coastal mountains; the population is largely Eskimo, with a European minority; fishing, hunting, and mining. Capital: Nuuk. Pop.: 55 117 (1993). Area: 2 175 600 sq. km (840 000 sq. miles). Danish name: **Grønland.** Greenlandic name: **Kalallit Nunaat.**
▸ 'Greenlander *n*

Greenland Sea ★ *n* the S part of the Arctic Ocean, off the NE coast of Greenland.

Greenland whale *n* another name for **bowhead.**

green leek *n* any of several Australian parrots with a green or mostly green plumage.

green light *n* **1** a signal to go, esp. a green traffic light. **2** permission to proceed with a project, etc. ◆ *vb* **greenlight, greenlights, greenlighting, greenlighted.** (*tr*) **3** to permit (a project, etc.) to proceed.

greenmail ('griːn,meɪl) *n* (esp. in the US) the practice of a company buying sufficient shares in another company to threaten takeover and making a quick profit as a result of the threatened company buying back its shares at a higher price.

green monkey disease *n* another name for **Marburg disease.**

Green Mountains ★ *pl n* a mountain range in E North America, extending from Canada through Vermont into W Massachusetts: part of the Appalachian system. Highest peak: Mount Mansfield, 1338 m (4393 ft).

Greenock ★ ('griːnək) *n* a port in SW Scotland, in

Inverclyde on the Firth of Clyde: shipbuilding and other marine industries. Pop.: 50 013 (1991).

Greenough ★ ('gri:nəʊ) n **George Bellas.** 1778–1855, British geologist, founder of the Geological Society of London.

green paper n (often caps.) (in Britain) a government document containing policy proposals to be discussed, esp. by Parliament.

Green Party n a political party whose policies are based on concern for the environment.

Greenpeace ('gri:n,pi:s) n a conservationist organization founded in 1971: members take active but nonviolent measures against what are regarded as threats to environmental safety, such as the dumping of nuclear waste at sea.

green pepper n the green unripe fruit of the sweet pepper, eaten raw or cooked.

green pound n a unit of account used in calculating Britain's contributions to and payments from the Community Agricultural Fund of the EU. See also **green** (sense 15).

Green River ★ n a river in the western US, rising in W central Wyoming and flowing south into Utah, east through NW Colorado, re-entering Utah before joining the Colorado River. Length: 1175 km (730 miles).

greenroom ('gri:n,ru:m, -,rʊm) n (esp. formerly) a backstage room in a theatre where performers may rest or receive visitors. [C18: prob. from its original colour]

greensand ('gri:n,sænd) n an olive-green sandstone consisting mainly of quartz and glauconite.

Greensboro ★ ('gri:nzbərə, -brə) n a city in N central North Carolina. Pop.: 196 167 (1994 est.).

greenshank ('gri:n,ʃæŋk) n a large European sandpiper with greenish legs and a slightly upturned bill.

greensickness ('gri:n,sɪknɪs) n an informal name for **chlorosis.**

greenstick fracture ('gri:n,stɪk) n a fracture in children in which the bone is partly bent and splinters only on the convex side of the bend. [C20: alluding to the similar way in which a green stick splinters]

greenstone ('gri:n,stəʊn) n 1 any basic dark green igneous rock. 2 a variety of jade formerly used in New Zealand by Maoris for ornaments and tools, now used for jewellery.

greensward ('gri:n,swɔ:d) n Arch. or literary. fresh green turf or an area of such turf.

green tea n a sharp tea made from tea leaves that have been dried quickly without fermenting.

green turtle n a mainly tropical edible turtle, with greenish flesh.

green-wellie n (modifier) characterizing or belonging to the upper-class set devoted to hunting, shooting, and fishing: the green-wellie brigade.

Greenwich ★ ('grɪnɪdʒ, -ɪtʃ, 'grɛn-) n a Greater London borough on the Thames: site of a Royal Naval College and of the original Royal Observatory designed by Christopher Wren (1675), accepted internationally as the prime meridian of longitude since 1884, and the basis of Greenwich Mean Time. Pop.: 212 200 (1994 est.). Area: 46 sq. km (18 sq. miles).

Greenwich Mean Time or **Greenwich Time** n mean solar time on the 0° meridian passing through Greenwich, England, measured from midnight: formerly a standard time in Britain and a basis for calculating times throughout most of the world, it has been replaced by an atomic timescale. See **universal time.** Abbrev.: **GMT.**

USAGE NOTE The name **Greenwich mean time** is ambiguous, having been measured from mean midday in astronomy up to 1925, and is not used for scientific purposes. It is generally and incorrectly used in the sense of **coordinated universal time**, an atomic timescale available since 1972 from broadcast signals, in addition to the sense of **universal time**, adopted internationally in 1928 as the name for GMT measured from midnight.

Greenwich Village ★ ('grɛnɪtʃ, 'grɪn-) n a part of New York City in the lower west side of Manhattan; traditionally the home of many artists and writers.

greenwood ('gri:n,wʊd) n a forest or wood when the leaves are green.

Greer ★ ('grɪə) n **Germaine.** born 1939, Australian writer and feminist. Her books include The Female Eunuch (1970) Sex and Destiny (1984), and The Whole Woman (1998).

greet[1] (gri:t) vb (tr) 1 to meet or receive with expressions of gladness or welcome. 2 to send a message of friendship to. 3 to receive in a specified manner: her remarks were greeted by silence. 4 to become apparent to: the smell of bread greeted him. [OE grētan]
▸ **'greeter** n

greet[2] (gri:t) vb Scot. or dialect. ◆ vb 1 (intr) to weep; lament. ◆ n 2 weeping; lamentation. [from OE grētan, N dialect var. of grætan]

greeting ('gri:tɪŋ) n 1 the act or an instance of welcoming or saluting on meeting. 2 (often pl) 2a an expression of friendly salutation. 2b (as modifier): a greetings card.

gregarious (grɪ'gɛərɪəs) adj 1 enjoying the company of others. 2 (of animals) living together in herds or flocks. 3 (of plants) growing close together. 4 of or characteristic of crowds or communities. [C17: from L, from grex flock]
▸ **gre'gariously** adv ▸ **gre'gariousness** n

Gregorian calendar (grɪ'gɔ:rɪən) n the revision of the Julian calendar introduced in 1582 by Pope Gregory XIII and still in force, whereby the ordinary year is made to consist of 365 days.

Gregorian chant n another name for **plainsong.**

Gregorian telescope n a type of reflecting astronomical telescope with a concave secondary mirror and the eyepiece set in the centre of the parabolic primary mirror. [C18: after J. Gregory (died 1675), Scot. mathematician]

Gregory ★ ('grɛgərɪ) n Lady (**Isabella**) **Augusta** (**Persse**). 1852–1932, Irish dramatist; a founder and director of the Abbey Theatre, Dublin.

Gregory I ★ n **Saint,** known as Gregory the Great. ?540–604 A.D., pope (590–604). He strengthened papal authority and appointed Saint Augustine missionary to England. Feast day: March 12 or Sept. 3.

Gregory VII ★ n **Saint,** monastic name Hildebrand. ?1020–85, pope (1073–85), who did much to reform abuses in the Church. His assertion of papal supremacy was opposed by the Holy Roman Emperor Henry IV, whom he excommunicated (1076). He was driven into exile when Henry captured Rome (1084). Feast day: May 25.

Gregory XIII ★ n 1502–85, pope (1572–85). He promoted the Counter-Reformation and founded seminaries. His reformed (Gregorian) calendar was issued in 1582.

Gregory of Tours ★ n **Saint.** ?538–?594 A.D., Frankish bishop and historian. His Historia Francorum is the chief source of knowledge of 6th-century Gaul. Feast day: Nov. 17.

gremial ('gri:mɪəl) n RC Church. a cloth spread upon the lap of a bishop when seated during Mass. [C17: from L gremium lap]

gremlin ('gremlɪn) n 1 an imaginary imp jokingly said to be responsible for mechanical troubles in aircraft, esp. in World War II. 2 any mischievous troublemaker. [C20: from ?]

Grenada ★ (grɛ'neɪdə) n an island state in the Caribbean, in the Windward Islands: formerly a British colony (1783–1967); since 1974 an independent state within the Commonwealth; occupied by US troops (1983–85); mainly agricultural. Official language: English. Religion: Christian majority. Currency: East Carib-

★ people and places

bean dollar. Capital: St George's. Pop.: 98 400 (1997). Area: 344 sq. km (133 sq. miles).
▶ Gre'nadian *n, adj*

grenade (grɪ'neɪd) *n* **1** a small container filled with explosive thrown by hand or fired from a rifle. **2** a sealed glass vessel that is thrown and shatters to release chemicals, such as tear gas. [C16: from F, from Sp.: pomegranate, from LL, from L *grānātus* seedy; see GRAIN]

grenadier (,grenə'dɪə) *n* **1** *Mil.* **1a** (in the British Army) a member of the senior regiment of infantry in the Household Brigade. **1b** (formerly) a member of a special formation, usually selected for strength and height. **1c** (formerly) a soldier trained to throw grenades. **2** any of various deep-sea fish, typically having a large head and a long tapering tail. [C17: from F; see GRENADE]

grenadine[1] (,grenə'di:n) *n* a light thin fabric of silk, wool, rayon, or nylon, used for dresses, etc. [C19: from F]

grenadine[2] (,grenə'di:n, 'grenə,di:n) *n* a syrup made from pomegranate juice, used as a sweetening and colouring agent in various drinks. [C19: from F: a little pomegranate; see GRENADE]

Grenadines ★ (,grenə'di:nz, 'grenə,di:nz) *pl n* **the**. a chain of about 600 islets in the Caribbean, part of the Windward Islands, extending for about 100 km (60 miles) between St Vincent and Grenada and divided administratively between the two states. Largest island: Carriacou.

Grendel ★ ('grend°l) *n* (in Old English legend) a man-eating monster defeated by the hero Beowulf.

Grenfell ★ ('grenfəl) *n* **Joyce**, real name *Joyce Irene Phipps*. 1910–79, British comedy actress and writer.

Grenoble ★ (grə'nəub°l; *French* grənɔblə) *n* a city in SE France, on the Isère River: university (1339). Pop.: 153 973 (1990).

Grenville ★ ('grenvɪl) *n* **1 George.** 1712–70, British statesman; prime minister (1763–65). His policy of taxing the American colonies precipitated the War of Independence. **2 Sir Richard.** ?1541–91, English naval commander. He was fatally wounded during a battle with a fleet of Spanish treasure ships. **3 William Wyndham**, Baron Grenville, son of George Grenville. 1759–1834, British statesman; prime minister (1806–07).

Gresham ★ ('greʃəm) *n* **Sir Thomas**. ?1519–79, English financier, who founded the Royal Exchange in London (1568).

Gresham's law *or* **theorem** *n* the economic hypothesis that bad money drives good money out of circulation; the superior currency will tend to be hoarded and the inferior will thus dominate the circulation. [C16: after Sir T. GRESHAM]

gressorial (gre'sɔːrɪəl) *or* **gressorious** *adj* **1** (of the feet of certain birds) specialized for walking. **2** (of birds, such as the ostrich) having such feet. [C19: from NL, from *gressus* having walked, from *gradī* to step]

Gretna Green ★ ('gretnə) *n* a village in S Scotland, in Dumfries and Galloway on the border with England: famous smithy where eloping couples were married by the blacksmith from 1754 until 1940, when such marriages were made illegal. Pop.: 3149 (1991).

Greville ★ ('grevɪl) *n* **Fulke** (fulk), 1st Baron Brooke. 1554–1628, English poet, writer, politician, and diplomat: Chancellor of the Exchequer (1614–22); author of *The Life of the Renowned Sir Philip Sidney* (1652).

grew (gru:) *vb* the past tense of **grow**.

grey *or US* **gray** (greɪ) *adj* **1** of a neutral tone, intermediate between black and white, that has no hue and reflects and transmits only a little light. **2** greyish in colour or having greyish marks. **3** dismal or dark, esp. from lack of light; gloomy. **4** conventional or dull, esp. in character or opinion. **5** having grey hair. **6** of or relating to people of middle age or above: *grey power*. **7** ancient; venerable. ◆ *n* **8** any of a group of grey tones. **9** grey cloth or clothing. **10** an animal, esp. a horse, that is grey or whitish. ◆ *vb* **11** to become or make grey. [OE *grǣg*]
▶ 'greyish *or US* 'grayish *adj* ▶ 'greyly *or US* 'grayly *adv*
▶ 'greyness *or US* 'grayness *n*

Grey ★ (greɪ) *n* **1 Charles**, 2nd Earl Grey. 1764–1845, British statesman. As Whig prime minister (1830–34), he carried the Reform Bill of 1832 and the bill for the abolition of slavery throughout the British Empire (1833). **2 Sir Edward**, 1st Viscount Grey of Fallodon. 1862–1933, British statesman; foreign secretary (1905–16). **3 Sir George**. 1812–98, British statesman and colonial administrator; prime minister of New Zealand. (1877–79). **4 Lady Jane**. 1537–54, queen of England (July 9–19, 1553); great-granddaughter of Henry VII. Her father-in-law, the Duke of Northumberland, persuaded Edward VI to alter the succession in her favour, but after ten days as queen she was imprisoned and later executed. **5 Zane**. 1875–1939, US author of Westerns, including *Riders of the Purple Sage* (1912).

grey area *n* **1** an area or part of something existing between two extremes and having mixed characteristics of both. **2** an area, situation, etc., lacking clearly defined characteristics.

greybeard *or US* **graybeard** ('greɪ,bɪəd) *n* **1** an old man, esp. a sage. **2** a large stoneware or earthenware jar or jug for spirits.

grey eminence *n* the English equivalent of *éminence grise*.

Grey Friar *n* a Franciscan friar.

greyhen ('greɪ,hen) *n* the female of the black grouse.

greyhound ('greɪ,haund) *n* a tall slender fast-moving breed of dog.

grey knight *n* *Inf.* an ambiguous intervener in a takeover battle, who makes a counterbid for the shares of the target company without having made his intentions clear. Cf. **black knight, white knight**.

greylag *or* **greylag goose** ('greɪ,læg) *n* a large grey Eurasian goose: the ancestor of many domestic breeds of goose. US spelling: **graylag**. [C18: from GREY + LAG[1], from its migrating later than other species]

grey market *n* **1** trade in newly-issued shares before they have been formally listed and traded on the Stock Exchange. **2** a practice in which supermarkets buy excess stock of branded goods from other retailers at a low margin and then sell them at discounted prices.

grey matter *n* **1** the greyish tissue of the brain and spinal cord, containing nerve cell bodies and fibres. **2** *Inf.* brains or intellect.

grey squirrel *n* a grey-furred squirrel, native to E North America but now widely established.

greywacke ('greɪ,wækə) *n* any dark sandstone or grit having a matrix of clay minerals. [C19: partial translation of G *Grauwacke*; see WACKE]

grey water *n* water that has been used for one purpose but can be used again for another without repurification (e.g. bathwater, which can be used to water plants).

grey wolf *n* another name for **timber wolf**.

grid (grɪd) *n* **1** See **gridiron**. **2** a network of horizontal and vertical lines superimposed over a map, building plan, etc., for locating points. **3** a grating consisting of parallel bars. **4 the grid**. the national network of transmission lines, pipes, etc., by which electricity, gas, or water is distributed. **5** Also called: **control grid**. *Electronics*. an electrode usually consisting of a cylindrical mesh of wires, that controls the flow of electrons between the cathode and anode of a valve. **6** See **starting grid**. **7** a plate in an accumulator that carries the active substance. **8** any interconnecting system of links: *the bus service formed a grid across the country*. [C19: back formation from GRIDIRON]

grid bias *n* the fixed voltage applied between the control grid and cathode of a valve.

griddle ('grɪd°l) *n* **1** Also called: **girdle**. *Brit.* a thick round iron plate with a half hoop handle over the top, for making scones, etc. **2** any flat heated surface, esp. on the top of a stove, for cooking food. ◆ *vb* **griddles, griddling, griddled**. **3** (*tr*) to cook (food) on a griddle. [C13: from OF *gridil*, from LL *crāticulum* (unattested) fine wickerwork; see GRILL]

griddlecake ('grɪd°l,keɪk) *n* another name for **drop scone**.

gridiron ('grɪd,aɪən) *n* **1** a utensil of parallel metal bars, used to grill meat, fish, etc. **2** any framework resembling this utensil. **3** a framework above the stage in a theatre from which suspended scenery, lights, etc., are manipulated. **4a** the field of play in American football. **4b** an informal name for **American football.** ◆ Often shortened to **grid.** [C13 *gredire*, ? a var. (through influence of *ire* IRON) of *gredile* GRIDDLE]

gridlock ('grɪd,lɒk) *Chiefly US.* ◆ *n* **1** obstruction of urban traffic caused by queues of vehicles forming across junctions and causing further queues to form in the intersecting streets. **2** a point in a dispute at which no agreement can be reached: *political gridlock.* ◆ *vb* **3** (*tr*) (of traffic) to block or obstruct (an area).

grief (griːf) *n* **1** deep or intense sorrow, esp. at the death of someone. **2** something that causes keen distress. **3** come to grief. *Inf.* to end unsuccessfully or disastrously. [C13: from Anglo-F *gref*, from *grever* to GRIEVE]

Grieg ★ (griːg) *n* Edvard (**Hagerup**) ('ɛdvard). 1843–1907, Norwegian composer. His works include the music for *Peer Gynt* (1876), a piano concerto, and many songs.

Grierson ★ ('grɪəs°n) *n* John. 1898–1972, Scottish film director. He coined the noun *documentary*; his *Industrial Britain* (1931) and *Song of Ceylon* (1934) are notable examples.

grievance ('griːv°ns) *n* **1** a real or imaginary wrong causing resentment and regarded as grounds for complaint. **2** a feeling of resentment or injustice at having been unfairly treated. [C15 *grevance*, from OF, from *grever* to GRIEVE]

grieve (griːv) *vb* grieves, grieving, grieved. to feel or cause to feel great sorrow or distress, esp. at the death of someone. [C13: from OF *grever*, from L *gravāre* to burden, from *gravis* heavy]
▶ '**griever** *n* ▶ '**grieving** *n, adj*

grievous ('griːvəs) *adj* **1** very severe or painful: *a grievous injury.* **2** very serious; heinous: *a grievous sin.* **3** showing or marked by grief. **4** causing great pain or suffering.
▶ '**grievously** *adv* ▶ '**grievousness** *n*

grievous bodily harm *n Criminal law.* serious injury caused by one person to another.

griffin ('grɪfɪn), **griffon,** or **gryphon** *n* a winged monster with an eagle-like head and the body of a lion. [C14: from OF *grifon*, from L *grȳphus*, from Gk *grups*, from *grupos* hooked]

Griffith ★ ('grɪfɪθ) *n* **1** Arthur. 1872–1922, Irish journalist and nationalist: founder of Sinn Féin (1905); president of the Irish Free State (1922). **2** D(avid Lewelyn) W(ark). 1875–1948, US film director and producer, noted for *The Birth of a Nation* (1915).

Griffith-Joyner ★ (-'dʒɔɪnə) *n* Florence, known as *Flojo.* 1959–98, US sprinter, winner of gold medals for the 100 m and 200 m at the 1988 Olympic Games.

griffon[1] ('grɪf°n) *n* **1** any of various small wire-haired breeds of dog, originally from Belgium. **2** a large vulture of Africa, S Europe, and SW Asia, having a pale plumage with black wings. [C19: from F: GRIFFIN]

griffon[2] ('grɪf°n) *n* a variant of **griffin.**

grifter ('grɪftə) *n Sl., chiefly US.* a petty criminal or gambler. [C20: a blend of GR(AFT)[2] (sense 2) + DRIFTER (sense 2)]

Grigioni ★ (gri'dʒoːni) *n* the Italian name for **Graubünden.**

grigri, gris-gris, or **greegree** ('griːgriː) *n, pl* grigris, gris-gris (-griːz) or greegrees. an African talisman, amulet, or charm. [of African origin]

grill (grɪl) *vb* **1** to cook (meat, etc.) by direct heat, as under a grill or over a hot fire, or (of meat, etc.) to be cooked in this way. Usual US and Canad. word: **broil. 2** (*tr; usually passive*) to torment with or as if with extreme heat: *the travellers were grilled by the scorching sun.* **3** (*tr*) *Inf.* to subject to insistent or prolonged questioning. ◆ *n* **4** a device with parallel bars of thin metal on which meat, etc., may be cooked by a fire; gridiron. **5** a device on a cooker that radiates heat downwards for grilling meat, etc. **6** food cooked by grilling. **7** See **grillroom.** [C17: from F *gril* gridiron, from L *crātīcula* fine wickerwork; see GRILLE]
▶ '**grilled** *adj* ▶ '**griller** *n*

grillage ('grɪlɪdʒ) *n* an arrangement of beams and cross-

beams used as a foundation on soft ground. [C18: from F, from *griller* to furnish with a grille]

grille or **grill** (grɪl) *n* **1** a framework, esp. of metal bars arranged to form an ornamental pattern, used as a screen or partition. **2** Also called: **radiator grille.** a grating that admits cooling air to the radiator of a motor vehicle. **3** a metal or wooden openwork grating used as a screen or divider. **4** a protective screen, usually plastic or metal, in front of the loudspeaker in a radio, record player, etc. [C17: from OF, from L *crātīcula* fine hurdlework, from *crātis* a hurdle]

grillroom ('grɪl,ruːm, -,rʊm) *n* a restaurant where grilled steaks and other meat are served.

grilse (grɪls) *n, pl* grilses or grilse. a young salmon that returns to fresh water after one winter in the sea. [C15 *grilles* (pl), from ?]

grim (grɪm) *adj* grimmer, grimmest. **1** stern; resolute: *grim determination.* **2** harsh or formidable in manner or appearance. **3** harshly ironic or sinister: *grim laughter.* **4** cruel, severe, or ghastly: *a grim accident.* **5** *Arch. or poetic.* fierce: *a grim warrior.* **6** *Inf.* unpleasant; disagreeable. [OE *grimm*]
▶ '**grimly** *adv* ▶ '**grimness** *n*

grimace (grɪ'meɪs) *n* **1** an ugly or distorted facial expression, as of wry humour, disgust, etc. ◆ *vb* grimaces, grimacing, grimaced. **2** (*intr*) to contort the face. [C17: from F, of Gmc origin; rel. to Sp. *grimazo* caricature]
▶ gri'**macer** *n*

Grimaldi ★ (grɪ'mɔːldɪ) *n* Joseph. 1779–1837, British actor, noted as a clown in pantomime.

grimalkin (grɪ'mælkɪn, -'mɔːl-) *n* **1** an old cat, esp. an old female cat. **2** a crotchety or shrewish old woman. [C17: from GREY + *malkin*, dim. of female name *Maud*]

grime (graɪm) *n* **1** dirt, soot, or filth, esp. when ingrained. ◆ *vb* grimes, griming, grimed. **2** (*tr*) to make dirty or coat with filth. [C15: from MDu. *grime*]
▶ '**grimy** *adj* ▶ '**griminess** *n*

Grimm ★ (grɪm) *n* Jakob Ludwig Karl ('jaːkɔp 'luːtvɪç karl), 1785–1863, and his brother, Wilhelm Karl ('vɪlhɛlm karl), 1786–1859, German philologists and folklorists, who collaborated on *Grimm's Fairy Tales* (1812–22) and began a German dictionary. Jakob is noted also for his *Deutsche Grammatik* (1819–37), in which he formulated the law named after him.

Grimsby ★ ('grɪmzbɪ) *n* a fishing port in E England, in North East Lincolnshire. Pop.: 90 703 (1991).

grin (grɪn) *vb* grins, grinning, grinned. **1** to smile with the lips drawn back revealing the teeth or express (something) by such a smile: *to grin a welcome.* **2** (*intr*) to draw back the lips revealing the teeth, as in a snarl or grimace. **3** grin and bear it. *Inf.* to suffer trouble or hardship without complaint. ◆ *n* **4** a broad smile. **5** a snarl or grimace. [OE *grennian*]
▶ '**grinning** *adj, n*

grind (graɪnd) *vb* grinds, grinding, ground. **1** to reduce or be reduced to small particles by pounding or abrading: *to grind corn.* **2** (*tr*) to smooth, sharpen, or polish by friction or abrasion: *to grind a knife.* **3** to scrape or grate together (two things, esp. the teeth) with a harsh rasping sound or (of such objects) to be scraped together. **4** (*tr; foll. by out*) to speak or say something in a rough voice. **5** (*tr; often foll. by down*) to hold down; oppress; tyrannize. **6** (*tr*) to operate (a machine) by turning a handle. **7** (*tr; foll. by out*) to produce in a routine or uninspired manner: *he ground out his weekly article for the paper.* **8** (*intr*) *Inf.* to study or work laboriously. ◆ *n* **9** *Inf.* laborious or routine work or study. **10** a specific grade of pulverization, as of coffee beans: *coarse grind.* **11** the act or sound of grinding. [OE *grindan*]
▶ '**grindingly** *adv*

Grindelwald ★ (*German* 'grɪndəlvalt) *n* a valley and resort in central Switzerland, in the Bernese Oberland: mountaineering centre, with the Wetterhorn and the Eiger nearby.

grinder ('graɪndə) *n* **1** a person who grinds, esp. one who grinds cutting tools. **2** a machine for grinding. **3** a molar tooth.

grindstone ('graɪnd,stəʊn) *n* **1a** a machine having a circular block of stone rotated for sharpening tools or grinding metal. **1b** the stone used in this machine. **1c** any stone used for sharpening; whetstone. **2 keep** *or* **have one's nose to the grindstone.** to work hard and perseveringly.

gringo ('grɪŋɡəʊ) *n, pl* **gringos.** a person from an English-speaking country: used as a derogatory term by Latin Americans. [C19: from Sp.: foreigner, prob. from *griego* Greek, hence an alien]

grip (ɡrɪp) *n* **1** the act or an instance of grasping and holding firmly: *he lost his grip on the slope.* **2** Also called: **handgrip.** the strength or pressure of such a grasp, as in a handshake. **3** the style or manner of grasping an object, such as a tennis racket. **4** understanding, control, or mastery of a subject, problem, etc. **5** a person who manoeuvres the cameras in a film or television studio. **6 get** *or* **come to grips.** (often foll. by *with*) **6a** to deal with (a problem or subject). **6b** to tackle (an assailant). **7** Also called: **handgrip.** a part by which an object is grasped; handle. **8** Also called: **handgrip.** a travelling bag or holdall. **9** See **hairgrip. 10** any device that holds by friction, such as certain types of brake. ♦ *vb* **grips, gripping, gripped. 11** to take hold of firmly or tightly, as by a clutch. **12** to hold the interest or attention of: *the thrilling performance gripped the audience.* [OE *gripe* grasp]
▶ 'gripper *n* ▶ 'gripping *adj*

gripe (ɡraɪp) *vb* **gripes, griping, griped. 1** (*intr*) *Inf.* to complain, esp. in a persistent nagging manner. **2** to cause sudden intense pain in the intestines of (a person) or (of a person) to experience this pain. **3** *Arch.* to clutch; grasp. **4** (*tr*) *Arch.* to afflict. ♦ *n* **5** (*usually pl*) a sudden intense pain in the intestines; colic. **6** *Inf.* a complaint or grievance. **7** *Now rare.* **7a** the act of gripping. **7b** a firm grip. **7c** a device that grips. [OE *grīpan*]
▶ 'griper *n*

Gripe Water *n Brit., trademark.* a solution given to infants to relieve colic.

grippe *or* **grip** (ɡrɪp) *n* a former name for **influenza.** [C18: from F *grippe*, from *gripper* to seize, of Gmc origin; see GRIP]

Griqualand East ★ ('ɡriːkwə,lænd, 'ɡrɪk-) *n* an area of central South Africa: settled in 1861 by Griquas led by Adam Kok III; annexed to the Cape in 1879; part of the Transkei (1903–94). Chief town: Kokstad. Area: 17 100 sq. km (6602 sq. miles).

Griqualand West ★ *n* an area of NW South Africa, north of the Orange river: settled after 1803 by the Griquas; annexed by the British in 1871 following a dispute with the Orange Free State; became part of the Cape Colony in 1880. Chief town: Kimberley. Area: 39 360 sq. km (15 197 sq. miles).

Gris ★ (*Spanish* ɡris) *n* **Juan** (xwan). 1887–1927, Spanish cubist painter, resident in France from 1906.

grisaille (ɡrɪˈzeɪl) *n* **1** a technique of monochrome painting in shades of grey, imitating the effect of relief. **2** a painting, stained-glass window, etc., in this manner. [C19: from F, from *gris* grey]

griseofulvin (,ɡrɪzɪəʊˈfʊlvɪn) *n* an antibiotic used to treat fungal infections of the skin and hair. [C20: from NL, ult. from Med. L *griseus* grey + L *fulvus* reddish-yellow]

grisette (ɡrɪˈzɛt) *n* (esp. formerly) a French working girl. [C18: from F, from grey fabric used for dresses, from *gris* grey]

gris-gris ('ɡriːɡriː) *n, pl* **gris-gris** (-ɡriːz). a variant spelling of **grigri.**

Grishun ★ (ɡriːˈʃʊn) *n* the Romansch name for **Graubünden.**

grisly ('ɡrɪzlɪ) *adj* **grislier, grisliest.** causing horror or dread; gruesome. [OE *grislic*]
▶ 'grisliness *n*

USAGE NOTE See at **grizzly.**

Grisons ★ (ɡrizɔ̃) *n* the French name for **Graubünden.**

grist (ɡrɪst) *n* **1a** grain intended to be or that has been ground. **1b** the quantity of such grain processed in one grinding. **2** *Brewing.* malt grains that have been cleaned

and cracked. **3 grist to** (*or* **for**) **the** (*or* **one's**) **mill.** anything that can be turned to profit or advantage. [OE *grist*]

gristle ('ɡrɪsəl) *n* cartilage, esp. when in meat. [OE *gristle*]
▶ 'gristly *adj* ▶ 'gristliness *n*

grit (ɡrɪt) *n* **1** small hard particles of sand, earth, stone, etc. **2** Also called: **gritstone.** any coarse sandstone that can be used as a grindstone or millstone. **3** indomitable courage, toughness, or resolution. ♦ *vb* **grits, gritting, gritted. 4** to clench or grind together (two objects, esp. the teeth). **5** to cover (a surface, such as icy roads) with grit. [OE *grēot*]
▶ 'gritter *n*

Grit (ɡrɪt) *n, adj Canad.* an informal word for **Liberal.**

grits (ɡrɪts) *pl n* **1** hulled or coarsely ground grain. **2** *US.* See **hominy grits.** [OE *grytt*]

gritty ('ɡrɪtɪ) *adj* **grittier, grittiest. 1** courageous; hardy; resolute. **2** of, like, or containing grit.
▶ 'grittily *adv* ▶ 'grittiness *n*

grizzle[1] ('ɡrɪzəl) *vb* **grizzles, grizzling, grizzled. 1** to make or become grey. ♦ *n* **2** a grey colour. **3** grey hair. [C15: from OF *grisel*, from *gris*, of Gmc origin]

grizzle[2] ('ɡrɪzəl) *vb* **grizzles, grizzling, grizzled.** (*intr*) *Inf.*, *chiefly Brit.* (esp. of a child) to fret; whine. [C18: of Gmc origin]
▶ 'grizzler *n*

grizzled ('ɡrɪzəld) *adj* **1** streaked or mixed with grey; grizzly. **2** having grey hair.

grizzly ('ɡrɪzlɪ) *adj* **grizzlier, grizzliest. 1** somewhat grey; grizzled. ♦ *n, pl* **grizzlies. 2** See **grizzly bear.**

USAGE NOTE *Grizzly* is sometimes wrongly used where *grisly* is meant: *a grisly* (not *grizzly*) *murder.*

grizzly bear *n* a variety of the brown bear, formerly widespread in W North America; its brown fur has cream or white tips on the back, giving a grizzled appearance. Often shortened to **grizzly.**

groan (ɡrəʊn) *n* **1** a prolonged stressed dull cry expressive of agony, pain, or disapproval. **2** a loud harsh creaking sound, as of a tree bending in the wind. **3** *Inf.* a grumble or complaint, esp. a persistent one. ♦ *vb* **4** to utter (low inarticulate sounds) expressive of pain, grief, disapproval, etc. **5** (*intr*) to make a sound like a groan. **6** (*intr*; usually foll. by *beneath* or *under*) to be weighed down (by) or suffer greatly (under). **7** (*intr*) *Inf.* to complain or grumble. [OE *grānian*]
▶ 'groaner *n* ▶ 'groaning *adj, n* ▶ 'groaningly *adv*

groat (ɡrəʊt) *n* an obsolete English silver coin worth four pennies. [C14: from MDu. *groot*, from MLow G *gros*, from Med. L (*denarius*) *grossus* thick (coin); see GROSCHEN]

groats (ɡrəʊts) *pl n* the hulled and crushed grain of oats, wheat, or certain other cereals. [OE *grot* particle]

grocer ('ɡrəʊsə) *n* a dealer in foodstuffs and other household supplies. [C15: from OF *grossier*, from *gros* large; see GROSS]

groceries ('ɡrəʊsərɪz) *pl n* merchandise, esp. foodstuffs, sold by a grocer.

grocery ('ɡrəʊsərɪ) *n, pl* **groceries.** the business or premises of a grocer.

Grodno ★ (*Russian* 'ɡrɔdnə) *n* a city in W Belarus, on the Neman River: part of Poland (1921–39); an industrial centre. Pop.: 301 000 (1996 est.).

grog (ɡrɒɡ) *n* **1** diluted spirit, usually rum, as an alcoholic drink. **2** *Austral. & NZ inf.* alcoholic drink in general, esp. spirits. [C18: from Old *Grog*, nickname of Edward Vernon (1684–1757), Brit. admiral, who in 1740 issued naval rum diluted with water; his nickname arose from his program cloak]

groggy ('ɡrɒɡɪ) *adj* **groggier, groggiest.** *Inf.* **1** dazed or staggering, as from exhaustion, blows, or drunkenness. **2** faint or weak.
▶ 'groggily *adv* ▶ 'grogginess *n*

grogram ('ɡrɒɡrəm) *n* a coarse fabric of silk, wool, or silk mixed with wool or mohair, often stiffened with gum, formerly used for clothing. [C16: from F *gros grain* coarse grain; see GROSGRAIN]

groin (grɔɪn) *n* **1** the depression or fold where the legs join the abdomen. **2** *Euphemistic.* the genitals, esp. the testicles. **3** a variant spelling (esp. US) of **groyne**. **4** *Archit.* a curved arris formed where two intersecting vaults meet. ◆ *vb* **5** (*tr*) *Archit.* to provide or construct with groins. [C15: ?from E *grynde* abyss]

grommet ('grɒmɪt) *or* **grummet** *n* **1** a ring of rubber or plastic or a metal eyelet designed to line a hole to prevent a cable or pipe passed through it from chafing. **2** *Med.* a small tube inserted into the eardrum in order to drain fluid from the middle ear, as in glue ear. [C15: from obs. F *gourmette* chain linking the ends of a bit, from *gourmer* bridle, from ?]

Gromyko ★ (*Russian* gra'mikə) *n* **Andrei Andreyevich** (an-'drjej an'drjejɪvitʃ). 1909–89, Soviet statesman and diplomat; foreign minister (1957–85); president (1985–88).

Groningen ★ ('grəʊnɪŋən; *Dutch* 'xroːnɪŋə) *n* **1** a province in the NE Netherlands: mainly agricultural. Capital: Groningen. Pop.: 556 757 (1988 est.). Area: 2336 sq. km (902 sq. miles). **2** a city in the NE Netherlands, capital of Groningen province. Pop.: 170 748 (1995 est.).

Grønland ★ ('grœnlan) *n* the Danish name for **Greenland**.

groom (gruːm, grʊm) *n* **1** a person employed to clean and look after horses. **2** See **bridegroom**. **3** any of various officers of a royal or noble household. **4** *Arch.* a male servant. ◆ *vb* (*tr*) **5** to make or keep (clothes, appearance, etc.) clean and tidy. **6** to rub down, clean, and smarten (a horse, dog, etc.). **7** to train or prepare for a particular task, occupation, etc.: *to groom someone for the Presidency*. [C13 *grom* manservant; ? rel. to OE *grōwan* to GROW]

groomsman ('gruːmzmən, 'grʊmz-) *n, pl* **groomsmen.** a man who attends the bridegroom at a wedding, usually the best man.

groove (gruːv) *n* **1** a long narrow channel or furrow, esp. one cut into wood by a tool. **2** the spiral channel in a gramophone record. **3** a settled existence, routine, etc., to which one is suited or accustomed. **4** *Dated sl.* an experience, event, etc., that is groovy. **5 in the groove.** 5a *Jazz.* playing well and apparently effortlessly, with a good beat, etc. **5b** *US.* fashionable. ◆ *vb* **grooves, grooving, grooved.** **6** (*tr*) to form or cut a groove in. **7** (*intr*) *Dated sl.* to enjoy oneself or feel in rapport with one's surroundings. **8** (*intr*) *Jazz.* to play well, with a good beat, etc. [C15: from obs. Du. *groeve*, of Gmc origin]

groovy ('gruːvɪ) *adj* **groovier, grooviest.** *Sl., often jocular.* attractive, fashionable, or exciting.

grope (grəʊp) *vb* **gropes, groping, groped. 1** (*intr*; usually foll. by *for*) to feel or search about uncertainly (for something) with the hands. **2** (*intr*; usually foll. by *for* or *after*) to search uncertainly or with difficulty (for a solution, answer, etc.). **3** (*tr*) to find (one's way) by groping. **4** (*tr*) *Sl.* to fondle the body of (someone) for sexual gratification. ◆ *n* **5** the act of groping. [OE *grāpian*]
▶ '**gropingly** *adv*

groper ('grəʊpə) *or* **grouper** *n, pl* **groper, gropers** *or* **grouper, groupers.** a large marine fish of warm and tropical seas. [C17: from Port. *garupa*, prob. from a South American Indian word]

Gropius ★ ('grəʊpɪəs) *n* **Walter.** 1883–1969, US architect, born in Germany. He founded (1919) and directed (1919–28) the Bauhaus in Germany. His buildings include the Fagus factory at Alfeld (1911).

Gros ★ (*French* gro) *n* Baron **Antoine Jean** (ɑ̃twan ʒɑ̃). 1771–1835, French painter, noted for his battle scenes.

grosbeak ('grəʊs,biːk, 'grɒs-) *n* any of various finches that have a massive powerful bill. [C17: from F *grosbec*, from OF *gros* large, thick + *bec* BEAK¹]

groschen ('grəʊʃən) *n, pl* **groschen. 1** an Austrian monetary unit worth one hundredth of a schilling. **2** a German coin worth ten pfennigs. **3** a former German silver coin. [C17: from G: alteration of MHG *grosse*, from Med. L (*denarius*) *grossus* thick (penny); see GROSS, GROAT]

grosgrain ('grəʊ,greɪn) *n* a heavy ribbed silk or rayon fabric or tape for trimming clothes, etc. [C19: from F *gros grain* coarse grain; see GROSS, GRAIN]

gros point ('grəʊ 'pɔɪnt; *French* gro pwɛ̃) *n* **1** a needlepoint stitch covering two horizontal and two vertical threads. **2** work done in this stitch. [OF: large point]

gross (grəʊs) *adj* **1** repellently or excessively fat or bulky. **2** with no deductions for expenses, tax, etc.; total: *gross sales.* Cf. **net².** **3** (of personal qualities, tastes, etc.) conspicuously coarse or vulgar. **4** obviously or exceptionally culpable or wrong; flagrant: *gross inefficiency.* **5** lacking in perception, sensitivity, or discrimination: *gross judgments.* **6** (esp. of vegetation) dense; thick; luxuriant. ◆ *n* **7** (*pl* **gross**). a unit of quantity equal to 12 dozen. **8** (*pl* **grosses**). **8a** the entire amount. **8b** the great majority. ◆ *interj* **9** *Sl.* an exclamation indicating disgust. ◆ *vb* (*tr*) **10** to earn as total revenue, before deductions for expenses, tax, etc. [C14: from OF *gros* large, from LL *grossus* thick]
▶ '**grossly** *adv* ▶ '**grossness** *n*

gross domestic product *n* the total value of all goods and services produced domestically by a nation during a year. It is equivalent to gross national product minus net investment incomes from foreign nations. Abbrev.: **GDP**.

Grosseteste ★ ('grəʊs,test) *n* **Robert.** ?1175–1253, English prelate and scholar; bishop of Lincoln (1235–53).

gross national product *n* the total value of all final goods and services produced annually by a nation. Abbrev.: **GNP**.

gross profit *n* *Accounting.* the difference between total revenue from sales and the total cost of purchases or materials, with an adjustment for stock.

Grosswardein ★ (groːsvar'dain) *n* the German name for **Oradea**.

gross weight *n* total weight of an article inclusive of the weight of the container and packaging.

Grosz ★ (grəʊs; *German* grɔs) *n* **George.** 1893–1959, German painter, in the US from 1932, whose works satirized German militarism.

grot (grɒt) *n* *Sl.* rubbish; dirt. [C20: from GROTTY]

Grote ★ (grəʊt) *n* **George.** 1794–1871, English historian, noted particularly for his *History of Greece* (1846–56).

grotesque (grəʊ'tesk) *adj* **1** strangely or fantastically distorted; bizarre. **2** of or characteristic of the grotesque in art. **3** absurdly incongruous; in a ludicrous context. ◆ *n* **4** a 16th-century decorative style in which parts of human, animal, and plant forms are distorted and mixed. **5** a decorative device, as in painting or sculpture, in this style. **6** *Printing.* the family of 19th-century sans serif display types. **7** any grotesque person or thing. [C16: from F, from OIt. (*pittura*) *grottesca* cave painting, from *grotta* cave; see GROTTO]
▶ gro'**tesquely** *adv* ▶ gro'**tesqueness** *n* ▶ gro'**tesquery** *or* gro'**tesquerie** *n*

Grotius ★ ('grəʊtɪəs) *n* **Hugo,** original name *Huig de Groot.* 1583–1645, Dutch jurist and statesman, whose *De Jure Belli ac Pacis* (1625) is regarded as the foundation of modern international law.
▶ '**Grotian** *adj*

grotto ('grɒtəʊ) *n, pl* **grottoes** *or* **grottos. 1** a small cave, esp. one with attractive features. **2** a construction in the form of a cave, esp. as in landscaped gardens during the 18th century. [C17: from OIt. *grotta*, from LL *crypta* vault; see CRYPT]

grotty ('grɒtɪ) *adj* **grottier, grottiest.** *Brit. sl.* **1** nasty or unattractive. **2** of poor quality or in bad condition. [C20: from GROTESQUE]

grouch (graʊtʃ) *Inf.* ◆ *vb* (*intr*) **1** to complain; grumble. ◆ *n* **2** a complaint, esp. a persistent one. **3** a person who is always grumbling. [C20: from obs. *grutch*, from OF *grouchier* to complain; see GRUDGE]
▶ '**grouchy** *adj* ▶ '**grouchily** *adv* ▶ '**grouchiness** *n*

ground¹ (graʊnd) *n* **1** the land surface. **2** earth or soil. **3** (*pl*) the land around a dwelling house or other building. **4** (*sometimes pl*) an area of land given over to a purpose: *football ground.* **5** land having a particular characteristic: *high ground.* **6** matter for consideration or debate; field of research or inquiry: *the report covered a lot of ground.* **7** a position or viewpoint, as in an argument or controversy (esp. in **give ground, hold, stand,** *or* **shift one's ground**). **8** position or advantage, as in a subject or competition (esp. in **gain ground, lose ground,** etc.). **9** (*often pl*) reason; justification: *grounds for complaint.* **10** *Arts.* **10a** the prepared surface applied to a wall, canvas, etc., to prevent it reacting with or absorbing the paint. **10b** the background of a painting against which the other parts of a work of art appear superimposed. **11a** the first coat of paint applied to a surface. **11b** (*as modifier*): *ground colour.* **12** the bottom of a river or the sea. **13** (*pl*) sediment or dregs, esp. from coffee. **14** *Chiefly Brit.* the floor of a room. **15** *Cricket.* the area from the popping crease back past the stumps, in which a batsman may legally stand. **16** *Electrical.* the usual US and Canad. word for **earth** (sense 8). **17 break new ground.** to do something that has not been done before. **18 common ground.** an agreed basis for identifying issues in an argument. **19 cut the ground from under someone's feet.** to anticipate someone's action or argument and thus make it irrelevant or meaningless. **20 (down) to the ground.** *Brit. inf.* completely; absolutely: *it suited him down to the ground.* **21 home ground.** a familiar area or topic. **22 into the ground.** beyond what is requisite or can be endured; to exhaustion. **23** (*modifier*) on or concerned with the ground: *ground frost; ground forces.* ♦ *vb* **24** (*tr*) to put or place on the ground. **25** (*tr*) to instruct in fundamentals. **26** (*tr*) to provide a basis or foundation for; establish. **27** (*tr*) to confine (an aircraft, pilot, etc.) to the ground. **28** (*tr*) to confine (a teenager) to the house as a punishment. **29** the usual US and Canad. word for **earth** (sense 13). **30** (*tr*) *Naut.* to run (a vessel) aground. **31** (*intr*) to hit or reach the ground. [OE *grund*]

ground² (graʊnd) *vb* **1** the past tense and past participle of **grind.** ♦ *adj* **2** having the surface finished, thickness reduced, or an edge sharpened by grinding. **3** reduced to fine particles by grinding.

groundage ('graʊndɪdʒ) *n Brit.* a fee levied on a vessel entering a port or anchored off a shore.

groundbait ('graʊnd,beɪt) *n Angling.* bait, such as bread or maggots, thrown into an area of water to attract fish.

ground bass (beɪs) *n Music.* a short melodic bass line that is repeated over and over again.

ground-breaking *adj* innovative: *a ground-breaking novel.*

ground control *n* **1** the personnel, radar, computers, etc., on the ground that monitor the progress of aircraft or spacecraft. **2** a system for feeding radio messages to an aircraft pilot to enable him to make a blind landing.

ground cover *n* dense low herbaceous plants and shrubs that grow over the surface of the ground.

ground elder *n* a widely naturalized Eurasian umbelliferous plant with white flowers and creeping underground stems. Also called: **bishop's weed, goutweed.**

ground floor *n* **1** the floor of a building level or almost level with the ground. **2 get in on the ground floor.** *Inf.* to be in a project, undertaking, etc., from its inception.

ground frost *n* the condition resulting from a temperature reading of 0°C or below on a thermometer in contact with a grass surface.

ground glass *n* **1** glass that has a rough surface produced by grinding, used for diffusing light. **2** glass in the form of fine particles produced by grinding, used as an abrasive.

groundhog ('graʊnd,hɒg) *n* another name for **woodchuck.**

grounding ('graʊndɪŋ) *n* a foundation, esp. the basic general knowledge of a subject.

ground ivy *n* a creeping or trailing Eurasian aromatic herbaceous plant with scalloped leaves and purplish-blue flowers.

groundless ('graʊndlɪs) *adj* without reason or justification: *his suspicions were groundless.*
▶ '**groundlessly** *adv* ▶ '**groundlessness** *n*

groundling ('graʊndlɪŋ) *n* **1** any animal or plant that lives close to the ground or at the bottom of a lake, river, etc. **2** (in Elizabethan theatre) a spectator standing in the yard in front of the stage and paying least. **3** a person on the ground as distinguished from one in an aircraft.

groundnut ('graʊnd,nʌt) *n* **1** a North American climbing leguminous plant with small edible underground tu-

bers. **2** the tuber of this plant. **3** *Brit.* another name for **peanut.**

ground plan *n* **1** a drawing of the ground floor of a building, esp. one to scale. **2** a preliminary or basic outline.

ground rule *n* a procedural or fundamental principle.

groundsel ('graʊnsəl) *n* any of certain plants of the composite family, esp. a Eurasian weed with heads of small yellow flowers. [OE, from *gundeswilge,* from *gund* pus + *swelgan* to swallow; after its use in poultices]

groundsheet ('graʊnd,ʃiːt) *n* a waterproof rubber, plastic, or polythene sheet placed on the ground in a tent, etc., to keep out damp.

groundsill ('graʊnd,sɪl) *n* a joist forming the lowest member of a timber frame. Also called: **ground plate.**

groundsman ('graʊndzmən) *n, pl* **groundsmen.** a person employed to maintain a sports ground, park, etc.

groundspeed ('graʊnd,spiːd) *n* the speed of an aircraft relative to the ground.

ground squirrel *n* a burrowing rodent resembling a chipmunk and occurring in North America, E Europe, and Asia. Also called: **gopher.**

groundswell ('graʊnd,swel) *n* **1** a considerable swell of the sea, often caused by a distant storm or earthquake. **2** a rapidly developing general feeling or opinion.

ground water *n* underground water that is held in the soil and in pervious rocks.

groundwork ('graʊnd,wɜːk) *n* **1** preliminary work as a foundation or basis. **2** the ground or background of a painting, etc.

ground zero *n* a point on the ground directly below the centre of a nuclear explosion.

group (gruːp) *n* **1** a number of persons or things considered as a collective unit. **2a** a number of persons bound together by common social standards, interests, etc. **2b** (*as modifier*): *group behaviour.* **3** a small band of players or singers, esp. of pop music. **4** a number of animals or plants considered as a unit because of common characteristics, habits, etc. **5** an association of companies under a single ownership and control. **6** two or more figures or objects forming a design in a painting or sculpture. **7** a military formation comprising complementary arms and services: *a brigade group.* **8** an air force organization of higher level than a squadron. **9** Also called: **radical.** *Chem.* two or more atoms that are bound together in a molecule and behave as a single unit: *a methyl group* -CH_3. **10** a vertical column of elements in the periodic table that all have similar electronic structures, properties, and valencies: *the halogen group.* **11** *Maths.* a set under an operation involving any two members of the set such that the set is closed, associative, and contains both an identity and the inverse of each member. **12** See **blood group.** ♦ *vb* **13** to arrange or place (things, people, etc.) in or into a group, or (of things, etc.) to form into a group. [C17: from F *groupe,* of Gmc origin; cf. It. *gruppo;* see CROP]

group captain *n* an officer holding commissioned rank senior to a wing commander but junior to an air commodore in the RAF and certain other air forces.

group dynamics *n* (*functioning as sing*) *Psychol.* a field of social psychology concerned with the nature of human groups, their development, and their interactions.

grouper ('gruːpə) *n* a variant spelling of **groper.**

groupie ('gruːpɪ) *n Sl.* **1** an ardent fan of a celebrity, esp. a girl who follows the members of a pop group on tour in order to have sexual relations with them. **2** an enthusiastic follower of some activity: *a political groupie.*

Group of Five *n* France, Japan, the UK, the US, and Germany acting as a group to stabilize their currency exchange rates. Abbrev.: **G5.**

Group of Seven *n* the seven leading industrial nations excepting Russia, i.e. Canada, France, Germany, Italy, Japan, the UK, and the US, whose heads of state and finance ministers meet regularly to coordinate economic policy. Abbrev.: **G7.**

Group of Seventy-Seven *n* the developing countries of the world. Abbrev.: **G77.**

Group of Ten *n* the ten nations who met in Paris in 1961 to arrange the special drawing rights of the IMF; Belgium, Canada, France, Italy, Japan, the Netherlands, Sweden, the UK, the US, and West Germany. Also called: **Paris Club.** Abbrev.: **G10.**

Group of Three *n* Japan, the US, and Germany, regarded as the largest industrialized nations. Abbrev.: **G3.**

Group of Twenty-Four *n* the twenty-four richest industrial countries of the world. Abbrev.: **G24.**

group practice *n* a group of doctors who together run a general practice.

group therapy *n Psychol.* the simultaneous treatment of a number of individuals who are brought together to share their problems in group discussion.

groupuscule ('gruːpə,skjuːl) *n Usually derog.* a small group within a political party or movement. [C20: a blend of GROUP + *corpuscule*; see CORPUSCLE]

groupware ('gruːp,wɛə) *n* software that enables a group of computers to work together, so that users may access shared files, exchange messages, etc.

grouse[1] (graʊs) *n, pl* **grouse** *or* **grouses.** a game bird occurring mainly in the N hemisphere, having a stocky body and feathered legs and feet. [C16: from ?]

grouse[2] (graʊs) *vb* **grouses, grousing, groused. 1** (*intr*) to grumble; complain. ◆ *n* **2** a persistent complaint. [C19: from ?]
▶ 'grouser *n*

grouse[3] (graʊs) *adj Austral. & NZ sl.* fine; excellent. [from ?]

grout (graʊt) *n* **1** a thin mortar for filling joints between tiles, masonry, etc. **2** a fine plaster used as a finishing coat. **3** (*pl*) sediment or dregs. ◆ *vb* **4** (*tr*) to fill (joints) or finish (walls, etc.) with grout. [OE *grūt*]
▶ 'grouter *n*

grove (grəʊv) *n* **1** a small wooded area. **2** a road lined with houses and trees, esp. in a suburban area. [OE *grāf*]

grovel ('grɒvəl) *vb* **grovels, grovelling, grovelled** *or US* **groveling, groveled.** (*intr*) **1** to humble or abase oneself, as in making apologies or showing respect. **2** to lie or crawl face downwards, as in fear or humility. **3** (often foll. by *in*) to indulge or take pleasure (in sensuality or vice). [C16: back formation from obs. *groveling* (adv), from ME *on grufe* on the face, of Scand. origin; see -LING[2]]
▶ 'groveller *or US* ,groveler *n*

Groves ★ (grəʊvz) *n* Sir **Charles.** 1915–92, British orchestral conductor.

grow (grəʊ) *vb* **grows, growing, grew, grown. 1** (of an organism or part of an organism) to increase in size or develop (hair, leaves, or other structures). **2** (*intr*; usually foll. by *out of* or *from*) to originate, as from an initial cause or source: *the federation grew out of the Empire.* **3** (*intr*) to increase in size, number, degree, etc.: *the population is growing rapidly.* **4** (*intr*) to change in length or amount in a specified direction: *some plants grow downwards.* **5** (*copula; may take an infinitive*) (esp. of emotions, physical states, etc.) to develop or come into existence or being gradually: *to grow cold.* **6** (*intr*; foll. by *together*) to be joined gradually by or as by growth. **7** (when *intr*, foll. by *with*) to become covered with a growth: *the path grew with weeds.* **8** to produce (plants) by controlling or encouraging their growth, esp. for home consumption or on a commercial basis. ◆ See also **grow into, grow on,** etc. [OE *grōwan*]
▶ 'growable *adj* ▶ 'grower *n*

grow bag *n* a plastic bag containing a sterile growing medium that enables a plant to be grown to full size in it, usually for one season only. [C20: from *Gro-bag*, trademark for the first ones marketed]

growing pains *pl n* **1** pains in muscles or joints sometimes experienced by growing children. **2** difficulties besetting a new enterprise in its early stages.

grow into *vb* (*intr, prep*) to become big or mature enough for: *clothes big enough for him to grow into.*

growl (graʊl) *vb* **1** (of animals, esp. when hostile) to utter (sounds) in a low inarticulate manner: *the dog growled.* **2** to utter (words) in a gruff or angry manner. **3** (*intr*) to make sounds suggestive of an animal growling: *the thun-*

der growled. ◆ *n* **4** the act or sound of growling. [C18: from earlier *grolle*, from OF *grouller* to grumble]
▶ 'growler *n*

grown (grəʊn) *adj* **a** developed or advanced: *fully grown.* **b** (*in combination*): *half-grown.*

grown-up *adj* **1** having reached maturity; adult. **2** suitable for or characteristic of an adult. ◆ *n* **3** an adult.

grow on *vb* (*intr, prep*) to become progressively more acceptable or pleasant to.

grow out of *vb* (*intr, adv + prep*) to become too big or mature for: *she soon grew out of her girlish ways.*

growth (grəʊθ) *n* **1** the process or act of growing. **2** an increase in size, number, significance, etc. **3** something grown or growing: *a new growth of hair.* **4** a stage of development: *a full growth.* **5** any abnormal tissue, such as a tumour. **6** (*modifier*) of, relating to, causing, or characterized by growth: *a growth industry; growth hormone.*

growth curve *n* a curve on a graph in which a variable is plotted against time to illustrate the growth of the variable.

grow up *vb* (*intr, adv*) **1** to reach maturity; become adult. **2** to come into existence; develop.

groyne *or esp. US* **groin** (grɔɪn) *n* a wall or jetty built out from a riverbank or seashore to control erosion. Also called: **spur, breakwater.** [C16: ?from OF *groign* snout, promontory]

Grozny ★ (*Russian* 'grɔznij) *n* a city in S Russia, capital of Chechenia: badly damaged in the war between Russian troops and Chechen separatists (1996–97); a major oil centre. Pop.: 364 000 (1993 est.).

grub (grʌb) *vb* **grubs, grubbing, grubbed. 1** (when *tr*, often foll. by *up* or *out*) to search for and pull up (roots, stumps, etc.) by digging in the ground. **2** to dig up the surface of (ground, soil, etc.), esp. to clear away roots, stumps, etc. **3** (*intr*; often foll. by *in* or *among*) to search carefully. **4** (*intr*) to work unceasingly, esp. at a dull task. ◆ *n* **5** the short tubular larva of certain insects, esp. beetles. **6** *Sl.* food; victuals. **7** a person who works hard, esp. in a dull plodding way. [C13: of Gmc origin; cf. OHG *grubilōn* to dig]
▶ 'grubber *n*

grubby ('grʌbɪ) *adj* **grubbier, grubbiest. 1** dirty; slovenly. **2** mean; beggarly. **3** infested with grubs.
▶ 'grubbily *adv* ▶ 'grubbiness *n*

grub screw *n* a small headless screw used to secure a sliding component in position.

grubstake ('grʌb,steɪk) *US & Canad. inf.* ◆ *n* **1** supplies provided for a prospector on the condition that the donor has a stake in any finds. ◆ *vb* **grubstakes, grubstaking, grubstaked.** (*tr*) **2** to furnish with such supplies. **3** to supply (a person) with a stake in a gambling game.
▶ 'grub,staker *n*

Grub Street *n* **1** a former street in London frequented by literary hacks and needy authors. **2** the world or class of literary hacks, etc. ◆ *adj also* **Grubstreet. 3** (*sometimes not cap.*) relating to or characteristic of hack literature.

grudge (grʌdʒ) *n* **1** a persistent feeling of resentment, esp. one due to an insult or injury. **2** (*modifier*) planned or carried out in order to settle a grudge: *a grudge fight.* ◆ *vb* **grudges, grudging, grudged. 3** (*tr*) to give unwillingly. **4** to feel resentful or envious about (someone else's success, etc.). [C15: from OF *grouchier* to grumble, prob. of Gmc origin]
▶ 'grudging *adj* ▶ 'grudgingly *adv*

gruel ('gruːəl) *n* a drink or thin porridge made by boiling meal, esp. oatmeal, in water or milk. [C14: from OF, of Gmc origin]

gruelling *or US* **grueling** ('gruːəlɪŋ) *adj* **1** extremely severe or tiring. ◆ *n* **2** *Inf.* a severe or tiring experience, esp. punishment. [C19: from obs. *gruel* (vb) to punish]

gruesome ('gruːsəm) *adj* inspiring repugnance and horror; ghastly. [C16: orig. Northern E and Scot., of Scand. origin]
▶ 'gruesomely *adv* ▶ 'gruesomeness *n*

gruff (grʌf) *adj* **1** rough or surly in manner, speech, etc. **2**

(of a voice, bark, etc.) low and throaty. [C16: orig. Scot., from Du. *grof*, of Gmc origin; rel. to OE *hrēof*]
► **'gruffly** *adv* ► **'gruffness** *n*

grumble ('grʌmb°l) *vb* **grumbles, grumbling, grumbled. 1** to utter (complaints) in a nagging way. **2** (*intr*) to make low rumbling sounds. ◆ *n* **3** a complaint. **4** a low rumbling sound. [C16: from MLow G *grommelen*, of Gmc origin]
► **'grumbler** *n* ► **'grumblingly** *adv* ► **'grumbly** *adj*

grumbling appendix *n Inf.* a condition in which the appendix causes intermittent pain or discomfort but appendicitis has not developed.

grummet ('grʌmɪt) *n* a variant of **grommet**.

grump (grʌmp) *Inf.* ◆ *n* **1** a surly or bad-tempered person. **2** (*pl*) a surly or morose mood (esp. in **have the grumps**). ◆ *vb* **3** (*intr*) to complain or grumble. [C18: dialect: surly remark, prob. imit.]

grumpy ('grʌmpɪ) *or* **grumpish** *adj* **grumpier, grumpiest.** peevish; sulky. [C18: from GRUMP + -Y[1]]
► **'grumpily** *or* **'grumpishly** *adv* ► **'grumpiness** *or* **'grumpishness** *n*

Grundy ('grʌndɪ) *n* a narrow-minded person who keeps critical watch on the propriety of others. [C18: after Mrs *Grundy*, the character in T. Morton's play *Speed the Plough* (1798)]
► **'Grundy,ism** *n* ► **'Grundyist** *or* **'Grundyite** *n*

Grünewald ★ (German 'gry:nəvalt) *n* **Matthias** (ma'ti:as), original name *Mathis Gothardt.* ?1470–1528, German painter.

grunge (grʌndʒ) *n* **1** *US sl.* dirt or rubbish. **2** a style of rock music originating in the US in the late 1980s, featuring a distorted guitar sound. **3** a deliberately untidy and uncoordinated fashion style. [C20: possibly a coinage imitating GRIME + SLUDGE]

grungy ('grʌndʒɪ) *adj* **grungier, grungiest. 1** *Sl.*, chiefly US & Canad. squalid, seedy, grotty. **2** (of pop music) characterized by a loud fuzzy guitar sound. [from ?]

grunion ('grʌnjən) *n* a Californian marine fish that spawns on beaches. [C20: prob. from Sp. *gruñón* a grunter]

grunt (grʌnt) *vb* **1** (*intr*) (esp. of pigs and some other animals) to emit a low short gruff noise. **2** (when *tr*, *may take a clause as object*) to express something gruffly: *he grunted his answer.* ◆ *n* **3** the characteristic low short gruff noise of pigs, etc., or a similar sound, as of disgust. **4** any of various mainly tropical marine fishes that utter a grunting sound when caught. [OE *grunnettan*, prob. imit.; cf. OHG *grunnizōn, grunni* moaning]
► **'grunter** *n*

Gruyère *or* **Gruyère cheese** ('gru:jɛə) *n* a hard flat whole-milk cheese, pale yellow in colour and with holes. [C19: after *Gruyère*, Switzerland, where it originated]

gr. wt. *abbrev.* for gross weight.

gryphon ('grɪf°n) *n* a variant of **griffin**.

grysbok ('graɪs,bɒk) *n* either of two small antelopes of central and southern Africa, having small straight horns. [C18: Afrik., from Du. *grijs* grey + *bok* BUCK[1]]

GS *abbrev. for:* **1** General Secretary. **2** General Staff.

GST (in New Zealand) *abbrev.* for goods and services tax.

G-string *n* **1** a piece of cloth worn by striptease artistes covering the pubic area and attached to a narrow waistband. **2** a strip of cloth attached to the front and back of a waistband and covering the loins. **3** *Music.* a string tuned to G.

G-suit *n* a close-fitting garment that is worn by the crew of high-speed aircraft and can be pressurized to prevent blackout during manoeuvres. [C20: from *g*(ravity) *suit*]

GSVQ (in Britain) *abbrev.* for General Scottish Vocational Qualification: the Scottish equivalent of GNVQ.

GT *abbrev.* for gran turismo: a touring car; usually a fast sports car with a hard fixed roof.

gtd *abbrev.* for guaranteed.

Guadalajara ★ (ˌgwɑːd°lə'hɑːrə; *Spanish* gwaðala'xara) *n* **1** a city in W Mexico, capital of Jalisco state: centre of the Indian slave trade until its abolition, declared here in 1810; two universities (1792 and 1935). Pop.: 1 650 042

(1990). **2** a city in central Spain, in New Castile. Pop.: 67 200 (1991).

Guadalcanal ★ (ˌgwɑːd°l'kə'næl; *Spanish* gwaðalka'nal) *n* a mountainous island in the SW Pacific, the largest of the Solomon Islands: under British protection until 1978; occupied by the Japanese (1942–43). Pop.: 59 064 (1996 est.). Area: 6475 sq. km (2500 sq. miles).

Guadalquivir ★ (ˌgwɑːd°l'kwɪ'vɪə; *Spanish* gwaðalki'βir) *n* the chief river of S Spain, rising in the Sierra de Segura and flowing west and southwest to the Gulf of Cádiz: navigable by ocean-going vessels to Seville. Length: 560 km (348 miles).

Guadalupe Hidalgo ★ (ˌgwɑːd°'lu:p hɪ'dælgəʊ; *Spanish* gwaða'lupe i'ðalɣo) *n* a city in central Mexico, northwest of Mexico City: became the foremost pilgrimage centre in the Americas after an Indian convert reported seeing a vision of the Virgin Mary here in 1531. Pop.: 535 332 (1990). Former name (1931–71): **Gustavo A. Madero.**

Guadeloupe ★ (ˌgwɑːd°'lu:p) *n* an overseas region of France in the E Caribbean, in the Leeward Islands, formed by the islands of Basse Terre and Grande Terre and their five dependencies. Capital: Basse-Terre. Pop.: 433 000 (1997). Area: 1780 sq. km (687 sq. miles).

Guadiana ★ (*Spanish* gwa'ðjana; *Portuguese* gwə'ðjənə) *n* a river in SW Europe, rising in S central Spain and flowing west, then south as part of the border between Spain and Portugal, to the Gulf of Cádiz. Length: 578 km (359 miles).

guaiacum ('gwaɪəkəm) *n* **1** any of a family of tropical American evergreen trees such as the lignum vitae. **2** the hard heavy wood of any of these trees. **3** a brownish resin obtained from the lignum vitae, used medicinally and in making varnishes. [C16: NL, from Sp. *guayaco*, of Amerind origin]

Guam ★ (gwɑːm) *n* an island in the N Pacific, the largest and southernmost of the Marianas: belonged to Spain from the 17th century until 1898, when it was ceded to the US; site of naval and air force bases. Capital: Agaña. Pop.: 133 152 (1990). Area: 541 sq. km (209 sq. miles).
► **Guamanian** (gwɑː'meɪnɪən) *n, adj*

Guanabara ★ (*Portuguese* gwənə'bara) *n* (until 1975) a state of SE Brazil, on the Atlantic and **Guanabara Bay**, now amalgamated with the state of Rio de Janeiro.

guanaco (gwɑː'nɑːkəʊ) *n, pl* **guanacos.** a cud-chewing South American mammal closely related to the domesticated llama. [C17: from Sp., from Quechuan *huanacu*]

Guanajuato ★ (*Spanish* gwana'xwato) *n* **1** a state of central Mexico, on the great central plateau: mountainous in the north, with fertile plains in the south; important mineral resources. Capital: Guanajuato. Pop.: 4 393 160 (1995 est.). Area: 30 588 sq. km (11 810 sq. miles). **2** a city in central Mexico, capital of Guanajuato state: founded in 1554, it became one of the world's richest silver-mining centres. Pop.: 113 580 (1990).

Guangdong ('gwæŋ'dʊŋ) *or* **Kwangtung** ★ *n* a province of SE China, on the South China Sea: includes the Leizhou Peninsula, with densely populated river valleys; the only true tropical climate in China. Capital: Canton. Pop.: 66 890 000 (1995 est.). Area: 197 100 sq. km (76 100 sq. miles).

Guangxi Zhuang Autonomous Region ('gwæŋ'si: 'dʒwæŋ) *or* **Kwangsi-Chuang Autonomous Region** ★ *n* an administrative division of S China: the least developed of Chinese regions. Capital: Nanning. Pop.: 44 930 000 (1995 est.). Area: 220 400 sq. km (85 100 sq. miles).

Guangzhou ★ ('gwæŋ'dzəʊ) *n* the Pinyin transliteration of the Chinese name for **Canton**.

guanine ('gwɑː ni:n, 'guːə,ni:n) *n* a white almost insoluble compound: one of the purine bases in nucleic acids. [C19: from GUANO + -INE[2]]

guano ('gwɑːnəʊ) *n, pl* **guanos. 1** the dried excrement of fish-eating sea birds, deposited in rocky coastal regions of South America: used as a fertilizer. **2** any similar but artificially produced fertilizer. [C17: from Sp., from Quechuan *huano* dung]

Guantánamo ★ (*Spanish* gwan'tanamo) *n* a city in SE

Cuba, on **Guantánamo Bay**: site of a US naval base. Pop.: 207 796 (1994 est.).

Guaporé ★ (*Portuguese* gwapo'rɛ) *n* **1** a river in W central South America, rising in SW Brazil and flowing northwest as part of the border between Brazil and Bolivia, to join the Mamoré River. Length: 1750 km (1087 miles). Spanish name: **Iténez**. **2** the former name (until 1956) of **Rondônia**.

Guarani (ˌgwɑːrə'niː) *n* **1** (*pl* **Guarani** *or* **Guaranis**) a member of a South American Indian people of Paraguay, S Brazil, and Bolivia. **2** the language of this people.

guarantee (ˌgærən'tiː) *n* **1** a formal assurance, esp. in writing, that a product, service, etc., will meet certain standards or specifications. **2** *Law.* a promise, esp. a collateral agreement, to answer for the debt, default, or miscarriage of another. **3a** a person, company, etc., to whom a guarantee is made. **3b** a person, company, etc., who gives a guarantee. **4** a person who acts as a guarantor. **5** something that makes a specified condition or outcome certain. **6** a variant spelling of **guaranty**. ◆ *vb* **guarantees, guaranteeing, guaranteed.** (*mainly tr*) **7** (*also intr*) to take responsibility for (someone else's debts, obligations, etc.). **8** to serve as a guarantee for. **9** to secure or furnish security for: *a small deposit will guarantee any dress.* **10** (usually foll. by *from* or *against*) to undertake to protect or keep secure, as against injury, loss, etc. **11** to ensure: *good planning will guarantee success.* **12** (*may take a clause as object or an infinitive*) to promise or make certain. [C17: ?from Sp. *garante* or F *garant*, of Gmc origin; cf. WARRANT]

guarantor (ˌgærən'tɔː) *n* a person who gives or is bound by a guarantee or guaranty; surety.

guaranty ('gærəntɪ) *n, pl* **guaranties. 1** a pledge of responsibility for fulfilling another person's obligations in case of that person's default. **2** a thing given or taken as security for a guaranty. **3** the act of providing security. **4** a person who acts as a guarantor. ◆ *vb* **guaranties, guarantying, guarantied. 5** a variant spelling of **guarantee**. [C16: from OF *garantie*, var. of *warantie*, of Gmc origin; see WARRANTY]

guard (gɑːd) *vb* **1** to watch over or shield (a person or thing) from danger or harm; protect. **2** to keep watch over (a prisoner or other potentially dangerous person or thing), as to prevent escape. **3** (*tr*) to control: *to guard one's tongue.* **4** (*intr*; usually foll. by *against*) to take precautions. **5** to control entrance and exit through (a gate, door, etc.). **6** (*tr*) to provide (machinery, etc.) with a device to protect the operator. **7** (*tr*) **7a** *Chess, cards.* to protect or cover (a chessman or card) with another. **7b** *Curling, bowling.* to protect or cover (a stone or bowl) by placing one's own stone or bowl between it and another player. ◆ *n* **8** a person or group who keeps a protecting, supervising, or restraining watch or control over people, such as prisoners, things, etc. Related adj: **custodial. 9** a person or group of people, such as soldiers, who form a ceremonial escort. **10** *Brit.* the official in charge of a train. **11a** the act or duty of protecting, restraining, or supervising. **11b** (*as modifier*): *guard duty.* **12** a device, part, or attachment on an object, such as a weapon or machine tool, designed to protect the user against injury. **13** anything that provides or is intended to provide protection: *a guard against infection.* **14** *Sport.* an article of light tough material worn to protect any of various parts of the body. **15** the posture of defence or readiness in fencing, boxing, cricket, etc. **16 mount guard. 16a** (of a sentry, etc.) to begin to keep watch. **16b** (with *over*) to take a protective or defensive stance (towards something). **17 off (one's) guard.** having one's defences down; unprepared. **18 on (one's) guard.** prepared to face danger, difficulties, etc. **19 stand guard.** (of a sentry, etc.) to keep watch. [C15: from OF, from *garder* to protect, of Gmc origin; see WARD]
▸ **'guarder** *n*

Guardafui ★ (ˌgwɑːdəˈfuːɪ) *n* **Cape.** a cape at the NE tip of Somalia, extending into the Indian Ocean.

guarded ('gɑːdɪd) *adj* **1** protected or kept under surveillance. **2** prudent, restrained, or noncommittal: *a guarded reply.*
▸ **'guardedly** *adv* ▸ **'guardedness** *n*

guard hair *n* any of the coarse hairs that form the outer fur in certain mammals.

guardhouse ('gɑːdˌhaʊs) *or* **guardroom** ('gɑːdˌruːm, -rʊm) *n Mil.* a building serving as headquarters for military police and in which military prisoners are detained.

Guardi ★ (*Italian* 'gwardi) *n* **Francesco** (fran'tʃesko). 1712–93, Venetian landscape painter.

guardian ('gɑːdɪən) *n* **1** one who looks after, protects, or defends: *the guardian of public morals.* **2** *Law.* someone legally appointed to manage the affairs of a person incapable of acting for himself, as a minor or person of unsound mind. ◆ *adj* **3** protecting or safeguarding.
▸ **'guardian,ship** *n*

Guardian Angels *pl n* vigilante volunteers who patrol the New York Underground and elsewhere, wearing red berets, to deter violent crime.

guard ring *n* **1** Also called: **keeper ring.** a ring worn to prevent another from slipping off the finger. **2** an electrode used to counteract distortion of the electric fields at the edges of other electrodes.

Guards (gɑːdz) *pl n* (esp. in European armies) any of various regiments responsible for ceremonial duties and, formerly, the protection of the head of state: *the Life Guards.*

guardsman ('gɑːdzmən) *n, pl* **guardsmen. 1** (in Britain) a member of a Guards battalion or regiment. **2** (in the US) a member of the National Guard. **3** a guard.

guard's van *n Railways, Brit. & NZ.* the van in which the guard travels, usually attached to the rear of a train. US and Canad. equivalent: **caboose.**

Guarneri (gwɑːˈnɪərɪ; *Italian* gwarˈnɛːri), **Guarnieri** (*Italian* gwarˈnjɛːri), *or* **Guarnerius** (gwɑːˈnɪərɪəs) *n, pl* **Guarneris, Guarnieris,** *or* **Guarneriuses. 1** an Italian family of 17th- and 18th-century violin-makers. **2** any violin made by a member of this family.

Guat. *abbrev. for* Guatemala.

Guatemala ★ (ˌgwɑːtəˈmɑːlə) *n* a republic in Central America: original Maya Indians conquered by the Spanish in 1523; became the centre of Spanish administration in Central America; gained independence and was annexed to Mexico in 1821, becoming an independent republic in 1839. Official language: Spanish. Religion: Roman Catholic majority. Currency: quetzal. Capital: Guatemala City. Pop.: 11 242 000 (1997). Area: 108 889 sq. km (42 042 sq. miles).
▸ ˌGuateˈmalan *adj, n*

Guatemala City ★ *n* the capital of Guatemala, in the southeast: founded in 1776 to replace the former capital, Antigua Guatemala, after an earthquake; university (1676). Pop.: 1 167 495 (1995).

guava ('gwɑːvə) *n* **1** any of various tropical American trees, grown esp. for their edible fruit. **2** the fruit of such a tree, having yellow skin and pink pulp. [C16: from Sp. *guayaba*, from a South American Indian word]

Guayaquil ★ (*Spanish* gwajaˈkil) *n* a port in W Ecuador: the largest city in the country and its chief port; university (1867). Pop.: 1 925 479 (1996 est.).

guayule (gwəˈjuːlɪ) *n* **1** a bushy shrub of the southwestern US. **2** rubber derived from the sap of this plant. [from American Sp., from Nahuatl *cuauhuli*, from *cuahuitl* tree + *uli* gum]

gubbins ('gʌbɪnz) *n* **1** (*functioning as sing*) an object of little value. **2** (*functioning as sing*) a small gadget. **3** (*functioning as pl*) odds and ends; rubbish. **4** (*functioning as sing*) a silly person. [C16 (meaning: fragments): from obs. *gobbon*]

gubernatorial (ˌgjuːbənəˈtɔːrɪəl, ˌguː-) *adj Chiefly US.* of or relating to a governor. [C18: from L *gubernātor* governor]

guddle ('gʌdᵊl) *Scot.* ◆ *vb* **guddles, guddling, guddled. 1** to catch (fish) by groping with the hands under the banks or stones of a stream. ◆ *n* **2** a muddle; confusion. [C19: from ?]

gudgeon[1] ('gʌdʒən) *n* **1** a small slender European freshwater fish with a barbel on each side of the mouth: used as bait by anglers. **2** any of various other fishes, such as the goby. **3** *Sl.* a person who is easy to trick or cheat.

◆ *vb* **4** (*tr*) *Sl.* to trick or cheat. [C15: from OF *gougon*, prob. from L *gōbius;* see GOBY]

gudgeon[2] ('gʌdʒən) *n* **1** the female or socket portion of a pinned hinge. **2** *Naut.* one of two or more looplike sockets, fixed to the transom of a boat, into which the pintles of a rudder are fitted. [C14: from OF *goujon,* ?from LL *gulbia* chisel]

gudgeon pin *n Brit.* the pin through the skirt of a piston in an internal-combustion engine, to which the little end of the connecting rod is attached. US and Canad. name: **wrist pin.**

Gudrun ('gʊdruːn), **Guthrun** ('gʊðruːn), *or* **Kudrun** ★ ('kudruːn) *n Norse myth.* the wife of Sigurd and, after his death, of Atli, whom she slew for his murder of her brother Gunnar. She corresponds to Kriemhild in the *Nibelungenlied.*

guelder-rose ('gɛldə,rəʊz) *n* a Eurasian shrub with clusters of white flowers and small red fruits. [C16: from Du. *geldersche roos,* from *Gelderland* or *Gelders,* province of Holland]

Guelders ★ ('gɛldəz) *n* another name for **Gelderland.**

Guelph ★ (gwelf) *n* a city in Canada, in SE Ontario. Pop.: 87 976 (1991).

guenon (gə'nɒn) *n* a slender agile Old World monkey inhabiting wooded regions of Africa and having long hind limbs and tail and long hair surrounding the face. [C19: from F, from ?]

guerdon ('gɜːdᵊn) *Poetic.* ◆ *n* **1** a reward or payment. ◆ *vb* **2** (*tr*) to give a guerdon to. [C14: from OF *gueredon,* of Gmc origin; final element infl. by L *dōnum* gift]

Guernica ★ (gɜː'niːkə, 'gɜːnɪkə; *Spanish* ger'nika) *n* a town in N Spain: formerly the seat of a Basque parliament; destroyed in 1937 by German bombers during the Spanish Civil War, an event depicted in one of Picasso's most famous paintings. Pop.: 16 378 (1989).

Guernsey ★ ('gɜːnzɪ) *n* **1** an island in the English Channel: the second largest of the Channel Islands, which, with Alderney and Sark, Herm, Jethou, and some islets, forms the bailiwick of Guernsey; finance, market gardening, dairy farming, and tourism. Capital: St Peter Port. Pop.: 58 867 (1991). Area: 63 sq. km (24.5 sq. miles). **2** a breed of dairy cattle producing rich creamy milk, originating from the island of Guernsey. **3** (*sometimes not cap.*) a seaman's knitted woollen sweater. **4** (*not cap.*) *Austral.* a sleeveless woollen shirt or jumper worn by a football player. **5 get a guernsey.** *Austral.* to be selected or gain recognition for something.

Guerrero ★ (*Spanish* ge'rrero) *n* a mountainous state of S Mexico, on the Pacific: rich mineral resources. Capital: Chilpancingo. Pop.: 2 915 497 (1995 est.). Area: 63 794 sq. km (24 631 sq. miles).

guerrilla *or* **guerilla** (gə'rɪlə) *n* **a** a member of an irregular usually politically motivated armed force that combats stronger regular forces. **b** (*as modifier*): *guerrilla warfare.* [C19: from Sp., dim. of *guerra* WAR]

guess (gɛs) *vb* (when *tr, may take a clause as object*) **1** (when *intr,* often foll. by *at* or *about*) to form or express an uncertain estimate or conclusion (about something), based on insufficient information: *guess what we're having for dinner.* **2** to arrive at a correct estimate of (something) by guessing: *he guessed my age.* **3** *Inf., chiefly US & Canad.* to believe, think, or suppose (something): *I guess I'll go now.* ◆ *n* **4** an estimate or conclusion arrived at by guessing: *a bad guess.* **5** the act of guessing. [C13: prob. from ON] ▸ **'guesser** *n*

guesstimate *or* **guestimate** *Inf.* ◆ *n* ('gɛstɪmɪt). **1** an estimate calculated mainly or only by guesswork. ◆ *vb* ('gɛstɪ,meɪt), **guesstimates, guesstimating, guesstimated.** (*tr*) **2** to form a guesstimate of.

guesswork ('gɛs,wɜːk) *n* **1** a set of conclusions, estimates, etc., arrived at by guessing. **2** the process of making guesses.

guest (gɛst) *n* **1** a person who is entertained, taken out to eat, etc., and paid for by another. **2a** a person who receives hospitality at the home of another. **2b** (*as modifier*): *the guest room.* **3a** a person who receives the hospitality of a government, establishment, or organization.

3b (*as modifier*): *a guest speaker.* **4a** an actor, contestant, entertainer, etc., taking part as a visitor in a programme in which there are also regular participants. **4b** (*as modifier*): *a guest appearance.* **5** a patron of a hotel, boarding house, restaurant, etc. ◆ *vb* **6** (*intr*) (in theatre and broadcasting) to be a guest: *to guest on a show.* [OE *giest* guest, stranger, enemy]

guest beer *n* a draught beer stocked by a bar, often for a limited period, in addition to its usual range.

guesthouse ('gɛst,haʊs) *n* a private home or boarding house offering accommodation.

guest rope *n Naut.* any line trailed over the side of a vessel as a convenience for boats drawing alongside, as an aid in towing, etc.

Guevara ★ (ge'vɑːrə; *Spanish* ge'βara) *n* **Ernesto** (ɛr'nesto), known as *Che Guevara.* 1928–67, Latin American politician and soldier, born in Argentina. He developed guerrilla warfare as a tool for revolution and was instrumental in Castro's victory in Cuba (1959): killed while training guerrillas in Bolivia.

guff (gʌf) *n Sl.* ridiculous or insolent talk. [C19: imit. of empty talk]

guffaw (gʌ'fɔː) *n* **1** a crude and boisterous laugh. ◆ *vb* **2** to laugh or express (something) in this way. [C18: imit.]

Guggenheim Museum ★ ('gʊgən,haɪm) *n* a museum of modern art in New York: designed by Frank Lloyd Wright (1956–59).

Guiana (gaɪ'ænə, gɪ'ɑːnə) *or* **The Guianas** ★ *n* a region of NE South America, including Guyana, Surinam, French Guiana, and the **Guiana Highlands** (largely in SE Venezuela and partly in N Brazil). Area: about 1 787 000 sq. km (690 000 sq. miles).
▸ **Guianese** (,gaɪə'niːz, ,gɪə-) *or* **Guianan** (gaɪ'ænən, gɪ'ɑːnən) *adj, n*

guidance ('gaɪdᵊns) *n* **1** leadership, instruction, or direction. **2a** counselling or advice on educational, vocational, or psychological matters. **2b** (*as modifier*): *the marriage-guidance counsellor.* **3** something that guides. **4** any process by which the flight path of a missile is controlled in flight.

guide (gaɪd) *vb* **guides, guiding, guided. 1** to lead the way for (a person). **2** to control the movement or course of (an animal, vehicle, etc.) by physical action; steer. **3** to supervise or instruct (a person). **4** (*tr*) to direct the affairs of (a person, company, nation, etc.). **5** (*tr*) to advise or influence (a person) in his standards or opinions: *let truth guide you.* ◆ *n* **6a** a person, animal, or thing that guides. **6b** (*as modifier*): *a guide dog.* **7** a person, usually paid, who conducts tour expeditions, etc. **8** a model or criterion, as in moral standards or accuracy. **9** Also called: **guidebook.** a handbook with information for visitors to a place. **10** a book that instructs or explains the fundamentals of a subject or skill. **11** any device that directs the motion of a tool or machine part. **12** a mark, sign, etc., that points the way. **13a** *Naval.* a ship in a formation used as a reference for manoeuvres. **13b** *Mil.* a soldier stationed to one side of a column or line to regulate alignment, show the way, etc. [C14: from (O)F *guider,* of Gmc origin]
▸ **'guidable** *adj* ▸ **'guider** *n*

Guide (gaɪd) *n* (*sometimes not cap.*) a member of an organization for girls equivalent to the Scouts. US equivalent: **Girl Scout.**

guided missile *n* a missile, esp. one that is rocket-propelled, having a flight path controlled either by radio signals or by internal preset or self-actuating homing devices.

guide dog *n* a dog that has been specially trained to accompany someone who is blind, enabling the blind person to move about safely.

guideline ('gaɪd,laɪn) *n* a principle put forward to set standards or determine a course of action.

guidepost ('gaɪd,pəʊst) *n* **1** a sign on a post by a road indicating directions. **2** a principle or guideline.

Guider ('gaɪdə) *n* (*sometimes not cap.*) a woman leader of a company of Guides or of a pack of Brownie Guides.

★ people and places

Guido d'Arezzo ★ (*Italian* 'gwi:do da'rettso) *n* ?995–?1050 A.D., Italian Benedictine monk and musical theorist: reputed inventor of solmization.

guidon ('gaɪdᵊn) *n* **1** a small pennant, used as a marker or standard, esp. by cavalry regiments. **2** the man or vehicle that carries this. [C16: from F, from OProvençal *guidoo*, from *guida* GUIDE]

Guienne *or* **Guyenne** ★ (*French* gɥijɛn) *n* a former province of SW France: formed, with Gascony, the duchy of Aquitaine during the 12th century.

guild *or* **gild** (gɪld) *n* **1** an organization, club, or fellowship. **2** (esp. in medieval Europe) an association of men sharing the same interests, such as merchants or artisans: formed for mutual aid and protection and to maintain craft standards. [C14: from ON; cf. *gjald* payment, *gildi* guild; rel. to OE *gield* offering, OHG *gelt* money]
▸ **'guildsman**, **'gildsman** *or* (*fem*) **'guildswoman**, **'gildswoman** *n*

guilder ('gɪldə) *or* **gulden** *n, pl* **guilders, guilder** *or* **guldens, gulden. 1** Also: **gilder, florin.** the standard monetary unit of the Netherlands, divided into 100 cents. **2** any of various former gold or silver coins of Germany, Austria, or the Netherlands. [C15: from MDu. *gulden*, lit.: GOLDEN]

Guildford ('gɪlfəd) *n* a town in S England, the administrative centre of Surrey: cathedral (1936–68); seat of the University of Surrey (1966). Pop.: 65 998 (1991).

guildhall ('gɪld,hɔːl) *n Brit.* **a** the hall of a guild or corporation. **b** a town hall.

guile (gaɪl) *n* clever or crafty character or behaviour. [C18: from OF *guile*, of Gmc origin; see WILE]
▸ **'guileful** *adj* ▸ **'guilefully** *adv* ▸ **'guilefulness** *n* ▸ **'guileless** *adj* ▸ **'guilelessly** *adv* ▸ **'guilelessness** *n*

Guilin ('gweɪ'lɪn), **Kweilin**, *or* **Kuei-lin** ★ *n* a city in S China, in Guangxi Zhuang AR on the Li River: noted for the unusual caves and formations of the surrounding karst scenery; trade and manufacturing centre. Pop.: 364 130 (1990 est.).

Guillaume de Lorris ★ (*French* gijom də lɔris) *n* 13th century, French poet who wrote the first 4058 lines of the allegorical romance, the *Roman de la rose*, continued by Jean de Meung.

guillemot ('gɪlɪ,mɒt) *n* a northern oceanic diving bird having a black-and-white plumage and long narrow bill. [C17: from F, dim. of *Guillaume* William]

guilloche (gɪ'lɒʃ) *n* an ornamental border with a repeating pattern of two or more interwoven wavy lines, as in architecture. [C19: from F: tool used in ornamental work, ?from *Guillaume* William]

guillotine *n* ('gɪlə,tiːn). **1a** a device for beheading persons, consisting of a weighted blade set between two upright posts. **1b** **the guillotine.** execution by this instrument. **2** a device for cutting or trimming sheet material, such as paper or sheet metal, consisting of a slightly inclined blade that descends onto the sheet. **3** a surgical instrument for removing tonsils, growths in the throat, etc. **4** (in Parliament, etc.) a form of closure under which a bill is divided into compartments, groups of which must be completely dealt with each day. ◆ *vb* (,gɪlə'tiːn), **guillotines, guillotining, guillotined.** (*tr*) **5** to behead (a person) by guillotine. **6** (in Parliament, etc.) to limit debate on (a bill, motion, etc.) by the guillotine. [C18: from F, after Joseph Ignace *Guillotin* (1738–1814), F physician, who advocated its use in 1789]
▸ **,guillo'tiner** *n*

guilt (gɪlt) *n* **1** the fact or state of having done wrong or committed an offence. **2** responsibility for a criminal or moral offence deserving punishment or a penalty. **3** remorse or self-reproach caused by feeling that one is responsible for a wrong or offence. **4** *Arch.* sin or crime. [OE *gylt*, from ?]

guiltless ('gɪltlɪs) *adj* free of all responsibility for wrongdoing or crime; innocent.
▸ **'guiltlessly** *adv* ▸ **'guiltlessness** *n*

guilty ('gɪltɪ) *adj* **guiltier, guiltiest. 1** responsible for an offence or misdeed. **2** *Law.* having committed an offence or adjudged to have done so: *the accused was found guilty*. **3** of, showing, or characterized by guilt.
▸ **'guiltily** *adv* ▸ **'guiltiness** *n*

guimpe (gɪmp) *n* a variant spelling of **gimp**.

Guin. *abbrev. for* Guinea.

guinea ('gɪnɪ) *n* **1a** a British gold coin taken out of circulation in 1813, worth 21 shillings. **1b** the sum of 21 shillings (1.05), still used in quoting professional fees. **2** See **guinea fowl.** [C16: the coin was orig. made of gold from Guinea]

Guinea ★ ('gɪnɪ) *n* **1** a republic in West Africa, on the Atlantic: established as the colony of French Guinea in 1890 and became an independent republic in 1958. Official language: French. Religion: Muslim majority and animist. Currency: Guinean franc of 100 cauris. Capital: Conakry. Pop.: 7 405 000 (1997). Area: 245 855 sq. km (94 925 sq. miles). **2** (formerly) the coastal region of West Africa, between Cape Verde and Namibe (formerly Moçâmedes; Angola): divided by a line of volcanic peaks into **Upper Guinea** (between The Gambia and Cameroon) and **Lower Guinea** (between Cameroon and S Angola). **3 Gulf of.** a large inlet of the S Atlantic on the W coast of Africa, extending from Cape Palmas, Liberia, to Cape Lopez, Gabon: contains two large bays, the Bight of Biafra and the Bight of Benin, separated by the Niger delta.
▸ **'Guinean** *adj, n*

Guinea-Bissau ★ *n* a republic in West Africa, on the Atlantic: first discovered by the Portuguese in 1446 and of subsequent importance in the slave trade; made a colony in 1879; became an independent republic in 1974. Official language: Portuguese; Cape Verde creole is widely spoken. Religion: animist majority and Muslim. Currency: peso. Capital: Bissau. Pop.: 1 179 000 (1997). Area: 36 125 sq. km (13 948 sq. miles). Former name (until 1974): **Portuguese Guinea.**

guinea fowl *or* **guinea** *n* a domestic fowl of Africa and SW Asia, having a dark plumage mottled with white, a naked head and neck, and a heavy rounded body.

guinea hen *n* a guinea fowl, esp. a female.

guinea pig *n* **1** a domesticated cavy, commonly kept as a pet and used in scientific experiments. **2** a person or thing used for experimentation. [C17: from ?]

Guinevere ('gwɪnɪ,vɪə), **Guenevere** ('gwɛnɪ,vɪə), *or* **Guinever** ★ ('gwɪnɪvə) *n* (in Arthurian legend) the wife of King Arthur and paramour of Lancelot.

Guinness ★ ('gɪnɪs) *n* Sir **Alec.** born 1914, British actor. His films include *The Bridge on the River Kwai* (1957) and his TV roles include Le Carré's George Smiley.

guipure (gɪ'pjuə) *n* **1** Also called: **guipure lace.** any of many types of heavy lace that have their pattern connected by threads, rather than supported on a net mesh. **2** a heavy corded trimming; gimp. [C19: from OF, from *guiper* to cover with cloth, of Gmc origin]

guise (gaɪz) *n* **1** semblance or pretence: *under the guise of friendship*. **2** external appearance in general. **3** *Arch.* manner or style of dress. [C13: from OF *guise*, of Gmc origin]

guising ('gaɪzɪŋ) *n* (in Scotland and N England) the practice or custom of disguising oneself in fancy dress, often with mask, and visiting people's houses, esp. at Halloween.
▸ **'guiser** *n*

guitar (gɪ'tɑː) *n* a plucked stringed instrument originating in Spain, usually having six strings, a flat sounding board with a circular sound hole in the centre, a flat back, and a fretted fingerboard. [C17: from Sp. *guitarra*, from Ar. *qītār*, from Gk: CITHARA]
▸ **gui'tarist** *n*

Guitry ★ (*French* gitri) *n* **Sacha** (saʃa). 1885–1957, French actor, dramatist, and film director, born in Russia: plays include *Nono* (1905).

Guiyang ('gweɪ'jæŋ), **Kweiyang**, *or* **Kuei-yang** ★ *n* a city in S China, capital of Guizhou province: reached by rail in 1959, with subsequent industrial growth. Pop.: 1 530 000 (1991 est.).

Guizhou ('gweɪ'dʒəʊ), **Kweichow**, *or* **Kueichou** ★ *n* a province of SW China, between the Yangtze and Xi Rivers: a high plateau. Capital: Guiyang. Pop.: 34 580 000 (1995 est.). Area: 174 000 sq. km (69 278 sq. miles).

★ people and places

Guizot ★ (*French* gizo) *n* François Pierre Guillaume (frɑ̃swa pjer gijom). 1787–1874, French statesman and historian. As chief minister (1840–48), his reactionary policies contributed to the outbreak of the revolution of 1848.

Gujarat *or* **Gujerat** ★ (ˌɡudʒəˈrɑːt) *n* **1** a state of W India: formed in 1960 from the N and W parts of Bombay State; one of India's most industrialized states. Capital: Gandhinagar. Pop.: 44 235 000 (1994 est.). Area: 196 024 sq. km (75 268 sq. miles). **2** a region of W India, north of the Narmada River: generally includes the areas north of Bombay city where Gujarati is spoken.

Gujranwala ★ (guːdʒˈrɑːnˌwʌlə) *n* a city in NE Pakistan: textile manufacturing. Pop.: 1 663 000 (1995 est.).

Gulag ('guːlæɡ) *n* **1** (formerly) the central administrative department of the Soviet security service, responsible for maintaining prisons and labour camps. **2** (*not cap.*) any system used to silence dissidents. [C20: from Russian *G(lavnoye) U(pravleniye Ispravitelno-Trudovykh) Lag(erei)* Main Administration for Corrective Labour Camps]

Gulbenkian ★ (ɡʊlˈbɛŋkɪən) *n* **1 Calouste Sarkis** (kæˈluːst ˈsɑːkɪz). 1869–1955, British industrialist, born in Turkey. He endowed the international Gulbenkian Foundation for the advancement of the arts, science, and education. **2** his son, **Nubar Sarkis** ('nuːbɑː 'sɑːkɪz). 1896–1972, British industrialist, diplomat, and philanthropist.

gulch (ɡʌltʃ) *n US & Canad.* a narrow ravine cut by a fast stream. [C19: from ?]

gulden ('ɡʊldⁿn) *n*, *pl* **guldens** *or* **gulden**. a variant of **guilder**.

Gülek Bogaz ★ (ɡuːˈlɛk bəʊˈɡɑːz) *n* the Turkish name for the **Cilician Gates**.

gules (ɡjuːlz) *adj* (*usually postpositive*), *n Heraldry*. red. [C14: from OF *gueules* red fur worn around the neck, from *gole* throat, from L *gula* GULLET]

gulf (ɡʌlf) *n* **1** a large deep bay. **2** a deep chasm. **3** something that divides or separates, such as a lack of understanding. **4** something that engulfs, such as a whirlpool. ◆ *vb* **5** (*tr*) to swallow up; engulf. [C14: from OF *golfe*, from It. *golfo*, from Gk *kolpos*]

Gulf ★ (ɡʌlf) *n* **the. 1** the Persian Gulf. **2** *Austral.* **2a** the Gulf of Carpentaria. **2b** (*modifier*) of, relating to, or adjoining the Gulf: *Gulf country.* **3** *NZ.* the Hauraki Gulf.

Gulf States ★ *pl n* **the. 1** the oil-producing states around the Persian Gulf: Iran, Iraq, Kuwait, Saudi Arabia, Bahrain, Qatar, the United Arab Emirates, and Oman. **2** the states of the US that border on the Gulf of Mexico: Alabama, Florida, Louisiana, Mississippi, and Texas.

Gulf Stream *n* a relatively warm ocean current flowing northeastwards from the Gulf of Mexico towards NW Europe. Also called: **North Atlantic Drift.**

Gulf War *n* **1** the war (1991) between US-led UN forces and Iraq, following Iraq's invasion of Kuwait. **2** See **Iran-Iraq War.**

Gulf War syndrome *n* a group of various debilitating symptoms experienced by many soldiers who served in the Gulf War of 1991. It is claimed to be associated with damage to the central nervous system, caused by exposure to pesticides containing organophosphates.

gulfweed ('ɡʌlfˌwiːd) *n* a brown seaweed having air bladders and forming dense floating masses in tropical Atlantic waters, esp. the Gulf Stream. Also called: **sargasso, sargasso weed.**

gull[1] (ɡʌl) *n* an aquatic bird such as the common gull or mew having long pointed wings, short legs, and a mostly white plumage. [C15: of Celtic origin]

gull[2] (ɡʌl) *Arch.* ◆ *n* **1** a person who is easily fooled or cheated. ◆ *vb* **2** (*tr*) to fool, cheat, or hoax. [C16: ?from dialect *gull* unfledged bird, prob. from *gul*, from ON *gulr* yellow]

gullet ('ɡʌlɪt) *n* **1** a less formal name for the **oesophagus. 2** the throat or pharynx. [C14: from OF *goulet*, dim. of *goule*, from L *gula* throat]

gullible ('ɡʌlɪbⁿl) *adj* easily taken in or tricked.
▸ ˌgulliˈbility *n* ▸ 'gullibly *adv*

gully *or* **gulley** ('ɡʌlɪ) *n*, *pl* **gullies** *or* **gulleys. 1** a channel or small valley, esp. one cut by heavy rainwater. **2** *NZ.* a bush-clad small valley. **3** *Cricket.* **3a** a fielding position

between the slips and point. **3b** a fielder in this position. ◆ *vb* **gullies, gullying, gullied** *or* **gulleys, gulleying, gulleyed. 4** (*tr*) to make channels in (the ground, sand, etc.). [C16: from F *goulet* neck of a bottle; see GULLET]

gulp (ɡʌlp) *vb* **1** (*tr*; often foll. by *down*) to swallow rapidly, esp. in large mouthfuls. **2** (*tr*; often foll. by *back*) to stifle or choke: *to gulp back sobs.* **3** (*intr*) to swallow air convulsively because of nervousness, surprise, etc. **4** (*intr*) to make a noise, as when swallowing too quickly. ◆ *n* **5** the act of gulping. **6** the quantity taken in a gulp. [C15: from MDu. *gulpen*, imit.]
▸ 'gulper *n* ▸ 'gulpingly *adv* ▸ 'gulpy *adj*

gum[1] (ɡʌm) *n* **1** any of various sticky substances that exude from certain plants, hardening on exposure to air and dissolving or forming viscous masses in water. **2** any of various products, such as adhesives, that are made from such substances. **3** any sticky substance used as an adhesive; mucilage; glue. **4** See **chewing gum, bubble gum,** and **gumtree. 5** *NZ.* See **kauri gum. 6** *Chiefly Brit.* a gumdrop. ◆ *vb* **gums, gumming, gummed. 7** to cover or become covered, clogged, or stiffened as with gum. **8** (*tr*) to stick together or in place with gum. **9** (*intr*) to emit or form gum. ◆ See also **gum up.** [C14: from OF *gomme*, from L *gummi*, from Gk *kommi*, from Egyptian *kemai*]

gum[2] (ɡʌm) *n* the fleshy tissue that covers the jawbones around the bases of the teeth. Technical name: **gingiva.** Related adj: **gingival.** [OE *gōma* jaw]

gum ammoniac *n* another name for **ammoniac.**

gum arabic *n* a gum exuded by certain acacia trees, used in the manufacture of ink, food thickeners, pills, emulsifiers, etc. Also called: **gum acacia.**

gumbo ('ɡʌmbəʊ) *n*, *pl* **gumbos.** *US.* **1** the mucilaginous pods of okra. **2** another name for **okra. 3** a soup or stew thickened with okra pods. **4** a fine soil in the W prairies that becomes muddy when wet. [C19: from Louisiana F *gombo*, of Bantu origin]

gumboil ('ɡʌmˌbɔɪl) *n* an abscess on the gums.

gumboots ('ɡʌmˌbuːts) *pl n* another name for **Wellington boots** (sense 1).

gum-digger *n NZ.* a person who digs for fossilized kauri gum in a gum-field, an area where it is found buried.

gumdrop ('ɡʌmˌdrɒp) *n* a small jelly-like sweet containing gum arabic and various colourings and flavourings. Also called (esp. *Brit.*): **gum.**

gummy[1] ('ɡʌmɪ) *adj* **gummier, gummiest. 1** sticky or tacky. **2** consisting of, coated with, or clogged by gum or a similar substance. **3** producing gum. [C14: from GUM[1] + -Y[1]]
▸ 'gumminess *n*

gummy[2] ('ɡʌmɪ) *adj* **gummier, gummiest. 1** toothless. ◆ *n*, *pl* **gummies. 2** Also called: **gummy shark.** *Austral.* a small crustacean-eating shark with flat crushing teeth. [C20: from GUM[2] + -Y[1]]

gum nut *n Austral.* the hardened seed container of the gumtree *Eucalyptus gummifera.*

gumption ('ɡʌmpʃən) *n Inf.* **1** *Brit.* common sense or resourcefulness. **2** initiative or courage. [C18: orig. Scot., from ?]

gum resin *n* a mixture of resin and gum obtained from various plants and trees.

gumtree ('ɡʌmˌtriː) *n* **1** any of various trees that yield gum, such as the eucalyptus, sweet gum, and sour gum. Sometimes shortened to **gum. 2 up a gumtree.** *Inf.* in a very awkward position; in difficulties.

gum up *vb* (*tr, adv*) **1** to cover, dab, or stiffen with gum. **2** *Inf.* to make a mess of; bungle (often in **gum up the works**).

gun (ɡʌn) *n* **1a** a weapon with a metallic tube or barrel from which a missile is discharged, usually by force of an explosion. It may be portable or mounted. **1b** (*as modifier*): *a gun barrel.* **2** the firing of a gun as a salute or signal, as in military ceremonial. **3** a member of or a place in a shooting party or syndicate. **4** any device used to project something under pressure: *a spray gun.* **5** *US sl.* an armed criminal; gunman. **6** *Austral. & NZ sl.* **6a** an expert. **6b** (*as modifier*): *a gun shearer.* **7** give it the gun. *Sl.* to increase speed, effort, etc., to a considerable or maximum degree. **8 go great guns.** *Sl.* to act or function with great speed, intensity, etc. **9 jump** *or* **beat the gun. 9a** (of a runner, etc.) to set off before the starting signal is given. **9b** *Inf.* to act prematurely. **10 stick to one's guns.** *Inf.* to maintain one's opinions or intentions in spite of opposition. ◆ *vb* **guns, gunning, gunned. 11** (when *tr*, often foll. by *down*) to shoot (someone) with a gun. **12** (*tr*) to press hard on the accelerator of (an engine): *to gun the engine.* **13** (*intr*) to hunt with a gun. ◆ See also **gun for. [C14:** prob. from a female pet name, from the Scand. name *Gunnhildr* (from ON *gunnr* war + *hildr* war)]

gunboat ('gʌn,bəʊt) *n* a small shallow-draft vessel carrying mounted guns and used by coastal patrols, etc.

gunboat diplomacy *n* diplomacy conducted by threats of military intervention.

guncotton ('gʌn,kɒtᵊn) *n* cellulose nitrate containing a relatively large amount of nitrogen: used as an explosive.

gun dog *n* **1** a dog trained to work with a hunter or gamekeeper, esp. in retrieving, pointing at, or flushing game. **2** a dog belonging to any breed adapted to these activities.

gunfight ('gʌn,faɪt) *n Chiefly US.* a fight between persons using firearms.
▸ **'gun,fighter** *n*

gunfire ('gʌn,faɪə) *n* **1** the firing of one or more guns, esp. when done repeatedly. **2** the use of guns, as contrasted with other military tactics.

gun for *vb* (*intr, prep*) **1** to search for in order to reprimand, punish, or kill. **2** to try earnestly for: *he was gunning for promotion.*

gunge (gʌndʒ) *Inf.* ◆ *n* **1** sticky, rubbery, or congealed matter. ◆ *vb* **gunges, gunging, gunged. 2** (*tr; usually passive*; foll. by *up*) to block or encrust with gunge; clog. **[C20:** imit., ? infl. by GOO & SPONGE]
▸ **'gungy** *adj*

gunk (gʌŋk) *n Inf.* slimy, oily, or filthy matter. **[C20:** ? imit.]

gunlock ('gʌn,lɒk) *n* the mechanism in some firearms that causes the charge to be exploded.

gunman ('gʌnmən) *n, pl* **gunmen. 1** a man armed with a gun, esp. unlawfully. **2** a man skilled with a gun.

gunmetal ('gʌn,metᵊl) *n* **1** a type of bronze containing copper, tin, and zinc. **2a** a dark grey colour. **2b** (*as adj*): *gunmetal chiffon.*

Gunn ★ (gʌn) *n* Thom(son William). born 1929, British poet resident in the US. His works include *Fighting Terms* (1954), *Jack Straw's Castle* (1976), and *The Man with Night Sweats* (1992).

Gunnar ★ ('gʊnɑː) *n Norse myth.* brother of Gudrun and husband of Brynhild, won for him by Sigurd. He corresponds to Gunther in the *Nibelungenlied.*

gunnel¹ ('gʌnᵊl) *n* any eel-like fish occurring in coastal regions of northern seas. **[C17:** from ?]

gunnel² ('gʌnᵊl) *n* a variant spelling of **gunwale.**

Gunnell ★ ('gʌnᵊl) *n* Sally. born 1966, English hurdler; Olympic gold medallist (1992).

gunner ('gʌnə) *n* **1** a serviceman who works with, uses, or specializes in guns. **2** *Naval.* (formerly) a warrant officer responsible for the training of gun crews, their performance in action, and accounting for ammunition. **3** (in the British Army) an artilleryman, esp. a private. **4** a person who hunts with a rifle or shotgun.

gunnery ('gʌnərɪ) *n* **1** the art and science of the efficient design and use of ordnance, esp. artillery. **2** guns collectively. **3** the use and firing of guns.

gunny ('gʌnɪ) *n, pl* **gunnies.** *Chiefly US.* **1** a coarse hardwearing fabric usually made from jute and used for sacks, etc. **2** Also called: **gunny sack.** a sack made from this fabric. **[C18:** from Hindi, from Sansk. *gōnī* sack, prob. of Dravidian origin]

gunplay ('gʌn,pleɪ) *n Chiefly US.* the use of firearms, as by criminals, etc.

gunpoint ('gʌn,pɔɪnt) *n* **1** the muzzle of a gun. **2 at gunpoint.** being under or using the threat of being shot.

gunpowder ('gʌn,paʊdə) *n* an explosive mixture of potassium nitrate, charcoal, and sulphur: used in time fuses and in fireworks.

gun room *n* **1** (esp. in the Royal Navy) the mess allocated to junior officers. **2** a room where guns are stored.

gunrunning ('gʌn,rʌnɪŋ) *n* the smuggling of guns and ammunition or other weapons of war into a country.
▸ **'gun,runner** *n*

gunshot ('gʌn,ʃɒt) *n* **1a** shot fired from a gun. **1b** (*as modifier*): *gunshot wounds.* **2** the range of a gun. **3** the shooting of a gun.

gunslinger ('gʌn,slɪŋə) *n Sl.* a gunfighter or gunman, esp. in the Old West.

gunsmith ('gʌn,smɪθ) *n* a person who makes or repairs firearms, esp. portable guns.

gunstock ('gʌn,stɒk) *n* the wooden handle or support to which is attached the barrel of a rifle.

Gunter ★ ('gʌntə) *n* Edmund. 1581–1626, English mathematician and astronomer, who invented various measuring instruments.

Gunter's chain *n Surveying.* a measuring chain 22 yards in length, or this length as a unit. **[C17:** after E. GUNTER]

Gunther ★ ('gʊntə) *n* (in the *Nibelungenlied*) a king of Burgundy, allied with Siegfried, who won for him his wife Brunhild. He corresponds to Gunnar in Norse mythology.

Guntur ★ (gʊn'tʊə) *n* a city in E India, in central Andhra Pradesh: founded by the French in the 18th century; ceded to Britain in 1788. Pop.: 471 051 (1991).

gunwale *or* **gunnel** ('gʌnᵊl) *n Naut.* the top of the side of a boat or ship. **[C15:** from GUN + WALE from its use to support guns]

gunyah ('gʌnjə) *n Austral.* a bush hut or shelter. **[C19:** from Abor.]

guppy ('gʌpɪ) *n, pl* **guppies.** a small brightly coloured freshwater fish of N South America and the Caribbean: a popular aquarium fish. **[C20:** after R. J. L. *Guppy*, 19th-cent. clergyman of Trinidad who first presented specimens to the British Museum]

Gurdjieff ★ ('gɜːdjɛf) *n* Georgei Ivanovitch. ?1877–1949, Russian mystic: founded a teaching centre in Paris (1922).

gurdwara ('gɜːdwɑːrə) *n* a Sikh place of worship. **[C20:** from Punjabi *gurduārā*, from Sansk. *guru* teacher + *dvāra* door]

gurgle ('gɜːgᵊl) *vb* **gurgles, gurgling, gurgled.** (*intr*) **1** (of liquids, esp. of streams, etc.) to make low bubbling noises when flowing. **2** to utter low throaty bubbling noises, esp. as a sign of contentment: *the baby gurgled with delight.* ◆ *n* **3** the act or sound of gurgling. **[C16:** ?from Vulgar L *gurgulāre*, from L *gurguliō* gullet]

Gurkha ('gɜːkə) *n* **1** a member of a Hindu people, descended from Brahmins and Rajputs, living chiefly in Nepal. **2** a member of a Gurkha regiment in the Indian or British army.

gurnard ('gɜːnəd) *or* **gurnet** ('gɜːnɪt) *n, pl* **gurnard, gurnards** *or* **gurnets, gurnets.** a European marine fish having a heavily armoured head and finger-like pectoral fins. **[C14:** from OF *gornard*, from *grognier* to grunt, from L *grunnīre*]

guru ('gʊruː, 'guːruː) *n* **1** a Hindu or Sikh religious teacher or leader, giving personal spiritual guidance to his disciples. **2** *Often derog.* a leader or chief theoretician of a movement, esp. a spiritual or religious cult. **3** *Often facetious.* a leading authority in a particular field: *a cricketing guru.* **[C17:** from Hindi *gurū*, from Sansk. *guruh* weighty]

gush (gʌʃ) *vb* **1** to pour out or cause to pour out suddenly and profusely, usually with a rushing sound. **2** to act or utter in an overeffusive, affected, or sentimental manner. ◆ *n* **3** a sudden copious flow or emission, esp. of liquid. **4** something that flows out or is emitted. **5** an extravagant and insincere expression of admiration, sentiment, etc. **[C14:** prob. imit.; cf. ON *gjósa*]
▸ **'gushing** *adj* ▸ **'gushingly** *adv*

gusher ('gʌʃə) *n* **1** a person who gushes, as in being effusive or sentimental. **2** something, such as a spurting oil well, that gushes.

gushy ('gʌʃɪ) *adj* **gushier, gushiest.** *Inf.* displaying excessive admiration or sentimentality.
▸ **'gushily** *adv* ▸ **'gushiness** *n*

★ people and places

gusset ('gʌsɪt) n **1** an inset piece of material used esp. to strengthen or enlarge a garment. **2** a triangular metal plate for strengthening a corner joist. ♦ vb **3** (tr) to put a gusset in (a garment). [C15: from OF gousset a piece of mail, dim. of gousse pod, from ?]
▶ 'gusseted adj

gust (gʌst) n **1** a sudden blast of wind. **2** a sudden rush of smoke, sound, etc. **3** an outburst of emotion. ♦ vb **4** (intr) to blow in gusts. [C16: from ON gustr; rel. to gjósa to GUSH; see GEYSER]

gustation (gʌ'steɪʃən) n the act of tasting or the faculty of taste. [C16: from L gustātiō, from gustāre to taste]
▶ 'gustatory ('gʌstətərɪ) adj

Gustavo A. Madero ★ (Spanish gus'taβo a ma'ðero) n the former name (1931–71) of **Guadalupe Hidalgo.**

Gustavus I ★ n (gu'stɑːvəs) n called Gustavus Vasa. ?1496–1560, king of Sweden (1523–60). He was elected king after driving the Danes from Sweden (1520–23).

Gustavus II ★ n See **Gustavus Adolphus.**

Gustavus VI ★ n title of Gustaf Adolf. 1882–1973, king of Sweden (1950–73).

Gustavus Adolphus (ə'dɒlfəs) or **Gustavus II** ★ n 1594–1632, king of Sweden (1611–32). He waged successful wars with Denmark, Russia, and Poland and in the Thirty Years' War led a Protestant army: killed at the battle of Lützen.

gusto ('gʌstəʊ) n vigorous enjoyment, zest, or relish: the aria was sung with great gusto. [C17: from Sp.: taste, from L gustus a tasting]

gusty ('gʌstɪ) adj **gustier, gustiest. 1** blowing in gusts or characterized by blustery weather: a gusty wind. **2** given to sudden outbursts, as of emotion.
▶ 'gustily adv ▶ 'gustiness n

gut (gʌt) n **1a** the lower part of the alimentary canal; intestine. **1b** the entire alimentary canal. Related adj: **visceral. 2** (often pl) the bowels or entrails, esp. of an animal. **3** Sl. the belly; paunch. **4** See **catgut. 5** a silky fibrous substance extracted from silkworms, used in the manufacture of fishing tackle. **6** a narrow channel or passage. **7** (pl) Inf. courage, willpower, or daring; forcefulness. **8** (pl) Inf. the essential part: the guts of a problem. ♦ vb **guts, gutting, gutted.** (tr) **9** to remove the entrails from (fish, etc.). **10** (esp. of fire) to destroy the inside of (a building). **11** to take out the central points of (an article, etc.), esp. in summary form. ♦ adj **12** Inf. instinctive, basic, or fundamental: a gut feeling; capital punishment is a gut issue. [OE gutt; rel. to gēotan to flow]

GUT (gʌt) n acronym for grand unified theory.

Gutenberg ★ ('guːt^ən,bɜːg; German 'guːtənberk) n **Johann** (jo'han), original name Johannes Gensfleisch. ?1398–1468, German printer; inventor of printing by movable type.

Gütersloh ★ (German 'gyːtərsloː) n a town in NW Germany, in North Rhine-Westphalia. Pop.: 83 400 (1989 est.).

Guthrie ★ ('gʌθrɪ) n **1** Samuel. 1782–1848, US chemist: invented percussion priming powder and a punch lock for exploding it, and discovered chloroform (1831). **2** Sir (**William**) Tyrone. 1900–71, British theatrical director. **3** **Woody,** full name Woodrow Wilson Guthrie. 1912–67, US folk singer and songwriter.

Guthrun ★ ('guðrʊn) n a variant of **Gudrun.**

gutless ('gʌtlɪs) adj Inf. lacking courage or determination.

gut reaction n the first, instinctive, reaction to a situation.

gutsy ('gʌtsɪ) adj **gutsier, gutsiest.** Sl. **1** gluttonous; greedy. **2** full of courage or boldness. **3** passionate; lusty.

gutta-percha ('gʌtə'pɜːtʃə) n **1** any of several tropical trees with leathery leaves. **2** a whitish rubber substance derived from the coagulated milky latex of any of these trees: used in electrical insulation and dentistry. [C19: from Malay getah gum + percha tree that produces it]

guttate ('gʌteɪt) adj Biol. (esp. of plants) covered with small drops or droplike markings. [C19: from L guttātus dappled, from gutta a drop]

gutted ('gʌtɪd) adj Inf. disappointed and upset.

gutter ('gʌtə) n **1** a channel along the eaves or on the roof of a building, used to collect and carry away rainwater. **2** a channel running along the kerb or the centre of a road to collect and carry away rainwater. **3** either of the two channels running parallel to a tenpin bowling lane. **4** Printing. the white space between the facing pages of an open book. **5** Surfing. a dangerous deep channel formed by currents and waves. **6 the gutter.** a povertystricken, degraded, or criminal environment. ♦ vb **7** (tr) to make gutters in. **8** (intr) to flow in a stream. **9** (intr) (of a candle) to melt away as the wax forms channels and runs down in drops. **10** (intr) (of a flame) to flicker and be about to go out. [C13: from Anglo-F goutiere, from OF goute a drop, from L gutta]
▶ 'guttering n

gutter press n the section of the popular press that seeks sensationalism in its coverage.

guttersnipe ('gʌtə,snaɪp) n a child who spends most of his time in the streets, esp. in a slum area.

guttural ('gʌtərəl) adj **1** Anat. of or relating to the throat. **2** Phonetics. pronounced in the throat or the back of the mouth. **3** raucous. ♦ n **4** Phonetics. a guttural consonant. [C16: from NL gutturālis, from L guttur gullet]
▶ 'gutturally adv

guy¹ (gaɪ) n **1** Inf. a man or youth. **2** Brit. a crude effigy of Guy Fawkes, usually made of old clothes stuffed with straw or rags, that is burnt on top of a bonfire on Guy Fawkes Day. **3** Brit. a person in shabby or ludicrously odd clothes. **4** (pl) Inf. persons of either sex. ♦ vb **5** (tr) to make fun of; ridicule. [C19: short for Guy FAWKES]

guy² (gaɪ) n **1** a rope, chain, wire, etc., for anchoring an object in position or for steadying or guiding it. ♦ vb **2** (tr) to anchor, steady, or guide with a guy or guys. [C14: prob. from Low G; cf. OF guie guide, from guier to GUIDE]

Guyana ★ (gaɪ'ænə) n a republic in NE South America, on the Atlantic: colonized chiefly by the Dutch in the 17th and 18th centuries; became a British colony in 1831 and an independent republic within the Commonwealth in 1966. Official language: English. Religions: Christian and Hindu. Currency: dollar. Capital: Georgetown. Pop.: 773 000 (1997). Area: about 215 000 sq. km (83 000 sq. miles). Former name (until 1966): **British Guiana.**
▶ **Guyanese** (,gaɪə'niːz) or **Guy'anan** adj, n

Guyenne ★ (French gɥijɛn) n a variant spelling of **Guienne.**

Guzmán Blanco ★ (Spanish guð'man 'blaŋko) n **Antonio** (an'tonjo). 1829–99, Venezuelan statesman; president (1873–77; 1879–84; 1886–87). He was virtual dictator of Venezuela from 1870 until his overthrow (1889).

guzzle ('gʌzˀl) vb **guzzles, guzzling, guzzled.** to consume (food or drink) excessively or greedily. [C16: from ?]
▶ 'guzzler n

Gwalior ★ ('gwɑːlɪˌɔː) n **1** a city in N central India, in Madhya Pradesh: built around the fort, which dates from before 525; industrial and commercial centre. Pop.: 690 765 (1991). **2** a former princely state of central India, established in the 18th century: merged with Madhya Bharat in 1948, which in turn merged with Madhya Pradesh in 1956.

Gwent ★ (gwɛnt) n a former (1974–96) county of SE Wales.

Gweru ★ ('gweɪruː) n a city in central Zimbabwe. Pop.: 124 735 (1992). Former name (until 1982): **Gwelo** ('gwiːləʊ).

Gwyn ★ (gwɪn) n **Nell,** original name Eleanor Gwynne. 1650–87, English actress; mistress of Charles II.

Gwynedd ★ ('gwɪnɛð) n a county of NW Wales, formed in 1974 from Anglesey, Caernarvonshire, part of Denbighshire, and most of Merionethshire, reorganized in 1996 and lost Anglesey and areas in the NE: the mainland is generally mountainous with many lakes, much of it lying in the Snowdonia National Park. Administrative centre: Caernarfon. Pop.: 118 005 (1996 est.). Area: 2550 sq. km (869 sq. miles).

gybe, gibe, or **jibe** (dʒaɪb) Naut. ♦ vb **gybes, gybing, gybed, gibes, gibing, gibed** or **jibes, jibing, jibed. 1** (intr) (of a fore-and-aft sail) to shift suddenly from one side of the vessel to the other when running before the wind. **2** to cause (a sailing vessel) to gybe or (of a sailing vessel) to undergo gybing. ◆ *n* **3** an instance of gybing. [C17: from obs. Du. *gijben* (now *gijpen*), from ?]

gym (dʒɪm) *n, adj* short for **gymnasium, gymnastics, gymnastic.**

gymkhana (dʒɪmˈkɑːnə) *n* **1** *Chiefly Brit.* an event in which horses and riders display skill and aptitude in various races and contests. **2** (in Anglo-India) a place providing sporting and athletic facilities. [C19: from Hindi *gend-khānā*, lit.: ball house]

gymnasium (dʒɪmˈneɪzɪəm) *n, pl* **gymnasiums** or **gymnasia** (-zɪə). **1** a large room or hall equipped with bars, weights, ropes, etc., for physical training. **2** (in various European countries) a secondary school that prepares pupils for university. [C16: from L: school for gymnastics, from Gk *gumnasion*, from *gumnazein* to exercise naked]

gymnast (ˈdʒɪmnæst) *n* a person who is skilled or trained in gymnastics.

gymnastic (dʒɪmˈnæstɪk) *adj* of, like, or involving gymnastics.
▸ **gym'nastically** *adv*

gymnastics (dʒɪmˈnæstɪks) *n* **1** (*functioning as sing*) practice or training in exercises that develop physical strength and agility or mental capacity. **2** (*functioning as pl*) gymnastic exercises.

gymno- *combining form.* naked, bare, or exposed: *gymnosperm.* [from Gk *gumnos* naked]

gymnosperm (ˈdʒɪmnəʊˌspɜːm, ˈgɪm-) *n* any seed-bearing plant in which the ovules are borne naked on open scales, which are often arranged in cones; any conifer or related plant. Cf. **angiosperm.**
▸ ˌgymno'spermous *adj*

gympie (ˈgɪmpɪ) *n* a tall Australian tree with stinging hairs on its leaves. Also: **nettle tree.**

gym shoe *n* another name for **plimsoll.**

gymslip (ˈdʒɪmˌslɪp) *n* a tunic or pinafore dress worn by schoolgirls, often part of a school uniform.

gyn- *combining form.* a variant of **gyno-** before a vowel.

gynaeco- or US **gyneco-** *combining form.* relating to women; female: *gynaecology.* [from Gk, from *gunē, gunaik-* woman, female]

gynaecology or US **gynecology** (ˌgaɪnɪˈkɒlədʒɪ) *n* the branch of medicine concerned with diseases and conditions specific to women.
▸ **gynaecological** (ˌgaɪnɪkəˈlɒdʒɪkʰl), **gynaeco'logic** or US **gyneco'logical, gyneco'logic** *adj* ▸ ˌgynae'cologist or US ˌgyne'cologist *n*

gynandromorph (dʒɪˈnændrəʊˌmɔːf, gaɪ-) *n* an abnormal organism, esp. an insect, that has both male and female physical characteristics.

gynandrous (dʒaɪˈnændrəs, gaɪ-) *adj* (of flowers such as the orchid) having the stamens and styles united in a column. [C19: from Gk *gunandros* of uncertain sex, from *gunē* woman + *anēr* man]

gyno- or before a vowel **gyn-** *combining form.* **1** relating to women; female: *gynarchy.* **2** denoting a female reproductive organ: *gynophore.* [from Gk, from *gunē* woman]

gynoecium, gynaeceum, or esp. US **gynecium** (dʒaɪˈniːsɪəm, gaɪ-) *n, pl* **gynoecia, gynaecea** or esp. US **gynecia** (-sɪə). the carpels of a flowering plant collectively. [C18: NL, from Gk *gunaikeion* women's quarters, from *gunaik-, gunē* woman + *-eion,* suffix indicating place]

gynophore (ˈdʒaɪnəʊˌfɔː, ˈgaɪ-) *n* a stalk in some plants that bears the gynoecium above the level of the other flower parts.

-gynous *adj combining form.* **1** of or relating to women or females: *androgynous; misogynous.* **2** relating to female organs: *epigynous.* [from NL, from Gk, from *gunē* woman]
▸ **-gyny** *n combining form.*

Györ ★ (*Hungarian* djøːr) *n* an industrial town in NW Hungary: medieval Benedictine abbey. Pop.: 127 000 (1996 est.).

gyp[1] or **gip** (dʒɪp) *Sl.* ◆ *vb* **gyps, gypping, gypped** or **gips, gipping, gipped. 1** (*tr*) to swindle, cheat, or defraud. ◆ *n* **2** an act of cheating. **3** a person who gyps. [C18: back formation from GYPSY]

gyp[2] or **gip** (dʒɪp) *n Brit. & NZ sl.* severe pain; torture: *his arthritis gave him gyp.* [C19: prob. a contraction of *gee up!;* see GEE[1]]

gyp[3] (dʒɪp) *n* a college servant at the universities of Cambridge or Durham. [C18: ?from obs. *gippo* scullion]

gypsophila (dʒɪpˈsɒfɪlə) *n* any of a Mediterranean genus of plants, having small white or pink fragrant flowers. [C18: NL, from Gk *gupsos* chalk + *philos* loving]

gypsum (ˈdʒɪpsəm) *n* a mineral consisting of hydrated calcium sulphate that occurs in sedimentary rocks and clay and is used principally in making plasters and cements, esp. plaster of Paris. Formula: $CaSO_4.2H_2O$. [C17: from L, from Gk *gupsos* chalk, plaster, cement, of Semitic origin]
▸ **gypseous** (ˈdʒɪpsɪəs) *adj*

Gypsy or **Gipsy** (ˈdʒɪpsɪ) *n, pl* **Gypsies** or **Gipsies.** (*sometimes not cap.*) **1a** a member of a people scattered throughout Europe and North America, who maintain a nomadic way of life in industrialized societies. They migrated from NW India about the 9th century onwards. **1b** (*as modifier*): *a Gypsy fortune-teller.* **2** the language of the Gypsies; Romany. **3** a person who looks or behaves like a Gypsy. [C16: from EGYPTIAN, since they were thought to have come orig. from Egypt]
▸ **'Gypsyish** or **'Gipsyish** *adj*

gypsy moth or **gipsy moth** *n* a European moth whose caterpillars are pests on deciduous trees.

gyrate *vb* (dʒaɪˈreɪt) **gyrates, gyrating, gyrated. 1** (*intr*) to rotate or spiral, esp. about a fixed point or axis. ◆ *adj* (ˈdʒaɪrɪt). **2** *Biol.* curved or coiled into a circle. [C19: from LL *gȳrāre,* from L *gȳrus* circle, from Gk *guros*]
▸ **gy'ration** *n* ▸ **gy'rator** *n* ▸ **gyratory** (ˈdʒaɪrətərɪ) *adj*

gyre (ˈdʒaɪə) *Chiefly literary.* ◆ *n* **1** a circular or spiral movement or path. **2** a ring, circle, or spiral. ◆ *vb* **gyres, gyring, gyred. 3** (*intr*) to whirl. [C16: from L *gȳrus* circle, from Gk *guros*]

gyrfalcon or **gerfalcon** (ˈdʒɜːˌfɔːlkən, -ˌfɔːkən) *n* a very large rare falcon of northern and arctic regions. [C14: from OF *gerfaucon,* ?from ON *geirfalki,* from *geirr* spear + *falki* falcon]

gyro (ˈdʒaɪrəʊ) *n, pl* **gyros. 1** See **gyrocompass. 2** See **gyroscope.**

gyro- or before a vowel **gyr-** *combining form.* **1** indicating rotating or gyrating motion: *gyroscope.* **2** indicating a gyrocompass: *gyrocompass.* [from Gk, from *guros* circle]

gyrocompass (ˈdʒaɪrəʊˌkʌmpəs) *n* a nonmagnetic compass that uses a motor-driven gyroscope to indicate true north.

gyrodyne (ˈdʒaɪrəʊˌdaɪn) *n* an aircraft that uses a powered rotor to take off and manoeuvre, but uses autorotation when cruising.

gyromagnetic (ˌdʒaɪrəʊmægˈnetɪk) *adj* of or caused by magnetic properties resulting from the spin of a charged particle, such as an electron.

gyroscope (ˈdʒaɪrəˌskəʊp) *n* a device containing a disc rotating on an axis that can turn freely in any direction so that the disc maintains the same orientation irrespective of the movement of the surrounding structure.
▸ **gyroscopic** (ˌdʒaɪrəˈskɒpɪk) *adj* ▸ **gyro'scopically** *adv*

gyrostabilizer or **gyrostabiliser** (ˌdʒaɪrəʊ-ˈsteɪbɪˌlaɪzə) *n* a gyroscopic device used to stabilize the rolling motion of a ship.

gyve (dʒaɪv) *Arch.* ◆ *vb* **gyves, gyving, gyved. 1** (*tr*) to shackle or fetter. ◆ *n* **2** (*usually pl*) fetter. [C13: from ?]

Hh

h or **H** (eɪtʃ) *n, pl* **h's, H's,** or **Hs. 1** the eighth letter of the English alphabet. **2** a speech sound represented by this letter. **3a** something shaped like an H. **3b** (*in combination*): *an H-beam.*

h *symbol for:* **1** *Physics.* Planck constant. **2** hecto-. **3** hour.

H *symbol for:* **1** *Chem.* hydrogen. **2** *Physics.* magnetic field strength. **3** *Electronics.* henry. **4** (on Brit. pencils, signifying degree of hardness of lead) hard.

h. or **H.** *abbrev. for:* **1** harbour. **2** height. **3** high. **4** hour. **5** hundred. **6** husband.

ha¹ or **hah** (hɑː) *interj* **1** an exclamation expressing derision, triumph, surprise, etc. **2** (*reiterated*) a representation of the sound of laughter.

ha² *symbol for* hectare.

Haakon VII ★ (ˈhɔːkɒn) *n* 1872–1957, king of Norway (1905–57). During the Nazi occupation of Norway (1940–45), he led Norwegian resistance from England.

haar (hɑː) *n Eastern Brit.* a cold sea mist or fog off the North Sea. [C17: rel. to Du. dialect *harig* damp]

Haarlem ★ (*Dutch* ˈhɑːrlɛm) *n* a city in the W Netherlands, capital of North Holland province. Pop.: 148 947 (1995 est.).

Hab. *Bible. abbrev. for* Habakkuk.

Habakkuk ★ (ˈhæbəkək) *n Old Testament.* **1** a Hebrew prophet. **2** the book containing his oracles and canticle.

Habana ★ (aˈβana) *n* the Spanish name for **Havana.**

habanera (ˌhæbəˈnɛərə) *n* **1** a slow Cuban dance in duple time. **2** a piece of music for this dance. [from Sp. *danza habanera* dance from Havana]

habeas corpus (ˈheɪbɪəs ˈkɔːpəs) *n Law.* a writ ordering a person to be brought before a court or judge, esp. so that the court may ascertain whether his detention is lawful. [C15: from the opening of the L writ, lit.: you may have the body]

haberdasher (ˈhæbəˌdæʃə) *n* **1** *Brit.* a dealer in small articles for sewing, such as buttons and ribbons. **2** *US.* a men's outfitter. [C14: from Anglo-F *hapertas* small items of merchandise, from ?]

haberdashery (ˈhæbəˌdæʃərɪ) *n, pl* **haberdasheries.** the goods or business kept by a haberdasher.

habergeon (ˈhæbədʒən) *n* a light sleeveless coat of mail worn in the 14th century under the plated hauberk. [C14: from OF *haubergeon* a little HAUBERK]

Haber process (ˈhɑːbə) *n* an industrial process for producing ammonia by reacting atmospheric nitrogen with hydrogen at high pressure and temperature in the presence of a catalyst. [after Fritz *Haber* (1868–1934), G chemist]

habiliment (həˈbɪlɪmənt) *n* (*often pl*) dress or attire. [C15: from OF *habillement*, from *habiller* to dress]

habilitate (həˈbɪlɪˌteɪt) *vb* **habilitates, habilitating, habilitated. 1** (*tr*) *US.* to equip and finance (a mine). **2** (*intr*) to qualify for office. [C17: from Med. L *habilitāre* to make fit, from L *habilitās* aptness]
▶ ha·bili·ta·tion *n*

habit (ˈhæbɪt) *n* **1** a tendency or disposition to act in a particular way. **2** established custom, usual practice, etc. **3** *Psychol.* a learned behavioural response to a particular situation. **4** mental disposition or attitude: *a good working habit of mind.* **5a** a practice or substance to which a person is addicted: *drink has become a habit with him.* **5b** the state of being dependent on something, esp. a drug. **6** *Bot., zool.* method of growth, type of existence, or general appearance: *a burrowing habit.* **7** the customary apparel of a particular occupation, rank, etc., now esp. the costume of a nun or monk. **8** Also called: **riding habit.** a woman's riding dress. ◆ *vb* **habits, habiting, habited.** (*tr*) **9** to clothe. **10** an archaic word for **inhabit.** [C13: from L *habitus* custom, from *habēre* to have]

habitable (ˈhæbɪtəbəl) *adj* able to be lived in.
▶ ˌhabitaˈbility or ˈhabitableness *n* ▶ ˈhabitably *adv*

habitant (ˈhæbɪtənt) *n* **1** a less common word for **inhabitant. 2a** an early French settler in Canada or Louisiana. **2b** a descendant of these settlers, esp. a farmer.

habitat (ˈhæbɪˌtæt) *n* **1** the natural home of an animal or plant. **2** the place in which a person, group, class, etc., is normally found. [C18: from L: it inhabits, from *habitāre* to dwell, from *habēre* to have]

habitation (ˌhæbɪˈteɪʃən) *n* **1** a dwelling place. **2** occupation of a dwelling place.

habit-forming *adj* tending to become a habit or addiction.

habitual (həˈbɪtjʊəl) *adj* **1** (*usually prenominal*) done or experienced regularly and repeatedly: *the habitual Sunday walk.* **2** (*usually prenominal*) by habit: *a habitual drinker.* **3** customary; usual.
▶ haˈbitually *adv* ▶ haˈbitualness *n*

habituate (həˈbɪtjʊˌeɪt) *vb* **habituates, habituating, habituated. 1** to accustom; make used to. **2** *US & Canad. arch.* to frequent.
▶ haˌbituˈation *n*

habitude (ˈhæbɪˌtjuːd) *n Rare.* habit; tendency.

habitué (həˈbɪtjʊˌeɪ) *n* a frequent visitor to a place. [C19: from F, from *habituer* to frequent]

Habsburg ★ (ˈhɑːpsbʊrk) *n* the German name for **Hapsburg.**

HAC *abbrev. for* Honourable Artillery Company.

hachure (hæˈʃʊə) *n* shading of short lines drawn on a relief map to indicate gradients. [C19: from F, from *hacher* to chop up]

hacienda (ˌhæsɪˈɛndə) *n* (in Spain or Spanish-speaking countries) **1a** a ranch or large estate. **1b** any substantial manufacturing establishment in the country. **2** the main house on such a ranch or establishment. [C18: from Sp., from L *facienda* things to be done, from *facere* to do]

hack¹ (hæk) *vb* **1** (when *intr*, usually foll. by *at* or *away*) to chop (at) roughly or violently. **2** to cut and clear (a way), as through undergrowth. **3** (in sport, esp. rugby) to foul (an opposing player) by kicking his shins. **4** (*intr*) to cough in short dry bursts. **5** (*tr*) to cut (a story, article, etc.) in a damaging way. **6** (*intr*; usually foll. by *into*) to manipulate a computer program skilfully, esp. to gain unauthorized access to another computer system. ◆ *n* **7** a cut or gash. **8** any tool used for shallow digging, such as a mattock or pick. **9** a chopping blow. **10** a dry spasmodic cough. **11** a kick on the shins, as in rugby. [OE *haccian*]

hack² (hæk) *n* **1** a horse kept for riding. **2** an old or overworked horse. **3** a horse kept for hire. **4** *Brit.* a country ride on horseback. **5** a drudge. **6** a person who produces mediocre literary work. **7** *US inf.* **7a** a cab driver. **7b** a taxi. ◆ *vb* **8** *Brit.* to ride (a horse) cross-country for pleasure. **9** (*tr*) *Inf.* to write (an article, etc.) in the manner of a hack. ◆ *adj* **10** (*prenominal*) banal, mediocre, or unoriginal: *hack writing.* [C17: short for HACKNEY]

hack³ (hæk) *n* **1** a rack used for fodder for livestock. **2** a board on which meat is placed for a hawk. **3** a pile or row of unfired bricks stacked to dry. [C16: var. of HATCH²]

hackamore (ˈhækəˌmɔː) *n US & NZ.* a rope or rawhide halter used for unbroken foals. [C19: from Sp. *jáquima* headstall, ult. from Ar. *shaqīmah*]

hackberry (ˈhækˌbɛrɪ) *n, pl* **hackberries. 1** an American tree having edible cherry-like fruits. **2** the fruit. [C18: var. of C16 *hagberry*, of Scand. origin]

hacker (ˈhækə) *n* **1** a person that hacks. **2** *Sl.* a computer fanatic, esp. one who through a personal computer breaks into the computer system of a company, government, etc.

hackery ('hækərɪ) n **1** *Ironic.* journalism; hackwork. **2** *Inf.* a variant of **hacking**[2].

hacking[1] ('hækɪŋ) *adj* (of a cough) harsh, dry, and spasmodic.

hacking[2] ('hækɪŋ) n the practice of gaining illegal access to a computer system.

hackle ('hæk³l) n **1** any of the long slender feathers on the neck of poultry and other birds. **2** *Angling.* parts of an artificial fly made from hackle feathers, representing the legs and sometimes the wings of a real fly. **3** a feathered ornament worn in the headdress of some Highland regiments. **4** a steel flax comb. ◆ *vb* **hackles, hackling, hackled.** *(tr)* **5** to comb (flax) using a hackle. [C15: *hakell* prob. from OE]

hackles ('hæk³lz) *pl n* **1** the hairs on the back of the neck and the back of a dog, cat, etc., which rise when the animal is angry or afraid. **2** anger or resentment: *to make one's hackles rise.*

hackney ('hæknɪ) n **1** a compact breed of harness horse with a high-stepping trot. **2** a coach or carriage that is for hire. **3** a popular term for **hack**[2] (sense 1). ◆ *vb* **4** *(tr; usually passive)* to make commonplace and banal by too frequent use. [C14: prob. after HACKNEY, where horses were formerly raised]

Hackney ★ ('hæknɪ) n a borough of NE Greater London: formed in 1965 from the former boroughs of Shoreditch, Stoke Newington, and Hackney; nearby are **Hackney Marshes**, the largest recreation ground in London. Pop.: 192 500 (1994 est.). Area: 19 sq. km (8 sq. miles).

hackneyed ('hæknɪd) *adj* used so often as to be trite, dull, and stereotyped.

hacksaw ('hæk,sɔ:) n a handsaw for cutting metal, with a blade in a frame under tension.

hackwork ('hæk,wɜ:k) n undistinguished literary work produced to order.

had (hæd) *vb* the past tense and past participle of **have.**

haddock ('hædək) n, *pl* **haddocks** or **haddock.** a North Atlantic gadoid food fish similar to but smaller than the cod. [C14: from ?]

hade (heɪd) *Geol.* ◆ n **1** the angle made to the vertical by the plane of a fault or vein. ◆ *vb* **hades, hading, haded. 2** *(intr)* to incline from the vertical. [C18: from ?]

hadedah ('hɑːdɪ,dɑː) n a large grey-green S. African ibis. [imit.]

Hades ('heɪdiːz) n **1** *Greek myth.* **1a** the underworld abode of the souls of the dead. **1b** Pluto, the god of the underworld. **2** *(often not cap.)* hell.

Hadhramaut or **Hadramaut** ★ ('hɑːdrəˈmɔːt) n a plateau region of the S Arabian Peninsula, in SE Yemen on the Indian Ocean; formerly in South Yemen: corresponds roughly to the former East Aden Protectorate. Area: about 151 500 sq. km (58 500 sq. miles).

Hadith ('hædɪθ, hɑːˈdiːθ) n the body of tradition about Mohammed and his followers. [Ar.]

hadj (hædʒ) n a variant spelling of **hajj.**

hadji ('hædʒɪ) n, *pl* **hadjis.** a variant spelling of **hajji.**

Hadlee ★ ('hædlɪ) n Sir **Richard (John).** born 1951, New Zealand cricketer.

hadn't ('hæd³nt) *contraction of* had not.

Hadrian ('heɪdrɪən) or **Adrian** ★ n Latin name *Publius Aelius Hadrianus.* 76–138 A.D., Roman emperor (117–138); adopted son and successor of Trajan. He codified Roman law.

Hadrian's Wall ★ n a fortified Roman wall, of which substantial parts remain, extending across N England from the Solway Firth to the mouth of the River Tyne. It was built in 120–123 A.D. on the orders of the emperor Hadrian as a defence against the N British tribes.

hadron ('hædrɒn) n an elementary particle capable of taking part in a strong nuclear interaction. [C20: from Gk *hadros* heavy, from *hadēn* enough + -ON]
▶ **hadˈronic** *adj*

hadst (hædst) *vb Arch.* or *dialect.* (used with the pronoun *thou*) a singular form of the past tense (indicative mood) of **have.**

haecceity (hɛkˈsiːɪtɪ, hiːk-) n, *pl* **haecceities.** *Philosophy.* the property that uniquely identifies an object. [C17: from Med. L *haecceitas,* lit.: thisness, from *haec,* fem. of *hic* this]

Haeckel ★ (German ˈhɛkəl) n **Ernst Heinrich** (ɛrnst ˈhaɪnrɪç). 1834–1919, German biologist and philosopher.
▶ **Haeckelian** (hɛˈkiːlɪən) *adj*

haem or US **heme** (hiːm) n *Biochem.* a complex red organic pigment containing ferrous iron, present in haemoglobin. [C20: from HAEMATIN]

haem- *combining form.* a variant of **haemo-** before a vowel. Also (US): **hem-.**

haemal or US **hemal** ('hiːməl) *adj* **1** of the blood. **2** denoting or relating to the region of the body containing the heart.

haematemesis or US **hematemesis** (,hiːməˈtɛmɪsɪs) n vomiting of blood, esp. as the result of a bleeding ulcer. [C19: from HAEMATO- + Gk *emesis* vomiting]

haematic or US **hematic** (hiːˈmætɪk) *adj* relating to, acting on, having the colour of, or containing blood. Also: **haemic** or US **hemic.**

haematin or US **hematin** ('hɛmətɪn, 'hiː-) n *Biochem.* a dark bluish or brownish pigment obtained by the oxidation of haem.

haematite or US **hematite** ('hiːmə,taɪt, 'hɛm-) n a variant spelling of **hematite.**

haemato- or before a vowel **haemat-** *combining form.* indicating blood: *haematology.* Also: **haemo-** or (US) **hemato-, hemat-, hemo-.** [from Gk *haima, haimat-* blood]

haematocrit or US **hematocrit** ('hɛmətəʊkrɪt, 'hiː-) n **1** a centrifuge for separating blood cells from plasma. **2** the ratio of the volume occupied by these cells, esp. the red cells, to the total volume of blood, expressed as a percentage. [C20: from HAEMATO- + *-crit,* from Gk *kritēs* judge, from *krinein* to separate]

haematology or US **hematology** (,hiːməˈtɒlədʒɪ) n the branch of medical science concerned with diseases of the blood.
▶ **haematologic** (,hiːmətəˈlɒdʒɪk), **haematoˈlogical** or US **hematoˈlogic, hematoˈlogical** *adj*

haematoma or US **hematoma** (,hiːməˈtəʊmə) n, *pl* **haematomas, haematomata** or US **hematomas, hematomata** (-mətə). *Pathol.* a tumour of clotted blood.

haematuria or US **hematuria** (,hiːməˈtjʊərɪə) n *Pathol.* the presence of blood or red blood cells in the urine.

-haemia or esp. US **-hemia** n *combining form.* variants of **-aemia.**

haemo-, haema-, or before a vowel **haem-** *combining form.* denoting blood. Also: (US) **hemo-, hema-,** or **hem-.** [from Gk *haima* blood]

haemocyanin or US **hemocyanin** (,hiːməʊˈsaɪənɪn) n a blue copper-containing respiratory pigment in crustaceans and molluscs that functions as haemoglobin.

haemocytometer or US **hemocytometer** (,hiːməʊsaɪˈtɒmɪtə) n *Med.* an apparatus for counting the number of cells in a quantity of blood.

haemodialysis or US **hemodialysis** (,hiːməʊdaɪˈælɪsɪs) n, *pl* **haemodialyses** or US **hemodialyses** (-,siːz). *Med.* the filtering of circulating blood through a membrane in an apparatus (**haemodialyser** or **artificial kidney**) to remove waste products: performed in cases of kidney failure. [C20: from HAEMO- + DIALYSIS]

haemoglobin or US **hemoglobin** (,hiːməʊˈɡləʊbɪn) n a protein that gives red blood cells their characteristic colour. It combines reversibly with oxygen and is thus very important in the transportation of oxygen to tissues. [C19: shortened from *haematoglobulin:* see HAEMATIN + GLOBULIN]

haemolysis (hɪˈmɒlɪsɪs), **haematolysis** (,hiːməˈtɒlɪsɪs) or US **hemolysis, hematolysis** n, *pl* **haemolyses, haematolyses** or US **hemolyses, hematolyses** (-,siːz). the disintegration of red blood cells, with the release of haemoglobin.
▶ **haemolytic** or US **hemolytic** (,hiːməʊˈlɪtɪk) *adj*

haemophilia or US **hemophilia** (,hiːməʊˈfɪlɪə) n an inheritable disease, usually affecting only males, charac-

terized by loss or impairment of the normal clotting ability of blood.
▶ ‚haemo'philiac or US ‚hemo'philiac n ▶ ‚haemo'philic or US ‚hemo'philic adj

haemoptysis or US **hemoptysis** (hɪ'mɒptɪsɪs) n, pl **haemoptyses** or US **hemoptyses** (-‚siːz). spitting or coughing up of blood, as in tuberculosis. [C17: from HAEMO- -ptysis, from Gk ptyein to spit]

haemorrhage or US **hemorrhage** ('hɛmərɪdʒ) n 1 profuse bleeding from ruptured blood vessels. 2 a steady or severe loss or depletion of resources, staff, etc. ◆ vb **haemorrhages, haemorrhaging, haemorrhaged** or US **hemorrhages, hemorrhaging, hemorrhaged.** 3 (intr) to bleed profusely. [C17: from L haemorrhagia; see HAEMO-, -RRHAGIA]

haemorrhoids or US **hemorrhoids** ('hɛmə‚rɔɪdz) pl n Pathol. swollen and twisted veins in the region of the anus. Nontechnical name: **piles.** [C14: from L haemorrhoidae (pl), from Gk, from haimorrhoos discharging blood, from haimo- HAEMO- + rhein to flow]
▶ ‚haemor'rhoidal or US ‚hemor'rhoidal adj

haemostasis or US **hemostasis** (‚hiːməʊ'steɪsɪs) n the stopping of bleeding or of blood circulation, as during a surgical operation. [C18: from NL, from HAEMO- + Gk stasis a standing still]
▶ ‚haemo'static or US ‚hemo'static adj

haemostat or US **hemostat** ('hiːməʊ‚stæt) n a surgical instrument or chemical agent that retards or stops bleeding.

haeremai ('haɪrə‚maɪ) NZ. ◆ sentence substitute. 1 an expression of greeting or welcome. ◆ n 2 the act of saying "haeremai". [C18: Maori, lit.: come hither]

Ha-erh-pin ★ ('haː'əˈpɪn) n transliteration of the Chinese name for **Harbin**.

hafiz ('haːfɪz) n Islam. 1 a title for a person who knows the Koran by heart. 2 the guardian of a mosque. [from Persian, from Ar., from hafiza to guard]

hafnium ('hæfnɪəm) n a bright metallic element found in zirconium ores. Symbol: Hf; atomic no.: 72; atomic wt.: 178.49. [C20: NL, after Hafnia, L name of Copenhagen + -IUM]

haft (haːft) n 1 the handle of an axe, knife, etc. ◆ vb 2 (tr) to provide with a haft. [OE hæft]

hag[1] (hæg) n 1 an unpleasant or ugly old woman. 2 a witch. 3 short for **hagfish.** [OE hægtesse witch]
▶ 'haggish adj

hag[2] (hæg) n Scot. & N English dialect. 1 a firm spot in a bog. 2 a soft place in a moor. [C13: from ON]

Hag. Bible. abbrev. for Haggai.

Hagar ★ ('heɪgaː, -gə) n Old Testament. an Egyptian maid of Sarah, who bore Ishmael to Abraham, Sarah's husband.

Hagen[1] ★ ('haːgən) n (in the Nibelungenlied) Siegfried's killer, who in turn is killed by Siegfried's wife, Kriemhild.

Hagen[2] ★ (German 'haːgən) n an industrial city in NW Germany, in North Rhine-Westphalia. Pop.: 213 747 (1995 est.).

Hagen[3] ★ ('heɪgən) n Walter. 1892–1969, US golfer.

hagfish ('hæg‚fɪʃ) n, pl **hagfish** or **hagfishes.** an eel-like marine vertebrate having a round sucking mouth and feeding on the tissues of other animals and on dead organic material.

Haggadah or **Haggodoh** (hə'gaːdə) n, pl **Haggadahs, Haggadas** or **Haggadoth** (hægə'dəʊt). Judaism. **a** a book containing the order of service of the traditional Passover meal. **b** the narrative of the Exodus from Egypt that constitutes the main part of that service. ◆ See also **Seder.** [C19: from Heb.: story, from hagged to tell]
▶ **haggadic** (hə'gædɪk, -'gaː-) adj

Haggai ★ ('hægeɪ‚aɪ) n Old Testament. 1 a Hebrew prophet, whose oracles are usually dated between August and December of 520 B.C. 2 the book in which these oracles are contained, chiefly concerned with the re-building of the Temple after the Exile. Douay spelling: **Aggeus** (ə'dʒiːəs).

haggard ('hægəd) adj 1 careworn or gaunt, as from anxiety or starvation. 2 wild or unruly. 3 (of a hawk) having

reached maturity in the wild before being caught. ◆ n 4 Falconry. a haggard hawk. [C16: from OF hagard, ? rel. to HEDGE]
▶ 'haggardly adv ▶ 'haggardness n

Haggard ★ ('hægəd) n Sir H(enry) Rider. 1856–1925, British author of romantic adventure stories, including King Solomon's Mines (1885).

haggis ('hægɪs) n a Scottish dish made from sheep's or calf's offal, oatmeal, suet, and seasonings boiled in a skin made from the animal's stomach. [C15: ?from haggen to HACK[1]]

haggle ('hæg°l) vb **haggles, haggling, haggled.** (intr; often foll. by over) to bargain or wrangle (over a price, terms of an agreement, etc.); barter. [C16: of Scand. origin]
▶ 'haggler n

hagio- or before a vowel **hagi-** combining form. indicating a saint, saints, or holiness: hagiography. [via LL from Gk, from hagios holy]

Hagiographa (‚hægɪ'ɒgrəfə) n the third of the three main parts into which the books of the Old Testament are divided in Jewish tradition (the other two parts being the Law and the Prophets).

hagiographer (‚hægɪ'ɒgrəfə) or **hagiographist** n 1 a person who writes about the lives of the saints. 2 one of the writers of the Hagiographa.

hagiography (‚hægɪ'ɒgrəfɪ) n, pl **hagiographies.** 1 the writing of the lives of the saints. 2 a biography that idealizes or idolizes its subject.
▶ **hagiographic** (‚hægɪə'græfɪk) or ‚hagio'graphical adj

hagiolatry (‚hægɪ'ɒlətrɪ) n worship or veneration of saints.

hagiology (‚hægɪ'ɒlədʒɪ) n, pl **hagiologies.** literature concerned with the lives and legends of saints.
▶ **hagiological** (‚hægɪə'lɒdʒɪk°l) adj ▶ ‚hagi'ologist n

hag-ridden adj tormented or worried, as if by a witch.

Hague[1] ★ (heɪg) n The. the seat of government of the Netherlands and the capital of South Holland province, situated about 3 km (2 miles) from the North Sea. Pop.: 442 105 (1995). Dutch names: 's Gravenhage, Den Haag.

Hague[2] ★ (heɪg) n William Jefferson. born 1961, British politician; leader of the Conservative party from 1997.

hah (haː) interj a variant spelling of ha[1].

ha-ha[1] ('haː'haː) or **haw-haw** ('hɔː'hɔː) interj 1 a representation of the sound of laughter. 2 an exclamation expressing derision, mockery, etc.

ha-ha[2] ('haː‚haː) or **haw-haw** ('hɔː‚hɔː) n a wall or other boundary marker that is set in a ditch so as not to interrupt the landscape. [C18: from F haha, prob. based on ha! ejaculation denoting surprise]

Hahn ★ (German haːn) n 1 Kurt (kurt). 1886–1974, German educationalist; escaped to Britain during the Nazi era, where he founded Gordonstoun School (1935) and helped to establish the Duke of Edinburgh's award scheme. 2 Otto ('ɔto). 1879–1968, German physicist: discovered the element protactinium with Meitner (1917); with Strassmann, demonstrated the nuclear fission of uranium when it is bombarded with neutrons: Nobel prize for chemistry 1944.

Hahnemann ★ (German 'haːnəman) n (Christian Friedrich) Samuel ('zaːmueːl). 1755–1843, German physician; founder of homeopathy.

hahnium ('haːnɪəm) n the former name for **hassium.**

Haidar Ali ★ ('haɪdər 'aːlɪ) n a variant spelling of **Hyder Ali.**

Haifa ('haɪfə) n a port in NW Israel, near Mount Carmel, on the Bay of Acre: Israel's chief port, with an oil refinery and other heavy industry. Pop.: 252 300 (1996 est.).

Haig ★ (heɪg) n Douglas, 1st Earl Haig. 1861–1928, British field marshal; commander in chief of the British forces in France and Flanders (1915–18).

haik or **haick** (haɪk, heɪk) n a traditional Arabian outer garment for the head and body. [C18: from Ar.]

haiku ('haɪkuː) or **hokku** ('hɒkuː) n, pl **haiku** or **hokku.** an epigrammatic Japanese verse form in 17 syllables. [from Japanese, from *hai* amusement + *ku* verse]

hail[1] (heɪl) *n* **1** small pellets of ice falling from cumulonimbus clouds when there are strong rising air currents. **2** a storm of such pellets. **3** words, ideas, missiles, etc., directed with force and in great quantity: *a hail of abuse.* ◆ *vb* **4** (*intr*; with *it* as subject) to be the case that hail is falling. **5** (often with *it* as subject) to fall or cause to fall as or like hail. [OE *hægl*]

hail[2] (heɪl) *vb* (*mainly tr*) **1** to greet, esp. enthusiastically: *the crowd hailed the actress with joy.* **2** to acclaim or acknowledge: *they hailed him as their hero.* **3** to attract the attention of by shouting or gesturing: *to hail a taxi.* **4** (*intr*; foll. by *from*) to be a native of: *she hails from India.* ◆ *n* **5** the act or an instance of hailing. **6** a distance across which one can attract attention (esp. in **within hail**). ◆ *sentence substitute.* **7** *Poetic.* an exclamation of greeting. [C12: from ON *heill* healthy]

Haile Selassie ★ (ˈhaɪlɪ səˈlæsɪ) *n* title of *Ras Tafari Makonnen*. 1892–1975, emperor of Ethiopia (1930–36; 1941–74). During the Italian occupation of Ethiopia (1936–41), he lived in exile in England: deposed 1974.

hail-fellow-well-met *adj* genial and familiar, esp. in an offensive or ingratiating way.

Hail Mary *n* **1** Also called: **Ave Maria**. *RC Church.* a prayer to the Virgin Mary, based on the salutations of the angel Gabriel (Luke 1:28) and Elizabeth (Luke 1:42) to her. **2** *American football sl.* a very long high pass into the end zone, made in the final seconds of a half or of a game.

Hailsham of St Marylebone ★ (ˈheɪlʃəm) *n* **Quintin (McGarel) Hogg**, Baron. born 1907, British Conservative politician; Lord Chancellor (1970–74; 1979–87). He renounced his viscountcy in 1963 when he made an unsuccessful bid for the Conservative Party leadership; he became a life peer in 1970.

hailstone (ˈheɪlˌstəʊn) *n* a pellet of hail.

hailstorm (ˈheɪlˌstɔːm) *n* a storm during which hail falls.

Hailwood ★ (ˈheɪlwʊd) *n* **Mike**, full name *Stanley Michael Bailey Hailwood*. 1940–81, British racing motorcyclist.

Hainan (ˈhaɪˈnæn) *or* **Hainan Tao** ★ (taʊ) *n* an island and province in the South China Sea, separated from the mainland of S China by **Hainan Strait**: part of Guangdong province until 1988; China's second largest offshore island. Pop.: 7 110 000 (1995 est.). Area: 33 572 sq. km (12 962 sq. miles).

Hainaut *or* **Hainault** ★ (French εno) *n* a province of SW Belgium: stretches from the Flanders Plain in the north to the Ardennes in the south. Capital: Mons. Pop.: 1 286 649 (1995 est.). Area: 3797 sq. km (1466 sq. miles).

Haiphong ★ (ˈhaɪˈfɒŋ) *n* a port in N Vietnam, on the Red River delta: a major industrial centre. Pop.: 783 133 (1992 est.).

hair (hεə) *n* **1** any of the threadlike structures that grow from follicles beneath the skin of mammals. **2** a growth of such structures, as on an animal's body, which helps prevent heat loss. **3** *Bot.* any threadlike outgrowth, such as a root hair. **4** a fabric made from the hair of some animals. **5** another word for **hair's-breadth**: *to lose by a hair.* **6** **get in someone's hair**. *Inf.* to annoy someone persistently. **7** **hair of the dog (that bit one)**. an alcoholic drink taken as an antidote to a hangover. **8** **keep your hair on!** *Brit. inf.* keep calm. **9** **let one's hair down**. to behave without reserve. **10** **not turn a hair**. to show no surprise, anger, fear, etc. **11** **split hairs**. to make petty and unnecessary distinctions. [OE *hær*]
▸ **'hairless** *adj* ▸ **'hair,like** *adj*

haircloth (ˈhεəˌklɒθ) *n* a cloth woven from horsehair, used (esp. formerly) in upholstery, etc.

haircut (ˈhεəˌkʌt) *n* **1** the act of cutting the hair. **2** the style in which hair has been cut.

hairdo (ˈhεəˌduː) *n, pl* **hairdos**. the arrangement of a person's hair, esp. after styling and setting.

hairdresser (ˈhεəˌdrεsə) *n* **1** a person whose business is cutting, dyeing, and arranging hair. **2** a hairdresser's establishment. ◆ Related adj: **tonsorial**.
▸ **'hair,dressing** *n*

-haired *adj* having hair as specified: *long-haired.*

hair gel *n* a preparation used in hair styling.

hairgrip (ˈhεəˌgrɪp) *n Chiefly Brit.* a small tightly bent metal hair clip. Also called (US, Canad., and NZ): **bobby pin**.

hairline (ˈhεəˌlaɪn) *n* **1** the natural margin formed by hair on the head. **2a** a very narrow line. **2b** (*as modifier*): *a hairline crack.*

hairline fracture *n* a very fine crack in a bone.

hairnet (ˈhεəˌnεt) *n* any of several kinds of light netting worn over the hair to keep it in place.

hairpiece (ˈhεəˌpiːs) *n* **1** a wig or toupee. **2** a section of extra hair attached to a woman's real hair to give it greater bulk or length.

hairpin (ˈhεəˌpɪn) *n* **1** a thin double-pronged pin used to fasten the hair. **2** (*modifier*) (esp. of a bend in a road) curving very sharply.

hair-raising *adj* inspiring horror; terrifying.

hair's-breadth *n* **a** a very short or imperceptible margin or distance. **b** (*as modifier*): *a hair's-breadth escape.*

hair shirt *n* **1** a shirt made of haircloth worn next to the skin as a penance. **2** a secret trouble or affliction.

hair slide *n* a hinged clip with a tortoiseshell, bone, or similar back, used to fasten a girl's hair.

hairsplitting (ˈhεəˌsplɪtɪŋ) *n* **1** the making of petty distinctions. ◆ *adj* **2** occupied with or based on petty distinctions.
▸ **'hair,splitter** *n*

hairspring (ˈhεəˌsprɪŋ) *n* a fine spiral spring in some timepieces which, in combination with the balance wheel, controls the timekeeping.

hairstreak (ˈhεəˌstriːk) *n* a small butterfly having fringed wings with narrow white streaks.

hairstyle (ˈhεəˌstaɪl) *n* a particular mode of arranging the hair.
▸ **'hair,stylist** *n*

hair trigger *n* **1** a trigger of a firearm that responds to very slight pressure. **2** *Inf.* any mechanism, reaction, etc., set in operation by slight provocation.

hairy (ˈhεərɪ) *adj* **hairier, hairiest. 1** covered with hair. **2** *Sl.* **2a** difficult or problematic. **2b** dangerous or exciting.
▸ **'hairiness** *n*

Haiti ★ (ˈheɪtɪ, hɑːˈiːtɪ) *n* **1** a republic occupying the W part of the island of Hispaniola in the Caribbean, the E part consisting of the Dominican Republic: ceded by Spain to France in 1697 and became one of the richest colonial possessions in the world, with numerous plantations; slaves rebelled under Toussaint L'Ouverture in 1793 and defeated the French; taken over by the US (1915–41) after long political and economic chaos; under the authoritarian regimes of François Duvalier (1957–71) and his son Jean-Claude Duvalier (1971–86); in 1991, following three military regimes, Jean-Bertrand Aristide was democratically elected but was deposed; in 1994, aided by the US military, he returned to power. Official languages: French and Haitian creole. Religions: Roman Catholic and voodoo. Currency: gourde. Capital: Port-au-Prince. Pop.: 6 611 000 (1997). Area: 27 749 sq. km (10 714 sq. miles). **2** a former name for **Hispaniola**.
▸ **Haitian** (ˈheɪʃən, hɑːˈiːʃən) *adj, n*

Haitink ★ (ˈhaɪˌtɪŋk) *n* **Bernard**. born 1929, Dutch orchestral conductor; received an honorary knighthood in 1977.

hajj *or* **hadj** (hædʒ) *n* the pilgrimage to Mecca that every Muslim is required to make at least once. [from Ar.]

hajji, hadji, *or* **haji** (ˈhædʒɪ) *n, pl* **hajjis, hadjis,** *or* **hajis. 1** a Muslim who has made a pilgrimage to Mecca: also used as a title. **2** a Christian who has visited Jerusalem.

haka (ˈhɑːkə) *n NZ.* **1** a Maori war chant accompanied by gestures. **2** a similar performance by, for instance, a rugby team.

hake (heɪk) *n, pl* **hake** *or* **hakes. 1** a gadoid food fish of the N hemisphere, having an elongated body with a large head and two dorsal fins. **2** a similar North American fish. [C15: ?from ON *haki* hook]

hakea (ˈhɑːkɪə, ˈheɪkɪə) *n* any shrub or tree of the Australian genus *Hakea*, having a hard woody fruit and

★ people and places

often yielding a useful wood. [C19: NL, after C. L. von *Hake* (died 1818), G botanist]

hakim *or* **hakeem** (hɑːˈkiːm) *n* **1** a Muslim judge, ruler, or administrator. **2** a Muslim physician. [C17: from Ar., from *hakama* to rule]

Hakluyt ★ (ˈhæklu:t) *n* **Richard**. ?1552–1616, English geographer, who compiled *The Principal Navigations, Voyages, and Discoveries of the English Nation* (1589).

Hakodate ★ (ˌhɑːkəʊˈdɑːteɪ) *n* a port in N Japan, on S Hokkaido: fishing industry and shipbuilding. Pop.: 298 868 (1995).

Halakah *or* **Halacha** (ˌhɑːləˈkɑː, həˈlɑːkə) *n* that part of traditional Jewish literature concerned with the law, as contrasted with Haggadah. [C19: from Heb.: way, from *hālakh* to go]
▶ **Halakic** *or* **Halachic** (həˈlækɪk) *adj*

halal *or* **hallal** (hɑːˈlɑːl) *n* **1** meat from animals that have been killed according to Muslim law. ◆ *adj* **2** of or relating to such meat: *a halal butcher*. ◆ *vb* **halals, hallalling, hallalled** *or* **hallals, hallalling, hallalled**. (*tr*) **3** to kill (animals) according to Muslim law. [from Ar.: lawful]

halation (həˈleɪʃən) *n Photog*. fogging usually seen as a bright ring surrounding a source of light. [C19: from HALO + -ATION]

halberd (ˈhælbəd) *or* **halbert** (ˈhælbət) *n* a weapon consisting of a long shaft with an axe blade and a pick, topped by a spearhead: used in 15th- and 16th-century warfare. [C15: from OF *hallebarde*, from MHG *helm* handle + *barde* axe]
▶ ˌhalberˈdier *n*

Halberstadt ★ (German ˈhalbərʃtat) *n* a town in central Germany, in Saxony-Anhalt: industrial centre noted for its historic buildings. Pop.: 47 500 (1989 est.).

halcyon (ˈhælsɪən) *adj* **1** peaceful, gentle, and calm. **2 halcyon days**. **2a** a fortnight of calm weather during the winter solstice. **2b** a period of peace and happiness. ◆ *n* **3** *Greek myth*. a fabulous bird associated with the winter solstice. **4** a poetic name for the **kingfisher**. [C14: from L *alcyon*, from Gk *alkuōn* kingfisher, from ?]

Haldane ★ (ˈhɔːldeɪn) *n* **1 J(ohn) B(urdon) S(anderson)**. 1892–1964, British biochemist, geneticist, and writer on science. **2** his father, **John Scott**. 1860–1936, British physiologist, noted for his research into industrial diseases. **3** his brother, **Richard Burdon**, 1st Viscount Haldane of Cloan. 1856–1928, British statesman and jurist; secretary of state for war (1905–12).

hale[1] (heɪl) *adj* healthy and robust (esp. in **hale and hearty**). [OE *hæl* WHOLE]
▶ ˈhaleness *n*

hale[2] (heɪl) *vb* **hales, haling, haled**. (*tr*) to pull or drag. [C13: from OF *haler*, of Gmc origin]
▶ ˈhaler *n*

Hale ★ (heɪl) *n* **1 George Ellery**. 1868–1938, US astronomer: invented the spectroheliograph. **2 Sir Matthew**. 1609–76, English judge and scholar; Lord Chief Justice (1671–76).

Haleakala ★ (ˌhɑːliːˌɑːkɑːˈlɑː) *n* a volcano in Hawaii, on E Mani Island. Height: 3057 m (10 032 ft). Area of crater: 49 sq. km (19 sq. miles). Depth of crater: 829 m (2720 ft).

Halesowen ★ (ˌheɪlzˈəʊɪn) *n* a town in W central England, in Dudley unitary authority, in the SW West Midlands. Pop.: 57 918 (1991).

Haley ★ (ˈheɪlɪ) *n* **Bill**, full name *William John Clifton Haley*. 1925–81, US rock-and-roll singer.

half (hɑːf) *n, pl* **halves** (hɑːvz). **1a** either of two equal or corresponding parts that together comprise a whole. **1b** a quantity equalling such a part: *half a dozen*. **2** half a pint, esp. of beer. **3** *Scot*. a small drink of spirits, esp. whisky. **4** *Football, hockey, etc*. the half of the pitch regarded as belonging to one team. **5** *Golf*. an equal score with an opponent. **6** (in various games) either of two periods of play separated by an interval. **7** a half-price ticket on a bus, etc. **8** short for **half-hour**. **9** *Sport*. short for **halfback**. **10** *Obs*. a half-year period. **11 by halves**. (used with a negative) without being thorough: *we don't do things by halves*. **12 go halves**. (often foll. by *on, in*, etc.) **12a** to share expenses. **12b** to share the whole amount (of something): *to go halves on an orange*. ◆ *determiner* **13a** being a

half or approximately a half: *half the kingdom*. **13b** (as *pron; functioning as sing or pl*): *half of them came*. ◆ *adj* **14** not perfect or complete: *he only did a half job on it*. ◆ *adv* **15** to the amount or extent of a half. **16** to a great amount or extent. **17** partially; to an extent. **18 by half**. to an excessive degree: *he's too arrogant by half*. **19 half two**, etc. *Inf*. 30 minutes after two o'clock, etc. **20 have half a mind to**. to have a vague intention to. **21 not half**. *Inf*. **21a** not in any way: *he's not half stupid*. **21b** *Brit*. very: *he isn't half stupid*. **21c** yes, indeed. [OE *healf*]

half- *prefix* **1** one of two equal parts: *half-moon*. **2** related through one parent only: *half-brother*. **3** not completely; partly: *half-hardy*.

half-and-half *n* **1** a mixture of half one thing and half another thing. **2** a drink consisting of equal parts of beer and stout, or equal parts of bitter and mild.

halfback (ˈhɑːfˌbæk) *n* **1** *Soccer*. any of three players positioned behind the line of forwards and in front of the fullbacks. **2** *Rugby*. either the scrum half or the stand-off half. **3** any of certain similar players in other team sports.

half-baked *adj* **1** insufficiently baked. **2** *Inf*. foolish; stupid. **3** *Inf*. poorly planned.

halfbeak (ˈhɑːfˌbiːk) *n* a marine and freshwater teleost fish having an elongated body with a short upper jaw and a long protruding lower jaw.

half-binding *n* a type of bookbinding in which the backs are bound in one material and the sides in another.

half-blood *n* **1a** the relationship between individuals having only one parent in common. **1b** an individual having such a relationship. **2** a less common name for a **half-breed**.
▶ ˌhalf-ˈblooded *adj*

half board *n* accommodation at a hotel, etc., that includes breakfast and one main meal. Also called: **demi-pension**.

half-boot *n* a boot reaching to the midcalf.

half-bottle *n* a bottle of spirits or wine that contains half the quantity of a standard bottle.

half-breed *n* **1** *Often offens*. a person whose parents are of different races, esp. the offspring of a White person and an American Indian. ◆ *adj also* **half-bred**. **2** of, relating to, or designating offspring of people or animals of different races or breeds.

half-brother *n* the son of either of one's parents by another partner.

half-butt *n* a snooker cue that is longer than an ordinary cue.

half-caste *n* **1** a person having parents of different races, esp. the offspring of a European and an Indian. ◆ *adj* **2** of, relating to, or designating such a person.

half-century *n* **1** a period of 50 years. **2** a score or grouping of 50: *he scored his first half-century for England*.

half-cock *n* **1** the halfway position of a firearm's hammer when the trigger is cocked by the hammer and the hammer cannot reach the primer to fire the weapon. **2 go off at half-cock** *or* **half-cocked**. to fail as a result of inadequate preparation or premature starting.

half-crown *n* a former British coin worth two shillings and sixpence (12½p). Also called: **half-a-crown**.

half-cut *adj Brit. sl*. rather drunk.

half-dozen *n* six.

half gainer *n* a type of dive in which the diver completes a half backward somersault to enter the water headfirst facing the diving board.

half-hardy *adj* (of a cultivated plant) able to survive out of doors except during severe frost.

half-hearted *adj* without enthusiasm or determination.
▶ ˌhalf-ˈheartedly *adv*

half-hitch *n* a knot made by passing the end of a piece of rope around itself and through the loop thus made.

half-hour *n* **1** a period of 30 minutes. **2** the point of time 30 minutes after the beginning of an hour.
▶ ˌhalf-ˈhourly *adv, adj*

half-hunter *n* a watch with a hinged lid in which a

small circular opening or crystal allows the approximate time to be read.

half landing *n* a landing halfway up a flight of stairs.

half-life *n* the time taken for half of the atoms in a radioactive material to undergo decay.

half-light *n* a dim light, as at dawn or dusk.

half-mast *n* the lower than normal position to which a flag is lowered on a mast as a sign of mourning.

half measure *n* (*often pl*) an inadequate measure or action; compromise.

half-moon *n* **1** the moon at first or last quarter when half its face is illuminated. **2** the time at which a half-moon occurs. **3** something shaped like a half-moon.

half-nelson *n* a wrestling hold in which a wrestler places an arm under one of his opponent's arms from behind and exerts pressure with his palm on the back of his opponent's neck.

half-note *n* the usual US name for **minim** (sense 2).

halfpenny *or* **ha'penny** ('heɪpnɪ, *for sense 1* 'hɑːfˌpenɪ) *n* **1** (*pl* **halfpennies** *or* **ha'pennies**) a small British coin worth half a new penny (withdrawn 1985). **2** (*pl* **halfpennies** *or* **ha'pennies**) an old British coin worth half an old penny. **3** (*pl* **halfpence**) something of negligible value.
  ▸ **halfpennyworth** *or* **ha'p'orth** ('heɪpəθ) *n*

half-pie *adj NZ inf.* ill planned; not properly thought out: *a half-pie scheme.* [from Maori *pai* good]

half-pint *n Sl.* a small or insignificant person.

half-plate *or* **half-print** *n Photog.* a size of plate measuring 6½ × 4½ inches.

half-rotten *adj* partially rotted or decomposed.

half seas over *adj Brit. inf.* drunk.

half-section *n Engineering.* a scale drawing of a section through a symmetrical object that shows only half the object.

half-sister *n* the daughter of either of one's parents by another partner.

half-size *n* any size, esp. in clothing, that is halfway between two sizes.

half-sole *n* a sole from the shank of a shoe to the toe.

half term *n Brit. education.* a short holiday midway through an academic term.

half-timbered *or* **half-timber** *adj* (of a building) having an exposed timber framework filled with brick, stone, or plastered laths, as in Tudor architecture.
  ▸ ˌhalf-ˈtimbering *n*

half-time *n Sport.* **a** a rest period between the two halves of a game. **b** (*as modifier*): *the half-time score.*

half-title *n* **1** the short title of a book as printed on the right-hand page preceding the title page. **2** a title on a separate page preceding a section of a book.

halftone ('hɑːfˌtəʊn) *n* **1** a process used to reproduce an illustration by photographing it through a fine screen to break it up into dots. **2** the print obtained. **3** *Music.* the usual US and Canad. name for **semitone.**

half-track *n* a vehicle with caterpillar tracks on the wheels that supply motive power only.

half-truth *n* a partially true statement intended to mislead.
  ▸ ˌhalf-ˈtrue *adj*

half volley *n Sport.* a stroke or shot in which the ball is hit immediately after it bounces.

halfway (ˌhɑːfˈweɪ) *adv, adj* **1** at or to half the distance. **2** in or of an incomplete manner. **3 meet halfway.** to compromise with.

halfway house *n* **1** a place to rest midway on a journey. **2** the halfway point in any progression. **3** a centre or hostel designed to facilitate the readjustment to private life of released prisoners, mental patients, etc.

halfwit ('hɑːfˌwɪt) *n* **1** a feeble-minded person. **2** a foolish or inane person.
  ▸ ˌhalf-ˈwitted *adj*

half-year *n* a period of six months.

halibut ('hælɪbət) *n, pl* **halibuts** *or* **halibut.** the largest flatfish: a dark green North Atlantic species that is a very important food fish. [C15: from *hali* HOLY (because it was eaten on holy days) + *butte* flat-fish, from MDu.]

Haliç ★ (ha'liːtʃ) *n* the Turkish name for the **Golden Horn.**

Halicarnassus ★ (ˌhælɪkɑːˈnæsəs) *n* a Greek colony on the SW coast of Asia Minor: one of the major Hellenistic cities.
  ▸ ˌHalicarˈnassian *adj*

halide ('hælaɪd) *or* **halid** ('hælɪd) *n* a binary compound containing a halogen atom or ion in combination with a more electropositive element.

Halifax[1] ★ ('hælɪˌfæks) *n* **1** a port in SE Canada, capital of Nova Scotia, on the Atlantic: founded in 1749 as a British stronghold. Pop.: 114 455 (1991). **2** a town in N England, in Calderdale, West Yorkshire: textiles. Pop.: 91 069 (1991).

Halifax[2] ★ ('hælɪˌfæks) *n* **1 Charles Montagu, Earl of Halifax.** 1661–1715, British statesman; founder of the National Debt (1692) and the Bank of England (1694). **2 Edward Frederick Lindley Wood, Earl of Halifax.** 1881–1959, British Conservative statesman. He was viceroy of India (1926–31), foreign secretary (1938–40), and ambassador to the US (1941–46).

halite ('hælaɪt) *n* a mineral consisting of sodium chloride in cubic crystalline form, occurring in sedimentary beds and dried salt lakes: an important source of table salt. Also called: **rock salt.** [C19: from NL *halītes*, from Gk *hals* salt + -ITE[2]]

halitosis (ˌhælɪˈtəʊsɪs) *n* the state or condition of having bad breath. [C19: NL, from L *hālitus* breath, from *hālāre* to breathe]

hall (hɔːl) *n* **1** a room serving as an entry area. **2** (*sometimes cap.*) a building for public meetings. **3** (*often cap.*) the great house of an estate; manor. **4** a large building or room used for assemblies, dances, etc. **5** a residential building, esp. in a university; hall of residence. **6a** a large room, esp. for dining, in a college or university. **6b** a meal eaten in this room. **7** the large room of a house, castle, etc. **8** *US & Canad.* a corridor into which rooms open. **9** (*often pl*) *Inf.* short for **music hall.** [OE *heall*]

Hall ★ (hɔːl) *n* **1 Charles Martin.** 1863–1914, US chemist: discovered the electrolytic process for producing aluminium. **2 Sir John.** 1824–1907, New Zealand statesman, born in England: prime minister of New Zealand (1879–82). **3 Sir Peter.** born 1930, British stage director: director of the Royal Shakespeare Company (1960–73) and of the National Theatre (1973–88). **4 (Marguerite) Radclyffe.** 1883–1943, British novelist. Her treatment of a lesbian theme in the novel *The Well of Loneliness* (1928) led to an obscenity trial.

Halle ★ (*German* 'halə) *n* a city in E central Germany, in Saxony-Anhalt, on the River Saale: early saltworks; a Hanseatic city in the late Middle Ages; university (1694). Pop.: 290 051 (1995 est.). Official name: **Halle an der Saale** (an der 'za:lə).

Hallé ★ ('hæleɪ) *n* Sir **Charles**, original name *Karl Hallé.* 1819–95, German conductor and pianist, in Britain from 1848. In 1857 he founded the Hallé Orchestra in Manchester.

hallelujah, halleluiah (ˌhælɪˈluːjə), *or* **alleluia** (ˌælɪˈluːjə) *interj* **1** an exclamation of praise to God. ◆ *n* **2** an exclamation of "Hallelujah". **3** a musical composition that uses the word *Hallelujah* as its text. [C16: from Heb. *hellēl* to praise + *yāh* the Lord]

Haller ★ (*German* 'halər) *n* **Albrecht von** ('albrɛçt fɔn). 1708–77, Swiss biologist: founder of experimental physiology.

Halley ★ ('hælɪ) *n* **Edmund.** 1656–1742, English astronomer and mathematician. He predicted the return of the comet now known as **Halley's comet.**

halliard ('hæljəd) *n* a variant spelling of **halyard.**

Hall-Jones ★ ('hɔːlˈdʒəʊnz) *n* Sir **William.** 1851–1936, New Zealand statesman, born in England: prime minister of New Zealand (1906).

hallmark ('hɔːlˌmɑːk) *n* **1** *Brit.* an official series of marks stamped by the London Guild of Goldsmiths on gold, silver, or platinum articles to guarantee purity, date of manufacture, etc. **2** a mark of authenticity or excellence. **3** an outstanding feature. ◆ *vb* **4** (*tr*) to stamp with or as

★ people and places

if with a hallmark. [C18: after Goldsmiths' *Hall* in London, where items were graded and stamped]

hallo (həˈləʊ) *sentence substitute, n* **1** a variant spelling of **hello**. ♦ *sentence substitute, n, vb* **2** a variant spelling of **halloo**.

halloo (həˈluː), **hallo,** or **halloa** (həˈləʊ) *sentence substitute*. **1** a shout to attract attention, esp. to call hounds at a hunt. ♦ *n, pl* **halloos, hallos,** or **halloas**. **2** a shout of "halloo". ♦ *vb* **halloos, hallooing, hallooed; hallos, halloing, halloed;** or **halloas, halloaing, halloaed. 3** to shout. **4** (*tr*) to urge on (dogs) with shouts. [C16: ? var. of *hallow* to encourage hounds by shouting]

hallow (ˈhæləʊ) *vb* (*tr*) **1** to consecrate or set apart as being holy. **2** to venerate as being holy. [OE *hālgian,* from *hālig* HOLY]
▸ **'hallower** *n*

hallowed (ˈhæləʊd; *liturgical* ˈhæləʊɪd) *adj* **1** set apart as sacred. **2** consecrated or holy.

Halloween or **Hallowe'en** (ˌhæləʊˈiːn) *n* the eve of All Saints' Day celebrated on Oct. 31; Allhallows Eve. [C18: see ALLHALLOWS, EVEN[2]]

hall stand or *esp.* US **hall tree** *n* a piece of furniture for hanging coats, hats, etc., on.

Hallstatt (ˈhælstæt) *adj* of a late Bronze Age culture extending from central Europe to Britain and lasting from the 9th to the 5th century B.C. [C19: after *Hallstatt,* Austrian village where remains were found]

hallucinate (həˈluːsɪˌneɪt) *vb* **hallucinates, hallucinating, hallucinated.** (*intr*) to experience hallucinations. [C17: from L *ālūcinārī* to wander in mind]
▸ **hal'luci,nator** *n*

hallucination (həˌluːsɪˈneɪʃən) *n* the alleged perception of an object when no object is present, occurring under hypnosis, in some mental disorders, etc.
▸ **hal'lucinatory** *adj*

hallucinogen (həˈluːsɪnəˌdʒɛn) *n* any drug that induces hallucinations.
▸ **hallucinogenic** (həˌluːsɪnəˈdʒɛnɪk) *adj*

hallux (ˈhæləks) *n* the first digit on the hind foot of a mammal, bird, reptile, or amphibian; the big toe of man. [C19: NL, from LL *allex* big toe]

hallway (ˈhɔːlˌweɪ) *n* a hall or corridor.

halm (hɑːm) *n* a variant spelling of **haulm.**

halma (ˈhælmə) *n* a board game in which players attempt to transfer their pieces from their own to their opponents' bases. [C19: from Gk *halma* leap]

Halmahera (ˌhælməˈhɪərə) *n* an island in NE Indonesia, the largest of the Moluccas: consists of four peninsulas enclosing three bays; mountainous and forested. Area: 17 780 sq. km (6865 sq. miles). Dutch name: Djailola.

Halmstad ★ (*Swedish* ˈhalmstɑːd) *n* a port in SW Sweden, on the Kattegat. Pop.: 83 080 (1994).

halo (ˈheɪləʊ) *n, pl* **haloes** or **halos. 1** a disc or ring of light around the head of an angel, saint, etc., as in painting. **2** the aura surrounding a famous or admired person, thing, or event. **3** a circle of light around the sun or moon, caused by the refraction of light by particles of ice. ♦ *vb* **haloes** or **halos, haloing, haloed. 4** to surround with or form a halo. [C16: from Med. L, from L *halōs* circular threshing floor, from Gk]

halogen (ˈhæləˌdʒɛn) *n* any of the chemical elements fluorine, chlorine, bromine, iodine, and astatine. They are all monovalent and readily form negative ions. [C19: from Swedish, from Gk *hals* salt + -GEN]
▸ **halogenous** (həˈlɒdʒɪnəs) *adj*

halogenate (ˈhæləˌdʒəˌneɪt) *vb* **halogenates, halogenating, halogenated.** *Chem.* to treat or combine with a halogen.
▸ **,halogen'ation** *n*

haloid (ˈhæləɪd) *Chem.* ♦ *adj* **1** derived from a halogen: *a haloid salt.* ♦ *n* **2** a compound containing halogen atoms in its molecules.

halon (ˈhæləɒn) *n* any of a class of chemical compounds derived from hydrocarbons by replacing one or more hydrogen atoms by bromine atoms and other hydrogen atoms by other halogen atoms (chlorine, fluorine, or iodine).

Hals ★ (*Dutch* hɑls) *n* **Frans** (frɑns). ?1580–1666, Dutch portrait and genre painter: his works include *The Laughing Cavalier* (1624).

Hälsingborg ★ (*Swedish* hɛlsɪŋˈbɔrj) *n* the former name (until 1971) of **Helsingborg.**

halt[1] (hɔːlt) *n* **1** an interruption or end to movement or progress. **2** *Chiefly Brit.* a minor railway station, without permanent buildings. **3 call a halt (to).** to put an end (to); stop. ♦ *n, sentence substitute.* **4** a command to halt, esp. as an order when marching. ♦ *vb* **5** to come or bring to a halt. [C17: from *to make halt,* translation of G *halt machen,* from *halten* to stop]

halt[2] (hɔːlt) *vb* (*intr*) **1** (esp. of verse) to falter or be defective. **2** to be unsure. **3** *Arch.* to be lame. ♦ *adj* **4** *Arch.* **4a** lame. **4b** (*as collective n*; preceded by *the*): *the halt.* [OE *healt* lame]

halter (ˈhɔːltə) *n* **1** headgear for a horse, usually with a rope for leading. **2** Also: **halterneck.** a style of woman's top fastened behind the neck and waist, leaving the back and arms bare. **3** a rope having a noose for hanging a person. **4** death by hanging. ♦ *vb* (*tr*) **5** to put on a halter. **6** to hang (someone). [OE *hælfter*]

haltere (ˈhæltɪə) *n, pl* **halteres** (hælˈtɪəriːz). one of a pair of short projections in dipterous insects that are modified hind wings, used for maintaining equilibrium during flight. [C18: from Gk *haltēres* (pl) hand-held weights used as balancers or to give impetus in leaping, from *hallesthai* to leap]

halting (ˈhɔːltɪŋ) *adj* **1** hesitant: *halting speech.* **2** lame.
▸ **'haltingly** *adv*

Halton ★ (ˈhɔːltən) *n* a unitary authority in NE England, in Greater Manchester. Pop.: 123 000 (1996 est.).

halvah, halva (ˈhælvɑː), or **halavah** (ˈhæləvɑː) *n* an Eastern sweetmeat made of honey and containing sesame seeds, nuts, etc. [from Yiddish *halva,* ult. from Ar. *halwā*]

halve (hɑːv) *vb* **halves, halving, halved.** (*mainly tr*) **1** to divide into two approximately equal parts. **2** to share equally. **3** (*also intr*) to reduce by half, as by cutting. **4** *Golf.* to take the same number of strokes on (a hole or round) as one's opponent. [OE *hielfan*]

halyard or **halliard** (ˈhæljəd) *n Naut.* a line for hoisting or lowering a sail, flag, or spar. [C14 *halier,* infl. by YARD[1]; see HALE[2]]

ham[1] (hæm) *n* **1** the part of the hindquarters of a pig between the hock and the hip. **2** the meat of this part. **3** *Inf.* the back of the leg above the knee. [OE *hamm*]

ham[2] (hæm) *n* **1** *Theatre, inf.* **1a** an actor who overacts or relies on stock gestures. **1b** overacting or clumsy acting. **1c** (*as modifier*): *a ham actor.* **2** *Inf.* a licensed amateur radio operator. ♦ *vb* **hams, hamming, hammed. 3** *Inf.* to overact. [C19: special use of HAM[1]; in some senses prob. infl. by AMATEUR]

Hama ★ (ˈhɑːmɑː) *n* a city in W Syria, on the Orontes River: an early Hittite settlement; famous for its huge water wheels, used for irrigation since the Middle Ages. Pop.: 229 000 (1992 est.). Biblical name: **Hamath.**

Hamadān or **Hamedān** ★ (ˈhæməˌdæn) *n* city in W central Iran, at an altitude of over 1830 m (6000 ft): changed hands several times from the 17th century between Iraq, Persia, and Turkey; trading centre. Pop.: 349 653 (1991).

hamadryad (ˌhæməˈdraɪəd) *n* **1** *Classical myth.* a nymph who inhabits a tree and dies with it. **2** another name for **king cobra.** [C14: from L *Hamādryas,* from Gk *Hamadruas,* from *hama* together with + *drus* tree]

hamadryas (ˌhæməˈdraɪəs) *n* a baboon of Arabia and NE Africa, having long silvery hair on the head, neck, and chest. [C19: via NL from L; see HAMADRYAD]

Hamamatsu ★ (ˌhæməˈmætsuː) *n* a city in central Japan, in S central Honshu: cotton textiles and musical instruments. Pop.: 561 568 (1995).

hamba (ˈhæmbə) *sentence substitute. S. African, usually offens.* go away; be off. [from a Bantu language, from *ukuttamba* to go]

Hamburg ★ (ˈhæmbɜːɡ) *n* a city-state and port in NW Germany, on the River Elbe: the largest port in Germany; a founder member of the Hanseatic League; became a free imperial city in 1510 and a state of the German empire in 1871; university (1919); extensive shipyards. Pop.: 1 705 872 (1995 est.).

hamburger ('hæm,bɜːɡə) *n* a cake of minced beef, often served in a bread roll. Also called: **beefburger**. [C20: from *Hamburger steak* (steak in the fashion of HAMBURG)]

hame (heɪm) *n* either of the two curved bars holding the traces of the harness, attached to the collar of a draught animal. [C14: from MDu. *hame*]

Hameln ★ (*German* 'haːməln) *n* an industrial town in N Germany, in Lower Saxony on the Weser River: famous for the legend of the Pied Piper (supposedly took place in 1284). Pop.: 57 640 (1989 est.). English name: **Hamelin** ('hæməlɪn, 'hæmlɪn).

Hamersley Range ★ ('hæməzlɪ) *n* a mountain range in N Western Australia: iron-ore deposits. Highest peak: 1236 m (4056 ft).

ham-fisted *or* **ham-handed** *adj Inf.* lacking dexterity or elegance; clumsy.

Hamhung *or* **Hamheung** ★ ('haːm'huŋ) *n* an industrial city in central North Korea: commercial and governmental centre of NE Korea during the Yi dynasty (1392–1910). Pop.: 701 000 (1987 est.).

Hamilcar Barca ★ (hæˈmɪlkaː 'baːkə, ˌhæmɪlˌkaː) *n* died ?228 B.C., Carthaginian general; father of Hannibal. He held command (247–41) during the first Punic War and established Carthaginian influence in Spain (237–?228).

Hamilton[1] ★ ('hæməltən) *n* **1** a port in central Canada, in S Ontario on Lake Ontario: iron and steel industry. Pop.: 318 499 (1991). **2** a city in New Zealand, on central North Island. Pop. (urban area): 156 500 (1995 est.). **3** a town in S Scotland, in South Lanarkshire near Glasgow. Pop.: 49 991 (1991). **4** the capital and chief port of Bermuda. Pop.: 1100 (1994 est.). **5** the former name of the **Churchill** River in Labrador.

Hamilton[2] ★ ('hæməltən) *n* **1 Alexander.** ?1757–1804, American statesman. He was a leader of the Federalists and as first secretary of the Treasury (1789–95) established a federal bank. **2 Lady Emma.** ?1765–1815, mistress of Viscount Nelson. **3 Sir William Rowan.** 1805–65, Irish mathematician.

Hamitic (hæˈmɪtɪk, hə-) *n* **1** a group of N African languages related to Semitic. ◆ *adj* **2** denoting or belonging to this group of languages. **3** denoting or characteristic of the Hamites, a group of peoples of N Africa, including the ancient Egyptians, supposedly descended from Noah's son Ham.

hamlet ('hæmlɪt) *n* a small village, esp. (in Britain) one without its own church. [C14: from OF *hamelet*, dim. of *hamel*, from *ham*, of Gmc origin]

Hamlyn ★ ('hæmlɪn) *n* Baron **Paul.** born 1926, British businessman and publisher.

Hamm ★ (*German* ham) *n* an industrial city in NW Germany, in North Rhine-Westphalia: a Hanse town from 1417; severely damaged in World War II. Pop.: 184 020 (1995 est.).

Hammarskjöld ★ ('hæmə,ʃuld; *Swedish* 'hamarʃœld) *n* **Dag (Hjalmar Agne Carl)** (daːg). 1905–61, Swedish statesman; secretary-general of the United Nations (1953–61): Nobel peace prize 1961.

hammer ('hæmə) *n* **1** a hand tool consisting of a heavy usually steel head held transversely on the end of a handle, used for driving in nails, etc. **2** any tool or device with a similar function, such as the striking head on a bell. **3** a power-driven striking tool, esp. one used in forging. **4** a part of a gunlock that strikes the primer or percussion cap when the trigger is pulled. **5** *Athletics.* **5a** a heavy metal ball attached to a flexible wire: thrown in competitions. **5b** the sport of throwing the hammer. **6** an auctioneer's gavel. **7** a device on a piano that is made to strike a string or group of strings causing them to vibrate. **8** *Anat.* the nontechnical name for **malleus**. **9 go under the hammer.** to be offered for sale by an auctioneer. **10 hammer and tongs.** with great effort or energy. **11 on someone's hammer.** *Austral. & NZ sl.* persistently demanding and critical of someone. ◆ *vb* **12** to strike or beat with or as if with a hammer. **13** (*tr*) to shape with or as if with a hammer. **14** (*tr;* foll. by *in* or *into*) to force (facts, ideas, etc.) into (someone) through constant repetition. **15** (*intr*) to feel or sound like hammering. **16** (*intr;* often foll. by *away*) to work at constantly. **17** (*tr*) *Brit.* to criticize severely. **18** (*tr*) *Inf.* to defeat. **19** (*tr*) *Stock Exchange.* **19a** to announce the default of (a member). **19b** to cause prices of (securities, the market, etc.) to fall by bearish selling. [OE *hamor*]
▸ 'hammer-,like *adj*

hammer and sickle *n* the emblem on the flag of the former Soviet Union, representing the industrial workers and the peasants respectively.

hammer beam *n* either of a pair of short horizontal beams that project from opposite walls to support arched braces and struts.

Hammerfest ★ (*Norwegian* 'hamərfest) *n* a port in N Norway, on the W coast of Kvalöy Island: the northernmost town in Europe, with uninterrupted daylight from May 17 to July 29 and no sun between Nov. 21 and Jan. 21; fishing and tourist centre. Pop.: 6900 (1991).

hammerhead ('hæmə,hed) *n* **1** a shark having a flattened hammer-shaped head. **2** a tropical African wading bird having a dark plumage and a long backward-pointing crest. **3** a large African fruit bat with a hammer-shaped muzzle.
▸ 'hammer,headed *adj*

hammerlock ('hæmə,lɒk) *n* a wrestling hold in which a wrestler twists his opponent's arm upwards behind his back.

hammer out *vb* (*tr, adv*) **1** to shape or remove with or as if with a hammer. **2** to settle or reconcile (differences, problems, etc.).

Hammersmith and Fulham ★ ('hæmə,smɪθ) *n* a borough of Greater London on the River Thames: established in 1965 by the amalgamation of Fulham and Hammersmith. Pop.: 156 600 (1994 est.). Area: 16 sq. km (6 sq. miles).

Hammerstein II ★ ('hæmə,staɪn) *n* **Oscar.** 1895–1960, US librettist and songwriter: collaborated with the composer Richard Rodgers in musicals such as *South Pacific* (1949) and *The Sound of Music* (1959).

hammertoe ('hæmə,təʊ) *n* a deformity causing the toe to be bent in a clawlike arch.

Hammett ★ ('hæmət) *n* **Dashiell** (də'ʃiːl). 1894–1961, US writer of such detective novels as *The Maltese Falcon* (1930) and *The Thin Man* (1932).

hammock ('hæmək) *n* a length of canvas, net, etc., suspended at the ends and used as a bed. [C16: from Sp. *hamaca*, from Amerind]

Hammond[1] ★ ('hæmənd) *n* a city in NW Indiana, adjacent to Chicago. Pop.: 82 837 (1994 est.).

Hammond[2] ★ ('hæmənd) *n* **1 Dame Joan.** 1912–96, Australian operatic singer, born in New Zealand. **2 Walter Reginald**, known as *Wally.* 1903–65, English cricketer. An all-rounder, he played for England 85 times between 1928 and 1946.

Hammurabi (ˌhæmʊ'raːbɪ) *or* **Hammurapi** ★ *n* ?18th century B.C., king of Babylonia; promulgator of one of the earliest known codes of law.

hammy ('hæmɪ) *adj* **hammier, hammiest.** *Inf.* **1** (of an actor) tending to overact. **2** (of a play, performance, etc.) overacted or exaggerated.

Hampden ★ ('hæmpdən, 'hæmdən) *n* **John.** 1594–1643, English statesman; one of the leaders of the Parliamentary opposition to Charles I.

hamper[1] ('hæmpə) *vb* **1** (*tr*) to prevent the progress or free movement of. ◆ *n* **2** *Naut.* gear aboard a vessel that, though essential, is often in the way. [C14: from ?; ? rel. to OE *hamm* enclosure, *hemm* HEM[1]]

hamper[2] ('hæmpə) *n* **1** a large basket, usually with a cover. **2** *Brit.* a selection of food and drink packed in a hamper or other container. [C14: var. of earlier *hanaper* a small basket, from OF, of Gmc origin]

Hampshire[1] ★ ('hæmp,ʃɪə, -ʃə) *n* a county of S England, on the English Channel: includes two unitary authorities; crossed by the **Hampshire Downs** and the South Downs, with the New Forest in the southwest and many prehistoric and Roman remains. Administrative centre: Winchester. Pop.: 1 605 700 (1994 est.). Area: 3777 sq. km (1458 sq. miles). Abbrev.: **Hants.**

Hampshire[2] ★ ('hæmpʃə) *n* Sir **Stuart.** born 1914, British philosopher.

Hampstead ★ ('hæmpstɪd) *n* a residential district in N London: part of the Greater London borough of Camden since 1965; nearby is **Hampstead Heath,** a popular recreation area.

Hampton[1] ★ ('hæmptən) *n* **1** a city in SE Virginia, on the harbour of **Hampton Roads** on Chesapeake Bay. Pop.: 139 628 (1994 est.). **2** a district of the Greater London borough of Richmond-upon-Thames, on the River Thames: famous for **Hampton Court Palace** (built in 1515 by Cardinal Wolsey).

Hampton[2] ★ ('hæmptən) *n* **1** Christopher James. born 1946, British playwright. **2** Lionel. 1913–96, US jazz-band leader and vibraphone player.

hamster ('hæmstə) *n* a Eurasian burrowing rodent having a stocky body, short tail, and cheek pouches: a popular pet. [C17: from G, from OHG *hamustro,* of Slavic origin]

hamstring ('hæm,strɪŋ) *n* **1** one of the tendons at the back of the knee. **2** the large tendon at the back of the hind leg of a horse, etc. ◆ *vb* **hamstrings, hamstringing, hamstrung.** (*tr*) **3** to cripple by cutting the hamstring of. **4** to thwart. [C16: HAM[1] + STRING]

Hamsun ★ (*Norwegian* 'hamsun) *n* Knut (knu:t), pen name of *Knut Pedersen.* 1859–1952, Norwegian novelist, whose works include *The Growth of the Soil* (1917): Nobel prize for literature 1920.

hamulus ('hæmjuləs) *n, pl* **hamuli** (-,laɪ). *Biol.* a hook or hooklike process, between the fore and hind wings of a bee. [C18: from L: a little hook, from *hāmus* hook]

Han[1] ★ (hæn) *n* **1** the imperial dynasty that ruled China for most of the time from 206 B.C. to 221 A.D., expanding its territory and developing its bureaucracy. **2** the Chinese people as contrasted with Mongols, Manchus, etc.

Han[2] ★ (hæn) *n* a river in E central China, rising in S Shaanxi and flowing southeast through Hubei to the Yangtze River at Wuhan. Length: about 1450 km (900 miles).

Hanau ★ (*German* 'ha:nau) *n* a city in central Germany, in Hesse east of Frankfurt am Main: a centre of the jewellery industry. Pop.: 84 420 (1989 est.).

Han Cities ★ *pl n* a group of three cities in E central China, in SE Hubei at the confluence of the Han and Yangtze Rivers: Hanyang, Hankow, and Wuchang; united in 1950 to form the conurbation of Wuhan, the capital of Hubei province.

Hancock ★ ('hænkɒk) *n* **1** Anthony John, known as *Tony.* 1924–68, British comedian, noted for his radio series *Hancock's Half Hour.* **2** John. 1737–93, American statesman; first signatory of the Declaration of Independence.

hand (hænd) *n* **1** the prehensile part of the body at the end of the arm, consisting of a thumb, four fingers, and a palm. Related adj: **manual. 2** the corresponding part in animals. **3** something resembling this in shape or function. **4a** the cards dealt in one round of a card game. **4b** a player holding such cards. **4c** one round of a card game. **5** agency or influence: *the hand of God.* **6** a part in something done: *he had a hand in the victory.* **7** assistance: *to give someone a hand.* **8** a pointer on a dial, indicator, or gauge, esp. on a clock. **9** acceptance or pledge of partnership, as in marriage. **10** a position indicated by its location to the side of an object or the observer: *on the right hand.* **11** a contrastive aspect, condition, etc.: *on the other hand.* **12** source or origin: *a story heard at third hand.* **13** a person, esp. one who creates something: *a good hand at painting.* **14** a manual worker. **15** a member of a ship's crew: *all hands on deck.* **16** a person's handwriting: *the letter was in his own hand.* **17** a round of applause: *give him a hand.* **18** a characteristic way of doing something: *the hand of a master.* **19** a unit of length equalling four inches, used for measuring the height of horses. **20** a cluster of bananas. **21** (*modifier*) **21a** of or involving the hand: *a hand grenade.* **21b** carried in or worn on the hand: *hand luggage.* **21c** operated by hand: *a hand drill.* **22**
(*in combination*) made by hand rather than machine: *hand-sewn.* **23 a free hand.** freedom to do as desired. **24 a hand's turn.** (*usually used with a negative*) a small amount of work: *he hasn't done a hand's turn.* **25 a heavy hand.** tyranny or oppression: *he ruled with a heavy hand.* **26 a high hand.** a dictatorial manner. **27 by hand. 27a** by manual rather than mechanical means. **27b** by messenger or personally: *the letter was delivered by hand.* **28 force someone's hand.** to force someone to act. **29 from hand to mouth. 29a** in poverty: *living from hand to mouth.* **29b** without preparation or planning. **30 hand and foot.** in all ways possible; completely: *they waited on him hand and foot.* **31 hand in glove.** in close association. **32 hand over fist.** steadily and quickly: *he makes money hand over fist.* **33 hold one's hand.** to stop or postpone a planned action or punishment. **34 hold someone's hand.** to support, help, or guide someone, esp. by giving sympathy. **35 in hand. 35a** under control. **35b** receiving attention. **35c** available in reserve. **35d** with deferred payment: *he works a week in hand.* **36 keep one's hand in.** to maintain a limited involvement in an activity so as to preserve one's proficiency at it. **37 (near) at hand.** very close, esp. in time. **38 on hand.** close by; present. **39 out of hand. 39a** beyond control. **39b** without reservation or deeper examination: *he condemned him out of hand.* **40 show one's hand.** to reveal one's stand, opinion, or plans. **41 take in hand.** to discipline; control. **42 throw one's hand in.** to give up a venture, game, etc. **43 to hand.** accessible. **44 try one's hand.** to attempt to do something. ◆ *vb* (*tr*) **45** to transmit or offer by the hand or hands. **46** to help or lead with the hand. **47** *Naut.* to furl (a sail). **48 hand it to someone.** to give credit to someone. ◆ See also **hand down, hand in,** etc., **hands.** [OE *hand*]

▶ **'handless** *adj*

handbag ('hænd,bæg) *n* **1** Also called: **bag, purse** (US and Canad.), **pocketbook** (chiefly US). a woman's small bag carried to contain personal articles. **2** a small suitcase that can be carried by hand.

handball ('hænd,bɔ:l) *n* **1** a game in which two teams of seven players try to throw a ball into their opponent's goal. **2** a game in which two or four people strike a ball against a wall with the hand. **3** *Soccer.* the offence committed when a player other than a goalkeeper in his own penalty area touches the ball with a hand. ◆ *vb* **4** *Australian Rules football.* to pass (the ball) with a blow of the fist.

handbarrow ('hænd,bærəʊ) *n* a flat tray for transporting loads, usually carried by two men.

handbill ('hænd,bɪl) *n* a small printed notice for distribution by hand.

handbook ('hænd,bʊk) *n* a reference book listing brief facts on a subject or place or directions for maintenance or repair, as of a car.

handbrake ('hænd,breɪk) *n* **1** a brake operated by a hand lever. **2** the lever that operates the handbrake.

handbrake turn *n* a turn sharply reversing the direction of a vehicle by speedily applying the handbrake while turning the steering wheel.

handbreadth ('hænd,bretθ, -,bredθ) *or* **hand's-breadth** *n* the width of a hand used as an indication of length.

h and c *abbrev. for* hot and cold (water).

handcart ('hænd,kɑːt) *n* a simple cart, usually with one or two wheels, pushed or drawn by hand.

handcraft ('hænd,krɑːft) *n* **1** another word for **handicraft.** ◆ *vb* **2** (*tr*) to make by handicraft. ▶ **'hand,crafted** *adj*

handcuff ('hænd,kʌf) *vb* **1** (*tr*) to put handcuffs on (a person); manacle. ◆ *n* **2** (*pl*) a pair of locking metal rings joined by a short bar or chain for securing prisoners, etc.

hand down *vb* (*tr, adv*) **1** to bequeath. **2** to pass (an outgrown garment) on from one member of a family to a younger one. **3** *US & Canad. law.* to announce (a verdict).

-handed *adj* of, for, or using a hand or hands as specified: *left-handed; a four-handed game of cards.*

Handel ★ ('hænd°l) *n* **George Frederick.** German name *Georg Friedrich Händel.* 1685–1759, German composer, resident in England, noted particularly for his oratorios,

---

★ people and places

including the *Messiah* (1741) and *Samson* (1743), 40 operas, and 12 concerti grossi.

handful ('hændful) *n, pl* **handfuls. 1** the amount or number that can be held in the hand. **2** a small number or quantity. **3** *Inf.* a person or thing difficult to manage or control.

handgun ('hænd,gʌn) *n US & Canad.* a firearm that can be fired with one hand, such as a pistol.

handicap ('hændɪ,kæp) *n* **1** something that hampers or hinders. **2a** a contest, esp. a race, in which competitors are given advantages or disadvantages of weight, distance, etc., in an attempt to equalize their chances. **2b** the advantage or disadvantage prescribed. **3** *Golf.* the number of strokes by which a player's averaged score exceeds par for the course. **4** any disability or disadvantage resulting from physical, mental, or social impairment or abnormality. ◆ *vb* **handicaps, handicapping, handicapped.** (*tr*) **5** to be a hindrance or disadvantage to. **6** to assign a handicap to. **7** to organize (a contest) by handicapping. [C17: prob. from *hand in cap*, a lottery game in which players drew forfeits from a cap or deposited money in it]
▶ '**handi,capper** *n*

handicapped ('hændɪ,kæpt) *adj* **1a** physically or mentally disabled. **1b** (*as collective n;* preceded by *the*): *the handicapped.* **2** (of a competitor) assigned a handicap.

handicraft ('hændɪ,krɑːft) *n* **1** skill in working with the hands. **2** a particular skill performed with the hands, such as weaving. **3** the work so produced. ◆ Also called: **handcraft.** [C15: changed from HANDCRAFT through infl. of HANDIWORK]

hand in *vb* (*tr, adv*) to return or submit (something, such as an examination paper).

handiwork ('hændɪ,wɜːk) *n* **1** work produced by hand. **2** the result of the action or endeavours of a person or thing. [OE *handgeweorc*, from HAND + *ge-* (collective prefix) + *weorc* WORK]

handkerchief ('hæŋkətʃɪf, -tʃiːf) *n* a small square of soft absorbent material carried and used to wipe the nose, etc.

handle ('hænd³l) *n* **1** the part of a utensil, drawer, etc., designed to be held in order to move, use, or pick up the object. **2** *Sl.* a person's name or title. **3** *CB radio.* a slang name for **call sign. 4** an excuse for doing something: *his background served as a handle for their mockery.* **5** the quality, as of textiles, perceived by feeling. **6** *NZ.* a glass beer mug with a handle. **7 fly off the handle.** *Inf.* to become suddenly extremely angry. ◆ *vb* **handles, handling, handled.** (*mainly tr*) **8** to hold, move, or touch with the hands. **9** to operate using the hands: *the boy handled the reins well.* **10** to control: *my wife handles my investments.* **11** to manage successfully: *a secretary must be able to handle clients.* **12** to discuss (a theme, subject, etc.). **13** to deal with in a specified way: *I was handled with great tact.* **14** to trade or deal in (specified merchandise). **15** (*intr*) to react in a specified way to operation: *the car handles well on bends.* [OE]
▶ '**handled** *adj* ▶ '**handling** *n*

handlebar moustache ('hænd³l,bɑː) *n* a bushy extended moustache with curled ends.

handlebars ('hænd³l,bɑːz) *pl n* (*sometimes sing*) a metal tube having its ends curved to form handles, used for steering a bicycle, etc.

handler ('hændlə) *n* **1** a person who trains and controls an animal, esp. a police dog. **2** the trainer or second of a boxer.

Handley Page ★ ('hændlɪ) *n* Sir **Frederick.** See (Sir Frederick Handley) **Page.**

handmade (,hænd'meɪd) *adj* made by hand, not by machine, esp. with care or craftsmanship.

handmaiden ('hænd,meɪd³n) *or* **handmaid** *n* **1** a person or thing that serves a useful but subordinate purpose. **2** *Arch.* a female servant.

hand-me-down *n Inf.* **1** something, esp. an outgrown garment, passed down from one person to another. **2** anything that has already been used by another.

hand-off *Rugby.* ◆ *n* **1** the act of warding off an oppos-

ing player with the open hand. ◆ *vb* **hand off. 2** (*tr, adv*) to ward off thus.

hand on *vb* (*tr, adv*) to pass to the next in a succession.

hand organ *n* another name for **barrel organ.**

hand-out *n* **1** clothing, food, or money given to a needy person. **2** a leaflet, free sample, etc., given out to publicize something. **3** a statement distributed to the press or an audience to confirm or replace an oral presentation. ◆ *vb* **hand out. 4** (*tr, adv*) to distribute.

hand over *vb* **1** (*tr, adv*) to surrender possession of; transfer. ◆ *n* **handover. 2** a transfer; surrender.

hand-pick *vb* (*tr*) to select with great care, as for a special job.
▶ ,**hand-'picked** *adj*

handrail ('hænd,reɪl) *n* a rail alongside a stairway, etc., to provide support.

hands (hændz) *pl n* **1** power or keeping: *your welfare is in his hands.* **2** Also called: **handling.** *Soccer.* the infringement of touching the ball with the hand or arm. **3 change hands.** to pass from the possession of one person to another. **4 hands down.** without effort; easily. **5 have one's hands full.** to be completely occupied. **5b** to be beset with problems. **6 have one's hands tied.** to be unable to act. **7 lay hands on** *or* **upon. 7a** to get possession of. **7b** to beat up; assault. **7c** to find. **7d** *Christianity.* to place hands on (someone) in order to confirm or ordain. **8 off one's hands.** for which one is no longer responsible. **9 on one's hands. 9a** for which one is responsible: *I've got too much on my hands to help.* **9b** to spare: *time on my hands.* **10 wash one's hands of.** to have nothing more to do with; refuse to accept responsibility for.

handsaw ('hænd,sɔː) *n* any saw for use in one hand only.

hand's-breadth *n* another name for **handbreadth.**

handsel *or* **hansel** ('hæns³l) *Arch. or dialect.* ◆ *n* **1** a gift for good luck at the beginning of a new year, new venture, etc. ◆ *vb* **handsels, handselling, handselled** *or* **hansels, hanselling, hanselled;** *or US* **handsels, handseling, handseled** *or* **hansels, hanseling, hanseled.** (*tr*) **2** to give a handsel to (a person). **3** to inaugurate. [OE *handselen* delivery into the hand]

handset ('hænd,set) *n* a telephone mouthpiece and earpiece mounted as a single unit.

handshake ('hænd,ʃeɪk) *n* the act of grasping and shaking a person's hand, as when being introduced or agreeing on a deal.

hands-off *adj* **1** (of a machine, device, etc.) without need of manual operation. **2** denoting a policy, etc., of deliberate noninvolvement: *a hands-off strategy towards industry.*

handsome ('hænsəm) *adj* **1** (of a man) good-looking. **2** (of a woman) fine-looking in a dignified way. **3** well-proportioned; stately: *a handsome room.* **4** liberal: *a handsome allowance.* **5** gracious or generous: *a handsome action.* [C15 *handsom* easily handled]
▶ '**handsomely** *adv* ▶ '**handsomeness** *n*

hands-on *adj* involving practical experience of equipment, etc.: *hands-on training in computing.*

handspring ('hænd,sprɪŋ) *n* a gymnastic feat in which a person starts from a standing position and leaps forwards or backwards into a handstand and then onto his feet.

handstand ('hænd,stænd) *n* the act of supporting the body on the hands in an upside-down position.

hand-to-hand *adj, adv* at close quarters.

hand-to-mouth *adj, adv* with barely enough money or food to satisfy immediate needs.

handwork ('hænd,wɜːk) *n* work done by hand rather than by machine.
▶ '**hand,worked** *adj*

handwriting ('hænd,raɪtɪŋ) *n* **1** writing by hand rather than by typing or printing. **2** a person's characteristic writing style: *that is in my handwriting.*
▶ '**hand,written** *adj*

handy ('hændɪ) *adj* **handier, handiest. 1** conveniently

★ people and places

within reach. **2** easy to handle or use. **3** skilful with one's hands.
▶ **'handily** adv ▶ **'handiness** n

Handy ★ ('hændɪ) n **W(illiam) C(hristopher)**. 1873–1958, US blues musician and songwriter, esp. noted for the song "St Louis Blues".

handyman ('hændɪˌmæn) n, pl **handymen**. a man employed to do or skilled in odd jobs, etc.

hanepoot ('hɑːnəˌpɔːt) n S. African. a kind of grape for eating or wine making. [from Du.]

hang (hæŋ) vb **hangs, hanging, hung**. **1** to fasten or be fastened from above, esp. by a cord, chain, etc. **2** to place or be placed in position so as to allow free movement: to hang a door. **3** (intr; sometimes foll. by over) to be suspended; hover: a pall of smoke hung over the city. **4** (intr; sometimes foll. by over) to threaten. **5** (intr) to be or remain doubtful (esp. in **hang in the balance**). **6** (p.t. & p.p. **hanged**) to suspend or be suspended by the neck until dead. **7** (tr) to decorate, furnish, or cover with something suspended. **8** (tr) to fasten to a wall: to hang wallpaper. **9** to exhibit or be exhibited in an art gallery, etc. **10** to droop or allow to droop: to hang one's head. **11** (of cloth, clothing, etc.) to drape, fall, or flow: her skirt hangs well. **12** (tr) to suspend (game such as pheasant) so that it becomes slightly decomposed and therefore more tasty. **13** (of a jury) to prevent or be prevented from reaching a verdict. **14** (p.t. & p.p. **hanged**) Sl. to damn or be damned: used in mild curses or interjections. **15** (intr) to pass slowly (esp. in **time hangs heavily**). **16 hang fire**. to be delayed or to procrastinate. ◆ n **17** the way in which something hangs. **18** (usually used with a negative) Sl. a damn: I don't care a hang. **19 get the hang of.** Inf. **19a** to understand the technique of doing something. **19b** to perceive the meaning of. ◆ See also **hang about, hang back**, etc. [OE hangian]

hang about or **around** vb (intr) **1** to waste time; loiter. **2** (adv; foll. by with) to frequent the company (of someone).

hangar ('hæŋə) n a large building for storing and maintaining aircraft. [C19: from F: shed, ?from Med. L angārium shed used as a smithy, from ?]

hang back vb (intr, adv; often foll. by from) to be reluctant to go forward or carry on.

Hangchow ★ ('hæŋ'dʒəʊ) n a variant transliteration of the Chinese name for **Hangzhou**.

hangdog ('hæŋˌdɒg) adj downcast, furtive, or guilty in appearance or manner.

hanger ('hæŋə) n **1a** any support, such as a peg or loop, on or by which something may be hung. **1b** See **coat hanger**. **2a** a person who hangs something. **2b** (in combination): paperhanger. **3** a type of dagger worn on a sword belt. **4** Brit. a wood on a steep hillside.

hanger-on n, pl **hangers-on**. a sycophantic follower or dependant.

hang-glider n an unpowered aircraft consisting of a large wing made of cloth or plastic stretched over a light framework from which the pilot hangs in a harness.
▶ **'hang-ˌgliding** n

hangi ('hʌŋi:) n NZ. **1** an open-air cooking pit. **2** the food cooked in it. **3** the social gathering at the resultant meal. [from Maori]

hang in vb (intr, prep) Inf., chiefly US & Canad. to persist: just hang in there for a bit longer.

hanging ('hæŋɪŋ) n **1a** the putting of a person to death by suspending the body by the neck. **1b** (as modifier): a hanging offence. **2** (often pl) a decorative drapery hung on a wall or over a window. ◆ adj **3** not supported from below; suspended. **4** undecided; still under discussion. **5** projecting downwards; overhanging. **6** situated on a steep slope. **7** (prenominal) given to issuing death sentences: a hanging judge.

Hanging Gardens of Babylon ★ n (in ancient Babylon) gardens, probably planted on terraces of a ziggurat: one of the Seven Wonders of the World.

hanging valley n Geog. a tributary valley entering a main valley at a much higher level because of overdeepening of the main valley, esp. by glacial erosion.

hangman ('hæŋmən) n, pl **hangmen**. an official who carries out a sentence of hanging.

hangnail ('hæŋˌneɪl) n a piece of skin torn away from, but still attached to, the base or side of a fingernail. [C17: from OE angnægl, from enge tight + nægl nail; infl. by HANG]

hang on vb (intr) **1** (adv) to continue or persist, esp. with effort or difficulty. **2** (adv) to grasp or hold. **3** (prep) to depend on: everything hangs on this deal. **4** (prep) Also: **hang onto, hang upon**. to listen attentively to. **5** (adv) Inf. to wait: hang on for a few minutes.

hang out vb (adv) **1** to suspend, be suspended, or lean. **2** (intr) Inf. to frequent a place. **3 let it all hang out.** Inf., chiefly US. **3a** to relax completely in an unassuming way. **3b** to act or speak freely. ◆ n **hang-out**. **4** Inf. a place that one frequents.

hangover ('hæŋˌəʊvə) n **1** the delayed aftereffects of drinking too much alcohol. **2** a person or thing left over from or influenced by a past age.

Hang Seng Index (hæŋ sɛŋ) n an index of share prices based on an average of 33 stocks quoted on the Hong Kong Stock Exchange. [name of a Hong Kong bank]

hang together vb (intr, adv) **1** to be cohesive or united. **2** to be consistent: your statements don't quite hang together.

Hanguk ★ ('hæn'guk) n the Korean name for **South Korea**.

hang up vb (adv) **1** (tr) to put on a hook, hanger, etc. **2** to replace (a telephone receiver) on its cradle at the end of a conversation. **3** (tr; usually passive; usually foll. by on) Inf. to cause to have an emotional or psychological preoccupation or problem: he's really hung up on his mother. ◆ n **hang-up**. Inf. **4** an emotional or psychological preoccupation or problem. **5** a persistent cause of annoyance.

Hangzhou ('hæŋ'dʒəʊ) or **Hangchow** ★ n a port in E China, capital of Zhejiang province, on **Hangzhou Bay** (an inlet of the East China Sea), at the foot of the Eye of Heaven Mountains: regarded by Marco Polo as the finest city in the world; seat of two universities (1927, 1959). Pop.: 1 340 000 (1991 est.).

hank (hæŋk) n **1** a loop, coil, or skein, as of rope. **2** Naut. a ringlike fitting that can be opened to admit a stay for attaching the luff of a sail. **3** a unit of measurement of cloth, such as a length of 840 yards (767 m) of cotton or 560 yards (512 m) of worsted yarn. [C15: from ON]

hanker ('hæŋkə) vb (foll. by for, after, or an infinitive) to have a yearning. [C17: prob. from Du. dialect hankeren]
▶ **'hankering** n

Hankow or **Han-k'ou** ★ ('hæn'kaʊ) n a former city in SE China, in SE Hubei at the confluence of the Han and Yangtze Rivers: one of the Han Cities; merged with Hanyang and Wuchang in 1950 to form the conurbation of Wuhan.

Hanks ★ (hæŋks) n **Tom**. born 1956, US film actor: his films include Forrest Gump (1994), Saving Private Ryan (1998), and You've Got Mail (1999).

hanky or **hankie** ('hæŋkɪ) n, pl **hankies**. Inf. short for **handkerchief**.

hanky-panky ('hæŋkɪ'pæŋkɪ) n Inf. **1** dubious or foolish behaviour. **2** illicit sexual relations. [C19: var. of HOCUS-POCUS]

Hannah ★ ('hænə) n Old Testament. the woman who gave birth to Samuel (I Samuel 1–2).

Hannibal ★ ('hænɪb'l) n 247–182 B.C., Carthaginian general; son of Hamilcar Barca. He commanded the Carthaginian army in the Second Punic War (218–201). After capturing Sagunto in Spain, he invaded Italy (218), crossing the Alps with an army of about 40 000 men and defeated the Romans. In 203 he was recalled to defend Carthage and was defeated by Scipio, later being forced into exile; committed suicide to avoid capture.

Hannover ★ (German ha'noːfər) n a city in N Germany, capital of Lower Saxony: capital of the kingdom of Hannover (1815–66); situated on the Mittelland Canal. Pop.: 525 763 (1995 est.). English spelling: **Hanover**.

Hanoi ★ (hæ'nɔɪ) n the capital of Vietnam, on the Red River: became capital of Tonkin in 1802, French Indochina in 1887, Vietnam in 1945, and North Vietnam (1954–75); university (1917); industrial centre. Pop.: 2 154 900 (1993 est.).

Hanover[1] ★ ('hænəuvə) *n* the English spelling of **Hannover.**

Hanover[2] ('hænəuvə) *n* **1** a princely house of Germany (1692–1815), the head of which succeeded to the British throne as George I in 1714. **2** the royal house of Britain (1714–1901).
▸ ˌHano'verian *adj, n*

Hansard ('hænsɑːd) *n* **1** the official verbatim report of the proceedings of the British Parliament. **2** a similar report kept by the Canadian House of Commons and other legislative bodies. [C19: after L. *Hansard* (1752–1828) and his descendants, who compiled the reports until 1889]

Hanse (hæns) *n* **1** a medieval guild of merchants. **2** a fee paid by the new members of a medieval trading guild. **3** another name for the **Hanseatic League**. [C12: of Gmc origin]
▸ Hanseatic (ˌhænsɪ'ætɪk) *adj*

Hanseatic League *n* a commercial organization of towns in N Germany formed in the mid-14th century to protect and control trade.

hansel ('hænsᵊl) *n*, *vb* a variant spelling of **handsel.**

hansom ('hænsəm) *n* (*sometimes cap.*) a two-wheeled one-horse carriage with a fixed hood. The driver sits on a high outside seat at the rear. Also called: **hansom cab.** [C19: after its designer J. A. *Hansom* (1803–82)]

hantavirus ('hæntəˌvaɪrəs) *n* any member of a genus of viruses that infect rodents and can be transmitted to humans, in whom they can cause kidney damage or respiratory disease. [C20: after the *Hantaan* river, South Korea]

Hants (hænts) *abbrev. for* Hampshire.

Hanukkah ('hɑːnəkə, -nuˌkɑː) *n* a variant of **Chanukah.**

Hanuman (ˌhʌnʊ'mɑːn) *n* **1** (*pl* **Hanumans**) another word for **entellus** (the monkey). **2** the monkey chief of Hindu mythology. [from Hindi, from Sansk. *hanumant* having (conspicuous) jaws, from *hanu* jaw]

Hanyang *or* **Han-yang** ★ ('hæn'jæŋ) *n* a former city in SE China, in SE Hubei at the confluence of the Han and Yangtze Rivers: one of the Han Cities; merged with Hankow and Wuchang in 1950 to form the conurbation of Wuhan.

hap (hæp) *Arch.* ◆ *n* **1** luck; chance. **2** an occurrence. ◆ *vb* **haps, happing, happed. 3** (*intr*) to happen. [C13: from ON *happ* good luck]

ha'penny ('heɪpnɪ) *n*, *pl* **ha'pennies.** *Brit.* a variant spelling of **halfpenny.**

haphazard (hæp'hæzəd) *adv, adj* **1** at random. ◆ *adj* **2** careless.
▸ hap'hazardly *adv* ▸ hap'hazardness *n*

hapless ('hæplɪs) *adj* unfortunate; wretched.
▸ 'haplessly *adv* ▸ 'haplessness *n*

haplography (hæp'lɒgrəfɪ) *n*, *pl* **haplographies.** the accidental omission of a letter or syllable which recurs, as in spelling *endodontics* as *endontics.* [C19: from Gk, from *haplous* single + -GRAPHY]

haploid ('hæplɔɪd) *Biol.* ◆ *adj* **1** (esp. of gametes) having a single set of unpaired chromosomes. ◆ *n* **2** a haploid cell or organism. [C20: from Gk *haploeidēs*, from *haplous* single]
▸ 'haploidy *n*

haplology (hæp'lɒlədʒɪ) *n* omission of a repeated occurrence of a sound or syllable in fluent speech, as for example in the pronunciation of *library* as ('laɪbrɪ).

haply ('hæplɪ) *adv* (*sentence modifier*) an archaic word for **perhaps.**

happen ('hæpᵊn) *vb* **1** (*intr*) to take place; occur. **2** (*intr*; foll. by *to*) (of some unforeseen event, esp. death) to fall to the lot (of): *if anything happens to me it'll be your fault.* **3** (*tr*) to chance (to be or do something): *I happen to know him.* **4** (*tr*; takes a clause as object) to be the case, esp. by chance: *it happens that I know him.* ◆ *adv, sentence substitute.* **5** N English dialect. another word for **perhaps.** [C14: see HAP, -EN[1]]

happening ('hæpənɪŋ, 'hæpnɪŋ) *n* **1** an event. **2** an improvised or spontaneous performance consisting of bizarre events. ◆ *adj* **3** *Inf.* fashionable and up-to-the-minute.

happen on *or* **upon** *vb* (*intr*; *prep*) to find by chance.

happy ('hæpɪ) *adj* **happier, happiest. 1** feeling or expressing joy; pleased. **2** willing: *I'd be happy to show you around.* **3** causing joy or gladness. **4** fortunate: *the happy position of not having to work.* **5** aptly expressed; appropriate: *a happy turn of phrase.* **6** (*postpositive*) *Inf.* slightly intoxicated. [C14: see HAP, -Y[1]]
▸ 'happily *adv* ▸ 'happiness *n*

happy event *n Inf.* the birth of a child.

happy-go-lucky *adj* carefree or easy-going.

happy hour *n* a period during which some public houses, bars, restaurants, etc., charge reduced prices.

happy hunting ground *n* **1** (in Amerind legend) the paradise to which a person passes after death. **2** a productive or profitable area to explore.

happy medium *n* a course or state that avoids extremes.

Hapsburg ★ ('hæps,bɜːg) *n* a German princely family founded by Albert, count of Hapsburg (1153). From 1440 to 1806, they ruled the Holy Roman Empire almost uninterruptedly and provided rulers for Austria, Spain, Hungary, Bohemia, etc. The line continued as the royal house of **Hapsburg-Lorraine,** ruling in Austria (1806–48) and Austria-Hungary (1848–1918). German name: **Habsburg.**

haptic ('hæptɪk) *adj* relating to or based on the sense of touch. [C19: from Gk, from *haptein* to touch]

hapuka *or* **hapuku** (həˈpuːkə, ˈhɑːpʊkə) *n NZ.* another name for **groper.** [from Maori]

hara-kiri (ˌhærəˈkɪrɪ) *or* **hari-kari** (ˌhærɪˈkɑːrɪ) *n* (formerly, in Japan) ritual suicide by disembowelment when disgraced or under sentence of death. Also called: **seppuku.** [C19: from Japanese, from *hara* belly + *kiri* cutting]

Harald I ★ ('hærəld) *n* called *Harald Fairhair.* ?850–933, first king of Norway: his rule caused emigration to the British Isles.

Harald III ★ *n* surname *Hardraade.* 1015–66, king of Norway (1047–66); invaded England (1066) and died at the battle of Stamford Bridge.

harangue (həˈræŋ) *vb* **harangues, haranguing, harangued. 1** to address (a person or crowd) in an angry, vehement, or forcefully persuasive way. ◆ *n* **2** a loud, forceful, or angry speech. [C15: from OF, from OIt. *aringa* public speech, prob. of Gmc origin]
▸ haˈranguer *n*

Harappa ★ (həˈræpə) *n* an ancient city in the Punjab in NW Pakistan: one of the centres of the Indus civilization that flourished from 2500 to 1700 B.C.; probably destroyed by Indo-European invaders.
▸ Haˈrappan *adj, n*

Harar *or* **Harrer** ★ ('hɑːrə) *n* a city in E Ethiopia: former capital of the Muslim state of Adal. Pop.: 122 932 (1994 est.).

Harare ★ (həˈrɑːrɪ) *n* the capital of Zimbabwe, in the northeast: University of Zimbabwe (1957); industrial and commercial centre. Pop.: 1 184 169 (1992). Former name (until 1982): **Salisbury.**

harass ('hærəs, həˈræs) *vb* (*tr*) to trouble, torment, or confuse by continual persistent attacks, questions, etc. [C17: from F *harasser*, var. of OF *harer* to set a dog on, of Gmc origin]
▸ 'harassed *adj* ▸ 'harassment *n*

Harbin ★ (hɑːˈbiːn, -ˈbɪn) *n* a city in NE China, capital of Heilongjiang province on the Songhua River: founded by the Russians in 1897; centre of tsarist activities after the October Revolution in Russia (1917). Pop.: 2 830 000 (1991 est.). Also called: **Ha-erh-pin.**

harbinger ('hɑːbɪndʒə) *n* **1** a person or thing that announces or indicates the approach of something; fore-runner. ◆ *vb* **2** (*tr*) to announce the approach or arrival of. [C12: from OF *herbergere*, from *herberge* lodging, from OSaxon]

harbour *or US* **harbor** ('hɑːbə) *n* **1** a sheltered port. **2** a place of refuge or safety. ◆ *vb* **3** (*tr*) to give shelter to: *to harbour a criminal*. **4** (*tr*) to maintain secretly: *to harbour a grudge*. **5** to shelter (a vessel) in a harbour or (of a vessel) to seek shelter. [OE *hereborg*, from *here* army + *beorg* shelter]

harbourage *or US* **harborage** ('hɑːbərɪdʒ) *n* shelter or refuge, as for a ship.

harbour master *n* an official in charge of a harbour.

hard (hɑːd) *adj* **1** firm or rigid. **2** toughened; not soft or smooth: *hard skin*. **3** difficult to do or accomplish: *a hard task*. **4** difficult to understand: *a hard question*. **5** showing or requiring considerable effort or application: *hard work*. **6** demanding: *a hard master*. **7** harsh; cruel: *a hard fate*. **8** inflicting pain, sorrow, or hardship: *hard times*. **9** tough or violent: *a hard man*. **10** forceful: *a hard knock*. **11** cool or uncompromising: *we took a long hard look at our profit factor*. **12** indisputable; real: *hard facts*. **13** *Chem.* (of water) impairing the formation of a lather: *hard water*. **14** practical, shrewd, or calculating: *he is a hard man in business*. **15** harsh: *hard light*. **16a** (of currency) in strong demand, esp. as a result of a good balance of payments situation. **16b** (of credit) difficult to obtain; tight. **17** (of alcoholic drink) being a spirit rather than a wine, beer, etc. **18** (of a drug) highly addictive. **19** *Physics*. (of radiation) having high energy and the ability to penetrate solids. **20** *Chiefly US*. (of goods) durable. **21** short for **hardcore**. **22** *Phonetics*. (not in technical use) denoting the consonants *c* and *g* when they are pronounced as in *cat* and *got*. **23a** heavily fortified. **23b** (of nuclear missiles) located underground. **24** politically extreme: *the hard left*. **25** *Brit. & NZ inf.* incorrigible or disreputable (esp. in **a hard case**). **26 a hard nut to crack**. **26a** a person not easily won over. **26b** a thing not easily done or understood. **27 hard by**. close by. **28 hard of hearing**. slightly deaf. **29 hard up**. *Inf.* **29a** in need of money. **29b** (foll. by *for*) in great need (of): *hard up for suggestions*. ◆ *adv* **30** with great energy, force, or vigour: *the team always played hard*. **31** as far as possible: *hard left*. **32** earnestly or intently: *she thought hard about the formula*. **33** with great intensity: *his son's death hit him hard*. **34** (foll. by *on*, *upon*, *by*, or *after*) close; near: *hard on his heels*. **35** (foll. by *at*) assiduously; devotedly. **36a** with effort or difficulty: *their victory was hard won*. **36b** (*in combination*): *hard-earned*. **37** slowly: *prejudice dies hard*. **38 go hard with**. to cause pain or difficulty to (someone). **39 hard put (to it)**. scarcely having the capacity (to do something). ◆ *n* **40** *Brit.* a roadway across a fore-shore. **41** *Sl.* hard labour. **42** *Taboo sl.* an erection of the penis (esp. in **get** or **have a hard on**). [OE *heard*]
▸ **'hardness** *n*

hard and fast *adj* (**hard-and-fast** *when prenominal*). (of rules, etc.) invariable or strict.

hardback ('hɑːd,bæk) *n* **1** a book with covers of cloth, cardboard, or leather. ◆ *adj* **2** *Also*: **casebound, hardbound, hardcover**. of or denoting a hardback or the publication of hardbacks.

hard-bitten *adj Inf.* tough and realistic.

hardboard ('hɑːd,bɔːd) *n* a thin stiff sheet made of compressed sawdust and wood pulp bound together under heat and pressure.

hard-boiled *adj* **1** (of an egg) boiled until solid. **2** *Inf.* **2a** tough, realistic. **2b** cynical.

hard card *n* a hard disk, mounted on a card, that can be added to a personal computer.

hard cash *n* money or payment in money, as opposed to payment by cheque, credit, etc.

hard coal *n* another name for **anthracite**.

hard copy *n* computer output printed on paper, as contrasted with machine-readable output such as magnetic tape.

hardcore ('hɑːd,kɔː) *n* **1** a style of rock music characterized by short fast songs with minimal melody and aggressive delivery. **2** a type of dance music with a very fast beat.

hard core *n* **1** the members of a group who form an intransigent nucleus resisting change. **2** material, such as broken stones, used to form a foundation for a road, etc. ◆ *adj* **hard-core**. **3** (of pornography) describing or depicting sexual acts in explicit detail. **4** extremely committed or fanatical: *a hard-core Communist*.

hard disk *n Computing*. a disk of rigid magnetizable material that is used to store data for computers: it is permanently mounted in its disk drive and usually has a storage capacity of a few gigabytes.

Hardecanute ★ ('hɑːdɪkə,njuːt) *n* a variant of **Harthacanute**.

harden ('hɑːdᵊn) *vb* **1** to make or become hard or harder; freeze, stiffen, or set. **2** to make or become tough or unfeeling. **3** to make or become stronger or firmer. **4** (*intr*) *Commerce*. (of prices, a market, etc.) to cease to fluctuate. **4b** (of price) to rise higher.
▸ **'hardener** *n*

Hardenberg ★ (*German* 'hardənbɛrk) *n* Friedrich von ('friːdrɪç fɔn). the original name of **Novalis**.

hardened ('hɑːdᵊnd) *adj* **1** rigidly set, as in a mode of behaviour. **2** toughened; seasoned.

harden off *vb* (*tr, adv*) to cause (plants) to become resistant to cold, frost, etc., by gradually exposing them to such conditions.

hard feeling *n* (*often pl; often used with a negative*) resentment; ill will: *no hard feelings?*

hard hat *n* **1** a hat made of a hard material for protection, worn esp. by construction workers, equestrians, etc. **2** *Inf., chiefly US*. a construction worker.

hard-headed *adj* tough, realistic, or shrewd; not moved by sentiment.

hardhearted (,hɑːd'hɑːtɪd) *adj* unkind or intolerant.
▸ **,hard'heartedness** *n*

Hardicanute ★ ('hɑːdɪkə,njuːt) *n* a variant of **Harthacanute**.

Hardie ★ ('hɑːdɪ) *n* (**James**) **Keir** (kɪə). 1856–1915, British Labour leader and politician, born in Scotland; the first parliamentary leader of the Labour Party.

hardihood ('hɑːdɪ,hʊd) *n* courage or daring.

Harding ★ ('hɑːdɪŋ) *n* **Warren G(amaliel)**. 1865–1923, 29th president of the US (1921–23).

hard labour *n Criminal law*. (formerly) the penalty of compulsory physical labour imposed in addition to a sentence of imprisonment.

hard landing *n* **1** a landing by a rocket or spacecraft in which the vehicle is destroyed on impact. **2** a solution to a problem, esp. an economic problem, that involves hardship.

hard line *n* an uncompromising course or policy.
▸ **,hard'liner** *n*

hardly ('hɑːdlɪ) *adv* **1** scarcely; barely: *we hardly knew the family*. **2** only just: *he could hardly hold the cup*. **3** *Often used ironically*. not at all: *he will hardly incriminate himself*. **4** with difficulty. **5** *Rare*. harshly or cruelly.

> **USAGE NOTE** Since *hardly, scarcely,* and *barely* already have negative force, it is redundant to use another negative in the same clause: *he had hardly had* (not *he hadn't hardly had*) *time to think; there was scarcely any* (not *scarcely no*) *bread left*.

hard-nosed *adj Inf.* tough, shrewd, and practical.

Hardouin Mansart ★ (*French* ardwɛ̃ mɑ̃sar) *n* See (Jules Hardouin) Mansart.

hard pad *n* (in dogs) an abnormal increase in the thickness of the foot pads: one of the clinical signs of canine distemper. See **distemper**[1].

hard palate *n* the anterior bony portion of the roof of the mouth.

hardpan ('hɑːd,pæn) *n* a hard impervious layer of clay below the soil.

hard paste *n* **a** porcelain made with kaolin and petuntse, of Chinese origin and made in Europe from the early 18th century. **b** (*as modifier*): *hard-paste porcelain.*

hard-pressed *adj* **1** in difficulties. **2** subject to severe competition or attack. **3** closely pursued.

hard rock *n* rhythmically simple rock music that is very loud.

hard sauce *n* another name for **brandy butter.**

hard science *n* one of the natural or physical sciences, such as physics, chemistry, biology, geology, or astronomy.
▸ **hard scientist** *n*

hard sell *n* an aggressive insistent technique of selling or advertising.

hard-shell *adj also* **hard-shelled. 1** *Zool.* having a shell or carapace that is thick, heavy, or hard. **2** *US.* strictly orthodox.

hardship ('hɑːdʃɪp) *n* **1** conditions of life difficult to endure. **2** something that causes suffering or privation.

hard shoulder *n Brit.* a surfaced verge running along the edge of a motorway for emergency stops.

hardtack ('hɑːd,tæk) *n* a kind of hard saltless biscuit, formerly eaten esp. by sailors as a staple aboard ship. Also called: **ship's biscuit, sea biscuit.**

hardtop ('hɑːd,tɒp) *n* a car with a metal or plastic roof that is sometimes detachable.

hardware ('hɑːd,wɛə) *n* **1** metal tools, implements, etc., esp. cutlery or cooking utensils. **2** *Computing.* the physical equipment used in a computer system, such as the central processing unit, peripheral devices, and memory. Cf. **software. 3** mechanical equipment, components, etc. **4** heavy military equipment, such as tanks and missiles. **5** *Inf.* a gun.

hard-wired *adj* (of a circuit or instruction) permanently wired into a computer, replacing separate software.

hardwood ('hɑːd,wʊd) *n* **1** the wood of any of numerous broad-leaved trees, such as oak, beech, ash, etc., as distinguished from the wood of a conifer. **2** any tree from which this wood is obtained.

hardy ('hɑːdɪ) *adj* **hardier, hardiest. 1** having or demanding a tough constitution; robust. **2** bold; courageous. **3** foolhardy; rash. **4** (of plants) able to live out of doors throughout the winter. [C13: from OF *hardi*, p.p. of *hardir* to become bold, of Gmc origin; cf. OE *hierdan* to HARDEN, ON *hertha*, OHG *herten*]
▸ **'hardily** *adv* ▸ **'hardiness** *n*

Hardy ★ ('hɑːdɪ) *n* **1** Oliver. See **Laurel and Hardy. 2** Thomas. 1840–1928, British writer; his novels set in his native Dorset, include *Far from the Madding Crowd* (1874), *Tess of the d'Urbervilles* (1891), and *Jude the Obscure* (1895).

hare (hɛə) *n, pl* **hares** *or* **hare. 1** a solitary mammal which is larger than a rabbit, has longer ears and legs, and lives in a shallow nest (form). **2 run with the hare and hunt with the hounds.** to be on good terms with both sides. **3 start a hare.** to raise a topic for conversation. ♦ *vb* **hares, haring, hared. 4** (*intr*; often foll. by *off, after,* etc.) *Brit. inf.* to run fast or wildly. [OE *hara*]
▸ **'hare,like** *adj*

Hare ★ (hɛə) *n* **1** Sir **David.** born 1947, British dramatist and theatre director: his plays include *Plenty* (1978) and *The Judas Kiss* (1998). **2 William.** 19th century, Irish murderer and body snatcher; associate of William Burke.

hare and hounds *n* (*functioning as sing*) a game in which certain players (**hares**) run across country scattering pieces of paper that the other players (**hounds**) follow in an attempt to catch the hares.

harebell ('hɛə,bɛl) *n* a N temperate plant having slender stems and leaves, and bell-shaped blue flowers.

harebrained *or* **hairbrained** ('hɛə,breɪnd) *adj* rash, foolish, or badly thought out.

Hare Krishna ('hɑːrɪ 'krɪʃnə) *n* **1** a Hindu sect devoted to a form of Hinduism (**Krishna Consciousness**) based on the worship of the god Krishna. **2** (*pl* **Hare Krishnas**) a member or follower of this sect. [C20: from Hindi, literally: Lord Krishna (vocative): the opening words of a sacred verse often chanted in public by adherents of the movement]

harelip ('hɛə,lɪp) *n* a congenital cleft or fissure in the

midline of the upper lip, resembling the cleft upper lip of a hare, often occurring with cleft palate.
▸ **'hare,lipped** *adj*

harem ('hɛərəm, hɑːˈriːm) *or* **hareem** (hɑːˈriːm) *n* **1** the part of an Oriental house reserved strictly for wives, concubines, etc. **2** a Muslim's wives and concubines collectively. **3** a group of female animals that are the mates of a single male. [C17: from Ar. *harīm* forbidden (place)]

hare's-foot *n* a plant that grows on sandy soils in Europe and NW Asia and has downy heads of white or pink flowers.

Harfleur ★ ('hɑːflɜː; *French* arflœr) *n* a port in N France, in the Seine-Maritime department: important centre in the Middle Ages. Pop.: 9700 (latest est.).

Hargeisa ★ (hɑːˈgeɪsə) *n* a city in NW Somalia: former capital of British Somaliland (1941–60); trading centre for nomadic herders. Pop.: 400 000 (1987 est.).

Hargreaves ★ ('hɑːgriːvz) *n* **James.** died 1778, English inventor of the spinning jenny.

haricot ('hærɪkəʊ) *n* a variety of French bean with light-coloured edible seeds, which can be dried and stored. [C17: from F, ?from Amerind]

Harijan ('hʌrɪdʒən) *n* a member of certain classes in India, formerly considered inferior and untouchable. [Hindi, lit.: man of God (so called by Mahatma Gandhi)]

hari-kari (,hærɪˈkɑːrɪ) *n* a non-Japanese variant spelling of **hara-kiri.**

Haringey ★ ('hærɪŋgeɪ) *n* a borough of N Greater London. Pop.: 212 300 (1994 est.). Area: 30 sq. km (12 sq. miles).

hark (hɑːk) *vb* (*intr; usually imperative*) to listen; pay attention. [OE *heorcnian* to HEARKEN]

hark back *vb* (*intr, adv*) to return to an earlier subject in speech or thought.

harken ('hɑːkən) *vb* a variant spelling (esp. US) of **hearken.**
▸ **'harkener** *n*

harl (hɑːl) *n Angling.* a variant of **herl.**

Harlech ★ ('hɑːlək) *n* a town in N Wales, in Gwynedd: noted for its ruined 13th-century castle overlooking Cardigan Bay: tourism. Pop.: 1233 (1991).

Harlem ★ ('hɑːləm) *n* a district of New York City, in NE Manhattan: now largely a Black ghetto.

harlequin ('hɑːlɪkwɪn) *n* **1** (*sometimes cap.*) *Theatre.* a stock comic character originating in the commedia dell'arte; the foppish lover of Columbine in the English harlequinade. He is usually represented in diamond-patterned multicoloured tights, wearing a black mask. **2** a clown or buffoon. ♦ *adj* **3** varied in colour or decoration. [C16: from OF *Herlequin, Hellequin* leader of band of demon horsemen]

harlequinade (,hɑːlɪkwɪˈneɪd) *n* **1** (*sometimes cap.*) *Theatre.* a play in which harlequin has a leading role. **2** buffoonery.

Harley ★ ('hɑːlɪ) *n* **Robert,** 1st Earl of Oxford. 1661–1724, British statesman; head of the government (1710–14), negotiated the treaty of Utrecht (1713).

Harley Street ★ *n* a street in central London famous for its large number of medical specialists' consulting rooms.

harlot ('hɑːlət) *n* a prostitute. [C13: from OF *herlot* rascal, from ?]
▸ **'harlotry** *n*

Harlow[1] ★ ('hɑːləʊ) *n* a town in SE England, in W Essex: designated a new town in 1947. Pop.: 74 629 (1991).

Harlow[2] ★ ('hɑːləʊ) *n* **Jean,** real name *Harlean Carpentier.* 1911–37, US film actress, whose films include *Hell's Angels* (1930) and *Bombshell* (1933).

harm (hɑːm) *n* **1** physical or mental injury. **2** moral wrongdoing. ♦ *vb* **3** (*tr*) to injure physically, morally, or mentally. [OE *hearm*]

harmattan (hɑːˈmætˈn) *n* a dry dusty wind from the Sahara blowing towards the W African coast. [C17: from native African language *haramata,* ?from Ar. *harām* forbidden thing; see HAREM]

★ people and places

harmful ('hɑːmfʊl) *adj* causing or tending to cause harm; injurious.
▸ **'harmfully** *adv*

harmless ('hɑːmlɪs) *adj* **1** not causing or tending to cause harm. **2** unlikely to annoy or worry people: *a harmless sort of man*.
▸ **'harmlessly** *adv*

harmonic (hɑː'mɒnɪk) *adj* **1** of, producing, or characterized by harmony; harmonious. **2** *Music*. of or belonging to harmony. **3** *Maths*. **3a** capable of expression in the form of sine and cosine functions. **3b** of or relating to numbers whose reciprocals form an arithmetic progression. **4** *Physics*. of or concerned with a harmonic or harmonics. ◆ *n* **5** *Physics, music*. a component of a periodic quantity, such as a musical tone, with a frequency that is an integral multiple of the fundamental frequency. **6** *Music*. (not in technical use) overtone. ◆ See also **harmonics**. [C16: from L *harmonicus* relating to HARMONY]
▸ **har'monically** *adv*

harmonica (hɑː'mɒnɪkə) *n* **1** Also called: **mouth organ**. a small wind instrument in which reeds of graduated lengths set into a metal plate enclosed in a narrow oblong box are made to vibrate by blowing and sucking. **2** See **glass harmonica**. [C18: from L *harmonicus* relating to HARMONY]

harmonic analysis *n* the representation of a periodic function by means of the summation and integration of simple trigonometric functions.

harmonic mean *n* the reciprocal of the arithmetic mean of the reciprocals of a set of specified numbers: the harmonic mean of 2, 3, and 4 is 3/ (½ + ⅓ + ¼) = 36/13.

harmonic minor scale *n* *Music*. a minor scale modified from the natural by the sharpening of the seventh degree.

harmonic motion *n* a periodic motion in which the displacement is symmetrical about a point or a periodic motion that is composed of such motions.

harmonic progression *n* a sequence of numbers whose reciprocals form an arithmetic progression, as 1, ½, ⅓, ...

harmonics (hɑː'mɒnɪks) *n* **1** (*functioning as sing*) the science of musical sounds and their acoustic properties. **2** (*functioning as pl*) the overtones of a fundamental note, as produced by lightly touching the string of a stringed instrument at one of its node points while playing.

harmonic series *n* **1** *Maths*. a series whose terms are in harmonic progression, as in 1 + ½ + ⅓ + ... **2** *Acoustics*. the series of tones with frequencies strictly related to one another and to the fundamental tone, as obtained by touching lightly the node points of a string while playing it.

harmonious (hɑː'məʊnɪəs) *adj* **1** (esp. of colours or sounds) fitting together well. **2** having agreement. **3** tuneful or melodious.

harmonist ('hɑːmənɪst) *n* **1** a person skilled in the art and techniques of harmony. **2** a person who combines and collates parallel narratives.

harmonium (hɑː'məʊnɪəm) *n* a musical keyboard instrument in which air from pedal-operated bellows causes the reeds to vibrate. [C19: from F, from *harmonie* HARMONY]

harmonize or **harmonise** ('hɑːmə,naɪz) *vb* **harmonizes, harmonizing, harmonized** or **harmonises, harmonising, harmonised. 1** to make or become harmonious. **2** (*tr*) *Music*. to provide a harmony for (a tune, etc.). **3** (*intr*) to sing in harmony, as with other singers. **4** to collate parallel narratives.
▸ **harmoni'zation** or **harmoni'sation** *n*

harmony ('hɑːmənɪ) *n, pl* **harmonies. 1** agreement in action, opinion, feeling, etc. **2** order or congruity of parts to their whole or to one another. **3** agreeable sounds. **4** *Music*. **4a** any combination of notes sounded simultaneously. **4b** the vertically represented structure of a piece of music. Cf. **melody** (sense 1b). **4c** the art or science concerned with combinations of chords. **5** a collation of parallel narratives, esp. of the four Gospels. [C14: from L *harmonia* concord of sounds, from Gk: harmony, from *harmos* a joint]

Harmsworth ★ ('hɑːmzwɜːθ) *n* **1** Alfred Charles William. See (Viscount) **Northcliffe. 2** Harold Sydney. See (1st Viscount) **Rothermere**.

harness ('hɑːnɪs) *n* **1** an arrangement of straps fitted to a draught animal in order that the animal can be attached to and pull a cart. **2** something resembling this, esp. for attaching something to the body: *a parachute harness*. **3** *Weaving*. the part of a loom that raises and lowers the warp threads. **4** *Arch*. armour. **5 in harness**. at one's routine work. ◆ *vb* (*tr*) **6** to put a harness on (a horse). **7** (usually foll. by *to*) to attach (a draught animal) to (a cart, etc.). **8** to control so as to employ the energy or potential power of: *to harness the atom*. **9** to equip with armour. [C13: from OF *harneis* baggage, prob. from ON *hernest* (unattested), from *herr* army + *nest* provisions]
▸ **'harnesser** *n*

harness race *n* *Horse racing*. a trotting or pacing race for horses pulling sulkies.

Harney Peak ★ ('hɑːnɪ) *n* a mountain in SW South Dakota: the highest peak in the Black Hills. Height: 2207 m (7242 ft).

Harold I ★ ('hærəld) *n* surname *Harefoot*. died 1040, king of England (1037–40); son of Canute.

Harold II ★ *n* ?1022–66, king of England (1066); son of Earl Godwin and successor of Edward the Confessor. His claim to the throne was disputed by William the Conqueror, who defeated him at the Battle of Hastings (1066).

harp (hɑːp) *n* **1** a large triangular plucked stringed instrument consisting of a soundboard connected to an upright pillar by means of a curved crossbar from which the strings extend downwards. ◆ *vb* (*intr*) **2** to play the harp. **3** (foll. by *on* or *upon*) to speak or write in a persistent and tedious manner. [OE *hearpe*]
▸ **'harper** or **'harpist** *n*

Harper's Ferry ★ ('hɑːpəz) *n* a village in NE West Virginia, at the confluence of the Potomac and Shenandoah Rivers: site of an arsenal seized by John Brown (1859). Pop.: 308 (1990).

harpoon (hɑː'puːn) *n* **1a** a barbed missile attached to a long cord and hurled or fired from a gun when hunting whales, etc. **1b** (*as modifier*): *a harpoon gun*. ◆ *vb* **2** (*tr*) to spear with or as if with a harpoon. [C17: prob. from Du. *harpoen*, from OF *harpon* clasp, ? of Scand. origin]
▸ **har'pooner** or **,harpoon'eer** *n*

harp seal *n* a brownish-grey North Atlantic and Arctic seal, having a dark mark on its back.

harpsichord ('hɑːpsɪ,kɔːd) *n* a horizontally strung stringed keyboard instrument, triangular in shape, with strings plucked by pivoted plectra mounted on jacks. [C17: from NL *harpichordium*, from LL *harpa* HARP + L *chorda* CHORD[1]]
▸ **'harpsi,chordist** *n*

harpy ('hɑːpɪ) *n, pl* **harpies**. a cruel grasping woman. [C16: from L *Harpyia*, from Gk *Harpuiai* the Harpies, lit.: snatchers, from *harpazein* to seize]

Harpy ('hɑːpɪ) *n, pl* **Harpies**. *Greek myth*. a ravenous creature with a woman's head and trunk and a bird's wings and claws.

harquebus ('hɑːkwɪbəs) *n, pl* **harquebuses**. a variant spelling of **arquebus**.

Harrer ★ ('hɑːrə) *n* a variant spelling of **Harar**.

harridan ('hærɪd⁹n) *n* a scolding old woman; nag. [C17: from ?; ? rel. to F *haridelle*, lit.: broken-down horse]

harrier[1] ('hærɪə) *n* **1** a person or thing that harries. **2** a diurnal bird of prey having broad wings and long legs and tail.

harrier[2] ('hærɪə) *n* **1** a smallish breed of hound used originally for hare-hunting. **2** a cross-country runner. [C16: from HARE[1] + -ER[1]; infl. by HARRIER[1]]

Harriman ★ ('hærɪmən) *n* W(illiam) Averell. 1891–1986, US diplomat: negotiated the Nuclear Test Ban Treaty with the Soviet Union (1963); governor of New York (1955–58).

Harris[1] ★ ('hærɪs) *n* the S part of the island of Lewis with Harris, in the Outer Hebrides. Pop.: (including Lewis) 23 390 (1981). Area: 500 sq. km (193 sq. miles).

Harris[2] ★ ('hærɪs) n 1 Sir **Arthur Travers**, known as *Bomber Harris*. 1892–1984, British air marshal. He was commander-in-chief of Bomber Command of the RAF (1942–45). 2 **Frank**. 1856–1931, British writer and journalist; his books include his autobiography *My Life and Loves* (1923–27) and *Contemporary Portraits* (1915–30). 3 **Joel Chandler**. 1848–1908, US writer; creator of Uncle Remus. 4 **Roy**. 1898–1979, US composer, esp. of orchestral and choral music.

Harrisburg ★ ('hærɪs,bɜːg) n a city in S Pennsylvania, on the Susquehanna River: the state capital. Pop.: 53 430 (1992 est.).

Harrison ★ ('hærɪs³n) n 1 **Benjamin**. 1833–1901, 23rd president of the US (1889–93). 2 **George**. born 1943, British rock singer, guitarist, and songwriter: a member of the Beatles (1962–70). 3 **Rex** (**Carey**). 1908–90, British actor. His many films include *Major Barbara* (1940) and *My Fair Lady* (1964). 4 **William Henry**. 1773–1841, 9th president of the US (1841); grandfather of Benjamin Harrison.

Harris Tweed n *Trademark*. a loose-woven tweed made in the Outer Hebrides.

Harrogate ★ ('hærəgɪt) n a town in N England, in North Yorkshire: a spa. Pop.: 66 178 (1991).

harrow ('hærəʊ) n 1 any of various implements used to level the ground, stir the soil, break up clods, destroy weeds, etc., in soil. ◆ vb (tr) 2 to draw a harrow over (land). 3 to distress; vex. [C13: from ON]
▶ 'harrower n ▶ 'harrowing adj

Harrow ★ ('hærəʊ) n a borough of NW Greater London; site of an English boys' public school founded in 1571 at **Harrow-on-the-Hill**, a part of this borough. Pop.: 210 300 (1994 est.). Area: 51 sq. km (20 sq. miles).
▶ **Harrovian** (hə'rəʊvɪən) adj, n

harrumph (hə'rʌmf) vb (intr) *Chiefly US & Canad*. to clear or make the noise of clearing the throat.

harry ('hærɪ) vb **harries**, **harrying**, **harried**. 1 (tr) to harass; worry. 2 to ravage (a town, etc.), esp. in war. [OE *hergian*; rel. to *here* army, ON *herja* to lay waste]

harsh (hɑːʃ) adj 1 rough or grating to the senses. 2 stern, severe, or cruel. [C16: prob. of Scand. origin]
▶ 'harshly adv ▶ 'harshness n

hart (hɑːt) n, pl **harts** or **hart**. the male of the deer, esp. the red deer aged five years or more. [OE *heorot*]

Hart ★ (hɑːt) n **Lorenz** ('lɒr³nz). 1895–1943, US lyricist: collaborated with Richard Rodgers in writing musicals.

hartal (hɑː'tɑːl) n (in India) the act of closing shops or suspending work, esp. in political protest. [C20: from Hindi *hartāl*, from *hāt* shop + *tālā* bolt for a door, from Sansk.]

Harte ★ (hɑːt) n (**Francis**) **Bret**. 1836–1902, US writer, noted for his sketches of Californian gold miners, such as *The Luck of Roaring Camp* (1870).

hartebeest ('hɑːtɪ,biːst) or **hartbeest** ('hɑːt,biːst) n either of two large African antelopes having an elongated muzzle, lyre-shaped horns, and a fawn-coloured coat. [C18: via Afrik. from Du.; see HART, BEAST]

Hartford ★ ('hɑːtfəd) n a port in central Connecticut, on the Connecticut River: the state capital. Pop.: 124 196 (1994 est.).

Harthacanute ('hɑːθəkə,njuːt), **Hardecanute**, or **Hardicanute** ★ n ?1019–42, king of Denmark (1035–42) and of England (1040–42); son of Canute.

Hartington ★ ('hɑːtɪŋtən) n **Lord**. See (8th Duke of) Devonshire.

Hartlepool ★ ('hɑːtlɪ,puːl) n 1 a port in NE England, in Co. Durham, on the North Sea: greatly enlarged in 1967 by its amalgamation with West Hartlepool; engineering, clothing, food processing. Pop.: 87 310 (1991). 2 a unitary authority in NE England, in Co. Durham. Pop.: 90 409 (1994 est.). Area: 93 sq. km (36 sq. miles).

Hartley ★ ('hɑːtlɪ) n 1 **David**. 1705–57, English philosopher and physician. In *Observations of Man* (1749) he introduced the theory of psychological associationism. 2 **L(eslie) P(oles)**. 1895–1972, British novelist. His novels include the trilogy *The Shrimp and the Anemone* (1944), *The Sixth Heaven* (1946), and *Eustace and Hilda* (1947).

Hartnell ★ ('hɑːtn³l) n Sir **Norman**. 1901–79, British couturier.

hartshorn ('hɑːts,hɔːn) n an obsolete name for **sal volatile**. [OE *heortes horn* hart's horn (formerly a chief source of ammonia)]

hart's-tongue n an evergreen Eurasian fern with narrow undivided fronds.

harum-scarum ('heərəm'skeərəm) adj, adv 1 in a reckless way or of a reckless nature. ◆ n 2 a person who is impetuous or rash. [C17: ?from *hare* (in obs. sense: harass) + *scare*, var. of STARE]

Harun al-Rashid ★ (hæ'ruːn 'ælrə'ʃiːd) n ?763–809 A.D., Abbasid caliph of Islam (786–809), whose court at Baghdad was idealized in the *Arabian Nights*.

haruspex (hə'rʌspeks) n, pl **haruspices** (hə'rʌspɪ,siːz). (in ancient Rome) a priest who practised divination, esp. by examining the entrails of animals. [C16: from L, prob. from *hīra* gut + *specere* to look]
▶ **haruspicy** (hə'rʌspɪsɪ) n

harvest ('hɑːvɪst) n 1 the gathering of a ripened crop. 2 the crop itself. 3 the season for gathering crops. 4 the product of an effort, action, etc.: *a harvest of love*. ◆ vb 5 to gather (a ripened crop) from (the place where it has been growing). 6 (tr) to receive (consequences). [OE *hærfest*]
▶ 'harvesting n

harvester ('hɑːvɪstə) n 1 a person who harvests. 2 a harvesting machine, esp. a combine harvester.

harvest home n 1 the bringing in of the harvest. 2 *Chiefly Brit*. a harvest supper.

harvestman ('hɑːvɪstmən) n, pl **harvestmen**. 1 a person engaged in harvesting. 2 Also called (US and Canad.): **daddy-longlegs**. an arachnid having a small rounded body and very long thin legs.

harvest moon n the full moon occurring nearest to the autumnal equinox.

harvest mouse n a very small reddish-brown Eurasian mouse inhabiting cornfields, hedgerows, etc.

Harvey ★ ('hɑːvɪ) n **William**. 1578–1657, English physician who discovered the mechanism of blood circulation.

Harwell ★ ('hɑː,wel) n a village in S England, in Oxfordshire: atomic research station (1947).

Harwich ★ ('hærɪtʃ) n a port in SE England, in NE Essex on the North Sea. Pop.: 18 436 (1991).

Haryana ★ (hər'jɑːnə) n a state of NE India, formed in 1966 from the Hindi-speaking parts of the state of Punjab. Capital: Chandigarh (shared with Punjab). Pop.: 17 925 000 (1994 est.). Area: 44 506 sq. km (17 182 sq. miles).

Harz or **Harz Mountains** ★ (hɑːts) pl n a range of wooded hills in central Germany, between the Rivers Weser and Elbe: source of many legends. Highest peak: Brocken, 1142 m (3746 ft).

has (hæz) vb (used with *he*, *she*, *it*, or a singular noun) a form of the present tense (indicative mood) of **have**.

has-been n *Inf*. a person or thing that is no longer popular, successful, effective, etc.

Hasdrubal ★ ('hæzdrʊb³l) n died 207 B.C., Carthaginian general: commanded the Carthaginian army in Spain (218–211); joined his brother Hannibal in Italy and was killed at the Metaurus.

Hašek ★ (Czech 'haʃɛk) n **Jaroslav** ('jarɔslaf). 1883–1923, Czech novelist and short-story writer; author of *The Good Soldier Schweik* (1923).

hash[1] (hæʃ) n 1 a dish of diced cooked meat, vegetables, etc., reheated in a sauce. 2 a reuse or rework of old material. 3 **make a hash of**. *Inf*. to mess up or destroy. 4 **settle someone's hash**. *Inf*. to subdue or silence someone. ◆ vb (tr) 5 to chop into small pieces. 6 to mess up. [C17: from OF *hacher* to chop up, from *hache* HATCHET]

hash[2] n *sl*. short for **hashish**.

Hashemite Kingdom of Jordan ★ ('hæʃɪ,maɪt) n the official name of **Jordan**.

hashish ('hæʃiːʃ, -ɪʃ) or **hasheesh** n a resinous extract of the dried flower tops of the female hemp plant, used as a hallucinogenic. See also **cannabis**. [C16: from Ar. *hashīsh* hemp]

haslet ('hæzlɪt) *or* **harslet** *n* a loaf of cooked minced pig's offal, eaten cold. [C14: from OF *hastelet* piece of spit-roasted meat, from *haste* spit, of Gmc origin]

hasn't ('hæz³nt) contraction of has not.

hasp (hɑːsp) *n* 1 a metal fastening consisting of a hinged strap with a slot that fits over a staple and is secured by a pin, bolt, or padlock. ♦ *vb* 2 (*tr*) to secure (a door, window, etc.) with a hasp. [OE *hæpse*]

Hassan II ★ (hæ'saːn, 'hæs³n) *n* born 1929, king of Morocco from 1961.

Hasselt ★ (*Flemish* 'hɒsəlt; *French* asɛlt) *n* a market town in E Belgium, capital of Limbourg province. Pop.: 67 486 (1995 est.).

Hassid ('hæsɪd) *n* a variant spelling of **Chassid**.

hassium ('hæsɪəm) *n* a synthetic element produced in small quantities by high-energy ion bombardment. Symbol: Hs; atomic no. 108. Former name: **hahnium**. [C20: from L, from HESSE[1], German state where it was discovered]

hassle ('hæs³l) *Inf.* ♦ *n* 1 a great deal of trouble. 2 a prolonged argument. ♦ *vb* **hassles, hassling, hassled**. 3 (*tr*) to cause annoyance or trouble to (someone); harass. 4 (*intr*) to quarrel or wrangle. [C20: from ?]

hassock ('hæsək) *n* 1 a firm upholstered cushion used for kneeling on, esp. in church. 2 a thick clump of grass. [OE *hassuc* matted grass]

hast (hæst) *vb Arch. or dialect.* (used with the pronoun *thou*) a singular form of the present tense (indicative mood) of **have**.

hastate ('hæsteɪt) *adj* (of a leaf) having a pointed tip and two outward-pointing lobes at the base. [C18: from L *hastātus*, from *hasta* spear]

haste (heɪst) *n* 1 speed, esp. in an action. 2 the act of hurrying in a careless manner. 3 a necessity for hurrying; urgency. 4 **make haste**. to hurry; rush. ♦ *vb* **hastes, hasting, hasted. 5** a poetic word for **hasten**. [C14: from OF *haste*, of Gmc origin]

hasten ('heɪs³n) *vb* 1 (*may take an infinitive*) to hurry or cause to hurry. 2 (*tr*) to be anxious (to say something). ► '**hastener** *n*

Hastings[1] ★ ('heɪstɪŋz) *n* 1 a port in SE England, in East Sussex on the English Channel: near the site of the **Battle of Hastings** (1066), in which William the Conqueror defeated King Harold; chief of the Cinque Ports. Pop.: 81 139 (1991). 2 a town in New Zealand, on E North Island: centre of a rich agricultural and fruit-growing region. Pop. (urban area): 58 700 (1995 est.).

Hastings[2] ★ ('heɪstɪŋz) *n* **Warren**. 1732–1818, British administrator in India; governor general of Bengal (1773–85). He was impeached by parliament (1788) on charges of corruption; acquitted in 1795.

hasty ('heɪstɪ) *adj* **hastier, hastiest.** 1 rapid; swift; quick. 2 excessively or rashly quick. 3 short-tempered. 4 showing irritation or anger: *hasty words*. ► '**hastily** *adv* ► '**hastiness** *n*

hat (hæt) *n* 1 a head covering, esp. one with a brim and a shaped crown. 2 *Inf.* a role or capacity. 3 **I'll eat my hat**. *Inf.* I will be greatly surprised if (something that proves me wrong) happens. 4 **keep (something) under one's hat**. to keep (something) secret. 5 **pass** (*or* **send**) **the hat round**. to collect money, as for a cause. 6 **take off one's hat**. to admire or congratulate. 7 **talk through one's hat**. 7a to talk foolishly. 7b to deceive or bluff. ♦ *vb* **hats, hatting, hatted. 8** (*tr*) to supply (a person, etc.) with a hat or put a hat on (someone). [OE *hætt*] ► '**hatless** *adj*

hatband ('hæt,bænd) *n* a band or ribbon around the base of the crown of a hat.

hatbox ('hæt,bɒks) *n* a box or case for a hat.

hatch[1] (hætʃ) *vb* 1 to cause (the young of various animals, esp. birds) to emerge from the egg or (of young birds, etc.) to emerge from the egg. 2 to cause (eggs) to break and release the fully developed young or (of eggs) to break and release the young animal within. 3 (*tr*) to contrive or devise (a scheme, plot, etc.). ♦ *n* 4 the act or pro-

cess of hatching. 5 a group of newly hatched animals. [C13: of Gmc origin]

hatch[2] (hætʃ) *n* 1 a covering for a hatchway. 2a short for **hatchway**. 2b a door in an aircraft or spacecraft. 3 Also called: **serving hatch**. an opening in a wall separating a kitchen from a dining area. 4 the lower half of a divided door. 5 a sluice in a dam, dyke, or weir. 6 **down the hatch**. *Sl.* (used as a toast) drink up! 7 **under hatches**. 7a below decks. 7b out of sight. 7c dead. [OE *hæcc*]

hatch[3] (hætʃ) *vb Drawing, engraving, etc.* to mark (a figure, etc.) with fine parallel or crossed lines to indicate shading. [C15: from OF *hacher* to chop, from *hache* HATCHET] ► '**hatching** *n*

hatch[4] (hætʃ) *n Inf.* short for **hatchback**.

hatchback ('hætʃ,bæk) *n* 1 a sloping rear end of a car having a single door that is lifted to open. 2 a car having such a rear end.

hatchery ('hætʃərɪ) *n, pl* **hatcheries**. a place where eggs are hatched under artificial conditions.

hatchet ('hætʃɪt) *n* 1 a short axe used for chopping wood, etc. 2 a tomahawk. 3 (*modifier*) of narrow dimensions and sharp features: *a hatchet face*. 4 **bury the hatchet**. to cease hostilities and become reconciled. [C14: from OF *hachette*, from *hache* axe, of Gmc origin]

hatchet job *n Inf.* a malicious or devastating verbal or written attack.

hatchet man *n Inf.* 1 a person carrying out unpleasant assignments for an employer or superior. 2 a severe or malicious critic.

hatchling ('hætʃlɪŋ) *n* a young animal that has newly emerged from the egg. [C19: from HATCH[1] + -LING[1]]

hatchment ('hætʃmənt) *n Heraldry.* a diamond-shaped tablet displaying the coat of arms of a dead person. [C16: changed from earlier use of *achievement* in this sense]

hatchway ('hætʃ,weɪ) *n* 1 an opening in the deck of a vessel to provide access below. 2 a similar opening in a wall, floor, ceiling, or roof.

hate (heɪt) *vb* **hates, hating, hated. 1** to dislike (something) intensely; detest. 2 (*intr*) to be unwilling (to be or do something). ♦ *n* 3 intense dislike. 4 *Inf.* a person or thing that is hated (esp. in **pet hate**). 5 (*modifier*) expressing or arousing feelings of hatred: *hate mail*. [OE *hatian*] ► '**hateable** *or* '**hatable** *adj* ► '**hater** *n*

hateful ('heɪtful) *adj* 1 causing or deserving hate; loathsome; detestable. 2 *Arch.* full of hate. ► '**hatefully** *adv* ► '**hatefulness** *n*

Hatfield ★ ('hæt,fiːld) *n* a market town in S central England, in Hertfordshire, with a new town of the same name built on the outskirts. Pop.: 31 104 (1991).

hath (hæθ) *vb Arch. or dialect.* (used with the pronouns *he, she,* or *it* or a singular noun) a form of the present tense (indicative mood) of **have**.

Hathaway ★ ('hæθə,weɪ) *n* **Anne**. ?1557–1623, wife of William Shakespeare.

Hathor ★ ('hæθɔː) *n* (in ancient Egyptian religion) the mother of Horus and goddess of creation. ► **Hathoric** (hæ'θɒrɪk, -'θɒr-) *adj*

hatred ('heɪtrɪd) *n* intense dislike; enmity.

Hatshepsut (hæt'ʃepsuːt) *or* **Hatshepset** ★ *n* queen of Egypt of the 18th dynasty (?1512–1482 B.C.), who built a temple at Deir el Bahri near Thebes.

hat stand *or* esp. *US* **hat tree** *n* a pole equipped with hooks for hanging up hats, etc.

hatter ('hætə) *n* 1 a person who makes and sells hats. 2 **mad as a hatter**. eccentric.

Hatteras ★ ('hætərəs) *n* **Cape**. a promontory off the E coast of North Carolina, on **Hatteras Island**, which is situated between Pamlico Sound and the Atlantic: known as the "Graveyard of the Atlantic" for its danger to shipping.

Hattersley ★ ('hætəzlɪ) *n* **Roy** (**Sydney George**), Baron Hattersley of Sparkbrook. born 1932, British Labour politician; deputy leader of the Labour Party (1983–92), shadow home secretary (1987–92).

hat trick *n* 1 *Cricket*. the achievement of a bowler in taking three wickets with three successive balls. **2** any achievement of three successive points, victories, etc.

hauberk ('hɔːbɜːk) *n* a long coat of mail, often sleeveless. [C13: from OF *hauberc*, of Gmc origin; cf. OHG *halsberc*, OE *healsbeorg*, from *heals* neck + *beorg* protection]

Haughey ★ ('hɔːxɪ; *Irish* 'hʌhiː) *n* **Charles James.** born 1925, Irish politician; leader of the Fianna Fáil party; prime minister of the Republic of Ireland (1979–81; 1982; 1987–92).

haughty ('hɔːtɪ) *adj* **haughtier, haughtiest.** having or showing arrogance. [C16: from OF *haut* lofty, from L *altus* high]
▶ '**haughtily** *adv* ▶ '**haughtiness** *n*

haul (hɔːl) *vb* **1** to drag (something) with effort. **2** (*tr*) to transport, as in a lorry. **3** *Naut.* to alter the course of (a vessel), esp. so as to sail closer to the wind. **4** (*intr*) *Naut.* (of the wind) to blow from a direction nearer the bow. ♦ *n* **5** the act of dragging with effort. **6** (esp. of fish) the amount caught at a single time. **7** something that is hauled. **8** the goods obtained from a robbery. **9** a distance of hauling or travelling. **10** the amount of a contraband seizure: *arms haul, drugs haul.* [C16: from OF *haler*, of Gmc origin]
▶ '**hauler** *n*

haulage ('hɔːlɪdʒ) *n* **1** the act or labour of hauling. **2** a rate or charge levied for the transportation of goods, esp. by rail.

haulier ('hɔːljə) *n* **1** *Brit.* a person or firm that transports goods by road. **2** a mine worker who conveys coal from the workings to the foot of the shaft.

haulm *or* **halm** (hɔːm) *n* **1** the stalks of beans, peas, potatoes, grasses, etc., collectively. **2** a single stem of such a plant. [OE *healm*]

haul up *vb* (*adv*) **1** (*tr*) *Inf.* to call to account or criticize. **2** *Naut.* to sail (a vessel) closer to the wind.

haunch (hɔːntʃ) *n* **1** the human hip or fleshy hindquarter of an animal. **2** the leg and loin of an animal, used for food. **3** *Archit.* the part of an arch between the impost and apex. [C13: from OF *hanche*; rel. to Sp., It. *anca*, of Gmc origin]

haunt (hɔːnt) *vb* **1** to visit (a person or place) in the form of a ghost. **2** (*tr*) to recur to (the memory, thoughts, etc.): *he was haunted by the fear of insanity.* **3** to visit (a place) frequently. **4** to associate with (someone) frequently. ♦ *n* **5** (*often pl*) a place visited frequently. **6** a place to which animals habitually resort for food, drink, shelter, etc. [C13: from OF *hanter*, of Gmc origin]

haunted ('hɔːntɪd) *adj* **1** frequented or visited by ghosts. **2** (*postpositive*) obsessed or worried.

haunting ('hɔːntɪŋ) *adj* **1** (of memories) poignant or persistent. **2** poignantly sentimental; eerily evocative.
▶ '**hauntingly** *adv*

Hauptmann ★ (*German* 'hauptman) *n* **Gerhart** ('geːrhart). 1862–1946, German naturalist and writer. His works include the drama *The Weavers* (1892): Nobel prize for literature 1912.

Hauraki Gulf ★ (hau'rækɪ) *n* an inlet of the Pacific in New Zealand, on the N coast of North Island.

Hausa ('hausə) *n* **1** (*pl* **Hausas** *or* **Hausa**) a member of a Negroid people of W Africa, living chiefly in N Nigeria. **2** the language of this people, widely used as a trading language throughout W Africa.

hausfrau ('haus,frau) *n* a German housewife. [G, from *Haus* house + *Frau* woman, wife]

Haussmann ★ (*French* osman) *n* **Georges-Eugène** (ʒɔrʒøʒɛn), Baron. 1809–91, French town planner, noted for his rebuilding of Paris.

hautboy ('əubɔɪ) *n* **1** a strawberry with large fruit. **2** an archaic word for **oboe.** [C16: from F *hautbois*, from *haut* high + *bois* wood, of Gmc origin]

haute couture French. (ot kutyr) *n* high fashion. [lit.: high dressmaking]

haute cuisine French. (ot kwizin) *n* high-class cooking. [lit.: high cookery]

haute école French. (ot ekɔl) *n* the classical art of riding. [lit.: high school]

Haute-Garonne ★ (*French* otgarɔn) *n* a department of SW France, in Midi-Pyrénées region. Capital: Toulouse. Pop.: 985 030 (1994 est.). Area: 6367 sq. km (2483 sq. miles).

Haute-Loire ★ (*French* otlwar) *n* a department of S central France, in Auvergne region. Capital: Le Puy. Pop.: 206 578 (1994 est.). Area: 5001 sq. km (1950 sq. miles).

Haute-Marne ★ (*French* otmarn) *n* a department of NE France, in Champagne-Ardenne region. Capital: Chaumont. Pop.: 200 240 (1994 est.). Area: 6257 sq. km (2440 sq. miles).

Haute-Normandie ★ (*French* otnɔrmãdi) *n* a region of NW France, on the English Channel: generally fertile and flat. Pop.: 1 773 704 (1994 est.).

Hautes-Alpes ★ (*French* otzalp) *n* a department of SE France in Provence-Alpes-Côte d'Azur region. Capital: Gap. Pop.: 118 220 (1994 est.). Area: 5643 sq. km (2201 sq. miles).

Haute-Saône ★ (*French* otson) *n* a department of E France, in Franche-Comté region. Capital: Vesoul. Pop.: 229 448 (1994 est.). Area: 5375 sq. km (2096 sq. miles).

Haute-Savoie ★ (*French* otsavwa) *n* a department of E France, in Rhône-Alpes region. Capital: Annecy. Pop.: 613 176 (1994 est.). Area: 4958 sq. km (1934 sq. miles).

Hautes-Pyrénées ★ (*French* otpirene) *n* a department of SW France, in Midi-Pyrénées region. Capital: Tarbes. Pop.: 223 840 (1994 est.). Area: 4534 sq. km (1768 sq. miles).

hauteur (əu'tɜː) *n* pride; haughtiness. [C17: from F, from *haut* high; see HAUGHTY]

Haute-Vienne ★ (*French* otvjɛn) *n* a department of W central France, in Limousin region. Capital: Limoges. Pop.: 355 524 (1994 est.). Area: 5555 sq. km (2166 sq. miles).

haut monde French. (o mõd) *n* high society. [lit.: high world]

Haut-Rhin ★ (*French* orɛ̃) *n* a department of E France in Alsace region. Capital: Colmar. Pop.: 693 135 (1994 est.). Area: 3566 sq. km (1377 sq. miles).

Hauts-de-Seine ★ (*French* odsɛn) *n* a department of N central France, in Île-de-France region just west of Paris: formed in 1964. Capital: Nanterre. Pop.: 1 403 463 (1994 est.). Area: 175 sq. km (68 sq. miles).

Havana ★ (hə'vænə) *n* the capital of Cuba, a port in the northwest on the Gulf of Mexico: the largest city in the Caribbean, founded in 1514 as San Cristóbal de la Habana by Diego Velásquez. Pop.: 2 241 000 (1995 est.). Spanish name: **Habana.**

Havana cigar *n* any of various cigars manufactured in Cuba, known esp. for their high quality. Also: **Havana.**

Havant ★ ('hæv°nt) *n* a market town in S England, in SE Hampshire. Pop.: 46 510 (1991).

have (hæv) *vb* **has, having, had.** (*mainly tr*) **1** to be in possession of; own: *he has two cars.* **2** to possess as a quality or attribute: *he has dark hair.* **3** to receive, take, or obtain: *she had a present; have a look.* **4** to hold in the mind: *to have an idea.* **5** to possess a knowledge of: *I have no German.* **6** to experience: *to have a shock.* **7** to suffer from: *to have a cold.* **8** to gain control of or advantage over: *you have me on that point.* **9** (*usually passive*) *Sl.* to cheat or outwit: *he was had by that dishonest salesman.* **10** (foll. by *on*) to exhibit (mercy, etc., towards): *to have a conversation.* **12** to arrange or hold: *to have a party.* **13** to cause, compel, or require to (be, do, or be done): *have my shoes mended.* **14** (takes an infinitive with *to*) used as an auxiliary to express compulsion or necessity: *I had to run quickly to escape him.* **15** to eat, drink, or partake of. **16** *Taboo sl.* to have sexual intercourse with. **17** (*used with a negative*) to tolerate or allow: *I won't have all this noise.* **18** to state or assert: *rumour has it that they will marry.* **19** to place: *I'll have the sofa in this room.* **20** to receive as a guest: *to have people to stay.* **21** to be pregnant with or bear (offspring). **22** (*takes a past participle*) used as an auxiliary to form compound tenses expressing completed action: *I have gone; I had gone.* **23 had rather** *or* **sooner.** to consider preferable that: *I had rather you left at once.* **24 have had it.** *Inf.* **24a** to be exhausted, defeated, or killed. **24b** to have lost one's last chance. **24c** to become unfashionable. **25**

have it away (*or* **off**). *Taboo, Brit. sl.* to have sexual intercourse. **26 have it so good.** to have so many material benefits. **27 have to do with.** **27a** to have dealings with. **27b** to be of relevance to. **28 let (someone) have it.** *Sl.* to launch an attack on (someone). ◆ *n* **29** (*usually pl*) *Inf.* a person or group in possession of wealth, security, etc.: *the haves and the have-nots.* ◆ See also **have at, have on,** etc. [OE *habban*]

have-a-go *adj Inf.* (of members of the public at the scene of a crime) intervening physically in an attempt to catch or thwart a criminal, esp. one who is armed: *a have-a-go pensioner.*

have at *vb* (*intr, prep*) *Arch.* to make an opening attack on, esp. in fencing.

Havel[1] ★ (*German* 'haːfəl) *n* a river in E Germany, flowing south to Berlin, then west and north to join the River Elbe. Length: about 362 km (225 miles).

Havel[2] (*Czech* 'havɛl) ★ *n* **Václav** ('vaːtslaf). born 1936, Czech dramatist and statesman; founder of the Civil Forum movement for political change: president of Czechoslovakia (1990–93); president of the Czech Republic from 1993. His plays include *Redevelopment* (1989).

havelock ('hævlɒk) *n* a light-coloured cover for a service cap with a flap extending over the back of the neck to protect the head and neck from the sun. [C19: after Sir H. *Havelock* (1795–1857), E general in India]

haven ('heɪvˈn) *n* **1** a harbour or other sheltered place for shipping. **2** a place of safety; shelter. ◆ *vb* **3** (*tr*) to shelter as in a haven. [OE *hæfen*, from ON *höfn*]

have-not *n* (*usually pl*) a person or group in possession of relatively little material wealth.

haven't ('hævˈnt) *contraction of* have not.

have on *vb* (*tr*) **1** (*usually adv*) to wear. **2** (*usually adv*) to have a commitment: *what does your boss have on this afternoon?* **3** (*adv*) *Inf.* to trick or tease (a person). **4** (*prep*) to have available (information, esp. when incriminating) about (a person).

have out *vb* (*tr, adv*) **1** to settle (a matter) or come to (a final decision), esp. by fighting or by frank discussion (often in **have it out**). **2** to have extracted or removed.

haver ('heɪvə) *vb* (*intr*) **1** *Scot. & N English dialect.* to babble; talk nonsense. **2** to dither. ◆ *n* **3** (*usually pl*) *Scot.* nonsense. [C18: from ?]

Havering ★ ('heɪvərɪŋ) *n* a borough of NE Greater London, formed in 1965 from Romford and Hornchurch (both previously in Essex). Pop.: 231 700 (1994 est.). Area: 120 sq. km (46 sq. miles).

haversack ('hævə,sæk) *n* a canvas bag for provisions or equipment, carried on the back or shoulder. [C18: from F *havresac*, from G *Habersack* oat bag, from OHG *habaro* oats + *Sack* SACK[1]]

haversine ('hævə,saɪn) *n* half the value of the versed sine. [C19: combination of *half* + *versed* + *sine*[1]]

have up *vb* (*tr, adv; usually passive*) to cause to appear for trial: *he was had up for breaking and entering.*

havildar ('hævɪl,daː) *n* a noncommissioned officer in the Indian army, equivalent in rank to sergeant. [C17: from Hindi, from Persian *hawāldār* one in charge]

havoc ('hævək) *n* **1** destruction; devastation; ruin. **2** *Inf.* confusion; chaos. **3 cry havoc.** *Arch.* to give the signal for pillage and destruction. **4 play havoc.** (often foll. by *with*) to cause a great deal of damage, distress, or confusion (to). [C15: from OF *havot* pillage, prob. of Gmc origin]

Havre ★ ('haːvrə; *French* avrə) *n* See **Le Havre.**

haw[1] (hɔː) *n* **1** the fruit of the hawthorn. **2** another name for **hawthorn.** [OE *haga*, identical with *haga* hedge]

haw[2] (hɔː) *n, interj* **1** an inarticulate utterance, as of hesitation, embarrassment, etc.; hem. ◆ *vb* **2** (*intr*) to make this sound. [C17: imit.]

haw[3] (hɔː) *n* the nictitating membrane of a horse or other domestic animal. [C15: from ?]

Hawaii ★ (haˈwaɪɪ) *n* a state of the US in the central Pacific, consisting of over 20 volcanic islands and atolls, including Hawaii, Maui, Oahu, Kauai, and Molokai: discovered by Captain Cook in 1778; annexed by the US in

1898; naval base at Pearl Harbor attacked by the Japanese in 1941, a major cause of US entry into World War II; became a state in 1959. Capital: Honolulu. Pop.: 1 183 723 (1996 est.). Area: 16 640 sq. km (6425 sq. miles). Former name: **Sandwich Islands.** Abbrevs: **Ha.** or (with zip code) **HI**
▸ Ha'waiian *adj, n*

Hawaiki ★ ('haːwaɪki:) *n NZ.* a legendary Pacific island from which the Maoris migrated to New Zealand by canoe. [Maori]

Hawes Water ★ (hɔːz) *n* a lake in NW England, in the Lake District: provides part of Manchester's water supply; extended by damming from 4 km (2.5 miles) to 6 km (4 miles).

hawfinch ('hɔː,fɪntʃ) *n* an uncommon European finch having a very stout bill.

Haw-Haw ★ ('hɔː,hɔː) *n* **Lord.** See (William) Joyce.

Hawick ★ ('hɔːɪk) *n* a town in SE Scotland, in S central Scottish Borders: knitwear industry. Pop.: 15 812 (1991).

hawk[1] (hɔːk) *n* **1** any of various diurnal birds of prey of the family Accipitridae, typically having short rounded wings and a long tail. **2** a person who supports war or warlike policies. Cf. **dove** (sense 2). **3** a ruthless or rapacious person. ◆ *vb* **4** (*intr*) to hunt with falcons, hawks, etc. **5** (*intr*) (of falcons or hawks) to fly in quest of prey. **6** to pursue or attack on the wing, as a hawk. [OE *hafoc*]
▸ 'hawking *n* ▸ 'hawkish *adj* ▸ 'hawk,like *adj*

hawk[2] (hɔːk) *vb* **1** to offer (goods) for sale, as in the street. **2** (*tr*; often foll. by *about*) to spread (news, gossip, etc.). [C16: back formation from HAWKER[1]]

hawk[3] (hɔːk) *vb* **1** (*intr*) to clear the throat noisily. **2** (*tr*) to force (phlegm, etc.) up from the throat. [C16: imit.]

hawk[4] (hɔːk) *n* a small square board with a handle underneath, for carrying wet mortar. Also called: **mortarboard.** [from ?]

Hawke ★ (hɔːk) *n* **Robert** (**James Lee**), known as *Bob*. born 1929, Australian statesman; prime minister of Australia (1983–91).

hawker[1] ('hɔːkə) *n* a person who travels from place to place selling goods. [C16: prob. from MLow G *hōker*, from *hōken* to peddle; see HUCKSTER]

hawker[2] ('hɔːkə) *n* a person who hunts with hawks, falcons, etc. [OE *hafecere*]

hawk-eyed *adj* **1** having extremely keen sight. **2** vigilant, watchful, or observant.

Hawking ★ ('hɔːkɪŋ) *n* **Stephen William.** born 1942, British physicist. Stricken with a progressive nervous disease since the 1960s, he has nevertheless been a leader in cosmological theory. His *A Brief History of Time* (1987) was a bestseller.

Hawkins ★ ('hɔːkɪnz) *n* **1 Coleman.** 1904–69, US jazz saxophonist. **2 Sir John.** 1532–95, English naval commander and slave trader, treasurer of the navy (1577–89); commander of a squadron in the fleet that defeated the Spanish Armada (1588).

hawk moth *n* any of various moths having long narrow wings and powerful flight, with the ability to hover over flowers when feeding from the nectar.

Hawks ★ (hɔːks) *n* **Howard** (**Winchester**). 1896–1977, US film director. His films include *Sergeant York* (1941) and *The Big Sleep* (1946).

hawksbill turtle *or* **hawksbill** ('hɔːks,bɪl) *n* a small tropical turtle with a hooked beaklike mouth: a source of tortoiseshell.

Hawksmoor ★ ('hɔːks,mɔː) *n* **Nicholas.** 1661–1736, English architect. His designs include All Souls', Oxford, and a number of London churches.

hawkweed ('hɔːk,wiːd) *n* a hairy plant with clusters of dandelion-like flowers.

Haworth[1] ★ ('hauəθ) *n* a village in N England, in West Yorkshire: home of Charlotte, Emily, and Anne Brontë. Pop.: 4956 (1991).

Haworth[2] ★ ('hauəθ) *n* **Sir Walter Norman.** 1883–1950, British biochemist, who shared the Nobel prize for chemistry (1937) for synthesizing ascorbic acid (vitamin C).

hawse (hɔːz) *n Naut.* **1** the part of the bows of a vessel where the hawseholes are. **2** short for **hawsehole** or **hawsepipe**. **3** the distance from the bow of an anchored vessel to the anchor. **4** the arrangement of port and starboard anchor ropes when a vessel is riding on both anchors. [C14: from earlier *halse,* prob. from ON *háls* neck, ship's bow]

hawsehole ('hɔːz,həʊl) *n Naut.* one of the holes in the upper part of the bows of a vessel through which the anchor ropes pass.

hawsepipe ('hɔːz,paɪp) *n Naut.* a strong metal pipe through which an anchor rope passes.

hawser ('hɔːzə) *n Naut.* a large heavy rope. [C14: from Anglo-F *hauceour,* from OF *haucier* to hoist, ult. from L *altus* high]

hawthorn ('hɔː,θɔːn) *n* any of various thorny trees or shrubs of a N temperate genus, having white or pink flowers and reddish fruits (haws). Also called (in Britain): **may, may tree, mayflower.** [OE *haguthorn,* from *haga* hedge + *thorn* thorn]

hay (heɪ) *n* **1a** grass, clover, etc., cut and dried as fodder. **1b** (*in combination*): *a hayfield.* **2 hit the hay.** *Sl.* to go to bed. **3 make hay of.** to throw into confusion. **4 make hay while the sun shines.** to take full advantage of an opportunity. **5 roll in the hay.** *Inf.* sexual intercourse or heavy petting. ◆ *vb* **6** to cut, dry, and store (grass, etc.) as fodder. [OE *hieg*]

Hay ★ (heɪ) *n* Will. 1888–1949, British music-hall comedian, who later starred in films, such as *Oh, Mr Porter!* (1937).

haybox ('heɪ,bɒks) *n* an airtight box full of hay used for cooking preheated food by retained heat.

haycock ('heɪ,kɒk) *n* a small cone-shaped pile of hay left in the field until dry.

Haydn ★ ('haɪd°n) *n* **1** (**Franz**) **Joseph** (German 'joːzɛf). 1732–1809, Austrian composer. His works include the oratorios *The Creation* (1796–98) and *The Seasons* (1798–1801), 104 symphonies, piano music, and string quartets. **2** his brother, (**Johann**) **Michael** (German 'mɪçaɛl). 1737–1806, Austrian composer, esp. of Church music.

Hayek ★ ('haɪɛk) *n* **Friedrich August von** (German 'friːdrɪç 'aʊgust fɒn). 1899–1992, British economist and political philosopher, born in Austria; shared the Nobel prize for economics 1974.

Hayes ★ (heɪz) *n* **Rutherford B**(irchard). 1822–93, 19th president of the US (1877–81).

hay fever *n* an allergic reaction to pollen, dust, etc., characterized by sneezing, runny nose, and watery eyes due to inflammation of the mucous membranes of the eyes and nose.

haymaker ('heɪ,meɪkə) *n* **1** a person who helps to cut, turn, or carry hay. **2** either of two machines, one designed to crush stems of hay, the other to break and bend them, in order to cause more rapid and even drying. **3** *Boxing sl.* a wild swinging punch.
▶ '**hay,making** *adj, n*

haymow ('heɪ,maʊ) *n* **1** a part of a barn where hay is stored. **2** a quantity of hay stored.

hayseed ('heɪ,siːd) *n* **1** seeds or fragments of grass or straw. **2** *US & Canad. inf., derog.* a yokel.

haystack ('heɪ,stæk) *or* **hayrick** *n* a large pile of hay, esp. one built in the open air and covered with thatch.

haywire ('heɪ,waɪə) *adj* (*postpositive*) *Inf.* **1** (of things) not functioning properly. **2** (of people) erratic or crazy. [C20: from the disorderly tangle of wire removed from bales of hay]

hazard ('hæzəd) *n* **1** exposure or vulnerability to injury, loss, etc. **2 at hazard.** at risk; in danger. **3** a thing likely to cause injury, etc. **4** *Golf.* an obstacle such as a bunker, a road, rough, water, etc. **5** chance; accident. **6** a gambling game played with two dice. **7** *Real Tennis.* **7a** the receiver's side of the court. **7b** one of the winning openings. **8** *Billiards.* a scoring stroke made either when a ball other than the striker's is pocketed (**winning hazard**) or the striker's cue ball itself (**losing hazard**). ◆ *vb* (*tr*) **9** to risk. **10**

to venture (an opinion, guess, etc.). **11** to expose to danger. [C13: from OF *hasard,* from Ar. *az-zahr* the die]

hazard lights *pl n* the indicator lights of a motor vehicle when flashing simultaneously to indicate that the vehicle is stationary and temporarily obstructing the traffic. Also called: **hazard warning lights, hazards.**

hazardous ('hæzədəs) *adj* **1** involving great risk. **2** depending on chance.
▶ '**hazardously** *adv* ▶ '**hazardousness** *n*

hazard warning device *n* an appliance fitted to a motor vehicle that operates the hazard lights.

haze[1] (heɪz) *n* **1** *Meteorol.* reduced visibility in the air as a result of condensed water vapour, dust, etc., in the atmosphere. **2** obscurity of perception, feeling, etc. ◆ *vb* **hazes, hazing, hazed. 3** (when *intr,* often foll. by *over*) to make or become hazy. [C18: back formation from HAZY]

haze[2] (heɪz) *vb* **hazes, hazing, hazed.** (*tr*) **1** *Chiefly US & Canad.* to subject (fellow students) to ridicule or abuse. **2** *Naut.* to harass with humiliating tasks. [C17: from ?]

hazel ('heɪz°l) *n* **1** Also called: **cob.** any of several shrubs of a N temperate genus, having edible rounded nuts. **2** the wood of any of these trees. **3** short for **hazelnut. 4a** a light yellowish-brown colour. **4b** (*as adj*): *hazel eyes.* [OE *hæsel*]

hazelhen ('heɪz°l,hɛn) *n* a European woodland gallinaceous bird with a speckled brown plumage and slightly crested crown.

hazelnut ('heɪz°l,nʌt) *n* the nut of a hazel shrub, having a smooth shiny hard shell. Also called: **filbert,** (Brit.) **cobnut, cob.**

Hazlitt ★ ('hæzlɪt) *n* **William.** 1778–1830, British critic and essayist: works include *Table Talk* (1821) and *The Plain Speaker* (1826).

hazy ('heɪzɪ) *adj* **hazier, haziest.** misty; indistinct; vague. [C17: from ?]
▶ '**hazily** *adv* ▶ '**haziness** *n*

Hb *symbol for* haemoglobin.

HB (on Brit. pencils) *symbol for* hard-black: denoting a medium-hard lead.

HBC *abbrev. for* Hudson's Bay Company.

HBM (in Britain) *abbrev. for* His (*or* Her) Britannic Majesty.

H-bomb *n* short for **hydrogen bomb.**

HC *abbrev. for:* **1** Holy Communion. **2** (in Britain) House of Commons.

HCF *or* **hcf** *abbrev. for* highest common factor.

HCG *abbrev. for* human chorionic gonadotrophin; a hormone produced by the placenta during pregnancy: its presence in the urine is used as the basis of most pregnancy tests.

hcp *abbrev. for* handicap.

HD *abbrev. for* heavy duty.

hdqrs *abbrev. for* headquarters.

HDTV *abbrev. for* high definition television.

he (hiː; *unstressed* iː) *pron* (*subjective*) **1** refers to a male person or animal. **2** refers to an indefinite antecedent such as *whoever* or *anybody: everybody can do as he likes.* **3** refers to a person or animal of unknown or unspecified sex: *a member may vote as he sees fit.* ◆ *n* **4a** a male person or animal. **4b** (*in combination*): *he-goat.* **5** (in children's play) another name for **tag**[2] (sense 1), **it** (sense 7). [OE *hē*]

He *the chemical symbol for* helium.

HE *abbrev. for:* **1** high explosive. **2** His Eminence. **3** His (*or* Her) Excellency.

head (hɛd) *n* **1** the upper or front part of the body in vertebrates, including man, that contains and protects the brain, eyes, mouth, nose, and ears. Related adj: **cephalic. 2** the corresponding part of an invertebrate animal. **3** something resembling a head in form or function, such as the top of a tool. **4a** the person commanding most authority within a group, organization, etc. **4b** (*as modifier*): *head buyer.* **4c** (*in combination*): *headmaster.* **5** the position of leadership or command. **6** the most forward part of a thing; front: *the head of a queue.* **7** the highest part of a thing; upper end: *the head of the pass.* **8** the froth on the top of a glass of beer. **9** aptitude, intelligence, and

emotions (esp. in **over one's head, lose one's head,** etc.): *she has a good head for figures.* **10** (*pl* **head**) a person or animal considered as a unit: *the show was two pounds per head; six hundred head of cattle.* **11** the head considered as a measure: *he's a head taller than his mother.* **12** *Bot.* **12a** a dense inflorescence such as that of the daisy. **12b** any other compact terminal part of a plant, such as the leaves of a cabbage. **13** a culmination or crisis (esp. in **bring** or **come to a head**). **14** the pus-filled tip or central part of a pimple, boil, etc. **15** the source of a river or stream. **16** (*cap. when part of a name*) a headland or promontory. **17** the obverse of a coin, usually bearing a portrait of the head of a monarch, etc. **18** a main point of an argument, discourse, etc. **19** (*often pl*) a headline or heading. **20** (*often pl*) *Naut.* a lavatory. **21** the taut membrane of a drum, tambourine, etc. **22a** the height of the surface of liquid above a specific point, esp. as a measure of the pressure at that point: *a head of four feet.* **22b** pressure of water, caused by height or velocity, measured in terms of a vertical column of water. **22c** any pressure: *a head of steam in the boiler.* **23** *Sl.* **23a** a person who regularly takes drugs, esp. LSD or cannabis. **23b** (*in combination*): *an acidhead.* **24** *Mining.* a road driven into the coalface. **25a** the terminal point of a route. **25b** (*in combination*): *railhead.* **26** a device on a turning or boring machine equipped with one or more cutting tools held to the work by this device. **27** **cylinder head.** See **cylinder** (sense 4). **28** an electromagnet that can read, write, or erase information on a magnetic medium, used in computers, tape recorders, etc. **29** *Inf.* short for **headmaster** *or* **headmistress.** **30** a narrow margin of victory (esp. in (**win**) **by a head**). **31** *Inf.* short for **headache. 32 bite** *or* **snap someone's head off.** to speak sharply to someone. **33 give someone** (*or* **something**) **his** (*or* **its**) **head. 33a** to allow a person greater freedom or responsibility. **33b** to allow a horse to gallop by lengthening the reins. **34 go to one's head. 34a** to make one dizzy or confused, as might an alcoholic drink. **34b** to make one conceited: *his success has gone to his head.* **35 head and shoulders above.** greatly superior to. **36 head over heels. 36a** turning a complete somersault. **36b** completely; utterly (esp. in **head over heels in love**). **37 hold up one's head.** to be unashamed. **38 keep one's head.** to remain calm. **39 keep one's head above water.** to manage to survive difficulties, esp. financial ones. **40 make head or tail of.** (*used with a negative*) to attempt to understand (a problem, etc.). **41 off** (*or* **out of**) **one's head.** *Sl.* insane or delirious. **42 on one's** (**own**) **head.** at a one's (own) risk or responsibility. **43 over someone's head. 43a** without a person in the obvious position being considered: *the graduate was promoted over the heads of several of his seniors.* **43b** without consulting a person in the obvious position but referring to a higher authority: *he went straight to the director, over the head of his immediate boss.* **43c** beyond a person's comprehension. **44 put** (**our, their,** etc.) **heads together.** *Inf.* to consult together. **45 take it into one's head.** to conceive a notion (to do something). **46 turn someone's head.** to make someone vain, conceited, etc. ◆ *vb* **47** (*tr*) to be at the front or top of: *to head the field.* **48** (*tr*; often foll. by *up*) to be in the commanding or most important position. **49** (often foll. by *for*) to go or cause to go (towards): *where are you heading?* **50** to turn or steer (a vessel) as specified: *to head into the wind.* **51** *Soccer.* to propel (the ball) by striking it with the head. **52** (*tr*) to provide with or be a head or heading for. **53** (*tr*) to cut the top branches or shoots off a tree or plant. **54** (*intr*) to form a head, as a plant. **55** (*intr*; often foll. by *in*) (of streams, rivers, etc.) to originate or rise. ◆ See also **head off, heads.** [OE *hēafod*]
▷ **¹headless** *adj* ▷ **¹head,like** *adj*

Head ★ (hɛd) *n* Edith. 1907–81, US dress designer: won many Oscars for her Hollywood film-costume designs.

-head *n combining form.* indicating a person having a preoccupation as specified: *breadhead.*

headache (ˈhɛd,eɪk) *n* **1** a continuous pain in the head. **2** *Inf.* any cause of worry, difficulty, or annoyance.
▷ **¹head,achy** *adj*

headband (ˈhɛd,bænd) *n* **1** a ribbon or band worn around the head. **2** a narrow cloth band attached to the top of the spine of a book for protection or decoration.

headbang (ˈhɛd,bæŋ) *vb* (*intr*) *Sl.* to nod one's head violently to the beat of heavy-metal rock music.

head-banger *n Sl.* **1** a heavy-metal rock fan. **2** a crazy or stupid person.

headboard (ˈhɛd,bɔːd) *n* a vertical board or terminal at the head of a bed.

head-butt *vb* (*tr*) **1** to strike (someone) deliberately with the head. ◆ *n* **head butt. 2** an act or an instance of deliberately striking someone with the head.

headdress (ˈhɛd,drɛs) *n* any head covering, esp. an ornate one or one denoting a rank.

headed (ˈhɛdɪd) *adj* **1a** having a head or heads. **1b** (*in combination*): *two-headed; bullet-headed.* **2** having a heading: *headed notepaper.*

header (ˈhɛdə) *n* **1** a machine that trims the heads from castings, forgings, etc., or one that forms heads, as in wire, to make nails. **2** a person who operates such a machine. **3** Also called: **header tank.** a reservoir that maintains a gravity feed or a static fluid pressure in an apparatus. **4** a brick or stone laid across a wall so that its end is flush with the outer surface. **5** the action of striking a ball with the head. **6** *Inf.* a headlong fall or dive.

headfirst (ˈhɛdˈfɜːst) *adj, adv* **1** with the head foremost; headlong. ◆ *adv* **2** rashly.

headgear (ˈhɛd,ɡɪə) *n* **1** a hat. **2** any part of a horse's harness that is worn on the head. **3** the hoisting mechanism at the pithead of a mine.

headguard (ˈhɛd,ɡɑːd) *n* a lightweight helmet-like piece of equipment worn to protect the head in various sports.

head-hunting *n* **1** the practice among certain peoples of removing the heads of slain enemies and preserving them as trophies. **2** *US sl.* the destruction or neutralization of political opponents. **3** (of a company or corporation) the recruitment of, or a drive to recruit, new high-level personnel, esp. in management or in specialist fields.
▷ **¹head-,hunter** *n*

heading (ˈhɛdɪŋ) *n* **1** a title for a page, chapter, etc. **2** a main division, as of a speech. **3** *Mining.* **3a** a horizontal tunnel. **3b** the end of such a tunnel. **4** the angle between the direction of an aircraft and a specified meridian, often due north. **5** the compass direction parallel to the keel of a vessel. **6** the act of heading.

headland *n* **1** (ˈhɛdlənd). a narrow area of land jutting out into a sea, lake, etc. **2** (ˈhɛd,lænd). a strip of land along the edge of an arable field left unploughed to allow space for machines.

headlight (ˈhɛd,laɪt) *or* **headlamp** *n* a powerful light, equipped with a reflector and attached to the front of a motor vehicle, etc.

headline (ˈhɛd,laɪn) *n* **1a** a phrase at the top of a newspaper or magazine article indicating the subject of the article, usually in larger and heavier type. **1b** a line at the top of a page giving the title, page number, etc. **2 hit the headlines.** to become prominent in the news. **3** (*usually pl*) the main points of a television or radio news broadcast, read out before the full broadcast. ◆ *vb* **headlines, headlining, headlined. 4** (*tr*) to furnish (a story or page) with a headline. **5** to have top billing (in).

headlong (ˈhɛd,lɒŋ) *adv, adj* **1** with the head foremost; headfirst. **2** with great haste. ◆ *adj* **3** *Arch.* (of slopes, etc.) very steep; precipitous.

headman (ˈhɛdmən) *n, pl* **headmen. 1** *Anthropol.* a chief or leader. **2** a foreman or overseer.

headmaster (ˌhɛdˈmɑːstə) *or* (*fem*) **headmistress** *n* the principal of a school.

headmost (ˈhɛd,məʊst) *adj* foremost.

head off *vb* (*tr, adv*) **1** to intercept and force to change direction. **2** to prevent or forestall.

head-on *adv, adj* **1** front foremost: *a head-on collision.* **2** with directness or without compromise: *in his usual head-on fashion.*

headphones (ˈhɛd,fəʊnz) *pl n* an electrical device consisting of two earphones held in position by a flexible metallic strap passing over the head. Informal name: **cans.**

headpiece (ˈhɛd,piːs) *n* **1** *Printing.* a decorative band at the top of a page, etc. **2** a helmet. **3** *Arch.* the intellect.

headpin ('hɛdˌpɪn) *n Tenpin bowling.* another word for **kingpin** (sense 2).

headquarters (ˌhɛd'kwɔːtəz) *pl n* (*sometimes functioning as sing*) **1** any centre from which operations are directed, as in the police. **2** a military formation comprising the commander and his staff. ◆ Abbrev.: **HQ, h.q.**

headrace ('hɛdˌreɪs) *n* a channel that carries water to a water wheel, turbine, etc.

headrest ('hɛdˌrɛst) *n* a support for the head, as on a dentist's chair or car seat.

head restraint *n* an adjustable support for the head, attached to a car seat, to prevent the neck from being jolted backwards sharply in the event of a crash or sudden stop.

headroom ('hɛdˌrʊm, -ˌruːm) *or* **headway** *n* the height of a bridge, room, etc.; clearance.

heads (hɛdz) *interj, adv* with the obverse side of a coin uppermost, esp. if it has a head on it: used as a call before tossing a coin.

headscarf ('hɛdˌskɑːf) *n, pl* **headscarves.** a scarf for the head, often worn tied under the chin.

headset ('hɛdˌsɛt) *n* a pair of headphones, esp. with a microphone attached.

headship ('hɛdʃɪp) *n* **1** the position or state of being a leader; command. **2** *Brit.* the position of headmaster or headmistress of a school.

headshrinker ('hɛdˌʃrɪŋkə) *n* **1** a slang name for **psychiatrist.** Often shortened to **shrink.** **2** a head-hunter who shrinks the heads of his victims.

headsman ('hɛdzmən) *n, pl* **headsmen.** (formerly) an executioner who beheaded condemned persons.

headstall ('hɛdˌstɔːl) *n* the part of a bridle that fits round a horse's head.

head start *n* an initial advantage in a competitive situation.

headstock ('hɛdˌstɒk) *n* the part of a machine that supports and transmits the drive.

headstone ('hɛdˌstəʊn) *n* **1** a memorial stone at the head of a grave. **2** *Archit.* another name for **keystone.**

headstream ('hɛdˌstriːm) *n* a stream that is the source or a source of a river.

headstrong ('hɛdˌstrɒŋ) *adj* **1** self-willed; obstinate. **2** (of an action) heedless; rash.

head-to-head *Inf.* ◆ *adj* **1** in direct competition. ◆ *n* **2** a competition involving two people, teams, etc.

head-up display *n* a projection of readings from instruments onto a windscreen, enabling a pilot or driver to see them without moving his eyes.

head voice *or* **register** *n* the high register of the human voice, in which the vibrations of sung notes are felt in the head.

headwaters ('hɛdˌwɔːtəz) *pl n* the tributary streams of a river in the area in which it rises.

headway ('hɛdˌweɪ) *n* **1** motion forward: *the vessel made no headway.* **2** progress: *he made no headway with the problem.* **3** another name for **headroom.** **4** the interval between consecutive trains, buses, etc., on the same route.

headwind ('hɛdˌwɪnd) *n* a wind blowing directly against the course of an aircraft or ship.

headword ('hɛdˌwɜːd) *n* a key word placed at the beginning of a line, paragraph, etc., as in a dictionary entry.

headwork ('hɛdˌwɜːk) *n* **1** mental work. **2** the ornamentation of the keystone of an arch.

heady ('hɛdɪ) *adj* **headier, headiest. 1** (of alcoholic drink) intoxicating. **2** strongly affecting the senses; extremely exciting. **3** rash; impetuous.
▸ **'headily** *adv* ▸ **'headiness** *n*

heal (hiːl) *vb* **1** to restore or be restored to health. **2** (*intr; often foll. by over or up*) (of a wound) to repair by natural processes, as by scar formation. **3** (*tr*) to cure (a disease or disorder). **4** to restore or be restored to friendly relations, harmony, etc. [OE *hǣlan*; see HALE¹, WHOLE]
▸ **'healer** *n* ▸ **'healing** *n, adj*

Healey ★ ('hiːlɪ) *n* Denis (Winston), Baron Healey. born 1917, British Labour politician; Chancellor of the Exchequer (1974–79); deputy leader of the Labour Party (1980–83).

Healy ★ ('hiːlɪ) *n* Ian. born 1964, Australian cricketer.

health (hɛlθ) *n* **1** the state of being bodily and mentally vigorous and free from disease. **2** the general condition of body and mind: *in poor health.* **3** the condition of any unit, society, etc.: *the economic health of a nation.* **4** a toast to a person. **5** (*modifier*) of or relating to food or other goods reputed to be beneficial to the eater: *health food.* **6** (*modifier*) of or relating to health: *health care; health service.* [OE *hǣlth;* rel. to *hāl* HALE¹]

health centre *n* (in Britain) premises providing health care for a local community and usually housing a group practice, nursing staff, a child-health clinic, etc.

health farm *n* a residential establishment, often in the country, visited by those who wish to improve their health by losing weight, eating health foods, taking exercise, etc.

health food *n* **a** food eaten for its alleged benefits to health, esp. fruit, vegetables, etc., that are organically grown, high in dietary fibre, and without additives. **b** (*modifier*): *a health-food shop.*

healthful ('hɛlθfʊl) *adj* a less common word for **healthy** (senses 1–3).

health salts *pl n* magnesium sulphate or similar salts taken as a mild laxative.

health visitor *n* (in Britain) a nurse employed by a district health authority to visit people in their homes and give help and advice on health and social welfare, esp. to mothers of preschool children, and to handicapped and elderly people.

healthy ('hɛlθɪ) *adj* **healthier, healthiest. 1** enjoying good health. **2** sound: *the company's finances are not very healthy.* **3** conducive to health. **4** indicating soundness of body or mind: *a healthy appetite.* **5** *Inf.* considerable: *a healthy sum.*
▸ **'healthily** *adv* ▸ **'healthiness** *n*

Heaney ★ ('hiːnɪ) *n* Seamus (Justin) ('ʃeɪməs). born 1939, Irish poet and critic, born in Northern Ireland. His collections include *Death of a Naturalist* (1966) and *The Spirit Level* (1996): Nobel prize for literature 1995.

heap (hiːp) *n* **1** a collection of articles or mass of material gathered in a pile. **2** (*often pl; usually foll. by of*) *Inf.* a large number or quantity. **3** *Inf.* a thing that is very old, unreliable, etc.: *the car was a heap.* ◆ *adv* **4 heaps.** (intensifier): *he was heaps better.* ◆ *vb* **5** (often foll. by *up* or *together*) to collect or be collected into or as if into a pile. **5** (*tr; often foll. by with, on,* or *upon*) to load (with) abundantly: *to heap with riches.* [OE *héap*]

hear (hɪə) *vb* **hears, hearing, heard** (hɜːd). **1** (*tr*) to perceive (a sound) with the sense of hearing. **2** (*tr; may take a clause as object*) to listen to: *did you hear what I said?* **3** (when *intr,* sometimes foll. by *of* or *about;* when *tr,* may take a clause as object) to be informed (of); receive information (about). **4** *Law.* to give a hearing to (a case). **5** (when *intr,* usually foll. by *of* and used with a negative) to listen (to) with favour, assent, etc.: *she wouldn't hear of it.* **6** (*intr;* foll. by *from*) to receive a letter (from). **7 hear! hear!** an exclamation of approval. **8 hear tell (of).** *Dialect.* to be told (about). [OE *hieran*]
▸ **'hearer** *n*

Heard and McDonald Islands ★ (hɜːd, mək'dɒnəld) *pl n* a group of islands in the S Indian Ocean: an external territory of Australia from 1947. Area: 412 sq. km (159 sq. miles).

hearing ('hɪərɪŋ) *n* **1** the sense by which sound is perceived. **2** an opportunity to be listened to. **3** the range within which sound can be heard; earshot. **4** the investigation of a matter by a court of law, esp. the preliminary inquiry into an indictable crime by magistrates.

hearing aid *n* a device for assisting the hearing of partially deaf people, typically a small battery-powered amplifier worn in or behind the ear. Also called: **deaf aid.**

hearing dog *n* a dog that has been specially trained to help deaf or partially deaf people by alerting them to such sounds as a ringing doorbell, an alarm, etc.

★ people and places

hearken or US (sometimes) **harken** ('hɑːkən) vb Arch. to listen to (something). [OE heorcnian]

hear out vb (tr, adv) to listen in regard to every detail and give a proper or full hearing to.

hearsay ('hɪəˌseɪ) n gossip; rumour.

hearsay evidence n Law. evidence based on what has been reported to a witness by others rather than what he has himself observed.

hearse (hɜːs) n a vehicle, such as a car or carriage, used to carry a coffin to the grave. [C14: from OF herce, from L hirpex harrow]

Hearst ★ (hɜːst) n **William Randolph**. 1863–1951, US newspaper publisher.

heart (hɑːt) n **1** the hollow muscular organ in vertebrates whose contractions propel the blood through the circulatory system. Related adj: **cardiac**. **2** the corresponding organ in invertebrates. **3** this organ considered as the seat of emotions, esp. love. **4** emotional mood: a change of heart. **5** tenderness or pity: you have no heart. **6** courage or spirit. **7** the most central part: the heart of the city. **8** the most important part: the heart of the matter. **9** (of vegetables, such as cabbage) the inner compact part. **10** the breast: she held him to her heart. **11** a dearly loved person: dearest heart. **12** a conventionalized representation of the heart, having two rounded lobes at the top meeting in a point at the bottom. **13a** a red heart-shaped symbol on a playing card. **13b** a card with one or more of these symbols or (when pl) the suit of cards so marked. **14** a fertile condition in land (esp. in **in good heart**). **15 after one's own heart**. appealing to one's own disposition or taste. **16 break one's** (or **someone's**) **heart**. to grieve (or cause to grieve) very deeply, esp. through love. **17 by heart**. by committing to memory. **18 eat one's heart out**. to brood or pine with grief or longing. **19 from (the bottom of) one's heart**. very sincerely or deeply. **20 have a change of heart**. to experience a profound change of outlook, attitude, etc. **21 have one's heart in one's mouth** (or throat). to be full of apprehension, excitement, or fear. **22 have one's heart in the right place**. to be kind, thoughtful, or generous. **23 have the heart**. (usually used with a negative) to have the necessary will, callousness, etc. (to do something): I didn't have the heart to tell him. **24 heart of hearts**. the depths of one's conscience or emotions. **25 heart of oak**. a brave person. **26 lose heart**. to become despondent or disillusioned (over something). **27 lose one's heart to**. to fall in love with. **28 set one's heart on**. to have as one's ambition to obtain; covet. **29 take heart**. to become encouraged. **30 take to heart**. to take seriously or be upset about. **31 wear one's heart on one's sleeve**. to show one's feelings openly. **32 with all one's heart**. very willingly. ◆ vb (intr) **33** (of vegetables) to form a heart. ◆ See also **hearts**. [OE heorte]

heartache ('hɑːtˌeɪk) n intense anguish or mental suffering.

heart attack n any sudden severe instance of abnormal heart functioning, esp. coronary thrombosis.

heartbeat ('hɑːtˌbiːt) n one complete pulsation of the heart.

heart block n impaired conduction of the impulse that regulates the heartbeat, resulting in a lack of coordination between the beating of the atria and the ventricles.

heartbreak ('hɑːtˌbreɪk) n intense and overwhelming grief, esp. through disappointment in love.
▶ 'heartˌbreaker n ▶ 'heartˌbreaking adj

heartburn ('hɑːtˌbɜːn) n a burning sensation beneath the breastbone caused by irritation of the oesophagus. Technical names: **cardialgia, pyrosis**.

-hearted adj having a heart or disposition as specified: cold-hearted; heavy-hearted.

hearten ('hɑːtªn) vb to make or become cheerful.
▶ 'heartening adj

heart failure n **1** a condition in which the heart is unable to pump an adequate amount of blood to the tissues. **2** sudden cessation of the heartbeat, resulting in death.

heartfelt ('hɑːtˌfɛlt) adj sincerely and strongly felt.

hearth (hɑːθ) n **1a** the floor of a fireplace, esp. one that extends outwards into the room. **1b** (as modifier): hearth rug. **2** this as a symbol of the home, etc. **3** the bottom part of a metallurgical furnace in which the molten metal is produced or contained. [OE heorth]

hearthstone ('hɑːθˌstəʊn) n **1** a stone that forms a hearth. **2** soft stone used (esp. formerly) to clean and whiten floors, steps, etc.

heartily ('hɑːtɪlɪ) adv **1** thoroughly or vigorously. **2** in a sincere manner.

heartland ('hɑːtˌlænd) n the central or most important region of a country or continent.

heartless ('hɑːtlɪs) adj unkind or cruel.
▶ 'heartlessly adv ▶ 'heartlessness n

heart-lung machine n a machine used to maintain the circulation and oxygenation of the blood during heart surgery.

heart-rending adj causing great mental pain and sorrow.
▶ 'heart-ˌrendingly adv

hearts (hɑːts) n (functioning as sing) a card game in which players must avoid winning tricks containing hearts or the queen of spades. Also called: **Black Maria**.

heart-searching n examination of one's feelings or conscience.

heartsease or **heart's-ease** ('hɑːtsˌiːz) n **1** another name for the **wild pansy**. **2** peace of mind.

heartsick ('hɑːtˌsɪk) adj deeply despondent.
▶ 'heartˌsickness n

heartstrings ('hɑːtˌstrɪŋz) pl n Often facetious. deep emotions. [C15: orig. referring to the tendons supposed to support the heart]

heart-throb n **1** an object of infatuation. **2** a heartbeat.

heart-to-heart adj **1** (esp. of a conversation) concerned with personal problems or intimate feelings. ◆ n **2** an intimate conversation.

heart-warming adj **1** pleasing; gratifying. **2** emotionally moving.

heartwood ('hɑːtˌwʊd) n the central core of dark hard wood in tree trunks, consisting of nonfunctioning xylem tissue that has become blocked with resins, tannins, and oils.

hearty ('hɑːtɪ) adj **heartier, heartiest**. **1** warm and unreserved in manner. **2** vigorous and heartfelt: hearty dislike. **3** healthy and strong (esp. in **hale and hearty**). **4** substantial and nourishing. ◆ n, pl **hearties**. Inf. **5** a comrade, esp. a sailor. **6** a vigorous sporting man: a rugby hearty.
▶ 'heartiness n

heat (hiːt) n **1** the energy transferred as a result of a difference in temperature. Related adjs.: **thermal, calorific**. **2** the sensation caused by heat energy; warmth. **3** the state of being hot. **4** hot weather: the heat of summer. **5** intensity of feeling: the heat of rage. **6** pressure: the political heat on the government over the economy. **7** the most intense part: the heat of the battle. **8** a period of sexual excitement in female mammals that occurs at oestrus. **9** Sport. **9a** a preliminary eliminating contest in a competition. **9b** a single section of a contest. **10** Sl. police activity after a crime: the heat is off. **11** Sl., chiefly US. criticism or abuse: he took a lot of heat for that mistake. **12 in the heat of the moment**. without pausing to think. **13 on** or **in heat**. **13a** Also: **in season**. (of some female mammals) sexually receptive. **13b** in a state of sexual excitement. ◆ vb **14** to make or become hot or warm. **15** to make or become excited or intense. [OE hætu]

heat barrier n another name for **thermal barrier**.

heat capacity n the heat required to raise the temperature of a substance by unit temperature interval under specified conditions.

heat death n Thermodynamics. the condition of any closed system when its total entropy is a maximum and it has no available energy. If the universe is a closed system it should eventually reach this state.

heated ('hiːtɪd) adj **1** made hot. **2** impassioned or highly emotional.
▶ 'heatedly adv

heat engine n an engine that converts heat energy into mechanical energy.

heater ('hiːtə) *n* **1** any device for supplying heat, such as a convector. **2** *US sl.* a pistol. **3** *Electronics.* a conductor carrying a current that indirectly heats the cathode in some types of valve.

heat exchanger *n* a device for transferring heat from one fluid to another without allowing them to mix.

heat exhaustion *n* a condition resulting from exposure to intense heat, characterized by dizziness, abdominal cramp, and prostration.

heath (hiːθ) *n* **1** *Brit.* a large open area, usually with sandy soil and scrubby vegetation, esp. heather. **2** Also called: **heather.** a low-growing evergreen shrub having small bell-shaped typically pink or purple flowers. **3** any of several heathlike plants, such as sea heath. [OE *hǣth*]
▸ 'heath,like *adj* ▸ 'heathy *adj*

Heath ★ (hiːθ) *n* **Edward (Richard George).** born 1916, British statesman; leader of the Conservative Party (1965–75); prime minister (1970–74).

heathen ('hiːðən) *n, pl* **heathens** *or* **heathen. 1** a person who does not acknowledge the God of Christianity, Judaism, or Islam; pagan. **2** an uncivilized or barbaric person. ◆ *adj* **3** irreligious; pagan. **4** uncivilized; barbaric. **5** of or relating to heathen peoples or their customs and beliefs. [OE *hǣthen*]
▸ 'heathendom *n* ▸ 'heathenism *or* 'heathenry *n*

heathenize *or* **heathenise** ('hiːðə,naɪz) *vb* **heathenizes, heathenizing, heathenized** *or* **heathenises, heathenising, heathenised.** to render or become heathen.

heather ('heðə) *n* **1** Also called: **ling, heath.** a low-growing evergreen Eurasian shrub that grows in dense masses on open ground and has clusters of small bell-shaped typically pinkish-purple flowers. **2** a purplish-red to pinkish-purple colour. ◆ *adj* **3** of a heather colour. **4** of or relating to interwoven yarns of mixed colours: *heather mixture.* [C14: orig. Scot. & N English, prob. from HEATH]
▸ 'heathery *adj*

Heath Robinson *adj* (of a mechanical device) absurdly complicated in design and having a simple function. [C20: after (William) *Heath Robinson* (1872–1944), Brit. cartoonist]

heating ('hiːtɪŋ) *n* **1** a device or system for supplying heat, esp. central heating, to a building. **2** the heat supplied.

heat pump *n* a device for extracting heat from a source and delivering it elsewhere at a higher temperature.

heat rash *n* a nontechnical name for **miliaria.**

heat-seeking *adj* (of a missile, detecting device, etc.) able to detect a source of heat, as from an aircraft engine: *a heat-seeking missile.*
▸ heat seeker *n*

heat shield *n* a coating or barrier for shielding from excessive heat, such as that experienced by a spacecraft on re-entry into the earth's atmosphere.

heat sink *n* **1** a metal plate designed to conduct and radiate heat from an electrical component. **2** a layer within the outer skin of high-speed aircraft to absorb heat.

heatstroke ('hiːt,strəʊk) *n* a condition resulting from prolonged exposure to intense heat, characterized by high fever.

heat-treat *vb* (*tr*) to apply heat to (a metal or alloy) in one or more temperature cycles to give it desirable properties.
▸ heat treatment *n*

heat wave *n* **1** a continuous spell of abnormally hot weather. **2** an extensive slow-moving air mass at a relatively high temperature.

heave (hiːv) *vb* **heaves, heaving, heaved** *or* **hove. 1** (*tr*) to lift or move with a great effort. **2** (*tr*) to throw (something heavy) with effort. **3** to utter (sounds) noisily or unhappily: *to heave a sigh.* **4** to rise and fall or cause to rise and fall heavily. **5** (*p.t. & p.p.* **hove**) *Naut.* **5a** to move or cause to move in a specified direction: *to heave in sight.* **5b** (*intr*) (of a vessel) to pitch or roll. **6** (*tr*) to displace (rock strata, etc.) in a horizontal direction. **7** (*intr*) to retch. ◆ *n* **8** the act of heaving. **9** a horizontal displacement of rock strata at a fault. ◆ See also **heave to, heaves.** [OE *hebban*]
▸ 'heaver *n*

heave-ho *interj* a sailors' cry, as when hoisting anchor.

heaven ('hevən) *n* **1** (*sometimes cap.*) *Christianity.* **1a** the abode of God and the angels. **1b** a state of communion with God after death. **2** (*usually pl*) the firmament surrounding the earth. **3** (in various mythologies) a place, such as Elysium or Valhalla, to which those who have died in the gods' favour are brought to dwell in happiness. **4** a place or state of happiness. **5** (*sing* or *pl; sometimes cap.*) God or the gods, used in exclamatory phrases: *for heaven's sake.* **6 move heaven and earth.** to do everything possible (to achieve something). [OE *heofon*]

heavenly ('hevənlɪ) *adj* **1** *Inf.* wonderful. **2** of or occurring in space: *a heavenly body.* **3** holy.
▸ 'heavenliness *n*

heavenward ('hevənwəd) *adj* **1** directed towards heaven or the sky. ◆ *adv* **2** Also **heavenwards.** towards heaven or the sky.

heaves (hiːvz) *n* (*functioning as sing or pl*) a chronic respiratory disorder of animals of the horse family, of unknown cause. Also called: **broken wind.**

heave to *vb* (*adv*) to stop (a vessel) or (of a vessel) to stop, as by trimming the sails, etc.

Heaviside ★ ('hevɪ,saɪd) *n* **Oliver.** 1850–1925, British physicist. Independently of Kennelly, he predicted (1902) the existence of the Heaviside layer; he also contributed to telegraphy.

Heaviside layer *n* another name for **E region** (of the ionosphere). [C20: after O. HEAVISIDE]

heavy ('hevɪ) *adj* **heavier, heaviest. 1** of comparatively great weight. **2** having a relatively high density: *lead is a heavy metal.* **3** great in yield, quality, or quantity: *heavy traffic.* **4** considerable: *heavy emphasis.* **5** hard to bear or fulfil: *heavy demands.* **6** sad or dejected: *heavy at heart.* **7** coarse or broad: *heavy features.* **8** (of soil) having a high clay content; cloggy. **9** solid or fat: *heavy legs.* **10** (of an industry) engaged in the large-scale complex manufacture of capital goods or extraction of raw materials. **11** serious; grave. **12** *Mil.* **12a** equipped with large weapons, armour, etc. **12b** (of guns, etc.) of a large and powerful type. **13** (of a syllable) having stress or accentuation. **14** dull and uninteresting: *a heavy style.* **15** prodigious: *a heavy drinker.* **16** (of cakes, etc.) insufficiently leavened. **17** deep and loud: *a heavy thud.* **18** (of music, literature, etc.) **18a** dramatic and powerful. **18b** not immediately comprehensible or appealing. **19** *Sl.* (of rock music) having a powerful beat; hard. **20** burdened: *heavy with child.* **21 heavy on.** *Inf.* using large quantities of: *this car is very heavy on petrol.* **22** clumsy and slow: *heavy going.* **23** cloudy or overcast: *heavy skies.* **24** not easily digestible: *a heavy meal.* **25** (of an element or compound) being or containing an isotope with greater atomic weight than that of the naturally occurring element: *heavy water.* **26** (of the going on a racecourse) soft and muddy. **27** *Sl.* using, or prepared to use, violence or brutality. ◆ *n, pl* **heavies. 28a** a villainous role. **28b** an actor who plays such a part. **29** *Mil.* **29a** a large fleet unit, esp. an aircraft carrier or battleship. **29b** a large piece of artillery. **30** (*usually pl*; often preceded by *the*) *Inf.* a serious newspaper: *the Sunday heavies.* **31** *Inf.* a heavyweight boxer, wrestler, etc. **32** *Sl.* a man hired to threaten violence or deter others by his presence. ◆ *adv* **33a** in a heavy manner; heavily: *time hangs heavy.* **33b** (*in combination*): *heavy-laden.* [OE *hefig*]
▸ 'heavily *adv* ▸ 'heaviness *n*

heavy-duty *n* (*modifier*) made to withstand hard wear, bad weather, etc.

heavy-handed *adj* **1** clumsy. **2** harsh and oppressive.
▸ ,heavy-'handedly *adv*

heavy-hearted *adj* sad; melancholy.

heavy hydrogen *n* another name for **deuterium.**

heavy metal *n* a type of rock music characterized by high volume, a driving beat, and extended guitar solos, often with violent, nihilistic, and misogynistic lyrics.

heavy middleweight *n* a professional wrestler weighing 177–187 pounds (81–85 kg).

heavy spar *n* another name for **barytes.**

heavy water *n* water that has been electrolytically decomposed to reduce the amount of normal hydrogen present and enrich it in deuterium in the form D_2O or HDO. See also **deuterium oxide**.

heavyweight ('hɛvɪ,weɪt) n **1** a person or thing that is heavier than average. **2a** a professional boxer weighing more than 175 pounds (79 kg). **2b** an amateur boxer weighing more than 81 kg (179 pounds). **3a** a professional wrestler weighing over 209 pounds (95 kg). **3b** an amateur wrestler weighing over 220 pounds (100kg). **4** Inf. an important or highly influential person.

Heb. or **Hebr.** abbrev. for: **1** Hebrew (language). **2** Bible. Hebrews.

Hebbel ★ (German 'hɛbəl) n **Christian Friedrich** ('krɪstɪan 'friːdrɪç). 1813–63, German dramatist and lyric poet; his major plays include the trilogy Die Nibelungen (1862).

hebdomadal (hɛb'dɒməd°l) adj weekly. [C18: from L, from Gk hebdomas seven (days), from hepta seven]

Hebe ★ ('hiːbɪ) n Greek myth. the goddess of youth and spring, daughter of Zeus and Hera and wife of Hercules.

Hebei ('hʌ'beɪ), **Hopeh,** or **Hopei** ★ n a province of NE China, on the Gulf of Chihli: important for the production of winter wheat, cotton, and coal. Capital: Shijiazhuang. Pop.: 63 880 000 (1995 est.). Area: 202 700 sq. km (79 053 sq. miles).

hebetate ('hɛbɪ,teɪt) adj **1** (of plant parts) having a blunt or soft point. ◆ vb hebetates, hebetating, hebetated. **2** Rare. to make or become blunted. [C16: from L hebetāre to make blunt, from hebes blunt]

Hebraic (hɪ'breɪɪk) or **Hebraical** adj of, relating to, or characteristic of the Hebrews or their language or culture.
▶ He'braically adv

Hebraism ('hiːbreɪ,ɪzəm) n a linguistic usage, custom, or other feature borrowed from or particular to the Hebrew language, or to the Jewish people or their culture.
▶ 'Hebraist n ▶ 'Hebra,ize or 'Hebra,ise vb

Hebrew ('hiːbruː) n **1** the ancient language of the Hebrews, revived as the official language of Israel. **2** a member of an ancient Semitic people claiming descent from Abraham; an Israelite. **3** Arch. or offens. a Jew. ◆ adj **4** of or relating to the Hebrews or their language. **5** Arch. or offens. Jewish. [C13: from OF Ebreu, ult. from Heb. 'ibhrī one from beyond (the river)]

Hebrews ('hiːbruːz) n (functioning as sing) a book of the New Testament.

Hebrides ★ ('hɛbrɪ,diːz) pl n the. a group of over 500 islands off the W coast of Scotland: separated by the North Minch, Little Minch, and the Sea of the Hebrides: the chief islands are Skye, Raasay, Rhum, Eigg, Coll, Tiree, Mull, Jura, Colonsay, and Islay (**Inner Hebrides**), and Lewis with Harris, North Uist, Benbecula, South Uist, and Barra (**Outer Hebrides**). Also called: **Western Isles**.
▶ ,Hebri'dean or Hebridian (hɛ'brɪdɪən) adj, n

Hebron ★ ('hɛbrɒn, 'hiː-) n a city in the West Bank: famous for the Haram, which includes the cenotaphs of Abraham and Sarah, Isaac and Rebecca, and Jacob and Leah. Pop.: 80 000 (1990 est.). Arabic name: **El Khalil**.

Hecate or **Hekate** ★ ('hɛkətɪ) n Greek myth. a goddess of the underworld.

hecatomb ('hɛkə,təʊm, -,tuːm) n **1** (in ancient Greece or Rome) any great public sacrifice and feast, originally one in which 100 oxen were sacrificed. **2** a great sacrifice. [C16: from L hecatombē, from Gk, from hekaton hundred + bous ox]

heck (hɛk) interj a mild exclamation of surprise, irritation, etc. [C19: euphemistic for hell]

heckelphone ('hɛkəl,fəʊn) n Music. a type of bass oboe. [C20: after W. Heckel (1856-1909), G inventor]

heckle ('hɛk°l) vb heckles, heckling, heckled. **1** to interrupt (a public speaker, etc.) by comments, questions, or taunts. **2** (tr) Also: hackle, hatchel. to comb (hemp or flax). ◆ n **3** an instrument for combing flax or hemp. [C15: N English & East Anglian form of HACKLE]
▶ 'heckler n

hectare ('hɛktɑː) n one hundred ares (10 000 square metres or 2.471 acres). Symbol: ha [C19: from F; see HECTO-, ARE²]

hectic ('hɛktɪk) adj **1** characterized by extreme activity or excitement. **2** associated with or symptomatic of tuberculosis (esp. in **hectic fever, hectic flush**). ◆ n **3** a hectic fever or flush. **4** Rare. a person who is consumptive. [C14: from LL hecticus, from Gk hektikos habitual, from hexis state, from ekhein to have]
▶ 'hectically adv

hecto- or before a vowel **hect-** prefix denoting 100: hectogram. Symbol: h [via F from Gk hekaton hundred]

hectog abbrev. for hectogram.

hectogram or **hectogramme** ('hɛktəʊ,græm) n one hundred grams (3.527 ounces). Symbol: hg

hectograph ('hɛktəʊ,grɑːf) n **1** a process for copying type or manuscript from a glycerine-coated gelatine master to which the original has been transferred. **2** a machine using this process.

hector ('hɛktə) vb **1** to bully or torment by teasing. ◆ n **2** a blustering bully. [C17: after HECTOR, in the sense: a bully]

Hector ★ ('hɛktə) n Classical myth. a son of King Priam of Troy, who was killed by Achilles.

Hecuba ★ ('hɛkjʊbə) n Classical myth. the wife of King Priam of Troy, and mother of Hector and Paris.

he'd (hiːd; unstressed iːd, hɪd, ɪd) contraction of he had or he would.

heddle ('hɛd°l) n one of a set of frames of vertical wires on a loom, each wire having an eye through which a warp thread can be passed. [OE hefeld chain]

hedera ('hɛdərə) n the genus name of ivy (sense 1). [L]

hedge (hɛdʒ) n **1** a row of shrubs or bushes forming a boundary. **2** a barrier or protection against something. **3** the act or a method of reducing the risk of loss on an investment, etc. **4** a cautious or evasive statement. **5** (as modifier) low, inferior, or illiterate: hedge priest. ◆ vb hedges, hedging, hedged. **6** (tr) to enclose or separate with or as if with a hedge. **7** (intr) to make or maintain a hedge. **8** (tr; often foll. by in, about, or around) to hinder or restrict. **9** (intr) to evade decision, esp. by making noncommittal statements. **10** (tr) to guard against the risk of loss in (a bet, etc.), esp. by laying bets with other bookmakers. **11** (intr) to protect against loss through future price fluctuations, as by investing in futures. [OE hecg]
▶ 'hedger n ▶ 'hedging n

hedge fund n a largely unregulated speculative fund which offers substantial returns for high-risk investments.

hedgehog ('hɛdʒ,hɒg) n a small nocturnal Old World mammal having a protective covering of spines on the back.

hedgehop ('hɛdʒ,hɒp) vb hedgehops, hedgehopping, hedgehopped. (intr) (of an aircraft) to fly close to the ground, as in crop spraying.
▶ 'hedge,hopping n, adj

hedgerow ('hɛdʒ,rəʊ) n a hedge of shrubs or low trees, esp. one bordering a field.

hedge sparrow n a small brownish European songbird. Also called: **dunnock**.

Hedjaz ★ (hiː'dʒæz) n a variant spelling of **Hejaz**.

hedonics (hiː'dɒnɪks) n (functioning as sing) **1** the branch of psychology concerned with the study of pleasant and unpleasant sensations. **2** (in philosophy) the study of pleasure.

hedonism ('hiːd°,nɪzəm, 'hɛd-) n **1** Ethics. **1a** the doctrine that moral value can be defined in terms of pleasure. **1b** the doctrine that the pursuit of pleasure is the highest good. **2** indulgence in sensual pleasures. [C19: from Gk hēdonē pleasure]
▶ ,hedon'istic adj ▶ 'hedonist n

-hedron n combining form. indicating a solid having a specified number of surfaces: tetrahedron. [from Gk -edron -sided, from hedra seat, base]
▶ **-hedral** adj combining form.

heebie-jeebies ('hiːbɪ'dʒiːbɪz) pl n the. Sl. apprehension and nervousness. [C20: coined by W. De Beck (1890–1942), American cartoonist]

heed (hiːd) n **1** careful attention; notice: to take heed. ◆ vb

2 to pay close attention to (someone or something). [OE *hēdan*]
▸ **'heedful** *adj* ▸ **'heedfully** *adv* ▸ **'heedfulness** *n*

heedless ('hi:dlɪs) *adj* taking no notice; careless or thoughtless.
▸ **'heedlessly** *adv* ▸ **'heedlessness** *n*

heehaw (ˌhi:'hɔ:) *interj* an imitation or representation of the braying sound of a donkey.

heel[1] (hi:l) *n* **1** the back part of the human foot. **2** the corresponding part in other vertebrates. **3** the part of a stocking, etc., designed to fit the heel. **4** the outer part of a shoe underneath the heel. **5** the end or back section of something: *the heel of a loaf.* **6** *Horticulture.* the small part of the parent plant that remains attached to a young shoot cut for propagation. **7** the back part of a golf club head where it bends to join the shaft. **8** *Sl.* a contemptible person. **9 at** (*or* **on**) **one's heels.** following closely. **10 down at heel. 10a** shabby or worn. **10b** slovenly. **11 kick** (*or* **cool**) **one's heels.** to wait or be kept waiting. **12 take to one's heels.** to run off. **13 to heel.** under control, as a dog walking by a person's heel. ◆ *vb* **14** (*tr*) to repair or replace the heel of (a shoe, etc.). **15** (*tr*) *Golf.* to strike (the ball) with the heel of the club. **16** to follow at the heels of (a person). [OE *hēla*]
▸ **'heelless** *adj*

heel[2] (hi:l) *vb* **1** (of a vessel) to lean over; list. ◆ *n* **2** inclined position from the vertical. [OE *hieldan*]

heelball ('hi:lˌbɔ:l) *n* **a** a mixture of beeswax and lampblack used by shoemakers to blacken the edges of heels and soles. **b** a similar substance used to take rubbings, esp. brass rubbings.

heeler ('hi:lə) *n* **1** *US.* See **ward heeler. 2** a person or thing that heels. **3** *Austral. & NZ.* a dog that herds cattle, etc., by biting at their heels.

heel in *vb* (*tr, adv*) to insert (cuttings, shoots, etc.) into the soil before planting to keep them moist.

heeltap ('hi:lˌtæp) *n* **1** a layer of leather, etc., in the heel of a shoe. **2** a small amount of alcoholic drink left at the bottom of a glass.

Heerlen ★ ('hɪələn; *Dutch* 'he:rlə) *n* a city in the SE Netherlands, in Limburg province: industrial centre of a coal-mining region. Pop.: 95 794 (1994).

Hefei ('hʌ'feɪ) *or* **Hofei** ★ *n* a city in SE China, capital of Anhui province: administrative and commercial centre in a rice- and cotton-growing region. Pop.: 1 000 000 (1991 est.).

heft (heft) *vb* (*tr*) *Brit. dialect. & US inf.* **1** to assess the weight of (something) by lifting. **2** to lift. ◆ *n* **3** weight. **4** *US.* the main part. [C19: prob. from HEAVE, by analogy with *thieve, theft, cleave, cleft*]

hefty ('heftɪ) *adj* **heftier, heftiest.** *Inf.* **1** big and strong. **2** characterized by vigour or force: *a hefty blow.* **3** bulky or heavy. **4** sizable; involving a large amount of money: *a hefty bill.*
▸ **'heftily** *adv*

Hegel ★ ('heɪɡ°l) *n* Georg Wilhelm Friedrich (ge'ɔrk 'vɪlhelm 'fri:drɪç). 1770–1831, German philosopher, whose views are expounded in *The Phenomenology of Mind* (1807).
▸ **Hegelian** (hɪ'ɡeɪlɪən, heɪ'ɡi:-) *adj* ▸ **He'gelianˌism** *n*

hegemony (hɪ'ɡemənɪ) *n, pl* **hegemonies.** ascendancy or domination of one power or state within a league, confederation, etc. [C16: from Gk *hēgemonia*, from *hēgemōn* leader, from *hēgeisthai* to lead]
▸ **hegemonic** (ˌheɡə'mɒnɪk) *adj*

Hegira *or* **Hejira** ('hedʒɪrə) *n* **1** the flight of Mohammed from Mecca to Medina in 622 A.D.; the starting point of the Muslim era. **2** the Muslim era itself. **3** (*often not cap.*) an emigration, escape, or flight. [C16: from Med. L, from Ar. *hijrah* emigration or flight]

Heidegger ★ (*German* 'haidəɡər) *n* Martin ('marti:n). 1889–1976, German existentialist philosopher: he expounded his system in *Being and Time* (1927).

Heidelberg ★ ('haid°lˌbɜːɡ; *German* 'haidəlberk) *n* a city in SW Germany, in NW Baden-Württemberg on the River Neckar: capital of the Palatinate from the 13th century until 1719; famous castle (begun in the 12th

century) and university (1386), the oldest in Germany. Pop.: 138 964 (1995 est.).

heifer ('hefə) *n* a young cow. [OE *heahfore*]

Heifetz ★ ('haɪfɪts) *n* Jascha ('jæʃə). 1901–87, US violinist, born in Russia.

heigh-ho ('heɪ'həʊ) *interj* an exclamation of weariness, surprise, or happiness.

height (haɪt) *n* **1** the vertical distance from the bottom of something to the top. **2** the vertical distance of a place above sea level. **3** relatively great altitude. **4** the topmost point; summit. **5** *Astron.* the angular distance of a celestial body above the horizon. **6** the period of greatest intensity: *the height of the battle.* **7** An extreme example: *the height of rudeness.* **8** (*often pl*) an area of high ground. [OE *hīehthu; see* HIGH]

heighten ('haɪt°n) *vb* to make or become higher or more intense.
▸ **'heightened** *adj*

height of land *n* *US & Canad.* a watershed.

Heilbronn ★ (*German* hail'brɔn) *n* a city in SW Germany, in N Baden-Württemberg on the River Neckar. Pop.: 122 253 (1995 est.).

Heilongjiang ('heɪˌlʊŋdʒaɪ'æŋ) *or* **Heilungkiang** ★ ('heɪˌlʊŋ'kjæŋ, -kaɪ'æŋ) *n* a province of NE China, in Manchuria: coal-mining, with placer gold in some rivers. Capital: Harbin. Pop.: 36 720 000 (1995 est.). Area: 464 000 sq. km (179 000 sq. miles).

Heilong Jiang ★ ('heɪ'lʊŋ dʒaɪ'æŋ) *n* the Pinyin transliteration of the Chinese name for the **Amur**.

Heimdall, Heimdal ('heɪmˌdɑːl), *or* **Heimdallr** ('heɪmˌdɑːlə) *n Norse myth.* the god of light and the dawn, and the guardian of the rainbow bridge Bifrost.

Heine ★ (*German* 'hainə) *n* Heinrich ('hainrɪç). 1797–1856, German poet and essayist, whose chief poetic work is *Das Buch der Lieder* (1827). Many of his poems have been set to music, notably by Schubert and Schumann.

Heinkel ★ (*German* 'haink°l) *n* Ernst Heinrich (ɛrnst 'hainrɪç). 1888–1958, German aircraft designer. His company provided many military aircraft in World Wars I and II, including the first jet-powered plane.

heinous ('heɪnəs, 'hi:-) *adj* evil; atrocious. [C14: from OF *haineus*, from *haine* hatred, of Gmc origin]
▸ **'heinously** *adv*

heir (ɛə) *n* **1** the person legally succeeding to all property of a deceased person. **2** any person or thing that carries on some tradition, circumstance, etc., from a forerunner. [C13: from OF, from L *hērēs*]
▸ **'heirdom** *or* **'heirship** *n*

heir apparent *n, pl* **heirs apparent.** a person whose right to succeed to certain property cannot be defeated, provided such person survives his ancestor.

heiress ('ɛərɪs) *n* **1** a woman who inherits or expects to inherit great wealth. **2** a female heir.

heirloom ('ɛəˌlu:m) *n* **1** an object that has been in a family for generations. **2** an item of personal property inherited in accordance with the terms of a will. [C15: from HEIR + *lome* tool; see LOOM[1]]

heir presumptive *n Property law.* a person who expects to succeed to an estate but whose right may be defeated by the birth of one nearer in blood to the ancestor.

Heisenberg ★ ('haɪz°nˌbɜːɡ; *German* 'haizənberk) *n* Werner Karl ('vɛrnər karl). 1901–76, German physicist. He contributed to quantum mechanics and formulated the uncertainty principle (1927): Nobel prize for physics 1932.

heist (haɪst) *Sl., chiefly US & Canad.* ◆ *n* **1** a robbery. ◆ *vb* **2** (*tr*) to steal. [var. of HOIST]

Heitler ★ (*German* 'haitlər) *n* Walter ('valtər). 1904–81, German physicist, noted for his work on chemical bonds.

Hejaz, Hedjaz, *or* **Hijaz** ★ (hi:'dʒæz) *n* a region of W Saudi Arabia, along the Red Sea and the Gulf of Aqaba: formerly an independent kingdom; united with Nejd in 1932 to form Saudi Arabia.

Hejira ('hedʒɪrə) *n* a variant spelling of **Hegira.**

Hekate ★ ('hekətɪ) *n* a variant spelling of **Hecate.**

★ people and places

Hekla ★ ('hɛklə) *n* a volcano in SW Iceland: several craters, with the last eruption in 1970. Height: 1491 m (4892 ft).

Hel (hɛl) *or* **Hela** ★ ('hɛlɑ:) *n Norse myth.* **1** the goddess of the dead. **2** the underworld realm of the dead.

held (hɛld) *vb* the past tense and past participle of **hold**[1].

Helen ★ ('hɛlɪn) *n Greek myth.* the beautiful daughter of Zeus and Leda, whose abduction by Paris from her husband Menelaus caused the Trojan War.

Helena[1] ★ ('hɛlɪnə) *n* a city in W Montana: the state capital. Pop.: 24 569 (1990).

Helena[2] ('hɛlənə) ★ *n* **Saint**. ?248–?328 A.D., Roman empress, mother of Constantine I. After converting to Christianity (313) she made a pilgrimage to the Holy Land (?326). Feast day: May 21.

helenium (hɛ'li:nɪəm) *n* a perennial garden plant with yellow, bronze, or crimson flowers. [from Gk *helenion* name of a plant]

Helgoland ★ ('hɛlgolant) *n* the German name for **Heligoland**.

heliacal rising (hɪ'laɪək[ə]l) *n* **1** the rising of a celestial object at the same time as the sun. **2** the date at which such a celestial object first becomes visible. [C17: from LL *hēliacus* relating to the sun, from Gk, from *hēlios* sun]

helianthemum (hi:lɪ'ænθəməm) *n* any of a genus of dwarf shrubs with brightly coloured flowers: often grown in rockeries. [from Gk *helios* sun + *anthemon* flower]

helianthus (,hi:lɪ'ænθəs) *n, pl* **helianthuses**. a plant of the composite family having large yellow daisy-like flowers with yellow, brown, or purple centres. [C18: NL, from Gk *hēlios* sun + *anthos* flower]

helical ('hɛlɪk[ə]l) *adj* of or like a helix; spiral.

helical gear *n* a gearwheel having the tooth form generated on a helical path about the axis of the wheel.

helices ('hɛlɪ,si:z) *n* a plural of **helix**.

helichrysum (,hɛlɪ'kraɪzəm) *n* any plant of the genus *Helichrysum*, whose flowers retain their shape and colour when dried. [C16: from L, from Gk, from *helix* spiral + *khrusos* gold]

helicoid ('hɛlɪ,kɔɪd) *adj* **1** *Biol.* shaped like a spiral: *a helicoid shell.* ◆ *n* **2** *Geom.* any surface resembling that of a screw thread.

helicon ('hɛlɪkən) *n* a bass tuba made to coil over the shoulder of a band musician. [C19: prob. from HELICON; associated with Gk *helix* spiral]

Helicon ★ ('hɛlɪkən) *n* a mountain in Greece, in Boeotia: location of the springs of Hippocrene and Aganippe, believed by the Ancient Greeks to be the source of poetic inspiration and the home of the Muses. Height: 1749 m (5738 ft). Modern Greek name: **Elikón**.

helicopter ('hɛlɪ,kɒptə) *n* an aircraft capable of hover, vertical flight, and horizontal flight in any direction. Most get their lift and propulsion from overhead rotating blades. [C19: from F, from Gk *helix* spiral + *pteron* wing]

helicopter gunship *n* a large heavily armed helicopter used for ground attack.

Heligoland ★ ('hɛlɪgəʊ,lænd) *n* a small island in the North Sea, one of the North Frisian Islands, separated from the coast of NW Germany by **Heligoland Bight**: administratively part of the German state of Schleswig-Holstein: a large island in early medieval times, now eroded to an area of about 150 hectares (380 acres); ceded by Britain to Germany in 1890 in exchange for Zanzibar. German name: **Helgoland**.

helio- *or before a vowel* **heli-** *combining form.* indicating the sun: *heliocentric.* [from Gk, from *hēlios* sun]

heliocentric (,hi:lɪəʊ'sɛntrɪk) *adj* **1** having the sun at its centre. **2** measured from or in relation to the sun.
  ▶ ,helio'centrically *adv*

Heliogabalus (hi:lɪəʊ'gæbələs) *or* **Elagabalus** ★ *n* original name *Varius Avitus Bassianus.* ?204–222 A.D., Roman emperor (218–222); notorious for his debauchery.

heliograph ('hi:lɪəʊ,grɑ:f) *n* **1** an instrument with mirrors and a shutter used for sending messages in Morse code by reflecting the sun's rays. **2** a device used to photograph the sun.
  ▶ ,heli'ography *n*

heliometer (,hi:lɪ'ɒmɪtə) *n* a refracting telescope used to determine angular distances between celestial bodies.
  ▶ ,heli'ometry *n*

heliopause ('hi:lɪəʊ,pɔ:z) *n* the region of space beyond the sun's magnetic field.

Heliopolis ★ (,hi:lɪ'ɒpəlɪs) *n* **1** (in ancient Egypt) a city near the apex of the Nile delta: a centre of sun worship. Ancient Egyptian name: **On.** **2** the Ancient Greek name for **Baalbek**.

heliopsis (,hɛlɪ'ɒpsɪs) *n* a perennial plant with yellow daisy-like flowers.

Helios ★ ('hi:lɪ,ɒs) *n Greek myth.* the god of the sun, who drove his chariot daily across the sky. Roman counterpart: **Sol**.

heliostat ('hi:lɪəʊ,stæt) *n* an astronomical instrument used to reflect the light of the sun in a constant direction.
  ▶ ,helio'static *adj*

heliotrope ('hi:lɪə,trəʊp, 'hɛljə-) *n* **1** any plant of the genus *Heliotropium*, esp. the South American variety, cultivated for its small fragrant purple flowers. **2a** a bluish-violet to purple colour. **2b** (*as adj*): *a heliotrope dress.* **3** another name for **bloodstone**. [C17: L, from *hēliotropium*, from Gk, from *hēlios* sun + *trepein* to turn]

heliotropism (,hi:lɪ'ɒtrə,pɪzəm) *n* the growth of a plant in response to the stimulus of sunlight.
  ▶ heliotropic (,hi:lɪəʊ'trɒpɪk) *adj*

heliport ('hɛlɪ,pɔ:t) *n* an airport for helicopters. [C20: from HELI(COPTER) + PORT[1]]

helium ('hi:lɪəm) *n* a very light nonflammable colourless odourless element that is an inert gas, occurring in certain natural gases. Symbol: He; atomic no.: 2; atomic wt.: 4.0026. [C19: NL, from HELIO- + -IUM; because first detected in the solar spectrum]

helix ('hi:lɪks) *n, pl* **helices** *or* **helixes**. **1** a spiral. **2** the incurving fold that forms the margin of the external ear. **3** another name for **volute** (sense 2). **4** any terrestrial mollusc of the genus *Helix*, including the garden snail. [C16: from L, from Gk: spiral; prob. rel. to Gk *helissein* to twist]

hell (hɛl) *n* **1** (*sometimes cap.*) *Christianity.* **1a** the place or state of eternal punishment of the wicked after death. **1b** forces of evil regarded as residing there. **2** (*sometimes cap.*) (in various religions and cultures) the abode of the spirits of the dead. **3** pain, extreme difficulty, etc. **4** *Inf.* a cause of such suffering: *war is hell.* **5** *US & Canad.* high spirits or mischievousness. **6** *Now rare.* a gambling house. **7** (**come**) **hell or high water**. *Inf.* whatever difficulties may arise. **8** **for the hell of it**. *Inf.* for the fun of it. **9** **from hell**. *Inf.* denoting a person or thing that is particularly bad or alarming: *job from hell.* **10** **give someone hell**. *Inf.* **10a** to give someone a severe reprimand or punishment. **10b** to be a source of torment to someone. **11** **hell for leather**. at great speed. **12** **hell to pay**. *Inf.* serious consequences, as of a foolish action. **13** **the hell**. *Inf.* **13a** (intensifier): used in such phrases as **what the hell**. **13b** an expression of strong disagreement: *the hell I will.* ◆ *interj* **14** *Inf.* an exclamation of anger, surprise, etc. [OE *hell*]

he'll (hi:l; *unstressed* i:l, hɪl, ɪl) *contraction of* he will *or* he shall.

hellacious (hɛ'leɪʃəs) *adj US sl.* **1** remarkable; horrifying. **2** wonderful; excellent. [C20: from HELL + -acious as in AUDACIOUS]

Helladic (hɛ'lædɪk) *adj* of or relating to the Bronze Age civilization that flourished about 2900 to 1100 B.C. on the Greek mainland and islands.

Hellas ★ ('hɛləs) *n* transliteration of the Ancient Greek name for Greece.

hellbent (,hɛl'bɛnt) *adj* (*postpositive;* foll. by *on*) *Inf.* strongly or rashly intent.

hellcat ('hɛl,kæt) *n* a spiteful fierce-tempered woman.

Helle ★ ('hɛlɪ) *n Greek myth.* a daughter of King Athamas, who was borne away with her brother Phrixus on the golden winged ram. She fell from its back and was drowned in the Hellespont. See also **Phrixus, Golden Fleece.**

hellebore ('hɛlɪ,bɔː) n 1 any plant of the Eurasian genus *Helleborus*, typically having showy flowers and poisonous parts. See also **Christmas rose. 2** any of various plants that yield alkaloids used in the treatment of heart disease. [C14: from Gk *helleboros*, from ?]

Hellen ★ ('hɛlɪn) n (in Greek legend) a Thessalian king and eponymous ancestor of the Hellenes.

Hellene ('heliːn) or **Hellenian** (hɛ'liːnɪən) n another name for a **Greek.**

Hellenic (hɛ'lɛnɪk, -'liː-) adj 1 of or relating to the ancient or modern Greeks or their language. 2 of or relating to ancient Greece or the Greeks of the classical period (776–323 B.C.). Cf. **Hellenistic.** ♦ n 3 the Greek language in its various ancient and modern dialects.

Hellenism ('hɛlɪ,nɪzəm) n 1 the principles, ideals, and pursuits associated with classical Greek civilization. 2 the spirit or national character of the Greeks. 3 imitation of or devotion to the culture of ancient Greece.
▸ **'Hellenist** n

Hellenistic (,hɛlɪ'nɪstɪk) or **Hellenistical** adj 1 characteristic of or relating to Greek civilization in the Mediterranean world, esp. from the death of Alexander the Great (323 B.C.) to the defeat of Antony and Cleopatra (30 B.C.). 2 of or relating to the Greeks or to Hellenism.
▸ **,Hellen'istically** adv

Hellenize or **Hellenise** ('hɛlɪ,naɪz) vb **Hellenizes, Hellenizing, Hellenized** or **Hellenises, Hellenising, Hellenised.** to make or become like the ancient Greeks.
▸ **,Helleni'zation** or **,Helleni'sation** n

Heller ★ ('hɛlə) n **Joseph.** born 1923, US novelist. His works include *Catch 22* (1961) and *Closing Time* (1994).

Helles ★ ('hɛlɪs) n **Cape.** a cape in NW Turkey, at the S end of the Gallipoli Peninsula.

Hellespont ★ ('hɛlɪ,spɒnt) n the ancient name for the **Dardanelles.**

hellfire ('hɛl,faɪə) n 1 the torment of hell, envisaged as eternal fire. 2 (*modifier*) characterizing sermons that emphasize this.

hellion ('hɛljən) n *Chiefly US inf.* a rowdy person, esp. a child; troublemaker. [C19: prob. from dialect *hallion* rogue, from ?]

hellish ('hɛlɪʃ) adj 1 of or resembling hell. 2 wicked; cruel. 3 *Inf.* very unpleasant. ♦ adv 4 *Brit. inf.* (intensifier): *a hellish good idea.*

Hellman ★ ('hɛlmən) n **Lillian.** 1905–84, US dramatist. Her works include the play *The Little Foxes* (1939) and the autobiographical *Scoundrel Time* (1976).

hello, hallo, or **hullo** (hɛ'ləʊ, hə-; 'hɛləʊ) *sentence substitute.* 1 an expression of greeting. 2 a call used to attract attention. 3 an expression of surprise. ♦ n, pl **hellos, hallos** or **hullos.** 4 the act of saying or calling "hello". [C19: see HOLLO]

Hell's Angel n a member of a motorcycle gang who typically dress in Nazi-style paraphernalia and are noted for their lawless behaviour.

helm¹ (hɛlm) n 1 *Naut.* **1a** the wheel or entire apparatus by which a vessel is steered. **1b** the position of the helm: that is, on the side of the keel opposite from that of the rudder. 2 a position of leadership or control (esp. in **at the helm**). ♦ vb 3 (*tr*) to steer. [OE *helma*]
▸ **'helmsman** n

helm² (hɛlm) n an archaic or poetic word for **helmet.** [OE *helm*]

Helmand ★ ('hɛlmənd) n a river in S Asia, rising in E Afghanistan and flowing generally southwest to a marshy lake, Hamun Helmand, on the border with Iran. Length: 1400 km (870 miles).

helmet ('hɛlmɪt) n 1 a piece of protective or defensive armour for the head worn by soldiers, policemen, firemen, divers, etc. See also **crash helmet, pith helmet. 2** *Biol.* a part or structure resembling a helmet, esp. the upper part of the calyx of certain flowers. [C15: from OF, dim. of *helme*, of Gmc origin]
▸ **'helmeted** adj

Helmholtz ★ (*German* 'hɛlmhɔlts) n Baron **Hermann Ludwig Ferdinand von** ('hɛrman 'luːtvɪç 'fɛrdɪnant fɔn). 1821–94, German physiologist and physicist: helped to establish the conservation of energy and invented the ophthalmoscope (1850).

helminth ('hɛlmɪnθ) n any parasitic worm, esp. a nematode or fluke. [C19: from Gk *helmins* parasitic worm]
▸ **hel'minthic** or **helminthoid** (hɛlmɪn'θɔɪd, hɛl'mɪnθɔɪd) adj

helminthiasis (,hɛlmɪn'θaɪəsɪs) n infestation of the body with parasitic worms. [C19: from NL, from Gk *helminthian* to be infested with worms]

Helmont ★ (*Flemish* 'hɛlmɔnt) n **Jean Baptiste van** (ʒɑ̃ batist van). 1577–1644, Flemish chemist and physician. He was the first to distinguish gases.

Héloïse ★ ('ɛləʊ,iːz; *French* elɔiz) n ?1101–64, pupil, mistress, and wife of Abelard.

helot ('hɛlət, 'hiː-) n 1 (*cap.*) (in ancient Sparta) a member of the class of serfs owned by the state. 2 a serf or slave. [C16: from L *Hēlōtēs*, from Gk *Heilōtes*, alleged to have meant orig.: inhabitants of Helos, who, after its conquest, were serfs of the Spartans]
▸ **'helotism** n ▸ **'helotry** n

help (hɛlp) vb 1 to assist (someone to do something), esp. by sharing the work, cost, or burden of something. 2 to alleviate the burden of (someone else) by giving assistance. 3 (*tr*) to assist (a person) to go in a specified direction: *help the old lady up.* 4 to contribute to: *to help the relief operations.* 5 to improve (a situation, etc.): *crying won't help.* 6 (*tr*; preceded by *can, could,* etc.; usually used with a negative) **6a** to refrain from: *we can't help wondering who he is.* **6b** (usually foll. by *it*) to be responsible for: *I can't help it if it rains.* 7 to alleviate (an illness, etc.). 8 (*tr*) to serve (a customer). 9 (*tr*; foll. by *to*) **9a** to serve (someone with food, etc.) (usually in **help oneself**). **9b** to provide (oneself with) without permission. 10 **cannot help but.** to be unable to do anything else except: *I cannot help but laugh.* 11 **so help me. 11a** on my honour. **11b** no matter what: *so help me, I'll get revenge.* ♦ n 12 the act of helping or being helped, or a person or thing that helps. **13a** a person hired for a job, esp. a farm worker or domestic servant. **13b** (*functioning as sing*) several employees collectively. 14 a remedy: *there's no help for it.* ♦ *sentence substitute.* 15 used to ask for assistance. ♦ See also **help out.** [OE *helpan*]
▸ **'helper** n

helpful ('hɛlpfʊl) adj giving help.
▸ **'helpfully** adv ▸ **'helpfulness** n

helping ('hɛlpɪŋ) n a single portion of food.

helping hand n assistance: *many people lent a helping hand in making arrangements.*

helpless ('hɛlplɪs) adj 1 unable to manage independently. 2 made weak: *they were helpless from giggling.*
▸ **'helplessly** adv ▸ **'helplessness** n

helpline ('hɛlp,laɪn) n a telephone line operated by a charitable organization for people in distress or by a commercial organization to provide information.

Helpmann ★ ('hɛlpmən) n Sir **Robert.** 1909–86, Australian ballet dancer and choreographer: his ballets include *Miracle in the Gorbals* (1944) and *Yugen* (1965).

helpmate ('hɛlp,meɪt) n a companion and helper, esp. a wife.

helpmeet ('hɛlp,miːt) n a less common word for **helpmate.** [C17: from *an helpe meet* (suitable) *for him* Genesis 2:18]

help out vb (adv) to assist, esp. by sharing the burden or cost of something with (another person).

Helsingborg ★ (*Swedish* helsɪŋ'bɔrj) n a port in SW Sweden, on the Sound opposite Helsingør, Denmark: changed hands several times between Denmark and Sweden, finally becoming Swedish in 1710; shipbuilding. Pop.: 114 339 (1996 est.). Former name (until 1971): **Hälsingborg.**

Helsingør ★ (*Danish* helsɛŋ'øːr) n a port in NE Denmark, in NE Zealand: site of Kronborg Castle (16th century), famous as the scene of Shakespeare's *Hamlet*. Pop.: 56 855 (1995). English name: **Elsinore.**

★ people and places

Helsinki ★ ('hɛlsɪŋkɪ, hɛl'sɪŋ-) n the capital of Finland, a port in the south on the Gulf of Finland: founded by Gustavus I of Sweden in 1550; replaced Turku as capital in 1812, while under Russian rule; university. Pop.: 532 053 (1997 est.). Swedish name: **Helsingfors** (hɛlsɪŋ'fɔrs).

helter-skelter ('hɛltə'skɛltə) adj 1 haphazard or careless. ◆ adv 2 in a helter-skelter manner. ◆ n 3 Brit. a high spiral slide, as at a fairground. 4 disorder. [C16: prob. imit.]

helve (hɛlv) n the handle of a hand tool such as an axe or pick. [OE hielfe]

Helvellyn ★ (hɛl'vɛlɪn) n a mountain in NW England, in the Lake District. Height: 950 m (3118 ft).

Helvetia ★ (hɛl'viːʃə) n 1 the Latin name for Switzerland. 2 a Roman province in central Europe (1st century B.C. to the 5th century A.D.), corresponding to part of S Germany and parts of W and N Switzerland.

Helvetian (hɛl'viːʃən) adj 1 Swiss. ◆ n 2 a native or citizen of Switzerland.

Helvétius ★ (hɛl'viːʃɪəs; French ɛlvesjys) n **Claude Adrien** (klod adriɛ̃). 1715–71, French philosopher. His chief work was De l'Esprit (1758).

hem[1] (hɛm) n 1 an edge to a piece of cloth, made by folding the raw edge under and stitching it down. 2 short for **hemline**. ◆ vb **hems, hemming, hemmed**. (tr) 3 to provide with a hem. 4 (usually foll. by in, around, or about) to enclose or confine. [OE hemm]
  ▸ 'hemmer n

hem[2] (hɛm) n, interj 1 a representation of the sound of clearing the throat, used to gain attention, etc. ◆ vb **hems, hemming, hemmed**. 2 (intr) to utter this sound. 3 hem (or hum) and haw. to hesitate in speaking.

he-man n, pl he-men. Inf. a strongly built muscular man.

hematite or **haematite** ('hɛmətaɪt, 'hiːm-) n a red, grey, or black mineral, found as massive beds and in veins and igneous rocks. It is the chief source of iron. Composition: iron (ferric) oxide. Crystal structure: hexagonal (rhombohedral). [C16: via L from Gk haimatitēs resembling blood, from haima blood]
  ▸ **hematitic** or **haematitic** (ˌhɛmə'tɪtɪk, ˌhiː-) adj

hemato- or before a vowel **hemat-** combining form. US variants of haemato-.

Hemel Hempstead ★ ('hɛməl 'hɛmstɪd) n a town in SE England, in W Hertfordshire: designated a new town in 1947. Pop.: 79 235 (1991).

hemeralopia (ˌhɛmərə'ləʊpɪə) n inability to see clearly in bright light. Nontechnical name: **day blindness**. [C18: NL, from Gk, from hēmera day + alaos blind + ōps eye]

hemerocallis (hɛmər'ɒkælɪs) n a N temperate plant with large funnel-shaped orange flowers: each single flower lasts for only one day. Also called: **day lily**. [C17: from Gk hēmera day + kallos beauty]

hemi- prefix half: hemicycle; hemisphere. [from L, from Gk hēmi-]

-hemia n combining form. a US variant of -aemia.

hemidemisemiquaver (ˌhɛmɪˌdɛmɪ'sɛmɪˌkweɪvə) n Music. a note having the time value of one sixty-fourth of a semibreve. Usual US & Canad. name: **sixty-fourth note**.

Hemingway ★ ('hɛmɪŋˌweɪ) n **Ernest**. 1899–1961, US writer. His novels include A Farewell to Arms (1929) and For Whom the Bell Tolls (1940): Nobel prize for literature 1954.

hemiplegia (ˌhɛmɪ'pliːdʒɪə) n paralysis of one side of the body.
  ▸ ˌhemi'plegic adj

hemipode ('hɛmɪˌpəʊd) n a small quail-like bird occurring in tropical and subtropical regions of the Old World. Also called: **button quail**.

hemipteran (hɪ'mɪptərən) n any hemipterous insect. [C19: from HEMI- + Gk pteron wing]

hemipterous (hɪ'mɪptərəs) adj of or belonging to a large order of insects having sucking or piercing mouthparts.

hemisphere ('hɛmɪˌsfɪə) n 1 one half of a sphere. 2a half of the terrestrial globe, divided into **northern** and **southern** hemispheres by the equator or into **eastern** and **western** hemispheres by some meridians, usually 0° and 180°. 2b a map or projection of one of the hemispheres. 3 Anat. short for **cerebral hemisphere**. 4 half of the cerebrum.
  ▸ **hemispheric** (ˌhɛmɪ'sfɛrɪk) or ˌhemi'spherical adj

hemistich ('hɛmɪˌstɪk) n Prosody. a half line of verse.

hemline ('hɛmˌlaɪn) n the level to which the hem of a skirt or dress hangs.

hemlock ('hɛmˌlɒk) n 1 an umbelliferous poisonous Eurasian plant having finely divided leaves, spotted stems, and small white flowers. 2 a poisonous drug derived from this plant. 3 Also called: **hemlock spruce**. a coniferous tree of North America and Asia. [OE hymlic]

hemo- combining form. a US variant of **haemo-**.

hemp (hɛmp) n 1 Also called: **cannabis, marijuana**. an Asian plant having tough fibres, deeply lobed leaves, and small greenish flowers. See also **Indian hemp**. 2 the fibre of this plant, used to make canvas, rope, etc. 3 any of several narcotic drugs obtained from some varieties of this plant, esp. from Indian hemp. [OE hænep]
  ▸ 'hempen or 'hemp,like adj

hemstitch ('hɛm,stɪtʃ) n 1 a decorative edging stitch, usually for a hem, in which the cross threads are stitched in groups. ◆ vb 2 to decorate (a hem, etc.) with hemstitches.

hen (hɛn) n 1 the female of any bird, esp. of the domestic fowl. 2 the female of certain other animals, such as the lobster. 3 Scot. dialect. a term of address used to women. [OE henn]

Henan ('hʌ'næn) or **Honan** ★ n a province of N central China: the chief centre of early Chinese culture; mainly agricultural (the largest wheat-producing province in China). Capital: Zhengzhou. Pop.: 90 270 000 (1995 est.).

henbane ('hɛnˌbeɪn) n a poisonous Mediterranean plant with sticky hairy leaves: yields the drug hyoscyamine.

hence (hɛns) sentence connector. 1 for this reason; therefore. ◆ adv 2 from this time: a year hence. 3 Arch. from here; away. ◆ sentence substitute. 4 Arch. begone! away! [OE hionane]

henceforth ('hɛns'fɔːθ), **henceforwards**, or **henceforward** adv from now on.

henchman ('hɛntʃmən) n, pl **henchmen**. 1 a faithful attendant or supporter. 2 Arch. a squire; page. [C14 hengestman, from OE hengest stallion + MAN]

hendeca- combining form. eleven: hendecagon; hendecasyllable. [from Gk hendeka, from hen, neuter of heis one + deka ten]

hendecagon (hɛn'dɛkəgən) n a polygon having 11 sides.
  ▸ **hendecagonal** (ˌhɛndɪ'kægənˑl) adj

hendecasyllable ('hɛndɛkəˌsɪləbˑl) n Prosody. a verse line of 11 syllables. [C18: from Gk]

Henderson ★ ('hɛndəsˑn) n **Arthur**. 1863–1935, British Labour politician. Foreign secretary (1929–31); Nobel peace prize 1934.

hendiadys (hɛn'daɪədɪs) n a rhetorical device by which two nouns joined by a conjunction are used instead of a noun and a qualifier, as in to run with fear and haste instead of to run with fearful haste. [C16: from Med. L, from Gk hen dia duoin, lit.: one through two]

Hendrix ★ ('hɛndrɪks) n **Jimi**, full name James Marshall Hendrix. 1942–70, US rock guitarist, singer, and songwriter. His recordings include "Purple Haze" (1967) and Are you Experienced? (1967).

Hendry ★ ('hɛndrɪ) n **Stephen**. born 1969, British snooker player: world champion 1990, 1992, 1994, 1995, and 1996.

henequen, henequin, or **heniquen** ('hɛnɪkɪn) n 1 an agave plant that is native to Mexico. 2 the fibre of this plant, used in making rope, twine, and coarse fabrics. [C19: from American Sp. henequén, prob. of Amerind origin]

henge (hɛndʒ) n a circular monument, often containing a circle of stones, dating from the Neolithic and Bronze Ages. [back formation from Stonehenge, site of important megalithic ruins on Salisbury Plain, S England]

Hengelo ★ (*Dutch* 'hɛŋəloː) *n* a city in the E Netherlands, in Overijssel province on the Twente Canal: industrial centre, esp. for textiles. Pop.: 77 514 (1994).

Hengist ★ ('hɛŋgɪst) *n* died ?488 A.D., a leader, with his brother Horsa, of the first Jutish settlers in Britain; he is thought to have conquered Kent (?455).

Hengyang ★ ('hɛŋ'jæŋ) *n* a city in SE central China, in Hunan province on the Xiang River. Pop.: 487 148 (1990 est.).

hen harrier *n* a common harrier that nests in marshes and open land.

henhouse ('hɛn,haʊs) *n* a coop for hens.

Henie ★ ('hɛnɪ) *n* **Sonja** ('sɒnjə). 1912–69, Norwegian figure-skater.

Henley-on-Thames ★ ('hɛnlɪ-) *n* a town in S England, in SE Oxfordshire on the River Thames: a riverside resort with an annual regatta. Pop.: 10 558 (1991). Often shortened to **Henley.**

henna ('hɛnə) *n* **1** a shrub or tree of Asia and N Africa. **2** a reddish dye obtained from the powdered leaves of this plant, used as a cosmetic and industrial dye. **3a** a reddish-brown colour. **3b** (*as adj*): *henna tresses.* ◆ *vb* **hennas, hennaing, hennaed. 4** (*tr*) to dye with henna. [C16: from Ar. *hinnā'*; see ALKANET]

hen night *n Inf.* a party for women only, esp. held for a woman shortly before she is married. Cf. **hen party, stag night.**

henotheism ('hɛnəʊθiː,ɪzəm) *n* the worship of one deity (of several) as the special god of one's family, clan, or tribe. [C19: from Gk *heis* one + *theos* god]
▸ **,henothe'istic** *adj*

hen party *n Inf.* a party at which only women are present. Cf. **hen night, stag night.**

henpeck ('hɛn,pɛk) *vb* (*tr*) (of a woman) to harass or torment (a man, esp. her husband) by persistent nagging.
▸ **'hen,pecked** *adj*

Henrietta Maria ★ (,hɛnrɪ'ɛtə mə'riːə) *n* 1609–69, queen of England (1625–49), the wife of Charles I; daughter of Henry IV of France. Her Roman Catholicism contributed to the unpopularity of the crown in the period leading to the Civil War.

henry ('hɛnrɪ) *n, pl* **henry, henries,** *or* **henrys.** the derived SI unit of electric inductance; the inductance of a closed circuit in which an emf of 1 volt is produced when the current varies uniformly at the rate of 1 ampere per second. Symbol: H [C19: after Joseph HENRY]

Henry ★ ('hɛnrɪ) *n* **1 Joseph.** 1797–1878, US physicist. He discovered the principle of electromagnetic induction independently of Faraday and constructed the first electromagnetic motor (1829). **2 Patrick.** 1736–99, American statesman, a leading opponent of British rule during the War of American Independence.

Henry I ★ *n* 1068–1135, king of England (1100–35) and duke of Normandy (1106–35); son of William the Conqueror: crowned in the absence of his elder brother, Robert II, duke of Normandy; conquered Normandy (1106).

Henry II ★ *n* **1** 1133–89, first Plantagenet king of England (1154–89): extended his Anglo-French domains and instituted judicial and financial reforms. His attempts to control the church were opposed by Becket. **2** 1519–59, king of France (1547–59); husband of Catherine de' Medici. He recovered Calais from the English (1558) and suppressed the Huguenots.

Henry III ★ *n* **1** 1207–72, king of England (1216–72); son of John. His incompetent rule provoked the second Barons' War (1264–67), during which he was captured by Simon de Montfort. **2** 1551–89, king of France (1574–89). He plotted the massacre of Huguenots on St Bartholomew's Day (1572) with his mother Catherine de' Medici, thus exacerbating the religious wars in France.

Henry IV ★ *n* **1** 1050–1106, Holy Roman Emperor (1084–1105) and king of Germany (1056–1105). He was excommunicated by Pope Gregory VII, whom he deposed (1084). **2** surnamed *Bolingbroke.* 1367–1413, first Lancastrian king of England (1399–1413); son of John of Gaunt: deposed Richard II (1399) and suppressed rebellions led by Owen Glendower and the Earl of Northumberland. **3** known as *Henry of Navarre.* 1553–1610, first Bourbon king of France (1589–1610). He obtained toleration for the Huguenots with the Edict of Nantes (1598) and restored prosperity to France following the religious wars (1562–98).

Henry V ★ *n* 1387–1422, king of England (1413–22); son of Henry IV. He defeated the French at the Battle of Agincourt (1415), conquered Normandy (1419), and was recognized as heir to the French throne (1420).

Henry VI ★ *n* 1421–71, last Lancastrian king of England (1422–61; 1470–71); son of Henry V. His weak rule was blamed for the loss by 1453 of all his possessions in France except Calais; from 1454 he suffered periods of insanity, which contributed to the outbreak of the Wars of the Roses (1455–85). He was deposed by Edward IV (1461) but was briefly restored to the throne (1470).

Henry VII ★ *n* 1457–1509, first Tudor king of England (1485–1509). He came to the throne (1485) after defeating Richard III at the Battle of Bosworth Field, ending the Wars of the Roses. Royal power and the prosperity of the country greatly increased during his reign.

Henry VIII ★ *n* 1491–1547, king of England (1509–47); second son of Henry VII. The declaration that his marriage to Catherine of Aragon was invalid and his marriage to Anne Boleyn (1533) precipitated the Act of Supremacy, making Henry supreme head of the Church in England. Anne Boleyn was executed (1536) and Henry subsequently married Jane Seymour, Anne of Cleves, Catherine Howard, and Catherine Parr.

Henryson ★ ('hɛnrɪsᵊn) *n* **Robert.** ?1430–?1506, Scottish poet. His works include *Testament of Cresseid* (1593) and the 13 *Moral Fables of Esope the Phrygian.*

Henry the Navigator ★ *n* 1394–1460, prince of Portugal, noted for his patronage of Portuguese voyages of exploration.

Henslowe ★ ('hɛnzləʊ) *n* **Philip.** died 1616, English theatre manager, noted also for his diary.

Henze ★ (*German* 'hɛntsə) *n* **Hans Werner** (hans 'vɛrnər). born 1926, German composer, whose works include the operas *The Stag King* (1956) and *Das verratene Meer* (1990) and the oratorio *The Raft of the Medusa* (1968).

hep (hɛp) *adj* **hepper, heppest.** *Sl.* an earlier word for **hip**[4].

heparin ('hɛpərɪn) *n* a polysaccharide, containing sulphate groups, present in most body tissues: an anticoagulant used in the treatment of thrombosis. [C20: from Gk *hēpar* the liver + -IN]

hepatic (hɪ'pætɪk) *adj* **1** of the liver. **2** having the colour of liver. ◆ *n* **3** any of various drugs for use in treating diseases of the liver. [C15: from L *hēpaticus,* from Gk *hēpar* liver]

hepatica (hɪ'pætɪkə) *n* a woodland plant of a N temperate genus, having three-lobed leaves and white, mauve, or pink flowers. [C16: from Med. L: liverwort, from L *hēpaticus* of the liver]

hepatitis (,hɛpə'taɪtɪs) *n* inflammation of the liver.

hepatitis A *n* a form of hepatitis caused by a virus transmitted in contaminated food or drink.

hepatitis B *n* a form of hepatitis caused by a virus transmitted by infected blood (as in transfusions), contaminated hypodermic needles, sexual contact, or by contact with any other body fluid. Former name: **serum hepatitis.**

hepatitis C *n* a form of hepatitis caused by a virus that is transmitted in the same ways as that responsible for hepatitis B. Former name: **non-A, non-B hepatitis.**

Hepburn ★ ('hɛp,bɜːn) *n* **Katharine.** born 1909, US film actress, whose films include *The Philadelphia Story* (1940), *The African Queen* (1951), *The Lion in Winter* (1968), and *On Golden Pond* (1981).

Hephaestus (hɪ'fiːstəs) *or* **Hephaistos** ★ (hɪ'faɪstɒs) *n Greek myth.* the lame god of fire and metal-working. Roman counterpart: **Vulcan.**

Hepplewhite ('hɛpᵊl,waɪt) *adj* of or in a style of ornamental and carved 18th-century English furniture. [C18: after George *Hepplewhite* (1727–86), E cabinet-maker]

hepta- *or before a vowel* **hept-** *combining form.* seven: *hep-tameter.* [from Gk]

heptad ('hɛptæd) *n* a group or series of seven. [C17: from Gk *heptas* seven]

heptagon ('hɛptəgən) *n* a polygon having seven sides.
▶ **heptagonal** (hɛp'tægən²l) *adj*

heptahedron (ˌhɛptə'hiːdrən) *n* a solid figure having seven plane faces.
▶ ˌhepta'hedral *adj*

heptameter (hɛp'tæmɪtə) *n Prosody.* a verse line of seven metrical feet.
▶ **heptametrical** (ˌhɛptə'mɛtrɪk²l) *adj*

heptane ('hɛpteɪn) *n* an alkane which is found in petroleum and used as an anaesthetic. [C19: from HEPTA- + -ANE, because it has seven carbon atoms]

heptarchy ('hɛptɑːkɪ) *n, pl* **heptarchies. 1** government by seven rulers. **2** the seven kingdoms into which Anglo-Saxon England is thought to have been divided from about the 7th to the 9th centuries A.D.
▶ **heptarch** *n* ▶ **hep'tarchic** *or* **hep'tarchal** *adj*

heptathlon (hɛp'tæθlɒn) *n* an athletic contest for women in which each athlete competes in seven different events. [C20: from HEPTA- + Gk *athlon* contest]
▶ **hep'tathlete** *n*

heptavalent (hɛp'tævələnt, ˌhɛptə'veɪlənt) *adj Chem.* having a valency of seven.

Hepworth ★ ('hɛpwəθ) *n* Dame **Barbara**. 1903–75, British sculptor of abstract works.

her (hɜː; *unstressed* hə, ə) *pron (objective)* **1** refers to a female person or animal: *he loves her.* **2** refers to things personified as feminine or traditionally to ships and nations. ◆ *determiner* **3** of, belonging to, or associated with her: *her hair.* [OE *hire,* genitive & dative of *hēo* SHE, fem. of *hē* HE]

> **USAGE NOTE**   See at **me¹**.

Hera *or* **Here** ★ ('hɪərə) *n Greek myth.* the queen of the Olympian gods and sister and wife of Zeus. Roman counterpart: **Juno.**

Heraclea ★ (ˌhɛrə'kliːə) *n* any of several ancient Greek colonies. The most famous is the S Italian site where Pyrrhus of Epirus defeated the Romans (280 B.C.).

Heracleides *or* **Heraclides of Pontus** ★ (ˌhɛrə'klaɪdiːz; 'pɒntəs) *n* ?390 B.C.–?322 B.C., Greek astronomer and philosopher: the first to state that the earth rotates on its axis.

Heracles *or* **Herakles** ★ ('hɛrəˌkliːz) *n* the usual name (in Greek) for **Hercules.**
▶ ˌHera'clean *or* ˌHera'klean *adj*

Heraclitus ★ (ˌhɛrə'klaɪtəs) *n* ?535–?475 B.C., Greek philosopher, who held that fire is the primordial substance.

Heraclius ★ (hə'rækliəs) *n* ?575–641 A.D., Byzantine emperor, who restored the Holy Cross to Jerusalem (629).

Herakleion *or* **Heraklion** ★ (*Greek* he'raːkliɔn) *n* a variant of **Iráklion.**

herald ('hɛrəld) *n* **1** a person who announces important news. **2** *Often literary.* a forerunner; harbinger. **3** the intermediate rank of heraldic officer, between king-of-arms and pursuivant. **4** (in the Middle Ages) an official at a tournament. ◆ *vb (tr)* **5** to announce publicly. **6** to precede or usher in. [C14: from OF *herault,* of Gmc origin]

heraldic (hɛ'rældɪk) *adj* of or relating to heraldry or heralds.
▶ **he'raldically** *adv*

heraldry ('hɛrəldrɪ) *n, pl* **heraldries. 1** the study concerned with the classification of armorial bearings, the tracing of genealogies, etc. **2** armorial bearings, insignia, etc. **3** the show and ceremony of heraldry.
▶ 'heraldist *n*

Herat ★ (he'ræt) *n* a city in NW Afghanistan, on the Hari Rud River: on the site of several ancient cities; at its height as a cultural centre in the 15th century. Pop.: 186 800 (1990 est.).

Hérault ★ (*French* ero) *n* a department of S France, in

Languedoc-Roussillon region. Capital: Montpellier. Pop.: 853 594 (1994 est.). Area: 6224 sq. km (2427 sq. miles).

herb (hɜːb; *US* ɜːrb) *n* **1** a plant whose aerial parts do not persist above ground at the end of the growing season; herbaceous plant. **2** any of various usually aromatic plants, such as parsley and rosemary, that are used in cookery and medicine. [C13: from OF *herbe,* from L *herba* grass, green plants]
▶ 'herbˌlike *adj* ▶ 'herby *adj*

herbaceous (hɜː'beɪʃəs) *adj* **1** designating or relating to plants that are fleshy as opposed to woody: *a herbaceous plant.* **2** (of petals and sepals) green and leaflike.

herbaceous border *n* a flower bed that contains perennials rather than annuals.

herbage ('hɜːbɪdʒ) *n* **1** herbaceous plants collectively, esp. the edible parts on which cattle, sheep, etc., graze. **2** the vegetation of pasture land; pasturage.

herbal ('hɜːb²l) *adj* **1** of herbs. ◆ *n* **2** a book describing the properties of plants.

herbalist ('hɜːb²lɪst) *n* **1** a person who grows or specializes in the use of herbs, esp. medicinal herbs. **2** (formerly) a descriptive botanist.

herbarium (hɜː'bɛərɪəm) *n, pl* **herbariums** *or* **herbaria** (-ɪə). **1** a collection of dried plants that are mounted and classified systematically. **2** a room, etc., in which such a collection is kept.

herb bennet ('bɛnɪt) *n* a Eurasian and N African plant with yellow flowers. Also called: **wood avens, bennet.** [from OF *herbe benoite,* lit.: blessed herb, from Med. L *herba benedicta*]

Herbert ★ ('hɜːbət) *n* **George.** 1593–1633, English Metaphysical poet. His chief work is *The Temple: Sacred Poems and Private Ejaculations* (1633).

herbicide ('hɜːbɪˌsaɪd) *n* a chemical that destroys plants, esp. one used to control weeds.

herbivore ('hɜːbɪˌvɔː) *n* **1** an animal that feeds on grass and other plants. **2** *Inf.* a liberal, idealistic, or nonmaterialistic person. [C19: from NL *herbivora* grass-eaters]
▶ her'bivorous *adj*

herb Paris ('pærɪs) *n, pl* **herbs Paris.** a Eurasian woodland plant with a whorl of four leaves and a solitary yellow flower. [C16: from Med. L *herba paris,* lit.: herb of a pair: because the four leaves on the stalk look like a true lovers' knot]

herb Robert ('rɒbət) *n, pl* **herbs Robert.** a low-growing N temperate plant with strongly scented divided leaves and small purplish flowers. [C13: from Med. L *herba Roberti* herb of Robert, prob. after St *Robert,* 11th-cent. F ecclesiastic]

Hercegovina ★ (*Serbo-Croat* 'hɛrtsɛgɔvina) *n* a variant of **Herzegovina.**

Herculaneum ★ (ˌhɜːkjʊ'leɪnɪəm) *n* an ancient city in SW Italy, of marked Greek character, on the S slope of Vesuvius: buried along with Pompeii by an eruption of the volcano (79 A.D.). Excavation has uncovered well-preserved streets, houses, etc.

herculean (ˌhɜːkjʊ'liːən) *adj* **1** requiring tremendous effort, strength, etc. **2** (*sometimes cap.*) resembling Hercules in strength, courage, etc.

Hercules ('hɜːkjʊˌliːz), **Heracles,** *or* **Herakles** ★ *n* **1** Also called: **Alcides.** *Classical myth.* a hero noted for his great strength, courage, and for the performance of twelve immense labours. **2** a man of outstanding strength or size.

herd¹ (hɜːd) *n* **1** a large group of mammals living and feeding together, esp. cattle. **2** *Often disparaging.* a large group of people. ◆ *vb* **3** to collect or be collected or as if into a herd. [OE *heord*]

herd² (hɜːd) *n* **1a** *Arch. or dialect.* a man who tends livestock; herdsman. **1b** (*in combination*): *goatherd.* ◆ *vb (tr)* **2** to drive forwards in a large group. **3** to look after (livestock). [OE *hirde:* see HERD¹]

herd instinct *n Psychol.* the inborn tendency to associate with others and follow the group's behaviour.

herdsman ('hɜːdzmən) *n, pl* **herdsmen.** *Chiefly Brit.* a person who breeds or cares for cattle or (rarely) other livestock. US equivalent: **herder.**

here (hɪə) *adv* **1** in, at, or to this place, point, case, or respect: *we come here every summer; here comes Roy.* **2 here and there.** at several places in or throughout an area. **3 here's to.** a formula used in proposing a toast to someone or something. **4 neither here nor there.** of no relevance or importance. ◆ *n* **5** this place or point: *they leave here tonight.* [OE *hēr*]

hereabouts ('hɪərə,baʊts) *or* **hereabout** *adv* in this region or neighbourhood.

hereafter (,hɪər'ɑːftə) *adv* **1** *Formal or law.* in a subsequent part of this document, matter, case, etc. **2** a less common word for **henceforth. 3** at some time in the future. **4** in a future life after death. ◆ *n* (usually preceded by *the*) **5** life after death. **6** the future.

hereat (,hɪər'æt) *adv Arch.* because of this.

hereby (,hɪə'baɪ) *adv* (used in official statements, etc.) by means of or as a result of this.

hereditable (hɪ'rɛdɪtəbᵊl) *adj* a less common word for **heritable.**
► he,redita'bility *n*

hereditament (,hɛrɪ'dɪtəmənt) *n Property law.* any kind of property capable of being inherited.

hereditary (hɪ'rɛdɪtərɪ, -trɪ) *adj* **1** of or denoting factors that can be transmitted genetically from one generation to another. **2** *Law.* **2a** descending to succeeding generations by inheritance. **2b** transmitted according to established rules of descent. **3** derived from one's ancestors; traditional: *hereditary feuds.*
► he'reditarily *adv* ► he'reditariness *n*

heredity (hɪ'rɛdɪtɪ) *n, pl* **heredities. 1** the transmission from one generation to another of genetic factors that determine individual characteristics. **2** the sum total of the inherited factors in an organism. [C16: from OF *heredite*, from L *hērēditās* inheritance; see HEIR]

Hereford ★ ('hɛrɪfəd) *n* **1** a city in W England, in Hereford and Worcester county on the River Wye: trading centre for agricultural produce; cathedral (begun 1079). Pop.: 54 326 (1991). **2** a hardy breed of beef cattle characterized by a red body, red and white head, and white markings.

Hereford and Worcester ★ *n* a county of the W Midlands of England, formed in 1974 from the two former separate counties minus a small area of NW Worcestershire: drained chiefly by the Rivers Wye and Severn: important agriculturally (esp. for fruit and cattle). Administrative centre: Worcester. Pop.: 699 900 (1994 est.). Area: 3926 sq. km (1516 sq. miles).

Herefordshire ★ ('hɛrɪfəd,ʃɪə, -fə) *n* a former county of W England, since 1974 part of Hereford and Worcester.

herein (,hɪər'ɪn) *adv* **1** *Formal or law.* in or into this place, thing, document, etc. **2** *Rare.* in this respect, circumstance, etc.

hereinafter (,hɪərɪn'ɑːftə) *adv Formal or law.* from this point on in this document, etc.

hereinto (,hɪər'ɪntuː) *adv Formal or law.* into this place, circumstance, etc.

hereof (,hɪər'ɒv) *adv Formal or law.* of or concerning this.

hereon (,hɪər'ɒn) *adv* an archaic word for **hereupon.**

heresiarch (hɪ'riːzɪ,ɑːk) *n* the leader or originator of a heretical movement or sect.

heresy ('hɛrəsɪ) *n, pl* **heresies. 1a** an opinion contrary to the orthodox tenets of a religious body. **1b** the act of maintaining such an opinion. **2** any belief that is or is thought to be contrary to official or established theory. **3** adherence to unorthodox opinion. [C13: from OF *eresie*, from LL, from L: sect, from Gk, from *hairein* to choose]

heretic ('hɛrɪtɪk) *n* **1** *Now chiefly RC Church.* a person who maintains beliefs contrary to the established teachings of his Church. **2** a person who holds unorthodox opinions in any field.
► **heretical** (hɪ'rɛtɪkᵊl) *adj* ► he'retically *adv*

hereto (,hɪə'tuː) *adv Formal or law.* to this place, thing, matter, document, etc.

heretofore (,hɪətu'fɔː) *adv Formal or law.* until now; before this time.

hereunder (,hɪər'ʌndə) *adv Formal or law.* **1** (in documents, etc.) below this; subsequently; hereafter. **2** under the terms or authority of this.

hereupon (,hɪərə'pɒn) *adv* **1** following immediately after this; at this stage. **2** *Formal or law.* upon this thing, point, subject, etc.

Hereward ★ ('hɛrɪwəd) *n* called *Hereward the Wake.* 11th-century Anglo-Saxon rebel, who defended the Isle of Ely against William the Conqueror (1070–71): a subject of many legends.

herewith (,hɪə'wɪð, -'wɪθ) *adv Formal.* together with this: *we send you herewith your statement of account.*

heriot ('hɛrɪət) *n* (in medieval England) a death duty paid by villeins and free tenants to their lord, often consisting of the dead man's best beast or chattel. [OE *heregeatwa*, from *here* army + *geatwa* equipment]

Herisau ★ (*German* 'heːrɪzau) *n* a town in NE Switzerland, capital of Appenzell Outer Rhodes demicanton. Pop.: 14 955 (1987).

heritable ('hɛrɪtəbᵊl) *adj* **1** capable of being inherited; inheritable. **2** *Chiefly law.* capable of inheriting. [C14: from OF, from *heriter* to INHERIT]
► ,herita'bility *n* ► 'heritably *adv*

heritage ('hɛrɪtɪdʒ) *n* **1** something inherited at birth. **2** anything that has been transmitted from the past or handed down by tradition. **3** the evidence of the past, such as historical sites, and the unspoilt natural environment, considered as the inheritance of present-day society. **4** *Law.* any property, esp. land, that by law has descended or may descend to an heir. [C13: from OF; see HEIR]

herl (hɜːl) *or* **harl** *n Angling.* **1** the barb or barbs of a feather, used to dress fishing flies. **2** an artificial fly dressed with such barbs. [C15: from MLow G *herle*, from ?]

Hermannstadt ★ ('hɛrmanʃtat) *n* the German name for **Sibiu.**

hermaphrodite (hɜː'mæfrə,daɪt) *n* **1** *Biol.* an animal or flower that has both male and female reproductive organs. **2** a person having both male and female sexual characteristics. **3** a person or thing in which two opposite qualities are combined. ◆ *adj* **4** having the characteristics of a hermaphrodite. [C15: from L *hermaphrodītus*, from Gk, after HERMAPHRODITUS]
► her,maphro'ditic *or* her,maphro'ditical *adj* ► her-'maphrodit,ism *n*

hermaphrodite brig *n* a sailing vessel with two masts, rigged square on the foremast and fore-and-aft on the aftermast.

Hermaphroditus ★ (hɜː,mæfrə'daɪtəs) *n Greek myth.* a son of Hermes and Aphrodite who merged with the nymph Salmacis to form one body.

hermeneutic (,hɜːmɪ'njuːtɪk) *or* **hermeneutical** *adj* **1** of or relating to the interpretation of Scripture. **2** interpretive.
► ,herme'neutically *adv*

hermeneutics (,hɜːmɪ'njuːtɪks) *n* (*functioning as sing*) **1** the science of interpretation, esp. of Scripture. **2** *Philosophy.* **2a** the study and interpretation of human behaviour and social institutions. **2b** (in existentialist thought) discussion of the purpose of life. [C18: from Gk *hermēneutikos* expert in interpretation, from *hermēneuein* to interpret, from ?]

Hermes ★ ('hɜːmiːz) *n Greek myth.* the messenger and herald of the gods; the divinity of commerce, cunning, theft, travellers, and rascals. He was represented as wearing winged sandals. Roman counterpart: **Mercury.**

Hermes Trismegistus ★ (,trɪsmə'dʒɪstəs) *n* a Greek name for the Egyptian god Thoth, credited with various works on mysticism and magic. [Gk: Hermes thrice-greatest]

hermetic (hɜː'mɛtɪk) *or* **hermetical** *adj* **1a** (of a seal) airtight. **1b** (of a vessel, etc.) sealed so as to be airtight. **2** of or relating to alchemy or other forms of ancient science: *the hermetic arts.* **3** esoteric or recondite. **4** hidden or

protected from the outside world: *the hermetic world of Vatican politics.* [C17: from Med. L *hermēticus* belonging to HERMES TRISMEGISTUS, traditionally the inventor of a magic seal]
▸ her'metically *adv*

hermit ('hɜːmɪt) *n* **1** one of the early Christian recluses. **2** any person living in solitude. [C13: from OF *hermite*, from LL, from Gk *erēmitēs* living in the desert, from *erēmos* lonely]
▸ her'mitic *or* her'mitical *adj*

hermitage ('hɜːmɪtɪdʒ) *n* **1** the abode of a hermit. **2** any retreat.

hermit crab *n* a small soft-bodied crustacean living in and carrying about the empty shells of whelks or similar molluscs.

Hermon ★ ('hɜːmən) *n Mount.* a mountain on the border between Lebanon and SW Syria, in the Anti-Lebanon Range: represented the NE limits of Israeli conquests under Moses and Joshua. Height: 2814 m (9232 ft).

Hermosillo ★ (*Spanish* ɛrmoʹsiʎo) *n* a city in NW Mexico, capital of Sonora state, on the Sonora River: university (1938); winter resort and commercial centre for an agricultural and mining region. Pop.: 406 417 (1990).

Hermoupolis ★ (hɜːʹmuːpəlɪs) *n* a port in Greece, capital of Cyclades department, on the E coast of Syros Island. Pop.: 14 115 (1981).

Herne ★ (*German* 'hɛrnə) *n* an industrial city in W Germany, in North Rhine-Westphalia, in the Ruhr on the Rhine-Herne Canal. Pop.: 180 029 (1995 est.).

hernia ('hɜːnɪə) *n, pl* **hernias** *or* **herniae** (-nɪˌiː). the projection of an organ or part through the lining of the cavity in which it is normally situated, esp. the intestine through the front wall of the abdominal cavity. Also called: **rupture.** [C14: from L]
▸ 'hernial *adj* ▸ 'herni,ated *adj*

hero ('hɪərəʊ) *n, pl* **heroes. 1** a man distinguished by exceptional courage, nobility, etc. **2** a man who is idealized for possessing superior qualities in any field. **3** *Classical myth.* a being of extraordinary strength and courage, often the offspring of a mortal and a god. **4** the principal male character in a novel, play, etc. [C14: from L *hērōs*, from Gk]

Hero[1] ★ ('hɪərəʊ) *n Greek myth.* a priestess of Aphrodite, who killed herself when her lover Leander drowned while swimming the Hellespont to visit her.

Hero[2] ('hɪərəʊ) *or* **Heron** ★ *n* 1st century A.D., Greek mathematician and inventor.

Herod ★ ('hɛrəd) *n* called *the Great.* ?73–4 B.C., king of Judaea (37–4); according to the New Testament he ordered the Massacre of the Innocents.

Herod Agrippa I ★ *n* 10 B.C.–44 A.D., king of Judaea (41–44), grandson of Herod (the Great). A friend of Caligula and Claudius, he imprisoned Saint Peter and executed Saint James.

Herod Agrippa II ★ *n* died ?93 A.D., king of territories in N Palestine (50–?93 A.D.). He presided (60) at the trial of Saint Paul and sided with the Roman authorities in the Jewish rebellion of 66.

Herod Antipas ★ ('æntɪˌpæs) *n* died ?40 A.D., tetrarch of Galilee and Peraea (4 B.C.–40 A.D.); son of Herod the Great. At the instigation of his wife Herodias, he ordered the execution of John the Baptist.

Herodias ★ (heʹrəʊdɪˌæs) *n* ?14 B.C. –?40 A.D., niece and wife of Herod Antipas and mother of Salome, whom she persuaded to ask for the head of John the Baptist. Her ambition led to the banishment of her husband.

Herodotus ★ (hɪʹrɒdətəs) *n* called *the Father of History.* ?485–?425 B.C., Greek historian, whose *History* records the events of the wars between the Greeks and the Persians (490–479).

heroic (hɪʹrəʊɪk) *or* **heroical** *adj* **1** of, like, or befitting a hero. **2** courageous but desperate. **3** treating of heroes and their deeds. **4** of or resembling the heroes of classical mythology. **5** (of language, manner, etc.) extravagant. **6** *Prosody.* of or resembling heroic verse. **7** (of the arts, esp. sculpture) larger than life-size; smaller than colossal.
▸ heʹroically *adv*

heroic age *n* the period in an ancient culture, when legendary heroes are said to have lived.

heroic couplet *n Prosody.* a verse form consisting of two rhyming lines in iambic pentameter.

heroics (hɪʹrəʊɪks) *pl n* **1** *Prosody.* short for **heroic verse. 2** extravagant or melodramatic language, behaviour, etc.

heroic verse *n Prosody.* a type of verse suitable for epic or heroic subjects, such as the classical hexameter or the French Alexandrine.

heroin ('hɛrəʊɪn) *n* a white bitter-tasting crystalline powder derived from morphine: a highly addictive narcotic. [C19: coined in G as a trademark, prob. from HERO, referring to its aggrandizing effect on the personality]

heroine ('hɛrəʊɪn) *n* **1** a woman possessing heroic qualities. **2** a woman idealized for possessing superior qualities. **3** the main female character in a novel, play, film, etc.

heroism ('hɛrəʊˌɪzəm) *n* the state or quality of being a hero.

heron ('hɛrən) *n* any of various wading birds having a long neck, slim body, and a plumage that is commonly grey or white. [C14: from OF *hairon*, of Gmc origin]

Heron ★ ('hɪərɒn) *n* a variant of **Hero**[2].

heronry ('hɛrənrɪ) *n, pl* **heronries.** a colony of breeding herons.

Herophilus ★ (hɪəʹrɒfɪləs) *n* died ?280 B.C., Greek anatomist in Alexandria. He distinguished sensory from motor nerves.

hero worship *n* **1** admiration for heroes or idealized persons. **2** worship by the ancient Greeks and Romans of heroes. ◆ *vb* **hero-worship, hero-worships, hero-worshipping, hero-worshipped** *or US* **hero-worships, hero-worshiping, hero-worshiped. 3** (*tr*) to feel admiration or adulation for.
▸ 'hero-ˌworshipper *or US* 'hero-ˌworshiper *n*

herpes ('hɜːpiːz) *n* any of several inflammatory diseases of the skin, esp. herpes simplex. [C17: via L from Gk, from *herpein* to creep]
▸ herpetic (hɜːʹpɛtɪk) *adj, n*

herpes simplex ('sɪmplɛks) *n* an acute viral disease characterized by formation of clusters of watery blisters, esp. on the lips or the genitals. See **cold sore, genital herpes.** [NL: simple herpes]

herpes zoster ('zɒstə) *n* a technical name for **shingles.** [NL: girdle herpes, from HERPES + Gk *zōstēr* girdle]

herpetology (ˌhɜːpɪʹtɒlədʒɪ) *n* the study of reptiles and amphibians. [C19: from Gk *herpeton* creeping animal]
▸ **herpetologic** (ˌhɜːpɪtəʹlɒdʒɪk) *or* ˌherpetoʹlogical *adj*

Herr (*German* hɛr) *n, pl* **Herren** ('hɛrən). a German man: used before a name as a title equivalent to *Mr.* [G, from OHG *herro* lord]

Herrenvolk *German.* ('hɛrənfɒlk) *n* a race, nation, or group, such as the Germans or Nazis as viewed by Hitler, believed by themselves to be superior to other races. Also called: **master race.** [lit.: master race, from *Herren,* pl. of HERR + *Volk* folk]

Herrick ★ ('hɛrɪk) *n* **Robert.** 1591–1674, English poet. His chief work is the *Hesperides* (1648).

herring ('hɛrɪŋ) *n, pl* **herrings** *or* **herring.** an important food fish of northern seas, having an elongated body covered with large silvery scales. [OE *hæring*]

herringbone ('hɛrɪŋˌbəʊn) *n* **1a** a pattern consisting of two or more rows of short parallel strokes slanting in alternate directions to form a series of zigzags. **1b** (*as modifier*): *a herringbone pattern.* **2** *Skiing.* a method of ascending a slope by walking with the skis pointing outwards and one's weight on the inside edges. ◆ *vb* **herringbones, herringboning, herringboned. 3** to decorate (textiles, brickwork, etc.) with herringbone. **4** (*intr*) *Skiing.* to ascend a slope in herringbone fashion.

herring gull *n* a common gull that has a white plumage with black-tipped wings.

Herriot ★ *n* **1** (*French* ɛrjo) **Édouard** (edwar). 1872–1957, French Radical statesman and writer; premier (1924–25; 1932). **2** ('hɛrɪət) **James.** real name *James Alfred Wight.* 1916–95, British veterinary surgeon and writer.

★ people and places

hers (hɜːz) *pron* **1** something or someone belonging to her: *hers is the nicest dress; that cat is hers.* **2 of hers.** belonging to her. [C14 *hires;* see HER]

Herschel ★ (ˈhɜːʃəl) *n* **1** Sir **John Frederick William.** 1792–1871, British astronomer. He discovered and catalogued over 525 nebulae and star clusters. **2** his father, Sir **William,** original name *Friedrich Wilhelm Herschel.* 1738–1822, British astronomer, born in Germany. He constructed a reflecting telescope and discovered the planet Uranus (1781).

herself (həˈsɛlf) *pron* **1a** the reflexive form of *she* or *her.* **1b** (intensifier): *the queen herself signed.* **2** (*preceded by a copula*) her normal self: *she looks herself again.*

Herstmonceux *or* **Hurstmonceux** ★ (ˈhɜːstmənˌsuː, -ˌsəu) *n* a village in S England, in E Sussex north of Eastbourne: 15th-century castle, site of the Royal Observatory, which was transferred from Greenwich between 1948 and 1958, until 1990.

Hertford ★ (ˈhɑːtfəd) *n* a town in SE England, administrative centre of Hertfordshire. Pop.: 21 665 (1991).

Hertfordshire ★ (ˈhɑːtfədˌʃɪə, -ʃə) *n* a county of S England, bordering on Greater London in the south: mainly low-lying, with the Chiltern Hills in the northwest; largely agricultural; expanding light industries, esp. in the new towns. Administrative centre: Hertford. Pop.: 1 005 400 (1994 est.). Area: 1634 sq. km (631 sq. miles).

Hertogenbosch ★ (*Dutch* hɛrtoːxənˈbɔs) *n* 's. See **'s Hertogenbosch.**

Herts (hɑːts) *abbrev. for* Hertfordshire.

hertz (hɜːts) *n, pl* **hertz.** the derived SI unit of frequency; the frequency of a periodic phenomenon that has a periodic time of 1 second; 1 cycle per second. Symbol: Hz [C20: after H. R. HERTZ]

Hertz ★ (hɜːts; *German* hɛrts) *n* **1** Gustav (ˈgʊstaf). 1887–1975, German physicist. His research with Franck provided evidence to support the quantum theory: they shared the Nobel prize for physics (1925). **2 Heinrich Rudolph** (ˈhainrɪç ˈruːdɔlf). 1857–94, German physicist; the first to produce electromagnetic waves artificially.
▸ **'Hertzian** *adj*

Hertzian wave *n* an electromagnetic wave with a frequency in the range from about 3×10^{10} hertz to about 1.5×10^{5} hertz. [C19: after H. R. HERTZ]

Hertzog ★ (ˈhɜːtsɒg) *n* **James Barry Munnik.** 1866–1942, South African statesman; prime minister (1924–39): founded the Nationalist Party (1913), advocating South African independence from Britain.

Hertzsprung-Russell diagram (ˈhɜːtssprʌŋˈrʌsˀl) *n* a graph in which the spectral types of stars are plotted against their absolute magnitudes. Stars fall into different groupings in different parts of the graph. [C20: after E. *Hertzsprung* (1873–1967), Danish astronomer, and H. N. *Russell* (1877–1957), US astronomer]

Herzegovina (ˌhɜːtsəgəʊˈviːnə) *or* **Hercegovina** ★ *n* a region of Bosnia-Herzegovina: originally under Austro-Hungarian rule; was part of the province of Bosnia-Herzegovina (1878), which became a constituent republic of Yugoslavia (1946–91).

Herzl ★ (*German* ˈhɛrtsəl) *n* **Theodor** (ˈteːodoːr). 1860–1904, Austrian writer, born in Hungary; founder of the Zionist movement.

Herzog ★ (*German* ˈhɛrtsoːk) *n* **1** Roman. born 1934, German politician; president of Germany from 1994. **2 Werner** (ˈvɛrnər). born 1942, German film director. His films include *Signs of Life* (1967) and *Scream from Stone* (1991).

he's (hiːz) *contraction of* he is *or* he has.

Heseltine ★ (ˈhɛzˀlˌtain) *n* **1** Michael (Ray Dibden). born 1933, British Conservative politician; deputy prime minister (1995–97). **2** Philip Arnold. See (Peter) **Warlock.**

Hesiod ★ (ˈhɛsɪˌɒd) *n* 8th century B.C., Greek poet. His complete extant works are the *Works and Days* and the *Theogony.*
▸ ˌHesi'odic *adj*

Hesione ★ (hɪˈsaɪəni) *n Greek myth.* daughter of King Laomedon, rescued by Hercules from a sea monster.

hesitant (ˈhɛzɪtˀnt) *adj* wavering, hesitating, or irresolute.
▸ 'hesitantly *adv*

hesitate (ˈhɛzɪˌteɪt) *vb* **hesitates, hesitating, hesitated.** (*intr*) **1** to be slow in acting; be uncertain. **2** to be reluctant (to do something). **3** to stammer or pause in speaking. [C17: from L *haesitāre,* from *haerēre* to cling to]
▸ **hesitancy** (ˈhɛzɪtˀnsɪ) *or* ˌhesi'tation *n* ▸ 'hesi,tatingly *adv*

Hesperia ★ (hɛˈspɪərɪə) *n* a poetic name used by the ancient Greeks for Italy and by the Romans for Spain or beyond. [L, from Gk: land of the west, from *hesperos* western]

Hesperian (hɛˈspɪərɪən) *adj* **1** *Poetic.* western. **2** of or relating to the Hesperides or Islands of the Blessed.

Hesperides ★ (hɛˈspɛrɪˌdiːz) *pl n Greek myth.* **1** the daughters of Hesperus, nymphs who kept watch with a dragon over the garden of the golden apples in the Islands of the Blessed. **2** (*functioning as sing*) the gardens themselves. **3** another name for the **Islands of the Blessed.**
▸ **Hesperidian** (ˌhɛspəˈrɪdɪən) *or* ˌHesper'idean *adj*

hesperidium (ˌhɛspəˈrɪdɪəm) *n Bot.* the fruit of citrus plants, in which the flesh consists of fluid-filled hairs and is protected by a tough rind. [C19: NL; alluding to the fruit in the garden of the HESPERIDES]

Hesperus (ˈhɛspərəs) *n* an evening star, esp. Venus. [from L, from Gk, from *hesperos* western]

Hess ★ (hɛs) *n* **1** Dame **Myra.** 1890–1965, British pianist. **2** (**Walther Richard**) **Rudolf** (ˈruːdɔlf). 1894–1987, German Nazi leader. He made a secret flight to Scotland (1941) to negotiate peace; later sentenced to life imprisonment at Nuremberg (1946); committed suicide. **3 Victor Francis.** 1883–1964, US physicist, born in Austria: investigated cosmic rays: shared the Nobel prize for physics (1936).

Hesse[1] ★ (hɛs) *n* a state of E central Germany, formed in 1945 from the former Prussian province of Hesse-Nassau and part of the former state of Hesse; part of West Germany until 1990. Capital: Wiesbaden. Pop.: 5 980 700 (1995 est.). Area: 21 111 sq. km (8151 sq. miles). German name: **Hessen** (ˈhɛsˀn).

Hesse[2] ★ (hɛs; *German* ˈhɛsə) *n* **Hermann** (ˈhɛrman). 1877–1962, German writer. His novels include *Steppenwolf* (1927) and *The Glass Bead Game* (1943): Nobel prize for literature 1946.

Hesse-Nassau ★ *n* a former province of Prussia, now part of the state of Hesse, Germany.

hessian (ˈhɛsɪən) *n* a coarse jute fabric similar to sacking. [C18: from HESSIAN]

Hessian (ˈhɛsɪən) *n* **1** a native or inhabitant of Hesse. **2** a Hessian soldier in any of the mercenary units of the British Army in the War of American Independence or the Napoleonic Wars. ◆ *adj* **3** of Hesse or its inhabitants.

Hessian fly *n* a small dipterous fly whose larvae damage wheat, barley, and rye. [C18: thought to have been introduced into America by Hessian soldiers]

hest (hɛst) *n* an archaic word for **behest.** [OE *hǽs*]

Hestia ★ (ˈhɛstɪə) *n Greek myth.* the goddess of the hearth. Roman counterpart: **Vesta.**

hetaera (hɪˈtɪərə) *or* **hetaira** (hɪˈtaɪrə) *n, pl* **hetaerae** (-ˈtɪəriː) *or* **hetairai** (-ˈtaɪraɪ). (esp. in ancient Greece) a prostitute, esp. an educated courtesan. [C19: from Gk *hetaira* concubine]

hetaerism (hɪˈtɪərɪzəm) *or* **hetairism** (hɪˈtaɪrɪzəm) *n* **1** the state of being a concubine. **2** *Sociol., anthropol.* a social system attributed to some primitive societies, in which women are communally shared.

hetero- *combining form.* other, another, or different: *heterosexual.* [from Gk *heteros* other]

heteroclite (ˈhɛtərəˌklaɪt) *adj* also **heteroclitic** (ˌhɛtərəˈklɪtɪk). **1** (esp. of the form of a word) irregular or unusual. ◆ *n* **2** an irregularly formed word. [C16: from LL *heteroclitus* declining irregularly, from Gk, from HETERO- + *klinein* to inflect]

heterocyclic (ˌhɛtərəʊˈsaɪklɪk, -ˈsɪk-) *adj* (of an organic compound) containing a closed ring of atoms, at least one of which is not a carbon atom.

heterodox (ˈhɛtərəʊˌdɒks) *adj* **1** at variance with estab-

---

★ people and places

lished or accepted doctrines or beliefs. **2** holding unorthodox opinions. [C17: from Gk *heterodoxos*, from HETERO- + *doxa* opinion]
► ˈheteroˌdoxy *n*

heterodyne (ˈhɛtərəʊˌdaɪn) *vb* **heterodynes, heterodyning, heterodyned. 1** *Electronics*. to combine by modulation (two alternating signals) to produce two signals having frequencies corresponding to the sum and the difference of the original frequencies. ◆ *adj* **2** produced by, operating by, or involved in heterodyning two signals.

heteroecious (ˌhɛtəˈriːʃəs) *adj* (of parasites) undergoing different stages of the life cycle on different host species. [from HETERO- + *-oecious*, from Gk *oikia* house]
► heteroˈecism (ˌhɛtəˈriːˌsɪzəm) *n*

heterogamete (ˌhɛtərəʊɡæˈmiːt) *n* a gamete that differs in size and form from the one with which it unites in fertilization.

heterogamy (ˌhɛtəˈrɒɡəmɪ) *n* **1** a type of sexual reproduction in which the gametes differ in both size and form. **2** a condition in which different types of reproduction occur in successive generations of an organism. **3** the presence of both male and female flowers in one inflorescence.
► ˌheterˈogamous *adj*

heterogeneous (ˌhɛtərəʊˈdʒiːnɪəs) *adj* **1** composed of unrelated parts. **2** not of the same type. [C17: from Med. L *heterogeneus*, from Gk, from HETERO- + *genos* sort]
► heterogeneity (ˌhɛtərəʊdʒɪˈniːɪtɪ) *or* ˌheteroˈgeneousness *n*

heterogony (ˌhɛtəˈrɒɡənɪ) *n* **1** *Biol.* the alternation of parthenogenetic and sexual generations in rotifers and similar animals. **2** the condition in plants, such as the primrose, of having flowers that differ from each other in the length of their stamens and styles.
► ˌheterˈogonous *adj*

heterologous (ˌhɛtəˈrɒləɡəs) *adj* **1** *Pathol.* designating cells or tissues not normally present in a particular part of the body. **2** differing in structure or origin.
► ˌheterˈology *n*

heteromerous (ˌhɛtəˈrɒmərəs) *adj Biol.* having parts that differ, esp. in number.

heteromorphic (ˌhɛtərəʊˈmɔːfɪk) *or* **heteromorphous** *adj Biol.* **1** differing from the normal form. **2** (esp. of insects) having different forms at different stages of the life cycle.
► ˌheteroˈmorphism *n*

heteronomous (ˌhɛtəˈrɒnɪməs) *adj* **1** subject to an external law. **2** (of parts of an organism) differing in the manner of growth, development, or specialization.
► ˌheterˈonomy *n*

heteronym (ˈhɛtərəʊˌnɪm) *n* one of two or more words pronounced differently but spelt alike: *the two English words spelt "bow" are heteronyms*. Cf. **homograph**. [C17: from LGk *heteronumos*, from Gk HETERO- + *onoma* name]

heterophyllous (ˌhɛtərəʊˈfɪləs, ˌhɛtəˈrɒfɪləs) *adj* having more than one type of leaf on the same plant.
► ˈheteroˌphylly *n*

heteropterous (ˌhɛtəˈrɒptərəs) *or* **heteropteran** *adj* of or belonging to a suborder of hemipterous insects, including bedbugs, water bugs, etc., in which the forewings are membranous but have leathery tips. [C19: from NL *Heteroptera*, from HETERO- + Gk *pteron* wing]

heterosexism (ˌhɛtərəʊˈsɛkˌsɪzəm) *n* discrimination on the basis of sexual orientation, practised by heterosexuals against homosexuals.
► heteroˈsexist *adj, n*

heterosexual (ˌhɛtərəʊˈsɛksjʊəl) *n* **1** a person who is sexually attracted to the opposite sex. ◆ *adj* **2** of or relating to heterosexuality.
► ˌheteroˌsexuˈality *n*

heterotaxis (ˌhɛtərəʊˈtæksɪs) *or* **heterotaxy** *n* an abnormal or asymmetrical arrangement of parts, as of the organs of the body.

heterotrophic (ˌhɛtərəʊˈtrɒfɪk) *adj* (of animals and some plants) using complex organic compounds to manufacture their own constituents. [C20:

from HETERO- + Gk *trophikos* concerning food, from *trophē* nourishment]
► ˈheteroˌtroph *n*

heterozygote (ˌhɛtərəʊˈzaɪɡəʊt) *n* an animal or plant that is heterozygous; a hybrid.

heterozygous (ˌhɛtərəʊˈzaɪɡəs) *adj Genetics.* (of an organism) having dissimilar alleles for any one gene: *heterozygous for eye colour.*

hetman (ˈhɛtmən) *n, pl* **hetmans.** an elected leader of the Cossacks. Also called: **ataman**. [C18: from Polish, from G *Hauptmann* headman]

het up *adj Inf.* angry; excited: *don't get het up.* [C19: from dialect p.p. of HEAT]

heuchera (ˈhɔɪkərə) *n* a North American shrub with red or pink flowers and ornamental foliage. [after J. H. *Heucher* (1677–1747), G botanist]

heuristic (hjʊəˈrɪstɪk) *adj* **1** helping to learn; guiding in investigation. **2** (of a method of teaching) allowing pupils to learn things for themselves. **3a** *Maths, science, philosophy.* using or obtained by exploration of possibilities rather than by following set rules. **3b** *Computing.* denoting a rule of thumb for solving a problem without the exhaustive application of an algorithm: *a heuristic solution.* ◆ *n* **4** (*pl*) the science of heuristic procedure. [C19: from NL *heuristicus*, from Gk *heuriskein* to discover]
► heuˈristically *adv*

Hevesy ★ (*Hungarian* ˈhɛvɛʃi) *n* Georg von (ˈɡeːɔrɡ fɔn). 1885–1966, Hungarian chemist; worked on radioactive tracing and, with D. Coster, discovered hafnium (1923): Nobel prize for chemistry 1943.

hew (hjuː) *vb* **hews, hewing, hewed, hewed** *or* **hewn. 1** to strike (something, esp. wood) with cutting blows, as with an axe. **2** (*tr;* often foll. by *out*) to carve from a substance. **3** (*tr;* often foll. by *away, off,* etc.) to sever from a larger portion. **4** (*intr;* often foll. by *to*) *US & Canad.* to conform. [OE *hēawan*]
► ˈhewer *n*

Hewish ★ (ˈhjuːɪʃ) *n* Antony. born 1924, British radio astronomer, helped to discover pulsars (1967): shared the Nobel prize for physics 1974.

hex[1] (hɛks) *n* **a** short for **hexadecimal (notation). b** (*as modifier*): *hex code.*

hex[2] (hɛks) *US & Canad. inf.* ◆ *vb* **1** (*tr*) to bewitch. ◆ *n* **2** an evil spell. **3** a witch. [C19: via Pennsylvania Du. from G *Hexe* witch, from MHG *hecse,* ?from OHG *hagzissa*]

hex. *abbrev. for:* **1** hexachord. **2** hexagon(al).

hexa- *or before a vowel* **hex-** *combining form.* six: *hexachord; hexameter.* [from Gk, from *hex* SIX]

hexachlorophene (ˌhɛksəˈklɔːrəfiːn) *n* an insoluble white bactericidal substance used in antiseptic soaps, deodorants, etc. Formula: $(C_6HCl_3OH)_2CH_2$.

hexachord (ˈhɛksəˌkɔːd) *n* (in medieval musical theory) any of three diatonic scales based upon C, F, and G, each consisting of six notes, from which solmization was developed.

hexad (ˈhɛksæd) *n* a group or series of six. [C17: from Gk *hexas,* from *hex* six]

hexadecane (ˈhɛksədeˌkeɪn, ˌhɛksəˈdɛkeɪn) *n* the systematic name for **cetane**.

hexadecanoic acid (ˌhɛksəˌdɛkəˈnəʊɪk) *n* the systematic name for **palmitic acid.**

hexadecimal notation *or* **hexadecimal** (ˌhɛksəˈdɛsɪməl) *n* a number system having a base 16; the symbols for the numbers 0 – 9 are the same as those used in the decimal system, and the numbers 10 – 15 are usually represented by the letters A – F. The system is used as a convenient way of representing the internal binary code of a computer.

hexagon (ˈhɛksəɡən) *n* a polygon having six sides.
► hexˈagonal *adj*

hexagram (ˈhɛksəˌɡræm) *n* a star-shaped figure formed by extending the sides of a regular hexagon to meet at six points.

hexahedron (ˌhɛksəˈhiːdrən) *n* a solid figure having six plane faces.
► ˌhexaˈhedral *adj*

★ people and places

hexameter (hɛk'sæmɪtə) n Prosody. **1** a verse line consisting of six metrical feet. **2** (in Greek and Latin epic poetry) a verse line of six metrical feet, of which the first four are usually dactyls or spondees, the fifth almost always a dactyl, and the sixth a spondee or trochee.
▸ **hexametric** (ˌhɛksə'mɛtrɪk) or ˌhexa'metrical adj

hexane ('hɛkseɪn) n a liquid alkane found in petroleum and used as a solvent. Formula: C_6H_{14}. [C19: from HEXA- + -ANE]

hexapla ('hɛksəplə) n an edition of the Old Testament compiled by Origen (?185–?254 A.D.), Christian theologian, containing six versions of the text. [C17: from Gk hexaploos sixfold]
▸ **'hexaplar** adj

hexapod ('hɛksəˌpɒd) n an insect.

hexavalent (ˌhɛksə'veɪlənt) adj Chem. having a valency of six. Also: **sexivalent.**

hexose ('hɛksəʊs, -əʊz) n a monosaccharide, such as glucose, that contains six carbon atoms per molecule.

hey (heɪ) interj **1** an expression indicating surprise, dismay, discovery, etc. **2 hey presto!** an exclamation used by conjurors to herald the climax of a trick. [C13: imit.]

heyday ('heɪˌdeɪ) n the time of most power, popularity, vigour, etc. [C16: prob. based on HEY]

Heyer ★ ('heɪə) n **Georgette.** 1902–74, British historical novelist and writer of detective stories.

Heyerdahl ★ (Norwegian 'heiərdɑːl) n **Thor** (tɔː). born 1914, Norwegian anthropologist. In 1947 he demonstrated that the Polynesians could have been migrants from South America, by sailing from Peru to the Pacific Islands of Tuamotu in the Kon-Tiki, a balsawood raft. DNA testing in the late 1990s indicated that such a migration did not actually take place.

Heysham ★ ('heɪʃəm) n a port in NW England, in NW Lancashire. Pop. (with Morecambe): 46 657 (1991).

Heywood[1] ★ ('heɪˌwʊd) n a town in NW England, in Greater Manchester near Bury. Pop.: 29 286 (1991).

Heywood[2] ★ ('heɪˌwʊd) n **1 John.** ?1497–?1580, English dramatist. **2 Thomas.** ?1574–1641, English dramatist, noted for his A Woman Killed with Kindness (1607).

Hezekiah ★ (ˌhɛzə'kaɪə) n a king of Judah ?715–?687 B.C., noted for his religious reforms (II Kings 18–19). Douay spelling: **Ezechias.** [from Heb. hizqīyyāhū God has strengthened]

hf abbrev. for half.

Hf the chemical symbol for hafnium.

HF or **h.f.** abbrev. for high frequency.

hg abbrev. for hectogram.

Hg the chemical symbol for mercury. [from NL hydrargyrum]

HG abbrev. for His (or Her) Grace.

hgt abbrev. for height.

HGV (formerly, in Britain) abbrev. for heavy goods vehicle.

HH abbrev. for: **1** His (or Her) Highness. **2** His Holiness (title of the Pope). ◆ **3.** (on Brit. pencils) symbol for double hard.

hi (haɪ) sentence substitute. an informal word for **hello.** [C20: prob. from how are you?]

HI abbrev. for: **1** Hawaii (state). **2** Hawaiian Islands.

Hialeah ★ (ˌhaɪə'liːə) n a city in SE Florida, near Miami: racetrack. Pop.: 194 120 (1994 est.).

hiatus (haɪ'eɪtəs) n, pl **hiatuses** or **hiatus. 1** (esp. in manuscripts) a break or interruption in continuity. **2** a break between adjacent vowels in the pronunciation of a word. [C16: from L: gap, cleft, from hiāre to gape]

hiatus hernia n protrusion of part of the stomach through the diaphragm at the oesophageal opening.

Hiawatha ★ (ˌhaɪə'wɒθə) n a 16th-century Onondaga Indian chief: credited with the organization of the Five Nations.

Hib (hɪb) n acronym for Haemophilus influenzae type b: a vaccine against a type of bacterial meningitis, administered to children.

hibachi (hɪ'bɑːtʃɪ) n a portable brazier for heating and cooking food. [from Japanese, from hi fire + bachi bowl]

hibakusha (hɪ'bɑːkuʃə) n, pl **hibakusha** or **hibakushas.** a survivor of either of the atomic-bomb attacks on Hiroshima and Nagasaki in 1945. [C20: from Japanese, from hibaku bombed + -sha -person]

hibernal (haɪ'bɜːnəl) adj of or occurring in winter. [C17: from L hībernālis, from hiems winter]

hibernate ('haɪbəˌneɪt) vb **hibernates, hibernating, hibernated. 1** (intr) (of some animals) to pass the winter in a dormant condition with metabolism greatly slowed down. **2** to cease from activity. [C19: from L hībernāre to spend the winter, from hibernus of winter]
▸ ˌhiber'nation n ▸ 'hiberˌnator n

Hibernia ★ (haɪ'bɜːnɪə) n the Roman name for Ireland: used poetically in later times.
▸ **Hi'bernian** adj, n

Hibernicism (haɪ'bɜːnɪˌsɪzəm) n an Irish expression, idiom, trait, custom, etc.

Hiberno- (haɪ'bɜːnəʊ) combining form. denoting Irish or Ireland: Hiberno-English.

hibiscus (hɪ'bɪskəs) n, pl **hibiscuses.** any plant of the chiefly tropical and subtropical genus Hibiscus, cultivated for its large brightly coloured flowers. [C18: from L, from Gk hibiskos marsh mallow]

hiccup ('hɪkʌp) n **1** a spasm of the diaphragm producing a sudden breathing in of air resulting in a characteristic sharp sound. **2** (pl) the state of having such spasms. **3** Inf. a minor difficulty. ◆ vb **hiccups, hiccuping, hiccuped** or **hiccups, hiccupping, hiccupped. 4** (intr) to make a hiccup or hiccups. **5** (tr) to utter with a hiccup. ◆ Also: **hiccough** ('hɪkʌp). [C16: imit.]

hic jacet Latin. (hɪk 'jækɛt) (on gravestones, etc.) here lies.

hick (hɪk) n Inf., chiefly US & Canad. a country bumpkin. [C16: after Hick, familiar form of Richard]

Hickok ★ ('hɪkɒk) n **James Butler,** known as **Wild Bill Hickok.** 1837–76, US frontiersman and marshal.

hickory ('hɪkərɪ) n, pl **hickories. 1** a tree of a chiefly North American genus having nuts with edible kernels and hard smooth shells. **2** the hard tough wood of this tree. [C17: ult. from Algonquian pawcohiccora food made from ground hickory nuts]

hid (hɪd) vb the past tense and a past participle of **hide**[1].

hidalgo (hɪ'dælgəʊ) n, pl **hidalgos.** a member of the lower nobility in Spain. [C16: from Sp., from OSp. fijo dalgo nobleman, from L filius son + dē of + aliquid something]

Hidalgo ★ (hɪ'dælgəʊ; Spanish i'ðalɣo) n a state of central Mexico: consists of a high plateau, with the Sierra Madre Oriental in the north and east; ancient remains of Teltec culture (at Tula); mineral resources. Capital: Pachuca. Pop.: 2 111 782 (1995 est.). Area: 20 987 sq. km (8103 sq. miles).

hidden ('hɪd²n) vb **1** a past participle of **hide**[1]. ◆ adj **2** concealed or obscured: a hidden cave; a hidden meaning.

hidden agenda n a hidden motive or intention behind an overt action, policy, etc.

hide[1] (haɪd) vb **hides, hiding, hid, hidden** or **hid. 1** to conceal (oneself or an object) from view or discovery: to hide a pencil; to hide from the police. **2** (tr) to obscure: clouds hid the sun. **3** (tr) to keep secret. **4** (tr) to turn (one's eyes, etc.) away. ◆ n **5** Brit. a place of concealment, usually disguised to appear as part of the natural environment, used by hunters, birdwatchers, etc. US and Canad. equivalent: **blind.** [OE hȳdan]
▸ **'hider** n

hide[2] (haɪd) n **1** the skin of an animal, either tanned or raw. **2** Inf. the human skin. ◆ vb **hides, hiding, hided. 3** (tr) Inf. to flog. [OE hȳd]

hide[3] (haɪd) n an obsolete Brit. land measure, varying from about 60 to 120 acres. [OE hīgid]

hide-and-seek or US, Canad., & Scot. **hide-and-go-seek** n a game in which one player covers his eyes while the others hide, and he then tries to find them.

hideaway ('haɪdəˌweɪ) n a hiding place or secluded spot.

hidebound ('haɪdˌbaʊnd) adj **1** restricted by petty rules,

★ people and places

a conservative attitude, etc. **2** (of cattle, etc.) having the skin closely attached to the flesh as a result of poor feeding.

hideous ('hɪdɪəs) *adj* **1** extremely ugly; repulsive. **2** terrifying and horrific. [C13: from OF *hisdos*, from *hisde* fear; from ?]
▸ **'hideously** *adv* ▸ **'hideousness** *n*

hide-out *n* a hiding place, esp. a remote place used by outlaws, etc.; hideaway.

hiding[1] ('haɪdɪŋ) *n* **1** the state of concealment: *in hiding.* **2 hiding place.** a place of concealment.

hiding[2] ('haɪdɪŋ) *n Inf.* a flogging; beating.

hidrosis (hɪ'drəʊsɪs) *n* a technical word for **perspiration** or **sweat.** [C18: via NL from Gk, from *hidrōs* sweat]
▸ **hidrotic** (hɪ'drɒtɪk) *adj*

hidy-hole or **hidey-hole** *n Inf.* a hiding place.

hie (haɪ) *vb* **hies, hieing** or **hying, hied.** *Arch.* or *poetic.* to hurry; speed. [OE *hīgian* to strive]

hierarch ('haɪə,rɑːk) *n* **1** a high priest. **2** a person at a high level in a hierarchy.
▸ **,hier'archal** *adj*

hierarchy ('haɪə,rɑːkɪ) *n, pl* **hierarchies. 1** a system of persons or things arranged in a graded order. **2** a body of persons in holy orders organized into graded ranks. **3** the collective body of those so organized. **4** a series of ordered groupings within a system, such as the arrangement of plants into classes, orders, etc. **5** government by a priesthood. [C14: from Med. L *hierarchia*, from LGk, from *hierarkhēs* high priest; see HIERO-, -ARCHY]
▸ **,hier'archical** or **,hier'archic** *adj* ▸ **'hier,archism** *n*

hieratic (,haɪə'rætɪk) *adj* **1** of priests. **2** of a cursive form of hieroglyphics used by priests in ancient Egypt. **3** of styles in art that adhere to certain fixed types, as in ancient Egypt. ◆ *n* **4** the hieratic script of ancient Egypt. [C17: from L *hierāticus*, from Gk, from *hiereus* priest]
▸ **,hier'atically** *adv*

hiero- or before a vowel **hier-** *combining form.* holy or divine: *hierarchy.* [from Gk, from *hieros* holy]

hieroglyphic (,haɪərə'glɪfɪk) *adj* also **hieroglyphical. 1** of or relating to a form of writing using picture symbols, esp. as used in ancient Egypt. **2** difficult to decipher. ◆ *n* also **hieroglyph. 3** a picture or symbol representing an object, concept, or sound. **4** a symbol that is difficult to decipher. [C16: from LL *hieroglyphicus*, from Gk, from HIERO- + *gluphē*, from *gluphein* to carve]
▸ **,hiero'glyphically** *adv*

hieroglyphics (,haɪərə'glɪfɪks) *n* (*functioning as sing* or *pl*) **1** a form of writing, esp. as used in ancient Egypt, in which pictures or symbols are used to represent objects, concepts, or sounds. **2** difficult or undecipherable writing.

Hieronymus ★ (,haɪə'rɒnɪməs) *n* **Eusebius** (juː'siːbɪəs). the Latin name of (Saint) **Jerome.**
▸ **Hieronymic** (,haɪərə'nɪmɪk) or **,Hiero'nymian** *adj*

hierophant ('haɪərə,fænt) *n* **1** (in ancient Greece) a high priest of religious mysteries. **2** a person who interprets esoteric mysteries. [C17: from LL *hierophanta*, from Gk, from HIERO- + *phainein* to reveal]
▸ **,hiero'phantic** *adj*

hi-fi ('haɪ,faɪ) *n Inf.* **1a** short for **high fidelity. 1b** (*as modifier*): *hi-fi equipment.* **2** a set of high-quality sound-reproducing equipment.

Higgins ★ ('hɪgɪnz) *n* **Alex**, known as *Hurricane Higgins.* born 1949, Northern Irish snooker player.

higgledy-piggledy ('hɪgᵊldɪ'pɪgᵊldɪ) *Inf.* ◆ *adj, adv* **1** in a jumble. ◆ *n* **2** a muddle.

high (haɪ) *adj* **1** being a relatively great distance from top to bottom; tall: *a high building.* **2** situated at a relatively great distance above sea level: *a high plateau.* **3** (*postpositive*) being a specified distance from top to bottom: *three feet high.* **4** extending from or performed at an elevation: *a high dive.* **5** (*in combination*) coming up to a specified level: *knee-high.* **6** being at its peak: *high noon.* **7** of greater than average height: *a high collar.* **8** greater than normal in intensity or amount: *a high wind; high mileage.* **9** (of sound) acute in pitch. **10** (of latitudes) relatively far north or south from the equator. **11** (of meat) slightly

decomposed, regarded as enhancing the flavour of game. **12** very important: *the high priestess.* **13** exalted in style or character: *high drama.* **14** expressing contempt or arrogance: *high words.* **15** elated; cheerful: *high spirits.* **16** *Inf.* being in a state of altered consciousness induced by alcohol, narcotics, etc. **17** *Inf.* overexcited: *by Christmas the children are high.* **18** luxurious or extravagant: *high life.* **19** advanced in complexity: *high finance.* **20** (of a gear) providing a relatively great forward speed for a given engine speed. **21** *Phonetics.* denoting a vowel whose articulation is produced by raising the tongue, such as the *ee* in *see* or *oo* in *moon.* **22** (*cap. when part of a name*) formal and elaborate: *High Mass.* **23** (*usually cap.*) relating to the High Church. **24** *Cards.* having a relatively great value in a suit. **25 high and dry.** stranded; destitute. **26 high and mighty.** *Inf.* arrogant. **27 high opinion.** a favourable opinion. ◆ *adv* **28** at or to a height: *he jumped high.* **29** in a high manner. **30** *Naut.* close to the wind with sails full. ◆ *n* **31** a high place or level. **32** *Inf.* a state of altered consciousness induced by alcohol, narcotics, etc. **33** another word for **anticyclone. 34 on high.** **34a** at a height. **34b** in heaven. [OE *hēah*]

High Arctic ★ *n* the regions of Canada, esp. the northern islands, within the Arctic Circle.

highball ('haɪ,bɔːl) *n Chiefly US.* a long iced drink consisting of spirits with soda water, etc.

highborn ('haɪ,bɔːn) *adj* of noble birth.

highboy ('haɪ,bɔɪ) *n US & Canad.* a tallboy.

highbrow ('haɪ,braʊ) *Often disparaging.* ◆ *n* **1** a person of scholarly and erudite tastes. ◆ *adj* also **highbrowed. 2** appealing to highbrows.

highchair ('haɪ,tʃeə) *n* a long-legged chair for a child, esp. one with a table-like tray.

High Church *n* **1** the party or movement within the Church of England stressing continuity with Catholic Christendom, the authority of bishops, and the importance of sacraments. ◆ *adj* **High-Church. 2** of or relating to this party or movement.
▸ **'High-'Churchman** *n*

high-class *adj* **1** of very good quality: *a high-class grocer.* **2** belonging to or exhibiting the characteristics of an upper social class.

high-coloured *adj* (of the complexion) deep red or purplish; florid.

high comedy *n* comedy set largely among cultured and articulate people and featuring witty dialogue.

high commissioner *n* the senior diplomatic representative sent by one Commonwealth country to another instead of an ambassador.

high country *n* (often preceded by *the*) *NZ.* sheep pastures in the foothills of the Southern Alps, New Zealand.

High Court *n* **1** Also called: **High Court of Justice.** (in England) the supreme court dealing with civil law cases. **2** (in Australia) the highest court of appeal, deciding esp. constitutional issues. **3** (in New Zealand) a court of law that is superior to a District Court. Former name: **Supreme Court.**

high definition television *n* a television system using 1000 or more scanning lines and a higher field repetition rate. Abbrev.: **HDTV.**

high-energy physics *n* (*functioning as sing*) another name for **particle physics.**

higher ('haɪə) *adj* **1** the comparative of **high.** ◆ *n* (*usually cap.*) (in Scotland) **2a** the advanced level of the Scottish Certificate of Education. **2b** (*as modifier*): *Higher Latin.* **3** a pass in a subject at Higher level: *she has four Highers.*

higher education *n* education and training at colleges, universities, etc.

higher mathematics *n* (*functioning as sing*) mathematics that is more abstract than normal arithmetic, algebra, geometry, and trigonometry.

higher-rate tax *n* (in Britain) a rate of income tax that is higher than the basic rate and becomes payable on taxable income in excess of a specified limit.

higher-up *n Inf.* a person of higher rank or in a superior position.

highest common factor *n* the largest number or

quantity that is a factor of each member of a group of numbers or quantities.

high explosive *n* an extremely powerful chemical explosive, such as TNT or gelignite.

highfalutin (ˌhaɪfəˈluːtɪn) *or* **highfaluting** *adj Inf.* pompous or pretentious. [C19: from HIGH + -*falutin*, ? var. of *fluting*, from FLUTE]

high fidelity *n* **a** the reproduction of sound using electronic equipment that gives faithful reproduction with little or no distortion. **b** (*as modifier*): *a high-fidelity amplifier.* ◆ Often shortened to **hi-fi.**

high-five *n Sl.* a gesture of greeting or congratulation in which two people slap raised right palms together.

high-flown *adj* extravagant or pretentious in conception or intention: *high-flown ideas.*

high-flyer *or* **high-flier** *n* **1** a person who is extreme in aims, ambition, etc. **2** a person of great ability, esp. in a career.
▸ ˌhigh-ˈflying *adj, n*

high frequency *n* a radio frequency lying between 30 and 3 megahertz. Abbrev.: **HF.**

High German *n* the standard German language, historically developed from the form of West Germanic spoken in S Germany.

high-handed *adj* tactlessly overbearing and inconsiderate.
▸ ˌhigh-ˈhandedness *n*

high-hat *Inf.* ◆ *adj* **1** snobbish and arrogant. ◆ *vb* **high-hats, high-hatting, high-hatted.** (*tr*) **2** *Chiefly US & Canad.* to treat in a snobbish or offhand way. ◆ *n* **3** a snobbish person.

high hurdles *n* (*functioning as sing*) a race in which competitors leap over hurdles 42 inches (107 cm) high.

highjack (ˈhaɪˌdʒæk) *vb, n* a less common spelling of **hijack.**
▸ ˈhighˌjacker *n*

high jump *n* **1** (*usually preceded by the*) an athletic event in which a competitor has to jump over a high bar. **2 be for the high jump.** *Brit. inf.* to be liable to receive a severe reprimand or punishment.
▸ **high jumper** *n* ▸ **high jumping** *n*

high-key *adj* (of a painting, etc.) having a predominance of light tones or colours. Cf. **low-key** (sense 3).

highland (ˈhaɪlənd) *n* **1** relatively high ground. **2** (*modifier*) of or relating to a highland.
▸ ˈhighlander *n*

Highland ★ (ˈhaɪlənd) *n* **1** a council area in N Scotland, formed in 1975 as Highland Region and reorganized in 1996. Administrative centre: Inverness. Pop.: 206 900 (1996 est.). Area: 25 149 sq. km (9710 sq. miles). **2** (*modifier*) of or denoting the Highlands of Scotland.
▸ ˈHighlander *n*

Highland cattle *n* a breed of cattle with shaggy reddish-brown hair and long horns.

Highland dress *n* **1** the historical costume including the plaid and kilt, of Highland clansmen and soldiers. **2** a modern version of this worn for formal occasions.

Highland fling *n* a vigorous Scottish solo dance.

Highland Games *n* (*functioning as sing or pl*) a meeting in which competitions in sport, piping, and dancing are held: originating in the Highlands of Scotland.

Highlands ★ (ˈhaɪləndz) *pl n* **the. 1a** the part of Scotland that lies to the northwest of the great fault that runs from Dumbarton to Stonehaven. **1b** a mountainous region of NW Scotland: distinguished by Gaelic culture. **2** (*often not cap.*) the highland region of any country.

high-level *adj* (of conferences, talks, etc.) involving very important people.

high-level language *n Computing.* a programming language that resembles natural language or mathematical notation and is designed to reflect the requirements of a problem.

high-level waste *n* high-activity radioactive waste, such as spent nuclear fuel, needing cooling for several decades before disposal. Cf. **intermediate-level waste, low-level waste.**

highlight (ˈhaɪˌlaɪt) *n* **1** an area of the lightest tone in a painting, photograph, etc. **2** Also called: **high spot.** the most exciting or memorable part or time. **3** (*pl*) a lightened or brightened effect produced in the hair by bleaching selected strands. ◆ *vb* (*tr*) **4** *Painting, photog. etc.* to mark with light tone. **5** to bring emphasis to. **6** to produce highlights in (the hair).

highlighter (ˈhaɪˌlaɪtə) *n* **1** a cosmetic cream or powder applied to the face to highlight the cheekbones, eyes etc. **2** a fluorescent felt-tip pen used as a marker to emphasize a section of text without obscuring it.

highly (ˈhaɪlɪ) *adv* **1** (intensifier): *highly disappointed.* **2** with great approbation: *we spoke highly of it.* **3** in a high position: *placed highly in class.* **4** at or for a high cost.

highly strung *or US & Canad.* **high-strung** *adj* tense and easily upset; excitable; nervous.

High Mass *n* a solemn and elaborate sung Mass.

high-minded *adj* **1** having or characterized by high moral principles. **2** *Arch.* arrogant; haughty.
▸ ˌhigh-ˈmindedness *n*

highness (ˈhaɪnɪs) *n* the condition of being high.

Highness (ˈhaɪnɪs) *n* (preceded by *Your, His,* or *Her*) a title used to address or refer to a royal person.

high-octane *adj* **1** (of petrol) having a high octane number. **2** *Inf.* dynamic, forceful, or intense: *high-octane drive and efficiency.*

high-pass filter *n Electronics.* a filter that transmits all frequencies above a specified value, attenuating frequencies below this value.

high-pitched *adj* **1** pitched high in tone. **2** (of a roof) having steeply sloping sides. **3** (of an argument, style, etc.) lofty or intense.

high-powered *adj* **1** (of an optical instrument or lens) having a high magnification. **2** dynamic and energetic; highly capable.

high-pressure *adj* **1** having, using, or designed to withstand pressure above normal. **2** *Inf.* (of selling) persuasive in an aggressive and persistent manner.

high priest *n* **1** *Bible.* the priest of highest rank who alone was permitted to enter the holy of holies of the Temple. **2** Also (fem): **high priestess.** the head of a cult.
▸ **high priesthood** *n*

high profile *n* a position or attitude characterized by a deliberate seeking of prominence or publicity.

high-rise *adj* **1** (*prenominal*) of or relating to a building that has many storeys, esp. one used for flats or offices: *a high-rise block.* ◆ *n* **2** a high-rise building.

high-risk *adj* (*prenominal*) denoting a group, part, etc., that is particularly subject to a danger.

highroad (ˈhaɪˌrəʊd) *n* **1** a main road; highway. **2** (*usually preceded by the*) the sure way: *the highroad to fame.*

high school *n* **1** *Brit.* another term for **grammar school. 2** *US, Canad., NZ, & Scot.* a secondary school.

high seas *pl n* (*sometimes sing*) the open seas, outside the jurisdiction of any one nation.

high season *n* the most popular time of year at a holiday resort, etc.

Highsmith ★ (ˈhaɪˌsmɪθ) *n* Patricia. 1921–95, US author of crime fiction. Her novels include *Strangers on a Train* (1950) and *Ripley's Game* (1974).

high-sounding *adj* another term for **high-flown.**

high-spirited *adj* vivacious, bold, or lively.
▸ ˌhigh-ˈspiritedness *n*

High Street *n* (*often not cap.; usually preceded by the*) *Brit.* the main street of a town, usually where the principal shops are situated.

high table *n* (*sometimes cap.*) the table in the dining hall of a school, college, etc., at which the principal teachers, fellows, etc., sit.

hightail (ˈhaɪˌteɪl) *vb* (*intr*) *Inf., chiefly US & Canad.* to go or move in a great hurry.

High Tatra ★ *n* another name for the **Tatra Mountains.**

high tea *n Brit.* See **tea** (sense 4b).

high tech (tɛk) *n* a variant spelling of **hi tech.**

igh technology *n* any type of sophisticated industrial process, esp. electronic.

igh-tension *n* (*modifier*) carrying or operating at a relatively high voltage.

igh tide *n* **1** the tide at its highest level. **2** a culminating point.

igh time *Inf.* ◆ *adv* **1** the latest possible time: *it's high time you left.* ◆ *n* **2** Also: **high old time.** an enjoyable and exciting time.

igh-toned *adj* **1** having a superior social, moral, or intellectual quality. **2** affectedly superior. **3** high in tone.

igh tops *pl n* training shoes that reach to above the ankles.

igh treason *n* an act of treason directly affecting a sovereign or state.

igh-up *n Inf.* a person who holds an important or influential position.

ighveld ('haɪ‚fɛlt) *n* **the.** the high grassland region of NE South Africa.

igh water *n* **1** another name for **high tide. 2** the state of any stretch of water at its highest level, as during a flood. ◆ Abbrev.: **HW.**

igh-water mark *n* **1** the level reached by sea water at high tide or by other stretches of water in flood. **2** the highest point.

ighway ('haɪ‚weɪ) *n* **1** a public road that all may use. **2** *Now chiefly US & Canad. except in legal contexts.* a main road, esp. one that connects towns. **3** a direct path or course.

ighway Code *n* (in Britain) a booklet compiled by the Department of Transport for the guidance of users of public roads.

ighwayman ('haɪweɪmən) *n, pl* **highwaymen.** (formerly) a robber, usually on horseback, who held up travellers on public roads.

high wire *n* a tightrope stretched high in the air for balancing acts.

High Wycombe ★ ('wɪkəm) *n* a town in S central England, in S Buckinghamshire: furniture industry. Pop.: 71 718 (1991).

HIH *abbrev. for* His (*or* Her) Imperial Highness.

hijack *or* **highjack** ('haɪ‚dʒæk) *vb* **1** (*tr*) to seize or divert (a vehicle or the goods it carries) while in transit: *to hijack an aircraft.* ◆ *n* **2** the act or an instance of hijacking. [C20: from ?]
▸ **'hi‚jacker** *or* **'high‚jacker** *n*

Hijaz ★ (hiː'dʒæz) *n* a variant spelling of **Hejaz.**

hike (haɪk) *vb* **hikes, hiking, hiked. 1** (*intr*) to walk a long way, usually for pleasure, esp. in the country. **2** (usually foll. by *up*) to pull or be pulled; hitch. **3** (*tr;* usually foll. by *up*) to raise (prices). ◆ *n* **4** a long walk. **5** a rise in price. [C18: from ?]
▸ **'hiker** *n*

hilarious (hɪ'lɛərɪəs) *adj* very funny. [C19: from L *hilaris* glad, from Gk *hilaros*]
▸ **hi'lariously** *adv* ▸ **hi'lariousness** *n*

hilarity (hɪ'lærɪtɪ) *n* mirth and merriment.

Hilary of Poitiers ★ ('hɪlərɪ) *n* **Saint.** ?315–?367 A.D., French bishop, an opponent of Arianism. Feast day: Jan. 13 or 14.

Hilary term *n* the spring term at Oxford University, the Inns of Court, and some other educational establishments. [C16: after Saint HILARY of Poitiers]

Hilbert ★ (*German* 'hɪlbərt) *n* **David.** (da:fɪt). 1862–1943, German mathematician, who made outstanding contributions to the theories of number fields and invariants and to geometry.

Hildebrand ★ ('hɪldə‚brænd) *n* the monastic name of **Gregory VII.**
▸ **‚Hilde'brandian** *adj, n* ▸ **'Hilde‚brandine** *adj*

Hildegard of Bingen ★ ('hɪldəgɑːd; 'bɪŋən) *n* **Saint.** 1098–1179, German abbess, poet, composer, and mystic.

Hildesheim ★ (*German* 'hɪldəshaɪm) *n* a city in N central Germany, in Lower Saxony: a member of the Hanseatic League. Pop.: 106 095 (1995 est.).

hill (hɪl) *n* **1a** a natural elevation of the earth's surface, less high or craggy than a mountain. **1b** (*in combination*): *a hillside.* **2a** a heap or mound. **2b** (*in combination*): *a dunghill.* **3** an incline; slope. **4 over the hill. 4a** *Inf.* beyond one's prime. **4b** *Mil. sl.* absent without leave or deserting. ◆ *vb* (*tr*) **5** to form into a hill. **6** to cover or surround with a heap of earth. [OE *hyll*]
▸ **'hilly** *adj*

Hill ★ (hɪl) *n* **1 Archibald Vivian.** 1886–1977, British biochemist, noted for his research into heat loss in muscle contraction: shared the Nobel prize for physiology or medicine (1922). **2 Damon Graham Devereux,** son of Graham Hill. born 1960, British motor-racing driver. **3 Geoffrey (William).** born 1932, British poet: his books include *King Log* (1968) and *The Triumph of Love* (1999). **4 Graham.** 1929–75, British motor-racing driver. **5 Octavia.** 1838–1912, British housing reformer; a founder of the National Trust. **6 Sir Rowland.** 1795–1879, British originator of the penny postage.

Hilla ★ ('hɪlə) *n* a market town in central Iraq, on a branch of the Euphrates: built partly of bricks from the nearby site of Babylon. Pop.: 268 834 (1987). Also called: **Al Hillah.**

Hillary ★ ('hɪlərɪ) *n* **Sir Edmund.** born 1919, New Zealand explorer and mountaineer. He was the first to reach the summit of Mount Everest (1953); New Zealand ambassador to India (1984–89).

hillbilly ('hɪl‚bɪlɪ) *n, pl* **hillbillies. 1** *Usually disparaging.* an unsophisticated person, esp. from the mountainous areas in the southeastern US. **2** another name for **country and western.** [C20: from HILL + *Billy* (the nickname)]

Hillel ★ ('hɪlel, -ləl) *n* ?60 B.C.–?9 A.D., rabbi, born in Babylonia; president of the Sanhedrin. He was the first to formulate principles of biblical interpretation.

Hiller ★ ('hɪlə) *n* **Dame Wendy.** born 1912, British actress. Her many films include *Pygmalion* (1938) and *Separate Tables* (1958).

Hilliard ★ ('hɪlɪəd) *n* **Nicholas.** 1537–1619, English miniaturist, esp. of portraits.

Hillingdon ★ ('hɪlɪŋdən) *n* a residential borough of W Greater London. Pop.: 243 000 (1994 est.). Area: 110 sq. km (43 sq. miles).

hillock ('hɪlək) *n* a small hill or mound. [C14 *hilloc*]
▸ **'hillocked** *or* **'hillocky** *adj*

hills (hɪlz) *pl n* **1 as old as the hills.** very old. **2 the.** a hilly and often remote region.

hill station *n* (in northern India, etc.) a settlement or resort at a high altitude.

hilt (hɪlt) *n* **1** the handle or shaft of a sword, dagger, etc. **2 to the hilt.** to the full. [OE]

hilum ('haɪləm) *n, pl* **hila** (-lə). *Bot.* a scar on a seed marking its point of attachment to the seed stalk. [C17: from L: trifle]

Hilversum ★ ('hɪlvəsəm; *Dutch* 'hɪlvərsym) *n* a city in the central Netherlands, in North Holland province: Dutch radio and television centre. Pop.: 84 213 (1994).

him (hɪm; *unstressed* ɪm) *pron* (*objective*) refers to a male person or animal: *they needed him; she baked him a cake; not him again!* [OE *him*, dative of *hē* HE]

HIM *abbrev. for* His (*or* Her) Imperial Majesty.

Himachal Pradesh ★ (hɪ'mɑːtʃəl prɑː'deʃ) *n* a state of N India, in the W Himalayas: rises to about 6700 m (22 000 ft) and is densely forested. Capital: Simla. Pop.: 5 530 000 (1994 est.). Area: 55 658 sq. km (21 707 sq. miles).

Himalayas ★ (‚hɪmə'leɪəz, hɪ'mɑːljəz) *pl n* **the.** a vast mountain system in S Asia, extending 2400 km (1500 miles) from Kashmir (west) to Assam (east), between the valleys of the Rivers Indus and Brahmaputra: covers most of Nepal, Sikkim, Bhutan, and the S edge of Tibet; the highest range in the world, with several peaks over

---

★ people and places

7500 m (25 000 ft). Highest peak: Mount Everest, 8848 m (29 028 ft).
> ˌHima'layan adj

himation (hɪ'mætɪˌɒn) n, pl **himatia** (-ɪə). (in ancient Greece) a cloak draped around the body. [C19: from Gk, from *heima* dress, from *hennunai* to clothe]

Himeji ★ ('hiːmeˌdʒiː) n a city in central Japan, on W Honshu: cotton textile centre. Pop.: 470 986 (1995).

Himmler ★ (*German* 'hɪmlər) n **Heinrich** ('haɪnrɪç). 1900–45, German Nazi leader, head of the SS and the Gestapo (1936–45); committed suicide.

Hims ★ (hɪmz) n a former name of **Homs**.

himself (hɪm'sɛlf; *medially often* ɪm'sɛlf) pron **1a** the reflexive form of *he* or *him*. **1b** (intensifier): *the king himself waved to me.* **2** (*preceded by a copula*) his normal self: *he seems himself once more.* [OE *him selfum*, dative sing of *hē self*; see HE, SELF]

Hinayana (ˌhiːnə'jɑːnə) n any of various early forms of Buddhism. [from Sansk., from *hīna* lesser + *yāna* vehicle]

Hinckley ★ ('hɪŋklɪ) n a town in central England, in Leicestershire. Pop.: 40 608 (1991 est.).

hind[1] (haɪnd) adj **hinder, hindmost** *or* **hindermost**. (*prenominal*) (esp. of parts of the body) situated at the back: *a hind leg.* [OE *hindan* at the back, rel. to G *hinten*]

hind[2] (haɪnd) n, pl **hinds** *or* **hind**. **1** the female of the deer, esp. the red deer when aged three years or more. **2** any of several marine fishes related to the groper. [OE *hind*]

hind[3] (haɪnd) n (formerly) **1** a simple peasant. **2** (in Scotland and N England) a skilled farm worker. **3** a steward. [OE *hīne*, from *hīgna*, genitive pl of *hīgan* servants]

Hindemith ★ (*German* 'hɪndəmɪt) n **Paul** (paul). 1895–1963, German composer and music theorist, who opposed the twelve-tone technique. His works include the song cycle *Das Marienleben* (1923) and the opera *Mathis der Maler* (1938).

Hindenburg[1] ★ ('hɪndənburk) n the German name for **Zabrze**.

Hindenburg[2] ★ ('hɪndənˌbɜːg; *German* 'hɪndənburk) n **Paul von Beneckendorff und von** (paul fɔn 'benəkəndɔrf unt fɔn). 1847–1934, German field marshal and statesman; president (1925–34). During World War I he directed German strategy.

hinder[1] ('hɪndə) vb **1** to be or get in the way of (someone or something); hamper. **2** (*tr*) to prevent. [OE *hindrian*]

hinder[2] ('haɪndə) adj (*prenominal*) situated at or further towards the back; posterior. [OE]

Hindi ('hɪndɪ) n **1** a language or group of dialects of N central India. See also **Hindustani**. **2** a formal literary dialect of this language, the official language of India. **3** a person whose native language is Hindi. [C18: from Hindi, from *Hind* India, from OPersian *Hindu* the river Indus]

hindmost ('haɪndˌməʊst) *or* **hindermost** ('hɪndəˌməʊst) adj furthest back; last.

Hindoo ('hɪnduː, hɪn'duː) n, pl **Hindoos**, adj an older spelling of **Hindu**.
> ˈHindooˌism n

hindquarter ('haɪndˌkwɔːtə) n **1** one of the two back quarters of a carcass of beef, lamb, etc. **2** (*pl*) the rear, esp. of a four-legged animal.

hindrance ('hɪndrəns) n **1** an obstruction or snag; impediment. **2** the act of hindering.

hindsight ('haɪndˌsaɪt) n **1** the ability to understand, after something has happened, what should have been done. **2** a firearm's rear sight.

Hindu ('hɪnduː, hɪn'duː) n, pl **Hindus**. **1** a person who adheres to Hinduism. **2** an inhabitant or native of Hindustan or India. ◆ adj **3** relating to Hinduism, Hindus, or India. [C17: from Persian *Hindū*, from *Hind* India; see HINDI]

Hinduism ('hɪnduːˌɪzəm) n the complex of beliefs and customs comprising the dominant religion of India, characterized by the worship of many gods, a caste system, belief in reincarnation, etc.

Hindu Kush ★ (kʊʃ, kuːʃ) pl n a mountain range in central Asia, extending about 800 km (500 miles) east from the Koh-i-Baba Mountains of central Afghanistan to the Pamirs. Highest peak: Tirich Mir, 7690 m (25 230 ft).

Hindustan ★ (ˌhɪndʊ'stɑːn) n **1** the land of the Hindus esp. India north of the Deccan and excluding Bengal. **2** the general area around the Ganges where Hindi is the predominant language. **3** the areas of India where Hinduism predominates, as contrasted with those areas where Islam predominates.

Hindustani (ˌhɪndʊ'stɑːnɪ) n **1** the dialect of Hindi spoken in Delhi: used as a lingua franca throughout India. **2** all the spoken forms of Hindi and Urdu considered together. ◆ adj **3** of or relating to these languages or Hindustan.

Hines ★ (haɪnz) n **Earl**, known as *Earl "Fatha" Hines*. 1905–83, US jazz pianist and songwriter.

hinge (hɪndʒ) n **1** a device for holding together two parts such that one can swing relative to the other. **2** a natural joint, such as the knee joint, that functions in only one plane. **3** a similar structure in invertebrate animals, such as the joint between the two halves of a bivalve shell. **4** something on which events, opinions, etc., turn. **5** Also called: **mount**. *Philately*. a small transparent strip of gummed paper for affixing a stamp to a page. ◆ vb **hinges, hinging, hinged**. **6** (*tr*) to fit a hinge to (something). **7** (*intr*; usually foll. by *on* or *upon*) to depend (on). **8** (*intr*) to hang or turn on or as if on a hinge. [C13: prob. of Gmc origin]
> **hinged** adj

hinny[1] ('hɪnɪ) n, pl **hinnies**. the sterile hybrid offspring of a male horse and a female donkey. [C19: from L *hinnus*, from Gk *hinnos*]

hinny[2] ('hɪnɪ) n *Scot. & N English dialect*. a term of endearment, esp. for a woman. [var. of HONEY]

Hi-NRG (ˌhaɪ'enədʒɪ) n a type of dance music, originating in the late 1980s, that has a very fast tempo and a strong beat. [C20: from HIGH + ENERGY]

hint (hɪnt) n **1** a suggestion given in an indirect or subtle manner. **2** a helpful piece of advice. **3** a small amount; trace. ◆ vb **4** (when *intr*, often foll. by *at*; when *tr*, *takes a clause as object*) to suggest indirectly. [C17: from ?]

hinterland ('hɪntəˌlænd) n **1** land lying behind something, esp. a coast or the shore of a river. **2** remote or undeveloped areas. **3** an area near and dependent on a large city, esp. a port. [C19: from G, from *hinter* behind + *land* LAND]

hip[1] (hɪp) n **1** (*often pl*) either side of the body below the waist and above the thigh. **2** another name for **pelvis** (sense 1). **3** short for **hip joint**. **4** the angle formed where two sloping sides of a roof meet. [OE *hype*]
> 'hipless adj

hip[2] (hɪp) n the berry-like brightly coloured fruit of a rose plant. Also called: **rosehip**. [OE *héopa*]

hip[3] (hɪp) interj an exclamation used to introduce cheers (in *hip, hip, hurrah*). [C18: from ?]

hip[4] (hɪp) adj **hipper, hippest**. *Sl*. **1** aware of or following the latest trends. **2** (*often postpositive*; foll. by *to*) informed (about). [var. of earlier *hep*]

hip bath n a portable bath in which the bather sits.

hipbone ('hɪpˌbəʊn) n the nontechnical name for **innominate bone**.

hip flask n a small metal flask for spirits, etc.

hip-hop ('hɪpˌhɒp) n a US pop culture movement of the 1980s comprising rap music, graffiti, and break dancing.

hip joint n the ball-and-socket joint that connects each leg to the trunk of the body.

Hipparchus ★ (hɪ'pɑːkəs) n **1** 2nd century B.C., Greek astronomer. He discovered the precession of the equinoxes, calculated the length of the solar year, and developed trigonometry. **2** died 514 B.C., tyrant of Athens (527–514).

hippeastrum (ˌhɪpɪ'æstrəm) n any plant of a South American genus cultivated for their large funnel-shaped typically red flowers. [C19: NL, from Gk *hippeus* knight + *astron* star]

hipped[1] (hɪpt) adj **1a** having a hip or hips. **1b** (*in combination*): *broad-hipped*. **2** (esp. of cows, sheep, etc.) having an injury to the hip, such as a dislocation. **3** *Archit.* having a hip or hips: *hipped roof.*

hipped² (hıpt) *adj* (*often postpositive;* foll. by *on*) *US & Canad. dated sl.* very enthusiastic. [C20: from HIP⁴]

hippie *n, pl* **hippies.** a variant of **hippy**¹.

hippo ('hıpəu) *n, pl* **hippos.** *Inf.* short for **hippopotamus.**

hippocampus (ˌhıpəu'kæmpəs) *n, pl* **hippocampi** (-paı). **1** a mythological sea creature with the forelegs of a horse and the tail of a fish. **2** any of various small sea fishes with a horselike head; sea horse. **3** an area of cerebral cortex that forms a ridge in the floor of the brain, which in cross section has the shape of a sea horse. It functions as part of the limbic system. [C16: from L, from Gk *hippos* horse + *kampos* a sea monster]

hippocras ('hıpəuˌkræs) *n* an old English drink of wine flavoured with spices. [C14 *ypocras*, from OF: HIPPOCRATES, prob. referring to a filter called *Hippocrates' sleeve*]

Hippocrates ★ (hı'pɒkrəˌtiːz) *n* ?460–?377 B.C., Greek physician, commonly regarded as the father of medicine.
  ▸ **Hippocratic** (ˌhıpəu'krætık) *or* **Hippo'cratical** *adj*

Hippocratic oath *n* an oath taken by a doctor to observe a code of medical ethics derived from that of Hippocrates.

Hippocrene ★ ('hıpəuˌkriːn, ˌhıpəu'kriːnı) *n* a spring on Mount Helicon in Greece, said to engender poetic inspiration. [C17: via L from Gk *hippos* horse + *krēnē* spring]
  ▸ **ˌHippo'crenian** *adj*

hippodrome ('hıpəˌdrəum) *n* **1** a music hall, variety theatre, or circus. **2** (in ancient Greece or Rome) an open-air course for horse and chariot races. [C16: from L *hippodromos*, from Gk *hippos* horse + *dromos* race]

hippogriff *or* **hippogryph** ('hıpəuˌgrıf) *n* a monster with a griffin's head, wings, and claws and a horse's body. [C17: from It. *ippogrifo*, from *ippo-* horse (from Gk) + *grifo* GRIFFIN]

Hippolyta (hı'pɒlıtə) *or* **Hippolyte** ★ (hı'pɒlıˌtiː) *n Greek myth.* a queen of the Amazons, slain by Hercules in battle for her belt, which he obtained as his ninth labour.

Hippolytus ★ (hı'pɒlıtəs) *n Greek myth.* a son of Theseus, killed after his stepmother Phaedra falsely accused him of raping her.
  ▸ **Hip'polytan** *adj*

Hippomenes (hı'pɒmıˌniːz) *n Greek myth.* the husband, in some traditions, of Atalanta.

hippopotamus (ˌhıpə'pɒtəməs) *n, pl* **hippopotamuses** *or* **hippopotami** (-ˌmaı). a very large gregarious mammal living in or around the rivers of tropical Africa. [C16: from L, from Gk: river horse, from *hippos* horse + *potamos* river]

Hippo Regius ★ ('hıpəu 'riːdʒıəs) *n* an ancient Numidian city, adjoining present-day Annaba, Algeria. Often shortened to **Hippo.**

hippy¹ *or* **hippie** ('hıpı) *n, pl* **hippies.** (esp. during the 1960s) a person whose behaviour, dress, use of drugs, etc., implies a rejection of conventional values. [C20: see HIP⁴]

hippy² ('hıpı) *adj* **hippier, hippiest.** *Inf.* (esp. of a woman) having large hips.

hip roof *n* a roof having sloping ends and sides.

hipster ('hıpstə) *n* **1** *Sl.,* now rare. **1a** an enthusiast of modern jazz. **1b** an outmoded word for **hippy**¹. **2** (*modifier*) (of trousers) cut so that the top encircles the hips.

hipsters ('hıpstəz) *pl n Brit.* trousers cut so that the top encircles the hips. Usual US word: **hip-huggers.**

Hiram ★ ('haıərəm) *n* 10th century B.C., king of Tyre, who supplied Solomon with materials and craftsmen for the building of the Temple (II Samuel 5:11; I Kings 5:1–18).

hircine ('hɜːsaın, -sın) *adj* **1** *Arch.* of or like a goat. **2** *Literary.* lascivious. [C17: from L *hircīnus,* from *hircus* goat]

hire ('haıə) *vb* **hires, hiring, hired.** (*tr*) **1** to acquire the temporary use of (a thing) or the services of (a person) in exchange for payment. **2** to employ (a person) for wages. **3** (often foll. by *out*) to provide (something) or the services

of (oneself or others) for payment, usually for an agreed period. **4** (foll. by *out*) *Chiefly Brit.* to pay independent contractors for (work to be done). ◆ *n* **5a** the act of hiring or the state of being hired. **5b** (*as modifier*): *a hire car.* **6** the price for a person's services or the temporary use of something. **7 for** *or* **on hire.** available for hire. [OE *hȳrian*]
  ▸ **'hirable** *or* **'hireable** *adj* ▸ **'hirer** *n*

hireling ('haıəlıŋ) *n Derog.* a person who works only for money. [OE *hȳrling*]

hire-purchase *n Brit.* a system in which a buyer takes possession of merchandise on payment of a deposit and completes the purchase by paying a series of instalments while the seller retains ownership until the final instalment is paid. Abbrev.: **HP, h.p.** US and Canad. equivalents: **installment plan, instalment plan.**

Hirohito ★ (ˌhıərəu'hiːtəu) *n* 1901–89, emperor of Japan 1926–89. In 1946 he became a constitutional monarch.

Hiroshige ★ (ˌhıərəu'ʃiːgeı) *n* **Ando** ('ɑːndəu). 1797–1858, Japanese artist, esp. of colour wood-block prints.

Hiroshima ★ (ˌhırɒ'ʃiːmə, hı'rɒʃımə) *n* a port in SW Japan, on SW Honshu on the delta of the Ota River: largely destroyed on August 6, 1945, by the first atomic bomb to be used in warfare, dropped by the US, which killed over 75 000 of its inhabitants. Pop.: 1 108 868 (1995).

Hirst ★ (hɜːst) *n* **Damien.** born 1965, British artist.

hirsute ('hɜːsjuːt) *adj* **1** covered with hair. **2** (of plants) covered with long but not stiff hairs. **3** (of a person) having long, thick, or untrimmed hair. [C17: from L *hirsūtus* shaggy]
  ▸ **'hirsuteness** *n*

his (hız; *unstressed* ız) *determiner* **1a** of, belonging to, or associated with him: *his knee; I don't like his being out so late.* **1b** (*as pron*): *his is on the left; that book is his.* **2 his and hers.** for a man and woman respectively. ◆ *pron* **3 of his.** belonging to him. [OE *his,* genitive of *hē* HE & of *hit* IT]

Hispania ★ (hı'speınıə) *n* the Iberian peninsula in the Roman world. [L *Hispania* Spain]

Hispanic (hı'spænık) *adj* **1** of or derived from Spain or the Spanish. ◆ *n* **2** *US.* a US citizen of Latin-American descent.
  ▸ **His'panicism** *n*

Hispaniola ★ (ˌhıspən'jəulə; *Spanish* ispa'ɲola) *n* the second largest island in the Caribbean, in the Greater Antilles: divided politically into Haiti and the Dominican Republic; discovered in 1492 by Christopher Columbus, who named it La Isla Española. Area: 18 703 sq. km (29 418 sq. miles). Former name: **Santo Domingo.**

hispid ('hıspıd) *adj Biol.* covered with stiff hairs or bristles. [C17: from L *hispidus* bristly]

hiss (hıs) *n* **1** a sound like that of a prolonged *s.* **2** such a sound as an exclamation of derision, contempt, etc. ◆ *vb* **3** (*intr*) to produce or utter a hiss. **4** (*tr*) to express with a hiss. **5** (*tr*) to show derision or anger towards (a speaker, performer, etc.) by hissing. [C14: imit.]

Hiss ★ (hıs) *n* **Alger** ('ældʒə). 1904–96, US politician: imprisoned (1950–54) for perjury in connection with alleged espionage activities.

hist (hıst) *interj* an exclamation used to attract attention or as a warning to be silent.

histamine ('hıstəˌmiːn) *n* an amine released by the body tissues in allergic reactions, causing irritation. [C20: from HIST- + AMINE]
  ▸ **histaminic** (ˌhıstə'mınık) *adj*

histo- *or before a vowel* **hist-** *combining form.* indicating animal or plant tissue: *histology; histochemistry.* [from Gk, from *histos* web]

histogenesis (ˌhıstəu'dʒenısıs) *n* the formation of tissues and organs from undifferentiated cells.
  ▸ **histogenetic** (ˌhıstəudʒə'netık) *or* **ˌhisto'genic** *adj*

histogram ('hıstəˌgræm) *n* a statistical graph that represents the frequency of values of a quantity by vertical rectangles of varying heights and widths. [C20: ?from HISTO(RY) + -GRAM]

histology (hı'stɒlədʒı) *n* the study of the tissues of an animal or plant.
  ▸ **histological** (ˌhıstə'lɒdʒık°l) *or* **ˌhisto'logic** *adj*

histolysis (hɪˈstɒlɪsɪs) *n* the disintegration of organic tissues.
▶ **histolytic** (ˌhɪstəˈlɪtɪk) *adj*

historian (hɪˈstɔːrɪən) *n* a person who writes or studies history, esp. one who is an authority on it.

historic (hɪˈstɒrɪk) *adj* **1** famous in history; significant. **2** *Linguistics.* (of Latin, Greek, or Sanskrit verb tenses) referring to past time.

> USAGE NOTE A distinction is usually made between *historic* (important, significant) and *historical* (pertaining to history): *a historic decision; a historical perspective.*

historical (hɪˈstɒrɪkᵊl) *adj* **1** belonging to or typical of the study of history: *historical methods.* **2** concerned with events of the past: *historical accounts.* **3** based on or constituting factual material as distinct from legend or supposition. **4** based on history: *a historical novel.* **5** occurring in history.
▶ **hisˈtorically** *adv*

> USAGE NOTE See at **historic.**

historical-cost accounting *n* a method of accounting that values assets at the original cost. In times of high inflation profits can be overstated. Cf. **current-cost accounting.**

historical linguistics *n* (*functioning as sing*) the study of language as it changes in the course of time.

historical present *n* the present tense used to narrate past events, employed for effect or in informal use, as in *a week ago I see this accident.*

historicism (hɪˈstɒrɪˌsɪzəm) *n* **1** the belief that natural laws govern historical events. **2** the doctrine that each period of history has its own beliefs and values inapplicable to any other. **3** excessive emphasis on history, past styles, etc.
▶ **hisˈtoricist** *n, adj*

historicity (ˌhɪstəˈrɪsɪtɪ) *n* historical authenticity.

historiographer (hɪˌstɔːrɪˈɒɡrəfə) *n* **1** a historian, esp. one concerned with historical method. **2** a historian employed to write the history of a group or public institution.
▶ **hiˌstoriˈography** *n*

history (ˈhɪstərɪ) *n, pl* **-ries. 1** a record or account of past events, developments, etc. **2** all that is preserved of the past, esp. in written form. **3** the discipline of recording and interpreting past events. **4** past events, esp. when considered as an aggregate. **5** an event in the past, esp. one that has been reduced in importance: *their quarrel was just history.* **6** the past, previous experiences, etc., of a thing or person: *the house had a strange history.* **7** a play that depicts historical events. **8** a narrative relating the events of a character's life: *the history of Joseph Andrews.* [C15: from L *historia*, from Gk: inquiry, from *historein* to narrate, from *histōr* judge]

histrionic (ˌhɪstrɪˈɒnɪk) *adj* **1** excessively dramatic or artificial: *histrionic gestures.* **2** *Now rare.* dramatic. ◆ *n* **3** (*pl*) melodramatic displays of temperament. **4** *Rare.* (*pl; functioning as sing*) dramatics. [C17: from LL *histriōnicus*, from L *histriō* actor]
▶ **ˌhistriˈonically** *adv*

hit (hɪt) *vb* **hits, hitting, hit.** (*mainly tr*) **1** (*also intr*) to deal (a blow) to (a person or thing); strike. **2** to come into violent contact with: *the car hit the tree.* **3** to strike with a missile: *to hit a target.* **4** to knock or bump: *I hit my arm on the table.* **5** to propel by striking: *to hit a ball.* **6** *Cricket.* to score (runs). **7** to affect (a person, place, or thing), esp. suddenly or adversely: *his illness hit his wife very hard.* **8** to reach: *unemployment hit a new high.* **9** to experience: *I've hit a slight snag here.* **10** *Sl.* to murder (a rival criminal) in fulfilment of an underworld vendetta. **11** *Inf.* to set out on: *let's hit the road.* **12** *Inf.* to arrive: *he will hit town tomorrow.* **13** *Inf., chiefly US & Canad.* to demand or request from: *he hit me for a pound.* **14 hit the bottle.** *Sl.* to drink an excessive amount of alcohol. ◆ *n* **15** an impact or collision. **16** a shot, blow, etc., that reaches its object. **17** an apt, witty, or telling remark. **18** *Inf.* **18a** a person or thing that gains wide appeal: *she's a hit with everyone.* **18b** (*as modifier*): *a hit record.* **19** *Inf.* a stroke of luck. **20** *Sl.* **20a** a murder carried out as the result of an underworld vendetta. **20b** (*as modifier*): *a hit squad.* **21** *Computing sl.* a single visit to a website. **22 make a hit with.** *Inf.* to make a favourable impression on. ◆ See also **hit off, hit on, hit out** [OE *hittan*, from ON *hitta*]
▶ **ˈhitter** *n*

Hitachi ★ (hɪˈtætʃɪ) *n* a city in Japan, in E Honshu: a centre of the electronics industry. Pop.: 199 241 (1995).

hit-and-miss *adj* *Inf.* random; haphazard: *a hit-and-miss affair; the technique is very hit and miss.* Also: **hit or miss.**

hit-and-run *adj* (*prenominal*) **1** denoting a motor-vehicle accident in which the driver leaves the scene without stopping to give assistance, inform the police, etc. **2** (of an attack, raid, etc.) relying on surprise allied to a rapid departure from the scene of operations: *hit-and-run tactics.*

hitch (hɪtʃ) *vb* **1** to fasten or become fastened with a knot or tie. **2** (*tr;* often foll. by *up*) to pull up (the trousers, etc.) with a quick jerk. **3** (*intr*) *Chiefly US.* to move in a halting manner. **4** (*tr; passive*) *Sl.* to marry (esp. in **get hitched**). **5** *Inf.* to obtain (a ride) by hitchhiking. ◆ *n* **6** an impediment or obstacle, esp. one that is temporary or minor. **7** a knot that can be undone by pulling against the direction of the strain that holds it. **8** a sudden jerk: *he gave it a hitch and it came loose.* **9** *Inf.* a ride obtained by hitchhiking. [C15: from ?]
▶ **ˈhitcher** *n*

Hitchcock ★ (ˈhɪtʃˌkɒk) *n* Sir **Alfred (Joseph).** 1899–1980, British film director, noted for his suspense films, such as *The Thirty-Nine Steps* (1935), *Psycho* (1960), and *The Birds* (1963).

hitchhike (ˈhɪtʃˌhaɪk) *vb* **hitchhikes, hitchhiking, hitchhiked.** (*intr*) to travel by obtaining free lifts in motor vehicles.
▶ **ˈhitchˌhiker** *n*

hi tech *or* **high tech** (tɛk) *n* **1** short for **high technology. 2** a style of interior design using features of industrial equipment. ◆ *adj* **hi-tech** *or* **high-tech. 3** designed for or using high technology. **4** of or in the interior design style. ◆ Cf. **low tech.**

hither (ˈhɪðə) *adv* **1** to or towards this place (esp. in **come hither**). **2 hither and thither.** this way and that, as in confusion. ◆ *adj* **3** *Arch. or dialect.* (of a side or part) nearer; closer. [OE *hider*]

hithermost (ˈhɪðəˌməʊst) *adj* *Now rare.* nearest to this place or in this direction.

hitherto (ˌhɪðəˈtuː) *adv, adj* until this time: *hitherto, there have been no problems; hitherto private aristocratic homes.*

Hitler ★ (ˈhɪtlə) *n* **1 Adolf** (ˈaːdɔlf). 1889–1945, German dictator, born in Austria. As president of the National Socialist German Workers' Party (Nazi party), he attempted to overthrow the government of Bavaria (1923); imprisoned, but eventually became chancellor of Germany (1933), transforming it into the Third Reich. He established concentration camps to exterminate the Jews, annexed (1938) Austria and Czechoslovakia, and invaded Poland (1939), which precipitated World War II; committed suicide. **2** a person who displays dictatorial characteristics.

Hitlerism (ˈhɪtləˌrɪzəm) *n* the policies, principles, and methods of the Nazi party as developed by Adolf Hitler.

hit list *n* *Inf.* **1** a list of people to be murdered: *a terrorist hit list.* **2** a list of targets to be eliminated in some way: *a hit list of pits to be closed.*

hit man *n* a hired assassin.

hit off *vb* **1** (*tr, adv*) to represent or mimic accurately. **2 hit it off with.** *Inf.* to have a good relationship with.

hit on *vb* (*prep*) **1** (*tr*) to discover unexpectedly or guess correctly. Also: **hit upon. 2** (*tr*) *US & Canad.* to make sexual advances to.

hit out *vb* (*intr, adv;* often foll. by *at*) **1** to direct blows forcefully and vigorously. **2** to make a verbal attack (upon someone).

> ★ people and places

Hittite ('hɪtaɪt) *n* **1** a member of an ancient people of Anatolia, who built a great empire in N Syria and Asia Minor in the second millennium B.C. **2** the extinct language of this people. ◆ *adj* **3** of or relating to this people, their civilization, or their language.

hit wicket *n Cricket.* an instance of a batsman breaking the wicket with the bat or a part of the body while playing a stroke and so being out.

HIV *abbrev. for* human immunodeficiency virus; the cause of AIDS.

hive (haɪv) *n* **1** a structure in which social bees live. **2** a colony of social bees. **3** a place showing signs of great industry (esp. in **a hive of activity**). **4** a teeming multitude. ◆ *vb* **hives, hiving, hived. 5** to cause (bees) to collect or (of bees) to collect inside a hive. **6** to live or cause to live in or as if in a hive. **7** (*tr*; often foll. by *up* or *away*) to store, esp. for future use. [OE *hȳf*]

hive off *vb* (*adv*) **1** to transfer or be transferred from a larger group or unit. **2** (*usually tr*) to transfer (profitable activities of a nationalized industry) back to private ownership.

hives (haɪvz) *n* (*functioning as sing or pl*) *Pathol.* a nontechnical name for **urticaria**. [C16: from ?]

hiya ('haɪjə, ˌhaɪ'jɑː) *sentence substitute.* an informal term of greeting. [C20: shortened from *how are you?*]

hl *abbrev. for* hectolitre.

HL (in Britain) *abbrev. for* House of Lords.

hm *symbol for* hectometre.

h'm (*spelling pron* hmmm) *interj* used to indicate hesitation, doubt, assent, pleasure, etc.

HM *abbrev. for:* **1** His (*or* Her) Majesty. **2** headmaster; headmistress.

HMAS *abbrev. for* His (*or* Her) Majesty's Australian Ship.

HMCS *abbrev. for* His (*or* Her) Majesty's Canadian Ship.

HMI (in Britain) *abbrev. for* His (*or* Her) Majesty's Inspector; a government official who examines and supervises schools.

H.M.S. *or* **HMS** *abbrev. for:* **1** His (*or* Her) Majesty's Service. **2** His (*or* Her) Majesty's Ship.

HMSO (in Britain) *abbrev. for* His (*or* Her) Majesty's Stationery Office.

HNC (in Britain) *abbrev. for* Higher National Certificate; a qualification recognized by many national technical and professional institutions.

HND (in Britain) *abbrev. for* Higher National Diploma; a qualification in technical subjects equivalent to a degree.

ho[1] (həʊ) *interj* **1** Also: **ho-ho.** an imitation or representation of a deep laugh. **2** an exclamation used to attract attention, etc. [C13: imit.]

ho[2] (həʊ) *n US Black sl.* a derogatory term for a woman. [C20: from Black or Southern US pronunciation of WHORE]

Ho *the chemical symbol for* holmium.

hoar (hɔː) *n* **1** short for **hoarfrost.** ◆ *adj* **2** *Rare.* covered with hoarfrost. **3** *Arch.* a poetic variant of **hoary.** [OE *hār*]

hoard (hɔːd) *n* **1** an accumulated store hidden away for future use. **2** a cache of ancient coins, etc. ◆ *vb* **3** to accumulate (a hoard). [OE *hord*]
▸ **'hoarder** *n*

> **USAGE NOTE** *Hoard* is sometimes wrongly written where *horde* is meant: *hordes* (not *hoards*) *of tourists.*

hoarding ('hɔːdɪŋ) *n* **1** Also called (esp. US and Canad.): **billboard.** a large board used for displaying advertising posters, as by a road. **2** a temporary wooden fence erected round a building or demolition site. [C19: from C15 *hoard* fence, from OF *hourd* palisade, of Gmc origin]

hoarfrost ('hɔːˌfrɒst) *n* a deposit of needle-like ice crystals formed on the ground by direct condensation at temperatures below freezing point. Also called: **white frost.**

hoarhound ('hɔːˌhaʊnd) *n* a variant spelling of **horehound.**

hoarse (hɔːs) *adj* **1** gratingly harsh in tone. **2** having a husky voice, as through illness, shouting, etc. [C14: from ON]
▸ **'hoarsely** *adv* ▸ **'hoarseness** *n*

hoarsen ('hɔːsᵊn) *vb* to make or become hoarse.

hoary ('hɔːrɪ) *adj* **hoarier, hoariest. 1** having grey or white hair. **2** white or whitish-grey in colour. **3** ancient or venerable.
▸ **'hoariness** *n*

hoatzin (həʊˈætsɪn) *n* a unique South American bird with clawed wing digits in the young. [C17: from American Sp., from Nahuatl *uatzin* pheasant]

hoax (həʊks) *n* **1** a deception, esp. a practical joke. ◆ *vb* **2** (*tr*) to deceive or play a joke on (someone). [C18: prob. from HOCUS]
▸ **'hoaxer** *n*

hob[1] (hɒb) *n* **1** the flat top part of a cooking stove, or a separate flat surface, containing hotplates or burners. **2** a shelf beside an open fire, for keeping kettles, etc., hot. **3** a steel pattern used in forming a mould or die in cold metal. [C16: var. of obs. *hubbe*; ? rel. to HUB]

hob[2] (hɒb) *n* **1** a hobgoblin or elf. **2 raise** *or* **play hob.** *US inf.* to cause mischief. **3** a male ferret. [C14: var. of *Rob*, short for *Robin* or *Robert*]

Hobart ★ ('həʊbɑːt) *n* a port in Australia, capital of the state of Tasmania on the estuary of the Derwent: natural harbour; University of Tasmania (1890). Pop.: 194 700 (1995 est.).

Hobbema ★ ('hɒbɪmə; *Dutch* 'hɔbəmɑː) *n* **Meindert** ('maɪndərt). 1638–1709, Dutch painter of peaceful landscapes, usually including a watermill.

Hobbes ★ (hɒbz) *n* **Thomas.** 1588–1679, English political philosopher. Best known for the *Leviathan* (1651).

hobbit ('hɒbɪt) *n* one of an imaginary race of half-size people living in holes. [C20: coined by J. R. R. Tolkien, with the meaning "hole-builder"]

hobble ('hɒbᵊl) *vb* **hobbles, hobbling, hobbled. 1** (*intr*) to walk with a lame awkward movement. **2** (*tr*) to fetter the legs of (a horse) in order to restrict movement. **3** (*intr*) to progress with difficulty. ◆ *n* **4** a strap, rope, etc., used to hobble a horse. **5** a limping gait. ◆ Also (for senses 2, 4): **hopple.** [C14: prob. from Low G]
▸ **'hobbler** *n*

hobbledehoy (ˌhɒbᵊldɪˈhɔɪ) *n* a clumsy or bad-mannered youth. [C16: from earlier *hobbard de hoy*, from ?]

Hobbs ★ (hɒbz) *n* Sir **John Berry**, known as *Jack Hobbs.* 1882–1963, British cricketer: scored 197 centuries.

hobby[1] ('hɒbɪ) *n, pl* **hobbies. 1** an activity pursued in spare time for pleasure or relaxation. **2** *Arch.* a small horse. **3** short for **hobbyhorse** (sense 1). **4** an early form of bicycle, without pedals. [C14 *hobyn*, prob. var. of name *Robin*]
▸ **'hobbyist** *n*

hobby[2] ('hɒbɪ) *n, pl* **hobbies.** any of several small Old World falcons. [C15: from OF *hobet*, from *hobe* falcon]

hobbyhorse ('hɒbɪˌhɔːs) *n* **1** a toy consisting of a stick with a figure of a horse's head at one end. **2** a rocking horse. **3** a figure of a horse attached to a performer's waist in a morris dance, etc. **4** a favourite topic (esp. in **on one's hobbyhorse**). [C16: from HOBBY[1], orig. a small horse; then generalized to apply to any pastime]

hobgoblin (ˌhɒbˈgɒblɪn) *n* **1** a mischievous goblin. **2** a bogey; bugbear. [C16: from HOB[2] + GOBLIN]

hobnail ('hɒbˌneɪl) *n* **a** a short nail with a large head for protecting the soles of heavy footwear. **b** (*as modifier*): *hobnail boots.* [C16: from HOB[1] (in archaic sense: peg) + NAIL]
▸ **'hob,nailed** *adj*

hobnob ('hɒbˌnɒb) *vb* **hobnobs, hobnobbing, hobnobbed.** (*intr*; often foll. by *with*) **1** to socialize or talk informally. **2** *Obs.* to drink (with). [C18: from *hob or nob* to drink to one another in turns, ult. from OE *habban* to HAVE + *nabban* not to have]

hobo ('həʊbəʊ) *n, pl* **hobos** *or* **hoboes.** *Chiefly US & Canad.* **1** a

tramp; vagrant. **2** a migratory worker. [C19 (US): from ?]
▶ 'hoboism n

Hoboken ★ ('həʊbəʊkən) n a city in N Belgium, in Antwerp province, on the River Scheldt. Pop.: 35 000 (latest est.).

Hobson's choice ('hɒbsⁿz) n the choice of taking what is offered or nothing at all. [C16: after Thomas Hobson (1544–1631), E liveryman who gave his customers no choice but had them take the nearest horse]

Hochhuth ★ (German 'hoːxhuːt) n **Rolf** (rɒlf). born 1933, Swiss dramatist. His best-known works are the controversial documentary drama *The Representative* (1963), on the papacy's attitude to the Jews in World War II, *Soldiers* (1967), and *Wessis in Weimar* (1992).

Ho Chi Minh ★ ('həʊ 'tʃiː 'mɪn) n original name *Nguyen That Tan*. 1890–1969, Vietnamese statesman; president of North Vietnam (1954–69). He headed the Vietminh (1941), which won independence for Vietnam from the French (1954).

Ho Chi Minh City ★ n a port in S Vietnam, 97 km (60 miles) from the South China Sea, on the Saigon River: captured by the French in 1859; merged with adjoining Cholon in 1932; capital of the former Republic of Vietnam (South Vietnam) from 1954 to 1976; university (1917); US headquarters during the Vietnam War. Pop.: 4 322 300 (1993 est.). Former name (until 1976): **Saigon**.

hock[1] (hɒk) n **1** the joint at the tarsus of a horse or similar animal, corresponding to the human ankle. ♦ vb **2** another word for **hamstring**. [C16: short for *hockshin*, from OE *hōhsinu* heel sinew]

hock[2] (hɒk) n any of several white wines from the German Rhine. [C17: short for obs. *hockamore* from G *Hochheimer*]

hock[3] (hɒk) *Inf., chiefly US & Canad.* ♦ vb **1** (tr) to pawn or pledge. ♦ n **2** the state of being in pawn. **3 in hock. 3a** in prison. **3b** in debt. **3c** in pawn. [C19: from Du. *hok* prison, debt]

hockey ('hɒkɪ) n **1** Also called (esp. US and Canad.): **field hockey**. a game played on a field by two opposing teams of 11 players each, who try to hit a ball into their opponents' goal using long sticks curved at the end. **2** See **ice hockey**. [C19: from earlier *hawkey*, from ?]

Hockney ★ ('hɒknɪ) n **David**. born 1937, British painter, known for his etchings, portraits, and paintings of aquatic themes.

hocus ('həʊkəs) vb **hocuses, hocusing, hocused** or **hocuses, hocussing, hocussed**. (tr) *Now rare*. **1** to trick. **2** to stupefy, esp. with a drug. **3** to drug (a drink).

hocus-pocus ('həʊkəs'pəʊkəs) n **1** trickery or chicanery. **2** an incantation used by conjurors or magicians. **3** conjuring skill. ♦ vb **hocus-pocuses, hocus-pocusing, hocus-pocused** or **hocus-pocuses, hocus-pocussing, hocus-pocussed**. **4** to deceive or trick (someone). [C17: ? dog Latin invented by jugglers]

hod (hɒd) n **1** an open wooden box attached to a pole, for carrying bricks, mortar, etc. **2** a tall narrow coal scuttle. [C14: ?from C13 dialect *hot*, from OF *hotte* pannier, prob. of Gmc origin]

Hodeida ★ (hɒ'deɪdə) n a port in N Yemen, on the Red Sea; formerly in North Yemen. Pop.: 155 100 (latest est.).

hodgepodge ('hɒdʒ,pɒdʒ) n a variant spelling (esp. US and Canad.) of **hotchpotch**.

Hodgkin ★ ('hɒdʒkɪn) n **1** Sir **Alan Lloyd**. 1914–98, British physiologist. With A. F. Huxley, he explained the conduction of nervous impulses: shared the Nobel prize for physiology or medicine (1963). **2** Dorothy Crowfoot. 1910–94, British chemist and crystallographer, who determined the three-dimensional structure of insulin: Nobel prize for chemistry (1964).

Hodgkin's disease n a malignant disease, a form of lymphoma, characterized by enlargement of the lymph nodes, spleen, and liver. [C19: after Thomas *Hodgkin* (1798–1866), London physician, who first described it]

hodograph ('hɒdə,grɑːf) n a curve of which the radius

vector represents the velocity of a moving particle. [C19: from Gk *hodos* way + -GRAPH]

hodometer (hɒ'dɒmɪtə) n another name for **odometer**.
▶ ho'dometry n

hoe (həʊ) n **1** any of several kinds of long-handled hand implement used to till the soil, weed, etc. ♦ vb **hoes, hoeing, hoed**. **2** to dig, scrape, weed, or till (surface soil) with or as if with a hoe. [C14: via OF *houe*, of Gmc origin]
▶ 'hoer n

hoedown ('həʊ,daʊn) n US & Canad. **1** a boisterous square dance. **2** a party at which hoedowns are danced.

Hoek van Holland ★ ('huːk fan 'hɒlant) n the Dutch name for the **Hook of Holland**.

Hofei ★ ('həʊ'feɪ) n a variant transliteration of the Chinese name for **Hefei**.

Hoffman ★ ('hɒfmən) n **Dustin** (**Lee**) born 1937, US actor. His films include *Midnight Cowboy* (1969), *Rain Man* (1989), and *Wag the Dog* (1998).

Hofmannsthal ★ (German 'hoːfmanstaːl) n **Hugo von** ('huːgo fɒn). 1874–1929, Austrian poet and dramatist, noted as the librettist for Richard Strauss's operas.

Hofuf ★ (hʊ'fuːf) n another name for **Al Hufuf**.

hog (hɒg) n **1** a domesticated pig, esp. a castrated male. **2** US & Canad. any mammal of the family Suidae; pig. **3** Also: **hogg**. *Dialect, Austral. & NZ.* another name for **hogget**. **4** *Inf.* a greedy person. **5 go the whole hog**. *Sl.* to do something thoroughly or unreservedly. ♦ vb **hogs, hogging, hogged**. (tr) **6** *Sl.* to take more than one's share of. **7** to arch (the back) like a hog. **8** to cut (the mane) of (a horse) very short. [OE *hogg*, of Celtic origin]
▶ 'hogger n ▶ 'hog,like adj

hogan ('həʊgən) n a wooden dwelling covered with earth, typical of the Navaho Indians of North America. [of Amerind origin]

Hogarth ★ ('həʊgaːθ) n **William**. 1697–1764, English engraver and painter. His engravings satirizing the vices and affectations of his age, include *A Rake's Progress* (1735) and *Marriage à la Mode* (1745).
▶ Ho'garthian adj

hogback ('hɒg,bæk) n **1** Also called: **hog's back**. a narrow ridge with steep sides. **2** *Archaeol.* a tomb with sloping sides.

hogfish ('hɒg,fɪʃ) n, pl **hogfish** or **hogfishes**. a wrasse that occurs in the Atlantic. The head of the male resembles a pig's snout.

Hogg ★ (hɒg) n **1** James, known as *the Ettrick Shepherd*. 1770–1835, Scottish writer. His works include the poems *The Queen's Wake* (1813) and the novel *The Confessions of a Justified Sinner* (1824). **2** Quintin. See (1st Baron) **Hailsham of St Marylebone**.

hogget ('hɒgɪt) n *Dialect, Austral. & NZ.* a young sheep that has yet to be sheared. Also: **hog, hogg**.

hoggish ('hɒgɪʃ) adj selfish, gluttonous, or dirty.

Hogmanay (,hɒgmə'neɪ) n (*sometimes not cap.*) New Year's Eve in Scotland. [C17: ?from Norman F *hoguinane*, from OF *aguillanneuf* a New Year's Eve gift]

hognose snake ('hɒg,nəʊz) n a North American nonvenomous snake that has a trowel-shaped snout and inflates its body when alarmed. Also called: **puff adder**.

hogshead ('hɒgz,hed) n **1** a unit of capacity, used esp. for alcoholic beverages. It has several values. **2** a large cask. [C14: from ?]

hogtie ('hɒg,taɪ) vb **hogties, hogtying, hogtied**. (tr) *Chiefly US.* **1** to tie together the legs or the arms and legs of. **2** to impede, hamper, or thwart.

hogwash ('hɒg,wɒʃ) n **1** *Inf.* nonsense. **2** pigswill.

hogweed ('hɒg,wiːd) n any of several coarse weedy plants.

Hohenlohe ★ ('həʊən,ləʊə; German hoːən'loːə) n **Chlodwig** ('kloːtvɪç), Prince of Hohenlohe-Schillingsfürst. 1819–1901, Prussian statesman; chancellor of the German empire (1894–1900).

Hohenstaufen ★ ('həʊən,ʃtaʊfən; German hoːən'ʃtaʊfən) n a German princely family that provided rulers of Germany (1138–1208, 1215–54), Sicily (1194–1268), and the Holy Roman Empire (1138–1254).

★ people and places

Hohenzollern ★ ('həʊən‚zɒlən; *German* hoːən'tsɔlərn) *n* a German noble family, the younger (Franconian) branch of which provided rulers of Brandenburg (1417–1701) and Prussia (1701–1918). The last kings of Prussia (1871–1918) were also emperors of Germany.

Hohhot ('hɒ'hɒt), **Huhehot**, *or* **Hu-ho-hao-t'e** ★ *n* a city in N China, capital of Inner Mongolia Autonomous Region (since 1954) and capital of the former Suiyüan province; Inner Mongolia University (1957). Pop.: 652 534 (1990 est.).

ho-hum ('həʊ'hʌm) *adj Inf.* lacking interest or inspiration; dull; mediocre: *a ho-hum collection of new releases.*

hoick (hɔɪk) *vb* to rise or raise abruptly and sharply. [C20: from ?]

hoi polloi ('hɔɪ pə'lɔɪ) *n* **the.** *Often derog.* the masses; common people. [Gk, lit.: the many]

hoist (hɔɪst) *vb* **1** (*tr*) to raise or lift up, esp. by mechanical means. ◆ *n* **2** any apparatus or device for hoisting. **3** the act of hoisting. **4** *Naut.* a group of signal flags. **5** the inner edge of a flag next to the staff. [C16: var. of *hoise*, prob. from Low G]
▸ **'hoister** *n*

hoity-toity (‚hɔɪtɪ'tɔɪtɪ) *adj Inf.* arrogant or haughty. [C17: rhyming compound based on C16 *hoit* to romp, from ?]

hokey cokey ('həʊkɪ 'kəʊkɪ) *n* a dance routine performed to a cockney song of the same name.

Hokkaido ★ (hɒ'kaɪdəʊ) *n* the second largest and northernmost of the four main islands of Japan, separated from Honshu by the Tsugaru Strait and from the island of Sakhalin, Russia, by La Pérouse Strait: constitutes an autonomous administrative division. Capital: Sapporo. Pop.: 5 692 000 (1995). Area: 78 508 sq. km (30 312 sq. miles).

hokonui (‚həʊkə'nuːi) *n NZ.* illicit whisky. [from *Hokonui*, district of Southland region, NZ]

hokum ('həʊkəm) *n Sl.*, chiefly *US & Canad.* **1** claptrap; bunk. **2** obvious or hackneyed material of a sentimental nature in a play, film, etc. [C20: prob. a blend of HOCUS-POCUS & BUNKUM]

Hokusai ★ ('həʊkuːˌsaɪ, ‚həʊkuː'saɪ) *n* **Katsushika** (‚kætsuː-'jiːkə). 1760–1849, Japanese artist.

Holarctic (həʊ'lɑːktɪk) *adj* of or denoting a zoogeographical region consisting of the entire arctic regions. [C19: from HOLO- + ARCTIC]

Holbein ★ (*German* 'hɒlbaɪn) *n* **1 Hans** (hans), known as *Holbein the Elder.* 1465–1524, German painter. **2** his son, **Hans,** known as *Holbein the Younger.* 1497–1543, German painter and engraver; court painter to Henry VIII of England (1536–43), noted for his portraits.

hold[1] (həʊld) *vb* **holds, holding, held.** **1** to have or keep (an object) with or within the hands, arms, etc.; clasp. **2** (*tr*) to support: *to hold a drowning man's head above water.* **3** to maintain or be maintained in a specified state: *to hold firm.* **4** (*tr*) to set aside or reserve: *they will hold our tickets until tomorrow.* **5** (when *intr*, usually used in commands) to restrain or be restrained from motion, action, departure, etc.: *hold that man until the police come.* **6** (*intr*) to remain fast or unbroken: *that cable won't hold much longer.* **7** (*intr*) (of the weather) to remain dry and bright. **8** (*tr*) to keep the attention of. **9** (*tr*) to engage in or carry on: *to hold a meeting.* **10** (*tr*) to have the ownership, possession, etc., of: *he holds a law degree; who's holding the ace?* **11** (*tr*) to have the use of or responsibility for: *to hold office.* **12** (*tr*) to have the capacity for: *the carton will hold eight books.* **13** (*tr*) to be able to control the outward effects of drinking beer, spirits, etc. **14** (often foll. by *to* or *by*) to remain or cause to remain committed (to): *hold him to his promise.* **15** (*tr; takes a clause as object*) to claim: *he holds that the theory is incorrect.* **16** (*intr*) to remain relevant, valid, or true: *the old philosophies don't hold nowadays.* **17** (*tr*) to consider in a specified manner: *I hold him very dear.* **18** (*tr*) to defend successfully: *hold the fort against the attack.* **19** (sometimes foll. by *on*) *Music.* to sustain the sound of (a note) throughout its specified duration. **20** (*tr*) *Computing.* to retain (data) in a storage device after copying onto another storage device or location. **21 hold (good) for.** to apply or be relevant to: *the same rules hold for everyone.* **22**

there is no holding him. he is so spirited that he cannot be restrained. ◆ *n* **23** the act or method of holding fast or grasping. **24** something to hold onto, as for support or control. **25** an object or device that holds fast or grips something else. **26** controlling influence: *she has a hold on him.* **27** a short pause. **28** a prison or a cell in a prison. **29** *Wrestling.* a way of seizing one's opponent. **30** *Music.* a pause or fermata. **31a** a tenure, esp. of land. **31b** (*in combination*): *freehold.* **32** *Arch.* a fortified place. **33 no holds barred.** all limitations removed. ◆ *See also* **hold back, hold down,** etc. [OE *healdan*]
▸ **'holdable** *adj*

hold[2] (həʊld) *n* the space in a ship or aircraft for storing cargo. [C16: var. of HOLE]

holdall ('həʊld‚ɔːl) *n Brit.* a large strong bag or basket. Usual *US* and *Canad.* name: **carryall.**

hold back *vb* (*adv*) **1** to restrain or be restrained. **2** (*tr*) to withhold: *he held back part of the payment.*

hold down *vb* (*tr, adv*) **1** to restrain or control. **2** *Inf.* to manage to retain or keep possession of: *to hold down two jobs at once.*

holder ('həʊldə) *n* **1** a person or thing that holds. **2a** a person who has possession or control of something. **2b** (*in combination*): *householder.* **3** *Law.* a person who has possession of a bill of exchange, cheque, or promissory note that he is legally entitled to enforce.

Hölderlin ★ (*German* 'hœldərliːn) *n* **Friedrich** ('friːdrɪç). 1770–1843, German poet, whose works include the poem *Menon's Lament for Diotima* and the novel *Hyperion* (1797–99).

holdfast ('həʊld‚fɑːst) *n* **1** the act of gripping strongly. **2** any device used to secure an object, such as a hook, clamp, etc. **3** the organ of attachment of a seaweed or related plant.

hold forth *vb* (*adv*) **1** (*intr*) to speak for a long time or in public. **2** (*tr*) to offer (an attraction or enticement).

hold in *vb* (*tr, adv*) **1** to curb, control, or keep in check. **2** to conceal (feelings).

holding ('həʊldɪŋ) *n* **1** land held under a lease. **2** (*often pl*) property to which the holder has legal title, such as land, stocks, shares, and other investments. **3** *Sport.* the obstruction of an opponent with the hands or arms, esp. in boxing. ◆ *adj* **4** *Austral. inf.* in funds; having money.

holding company *n* a company with controlling shareholdings in one or more other companies.

holding operation *n* a plan or procedure devised to prolong the existing situation.

holding paddock *n Austral. & NZ.* a paddock in which cattle or sheep are kept temporarily, as before shearing, etc.

holding pattern *n* the oval or circular path of an aircraft flying around an airport awaiting permission to land.

hold off *vb* (*adv*) **1** (*tr*) to keep apart or at a distance. **2** (*intr; often foll. by from*) to refrain (from doing something).

hold on *vb* (*intr, adv*) **1** to maintain a firm grasp. **2** to continue or persist. **3** (foll. by *to*) to keep or retain: *hold on to those stamps as they'll soon be valuable.* **4** *Inf.* to keep a telephone line open. ◆ *sentence substitute.* **5** *Inf.* stop! wait!

hold out *vb* (*adv*) **1** (*tr*) to offer. **2** (*intr*) to last or endure. **3** (*intr*) to continue to stand firm, as a person refusing to succumb to persuasion. **4** *Chiefly US.* to withhold (something due). **5 hold out for.** to wait patiently for (the fulfilment of one's demands). **6 hold out on.** *Inf.* to keep from telling (a person) some important information.

hold over *vb* (*tr, mainly adv*) **1** to defer or postpone. **2** (*prep*) to intimidate (a person) with (a threat).

hold-up *n* **1** a robbery, esp. an armed one. **2** a delay; stoppage. ◆ *vb* **hold up.** (*tr, adv*) **3.** to delay; hinder. **4** to support. **5** to waylay in order to rob, esp. using a weapon. **6** to exhibit or present.

hold with *vb* (*intr, prep*) to support; approve of.

hole (həʊl) *n* **1** an area hollowed out in a solid. **2** an opening in or through something. **3** an animal's burrow. **4** *Inf.* an unattractive place, such as a town. **5** a fault (esp. in **pick holes in**). **6** *Sl.* a difficult and embarrassing situa-

tion. **7** the cavity in various games into which the ball must be thrust. **8** (on a golf course) **8a** each of the divisions of a course (usually 18) represented by the distance between the tee and a green. **8b** the score made in striking the ball from the tee into the hole. **9** *Physics.* a vacancy in a nearly full band of quantum states of electrons in a semiconductor or an insulator. Under the action of an electric field holes behave as carriers of positive charge. **10 hole in the wall.** *Inf.* a small dingy place, esp. one difficult to find. **11 in holes.** so worn as to be full of holes. **12 make a hole in.** to consume or use a great amount of (food, drink, money, etc.). ◆ *vb* **holes, holing, holed. 13** to make a hole or holes in (something). **14** (when *intr,* often foll. by *out*) *Golf.* to hit (the ball) into the hole. [OE *hol*]
▷ **'holey** *adj*

hole-and-corner *adj* (*usually prenominal*) *Inf.* furtive or secretive.

hole in one *n Golf.* a shot from the tee that finishes in the hole. Also (esp. US): **ace.**

hole in the heart *n* a defect of the heart in which there is an abnormal opening in any of the walls dividing the four heart chambers.

hole up *vb* (*intr, adv*) **1** (of an animal) to hibernate. **2** *Inf.* to hide or remain secluded.

Holguín ★ (*Spanish* ɔl'yin) *n* a city in NE Cuba, in Holguín province: trading centre. Pop.: 242 085 (1994 est.).

Holi ('həʊlɪ) *n* a Hindu spring festival, celebrated for two to five days, commemorating Krishna's dalliance with the cowgirls. Bonfires are lit and coloured powder and water thrown over celebrants. [after *Holika,* legendary female demon]

-holic *suffix forming noun* indicating desire for or dependence on; *workaholic; chocoholic.* [C20: abstracted from (*alco*)*holic*]

holiday ('hɒlɪ,deɪ) *n* **1** (*often pl*) *Chiefly Brit.* a period in which a break is taken from work or studies for rest, travel, or recreation. US and Canad. word: **vacation. 2** a day on which work is suspended by law or custom, such as a religious festival, bank holiday, etc. Related adj: **ferial.** ◆ *vb* **3** (*intr*) *Chiefly Brit.* to spend a holiday. [OE *hāligdæg,* lit.: holy day]

Holiday ★ ('hɒlɪ,deɪ) *n* **Billie.** real name *Eleanora Fagan;* known as *Lady Day.* 1915–59, US jazz singer.

holiday camp *n Brit.* a place, esp. one at the seaside, providing accommodation, recreational facilities, etc., for holiday-makers.

holiday-maker *n Brit.* a person who goes on holiday. US and Canad. equivalents: **vacationer, vacationist.**

holily ('həʊlɪlɪ) *adv* in a holy, devout, or sacred manner.

holiness ('həʊlɪnɪs) *n* the state or quality of being holy.

Holiness ('həʊlɪnɪs) *n* (preceded by *His* or *Your*) a title reserved for the pope.

Holinshed ('hɒlɪnʃed) or **Holingshed** ★ *n* **Raphael.** died ?1580, English chronicler. His *Chronicles of England, Scotland, and Ireland* (1577) provided material for Shakespeare's plays.

holism ('həʊlɪzəm) *n* **1** any doctrine that a system may have properties over and above those of its parts and their organization. **2** (in medicine) the consideration of the complete person in the treatment of disease. [C20: from HOLO- + -ISM]
▷ **ho'listic** *adj*

Holkar State ★ (hɒl'kɑː) *n* a former state of central India, ruled by the Holkar dynasty of Maratha rulers of Indore (18th century until 1947).

holland ('hɒlənd) *n* a coarse linen cloth. [C15: after HOLLAND, where it was made]

Holland[1] ★ ('hɒlənd) *n* **1** another name for the **Netherlands. 2** a county of the Holy Roman Empire, corresponding to the present-day North and South Holland provinces of the Netherlands. **3 Parts of.** an area in E England constituting a former administrative division of Lincolnshire.

Holland[2] ★ ('hɒlənd) *n* Sir **Sidney George.** 1893–1961, New Zealand statesman; prime minister of New Zealand (1949–57).

hollandaise sauce (,hɒlən'deɪz, 'hɒlən,deɪz) *n* a rich sauce of egg yolks, butter, vinegar, etc. [C19: from F *sauce hollandaise* Dutch sauce]

Hollandia ★ (hɒ'lændɪə) *n* a former name of **Jayapura.**

Hollands ('hɒləndz) *n* (*functioning as sing*) Dutch gin, often sold in stone bottles. [C18: from Du. *hollandsch genever*]

holler ('hɒlə) *Inf.* ◆ *vb* **1** to shout or yell (something). ◆ *n* **2** a shout; call. [var. of C16 *hollow,* from *holla,* from F *holà* stop! (lit.: ho there!)]

hollo ('hɒləʊ) or **holla** ('hɒlə) *n, pl* **hollos** or **hollas,** *interj* **1** a cry for attention, or of encouragement. ◆ *vb* **2** (*intr*) to shout. [C16: from F *holà* ho there!]

hollow ('hɒləʊ) *adj* **1** having a hole or space within; not solid. **2** having a sunken area; concave. **3** deeply set: *hollow cheeks.* **4** (of sounds) as if resounding in a hollow place. **5** without substance or validity. **6** hungry or empty. **7** insincere; cynical. ◆ *adv* **8 beat** (**someone**) **hollow.** *Brit. inf.* to defeat thoroughly. ◆ *n* **9** a cavity, opening, or space in or within something. **10** a depression in the land. ◆ *vb* (often foll. by *out,* usually when *tr*) **11** to make or become hollow. **12** to form (a hole, cavity, etc.) or (of a hole, etc.) to be formed. [C12: from *holu,* inflected form of OE *holh* cave]
▷ **'hollowly** *adv* ▷ **'hollowness** *n*

hollow-eyed *adj* with the eyes appearing to be sunk into the face, as from excessive fatigue.

holly ('hɒlɪ) *n, pl* **hollies. 1** a tree or shrub having bright red berries and shiny evergreen leaves with prickly edges. **2** its branches, used for Christmas decorations. **3 holly oak.** another name for **holm oak.** [OE *holegn*]

Holly ★ ('hɒlɪ) *n* **Buddy.** real name *Charles Harden Holley.* 1936–59, US rock-and-roll singer, guitarist, and songwriter. His hits include "That'll be the Day" (1957) and "Peggy Sue" (1957).

hollyhock ('hɒlɪ,hɒk) *n* a tall plant with stout hairy stems and spikes of white, yellow, red, or purple flowers. Also called (US): **rose mallow.** [C16: from HOLY + *hock,* from OE *hoc* mallow]

Hollywood ★ ('hɒlɪ,wʊd) *n* **1** a NW suburb of Los Angeles, California: centre of the US film industry. Pop.: 250 000 (1985 est.). **2a** the US film industry. **2b** (*as modifier*): *a Hollywood star.*

holm[1] (həʊm) *n Dialect, chiefly northwestern English.* **1** an island in a river or lake. **2** low flat land near a river. [OE *holm* sea, island]

holm[2] (həʊm) *n* **1** short for **holm oak. 2** *Chiefly Brit.* a dialect word for **holly.** [C14: var. of obs. *holin,* from OE *holegn* holly]

Holmes ★ (həʊmz) *n* **1 Oliver Wendell.** 1809–94, US author, esp. of humorous essays, such as *The Autocrat of the Breakfast Table* (1858). **2** his son, **Oliver Wendell.** 1841–1935, US jurist.

holmium ('hɒlmɪəm) *n* a malleable silver-white metallic element of the lanthanide series. Symbol: Ho; atomic no.: 67; atomic wt.: 164.93. [C19: from NL *Holmia* Stockholm]

holm oak *n* an evergreen Mediterranean oak tree with prickly leaves resembling holly. Also called: **holm, holly oak, ilex.**

holo- *or before a vowel* **hol-** *combining form.* whole or wholly: *holograph.* [from Gk *holos*]

holocaust ('hɒlə,kɔːst) *n* **1** great destruction or loss of life or the source of such destruction, esp. fire. **2** (*usually cap.*) **the.** the mass murder of some six million European Jews by the Germans during World War II. **3** a rare word for **burnt offering.** [C13: from LL *holocaustum* whole burnt offering, from Gk, from HOLO- + *kaiein* to burn]

Holocene ('hɒlə,siːn) *adj* **1** of, denoting, or formed in the second and most recent epoch of the Quaternary period, which began 10 000 years ago. ◆ *n* **2 the.** the Holocene epoch or rock series. ◆ Also: **Recent.**

Holofernes ★ (,hɒlə'fɜːniːz, hə'lɒfə,niːz) *n* the Assyrian general, who was killed by the biblical heroine Judith.

hologram ('hɒlə,græm) *n* a photographic record produced by illuminating the object with coherent light (as from a laser) and, without using lenses, exposing a film to light reflected from this object and to a direct beam of coherent light. When interference patterns on the film are illuminated by the coherent light a three-dimensional image is produced.

holograph ('hɒlə,grɑːf) *n* a book or document handwritten by its author; original manuscript; autograph.

holography (hɒ'lɒgrəfɪ) *n* the science or practice of producing holograms.
▶ **holographic** (,hɒlə'græfɪk) *adj* ▶ ,holo'**graphically** *adv*

holohedral (,hɒlə'hiːdrəl) *adj* (of a crystal) exhibiting all the planes required for the symmetry of the crystal system.

holophytic (,hɒlə'fɪtɪk) *adj* (of plants) capable of synthesizing their food from inorganic molecules, esp. by photosynthesis.

holothurian (,hɒlə'θjʊərɪən) *n* **1** an echinoderm of the class *Holothuroidea*, having a leathery elongated body with a ring of tentacles around the mouth. ◆ *adj* **2** of the *Holothuroidea*. [C19: from NL *Holothūria*, name of type genus, from L: water polyp, from Gk, from ?]

hols (hɒlz) *pl n Brit. school sl.* holidays.

Holst ★ (həʊlst) *n* **Gustav (Theodore)**. 1874–1934, English composer. His works include operas, choral music, and orchestral music such as the suite *The Planets* (1917).

Holstein ★ (*German* 'hɔljtain) *n* a region of N Germany, in S Schleswig-Holstein: in early times a German duchy of Saxony; became a duchy of Denmark in 1474; finally incorporated into Prussia in 1866.

holster ('həʊlstə) *n* a sheathlike leather case for a pistol, attached to a belt or saddle. [C17: via Du., of Gmc origin]

holt[1] (həʊlt) *n Arch. or poetic.* a wood or wooded hill. [OE *holt*]

holt[2] (həʊlt) *n* the lair of an animal, esp. an otter. [C16: from HOLD[1]]

Holt ★ (həʊlt) *n* **Harold Edward**. 1908–67, Australian statesman; prime minister (1966–67); believed drowned.

holy ('həʊlɪ) *adj* **holier, holiest. 1** of or associated with God or a deity; sacred. **2** endowed or invested with extreme purity. **3** devout or virtuous. **4** holier-than-thou. ◆ *n, pl* **holies. 5** a sacred place. [OE *hālig, hǣlig*]

Holy City ★ *n the*. **1** Jerusalem, esp. when regarded as the focal point of the religions of Judaism, Christianity, or Islam. **2** *Christianity*. heaven regarded as the perfect counterpart of Jerusalem. **3** any city regarded as especially sacred by a particular religion.

Holy Communion *n* **1** the celebration of the Eucharist. **2** the consecrated elements.

holy day *n* a day on which a religious festival is observed.

Holy Father *n RC Church*. the pope.

Holy Ghost *n* another name for the **Holy Spirit**.

Holy Grail *n* **1** Also called: **Grail, Sangraal**. (in medieval legend) the bowl used by Jesus at the Last Supper. It was brought to Britain by Joseph of Arimathea, where it became the quest of many knights. **2** *Inf*. any desired ambition or goal: *the Holy Grail of infrared astronomy*. [C14: *grail* from OF *graal*, from Med. L *gradālis* bowl, from ?]

Holyhead ★ ('hɒlɪ,hɛd) *n* a port in NW Wales, in Anglesey; the chief town of Holy Island. Pop.: 11 796 (1991).

Holy Island ★ *n* **1** Also called: **Lindisfarne**. an island off the NE coast of Northumberland, site of a monastery founded by St Aidan in 635. **2** an island off NW Anglesey. Area: about 62 sq. km (24 sq. miles).

Holy Land ★ *n the*. another name for Palestine.

Holyoake ★ ('həʊlɪ,əʊk) *n* **Sir Keith Jacka**. 1904–83, New Zealand politician; prime minister (1957; 1960–72); governor general (1977–80).

holy of holies *n* **1** any place of special sanctity. **2** (*cap.*) the innermost compartment of the Jewish tabernacle, where the Ark was enshrined.

holy orders *pl n* **1** the sacrament whereby a person is ad-

mitted to the Christian ministry. **2** the grades of the Christian ministry. **3** the status of an ordained Christian minister.

Holy Roman Empire *n* the complex of European territories under the rule of the Frankish or German king who bore the title of Roman emperor, beginning with the coronation of Charlemagne in 800 A.D.

Holy Scripture *n* another term for **Scripture**.

Holy See *n RC Church*. **1** the see of the pope as bishop of Rome. **2** the Roman curia.

Holy Spirit *n Christianity*. the third person of the Trinity. Also called: **Holy Ghost**.

holystone ('həʊlɪ,stəʊn) *n* **1** a soft sandstone used for scrubbing the decks of a vessel. ◆ *vb* **holystones, holystoning, holystoned. 2** (*tr*) to scrub (a vessel's decks) with a holystone. [C19: ?from its being used in a kneeling position]

holy synod *n* the governing body of any of the Orthodox Churches.

holy water *n* water that has been blessed by a priest for use in symbolic rituals of purification.

Holy Week *n* the week preceding Easter Sunday.

Holy Willie ('wɪlɪ) *n* a person who is hypocritically pious. [C18: from Burns' *Holy Willie's Prayer*]

Holy Writ *n* another term for **Scripture**.

homage ('hɒmɪdʒ) *n* **1** a public show of respect or honour towards someone or something (esp. in **pay** *or* **do homage to**). **2** (in feudal society) the act of respect and allegiance made by a vassal to his lord. [C13: from OF, from *home* man, from L *homo*]

homburg ('hɒmbɜːg) *n* a man's hat of soft felt with a dented crown and a stiff upturned brim. [C20: after *Homburg*, in Germany, where orig. made]

home (həʊm) *n* **1** the place where one lives. **2** a house or other dwelling. **3** a family or other group living in a house. **4** a person's country, city, etc., esp. viewed as a birthplace or a place dear to one. **5** the habitat of an animal. **6** the place where something is invented, founded, or developed. **7** a building or organization set up to care for people in a certain category, such as orphans, the aged, etc. **8** *Sport*. one's own ground: *the match is at home*. **9a** the objective towards which a player strives in certain sports. **9b** an area where a player is safe from attack. **10 a home from home**. a place other than one's own home where one can be at ease. **11 at home. 11a** in one's own home or country. **11b** at ease. **11c** giving an informal party at one's own home. **12 at home in, on,** *or* **with**. familiar with. **13 home and dry**. *Brit. sl.* definitely safe or successful. Austral. and NZ equivalent: **home and hosed. 14 near home**. concerning one deeply. ◆ *adj* (*usually prenominal*) **15** of one's home, country, etc.; domestic. **16** (of an activity) done in one's house: *home taping*. **17** *Sport*. relating to one's own ground: *a home game*. **18** *US*. central; principal: *the company's home office*. ◆ *adv* **19** to or at home: *I'll be home tomorrow*. **20** to or on the point. **21** to the fullest extent: *hammer the nail home*. **22 bring home to. 22a** to make clear to. **22b** to place the blame on. **23 nothing to write home about**. *Inf*. of no particular interest: *the film was nothing to write home about*. ◆ *vb* **homes, homing, homed. 24** (*intr*) (of birds and other animals) to return home accurately from a distance. **25** (often foll. by *in on* or *onto*) to direct or be directed onto a point or target, esp. by automatic navigational aids. **26** to send or go home. **27** (*tr*) to furnish with a home. **28** (*intr*; often foll. by *in on* or *in on*) to be directed towards a goal, target, etc. [OE *hām*]

Home ★ (hjuːm) *n* **Baron**. See (Baron) **Home of the Hirsel**.

home-alone *adj Inf*. (esp. of a young child) left in a house, flat, etc., unattended.

home banking *n* a system whereby a person at home or in an office can use a computer with a modem to call up information from a bank or to transfer funds electronically.

homeboy ('həʊm,bɔɪ) *n Sl., chiefly US*. **1** a close friend. **2** a person from one's home town or neighbourhood. **3** a member of a neighbourhood gang. [C20: US rap-music usage]
▶ '**home,girl** *fem n*

home-brew *n* **1** a beer or other alcoholic drink brewed at home rather than commercially. **2** *Canad. inf.* a professional football player who was born in Canada and is not an import.
▶ **home-'brewed** *adj*

homecoming ('həʊm,kʌmɪŋ) *n* **1** the act of coming home. **2** *US.* an annual celebration held by a university, college, or school for former students.

Home Counties ★ *pl n* the counties surrounding London.

home economics *n* (*functioning as sing or pl*) the study of diet, budgeting, child care, and other subjects concerned with running a home.

home farm *n Brit.* (esp. formerly) a farm attached to and providing food for a large country house.

Home Guard *n* a volunteer part-time military force recruited to defend the United Kingdom in World War II.

home help *n Brit.* a woman employed, esp. by a local authority, to do housework in a person's home. NZ equivalent: **home aid.**

homeland ('həʊm,lænd) *n* **1** the country in which one lives or was born. **2** the official name for a **Bantustan.**

homeless ('həʊmlɪs) *adj* **a** having nowhere to live. **b** (*as collective n; preceded by the*): *the homeless.*
▶ **'homelessness** *n*

homely ('həʊmlɪ) *adj* **homelier, homeliest. 1** characteristic of or suited to the ordinary home; unpretentious. **2** (of a person) **2a** *Brit.* warm and domesticated. **2b** *Chiefly US & Canad.* plain.
▶ **'homeliness** *n*

home-made *adj* **1** (esp. of foods) made at home or on the premises, esp. of high quality ingredients. **2** crudely fashioned.

homeo-, homoeo-, *or* **homoio-** *combining form.* like or similar: *homeomorphism.* [from L *homoeo-*, from Gk *homoio-*, from *homos* same]

Home Office *n Brit. government.* the department responsible for the maintenance of law and order, and all other domestic affairs not assigned to another department.

Home of the Hirsel ★ ('hɜːsəl) *n* Baron, title of *Sir Alec Douglas-Home,* formerly 14th Earl of Home. 1903–95, British Conservative statesman: he renounced his earldom to become prime minister (1963–64); foreign secretary (1970–74).

homeopathy *or* **homoeopathy** (,həʊmɪ'ɒpəθɪ) *n* a method of treating disease by the use of small amounts of a drug that, in healthy persons, produces symptoms similar to those of the disease being treated.
▶ **homeopathic** *or* **homoeopathic** (,həʊmɪə'pæθɪk) *adj*
▶ **homeopathist, homoeopathist** (,həʊmɪ'ɒpəθɪst) *or* **homeopath, homoeopath** ('həʊmɪə,pæθ) *n*

homeostasis *or* **homoeostasis** (,həʊmɪəʊ'steɪsɪs) *n* **1** the maintenance of metabolic equilibrium within an animal by a tendency to compensate for disrupting changes. **2** the maintenance of equilibrium within a social group, person, etc.

homeowner ('həʊm,əʊnə) *n* a person who owns the house in which he or she lives.
▶ **home'ownership** *n*

home page *n Computing.* (on a website) the main document relating to an individual or an institution that provides introductory information about a website with links to the actual details of services or information provided.

homer ('həʊmə) *n* a homing pigeon.

Homer ★ ('həʊmə) *n* c. 800 B.C., Greek poet to whom are attributed the *Iliad* and the *Odyssey*: it is thought that he was born on the island of Chios and was blind.

Homeric (həʊ'mɛrɪk) *adj* **1** of, relating to, or resembling Homer or his poems. **2** imposing or heroic.

home rule *n* **1** self-government, esp. in domestic affairs. **2** the partial autonomy sometimes granted to a national minority or a colony.

Home Secretary *n Brit. government.* the head of the Home Office.

homesick ('həʊm,sɪk) *adj* depressed or melancholy at being away from home and family.
▶ **'home,sickness** *n*

homespun ('həʊm,spʌn) *adj* **1** having plain or unsophisticated character. **2** woven or spun at home. ◆ *n* **3** cloth made at home or made of yarn spun at home.

homestead ('həʊm,stɛd, -stɪd) *n* **1** a house or estate and the adjoining land, buildings, etc., esp. a farm. **2** (in the US) a house and adjoining land designated by the owner as his fixed residence and exempt under the homestead laws from seizure and forced sale for debts. **3** (in western Canada) a piece of land granted to a settler by the federal government. **4** *Austral. & NZ.* (on a sheep or cattle station) the owner's or manager's residence; in New Zealand, the term includes all outbuildings.

Homestead Act *n* **1** an act passed by the US Congress in 1862 making available to settlers 160-acre tracts of public land for cultivation. **2** (in Canada) a similar act passed by the Canadian Parliament in 1872.

homesteader ('həʊm,stɛdə) *n US and Canad.* a person who possesses land under a homestead law.

homestead law *n* (in the US and Canada) any of various laws conferring privileges on owners of homesteads.

home straight *n* **1** *Horse racing.* the section of a racecourse forming the approach to the finish. **2** the final stage of an undertaking. ◆ Also (chiefly US): **home stretch.**

home truth *n* (*often pl*) an unpleasant fact told to a person about himself.

home unit *n Austral. & NZ.* a self-contained residence which is part of a series of similar residences. Often shortened to **unit.**

homeward ('həʊmwəd) *adj* **1** going home. **2** (of a voyage, etc.) returning to the home port. ◆ *adv also* **homewards. 3** towards home.

homework ('həʊm,wɜːk) *n* **1** school work done at home. **2** any preparatory study. **3** work done at home for pay.

homey ('həʊmɪ) *adj* **homier, homiest.** a variant spelling (esp. US) of **homy.**
▶ **'homeyness** *n*

homicide ('hɒmɪ,saɪd) *n* **1** the killing of a human being by another person. **2** a person who kills another. [C14: from OF, from L *homo* man + *caedere* to slay]
▶ **,homi'cidal** *adj*

homiletics (,hɒmɪ'lɛtɪks) *n* (*functioning as sing*) the art of preaching or writing sermons. [C17: from Gk *homilētikos* cordial, from *homilein*; see HOMILY]

homily ('hɒmɪlɪ) *n, pl* **homilies. 1** a sermon. **2** moralizing talk or writing. [C14: from Church L *homīlia*, from Gk: discourse, from *homilein* to converse with, from *homilos* crowd, from *homou* together + *ilē* crowd]
▶ **,homi'letic** *adj* ▶ **'homilist** *n*

homing ('həʊmɪŋ) *n* (*modifier*) **1** *Zool.* relating to the ability to return home after travelling great distances. **2** (of an aircraft, missile, etc.) capable of guiding itself onto a target.

homing pigeon *n* any breed of pigeon developed for its homing instinct, used for racing. Also called: **homer.**

hominid ('hɒmɪnɪd) *n* **1** any primate of the family Hominidae, which includes modern man (*Homo sapiens*) and the extinct precursors of man. ◆ *adj* **2** of or belonging to the Hominidae. [C19: via NL from L *homo* man + -ID[1]]

hominoid ('hɒmɪ,nɔɪd) *adj* **1** of or like man; manlike. **2** of or belonging to the primate family, which includes the anthropoid apes and man. ◆ *n* **3** a hominoid animal. [C20: from L *homin-, homo* man + -OID]

hominy ('hɒmɪnɪ) *n Chiefly US.* coarsely ground maize prepared as a food by boiling in milk or water. [C17: prob. of Algonquian origin]

hominy grits *pl n US.* finely ground hominy.

homo ('həʊməʊ) *n, pl* **homos.** *Inf., derog.* short for **homosexual.**

Homo ('həʊməʊ) *n* a genus of hominids including modern man (see *Homo sapiens*) and several extinct species of primitive man. [L: man]

homo- *combining form.* same or like: *homologous; homosexual.* [via L from Gk *homos* same]

homocyclic (ˌhəʊməʊˈsaɪklɪk) *adj* (of a chemical compound) containing a closed ring of atoms of the same kind, esp. carbon atoms.

homoeo- *combining form.* a variant of **homeo-**.

homogamy (hɒˈmɒgəmɪ) *n* 1 a condition in which all the flowers of an inflorescence are either of the same sex or hermaphrodite. 2 the maturation of the anthers and stigmas at the same time, ensuring self-pollination.
  ▸ ho'mogamous *adj*

homogeneous (ˌhəʊməˈdʒiːnɪəs, ˌhɒm-) *adj* 1 composed of similar or identical parts or elements. 2 of uniform nature. 3 similar in kind or nature. 4 *Maths.* containing terms of the same degree with respect to all the variables, as in $x^2 + 2xy + y^2$.
  ▸ ,homo'geneousness *n*

homogenize or **homogenise** (hɒˈmɒdʒɪˌnaɪz) *vb* **homogenizes, homogenizing, homogenized** or **homogenises, homogenising, homogenised.** 1 (*tr*) to break up the fat globules in (milk or cream) so that they are evenly distributed. 2 to make or become homogeneous.
  ▸ ho,mogeni'zation or ho,mogeni'sation *n* ▸ ho'moge,nizer or ho'moge,niser *n*

homogenous (hɒˈmɒdʒɪnəs) *adj* of, relating to, or exhibiting homogeny.

homogeny (hɒˈmɒdʒɪnɪ) *n Biol.* similarity in structure because of common ancestry. [C19: from Gk *homogeneia* community of origin, from *homogenēs* of the same kind]

homograph ('hɒməˌɡrɑːf) *n* one of a group of words spelt in the same way but having different meanings.
  ▸ ,homo'graphic *adj*

homoiothermic (həʊˌmɔɪəˈθɜːmɪk) or **homothermal** (ˌhəʊməʊˈθɜːməl, ˌhɒm-) *adj* having a constant body temperature, usually higher than the temperature of the surroundings; warm-blooded.
  ▸ ho'moio,thermy or 'homo,thermy *n*

homologize or **homologise** (hɒˈmɒləˌdʒaɪz) *vb* **homologizes, homologizing, homologized** or **homologises, homologising, homologised.** to be, show to be, or make homologous.

homologous (hɒˈmɒləgəs, hɒ-), **homological** (ˌhəʊməˈlɒdʒɪkəl, ˌhɒm-), or **homologic** *adj* 1 having a related or similar position, structure, etc. 2 *Biol.* (of organs and parts) having the same evolutionary origin but different functions: *the wing of a bat and the paddle of a whale are homologous.*
  ▸ ,homo'logically *adv* ▸ 'homo,logue or US (sometimes) 'homolog *n*

homology (hɒˈmɒlədʒɪ) *n, pl* **homologies.** the condition of being homologous. [C17: from Gk *homologia* agreement, from *homologos* agreeing, from HOMO- + *legein* to speak]

homolosine projection (hɒˈmɒləˌsaɪn) *n* a map projection of the world on which the oceans are distorted to allow for greater accuracy in representing the continents. [C20: from Gk *homologos* agreeing + SINE[1]]

homomorphism (ˌhəʊməʊˈmɔːfɪzəm, ˌhɒm-) or **homomorphy** *n Biol.* similarity in form.
  ▸ ,homo'morphic or ,homo'morphous *adj*

homonym ('hɒmənɪm) *n* 1 one of a group of words spelt in the same way but having different meanings. Cf. **homograph, homophone.** 2 *Biol.* a specific or generic name that has been used for two or more different organisms. [C17: from L *homōnymum*, from Gk, from *homōnumos* of the same name; see HOMO-, -ONYM]
  ▸ ,homo'nymic or ho'monymous *adj*

homophobia (ˌhəʊməʊˈfəʊbɪə) *n* intense hatred or fear of homosexuals or homosexuality. [C20: from HOMO- (SEXUAL) + -PHOBIA]
  ▸ 'homo,phobe *n* ▸ ,homo'phobic *adj*

homophone ('hɒməˌfəʊn) *n* 1 one of a group of words pronounced in the same way but differing in meaning or spelling or both, as *bear* and *bare*. 2 a written letter or

combination of letters that represents the same speech sound as another: *"ph" is a homophone of "f"*.

homophonic (ˌhɒməˈfɒnɪk) *adj* of or relating to music in which the parts move together rather than exhibit individual rhythmic independence.

homopterous (həʊˈmɒptərəs) or **homopteran** *adj* of or belonging to a suborder of hemipterous insects having wings of a uniform texture held over the back at rest. [C19: from Gk *homopteros*, from HOMO- + *pteron* wing]

Homo sapiens ('sæpɪˌenz) *n* the specific name of modern man; the only extant species of the genus *Homo*. This species also includes some extinct types of primitive man, such as Cro-Magnon man. [NL, from L *homo* man + *sapiens* wise]

homosexual (ˌhəʊməʊˈseksjʊəl, ˌhɒm-) *n* 1 a person who is sexually attracted to members of the same sex.
  ♦ *adj* 2 of or relating to homosexuals or homosexuality. 3 of or relating to the same sex.

homosexuality (ˌhəʊməʊˌseksjʊˈælɪtɪ, ˌhɒm-) *n* sexual attraction to or sexual relations with members of the same sex.

homozygote (ˌhəʊməʊˈzaɪgəʊt) *n* an animal or plant that is homozygous and breeds true to type.
  ▸ **homozygotic** (ˌhəʊməʊzaɪˈgɒtɪk) *adj*

homozygous (ˌhəʊməʊˈzaɪgəs) *adj Genetics.* (of an organism) having identical alleles for any one gene: *these two fruit flies are homozygous for red eye colour.*

Homs (hɒms) or **Hums** ★ (hums) *n* a city in W Syria, near the Orontes River: important in Roman times as the capital of Phoenicia-Lebanesia. Pop.: 644 204 (1994 est.). Ancient name: **Emesa** ('ɛmɛsə). Former name: **Hims.**

homunculus (hɒˈmʌŋkjʊləs) *n, pl* **homunculi** (-ˌlaɪ). a miniature man; midget. Also called: **homuncule** (həʊˈmʌŋkjuːl). [C17: from L, dim. of *homo* man]
  ▸ ho'muncular *adj*

homy or *esp. US* **homey** ('həʊmɪ) *adj* **homier, homiest.** like a home; cosy.
  ▸ 'hominess or *esp. US* 'homeyness *n*

hon. *abbrev. for:* 1 honorary. 2 honourable.

Hon. *abbrev. for* Honourable (title).

Honan ★ ('həʊ'næn) *n* a variant transliteration of the Chinese name for **Henan.**

honcho ('hɒntʃəʊ) *n, pl* **honchos.** *Inf., chiefly US.* the person in charge; the boss. [C20: from Japanese *han'chō* group leader]

Hond. *abbrev. for* Honduras.

Hondo ★ ('hɒndəʊ) *n* another name for **Honshu.**

Honduras ★ (hɒnˈdjʊərəs) *n* 1 a republic in Central America: an early centre of Mayan civilization; colonized by the Spanish from 1524 onwards; gained independence in 1821. Official language: Spanish; English is also widely spoken. Religion: Roman Catholic majority. Currency: lempira. Capital: Tegucigalpa. Pop.: 5 823 000 (1997). Area: 112 088 sq. km (43 277 sq. miles). 2 Gulf of. an inlet of the Caribbean, on the coasts of Honduras, Guatemala, and Belize.
  ▸ Hon'duran *adj,*

hone (həʊn) *n* 1 a fine whetstone for sharpening. ♦ *vb* **hones, honing, honed.** 2 (*tr*) to sharpen or polish with or as if with a hone. [OE *hān* stone]

> **USAGE NOTE** *Hone* is sometimes wrongly used where *home* is meant: *this device makes it easier to home in on* (not *hone in on*) *the target.*

Honecker ★ (*German* 'hɔːnɛkər) *n* **Erich** ('eːrɪç). 1912–94, German statesman; head of state of East Germany (1976–89).

Honegger ★ ('hɒnɪgə; *French* ɔnɛgɛr) *n* **Arthur** (artyr). 1892–1955, French composer, one of Les Six. His works include the oratorio *King David* (1921) and *Pacific 231* (1924) for orchestra.

honest ('ɒnɪst) *adj* 1 not given to lying, cheating, stealing, etc.; trustworthy. 2 not false or misleading; genuine. 3 just or fair: *honest wages.* 4 characterized by sincerity: *an* *honest appraisal.* **5** without pretensions: *honest farmers.* **6** *Arch.* (of a woman) respectable. **7 honest broker.** a mediator in disputes, esp. international ones. **8 make an honest woman of.** to marry (a woman, esp. one who is pregnant) to prevent scandal. [C13: from OF *honeste*, from L *honestus* distinguished, from *honōs* HONOUR]

honestly ('ɒnɪstlɪ) *adv* **1** in an honest manner. **2** (intensifier): *I honestly don't believe it.*

honesty ('ɒnɪstɪ) *n, pl* **honesties. 1** the condition of being honest. **2** *Arch.* virtue or respect. **3** Also called: **moonwort, satinpod.** a purple-flowered European plant cultivated for its flattened silvery pods, which are used for indoor decoration.

honey ('hʌnɪ) *n* **1** a sweet viscid substance made by bees from nectar and stored in their nests or hives as food. **2** anything that is sweet or delightful. **3** (*often cap.*) *Chiefly US & Canad.* a term of endearment. **4** *Inf., chiefly US & Canad.* something very good of its kind. ◆ *vb* **honeys, honeying, honeyed. 5** (*tr*) to sweeten with or as if with honey. **6** (often foll. by *up*) to talk to (someone) in a flattering way. [OE *huneg*]
▶ **'honey-,like** *adj*

honey badger *n* another name for **ratel.**

honeybee ('hʌnɪ,biː) *n* any of various social bees widely domesticated as a source of honey and beeswax. Also called: **hive bee.**

honey buzzard *n* a common European bird of prey having broad wings and a typically dull brown plumage with white-streaked underparts.

honeycomb ('hʌnɪ,kəʊm) *n* **1** a waxy structure, constructed by bees in a hive, that consists of adjacent hexagonal cells in which honey is stored, eggs are laid, and larvae develop. **2** something resembling this in structure. **3** *Zool.* another name for **reticulum** (sense 2). ◆ *vb* (*tr*) **4** to pierce with holes, cavities, etc. **5** to permeate: *honeycombed with spies.*

honey creeper *n* a small tropical American songbird having a slender downward-curving bill and feeding on nectar.

honeydew ('hʌnɪ,djuː) *n* **1** a sugary substance excreted by aphids and similar insects. **2** a similar substance exuded by certain plants.

honeydew melon *n* a variety of muskmelon with a smooth greenish-white rind and sweet greenish flesh.

honey-eater ('hʌnɪ,iːtə) *n* a small Australasian songbird having a downward-curving bill and a brushlike tongue specialized for extracting nectar from flowers.

honeyed *or* **honied** ('hʌnɪd) *adj Poetic.* **1** flattering or soothing. **2** made sweet or agreeable: *honeyed words.* **3** full of honey.

honey guide *n* a small bird inhabiting tropical forests of Africa and Asia and feeding on beeswax, honey, and insects.

honeymoon ('hʌnɪ,muːn) *n* **1** a holiday taken by a newly married couple. **2** a holiday considered to resemble a honeymoon: *a second honeymoon.* **3** the early, usually calm period of a relationship or enterprise. ◆ *vb* **4** (*intr*) to take a honeymoon. [C16: traditionally explained as an allusion to the feelings of married couples as changing with the phases of the moon]
▶ **'honey,mooner** *n*

honeysuckle ('hʌnɪ,sʌkˀl) *n* **1** a temperate climbing shrub with fragrant white, yellow, or pink tubular flowers. **2** any of various Australian trees or shrubs of the genus *Banksia*, having flowers in dense spikes. [OE *hunigsūce*, from HONEY + SUCK]

honeytrap ('hʌnɪ,træp) *n Inf.* a scheme in which a victim is lured into a compromising sexual situation that provides the opportunity for blackmail.

Hong Kong ★ ('hɒŋ 'kɒŋ) *n* **1** a Special Administrative Region of S China, with some autonomy; formerly a British Crown Colony: consists of Hong Kong Island, leased by China to Britain (1842–1997), Kowloon Peninsula, Stonecutters Island, the New Territories (mainland), leased by China in 1898 for a 99-year period, and over 230 small islands; important entrepôt trade and manufacturing centre, esp. for textiles and other con-

sumer goods; university (1912). Pop.: 6 491 000 (1997). Area: 1046 sq. km (404 sq. miles). **2** an island in Hong Kong, south of Kowloon Peninsula: contains the former colonial capital, Victoria. Pop.: 996 183 (latest est.). Area: 75 sq. km (29 sq. miles).

Hong-wu ('hɒŋ'wuː) *or* **Hung-wu** ★ *n* title of *Chu Yuan Zhang* (or *Chu Yüan-Chang*), 1328–98, first emperor (1368–98) of the Ming dynasty, uniting China under his rule by 1382.

Hong Xiu Quan ('hɒŋ 'ʃjuː 'tʃwɑːn) *or* **Hung Hsiu-ch'uan** ★ *n* 1814–64, Chinese religious leader and revolutionary. Claiming (1851) to be Christ's brother, he led the Taiping rebellion; committed suicide.

Honiara ★ (,həʊnɪˈɑːrə) *n* the capital of the Solomon Islands, on NW Guadalcanal Island. Pop.: 43 643 (1996 est.).

honk (hɒŋk) *n* **1** a representation of the sound made by a goose. **2** any sound resembling this, esp. a motor horn. **3** *Brit. & Austral. sl.* a bad smell. ◆ *vb* **4** to make or cause (something) to make such a sound. **5** (*intr*) *Brit. sl.* to vomit. **6** (*intr*) *Brit. & Austral. sl.* to have a bad smell.

honky ('hɒŋkɪ) *n, pl* **honkies.** *Derog. sl., chiefly US.* a White man or White men collectively. [C20: from ?]

honky-tonk ('hɒŋkɪ,tɒŋk) *n* **1** *US & Canad. sl.* a cheap disreputable nightclub, bar, etc. **2a** a style of ragtime piano playing, esp. on a tinny-sounding piano. **2b** (*as modifier*): *honky-tonk music.* [C19: rhyming compound based on HONK]

Honolulu ★ (,hɒnəˈluːluː) *n* a port in Hawaii, on S Oahu Island: the state capital. Pop.: 385 881 (1994 est.).

honorarium (,ɒnəˈrɛərɪəm) *n, pl* **honorariums** *or* **honoraria** (-rɪə). a fee paid for a nominally free service. [C17: from L: something presented on being admitted to a post of HONOUR]

honorary ('ɒnərərɪ) *adj* (*usually prenominal*) **1a** held or given only as an honour, without the normal privileges or duties: *an honorary degree.* **1b** (of a secretary, treasurer, etc.) unpaid. **2** having such a position or title. **3** depending on honour rather than legal agreement.

honorific (,ɒnəˈrɪfɪk) *adj* **1** showing respect. **2a** (of a pronoun, verb inflection, etc.) indicating the speaker's respect for the addressee. **2b** (*as n*): *a Japanese honorific.*
▶ **,honor'ifically** *adv*

honour *or US* **honor** ('ɒnə) *n* **1** personal integrity; allegiance to moral principles. **2a** fame or glory. **2b** a person who wins this for his country, school, etc. **3** (*often pl*) great respect, esteem, etc., or an outward sign of this. **4** (*often pl*) high or noble rank. **5** a privilege or pleasure: *it is an honour to serve you.* **6** a woman's chastity. **7a** *Bridge, etc.* any of the top five cards in a suit or any of the four aces at no trumps. **7b** *Whist.* any of the top four cards. **8** *Golf.* the right to tee off first. **9 in honour bound.** under a moral obligation. **10 in honour of.** out of respect for. **11 on one's honour.** on the pledge of one's word or good name. ◆ *vb* (*tr*) **12** to hold in respect. **13** to show courteous behaviour towards. **14** to worship. **15** to confer a distinction upon. **16** to accept and then pay when due (a cheque, draft, etc.). **17** to keep (one's promise); fulfil (a previous agreement). **18** to bow or curtsy to (one's dancing partner). [C12: from OF *onor*, from L *honor* esteem]

Honour ('ɒnə) *n* (preceded by *Your, His,* or *Her*) a title used to address or refer to certain judges.

honourable *or US* **honorable** ('ɒnərəbˀl) *adj* **1** possessing or characterized by high principles. **2** worthy of honour or esteem. **3** consistent with or bestowing honour.
▶ **'honourably** *or US* **'honorably** *adv*

Honourable *or US* **Honorable** ('ɒnərəbˀl) *adj* (*prenominal*) **the.** a title of respect placed before a name: used of various officials in the English-speaking world, as a courtesy title in Britain for the children of certain peers, and in Parliament by one member speaking of another. Abbrev.: **Hon.**

honours *or US* **honors** ('ɒnəz) *pl n* **1** observances of respect. **2** (*often cap.*) **2a** (in a university degree course) a rank of the highest academic standard. **2b** (*as modifier*): *an honours degree.* Abbrev.: **Hons. 3** a high mark awarded for an examination; distinction. **4 do the honours.** to serve as host or hostess. **5 last** (*or* **funeral**) **honours.** observances

---

★ people and places

of respect at a funeral. **6 military honours.** ceremonies performed by troops in honour of royalty, at the burial of an officer, etc.

honours of war *pl n Mil.* the honours granted by the victorious to the defeated, esp. as of marching out with all arms and flags flying.

Honshu ★ ('hɒnʃuː) *n* the largest of the four main islands of Japan, between the Pacific and the Sea of Japan; regarded as the Japanese mainland; includes a number of offshore islands and contains most of the main cities. Pop.: 100 995 000 (1995). Area: 230 448 sq. km (88 976 sq. miles). Also called: **Hondo**.

hooch *or* **hootch** (huːtʃ) *n Inf., chiefly US & Canad.* alcoholic drink, esp. illicitly distilled spirits. [C20: of Amerind origin, *Hootchinoo*, name of a tribe that distilled a type of liquor]

Hooch *or* **Hoogh** ★ (huːtʃ; *Dutch* hoːx) *n* Pieter de ('piːtər də). 1629–?1684, Dutch genre painter.

hood[1] (hʊd) *n* **1** a loose head covering either attached to a cloak or coat or made as a separate garment. **2** something resembling this in shape or use. **3** the US and Canad. name for **bonnet** (of a car). **4** the folding roof of a convertible car. **5** a hoodlike garment worn over an academic gown, indicating its wearer's degree and university. **6** *Biol.* a hoodlike structure, such as the fold of skin on the head of a cobra ◆ *vb* **7** (*tr*) to cover with or as if with a hood. [OE *hōd*]
▸ '**hood,like** *adj*

hood[2] (hʊd) *n Sl.* short for **hoodlum.**

Hood ★ (hʊd) *n* **1** Robin. See **Robin Hood. 2** Samuel, 1st Viscount. 1724–1816, British admiral. **3** Thomas. 1799–1845, British poet and humorist.

-hood *suffix forming nouns.* **1** indicating state or condition: *manhood.* **2** indicating a body of persons: *knighthood; priesthood.* [OE *-hād*]

hooded ('hʊdɪd) *adj* **1** covered with, having, or shaped like a hood. **2** (of eyes) having heavy eyelids that appear to be half closed.

hooded crow *n* a crow that has a grey body and black head, wings, and tail. Also called (Scot.): **hoodie** ('hʊdɪ), **hoodie crow.**

hoodlum ('huːdləm) *n* **1** a petty gangster. **2** a lawless youth. [C19: ?from Southern G *Haderlump* ragged good-for-nothing]

hoodman-blind (,hʊdmən'blaɪnd) *n Brit., arch.* blind man's buff.

hoodoo ('huːduː) *n, pl* **hoodoos. 1** a variant of **voodoo. 2** *Inf.* a person or thing that brings bad luck. **3** *Inf.* bad luck. ◆ *vb* **hoodoos, hoodooing, hoodooed. 4** (*tr*) *Inf.* to bring bad luck to.

hoodwink ('hʊd,wɪŋk) *vb* (*tr*) **1** to dupe; trick. **2** *Obs.* to cover or hide. [C16: orig., to cover the eyes with a hood, blindfold]

hooey ('huːɪ) *n, interj Sl.* nonsense. [C20: from ?]

hoof (huːf) *n, pl* **hooves** *or* **hoofs. 1a** the horny covering of the end of the foot in the horse, deer, and all other ungulate mammals. **1b** (*in combination*): *a hoofbeat.* Related adj: **ungular. 2** the foot of an ungulate mammal. **3** a hoofed animal. **4** *Facetious.* a person's foot. **5 on the hoof. 5a** (of livestock) alive. **5b** in an impromptu manner: *he did his thinking on the hoof.* ◆ *vb* **6 hoof it.** *Sl.* **6a** to walk. **6b** to dance. [OE *hōf*]
▸ '**hoofed** *adj*

hoofer ('huːfə) *n Sl.* a professional dancer.

Hoogh ★ (*Dutch* hoːx) *n* See (Pieter de) **Hooch.**

Hooghly ★ ('huːglɪ) *n* a river in NE India, in West Bengal: the westernmost and commercially most important channel by which the River Ganges enters the Bay of Bengal. Length: 232 km (144 miles).

hoo-ha ('huː,hɑː) *n* a noisy commotion or fuss. [C20: from ?]

hook (hʊk) *n* **1** a curved piece of material, usually metal, used to suspend, hold, or pull something. **2** short for **fish-hook. 3** a trap or snare. **4** something resembling a hook in design or use. **5a** a sharp bend, esp. in a river. **5b** a sharply curved spit of land. **6** *Boxing.* a short swinging blow delivered with the elbow bent. **7** *Cricket.* a shot in

which the ball is hit square on the leg side with the bat held horizontally. **8** *Golf.* a shot that causes the ball to go to the player's left. **9** a hook-shaped stroke used in writing, such as a part of a letter extending above or below the line. **10** *Music.* a stroke added to the stem of a note to indicate time values shorter than a crotchet. **11** a sickle. **12** *Naut.* an anchor. **13 by hook or (by) crook.** by any means. **14 hook, line, and sinker.** *Inf.* completely: *he fell for it hook, line, and sinker.* **15 off the hook.** *Sl.* free from obligation or guilt. **16 sling one's hook.** *Brit. sl.* to leave. ◆ *vb* **17** (often foll. by *up*) to fasten or be fastened with or as if with a hook or hooks. **18** (*tr*) to catch (something, such as a fish) on a hook. **19** to curve like or into the shape of a hook. **20** (*tr*) to make (a rug) by hooking yarn through a stiff fabric backing with a special instrument. **21** *Boxing.* to hit (an opponent) with a hook. **22** *Cricket, etc.* to play (a ball) with a hook. **23** *Rugby.* to obtain and pass (the ball) backwards from a scrum, using the feet. **24** (*tr*) *Sl.* to steal. [OE *hōc*]
▸ '**hook,like** *adj*

hookah *or* **hooka** ('hʊkə) *n* an oriental pipe for smoking marijuana, tobacco, etc., consisting of one or more long flexible stems connected to a container of water or other liquid through which smoke is drawn and cooled. Also called: **hubble-bubble, water pipe.** [C18: from Ar. *huqqah*]

Hooke ★ (hʊk) *n* **Robert.** 1635–1703, English physicist and inventor. He formulated Hooke's law (1678), built the first Gregorian telescope, and invented a balance spring.

hooked (hʊkt) *adj* **1** bent like a hook. **2** having a hook or hooks. **3** caught or trapped. **4** a slang word for **married. 5** *Sl.* addicted to a drug. **6** (often foll. by *on*) obsessed (with).

hooker ('hʊkə) *n* **1** a person or thing that hooks. **2** *Sl.* a prostitute. **3** *Rugby.* the central forward in the front row of a scrum.

Hooke's law *n* the principle that the stress imposed on a solid is directly proportional to the strain produced, within the elastic limit. [C18: after R. HOOKE]

Hook of Holland ★ *n* the. **1** a cape on the SW coast of the Netherlands, in South Holland province. **2** a port on this cape. ◆ *Dutch name:* **Hoek van Holland.**

hook-up *n* **1** the contact of an aircraft in flight with the refuelling hose of a tanker aircraft. **2** an alliance or relationship. **3** the linking of broadcasting equipment or stations to transmit a special programme. ◆ *vb* **hook up** (*adv*). **4** to connect (two or more people or things).

hookworm ('hʊk,wɜːm) *n* any of various parasitic bloodsucking worms which cause disease. They have hooked mouthparts and enter their hosts by boring through the skin. Cf. **ancylostomiasis.**

hooky *or* **hookey** ('hʊkɪ) *n Inf., chiefly US, Canad., & NZ.* truancy, usually from school (esp. in **play hooky**). [C20: ?from *hook* it to escape]

hooligan ('huːlɪgən) *n Sl.* a rough lawless young person. [C19: ? var. of *Houlihan*, Irish surname]
▸ '**hooliganism** *n*

hoop[1] (huːp) *n* **1** a rigid circular band of metal or wood. **2** something resembling this. **3** a band of iron that holds the staves of a barrel together. **4** a child's toy shaped like a hoop and rolled on the ground or whirled around the body. **5** *Croquet.* any of the iron arches through which the ball is driven. **6a** a light curved frame to spread out a skirt. **6b** (*as modifier*): *a hoop skirt.* **7** *Basketball.* the round metal frame to which the net is attached to form the basket. **8** a large ring through which performers or animals jump. **9 go or be put through the hoop.** to be subjected to an ordeal. [OE *hōp*]
▸ '**hooped** *adj*

hoop[2] (huːp) *n, vb* a variant spelling of **whoop.**

hoopla ('huːplɑː) *n* **1** *Brit.* a fairground game in which a player tries to throw a hoop over an object and so win it. **2** *US & Canad. sl.* **2a** noise; bustle. **2b** nonsense; ballyhoo. [C20: see WHOOP, LA[2]]

hoopoe ('huːpuː) *n* an Old World bird having a pinkish-brown plumage with black-and-white wings and an erectile crest. [C17: from earlier *hoopoop*, imit.]

hoop pine *n* a fast-growing timber tree of Australia having rough bark with hooplike cracks around the trunk and branches.

hooray (huːˈreɪ) *interj, n, vb* **1** a variant spelling of **hurrah.** ◆ *sentence substitute.* **2** Also: **hooroo** (huːˈruː). *Austral. & NZ.* cheerio.

Hooray Henry (ˈhuːˌreɪ ˈhɛnrɪ) *n, pl* **Hooray Henries** *or* **Hooray Henrys.** a young upper-class man, often with affectedly hearty voice and manners. Sometimes shortened to **Hooray.**

hoosegow *or* **hoosgow** (ˈhuːsɡaʊ) *n US.* a slang word for **jail.** [C20: from Mexican Sp. *jusgado* prison, from Sp.: court of justice, ult. from L *judex* a JUDGE]

hoot[1] (huːt) *n* **1** the mournful wavering cry of some owls. **2** a similar sound, such as that of a train whistle. **3** a jeer of derision. **4** *Inf.* an amusing person or thing. ◆ *vb* **5** (often foll. by *at*) to jeer or yell (something) contemptuously (at someone). **6** (*tr*) to drive (speakers, actors on stage, etc.) off by hooting. **7** (*intr*) to make a hoot. **8** (*intr*) *Brit.* to blow a horn. [C13 *hoten*, imit.]

hoot[2] (huːt) *n Austral. & NZ.* a slang word for **money.** [from Maori *utu* price]

hootenanny (ˈhuːtⁿˌnænɪ) *or* **hootnanny** (ˈhuːtˌnænɪ) *n, pl* **hootenannies** *or* **hootnannies.** *US & Canad.* an informal performance by folk singers. [C20: from ?]

hooter (ˈhuːtə) *n Chiefly Brit.* **1** a person or thing that hoots, esp. a car horn. **2** *Sl.* a nose.

Hoover[1] (ˈhuːvə) *n* **1** *Trademark.* a type of vacuum cleaner. ◆ *vb* (*usually not cap.*) **2** to vacuum-clean (a carpet, etc.). **3** (*tr*; often foll. by *up*) to consume or dispose of (something) quickly and completely: *he hoovered up his grilled fish.*

Hoover[2] ★ (ˈhuːvə) *n* **1** **Herbert (Clark).** 1874–1964, US statesman; 31st president of the US (1929–33). He organized relief for Europe during and after World War I. **2** **J(ohn) Edgar.** 1895–1972, US lawyer: director of the FBI (1924–72).

Hoover Dam ★ *n* a dam in the western US, on the Colorado River on the border between Nevada and Arizona; forms Lake Mead. Height: 222 m (727 ft). Length: 354 m (1180 ft). Former name (1933–47): **Boulder Dam.**

hooves (huːvz) *n* a plural of **hoof.**

hop[1] (hɒp) *vb* **hops, hopping, hopped. 1** (*intr*) to jump forwards or upwards on one foot. **2** (*intr*) (esp. of frogs, birds, etc.) to move forwards in short jumps. **3** (*tr*) to jump over. **4** (*intr*) *Inf.* to move quickly (in, on, out of, etc.): *hop on a bus.* **5** (*tr*) *Inf.* to cross (an ocean) in an aircraft. **6** (*tr*) *US & Canad. inf.* to travel by means of: *he hopped a train to Chicago.* **7** (*intr*) another word for **limp**[1] (senses 1 and 2). **8 hop it** (*or* **off**). *Brit. sl.* to go away. ◆ *n* **9** the act or an instance of hopping. **10** *Inf.* an informal dance. **11** *Inf.* a trip, esp. in an aircraft. **12 on the hop.** *Inf.* **12a** active or busy. **12b** *Brit.* unawares or unprepared. [OE *hoppian*]

hop[2] (hɒp) *n* **1** a climbing plant which has green conelike female flowers and clusters of small male flowers. **2 hop garden.** a field of hops. **3** *Obs. sl.* opium or any other narcotic drug. ◆ See also **hops.** [C15: from MDu. *hoppe*]

hope (həʊp) *n* **1** (*sometimes pl*) a feeling of desire for something and confidence in the possibility of its fulfilment: *his hope for peace was justified.* **2** a reasonable ground for this feeling: *there is still hope.* **3** a person or thing that gives cause for hope. **4** a thing, situation, or event that is desired: *my hope is that prices will fall.* **5 not a hope** *or* **some hope.** used ironically to express little confidence that expectations will be fulfilled. ◆ *vb* **hopes, hoping, hoped. 6** (*tr; takes a clause as object or an infinitive*) to desire (something) with some possibility of fulfilment: *I hope to tell you.* **7** (*intr*; often foll. by *for*) to have a wish. **8** (*tr; takes a clause as object*) to trust or believe: *we hope that this is satisfactory.* [OE *hopa*]

Hope ★ (həʊp) *n* **1 Anthony,** real name *Sir Anthony Hope Hawkins.* 1863–1933, British novelist; author of *The Prisoner of Zenda* (1894). **2 Bob,** real name *Leslie Townes Hope.* born 1903, US comedian, born in England. His films in-

clude *Road to Morocco* (1942) and *The Paleface* (1947): awarded an honorary knighthood in 1998.

hope chest *n* the US, Canad., and NZ name for **bottom drawer.**

hopeful (ˈhəʊpfʊl) *adj* **1** having or expressing hope. **2** inspiring hope; promising. ◆ *n* **3** a person considered to be on the brink of success (esp. in **a young hopeful**). ► **ˈhopefulness** *n*

hopefully (ˈhəʊpfʊlɪ) *adv* **1** in a hopeful manner. **2** *Inf.* it is hoped: *hopefully they will be married soon.*

> **USAGE NOTE**   The use of *hopefully* to mean *it is hoped* used to be considered incorrect by some people but has now become acceptable in informal contexts.

Hopeh *or* **Hopei** ★ (ˈhəʊˈpeɪ) *n* a variant transliteration of the Chinese name for **Hebei.**

hopeless (ˈhəʊplɪs) *adj* **1** having or offering no hope. **2** impossible to solve. **3** unable to learn, function, etc. **4** *Inf.* without skill or ability. ► **ˈhopelessly** *adv* ► **ˈhopelessness** *n*

Hopi (ˈhəʊpɪ) *n* **1** (*pl* **Hopis** *or* **Hopi**) a member of a North American Indian people of NE Arizona. **2** the language of this people. [from Hopi *Hópi* peaceful]

Hopkins ★ (ˈhɒpkɪnz) *n* **1 Sir Anthony.** born 1937, Welsh actor: his films include *The Silence of the Lambs* (1991) and *Meet Joe Black* (1999). **2 Sir Frederick Gowland** (ˈɡaʊlənd). 1861–1947, British biochemist, who pioneered research into vitamins: shared the Nobel prize for physiology or medicine (1929). **3 Gerard Manley.** 1844–89, British poet and Jesuit priest.

hoplite (ˈhɒplaɪt) *n* (in ancient Greece) a heavily armed infantryman. [C18: from Gk *hoplitēs*, from *hoplon* weapon, from *hepein* to prepare]

hopper (ˈhɒpə) *n* **1** a person or thing that hops. **2** a funnel-shaped reservoir from which solid materials can be discharged into a receptacle below, esp. for feeding fuel to a furnace, loading a truck, etc. **3** a machine used for picking hops. **4** any of various long-legged hopping insects. **5** an open-topped railway truck for loose minerals, etc., unloaded through doors on the underside. **6** *S. African.* another name for **cocopan.** **7** *Computing.* a device for holding punched cards and feeding them to a card reader.

hopping (ˈhɒpɪŋ) *adv* **hopping mad.** in a terrible rage.

hops (hɒps) *pl n* the dried flowers of the hop plant, used to give a bitter taste to beer.

hopsack (ˈhɒpˌsæk) *n* **1** a roughly woven fabric of wool, cotton, etc., used for clothing. **2** Also called: **hopsacking.** a coarse fabric used for bags, etc., made generally of hemp or jute.

hopscotch (ˈhɒpˌskɒtʃ) *n* a children's game in which a player throws a small stone or other object to land in one of a pattern of squares marked on the ground and then hops over to it to pick it up. [C19: HOP[1] + SCOTCH[1]]

Horace ★ (ˈhɒrɪs) *n* Latin name *Quintus Horatius Flaccus.* 65–8 B.C., Roman poet and satirist: his verse includes the lyrics in the *Epodes* and the *Odes,* the *Epistles* and *Satires,* and the *Ars Poetica.*

Horae ★ (ˈhɔːriː) *pl n Classical myth.* the goddesses of the seasons. Also called: **the Hours.** [L: hours]

horary (ˈhɔːrərɪ) *adj Arch.* **1** relating to the hours. **2** hourly. [C17: from Med. L *hōrārius,* from L *hora*]

Horatian (həˈreɪʃən) *adj* of, relating to, or characteristic of Horace or his poetry.

Horatius Cocles ★ (hɒˈreɪʃɪəs ˈkəʊkliːz) *n* a legendary Roman hero of the 6th century B.C., who defended a bridge over the Tiber against Lars Porsena.

horde (hɔːd) *n* **1** a vast crowd; throng; mob. **2** a nomadic group of people, esp. an Asiatic group. **3** a large moving mass of animals, esp. insects. [C16: from Polish *horda,* from Turkish *ordū* camp]

Hordern ★ ('hɔːdən) *n* Sir **Michael (Murray)**. 1911–95, British actor.

Horeb ★ ('hɔːrɛb) *n Bible*. a mountain, probably Mount Sinai.

horehound *or* **hoarhound** ('hɔːˌhaʊnd) *n* a downy herbaceous Old World plant with small white flowers that contain a bitter juice formerly used as a cough medicine and flavouring.   [OE *hārhūne*, from *hār* grey + *hūne* horehound, from ?]

horizon (hə'raɪz°n) *n* **1** Also called: **visible horizon, apparent horizon.** the apparent line that divides the earth and the sky. **2** *Astron.* **2a** Also called: **sensible horizon.** the circular intersection with the celestial sphere of the plane tangential to the earth at the position of the observer. **2b** Also called: **celestial horizon.** the great circle on the celestial sphere, the plane of which passes through the centre of the earth and is parallel to the sensible horizon. **3** the range or limit of scope, interest, knowledge, etc. **4** a layer of rock within a stratum that has a particular composition by which the stratum may be dated.   [C14: from L, from Gk *horizōn kuklos* limiting circle, from *horizein* to limit]

horizontal (ˌhɒrɪ'zɒnt°l) *adj* **1** parallel to the plane of the horizon; level; flat. **2** of or relating to the horizon. **3** in a plane parallel to that of the horizon. **4** applied uniformly to all members of a group. **5** *Econ.* relating to identical stages of commercial activity: *horizontal integration.*   ◆ *n* **6** a horizontal plane, position, line, etc.
▶ ˌhorizon'tality *n* ▶ ˌhori'zontally *adv*

horizontal bar *n Gymnastics.* a raised bar on which swinging and vaulting exercises are performed.

hormone ('hɔːməʊn) *n* **1** a chemical substance produced in an endocrine gland and transported in the blood to a certain tissue, on which it exerts a specific effect. **2** an organic compound produced by a plant that is essential for growth. **3** any synthetic substance having the same effects.   [C20: from Gk *hormōn*, from *horman* to stir up, from *hormē* impulse]
▶ hor'monal *adj*

hormone replacement therapy *n* a form of oestrogen treatment used to control menopausal symptoms and in the prevention of osteoporosis. Abbrev.: **HRT.**

Hormuz (hɔː'muːz, 'hɔːmʌz) *or* **Ormuz** ★ *n* an island off the SE coast of Iran, in the **Strait of Hormuz**: ruins of the ancient city of Hormuz, a major trading centre in the Middle Ages. Area: about 41 sq. km (16 sq. miles).

horn (hɔːn) *n* **1** either of a pair of permanent bony outgrowths on the heads of cattle, antelopes, etc. **2** the outgrowth from the nasal bone of a rhinoceros, consisting of a mass of fused hairs. **3** any hornlike projection, such as the eyestalk of a snail. **4** the antler of a deer. **5a** the constituent substance, mainly keratin, of horns, hooves, etc. **5b** (*in combination*): *horn-rimmed spectacles.* **6** a container or device made from this substance or an artificial substitute: *a drinking horn.* **7** an object resembling a horn in shape, such as a cornucopia. **8** a primitive musical wind instrument made from horn. **9** any musical instrument consisting of a pipe or tube of brass fitted with a mouthpiece. See **French horn, cor anglais. 10** *Jazz sl.* any wind instrument. **11a** a device for producing a warning or signalling noise. **11b** (*in combination*): *a foghorn.* **12** (*usually pl*) the imaginary hornlike parts formerly supposed to appear on the forehead of a cuckold. **13a** a hollow conical device coupled to a gramophone to control the direction and quality of the sound. **13b** a similar device attached to an electrical loudspeaker, esp. in a public-address system. **14** a stretch of land or water shaped like a horn. **15** *Brit. taboo sl.* an erection of the penis.   ◆ *vb* (*tr*) **16** to provide with a horn or horns. **17** to gore or butt with a horn. **18** to remove or shorten the horns of (cattle, etc.).   ◆ See also **horn in.** [OE]
▶ **horned** *adj* ▶ 'hornless *adj*

Horn ★ (hɔːn) *n* Cape. See **Cape Horn.**

hornbeam ('hɔːnˌbiːm) *n* **1** a tree of Europe and Asia having smooth grey bark and hard white wood. **2** its wood.   ◆ Also called: **ironwood.** [C14: from HORN + BEAM, referring to its tough wood]

hornbill ('hɔːnˌbɪl) *n* a bird of tropical Africa and Asia, having a very large bill with a basal bony protuberance.

hornblende ('hɔːnˌblɛnd) *n* a mineral of the amphibole group consisting of the aluminium silicates of calcium, sodium, magnesium, and iron: varies in colour from green to black.   [C18: from G *Horn* horn + BLENDE]

hornbook ('hɔːnˌbʊk) *n* a page bearing a religious text or the alphabet, held in a frame with a thin window of horn over it.

horned toad *or* **lizard** *n* a small insectivorous burrowing lizard inhabiting desert regions of America, having a flattened toadlike body covered with spines.

horned viper *n* a venomous snake that occurs in desert regions of N Africa and SW Asia and has a small horny spine above each eye.

hornet ('hɔːnɪt) *n* **1** any of various large social wasps that can inflict a severe sting. **2 hornet's nest.** a strongly unfavourable reaction (often in **stir up a hornet's nest**).   [OE *hyrnetu*]

horn in *vb* (*intr, adv*; often foll. by *on*) *Sl.* to interrupt or intrude.

Horn of Africa ★ *n* a region of NE Africa, comprising Somalia and adjacent territories.

horn of plenty *n* another term for **cornucopia.**

hornpipe ('hɔːnˌpaɪp) *n* **1** an obsolete reed instrument with a mouthpiece made of horn. **2** an old British solo dance to a hornpipe accompaniment, traditionally performed by sailors. **3** a piece of music for such a dance.

hornswoggle ('hɔːnˌswɒg°l) *vb* **hornswoggles, hornswoggling, hornswoggled.** (*tr*) *Sl.* to cheat or trick; bamboozle.   [C19: from ?]

horny ('hɔːnɪ) *adj* **hornier, horniest. 1** of, like, or hard as horn. **2** having a horn or horns. **3** *Sl.* **3a** sexually aroused. **3b** provoking or intended to provoke sexual arousal. **3c** sexually eager or lustful.
▶ 'horniness *n*

horologe ('hɒrəˌlɒdʒ) *n* a rare word for **timepiece.**   [C14: from L *hōrologium*, from Gk *hōrologion*, from *hōra* HOUR + *-logos* from *legein* to tell]

horologist (hɒ'rɒlədʒɪst) *or* **horologer** *n* a person skilled in horology.

horology (hɒ'rɒlədʒɪ) *n* the art or science of making timepieces or of measuring time.
▶ horologic (ˌhɒrə'lɒdʒɪk) *or* ˌhoro'logical *adj*

horoscope ('hɒrəˌskəʊp) *n* **1** the prediction of a person's future based on zodiacal data for the time of birth. **2** the configuration of the planets, sun, and moon in the sky at a particular moment. **3** a diagram showing the positions of the planets, sun, moon, etc., at a particular time and place.   [OE *horoscopus*, from L, from Gk *hōroskopos*, from *hōra* HOUR + -SCOPE]
▶ horoscopic (ˌhɒrə'skɒpɪk) *adj* ▶ horoscopy (hɒ'rɒskəpɪ) *n*

Horowitz ★ ('hɒrəvɪts) *n* Vladimir ('vlædɪmɪə). 1904–89, Russian pianist, in the US from 1928.

horrendous (hɒ'rɛndəs) *adj* another word for **horrific.**   [C17: from L *horrendus* fearful, from *horrēre* to bristle, shudder, tremble; see HORROR]
▶ hor'rendously *adv*

horrible ('hɒrɪb°l) *adj* **1** causing horror; dreadful. **2** disagreeable. **3** *Inf.* cruel or unkind.   [C14: via OF from L *horribilis*, from *horrēre* to tremble]
▶ 'horribleness *n* ▶ 'horribly *adv*

horrid ('hɒrɪd) *adj* **1** disagreeable; unpleasant: *a horrid meal.* **2** repulsive or frightening. **3** *Inf.* unkind.   [C16 (in the sense: bristling, shaggy): from L *horridus* prickly, from *horrēre* to bristle]
▶ 'horridly *adv* ▶ 'horridness *n*

horrific (hɒ'rɪfɪk, hə-) *adj* provoking horror; horrible.
▶ hor'rifically *adv*

horrify ('hɒrɪ,faɪ) *vb* **horrifies, horrifying, horrified.** (*tr*) **1** to cause feelings of horror in; terrify. **2** to shock greatly.
▶ ,horrifi'cation *n* ▶ 'horri,fied *adj* ▶ 'horri,fying *adj* ▶ 'horri,fyingly *adv*

horripilation (hɒ,rɪpɪ'leɪʃən) *n Physiol.* a technical name for **goose flesh.** [C17: from LL *horripilātiō* a bristling, from L *horrēre* to stand on end + *pilus* hair]

horror ('hɒrə) *n* **1** extreme fear; terror; dread. **2** intense hatred. **3** (*often pl*) a thing or person causing fear, loathing, etc. **4** (*modifier*) having a frightening subject: *a horror film.* [C14: from L: a trembling with fear]

horrors ('hɒrəz) *pl n* **1** *Sl.* a fit of depression or anxiety. **2** *Inf.* See **delirium tremens.** ◆ *interj* **3** an expression of dismay, sometimes facetious.

Horsa ★ ('hɔːsə) *n* died ?455 A.D., leader, with his brother Hengist, of the first Jutish settlers in Britain. See also **Hengist.**

hors de combat *French.* (ɔr də kɔ̃ba) *adj* (*postpositive*), *adv* disabled or injured. [lit.: out of (the) fight]

hors d'oeuvre (ɔː 'dɜːvr) *n, pl* **hors d'oeuvre** *or* **hors d'oeuvres** ('dɜːvr). an appetizer, usually served before the main meal. [C18: from F, lit.: outside the work]

horse (hɔːs) *n* **1** a solid-hoofed, herbivorous, domesticated mammal used for draught work and riding. Related adj: **equine. 2** the adult male of this species; stallion. **3 wild horse.** another name for **Przewalski's horse. 4** (*functioning as pl*) horsemen, esp. cavalry: *a regiment of horse.* Also called: **buck.** *Gymnastics.* a padded apparatus on legs, used for vaulting, etc. **6** a narrow board supported by a pair of legs at each end, used as a frame for sawing or as a trestle, barrier, etc. **7** a contrivance on which a person may ride and exercise. **8** a slang word for **heroin. 9** *Mining.* a mass of rock within a vein of ore. **10** *Naut.* a rod, rope, or cable, fixed at the ends, along which something may slide; traveller. **11** *Inf.* short for **horsepower. 12** (*modifier*) drawn by a horse or horses: *a horse cart.* **13 a horse of another or a different colour.** a completely different topic, argument, etc. **14 be** (*or* **get**) **on one's high horse.** *Inf.* to act disdainfully aloof. **15 hold one's horses.** to restrain oneself. **16 horses for courses.** a policy, course of action, etc. modified slightly to take account of special circumstances without departing in essentials from the original. **17 the horse's mouth.** the most reliable source. ◆ *vb* **horses, horsing, horsed. 18** (*tr*) to provide with a horse or horses. **19** to put or be put on horseback. [OE *hors*]
▶ 'horse,like *adj*

horse around *or* **about** *vb* (*intr, adv*) *Inf.* to indulge in horseplay.

horseback ('hɔːs,bæk) *n* **a** a horse's back (esp. in **on horseback**). **b** *Chiefly US.* (*as modifier*): *horseback riding.*

horsebox ('hɔːs,bɒks) *n Brit.* a van or trailer used for carrying horses.

horse brass *n* a decorative brass ornament, originally attached to a horse's harness.

horse chestnut *n* **1** a tree having palmate leaves, erect clusters of white, pink, or red flowers, and brown shiny inedible nuts enclosed in a spiky bur. **2** Also called: **conker.** the nut of this tree. [C16: from its having been used in the treatment of respiratory disease in horses]

horseflesh ('hɔːs,fleʃ) *n* **1** horses collectively. **2** the flesh of a horse, esp. edible horse meat.

horsefly ('hɔːs,flaɪ) *n, pl* **horseflies.** a large stout-bodied dipterous fly, the female of which sucks the blood of mammals, esp. horses, cattle, and man. Also called: **gadfly, cleg.**

horsehair ('hɔːs,heə) *n* hair taken chiefly from the tail or mane of a horse, used in upholstery and for fabric, etc.

horsehide ('hɔːs,haɪd) *n* **1** the hide of a horse. **2** leather made from this hide.

horse latitudes *pl n Naut.* the latitudes near 30°N or 30°S at sea, characterized by baffling winds, calms, and high barometric pressure. [C18: referring either to the high mortality of horses on board ship in these latitudes or to *dead horse* (nautical slang: advance pay), which sailors expected to work off by this stage of a voyage]

horse laugh *n* a coarse or raucous laugh.

horseleech ('hɔːs,liːtʃ) *n* **1** any of several large carnivo-

rous freshwater leeches. **2** an archaic name for a veterinary surgeon.

horse mackerel *n* **1** Also called: **scad.** a mackerel-like fish of European Atlantic waters, with a row of bony scales along the lateral line. Sometimes called (US): **saurel. 2** any of various large tunnies or related fishes.

horseman ('hɔːsmən) *n, pl* **horsemen. 1** a person skilled in riding. **2** a person who rides a horse.
▶ 'horseman,ship *n* ▶ 'horse,woman *fem n*

horse mushroom *n* a large edible mushroom, with a white cap and greyish gills.

Horsens ★ (*Danish* 'hɔrsəns) *n* a port in Denmark, in E Jutland at the head of **Horsens Fjord.** Pop.: 55 252 (1995).

horse pistol *n* a large holstered pistol formerly carried by horsemen.

horseplay ('hɔːs,pleɪ) *n* rough or rowdy play.

horsepower ('hɔːs,pauə) *n* an fps unit of power, equal to 550 foot-pounds per second (equivalent to 745.7 watts). Abbrev.: **HP, h.p.**

horseradish ('hɔːs,rædɪʃ) *n* a coarse Eurasian plant cultivated for its thick white pungent root, which is ground and combined with vinegar, etc., to make a sauce.

horse sense *n* another term for **common sense.**

horseshoe ('hɔːs,ʃuː) *n* **1** a piece of iron shaped like a U nailed to the underside of the hoof of a horse to protect the soft part of the foot: commonly thought to be a token of good luck. **2** an object of similar shape.

horseshoe bat *n* any of numerous large-eared Old World bats with a fleshy growth around the nostrils, used in echolocation.

horseshoe crab *n* a marine arthropod of North America and Asia, having a rounded heavily armoured body with a long pointed tail. Also called: **king crab.**

horsetail ('hɔːs,teɪl) *n* **1** a plant having jointed stems with whorls of small dark toothlike leaves and producing spores within conelike structures at the tips of the stems. **2** a stylized horse's tail formerly used as the emblem of a pasha.

horse trading *n* shrewd bargaining.

horsewhip ('hɔːs,wɪp) *n* **1** a whip, usually with a long thong, used for managing horses. ◆ *vb* **horsewhips, horsewhipping, horsewhipped. 2** (*tr*) to flog with such a whip.
▶ 'horse,whipper *n*

horsey *or* **horsy** ('hɔːsɪ) *adj* **horsier, horsiest. 1** of or relating to horses: *a horsey smell.* **2** dealing with or devoted to horses. **3** like a horse: *a horsey face.*
▶ 'horsily *adv* ▶ 'horsiness *n*

horst (hɔːst) *n* a ridge of land that has been forced upwards between two parallel faults. [C20: from G *Horst* thicket]

Horta ★ (*Portuguese* 'ɔrtə) *n* a port in the Azores, on the SE coast of Fayal Island.

hortatory ('hɔːtətərɪ) *or* **hortative** ('hɔːtətɪv) *adj* tending to exhort; encouraging. [C16: from LL *hortātōrius*, from L *hortārī* to EXHORT]
▶ hor'tation *n* ▶ 'hortatorily *or* 'hortatively *adv*

Hortense ★ (*French* ɔrtɑ̃s) *n* See (Eugénie Hortense de) **Beauharnais.**

Horthy ★ (*Hungarian* 'horti) *n* **Miklós** ('mikloːʃ), full name *Horthy de Nagybánya.* 1868–1957, Hungarian admiral: suppressed Kun's Communist republic (1919); regent of Hungary (1920–44).

horticulture ('hɔːtɪ,kʌltʃə) *n* the art or science of cultivating gardens. [C17: from L *hortus* garden + CULTURE; cf. AGRICULTURE]
▶ ,horti'cultural *adj* ▶ ,horti'culturalist *or* ,horti'culturist *n*

Horus ★ ('hɔːrəs) *n* a solar god of Egyptian mythology, usually depicted with a falcon's head. [via LL from Gk *Hōros*, from Egyptian *Hur* hawk]

Hos. *Bible. abbrev.* for Hosea.

hosanna (həʊ'zænə) *interj* an exclamation of praise, esp. one to God. [OE *osanna*, via LL from Gk, from Heb. *hōshī 'āh nnā* save now, we pray]

hose¹ (həʊz) *n* **1** a flexible pipe, for conveying a liquid or gas. ◆ *vb* **hoses, hosing, hosed. 2** (sometimes foll. by *down*)

★ **people and places**

to wash, water, or sprinkle (a person or thing) with or as if with a hose. [C15: later use of HOSE²]

hose² (həʊz) *n*, *pl* **hose** or **hosen** ('həʊz°n). **1** stockings, socks, and tights collectively. **2** *History.* a man's garment covering the legs and reaching up to the waist. **3 half-hose.** socks. [OE *hosa*]

Hosea ★ (həʊ'zɪə) *n Old Testament.* **1** a Hebrew prophet of the 8th century B.C. **2** the book containing his oracles.

hosier ('həʊzɪə) *n* a person who sells stockings, etc.

hosiery ('həʊzɪərɪ) *n* stockings, socks, and knitted underclothing collectively.

hospice ('hɒspɪs) *n* **1** a nursing home that specializes in caring for the terminally ill. **2** *Arch.* a place of shelter for travellers, esp. one kept by a monastic order. [C19: from F, from L *hospitium* hospitality, from *hospes* guest]

hospitable ('hɒspɪtəb°l, hɒ'spɪt-) *adj* **1** welcoming to guests or strangers. **2** fond of entertaining. [C16: from Med. L *hospitāre* to receive as a guest, from L *hospes* guest] ▸ **'hospitableness** *n* ▸ **'hospitably** *adv*

hospital ('hɒspɪt°l) *n* **1** an institution for the medical or psychiatric care and treatment of patients. **2** (*modifier*) having the function of a hospital: *a hospital ship.* **3** a repair shop for something specified: *a dolls' hospital.* **4** *Arch.* a charitable home, hospice, or school. [C13: from Med. L *hospitāle* hospice, from L *hospes* guest]

Hospitalet ★ (*Spanish* ɔspita'let) *n* a city in NE Spain, a SW suburb of Barcelona. Pop.: 266 242 (1994 est.).

hospitality (ˌhɒspɪ'tælɪtɪ) *n*, *pl* **hospitalities.** kindness in welcoming strangers or guests.

hospitality suite *n* a room or suite, as at a conference, where free drinks are offered.

hospitalize or **hospitalise** ('hɒspɪtəˌlaɪz) *vb* **hospitalizes, hospitalizing, hospitalized** or **hospitalises, hospitalising, hospitalised.** (*tr*) to admit or send (a person) into a hospital. ▸ ˌhospitali'zation or ˌhospitali'sation *n*

hospitaller or US **hospitaler** ('hɒspɪtələ) *n* a person, esp. a member of certain religious orders, dedicated to hospital work, ambulance services, etc. [C14: from OF *hospitalier*, from Med. L, from *hospitāle* hospice; see HOSPITAL]

Hospitaller or US **Hospitaler** ('hɒspɪtələ) *n* a member of the order of the Knights Hospitallers.

host¹ (həʊst) *n* **1** a person who receives or entertains guests, esp. in his own home. **2a** a country or organization which provides facilities for and receives visitors to an event. **2b** (*as modifier*): *the host nation.* **3** the compere of a show or television programme. **4** *Biol.* **4a** an animal or plant that supports a parasite. **4b** an animal into which tissue is experimentally grafted. **5** *Computing.* a computer that is connected to others on a network. **6** the owner or manager of an inn. ♦ *vb* **7** to be the host of (a party, programme, etc.): *to host one's own show.* [C13: from F *hoste*, from L *hospes* guest]

host² (həʊst) *n* **1** a great number; multitude. **2** an archaic word for **army.** [C13: from OF *hoste*, from L *hostis* stranger]

Host (həʊst) *n Christianity.* the wafer of unleavened bread consecrated in the Eucharist. [C14: from OF *oiste*, from L *hostia* victim]

hosta ('hɒstə) *n* a plant cultivated esp. for its ornamental foliage. [C19: NL, after N. T. *Host* (1761–1834), Austrian physician]

hostage ('hɒstɪdʒ) *n* **1** a person held as a security or pledge or to be ransomed, exchanged for prisoners, etc. **2** the state of being held as a hostage. **3** any security or pledge. **4 give hostages to fortune.** to place oneself in a position in which misfortune may strike through the loss of what one values most. [C13: from OF, from *hoste* guest]

hostel ('hɒst°l) *n* **1** a building providing overnight accommodation, as for homeless people. **2** See **youth hostel**. **3** *Brit.* a supervised lodging house for nurses, workers, etc. **4** *Arch.* another word for **hostelry.** [C13: from OF, from Med. L *hospitāle* hospice; see HOSPITAL]

hosteller or US **hosteler** ('hɒstələ) *n* **1** a person who stays at youth hostels. **2** an archaic word for **innkeeper.**

hostelling or US **hosteling** ('hɒstəlɪŋ) *n* the practice of staying at youth hostels when travelling.

hostelry ('hɒstəlrɪ) *n*, *pl* **hostelries.** *Arch.* or *facetious.* an inn.

hostess ('həʊstɪs) *n* **1** a woman acting as host. **2** a woman who receives and entertains patrons of a club, restaurant, etc. **3** See **air hostess.**

hostile ('hɒstaɪl) *adj* **1** antagonistic; opposed. **2** of or relating to an enemy. **3** unfriendly. [C16: from L *hostīlis*, from *hostis* enemy] ▸ **'hostilely** *adv*

hostility (hɒ'stɪlɪtɪ) *n*, *pl* **hostilities.** **1** enmity. **2** an act expressing enmity. **3** (*pl*) fighting; warfare.

hostler ('ɒslə) *n* a variant (esp. Brit.) of **ostler.**

hot (hɒt) *adj* **hotter, hottest.** **1** having a relatively high temperature. **2** having a temperature higher than desirable. **3** causing a sensation of bodily heat. **4** causing a burning sensation on the tongue: *a hot curry.* **5** expressing or feeling intense emotion, such as anger or lust. **6** intense or vehement. **7** recent; new: *hot from the press.* **8** *Ball games.* (of a ball) thrown or struck hard, and so difficult to respond to. **9** much favoured: *a hot favourite.* **10** *Inf.* having a dangerously high level of radioactivity. **11** *Sl.* stolen or otherwise illegally obtained. **12** *Sl.* (of people) being sought by the police. **13** (of a colour) intense; striking: *hot pink.* **14** following closely: *hot on the scent.* **15** *Inf.* at a dangerously high electric potential. **16** *Sl.* good (esp. in **not so hot**). **17** *Jazz sl.* arousing great excitement by inspired improvisation, strong rhythms, etc. **18** *Inf.* dangerous or unpleasant (esp. in **make it hot for someone**). **19** (in various games) very near the answer. **20** *Metallurgy.* (of a process) at a sufficiently high temperature for metal to be in a soft workable state. **21** *Austral. & NZ inf.* (of a price, etc.) excessive. **22 hot on.** *Inf.* **22a** very severe: *the police are hot on drunk drivers.* **22b** particularly knowledgeable about. **23 hot under the collar.** *Inf.* aroused with anger, annoyance, etc. **24 in hot water.** *Inf.* in trouble. ♦ *adv* **25** in a hot manner; hotly. ♦ See also **hots, hot up.** [OE *hāt*] ▸ **'hotly** *adv* ▸ **'hotness** *n* ▸ **'hottish** *adj*

hot air *n Inf.* empty and usually boastful talk.

Hotan ('həʊ'tæn), **Hotien,** or **Ho-t'ien** ★ ('həʊ'tjen) *n* **1** an oasis in W China, in the Taklimakan Shamo desert of central Xinjiang Uygur Autonomous Region, around the seasonal Hotan River. **2** the chief town of this oasis, situated at the foot of the Kunlun Mountains. Pop.: 71 600 (1986 est.). Also called: **Khotan, Hetian.**

hotbed ('hɒtˌbed) *n* **1** a glass-covered bed of soil, usually heated, for propagating plants, forcing early vegetables, etc. **2** a place offering ideal conditions for the growth of an idea, activity, etc., esp. one considered bad.

hot-blooded *adj* **1** passionate or excitable. **2** (of a horse) being of thoroughbred stock.

hotchpotch ('hɒtʃˌpɒtʃ) or *esp.* US & Canad. **hodge-podge** *n* **1** a jumbled mixture. **2** a thick soup or stew. [C15: var. of *hotchpot* from OF, from *hocher* to shake + POT¹]

hot cross bun *n* a yeast bun marked with a cross and traditionally eaten on Good Friday.

hot desking ('deskɪŋ) *n* the practice of not assigning permanent desks in a workplace, so that employees may work at any available desk.

hot dog¹ *n* a sausage, esp. a frankfurter, usually served hot in a long roll split lengthways. [C20: from the supposed resemblance of the sausage to a dachshund]

hot dog² *n* **1** *Chiefly US.* a person who performs showy acrobatic manoeuvres when skiing or surfing. ♦ *vb* **hot-dog, hot-dogs, hot-dogging, hot-dogged.** **2** (*intr*) to perform a series of manoeuvres in skiing, surfing, etc.

hotel (həʊ'tel) *n* a commercially run establishment providing lodging and usually meals for guests and often containing a public bar. [C17: from F *hôtel*, from OF *hostel*; see HOSTEL]

hotelier (hɒ'teljeɪ) *n* an owner or manager of one or more hotels.

hotel ship *n* an accommodation barge anchored near an oil production rig.

hot flush or US **hot flash** n a sudden unpleasant hot feeling experienced by menopausal women.

hotfoot ('hɒt,fʊt) adv with all possible speed.

hothead ('hɒt,hed) n an excitable person.

hot-headed adj impetuous, rash, or hot-tempered.
► ,hot-'headedness n

hothouse ('hɒt,haʊs) n **1a** a greenhouse in which the temperature is maintained at a fixed level. **1b** (as modifier): a hothouse plant. **2a** an environment that encourages rapid development. **2b** (as modifier): a hothouse atmosphere. **3** (modifier) Inf., often disparaging. sensitive or delicate: a hothouse temperament.

Hotien or **Ho-t'ien** ★ ('həʊ'tjɛn) n a variant transliteration of the Chinese name for **Hotan**.

hot key n Computing. a single key on the keyboard of a computer which carries out a series of commands.

hotline ('hɒt,laɪn) n **1** a direct telephone, teletype, or other communications link between heads of government, etc., for emergency use. **2** any such direct line kept for urgent use.

hot link n Computing. a word or phrase in a hypertext document that can be selected to access additional information.

hot money n capital that is transferred from one financial centre to another seeking the best opportunity for short-term gain.

hotplate ('hɒt,pleɪt) n **1** an electrically heated plate on a cooker or one set into a working surface. **2** a portable device on which food can be kept warm.

hotpot ('hɒt,pɒt) n **1** Brit. a casserole covered with a layer of potatoes. **2** Austral. sl. a heavily backed horse.

hot potato n Sl. a delicate or awkward matter.

hot-press n **1** a machine for applying a combination of heat and pressure to give a smooth surface to paper, to express oil from it, etc. ◆ vb **2** (tr) to subject (paper, cloth, etc.) to such a process.

hot rod n a car with an engine that has been radically modified to produce increased power.

hots (hɒts) pl n the. Sl. intense sexual desire; lust (esp. in the phrase **have the hots for (someone)**).

hot seat n **1** Inf. a difficult or dangerous position. **2** US. a slang term for **electric chair**.

hot spot n **1** an area of potential violence. **2** a lively nightclub. **3** any local area of high temperature in a part of an engine, etc. **4** Med. **4a** a small area on the surface or within a body with an exceptionally high level of radioactivity or of some chemical or mineral considered harmful. **4b** a similar area that generates an abnormal amount of heat, as revealed by thermography.

hot spring n a natural spring of mineral water at 21°C (70°F) or above, found in areas of volcanic activity. Also called: **thermal spring**.

hotspur ('hɒt,spɜː) n an impetuous or fiery person. [C15: from HOTSPUR]

Hotspur ★ ('hɒt,spɜː) n **Harry.** nickname of (Sir Henry) Percy.

hot stuff n Inf. **1** a person, object, etc., considered important, attractive, etc. **2** a pornographic or erotic book, play, film, etc.

Hottentot ('hɒt³n,tɒt) n another name for **Khoikhoi**.

hotting ('hɒtɪŋ) n Inf. the practice of stealing fast cars and putting on a show of skilful but dangerous driving.
► 'hotter n

hot up vb **hots, hotting, hotted.** (adv) Inf. **1** to make or become more exciting, active, or intense. **2** (tr) another term for **soup up**.

hot-water bottle n a receptacle now usually made of rubber, designed to be filled with hot water and used for warming a bed.

hot-wire vb **hot-wires, hot-wiring, hot-wired.** (tr) Sl. to start the engine of (a motor vehicle) by bypassing the ignition switch.

Houdini ★ (huː'diːnɪ) n **Harry,** real name Ehrich Weiss. 1874–1926, US magician and escapologist.

Houdon ★ (French udɔ̃) n **Jean Antoine** (ʒɑ̃ ɑ̃twan). 1741–1828, French neoclassical portrait sculptor.

hough (hɒk) Brit. ◆ n **1** a variant of **hock**[1]. ◆ vb **2** to hamstring (cattle, horses, etc.). [C14: from OE hōh heel]

Houghton-le-Spring ★ ('haʊt³nlə'sprɪŋ) n a town in N England, in Sunderland, E Tyne and Wear: coal-mining. Pop.: 35 100 (1991).

hound (haʊnd) n **1a** any of several breeds of dog used for hunting. **1b** (in combination): a deerhound. **2** a dog, esp. one regarded as annoying. **3** a despicable person. **4** (in hare and hounds) a runner who pursues a hare. **5** Sl., chiefly US & Canad. an enthusiast. **6 ride to hounds** or **follow the hounds.** to take part in a fox hunt. **7 the hounds.** a pack of foxhounds, etc. ◆ vb (tr) **8** to pursue relentlessly. **9** to urge on. [OE hund]
► 'hounder n

hound's-tongue n a plant which has small reddish-purple flowers and spiny fruits. Also called: **dog's-tongue**. [OE hundestunge, translation of L cynoglōssos, from Gk, from kuōn dog + glōssa tongue; referring to the shape of its leaves]

hound's-tooth check n a pattern of broken or jagged checks, esp. on cloth. Also called: **dog's-tooth check, dog-tooth check**.

Hounslow ★ ('haʊnzləʊ) n a borough of Greater London, on the River Thames: site of London's first civil airport (1919). Pop.: 202 700 (1994 est.). Area: 59 sq. km (23 sq. miles).

Houphouet-Boigny ★ (French ufwɛbwaɲi) n **Félix** (feliks). 1905–93, Côte d'Ivoire statesman; president (1960–93).

hour ('aʊə) n **1** a period of time equal to 3600 seconds; 1/24th of a calendar day. Related adj: **horary. 2** any of the points on the face of a timepiece that indicate intervals of 60 minutes. **3** the time. **4** the time allowed for or used for something: lunch hour. **5** a special moment: our finest hour. **6** the distance covered in an hour: we live an hour away. **7** Astron. an angular measurement of right ascension equal to 15° or a 24th part of the celestial equator. **8 one's last hour.** the time of one's death. **9 the hour.** an exact number of complete hours: the bus leaves on the hour. ◆ See also **hours**. [C13: from OF hore, from L hōra, from Gk: season]

hour circle n a great circle on the celestial sphere passing through the celestial poles and a specified point, such as a star.

hourglass ('aʊə,glɑːs) n **1** a device consisting of two transparent chambers linked by a narrow channel, containing a quantity of sand that takes a specified time to trickle from one chamber to the other. **2** (modifier) well-proportioned with a small waist: an hourglass figure.

hour hand n the pointer on a timepiece that indicates the hour.

houri ('hʊərɪ) n, pl **houris. 1** (in Muslim belief) any of the nymphs of Paradise. **2** any alluring woman. [C18: from F, from Persian, from Ar. hūr, pl. of haurā' woman with dark eyes]

hourly ('aʊəlɪ) adj **1** of, occurring, or done every hour. **2** done in or measured by the hour: an hourly rate. **3** continual or frequent. ◆ adv **4** every hour. **5** at any moment.

hours ('aʊəz) pl n **1** a period regularly appointed for work, etc. **2** one's times of rising and going to bed: he keeps late hours. **3 till all hours.** until very late. **4** an indefinite time. **5** RC Church. Also called: **canonical hours. 5a** the seven times of the day laid down for the recitation of the prayers of the divine office. **5b** the prayers recited at these times.

Hours ★ (aʊəz) pl n another word for the **Horae**.

house n (haʊs), pl **houses** ('haʊzɪz). **1a** a building used as a home; dwelling. **1b** (as modifier): house dog. **2** the people present in a house. **3a** a building for some specific purpose. **3b** (in combination): a schoolhouse. **4** (often cap.) a family or dynasty: the House of York. **5a** a commercial company: a publishing house. **5b** (as modifier): a house journal. **6** a legislative body. **7** a quorum in such a body (esp. in **make a house**). **8** a dwelling for a religious community. **9** Astrol. any of the 12 divisions of the zodiac. **10** any of several divisions of a large school. **11** a hotel, restaurant, club, etc., or the management of such an establishment.

★ people and places

12 (*modifier*) (of wine) sold unnamed by a restaurant, at a lower price than wines specified on the wine list: *the house red*. **13** the audience in a theatre or cinema. **14** an informal word for **brothel**. **15** a hall in which a legislative body meets. **16** See **full house**. **17** *Naut.* any structure or shelter on the weather deck of a vessel. **18 bring the house down**. *Theatre*. to win great applause. **19 like a house on fire**. *Inf.* very well. **20 on the house**. (usually of drinks) paid for by the management of the hotel, bar, etc. **21 put one's house in order**. to settle or organize one's affairs. **22 safe as houses**. *Brit.* very secure. ◆ *vb* (hauz), **houses, housing, housed**. **23** (*tr*) to provide with or serve as accommodation. **24** to give or receive lodging. **25** (*tr*) to contain or cover; protect. **26** (*tr*) to fit (a piece of wood) into a mortise, etc. [OE *hūs*]
▶ 'houseless *adj*

house agent *n Brit.* another name for **estate agent**.

house arrest *n* confinement to one's own home rather than in prison.

houseboat ('haus,bəut) *n* a stationary boat or barge used as a home.

housebound ('haus,baund) *adj* unable to leave one's house because of illness, injury, etc.

housebreaking ('haus,breikiŋ) *n Criminal law*. the act of entering a building as a trespasser for an unlawful purpose. Assimilated with burglary (1968).
▶ 'house,breaker *n*

housecoat ('haus,kəut) *n* a woman's loose robelike informal garment.

house-craft *n* skill in domestic management.

housefly ('haus,flai) *n, pl* **houseflies**. a common dipterous fly that frequents human habitations, spreads disease, and lays its eggs in carrion, decaying vegetables, etc.

household ('haus,həuld) *n* **1** the people living together in one house. **2** (*modifier*) relating to the running of a household: *household management*.

householder ('haus,həuldə) *n* a person who owns or rents a house.
▶ 'house,holder,ship *n*

household name *or* **word** *n* a person or thing that is very well known.

housekeeper ('haus,ki:pə) *n* a person, esp. a woman, employed to run a household.

housekeeping ('haus,ki:piŋ) *n* **1** the running of a household. **2** money allotted for this. **3** general maintenance as of records, data, etc., in an organization.

houseleek ('haus,li:k) *n* an Old World plant which has a rosette of succulent leaves and pinkish flowers: grows on walls.

house lights *pl n* the lights in the auditorium of a theatre, cinema, etc.

housemaid ('haus,meid) *n* a girl or woman employed to do housework, esp. one who is resident in the household.

housemaid's knee *n* inflammation and swelling of the bursa in front of the kneecap, caused esp. by constant kneeling on a hard surface. Technical name: **prepatellar bursitis**.

houseman ('hausmən) *n, pl* **housemen**. *Med.* a junior doctor who is a member of the medical staff of a hospital. US and Canad. equivalent: **intern**.

house martin *n* a Eurasian swallow with a forked tail.

house mouse *n* any of various greyish mice, a common household pest in most parts of the world.

House music *or* **House** *n* a type of disco music of the late 1980s, based on funk, with fragments of other recordings edited in electronically.

House of Assembly *n* a legislative assembly or the lower chamber of such an assembly.

house of cards *n* **1** a tiered structure created by balancing playing cards on their edges. **2** an unstable situation, etc.

House of Commons *n* (in Britain, Canada, etc.) the lower chamber of Parliament.

house of correction *n* (formerly) a place of confinement for persons convicted of minor offences.

house of ill repute *or* **ill fame** *n* a euphemistic name for **brothel**.

House of Keys *n* the lower chamber of the legislature of the Isle of Man.

House of Lords *n* (in Britain) the upper chamber of Parliament, composed of the peers of the realm.

House of Representatives *n* **1** (in the US) the lower chamber of Congress, or of many state legislatures. **2** (in Australia) the lower chamber of Parliament. **3** the sole chamber of New Zealand's Parliament.

houseparent ('haus,pɛərənt) *n* a person in charge of the welfare of a group of children in an institution.

house party *n* **1** a party, usually in a country house, at which guests are invited to stay for several days. **2** the guests who are invited.

house plant *n* a plant that can be grown indoors.

house-proud *adj* proud of the appearance, cleanliness, etc., of one's house, sometimes excessively so.

houseroom ('haus,rum, -,ru:m) *n* **1** room for storage or lodging. **2 give (something) houseroom**. (*used with a negative*) to have or keep (something) in one's house.

Houses of Parliament ★ *n* (in Britain) **1** the building in which the House of Commons and the House of Lords assemble. **2** these two chambers considered together.

house sparrow *n* a small Eurasian bird, now established in North America and Australia. It has a brown plumage with grey underparts. Also called (US): **English sparrow**.

housetop ('haus,tɒp) *n* **1** the roof of a house. **2 proclaim from the housetops**. to announce (something) publicly.

house-train *vb* (*tr*) *Brit.* to train (pets) to urinate and defecate outside the house.
▶ 'house-,trained *adj*

house-warming *n* a party given after moving into a new home.

housewife *n, pl* **housewives**. **1** ('haus,waif). a woman who keeps house. **2** ('hʌzif). Also called: **hussy, huswife**. *Chiefly Brit.* a small sewing kit.
▶ **housewifery** ('haus,wifəri) *n* ▶ 'housewifely *adj*

housework ('haus,wɜ:k) *n* the work of running a home, such as cleaning, cooking, etc.

housey-housey ('hausi'hausi) *n* another name for **bingo** or **lotto**. [C20: from the cry of "house!" shouted by the winner, prob. from FULL HOUSE]

housing[1] ('hauziŋ) *n* **1a** houses collectively. **1b** (*as modifier*): *a housing problem*. **2** the act of providing with accommodation. **3** a hole or slot made in one wooden member to receive another. **4** a part designed to contain or support a component or mechanism: *a wheel housing*.

housing[2] ('hauziŋ) *n* (*often pl*) *Arch.* another word for **trappings** (sense 2). [C14: from OF *houce* covering, of Gmc origin]

housing estate *n* a planned area of housing, often with its own shops and other amenities.

housing scheme *n* a local-authority housing estate. Often shortened to **scheme**.

Housman ★ ('hausmən) *n* **A**(lfred) **E**(dward). 1859–1936, British poet and classical scholar, author of *A Shropshire Lad* (1896) and *Last Poems* (1922).

Houston ★ ('hju:stən) *n* an inland port in SE Texas, linked by the **Houston Ship Canal** to the Gulf of Mexico and the Gulf Intracoastal Waterway: capital of the Republic of Texas (1837–39; 1842–45); site of the Manned Spacecraft Center (1964). Pop.: 1 702 086 (1994 est.).

hove (həuv) *vb Chiefly naut.* a past tense and past participle of **heave**.

Hove ★ (həuv) *n* a town and resort in S England, in East Sussex adjoining Brighton. Pop.: 67 602 (1991).

hovel ('hɒv[ə]l) *n* **1** a ramshackle dwelling place. **2** an open shed for livestock, carts, etc. **3** the conical building enclosing a kiln. [C15: from ?]

hover ('hɒvə) *vb* (*intr*) **1** to remain suspended in one place. **2** (of certain birds, esp. hawks) to remain in one place in the air by rapidly beating the wings. **3** to linger

uncertainly. **4** to be in a state of indecision. ◆ *n* **5** the act of hovering. [C14: *hoveren*, var. of *hoven*, from ?]
▸ **'hoverer** *n*

hovercraft ('hɒvəˌkrɑːft) *n* a vehicle that is able to travel across both land and water on a cushion of air.

hover fly *n* a dipterous fly with a hovering flight.

hoverport ('hɒvəˌpɔːt) *n* a port for hovercraft.

hovertrain ('hɒvəˌtreɪn) *n* a train that moves over a concrete track and is supported by a cushion of air supplied by powerful fans.

how (haʊ) *adv* **1** in what way?: *how did it happen?* Also used in indirect questions: *tell me how he did it.* **2** to what extent?: *how tall is he?* **3** how good? how well? what...like?: *how did she sing?* **4 and how!** (intensifier) very much so! **5 how about?** used to suggest something: *how about a cup of tea?* **6 how are you?** what is your state of health? **7 how come?** *Inf.* what is the reason (that)?: *how come you told him?* **8 how's that? 8a** what is your opinion? **8b** *Cricket.* Also written: **howzat** (haʊ'zæt). (an appeal to the umpire) is the batsman out? **9 how now?** *or* **how so?** *Arch.* what is the meaning of this? **10** in whatever way: *do it how you wish.* ◆ *n* **11** the way a thing is done: *the how of it.* [OE *hū*]

Howard ★ ('haʊəd) *n* **1 Catherine.** ?1521–42, fifth wife of Henry VIII of England; beheaded. **2 Charles,** Lord Howard of Effingham and 1st Earl of Nottingham. 1536–1624, Lord High Admiral of England (1585–1618). He commanded the fleet that defeated the Spanish Armada (1588). **3** Sir **Ebenezer.** 1850–1928, British town planner, who introduced garden cities. **4 Henry.** See (Earl of) **Surrey. 5 John.** 1726–90, British prison reformer. **6 John Winston.** born 1939, Australian politician; prime minister of Australia from 1996. **7 Leslie,** real name *Leslie Howard Stainer.* 1890–1943, British actor of Hungarian descent. His films include *Gone With the Wind* (1939). **8 Michael.** born 1941, British Conservative politician; home secretary (1993–97). **9 Trevor.** 1916–88, British actor. His films include *Brief Encounter* (1946), *The Third Man* (1949), and *White Mischief* (1987).

howbeit (haʊ'biːɪt) *Arch.* ◆ *sentence connector.* **1** however. ◆ *conj* **2** (subordinating) though; although.

howdah ('haʊdə) *n* a seat for riding on an elephant's back, esp. one with a canopy. [C18: from Hindi *haudah*, from Ar. *haudaj* load carried by elephant or camel]

how do you do *sentence substitute.* **1** a formal greeting said by people who are being introduced to each other. ◆ *n* **how-do-you-do. 2** *Inf.* a difficult situation.

howdy ('haʊdɪ) *sentence substitute. Chiefly US.* an informal word for **hello.** [C16: from *how d'ye do*]

Howe ★ (haʊ) *n* **1 Elias.** 1819–67, US inventor of the sewing machine (1846). **2 Howe of Aberavon,** Baron, title of (*Richard Edward*) *Geoffrey Howe.* born 1926, British Conservative politician; Chancellor of the Exchequer (1979–83); foreign secretary (1983–89); deputy prime minister (1984–90). **3 Richard,** 4th Viscount Howe. 1726–99, British admiral: served (1776–78) in the War of American Independence, winning the Battle of the Glorious First of June (1794). **4** his brother, **William,** 5th Viscount Howe. 1729–1814, British general; commander in chief (1776–78) of British forces in the War of American Independence.

Howel Dda ★ ('haʊəl 'ðɑː) *n* a variant of **Hywel Dda.**

however (haʊ'ɛvə) *sentence connector.* **1** still; nevertheless. **2** on the other hand; yet. ◆ *adv* **3** by whatever means. **4** (*used with adjectives of quantity or degree*) no matter how: *however long it takes, finish it.* **5** an emphatic form of **how** (sense 1).

howitzer ('haʊɪtsə) *n* a cannon having a short barrel with a low muzzle velocity and a steep angle of fire. [C16: from Du. *houwitser*, from G, from Czech *houfnice* stone-sling]

howl (haʊl) *n* **1** a long plaintive cry characteristic of a wolf or hound. **2** a similar cry of pain or sorrow. **3** a prolonged outburst of laughter. **4** *Electronics.* an unwanted high-pitched sound produced by a sound-producing system as a result of feedback. ◆ *vb* **5** to express in a howl or utter such cries. **6** (*intr*) (of the wind, etc.) to

make a wailing noise. **7** (*intr*) *Inf.* to shout or laugh. [C14: *houlen*]

Howland Island ★ ('haʊlənd) *n* a small island in the central Pacific, near the equator northwest of Phoenix Island: US airfield. Area: 2.6 sq. km (1 sq. mile).

howl down *vb* (*tr, adv*) to prevent (a speaker) from being heard by shouting disapprovingly.

howler ('haʊlə) *n* **1** Also called: **howler monkey.** a large New World monkey inhabiting tropical forests in South America and having a loud howling cry. **2** *Inf.* a glaring mistake. **3** a person or thing that howls.

howling ('haʊlɪŋ) *adj* (*prenominal*) *Inf.* (intensifier): *a howling success; a howling error.*

Howlin' Wolf ★ ('haʊlɪn) *n* real name *Chester Burnett.* 1910–76, US blues singer and songwriter.

Howrah ★ ('haʊrə) *n* an industrial city in E India, on the Hooghly River opposite Calcutta. Pop.: 950 435 (1991).

howsoever (ˌhaʊsəʊ'ɛvə) *sentence connector, adv* a less common word for **however.**

how-to *adj* (of a book or guide) giving basic instructions to the lay person on how to do or make something: *a how-to book on carpentry.*

Hoxha ★ (*Albanian* 'hodʒa) *n* **Enver** ('ɛmvər). 1908–85, Albanian statesman: founded the Albanian Communist Party in 1941 and was its first secretary (1954–85).

hoy[1] (hɔɪ) *n Naut.* **1** a freight barge. **2** a coastal fishing and trading vessel used during the 17th and 18th centuries. [C15: from MDu. *hoei*]

hoy[2] (hɔɪ) *interj* a cry used to attract attention or drive animals. [C14: var. of HEY]

hoya ('hɔɪə) *n* any plant of the genus *Hoya,* of E Asia and Australia, esp. the waxplant. [C19: after Thomas *Hoy* (died 1821), E gardener]

hoyden *or* **hoiden** ('hɔɪdᵊn) *n* a wild boisterous girl; tomboy. [C16: ?from MDu. *heidijn* heathen]
▸ **'hoydenish** *or* **'hoidenish** *adj*

Hoylake ★ ('hɔɪˌleɪk) *n* a town and resort in NW England, in Merseyside on the Irish Sea. Pop.: 25 554 (1991).

Hoyle[1] (hɔɪl) *n* an authoritative book of rules for card games. [after Sir Edmund *Hoyle,* 18th-cent. E authority on games, its compiler]

Hoyle[2] ★ (hɔɪl) *n* Sir **Fred.** born 1915, British astronomer and writer: his books include *The Nature of the Universe* (1950) and *Frontiers of Astronomy* (1955), and science-fiction writings.

HP *abbrev. for:* **1** *Brit.* hire-purchase. **2** horsepower. **3** high pressure. ◆ Also **4** (in Britain) Houses of Parliament. (for senses 1–3): **h.p.**

HPV *abbrev. for* human papilloma virus.

HQ *or* **h.q.** *abbrev. for* headquarters.

hr *abbrev. for* hour.

Hradec Králové ★ (*Czech* 'hradɛts 'krɑːlɔvɛː) *n* a town in the N Czech Republic, on the Elbe River. Pop.: 100 671 (1995 est.). German name: **Königgrätz.**

HRH *abbrev. for* His (*or* Her) Royal Highness.

HRT *abbrev. for* hormone replacement therapy.

Hrvatska ★ ('hrvaːtskaː) *n* the Serbo-Croat name for **Croatia.**

HS (in Britain) *abbrev. for* Home Secretary.

HSH *abbrev. for* His (*or* Her) Serene Highness.

Hsi ★ (jiː) *n* a variant spelling of **Xi.**

Hsia Kuei ★ ('ʃjɑː 'kweɪ) *n* a variant spelling of **Xia Gui.**

Hsia-men ★ ('ʃjɑː'mɛn) *n* a transliteration of the modern Chinese name for **Amoy.**

Hsian ★ (ʃjɑːn) *n* a variant transliteration of the Chinese name for **Xi An.**

Hsiang ★ (ʃjɑːŋ) *n* a variant transliteration of the Chinese name for **Xiang.**

Hsin-hai-lien ★ ('ʃɪn'haɪ'ljɛn) *n* a variant transliteration of the Chinese name of **Lianyungang.**

Hsining ★ ('ʃiː'nɪŋ) *n* a variant transliteration of the Chinese name for **Xining.**

Hsinking ★ ('ʃɪn'kɪŋ) *n* the former name (1932–45) of **Changchun.**

★ people and places

Hsüan T'ung ★ ('ʃwɑːn 'tʊŋ) *n* a variant transliteration of the Chinese name for **Xuan-tong.**

Hsü-chou ★ ('ʃuː'tʃəʊ) *n* a variant transliteration of the Chinese name for **Xuzhou.**

ht *abbrev. for* height.

HT *Physics. abbrev. for* high tension.

HTLV *abbrev. for* human T-cell lymphotropic virus: any one of a family of viruses that cause certain rare human diseases in the T-cells. HTLV-III was an early name for the AIDS virus.

HTML *abbrev. for* hypertext markup language: a text description language that is used for electronic publishing, esp. on the World Wide Web.

HTTP *abbrev. for* hypertext transfer protocol, used esp. on the World Wide Web. See also **hypertext.**

Hua Guo Feng ('hwa: gwəʊ 'fɛʃ) *or* **Hua Kuo-feng** ★ ('hwa: kwəʊ'fɛŋ) *n* born *c.* 1920, Chinese Communist statesman; prime minister of China 1976–80.

Huainan ★ ('hwaɪ'næn) *n* a city in E China, in Anhui province north of Hefei. Pop.: 1 200 000 (1991 est.).

Huambo ★ (*Portuguese* 'wambu) *n* a town in central Angola: designated by the Portuguese as the future capital of the country. Pop.: 400 000 (1995 est.). Former name (1928–73): **Nova Lisboa.**

Huang Hai ★ ('hwæŋ 'haɪ) *n* the Pinyin transliteration of the Chinese name for the **Yellow Sea.**

Huang Ho ★ ('hwæŋ 'həʊ) *n* the Pinyin transliteration of the Chinese name for the **Yellow River.**

Huang Hua ★ ('hwæŋ 'hwa:) *n* born 1913, Chinese Communist statesman; minister for foreign affairs (1976–83).

Huáscar ★ (*Spanish* uas'kar) *n* died 1533, Inca ruler (1525–33): murdered by his half brother Atahualpa.

Huascarán (*Spanish* uaska'ran) *or* **Huascán** ★ (*Spanish* uas'kan) *n* an extinct volcano in W Peru, in the Peruvian Andes: the highest peak in Peru; avalanche in 1962 killed over 3000 people. Height: 6768 m (22 205 ft).

hub (hʌb) *n* **1** the central portion of a wheel, propeller, fan, etc., through which the axle passes. **2** the focal point. [C17: prob. var. of HOB¹]

hub-and-spoke *n* (*modifier*) denoting a method of organizing intercontinental air traffic in which one major airport is used as a feeder for local airports. Sometimes shortened to **hub.**

Hubble ★ ('hʌbʲl) *n* **Edwin Powell.** 1889–1953, US astronomer, noted for his investigations of nebulae and the recession of the galaxies.

hubble-bubble ('hʌbʲl'bʌbʲl) *n* **1** another name for **hookah. 2** turmoil. **3** a gargling sound. [C17: rhyming jingle based on BUBBLE]

Hubble's law *n Astron.* a law stating that the velocity of recession of a galaxy is proportional to its distance from the observer. [C20: after E. P. HUBBLE]

Hubble telescope *n* a telescope launched into orbit around the earth in 1990 to provide information about the universe.

hubbub ('hʌbʌb) *n* **1** a confused noise of many voices. **2** tumult; uproar. [C16: prob. from Irish *hooboobbes*]

hubby ('hʌbɪ) *n, pl* **hubbies.** an informal word for **husband.** [C17: by shortening and altering]

hubcap ('hʌb,kæp) *n* a cap fitting over the hub of a wheel.

Hubei ('huː'beɪ), **Hupeh,** *or* **Hupei** ★ *n* a province of central China: low-lying with many lakes. Capital: Wuhan. Pop.: 57 190 000 (1995 est.). Area: 187 500 sq. km (72 394 sq. miles).

Hubli ('huːblɪ) *n* a city in W India, in NW Mysore: incorporated with Dharwar in 1961; educational and trading centre. Pop. (with Dharwar): 648 298 (1991).

hubris ('hjuːbrɪs) *n* **1** pride or arrogance. **2** (in Greek tragedy) ambition, arrogance, etc., ultimately causing the transgressor's ruin. [C19: from Gk]
  ▸ **hu'bristic** *adj*

huckaback ('hʌkə,bæk) *n* a coarse absorbent linen or

cotton fabric used for towels, etc. Also: **huck** (hʌk). [C17: from ?]

huckleberry ('hʌkʲl,bɛrɪ) *n, pl* **huckleberries. 1** an American shrub having edible dark blue berries. **2** the fruit of this shrub. **3** a Brit. name for **whortleberry** (sense 1,2). [C17: prob. var. of *hurtleberry,* from ?]

huckster ('hʌkstə) *n* **1** a person who uses aggressive or questionable methods of selling. **2** *Now rare.* a person who sells small articles or fruit in the street. **3** *US.* a person who writes for radio or television advertisements. ◆ *vb* **4** (*tr*) to peddle. **5** (*tr*) to sell or advertise aggressively or questionably. **6** to haggle (over). [C12: ?from MDu. *hoekster,* from *hoeken* to carry on the back]

Huddersfield ★ ('hʌdəz,fiːld) *n* a town in N England, in West Yorkshire on the River Colne: textile industry. Pop.: 143 726 (1991).

huddle ('hʌdʲl) *n* **1** a heaped or crowded mass of people or things. **2** *Inf.* a private or impromptu conference (esp. in **go into a huddle**). ◆ *vb* **huddles, huddling, huddled. 3** to crowd or nestle closely together. **4** (often foll. by *up*) to hunch (oneself), as through cold. **5** (*intr*) *Inf.* to confer privately. **6** (*tr*) *Chiefly Brit.* to do (something) in a careless way. **7** (*tr*) *Rare.* to put on (clothes) hurriedly. [C16: from ?; cf. ME *hoderen* to wrap up]
  ▸ **'huddler** *n*

Huddleston ★ ('hʌdʲlstən) *n* **Trevor.** 1913–98, British prelate; suffragan bishop of Stepney (1968–78) and bishop of Mauritius (1978–83); president of the Anti-Apartheid Movement (1981–94).

Hudson ★ ('hʌdsən) *n* **1 Henry.** died 1611, English navigator: he explored the Hudson River (1609) and Hudson Bay (1610), where his crew mutinied and cast him adrift to die. **2 W(illiam) H(enry).** 1841–1922, British naturalist and novelist, born in Argentina, noted esp. for his romance *Green Mansions* (1904) and the autobiographical *Far Away and Long Ago* (1918).

Hudson Bay ★ *n* an inland sea in NE Canada: linked with the Atlantic by **Hudson Strait;** the S extension forms James Bay; discovered in 1610 by Henry Hudson. Area (excluding James Bay): 647 500 sq. km (250 000 sq. miles).

Hudson River ★ *n* a river in E New York State, flowing generally south into Upper New York Bay: linked to the Great Lakes, the St Lawrence Seaway, and Lake Champlain by the New York State Barge Canal and the canalized Mohawk River. Length: 492 km (306 miles).

hue (hjuː) *n* **1** the attribute of colour that enables an observer to classify it as red, blue, etc., and excludes white, black, and grey. **2** a shade of a colour. **3** aspect: *a different hue on matters.* [OE *hīw* beauty]
  ▸ **hued** *adj*

Hué ★ (*French* ɥe) *n* a port in central Vietnam, on the delta of the **Hué River** near the South China Sea: former capital of the kingdom of Annam, of French Indochina (1883–1946), and of Central Vietnam (1946–54). Pop.: 219 149 (1992 est.).

hue and cry *n* **1** (formerly) the pursuit of a suspected criminal with loud cries in order to raise the alarm. **2** any loud public outcry. [C16: from Anglo-F *hut et cri,* from OF *hue* outcry, from *hu!* shout of warning + *cri* CRY]

Huelva ★ (*Spanish* 'welβa) *n* a port in SW Spain, between the estuaries of the Odiel and Tinto Rivers: exports copper and other ores. Pop.: 145 049 (1994 est.).

Huesca ★ (*Spanish* 'ueska) *n* a city in NE Spain: Roman town, site of Quintus Sertorius' school (76 B.C.); 15th-century cathedral and ancient palace of Aragonese kings. Pop.: 50 020 (1991). Latin name: **Osca** ('ɒska).

huff (hʌf) *n* **1** a passing mood of anger or pique. in **in a huff).** ◆ *vb* **2** to make or become angry or resentful. **3** (*intr*) to blow or puff heavily. **4** Also: **blow.** *Draughts.* to remove (an opponent's draught) from the board for failure to make a capture. **5** (*tr*) *Obs.* to bully. **6 huffing and puffing.** empty threats or objections: bluster. [C16: imit.; cf. PUFF]
  ▸ **'huffish** *or* **'huffy** *adj* ▸ **'huffily** *or* **'huffishly** *adv*

Hufuf ★ (hu'fuːf) *n* See **Al Hufuf.**

hug (hʌg) *vb* **hugs, hugging, hugged.** (*mainly tr*) **1** (*also intr*) to clasp tightly, usually with affection; embrace. **2** to keep

close to a shore, kerb, etc. **3** to cling to (beliefs, etc.); cherish. **4** to congratulate (oneself). ◆ *n* **5** a tight or fond embrace. [C16: prob. of Scand. origin]
▸ **'huggable** *adj*

huge (hju:dʒ) *adj* extremely large. [C13: from OF *ahuge*, from ?]
▸ **'hugely** *adv* ▸ **'hugeness** *n*

hugger-mugger ('hʌgə,mʌgə) *n* **1** confusion. **2** *Rare.* secrecy. ◆ *adj, adv Arch.* **3** with secrecy. **4** in confusion. ◆ *vb Obs.* **5** (*tr*) to keep secret. **6** (*intr*) to act secretly. [C16: from ?]

Huggins ★ ('hʌgɪnz) *n* Sir **William**. 1824–1910, British astronomer, who used spectroscopy to discover the red shift in stellar spectra.

Hugh Capet ★ ('hju: 'kæpɪt, 'keɪpɪt) *n* See (Hugh) **Capet**.

Hughes ★ (hju:z) *n* **1** Howard. 1905–76, US industrialist, aviator, and film producer. **2** Richard (**Arthur Warren**). 1900–76, British novelist. He wrote *A High Wind in Jamaica* (1929) and *The Fox in the Attic* (1961). **3** Ted. 1930–98, British poet: his works include *The Hawk in the Rain* (1957) and *Birthday Letters* (1998); poet laureate (1984–98). **4** Thomas. 1822–96, British novelist; author of *Tom Brown's Schooldays* (1857).

Hughie ★ ('hju:ɪ) *n Austral. & NZ inf.* the god of rain and of surf (esp. in the phrases **send her down, Hughie!**, **send 'em up, Hughie!**).

Hugo ★ ('hju:gəʊ; *French* ygo) *n* Victor (**Marie**) (viktɔr). 1802–85, French writer and leader of the romantic movement in France. His works include the verse *Les Feuilles d'automne* (1831), the novel *Les Misérables* (1862), and the play *Ruy Blas* (1838).

Huguenot ('hju:gə,nəʊ, -,nɒt) *n* **1** a French Calvinist, esp. of the 16th or 17th centuries. ◆ *adj* **2** designating the French Protestant Church. [C16: from F, from Genevan dialect *eyguenot* one who opposed annexation by Savoy, ult. from Swiss G *Eidgenoss* confederate]

huh (*spelling pron* hʌ) *interj* an exclamation of derision, bewilderment, inquiry, etc.

Huhehot (,hu:hɪ'hɒt ,hu:ɪ-) *or* **Hu-ho-hao-t'e** ★ (,hu:həʊhaʊ'teɪ) *n* a variant transliteration of the Chinese name for **Hohhot**.

huhu ('hu:hu:) *n* a New Zealand beetle with a hairy body. [from Maori]

hui ('hu:ɪ) *n NZ.* **1** a Maori social gathering. **2** *Inf.* any party. [from Maori]

huia ('hʊɪjə) *n* an extinct New Zealand bird, prized by early Maoris for its distinctive tail feathers. [from Maori]

hula ('hu:lə) *or* **hula-hula** *n* a Hawaiian dance performed by a woman. [from Hawaiian]

Hula Hoop *n Trademark.* a light hoop that is whirled around the body by movements of the waist and hips.

hulk (hʌlk) *n* **1** the body of an abandoned vessel. **2** *Disparaging.* a large or unwieldy vessel. **3** *Disparaging.* a large ungainly person or thing. **4** (*often pl*) the hull of a ship, used as a storehouse, etc., or (esp. in 19th-century Britain) as a prison. [OE *hulc*, from Med. L *hulca*, from Gk *holkas* barge, from *helkein* to tow]

hulking ('hʌlkɪŋ) *adj* big and ungainly.

hull (hʌl) *n* **1** the main body of a vessel, tank, etc. **2** the outer covering of a fruit or seed. **3** the calyx at the base of a strawberry, raspberry, or similar fruit. **4** the outer casing of a missile, rocket, etc. ◆ *vb* **5** to remove the hulls from (fruit or seeds). **6** (*tr*) to pierce the hull of (a vessel, tank, etc.). [OE *hulu*]

Hull[1] ★ (hʌl) *n* **1** a port in NE England: the largest fishing port in Britain; university (1929). Pop.: 310 636 (1991). Official name: **Kingston upon Hull**. **2** a city in SE Canada, in SW Quebec on the River Ottawa: a centre of the timber trade and associated industries. Pop.: 60 707 (1991).

Hull[2] ★ (hʌl) *n* **Cordell** (,kɔː'dɛl). 1871–1955, US statesman; secretary of state (1933–44). He helped to found the U.N.: Nobel peace prize 1945.

hullabaloo *or* **hullaballoo** (,hʌləbə'lu:) *n, pl* **hullabaloos** *or* **hullaballoos.** loud confused noise; commotion. [C18: ?from HALLO + Scot. *baloo* lullaby]

hullo (hʌ'ləʊ) *sentence substitute, n* a variant spelling of **hello**.

hum (hʌm) *vb* **hums, humming, hummed.** (*intr*) **1** to make a low continuous vibrating sound. **2** (of a person) to sing with the lips closed. **3** to utter an indistinct sound, as in hesitation; hem. **4** *Inf.* to be in a state of feverish activity. **5** *Brit. & Irish sl.* to smell unpleasant. **6** **hum and haw.** See **hem**[2] (sense 3). ◆ *n* **7** a low continuous murmuring sound. **8** *Electronics.* an undesired low-frequency noise in the output of an amplifier or receiver. ◆ *interj, n* **9** an indistinct sound of hesitation, embarrassment, etc.; hem. [C14: imit.]

human ('hju:mən) *adj* **1** of or relating to mankind: *human nature.* **2** consisting of people: *a human chain.* **3** having the attributes of man as opposed to animals, divine beings, or machines: *human failings.* **4a** kind or considerate. **4b** natural. ◆ *n* **5** a human being; person. [C14: from L *hūmānus*; rel. to L *homō* man]
▸ **'humanness** *n*

human being *n* a member of any of the races of *Homo sapiens*; person; man, woman, or child.

humane (hju:'meɪn) *adj* **1** characterized by kindness, sympathy, etc. **2** inflicting as little pain as possible: *a humane killing.* **3** civilizing or liberal: *humane studies.* [C16: var. of HUMAN]
▸ **hu'manely** *adv* ▸ **hu'maneness** *n*

human interest *n* (in a newspaper story, etc.) reference to individuals and their emotions, sometimes from exploitative motives.

humanism ('hju:mə,nɪzəm) *n* **1** the rejection of religion in favour of a belief in the advancement of humanity by its own efforts. **2** (*often cap.*) a cultural movement of the Renaissance, based on classical studies. **3** interest in the welfare of people.
▸ **'humanist** *n* ▸ **,human'istic** *adj*

humanitarian (hju:,mænɪ'tɛərɪən) *adj* **1** having the interests of mankind at heart. ◆ *n* **2** a philanthropist.
▸ **hu,mani'tarianism** *n*

humanity (hju:'mænɪtɪ) *n, pl* **humanities.** **1** the human race. **2** the quality of being human. **3** kindness or mercy. **4** (*pl;* usually preceded by *the*) the study of literature, philosophy, and the arts, esp. study of Ancient Greece and Rome.

humanize *or* **humanise** ('hju:mə,naɪz) *vb* **humanizes, humanizing, humanized** *or* **humanises, humanising, humanised.** **1** to make or become human. **2** to make or become humane.
▸ **,humani'zation** *or* **,humani'sation** *n*

humankind (,hju:mən'kaɪnd) *n* the human race; humanity.

USAGE NOTE See at **mankind**.

---

humanly ('hju:mənlɪ) *adv* **1** by human powers or means. **2** in a human or humane manner.

human nature *n* the qualities common to humanity, esp. with reference to human weakness.

humanoid ('hju:mə,nɔɪd) *adj* **1** like a human being in appearance. ◆ *n* **2** a being with human rather than anthropoid characteristics. **3** (in science fiction) a robot or creature resembling a human being.

human papilloma virus *n* any of a class of viruses that cause tumours, including warts, in humans. Certain strains have been implicated as a cause of cervical cancer. Abbrev.: **HPV**.

human rights *pl n* the rights of individuals to liberty, justice, etc.

Humber ★ ('hʌmbə) *n* an estuary in NE England, into which flow the Rivers Ouse and Trent: flows east into the North Sea; navigable for large ocean-going ships as far as Hull; crossed by the **Humber Bridge** (1981), the world's longest single-span suspension bridge with a main span of 1410 m (4626 ft). Length: 64 km (40 miles).

Humberside ★ ('hʌmbə,saɪd) *n* a former county of N England around the Humber estuary, formed in 1974 and replaced by four unitary authorities in 1996.

★ people and places

humble ('hʌmbᵊl) adj **1** conscious of one's failings. **2** unpretentious; lowly: *a humble cottage; my humble opinion.* **3** deferential or servile. ♦ *vb* **humbles, humbling, humbled.** (*tr*) **4** to cause to become humble; humiliate. **5** to lower in status. [C13: from OF, from L *humilis* low, from *humus* the ground]
▶ '**humbleness** *n* ▶ '**humbly** *adv*

humblebee ('hʌmbᵊl,bi:) *n* another name for the **bumblebee.** [C15: rel. to MDu. *hommel* bumblebee, OHG *humbal*]

humble pie *n* **1** (formerly) a pie made from the heart, entrails, etc., of a deer. **2 eat humble pie.** to be forced to behave humbly; be humiliated. [C17: earlier *an umble pie,* by mistaken word division from *a numble pie,* from *numbles* offal of a deer, ult. from L *lumbulus* a little loin]

Humboldt ★ ('hʌmbəʊlt; *German* 'humbɔlt) *n* **1** Baron **(Friedrich Heinrich) Alexander von** (aleˈksandər fɔn). 1769–1859, German scientist, who explored in Central and South America (1799–1804). **2** his brother, Baron **(Karl) Wilhelm von** ('vɪlhɛlm fɔn). 1767–1835, German philologist and educational reformer.

humbug ('hʌm,bʌg) *n* **1** a person or thing that deceives. **2** nonsense. **3** *Brit.* a hard boiled sweet, usually having a striped pattern. ♦ *vb* **humbugs, humbugging, humbugged. 4** to cheat or deceive (someone). [C18: from ?]
▶ '**hum,bugger** *n* ▶ '**hum,buggery** *n*

humdinger ('hʌm,dɪŋə) *n Sl.* an excellent person or thing. [C20: from ?]

humdrum ('hʌm,drʌm) adj **1** ordinary; dull. ♦ *n* **2** a monotonous routine, task, or person. [C16: rhyming compound, prob. based on HUM]

Hume ★ (hju:m) *n* **1** (George) Basil. born 1923, British Roman Catholic Benedictine monk and cardinal; archbishop of Westminster from 1976. **2 David.** 1711–76, Scottish empiricist philosopher, economist, and historian, who believed that human knowledge is restricted to that which can be perceived by the senses. His works include *A Treatise of Human Nature* (1740) and *An Enquiry concerning the Principles of Morals* (1751). **3 John.** born 1937, Northern Irish politician; leader of the Social Democratic and Labour party from 1979: awarded the Nobel peace prize with David Trimble in 1998 for his role in the Northern Irish peace settlement.
▶ '**Humism** *n*

humectant (hju:ˈmɛktənt) adj **1** producing moisture. ♦ *n* **2** a substance added to another to keep it moist. [C17: from L *ūmectāre* to wet, from *ūmēre* to be moist]

humerus ('hju:mərəs) *n, pl* **humeri** (-mə,raɪ). **1** the bone that extends from the shoulder to the elbow in man. **2** the corresponding bone in other vertebrates. [C17: from L *umerus;* rel. to Gothic *ams* shoulder, Gk *ōmos*]
▶ '**humeral** *adj*

humid ('hju:mɪd) adj moist; damp. [C16: from L *ūmidus,* from *ūmēre* to be wet]
▶ '**humidly** *adv* ▶ '**humidness** *n*

humidex ('hju:mɪ,dɛks) *n Canad.* an index of discomfort showing the combined effect of humidity and temperature.

humidify (hju:ˈmɪdɪ,faɪ) *vb* **humidifies, humidifying, humidified.** (*tr*) to make (air, etc.) humid or damp.
▶ hu,midifi'cation *n* ▶ hu'midi,fier *n*

humidity (hju:ˈmɪdɪtɪ) *n* **1** dampness. **2** a measure of the amount of moisture in the air.

humidor ('hju:mɪ,dɔ:) *n* a humid place or container for storing cigars, tobacco, etc.

humify ('hju:mɪ,faɪ) *vb* **humifies, humifying, humified.** to convert or be converted into humus.
▶ ,humifi'cation *n*

humiliate (hju:ˈmɪlɪ,eɪt) *vb* **humiliates, humiliating, humiliated.** (*tr*) to lower or hurt the dignity or pride of. [C16: from LL *humiliāre,* from L *humilis* HUMBLE]
▶ hu'mili,atingly *adv* ▶ hu,mili'ation *n* ▶ hu'mili,ator *n*

humility (hju:ˈmɪlɪtɪ) *n, pl* **humilities.** the state or quality of being humble.

Hummel ★ ('hʊməl) *n* Johann Nepomuk (joˈhan 'ne:po-mʊk). 1778–1837, German composer and pianist.

hummingbird ('hʌmɪŋ,bɜːd) *n* a very small American bird having a brilliant iridescent plumage, long slender bill, and wings specialized for very powerful vibrating flight.

hummock ('hʌmək) *n* **1** a hillock; knoll. **2** a ridge or mound of ice in an ice field. **3** *Chiefly southern US.* a wooded area lying above the level of an adjacent marsh. [C16: from ?; cf. HUMP]
▶ '**hummocky** *adj*

hummus *or* **houmous** ('hʊməs) *n* a creamy dip originating in the Middle East, made from puréed chickpeas. [from Turkish *humus*]

humoral ('hju:mərəl) adj **1** *Immunol.* denoting or relating to a type of immunity caused by free antibodies circulating in the blood. **2** *Obs.* of or relating to the four bodily fluids (humours).

humoresque (,hju:məˈrɛsk) *n* a short lively piece of music. [C19: from G *Humoreske,* ult. from E HUMOUR]

humorist ('hju:mərɪst) *n* a person who acts, speaks, or writes in a humorous way.

humorous ('hju:mərəs) adj **1** funny; comical; amusing. **2** displaying or creating humour.
▶ '**humorously** *adv* ▶ '**humorousness** *n*

humour *or US* **humor** ('hju:mə) *n* **1** the quality of being funny. **2** Also called: **sense of humour.** the ability to appreciate or express that which is humorous. **3** situations, speech, or writings that are humorous. **4a** a state of mind; mood. **4b** (*in combination*): *good humour.* **5** temperament or disposition. **6** a caprice or whim. **7** any of various fluids in the body: *aqueous humour.* **8** Also called: **cardinal humour.** *Arch.* any of the four bodily fluids (blood, phlegm, choler or yellow bile, melancholy or black bile) formerly thought to determine emotional and physical disposition. **9 out of humour.** in a bad mood. ♦ *vb* (*tr*) **10** to gratify; indulge: *he humoured the boy's whims.* **11** to adapt oneself to: *to humour someone's fantasies.* [C14: from L *humor* liquid; rel. to L *ūmēre* to be wet]
▶ '**humourless** *or US* '**humorless** *adj*

hump (hʌmp) *n* **1** a rounded protuberance or projection. **2** a rounded deformity of the back, consisting of a spinal curvature. **3** a rounded protuberance on the back of a camel or related animal. **4 the hump.** *Brit. inf.* a fit of sulking. ♦ *vb* **5** to form or become a hump; hunch; arch. **6** (*tr*) *Sl.* to carry or heave. **7** *Taboo sl.* to have sexual intercourse with (someone). [C18: prob. from earlier *humpbacked*]
▶ '**humpy** *adj*

humpback ('hʌmp,bæk) *n* **1** another word for **hunchback. 2** Also called: **humpback whale.** a large whalebone whale with a humped back and long flippers. **3** a Pacific salmon, the male of which has a humped back. **4** Also: **humpback bridge.** *Brit.* a road bridge having a sharp incline and decline and usually a narrow roadway. [C17: alteration of earlier *crumpbacked,* ? infl. by HUNCHBACK]
▶ '**hump,backed** *adj*

Humperdinck ★ (*German* 'hʊmpərdɪŋk) *n* **Engelbert** ('ɛŋəlbɛrt). 1854–1921, German composer, esp. of operas, including *Hansel and Gretel* (1893).

humph (*spelling pron* hʌmf) *interj* an exclamation of annoyance, indecision, etc.

Humphrey ★ ('hʌmfrɪ) *n* **Duke.** See (Humphrey, Duke of) **Gloucester.**

Humphreys Peak ★ ('hʌmfrɪz) *n* a mountain in N central Arizona, in the San Francisco Peaks: the highest peak in the state. Height: 3862 m (12 670 ft).

Humphries ★ ('hʌmfrɪz) *n* (John) **Barry.** born 1934, Australian comic actor and writer, best known for creating the character Dame Edna Everage.

humpty dumpty ('hʌmptɪ 'dʌmptɪ) *n, pl* **humpty dumpties.** *Chiefly Brit.* **1** a short fat person. **2** a person or thing that once broken cannot be mended. [C18: from the nursery rhyme *Humpty Dumpty*]

humpy ('hʌmpɪ) *n, pl* **humpies.** *Austral.* a primitive hut. [C19: from Abor.]

Hums ★ (hʊms) *n* a variant of **Homs.**

humus ('hjuːməs) *n* a dark brown or black colloidal mass of partially decomposed organic matter in the soil. It improves the fertility and water retention of the soil. [C18: from L: soil]

USAGE NOTE Avoid confusion with **hummus.**

Hun (hʌn) *n, pl* **Huns** *or* **Hun. 1** a member of any of several Asiatic nomadic peoples who dominated much of Asia and E Europe from before 300 B.C., invading the Roman Empire in the 4th and 5th centuries A.D. **2** *Inf.* (esp. in World War I) a derogatory name for a **German. 3** *Inf.* a vandal. [OE *Hūnas*, from LL *Hūnī*, from Turkish *Hun-yü*] ▶ '**Hunnish** *adj* ▶ '**Hun,like** *adj*

Hunan ★ ('huːˈnæn) *n* a province of S China, between the Yangtze River and the Nan Ling Mountains: drained chiefly by the Xiang and Yüan Rivers; valuable mineral resources. Capital: Changsha. Pop.: 63 550 000 (1995 est.). Area: 210 500 sq. km (82 095 sq. miles).

hunch (hʌntʃ) *n* **1** an intuitive guess or feeling. **2** another word for **hump. 3** a lump or large piece. ◆ *vb* **4** to draw (oneself or a part of the body) up or together. **5** (*intr*; usually foll. by *up*) to sit in a hunched position. [C16: from ?]

hunchback ('hʌntʃ,bæk) *n* **1** a person having an abnormal curvature of the spine. **2** such a curvature. ◆ Also called: **humpback.** [C18: from earlier *hunchbacked*] ▶ '**hunch,backed** *adj*

hundred ('hʌndrəd) *n, pl* **hundreds** *or* **hundred. 1** the cardinal number that is the product of ten and ten; five score. **2** a numeral, 100, C, etc., representing this number. **3** (*often pl*) a large but unspecified number, amount, or quantity. **4** (*pl*) the 100 years of a specified century: *in the sixteen hundreds.* **5** something representing, represented by, or consisting of 100 units. **6** *Maths.* the position containing a digit representing that number followed by two zeros: *in 4376, 3 is in the hundred's place.* **7** an ancient division of a county. ◆ *determiner* **8** amounting to or approximately a hundred: *a hundred reasons for that.* [OE] ▶ '**hundredth** *adj,* n

hundreds and thousands *pl n* tiny beads of coloured sugar, used in decorating cakes, etc.

hundredweight ('hʌndrəd,weɪt) *n, pl* **hundredweights** *or* **hundredweight. 1** Also called: **long hundredweight.** *Brit.* a unit of weight equal to 112 pounds (50.802 kg). **2** Also called: **short hundredweight.** *US & Canad.* a unit of weight equal to 100 pounds (45.359 kg). **3** Also called: **metric hundredweight.** a metric unit of weight equal to 50 kilograms. ◆ Abbrev. (for senses 1, 2): **cwt.**

hung (hʌŋ) *vb* **1** the past tense and past participle of **hang** (except in the sense of *to execute*). ◆ *adj* **2** (of a political party, jury, etc.) not having a majority: *a hung parliament.* **3 hung over.** *Inf.* suffering from the effects of a hangover. **4 hung up.** *Sl.* **4a** impeded by some difficulty or delay. **4b** emotionally disturbed. **5 hung up on.** *Sl.* obsessively interested in.

Hung. *abbrev. for:* **1** Hungarian. **2** Hungary.

Hungarian (hʌŋˈgɛərɪən) *n* **1** the official language of Hungary, also spoken in Romania and elsewhere, belonging to the Finno-Ugric family. **2** a native, inhabitant, or citizen of Hungary. ◆ *adj* **3** of or relating to Hungary, its people, or their language. ◆ Cf. **Magyar.**

Hungary ★ ('hʌŋgərɪ) *n* a republic in central Europe: Magyars first unified under Saint Stephen, the first Hungarian king (1001–38); taken by the Hapsburgs from the Turks at the end of the 17th century; gained autonomy with the establishment of the dual monarchy of Austria-Hungary (1867) and became a republic in 1918; passed under Communist control in 1949; a popular rising in 1956 was suppressed by Soviet troops; democracy replaced Communism in 1989 after mass protests. It consists chiefly of the Middle Danube basin and plains. Official language: Hungarian. Religion: Christian majority. Currency: forint. Capital: Budapest. Pop.: 10 157 000 (1997). Area: 93 030 sq. km (35 919 sq. miles). Hungarian name: **Magyarország.**

hunger ('hʌŋgə) *n* **1** a feeling of emptiness or weakness induced by lack of food. **2** desire or craving: *hunger for a woman.* ◆ *vb* **3** (*intr*; usually foll. by *for* or *after*) to have a great appetite or desire (for). [OE]

hunger march *n* a procession of protest or demonstration, esp. by the unemployed.

hunger strike *n* a voluntary fast undertaken, usually by a prisoner, as a means of protest. ▶ **hunger striker** *n*

Hung Hsiu-ch'uan ★ ('hʌŋ 'ʃjuːˈtʃwɑːn) *n* a variant of **Hong Xiu Quan.**

Hungnam ★ (,hʊŋˈnæm) *n* a port in E North Korea, on the Sea of Japan southeast of Hamhung. Pop.: 260 000 (latest est.).

hungry ('hʌŋgrɪ) *adj* **hungrier, hungriest. 1** desiring food. **2** (*postpositive*; foll. by *for*) having a craving, desire, or need (for). **3** expressing or appearing to express greed, craving, or desire. **4** lacking fertility; poor. **5** *Austral. & NZ.* greedy; mean. **6** *NZ.* (of timber) dry and bare. ▶ '**hungrily** *adv* ▶ '**hungriness** *n*

Hung-wu ★ ('hʌŋ 'wuː) *n* a variant of **Hong-wu.**

hunk (hʌŋk) *n* **1** a large piece. **2** *Sl.* a sexually attractive man. [C19: prob. rel. to Flemish *hunke*]

hunkers ('hʌŋkəz) *pl n* haunches. [C18: from ?]

hunky-dory (,hʌŋkɪ'dɔːrɪ) *adj Inf.* very satisfactory; fine. [C20: from ?]

hunt (hʌnt) *vb* **1** to seek out and kill (animals) for food or sport. **2** (*intr*; often foll. by *for*) to search (for): *to hunt for a book.* **3** (*tr*) to use (hounds, horses, etc.) in the pursuit of wild animals, game, etc.: *to hunt a pack of hounds.* **4** (*tr*) to search (country) to hunt game, etc.: *to hunt the parkland.* **5** (*tr*; often foll. by *down*) to track diligently so as to capture: *to hunt down a criminal.* **6** (*tr*; usually passive) to persecute; hound. **7** (*intr*) (of a gauge indicator, etc.) to oscillate about a mean value or position. **8** (*intr*) (of an aircraft, rocket, etc.) to oscillate about a flight path or course axis. ◆ *n* **9** the act or an instance of hunting. **10** chase or search, esp. of animals. **11** the area of a hunt. **12** a party or institution organized for the pursuit of wild animals, esp. for sport. **13** the members of such a party or institution. [OE *huntian*]

Hunt ★ (hʌnt) *n* **1** (**William**) **Holman** ('həʊlmən). 1827–1910, British painter; a founder of the Pre-Raphaelite Brotherhood (1848). **2** (**Henry Cecil**) **John,** Baron. 1910–98, British army officer, who planned and led the first successful Everest ascent (1953). **3** (**James Henry**) **Leigh.** 1784–1859, British poet and essayist.

huntaway ('hʌntə,weɪ) *n NZ.* a dog trained to drive sheep at a long distance from the shepherd.

hunted ('hʌntɪd) *adj* harassed: *a hunted look.*

hunter ('hʌntə) *n* **1** a person or animal that seeks out and kills or captures game. Fem.: **huntress** ('hʌntrɪs). **2a** a person who looks diligently for something. **2b** (*in combination*): *a fortune-hunter.* **3** a specially bred horse used in hunting, characterized by strength and stamina. **4** a watch with a hinged metal lid or case (**hunting case**) to protect the crystal.

hunter-killer *adj* denoting a type of submarine designed and equipped to pursue and destroy enemy craft.

hunter's moon *n* the full moon following the harvest moon.

hunting ('hʌntɪŋ) *n* **a** the pursuit and killing or capture of wild animals, regarded as a sport. **b** (*as modifier*): *hunting lodge.*

Huntingdon[1] ★ ('hʌntɪŋdən) *n* a town in E central England, in Cambridgeshire: birthplace of Oliver Cromwell. Pop. (with Godmanchester): 15 575 (1991).

Huntingdon[2] ★ ('hʌntɪŋdən) *n* **Selina,** Countess of Huntingdon. 1707–91, British religious leader, who founded a Calvinistic Methodist sect.

Huntingdonshire ★ ('hʌntɪŋdən,ʃɪə, -ʃə) *n* (until 1974) a former county of E England, now part of Cambridgeshire.

hunting horn *n* a long straight metal tube with a flared end, used in giving signals in hunting.

Huntington's disease ('hʌntɪŋtənz) *n* a hereditary

★ people and places

form of chorea associated with progressive dementia. Former name: **Huntington's chorea**. [after G. *Huntington* (1850–1916), US physician]

huntsman ('hʌntsmən) *n, pl* **huntsmen**. **1** a person who hunts. **2** a person who trains hounds, beagles, etc., and manages during a hunt.

Huntsville ★ ('hʌntsvɪl) *n* a city in NE Alabama: spaceflight and guided-missile research centre. Pop.: 160 325 (1994 est.).

Huon pine ('hjuːɒn) *n* a tree of Australasia, SE Asia, and Chile, with scalelike leaves and cup-shaped berry-like fruits. [after the *Huon* River, Tasmania]

Hupeh or **Hupei** ★ ('xuː'peɪ) *n* a variant transliteration of the Chinese name for **Hubei**.

Hurd ★ (hɜːd) *n* **Douglas (Richard)**, Baron Hurd of Westwell. born 1930, British Conservative politician; home secretary (1985–89); foreign secretary (1989–95).

hurdle ('hɜːdªl) *n* **1a** *Athletics.* one of a number of light barriers over which runners leap in certain events. **1b** a low barrier used in certain horse races. **2** an obstacle: *the next hurdle in his career.* **3** a light framework of interlaced osiers, etc., used as a temporary fence. **4** a sledge on which criminals were dragged to their executions. ◆ *vb* **hurdles, hurdling, hurdled. 5** to jump (a hurdle). **6** (*tr*) to surround with hurdles. **7** (*tr*) to overcome. [OE *hyrdel*]
▶ **'hurdler** *n*

hurdy-gurdy ('hɜːdɪ'gɜːdɪ) *n, pl* **hurdy-gurdies**. any mechanical musical instrument, such as a barrel organ. [C18: rhyming compound, prob. imit.]

hurl (hɜːl) *vb* (*tr*) **1** to throw with great force. **2** to utter with force; yell: *to hurl insults.* ◆ *n* **3** the act of hurling. [C13: prob. imit.]

hurling ('hɜːlɪŋ) or **hurley** *n* a traditional Irish game resembling hockey, played with sticks and a ball between two teams of 15 players.

hurly-burly ('hɜːlɪ'bɜːlɪ) *n, pl* **hurly-burlies**. confusion or commotion. [C16: from earlier *hurling and burling*, rhyming phrase based on *hurling* in obs. sense of uproar]

Huron ★ ('hjʊərən) *n* **1 Lake**. a lake in North America, between the US and Canada: the second largest of the Great Lakes. Area: 59 570 sq. km (23 000 sq. miles). **2** (*pl* **Hurons** or **Huron**) a member of a North American Indian people formerly living in the region east of Lake Huron. **3** the Iroquoian language of this people.

hurrah (hʊ'rɑː), **hooray** (huː'reɪ), or **hurray** (hʊ'reɪ) *interj, n* **1** a cheer of joy, victory, etc. ◆ *vb* **2** to shout "hurrah". [C17: prob. from G *hurra*; cf. HUZZAH]

hurricane ('hʌrɪkªn) *n* **1** a severe, often destructive storm, esp. a tropical cyclone. **2** a wind of force 12 on the Beaufort scale, with speeds over 72 mph. [C16: from Sp. *huracán*, of Amerind origin, from *hura* wind]

hurricane deck *n* a ship's deck that is covered by a light deck as a sunshade.

hurricane lamp *n* a paraffin lamp with a glass covering. Also called: **storm lantern**.

hurried ('hʌrɪd) *adj* performed with great or excessive haste.
▶ **'hurriedly** *adv* ▶ **'hurriedness** *n*

hurry ('hʌrɪ) *vb* **hurries, hurrying, hurried. 1** (*intr*; often foll. by *up*) to hasten; rush. **2** (*tr*; often foll. by *along*) to speed up the completion, progress, etc., of. ◆ *n* **3** haste. **4** urgency or eagerness. **5 in a hurry.** *Inf.* **5a** easily: *you won't beat him in a hurry.* **5b** willingly: *we won't go there again in a hurry.* [C16 *horyen*, prob. imit.]

hurst (hɜːst) *n Arch.* **1** a wood. **2** a sandbank. [OE *hyrst*]

Hurstmonceux ★ ('hɜːstmən,suː, -,səu) *n* a variant spelling of **Herstmonceux**.

hurt (hɜːt) *vb* **hurts, hurting, hurt. 1** (*tr*) to cause physical pain to (someone or something). **2** (*tr*) to cause emotional pain or distress to (someone). **3** to produce a painful sensation in (someone): *the bruise hurts.* **4** (*intr*) *Inf.* to feel pain. ◆ *n* **5** physical or mental pain or suffering. **6** a wound, cut, or sore. **7** damage or injury; harm. ◆ *adj* **8** injured or pained: *a hurt knee; a hurt look.* [C12 *hurten* to hit, from OF *hurter* to knock against, prob. of Gmc origin]

hurtful ('hɜːtful) *adj* causing distress or injury: *to say hurtful things.*
▶ **'hurtfully** *adv*

hurtle ('hɜːtªl) *vb* **hurtles, hurtling, hurtled.** to project or be projected very quickly, noisily, or violently. [C13 *hurtlen*, from *hurten* to strike; see HURT]

Hus ★ (*Czech* hus) *n* **Jan** (jan). the Czech name of (John) **Huss**.

Husain ★ (hu'seɪn, -'saɪn) *n* **1** ?629–680 A.D., Islamic caliph, the son of Ali and Fatima and the grandson of Mohammed. **2** a variant spelling of **Hussein**.

husband ('hʌzbənd) *n* **1** a woman's partner in marriage. **2** *Arch.* a manager of an estate. ◆ *vb* **3** to manage or use (resources, finances, etc.) thriftily. **4** (*tr*) *Arch.* to find a husband for. **5** (*tr*) *Obs.* to till (the soil). [OE *hūsbonda*, from ON *hūsbōndi*, from *hūs* house + *bōndi* one who has a household]
▶ **'husbander** *n*

husbandman ('hʌzbəndmən) *n, pl* **husbandmen**. *Arch.* a farmer.

husbandry ('hʌzbəndrɪ) *n* **1** farming, esp. when regarded as a science, skill, or art. **2** management of affairs and resources.

Husein ibn-Ali ★ (hu'seɪn 'ɪbªn'ɑːlɪ, -'ælɪ, hu'saɪn) *n* 1856–1931, first king of Hejaz (1916–24): initiated the Arab revolt against the Turks (1916–18); forced to abdicate by ibn-Saud.

hush (hʌʃ) *vb* **1** to make or become silent; quieten; soothe. ◆ *n* **2** stillness; silence. ◆ *interj* **3** a plea or demand for silence. [C16: prob. from earlier *husht* quiet!, the *-t* being thought to indicate a past participle]
▶ **hushed** *adj*

hushaby ('hʌʃə,baɪ) *interj* **1** used in quietening a baby or child to sleep. ◆ *n, pl* **hushabies. 2** a lullaby. [C18: from HUSH + *by*, as in BYE-BYES]

hush-hush *adj Inf.* (esp. of official work, documents, etc.) secret; confidential.

hush money *n Sl.* money given to a person to ensure that something is kept secret.

hush up *vb* (*tr, adv*) to suppress information or rumours about.

husk (hʌsk) *n* **1** the external green or membranous covering of certain fruits and seeds. **2** any worthless outer covering. ◆ *vb* **3** (*tr*) to remove the husk from. [C14: prob. based on MDu. *huusken* little house, from *hūs* house]

husky[1] ('hʌskɪ) *adj* **huskier, huskiest. 1** (of a voice, utterance, etc.) slightly hoarse or rasping. **2** of or containing husks. **3** *Inf.* big and strong. [C19: prob. from HUSK, from the toughness of a corn husk]
▶ **'huskily** *adv* ▶ **'huskiness** *n*

husky[2] ('hʌskɪ) *n, pl* **huskies. 1** a breed of Arctic sled dog with a thick dense coat, pricked ears, and a curled tail. **2** *Canad. sl.* **2a** a member of the Inuit people. **2b** their language. [C19: prob. based on ESKIMO]

Huss ★ (hʌs) *n* **John**, Czech name *Jan Hus.* ?1372–1415, Bohemian religious reformer. Influenced by Wycliffe, he anticipated the Reformation by denouncing Church doctrines. His death at the stake precipitated the Hussite wars.

hussar (hu'zɑː) *n* **1** a member of any of various light cavalry regiments, renowned for their elegant dress. **2** a Hungarian horseman of the 15th century. [C15: from Hungarian *huszár* hussar, formerly freebooter, ult. from OIt. *corsaro* CORSAIR]

Hussein ★ (hu'seɪn) *n* **1** Also: **Husain**. 1935–99, king of Jordan (1952–99). **2 Saddam** (sæ'dæm). born 1937, Iraqi politician: president of Iraq from 1979. He led Iraq into the Iran-Iraq War (1980–88) and the Gulf War (1991).

Husserl ★ (*German* 'husərl) *n* **Edmund** ('etmunt). 1859–1938, German philosopher; founder of phenomenology.

Hussite ('hʌsaɪt) *n* **1** an adherent of the ideas of John Huss or a member of the movement initiated by him. ◆ *adj* **2** of or relating to John Huss, his teachings, followers, etc.
▶ **'Hussitism** *n*

hussy ('hʌsɪ, -zɪ) *n, pl* **hussies**. *Contemptuous.* a shameless or promiscuous woman. [C16 (in the sense: housewife): from *hussif* HOUSEWIFE]

hustings ('hʌstɪŋz) *n* (*functioning as pl or sing*) **1** *Brit*. (before 1872) the platform on which candidates were nominated for Parliament and from which they addressed the electors. **2** the proceedings at a parliamentary election. [C11: from ON *hūsthing*, from *hūs* HOUSE + *thing* assembly]

hustle ('hʌsˀl) *vb* **hustles, hustling, hustled. 1** to shove or crowd (someone) roughly. **2** to move hurriedly or furtively: *he hustled her out of sight.* **3** (*tr*) to deal with hurriedly: *to hustle legislation through.* **4** *Sl.* to obtain (something) forcefully. **5** *US & Canad. sl.* (of procurers and prostitutes) to solicit. ◆ *n* **6** an instance of hustling. [C17: from Du. *husselen* to shake, from MDu. *hutsen*]
▶ **'hustler** *n*

Huston ★ ('hjuːstˀn) *n* **John.** 1906–87, US film director. His films include *The Treasure of the Sierra Madre* (1947), *The African Queen* (1951), and *The Dead* (1987).

hut (hʌt) *n* **1** a small house or shelter. ◆ *vb* **huts, hutting, hutted. 2** to furnish with or live in a hut. [C17: from F *hutte*, of Gmc origin]
▶ **'hut,like** *adj*

hutch (hʌtʃ) *n* **1** a cage, usually of wood and wire mesh, for small animals. **2** *Inf., derog.* a small house. **3** a cart for carrying ore. [C14 *hucche*, from OF *huche*, from Med. L *hutica*, from ?]

hutment ('hʌtmənt) *n* *Chiefly mil.* a number or group of huts.

Hutton ★ ('hʌtˀn) *n* **1 James.** 1726–97, Scottish geologist, regarded as the founder of modern geology. **2** Sir **Leonard,** known as Len *Hutton.* 1916–90, English cricketer.

Huxley ★ ('hʌkslɪ) *n* **1** Aldous **(Leonard)** ('ɔːldəs). 1894–1963, British writer, noted for his novel *Brave New World* (1932). **2** his half-brother, Sir **Andrew Fielding,** born 1917, British biologist: noted for his research into the transmission of nerve impulses; shared Nobel prize for physiology or medicine (1963). **3** brother of Aldous, Sir **Julian (Sorrel).** 1887–1975, British biologist; first director-general of UNESCO (1946–48). His works include *Essays of a Biologist* (1923). **4** their grandfather, **Thomas Henry.** 1825–95, British biologist, the leading exponent of Darwin's theory of evolution; his works include *Evolution and Ethics* (1893).

Hu Yaobang ★ ('xuː jaʊ'bɑːŋ) *n* 1915–89, Chinese statesman; leader of the Chinese Communist Party (1981–87).

Huygens ★ ('haɪgənz; *Dutch* 'hœixəns) *n* **Christiaan** ('kristiːˌɑːn). 1629–95, Dutch physicist: first formulated the wave theory of light.

Huysmans ★ (*French* ɥismɑ̃s) *n* **Joris Karl** (ʒɔris karl). 1848–1907, French novelist of the Decadent school, whose works include *À rebours* (1884).

huzzah (hə'zɑː) *interj, n, vb* an archaic word for **hurrah.** [C16: from ?]

HV *or* **h.v.** *abbrev. for* high voltage.

Hwange ★ ('hwæŋɡeɪ) *n* a town in W Zimbabwe: coal mines. Pop.: 40 000 (1989 est.). Former name (until 1982): **Wankie.**

Hwang Hai ★ ('wæŋ 'haɪ) *n* a variant transliteration of the Chinese name for the **Yellow Sea.**

Hwang Ho ★ ('wæŋ 'həʊ) *n* a variant transliteration of the Chinese name for the **Yellow River.**

HWM *abbrev. for* high-water mark.

hwyl ('huːɪl) *n* emotional fervour, as in the recitation of poetry. [C19: Welsh]

hyacinth ('haɪəsɪnθ) *n* **1** any plant of the Mediterranean genus *Hyacinthus,* esp. a cultivated variety having a thick flower stalk bearing bell-shaped fragrant flowers. **2** the flower or bulb of such a plant. **3** any similar plant, such as the grape hyacinth. **4** Also called: **jacinth.** a reddish transparent variety of the mineral zircon, used as a gemstone. **5a** any of the varying colours of the hyacinth flower or stone. **5b** (*as adj*): *hyacinth eyes.* [C16: from L *hyacinthus,* from Gk *huakinthos*]
▶ **,hya'cinthine** *adj*

Hyacinthus ★ (ˌhaɪə'sɪnθəs) *n* *Greek myth.* a youth beloved of Apollo and inadvertently killed by him. At the spot where the youth died, Apollo caused a flower to grow.

Hyades[1] ('haɪəˌdiːz) *pl n* an open cluster of stars in the constellation Taurus, formerly believed to bring rain when they rose with the sun. [C16: via L from Gk *huades,* ?from *huein* to rain]

Hyades[2] ★ ('haɪəˌdiːz) *pl n* *Greek myth.* seven nymphs, daughters of Atlas, whom Zeus placed among the stars after death.

hyaena (haɪ'iːnə) *n* a variant spelling of **hyena.**

hyaline ('haɪəlɪn) *adj* *Biol.* clear and translucent, as a common type of cartilage. [C17: from LL *hyalinus,* from Gk, from *hualos* glass]

hyalite ('haɪəˌlaɪt) *n* a clear and colourless variety of opal in globular form.

hyaloid ('haɪəˌlɔɪd) *adj* *Anat., zool.* clear and transparent; hyaline. [C19: from Gk *hualoeidēs*]

hyaloid membrane *n* the delicate transparent membrane enclosing the vitreous humour of the eye.

hybrid ('haɪbrɪd) *n* **1** an animal or plant resulting from a cross between genetically unlike individuals; usually sterile. **2** anything of mixed ancestry. **3** a word, part of which is derived from one language and part from another, such as *monolingual.* ◆ *adj* **4** denoting or being a hybrid; of mixed origin. [C17: from L *hibrida* offspring of a mixed union (human or animal)]
▶ **'hybridism** *n* ▶ **hy'bridity** *n*

hybrid computer *n* a computer that uses both analogue and digital techniques.

hybridize *or* **hybridise** ('haɪbrɪˌdaɪz) *vb* **hybridizes, hybridizing, hybridized** *or* **hybridises, hybridising, hybridised.** to produce or cause to produce hybrids; crossbreed.
▶ **,hybridi'zation** *or* **,hybridi'sation** *n*

hybridoma (ˌhaɪbrɪ'dəʊmə) *n* a hybrid cell formed by the fusion of two different types of cell, esp. one capable of producing antibodies fused with an immortal tumour cell. [C20: from HYBRID + -OMA]

hybrid vigour *n* *Biol.* the increased size, strength, etc., of a hybrid as compared to either of its parents. Also called: **heterosis.**

hydatid ('haɪdətɪd) *n* **1** a large bladder containing encysted larvae of the tapeworm *Echinococcus:* causes serious disease in man. **2** Also called: **hydatid cyst.** a sterile fluid-filled cyst produced in man and animals during infestation by *Echinococcus* larval forms. [C17: from Gk *hudatis* watery vesicle, from *hudōr, hudat-* water]

Hyde[1] ★ (haɪd) *n* a town in NW England, in Tameside, in E Greater Manchester; textiles, footwear, engineering. Pop.: 30 666 (1991).

Hyde[2] ★ (haɪd) *n* **1 Douglas.** 1860–1949, Irish scholar and author; first president of Eire (1938–45). **2 Edward.** See (1st Earl of) **Clarendon.**

Hyde Park ★ *n* a park in W central London: popular for open-air meetings.

Hyderabad ★ ('haɪdərəˌbɑːd, -ˌbæd, ˌhaɪdrə-) *n* **1** a city in S central India, capital of Andhra Pradesh state and capital of former Hyderabad state; university (1918). Pop.: 3 145 939 (1991). **2** a former state of S India: divided in 1956 between the states of Andhra Pradesh, Mysore, and Maharashtra. **3** a city in SW Pakistan, on the River Indus: seat of the University of Sind (1947). Pop.: 800 000 (latest est.).

Hyder Ali *or* **Haidar Ali** ★ ('haɪdər 'ɑːlɪ) *n* 1722–82, Indian ruler of Mysore (1766–82), who waged two wars against the British in India (1767–69; 1780–82).

hydr- *combining form.* a variant of **hydro-** before a vowel.

hydra ('haɪdrə) *n, pl* **hydras** *or* **hydrae** (-driː). **1** a freshwater coelenterate in which the body is a slender polyp with tentacles around the mouth. **2** a persistent trouble or evil. [C16: from L, from Gk *hudra* water serpent]

Hydra ★ ('haɪdrə) *n* *Greek myth.* a monster with nine heads, each of which, when struck off, was replaced by two new ones.

hydracid (haɪ'dræsɪd) *n* an acid, such as hydrochloric acid, that does not contain oxygen.

hydrangea (haɪ'dreɪndʒə) *n* a shrub or tree of an Asian

★ people and places

and American genus cultivated for their large clusters of white, pink, or blue flowers. [C18: from NL, from Gk *hudōr* water + *angeion* vessel: prob. from the cup-shaped fruit]

hydrant ('haɪdrənt) *n* an outlet from a water main, usually an upright pipe with a valve attached, from which water can be tapped for fighting fires, etc. [C19: from HYDRO- + -ANT]

hydrate ('haɪdreɪt) *n* **1** a chemical compound containing water that is chemically combined with a substance. **2** a crystalline chemical compound containing weakly bound water molecules. ◆ *vb* **hydrates, hydrating, hydrated.** **3** to undergo or cause to undergo treatment or impregnation with water.
▸ **hy'dration** *n* ▸ **'hydrator** *n*

hydrated ('haɪdreɪtɪd) *adj* (of a compound) chemically bonded to water molecules.

hydraulic (haɪ'drɒlɪk) *adj* **1** operated by pressure transmitted through a pipe by a liquid, such as water or oil. **2** of or employing liquids in motion. **3** of hydraulics. **4** hardening under water: *hydraulic cement.* [C17: from L *hydraulicus,* from Gk *hudraulikos,* from *hudraulos* water organ, from HYDRO- + *aulos* pipe]
▸ **hy'draulically** *adv*

hydraulic brake *n* a type of brake, used in motor vehicles, in which the braking force is transmitted from the brake pedal to the brakes by a liquid under pressure.

hydraulic coupling *n* another name for **torque converter.**

hydraulic press *n* a press that utilizes liquid pressure to enable a small force applied to a small piston to produce a large force on a larger piston.

hydraulic ram *n* **1** the larger or working piston of a hydraulic press. **2** a form of water pump utilizing the kinetic energy of running water to provide static pressure to raise water to a reservoir higher than the source.

hydraulics (haɪ'drɒlɪks) *n* (*functioning as sing*) another name for **fluid mechanics.**

hydraulic suspension *n* a system of motor-vehicle suspension using hydraulic members, often with hydraulic compensation between front and rear systems (**hydroelastic suspension**).

hydrazine ('haɪdrə,ziːn, -zɪn) *n* a colourless liquid made from sodium hypochlorite and ammonia: used as a rocket fuel. Formula: N_2H_4. [C19: from HYDRO- + AZO + -INE²]

hydric ('haɪdrɪk) *adj* **1** of or containing hydrogen. **2** containing or using moisture.

hydride ('haɪdraɪd) *n* any compound of hydrogen with another element.

hydrilla (haɪ'drɪlə) *n* a type of underwater aquatic weed that was introduced from Asia into the south US, where it has become a serious problem, choking fish and hindering navigation. [C20: NL, prob. from L *hydra:* see HYDRA]

hydriodic acid (,haɪdrɪ'ɒdɪk) *n* a solution of hydrogen iodide in water: a strong acid. [C19: from HYDRO- + IODIC]

hydro¹ ('haɪdrəʊ) *n, pl* **hydros.** Brit. (esp. formerly) a hotel or resort, often near a spa, offering facilities for hydropathic treatment.

hydro² ('haɪdrəʊ) *adj* **1** short for **hydroelectric.** ◆ *n* **2** a Canadian name for **electricity.**

Hydro ('haɪdrəʊ) *n* (esp. in Canada) a hydroelectric power company or board.

hydro- *or sometimes before a vowel* **hydr-** *combining form.* **1** indicating water or fluid: *hydrodynamics.* **2** indicating hydrogen in a chemical compound: *hydrochloric acid.* **3** indicating a hydroid: *hydrozoan.* [from Gk *hudōr* water]

hydrobromic acid (,haɪdrəʊ'brəʊmɪk) *n* a solution of hydrogen bromide in water: a strong acid.

hydrocarbon (,haɪdrəʊ'kɑːbᵊn) *n* any organic compound containing only carbon and hydrogen.

hydrocele ('haɪdrəʊ,siːl) *n* an abnormal collection of fluid in any saclike space.

hydrocephalus (,haɪdrəʊ'sefələs) *or* **hydrocephaly**

(,haɪdrəʊ'sefəlɪ) *n* accumulation of cerebrospinal fluid within the ventricles of the brain because its normal outlet has been blocked by congenital malformation or disease. Nontechnical name: **water on the brain.**
▸ **hydrocephalic** (,haɪdrəʊse'fælɪk) *or* ,**hydro'cephalous** *adj*

hydrochloric acid (,haɪdrə'klɒrɪk) *n* a solution of hydrogen chloride in water: a strong acid used in many industrial and laboratory processes.

hydrochloride (,haɪdrə'klɔːraɪd) *n* a quaternary salt formed by the addition of hydrochloric acid to an organic base.

hydrocyanic acid (,haɪdrəʊsaɪ'ænɪk) *n* another name for **hydrogen cyanide.**

hydrodynamics (,haɪdrəʊdaɪ'næmɪks, -dɪ-) *n* (*functioning as sing*) the branch of science concerned with the mechanical properties of fluids, esp. liquids. Also called: **hydromechanics.**

hydroelastic suspension (,haɪdrəʊɪ'læstɪk) *n* See **hydraulic suspension.**

hydroelectric (,haɪdrəʊɪ'lektrɪk) *adj* **1** generated by the pressure of falling water: *hydroelectric power.* **2** of the generation of electricity by water pressure: *a hydroelectric scheme.*
▸ **hydroelectricity** (,haɪdrəʊɪlek'trɪsɪtɪ) *n*

hydrofluoric acid (,haɪdrəʊflu'ɒrɪk) *n* a solution of hydrogen fluoride in water: a strong acid that attacks glass.

hydrofoil ('haɪdrə,fɔɪl) *n* **1** a fast light vessel the hull of which is raised out of the water on one or more pairs of fixed vanes. **2** any of these vanes.

hydroforming ('haɪdrəʊ,fɔːmɪŋ) *n* **1** *Chem.* the catalytic reforming of petroleum to increase the proportion of aromatic and branched-chain hydrocarbons. **2** *Engineering.* a forming process in which a metal is shaped by a punch forced against a die, consisting of a flexible bag containing a fluid.

hydrogen ('haɪdrɪdʒən) *n* **a** a flammable colourless gas that is the lightest and most abundant element in the universe. It occurs in water and in most organic compounds. Symbol: H; atomic no.: 1; atomic wt.: 1.007 94. **b** (*as modifier*): *hydrogen bomb.* [C18: from F *hydrogène,* from HYDRO- + -GEN; because its combustion produces water]
▸ **hydrogenous** (haɪ'drɒdʒɪnəs) *adj*

hydrogenate ('haɪdrədʒɪ,neɪt, haɪ'drɒdʒɪ,neɪt) *vb* **hydrogenates, hydrogenating, hydrogenated.** to undergo or cause to undergo a reaction with hydrogen: *to hydrogenate ethylene.*
▸ ,**hydrogen'ation** *n*

hydrogen bomb *n* a type of bomb in which energy is released by fusion of hydrogen nuclei to give helium nuclei. The energy required to initiate the fusion is provided by the detonation of an atomic bomb, which is surrounded by a hydrogen-containing substance. Also called: **H-bomb.**

hydrogen bond *n* a weak chemical bond between an electronegative atom, such as fluorine, oxygen, or nitrogen, and a hydrogen atom bound to another electronegative atom.

hydrogen bromide *n* **1** a colourless pungent gas used in organic synthesis. Formula: HBr. **2** an aqueous solution of hydrogen bromide; hydrobromic acid.

hydrogen carbonate *n* another name for **bicarbonate.**

hydrogen chloride *n* **1** a colourless pungent corrosive gas obtained by the action of sulphuric acid on sodium chloride: used in making vinyl chloride and other organic chemicals. Formula: HCl. **2** an aqueous solution of hydrogen chloride; hydrochloric acid.

hydrogen cyanide *n* a colourless poisonous liquid with a faint odour of bitter almonds. It forms prussic acid in aqueous solution and is used for making plastics and as a war gas. Formula: HCN. Also called: **hydrocyanic acid.**

hydrogen fluoride *n* **1** a colourless poisonous corrosive gas or liquid made by reaction between calcium fluoride and sulphuric acid: used as a fluorinating agent and catalyst. Formula: HF. **2** an aqueous solution of hydrogen fluoride; hydrofluoric acid.

hydrogen iodide *n* **1** a colourless poisonous corrosive gas obtained by a catalysed reaction between hydrogen and iodine vapour: used in making iodides. Formula HI. **2** an aqueous solution of this gas; hydriodic acid.

hydrogen ion *n* an ionized hydrogen atom, occurring in aqueous solutions of acids; proton. Formula: H⁺.

hydrogenize *or* **hydrogenise** ('haɪdrədʒɪ,naɪz, haɪ'drɒdʒɪ,naɪz) *vb* **hydrogenizes, hydrogenizing, hydrogenized** *or* **hydrogenises, hydrogenising, hydrogenised.** a variant of **hydrogenate.**

hydrogen peroxide *n* a colourless oily unstable liquid used as a bleach and as an oxidizer in rocket fuels. Formula: H_2O_2.

hydrogen sulphide *n* a colourless poisonous gas with an odour of rotten eggs. Formula: H_2S. Also called: **sulphuretted hydrogen.**

hydrography (haɪ'drɒɡrəfɪ) *n* the study, surveying, and mapping of the oceans, seas, and rivers.
  ▶ hy'**drographer** *n* ▶ **hydrographic** (,haɪdrə'ɡræfɪk) *adj*

hydroid ('haɪdrɔɪd) *adj* **1** of or relating to the *Hydroida,* an order of hydrozoan coelenterates that have the polyp phase dominant. **2** having or consisting of hydra-like polyps. ◆ *n* **3** a hydroid colony or individual.

hydrokinetics (,haɪdrəʊkɪ'netɪks, -kaɪ-) *n (functioning as sing)* the branch of science concerned with the behaviour and properties of fluids in motion. Also called: **hydrodynamics.**

hydrolase ('haɪdrə,leɪz) *n* an enzyme that controls hydrolysis.

hydrology (haɪ'drɒlədʒɪ) *n* the study of the distribution, conservation, use, etc., of the water of the earth and its atmosphere.
  ▶ **hydrological** (,haɪdrə'lɒdʒɪkᵊl) *adj* ▶ hy'**drologist** *n*

hydrolyse *or US* **hydrolyze** ('haɪdrə,laɪz) *vb* **hydrolyses, hydrolysing, hydrolysed** *or US* **hydrolyzes, hydrolyzing, hydrolyzed.** to subject to or undergo hydrolysis.

hydrolysis (haɪ'drɒlɪsɪs) *n* a chemical reaction in which a compound reacts with water to produce other compounds.
  ▶ **hydrolytic** (,haɪdrə'lɪtɪk) *adj*

hydrolyte ('haɪdrə,laɪt) *n* a substance subjected to hydrolysis.

hydromel ('haɪdrəʊ,mɛl) *n Arch.* another word for **mead** (the drink). [C15: from L, from Gk *hudromeli,* from HYDRO- + *meli* honey]

hydrometer (haɪ'drɒmɪtə) *n* an instrument for measuring the relative density of a liquid.
  ▶ **hydrometric** (,haɪdrəʊ'metrɪk) *or* ,**hydro'metrical** *adj*

hydronaut ('haɪdrəʊ,nɔːt) *n US Navy.* a person trained to operate deep submergence vessels. [C20: from Gk, from HYDRO- + *-naut,* as in *astronaut*]

hydropathy (haɪ'drɒpəθɪ) *n* a pseudoscientific method of treating disease by the use of large quantities of water both internally and externally.
  ▶ **hydropathic** (,haɪdrəʊ'pæθɪk) *adj*

hydrophilic (,haɪdrəʊ'fɪlɪk) *adj Chem.* tending to dissolve in, mix with, or be wetted by water: *a hydrophilic colloid.*
  ▶ **hydrophile** ('haɪdrəʊ,faɪl) *n*

hydrophobia (,haɪdrə'fəʊbɪə) *n* **1** another word for **rabies. 2** a fear of drinking fluids, esp. that of a person with rabies, because of painful spasms when trying to swallow.
  ▶ ,**hydro'phobic** *adj*

hydrophone ('haɪdrə,fəʊn) *n* an electroacoustic transducer that converts sound travelling through water into electrical oscillations.

hydrophyte ('haɪdrəʊ,faɪt) *n* a plant that grows only in water or very moist soil.

hydroplane ('haɪdrəʊ,pleɪn) *n* **1** a motorboat equipped with hydrofoils or with a shaped bottom that raises its hull out of the water at high speeds. **2** an attachment to an aircraft to enable it to glide along the surface of the water. **3** another name for a **seaplane. 4** a horizontal vane

on the hull of a submarine for controlling its vertical motion. ◆ *vb* **hydroplanes, hydroplaning, hydroplaned. 5** *(intr)* (of a boat) to rise out of the water in the manner of a hydroplane.

hydroponics (,haɪdrəʊ'pɒnɪks) *n (functioning as sing)* a method of cultivating plants by growing them in gravel, etc., through which water containing dissolved inorganic nutrient salts is pumped. [C20: from HYDRO- + (*geo*)*ponics* science of agriculture]
  ▶ ,**hydro'ponic** *adj* ▶ ,**hydro'ponically** *adv*

hydropower ('haɪdrəʊ,paʊə) *n* hydroelectric power.

hydroquinone (,haɪdrəʊkwɪ'nəʊn) *or* **hydroquinol** (,haɪdrəʊ'kwɪnɒl) *n* a white crystalline soluble phenol used as a photographic developer.

hydrosphere ('haɪdrə,sfɪə) *n* the watery part of the earth's surface, including oceans, lakes, water vapour in the atmosphere, etc.

hydrostatics (,haɪdrəʊ'stætɪks) *n (functioning as sing)* the branch of science concerned with the mechanical properties and behaviour of fluids that are not in motion.
  ▶ ,**hydro'static** *adj*

hydrotherapeutics (,haɪdrəʊ,θerə'pjuːtɪks) *n (functioning as sing)* the branch of medical science concerned with hydrotherapy.

hydrotherapy (,haɪdrəʊ'θerəpɪ) *n Med.* the treatment of certain diseases by the application of water, esp. by exercising in water to mobilize stiff joints or strengthen weak muscles.

hydrothermal (,haɪdrəʊ'θɜːməl) *adj* of or relating to the action of water under conditions of high temperature, esp. in forming rocks.

hydrotropism (haɪ'drɒtrə,pɪzəm) *n* the directional growth of plants in response to the stimulus of water.

hydrous ('haɪdrəs) *adj* containing water.

hydrovane ('haɪdrəʊ,veɪn) *n* a vane on a seaplane conferring stability on water (a sponson) or facilitating take-off (a hydrofoil).

hydroxide (haɪ'drɒksaɪd) *n* **1** a base or alkali containing the ion OH⁻. **2** any compound containing an -OH group.

hydroxy (haɪ'drɒksɪ) *adj* (of a chemical compound) containing one or more hydroxyl groups. [C19: HYDRO- + OXY(GEN)]

hydroxyl (haɪ'drɒksɪl) *n (modifier)* of, consisting of, or containing the monovalent group -OH or the ion OH⁻: *a hydroxyl group or radical.*

hydroxytryptamine (haɪ,drɒksɪ'trɪptə,miːn) *n* 5-hydroxytryptamine: another name for **serotonin.** Abbrev.: **5HT.**

hydrozoan (,haɪdrəʊ'zəʊən) *n* **1** any coelenterate of the class *Hydrozoa,* which includes the hydra and the Portuguese man-of-war. ◆ *adj* **2** of the *Hydrozoa.*

hyena *or* **hyaena** (haɪ'iːnə) *n* any of several long-legged carnivorous doglike mammals such as the spotted or laughing hyena, of Africa and S Asia. [C16: from Med. L, from L *hyaena,* from Gk, from *hus* hog]
  ▶ hy'**enic** *or* hy'**aenic** *adj*

Hygeia ★ (haɪ'dʒiːə) *n* the Greek goddess of health.
  ▶ Hy'**geian** *adj*

hygiene ('haɪdʒiːn) *n* **1** Also called: **hygienics.** the science concerned with the maintenance of health. **2** clean or healthy practices or thinking: *personal hygiene.* [C18: from NL *hygiēna,* from Gk *hugieinē,* from *hugiēs* healthy]

hygienic (haɪ'dʒiːnɪk) *adj* promoting health or cleanliness; sanitary.
  ▶ hy'**gienically** *adv*

hygienics (haɪ'dʒiːnɪks) *n (functioning as sing)* another word for **hygiene** (sense 1).

hygienist ('haɪdʒiːnɪst) *n* a person skilled in the practice of hygiene.

hygro- *or before a vowel* **hygr-** *combining form.* indicating moisture: *hygrometer.* [from Gk *hugros* wet]

hygrometer (haɪ'grɒmɪtə) *n* any of various instruments for measuring humidity.
  ▶ **hygrometric** (,haɪgrə'metrɪk) *adj*

★ people and places

hygrophyte ('haɪgrə,faɪt) *n* any plant that grows in wet or waterlogged soil.
▸ **hygrophytic** (,haɪgrə'fɪtɪk) *adj*

hygroscope ('haɪgrə,skəʊp) *n* any device that indicates the humidity of the air without necessarily measuring it.

hygroscopic (,haɪgrə'skɒpɪk) *adj* (of a substance) tending to absorb water from the air.
▸ ,**hygro'scopically** *adv*

hying ('haɪɪŋ) *vb* a present participle of **hie**.

hyla ('haɪlə) *n* a tree frog of tropical America. [C19: from NL, from Gk *hulē* forest]

hylomorphism (,haɪlə'mɔːfɪzəm) *n* the philosophical doctrine that identifies matter with the first cause of the universe.

hylozoism (,haɪlə'zəʊɪzəm) *n* the philosophical doctrine that life is one of the properties of matter. [C17: from Gk *hulē* wood, matter + *zōē* life]

hymen ('haɪmɛn) *n Anat.* a fold of mucous membrane that partly covers the entrance to the vagina and is usually ruptured when sexual intercourse takes place for the first time. [C17: from Gk: membrane]
▸ '**hymenal** *adj*

Hymen ★ ('haɪmɛn) *n* the Greek and Roman god of marriage.

hymeneal (,haɪmɛ'niːəl) *adj* **1** *Chiefly poetic.* of or relating to marriage. ◆ *n* **2** a wedding song or poem.

hymenopteran (,haɪmɪ'nɒptərən) *or* **hymenopteron** *n, pl* **hymenopterans, hymenoptera** (-tərə), *or* **hymenopterons.** any hymenopterous insect.

hymenopterous (,haɪmɪ'nɒptərəs) *adj* of or belonging to an order of insects, including bees, wasps, and ants, having two pairs of membranous wings. [C19: from Gk *humenopteros* membrane wing; see HYMEN, -PTEROUS]

Hymettus ★ (haɪ'mɛtəs) *n* a mountain in SE Greece, in Attica east of Athens: famous for its marble and for honey. Height: 1032 m (3386 ft). Modern Greek name: **Imittós.**
▸ **Hy'mettian** *or* **Hy'mettic** *adj*

hymn (hɪm) *n* **1** a Christian song of praise sung to God or a saint. **2** a similar song praising other gods, a nation, etc. ◆ *vb* **3** to express (praises, thanks, etc.) by singing hymns. [C13: from L *hymnus*, from Gk *humnos*]
▸ **hymnic** ('hɪmnɪk) *adj*

hymnal ('hɪmn³l) *n* **1** Also: **hymn book.** a book of hymns. ◆ *adj* **2** of, relating to, or characteristic of hymns.

hymnody ('hɪmnədɪ) *n* **1** the composition or singing of hymns. **2** hymns collectively. ◆ Also called: **hymnology.** [C18: from Med. L *hymnōdia*, from Gk, from *humnōidein*, from HYMN + *aeidein* to sing]

hymnology (hɪm'nɒlədʒɪ) *n* **1** the study of hymn composition. **2** another word for **hymnody.**
▸ **hym'nologist** *n*

hyoid ('haɪɔɪd) *adj* of or relating to the **hyoid bone,** the horseshoe-shaped bone that lies at the base of the tongue. [C19: from NL *hyoïdes*, from Gk *huoeidēs* having the shape of the letter UPSILON, from *hu* upsilon + -OID]

hyoscine ('haɪə,siːn) *n* another name for **scopolamine.** [C19: from *huosc(yamus)* a medicinal plant + -INE[2]; see HYOSCYAMINE]

hyoscyamine (,haɪə'saɪə,miːn) *n* a poisonous alkaloid occurring in henbane and related plants: used in medicine. [C19: from NL, from Gk *huoskuamos* (from *hus* pig + *kuamos* bean) + AMINE]

hyp. *abbrev. for:* **1** hypotenuse. **2** hypothesis. **3** hypothetical.

hypaethral *or US* **hypethral** (hɪ'piːθrəl, haɪ-) *adj* (esp. of a classical temple) having no roof. [C18: from L *hypaethrus* uncovered, from Gk, from HYPO- + *aithros* clear sky]

hypallage (haɪ'pælə,dʒiː) *n Rhetoric.* a figure of speech in which the natural relations of two words in a statement are interchanged, as in *the fire spread the wind.* [C16: via LL from Gk *hupallagē*, from HYPO- + *allassein* to exchange]

Hypatia ★ (haɪ'peɪʃɪə) *n* died 415 A.D., Neo-Platonist philosopher and politician, who lectured at Alexandria. She was murdered by a Christian mob.

hype[1] (haɪp) *Sl.* ◆ *n* **1** an intensive or exaggerated publicity or sales promotion. **2** a deception or racket. ◆ *vb* **hypes, hyping, hyped.** **3** (*tr*) to market or promote (a product) using intensive or exaggerated publicity. [C20: from ?]

hype[2] (haɪp) *Sl.* ◆ *n* **1** a hypodermic needle or injection. ◆ *vb* **hypes, hyping, hyped. 2** (*intr*; usually foll. by *up*) to inject oneself with a drug. **3** (*tr*) to stimulate artificially or excite. [C20: shortened from HYPODERMIC]

hyped up *adj Sl.* stimulated or excited by or as if by the effect of a stimulating drug.

hyper ('haɪpə) *adj Inf.* overactive; overexcited. [C20: prob. independent use of HYPER-]

hyper- *prefix* **1** above, over, or in excess: *hypercritical.* **2** denoting an abnormal excess: *hyperacidity.* **3** indicating that a chemical compound contains a greater than usual amount of an element: *hyperoxide.* [from Gk *huper* over]

hyperacidity (,haɪpərə'sɪdɪtɪ) *n* excess acidity of the gastrointestinal tract, esp. the stomach, producing a burning sensation.

hyperactive (,haɪpər'æktɪv) *adj* abnormally active.
▸ ,**hyperac'tivity** *n*

hyperaemia *or US* **hyperemia** (,haɪpər'iːmɪə) *n Pathol.* an excessive amount of blood in an organ or part.

hyperaesthesia *or US* **hyperesthesia** (,haɪpəriːs'θiːzɪə) *n Pathol.* increased sensitivity of any of the sense organs.
▸ **hyperaesthetic** *or US* **hyperesthetic** (,haɪpəriːs'θɛtɪk) *adj*

hyperbaton (haɪ'pɜːbə,tɒn) *n Rhetoric.* a figure of speech in which the normal order of words is reversed, as in *cheese I love.* [C16: via L from Gk, lit.: an overstepping, from HYPER- + *bainein* to step]

hyperbola (haɪ'pɜːbələ) *n, pl* **hyperbolas** *or* **hyperbole** (-,liː). a conic section formed by a plane that cuts both bases of a cone: it consists of two branches asymptotic to two intersecting fixed lines. [C17: from Gk *huperbolē*, lit.: excess, extravagance, from HYPER- + *ballein* to throw]

hyperbole (haɪ'pɜːbəlɪ) *n* a deliberate exaggeration used for effect: *he embraced her a thousand times.* [C16: from Gk, from HYPER- + *bolē*, from *ballein* to throw]
▸ **hy'perbolism** *n*

hyperbolic (,haɪpə'bɒlɪk) *or* **hyperbolical** *adj* **1** of a hyperbola. **2** *Rhetoric.* of a hyperbole.
▸ ,**hyper'bolically** *adv*

hyperbolic function *n* any of a group of functions of an angle expressed as a relationship between the distances of a point on a hyperbola to the origin and to the coordinate axes.

hyperbolize *or* **hyperbolise** (haɪ'pɜːbə,laɪz) *vb* **hyperbolizes, hyperbolizing, hyperbolized** *or* **hyperbolises, hyperbolising, hyperbolised.** to express (something) by means of hyperbole.

hyperboloid (haɪ'pɜːbə,lɔɪd) *n* a geometric surface consisting of one sheet, or of two sheets separated by a finite distance, whose sections parallel to the three coordinate planes are hyperbolas or ellipses.

Hyperborean ★ (,haɪpə'bɔːrɪən) *n* **1** *Greek myth.* one of a people believed to have lived beyond the North Wind in a sunny land. **2** an inhabitant of the extreme north. ◆ *adj* **3** (*sometimes not cap.*) of or relating to the extreme north. [C16: from L *hyperboreus*, from Gk, from HYPER- + *Boreas* the north wind]

hypercharge ('haɪpə,tʃɑːdʒ) *n* a property of baryons that is used to account for the absence of certain strong interaction decays.

hypercholesterolaemia *or US* **hypercholesterolemia** (,haɪpəkə,lɛstərɒl'iːmɪə) *n* the condition of having high levels of cholesterol in the blood, predisposing to atherosclerosis of the coronary arteries.

hypercorrect (,haɪpəkə'rɛkt) *adj* **1** excessively correct or fastidious. **2** resulting from or characterized by hypercorrection.

hypercorrection (,haɪpəkə'rɛkʃən) *n* a mistaken correction to text or speech made through a desire to avoid nonstandard pronunciation or grammar: *"between you and I" is a hypercorrection of "between you and me."*

hypercritical (ˌhaɪpəˈkrɪtɪkªl) *adj* excessively or severely critical.
▸ ˌhyperˈcritically *adv*

hyperfocal distance (ˌhaɪpəˈfəʊkªl) *n* the distance from a camera lens to the point beyond which all objects appear sharp and clearly defined.

hyperglycaemia *or US* **hyperglycemia** (ˌhaɪpəglaɪˈsiːmɪə) *n Pathol.* an abnormally large amount of sugar in the blood. [C20: from HYPER- + GLYCO- + -AEMIA]
▸ ˌhyperglyˈcaemic *or US* ˌhyperglyˈcemic *adj*

hypergolic (ˌhaɪpəˈgɒlɪk) *adj* (of a rocket fuel) able to ignite spontaneously on contact with an oxidizer. [C20: from G *Hypergol* (?from HYP(ER-) + ERG¹ + -OL²) + -IC]

hypericum (haɪˈperɪkəm) *n* any herbaceous plant or shrub of the temperate genus *Hypericum*. See **rose of Sharon, Saint John's wort.** [C16: via L from Gk *hupereikon*, from HYPER- + *ereikē* heath]

hyperinflation (ˌhaɪpəɪnˈfleɪʃən) *n* an extremely high level of inflation (with price rises of 50 percent per month), often involving social disorder.

Hyperion ★ (haɪˈpɪərɪən) *n Greek myth.* a Titan, son of Uranus and Gaea, father of Helios (sun), Selene (moon), and Eos (dawn).

hypermarket (ˈhaɪpəˌmɑːkɪt) *n Brit.* a huge self-service store, usually built on the outskirts of a town. [C20: translation of F *hypermarché*]

hypermedia (ˈhaɪpəˌmiːdɪə) *n* computer software and hardware that allows users to interact with text, graphics, sound, and video, each of which can be accessed from within any of the others. Cf. **hypertext.**

hypermetropia (ˌhaɪpəmɪˈtrəʊpɪə) *or* **hypermetropy** (ˌhaɪpəˈmetrəpɪ) *n Pathol.* a variant of **hyperopia.** [C19: from Gk *hupermetros* beyond measure (from HYPER- + *metron* measure) + -OPIA]

hyperon (ˈhaɪpəˌrɒn) *n Physics.* any baryon that is not a nucleon. [C20: from HYPER- + -ON]

hyperopia (ˌhaɪpəˈrəʊpɪə) *n* inability to see near objects clearly because the images received by the eye are focused behind the retina; long-sightedness.
▸ **hyperopic** (ˌhaɪpəˈrɒpɪk) *adj*

hyperphysical (ˌhaɪpəˈfɪzɪkªl) *adj* beyond the physical; supernatural or immaterial.

hyperpyrexia (ˌhaɪpəpaɪˈreksɪə) *n Pathol.* an extremely high fever, with a temperature of 41°C (106°F) or above.

hypersensitive (ˌhaɪpəˈsensɪtɪv) *adj* 1 having unduly vulnerable feelings. 2 abnormally sensitive to an allergen, a drug, or other agent.
▸ ˌhyperˈsensitiveness *or* ˌhyperˌsensiˈtivity *n*

hypersonic (ˌhaɪpəˈsɒnɪk) *adj* concerned with or having a velocity of at least five times that of sound in the same medium under the same conditions.
▸ ˌhyperˈsonics *n*

hyperspace (ˈhaɪpəˌspeɪs) *n* 1 *Maths.* space having more than three dimensions. 2 (in science fiction) a theoretical dimension within which conventional space-time relationship does not apply.

hypersthene (ˈhaɪpəˌsθiːn) *n* a green, brown, or black pyroxene mineral. [C19: from HYPER- + Gk *sthenos* strength]

hypertension (ˌhaɪpəˈtenʃən) *n Pathol.* abnormally high blood pressure.
▸ **hypertensive** (ˌhaɪpəˈtensɪv) *adj, n*

hypertext (ˈhaɪpəˌtekst) *n* computer software and hardware that allows users to create, store, and view text and move between related items easily and in a nonsequential way.

hyperthermia (ˌhaɪpəˈθɜːmɪə) *or* **hyperthermy** (ˌhaɪpəˈθɜːmɪ) *n Pathol.* a variant of **hyperpyrexia.**
▸ ˌhyperˈthermal *adj*

hyperthyroidism (ˌhaɪpəˈθaɪrɔɪˌdɪzəm) *n* overproduction of thyroid hormone by the thyroid gland, causing nervousness, insomnia, and sensitivity to heat.
▸ ˌhyperˈthyroid *adj, n*

hypertonic (ˌhaɪpəˈtɒnɪk) *adj* 1 (esp. of muscles) being in a state of abnormally high tension. 2 (of a solution) having a higher osmotic pressure than that of a specified solution.

hypertrophy (haɪˈpɜːtrəfɪ) *n, pl* **hypertrophies. 1** enlargement of an organ or part resulting from an increase in the size of the cells. ◆ *vb* **hypertrophies, hypertrophying, hypertrophied. 2** to undergo or cause to undergo this condition.

hyperventilation (ˌhaɪpəˌventɪˈleɪʃən) *n* an increase in the rate of breathing, sometimes resulting in cramp and dizziness.
▸ ˌhyperˈventiˌlate *vb*

hypha (ˈhaɪfə) *n, pl* **hyphae** (-fiː). any of the filaments that constitute the body (mycelium) of a fungus. [C19: from NL, from Gk *huphē* web]
▸ ˈhyphal *adj*

hyphen (ˈhaɪfªn) *n* 1 the punctuation mark (-), used to separate parts of compound words, to link the words of a phrase, and between syllables of a word split between two consecutive lines. ◆ *vb* 2 (*tr*) another word for **hyphenate.** [C17: from LL (meaning: the combining of two words), from Gk *huphen* (adv) together, from HYPO- + *heis* one]

hyphenate (ˈhaɪfªˌneɪt) *vb* **hyphenates, hyphenating, hyphenated.** (*tr*) to separate (words, etc.) with a hyphen.
▸ ˌhyphenˈation *n*

hyphenated (ˈhaɪfªˌneɪtɪd) *adj* 1 containing or linked with a hyphen. 2 *Chiefly US.* having a nationality denoted by a hyphenated word: *Irish-American.*

hypno- *or before a vowel* **hypn-** *combining form.* 1 indicating sleep: *hypnopaedia.* 2 relating to hypnosis: *hypnotherapy.* [from Gk *hupnos* sleep]

hypnoid (ˈhɪpˌnɔɪd) *or* **hypnoidal** (hɪpˈnɔɪdªl) *adj Psychol.* of or relating to a state resembling sleep or hypnosis.

hypnology (hɪpˈnɒlədʒɪ) *n Psychol.* the study of sleep and hypnosis.
▸ hypˈnologist *n*

hypnopaedia (ˌhɪpnəʊˈpiːdɪə) *n* the learning of lessons heard during sleep. [C20: from HYPNO- + Gk *paideia* education]

hypnopompic (ˌhɪpnəʊˈpɒmpɪk) *adj Psychol.* relating to the state existing between sleep and full waking, characterized by the persistence of dreamlike imagery. [C20: from HYPNO- + Gk *pompē* a sending forth, escort + -IC]

Hypnos ★ (ˈhɪpnɒs) *n Greek myth.* the god of sleep. Roman counterpart: **Somnus.** Cf. **Morpheus.** [Gk: sleep]

hypnosis (hɪpˈnəʊsɪs) *n, pl* **hypnoses** (-siːz). an artificially induced state of relaxation and concentration in which deeper parts of the mind become more accessible.

hypnotherapy (ˌhɪpnəʊˈθerəpɪ) *n* the use of hypnosis in the treatment of emotional and psychogenic problems.
▸ ˌhypnoˈtherapist *n*

hypnotic (hɪpˈnɒtɪk) *adj* 1 of or producing hypnosis or sleep. 2 (of a person) susceptible to hypnotism. ◆ *n* 3 a drug that induces sleep. 4 a person susceptible to hypnosis. [C17: from LL *hypnōticus*, from Gk, from *hupnoun* to put to sleep, from *hupnos* sleep]
▸ hypˈnotically *adv*

hypnotism (ˈhɪpnəˌtɪzəm) *n* 1 the scientific study and practice of hypnosis. 2 the process of inducing hypnosis.
▸ ˈhypnotist *n*

hypnotize *or* **hypnotise** (ˈhɪpnəˌtaɪz) *vb* **hypnotizes, hypnotizing, hypnotized** *or* **hypnotises, hypnotising, hypnotised.** (*tr*) 1 to induce hypnosis in (a person). 2 to charm or beguile; fascinate.
▸ ˌhypnotiˈzation *or* ˌhypnotiˈsation *n* ▸ ˈhypnoˌtizer *or* ˈhypnoˌtiser *n*

hypo¹ (ˈhaɪpəʊ) *n* short for **hyposulphite.** [C19]

hypo² (ˈhaɪpəʊ) *n, pl* **hypos.** *Inf.* short for **hypodermic syringe.**

hypo- *or before a vowel* **hyp-** *prefix* 1 beneath or below: *hypodermic.* 2 lower: *hypogastrium.* 3 less than; denoting a deficiency: *hypothyroid.* 4 indicating that a chemical compound contains an element in a lower oxidation state than usual: *hypochlorous acid.* [from Gk, from *hupo* under]

hypoallergenic (ˌhaɪpəʊˌæləˈdʒenɪk) *adj* (of cosmetics, earrings, etc.) not likely to cause an allergic reaction.

★ people and places

hypoblast ('haɪpə,blæst) n Embryol. the inner layer of an embryo at an early stage of development that becomes the endoderm.

hypocaust ('haɪpə,kɔːst) n an ancient Roman heating system in which hot air circulated under the floor and between double walls. [C17: from L hypocaustum, from Gk, from hupokaiein to light a fire beneath, from HYPO- + kaiein to burn]

hypocentre ('haɪpəʊ,sɛntə) n the point immediately below the centre of explosion of a nuclear bomb. Also called: **ground zero**.

hypochlorite (,haɪpə'klɔːraɪt) n any salt or ester of hypochlorous acid.

hypochlorous acid (,haɪpə'klɔːrəs) n an unstable acid known only in solution and in the form of its salts: a strong oxidizing and bleaching agent. Formula: HOCl.

hypochondria (,haɪpə'kɒndrɪə) n chronic abnormal anxiety concerning the state of one's health. Also called: **hypochondriasis** (,haɪpəkɒn'draɪəsɪs). [C18: from LL: abdomen, supposedly the seat of melancholy, from Gk, from hupokhondrios, from HYPO- + khondros cartilage]

hypochondriac (,haɪpə'kɒndrɪ,æk) n 1 a person suffering from hypochondria. ◆ adj also **hypochondriacal** (,haɪpəkɒn'draɪək³l). 2 relating to or suffering from hypochondria.

hypocorism (haɪ'pɒkə,rɪzəm) n a pet name, esp. one using a diminutive affix: "Sally" is a hypocorism for "Sarah". [C19: from Gk hupo-korisma, from hupo-korizesthai to use pet names, from hypo- beneath + korizesthai, from korē girl, koros boy]
▸ **hypocoristic** (,haɪpəkɒ'rɪstɪk) adj

hypocotyl (,haɪpə'kɒtɪl) n the part of an embryo plant between the cotyledons and the radicle. [C19: from HYPO- + COTYL(EDON)]

hypocrisy (hɪ'pɒkrəsɪ) n, pl **hypocrisies**. 1 the practice of professing standards, beliefs, etc., contrary to one's real character or actual behaviour. 2 an act or instance of this.

hypocrite ('hɪpəkrɪt) n a person who pretends to be what he is not. [C13: from OF ipocrite, via LL from Gk hupokritēs one who plays a part, from hupokrinein to feign, from krinein to judge]
▸ **hypo'critical** adj ▸ **hypo'critically** adv

hypocycloid (,haɪpə'saɪklɔɪd) n a curve described by a point on the circumference of a circle as the circle rolls around the inside of a fixed coplanar circle.
▸ **hypocy'cloidal** adj

hypodermic (,haɪpə'dɜːmɪk) adj 1 of or relating to the region of the skin beneath the epidermis. 2 injected beneath the skin. ◆ n 3 a hypodermic syringe or needle. 4 a hypodermic injection.
▸ **hypo'dermically** adv

hypodermic syringe n Med. a type of syringe consisting of a hollow cylinder, usually of glass or plastic, a tightly fitting piston, and a hollow needle (**hypodermic needle**), used for withdrawing blood samples, etc.

hypodermis (,haɪpə'dɜːmɪs) or **hypoderm** n 1 Bot. a layer of thick-walled supportive or water-storing cells beneath the epidermis in some plants. 2 Zool. the epidermis of arthropods, annelids, etc. [C19: from HYPO- + EPIDERMIS]

hypogastrium (,haɪpə'gæstrɪəm) n, pl **hypogastria** (-trɪə). Anat. the lower front central region of the abdomen. [C17: from NL, from Gk hupogastrion, from HYPO- + gastrion, dim. of gastēr stomach]

hypogeal (,haɪpə'dʒiːəl) or **hypogeous** adj occurring or living below the surface of the ground. [C19: from L hypogēus, from Gk, from HYPO- + gē earth]

hypogene ('haɪpə,dʒiːn) adj formed or originating beneath the surface of the earth.

hypogeum (,haɪpə'dʒiːəm) n, pl **hypogea** (-'dʒiːə). an underground vault, esp. one used for burials. [C18: from L, from Gk hupogeion; see HYPOGEAL]

hypoid gear ('haɪpɔɪd) n a gear having a tooth form generated by a hypocycloidal curve. [C20: hypoid, shortened from HYPOCYCLOID]

hyponasty ('haɪpə,næstɪ) n increased growth of the lower surface of a plant part, resulting in an upward bending of the part.
▸ **hypo'nastic** adj

hypophosphate (,haɪpə'fɒsfeɪt) n any salt or ester of hypophosphoric acid.

hypophosphite (,haɪpə'fɒsfaɪt) n any salt of hypophosphorous acid.

hypophosphoric acid (,haɪpəfɒs'fɒrɪk) n a tetrabasic acid produced by the slow oxidation of phosphorus in moist air. Formula: $H_4P_2O_6$.

hypophosphorous acid (,haɪpə'fɒsfərəs) n a monobasic acid and a reducing agent. Formula: H_3PO_2.

hypophysis (haɪ'pɒfɪsɪs) n, pl **hypophyses** (-,siːz). the technical name for **pituitary gland**. [C18: from Gk: outgrowth, from HYPO- + phuein to grow]
▸ **hypophyseal** or **hypophysial** (,haɪpə'fɪzɪəl, haɪ,pɒfɪ'sɪəl) adj

hypostasis (haɪ'pɒstəsɪs) n, pl **hypostases** (-,siːz). 1 Metaphysics. the essential nature of a substance. 2 Christianity. 2a any of the three persons of the Godhead. 2b the one person of Christ in which the divine and human natures are united. 3 the accumulation of blood in an organ or part as the result of poor circulation. [C16: from LL: substance, from Gk hupostasis foundation, from huphistasthai, from HYPO- + histanai to cause to stand]
▸ **hypostatic** (,haɪpə'stætɪk) or **hypo'statical** adj

hypostyle ('haɪpəʊ,staɪl) adj 1 having a roof supported by columns. ◆ n 2 a building constructed in this way.

hyposulphite (,haɪpə'sʌlfaɪt) n another name for **sodium thiosulphate**, esp. when used as a photographic fixer. Often shortened to **hypo**.

hyposulphurous acid (,haɪpə'sʌlfərəs) n an unstable acid known only in solution: a powerful reducing agent. Formula $H_2S_2O_4$.

hypotension (,haɪpəʊ'tɛnʃən) n Pathol. abnormally low blood pressure.
▸ **hypotensive** (,haɪpəʊ'tɛnsɪv) adj

hypotenuse (haɪ'pɒtɪ,njuːz) n the side in a right-angled triangle that is opposite the right angle. Abbrev.: **hyp**. [C16: from L hypotēnūsa, from Gk hupoteinousa grammē subtending line, from HYPO- + teinein to stretch]

hypothalamus (,haɪpə'θæləməs) n, pl **hypothalami** (-,maɪ). a neural control centre at the base of the brain, concerned with hunger, thirst, satiety, and other autonomic functions.
▸ **hypothalamic** (,haɪpəθə'læmɪk) adj

hypothec (haɪ'pɒθɪk) n Roman & Scots Law. a charge on property in favour of a creditor. [C16: from LL hypotheca, from Gk hupothēkē pledge, from hupotithenai to deposit as a security, from HYPO- + tithenai to place]

hypothecate (haɪ'pɒθɪ,keɪt) vb **hypothecates, hypothecating, hypothecated**. (tr) Law. to pledge (personal property or a ship) as security for a debt without transferring possession or title.
▸ **hy,pothe'cation** n ▸ **hy'pothe,cator** n

hypothermia (,haɪpəʊ'θɜːmɪə) n 1 Pathol. an abnormally low body temperature, as induced in the elderly by exposure to cold weather. 2 Med. the intentional reduction of normal body temperature to reduce the patient's metabolic rate.

hypothesis (haɪ'pɒθɪsɪs) n, pl **hypotheses** (-,siːz). 1 a suggested explanation for a group of facts or phenomena, either accepted as a basis for further verification (**working hypothesis**) or accepted as likely to be true. 2 an assumption used in an argument; supposition. [C16: from Gk, from hupotithenai to propose, lit.: put under; see HYPO-, THESIS]
▸ **hy'pothesist** n

hypothesize or **hypothesise** (haɪ'pɒθɪ,saɪz) vb **hypothesizes, hypothesizing, hypothesized** or **hypothesises, hypothesising, hypothesised**. to form or assume as a hypothesis.
▸ **hy'pothe,sizer** or **hy'pothe,siser** n

hypothetical (,haɪpə'θɛtɪk³l) or **hypothetic** adj 1 having the nature of a hypothesis. 2 assumed or thought to exist. 3 Logic. another word for **conditional** (sense 3).
▸ **hypo'thetically** adv

hypothyroidism (ˌhaɪpəʊˈθaɪrɔɪˌdɪzəm) *n Pathol.* **1** insufficient production of thyroid hormones by the thyroid gland. **2** any disorder, such as cretinism or myxoedema, resulting from this.
▸ ˌhypoˈthyroid *n, adj*

hypotonic (ˌhaɪpəˈtɒnɪk) *adj Pathol.* (of muscles) lacking normal tone or tension. **2** (of a solution) having a lower osmotic pressure than that of a specified solution.

hypoxia (haɪˈpɒksɪə) *n* deficiency in the amount of oxygen delivered to the body tissues. [C20: from HYPO- + OXY-^{2} + -IA]
▸ **hypoxic** (haɪˈpɒksɪk) *adj*

Hypsilantis *or* **Hypsilantes** ★ (*Greek* ˌipsiˈlandis) *n* variants of **Ypsilanti**.

hypso- *or before a vowel* **hyps-** *combining form.* indicating height: *hypsometry.* [from Gk *hupsos*]

hypsography (hɪpˈsɒgrəfɪ) *n* the scientific study and mapping of the earth's topography above sea level.

hypsometer (hɪpˈsɒmɪtə) *n* **1** an instrument for measuring altitudes by determining the boiling point of water at a given altitude. **2** any instrument used to calculate the heights of trees by triangulation.

hypsometry (hɪpˈsɒmɪtrɪ) *n* (in mapping) the establishment of height above sea level.

hyrax (ˈhaɪræks) *n, pl* **hyraxes** *or* **hyraces** (ˈhaɪrəˌsiːz). any of various agile herbivorous mammals of Africa and SW Asia. They resemble rodents but have feet with hooflike toes. Also called: **dassie**. [C19: from NL, from Gk *hurax* shrewmouse]

Hyrcania ★ (hɜːˈkeɪnɪə) *n* an ancient district of Asia, southeast of the Caspian Sea.
▸ **Hyrˈcanian** *adj*

hyssop (ˈhɪsəp) *n* **1** a widely cultivated Asian plant with spikes of small blue flowers and aromatic leaves, used as a condiment and in perfumery and folk medicine. **2** a Biblical plant, used for sprinkling in the ritual practices of the Hebrews. [OE *ysope*, from L *hyssōpus*, from Gk *hussōpos*, of Semitic origin]

hysterectomy (ˌhɪstəˈrɛktəmɪ) *n, pl* **hysterectomies.** surgical removal of the uterus.

hysteresis (ˌhɪstəˈriːsɪs) *n Physics.* the lag in a variable property of a system with respect to the effect producing it as this effect varies, esp. the phenomenon in which the magnetic induction of a ferromagnetic material lags behind the changing external field. [from Gk *husterēsis*, from *husteros* coming after]
▸ **hysteretic** (ˌhɪstəˈrɛtɪk) *adj*

hysteresis loop *n* a closed curve showing the variation of the magnetic induction of a ferromagnetic material with the external magnetic field producing it, when this field is changed through a complete cycle.

hysteria (hɪˈstɪərɪə) *n* **1** a mental disorder characterized by emotional outbursts and, often, symptoms such as paralysis. **2** any frenzied emotional state, esp. of laughter or crying. [C19: from NL, from L *hystericus* HYSTERIC]

hysteric (hɪˈstɛrɪk) *n* **1** a hysterical person. ◆ *adj* **2** hysterical. [C17: from L *hystericus*, lit.: of the womb, from Gk, from *hustera* womb; from the belief that hysteria in women originated in disorders of the womb]

hysterical (hɪˈstɛrɪkᵊl) *adj* **1** suggesting hysteria: *hysterical cries.* **2** suffering from hysteria. **3** *Inf.* wildly funny.
▸ **hysˈterically** *adv*

hysterics (hɪˈstɛrɪks) *n (functioning as pl or sing)* **1** an attack of hysteria. **2** *Inf.* wild uncontrollable bursts of laughter.

hystero- *or before a vowel* **hyster-** *combining form.* the uterus: *hysterectomy.* [from Gk *hustera* womb]

hysteron proteron (ˈhɪstəˌrɒn ˈprɒtəˌrɒn) *n* **1** *Logic.* a fallacious argument in which the proposition to be proved is assumed as a premise. **2** *Rhetoric.* a figure of speech in which the normal order of two sentences, clauses, etc., is reversed: *bred and born* (for *born and bred*). [C16: from LL, from Gk *husteron proteron* the latter (placed as) former]

hystricomorph (hɪˈstraɪkəʊˌmɔːf) *n* **1** any rodent of the suborder *Hystricomorpha*, which includes porcupines, cavies, agoutis, and chinchillas. ◆ *adj* also: **hystricomorphic** (hɪˌstraɪkəʊˈmɔːfɪk) **2** of the *Hystricomorpha*. [C19: from L *hystrix* porcupine, from Gk *hustrix*]

Hywel Dda *or* **Howel Dda** ★ (ˈhaʊəl ˈdɑː) *n* known as *Hywel the Good.* died 950 A.D., Welsh prince. He united S and N Wales and codified Welsh law.

Hz *symbol for* hertz.

Ii

i or **I** (aɪ) n, pl **i's**, **I's**, or **Is**. **1** the ninth letter and third vowel of the English alphabet. **2** any of several speech sounds represented by this letter. **3a** something shaped like an I. **3b** (in combination): an I-beam.

i symbol for the imaginary number √–1.

I¹ (aɪ) pron (subjective) refers to the speaker or writer. [C12: from OE ic; cf. OSaxon ik, OHG ih, Sansk. ahám]

I² symbol for: **1** Chem. iodine. **2** Physics. current. **3** Physics. isospin. ◆ **4** the Roman numeral for one. See **Roman numerals**.

I. abbrev. for: **1** Independence. **2** Independent. **3** Institute. **4** International. **5** Island; Isle.

Ia. or **IA** abbrev. for Iowa.

-ia suffix forming nouns. **1** in place names: Columbia. **2** in names of diseases: pneumonia. **3** in words denoting condition or quality: utopia. **4** in names of botanical genera and zoological classes: Reptilia. **5** in collective nouns borrowed from Latin: regalia. [(for senses 1–4) NL, from L & Gk, suffix of fem nouns; (for sense 5) from L, neuter pl suffix]

IAA abbrev. for indoleacetic acid.

IAEA abbrev. for International Atomic Energy Agency.

-ial suffix forming adjectives. of or relating to: managerial. [from L -iālis, adj. suffix; cf. -AL¹]

iamb ('aɪæm, 'aɪæmb) or **iambus** (aɪ'æmbəs) n, pl **iambs**, **iambi** (aɪ'æmbaɪ), or **iambuses**. Prosody. **1** a metrical foot of two syllables, a short one followed by a long one. **2** a line of verse of such feet. [C19 iamb, from C16 iambus, from L, from Gk iambos]

iambic (aɪ'æmbɪk) Prosody. ◆ adj **1** of, relating to, or using an iamb. **2** (in Greek literature) denoting a satirical verse written in iambs. ◆ n **3** a metrical foot, line, or stanza consisting of iambs. **4** an ancient Greek satirical verse written in iambs.

-ian suffix. a variant of **-an**: Etonian. [from L -iānus]

-iana suffix forming nouns. a variant of **-ana**.

IAP abbrev. for Internet access provider.

Iaşi ★ (Romanian 'iaʃj) n a city in NE Romania: capital of Moldavia (1565–1859); university (1860). Pop.: 337 643 (1993 est.). German name: **Jassy**.

-iasis or **-asis** n combining form. (in medicine) indicating a diseased condition: psoriasis. Cf. **-osis** (sense 2). [from NL, from Gk, suffix of action]

IATA (aɪ'ɑːtə, iː'ɑːtə) n acronym for International Air Transport Association.

-iatrics n combining form. indicating medical care or treatment: paediatrics. [C19: from Gk, from iasthai to heal]

iatrogenic (aɪˌætrəʊ'dʒenɪk) adj Med. (of an illness) induced in a patient as the result of a physician's action. ▸ **iatrogenicity** (aɪˌætrəʊdʒɪ'nɪsɪtɪ) n

-iatry n combining form. indicating healing or medical treatment: psychiatry. Cf. **-iatrics**. [from NL -iatria, from Gk iatreia the healing art, from iatros healer, physician] ▸ **-iatric** adj combining form.

IBA (in Britain) abbrev. for Independent Broadcasting Authority.

Ibadan ★ (ɪ'bædⁿn) n a city in SW Nigeria, capital of Oyo state: university (1948). Pop.: 1 365 000 (1995 est.).

Ibagué ★ (Spanish iβa'ye) n a city in W central Colombia. Pop.: 346 632 (1995 est.).

I-beam n a rolled steel joist or a girder with a cross section in the form of a capital I.

Ibarruri ★ (Spanish i'βarruri) n **Dolores** (do'lores). real name (La) **Pasionaria**.

Iberia ★ (aɪ'bɪərɪə) n **1** the Iberian Peninsula. **2** an ancient region south of the Caucasus in central Asia, corresponding approximately to present-day Georgia.

Iberian (aɪ'bɪərɪən) n **1** a member of a group of ancient Caucasoid peoples who inhabited the Iberian Peninsula, in classical times. **2** a native or inhabitant of the Iberian Peninsula; a Spaniard or Portuguese. **3** a native or inhabitant of ancient Iberia. ◆ adj **4** relating to the pre-Roman peoples of the Iberian Peninsula or of Caucasian Iberia. **5** of or relating to the Iberian Peninsula, its inhabitants, or any of their languages.

Iberian Peninsula ★ n a peninsula of SW Europe, occupied by Spain and Portugal.

iberis (aɪ'bɪərɪs) n any of various Mediterranean plants with white, lilac, or purple flowers. Also called: **candytuft**. [from Gk ibēris pepperwort]

Ibert ★ (French iber) n **Jacques** (**François Antoine**) (ʒak). 1890–1962, French composer; his works include the humorous orchestral Divertissement (1930).

ibex ('aɪbeks) n, pl **ibexes**, **ibices** ('ɪbɪˌsiːz, 'aɪ-), or **ibex**. any of three species of wild goat of mountainous regions of Europe, Asia, and North Africa, having large backward-curving horns. [C17: from L: chamois]

ibid. or **ib.** (referring to a book, etc., previously cited) abbrev. for ibidem. [L: in the same place]

ibis ('aɪbɪs) n, pl **ibises** or **ibis**. any of various wading birds such as the sacred ibis, that occur in warm regions and have a long thin down-curved bill. [C14: via L from Gk, from Egyptian hby]

Ibiza or **Iviza** ★ (Spanish i'βiθa) n **1** a Spanish island in the W Mediterranean, one of the Balearic Islands: hilly, with a rugged coast; tourism. Pop.: 45 000 (1986). Area: 541 sq. km (209 sq. miles). **2** the capital of Ibiza, a port on the south of the island. Pop.: 16 000 (latest est.).

-ible suffix forming adjectives. a variant of **-able**. ▸ **-ibly** suffix forming adverbs. ▸ **-ibility** suffix forming nouns.

ibn-Rushd ★ (ˌɪbⁿn'ruʃt) n the Arabic name of **Averroës**.

ibn-Saud ★ (ˌɪbⁿn'saʊd) n **Abdul-Aziz** (æb'dulæ'ziːz). 1880–1953, first king of Saudi Arabia (1932–53).

ibn-Sina ★ (ˌɪbⁿn'siːnə) n the Arabic name of **Avicenna**.

Ibo or **Igbo** ('iːbəʊ) n **1** (pl **Ibos** or **Ibo**) a member of a Negroid people of W Africa, living in S Nigeria. **2** their language, belonging to the Niger-Congo family.

Ibrahim Pasha ★ (ˌɪbrə'hiːm 'pɑːʃə) n 1789–1848, Albanian general; son of Mehemet Ali, whom he succeeded as viceroy of Egypt (1848).

IBRD abbrev. for International Bank for Reconstruction and Development (the World Bank).

Ibsen ★ ('ɪbsən) n **Henrik** ('henrɪk). 1828–1906, Norwegian dramatist and poet. After his early verse plays Brand (1866) and Peer Gynt (1867), he began the series of social dramas in prose, including A Doll's House (1879), Ghosts (1881), and The Wild Duck (1886), which have had a profound influence on modern drama. His later plays, such as Hedda Gabler (1890) and The Master Builder (1892), are more symbolic.

ibuprofen (aɪ'bjuːˌprəʊfen) n a drug that relieves pain and reduces inflammation: used to treat arthritis and muscular strains.

i/c abbrev. for: **1** in charge (of). **2** internal combustion.

-ic suffix forming adjectives. **1** of, relating to, or resembling: periodic. See also **-ical**. **2** (in chemistry) indicating that an element is chemically combined in the higher of two possible valence states: ferric. Cf. **-ous** (sense 2). [from L -icus or Gk -ikos; -ic also occurs in nouns that represent a substantive use of adjectives (magic) and in nouns borrowed directly from L or Gk (critic, music)]

Içá ★ ('iːsɑː; Portuguese i'sa) n the Brazilian part of the **Putumayo River**.

ICA abbrev. for: **1** (in Britain) Institute of Contemporary Arts. **2** Institute of Chartered Accountants.

-ical *suffix forming adjectives.* a variant of **-ic**, but having a less literal application than corresponding adjectives ending in *-ic: economical.* [from L *-icālis*]
▸ **-ically** *suffix forming adverbs.*

ICAO *abbrev. for* International Civil Aviation Organization.

Icaria ★ (aɪˈkɛərɪə, ɪ-) *n* a Greek island in the Aegean Sea, in the Southern Sporades group. Area: 256 sq. km (99 sq. miles). Modern Greek name: **Ikaría.** Also called: **Nikaria.**

Icarian Sea ★ (aɪˈkɛərɪən, ɪ-) *n* the part of the Aegean Sea between the islands of Patmos and Leros and the coast of Asia Minor, where, according to legend, Icarus fell into the sea.

Icarus ★ (ˈɪkərəs, ˈaɪ-) *n Greek myth.* the son of Daedalus, with whom he escaped from Crete, flying with wings made of wax and feathers. Heedless of his father's warning he flew too near the sun, causing the wax to melt, and fell into the Aegean and drowned.

ICBM *abbrev. for* intercontinental ballistic missile: a missile with a range greater than 5550 km.

ice (aɪs) *n* **1** water in the solid state, formed by freezing liquid water. Related adj: **glacial. 2** a portion of ice cream. **3** *Sl.* a diamond or diamonds. **4** *Sl.* a concentrated and highly potent form of methamphetamine with dangerous side effects. **5 break the ice.** to relieve shyness, etc., esp. between strangers. **5b** to be the first of a group to do something. **6 on ice.** in abeyance; pending. **7 on thin ice.** unsafe; vulnerable. ◆ *vb* **ices, icing, iced. 8** (often foll. by *up, over,* etc.) to form ice; freeze. **9** (*tr*) to mix with ice or chill (a drink, etc.). **10** (*tr*) to cover (a cake, etc.) with icing. [OE *īs*]
▸ **iced** *adj*

ICE (in Britain) *abbrev. for* Institution of Civil Engineers.

Ice. *abbrev. for* Iceland(ic).

ice age *n* another name for **glacial period.**

ice axe *n* a light axe used by mountaineers for cutting footholds in ice.

ice bag *n* a waterproof bag used as an ice pack.

iceberg (ˈaɪsbɜːɡ) *n* **1** a large mass of ice floating in the sea. **2 tip of the iceberg.** the small visible part of something, esp. a problem, that is much larger. **3** *Sl., chiefly US.* a person considered to have a cold or reserved manner. [C18: prob. part translation of MDu. *ijsberg* ice mountain; cf. Norwegian *isberg*]

iceberg lettuce *n* a type of lettuce with very crisp pale leaves tightly enfolded.

iceblink (ˈaɪsˌblɪŋk) *n* a reflected glare in the sky over an ice field. Also called: **blink.**

icebound (ˈaɪsˌbaʊnd) *adj* covered or made immobile by ice; frozen in: *an icebound ship.*

icebox (ˈaɪsˌbɒks) *n* **1** a compartment in a refrigerator for storing or making ice. **2** an insulated cabinet packed with ice for storing food. **3** a US and Canad. name for **refrigerator.**

icebreaker (ˈaɪsˌbreɪkə) *n* **1** Also called: **iceboat.** a vessel with a reinforced bow for breaking up the ice in bodies of water. **2** a device for breaking ice into smaller pieces. **3** something intended to relieve shyness between strangers.

icecap (ˈaɪsˌkæp) *n* a thick mass of glacial ice that permanently covers an area, such as the polar regions or the peak of a mountain.

ice cream *n* a sweetened frozen liquid, made from cream, milk, or a custard base, flavoured in various ways.

ice dance *n* any of a number of dances, mostly based on ballroom dancing, performed by a couple skating on ice.
▸ **ice dancer** *n* ▸ **ice dancing** *n*

icefall (ˈaɪsˌfɔːl) *n* a steep part of a glacier that resembles a frozen waterfall.

ice field *n* **1** a large ice floe. **2** a large mass of ice permanently covering an extensive area of land.

ice floe *n* a sheet of ice, of variable size, floating in the sea. See also **ice field** (sense 1).

ice hockey *n* a game played on ice by two teams wearing skates, who try to propel a flat puck into their opponents' goal with long sticks.

ice house *n* a building for storing ice.

İçel ★ (iːˈtʃel) *n* another name for **Mersin.**

Icel. *abbrev. for* Iceland(ic).

Iceland ★ (ˈaɪslənd) *n* an island republic in the N Atlantic, regarded as part of Europe: settled by Norsemen, who established a legislative assembly in 930; under Danish rule (1380–1918); gained independence in 1918 and became a republic in 1944; contains large areas of glaciers, snowfields, and lava beds with many volcanoes and hot springs (the chief source of domestic heat); inhabited chiefly along the SW coast. The economy is based largely on fishing. Official language: Icelandic. Official religion: mostly Lutheran. Currency: krona. Capital: Reykjavik. Pop.: 271 000 (1997). Area: 102 828 sq. km (39 702 sq. miles).

Icelander (ˈaɪslændə, ˈaɪsləndə) *n* a native or inhabitant of Iceland.

Icelandic (aɪsˈlændɪk) *adj* **1** of or relating to Iceland, its people, or their language. ◆ *n* **2** the official language of Iceland.

Iceland poppy *n* any of various arctic poppies with white or yellow nodding flowers.

Iceland spar *n* a pure transparent variety of calcite with double-refracting crystals.

ice lolly *n Brit. inf.* a water ice or an ice cream on a stick. Also called: **lolly.**

ice pack *n* **1** a bag or folded cloth containing ice, applied to a part of the body to reduce swelling, etc. **2** another name for **pack ice. 3** a sachet containing a gel that retains its temperature for an extended period of time, used esp. in cool bags.

ice pick *n* a pointed tool used for breaking ice.

ice plant *n* a low-growing plant of southern Africa, with fleshy leaves covered with icelike hairs and pink or white rayed flowers.

ice point *n* the temperature at which a mixture of ice and water are in equilibrium at a pressure of one atmosphere. It is 0° on the Celsius scale and 32° on the Fahrenheit scale. Cf. **steam point.**

ice sheet *n* a thick layer of ice covering a large area of land for a long time, esp. the layer that covered much of the N hemisphere during the last glacial period.

ice shelf *n* a thick mass of ice that is permanently attached to the land but projects into and floats on the sea.

ice skate *n* **1** a boot having a steel blade fitted to the sole to enable the wearer to glide over ice. **2** the steel blade on such a boot. ◆ *vb* **ice-skate, ice-skates, ice-skating, ice-skated. 3** (*intr*) to glide over ice on ice skates.
▸ **ice-ˌskater** *n*

ice station *n* a scientific research station in polar regions, where ice movement, weather, and environmental conditions are monitored.

Ichang *or* **I-ch'ang** ★ (ˈiːˈtʃæŋ) *n* a variant transliteration of the Chinese name of **Yichang.**

IChemE *abbrev. for* Institution of Chemical Engineers.

I Ching (ˈiː ˈtʃɪŋ) *n* an ancient Chinese book of divination and a source of Confucian and Taoist philosophy.

ichneumon (ɪkˈnjuːmən) *n* a mongoose of Africa and S Europe, having greyish-brown speckled fur. [C16: via L from Gk, lit.: tracker, hunter, from *ikhneuein* to track, from *ikhnos* a footprint; so named from the animal's alleged ability to locate the eggs of crocodiles]

ichneumon fly *or* **wasp** *n* any hymenopterous insect whose larvae are parasitic in caterpillars and other insect larvae.

ichnography (ɪkˈnɒɡrəfɪ) *n* **1** the art of drawing ground plans. **2** the ground plan of a building. [C16: from L, from Gk *ikhnos* trace, track]
▸ **ichnographic** (ˌɪknəˈɡræfɪk) *or* **ˌichnoˈgraphical** *adj*

ichor (ˈaɪkɔː) *n* **1** *Greek myth.* the fluid said to flow in the veins of the gods. **2** *Pathol.* a foul-smelling watery discharge from a wound or ulcer. [C17: from Gk *ikhōr*, from ?]
▸ **ˈichorous** *adj*

★ people and places

ichthyo- *or before a vowel* **ichthy-** *combining form.* indicating or relating to fishes: *ichthyology.* [from L, from Gk *ikhthus* fish]

ichthyoid (ˈɪkθɪˌɔɪd) *adj also* **ichthyoidal. 1** resembling a fish. ◆ *n* **2** a fishlike vertebrate.

ichthyology (ˌɪkθɪˈɒlədʒɪ) *n* the study of fishes.
▶ **ichthyologic** (ˌɪkθɪəˈlɒdʒɪk) *or* ˌ**ichthyoˈlogical** *adj*
▶ ˌ**ichthyˈologist** *n*

ichthyosaur (ˈɪkθɪəˌsɔː) *or* **ichthyosaurus** (ˌɪkθɪəˈsɔːrəs) *n, pl* **ichthyosaurs, ichthyosauruses,** *or* **ichthyosauri** (-ˈsɔːraɪ). an extinct marine Mesozoic reptile which had a porpoise-like body with dorsal and tail fins and paddle-like limbs. See also **plesiosaur.**

ichthyosis (ˌɪkθɪˈəʊsɪs) *n* a congenital disease in which the skin is coarse, dry, and scaly.
▶ **ichthyotic** (ˌɪkθɪˈɒtɪk) *adj*

ICI *abbrev. for* Imperial Chemical Industries.

-ician *suffix forming nouns.* indicating a person skilled or involved in a subject or activity: *physician; beautician.* [from F *-icien;* see -IC, -IAN]

icicle (ˈaɪsɪkᵊl) *n* a hanging spike of ice formed by the freezing of dripping water. [C14: from ICE + *ickel,* from OE *gicel* icicle, rel. to ON *jökull* glacier]

icing (ˈaɪsɪŋ) *n* **1** *Also (esp. US and Canad.):* **frosting.** a sugar preparation, variously flavoured and coloured, for coating and decorating cakes, etc. **2 icing on the cake** any unexpected extra or bonus. **3** the formation of ice, as on a ship, due to the freezing of moisture in the atmosphere.

icing sugar *n Brit.* a very finely ground sugar used for icings, confections, etc. US term: **confectioners' sugar.**

icon *or* **ikon** (ˈaɪkɒn) *n* **1** a representation of Christ or a saint, esp. one painted in oil on a wooden panel in the traditional Byzantine style and venerated in the Eastern Church. **2** an image, picture, etc. **3** a symbol resembling or analogous to the thing it represents. **4** a person regarded as a sex symbol or as a symbol of a belief or cultural movement. **5** a pictorial representation of a facility available on a computer that can be implemented by a cursor rather than by a textual instruction. [C16: from L, from Gk *eikōn* image, from *eikenai* to be like]

Iconium ★ (aɪˈkəʊnɪəm) *n* the ancient name for **Konya.**

icono- *or before a vowel* **icon-** *combining form.* indicating an image or likeness: *iconology.*

iconoclast (aɪˈkɒnəˌklæst) *n* **1** a person who attacks established or traditional concepts, principles, etc. **2a** a destroyer of religious images or objects. **2b** an adherent of a heretical iconoclastic movement within the Greek Orthodox Church from 725 to 842 A.D. [C16: from LL, from LGk *eikonoklastes,* from *eikōn* icon + *klastes* breaker]
▶ i,cono'clastic *adj* ▶ i'cono,clasm *n*

iconography (ˌaɪkɒˈnɒɡrəfɪ) *n, pl* **iconographies. 1a** the symbols used in a work of art. **1b** the conventional significance attached to such symbols. **2** a collection of pictures of a particular subject. **3** the representation of the subjects of icons or portraits, esp. on coins.
▶ ˌi**co'nographer** *n* ▶ **iconographic** (aɪˌkɒnəˈɡræfɪk) *or* i,cono'graphical *adj*

iconolatry (ˌaɪkɒˈnɒlətrɪ) *n* the worship of icons as idols.
▶ ˌi**co'nolater** *n* ▶ ˌi**co'nolatrous** *adj*

iconology (ˌaɪkɒˈnɒlədʒɪ) *n* **1** the study of icons. **2** icons collectively. **3** the symbolic representation of icons.
▶ **iconological** (aɪˌkɒnəˈlɒdʒɪkᵊl) *adj* ▶ ˌi**co'nologist** *n*

iconoscope (aɪˈkɒnəˌskəʊp) *n* a television camera tube in which an electron beam scans a surface, converting an optical image into electrical pulses.

iconostasis (ˌaɪkəʊˈnɒstəsɪs) *or* **iconostas** (aɪˈkɒnəˌstæs) *n, pl* **iconostases** (ˌaɪkəʊˈnɒstəˌsiːz *or* aɪˈkɒnəˌstæsɪz). *Eastern Church.* a screen with doors and with icons set in tiers, which separates the sanctuary from the nave. [C19: Church L, from LGk *eikonostasion* shrine, lit.: area where images are placed, from *icono-* + *histanai* to stand]

icosahedron (ˌaɪkəsəˈhiːdrən) *n, pl* **icosahedrons** *or* **icosahedra** (-drə). a solid figure having 20 faces. [C16: from Gk, from *eikosi* twenty + *-edron* -HEDRON]
▶ ˌ**icosa'hedral** *adj*

-ics *suffix forming nouns; functioning as sing* **1** indicating a

science, art, or matters relating to a particular subject: *politics.* **2** indicating certain activities: *acrobatics.* [pl. of *-ic,* representing L *-ica,* from Gk *-ika*]

Ictinus ★ (ɪkˈtaɪnəs) *n* 5th century B.C., Greek architect, who designed the Parthenon with Callicrates.

ictus (ˈɪktəs) *n, pl* **ictuses** *or* **ictus. 1** *Prosody.* metrical or rhythmic stress in verse feet, as contrasted with the stress accent on words. **2** *Med.* a sudden attack or stroke. [C18: from L *icere* to strike]
▶ ˈ**ictal** *adj*

ICU *abbrev. for* intensive care unit.

icy (ˈaɪsɪ) *adj* **icier, iciest. 1** made of, covered with, or containing ice. **2** resembling ice. **3** freezing or very cold. **4** cold or reserved in manner; aloof.
▶ ˈ**icily** *adv* ▶ ˈ**iciness** *n*

id (ɪd) *n Psychoanal.* the primitive instincts and energies in the unconscious mind that, modified by the ego and the superego, underlie all psychic activity. [C20: NL, from L: it; used to render G *Es*]

ID *abbrev. for:* **1** Idaho. **2** identification. **3** *Also:* **i.d.** intradermal(ly).

id. *abbrev. for* idem.

Id. *abbrev. for* Idaho.

I'd (aɪd) *contraction of* I had *or* I would.

-id[1] *suffix forming nouns and adjectives.* indicating members of a zoological family: *cyprinid.* [from NL *-idae* or *-ida,* from Gk *-idēs* suffix indicating offspring]

-id[2] *suffix forming nouns.* a variant of **-ide.**

Ida ★ (ˈaɪdə) *n* **Mount. 1** a mountain in central Crete: the highest on the island; in ancient times associated with the worship of Zeus. Height: 2456 m (8057 ft). Modern Greek name: **Idhi. 2** a mountain in NW Turkey, southeast of the site of ancient Troy. Height: 1767 m (5797 ft). Turkish name: **Kaz Daği.**

IDA *abbrev. for* International Development Association.

-idae *suffix forming plural proper nouns.* indicating names of zoological families: *Felidae.* [NL, from L, from Gk *-idai,* suffix indicating offspring]

Idaho ★ (ˈaɪdəˌhəʊ) *n* a state of the northwestern US: consists chiefly of ranges of the Rocky Mountains, with the Snake River basin in the south; important for agriculture (**Idaho potatoes**), livestock, and silver-mining. Capital: Boise. Pop.: 1 189 251 (1996 est.). Area: 216 413 sq. km (83 557 sq. miles). Abbrevs.: **Id., Ida.,** or (with zip code) **ID**
▶ ˈ**Ida,hoan** *adj, n*

-ide *or* **-id** *suffix forming nouns.* **1** (*added to the combining form of the nonmetallic or electronegative elements*) indicating a binary compound: *sodium chloride.* **2** indicating an organic compound derived from another: *acetanilide.* **3** indicating one of a class of compounds or elements: *peptide.* [from G *-id,* from F *oxide* OXIDE, based on the suffix of *acide* ACID]

idea (aɪˈdɪə) *n* **1** any product of mental activity; thought. **2** the thought of something: *the idea appals me.* **3** a belief; opinion. **4** a scheme, intention, plan, etc. **5** a vague notion; inkling: *he had no idea of the truth.* **6** a person's conception of something: *her idea of honesty is not the same as mine.* **7** significance or purpose: *the idea of the game is to discover the murderer.* **8** *Philosophy.* **8a** an immediate object of thought or perception. **8b** (*sometimes cap.*) (in Plato) the universal essence or archetype of any class of things or concepts. **9 get ideas.** to become ambitious, restless, etc. **10 not one's idea of.** not what one regards as (hard work, a holiday, etc.). **11 that's an idea.** that is worth considering. **12 the very idea!** that is preposterous, unreasonable, etc. [C16: via LL from Gk: model, notion, from *idein* to see]

> **USAGE NOTE** It is usually considered correct to say that someone has the *idea of doing* something, rather than *the idea to do it: he had the idea of taking* (not *the idea to take) a* short holiday.

ideal (aɪˈdɪəl) *n* **1** a conception of something that is perfect. **2** a person or thing considered to represent perfec-

tion. **3** something existing only as an idea. **4** a pattern or model, esp. of ethical behaviour. ◆ *adj* **5** conforming to an ideal. **6** of, involving, or existing in the form of an idea. **7** *Philosophy*. **7a** of or relating to a highly desirable and possible state of affairs. **7b** of or relating to idealism.
▸ i'**deally** *adv* ▸ i'**dealness** *n*

ideal element *n* any element added to a mathematical theory in order to eliminate special cases. The ideal element i = √–1 allows all algebraic equations to be solved.

ideal gas *n* a hypothetical gas which obeys Boyle's law exactly at all temperatures and pressures, and which has internal energy that depends only upon the temperature.

idealism (aɪ'dɪə‚lɪzəm) *n* **1** belief in or pursuance of ideals. **2** the tendency to represent things in their ideal forms, rather than as they are. **3** *Philosophy*. the doctrine that material objects and the external world do not exist in reality, but are creations of the mind. Cf. **materialism**.
▸ i'**dealist** *n* ▸ i‚deal'**istic** *adj* ▸ i‚deal'**istically** *adv*

idealize *or* **idealise** (aɪ'dɪə‚laɪz) *vb* **idealizes, idealizing, idealized** *or* **idealises, idealising, idealised. 1** to consider or represent (something) as ideal. **2** (*tr*) to portray as ideal; glorify. **3** (*intr*) to form an ideal or ideals.
▸ i‚deali'**zation** *or* i‚deali'**sation** *n* ▸ i'**deal‚izer** *or* i'**deal‚iser** *n*

idée fixe *French*. (ide fiks) *n, pl* **idées fixes** (ide fiks). a fixed idea; obsession.

idem *Latin*. ('aɪdɛm, 'ɪdɛm) *pron, adj* the same: used to refer to an article, chapter, etc., previously cited.

identic (aɪ'dɛntɪk) *adj Diplomacy*. (esp. of opinions expressed by two or more governments) having the same wording or intention regarding another power.

identical (aɪ'dɛntɪk°l) *adj* **1** being the same: *we got the identical hotel room as last year*. **2** exactly alike or equal. **3** designating either or both of a pair of twins of the same sex who developed from a single fertilized ovum that split into two. Cf. **fraternal** (sense 3). **[C17: from Med. L identicus, from L idem the same]**
▸ i'**dentically** *adv*

identification (aɪ‚dɛntɪfɪ'keɪʃən) *n* **1** the act of identifying or the state of being identified. **2a** something that identifies a person or thing. **2b** (*as modifier*): *an identification card*. **3** *Psychol*. **3a** the process of recognizing specific objects as the result of remembering. **3b** the process by which one incorporates aspects of another person's personality. **3c** the transferring of a response from one situation to another because the two bear similar features.

identification parade *n* a group of persons, including one suspected of a crime, assembled for the purpose of discovering whether a witness can identify the suspect.

identify (aɪ'dɛntɪ‚faɪ) *vb* **identifies, identifying, identified.** (*mainly tr*) **1** to prove or recognize as being a certain person or thing; determine the identity of. **2** to consider as the same or equivalent. **3** (*also intr; often foll. by with*) to consider (oneself) as similar to another. **4** to determine the taxonomic classification of (a plant or animal). **5** (*intr; usually foll. by with*) *Psychol*. to engage in identification.
▸ i'**denti‚fiable** *adj* ▸ i'**denti‚fiableness** *n* ▸ i'**denti‚fier** *n*

Identikit (aɪ'dɛntɪ‚kɪt) *n Trademark*. **1a** a set of transparencies of typical facial characteristics that can be superimposed on one another to build up a picture of a person sought by the police. **1b** (*as modifier*): *an Identikit picture*. **2** (*modifier*) artificially created by copying different elements in an attempt to form a whole: *an Identikit pop group*.

identity (aɪ'dɛntɪtɪ) *n, pl* **identities. 1** the state of having unique identifying characteristics. **2** the individual characteristics by which a person or thing is recognized. **3** the state of being the same in nature, quality, etc.: *linked by the identity of their tastes*. **4** the state of being the same as a person or thing described or known: *the identity of the stolen goods was soon established*. **5** *Maths*. **5a** an equation that is valid for all values of its variables, as in $(x - y)(x + y) = x^2 - y^2$. Often denoted by the symbol ≡. **5b** Also called: **identity element**. a member of a set that when operating on another member, x, produces that member x: the identity for multiplication of numbers is 1 since

$x.1 = 1.x = x$. **6** *Logic*. the relationship between an object and itself. **7** *Austral. inf*. a well-known local person; figure: *a Barwidgee identity*. **8** *Austral. & NZ inf*. an eccentric; character: *an old identity in the town*. **[C16: from LL identitās, from L idem the same]**

identity card *n* a card that establishes a person's identity, esp. one issued to all members of the population in wartime, to the staff of an organization, etc.

ideo- *combining form*. of or indicating idea or ideas: *ideology*. **[from F idéo-, from Gk idea IDEA]**

ideogram ('ɪdɪəʊ‚græm) *or* **ideograph** ('ɪdɪəʊ‚grɑːf) *n* **1** a sign or symbol, used in a writing system such as that of China, that directly represents a concept or thing, rather than a word for it. **2** any graphic sign or symbol, such as % or &.

ideography (‚ɪdɪ'ɒgrəfɪ) *n* the use of ideograms to communicate ideas.

ideology (‚aɪdɪ'ɒlədʒɪ) *n, pl* **ideologies. 1** a body of ideas that reflects the beliefs of a nation, political system, class, etc. **2** speculation that is imaginary or visionary. **3** the study of the nature and origin of ideas.
▸ **ideological** (‚aɪdɪə'lɒdʒɪk°l) *or* **ideo'logic** *adj* ▸ ‚ideo-'**logically** *adv* ▸ ‚ide'**ologist** *or* '**ideo‚logue** *n*

ides (aɪdz) *n (functioning as sing)* (in the Roman calendar) the 15th day in March, May, July, and October and the 13th day of each other month. **[C15: from OF, from L īdūs (pl), from ?]**

id est *Latin*. ('ɪd 'ɛst) the full form of **i.e.**

Idhi ★ ('ɪðɪ) *n* a transliteration of the Modern Greek name for (Mount) **Ida** (sense 1).

idiocy ('ɪdɪəsɪ) *n, pl* **idiocies. 1** (*not in technical usage*) severe mental retardation. **2** foolishness; stupidity. **3** a foolish act or remark.

idiom ('ɪdɪəm) *n* **1** a group of words whose meaning cannot be predicted from the constituent words: (*It was raining*) *cats and dogs*. **2** linguistic usage that is grammatical and natural to native speakers. **3** the characteristic vocabulary or usage of a specific human group or subject. **4** the characteristic artistic style of an individual, school, etc. **[C16: from L idiōma peculiarity of language, from Gk idios private, separate]**
▸ **idiomatic** (‚ɪdɪə'mætɪk) *adj* ▸ **idio'matically** *adv*

idiosyncrasy (‚ɪdɪəʊ'sɪŋkrəsɪ) *n, pl* **idiosyncrasies. 1** a tendency, type of behaviour, etc., of a person; quirk. **2** the composite physical or psychological make-up of a person. **3** an abnormal reaction of an individual to specific foods, drugs, etc. **[C17: from Gk, from idios private, separate + sunkrasis mixture, temperament]**
▸ **idiosyncratic** (‚ɪdɪəʊsɪŋ'krætɪk) *adj* ▸ ‚idiosyn'**cratically** *adv*

idiot ('ɪdɪət) *n* **1** a person with severe mental retardation. **2** a foolish or senseless person. **[C13: from L idiōta ignorant person, from Gk idiōtēs private person, ignoramus]**

idiot board *n* a slang name for **Autocue**.

idiot box *n Sl*. a television set.

idiotic (‚ɪdɪ'ɒtɪk) *adj* of or resembling an idiot; foolish; senseless.
▸ ‚idi'**otically** *adv*

idiot savant ('iːdjəʊ sæ'vɑ̃, 'ɪdɪət 'sævɒnt) *n, pl* **idiots savants** ('iːdjəʊ sæ'vɑ̃) *or* **idiot savants**. a person of subnormal intelligence who performs brilliantly at some specialized intellectual task.

idiot tape *n Computing*. a tape that prints out information in a continuous stream, with no line breaks.

idle ('aɪd°l) *adj* **1** unemployed or unoccupied; inactive. **2** not operating or being used. **3** (of money) not used to earn interest, etc. **4** not wanting to work; lazy. **5** (*usually prenominal*) frivolous or trivial: *idle pleasures*. **6** ineffective or powerless; vain. **7** without basis; unfounded. ◆ *vb* **idles, idling, idled. 8** (when *tr*, often foll. by *away*) to waste or pass (time) fruitlessly or inactively. **9** (*intr*) (of a shaft, etc.) to turn without doing useful work. **10** (*intr*) (of an engine) to run at low speed with the transmission disengaged. **[OE īdel]**
▸ '**idleness** *n* ▸ '**idly** *adv*

idle pulley *or* **idler pulley** *n* a freely rotating pulley used to control the tension or direction of a belt. Also called: **idler**.

idler ('aɪdlə) n 1 a person who idles. 2 another name for **idle pulley** or **idle wheel**.

idle wheel n a gearwheel interposed between two others to transmit torque without changing the direction of rotation or the velocity ratio. Also called: **idler**.

idol ('aɪdªl) n 1 a material object that is worshipped as a god. 2 Christianity, Judaism. any being (other than the one God) to which divine honour is paid. 3 a person who is revered, admired, or highly loved. [C13: from LL, from L: image, from Gk, from eidos shape, form]

idolatry (aɪ'dɒlətrɪ) n 1 the worship of idols. 2 great devotion or reverence.
▸ i'**dolater** n or i'**dolatress** fem n ▸ i'**dolatrous** adj

idolize or **idolise** ('aɪdə,laɪz) vb idolizes, idolizing, idolized or idolises, idolising, idolised. 1 (tr) to admire or revere greatly. 2 (tr) to worship as an idol. 3 (intr) to worship idols.
▸ ,idoli'**zation** or ,idoli'**sation** n ▸ '**idol,izer** or '**idol,iser** n

idolum (ɪ'dəʊləm) n 1 a mental picture; idea. 2 a false idea; fallacy. [C17: from L: IDOL]

Idomeneus ★ (aɪ'dɒmɪˌnjuːs) n Greek myth. a king of Crete who fought on the Greek side in the Trojan War.

IDP abbrev. for integrated data processing.

Idun ('iːdʊn) or **Ithunn** ★ n Norse myth. the goddess of spring who guarded the apples that kept the gods eternally young; wife of Bragi.

idyll or US (sometimes) **idyl** ('ɪdɪl) n 1 a poem or prose work describing an idealized rural life, pastoral scenes, etc. 2 a charming or picturesque scene or event. 3 a piece of music with a pastoral character. [C17: from L, from Gk eidullion, from eidos shape, (literary) form]
▸ i'**dyllic** adj ▸ i'**dyllically** adv

IE abbrev. for Indo-European (languages).

i.e. abbrev. for id est. [L: that is (to say); in other words]

-ie suffix forming nouns. a variant of -y²: groupie.

IEE abbrev. for Institution of Electrical Engineers.

Ieper ★ ('iːpər) n the Flemish name for **Ypres**.

-ier suffix forming nouns. a variant of -eer: brigadier. [from OE -ere -ER¹ or (in some words) from OF -ier, from L -ārius -ARY]

Ieyasu ★ (,iːjeˈjɑːsuː) n a variant spelling of (Tokugawa) **Iyeyasu**.

if (ɪf) conj (subordinating) 1 in case that, or on condition that: if you try hard it might work. 2 used to introduce an indirect question. In this sense, if approaches the meaning of whether. 3 even though: an attractive if awkward girl. 4a used to introduce expressions of desire, with only: if I had only known. 4b used to introduce exclamations of surprise, dismay, etc.: if this doesn't top everything! ♦ n 5 an uncertainty or doubt: the big if is whether our plan will work. 6 a condition or stipulation: I won't have any ifs or buts. [OE gif]

IF or **i.f.** Electronics. abbrev. for intermediate frequency.

IFA abbrev. for independent financial adviser.

IFC abbrev. for International Finance Corporation.

Ife ★ ('iːfɪ) n a town in W central Nigeria: one of the largest and oldest Yoruba towns; university (1961); centre of the cocoa trade. Pop.: 289 500 (1995 est.).

-iferous suffix forming adjectives. containing or yielding: carboniferous.

iffy ('ɪfɪ) adj iffier, iffiest. Inf. uncertain or subject to contingency. [C20: from IF + -Y¹]

Ifni ★ (Spanish 'ifni) n a former Spanish province in S Morocco, on the Atlantic: returned to Morocco in 1969.

IFS abbrev. for Irish Free State (now called Republic of Ireland).

-ify suffix forming verbs. a variant of -fy: intensify.
▸ **-ification** suffix forming nouns.

Igbo ('iːbəʊ) n, pl igbo or igbos. a variant spelling of **Ibo**.

Igdrasil ★ ('ɪgdrəsɪl) n a variant spelling of **Yggdrasil**.

igloo or **iglu** ('ɪgluː) n, pl igloos or iglus. 1 a dome-shaped Eskimo house, built of blocks of solid snow. 2 a hollow

made by a seal in the snow over its breathing hole in the ice. [C19: from Eskimo igdlu house]

Ignatius ★ (ɪgˈneɪʃəs) n Saint, surnamed Theophorus. died ?110 A.D., bishop of Antioch. His seven letters, written on his way to his martyrdom in Rome, give valuable insight into the early Christian Church. Feast day: Oct. 17 or Dec. 17 or 20.

Ignatius Loyola ★ (lɔɪˈəʊlə) n Saint. 1491–1556, Spanish ecclesiastic. He founded the Society of Jesus (1534) and was its first general (1541–56). His Spiritual Exercises (1548) remains the manual for training Jesuits. Feast day: July 31.

igneous ('ɪgnɪəs) adj 1 (of rocks) derived from magma or lava that has solidified on or below the earth's surface. 2 of or relating to fire. [C17: from L igneus fiery, from ignis fire]

ignis fatuus ('ɪgnɪs 'fætjʊəs) n, pl ignes fatui ('ɪgniːz 'fætjuˌaɪ). another name for **will-o'-the-wisp**. [C16: from Med. L, lit.: foolish fire]

ignite (ɪgˈnaɪt) vb ignites, igniting, ignited. 1 to catch fire or set fire to; burn or cause to burn. 2 (tr) Chem. to heat strongly. [C17: from L, from ignis fire]
▸ igˈnitable or igˈnitible adj ▸ ig,nitaˈbility or ig,nitiˈbility n
▸ igˈniter n

ignition (ɪgˈnɪʃən) n 1 the act or process of initiating combustion. 2 the process of igniting the fuel in an internal-combustion engine. 3 (preceded by the) the devices used to ignite the fuel in an internal-combustion engine.

ignition coil n an induction coil that supplies the high voltage to the sparking plugs on an internal-combustion engine.

ignition key n the key used in a motor vehicle to turn the switch that connects the battery to the ignition system.

ignitron (ɪgˈnaɪtrɒn, 'ɪgnɪˌtrɒn) n a rectifier controlled by a subsidiary electrode, the igniter, partially immersed in a mercury cathode. A current passed between igniter and cathode forms a hot spot sufficient to strike an arc between cathode and anode. [C20: from igniter + ELECTRON]

ignoble (ɪgˈnəʊbªl) adj 1 dishonourable; base; despicable. 2 of low birth or origins; humble; common. 3 of low quality; inferior. [C16: from L, from IN-¹ + OL gnōbilis NOBLE]
▸ ,ignoˈbility or igˈnobleness n ▸ igˈnobly adv

ignominy ('ɪgnəˌmɪnɪ) n, pl ignominies. 1 disgrace or public shame; dishonour. 2 a cause of disgrace; a shameful act. [C16: from L ignōminia disgrace, from ig- (see IN-²) + nōmen name, reputation]
▸ ,ignoˈminious adj ▸ ,ignoˈminiously adv ▸ ,ignoˈminiousness n

ignoramus (,ɪgnəˈreɪməs) n, pl ignoramuses. an ignorant person; fool. [C16: from legal L, lit.: we have no knowledge of, from L ignōrāre to be ignorant of; see IGNORE; modern usage originated from use of Ignoramus as the name of an unlettered lawyer in a play by G. Ruggle, 17th-century E dramatist]

ignorance ('ɪgnərəns) n lack of knowledge, information, or education; the state of being ignorant.

ignorant ('ɪgnərənt) adj 1 lacking in knowledge or education; unenlightened. 2 (postpositive; often foll. by of) lacking in awareness or knowledge (of): ignorant of the law. 3 resulting from or showing lack of knowledge or awareness: an ignorant remark.
▸ '**ignorantly** adv

ignore (ɪgˈnɔː) vb ignores, ignoring, ignored. (tr) to fail or refuse to notice; disregard. [C17: from L ignōrāre not to know, from ignārus ignorant of]
▸ igˈnorer n

Iguaçú or **Iguassú** ★ (Portuguese iguaˈsu) n a river in SE South America, rising in S Brazil and flowing west to join the Paraná River, forming part of the border between Brazil and Argentina. Length: 1200 km (745 miles).

Iguaçú Falls ★ n a waterfall on the border between Brazil and Argentina, on the Iguaçú River: divided into hundreds of separate falls by forested rocky islands. Width: about 4 km (2.5 miles). Height: 82 m (269 ft).

iguana (ɪˈgwɑːnə) *n* either of two large tropical American arboreal herbivorous lizards, esp. the common iguana, having a greyish-green body with a row of spines along the back. [C16: from Sp., from S Amerind *iwana*]
▶ **iˈguanian** *n, adj*

iguanodon (ɪˈgwɑːnəˌdɒn) *n* a massive herbivorous long-tailed bipedal dinosaur common in Europe and N Africa in Jurassic and Cretaceous times. [C19: NL, from IGUANA + Gk *odōn* tooth]

IHC (in New Zealand) *abbrev. for* intellectually handicapped child.

IHS the first three letters of the name Jesus in Greek (ΙΗΣΟΥΣ), often used as a Christian emblem.

IJssel *or* **Yssel** ★ (ˈaɪsᵊl; *Dutch* ˈeisəl) *n* a river in the central Netherlands: a distributary of the Rhine, flowing north to the IJsselmeer. Length: 116 km (72 miles).

Ikaría ★ (ikaˈria) *n* a transliteration of the Modern Greek name for **Icaria**.

ikat (ˈiːkæt) *n* a method of creating patterns in fabric by tie-dyeing the yarn before weaving. [C20: from Malay, lit.: to tie, bind]

ikebana (ˌiːkəˈbɑːnə) *n* the Japanese decorative art of flower arrangement.

Ikeja ★ (ɪˈkeɪjə) *n* a town in SW Nigeria, capital of Lagos state: residential and industrial suburb of Lagos. Pop.: 63 870 (latest est.).

Ikhnaton ★ (ɪkˈnɑːtən) *n* a variant of **Akhenaten**.

ikon (ˈaɪkɒn) *n* a variant spelling of **icon**.

IL *abbrev. for* Illinois.

il- *prefix* a variant of **in-**¹ and **in-**² before *l*.

-ile *or* **-il** *suffix forming adjectives and nouns.* indicating capability, liability, or a relationship with something: *agile; juvenile.* [via F from L or directly from L *-ilis*]
▶ **-ility** *suffix forming nouns.*

Île-de-France ★ (*French* ildəfrɑ̃s) *n* **1** a region of N France, in the Paris Basin: part of the duchy of France in the 10th century. **2** a former name (1715–1810) for **Mauritius**.

Île du Diable ★ (il dy djɑblə) *n* the French name for **Devil's Island**.

ileitis (ˌɪlɪˈaɪtɪs) *n* inflammation of the ileum.

ileostomy (ˌɪlɪˈɒstəmɪ) *n, pl* **ileostomies**. the surgical formation of a permanent opening through the abdominal wall into the ileum.

Îles Comores ★ (il kɔmɔr) *n* the French name for the **Comoros**.

Îles du Salut ★ (il dy saly) *n* the French name for the **Safety Islands**.

Ilesha ★ (ɪˈleɪʃə) *n* a town in W Nigeria. Pop.: 369 000 (1995 est.).

Îles Mascareignes ★ (il maskarɛɲ) *n* the French name for the **Mascarene Islands**.

Îles sous le Vent ★ (il su lə vɑ̃) *n* the French name for the **Leeward Islands** (sense 3).

ileum (ˈɪlɪəm) *n* the part of the small intestine between the jejunum and the caecum. [C17: NL, from L *īlium, īleum* flank, groin, from ?]
▶ **ˈileˌac** *adj*

ilex (ˈaɪlɛks) *n* **1** any of a genus of trees or shrubs such as the holly and inkberry. **2** another name for the **holm oak**. [C16: from L]

Ilia ★ (ˈɪlɪə) *n* (in Roman legend) the daughter of Aeneas and Lavinia, who, according to some traditions, was the mother of Romulus and Remus. See also **Rhea Silvia**.

Ilía ★ (iˈlia) *n* a transliteration of the Modern Greek name for **Elia**¹.

Iliamna ★ (ˌɪlɪˈæmnə) *n* **1** a lake in SW Alaska: the largest lake in Alaska. Length: about 130 km (80 miles). Width: 40 km (25 miles). **2** a volcano in SW Alaska, northwest of Iliamna Lake. Height: 3076 m (10 092 ft).

Iligan ★ (ɪˈliːgən) *n* a city in the Philippines, a port on the N coast of Mindanao. Pop.: 209 639 (1994 est.).

Ilion ★ (ˈɪlɪən) *n* a transliteration of the Greek name for ancient **Troy**.

ilium (ˈɪlɪəm) *n, pl* **ilia** (-ɪə). the uppermost and widest of the three sections of the hipbone.

Ilium ★ (ˈɪlɪəm) *n* the Latin name for ancient **Troy**.

ilk (ɪlk) *n* **1** a type; class; sort (esp. in **of that, his,** etc., **ilk**): *people of that ilk should not be allowed here.* **2** of that ilk. *Scot.* of the same name: to indicate that the person is laird of the place named: *Moncrieff of that ilk.* [OE *ilca* the same family, same kind]

> **USAGE NOTE**   Although the use of *ilk* in sense 1 is sometimes condemned as being the result of a misunderstanding of the original Scottish expression *of that ilk,* it is nevertheless well established and generally acceptable.

Ilkeston ★ (ˈɪlkɪstən) *n* a town in N central England, in SE Derbyshire. Pop.: 35 134 (1991).

Ilkley ★ (ˈɪlklɪ) *n* a town in N England, in West Yorkshire: nearby is **Ilkley Moor** (to the south). Pop.: 13 530 (1991).

ill (ɪl) *adj* **worse, worst. 1** (*usually postpositive*) not in good health; sick. **2** characterized by or intending harm, etc.; hostile: *ill deeds.* **3** causing pain, harm, adversity, etc. **4** ascribing or imputing evil to something referred to: *ill repute.* **5** promising an unfavourable outcome; unpropitious: *an ill omen.* **6** harsh; lacking kindness: *ill will.* **7** not up to an acceptable standard; faulty: *ill manners.* **8** ill at ease. unable to relax; uncomfortable. ◆ *n* **9** evil or harm; misfortune; trouble. **10** a mild disease. ◆ *adv* **11** badly: *the title ill befits him.* **12** with difficulty; hardly: *he can ill afford the money.* **13** not rightly: *he ill deserves such good fortune.* [C11 (in the sense: evil): from ON *illr* bad]

ill. *abbrev. for:* **1** illustrated. **2** illustration.

Ill. *abbrev. for* Illinois.

I'll (aɪl) *contraction of* I will *or* I shall.

ill-advised *adj* **1** acting without reasonable care or thought: *you would be ill-advised to sell your house now.* **2** badly thought out; not or insufficiently considered: *an ill-advised plan of action.*
▶ **ill-advisedly** (ˌɪlədˈvaɪzɪdlɪ) *adv*

ill-affected *adj* (often foll. by *towards*) not well disposed; disaffected.

Illampu ★ (*Spanish* iʎamˈpu) *n* one of the two peaks of Mount **Sorata**.

ill-assorted *adj* badly matched; incompatible.

illative (ɪˈleɪtɪv) *adj* **1** relating to inference; inferential. **2** *Grammar.* denoting a word or morpheme used to signal inference, for example *so* or *therefore.* **3** (esp. in Finnish grammar) denoting a case of nouns expressing a relation of motion or direction, usually translated by *into* or *towards.* ◆ *n* **4** *Grammar.* **4a** the illative case. **4b** an illative word or speech element. [C16: from LL *illātīvus* inferring, concluding]
▶ **ilˈlatively** *adv*

Illawarra ★ (ˌɪləˈwɒrə) *n* **1** a coastal district of E Australia, in S New South Wales. Pop.: 359 600 (1993). **2** an Australian breed of shorthorn dairy cattle noted for its high milk yield and ability to survive on poor pastures.

ill-bred *adj* badly brought up; lacking good manners.
▶ **ˌill-ˈbreeding** *n*

ill-considered *adj* done without due consideration; not thought out: *an ill-considered decision.*

ill-defined *adj* imperfectly defined; having no clear outline.

ill-disposed *adj* (often foll. by *towards*) not kindly disposed.

Ille-et-Vilaine ★ (*French* ilevilɛn) *n* a department of NW France, in E Brittany. Capital: Rennes. Pop.: 832 882 (1994 est.). Area: 6992 sq. km (2727 sq. miles).

illegal (ɪˈliːgᵊl) *adj* **1** forbidden by law; unlawful; illicit. **2** unauthorized or prohibited by a code of official or accepted rules. ◆ *n* **3** a person who has entered or attempted to enter a country illegally.
▶ **ilˈlegally** *adv* ▶ **ˌilleˈgality** *n*

★ people and places

illegible (ɪˈlɛdʒɪbᵊl) *adj* unable to be read or deciphered.
► il,legiˈbility *or* ilˈlegibleness *n* ► ilˈlegibly *adv*

illegitimate (,ɪlɪˈdʒɪtɪmɪt) *adj* **1a** born of parents who were not married to each other at the time of birth; bastard. **1b** occurring outside marriage: *of illegitimate birth.* **2** illegal; unlawful. **3** contrary to logic; incorrectly reasoned. ◆ *n* **4** an illegitimate person; bastard.
► ,illeˈgitimacy *or* ,illeˈgitimateness *n* ► ,illeˈgitimately *adv*

ill-fated *adj* doomed or unlucky.

ill-favoured *adj* **1** unattractive or repulsive in appearance; ugly. **2** disagreeable or objectionable.
► ,illˈfavouredly *adv* ► ,illˈfavouredness *n*

ill feeling *n* hostile feeling; animosity.

ill-founded *adj* not founded on true or reliable premises; unsubstantiated.

ill-gotten *adj* obtained dishonestly or illegally (esp. in **ill-gotten gains**).

ill humour *n* a disagreeable or sullen mood; bad temper.
► ,illˈhumoured *adj* ► ,illˈhumouredly *adv*

illiberal (ɪˈlɪbərəl) *adj* **1** narrow-minded; prejudiced; bigoted; intolerant. **2** not generous; mean. **3** lacking in culture or refinement.
► il,liberˈality *n* ► ilˈliberally *adv*

Illich ★ (ˈɪlɪtʃ) *n* Ivan. born 1926. US teacher and writer, born in Austria. His books include *Deschooling Society* (1971) and *Medical Nemesis* (1975).

illicit (ɪˈlɪsɪt) *adj* **1** another word for **illegal**. **2** not allowed or approved by common custom, rule, or standard: *illicit sexual relations.*
► ilˈlicitly *adv* ► ilˈlicitness *n*

Illimani ★ (*Spanish* iʎiˈmani) *n* a mountain in W Bolivia, in the Andes near La Paz. Height: 6882 m (22 580 ft).

illimitable (ɪˈlɪmɪtəbᵊl) *adj* limitless; boundless.
► il,limitaˈbility *or* ilˈlimitableness *n*

Illinois ★ (,ɪlɪˈnɔɪ) *n* **1** a state of the N central US, in the Midwest: consists of level prairie crossed by the Illinois and Kaskaskia Rivers; mainly agricultural. Capital: Springfield. Pop.: 11 846 544 (1996 est.). Area: 144 858 sq. km (55 930 sq. miles). Abbrevs.: **Ill.** or (with zip code) **IL 2** a river in Illinois, flowing SW to the Mississippi. Length: 439 km (273 miles).
► **Illinoisan** (,ɪlɪˈnɔɪən), **Illinoian** (,ɪlɪˈnɔɪən), *or* **Illinoisian** (,ɪlɪˈnɔɪzɪən) *n, adj*

illiterate (ɪˈlɪtərɪt) *adj* **1** unable to read and write. **2** violating accepted standards in reading and writing: *an illiterate scrawl.* **3** uneducated, ignorant, or uncultured: *scientifically illiterate.* ◆ *n* **4** an illiterate person.
► ilˈliteracy *or* ilˈliterateness *n* ► ilˈliterately *adv*

ill-judged *adj* rash; ill-advised.

ill-mannered *adj* having bad manners; rude; impolite.
► ,illˈmanneredly *adv*

ill-natured *adj* naturally unpleasant and mean.
► ,illˈnaturedly *adv* ► ,illˈnaturedness *n*

illness (ˈɪlnɪs) *n* **1** a disease or indisposition; sickness. **2** a state of ill health.

illogical (ɪˈlɒdʒɪkᵊl) *adj* **1** characterized by lack of logic; senseless or unreasonable. **2** disregarding logical principles.
► illogicality (ɪ,lɒdʒɪˈkælɪtɪ) *or* ilˈlogicalness *n* ► ilˈlogically *adv*

ill-starred *adj* unlucky; unfortunate; ill-fated.

ill temper *n* bad temper; irritability.
► ,illˈtempered *adj* ► ,illˈtemperedly *adv*

ill-timed *adj* occurring at or planned for an unsuitable time.

ill-treat *vb* (*tr*) to behave cruelly or harshly towards; misuse; maltreat.
► ,illˈtreatment *n*

illuminance (ɪˈluːmɪnəns) *n* the luminous flux incident on unit area of a surface. Sometimes called: **illumination**. Cf. **irradiance**.

illuminant (ɪˈluːmɪnənt) *n* **1** something that provides or gives off light. ◆ *adj* **2** giving off light; illuminating.

illuminate *vb* (ɪˈluːmɪ,neɪt), **illuminates, illuminating, illumi-**

nated. **1** (*tr*) to throw light in or into; light up. **2** (*tr*) to make easily understood; clarify. **3** to adorn, decorate, or be decorated with lights. **4** (*tr*) to decorate (a letter, etc.) by the application of colours, gold, or silver. **5** (*intr*) to become lighted up. ◆ *adj* (ɪˈluːmɪnɪt, -,neɪt). **6** *Arch.* made clear or bright with light. ◆ *n* (ɪˈluːmɪnɪt, -,neɪt). **7** a person who claims to have special enlightenment. [C16: from L *illūmināre* to light up, from *lūmen* light]
► ilˈlumi,nating *adj* ► ilˈluminative *adj* ► ilˈlumi,nator *n*

illuminati (ɪ,luːmɪˈnɑːtiː) *pl n, sing* **illuminato** (-təʊ). **1** a group of persons claiming exceptional enlightenment on some subject, esp. religion. **2** (*cap.*) any of several groups of illuminati, esp. in 18th-century France and Bavaria or 16th-century Spain. [C16: from L, lit.: the enlightened ones, from *illūmināre* to ILLUMINATE]

illumination (ɪ,luːmɪˈneɪʃən) *n* **1** the act of illuminating or the state of being illuminated. **2** a source of light. **3** (*often pl*) *Chiefly Brit.* a light or lights used as decoration in streets, parks, etc. **4** spiritual or intellectual enlightenment; insight or understanding. **5** the act of making understood; clarification. **6** decoration in colours, gold, or silver used on some manuscripts. **7** *Physics.* another name (not in technical usage) for **illuminance**.

illumine (ɪˈluːmɪn) *vb* **illumines, illumining, illumined.** a literary word for **illuminate**. [C14: from L *illūmināre* to make light]
► ilˈluminable *adj*

ill-use *vb* (ˈɪlˈjuːz), **ill-uses, ill-using, ill-used. 1** to use badly or cruelly; abuse; maltreat. ◆ *n* (ˈɪlˈjuːs), *also* **ill-usage. 2** harsh or cruel treatment; abuse.

illusion (ɪˈluːʒən) *n* **1** a false appearance or deceptive impression of reality: *the mirror gives an illusion of depth.* **2** a false or misleading perception or belief; delusion. **3** *Psychol.* a perception that is not true to reality, having been altered subjectively in the mind of the perceiver. See also **hallucination**. [C14: from L *illūsiō* deceit, from *illūdere* to sport with, from *ludus* game]
► ilˈlusionary *or* ilˈlusional *adj* ► ilˈlusioned *adj*

illusionism (ɪˈluːʒə,nɪzəm) *n* **1** *Philosophy.* the doctrine that the external world exists only in illusory sense perceptions. **2** the use of highly illusory effects in art.

illusionist (ɪˈluːʒənɪst) *n* **1** a person given to illusions; visionary; dreamer. **2** *Philosophy.* a person who believes in illusionism. **3** an artist who practises illusionism. **4** a conjuror; magician.
► il,lusionˈistic *adj*

illusory (ɪˈluːsərɪ) *or* **illusive** (ɪˈluːsɪv) *adj* producing or based on illusion; deceptive or unreal.
► ilˈlusorily *adv* ► ilˈlusoriness *n*

> **USAGE NOTE**   *Illusive* is sometimes wrongly used where *elusive* is meant: *they fought hard, but victory remained elusive* (not *illusive*).

illust. *or* **illus.** *abbrev. for:* **1** illustrated. **2** illustration.

illustrate (ˈɪlə,streɪt) *vb* **illustrates, illustrating, illustrated. 1** to clarify or explain by use of examples, analogy, etc. **2** (*tr*) to be an example of. **3** (*tr*) to explain or decorate (a book, text, etc.) with pictures. [C16: from L, from *lustrāre* to purify, brighten; see LUSTRUM]
► ˈillus,trative *adj* ► ˈillus,trator *n*

illustration (,ɪləˈstreɪʃən) *n* **1** pictorial matter used to explain or decorate a text. **2** an example: *an illustration of his ability.* **3** the act of illustrating or the state of being illustrated.
► ,illusˈtrational *adj*

illustrious (ɪˈlʌstrɪəs) *adj* **1** of great renown; famous and distinguished. **2** glorious or great: *illustrious deeds.* [C16: from L *illustris* bright, famous, from *illustrāre* to make light; see ILLUSTRATE]
► ilˈlustriously *adv* ► ilˈlustriousness *n*

ill will *n* hostile feeling; enmity; antagonism.

Illyria ★ (ɪˈlɪərɪə) *n* an ancient region of uncertain boundaries on the E shore of the Adriatic Sea, including parts of present-day Croatia, Montenegro, and Albania.
► Ilˈlyrian *adj, n*

★ people and places

Illyricum ★ (ɪ'lɪərɪkəm) *n* a Roman province founded after 168 B.C., based on the coastal area of Illyria.

Ilmen ★ ('ɪlmən) *n* **Lake**. a lake in NW Russia, in the Novgorod Region: drains through the Volkhov River into Lake Ladoga. Area: between 780 sq. km (300 sq. miles) and 2200 sq. km (850 sq. miles), according to the season.

ILO *abbrev. for* International Labour Organisation.

Iloilo ★ (ˌiːlə'iːləʊ) *n* a port in the W central Philippines, on SE Panay Island. Pop.: 302 200 (1994 est.).

Ilorin ★ (ɪ'lɒrɪn) *n* a city in W Nigeria, capital of Kwara state: agricultural trade centre. Pop.: 464 000 (1995 est.).

Ilyushin ★ (*Russian* ilj'uʃin) *n* **Sergei Vladimirovich** (sɪr'jej vla'dimirəvitʃ). 1894–1977, Soviet aircraft designer.

IM *or* **i.m.** *abbrev. for* intramuscular(ly).

I'm (aɪm) *contraction of* I am.

im- *prefix* a variant of **in-**[1] and **in-**[2] before *b*, *m*, and *p*.

image ('ɪmɪdʒ) *n* **1** a representation or likeness of a person or thing, esp. in sculpture. **2** an optically formed reproduction of an object, such as one formed by a lens or mirror. **3** a person or thing that resembles another closely; double or copy. **4** a mental picture; idea produced by the imagination. **5** the personality presented to the public by a person, organization, etc.: *a politician's image*. **6** the pattern of light that is focused onto the retina. **7** *Psychol.* the mental experience of something that is not immediately present to the senses, often involving memory. See also **imagery**. **8** a personification of a specified quality; epitome: *the image of good breeding*. **9** a mental picture or association of ideas evoked in a literary work. **10** a figure of speech such as a simile or metaphor. ◆ *vb* **images, imaging, imaged**. (*tr*) **11** to picture in the mind; imagine. **12** to make or reflect an image of. **13** to project or display on a screen, etc. **14** to portray or describe. **15** to be an example or epitome of; typify. [C13: from OF *imagene*, from L *imāgō* copy, representation; rel. to L *imitārī* to IMITATE]
▸ **'imageable** *adj* ▸ **'imageless** *adj*

image converter *or* **tube** *n* an electronic device that converts an invisible image, esp. one formed by X-rays, into an image that is visible on a fluorescent screen.

image enhancement *n* a method of improving the definition of a video picture by a computer program which reduces the lowest grey values to black and the highest to white: used for pictures from microscopes, surveillance cameras, and scanners.

image intensifier *or* **tube** *n* any of various devices for amplifying the intensity of an optical image, sometimes used in conjunction with an image converter.

image orthicon *n* a television camera tube in which electrons, emitted from a surface in proportion to the intensity of the incident light, are focused onto the target causing secondary emission of electrons.

imagery ('ɪmɪdʒrɪ, -dʒərɪ) *n*, *pl* **imageries**. **1** figurative or descriptive language in a literary work. **2** images collectively. **3** *Psychol.* **3a** the materials or general processes of the imagination. **3b** the characteristic kind of mental images formed by a particular individual. See also **image** (sense 7), **imagination** (sense 1).

image tube *n* another name for **image converter** or **image intensifier**.

imaginary (ɪ'mædʒɪnərɪ, -dʒɪnrɪ) *adj* **1** existing in the imagination; unreal; illusory. **2** *Maths.* involving or containing imaginary numbers.
▸ **im'aginarily** *adv*

imaginary number *n* any complex number of the form $a + ib$, where b is not zero and $i = \sqrt{-1}$.

imagination (ɪˌmædʒɪ'neɪʃən) *n* **1** the faculty or action of producing ideas, esp. mental images of what is not present or has not been experienced. **2** mental creative ability. **3** the ability to deal resourcefully with unexpected or unusual problems, circumstances, etc.

imaginative (ɪ'mædʒɪnətɪv) *adj* **1** produced by or indicative of a creative imagination. **2** having a vivid imagination.
▸ **im'aginatively** *adv* ▸ **im'aginativeness** *n*

imagine (ɪ'mædʒɪn) *vb* **imagines, imagining, imagined**. **1**

(when *tr*, may take a clause as object) to form a mental image of. **2** (when *tr*, may take a clause as object) to think, believe, or guess. **3** (*tr*; takes a clause as object) to suppose; assume: *I imagine he'll come*. **4** (*tr*; takes a clause as object) to believe without foundation: *he imagines he knows the whole story*. [C14: from L *imāginārī* to fancy, picture mentally, from *imāgō* likeness; see IMAGE]
▸ **im'aginable** *adj* ▸ **im'aginably** *adv* ▸ **im'aginer** *n*

imagism ('ɪmɪˌdʒɪzəm) *n* an early 20th-century poetic movement, advocating the use of ordinary speech and the precise presentation of images.
▸ **'imagist** *n*, *adj* ▸ ˌimag'istic *adj*

imago (ɪ'meɪgəʊ) *n*, *pl* **imagoes** *or* **imagines** (ɪ'mædʒəˌniːz). **1** an adult sexually mature insect. **2** *Psychoanal.* an idealized image of another person, usually a parent, carried in the unconscious. [C18: from NL, from L: likeness]

imam (ɪ'mɑːm) *or* **imaum** (ɪ'mɑːm, ɪ'mɔːm) *n Islam*. **1** a leader of congregational prayer in a mosque. **2** a caliph, as leader of a Muslim community. **3** any of a succession of Muslim religious leaders regarded by their followers as divinely inspired. [C17: from Ar.: leader]

imamate (ɪ'mɑːmeɪt) *n Islam*. **1** the region or territory governed by an imam. **2** the office, rank, or period of office of an imam.

imbalance (ɪm'bæləns) *n* a lack of balance, as in emphasis, proportion, etc.: *the political imbalance of the programme*.

imbecile ('ɪmbɪˌsiːl, -, saɪl) *n* **1** *Psychol.* a person of very low intelligence (IQ of 25 to 50). **2** *Inf.* an extremely stupid person; dolt. ◆ *adj also* **imbecilic** (ˌɪmbɪ'sɪlɪk). **3** of or like an imbecile; mentally deficient; feeble-minded. **4** stupid or senseless: *an imbecile thing to do*. [C16: from L *imbēcillus* feeble (physically or mentally)]
▸ **'imbe,cilely** *or* ˌimbe'cilically *adv* ▸ ˌimbe'cility *n*

imbed (ɪm'bed) *vb* **imbeds, imbedding, imbedded**. a less common spelling of **embed**.

imbibe (ɪm'baɪb) *vb* **imbibes, imbibing, imbibed**. **1** to drink (esp. alcoholic drinks). **2** *Literary*. to take in or assimilate (ideas, etc.): *to imbibe the spirit of the Renaissance*. **3** (*tr*) to take in as if by drinking: *to imbibe fresh air*. **4** to absorb or cause to absorb liquid or moisture; assimilate or saturate. [C14: from L *imbibere*, from *bibere* to drink]
▸ **im'biber** *n*

imbricate *adj* ('ɪmbrɪkɪt, -, keɪt), *also* **imbricated**. **1** *Archit.* relating to or having tiles, shingles, or slates that overlap. **2** (of leaves, scales, etc.) overlapping each other. ◆ *vb* ('ɪmbrɪˌkeɪt), **imbricates, imbricating, imbricated**. **3** (*tr*) to decorate with a repeating pattern resembling scales or overlapping tiles. [C17: from L *imbricāre* to cover with overlapping tiles, from *imbrex* pantile]
▸ **'imbricately** *adv* ▸ ˌimbri'cation *n*

imbroglio (ɪm'brəʊlɪˌəʊ) *n*, *pl* **imbroglios**. **1** a confused or perplexing political or interpersonal situation. **2** *Obs.* a confused heap; jumble. [C18: from It., from *imbrogliare* to confuse, EMBROIL]

Imbros ★ ('ɪmbrəs) *n* a Turkish island in the NE Aegean Sea, west of the Gallipoli Peninsula: occupied by Greece (1912–14) and Britain (1914–23). Area: 280 sq. km (108 sq. miles). Turkish name: **Imroz**.

imbrue (ɪm'bruː) *vb* **imbrues, imbruing, imbrued**. (*tr*) *Rare*. **1** to stain, esp. with blood. **2** to permeate or impregnate. [C15: from OF *embreuver*, from L *imbibere* to IMBIBE]
▸ **im'bruement** *n*

imbue (ɪm'bjuː) *vb* **imbues, imbuing, imbued**. (*tr*; usually foll. by *with*) **1** to instil or inspire (with ideals, principles, etc.). **2** *Rare*. to soak, esp. with dye, etc. [C16: from L *imbuere* to stain, accustom]
▸ **im'buement** *n*

IMechE *abbrev. for* Institution of Mechanical Engineers.

IMF *abbrev. for* International Monetary Fund.

Imhotep ★ (ɪm'həʊtɛp) *n* c 2600 B.C., Egyptian physician and architect. After his death he was worshipped as a god; the Greeks identified him with Asclepius.

imit. *abbrev. for* **1** imitation. **2** imitative.

imitate ('ɪmɪˌteɪt) *vb* **imitates, imitating, imitated**. (*tr*) **1** to try to follow the manner, style, etc., of or take as a model: *many writers imitated the language of Shakespeare*. **2** to pre-

tend to be or to impersonate, esp. for humour; mimic. **3** to make a copy or reproduction of; duplicate. [C16: from L *imitārī*; see IMAGE]
▸ **imitable** ('ɪmɪtəb³l) *adj* ▸ ˌimita'bility *n* ▸ 'imiˌtator *n*

imitation (ˌɪmɪ'teɪʃən) *n* **1** the act or practice of imitating; mimicry. **2** an instance or product of imitating, such as a copy of the manner of a person; impression. **3a** a copy of a genuine article; counterfeit. **3b** (*as modifier*): *imitation jewellery.* **4** *Music.* the repetition of a phrase or figure in one part after its appearance in another, as in a fugue.
▸ ˌimi'tational *adj*

imitative ('ɪmɪtətɪv) *adj* **1** imitating or tending to copy. **2** characterized by imitation. **3** copying or reproducing an original, esp. in an inferior manner: *imitative painting.* **4** another word for **onomatopoeic.**
▸ 'imitatively *adv* ▸ 'imitativeness *n*

Imittós ★ (ˌimi'tɒs) *n* a transliteration of the Modern Greek name for **Hymettus.**

immaculate (ɪ'mækjʊlɪt) *adj* **1** completely clean; extremely tidy: *his clothes were immaculate.* **2** completely flawless, etc.: *an immaculate rendering of the symphony.* **3** morally pure; free from sin or corruption. **4** *Biol.* with no spots or markings. [C15: from L, from IM- (not) + *macula* blemish]
▸ im'maculacy *or* im'maculateness *n* ▸ im'maculately *adv*

Immaculate Conception *n Christian theol., RC Church.* the doctrine that the Virgin Mary was conceived without any stain of original sin.

immanent ('ɪmənənt) *adj* **1** existing, operating, or remaining within; inherent. **2** (of God) present throughout the universe. [C16: from L *immanēre* to remain in]
▸ 'immanence *or* 'immanency *n* ▸ 'immanently *adv* ▸ 'immanenˌtism *n*

Immanuel *or* **Emmanuel ★** (ɪ'mænjʊəl) *n Bible.* the child whose birth was foretold by Isaiah (Isaiah 7:14) and who in Christian tradition is identified with Jesus. [from Heb. *'immānū'ēl*, lit.: God with us]

immaterial (ˌɪmə'tɪərɪəl) *adj* **1** of no real importance; inconsequential. **2** not formed of matter; incorporeal; spiritual.
▸ ˌimma,teri'ality *n* ▸ ˌimma'terially *adv*

immaterialism (ˌɪmə'tɪərɪəˌlɪzəm) *n Philosophy.* the doctrine that the material world exists only in the mind.
▸ ˌimma'terialist *n*

immature (ˌɪmə'tjʊə, -'tʃʊə) *adj* **1** not fully grown or developed. **2** deficient in maturity; lacking wisdom, insight, emotional stability, etc.
▸ ˌimma'turely *adv* ▸ ˌimma'turity *or* ˌimma'tureness *n*

immeasurable (ɪ'mɛʒərəb³l) *adj* incapable of being measured, esp. by virtue of great size; limitless.
▸ imˌmeasura'bility *or* im'measurableness *n* ▸ im'measurably *adv*

immediate (ɪ'miːdɪət) *adj* (*usually prenominal*) **1** taking place or accomplished without delay: *an immediate reaction.* **2** closest or most direct in effect or relationship: *the immediate cause of his downfall.* **3** having no intervening medium; direct in effect: *an immediate influence.* **4** contiguous in space, time, or relationship: *our immediate neighbour.* **5** present; current: *the immediate problem is food.* **6** *Philosophy.* of or relating to a concept that is directly known or intuited. [C16: from Med. L, from L IM- (not) + *mediāre* to be in the middle; see MEDIATE]
▸ im'mediacy *or* im'mediateness *n*

immediately (ɪ'miːdɪətlɪ) *adv* **1** without delay or intervention; at once; instantly. **2** very closely or directly: *this immediately concerns you.* **3** near or close by: *somewhere immediately in this area.* ◆ *conj* **4** (*subordinating*) *Chiefly Brit.* as; as soon as: *immediately he opened the door, there was a gust of wind.*

immemorial (ˌɪmɪ'mɔːrɪəl) *adj* originating in the distant past; ancient (postpositive in **time immemorial**). [C17: from Med. L, from L IM- (not) + *memoria* MEMORY]
▸ ˌimme'morially *adv*

immense (ɪ'mɛns) *adj* **1** unusually large; huge; vast. **2** without limits; immeasurable. **3** *Inf.* very good; excellent. [C15: from L *immensus*, lit.: unmeasured, from IM- (not) + *mētīrī* to measure]
▸ im'mensely *adv* ▸ im'menseness *n*

immensity (ɪ'mɛnsɪtɪ) *n, pl* **immensities. 1** the state of being immense; vastness; enormity. **2** enormous expanse, distance, or volume. **3** *Inf.* a huge amount: *an immensity of wealth.*

immerse (ɪ'mɜːs) *vb* **immerses, immersing, immersed.** (*tr*) **1** (often foll. by *in*) to plunge or dip into liquid. **2** (*often passive*; often foll. by *in*) to involve deeply; engross: *to immerse oneself in a problem.* **3** to baptize by dipping the whole body into water. [C17: from L *immergere*, from IM- (in) + *mergere* to dip]
▸ im'mersible *adj* ▸ im'mersion *n*

immerser (ɪ'mɜːsə) *n* an informal term for **immersion heater.**

immersion heater *n* an electrical device, usually thermostatically controlled, for heating the liquid in which it is immersed, esp. as a fixture in a domestic hot-water tank.

immigrant ('ɪmɪgrənt) *n* **1a** a person who immigrates. **1b** (*as modifier*): *an immigrant community.* **2** *Brit.* a person who has been settled in a country of which he is not a native for less than ten years.

immigrate ('ɪmɪˌgreɪt) *vb* **immigrates, immigrating, immigrated. 1** (*intr*) to come to a place or country of which one is not a native in order to settle there. **2** (*tr*) to introduce or bring in as an immigrant. [C17: from L *immigrāre* to go into]
▸ ˌimmi'gration *n* ▸ 'immiˌgrator *n* ▸ 'immiˌgratory *adj*

imminent ('ɪmɪnənt) *adj* **1** liable to happen soon; impending. **2** *Obs.* overhanging. [C16: from L *imminēre* to project over; rel. to *mons* mountain]
▸ 'imminence *n* ▸ 'imminently *adv*

Immingham ★ ('ɪmɪŋəm) *n* a port in NE England, in North East Lincolnshire: docks opened in 1912, principally for the exporting of coal; now handles chiefly bulk materials, esp. imported iron ore. Pop.: 12 278 (1991).

immiscible (ɪ'mɪsɪb³l) *adj* (of liquids) incapable of being mixed: *oil and water are immiscible.*
▸ imˌmisci'bility *n* ▸ im'miscibly *adv*

immitigable (ɪ'mɪtɪgəb³l) *adj Rare.* unable to be mitigated.
▸ imˌmitiga'bility *n* ▸ im'mitigably *adv*

immobile (ɪ'məʊbaɪl) *adj* **1** not moving; motionless. **2** not able to move or be moved; fixed.
▸ immobility (ˌɪməʊ'bɪlɪtɪ) *n*

immobilize *or* **immobilise** (ɪ'məʊbɪˌlaɪz) *vb* **immobilizes, immobilizing, immobilized** *or* **immobilises, immobilising, immobilised.** (*tr*) **1** to make immobile: *to immobilize a car.* **2** *Finance.* to convert (circulating capital) into fixed capital.
▸ imˌmobili'zation *or* imˌmobili'sation *n* ▸ im'mobiˌlizer *or* im'mobiˌliser *n*

immoderate (ɪ'mɒdərɪt, ɪ'mɒdrɪt) *adj* lacking in moderation; excessive: *immoderate demands.*
▸ im'moderately *adv* ▸ imˌmoder'ation *or* im'moderateness *n*

immodest (ɪ'mɒdɪst) *adj* **1** indecent, esp. with regard to sexual propriety; improper. **2** bold, impudent, or shameless.
▸ im'modestly *adv* ▸ im'modesty *n*

immolate ('ɪməˌleɪt) *vb* **immolates, immolating, immolated.** (*tr*) **1** to kill or offer as a sacrifice, esp. by fire. **2** *Literary.* to sacrifice (something highly valued). [C16: from L *immolāre* to sprinkle an offering with sacrificial meal, sacrifice; see MILL]
▸ ˌimmo'lation *n* ▸ 'immoˌlator *n*

immoral (ɪ'mɒrəl) *adj* **1** transgressing accepted moral rules; corrupt. **2** sexually dissolute; profligate or promiscuous. **3** unscrupulous or unethical: *immoral trading.* **4** tending to corrupt or resulting from corruption: *immoral earnings.*
▸ im'morally *adv*

immorality (ˌɪmə'rælɪtɪ) *n, pl* **immoralities. 1** the quality or state of being immoral. **2** immoral behaviour, esp. in sexual matters; licentiousness; promiscuity. **3** an immoral act.

immortal (ɪ'mɔːt³l) *adj* **1** not subject to death or decay; having perpetual life. **2** having everlasting fame; remem-

bered throughout time. **3** everlasting; perpetual; constant. **4** of or relating to immortal beings or concepts. ◆ *n* **5** an immortal being. **6** (*often pl*) a person who is remembered enduringly, esp. an author.
▸ ˌimmorˈtality *n* ▸ imˈmortally *adv*

immortalize *or* **immortalise** (ɪˈmɔːtəˌlaɪz) *vb* **immortalizes, immortalizing, immortalized** *or* **immortalises, immortalising, immortalised**. (*tr*) **1** to give everlasting fame to, as by treating in a literary work: *Macbeth was immortalized by Shakespeare*. **2** to give immortality to.
▸ imˌmortaliˈzation *or* imˌmortaliˈsation *n* ▸ imˈmortalˌizer *or* imˈmortalˌiser *n*

immortelle (ˌɪmɔːˈtɛl) *n* any of various composite plants that retain their colour when dried. Also called: **everlasting**. [C19: from F (*fleur*) *immortelle* everlasting (flower)]

immovable *or* **immoveable** (ɪˈmuːvəbᵊl) *adj* **1** unable to move or be moved; immobile. **2** unable to be diverted from one's intentions; steadfast. **3** unaffected by feeling; impassive. **4** unchanging; unalterable. **5** (of feasts, etc.) on the same date every year. **6** *Law*. **6a** (of property) not liable to be removed; fixed. **6b** of or relating to immovable property.
▸ imˌmovaˈbility, imˌmoveaˈbility *or* imˈmovableness, imˈmoveableness *n* ▸ imˈmovably *or* imˈmoveably *adv*

immune (ɪˈmjuːn) *adj* **1** protected against a specific disease by inoculation or as the result of innate or acquired resistance. **2** relating to or conferring immunity: *an immune body* (see **antibody**). **3** (*usually postpositive; foll. by to*) unsusceptible (to) or secure (against): *immune to inflation*. **4** exempt from obligation, penalty, etc. ◆ *n* **5** an immune person or animal. [C15: from L *immūnis* exempt from a public service]

immune response *n* the reaction of an organism's body to foreign materials (antigens), including the production of antibodies.

immunity (ɪˈmjuːnɪtɪ) *n, pl* **immunities**. **1** the ability of an organism to resist disease, either through the activities of specialized blood cells or antibodies produced by them in response to natural exposure or inoculation (**active immunity**) or by the injection of antiserum or the transfer of antibodies from a mother to her baby via the placenta or breast milk (**passive immunity**). See also **acquired immunity, natural immunity**. **2** freedom from obligation or duty, esp. exemption from tax, legal liability, etc.

immunize *or* **immunise** (ˈɪmjuˌnaɪz) *vb* **immunizes, immunizing, immunized** *or* **immunises, immunising, immunised**. (*tr*) to make immune, esp. by inoculation.
▸ ˌimmuniˈzation *or* ˌimmuniˈsation *n* ▸ ˈimmuˌnizer *or* ˈimmuˌniser *n*

immuno- *or before a vowel* **immun-** *combining form*. indicating immunity or immune: *immunology*.

immunoassay (ˌɪmjʊnəʊˈæseɪ) *n Immunol*. a technique of identifying a substance, esp. a protein, through its action as an antigen.

immunocompromised (ˌɪmjʊnəʊˈkɒmprəmaɪzd) *adj* having an impaired immune system and therefore incapable of an effective immune response, usually as a result of disease, such as AIDS, that damages the immune system.

immunodeficiency (ˌɪmjʊnəʊdɪˈfɪʃənsɪ) *n* a deficiency in or breakdown of a person's immune system.

immunogenic (ˌɪmjʊnəʊˈdʒɛnɪk) *adj* causing or producing immunity or an immune response.
▸ ˌimmunoˈgenically *adv*

immunoglobulin (ˌɪmjʊnəʊˈɡlɒbjʊlɪn) *n* any of five classes of proteins, all of which show antibody activity.

immunology (ˌɪmjʊˈnɒlədʒɪ) *n* the branch of biological science concerned with the study of immunity.
▸ **immunologic** (ˌɪmjʊnəˈlɒdʒɪk) *or* ˌimmunoˈlogical *adj* ▸ ˌimmunoˈlogically *adv* ▸ ˌimmuˈnologist *n*

immunoreaction (ˌɪmjʊnəʊrɪˈækʃən) *n* the reaction between an antigen and its antibody.

immunosuppression (ˌɪmjʊnəʊsəˈprɛʃən) *n* medical suppression of the body's immune system, esp. in order to reduce the likelihood of rejection of a transplanted organ.
▸ ˌimmunosupˈpressant *n, adj*

immunosuppressive (ˌɪmjʊnəʊsəˈprɛsɪv) *n* **1** any drug that lessens the body's rejection, esp. of a transplanted organ. ◆ *adj* **2** of or relating to such a drug.

immunotherapy (ˌɪmjʊnəʊˈθɛrəpɪ) *n* the treatment of disease by stimulating or modifying the immune response.
▸ **immunotherapeutic** (ˌɪmjʊnəʊˌθɛrəˈpjuːtɪk) *adj*

immure (ɪˈmjʊə) *vb* **immures, immuring, immured**. (*tr*) **1** *Arch. or literary*. to enclose within or as if within walls; imprison. **2** to shut (oneself) away from society. [C16: from Med. L, from L IM- (in) + *mūrus* wall]
▸ imˈmurement *n*

immutable (ɪˈmjuːtəbᵊl) *adj* unchanging through time; unalterable; ageless: *immutable laws*.
▸ imˌmutaˈbility *or* imˈmutableness *n*

Imo ★ (ˈiːməʊ) *n* a state of SE Nigeria, formed in 1976 from part of East-Central State. Capital: Owerri. Pop.: 2 560 064 (1992 est.). Area: 5530 sq. km (2135 sq. miles).

imp (ɪmp) *n* **1** a small demon or devil; mischievous sprite. **2** a mischievous child. ◆ *vb* **3** (*tr*) *Falconry*. to insert new feathers in order to repair (the wing of a falcon). [OE *impa* bud, graft, hence offspring, child, from *impian* to graft]

imp. *abbrev. for*: **1** imperative. **2** imperfect. **3** imperial. **4** impersonal. **5** import. **6** importer.

impact *n* (ˈɪmpækt). **1** the act of one body, etc., striking another; collision. **2** the force with which one thing hits another. **3** the impression made by an idea, social group, etc. ◆ *vb* (ɪmˈpækt). **4** to drive or press (an object) firmly into (another object, thing, etc.) or (of two objects) to be driven or pressed firmly together. **5** to have an impact or strong effect (on). [C18: from L *impactus* pushed against, fastened on, from *impingere* to thrust at, from *pangere* to drive in]
▸ imˈpaction *n*

impacted (ɪmˈpæktɪd) *adj* **1** (of a tooth) unable to erupt, esp. because of being wedged against another tooth below the gum. **2** (of a fracture) having the jagged broken ends wedged into each other.

impair (ɪmˈpɛə) *vb* (*tr*) to reduce or weaken in strength, quality, etc.: *his hearing was impaired by an accident*. [C14: from OF *empeirer* to make worse, from LL, from L *pēior* worse; see PEJORATIVE]
▸ imˈpairable *adj* ▸ imˈpairer *n* ▸ imˈpairment *n*

impala (ɪmˈpɑːlə) *n, pl* **impalas** *or* **impala**. an antelope of southern and eastern Africa, having lyre-shaped horns and able to move with enormous leaps. [from Zulu]

impale *or* **empale** (ɪmˈpeɪl) *vb* **impales, impaling, impaled**. (*tr*) **1** (*often foll. by on, upon,* or *with*) to pierce with a sharp instrument: *they impaled his severed head on a spear*. **2** *Heraldry*. to charge (a shield) with two coats of arms placed side by side. [C16: from Med. L, from L IM- (in) + *pālus* PALE²]
▸ imˈpalement *or* emˈpalement *n*

impalpable (ɪmˈpælpəbᵊl) *adj* **1** imperceptible, esp. to the touch: *impalpable shadows*. **2** difficult to understand; abstruse.
▸ imˌpalpaˈbility *n* ▸ imˈpalpably *adv*

impanel (ɪmˈpænᵊl) *vb* **impanels, impanelling, impanelled** *or US* **impanels, impaneling, impaneled**. a variant spelling (esp. US) of **empanel**.
▸ imˈpanelment *n*

impart (ɪmˈpɑːt) *vb* (*tr*) **1** to communicate (information, etc.); relate. **2** to give or bestow (an abstract quality): *to impart wisdom*. [C15: from OF, from L, from IM- (in) + *partīre* to share, from *pars* part]
▸ imˈpartable *adj* ▸ ˌimparˈtation *or* imˈpartment *n*

impartial (ɪmˈpɑːʃəl) *adj* not prejudiced towards or against any particular side; fair; unbiased.
▸ imˌpartiˈality *or* imˈpartialness *n* ▸ imˈpartially *adv*

impartible (ɪmˈpɑːtəbᵊl) *adj Law*. (of land, an estate, etc.) incapable of partition; indivisible.
▸ imˌpartiˈbility *n* ▸ imˈpartibly *adv*

impassable (ɪmˈpɑːsəbᵊl) *adj* (of terrain, roads, etc.) not able to be travelled through or over.
▸ imˌpassaˈbility *or* imˈpassableness *n* ▸ imˈpassably *adv*

impasse (æmˈpɑːs, ˈæmpɑːs) *n* a situation in which progress is blocked; an insurmountable difficulty; stalemate. [C19: from F; see IM-, PASS]

impassible (ɪmˈpæsəbªl) *adj Rare.* **1** not susceptible to pain or injury. **2** impassive or unmoved.
▶ im,passi'bility *or* im'passibleness *n* ▶ im'passibly *adv*

impassion (ɪmˈpæʃən) *vb (tr)* to arouse the passions of; inflame.

impassioned (ɪmˈpæʃənd) *adj* filled with passion; fiery; inflamed: *an impassioned appeal.*
▶ im'passionedly *adv* ▶ im'passionedness *n*

impassive (ɪmˈpæsɪv) *adj* **1** not revealing or affected by emotion; reserved. **2** calm; serene; imperturbable.
▶ im'passively *adv* ▶ im'passiveness *or* impassivity (,ɪmpæˈsɪvɪtɪ) *n*

impasto (ɪmˈpæstəʊ) *n* **1** paint applied thickly, so that brush marks are evident. **2** the technique of painting in this way. [C18: from It., from *impastare*, from *pasta* PASTE]

impatience (ɪmˈpeɪʃəns) *n* **1** lack of patience; intolerance of or irritability with anything that impedes or delays. **2** restless desire for change and excitement.

impatiens (ɪmˈpeɪʃɪˌɛnz) *n, pl* **impatiens.** a plant with explosive pods, such as balsam, touch-me-not, and busy Lizzie. [C18: NL from L: impatient; from the fact that the ripe pods burst open when touched]

impatient (ɪmˈpeɪʃənt) *adj* **1** lacking patience; easily irritated at delay, etc. **2** exhibiting lack of patience. **3** (*postpositive;* foll. by *of*) intolerant (of) or indignant (at): *impatient of indecision.* **4** (*postpositive;* often foll. by *for*) restlessly eager (for *or* to do something).
▶ im'patiently *adv*

impeach (ɪmˈpiːtʃ) *vb (tr)* **1** *Criminal law.* to bring a charge or accusation against. **2** *Brit. criminal law.* to accuse of a crime against the state. **3** *Chiefly US.* to charge (a public official) with an offence committed in office. **4** to challenge or question (a person's honesty, etc.). [C14: from OF, from LL *impedicāre* to entangle, catch, from L IM- (in) + *pedica* a fetter, from *pēs* foot]
▶ im'peachable *adj* ▶ im'peachment *n*

impeccable (ɪmˈpɛkəbªl) *adj* **1** without flaw or error; faultless: *an impeccable record.* **2** *Rare.* incapable of sinning. [C16: from LL *impeccābilis* sinless, from L IM- (not) + *peccāre* to sin]
▶ im,pecca'bility *n* ▶ im'peccably *adv*

impecunious (,ɪmpɪˈkjuːnɪəs) *adj* without money; penniless. [C16: from IM- (not) + from L *pecūniōsus* wealthy, from *pecūnia* money]
▶ ,impe'cuniously *adv* ▶ ,impe'cuniousness *or* impecuniosity (,ɪmpɪkjuːnɪˈɒsɪtɪ) *n*

impedance (ɪmˈpiːdªns) *n* **1** a measure of the opposition to the flow of an alternating current equal to the square root of the sum of the squares of the resistance and the reactance, expressed in ohms. **2** the ratio of the sound pressure in a medium to the rate of alternating flow through a specified surface due to the sound wave. **3** the ratio of the mechanical force to the velocity of the resulting vibration.

impede (ɪmˈpiːd) *vb* **impedes, impeding, impeded.** (*tr*) to restrict or retard in action, progress, etc.; obstruct. [C17: from L *impedīre* to hinder, lit.: shackle the feet, from *pēs* foot]
▶ im'peder *n* ▶ im'pedingly *adv*

impediment (ɪmˈpɛdɪmənt) *n* **1** a hindrance or obstruction. **2** a physical defect, esp. one of speech, such as a stammer. **3** (*pl* **impediments** *or* **impedimenta** (-ˈmɛntə)) *Law.* an obstruction to the making of a contract, esp. one of marriage.
▶ im,pedi'mental *or* im,pedi'mentary *adj*

impedimenta (ɪm,pɛdɪˈmɛntə) *pl n* **1** any objects that impede progress, esp. the baggage and equipment carried by an army. **2** a plural of **impediment** (sense 3). [C16: from L, pl of *impedīmentum* hindrance; see IMPEDE]

impel (ɪmˈpɛl) *vb* **impels, impelling, impelled.** (*tr*) **1** to urge or force (a person) to an action; constrain or motivate. **2** to push, drive, or force into motion. [C15: from L *impellere* to push against, drive forward]
▶ im'pellent *n, adj*

impeller (ɪmˈpɛlə) *n* the vaned rotating disc of a centrifugal pump, compressor, etc.

impend (ɪmˈpɛnd) *vb (intr)* **1** (esp. of something threatening) to be imminent. **2** (foll. by *over*) *Rare.* to be suspended; hang. [C16: from L *impendēre* to overhang, from *pendēre* to hang]
▶ im'pendence *or* im'pendency *n* ▶ im'pending *adj*

impenetrable (ɪmˈpɛnɪtrəbªl) *adj* **1** incapable of being pierced through or penetrated: *an impenetrable forest.* **2** incapable of being understood; incomprehensible. **3** incapable of being seen through: *impenetrable gloom.* **4** not susceptible to ideas, influence, etc.: *impenetrable ignorance.* **5** *Physics.* (of a body) incapable of occupying the same space as another body.
▶ im,penetra'bility *n* ▶ im'penetrableness *n* ▶ im'penetrably *adv*

impenitent (ɪmˈpɛnɪtənt) *adj* not sorry or penitent; unrepentant.
▶ im'penitence, im'penitency, *or* im'penitentness *n* ▶ im'penitently *adv* ·

imper. *abbrev. for* imperative.

imperative (ɪmˈpɛrətɪv) *adj* **1** extremely urgent or important; essential. **2** peremptory or authoritative: *an imperative tone of voice.* **3** *Also:* **imperatival** (ɪm,pɛrəˈtaɪvªl). *Grammar.* denoting a mood of verbs used in giving orders, making requests, etc. ♦ *n* **4** something that is urgent or essential. **5** an order or command. **6** *Grammar.* **6a** the imperative mood. **6b** a verb in this mood. [C16: from LL, form L *imperāre* to command]
▶ im'peratively *adv* ▶ im'perativeness *n*

imperator (,ɪmpəˈrɑːtɔː) *n* (in ancient Rome) a title bestowed upon generals and, later, emperors. [C16: from L: commander, from *imperāre* to command]
▶ imperatorial (ɪm,pɛrəˈtɔːrɪəl) *adj* ▶ ,impe'rator,ship *n*

imperceptible (,ɪmpəˈsɛptɪbªl) *adj* too slight, subtle, gradual, etc., to be perceived.
▶ ,imper,cepti'bility *or* ,imper'ceptibleness *n* ▶ ,imper'ceptibly *adv*

imperceptive (,ɪmpəˈsɛptɪv) *adj, also* **impercipient** (,ɪmpəˈsɪpɪənt). lacking in perception; obtuse.
▶ ,imper'ception *n* ▶ ,imper'ceptively *adv* ▶ ,imper'ceptiveness *or* ,imper'cipience *n*

imperf. *abbrev. for:* **1** *Also:* **impf.** imperfect. **2** (of stamps) imperforate.

imperfect (ɪmˈpɜːfɪkt) *adj* **1** exhibiting or characterized by faults, mistakes, etc.; defective. **2** not complete or finished; deficient. **3** *Grammar.* denoting a tense of verbs used most commonly in describing continuous or repeated past actions or events. **4** *Law.* legally unenforceable. **5** *Music.* **5a** proceeding to the dominant from the tonic, subdominant, or any chord other than the dominant. **5b** of or relating to all intervals other than the fourth, fifth, and octave. Cf. **perfect** (sense 9). ♦ *n* **6** *Grammar.* **6a** the imperfect tense. **6b** a verb in this tense.
▶ im'perfectly *adv* ▶ im'perfectness *n*

imperfection (,ɪmpəˈfɛkʃən) *n* **1** the condition or quality of being imperfect. **2** a fault or defect.

imperfective (,ɪmpəˈfɛktɪv) *Grammar.* ♦ *adj* **1** denoting an aspect of the verb to indicate that the action is in progress without regard to its completion. Cf. **perfective.** ♦ *n* **2a** the imperfective aspect of a verb. **2b** a verb in this aspect.
▶ ,imper'fectively *adv*

imperforate (ɪmˈpɜːfərɪt, -,reɪt) *adj* **1** not perforated. **2** (of a postage stamp) not provided with perforation or any other means of separation. **3** *Anat.* without the normal opening.
▶ im,perfo'ration *n*

imperial (ɪmˈpɪərɪəl) *adj* **1** of or relating to an empire, emperor, or empress. **2** characteristic of an emperor; majestic; commanding. **3** exercising supreme authority; imperious. **4** (esp. of products) of a superior size or quality. **5** (*usually prenominal*) (of weights, measures, etc.) conforming to standards legally established in Great Britain. ♦ *n* **6** a book size, esp. 7½ by 11 inches or 11 by 15 inches. **7** a size of writing paper, 23 by 31 inches (US and Canad.) or 22 by 30 inches (Brit.). **8** *US.* **8a** the top of a carriage. **8b** a luggage case carried there. **9** a small

tufted beard popularized by the French emperor Napoleon III. **10** a wine bottle holding the equivalent of eight normal bottles. [C14: from LL, from L *imperium* command, authority, empire]
▸ im'perially *adv* ▸ im'perialness *n*

imperialism (ɪmˈpɪərɪəˌlɪzəm) *n* **1** the policy or practice of extending a state's rule over other territories. **2** the extension or attempted extension of authority, influence, power, etc., by any person, country, institution, etc.: *cultural imperialism*. **3** a system of imperial government or rule by an emperor. **4** the spirit, character, authority, etc., of an empire.
▸ im'perialist *adj, n* ▸ im,perial'istic *adj* ▸ im,perial-'istically *adv*

imperil (ɪmˈpɛrɪl) *vb* imperils, imperilling, imperilled *or US* imperils, imperiling, imperiled. (*tr*) to place in danger or jeopardy; endanger.
▸ im'perilment *n*

imperious (ɪmˈpɪərɪəs) *adj* **1** domineering; overbearing. **2** *Rare.* urgent. [C16: from L, from *imperium* command, power]
▸ im'periously *adv* ▸ im'periousness *n*

imperishable (ɪmˈpɛrɪʃəbəl) *adj* **1** not subject to decay or deterioration. **2** not likely to be forgotten: *imperishable truths.*
▸ im,perisha'bility *or* im'perishableness *n* ▸ im'perishably *adv*

impermanent (ɪmˈpɜːmənənt) *adj* not permanent; fleeting.
▸ im'permanence *or* im'permanency *n* ▸ im'permanently *adv*

impermeable (ɪmˈpɜːmɪəbəl) *adj* (of a substance) not allowing the passage of a fluid through interstices; not permeable.
▸ im,permea'bility *or* im'permeableness *n* ▸ im'permeably *adv*

impermissible (ˌɪmpəˈmɪsɪbəl) *adj* not permissible; not allowed.
▸ ,imper,missi'bility *n*

impersonal (ɪmˈpɜːsənəl) *adj* **1** without reference to any individual person; objective: *an impersonal assessment.* **2** devoid of human warmth or sympathy; cold: *an impersonal manner.* **3** not having human characteristics: *an impersonal God.* **4** *Grammar.* (of a verb) having no logical subject: *it is raining.* **5** *Grammar.* (of a pronoun) not denoting a person.
▸ im,person'ality *n* ▸ im'personally *adv*

impersonalize *or* **impersonalise** (ɪmˈpɜːsənəˌlaɪz) *vb* impersonalizes, impersonalizing, impersonalized *or* impersonalises, impersonalising, impersonalised. (*tr*) to make impersonal, esp. to rid of such human characteristics as sympathy, etc.; dehumanize.
▸ im,personali'zation *or* im,personali'sation *n*

impersonate (ɪmˈpɜːsəˌneɪt) *vb* impersonates, impersonating, impersonated. (*tr*) **1** to pretend to be (another person). **2** to imitate the character, mannerisms, etc., of (another person). **3** *Rare.* to play the part or character of. **4** an archaic word for **personify.**
▸ im,person'ation *n* ▸ im'person,ator *n*

impertinence (ɪmˈpɜːtɪnəns) *or* **impertinency** *n* **1** disrespectful behaviour or language; rudeness; insolence. **2** an impertinent act, gesture, etc. **3** *Rare.* lack of pertinence; irrelevance; inappropriateness.

impertinent (ɪmˈpɜːtɪnənt) *adj* **1** rude; insolent; impudent. **2** irrelevant or inappropriate. [C14: from L *impertinēns* not belonging, from L IM- (not) + *pertinēre* to be relevant; see PERTAIN]
▸ im'pertinently *adv*

imperturbable (ˌɪmpəˈtɜːbəbəl) *adj* not easily perturbed; calm; unruffled.
▸ ,imper,turba'bility *or* ,imper'turbableness *n* ▸ ,imper-'turbably *adv*

impervious (ɪmˈpɜːvɪəs) *or* **imperviable** *adj* **1** not able to be penetrated, as by water, light, etc.; impermeable. **2** (*often postpositive*; foll. by *to*) not able to be influenced (by) or not receptive (to): *impervious to argument.*
▸ im'perviously *adv* ▸ im'perviousness *n*

impetigo (ˌɪmpɪˈtaɪɡəʊ) *n* a contagious pustular skin disease. [C16: from L: scabby eruption, from *impetere* to assail; see IMPETUS; for form, cf. VERTIGO]
▸ impetiginous (ˌɪmpɪˈtɪdʒɪnəs) *adj*

impetuous (ɪmˈpɛtjʊəs) *adj* **1** liable to act without consideration; rash; impulsive. **2** resulting from or characterized by rashness or haste. **3** *Poetic.* moving with great force or violence; rushing: *the impetuous stream hurtled down the valley.* [C14: from LL *impetuōsus* violent; see IMPETUS]
▸ im'petuously *adv* ▸ im'petuousness *or* impetuosity (ɪmˌpɛtjʊˈɒsɪtɪ) *n*

impetus (ˈɪmpɪtəs) *n, pl* impetuses. **1** an impelling movement or force; incentive or impulse; stimulus. **2** *Physics.* the force that sets a body in motion or that tends to resist changes in a body's motion. [C17: from L: attack, from *impetere* to assail, from IM- (in) + *petere* to make for, seek out]

impf. *or* **imperf.** *abbrev. for* imperfect.

Imphal ★ (ɪmˈfɑːl, ˈɪmfəl) *n* a city in NE India, capital of Manipur Territory, on the Manipur River: formerly the seat of the Manipur kings: site of a major Anglo-Indian victory over the Japanese (1944), which was a turning point in the British recovery of Burma (now Myanmar). Pop.: 198 535 (1991).

impi (ˈɪmpɪ) *n, pl* impi *or* impies. a group of Bantu warriors. [C19: from Zulu]

impiety (ɪmˈpaɪɪtɪ) *n, pl* impieties. **1** lack of reverence or proper respect for a god. **2** any lack of proper respect. **3** an impious act.

impinge (ɪmˈpɪndʒ) *vb* impinges, impinging, impinged. **1** (*intr*; usually foll. by *on* or *upon*) to encroach or infringe; trespass: *to impinge on someone's time.* **2** (*intr*; usually foll. by *on, against,* or *upon*) to collide (with); strike. [C16: from L *impingere* to drive at, dash against, from *pangere* to fasten, drive in]
▸ im'pingement *n* ▸ im'pinger *n*

impious (ˈɪmpɪəs) *adj* **1** lacking piety or reverence for a god. **2** lacking respect; undutiful.
▸ 'impiously *adv* ▸ 'impiousness *n*

impish (ˈɪmpɪʃ) *adj* of or like an imp; mischievous.
▸ 'impishly *adv* ▸ 'impishness *n*

implacable (ɪmˈplækəbəl) *adj* **1** incapable of being placated or pacified; unappeasable. **2** inflexible; intractable.
▸ im,placa'bility *n* ▸ im'placably *adv*

implant *vb* (ɪmˈplɑːnt). (*tr*) **1** to inculcate; instil: *to implant sound moral principles.* **2** to plant or embed; infix; entrench. **3** *Surgery.* to graft or insert (a tissue, hormone, etc.) into the body. ◆ *n* (ˈɪmplɑːnt). **4** anything implanted, esp. surgically, such as a tissue graft or hormone.
▸ ,implan'tation *n*

implausible (ɪmˈplɔːzəbəl) *adj* not plausible; provoking disbelief; unlikely.
▸ im,plausi'bility *or* im'plausibleness *n* ▸ im'plausibly *adv*

implement *n* (ˈɪmplɪmənt). **1** a piece of equipment; tool or utensil: *gardening implements.* **2** a means to achieve a purpose; agent. ◆ *vb* (ˈɪmplɪˌmɛnt). (*tr*) **3** to carry out; put into action: *to implement a plan.* **4** *Rare.* to supply with tools. [C17: from LL *implēmentum*, lit.: a filling up, from L *implēre* to fill up, satisfy, fulfil]
▸ ,imple'mental *adj* ▸ ,implemen'tation *n*

implicate (ˈɪmplɪˌkeɪt) *vb* implicates, implicating, implicated. (*tr*) **1** to show to be involved, esp. in a crime. **2** to imply: *his protest implicated censure by the authorities.* **3** *Rare.* to entangle. [C16: from L *implicāre* to involve, from *plicāre* to fold]
▸ implicative (ɪmˈplɪkətɪv) *adj* ▸ im'plicatively *adv*

implication (ˌɪmplɪˈkeɪʃən) *n* **1** the act of implicating. **2** something that is implied. **3** *Logic.* a relation between two propositions, such that the second can be logically deduced from the first.

implicit (ɪmˈplɪsɪt) *adj* **1** not explicit; implied; indirect. **2** absolute and unreserved; unquestioning: *implicit trust.* **3** (when *postpositive*, foll. by *in*) contained or inherent: *to bring out the anger implicit in the argument.* [C16: from L *implicitus*, var. of *implicātus* interwoven; see IMPLICATE]
▸ im'plicitly *adv* ▸ im'plicitness *n*

implied (ɪm'plaɪd) *adj* hinted at or suggested; not directly expressed: *an implied criticism*.

implode (ɪm'pləʊd) *vb* **implodes, imploding, imploded.** to collapse inwards. Cf. **explode.** [C19: from IM- + (EX)PLODE]

implore (ɪm'plɔː) *vb* **implores, imploring, implored.** (*tr*) to beg or ask (someone) earnestly (to do something); plead with; beseech; supplicate. [C16: from L *implōrāre*, from IM- + *plōrāre* to bewail]
► **implo'ration** *n* ► **im'ploratory** *adj* ► **im'ploringly** *adv*

imply (ɪm'plaɪ) *vb* **implies, implying, implied.** (*tr; may take a clause as object*) **1** to express or indicate by a hint; suggest. **2** to suggest or involve as a necessary consequence. [C14: from OF *emplier*, from L; see IMPLICATE]

> **USAGE NOTE** See at **infer.**

impolder (ɪm'pəʊldə) *or* **empolder** *vb* to make into a polder; reclaim (land) from the sea. [C19: from Du. *inpolderen*, see IN-², POLDER]

impolite (ˌɪmpə'laɪt) *adj* discourteous; rude.
► **ˌimpo'litely** *adv* ► **ˌimpo'liteness** *n*

impolitic (ɪm'pɒlɪtɪk) *adj* not politic or expedient; unwise.
► **im'politicly** *adv*

imponderable (ɪm'pɒndərəb³l, -drəb³l) *adj* **1** unable to be weighed or assessed. ◆ *n* **2** something difficult or impossible to assess.
► **im,pondera'bility** *or* **im'ponderableness** *n* ► **im'ponderably** *adv*

import *vb* (ɪm'pɔːt, 'ɪmpɔːt). **1** to buy or bring in (goods or services) from a foreign country. **2** (*tr*) to bring in from an outside source: *to import foreign words into the language*. **3** *Rare.* to signify; mean: *to import doom*. ◆ *n* ('ɪmpɔːt). **4** (*often pl*) **4a** goods or services that are bought from foreign countries. **4b** (*as modifier*): *an import licence*. **5** importance: *a man of great import*. **6** meaning. **7** *Inf.* a sportsman or -woman who is not native to the country in which he or she plays. [C15: from L *importāre* to carry in]
► **im'portable** *adj* ► **im'porter** *n*

importance (ɪm'pɔːt³ns) *n* **1** the state of being important; significance. **2** social status; standing; esteem: *a man of importance*. **3** *Obs.* **3a** meaning or signification. **3b** an important matter. **3c** importunity.

important (ɪm'pɔːt³nt) *adj* **1** of great significance or value; outstanding. **2** of social significance; notable; eminent; esteemed: *an important man in the town*. **3** (when postpositive, usually foll. by *to*) of great concern (to); valued highly (by): *your wishes are important to me*. [C16: from OIt., from Med. L *importāre* to signify, be of consequence, from L: to carry in]
► **im'portantly** *adv*

> **USAGE NOTE** The use of *more importantly* as in *more importantly, the local council is opposed to this proposal* has become very common, but many people still prefer to use *more important*.

importation (ˌɪmpɔː'teɪʃən) *n* **1** the act, business, or process of importing goods or services. **2** an imported product or service.

importunate (ɪm'pɔːtjʊnɪt) *adj* **1** persistent or demanding; insistent. **2** *Rare.* troublesome; annoying.
► **im'portunately** *adv* ► **im'portunateness** *n*

importune (ɪm'pɔːtjuːn, ˌɪmpɔː'tjuːn) *vb* **importunes, importuning, importuned.** (*tr*) **1** to harass with persistent requests; demand of (someone) insistently. **2** to beg or persistently; request with insistence. [C16: from L *importūnus* tiresome, from *im-* IN-¹ + *-portūnus* as in *opportūnus* OPPORTUNE]
► **im'portunely** *adv* ► **im'portuner** *n* ► **impor'tunity** *or* **im'portunacy** *n*

impose (ɪm'pəʊz) *vb* **imposes, imposing, imposed.** (usually foll. by *on* or *upon*) **1** (*tr*) to establish as something to be obeyed or complied with; enforce. **2** to force (oneself, one's presence, etc.) on others; obtrude. **3** (*intr*) to take advantage, as of a person or quality: *to impose on someone's kindness*. **4** (*tr*) *Printing.* to arrange (pages, type, etc.) in a chase so that the pages will be in the correct order. **5** (*tr*) to pass off deceptively; foist. [C15: from OF, from L *impōnere* to place upon, from *pōnere* to place, set]
► **im'posable** *adj* ► **im'poser** *n*

imposing (ɪm'pəʊzɪŋ) *adj* grand or impressive: *an imposing building*.
► **im'posingly** *adv* ► **im'posingness** *n*

imposition (ˌɪmpə'zɪʃən) *n* **1** the act of imposing. **2** something imposed unfairly on someone. **3** a task set as a school punishment. **4** the arrangement of pages for printing.

impossibility (ɪm,pɒsə'bɪlɪtɪ, ˌɪmpɒs-) *n, pl* **impossibilities. 1** the state or quality of being impossible. **2** something that is impossible.

impossible (ɪm'pɒsəb³l) *adj* **1** incapable of being done, undertaken, or experienced. **2** incapable of occurring or happening. **3** absurd or inconceivable; unreasonable. **4** *Inf.* intolerable; outrageous: *those children are impossible*.
► **im'possibleness** *n* ► **im'possibly** *adv*

impossible figure *n* a picture of an object that at first sight looks three-dimensional but cannot be a two-dimensional projection of a real three-dimensional object, for example a picture of a staircase that re-enters itself while appearing to ascend continuously.

impost¹ ('ɪmpəʊst) *n* **1** a tax, esp. a customs duty. **2** the weight that a horse must carry in a handicap race. ◆ *vb* **3** (*tr*) *US.* to classify (imported goods) according to the duty payable on them. [C16: from Med. L *impostus* tax, from L *impositus* imposed; see IMPOSE]
► **'imposter** *n*

impost² ('ɪmpəʊst) *n Archit.* a member at the top of a column that supports an arch. [C17: from F *imposte*, from L *impositus* placed upon; see IMPOSE]

impostor *or* **imposter** (ɪm'pɒstə) *n* a person who deceives others, esp. by assuming a false identity; charlatan. [C16: from LL: deceiver; see IMPOSE]

imposture (ɪm'pɒstʃə) *n* the act or an instance of deceiving others, esp. by assuming a false identity. [C16: from F, from LL, from L *impōnere*; see IMPOSE]
► **impostrous** (ɪm'pɒstrəs) *or* **impostorous** (ɪm'pɒstərəs) *adj*

impotent ('ɪmpətənt) *adj* **1** (when *postpositive*, often takes an infinitive) lacking sufficient strength; powerless. **2** (esp. of males) unable to perform sexual intercourse.
► **'impotence** *or* **'impotency** *n* ► **'impotently** *adv*

impound (ɪm'paʊnd) *vb* (*tr*) **1** to confine (animals, etc.) in a pound. **2** to take legal possession of (a document, evidence, etc.). **3** to collect (water) in a reservoir or dam.
► **im'poundable** *adj* ► **im'poundage** *or* **im'poundment** *n* ► **im'pounder** *n*

impoverish (ɪm'pɒvərɪʃ) *vb* (*tr*) **1** to make poor or diminish the quality of: *to impoverish society by cutting the grant to the arts*. **2** to deprive (soil, etc.) of fertility. [C15: from OF *empovrir*, from *povre* POOR]
► **im'poverishment** *n*

impracticable (ɪm'præktɪkəb³l) *adj* **1** incapable of being put into practice or accomplished; not feasible. **2** unsuitable for a desired use; unfit.
► **im,practica'bility** *or* **im'practicableness** *n* ► **im'practicably** *adv*

impractical (ɪm'præktɪk³l) *adj* **1** not practical or workable: *an impractical solution*. **2** not given to practical matters or gifted with practical skills.
► **im,practi'cality** *or* **im'practicalness** *n* ► **im'practically** *adv*

imprecate ('ɪmprɪˌkeɪt) *vb* **imprecates, imprecating, imprecated. 1** (*intr*) to swear or curse. **2** (*tr*) to invoke or bring down (evil, a curse, etc.). [C17: from L *imprecārī* to invoke, from *im-* IN-² + *precārī* to PRAY]
► **ˌimpre'cation** *n* ► **'impre,catory** *adj*

imprecise (ˌɪmprɪ'saɪs) *adj* not precise; inexact or inaccurate.
► **ˌimpre'cisely** *adv* ► **imprecision** (ˌɪmprɪ'sɪʒən) *or* **ˌimpre'ciseness** *n*

impregnable¹ (ɪm'prɛgnəb³l) *adj* **1** unable to be broken

into or taken by force: *an impregnable castle*. **2** unshakable: *impregnable self-confidence*. **3** incapable of being refuted: *an impregnable argument*. [C15 *imprenable*, from OF, from IM- (not) + *prenable* able to be taken, from *prendre* to take]
▸ im,pregna'bility *n* ▸ im'pregnably *adv*

impregnable[2] (ɪmˈprɛgnəbᵊl) *or* **impregnatable** (ˌɪmprɛgˈneɪtəbᵊl) *adj* able to be impregnated; fertile.

impregnate *vb* (ˈɪmprɛgˌneɪt), **impregnates, impregnating, impregnated**. (*tr*) **1** to saturate, soak, or infuse. **2** to imbue or permeate; pervade. **3** to cause to conceive; make pregnant; fertilize. **4** to make (land, soil, etc.) fruitful. ◆ *adj* (ɪmˈprɛgnɪt, -ˌneɪt). **5** pregnant or fertilized. [C17: from LL, from L *im-* IN-[2] + *praegnans* PREGNANT]
▸ ,impreg'nation *n* ▸ im'pregnator *n*

impresario (ˌɪmprəˈsɑːrɪˌəʊ) *n, pl* **impresarios.** the director or manager of an opera, ballet, etc. [C18: from It., lit.: one who undertakes]

imprescriptible (ˌɪmprɪˈskrɪptəbᵊl) *adj Law.* immune or exempt from prescription.
▸ ,impre,scripti'bility *n* ▸ ,impre'scriptibly *adv*

impress[1] *vb* (ɪmˈprɛs). (*tr*) **1** to make an impression on; have a strong, lasting, or favourable effect on: *I am impressed by your work*. **2** to produce (an imprint, etc.) by pressure in or on (something): *to impress a seal in wax*. **3** (often foll. by *on*) to stress (something to a person); urge; emphasize. **4** to exert pressure on; press. ◆ *n* (ˈɪmprɛs). **5** the act or an instance of impressing. **6** a mark, imprint, or effect produced by impressing. [C14: from L *imprimere* to press into, imprint]
▸ im'presser *n* ▸ im'pressible *adj*

impress[2] *vb* (ɪmˈprɛs). **1** to commandeer or coerce (men or things) into government service; press-gang. ◆ *n* (ˈɪmprɛs). **2** the act of commandeering or coercing into government service. [C16: see *im-* IN-[2], PRESS[2]]

impression (ɪmˈprɛʃən) *n* **1** an effect produced in the mind by a stimulus; sensation: *he gave the impression of wanting to help*. **2** an imprint or mark produced by pressing. **3** a vague idea, consciousness, or belief: *I had the impression we had met before*. **4** a strong, favourable, or remarkable effect. **5** the act of impressing or the state of being impressed. **6** *Printing.* **6a** the act, process, or result of printing from type, plates, etc. **6b** the total number of copies of a publication printed at one time. **7** an imprint of the teeth and gums for preparing crowns, dentures, etc. **8** an imitation or impersonation.
▸ im'pressional *adj* ▸ im'pressionally *adv*

impressionable (ɪmˈprɛʃənəbᵊl, -ˈprɛʃnə-) *adj* easily influenced or characterized by susceptibility to influence: *an impressionable age*.
▸ im,pressiona'bility *or* im'pressionableness *n*

impressionism (ɪmˈprɛʃəˌnɪzəm) *n* (*often cap.*) a 19th-century movement in French painting, having the aim of objectively recording experience by a system of fleeting impressions, esp. of natural light.
▸ im'pressionist *n*

impressive (ɪmˈprɛsɪv) *adj* capable of impressing, esp. by size, magnificence, etc.; awe-inspiring; commanding.
▸ im'pressively *adv* ▸ im'pressiveness *n*

imprest (ɪmˈprɛst) *n* **1** a fund of cash from which a department, etc., pays incidental expenses, topped up periodically from central funds. **2** *Chiefly Brit.* an advance from government funds for some public business or service. [C16: prob. from It. *imprestare* to lend, from L *in-* towards + *praestāre* to pay, from *praestō* at hand; see PRESTO]

imprimatur (ˌɪmprɪˈmeɪtə, -ˈmɑː-) *n* **1** sanction or approval for something to be printed. **2** *RC Church.* a licence certifying the Church's approval. [C17: NL, lit.: let it be printed]

imprint *n* (ˈɪmprɪnt). **1** a mark or impression produced by pressure, printing, or stamping. **2** a characteristic mark or indication; stamp: *the imprint of great sadness on his face*. **3a** the publisher's name and address, often with the date of publication, printed in a book, usually on the title page or the verso title page. **3b** the printer's name and address on any printed matter. ◆ *vb* (ɪmˈprɪnt). (*tr*) **4** to produce (a mark, impression, etc.) on (a surface) by

pressure, printing, or stamping: *to imprint a seal on wax*. **5** to establish firmly; impress: *to imprint the details on one's mind*. **6** to cause (a young animal) to undergo the process of imprinting: *chicks can be imprinted on human beings*.

imprinting (ɪmˈprɪntɪŋ) *n* the development in young animals of recognition of and attraction to members of their own species or surrogates.

imprison (ɪmˈprɪzən) *vb* (*tr*) to confine in or as if in prison.
▸ im'prisonment *n*

improbable (ɪmˈprɒbəbᵊl) *adj* not likely or probable; doubtful; unlikely.
▸ im,proba'bility *or* im'probableness *n* ▸ im'probably *adv*

improbity (ɪmˈprəʊbɪtɪ) *n, pl* **improbities.** dishonesty, wickedness, or unscrupulousness.

impromptu (ɪmˈprɒmptjuː) *adj* **1** unrehearsed; spontaneous. **2** produced or done without care or planning; improvised. ◆ *adv* **3** in a spontaneous or improvised way: *he spoke impromptu*. ◆ *n* **4** something that is impromptu. **5** a short piece of instrumental music, sometimes improvisatory in character. [C17: from F, from L *in promptū* in readiness, from *promptus* (adj) ready, PROMPT]

improper (ɪmˈprɒpə) *adj* **1** lacking propriety; not seemly. **2** unsuitable for a certain use or occasion; inappropriate. **3** irregular or abnormal.
▸ im'properly *adv* ▸ im'properness *n*

improper fraction *n* a fraction in which the numerator is greater than the denominator, as 7/6.

impropriate *vb* (ɪmˈprəʊprɪˌeɪt), **impropriates, impropriating, impropriated.** **1** (*tr*) to transfer (property, rights, etc.) from the Church into lay hands. ◆ *adj* (ɪmˈprəʊprɪt, -ˌeɪt). **2** transferred in this way. [C16: from Med. L *impropriāre* to make one's own, from L *in-*[2] + *propriāre* to APPROPRIATE]
▸ im,propri'ation *n* ▸ im'propri,ator *n*

impropriety (ˌɪmprəˈpraɪɪtɪ) *n, pl* **improprieties. 1** lack of propriety; indecency; indecorum. **2** an improper act or use. **3** the state of being improper.

improve (ɪmˈpruːv) *vb* **improves, improving, improved. 1** to make or become better in quality; ameliorate. **2** (*tr*) to make (buildings, land, etc.) more valuable by additions or betterment. **3** (*intr*; usually foll. by *on* or *upon*) to achieve a better standard or quality in comparison (with): *to improve on last year's crop*. [C16: from Anglo-F *emprouer* to turn to profit, from LL *prōde* beneficial, from L *prōdesse* to be advantageous]
▸ im'provable *adj* ▸ im,prova'bility *or* im'provableness *n* ▸ im'prover *n*

improvement (ɪmˈpruːvmənt) *n* **1** the act of improving or the state of being improved. **2** something that improves, esp. an addition or alteration. **3** (*usually pl*) *Austral. & NZ.* a building, etc., on a piece of land, adding to its value.

improvident (ɪmˈprɒvɪdənt) *adj* **1** not provident; thriftless, imprudent, or prodigal. **2** heedless or incautious; rash.
▸ im'providence *n* ▸ im'providently *adv*

improvise (ˈɪmprəˌvaɪz) *vb* **improvises, improvising, improvised. 1** to perform or make quickly from materials and sources available, without previous planning. **2** to perform (a poem, play, piece of music, etc.), composing as one goes along. [C19: from F, from It., from L *imprōvīsus* unforeseen, from *prōvidēre* to foresee; see PROVIDE]
▸ 'impro,viser *n* ▸ ,improvi'sation *n* ▸ improvisatory (ˌɪmprəˈvaɪzətərɪ, -ˈvɪz-, ˌɪmprəvaɪzˈeɪtərɪ) *adj*

imprudent (ɪmˈpruːdᵊnt) *adj* not prudent; rash, heedless, or indiscreet.
▸ im'prudence *n* ▸ im'prudently *adv*

impudence (ˈɪmpjʊdəns) *or* **impudency** *n* **1** the quality of being impudent. **2** an impudent act or statement. [C14: from L *impudēns* shameless]

impudent (ˈɪmpjʊdənt) *adj* **1** mischievous, impertinent, or disrespectful. **2** *Obs.* immodest.
▸ 'impudently *adv* ▸ 'impudentness *n*

impugn (ɪmˈpjuːn) *vb* (*tr*) to challenge or attack as false;

★ people and places

criticize. [C14: from OF, from L *impugnāre* to fight against, attack]
▸ im'**pugnable** *adj* ▸ im'**pugnment** *n* ▸ im'**pugner** *n*

impulse ('ɪmpʌls) *n* **1** an impelling force or motion; thrust; impetus. **2** a sudden desire, whim, or inclination. **3** an instinctive drive; urge. **4** tendency; current; trend. **5** *Physics.* **5a** the product of the average magnitude of a force acting on a body and the time for which it acts. **5b** the change in the momentum of a body as a result of a force acting upon it. **6** *Physiol.* See **nerve impulse. 7 on impulse.** spontaneously or impulsively. [C17: from L *impulsus* a pushing against, incitement, from *impellere* to strike against; see IMPEL]

impulse buying *n* the buying of merchandise prompted by a whim.
▸ **impulse buyer** *n*

impulsion (ɪm'pʌlʃən) *n* **1** the act of impelling or the state of being impelled. **2** motion produced by an impulse; propulsion. **3** a driving force; compulsion.

impulsive (ɪm'pʌlsɪv) *adj* **1** characterized by actions based on sudden desires, whims, or inclinations: *an impulsive man.* **2** based on emotional impulses or whims; spontaneous. **3** forceful, inciting, or impelling. **4** (of physical forces) acting for a short time; not continuous. **5** (of a sound) brief, loud, and having a wide frequency range.
▸ im'**pulsively** *adv* ▸ im'**pulsiveness** *n*

impundulu ('ɪmpun,dulu) *n S. African.* a mythical bird often associated with witchcraft. [from Bantu]

impunity (ɪm'pjuːnɪtɪ) *n, pl* **impunities. 1** exemption or immunity from punishment, recrimination, or other unpleasant consequences. **2 with impunity.** with no care or heed for such consequences. [C16: from L, from *impūnis* unpunished, from IM- (not) + *poena* punishment]

impure (ɪm'pjʊə) *adj* **1** not pure; combined with something else; tainted or sullied. **2** (in certain religions) ritually unclean. **3** (of a colour) mixed with another colour. **4** of more than one origin or style, as of architecture.
▸ im'**purely** *adv* ▸ im'**pureness** *n*

impurity (ɪm'pjʊərɪtɪ) *n, pl* **impurities. 1** the quality of being impure. **2** an impure thing, constituent, or element: *impurities in the water.* **3** *Electronics.* a small quantity of an element added to a pure semiconductor crystal to control its electrical conductivity.

impute (ɪm'pjuːt) *vb* **imputes, imputing, imputed.** (*tr*) **1** to attribute or ascribe (something dishonest or dishonourable) to a person. **2** to attribute to a source or cause: *I impute your success to nepotism.* **3** *Commerce.* to give (a notional value) to goods, etc., when the real value is unknown. [C14: from L, from IM- + *putāre* to think, calculate]
▸ ,impu'**tation** *n* ▸ im'**putative** *adj* ▸ im'**puter** *n* ▸ im'**putable** *adj*

Imran Khan ★ ('ɪmrɑːn 'kɑːn) *n* full name *Imran Ahmad Khan Niazi.* born 1952, Pakistani cricketer: played for Worcestershire (1971–76) and Sussex from 1977; captained Pakistan (1982–84; 1985–87; 1988–92).

Imroz ★ ('ɪmrɒz) *n* the Turkish name for **Imbros.**

IMunE *abbrev. for* Institution of Municipal Engineers.

in (ɪn) *prep* **1** inside; within: *no smoking in the auditorium.* **2** at a place where there is: *in the shade.* **3** indicating a state, situation, or condition: *in silence.* **4** when (a period of time) has elapsed: *return in one year.* **5** using: *written in code.* **6** concerned with, esp. as an occupation: *in journalism.* **7** while or by performing the action of: *in crossing the street he was run over.* **8** used to indicate purpose: *in honour of the king.* **9** (of certain animals) pregnant with: *in calf.* **10** a variant of **into:** *she fell in the water.* **11 have it in one.** (often foll. by an infinitive) to have the ability (to do something). **12 in that or in so far as.** (*conj*) because or to the extent that: *I regret my remark in that it upset you.* **13 nothing in it.** no difference or interval between two things. ◆ *adv* (*particle*) **14** in or into a particular place; inward or indoors: *come in.* **15** so as to achieve office or power: *Labour got in at the last election.* **16** so as to enclose: *block in.* **17** (in certain games) so as to take one's turn of the play: *you have to get the other side out before you go in.* **18** *NZ.* competing: *you've got to be in to win.* **19** *Brit.* (of a fire) alight. **20** (in combination) indicating an activity or gathering: *teach-in; work-in.* **21 in at.** present at (the beginning, end, etc.). **22 in for.** about to be affected by (something, esp. something unpleasant): *you're in for a shock.* **23 in on.** acquainted with or sharing in: *I was in on all his plans.* **24 in with.** associated with; friendly with; regarded highly by. **25 have (got) it in for.** to wish or intend harm towards. ◆ *adj* **26** (*stressed*) fashionable; modish: *the in thing to do.* ◆ *n* **27 ins and outs.** intricacies or complications; details. [OE]

In *the chemical symbol for* indium.

in. *abbrev. for* inch(es).

in-¹, il-, im-, *or* **ir-** *prefix* **a** not; non-: *incredible; illegal; imperfect; irregular.* **b** lack of: *inexperience.* Cf. **un-.** [from L *in-*; rel. to *ne-, nōn* not]

in-², il-, im-, *or* **ir-** *prefix* **1** in; into; towards; within; on: *infiltrate; immigrate.* **2** having an intensive or causative function: *inflame; imperil.* [from IN (prep, adv)]

-in *suffix forming nouns.* **1** indicating a neutral organic compound, including proteins, glucosides, and glycerides: *insulin; tripalmitin.* **2** indicating an enzyme in certain nonsystematic names: *pepsin.* **3** indicating a pharmaceutical substance: *penicillin; aspirin.* **4** indicating a chemical substance in certain nonsystematic names: *coumarin.* [from NL *-ina*; cf. -INE²]

in absentia *Latin.* (ɪn æb'sɛntɪə) *adv* in the absence of (someone indicated).

inaccessible (,ɪnæk'sɛsəbᵊl) *adj* not accessible; unapproachable.
▸ ,inac,cessi'**bility** *or* ,inac'**cessibleness** *n* ▸ ,inac'**cessibly** *adv*

inaccuracy (ɪn'ækjʊrəsɪ) *n, pl* **inaccuracies. 1** lack of accuracy; imprecision. **2** an error, mistake, or slip.
▸ in'**accurate** *adj*

inaction (ɪn'ækʃən) *n* lack of action; idleness; inertia.

inactivate (ɪn'æktɪ,veɪt) *vb* **inactivates, inactivating, inactivated.** (*tr*) to render inactive.
▸ in,acti'**vation** *n*

inactive (ɪn'æktɪv) *adj* **1** idle or inert; not active. **2** sluggish or indolent. **3** *Mil.* of or relating to persons or equipment not in active service. **4** *Chem.* (of a substance) having little or no reactivity.
▸ in'**actively** *adv* ▸ ,inac'**tivity** *n*

inadequate (ɪn'ædɪkwɪt) *adj* **1** not adequate; insufficient. **2** not capable; lacking.
▸ in'**adequacy** *n* ▸ in'**adequately** *adv*

inadvertence (,ɪnəd'vɜːtᵊns) *or* **inadvertency** *n* **1** lack of attention; heedlessness. **2** an oversight; slip.

inadvertent (,ɪnəd'vɜːtᵊnt) *adj* **1** failing to act carefully or considerately; inattentive. **2** resulting from heedless action; unintentional.
▸ ,inad'**vertently** *adv*

-inae *suffix forming plural proper nouns.* occurring in names of zoological subfamilies: *Felinae.* [NL, from L, fem pl of *-īnus* -INE¹]

inalienable (ɪn'eɪljənəbᵊl) *adj* not able to be transferred to another; not alienable: *the inalienable rights of the citizen.*
▸ in,aliena'**bility** *or* in'**alienableness** *n* ▸ in'**alienably** *adv*

inalterable (ɪn'ɔːltərəbᵊl) *adj* not alterable; unalterable.
▸ in,altera'**bility** *or* in'**alterableness** *n* ▸ in'**alterably** *adv*

inamorata (ɪn,æmə'rɑːtə, ,ɪnæmə-) *or* (*masc*) **inamorato** (ɪn,æmə'rɑːtəʊ, ,ɪnæmə-) *n, pl* **inamoratas** *or* (*masc*) **inamoratos.** a person with whom one is in love; lover. [C17: from It., from *innamorare* to cause to fall in love, from *amore* love, from L *amor*]

inane (ɪ'neɪn) *adj* **1** senseless, unimaginative, or empty; unintelligent: *inane remarks.* ◆ *n* **2** *Arch.* something empty or vacant, esp. the void of space. [C17: from L *inānis* empty]
▸ in'**anely** *adv*

inanimate (ɪn'ænɪmɪt) *adj* **1** lacking the qualities of living beings; not animate: *inanimate objects.* **2** lacking any sign of life or consciousness; appearing dead. **3** lacking vitality; dull.
▸ in'**animately** *adv* ▸ in'**animateness** *or* **inanimation** (ɪn,ænɪ'meɪʃən) *n*

inanition (,Ina'nIʃən) *n* **1** exhaustion resulting from lack of food. **2** mental, social, or spiritual weakness or lassitude. [C14: from LL *inānītio* emptiness, from L *inānis* empty; see INANE]

inanity (I'nænItI) *n, pl* **inanities. 1** lack of intelligence or imagination; senselessness; silliness. **2** a senseless action, remark, etc. **3** an archaic word for **emptiness.**

inapposite (In'æpəzIt) *adj* not appropriate or pertinent; unsuitable.
▸ in'appositely *adv* ▸ in'appositeness *n*

inapt (In'æpt) *adj* **1** not apt or fitting; inappropriate. **2** lacking skill; inept.
▸ in'apti,tude *or* in'aptness *n* ▸ in'aptly *adv*

inarch (In'ɑ:tʃ) *vb* (*tr*) to graft (a plant) by uniting stock and scion while both are still growing independently.

inasmuch as (,Inəz'mʌtʃ) *conj* (*subordinating*) **1** in view of the fact that; seeing that; since. **2** to the extent or degree that; in so far as.

inaugural (In'ɔ:gjυrəl) *adj* **1** characterizing or relating to an inauguration. ◆ *n* **2** a speech made at an inauguration, esp. by a president of the US.

inaugurate (In'ɔ:gju,reIt) *vb* **inaugurates, inaugurating, inaugurated.** (*tr*) **1** to commence officially or formally; initiate. **2** to place in office formally and ceremonially; induct. **3** to open ceremonially; dedicate formally: *to inaugurate a factory.* [C17: from L *inaugurāre*, lit.: to take omens, practise augury, hence to install in office after taking auguries; see IN-², AUGUR]
▸ in,augu'ration *n* ▸ in'augu,rator *n* ▸ **inauguratory** (In'ɔ:gjυrətərI, -trI) *adj*

in-between *adj* intermediate: *he's at the in-between stage, neither a child nor an adult.*

inboard ('In,bɔ:d) *adj* **1** (esp. of a boat's motor or engine) situated within the hull. **2** situated between the wing tip of an aircraft and its fuselage: *an inboard engine.* ◆ *adv* **3** towards the centre line of or within a vessel, aircraft, etc.

inborn ('In'bɔ:n) *adj* existing from birth; congenital; innate.

inbred ('In'brɛd) *adj* **1** produced as a result of inbreeding. **2** deeply ingrained; innate: *inbred good manners.*

inbreed ('In'bri:d) *vb* **inbreeds, inbreeding, inbred. 1** to breed from unions between closely related individuals, esp. over several generations. **2** (*tr*) to develop within; engender.
▸ 'in'breeding *n, adj*

in-built *adj* built-in, integral.

inc. *abbrev. for:* **1** including. **2** inclusive. **3** income. **4** increase.

Inc. (esp. US) *abbrev. for* incorporated.

Inca ('Iŋkə) *n, pl* **Inca** *or* **Incas. 1** a member of a South American Indian people whose empire centred on Peru lasted from about 1100 A.D. to the Spanish conquest in the early 1530s. **2** the language of the Incas. See also **Quechua.** [C16: from Sp., from Quechua *inka* king]
▸ **Incan** *adj*

incalculable (In'kælkjυləb°l) *adj* beyond calculation; unable to be predicted or determined.
▸ in,calcula'bility *n* ▸ in'calculably *adv*

incandesce (,Inkæn'dɛs) *vb* **incandesces, incandescing, incandesced.** (*intr*) to make or become incandescent.

incandescent (,Inkæn'dɛsªnt) *adj* **1** emitting light as a result of being heated; red-hot or white-hot. **2** *Inf.* extremely angry. [C18: from L *incandescere* to become hot, glow, from *candēre* to be white; see CANDID]
▸ ,incan'descently *adv* ▸ ,incan'descence *n*

incandescent lamp *n* a source of light that contains a heated solid, such as an electrically heated filament.

incantation (,Inkæn'teIʃən) *n* **1** ritual recitation of magic words or sounds. **2** the formulaic words or sounds used; a magic spell. [C14: from LL *incantātio* an enchanting, from *incantare* to repeat magic formulas, from L, from IN-² + *cantāre* to sing; see ENCHANT]
▸ ,incan'tational *or* in'cantatory *adj*

incapacitate (,Inkə'pæsI,teIt) *vb* **incapacitates, incapacitating, incapacitated.** (*tr*) **1** to deprive of power, strength, or

capacity; disable. **2** to deprive of legal capacity or eligibility.
▸ ,inca,paci'tation *n*

incapacity (,Inkə'pæsItI) *n, pl* **incapacities. 1** lack of power, strength, or capacity; inability. **2** *Law.* legal disqualification or ineligibility.

in-car *adj* (of hi-fi equipment, etc.) installed inside a car.

incarcerate (In'kɑ:sə,reIt) *vb* **incarcerates, incarcerating, incarcerated.** (*tr*) to confine or imprison. [C16: from Med. L, from L IN-² + *carcer* prison]
▸ in,carcer'ation *n* ▸ in'carcer,ator *n*

incarnadine (In'kɑ:nə,daIn) *Arch. or literary.* ◆ *vb* **incarnadines, incarnadining, incarnadined. 1** (*tr*) to tinge or stain with red. ◆ *adj* **2** of a pinkish or reddish colour similar to that of flesh or blood. [C16: from F *incarnadin* flesh-coloured, from It., from LL *incarnātus* made flesh, INCARNATE]

incarnate *adj* (In'kɑ:nIt, -neIt). (*usually immediately postpositive*) **1** possessing bodily form, esp. the human form: *a devil incarnate.* **2** personified or typified: *stupidity incarnate.* ◆ *vb* (In'kɑ:neIt). **incarnates, incarnating, incarnated.** (*tr*) **3** to give a bodily or concrete form to. **4** to be representative or typical of. [C14: from LL *incarnāre* to make flesh, from L IN-² + *carō* flesh]

incarnation (,Inkɑ:'neIʃən) *n* **1** the act of manifesting or state of being manifested in bodily form, esp. human form. **2** a bodily form assumed by a god, etc. **3** a person or thing that typifies or represents some quality, idea, etc.

Incarnation (,Inkɑ:'neIʃən) *n Christian theol.* the assuming of a human body by the Son of God.

incarvillea (,Inkɑ:'vIlIə) *n* any of various perennials with pink flowers and pinnate leaves. Also called: **Chinese trumpet flower.** [C18: after Pierre d'*Incarville*, F missionary in China]

incase (In'keIs) *vb* **incases, incasing, incased.** a variant spelling of **encase.**
▸ in'casement *n*

incautious (In'kɔ:ʃəs) *adj* not careful or cautious.
▸ in'cautiously *adv* ▸ in'cautiousness *or* in'caution *n*

incendiary (In'sɛndIərI) *adj* **1** of or relating to the illegal burning of property, goods, etc. **2** tending to create strife, violence, etc. **3** (of a substance) capable of catching fire or burning readily. ◆ *n, pl* **incendiaries. 4** a person who illegally sets fire to property, goods, etc.; arsonist. **5** (esp. formerly) a person who stirs up civil strife, violence, etc.; agitator. **6** Also called: **incendiary bomb.** a bomb that is designed to start fires. **7** an incendiary substance, such as phosphorus. [C17: from L, from *incendium* fire, from *incendere* to kindle]
▸ in'cendia,rism *n*

incense¹ ('InsƐns) *n* **1** any of various aromatic substances burnt for their fragrant odour, esp. in religious ceremonies. **2** the odour or smoke so produced. **3** any pleasant fragrant odour; aroma. ◆ *vb* **incenses, incensing, incensed. 4** to burn incense in honour of (a deity). **5** (*tr*) to perfume or fumigate with incense. [C13: from OF *encens,* from Church L *incensum,* from L *incendere* to kindle]

incense² (In'sɛns) *vb* **incenses, incensing, incensed.** (*tr*) to enrage greatly. [C15: from L *incensus* set on fire, from *incendere* to kindle]
▸ in'censement *n*

incensory ('InsɛnsərI) *n, pl* **incensories.** a less common name for **censer.** [C17: from Med. L *incensorium*]

incentive (In'sɛntIv) *n* **1** a motivating influence; stimulus. **2a** an additional payment made to employees to increase production. **2b** (*as modifier*): *an incentive scheme.* ◆ *adj* **3** serving to incite to action. [C15: from LL, from L: striking up, setting the tune, from *incinere* to sing]

incept (In'sɛpt) *vb* (*tr*) **1** (of organisms) to ingest (food). **2** *Brit.* (formerly) to take a master's or doctor's degree at a university. [C19: from L *inceptus* begun, attempted, from *incipere* to begin, take in hand]
▸ in'ceptor *n*

inception (In'sɛpʃən) *n* the beginning, as of a project or undertaking.

inceptive (In'sɛptIv) *adj* **1** beginning; incipient; initial. **2**

Also called: **inchoative.** *Grammar.* denoting a verb used to indicate the beginning of an action. ◆ *n* **3** *Grammar.* an inceptive verb.
▶ in'ceptively *adv*

incertitude (ɪnˈsɜːtɪˌtjuːd) *n* **1** uncertainty; doubt. **2** a state of mental or emotional insecurity.

incessant (ɪnˈsesənt) *adj* not ceasing; continual. [C16: from LL, from L IN-¹ + *cessāre* to CEASE]
▶ in'cessancy *n* ▶ in'cessantly *adv*

incest (ˈɪnsest) *n* sexual intercourse between two persons who are too closely related to marry. [C13: from L, from IN-¹ + *castus* CHASTE]

incestuous (ɪnˈsestjʊəs) *adj* **1** relating to or involving incest: *an incestuous union.* **2** guilty of incest. **3** resembling incest in excessive or claustrophobic intimacy.
▶ in'cestuously *adv* ▶ in'cestuousness *n*

inch¹ (ɪntʃ) *n* **1** a unit of length equal to one twelfth of a foot or 0.0254 metre. **2** *Meteorol.* **2a** an amount of precipitation that would cover a surface with water one inch deep. **2b** a unit of pressure equal to a mercury column one inch high in a barometer. **3** a very small distance, degree, or amount. **4** *every inch.* in every way; completely: *every inch an aristocrat.* **5** *inch by inch.* gradually; little by little. **6** *within an inch of one's life.* almost to death. ◆ *vb* **7** to move or be moved very slowly or in very small steps: *the car inched forward.* **8** (*tr*; foll. by *out*) to defeat (someone) by a very small margin. [OE *ynce*; see OUNCE¹]

inch² (ɪntʃ) *n Scot. & Irish.* a small island. [C15: from Gaelic *innis* island; cf. Welsh *ynys*]

inchoate *adj* (ɪnˈkəʊeɪt, -ˈkəʊɪt). **1** just beginning; incipient. **2** undeveloped; immature; rudimentary. ◆ *vb* (ɪnˈkəʊeɪt), **inchoates, inchoating, inchoated.** (*tr*) **3** to begin. [C16: from L *incohāre* to make a beginning, lit.: to hitch up, from IN-² + *cohum* yokestrap]
▶ in'choately *adv* ▶ in'choateness *n* ▶ ˌinchoˈation *n*
▶ inchoative (ɪnˈkəʊətɪv) *adj*

Inchon or **Incheon** ★ (ˈɪntʃɒn) *n* a port in W South Korea, on the Yellow Sea: the chief port for Seoul: site of a major strategic amphibious assault by UN troops, liberating Seoul (Sept. 15, 1950). Pop.: 2 307 618 (1995). Former name: **Chemulpo.**

inchworm (ˈɪntʃˌwɜːm) *n* another name for **measuring worm.**

incidence (ˈɪnsɪdəns) *n* **1** degree, extent, or frequency of occurrence; amount: *a high incidence of death from pneumonia.* **2** the act or manner of impinging on or affecting by proximity or influence. **3** *Physics.* the arrival of a beam of light or particles at a surface. See also **angle of incidence. 4** *Geom.* the partial coincidence of two configurations, such as a point on a circle.

incident (ˈɪnsɪdənt) *n* **1** a definite occurrence; event. **2** a minor, subsidiary, or related event. **3** a relatively insignificant event that might have serious consequences. **4** a public disturbance. ◆ *adj* **5** (*postpositive*; foll. by *to*) related (to) or dependent (on). **6** (when *postpositive*, often foll. by *to*) having a subsidiary or minor relationship (with). **7** (esp. of a beam of light or particles) arriving at or striking a surface. [C15: from Med. L, from L *incidere,* lit.: to fall into, hence befall, happen]

incidental (ˌɪnsɪˈdentəl) *adj* **1** happening in connection with or resulting from something more important; casual or fortuitous. **2** (*postpositive*; foll. by *to*) found in connection (with); related (to). **3** (*postpositive*; foll. by *upon*) caused (by). **4** occasional or minor: *incidental expenses.* ◆ *n* **5** (*often pl*) a minor expense, event, or action.
▶ ˌinciˈdentalness *n*

incidentally (ˌɪnsɪˈdentəlɪ) *adv* **1** as a subordinate or chance occurrence. **2** (*sentence modifier*) by the way.

incidental music *n* background music for a film, etc.

incinerate (ɪnˈsɪnəˌreɪt) *vb* **incinerates, incinerating, incinerated.** to burn up completely; reduce to ashes. [C16: from Med. L, from L IN-² + *cinis* ashes]
▶ inˌcinerˈation *n*

incinerator (ɪnˈsɪnəˌreɪtə) *n* a furnace or apparatus for incinerating something, esp. refuse.

incipient (ɪnˈsɪpɪənt) *adj* just starting to be or happen;

beginning. [C17: from L, from *incipere* to begin, take in hand]
▶ in'cipience or in'cipiency *n* ▶ in'cipiently *adv*

incise (ɪnˈsaɪz) *vb* **incises, incising, incised.** (*tr*) to produce (lines, a design, etc.) by cutting into the surface of (something) with a sharp tool. [C16: from L *incīdere* to cut into]

incision (ɪnˈsɪʒən) *n* **1** the act of incising. **2** a cut, gash, or notch. **3** a cut made with a knife during a surgical operation.

incisive (ɪnˈsaɪsɪv) *adj* **1** keen, penetrating, or acute. **2** biting or sarcastic; mordant: *an incisive remark.* **3** having a sharp cutting edge: *incisive teeth.*
▶ in'cisively *adv* ▶ in'cisiveness *n*

incisor (ɪnˈsaɪzə) *n* a chisel-edged tooth at the front of the mouth.

incite (ɪnˈsaɪt) *vb* **incites, inciting, incited.** (*tr*) to stir up or provoke to action. [C15: from L, from IN-² + *citāre* to excite]
▶ ˌinciˈtation *n* ▶ in'citement *n* ▶ in'citer *n* ▶ in'citingly *adv*

incivility (ˌɪnsɪˈvɪlɪtɪ) *n, pl* **incivilities. 1** lack of civility or courtesy; rudeness. **2** an impolite or uncivil act or remark.

incl. *abbrev. for:* **1** including. **2** inclusive.

inclement (ɪnˈklemənt) *adj* **1** (of weather) stormy, severe, or tempestuous. **2** severe or merciless.
▶ in'clemency *n* ▶ in'clemently *adv*

inclination (ˌɪnklɪˈneɪʃən) *n* **1** (often foll. by *for, to, towards,* or an infinitive) a particular disposition, esp. a liking; tendency: *I've no inclination for such dull work.* **2** the degree of deviation from a particular plane, esp. a horizontal or vertical plane. **3** a sloping or slanting surface; incline. **4** the act of inclining or the state of being inclined. **5** the act of bowing or nodding the head. **6** another name for **dip** (sense 24).
▶ ˌincliˈnational *adj*

incline *vb* (ɪnˈklaɪn), **inclines, inclining, inclined. 1** to deviate from a particular plane, esp. a vertical or horizontal plane; slope or slant. **2** (when *tr,* may take an infinitive) to be disposed or cause to be disposed (towards some attitude or to do something). **3** to bend or lower (part of the body, esp. the head), as in a bow or in order to listen. **4** *incline one's ear.* to listen favourably (to). ◆ *n* (ˈɪnklaɪn, ɪnˈklaɪn) a sloping surface or slope; gradient. [C13: from L *inclīnāre* to cause to lean, from *clīnāre* to bend; see LEAN¹]
▶ in'clined *adj* ▶ in'cliner *n*

inclined plane *n* a plane whose angle to the horizontal is less than a right angle.

inclinometer (ˌɪnklɪˈnɒmɪtə) *n* an aircraft instrument that indicates the angle an aircraft makes with the horizontal.

inclose (ɪnˈkləʊz) *vb* **incloses, inclosing, inclosed.** a less common spelling of **enclose.**
▶ in'closure *n*

include (ɪnˈkluːd) *vb* **includes, including, included.** (*tr*) **1** to have as contents or part of the contents; be made up of or contain. **2** to add as part of something else; put in as part of a set, group, or category. **3** to contain as a secondary or minor ingredient or element. [C15 (in the sense: to enclose): from L, from IN-² + *claudere* to close]
▶ in'cludable or in'cludible *adj*

include out *vb* (*tr, adv*) *Inf.* to exclude: *you can include me out of that deal.*

inclusion (ɪnˈkluːʒən) *n* **1** the act of including or the state of being included. **2** something included.

inclusion body *n Pathol.* any of the small particles found in cells infected with certain viruses.

inclusive (ɪnˈkluːsɪv) *adj* **1** (*postpositive*; foll. by *of*) considered together (with): *capital inclusive of profit.* **2** (*postpositive*) including the limits specified: *Monday to Friday inclusive.* **3** comprehensive. **4** *Logic.* (of a disjunction) true if at least one of its component propositions is true.
▶ in'clusively *adv* ▶ in'clusiveness *n*

inclusive language *n* language that avoids the use of expressions or words that might be considered to exclude particular groups of people, esp. gender-specific words, such as "man", "mankind", and masculine pronouns, in contexts that could exclude women.

incognito (ˌɪnkɒɡˈniːtəʊ, ɪnˈkɒɡnɪtəʊ) *or (fem)* **incognita** *adv, adj (postpositive)* **1** under an assumed name or appearance; in disguise. ◆ *n, pl* **incognitos** *or (fem)* **incognitas**. **2** a person who is incognito. **3** the assumed name or disguise of such a person. [C17: from It., from L *incognitus* unknown]

incognizant (ɪnˈkɒɡnɪzənt) *adj (when postpositive, often foll. by of)* unaware (of).
▶ **in'cognizance** *n*

incoherent (ˌɪnkəʊˈhɪərənt) *adj* **1** lacking in clarity or organization; disordered. **2** unable to express oneself clearly; inarticulate. **3** *Physics.* (of two or more waves) having the same frequency but not the same phase: *incoherent light.*
▶ ˌinco'herently *adv* ▶ ˌinco'herence *or* ˌinco'herency *n*

income ('ɪnkʌm, 'ɪnkəm) *n* **1** the amount of monetary or other returns, either earned or unearned, accruing over a given period of time. **2** receipts; revenue. [C13 (in the sense: arrival, entrance): from OE *incumen* a coming in]

incomer ('ɪnkʌmə) *n* a person who comes to live in a place in which he was not born.

incomes policy *n* an economic policy that attempts to reduce or control inflation by limiting incomes.

income support *n* (in Britain) a social security payment for people on very low incomes.

income tax *n* a personal tax levied on annual income subject to certain deductions.

incoming ('ɪnˌkʌmɪŋ) *adj* **1** coming in; entering. **2** about to come into office; succeeding. **3** (of interest, dividends, etc.) being received; accruing. ◆ *n* **4** the act of coming in; entrance. **5** (*usually pl*) income or revenue.

incommensurable (ˌɪnkəˈmɛnʃərəbəl) *adj* **1** incapable of being judged, measured, or considered comparatively. **2** (*postpositive*; foll. by *with*) not in accordance; incommensurate. **3** *Maths.* not having a common factor other than 1, such as 2 and √−5. ◆ *n* **4** something incommensurable.
▶ ˌincomˌmensura'bility *n* ▶ ˌincom'mensurably *adv*

incommensurate (ˌɪnkəˈmɛnʃərɪt) *adj* **1** (when *postpositive*, often foll. by *with*) not commensurate; disproportionate. **2** incommensurable.
▶ ˌincom'mensurately *adv* ▶ ˌincom'mensurateness *n*

incommode (ˌɪnkəˈməʊd) *vb* **incommodes, incommoding, incommoded.** (*tr*) to bother, disturb, or inconvenience. [C16: from L *incommodāre* to be troublesome, from *incommodus* inconvenient; see COMMODE]

incommodious (ˌɪnkəˈməʊdɪəs) *adj* **1** insufficiently spacious; cramped. **2** troublesome or inconvenient.
▶ ˌincom'modiously *adv*

incommodity (ˌɪnkəˈmɒdɪtɪ) *n, pl* **incommodities.** anything that causes inconvenience.

incommunicado (ˌɪnkəˌmjuːnɪˈkɑːdəʊ) *adv, adj (postpositive)* deprived of communication with other people, as while in solitary confinement. [C19: from Sp., from *incomunicar* to deprive of communication; see IN-[1], COMMUNICATE]

incomparable (ɪnˈkɒmpərəbəl, -prəbəl) *adj* **1** beyond or above comparison; matchless; unequalled. **2** lacking a basis for comparison; not having qualities or features that can be compared.
▶ inˌcompara'bility *or* in'comparableness *n* ▶ in'comparably *adv*

incompatible (ˌɪnkəmˈpætəbəl) *adj* **1** incapable of living or existing together in harmony; conflicting. **2** opposed in nature or quality; inconsistent. **3** *Med.* (esp. of two drugs or two types of blood) incapable of being combined or used together; antagonistic. **4** *Logic.* (of two propositions) unable to be both true at the same time. **5** (of plants) incapable of self-fertilization. ◆ *n* **6** (*often pl*) a person or thing that is incompatible with another.
▶ inˌcompati'bility *or* in'compatibleness *n* ▶ inˌcom'patibly *adv*

incompetent (ɪnˈkɒmpɪtənt) *adj* **1** not possessing the necessary ability, skill, etc., to do or carry out a task; in-

capable. **2** marked by lack of ability, skill, etc. **3** *Law.* not legally qualified: *an incompetent witness.* ◆ *n* **4** an incompetent person.
▶ in'competence *or* in'competency *n* ▶ in'competently *adv*

incomplete (ˌɪnkəmˈpliːt) *adj* **1** not complete or finished. **2** not completely developed; imperfect.
▶ ˌincom'pletely *adv* ▶ ˌincom'pleteness *or* ˌincom'pletion *n*

incomprehensible (ˌɪnkɒmprɪˈhɛnsəbəl, ɪnˌkɒm-) *adj* **1** incapable of being understood; unintelligible. **2** *Archaic.* limitless; boundless.
▶ ˌincompreˌhensi'bility *or* ˌincompre'hensibleness *n* ▶ ˌincompre'hensibly *adv*

inconceivable (ˌɪnkənˈsiːvəbəl) *adj* incapable of being conceived, imagined, or considered.
▶ ˌinconˌceiva'bility *or* ˌincon'ceivableness *n* ▶ ˌincon'ceivably *adv*

inconclusive (ˌɪnkənˈkluːsɪv) *adj* not conclusive or decisive; not finally settled; indeterminate.
▶ ˌincon'clusively *adv* ▶ ˌincon'clusiveness *n*

incongruous (ɪnˈkɒŋɡrʊəs) *or* **incongruent** *adj* **1** (when *postpositive*, foll. by *with* or *to*) incompatible with (what is suitable); inappropriate. **2** containing disparate or discordant elements or parts.
▶ in'congruously *adv* ▶ in'congruousness *or* incongruity (ˌɪnkɒŋˈɡruːɪtɪ) *n*

inconnu ('ɪnkənjuː, ɪnˈkɒnuː) *n Canad.* a whitefish of Far Northern waters. [C19: from F, lit: unknown]

inconsequential (ˌɪnkɒnsɪˈkwɛnʃəl, ɪnˌkɒn-) *or* **inconsequent** (ɪnˈkɒnsɪkwənt) *adj* **1** not following logically as a consequence. **2** trivial or insignificant. **3** not in a logical sequence; haphazard.
▶ ˌinconseˌquenti'ality, ˌinconse'quentialness, *or* in'consequence *n* ▶ ˌinconse'quentially *or* in'consequently *adv*

inconsiderable (ˌɪnkənˈsɪdərəbəl) *adj* **1** relatively small. **2** not worthy of consideration; insignificant.
▶ ˌincon'siderableness *n* ▶ ˌincon'siderably *adv*

inconsiderate (ˌɪnkənˈsɪdərɪt) *adj* lacking in care or thought for others; thoughtless.
▶ ˌincon'siderately *adv* ▶ ˌincon'siderateness *or* ˌinconˌsider'ation *n*

inconsistency (ˌɪnkənˈsɪstənsɪ) *n, pl* **inconsistencies. 1** lack of consistency or agreement; incompatibility. **2** an inconsistent feature or quality.

inconsistent (ˌɪnkənˈsɪstənt) *adj* **1** lacking in consistency, agreement, or compatibility; at variance. **2** containing contradictory elements. **3** irregular or fickle in behaviour or mood. **4** *Logic.* (of a set of propositions) enabling an explicit contradiction to be validly derived.
▶ ˌincon'sistently *adv*

inconsolable (ˌɪnkənˈsəʊləbəl) *adj* incapable of being consoled or comforted; disconsolate.
▶ ˌinconˌsola'bility *or* ˌincon'solableness *n* ▶ ˌincon'solably *adv*

inconsonant (ɪnˈkɒnsənənt) *adj* lacking in harmony or compatibility; discordant.
▶ in'consonance *n* ▶ in'consonantly *adv*

inconspicuous (ˌɪnkənˈspɪkjʊəs) *adj* not easily noticed or seen; not prominent or striking.
▶ ˌincon'spicuously *adv* ▶ ˌincon'spicuousness *n*

incontinent[1] (ɪnˈkɒntɪnənt) *adj* **1** relating to or exhibiting involuntary urination or defecation. **2** lacking in restraint or control, esp. sexually. **3** (foll. by *of*) having little or no control (over). **4** unrestrained; uncontrolled. [C14: from OF, from L, from IN-[1] + *continere* to hold, restrain]
▶ in'continence *n* ▶ in'continently *adv*

incontinent[2] (ɪnˈkɒntɪnənt) *or* **incontinently** *adv* obsolete words for **immediately**. [C15: from LL *in continenti tempore*, lit.: in continuous time, that is, with no interval]

incontrovertible (ˌɪnkɒntrəˈvɜːtəbəl, ɪnˌkɒn-) *adj* incapable of being contradicted or disputed; undeniable.
▶ ˌincontroˌverti'bility *n* ▶ ˌincontro'vertibly *adv*

inconvenience (ˌɪnkənˈviːnjəns, -ˈviːnɪəns) *n* **1** the state or quality of being inconvenient. **2** something inconvenient; a hindrance, trouble, or difficulty. ◆ *vb* **3** (*tr*) to cause inconvenience to; trouble or harass.

inconvenient (ˌɪnkən'viːnjənt, -'viːnɪənt) *adj* not convenient; troublesome, awkward, or difficult.
▸ ˌincon'veniently *adv*

incorporate *vb* (ɪn'kɔːpəˌreɪt), **incorporates, incorporating, incorporated. 1** to include or be included as a part or member of a united whole. **2** to form a united whole or mass; merge or blend. **3** to form into a corporation or other organization with a separate legal identity. ◆ *adj* (ɪn'kɔːpərɪt, -prɪt). **4** combined into a whole; incorporated. **5** formed into or constituted as a corporation. [C14 (in the sense: put into the body of something else): from LL *incorporāre* to embody, from L IN-[2] + *corpus* body]
▸ in'corpoˌrated *adj* ▸ in,corpo'ration *n* ▸ in'corporative *adj*

incorporeal (ˌɪnkɔː'pɔːrɪəl) *adj* **1** without material form, body, or substance. **2** spiritual or metaphysical. **3** *Law.* having no material existence but existing by reason of its annexation of something material: *an incorporeal hereditament.*
▸ ˌincor'poreally *adv* ▸ **incorporeity** (ɪnˌkɔːpə'riːɪtɪ) *or* ˌincorpore'ality *n*

incorrect (ˌɪnkə'rekt) *adj* **1** false; wrong: *an incorrect calculation.* **2** not fitting or proper: *incorrect behaviour.*
▸ ˌincor'rectly *adv* ▸ ˌincor'rectness *n*

incorrigible (ɪn'kɒrɪdʒəb°l) *adj* **1** beyond correction, reform, or alteration. **2** firmly rooted; ineradicable. ◆ *n* **3** a person or animal that is incorrigible.
▸ in,corrigi'bility *or* in'corrigibleness *n* ▸ in'corrigibly *adv*

incorruptible (ˌɪnkə'rʌptəb°l) *adj* **1** incapable of being corrupted; honest; just. **2** not subject to decay or decomposition.
▸ ˌincor,rupti'bility *n* ▸ ˌincor'ruptibly *adv*

incr. *abbrev. for:* **1** increase. **2** increased. **3** increasing.

incrassate *adj* (ɪn'kræsɪt, -eɪt), *also* **incrassated. 1** *Biol.* thickened or swollen. ◆ *vb* (ɪn'kræseɪt), **incrassates, incrassating, incrassated. 2** *Obs.* to make or become thicker. [C17: from LL, from L *crassus* thick, dense]
▸ ˌincras'sation *n*

increase *vb* (ɪn'kriːs), **increases, increasing, increased. 1** to make or become greater in size, degree, frequency, etc.; grow or expand. ◆ *n* ('ɪnkriːs). **2** the act of increasing; augmentation. **3** the amount by which something increases. **4 on the increase.** increasing, esp. becoming more frequent. [C14: from OF *encreistre*, from L, from IN-[2] + *crēscere* to grow]
▸ in'creasable *adj* ▸ **increasedly** (ɪn'kriːsɪdlɪ) *or* in'creasingly *adv* ▸ in'creaser *n*

incredible (ɪn'kredəb°l) *adj* **1** beyond belief or understanding; unbelievable. **2** *Inf.* marvellous; amazing.
▸ in,credi'bility *or* in'credibleness *n* ▸ in'credibly *adv*

incredulity (ˌɪnkrɪ'djuːlɪtɪ) *n* lack of belief; scepticism.

incredulous (ɪn'kredjʊləs) *adj* (often foll. by *of*) not prepared or willing to believe (something); unbelieving.
▸ in'credulously *adv* ▸ in'credulousness *n*

increment ('ɪnkrɪmənt) *n* **1** an increase or addition, esp. one of a series. **2** the act of increasing; augmentation. **3** *Maths.* a small positive or negative change in a variable or function. [C15: from L *incrēmentum* growth, INCREASE]
▸ **incremental** (ˌɪnkrɪ'ment°l) *adj*

incremental plotter *n* a device that plots graphs on paper from computer-generated instructions.

incriminate (ɪn'krɪmɪˌneɪt) *vb* **incriminates, incriminating, incriminated.** (*tr*) **1** to imply or suggest the guilt or error of (someone). **2** to charge with a crime or fault. [C18: from LL *incrīmināre* to accuse, from L *crīmen* accusation; see CRIME]
▸ in,crimi'nation *n* ▸ in'crimi,nator *n* ▸ in'criminatory *adj*

incrust (ɪn'krʌst) *vb* a variant spelling of **encrust.**
▸ in'crustant *n, adj* ▸ ˌincrus'tation *n*

incubate ('ɪnkjʊˌbeɪt) *vb* **incubates, incubating, incubated. 1** (of birds) to supply (eggs) with heat for their development, esp. by sitting on them. **2** to cause (bacteria, etc.) to develop, esp. in an incubator or culture medium. **3** (*intr*) (of embryos, etc.) to develop in favourable conditions, esp. in an incubator. **4** (*intr*) (of disease germs) to

remain inactive in an animal or human before causing disease. **5** to develop gradually; foment or be fomented. [C18: from L *incubāre* to lie upon, hatch, from IN-[2] + *cubāre* to lie down]
▸ ˌincu'bation *n* ▸ ˌincu'bational *adj* ▸ 'incu,bative *or* 'incu,batory *adj*

incubation period *n Med.* the time between exposure to an infectious disease and the appearance of the first signs or symptoms.

incubator ('ɪnkjʊˌbeɪtə) *n* **1** *Med.* an apparatus for housing prematurely born babies until they are strong enough to survive. **2** a container in which birds' eggs can be artificially hatched or bacterial cultures grown. **3** a person, animal, or thing that incubates.

incubus ('ɪnkjʊbəs) *n, pl* **incubi** (-ˌbaɪ) *or* **incubuses. 1** a demon believed in folklore to have sexual intercourse with sleeping women. Cf. **succubus. 2** something that oppresses or disturbs greatly, esp. a nightmare or obsession. [C14: from LL, from L *incubāre* to lie upon; see INCUBATE]

inculcate ('ɪnkʌlˌkeɪt, ɪn'kʌlkeɪt) *vb* **inculcates, inculcating, inculcated.** (*tr*) to instil by insistent repetition. [C16: from L *inculcāre* to tread upon, ram down, from IN-[2] + *calcāre* to trample, from *calx* heel]
▸ ˌincul'cation *n* ▸ 'incul,cator *n*

inculpate ('ɪnkʌlˌpeɪt, ɪn'kʌlpeɪt) *vb* **inculpates, inculpating, inculpated.** (*tr*) to incriminate; cause blame to be imputed to. [C18: from LL, from L *culpāre* to blame, from *culpa* fault, blame]
▸ ˌincul'pation *n* ▸ **inculpative** (ɪn'kʌlpətɪv) *or* **inculpatory** (ɪn'kʌlpətərɪ, -trɪ) *adj*

incumbency (ɪn'kʌmbənsɪ) *n, pl* **incumbencies. 1** the state or quality of being incumbent. **2** the office, duty, or tenure of an incumbent.

incumbent (ɪn'kʌmbənt) *adj* **1** *Formal.* (often *postpositive* and foll. by *on* or *upon* and an infinitive) morally binding; obligatory: *it is incumbent on me to attend.* **2** (usually *postpositive* and foll. by *on*) resting or lying (on). **3** (usually *prenominal*) occupying or holding an office. ◆ *n* **4** a person who holds an office, esp. a clergyman holding a benefice. [C16: from L *incumbere* to lie upon, devote one's attention to]

incunabula (ˌɪnkjʊ'næbjʊlə) *pl n, sing* **incunabulum** (-ləm). **1** any book printed before 1500. **2** the earliest stages of something; beginnings. [C19: from L, orig.: swaddling clothes, hence beginnings, from IN-[2] + *cūnābula* cradle]
▸ ˌincu'nabular *adj*

incur (ɪn'kɜː) *vb* **incurs, incurring, incurred.** (*tr*) **1** to make oneself subject to (something undesirable); bring upon oneself. **2** to run into or encounter. [C16: from L *incurrere* to run into, from *currere* to run]
▸ in'currable *adj*

incurable (ɪn'kjʊərəb°l) *adj* **1** (esp. of a disease) not curable; unresponsive to treatment. ◆ *n* **2** a person having an incurable disease.
▸ in,cura'bility *or* in'curableness *n* ▸ in'curably *adv*

incurious (ɪn'kjʊərɪəs) *adj* not curious; indifferent or uninterested.
▸ **incuriosity** (ɪnˌkjʊərɪ'ɒsɪtɪ) *or* in'curiousness *n* ▸ in'curiously *adv*

incursion (ɪn'kɜːʃən) *n* **1** a sudden invasion, attack, or raid. **2** the act of running or leaking into; penetration. [C15: from L *incursiō* onset, attack, from *incurrere* to run into; see INCUR]
▸ **incursive** (ɪn'kɜːsɪv) *adj*

incus ('ɪŋkəs) *n, pl* **incudes** (ɪn'kjuːdiːz). the central of the three small bones in the middle ear of mammals. Cf. **malleus, stapes.** [C17: from L: anvil, from *incūdere* to forge]

incuse (ɪn'kjuːz) *n* **1** a design stamped or hammered onto a coin. ◆ *vb* **incuses, incusing, incused. 2** to impress (a coin) with a design by hammering or stamping. ◆ *adj* **3** stamped or hammered onto a coin. [C19: from L *incūsus* hammered; see INCUS]

Ind ★ (ɪnd) *n* **1** a poetic name for **India. 2** an obsolete name for the **Indies.**

ind. *abbrev. for:* **1** independence. **2** independent. **3** index. **4** indicative. **5** indirect. **6** industrial. **7** industry.

Ind. *abbrev. for:* **1** Independent. **2** India. **3** Indian. **4** Indies.

indaba (ɪnˈdɑːbə) *n* **1** (among Bantu peoples of southern Africa) a meeting to discuss a serious topic. **2** *S. African inf.* a matter of concern or for discussion. [C19: from Zulu: topic]

indebted (ɪnˈdɛtɪd) *adj* (*postpositive*) **1** owing gratitude for help, favours, etc.; obligated. **2** owing money.

indebtedness (ɪnˈdɛtɪdnɪs) *n* **1** the state of being indebted. **2** the total of a person's debts.

indecency (ɪnˈdiːsənsɪ) *n, pl* **indecencies**. **1** the state or quality of being indecent. **2** an indecent act, etc.

indecent (ɪnˈdiːsᵊnt) *adj* **1** offensive to standards of decency, esp. in sexual matters. **2** unseemly or improper (esp. in **indecent haste**).
▸ **inˈdecently** *adv*

indecent assault *n* the offence of subjecting a person to a form of sexual activity, other than rape, against his or her will.

indecent exposure *n* the offence of indecently exposing one's body in public, esp. the genitals.

indecisive (ˌɪndɪˈsaɪsɪv) *adj* **1** (of a person) vacillating; irresolute. **2** not decisive or conclusive.
▸ ˌindeˈcision *or* ˌindeˈcisiveness *n* ▸ ˌindeˈcisively *adv*

indecorum (ˌɪndɪˈkɔːrəm) *n* lack of decorum; unseemliness.
▸ **inˈdecorous** *adj*

indeed (ɪnˈdiːd) (*sentence connector*). **1** certainly; actually: *indeed, it may never happen.* ◆ *adv* **2** (intensifier): *that is indeed amazing.* **3** or rather; what is more: *a comfortable, indeed wealthy family.* ◆ *interj* **4** an expression of doubt, surprise, etc.

indef. *abbrev. for* indefinite.

indefatigable (ˌɪndɪˈfætɪɡəᵊl) *adj* unable to be tired out; unflagging. [C16: from L, from *fatīgāre* to tire]
▸ ˌindeˌfatigaˈbility *n* ▸ ˌindeˈfatigably *adv*

indefeasible (ˌɪndɪˈfiːzəᵊl) *adj Law.* not liable to be annulled or forfeited.
▸ ˌindeˌfeasiˈbility *n* ▸ ˌindeˈfeasibly *adv*

indefensible (ˌɪndɪˈfɛnsəᵊl) *adj* **1** not justifiable or excusable. **2** capable of being disagreed with; untenable. **3** incapable of defence against attack.
▸ ˌindeˌfensiˈbility *n* ▸ ˌindeˈfensibly *adv*

indefinite (ɪnˈdɛfɪnɪt) *adj* **1** not certain or determined; unsettled. **2** without exact limits; indeterminate: *an indefinite number.* **3** vague or unclear. **4** in traditional logic, a proposition in which it is not stated whether the subject is universal or particular, as in *men are mortal.*
▸ **inˈdefinitely** *adv* ▸ **inˈdefiniteness** *n*

indefinite article *n Grammar.* a determiner that expresses nonspecificity of reference, such as *a, an,* or *some.*

indehiscent (ˌɪndɪˈhɪsᵊnt) *adj* (of fruits, etc.) not dehiscent; not opening to release seeds, etc.
▸ ˌindeˈhiscence *n*

indelible (ɪnˈdɛlɪbᵊl) *adj* **1** incapable of being erased or obliterated. **2** making indelible marks: *indelible ink.* [C16: from L, from IN-¹ + *delēre* to destroy]
▸ inˌdeliˈbility *or* inˈdelibleness *n* ▸ inˈdelibly *adv*

indelicate (ɪnˈdɛlɪkɪt) *adj* **1** coarse, crude, or rough. **2** offensive, embarrassing, or tasteless.
▸ inˈdelicacy *or* inˈdelicateness *n* ▸ inˈdelicately *adv*

indemnify (ɪnˈdɛmnɪˌfaɪ) *vb* **indemnifies, indemnifying, indemnified.** (*tr*) **1** to secure against future loss, damage, or liability; give security for; insure. **2** to compensate for loss, etc.; reimburse.
▸ inˌdemnifiˈcation *n* ▸ inˈdemniˌfier *n*

indemnity (ɪnˈdɛmnɪtɪ) *n, pl* **indemnities. 1** compensation for loss or damage; reimbursement. **2** protection or insurance against future loss or damage. **3** legal exemption from penalties incurred through one's acts or defaults. **4** *Canad.* the annual salary paid by the government to a member of Parliament or of a provincial legislature. [C15: from LL, from *indemnis* uninjured, from L IN-¹ + *damnum* damage]

indene (ˈɪndiːn) *n* a colourless liquid hydrocarbon obtained from coal tar and used in making synthetic resins. Formula: C_9H_8. [C20: from INDOLE + -ENE]

indent¹ *vb* (ɪnˈdɛnt). (*mainly tr*) **1** to place (written matter, etc.) in from the margin. **2** to cut (a document in duplicate) so that the irregular lines may be matched. **3** *Chiefly Brit.* (in foreign trade) to place an order for (foreign goods). **4** (when *intr*, foll. by *for, on,* or *upon*) *Chiefly Brit.* to make an order on (a source or supply) or for (something). **5** to notch (an edge, border, etc.); make jagged. **6** to bind (an apprentice, etc.) by indenture. ◆ *n* (ˈɪnˌdɛnt). *Chiefly Brit.* **7** (in foreign trade) an order for foreign merchandise. **8** an official order for goods. [C14: from OF *endenter,* from EN-¹ + *dent* tooth, from L *dēns*]
▸ inˈdenter *or* inˈdentor *n*

indent² *vb* (ɪnˈdɛnt). **1** (*tr*) to make a dent or depression in. ◆ *n* (ˈɪnˌdɛnt). **2** a dent or depression. [C15: from IN-² + DENT]

indentation (ˌɪndɛnˈteɪʃən) *n* **1** a hollowed, notched, or cut place, as on an edge or on a coastline. **2** a series of hollows, notches, or cuts. **3** the act of indenting or the condition of being indented. **4** Also: **indention, indent.** the leaving of space or the amount of space left between a margin and the start of an indented line.

indention (ɪnˈdɛnʃən) *n* another word for **indentation** (sense 4).

indenture (ɪnˈdɛntʃə) *n* **1** any deed, contract, or sealed agreement between two or more parties. **2** (formerly) a deed drawn up in duplicate, each part having correspondingly indented edges for identification and security. **3** (*often pl*) a contract between an apprentice and his master. **4** a less common word for **indentation.** ◆ *vb* **indentures, indenturing, indentured. 5** (*intr*) to enter into an agreement by indenture. **6** (*tr*) to bind (an apprentice, servant, etc.) by indenture.
▸ inˈdentureˌship *n*

independence (ˌɪndɪˈpɛndəns) *n* the state or quality of being independent. Also: **independency.**

Independence ★ (ˌɪndɪˈpɛndəns) *n* a city in W Missouri, near Kansas City: starting point for the Santa Fe, Oregon, and California Trails (1831–44). Pop.: 111 669 (1994 est.).

independency (ˌɪndɪˈpɛndənsɪ) *n, pl* **independencies. 1** a territory or state free from the control of any other power. **2** another word for **independence.**

independent (ˌɪndɪˈpɛndənt) *adj* **1** free from control in action, judgment, etc.; autonomous. **2** not dependent on anything else for function, validity, etc.; separate. **3** not reliant on the support, esp. financial support, of others. **4** capable of acting for oneself or on one's own: *a very independent little girl.* **5** providing a large unearned sum towards one's support (esp. in **independent income, independent means**). **6** living on an unearned income. **7** *Maths.* (of a system of equations) not linearly dependent. See also **independent variable. 8** *Logic.* (of two or more propositions) unrelated. ◆ *n* **9** an independent person or thing. **10** a person who is not affiliated to or who acts independently of a political party.
▸ ˌindeˈpendently *adv*

Independent (ˌɪndɪˈpɛndənt) *Christianity.* ◆ *n* **1** (in England) a member of the Congregational Church. ◆ *adj* **2** of or relating to the Congregational Church.

independent clause *n Grammar.* a main or coordinate clause.

independent school *n* **1** (in Britain) a school that is neither financed nor controlled by the government or local authorities. **2** (in Australia) a school that is not part of the state system.

independent variable *n* a variable in a mathematical equation or statement whose value determines that of the dependent variable: in $y = f(x)$, x is the independent variable.

in-depth *adj* detailed and thorough: *an in-depth study.*

indescribable (ˌɪndɪˈskraɪbəᵊl) *adj* beyond description; too intense, extreme, etc., for words.
▸ ˌindeˌscribaˈbility *n* ▸ ˌindeˈscribably *adv*

indestructible (ˌɪndɪˈstrʌktəᵊl) *adj* incapable of being destroyed; very durable.
▸ ˌindeˌstructiˈbility *or* ˌindeˈstructibleness *n* ▸ ˌindeˈstructibly *adv*

indeterminate (ˌɪndɪˈtɜːmɪnɪt) *adj* **1** uncertain in extent, amount, or nature. **2** not definite; inconclusive: *an indeterminate reply.* **3** unable to be predicted, calculated, or deduced. **4** *Maths.* **4a** having no numerical meaning, as 0/0. **4b** (of an equation) having more than one variable and an unlimited number of solutions.
▶ ˌindeˈterminacy *or* ˌindeˈterminateness *n* ▶ ˌindeˈterminately *adv*

indeterminism (ˌɪndɪˈtɜːmɪˌnɪzəm) *n* the philosophical doctrine that behaviour is not entirely determined by motives.
▶ ˌindeˈterminist *n, adj* ▶ ˌindeˌterminˈistic *adj*

index (ˈɪndɛks) *n, pl* **indexes** *or* **indices** (-dɪˌsiːz). **1** an alphabetical list of persons, subjects, etc., mentioned in a printed work, usually at the back, and indicating where they are referred to. **2** See **thumb index.** **3** *Library science.* a systematic list of book titles or authors' names, giving cross-references and the location of each book; catalogue. **4** an indication, sign, or token. **5** a pointer, needle, or other indicator, as on an instrument. **6** *Maths.* **6a** another name for **exponent** (sense 4). **6b** a number or variable placed as a superscript to the left of a radical sign indicating the root to be extracted, as in $^3\sqrt{8} = 2$. **7** a numerical scale by means of which levels of the cost of living can be compared with some base number. **8** a number or ratio indicating a specific characteristic, property, etc.: *refractive index.* **9** Also called: **fist.** a printer's mark, ☞ used to indicate notes, paragraphs, etc. ◆ *vb* (*tr*) **10** to put an index in (a book). **11** to enter (a word, item, etc.) in an index. **12** to point out; indicate. **13** to make index-linked. **14** to move (a machine, etc.) so that an operation will be repeated at certain defined intervals. [C16: from L: pointer, hence forefinger, title, index, from *indicāre* to disclose, show; see INDICATE]
▶ ˈindexer *n*

indexation (ˌɪndɛkˈseɪʃən) *or* **index-linking** *n* the act of making wages, interest rates, etc., index-linked.

index case *n Med.* the first case of a disease.

index finger *n* the finger next to the thumb. Also called: **forefinger.**

index fossil *n* a fossil species that characterizes and is used to delimit a geological zone. Also called: **zone fossil.**

index futures *pl n* a form of financial futures based on projected movements of a share price index, such as the Financial Times Stock Exchange 100 Share Index.

indexical (ɪnˈdɛksɪkᵊl) *adj* **1** arranged as or relating to an index or indexes. ◆ *n* **2** Also called: **deictic.** *Logic, linguistics.* a term whose reference depends on the context of utterance, such as *I, you, here, now,* or *tomorrow.*

Index Librorum Prohibitorum *Latin.* (ˈɪndɛks laɪˈbrɔːrʊm prəʊˌhɪbɪˈtɔːrʊm) *n RC Church.* (formerly) an official list of proscribed books. Often called: **the Index.** [C17, lit.: list of forbidden books]

index-linked *adj* (of wages, interest rates, etc.) directly related to the cost-of-living index and rising or falling accordingly.

index number *n Statistics.* a statistic indicating the relative change occurring in the price or value of a commodity or in a general economic variable, with reference to a previous base period conventionally given the number 100.

India ★ (ˈɪndɪə) *n* **1** a republic in S Asia: history dates from the Indus Valley civilization (3rd millennium B.C.); came under British supremacy in 1763 and passed to the British Crown in 1858; nationalist movement arose under Gandhi (1869–1948); Indian subcontinent divided into Pakistan (Muslim) and India (Hindu) in 1947; became a republic within the Commonwealth in 1950. It consists chiefly of the Himalayas, rising over 7500 m (25 000 ft) in the extreme north, the Ganges plain in the north, the Thar Desert in the northwest, the Chota Nagpur plateau in the northeast, and the Deccan Plateau in the south. Official and administrative languages: Hindi and English; each state has its own language. Religion: Hindu majority, Muslim minority. Currency: rupee. Capital: New Delhi. Pop.: 967 613 000 (1997). Area: 3 268 100 sq. km (1 261 813 sq. miles). Hindi name: **Bharat. 2** *Communications.* a code word for the letter *i.*

Indiaman (ˈɪndɪəmən) *n, pl* **Indiamen.** (formerly) a merchant ship engaged in trade with India.

Indian (ˈɪndɪən) *n* **1** a native or inhabitant of the Republic of India or a descendant of one. **2** an American Indian. **3** (*not in scholarly usage*) any of the languages of the American Indians. ◆ *adj* **4** of or relating to India, its inhabitants, or any of their languages. **5** of or relating to the American Indians or any of their languages.

Indiana ★ (ˌɪndɪˈænə) *n* a state of the N central US, in the Midwest: consists of an undulating plain, with sand dunes and lakes in the north and limestone caves in the south. Capital: Indianapolis. Pop.: 5 840 528 (1996 est.). Area: 93 491 sq. km (36 097 sq. miles). Abbrevs.: **Ind.** or (with zip code) **IN**
▶ ˌIndiˈanian *adj, n*

Indianapolis ★ (ˌɪndɪəˈnæpəlɪs) *n* a city in central Indiana: the state capital. Pop.: 752 279 (1994 est.).

Indian club *n* a bottle-shaped club, usually used in pairs by gymnasts, jugglers, etc.

Indian corn *n* another name for **maize** (sense 1).

Indian Desert ★ *n* another name for the **Thar Desert.**

Indian Empire ★ *n* British India and the Indian states under indirect British control, which gained independence as India and Pakistan in 1947.

Indian file *n* another term for **single file.**

Indian hemp *n* another name for **hemp,** esp. the variety *Cannabis indica,* from which several narcotic drugs are obtained.

Indian ink *or esp. US & Canad.* **India ink** *n* **1** a black pigment made from a mixture of lampblack and a binding agent such as gelatine or glue: usually formed into solid cakes and sticks. **2** a black liquid ink made from this pigment. ◆ Also called: **China ink, Chinese ink.**

Indian list *n Inf.* (in Canada) a list of persons to whom spirits may not be sold.

Indian meal *n* another name for **corn meal.**

Indian Ocean ★ *n* an ocean bordered by Africa in the west, Asia in the north, and Australia in the east and merging with the Antarctic Ocean in the south. Average depth: 3900 m (13 000 ft). Greatest depth (off the Sunda Islands): 7450 m (24 442 ft). Area: about 73 556 000 sq. km (28 400 000 sq. miles).

Indian rope-trick *n* the supposed Indian feat of climbing an unsupported rope.

Indian States and Agencies ★ *pl n* another name for the **Native States.**

Indian summer *n* **1** a period of unusually warm weather in the late autumn. **2** a period of tranquillity or of renewed productivity towards the end of something, esp. a person's life. [orig. US: prob. so named because it was first noted in Amerind regions]

Indian Territory ★ *n* the territory established in the early 19th century in present-day Oklahoma, where Indians were forced to settle by the US government. The last remnant was integrated into the new state of Oklahoma in 1907.

Indian tobacco *n* a poisonous North American plant with small pale bell-shaped blue flowers and rounded inflated seed capsules.

India paper *n* a thin soft opaque printing paper originally made in the Orient.

India rubber *n* another name for **rubber**¹ (sense 1).

Indic (ˈɪndɪk) *adj* **1** denoting, belonging to, or relating to a branch of Indo-European consisting of certain languages of India, including Sanskrit, Hindi and Urdu. ◆ *n* **2** this group of languages. ◆ Also: **Indo-Aryan.**

indicate (ˈɪndɪˌkeɪt) *vb* **indicates, indicating, indicated.** (*tr*) **1** (*may take a clause as object*) to be or give a sign or symptom of; imply: *cold hands indicate a warm heart.* **2** to point out or show. **3** (*may take a clause as object*) to state briefly; suggest. **4** (of instruments) to show a reading of. **5** (*usually passive*) to recommend or require: *surgery seems to be indicated for this patient.* [C17: from L *indicāre* to point out, from IN-² + *dicāre* to proclaim; cf. INDEX]
▶ ˈindiˌcatable *adj* ▶ **indicatory** (ɪnˈdɪkətərɪ, -trɪ) *adj*

indication (ˌɪndɪˈkeɪʃən) *n* **1** something that serves to indicate or suggest; sign: *an indication of foul play*. **2** the degree or quantity represented on a measuring instrument or device. **3** the action of indicating. **4** something that is indicated as advisable, necessary, or expedient.

indicative (ɪnˈdɪkətɪv) *adj* **1** (*usually postpositive*; foll. by *of*) serving as a sign; suggestive: *indicative of trouble ahead*. **2** *Grammar*. denoting a mood of verbs used chiefly to make statements. ◆ *n* **3** *Grammar*. **3a** the indicative mood. **3b** a verb in the indicative mood. ◆ Abbrev.: **indic**.
▸ in'dicatively *adv*

indicator (ˈɪndɪˌkeɪtə) *n* **1** something that provides an indication, esp. of trends. See **economic indicator. 2** a device to attract attention, such as the pointer of a gauge or a warning lamp. **3** an instrument that displays certain operating conditions in a machine, such as a gauge showing temperature, etc. **4** a device that registers something, such as the movements of a lift, or that shows information, such as train departure times. **5** Also called: **blinker.** a device for indicating that a motor vehicle is about to turn left or right, esp. two pairs of lights that flash. **6** a delicate measuring instrument used to determine small differences in the height of mechanical components. **7** *Chem.* a substance used to indicate the completion of a chemical reaction, usually by a change of colour. **8** Also called: **indicator species.** *Ecology.* a plant or animal species that thrives only under particular environmental conditions and therefore indicates these conditions where it is found.

indices (ˈɪndɪˌsiːz) *n* a plural of **index.**

indicia (ɪnˈdɪʃɪə) *pl n, sing* **indicium** (-ʃɪəm). distinguishing markings or signs; indications. [C17: from L, pl of *indicium* a notice, from INDEX]
▸ in'dicial *adj*

indict (ɪnˈdaɪt) *vb* (*tr*) to charge (a person) with crime, esp. formally in writing; accuse. [C14: alteration of *enditen* to INDITE]
▸ ˌindict'ee *n* ▸ in'dicter *or* in'dictor *n* ▸ in'dictable *adj*

USAGE NOTE See at **indite.**

---

indictment (ɪnˈdaɪtmənt) *n Criminal law.* **1** a formal written charge of crime formerly referred to and presented on oath by a grand jury. **2** any formal accusation of crime. **3** the act of indicting or the state of being indicted.

indie (ˈɪndɪ) *n Inf.* **a** an independent record company. **b** (*as modifier*): *the indie charts.*

Indies ★ (ˈɪndɪz) *n* **the. 1** the territories of S and SE Asia included in the East Indies, India, and Indochina. **2** See **East Indies. 3** See **West Indies.**

indifference (ɪnˈdɪfrəns, -fərəns) *n* **1** the fact or state of being indifferent; lack of care or concern. **2** lack of quality; mediocrity. **3** lack of importance; insignificance.

indifferent (ɪnˈdɪfrənt, -fərənt) *adj* **1** (often foll. by *to*) showing no care or concern; uninterested: *he was indifferent to my pleas.* **2** unimportant; immaterial. **3a** of only average or moderate size, extent, quality, etc. **3b** not at all good; poor. **4** showing or having no preferences; impartial. [C14: from L *indifferēns* making no distinction]
▸ in'differently *adv*

indifferentism (ɪnˈdɪfrənˌtɪzəm, -fərən-) *n* systematic indifference, esp. in matters of religion.
▸ in'differentist *n*

indigenous (ɪnˈdɪdʒɪnəs) *adj* (when *postpositive*, foll. by *to*) **1** originating or occurring naturally (in a country, etc.); native. **2** innate (to); inherent (in). [C17: from L *indigenus*, from *indi-* in + *gignere* to beget]
▸ in'digenously *adv* ▸ in'digenousness *n*

indigent (ˈɪndɪdʒənt) *adj* **1** so poor as to lack even necessities; very needy. **2** (usually foll. by *of*) *Arch.* lacking (in) or destitute (of). ◆ *n* **3** an impoverished person. [C14: from L *indigēre* to need, from *egēre* to lack]
▸ 'indigence *n* ▸ 'indigently *adv*

indigestible (ˌɪndɪˈdʒɛstəbᵊl) *adj* **1** incapable of being digested or difficult to digest. **2** difficult to understand or absorb mentally: *an indigestible book.*
▸ ˌindiˌgesti'bility *n* ▸ ˌindi'gestibly *adv*

indigestion (ˌɪndɪˈdʒɛstʃən) *n* difficulty in digesting food, accompanied by abdominal pain, heartburn, and belching.

indignant (ɪnˈdɪgnənt) *adj* feeling or showing indignation. [C16: from L *indignārī* to be displeased with]
▸ in'dignantly *adv*

indignation (ˌɪndɪgˈneɪʃən) *n* anger aroused by something felt to be unfair, unworthy, or wrong.

indignity (ɪnˈdɪgnɪtɪ) *n, pl* **indignities.** injury to one's self-esteem or dignity; humiliation.

indigo (ˈɪndɪˌgəʊ) *n, pl* **indigos** *or* **indigoes. 1** a blue vat dye originally obtained from plants but now made synthetically. **2** any of various leguminous tropical plants, such as the anil, that yield this dye. **3a** any of a group of colours that have the same blue-violet hue; a spectral colour. **3b** (*as adj*): *an indigo rug.* [C16: from Sp. *indico*, via L from Gk *Indikos* of India]
▸ indigotic (ˌɪndɪˈgɒtɪk) *adj*

indigo blue *n, adj* (**indigo-blue** *when prenominal*). the full name for **indigo** (the colour and the dye).

indirect (ˌɪndɪˈrɛkt) *adj* **1** deviating from a direct course or line; roundabout; circuitous. **2** not coming as a direct effect or consequence; secondary: *indirect benefits.* **3** not straightforward, open, or fair; devious or evasive.
▸ ˌindi'rectly *adv* ▸ ˌindi'rectness *n*

indirect costs *pl n* another name for **overheads.**

indirection (ˌɪndɪˈrɛkʃən) *n* **1** indirect procedure, courses, or methods. **2** lack of direction or purpose; aimlessness. **3** indirect dealing; deceit.

indirect lighting *n* reflected or diffused light from a concealed source.

indirect object *n Grammar.* a noun, pronoun, or noun phrase indicating the recipient or beneficiary of the action of a verb and its direct object, as *John* in the sentence *I bought John a newspaper.*

indirect proof *n Logic, maths.* proof of a conclusion by showing its negation to be self-contradictory. Cf. **direct** (sense 17).

indirect question *n* a question reported in indirect speech, as in *She asked why you came.*

indirect speech *or esp. US* **indirect discourse** *n* the reporting of something said or written by conveying what was meant rather than repeating the exact words, as in the sentence *He said I looked happy* as opposed to *He said to me, "You look happy."* Also called: **reported speech.**

indirect tax *n* a tax levied on goods or services rather than on individuals or companies.

indiscreet (ˌɪndɪˈskriːt) *adj* not discreet; imprudent or tactless.
▸ ˌindis'creetly *adv* ▸ ˌindis'creetness *n*

indiscrete (ˌɪndɪˈskriːt) *adj* not divisible or divided into parts.

indiscretion (ˌɪndɪˈskrɛʃən) *n* **1** the characteristic or state of being indiscreet. **2** an indiscreet act, remark, etc.

indiscriminate (ˌɪndɪˈskrɪmɪnɪt) *adj* **1** lacking discrimination or careful choice; random or promiscuous. **2** jumbled; confused.
▸ ˌindis'criminately *adv* ▸ ˌindis'criminateness *n*
▸ ˌindisˌcrimi'nation *n*

indispensable (ˌɪndɪˈspɛnsəbᵊl) *adj* **1** absolutely necessary; essential. **2** not to be disregarded or escaped: *an indispensable role.* ◆ *n* **3** an indispensable person or thing.
▸ ˌindisˌpensa'bility *or* ˌindis'pensableness *n* ▸ ˌindis'pensably *adv*

indispose (ˌɪndɪˈspəʊz) *vb* **indisposes, indisposing, indisposed.** (*tr*) **1** to make unwilling or opposed; disincline. **2** to cause to feel ill. **3** to make unfit (for something or to do something).

indisposed (ˌɪndɪˈspəʊzd) *adj* **1** sick or ill. **2** unwilling. [C15: from L *indispositus* disordered]
▸ indisposition (ˌɪndɪspəˈzɪʃən) *n*

indisputable (ˌɪndɪˈspjuːtəbᵊl) *adj* beyond doubt; not open to question.
▸ ˌindisˌputa'bility *or* ˌindis'putableness *n* ▸ ˌindis'putably *adv*

★ people and places

indissoluble (ˌɪndɪˈsɒljuˑbəl) *adj* incapable of being dissolved or broken; permanent.
  ▸ ˌindisˈsolubly *adv*

indistinct (ˌɪndɪˈstɪŋkt) *adj* incapable of being clearly distinguished, as by the eyes, ears, or mind; not distinct.
  ▸ ˌindisˈtinctly *adv* ▸ ˌindisˈtinctness *n*

indistinguishable (ˌɪndɪˈstɪŋgwɪʃəbəl) *adj* **1** (*often postpositive*; foll. by *from*) identical or very similar (to): *twins indistinguishable from one another.* **2** not easily perceptible; indiscernible.
  ▸ ˌindisˌtinguishaˈbility *or* ˌindisˈtinguishableness *n*
  ▸ ˌindisˈtinguishably *adv*

indite (ɪnˈdaɪt) *vb* **indites, inditing, indited.** (*tr*) *Arch.* to write. [C14: from OF *enditer*, from L *indīcere* to declare, from IN-² + *dīcere* to say]
  ▸ inˈditement *n* ▸ inˈditer *n*

> **USAGE NOTE** *Indite* and *inditement* are sometimes wrongly used where *indict* and *indictment* are meant: *he was indicted* (not *indited*) *for fraud.*

indium (ˈɪndɪəm) *n* a rare soft silvery metallic element associated with zinc ores: used in alloys, electronics, and electroplating. Symbol: In; atomic no.: 49; atomic wt.: 114.82. [C19: NL, from INDIGO + -IUM]

individual (ˌɪndɪˈvɪdjuəl) *adj* **1** of, relating to, characteristic of, or meant for a single person or thing. **2** separate or distinct, esp. from others of its kind; particular: *please mark the individual pages.* **3** characterized by unusual and striking qualities; distinctive. **4** *Obs.* indivisible; inseparable. ◆ *n* **5** a single person, esp. when regarded as distinct from others. **6** *Biol.* a single animal or plant, esp. as distinct from a species. **7** *Inf.* a person: *a most obnoxious individual.* [C15: from Med. L, from L *indīviduus* indivisible, from IN-¹ + *dīvidere* to DIVIDE]
  ▸ ˌindiˈvidually *adv*

individualism (ˌɪndɪˈvɪdjuəˌlɪzəm) *n* **1** the principle of asserting one's independence and individuality; egoism. **2** an individual quirk. **3** another word for **laissez faire** (sense 1). **4** *Philosophy.* the doctrine that only individual things exist.
  ▸ ˌindiˈvidualist *n*

individuality (ˌɪndɪˌvɪdjuˈælɪtɪ) *n, pl* **individualities. 1** distinctive or unique character or personality: *a work of great individuality.* **2** the qualities that distinguish one person or thing from another; identity. **3** the state or quality of being a separate entity; discreteness.

individualize *or* **individualise** (ˌɪndɪˈvɪdjuəˌlaɪz) *vb* **individualizes, individualizing, individualized** *or* **individualises, individualising, individualised.** (*tr*) **1** to make or mark as individual or distinctive in character. **2** to consider or treat individually; particularize. **3** to make or modify so as to meet the special requirements of a person.
  ▸ ˌindiˌvidualiˈzation *or* ˌindiˌvidualiˈsation *n* ▸ ˌindiˈvidualˌizer *or* ˌindiˈvidualˌiser *n*

individuate (ˌɪndɪˈvɪdjuˌeɪt) *vb* **individuates, individuating, individuated.** (*tr*) **1** to give individuality or an individual form to. **2** to distinguish from others of the same species or group; individualize.
  ▸ ˌindiˈviduˌator *n*

indivisible (ˌɪndɪˈvɪzəbəl) *adj* **1** unable to be divided. **2** *Maths.* leaving a remainder when divided by a given number.
  ▸ ˌindiˌvisiˈbility *n* ▸ ˌindiˈvisibly *adv*

Indo- (ˈɪndəʊ) *combining form.* denoting India or Indian: *Indo-European.*

Indochina *or* **Indo-China** ★ (ˌɪndəʊˈtʃaɪnə) *n* **1** Also called: **Farther India.** a peninsula in SE Asia, between India and China: consists of Myanmar, Thailand, Laos, Cambodia, Vietnam, and Malaysia. **2** the former French colonial possessions of Cochin China, Annam, Tonkin, Laos, and Cambodia.
  ▸ ˈIndochiˈnese *or* ˈIndo-Chiˈnese *adj, n*

indoctrinate (ɪnˈdɒktrɪˌneɪt) *vb* **indoctrinates, indoctrinating, indoctrinated.** (*tr*) **1** to teach (a person or group of peo-

ple) systematically to accept doctrines, esp. uncritically. **2** *Rare.* to instruct.
  ▸ inˌdoctriˈnation *n* ▸ inˈdoctriˌnator *n*

Indo-European *adj* **1** denoting, belonging to, or relating to a family of languages that includes English: characteristically marked, esp. in the older languages, such as Latin, by inflection showing gender, number, and case. **2** denoting or relating to the hypothetical parent language of this family, primitive Indo-European. **3** denoting, belonging to, or relating to any of the peoples speaking these languages. ◆ *n* **4** the Indo-European family of languages. **5** the reconstructed hypothetical parent language of this family. ◆ Also (*obs.*): **Indo-Germanic.**

Indo-Iranian *adj* **1** of or relating to the Indic and Iranian branches of the Indo-European family of languages. ◆ *n* **2** this group of languages, sometimes considered as forming a single branch of Indo-European.

indole (ˈɪndəʊl) *or* **indol** (ˈɪndəʊl, -dɒl) *n* a white or yellowish crystalline heterocyclic compound extracted from coal tar and used in perfumery, medicine, and as a flavouring agent. [C19: from IND(IGO) + -OLE¹]

indolent (ˈɪndələnt) *adj* **1** disliking work or effort; lazy; idle. **2** *Pathol.* causing little pain: *an indolent tumour.* **3** (esp. of a painless ulcer) slow to heal. [C17: from L *indolēns* not feeling pain, from IN-¹ + *dolēre* to grieve, cause distress]
  ▸ ˈindolence *n* ▸ ˈindolently *adv*

indomitable (ɪnˈdɒmɪtəbəl) *adj* (of courage, pride, etc.) difficult or impossible to defeat or subdue. [C17: from LL, from L *indomitus* untameable, from *domāre* to tame]
  ▸ inˌdomitaˈbility *or* inˈdomitableness *n* ▸ inˈdomitably *adv*

Indonesia ★ (ˌɪndəʊˈniːzɪə) *n* a republic in SE Asia, in the Malay Archipelago, consisting of the main islands of Sumatra, Java and Madura, Bali, Sulawesi (Celebes), Lombok, Sumbawa, Flores, the Moluccas, Timor, part of Borneo (Kalimantan), Irian Jaya, and over 3000 small islands in the Indian and Pacific Oceans: became the Dutch East Indies in 1798; declared independence in 1945; became a republic in 1950. Official language: Bahasa Indonesia. Religion: mostly Muslim. Currency: rupiah. Capital: Jakarta. Pop.: 199 544 000 (1997). Area: 1 919 317 sq. km (741 052 sq. miles). Former names (1798–1945): **Dutch East Indies, Netherlands East Indies.**

Indonesian (ˌɪndəʊˈniːzɪən) *adj* **1** of or relating to Indonesia, its people, or their language. ◆ *n* **2** a native or inhabitant of Indonesia.

indoor (ˈɪnˌdɔː) *adj* (*prenominal*) of, situated in, or appropriate to the inside of a house or other building: *an indoor pool; indoor amusements.*

indoors (ˌɪnˈdɔːz) *adv, adj* (*postpositive*) inside or into a house or other building.

Indore ★ (ɪnˈdɔː) *n* **1** a city in central India, in W Madhya Pradesh. Pop.: 1 091 674 (1991). **2** a former state of central India: became part of Madhya Bharat in 1948, which in turn became part of Madhya Pradesh in 1956.

indorse (ɪnˈdɔːs) *vb* **indorses, indorsing, indorsed.** a variant spelling of **endorse.**

Indra ★ (ˈɪndrə) *n Hinduism.* the most celebrated god of the Rig-Veda, governing the weather and dispensing rain.

indraught *or US* **indraft** (ˈɪnˌdrɑːft) *n* **1** the act of drawing or pulling in. **2** an inward flow, esp. of air.

indrawn (ˌɪnˈdrɔːn) *adj* **1** drawn or pulled in. **2** inward-looking or introspective.

Indre ★ (French ɛ̃drə) *n* a department of central France in the Centre region. Capital: Châteauroux. Pop.: 234 531 (1994 est). Area: 6906 sq. km (2693 sq. miles).

Indre-et-Loire ★ (French ɛ̃drelwar) *n* a department of W central France in the Centre region: contains many famous châteaux along the Loire. Capital: Tours. Pop.: 543 973 (1994 est.). Area: 6158 sq. km (2402 sq. miles).

indris (ˈɪndrɪs) *or* **indri** (ˈɪndrɪ) *n, pl* **indris. 1** a large Madagascan arboreal lemuroid primate with thick silky fur patterned in black, white, and fawn. **2** **woolly indris.** a related nocturnal Madagascan animal with thick grey-brown fur and a long tail. [C19: from F: lemur, from native word *indry!* look! mistaken for the animal's name]

indubitable (ɪnˈdjuːbɪtəbªl) *adj* incapable of being doubted; unquestionable. [C18: from L, from IN-[1] + *dubitāre* to doubt]
▸ in'**dubitably** *adv*

induce (ɪnˈdjuːs) *vb* **induces, inducing, induced.** (*tr*) **1** (often foll. by an infinitive) to persuade or use influence on. **2** to cause or bring about. **3** *Med.* to initiate or hasten (labour), as by administering a drug to stimulate uterine contractions. **4** *Logic, obs.* to assert or establish (a general proposition, etc.) by induction. **5** to produce (an electromotive force or electrical current) by induction. **6** to transmit (magnetism) by induction. [C14: from L *indūcere* to lead in]
▸ in'**ducer** *n* ▸ in'**ducible** *adj*

inducement (ɪnˈdjuːsmənt) *n* **1** the act of inducing. **2** a means of inducing; persuasion; incentive. **3** *Law.* the introductory part that leads up to and explains the matter in dispute.

induct (ɪnˈdʌkt) *vb* (*tr*) **1** to bring in formally or install in an office, place, etc.; invest. **2** (foll. by *into*) to initiate in knowledge (of). **3** *US.* to enlist for military service. **4** *Physics.* another word for **induce** (senses 5, 6). [C14: from L *inductus* led in, p.p. of *indūcere* to introduce; see IN-DUCE]

inductance (ɪnˈdʌktəns) *n* **1** the property of an electric circuit as a result of which an electromotive force is created by a change of current in the same or in a neighbouring circuit. **2** a component, such as a coil, in an electrical circuit, the main function of which is to produce inductance.

induction (ɪnˈdʌkʃən) *n* **1** the act of inducting or state of being inducted. **2** the act of inducing. **3** (in an internal-combustion engine) the drawing in of mixed air and fuel from the carburettor to the cylinder. **4** *Logic.* **4a** a process of reasoning by which a general conclusion is drawn from a set of premises, based mainly on experience or experimental evidence. **4b** a conclusion reached by this process of reasoning. **5** the process by which electrical or magnetic properties are transferred, without physical contact, from one circuit or body to another. See also **inductance**. **6** *Maths.* a method of proving a proposition P(n) by showing that it is true for all preceding values of n and for $n + 1$. **7a** a formal introduction or entry into an office or position. **7b** (*as modifier*): induction course. **8** *US.* the enlistment of a civilian into military service.
▸ in'**ductional** *adj*

induction coil *n* **1** any coil of wire used to introduce inductance into a circuit. **2** another name for **ignition coil**.

induction heating *n* the heating of a conducting material as a result of the electric currents induced in it by an externally applied alternating magnetic field.

induction loop system *n* an electronic system enabling partially deaf people to hear dialogue and sound in theatres, cinemas, etc. Often shortened to **induction loop.**

induction motor *n* a type of electric motor in which an alternating supply fed to the windings of the stator creates a magnetic field that induces a current in the windings of the rotor. Rotation of the rotor results from the interaction of the magnetic field created by the rotor current with the field of the stator.

inductive (ɪnˈdʌktɪv) *adj* **1** relating to or operated by electrical or magnetic induction: *an inductive reactance.* **2** *Logic, maths.* of, relating to, or using induction: *inductive reasoning.* **3** serving to induce or cause.
▸ in'**ductively** *adv* ▸ in'**ductiveness** *n*

inductor (ɪnˈdʌktə) *n* **1** a person or thing that inducts. **2** another name for an **inductance** (sense 2).

indue (ɪnˈdjuː) *vb* **indues, induing, indued.** a variant spelling of **endue.**

indulge (ɪnˈdʌldʒ) *vb* **indulges, indulging, indulged. 1** (when *intr*, often foll. by *in*) to yield to or gratify (a whim or desire for): *to indulge in new clothes.* **2** (*tr*) to yield to the wishes of; pamper: *to indulge a child.* **3** (*tr*) to allow (oneself) the pleasure of something: *he indulged himself.* **4**

(*intr*) *Inf.* to take alcoholic drink, esp. to excess. [C17: from L *indulgēre* to concede]
▸ in'**dulger** *n* ▸ in'**dulgingly** *adv*

indulgence (ɪnˈdʌldʒəns) *n* **1** the act of indulging or state of being indulgent. **2** a pleasure, habit, etc., indulged in; extravagance. **3** liberal or tolerant treatment. **4** something granted as a favour or privilege. **5** *RC Church.* a remission of the temporal punishment for sin after its guilt has been forgiven. **6** Also called: **Declaration of Indulgence.** a royal grant during the reigns of Charles II and James II of England giving Nonconformists and Roman Catholics a measure of religious freedom.

indulgent (ɪnˈdʌldʒənt) *adj* showing or characterized by indulgence.
▸ in'**dulgently** *adv*

induna (ɪnˈduːnə) *n* (in South Africa) a Black African overseer in a factory, mine, etc. [C20: from Zulu *nduna* an official]

indurate *vb* (ˈɪndjʊˌreɪt), **indurates, indurating, indurated. 1** to make or become hard or callous. **2** to make or become hardy. ◆ *adj* (ˈɪndjʊrɪt). **3** hardened, callous, or unfeeling. [C16: from L *indūrāre* to make hard; see ENDURE]
▸ ˌindu'**ration** *n* ▸ ˈindu,**rative** *adj*

Indus ★ (ˈɪndəs) *n* a river in S Asia, rising in SW Tibet in the Kailas Range of the Himalayas and flowing northwest through Kashmir, then southwest across Pakistan to the Arabian Sea: important throughout history, esp. for the Indus Civilization (about 3000 to 1500 B.C.), and for irrigation. Length: about 2900 km (1800 miles).

indusium (ɪnˈdjuːzɪəm) *n, pl* **indusia** (-zɪə). **1** a membranous outgrowth on the undersurface of fern leaves that protects the developing spores. **2** an enveloping membrane, such as the amnion. [C18: NL, from L: tunic, from *induere* to put on]
▸ in'**dusial** *adj*

industrial (ɪnˈdʌstrɪəl) *adj* **1** of, relating to, or derived from industry. **2** employed in industry: *the industrial workforce.* **3** relating to or concerned with workers in industry: *industrial conditions.* **4** used in industry: *industrial chemicals.*
▸ in'**dustrially** *adv*

industrial action *n Brit.* any action, such as a strike or go-slow, taken by employees in industry to protest against working conditions, etc.

industrial archaeology *n* the study of industrial machines, works, etc. of the past.

industrial design *n* the art or practice of designing any object for manufacture.
▸ **industrial designer** *n*

industrial diamond *n* a small often synthetic diamond, valueless as a gemstone, used in cutting tools, abrasives, etc.

industrial disease *n* any disease to which workers in a particular industry are prone.

industrial espionage *n* attempting to obtain trade secrets by dishonest means, as by telephone- or computer-tapping, infiltration of a competitor's workforce, etc.

industrial estate *n Brit.* another name for **trading estate.** US equivalent: **industrial park.**

industrialism (ɪnˈdʌstrɪəˌlɪzəm) *n* an organization of society characterized by large-scale mechanized manufacturing industry rather than trade, farming, etc.

industrialist (ɪnˈdʌstrɪəlɪst) *n* a person who has a substantial interest in the ownership or control of industrial enterprise.

industrialize *or* **industrialise** (ɪnˈdʌstrɪəˌlaɪz) *vb* **dustrializes, industrializing, industrialized** *or* **industrialises, industrialising, industrialised. 1** (*tr*) to develop industry on an extensive scale in (a country, region, etc.). **2** (*intr*) (of a country, region, etc.) to undergo the development of industry on an extensive scale.
▸ in,**dustriali'zation** *or* in,**dustriali'sation** *n*

industrial medicine *n* the study and practice of the health care of employees of large organizations.

industrial relations *n* **1** (*functioning as pl*) relations between the employers and employees in an industrial enterprise. **2** (*functioning as sing*) the management of such relations.

Industrial Revolution *n* **the.** the transformation in the 18th and 19th centuries of Britain and other countries into industrial nations.

industrial tribunal *n* a tribunal that rules on disputes between employers and employees regarding unfair dismissal, redundancy, etc.

industrious (ɪn'dʌstrɪəs) *adj* hard-working, diligent, or assiduous.
 ▶ in'dustriously *adv* ▶ in'dustriousness *n*

industry ('ɪndəstrɪ) *n, pl* **industries. 1** organized economic activity concerned with manufacture, processing of raw materials, or construction. **2** a branch of commercial enterprise concerned with the output of a specified product: *the steel industry*. **3a** industrial ownership and management interests collectively. **3b** manufacturing enterprise collectively, as opposed to agriculture. **4** diligence; assiduity. [C15: from L *industria* diligence, from *industrius* active, from ?]

indwell (ɪn'dwɛl) *vb* **indwells, indwelling, indwelt. 1** (*tr*) (of a spirit, principle, etc.) to inhabit; suffuse. **2** (*intr*) to dwell; exist.
 ▶ in'dweller *n*

Indy, d' ★ (*French* dēdi) *n* Vincent (vɛ̃sā). See (Vincent) **d'Indy**.

Ine ★ ('ɪnə, 'ɪnɪ) *n* died after 726, king of Wessex (688–726).

-ine[1] *suffix forming adjectives.* **1** of, relating to, or belonging to: *saturnine*. **2** consisting of or resembling: *crystalline*. [from L *-īnus*, from Gk *-inos*]

-ine[2] *suffix forming nouns.* **1** indicating a halogen: *chlorine*. **2** indicating a nitrogenous organic compound, including amino acids, alkaloids, and certain other bases: *nicotine*. **3** Also: **-in.** indicating a chemical substance in certain nonsystematic names: *glycerine*. **4** indicating a mixture of hydrocarbons: *benzine*. **5** indicating feminine form: *heroine*. [via F from L *-ina* (from *-inus*) and Gk *-inē*]

inebriate *vb* (ɪn'iːbrɪˌeɪt), **inebriates, inebriating, inebriated.** (*tr*) **1** to make drunk; intoxicate. **2** to arouse emotionally; make excited. ◆ *n* (ɪn'iːbrɪt). **3** a person who is drunk, esp. habitually. ◆ *adj* (ɪn'iːbrɪt), *also* **inebriated. 4** drunk, esp. habitually. [C15: from L, from IN-[2] + *ēbriāre* to intoxicate, from *ēbrius* drunk]
 ▶ in'ebri'ation *n* ▶ in'ebriety (ˌɪnɪ'braɪɪtɪ) *n*

inedible (ɪn'ɛdɪb°l) *adj* not fit to be eaten.
 ▶ in,edi'bility *n*

ineducable (ɪn'ɛdjʊkəb°l) *adj* incapable of being educated, esp. on account of mental retardation.
 ▶ in,educa'bility *n*

ineffable (ɪn'ɛfəb°l) *adj* **1** too great or intense to be expressed in words; unutterable. **2** too sacred to be uttered. **3** indescribable; indefinable. [C15: from L, from IN-[1] + *effābilis*, from *fārī* to speak]
 ▶ in,effa'bility *or* in'effableness *n* ▶ in'effably *adv*

ineffective (ˌɪnɪ'fɛktɪv) *adj* **1** having no effect. **2** incompetent or inefficient.
 ▶ ,inef'fectively *adv* ▶ ,inef'fectiveness *n*

ineffectual (ˌɪnɪ'fɛktjʊəl) *adj* **1** having no effect or an inadequate effect. **2** lacking in power or forcefulness; impotent: *an ineffectual ruler.*
 ▶ ,inef,fectu'ality *or* ,inef'fectualness *n* ▶ ,inef'fectually *adv*

inefficacious (ˌɪnɛfɪ'keɪʃəs) *adj* failing to produce the desired effect.
 ▶ ,ineffi'caciously *adv* ▶ **inefficacy** (ɪn'ɛfɪkəsɪ), ,ineffi-'caciousness, *or* **inefficacity** (ˌɪnɛfɪ'kæsɪtɪ) *n*

inefficient (ˌɪnɪ'fɪʃənt) *adj* **1** unable to perform a task or function to the best advantage; wasteful or incompetent. **2** unable to produce the desired result.
 ▶ ,inef'ficiency *n* ▶ ,inef'ficiently *adv*

ineligible (ɪn'ɛlɪdʒəb°l) *adj* (often foll. by *for* or an infinitive) not fit or qualified: *ineligible for a grant; ineligible to vote*. ◆ *n* **2** an ineligible person.
 ▶ in,eligi'bility *or* in'eligibleness *n* ▶ in'eligibly *adv*

ineluctable (ˌɪnɪ'lʌktəb°l) *adj* (esp. of fate) incapable of

being avoided; inescapable. [C17: from L, from IN-[1] + *ēluctārī* to escape, from *luctārī* to struggle]
 ▶ ,ine,lucta'bility *n* ▶ ,ine'luctably *adv*

inept (ɪn'ɛpt) *adj* **1** awkward, clumsy, or incompetent. **2** not suitable, appropriate, or fitting; out of place. [C17: from L *ineptus*, from IN-[1] + *aptus* fitting]
 ▶ in'epti,tude *n* ▶ in'eptly *adv* ▶ in'eptness *n*

inequable (ɪn'ɛkwəb°l) *adj* **1** uneven. **2** not uniform. **3** changeable.

inequality (ˌɪnɪ'kwɒlɪtɪ) *n, pl* **inequalities. 1** the state or quality of being unequal; disparity. **2** an instance of disparity. **3** lack of smoothness or regularity. **4** social or economic disparity. **5** *Maths.* **5a** a statement indicating that the value of one quantity or expression is not equal to another. **5b** the relation of being unequal. **6** *Astron.* a departure from uniform orbital motion.

inert (ɪn'ɜːt) *adj* **1** having no inherent ability to move or to resist motion. **2** inactive, lazy, or sluggish. **3** having only a limited ability to react chemically; unreactive. [C17: from L *iners* unskilled, from IN-[1] + *ars* skill; see ART[1]]
 ▶ in'ertly *adv* ▶ in'ertness *n*

inert gas *n* **1** any of the unreactive gaseous elements helium, neon, argon, krypton, xenon, and radon. **2** (loosely) any gas, such as carbon dioxide, that is nonoxidizing.

inertia (ɪn'ɜːʃə, -ʃɪə) *n* **1** the state of being inert; disinclination to move or act. **2** *Physics.* **2a** the tendency of a body to preserve its state of rest or uniform motion unless acted upon by an external force. **2b** an analogous property of other physical quantities that resist change: *thermal inertia.*
 ▶ in'ertial *adj*

inertial guidance *or* **navigation** *n* a method of controlling the flight path of a missile by instruments contained within it.

inertial mass *n* the mass of a body as determined by its momentum, as opposed to the extent to which it responds to the force of gravity. Cf. **gravitational mass.**

inertia-reel seat belt *n* a type of car seat belt in which the belt is free to unwind from a metal drum except when the drum locks as a result of rapid change of velocity.

inertia selling *n* the illegal practice of sending unrequested goods to householders, followed by a bill for the goods if they do not return them.

inescapable (ˌɪnɪ'skeɪpəb°l) *adj* incapable of being escaped or avoided.
 ▶ ,ines'capably *adv*

inestimable (ɪn'ɛstɪməb°l) *adj* **1** not able to be estimated; immeasurable. **2** of immeasurable value.
 ▶ in,estima'bility *or* in'estimableness *n* ▶ in'estimably *adv*

inevitable (ɪn'ɛvɪtəb°l) *adj* **1** unavoidable. **2** sure to happen; certain. ◆ *n* **3** (often preceded by *the*) something that is unavoidable. [C15: from L, from IN-[1] + *ēvītāre* to shun, from *vītāre* to avoid]
 ▶ in,evita'bility *or* in'evitableness *n* ▶ in'evitably *adv*

inexcusable (ˌɪnɪk'skjuːzəb°l) *adj* not able to be excused or justified.
 ▶ ,inex,cusa'bility *or* ,inex'cusableness *n* ▶ ,inex'cusably *adv*

inexhaustible (ˌɪnɪg'zɔːstəb°l) *adj* **1** incapable of being used up; endless. **2** incapable or apparently incapable of becoming tired; tireless.
 ▶ ,inex,hausti'bility *n* ▶ ,inex'haustibly *adv*

inexorable (ɪn'ɛksərəb°l) *adj* **1** not able to be moved by entreaty or persuasion. **2** relentless. [C16: from L, from IN-[1] + *exōrāre* to prevail upon, from *ōrāre* to pray]
 ▶ in,exora'bility *n* ▶ in'exorably *adv*

inexpensive (ˌɪnɪk'spɛnsɪv) *adj* not expensive; cheap.
 ▶ ,inex'pensively *adv* ▶ ,inex'pensiveness *n*

inexperience (ˌɪnɪk'spɪərɪəns) *n* lack of experience or of the knowledge and understanding derived from experience.
 ▶ ,inex'perienced *adj*

inexpiable (ɪn'ɛkspɪəb°l) *adj* **1** incapable of being expiated; unpardonable. **2** *Arch.* implacable.
 ▶ in'expiableness *n*

inexplicable (ˌɪnɪkˈsplɪkəb°l, ɪnˈɛksplɪkəb°l) *adj* not capable of explanation; unexplained.
▸ ˌinexplicaˈbility *n* ▸ ˌinexˈplicably *adv*

in extenso *Latin.* (ɪn ɪkˈstɛnsəʊ) *adv* at full length.

in extremis *Latin.* (ɪn ɪkˈstriːmɪs) *adv* **1** in extremity; in dire straits. **2** at the point of death. [lit.: in the furthest reaches]

inextricable (ˌɪnɛksˈtrɪkəb°l) *adj* **1** not able to be escaped from: *an inextricable dilemma.* **2** not able to be disentangled, etc.: *an inextricable knot.* **3** extremely involved or intricate.
▸ ˌinextricaˈbility *or* ˌinexˈtricableness *n* ▸ ˌinexˈtricably *adv*

inf. *abbrev. for:* **1** *Also:* **Inf.** infantry. **2** inferior. **3** infinitive. **4** informal. **5** information.

infallible (ɪnˈfæləb°l) *adj* **1** not fallible; not liable to error. **2** not liable to failure; certain; sure: *an infallible cure.* ◆ *n* **3** a person or thing that is incapable of error or failure.
▸ inˌfalliˈbility *or* inˈfallibleness *n* ▸ inˈfallibly *adv*

infamous (ˈɪnfəməs) *adj* **1** having a bad reputation; notorious. **2** causing or deserving a bad reputation; shocking: *infamous conduct.*
▸ ˈinfamously *adv* ▸ ˈinfamousness *n*

infamy (ˈɪnfəmɪ) *n, pl* **infamies. 1** the state or condition of being infamous. **2** an infamous act or event. [C15: from L *infāmis* of evil repute, from IN-[1] + *fāma* FAME]

infancy (ˈɪnfənsɪ) *n, pl* **infancies. 1** the state or period of being an infant; childhood. **2** an early stage of growth or development. **3** infants collectively. **4** the period of life prior to attaining legal majority; minority nonage.

infant (ˈɪnfənt) *n* **1** a child at the earliest stage of its life; baby. **2** *Law.* another word for **minor** (sense 9). **3** *Brit.* a young schoolchild. **4** a person who is beginning or inexperienced in an activity. **5** (*modifier*) **5a** of or relating to young children or infancy. **5b** designed or intended for young children. ◆ *adj* **6** in an early stage of development; nascent: *an infant science.* **7** *Law.* of or relating to the legal status of infancy. [C14: from L *infāns*, lit.: speechless, from IN-[1] + *fārī* to speak]
▸ ˈinfantˌhood *n*

infanta (ɪnˈfæntə) *n* (formerly) **1** a daughter of a king of Spain or Portugal. **2** the wife of an infante. [C17: from Sp. or Port., fem of INFANTE]

infante (ɪnˈfæntɪ) *n* (formerly) a son of a king of Spain or Portugal, esp. one not heir to the throne. [C16: from Sp. or Port., lit.: INFANT]

infanticide (ɪnˈfæntɪˌsaɪd) *n* **1** the killing of an infant. **2** the practice of killing newborn infants, still prevalent in some primitive tribes. **3** a person who kills an infant.
▸ inˌfantiˈcidal *adj*

infantile (ˈɪnfənˌtaɪl) *adj* **1** like a child in action or behaviour; childishly immature; puerile. **2** of, relating to, or characteristic of infants or infancy. **3** in an early stage of development.
▸ infantility (ˌɪnfənˈtɪlɪtɪ) *n*

infantile paralysis *n* a former name for **poliomyelitis.**

infantilism (ɪnˈfæntɪˌlɪzəm) *n* **1** *Psychol.* a condition in which an older child or adult is mentally or physically undeveloped. **2** childish speech; baby talk.

infantry (ˈɪnfəntrɪ) *n, pl* **infantries. a** soldiers or units of soldiers who fight on foot with small arms. **b** (*as modifier*): *an infantry unit.* [C16: from It. *infanteria*, from *infante* boy, foot soldier; see INFANT]

infantryman (ˈɪnfəntrɪmən) *n, pl* **infantrymen. a** soldier belonging to the infantry.

infant school *n* (in England and Wales) a school for children aged between 5 and 7.

infarct (ɪnˈfɑːkt) *n* a localized area of dead tissue resulting from obstruction of the blood supply to that part. *Also called:* **infarction.** [C19: via NL from L *infarctus* stuffed into, from *farcīre* to stuff]
▸ inˈfarcted *adj*

infatuate *vb* (ɪnˈfætjʊˌeɪt), **infatuates, infatuating, infatuated.** (*tr*) **1** to inspire or fill with foolish, shallow, or extravagant passion. **2** to cause to act foolishly. ◆ *n* (ɪnˈfætjʊɪt,

-ˌeɪt). **3** *Literary.* a person who is infatuated. [C16: from L *infatuāre*, from IN-[2] + *fatuus* FATUOUS]
▸ inˌfatuˈation *n*

infatuated (ɪnˈfætjʊˌeɪtɪd) *adj* (often foll. by *with*) possessed by a foolish or extravagant passion, esp. for another person.

infect (ɪnˈfɛkt) *vb* (*mainly tr*) **1** to cause infection in; contaminate (an organism, wound, etc.) with pathogenic microorganisms. **2** (*also intr*) to affect or become affected with a communicable disease. **3** to taint, pollute, or contaminate. **4** to affect, esp. adversely, as if by contagion. **5** (*also intr*) *Computing.* to affect or become affected with a computer virus. ◆ *adj* **6** *Arch.* contaminated or polluted with or as if with a disease; infected. [C14: from L *inficere* to dip into, stain, from *facere* to make]
▸ inˈfector *or* inˈfecter *n*

infection (ɪnˈfɛkʃən) *n* **1** invasion of the body by pathogenic microorganisms. **2** the resulting condition in the tissues. **3** an infectious disease. **4** the act of infecting or state of being infected. **5** an agent or influence that infects. **6** persuasion or corruption, as by ideas, perverse influences, etc.

infectious (ɪnˈfɛkʃəs) *adj* **1** (of a disease) capable of being transmitted. **2** (of a disease) caused by microorganisms, such as bacteria, viruses, or protozoa. **3** causing or transmitting infection. **4** tending or apt to spread, as from one person to another: *infectious mirth.*
▸ inˈfectiously *adv* ▸ inˈfectiousness *n*

infectious hepatitis *n* any form of hepatitis caused by viruses. See **hepatitis A, hepatitis B, non-A, non-B hepatitis.**

infectious mononucleosis *n* an acute infectious disease, caused by a virus (**Epstein-Barr virus**), characterized by fever, sore throat, swollen and painful lymph nodes, and abnormal lymphocytes in the blood. *Also called:* **glandular fever.**

infective (ɪnˈfɛktɪv) *adj* **1** capable of causing infection. **2** a less common word for **infectious.**
▸ inˈfectively *adv* ▸ inˈfectiveness *n*

infelicity (ˌɪnfɪˈlɪsɪtɪ) *n, pl* **infelicities. 1** unhappiness; misfortune. **2** an instance of bad luck or mischance. **3** something, esp. a remark or expression, that is inapt or inappropriate.
▸ ˌinfeˈlicitous *adj*

infer (ɪnˈfɜː) *vb* **infers, inferring, inferred.** (when *tr, may take a clause as object*) **1** to conclude (a state of affairs, supposition, etc.) by reasoning from evidence; deduce. **2** (*tr*) to have or lead to as a necessary or logical consequence; indicate. **3** (*tr*) to hint or imply. [C16: from L *inferre* to bring into, from *ferre* to bear, carry]
▸ inˈferable *or* inˈferrable *adj* ▸ inˈferrer *n*

> **USAGE NOTE** The use of *infer* to mean *imply* is common in both speech and writing, but is regarded by many people as incorrect.

inference (ˈɪnfərəns, -frəns) *n* **1** the act or process of inferring. **2** an inferred conclusion, deduction, etc. **3** process of reasoning from premises to a conclusion. **4** *Logic.* the specific mode of reasoning used.

inferential (ˌɪnfəˈrɛnʃəl) *adj* of, relating to, or derived from inference.
▸ ˌinferˈentially *adv*

inferior (ɪnˈfɪərɪə) *adj* **1** lower in value or quality. **2** lower in rank, position, or status; subordinate. **3** not of the best; mediocre; commonplace. **4** lower in position; situated beneath. **5** (of a plant ovary) situated below the other floral parts. **6** *Astron.* orbiting between the sun and the earth: *an inferior planet.* **6b** lying below the horizon. **7** *Printing.* (of a character) printed at the foot of an ordinary character. ◆ *n* **8** an inferior person. **9** *Printing.* an inferior character. [C15: from L: lower, from *inferus* low]
▸ inferiority (ɪnˌfɪərɪˈɒrɪtɪ) *n* ▸ inˈferiorly *adv*

inferiority complex *n* *Psychiatry.* a disorder arising from the conflict between the desire to be noticed and the fear of being humiliated, characterized by aggressiveness or withdrawal into oneself.

★ people and places

nfernal (ɪnˈfɜːnᵊl) *adj* **1** of or relating to an underworld of the dead. **2** deserving or befitting hell; diabolic; fiendish. **3** *Inf.* irritating; confounded. [C14: from LL, from *infernus* hell, from L (adj): lower, hellish; rel. to L *inferus* low]
▶ ˌinferˈnality *n* ▶ inˈfernally *adv*

nfernal machine *n Arch.* an explosive device (usually disguised) or booby trap.

nferno (ɪnˈfɜːnəʊ) *n, pl* **infernos. 1** (*sometimes cap.*; usually preceded by *the*) hell; the infernal region. **2** any place or state resembling hell, esp. a conflagration. [C19: from It., from LL *infernus* hell]

nfertile (ɪnˈfɜːtaɪl) *adj* **1** not capable of producing offspring; sterile. **2** (of land) not productive; barren.
▶ inˈfertilely *adv* ▶ **infertility** (ˌɪnfəˈtɪlɪtɪ) *n*

nfest (ɪnˈfɛst) *vb* (*tr*) **1** to inhabit or overrun in unpleasantly large numbers. **2** (of parasites such as lice) to invade and live on or in (a host). [C15: from L *infestāre* to molest, from *infestus* hostile]
▶ ˌinfesˈtation *n* ▶ inˈfester *n*

nfeudation (ˌɪnfjuˈdeɪʃən) *n History.* **1** (in feudal society) the act of putting a vassal in possession of a fief. **2** the granting of tithes to laymen.

infidel (ˈɪnfɪdᵊl) *n* **1** a person who has no religious belief; unbeliever. ◆ *adj* **2** rejecting a specific religion, esp. Christianity or Islam. **3** of or relating to unbelievers or unbelief. [C15: from Med. L, from L (adj): unfaithful, from IN-¹ + *fidēlis* faithful; see FEALTY]

infidelity (ˌɪnfɪˈdɛlɪtɪ) *n, pl* **infidelities. 1** lack of faith or constancy, esp. sexual faithfulness. **2** lack of religious faith; disbelief. **3** an act or instance of disloyalty.

infield (ˈɪnˌfiːld) *n* **1** *Cricket.* the area of the field near the pitch. Cf. **outfield** (sense 1). **2** *Baseball.* the area of the playing field enclosed by the base lines. **3** *Agriculture.* the part of a farm nearest to the farm buildings.
▶ ˈinˌfielder *n*

infighting (ˈɪnˌfaɪtɪŋ) *n* **1** *Boxing.* combat at close quarters in which proper blows are inhibited. **2** intense competition, as between members of an organization.
▶ ˈinˌfighter *n*

infill (ˈɪnfɪl) *or* **infilling** (ˈɪnfɪlɪŋ) *n* **1** the act of filling or closing gaps, etc., in something, such as a row of buildings. **2** material used to fill a cavity, gap, hole, etc.

infiltrate (ˈɪnfɪlˌtreɪt) *vb* **infiltrates, infiltrating, infiltrated. 1** to undergo the process in which a fluid passes into the pores or interstices of a solid; permeate. **2** *Mil.* to pass undetected through (an enemy-held line or position). **3** to gain or cause to gain entrance or access surreptitiously: *they infiltrated the party structure.* ◆ *n* **4** something that infiltrates. [C18: from IN-² + FILTRATE]
▶ ˌinfilˈtration *n* ▶ ˈinfilˌtrative *adj* ▶ ˈinfilˌtrator *n*

infin. *abbrev.* for infinitive.

infinite (ˈɪnfɪnɪt) *adj* **1a** having no limits or boundaries in time, space, extent, or magnitude. **1b** (*as n*; preceded by *the*): *the infinite.* **2** extremely or immeasurably great or numerous: *infinite wealth.* **3** all-embracing, absolute, or total: *God's infinite wisdom.* **4** *Maths.* having an unlimited or uncountable number of digits, factors, terms, etc.
▶ ˈinfinitely *adv* ▶ ˈinfiniteness *n*

infinitesimal (ˌɪnfɪnɪˈtɛsɪməl) *adj* **1** infinitely or immeasurably small. **2** *Maths.* of, relating to, or involving a small change in the value of a variable that approaches zero as a limit. ◆ *n* **3** *Maths.* an infinitesimal quantity.
▶ ˌinfiniˈtesimally *adv*

infinitesimal calculus *n* another name for **calculus** (sense 1).

infinitive (ɪnˈfɪnɪtɪv) *n Grammar.* a form of the verb not inflected for grammatical categories such as tense and person and used without an overt subject. In English, the infinitive usually consists of the word *to* followed by the verb.
▶ **infinitival** (ˌɪnfɪnɪˈtaɪvᵊl) *adj* ▶ inˈfinitively *or* ˌinfiˈnitively *adv*

infinitude (ɪnˈfɪnɪˌtjuːd) *n* **1** the state or quality of being infinite. **2** an infinite extent, quantity, degree, etc.

infinity (ɪnˈfɪnɪtɪ) *n, pl* **infinities. 1** the state or quality of being infinite. **2** endless time, space, or quantity. **3** an in-

finitely or indefinitely great number or amount. **4** *Maths.* **4a** the concept of a value greater than any finite numerical value. **4b** the reciprocal of zero. **4c** the limit of an infinite sequence of numbers.

infirm (ɪnˈfɜːm) *adj* **1a** weak in health or body, esp. from old age. **1b** (*as collective n*; preceded by *the*): *the infirm.* **2** lacking moral certainty; indecisive or irresolute. **3** not stable, sound, or secure: *an infirm structure.* **4** *Law.* (of a law, etc.) lacking legal force; invalid.
▶ inˈfirmly *adv* ▶ inˈfirmness *n*

infirmary (ɪnˈfɜːmərɪ) *n, pl* **infirmaries.** a place for the treatment of the sick or injured; hospital.

infirmity (ɪnˈfɜːmɪtɪ) *n, pl* **infirmities. 1** the state or quality of being infirm. **2** physical weakness or debility; frailty. **3** a moral flaw or failing.

infix *vb* (ɪnˈfɪks, ˈɪnˌfɪks). **1** (*tr*) to fix firmly in. **2** (*tr*) to instil or inculcate. **3** *Grammar.* to insert (an affix) into the middle of a word. ◆ *n* (ˈɪnˌfɪks). **4** *Grammar.* an affix inserted into the middle of a word.
▶ ˌinfixˈation *or* infixion (ɪnˈfɪkʃən) *n*

in flagrante delicto (ɪn fləˈɡrænti dɪˈlɪktəʊ) *adv Chiefly law.* while committing the offence; red-handed. Also: **flagrante delicto.** [L, lit.: with the crime still blazing]

inflame (ɪnˈfleɪm) *vb* **inflames, inflaming, inflamed. 1** to arouse or become aroused to violent emotion. **2** (*tr*) to increase or intensify; aggravate. **3** to produce inflammation in (a tissue, organ, or part) or (of a tissue, etc.) to become inflamed. **4** to set or be set on fire. **5** (*tr*) to cause to redden.
▶ inˈflamer *n*

inflammable (ɪnˈflæməbᵊl) *adj* **1** liable to catch fire; flammable. **2** readily aroused to anger or passion. ◆ *n* **3** something that is liable to catch fire.
▶ inˌflammaˈbility *or* inˈflammableness *n* ▶ inˈflammably *adv*

USAGE NOTE See at **flammable.**

---

inflammation (ˌɪnfləˈmeɪʃən) *n* **1** the reaction of living tissue to injury or infection, characterized by heat, redness, swelling, and pain. **2** the act of inflaming or the state of being inflamed.

inflammatory (ɪnˈflæmətərɪ, -trɪ) *adj* **1** characterized by or caused by inflammation. **2** tending to arouse violence, strong emotion, etc.
▶ inˈflammatorily *adv*

inflatable (ɪnˈfleɪtəbᵊl) *n* **1** any of various large air-filled objects made of strong plastic or rubber. ◆ *adj* **2** capable of being inflated.

inflate (ɪnˈfleɪt) *vb* **inflates, inflating, inflated. 1** to expand or cause to expand by filling with gas or air. **2** (*tr*) to cause to increase excessively; puff up; swell: *to inflate one's opinion of oneself.* **3** (*tr*) to cause inflation of (prices, money, etc.). **4** (*tr*) to raise in spirits; elate. **5** (*intr*) to undergo economic inflation. [C16: from L *inflāre* to blow into, from *flāre* to blow]
▶ inˈflatedly *adv* ▶ inˈflatedness *n* ▶ inˈflater *or* inˈflator *n*

inflation (ɪnˈfleɪʃən) *n* **1** the act of inflating or state of being inflated. **2** *Econ.* a progressive increase in the general level of prices brought about by an expansion in demand or the money supply or by autonomous increases in costs. Cf. **reflation. 3** *Inf.* the rate of increase of prices. **4** *Astron.* a very fast expansion of the universe occurring immediately after the big bang, postulated in certain models of the universe (**inflationary universes**) to account for the present distribution of matter.
▶ inˈflationary *adj*

inflationary spiral *n* a self-sustaining form of inflation in which a rise in prices generates a wage demand, causing a further price rise and a further wage demand.

inflationism (ɪnˈfleɪʃəˌnɪzəm) *n* the policy of inflation through expansion of the supply of money and credit.
▶ inˈflationist *n, adj*

inflect (ɪnˈflɛkt) *vb* **1** *Grammar.* to change (the form of a word) by inflection. **2** (*tr*) to change (the voice) in tone or pitch; modulate. **3** (*tr*) to cause to deviate from a

straight or normal line or course; bend. [C15: from L *inflectere* to curve round, alter, from *flectere* to bend]
▸ in'flectedness *n* ▸ in'flective *adj* ▸ in'flector *n*

inflection *or* **inflexion** (ɪnˈflɛkʃən) *n* **1** modulation of the voice. **2** *Grammar.* a change in the form of a word, signalling change in such grammatical functions as tense, person, gender, number, or case. **3** an angle or bend. **4** the act of inflecting or the state of being inflected. **5** *Maths.* a change in curvature from concave to convex or vice versa.
▸ in'flectional *or* in'flexional *adj* ▸ in'flectionally *or* in-'flexionally *adv* ▸ in'flectionless *or* in'flexionless *adj*

inflexible (ɪnˈflɛksəbᵊl) *adj* **1** not flexible; rigid; stiff. **2** obstinate; unyielding. **3** without variation; unalterable; fixed. [C14: from L *inflexībilis*; see INFLECT]
▸ in,flexi'bility *or* in'flexibleness *n* ▸ in'flexibly *adv*

inflict (ɪnˈflɪkt) *vb* (*tr*) **1** (often foll. by *on* or *upon*) to impose (something unwelcome, such as pain, oneself, etc.). **2** to deal out (blows, lashes, etc.). [C16: from L *inflīgere* to strike (something) against, dash against, from *flīgere* to strike]
▸ in'flictable *adj* ▸ in'flicter *or* in'flictor *n* ▸ in'fliction *n*

in-flight *adj* provided during flight in an aircraft: *in-flight entertainment.*

inflorescence (ˌɪnflɔːˈrɛsəns) *n* **1** the part of a plant that consists of the flower-bearing stalks. **2** the arrangement of the flowers on the stalks. **3** the process of flowering; blossoming. [C16: from NL, from LL, from *flōrescere* to bloom]
▸ inflo'rescent *adj*

inflow (ˈɪnˌfləʊ) *n* **1** something, such as a liquid or gas, that flows in. **2** Also called: **inflowing**. the act of flowing in; influx.

influence (ˈɪnfluəns) *n* **1** an effect of one person or thing on another. **2** the power of a person or thing to have such an effect. **3** power resulting from ability, wealth, position, etc. **4** a person or thing having influence. **5** *Astrol.* an ethereal fluid regarded as emanating from the stars and affecting a person's future. **6 under the influence.** *Inf.* drunk. ◆ *vb* **influences, influencing, influenced.** (*tr*) **7** to persuade or induce. **8** to have an effect upon (actions, events, etc.); affect. [C14: from Med. L *influentia* emanation of power from the stars, from L *influere* to flow into, from *fluere* to flow]
▸ 'influenceable *adj* ▸ 'influencer *n*

influent (ˈɪnfluənt) *adj also* **inflowing**. **1** flowing in. ◆ *n* **2** something flowing in, esp. a tributary. **3** *Ecology.* an organism that has a major effect on its community.

influential (ˌɪnfluˈɛnʃəl) *adj* having or exerting influence.
▸ ,influ'entially *adv*

influenza (ˌɪnfluˈɛnzə) *n* a highly contagious viral disease characterized by fever, muscular aches and pains, and inflammation of the respiratory passages. [C18: from It., lit.: INFLUENCE, hence, incursion, epidemic (first applied to influenza in 1743)]
▸ ,influ'enzal *adj*

influx (ˈɪnˌflʌks) *n* **1** the arrival or entry of many people or things. **2** the act of flowing in; inflow. **3** the mouth of a stream or river. [C17: from LL *influxus*, from *influere*; see INFLUENCE]

info (ˈɪnfəʊ) *n Inf.* short for **information**.

infold (ɪnˈfəʊld) *vb* (*tr*) a variant of **enfold**.

inform (ɪnˈfɔːm) *vb* **1** (*tr*; often foll. by *of* or *about*) to give information to; tell. **2** (*tr*; often foll. by *of* or *about*) to make conversant (with). **3** (*intr*; often foll. by *against* or *on*) to give information regarding criminals, to the police, etc. **4** (*tr*) to give form to. **5** (*tr*) to impart some essential or formative characteristic to. **6** (*tr*) to animate or inspire. [C14: from L *informāre* to give form to, describe, from *formāre* to FORM]
▸ in'formable *adj*

informal (ɪnˈfɔːməl) *adj* **1** not of a formal, official, or stiffly conventional nature. **2** appropriate to everyday life or use. **3** denoting or characterized by idiom, vocabulary, etc., appropriate to conversational language rather than formal written language. **4** denoting a

second-person pronoun in some languages used when the addressee is regarded as a friend or social inferior.
▸ in'formally *adv*

informality (ˌɪnfɔːˈmælɪtɪ) *n, pl* **informalities. 1** the condition or quality of being informal. **2** an informal act.

informal vote *n Austral. & NZ.* an invalid vote or ballot.

informant (ɪnˈfɔːmənt) *n* a person who gives information.

information (ˌɪnfəˈmeɪʃən) *n* **1** knowledge acquired through experience or study. **2** knowledge of specific and timely events or situations; news. **3** the act of informing or the condition of being informed. **4a** an office, agency, etc., providing information. **4b** (*as modifier*): *information service.* **5** a charge or complaint made before justices of the peace, usually on oath, to institute summary criminal proceedings. **6** *Computing.* **6a** the meaning given to data by the way it is interpreted. **6b** another word for **data** (sense 2).
▸ ,infor'mational *adj*

information retrieval *n Computing.* the process of recovering information from stored data.

information superhighway *n* **1** the concept of a worldwide network of computers capable of transferring all types of digital information at high speed. **2** another name for the **Internet**. ◆ Also called: **information highway**.

information technology *n* the production, storage, and communication of information using computers, etc.

information theory *n* a collection of mathematical theories concerned with coding, transmitting, storing, retrieving, and decoding information.

informative (ɪnˈfɔːmətɪv) *or* **informatory** *adj* providing information; instructive.
▸ in'formatively *adv* ▸ in'formativeness *n*

informed (ɪnˈfɔːmd) *adj* **1** having much knowledge or education; learned or cultured. **2** based on information: *an informed judgment.*

informer (ɪnˈfɔːmə) *n* **1** a person who informs against someone, esp. a criminal. **2** a person who provides information.

infotainment (ˌɪnfəʊˈteɪnmənt) *n* (in television) the practice of presenting serious or instructive subjects in a style designed primarily to be entertaining. [C20: from INFO + (ENTER)TAINMENT]

infra- *prefix* below; beneath; after: *infrasonic.* [from L *infrā*]

infract (ɪnˈfrækt) *vb* (*tr*) to violate or break (a law, etc.). [C18: from L *infractus* broken off; see INFRINGE]
▸ in'fraction *n* ▸ in'fractor *n*

infra dig (ˈɪnfrə ˈdɪg) *adj* (*postpositive*) *Inf.* beneath one's dignity. [C19: from L *infrā dignitātem*]

infrangible (ɪnˈfrændʒɪbᵊl) *adj* **1** incapable of being broken. **2** not capable of being violated or infringed. [C16: from LL, from L IN-¹ + *frangere* to break]
▸ in,frangi'bility *or* in'frangibleness *n* ▸ in'frangibly *adv*

infrared (ˌɪnfrəˈrɛd) *n* **1** the part of the electromagnetic spectrum with a longer wavelength than light but a shorter wavelength than radio waves. ◆ *adj* **2** of, relating to, using, or consisting of radiation lying within the infrared.

infrared astronomy *n* the study of radiations from space in the infrared region of the electromagnetic spectrum.

infrared photography *n* photography using film with an emulsion that is sensitive to infrared light, enabling it to be used in dark or misty conditions.

infrasound (ˈɪnfrəˌsaʊnd) *n* soundlike waves having a frequency below the audible range, i.e. below about 16 Hz.
▸ **infrasonic** (ˌɪnfrəˈsɒnɪk) *adj*

infrastructure (ˈɪnfrəˌstrʌktʃə) *n* **1** the basic structure of an organization, system, etc. **2** the stock of fixed capital equipment in a country, including factories, roads, schools, etc., considered as a determinant of economic growth.

★ people and places

nfrequent (ɪnˈfriːkwənt) *adj* rarely happening or present; only occasional.
▸ in'frequency *or* in'frequence *n* ▸ in'frequently *adv*

nfringe (ɪnˈfrɪndʒ) *vb* **infringes, infringing, infringed. 1** (*tr*) to violate or break (a law, agreement, etc.). **2** (*intr*; foll. by *on* or *upon*) to encroach or trespass. [C16: from L *infringere* to break off, from *frangere* to break]
▸ in'fringement *n* ▸ in'fringer *n*

nfundibular (ˌɪnfʌnˈdɪbjʊlə) *adj* funnel-shaped. [C18: from L *infundibulum* funnel]

nfuriate *vb* (ɪnˈfjʊərɪˌeɪt), **infuriates, infuriating, infuriated. 1** (*tr*) to anger; annoy. ◆ *adj* (ɪnˈfjʊərɪɪt). **2** *Arch.* furious. [C17: from Med. L *infuriāre* (vb); see IN-², FURY]
▸ in'furi,ating *adj* ▸ in'furi,atingly *adv*

nfuse (ɪnˈfjuːz) *vb* **infuses, infusing, infused. 1** (*tr*; often foll. by *into*) to instil or inculcate. **2** (*tr*; foll. by *with*) to inspire; emotionally charge. **3** to soak or be soaked so as to extract flavour or other properties. **4** *Rare.* (foll. by *into*) to pour. [C15: from L *infundere* to pour into]
▸ in'fuser *n*

nfusible[1] (ɪnˈfjuːzəbˀl) *adj* not fusible; not easily melted; having a high melting point. [C16: from IN-¹ + FUSIBLE]
▸ in,fusi'bility *or* in'fusibleness *n*

nfusible[2] (ɪnˈfjuːzəbˀl) *adj* capable of being infused. [C17: from INFUSE + -IBLE]
▸ in,fusi'bility *or* in'fusibleness *n*

nfusion (ɪnˈfjuːʒən) *n* **1** the act of infusing. **2** something infused. **3** an extract obtained by soaking.
▸ infusive (ɪnˈfjuːsɪv) *adj*

nfusorian (ˌɪnfjuˈzɔːrɪən) *Obs.* ◆ *n* **1** any of the microscopic organisms, such as protozoans, found in infusions of organic material. ◆ *adj* **2** of or relating to infusorians. [C18: from NL *Infusoria* former class name; see INFUSE]
▸ ,infu'sorial *adj*

-ing[1] *suffix forming nouns.* **1** (*from verbs*) the action of, process of, result of, or something connected with the verb: *meeting; winnings.* **2** (*from other nouns*) something used in, consisting of, involving, etc.: *tubing; soldiering.* **3** (*from other parts of speech*): *an outing.* [OE -*ing*, -*ung*]

-ing[2] *suffix.* **1** forming the present participle of verbs: *walking; believing.* **2** forming participial adjectives: *a sinking ship.* **3** forming adjectives not derived from verbs: *swashbuckling.* [ME -*ing*, -*inde*, from OE -*ende*]

-ing[3] *suffix forming nouns.* a person or thing having a certain quality or being of a certain kind: *sweeting; whiting.* [OE -*ing*; rel. to ON -*ingr*]

ingather (ɪnˈɡæðə) *vb* (*tr*) to gather together or in (a harvest, etc.).
▸ in'gatherer *n*

Inge ★ (ɪŋ) *n* **William Ralph**, known as *the Gloomy Dean.* 1860–1954, British theologian, noted for his pessimism; dean of St Paul's Cathedral (1911–34).

ingeminate (ɪnˈdʒɛmɪˌneɪt) *vb* **ingeminates, ingeminating, ingeminated.** (*tr*) *Rare.* to repeat; reiterate. [C16: from L *ingemināre* to redouble, from IN-² + *gemināre* to GEMINATE]

Ingenhousz ★ (Dutch ˈɪŋənhuːs) *n* **Jan** (jɑn). 1730–99, Dutch plant physiologist and physician, who discovered photosynthesis.

ingenious (ɪnˈdʒiːnjəs, -nɪəs) *adj* possessing or done with ingenuity; skilful or clever. [C15: from L, from *ingenium* natural ability; see ENGINE]
▸ in'geniously *adv* ▸ in'geniousness *n*

ingénue (ˌænʒeɪˈnjuː) *n* an artless, innocent, or inexperienced girl or young woman. [C19: from F, fem of *ingénu* INGENUOUS]

ingenuity (ˌɪndʒɪˈnjuːɪtɪ) *n, pl* **ingenuities. 1** inventive talent; cleverness. **2** an ingenious device, act, etc. **3** *Arch.* frankness; candour. [C16: from L *ingenuitās* a freeborn condition, outlook consistent with such a condition, from *ingenuus* native, freeborn (see INGENUOUS); meaning infl. by INGENIOUS]

ingenuous (ɪnˈdʒɛnjʊəs) *adj* **1** naive, artless, or innocent. **2** candid; frank; straightforward. [C16: from L *ingenuus* freeborn, virtuous, from IN-² + *gignere* to beget]
▸ in'genuously *adv* ▸ in'genuousness *n*

ingest (ɪnˈdʒɛst) *vb* (*tr*) to take (food or liquid) into the body. [C17: from L *ingerere* to put into, from IN-² + *gerere* to carry; see GEST]
▸ in'gestible *adj* ▸ in'gestion *n* ▸ in'gestive *adj*

ingle (ˈɪŋɡˀl) *n Arch. or dialect.* a fire in a room or a fireplace. [C16: prob. from Scot. Gaelic *aingeal* fire]

Ingleborough ★ (ˈɪŋɡˀlbərə, -brə) *n* a mountain in N England, in North Yorkshire: potholes. Height: 723 m (2373 ft).

inglenook (ˈɪŋɡˀl,nʊk) *n Brit.* a corner by a fireplace; chimney corner.

ingoing (ˈɪnˌɡəʊɪŋ) *adj* going in; entering.

Ingolstadt ★ (German ˈɪŋɡɔlʃtat) *n* a city in S central Germany, in Bavaria on the River Danube: oil-refining. Pop.: 110 910 (1995 est.).

ingot (ˈɪŋɡət) *n* a piece of cast metal obtained from a mould in a form suitable for storage, etc. [C14: ?from IN-² + OE *goten*, p.p. of *geotan* to pour]

ingraft (ɪnˈɡrɑːft) *vb* a variant spelling of **engraft.**
▸ in'graftment *or* ,ingraf'tation *n*

ingrain *or* **engrain** (ɪnˈɡreɪn). (*tr*) **1** to impress deeply on the mind or nature; instil. **2** *Arch.* to dye into the fibre of (a fabric). ◆ *adj* (ˈɪnˌɡreɪn). **3** (of woven or knitted articles) made of dyed yarn or of fibre that is dyed before being spun into yarn. ◆ *n* (ˈɪnˌɡreɪn). **4** a carpet made from ingrained yarn. [C18: from *dyed in grain* dyed with kermes through the fibre]

ingrained *or* **engrained** (ɪnˈɡreɪnd) *adj* **1** deeply impressed or instilled. **2** (*prenominal*) complete or inveterate; utter. **3** (esp. of dirt) worked into or through the fibre, pores, etc.
▸ ingrainedly *or* engrainedly (ɪnˈɡreɪnɪdlɪ) *adv* ▸ in'grainedness *or* en'grainedness *n*

ingrate (ˈɪnɡreɪt, ɪnˈɡreɪt) *Arch.* ◆ *n* **1** an ungrateful person. ◆ *adj* **2** ungrateful. [C14: from L *ingrātus* (adj), from IN-¹ + *grātus* GRATEFUL]
▸ 'ingrately *adv*

ingratiate (ɪnˈɡreɪʃɪˌeɪt) *vb* **ingratiates, ingratiating, ingratiated.** (*tr*; often foll. by *with*) to place (oneself) purposely in the favour (of another). [C17: from L, from IN-² + *grātia* grace, favour]
▸ in'grati,ating *or* in'gratiatory *adj* ▸ in'grati,atingly *adv* ▸ in,grati'ation *n*

ingredient (ɪnˈɡriːdɪənt) *n* a component of a mixture, compound, etc., esp. in cooking. [C15: from L *ingrediēns* going into, from *ingredī* to enter; see INGRESS]

Ingres ★ (French ɛ̃ɡrə) *n* **Jean Auguste Dominique** (ʒɑ̃ oɡyst dɔminik). 1780–1867, French classical painter, noted for his draughtsmanship.

ingress (ˈɪnɡres) *n* **1** the act of going or coming in; an entering. **2** a way in; entrance. **3** the right or permission to enter. [C15: from L *ingressus*, from *ingredī* to go in, from *gradī* to step, go]
▸ ingression (ɪnˈɡreʃən) *n*

in-group *n Sociol.* a highly cohesive and relatively closed social group characterized by the preferential treatment reserved for its members.

ingrowing (ˈɪnˌɡrəʊɪŋ) *adj* **1** (esp. of a toenail) growing abnormally into the flesh. **2** growing within or into.
▸ 'in,growth *n*

ingrown (ˈɪnˌɡrəʊn, ɪnˈɡrəʊn) *adj* **1** (esp. of a toenail) grown abnormally into the flesh; covered by adjacent tissues. **2** grown within; native; innate.

inguinal (ˈɪŋɡwɪnˀl) *adj Anat.* of or relating to the groin. [C17: from L *inguinālis*, from *inguen* groin]

ingulf (ɪnˈɡʌlf) *vb* (*tr*) a variant of **engulf.**

ingurgitate (ɪnˈɡɜːdʒɪˌteɪt) *vb* **ingurgitates, ingurgitating, ingurgitated.** to swallow (food, etc.) greedily or in excess. [C16: from L *ingurgitāre* to flood, from IN-² + *gurges* abyss]
▸ in,gurgi'tation *n*

Ingushetia ★ (ˌɪnɡuːˈʃetɪə) *n* an administrative division of S Russia: part of the former Checheno-Ingush Autonomous Republic, which was split into Ingushetia and Chechenia in 1992. Capital: Nazran (a new capital, Magas, is under construction). Pop. (including Chechenia): 1 185 000 (1995 est.). Area (including Chechenia): 19 300 sq. km (7450 sq. miles). Also called: **Ingush Republic** (ˌɪŋɡuːʃ).

★ people and places

inhabit (ɪn'hæbɪt) vb **inhabits, inhabiting, inhabited.** (tr) to live or dwell in; occupy. [C14: from L inhabitāre, from habitāre to dwell]
▸ in'habitable adj ▸ in,habita'bility n ▸ in,habi'tation n

inhabitant (ɪn'hæbɪtənt) n a person or animal that is a permanent resident of a particular place or region.
▸ in'habitancy or in'habitance n

inhalant (ɪn'heɪlənt) adj **1** (esp. of a medicinal preparation) inhaled for its therapeutic effect. **2** inhaling. ♦ n **3** an inhalant medicinal preparation.

inhale (ɪn'heɪl) vb **inhales, inhaling, inhaled.** to draw (breath, etc.) into the lungs; breathe in. [C18: from IN-² + L halāre to breathe]
▸ ,inha'lation n

inhaler (ɪn'heɪlə) n **1** a device for breathing in therapeutic vapours, esp. one for relieving nasal congestion. **2** a person who inhales.

Inhambane ★ (,ɪnjəm'bɑːnə) n a port in SE Mozambique on an inlet of the Mozambique Channel (**Inhambane Bay**). Pop.: 64 274 (1986).

inhere (ɪn'hɪə) vb **inheres, inhering, inhered.** (intr; foll. by in) to be an inseparable part (of). [C16: from L inhaerēre to stick in, from haerēre to stick]

inherent (ɪn'hɪərənt, -'her-) adj existing as an inseparable part; intrinsic.
▸ in'herently adv

inherit (ɪn'herɪt) vb **inherits, inheriting, inherited. 1** to receive (property, etc.) by succession or under a will. **2** (intr) to succeed as heir. **3** (tr) to possess (a characteristic) through genetic transmission. **4** (tr) to receive (a position, etc.) from a predecessor. [C14: from OF enheriter, from LL inhērēditāre to appoint an heir, from L hērēs HEIR]
▸ in'herited adj ▸ in'heritor n ▸ in'heritress or in'heritrix fem n

inheritable (ɪn'herɪtəb³l) adj **1** capable of being transmitted by heredity from one generation to a later one. **2** capable of being inherited. **3** Rare. having the right to inherit.
▸ in,herita'bility or in'heritableness n ▸ in'heritably adv

inheritance (ɪn'herɪtəns) n **1** Law. **1a** hereditary succession to an estate, title, etc. **1b** the right of an heir to succeed on the death of an ancestor. **1c** something that may legally be transmitted to an heir. **2** the act of inheriting. **3** something inherited; heritage. **4** the derivation of characteristics of one generation from an earlier one by heredity.

inheritance tax n **1** (in Britain) a tax introduced in 1986 to replace capital transfer tax, consisting of a percentage levied on that part of an inheritance exceeding a specified allowance. **2** (in the US) a state tax imposed on an inheritance according to its size and the relationship of the beneficiary to the deceased.

inhibit (ɪn'hɪbɪt) vb **inhibits, inhibiting, inhibited.** (tr) **1** to restrain or hinder (an impulse, desire, etc.). **2** to prohibit, forbid, or prevent. **3** to stop, prevent, or decrease the rate of (a chemical reaction). [C15: from L inhibēre to restrain, from IN-² + habēre to have]
▸ in'hibitable adj ▸ in'hibitive or in'hibitory adj

inhibition (,ɪnɪ'bɪʃən, ,ɪnhɪ-) n **1** the act of inhibiting or the condition of being inhibited. **2** Psychol. a mental state or condition in which the varieties of expression and behaviour of an individual become restricted. **3** the process of stopping or retarding a chemical reaction. **4** Physiol. the suppression of the function or action of an organ or part, as by stimulation of its nerve supply.

inhibitor (ɪn'hɪbɪtə) n **1** Also: **inhibiter.** a person or thing that inhibits. **2** a substance that retards or stops a chemical reaction. **3** Biochem. **3a** a substance that inhibits the action of an enzyme. **3b** a substance that inhibits a metabolic or physiological process: a plant growth inhibitor.

inhospitable (ɪn'hɒspɪtəb³l, ,ɪnhɒ'spɪt-) adj **1** not hospitable; unfriendly. **2** (of a region, an environment, etc.) lacking a favourable climate, terrain, etc.
▸ in'hospitableness n ▸ in'hospitably adv

in-house adj, adv within an organization or group: an in-house job; the job was done in-house.

inhuman (ɪn'hjuːmən) adj **1** Also: **inhumane** (,ɪnhjuː'meɪn). lacking humane feelings, such as sympathy, understanding, etc.; cruel; brutal. **2** not human.
▸ ,inhu'manely adv ▸ in'humanly adv ▸ in'humanness n

inhumanity (,ɪnhjuː'mænɪtɪ) n, pl **inhumanities. 1** lack of humane qualities. **2** an inhumane act, decision, etc.

inhume (ɪn'hjuːm) vb **inhumes, inhuming, inhumed.** (tr) to inter; bury. [C17: from L, from IN-² + humus ground]
▸ ,inhu'mation n ▸ in'humer n

inimical (ɪ'nɪmɪk³l) adj **1** adverse or unfavourable. **2** not friendly; hostile. [C17: from LL, from inimīcus, from IN- + amīcus friendly; see ENEMY]
▸ in'imically adv ▸ in'imicalness or in,imi'cality n

inimitable (ɪ'nɪmɪtəb³l) adj incapable of being duplicated or imitated; unique.
▸ in,imita'bility or in'imitableness n ▸ in'imitably adv

iniquity (ɪ'nɪkwɪtɪ) n, pl **iniquities. 1** lack of justice or righteousness; wickedness; injustice. **2** a wicked act; sin. [C14: from L, from inīquus unfair, from IN-¹ + aequus even, level; see EQUAL]
▸ in'iquitous adj ▸ in'iquitously adv ▸ in'iquitousness n

initial (ɪ'nɪʃəl) adj **1** of, at, or concerning the beginning. ♦ n **2** the first letter of a word, esp. a person's name. **3** Printing. a large letter set at the beginning of a chapter or work. **4** Bot. a cell from which tissues and organs develop by division and differentiation. ♦ vb **initials, initialling, initialled** or US **initials, initialing, initialed. 5** (tr) to sign with one's initials, esp. to indicate approval; endorse. [C16: from L initiālis of the beginning, from initium beginning lit.: an entering upon, from inīre to go in]
▸ in'itialer or in'itialler n ▸ in'itially adv

initialize or **initialise** (ɪ'nɪʃə,laɪz) vb **initializes, initializing, initialized** or **initialises, initialising, initialised.** (tr) to assign an initial value to (a variable or storage location) in a computer program.
▸ in,itiali'zation or in,itiali'sation n

initiate vb (ɪ'nɪʃɪ,eɪt) **initiates, initiating, initiated.** (tr) **1** to begin or originate. **2** to accept (new members) into an organization such as a club, through often secret ceremonies. **3** to teach fundamentals to. ♦ adj (ɪ'nɪʃɪɪt, -,eɪt). **4** initiated; begun. ♦ n (ɪ'nɪʃɪɪt, -,eɪt). **5** a person who has been initiated, esp. recently. **6** a beginner; novice. [C17: from L initiāre (vb), from initium; see INITIAL]
▸ in'itiatory adj

initiation (ɪ,nɪʃɪ'eɪʃən) n **1** the act of initiating or the condition of being initiated. **2** the ceremony, often secret, initiating new members into an organization.

initiative (ɪ'nɪʃɪətɪv, -'nɪʃətɪv) n **1** the first step or action of a matter; commencing move: a peace initiative. **2** the right or power to begin or initiate something: he has the initiative. **3** the ability or attitude required to begin or initiate something. **4** Government. the right of citizens to introduce legislation, etc., in a legislative body, as in Switzerland. **5 on one's own initiative.** without being prompted. ♦ adj **6** of or concerning initiation or serving to initiate; initiatory.
▸ in'itiatively adv

initiator (ɪ'nɪʃɪ,eɪtə) n **1** a person or thing that initiates. **2** Chem. a substance that starts a chain reaction. **3** Chem. a very sensitive explosive used in detonators.

inject (ɪn'dʒɛkt) vb (tr) **1** Med. to introduce (a fluid) into the body (of a person or animal) by means of a syringe. **2** (foll. by into) to introduce (a new aspect or element): to inject humour into a scene. **3** to interject (a comment, idea, etc.). [C17: from injicere to throw in, from jacere to throw]
▸ in'jectable adj ▸ in'jector n

injection (ɪn'dʒɛkʃən) n **1** fluid injected into the body, esp. for medicinal purposes. **2** something injected. **3** the act of injecting. **4a** the act or process of introducing fluid under pressure, such as fuel into the combustion chamber of an engine. **4b** (as modifier): injection moulding.
▸ in'jective adj

injunction (ɪn'dʒʌŋkʃən) n **1** Law. an instruction or order issued by a court to a party to an action, esp. to refrain from some act. **2** a command, admonition, etc. **3** the act of enjoining. [C16: from LL, from L injungere ENJOIN]
▸ in'junctive adj ▸ in'junctively adv

★ people and places

injure ('ɪndʒə) *vb* **injures, injuring, injured.** (*tr*) **1** to cause physical or mental harm or suffering to; hurt or wound. **2** to offend, esp. by an injustice. [C16: back formation from INJURY]
▸ **'injurable** *adj* ▸ **'injured** *adj* ▸ **'injurer** *n*

injurious (ɪn'dʒʊərɪəs) *adj* **1** causing damage or harm; deleterious; hurtful. **2** abusive, slanderous, or libellous.
▸ **in'juriously** *adv* ▸ **in'juriousness** *n*

injury ('ɪndʒərɪ) *n, pl* **injuries. 1** physical damage or hurt. **2** a specific instance of this: *a leg injury*. **3** harm done to a reputation. **4** *Law*. a violation or infringement of another person's rights that causes him harm and is actionable at law. [C14: from L *injūria* injustice, wrong, from *injūriōsus* acting unfairly, wrongful, from IN-[1] + *jūs* right]

injury time *n Soccer, rugby, etc.* extra playing time added on to compensate for time spent attending to injured players during the match. Also called: **stoppage time.**

injustice (ɪn'dʒʌstɪs) *n* **1** the condition or practice of being unjust or unfair. **2** an unjust act.

ink (ɪŋk) *n* **1** a fluid or paste used for printing, writing, and drawing. **2** a dark brown fluid ejected into the water for self-concealment by an octopus or related mollusc. ◆ *vb* (*tr*) **3** to mark with ink. **4** to coat (a printing surface) with ink. [C13: from OF *enque*, from LL *encaustum* a purplish-red ink, from Gk *enkauston* purple ink, from *enkaustos* burnt in, from *enkaiein* to burn in; see EN-[2], CAUSTIC]
▸ **'inker** *n*

Inkatha (ɪn'kɑːtə) *n* a South African political party; originally a Zulu organization founded in 1975 as a paramilitary group seeking nonracial democracy; won four seats in democratic multiracial elections in 1994. [C20: Zulu name for the grass coil used by Zulu women carrying loads on their heads]

inkblot ('ɪŋk,blɒt) *n* a patch of ink accidentally or deliberately spilled. Ten such patches, of different shapes, are used in the Rorschach test.

ink-cap *n* any of several saprotrophic fungi whose caps disintegrate into a black inky fluid after the spores mature.

Inkerman ★ ('ɪŋkəmən; *Russian* ɪnkɪr'man) *n* a village in the Ukraine, in the S Crimea east of Sevastopol: scene of a battle during the Crimean War in which British and French forces defeated the Russians (1854).

inkhorn ('ɪŋk,hɔːn) *n* (formerly) a small portable container for ink, usually made from horn.

ink in *vb* (*adv*) **1** (*tr*) to use ink to go over pencil lines in (a drawing). **2** to apply ink to (a printing surface) in preparing to print from it. **3** to arrange or confirm definitely.

inkling ('ɪŋklɪŋ) *n* a slight intimation or suggestion; suspicion. [C14: prob. from *inclen* to hint at]

inkstand ('ɪŋk,stænd) *n* a stand or tray on which are kept writing implements and containers for ink.

inkwell ('ɪŋk,wɛl) *n* a small container for pen ink, often let into the surface of a desk.

inky ('ɪŋkɪ) *adj* **inkier, inkiest. 1** resembling ink, esp. in colour; dark or black. **2** of, containing, or stained with ink.
▸ **'inkiness** *n*

INLA *abbrev. for* Irish National Liberation Army.

inlaid ('ɪn,leɪd, ɪn'leɪd) *adj* **1** set in the surface, as a design in wood. **2** having such a design or inlay: *an inlaid table*.

inland *adj* ('ɪnlənd). **1** of or located in the interior of a country or region away from a sea or border. **2** *Chiefly Brit.* operating within a country or region; domestic; not foreign. ◆ *n* ('ɪn,lænd, -lənd). **3** the interior of a country or region. ◆ *adv* ('ɪn,lænd, -lənd). **4** towards or into the interior of a country or region.
▸ **'inlander** *n*

Inland Revenue *n* (in Britain and New Zealand) a government board that administers and collects major direct taxes, such as income tax.

Inland Sea ★ *n* a sea in SW Japan, between the islands of Honshu, Shikoku, and Kyushu. Japanese name: **Seto Naikai.**

in-law *n* **1** a relative by marriage. ◆ *adj* **2** (*postpositive; in combination*) related by marriage: *a father-in-law*. [C19: back formation from *father-in-law*, etc.]

inlay *vb* (ɪn'leɪ), **inlays, inlaying, inlaid.** (*tr*) **1** to decorate (an article, esp. of furniture) by inserting pieces of wood, ivory, etc., into slots in the surface. ◆ *n* ('ɪn,leɪ). **2** *Dentistry*. a filling inserted into a cavity and held in position by cement. **3** decoration made by inlaying. **4** an inlaid article, surface, etc.
▸ **'in,layer** *n*

inlet *n* ('ɪn,lɛt). **1** a narrow inland opening of the coastline. **2** an entrance or opening. **3** the act of letting someone or something in. **4** something let in or inserted. **5a** a passage or valve through which a substance, esp. a fluid, enters a machine. **5b** (*as modifier*): *an inlet valve*. ◆ *vb* (ɪn'lɛt), **inlets, inletting, inlet. 6** (*tr*) to insert or inlay.

inlier ('ɪn,laɪə) *n* an outcrop of rocks that is entirely surrounded by younger rocks.

in-line skate *n* another name for **Rollerblade.**

in loco parentis *Latin.* (ɪn 'ləʊkəʊ pə'rɛntɪs) in place of a parent: said of a person acting in a parental capacity.

inly ('ɪnlɪ) *adv Poetic.* inwardly; intimately.

inmate ('ɪn,meɪt) *n* a person who is confined to an institution such as a prison or hospital.

in medias res *Latin.* (ɪn 'miːdɪ,æs 'reɪs) in or into the middle of events or a narrative. [lit.: into the midst of things, taken from a passage in Horace's *Ars Poetica*]

in memoriam (ɪn mɪ'mɔːrɪəm) in memory of: used in obituaries, epitaphs, etc. [L]

inmost ('ɪn,məʊst) *adj* another word for **innermost.**

inn (ɪn) *n* a pub or small hotel providing food and accommodation.

Inn ★ (ɪn) *n* a river in central Europe, rising in Switzerland in Graubünden and flowing northeast through Austria and Bavaria to join the River Danube at Passau: forms part of the border between Austria and Germany. Length: 514 km (319 miles).

innards ('ɪnədz) *pl n Inf.* **1** the internal organs of the body, esp. the viscera. **2** the interior parts of anything, esp. the working parts. [C19: colloquial var. of *inwards*]

innate (ɪ'neɪt, 'ɪneɪt) *adj* **1** existing from birth; congenital; inborn. **2** being an essential part of the character of a person or thing. **3** instinctive; not learned: *innate capacities*. **4** *Philosophy*. (of ideas) present in the mind before any experience and knowable by pure reason. [C15: from L, from *innascī* to be born in, from *nascī* to be born]
▸ **in'nately** *adv* ▸ **in'nateness** *n*

inner ('ɪnə) *adj* (*prenominal*) **1** being or located further inside: *an inner room*. **2** happening or occurring inside. **3** relating to the soul, mind, spirit, etc. **4** more profound or obscure; less apparent: *the inner meaning*. **5** exclusive or private: *inner regions of the party*. ◆ *n* **6** *Archery*. **6a** the red innermost ring on a target. **6b** a shot which hits this ring.
▸ **'innerly** *adv* ▸ **'innerness** *n*

inner bar *n the. Brit.* all Queen's or King's Counsel collectively.

inner child *n Psychol.* the part of the psyche that retains feelings as they were experienced in childhood.

inner city *n* a the parts of a city in or near its centre, esp. when associated with poverty, substandard housing, etc. **b** (*as modifier*): *inner-city schools*.

Inner Hebrides ★ *pl n* See **Hebrides.**

inner man *or* (*fem*) **inner woman** *n* **1** the mind or soul. **2** *Jocular.* the stomach or appetite.

Inner Mongolia ★ *n* an autonomous region of NE China: consists chiefly of the Mongolian plateau, with the Gobi Desert in the north and the Great Wall of China in the south. Capital: Hohhot. Pop.: 22 600 000 (1995 est.). Area: 1 177 500 sq. km (459 225 sq. miles).

innermost ('ɪnə,məʊst) *adj* **1** being or located furthest within; central. **2** intimate; private.

inner tube *n* an inflatable rubber tube that fits inside a pneumatic tyre casing.

innervate ('ɪnɜː,veɪt) *vb* **innervates, innervating, innervated.** (*tr*) **1** to supply nerves to (a bodily organ or part). **2** to stimulate (a bodily organ or part) with nerve impulses.
▸ **,inner'vation** *n*

innings ('ɪnɪŋz) *n* **1** (*functioning as sing*) *Cricket, etc.* **1a** the batting turn of a player or team. **1b** the runs scored during such a turn. **2** (*sometimes sing*) a period of opportunity or action.

Inniskilling ★ (ˌɪnɪsˈkɪlɪŋ) *n* the former name of **Enniskillen.**

innkeeper ('ɪnˌkiːpə) *n* an owner or manager of an inn.

innocence ('ɪnəsəns) *n* the quality or state of being innocent. Archaic word: **innocency** ('ɪnəsənsɪ). [C14: from L *innocentia* harmlessness, from *innocēns* blameless, from IN-¹ + *nocēre* to hurt]

innocent ('ɪnəsənt) *adj* **1** not corrupted or tainted with evil; sinless; pure. **2** not guilty of a particular crime; blameless. **3** (*postpositive*; foll. by *of*) free (of); lacking: *innocent of all knowledge of history*. **4a** harmless or innocuous: *an innocent game*. **4b** not cancerous: *an innocent tumour*. **5** credulous, naive, or artless. **6** simple-minded; slow-witted. ◆ *n* **7** an innocent person, esp. a young child or an ingenuous adult. **8** a simple-minded person; simpleton. ▸ '**innocently** *adv*

Innocent II ★ ('ɪnəsənt) *n* original name *Gregorio Papareschi*. died 1143, pope (1130–43). He condemned Abelard's teachings.

Innocent III ★ *n* original name *Giovanni Lotario de' Conti*. ?1161–1216, pope (1198–1216), under whom the temporal power of the papacy reached its height. He instituted the Fourth Crusade (1202) and a crusade against the Albigenses (1208), and called the fourth Lateran Council (1215).

Innocent IV ★ *n* original name *Sinibaldo de' Fieschi*. died 1254, pope (1243–54); an unrelenting enemy of Emperor Frederick II and his heirs.

innocuous (ɪˈnɒkjʊəs) *adj* having little or no adverse or harmful effect; harmless. [C16: from L *innocuus* harmless, from IN-¹ + *nocēre* to harm] ▸ in'**nocuously** *adv* ▸ in'**nocuousness** *or* **innocuity** (ˌɪnəˈkjuːɪtɪ) *n*

innominate bone (ɪˈnɒmɪnɪt) *n* either of the two bones that form the sides of the pelvis, consisting of the ilium, ischium, and pubis. Nontechnical name: **hipbone.**

innovate ('ɪnəˌveɪt) *vb* **innovates, innovating, innovated.** to invent or begin to apply (methods, ideas, etc.). [C16: from L *innovāre* to renew, from IN-² + *novāre* to make new, from *novus* new] ▸ '**inno**ˌ**vative** *or* '**inno**ˌ**vatory** *adj* ▸ '**inno**ˌ**vator** *n*

innovation (ˌɪnəˈveɪʃən) *n* **1** something newly introduced, such as a new method or device. **2** the act of innovating. ▸ ˌinno'**vational** *adj* ▸ ˌinno'**vationist** *n*

Innsbruck ★ ('ɪnzbrʊk) *n* a city in W Austria, on the River Inn at the foot of the Brenner Pass: tourist centre. Pop.: 118 112 (1991).

innuendo (ˌɪnjuˈɛndəʊ) *n, pl* **innuendos** *or* **innuendoes. 1** an indirect or subtle reference, esp. one made maliciously or indicating criticism or disapproval; insinuation. **2** *Law.* (in an action for defamation) an explanation of the construction put upon words alleged to be defamatory where this meaning is not apparent. [C17: from L, lit.: by hinting, from *innuere* to convey by a nod, from IN-² + *nuere* to nod]

Innuit ('ɪnjuːɪt) *n* a variant spelling of **Inuit.**

innumerable (ɪˈnjuːmərəbəl, ɪˈnjuːmrəbəl) *or* **innumerous** *adj* so many as to be uncountable; extremely numerous. ▸ in,numera'**bility** *or* in'**numerableness** *n* ▸ in'**numerably** *adv*

innumerate (ɪˈnjuːmərɪt) *adj* **1** having neither knowledge nor understanding of mathematics or science. ◆ *n* **2** an innumerate person. ▸ in'**numeracy** *n*

inoculate (ɪˈnɒkjʊˌleɪt) *vb* **inoculates, inoculating, inoculated. 1** to introduce (the causative agent of a disease) into the body in order to induce immunity. **2** (*tr*) to introduce (microorganisms, esp. bacteria) into (a culture medium). **3** (*tr*) to cause to be influenced or imbued, as with ideas. [C15: from L *inoculāre* to implant, from IN-² + *oculus* eye, bud] ▸ in,ocu'**lation** *n* ▸ in'**oculative** *adj* ▸ in'**ocu**ˌ**lator** *n*

inoculum (ɪˈnɒkjʊləm) *or* **inoculant** *n, pl* **inocula** (-lə) *or* **inoculants.** *Med.* the substance used in giving an inoculation. [C20: NL; see INOCULATE]

in-off *n Billiards.* a shot that goes into a pocket after striking another ball.

Inönü ('iːnɔːˌnu, ˌɪnɔːˈnuː) *n* **Ismet** (ɪsˈmɛt, 'ɪsmɛt). 1884–1973, Turkish statesman; president of Turkey (1938–50) and prime minister (1923–37; 1961–65).

inoperable (ɪnˈɒpərəbəl, -'ɒprə-) *adj* **1** incapable of being implemented and operated. **2** *Surgery.* not suitable for operation without risk, esp. because of metastasis. ▸ in,opera'**bility** *or* in'**operableness** *n* ▸ in'**operably** *adv*

inordinate (ɪnˈɔːdɪnɪt) *adj* **1** exceeding normal limits; immoderate. **2** unrestrained, as in behaviour or emotion; intemperate. **3** irregular or disordered. [C14: from L *inordinātus* disordered, from IN-¹ + *ordināre* to put in order] ▸ in'**ordinacy** *or* in'**ordinateness** *n* ▸ in'**ordinately** *adv*

inorganic (ˌɪnɔːˈɡænɪk) *adj* **1** not having the structure or characteristics of living organisms; not organic. **2** relating to or denoting chemical compounds that do not contain carbon. **3** not having a system, structure, or ordered relation of parts; amorphous. **4** not resulting from or produced by growth; artificial. ▸ ˌinor'**ganically** *adv*

inorganic chemistry *n* the branch of chemistry concerned with the elements and all their compounds except those containing carbon.

inosculate (ɪnˈɒskjuˌleɪt) *vb* **inosculates, inosculating, inosculated. 1** *Physiol.* (of small blood vessels) to communicate by anastomosis. **2** to unite or be united so as to be continuous; blend. **3** to intertwine or cause to intertwine. [C17: from IN-² + L *ōsculāre* to equip with an opening, from *ōsculum*, dim. of *ōs* mouth] ▸ in,oscu'**lation** *n*

inositol (ɪˈnəʊsɪˌtɒl) *n* a cyclic alcohol, one isomer of which (*i*-inositol) is present in yeast and is a growth factor for some organisms. [C19: from Gk *in-, is* sinew + -OSE² + -ITE¹ + -OL¹]

inpatient ('ɪnˌpeɪʃənt) *n* a patient living in the hospital where he is being treated.

in perpetuum *Latin.* (ɪn pɜːˈpetjuəm) forever.

input ('ɪnˌpʊt) *n* **1** the act of putting in. **2** that which is put in. **3** (*often pl*) a resource required for industrial production, such as capital goods, etc. **4** *Electronics.* the signal or current fed into a component or circuit. **5** *Computing.* the data fed into a computer from a peripheral device. **6** (*modifier*) of or relating to electronic, computer, or other input: *input program*. ◆ *vb* **inputs, inputting, input. 7** (*tr*) to insert (data) into a computer.

input/output *n Computing.* **1** the data or information passed into or out of a computer. **2** (*modifier*) concerned with or relating to such passage of data or information.

inquest ('ɪnˌkwɛst) *n* **1** an inquiry, esp. into the cause of an unexplained, sudden, or violent death, held by a coroner, in certain cases with a jury. **2** *Inf.* any inquiry or investigation. [C13: from Med. L, from L IN-² + *quaesītus* investigation, from *quaerere* to examine]

inquietude (ɪnˈkwaɪɪˌtjuːd) *n* restlessness, uneasiness, or anxiety. ▸ **inquiet** (ɪnˈkwaɪət) *adj* ▸ in'**quietly** *adv*

inquiline ('ɪnkwɪˌlaɪn) *n* **1** an animal that lives in close association with another animal without harming it. See also **commensal** (sense 1). ◆ *adj* **2** of or living as an inquiline. [C17: from L *inquilīnus* lodger, from IN-² + *colere* to dwell] ▸ **inquilinous** (ˌɪnkwɪˈlaɪnəs) *adj*

inquire *or* **enquire** (ɪnˈkwaɪə) *vb* **inquires, inquiring, inquired** *or* **enquires, enquiring, enquired. 1a** to seek information (about); ask: *she inquired his age; she inquired about rates of pay*. **1b** (*intr*; foll. by *of*) to ask (a person) for information: *I'll inquire of my aunt when she is coming*. **2** (*intr*; often foll. by *into*) to make a search or investigation. [C13: from L *inquīrere*, from IN-² + *quaerere* to seek] ▸ in'**quirer** *or* en'**quirer** *n* ▸ in'**quiry** *or* en'**quiry** *n*

inquisition (ˌɪnkwɪˈzɪʃən) *n* **1** the act of inquiring deeply or searchingly; investigation. **2** a deep or searching in-

quiry, esp. a ruthless official investigation in order to suppress revolt or root out the unorthodox. **3** an official inquiry, esp. one held by a jury before an officer of the Crown. [C14: from legal L *inquīsītiō*, from *inquīrere* to seek for; see INQUIRE]
▶ ˌinqui'sitional *adj* ▶ ˌinqui'sitionist *n*

Inquisition (ˌɪnkwɪ'zɪʃən) *n History.* a judicial institution of the Roman Catholic Church (1232–1820) founded to suppress heresy.

inquisitive (ɪn'kwɪzɪtɪv) *adj* **1** excessively curious, esp. about the affairs of others; prying. **2** eager to learn; inquiring.
▶ in'quisitively *adv* ▶ in'quisitiveness *n*

inquisitor (ɪn'kwɪzɪtə) *n* **1** a person who inquires, esp. deeply, searchingly, or ruthlessly. **2** (*often cap.*) an official of the ecclesiastical court of the Inquisition.

inquisitorial (ɪnˌkwɪzɪ'tɔːrɪəl) *adj* **1** of, relating to, or resembling inquisition or an inquisitor. **2** offensively curious; prying. **3** *Law.* denoting criminal procedure in which one party is both prosecutor and judge, or in which the trial is held in secret. Cf. **accusatorial** (sense 2).
▶ inˌquisi'torially *adv* ▶ inˌquisi'torialness *n*

inquorate (ɪn'kwɔːˌreɪt) *adj Brit.* not consisting of or being a quorum: *this meeting is inquorate.*

in re (ɪn 'reɪ) *prep* in the matter of: used esp. in bankruptcy proceedings. [C17: from L]

INRI *abbrev. for* Iesus Nazarenus Rex Iudaeorum (the inscription placed over Christ's head during the Crucifixion). [L: Jesus of Nazareth, King of the Jews]

inro ('ɪnrəʊ) *n, pl* **inro.** a set of small lacquer boxes formerly worn hung from the belt by Japanese men and used to carry medicines, seals, etc.

inroad ('ɪnˌrəʊd) *n* **1** an invasion or hostile attack; raid or incursion. **2** an encroachment or intrusion.

inrush ('ɪnˌrʌʃ) *n* a sudden usually overwhelming inward flow or rush; influx.
▶ 'in,rushing *n, adj*

ins. *abbrev. for:* **1** inches. **2** insulated. **3** insurance.

insane (ɪn'seɪn) *adj* **1a** mentally deranged; crazy; of unsound mind. **1b** (*as collective n;* preceded by *the*): *the insane.* **2** characteristic of a person of unsound mind: *an insane stare.* **3** irresponsible; very foolish; stupid.
▶ in'sanely *adv* ▶ in'saneness *n*

insanitary (ɪn'sænɪtərɪ, -trɪ) *adj* not sanitary; dirty or infected.

insanity (ɪn'sænɪtɪ) *n, pl* **insanities. 1** relatively permanent disorder of the mind; state or condition of being insane. **2** utter folly; stupidity.

insatiable (ɪn'seɪʃəbᵊl, -ʃɪə-) *or* **insatiate** (ɪn'seɪʃɪɪt) *adj* not able to be satisfied; greedy or unappeasable.
▶ inˌsatia'bility *or* in'satiateness *n* ▶ in'satiably *or* in'satiately *adv*

inscape ('ɪnskeɪp) *n* the essential inner nature of a person, object, etc. [C19: from IN-² + -*scape,* as in LANDSCAPE; coined by Gerard Manley HOPKINS]

inscribe (ɪn'skraɪb) *vb* **inscribes, inscribing, inscribed.** (*tr*) **1** to make, carve, or engrave (writing, letters, etc.) on (a surface such as wood, stone, or paper). **2** to enter (a name) on a list or in a register. **3** to sign one's name on (a book, etc.) before presentation to another person. **4** to draw (a geometric construction) inside another construction so that the two are in contact but do not intersect. [C16: from L *inscrībere;* see INSCRIPTION]
▶ in'scribable *adj* ▶ in'scribableness *n* ▶ in'scriber *n*

inscription (ɪn'skrɪpʃən) *n* **1** something inscribed, esp. words carved or engraved on a coin, tomb, etc. **2** a signature or brief dedication in a book or on a work of art. **3** the act of inscribing. [C14: from L *inscriptiō* a writing upon, from *inscrībere* to write upon, from IN-² + *scrībere* to write]
▶ in'scriptional *or* in'scriptive *adj* ▶ in'scriptively *adv*

inscrutable (ɪn'skruːtəbᵊl) *adj* mysterious or enigmatic; incomprehensible. [C15: from LL, from L IN-¹ + *scrūtārī* to examine]
▶ inˌscruta'bility *or* in'scrutableness *n* ▶ in'scrutably *adv*

insect ('ɪnsɛkt) *n* **1** any of a class of small air-breathing arthropods, having a body divided into head, thorax,

and abdomen, three pairs of legs, and (in most species) two pairs of wings. **2** (loosely) any similar invertebrate, such as a spider, tick, or centipede. **3** a contemptible, loathsome, or insignificant person. [C17: from L *insectum* (animal that has been) cut into, insect, from *insecāre,* from IN-² + *secāre* to cut]
▶ in'sectile *adj* ▶ 'insect-ˌlike *adj*

insectarium (ˌɪnsɛk'tɛərɪəm) *or* **insectary** (ɪn'sɛktərɪ) *n, pl* **insectariums, insectaria** (-'tɛərɪə), *or* **insectaries.** a place where living insects are kept, bred, and studied.

insecticide (ɪn'sɛktɪˌsaɪd) *n* a substance used to destroy insect pests.
▶ inˌsecti'cidal *adj*

insectivore (ɪn'sɛktɪˌvɔː) *n* **1** any of an order of placental mammals, being typically small, with simple teeth, and feeding on invertebrates. The group includes shrews, moles, and hedgehogs. **2** any animal or plant that derives nourishment from insects.
▶ ˌinsec'tivorous *adj*

insecure (ˌɪnsɪ'kjʊə) *adj* **1** anxious or afraid; not confident or certain. **2** not adequately protected: *an insecure fortress.* **3** unstable or shaky.
▶ ˌinse'curely *adv* ▶ ˌinse'cureness *n* ▶ ˌinse'curity *n*

inselberg ('ɪnzᵊlˌbɜːg) *n* an isolated rocky hill rising abruptly from a flat plain. [from G, from *Insel* island + *Berg* mountain]

inseminate (ɪn'sɛmɪˌneɪt) *vb* **inseminates, inseminating, inseminated.** (*tr*) **1** to impregnate (a female) with semen. **2** to introduce (ideas or attitudes) into the mind of (a person or group). [C17: from L *insēmināre,* from IN-² + *sēmināre* to sow, from *sēmen* seed]
▶ inˌsemi'nation *n* ▶ in'semiˌnator *n*

insensate (ɪn'sɛnseɪt, -sɪt) *adj* **1** lacking sensation or consciousness. **2** insensitive; unfeeling. **3** foolish; senseless.
▶ in'sensately *adv* ▶ in'sensateness *n*

insensible (ɪn'sɛnsəbᵊl) *adj* **1** lacking sensation or consciousness. **2** (foll. by *of* or *to*) unaware (of) or indifferent (to): *insensible to suffering.* **3** thoughtless or callous. **4** a less common word for **imperceptible.**
▶ inˌsensi'bility *or* in'sensibleness *n* ▶ in'sensibly *adv*

insensitive (ɪn'sɛnsɪtɪv) *adj* **1** lacking sensitivity; unfeeling. **2** lacking physical sensation. **3** (*postpositive;* foll. by *to*) not sensitive (to) or affected (by): *insensitive to radiation.*
▶ in'sensitively *adv* ▶ in'sensitiveness *or* inˌsensi'tivity *n*

insentient (ɪn'sɛnʃɪənt) *adj* lacking consciousness or senses; inanimate.
▶ in'sentience *n*

inseparable (ɪn'sɛpərəbᵊl, -'sɛprə-) *adj* incapable of being separated or divided.
▶ inˌsepara'bility *or* in'separableness *n* ▶ in'separably *adv*

insert *vb* (ɪn'sɜːt). (*tr*) **1** to put in or between; introduce. **2** to introduce into text, as in a newspaper; interpolate. ◆ *n* ('ɪnsɜːt). **3** something inserted. **4** Also called: **inset. 4a** a folded section placed in another for binding in with a book. **4b** a printed sheet, esp. one bearing advertising, placed loose between the leaves of a book, periodical, etc. [C16: from L *inserere* to plant in, from IN-² + *serere* to join]
▶ in'sertable *adj* ▶ in'serter *n*

insertion (ɪn'sɜːʃən) *n* **1** the act of inserting or something that is inserted. **2** a word, sentence, correction, etc., inserted into text, such as a newspaper. **3** a strip of lace, embroidery, etc., between two pieces of material. **4** *Anat.* the point or manner of attachment of a muscle to the bone that it moves.
▶ in'sertional *adj*

in-service *adj* denoting training that is given to employees during the course of employment: *an in-service course.*

insessorial (ˌɪnsɛ'sɔːrɪəl) *adj* **1** (of feet or claws) adapted for perching. **2** (of birds) having insessorial feet. [C19: from NL *Insessōrēs* birds that perch, from L: perchers, from *insidēre* to sit upon]

inset *vb* (ɪn'sɛt). **insets, insetting, inset. 1** (*tr*) to set or place in or within; insert. ◆ *n* ('ɪnˌsɛt). **2** something inserted. **3** *Printing.* **3a** a small map or diagram set within the borders of a larger one. **3b** another name for **insert** (sense 4).

4 a piece of fabric inserted into a garment, as to shape it or for decoration.
▶ 'in,setter *n*

inshallah (ɪnˈʃælə) *sentence substitute. Islam.* if Allah wills it. [C19: from Ar.]

inshore (ˈɪnˈʃɔː) *adj* **1** in or on the water, but close to the shore: *inshore weather*. ◆ *adv, adj* **2** towards the shore from the water: *an inshore wind; we swam inshore*.

inside *n* (ˈɪnˈsaɪd). **1** the interior; inner or enclosed part or surface. **2** the side of a path away from the road or adjacent to a wall. **3** (*also pl*) *Inf.* the internal organs of the body, esp. the stomach and bowels. **4 inside of.** in a period of time less than; within. **5 inside out.** with the inside facing outwards. **6 know (something) inside out.** to know thoroughly or perfectly. ◆ *prep* (ˌɪnˈsaɪd). **7** in or to the interior of; within or to within; on the inside of. ◆ *adj* (ˈɪnˌsaɪd). **8** on or of an interior; on the inside: *an inside door*. **9** (*prenominal*) arranged or provided by someone within an organization or building, esp. illicitly: *the raid was an inside job; inside information*. ◆ *adv* (ˌɪnˈsaɪd). **10** within or to within a thing or place; indoors. **11** *Sl.* in or into prison.

USAGE NOTE See at **outside.**

---

inside job *n Inf.* a crime committed with the assistance of someone associated with the victim.

inside lane *n Athletics.* the inside, and therefore the shortest, route around a circular or oval multi-lane running track.

insider (ˌɪnˈsaɪdə) *n* **1** a member of a specified group. **2** a person with access to exclusive information.

insider dealing *or* **trading** *n* the illegal practice of a person on the Stock Exchange or in some branches of the Civil Service taking advantage of early confidential information in order to deal in shares for personal profit.
▶ **insider dealer** *or* **trader** *n*

insidious (ɪnˈsɪdɪəs) *adj* **1** stealthy, subtle, cunning, or treacherous. **2** working in a subtle or apparently innocuous way, but nevertheless deadly: *an insidious illness*. [C16: from L *insidiōsus* cunning, from *insidiae* an ambush, from *insidēre* to sit in]
▶ in'sidiously *adv* ▶ in'sidiousness *n*

insight (ˈɪnˌsaɪt) *n* **1** the ability to perceive clearly or deeply; penetration. **2** a penetrating and often sudden understanding, as of a complex situation or problem. **3** *Psychol.* the capacity for understanding one's own or another's mental processes. **4** *Psychiatry.* the ability to understand one's own problems.
▶ 'in,sightful *adj*

insignia (ɪnˈsɪgnɪə) *n, pl* **insignias** *or* **insignia. 1** a badge or emblem of membership, office, or dignity. **2** a distinguishing sign or mark. [C17: from L: badges, from *insignis* distinguished by a mark, prominent, from IN-² + *signum* mark]

insignificant (ˌɪnsɪgˈnɪfɪkənt) *adj* **1** having little or no importance; trifling. **2** almost or relatively meaningless. **3** small or inadequate: *an insignificant wage*. **4** not distinctive in character, etc.
▶ ,insig'nificance *or* ,insig'nificancy *n* ▶ ,insig'nificantly *adv*

insincere (ˌɪnsɪnˈsɪə) *adj* lacking sincerity; hypocritical.
▶ ,insin'cerely *adv* ▶ insincerity (ˌɪnsɪnˈsɛrɪtɪ) *n*

insinuate (ɪnˈsɪnjʊˌeɪt) *vb* **insinuates, insinuating, insinuated. 1** (*may take a clause as object*) to suggest by indirect allusion, hints, innuendo, etc. **2** (*tr*) to introduce subtly or deviously. **3** (*tr*) to cause (someone, esp. oneself) to be accepted by gradual approaches or manoeuvres. [C16: from L *insinuāre* to wind one's way into, from IN-² + *sinus* curve]
▶ in'sinuative *or* in'sinuatory *adj* ▶ in'sinu,ator *n*

insinuation (ɪnˌsɪnjʊˈeɪʃən) *n* **1** an indirect or devious hint or suggestion. **2** the act or practice of insinuating.

insipid (ɪnˈsɪpɪd) *adj* **1** lacking spirit or interest; boring.

2 lacking taste; unpalatable. [C17: from L, from IN-¹ + *sapidus* full of flavour, SAPID]
▶ ,insi'pidity *or* in'sipidness *n* ▶ in'sipidly *adv*

insist (ɪnˈsɪst) *vb* (when *tr*, takes a clause as object; when *intr*, usually foll. by *on* or *upon*) **1** to make a determined demand (for): *he insisted on his rights*. **2** to express a convinced belief (in) or assertion (of). [C16: from L *insistere* to stand upon, urge, from IN-² + *sistere* to stand]
▶ in'sister *n* ▶ in'sistingly *adv*

insistent (ɪnˈsɪstənt) *adj* **1** making continual and persistent demands. **2** demanding notice or attention; compelling: *the insistent cry of a bird*.
▶ in'sistence *or* in'sistency *n* ▶ in'sistently *adv*

in situ Latin. (ɪn ˈsɪtjuː) *adv, adj* (*postpositive*) in the natural, original, or appropriate position.

in so far as *or* **insofar as** (ˌɪnsəʊˈfɑː) *adv* to the degree or extent that.

insolation (ˌɪnsəʊˈleɪʃən) *n* **1** the quantity of solar radiation falling upon a body or planet, esp. per unit area. **2** exposure to the sun's rays. **3** another name for **sunstroke.**

insole (ˈɪnˌsəʊl) *n* **1** the inner sole of a shoe or boot. **2** a loose additional inner sole used to give extra warmth or to make a shoe fit.

insolent (ˈɪnsələnt) *adj* impudent or disrespectful. [C14: from L, from IN-¹ + *solēre* to be accustomed]
▶ 'insolence *n* ▶ 'insolently *adv*

insoluble (ɪnˈsɒljʊbᵊl) *adj* **1** incapable of being dissolved; incapable of forming a solution, esp. in water. **2** incapable of being solved.
▶ in,solu'bility *or* in'solubleness *n* ▶ in'solubly *adv*

insolvent (ɪnˈsɒlvənt) *adj* **1** having insufficient assets to meet debts and liabilities; bankrupt. **2** of or relating to bankrupts or bankruptcy. ◆ *n* **3** a person who is insolvent; bankrupt.
▶ in'solvency *n*

insomnia (ɪnˈsɒmnɪə) *n* chronic inability to fall asleep or to enjoy uninterrupted sleep. [C18: from L, from *insomnis* sleepless, from *somnus* sleep]
▶ in'somni,ac *n, adj* ▶ in'somnious *adj*

insomuch (ˌɪnsəʊˈmʌtʃ) *adv* **1** (foll. by *as* or *that*) to such an extent or degree. **2** (foll. by *as*) because of the fact (that); inasmuch (as).

insouciant (ɪnˈsuːsɪənt) *adj* carefree or unconcerned; light-hearted. [C19: from F, from IN-¹ + *souciant* worrying, from *soucier* to trouble, from L *sollicitāre*]
▶ in'souciance *n* ▶ in'souciantly *adv*

inspan (ɪnˈspæn) *vb* **inspans, inspanning, inspanned.** (*tr*) *Chiefly S. African.* **1** to harness (animals) to (a vehicle); yoke. **2** to press (people) into service. [C19: from Afrik., from MDu. *inspannen*, from *spannen* to stretch]

inspect (ɪnˈspɛkt) *vb* (*tr*) **1** to examine closely, esp. for faults or errors. **2** to scrutinize officially (a document, military personnel on ceremonial parade, etc.). [C17: from L *inspicere*, from *specere* to look]
▶ in'spectable *adj* ▶ in'spection *n* ▶ in'spective *adj*

inspector (ɪnˈspɛktə) *n* **1** a person who inspects, esp. an official who examines for compliance with regulations, standards, etc. **2** a police officer ranking below a superintendent and above a sergeant.
▶ in'spectoral *or* inspectorial (ˌɪnspɛkˈtɔːrɪəl) *adj* ▶ in'spector,ship *n*

inspectorate (ɪnˈspɛktərɪt) *n* **1** the office, rank, or duties of an inspector. **2** a body of inspectors. **3** a district under an inspector.

inspiration (ˌɪnspɪˈreɪʃən) *n* **1** stimulation or arousal of the mind, feelings, etc., to special activity or creativity. **2** the state or quality of being so stimulated or aroused. **3** someone or something that causes this state. **4** an idea or action resulting from such a state. **5** the act or process of inhaling; breathing in.

inspiratory (ɪnˈspaɪərətərɪ, -trɪ) *adj* of or relating to inhalation or the drawing in of air.

inspire (ɪnˈspaɪə) *vb* **inspires, inspiring, inspired. 1** to exert a stimulating or beneficial effect upon (a person, etc.); animate or invigorate. **2** (*tr;* foll. by *with* or *to;* may take an *infinitive*) to arouse (with a particular emotion or to a particular action); stir. **3** (*tr*) to prompt or instigate; give

---

★ **people and places**

rise to. **4** (*tr; often passive*) to guide or arouse by divine influence or inspiration. **5** to take or draw (air, gas, etc.) into the lungs; inhale. **6** (*tr*) *Arch.* to breathe into or upon. [C14 (in the sense: to breathe upon, blow into): from L *inspīrāre*, from *spīrāre* to breathe]
▸ **in'spirable** *adj* ▸ **in'spirative** *adj* ▸ **in'spirer** *n* ▸ **in'spiringly** *adv*

inspirit (ɪn'spɪrɪt) *vb* (*tr*) to fill with vigour; inspire.
▸ **in'spiriter** *n* ▸ **in'spiriting** *adj* ▸ **in'spiritment** *n*

inspissate (ɪn'spɪseɪt) *vb* **inspissates, inspissating, inspissated.** *Arch.* to thicken, as by evaporation. [C17: from LL *inspissātus* thickened, from L, from *spissus* thick]
▸ **,inspis'sation** *n* ▸ **'inspis,sator** *n*

inst. *abbrev. for:* **1** instant (this month). **2** instantaneous. **3** instrumental.

Inst. *abbrev. for:* **1** Institute. **2** Institution.

instability (,ɪnstə'bɪlɪtɪ) *n, pl* **instabilities. 1** lack of stability or steadiness. **2** tendency to variable or unpredictable behaviour.

install *or* **instal** (ɪn'stɔːl) *vb* **installs** *or* **instals, installing, installed.** (*tr*) **1** to place (equipment) in position and connect and adjust for use. **2** to transfer (computer software) from a distribution file to a permanent location on disk, and prepare it for its particular environment and application. **3** to put in a position, rank, etc. **4** to settle (a person, esp. oneself) in a position or state: *she installed herself in an armchair.* [C16: from Med. L *installāre*, from IN-[2] + *stallum* STALL[1]]
▸ **in'staller** *n*

installation (,ɪnstə'leɪʃən) *n* **1** the act of installing or the state of being installed. **2** a large device, system, or piece of equipment that has been installed.

installment plan *or esp. Canad.* **instalment plan** *n* the US and Canad. name for **hire-purchase.**

instalment *or US* **installment** (ɪn'stɔːlmənt) *n* **1** one of the portions into which a debt is divided for payment at specified intervals over a fixed period. **2** a portion of something that is issued, broadcast, or published in parts. [C18: from obs. *estallment*, prob. from OF *estaler* to fix, from *estal* something fixed, from OHG *stal* STALL[1]]

instance ('ɪnstəns) *n* **1** a case or particular example. **2 for instance.** for or as an example. **3** a specified stage in proceedings; step (in **in the first, second,** etc., **instance**). **4** urgent request or demand (esp. in **at the instance of**). ◆ *vb* **instances, instancing, instanced.** (*tr*) **5** to cite as an example. [C14 (in the sense: case, example): from Med. L *instantia* example, (in the sense: urgency) from L: a being close upon, from *instāns* urgent; see INSTANT]

instant ('ɪnstənt) *n* **1** a very brief time; moment. **2** a particular moment or point in time: *at the same instant.* **3 on the instant.** immediately; without delay. ◆ *adj* **4** immediate; instantaneous. **5** (esp. of foods) prepared or designed for preparation with very little time and effort: *instant coffee.* **6** urgent or imperative. **7** (*postpositive*) of the present month: *a letter of the 7th instant.* Abbrev.: **inst.** [C15: from L *instāns*, from *instāre* to be present, press closely, from IN-[2] + *stāre* to stand]

instantaneous (,ɪnstən'teɪnɪəs) *adj* **1** occurring with almost no delay; immediate. **2** happening or completed within a moment: *instantaneous death.*
▸ **,instan'taneously** *adv* ▸ **,instan'taneousness** *or* **instantaneity** (ɪn,stæntə'niːɪtɪ) *n*

instanter (ɪn'stæntə) *adv Law.* without delay; the same day or within 24 hours. [C17: from L: urgently, from *instāns* INSTANT]

instantly ('ɪnstəntlɪ) *adv* **1** immediately; at once. **2** *Arch.* urgently or insistently.

instar ('ɪnstɑː) *n* the stage in the development of an insect between any two moults. [C19: NL from L: image]

instate (ɪn'steɪt) *vb* **instates, instating, instated.** (*tr*) to place in a position or office; install.
▸ **in'statement** *n*

instead (ɪn'sted) *adv* **1** as a replacement, substitute, or alternative. **2 instead of.** (*prep*) in place of or as an alternative to. [C13: from *in stead* in place]

instep ('ɪn,step) *n* **1** the middle section of the human foot, forming the arch between the ankle and toes. **2** the part of a shoe, stocking, etc., covering this. [C16: prob. from IN-[2] + STEP]

instigate ('ɪnstɪ,geɪt) *vb* **instigates, instigating, instigated.** (*tr*) **1** to bring about, as by incitement: *to instigate rebellion.* **2** to urge on to some drastic or unadvisable action. [C16: from L *instīgāre* to incite]
▸ **,insti'gation** *n* ▸ **'insti,gative** *adj* ▸ **'insti,gator** *n*

instil *or US* **instill** (ɪn'stɪl) *vb* **instils** *or US* **instills, instilling, instilled.** (*tr*) **1** to introduce gradually; implant or infuse. **2** *Rare.* to pour in or inject in drops. [C16: from L *instillāre* to pour in a drop at a time, from *stillāre* to drip]
▸ **in'stiller** *n* ▸ **in'stilment,** *US* **in'stillment,** *or* **,instil'lation** *n*

instinct *n* ('ɪnstɪŋkt). **1** the innate capacity of an animal to respond to a given stimulus in a relatively fixed way. **2** inborn intuitive power. ◆ *adj* (ɪn'stɪŋkt). **3** (*postpositive; often foll. by with*) *Rare.* **3a** animated or impelled (by). **3b** imbued or infused (with). [C15: from L *instinctus* roused, from *instinguere* to incite]

instinctive (ɪn'stɪŋktɪv) *adj* **1** of, relating to, or resulting from instinct. **2** conditioned so as to appear innate: *an instinctive movement in driving.*
▸ **in'stinctively** *adv*

instinctual (ɪn'stɪŋktjʊəl) *adj* of or pertaining to instinct.
▸ **in'stinctually** *adv*

institute ('ɪnstɪ,tjuːt) *vb* **institutes, instituting, instituted.** (*tr*) **1** to organize; establish. **2** to initiate: *to institute a practice.* **3** to establish in a position or office; induct. ◆ *n* **4** an organization founded for particular work, such as education, promotion of the arts, or scientific research. **5** the building where such an organization is situated. **6** something instituted, esp. a rule, custom, or precedent. [C16: from L *instituere*, from *statuere* to place]
▸ **'insti,tutor** *or* **'insti,tuter** *n*

institutes ('ɪnstɪ,tjuːts) *pl n* a digest or summary, esp. of laws.

institution (,ɪnstɪ'tjuːʃən) *n* **1** the act of instituting. **2** an organization or establishment founded for a specific purpose, such as a hospital or college. **3** the building where such an organization is situated. **4** an established custom, law, or relationship in a society or community. **5** Also called: **institutional investor.** a large organization, such as an insurance company or pension fund, that has substantial sums to invest on a stock exchange. **6** *Inf.* a constant feature or practice: *Jones's drink at the bar was an institution.* **7** the appointment of an incumbent to an ecclesiastical office or pastoral charge.
▸ **,insti'tutionary** *adj*

institutional (,ɪnstɪ'tjuːʃənᵊl) *adj* **1** of, relating to, or characteristic of institutions. **2** dull, routine, and uniform: *institutional meals.* **3** relating to principles or institutes, esp. of law.
▸ **,insti'tutionally** *adv* ▸ **,insti'tutiona,lism** *n*

institutionalize *or* **institutionalise** (,ɪnstɪ'tjuːʃənə,laɪz) *vb* **institutionalizes, institutionalizing, institutionalized** *or* **institutionalises, institutionalising, institutionalised. 1** (*tr; often passive*) to subject to the deleterious effects of confinement in an institution. **2** (*tr*) to place in an institution. **3** to make or become an institution.
▸ **,insti,tutionali'zation** *or* **,insti,tutionali'sation** *n*

in-store *adj* available within a department store: *in-store banking facilities.*

instruct (ɪn'strʌkt) *vb* (*tr*) **1** to direct to do something; order. **2** to teach (someone) how to do (something). **3** to furnish with information; apprise. **4** *Law, chiefly Brit.* (esp. of a client) to his solicitor or a solicitor to a barrister) to give relevant facts or information to. [C15: from L *instruere* to construct, equip, teach, from *struere* to build]
▸ **in'structible** *adj*

instruction (ɪn'strʌkʃən) *n* **1** a direction; order. **2** the process or act of imparting knowledge; teaching; education. **3** *Computing.* a part of a program consisting of a coded command to the computer to perform a specified function.
▸ **in'structional** *adj*

instructions (ɪn'strʌkʃənz) *pl n* **1** directions, orders, or recommended rules for guidance, use, etc. **2** *Law.* the facts and details relating to a case given by a client to his solicitor or by a solicitor to a barrister.

instructive (ɪn'strʌktɪv) *adj* serving to instruct or enlighten; conveying information.
▸ in'structively *adv* ▸ in'structiveness *n*

instructor (ɪn'strʌktə) *n* **1** someone who instructs; teacher. **2** *US & Canad.* a university teacher ranking below assistant professor.
▸ in'structorship *n* ▸ instructress (ɪn'strʌktrɪs) *fem n*

instrument *n* ('ɪnstrəmənt). **1** a mechanical implement or tool, esp. one used for precision work. **2** *Music.* any of various contrivances or mechanisms that can be played to produce musical tones or sounds. **3** an important factor or agency in something: *her evidence was an instrument in his arrest.* **4** *Inf.* a person used by another to gain an end; dupe. **5** a measuring device, such as a pressure gauge. **6a** a device or system for use in navigation or control, esp. of aircraft. **6b** (*as modifier*): *instrument landing.* **7** a formal legal document. ◆ *vb* ('ɪnstrə,mɛnt). (*tr*) **8** another word for **orchestrate** (sense 1). **9** to equip with instruments. [C13: from L *instrūmentum* tool, from *instruere* to erect, furnish; see INSTRUCT]

instrumental (,ɪnstrə'mɛntªl) *adj* **1** serving as a means or influence; helpful. **2** of, relating to, or characterized by an instrument. **3** played by or composed for musical instruments. **4** *Grammar.* denoting a case of nouns, etc. indicating the instrument used in performing an action, usually using the prepositions *with* or *by means of.* ◆ *n* **5** a piece of music composed for instruments rather than for voices. **6** *Grammar.* the instrumental case.
▸ ,instrumen'tality *n* ▸ ,instru'mentally *adv*

instrumentalist (,ɪnstrə'mɛntəlɪst) *n* a person who plays a musical instrument.

instrumentation (,ɪnstrəmɛn'teɪʃən) *n* **1** the instruments specified in a musical score or arrangement. **2** another word for **orchestration. 3** the study of the characteristics of musical instruments. **4** the use of instruments or tools.

instrument panel *or* **board** *n* **1** a panel on which instruments are mounted, as on a car. See also **dashboard. 2** an array of instruments, gauges, etc., mounted to display the condition or performance of a machine.

insubordinate (,ɪnsə'bɔːdɪnɪt) *adj* **1** not submissive to authority; disobedient or rebellious. **2** not in a subordinate position or rank. ◆ *n* **3** an insubordinate person.
▸ ,insub'ordinately *adv* ▸ ,insub,ordi'nation *n*

insubstantial (,ɪnsəb'stænʃəl) *adj* **1** not substantial; flimsy, tenuous, or slight. **2** imaginary; unreal.
▸ ,insub,stanti'ality *n* ▸ ,insub'stantially *adv*

insufferable (ɪn'sʌfərəbªl) *adj* intolerable; unendurable.
▸ in'sufferableness *n* ▸ in'sufferably *adv*

insufficiency (,ɪnsə'fɪʃənsɪ) *n* **1** Also: ,insuf'ficience. the state of being insufficient. **2** *Pathol.* failure in the functioning of an organ, tissue, etc.: *cardiac insufficiency.*

insufficient (,ɪnsə'fɪʃənt) *adj* not sufficient; inadequate or deficient.
▸ ,insuf'ficiently *adv*

insufflate ('ɪnsʌ,fleɪt) *vb* insufflates, insufflating, insufflated. **1** (*tr*) to breathe or blow (something) into (a room, area, etc.). **2** *Med.* to blow (air, medicated powder, etc.) into a body cavity. **3** (*tr*) to breathe or blow upon (someone or something) as a ritual or sacramental act.
▸ ,insuf'flation *n* ▸ 'insuf,flator *n*

insular ('ɪnsjʊlə) *adj* **1** of, relating to, or resembling an island. **2** remote, detached, or aloof. **3** illiberal or narrow-minded. **4** isolated or separated. [C17: from LL, from L *insula* island]
▸ 'insularism *or* insularity (,ɪnsjʊ'lærɪtɪ) *n* ▸ 'insularly *adv*

insulate ('ɪnsjʊ,leɪt) *vb* insulates, insulating, insulated. (*tr*) **1** to prevent the transmission of electricity, heat, or sound to or from (a body or device) by surrounding with a nonconducting material. **2** to isolate or detach. [C16: from LL *insulātus* made into an island]

insulation (,ɪnsjʊ'leɪʃən) *n* **1** Also: **insulant.** material used to insulate a body or device. **2** the act or process of insulating.

insulator ('ɪnsjʊ,leɪtə) *n* any material or device that insulates, esp. a material with a very low electrical conductivity or thermal conductivity.

insulin ('ɪnsjʊlɪn) *n* a protein hormone, secreted in the pancreas by the islets of Langerhans, that controls the concentration of glucose in the blood. [C20: from NL *insula* islet (of the pancreas) + -IN]

insult *vb* (ɪn'sʌlt). (*tr*) **1** to treat, mention, or speak to rudely; offend; affront. ◆ *n* ('ɪnsʌlt). **2** an offensive or contemptuous remark or action; affront; slight. **3** a person or thing producing the effect of an affront: *some television is an insult to intelligence.* **4** *Med.* an injury or trauma. [C16: from L *insultāre* to jump upon]
▸ in'sulter *n*

insuperable (ɪn'suːpərəbªl, -prəbªl, -'sjuː-) *adj* incapable of being overcome; insurmountable.
▸ in,supera'bility *n* ▸ in'superably *adv*

insupportable (,ɪnsə'pɔːtəbªl) *adj* **1** incapable of being endured; intolerable; insufferable. **2** incapable of being supported or justified; indefensible.
▸ ,insup'portableness *n* ▸ ,insup'portably *adv*

insurance (ɪn'ʃʊərəns, -'ʃɔː-) *n* **1a** the act, system, or business of providing financial protection against specified contingencies, such as death, loss, or damage. **1b** the state of having such protection. **1c** Also called: **insurance policy.** the policy providing such protection. **1d** the pecuniary amount of such protection. **1e** the premium payable in return for such protection. **1f** (*as modifier*): *insurance agent; insurance broker; insurance company.* **2** a means of protecting or safeguarding against risk or injury.

insure (ɪn'ʃʊə, -'ʃɔː) *vb* insures, insuring, insured. **1** (often foll. by *against*) to guarantee or protect (against risk, loss, etc.). **2** (often foll. by *against*) to issue (a person) with an insurance policy or take out an insurance policy (on): *his house was heavily insured against fire.* **3** a variant spelling (esp. US) of **ensure.** ◆ Also (rare) (for senses 1, 2): **ensure.**
▸ in'surable *adj* ▸ in,sura'bility *n*

insured (ɪn'ʃʊəd, -'ʃɔːd) *adj* **1** covered by insurance: *an insured risk.* ◆ *n* **2** the person, persons, or organization covered by an insurance policy.

insurer (ɪn'ʃʊərə, -'ʃɔː-) *n* **1** a person or company offering insurance policies in return for premiums. **2** a person or thing that insures.

insurgence (ɪn'sɜːdʒəns) *n* rebellion, uprising, or riot.

insurgent (ɪn'sɜːdʒənt) *adj* **1** rebellious or in revolt, as against a government in power or the civil authorities. ◆ *n* **2** a person who takes part in an uprising or rebellion; insurrectionist. [C18: from L *insurgēns* rising upon or against, from *surgere* to rise]
▸ in'surgency *n*

insurmountable (,ɪnsə'maʊntəbªl) *adj* incapable of being overcome; insuperable.
▸ ,insur,mounta'bility *or* ,insur'mountableness *n* ▸ ,insur'mountably *adv*

insurrection (,ɪnsə'rɛkʃən) *n* the act or an instance of rebelling against a government in power or the civil authorities; insurgency. [C15: from LL *insurrectiō*, from *insurgere* to rise up]
▸ ,insur'rectional *adj* ▸ ,insur'rectionary *n, adj* ▸ ,insur'rectionist *n, adj*

int. *abbrev. for:* **1** interest. **2** interior. **3** internal. **4** Also: **Int.** international.

intact (ɪn'tækt) *adj* untouched or unimpaired; left complete or perfect. [C15: from L *intactus* not touched, from *tangere* to touch]
▸ in'tactness *n*

intaglio (ɪn'tɑːlɪ,əʊ) *n, pl* intaglios *or* intagli (-lji:). **1** a seal, gem, etc., ornamented with a sunken or incised design. **2** the art or process of incised carving. **3** a design, figure, or ornamentation carved, engraved, or etched into the surface of the material used. **4** any of various printing techniques using an etched or engraved plate. **5** an incised die used to make a design in relief. [C17: from It., from *intagliare* to engrave, from *tagliare* to cut, from LL *tāliāre; see* TAILOR]
▸ intaglied (ɪn'tɑːlɪ,ɛrtɪd) *adj*

intake ('ɪn,teɪk) *n* **1** a thing or a quantity taken in: *an in-*

take of students. **2** the act of taking in. **3** the opening through which fluid enters a duct or channel, esp. the air inlet of a jet engine. **4** a ventilation shaft in a mine. **5** a contraction or narrowing: *an intake in a garment.*

intangible (ɪn'tændʒɪbʰl) *adj* **1** incapable of being perceived by touch; impalpable. **2** imprecise or unclear to the mind: *intangible ideas.* **3** (of property or a business asset) saleable though not possessing intrinsic productive value. ◆ *n* **4** something that is intangible.
▸ in,tangi'bility *n* ▸ in'tangibly *adv*

intarsia (ɪn'tɑːsɪə) *or* **tarsia** *n* **1** a decorative mosaic of inlaid wood of a style developed in the Italian Renaissance. **2** (in knitting) **2a** an individually worked motif. **2b** the method of knitting blocks of colour in place to create such a pattern. [C19: changed from It. *intarsio*]

integer ('ɪntɪdʒə) *n* **1** any rational number that can be expressed as the sum or difference of a finite number of units, as 1, 2, 3, etc. **2** an individual entity or whole unit. [C16: from L: untouched, from *tangere* to touch]

integral ('ɪntɪgrəl, ɪn'tɛgrəl) *adj* **1** (often foll. by *to*) being an essential part (of); intrinsic (to). **2** intact; entire. **3** formed of constituent parts; united. **4** *Maths.* **4a** of or involving an integral. **4b** involving or being an integer. ◆ *n* **5** *Maths.* the sum of a large number of infinitesimally small quantities, summed either between stated limits (**definite integral**) or in the absence of limits (**indefinite integral**). **6** a complete thing; whole. [C17: from L *integrāre*; see INTEGER]
▸ **integrality** (,ɪntɪ'grælɪtɪ) *n* ▸ **integrally** *adv*

integral calculus *n* the branch of calculus concerned with the determination of integrals (**integration**) and their application to the solution of differential equations.

integrand ('ɪntɪ,grænd) *n* a mathematical function to be integrated. [C19: from L: to be integrated]

integrant ('ɪntəgrənt) *adj* **1** part of a whole; integral; constituent. ◆ *n* **2** an integrant part.

integrate *vb* ('ɪntɪ,greɪt), **integrates, integrating, integrated.** **1** to make or be made into a whole; incorporate or be incorporated. **2** (*tr*) to designate (a school, park, etc.) for use by all races or groups; desegregate. **3** to amalgamate or mix (a racial or religious group) with an existing community. **4** *Maths.* to determine the integral of a function or variable. ◆ *adj* ('ɪntɪgrɪt). **5** made up of parts; integrated. [C17: from L *integrāre*; see INTEGER]
▸ **integrable** ('ɪntəgrəbʰl) *adj* ▸ ,integra'bility *n* ▸ ,inte-'gration *n* ▸ 'inte,grative *adj*

integrated circuit *n* a very small electronic circuit consisting of an assembly of elements made from a chip of semiconducting material.

integrity (ɪn'tɛgrɪtɪ) *n* **1** adherence to moral principles; honesty. **2** the quality of being unimpaired; soundness. **3** unity; wholeness. [C15: from L *integritās*; see INTEGER]

integument (ɪn'tɛgjʊmənt) *n* any outer protective layer or covering, such as a cuticle, seed coat, rind, or shell. [C17: from L *integumentum*, from *tegere* to cover]
▸ in,tegu'mental *or* in,tegu'mentary *adj*

intellect ('ɪntɪ,lɛkt) *n* **1** the capacity for understanding, thinking, and reasoning. **2** a mind or intelligence, esp. a brilliant one: *his intellect is wasted on that job.* **3** *Inf.* a person possessing a brilliant mind; brain. [C14: from L *intellectus* comprehension, from *intellegere* to understand; see INTELLIGENCE]
▸ ,intel'lective *adj* ▸ ,intel'lectively *adv*

intellection (,ɪntɪ'lɛkʃən) *n* **1** mental activity; thought. **2** an idea or thought.

intellectual (,ɪntɪ'lɛktʃʊəl) *adj* **1** of or relating to the intellect. **2** appealing to or characteristic of people with a developed intellect: *intellectual literature.* **3** expressing or enjoying mental activity. ◆ *n* **4** a person who enjoys mental activity and has highly developed tastes in art, etc. **5** a person who uses his intellect. **6** a highly intelligent person.
▸ ,intel,lectu'ality *or* ,intel'lectualness *n* ▸ ,intel'lectual-,ize *or* ,intel'lectual,ise *vb* ▸ ,intel'lectually *adv*

intellectualism (,ɪntɪ'lɛktʃʊə,lɪzəm) *n* **1** development and exercise of the intellect. **2** *Philosophy.* the doctrine that reason is the ultimate criterion of knowledge.
▸ ,intel'lectualist *n, adj* ▸ ,intel,lectual'istic *adj*

intellectual property *n* an intangible asset, such as a copyright or patent.

intelligence (ɪn'tɛlɪdʒəns) *n* **1** the capacity for understanding; ability to perceive and comprehend meaning. **2** *Old-fashioned.* news; information. **3** military information about enemies, spies, etc. **4** a group or department that gathers or deals with such information. **5** (*often cap.*) an intelligent being, esp. one that is not embodied. **6** (*modifier*) of or relating to intelligence: *an intelligence network.* [C14: from L *intellegentia*, from *intellegere* to discern, lit.: to choose between, from INTER- + *legere* to choose]
▸ in,telli'gential *adj*

intelligence quotient *n* a measure of the intelligence of an individual. The quotient is derived by dividing an individual's mental age by his chronological age and multiplying the result by 100. Abbrev.: **IQ.**

intelligence test *n* any of a number of tests designed to measure a person's mental skills.

intelligent (ɪn'tɛlɪdʒənt) *adj* **1** having or indicating intelligence; clever. **2** indicating high intelligence; perceptive: *an intelligent guess.* **3** (of computerized functions, weapons, etc.) able to initiate or modify action in the light of ongoing events. **4** (*postpositive;* foll. by *of*) *Arch.* having knowledge or information.
▸ in'telligently *adv*

intelligent card *n* another name for **smart card.**

intelligentsia (ɪn,tɛlɪ'dʒɛntsɪə) *n* (usually preceded by *the*) the educated or intellectual people in a society or community. [C20: from Russian *intelligentsiya*, from L *intellegentia* INTELLIGENCE]

intelligible (ɪn'tɛlɪdʒəbʰl) *adj* **1** able to be understood; comprehensible. **2** *Philosophy.* capable of being apprehended by the mind or intellect alone. [C14: from L *intellegibilis*; see INTELLECT]
▸ in,telli'gibility *n* ▸ in'telligibly *adv*

intemperate (ɪn'tɛmpərɪt, -prɪt) *adj* **1** consuming alcoholic drink habitually or to excess; immoderate. **2** unrestrained: *intemperate rage.* **3** extreme or severe: *an intemperate climate.*
▸ in'temperance *or* in'temperateness *n* ▸ in'temperately *adv*

intend (ɪn'tɛnd) *vb* **1** (*may take a clause as object*) to propose or plan (something or to do something); have in mind; mean. **2** (*tr;* often foll. by *for*) to design or destine (for a certain purpose, person, etc.). **3** (*tr*) to mean to express or indicate: *what do his words intend?* **4** (*intr*) to have a purpose as specified; mean: *he intends well.* [C14: from L *intendere* to stretch forth, give one's attention to, from *tendere* to stretch]
▸ in'tender *n*

intendancy (ɪn'tɛndənsɪ) *n* **1** the position or work of an intendant. **2** intendants collectively.

intendant (ɪn'tɛndənt) *n* a senior administrator; superintendent or manager.

intended (ɪn'tɛndɪd) *adj* **1** planned or future. ◆ *n* **2** *Inf.* a person whom one is to marry; fiancé or fiancée.

intense (ɪn'tɛns) *adj* **1** of extreme force, strength, degree, or amount: *intense heat.* **2** characterized by deep or forceful feelings: *an intense person.* [C14: from L *intensus* stretched, from *intendere* to stretch out]
▸ in'tensely *adv* ▸ in'tenseness *n*

> **USAGE NOTE** *Intense* is sometimes wrongly used where *intensive* is meant: *the land is under intensive* (not *intense*) *cultivation. Intensely* is sometimes wrongly used where *intently* is meant: *he listened intently* (not *intensely*).

intensifier (ɪn'tɛnsɪ,faɪə) *n* **1** a person or thing that intensifies. **2** a word, esp. an adjective or adverb, that serves to intensify the meaning of the word or phrase that it modifies. **3** a substance, esp. one containing silver or uranium, used to increase the density of a photographic film or plate.

intensify (ɪn'tɛnsɪ,faɪ) *vb* **intensifies, intensifying, intensi-**

fied. **1** to make or become intense or more intense. **2** (*tr*) to increase the density of (a photographic film or plate).
▶ in,tensifi'cation *n*

intension (ɪnˈtɛnʃən) *n Logic.* the set of characteristics or properties that distinguish the referent or referents of a given word.
▶ in'tensional *adj*

intensity (ɪnˈtɛnsɪtɪ) *n, pl* **intensities. 1** the state or quality of being intense. **2** extreme force, degree, or amount. **3** *Physics.* **3a** a measure of field strength or of the energy transmitted by radiation. **3b** (of sound in a specified direction) the average rate of flow of sound energy for one period through unit area at right angles to the specified direction.

intensive (ɪnˈtɛnsɪv) *adj* **1** of, relating to, or characterized by intensity: *intensive training.* **2** (*usually in combination*) using one factor of production proportionately more than others, as specified: *capital-intensive; labour-intensive.* **3** *Agriculture.* involving or farmed using large amounts of capital or labour to increase production from a particular area. Cf. **extensive** (sense 3). **4** denoting or relating to a grammatical intensifier. **5** denoting or belonging to a class of pronouns used to emphasize a noun or personal pronoun. **6** of or relating to intension. ◆ *n* **7** an intensifier or intensive pronoun or grammatical construction.
▶ in'tensively *adv* ▶ in'tensiveness *n*

intensive care *n* **1** extensive and continuous care provided for an acutely ill patient in a hospital. **2** the unit in which this care is provided; intensive-care unit.

intent (ɪnˈtɛnt) *n* **1** something that is intended; aim; purpose; design. **2** the act of intending. **3** *Law.* the will or purpose with which one does an act. **4** implicit meaning; connotation. **5 to all intents and purposes.** for all practical purposes; virtually. ◆ *adj* **6** firmly fixed; determined; concentrated: *an intent look.* **7** (*postpositive*; usually foll. by *on* or *upon*) having the fixed intention (of); directing one's mind or energy (to): *intent on committing a crime.* [C13 in the sense: intention): from LL *intentus* aim, from L: a stretching out; see INTEND]
▶ in'tently *adv* ▶ in'tentness *n*

intention (ɪnˈtɛnʃən) *n* **1** a purpose or goal; aim: *it is his intention to reform.* **2** *Med.* a natural healing process in which the edges of a wound cling together with no tissue between (**first intention**), or in which the edges adhere with tissue between (**second intention**). **3** (*usually pl*) design or purpose with respect to a proposal of marriage (esp. in **honourable intentions**).

intentional (ɪnˈtɛnʃən²l) *adj* **1** performed by or expressing intention; deliberate. **2** of or relating to intention or purpose.
▶ in,tention'ality *n* ▶ in'tentionally *adv*

inter (ɪnˈtɜː) *vb* **inters, interring, interred.** (*tr*) to place (a body, etc.) in the earth; bury, esp. with funeral rites. [C14: from OF *enterrer*, from L IN-² + *terra* earth]

inter- *prefix* **1** between or among: *international.* **2** together, mutually, or reciprocally: *interdependent; interchange.* [from L]

interact (ˌɪntərˈækt) *vb* (*intr*) to act on or in close relation with each other.

interaction (ˌɪntəˈrækʃən) *n* **1** a mutual or reciprocal action. **2** *Physics.* the transfer of energy between elementary particles, between a particle and a field, or between fields. See **fundamental interaction**.

interactive (ˌɪntərˈæktɪv) *adj* **1** allowing or relating to continuous two-way transfer of information between a user and the central point of a communication system, such as a computer or television. **2** (of two or more persons, forces, etc.) acting upon or in close relation with each other; interacting.

inter alia *Latin.* (ˈɪntər ˈeɪlɪə) *adv* among other things.

interbreed (ˌɪntəˈbriːd) *vb* **interbreeds, interbreeding, interbred. 1** to breed within a single family or strain so as to produce particular characteristics in the offspring. **2** another term for **crossbreed** (sense 1).

interbroker dealer (ˌɪntəˈbrəʊkə) *n Stock Exchange.* a specialist who matches the needs of different market makers and facilitates dealings between them.

intercalary (ɪnˈtɜːkələrɪ) *adj* **1** (of a day, month, year, etc.) inserted in the calendar. **2** (of a particular year) having one or more days inserted. **3** inserted, introduced, or interpolated. [C17: from L *intercalārius*; see INTERCALATE]

intercalate (ɪnˈtɜːkəˌleɪt) *vb* **intercalates, intercalating, intercalated.** (*tr*) **1** to insert (one or more days) into the calendar. **2** to interpolate or insert. [C17: from L *intercalāre* to insert, proclaim that a day has been inserted, from INTER- + *calāre* to proclaim]
▶ in,terca'lation *n* ▶ in'tercalative *adj*

intercede (ˌɪntəˈsiːd) *vb* **intercedes, interceding, interceded.** (*intr*; often foll. by *in*) to come between parties or act as mediator or advocate: *to intercede in the strike.* [C16: from L *intercēdere*, from INTER- + *cēdere* to move]
▶ ˌinter'ceder *n*

intercensal (ˌɪntəˈsɛnsəl) *adj* (of population figures, etc.) estimated at a time between official censuses. [C19: from INTER- + *censal*, irregularly formed from CENSUS]

intercept *vb* (ˌɪntəˈsɛpt). (*tr*) **1** to stop, deflect, or seize on the way from one place to another; prevent from arriving or proceeding. **2** *Sport.* to seize or cut off (a pass) on its way from one opponent to another. **3** *Maths.* to cut off, mark off, or bound (some part of a line, curve, plane, or surface). ◆ *n* (ˈɪntəˌsɛpt). **4** *Maths.* **4a** a point at which two figures intersect. **4b** the distance from the origin to the point at which a line, curve, or surface cuts a coordinate axis. **5** *Sport, US & Canad.* the act of intercepting an opponent's pass. [C16: from L *intercipere* to seize before arrival, from INTER- + *capere* to take]
▶ ˌinter'ception *n* ▶ ˌinter'ceptive *adj*

interceptor *or* **intercepter** (ˌɪntəˈsɛptə) *n* **1** a person or thing that intercepts. **2** a fast highly manoeuvrable fighter aircraft used to intercept enemy aircraft.

intercession (ˌɪntəˈsɛʃən) *n* **1** the act or an instance of interceding. **2** the act of interceding or offering petitionary prayer to God on behalf of others. **3** such petitionary prayer. [C16: from L *intercessio*; see INTERCEDE]
▶ ˌinter'cessional *or* ˌinter'cessory *adj* ▶ ˌinter'cessor *n* ▶ ˌinterces'sorial *adj*

interchange *vb* (ˌɪntəˈtʃeɪndʒ). **interchanges, interchanging, interchanged. 1** to change places or cause to change places; alternate; exchange; switch. ◆ *n* (ˈɪntəˌtʃeɪndʒ). **2** the act of interchanging; exchange or alternation. **3** a motorway junction of interconnecting roads and bridges designed to prevent streams of traffic crossing one another.
▶ ˌinter'changeable *adj* ▶ ˌinter,changea'bility *or* ˌinter'changeableness *n* ▶ ˌinter'changeably *adv*

Intercity (ˌɪntəˈsɪtɪ) *adj* (in Britain) *Trademark.* denoting a fast train or passenger rail service, esp. between main towns.

intercom (ˈɪntəˌkɒm) *n Inf.* an internal telephone system for communicating within a building, aircraft, etc. [C20: short for INTERCOMMUNICATION]

intercommunicate (ˌɪntəkəˈmjuːnɪˌkeɪt) *vb* **intercommunicates, intercommunicating, intercommunicated.** (*intr*) **1** to communicate mutually. **2** to interconnect, as two rooms, etc.
▶ ˌintercom'municable *adj* ▶ ˌintercom,muni'cation *n* ▶ ˌintercom'municative *adj*

intercommunion (ˌɪntəkəˈmjuːnjən) *n* association between Churches, involving esp. mutual reception of Holy Communion.

intercontinental (ˌɪntəˌkɒntɪˈnɛnt²l) *adj* travelling between or linking continents.

interconvertible (ˌɪntəkənˈvɜːtɪb²l) *adj* (of two or more things) capable of being converted into each other.

intercostal (ˌɪntəˈkɒst²l) *adj Anat.* between the ribs: *intercostal muscles.* [C16: via NL from L INTER- + *costa* rib]

intercourse (ˈɪntəˌkɔːs) *n* **1** See **sexual intercourse. 2** communication or exchange between individuals; mutual dealings. [C15: from Med. L *intercursus* business, from L *intercurrere* to run between]

intercurrent (ˌɪntəˈkʌrənt) *adj* **1** occurring during or in

between; intervening. **2** *Pathol.* (of a disease) occurring during the course of another disease.
▸ ˌinterˈcurrence *n*

nterdependent (ˌɪntədɪˈpɛndənt) *adj* (of two or more things) dependent on each other.

nterdict *n* (ˈɪntəˌdɪkt). **1** *RC Church.* the exclusion of a person in a particular place from certain sacraments, although not from communion. **2** *Civil law.* any order made by a court or official prohibiting an act. **3** *Scots Law.* an order having the effect of an injunction. ◆ *vb* (ˌɪntəˈdɪkt). (*tr*) **4** to place under legal or ecclesiastical sanction; prohibit; forbid. **5** *Mil.* to destroy (an enemy's lines of communication) by firepower. [C13: from L *interdictum* prohibition, from *interdīcere* to forbid, from INTER- + *dīcere* to say]
▸ ˌinterˈdiction *n* ▸ ˌinterˈdictive *or* ˌinterˈdictory *adj*
▸ ˌinterˈdictively *adv* ▸ ˌinterˈdictor *n*

nterdigitate (ˌɪntəˈdɪdʒɪˌteɪt) *vb* **interdigitates, interdigitating, interdigitated.** (*intr*) to interlock like the fingers of clasped hands. [C19: from INTER- + L *digitus* (see DIGIT) + -ATE¹]

nterdisciplinary (ˌɪntəˈdɪsɪˌplɪnərɪ) *adj* involving two or more academic disciplines.

nterest (ˈɪntrɪst, -tərɪst) *n* **1** the sense of curiosity about or concern with something or someone. **2** the power of stimulating such a sense: *to have great interest.* **3** the quality of such stimulation. **4** something in which one is interested; a hobby or pursuit. **5** (*often pl*) benefit; advantage: *in one's own interest.* **6** (*often pl*) a right, share, or claim, esp. in a business or property. **7a** a charge for the use of credit or borrowed money. **7b** such a charge expressed as a percentage per time unit of the sum borrowed or used. **8** (*often pl*) a section of a community, etc., whose members have common aims: *the landed interest.* **9 declare an interest.** to make known one's connection, esp. a prejudicial connection, with an affair. ◆ *vb* (*tr*) **10** to arouse or excite the curiosity or concern of. **11** to cause to become involved in something; concern. [C15: from L: it concerns, from *interesse,* from INTER- + *esse* to be]

nterested (ˈɪntrɪstɪd, -tərɪs-) *adj* **1** showing or having interest. **2** (*usually prenominal*) personally involved or implicated: *the interested parties met to discuss the business.*
▸ ˈinterestedly *adv* ▸ ˈinterestedness *n*

nteresting (ˈɪntrɪstɪŋ, -tərɪs-) *adj* inspiring interest; absorbing.
▸ ˈinterestingly *adv* ▸ ˈinterestingness *n*

nterest-rate futures *pl n* financial futures based on projected movements of interest rates.

nterface *n* (ˈɪntəˌfeɪs). **1** *Physical chem.* a surface that forms the boundary between two liquids or chemical phases. **2** a common point or boundary between two things. **3** an electrical circuit linking one device, esp. a computer, with another. ◆ *vb* (ˌɪntəˈfeɪs). **interfaces, interfacing, interfaced. 4** (*tr*) to design or adapt the input and output configurations of (two electronic devices) so that they may work together compatibly. **5** to be an interface (with). **6** to be interactive (with).
▸ **interfacial** (ˌɪntəˈfeɪʃəl) *adj* ▸ ˌinterˈfacially *adv*

nterfacing (ˈɪntəˌfeɪsɪŋ) *n* **1** a piece of fabric sewn beneath the facing of a garment, usually at the inside of the neck, armholes, etc., to give shape and firmness. **2** another name for **interlining.**

nterfere (ˌɪntəˈfɪə) *vb* **interferes, interfering, interfered.** (*intr*) **1** (often foll. by *in*) to interpose, esp. meddlesomely or unwarrantedly; intervene. **2** (often foll. by *with*) to come between or into opposition; hinder. **3** (foll. by *with*) *Euphemistic.* to assault sexually. **4** to strike one against the other, as a horse's legs. **5** *Physics.* to cause or produce interference. [C16: from OF *s'entreferir* to collide, from *entre-* INTER- + *ferir* to strike, from L *ferīre*]
▸ ˌinterˈfering *adj*

nterference (ˌɪntəˈfɪərəns) *n* **1** the act or an instance of interfering. **2** *Physics.* the process in which two or more coherent waves combine to form a resultant wave in which the displacement at any point is the vector sum of the displacements of the individual waves. **3** any undesired signal that tends to interfere with the reception of radio waves.
▸ **interferential** (ˌɪntəfəˈrɛnʃəl) *adj*

interferometer (ˌɪntəfəˈrɒmɪtə) *n Physics.* any acoustic, optical, or microwave instrument that uses interference patterns to make accurate measurements of wavelength, distance, etc.
▸ **interferometric** (ˌɪntəˌfɛrəˈmɛtrɪk) *adj* ▸ ˌinterˌferoˈmetrically *adv* ▸ ˌinterferˈometry *n*

interferon (ˌɪntəˈfɪərɒn) *n Biochem.* any of a family of proteins made by cells in response to virus infection that prevent the growth of the virus. [C20: from INTERFERE + -ON]

interfuse (ˌɪntəˈfjuːz) *vb* **interfuses, interfusing, interfused. 1** to diffuse or mix throughout or become so diffused or mixed; intermingle. **2** to blend or fuse or become blended or fused.
▸ ˌinterˈfusion *n*

intergovernmental (ˌɪntəˌɡʌvənˈmɛnt°l) *adj* conducted between or involving two or more governments.

interim (ˈɪntərɪm) *adj* **1** (*prenominal*) temporary, provisional, or intervening: *interim measures to deal with the emergency.* ◆ *n* **2** (usually preceded by *the*) the intervening time; the meantime (esp. in **in the interim**). ◆ *adv* **3** *Rare.* meantime. [C16: from L: meanwhile]

interior (ɪnˈtɪərɪə) *n* **1** a part, surface, or region that is inside or on the inside: *the interior of Africa.* **2** inner character or nature. **3** a film or scene shot inside a building, studio, etc. **4** a picture of the inside of a room or building, as in a painting or stage design. **5** the inside of a building or room, with respect to design and decoration. ◆ *adj* **6** of, situated on, or suitable for the inside; inner. **7** coming or acting from within; internal. **8** of or involving a nation's domestic affairs; internal. **9** (esp. of one's spiritual or mental life) secret or private; not observable. [C15: from L (adj), comp. of *inter* within]
▸ inˈteriorly *adv*

interior angle *n* an angle of a polygon contained between two adjacent sides.

interior decoration *n* **1** the colours, furniture, etc., of the interior of a house, etc. **2** Also called: **interior design.** the art or business of planning the interiors of houses, etc.
▸ **interior decorator** *n*

interiorize *or* **interiorise** (ɪnˈtɪərɪəˌraɪz) *vb* **interiorizes, interiorizing, interiorized** *or* **interiorises, interiorising, interiorised.** (*tr*) another word for **internalize.**

interj. *abbrev. for* interjection.

interject (ˌɪntəˈdʒɛkt) *vb* (*tr*) to interpose abruptly or sharply; interrupt with; throw in: *she interjected clever remarks.* [C16: from L *interjicere* to place between, from *jacere* to throw]
▸ ˌinterˈjector *n*

interjection (ˌɪntəˈdʒɛkʃən) *n* **1** the act of interjecting. **2** a word or phrase that is used in syntactic isolation and that expresses sudden emotion; expletive. Abbrev.: **interj.**
▸ ˌinterˈjectional *or* ˌinterˈjectory *adj* ▸ ˌinterˈjectionally *adv*

Interlaken ★ (ˈɪntəˌlɑːkən) *n* a town and resort in central Switzerland, situated between Lakes Brienz and Thun on the River Aar. Pop.: 4900 (1987 est.).

interlard (ˌɪntəˈlɑːd) *vb* (*tr*) **1** to scatter thickly in or between; intersperse: *to interlard one's writing with foreign phrases.* **2** to occur frequently in; be scattered in or through: *foreign phrases interlard his writings.*

interlay (ˌɪntəˈleɪ) *vb* **interlays, interlaying, interlaid.** (*tr*) to insert (layers) between; interpose.

interleaf (ˈɪntəˌliːf) *n, pl* **interleaves.** a blank leaf inserted between the leaves of a book.

interleave (ˌɪntəˈliːv) *vb* **interleaves, interleaving, interleaved.** (*tr*) **1** (often foll. by *with*) to interspersed (with), esp. alternately, as the illustrations in a book (with protective leaves). **2** to provide (a book) with blank leaves for notes, etc., or to protect illustrations.

interleukin (ˌɪntəˈluːkɪn) *n* a substance extracted from white blood cells that stimulates their activity against infection and may be used to combat some forms of cancer.

interline¹ (ˌɪntəˈlaɪn) *or* **interlineate** (ˌɪntəˈlɪnɪˌeɪt) *vb*

interlines, interlining, interlined or **interlineates, interlineating, interlineated.** (*tr*) to write or print (matter) between the lines of (a text, book, etc.).
▶ ˈinterˌlining or ˌinterˌlineˈation *n*

interline[2] (ˌɪntəˈlaɪn) *vb* **interlines, interlining, interlined.** (*tr*) to provide (a part of a garment) with a second lining, esp. of stiffened material.
▶ ˈinterˌliner *n*

interlinear (ˌɪntəˈlɪnɪə) or **interlineal** *adj* **1** written or printed between lines of text. **2** written or printed with the text in different languages or versions on alternate lines.
▶ ˌinterˈlinearly or ˌinterˈlineally *adv*

interlining (ˈɪntəˌlaɪnɪŋ) *n* the material used to interline parts of garments, now often made of reinforced paper.

interlock *vb* (ˌɪntəˈlɒk). **1** to join or be joined firmly, as by a mutual interconnection of parts. ◆ *n* (ˈɪntəˌlɒk). **2** the act of interlocking or the state of being interlocked. **3** a device, esp. one operated electromechanically, used in a logic circuit to prevent an activity being initiated unless preceded by certain events. **4** a closely knitted fabric. ◆ *adj* **5** closely knitted.
▶ ˈinterˌlocker *n*

interlocutor (ˌɪntəˈlɒkjʊtə) *n* **1** a person who takes part in a conversation. **2** the man in the centre of a troupe of minstrels who engages the others in talk or acts as announcer. **3** *Scots Law.* a decree by a judge.
▶ ˌinterˈlocutress, ˌinterˈlocutrice, or ˌinterˈlocutrix *fem n*

interlocutory (ˌɪntəˈlɒkjʊtərɪ, -trɪ) *adj* **1** *Law.* pronounced during the course of proceedings; provisional: *an interlocutory injunction.* **2** interposed, as into a conversation, narrative, etc. **3** of, relating to, or characteristic of dialogue.
▶ ˌinterˈlocutorily *adv*

interloper (ˈɪntəˌləʊpə) *n* **1** an intruder. **2** a person who introduces himself into professional or social circles where he does not belong. **3** a person who interferes in matters that are not his concern. [C17: from INTER- + *loper*, from MDu. *loopen* to leap]
▶ ˈinterˌlope *vb* (*intr*)

interlude (ˈɪntəˌluːd) *n* **1** a period of time or different activity between longer periods, processes, or events; episode or interval. **2** *Theatre.* a short dramatic piece played separately or as part of a longer entertainment, common in 16th-century England. **3** a brief piece of music, dance, etc., given between the sections of another performance. [C14: from Med. L, from L INTER- + *lūdus* play]

intermarry (ˌɪntəˈmærɪ) *vb* **intermarries, intermarrying, intermarried.** (*intr*) **1** (of different races, religions, etc.) to become connected by marriage. **2** to marry within one's own family, clan, group, etc.
▶ ˌinterˈmarriage *n*

intermediary (ˌɪntəˈmiːdɪərɪ) *n, pl* **intermediaries. 1** a person who acts as a mediator or agent between parties. **2** something that acts as a medium or means. ◆ *adj* **3** acting as an intermediary. **4** situated, acting, or coming between.

intermediate *adj* (ˌɪntəˈmiːdɪɪt). **1** occurring or situated between two points, extremes, places, etc.; in between. **2** (of a class, course, etc.) suitable for learners with some degree of skill or competence. ◆ *n* (ˌɪntəˈmiːdɪɪt). **3** something intermediate. **4** a substance formed during one of the stages of a chemical process before the desired product is obtained. ◆ *vb* (ˌɪntəˈmiːdɪˌeɪt), **intermediates, intermediating, intermediated. 5** (*intr*) to act as an intermediary or mediator. [C17: from Med. L *intermediāre* to intervene, from L INTER- + *medius* middle]
▶ ˌinterˈmediacy or ˌinterˈmediateness *n* ▶ ˌinterˈmediately *adv* ▶ ˌinterˌmediˈation *n* ▶ ˌinterˈmediˌator *n*

intermediate-acting *adj* (of a drug) intermediate in its effects between long- and short-acting drugs. Cf. **long-acting, short-acting.**

intermediate frequency *n Electronics.* the frequency to which the signal carrier frequency is changed in a superheterodyne receiver and at which most of the amplification takes place.

intermediate-level waste *n* radioactive waste material, such as reactor components, that can be mixed with concrete and safely stored in steel drums in deep mines or beneath the seabed in concrete chambers. Cf. **high-level waste, low-level waste.**

intermediate vector boson *n Physics.* a hypothetical particle believed to mediate the weak interaction between elementary particles.

interment (ɪnˈtɜːmənt) *n* burial, esp. with ceremonial rites.

intermezzo (ˌɪntəˈmetsəʊ) *n, pl* **intermezzos** or **intermezzi** (-tsiː). **1** a short piece of instrumental music composed for performance between the acts or scenes of an opera, drama, etc. **2** an instrumental piece either inserted between two longer movements in an extended composition or intended for independent performance. [C19: from It., from LL *intermedium* interval; see INTERMEDIATE]

interminable (ɪnˈtɜːmɪnəbʰl) *adj* endless or seemingly endless because of monotony or tiresome length.
▶ inˈterminableness *n* ▶ inˈterminably *adv*

intermission (ˌɪntəˈmɪʃən) *n* **1** an interval, as between parts of a film, etc. **2** a period between events or activities; pause. **3** the act of intermitting or the state of being intermitted. [C16: from L, from *intermittere* to INTERMIT]
▶ ˌinterˈmissive *adj*

intermit (ˌɪntəˈmɪt) *vb* **intermits, intermitting, intermitted.** to suspend (activity) or (of activity) to be suspended temporarily or at intervals. [C16: from L *intermittere* to leave off, from INTER- + *mittere* to send]
▶ ˌinterˈmittor *n*

intermittent (ˌɪntəˈmɪtʰnt) *adj* occurring occasionally or at regular or irregular intervals; periodic.
▶ ˌinterˈmittence or ˌinterˈmittency *n* ▶ ˌinterˈmittently *adv*

intermix (ˌɪntəˈmɪks) *vb* **1** (*tr*) to mix (ingredients, liquids, etc.) together. **2** (*intr*) to become or have the capacity to become combined, joined, etc.

intermixture (ˌɪntəˈmɪkstʃə) *n* **1** the act of intermixing or state of being intermixed. **2** an additional ingredient.

intern *vb* **1** (ɪnˈtɜːn). (*tr*) to detain or confine within a country or a limited area, esp. during wartime. **2** (ˈɪntɜːn). (*intr*) *Chiefly US.* to serve or train as an intern. ◆ *n* (ˈɪntɜːn). **3** another word for **internee. 4** Also: **interne.** the approximate US and Canad. equivalent of **houseman. 5** Also: **interne.** *Chiefly US.* a student teacher. **6** Also: **interne.** *Chiefly US.* a student or recent graduate undergoing practical training in a working environment. [C19: from L *internus* internal]
▶ inˈternment *n* ▶ ˈinternship or ˈinterneship *n*

internal (ɪnˈtɜːnʰl) *adj* **1** of, situated on, or suitable for the inside; inner. **2** coming or acting from within; interior. **3** involving the spiritual or mental life; subjective. **4** of or involving a nation's domestic as opposed to foreign affairs. **5** situated within, affecting, or relating to the inside of the body. ◆ *n* **6** *Euphemistic.* a medical examination of the vagina or uterus. [C16: from Med. L, from LL *internus* inward]
▶ inˈternality or inˈternalness *n* ▶ inˈternally *adv*

internal-combustion engine *n* a heat engine in which heat is supplied by burning the fuel in the working fluid (usually air).

internal energy *n* the thermodynamic property of a system that changes by an amount equal to the work done on the system when it suffers an adiabatic change.

internalize or **internalise** (ɪnˈtɜːnəˌlaɪz) *vb* **internalizes, internalizing, internalized** or **internalises, internalising, internalised.** (*tr*) *Psychol., sociol.* to make internal, esp. to incorporate within oneself (values, attitudes, etc.) through learning or socialization. Also: **interiorize.**
▶ inˌternaliˈzation or inˌternaliˈsation *n*

internal market *n* a system in which goods and services are sold by the provider to a range of purchasers within the same organization, who compete to establish the price of the product.

internal medicine *n* the branch of medical science concerned with the diagnosis and nonsurgical treatment of disorders of the internal structures of the body.

international (ˌɪntəˈnæʃənʰl) *adj* **1** of, concerning, or involving two or more nations or nationalities. **2** established by, controlling, or legislating for several nations:

★ people and places

an international court. **3** available for use by all nations: *international waters.* ◆ *n* **4** *Sport.* **4a** a contest between two national teams. **4b** a member of a national team.
▶ ˌinterˈnationˈality *n* ▶ ˌinterˈnationally *adv*

nternational (ˌɪntəˈnæʃənˀl) *n* **1** any of several international socialist organizations, esp. **First International** (1864–76) and **Second International** (1889 until World War I). **2** a member of any of these organizations.

nternational Atomic Time *n* the scientific standard of time based on the SI unit, the second, used to synchronize the time standards of the major nations. Abbrev.: **TAI.**

nternational Bank for Reconstruction and Development *n* the official name for the **World Bank.**

nternational Court of Justice *n* a court established in the Hague, in the Netherlands, to settle disputes brought by nations that are parties to the Statute of the Court. Also called: **World Court.**

nternational Date Line *n* the line approximately following the 180° meridian from Greenwich on the east side of which the date is one day earlier than on the west.

nternationalism (ˌɪntəˈnæʃənəˌlɪzəm) *n* **1** the ideal or practice of cooperation and understanding between nations. **2** the state or quality of being international.
▶ ˌinterˈnationalist *n*

nternationalize *or* **internationalise** (ˌɪntəˈnæʃənəˌlaɪz) *vb* **internationalizes, internationalizing, internationalized** *or* **internationalises, internationalising, internationalised.** (*tr*) **1** to make international. **2** to put under international control.
▶ ˌinterˌnationaliˈzation *or* ˌinterˌnationaliˈsation *n*

nternational law *n* the body of rules generally recognized by civilized nations as governing their conduct towards each other.

International Modernism *n* See **International Style.**

International Phonetic Alphabet *n* a series of signs and letters for the representation of human speech sounds. It is based on the Roman alphabet but supplemented by modified signs or symbols from other writing systems.

International Practical Temperature Scale *n* a temperature scale adopted by international agreement in 1968 based on thermodynamic temperature and using experimental values to define 11 fixed points.

International Style *or* **Modernism** *n* an architectural style of the 1920s that used cubic forms, large windows, and modern materials.

International Telecommunications Union *n* a special agency of the United Nations, founded in 1947, that is responsible for the international allocation and registration of frequencies for communications and the regulation of telegraph, telephone, and radio services.

interne (ˈɪntɜːn) *n* a variant spelling of **intern** (senses 4, 5, 6).

internecine (ˌɪntəˈniːsaɪn) *adj* **1** mutually destructive or ruinous; maiming both or all sides: *internecine war.* **2** of or relating to slaughter or carnage; bloody. **3** of or involving conflict within a group or organization. [C17: from L, from *internecāre* to destroy, from *necāre* to kill]

internee (ˌɪntɜːˈniː) *n* a person who is interned, esp. an enemy citizen in wartime or a terrorism suspect.

Internet (ˈɪntəˌnɛt) *n* **the.** the single worldwide computer network that interconnects other computer networks, on which end-user services, such as World Wide Web sites or data archives, are located, enabling data and other information to be exchanged. Also called: the **Net.**

internist (ˈɪntɜːnɪst, ɪnˈtɜːnɪst) *n* a physician who specializes in internal medicine.

interpellate (ɪnˈtɜːpəˌleɪt) *vb* **interpellates, interpellating, interpellated.** (*tr*) *Parliamentary procedure.* (in European legislatures) to question (a member of the government) on a point of government policy, often interrupting the business of the day. [C16: from L *interpellāre* to disturb, from INTER- + *pellere* to push]
▶ inˌterpelˈlation *n* ▶ inˈterpelˌlator *n*

interpenetrate (ˌɪntəˈpɛnɪˌtreɪt) *vb* **interpenetrates, inter-**

penetrating, interpenetrated. 1 to penetrate (something) thoroughly; pervade. **2** to penetrate each other or one another mutually.
▶ ˌinterˈpenetrable *adj* ▶ ˌinterˈpenetrant *adj* ▶ ˌinterˌpeneˈtration *n* ▶ ˌinterˈpenetrative *adj* ▶ ˌinterˈpenetratively *adv*

interplay (ˈɪntəˌpleɪ) *n* reciprocal and mutual action and reaction, as in circumstances, events, or personal relations.

interpleader (ˌɪntəˈpliːdə) *n* *Law.* **1** a process by which a person holding money claimed by two or more parties and having no interest in it himself can require the claimants to litigate with each other. **2** a person who interpleads.

Interpol (ˈɪntəˌpɒl) *n* *acronym for* International Criminal Police Organization, an association of over 100 national police forces, devoted to fighting international crime.

interpolate (ɪnˈtɜːpəˌleɪt) *vb* **interpolates, interpolating, interpolated. 1** to insert or introduce (a comment, passage, etc.) into (a conversation, text, etc.) **2** to falsify or alter (a text, manuscript, etc.) by the later addition of (material, esp. spurious passages). **3** (*intr*) to make additions, interruptions, or insertions. **4** *Maths.* to estimate (a value of a function) between the values already known or determined. Cf. **extrapolate** (sense 1). [C17: from L *interpolāre* to give a new appearance to]
▶ inˈterpoˌlater *or* inˈterpoˌlator *n* ▶ inˈterpolative *adj*

interpose (ˌɪntəˈpəuz) *vb* **interposes, interposing, interposed. 1** to put or place between or among other things. **2** to introduce (comments, questions, etc.) into a speech or conversation; interject. **3** to exert or use influence or action in order to alter or intervene in (a situation). [C16: from OF, from L *interpōnere*, from INTER- + *pōnere* to put]
▶ ˌinterˈposal *n* ▶ ˌinterˈposer *n* ▶ ˌinterpoˈsition *n*

interpret (ɪnˈtɜːprɪt) *vb* **1** (*tr*) to clarify or explain the meaning of; elucidate. **2** (*tr*) to construe the significance or intention of. **3** (*tr*) to convey the spirit or meaning of (a poem, song, etc.) in performance. **4** (*intr*) to act as an interpreter; translate orally. [C14: from L *interpretārī*, from *interpres* negotiator, one who explains]
▶ inˈterpretable *adj* ▶ inˌterpretaˈbility *or* inˈterpretableness *n* ▶ inˈterpretably *adv* ▶ inˈterpretive *adj*

interpretation (ɪnˌtɜːprɪˈteɪʃən) *n* **1** the act or process of interpreting or explaining; elucidation. **2** the result of interpreting; an explanation. **3** a particular view of an artistic work, esp. as expressed by stylistic individuality in its performance. **4** explanation, as of a historical site, provided by the use of original objects, visual display material, etc.
▶ inˌterpreˈtational *adj*

interpreter (ɪnˈtɜːprɪtə) *n* **1** a person who translates orally from one language into another. **2** a person who interprets the work of others. **3** *Computing.* a program that translates a statement in a source program to machine code and executes it before translating and executing the next statement.
▶ inˈterpretership *n* ▶ inˈterpretress *fem n*

interpretive centre *n* (at a historical site, etc.) a building that provides interpretation of the site through a variety of media, such as video displays and exhibitions, and, often, includes facilities such as refreshment rooms.

interregnum (ˌɪntəˈrɛgnəm) *n, pl* **interregnums** *or* **interregna** (-nə) **1** an interval between two reigns, governments, etc. **2** any period in which a state lacks a ruler, government, etc. **3** a period of absence of some control, authority, etc. **4** a gap in a continuity. [C16: from L, from INTER- + *regnum* REIGN]
▶ ˌinterˈregnal *adj*

interrelate (ˌɪntərɪˈleɪt) *vb* **interrelates, interrelating, interrelated.** to place in or come into a mutual or reciprocal relationship.
▶ ˌinterreˈlation *n* ▶ ˌinterreˈlationˌship *n*

interrogate (ɪnˈtɛrəˌgeɪt) *vb* **interrogates, interrogating, interrogated.** to ask questions (of), esp. to question (a witness in court, spy, etc.) closely. [C15: from L *interrogāre*, from *rogāre* to ask]
▶ inˈterroˌgator *n*

interrogation (ɪnˌtɛrəˈgeɪʃən) *n* **1** the technique, practice, or an instance of interrogating. **2** a question or query. **3** *Telecomm.* the transmission of one or more triggering pulses to a transponder.
▸ **inˌterroˈgational** *adj*

interrogation mark *n* a less common term for **question mark.**

interrogative (ˌɪntəˈrɒgətɪv) *adj* **1** asking or having the nature of a question. **2** denoting a form or construction used in asking a question. **3** denoting or belonging to a class of words, such as *which* and *whom*, that serve to question which individual referent is intended. ◆ *n* **4** an interrogative word, phrase, sentence, or construction. **5** a question mark.
▸ ˌinterˈrogatively *adv*

interrogatory (ˌɪntəˈrɒgətərɪ, -trɪ) *adj* **1** expressing or involving a question. ◆ *n, pl* **interrogatories. 2** a question or interrogation.

interrupt (ˌɪntəˈrʌpt) *vb* **1** to break the continuity of (an action, event, etc.) or hinder (a person) by intrusion. **2** (*tr*) to cease to perform (some action). **3** (*tr*) to obstruct (a view, etc.). **4** to prevent or disturb (a conversation, discussion, etc.) by questions, interjections, or comment. [C15: from L *interrumpere*, from INTER- + *rumpere* to break]
▸ ˌinterˈruptible *adj* ▸ ˌinterˈruptive *adj* ▸ ˌinterˈruptively *adv* ▸ ˌinterˈrupted *adj*

interrupted screw *n* a screw with a slot cut into the thread, esp. one used in the breech of some guns permitting both engagement and release of the block by a partial turn of the screw.

interrupter *or* **interruptor** (ˌɪntəˈrʌptə) *n* **1** a person or thing that interrupts. **2** an electromechanical device for opening and closing an electric circuit.

interruption (ˌɪntəˈrʌpʃən) *n* **1** something that interrupts, such as a comment, question, or action. **2** an interval or intermission. **3** the act of interrupting or the state of being interrupted.

interscholastic (ˌɪntəskəˈlæstɪk) *adj* **1** (of sports events, competitions, etc.) occurring between two or more schools. **2** representative of various schools.

intersect (ˌɪntəˈsɛkt) *vb* **1** to divide, cut, or mark off by passing through or across. **2** (esp. of roads) to cross (each other). **3** *Maths.* (often foll. by *with*) to have one or more points in common (with another configuration). [C17: from L *intersecāre* to divide, from INTER- + *secāre* to cut]

intersection (ˌɪntəˈsɛkʃən, ˈɪntəˌsɛk-) *n* **1** a point at which things intersect, esp. a road junction. **2** the act of intersecting or the state of being intersected. **3** *Maths.* **3a** a point or set of points common to two or more geometric configurations. **3b** Also called: **product.** the set of elements that are common to two sets. **3c** the operation that yields that set from a pair of given sets.
▸ ˌinterˈsectional *adj*

intersex (ˈɪntəˌsɛks) *n Zool.* an individual with characteristics intermediate between those of a male and a female.

intersexual (ˌɪntəˈsɛksjʊəl) *adj* **1** occurring or existing between the sexes. **2** relating to or being an intersex.
▸ ˌinterˈsexuˈality *n* ▸ ˌinterˈsexually *adv*

interspace *vb* (ˌɪntəˈspeɪs), **interspaces, interspacing, interspaced. 1** (*tr*) to make or occupy a space between. ◆ *n* (ˈɪntəˌspeɪs). **2** space between or among things.
▸ ˌinterˈspatial *adj* ▸ ˌinterˈspatially *adv*

intersperse (ˌɪntəˈspɜːs) *vb* **intersperses, interspersing, interspersed.** (*tr*) **1** to scatter or distribute among, between, or on. **2** to diversify (something) with other things scattered here and there. [C16: from L *interspargere*, from INTER- + *spargere* to sprinkle]
▸ ˌinterˈspersedly (ˌɪntəˈspɜːsɪdlɪ) *adv* ▸ **interspersion** (ˌɪntəˈspɜːʃən) *or* ˌinterˈspersal *n*

interstate (ˈɪntəˌsteɪt) *n US.* a motorway crossing between states.

interstellar (ˌɪntəˈstɛlə) *adj* between or among stars.

interstice (ɪnˈtɜːstɪs) *n* (*usually pl*) **1** a minute opening or crevice between things. **2** *Physics.* the space between adjacent atoms in a crystal lattice. [C17: from L *interstitium* interval, from *intersistere*, from INTER- + *sistere* to stand]

interstitial (ˌɪntəˈstɪʃəl) *adj* **1** of or relating to an interstice or interstices. **2** *Physics.* forming or occurring in an interstice: *an interstitial atom.* **3** *Anat., zool.* occurring in the spaces between organs, tissues, etc.: *interstitial cells.* ◆ *n* **4** *Chem.* an atom or ion situated in the interstices of a crystal lattice.
▸ ˌinterˈstitially *adv*

intertrigo (ˌɪntəˈtraɪgəʊ) *n* chafing between two skin surfaces, as at the armpit. [C18: from INTER- + *-trigo*, from L *terere* to rub]

interval (ˈɪntəvəl) *n* **1** the period of time between two events, instants, etc. **2** the distance between two points, objects, etc. **3** a pause or interlude, as between periods of intense activity. **4** *Brit.* a short period between parts of a play, etc.; intermission. **5** *Music.* the difference of pitch between two notes, either sounded simultaneously or in succession as in a musical part. **6** the ratio of the frequencies of two sounds. **7 at intervals. 7a** occasionally or intermittently. **7b** with spaces between. [C13: from L *intervallum*, lit.: space between two palisades, from INTER- + *vallum* palisade]
▸ **intervallic** (ˌɪntəˈvælɪk) *adj*

intervene (ˌɪntəˈviːn) *vb* **intervenes, intervening, intervened.** (*intr*) **1** (often foll. by *in*) to take a decisive or intrusive role (in) in order to determine events. **2** (foll. by *in* or *between*) to come or be (among or between). **3** (of a period of time) to occur between events or points in time. **4** (of an event) to disturb or hinder a course of action. **5** *Econ.* to take action to affect the market forces of an economy, esp. to maintain the stability of a currency. **6** *Law.* to interpose and become a party to a legal action between others, esp. in order to protect one's interests. [C16: from L *intervenīre* to come between]
▸ ˌinterˈvener *or* ˌinterˈvenor *n*

intervention (ˌɪntəˈvɛnʃən) *n* **1** an act of intervening. **2** any interference in the affairs of others, esp. by one state in the affairs of another. **3** *Econ.* the action of a central bank in supporting the international value of a currency by buying large quantities of the currency to keep the price up. **4** *Commerce.* the action of the EU in buying up surplus produce when the market price drops to a certain value.

interventionist (ˌɪntəˈvɛnʃənɪst) *adj* **1** of, relating to, or advocating intervention, esp. in order to achieve a policy objective. ◆ *n* **2** a person or state that pursues a policy of intervention.

intervertebral disc (ˌɪntəˈvɜːtɪbrəl) *n* any of the cartilaginous discs between individual vertebrae, acting as shock absorbers.

interview (ˈɪntəˌvjuː) *n* **1** a conversation with or questioning of a person, usually conducted for television or a newspaper. **2** a formal discussion, esp. one in which an employer assesses a job applicant. ◆ *vb* **3** to conduct an interview with (someone). [C16: from OF *entrevue*]
▸ ˌinterviewˈee *n* ▸ ˈinterˌviewer *n*

inter vivos *Latin.* (ˈɪntə ˈviːvɒs) *adj Law.* between living people: *an inter vivos gift.*

interwar (ˌɪntəˈwɔː) *adj* of or happening in the period between World War I and World War II.

intestate (ɪnˈtesteɪt, -tɪt) *adj* **1a** (of a person) not having made a will. **1b** (of property) not disposed of by will. ◆ *n* **2** a person who dies without having made a will. [C14: from L *intestātus*, from IN-¹ + *testārī* to bear witness, make a will, from *testis* a witness]
▸ inˈtestacy *n*

intestine (ɪnˈtestɪn) *n* the part of the alimentary canal between the stomach and the anus. See **large intestine, small intestine.** [C16: from L *intestīnum* gut, from *intestīnus* internal, from *intus* within]
▸ **intestinal** (ɪnˈtestɪnˀl, ˌɪntesˈtaɪnˀl) *adj*

inti (ˈɪntɪ) *n* a former monetary unit of Peru. [C20: from Quechua]

intifada (ˌɪntɪˈfɑːdə) *n* the Palestinian uprising against Israel in the West Bank and Gaza Strip that started at the end of 1987. [C20: Ar., lit.: uprising]

intimacy (ˈɪntɪməsɪ) *n, pl* **intimacies. 1** close or warm friendship or understanding; personal relationship. **2** (*often pl*) *Euphemistic.* sexual relations.

★ people and places

ntimate[1] ('ɪntɪmɪt) *adj* **1** characterized by a close or warm personal relationship: *an intimate friend*. **2** deeply personal, private, or secret. **3** (*often postpositive; foll. by* with) *Euphemistic*. having sexual relations (with). **4** (*postpositive;* foll. by *with*) having a deep or unusual knowledge (of). **5** having a friendly, warm, or informal atmosphere: *an intimate nightclub*. **6** of or relating to the essential part or nature of something; intrinsic. ◆ *n* **7** a close friend. [C17: from L *intimus* very close friend, from (adj): innermost, from *intus* within]
▸ **'intimately** *adv* ▸ **'intimateness** *n*

ntimate[2] ('ɪntɪˌmeɪt) *vb* **intimates, intimating, intimated.** (*tr; may take a clause as object*) **1** to hint; suggest. **2** to proclaim; make known. [C16: from LL *intimāre* to proclaim, from L *intimus* innermost]
▸ **'intiˌmater** *n* ▸ **ˌinti'mation** *n*

ntimidate (ɪn'tɪmɪˌdeɪt) *vb* **intimidates, intimidating, intimidated.** (*tr*) **1** to make timid or frightened; scare. **2** to discourage, restrain, or silence unscrupulously, as by threats. [C17: from Med. L *intimidāre*, from L IN-[2] + *timidus* fearful, from *timor* fear]
▸ **in'timiˌdating** *adj* ▸ **inˌtimi'dation** *n* ▸ **in'timiˌdator** *n*

ntinction (ɪn'tɪŋkʃən) *n Christianity*. the practice of dipping the Eucharistic bread into the wine at Holy Communion. [C16: from LL *intinctiō* a dipping in, from L *tingere* to dip]

ntitule (ɪn'tɪtjuːl) *vb* **intitules, intituling, intituled.** (*tr*) *Parliamentary procedure.* (in Britain) to entitle (an Act). [C15: from OF *intituler*, from L *titulus* TITLE]

ntl *abbrev. for* international.

nto ('ɪntuː; *unstressed* 'ɪntə) *prep* **1** to the interior or inner parts of: *to look into a case.* **2** to the middle or midst of so as to be surrounded by: *into the bushes.* **3** against; up against: *he drove into a wall.* **4** used to indicate the result of a change: *he changed into a monster.* **5** *Maths.* used to indicate a dividend: *three into six is two.* **6** *Inf.* interested or enthusiastically involved in: *I'm really into Freud.*

ntonation (ˌɪntəʊ'neɪʃən) *n* **1** the sound pattern of phrases and sentences produced by pitch variation in the voice. **2** the act or manner of intoning. **3** an intoned, chanted, or monotonous utterance; incantation. **4** *Music.* the opening of a piece of plainsong, sung by a soloist. **5** *Music.* the capacity to play or sing in tune.
▸ ˌinto'national *adj*

ntone (ɪn'təʊn) *or* **intonate** *vb* **intones, intoning, intoned** *or* **intonates, intonating, intonated.** **1** to utter, recite, or sing (a chant, prayer, etc.) in a monotonous or incantatory tone. **2** (*intr*) to speak with a particular or characteristic intonation or tone. **3** to sing (the opening phrase of a psalm, etc.) in plainsong. [C15: from Med. L *intonare*, from IN-[2] + TONE]
▸ **in'toner** *n*

in toto *Latin.* (ɪn 'təʊtəʊ) *adv* totally; entirely.

ntoxicant (ɪn'tɒksɪkənt) *n* **1** anything that causes intoxication. ◆ *adj* **2** causing intoxication.

ntoxicate (ɪn'tɒksɪˌkeɪt) *vb* **intoxicates, intoxicating, intoxicated.** (*tr*) **1** (of an alcoholic drink) to produce in (a person) a state ranging from euphoria to stupor; make drunk; inebriate. **2** to stimulate, excite, or elate so as to overwhelm. **3** (of a drug, etc.) to poison. [C16: from Med. L, from *intoxicāre* to poison, from L *toxicum* poison; see TOXIC]
▸ **in'toxicable** *adj* ▸ **in'toxiˌcating** *adj* ▸ **in'toxiˌcatingly** *adv*

ntoxication (ɪnˌtɒksɪ'keɪʃən) *n* **1** drunkenness; inebriation. **2** great elation. **3** the act of intoxicating. **4** poisoning.

ntr. *abbrev. for* intransitive.

ntra- *prefix* within; inside: *intrastate; intravenous.* [from L *intrā* within; see INTERIOR]

Intracoastal Waterway ★ (ˌɪntrə'kəʊstᵊl) *n short for* Atlantic Intracoastal Waterway.

ntractable (ɪn'træktəbᵊl) *adj* **1** difficult to influence or direct: *an intractable disposition.* **2** (of a problem, illness, etc.) difficult to solve, alleviate, or cure.
▸ **inˌtracta'bility** *or* **in'tractableness** *n* ▸ **in'tractably** *adv*

ntradermal (ˌɪntrə'dɜːməl) *adj* within the skin: *an*

---

intradermal injection. Abbrevs. (esp. of an injection): **ID, i.d.**
▸ ˌintra'dermally *adv*

intrados (ɪn'treɪdɒs) *n, pl* **intrados** *or* **intradoses.** *Archit.* the inner curve or surface of an arch. [C18: from F, from INTRA- + *dos* back, from L *dorsum*]

intramural (ˌɪntrə'mjʊərəl) *adj Education, chiefly US & Canad.* operating within or involving those in a single establishment.
▸ ˌintra'murally *adv*

intramuscular (ˌɪntrə'mʌskjuːlə) *adj* within a muscle: *an intramuscular injection.* Abbrevs. (esp. of an injection): **IM, i.m.**
▸ ˌintra'muscularly *adv*

intranet ('ɪntrəˌnet) *n Computing.* an internal network that makes use of Internet technology. [C20: INTRA- + NET (sense 8), modelled on INTERNET]

intrans. *abbrev. for* intransitive.

intransigent (ɪn'trænsɪdʒənt) *adj* **1** not willing to compromise; obstinately maintaining an attitude. ◆ *n* **2** an intransigent person, esp. in politics. [C19: from Sp. *los intransigentes* the uncompromising (ones), a name adopted by certain political extremists, from IN-[1] + *transigir* to compromise, from L *transigere* to settle; see TRANSACT]
▸ **in'transigence** *or* **in'transigency** *n* ▸ **in'transigently** *adv*

intransitive (ɪn'trænsɪtɪv) *adj* **1a** denoting a verb that does not require a direct object: *"to faint" is an intransitive verb.* **1b** (*as n*) such a verb. **2** denoting an adjective or noun that does not require any particular noun phrase as a referent. **3** having the property that if it holds between one argument and a second, and between the second and a third, it must fail to hold between the first and third: *"being the mother of" is an intransitive relation.*
◆ Cf. **transitive.**
▸ **in'transitively** *adv* ▸ **inˌtransi'tivity** *or* **in'transitiveness** *n*

intrapreneur (ˌɪntrəprə'nɜː) *n* a person who while remaining within a larger organization uses entrepreneurial skills to develop a new product or line of business as a subsidiary of the organization. [C20: from INTRA- + (ENTRE)PRENEUR]

intrauterine (ˌɪntrə'juːtəraɪn) *adj* within the womb.

intrauterine device *n* a metal or plastic device, in the shape of a loop, coil, or ring, inserted into the uterus to prevent conception. Abbrev.: **IUD.**

intravenous (ˌɪntrə'viːnəs) *adj Anat.* within a vein: *an intravenous injection.* Abbrevs. (esp. of an injection): **IV, i.v.**
▸ ˌintra'venously *adv*

in-tray *n* a tray for incoming papers, etc., requiring attention.

intrench (ɪn'trentʃ) *vb* a less common spelling of **entrench.**
▸ **in'trencher** *n* ▸ **in'trenchment** *n*

intrepid (ɪn'trepɪd) *adj* fearless; daring; bold. [C17: from L *intrepidus*, from IN-[1] + *trepidus* fearful]
▸ **in'trepidity** *n* ▸ **in'trepidly** *adv*

intricate ('ɪntrɪkɪt) *adj* **1** difficult to understand; obscure; complex; puzzling. **2** entangled or involved: *intricate patterns.* [C15: from L *intrīcāre* to entangle, perplex, from IN-[1] + *trīcae* trifles, perplexities]
▸ **'intricacy** *or* **'intricateness** *n* ▸ **'intricately** *adv*

intrigue *vb* (ɪn'triːg), **intrigues, intriguing, intrigued.** **1** (*tr*) to make interested or curious. **2** (*intr*) to make secret plots or employ underhand methods; conspire. **3** (*intr;* often foll. by *with*) to carry on a clandestine love affair. ◆ *n* (ɪn'triːg, 'ɪntriːg). **4** the act or an instance of secret plotting, etc. **5** a clandestine love affair. **6** the quality of arousing interest or curiosity; beguilement. [C17: from F *intriguer*, from It., from L *intrīcāre;* see INTRICATE]
▸ **in'triguer** *n* ▸ **in'triguingly** *adv*

intrinsic (ɪn'trɪnsɪk) *or* **intrinsical** *adj* **1** of or relating to the essential nature of a thing; inherent. **2** *Anat.* situated within or peculiar to a part: *intrinsic muscles.* [C15: from LL *intrinsecus* from L, inwardly, from *intrā* within + *secus* alongside]
▸ **in'trinsically** *adv*

intro ('ɪntrəʊ) *n, pl* **intros.** *Inf.* short for **introduction.**

---

intro. *or* **introd.** *abbrev. for:* **1** introduction. **2** introductory.

intro- *prefix* in, into, or inward: *introvert.* [from L *intrō* inwardly, within]

introduce (ˌɪntrə'djuːs) *vb* **introduces, introducing, introduced.** (*tr*) **1** (often foll. by *to*) to present (someone) by name (to another person). **2** (foll. by *to*) to cause to experience for the first time: *to introduce a visitor to beer.* **3** to present for consideration or approval, esp. before a legislative body: *to introduce a bill in parliament.* **4** to bring in; establish: *to introduce decimal currency.* **5** to present (a radio or television programme, etc.) verbally. **6** (foll. by *with*) to start: *he introduced his talk with some music.* **7** (often foll. by *into*) to insert or inject: *he introduced the needle into his arm.* **8** to place (members of a plant or animal species) in a new environment with the intention of producing a resident breeding population. [C16: from L *intrōdūcere* to bring inside]
▸ ˌintro'ducer *n* ▸ ˌintro'ducible *adj*

introduction (ˌɪntrə'dʌkʃən) *n* **1** the act of introducing or fact of being introduced. **2** a presentation of one person to another or others. **3** a means of presenting a person to another person, such as a letter of introduction or reference. **4** a preliminary part, as of a book. **5** *Music.* an opening passage in a movement or composition that precedes the main material. **6** a basic or elementary work of instruction, reference, etc.

introductory (ˌɪntrə'dʌktəri, -tri) *adj* serving as an introduction; preliminary; prefatory.

introit ('ɪntrɔɪt) *n RC Church, Church of England.* a short prayer said or sung as the celebrant is entering the sanctuary to celebrate Mass or Holy Communion. [C15: from Church L *introitus* introit, from L: entrance, from *introīre* to go in]
▸ in'troital *adj*

intromit (ˌɪntrə'mɪt) *vb* **intromits, intromitting, intromitted.** (*tr*) *Rare.* to enter or insert. [C15: from L *intrōmittere* to send in]
▸ ˌintro'missible *adj* ▸ ˌintro'mission *n* ▸ ˌintro'mittent *adj*

introspection (ˌɪntrə'spekʃən) *n* the examination of one's own thoughts, impressions, and feelings. [C17: from L *intrōspicere* to look within]
▸ ˌintro'spective *adj* ▸ ˌintro'spectively *adv*

introversion (ˌɪntrə'vɜːʃən) *n Psychol.* the directing of interest inwards towards one's own thoughts and feelings rather than towards the external world or making social contacts.
▸ ˌintro'versive *or* ˌintro'vertive *adj*

introvert *n* ('ɪntrəˌvɜːt). **1** *Psychol.* a person prone to introversion. ◆ *adj* ('ɪntrəˌvɜːt). **2** Also: **introverted.** characterized by introversion. ◆ *vb* (ˌɪntrə'vɜːt). **3** (*tr*) *Pathol.* to turn (a hollow organ or part) inside out. [C17: see INTRO-, INVERT]

intrude (ɪn'truːd) *vb* **intrudes, intruding, intruded.** **1** (often foll. by *into, on,* or *upon*) to put forward or interpose (oneself, one's views, something) abruptly or without invitation. **2** *Geol.* to force or thrust (molten magma) between solid rocks. [C16: from L *intrūdere* to thrust in]
▸ in'truder *n* ▸ in'trudingly *adv*

intrusion (ɪn'truːʒən) *n* **1** the act or an instance of intruding; an unwelcome visit, etc.: *an intrusion on one's privacy.* **2a** the movement of magma into spaces in the overlying strata to form igneous rock. **2b** any igneous rock formed in this way. **3** *Property law.* an unlawful entry onto land by a stranger after determination of a particular estate of freehold.
▸ in'trusional *adj*

intrusive (ɪn'truːsɪv) *adj* **1** characterized by intrusion or tending to intrude. **2** (of igneous rocks) formed by intrusion. **3** *Phonetics.* relating to or denoting a speech sound that is introduced into a word or piece of connected speech for a phonetic reason.
▸ in'trusively *adv* ▸ in'trusiveness *n*

intrust (ɪn'trʌst) *vb* a less common spelling of **entrust.**

intubate ('ɪntjuˌbeɪt) *vb* **intubates, intubating, intubated.** (*tr*) *Med.* to insert a tube into (a hollow organ).
▸ ˌintu'bation *n*

intuit (ɪn'tjuːɪt) *vb* **intuits, intuiting, intuited.** to know or discover by intuition.
▸ in'tuitable *adj*

intuition (ˌɪntjʊ'ɪʃən) *n* **1** knowledge or belief obtained neither by reason nor perception. **2** instinctive knowledge or belief. **3** a hunch or unjustified belief. [C15: from LL *intuitiō* a contemplation, from L *intuērī* to gaze upon, from *tuērī* to look at]
▸ in'tuitional *adj* ▸ in'tuitionally *adv*

intuitionism (ˌɪntjʊ'ɪʃəˌnɪzəm) *or* **intuitionalism** *Philosophy.* **1** the doctrine that knowledge is acquired primarily by intuition. **2** the theory that the solution to moral problems can be discovered by intuition. **3** the doctrine that external objects are known to be real by intuition.
▸ ˌintu'itionist *or* ˌintu'itionalist *n*

intuitive (ɪn'tjuːɪtɪv) *adj* **1** resulting from intuition: *an intuitive awareness.* **2** of, characterized by, or involving intuition.
▸ in'tuitively *adv* ▸ in'tuitiveness *n*

intumesce (ˌɪntjʊ'mes) *vb* **intumesces, intumescing, intumesced.** (*intr*) to swell. [C18: from L *intumescere*, from *tumescere* to begin to swell, from *tumēre* to swell]
▸ ˌintu'mescence *n*

intussusception (ˌɪntəssə'sepʃən) *n* **1** *Pathol.* the telescoping of one section of the intestinal tract into a lower section. **2** *Biol.* growth in the surface area of a cell by the deposition of new particles between the existing particles of the cell wall. [C18: from L *intus* within + *susceptiō* a taking up]

Inuit *or* **Innuit** ('ɪnjuːɪt) *n, pl* **Inuit, Inuits** *or* **Innuit, Innuits** an Eskimo of North America or Greenland, as distinguished from one from Asia or the Aleutian Islands. [from Eskimo *inuit* people, pl of *inuk* a man]

Inuktitut (ɪ'nʊktɪˌtut) *n Canad.* the language of the Inuit Eskimo. [from Eskimo *inuk* man + *titut* speech]

inunction (ɪn'ʌŋkʃən) *n* **1** the application of an ointment to the skin, esp. by rubbing. **2** the ointment so used. **3** the act of anointing; anointment. [C15: from L *inunguere* to anoint, from *unguere;* see UNCTION]

inundate ('ɪnʌnˌdeɪt) *vb* **inundates, inundating, inundated.** (*tr*) **1** to cover completely with water; overflow; flood: *to be inundated with requests.* [C17: from L *inundāre*, from *unda* wave]
▸ 'inundant *or* in'undatory *adj* ▸ ˌinun'dation *n* ▸ 'inunˌdator *n*

inure *or* **enure** (ɪ'njʊə) *vb* **inures, inuring, inured** *or* **enures, enuring, enured.** **1** (*tr; often passive;* often foll. by *to*) to cause to accept or become hardened to; habituate. **2** (*intr*) (esp. of a law, etc.) to come into operation; take effect. [C15: *enuren* to accustom, from *ure* use, from OF *euvre* custom, work, from L *opera* works]
▸ in'urement *or* en'urement *n*

in utero *Latin.* (ɪn 'juːtərəʊ) *adv, adj* in the uterus.

inv. *abbrev. for:* **1** invented. **2** inventor. **3** invoice.

in vacuo *Latin.* (ɪn 'vækjuˌəʊ) *adv* in a vacuum.

invade (ɪn'veɪd) *vb* **invades, invading, invaded.** **1** to enter (a country, territory, etc.) by military force. **2** (*tr*) to occupy in large numbers; overrun; infest. **3** (*tr*) to trespass or encroach upon (privacy, etc.). **4** (*tr*) to enter and spread throughout, esp. harmfully; pervade. [C15: from L *invādere*, from *vādere* to go]
▸ in'vadable *adj* ▸ in'vader *n*

invaginate *vb* (ɪn'vædʒɪˌneɪt), **invaginates, invaginating, invaginated.** **1** *Pathol.* to push one section of (a tubular organ or part) back into itself so that it becomes ensheathed. **2** (*intr*) (of the outer layer of an organism or part) to undergo this process. ◆ *adj* (ɪn'vædʒɪnɪt, -ˌneɪt). **3** (of an organ or part) folded back upon itself. [C19 from Med. L *invāgināre*, from L IN-[2] + *vāgīna* sheath]
▸ in'vaginable *adj* ▸ inˌvagi'nation *n*

invalid[1] ('ɪnvəˌliːd, -lɪd) *n* **1a** a person suffering from disablement or chronic ill health. **1b** (*as modifier*): *an invalid chair.* ◆ *adj* **2** suffering from or disabled by injury, sickness, etc. ◆ *vb* (*tr*) **3** to cause to become an invalid; disable. **4** (*often passive; usually foll. by out*) *Chiefly Brit.* to require (a member of the armed forces) to retire from ac-

tive service through wounds or illness. [C17: from L *invalidus* infirm, from IN-[1] + *validus* strong]
▸ **invalidity** (ˌɪnvəˈlɪdɪtɪ) *n*

invalid[2] (ɪnˈvælɪd) *adj* **1** not valid; having no cogency or legal force. **2** *Logic.* (of an argument) having a conclusion that does not follow from the premises. [C16: from Med. L *invalidus* without legal force; see INVALID[1]]
▸ **ˌinvaˈlidity** *or* **inˈvalidness** *n* ▸ **inˈvalidly** *adv*

invalidate (ɪnˈvælɪˌdeɪt) *vb* **invalidates, invalidating, invalidated.** (*tr*) **1** to render weak or ineffective (an argument). **2** to take away the legal force or effectiveness of; annul (a contract).
▸ **inˌvaliˈdation** *n* ▸ **inˈvaliˌdator** *n*

invaluable (ɪnˈvæljʊəbᵊl) *adj* having great value that is impossible to calculate; priceless.
▸ **inˈvaluableness** *n* ▸ **inˈvaluably** *adv*

Invar (ɪnˈvɑː) *n Trademark.* an alloy containing iron, nickel, and carbon. It has a very low coefficient of expansion and is used for the balance springs of watches, etc. [C20: shortened from INVARIABLE]

invariable (ɪnˈvɛərɪəbᵊl) *adj* **1** not subject to alteration; unchanging. ♦ *n* **2** a mathematical quantity having an unchanging value; a constant.
▸ **inˌvariaˈbility** *or* **inˈvariableness** *n* ▸ **inˈvariably** *adv*

invariant (ɪnˈvɛərɪənt) *Maths.* ♦ *n* **1** an entity, quantity, etc., that is unaltered by a particular transformation of coordinates. ♦ *adj* **2** (of a relationship or a property of a function, configuration, or equation) unaltered by a particular transformation of coordinates.
▸ **inˈvariance** *or* **inˈvariancy** *n*

invasion (ɪnˈveɪʒən) *n* **1** the act of invading with armed forces. **2** any encroachment or intrusion: *an invasion of rats.* **3** the onset or advent of something harmful, esp. of a disease. **4** *Pathol.* the spread of cancer from its point of origin into surrounding tissues. **5** the movement of plants to an area to which they are not native.

invasive (ɪnˈveɪsɪv) *adj* **1** of or relating to an invasion, intrusion, etc. **2** (of surgery) involving making a relatively large incision in the body to gain access to the target of the surgery.

invective (ɪnˈvɛktɪv) *n* **1** vehement accusation or denunciation, esp. of a bitterly abusive or sarcastic kind. ♦ *adj* **2** characterized by or using abusive language, bitter sarcasm, etc. [C15: from LL *invectīvus* reproachful, from L *invectus* carried in; see INVEIGH]
▸ **inˈvectively** *adv* ▸ **inˈvectiveness** *n*

inveigh (ɪnˈveɪ) *vb* (*intr*; foll. by *against*) to speak with violent or invective language; rail. [C15: from L *invehī*, lit.: to be carried in, hence, assail physically or verbally]
▸ **inˈveigher** *n*

inveigle (ɪnˈviːgᵊl, -ˈveɪ-) *vb* **inveigles, inveigling, inveigled.** (*tr*; often foll. by *into* or an infinitive) to lead (someone into a situation) or persuade (to do something) by cleverness or trickery; cajole. [C15: from OF *avogler* to blind, deceive, from *avogle* blind, from Med. L *ab oculis* without eyes]
▸ **inˈveiglement** *n* ▸ **inˈveigler** *n*

invent (ɪnˈvɛnt) *vb* **1** to create or devise (new ideas, machines, etc.). **2** to make up (falsehoods, etc.); fabricate. [C15: from L *invenīre* to find, come upon]
▸ **inˈventable** *adj*

invention (ɪnˈvɛnʃən) *n* **1** the act or process of inventing. **2** something that is invented. **3** *Patent law.* the discovery or production of some new or improved process or machine. **4** creative power or ability; inventive skill. **5** *Euphemistic.* a fabrication; lie. **6** *Music.* a short piece consisting of two or three parts usually in imitative counterpoint.
▸ **inˈventional** *adj* ▸ **inˈventionless** *adj*

inventive (ɪnˈvɛntɪv) *adj* **1** skilled or quick at contriving; ingenious; resourceful. **2** characterized by inventive skill: *an inventive programme of work.* **3** of or relating to invention.
▸ **inˈventively** *adv* ▸ **inˈventiveness** *n*

inventor (ɪnˈvɛntə) *n* a person who invents, esp. as a profession.
▸ **inˈventress** *fem n*

inventory (ˈɪnvəntərɪ, -trɪ) *n, pl* **inventories. 1** a detailed

list of articles, goods, property, etc. **2** (*often pl*) *Accounting, chiefly US.* **2a** the amount or value of a firm's current assets that consist of raw materials, work in progress, and finished goods; stock. **2b** such assets individually. ♦ *vb* **inventories, inventorying, inventoried. 3** (*tr*) to enter (items) in an inventory; make a list of. [C16: from Med. L *inventōrium;* see INVENT]
▸ **ˈinventoriable** *adj* ▸ **ˌinvenˈtorial** *adj* ▸ **ˌinvenˈtorially** *adv*

Inveraray ★ (ˌɪnvəˈrɛərɪ) *n* a town in W Scotland, in Argyll and Bute: Inveraray Castle is the seat of the Dukes of Argyll. Pop.: 512 (1991).

Invercargill ★ (ˌɪnvəˈkɑːgɪl) *n* a city in New Zealand, on South Island: regional trading centre for sheep and agricultural products. Pop.: 51 600 (1995 est.).

Inverclyde ★ (ˌɪnvəˈklaɪd) *n* a council area of W central Scotland. Administrative centre: Greenock. Pop.: 89 990 (1996 est.). Area: 162 sq. km (63 sq. miles).

Inverness ★ (ˌɪnvəˈnɛs) *n* **1** a town in N Scotland, administrative centre of Highland: tourism and specialized engineering. Pop.: 41 234 (1991). **2** (*sometimes not cap.*) an overcoat with a removable cape.

Inverness-shire ★ (ˌɪnvəˈnɛsˌʃɪə, -ʃə) *n* (until 1975) a county of NW Scotland, now part of Highland.

inverse (ɪnˈvɜːs, ˈɪnvɜːs) *adj* **1** opposite or contrary in effect, sequence, direction, etc. **2** *Maths.* **2a** (of a relationship) containing two variables such that an increase in one results in a decrease in the other. **2b** (of an element) operating on a specified member of a set to produce the identity of the set: *the additive inverse element of x is –x.* **3** (*usually prenominal*) upside-down; inverted: *in an inverse position.* ♦ *n* **4** *Maths.* an inverse element. [C17: from L *inversus,* from *invertere* to INVERT]
▸ **inˈversely** *adv*

inverse function *n* a function whose independent variable is the dependent variable of a given trigonometric or hyperbolic function: *the inverse function of* sin *x is* arcsin *y* (*also written* $\sin^{-1}y$).

inversion (ɪnˈvɜːʃən) *n* **1** the act of inverting or state of being inverted. **2** something inverted, esp. a reversal of order, mutual functions, etc.: *an inversion of their previous relationship.* **3** Also: **anastrophe.** *Rhetoric.* the reversal of a normal order of words, as in the phrase *Weeping left she sorrowfully.* **4** *Chem.* **4a** the conversion of a dextrorotatory solution of sucrose into a laevorotatory solution of glucose and fructose by hydrolysis. **4b** any similar reaction in which the optical properties of the reactants are opposite to those of the products. **5** *Music.* **5a** the process or result of transposing the notes of a chord such that the root, originally in the bass, is placed in an upper part. **5b** the modification of an interval in which the higher note becomes the lower or the lower one the higher. **6** *Pathol.* abnormal positioning of an organ or part, as in being upside down or turned inside out. **7** *Psychiatry.* **7a** the adoption of the role or characteristics of the opposite sex. **7b** another word for **homosexuality. 8** *Meteorol.* an abnormal condition in which the layer of air next to the earth's surface is cooler than an overlying layer. **9** *Computing.* an operation by which each digit of a binary number is changed to the alternative digit, as 10110 to 01001.
▸ **inˈversive** *adj*

invert *vb* (ɪnˈvɜːt). **1** to turn or cause to turn upside down or inside out. **2** (*tr*) to reverse in effect, sequence, direction, etc. **3** (*tr*) *Phonetics.* to turn (the tip of the tongue) up and back to pronounce (a speech sound). ♦ *n* (ˈɪnvɜːt). **4** *Psychiatry.* **4a** a person who adopts the role of the opposite sex. **4b** another word for **homosexual. 5** *Archit.* **5a** the lower inner surface of a drain, sewer, etc. **5b** an arch that is concave upwards, esp. one used in foundations. [C16: from L *invertere,* from IN-[2] + *vertere* to turn]
▸ **inˈvertible** *adj* ▸ **inˌvertiˈbility** *n*

invertase (ɪnˈvɜːteɪz) *n* an enzyme, occurring in the intestinal juice of animals and in yeasts, that hydrolyses sucrose to glucose and fructose.

invertebrate (ɪnˈvɜːtɪbrɪt, -ˌbreɪt) *n* **1** any animal lacking a backbone, including all species not classified as vertebrates. ◆ *adj also* **invertebral. 2** of, relating to, or designating invertebrates.

inverted comma *n* another term for **quotation mark.**

inverted mordent *n Music.* a melodic ornament consisting of the rapid alternation of a principal note with a note one degree higher.

inverter *or* **invertor** (ɪnˈvɜːtə) *n* any device for converting a direct current into an alternating current.

invert sugar *n* a mixture of fructose and glucose obtained by the inversion of sucrose.

invest (ɪnˈvɛst) *vb* **1** (often foll. by *in*) to lay out (money or capital in an enterprise) with the expectation of profit. **2** (*tr;* often foll. by *in*) to devote (effort, resources, etc., to a project). **3** (*tr;* often foll. by *in* or *with*) *Arch.* or *ceremonial.* to clothe or adorn (in some garment, esp. the robes of an office). **4** (*tr;* often foll. by *in*) to install formally or ceremoniously (in an official position, rank, etc.). **5** (*tr;* foll. by *in* or *with*) to place (power, authority, etc., in) or provide (with power or authority): *to invest new rights in the monarchy.* **6** (*tr; usually passive;* foll. by *in* or *with*) to provide or endow (a person with qualities, characteristics, etc.). **7** (*tr;* foll. by *with*) *Usually poetic.* to cover or adorn, as if with a coat or garment: *when spring invests the trees with leaves.* **8** (*tr*) *Rare.* to surround with military forces; besiege. **9** (*intr;* foll. by *in*) *Inf.* to purchase; buy. [C16: from Med. L *investīre* to clothe, from L, from *vestīre,* from *vestis* a garment]
▸ in'vestable *or* in'vestible *adj* ▸ in'vestor *n*

investigate (ɪnˈvɛstɪˌɡeɪt) *vb* **investigates, investigating, investigated.** to inquire into (a situation or problem, esp. a crime or death) thoroughly; examine systematically, esp. in order to discover the truth. [C16: from L *vestīgāre* to search after, from IN-² + *vestīgium* track; see VESTIGE]
▸ in'vesti,gative *or* in'vestigatory *adj* ▸ in'vesti,gator *n*

investigation (ɪnˌvɛstɪˈɡeɪʃə) *n* the act or process of investigating; a careful search or examination in order to discover facts, etc.

investiture (ɪnˈvɛstɪtʃə) *n* **1** the act of presenting with a title or with the robes and insignia of an office or rank. **2** (in feudal society) the formal bestowal of the possessory right to a fief.
▸ in'vestitive *adj*

investment (ɪnˈvɛstmənt) *n* **1a** the act of investing money. **1b** the amount invested. **1c** an enterprise, asset, etc., in which money is or can be invested. **2a** the act of investing effort, resources, etc. **2b** the amount invested. **3** *Biol.* the outer layer or covering of an organ, part, or organism. **4** a less common word for **investiture** (sense 1). **5** the act of investing or state of being invested, as with an official robe, specific quality, etc. **6** *Rare.* the act of besieging with military forces, works, etc.

investment analyst *n* a specialist in forecasting the prices of stocks and shares.

investment bond *n* a single-premium life-assurance policy in which a fixed sum is invested in an asset-backed fund.

investment trust *n* a financial enterprise that invests its subscribed capital in securities for its investors' benefit.

inveterate (ɪnˈvɛtərɪt) *adj* **1** long established, esp. so as to be deep-rooted or ingrained: *an inveterate feeling of hostility.* **2** (*prenominal*) confirmed in a habit or practice, esp. a bad one; hardened. [C16: from L *inveterātus* of long standing, from *inveterāre* to make old, from IN-² + *vetus* old]
▸ in'veteracy *n* ▸ in'veterately *adv*

invidious (ɪnˈvɪdɪəs) *adj* **1** incurring or tending to arouse resentment, unpopularity, etc.: *an invidious task.* **2** (of comparisons or distinctions) unfairly or offensively discriminating. [C17: from L *invidiōsus* full of envy, from *invidia* ENVY]
▸ in'vidiously *adv* ▸ in'vidiousness *n*

invigilate (ɪnˈvɪdʒɪˌleɪt) *vb* **invigilates, invigilating, invigilated.** (*intr*) **1** *Brit.* to watch examination candidates, esp. to prevent cheating. US word: **proctor. 2** *Arch.* to keep watch. [C16: from L *invigilāre* to watch over; see VIGIL]
▸ in,vigi'lation *n* ▸ in'vigi,lator *n*

invigorate (ɪnˈvɪɡəˌreɪt) *vb* **invigorates, invigorating, invigorated.** (*tr*) to give vitality and vigour to; animate; brace; refresh: *to be invigorated by fresh air.* [C17: from IN-² + L *vigor* VIGOUR]
▸ in'vigor,ating *adj* ▸ in,vigor'ation *n* ▸ in'vigorative *adj* ▸ in'vigor,ator *n*

invincible (ɪnˈvɪnsəbʰl) *adj* incapable of being defeated; unconquerable. [C15: from LL *invincibilis,* from L IN-¹ + *vincere* to conquer]
▸ in,vinci'bility *or* in'vincibleness *n* ▸ in'vincibly *adv*

inviolable (ɪnˈvaɪələbʰl) *adj* that must not or cannot be transgressed, dishonoured, or broken; to be kept sacred: *an inviolable oath.*
▸ in,viola'bility *n* ▸ in'violably *adv*

inviolate (ɪnˈvaɪəlɪt, -ˌleɪt) *adj* **1** free from violation, injury, disturbance, etc. **2** a less common word for **inviolable.**
▸ in'violacy *or* in'violateness *n* ▸ in'violately *adv*

invisible (ɪnˈvɪzəbʰl) *adj* **1** not visible; not able to be perceived by the eye: *invisible rays.* **2** concealed from sight; hidden. **3** not easily seen or noticed: *invisible mending.* **4** kept hidden from public view; secret. **5** *Econ.* of or relating to services, such as insurance and freight, rather than goods: *invisible earnings.* ◆ *n* **6** *Econ.* an invisible item of trade; service.
▸ in,visi'bility *or* in'visibleness *n* ▸ in'visibly *adv*

invitation (ˌɪnvɪˈteɪʃən) *n* **1a** the act of inviting, such as an offer of entertainment or hospitality. **1b** (*as modifier*): *an invitation race.* **2** the act of enticing or attracting; allurement.

invite *vb* (ɪnˈvaɪt), **invites, inviting, invited.** (*tr*) **1** to ask (a person) in a friendly or polite way (to do something, attend an event, etc.). **2** to make a request for, esp. publicly or formally: *to invite applications.* **3** to bring on or provoke; give occasion for: *you invite disaster by your actions.* **4** to welcome or tempt. ◆ *n* (ˈɪnvaɪt). **5** *Inf.* an invitation. [C16: from L *invītāre* to invite, entertain]
▸ in'viter *n*

inviting (ɪnˈvaɪtɪŋ) *adj* tempting; alluring; attractive.
▸ in'vitingness *n*

in vitro (ɪn ˈviːtrəʊ) *adv, adj* (of biological processes or reactions) made to occur outside the body of the organism in an artificial environment. [NL, lit.: in glass]

in vitro fertilization *n* a technique enabling some women who are unable to conceive to bear children. Egg cells removed from a woman's ovary are fertilized by sperm in vitro; some of the resulting fertilized egg cells are then implanted into her uterus. Abbrev.: **IVF.**

in vivo (ɪn ˈviːvəʊ) *adv, adj* (of biological processes or experiments) occurring or carried out in the living organism. [NL, lit.: in a living (thing)]

invocation (ˌɪnvəˈkeɪʃən) *n* **1** the act of invoking or calling upon some agent for assistance. **2** a prayer asking God for help, forgiveness, etc. **3** an appeal for inspiration from a Muse or deity at the beginning of a poem. **4a** the act of summoning a spirit from another world by ritual incantation or magic. **4b** the incantation used in this act.
▸ ,invo'cational *adj* ▸ invocatory (ɪnˈvɒkətərɪ, -trɪ) *adj*

invoice (ˈɪnvɔɪs) *n* **1** a document issued by a seller to a buyer listing the goods or services supplied and stating the sum of money due. **2** *Rare.* a consignment of invoiced merchandise. ◆ *vb* **invoices, invoicing, invoiced. 3** (*tr*) **3a** to present (a customer, etc.) with an invoice. **3b** to list (merchandise sold) on an invoice. [C16: from earlier *invoyes,* from OF *envois,* pl. of *envoi* message; see ENVOY¹]

invoke (ɪnˈvəʊk) *vb* **invokes, invoking, invoked.** (*tr*) **1** to call upon (an agent, esp. God or another deity) for help, inspiration, etc. **2** to put (a law, penalty, etc.) into use: *the union invoked the dispute procedure.* **3** to appeal to (an outside authority) for confirmation, corroboration, etc. **4** to implore or beg (help, etc.). **5** to summon (a spirit, etc.); conjure up. [C15: from L *invocāre* to appeal to, from *vocāre* to call]
▸ in'vocable *adj* ▸ in'voker *n*

USAGE NOTE   *Invoke* is sometimes wrongly used where *evoke* is meant: *this proposal evoked* (not *invoked*) *a strong reaction.*

★ people and places

involucre ('ɪnvə.luːkə) or **involucrum** (.ɪnvə'luːkrəm) *n*, *pl* **involucres** or **involucra** (-krə). a ring of bracts at the base of an inflorescence. [C16 (in the sense: envelope): from NL *involucrum*, from L: wrapper, from *involvere* to wrap]
▶ .invo'lucral *adj* ▶ .invo'lucrate *adj*

involuntary (ɪn'vɒləntərɪ, -trɪ) *adj* **1** carried out without one's conscious wishes; not voluntary; unintentional. **2** *Physiol.* (esp. of a movement or muscle) performed or acting without conscious control.
▶ in'voluntarily *adv* ▶ in'voluntariness *n*

involute *adj* ('ɪnvə.luːt), *also* **involuted. 1** complex, intricate, or involved. **2** *Bot.* (esp. of petals, leaves, etc., in bud) having margins that are rolled inwards. **3** (of certain shells) closely coiled so that the axis is obscured. ♦ *n* ('ɪnvə.luːt). **4** *Geom.* the curve described by the free end of a thread as it is wound around another curve, the **evolute**, such that its normals are tangential to the evolute. ♦ *vb* (.ɪnvə'luːt), **involutes, involuting, involuted. 5** (*intr*) to become involute. [C17: from L *involūtus*, from *involvere*; see INVOLVE]
▶ 'invo.lutely *adv* ▶ .invo'lutedly *adv*

involution (.ɪnvə'luːʃən) *n* **1** the act of involving or complicating or the state of being involved or complicated. **2** something involved or complicated. **3** *Zool.* degeneration or structural deformation. **4** *Biol.* an involute formation or structure. **5** *Physiol.* reduction in size of an organ or part, as of the uterus following childbirth or as a result of ageing. **6** an algebraic operation in which a number, expression, etc., is raised to a specified power.
▶ .invo'lutional *adj*

involve (ɪn'vɒlv) *vb* **involves, involving, involved.** (*tr*) **1** to include or contain as a necessary part. **2** to have an effect on; spread to: *the investigation involved many innocent people*. **3** (*often passive*: usually foll. by *in* or *with*) to concern or associate significantly: *many people were involved in the crime*. **4** (*often passive*) to make complicated; tangle. **5** *Rare, often poetic.* to wrap or surround. **6** *Maths, obs.* to raise to a specified power. [C14: from L *involvere* to surround, from IN-² + *volvere* to roll]
▶ in'volvement *n* ▶ in'volver *n*

invulnerable (ɪn'vʌlnərəbᵊl, -'vʌlnrəbᵊl) *adj* **1** incapable of being wounded, hurt, damaged, etc. **2** incapable of being damaged or captured: *an invulnerable fortress*.
▶ in.vulnera'bility or in'vulnerableness *n* ▶ in'vulnerably *adv*

inward ('ɪnwəd) *adj* **1** going or directed towards the middle of or into something. **2** situated within; inside. **3** of, relating to, or existing in the mind or spirit: *inward meditation*. **4** of one's own country or a specific country: *inward investment*. ♦ *adv* **5** a variant of **inwards**. ♦ *n* **6** the inward part; inside.
▶ 'inwardness *n*

inwardly ('ɪnwədlɪ) *adv* **1** within the private thoughts or feelings; secretly. **2** not aloud: *to laugh inwardly*. **3** with reference to the inside or inner part; internally.

inwards *adv* ('ɪnwədz), *also* **inward. 1** towards the interior or middle of something. **2** in, into, or towards the mind or spirit. ♦ *pl n* ('ɪnədz). **3** a variant of **innards** (sense 1).

inweave (ɪn'wiːv) *vb* **inweaves, inweaving, inwove** or **inweaved; inwoven** or **inweaved.** (*tr*) to weave together into or as if into a design, fabric, etc.

inwrap (ɪn'ræp) *vb* **inwraps, inwrapping, inwrapped.** a less common spelling of **enwrap**.

inwrought (.ɪn'rɔːt) *adj* **1** worked or woven into material, esp. decoratively. **2** *Rare.* blended with other things.

in-your-face *adj Sl.* aggressive and confrontational: *provocative in-your-face activism*.

Io¹ ★ ('aɪəʊ) *n Greek myth.* a maiden loved by Zeus and turned into a white heifer by either Zeus or Hera.

Io² *the chemical symbol for* ionium.

Ioánnina (*Greek* jɔ'anina) or **Yanina** ★ *n* a city in NW Greece: belonged to the Serbs (1349–1430) and then the Turks (until 1913); seat of Ali Pasha, the "Lion of Janina", from 1788 to 1822. Pop.: 56 496 (1991 est.). Serbian name: **Janina**.

IOC *abbrev. for* International Olympic Committee.

iodic (aɪ'ɒdɪk) *adj* of or containing iodine, esp. in the pentavalent state.

iodide ('aɪə.daɪd) *n* **1** a salt of hydriodic acid, containing the iodide ion, I⁻. **2** a compound containing an iodine atom, such as methyl iodide (iodomethane).

iodine ('aɪə.diːn) *n* a bluish-black element of the halogen group that sublimates into a violet irritating gas. Its compounds are used in medicine and photography and in dyes. The radioisotope **iodine-131** is used in the treatment of thyroid disease. Symbol: I; atomic no.: 53; atomic wt.: 126.90. [C19: from F *iode*, from Gk *iōdēs* rust-coloured, but mistaken as violet-coloured, from *ion* violet]

iodize or **iodise** ('aɪə.daɪz) *vb* **iodizes, iodizing, iodized** or **iodises, iodising, iodised.** (*tr*) to treat or react with iodine or an iodine compound. Also: **iodate.**
▶ .iodi'zation or .iodi'sation *n* ▶ 'io.dizer or 'io.diser *n*

iodoform (aɪ'ɒdə.fɔːm) *n* a yellow crystalline solid made by heating alcohol with iodine and an alkali: used as an antiseptic. Formula: CHI₃. Systematic name: **triiodomethane.**

iodopsin (.aɪə'dɒpsɪn) *n* a violet light-sensitive pigment in the cones of the retina of the eye. See also **rhodopsin.**

IOM *abbrev. for* Isle of Man.

ion ('aɪən, -ɒn) *n* an electrically charged atom or group of atoms formed by the loss or gain of one or more electrons. See also **cation, anion.** [C19: from Gk, lit.: going, from *ienai* to go]

-ion *suffix forming nouns.* indicating an action, process, or state: *creation; objection.* Cf. **-ation, -tion.** [from L *-iōn-, -io*]

Iona ★ (aɪ'əʊnə) *n* an island off the W coast of Scotland, in the Inner Hebrides: site of St Columba's monastery (founded in 563) and an important early centre of Christianity. Area: 854 ha (2112 acres).

Ionesco ★ (.iːə'neskəʊ; *French* jɔnesko) *n* **Eugène** (øʒɛn) 1912–94, French dramatist, born in Romania; a leading exponent of the theatre of the absurd. His plays include *The Bald Prima Donna* (1950) and *Rhinoceros* (1960).

ion exchange *n* the process in which ions are exchanged between a solution and an insoluble solid, usually a resin. It is used to soften water.

Ionia ★ (aɪ'əʊnɪə) *n* an ancient region of W central Asia Minor, including adjacent Aegean islands: colonized by Greeks in about 1100 B.C.
▶ I'onian *adj, n*

Ionian Islands ★ *pl n* a group of Greek islands in the Ionian Sea, consisting of Corfu, Cephalonia, Zante, Levkas, Ithaca, Cythera, and Paxos: ceded to Greece in 1864. Pop.: 193 734 (1991). Area: 2307 sq. km (891 sq. miles).

Ionian Sea ★ *n* the part of the Mediterranean Sea between SE Italy, E Sicily, and Greece.

ionic (aɪ'ɒnɪk) *adj* of, relating to, or occurring in the form of ions.

Ionic (aɪ'ɒnɪk) *adj* **1** of, denoting, or relating to one of the five classical orders of architecture, characterized by fluted columns and capitals with scroll-like ornaments. **2** of or relating to Ionia, on the coast of Asia Minor, its inhabitants or their dialect of Ancient Greek. ♦ *n* **3** one of four chief dialects of Ancient Greek; the dialect spoken in Ionia.

ionium (aɪ'əʊnɪəm) *n Obs.* a naturally occurring radioisotope of thorium with a mass number of 230. Symbol: Io [C20: from NL]

ionization or **ionisation** (.aɪənaɪ'zeɪʃən) *n* **a** the formation of ions as a result of a chemical reaction, high temperature, electrical discharge, or radiation. **b** (*as modifier*): *ionization temperature.*

ionize or **ionise** ('aɪə.naɪz) *vb* **ionizes, ionizing, ionized** or **ionises, ionising, ionised.** to change or become changed into ions.
▶ 'ion.izable or 'ion.isable *adj* ▶ 'ion.izer or 'ion.iser *n*

ionosphere (aɪ'ɒnə.sfɪə) *n* a region of the earth's atmosphere, extending from about 60 to 1000 km above the earth's surface, in which there is a high concentration of free electrons formed as a result of ionizing radiation entering the atmosphere from space.
▶ **ionospheric** (aɪ.ɒnə'sfɛrɪk) *adj*

★ people and places

iota (aɪˈəʊtə) n **1** the ninth letter in the Greek alphabet (Ι, ι), a vowel or semivowel. **2** (usually used with a negative) a very small amount; jot (esp. in **not one** or **an iota**). [C16: via L from Gk, of Semitic origin]

IOU n a written promise or reminder to pay a debt. [C17: representing *I owe you*]

-ious suffix forming adjectives from nouns. characterized by or full of: suspicious. [from L -ius & -iōsus full of]

IOW abbrev. for Isle of Wight.

Iowa ★ (ˈaɪəʊə) n a state of the N central US, in the Midwest: consists of rolling plains crossed by many rivers, with the Missouri forming the western border and the Mississippi the eastern. Capital: Des Moines. Pop.: 2 851 792 (1996 est.). Area: 144 887 sq. km (55 941 sq. miles). Abbrevs.: **Ia.** or (with zip code) **IA**
▸ **ˈIowan** adj, n

IPA abbrev. for International Phonetic Alphabet.

ipecacuanha (ˌɪpɪˌkækjʊˈænə) or **ipecac** (ˈɪpɪˌkæk) n **1** a low-growing South American shrub. **2** a drug prepared from the dried roots of this plant, used as a purgative and emetic. [C18: from Port., from Amerind *ipekaaguéne*, from *ipeh* low + *kaa* leaves + *guéne* vomit]

Iphigenia ★ (ˌɪfɪdʒɪˈnaɪə) n Greek myth. the daughter of Agamemnon, taken by him to be sacrificed to Artemis, who saved her life and made her a priestess.

I-pin ★ (ˈiːˈbɪn) n a variant transliteration of the Chinese name for **Yibin**.

Ipoh ★ (ˈiːpəʊ) n a city in Malaysia, capital of Perak state: tin-mining centre. Pop.: 382 633 (1991).

ipomoea (ˌɪpəˈmɪə, ˌaɪ-) n **1** any tropical or subtropical plant, such as the morning-glory, sweet potato, and jalap, having trumpet-shaped flowers. **2** the dried root of a Mexican species which yields a cathartic resin. [C18: NL, from Gk *ips* worm + *homoios* like]

ippon (ˈɪpɒn) n Judo & karate. a winning point awarded in a sparring competition for a perfectly executed technique. [C20: Japanese, lit.: one point]

Ipsambul ★ (ˌɪpsæmˈbuːl) n another name for **Abu Simbel**.

ipse dixit Latin. (ˈɪpseɪ ˈdɪksɪt) n an arbitrary and unsupported assertion. [C16, lit.: he himself said it]

ipso facto (ˈɪpsəʊ ˈfæktəʊ) adv by that very fact or act. [from L]

Ipsus ★ (ˈɪpsəs) n an ancient town in Asia Minor, in S Phrygia: site of a decisive battle (301 B.C.) in the Wars of the Diadochi in which Lysimachus and Seleucus defeated Antigonus and Demetrius.

Ipswich ★ (ˈɪpswɪtʃ) n a town in E England, administrative centre of Suffolk, at the head of the Orwell estuary: manufactures agricultural and industrial machinery. Pop.: 130 157 (1991).

IQ abbrev. for intelligence quotient.

Iqaluit ★ (ɪˈkæluːɪt) n a town in N Canada. Former name: **Frobisher Bay**.

Iqbal ★ (ˈɪkbal) n Sir **Muhammad** (mʊˈhæməd). 1875–1938, Indian Muslim poet, philosopher, and political leader, who advocated the establishment of separate nations for Indian Hindus and Muslims and is generally regarded as the originator of Pakistan.

Iquique ★ (Spanish iˈkike) n a port in N Chile: oil refineries. Pop.: 152 592 (1995 est.).

Iquitos ★ (Spanish iˈkitos) n an inland port in NE Peru, on the Amazon 3703 km (2300 miles) from the Atlantic: head of navigation for steamers. Pop.: 274 759 (1993).

Ir the chemical symbol for iridium.

Ir. abbrev. for: **1** Ireland. **2** Irish.

ir- prefix a variant of **in-¹** and **in-²** before r.

IRA abbrev. for Irish Republican Army.

irade (ɪˈrɑːdɛ) n a written edict of a Muslim ruler. [C19: from Turkish: will, from Ar. *irādah*]

Iráklion ★ (Greek iˈraklion) n a port in Greece, in N Crete: former capital of Crete (until 1841); ruled by Venetians (13th–17th centuries). Pop.: 117 167 (1991). Italian name: **Candia**. Also called: **Heraklion, Herakleion**.

Iran ★ (ɪˈrɑːn) n a republic in SW Asia, between the Caspian Sea and the Persian Gulf: consists chiefly of a high central desert plateau almost completely surrounded by mountains, a semitropical fertile region along the Caspian coast, and a hot and dry area beside the Persian Gulf. Oil is the most important export. Official language: Farsi (Persian). Official religion: Muslim. Currency: rial. Capital: Tehran. Pop.: 62 304 000 (1997). Area: 1 647 050 sq. km (635 932 sq. miles). Former name (until 1935): **Persia**. Official name: **Islamic Republic of Iran**. See also **Persian Empire**.

Iranian (ɪˈreɪnɪən) n **1** a native or inhabitant of Iran. **2** a branch of the Indo-European family of languages, including Persian. **3** the modern Persian language. ◆ adj **4** relating to or characteristic of Iran, its inhabitants, or their language; Persian. **5** belonging to or relating to the Iranian branch of Indo-European.

Iran-Iraq War n the indecisive war (1980–88) fought by Iran and Iraq, following the Iraqi invasion of disputed border territory in Iran. Also called: **Gulf War**.

Iraq ★ (ɪˈrɑːk) n a republic in SW Asia, on the Persian Gulf: coextensive with ancient Mesopotamia; became a British mandate in 1920, independent in 1932, and a republic in 1958; the Iraqi invasion of Kuwait (1990) led to the Gulf War (1991), in which Iraq was defeated by US-led UN forces. It consists chiefly of the mountains of Kurdistan in the northeast, part of the Syrian Desert, and the lower basin of the Rivers Tigris and Euphrates. Oil is the major export. Official language: Arabic; Kurdish is also spoken. Official religion: Muslim. Currency: dinar. Capital: Baghdad. Pop.: 22 219 000 (1997). Area: 438 446 sq. km (169 284 sq. miles).
▸ **Iraqi** (ɪˈrɑːkɪ) adj, n

irascible (ɪˈræsɪbᵊl) adj **1** easily angered; irritable. **2** showing irritability: an irascible action. [C16: from LL *īrascibilis*, from L *īra* anger]
▸ **i,rasci'bility** or **i'rascibleness** n ▸ **i'rascibly** adv

irate (aɪˈreɪt) adj **1** incensed with anger; furious. **2** marked by extreme anger: an irate letter. [C19: from L *īrātus* enraged, from *īrascī* to be angry]
▸ **i'rately** adv

Irbid ★ (ˈɪrbɪd) n a town in NW Jordan. Pop.: 208 201 (1994).

Irbil ★ (ˈɪəbɪl) n a variant of **Erbil**.

IRBM abbrev. for intermediate-range ballistic missile.

ire (ˈaɪə) n Literary. anger; wrath. [C13: from OF, from L *īra*]
▸ **'ireful** adj ▸ **'irefulness** n

Ire. abbrev. for Ireland.

Ireland¹ ★ (ˈaɪələnd) n **1** an island off NW Europe: part of the British Isles, separated from Britain by the North Channel, the Irish Sea, and St George's Channel; large areas of peat bog, with mountains that rise over 900 m (3000 ft) in the southwest and several large lakes. It was conquered by England in the 16th and early 17th centuries and ruled as a dependency until 1801, when it was united with Great Britain until its division in 1921 into the Irish Free State and Northern Ireland. Latin name: **Hibernia**. **2 Republic of.** Also called: **Irish Republic, Southern Ireland**. a republic in NW Europe occupying most of Ireland: established as the Irish Free State (a British dominion) in 1921 and declared a republic in 1949; a member of the European Union. Official languages: Irish (Gaelic) and English. Currency: punt and euro. Capital: Dublin. Pop.: 3 644 000 (1997). Area: 70 282 sq. km (27 136 sq. miles). Gaelic name: **Eire**. ◆ See also **Northern Ireland**.

Ireland² ★ (ˈaɪələnd) n John (Nicholson). 1879–1962, British composer, esp. of songs.

irenic, eirenic (aɪˈriːnɪk, -ˈrɛn-) or **irenical, eirenical** adj tending to conciliate or promote peace. [C19: from Gk *eirēnikos*, from *eirēnē* peace]
▸ **i'renically** or **ei'renically** adv

Ireton ★ (ˈaɪətᵊn) n Henry. 1611–51, English Parliamentarian general in the Civil War; son-in-law of Oliver Cromwell. His plan for a constitutional monarchy was rejected by Charles I (1647), whose death warrant he signed; lord deputy of Ireland (1650–51).

Irian Barat ★ (ˈɪərɪən ˈbærɑːt) n the former Indonesian name for **Irian Jaya**.

★ people and places

Irian Jaya ★ *n* the W part of the island of New Guinea: formerly under Dutch rule, becoming a province of Indonesia in 1963. Capital: Jayapura. Pop.: 1 956 300 (1995 est.). Area: 416 990 sq. km (161 000 sq. miles). Former names (until 1963): **Dutch New Guinea, Netherlands New Guinea.** English name: **West Irian.**

iridaceous (ˌɪrɪˈdeɪʃəs, ˌaɪ-) *adj* of, relating to, or belonging to the family of monocotyledonous plants, including the iris, having swordlike leaves and showy flowers.

iridescent (ˌɪrɪˈdɛsᵊnt) *adj* displaying a spectrum of colours that shimmer and change due to interference and scattering as the observer's position changes. [C18: from L *irid-* iris + -ESCENT]
▸ ˌiriˈdescence *n* ▸ ˌiriˈdescently *adv*

iridium (aɪˈrɪdɪəm, ɪˈrɪd-) *n* a very hard yellowish-white transition element that is the most corrosion-resistant metal known. It occurs in platinum ores and is used as an alloy with platinum. Symbol: Ir; atomic no.: 77; atomic wt.: 192.2. [C19: NL, from L *irid-* iris + -IUM; from its colourful appearance when dissolving in certain acids]

iris (ˈaɪrɪs) *n, pl* **irises** *or* **irides** (ˈaɪrɪˌdiːz, ˈɪrɪ-). **1** the coloured muscular diaphragm that surrounds and controls the size of the pupil of the eye. **2** Also called: **fleur-de-lys.** any iridaceous plant having brightly coloured flowers composed of three petals and three drooping sepals. **3** a poetic word for **rainbow. 4** short for **iris diaphragm.** [C14: from L: rainbow, iris (flower), crystal, from Gk]

Iris ★ (ˈaɪrɪs) *n* the goddess of the rainbow along which she travelled to earth as a messenger of the gods.

iris diaphragm *n* an adjustable diaphragm that regulates the amount of light entering an optical instrument, esp. a camera.

Irish (ˈaɪrɪʃ) *adj* **1** of, relating to, or characteristic of Ireland, its people, their Celtic language, or their dialect of English. **2** *Inf. offens.* ludicrous or illogical. ◆ *n* **3 the Irish.** (functioning as pl) the natives or inhabitants of Ireland. **4** another name for **Irish Gaelic. 5** the dialect of English spoken in Ireland.

Irish coffee *n* hot coffee mixed with Irish whiskey and topped with double cream.

Irish Free State ★ *n* a former name for the (Republic of) **Ireland** (1921–37).

Irish Gaelic *n* the Goidelic language of the Celts of Ireland, now spoken mainly along the west coast; an official language of the Republic of Ireland since 1921.

Irishman (ˈaɪrɪʃmən) *or* (fem) **Irishwoman** *n, pl* **Irishmen** *or* **Irishwomen.** a native or inhabitant of Ireland.

Irish pipes *pl n* another name for **uillean pipes.**

Irish Republic ★ *n* See **Ireland**¹ (sense 2).

Irish Republican Army *n* a militant organization of Irish nationalists founded with the aim of striving for a united independent Ireland by means of guerrilla warfare. Abbrev.: **IRA.**

Irish Sea ★ *n* an arm of the North Atlantic Ocean between Great Britain and Ireland.

Irish stew *n* a stew made of mutton, lamb, or beef, with potatoes, onions, etc.

Irish wolfhound *n* a large breed of hound with a rough thick coat.

iritis (aɪˈraɪtɪs) *n* inflammation of the iris of the eye.
▸ iritic (aɪˈrɪtɪk) *adj*

irk (ɜːk) *vb* (tr) to irritate, vex, or annoy. [C13 *irken* to grow weary]

irksome (ˈɜːksəm) *adj* causing vexation, annoyance, or boredom; troublesome or tedious.
▸ ˈirksomely *adv* ▸ ˈirksomeness *n*

Irkutsk ★ (Russian irˈkutsk) *n* a city in S Russia: situated on the Trans-Siberian railway; university (1918); one of the largest industrial centres in Siberia, esp. for heavy engineering. Pop.: 585 000 (1995 est.).

IRO *abbrev. for:* **1** (in Britain) Inland Revenue Office. **2** International Refugee Organization.

iron (ˈaɪən) *n* **1a** a malleable ductile silvery-white ferromagnetic metallic element. It is widely used for structural and engineering purposes. Symbol: Fe; atomic no.:

26; atomic wt.: 55.847. Related adjs.: **ferric, ferrous.** Related prefix: **ferro-. 1b** (as modifier): *iron railings.* **2** any of certain tools or implements made of iron or steel, esp. for use when hot: *a grappling iron; a soldering iron.* **3** an appliance for pressing fabrics using dry heat or steam, esp. a small electrically heated device with a handle and a weighted flat bottom. **4** any of various golf clubs with metal heads, numbered from 1 to 10 according to the slant of the face. **5** a splintlike support for a malformed leg. **6** great hardness, strength, or resolve: *a will of iron.* **7 strike while the iron is hot.** to act at an opportune moment. ◆ *adj* **8** very hard, immovable, or implacable: *iron determination.* **9** very strong; extremely robust: *an iron constitution.* **10** cruel or unyielding: *he ruled with an iron hand.* ◆ *vb* **11** to smooth (clothes or fabric) by removing (creases or wrinkles) using a heated iron; press. **12** (tr) to furnish or overlay with iron. **13** (tr) *Rare.* to place (a prisoner) in irons. ◆ See also **iron out, irons.** [OE *īren*]
▸ ˈironer *n* ▸ ˈironless *adj* ▸ ˈiron,like *adj*

Iron Age *n* **a** the period following the Bronze Age characterized by the extremely rapid spread of iron tools and weapons. **b** (as modifier): *an Iron-Age weapon.*

ironbark (ˈaɪənˌbɑːk) *n* any of several Australian eucalyptus trees that have hard rough bark.

ironbound (ˈaɪənˌbaʊnd) *adj* **1** bound with iron. **2** unyielding; inflexible. **3** (of a coast) rocky; rugged.

Iron Chancellor ★ *n the.* nickname of (Prince Otto Eduard Leopold von) **Bismarck.**

ironclad *adj* (ˌaɪənˈklæd). **1** covered or protected with iron: *an ironclad warship.* **2** inflexible; rigid: *an ironclad rule.* ◆ *n* (ˈaɪənˌklæd). **3** a large wooden 19th-century warship with armoured plating.

Iron Curtain *n* **1** (formerly) **1a** the guarded border between the countries of the Soviet bloc and the rest of Europe. **1b** (as modifier): *Iron Curtain countries.* **2** (sometimes not caps.) any barrier that separates communities or ideologies.

Iron Gate *or* **Iron Gates** ★ *n* a gorge of the River Danube on the border between Romania and Yugoslavia. Length: 3 km (2 miles). Romanian name: **Porţile de Fier.**

iron hand *n* harsh or rigorous control; overbearing or autocratic force.

iron horse *n Arch.* a steam-driven railway locomotive.

ironic (aɪˈrɒnɪk) *or* **ironical** *adj* of, characterized by, or using irony.
▸ iˈronically *adv* ▸ iˈronicalness *n*

ironing (ˈaɪənɪŋ) *n* **1** the act of ironing washed clothes. **2** clothes, etc., that are to be or that have been ironed.

ironing board *n* a board, usually on legs, with a suitable covering on which to iron clothes.

iron lung *n* an airtight metal cylinder enclosing the entire body up to the neck and providing artificial respiration.

iron maiden *n* a medieval instrument of torture, consisting of a hinged case (often shaped in the form of a woman) lined with iron spikes, which was forcibly closed on the victim.

iron man *n Austral.* **1** an event at a surf carnival in which contestants compete at swimming, surfing, running, etc. **2** a participant in such an event.

ironmaster (ˈaɪənˌmɑːstə) *n Brit.* a manufacturer of iron.

ironmonger (ˈaɪənˌmʌŋgə) *n Brit.* a dealer in metal utensils, hardware, locks, etc. US and Canad. equivalent: **hardware dealer.**
▸ ˈiron,mongery *n*

iron out *vb* (tr, adv) **1** to smooth, using a heated iron. **2** to put or settle (a problem or difficulty) as a result of negotiations or discussions. **3** *Austral. inf.* to knock unconscious.

iron pyrites (ˈpaɪraɪts) *n* another name for **pyrite.**

iron rations *pl n* emergency food supplies, esp. for military personnel in action.

irons (ˈaɪənz) *pl n* **1** fetters or chains (often in **in** *or* **into irons**). **2 have several irons in the fire.** to be involved in many projects, etc.

Irons ★ (ˈaɪənz) *n* **Jeremy.** born 1948, British film and stage actor. His films include *The French Lieutenant's Woman* (1981) and *House of the Spirits* (1993).

Ironside ★ ('aɪənˌsaɪd) *n* nickname of **Edmund II** of England.

ironsides ('aɪənˌsaɪdz) *n* **1** a person with great stamina or resistance. **2** an ironclad ship. **3** (*often cap.*) (in the English Civil War) **3a** the cavalry regiment trained and commanded by Oliver Cromwell. **3b** Cromwell's entire army.

ironstone ('aɪənˌstəʊn) *n* **1** any rock consisting mainly of an iron-bearing ore. **2** a tough durable earthenware.

ironware ('aɪənˌwɛə) *n* domestic articles made of iron.

ironwood ('aɪənˌwʊd) *n* **1** any of various trees, such as hornbeam, that have very hard wood. **2** a Californian rosaceous tree with very hard wood. **3** any of various other trees with hard wood, such as the mopani. **4** the wood of any of these trees.

ironwork ('aɪənˌwɜːk) *n* **1** work done in iron, esp. decorative work. **2** the craft or practice of working in iron.

ironworks ('aɪənˌwɜːks) *n* (*sometimes functioning as sing*) a building in which iron is smelted, cast, or wrought.

irony[1] ('aɪrənɪ) *n, pl* **ironies. 1** the humorous or mildly sarcastic use of words to imply the opposite of what they normally mean. **2** an instance of this, used to draw attention to some incongruity or irrationality. **3** incongruity between what is expected to be and what actually is, or a situation or result showing such incongruity. **4** See **dramatic irony. 5** *Philosophy.* See **Socratic irony.** [C16: from L, from Gk *eirōneia*, from *eirōn* dissembler, from *eirein* to speak]

irony[2] ('aɪənɪ) *adj* of, resembling, or containing iron.

Iroquois ('ɪrəˌkwɔɪ) *n* **1** (*pl* **Iroquois**) a member of a confederacy of North American Indian tribes formerly living in and around New York State. **2** any of the languages of these people.
　▶ ˌIro'quoian *adj*

irradiance (ɪ'reɪdɪəns) *n* the radiant flux incident on unit area of a surface. Also: **irradiation.** Cf. **illuminance.**

irradiate (ɪ'reɪdɪˌeɪt) *vb* **irradiates, irradiating, irradiated. 1** (*tr*) *Physics.* to subject to or treat with light or other electromagnetic radiation or with beams of particles. **2** (*tr*) to expose (food) to electromagnetic radiation to kill bacteria and retard deterioration. **3** (*tr*) to make clear or bright intellectually or spiritually; illumine. **4** a less common word for **radiate** (sense 1). **5** (*intr*) *Obs.* to become radiant.
　▶ ir'radiˌation *n* ▶ ir'radiative *adj* ▶ ir'radiˌator *n*

irrational (ɪ'ræʃənᵊl) *adj* **1** inconsistent with reason or logic; illogical; absurd. **2** incapable of reasoning. **3a** *Maths.* (of an equation, etc.) containing one or more variables in irreducible radical form or raised to a fractional power: $\sqrt{(x^2 + 1)} = x^{5/3}$. **3b** (*as n*): *an irrational.*
　▶ ir,ration'ality *n* ▶ ir'rationally *adv*

irrational number *n* any real number that cannot be expressed as the ratio of two integers, such as π.

Irrawaddy ★ (ˌɪrə'wɒdɪ) *n* the main river in Myanmar, rising in the north in two headstreams and flowing south through the whole length of Myanmar, to enter the Andaman Sea by nine main mouths. Length: 2100 km (1300 miles).

irreclaimable (ˌɪrɪ'kleɪməbᵊl) *adj* not able to be reclaimed.
　▶ ˌirre,claima'bility *or* ˌirre'claimableness *n* ▶ ˌirre-'claimably *adv*

irreconcilable (ɪ'rɛkᵊnˌsaɪləbᵊl, ɪˌrɛkᵊn'saɪ-) *adj* **1** not able to be reconciled; uncompromisingly conflicting; incompatible. ◆ *n* **2** a person or thing that is implacably hostile or uncompromisingly opposed. **3** (*usually pl*) one of various principles, ideas, etc., that are incapable of being brought into agreement.
　▶ ir,recon,cila'bility *or* ir'recon,cilableness *n* ▶ ir'recon-,cilably *adv*

irrecoverable (ˌɪrɪ'kʌvərəbᵊl, -'kʌvrə-) *adj* **1** not able to be recovered or regained. **2** not able to be remedied or rectified.
　▶ ˌirre'coverableness *n* ▶ ˌirre'coverably *adv*

irredeemable (ˌɪrɪ'diːməbᵊl) *adj* **1** (of bonds, shares, etc.) without a date of redemption of capital; incapable of being bought back directly or paid off. **2** (of paper money) not convertible into specie. **3** (of a loss) not able to be recovered; irretrievable. **4** not able to be improved or rectified; irreparable.
　▶ ˌirre,deema'bility *or* ˌirre'deemableness *n* ▶ ˌirre-'deemably *adv*

irredentist (ˌɪrɪ'dɛntɪst) *n* **1** (*sometimes cap.*) a person, esp. a member of a 19th-century Italian association, who favours the acquisition of territory that was once part of his country or is considered to have been. ◆ *adj* **2** of or relating to irredentists or their policies. [C19: from It. *irredentista*, from *ir-* IN-[1] + *redento* redeemed, from L *redemptus* bought back; see REDEEM]
　▶ ˌirre'dentism *n*

irreducible (ˌɪrɪ'djuːsɪbᵊl) *adj* **1** not able to be reduced or lessened. **2** not able to be brought to a simpler or reduced form. **3** *Maths.* (of a polynomial) unable to be factorized into polynomials of lower degree, as ($x^2 + 1$).
　▶ ˌirre,duci'bility *n* ▶ ˌirre'ducibly *adv*

irrefragable (ɪ'rɛfrəgəbᵊl) *adj* not able to be denied or refuted. [C16: from LL *irrefrāgābilis*, from L *ir-* + *refrāgārī* to resist]
　▶ ir,refraga'bility *or* ir'refragableness *n* ▶ ir'refragably *adv*

irrefrangible (ˌɪrɪ'frændʒəbᵊl) *adj* **1** not to be broken or transgressed; inviolable. **2** *Physics.* incapable of being refracted.
　▶ ˌirre,frangi'bility *or* ˌirre'frangibleness *n* ▶ ˌirre-'frangibly *adv*

irrefutable (ɪ'rɛfjʊtəbᵊl, ˌɪrɪ'fjuːtəbᵊl) *adj* impossible to deny or disprove; incontrovertible.
　▶ ir,refuta'bility *n* ▶ ir'refutably *adv*

irreg. *abbrev. for* irregular(ly).

irregular (ɪ'rɛgjʊlə) *adj* **1** lacking uniformity or symmetry; uneven in shape, position, arrangement, etc. **2** not occurring at expected or equal intervals: *an irregular pulse.* **3** differing from the normal or accepted practice or routine; unconventional. **4** (of the formation, inflections, or derivations of a word) not following the usual pattern of formation in a language. **5** of or relating to guerrillas or volunteers not belonging to regular forces: *irregular troops.* **6** (of flowers) having any of their petals differing in size, shape, etc. **7** *US.* (of merchandise) not up to the manufacturer's standards or specifications; imperfect. ◆ *n* **8** a soldier not in a regular army. **9** (*often pl*) *US.* imperfect or flawed merchandise.
　▶ ir,regu'larity *n* ▶ ir'regularly *adv*

irrelevant (ɪ'rɛləvənt) *adj* not relating or pertinent to the matter at hand.
　▶ ir'relevance *or* ir'relevancy *n* ▶ ir'relevantly *adv*

irreligion (ˌɪrɪ'lɪdʒən) *n* **1** lack of religious faith. **2** indifference or opposition to religion.
　▶ ˌirre'ligionist *n* ▶ ˌirre'ligious *adj* ▶ ˌirre'ligiously *adv* ▶ ˌirre'ligiousness *n*

irremediable (ˌɪrɪ'miːdɪəbᵊl) *adj* not able to be remedied; incurable or irreparable.
　▶ ˌirre'mediableness *n* ▶ ˌirre'mediably *adv*

irremissible (ˌɪrɪ'mɪsᵊbᵊl) *adj* **1** unpardonable; inexcusable. **2** that must be done, as through duty or obligation.
　▶ ˌirre,missi'bility *or* ˌirre'missibleness *n* ▶ ˌirre'missibly *adv*

irremovable (ˌɪrɪ'muːvəbᵊl) *adj* not able to be removed.
　▶ ˌirre,mova'bility *n* ▶ ˌirre'movably *adv*

irreparable (ɪ'rɛpərəbᵊl, ɪ'rɛprəbᵊl) *adj* not able to be repaired or remedied; beyond repair.
　▶ ir,repara'bility *or* ir'reparableness *n* ▶ ir'reparably *adv*

irreplaceable (ˌɪrɪ'pleɪsəbᵊl) *adj* not able to be replaced: *an irreplaceable antique.*
　▶ ˌirre'placeably *adv*

irrepressible (ˌɪrɪ'prɛsᵊbᵊl) *adj* not capable of being repressed, controlled, or restrained.
　▶ ˌirre,pressi'bility *or* ˌirre'pressibleness *n* ▶ ˌirre-'pressibly *adv*

irreproachable (ˌɪrɪ'prəʊtʃəbᵊl) *adj* not deserving reproach; blameless.
　▶ ˌirre,proacha'bility *or* ˌirre'proachableness *n* ▶ ˌirre-'proachably *adv*

irresistible (ˌɪrɪˈzɪstəbəl) *adj* **1** not able to be resisted or refused; overpowering: *an irresistible impulse.* **2** very fascinating or alluring: *an irresistible woman.*
▸ ˌirreˌsistiˈbility *or* ˌirreˈsistibleness *n* ▸ ˌirreˈsistibly *adv*

irresolute (ɪˈrɛzəˌluːt) *adj* lacking resolution; wavering; hesitating.
▸ irˈresoˌlutely *adv* ▸ irˈresoˌluteness *or* irˌresoˈlution *n*

irrespective (ˌɪrɪˈspɛktɪv) *adj* **1** irrespective of. without taking account of; regardless of. ◆ *adv* **2** *Inf.* regardless; without due consideration: *he carried on with his plan irrespective.*
▸ ˌirreˈspectively *adv*

irresponsible (ˌɪrɪˈspɒnsəbəl) *adj* **1** not showing or done with due care for the consequences of one's actions or attitudes; reckless. **2** not capable of bearing responsibility.
▸ ˌirreˌsponsiˈbility *or* ˌirreˈsponsibleness *n* ▸ ˌirreˈsponsibly *adv*

irresponsive (ˌɪrɪˈspɒnsɪv) *adj* not responsive.
▸ ˌirreˈsponsively *adv* ▸ ˌirreˈsponsiveness *n*

irretrievable (ˌɪrɪˈtriːvəbəl) *adj* not able to be retrieved, recovered, or repaired.
▸ ˌirreˌtrievaˈbility *n* ▸ ˌirreˈtrievably *adv*

irreverence (ɪˈrɛvərəns, ɪˈrɛvrəns) *n* **1** lack of due respect or veneration; disrespect. **2** a disrespectful remark or act.
▸ irˈreverent *or* irˌreveˈrential *adj* ▸ irˈreverently *adv*

irreversible (ˌɪrɪˈvɜːsəbəl) *adj* **1** not able to be reversed: *the irreversible flow of time.* **2** not able to be revoked or repealed; irrevocable. **3** *Chem., physics.* capable of changing or producing a change in one direction only: *an irreversible reaction.*
▸ ˌirreˌversiˈbility *or* ˌirreˈversibleness *n* ▸ ˌirreˈversibly *adv*

irrevocable (ɪˈrɛvəkəbəl) *adj* not able to be revoked, changed, or undone.
▸ irˌrevocaˈbility *or* irˈrevocableness *n* ▸ irˈrevocably *adv*

irrigate (ˈɪrɪˌgeɪt) *vb* **irrigates, irrigating, irrigated. 1** to supply (land) with water by means of artificial canals, etc., esp. to promote the growth of food crops. **2** *Med.* to bathe or wash out (a bodily part, cavity, or wound). **3** (*tr*) to make fertile, fresh, or vital by or as if by watering. [C17: from L *irrigāre*, from *rigāre* to moisten, conduct water]
▸ ˈirrigable *adj* ▸ ˌirriˈgation *n* ▸ ˈirriˌgative *adj* ▸ ˈirriˌgator *n*

irritable (ˈɪrɪtəbəl) *adj* **1** quickly irritated; easily annoyed; peevish. **2** (of all living organisms) capable of responding to such stimuli as heat, light, and touch. **3** *Pathol.* abnormally sensitive.
▸ ˌirritaˈbility *n* ▸ ˈirritableness *n* ▸ ˈirritably *adv*

irritable bowel syndrome *n Med.* a chronic condition of recurring abdominal pain with constipation or diarrhoea or both.

irritant (ˈɪrɪtənt) *adj* **1** causing irritation; irritating. ◆ *n* **2** something irritant.
▸ ˈirritancy *n*

irritate (ˈɪrɪˌteɪt) *vb* **irritates, irritating, irritated. 1** to annoy or anger (someone). **2** (*tr*) *Biol.* to stimulate (an organism or part) to respond in a characteristic manner. **3** (*tr*) *Pathol.* to cause (a bodily organ or part) to become excessively stimulated, resulting in inflammation, tenderness, etc. [C16: from L *irrītāre* to provoke]
▸ ˈirriˌtator *n*

irritation (ˌɪrɪˈteɪʃən) *n* **1** something that irritates. **2** the act of irritating or the condition of being irritated.
▸ ˈirriˌtative *adj*

irrupt (ɪˈrʌpt) *vb* (*intr*) **1** to enter forcibly or suddenly. **2** (of a plant or animal population) to enter a region suddenly and in very large numbers. **3** (of a population) to increase suddenly and greatly. [C19: from L *irrumpere* to rush into, invade, from *rumpere* to break, burst]
▸ irˈruption *n* ▸ irˈruptive *adj*

Irtysh *or* **Irtish** ★ (ɪəˈtɪʃ) *n* a river in central Asia, rising in China in the Altai Mountains and flowing west through Kazakhstan, then northwest into Russia to join the Ob River as its chief tributary. Length: 4444 km (2760 miles).

Irvine ★ (ˈɜːvɪn) *n* a town on the W coast of Scotland, the administrative centre of North Ayrshire: designated a new town in 1966. Pop.: 32 988 (1991).

Irving ★ (ˈɜːvɪŋ) *n* **1** Sir Henry. real name *John Henry Brodribb.* 1838–1905, English actor and manager of the Lyceum Theatre in London (1878–1902). **2** Washington. 1783–1859, US essayist and short-story writer, noted for *The Sketch Book of Geoffrey Crayon* (1820), which contains the stories *Rip Van Winkle* and *The Legend of Sleepy Hollow.*

is (ɪz) *vb* (used with *he, she, it,* and with singular nouns) a form of the present tense (indicative mood) of **be**. [OE]

Is. *abbrev. for:* **1** Also: **Isa.** *Bible.* Isaiah. **2** Island(s) *or* Isle(s).

is- *combining form.* a variant of **iso-** before a vowel: *isentropic.*

ISA (ˈaɪsə) *n acronym for* individual savings account: a tax-free savings scheme introduced in the UK in 1999.

Isaac ★ (ˈaɪzək) *n* an Old Testament patriarch, the son of Abraham and Sarah and father of Jacob and Esau (Genesis 17; 21–27).

Isabella ★ (ˌɪzəˈbɛlə) *n* original name *Elizabeth Farnese.* 1692–1766, second wife (1714–46) of Philip V of Spain and mother of Charles III of Spain.

Isabella I ★ *n* known as *Isabella the Catholic.* 1451–1504, queen of Castile (1474–1504) and, with her husband, Ferdinand V, joint ruler of Castile and Aragon (1479–1504).

Isabella II ★ *n* 1830–1904, queen of Spain (1833–68), whose accession precipitated the first Carlist war (1833–39). She was deposed in a revolution.

Isabella of France ★ *n* 1292–1358, wife (1308–27) of Edward II of England, whom, aided by her lover, Roger de Mortimer, she deposed; mother of Edward III.

isagogics (ˌaɪsəˈgɒdʒɪks) *n* introductory studies, esp. in the history of the Bible. [C19: from L, from Gk, from *eisagein* to introduce, from *eis-* into + *agein* to lead]

Isaiah ★ (aɪˈzaɪə) *n Old Testament.* **1** the first of the major Hebrew prophets, who lived in the 8th century B.C. **2** the book of his and others' prophecies.

isallobar (aɪˈsæləˌbɑː) *n* a line on a map connecting places with equal pressure changes.

Isar ★ (ˈiːzɑː) *n* a river in central Europe, rising in W Austria and flowing generally northeast through S Germany into the Danube. Length: over 260 km (160 miles).

isatin (ˈaɪsətɪn) *or* **isatine** (ˈaɪsəˌtiːn) *n* a yellowish-red crystalline compound soluble in hot water, used for the preparation of vat dyes. [C19: from L *isatis* woad + -IN]
▸ ˌisaˈtinic *adj*

Isauria ★ (aɪˈsɔːrɪə) *n* an ancient district of S central Asia Minor, chiefly on the N slopes of the W Taurus Mountains.
▸ Iˈsaurian *adj, n*

ISBN *abbrev. for* International Standard Book Number.

Iscariot ★ (ɪˈskærɪət) *n* See **Judas** (Iscariot).

ischaemia *or* **ischemia** (ɪˈskiːmɪə) *n Pathol.* an inadequate supply of blood to an organ or part, as from an obstructed blood flow. [C19: from Gk *iskhein* to restrict, + -AEMIA]
▸ ischaemic *or* ischemic (ɪˈskɛmɪk) *adj*

Ischia ★ (ˈiːskjɑː, ˈɪskɪə) *n* a volcanic island in the Tyrrhenian Sea, at the N end of the Bay of Naples. Area: 47 sq. km (18 sq. miles).

ischium (ˈɪskɪəm) *n, pl* **ischia** (-kɪə). one of the three sections of the hipbone, situated below the ilium. [C17: from L: hip joint, from Gk *iskhion*]
▸ ˈischial *adj*

-ise *suffix forming verbs.* a variant of **-ize.**

USAGE NOTE	See at **-ize.**

isentropic (ˌaɪsɛnˈtrɒpɪk) *adj* having or taking place at constant entropy.

Isère ★ (*French* izɛr) *n* **1** a department of SE France, in Rhône-Alpes region. Capital: Grenoble. Pop.: 1 060 252 (1994 est.). Area: 7904 sq. km (3083 sq. miles). **2** a river

★ people and places

in SE France, rising in the Graian Alps and flowing west and southwest to join the River Rhône near Valence. Length: 290 km (180 miles).

Iseult, Yseult (ɪ'suːlt), *or* **Isolde** ★ (ɪ'zəuldə) *n* (in Arthurian legend) **1** an Irish princess wed to Mark, king of Cornwall, but in love with his knight Tristan. **2** (in another account) the daughter of the king of Brittany, married to Tristan.

Isfahan (ˌɪsfəˈhɑːn) *or* **Eşfahān** ★ *n* a city in central Iran: the second largest city in the country; capital of Persia in the 11th century and from 1598 to 1722. Pop.: 1 127 030 (1991). Ancient name: **Aspadana** (ˌæspəˈdɑːnə).

-ish *suffix forming adjectives*. **1** of or belonging to a nationality: *Scottish*. **2** *Often derog*. having the manner or qualities of; resembling: *slavish*; *boyish*. **3** somewhat; approximately: *yellowish*; *sevenish*. **4** concerned or preoccupied with: *bookish*. [OE *-isc*]

Isherwood ★ (ˈɪʃəˌwʊd) *n* **Christopher**, full name *Christopher William Bradshaw-Isherwood*. 1904–86, US novelist and dramatist, born in England. His works include the novel *Goodbye to Berlin* (1939) and three verse plays written in collaboration with W. H. Auden.

Ishiguro ★ (ˌɪʃɪˈɡuːrəu) *n* **Kazuo** (kæˈzuːəu). born 1954, British novelist, born in Japan. His novels include *An Artist of the Floating World* (1986) and the Booker-prizewinning *The Remains of the Day* (1989).

Ishmael ★ (ˈɪʃmeɪəl) *n* **1** the son of Abraham and Hagar, Sarah's handmaid: the ancestor of 12 Arabian tribes (Genesis 21:8–21; 25:12–18). **2** a bandit chieftain, who defied the Babylonian conquerors of Judah and assassinated the governor appointed by Nebuchadnezzar (II Kings 25:25; Jeremiah 40:13–41:18). **3** *Rare*. an outcast.

Ishtar ★ (ˈɪʃtɑː) *n* the principal goddess of the Babylonians and Assyrians; divinity of love, fertility, and war.

Isidore of Seville ★ (ˈɪzɪdɔː) *n* **Saint**, Latin name *Isidorus Hispalensis*. ?560–636 A.D., Spanish archbishop and scholar, noted for his *Etymologies*, an encyclopedia. Feast day: April 4.

isinglass (ˈaɪzɪŋˌɡlɑːs) *n* **1** a gelatine made from the air bladders of freshwater fish, used as a clarifying agent and adhesive. **2** another name for **mica**. [C16: from MDu. *huysenblase*, lit.: sturgeon bladder; infl. by E GLASS]

Isis[1] ★ (ˈaɪsɪs) *n* the local name for the River Thames at Oxford.

Isis[2] ★ (ˈaɪsɪs) *n* an ancient Egyptian fertility goddess, usually depicted as a woman with a cow's horns, between which was the disc of the sun; wife and sister of Osiris.

Iskenderun ★ (ɪsˈkɛndəˌruːn) *n* a port in S Turkey, on the **Gulf of Iskenderun**. Pop.: 156 800 (1994 est.). Former name: **Alexandretta**.

Isl. *abbrev. for*: **1** Island. **2** Isle.

Islam (ˈɪzlɑːm) *n* **1** Also called: **Islamism**. the religion of Muslims, teaching that there is only one God and that Mohammed is his prophet; Mohammedanism. **2a** Muslims collectively and their civilization. **2b** the countries where the Muslim religion is predominant. [C19: from Ar.: surrender (to God), from *aslama* to surrender]
▸ **Is'lamic** *adj*

Islamabad ★ (ɪzˈlɑːməˌbɑːd) *n* the capital of Pakistan, in the north on the Potwar Plateau: site chosen in 1959; surrounded by the Capital Territory of Islamabad for 909 sq. km (351 sq. miles). Pop.: 204 364 (1995 est.).

Islamist (ˈɪzˌləmɪst) *adj* **1** supporting or advocating Islamic fundamentalism. ◆ *n* **2** a supporter or advocate of Islamic fundamentalism.

Islamize *or* **Islamise** (ˈɪzləˌmaɪz) *vb* **Islamizes, Islamizing, Islamized** *or* **Islamises, Islamising, Islamised**. (*tr*) to convert or subject to the influence of Islam.
▸ ˌIslami'zation *or* ˌIslami'sation *n*

island (ˈaɪlənd) *n* **1** a mass of land that is surrounded by water and is smaller than a continent. **2** something isolated, detached, or surrounded: *a traffic island*. **3** *Anat*. a part, structure, or group of cells distinct in constitution from its surroundings. ◆ Related adj: **insular**.
◆ *vb* (*tr*) *Rare*. **4** to cause to become an island. **5** to inter-

sperse with islands. **6** to place on an island; insulate; isolate. [OE *īgland*]
▸ 'island-ˌlike *adj*

islander (ˈaɪləndə) *n* a native or inhabitant of an island.

Islands ★ (ˈaɪləndz) *pl n* NZ. **the**. the islands of the South Pacific.

Islands of the Blessed ★ *pl n Greek myth*. lands where the souls of heroes and good men were taken after death. Also called: **Hesperides**.

island universe *n* a former name for **galaxy**.

Islay ★ (ˈaɪlə, ˈaɪleɪ) *n* an island off the W coast of Scotland: the southernmost of the Inner Hebrides; separated from the island of Jura by the **Sound of Islay**. Pop.: 3500 (latest est.). Area: 606 sq. km (234 sq. miles).

isle (aɪl) *n Poetic except when cap. and part of place name*. an island, esp. a small one. [C13: from OF, from L *insula* island]

Isle of Dogs ★ *n* See (Isle of) **Dogs**.

Isle of Man ★ *n* See (Isle of) **Man**.

Isle of Pines ★ *n* the former name of the (Isle of) **Youth**.

Isle of Sheppey ★ *n* See (Isle of) **Sheppey**.

Isle of Wight ★ *n* See (Isle of) **Wight**.

Isle of Youth ★ *n* See (Isle of) **Youth**.

Isle Royale ★ (ˈrɔɪəl) *n* an island in the northeast US, in NW Lake Superior: forms, with over 100 surrounding islands, **Isle Royale National Park**. Area: 541 sq. km (209 sq. miles).

islet (ˈaɪlɪt) *n* a small island. [C16: from OF *islette*; see ISLE]

islets *or* **islands of Langerhans** (ˈlæŋəˌhæns) *pl n* small groups of endocrine cells in the pancreas that secrete insulin. [C19: after Paul *Langerhans* (1847–88), G physician]

Islington ★ (ˈɪzlɪŋtən) *n* a borough of N Greater London. Pop.: 175 200 (1994 est.). Area: 16 sq. km (6 sq. miles).

ism (ˈɪzəm) *n Inf., often derog*. an unspecified doctrine, system, or practice.

-ism *suffix forming nouns*. **1** indicating an action, process, or result: *criticism*. **2** indicating a state or condition: *paganism*. **3** indicating a doctrine, system, or body of principles and practices: *Leninism; spiritualism*. **4** indicating behaviour or a characteristic quality: *heroism*. **5** indicating a characteristic usage, esp. of a language: *Scotticism*. **6** indicating prejudice on the basis specified: *sexism; ageism*. [from OF *-isme*, from L *-ismus*, from Gk *-ismos*]

Ismaili *or* **Isma'ili** (ˌɪzmɑːˈiːlɪ) *n Islam*. **1** a Shiah sect whose adherents believe that Ismail, son of the sixth imam, was the rightful seventh imam. **2** a member of this sect.

Ismailia ★ (ˌɪzmaɪˈliːə) *n* a city in NE Egypt, on the Suez Canal: founded in 1863 by the former Suez Canal Company; devastated by Israeli troops in the October War (1973). Pop.: 255 000 (1992 est.).

Ismail Pasha ★ (ˌɪzmɑːˈiːl ˈpɑːʃə) *n* 1830–95, viceroy (1863–66) and khedive (1867–79) of Egypt, who brought his country close to bankruptcy. He was forced to submit to Anglo-French financial control (1876) and to abdicate (1879).

isn't (ˈɪzᵊnt) *contraction of* is not.

ISO *abbrev. for*: **1** International Standards Organization. **2** Imperial Service Order (a Brit. decoration).

iso- *or before a vowel* **is-** *combining form*. **1** equal or identical: *isomagnetic*. **2** indicating that a chemical compound is an isomer of a specified compound: *isobutane*. [from Gk *isos* equal]

isobar (ˈaɪsəʊˌbɑː) *n* **1** a line on a map connecting places of equal atmospheric pressure, usually reduced to sea level for purposes of comparison, at a given time or period. **2** *Physics*. any two or more atoms that have the same mass number but different atomic numbers. Cf. **isotope**. [C19: from Gk *isobarēs* of equal weight]
▸ ˌiso'baric *adj* ▸ 'isobar,ism *n*

isobutene (ˌaɪsəʊˈbjuːtiːn) *n* a colourless gas used in the manufacture of synthetic rubber.

isocheim *or* **isochime** (ˈaɪsəʊˌkaɪm) *n* a line on a map

connecting places with the same mean winter temperature. Cf. **isothere**. [C19: from ISO- + Gk *kheima* winter weather]
> ‚iso'cheimal *or* ‚iso'chimal *adj*

sochronal (aɪ'sɒkrən³l) *or* **isochronous** *adj* **1** having the same duration; equal in time. **2** occurring at equal time intervals; having a uniform period of vibration. [C17: from NL, from Gk *isokhronos*, from ISO- + *khronos* time]
> i'sochronally *or* i'sochronously *adv* ▸ i'sochro‚nism *n*

soclinal (‚aɪsəʊ'klaɪn³l) *or* **isoclinic** (‚aɪsəʊ'klɪnɪk) *adj* **1** sloping in the same direction and at the same angle. **2** *Geol.* (of folds) having limbs that are parallel to each other. ◆ *n* **3** Also: **isocline, isoclinal line**. an imaginary line connecting points on the earth's surface having equal angles of magnetic dip.

socline ('aɪsəʊ‚klaɪn) *n* **1** a series of rock strata with isoclinal folds. **2** another name for **isoclinal** (sense 3).

socrates ★ (aɪ'sɒkrə‚tiːz) *n* 436–338 B.C., Athenian rhetorician and teacher.

sodynamic (‚aɪsəʊdaɪ'næmɪk) *adj Physics.* **1** having equal force or strength. **2** of or relating to an imaginary line on the earth's surface connecting points of equal magnetic intensity.

sogeotherm (‚aɪsəʊ'dʒiː‚əʊ‚θɜːm) *n* an imaginary line below the surface of the earth connecting points of equal temperature.
> ‚iso‚geo'thermal *or* ‚iso‚geo'thermic *adj*

sogloss ('aɪsəʊ‚glɒs) *n* a line drawn on a map around the area in which a linguistic feature is to be found.
> ‚iso'glossal *or* ‚iso'glottic *adj*

isogonic (‚aɪsəʊ'gɒnɪk) *or* **isogonal** (aɪ'sɒgən³l) *adj* **1** *Maths.* having, making, or involving equal angles. ◆ *n* **2** Also called: **isogonic line, isogonal line, isogone**. *Physics.* an imaginary line connecting points on the earth's surface having equal magnetic declination.

isohel ('aɪsəʊ‚hel) *n* a line on a map connecting places with an equal period of sunshine. [C20: from ISO- + Gk *hēlios* sun]

isohyet (‚aɪsəʊ'haɪɪt) *n* a line on a map connecting places having equal rainfall. [C19: from ISO- + -*hyet*, from Gk *huetos* rain]

isolate *vb* ('aɪsə‚leɪt), **isolates, isolating, isolated**. (*tr*) **1** to place apart; cause to be alone. **2** *Med.* to quarantine (a person or animal) having a contagious disease. **3** to obtain (a compound) in an uncombined form. **4** to obtain pure cultures of (bacteria, esp. those causing a particular disease). **5** *Electronics*. to prevent interaction between (circuits, components, etc.); insulate. ◆ *n* ('aɪsəlɪt). **6** an isolated person or group. [C19: back formation from *isolated*, via It. from L *insulātus*, lit.: made into an island]
> 'isolable *adj* ▸ 'isola'bility *n* ▸ 'iso‚lator *n* ▸ ‚iso'lation *n*

isolationism (‚aɪsə'leɪʃə‚nɪzəm) *n* **1** a policy of nonparticipation in or withdrawal from international affairs. **2** an attitude favouring such a policy.
> ‚iso'lationist *n, adj*

Isolde ★ (i'zɒldə) *n* the German name of **Iseult**.

isomer ('aɪsəmə) *n* **1** *Chem.* a compound that exhibits isomerism with one or more other compounds. **2** *Physics*. a nuclide that exhibits isomerism with one or more other nuclides.
> ‚iso'meric (‚aɪsə'merɪk) *adj*

isomerism (aɪ'sɒmə‚rɪzəm) *n* **1** the existence of two or more compounds having the same molecular formula but a different arrangement of atoms. **2** the existence of two or more nuclides having the same atomic numbers and mass numbers but different energy states.

isomerous (aɪ'sɒmərəs) *adj* (of flowers) having floral whorls with the same number of parts.

isometric (‚aɪsəʊ'metrɪk) *adj also* **isometrical**. **1** having equal dimensions or measurements. **2** *Physiol.* of or relating to muscular contraction that does not produce shortening of the muscle. **3** (of a crystal or system of crystallization) having three mutually perpendicular equal axes. **4** (of a method of projecting a drawing in three dimensions) having the three axes equally in-

clined and all lines drawn to scale. ◆ *n* **5** Also called: **isometric drawing**. a drawing made in this way. [C19: from Gk *isometria*]
> ‚iso'metrically *adv*

isometrics (‚aɪsəʊ'metrɪks) *n* (*functioning as sing*) physical exercise involving isometric contraction of muscles.

isomorphism (‚aɪsəʊ'mɔː‚fɪzəm) *n* **1** *Biol.* similarity of form, as in different generations of the same life cycle. **2** *Chem.* the existence of two or more substances of different composition in a similar crystalline form. **3** *Maths*. a one-to-one correspondence between the elements of two or more sets, such as those of Arabic and Roman numerals.
> 'iso‚morph *n* ▸ ‚iso'morphic *or* ‚iso'morphous *adj*

isopleth ('aɪsəʊ‚pleθ) *n* a line on a map connecting places registering the same amount or ratio of some geographical, etc. phenomenon. [C20: from Gk *isoplēthēs* equal in number, from ISO- + *plēthos* multitude]

isopod ('aɪsəʊ‚pɒd) *n* a crustacean, such as the woodlouse, in which the body is flattened.
> **isopodan** (aɪ'sɒpədən) *or* i'sopodous *adj*

isoprene ('aɪsəʊ‚priːn) *n* a colourless volatile liquid with a penetrating odour: used in making synthetic rubbers. Formula: $CH_2:C(CH_3)CH:CH_2$. Systematic name: **methylbuta-1,3-diene**. [C20: from ISO- + PR(OPYL) + -ENE]

isopteran (aɪ'sɒptərən) *n, pl* **isopterans** *or* **isoptera** (-tərə). **1** any of an order of insects having two pairs of wings equal in size: comprises the termites. ◆ *adj also* **isopterous**. **2** of, relating to, or belonging to this order. [C19: from NL, from ISO- + Gk *pteron* wing]

ISO rating *n Photog*. a classification of film speed in which a doubling of the ISO number represents a doubling in sensitivity; for example, ISO 400 film requires half the exposure of ISO 200 under the same conditions. The system uses identical numbers to the obsolete ASA rating. [C20: from International Standards Organization]

isosceles (aɪ'sɒsɪ‚liːz) *adj* (of a triangle) having two sides of equal length. [C16: from LL, from Gk, from ISO- + *skelos* leg]

isoseismal (‚aɪsəʊ'saɪzməl) *adj* **1** of or relating to equal intensity of earthquake shock. ◆ *n* **2** a line on a map connecting points at which earthquake shocks are of equal intensity. ◆ Also: **isoseismic**.

isostasy (aɪ'sɒstəsɪ) *n* the state of balance which sections of the earth's lithosphere are thought ultimately to achieve when the vertical forces upon them remain unchanged. If a section is loaded as by ice, it slowly subsides. If a section is reduced in mass, as by erosion, it slowly rises. [C19: ISO- + -*stasy*, from Gk *stasis* a standing]
> **isostatic** (‚aɪsəʊ'stætɪk) *adj*

isothere ('aɪsəʊ‚θɪə) *n* a line on a map linking places of equal mean summer temperature. Cf. **isocheim**. [C19: from ISO- + Gk *theros* summer]
> **isotheral** (aɪ'sɒθərəl) *adj*

isotherm ('aɪsəʊ‚θɜːm) *n* **1** a line on a map linking places of equal temperature. **2** *Physics*. a curve on a graph that connects points of equal temperature. ◆ Also called: **isothermal, isothermal line**.

isothermal (‚aɪsəʊ'θɜːməl) *adj* **1** (of a process or change) taking place at constant temperature. **2** of or relating to an isotherm. ◆ *n* **3** another word for **isotherm**.
> ‚iso'thermally *adv*

isotonic (‚aɪsəʊ'tɒnɪk) *adj* **1** *Physiol.* (of two or more muscles) having equal tension. **2** (of a drink) designed to replace the fluid and salts lost from the body during strenuous exercise. **3** Also: **isosmotic**. (of two solutions) having the same osmotic pressure, commonly have physiological osmotic pressure. Cf. **hypertonic, hypotonic**.
> **isotonicity** (‚aɪsəʊtəʊ'nɪsɪtɪ) *n*

isotope ('aɪsə‚təʊp) *n* one of two or more atoms with the same atomic number that contain different numbers of neutrons. [C20: from ISO- + Gk *topos* place]
> **isotopic** (‚aɪsə'tɒpɪk) *adj* ▸ ‚iso'topically *adv* ▸ **isotopy** (aɪ'sɒtəpɪ) *n*

isotropic (‚aɪsəʊ'trɒpɪk) *or* **isotropous** (aɪ'sɒtrəpəs) *adj*

1 having uniform physical properties in all directions. **2** *Biol.* not having predetermined axes: *isotropic eggs.*
▶ ˌiso'tropically *adv* ▶ i'sotropy *n*

ISP *abbrev. for* Internet service provider.

I-spy *n* a game in which one player specifies the initial letter of the name of an object that he can see, which the other players then try to guess.

Israel ★ ('ɪzreɪəl, -rɪəl) *n* **1** a republic in SW Asia, on the Mediterranean Sea: established in 1948, in the former British mandate of Palestine, as a primarily Jewish state; disputes with Arab neighbours, who did not recognize Israel, erupted into full-scale wars in 1949, 1956, 1967 (the Six Day War), and 1973 (the Yom Kippur War). In 1993 Israel agreed to grant autonomy to the West Bank and Gaza Strip in a peace deal with the PLO. Official languages: Hebrew and Arabic. Religion: Jewish majority, Muslim and Christian minorities. Currency: shekel. Capital: Jerusalem (international recognition withheld: UN recognized capital: Tel Aviv). Pop.: 5 652 000 (1997). Area (including Golan Heights and East Jerusalem): 21 946 sq. km (8473 sq. miles). **2a** the ancient kingdom of the 12 Hebrew tribes at the SE end of the Mediterranean. **2b** the kingdom in the N part of this region formed by the ten northern tribes of Israel in the 10th century B.C. and destroyed by the Assyrians in 721 B.C.

Israeli (ɪz'reɪlɪ) *n, pl* **Israelis** *or* **Israeli. 1** a citizen or inhabitant of the state of Israel. ◆ *adj* **2** of or relating to the state of Israel or its inhabitants.

Israelite ('ɪzrɪəˌlaɪt, -rə-) *n* **1** *Bible.* a member of the ethnic group claiming descent from Jacob; a Hebrew. **2** a member of any of various Christian sects who regard themselves as God's chosen people. **3** an archaic word for a Jew.

Issachar ★ ('ɪsəˌkɑː) *n Old Testament.* **1** the fifth son of Jacob by his wife Leah (Genesis 30:17–18). **2** the tribe descended from this patriarch. **3** the territory of this tribe.

Issigonis ★ (ˌɪsɪ'gəʊnɪs) *n* Sir Alec (**Arnold Constantine**). 1906–88, British car designer born in Smyrna. He is noted for his designs for the Morris Minor (1948) and the Mini (1959).

issuance ('ɪʃjʊəns) *n* the act of issuing.

issue ('ɪʃjuː) *n* **1** the act of sending or giving out something; supply; delivery. **2** something issued; an edition of stamps, a magazine, etc. **3** the number of identical items, such as banknotes or shares in a company, that become available at a particular time. **4** the act of emerging; outflow; discharge. **5** something flowing out, such as a river. **6** a place of outflow; outlet. **7** the descendants of a person; offspring; progeny. **8** a topic of interest or discussion. **9** an important subject requiring a decision. **10** an outcome or consequence; result. **11** *Pathol.* discharge from a wound. **12** *Law.* the matter remaining in dispute between the parties to an action after the pleadings. **13** the yield from or profits arising out of land or other property. **14 at issue.** under discussion. **14a** under discussion. **14b** in disagreement. **15 force the issue.** to compel decision on some matter. **16 join issue.** to join in controversy. **17 take issue.** to disagree. ◆ *vb* **issues, issuing, issued. 18** to come forth or emerge or cause to come forth or emerge. **19** to publish or deliver (a newspaper, magazine, etc.). **20** (*tr*) to make known or announce. **21** (*intr*) to originate or proceed. **22** (*intr*) to be a consequence; result. **23** (*intr*; foll. by *in*) to end or terminate. **24** (*tr*) (foll. by *with*) to supply officially (with). [C13: from OF *eissue* way out, from *eissir* to go out, from L *exīre*]
▶ 'issuable *adj* ▶ 'issuer *n*

issue price *n Stock Exchange.* the price at which a new issue of shares is offered to the public.

Issus ★ ('ɪsəs) *n* an ancient town in S Asia Minor, in Cilicia north of present-day Iskenderun: scene of a battle (333 B.C.) in which Alexander the Great defeated the Persians.

Issyk-Kul ★ (*Russian* is'sik'kulj) *n* a lake in NE Kyrgyzstan in the Tian Shan mountains, at an altitude of 1609 m (5280 ft): one of the largest mountain lakes in the world. Area: 6200 sq. km (2390 sq. miles).

-ist *suffix.* **1** (*forming nouns*) a person who performs a cer-

tain action or is concerned with something specified: *motorist; soloist.* **2** (*forming nouns*) a person who practises in a specific field: *physicist.* **3** (*forming nouns and adjectives*) a person who advocates a particular doctrine, system, etc., or relating to such a person or the doctrine advocated: *socialist.* **4** (*forming nouns and adjectives*) a person characterized by a specified trait, tendency, etc., or relating to such a person or trait: *purist.* **5** (*forming nouns and adjectives*) a person who is prejudiced on the basis specified: *sexist; ageist.* [via OF from L *-ista, -istēs,* from Gk *-istēs*]

Istanbul ★ (ˌɪstæn'buːl) *n* a port in NW Turkey, on the western (European) shore of the Bosporus: the largest city in Turkey; founded in about 660 B.C. by Greeks; refounded by Constantine the Great in 330 A.D. as the capital of the Eastern Roman Empire; taken by the Turks in 1453 and remained capital of the Ottoman Empire until 1922; industrial centre for shipbuilding, textiles, etc. Pop.: 7 615 500 (1994 est.). Ancient name: **Byzantium.** Former name (330–1926): **Constantinople.**

isthmian ('ɪsθmɪən) *adj* relating to or situated in an isthmus.

isthmus ('ɪsməs) *n, pl* **isthmuses** *or* **isthmi** (-maɪ). **1** a narrow strip of land connecting two relatively large land areas. **2** *Anat.* **2a** a narrow band of tissue connecting two larger parts of a structure. **2b** a narrow passage connecting two cavities. [C16: from L, from Gk *isthmos*]
▶ 'isthmoid *adj*

-istic *suffix forming adjectives.* equivalent to a combination of **-ist** and **-ic** but in some words having a less specific or literal application and sometimes a mildly pejorative force, as compared with corresponding adjectives ending in **-ist**: *communistic; impressionistic.* [from L *-isticus,* from Gk *istikos*]

istle ('ɪstlɪ) *or* **ixtle** *n* a fibre obtained from various tropical American agave and yucca trees used in making carpets, cord, etc. [C19: from Mexican Sp. *ixtle,* from Amerind *ichtli*]

Istria ★ ('ɪstrɪə) *n* a peninsula in the N Adriatic Sea: passed from Italy to Yugoslavia (except for Trieste) in 1947 and to Croatia in 1991.
▶ 'Istrian *n, adj*

it (ɪt) *pron* (*subjective or objective*) **1** refers to a nonhuman, animal, plant, or inanimate thing, or sometimes to a small baby: *it looks dangerous; give it a bone.* **2** refers to an unspecified or implied antecedent or to a previous or understood clause, phrase, etc.: *it is impossible; I knew it.* **3** used to represent human life or experience in respect of the present situation: *how's it going? I've had it; to brazen it out.* **4** used as a formal subject (or object), referring to a following clause, phrase, or word: *it helps to know the truth; I consider it dangerous to go on.* **5** used in the nominative as the formal grammatical subject of impersonal verbs: *it is raining; it hurts.* **6** (used as complement with *be*) *Inf.* the crucial or ultimate point: *the steering failed and I thought that was it.* ◆ *n* **7** (in children's games) the player whose turn it is to try to touch another. **8** *Inf.* **8a** sexual intercourse. **8b** sex appeal. **9** *Inf.* a desirable quality or ability: *he's really got it.* [OE *hit*]

IT *abbrev. for* information technology.

It. *abbrev. for:* **1** Italian. **2** Italy.

i.t.a. *or* **ITA** *abbrev. for* initial teaching alphabet, a partly phonetic alphabet used to teach reading.

ital. *abbrev. for* italic.

Ital. *abbrev. for:* **1** Italian. **2** Italy.

Italia ★ (i'taːlja) *n* the Italian name for **Italy.**

Italian (ɪ'tæljən) *n* **1** the official language of Italy and one of the official languages of Switzerland. **2** a native or inhabitant of Italy or a descendant of one. ◆ *adj* **3** relating to, denoting, or characteristic of Italy, its inhabitants, or their language.

Italianate (ɪ'tæljənɪt, -ˌneɪt) *or* **Italianesque** *adj* Italian in style or character.

Italian East Africa ★ *n* a former Italian territory in E Africa, formed in 1936 from the possessions of Eritrea, Italian Somaliland, and Ethiopia: taken by British forces in 1941.

★ people and places

talian Somaliland ★ *n* a former Italian colony in E Africa, united with British Somaliland in 1960 to form the independent republic of Somalia.

talic (ɪ'tælɪk) *adj* **1** Also: **Italian**. of, relating to, or denoting a style of handwriting with the letters slanting to the right. **2** of, relating to, or denoting a style of printing type modelled on this, chiefly used to indicate emphasis, a foreign word, etc. Cf. **roman**. ◆ *n* **3** (*often pl*) italic type or print. [C16 (after an edition of Virgil (1501) printed in Venice and dedicated to Italy): from L *Italicus* of Italy, from Gk *Italikos*]

talic (ɪ'tælɪk) *n* **1** a branch of the Indo-European family of languages that includes many of the ancient languages of Italy. ◆ *adj* **2** denoting, relating to, or belonging to this group of languages, esp. the extinct ones.

talicize *or* **italicise** (ɪ'tælɪ,saɪz) *vb* **italicizes, italicizing, italicized** *or* **italicises, italicising, italicised**. **1** to print (textual matter) in italic type. **2** (*tr*) to underline (words, etc.) with a single line to indicate italics.
▸ i,talici'zation *or* i,talici'sation *n*

taly ★ ('ɪtəlɪ) *n* a republic in S Europe, occupying a peninsula in the Mediterranean between the Tyrrhenian and the Adriatic Seas, with the islands of Sardinia and Sicily to the west: first united under the Romans but became fragmented into numerous political units in the Middle Ages; united kingdom proclaimed in 1861; under the dictatorship of Mussolini (1922–43); became a republic in 1946; a member of the European Union. It is generally mountainous, with the Alps in the north and the Apennines running the length of the peninsula. Official language: Italian. Religion: Roman Catholic majority. Currency: lira and euro. Capital: Rome. Pop.: 57 510 000 (1997). Area: 301 247 sq. km (116 312 sq. miles). Italian name: **Italia**.

TC (in Britain) *abbrev. for* Independent Television Commission.

tch (ɪtʃ) *n* **1** an irritation or tickling sensation of the skin causing a desire to scratch. **2** a restless desire. **3** any skin disorder, such as scabies, characterized by intense itching. ◆ *vb* (*intr*) **4** to feel or produce an irritating or tickling sensation. **5** to have a restless desire (to do something). **6 have itchy feet**. to be restless; have a desire to travel. **7 itching palm**. a grasping nature; avarice. [OE *gīccean*]
▸ 'itchy *adj* ▸ 'itchiness *n*

-ite[1] *suffix forming nouns*. **1** a native or inhabitant of: *Israelite*. **2** a follower or advocate of; a member of a group: *Luddite; labourite*. **3** (in biology) indicating a division of a body or organ: *somite*. **4** indicating a mineral or rock: *nephrite; peridotite*. **5** indicating a commercial product: *vulcanite*. [via L *-ita* from Gk *-itēs* or directly from Gk]

-ite[2] *suffix forming nouns*. indicating a salt or ester of an acid having a name ending in *-ous*: *a nitrite is a salt of nitrous acid*. [from F, arbitrary alteration of -ATE[1]]

tem *n* ('aɪtəm). **1** a thing or unit, esp. included in a list or collection. **2** *Book-keeping*. an entry in an account. **3** a piece of information, detail, or note: *a news item*. **4** *Inf.* two people having a romantic or sexual relationship. ◆ *vb* ('aɪtəm). **5** (*tr*) *Arch.* to itemize. ◆ *adv* ('aɪtəm). **6** likewise; also. [C14 (adv) from L: in like manner]

temize *or* **itemise** ('aɪtə,maɪz) *vb* **itemizes, itemizing, itemized** *or* **itemises, itemising, itemised**. (*tr*) to put on a list or make a list of.
▸ ,itemi'zation *or* ,itemi'sation *n* ▸ 'item,izer *or* 'item,iser *n*

ténez ★ (i'teneθ) *n* the Spanish name for the **Guaporé**.

terate ('ɪtə,reɪt) *vb* **iterates, iterating, iterated**. (*tr*) to say or do again. [C16: from L *iterāre*, from *iterum* again]
▸ 'iterant *adj* ▸ ,iter'ation *n* ▸ 'iterative *adj*

thaca ★ ('ɪθəkə) *n* a Greek island in the Ionian Sea, the smallest of the Ionian Islands: regarded as the home of Homer's Odyssaus. Area: 93 sq. km (36 sq. miles). Modern Greek name: **Itháki** (i'θaki).
▸ 'Ithacan *n, adj*

thunn ★ ('ɪðʊn) *n* a variant of **Idun**.

tinerancy (ɪ'tɪnərənsɪ, aɪ-) *or* **itineracy** *n* **1** the act of itinerating. **2** *Chiefly Methodist Church*. the system of appointing a minister to a circuit of churches or chapels. **3** itinerants collectively.

itinerant (ɪ'tɪnərənt, aɪ-) *adj* **1** itinerating. **2** working for a short time in various places, esp. as a casual labourer. ◆ *n* **3** an itinerant worker or other person. [C16: from LL *itinerārī* to travel, from L *iter* a journey]
▸ i'tinerantly *adv*

itinerary (aɪ'tɪnərərɪ, ɪ-) *n, pl* **itineraries**. **1** a plan or line of travel; route. **2** a record of a journey. **3** a guidebook for travellers. ◆ *adj* **4** of or relating to travel or routes of travel.

itinerate (aɪ'tɪnə,reɪt, ɪ-) *vb* **itinerates, itinerating, itinerated**. (*intr*) to travel from place to place.
▸ i,tiner'ation *n*

-itis *suffix forming nouns*. **1** indicating inflammation of a specified part: *tonsillitis*. **2** *Inf.* indicating a preoccupation with or imaginary condition of illness caused by: *computeritis; telephonitis*. [NL, from Gk, fem of *-itēs* belonging to]

it'll ('ɪt°l) *contraction of* it will or it shall.

Ito ★ ('i:təʊ) *n* Prince **Hirobumi** (,hɪərə'bu:mɪ). 1841–1909, Japanese statesman; premier (1884–88; 1892–96; 1898; 1900–01). He led the movement to modernize Japan and helped to draft the Meiji constitution (1889); assassinated.

ITO *abbrev. for* International Trade Organization.

-itol *suffix forming nouns*. indicating that certain chemical compounds are alcohols containing two or more hydroxyl groups: *inisitol; sorbitol*. [from -ITE[2] + -OL[1]]

its (ɪts) *determiner* **a** of, belonging to, or associated in some way with it: *its left rear wheel; I can see its logical consequence*. **b** (*as pronoun*): *each town claims its is the best*.

it's (ɪts) *contraction of* it is or it has.

itself (ɪt'sɛlf) *pron* **1a** the reflexive form of **it**. **1b** (intensifier): *even the money itself won't convince me*. **2** (*preceded by a copula*) its normal or usual self: *my cat doesn't seem itself these days*.

itsy-bitsy ('ɪtsɪ'bɪtsɪ) *or* **itty-bitty** ('ɪtɪ'bɪtɪ) *adj Inf.* very small; tiny. [C20: baby talk alteration of *little bit*]

ITU *abbrev. for:* **1** Intensive Therapy Unit. **2** International Telecommunications Union.

ITV (in Britain) *abbrev. for* Independent Television.

-ity *suffix forming nouns*. indicating state or condition: *technicality*. [from OF *-ite*, from L *-itās*]

IU *abbrev. for:* **1** immunizing unit. **2** international unit.

IU(C)D *abbrev. for* intrauterine (contraceptive) device.

Iulus ★ (aɪ'ju:ləs) *n* **1** another name for **Ascanius**. **2** the son of Ascanius, founder of the Julian gens or clan.

-ium *or sometimes* **-um** *suffix forming nouns*. **1** indicating a metallic element: *platinum; barium*. **2** (in chemistry) indicating groups forming positive ions: *ammonium chloride; hydroxonium ion*. **3** indicating a biological structure: *syncytium*. [NL, from L, from Gk *-ion*, dim. suffix]

i.v. *abbrev. for:* **1** initial velocity. **2** Also: **IV**. intravenous(ly).

Ivan III ★ ('aɪvən) *n* known as *Ivan the Great*. 1440–1505, grand duke of Muscovy (1462–1505). He expanded Muscovy by conquest, defeated the Tatars (1480), and assumed the title of Ruler of all Russia (1472).

Ivan IV ★ *n* known as *Ivan the Terrible*. 1530–84, grand duke of Muscovy (1533–47) and first tsar of Russia (1547–84). He conquered Kazan (1552), Astrakhan (1556), and Siberia (1581), but was defeated by Poland in the Livonian War (1558–82) after which his rule became increasingly oppressive.

Ivanovo ★ (*Russian* ɪ'vanəvə) *n* a city in W central Russia, on the Uvod River: a major textile centre. Pop.: 474 000 (1995 est.). Former name (1871–1932): **Ivanovo-Voznessensk** (-vəznɪ'sjensk).

I've (aɪv) *contraction of* I have.

-ive *suffix*. **1** (*forming adjectives*) indicating a tendency, inclination, character, or quality: *divisive; festive; massive*. **2** (*forming nouns of adjectival origin*): *detective; expletive*. [from L *-īvus*]

Ives (aɪvz) *n* **1 Charles Edward**. 1874–1954, US composer, noted for his innovative use of polytonality, polyrhythms, and quarter tones. His works include five symphonies, chamber music, and songs. **2 Frederick**

Eugene. 1856–1937, US inventor of halftone photography.

IVF *abbrev. for* in vitro fertilization.

ivied ('aɪvɪd) *adj* covered with ivy.

Iviza ★ (*Spanish* i'βiθa) *n* a variant spelling of **Ibiza.**

Ivorian (aɪ'vɔːrɪən) *n* **1** a native or inhabitant of the Côte d'Ivoire. ♦ *adj* **2** of or relating to the Côte d'Ivoire or its inhabitants.

ivories ('aɪvərɪz, -vrɪz) *pl n Sl.* **1** the keys of a piano. **2** billiard balls. **3** another word for **teeth. 4** another word for **dice.**

ivory ('aɪvərɪ, -vrɪ) *n, pl* **ivories. 1a** a hard smooth creamy white variety of dentine that makes up a major part of the tusks of elephants and walruses. **1b** (*as modifier*): *ivory ornaments.* **2** a tusk made of ivory. **3a** a yellowish-white colour; cream. **3b** (*as adj*): *ivory shoes.* **4** a substance resembling elephant tusk. **5** an ornament, etc., made of ivory. **6 black ivory.** *Obs.* Black slaves collectively. [C13: from OF, from L *evoreus* made of ivory, from *ebur* ivory]
▸ **'ivory-,like** *adj*

Ivory ★ ('aɪvərɪ) *n* **James.** born 1928, US film director. With the producer Ismael Merchant, his films include *Shakespeare Wallah* (1964), *A Room With a View* (1986), *The Remains of the Day* (1993), and *A Soldier's Daughter Never Cries* (1998).

ivory black *n* a black pigment obtained by grinding charred scraps of ivory in oil.

Ivory Coast ★ *n* **the.** the former name (until 1986) of **Côte d'Ivoire.**

ivory nut *n* **1** the seed of the ivory palm, which contains an ivory-like substance used to make buttons, etc. **2** any similar seed from other palms. ♦ Also called: **vegetable ivory.**

ivory tower ('taʊə) *n* a seclusion or remoteness of attitude regarding problems, everyday life, etc. **b** (*as modifier*): *ivory-tower aestheticism.*
▸ **,ivory-'towered** *adj*

ivorywood ('aɪvərɪ,wʊd) *n* **1** the yellowish-white wood of an Australian tree, used for engraving, inlaying, and turnery. **2** the tree itself.

IVR *abbrev. for* International Vehicle Registration.

ivy ('aɪvɪ) *n, pl* **ivies. 1** a woody climbing or trailing plant having lobed evergreen leaves and black berry-like fruits. **2** any of various other climbing or creeping plants, such as poison ivy and ground ivy. [OE *īfig*]
▸ **'ivy-,like** *adj*

Iwo ★ ('iːwəʊ) *n* a city in SW Nigeria. Pop.: 353 000 (1995 est.).

Iwo Jima ★ ('dʒiːmə) *n* an island in the W Pacific, about 1100 km (700 miles) south of Japan: one of the Volcano

Islands; scene of prolonged fighting between US and Japanese forces until taken by the US in 1945; returned to Japan in 1968. Area: 20 sq. km (8 sq. miles).

IWW *abbrev. for* Industrial Workers of the World.

ixia ('ɪksɪə) *n* an iridaceous plant of southern Africa, having showy ornamental funnel-shaped flowers. [C18: NL from Gk *ixos* mistletoe]

Ixion ★ (ɪk'saɪən) *n Greek myth.* a Thessalian king punished for his love of Hera by being bound to a perpetually revolving wheel.
▸ **Ixionian** (,ɪksɪ'əʊnɪən) *adj*

Ixtaccihuatl *or* **Iztaccihuatl** ★ (,iːstək'siːwətᵊl) *n* a dormant volcano in central Mexico, southeast of Mexico City. Height: (central peak) 5286 m (17 342 ft).

ixtle ('ɪkstlɪ, 'ɪst-) *n* a variant spelling of **istle.**

Iyeyasu *or* **Ieyasu** ★ (,iːjeɪ'jɑːsuː) *n* **Tokugawa** (,tɒkuː'gɑːwə). 1542–1616, Japanese general and statesman; founder of the Tokugawa shogunate (1603–1867).

izard ('ɪzəd) *n* (esp. in the Pyrenees) another name for **chamois.**

-ize *or* **-ise** *suffix forming verbs.* **1** to cause to become, resemble, or agree with: *legalize.* **2** to become; change into crystallize. **3** to affect in a specified way; subject to: *hypnotize.* **4** to act according to some practice, principle, policy, etc.: *economize.* [from OF *-iser*, from LL *-izāre*, from Gk *-izein*]

USAGE NOTE In Britain and the US *-ize* is the preferred ending for many verbs, but *-ise* is equally acceptable in British English. Certain words (chiefly those not formed by adding the suffix to an existing word) are, however, always spelt with *-ise* in both Britain and the US: *advertise, revise.*

Izetbegović ★ (,ɪzət'bɛgəvɪtʃ) *n* **Alija** ('æljə). born 1925, Bosnia-Herzegovinan politician; president since independence in 1992.

Izhevsk ★ (*Russian* i'ʒefsk) *n* an industrial city in central Russia, capital of the Udmurt Republic. Pop.: 654 000 (1995 est.).

Izmir ★ ('ɪzmɪə) *n* a port in W Turkey, on the **Gulf of Izmir:** the third largest city in the country; university (1955). Pop.: 1 985 300 (1994 est.). Former name: **Smyrna.**

Izmit ★ ('ɪzmɪt) *n* a town in NW Turkey, on the **Gulf of Izmit.** Pop.: 275 800 (1994 est.).

Iznik ★ (ɪz'nɪk) *n* the modern Turkish name of **Nicaea.**

Iztaccihuatl ★ (,iːstək'siːwətᵊl) *n* a variant spelling of **Ixtaccihuatl.**

Jj

j *or* **J** (dʒeɪ) *n*, *pl* **j's**, **J's**, *or* **Js**. **1** the tenth letter of the English alphabet. **2** a speech sound represented by this letter.

j *symbol for:* **1** *Maths.* the unit vector along the *y*-axis. **2** the imaginary number √–1.

J *symbol for:* **1** current density. **2** *Cards.* jack. **3** joule(s).

J. *abbrev. for:* **1** Journal. **2** (*pl* **JJ.**) Judge. **3** (*pl* **JJ.**) Justice.

jab (dʒæb) *vb* **jabs, jabbing, jabbed**. **1** to poke or thrust sharply. **2** to strike with a quick short blow or blows. ♦ *n* **3** a sharp poke or stab. **4** a quick short blow. **5** *Inf.* an injection: *polio jabs.* [C19: orig. Scot. var. of JOB]
▶ **'jabbing** *adj*

Jabalpur *or* **Jubbulpore** ★ (ˌdʒʌbəl'puə) *n* a city in central India, in central Madhya Pradesh. Pop.: 741 927 (1991).

jabber ('dʒæbə) *vb* **1** to speak or say rapidly, incoherently, and without making sense; chatter. ♦ *n* **2** such talk. [C15: imit.]

jabberwocky ('dʒæbəˌwɒkɪ) *n* nonsensical writing or speech. [C19: coined by Lewis Carroll as the title of a poem in *Through the Looking Glass* (1871)]

Jabir ibn Hayyan ★ ('dʒɑːbɪə 'ɪbⁿ hɑːˈjɑːn) *n* ?721–?815. Arab alchemist, whose works were esteemed by later alchemists.

jabiru ('dʒæbɪˌruː) *n* **1** a large white tropical American stork with a dark naked head and a dark bill. **2** Also called: **black-necked stork, policeman bird.** a large Australian stork, having a white plumage, dark green back and tail, and red legs. **3** another name for **saddlebill**. [C18: via Port., of Amerind origin]

jabot ('ʒæbəʊ) *n* a frill or ruffle on the breast or throat of a garment. [C19: from F: bird's crop, jabot]

jaçana (ˌʒɑːsəˈnɑː, ˌdʒæ-) *n* a bird of tropical and subtropical marshy regions, having long legs and very long toes that enable walking on floating plants. [C18: from Port., of Amerind origin, from *jasaná*]

jacaranda (ˌdʒækəˈrændə) *n* **1** a tropical American tree having fernlike leaves and pale purple flowers and widely cultivated in temperate areas of Australia. **2** the fragrant ornamental wood of this tree. **3** any of several related or similar trees or their wood. [C18: from Port., of Amerind origin, from *yacarandá*]

jacaré ('dʒækəˌreɪ) *n* another name for **cayman**. [C18: from Port., of Amerind origin]

jacinth ('dʒæsɪnθ) *n* another name for **hyacinth** (sense 4). [C13: from Med. L *jacinthus*, from L *hyacinthus* plant, precious stone; see HYACINTH]

jack (dʒæk) *n* **1** a man or fellow. **2** a sailor. **3** the male of certain animals, esp. of the ass or donkey. **4** a mechanical or hydraulic device for exerting a large force, esp. to raise a heavy weight such as a motor vehicle. **5** any of several mechanical devices that replace manpower, such as a contrivance for rotating meat on a spit. **6** one of four playing cards in a pack, one for each suit; knave. **7** *Bowls.* a small usually white bowl at which the players aim with their own bowls. **8** *Electrical engineering.* a female socket with two or more terminals designed to receive a male plug (**jack plug**) that either makes or breaks the circuit or circuits. **9** a flag, esp. a small flag flown at the bow of a ship indicating the ship's nationality. **10** a part of the action of a harpsichord, consisting of a fork-shaped device on the end of a pivoted lever on which a plectrum is mounted. **11a** any of various tropical and subtropical fishes. **11b** an immature pike. **12** Also called: **jackstone**. one of the pieces used in the game of jacks. **13** *US.* a slang word for **money**. **14** every man jack. everyone without exception. **15** the jack. *Austral. sl.* syphilis. ♦ *adj* **16** *Austral. sl.* tired or fed up (esp. in **be jack of something**). ♦ *vb* **17** (*tr*) to lift or push (an object) with a jack. ♦ See also **jack in, jack up**. [C16 *jakke*, var. of *Jankin*, dim. of *John*]

Jack (dʒæk) *n* **I'm all right, Jack**. *Brit. inf.* a remark indicating smug and complacent selfishness.

jackal ('dʒækɔːl) *n* **1** any of several African or S Asian mammals closely related to the dog, having long legs and pointed ears and muzzle: they are predators and carrion-eaters. **2** a person who does menial tasks for another. [C17: from Turkish, from Persian, from Sansk. *srgāla*]

jackanapes ('dʒækəˌneɪps) *n* (*functioning as sing*) **1** a conceited impertinent person. **2** a mischievous child. **3** *Arch.* a monkey. [C16: var. of *Jakken-apes*, lit.: Jack of the ape, nickname of William de la Pole (1396–1450), first Duke of Suffolk, whose badge showed an ape's ball and chain]

jackass ('dʒækˌæs) *n* **1** a male donkey. **2** a fool. [C18: from JACK (male) + ASS¹]

jackboot ('dʒækˌbuːt) *n* **1** an all-leather military boot, extending up to or above the knee. **2** authoritarian rule or behaviour.
▶ **'jack,booted** *adj*

jackdaw ('dʒækˌdɔː) *n* a large Eurasian bird, related to the crow, having a black and dark grey plumage: noted for its thieving habits. [C16: from JACK + *daw*, obs. name for jackdaw]

jackeroo *or* **jackaroo** (ˌdʒækəˈruː) *n*, *pl* **jackeroos** *or* **jackaroos**. *Austral. inf.* a novice on a sheep or cattle station. [C19: from JACK + (KANG)AROO]

jacket ('dʒækɪt) *n* **1** a short coat, esp. one that is hip-length and has a front opening and sleeves. **2** something that resembles this: *a life jacket.* **3** any exterior covering or casing, such as the insulating cover of a boiler. **4** See **dust jacket**. **5a** the skin of a baked potato. **5b** (*as modifier*): *jacket potatoes.* **6** *Oil industry.* the support structure, esp. the legs, of an oil platform. ♦ *vb* **7** (*tr*) to put a jacket on (someone or something). [C15: from OF *jaquet* short jacket, from *jacque* peasant, from *Jacques* James]
▶ **'jacketed** *adj*

Jack Frost *n* a personification of frost.

Jackie *or* **Jacky** ('dʒækɪ) *n*, *pl* **Jackies**. *Austral. offens. sl.* **1** a native Australian. **2** native Australians collectively. **3 sit up like Jackie**. to sit bolt upright, esp. cheekily.

jack in *vb* (*tr, adv*) *Sl.* to abandon or leave (an attempt or enterprise).

jack-in-office *n* a self-important petty official.

jack-in-the-box *n*, *pl* **jack-in-the-boxes** *or* **jacks-in-the-box**. a toy consisting of a figure on a compressed spring in a box, which springs out when the lid is opened.

Jack Ketch (kɛtʃ) *n Brit. arch.* a hangman. [C18: after *John Ketch* (died 1686), public executioner in England]

jackknife ('dʒækˌnaɪf) *n*, *pl* **jackknives**. **1** a knife with the blade pivoted to fold into a recess in the handle. **2** a former name for a type of dive in which the diver bends at the waist in midair; forward pike dive. ♦ *vb* **jackknifing, jackknifed**. (*intr*) **3** (of an articulated lorry) to go out of control in such a way that the trailer swings round at an angle to the tractor.

Jacklin ★ ('dʒæklɪn) *n* Tony, full name *Anthony Jacklin*. born 1944. British golfer: won the British Open Championship (1969) and the US Open Championship (1970).

jack of all trades *n*, *pl* **jacks of all trades**. a person who undertakes many different kinds of work.

jack-o'-lantern *n* **1** a lantern made from a hollowed pumpkin, which has holes cut in it to represent a human face. **2** a will-o'-the-wisp.

jack plane *n* a carpenter's plane, usually with a wooden body, used for rough planing of timber.

jack plug *n* See **jack** (sense 8).

jackpot ('dʒækˌpɒt) *n* **1** any large prize, kitty, or accumulated stake that may be won in gambling. **2 hit the jackpot**.

2a to win a jackpot. **2b** *Inf.* to achieve great success, esp. through luck. [C20: prob. from JACK (playing card) + POT¹]

jack rabbit *n* any of various W North American hares having long hind legs and large ears. [C19: shortened from *jackass-rabbit*, referring to its long ears]

Jack Robinson ('rɒbɪnsən) *n* **before you could** (*or* **can**) **say Jack Robinson.** extremely quickly or suddenly.

Jack Russell ('rʌs³l) *n* a small short-legged terrier having a white coat with tan, black, or lemon markings. [after John *Russell* (1795-1883), E clergyman who developed the breed]

jacks (dʒæks) *n* (*functioning as sing*) a game in which bone, metal, or plastic pieces (**jackstones**) are thrown and then picked up between bounces of a small ball or throws of another piece (the **jack**). [C19: shortened from *jackstones*, var. of *checkstones* pebbles]

jacksie *or* **jacksy** ('dʒæksɪ) *n, pl* **jacksies.** *Brit. sl.* the buttocks or anus. Also: **jaxie, jaxy.** [C19: ? from JACK]

jacksnipe ('dʒæk,snaɪp) *n, pl* **jacksnipe** *or* **jacksnipes.** a small Eurasian short-billed snipe.

Jackson¹ ★ ('dʒæksən) *n* a city in and state capital of Mississippi, on the Pearl River. Pop.: 193 097 (1994 est.).

Jackson² ★ ('dʒæksən) *n* **1 Andrew.** 1767-1845, US statesman, general, and lawyer; seventh president of the US (1829-37). He became a national hero after successfully defending New Orleans from the British (1815). During his administration the national debt was fully paid off. **2 Glenda.** born 1936, British stage and film actress. Her films include *Women in Love* (1969) and *A Touch of Class* (1972); became a Labour MP in 1992. **3 Jesse (Louis).** born 1941, US Democrat politician; Black campaigner for minority rights. **4 Michael (Joe).** born 1958, US pop singer, lead vocalist with the Jacksons (originally the Jackson 5) (1969-86). His solo albums include *Thriller* (1982) and *Bad* (1984). **5 Thomas Jonathan**, known as *Stonewall Jackson*. 1824-63, Confederate general in the American Civil War, in command at the first Battle of Bull Run (1861).

Jacksonville ★ ('dʒæksən,vɪl) *n* a port in NE Florida: the leading commercial centre of the southeast. Pop.: 665 070 (1994 est.).

jackstraws ('dʒæk,strɔːz) *n* (*functioning as sing*) another name for **spillikins.**

Jack Tar *n* Now chiefly literary. a sailor.

Jack the Ripper ★ *n* an unidentified murderer who killed at least seven prostitutes in London's East End between August and November 1888.

jack up *vb* (*adv*) **1** (*tr*) to increase (prices, salaries, etc.). **2** (*tr*) to raise an object, such as a car, with or as with a jack. **3** (*intr*) *Sl.* to inject oneself with a drug. **4** (*intr*) *Austral. inf.* to refuse to comply.

Jacob ★ ('dʒeɪkəb) *n* Old Testament. the son of Isaac, twin brother of Esau, and father of the twelve patriarchs of Israel.

Jacobean (,dʒækə'bɪən) *adj* **1** History. relating to James I of England or to the period of his rule (1603-25). **2** of or relating to the style of furniture current at this time, characterized by the use of dark brown carved oak. **3** relating to or having the style of architecture used in England during this period. [C18: from NL, from *Jacōbus* James]

Jacobi ★ *n* **1** ('dʒækəbɪ). **Derek (George).** born 1938, British actor. **2** (*German* ja'koːbi). **Karl Gustav Jacob** (karl 'gustaf 'jaːkɔp). 1804-51, German mathematician.

Jacobin ('dʒækəbɪn) *n* **1** a member of the most radical club founded during the French Revolution, which instituted the Reign of Terror. **2** an extreme political radical. **3** a French Dominican friar. ◆ *adj* **4** of or relating to the Jacobins or their policies. [C14: from OF, from Med. L *Jacōbīnus*, from LL *Jacōbus* James; the political club orig. met in the convent near the church of *St Jacques* in 1789]

▸ ,Jaco'binic *or* ,Jaco'binical *adj* ▸ 'Jacobinism *n*

Jacobite ('dʒækə,baɪt) *n* Brit. history. an adherent of James II after his overthrow in 1688, or of his descen-

dants in their attempts to regain the throne. [C17: from LL *Jacōbus* James + -ITE¹]

▸ **Jacobitic** (,dʒækə'bɪtɪk) *adj*

Jacobsen ★ (*Danish* 'jakɔbsən) *n* **Arne** ('aːnə). 1902-71, Danish architect and designer. His buildings include the Town Hall at Rodovre (1955).

Jacob's ladder *n* **1** Old Testament. the ladder reaching up to heaven that Jacob saw in a dream (Genesis 28:12-17). **2** a ladder made of wooden or metal steps supported by ropes or chains. **3** a North American plant with blue flowers and a ladder-like arrangement of leaves.

Jacob's staff *n* a medieval instrument for measuring heights and distances.

jaconet ('dʒækənɪt) *n* a light cotton fabric used for clothing, etc. [C18: from Urdu *jagannāthī*, from *Jagannāthpūrī*, India, where orig. made]

Jacquard ('dʒækɑːd, dʒə'kɑːd) *n* **1** Also called: **Jacquard weave.** a fabric in which the design is incorporated into the weave. **2** Also called: **Jacquard loom.** the loom that produces this fabric. [C19: after Joseph M. *Jacquard* (1752-1834), F inventor]

jactation (dʒæk'teɪʃən) *n* **1** Rare. the act of boasting. **2** Pathol. another word for **jactitation.** [C16: from L *jactātiō* bragging, from *jactāre* to flourish, from *jacere* to throw]

jactitation (,dʒæktɪ'teɪʃən) *n* **1** the act of boasting. **2** a false assertion that one is married to another, formerly actionable at law. **3** Pathol. restless tossing in bed, characteristic of severe fevers. [C17: from Med. L, from L *jacitāre* to utter publicly, from *jactitāre* to toss about; see JACTATION]

Jacuzzi (dʒə'kuːzɪ) *n* Trademark. **1** a device which swirls water in a bath. **2** a bath containing such a device. [C20: from *Candido* and *Roy Jacuzzi*, who developed and marketed it]

jade¹ (dʒeɪd) *n* **1** a semiprecious stone which varies in colour from white to green and is used for making ornaments and jewellery. **2a** the green colour of jade. **2b** (*as adj*): *a jade skirt.* [C18: from F, from It. *giada*, from obs. Sp. *piedra de ijada* colic stone (lit.: stone of the flank, because it was believed to cure renal colic)]

jade² (dʒeɪd) *n* **1** an old overworked horse. **2** Derog., facetious. a woman considered to be disreputable. ◆ *vb* **jades, jading, jaded. 3** to exhaust or make exhausted from work or use. [C14: from ?]

▸ 'jadish *adj*

jaded ('dʒeɪdɪd) *adj* **1** exhausted or dissipated. **2** satiated.

▸ 'jadedly *adv* ▸ 'jadedness *n*

jadeite ('dʒeɪdaɪt) *n* a green or white mineral, a variety of jade, consisting of sodium aluminium silicate in monoclinic crystalline form.

Jadotville ★ (*French* ʒadovil) *n* the former name of Likasi.

j'adoube French. (ʒadub) *interj* Chess. an expression of an intention to touch a piece in order to adjust its placement rather than to make a move. [lit.: I adjust]

Jael ★ ('dʒeɪəl) *n* Old Testament. the woman who killed Sisera when he took refuge in her tent (Judges 4:17-21).

Jaén ★ (xa'en) *n* a city in S Spain. Pop.: 112 772 (1994 est.).

Jaffa ★ ('dʒæfə, 'dʒɑː-) *n* **1** a port in W Israel, on the Mediterranean: incorporated into Tel Aviv in 1950; an old Canaanite city. Biblical name: **Joppa.** Hebrew name: **Yafo. 2** a large variety of orange, grown esp. in Israel, having a thick skin.

Jaffna ★ ('dʒæfnə) *n* a port in N Sri Lanka: for many centuries the capital of a Tamil kingdom. Pop.: 129 000 (1990 est.).

jag¹ (dʒæg) *vb* **jags, jagging, jagged. 1** (*tr*) to cut unevenly. **2** Austral. to catch (fish) by impaling on an unbaited hook. ◆ *n* **3** Scot. an informal word for **jab** (senses 3, 5). **4** a jagged notch or projection. [C14: from ?]

jag² (dʒæg) *n Sl.* **1a** intoxication from drugs or alcohol. **1b** a bout of drinking or drug taking. **2** a period of uncontrolled activity: *a crying jag.* [of unknown origin]

jagged ('dʒæɡɪd) *adj* having sharp projecting notches.

▸ 'jaggedly *adv*

Jagger ★ ('dʒægə) n **Mick**, full name *Michael Philip Jagger*. born 1943, British rock singer and songwriter: lead vocalist with the Rolling Stones.

jaggy ('dʒægɪ) adj **jaggier, jaggiest. 1** a less common word for jagged. **2** *Scot.* prickly.

jaguar ('dʒægjuə) n a large feline mammal of S North America, Central America, and N South America, similar to the leopard but with larger spots on its coat. [C17: from Port., from Guarani *yaguara*]

Jahwism ('jɑː,wɪzᵊm) or **Jahvism** ★ ('jɑː,vɪzəm) n a variant of Yahwism or Yahvism.
▸ **Jah'wistic** or **Jah'vistic** adj

jai alai ('haɪ 'laɪ, 'haɪ ə,laɪ) n a version of pelota played by two or four players. [via Sp. from Basque, from *jai* game + *alai* merry]

jail or **gaol** (dʒeɪl) n **1** a place for the confinement of persons convicted and sentenced to imprisonment or of persons awaiting trial. ◆ vb **2** (tr) to confine in prison. [C13: from OF *jaiole* cage, from Vulgar L *caveola* (unattested), from L *cavea* enclosure]

jailbird or **gaolbird** ('dʒeɪl,bɜːd) n a person who is or has been confined to jail, esp. repeatedly; convict.

jailbreak or **gaolbreak** ('dʒeɪl,breɪk) n an escape from jail.

jailer, jailor, or **gaoler** ('dʒeɪlə) n a person in charge of prisoners in a jail.

Jain (dʒaɪn) or **Jaina** ('dʒaɪnə) n **1** an adherent of Jainism. ◆ adj **2** of or relating to Jainism. [C19: from Hindi *jaina* saint, lit.: overcomer, from Sansk.]

Jainism ('dʒaɪ,nɪzəm) n an ancient Hindu religion, characterized by the belief that the material world is progressing endlessly in a series of cycles.
▸ **'Jainist** n, adj

Jaipur ★ (dʒaɪ'pʊə) n a city of great beauty in N India, capital of Rajasthan state: University of Rajasthan (1947). Pop.: 1 458 183 (1991).

Jakarta or **Djakarta** ★ (dʒə'kɑːtə) n the capital of Indonesia, in N West Java: founded in 1619 and ruled by the Dutch until 1945; the chief trading centre of the East in the 17th century; University of Indonesia (1947). Pop.: 8 259 266 (1990). Former name (until 1949): **Batavia**.

jake (dʒeɪk) adj Austral. & NZ sl. all right; fine: *she's jake.* [from ?]

Jalandhar ★ ('dʒæləndə) n a city in NW India, in central Punjab. Pop.: 509 510 (1991).

jalap or **jalop** ('dʒæləp) n **1** a Mexican climbing plant. **2** the dried and powdered root of any of these plants, used as a purgative. [C17: from F, from Mexican Sp. *jalapa*]
▸ **jalapic** (dʒə'læpɪk) adj

Jalapa ★ (*Spanish* xa'lapa) n a city in E central Mexico, capital of Veracruz State, at an altitude of 1427 m (4681 ft): resort. Pop.: 288 331 (1990).

jalapeño (dʒælə'piːnəʊ; *Spanish* xala'penjo) n, pl **jalapeñofños.** a type of red capsicum with a hot taste used in Mexican cookery. [Mexican Sp.]

Jalisco ★ (*Spanish* xa'lisko) n a state of W Mexico, on the Pacific: crossed by the Sierra Madre; valuable mineral resources. Capital: Guadalajara. Pop.: 5 990 054 (1995 est.). Area: 80 137 sq. km (30 934 sq. miles).

jalopy or **jaloppy** (dʒə'lɒpɪ) n, pl **jalopies** or **jaloppies.** Inf. a dilapidated old car. [C20: from ?]

jalousie ('ʒælʊ,ziː) n **1** a window blind or shutter constructed from angled slats of wood, etc. **2** a window made of angled slats of glass. [C19: from OF *gelosie* latticework screen]

jam¹ (dʒæm) vb **jams, jamming, jammed. 1** (tr) to cram or wedge into or against something: *to jam paper into an incinerator.* **2** (tr) to crowd or pack: *cars jammed the roads.* **3** to make or become stuck or locked. **4** (tr; often foll. by *on*) to activate suddenly (esp. in **jam on the brakes**). **5** (tr) to block; congest. **6** (tr) to crush or squeeze. **7** Radio. to prevent the clear reception of (radio communications) by transmitting other signals on the same frequency. **8** (intr) Sl. to play in a jam session. ◆ n **9** a crowd or congestion in a confined space: *a traffic jam.* **10** the act of jamming or the state of being jammed. **11** Inf. a predica-

ment: *to help a friend out of a jam.* **12** See **jam session**. [C18: prob. imit.]
▸ **'jammer** n

jam² (dʒæm) n **1** a preserve containing fruit, which has been boiled with sugar until the mixture sets. **2** Sl. something desirable: *you want jam on it.* [C18: ?from JAM¹ (the act of squeezing)]

Jam. abbrev. for: **1** Jamaica. **2** Bible. James.

Jamaica ★ (dʒə'meɪkə) n an island and state of the Caribbean: colonized by the Spanish from 1494 onwards, large numbers of Black slaves being imported; captured by the British in 1655 and established as a colony in 1866; gained full independence in 1962; a member of the Commonwealth. Exports: chiefly bauxite and alumina, sugar, and bananas. Official language: English. Religion: Protestant majority. Currency: Jamaican dollar. Capital: Kingston. Pop.: 2 536 000 (1997). Area: 10 992 sq. km (4244 sq. miles).
▸ **Ja'maican** n, adj

jamb or **jambe** (dʒæm) n a vertical side member of a doorframe, window frame, or lining. [C14: from OF *jambe* leg, jamb, from LL *gamba* hoof, from Gk *kampē* joint]

Jambi or **Djambi** ★ ('dʒæmbɪ) n a port in W Indonesia, in SE Sumatra on the Hari River. Pop.: 301 359 (1990). Also called: **Telanaipura**.

jamboree (,dʒæmbə'riː) n **1** a large and often international gathering of Scouts. **2** a party or celebration. [C19: from ?]

James ★ (dʒeɪmz) n **1** *New Testament.* **1a** known as *James the Great.* one of the twelve apostles, a son of Zebedee and brother to John the apostle (Matthew 4:21). **1b** known as *James the Less.* one of the twelve apostles, son of Alphaeus (Matthew 10:3). Feast day: May 3 or Oct. 9. **1c** known as *James the brother of the Lord.* a brother or close relative of Jesus (Mark 6:3; Galatians 1:19). Feast day: Oct. 23. **1d** the book ascribed to his authorship (in full **The Epistle of James**). **2** Henry. 1843–1916, British writer and critic, born in the US. Among his novels are *Washington Square* (1880), *The Ambassadors* (1903), and *The Golden Bowl* (1904). **3** Jesse (**Woodson**). 1847–82, US outlaw. **4** P(hyllis) D(orothy), Baroness James of Holland Park. born 1920, British detective novelist. Her books include *Death of an Expert Witness* (1977) and *A Certain Justice* (1997). **5** William, brother of Henry James. 1842–1910, US philosopher and psychologist, whose books include *Essays in Radical Empiricism* (1912) and *The Varieties of Religious Experience* (1902).

James I ★ n **1** 1394–1437, king of Scotland (1406–37), second son of Robert III. **2** 1566–1625, king of England and Ireland (1603–25) and, as James VI, king of Scotland (1567–1625), in succession to Elizabeth I of England and his mother, Mary Queen of Scots, respectively. He alienated Parliament by his assertion of the divine right of kings and his subservience to Spain.

James II ★ n **1** 1430–60, king of Scotland (1437–60), son of James I. **2** 1633–1701, king of England, Ireland, and, as James VII, of Scotland (1685–88); son of Charles I. His pro-Catholic sympathies and arbitrary rule caused the Whigs and Tories to unite in inviting his eldest surviving daughter, Mary, and her husband, William of Orange, to take the throne. James was defeated at the Boyne (1690) when he attempted to regain the throne.

James III ★ n 1451–88, king of Scotland (1460–88), son of James II.

James IV ★ n 1473–1513, king of Scotland (1488–1513), son of James III; he invaded England (1496) in support of Perkin Warbeck; he was killed at Flodden.

James V ★ n 1512–42, king of Scotland (1513–42), son of James IV.

James VI ★ n title as king of Scotland of **James I** of England and Ireland.

James VII ★ n title as king of Scotland of **James II** of England and Ireland.

James Bay ★ n the S arm of Hudson Bay, in central Canada. Area: 108 780 sq. km (42 000 sq. miles).

Jameson ★ ('dʒeɪmsᵊn) n Sir **Leander Starr**. 1853–1917, British administrator in South Africa, who led an expedition into the Transvaal in 1895 in an unsuccessful attempt to topple its Boer regime (the **Jameson Raid**); prime minister of Cape Colony (1904–08).

Jamestown ★ ('dʒeɪmz,taʊn) *n* a ruined village in E Virginia, on **Jamestown Island** (a peninsula in the James River): the first permanent settlement by the English in America (1607); capital of Virginia (1607–98); abandoned in 1699.

Jammu ★ ('dʒʌmuː) *n* a city in N India, winter capital of the state of Jammu and Kashmir. Pop.: 207 000 (latest est.).

Jammu and Kashmir ★ *n* the official name for the part of **Kashmir** under Indian control.

jammy ('dʒæmɪ) *adj* **jammier, jammiest.** *Brit. sl.* **1** pleasant; desirable. **2** lucky.

Jamnagar ★ ('dʒæmnəgə) *n* a city in India, in Gujarat: noted for its palaces and temples: cement, pottery, textiles. Pop.: 294 344 (1989).

jam-packed *adj* packed or filled to capacity.

jam session *n Sl.* an unrehearsed or improvised performance by jazz or rock musicians. [C20: prob. from JAM[1]]

Jamshedpur ★ (,dʒʌmʃɛd'pʊə) *n* a city in NE India, in SE Bihar: large iron and steel works (1907–11); a major industrial centre. Pop.: 461 000 (1991).

Jamshid *or* **Jamshyd** ★ (dʒæm'ʃiːd) *n Persian myth.* a ruler of the peris who was punished for bragging that he was immortal by being changed into human form. He then became a great king of Persia. See also **peri.**

Jan. *abbrev. for* January.

Janáček ★ (*Czech* 'jana:tʃɛk) *n* Leoš ('lɛoʃ). 1854–1928, Czech composer. His music is influenced by Czech folksong and speech rhythms. His works include the operas *Jenufa* (1904) and *The Cunning Little Vixen* (1924) as well as orchestral and chamber music and songs.

Jandal ('dʒændəl) *n NZ trademark.* a kind of sandal with a strip of material between the big toe and the other toes and over the foot.

Janet ★ (*French* ʒanɛ) *n* Pierre Marie Félix (pjɛr mari feliks). 1859–1947, French psychologist and neurologist, noted particularly for his work on the origins of hysteria.

jangle ('dʒæŋgᵊl) *vb* **jangles, jangling, jangled.** **1** to sound or cause to sound discordantly, harshly, or unpleasantly. **2** (*tr*) to produce a jarring effect on: *the accident jangled his nerves.* **3** *Arch.* to wrangle. ♦ *n* **4** a harsh unpleasant ringing noise. **5** an argument or quarrel. [C13: from OF *jangler*, of Gmc origin]
▶ '**jangler** *n*

Janiculum ★ (dʒə'nɪkjʊləm) *n* a hill in Rome across the River Tiber from the Seven Hills.

Janina ★ ('jani:na) *n* the Serbian name for **Ioánnina.**

janissary ('dʒænɪsərɪ) *or* **janizary** ('dʒænɪzərɪ) *n, pl* **janissaries** *or* **janizaries.** an infantryman in the Turkish army, originally a member of the sovereign's guard, from the 14th to the 19th century. [C16: from F, from It., from Turkish *yeniçeri*, from *yeni* new + *çeri* soldiery]

janitor ('dʒænɪtə) *n* **1** *Scot., US, & Canad.* the caretaker of a building, esp. a school. **2** *Chiefly US & Canad.* a person employed to clean and maintain a building. [C17: L: doorkeeper, from *jānua* door, from *jānus* covered way]
▶ janitorial (,dʒænɪ'tɔːrɪəl) *adj*

Jan Mayen ★ ('jæn 'maɪən) *n* an island in the Arctic Ocean, between Greenland and N Norway: volcanic, with large glaciers; former site of Dutch whaling stations; annexed to Norway in 1929. Area: 373 sq. km (144 sq. miles).

Jansen ★ ('dʒænsᵊn) *n* Cornelis (kɔ:'ni:lɪs). Latin name *Cornelius Jansenius.* 1585–1638, Dutch Roman Catholic theologian. In *Augustinus* (1640) he defended the teachings of St Augustine.

Jansenism ('dʒænsə,nɪzəm) *n RC Church.* the doctrine of Cornelis Jansen and his disciples, who believed in predestination and denied free will.
▶ 'Jansenist *n, adj* ▶ ,Jansen'istic *adj*

jansky ('dʒænskɪ) *n, pl* **janskys.** (in radio astronomy) a unit used to measure the intensity of radio waves. Also called: **flux unit.** [C20: after Karl G. *Jansky* (1905–50), US electrical engineer]

January ('dʒænjʊərɪ) *n, pl* **Januaries.** the first month of the year, consisting of 31 days. [C14: from L *Jānuārius*]

Janus ★ ('dʒeɪnəs) *n* the Roman god of doorways, passages, and bridges. In art he is depicted with two heads facing opposite ways. [C16: from L, from *jānus* archway]

Jap. *abbrev. for* Japan(ese).

japan (dʒə'pæn) *n* **1** a glossy black lacquer originally from the Orient, used on wood, metal, etc. **2** work decorated and varnished in the Japanese manner. ♦ *vb* **japans, japanning, japanned.** **3** (*tr*) to lacquer with japan or any similar varnish.

Japan ★ (dʒə'pæn) *n* an archipelago and empire in E Asia, extending for 3200 km (2000 miles) between the Sea of Japan and the Pacific and consisting of the main islands of Hokkaido, Honshu, Shikoku, and Kyushu and over 3000 smaller islands: feudalism abolished in 1871, followed by industrialization and expansion of territories, esp. during World Wars I and II, when most of SE Asia came under Japanese control; dogma of the emperor's divinity abolished in 1946 under a new democratic constitution; rapid economic growth has made Japan the most industrialized nation in the Far East. Official language: Japanese. Religion: Shintoist majority, large Buddhist minority. Currency: yen. Capital: Tokyo. Pop.: 126 110 000 (1997). Area: 369 660 sq. km (142 726 sq. miles). Japanese names: Nippon, Nihon.

Japan Current ★ *n* a warm ocean current flowing northeastwards off the E coast of Japan towards the North Pacific. Also called: Kuroshio.

Japanese (,dʒæpə'niːz) *adj* **1** of or characteristic of Japan, its people, or their language. ♦ *n* **2** (*pl* **Japanese**) a native or inhabitant of Japan. **3** the official language of Japan.

Japanese stranglehold *n* a wrestling hold in which an opponent's arms exert pressure on his own windpipe.

jape (dʒeɪp) *n* **1** a jest or joke. ♦ *vb* **japes, japing, japed. 2** to joke or jest (about). [C14: ?from OF *japper* to yap, imit.]
▶ 'japer *n* ▶ 'japery *n*

Japheth ★ ('dʒeɪfɛθ) *n Old Testament.* the second son of Noah, traditionally regarded as the ancestor of a number of non-Semitic nations (Genesis 10:1–5).

Japlish ('dʒæplɪʃ) *n* the adoption and adaptation of English words into the Japanese language. [C20: from a blend of JAPANESE + ENGLISH]

japonica (dʒə'pɒnɪkə) *n* **1** Also called: Japanese quince. a Japanese shrub cultivated for its red flowers and yellowish fruit. **2** another name for the **camellia.** [C19: from NL, fem of *japonicus* Japanese, from *Japonia* JAPAN]

Japurá ★ (*Portuguese* ʒapu'ra) *n* a river in NW South America, rising in SW Colombia and flowing southeast across Colombia and Brazil to join the Amazon near Tefé: known as the Caquetá in Colombia. Length: about 2800 km (1750 miles). Spanish name: Yapurá.

Jaques-Dalcroze ★ (*French* ʒakdalkroz) *n* Émile (emil). 1865–1950, Swiss composer and teacher: invented eurythmics.

jar[1] (dʒɑ:) *n* **1** a wide-mouthed container that is usually cylindrical, made of glass or earthenware, and without handles. **2** Also: **jarful.** the contents or quantity contained in a jar. **3** *Brit. inf.* a glass of beer. [C16: from OF *jarre, jarra,* from Ar. *jarrah* large earthen vessel]

jar[2] (dʒɑ:) *vb* **jars, jarring, jarred. 1** to vibrate or cause to vibrate. **2** to make or cause to make a harsh discordant sound. **3** (often foll. by *on*) to have a disturbing or painful effect (on the nerves, mind, etc.). **4** (*intr*) to disagree or clash. ♦ *n* **5** a jolt or shock. **6** a harsh discordant sound. [C16: prob. imit.]
▶ 'jarring *adj* ▶ 'jarringly *adv*

jar[3] (dʒɑ:) *n* on a (*or* the) jar. (of a door) slightly open; ajar. [C17 (in the sense: turn): from earlier *char,* from OF *cierran* to turn]

jardinière (,ʒɑːdɪ'njɛə) *n* **1** an ornamental pot or trough for plants. **2** a garnish of fresh vegetables for a dish of

★ people and places

meat. [C19: from F, fem of *jardinier* gardener, from *jardin* GARDEN]

jargon ('dʒɑːgən) *n* **1** specialized language concerned with a particular subject, culture, or profession. **2** language characterized by pretentious vocabulary or meaning. **3** gibberish. [C14: from OF, ? imit.]

jarl (jɑːl) *n Medieval history*. a Scandinavian chieftain or noble. [C19: from ON]
▸ **'jarldom** *n*

jarrah ('dʒærə) *n* an Australian eucalyptus tree that yields a valuable timber. [from Abor.]

Jarrett ★ ('dʒærɪt) *n* **Keith**. born 1945, US jazz pianist and composer.

Jarrow ★ ('dʒærəʊ) *n* a port in NE England, in South Tyneside: ruined monastery where the Venerable Bede lived and died; its unemployed marched on London in the 1930s; shipyards, oil installations, iron and steel works. Pop.: 29 325 (1991 est.).

Jarry ★ (*French* ʒari) *n* **Alfred** (alfrɛd). 1873–1907, French dramatist and poet, who initiated the theatre of the absurd with his play *Ubu Roi* (1896).

Jaruzelski ★ (*Polish* jaru:'ʒɛlski) *n* **Wojciech** ('vɔɪtʃɛk). born 1923, Polish statesman and soldier; prime minister (1981–85); head of state (1985–90; as president from 1989).

Jas. *abbrev. for* James.

jasmine ('dʒæsmɪn, 'dʒæz-) *n* **1** Also called: **jessamine**. any tropical or subtropical oleaceous shrub or climbing plant widely cultivated for their white, yellow, or red fragrant flowers. **2** any of several other shrubs with fragrant flowers, such as the Cape jasmine, yellow jasmine, and frangipani (**red jasmine**). [C16: from OF *jasmin*, from Ar., from Persian *yāsmīn*]

Jason ★ ('dʒeɪsⁿn) *n Greek myth.* the hero who led the Argonauts in quest of the Golden Fleece. He became the husband of Medea, whom he later abandoned for Glauce.

jaspé ('dʒæspeɪ) *adj* resembling jasper; variegated. [C19: from F, from *jasper* to marble]

jasper ('dʒæspə) *n* **1** an opaque impure form of quartz, red, yellow, brown, or dark green in colour, used as a gemstone and for ornamental decoration. **2** Also called: **jasper ware**. a dense hard stoneware. [C14: from OF *jaspe*, from L *jaspis*, from Gk *iaspis*, of Semitic origin]

Jasper National Park ('dʒæspə) ★ *n* a national park in SW Canada, in W Alberta in the Rockies: wildlife sanctuary. Area: 10 900 sq. km (4200 sq. miles).

Jaspers ★ (*German* 'jaspərs) *n* **Karl** (karl). 1883–1969, German existentialist philosopher.

Jassy ★ ('jasi) *n* the German name for Iaşi.

jato ('dʒeɪtəʊ) *n, pl* **jatos**. *Aeronautics.* jet-assisted takeoff. [C20: from *j(et-)a(ssisted) t(ake)o(ff)*]

jaundice ('dʒɔːndɪs) *n* **1** Also called: **icterus**. yellowing of the skin due to the abnormal presence of bile pigments in the blood, as in hepatitis. **2** jealousy, envy, and ill humour. ◆ *vb* **jaundices, jaundicing, jaundiced**. **3** to distort (the judgment, etc.) adversely: *jealousy had jaundiced his mind*. **4** (*tr*) to affect with or as if with jaundice. [C14: from OF *jaunisse*, from *jaune* yellow, from L *galbinus* yellowish]

jaunt (dʒɔːnt) *n* **1** a short pleasurable excursion; outing. ◆ *vb* **2** (*intr*) to go on such an excursion. [C16: from ?]

jaunting car *n* a light two-wheeled one-horse car, formerly widely used in Ireland.

jaunty ('dʒɔːntɪ) *adj* **jauntier, jauntiest**. **1** sprightly and cheerful: *a jaunty step*. **2** smart; trim: *a jaunty hat*. [C17: from F *gentil* noble; see GENTEEL]
▸ **'jauntily** *adv* ▸ **'jauntiness** *n*

Jaurès ★ (*French* ʒɔrɛs) *n* **Jean Léon** (ʒɑ̃ leɔ̃). 1859–1914, French politician and writer, who founded the socialist paper *l'Humanité* (1904), and united the French socialist movement into a single party (1905); assassinated.

Java¹ ('dʒɑːvə) ★ *n* an island of Indonesia, south of Borneo, from which it is separated by the **Java Sea**: politically the most important island of Indonesia; it consists chiefly of active volcanic mountains and is densely for-

ested. It came under Dutch control in 1596 and became part of Indonesia in 1949. It is one of the most densely populated areas in the world. Capital: Jakarta. Pop. (with Madura): 102 910 500 (1995 est.). Area: 132 174 sq. km (51 032 sq. miles).
▸ **'Javan** *n, adj*

Java² ('dʒɑːvə) *n Trademark.* a programming language especially applicable to the World Wide Web. [C20: named after *Java* coffee, said to have been consumed in large quantities by the language's creators]

Java man *n* a type of primitive man, *Homo erectus*, that lived in the middle Palaeolithic Age in Java.

Javanese (,dʒɑːvə'niːz) *adj* **1** of or relating to the island of Java. ◆ *n* **2** (*pl* **Javanese**) a native or inhabitant of Java. **3** the Malayo-Polynesian language of Java.

Javari or **Javary** ★ (*Portuguese* ʒava'ri) *n* a river in South America, flowing northeast as part of the border between Peru and Brazil to join the Amazon. Length: about 1050 km (650 miles). Spanish name: **Yavarí**.

javelin ('dʒævlɪn) *n* **1** a long pointed spear thrown as a weapon or in competitive field events. **2 the javelin**. the event or sport of throwing the javelin. [C16: from OF *javeline*, var. of *javelot*, of Celtic origin]

jaw (dʒɔː) *n* **1** the part of the skull of a vertebrate that frames the mouth and holds the teeth. **2** the corresponding part of an invertebrate, esp. an insect. **3** a pair or either of a pair of hinged or sliding components of a machine or tool designed to grip an object. **4** *Sl.* **4a** impudent talk. **4b** idle conversation. **4c** a lecture. ◆ *vb* **5** (*intr*) *Sl.* **5a** to chat; gossip. **5b** to lecture. [C14: prob. from OF *joue* cheek]

Jawara ★ ('dʒɑːwərə) *n* Sir **Dawda** ('dɔːdə). born 1924, Gambian statesman; president of The Gambia (1970–94).

jawbone ('dʒɔː,bəʊn) *n* a nontechnical name for **mandible** or (less commonly) **maxilla**.

jawbreaker ('dʒɔː,breɪkə) *n* **1** a device having hinged jaws for crushing rocks and ores. **2** *Inf.* a word that is hard to pronounce.
▸ **'jaw,breaking** *adj*

jaws (dʒɔːz) *pl n* **1** the narrow opening of some confined place such as a gorge. **2 the jaws**. a dangerously close position: *the jaws of death*.

Jaxartes ★ (dʒæk'sɑːtiːz) *n* the ancient name for **Syr Darya**.

jay (dʒeɪ) *n* **1** a passerine bird related to the crow having a pinkish-brown body, blue-and-black wings, and a black-and-white crest. **2** a foolish or gullible person. [C13: from OF *jai*, from LL *gāius*, ?from name *Gāius*]

Jay ★ (dʒeɪ) *n* **John**. 1745–1829, American statesman, jurist, and diplomat; first chief justice of the Supreme Court (1789–95). He negotiated the treaty with Great Britain (**Jay's treaty**, 1794), that settled outstanding disputes.

Jaya ('dʒɑːjə) or **Djaja** ★ *n* **Mount**. a mountain in E Indonesia, in Irian Jaya in the Sudirman Range: the highest mountain in New Guinea. Height: 5039 m (16 532 ft). Former names: (Mount) **Carstensz, Sukarno Peak**.

Jayapura (,dʒɑːjaː'pʊərə) or **Djajapura** ★ *n* a port in NE Indonesia, capital of Irian Jaya, on the N coast. Pop.: 150 000 (latest est.). Former names: **Sukarnapura, Kotabaru, Hollandia**.

Jayawardene ★ (,dʒeɪəˈwɑːdɪnə) *n* **Junius Richard**. 1906–96, Sri Lankan statesman; prime minister (1977–78) and first president of Sri Lanka (1978).

Jaycee ('dʒeɪ'siː) *n US, Canad., Austral., & NZ.* a young person who belongs to a junior chamber of commerce. [C20: from *J(unior) C(hamber)*]

jaywalk ('dʒeɪˌwɔːk) *vb* (*intr*) to cross or walk in a street recklessly or illegally. [C20: from JAY (sense 2)]
▸ **'jay,walker** *n* ▸ **'jay,walking** *n*

jazz (dʒæz) *n* **1a** music of US Black origin, characterized by syncopated rhythms, solo and group improvisation, and a variety of harmonic idioms and instrumental techniques. **1b** (*as modifier*): *a jazz band*. **1c** (*in combination*): *a jazzman*. **2** *Sl.* rigmarole: *legal papers and all that*

★ people and places

jazz. ◆ *vb* **3** (*intr*) to play or dance to jazz music. [C20: from ?]
▸ ¹**jazzy** *adj* ▸ ¹**jazzily** *adv* ▸ ¹**jazziness** *n*

jazz up *vb* (*tr, adv*) *Inf.* **1** to imbue (a piece of music) with jazz qualities, esp. by playing at a quicker tempo. **2** to make more lively or appealing.

JC *abbrev. for:* **1** Jesus Christ. **2** Julius Caesar.

JCB *n Trademark.* a type of construction machine with a hydraulically operated shovel on the front and an excavator arm on the back. [from the initials of *J*(oseph) *C*(yril) *B*(amford) (born 1916), its Brit. manufacturer]

jealous ('dʒɛləs) *adj* **1** suspicious or fearful of being displaced by a rival. **2** (often *postpositive* and foll. by *of*) resentful (of) or vindictive (towards). **3** (often *postpositive* and foll. by *of*) possessive and watchful in the protection (of): *jealous of one's reputation.* **4** characterized by or resulting from jealousy. **5** *Obsolete except in Biblical use.* demanding exclusive loyalty: *a jealous God.* [C13: from OF *gelos*, from Med. L, from LL *zēlus* emulation, from Gk *zēlos* ZEAL]
▸ ¹**jealously** *adv*

jealousy ('dʒɛləsɪ) *n, pl* **jealousies.** the state or quality of being jealous.

jean (dʒiːn) *n* a tough twill-weave cotton fabric used for hard-wearing trousers, overalls, etc. [C16: short for *jean fustian*, from *Gene* GENOA]

Jean ★ (*French* ʒɑ̃) *n* born 1921, grand duke of Luxembourg from 1964.

Jean Baptiste (*French* ʒɑ̃bɑtist) *n Canad. sl.* a French Canadian. [F: John the Baptist, traditional patron saint of French Canada]

Jean de Meung ★ (*French* ʒɑ̃ də mœ̃) *n* real name *Jean Clopinel.* ?1250–?1305, French poet, who continued Guillaume de Lorris' *Roman de la Rose.*

Jeanne d'Arc ★ (ʒɑn dark) *n* the French name of **Joan of Arc.**

Jean Paul ★ (*French* ʒɑ̃ pɔl) *n* real name *Johann Paul Friedrich Richter.* 1763–1825, German novelist.

jeans (dʒiːnz) *pl n* trousers for casual wear, made esp. of denim or corduroy. [pl. of JEAN]

Jeans ★ (dʒiːnz) *n* Sir **James Hopwood.** 1877–1946, British astronomer, physicist, and mathematician, best known for his popular books on astronomy.

Jebel Musa ★ ('dʒɛbᵊl 'muːsə) *n* a mountain in NW Morocco, near the Strait of Gibraltar: one of the Pillars of Hercules. Height: 850 m (2790 ft).

Jedda ★ ('dʒɛdə) *n* another name for **Jidda.**

Jeep (dʒiːp) *n Trademark.* a small road vehicle with four-wheel drive. [C20: ?from *GP*, for *general-purpose* (*vehicle*), infl. by Eugene the *Jeep*, creature in a comic strip by E. C. Segar]

jeepers *or* **jeepers creepers** ('dʒiːpəz 'kriːpəz) *interj US sl.* a mild exclamation of surprise. [C20: euphemism for *Jesus*]

jeer (dʒɪə) *vb* **1** (often foll. by *at*) to laugh or scoff (at a person or thing). ◆ *n* **2** a remark or cry of derision. [C16: from ?]
▸ ¹**jeerer** *n* ▸ ¹**jeering** *adj, n* ▸ ¹**jeeringly** *adv*

Jefferson ★ ('dʒɛfəsᵊn) *n* **Thomas.** 1743–1826, US statesman: secretary of state (1790–93); third president (1801–09). He was the chief drafter of the Declaration of Independence (1776), the chief opponent of the centralizing policies of the Federalists under Hamilton, and effected the Louisiana Purchase (1803).
▸ **Jeffersonian** (ˌdʒɛfə'səʊnɪən) *adj, n*

Jefferson City ★ *n* a city in central Missouri, the state capital, on the Missouri River. Pop.: 35 481 (1990).

Jeffrey ★ ('dʒɛfrɪ) *n* **Francis,** Lord. 1773–1850, Scottish judge and literary critic. As editor of the *Edinburgh Review* (1803–29), he severely criticized the romantic poets, esp. Wordsworth.

Jeffreys ★ ('dʒɛfrɪz) *n* **George,** 1st Baron Jeffreys of Wem. ?1645–89, English judge, notorious for his brutality at the "Bloody Assizes" (1685), where those involved in Monmouth's rebellion were tried.

jehad (dʒɪ'hæd) *n* a variant spelling of **jihad.**

Jehol ★ (dʒə'hɒl) *n* **1** a former province of NE China, north of the Great Wall: divided among Hebei, Liaoning, and Inner Mongolia in 1956. Area: 192 380 sq. km (74 278 sq. miles). **2** a region of NE China, in Hebei and Liaoning provinces: mountainous.

Jehoshaphat ★ (dʒɪ'hɒʃəˌfæt, -'hɒʃ-) *n Old Testament.* **1** the king of Judah (?873–?849 B.C.) (I Kings 22:41–50). **2 Valley of Jehoshaphat.** the site of Jehovah's apocalyptic judgment upon the nations (Joel 4:14).

Jehovah ★ (dʒɪ'həʊvə) *n Old Testament.* the personal name of God, revealed to Moses on Mount Horeb (Exodus 3). [C16: from Med. L, from Heb. YHVH YAHWEH]

Jehovah's Witness *n* a member of a Christian Church of American origin, the followers of which believe that the end of the present world system of government is near.

Jehu ★ ('dʒiːhjuː) *n* **1** *Old Testament.* the successor to Ahab as king of Israel. **2** *Humorous.* a reckless driver.

jejune (dʒɪ'dʒuːn) *adj* **1** naive; unsophisticated. **2** insipid; dull. **3** lacking nourishment. [C17: from L *jējūnus* hungry, empty]
▸ je'**junely** *adv* ▸ je'**juneness** *n*

jejunum (dʒɪ'dʒuːnəm) *n* the part of the small intestine between the duodenum and the ileum. [C16: from L, from *jējūnus* empty; from the belief that the jejunum is empty after death]

Jekyll ★ ('dʒɛkᵊl) *n* **Gertrude.** 1843–1932, British landscape gardener: noted for her simplicity of design and use of indigenous plants.

Jekyll and Hyde *n* **a** a person with two distinct personalities, one good, the other evil. **b** (*as modifier*): *a Jekyll-and-Hyde personality.* [C19: after the principal character of Robert Louis Stevenson's novel *The Strange Case of Dr Jekyll and Mr Hyde* (1886)]

jell *or* **gel** ('dʒɛl) *vb* **1** to make or become gelatinous; congeal. **2** (*intr*) to assume definite form: *his ideas have jelled.* [C19: back formation from JELLY¹]

jellaba *or* **jellabah** ('dʒɛləbə) *n* a variant spelling of **djellaba.**

Jellicoe ★ ('dʒɛlɪˌkəʊ) *n* **John Rushworth,** 1st Earl Jellicoe. 1859–1935, British admiral, who commanded the Grand Fleet at the Battle of Jutland (1916), which incapacitated the German fleet for the rest of World War I.

jellies ('dʒɛlɪz) *pl n Brit. sl.* gelatine capsules of temazepam, dissolved and injected as a recreational drug. [C20: shortened from GELATINE]

jellify ('dʒɛlɪˌfaɪ) *vb* **jellifies, jellifying, jellified.** to make into or become jelly.
▸ ˌjellifi'**cation** *n*

jelly¹ ('dʒɛlɪ) *n, pl* **jellies.** **1** a fruit-flavoured clear dessert set with gelatine. **2** a preserve made from the juice of fruit boiled with sugar and used as jam. **3** a savoury food preparation set with gelatine or with gelatinous stock: *calf's-foot jelly.* ◆ *vb* **jellies, jellying, jellied. 4** to jellify. [C14: from OF *gelee* frost, jelly, from *geler* to set hard, from L, from *gelu* frost]
▸ ¹**jellied** *adj* ▸ ¹**jelly-ˌlike** *adj*

jelly² ('dʒɛlɪ) *n Brit.* a slang name for **gelignite.**

jelly baby *n Brit.* a small sweet made from a gelatinous substance formed to resemble a baby.

jellyfish ('dʒɛlɪˌfɪʃ) *n, pl* **jellyfish** *or* **jellyfishes. 1** any marine coelenterate having a gelatinous umbrella-shaped body with trailing tentacles. **2** *Inf.* a weak indecisive person.

jelly fungus *n* a fungus that grows on trees and has a jelly-like consistency when wet.

Jemappes ★ (*French* ʒəmap) *n* a town in SW Belgium, in Hainaut province west of Mons: scene of a battle (1792) during the French Revolutionary Wars, in which the French defeated the Austrians. Pop.: 18 100 (latest est.).

jemmy ('dʒɛmɪ) *or US* **jimmy** *n, pl* **jemmies** *or US* **jimmies. 1** a short steel crowbar used, esp. by burglars, for forcing doors and windows. ◆ *vb* **jemmies, jemmying, jemmied** *or US* **jimmies, jimmying, jimmied. 2** (*tr*) to prise (something) open with a jemmy. [C19: from the pet name for *James*]

Jena ★ (*German* 'jeːna) *n* a city in S East Germany, in Thuringia: university (1558), at which Hegel and Schiller taught; site of the battle (1806) in which Napoleon Bonaparte defeated the Prussians; optical and precision instrument industry. Pop.: 102 204 (1995 est.).

Jenghis Khan ★ ('dʒɛŋgɪs 'kɑːn) *n* See **Genghis Khan**.

Jenkins ★ ('dʒɛŋkɪnz) *n* **Roy** (**Harris**), Baron Jenkins of Hillhead. born 1920, British Social Democrat politician; president of the Common Market Commission (1977–80); originally a Labour politician; cofounder of the Social Democratic Party (1981); leader of party (1982–83); Chancellor of Oxford University from 1987.

Jenner ★ ('dʒɛnə) *n* **1 Edward.** 1749–1823, British physician, who discovered vaccination by showing that injections of cowpox virus produce immunity against smallpox (1796). **2 Sir William.** 1815–98, British physician and pathologist, who distinguished between typhus and typhoid fevers (1849).

jennet, genet, *or* **gennet** ('dʒɛnɪt) *n* a small Spanish riding horse. [C15: from OF *genet*, from Catalan *ginet*, horse used by the *Zenete*, from Ar. *Zanātah* the Zenete, a Moorish people renowned for their horsemanship]

jenny ('dʒɛnɪ) *n, pl* **jennies. 1** a machine for turning up the edge of a piece of sheet metal in preparation for making a joint. **2** the female of certain animals or birds, esp. a donkey, ass, or wren. **3** short for **spinning jenny. 4** *Billiards, etc.* an in-off. [C17: from name *Jenny*, dim. of *Jane*]

Jensen ★ (*Danish* 'jɛnsən) *n* **Johannes Vilhelm** (jo'hanəs 'vɪlhelm). 1873–1950, Danish novelist, poet, and essayist: best known for his novel sequence *The Long Journey* (1908–22). Nobel prize for literature 1944.

jeopardize *or* **jeopardise** ('dʒɛpə,daɪz) *vb* **jeopardizes, jeopardizing, jeopardized** *or* **jeopardises, jeopardising, jeopardised.** (*tr*) **1** to risk; hazard: *he jeopardized his job by being persistently unpunctual*. **2** to put in danger.

jeopardy ('dʒɛpədɪ) *n* (usually preceded by *in*) **1** danger of injury, loss, death, etc.: *his health was in jeopardy*. **2** *Law.* danger of being convicted and punished for a criminal offence. [C14: from OF *jeu parti*, lit.: divided game, hence uncertain issue, from *jeu* game, from L *jocus* joke, game + *partir* to divide]

Jephthah ★ ('dʒɛfθə) *n Old Testament.* a judge of Israel, who sacrificed his daughter in fulfilment of a vow (Judges 11:12–40). Douay spelling: **Jephte** ('dʒɛftə).

jequirity (dʒɪ'kwɪrɪtɪ) *n, pl* **jequirities.** a tropical climbing plant with scarlet black-spotted seeds used as beads, and roots used as a substitute for liquorice. Also called: **Indian liquorice.** [C19: from Port. *jequiriti*, of Amerind origin, from *jekiriti*]

Jer. *Bible. abbrev. for* Jeremiah.

jerbil ('dʒɜːbɪl) *n* a variant spelling of **gerbil.**

jerboa (dʒɜː'bəʊə) *n* any small nocturnal burrowing rodent inhabiting dry regions of Asia and N Africa, having long hind legs specialized for jumping. [C17: from NL, from Ar. *yarbū'*]

jeremiad (,dʒɛrɪ'maɪəd) *n* a long mournful lamentation or complaint. [C18: from F *jérémiade*, referring to the Lamentations of Jeremiah in the Old Testament]

Jeremiah ★ (,dʒɛrɪ'maɪə) *n* **1** *Old Testament.* **1a** a major prophet of Judah from about 626 to 587 B.C. **1b** the book containing his oracles. **2** a person who habitually prophesies doom or denounces contemporary society.

jerepigo (,dʒɛrɪ'pɪgəʊ) *n S. African.* a sweet white or red sherry-type wine. [from Port. *cheripiga* an adulterant for port wine]

Jerez ★ (*Spanish* xe'reθ) *n* a town in SW Spain: famous for the making of sherry. Pop.: 190 390 (1994 est.). Official name: **Jerez de la Frontera** (xe'reð ðe la frɔn'tera). Former name: **Xeres.**

Jericho ★ ('dʒɛrɪ,kəʊ) *n* a village in the West Bank near the N end of the Dead Sea, 251 m (825 ft) below sea level: on the site of an ancient city, the first place to be taken by the Israelites under Joshua after entering the Promised Land in the 14th century B.C. (Joshua 6).

jerk¹ (dʒɜːk) *vb* **1** to move or cause to move with an irregular or spasmodic motion. **2** to throw, twist, pull, or push (something) abruptly or spasmodically. **3** (*tr;* often foll. by *out*) to utter (words, etc.) in a spasmodic or breathless manner. ◆ *n* **4** an abrupt or spasmodic movement. **5** an irregular jolting motion: *the car moved with a jerk*. **6** (*pl*)

Also called: **physical jerks.** *Brit. inf.* physical exercises. **7** *Sl., chiefly US & Canad.* a stupid or ignorant person. [C16: prob. var. of *yerk* to pull stitches tight]
▶ **'jerker** *n*

jerk² (dʒɜːk) *vb* (*tr*) **1** to preserve beef, etc., by cutting into thin strips and drying in the sun. ◆ *n* **2** Also called: **jerky.** jerked meat. [C18: back formation from *jerky*, from Sp. *charqui*, from Quechuan]

jerkin ('dʒɜːkɪn) *n* **1** a sleeveless short jacket worn by men or women. **2** a man's sleeveless fitted jacket, often made of leather, worn in the 16th and 17th centuries. [C16: from ?]

jerk off *or US* **jack off** *vb* (*adv often reflexive*) *Taboo sl.* (of a male) to masturbate.

jerky ('dʒɜːkɪ) *adj* **jerkier, jerkiest.** characterized by jerks.
▶ **'jerkily** *adv* ▶ **'jerkiness** *n*

jeroboam (,dʒɛrə'bəʊəm) *n* a wine bottle holding the equivalent of four normal bottles. [C19: allusion to JEROBOAM, a "mighty man of valour" (I Kings 11:28) who "made Israel to sin" (I Kings 14:16)]

Jeroboam ★ (,dʒɛrə'bəʊəm) *n Old Testament.* **1** the first king of the northern kingdom of Israel (?922–?901 B.C.). **2** king of the northern kingdom of Israel (?786–?746 B.C.).

Jerome ★ (dʒə'rəʊm) *n* **1 Saint.** Latin name *Eusebius Hieronymus.* ?347–?420 A.D., Christian monk and scholar, whose outstanding work was the production of the Vulgate. Feast day: Sept. 30. **2 Jerome K(lapka).** 1859–1927, English humorous writer; author of *Three Men in a Boat* (1889).

jerry ('dʒɛrɪ) *n, pl* **jerries.** *Brit.* an informal word for **chamber pot.**

Jerry ('dʒɛrɪ) *n, pl* **Jerries.** *Brit. sl.* **1** a German, esp. a German soldier. **2** the Germans collectively.

jerry-build *vb* **jerry-builds, jerry-building, jerry-built.** (*tr*) to build (houses, flats, etc.) badly using cheap materials.
▶ **'jerry-,builder** *n*

jerry can *n* a flat-sided can with a capacity of between 4.5 and 5 gallons used for storing or transporting liquids, esp. motor fuel. [C20: from JERRY]

jersey ('dʒɜːzɪ) *n* **1** a knitted garment covering the upper part of the body. **2a** a machine-knitted slightly elastic cloth of wool, silk, nylon, etc., used for clothing. **2b** (*as modifier*): *a jersey suit.* **3** a football shirt. [C16: from JERSEY, from the woollen sweaters worn by the fishermen]

Jersey ★ ('dʒɜːzɪ) *n* **1** an island in the English Channel, the largest of the Channel Islands: forms, with two other islands, the bailiwick of Jersey; colonized from Normandy in the 11th century and still officially French-speaking; noted for finance, market gardening, dairy farming, and tourism. Capital: St Helier. Pop.: 84 082 (1991). Area: 116 sq. km (45 sq. miles). **2** a breed of dairy cattle producing milk with a high butterfat content, originating from the island of Jersey.

Jersey City ★ *n* an industrial city in NE New Jersey, opposite Manhattan on a peninsula between the Hudson and Hackensack Rivers: part of the Port of New York; site of one of the greatest railway terminals in the world. Pop.: 226 022 (1994 est.).

Jerusalem ★ (dʒə'ruːsələm) *n* **1** the capital of Israel (recognition of this has been withheld by a number of countries pending completion of negotiations on Palestinian autonomy), situated in the Judaean hills: became capital of the Hebrew kingdom after its capture by David around 1000 B.C.; destroyed by Nebuchadnezzar of Babylon in 586 B.C.; taken by the Romans in 63 B.C.; devastated in 70 A.D. and 135 A.D. during the Jewish rebellions against Rome; fell to the Arabs in 637 and to the Seljuk Turks in 1071; ruled by Crusaders from 1099 to 1187 and by the Egyptians and Turks until conquered by the British (1917); centre of the British mandate of Palestine from 1920 to 1948, when the Arabs took the old city and the Jews held the new city; unified after the Six Day War (1967) under the Israelis; the holy city of Jews, Christians, and Muslims. Pop.: 591 400 (1996 est.). **2 the New Jerusalem.** *Christianity.* **2a** Heaven. **2b** any ideal city.

Jerusalem artichoke *n* **1** a North American sunflower widely cultivated for its underground edible tubers. **2** the tuber of this plant, which is eaten as a vegetable. [C17: by folk etymology from It. *girasole articiocco; see* GIRASOL]

Jervis Bay ★ ('dʒɑːvɪs) *n* an inlet of the Pacific in SE Australia, on the coast of S New South Wales: part of the Australian Capital Territory: site of the Royal Australian Naval College.

Jespersen ★ ('jespəs³n, 'dʒes-) *n* (Jens) Otto (Harry). 1860–1943, Danish philologist: author of *Modern English Grammar* (1909–31).

jess (dʒes) *n Falconry.* a short leather strap, one end of which is permanently attached to the leg of a hawk or falcon. [C14: from OF *ges,* from L *jactus* a throw, from *jacere* to throw]
► **jessed** *adj*

jessamine ('dʒesəmɪn) *n* another name for **jasmine** (sense 1).

Jesse ★ ('dʒesɪ) *n Old Testament.* the father of David (I Samuel 16).

Jesselton ★ ('dʒesəltən) *n* the former name of **Kota Kinabalu.**

jessie ('dʒesɪ) *n Sl.* an effeminate, weak, or cowardly boy or man.

jest (dʒest) *n* **1** something done or said for amusement; joke. **2** playfulness; fun: *to act in jest.* **3** a jeer or taunt. **4** an object of derision. ◆ *vb* **5** to act or speak in an amusing or frivolous way. **6** to make fun of (a person or thing). [C13: var. of GEST]
► **'jesting** *adj, n* ► **'jestingly** *adv*

jester ('dʒestə) *n* a professional clown employed by a king or nobleman during the Middle Ages.

Jesu ★ ('dʒiːzjuː) *n* a poetic name for or vocative form of **Jesus.** [C17: from LL, vocative of JESUS]

Jesuit ('dʒezjʊɪt) *n* **1** a member of a Roman Catholic religious order (the **Society of Jesus**) founded by Ignatius Loyola in 1534 with the aim of defending Catholicism against the Reformation. **2** (*sometimes not cap.*) *Inf., offens.* a person given to subtle and equivocating arguments. [C16: from NL *Jēsuita,* from LL *Jēsus* + *-ita* -ITE¹]
► **,Jesu'itical** *adj*

Jesus ★ ('dʒiːzəs) *n* **1** Also called: **Jesus Christ, Jesus of Nazareth.** ?4 B.C.–?29 A.D., founder of Christianity, born in Bethlehem and brought up in Nazareth as a Jew. He is believed by Christians to be the Son of God and to have been miraculously conceived by the Virgin Mary. After the Last Supper with his disciples, he was betrayed by Judas and crucified. Christians believe that he rose from his tomb after three days, appeared to his disciples several times, and ascended to Heaven after 40 days. **2** *Son of Sirach.* 3rd century B.C., author of the Apocryphal book of Ecclesiasticus. ◆ *interj also* **Jesus wept.** **3** *Taboo sl.* used to express intense surprise, dismay, etc. [via L from Gk *Iēsous,* from Heb. *Yeshūa',* shortened from *Yehōshūa'* God is help, JOSHUA]

Jesus freak *n Inf.* a vociferous Christian, esp. one who is evangelical and belongs to a community.

jet¹ (dʒet) *n* **1** a thin stream of liquid or gas forced out of a small aperture. **2** an outlet or nozzle for emitting such a stream. **3** a jet-propelled aircraft. ◆ *vb* **jets, jetting, jetted.** **4** to issue or cause to issue in a jet: *water jetted from the hose.* **5** to transport or be transported by jet aircraft. [C16: from OF *jeter* to throw, from L *jactāre* to toss about]

jet² (dʒet) *n* **a** a hard black variety of lignite that takes a brilliant polish and is used for jewellery, etc. **b** (*as modifier*): *jet earrings.* [C14: from OF *jaiet,* from L, from Gk *lithos gagatēs* stone of *Gagai,* a town in Lycia, Asia Minor]

jet black *n* **a** a deep black colour. **b** (*as adj*): *jet-black hair.*

jeté (ʒə'teɪ) *n Ballet.* a step in which the dancer springs from one leg and lands on the other. [F, lit.: thrown, from *jeter;* see JET¹]

jet engine *n* a gas turbine, esp. one fitted to an aircraft.

Jethro ★ ('dʒeθrəʊ) *n Old Testament.* a Midianite priest, the father-in-law of Moses (Exodus 3:1; 4:18).

jet lag *n* a general feeling of fatigue, disorientation, or nausea often experienced by air travellers after long journeys.

jet-propelled *adj* **1** driven by jet propulsion. **2** *Inf.* very fast.

jet propulsion *n* **1** propulsion by means of a jet of fluid. **2** propulsion by means of a gas turbine, esp. when the exhaust gases provide the propulsive thrust.

jetsam ('dʒetsəm) *n* **1** that portion of the cargo of a vessel thrown overboard to lighten her, as during a storm. Cf. **flotsam** (sense 1). **2** another word for **flotsam** (sense 2). [C16: shortened from JETTISON]

jet set *n* **a** a rich and fashionable social set, the members of which travel widely for pleasure. **b** (*as modifier*): *jet-set travellers.*
► **'jet-,setter** *n* ► **'jet-,setting** *n, adj*

jet ski *n* **1** a small self-propelled vehicle for one person resembling a scooter, which skims across water on a flat keel, and is steered by means of handlebars. ◆ *vb* **jet-ski, jet-skis, jet-skiing, jet-skied** *or* **jet ski'd.** (*intr*) **2** to ride a jet ski.
► **jet skier** *n* ► **jet skiing** *n*

jet stream *n* **1** *Meteorol.* a narrow belt of high-altitude winds moving east at high speeds. **2** the jet of exhaust gases produced by a gas turbine, etc.

jettison ('dʒetɪs³n, -z³n) *vb* **jettisons, jettisoning, jettisoned.** (*tr*) **1** to abandon: *to jettison old clothes.* **2** to throw overboard. ◆ *n* **3** another word for **jetsam** (sense 1). [C15: from OF, ult. from L *jactātiō* a tossing about]

jetton ('dʒet³n) *n* a counter or token, esp. a chip used in such gambling games as roulette. [C18: from F *jeton,* from *jeter* to cast up (accounts); see JET¹]

jetty ('dʒetɪ) *n, pl* **jetties.** **1** a structure built from a shore out into the water to direct currents or protect a harbour. **2** a landing pier; dock. [C15: from OF *jetee* projecting part, lit.: something thrown out, from *jeter* to throw]

jeu d'esprit (French ʒø despri) *n, pl* **jeux d'esprit** (ʒø despri). a light-hearted display of wit or cleverness, esp. in literature. [lit.: play of spirit]

Jevons ★ ('dʒev³nz) *n* William Stanley. 1835–82, British economist and logician: author of *The Theory of Political Economy* (1871).

Jew (dʒuː) *n* **1** a member of the Semitic people who are descended from the ancient Israelites. **2** a person whose religion is Judaism. [C12: from OF *juiu,* from L *jūdaeus,* from Gk *ioudaios,* from Heb., from *yehūdāh* JUDAH]

jewel ('dʒuːəl) *n* **1** a precious or semiprecious stone; gem. **2** a person or thing resembling a jewel in preciousness, brilliance, etc. **3** a gemstone used as a bearing in a watch. **4** a piece of jewellery. ◆ *vb* **jewels, jewelling, jewelled** *or US* **jewels, jeweling, jeweled.** **5** (*tr*) to fit or decorate with a jewel or jewels. [C13: from OF *jouel,* ?from *jeu* game, from L *jocus*]

jewelfish ('dʒuːəl,fɪʃ) *n, pl* **jewelfish** *or* **jewelfishes.** a beautifully coloured and popular aquarium fish native to Africa.

jeweller *or US* **jeweler** ('dʒuːələ) *n* a person whose business is the cutting or setting of gemstones or the making or selling of jewellery.

jeweller's rouge *n* a finely powdered form of ferric oxide used as a metal polish.

jewellery *or US* **jewelry** ('dʒuːəlrɪ) *n* objects that are worn for personal adornment, such as rings, necklaces, etc., considered collectively.

Jewess ('dʒuːɪs) *n* a Jewish girl or woman.

jewfish ('dʒuː,fɪʃ) *n, pl* **jewfish** *or* **jewfishes.** **1** any of various large dark fishes of warm or tropical seas. **2** *Austral.* a freshwater catfish. [C17: from ?]

Jewish ('dʒuːɪʃ) *adj* of or characteristic of Jews.
► **'Jewishly** *adv* ► **'Jewishness** *n*

Jewish Autonomous Region ★ *n* an administrative division of SE Russia, in E Siberia: colonized by Jews in 1928; largely agricultural. Capital: Birobidzhan. Pop.: 216 000 (1995 est.). Area: 36 000 sq. km (13 895 sq. miles). Also called: **Birobidzhan, Birobijan.**

Jew lizard *n* a large Australian lizard with spiny scales round its neck.

Jewry ('dʒʊərɪ) *n, pl* **Jewries.** **1a** Jews collectively. **1b** the

Jewish religion or culture. **2** a quarter of a town inhabited by Jews.

jew's-ear *n* a pinky-red fungus.

jew's-harp *n* a musical instrument consisting of a small lyre-shaped metal frame held between the teeth, with a steel tongue plucked with the finger.

Jezebel ★ ('dʒɛzə,bɛl) *n* **1** *Old Testament.* the wife of Ahab, king of Israel. **2** (*sometimes not cap.*) a shameless or scheming woman.

Jezreel ★ ('dʒɛzrɪəl) *n* **Plain of.** another name for **Esdraelon**.
▷ **'Jezreel,ite** *n*

JFK *abbrev. for* John Fitzgerald Kennedy.

Jhabvala ★ (dʒæb'vɑːlə) *n* **Ruth Prawer**, original name *Ruth Prawer.* born 1927, British writer living in India and the US, born in Germany to Polish parents: author of the Booker-prizewinning novel *Heat and Dust* (1975).

Jhansi ★ (dʒɑːnsɪ) *n* a city in central India, in SW Uttar Pradesh: scene of a mutiny against the British in 1857. Pop.: 300 850 (1991).

Jhelum ★ ('dʒiːləm) *n* a river in Pakistan and Kashmir, rising in W central Kashmir and flowing northwest through the Vale of Kashmir, then southwest into N West Punjab to join the Chenab River: important for irrigation, having the Mangla Dam (Pakistan), completed in 1967. Length: about 720 km (450 miles).

JHVH *or* **JHWH** *Old Testament.* a variant of **YHVH**.

Jiang Qing ('dʒæŋ 'tʃɪŋ) *or* **Chiang Ch'ing** ★ *n* c. 1913–91, Chinese Communist actress and politician; widow of Mao Tse-tung and a leading member of the Gang of Four.

Jiangsu ('dʒæŋ'suː) *or* **Kiangsu** ★ *n* a province of E China, on the Yellow Sea: consists mostly of the marshy delta of the Yangtze River, with some of China's largest cities and most densely populated areas. Capital: Nanjing. Pop.: 70 210 000 (1995 est.). Area: 102 200 sq. km (39 860 sq. miles).

Jiangxi ('dʒæŋ'ji:) *or* **Kiangsi** ★ *n* a province of SE central China, in the basins of the Kan River and the Poyang Lake: mineral resources include coal and tungsten. Capital: Nanchang. Pop.: 40 150 000 (1995 est.). Area: 164 800 sq. km (64 300 sq. miles).

Jiang Zemin ★ ('dʒjæŋ ʒeɪ'mɪn) *n* born 1926, Chinese Communist politician: president of China from 1993.

Jiazhou ('dʒjæ'dʒəu) *or* **Kiaochow** ★ *n* a territory of NE China, in SE Shandong province, surrounding **Jiazhou Bay** (an inlet of the Yellow Sea): leased to Germany from 1898 to 1914. Area: about 520 sq. km (200 sq. miles).

jib[1] (dʒɪb) *n* **1** *Naut.* any triangular sail set forward of the foremast of a vessel. **2 cut of someone's jib.** someone's manner, style, etc. [C17: from ?]

jib[2] (dʒɪb) *vb* **jibs, jibbing, jibbed.** (*intr*) *Chiefly Brit.* **1** (often foll. by *at*) to be reluctant (to). **2** (of an animal) to stop short and refuse to go forwards. **3** *Naut.* a variant of **gybe**. [C19: from ?]
▷ **'jibber** *n*

jib[3] (dʒɪb) *n* the projecting arm of a crane or the boom of a derrick. [C18: prob. based on GIBBET]

jib boom *n* *Naut.* a spar forming an extension of the bowsprit.

jibe[1] (dʒaɪb) *or* **jib** (dʒɪb) *vb* **jibes, jibing, jibed** *or* **jibs, jibbing, jibbed.** *n Naut.* a variant of **gybe**.

jibe[2] (dʒaɪb) *vb* **jibes, jibing, jibed.** a variant spelling of **gibe**[1].

jibe[3] (dʒaɪb) *vb* **jibes, jibing, jibed.** (*intr*) *Inf.* to agree; accord; harmonize. [C19: from ?]

Jibouti *or* **Jibuti** ★ (dʒɪ'buːtɪ) *n* variant spellings of **Djibouti**.

Jidda ('dʒɪdə) *or* **Jedda** ★ *n* a port in W Saudi Arabia on the Red Sea: the diplomatic capital of the country; the port of entry for Mecca, 80 km (50 miles) east. Pop.: 1 500 000 (1991 est.).

jiffy ('dʒɪfɪ) *or* **jiff** *n, pl* **jiffies** *or* **jiffs.** *Inf.* a very short time: *wait a jiffy.* [C18: from ?]

Jiffy bag *n Trademark.* a large padded envelope.

jig (dʒɪg) *n* **1** any of several old rustic kicking and leaping dances. **2** a piece of music composed for or in the rhythm of this dance. **3** a mechanical device designed to hold and locate a component during machining. **4** *Angling.* any of various spinning lures that wobble when drawn through the water. **5** Also called: **jigger**. *Mining.* a device for separating ore or coal from waste material by agitation in water. ◆ *vb* **jigs, jigging, jigged. 6** to dance (a jig). **7** to jerk or cause to jerk up and down rapidly. **8** (often foll. by *up*) to fit or be fitted in a jig. **9** (*tr*) to drill or cut (a workpiece) in a jig. **10** (*tr*) *Mining.* to separate ore or coal from waste material using a jig. [C16: from ?]

Jigawa ★ (,dʒɪ'gɑːwə) *n* a state of N Nigeria. Capital: Dutse. Pop.: 2 829 929 (1991). Area (including Kano state): 43 285 sq. km (16 712 sq. miles).

jigger[1] ('dʒɪgə) *n* **1** a person or thing that jigs. **2** *Golf.* (formerly) a club, an iron, usually No. 4. **3** any of a number of mechanical devices having a vibratory motion. **4** a light lifting tackle used on ships. **5** a small glass, esp. for whisky. **6** *Billiards.* another word for **bridge**[1] (sense 11). **7** *NZ.* a light hand- or power-propelled vehicle used on railway lines.

jigger[2] *or* **jigger flea** ('dʒɪgə) *n* another name for the **chigoe** (sense 1).

jiggered ('dʒɪgəd) *adj* (*postpositive*) *Inf.* damned; blowed: *I'm jiggered if he'll get away with it.* [C19: prob. euphemism for *buggered;* see BUGGER]

jiggermast ('dʒɪgə,mɑːst) *n Naut.* any small mast on a sailing vessel.

jiggery-pokery ('dʒɪgərɪ'pəukərɪ) *n Inf., chiefly Brit.* dishonest or deceitful behaviour. [C19: from Scot. dialect *joukery-pawkery*]

jiggle ('dʒɪgᵊl) *vb* **jiggles, jiggling, jiggled. 1** to move or cause to move up and down or to and fro with a short jerky motion. ◆ *n* **2** a short jerky motion. [C19: frequentative of JIG]
▷ **'jiggly** *adj*

jigsaw ('dʒɪg,sɔː) *n* **1** a mechanical saw with a fine steel blade for cutting intricate curves in sheets of material. **2** See **jigsaw puzzle**. [C19: from JIG to jerk up and down rapidly) + SAW[1]]

jigsaw puzzle *n* a puzzle in which the player has to reassemble a picture that has been cut into irregularly shaped interlocking pieces.

jihad *or* **jehad** (dʒɪ'hæd) *n Islam.* a holy war against infidels undertaken by Muslims. [C19: from Ar. *jihād* a conflict]

Jilin ('dʒiː'lɪn) *or* **Kirin** ★ *n* **1** a province of NE China, in central Manchuria. Capital: Changchun. Pop.: 25 740 000 (1995 est.). Area: 187 000 sq. km (72 930 sq. miles). **2** Also called: **Chi-lin** ('tʃiː'lɪn). a river port in NE China, in N central Jilin province on the Songhua River. Pop.: 1 270 000 (1991 est.).

Jilong ★ ('dʒiː'lʊŋ) *n* the Pinyin transliteration of the Chinese name for **Chilung**.

jilt (dʒɪlt) *vb* **1** (*tr*) to leave or reject (a lover), esp. without previous warning. ◆ *n* **2** a woman who jilts a lover. [C17: from dialect *jillet* flighty girl, dim. of name *Gill*]

jim crow ('dʒɪm 'krəu) *n* (*often caps.*) *US.* **1a** the policy or practice of segregating Blacks. **1b** (*as modifier*): *jim-crow laws.* **2** a derogatory term for **Black**[1]. **3** an implement for bending iron bars or rails. [C19: from *Jim Crow,* name of song used as the basis of an act by Thomas Rice (1808–60), US entertainer]
▷ **jim-'crowism** *n*

Jiménez ★ (*Spanish* xi'meneθ) *n* **Juan Ramón** (xwan ra'mɔn). 1881–1958, Spanish lyric poet. His most famous work is *Platero y yo* (1917), a prose poem: Nobel prize for literature 1956.

Jiménez de Cisneros ★ (*Spanish* xi'meneð ðe θiz'neros) *n* **Francisco** (fran'θisko). 1436–1517, Spanish cardinal and statesman: regent of Castile (1506–07) and Spain (1516–17) and grand inquisitor for Castile and León (1507–17). Also called: **Ximenes de Cisneros, Ximenez de Cisneros**.

jimjams ('dʒɪm,dʒæmz) *pl n* **1** *Sl.* delirium tremens. **2** a state of nervous tension or anxiety. **3** *Inf.* pyjamas. [C19: whimsical formation based on JAM[1]]

jimmy ('dʒɪmɪ) *n, pl* **jimmies,** *vb* **jimmies, jimmying, jimmied.** a US variant of **jemmy.**

Jinan (dʒiː'næn), **Chinan,** *or* **Tsinan** ★ *n* an industrial city in NE China, capital of Shandong province; probably over 3000 years old. Pop.: 2 320 000 (1991 est.).

Jingdezhen ('dʒɪŋ'dedʒen), **Fowliang,** *or* **Fou-liang** ★ *n* a city in SE China, in NE Jiangxi province east of Lake Poyang: famous for its porcelain industry, established in the sixth century. Pop.: 281 183 (1990 est.).

Jinghis Khan ★ ('dʒɪŋgɪs 'kɑːn) *n* See **Genghis Khan.**

jingle ('dʒɪŋgⁱl) *vb* **jingles, jingling, jingled. 1** to ring or cause to ring lightly and repeatedly. **2** (*intr*) to sound in a manner suggestive of jingling: *a jingling verse.* ◆ *n* **3** a sound of metal jingling. **4** a rhythmic verse, etc., esp. one used in advertising. [C16: prob. imit.]
▸ 'jingly *adj*

jingo ('dʒɪŋgəʊ) *n, pl* **jingoes. 1** a loud and bellicose patriot. **2** jingoism. **3 by jingo.** an exclamation of surprise. [C17: orig. ? euphemism for *Jesus*; applied to bellicose patriots after the use of *by Jingo!* in a 19th-cent. song]

jingoism ('dʒɪŋgəʊˌɪzəm) *n* the belligerent spirit or foreign policy of jingoes.
▸ 'jingoist *n, adj* ▸ ˌjingo'istic *adj*

Jinja ★ ('dʒɪndʒə) *n* a town in Uganda, on the N shore of Lake Victoria. Pop.: 60 979 (1991).

Jinjiang ('dʒɪn'dʒjæŋ), **Chinkiang,** *or* **Chengchiang** ★ *n* a port in E China, in S Jiangsu at the confluence of the Yangtze River and the Grand Canal. Pop.: 368 316 (1990 est.).

jink (dʒɪŋk) *vb* **1** (*intr*) to move swiftly or turn in order to dodge. ◆ *n* **2** a jinking movement. [C18: of Scot. origin, imit. of swift movement]

jinker ('dʒɪŋkə) *n Austral.* a vehicle for transporting timber, consisting of a tractor and two sets of wheels for supporting the logs. [from ?]

jinks (dʒɪŋks) *pl n* boisterous or mischievous play (esp. in **high jinks**). [C18: from ?]

jinn (dʒɪn) *n* (*often functioning as sing*) the plural of **jinni.**

Jinnah ★ ('dʒɪnə) *n* **Mohammed Ali.** 1876–1948, Indian Muslim statesman. He campaigned for the partition of India into separate Hindu and Muslim states, becoming first governor general of Pakistan (1947–48).

jinni, jinnee, *or* **djinni** (dʒɪ'niː) *n, pl* **jinn** *or* **djinn** (dʒɪn). a being or spirit in Muslim belief who could assume human or animal form and influence man by supernatural powers. [C17: from Ar.]

jinrikisha, jinricksha, *or* **jinrickshaw** (dʒɪn'rɪkʃɔː) *n* another name for **rickshaw.** [C19: from Japanese, from *jin* man + *riki* power + *sha* carriage]

jinx (dʒɪŋks) *n* **1** an unlucky force, person, or thing. ◆ *vb* **2** (*tr*) to be or put a jinx on. [C20: ?from NL *Jynx,* genus name of the wryneck, from Gk *iunx* wryneck, a bird used in magic]

Jinzhou ('dʒɪn'dʒəʊ), **Chin-Chou,** *or* **Chin-chow** ★ *n* a city in NE China, in SW Liaoning province. Pop.: 569 518 (1990 est.). Former name (1913–47): **Chin-hsien.**

JIT *abbrev. for* just-in-time.

jitter ('dʒɪtə) *Inf.* ◆ *vb* **1** (*intr*) to be anxious or nervous. ◆ *n* **2 the jitters.** nervousness and anxiety. [C20: from ?]
▸ 'jittery *adj* ▸ 'jitteriness *n*

jitterbug ('dʒɪtəˌbʌɡ) *n* **1** a fast jerky American dance, usually to a jazz accompaniment, that was popular in the 1940s. **2** a person who dances the jitterbug. ◆ *vb* **jitterbugs, jitterbugging, jitterbugged. 3** (*intr*) to perform such a dance.

jiujitsu *or* **jiujutsu** (dʒuː'dʒɪtsuː) *n* a variant spelling of **jujitsu.**

jive (dʒaɪv) *n* **1** a style of lively and jerky dance, popular esp. in the 1940s and 1950s. **2** *Sl., chiefly US.* **2a** misleading or deceptive talk. **2b** (*as modifier*): *jive talk.* ◆ *vb* **jives, jiving, jived. 3** (*intr*) to dance the jive. **4** *Sl., chiefly US.* to mislead; tell lies (to). [C20: from ?]
▸ 'jiver *n*

Joab ★ ('dʒəʊæb) *n Old Testament.* the successful commander of King David's forces and the slayer of Abner and Absalom (II Samuel 2:18–23; 3:24–27; 18:14–15).

Joachim ★ *n* **1** ('jɔːaxɪm). **Joseph** ('jɔːzef). 1831–1907, Hungarian violinist and composer. **2** ('dʒəʊəkɪm). **Saint.** 1st century B.C., traditionally the father of the Virgin Mary; feast day: July 25 or Sept. 9.

Joan ★ (dʒəʊn) *n* **1** known as *the Fair Maid of Kent.* 1328–85, wife of Edward the Black Prince; mother of Richard II. **2 Pope.** legendary female pope, first mentioned in the 13th century: said to have disguised herself as a man and to have died in childbirth.

Joan of Arc ★ *n* **Saint,** known as *the Maid of Orléans;* French name *Jeanne d'Arc.* ?1412–31, French national heroine, who led the army that relieved Orléans in the Hundred Years' War, enabling Charles VII to be crowned at Reims (1429). After being captured (1430), she was burnt at the stake as a heretic. She was canonized in 1920. Feast day: May 30.

João Pessoa ★ (*Portuguese* 'ʒuɐ̃um pe'soa) *n* a port in NE Brazil, capital of Paraíba state. Pop.: 497 306 (1991).

job (dʒɒb) *n* **1** an individual piece of work or task. **2** an occupation. **3** an object worked on or a result produced from working. **4** a duty or responsibility: *her job was to cook the dinner.* **5** *Inf.* a difficult task or problem: *I had a job to contact him.* **6** a state of affairs: *make the best of a bad job.* **7** *Inf.* a particular type of something: *a four-wheel drive job.* **8** *Inf.* a crime, esp. a robbery. **9** *Computing.* a unit of work for a computer. **10 jobs for the boys.** jobs given to or created for allies or favourites. **11 just the job.** exactly what was required. **12 on the job.** actively engaged in one's employment. ◆ *vb* **jobs, jobbing, jobbed. 13** (*intr*) to work by the piece or at casual jobs. **14** to make a private profit out of (a public office, etc.). **15** (*intr;* usually foll. by *in*) **15a** to buy and sell (goods or services) as a middleman: *he jobs in government surplus.* **15b** *Brit.* to buy and sell stocks and shares as a stockjobber. **16** *Austral. sl.* to punch. [C16: from ?]
▸ 'jobless *adj*

Job ★ (dʒəʊb) *n* **1** *Old Testament.* **1a** a Jewish patriarch, who maintained his faith in spite of the afflictions sent by God to test him. **1b** the book containing Job's pleas to God under these afflictions, attempted explanations of them by his friends, and God's reply to him. **2** any person who withstands great suffering without despairing.

jobber ('dʒɒbə) *n* **1** *Brit.* short for **stockjobber** (sense 1). See also **market maker. 2** a person who jobs.

jobbery ('dʒɒbərɪ) *n* the practice of making private profit out of a public office.

jobbing ('dʒɒbɪŋ) *adj* working by the piece, not regularly employed: *a jobbing gardener.*

Jobcentre ('dʒɒbˌsentə) *n Brit.* any of a number of government offices usually having premises situated in or near the main shopping area of a town in which people seeking jobs can consult displayed advertisements.

Jobclub ('dʒɒbˌklʌb) *n* a group of unemployed people organized through a Jobcentre, which meets every weekday and is given advice on job seeking to increase its members' chances of finding employment.

job description *n* a formal description of the duties and responsibilities involved in a job, esp. as given to applicants for the job.

job lot *n* **1** a miscellaneous collection of articles sold as a lot. **2** a collection of cheap or trivial items.

job satisfaction *n* the extent to which the desires and hopes of a worker are fulfilled as a result of his work.

Job's comforter *n* a person who, while purporting to give sympathy, succeeds only in adding to distress.

jobseeker's allowance ('dʒɒbˌsiːkəz) *n* (in Britain) a National Insurance or social security payment for unemployed people; replaced unemployment benefit in 1996. Abbrev.: **JSA.**

job sharing *n* the division of a job between two or more people such that each covers the same job for complementary parts of the day or week.
▸ **job share** *n*

jobsworth ('dʒɒbzˌwɜːθ) *n Inf.* a person in a position of minor authority who invokes the letter of the law in

---

★ people and places

order to avoid any action requiring initiative, cooperation, etc. [C20: from *it's more than my job's worth to...*]

Jocasta ★ (dʒəʊˈkæstə) *n Greek myth.* a queen of Thebes, the wife of Laius, who married Oedipus without either of them knowing he was her son.

Jochum ★ (*German* 'jɔxum) *n* **Eugen** ('ɔygeːn). 1902–87, German orchestral conductor.

jock (dʒɒk) *n Inf.* **1** short for **disc jockey. 2** short for **jockey. 3** short for **jockstrap.**

Jock (dʒɒk) *n* a slang word or term of address for a **Scot.**

jockey ('dʒɒkɪ) *n* **1** a person who rides horses in races, esp. as a profession. ◆ *vb* **2a** (*tr*) to ride (a horse) in a race. **2b** (*intr*) to ride as a jockey. **3** (*intr:* often foll. by *for*) to try to obtain an advantage by manoeuvring (esp. in **jockey for position**). **4** to trick or cheat (a person). [C16 (in the sense: lad): from name *Jock* + -EY]

jockstrap ('dʒɒk,stræp) *n* an elasticated belt with a pouch worn by men, esp. athletes, to support the genitals. Also called: **athletic support.** [C20: from sl. *jock* penis + STRAP]

jocose (dʒəˈkəʊs) *adj* characterized by humour. [C17: from L *jocōsus* given to jesting, from *jocus* joke]
▸ jo'cosely *adv* ▸ jocosity (dʒəˈkɒsɪtɪ) *n*

jocular ('dʒɒkjʊlə) *adj* **1** characterized by joking and good humour. **2** meant lightly or humorously. [C17: from L *joculāris*, from *joculus* little JOKE]
▸ jocularity (,dʒɒkjʊ'lærɪtɪ) *n* ▸ 'jocularly *adv*

jocund ('dʒɒkənd) *adj* of a humorous temperament; merry. [C14: from LL *jocundus*, from L *jūcundus* pleasant, from *juvāre* to please]
▸ jocundity (dʒəˈkʌndɪtɪ) *n* ▸ 'jocundly *adv*

Jodhpur ★ (,dʒɒd'pʊə) *n* **1** a former state of NW India, one of the W Rajputana states: now part of Rajasthan. **2** a walled city in NW India, in W Rajasthan: university (1962). Pop.: 666 279 (1991).
▸ Jodhpuri (,dʒɒd'pʊərɪ) *adj*

jodhpurs ('dʒɒdpəz) *pl n* riding breeches, loose-fitting around the thighs and tight-fitting from the knees to the ankles. [C19: from JODHPUR]

Jodl ★ (*German* 'joːdəl) *n* **Alfred** ('alfreːt). 1890–1946, German general, largely responsible for German strategy during World War II: executed as a war criminal.

Joe Blake (,dʒəʊ 'bleɪk) *n Austral. sl.* **1** a snake. **2 the Joe Blakes.** the DT's.

Joe Bloggs ('blɒgz) *n Brit. sl.* an average or typical man. US, Canad., and Austral. equivalent: **Joe Blow.** See also **Joe Six-Pack.**

Joel ★ ('dʒəʊəl) *n Old Testament.* **1** a Hebrew prophet. **2** the book containing his oracles.

Joe Public *n Sl.* the general public.

joes (dʒəʊz) *pl n* **the.** *Austral. inf.* a fit of depression. [short for *the Joe Blakes*]

Joe Six-Pack *n US sl.* an average or typical man.

joey ('dʒəʊɪ) *n Austral. inf.* **1** a young kangaroo. **2** a young animal or child. [C19: from Abor.]

Joffre ★ (*French* ʒɔfrə) *n* **Joseph Jacques Césaire** (ʒɔzef ʒak sezɛr). 1852–1931, French marshal. He commanded the French army (1914–16) and was largely responsible for the Allies' victory at the Marne (1914), which halted the German advance on Paris.

jog (dʒɒg) *vb* **jogs, jogging, jogged. 1** (*intr*) to run or move slowly or at a jog trot, esp. for physical exercise. **2** (*intr;* foll. by *on* or *along*) to continue in a plodding way. **3** (*tr*) to jar or nudge slightly. **4** (*tr*) to remind: *jog my memory.* ◆ *n* **5** the act of jogging. **6** a slight jar or nudge. **7** a jogging motion; trot. [C14: prob. var. of *shog* to shake]

jogger ('dʒɒgə) *n* **1** a person who runs at a jog trot over some distance for exercise. **2** *NZ.* a cart with rubber tyres used on farms.

jogger's nipple *n Inf.* painful inflammation of the nipple, caused by friction with a garment when running for long distances.

jogging ('dʒɒgɪŋ) *n* a slow run or trot, esp. as a keep-fit exercise.

joggle ('dʒɒg²l) *vb* **joggles, joggling, joggled. 1** to shake or move (someone or something) with a slightly jolting

motion. **2** (*tr*) to join or fasten (two pieces of building material) by means of a joggle. ◆ *n* **3** the act of joggling. **4** a slight irregular shake. **5** a joint between two pieces of building material by means of a projection on one piece that fits into a notch in the other. [C16: frequentative of JOG]
▸ 'joggler *n*

Jogjakarta ★ (,dʒɒgjɑː'kɑːtɑː, ,dʒɒg-) *n* a variant spelling of **Yogyakarta.**

jog trot *n* **1** an easy bouncy gait, esp. of a horse, midway between a walk and a trot. **2** a regular way of living or doing something.

Johannesburg ★ (dʒəʊ'hænɪs,bɜːg) *n* a city in NE South Africa, in Gauteng province: South Africa's largest city and chief industrial centre; grew with the establishment of the gold-mining industry in 1886; University of Witwatersrand (1922). Pop.: 1 712 507 (1991).

john (dʒɒn) *n Chiefly US & Canad.* a slang word for **lavatory.** [C20: special use of the name]

John ★ (dʒɒn) *n* **1** *New Testament.* **1a** the apostle John, the son of Zebedee, identified with the author of the fourth Gospel, three epistles, and the book of Revelation. Feast day: Sept. 26 or Dec. 27. **1b** the fourth Gospel. **1c** any of three epistles (in full **The First, Second,** and **Third Epistles of John**). **2** See **John the Baptist. 3** known as *John Lackland.* 1167–1216, king of England (1199–1216); son of Henry II. He succeeded to the throne on the death of his brother Richard I, having previously tried to usurp the throne. In 1215 he signed the Magna Carta. **4 Augustus** (**Edwin**). 1878–1961, British painter, esp. of portraits. **5 Barry.** born 1945, Welsh Rugby Union footballer: half-back for Wales (1966–72) and the British Lions (1968–71). **6** Sir **Elton** (**Hercules**). original name *Reginald Dwight.* born 1947, British singer, composer, and pianist.

John I ★ *n* called *the Great.* 1357–1433, king of Portugal (1385–1433). He secured independence for Portugal by his victory over Castile (1385) and initiated Portuguese overseas expansion.

John II ★ *n* called *the Good.* 1319–64, king of France (1350–64): captured by the English at Poitiers (1356) and forced to sign treaties (1360) surrendering SW France to England.

John III ★ *n* surnamed *Sobieski.* 1624–96, king of Poland (1674–96). He raised the Turkish siege of Vienna (1683).

John IV ★ *n* called *the Fortunate.* 1604–56, king of Portugal (1640–56). As duke of Braganza he led a revolt against Spanish rule and became king: lost most of Portugal's Asian possessions to the Dutch.

John XXII ★ *n* original name *Jacques Duèse.* ?1244–1334, pope (1316–34), residing at Avignon: involved in a long conflict with the Holy Roman Emperor Louis IV and opposed the Franciscan Spirituals.

John XXIII ★ *n* original name *Angelo Giuseppe Roncalli.* 1881–1963, pope (1958–63). He summoned the second Vatican Council (1962–65).

John Barleycorn *n Usually humorous.* the personification of alcoholic drink.

John Bull *n* **1** a personification of England or the English people. **2** a typical Englishman. [C18: name of a character intended to be representative of the English nation in *The History of John Bull* (1712) by John Arbuthnot]

John Chrysostom ★ ('krɪsəstəm) *n* **Saint.** ?345–407 A.D., Greek bishop and theologian; one of the Fathers of the Greek Church, noted for his eloquence. Feast day: Sept. 13.

John Doe *n* See **Doe.**

John Dory ('dɔːrɪ) *n* a European dory (the fish), having a deep compressed body and massive mobile jaws. [C18: from name *John* + DORY¹; on the model of DOE]

John Hop *n Austral. sl.* a policeman. [rhyming sl. for COP¹]

johnny ('dʒɒnɪ) *n, pl* **johnnies.** *Brit. inf.* (*often cap.*) a man or boy; chap.

Johnny Canuck ('dʒɒnɪ kə'nʌk) *n Canad.* **1** an informal name for a **Canadian. 2** a personification of Canada.

Johnny-come-lately *n, pl* **Johnny-come-latelies** *or*

Johnnies-come-lately. *Sl.* a brash newcomer, novice, or recruit.

John of Austria ★ *n* called *Don John*. 1547–78, Spanish general: defeated the Turks at Lepanto (1571).

John of Damascus ★ *n* Saint. ?675–749 A.D., Syrian theologian, who defended the veneration of icons and images against the iconoclasts. Feast day: Dec. 4.

John of Gaunt ★ (gɔːnt) *n* Duke of Lancaster. 1340–99, son of Edward III: virtual ruler of England during the last years of his father's reign and during Richard II's minority. [*Gaunt*, variant of GHENT, where he was born]

John of Leyden ★ ('laɪdᵊn) *n* original name *Jan Bockelson*. ?1509–36, Dutch Anabaptist leader. He established a theocracy in Münster (1534) but was tortured to death after the city was recaptured (1535) by its prince bishop.

John of Salisbury ★ *n* died 1180, English ecclesiastic and scholar; bishop of Chartres (1176–80). He supported Thomas à Becket against Henry II.

John of the Cross ★ *n* Saint. original name *Juan de Yepis y Alvarez*. 1542–91, Spanish Carmelite monk, poet, and mystic. He founded the Discalced Carmelites with Saint Teresa (1568). Feast day: Dec. 14.

John o'Groats ★ (ə'grəʊts) *n* a village at the northeasternmost tip of the Scottish mainland: considered to be the northernmost point of the mainland of Great Britain although Dunnet Head, slightly to the west, lies further north. See also **Land's End.**

John Paul I ★ *n* original name *Albino Luciani*. 1912–78, pope (1978); reigned only 33 days.

John Paul II ★ *n* original name *Karol Wojtyla*. born 1920, pope from 1978, born in Poland: the first non-Italian to be elected since 1522.

Johns ★ (dʒɒnz) *n* **Jasper.** born 1930, US artist, noted for his collages and constructions.

Johnson ★ ('dʒɒnsᵊn) *n* **1 Amy.** 1903–41, British flyer, whose record flights included those to Australia (1930) and to Cape Town and back (1936). **2 Andrew.** 1808–75, US Democrat statesman; 17th president of the US (1865–69): he was elected vice president under the Republican Abraham Lincoln and took office following Lincoln's assassination. **3 Jack.** 1878–1946, US boxer; world heavyweight champion (1908–15). **4 Lyndon Baines,** known as *LBJ*. 1908–73, US Democrat statesman; 36th president of the US (1963–69). He lost popularity by increasing US involvement in the Vietnam War. **5 Michael (Duane).** born 1967, US sprinter. **6 Robert.** ?1898–1937, US blues singer and guitarist. **7 Samuel,** known as *Dr Johnson*. 1709–84, British lexicographer and critic. His fame rests on his *Dictionary* (1755) and Boswell's biography of him.

Johnsonian (dʒɒn'səʊnɪən) *adj* of, relating to, or characteristic of Samuel Johnson, his works, or his style of writing.

John the Baptist ★ *n* Saint. *New Testament*. the son of Zacharias and Elizabeth and the cousin and forerunner of Jesus, whom he baptized. He was beheaded by Herod (Matthew 14:1–2). Feast day: June 24.

John Thomas *n Sl.* a euphemistic name for **penis.**

Johore ★ (dʒəʊ'hɔː) *n* a state of Malaysia, on the S Malay Peninsula: mostly forested, with large swamps; bauxite-and iron-mining. Capital: Johore Bahru. Pop.: 2 106 700 (1993 est.). Area: 18 984 sq. km (7330 sq. miles).

Johore Bahru ★ ('bɑːruː) *n* a city in S Malaysia, capital of Johore state: important trading centre, situated at the sole crossing point of **Johore Strait** (between Malaya and Singapore Island). Pop.: 328 646 (1991).

joie de vivre *French*. (ʒwa də vivrə) *n* joy of living; enjoyment of life; ebullience.

join (dʒɔɪn) *vb* **1** to come or bring together. **2** to become a member of (a club, etc.). **3** (*intr*; often foll. by *with*) to become associated or allied. **4** (*intr*; usually foll. by *in*) to take part. **5** (*tr*) to meet (someone) as a companion. **6** (*tr*) to become part of. **7** (*tr*) to unite (two people) in marriage. **8** (*tr*) *Geom.* to connect with a straight line or a curve. **9 join hands. 9a** to hold one's own hands together. **9b** (of two people) to hold each other's hands. **9c** (usu-

ally foll. by *with*) to work together in an enterprise. ◆ **10** a joint; seam. **11** the act of joining. ◆ See also **join up.** [C13: from OF, from L *jungere* to yoke]

joinder ('dʒɔɪndə) *n* **1** the act of joining, esp. in legal contexts. **2** *Law.* **2a** (in pleading) the stage at which the parties join issue (**joinder of issue**). **2b** the joining of two or more persons as coplaintiffs or codefendants (**joinder of parties**). [C17: from F *joindre* to JOIN]

joiner ('dʒɔɪnə) *n* **1** *Chiefly Brit.* a person skilled in making finished woodwork, such as windows and stairs. **2** a person or thing that joins. **3** *Inf.* a person who joins many clubs, etc.

joinery ('dʒɔɪnərɪ) *n* **1** the skill or craft of a joiner. **2** work made by a joiner.

joint (dʒɔɪnt) *n* **1** a junction of two or more parts or objects. **2** *Anat.* the junction between two or more bones. **3** the point of connection between movable parts in in vertebrates. **4** the part of a plant stem from which a branch or leaf grows. **5** one of the parts into which a carcass of meat is cut by the butcher, esp. for roasting. **6** *Geol.* a crack in a rock along which no displacement has occurred. **7** *Sl.* **7a** a bar or nightclub. **7b** *Often facetious.* a dwelling or meeting place. **8** *Sl.* a cannabis cigarette. **9 out of joint. 9a** dislocated. **9b** out of order. ◆ *adj* **10** shared by or belonging to two or more: *joint property*. **11** created by combined effort. **12** sharing with others or with one another: *joint rulers*. ◆ *vb* (*tr*) **13** to provide with or fasten by a joint or joints. **14** to plane the edge of (a board, etc. into the correct shape for a joint. **15** to cut or divide (meat, etc.) into joints.
▶ 'jointed *adj* ▶ 'jointly *adv*

joint account *n* a bank account registered in the name of two or more persons, any of whom may make deposits and withdrawals.

joint stock *n* capital funds held in common and usually divided into shares.

joint-stock company *n* **1** *Brit.* a business enterprise characterized by the sharing of ownership between shareholders, whose liability is limited. **2** *US.* a business enterprise whose owners are issued shares of transferable stock but do not enjoy limited liability.

jointure ('dʒɔɪntʃə) *n Law.* **a** a provision made by a husband for his wife by settling property upon her at marriage for her use after his death. **b** the property so settled. [C14: from OF, from L *junctūra* a joining]

join up *vb* (*adv*) **1** (*intr*) to become a member of a military or other organization; enlist. **2** (often foll. by *with*) to unite or connect.

Joinville ★ (*French* ʒwẽvil) *n* **Jean de** (ʒɑ̃ də). ?1224–1317, French chronicler, noted for his *Histoire de Saint Louis* (1309).

joist (dʒɔɪst) *n* a beam made of timber, steel, or reinforced concrete, used in the construction of floors, roofs, etc. [C14: from OF *giste* beam supporting a bridge, from Vulgar L *jacitum* (unattested) support, from *jacēre* to lie]

jojoba (həʊ'həʊbə) *n* a shrub or small tree of SW North America having edible seeds containing a valuable oil that is used in cosmetics.

joke (dʒəʊk) *n* **1** a humorous anecdote. **2** something that is said or done for fun. **3** a ridiculous or humorous circumstance. **4** a person or thing inspiring ridicule or amusement. **5 no joke.** something very serious. ◆ *vb* **6** (*intr*) to tell jokes. **7** (*intr*) to speak or act facetiously. **8** to make fun of (someone). **9 joking apart.** seriously: said after there has been joking in a discussion. [C17: from L *jocus* a jest]
▶ 'jokey *or* 'joky *adj* ▶ 'jokingly *adv*

joker ('dʒəʊkə) *n* **1** a person who jokes, esp. in an obnoxious manner. **2** *Sl., often derog.* a person: *who does that joke think he is?* **3** an extra playing card in a pack, which in many card games can rank above any other card.

Jokjakarta ★ (,dʒəʊkjə'kɑːtə, ,dʒɒk-) *n* a variant spelling of **Yogyakarta.**

Joliot-Curie ★ (*French* ʒɔljɔkyri) *n* **Jean-Frédéric** (ʒɑ̃ frederik), 1900–58, and his wife, **Irène** (irɛn), 1897–1956, French physicists: shared the Nobel prize for chemistry in 1935 for discovering artificial radioactivity.

★ people and places

jollify ('dʒɒlɪˌfaɪ) *vb* **jollifies, jollifying, jollified.** to be or cause to be jolly.
▸ **ˌjolliˈfication** *n*

jollity ('dʒɒlɪtɪ) *n, pl* **jollities.** the condition of being jolly.

jolly ('dʒɒlɪ) *adj* **jollier, jolliest. 1** full of good humour. **2** having or provoking gaiety and merrymaking. **3** pleasing. ◆ *adv* **4** *Brit.* (intensifier): *you're jolly nice.* ◆ *vb* **jollies, jollying, jollied.** (*tr*) *Inf.* **5** (often foll. by *up* or *along*) to try to make or keep (someone) cheerful. **6** to make goodnatured fun of. [C14: from OF *jolif*, prob. from ON *jōl* YULE]
▸ **ˈjolliness** *n*

jolly boat *n* a small boat used as a utility tender for a vessel. [C18 *jolly* prob. from Danish *jolle* YAWL]

Jolly Roger *n* the traditional pirate flag, consisting of a white skull and crossbones on a black field.

Jolo ★ (həʊˈləʊ) *n* an island in the SW Philippines: the main island of the Sulu Archipelago. Pop.: 360 588 (1980). Area: 893 sq. km (345 sq. miles).

Jolson ★ ('dʒəʊlsən) *n* **Al,** real name *Asa Yoelson.* 1886–1950, US singer and film actor, born in Russia; star of the first talking picture *The Jazz Singer* (1927).

jolt (dʒəʊlt) *vb* **1** (*tr*) to bump against with a jarring blow. **2** to move in a jolting manner. **3** (*tr*) to surprise or shock. ◆ *n* **4** a sudden jar or blow. **5** an emotional shock. [C16: prob. blend of dialect *jot* to jerk & dialect *joll* to bump]

Jon. *Bible. abbrev. for* Jonah.

Jonah ('dʒəʊnə) *or* **Jonas** ★ ('dʒəʊnəs) *n* **1** *Old Testament.* a Hebrew prophet who, having been thrown overboard from a ship was swallowed by a great fish and vomited onto dry land. **2** a person believed to bring bad luck to those around him.

Jonathan ★ *n Old Testament.* the son of Saul and David's close friend, who was killed in battle (I Samuel 31; II Samuel 1:19–26).

Jones (dʒəʊnz) *n* **1 Daniel.** 1881–1967, British phonetician. **2 Daniel.** 1912–93, Welsh composer. He wrote nine symphonies and much chamber music. **3 David.** 1895–1974, British artist and writer: his literary works include the novel *In Parenthesis* (1937) and the poem *The Anathemata* (1952). **4 Inigo** ('ɪnɪgəʊ). 1573–1652, English architect, who introduced Palladianism to England. **5 John Paul.** 1747–92, US naval commander in the War of Independence. **7 Robert Tyre,** known as *Bobby Jones.* 1902–71, US golfer.

Jongkind ★ (*Dutch* 'jɒŋkɪnt) *n* **Johann Barthold** (joːˈhɑn 'bɑrtɔlt). 1819–91, Dutch landscape painter and etcher.

jongleur (*French* ʒɔ̃glœr) *n* (in medieval France) an itinerant minstrel. [C18: from OF *jogleour*, from L *joculātor* jester]

Jönköping ★ (*Swedish* 'jœntʃøˌpiŋ) *n* a city in S Sweden, on the S shore of Lake Vättern: scene of the conclusion of peace between Sweden and Denmark in 1809. Pop.: 115 429 (1996 est.).

jonquil ('dʒɒŋkwɪl) *n* a Eurasian variety of narcissus with long fragrant yellow or white short-tubed flowers. [C17: from F *jonquille*, from Sp. *junquillo*, dim. of *junco* reed]

Jonson ★ ('dʒɒnsən) *n* **Ben.** 1572–1637, English dramatist and poet. His plays include *Volpone* (1606) and *Bartholomew Fair* (1614); he also wrote court masques.

Joplin ★ ('dʒɒplɪn) *n* **1 Janis.** 1943–70, US rock singer. **2 Scott.** 1868–1917, US pianist and composer: creator of ragtime.

Joppa ★ ('dʒɒpə) *n* the biblical name of **Jaffa,** the port from which Jonah embarked (Jonah 1:3).

Jordaens ★ (*Flemish* jɔrˈdɑːns) *n* **Jacob** ('jaːkɔp). 1593–1678, Flemish painter.

Jordan[1] ★ ('dʒɔːd²n) *n* **1** a kingdom in SW Asia: coextensive with the biblical Moab, Gilead, and Edom; made a League of Nations mandate and emirate under British control in 1922 and became an independent kingdom in 1946; territories west of the River Jordan and the Jordanian part of Jerusalem were occupied by Israel after the war of 1967. It contains part of the Great Rift Valley and consists mostly of desert. Official language: Arabic. Official religion: (Sunni) Muslim. Currency: dinar. Capital: Amman. Pop.: 4 522 000 (1997). Area: 89 185 sq. km (34 434 sq. miles). Official name: **Hashemite Kingdom of Jordan.** Former name (1922–49): **Trans-Jordan. 2** the chief and only perennial river of Israel and Jordan, rising in several headstreams in Syria and Lebanon, and flowing south through the Sea of Galilee to the Dead Sea: occupies the N end of the Great Rift Valley system and lies mostly below sea level. Length: over 320 km (200 miles).
▸ **Jordanian** (dʒɔːˈdeɪnɪən) *adj, n*

Jordan[2] ★ ('dʒɔːd²n) *n* **Michael Jeffrey.** born 1963, US basketball and baseball player.

jorum ('dʒɔːrəm) *n* a large drinking bowl or vessel or its contents. [C18: prob. after *Jorum,* who brought vessels of silver, gold, and brass to King David (II Samuel 8:10)]

Jos ★ (dʒɒs) *n* a city in central Nigeria, capital of Plateau state on the **Jos Plateau:** major centre of the tin-mining industry. Pop.: 201 200 (1995 est.).

Joseph ★ ('dʒəʊzɪf) *n* **1** *Old Testament.* **1a** the eleventh son of Jacob and one of the 12 patriarchs of Israel (Genesis 30:2–24). **1b** either or both of two tribes descended from his sons Ephraim and Manasseh. **2 Saint.** *New Testament.* the husband of Mary the mother of Jesus (Matthew 1:16–25). Feast day: Mar. 19.

Joseph II ★ *n* 1741–90, Holy Roman emperor (1765–90); son of Francis I. He ruled Austria jointly with his mother, Maria Theresa, until her death (1780). He abolished serfdom and asserted his independence from the pope.

Joseph Bonaparte Gulf ★ *n* an inlet of the Timor Sea in N Australia. Width: 360 km (225 miles).

Joséphine ★ ('dʒəʊzəˌfiːn) *n* **Empress,** previous name *Joséphine de Beauharnais;* real name *Marie Joséphine Tascher de la Pagerie.* 1763–1814, empress of France as wife (1796–1809) of Napoleon Bonaparte.

Joseph of Arimathea ★ (ˌærɪməˈθiːə) *n Saint. New Testament.* a wealthy member of the Sanhedrin, who obtained the body of Jesus after the Crucifixion and laid it in his own tomb (Matthew 27:57–60). Feast day: Mar. 17 or July 31.

Josephus ★ (dʒəʊˈsiːfəs) *n* **Flavius** ('fleɪvɪəs). real name *Joseph ben Matthias.* ?37–?100 A.D., Jewish historian and general; author of *Antiquities of the Jews.*

josh (dʒɒʃ) *Sl., chiefly US & Canad.* ◆ *vb* **1** to tease (someone) in a bantering way. ◆ *n* **2** a teasing joke. [C19: ?from JOKE, infl. by BOSH]
▸ **ˈjosher** *n*

Josh. *Bible. abbrev. for* Joshua.

Joshua ★ ('dʒɒʃjʊə) *n Old Testament.* **1** Moses' successor, who led the Israelites in the conquest of Canaan. **2** the book recounting his deeds. Douay spelling: **Josue** ('dʒɒsjuː).

Josiah ★ (dʒəʊˈsaɪə) *n* died ?609 B.C., king of Judah (?640–?609). After the discovery of a book of law (probably Deuteronomy) in the Temple he began a programme of religious reform. Douay spelling: **Josias** (dʒəʊˈsaɪəs).

Josquin des Prés ★ (*French* ʒɔskɛ̃ de pre) *n* See **des Prés.**

joss (dʒɒs) *n* a Chinese deity worshipped in the form of an idol. [C18: from pidgin E, from Port. *deos* god, from L *deus*]

joss house *n* a Chinese temple or shrine where an idol or idols are worshipped.

joss stick *n* a stick of dried perfumed paste, giving off a fragrant odour when burnt as incense.

jostle ('dʒɒs²l) *vb* **jostles, jostling, jostled. 1** to bump or push (someone) roughly. **2** to come or bring into contact. **3** to force (one's way) by pushing. ◆ *n* **4** the act of jostling. **5** a rough bump or push. [C14: see JOUST]

jot (dʒɒt) *vb* **jots, jotting, jotted. 1** (*tr;* usually foll. by *down*) to write a brief note of. ◆ *n* **2** (*used with a negative*) a little bit (in **not care** (*or* **give**) **a jot**). [C16: from L *jota,* from Gk *iōta,* of Semitic origin]

jota (*Spanish* 'xɒtə) *n* a Spanish dance in fast triple time. [Sp., prob. from OSp. *sota,* from *sotar* to dance, from L *saltāre*]

jotter ('dʒɒtə) *n* a small notebook.

jotting ('dʒɒtɪŋ) *n* something jotted down.

Jotun or **Jotunn** ★ ('jɔːtʊn) n Norse myth. any of a race of giants. [from ON jötunn giant; related to EAT]

Jotunheim or **Jotunnheim** ★ ('jɔːtʊn,heɪm) n Norse myth. the home of the giants in the northeast of Asgard. [from ON, from jötunn giant + heimr world, HOME]

joual (ʒwaːl) n nonstandard Canadian French dialect, esp. as associated with ill-educated speakers. [from the pronunciation in this dialect of F cheval horse]

joule (dʒuːl) n the derived SI unit of work or energy; the work done when the point of application of a force of 1 newton is displaced through a distance of 1 metre in the direction of the force. Symbol: J [C19: after J. P. JOULE]

Joule ★ (dʒuːl) n James Prescott. 1818–89, British physicist, who contributed to the study of heat and electricity.

jounce (dʒaʊns) vb **jounces, jouncing, jounced. 1** to shake or jolt or cause to shake or jolt. ◆ n **2** a shake; bump. [C15: prob. from dialect joll to bump + BOUNCE]

journal ('dʒɜːnᵊl) n **1** a newspaper or periodical. **2** a book in which a daily record of happenings, etc., is kept. **3** an official record of the proceedings of a legislative body. **4** Book-keeping. one of several books in which transactions are initially recorded to facilitate subsequent entry in the ledger. **5** Machinery. the part of a shaft or axle in contact with or enclosed by a bearing. [C14: from OF: daily, from L diurnālis; see DIURNAL]

journal box n Machinery. a case enclosing or supporting a journal.

journalese (,dʒɜːnᵊl'iːz) n Derog. a superficial style of writing regarded as typical of newspapers, etc.

journalism ('dʒɜːnᵊl,ɪzəm) n **1** the profession or practice of reporting about, photographing, or editing news stories for one of the mass media. **2** newspapers and magazines collectively.

journalist ('dʒɜːnᵊlɪst) n **1** a person whose occupation is journalism. **2** a person who keeps a journal.
▸ ,journa'listic adj ▸ ,journa'listically adv

journalize or **journalise** ('dʒɜːnᵊl,aɪz) vb **journalizes, journalizing, journalized** or **journalises, journalising, journalised.** to record (daily events) in a journal.
▸ ,journali'zation or ,journali'sation n

journey ('dʒɜːnɪ) n **1** a travelling from one place to another. **2a** the distance travelled in a journey. **2b** the time taken to make a journey. ◆ vb **3** (intr) to make a journey. [C13: from OF journee a day, a day's travelling, from L diurnum day's portion]
▸ 'journeyer n

journeyman ('dʒɜːnɪmən) n, pl **journeymen. 1** a craftsman, artisan, etc., who is qualified to work at his trade in the employment of another. **2** a competent workman. [C15: from JOURNEY (in obs. sense: a day's work) + MAN]

joust (dʒaʊst) History. ◆ n **1** a combat between two mounted knights tilting against each other with lances. ◆ vb **2** (intr; often foll. by against or with) to encounter or engage in such a tournament: he jousted with five opponents. [C13: from OF, from jouster to fight on horseback, from Vulgar L juxtāre (unattested) to come together, from L juxtā close]
▸ 'jouster n

Jove ★ (dʒəʊv) n **1** another name for **Jupiter**[1]. **2 by Jove.** an exclamation of surprise or excitement. [C14: from OL Jovis Jupiter]
▸ 'Jovian n

jovial ('dʒəʊvɪəl) adj having or expressing convivial humour. [C16: from L joviālis of (the planet) Jupiter, considered by astrologers to foster good humour]
▸ joviality (,dʒəʊvɪ'ælɪtɪ) n ▸ 'jovially adv

Jovian ★ ('dʒəʊvɪən) n full name Flavius Claudius Jovianus. ?331–364 A.D., Roman emperor (363–64): he made peace with Persia, relinquishing Roman provinces beyond the Tigris, and restored privileges to the Christians.

Jowett ★ ('dʒaʊɪt) n Benjamin. 1817–93, British classical scholar and educator: translated the works of Plato.

jowl[1] (dʒaʊl) n **1** the jaw, esp. the lower one. **2** (often pl) a cheek. **3 cheek by jowl.** See **cheek**. [OE ceafl jaw]
▸ jowled adj

jowl[2] (dʒaʊl) n **1** fatty flesh hanging from the lower jaw. **2** a similar fleshy part in animals, such as the dewlap of a bull. [OE ceole throat]

joy (dʒɔɪ) n **1** a deep feeling or condition of happiness or contentment. **2** something causing such a feeling. **3** an outward show of pleasure or delight. **4** Brit. inf. success; satisfaction: I went for a loan, but got no joy. ◆ vb Chiefly poetic. **5** (intr) to feel joy. **6** (tr) to gladden. [C13: from OF, from L gaudium joy, from gaudēre to be glad]

Joyce ★ (dʒɔɪs) n **1 James (Augustine Aloysius).** 1882–1941, Irish writer. He influenced the development of the novel, esp. by his stream of consciousness technique and coined words. His works include the novels Ulysses (1922) and Finnegans Wake (1939) and the short stories Dubliners (1914). **2 William,** known as Lord Haw-Haw 1906–46, British broadcaster of Nazi propaganda to Britain; executed for treason.

Joycean ('dʒɔɪsɪən) adj **1** of, relating to, or like, James Joyce or his works. ◆ n **2** a student or admirer of Joyce or his works.

joyful ('dʒɔɪfʊl) adj **1** full of joy; elated. **2** expressing or producing joy: a joyful look; a joyful occasion.
▸ 'joyfully adv ▸ 'joyfulness n

joyless ('dʒɔɪlɪs) adj having or producing no joy or pleasure.
▸ 'joylessly adv ▸ 'joylessness n

joyous ('dʒɔɪəs) adj **1** having a happy nature or mood. **2** joyful.
▸ 'joyously adv

joyride ('dʒɔɪ,raɪd) n **1** a ride taken for pleasure in a car, esp. in a stolen car driven recklessly. ◆ vb **joy-ride, joy-rides, joy-riding, joy-rode, joy-ridden. 2** (intr) to take such a ride.
▸ 'joy,rider n ▸ 'joyriding n

joystick ('dʒɔɪ,stɪk) n **1** Inf. the control stick of an aircraft, machine, etc. **2** Computing. a lever for controlling the movement of a cursor on a screen.

JP abbrev. for Justice of the Peace.

J/psi particle n a type of elementary particle thought to be formed from charmed quarks.

Jr or **jr** abbrev. for junior.

JSA (in Britain) abbrev. for jobseeker's allowance.

Juan Carlos ★ (Spanish xwan 'karlɔs) n born 1938, king of Spain from 1975. He was nominated by Franco as the first king of the restored monarchy to follow Franco's death.

Juan de Fuca ★ ('dʒuːən dɪ 'fjuːkə; Spanish xwan de 'fuka) n **Strait of.** a strait between Vancouver Island (Canada) and NW Washington (US). Length: about 129 km (80 miles). Width: about 24 km (15 miles).

Juan Fernández Islands ★ ('dʒuːən fə'nændɛz; Spanish xwan fer'nandeθ) pl n a group of three islands in the S Pacific Ocean, administered by Chile: volcanic and wooded. Area: about 180 sq. km (70 sq. miles).

Juantorena ★ (Spanish xwanto'rena) n **Alberto** (al'βɛrto) born 1951, Cuban runner: won the 400 metres and the 800 metres in the 1976 Olympic Games.

Juárez[1] ★ (Spanish 'xwareθ) n short for **Ciudad Juárez.**

Juárez[2] ★ (Spanish 'xwareθ) n **Benito Pablo** (be'nito 'paβlo). 1806–72, Mexican statesman. As president (1861–65; 1867–72) he thwarted Napoleon III's attempt to impose an empire under Maximilian.

Juba ★ ('dʒuːbə) n a river in NE Africa, rising in S central Ethiopia and flowing south across Somalia to the Indian Ocean: the chief river of Somalia. Length: about 1660 km (1030 miles).

Jubal ★ ('dʒuːbᵊl) n Old Testament. the alleged inventor of musical instruments (Genesis 4:21).

jubbah ('dʒʊbə) n a long loose outer garment with wide sleeves, worn by Muslim men and women, esp. in India [C16: from Ar.]

Jubbulpore ★ (,dʒʌbᵊl'pʊə) n a variant spelling of Jabalpur.

jube (dʒuːb) n Austral. & NZ inf. any jelly-like sweet [C20: shortened from JUJUBE]

jubilant ('dʒuːbɪlənt) adj feeling or expressing great joy

[C17: from L, from *jūbilāre* to give a joyful cry, from *jūbilum* a shout]
▶ **'jubilance** *n* ▶ **'jubilantly** *adv*

jubilate ('dʒu:bɪ,leɪt) *vb* jubilates, jubilating, jubilated. (*intr*)
1 to have or express great joy; rejoice. **2** to celebrate a jubilee. [C17: from L *jūbilāre*; see JUBILANT]

jubilation (,dʒu:bɪ'leɪʃən) *n* a feeling of great joy and celebration.

jubilee ('dʒu:bɪ,li:) *n* **1** a time or season for rejoicing. **2** a special anniversary, esp. a 25th or 50th one. **3** *RC Church.* a specially appointed period in which special indulgences are granted. **4** *Old Testament.* a year that was to be observed every 50th year, during which Hebrew slaves were to be liberated, etc. **5** a less common word for **jubilation.** [C14: from OF *jubile*, from LL *jubilaeus*, from LGk, from Heb. *yōbhēl* ram's horn, used for the proclamation of the year of jubilee]

Jud. *Bible. abbrev. for:* **1** Also: **Judg.** Judges. **2** Judith.

Judaea *or* **Judea** ★ (dʒu:'dɪə) *n* the S division of ancient Palestine, succeeding the kingdom of Judah: a Roman province during the time of Christ.
▶ **Ju'daean** *or* **Ju'dean** *adj, n*

Judah ★ ('dʒu:də) *n Old Testament.* **1** the fourth son of Jacob, one of whose descendants was to be the Messiah (Genesis 29:35; 49:8–12). **2** the tribe descended from him. **3** the tribal territory of his descendants which became the nucleus of David's kingdom and, after the kingdom had been divided into Israel and Judah, the southern kingdom of Judah, with Jerusalem as its centre. Douay spelling: **Juda.**

Judah ha-Levi ★ (hɑ:'li:vaɪ) *n* ?1075–1141, Jewish poet and philosopher, born in Spain; his works include the *Sefer ha-Kuzari.*

Judah ha-Nasi ★ (hɑ:nɑ:'si:) *n* ?135–?220 A.D., rabbi and patriarch of the Sanhedrin, who compiled the Mishnah.

Judaic (dʒu:'deɪɪk) *adj* of or relating to the Jews or Judaism.
▶ **Ju'daically** *adv*

Judaism ('dʒu:deɪ,ɪzəm) *n* **1** the religion of the Jews, based on the Old Testament and the Talmud and having as its central point a belief in one God. **2** the religious and cultural traditions of the Jews.
▶ **,Juda'istic** *adj*

Judaize *or* **Judaise** ('dʒu:deɪ,aɪz) *vb* Judaizes, Judaizing, Judaized *or* Judaises, Judaising, Judaised. **1** to conform or bring into conformity with Judaism. **2** (*tr*) to convert to Judaism.
▶ **,Judai'zation** *or* **,Judai'sation** *n*

Judas ★ ('dʒu:dəs) *n New Testament.* the apostle who betrayed Jesus to his enemies for 30 pieces of silver (Luke 22:3–6, 47–48). Full name: **Judas Iscariot. 2** a person who betrays a friend; traitor. **3** a brother or relative of James and also of Jesus (Matthew 13:55).

Judas Maccabaeus ★ (,mækə'bi:əs) *n* Jewish leader, whose revolt (166–161 B.C.) against the Seleucid kingdom of Antiochus IV (Epiphanes) enabled him to recapture Jerusalem and rededicate the Temple.

Judas tree *n* small Eurasian leguminous tree with pinkish-purple flowers that bloom before the leaves appear.

judder ('dʒʌdə) *Inf., chiefly Brit.* ♦ *vb* **1** (*intr*) to shake or vibrate. ♦ *n* **2** abnormal vibration in a mechanical system. **3** a juddering motion. [prob. blend of JAR² + SHUDDER]

Jude ★ (dʒu:d) *n* **1** a book of the New Testament (in full **The Epistle of Jude). 2** *Saint.* Also called: **Judas.** the author of this, stated to be the brother of James (Jude 1) and almost certainly identical with Thaddaeus (Matthew 10:2–4). Feast day: June 19 or Oct. 28.

Judea ★ (dʒu:'dɪə) *n* a variant spelling of **Judaea.**

judge (dʒʌdʒ) *n* **1** a public official with authority to hear cases in a court of law and pronounce judgment upon them. **2** a person who is appointed to determine the result of contests or competitions. **3** a person qualified to comment critically: *a good judge of antiques.* **4** a leader of the peoples of Israel from Joshua's death to the accession of Saul. ♦ *vb* judges, judging, judged. **5** to hear and decide upon (a case at law). **6** (*tr*) to pass judgment on. **7**

(when *tr, may take a clause as object or an infinitive*) to decide (something) after inquiry. **8** to determine the result of (a contest or competition). **9** to appraise (something) critically. **10** (*tr; takes a clause as object*) to believe something to be the case. [C14: from OF, from L *jūdicāre* to pass judgment, from *jūdex* a judge]
▶ **'judge,like** *adj* ▶ **'judger** *n* ▶ **'judgeship** *n*

judge advocate *n, pl* judge advocates. an officer who superintends proceedings at a military court martial.

judges' rules *pl n* (in English law) a set of rules, not legally binding, governing the behaviour of police towards suspects.

judgment *or* **judgement** ('dʒʌdʒmənt) *n* **1** the faculty of being able to make critical distinctions and achieve a balanced viewpoint. **2a** the verdict pronounced by a court of law. **2b** an obligation arising as a result of such a verdict, such as a debt. **2c** (*as modifier*): *a judgment debtor.* **3** the formal decision of one or more judges at a contest or competition. **4** a particular decision formed in a case in dispute or doubt. **5** an estimation: *a good judgment of distance.* **6** criticism or censure. **7** against one's better judgment. contrary to a preferred course of action. **8** in someone's judgment. in someone's opinion. **9** sit in judgment. **9a** to preside as judge. **9b** to assume the position of critic.

Judgment ('dʒʌdʒmənt) *n* **1** the estimate by God of the ultimate worthiness or unworthiness of the individual or of all mankind. **2** God's subsequent decision determining the final destinies of all individuals.

judgmental *or* **judgemental** (dʒʌdʒ'mentʰl) *adj* of or denoting an attitude in which judgments about other people's conduct are made.

Judgment Day *n* the occasion of the Last Judgment by God at the end of the world. Also called: **Day of Judgment.** See **Last Judgment.**

judicatory ('dʒu:dɪkətərɪ) *adj* **1** of or relating to the administration of justice. ♦ *n* **2** a court of law. **3** the administration of justice.

judicature ('dʒu:dɪkətʃə) *n* **1** the administration of justice. **2** the office, function, or power of a judge. **3** the extent of authority of a judge. **4** a body of judges; judiciary. **5** a court of justice or such courts collectively.

judicial (dʒu:'dɪʃəl) *adj* **1** of or relating to the administration of justice. **2** of or relating to judgment in a court of law or to a judge exercising this function. **3** allowed or enforced by a court of law: *judicial separation.* **4** having qualities appropriate to a judge. **5** giving or seeking judgment. [C14: from L *jūdiciālis* belonging to the law courts, from *jūdicium* judgment, from *jūdex* a judge]
▶ **ju'dicially** *adv*

judiciary (dʒu:'dɪʃɪərɪ) *adj* **1** of or relating to courts of law, judgment, or judges. ♦ *n, pl* judiciaries. **2** the branch of the central authority in a state concerned with the administration of justice. **3** the system of courts in a country. **4** the judges collectively.

judicious (dʒu:'dɪʃəs) *adj* having or proceeding from good judgment.
▶ **ju'diciously** *adv* ▶ **ju'diciousness** *n*

Judith ★ ('dʒu:dɪθ) *n* **1** the heroine of one of the books of the Apocrypha, who saved her native town by decapitating Holofernes. **2** the book recounting this episode.

judo ('dʒu:dəʊ) *n* **a** the modern sport derived from jujitsu, in which the object is to force an opponent to submit using the minimum of physical effort. **b** (*as modifier*): *a judo throw.* [Japanese, from *jū* gentleness + *dō* way]
▶ **'judoist** *n*

Judy ('dʒu:dɪ) *n, pl* Judies. **1** the wife of Punch in the children's puppet show *Punch and Judy.* See **Punch. 2** (*often not cap.*) *Brit. sl.* a girl.

jug (dʒʌg) *n* **1** a vessel for holding or pouring liquids, usually having a handle and a lip. US equivalent: **pitcher. 2** *Austral. & NZ.* a container in which water is boiled, esp. an electric kettle. **3** *US.* a large vessel with a narrow mouth. **4** Also called: **jugful.** the amount of liquid held by a jug. **5** *Brit. inf.* a glass of beer. **6** *Sl.* jail. ♦ *vb* jugs, jugging, jugged. **7** to stew or boil (meat, esp. hare) in an earthenware container. **8** (*tr*) *Sl.* to put in jail. [C16: prob. from *Jug,* nickname from name *Joan*]

jugate ('dʒu:geɪt, -gɪt) *adj* (esp. of compound leaves) having parts arranged in pairs. [C19: from NL *jugātus* (unattested), from L *jugum* a yoke]

juggernaut (ˈdʒʌgəˌnɔːt) *n* **1** any terrible force, esp. one that demands complete self-sacrifice. **2** *Brit.* a very large heavy lorry. [C17: from Hindi, from Sansk. *Jagannātha* lord of the world: devotees supposedly threw themselves under a cart carrying *Juggernaut*, an idol of Krishna]

juggins (ˈdʒʌgɪnz) *n* (*functioning as sing*) *Brit. inf.* a silly person. [C19: special use of the surname *Juggins*]

juggle (ˈdʒʌgəl) *vb* **juggles, juggling, juggled. 1** to throw and catch (several objects) continuously so that most are in the air all the time. **2** to manipulate (facts, etc.) so as to give a false picture. **3** (*tr*) to keep (several activities) in progress, esp. with difficulty. ◆ *n* **4** an act of juggling. [C14: from OF *jogler* to perform as a jester, from L, from *jocus* a jest]
▸ ˈjuggler *n*

Jugoslavia ★ (ˌjuːgəʊˈslɑːvɪə) *n* a variant spelling of **Yugoslavia.**
▸ ˈJugoˌslav *or* ˌJugoˈslavian *adj, n*

jugular (ˈdʒʌgjʊlə) *adj* **1** of, relating to, or situated near the throat or neck. ◆ *n* **2** Also called: **jugular vein.** any of the large veins in the neck carrying blood to the heart from the head. [C16: from LL, from L *jugulum* throat]

Jugurtha ★ (dʒuːˈgɜːθə) *n* died 104 B.C., king of Numidia (?112–104), who waged war against the Romans (the **Jugurthine War,** 112–105) and was defeated and executed.

juice (dʒuːs) *n* **1** any liquid that occurs naturally in or is secreted by plant or animal tissue: *the juice of an orange.* **2** *Inf.* **2a** petrol. **2b** electricity. **2c** alcoholic drink. **3** vigour or vitality. [C13: from OF *jus*, from L]
▸ ˈjuiceless *adj*

juice up *vb* (*tr, adv*) *US sl.* to make lively: *to juice up a party.*

juicy (ˈdʒuːsɪ) *adj* **juicier, juiciest. 1** full of juice. **2** provocatively interesting; spicy: *juicy gossip.* **3** profitable: *a juicy contract.*
▸ ˈjuicily *adv* ▸ ˈjuiciness *n*

Juiz de Fora ★ (Portuguese ʒuˈiʃ di ˈfɔrə) *n* a city in SE Brazil, in Minas Gerais state on the Rio de Janeiro–Belo Horizonte railway: textiles. Pop.: 377 538 (1991).

jujitsu, jujutsu, *or* **jiujutsu** (dʒuːˈdʒɪtsuː) *n* the traditional Japanese system of unarmed self-defence perfected by the samurai. See also **judo.** [C19: from Japanese, from *jū* gentleness + *jutsu* art]

juju (ˈdʒuːdʒuː) *n* **1** an object superstitiously revered by certain West African peoples and used as a charm or fetish. **2** the power associated with a juju. [C19: prob. from Hausa *djudju* evil spirit, fetish]

jujube (ˈdʒuːdʒuːb) *n* **1** any of several Old World spiny trees that have small yellowish flowers and dark red edible fruits. **2** the fruit of any of these trees. **3** a chewy sweet made of flavoured gelatine and sometimes medicated to soothe sore throats. [C14: from Med. L *jujuba*, modification of L *zīzyphum*, from Gk *zizuphon*]

jukebox (ˈdʒuːkˌbɒks) *n* a coin-operated machine, usually found in pubs, clubs, etc., that contains records, CDs, or videos, which are played when selected by a customer. [C20: from Gullah (an African-American language) *juke* bawdy (as in *juke house* brothel) + BOX¹]

jukskei (ˈjukˌskeɪ) *n* a South African game in which a peg is thrown over a fixed distance at a stake driven into the ground. [from Afrik. *juk* yoke + *skei* pin]

julep (ˈdʒuːlɪp) *n* **1** a sweet drink, variously prepared and sometimes medicated. **2** *Chiefly US.* short for **mint julep.** [C14: from OF, from Ar. *julāb*, from Persian, from *gul* rose + *āb* water]

Julian ★ (ˈdʒuːlɪən, -lɪən) *n* known as *Julian the Apostate*; Latin name *Flavius Claudius Julianus.* 331–363 A.D., Roman emperor (361–363), who attempted to revive paganism while remaining tolerant to Christians and Jews.

Juliana ★ (ˌdʒuːlɪˈɑːnə; *Dutch* jyːliːˈaːnaː) *n* full name *Juliana Louise Emma Marie Wilhelmina.* born 1909, queen of the Netherlands (1948–80). She abdicated in favour of her eldest daughter Beatrix.

Julian Alps ★ *pl n* a mountain range in Slovenia: an E range of the Alps.

Julian calendar *n* the calendar introduced by Julius Caesar in 46 B.C., in which leap years occurred every fourth year and in every centenary year. Cf. **Gregorian calendar.**

Julian of Norwich ★ *n* ?1342–?1413, English mystic and anchoress: best known for the *Revelations of Divine Love* describing her visions.

julienne (ˌdʒuːlɪˈen) *adj* **1** (of vegetables) cut into thin shreds. ◆ *n* **2** a clear consommé to which such vegetables have been added. [F, from name *Jules, Julien,* or *Julienne*]

Julius II ★ (ˈdʒuːlɪəs, -lɪəs) *n* original name *Guiliano della Rovere.* 1443–1513, pope (1503–13). He completed the restoration of the Papal States to the Church, began the building of St Peter's, Rome (1506), and patronized Michelangelo and Raphael.

Julius Caesar ★ *n* See **Caesar.**

Jullundur ★ (ˈdʒʌləndə) *n* the former name of **Jalandhar.**

July (dʒuːˈlaɪ) *n, pl* **Julies.** the seventh month of the year, consisting of 31 days. [C13: from Anglo-F *julie*, from L *Jūlius*, after Gaius *Julius* CAESAR, in whose honour it was named]

jumble (ˈdʒʌmbəl) *vb* **jumbles, jumbling, jumbled. 1** to mingle (objects, etc.) in a state of disorder. **2** (*tr; usually passive*) to remember in a confused form. ◆ *n* **3** a disordered mass, state, etc. **4** *Brit.* articles donated for a jumble sale. [C16: from ?]
▸ ˈjumbly *adj*

jumble sale *n* a sale of miscellaneous articles, usually second-hand, in aid of charity. US and Canad. equivalent: **rummage sale.**

jumbo (ˈdʒʌmbəʊ) *n, pl* **jumbos. 1** *Inf.* **1a** a very large person or thing. **1b** (*as modifier*): *a jumbo box of detergent.* **2** See **jumbo jet.** [C19: after a famous elephant exhibited by P. T. Barnum, from Swahili *jumbe* chief]

jumbo jet *n Inf.* a type of large jet-propelled airliner that carries several hundred passengers.

jumbo pack *n* **1** the promotion of bulk sales of small unit items, such as confectionery, by packing several in one wrapping, usually with a unit price reduction. **2** such a package of items.

jumbuck (ˈdʒʌmˌbʌk) *n Austral.* an informal word for **sheep.** [C19: from Abor.]

Jumna ★ (ˈdʒʌmnə) *n* a river in N India, rising in Uttar Pradesh in the Himalayas and flowing south and southeast to join the Ganges just below Allahabad (a confluence held sacred by Hindus). Length: 1385 km (860 miles).

jump (dʒʌmp) *vb* **1** (*intr*) to leap or spring clear of the ground or other surface by using the muscles in the legs and feet. **2** (*tr*) to leap over or clear (an obstacle): *to jump a gap.* **3** (*tr*) to cause to leap over an obstacle: *to jump a horse over a hedge.* **4** (*intr*) to move or proceed hastily (into, onto, out of, etc.): *she jumped into a taxi.* **5** (*tr*) *Inf.* to board so as to travel illegally on: *he jumped the train as it was leaving.* **6** (*intr*) to parachute from an aircraft. **7** (*intr*) to jerk or start, as with astonishment, surprise, etc. **8** to rise or cause to rise suddenly or abruptly. **9** to pass or skip over (intervening objects or matter): *she jumped a few lines and then continued reading.* **10** (*intr*) to change from one thing to another, esp. from one subject to another. **11** *Draughts.* to capture (an opponent's piece) by moving one of one's own pieces over it to an unoccupied square. **12** (*intr*) *Bridge.* to bid in response to one's partner at a higher level than is necessary, to indicate a strong hand. **13** (*tr*) to come off (a track, etc.): *the locomotive jumped the rails.* **14** (*intr*) (of the stylus of a record player) to be jerked out of the groove. **15** (*intr*) *Sl.* to be lively: *the party was jumping.* **16** (*tr*) *Inf.* to attack without warning: *thieves jumped the old man.* **17** (*tr*) *Inf.* (of a driver or a motor vehicle) to pass through (a red traffic light) or move away from (traffic lights) before they change to green. **18 jump down someone's throat.** *Inf.* to address or reply to someone sharply. **19 jump ship.** to desert, esp. to leave a ship in which one is legally bound to serve. **20 jump the queue.** *Inf.* to obtain some advantage out of turn or unfairly. **21 jump to it.** *Inf.* to begin something quickly and efficiently. ◆ *n* **22** an act or instance of jumping. **23** a space, distance, or obstacle to be jumped or that has been jumped. **24** a descent by parachute from an aircraft. **25** *Sport.* any of several contests involving a jump: *the high jump.* **26** a sudden rise: *the jump in prices last month.* **27** a sudden or abrupt transition. **28** a sudden jerk or involuntary muscular spasm, esp. as a reaction of surprise. **29** a step or degree: *one jump ahead.* **30** *Draughts.* a move that captures an opponent's piece by jumping over it. **31** *Films.* **31a** a break in continuity in the normal sequence of shots. **31b** (*as modifier*): *a jump cut.* **32 on the jump.** *Inf.,* chiefly US & Canad. **32a** in a hurry. **32b** busy. **33 take a running jump.** *Brit. inf.* a contemptuous expression of dismissal. ◆ See also **jump at, jump-off,** etc. [C16: prob. imit.]

jump at *vb* (*intr, prep*) to be glad to accept: *I would jump at the chance of going.*

jumped-up *adj Inf.* suddenly risen in significance, esp. when appearing arrogant.

jumper[1] ('dʒʌmpə) *n* **1** *Chiefly Brit.* a knitted or crocheted garment covering the upper part of the body. **2** the US and Canad. term for **pinafore dress.** [C19: from obs. *jump* man's loose jacket, var. of *jupe,* from OF, from Ar. *jubbah* long cloth coat]

jumper[2] ('dʒʌmpə) *n* **1** a boring tool that works by repeated impact, such as a steel bit in a drill used in boring rock. **2** Also called: **jumper cable, jumper lead.** a short length of wire used to make a connection, usually temporarily. **3** a person or animal that jumps.

jumping bean *n* a seed of any of several Mexican plants that contains a moth caterpillar whose movements cause it to jerk about.

jumping jack *n* a toy figure of a man with jointed limbs that can be moved by pulling attached strings.

jump jet *n Inf.* a fixed-wing jet aircraft that is capable of landing and taking off vertically.

jump jockey *n Brit. inf.* a jockey riding in a steeplechase, as opposed to racing on the flat.

jump leads (liːdz) *pl n* two heavy cables fitted with crocodile clips used to start a motor vehicle with a discharged battery by connecting the battery to an external battery.

jump-off *n* **1** an extra round in a showjumping contest when two or more horses are equal first, deciding the winner. ◆ *vb* **jump off. 2** (*intr, adv*) to engage in a jump-off.

jump on *vb* (*intr, prep*) *Inf.* to reprimand or attack suddenly and forcefully.

jump seat *n* **1** a folding seat on some aircraft for an additional crew member. **2** *Brit.* a folding seat in a motor vehicle.

jump-start *vb* **1** to start the engine of (a car) by pushing or rolling it and then engaging the gears or (of a car) to start in this way. ◆ *n* **2** the act of starting a car in this way. ◆ Also called (Brit.): **bump-start.**

jump suit *n* a one-piece garment of combined trousers and jacket or shirt.

jumpy ('dʒʌmpɪ) *adj* **jumpier, jumpiest. 1** nervous or apprehensive. **2** moving jerkily or fitfully.
▶ '**jumpily** *adv* ▶ '**jumpiness** *n*

Jun. *abbrev. for:* **1** June. **2** Also: **jun.** junior.

Junagadh ★ (ˌdʒuːnə'gæd) *n* a town in India, in Gujarat: noted for its Buddhist caves and temples. Pop.: 130 484 (1991).

junco ('dʒʌŋkəʊ) *n, pl* **juncos** or **juncoes.** a North American bunting having a greyish plumage. [C18: from Sp.: a rush, from L *juncus* rush]

junction ('dʒʌŋkʃən) *n* **1** a place where several routes, lines, or roads meet, link, or cross each other: *a railway junction.* **2** a point on a motorway where traffic may leave or join it. **3** *Electronics.* **3a** a contact between two different metals or other materials: *a thermocouple junction.* **3b** a transition region in a semiconductor. **4** the act of joining or the state of being joined. [C18: from L *junctiō* a joining, from *jungere* to join]

junction box *n* an earthed enclosure within which wires or cables can be safely connected.

junction transistor *n* a bipolar transistor consisting of

two p-n junctions combined to form either an n-p-n or a p-n-p transistor.

juncture ('dʒʌŋktʃə) *n* **1** a point in time, esp. a critical one (often in **at this juncture**). **2** *Linguistics.* the set of phonological features signalling a division between words, such as those that distinguish *a name* from *an aim.* **3** a less common word for **junction.**

Jundiaí ★ (Portuguese ʒundia'i) *n* an industrial city in SE Brazil, in São Paulo state. Pop.: 253 177 (1991).

June (dʒuːn) *n* the sixth month of the year, consisting of 30 days. [OE *iunius,* from L *junius,* prob. from *Junius* name of Roman gens]

Juneau ★ ('dʒuːnəʊ) *n* a port in SE Alaska: state capital. Pop.: 26 751 (1990).

Jung ★ (jʊŋ) *n* **Carl Gustav** (German karl 'gustaf). 1875–1961, Swiss psychologist who developed the concepts of the collective unconscious and of the extrovert and introvert types.
▶ '**Jungian** *adj*

Jungfrau ★ (German 'jʊŋfrau) *n* a mountain in S Switzerland, in the Bernese Alps south of Interlaken. Height: 4158 m (13 642 ft).

Junggar Pendi ('dʒʊŋ'geər 'pɛn'diː), **Dzungaria,** or **Zungaria** ★ *n* an arid region of W China, in N Xinjiang Uygur between the Altai Mountains and the Tian Shan.

jungle ('dʒʌŋgəl) *n* **1** an equatorial forest area with luxuriant vegetation. **2** any dense or tangled thicket or growth. **3** a place of intense or ruthless struggle for survival: *the concrete jungle.* **4** a type of fast electronic dance music, originating in the early 1990s, which combines elements of techno and ragga. [C18: from Hindi, from Sansk. *jāngala* wilderness]
▶ '**jungly** *adj*

jungle fever *n* a serious malarial fever occurring in the East Indies.

jungle fowl *n* **1** any small gallinaceous bird of S and SE Asia, the males of which (**junglecock**) have an arched tail and a combed and wattled head. **2** *Austral.* any of several megapodes.

jungle juice *n Sl.* alcoholic liquor.

junior ('dʒuːnjə) *adj* **1** lower in rank or length of service; subordinate. **2** younger in years. **3** of or relating to youth or childhood. **4** *Brit.* of schoolchildren between the ages of 7 and 11 approximately. **5** *US.* of or designating the third year of a four-year course at college or high school. ◆ *n* **6** *Law.* (in England) any barrister below the rank of Queen's Counsel. **7** a junior person. **8** *Brit.* a junior schoolchild. **9** *US.* a junior student. [C17: from L: younger, from *juvenis* young]

Junior ('dʒuːnjə) *adj* being the younger: usually used after a name to distinguish the son from the father: *Charles Parker, Junior.* Abbrev.: **Jnr, Jr, Jun., Junr.**

junior common room *n* (in certain universities and colleges) a common room for the use of students.

junior lightweight *n* **a** a professional boxer weighing 126–130 pounds (57–59 kg). **b** (*as modifier*): *a junior-lightweight bout.*

junior middleweight *n* **a** a professional boxer weighing 147–154 pounds (66.5–70 kg). **b** (*as modifier*): *the junior-middleweight championship.*

junior school *n* (in England and Wales) a school for children aged between 7 and 11.

junior technician *n* a rank in the Royal Air Force comparable to that of private in the army.

junior welterweight *n* **a** a professional boxer weighing 135–140 pounds (61–63.5 kg). **b** (*as modifier*): *a junior-welterweight fight.*

juniper ('dʒuːnɪpə) *n* a coniferous shrub or small tree of the N hemisphere having purple berry-like cones. The cones of the **common** or **dwarf juniper** are used as a flavouring in making gin. [C14: from L *jūniperus,* from ?]

junk[1] (dʒʌŋk) *n* **1** discarded objects, etc., collectively. **2** *Inf.* **2a** rubbish generally. **2b** nonsense: *the play was absolute junk.* **3** *Sl.* any narcotic drug, esp. heroin. ◆ *vb* **4** (*tr*) *Inf.* to discard as junk. [C15 *jonke* old useless rope]

junk² (dʒʌŋk) *n* a sailing vessel used in Chinese waters and characterized by a very high poop, flat bottom, and square sails supported by battens. [C17: from Port. *junco*, from Javanese *jon*]

junk bond *n Finance.* a security that offers a high yield but often involves a high risk of default.

Junker ('juŋkə) *n* **1** *History.* any of the aristocratic land-owners of Prussia. **2** an arrogant German army officer or official. **3** (formerly) a young German nobleman. [C16: from G, from OHG *junchērro* young lord]
▸ **'Junkerdom** *n*

Junkers ★ ('juŋkəz) *n* Hugo. 1859–1935, German aircraft designer; his aircraft were used in both World Wars.

junket ('dʒʌŋkɪt) *n* **1** a sweet dessert made of flavoured milk set to a curd with rennet. **2** a feast. **3** an excursion, esp. one made for pleasure at public expense. ◆ *vb* **4** to have or entertain with a feast. **5** (*intr*) (of a public official, etc.) to go on a junket. [C14 (in the sense: rush basket, hence custard served on rushes): from OF (dialect) *jonquette*, from *jonc* rush, from L *juncus* reed]
▸ **'junketing** *n*

junk food *n* food which is eaten in addition to or in-stead of regular meals, and which often has a low nutritional value.

junkie *or* **junky** ('dʒʌŋkɪ) *n, pl* **junkies.** an informal word for **drug addict.**

junk mail *n* unsolicited mail advertising goods or ser-vices.

junk shop *n* a shop selling miscellaneous second-hand goods and sometimes antiques.

Juno ★ ('dʒu:nəʊ) *n* **1** (in Roman tradition) the queen of the Olympian gods. Greek counterpart: **Hera. 2** a woman of stately bearing and regal beauty.

junta ('dʒʌntə, 'hʊntə) *n* (*functioning as sing or pl*) **1** a group of military officers holding the power in a coun-try, esp. after a coup d'état. **2** Also called: **junto.** a small group of men. **3** a legislative or executive council in some parts of Latin America. [C17: from Sp.: council, from L, from *jungere* to join]

junto ('dʒʌntəʊ) *n, pl* **juntos.** a variant of **junta** (sense 2). [C17]

Jupiter¹ ★ ('dʒu:pɪtə) *n* (in Roman tradition) the king and ruler of the Olympian gods. Also called: **Jove.**

Jupiter² ('dʒu:pɪtə) *n* the largest of the planets and the fifth from the sun.

Jura ★ ('dʒʊərə) *n* **1** a department of E France, in Franche-Comté region. Capital: Lons-le-Saunier. Pop.: 251 853 (1994 est.). Area: 5055 sq. km (1971 sq. miles). **2** a can-ton of Switzerland, bordering the French frontier: formed in 1979 from part of Bern. Capital: Delémont. Pop.: 68 979 (1995 est.). Area: 838 sq. km (323 sq. miles). **3** an island off the W coast of Scotland, in the Inner Hebrides, separated from the mainland by the **Sound of Jura.** Pop. (with Colonsay): 250 (latest est.). Area: 381 sq. km (147 sq. miles). **4** a mountain range in W central Eu-rope, between the Rivers Rhine and Rhône: mostly in E France, extending into W Switzerland. **5** a range of mountains in the NE quadrant of the moon lying on the N border of the Mare Imbrium.

Jurassic (dʒʊ'ræsɪk) *adj* **1** of or formed in the second pe-riod of the Mesozoic era, during which dinosaurs and ammonites flourished. ◆ *n* **2** **the.** the Jurassic period or rock system. [C19: from F *jurassique*, after the Jura (Mountains)]

jurat ('dʒʊəræt) *n* **1** *Law.* a statement at the foot of an affi-davit, naming the parties, stating when, where, and be-fore whom it was sworn, etc. **2** (in England) a municipal officer of the Cinque Ports. **3** (in France and the Channel Islands) a magistrate. [C16: from Med. L *jūrātus* one who has been sworn, from L *jūrāre* to swear]

juridical (dʒʊ'rɪdɪkəl) *adj* of or relating to law or to the administration of justice; legal. [C16: from L, from *iūs* law + *dicere* to say]
▸ **ju'ridically** *adv*

jurisdiction (ˌdʒʊərɪs'dɪkʃən) *n* **1** the right or power to administer justice and to apply laws. **2** the exercise or ex-tent of such right or power. **3** authority in general.

[C13: from L *jūrisdictiō* administration of justice, from *jus* law + DICTION]
▸ ˌjuris'dictional *adj*

jurisprudence (ˌdʒʊərɪs'pru:dⁿns) *n* **1** the science or philosophy of law. **2** a system or body of law. **3** a branch of law: *medical jurisprudence.* [C17: from L *jūris prūdentia,* from *jus* law + PRUDENCE]
▸ **jurisprudential** (ˌdʒʊərɪspru:'dɛnʃəl) *adj*

jurist ('dʒʊərɪst) *n* a person versed in the science of law, esp. Roman or civil law. [C15: from F *juriste,* from Med. L *jūrista*]

juristic (dʒʊ'rɪstɪk) *or* **juristical** *adj* **1** of or relating to jurists. **2** of or characteristic of the study of law or the legal profession.

juror ('dʒʊərə) *n* **1** a member of a jury. **2** a person who takes an oath. [C14: from Anglo-F *jurour,* from OF *jurer* to take an oath, from L *jūrāre*]

Juruá ★ (*Portuguese* ʒu'rua) *n* a river in South America, ris-ing in E central Peru and flowing northeast across NW Brazil to join the Amazon. Length: 1900 km (1200 miles).

jury¹ ('dʒʊərɪ) *n, pl* **juries. 1** a group of, usually, twelve peo-ple sworn to deliver a true verdict according to the evi-dence upon a case presented in a court of law. **2** a body of persons appointed to judge a competition and award prizes. [C14: from OF *juree,* from *jurer* to swear]

jury² ('dʒʊərɪ) *adj Chiefly naut.* (*in combination*) makeshift: *jury-rigged.* [C17: from ?]

jury box *n* an enclosure where the jury sits in court.

juryman ('dʒʊərɪmən) *or* (*fem*) **jurywoman** *n, pl* **jury-men** *or* **jurywomen.** a member of a jury.

jury-rigged *adj Chiefly naut.* set up in a makeshift man-ner.

just *adj* (dʒʌst). **1a** fair or impartial in action or judgment. **1b** (*as collective n; preceded by the*): *the just.* **2** conforming to high moral standards; honest. **3** consistent with jus-tice: *a just action.* **4** rightly applied or given: *a just reward.* **5** legally valid; lawful: *a just inheritance.* **6** well-founded: *just criticism.* **7** correct or true: *a just account.* ◆ *adv* (dʒʌst; *unstressed* dʒəst). **8** used with forms of *have* to indicate an action performed in the very recent past: *I have just closed the door.* **9** at this very instant: *he's just coming in to land.* **10** no more than; only: *just an ordinary car.* **11** exactly: *that's just what I mean.* **12** barely: *he just got there in time.* **13** just about. **13a** at the point of starting (to do something). **13b** almost: *I've just about had enough.* **14** just a moment, sec-ond, *or* minute. an expression requesting the hearer to wait or pause for a brief period of time. **15** just so. arranged with precision. [C14: from L *jūstus* righteous, from *jūs* justice]
▸ **'justly** *adv* ▸ **'justness** *n*

> **USAGE NOTE** The use of *just* with *exactly* (*it's just exactly what they want*) is redundant and should be avoided: *it's exactly what they want.*

justice ('dʒʌstɪs) *n* **1** the quality or fact of being just. **2** *Ethics.* the principle of fairness that like cases should be treated alike. **3** the administration of law according to prescribed and accepted principles. **4** conformity to the law. **5** a judge of the Supreme Court of Judicature. **6** short for **justice of the peace. 7** good reason (esp. in **with justice**). **8** bring to justice. to capture, try, and usually pun-ish (a criminal, etc.). **9** do justice to. **9a** to show to full ad-vantage. **9b** to show full appreciation of by action. **9c** to treat or judge fairly. **10** do oneself justice. to make full use of one's abilities. [C12: from OF, from L *jūstitia,* from *justus* JUST]
▸ **'justice,ship** *n*

justice of the peace *n* a lay magistrate whose func-tion is to preserve the peace in his area and try sum-marily such cases as are within his jurisdiction.

justiciar (dʒʌ'stɪʃɪˌɑ:) *n English legal history.* the chief po-litical and legal officer from the time of William I to that of Henry III, who deputized for the king in his absence. Also called: **justiciary.**
▸ **jus'ticiar,ship** *n*

justiciary (dʒʌ'stɪʃɪərɪ) *adj* **1** of or relating to the administration of justice. ◆ *n, pl* **justiciaries**. **2** an officer or administrator of justice; judge.

justifiable ('dʒʌstɪ,faɪəb³l) *adj* capable of being justified.
▶ ,justi,fia'bility *n* ▶ 'justi,fiably *adv*

justifiable homicide *n* lawful killing, as in the execution of a death sentence.

justification (,dʒʌstɪfɪ'keɪʃən) *n* **1** reasonable grounds for complaint, defence, etc. **2** proof, vindication, or exculpation. **3** *Christian theol.* **3a** the act of justifying. **3b** the process of being justified or the condition of having been justified.
▶ 'justifi,catory *adj*

justify ('dʒʌstɪ,faɪ) *vb* **justifies, justifying, justified.** (*mainly tr*) **1** (*often passive*) to prove or see to be just or valid; vindicate. **2** to show to be reasonable: *his behaviour justifies our suspicion.* **3** to declare or show to be free from blame or guilt. **4** *Law.* to show good reason in court for (some action taken). **5** (*also intr*) *Printing, computing.* to adjust the spaces between words in (a line of type or data) so that it is of the required length or (of a line of type or data) to fit exactly. **6a** *Protestant theol.* to declare righteous by the imputation of Christ's merits to the sinner. **6b** *RC theol.* to change from sinfulness to righteousness by the transforming effects of grace. **7** (*also intr*) *Law.* to prove (a person) to have sufficient means to act as surety, etc., or (of a person) to qualify to provide bail or surety. [C14: from OF *justifier*, from L *justificāre*, from *jūstus* JUST + *facere* to make]
▶ 'justi,fier *n*

Justinian I ★ (dʒʌ'stɪnɪən) *n* called *the Great*; Latin name *Flavius Anicius Justinianus.* 483–565 A.D., Byzantine emperor (527–565). He recovered North Africa, SE Spain, and Italy, largely owing to his generals, such as Belisarius. He sponsored the Justinian Code.

Justinian Code *n* a compilation of Roman imperial law made by order of Justinian I (483–565 A.D.), Byzantine emperor. *n* a compilation of Roman imperial law made by order of Justinian I.

Justin Martyr ★ ('dʒʌstɪn) *n* **Saint.** ?100–?165 A.D., Christian apologist and philosopher. Feast day: June 1.

just-in-time *adj* denoting or relating to an industrial method in which waste, queues, bottlenecks, etc., are eliminated or reduced by producing production-line components, etc., and by delivering materials just before they are needed. Abbrev.: **JIT.**

justle ('dʒʌs³l) *vb* **justles, justling, justled.** a less common word for **jostle.**

jut (dʒʌt) *vb* **juts, jutting, jutted. 1** (*intr*; often foll. by *out*) to stick out or overhang beyond the surface or main part. ◆ *n* **2** something that juts out. [C16: var. of JET¹]
▶ 'jutting *adj*

jute (dʒuːt) *n* **1** either of two Old World tropical yellow-flowered herbaceous plants, cultivated for their strong fibre. **2** this fibre, used in making sacks, rope, etc. [C18: from Bengali *jhuto*, from Sansk. *jūta* braid of hair]

Jutland ★ ('dʒʌtlənd) *n* a peninsula of N Europe: forms the continental portion of Denmark and geographically includes the N part of the German province of Schleswig-Holstein, while politically it includes only the mainland of Denmark and the islands north of Limfjorden; a major but inconclusive naval battle was fought off its NW coast in 1916 between the British and German fleets. Danish name: **Jylland.**
▶ 'Jutlander *n*

juv. *abbrev. for* juvenile.

Juvenal ★ ('dʒuːvɪn³l) *n* Latin name *Decimus Junius Juvenalis.* ?60–?140 A.D., Roman satirist, who denounced the vices of imperial Rome.

juvenescence (,dʒuːvɪ'nɛsəns) *n* **1** youth or immaturity. **2** the act or process of growing from childhood to youth.
▶ ,juve'nescent *adj*

juvenile ('dʒuːvɪ,naɪl) *adj* **1** young, youthful, or immature. **2** suitable or designed for young people: *juvenile pastimes.* ◆ *n* **3** a juvenile person, animal, or plant. **4** an actor who performs youthful roles. **5** a book intended for young readers. [C17: from L *juvenīlis* youthful, from *juvenis* young]
▶ 'juve,nilely *adv*

juvenile court *n* a court that deals with juvenile offenders and children beyond parental control or in need of care.

juvenile delinquency *n* antisocial or criminal conduct by juvenile delinquents.

juvenile delinquent *n* a child or young person guilty of some offence, act of vandalism, or antisocial behaviour and who may be brought before a juvenile court.

juvenilia (,dʒuːvɪ'nɪlɪə) *n* works of art, literature, or music produced in youth, before the artist, author, or composer has formed a mature style. [C17: from L, lit.: youthful things]

juxtapose (,dʒʌkstə'pəʊz) *vb* **juxtaposes, juxtaposing, juxtaposed.** (*tr*) to place close together or side by side. [C19: back formation from *juxtaposition*, from L *juxta* next to + POSITION]
▶ ,juxtapo'sition *n* ▶ ,juxtapo'sitional *adj*

Jylland ★ ('jylan) *n* the Danish name for **Jutland.**

★ people and places

Kk

k or **K** (keɪ) n, pl **k's, K's,** or **Ks. 1** the 11th letter and 8th consonant of the English alphabet. **2** a speech sound represented by this letter, usually a voiceless velar stop, as in *kitten*.

k symbol for: **1** kilo(s). **2** Maths. the unit vector along the z-axis.

K symbol for: **1** Kelvin(s). **2** Chess. king. **3** Chem. potassium. [from NL *kalium*] **4** Physics. kaon. **5** Currency. **5a** kina. **5b** kip. **5c** kopeck. **5d** kwacha. **5e** kyat. **6** one thousand. [from KILO-] **7** Computing. **7a** a unit of 1024 words, bits, or bytes. **7b** (not in technical usage) 1000.

K or **K.** abbrev. for Köchel: indicating the serial number in the catalogue of the works of Mozart made by Ludwig von Köchel, 1800–77.

k. abbrev. for: **1** karat. **2** Also: **K.** king.

K2 ★ n a mountain in the Karakoram Range on the Kashmir-Xinjiang Uygur AR border: the second highest mountain in the world. Height: 8611 m (28 250 ft). Also called: **Godwin Austen, Dapsang.**

Kaaba or **Caaba** ★ (ˈkɑːbə) n a cube-shaped building in Mecca, the most sacred Muslim pilgrim shrine, into which is built the black stone believed to have been given by Gabriel to Abraham. [from Ar. *ka'bah*, from *ka'b* cube]

kabaddi (kəˈbɑːdɪ) n a game played between two teams of seven players, in which individuals take turns to chase and try to touch members of the opposing team without being captured by them. [Tamil]

Kabalega Falls ★ (ˌkɑːbəˈleɪɡə) pl n rapids on the lower Victoria Nile, about 35 km (22 miles) east of Lake Albert, where the Nile drops 120 m (400 ft).

Kabardino-Balkar Republic ★ (ˈkæbəˌdiːnəʊˈbælkə) n a constituent republic of S Russia, on the N side of the Caucasus Mountains. Capital: Nalchik. Pop.: 787 000 (1995 est.). Area: 12 500 sq. km (4825 sq. miles). Also called: **Kabardino-Balkaria** (kæbəˌdiːnəʊbælˈkɑːrɪə).

kabbala or **kabala** (kəˈbɑːlə) n variant spellings of **cabbala.**

Kabila ★ (kæˈbiːlə) n **Laurent** (French lorã). born 1940, Zaïrese (now Congolese) politician and guerrilla leader: president of the Democratic Republic of the Congo from 1997.

kabuki (kæˈbuːkɪ) n a form of Japanese drama based on legends and characterized by elaborate costumes and the use of male actors. [Japanese, from *ka* singing + *bu* dancing + *ki* art]

Kabul (kəˈbʊl, ˈkɑːbᵊl) n **1** the capital of Afghanistan, in the northeast of the country at an altitude of 1800 m (5900 ft) on the **Kabul River**: over 3000 years old, with a strategic position commanding passes through the Hindu Kush and main routes to the Khyber Pass; destroyed and rebuilt many times; capital of the Mogul Empire from 1504 until 1738 and of Afghanistan from 1773; university (1932). Pop.: 700 000 (1993 est.). **2** a river in Afghanistan and Pakistan, rising in the Hindu Kush and flowing east into the Indus at Attock, Pakistan. Length: 700 km (435 miles).

Kabyle (kəˈbaɪl) n **1** (pl **Kabyles** or **Kabyle**) a member of a Berber people in Tunisia and Algeria. **2** the dialect of Berber spoken by this people. [C19: from Ar. *qabā'il*, pl. of *qabīlah* tribe]

Kádár ★ (Hungarian ˈkɑːdɑːr) n **János** (ˈjɑːnoʃ). 1912–89, Hungarian statesman; Communist prime minister of Hungary (1956–58; 1961–65) and first secretary of the Communist Party (1956–88).

kadi (ˈkɑːdɪ, ˈkeɪdɪ) n, pl **kadis.** a variant spelling of **cadi.**

Kaduna ★ (kəˈduːnə) n **1** a state of N Nigeria. Capital: Kaduna. Pop.: 4 088 239 (1992 est.). Area: 46 053 sq. km (17 781 sq. miles). Former name (until 1976): **North-Central State. 2** a city in N central Nigeria, capital of Kaduna state on the **Kaduna River** (a principal tributary of the Niger). Pop.: 333 600 (1995 est.).

Kaesöng ★ (ˈkæˌsʌŋ) n a city in SW North Korea: former capital of Korea (938–1392). Pop.: 120 000 (1987 est.).

Kaffir or **Kafir** (ˈkæfə) n, pl **Kaffirs** or **Kaffir, Kafirs** or **Kafir. 1** Offens. **1a** (in southern Africa) any Black African. **1b** (as modifier): *Kaffir farming.* **2** a former name for the **Xhosa** language. [C19: from Ar. *kāfir* infidel, from *kafara* to deny]

kaffir beer n S. African. beer made from sorghum (kaffir corn) or millet.

kaffirboom (ˈkæfəˌbʊəm) n a S. African deciduous flowering tree. [from KAFFIR + Afrik. *boom* tree]

kaffir corn n a southern African variety of sorghum, cultivated in dry regions for its grain and as fodder. Sometimes shortened to **kaffir.**

Kaffraria ★ (kæˈfrɛərɪə) n a former region of central South Africa: inhabited chiefly by the Kaffirs; British Kaffraria was a crown colony established in 1853 in the southwest of the region and annexed to Cape Colony in 1865.
  ► **Kafˈfrarian** adj, n

Kafir (ˈkæfə) n, pl **Kafirs** or **Kafir. 1** a member of a people inhabiting E Afghanistan. **2** a variant spelling of **Kaffir.** [C19: from Ar.; see KAFFIR]

Kafiristan ★ (ˌkæfɪrɪˈstɑːn) n the former name of **Nuristan.**

Kafka ★ (ˈkæfkə; Czech ˈkafka) n **Franz** (frants). 1883–1924, Czech writer, born in Prague (then in Bohemia) of German Jewish parents, writing in German. His nightmarish novels *The Trial* (1925) and *The Castle* (1926), were published posthumously against his wishes.
  ► **Kafkaesque** (ˌkæfkəˈɛsk) adj

kaftan or **caftan** (ˈkæftæn) n **1** a long coatlike garment, usually with a belt, worn in the East. **2** an imitation of this, worn esp. by women, consisting of a loose dress with long wide sleeves. [C16: from Turkish *qaftān*]

Kagera ★ (kæˈɡɛrə) n a river in E Africa, rising in headstreams on the border between Tanzania and Rwanda and flowing east to Lake Victoria: the most remote headstream of the Nile and largest tributary of Lake Victoria. Length: about 480 km (300 miles).

Kagoshima ★ (ˌkæɡɒˈʃiːmə) n a port in SW Japan, on S Kyushu. Pop.: 546 294 (1995).

kagoul (kəˈɡuːl) n a variant spelling of **cagoule.**

kahawai (ˈkɑːhəwaɪ, ˈkɑːwaɪ) n a New Zealand food and game fish. [from Maori]

Kahn ★ (kɑːn) n **1 Herman.** 1922–83, US mathematician and futurologist; director of the Hudson Institute (1961–83). **2 Louis I(sadore).** 1901–74, US architect, noted for his art museums at Yale (1951–53) and New Haven (1969–74).

kai (kaɪ) n NZ inf. food. [from Maori]

kaiak (ˈkaɪæk) n a variant spelling of **kayak.**

Kaieteur Falls ★ (ˌkaɪəˈtʊə) pl n a waterfall in Guyana, on the Potaro River. Height: 226 m (741 ft). Width: about 107 m (350 ft).

Kaifeng ★ (ˈkaɪˈfɛŋ) n a city in E China, in N Henan on the Yellow River: one of the oldest cities in China and its capital (as Pien-liang) from 907 to 1126. Pop.: 507 763 (1990 est.).

kail (keɪl) n a variant spelling of **kale.**

kai moana (məʊˈɑːnə) n NZ. seafood. [Maori]

kainite (ˈkaɪnaɪt) n a white mineral consisting of potassium chloride and magnesium sulphate: a fertilizer and source of potassium salts. [C19: from G *Kainit*, from Gk *kainos* new + -ITE[1]]

Kairouan (French kɛrwã), **Kairwan,** or **Qairwan**

| ★ people and places |

Kaiser (kaɪə'wɑːn) *n* a city in NE Tunisia: one of the holy cities of Islam; pilgrimage and trading centre. Pop.: 102 600 (1994).

Kaiser[1] ('kaɪzə) *n* (*sometimes not cap.*) *History.* **1** any of the three German emperors. **2** *Obs.* any Austro-Hungarian emperor. [C16: from G, ult. from L *Caesar* emperor]

Kaiser[2] ★ (*German* 'kaizər) *n* **Georg** ('geːɔrk). 1878–1945, German expressionist dramatist.

Kaiserslautern ★ (*German* kaizərs'lautərn) *n* a city in W Germany, in S Rhineland-Palatinate. Pop.: 101 910 (1995 est.).

kaizen *Japanese.* (kaɪ'zɛn) *n* a philosophy of continuous improvement of working practices that underlies total quality management and just-in-time business techniques. [lit.: improvement]

kaka ('kɑːkə) *n* a New Zealand parrot with a long compressed bill. [C18: from Maori, ? imit. of its call]

kaka beak *n* a New Zealand shrub with beaklike red flowers. [from KAKA]

kakapo ('kɑːkəˌpəʊ) *n, pl* **kakapos.** a ground-living nocturnal parrot of New Zealand, resembling an owl. [C19: from Maori, lit.: night kaka]

kakemono (ˌkækɪ'məʊnəʊ) *n, pl* **kakemonos.** a Japanese paper or silk wall hanging, usually long and narrow, with a picture or inscription on it. [C19: from Japanese, from *kake* hanging + *mono* thing]

Kalaalit Nunaat ★ (kə'lɑːlɪt 'nuːnɑːt) *n* the Greenlandic name for **Greenland.**

kala-azar (ˌkɑːləə'zɑː) *n* a tropical infectious disease caused by a protozoan in the liver, spleen, etc. [C19: from Assamese *kālā* black + *āzār* disease]

Kalahari ★ (ˌkælə'hɑːrɪ) *n* **the.** an extensive arid plateau of South Africa, Namibia, and Botswana: inhabited by Bushmen. Also called: **Kalahari Desert.**

Kalamazoo ★ (ˌkæləmə'zuː) *n* a city in SW Michigan, midway between Detroit and Chicago. Pop.: 81 644 (1994 est.).

Kalashnikov (kə'læʃnɪˌkɒf) *n* a Russian-made automatic rifle. See also **AK-47.** [C20: after Mikhail *Kalashnikov* (born 1919), its designer]

Kalat *or* **Khelat** ★ (kə'lɑːt) *n* a region of SW Pakistan, in S Baluchistan: formerly a princely state ruled by the Khan of Kalat, which joined Pakistan in 1948.

kale *or* **kail** (keɪl) *n* **1** a cultivated variety of cabbage with crinkled leaves. **2** *Scot.* a cabbage. ♦ Cf. **sea kale.** [OE *cāl*]

kaleidoscope (kə'laɪdəˌskəʊp) *n* **1** an optical toy for producing symmetrical patterns by multiple reflections in inclined mirrors enclosed in a tube. Loose pieces of coloured glass, paper, etc., are placed between transparent plates at the far end of the tube, which is rotated to change the pattern. **2** any complex pattern of frequently changing shapes and colours. [C19: from Gk *kalos* beautiful + *eidos* form + -SCOPE]

▶ **kaleidoscopic** (kəˌlaɪdə'skɒpɪk) *adj*

kalends ('kælɪndz) *pl n* a variant spelling of **calends.**

Kalevala (ˌkɑːlə'vɑːlə) *n Finnish legend.* **1** the land of the hero Kaleva, who performed legendary exploits. **2** the Finnish national epic in which these exploits are recounted. [Finnish, from *kaleva* of a hero + *-la* home]

kaleyard *or* **kailyard** ('keɪlˌjɑːd; *Scot.* -ˌjard) *n Scot.* a vegetable garden. [C19: lit.: cabbage garden]

kaleyard school *or* **kailyard school** *n* a group of writers who depicted the homely aspects of life in the Scottish Lowlands. The best-known contributor was J. M. Barrie.

Kalgan ★ ('kɑːl'ɡɑːn) *n* a former name of **Zhangjiakou.**

Kalgoorlie ★ (kæl'ɡuːlɪ) *n* a city in Western Australia, adjoining the town of Boulder: a centre of the Coolgardie gold rushes of the early 1890s; declining gold resources superseded by the discovery of nickel ore in 1966. Pop.: 26 079 (including Boulder) (1991).

Kali ★ ('kɑːlɪ) *n* the Hindu goddess of destruction, consort of Siva. Her cult was characterized by savagery and cannibalism.

Kalidasa ★ (ˌkælɪ'dɑːsə) *n* ?5th century A.D., Indian dramatist, noted for his verse drama *Sakuntala.*

kalied ('keɪlaɪd) *adj N English dialect.* drunk.

Kalimantan ★ (ˌkælɪ'mæntən) *n* the Indonesian name for Borneo: applied to the Indonesian part of the island only, excluding the Malaysian states of Sabah and Sarawak and the sultanate of Brunei. Pop.: 6 723 086 (1980).

Kalinin[1] ★ (*Russian* ka'linin) *n* the former name (1932–91) of **Tver.**

Kalinin[2] ★ (*Russian* ka'linin) *n* **Mikhail Ivanovich** (mixa'il i'vanəvitʃ). 1875–1946, Soviet statesman: titular head of state (1919–46); a founder of *Pravda* (1912).

Kaliningrad ★ (*Russian* kəlinin'grat) *n* a port in W Russia, on the Pregolya River: an exclave of Russian territory between Poland and Lithuania: severely damaged in World War II as the chief German naval base on the Baltic; ceded to the Soviet Union in 1945 and now Russia's chief Baltic naval base. Pop.: 419 000 (1995 est.). Former name (until 1946): **Königsberg.**

Kalisz ★ (*Polish* 'kaliʃ) *n* a town in central Poland, on an island in the Prosna River: textile industry. Pop.: 106 800 (1995 est.). Ancient name: **Calissia** (kə'lɪsɪə).

Kalmar ★ (*Swedish* 'kalmar) *n* a port in SE Sweden, partly on the mainland and partly on a small island in the **Sound of Kalmar,** opposite Öland: scene of the signing of the Union of Kalmar, which united Sweden, Denmark, and Norway into a single monarchy (1397–1523). Pop.: 58 070 (1994).

kalmia ('kælmɪə) *n* an evergreen North American ericaceous shrub having showy clusters of white or pink flowers. [C18: after Peter *Kalm* (1715–79), Swedish botanist and pupil of Linnaeus]

Kalmuck ('kælmʌk) *or* **Kalmyk** ('kælmɪk) *n* **1** (*pl* **Kalmucks, Kalmuck** *or* **Kalmyks, Kalmyk**) a member of a Mongoloid people of Buddhist tradition, who migrated from W China to Russia in the 17th century. **2** the language of this people.

Kalmuck *or* **Kalmyk Republic** ★ *n* a constituent republic of Russia, on the Caspian Sea: became subject to Russia in 1646. Capital: Elista. Pop.: 320 000 (1995 est.). Area: 76 100 sq. km (29 382 sq. miles). Also called: **Kalmykia** (ˌkæl'mɪkɪə).

kalong ('kɑːlɒŋ) *n* a fruit bat of the Malay Archipelago; a flying fox. [Javanese]

kalpa ('kælpə) *n* (in Hindu cosmology) a period in which the universe experiences a cycle of creation and destruction. [C18: Sansk.]

Kaluga ★ (*Russian* ka'luɡə) *n* a city in central Russia, on the Oka River. Pop.: 347 000 (1995 est.).

Kama[1] ★ (*Russian* 'kamə) *n* a river in central Russia, rising in the Ural Mountains and flowing to the River Volga, of which it is the largest tributary. Length: 2030 km (1260 miles).

Kama[2] ★ ('kɑːmə) *n* the Hindu god of love. [from Sansk.]

Kamakura ★ (ˌkæmə'kuərə) *n* a city in central Japan, on S Honshu: famous for its Great Buddha (Daibutsu), a 13th-century bronze, 15 m (49 ft) high. Pop.: 170 319 (1995).

Kamasutra (ˌkɑːmə'suːtrə) *n* **the.** an ancient Hindu text on erotic pleasure. [Sansk.: book on love, from *kāma* love + *sūtra* thread]

Kamchatka ★ (*Russian* kam'tʃatkə) *n* a peninsula in E Russia, between the Sea of Okhotsk and the Bering Sea. Length: about 1200 km (750 miles).

▶ **Kam'chatkan** *adj, n*

kame (keɪm) *n* an irregular mound or ridge of gravel, sand, etc., deposited by water derived from melting glaciers. [C19: Scot. & N English var. of COMB]

Kamensk-Uralski ★ (*Russian* 'kamɪnsku'raljskij) *n* an industrial city in S Russia. Pop.: 197 000 (1995 est.).

Kamerlingh-Onnes ★ (*Dutch* 'kaːmərlɪŋ'ɔnəs) *n* **Heike** ('hɛikə). 1853–1926, Dutch physicist: a discoverer (1911) of superconductivity. Nobel prize for physics 1913.

★ people and places

Kamerun ★ ('kaməruːn) *n* the German name for **Cameroon.**

Kamet ★ ('kɑːmɛt, 'kʌmeɪt) *n* a mountain in N India, in Uttar Pradesh in the Himalayas. Height: 7756 m (25 447 ft).

kamikaze (,kæmɪ'kɑːzɪ) *n* **1** (*often cap.*) (in World War II) one of a group of Japanese pilots who performed suicidal missions. **2** (*modifier*) (of an action) undertaken or (of a person) undertaking an action in the knowledge that it will result in the death of the person performing it in order to inflict maximum damage on an enemy: *a kamikaze attack.* **3** (*modifier*) extremely foolhardy and possibly self-defeating: *kamikaze prices.* [C20: from Japanese, from *kami* divine + *kaze* wind]

kamilaroi ('kæmələˌrɔɪ) *n* an Australian Aboriginal language formerly used in NW New South Wales.

Kamloops trout ('kæmluːps) *n* a variety of rainbow trout common in British Columbia.

Kampala ★ (kæm'pɑːlə) *n* the capital and largest city of Uganda, on Lake Victoria: Makerere University (1961). Pop.: 773 500 (1991).

kampong ('kæmpɒŋ) *n* (in Malaysia) a village. [C19: from Malay]

Kampuchea ★ (,kæmpu'tʃɪə) *n* the name from 1976 until 1989 of Cambodia, chosen by the Khmer Rouge (communist) government in 1976. During the Vietnamese occupation of Cambodia (1976–89) exiled Cambodian factions, including the Khmer Rouge, formed the Coalition Government of Democratic Kampuchea (CGDK). The pro-Vietnamese government reverted to the name Cambodia in 1989, and all factions of the CGDK except the Khmer Rouge participated in democratic elections in Cambodia in 1993. See also **Cambodia.**
▸ ˌKampu'chean *adj, n*

Kan. *abbrev. for* Kansas.

Kanak (kə'næk) *n* a native or inhabitant of New Caledonia who seeks independence from France. [C20: from Hawaiian: man]

Kanaka (kə'nækə) *n* **1** a native Hawaiian. **2** (*often not cap.*) *Austral.* any native of the South Pacific islands, esp. (formerly) one abducted to work in Australia. [C19: from Hawaiian: man]

Kananga ★ (kə'næŋgə) *n* a city in SW Democratic Republic of the Congo: a commercial centre on the railway from Lubumbashi to Port Francqui. Pop.: 393 030 (1994 est.). Former name (until 1966): **Luluabourg.**

Kanara *or* **Canara** (kə'nɑːrə) *n* a region of SW India, in Karnataka on the Deccan Plateau and the W Coast. Area: about 155 000 sq. km (60 000 sq. miles).

Kanarese *or* **Canarese** (,kænə'riːz) *n* **1** (*pl* **Kanarese** *or* **Canarese**) a member of a people of S India living chiefly in Kanara. **2** the language of this people.

Kanazawa ★ (,kænə'zɑːwə) *n* a port in Japan, on W Honshu: textile and porcelain industries. Pop.: 453 977 (1995).

kanban *Japanese.* ('kænbæn) *n* **1** a just-in-time manufacturing process in which the movements of materials through a process are recorded on specially designed cards. **2** any of the cards used for ordering materials in such a system. [lit.: advertisement hoarding]

Kanchenjunga ★ (,kæntʃən'dʒʌŋgə) *n* a variant spelling of **Kangchenjunga.**

Kanchipuram ★ (kɑːn'tʃiːpərəm) *n* a city in SE India, in Tamil Nadu: a sacred Hindu town known as "the Benares of the South"; textile industries. Pop.: 144 955 (1991).

Kandahar ★ (,kændə'hɑː) *n* a city in S Afghanistan: an important trading centre, built by Ahmad Shah Durrani (1724–73) as his capital on the site of several former cities. Pop.: 237 500 (1990 est.).

Kandinsky ★ (*Russian* kan'dinskij) *n* **Vasili** (va'silij). 1866–1944, Russian expressionist painter and theorist; a founder of *der Blaue Reiter* (a group of German expressionist painters).

Kandy ★ ('kændɪ) *n* a city in central Sri Lanka: capital of the kingdom of Kandy from 1480 until 1815, when oc-cupied by the British; sacred Buddhist temple; University of Sri Lanka. Pop.: 104 000 (1990 est.).

kanga *or* **khanga** ('kæŋgə) *n* a piece of gaily decorated thin cotton cloth used as a woman's garment, originally in E Africa. [from Swahili]

kangaroo (,kæŋgə'ruː) *n, pl* **kangaroos. 1** a large herbivorous marsupial of Australia and New Guinea, having large powerful hind legs used for leaping, and a long thick tail. **2** (*usually pl*) *Stock Exchange.* an Australian share, esp. in mining, land, or a tobacco company. [C18: prob. from Abor.]
▸ ˌkanga'roo-ˌlike *adj*

kangaroo closure *n Parliamentary procedure.* a form of closure in which the chairman or speaker selects certain amendments for discussion and excludes others.

kangaroo court *n* an irregular court, esp. one set up by strikers to judge strikebreakers.

Kangaroo Island ★ *n* an island in the Indian Ocean, off South Australia. Area: 4350 sq. km (1680 sq. miles).

kangaroo paw *n* any of various Australian plants having green-and-red hairy flowers.

kangaroo rat *n* **1** a small leaping rodent related to the squirrels and inhabiting desert regions of North America, having a stocky body and very long hind legs and tail. **2** Also called: **kangaroo mouse.** any of several leaping Australian rodents.

Kangchenjunga, Kanchenjunga (,kæntʃən'dʒʌŋgə), *or* **Kinchinjunga** ★ *n* a mountain on the border between Nepal and Sikkim, in the Himalayas: the third highest mountain in the world. Height: 8598 m (28 208 ft).

kanji ('kændʒɪ) *n, pl* **kanji** *or* **kanjis. 1** a Japanese writing system using characters mainly derived from Chinese ideograms. **2** a character in this system. [Japanese, from Chinese *han* Chinese + *zi* character]

Kano ★ ('kɑːnəʊ, 'keɪnəʊ) *n* **1** a state of N Nigeria: consists of wooded savanna in the south and scrub vegetation in the north. Capital: Kano. Pop.: 5 801 001 (1992 est.). Area: 20 131 sq. km (7773 sq. miles). **2** a city in N Nigeria, capital of Kano state: transport and market centre. Pop.: 594 800 (1991 est.).

Kanpur ★ (kɑːn'pʊə) *n* an industrial city in NE India, in S Uttar Pradesh on the River Ganges: scene of the massacre by Nana Sahib of British soldiers and European families and his later defeat by British forces in 1857. Pop.: 1 874 409 (1991). Former name: **Cawnpore.**

Kans. *abbrev. for* Kansas.

Kansas ★ ('kænzəs) *n* a state of the central US: consists of undulating prairie, drained chiefly by the Arkansas, Kansas, and Missouri Rivers; mainly agricultural. Capital: Topeka. Pop.: 2 572 150 (1996 est.). Area: 213 096 sq. km (82 277 sq. miles). Abbrevs.: **Kan., Kans.,** or (with zip code) **KS**

Kansas City ★ *n* **1** a city in W Missouri, at the confluence of the Missouri and Kansas Rivers: important centre of livestock and meat-packing industry. Pop.: 443 878 (1994 est.). **2** a city in NE Kansas, adjacent to Kansas City, Missouri. Pop.: 142 630 (1994 est.).

Kansu ★ ('kæn'suː) *n* a variant transliteration of the Chinese name for **Gansu.**

Kant ★ (kænt; *German* kant) *n* **Immanuel** (ɪ'maːnueːl). 1724–1804, German idealist philosopher. His main works are the *Critique of Pure Reason* (1781) and the *Critique of Practical Reason* (1788).
▸ 'Kantian *adj* ▸ 'Kantianˌism *or* 'Kantism *n*

KANU ('kɑːnuː) *n acronym for* Kenya African National Union.

Kaohsiung *or* **Kao-hsiung** ★ ('kau'ʃjʊŋ) *n* a variant transliteration of the Chinese name for **Gaoxiong.**

Kaolack ★ ('kɑːəʊˌlæk, 'kaʊlæk) *n* a port in SW Senegal, on the Saloum River. Pop.: 193 115 (1994 est.).

kaolin ('keɪəlɪn) *n* a fine white clay used for the manufacture of hard-paste porcelain and bone china and in medicine as a poultice. Also called: **china clay.** [C18: from F, from Chinese *Kaoling* Chinese mountain where supplies for Europe were first obtained]
▸ ˌkao'linic *adj* ▸ 'kaolinˌize *or* 'kaolinˌise *vb*

kaon ('keɪɒn) *n* a meson that has a rest mass of about 996 or 964 electron masses. Also called: **K-meson.** [C20 *ka* representing the letter *k* + (MES)ON]

kapellmeister (kæ'pɛl,maɪstə) *n* a variant spelling of **capellmeister.**

Kapfenberg ★ (*German* 'kapfənbɛrk) *n* an industrial town in E Austria, in Styria. Pop.: 23 490 (1991).

Kapil Dev ★ ('kæpɪl 'dɛv) *n* (**Ramlal) Nikhanj** (nɪ'kænd͡ʒ). born 1959, Indian cricketer: captain of India (1983–84).

Kapitza ★ (kə'pitsa) *n* **Piotr Leonidovich** ('pjɔt°r liə'nidovitʃ). 1894–1984, Russian physicist. He worked in England and the Soviet Union, mainly in cryogenics; Nobel prize for physics in 1978.

kapok ('keɪpɒk) *n* a silky fibre obtained from the hairs covering the seeds of a tropical tree (**kapok tree**): used for stuffing pillows, etc. [C18: from Malay]

Kaposi's sarcoma (kæ'pəʊsɪz) *n* a form of skin cancer found in Africans and more recently in victims of AIDS. [C20: after Moritz Kohn *Kaposi* (1837–1902), Austrian dermatologist who first described the sores that characterize the disease]

kappa ('kæpə) *n* the tenth letter in the Greek alphabet (K, κ). [Gk, of Semitic origin]

kaput (kæ'pʊt) *adj* (*postpositive*) *Inf.* ruined, broken, or not functioning. [C20: from G *kaputt* done for]

karabiner (,kærə'bi:nə) *n* *Mountaineering.* a metal clip with a spring for attaching to a piton, belay, etc. Also called: **snaplink, krab.** [shortened from G *Karabinerhaken,* lit.: carbine hook]

Karachai-Cherkess Republic ★ (kərʌ'tʃaɪtʃeə'kɛs) *n* a constituent republic of W Russia, on the N side of the Caucasus Mountains. Capital: Cherkessk. Pop.: 435 000 (1995 est.). Area: 14 100 sq. km (5440 sq. miles). Also called: **Karachayevo-Cherkess Republic** (kərʌ'tʃaɪevəʊtʃeə'kɛs), **Karachai-Cherkessia** (kærə,tʃaɪtʃeə'kɛsɪə).

Karachi (kə'rɑːtʃɪ) *n* a port in S Pakistan, on the Arabian Sea: capital of Pakistan (1947–60); university (1950); chief port: commercial and industrial centre. Pop.: 9 863 000 (1995 est.).

Karafuto ★ (,kɑːrɑː'fuːtɔ) *n* transliteration of the Japanese name for **Sakhalin.**

Karaganda ★ (*Russian* kərəgan'da) *n* a city in E central Kazakhstan: a major coal-mining and industrial centre. Pop.: 573 700 (1995 est.). Also called: **Qaraghandy.**

Karajan ★ (*German* 'ka:rajan) *n* **Herbert von** ('hɛrbɛrt fɔn). 1908–89, Austrian conductor.

Kara-Kalpak Autonomous Republic ★ (kə'rɑːkəl'pɑːk) *n* an administrative division of NW Uzbekistan, on the Aral Sea: came under Russian rule by stages from 1873 onwards until Uzbekistan became independent. Capital: Nukus. Pop.: 1 343 000 (1993 est.). Area: 165 600 sq. km (63 900 sq. miles). Also called: **Kara-Kalpakia** (kə'rɑːkəl'pɑːkɪə), **Kara-Kalpakstan** (kə'rɑːkəl-,pɑːk'stæn, -'stɑːn).

Karakoram *or* **Karakorum** ★ (,kærə'kɔːrəm) *n* a mountain system in N Kashmir, extending for about 480 km (300 miles) from northwest to southeast: contains the second highest peak in the world (K2); the range is crossed by several high passes, notably the **Karakoram Pass,** 5575 m (18 290 ft).

Karakorum ★ (,kærə'kɔːrəm) *n* a ruined city in Mongolia; ancient capital (1220–67), founded by Ghenghis Khan, of the Mongolian empire: destroyed in 1388.

karakul *or* **caracul** ('kærək°l) *n* **1** a breed of sheep of central Asia having coarse black, grey, or brown hair: the lambs have soft curled hair. **2** the fur prepared from these lambs. ◆ See also **Persian lamb.** [C19: from Russian, from the name of a region in Bukhara where the sheep originated]

Kara Kum ★ (*Russian* kərɑ 'kum) *n* a desert in Turkmenistan, covering most of the country: extensive areas now irrigated. Area: about 300 000 sq. km (120 000 sq. miles).

Karamanlis ★ (*Greek* karaman'lis) *n* **Konstantinos** (kɔnstan'tinos). 1907–98, Greek statesman; prime minister of Greece (1955–58; 1958–61; 1961–63; 1974–80); president of Greece (1980–85; 1990–95).

karaoke (,kɑːrə'əʊkɪ) *n* **a** an entertainment of Japanese origin in which people take it in turns to sing well-known songs over a prerecorded backing tape. **b** (*as modifier*): *a karaoke bar.* [from Japanese, from *kara* empty + *ōkesutora* orchestra]

Kara Sea ★ ('kɑːrə) *n* a shallow arm of the Arctic Ocean off the N coast of Russia: ice-free for about three months of the year.

karat ('kærət) *n* the usual US and Canad. spelling of **carat** (sense 2).

karate (kə'rɑːtɪ) *n* **a** a traditional Japanese system of unarmed combat, employing smashes, chops, kicks, etc., made with the hands, feet, elbows, or legs. **b** (*as modifier*): *karate chop.* [Japanese, lit.: empty hand]

karateka (kə'rɑːtɪ,kɑː) *n* a competitor or expert in karate. [Japanese; see KARATE]

Karbala ('kɑːbələ) *or* **Kerbela** ★ *n* a town in central Iraq: the chief holy city of Iraq and centre of Shiah Muslim pilgrimage; burial place of Mohammed's grandson Husain. Pop.: 296 705 (1987).

Karelia ★ (kə'riːlɪə; *Russian* ka'reljə) *n* **1** a region of NE Europe, formerly in Finland but annexed in several stages by the former Soviet Union: corresponds roughly to the Karelian Republic in Russia. **2** another name for the **Karelian Republic.**
▸ **Ka'relian** *adj, n*

Karelian Republic ★ (kə'riːlɪən) *n* a constituent republic of NW Russia between the White Sea and Lakes Onega and Ladoga. Capital: Petrozavodsk. Pop.: 789 000 (1995 est.). Area: 172 400 sq. km (66 560 sq. miles). Also called: **Karelia.**

Karelian Isthmus ★ *n* a strip of land, now in Russia, between the Gulf of Finland and Lake Ladoga: annexed by the former Soviet Union after the Russo-Finnish War (1939–40).

Kariba ★ (kə'riːbə) *n* **Lake.** a lake on the Zambia-Zimbabwe border, created by the building of the **Kariba Dam** across the Zambezi for hydroelectric power. Length: 282 km (175 miles).

Karitane (,kærɪ'tɑːne) *n* *NZ.* a nurse for babies; nanny. [from former child-care hospital at *Karitane,* New Zealand]

Karl-Marx-Stadt ★ (*German* karl'marksʃtat) *n* the former name (1953–90) of **Chemnitz.**

Karloff ★ ('kɑːlɒf) *n* **Boris,** real name *William Pratt.* 1887–1969, British film actor, known for his roles in horror films.

Karlovy Vary ★ (*Czech* 'karlɒvi 'vari) *n* a city in the W Czech Republic, at the confluence of the Tepla and Ohře Rivers: warm mineral springs. Pop.: 56 290 (1991). German name: **Karlsbad** *or* **Carlsbad** ('karlsbaːt).

Karlskrona ★ (*Swedish* kɑːrls'kruːnə) *n* a port in S Sweden: Sweden's main naval base since 1680. Pop.: 60 642 (1994).

Karlsruhe ★ (*German* 'karlsruːə) *n* a city in SW Germany, in Baden-Württemberg: capital of the former Baden state. Pop.: 277 011 (1995 est.).

karma ('kɑːmə) *n* **1** *Hinduism, Buddhism.* the principle of retributive justice determining a person's state of life and the state of his reincarnations as the effect of his past deeds. **2** destiny or fate. **3** *Inf.* an aura or quality that a person, place, or thing is felt to have. [C19: from Sansk.: action, effect, from *karoti* he does]
▸ **'karmic** *adj*

Karnak ★ ('kɑːnæk) *n* a village in E Egypt, on the Nile: site of the N part of the ruins of ancient Thebes.

Karnataka ★ (kə'nɑːtəkə) *n* a state of S India, on the Arabian Sea: consists of a narrow coastal plain rising to the South Deccan plateau; mainly agricultural. Capital: Bangalore. Pop.: 44 977 201 (1991). Area: 191 791 sq. km (74 051 sq. miles). Former name (1956–73): **Mysore.**

Kärnten ★ ('kɛrntən) *n* the German name for **Carinthia.**

Karoo *or* **Karroo** ★ (kə'ruː) *n, pl* **Karoos** *or* **Karroos.** (*often not cap.*) **1** any of several high arid plateaus in South Africa, esp. the **Central Karoo** and the **Little Karoo.** The highveld, north of the Great Karoo, is sometimes called the **Northern Karoo. 2** a period or rock system in S Africa equivalent to the period or system extending from the Upper Carboniferous to the Lower Jurassic: divided into **Lower** and **Upper Karoo.** ◆ *adj* **3** of, denoting or formed in the Karoo period. [C18: from Afrik. *karo*, probably from Khoikhoi *garo* desert]

kaross (kə'rɒs) *n* a garment of skins worn by indigenous peoples in southern Africa. [C18: from Afrik. *karos*, ?from Du., from F *cuirasse* CUIRASS]

Karpov ★ (*Russian* 'karpəf) *n* **Anatoly** (ana'təlij). born 1951, Russian chess player: world champion (1975–85; 1993).

karri ('kɑːrɪ) *n, pl* **karris. 1** an Australian eucalyptus tree. **2** the durable dark red wood of this tree, used for construction, etc. [from Abor.]

karst (kɑːst) *n* (*modifier*) denoting the characteristic scenery of a limestone region, including underground streams, gorges, etc. [C19: G, from *Karst*, limestone plateau near Trieste]

kart (kɑːt) *n* a light low-framed vehicle with small wheels and engine used for recreational racing (**karting**). Also called: **go-cart, go-kart.**

karyo- or **caryo-** *combining form.* indicating the nucleus of a cell. [from NL, from Gk *karuon* kernel]

karyotype ('kærɪə,taɪp) *n* **1** the appearance of the chromosomes in a somatic cell of an individual or species, with reference to their number, size, shape, etc. ◆ *vb* **karyotypes, karyotyping, karyotyped.** (*tr*) **2** to determine the karyotype of (a cell).
▶ **karyotypic** (,kærɪə'tɪpɪk) or ,**karyo'typical** *adj*

Kasai ★ (kɑː'saɪ) *n* a river in SW Africa, rising in central Angola and flowing east then north as part of the border between Angola and the Democratic Republic of the Congo, continuing northwest to the River Congo. Length: 2154 km (1338 miles).

kasbah or **casbah** ('kæzbɑː) *n* (*sometimes cap.*) **1** the citadel of any of various North African cities. **2** the quarter in which a kasbah is located. [from Ar. *kaṣba* citadel]

kasha ('kɑːʃə) *n* a dish originating in Eastern Europe, consisting of boiled or baked buckwheat. [from Russian]

Kashi (kɑː'ʃiː) or **Kashgar** ★ ('kɑːʃ'gɑː) *n* an oasis city in W China, in W Xinjiang Uygur AR. Pop.: 174 570 (1990 est.).

Kashmir ★ (kæʃ'mɪə) *n* a region of SW central Asia: from the 16th century ruled by the Moguls, Afghanis, Sikhs, and British successively; since 1947 disputed between India, Pakistan, and China; 84 000 sq. km (33 000 sq. miles) in the northwest are held by Pakistan and known as Azad Kashmir (Free Kashmir); 42 735 sq. km (16 496 sq. miles) in the east are held by China; the remainder was in 1956 officially incorporated into India as the state of Jammu and Kashmir; traversed by the Himalaya and Karakoram mountain ranges and the Rivers Jhelum and Indus; a fruit-growing and cattle-grazing region, with a woollen industry. Capitals: (Azad Kashmir) Muzaffarabad; (Jammu and Kashmir) Srinagar (summer), Jammu (winter).
▶ **Kash'miri** *adj, n* ▶ **Kash'mirian** *adj, n*

kashruth or **kashrut** *Hebrew.* (kaʃ'ruːt) *n* **1** the condition of being fit for ritual use in general. **2** the system of dietary laws that requires ritual slaughter, the complete separation of milk and meat, and the prohibition of such foods as pig meat and shell fish. ◆ See also **kosher** (sense 1). [lit.: appropriateness]

Kasparov ★ ('kæspərɒf) *n* **Gary** ('gærɪ), real name *Gary Weinstein*. born 1963, Russian chess player, born in Azerbaijan: world champion (1985–93).

Kassa ('kɒʃɒ) *n* the Hungarian name for **Košice.**

Kassala ★ (kə'sɑːlə) *n* a city in the E Sudan: founded as a fort by the Egyptians in 1834. Pop.: 234 270 (1993).

Kassel or **Cassel** ★ (*German* 'kasəl) *n* a city in central Germany, in Hesse: capital of Westphalia (1807–13) and of the Prussian province of Hesse-Nassau (1866–1945). Pop.: 201 789 (1995 est.).

kata ('kætə) *n* an exercise consisting of a sequence of the specific movements of a martial art, used in training and designed to show skill in technique. [C20: Japanese, lit.: shape, pattern]

kata- *prefix* a variant spelling of **cata-.**

katabatic (,kætə'bætɪk) *adj* (of winds) blowing downhill through having become denser with cooling.

Katanga ★ (kə'tæŋɡə) *n* the former name (until 1972) o[f] **Shaba.**

Katar ★ (kæ'tɑː) *n* a variant spelling of **Qatar.**

Kathiawar ★ (,kætɪə'wɑː) *n* a large peninsula of W India in Gujarat between the Gulf of Kutch and the Gulf o[f] Cambay. Area: about 60 690 sq. km (23 430 sq. miles).

Katmai ★ ('kætmaɪ) *n* **Mount.** a volcano in SW Alaska, i[n] the Aleutian Range: erupted in 1912 forming the Valle[y] of Ten Thousand Smokes, a region with numerou[s] fumaroles; established as **Katmai National Monument** 10 917 sq. km (4215 sq. miles), in 1918. Height: 2100 m (7000 ft). Depth of crater: 1130 m (3700 ft). Width o[f] crater: about 4 km (2.5 miles).

Katmandu or **Kathmandu** ★ (,kætmæn'duː) *n* the capital of Nepal, in the east at the confluence of the Baghmati and Vishnumati Rivers. Pop.: 535 000 (199[0] est.).

Katowice ★ (*Polish* katɔ'vitsɛ) *n* an industrial city in S Poland. Pop.: 355 100 (1995 est.). Former name (1953–56): **Stalinogrod.**

Katrine ★ ('kætrɪn) *n* **Loch.** a lake in central Scotland, eas[t] of Loch Lomond: noted for its associations with Si[r] Walter Scott's *Lady of the Lake.* Length: about 13 km (8 miles).

Katsina ★ (kæt'siːnə) *n* a city in N Nigeria, in Kaduna state: a major intellectual and cultural centre of the Hausa people (16th–18th centuries). Pop.: 201 50[0] (1995 est.).

Kattegat or **Cattegat** ★ ('kætɪ,ɡæt) *n* a strait betwee[n] Denmark and Sweden: linked by the Sound, the Grea[t] Belt, and the Little Belt with the Baltic Sea and by th[e] Skagerrak with the North Sea.

katydid ('keɪtɪ,dɪd) *n* a green long-horned grasshoppe[r] living on the foliage of trees in North America. [C18[:] imit.]

Katz ★ (kæts) *n* Sir **Bernard.** born 1911, Britis[h] neurophysiologist, born in Germany. Shared the Nobe[l] prize for physiology or medicine (1970) with Juliu[s] Axelrod and Ulf von Euler.

Kauai ★ (kɑː'wɑːiː) *n* a volcanic island in NW Hawai[i] northwest of Oahu. Chief town: Lihue. Pop.: 50 69[0] (1990). Area: 1433 sq. km (553 sq. miles).

Kauffmann ★ (*German* 'kaʊfman) *n* **Angelica** (aŋ'ɡeːlika) 1741–1807, Swiss painter, who worked chiefly in Eng[-] land.

Kaufman ★ ('kɔːfmən) *n* **1** George S(imon). 1889–1961, U[S] dramatist who, with Moss Hart, wrote many Broadwa[y] comedy hits.

kaumatua (kaʊ'mɑːtuːə) *n* NZ. a senior member of [a] tribe; elder. [Maori]

Kaunas ★ ('kaʊnəs) *n* a city in S central Lithuania at th[e] confluence of the Neman and Viliya Rivers: ceded by Po[-] land to Russia in 1795; the provisional capital of Lithua[-] nia (1920–40); part of the Soviet Union (1944–91[)] university (1922). Pop.: 429 000 (1993 est.). Russia[n] name: **Kovno.**

Kaunda ★ (kɑː'ʊndə) *n* **Kenneth** (**David**). born 1924, Zam[-] bian statesman. He led his country into independenc[e] and became its first president (1964–91).

kauri ('kaʊrɪ) *n, pl* **kauris. 1** a New Zealand coniferous tre[e] with oval leaves and round cones. **2** the wood or resin o[f] this tree. [C19: from Maori]

kauri gum *n* the fossil resin of the kauri tree.

kava ('kɑːvə) *n* **1** a Polynesian shrub. **2** a drink prepare[d] from the aromatic roots of this shrub. [C18: from Poly[-] nesian: bitter]

Kaválla ★ (kə'vælə; *Greek* ka'vala) *n* a port in E Greece, o[n] the **Bay of Kaválla:** an important Macedonian fortress o[f] the Byzantine empire; ceded to Greece by Turkey afte[r] the Balkan War (1912–13). Pop.: 58 576 (1991). Ancie[nt] name: **Neapolis** (,nɪ'æpɒlɪs).

Kavir Desert ★ (kæ'vɪə) *n* another name for the **Dasht-Kavir.**

Kawasaki ★ (ˌkɑːwəˈsɑːkɪ) *n* a port in central Japan, on SE Honshu: heavy industries. Pop.: 1 202 811 (1995).

Kawasaki's disease *n* a disease of children that causes a rash, fever, and swelling of the lymph nodes and often damages the heart muscle. [C20: after T. *Kawasaki*, Japanese physician who first described it]

Kay ★ (keɪ) *n* **Sir.** (in Arthurian legend) the braggart foster brother and steward of King Arthur.

kayak *or* **kaiak** (ˈkaɪæk) *n* **1** a canoe-like boat used by Eskimos, consisting of a frame covered with animal skins. **2** a fibreglass or canvas-covered canoe of similar design. [C18: from Eskimo]

kayo *or* **KO** (ˈkeɪˈəʊ) *n, pl* **kayos, vb kayos, kayoing, kayoed.** *Boxing, sl.* another term for **knockout** or **knock out.** [C20: from the initial letters of *knock out*]

Kayseri ★ (ˌkaɪsɛˈriː; *Turkish* ˈkaɪseri) *n* a city in central Turkey: in ancient times the chief city of Cappadocia. Pop.: 454 000 (1994 est.). Ancient name: **Caesarea Mazaca** (ˌməˈzækə).

Kazakh *or* **Kazak** (kəˈzɑːk, kɑː-) *n* **1** (*pl* **Kazakhs** *or* **Kazaks**) a member of a Mongoloid people of Kazakhstan. **2** the official language of Kazakhstan.

Kazakhstan *or* **Kazakstan** ★ (ˌkɑːzɑːkˈstæn, -ˈstɑːn) *n* a republic in central Asia: conquered by Mongols in the 13th century; came under Russian control in the 18th and 19th centuries; a Soviet republic from 1936 until it gained independence in 1991. It is agricultural, but has rich mineral deposits. Official language: Kazakh. Religion: believers are mostly Muslim or Christian. Official currency: tenge. Capital: Astana. Pop.: 16 554 000 (1997). Area: 2 715 100 sq. km (1 048 030 sq. miles).

Kazan[1] ★ (kəˈzæn, -ˈzɑːn; *Russian* kaˈzanj) *n* a city in W Russia, capital of the Tatar Autonomous Republic on the River Volga: capital of an independent khanate in the 15th century; university (1804); an industrial centre. Pop.: 1 085 000 (1995 est.).

Kazan[2] ★ (kəˈzɑːn) *n* **Elia** (ˈiːljə), real name *Elia Kazanjoglous.* born 1909, US film director and writer, born in Turkey. His films include *Gentleman's Agreement* (1947), *On the Waterfront* (1954), and *East of Eden* (1955).

Kazan Retto ★ (kɑːˈzɑːn ˈrɛtəʊ) *n* transliteration of the Japanese name for the **Volcano Islands.**

Kazantzakis ★ (*Greek* kazanˈdzakis) *n* **Nikos** (ˈnikɔs). 1885–1957, Greek writer, noted particularly for his novels *Zorba the Greek* (1946) and *Christ Recrucified* (1954).

Kazbek ★ (kɑːzˈbɛk) *n* **Mount.** an extinct volcano in N Georgia, in the Caucasus Mountains. Height: 5047 m (16 558 ft).

Kaz Daği ★ (ˈkɑz ˈdɑɡ) *n* the Turkish name for (Mount) **Ida** (sense 2).

kazoo (kəˈzuː) *n, pl* **kazoos.** a cigar-shaped musical instrument of metal or plastic with a membranous diaphragm of thin paper that vibrates with a nasal sound when the player hums into it. [C20: prob. imit.]

KB (in Britain) *abbrev. for:* **1** King's Bench. **2** *Computing.* kilobyte.

KBE *abbrev. for* Knight (Commander of the Order) of the British Empire.

kbyte *Computing. abbrev. for* kilobyte.

kc *abbrev. for* kilocycle.

KC (in Britain) *abbrev. for:* **1** King's Counsel. **2** Kennel Club.

kcal *abbrev. for* kilocalorie.

KCB *abbrev. for* Knight Commander of the Bath (a Brit. title).

KCMG *abbrev. for* Knight Commander (of the Order) of St Michael and St George (a Brit. title).

KE *abbrev. for* kinetic energy.

kea (ˈkɛə) *n* a large New Zealand parrot with a brownish-green plumage. [C19: from Maori, imit. of its call]

Kéa ★ (ˈkɛə) *n* transliteration of the Modern Greek name for **Keos.**

Kean ★ (kiːn) *n* **Edmund.** ?1789–1833, British actor, noted for his Shakespearean roles.

Keating ★ (ˈkiːtɪŋ) *n* **Paul (John).** born 1944, Australian statesman; prime minister (1991–96).

Keaton ★ (ˈkiːtⁿn) *n* **Buster,** real name *Joseph Francis Keaton.* 1895–1966, US film comedian known for his role in *The Navigator* (1924) and *Steamboat Bill Junior* (1927).

Keats ★ (kiːts) *n* **John.** 1795–1821, British poet. His best known poetry is contained in *Lamia and other Poems* (1820), which includes "The Eve of St Agnes" and the odes "On a Grecian Urn", "To a Nightingale", and "To Psyche".

kebab (kəˈbæb) *n* a dish consisting of small pieces of meat, tomatoes, onions, etc., grilled on skewers. Also called: **shish kebab.** [C17: from Ar. *kabāb* roast meat]

Keble ★ (ˈkiːbⁿl) *n* **John.** 1792–1866, British clergyman, who helped to inspire the Oxford Movement.

kecks *or* **keks** (kɛks) *pl n N English dialect.* trousers. [C19: from obs. *kicks* breeches]

Kecskemét ★ (*Hungarian* ˈkɛtʃkɛmeːt) *n* a city in central Hungary: vineyards and fruit farms. Pop.: 105 000 (1996 est.).

Kedah ★ (ˈkɛdə) *n* a state of NW Malaysia; the chief exports are rice, and rubber. Capital: Alor Star. Pop.: 1 412 000 (1993 est.). Area: 9425 sq. km (3639 sq. miles).

kedge (kɛdʒ) *Naut.* ◆ *vb* **kedges, kedging, kedged. 1** to draw (a vessel) along by hauling in on the cable of a light anchor, or (of a vessel) to be drawn in this fashion. ◆ *n* **2** a light anchor, used esp. for kedging. [C15: from *caggen* to fasten]

kedgeree (ˌkɛdʒəˈriː) *n Chiefly Brit.* a dish consisting of rice, cooked flaked fish, and hard-boiled eggs. [C17: from Hindi, from Sansk. *khiccā*]

Kediri ★ (kɪˈdɪərɪ) *n* a city in Indonesia, in E Java: commercial centre. Pop.: 235 602 (1990).

Kedron (ˈkɛdrɒn) *or* **Kidron** ★ *n Bible.* a ravine under the eastern wall of Jerusalem.

Keegan ★ (ˈkiːgən) *n* **Kevin.** born 1951, English footballer; manager of Newcastle United (1992–97).

keek (kiːk) *n, vb* a Scot. word for **peep**[1]. [C18: prob. from MDu. *kīken* to look]

keel[1] (kiːl) *n* **1** one of the main longitudinal structural members of a vessel to which the frames are fastened. **2 on an even keel.** well-balanced; steady. **3** any structure corresponding to or resembling the keel of a ship. **4** *Biol.* a ridgelike part; carina. ◆ *vb* **5** to capsize. ◆ See also **keel over.** [C14: from ON *kjǫlr*]

keel[2] (kiːl) *n Eastern English dialect.* **1** a flat-bottomed vessel, esp. one used for carrying coal. **2** a measure of coal. [C14 *kele,* from MDu. *kiel*]

keelage (ˈkiːlɪdʒ) *n* a fee charged by certain ports to allow a ship to dock.

keelhaul (ˈkiːlˌhɔːl) *vb (tr)* **1** to drag (a person) by a rope from one side of a vessel to the other through the water under the keel. **2** to rebuke harshly. [C17: from Du. *kielhalen;* see KEEL[1], HAUL]

Keeling Islands ★ (ˈkiːlɪŋ) *pl n* another name for the **Cocos Islands.**

keel over *vb (adv)* **1** to turn upside down; capsize. **2** *(intr) Inf.* to collapse suddenly.

keelson (ˈkɛlsən, ˈkiːl-) *or* **kelson** *n* a longitudinal beam fastened to the keel of a vessel for strength and stiffness. [C17: prob. from Low G *kielswin* keel swine, ult. of Scand. origin]

Keelung ★ (ˈkiːˈlʊŋ) *n* another name for **Chilung.**

keen[1] (kiːn) *adj* **1** eager or enthusiastic. **2** *(postpositive; foll. by on)* fond (of); devoted (to): *keen on golf.* **3** intellectually acute: *a keen wit.* **4** (of sight, smell, hearing, etc.) capable of recognizing fine distinctions. **5** having a sharp cutting edge or point. **6** extremely cold and penetrating: *a keen wind.* **7** intense or strong: *a keen desire.* **8** *Chiefly Brit.* extremely low so as to be competitive: *keen prices.* [OE *cēne*]
▶ ˈ**keenly** *adv* ▶ ˈ**keenness** *n*

keen[2] (kiːn) *vb (intr)* **1** to lament the dead. ◆ *n* **2** a dirge or lament for the dead. [C19: from Irish Gaelic *caoine,* from OIrish *coínim* I wail]
▶ ˈ**keener** *n*

keep (ki:p) *vb* **keeps, keeping, kept. 1** (*tr*) to have or retain possession of. **2** (*tr*) to have temporary possession or charge of: *keep my watch for me*. **3** (*tr*) to store in a customary place: *I keep my books in the desk.* **4** to remain or cause to remain in a specified state or condition: *keep ready.* **5** to continue or cause to continue: *keep in step.* **6** (*tr*) to have or take charge or care of: *keep the shop for me till I return.* **7** (*tr*) to look after or maintain for use, pleasure, etc.: *to keep chickens.* **8** (*tr*) to provide for the upkeep or livelihood of. **9** (*tr*) to support financially, esp. in return for sexual favours. **10** to confine or detain or be confined or detained. **11** to withhold or reserve or admit of withholding or reserving: *your news will keep.* **12** (*tr*) to refrain from divulging or violating: *to keep a secret.* **13** to preserve or admit of preservation. **14** (*tr*; sometimes foll. by *up*) to observe with due rites or ceremonies. **15** (*tr*) to maintain by writing regular records in: *to keep a diary.* **16** (when *intr*, foll. by *in, on, to,* etc.) to stay in, on, or at (a place or position): *keep to the path.* **17** (*tr*) to associate with (esp. in **keep bad company**). **18** (*tr*) to maintain in existence: *to keep court in the palace.* **19** (*tr*) *Chiefly Brit.* to have habitually in stock: *this shop keeps all kinds of wool.* **20 how are you keeping?** how are you? ◆ *n* **21** living or support. **22** *Arch.* charge or care. **23** Also called: **dungeon, donjon.** the main tower within the walls of a medieval castle or fortress. **24 for keeps.** *Inf.* **24a** permanently. **24b** for the winner or possessor to keep permanently. ◆ See also **keep at, keep away,** etc. [OE *cēpan* to observe]

keep at *vb* (*prep*) **1** (*intr*) to persist in. **2** (*tr*) to constrain (a person) to continue doing (a task).

keep away *vb* (*adv*; often foll. by *from*) to refrain or prevent from coming (near).

keep back *vb* (*adv*; often foll. by *from*) **1** (*tr*) to refuse to reveal or disclose. **2** to prevent or be prevented from advancing, entering, etc.

keep down *vb* (*adv*, mainly *tr*) **1** to repress. **2** to restrain or control: *he had difficulty keeping his anger down.* **3** to cause not to increase or rise. **4** (*intr*) to lie low. **5** not to vomit.

keeper ('ki:pə) *n* **1** a person in charge of animals, esp. in a zoo. **2** a person in charge of a museum, collection, or section of a museum. **3** a person in charge of other people, such as a warder in a jail. **4** See **goalkeeper, wicketkeeper, gamekeeper, park keeper. 5** a person who keeps something. **6** a bar placed across the poles of a permanent magnet to close the magnetic circuit when it is not in use.

keep fit *n* exercises designed to promote physical fitness if performed regularly.

keep from *vb* (*prep*) **1** (foll. by a gerund) to prevent or restrain (oneself or another); refrain or cause to refrain. **2** (*tr*) to protect or preserve from.

keeping ('ki:pɪŋ) *n* **1** conformity or harmony (esp. in **in** or **out of keeping**). **2** charge or care: *valuables in the keeping of a bank.*

keepnet ('ki:p,nɛt) *n* a net strung on wire hoops and sealed at one end, suspended in water by anglers to keep alive the fish they have caught.

keep off *vb* **1** to stay or cause to stay at a distance (from). **2** (*prep*) not to eat or drink or to prevent from eating or drinking. **3** (*prep*) to avoid or cause to avoid (a topic).

keep on *vb* (*adv*) **1** to continue or persist in (doing something): *keep on running.* **2** (*tr*) to continue to wear. **3** (*tr*) to continue to employ: *the firm kept on only ten men.* **4** (*intr*; foll. by *about*) to persist in talking (about). **5** (*intr*; foll. by *at*) to nag (a person).

keep out *vb* (*adv*) **1** to remain or cause to remain outside. **2 keep out of. 2a** to remain or cause to remain unexposed to. **2b** to avoid or cause to avoid: *keep out of his way.*

keepsake ('ki:p,seɪk) *n* a gift that evokes memories of a person or event.

keep to *vb* (*prep*) **1** to adhere to or stand by or cause to adhere to or stand by. **2** to confine or be confined to. **3 keep oneself to oneself.** to avoid the society of others. **4 keep oneself. 4a** (*intr*) to avoid the society of others. **4b** (*tr*) to refrain from sharing or disclosing.

keep up *vb* (*adv*) **1** to maintain (prices, one's morale) at the present level. **2** (*intr*; often foll. by *with*) to maintain a pace or rate set by another. **3** (*intr*; often foll. by

with) to remain informed: *to keep up with developments.* **4** (*tr*) to maintain in good condition. **5** (*tr*) to hinder (a person) from going to bed at night. **6 keep it up.** to continue a good performance. **7 keep up with.** to remain in contact with, esp. by letter. **8 keep up with (the Joneses).** *Inf.* to compete with (one's neighbours) in material possessions, etc.

Keewatin ★ (ki:'weɪtɪn) *n* a former administrative district of the Northwest Territories of Canada stretching from the district of Mackenzie to Hudson Bay: mostly tundra: became part of Nunavut in 1999. Area: 590 930 sq. km (228 160 sq. miles).

kef (kɛf) *n* a variant spelling of **kif.**

keffiyeh (kɛ'fi:jə), **kaffiyeh,** *or* **kufiyah** *n* a cotton headdress worn by Arabs. [C19: from Ar., ?from LL *cofea* COIF]

Keflavík ★ ('kɛfləvɪk) *n* a port in SW Iceland: NATO airbase, fishing. Pop.: 7627 (1994).

keg (kɛg) *n* **1** a small barrel with a capacity of between five and ten gallons. **2** *Brit., Austral., & NZ.* an aluminium container in which beer is transported and stored [C17: var. of ME *kag*, of Scand. origin]

Keighley ★ ('ki:θlɪ) *n* a town in N England, in Bradford unitary authority, West Yorkshire on the River Aire: textile industry. Pop.: 49 567 (1991).

Keijo ★ ('keɪ'dʒəʊ) *n* transliteration of the Japanese name for Seoul.

Keitel ★ (*German* 'kaɪtəl) *n* **Wilhelm** ('vɪlhɛlm). 1882-1946, German field marshal; chief of the armed forces (1938–45); convicted at the Nuremberg trials and executed.

Kekkonen ★ (*Finnish* 'kɛkkɔnɛn) *n* **Urho** ('urhɔ). (1900-86), Finnish statesman; president (1956–81).

keks (kɛks) *pl n* a variant spelling of **kecks.**

Kekulé von Stradonitz ★ (*German* 'ke:kule fɔr 'ʃtraːdɔnɪts) *n* (**Friedrich**) **August** ('august). 1829–96, German chemist. He elucidated valence and the structure of benzene (**Kekulé structure**).

Kelantan ★ (kə'læntən, kɪ,læn'tæn) *n* a state of NE Malaysia: under Thai control until it came under the British in 1909; produces rice and rubber. Capital: Kota Bharu Pop.: 1 221 700 (1993 est.). Area: 14 930 sq. km (5765 sq. miles).

Keller ★ ('kɛlə) *n* **Helen (Adams).** 1880–1968, US author and lecturer. Blind and deaf from infancy, she learned to read, write, and speak and worked for the handicapped.

Kells ★ (kɛlz) *n* a town in the Republic of Ireland, in Co Meath: *The Book of Kells,* an illuminated manuscript of the Gospels, was produced at the monastery here in the 8th century. Pop.: 2187 (1991).

Kelly ★ ('kɛlɪ) *n* **1 Gene,** full name *Eugene Curran Kelly* 1912–96, US dancer and film actor. His many films include *An American in Paris* (1951) and *Singin' in the Rain* (1952). **2 Grace.** 1929–82, US film actress, whose films included *High Noon* (1952) and *High Society* (1956). She married Prince Rainier III of Monaco in 1956 and died following a car crash. **3 Ned.** 1855–80, Australian horse thief and bushranger: captured by the police and hanged.

Kelman ★ ('kɛlmən) *n* **James.** born 1946, Scottish novelist; his novels include the Booker prizewinner *How Late It Was, How Late* (1994).

keloid ('ki:lɔɪd) *n Pathol.* a hard raised growth of scar tissue at the site of an injury. [C19: from Gk *khēlē* claw]

kelp (kɛlp) *n* **1** any large brown seaweed. **2** the ash of such seaweed, used as a source of iodine and potash. [C14 from ?]

kelpie[1] *or* **kelpy** ('kɛlpɪ) *n, pl* **kelpies.** an Australian breed of sheepdog having a coat of various colours and erect ears. [named after a particular specimen of the breed, c 1870]

kelpie[2] ('kɛlpɪ) *n* (in Scottish folklore) a water spirit in th form of a horse. [C18: prob. rel. to Scot. Gaelic *cailpeac* heifer, from ?]

kelson ('kɛlsən) *n* a variant spelling of **keelson.**

★ people and places

kelt (kɛlt) *n* a salmon that has recently spawned. [C14: from ?]

Kelt (kɛlt) *n* a variant spelling of **Celt**.

kelter ('kɛltə) *n* a variant of **kilter**.

kelvin ('kɛlvɪn) *n* the basic SI unit of thermodynamic temperature; the fraction 1/273.16 of the thermodynamic temperature of the triple point of water. Symbol: K

Kelvin ★ ('kɛlvɪn) *n* **William Thomson**, 1st Baron Kelvin. 1824–1907, British physicist, noted for his work in thermodynamics and pioneering undersea telegraphy.

Kelvin scale *n* a thermodynamic temperature scale in which the zero is absolute zero. Originally the degree was equal to that on the Celsius scale but it is now defined so that the triple point of water is exactly 273.16 kelvins.

Kemal Atatürk ★ (kɛ'mɑːl 'ætə,tɜːk) *n* See **Atatürk**.
▶ **Ke'malism** *n* ▶ **Ke'malist** *n, adj*

Kemerovo ★ (*Russian* 'kjɛmɪrəvə) *n* a city in S Russia: a coal-mining centre with chemical plants. Pop.: 503 000 (1995 est.). Former name (until 1932): **Shcheglovsk**.

Kempe ★ (*German* 'kɛmpə) *n* **Rudolf** ('ruːdɔlf). 1910–76, German conductor.

Kempis ★ ('kɛmpɪs) *n* **Thomas à**. ?1380–1471, German Augustinian monk, thought to be the author of *The Imitation of Christ*.

kempt (kɛmpt) *adj* (of hair) tidy; combed. See also **unkempt**. [C20: back formation from *unkempt*; orig. p.p. of dialect *kemb* to COMB]

ken (kɛn) *n* **1** range of knowledge (esp. in **beyond** *or* **in one's ken**). ◆ *vb* **kens, kenning, kenned** *or* **kent**. **2** *Scot. & northern English dialect*. to know. **3** *Scot. & northern English dialect*. to understand. [OE *cennan*]

Ken. *abbrev.* for Kentucky.

Kendal ★ ('kɛnd°l) *n* a town in NW England, in Cumbria: a gateway town to the Lake District, with an ancient woollen industry. Pop.: 25 461 (1991).

Kendall ★ ('kɛnd°l) *n* **Edward Calvin**. 1886–1972, US biochemist, who isolated the hormone thyroxine (1916). He shared the Nobel prize for physiology or medicine (1950).

kendo (kɛndəu) *n* the Japanese art of fencing with pliable bamboo staves or, sometimes, real swords. [Japanese, lit.: way of the sword, from *ken* sword + *do* way]

Kendrew ★ ('kɛndruː) *n* Sir **John Cowdery**. 1917–97, British biochemist. He discovered the structure of myoglobin, for which he shared a Nobel Prize (1962) with Max Perutz.

Keneally ★ (kə'nɪəlɪ) *n* **Thomas (Michael)**. born 1935, Australian writer. His novels include the Booker prizewinner *Schindler's Ark* (1982), *The Playmaker* (1987), and *The Great Shame* (1998).

Kenilworth ★ ('kɛnɪl,wɜːθ) *n* a town in central England, in Warwickshire: ruined 12th-century castle, subject of Sir Walter Scott's novel *Kenilworth*. Pop.: 21 623 (1991).

Kénitra ★ (*French* kenitra) *n* another name for **Mina Hassan Tani**.

Kennedy[1] ★ ('kɛnɪdɪ) *n* **Cape**. a former name (1963–73) of (Cape) **Canaveral**.

Kennedy[2] ★ ('kɛnɪdɪ) *n* **1 Edward (Moore)**, known as *Ted*. born 1932, US Democrat politician: brother of J.F. Kennedy; senator since 1962. **2 John Fitzgerald**, known as *JFK*. 1917–63, US Democrat statesman; 35th president of the US (1961–63), the first Roman Catholic and the youngest man to be president. He demanded the withdrawal of Soviet missiles from Cuba (1962); assassinated. **3 Nigel (Paul)**. born 1956, British violinist. **4 Robert (Francis)**. 1925–68, US Democrat statesman: brother of J. F. Kennedy; attorney general (1961–64) and senator for New York (1965–68); assassinated.

kennel ('kɛn°l) *n* **1** a hutlike shelter for a dog. US name: **doghouse**. **2** (*usually pl*) an establishment where dogs are bred, trained, boarded, etc. **3** a hovel. **4** a pack of hounds. ◆ *vb* **kennels, kennelling, kennelled** *or* US **kennels, kenneling, kenneled**. **5** to keep or stay in a kennel. [C14: from OF, from Vulgar L *canīle* (unattested), from L *canis* dog]

Kennelly ★ ('kɛnəlɪ) *n* **Arthur Edwin**. 1861–1939, US electrical engineer: he predicted the existence of an ionized layer in the upper atmosphere, known as the Kennelly-Heaviside layer.

Kenneth I ★ ('kɛnɪθ) *n* surnamed *MacAlpine*. died 858, king of the Scots of Dalriada and of the Picts (?844–858): considered the first Scottish king.

kenning ('kɛnɪŋ) *n* a conventional metaphoric name for something, esp. in Old Norse and Old English poetry. [C14: from ON, from *kenna*; see KEN]

Kenny ★ ('kɛnɪ) *n* **Yvonne**. born 1950, Australian opera singer.

Kensington and Chelsea ★ ('kɛnzɪŋtən) *n* a borough of Greater London, on the River Thames: **Kensington Palace** (17th century) and gardens. Pop.: 151 500 (1994 est.). Area: 12 sq. km (5 sq. miles).

kenspeckle ('kɛn,spɛk°l) *adj Scot.* easily seen or recognized. [C18: from dialect *kenspeck*, of Scand. origin]

Kent[1] ★ (kɛnt) *n* a county of SE England, on the English Channel: the first part of Great Britain to be colonized by the Romans; one of the seven kingdoms of Anglo-Saxon England until absorbed by Wessex in the 9th century A.D. Apart from the Downs it is mostly low-lying and agricultural, specializing in fruit and hops. Administrative centre: Maidstone. Pop.: 1 546 300 (1994 est.). Area: 3731 sq. km (1440 sq. miles).
▶ **'Kentish** *adj*

Kent[2] ★ (kɛnt) *n* **William**. ?1685–1748, English architect and landscape gardener.

Kentucky ★ (kɛn'tʌkɪ) *n* **1** a state of the S central US: consists of an undulating plain in the west, the Bluegrass region in the centre, the Tennessee and Ohio River basins in the southwest, and the Appalachians in the east. Capital: Frankfort. Pop.: 3 883 723 (1996 est.). Area: 102 693 sq. km (39 650 sq. miles). Abbrevs.: **Ken., Ky.** or (with zip code) **KY**. **2** a river in central Kentucky, rising in the Cumberland Mountains and flowing northwest to the Ohio River. Length: 417 km (259 miles).
▶ **Ken'tuckian** *adj, n*

Kenya ★ ('kɛnjə, 'kiːnjə) *n* **1** a republic in E Africa, on the Indian Ocean: became a British protectorate in 1895 and a colony in 1920; gained independence in 1963 and is a member of the Commonwealth. Coffee constitutes about a third of the total export. Official languages: Swahili and English. Religions: animist and Christian. Currency: shilling. Capital: Nairobi. Pop.: 28 803 000 (1997). Area: 582 647 sq. km (224 960 sq. miles). **2 Mount**. an extinct volcano in central Kenya: the second highest mountain in Africa; girth at 2400 m (8000 ft) is about 150 km (95 miles). The regions above 3200 m (10 500 ft) constitute **Mount Kenya National Park**. Height: 5200 m (17 058 ft).
▶ **'Kenyan** *adj, n*

Kenyatta ★ (kɛn'jætə) *n* **Jomo** ('dʒəuməu). ?1891–1978, Kenyan statesman: imprisoned as a suspected leader of the Mau Mau revolt (1953–59); elected president of the Kenya African National Union (1961); prime minister of independent Kenya (1963) and president (1964–78).

Keos ★ ('keɪɒs) *n* an island in the Aegean Sea, in the NW Cyclades. Pop.: 1700 (latest est.). Area: 174 sq. km (67 sq. miles). Italian name: **Zea**. Modern Greek name: **Kéa**.

Kephallinía ★ (,kɛfali'nia; *English* ,kɛfə'liːnɪə) *n* transliteration of the Modern Greek name for **Cephalonia**.

kepi ('keɪpɪ) *n, pl* **kepis**. a military cap with a circular top and a horizontal peak. [C19: from F *képi*, from G (Swiss dialect) *käppi* a little cap, from *kappe* CAP]

Kepler ★ ('kɛplə) *n* **Johannes** (jo'hanəs). 1571–1630, German astronomer. As discoverer of Kepler's laws he is regarded as one of the founders of modern astronomy.

Kepler's laws *pl n* three laws of planetary motion published by Johan Kepler between 1609 and 1619. They deal with the shape of a planet's orbit, the constant velocity of the planet in orbit, and the relationship between the length of a planetary year and the distance from the sun.

kept (kɛpt) *vb* **1** the past tense and past participle of **keep**. **2 kept woman**. *Censorious*. a woman maintained by a man as his mistress.

Kerala ★ ('kɛrələ, kə'rɑːlə) n a state of SW India, on the Arabian Sea: formed in 1956, it includes the former state of Travancore-Cochin; has the highest population density of any Indian state. Capital: Trivandrum. Pop.: 30 555 000 (1994 est.). Area: 38 863 sq. km (15 005 sq. miles).

keratin ('kɛrətɪn) n a fibrous protein that occurs in the outer layer of the skin and in hair, nails, hooves, etc.

keratose ('kɛrə,təʊs, -,təʊz) adj (esp. of certain sponges) having a horny skeleton. [C19: from Gk keras horn + -OSE¹]

kerb or US & Canad. **curb** (kɜːb) n a line of stone or concrete forming an edge between a pavement and a roadway. [C17: from OF courbe bent, from L curvus; see CURVE]
▶ 'kerbing n

kerb crawling n the act of driving slowly beside the pavement seeking to entice someone into the car for sexual purposes.
▶ kerb crawler n

kerb drill n a pedestrian's procedure for crossing a road safely, esp. as taught to children.

Kerbela ★ ('kɜːbələ) n a variant of **Karbala**.

kerbstone or US & Canad. **curbstone** ('kɜːb,stəʊn) n one of a series of stones that form a kerb.

Kerch ★ (Russian kjertʃ) n a port in the S Ukraine, on the **Kerch Peninsula** and the **Strait of Kerch** (linking the Black Sea with the Sea of Azov): founded as a Greek colony B.C. in the 6th century B.C.; ceded to Russia in 1774; iron-mining, steel production, and fishing. Pop.: 175 000 (1996 est.).

kerchief ('kɜːtʃɪf) n a piece of cloth worn over the head. [C13: from OF, from covrir to COVER + chef head]
▶ 'kerchiefed adj

kerel ('kɛərəl) n S. African. a young man. [from Afrik. kêrel; cf. OE ceorl]

Kerenski or **Kerensky** ★ (kə'rɛnskɪ; Russian 'kjerinskij) n **Aleksandr Fyodorovich** (alık'sandr 'fjɔdərəvitʃ). 1881–1970, Russian liberal revolutionary leader; prime minister (July–October 1917): overthrown by the Bolsheviks.

kerf (kɜːf) n the cut made by a saw, an axe, etc. [OE cyrf a cutting]

kerfuffle (kə'fʌfᵊl) n Inf., chiefly Brit. commotion; disorder. [from Scot. curfuffle, carfuffle, from Scot. Gaelic car twist, turn + fuffle to disarrange]

Kerguelen ★ ('kɜːgɪlɪn) n an archipelago in the S Indian Ocean: consists of one large volcanic island (Kerguelen or Desolation Island) and 300 small islands; part of the French Southern and Antarctic Territories.

Kerkrade ★ (Dutch 'kɛrkraːdə) n a town in the SE Netherlands, in Limburg: one of the oldest coal-mining centres in Europe. Pop.: 52 848 (1994).

Kérkyra ★ ('kɛrkira) n transliteration of the Modern Greek name for **Corfu**.

Kerman ★ (keə'mɑːn) n a city in SE Iran: carpet-making centre. Pop.: 311 643 (1991).

Kermanshah ★ (,kɜːmæn'ʃɑː) n the former name (until 1987) of **Bakhtaran**.

kermes ('kɜːmɪz) n 1 the dried bodies of female scale insects used as a red dyestuff. 2 a small evergreen Eurasian oak tree: the host plant of kermes scale insects. [C16: from F, from Ar. qirmiz, from Sansk. krmija- red dye, lit.: produced by a worm]

kermis or **kirmess** ('kɜːmɪs) n 1 (formerly, esp. in Holland and northern Germany) an annual country festival. 2 US & Canad. a similar event held to collect money for charity. [C16: from MDu., from kerc church + misse MASS; orig. a festival held to celebrate the dedication of a church]

kern¹ or **kerne** (kɜːn) n the part of the character on a piece of printer's type that projects beyond the body. [C17: from F carne corner of type, ult. from L cardō hinge]

kern² (kɜːn) n 1 a lightly armed foot soldier in medieval Ireland or Scotland. 2 Arch. a loutish peasant. [C14: from MIrish cethern band of foot soldiers, from cath battle]

Kern ★ (kɜːn) n **Jerome** (**David**). 1885–1945, US songwriter and composer of musicals, including Show Boat (1927).

kernel ('kɜːnᵊl) n 1 the edible seed of a nut or fruit within the shell or stone. 2 the grain of a cereal, esp. wheat, consisting of the seed in a hard husk. 3 the central or essential part of something. [OE cyrnel a little seed, from corn seed]
▶ 'kernel-less adj

kerosene or **kerosine** ('kɛrə,siːn) n 1 another name (esp. US, Canad., Austral., & NZ) for **paraffin** (sense 1). 2 the general name for paraffin as a fuel for jet aircraft. [C19: from Gk kēros wax + -ENE]

USAGE NOTE The spelling kerosine is now the preferred form in technical and industrial usage.

Kerouac ★ ('kɛru,æk) n **Jack**, real name Jean-Louis Lebris de Kérouac. 1922–69, US novelist and poet of the Beat Generation. His works include On the Road (1957) and Big Sur (1962).

Kerr ★ (kɜː) n Sir **John Robert**. 1914–91, Australian public servant. As governor general of Australia (1974–77), he dismissed the Labor prime minister Gough Whitlam (1975).

Kerry ★ ('kɛrɪ) n a county of SW Republic of Ireland, in W Munster province: mostly mountainous (including the highest peaks in Ireland), with a deeply indented coast and many offshore islands. County town: Tralee. Pop.: 121 894 (1991). Area: 4701 sq. km (1815 sq. miles).

kersey ('kɜːzɪ) n a twilled woollen cloth with a cotton warp. [C14: prob. from Kersey, village in Suffolk]

kerseymere ('kɜːzɪ,mɪə) n a fine soft woollen cloth of twill weave. [C18: from KERSEY + (cassi)mere, var. of CASHMERE]

Kesey ★ ('kiːzɪ) n **Ken**. born 1935, US novelist, best known for One Flew Over the Cuckoo's Nest (1962).

Kesselring ★ ('kɛsᵊlrɪŋ) n **Albert** ('albɛrt). 1885–1960, German field marshal. He commanded the Luftwaffe (1939–40), and was supreme commander in Italy (1943–45) and on the western front (1945).

Kesteven ★ ('kɛstɪvᵊn, kɛ'stiːvᵊn) n **Parts of.** an area in E England constituting a former administrative division of Lincolnshire.

kestrel ('kɛstrəl) n any of several small falcons that feed on small mammals and tend to hover against the wind. [C15: changed from OF cresserele, from cressele rattle, from Vulgar L crepicella (unattested), from L, from crepāre to rustle]

Keswick ★ ('kɛzɪk) n a market town in NW England, in Cumbria in the Lake District: tourist centre. Pop.: 4836 (1991).

ketch (kɛtʃ) n a two-masted sailing vessel, fore-and-aft rigged, with a tall mainmast. [C15 cache, prob. from cacchen to hunt; see CATCH]

ketchup ('kɛtʃəp), **catchup**, or **catsup** n any of various sauces containing vinegar: tomato ketchup. [C18: from Chinese kōetsiap brine of pickled fish, from kōe seafood + tsiap sauce]

ketone ('kiːtəʊn) n any of a class of compounds with the general formula R'COR, where R and R' are alkyl or aryl groups. [C19: from G, from Aketon ACETONE]
▶ **ketonic** (kɪ'tɒnɪk) adj

ketone body n Biochem. any of three compounds produced when fatty acids are broken down in the liver to provide a source of energy. Excess ketone bodies are present in the blood and urine of people unable to use glucose as an energy source, as in diabetes.

Kettering ★ ('kɛtərɪŋ) n a town in central England, in Northamptonshire: footwear industry. Pop.: 47 186 (1991).

kettle ('kɛtᵊl) n 1 a metal container with a handle and spout for boiling water. 2 any of various metal containers for heating liquids, cooking fish, etc. 3 a large metal vessel designed to withstand high temperatures, used in various industrial processes such as refining and brew-

★ people and places

ing. [C13: from ON *ketill*, ult. from L *catillus* a little pot, from *catīnus* pot]

kettledrum ('ket^əl,drʌm) *n* a percussion instrument of definite pitch, consisting of a hollow bowl-like hemisphere covered with a skin or membrane, supported on a tripod. The pitch may be adjusted by means of screws, which alter the tension of the skin.
▶ '**kettle,drummer** *n*

kettle hole *n* a round hollow formed by the melting of a mass of buried ice.

kettle of fish *n* 1 a situation; state of affairs (often used ironically in **a pretty** or **fine kettle of fish**). 2 case; matter for consideration: *that's quite a different kettle of fish*.

Kevlar ('kev,lɑː) *n Trademark.* a synthetic fibre, consisting of long-chain polyamides, having high tensile strength and temperature resistance.

Kew ★ (kjuː) *n* part of the Greater London borough of Richmond-upon-Thames, on the River Thames: famous for **Kew Gardens** (the Royal Botanic Gardens), established in 1759 and given to the nation in 1841.

key[1] (kiː) *n* 1 a metal instrument, usually of a specifically contoured shape, that is made to fit a lock and, when rotated, operates the lock's mechanism. 2 any instrument that is rotated to operate a valve, clock winding mechanism, etc. 3 a small metal peg or wedge inserted to prevent relative motion. 4 any of a set of buttons operating a typewriter, computer, etc. 5 any of the visible parts of the lever mechanism of a musical keyboard instrument that when depressed cause the instrument to sound. **6a** Also called: **tonality.** any of the 24 major and minor diatonic scales considered as a corpus of notes upon which a piece of music draws for its tonal framework. **6b** the main tonal centre in an extended composition: *a symphony in the key of F major.* 7 something that is crucial in providing an explanation or interpretation. 8 (*modifier*) of great importance: *a key issue.* 9 a means of achieving a desired end: *the key to happiness.* 10 a means of access or control: *Gibraltar is the key to the Mediterranean.* 11 a list of explanations of symbols, codes, etc. 12 a text that explains or gives information about a work of literature, art, or music. 13 *Electrical engineering.* a hand-operated switch that is pressed to transmit coded signals, esp. Morse code. 14 the grooving or scratching of a surface or the application of a rough coat of plaster, etc., to provide a bond for a subsequent finish. 15 pitch: *he spoke in a low key.* 16 a mood or style: *a poem in a melancholic key.* 17 short for **keystone** (sense 1). 18 *Bot.* any dry winged fruit, esp. that of the ash. ◆ *vb* (mainly tr) 19 (foll. by *to*) to harmonize (with): *to key one's actions to the prevailing mood.* 20 to adjust or fasten with a key or some similar device. 21 to provide with a key or keys. 22 (*also intr*) another word for **keyboard** (sense 3). 23 to include a distinguishing device in (an advertisement, etc.), so that responses to it can be identified. 24 (*also intr*) to groove, scratch, or apply a rough coat of plaster, etc., to (a surface) to provide a bond for a subsequent finish. ◆ See also **key in**, **key up.** [OE *cǣg*]
▶ '**keyless** *adj*

key[2] (kiː) *n* a variant spelling of **cay.**

keyboard ('kiː,bɔːd) *n* **1a** a set of keys, usually hand-operated, as on a piano, typewriter, or typesetting machine. **1b** (*as modifier*): *a keyboard instrument.* 2 (*pl*) electronic keyboard instruments: *John plays keyboards for the band.* ◆ *vb* 3 (*tr*) to set (a text) in type by using a keyboard machine.
▶ '**key,boarder** *n*

key grip *n* the person in charge of moving and setting up camera tracks and scenery in a film or television studio.

keyhole ('kiː,həʊl) *n* an aperture in a door or a lock case through which a key may be passed to engage the lock mechanism.

keyhole surgery *n* surgery carried out through a very small incision.

key in *vb* (tr, adv) to enter (information or instructions) in a computer or other device by means of a keyboard or keypad.

key-man assurance *n* an assurance policy taken out,

esp. by a small company, on the life of a senior executive whose death would create a serious loss.

key money *n* a fee payment required from a new tenant of a house or flat before he moves in.

Keynes ★ (keɪnz) *n* **John Maynard,** 1st Baron Keynes. 1883–1946, British economist. His most influential work was *The General Theory of Employment, Interest and Money* (1936). He helped to found the International Monetary Fund and the World Bank.
▶ '**Keynesian** *adj, n* ▶ '**Keynesian,ism** *n*

keynote ('kiː,nəʊt) *n* **1a** a central or determining principle in a speech, literary work, etc. **1b** (*as modifier*): *a keynote speech.* 2 the note upon which a scale or key is based; tonic. ◆ *vb* **keynotes, keynoting, keynoted.** (*tr*) 3 to deliver a keynote address to (a political convention, etc.).

keypad ('kiː,pæd) *n* a small panel with a set of buttons for operating a teletext system, electronic calculator, etc.

key punch *n* 1 Also called: **card punch.** a device having a keyboard that is operated manually to transfer data onto punched cards, paper tape, etc. ◆ *vb* **key-punch.** 2 to transfer (data) by using a key punch.

key signature *n Music.* a group of sharps or flats appearing at the beginning of each stave line to indicate the key in which a piece, section, etc., is to be performed.

key stage *n Brit. education.* any one of four broad age-group divisions (5–7; 7–11; 11–14; 14–16) to which each level of the National Curriculum applies.

keystone ('kiː,stəʊn) *n* 1 the central stone at the top of an arch or the top stone of a dome or vault. 2 something that is necessary to connect other related things.

key up *vb* (tr, adv) to raise the intensity, excitement, tension, etc., of.

kg 1 *abbrev. for* keg. ◆ 2 *symbol for* kilogram.

KG *abbrev. for* Knight of the Order of the Garter (a Brit. title).

KGB *abbrev. for* the former Soviet secret police, founded in 1954. [from Russian *Komitet gosudarstvennoi bezopasnosti* State Security Committee]

Khabarovsk ★ (*Russian* xa'barəfsk) *n* a port in E Russia, on the Amur River: the administrative centre of the whole Soviet Far Eastern territory until 1938; a major industrial centre. Pop.: 618 000 (1995 est.).

Khachaturian ★ (,kɑːtʃə'tʊərɪən; *Russian* xətʃətu'rjan) *n* **Aram Ilich** ('arəm ilj'jitʃ). 1903–78, Russian composer. His works include a piano concerto and the ballets *Gayaneh* (1942) and *Spartacus* (1954).

khaddar ('kɑːdə) *or* **khadi** ('kɑːdɪ) *n* a cotton cloth of plain weave, produced in India. [from Hindi *khādar*]

Khakass Republic ★ (kə'kæs) *n* a constituent republic of S central Russia, in the Krasnoyarsk Territory: formed in 1930. Capital: Abakan. Pop.: 583 000 (1995 est.). Area: 61 900 sq. km (23 855 sq. miles). Also called: **Khakassia** (kə'kæsɪə; *Russian* xə'kəsjə).

khaki ('kɑːkɪ) *n, pl* **khakis. 1** a dull yellowish-brown colour. **2a** a hard-wearing fabric of this colour, used esp. for military uniforms. **2b** (*as modifier*): *a khaki jacket.* [C19: from Urdu, from Persian: dusty, from *khāk* dust]

Khalid ibn Abdul Aziz ★ ('kɑːlɪd 'ɪbʔn 'æbdʊl ə'ziːz) *n* 1913–82, king and President of the Council of Ministers of Saudi Arabia (1975–82).

khalif ('keɪlɪf) *n* a variant spelling of **caliph.**

Khalkidíki ★ (xalkiði'ki) *n* transliteration of the Modern Greek name for **Chalcidice.**

Khalkís ★ (xal'kis) *n* transliteration of the Modern Greek name for **Chalcis.**

Khalsa ('kælsə) *n* an order of the Sikh religion, founded (1699) by Guru Gobind Singh.

Khama ★ ('kɑːmə) *n* Sir **Seretse** (sə'rɛtsɪ). 1921–80, Botswanan statesman; first president of Botswana (1966–80).

khan[1] (kɑːn) *n* **1a** (formerly) a title borne by medieval Chinese emperors and Mongol and Turkic rulers. **1b** such a ruler. 2 a title of respect borne by important personages in Afghanistan and central Asia. [C14: from OF,

from Med. L, from Turkish *khān*, contraction of *khāqān* ruler]
▶ 'khanate *n*

khan[2] (kɑːn) *n* an inn in Turkey, etc.; caravanserai. [C14: via Ar. from Persian]

Khan ★ (kɑːn) *n* Imran. See **Imran Khan**.

Khaniá ★ (xaˈnja) *n* transliteration of the Modern Greek name for **Canea**.

Kharkov ★ (*Russian* ˈxarjkəf) *n* a city in the E Ukraine: capital of the Ukrainian Soviet Socialist Republic from 1917 until 1934; university (1805). Pop.: 1 555 000 (1996 est.).

Khartoum *or* **Khartum** ★ (kɑːˈtuːm) *n* the capital of the Sudan, at the junction of the Blue and the White Nile: with adjoining Khartoum North and Omdurman, the largest conurbation in the country; destroyed by the Mahdists in 1885 when General Gordon was killed; seat of the Anglo-Egyptian government of the Sudan until 1954, then capital of the new republic. Pop.: 924 505 (1993).

Khayyám ★ (kaɪˈɑːm) *n* Omar. See **Omar Khayyám**.

khedive (kɪˈdiːv) *n* the viceroy of Egypt under Ottoman suzerainty (1867–1914). [C19: from F, from Turkish, from Persian *khidīw* prince]
▶ **khe'dival** *or* **khe'divial** *adj*

Khelat ★ (kəˈlɑːt) *n* a variant spelling of **Kalat**.

Kherson ★ (*Russian* xɪrˈsɒn) *n* a port in the S Ukraine, on the Dnieper River near the Black Sea: shipyards. Pop.: 363 000 (1996 est.).

Khingan Mountains ★ (ˈʃɪŋˈɑːn) *pl n* a mountain system of NE China, in W Manchuria. Highest peak: 2034 m (6673 ft).

Khíos ★ (ˈçiɒs) *n* transliteration of the Modern Greek name for **Chios**.

Khirbet Qumran ★ (ˈkɪəbet ˈkumrɑːn) *n* an archaeological site in NW Jordan, near the NW shore of the Dead Sea: includes the caves where the Dead Sea Scrolls were found.

Khmer (kmɛə) *n* **1** a member of a people of Cambodia, noted for a civilization that flourished from about 800 A.D. to about 1370. **2** the language of this people: the official language of Cambodia. ◆ *adj* **3** of or relating to this people or their language.
▶ **'Khmerian** *adj*

Khmer Republic ★ *n* the former official name (1970–76) of **Cambodia**.

Khoikhoi (kɔɪˈkɔɪ *or* xɔɪˈxɔɪ) *n* **1** a member of a Southern African people who formerly occupied the region around the Cape of Good Hope and are now almost extinct. **2** any of the languages of this people.

Khojent, Khodzhent (*Russian* xadˈʒɛnt), *or* **Khujand** ★ (*Russian* xuˈʒænd) *n* a town in Tajikistan, on the Syr Darya River: one of the oldest towns in central Asia; textile industries. Pop.: 164 500 (1991 est.). Former name (1936–91) **Leninabad**.

Khomeini ★ (ˈxɒmerˈniː) *n* **Ruholla** (ˈruhɒˈlɑː), known as *Ayatollah Khomeini*. 1900–89, Iranian Shiite Muslim religious leader. Following the overthrow of the shah of Iran (1979) he returned from exile and instituted an Islamic republic. His rule saw deteriorating relations with the West and war (1980–88) with Iraq.

Khotan ★ (ˈkəuˈtɑːn) *n* another name for **Hotan**.

Khrushchev ★ (kruːsˈtʃɒf, ˈkrustʃɒf; *Russian* xruˈʃtʃɒf) *n* **Nikita Sergeyevich** (nɪˈkitə sɪrˈgjejrvɪtʃ). 1894–1971, Soviet statesman; premier of the Soviet Union (1958–64), when he pursued a policy of peaceful coexistence with the West, but alienated Communist China. He was removed from office in 1964.

Khufu ★ (ˈkuːfuː) *n* the original name of **Cheops**.

Khulna ★ (ˈkʊlnɑː) *n* a city in S Bangladesh. Pop.: 731 000 (1991).

Khyber Pass ★ (ˈkaɪbə) *n* a narrow pass over the Safed Koh Range between Afghanistan and Pakistan, over which came the Persian, Greek, Tatar, Mogul, and Afghan invasions of India; scene of bitter fighting between the British and Afghans (1838–42, 1878–80).

Length: about 53 km (33 miles). Highest point: 1072 m (3518 ft).

kHz *symbol for* kilohertz.

kiang (kɪˈæŋ) *n* a variety of the wild ass that occurs in Tibet and surrounding regions. [C19: from Tibetan *rkyan*]

Kiangsi ★ (ˈkjænˈsiː) *n* a variant transliteration of the Chinese name for **Jiangxi**.

Kiangsu ★ (ˈkjænˈsuː) *n* a variant transliteration of the Chinese name for **Jiangsu**.

Kiaochow ★ (ˈkjauˈtʃau) *n* a variant transliteration of the Chinese name for **Jiazhou**.

kia ora (ˌkiə ˈɔːrə) *sentence substitute*. NZ. greetings! good luck! [Maori, lit.: be well!]

kibble[1] (ˈkɪbəl) *n Brit.* a bucket used in wells or in mining for hoisting. [C17: from G *kübel*, ult. from Med. L *cuppa* CUP]

kibble[2] (ˈkɪbəl) *vb* kibbles, kibbling, kibbled. (*tr*) to grind into small pieces. [C18: from ?]

kibbutz (kɪˈbuts) *n, pl* kibbutzim (ˌkɪbutˈsiːm). a collective agricultural settlement in modern Israel, owned and administered communally by its members. [C20: from Mod. Heb. *qibbūs* gathering, from Heb. *qibbūtz*]

kibe (kaɪb) *n* a chilblain, esp. an ulcerated one on the heel. [C14: prob. from Welsh *cibi*, from ?]

kiblah (ˈkɪblɑː) *n Islam*. the direction of Mecca, to which Muslims turn in prayer. [C18: from Ar. *qiblah* that which is placed opposite]

kibosh (ˈkaɪbɒʃ) *n* put the kibosh on. *Sl.* to put a stop to; prevent from continuing; halt. [C19: from ?]

kick (kɪk) *vb* **1** (*tr*) to drive or impel with the foot. **2** (*tr*) to hit with the foot or heel. **3** (*intr*) to strike out or thrash about with the feet, as in fighting or swimming. **4** (*intr*) to raise a leg high, as in dancing. **5** (of a gun, etc.) to recoil or strike in recoiling when fired. **6** (*tr*) *Rugby*. to make (a conversion or a drop goal) by means of a kick. **7** (*tr*) *Soccer*. to score (a goal) by a kick. **8** (*intr*) *Athletics*. to put on a sudden spurt. **9** (*intr*) to make a sudden violent movement. **10** (*intr*; sometimes foll. by *against*) *Inf.* to object or resist. **11** (*intr*) *Inf.* to be active and in good health (esp. in **alive and kicking**). **12** *Inf.* to change gear in a car: *he kicked into third.* **13** (*tr*) *Inf.* to free oneself of (an addiction, etc.): *he tried to kick the habit.* **14** kick up one's heels. *Inf.* to enjoy oneself without inhibition. ◆ *n* **15** a thrust or blow with the foot. **16** any of certain rhythmic leg movements used in swimming. **17** the recoil of a gun or other firearm. **18** *Inf.* exciting quality or effect (esp. in **get a kick out of, for kicks**). **19** *Athletics*. a sudden spurt, acceleration, or boost. **20** a sudden violent movement. **21** *Inf.* the sudden stimulating effect of strong alcoholic drink or certain drugs. **22** *Inf.* power or force. **23** kick in the teeth. *Sl.* a humiliating rebuff. ◆ See also **kick about, kickback**, etc. [C14 *kiken*, ?from ON]
▶ **'kickable** *adj*

kick about *or* **around** *vb* (*mainly adv*) *Inf.* **1** (*tr*) to treat harshly. **2** (*tr*) to discuss (ideas, etc.) informally. **3** (*intr*) to wander aimlessly. **4** (*intr*) to lie neglected or forgotten.

kickback (ˈkɪkˌbæk) *n* **1** a strong reaction. **2** part of an income paid to a person in return for an opportunity to make a profit, often by some illegal arrangement. ◆ *vb* **kick back**. (*adv*) **3** (*intr*) to have a strong reaction. **4** (*intr*) (esp. of a gun) to recoil. **5** to pay a kickback to (someone).

kick boxing *n* a martial art that resembles boxing but permits blows with the feet as well as punches.

kickdown (ˈkɪkˌdaun) *n* a method of changing gear in a car with automatic transmission, by fully depressing the accelerator.

kicker (ˈkɪkə) *n* **1** a person or thing that kicks. **2** *US & Canad. sl.* a hidden or unexpected factor.

kick in *vb* (*adv*) **1** (*intr*) to start or become activated. **2** (*tr*) *Chiefly Austral. & NZ inf.* to contribute.

kick off *vb* (*intr, adv*) **1** to start play in a game of football by kicking the ball from the centre of the field. **2** *Inf.* to commence (a discussion, job, etc.). ◆ *n* kickoff. **3a** a place kick from the centre of the field in a game of foot-

★ people and places

ball. **3b** the time at which the first such kick is due to take place.

kick on vb (adv) Inf. to continue.

kick out vb (tr, adv) Inf. to eject or dismiss.

kickshaw ('kɪk,ʃɔː) or **kickshaws** n 1 a valueless trinket. 2 Arch. a small exotic delicacy. [C16: back formation from kickshaws, by folk etymology from F quelque chose something]

kickstand ('kɪk,stænd) n a short metal bar attached to the frame of a motorcycle or bicycle, which when kicked into a vertical position holds the stationary vehicle upright.

kick-start ('kɪk,stɑːt) vb (tr) 1 to start (an engine, esp. of a motorcycle) by means of a pedal that is kicked downwards. 2 Inf. to make (something) active, functional, or productive again. ♦ n 3 an action or event resulting in the reactivation of something.
▸ 'kick-,starter n

kick up vb (adv) Inf. to cause (trouble, etc.).

kick upstairs vb (tr, adv) Inf. to promote to a higher but effectively powerless position.

kid[1] (kɪd) n 1 the young of a goat or of a related animal, such as an antelope. 2 soft smooth leather made from the hide of a kid. 3 Inf. 3a a young person; child. 3b (modifier) younger or being still a child: kid brother. ♦ vb kids, kidding, kidded. 4 (of a goat) to give birth to (young). [C12: from ON]
▸ 'kiddishness n ▸ 'kid,like adj

kid[2] (kɪd) vb kids, kidding, kidded. Inf. (sometimes foll. by on or along) 1 (tr) to tease or deceive for fun. 2 (intr) to behave or speak deceptively for fun. 3 (tr) to fool (oneself) into believing (something): don't kid yourself that no-one else knows. [C19: prob. from KID[1]]
▸ 'kidder n ▸ 'kiddingly adv

Kid ★ (kɪd) n Thomas. a variant spelling of (Thomas) Kyd.

Kidd ★ (kɪd) n William, known as Captain Kidd. 1645–1701, Scottish pirate and murderer; hanged.

Kidderminster ★ ('kɪdə,mɪnstə) n 1 a town in W central England, in NE Hereford and Worcester on the River Stour: carpet industry. Pop.: 54 644 (1991). 2 a type of ingrain reversible carpet originally made at Kidderminster.

kiddy or **kiddie** ('kɪdɪ) n, pl kiddies. Inf. an affectionate word for child.

kid glove n 1 a glove made of kidskin. 2 handle with kid gloves. to treat with great tact or caution. ♦ adj kidglove. 3 overdelicate. 4 diplomatic; tactful: a kidglove approach.

kidnap ('kɪdnæp) vb kidnaps, kidnapping, kidnapped or US kidnaps, kidnaping, kidnaped. (tr) to carry off and hold (a person), usually for ransom. [C17: KID[1] + obs. nap to steal; see NAB]
▸ 'kidnapper n

kidney ('kɪdnɪ) n 1 either of two bean-shaped organs at the back of the abdominal cavity in man. They filter waste products from the blood, which are excreted as urine. Related adj: renal. 2 the corresponding organ in other animals. 3 the kidneys of certain animals used as food. 4 class, type, or disposition (esp. in of the same or a different kidney). [C14: from ?]

kidney bean n 1 any of certain bean plants having kidney-shaped seeds, esp. the scarlet runner. 2 the seed of any of these beans.

kidney machine n a machine carrying out the functions of a kidney, esp. used in haemodialysis.

kidney stone n 1 Pathol. a hard mass formed in the kidney, usually composed of oxalates, phosphates, and carbonates. Related name for nephrite.

kidology (kɪ'dɒlədʒɪ) n Brit. inf. the practice of bluffing or deception. [C20: from KID[2] + ology a science]

Kidron ★ ('kiːdrən) n a variant of Kedron.

kidskin ('kɪd,skɪn) n a soft smooth leather made from the hide of a young goat. Often shortened to kid.

kids' stuff n Sl. 1 something considered fit only for children. 2 something considered easy.

kidstakes ('kɪd,steɪks) pl n Austral. inf. pretence; nonsense: cut the kidstakes!

kie kie ('kiːɛ kiːɛ) n a New Zealand climbing plant with edible bracts. [from Maori]

Kiel ★ (kiːl) n a port in N Germany, capital of Schleswig-Holstein state, on the **Kiel Canal** (connecting the North Sea with the Baltic): joined the Hanseatic League in 1284; became part of Denmark in 1773 and passed to Prussia in 1866; an important naval base in World Wars I and II; shipbuilding and engineering industries. Pop.: 246 586 (1995 est.).

Kielce ★ (Polish 'kjeltsɛ) n an industrial city in S Poland. Pop.: 213 800 (1995 est.).

Kierkegaard ★ ('kɪəkə,gɑːd; Danish 'kirgəgɔːr) n Søren Aabye ('sœːrə 'ɔːby). 1813–55, Danish philosopher, who rejected organized Christianity and anticipated the existentialists. His works include Either/Or (1843) and The Sickness unto Death (1849).
▸ ,Kierke'gaardian adj

kieselguhr ('kiːzl,guə) n an unconsolidated form of diatomite. [C19: from G Kieselgur, from Kiesel flint + Gur loose earthy deposit]

Kiev ★ ('kiːɛf; Russian 'kijɪf) n the capital of the Ukraine, on the Dnieper River: formed the first Russian state by the late 9th century; university (1834). Pop.: 2 630 000 (1996 est.).

kif (kɪf, kiːf), **kef**, or **kief** (kiːf) n 1 another name for marijuana. 2 any drug that when smoked is capable of producing a euphoric condition. 3 the euphoric condition produced by smoking marijuana. [C20: from Ar. kayf pleasure]

Kigali ★ (kɪ'gɑːlɪ) n the capital of Rwanda, in the central part. Pop.: 232 733 (1991).

kike (kaɪk) n US & Canad. sl. an offensive word for Jew. [C20: prob. var. of kiki, reduplication of -ki, common name-ending among Jews from Slavic countries]

Kikládhes ★ (ki'klaðes) n transliteration of the Modern Greek name for Cyclades.

Kilauea ★ (,kiːlɑːuː'eɪə) n a crater on the E side of Mauna Loa volcano, on SE Hawaii Island: the world's largest active crater. Height: 1247 m (4090 ft). Width: 3 km (2 miles).

Kildare ★ (kɪl'dɛə) n a county of E Republic of Ireland, in Leinster province: mostly low-lying and fertile. County town: Naas. Pop.: 122 656 (1991). Area: 1694 sq. km (654 sq. miles).

kilderkin ('kɪldəkɪn) n 1 an obsolete unit of liquid capacity equal to 16 or 18 Imperial gallons or of dry capacity equal to 16 or 18 wine gallons. 2 a cask capable of holding a kilderkin. [C14: from MDu. kindekijn, from kintal hundredweight, from Med. L quintale]

kilim (kɪ'liːm, 'kiːlɪm) n a pileless woven rug of intricate design made in the Middle East. [C19: from Turkish, from Persian kilīm]

Kilimanjaro ★ (,kɪlɪmən'dʒɑːrəʊ) n a volcanic massif in N Tanzania: the highest peak in Africa; extends from east to west for 80 km (50 miles). Height: 5895 m (19 340 ft).

Kilkenny ★ (kɪl'kɛnɪ) n 1 a county of SE Republic of Ireland, in Leinster province: mostly agricultural. County town: Kilkenny. Pop.: 73 635 (1991). Area: 2062 sq. km (796 sq. miles). 2 a market town in SE Republic of Ireland, county town of Co. Kilkenny: capital of the ancient kingdom of Ossory. Pop.: 9500 (latest est.).

kill (kɪl) vb (mainly tr) 1 (also intr; when tr, sometimes foll. by off) to cause the death of (a person or animal). 2 to put an end to: to kill someone's interest. 3 to occupy (time) by doing something unimportant, esp. while waiting for something. 4 to deaden (sound). 5 Inf. to tire out: the effort killed him. 6 Inf. to cause to suffer pain or discomfort: my shoes are killing me. 7 Inf. to quash or veto: the bill was killed in the House of Lords. 8 Inf. to switch off; stop. 9 (also intr) Inf. to overcome with attraction, laughter, surprise, etc.: she was dressed to kill. 10 Tennis, squash, etc. to hit (a ball) so hard or so accurately that the opponent cannot return it. 11 Soccer. to bring (a moving ball) under control. 12 kill oneself. Inf. to overexert oneself: don't kill yourself. 13 kill two birds with one stone. to achieve two results with one action. ♦ n 14 the act of causing death, esp. at the end of a hunt, bullfight, etc. 15 the animal or animals killed during a hunt. **16** *NZ.* a seasonal tally of the number of stock killed at a meatworks. **17** the destruction of a battleship, tank, etc. **18 in at the kill.** present at the end of some undertaking. [C13 *cullen;* see QUELL]

Killarney ★ (kɪˈlɑːnɪ) *n* a town in SW Republic of Ireland, in Co. Kerry: a tourist centre near the **Lakes of Killarney.** Pop.: 7250 (1991).

killdeer (ˈkɪlˌdɪə) *n, pl* **killdeer** or **killdeers.** a large brown-and-white North American plover with two black breast bands. [C18: imit.]

killer (ˈkɪlə) *n* **1a** a person or animal that kills, esp. habitually. **1b** *(as modifier): a killer shark.* **2** something, esp. a task or activity, that is particularly taxing or exhausting. **3** *Austral. & NZ.* a farm animal selected to be killed for food.

killer bee *n* an African honeybee, or one of its hybrids originating in Brazil, that is extremely aggressive when disturbed.

killer cell *n* a type of white blood cell that is able to kill cells, such as cancer cells and cells infected with viruses.

killer whale *n* a predatory black-and-white toothed whale most common on cold seas.

killick (ˈkɪlɪk) or **killock** (ˈkɪlək) *n Naut.* a small anchor, esp. one made of a heavy stone. [C17: from ?]

Killiecrankie ★ (ˌkɪlɪˈkræŋkɪ) *n* a pass in central Scotland, in the Grampians: scene of a battle (1689) in which the Jacobites defeated William III's forces but lost their leader, Viscount Dundee.

killifish (ˈkɪlɪˌfɪʃ) *n, pl* **killifish** or **killifishes.** any of various chiefly American minnow-like fishes of fresh and brackish waters: used to control mosquitoes and as anglers' bait. [C19: from MDu. *kille* river + FISH]

killing (ˈkɪlɪŋ) *Inf.* ◆ *adj* **1** very tiring: *a killing pace.* **2** extremely funny. **3** causing death; fatal. ◆ *n* **4** the act of causing death; slaying. **5** a sudden stroke of success, usually financial, as in speculations on the stock market (esp. in **make a killing**).

killjoy (ˈkɪlˌdʒɔɪ) *n* a person who spoils other people's pleasure.

Kilmarnock ★ (kɪlˈmɑːnək) *n* a town in SW Scotland, the administrative centre of East Ayrshire: associations with Robert Burns; engineering and textile industries; whisky blending. Pop.: 44 307 (1991).

kiln (kɪln) *n* a large oven for burning, drying, or processing something, such as porcelain or bricks. [OE *cylen,* from LL *culīna* kitchen, from L *coquere* to COOK]

kilo (ˈkiːləu) *n, pl* **kilos.** short for **kilogram** or **kilometre.**

kilo- *prefix* **1** denoting 10^3 (1000): *kilometre.* Symbol: k **2** (in computers) denoting 2^{10} (1024): *kilobyte:* in computer usage, *kilo-* is restricted to sizes of storage (e.g. *kilobit*) when it means 1024; in other computer contexts it retains its usual meaning of 1000. [from F, from Gk *khilioi* thousand]

kilobyte (ˈkɪləˌbaɪt) *n Computing.* 1024 bytes. Abbrev.: **KB, kbyte.** See also **kilo-** (sense 2).

kilocalorie (ˈkɪləuˌkælərɪ) *n* another name for **Calorie.**

kilocycle (ˈkɪləuˌsaɪkᵊl) *n* short for kilocycle per second: a former unit of frequency equal to 1 kilohertz.

kilogram (ˈkɪləuˌgræm) *n* **1** one thousand grams. **2** the basic SI unit of mass, equal to the mass of the international prototype held by the *Bureau International des Poids et Mesures.* Symbol: kg

kilohertz (ˈkɪləuˌhɜːts) *n* one thousand hertz; one thousand cycles per second. Symbol: kHz

kilolitre (ˈkɪləˌliːtə) *n* one thousand litres. Symbol: kl

kilometre or *US* **kilometer** (ˈkɪləˌmiːtə, kɪˈlɒmɪtə) *n* one thousand metres. Symbol: km
▸ **kilometric** (ˌkɪləuˈmetrɪk) *adj*

kiloton (ˈkɪləuˌtʌn) *n* **1** one thousand tons. **2** an explosive power, esp. of a nuclear weapon, equal to the power of 1000 tons of TNT. Abbrev.: **kt.**

kilovolt (ˈkɪləuˌvəult) *n* one thousand volts. Symbol: kV

kilowatt (ˈkɪləuˌwɒt) *n* one thousand watts. Symbol: kW

kilowatt-hour *n* a unit of energy equal to the work

done by a power of 1000 watts in one hour. Symbol: kWh

kilt (kɪlt) *n* **1** a knee-length pleated skirt, esp. one in tartan, as worn by men in Highland dress. ◆ *vb* (*tr*) **2** to tuck (the skirt) up around one's body. **3** to put pleats in (cloth, etc.). [C18: of Scand. origin]
▸ **'kilted** *adj*

kilter (ˈkɪltə) or **kelter** *n* working order (esp. in **out of kilter**). [C17: from ?]

Kilung ★ (ˈkiːˈlʊŋ) *n* another name for **Chilung.**

Kilvert ★ (ˈkɪlvət) *n* **Francis.** 1840–79, British clergyman and diarist. His diary (published 1938–40) gives a vivid account of life in the Welsh Marches in the 1870s.

Kimberley ★ (ˈkɪmbəlɪ) *n* **1** a city in central South Africa: besieged (1899–1900) for 126 days during the Boer War; diamond-mining and -marketing centre, with heavy engineering works. Pop.: 183 000 (1995 est.). **2** Also called: **the Kimberleys.** a plateau region of NW Australia, in N Western Australia: consists of rugged mountains surrounded by grassland. Area: about 360 000 sq. km (140 000 sq. miles).

kimberlite (ˈkɪmbəˌlaɪt) *n* an intrusive igneous rock consisting largely of peridotite and often containing diamonds. [C19: from KIMBERLEY + -ITE¹]

Kim Il Sung ★ (ˌkim il ˈsʌŋ) *n* 1912–94, North Korean statesman and marshal; prime minister (1948–72) and president (1972–94) of North Korea.

kimono (kɪˈməunəu) *n, pl* **kimonos.** a loose sashed ankle-length garment with wide sleeves, worn in Japan. [C19: from Japanese: clothing, from *kiru* to wear + *mono* thing]
▸ **ki'monoed** *adj*

kin (kɪn) *n* **1** a person's relatives collectively. **2** a class or group with similar characteristics. **3** See **next of kin.** ◆ *adj* **4** *(postpositive)* related by blood. [OE *cyn*]

-kin *suffix forming nouns.* small: *lambkin.* [from MDu., of West Gmc origin]

Kinabalu ★ (ˌkɪnəbəˈluː) *n* a mountain in Malaysia, on N Borneo in central Sabah: the highest peak in Borneo. Height: 4125 m (13 533 ft).

kinaesthesia (ˌkɪnɪsˈθiːzɪə) or *US* **kinesthesia** *n* the sensation by which bodily position, weight, muscle tension, and movement are perceived. [C19: from NL, from Gk *kinein* to move + AESTHESIA]
▸ **kinaesthetic** or *US* **kinesthetic** (ˌkɪnɪsˈθetɪk) *adj*

Kincardineshire ★ (kɪnˈkɑːdɪnˌʃɪə, -ʃə) *n* a historic county of E Scotland, now part of Aberdeenshire. Also called: **the Mearns.**

Kinchinjunga ★ (ˌkɪntʃɪnˈdʒʌŋgə) *n* a variant of **Kangchenjunga.**

kincob (ˈkɪŋkɒb) *n* a fine silk fabric embroidered with threads of gold or silver, of a kind made in India. [C18: from Urdu *kimkhāb*]

kind¹ (kaɪnd) *adj* **1** having a friendly nature or attitude. **2** helpful to others or to another: *a kind deed.* **3** considerate or humane. **4** cordial; courteous (esp. in **kind regards**). **5** pleasant; mild: *a kind climate.* **6** *Inf.* beneficial or not harmful. [OE *gecynde* natural, native]

kind² (kaɪnd) *n* **1** a class or group having characteristics in common; sort; type: *two of a kind.* **2** an instance or example of a class or group, esp. a rudimentary one: *heating of a kind.* **3** essential nature or character: *the difference is one of kind rather than degree.* **4** *Arch.* nature; the natural order. **5 in kind. 5a** (of payment) in goods or produce rather than in money. **5b** with something of the same sort: *to return an insult in kind.* [OE *gecynd* nature]

> **USAGE NOTE** The mixture of plural and singular constructions, although often used informally with *kind* and *sort,* should be avoided in serious writing: *children enjoy those kinds* (not *those kind*) *of stories; these sorts* (not *these sort*) *of distinctions are becoming blurred.*

kindergarten (ˈkɪndəˌgɑːtᵊn) *n* a class or small school for young children, usually between the ages of four and six. [C19: from G, lit.: children's garden]

★ people and places

kind-hearted *adj* kindly, readily sympathetic.
► ˌkind-ˈheartedly *adv* ► ˌkind-ˈheartedness *n*

kindle ('kɪnd°l) *vb* **kindles, kindling, kindled. 1** to set alight or start to burn. **2** to arouse or be aroused: *the project kindled his interest.* **3** to make or become bright. [C12: from ON *kynda*, infl. by ON *kyndill* candle]
► 'kindler *n*

kindling ('kɪndlɪŋ) *n* material for starting a fire, such as dry wood, straw, etc.

kindly ('kaɪndlɪ) *adj* **kindlier, kindliest. 1** having a sympathetic or warm-hearted nature. **2** motivated by warm and sympathetic feelings. **3** pleasant: *a kindly climate.* **4** *Arch.* natural; normal. ♦ *adv* **5** in a considerate or humane way. **6** with tolerance: *he kindly forgave my rudeness.* **7** cordially: *he greeted us kindly.* **8** please (often used to express impatience or formality): *will you kindly behave yourself!* **9** *Arch.* appropriately. **10 not take kindly to.** to react unfavourably towards.
► 'kindliness *n*

kindness ('kaɪndnɪs) *n* **1** the practice or quality of being kind. **2** a kind or helpful act.

kindred ('kɪndrɪd) *adj* **1** having similar or common qualities, origin, etc. **2** related by blood or marriage. **3 kindred spirit.** a person with whom one has something in common. ♦ *n* **4** relationship by blood. **5** similarity in character. **6** a person's relatives collectively. [C12 *kinred*, from KIN + -red, from OE *ræden* rule, from *rædan* to rule]

kine (kaɪn) *n (functioning as pl)* an archaic word for cows or cattle. [OE *cȳna* of cows, from *cū* COW¹]

kinematics (ˌkɪnɪˈmætɪks) *n (functioning as sing)* the study of the motion of bodies without reference to mass or force. [C19: from Gk *kinēma* movement; see CINEMA, -ICS]
► ˌkineˈmatic *adj* ► ˌkineˈmatically *adv*

kinematograph (ˌkɪnɪˈmætəˌɡrɑːf) *n* a variant spelling of cinematograph.

kinesics (kɪˈniːsɪks) *n (functioning as sing)* the study of the role of body movements, such as winking, shrugging, etc., in communication.

kinesis (kɪˈniːsɪs, kaɪ-) *n Biol.* the nondirectional movement of an organism or cell in response to a stimulus, the rate of movement being dependent on the strength of the stimulus.

kinesthesia (ˌkɪnɪsˈθiːzɪə) *n* the usual US spelling of kinaesthesia.

kinetic (kɪˈnɛtɪk) *adj* relating to or caused by motion. [C19: from Gk *kinētikos*, from *kinein* to move]
► kiˈnetically *adv*

kinetic art *n* art, esp. sculpture, that moves or has moving parts.

kinetic energy *n* the energy of motion of a body equal to the work it would do if it were brought to rest. It is equal to the product of the increase of mass caused by motion times the square of the speed of light.

kinetics (kɪˈnɛtɪks, kaɪ-) *n (functioning as sing)* **1** another name for **dynamics** (sense 2). **2** the branch of mechanics, including both dynamics and kinematics, concerned with the study of bodies in motion. The branch of dynamics that excludes the study of bodies at rest.

kinetic theory (of gases) *n the.* a theory of gases postulating that they consist of particles moving at random and undergoing elastic collisions.

kinfolk ('kɪnˌfəʊk) *pl n Chiefly US & Canad.* another word for kinsfolk.

king (kɪŋ) *n* **1** a male sovereign prince who is the official ruler of an independent state; monarch. Related adjs.: **royal, regal. 2a** a ruler or chief: *king of the fairies.* **2b** *(in combination)*: *the pirate king.* **3** a person, animal, or thing considered as the best or most important of its kind. **4** any of four playing cards in a pack, one for each suit, bearing the picture of a king. **5** the most important chess piece. **6** *Draughts.* a piece that has moved entirely across the board and has been crowned, after which it may move backwards as well as forwards. **7 king of kings. 7a** God. **7b** a title of any of various oriental monarchs. ♦ *vb (tr)* **8** to make (someone) a king. **9 king it.** to act in a superior fashion. [OE *cyning*]
► 'kingˌhood *n* ► 'kingˌlike *adj*

King ★ (kɪŋ) *n* **1 B.B.**, real name *Riley B. King.* born 1925, US blues singer and guitarist. **2 Billie Jean** (née *Moffitt*). born 1943, US tennis player: Wimbledon champion 1966–68, 1972–73, and 1975; US champion 1967, 1971–72, and 1974. **3 Martin Luther.** 1929–68, US Baptist minister and civil-rights leader. He advocated nonviolence in his campaigns against the segregation of Black people in the South: assassinated: Nobel Peace Prize 1964. **4 William Lyon Mackenzie.** 1874–1950, Canadian Liberal statesman; prime minister (1921–26; 1926–30; 1935–48).

kingbird ('kɪŋˌbɜːd) *n* any of several large American flycatchers.

kingbolt ('kɪŋˌbəʊlt) *or* **king rod** *n* **a** the pivot bolt that connects the body of a horse-drawn carriage to the front axle and provides the steering joint. **b** a similar bolt placed between a railway carriage and the bogies.

King Charles spaniel *n* a toy breed of spaniel with a short turned-up nose and a domed skull. [C17: after Charles II of England, who popularized the breed]

king cobra *n* a very large venomous tropical Asian snake that extends its neck into a hood when alarmed. Also called: **hamadryad.**

King Country ★ *n the.* an area in the centre of the North Island, New Zealand: home of the King Movement, a nineteenth-century Maori separatist movement.

king crab *n* another name for the **horseshoe crab.**

kingcup ('kɪŋˌkʌp) *n Brit.* any of several yellow-flowered plants, esp. the marsh marigold.

kingdom ('kɪŋdəm) *n* **1** a territory, state, people, or community ruled or reigned over by a king or queen. **2** any of the three groups into which natural objects may be divided: the animal, plant, and mineral kingdoms. **3** *Biol.* any of the major categories into which living organisms are classified. Modern systems recognize five kingdoms: *Prokaryotae* (bacteria), *Protoctista* (algae, protozoans, etc.), *Fungi, Plantae,* and *Animalia.* **4** *Theol.* the eternal sovereignty of God. **5** an area of activity: *the kingdom of the mind.*

kingdom come *n* **1** the next world. **2** *Inf.* the end of the world (esp. in **until kingdom come**). **3** *Inf.* unconsciousness.

kingfish ('kɪŋˌfɪʃ) *n, pl* **kingfish** *or* **kingfishes. 1** a marine food and game fish occurring in warm American Atlantic coastal waters. **2** *Austral.* any of various types of trevally, mulloway, and barracouta. **3** any of various other large food fishes, esp. the Spanish mackerel.

kingfisher ('kɪŋˌfɪʃə) *n* a bird which has a greenish-blue and orange plumage, a large head, short tail, and long sharp bill, and feeds on fish. [C15: orig. *king's fisher*]

King James Version *or* **Bible** *n the.* another name for the **Authorized Version.**

kingklip ('kɪŋˌklɪp) *n* an edible eel-like marine fish. [from Afrik., from Du. *koning* king + *klip* rock]

kinglet ('kɪŋlɪt) *n* **1** *Often derog.* the king of a small or insignificant territory. **2** *US & Canad.* any of various small warblers having a black-edged yellow crown.

kingly ('kɪŋlɪ) *adj* **kinglier, kingliest. 1** appropriate to a king. **2** royal. ♦ *adv* **3** *Poetic or arch.* in a manner appropriate to a king.
► 'kingliness *n*

kingmaker ('kɪŋˌmeɪkə) *n* a person who has control over appointments to positions of authority.

king-of-arms *n, pl* **kings-of-arms. 1** the highest rank of heraldic officer. **2** a person holding this rank.

king of the castle *n Chiefly Brit.* a children's game in which each child attempts to stand alone on a mound by pushing other children off it.

king penguin *n* a large New Zealand subantarctic penguin.

kingpin ('kɪŋˌpɪn) *n* **1** the most important person in an organization. **2** Also called (Brit.): **swivel pin.** a pivot pin that provides a steering joint in a motor vehicle by securing the stub axle to the axle beam. **3** *Tenpin bowling.* the front pin in the triangular arrangement of the ten pins. **4** (in ninepins) the central pin in the diamond pattern of the nine pins.

king post *n* a vertical post connecting the apex of a triangular roof truss to the tie beam.

King's Bench *n* (when the sovereign is male) another name for **Queen's Bench.**

King's Counsel *n* (when the sovereign is male) another name for **Queen's Counsel.**

King's English *n* (esp. when the British sovereign is male) standard Southern British English.

king's evidence *n* (when the sovereign is male) another name for **queen's evidence.**

king's evil *n* the. *Pathol.* a former name for **scrofula.** [C14: from the belief that the king's touch would heal scrofula]

Kingsford-Smith ★ ('kɪŋzfəd'smɪθ) *n* Sir **Charles** (**Edward**). 1897–1935, Australian aviator and pioneer (with Charles Ulm) of trans-Pacific and trans-Tasman flights.

king's highway *n* (in Britain, esp. when the sovereign is male) any public road or right of way.

kingship ('kɪŋʃɪp) *n* **1** the position or authority of a king. **2** the skill of ruling as a king.

king-size *or* **king-sized** *adj* larger or longer than a standard size.

Kingsley ★ ('kɪŋzlɪ) *n* **1 Ben.** born 1943, British actor, whose films include *Gandhi* (1982). **2 Charles.** 1819–75, British clergyman and author. His works include the novels *Westward Ho!* (1855), *Hereward the Wake* (1866), and *The Water Babies* (1863). **3** his brother, **Henry.** 1830–76, British novelist and journalist, who spent some time in Australia. His works include the Anglo-Australian novel *The Recollections of Geoffrey Hamlyn* (1859).

King's Lynn ★ ('kɪŋz 'lɪn) *n* a market town in E England, in Norfolk on the estuary of the Great Ouse near the Wash: a leading port in the Middle Ages. Pop.: 41 281 (1991). Also called: **Lynn, Lynn Regis.**

Kingston ★ ('kɪŋstən) *n* **1** the capital and chief port of Jamaica, on the SE coast: University of the West Indies. Pop.: 103 771 (1991). **2** a port in SE Canada, in SE Ontario: the chief naval base of Lake Ontario and a large industrial centre; university (1841). Pop.: 56 597 (1991). **3** short for **Kingston upon Thames.**

Kingston upon Hull ★ *n* **1** the official name of **Hull**¹. **2** a unitary authority in NE England, in the East Riding of Yorkshire. Pop.: 265 000 (1994 est.). Area: 71 sq. km (27 sq. miles).

Kingston upon Thames ★ *n* a borough of SW Greater London, on the River Thames: formed in 1965 by the amalgamation of several former boroughs of Surrey. Pop.: 138 500 (1994 est.). Area: 38 sq. km (15 sq. miles).

Kingstown ★ ('kɪŋz,taʊn) *n* the capital of St Vincent and the Grenadines: a port and resort. Pop.: 15 466 (1991).

kinin ('kaɪnɪn) *n* **1** any of a group of polypeptides in the blood that cause dilation of the blood vessels. **2** *Bot.* another name for **cytokinin.** [C20: from Gk *kin(ēma)* motion + -IN]

kink (kɪŋk) *n* **1** a sharp twist or bend in a wire, rope, hair, etc. **2** a crick in the neck or similar muscular spasm. **3** a flaw or minor difficulty in some undertaking. **4** a flaw or idiosyncrasy of personality. ★ [C17: from Du.: a curl in a rope]

kinkajou ('kɪŋkə,dʒu:) *n* an arboreal fruit-eating mammal of Central and South America, with a long prehensile tail. Also called: **honey bear.** [C18: from F *quincajou*, from Algonquian]

kinky ('kɪŋkɪ) *adj* **kinkier, kinkiest. 1** *Sl.* given to unusual, abnormal, or deviant sexual practices. **2** *Inf.* exhibiting unusual idiosyncrasies of personality. **3** *Inf.* attractive or provocative in a bizarre way: *kinky clothes.* **4** tightly looped, as a wire or rope. **5** tightly curled, as hair.
▸ **'kinkily** *adv* ▸ **'kinkiness** *n*

Kinnock ★ ('kɪnək) *n* **Neil** (**Gordon**). born 1942, British Labour politician, born in Wales; leader of the Labour Party (1983–92); European Commissioner (1994–99).

kino ('ki:nəʊ) *n* a dark red resin obtained from various tropical plants, esp. an Indian leguminous tree, used as an astringent and in tanning. [C18: of West African origin]

Kinross-shire ★ (kɪn'rɒs,ʃɪə, -ʃə) *n* a historic county of E central Scotland, now part of Perth and Kinross.

kin selection *n Biol.* natural selection resulting from altruistic behaviour by animals towards members of the same species, esp. their offspring or other relatives.

Kinsey ★ ('kɪnzɪ) *n* **Alfred Charles.** 1894–1956, US zoologist, who directed a survey of human sexual behaviour.

kinsfolk ('kɪnz,fəʊk) *pl n* one's family or relatives.

Kinshasa ★ (kɪn'ʃɑːzə, -'ʃɑːsə) *n* the capital of the Democratic Republic of the Congo, on the River Congo opposite Brazzaville: became capital of the Belgian Congo in 1929 and of Zaïre in 1960; university (1954). Pop.: 4 655 313 (1994 est.). Former name (until 1966): **Léopoldville.**

kinship ('kɪnʃɪp) *n* **1** blood relationship. **2** the state of having common characteristics.

kinsman ('kɪnzmən) *n, pl* **kinsmen.** a blood relation or a relation by marriage.
▸ **'kins,woman** *fem n*

kiosk ('ki:ɒsk) *n* **1** a small sometimes movable booth from which cigarettes, newspapers, sweets, etc., are sold. **2** *Chiefly Brit.* a telephone box. **3** (in Turkey, Iran, etc.) a light open-sided pavilion. [C17: from F *kiosque* bandstand, from Turkish, from Persian *kūshk* pavilion]

Kioto ★ (kɪ'əʊtəʊ, 'kjəʊ-) *n* a variant spelling of **Kyoto.**

kip¹ (kɪp) *Brit. sl.* ♦ *n* **1** sleep or slumber: *to get some kip.* **2** a bed or lodging. ♦ *vb* **kips, kipping, kipped.** (*intr*) **3** to sleep or take a nap. **4** (foll. by *down*) to prepare for sleep. [C18: from ?]

kip² (kɪp) *or* **kipskin** *n* the hide of a young animal, esp. a calf or lamb. [C16: from MDu. *kipp*]

kip³ (kɪp) *n Austral.* a small board used to spin the coins in two-up. [C19: from Brit. dialect *kep* to catch]

Kipling ★ ('kɪplɪŋ) *n* (**Joseph**) **Rudyard** ('rʌdjəd). 1865–1936, British poet, short-story writer, and novelist, born in India. His works include *Barrack-Room Ballads* (1892), the two *Jungle Books* (1894, 1895), *Stalky and Co.* (1899), *Kim* (1901), and the *Just So Stories* (1902): Nobel prize for literature 1907.

kipper ('kɪpə) *n* **1** a fish, esp. a herring, that has been cleaned, salted, and smoked. **2** a male salmon during the spawning season. ♦ *vb* **3** (*tr*) to cure (herrings or other fish) by salting and smoking. [OE *cypera*, ?from *coper* COPPER¹, referring to its colour]

kir (kɛə; *French* kir) *n* a drink made from dry white wine and cassis. [after Canon F. *Kir* (1876–1968), mayor of Dijon, who is said to have invented it]

kirby grip ('kɜːbɪ) *n Trademark.* a type of hairgrip with one straight and one wavy side.

Kirchhoff ★ (*German* 'kɪrçhɔf) *n* **Gustav Robert** ('gustaf 'roːbɛrt). 1824–87, German physicist. With Bunsen he developed spectrum analysis and discovered caesium (1860) and rubidium (1861): also worked on electrical networks.

Kirghiz *or* **Kirgiz** ★ ('kɜːgɪz) *n* variant spellings of **Kyrgyz.**

Kirghizia *or* **Kirgizia** ★ (kɜː'gɪzɪə) *n* another name for **Kyrgyzstan.**

Kiribati ★ (,kɪrɪ'bætɪ) *n* an independent republic in the W Pacific: comprises 33 islands including Banaba (Ocean Island), the Gilbert and Phoenix Islands, and eight of the Line Islands; part of the British colony of the Gilbert and Ellice Islands until 1975; became self-governing in 1977 and gained full independence in 1979; a member of the Commonwealth. Official language: English; I-Kiribati (Gilbertese) is widely spoken. Religion: Christian majority. Currency: Australian dollar. Capital: Bairiki islet, in Tarawa atoll. Pop.: 82 400 (1997). Area: 684 sq. km (264 sq. miles).

Kirin ★ ('ki:'rɪn) *n* a variant transliteration of the Chinese name for **Jilin.**

Kiritimati ★ ('kɪrɪtɪ'mɑːtɪ) *n* an island in the central Pacific, in Kiribati: one of the Line Islands; the largest atoll in the world. Pop.: 2537 (1990). Former name: **Christmas Island.**

kirk (kɜːk) *n* **1** a Scottish word for **church. 2** a Scottish church. [C12: from ON *kirkja*, from OE *cirice* CHURCH]

★ people and places

Kirk ★ (kɜːk) *n* Norman. 1923–74, prime minister of New Zealand (1972–74).

Kirkby ★ ('kɜːbɪ) *n* a town in NW England, in Knowsley, in Merseyside. Pop.: 43 017 (1991).

Kirkcaldy ★ (kɜː'kɔːdɪ) *n* a port in E Scotland, in SE Fife on the Firth of Forth. Pop.: 47 155 (1991).

Kirkcudbrightshire ★ (kɜː'kuːbrɪˌʃɪə, -'ʃɪə) *n* a historic county of SW Scotland, now part of Dumfries and Galloway region.

Kirklees ★ (ˌkɜːk'liːz) *n* a unitary authority in N England, in West Yorkshire. Pop.: 386 900 (1994 est.). Area: 410 sq. km (158 sq. miles).

Kirkpatrick ★ (kɜː'kpætrɪk) *n* Mount. a mountain in Antarctica, in S Victoria Land in the Queen Alexandra Range. Height: 4528 m (14 856 ft).

kirk session *n* the lowest court of the Presbyterian Church.

Kirkuk ★ (kɜː'kuk, 'kɜːkuk) *n* a city in NE Iraq: centre of a rich oilfield with pipelines to the Mediterranean. Pop.: 418 624 (1987).

Kirkwall ★ ('kɜːkˌwɔːl) *n* a town on the N coast of Mainland in the Orkney Islands: administrative centre of the island authority of Orkney: cathedral built by Norsemen (begun in 1137). Pop.: 6469 (1991).

kirmess ('kɜːmɪs) *n* a variant spelling of **kermis**.

Kirov[1] ★ ('kɪərɒf; *Russian* 'kiraf) *n* a city in NW Russia, on the Vyatka River: an early trading centre; engineering industries. Pop.: 464 000 (1995 est.). Former name (1780–1934): **Vyatka**.

Kirov[2] ★ ('kɪərɒf; *Russian* 'kiraf) *n* Sergei Mironovich (sɪr'gjej mi'rɒnəvɪtʃ). 1888–1934, Soviet politician. His assassination was the start for Stalin's purge of the Communist Party (1934–38).

Kirovabad ★ (*Russian* kirəva'bat) *n* the former name (1935–91) of **Gandzha**.

Kirovograd ★ (*Russian* kirəva'grat) *n* a city in the S central Ukraine, on the Ingul River: manufacturing centre of a rich agricultural area. Pop.: 276 000 (1996 est.). Former names: **Yelisavetgrad** (until 1924), **Zinovievsk** (1924–36).

Kirsch (kɪəʃ) or **Kirschwasser** ('kɪəʃˌvɑːsə) *n* a brandy distilled from cherries, made chiefly in the Black Forest in Germany. [G *Kirschwasser* cherry water]

kirtle ('kɜːt⁰l) *n* Arch. 1 a woman's skirt or dress. 2 a man's coat. [OE *cyrtel*, prob. from *cyrtan* to shorten, ult. from L *curtus* cut short]

Kiruna ★ (*Swedish* 'kiːruna) *n* a town in N Sweden: iron-mining centre. Pop.: 26 150 (1990).

Kisangani ★ (ˌkiːsæŋ'gɑːnɪ) *n* a city in N Democratic Republic of the Congo, at the head of navigation of the River Congo below Stanley Falls: Université Libre du Congo (1963). Pop.: 417 517 (1994 est.). Former name (until 1966): **Stanleyville**.

Kishinev ★ (*Russian* kiʃi'njɔf) *n* the capital of Moldova, on the Byk River: manufacturing centre of a rich agricultural region; university (1945). Pop.: 662 000 (1994 est.). Romanian name: **Chişinău**.

Kismayu ★ (kɪs'mɑːjuː) *n* another name for **Chisimaio**.

ismet ('kɪzmet, 'kɪs-) *n* 1 Islam. the will of Allah. 2 fate or destiny. [C19: from Turkish, from Persian *qismat*, from Ar. *qasama* he divided]

iss (kɪs) *vb* 1 (*tr*) to touch with the lips or press the lips against as an expression of love, greeting, respect, etc. 2 (*intr*) to join lips with another person in an act of love or desire. 3 to touch (each other) lightly. 4 Billiards. (of balls) to touch (each other) lightly while moving. ♦ *n* 5 a caress with the lips. 6 a light touch. [OE *cyssan*, from *coss*]
▶ '**kissable** *adj*

issagram ('kɪsəˌgræm) *n* a greetings service in which a person is employed to present greetings by kissing the person celebrating. [C20: blend of *kiss* and *telegram*]

iss-and-tell *n* (*modifier*) denoting the practice of publicizing one's former sexual relationship with a celebrity, esp. in the tabloid press: *a kiss-and-tell interview*.

kiss curl *n* Brit. a circular curl of hair pressed flat against the cheek or forehead.

kisser ('kɪsə) *n* 1 a person who kisses, esp. in a way specified. 2 a slang word for **mouth** or **face**.

Kissinger ★ ('kɪsɪndʒə) *n* Henry (Alfred). born 1923, US academic and diplomat, born in Germany; assistant to President Nixon for national security affairs (1969–75); Secretary of State (1973–77): shared the Nobel peace prize 1973.

kissing gate *n* a gate set in a U- or V-shaped enclosure, allowing only one person to pass through at a time.

kiss of life *n* the. mouth-to-mouth resuscitation in which a person blows gently into the mouth of an unconscious person, allowing the lungs to deflate after each blow.

kist (kɪst) *n* S. African. a large wooden chest in which linen is stored, esp. one used to store a bride's trousseau. [from Afrik., from Du.: CHEST]

Kistna ★ ('kɪstnə) *n* another name for the (River) **Krishna**.

Kisumu ★ (kɪ'suːmuː) *n* a port in W Kenya, in Nyanza province on the NE shore of Lake Victoria: fishing and trading centre. Pop.: 201 100 (1991 est.).

kit[1] (kɪt) *n* 1 a set of tools, supplies, etc., for use together or for a purpose: *a first-aid kit*. 2 the case or container for such a set. 3 a set of pieces of equipment sold ready to be assembled. 4a clothing and other personal effects, esp. those of a traveller or soldier: *safari kit*. 4b Inf. clothing in general (esp. in the phrase **get one's kit off**). ♦ See also **kit out**. [C14: from MDu. *kitte* tankard]

kit[2] (kɪt) *n* NZ. a string bag for shopping. [from Maori *kete*]

Kitaj ★ ('kaɪtæʒ) *n* R. B. born 1932, US painter working in Britain, noted for such large figurative works as *If Not, Not* (1976).

Kitakyushu ★ (ˌkiːtə'kjuːʃuː) *n* a port in Japan, on N Kyushu: formed in 1963 by the amalgamation of the cities of Wakamatsu, Yahata, Tobata, Kokura, and Moji; one of Japan's largest industrial centres. Pop.: 1 019 562 (1995).

kitbag ('kɪtˌbæg) *n* a canvas or other bag for a serviceman's kit.

kitchen ('kɪtʃɪn) *n* a a room or part of a building equipped for preparing and cooking food. b (*as modifier*): *a kitchen table*. [OE *cycene*, ult. from LL *coquīna*, from L *coquere* to COOK]

kitchen cabinet *n* a group of unofficial advisers to a political leader, esp. when considered to be more influential than the offical cabinet.

Kitchener[1] ★ ('kɪtʃɪnə) *n* an industrial town in SE Canada, in S Ontario: founded in 1806 as Dutch Sand Hills, it was renamed Berlin in 1830 and Kitchener in 1916. Pop.: 168 282 (1991).

Kitchener[2] ★ ('kɪtʃɪnə) *n* Horatio Herbert, 1st Earl Kitchener of Khartoum. 1850–1916, British field marshal. As head of the Egyptian army (1892–98), he expelled the Mahdi from the Sudan (1898) and commanded British forces (1900–02) in the Boer War and later (1902–09) in India. He became war minister (1914–16) but drowned on his way to Russia.

kitchenette (ˌkɪtʃɪ'net) *n* a small kitchen or part of a room equipped for use as a kitchen.

kitchen garden *n* a garden where vegetables and sometimes also fruit are grown.

kitchen midden *n* Archaeol. the site of a large mound of domestic refuse marking a prehistoric settlement.

kitchen police *pl n* US soldiers who have been detailed to work in the kitchen, esp. as a punishment.

kitchen sink *n* 1 a sink in a kitchen for washing dishes, vegetables, etc. 2 (*modifier*) denoting a type of drama or painting of the 1950s depicting sordid reality.

kitchen tea *n* Austral. & NZ. a party held before a wedding to which guests bring items of kitchen equipment as wedding presents.

kitchenware ('kɪtʃɪnˌweə) *n* pots and pans, knives, forks, spoons, etc., used in the kitchen.

kite (kaɪt) *n* 1 a light frame covered with a thin material flown in the wind at the end of a length of string. **2** *Brit. sl.* an aeroplane. **3** (*pl*) *Naut.* any of various light sails set in addition to the working sails of a vessel. **4** a bird of prey having a long forked tail and long broad wings and usually preying on small mammals and insects. **5** *Arch.* a person who preys on others. **6** *Commerce.* a negotiable paper drawn without any actual transaction or assets and designed to obtain money on credit, give an impression of affluence, etc. ◆ *vb* **kites, kiting, kited. 7** to issue (fictitious papers) to obtain credit or money. **8** (*intr*) to soar and glide. [OE *cȳta*]

Kite mark *n Brit.* the official mark of quality and reliability, in the form of a kite, on articles approved by the British Standards Institution.

kith (kɪθ) *n* **kith and kin.** one's friends and relations. [OE *cȳthth*; see UNCOUTH]

Kíthira ★ ('kiθira) *n* transliteration of the Modern Greek name for **Cythera.**

kit out *or* **up** *vb* **kits, kitting, kitted.** (*tr, adv*) *Chiefly Brit.* to provide with (a kit of personal effects and necessities).

kitsch (kɪtʃ) *n* tawdry, vulgarized, or pretentious art, literature, etc., usually with popular appeal. [C20: from G]
▸ **'kitschy** *adj*

kitten ('kɪtᵊn) *n* **1** a young cat. **2 have kittens.** *Brit. inf.* to react with disapproval, anxiety, etc.: *she had kittens when she got the bill.* ◆ *vb* **3** (of cats) to give birth to (young). [C14: from OF *caton*, from CAT; prob. infl. by ME *kiteling*]

kittenish ('kɪtᵊnɪʃ) *adj* **1** like a kitten; lively. **2** (of a woman) flirtatious, esp. coyly flirtatious.

kittiwake ('kɪtɪ,weɪk) *n* either of two oceanic gulls having pale grey black-tipped wings and a square-cut tail. [C17: imit.]

kitty[1] ('kɪtɪ) *n, pl* **kitties.** a diminutive or affectionate name for a **kitten** or **cat.** [C18]

kitty[2] ('kɪtɪ) *n, pl* **kitties. 1** the pool of bets in certain gambling games. **2** any shared fund of money. **3** (in bowls) the jack. [C19: see KIT[1]]

kitty-cornered *adj* a variant of **cater-cornered.**

Kitty Hawk ★ ('kɪtɪ ,hɔːk) *n* a village in NE North Carolina, near Kill Devil Hill, where the Wright brothers made the first aeroplane flight in the US (1903).

Kitwe ★ ('kɪtweɪ) *n* a city in N Zambia: commercial centre of the Copper Belt. Pop.: 338 207 (1990).

Kitzbühel ★ ('kɪts,buːəl) *n* a town in W Austria, in the Tirol: centre for winter sports. Pop.: 8223 (1991).

Kiushu ★ ('kjuːʃuː) *n* a variant spelling of **Kyushu.**

Kivu ★ ('kiːvuː) *n* **Lake.** a lake in central Africa, between the Democratic Republic of the Congo and Rwanda at an altitude of 1460 m (4790 ft). Area: 2698 sq. km (1042 sq. miles). Depth: (maximum) 475 m (1558 ft).

Kiwano (kɪ'wɑːnəʊ) *n, pl* **Kiwanos.** *Trademark.* an edible oval fruit of the passionflower family, having a golden spiky skin, juicy green pulp and many seeds.

kiwi ('kiːwiː) *n, pl* **kiwis. 1** a nocturnal flightless New Zealand bird having a long beak, stout legs, and weakly barbed feathers. **2** *Inf. except in NZ.* a New Zealander. **3** *NZ inf.* a lottery. [C19: from Maori, imit.: NZ sense from the *Golden Kiwi Lottery*]

kiwi fruit *n* the fuzzy edible fruit of an Asian climbing plant. Also called: **Chinese gooseberry.**

Kizil Irmak ★ (kɪ'zɪl ɪə'mɑːk) *n* a river in Turkey, rising in the Kizil Dag and flowing southwest, northwest, and northeast to the Black Sea: the longest river in Asia Minor. Length: about 1150 km (715 miles). Ancient name: **Halys** ('heɪlɪs).

KKK *abbrev. for* Ku Klux Klan.

Klagenfurt ★ (*German* 'klɑːɡənfʊrt) *n* a city in S Austria, capital of Carinthia province: tourist centre. Pop.: 89 415 (1991).

Klaipeda ★ (*Russian* 'klajpɪdə) *n* a port in Lithuania on the Baltic: shipbuilding. Pop.: 206 400 (1993 est.). German name: **Memel.**

Klan (klæn) *n* (usually preceded by *the*) short for **Ku Klux Klan.**
▸ **'Klanism** *n*

klaxon ('klæksᵊn) *n* a type of loud horn formerly used on motor vehicles. [C20: former trademark]

Kléber ★ (*French* kleber) *n* **Jean Baptiste** (ʒɑ̃ batist). 1753–1800, French general, who succeeded Napoleon as commander in Egypt (1799); assassinated.

Klee ★ (*German* kleː) *n* **Paul** (paul). 1879–1940, Swiss painter and etcher. A founder member of *der Blaue Reiter* (a group of German expressionist painters), he subsequently evolved an intensely personal style of unusual fantasy and wit.

Kleenex ('kliːnɛks) *n, pl* **Kleenex** *or* **Kleenexes.** *Trademark.* a kind of soft paper tissue, used esp. as a handkerchief.

Klein ★ (klaɪn) *n* **1 Calvin** (*Richard*). born 1942, US fashion designer. **2 Melanie.** 1882–1960, Austrian psychoanalyst resident in England (from 1926).

Klein bottle (klaɪn) *n Maths.* a three-dimensional surface formed by inserting the smaller end of an open tapered tube through the surface of the tube and making this end stretch to fit the other end. [after Felix *Klein* (1849–1925), G mathematician]

Kleist ★ (klaɪst) *n* (Bernd) **Heinrich** (**Wilhelm**) **von** ('haɪnrɪç fɒn). 1777–1811, German writer. His plays include *The Broken Pitcher* (1808).

Klemperer ★ ('klɛmpərə) *n* **Otto.** 1885–1973, Israeli conductor, born in Germany.

kleptomania (,klɛptəʊ'meɪnɪə) *n Psychol.* a strong impulse to steal, esp. when there is no obvious motivation. [C19: *klepto-* from Gk, from *kleptein* to steal + -MANIA]
▸ **,klepto'mani,ac** *n*

klieg light (kliːɡ) *n* an intense carbon-arc light used in producing films. [C20: after John H. *Kliegl* (1869–1959) & his brother Anton (1872–1927), German-born American inventors]

Kline ★ (klaɪn) *n* **Franz** (fræns). 1910–62, US abstract expressionist painter.

klipspringer ('klɪp,sprɪŋə) *n* a small agile antelope inhabiting rocky regions of Africa south of the Sahara. [C18: from Afrik., from Du. *klip* rock + *springer*, from *springen* to SPRING]

Klondike ★ ('klɒndaɪk) *n* **1** a region of NW Canada, in the Yukon in the basin of the Klondike River: site of rich gold deposits, discovered in 1896 but largely exhausted by 1910. Area: about 2100 sq. km (800 sq. miles). **2** a river in NW Canada, rising in the Yukon and flowing west to the Yukon River. Length: about 145 km (90 miles).

kloof (kluːf) *n* a mountain pass or gorge in southern Africa. [C18: from Afrik., from MDu. *clove* a cleft]

klystron ('klɪstrɒn) *n* an electron tube for the amplification or generation of microwaves. [C20: *klys-*, from Gk *kluzein* to wash over + -TRON]

km *symbol for* kilometre.

K-meson *n* another name for **kaon.**

knack (næk) *n* **1** a skilful, ingenious, or resourceful way of doing something. **2** a particular talent or aptitude, esp. an intuitive one. [C14: prob. var. of *knak* sharp knock, imit.]

knacker ('nækə) *Brit.* ◆ *n* **1** a person who buys up old horses for slaughter. **2** a person who buys up old buildings and breaks them up for scrap. **3** *Irish sl.* a despicable person. ◆ *vb* **4** (*tr; usually passive*) *Sl.* to tire. [C16: prob. from *nacker* saddler, prob. of Scand. origin]
▸ **'knackery** *n*

knacker's yard *n Brit.* **1** a slaughterhouse for horses. **2** *Inf.* destruction because of being beyond all usefulness (esp. in the phrase **ready for the knacker's yard**).

knag (næg) *n* **1** a knot in wood. **2** a wooden peg. [C15 ?from Low G *knagge*]

knap (næp) *vb* **knaps, knapping, knapped.** (*tr*) *Dialect.* to hit or chip. [C15 (in the sense: to strike with a sharp sound): imit.]
▸ **'knapper** *n*

knapping hammer *n* a hammer used for breaking and shaping stones.

knapsack ('næp,sæk) *n* a canvas or leather bag carried

★ people and places

strapped on the back or shoulder. [C17: from Low G, prob. from *knappen* to bite + *sack* bag]

knapweed ('næp,wiːd) *n* any of several plants having purplish thistle-like flowers. [C15 *knopwed*, from *knop* of Gmc origin + WEED]

knar (nɑː) *n* a variant of **knur**. [C14 *knarre* rough stone, knot on a tree]

knave (neɪv) *n* 1 *Arch.* a dishonest man. 2 another word for **jack** (the playing card). 3 *Obs.* a male servant. [OE *cnafa*]
▶ 'knavish *adj*

knavery ('neɪvərɪ) *n, pl* **knaveries**. 1 a deceitful or dishonest act. 2 dishonest conduct; trickery.

knead (niːd) *vb* 1 to work and press (a soft substance, such as bread dough) into a uniform mixture with the hands. 2 to squeeze or press with the hands. 3 to make by kneading. [OE *cnedan*]
▶ 'kneader *n*

knee (niː) *n* 1 the joint of the human leg connecting the tibia and fibula with the femur and protected in front by the patella. Technical name: **genu**. 2a the area surrounding and above this joint. 2b (*modifier*) reaching or covering the knee: *knee socks*. 3 the upper surface of a sitting person's thigh: *the child sat on her mother's knee*. 4 a corresponding or similar part in other vertebrates. 5 the part of a garment that covers the knee. 6 anything resembling a knee in action or shape. 7 any of the hollow rounded protuberances that project upwards from the roots of the swamp cypress. 8 **bend** *or* **bow the knee**. to kneel or submit. 9 **bring someone to his knees**. to force someone into submission. ◆ *vb* **knees, kneeing, kneed**. 10 (*tr*) to strike, nudge, or push with the knee. [OE *cnēow*]

kneecap ('niː,kæp) *n* 1 *Anat.* a nontechnical name for **patella**. ◆ *vb* **kneecaps, kneecapping, kneecapped**. (*tr*) 2 (esp. of certain terrorist groups) to shoot (a person) in the kneecap.

knee-deep *adj* 1 so deep as to reach or cover the knees. 2 (*postpositive; often foll. by in*) 2a sunk or covered to the knees: *knee-deep in sand*. 2b deeply involved: *knee-deep in work*.

knee-high *adj* another word for **knee-deep** (sense 1).

kneehole ('niː,həʊl) *n* a space for the knees, esp. under a desk.

knee jerk *n* 1 *Physiol.* an outward reflex kick of the lower leg caused by a sharp tap on the tendon just below the kneecap. ◆ *modifier*. **kneejerk**. 2 made or occurring as a predictable and automatic response, without thought: *a kneejerk reaction*.

kneel (niːl) *vb* **kneels, kneeling, knelt** *or* **kneeled**. 1 (*intr*) to rest, fall, or support oneself on one's knees. ◆ *n* 2 the act or position of kneeling. [OE *cnēowlian*; see KNEE]
▶ 'kneeler *n*

knees-up *n, pl* **knees-ups**. *Brit. inf.* a lively party. [C20: after popular song *Knees-up, Mother Brown!*]

knell (nɛl) *n* 1 the sound of a bell rung to announce a death or a funeral. 2 something that precipitates or indicates death or destruction. ◆ *vb* 3 (*intr*) to ring a knell. 4 (*tr*) to proclaim by or as if by a tolling bell. [OE *cnyll*]

Kneller ★ ('nɛlə) *n* Sir **Godfrey**. ?1646–1723, portrait painter at the English court, born in Germany.

knelt (nɛlt) *vb* a past tense and past participle of **kneel**.

Knesset ('knɛsɪt) *n* the representative assembly of Israel. [C20: Heb., lit.: gathering]

knew (njuː) *vb* the past tense of **know**.

knickerbocker glory ('nɪkə,bɒkə) *n* a rich confection consisting of layers of ice cream, jelly, cream, and fruit, served in a tall glass.

knickerbockers ('nɪkə,bɒkəz) *pl n* baggy breeches fastened with a band at the knee or above the ankle. Also called (US): **knickers**. [C19: regarded as the traditional dress of the Du. settlers in America; after Diedrich *Knickerbocker*, fictitious author of Washington Irving's *History of New York* (1809)]

knickers ('nɪkəz) *pl n* an undergarment for women covering the lower trunk and sometimes the thighs and having separate legs or leg-holes. [C19: contraction of KNICKERBOCKERS]

knick-knack *or* **nick-nack** ('nɪk,næk) *n* 1 a cheap ornament. 2 an ornamental article of furniture, dress, etc. [C17: by reduplication from *knack*, in obs. sense: toy]

knife (naɪf) *n, pl* **knives** (naɪvz). 1 a cutting instrument consisting of a sharp-edged blade of metal fitted into a handle or onto a machine. 2 a similar instrument used as a weapon. 3 **have one's knife in someone**. to have a grudge against someone. 4 **under the knife**. undergoing a surgical operation. ◆ *vb* **knifes, knifing, knifed**. (*tr*) 5 to stab or kill with a knife. 6 to betray or depose in an underhand way. [OE *cnīf*]
▶ 'knife,like *adj*

knife edge *n* 1 the sharp cutting edge of a knife. 2 any sharp edge, esp. an arête. 3 a sharp-edged wedge of hard material on which the beam of a balance pivots. 4 a critical point.

knight (naɪt) *n* 1 (in medieval Europe) 1a (originally) a person who served his lord as a mounted and heavily armed soldier. 1b (later) a gentleman with the military and social standing of this rank. 2 (in modern times) a person invested by a sovereign with a nonhereditary rank and dignity usually in recognition of personal services, achievements, etc. 3 a chess piece, usually shaped like a horse's head. 4 a heroic champion of a lady or of a cause or principle. 5 a member of the Roman class below the senators. ◆ *vb* 6 (*tr*) to make (a person) a knight. [OE *cniht* servant]

Knight ★ (naɪt) *n* Dame **Laura**. 1887–1970, British painter.

knight errant *n, pl* **knights errant**. (esp. in medieval romance) a knight who wanders in search of deeds of courage, chivalry, etc.
▶ **knight errantry** *n*

knighthood ('naɪthʊd) *n* 1 the order, dignity, or rank of a knight. 2 the qualities of a knight.

knightly ('naɪtlɪ) *adj* of, relating to, resembling, or befitting a knight.
▶ 'knightliness *n*

knight of the road *n Inf. or facetious*. 1 a tramp. 2 a commercial traveller. 3 a lorry driver.

Knights Hospitallers *pl n* a military Christian religious order founded about the time of the first crusade (1096–99).

Knight Templar *n, pl* **Knights Templars** *or* **Knights Templar**. another term for **Templar**.

kniphofia (nɪf'əʊfɪə) *n* the Latin name for **red-hot poker**. [C19: after Johann Hieronymus *Kniphof* (1704–63), G professor of medicine]

knit (nɪt) *vb* **knits, knitting, knitted** *or* **knit**. 1 to make (a garment, etc.) by looping and entwining (wool) by hand by means of long eyeless needles (**knitting needles**) or by machine (**knitting machine**). 2 to join or be joined together closely. 3 to draw (the brows) together or (of the brows) to come together, as in frowning or concentrating. 4 (of a broken bone) to join together; heal. ◆ *n* 5a a fabric made by knitting. 5b (*in combination*): *a heavy knit*. [OE *cnyttan* to tie in]
▶ 'knitter *n*

knitting ('nɪtɪŋ) *n* knitted work or the process of producing it.

knitwear ('nɪt,wɛə) *n* knitted clothes, esp. sweaters.

knives (naɪvz) *n* the plural of **knife**.

knob (nɒb) *n* 1 a rounded projection from a surface, such as a lump on a tree trunk. 2 a handle of a door, drawer, etc., esp. one that is rounded. 3 a round hill or knoll. ◆ *vb* **knobs, knobbing, knobbed**. 4 (*tr*) to supply or ornament with knobs. 5 (*intr*) to bulge. [C14: from MLow G *knobbe* knot in wood]
▶ 'knobbly *adj* ▶ 'knobby *adj* ▶ 'knob,like *adj*

knobkerrie ('nɒb,kɛrɪ), **knobkierie**, *or* **knobstick** *n* a stick with a round knob at the end, used as a club or missile by South African tribesmen. [C19: from Afrik., from *knop* knob, from MDu. *cnoppe* + *kierie* stick, from Khoikhoi *kīrri*]

knock (nɒk) *vb* 1 (*tr*) to give a blow or push to. 2 (*intr*) to rap sharply with the knuckles, a hard object, etc.: *to knock at the door*. 3 (*tr*) to make or force by striking: *to* *knock a hole in the wall.* **4** (*intr*; usually foll. by *against*) to collide (with). **5** (*tr*) to bring into a certain condition by hitting: *to knock someone unconscious.* **6** (*tr*) *Inf.* to criticize adversely. **7** (*intr*) Also: **pink.** (of an internal-combustion engine) to emit a metallic noise as a result of faulty combustion. **8** (*intr*) (of a bearing, esp. one in an engine) to emit a regular characteristic sound as a result of wear. **9** *Brit. sl.* to have sexual intercourse with (a person). **10** **knock (a person) into the middle of next week.** *Inf.* to hit (a person) with a very heavy blow. **11 knock on the head. 11a** to daze or kill (a person) by striking on the head. **11b** to prevent the further development of (a plan). ◆ *n* **12a** a blow, push, or rap: *he gave the table a knock.* **12b** the sound so caused. **13** the sound of knocking in an engine or bearing. **14** *Inf.* a misfortune, rebuff, or setback. **15** *Inf.* criticism. ◆ See also **knock about, knock back,** etc. [OE *cnocian,* imit.]

knock about *or* **around** *vb* **1** (*intr, adv*) to wander about aimlessly. **2** (*intr, prep*) to travel about, esp. as resulting in varied experience: *he's knocked about the world.* **3** (*intr, adv*; foll. by *with*) to associate. **4** (*tr, adv*) to treat brutally: *he knocks his wife about.* **5** (*tr, adv*) to consider or discuss informally. ◆ *adj* **knockabout. 6** tough; boisterous: *knockabout farce.*

knock back *vb* (*tr, adv*) *Inf.* **1** to drink, esp. quickly. **2** to cost. **3** to reject or refuse. **4** to shock; disconcert. ◆ *n* **knock-back. 5** *Sl.* a refusal or rejection. **6** *Prison sl.* failure to obtain parole.

knock down *vb* (*tr, adv*) **1** to strike to the ground with a blow, as in boxing. **2** (in auctions) to declare (an article) sold. **3** to demolish. **4** to dismantle for ease of transport. **5** *Inf.* to reduce (a price, etc.). **6** *Austral. sl.* to spend (a cheque). **7** *Austral. sl.* to drink. ◆ *adj* **knockdown.** (*prenominal*) **8** powerful: *a knockdown blow.* **9** *Chiefly Brit.* cheap: *a knockdown price.* **10** easily dismantled: *knockdown furniture.*

knocker ('nɒkə) *n* **1** an object, usually made of metal, attached to a door by a hinge and used for knocking. **2** *Inf.* a person who finds fault or disparages. **3** (*usually pl*) *Sl.* a female breast. **4** a person or thing that knocks. **5 on the knocker.** *Inf.* promptly: *you pay on the knocker here.*

knocking copy *n* publicity material designed to denigrate a competing product.

knocking-shop *n Brit.* a slang word for **brothel.**

knock-knee *n* a condition in which the legs are bent inwards causing the knees to touch when standing.
▸ ˌknock-'kneed *adj*

knock off *vb* (*mainly adv*) **1** (*intr, also prep*) *Inf.* to finish work: *we knocked off an hour early.* **2** (*tr*) *Inf.* to make or do hastily or easily: *to knock off a novel in a week.* **3** (*tr; also prep*) *Inf.* to reduce the price of (an article). **4** (*tr*) *Sl.* to kill. **5** (*tr*) *Sl.* to rob or steal: *to knock off a bank.* **6** (*tr*) *Sl.* to stop doing something, used as a command: *knock it off!*

knock-on *Rugby.* ◆ *n* **1** the infringement of playing the ball forward with the hand or arm. ◆ *vb* **knock on.** (*adv*) **2** to play (the ball) forward with the hand or arm.

knock-on effect *n* the indirect result of an action: *the number of redundancies was not great but there were as many again from the knock-on effect.*

knockout ('nɒk.aʊt) *n* **1** the act of rendering unconscious. **2** a blow that renders an opponent unconscious. **3a** a competition in which competitors are eliminated progressively. **3b** (*as modifier*): *a knockout contest.* **4** *Inf.* a person or thing that is overwhelmingly impressive or attractive: *she's a knockout.* ◆ *vb* **knock out.** (*tr, adv*) **5** to render unconscious, esp. by a blow. **6** *Boxing.* to defeat (an opponent) by a knockout. **7** to destroy or injure badly. **8** to eliminate, esp. in a knockout competition. **9** *Inf.* to overwhelm or amaze: *I was knocked out by that new song.* **10 knock the bottom out of.** *Inf.* to invalidate (an argument).

knockout drops *pl n Sl.* a drug secretly put into someone's drink to cause stupefaction. ◆ See also **Mickey Finn.**

knock up *vb* (*adv, mainly tr*) **1** Also: **knock together.** *Inf.* to assemble quickly: *to knock up a set of shelves.* **2** *Brit. inf.* to waken; rouse: *to knock someone up early.* **3** *Sl.* to make pregnant. **4** *Brit. inf.* to exhaust. **5** *Cricket.* to score (runs). **6**

(*intr*) *Tennis, squash, etc.* to practise, esp. before a match. ◆ *n* **knock-up. 7** a practice session at tennis, squash, etc.

knoll (nəʊl) *n* a small rounded hill. [OE *cnoll*]
▸ 'knolly *adj*

Knossos *or* **Cnossus** ★ ('nɒsəs, 'knɒs-) *n* a ruined city in N central Crete: remains of the Minoan Bronze Age civilization.

knot[1] (nɒt) *n* **1** any of various fastenings formed by looping and tying a piece of rope, cord, etc., in upon itself or to another piece of rope. **2** a prescribed method of tying a particular knot. **3** a tangle, as in hair or string. **4** a decorative bow, as of ribbon. **5** a small cluster or huddled group. **6** a tie or bond: *the marriage knot.* **7** a difficult problem. **8a** a hard mass of wood where a branch joins the trunk of a tree. **8b** a cross section of this visible on a piece of timber. **9** a sensation of constriction, caused by tension or nervousness: *his stomach was tying itself in knots.* **10** *Pathol.* a lump of vessels or fibres formed in a part, as in a muscle. **11** a unit of velocity used by ships and aircraft, being one nautical mile (about 1.15 statute miles or 1.85 km) per hour. **12 at a rate of knots.** very fast. **13 tie (someone) in knots.** to completely perplex (someone). ◆ *vb* **knots, knotting, knotted. 14** (*tr*) to tie or fasten in a knot. **15** to form or cause to form into a knot. **16** (*tr*) to entangle or become entangled. **17** (*tr*) to make (an article or design) by tying thread in ornamental knots. [OE *cnotta*]
▸ 'knotted *adj* ▸ 'knotter *n* ▸ 'knotless *adj*

knot[2] (nɒt) *n* a small northern sandpiper with a short bill and grey plumage. [C15: from ?]

knot garden *n* (esp. formerly) a formal garden of intricate design.

knotgrass ('nɒt.grɑːs) *n* **1** Also called: **allseed.** a weed whose small green flowers produce numerous seeds. **2** any of several related plants.

knothole ('nɒt.həʊl) *n* a hole in a piece of wood where a knot has been.

knotty ('nɒtɪ) *adj* **knottier, knottiest. 1** (of wood, rope, etc.) full of or characterized by knots. **2** extremely difficult or intricate.

knout (naʊt) *n* a stout whip used formerly in Russia as an instrument of punishment. [C17: from Russian *knut,* of Scand. origin]

know (nəʊ) *vb* **knows, knowing, knew, known.** (*mainly tr*) **1** (*also intr; may take a clause as object*) to be or feel certain of the truth or accuracy of (a fact, etc.). **2** to be acquainted or familiar with: *she's known him five years.* **3** to have a familiarity or grasp of: *he knows French.* **4** (*also intr; may take a clause as object*) to understand, be aware of, or perceive (facts, etc.): *he knows the answer now.* **5** (foll. by *how*) to be sure or aware of (how to be or do something). **6** to experience, esp. deeply: *to know poverty.* **7** to be intelligent, informed, or sensible enough (to do something). **8** (*may take a clause as object*) to be able to distinguish or discriminate. **9** *Arch.* to have sexual intercourse with. **10 know what's what.** to know how one thing or things in general work. **11 you never know.** things are uncertain. ◆ *n* **12 in the know.** *Inf.* aware or informed. [OE *gecnāwan*]
▸ 'knowable *adj* ▸ 'knower *n*

know-all *n Inf., disparaging.* a person who pretends to or appears to know a great deal.

know-how *n Inf.* **1** ingenuity, aptitude, or skill. **2** commercial and saleable knowledge of how to do a particular thing.

knowing ('nəʊɪŋ) *adj* **1** suggesting secret knowledge. **2** wise, shrewd, or clever. **3** deliberate. ◆ *n* **4 there is no knowing.** one cannot tell.
▸ 'knowingly *adv* ▸ 'knowingness *n*

knowledge ('nɒlɪdʒ) *n* **1** the facts or experiences known by a person or group of people. **2** the state of knowing. **3** consciousness or familiarity gained by experience or learning. **4** erudition or informed learning. **5** specific information about a subject. **6 to my knowledge. 6a** as understand it. **6b** as I know.

knowledgeable *or* **knowledgable** ('nɒlɪdʒəbᵊl) *adj* possessing or indicating much knowledge.
▸ 'knowledgeably *or* 'knowledgably *adv*

★ people and places

known (nəʊn) *vb* **1** the past participle of **know**. ♦ *adj* **2** identified: *a known criminal*.

Knowsley ★ ('nəʊzlɪ) *n* a unitary authority in NW England, in Merseyside. Pop.: 154 000 (1994 est.). Area: 97 sq. km (38 sq. miles).

Knox ★ (nɒks) *n* **John.** ?1514–72, Scottish theologian and historian. After exile in England and on the Continent (1547–59), he returned to Scotland in 1559 and established the Presbyterian Church of Scotland (1560). His chief historical work was the *History of the Reformation in Scotland* (1586).

Knox-Johnston ★ (,nɒks'dʒɒnstən) *n* Sir **Robin (William Robert Patrick).** born 1939, British yachtsman. He was the first to sail round the world alone nonstop (1968–69).

Knoxville ★ ('nɒksvɪl) *n* an industrial city in E Tennessee, on the Tennessee River: state capital (1796–1812; 1817–19). Pop.: 169 311 (1994 est.).

knuckle ('nʌkᵊl) *n* **1** a joint of a finger, esp. that connecting a finger to the hand. **2** a joint of veal, pork, etc., consisting of the part of the leg below the knee joint. **3 near the knuckle.** *Inf.* approaching indecency. ♦ *vb* **knuckles, knuckling, knuckled. 4** (*tr*) to rub or press with the knuckles. **5** (*intr*) to keep the knuckles on the ground while shooting a marble. ♦ See also **knuckle down, knuckle under.** [C14]
▶ 'knuckly *adj*

knucklebones ('nʌkᵊl,bəʊnz) *n* (*functioning as sing*) a less common name for **jacks** (the game).

knuckle down *vb* (*intr, adv*) *Inf.* to apply oneself diligently: *to knuckle down to some work.*

knuckle-duster *n* (*often pl*) a metal bar fitted over the knuckles, often with holes for the fingers, for inflicting injury by a blow with the fist.

knucklehead ('nʌkᵊl,hed) *n Inf.* a fool; idiot.
▶ 'knuckle,headed *adj*

knuckle under *vb* (*intr, adv*) to give way under pressure or authority; yield.

knur, knurr (nɜː), or **knar** *n* a knot or protuberance in a tree trunk or in wood. [C16 *knor*; cf. KNAR]

knurl or **nurl** (nɜːl) *vb* (*tr*) **1** to impress with a series of fine ridges or serrations. ♦ *n* **2** a small ridge, esp. one of a series. [C17: prob. from KNUR]

Knut (kə'njuːt) *n* a variant spelling of **Canute**.

KO or **k.o.** ('keɪ'əʊ) *vb* **KO's, KO'ing, KO'd** or **k.o.'s, k.o.'ing, k.o.'d,** *n, pl* **KO's** or **k.o.'s.** a slang term for **knockout** or **knock out**.

koala or **koala bear** (kəʊ'ɑːlə) *n* a slow-moving Australian arboreal marsupial, having dense greyish fur and feeding on eucalyptus leaves. Also called (Austral.): **native bear.** [from Abor.]

koan ('kəʊæn) *n* (in Zen Buddhism) a problem that admits no logical solution. [from Japanese]

Kobarid ★ ('kəʊbə,riːd; *Serbo-Croat* 'kɔba,rid) *n* a village in Slovenia, on the Isonzo River: part of Italy until 1947; scene of the defeat of the Italians by Austro-German forces (1917). Italian name: **Caporetto.**

Kobe ★ ('kəʊbɪ) *n* a port in S Japan, on S Honshu on Osaka Bay: formed in 1889 by the amalgamation of Hyogo and Kobe; a major industrial complex, producing ships, steel, and rubber goods. Pop.: 1 423 830 (1995).

København ★ (købən'haun) *n* the Danish name for **Copenhagen.**

Koblenz or **Coblenz** ★ (kəʊ'blɛnts; *German* 'koːblɛnts) *n* a city in W central Germany, in the Rhineland-Palatinate at the confluence of the Rivers Moselle and Rhine: ruled by the archbishop-electors of Trier from 1018 until occupied by the French in 1794; passed to Prussia in 1815, becoming capital of the Rhine Province (1824–1945) and of the Rhineland-Palatinate (1946–50); wine trade centre. Pop.: 109 550 (1995 est.). Latin name: **Confluentes** (,kɒnflʊ'ɛntiːz).

kobold ('kɒbəʊld) *n German myth.* **1** a mischievous household sprite. **2** a spirit that haunts mines. [C19: from G; see COBALT]

Koch ★ (*German* kɔx) *n* **Robert** ('roːbɛrt). 1843–1910, German bacteriologist, who isolated the anthrax bacillus

(1876), the tubercle bacillus (1882), and the cholera bacillus (1883): Nobel prize for physiology or medicine 1905.

Kochi ★ (kəʊ'tʃiː) *n* a port in SW Japan, on central Shikoku on Urado Bay. Pop.: 322 077 (1995 est.).

kochia ('kɒʃiːə) *n* an annual plant with ornamental foliage that turns purple-red in late summer. [C19: after W.D.J. *Koch*, G botanist]

Kodály ★ (*Hungarian* 'koda:j) *n* **Zoltán** ('zolta:n). 1882–1967, Hungarian composer. His works include the comic opera *Háry János* (1926) and *Psalmus Hungaricus* (1923) for chorus and orchestra.

Kodiak ★ ('kəʊdɪ,æk) *n* an island in S Alaska, in the Gulf of Alaska: site of the first European settlement in Alaska, made by Russians in 1784. Pop.: 13 309 (1990). Area: 8974 sq. km (3465 sq. miles).

Kodiak bear or **Kodiak** *n* a large variety of the brown bear inhabiting the W coast of Alaska and neighbouring islands, esp. Kodiak.

koeksister ('kuk,sɪstə) *n S. African.* a plaited doughnut deep-fried and soaked in syrup. [Afrik. but possibly of Malay origin]

koel ('kəʊəl) *n* any of several parasitic cuckoos of S and SE Asia and Australia. [C19: from Hindi, from Sansk. *kokila*]

Koestler ★ ('kɜːstlə) *n* **Arthur.** 1905–83, British writer, born in Hungary. His works include the novel *Darkness at Noon* (1940) and the nonfiction *The Sleepwalkers* (1959) and *The Ghost in the Machine* (1967), which reflect his interest in science and philosophy.

Kofu ★ ('kəʊfuː) *n* a city in central Japan, on S Honshu. Pop.: 201 123 (1995 est.).

Kogi ★ ('kəʊgɪ) *n* a state of W Nigeria. Capital: Lokoja: Pop.: 2 099 046 (1991).

koha ('kəʊhə) *n NZ.* a gift or donation. [Maori]

Kohima ★ ('kəʊhɪ,mɑː) *n* a city in NE India, capital of Nagaland, near the Burmese border: centre of fierce fighting in World War II, when it was surrounded by the Japanese but not captured (1944). Pop.: 53 122 (1991).

kohl (kəʊl) *n* a cosmetic powder used, originally esp. in Muslim and Asian countries, to darken the area around the eyes. [C18: from Ar. *kohl*; see ALCOHOL]

Kohl ★ (kəʊl) *n* **Helmut** ('hɛlmuːt). born 1930, German statesman: chancellor of West Germany (1982–90) and of Germany (1990–98).

Köhler ★ (*German* 'køːlər) *n* **Wolfgang** ('vɔlfɡaŋ). 1887–1967, German psychologist: exponent of Gestalt psychology.

kohlrabi (kəʊl'rɑːbɪ) *n, pl* **kohlrabies.** a cultivated variety of cabbage whose thickened stem is eaten as a vegetable. Also called: **turnip cabbage.** [C19: from G, from It. *cavoli rape* (pl), from *cavolo* cabbage (from L *caulis*) + *rapa* turnip (from L)]

koi (kɔɪ) *n* any of various ornamental forms of the common carp. [Japanese]

koine ('kɔɪniː) *n* a common language among speakers of different languages; lingua franca. [from Gk *koinē dialektos* common language]

Koine ('kɔɪniː) *n* (*sometimes not cap.*) **the.** the ancient Greek dialect that was the lingua franca of the empire of Alexander the Great and in Roman times.

Kokand ★ (*Russian* ka'kant) *n* a city in NE Uzbekistan, in the Fergana valley. Pop.: 184 000 (1996).

kokanee (kəʊ'kænɪ) *n* a landlocked salmon of lakes in W North America: a variety of sockeye. [prob. from *Kokanee* Creek, in SE British Columbia]

Koko Nor ('kəʊ'kəʊ 'nɔː) or **Kuku Nor** ★ *n* a lake in W China, in Qinghai province in the NE Tibetan Highlands at an altitude of about 3000 m (10 000 ft): the largest lake in China. Area: about 4100 sq. km (1600 sq. miles). Chinese name: **Qinghai.**

Kokoschka ★ (*German* ko'kɔʃka, 'kɔkɔʃka) *n* **Oskar** ('ɔskar). 1886–1980, Austrian expressionist painter.

Kokura ★ (,kəʊkə'rɑː) *n* a former city in SW Japan, on N Kyushu: merged with adjacent townships in 1963 to form the new city of **Kitakyushu.**

kola ('kəʊlə) *n* a variant spelling of **cola**.

kola nut *n* a variant spelling of **cola nut**.

Kola Peninsula ★ ('kəʊlə) *n* a peninsula of NW Russia, between the Barents and White Seas: forms most of the Murmansk Region. Area: about 130 000 sq. km (50 000 sq. miles).

Kolar Gold Fields ★ (kəʊ'lɑː) *n* a city in S India, in SE Karnataka: a major gold-mining centre since 1881. Pop.: 83 219 (1991 est.).

Kolding ★ (*Danish* 'kɔleŋ) *n* a port in Denmark, in E Jutland at the head of **Kolding Fjord** (an inlet of the Little Belt). Pop.: 59 558 (1995).

Kolhapur ★ (ˌkəʊlhɑː'pʊə) *n* a city in W India, in S Maharashtra: university (1963). Pop.: 406 370 (1991).

kolinsky (kə'lɪnskɪ) *n, pl* **kolinskies. 1** any of various Asian minks. **2** the rich tawny fur of this animal. [C19: from Russian *kolinski* of Kola: see KOLA PENINSULA]

kolkhoz (kɒl'hɔːz) *n* a Russian collective farm. [C20: from Russian, short for *kollektivnoe khozyaistvo* collective farm]

Kolmar ★ ('kɒlmar) *n* the German name for **Colmar**.

Kolmogorov ★ (ˌkɒlmɒ'gɔːrɒf) *n* **Andrei Nikolaevich** (an'drjej nika'lajəvitʃ). 1903–87, Soviet mathematician, who made important contributions to the theoretical foundations of probability.

Köln ★ (kœln) *n* the German name for **Cologne**.

Kol Nidre (kɔːl 'nɪdreɪ) *n Judaism.* **1** the evening service with which Yom Kippur begins. **2** the opening prayer of that service. [Aramaic *kōl nidhrē* all the vows; the prayer's opening words]

Kolomna ★ (*Russian* ka'lɒmnə) *n* a city in W central Russia, at the confluence of the Moskva and Oka Rivers: railway engineering centre. Pop.: 154 000 (1995 est.).

Kolyma ★ (*Russian* kəli'ma) *n* a river in NE Russia, rising in the Kolyma Mountains north of the Sea of Okhotsk and flowing generally north to the East Siberian Sea. Length: 2600 km (1615 miles).

Kolyma Range ★ *n* a mountain range in NE Russia, in NE Siberia, extending about 1100 km (700 miles) between the Kolyma River and the Sea of Okhotsk. Highest peak: 1862 m (6109 ft).

Komati ★ (kə'mɑːtɪ, 'kəʊmətɪ) *n* a river in southern Africa, rising in E South Africa and flowing east through Swaziland and Mozambique to the Indian Ocean at Delagoa Bay. Length: about 800 km (500 miles).

komatik ('kəʊmætɪk) *n* a sledge having wooden runners and crossbars bound with rawhide, used by Eskimos. [C20: from Eskimo]

Komi Republic ★ ('kəʊmɪ) *n* a constituent republic of NW Russia: annexed by the princes of Moscow in the 14th century. Capital: Syktyvkar. Pop.: 1 203 000 (1995 est.). Area: 415 900 sq. km (160 540 sq. miles).

Kommunarsk ★ (*Russian* kəmu'narsk) *n* the former (until 1992) name of **Alchevsk**.

Kommunizma Peak ★ (*Russian* kəmu'njizmə) *n* a mountain in SE Tajikistan, in the Pamirs: the highest mountain in the former Soviet Union. Height: 7495 m (24 590 ft). Former name: **Stalin Peak**.

Komsomolsk ★ (*Russian* kəmsa'mɒljsk) *n* an industrial city in W Russia, on the Amur River: built by members of the Komsomol (Communist youth league) in 1932. Pop.: 309 000 (1995 est.).

Konakry *or* **Konakri** ★ (*French* kɒnakri) *n* variant spellings of **Conakry**.

Kongur Shan ('kʊngʊə 'ʃæn), **Kungur**, *or* **Qungur** ★ *n* a mountain in China, in W Xinjiang Uygur: the highest peak in the Pamirs. Height: 7719 m (25 325 ft).

Kong Zi ★ ('kʊŋ ziː) *n* the Pinyin transliteration of the Chinese name for **Confucius**.

Königgrätz ★ (kø:nɪç'grɛːts) *n* the German name for **Hradec Králové**.

Königsberg ★ (kɜːnɪgz,bɜːg; *German* 'kø:nɪçsbɛrk) *n* the former name (until 1946) of **Kaliningrad**.

Königshütte ★ ('kø:nɪçshytə) *n* the German name for **Chorzów**.

Konstanz ★ ('kɒnstants) *n* the German name for **Constance**.

Konya *or* **Konia** ★ ('kɔːnjɑː) *n* a city in SW central Turkey: in ancient times a Phrygian city and capital of Lycaonia. Pop.: 576 000 (1994 est.). Ancient name: **Iconium**.

koodoo ('kuːduː) *n* a variant spelling of **kudu**.

kook (kuːk) *n US & Canad. inf.* an eccentric or foolish person. [C20: prob. from CUCKOO]
  ▸ **'kooky** *or* **'kookie** *adj*

kookaburra ('kʊkə,bʌrə) *n* a large Australian kingfisher with a cackling cry. Also called: **laughing jackass**. [C19: from Abor.]

Kooning ★ ('kuːnɪŋ) *n* **Willem de** ('wɪləm də). 1904–97, US abstract expressionist painter, born in Holland.

Kootenay *or* **Kootenai** ★ ('kuːt°niː, 'kuːtneɪ) *n* a river in W North America, rising in SE British Columbia and flowing south into NW Montana, then north into Idaho before re-entering British Columbia, broadening into **Kootenay Lake**, then flowing to the Columbia River. Length: 655 km (407 miles).

kopeck *or* **copeck** ('kəʊpɛk) *n* a monetary unit of Russia and Belarus worth one hundredth of a rouble: coins are still used as tokens for coin-operated machinery although the kopeck itself is virtually valueless. [Russian *kopeika*, from *kopye* lance]

Kopeisk *or* **Kopeysk** ★ (*Russian* ka'pjejsk) *n* a city in SW central Russia, in Chelyabinsk province: lignite mining. Pop.: 78 300 (1991 est.). Former name: **Kopi** ('kɒpi).

koppie *or* **kopje** ('kɒpɪ) *n* (in southern Africa) a small isolated hill. [C19: from Afrik., from Du. *kopje*, lit.: a little head, from *kop* head]

kora ('kɔːrə) *n* a West African instrument with twenty-one strings, combining features of the harp and the lute.

Koran (kɔː'rɑːn) *n* the sacred book of Islam, believed by Muslims to be the infallible word of God dictated to Mohammed. Also: **Qur'an**. [C17: from Ar. *qur'ān* reading, book]
  ▸ **Ko'ranic** *adj*

Korbut ★ (*Russian* 'kɔrbut) *n* **Olga** ('ɔljgə). born 1955, Soviet gymnast.

Korçë ★ (*Albanian* 'kortʃə) *n* a market town in SE Albania. Pop.: 67 100 (1991 est.).

Korchnoi ★ ('kɔːtʃˌnɔɪ) *n* **Victor**. born 1931, Soviet-born chess player: Soviet champion 1960, 1962, and 1964: defected to the West in 1976.

Korda ★ ('kɔːdə) *n* **Sir Alexander**, real name *Sandor Kellner*. 1893–1956, British film producer and director, born in Hungary: his films include *The Scarlet Pimpernel* (1934) and *The Third Man* (1949).

Kordofan ★ (ˌkɔːdəʊ'fæn) *n* a region of the central Sudan: consists of a plateau with rugged uplands (the Nuba Mountains). Area: 380 548 sq. km (146 930 sq. miles).

Korea ★ (kə'riːə) *n* a former country in E Asia, now divided into two separate countries, North Korea and South Korea. Korea occupied the peninsula between the Sea of Japan and the Yellow Sea: an isolated vassal of China for three centuries until the opening of ports to foreign trade in 1876; annexed to Japan in 1910 and divided in 1945 into two occupation zones (Russian in the north, American in the south), which became North Korea and South Korea in 1948: the Korean War (1950–53), in which US-led UN forces backed the South and China backed the North, ended with the country still divided. See **North Korea, South Korea**.
  ▸ **Ko'rean** *adj, n*

Korea Strait ★ *n* a strait between South Korea and SW Japan, linking the Sea of Japan with the East China Sea.

korfball ('kɔːf,bɔːl) *n* a game similar to basketball, in which each team consists of six men and six women. [C20: from Du. *korfbal* basketball]

Kórinthos ★ ('kɒrinθɒs) *n* transliteration of the Modern Greek name for **Corinth**.

korma ('kɔːmə) *n* an Indian dish consisting of meat or vegetables braised with stock, yogurt, or cream. [from Urdu]

★ people and places

Korsakoffian (ˌkɔːsəˈkɒfɪən) *adj* **1** relating to or suffering from **Korsakoff's psychosis**, a mental illness involving severe confusion and inability to retain recent memories, usually caused by alcoholism. ◆ *n* **2** a person suffering from Korsakoff's psychosis. [C19: after Sergei *Korsakoff* (1854–1900), Russian neuropsychiatrist]

Korzybski ★ (kɔːˈzɪbskɪ) *n* **Alfred** (**Habdank Skarbek**). 1879–1950, US originator of the theory and study of general semantics, born in Poland.

Kos *or* **Cos** ★ (kɒs) *n* an island in the SE Aegean Sea, in the Greek Dodecanese Islands: separated from SW Turkey by the **Kos Channel**; settled in ancient times by Dorians and became famous for literature and medicine. Pop.: 21 000 (latest est.). Area: 282 sq. km (109 sq. miles).

Kosciusko ★ (ˌkɒsɪˈʌskəʊ) *n* **Mount.** a mountain in Australia, in SE New South Wales in the Australian Alps: the highest peak in Australia. Height: 2230 m (7316 ft).

kosher (ˈkəʊʃə) *adj* **1** *Judaism.* conforming to religious law; fit for use: esp. (of food) prepared in accordance with the dietary laws. **2** *Inf.* **2a** genuine or authentic. **2b** legitimate. [C19: from Yiddish, from Heb. *kāshēr* proper]

Košice ★ (*Czech* ˈkɔʃitsɛ) *n* a city in E Slovakia: passed from Hungary to Czechoslovakia in 1920 and to Slovakia in 1993. Pop.: 239 927 (1995 est.). Hungarian name: **Kassa**.

Kosovo-Metohija ★ (*Serbo-Croat* ˈkɔsɔvɔmɛˌtɔhija) *n* a region in S central Yugoslavia, in SW Serbia: became an autonomous region in 1946; chiefly Albanian in population, it was deprived of its autonomous status by Serbia after declaring independence in 1990: mainly a plateau. Capital: **Priština**. Pop.: 1 989 000 (1995 est.). Area: 10 887 sq. km (4203 sq. miles).

Kossoff ★ (ˈkɒsɒf) *n* **Leon.** born 1926, British painter, esp. of London scenes.

Kossuth (*Hungarian* ˈkoʃuːt) *n* **Lajos** (ˈlɔjoʃ). 1802–94, Hungarian statesman. He led the revolution against Austria (1848) and was provisional governor (1849), but he fled when the revolt was suppressed (1849).

Kostroma ★ (*Russian* kəstrɑˈma) *n* a city in W central Russia, on the River Volga: fought over bitterly by Novgorod, Tver, and Moscow, until annexed by Moscow in 1523; textile centre. Pop.: 285 000 (1995 est.).

Kosygin ★ (*Russian* kaˈsigin) *n* **Aleksei Nikolayevich** (alɪkˈsjej nikaˈlajɪvitʃ). 1904–80, Soviet statesman; premier of the Soviet Union (1964–80).

Kota *or* **Kotah** ★ (ˈkəʊtə) *n* a city in NW India, in Rajasthan, on the Chambal River: textile industry. Pop.: 537 371 (1991).

Kotabaru ★ (ˌkəʊtəˈbɑːruː) *n* a former name of **Jayapura**.

Kota Bharu *or* **Bahru** ★ (ˈkəʊtə ˈbɑːruː) *n* a port in NE Peninsular Malaysia: capital of Kelantan state on the delta of the Kelantan River. Pop.: 219 713 (1991).

Kota Kinabalu ★ (ˈkəʊtə ˌkɪnəbəˈluː) *n* a port in Malaysia, capital of Sabah state on the South China Sea: exports timber and rubber. Pop.: 208 484 (1991). Former name: **Jesselton**.

koto (ˈkəʊtəʊ) *n, pl* **kotos.** a Japanese stringed instrument. [Japanese]

kotuku (ˈkəʊtuːkuː) *n, pl* **kotuku.** *NZ.* a white heron having brilliant white plumage, black legs and yellow eyes and bill. [Maori]

kouprey (ˈkuːpreɪ) *n* a large wild member of the cattle tribe, of SE Asia, having a blackish-brown body and white legs: an endangered species. [C20: from F, from Cambodian, from Pali *gō* cow + Khmer *brai* forest]

Kovno ★ (ˈkɒvnə) *n* transliteration of the Russian name for **Kaunas**.

Kovrov ★ (*Russian* kavˈrɔf) *n* a city in W central Russia, on the Klyazma River: textiles and heavy engineering. Pop.: 162 000 (1995 est.).

Koweit ★ (kəʊˈweɪt) *n* a variant of **Kuwait**.

kowhai (ˈkɔːwaɪ) *n, pl* **kowhais.** *NZ.* a small leguminous tree of New Zealand and Chile with clusters of yellow flowers. [C19: from Maori]

Kowloon ★ (ˈkaʊˈluːn) *n* **1** a peninsula of SE China, opposite Hong Kong Island: part of the former British colony of Hong Kong. Area: 10 sq. km (3.75 sq. miles). **2** a port in Hong Kong, on Kowloon Peninsula. Pop.: 1 990 000 (1994 est.).

kowtow (ˌkaʊˈtaʊ) *vb* (*intr*) **1** to touch the forehead to the ground as a sign of deference: a former Chinese custom. **2** (often foll. by *to*) to be servile (towards). ◆ *n* **3** the act of kowtowing. [C19: from Chinese, from *k'o* to strike, knock + *t'ou* head]

Kozhikode ★ (ˌkəʊʒɪˈkəʊd) *n* a port in SW India, in W Kerala on the Malabar coast: important European trading post (1511–1765): formerly calico-manufacturing. Pop.: 420 000 (1991). Former name: **Calicut**.

Kr 1 *Currency. symbol for:* **1a** krona. **1b** krone. **2** *the chemical symbol for* krypton.

kr. *abbrev. for:* **1** krona. **2** krone.

Kra ★ (krɑː) *n* **Isthmus of.** an isthmus of SW Thailand, between the Bay of Bengal and the Gulf of Siam: the narrowest part of the Malay Peninsula. Width: about 56 km (35 miles).

kraal (krɑːl) *n S. African.* **1** a hut village in southern Africa, esp. one surrounded by a stockade. **2** an enclosure for livestock. [C18: from Afrik., from Port. *curral* pen]

Krafft-Ebing ★ (*German* ˈkraftˈeːbɪŋ) *n* **Richard** (ˈrɪçart), Baron von Krafft-Ebing. 1840–1902, German neurologist, who pioneered the study of sexual behaviour in *Psychopathia Sexualis* (1886).

kraft (krɑːft) *n* strong wrapping paper. [G: force]

Kragujevac ★ (*Serbo-Croat* ˈkragujevats) *n* a town in E central Yugoslavia, in Serbia; capital of Serbia (1818–39); automobile industry. Pop.: 147 305 (1991).

krait (kraɪt) *n* any nonaggressive brightly coloured venomous snake of S and SE Asia. [C19: from Hindi *karait*, from ?]

Krakatoa (ˌkrɑːkəˈtəʊə, ˌkrækəˈtaʊə) *or* **Krakatau** ★ (ˌkrɑːkəˈtaʊ, ˌkrækəˈtaʊ) *n* a volcanic island in Indonesia, in the Sunda Strait between Java and Sumatra: partially destroyed by its eruption in 1883, the greatest in recorded history. Further eruptions 44 years later formed a new island, **Anak Krakatau** ("Child of Krakatau"). Also called: **Rakata**.

Krakau ★ (ˈkraˌkau) *n* the German name for **Cracow**.

kraken (ˈkrɑːkən) *n* a legendary sea monster of gigantic size believed to dwell off the coast of Norway. [C18: from Norwegian, from ?]

Kraków ★ (ˈkrakuf) *n* the Polish name for **Cracow**.

Kramatorsk ★ (*Russian* krəmaˈtɔrsk) *n* a city in the E Ukraine: a major industrial centre of the Donets Basin. Pop.: 197 000 (1996 est.).

Kranj ★ (kraːnj) *n* the Slovene name for **Carniola**.

krans (krɑːns) *n S. African.* a sheer rock face; precipice. [C18: from Afrik.]

Krasnodar ★ (*Russian* krəsnaˈdar) *n* an industrial city in SW Russia, on the Kuban River. Pop.: 646 000 (1995 est.). Former name (until 1920): **Yekaterinodar**.

Krasnoyarsk ★ (*Russian* krəsnaˈjarsk) *n* a city in E central Russia, on the Yenisei River: the country's largest hydroelectric power station is nearby. Pop.: 869 000 (1995 est.).

Krebs ★ (krɛbz) *n* **Sir Hans Adolf.** 1900–81, British biochemist, born in Germany, who shared a Nobel prize for physiology or medicine (1953) for the discovery of the **Krebs cycle**, a cycle of metabolic reactions.

Krefeld ★ (ˈkreːfɛld; *German* ˈkreːfɛlt) *n* a city in W Germany, in W North Rhine-Westphalia: textile industries. Pop.: 249 662 (1995 est.).

Kreisler ★ (*German* ˈkraɪslər) *n* **Fritz** (frɪts). 1875–1962, US violinist, born in Austria.

Kremenchug ★ (*Russian* krɪmɪnˈtʃuk) *n* an industrial city in the E central Ukraine, on the Dnieper River. Pop.: 246 000 (1996 est.).

kremlin (ˈkrɛmlɪn) *n* the citadel of any Russian city. [C17: from obs. G *Kremelin*, from Russian *kreml*]

Kremlin ★ (ˈkrɛmlɪn) *n* **1** the 12th-century citadel in Moscow, containing the offices of the Russian government. **2** (formerly) the central government of the Soviet Union.

Krems ★ (*German* krɛms) *n* a town in NE Austria, in Lower Austria on the River Danube. Pop.: 22 830 (1991).

Kriemhild ('kriːmhɪlt) *or* **Kriemhilde** ★ ('kriːm,hɪldə) *n* (in the *Nibelungenlied*) the wife of Siegfried. She corresponds to Gudrun in Norse mythology.

krill (krɪl) *n, pl* **krill.** any small shrimplike marine crustacean: the principal food of whalebone whales. [C20: from Norwegian *kril* young fish]

krimmer ('krɪmə) *n* a tightly curled light grey fur obtained from the skins of lambs from Crimea in the Ukraine. [C20: from G, from *Krim* Crimea]

Kriol ('kriːɒl) *n* a creole language used by Aboriginal communities in the northern regions of Australia, developed from Northern Territory pidgin.

kris (krɪs) *n* a Malayan and Indonesian stabbing or slashing knife with a scalloped edge. Also called: **crease, creese.** [C16: from Malay]

Krishna[1] ★ ('krɪʃnə) *n* a river in S India, rising in the Western Ghats and flowing generally southeast to the Bay of Bengal. Length: 1300 km (800 miles). Also called: **Kistna.**

Krishna[2] ★ ('krɪʃnə) *n Hinduism.* the most celebrated of the Hindu deities, whose life story is told in the *Mahabharata.* [via Hindi from Sansk., lit.: dark, black]
▸ **'Krishnaism** *n*

Krishna Menon ★ ('kriːʃnə 'mɛnən) *n* Vengalil Krishnan ('vɛŋgəlɪl 'kriːʃnən). See (Vengalil Krishnan Krishna) **Menon.**

Kristiania ★ (,krɪstɪ'ɑːnɪə) *n* a former name (1877–1924) of **Oslo.**

Kristiansand *or* **Christiansand** ★ ('krɪstʃən,sænd; *Norwegian* kristian'san) *n* a port in S Norway, on the Skagerrak: shipbuilding. Pop.: 65 543 (1990).

Kristiansen ★ ('krɪstʃənsən) *n* **Ingrid.** born 1956, Norwegian long-distance runner.

Kristianstad ★ ('krɪstʃən,stɑːd; *Swedish* kriʃ'anstɑːd) *n* a town in S Sweden: founded in 1614 as a Danish fortress, it was acquired by Sweden in 1678. Pop.: 73 543 (1994).

Kríti ★ ('kriti) *n* transliteration of the Modern Greek name for **Crete.**

Krivoy Rog ★ (*Russian* kri'vɔj 'rɔk) *n* a city in the SE Ukraine: founded in the 17th century by Cossacks; iron-mining centre; iron- and steelworks. Pop.: 720 000 (1996 est.).

krona ('krəʊnə) *n, pl* **kronor** (-nə). the standard monetary unit of Sweden.

króna ('krəʊnə) *n, pl* **krónur** (-nə). the standard monetary unit of Iceland.

krone ('krəʊnə) *n, pl* **kroner** (-nə). **1** the standard monetary unit of Denmark. **2** the standard monetary unit of Norway. [C19: from Danish or Norwegian, ult. from L *corōna* CROWN]

Kronos ★ ('krəʊnɒs) *n* a variant of **Cronus.**

Kronstadt ★ *n* **1** (*Russian* kran'ʃtat). a port in NW Russia, on Kotlin island in the Gulf of Finland: naval base. Pop.: 44 400 (1994 est.). **2** ('kroːnʃtat). the German name for **Brașov.**

Kropotkin ★ (*Russian* kra'pɒtkin) *n* Prince **Peter,** Russian name *Pyotr Alexeyevich.* 1842–1921, Russian anarchist: his books include *Modern Science and Anarchism* (1903).

Kruger ★ ('kruːgə) *n* **Stephanus Johannes Paulus** ('stefɑnus jəʊ'hænɪs 'pɔːlus), known as **Oom Paul.** 1825–1904, Boer statesman; president of the Transvaal (1883–1900). His denial of civil rights to the Uitlanders led to the Boer War (1899–1902).

Kruger National Park ★ *n* a wildlife sanctuary in NE South Africa: the world's largest game reserve. Area: over 21 700 sq. km (8400 sq. miles).

Krugerrand ('kruːgə,rænd) *n* a one-ounce gold coin minted in South Africa for investment only. [C20: from Paul KRUGER + RAND[1]]

Krugersdorp ★ ('kruːgəz,dɔːp) *n* a city in NE African, on the Witwatersrand, at an altitude of 1722 m

(5650 ft): a gold-, manganese-, and uranium-mining centre. Pop.: 74 000 (latest est.).

krummhorn ('krʌm,hɔːn) *or* **crumhorn** *n* a medieval wind instrument consisting of an upward-curving tube blown through a double reed.

Krupp ★ (krʊp, krʌp) *n* a German family of steel and armaments manufacturers, including **Alfred,** 1812–87, his son **Friedrich Alfred,** 1854–1902, and the latter's son-in-law, **Gustav Krupp von Bohlen und Halbach,** 1870–1950.

Krušné Hory ★ ('kruʃne 'hɔrɪ) *n* the Czech name for the **Erzgebirge.**

Krym *or* **Krim** ★ (krɪm) *n* transliteration of the Russian name for **Crimea.**

krypton ('krɪptɒn) *n* an inert gaseous element occurring in trace amounts in air and used in fluorescent lights and lasers. Symbol: Kr; atomic no.: 36; atomic wt.: 83.80. [C19: from Gk, from *kruptos* hidden]

krytron ('kraɪtrɒn) *n Electronics.* a type of fast electronic gas-discharge switch, used as a trigger in nuclear weapons.

KS *abbrev. for* Kansas.

Kshatriya ('kʃætrɪə) *n* a member of the second of the four main Hindu castes, the warrior caste. [C18: from Sansk., from *kshatra* rule]

kt *abbrev. for:* **1** karat. **2** *Naut.* knot.

Kt 1 Also: **knt.** *abbrev. for* Knight. **2** Also: **N.** *Chess. symbol for* knight.

Kuala Lumpur ★ ('kwɑːlə 'lʊmpʊə, -pə) *n* the capital of Malaysia, in the SW Malay Peninsula: became capital of the Federated Malay States in 1895, and of Malaysia in 1963; capital of Selangor state from 1880 to 1973, when it was made a federal territory. Pop.: 1 145 075 (1991).

Kuban ★ (*Russian* ku'banj) *n* a river in SW Russia, rising in the Caucasus Mountains and flowing north and northwest to the Sea of Azov. Length: 906 km (563 miles).

Kubelik ★ (*Czech* 'kubɛliːk) *n* **Raphael** ('raːfæl). 1914–96, Czech conductor and composer.

Kublai Khan ★ ('kuːblaɪ 'kɑːn) *n* ?1216–94, Mongol emperor of China: grandson of Genghis Khan. He completed his grandfather's conquest of China and founded the Yuan dynasty (1279–1368).

Kubrick ★ ('kjuːbrɪk) *n* **Stanley.** 1928–99, US film writer and director. His films include *2001: A Space Odyssey* (1968), *A Clockwork Orange* (1971), *Full Metal Jacket* (1987), and *Eyes Wide Shut* (1999).

Kuch Bihar ★ ('kuːtʃ bɪ'hɑː) *n* a variant spelling of **Cooch Behar.**

Kuching ★ ('kuːtʃɪŋ) *n* a port in E Malaysia, capital of Sarawak state, on the Sarawak River 24 km (15 miles) from its mouth. Pop.: 147 729 (1991).

kudos ('kjuːdɒs) *n* (*functioning as sing*) acclaim, glory, or prestige. [C18: from Gk]

kudu *or* **koodoo** ('kuːduː) *n* either of two spiral-horned antelopes (**greater kudu** *or* **lesser kudu**), which inhabit the bush of Africa. [C18: from Afrik. *koedoe,* prob. from Khoi]

Kuenlun ★ ('kʊn'lʊn) *n* a variant spelling of **Kunlun.**

Kuibyshev *or* **Kuybyshev** ★ (*Russian* 'kujbɪʃəf) *n* former name (1935–91) of **Samara.**

Ku Klux Klan (,kuː klʌks 'klæn) *n* **1** a secret organization of White Southerners formed after the US Civil War to fight Black emancipation. **2** a secret organization of White Protestant Americans, mainly in the South, who use violence against Blacks, Jews, etc. [C19 *Ku Klux,* prob. based on Gk *kuklos* CIRCLE + *Klan* CLAN]
▸ **Ku Klux Klanner** ('klænə) *n*

kukri ('kʊkrɪ) *n, pl* **kukris.** a knife with a curved blade that broadens towards the point, esp. as used by Gurkhas. [from Hindi]

Kuku Nor ★ ('kuː'kuː 'nɔː) *n* a variant of **Koko Nor.**

kulak ('kuːlæk) *n* (in Russia after 1906) a member of the class of peasants who became proprietors of their own farms. In 1929 Stalin initiated their liquidation. [C19: from Russian: fist, hence, tightfisted person]

★ people and places

kulfi ('kulfɪ) *n* an Indian dessert that resembles ice cream flavoured with nuts and cardamom seeds.

Kulun ★ ('kuːˈluːn) *n* the Chinese name for **Ulan Bator.**

Kum ★ (kum) *n* a variant spelling of **Qom.**

Kumamoto ★ (ˌkuməˈməutəu) *n* a city in SW Japan, on W central Kyushu: Kumamoto Medical University (1949). Pop.: 650 322 (1995).

Kumaratunge ★ (ˌkuməˈrætuŋgə) *n* **Chandrika** ('tʃun,drɪkə) **Bandaranaike.** born 1945, Sri Lankan politician: president from 1994.

Kumasi ★ (kuːˈmæsɪ) *n* a city in S Ghana: seat of Ashanti kings since 1663; university (1961); market town for a cocoa-producing region. Pop.: 385 192 (1988 est.).

Kumayri ★ (ˌkumarˈrɪ) *n* a city in NW Armenia. Pop.: 120 000 (1989). Former names: **Aleksandropol** (1840–1924), **Leninakan** (1924–91).

kumera *or* **kumara** ('kuːmərə) *n* NZ. the sweet potato. [from Maori]

kumiss *or* **koumiss** ('kuːmɪs) *n* a drink made from fermented mare's or other milk, drunk by certain Asian tribes. [C17: from Russian *kumys*]

kumite ('kuːmɪˌteɪ) *n* Karate, etc. freestyle sparring or fighting. [C20: Japanese, lit.: sparring]

kümmel ('kuməl) *n* a German liqueur flavoured with aniseed and cumin. [C19: from G, from OHG *kumil*, prob. var. of CUMIN CUMIN]

kumquat *or* **cumquat** ('kʌmkwɒt) *n* **1** a small Chinese citrus tree. **2** the small round orange fruit of such a tree, with a sweet rind, used in preserves and confections. [C17: from Mandarin Chinese *chin chü* golden orange]

Kun ★ (kuːn) *n* **Béla** ('beːlɔ). 1886–?1937, Hungarian Communist, president of the Communist republic in Hungary (1919). Forced into exile, he died in a Stalinist purge.

Kundera ★ ('kʌndərə) *n* **Milan.** born 1929, Czech novelist living in France. His novels include *The Book of Laughter and Forgetting* (1979) and *Slowness* (1996).

Küng ★ (*German* kyŋ) *n* **Hans** (hans). born 1928, Swiss Roman Catholic theologian. His books include *On Being a Christian* (1976) and *Does God Exist?* (1980); his licence to teach was withdrawn (1979).

kung fu ('kʌŋ 'fuː) *n* a Chinese martial art combining principles of karate and judo. [from Chinese: martial art]

K'ung Fu-tse ★ ('kuŋ 'fuːˈtseɪ) *n* the Chinese name for **Confucius.**

Kungur ★ ('kungʊə) *n* a variant transliteration of the Chinese name for **Kongur Shan.**

Kunlun, Kuenlun, *or* **Kwenlun** ★ ('kun'lun) *n* a mountain range in China, between the Tibetan plateau and the Tarim Basin, extending over 1600 km (1000 miles) east from the Pamirs: the largest mountain system of Asia. Highest peak: Ulugh Muztagh, 7723 m (25 338 ft).

Kunming *or* **K'un-ming** ★ ('kun'mɪŋ) *n* a city in SW China, capital of Yunnan province, near Lake Tien: important during World War II as a Chinese military centre, American air base, and transport terminus for the Burma Road; Yunnan University (1934). Pop.: 1 520 000 (1991 est.).

Kuopio ★ (*Finnish* 'kwɔpjɔ) *n* a city in S central Finland. Pop.: 83 955 (1994).

Kura ★ (kuˈrɑː) *n* a river in W Asia, rising in NE Turkey and flowing across Georgia and Azerbaijan to the Caspian Sea. Length: 1515 km (941 miles).

kurchatovium (ˌkɜːtʃəˈtəuvɪəm) *n* another name for **rutherfordium,** esp. as used in the former Soviet Union. [C20: from Russian, after I. V. *Kurchatov* (1903–60), Soviet physicist]

Kurd (kɜːd) *n* a member of a nomadic people living chiefly in E Turkey, N Iraq, and W Iran.

Kurdish ('kɜːdɪʃ) *n* **1** the language of the Kurds. ◆ *adj* **2** of or relating to the Kurds or their language.

Kurdistan, Kurdestan, *or* **Kordestan** ★ (ˌkɜːdɪˈstɑːn) *n* a large plateau and mountainous region,

between the Caspian Sea and the Black Sea, south of the Caucasus. Area: over 29 000 sq. km (74 000 sq. miles).

Kure ★ (kuˈreɪ) *n* a port in SW Japan, on SW Honshu: a naval base; shipyards. Pop.: 209 477 (1995 est.).

Kurgan ★ (*Russian* kur'gan) *n* a city in W central Russia, on the Tobol River: industrial centre for an agricultural region. Pop.: 363 000 (1995 est.).

kuri ('kuːrɪ) *n, pl* **kuris.** NZ. a mongrel dog. Also called: **goorie.** [Maori]

Kuril Islands *or* **Kurile Islands** ★ (kuˈriːl) *pl n* a chain of 56 volcanic islands off the NE coast of Asia, extending for 1200 km (750 miles) from the S tip of the Kamchatka Peninsula to NE Hokkaido. Area: 14 990 sq. km (6020 sq. miles). Japanese name: **Chishima.**

Kurosawa ★ (ˌkuərəˈsɑːwə) *n* **Akira** (əˈkɪərə). 1910–98, Japanese film director. His works include *Rashomon* (1950), *The Seven Samurai* (1954), *Ran* (1985), and *Madadayo* (1993).

Kuroshio ★ (kəˈrəuʃɪ,əu) *n* another name for **Japan Current.**

kurrajong *or* **currajong** ('kʌrə,dʒɒŋ) *n* any of various Australian trees or shrubs, esp. one that yields a tough durable fibre. [C19: from Abor.]

kursaal ('kɜːzˀl) *n* a public room at a health resort. [from G, lit.: cure room]

Kursk ★ (*Russian* kursk) *n* a city in W Russia: industrial centre of an agricultural region: scene of a major Soviet victory (1943). Pop.: 442 000 (1995 est.).

kurtosis (kəˈtəusɪs) *n Statistics.* a measure of the concentration of a distribution around its mean. [from Gk, from *kurtos* arched]

kuru ('kuru:) *n* a degenerative disease of the nervous system, restricted to certain tribes in New Guinea, marked by loss of muscular control and thought to be caused by a slow virus. [C20: from a native name]

Kush ★ (kʌʃ, kuʃ) *n* a variant spelling of **Cush.**

Kuskokwim ★ ('kʌskə,kwɪm) *n* a river in SW Alaska, rising in the Alaska Range and flowing generally southwest to **Kuskokwim Bay,** an inlet of the Bering Sea. Length: about 970 km (600 miles).

Kutaisi ★ (*Russian* kuta'isi) *n* an industrial city in W Georgia, on the Rioni River: one of the oldest towns of the Caucasus. Pop.: 238 200 (1991 est.).

Kutch *or* **Cutch** ★ (kʌtʃ) *n* **1** a former state of W India, on the **Gulf of Kutch** (an inlet of the Arabian Sea): part of Gujarat state since 1960. **2 Rann of.** an extensive salt waste in W central India, and S Pakistan: consists of the Great Rann in the north and the Little Rann in the southeast; seasonal alternation between marsh and desert; some saltworks. In 1968 an international tribunal awarded about 10 per cent of the border area to Pakistan. Area: 23 000 sq. km (9000 sq. miles).

Kutuzov ★ (*Russian* ku'tuzəf) *n* Prince **Mikhail Ilarionovich** (mixa'il iləri'ɔnəvitʃ). 1745–1813, Russian field marshal, who harried Napoleon's army on their retreat from Moscow (1812–13).

Kuwait (kuˈweɪt) *or* **Koweit** ★ *n* **1** a state on the NW coast of the Persian Gulf: came under British protection in 1899 and gained independence in 1961; invaded by Iraq in 1990 and liberated by US-led forces in 1991 following the Gulf War: mainly desert. The economy is dependent on oil. Official language: Arabic. Official religion: Muslim. Currency: dinar. Capital: Kuwait. Pop.: 1 809 000 (1997). Area: 24 280 sq. km (9375 sq. miles). **2** the capital of Kuwait: a port on the Persian Gulf. Pop.: 31 241 (1993 est.).

▶ **Ku'waiti** *or* **Ko'weiti** *adj, n*

Kuznets ★ ('kuznɪts) *n* **Simon.** 1901–85, US economist born in Russia. His books include *Economic Growth of Nations* (1971): Nobel Prize for economics (1971).

Kuznetsk Basin (*Russian* kuz'njetsk) *or* **Kuzbass** ★ (*Russian* kuz'bas) *n* a region of S Russia, in the Kemerovo Region of W Siberia: the richest coalfield in the country, with important reserves of iron ore. Chief industrial centre: Novokuznetsk. Area: about 69 900 sq. km (27 000 sq. miles).

Kvaløy ★ (*Norwegian* 'kvaːlœj) *n* two islands in the Arctic

Ocean, off the N coast of Norway: **North Kvaløy**, 329 sq. km (127 sq. miles), and **South Kvaløy**, 735 sq. km (284 sq. miles).

kvass (kvɑːs) n an alcoholic drink of low strength made in Russia and E Europe from cereals and stale bread. [C16: from Russian *kvas*]

kvetch (kvɛtʃ) vb (intr) Sl., chiefly US. to complain or grumble, esp. incessantly. [C20: from Yiddish *kvetshn*, lit.: to squeeze, press]

kW abbrev. for kilowatt.

kwacha ('kwɑːtʃɑː) n **1** the standard monetary unit of Zambia. **2** the standard monetary unit of Malawi. [from a native word in Zambia]

Kwajalein ★ ('kwɑːdʒəˌleɪn) n an atoll in the W Pacific, in the W Marshall Islands, in the central part of the Ralik Chain. Length: about 125 km (78 miles).

Kwangchow ★ ('kwæŋ'tʃaʊ) n a variant transliteration of the Chinese name for **Canton**.

Kwangchowan ★ ('kwæŋ'tʃaʊ'wɑːn) n a territory of SE China, in SW Kwantung province: leased to France as part of French Indochina from 1898 to 1945. Area: 842 sq. km (325 sq. miles).

Kwangju ★ ('kwæŋ'dʒuː) n a city in SW South Korea: an important military base during the Korean War; cotton textile industry. Pop.: 1 257 504 (1995).

Kwangsi-Chuang Autonomous Region ★ ('kwæŋ'siː'tʃwæŋ) n a variant transliteration of the Chinese name for **Guangxi Zhuang Autonomous Region**.

Kwangtung ★ ('kwæŋ'tʊŋ) n a variant transliteration of the Chinese name for **Guangdong**.

Kwantung Leased Territory ★ ('kwæn'tʊŋ) n a strategic territory of NE China, at the S tip of the Liaotung Peninsula of Manchuria: leased forcibly by Russia in 1898; taken over by Japan in 1905; occupied by the Soviet Union in 1945 and subsequently returned to China on the condition of shared administration; made part of Liaoning province by China in 1954. Area: about 3400 sq. km (1300 sq. miles). Also called: **Kuan-tung**.

Kwara ★ ('kwɑːrə) n a state of W Nigeria: mainly wooded savanna. Capital: Ilorin. Pop.: 1 613 501 (1992 est.). Area: 36 825 sq. km (14 218 sq. miles).

kwashiorkor (ˌkwæʃɪ'ɔːkə) n severe malnutrition of infants and young children, resulting from dietary deficiency of protein. [C20: from native word in Ghana]

Kwazulu ★ (kwɑː'zuːluː) n (formerly) a Bantu homeland in South Africa, replaced in 1994 by KwaZulu/Natal.

KwaZulu/Natal ★ (kwɑːˌzuːluːnə'tæl, -'tɑːl) n a province of NE South Africa. Capital: Ulundi. Pop.: 8 713 100 (1995 est.). Area: 92 180 sq. km (35 591 sq. miles).

Kweichow or **Kueichou** ★ ('kwei'tʃaʊ) n a variant transliteration of the Chinese name for **Guizhou**.

Kweilin or **Kuei-lin** ★ ('kwei'lɪn) n a variant transliteration of the Chinese name for **Guilin**.

Kweisui ★ ('kwei'swei) n the former name of **Hohhot**.

Kweiyang or **Kuei-yang** ★ ('kwei'jæŋ) n a variant transliteration of the Chinese name for **Guiyang**.

kWh abbrev. for kilowatt-hour.

KWIC (kwɪk) n acronym for key word in context (esp. in **KWIC index**).

KWOC (kwɒk) n acronym for key word out of context.

Ky ★ (kiː) n **Nguyen Kao** (ⁿŋ'guːjen 'kaʊ). born 1930, Vietnamese military and political leader: premier of South Vietnam (1965–67); vice president (1967–69).

Ky. or **KY** abbrev. for Kentucky.

kyanite ('kaɪəˌnaɪt) n a variant spelling of **cyanite**.
▶ **kyanitic** (ˌkaɪə'nɪtɪk) adj

kyanize or **kyanise** ('kaɪəˌnaɪz) vb kyanizes, kyanizing, kyanized or kyanises, kyanising, kyanised. (tr) to treat (timber) with corrosive sublimate to make it resistant to decay. [C19: after J.H. *Kyan* (died 1850), Brit. inventor of the process]
▶ ˌkyani'zation or ˌkyani'sation n

Kyd or **Kid** ★ (kɪd) n **Thomas**. 1558–94, English dramatist, noted for his play *The Spanish Tragedy* (1586).

kyle (kaɪl) n Scot. (esp. in place names) a narrow strait or channel: *Kyle of Lochalsh*. [C16: from Gaelic *caol* narrow]

kylie or **kiley** ('kaɪlɪ) n Austral. a boomerang that is flat on one side and convex on the other. [C19: from Abor.]

kyloe ('kaɪləʊ) n a breed of small long-horned long-haired beef cattle from NW Scotland. [C19: from ?]

kymograph ('kaɪməˌɡrɑːf) n a rotatable drum for holding paper on which a tracking stylus continuously records variations in sound waves, blood pressure, respiratory movements, etc. [C20: from Gk *kuma* wave + -GRAPH]
▶ ˌkymo'graphic adj

Kymric ('kɪmrɪk) n, adj a variant spelling of **Cymric**.

Kymry ('kɪmrɪ) pl n a variant spelling of **Cymry**.

Kynewulf ★ ('kɪnəˌwʊlf) n a variant spelling of **Cynewulf**.

Kyongsong ★ ('kjɔːŋ'sɔːŋ) n another name for **Seoul**.

Kyoto or **Kioto** ★ (kɪ'əʊtəʊ, 'kjəʊ-) n a city in central Japan, on S Honshu: the capital of Japan from 794 to 1868; cultural centre, with two universities (1875, 1897). Pop.: 1 463 601 (1995).

kyphosis (kaɪ'fəʊsɪs) n Pathol. backward curvature of the thoracic spine, of congenital origin or resulting from injury or disease. [C19: from NL, from Gk *kuphōsis*, from *kuphos* humpbacked]
▶ **kyphotic** (kaɪ'fɒtɪk) adj

Kyrgyz ('kɪəɡɪz) n **1** (pl **Kyrgyz**) a member of a Mongoloid people of central Asia, inhabiting Kyrgyzstan and a vast area of central Siberia. **2** the language of this people, belonging to the Turkic branch of the Altaic family. Also: **Kirghiz, Kirgiz**.

Kyrgyzstan, Kirghizstan, or **Kirgizstan** ★ ('kɜːɡɪzˌstɑːn, -ˌstæn) n a republic in central Asia: came under Russian rule in the 19th century, became a Soviet republic in 1936 and gained independence in 1991; it has deposits of minerals, oil, and gas. Official languages: Kirghiz and Russian. Religion: nonreligious, Muslim. Currency: som. Capital: Bishkek. Pop.: 4 595 000 (1997). Area: 198 500 sq. km (76 460 sq. miles). Also called: **Kirghizia, Kirgizia**.

Kyrgyz Steppe ★ n a vast steppe region in central Kazakhstan. Also called: (the) **Steppes**.

Kyrie eleison ('kɪrɪ ə'leɪsⁿn) n **1** a formal invocation used in the liturgies of the Roman Catholic, Greek Orthodox, and Anglican Churches. **2** a musical setting of this. Often shortened to **Kyrie**. [C14: via LL from LGk *kurie, eleēson* Lord, have mercy]

Kythera ★ ('kɪθɪrə) n a variant spelling of **Cythera**.

kyu (kjuː) n Judo. one of the student grades for inexperienced competitors. [from Japanese]

Kyushu or **Kiushu** ★ ('kjuːʃuː) n an island of SW Japan: the southernmost of Japan's four main islands, with over 300 surrounding small islands; coalfield and chemical industries. Chief cities: Fukuoka, Kitakyushu, and Nagasaki. Pop.: 13 424 000 (1995). Area: 35 659 sq. km (13 768 sq. miles).

Kyzyl Kum ★ (Russian kiˈzil ˈkum) n a desert in Kazakhstan and Uzbekistan.

★ people and places

Ll

l *or* **L** (ɛl) *n, pl* **l's, L's,** *or* **Ls. 1** the 12th letter of the English alphabet. **2** a speech sound represented by this letter. **3a** something shaped like an L. **3b** (*in combination*): *an L-shaped room.*

l *symbol for litre.*

L *symbol for:* **1** lambert(s). **2** large. **3** Latin. **4** (on British motor vehicles) learner driver. **5** *Physics.* length. **6** live. **7** Usually written: £, pound. [L *libra*]. **8** lire. **9** *Electronics.* inductor (in circuit diagrams). **10** *Physics.* **10a** latent heat. **10b** self-inductance. **11** the Roman numeral for 50. See **Roman numerals.**

L. *or* **l.** *abbrev. for:* **1** lake. **2** law. **3** leaf. **4** league. **5** left. **6** length. **7** (*pl* **LL** *or* **ll.**) line. **8** link. **9** low.

L. *abbrev. for:* **1** *Politics.* Liberal. **2** (in titles) Licentiate. **3** Linnaeus.

la (lɑː) *n Music.* the syllable used in the fixed system of solmization for the note A. [C14: see GAMUT]

la[2] (lɔː) *interj* an exclamation of surprise or emphasis. [OE *lā* lo]

La the chemical symbol for lanthanum.

laager ('lɑːgə) *n* **1** (in Africa) a camp, esp. one defended by a circular formation of wagons. **2** *Mil.* a place where armoured vehicles are parked. ◆ *vb* **3** to form (wagons) into a laager. **4** (*tr*) to park (armoured vehicles) in a laager. [C19: from Afrik. *lager*, via G from OHG *legar* bed, lair]

Laaland ★ (*Danish* 'lɔlan) *n* a variant spelling of **Lolland.**

lab (læb) *n Inf.* short for **laboratory.**

lab. *abbrev. for:* **1** laboratory. **2** labour.

Lab. *abbrev. for:* **1** *Politics.* Labour. **2** Labrador.

Laban ★ ('leɪb²n) *n Old Testament.* the father-in-law of Jacob, father of Leah and Rachel (Genesis 29:16).

Labe ★ ('labɛ) *n* the Czech name for the (River) **Elbe.**

label ('leɪb²l) *n* **1** a piece of paper, card, or other material attached to an object to identify it or give instructions or details concerning its ownership, use, nature, destination, etc.; tag. **2** a brief descriptive phrase or term given to a person, group, school of thought, etc.: *the label "Romantic" is applied to many different kinds of poetry.* **3** a word or phrase heading a piece of text to indicate or summarize its contents. **4** a trademark or company or brand name on certain goods, esp. on gramophone records. **5** *Computing.* a group of characters appended to a statement in a program to allow it to be identified. **6** *Chem.* a radioactive element used in a compound to trace the mechanism of a chemical reaction. ◆ *vb* **labels, labelling, labelled** *or US* **labels, labeling, labeled.** (*tr*) **7** to fasten a label to. **8** to mark with a label. **9** to describe or classify in a word or phrase: *to label someone a liar.* **10** to make (one or more atoms in a compound) radioactive, for use in determining the mechanism of a reaction. [C14: from OF, from Gmc]
▸ **'labeller** *n*

labia ('leɪbɪə) *n* the plural of **labium.**

labial ('leɪbɪəl) *adj* **1** of, relating to, or near lips or labia. **2** *Music.* producing sounds by the action of an air stream over a narrow liplike fissure, as in a flue pipe of an organ. **3** *Phonetics.* relating to a speech sound whose articulation involves movement or use of the lips. ◆ *n* **4** Also called: **labial pipe.** *Music.* an organ pipe with a liplike fissure. **5** *Phonetics.* a speech sound such as English *p* or *m*, whose articulation involves movement or use of the lips. [C16: from Med. L *labiālis*, from L *labium* lip]
▸ **'labially** *adv*

labiate ('leɪbɪˌeɪt, -ɪt) *n* **1** any plant of the family *Labiatae*, having square stems, aromatic leaves, and a two-lipped corolla: includes mint, thyme, sage, rosemary, etc. ◆ *adj* **2** of, relating to, or belonging to the family *Labiatae*. [C18: from NL *labiātus*, from L *labium* lip]

Labiche ★ (*French* labiʃ) *n* **Eugène Marin** (øʒɛn marɛ̃). 1815–88, French dramatist, noted for his farces, which include *Le Chapeau de paille d'Italie* (1851) and *Le Voyage de Monsieur Perrichon* (1860).

labile ('leɪbɪl) *adj Chem.* (of a compound) prone to chemical change. [C15: via LL *lābilis*, from L *lābī* to slide]
▸ **lability** (lə'bɪlɪtɪ) *n*

labiodental (ˌleɪbɪəʊ'dɛnt²l) *Phonetics.* ◆ *adj* **1** pronounced by bringing the bottom lip into contact with the upper teeth, as for *f* in *fat, puff.* ◆ *n* **2** a labiodental consonant. [C17: from L LABIUM + DENTAL]

labium ('leɪbɪəm) *n, pl* **labia** (-bɪə). **1** a lip or liplike structure. **2** any one of the four lip-shaped folds of the female vulva, comprising an outer pair (**labia majora**) and an inner pair (**labia minora**). [C16: NL, from L.: lip]

laboratory (lə'bɒrətərɪ, -trɪ; *US.* 'læbrəˌtɔːrɪ) *n, pl* **laboratories. 1a** a building or room equipped for conducting scientific research or for teaching practical science. **1b** (*as modifier*): *laboratory equipment.* **2** a place where chemicals or medicines are manufactured. ◆ Often shortened to **lab.** [C17: from Med. L *labōrātōrium* workshop, from L *labōrāre* to LABOUR]

Labor Day *n* **1** a public holiday in the US and Canada in honour of labour, held on the first Monday in September. **2** a public holiday in Australia, observed on different days in different states.

laborious (lə'bɔːrɪəs) *adj* **1** involving great exertion or long effort. **2** given to working hard. **3** (of literary style, etc.) not fluent.
▸ **la'boriously** *adv* ▸ **la'boriousness** *n*

Labor Party *n* one of the chief political parties of Australia, generally supporting the interests of organized labour.

labour *or US & sometimes Canad.* **labor** ('leɪbə) *n* **1** productive work, esp. physical toil done for wages. **2a** the people, class, or workers involved in this, esp. in contrast to management, capital, etc. **2b** (*as modifier*): *labour relations.* **3a** difficult or arduous work or effort. **3b** (*in combination*): *labour-saving.* **4** a particular job or task, esp. of a difficult nature. **5a** the process or effort of childbirth or the time during which this takes place. **5b** (*as modifier*): *labour pain; labour ward.* ◆ *vb* **6** (*intr*) to perform labour; work. **7** (*intr*; foll. by *for*, etc.) to strive or work hard (for something). **8** (*intr*; usually foll. by *under*) to be burdened (by) or be at a disadvantage (because of): *to labour under a misapprehension.* **9** (*intr*) to make one's way with difficulty. **10** (*tr*) to deal with too persistently: *to labour a point.* **11** (*intr*) (of a woman) to be in labour. **12** (*intr*) (of a ship) to pitch and toss. [C13: via OF from L *labor*]

labour camp *n* **1** a penal colony involving forced labour. **2** a camp for migratory labourers.

Labour Day *n* a public holiday in many countries in honour of labour, usually held on May 1.

laboured *or US & sometimes Canad.* **labored** ('leɪbəd) *adj* **1** (of breathing) performed with difficulty. **2** showing effort; contrived; lacking grace or fluency.

labourer *or US & sometimes Canad.* **laborer** ('leɪbərə) *n* a person engaged in physical work, esp. unskilled work.

labour exchange *n Brit.* a former name for the **employment office.**

labour-intensive *adj* of or denoting a task, organization, industry, etc., in which a high proportion of the costs are due to wages, salaries, etc.

Labourite ('leɪbəˌraɪt) *n* an adherent of the Labour Party.

Labour Party *n* **1** a British political party, formed in 1900 as an amalgam of various trade unions and socialist groups, generally supporting the interests of organized labour and advocating democratic socialism and social equality. **2** any similar party in any of various other countries.

Labrador ★ ('læbrə,dɔ:) *n* **1** Also called: **Labrador-Ungava.** a large peninsula of NE Canada, on the Atlantic, the Gulf of St Lawrence, Hudson Strait, and Hudson Bay: contains most of the province of Quebec and the mainland part of Newfoundland; geologically part of the Canadian Shield. Area: 1 619 000 sq. km (625 000 sq. miles). **2** Also called: **Coast of Labrador.** a region of NE Canada, on the Atlantic and consisting of the mainland part of Newfoundland province. **3** (*often not cap.*) short for **Labrador retriever.**

Labrador retriever *n* a powerfully-built variety of retriever with a short dense usually black or golden-brown coat. Often shortened to **Labrador.**

labret ('leɪbrɛt) *n* a piece of bone, shell, etc., inserted into the lip as an ornament by certain peoples. [C19: from L *labrum* lip]

labrum ('leɪbrəm, 'læb-) *n, pl* **labra** (-brə). a lip or liplike part, such as the cuticular plate forming the upper lip of insects. [C19: NL, from L]

La Bruyère ★ (*French* la bryjɛr) *n* **Jean de** (ʒɑ̃ də). 1645–96, French moralist, noted for his *Caractères* (1688), satirical studies of contemporary figures.

Labuan ★ (lə'bu:ən) *n* an island in Malaysia, off the NW coast of Borneo: part of the Straits Settlements until 1946, when transferred to North Borneo. Chief town: Victoria. Area: 98 sq. km (38 sq. miles).

laburnum (lə'bɜ:nəm) *n* any tree or shrub of a Eurasian genus having clusters of yellow drooping flowers: all parts of the plant are poisonous. [C16: NL, from L]

labyrinth ('læbərɪnθ) *n* **1** a mazelike network of tunnels, chambers, or paths, either natural or man-made. **2** any complex or confusing system of streets, passages, etc. **3** a complex or intricate situation. **4** any system of interconnecting cavities, esp. those comprising the internal ear. **5** *Electronics.* an enclosure behind a high-performance loudspeaker, consisting of a series of air chambers designed to absorb unwanted sound waves. [C16: via L from Gk *laburinthos*, from ?]

labyrinthine (,læbə'rɪnθaɪn) *adj* **1** of or relating to a labyrinth. **2** resembling a labyrinth in complexity.

lac[1] (læk) *n* a resinous substance secreted by certain insects (**lac insects**), used in the manufacture of shellac. [C16: from Du. *lak* or F *laque*, from Hindi *lākh* resin, ult. from Sansk. *lākshā*]

lac[2] (lɑ:k) *n* a variant spelling of **lakh.**

Lacan ★ (*French* lakɑ̃) *n* **Jacques** (ʒak). 1901–81, French psychoanalyst, who reinterpreted Freud in terms of structural linguistics: an important influence on structuralist thought.

Laccadive, Minicoy, and Amindivi Islands ★ ('lækədɪv, 'mɪnɪ,kɔɪ, ,amən'di:vi:) *pl n* the former name (until 1973) of the **Lakshadweep Islands.**

laccolith ('lækəlɪθ) *or* **laccolite** ('lækə,laɪt) *n* a dome of igneous rock between two layers of older sedimentary rock. [C19: from Gk *lakkos* cistern + -LITH]

lace (leɪs) *n* **1** a delicate decorative fabric made from cotton, silk, etc., woven in an open web of different symmetrical patterns and figures. **2** a cord or string drawn through eyelets or around hooks to fasten a shoe or garment. **3** ornamental braid often used on military uniforms, etc. ◆ *vb* **laces, lacing, laced.** (*tr*) **4** to fasten (shoes, etc.) with a lace. **5** to draw (a cord or thread) through holes, eyes, etc., as when tying shoes. **6** to compress the waist of (someone), as with a corset. **7** to add a small amount of alcohol or drugs to (food or drink). **8** (*usually passive* and foll. *by with*) to streak or mark with lines or colours: *the sky was laced with red.* **9** to intertwine; interlace. **10** *Inf.* to give a sound beating to. [C13 *las*, from OF *laz*, from L *laqueus* noose]

lacebark ('leɪsbɑ:k) *n* another name for **ribbonwood.**

Lacedaemon ★ (,læsɪ'di:mən) *n* another name for **Sparta** or **Laconia.**
► **Lacedae'monian** *adj, n*

lacerate *vb* ('læsə,reɪt), **lacerates, lacerating, lacerated.** (*tr*) **1** to tear (the flesh, etc.) jaggedly. **2** to hurt or harrow (the

feelings, etc.). ◆ *adj* ('læsə,reɪt, -rɪt). **3** having edges that are jagged: *lacerate leaves.* [C16: from L *lacerāre* to tear, from *lacer* mangled]
► ,lace'ration *n*

lace up *vb* **1** (*tr, adv*) to tighten or fasten (clothes or footwear) with laces. ◆ *adj* **lace-up. 2** (of footwear) to be fastened with laces. ◆ *n* **lace-up. 3** a lace-up shoe or boot.

lacewing ('leɪs,wɪŋ) *n* any of various insects, esp. the green lacewings and brown lacewings, having lacy wings and preying on aphids and similar pests.

laches ('lætʃɪz) *n Law.* negligence or unreasonable delay in pursuing a legal remedy. [C14 *lachesse*, via OF *lasche* slack, from L *laxus* LAX]

Lachesis ★ ('lækɪsɪs) *n Greek myth.* one of the three Fates. [via L from Gk, from *lakhesis* destiny, from *lakhein* to befall by lot]

Lachlan ★ ('lɒklən) *n* a river in SE Australia, rising in central New South Wales and flowing northwest then southwest to the Murrumbidgee River. Length: about 1450 km (900 miles). [named after *Lachlan* Macquarie, governor of New South Wales (1809–21)]

lachrymal ('lækrɪməl) *adj* a variant spelling of **lacrimal.**

lachrymatory ('lækrɪmətərɪ, -trɪ) *n, pl* **lachrymatories.** a small vessel found in ancient tombs, formerly thought to hold the tears of mourners. ◆ *adj* **2** a variant spelling of **lacrimatory.**

lachrymose ('lækrɪ,məʊs) *adj* **1** given to weeping; tearful. **2** mournful; sad. [C17: from L, from *lacrima* a tear]
► 'lachry,mosely *adv*

lacing ('leɪsɪŋ) *n* **1** *Chiefly Brit.* a course of bricks, stone, etc., for strengthening a rubble or flint wall. **2** another word for **lace** (senses 2, 3). **3** *Inf.* a severe beating.

laciniate (lə'sɪnɪ,eɪt, -ɪt) *or* **laciniated** *adj* **1** *Biol.* jagged: *a laciniate leaf.* **2** having a fringe. [C17: from L *lacinia* flap]
► la,cini'ation *n*

lack (læk) *n* **1** an insufficiency, shortage, or absence of something required or desired. **2** something that is required but is absent or in short supply. ◆ *vb* **3** (when *intr*, often foll. *by in* or *for*) to be deficient (in) or have need (of). [C12: rel. to MDu. *laken* to be wanting]

lackadaisical (,lækə'deɪzɪkʰl) *adj* **1** lacking vitality and purpose. **2** lazy, esp. in a dreamy way. [C18: from earlier *lackadaisy*]
► ,lacka'daisically *adv*

lackey ('lækɪ) *n* **1** a servile follower; hanger-on. **2** a liveried male servant or valet. **3** a person who is treated like a servant. ◆ *vb* **4** (when *intr*, often foll. *by for*) to act as a lackey (to). [C16: via F *laquais*, from OF, ?from Catalan *lacayo, alacayo*]

lacklustre *or US* **lackluster** ('læk,lʌstə) *adj* lacking force, brilliance, or vitality.

Laclos ★ (*French* laklo) *n* **Pierre Choderlos de** (pjɛr ʃɔdɛrlo də). 1741–1803, French soldier and writer, noted for his novel in epistolary form *Les Liaisons dangereuses* (1782).

Laconia ★ (lə'kəʊnɪə) *n* an ancient country of S Greece, in the SE Peloponnese, of which Sparta was the capital: corresponds to the present-day department of Lakonia.
► La'conian *n, adj*

laconic (lə'kɒnɪk) *adj* (of a person's speech) using few words; terse. [C16: via L from Gk *Lakōnikos*, from *Lakōn* Laconian, Spartan; referring to the Spartans' terseness of speech]
► la'conically *adv*

La Coruña ★ (*Spanish* la ko'ruɲa) *n* a port in NW Spain, on the Atlantic: point of departure for the Spanish Armada (1588); site of the defeat of the French by the English under Sir John Moore in the Peninsular War (1809). Pop.: 255 087 (1994 est.). English name: **Corunna.**

lacquer ('lækə) *n* **1** a hard glossy coating made by dissolving cellulose derivatives or natural resins in a volatile solvent. **2** a black resinous substance, obtained from certain trees (**lacquer trees**), used to give a hard glossy finish to wooden furniture. **3** Also called: **hair lacquer.** a mixture of shellac and alcohol for spraying onto the hair to hold a style in place. **4** *Art.* decorative objects coated with such lacquer, often inlaid. ◆ *vb* (*tr*) **5** to apply lac-

★ people and places

quer to. [C16: from obs. F *lacre* sealing wax, from Port. *laca* LAC[1]]
► 'lacquerer *n*

acrimal, lachrymal, *or* **lacrymal** ('lækrɪməl) *adj* of or relating to tears or to the glands that secrete tears. [C16: from Med. L, from L *lacrima* a tear]

acrimation (,lækrɪ'meɪʃən) *n* the secretion of tears.

acrimatory, lachrymatory, *or* **lacrymatory** ('lækrɪmətərɪ, -trɪ) *adj* of, causing, or producing tears.

acrosse (lə'krɒs) *n* a ball game invented by American Indians, now played by two teams who try to propel a ball into each other's goal by means of long-handled pouched sticks (**lacrosse sticks**). [C19: Canad. F: the hooked stick, crosier]

actam ('læktæm) *n Chem.* any of a group of cyclic amides, derived from amino acids, having the characteristic group -CONH-. [C20: from LACTO- + AM(IDE)]

lactate[1] ('lækteɪt) *n* an ester or salt of lactic acid. [C18]

lactate[2] (læk'teɪt) *vb* **lactates, lactating, lactated.** (*intr*) (of mammals) to produce or secrete milk.

lactation (læk'teɪʃən) *n* **1** the secretion of milk from the mammary glands after parturition. **2** the period during which milk is secreted.

lacteal ('læktɪəl) *adj* **1** of, relating to, or resembling milk. **2** (of lymphatic vessels) conveying or containing chyle. ◆ *n* **3** any of the lymphatic vessels conveying chyle from the small intestine to the thoracic duct. [C17: from L *lacteus* of milk, from *lac* milk]

lactescent (læk'tes°nt) *adj* **1** (of plants and certain insects) secreting a milky fluid. **2** milky or becoming milky. [C18: from L, from *lactescēre* to become milky, from *lact-, lac* milk]
► lac'tescence *n*

lactic ('læktɪk) *adj* relating to or derived from milk. [C18: from L *lact-, lac* milk]

lactic acid *n* a colourless syrupy carboxylic acid found in sour milk and many fruits and used as a preservative (**E270**) for foodstuffs. Formula: $CH_3CH(OH)COOH$. Systematic name: **2-hydroxypropanoic acid.**

lactiferous (læk'tɪfərəs) *adj* producing, conveying, or secreting milk or a milky fluid. [C17: from L *lactifer*, from *lact-, lac* milk]

lacto- ('læktəʊ) *or before a vowel* **lact-** *combining form.* indicating milk: *lactobacillus*. [from L *lact-, lac* milk]

lactose ('læktəʊs, -təʊz) *n* a white crystalline sugar occurring in milk and used in pharmaceuticals and baby foods. Formula: $C_{12}H_{22}O_{11}$.

lacto-vegetarian *n* a vegetarian whose diet includes dairy produce.

La Cumbre ★ (lə 'kuːmbreɪ) *n* another name for the Uspallata Pass.

lacuna (lə'kjuːnə) *n, pl* **lacunae** (-niː) *or* **lacunas. 1** a gap or space, esp. in a book or manuscript. **2** *Biol.* a cavity or depression, such as any of the spaces in the matrix of bone. [C17: from L *lacūna* pool, cavity, from *lacus* lake]
► la'cunose, la'cunal, la'cunar, *or* la'cunary *adj*

lacustrine (lə'kʌstraɪn) *adj* **1** of or relating to lakes. **2** living or growing in or on the shores of a lake. [C19: from It. *lacustre*, from L *lacus* lake]

lacy ('leɪsɪ) *adj* **lacier, laciest.** made of or resembling lace.
► 'lacily *adv* ► 'laciness *n*

lad (læd) *n* **1** a boy or young man. **2** *Inf.* a familiar form of address for any male. **3** a lively or dashing man or youth (esp. in **a bit of a lad**). **4** *Brit.* a boy or man who looks after horses. [C13 *ladde*; ?from ON]

ladanum ('lædənəm) *n* a dark resinous juice obtained from various rockroses: used in perfumery. [C16: L from Gk, from *lēdon* rockrose]

ladder ('lædə) *n* **1** a portable framework of wood, metal, rope, etc., in the form of two long parallel members connected by rungs or steps fixed to them at right angles, for climbing up or down. **2** any hierarchy conceived of as having a series of ascending stages, levels, etc.: *the social ladder*. **3** Also called: **run.** *Chiefly Brit.* a line of connected stitches that have come undone in knitted material, esp. stockings. ◆ *vb* **4** *Chiefly Brit.* to cause a line of intercon-

nected stitches in (stockings, etc.) to undo, as by snagging, or, (of a stocking) to come undone in this way. [OE *hlædder*]

ladder back *n* a type of chair in which the back is constructed of horizontal slats between two uprights.

laddie ('lædɪ) *n Chiefly Scot.* a familiar term for a male, esp. a boy; lad.

laddish ('lædɪʃ) *adj Inf., usually derog.* characteristic of male adolescents or young men, esp. by being rowdy, macho, or immature: *laddish behaviour.*

lade (leɪd) *vb* **lades, lading, laded; laden** *or* **laded. 1** to put cargo or freight on board (a ship, etc.) or (of a ship, etc.) to take on cargo or freight. **2** (*tr; usually passive* and foll. by *with*) to burden or oppress. **3** (*tr; usually passive* and foll. by *with*) to fill or load. **4** to remove (liquid) with or as if with a ladle. [OE *hladen* to load]

laden ('leɪd°n) *vb* **1** a past participle of **lade.** ◆ *adj* **2** weighed down with a load; loaded. **3** encumbered; burdened.

la-di-da, lah-di-dah, *or* **la-de-da** (,lɑːdiː'dɑː) *adj Inf.* affecting exaggeratedly genteel manners or speech. [C19: mockingly imit. of affected speech]

ladies *or* **ladies' room** *n* (*functioning as sing*) *Inf.* a women's public lavatory.

lading ('leɪdɪŋ) *n* a load; cargo; freight.

Ladislaus I ('lædɪs,lɔːs) *or* **Ladislas** ★ ('lædɪs,læs) *n* **Saint.** 1040–95, king of Hungary (1077–95). He extended his country's boundaries and suppressed paganism. Feast day: June 27.

ladle ('leɪd°l) *n* **1** a long-handled spoon having a deep bowl for serving or transferring liquids. **2** a large bucket-shaped container for transferring molten metal. ◆ *vb* **ladles, ladling, ladled. 3** (*tr*) to serve out as with a ladle. [OE *hlædel*, from *hladan* to draw out]
► 'ladleful *n*

ladle out *vb* (*tr, adv*) *Inf.* to distribute (money, gifts, etc.) generously.

Ladoga ★ (*Russian* 'ladəgə) *n* **Lake.** a lake in NW Russia, in the SW Karelian Republic: the largest lake in Europe; it drains through the River Neva into the Gulf of Finland. Area: about 18 000 sq. km (7000 sq. miles). Russian name: **Ladozhskoye Ozero** ('ladəʃskəjə 'ɒzɪrə).

Ladrone Islands ★ (lə'drəʊn) *pl n* the former name (1521–1668) of the **Mariana Islands.**

lady ('leɪdɪ) *n, pl* **ladies. 1** a woman regarded as having the characteristics of a good family and high social position. **2a** a polite name for a woman. **2b** (*as modifier*): *a lady doctor.* **3** an informal name for **wife. 4 lady of the house.** the female head of the household. **5** *History.* a woman with proprietary rights and authority, as over a manor. [OE *hlæfdīge*, from *hlāf* bread + *dīge* kneader, rel. to *dāh* dough]

Lady ('leɪdɪ) *n, pl* **Ladies. 1** (in Britain) a title of honour borne by various classes of women of the peerage. **2 my lady.** a term of address to holders of the title Lady. **3 Our Lady.** a title of the Virgin Mary.

ladybird ('leɪdɪ,bɜːd) *n* any of various small brightly coloured beetles, esp. one having red elytra with black spots. [C18: after *Our Lady*, the Virgin Mary]

lady bountiful *n* an ostentatiously charitable woman. [C19: after a character in George Farquhar's play *The Beaux' Stratagem* (1707)]

Lady Chapel *n* a chapel within a church or cathedral, dedicated to the Virgin Mary.

Lady Day *n* March 25, the feast of the Annunciation of the Virgin Mary. Also called: **Annunciation Day.**

lady-in-waiting *n, pl* **ladies-in-waiting.** a lady who attends a queen or princess.

lady-killer *n Inf.* a man who is, or believes he is, irresistibly fascinating to women.

ladylike ('leɪdɪ,laɪk) *adj* like or befitting a lady in manners and bearing; refined and fastidious.

ladylove ('leɪdɪ,lʌv) *n Now rare.* a beloved woman.

Lady Macbeth strategy *n* a strategy in a takeover battle in which a third party makes a bid acceptable to the target company, appearing to act as a white knight but subsequently joining forces with the original (unwelcome) bidder. [C20: after *Lady Macbeth* in Shakespeare's *Macbeth* (1605)]

lady mayoress *n Brit.* the wife of a lord mayor.

Lady of the Lake ★ *n* (in Arthurian legend) a mysterious supernatural being sometimes identified with **Vivian**.

lady's bedstraw *n* a Eurasian plant with clusters of small yellow flowers.

lady's finger *n* another name for **bhindi**.

Ladyship ('leɪdɪʃɪp) *n* (preceded by *your* or *her*) a title used to address or refer to any peeress except a duchess.

Ladysmith ★ ('leɪdɪˌsmɪθ) *n* a city in E South Africa: besieged by Boers for four months (1899–1900) during the Boer War. Pop.: 56 599 (1989).

lady's-slipper *n* any of various orchids having reddish or purple flowers.

lady's-smock *n* a N temperate plant with white or rose-pink flowers. Also called: **cuckooflower**.

Laënnec ★ (*French* laɛnɛk) *n* **René Théophile Hyacinthe** (rəne teɔfil jasɛt). 1781–1826, French physician, who invented the stethoscope.

Laertes ★ (leɪˈɜːtiːz) *n Greek myth.* the father of Odysseus.

laevo- *or US* **levo-** *combining form.* **1** on or towards the left: *laevorotatory*. **2** (in chemistry) denoting a laevorotatory compound. [from L *laevus* left]

laevorotation (ˌliːvəʊrəʊˈteɪʃən) *n* **1** a rotation to the left. **2** an anticlockwise rotation of the plane of polarization of plane-polarized light as a result of its passage through a crystal, liquid, or solution. ♦ Cf. **dextrorotation**.
 ▸ **laevorotatory** (ˌliːvəʊˈrəʊtətərɪ) *adj*

Lafayette *or* **La Fayette** ★ (*French* lafajɛt) *n* **1 Marie Joseph Paul Yves Roch Gilbert du Motier** (mari ʒɔzɛf pɔl iv rɔk ʒilbɛr dy mɔtje), Marquis de Lafayette. 1757–1834, French general and statesman. He fought on the side of the colonists in the War of American Independence and played a leading part in the French Revolution and the revolution of 1830. **2 Marie-Madeleine** (marimadlɛn), Comtesse de Lafayette. 1634–93, French novelist.

Laffer curve ('læfə) *n Econ.* a graph showing government tax revenue plotted against percentage tax rates; it illustrates that a cut in a high tax rate can increase government revenue. [C20: after Arthur *Laffer* (born 1940), US economist]

La Fontaine ★ (*French* la fɔ̃tɛn) *n* **Jean de** (ʒɑ̃ də). 1621–95, French poet, famous for his *Fables* (1668–94).

Laforgue ★ (*French* lafɔrg) *n* **Jules** (ʒyl). 1860–87, French symbolist poet and an originator of free verse.

LAFTA ('læftə) *n acronym for* Latin American Free Trade Area, the name before 1981 of the Latin American Integration Association. See **LAIA**.

lag[1] (læg) *vb* **lags, lagging, lagged.** (*intr*) **1** (often foll. by *behind*) to hang (back) or fall (behind) in movement, progress, development, etc. **2** to fall away in strength or intensity. ♦ *n* **3** the act or state of slowing down or falling behind. **4** the interval of time between two events, esp. between an action and its effect. [C16: from ?]

lag[2] (læg) *Sl.* ♦ *n* **1** a convict or ex-convict (esp. in **old lag**). **2** a term of imprisonment. ♦ *vb* **lags, lagging, lagged. 3** (*tr*) to arrest or put in prison. [C19: from ?]

lag[3] (læg) *vb* **lags, lagging, lagged. 1** (*tr*) to cover (a pipe, cylinder, etc.) with lagging to prevent loss of heat. ♦ *n* **2** the insulating casing of a steam cylinder, boiler, etc. **3** a stave. [C17: of Scand. origin]

lagan ('lægᵊn) *n* goods or wreckage on the sea bed, sometimes attached to a buoy to permit recovery. [C16: from OF *lagan*, prob. of Gmc origin]

lager ('lɑːgə) *n* a light-bodied effervescent beer, fermented in a closed vessel using yeasts that sink to the bottom of the brew. [C19: from G *Lagerbier* beer for storing, from *Lager* storehouse]

Lagerkvist ★ (*Swedish* 'lɑːgərkvist) *n* **Pär** (**Fabian**) (pæːr). 1891–1974, Swedish novelist and dramatist. His novels include *Barabbas* (1950): Nobel prize for literature 1951.

Lagerlöf ★ (*Swedish* 'lɑːgərlœːv) *n* **Selma** ('sɛlma). 1858–1940, Swedish novelist, noted esp. for her children's

classic *The Wonderful Adventures of Nils* (1906–07): Nobel prize for literature 1909.

lager lout *n* a rowdy or aggressive young drunk male.

laggard ('lægəd) *n* **1** a person who lags behind. ♦ *adj* **2** *Rare.* sluggish, slow, or dawdling.
 ▸ '**laggardly** *adj, adv* ▸ '**laggardness** *n*

lagging ('lægɪŋ) *n* **1** insulating material wrapped around pipes, boilers, etc., or laid in a roof loft, to prevent loss of heat. **2** the act or process of applying lagging.

lagomorph ('lægəʊˌmɔːf) *n* any placental mammal having two pairs of upper incisors specialized for gnawing, such as rabbits and hares. [C19: via NL from Gk *lagōs* hare; see -MORPH]

lagoon (ləˈguːn) *n* **1** a body of water cut off from the open sea by coral reefs or sand bars. **2** any small body of water, esp. one adjoining a larger one. [C17: from It. *laguna*, from L *lacūna* pool; see LACUNA]

Lagoon Islands ★ *pl n* a former name of **Tuvalu**.

Lagos ★ ('leɪgɒs) *n* **1** the former capital and chief port of Nigeria, on the Bight of Benin: first settled in the sixteenth century; a slave market until the nineteenth century; ceded to Britain (1861); university (1962). Pop.: 1 484 000 (1995 est.). **2** a state of SW Nigeria. Capital: Ikeja. Pop.: 5 847 355 (1992 est.). Area: 3345 sq. km (1292 sq. miles).

Lagrange ★ (*French* lagrɑ̃ʒ) *n* **Comte Joseph Louis** (ʒozɛf lwi). 1736–1813, French mathematician and astronomer.
 ▸ **Lagrangian** (ləˈgreɪndʒɪən) *adj*

Lagrangian point *n Astron.* one of five points in the plane of revolution of two bodies in orbit around their common centre of gravity, at which a third body of negligible mass can remain in equilibrium with respect to the other two bodies. [after J. L. LAGRANGE]

La Granja ★ (*Spanish* la 'granxa) *n* another name for **San Ildefonso**.

La Guaira *or* **La Guayra** ★ (*Spanish* la 'gwaira) *n* the chief seaport of Venezuela, on the Caribbean. Pop.: 26 669 (1990 est.).

La Guardia ★ (lə 'gwɑːdɪə) *n* **Fiorello H(enry)** (ˌfɪəˈrɛləʊ). 1882–1947, US politician and mayor of New York (1933–45).

lah (lɑː) *n Music.* (in tonic sol-fa) the sixth note of any major scale; submediant. [C14: later variant of *la*; see GAMUT]

lahar ('lɑːhɑː) *n* a landslide of volcanic debris mixed with water down the sides of a volcano, usually precipitated by heavy rainfall. [C20: from Javanese: lava]

lah-di-dah (ˌlɑːdiːˈdɑː) *adj, n Inf.* a variant spelling of **la-di-da**.

Lahore ★ (ləˈhɔː) *n* a city in NE Pakistan: capital of the former province of West Pakistan (1955–70); University of the Punjab (1882). Pop.: 5 085 000 (1995 est.).

Lahti ★ (*Finnish* 'lɑhti) *n* a town in S Finland: site of the main Finnish radio and television stations; furniture industry. Pop.: 94 706 (1994).

LAIA *abbrev. for* Latin American Integration Association (before 1981, known as the Latin American Free Trade Area). An economic group, its members are Argentina, Bolivia, Brazil, Chile, Colombia, Ecuador, Mexico, Paraguay, Peru, Uruguay, and Venezuela.

Laibach ★ ('laibax) *n* the German name for **Ljubljana**.

laic ('leɪɪk) *adj also* **laical. 1** of or involving the laity; secular. ♦ *n* **2** a rare word for **layman**. [C15: from LL *laicus* LAY[3]]
 ▸ '**laically** *adv*

laicize *or* **laicise** ('leɪɪˌsaɪz) *vb* **laicizes, laicizing, laicized** *or* **laicises, laicising, laicised.** (*tr*) to withdraw clerical or ecclesiastical character or status from (an institution, building, etc.).
 ▸ ˌ**laici'zation** *or* ˌ**laici'sation** *n*

laid (leɪd) *vb* the past tense and past participle of **lay**[1].

laid-back *adj* relaxed in style or character; easy-going and unhurried.

laid paper *n* paper with a regular mesh impressed upon it.

★ people and places

_ailat-ul-Qadr (ˌleɪlætʊlˈkɑːdə) *n* a night of study and prayer observed annually by Muslims to mark the communication of the Koran: it usually follows the 27th day of Ramadan. [from Ar.: night of determination]

_ain (leɪn) *vb* the past participle of **lie**[2].

_aine (leɪn) *n* **Cleo**, full name *Clementina Dinah Laine*. born 1927, British jazz singer, noted esp. for her recordings with her husband John Dankworth.

_aing ★ (læŋ) *n* **R(onald) D(avid)**. 1927–89, Scottish psychiatrist; his books include *The Divided Self* (1960) and the poems *Knots* (1970).

_aingian (ˈlæŋɪən) *adj* **1** of or based on R. D. Laing's theory that mental illnesses can be responses to stress in family and social situations.   ◆ *n* **2** a follower or adherent of Laing's teaching.

_air[1] (lɛə) *n* **1** the resting place of a wild animal. **2** *Inf.* a place of seclusion or hiding.   ◆ *vb* **3** (*intr*) (esp. of a wild animal) to retreat to or rest in a lair. **4** (*tr*) to drive or place (an animal) in a lair. [OE *leger*]

_air[2] (lɛə) *Austral. sl.*   ◆ *n* **1** a flashy man who shows off.   ◆ *vb* **2** (*intr*; foll. by *up* or *around*) to behave or dress like a lair. [?from LEER]

_aird (lɛəd) *n* *Scot.* a landowner, esp. of a large estate. [C15: Scot. var. of LORD]

_aissez faire *or* **laisser faire** *French*. (ˌleseɪ ˈfɛə) *n* **1a** Also called: **individualism**. the doctrine of unrestricted freedom in commerce, esp. for private interests. **1b** (*as modifier*): *a laissez-faire economy*. **2** indifference or noninterference, esp. in the affairs of others. [F, lit.: let (them) act]

_aissez passer (ˌleseɪ ˈpæseɪ) *n* a permit allowing someone to pass, cross a frontier, etc. [F, lit.: let (them) pass]

_aity (ˈleɪtɪ) *n* **1** laymen, as distinguished from clergymen. **2** all people not of a specific occupation. [C16: from LAY[3]]

_aius ★ (ˈlaɪəs) *n* *Greek myth.* a king of Thebes, killed by his son Oedipus, who did not know of their relationship.

_ake[1] (leɪk) *n* **1** an expanse of water entirely surrounded by land and unconnected to the sea except by rivers or streams. Related adj: **lacustrine**. **2** anything resembling this. **3** a surplus of a liquid commodity: *a wine lake*. [C13: *lac*, via OF from L *lacus* basin]

_ake[2] (leɪk) *n* **1** a bright pigment produced by the combination of an organic colouring matter with an inorganic compound, usually a metallic salt, oxide, or hydroxide. **2** a red dye obtained by combining a metallic compound with cochineal. [C17: var. of LAC[1]]

_ake District ★ *n* a region of lakes and mountains in NW England, in Cumbria: includes England's largest lake (Windermere) and highest mountain (Scafell Pike); national park; literary associations (the Lake Poets); tourist region. Also called: **Lakeland, the Lakes**.

_ake dwelling *n* a dwelling, esp. in prehistoric villages, constructed on platforms supported by wooden piles driven into the bottom of a lake.
▸ **lake dweller** *n*

_akeland ★ (ˈleɪkˌlænd) *n* **1** another name for the **Lake District**.   ◆ *adj* **2** of or relating to the Lake District.

_akeland terrier *n* a wire-haired breed of terrier, originally from the Lake District.

_ake of the Woods ★ *n* a lake in N central North America, mostly in W Northern Ontario, Canada: fed chiefly by the Rainy River; drains into Lake Winnipeg by the Winnipeg River; many islands; tourist region. Area: 3846 sq. km (1485 sq. miles).

_ake Poets *pl n* the English poets Wordsworth, Coleridge, and Southey, who lived in and drew inspiration from the Lake District at the beginning of the 19th century.

_ake Success ★ *n* a village in SE New York State, on W Long Island: headquarters of the United Nations Security Council from 1946 to 1951. Pop.: 2450 (1990 est.).

_ake trout *n* a yellow-spotted char of the Great Lakes region of Canada.

_akh *or* **lac** (lɑːk) *n* (in India) the number 100 000, esp. re-

ferring to this sum of rupees. [C17: from Hindi *lākh*, ult. from Sansk. *lakshā* a sign]

Lakshadweep Islands ★ (lækˈʃædwiːp) *pl n* a group of 26 coral islands and reefs in the Arabian Sea, off the SW coast of India: a union territory of India since 1956. Administrative centre: Kavaratti Island. Pop.: 56 000 (1994 est.). Area: 28 sq. km (11 sq. miles). Former name (until 1973): **Laccadive, Minicoy, and Amindivi Islands**.

-lalia *n combining form*. indicating a speech defect or abnormality: *echolalia*. [NL, from Gk *lalia* chatter, from *lalein* to babble]

La Línea ★ (Spanish la ˈlinea) *n* a town in SW Spain, on the Bay of Gibraltar. Pop.: 57 000 (latest est.). Official name: **La Línea de la Concepción** (ðe la ˌkɒnθepˈθjon).

Lalique ★ (*French* lalik) *n* **René (Jules)** (rəne). 1860–1945, French Art-Nouveau jeweller, glass-maker, and designer: noted esp. for his frosted glassware.

Lallans (ˈlælənz) *or* **Lallan** (ˈlælən) *n* **1** a literary version of the variety of English spoken in the Lowlands of Scotland. **2** (*modifier*) of or relating to the Lowlands of Scotland or their dialects. [Scot. var. of *Lowlands*]

lallation (læˈleɪʃən) *n* *Phonetics*. a defect of speech consisting of the pronunciation of (r) as (l). [C17: from L *lallāre* to sing lullaby, imit.]

Lalo ★ (ˈlɑːləʊ) *n* (**Victor-Antoine-**)**Édouard** (edwar). 1823–92, French composer of Spanish descent. His works include the *Symphonie espagnole* (1873).

lam[1] (læm) *vb* **lams, lamming, lammed**. *Sl.* **1** (*tr*) to thrash or beat. **2** (*intr*; usually foll. by *into* or *out*) to make a sweeping stroke or blow. [C16: from Scand.]

lam[2] (læm) *n* *US & Canad. sl.* **1** a sudden flight or escape, esp. to avoid arrest. **2 on the lam**. making an escape. [C19: ? from LAM[1] (hence, to be off)]

Lam. *Bible. abbrev. for* Lamentations.

lama (ˈlɑːmə) *n* a priest or monk of Lamaism. [C17: from Tibetan *blama*]

Lamaism (ˈlɑːməˌɪzəm) *n* the Mahayana form of Buddhism of Tibet and Mongolia.
▸ **ˈLamaist** *n, adj* ▸ **ˌLamaˈistic** *adj*

La Mancha ★ (*Spanish* la ˈmantʃa) *n* a plateau of central Spain, between the mountains of Toledo and the hills of Cuenca: traditionally associated with episodes in *Don Quixote*. Average height: 600 m (2000 ft).

La Manche ★ (*French* la mãʃ) *n* See **Manche** (sense 2).

Lamarck ★ (*French* lamark) *n* **Jean Baptiste Pierre Antoine de Monet** (ʒã batist pjɛr ãtwan də mɔne), Chevalier de Lamarck. 1744–1829, French naturalist. He outlined his theory of organic evolution (Lamarckism) in *Philosophie zoologique* (1809).
▸ **Laˈmarckian** *adj, n*

Lamarckism (lɑːˈmɑːkɪzəm) *n* the theory of organic evolution proposed by Lamarck, based on the principle that characteristics of an organism modified during its lifetime are inheritable.

Lamartine ★ (*French* lamartin) *n* **Alphonse Marie Louis de Prat de** (alfõs mari lwi də pra də). 1790–1869, French romantic poet, historian, and statesman: his works include *Méditations poétiques* (1820) and *Histoire des Girondins* (1847).

lamasery (ˈlɑːməsərɪ) *n, pl* **lamaseries**. a monastery of lamas. [C19: from F *lamaserie*, from LAMA + F *-serie*, from Persian *serāī* palace]

lamb (læm) *n* **1** the young of a sheep. **2** the meat of a young sheep. **3** a person, esp. a child, who is innocent, meek, good, etc. **4** a person easily deceived.   ◆ *vb* **5** (*intr*) (of a ewe) to give birth. **6** (*intr*) (of a shepherd) to tend the ewes and newborn lambs at lambing time. [OE *lamb*, from Gmc]
▸ **ˈlambˌlike** *adj*

Lamb[1] ★ (læm) *n* **the**. a title given to Christ in the New Testament.

Lamb[2] ★ (læm) *n* **1 Charles**, pen name *Elia*. 1775–1834, British essayist and critic. He collaborated with his sister Mary on *Tales from Shakespeare* (1807). His other works include the largely autobiographical *Essays of Elia* (1823; 1833). **2 William**. See (2nd Viscount) **Melbourne**. **3 Willis**

Eugene. born 1913, US physicist. He detected the small difference in energy between two states of the hydrogen atom (**Lamb shift**). Nobel prize for physics 1955.

lambada (læm'bɑːdə) *n* **1** an erotic dance, originating in Brazil, performed by two people who hold each other closely and gyrate their hips in synchronized movements. **2** the music that accompanies the lambada, combining salsa, calypso, and reggae. [C20: from Port., lit.: the snapping of a whip]

Lambaréné ★ (*French* lãbarene) *n* a town in W Gabon on the Ogooué River: site of the hospital built by Albert Schweitzer, who died and was buried there (1965). Pop.: 50 000 (1985 est.).

lambast (læm'bæst) *or* **lambaste** (læm'beɪst) *vb* **lambasts, lambasting, lambasted** *or* **lambastes, lambasting, lambasted.** (*tr*) **1** to beat or whip severely. **2** to reprimand or scold. [C17: ?from LAM + BASTE³]

lambda ('læmdə) *n* the 11th letter of the Greek alphabet (Λ, λ). [C14: from Gk, from Semitic]

lambent ('læmbənt) *adj* **1** (esp. of a flame) flickering softly over a surface. **2** glowing with soft radiance. **3** (of wit or humour) light or brilliant. [C17: from the present participle of L *lambere* to lick]
  ▸ 'lambency *n* ▸ 'lambently *adv*

lambert ('læmbət) *n* the cgs unit of illumination, equal to 1 lumen per square centimetre. Symbol: L [C20: after J. H. *Lambert* (1728–77), G mathematician & physicist]

Lambert ★ ('læmbət) *n* Constant. 1905–51, British composer and conductor. His works include much ballet music and the choral *The Rio Grande* (1929).

Lambeth ★ ('læmbəθ) *n* a borough of S Greater London, on the Thames: contains **Lambeth Palace** (the London residence of the Archbishop of Canterbury). Pop.: 260 700 (1994 est.). Area: 27 sq. km (11 sq. miles).

lambing ('læmɪŋ) *n* **1** the birth of lambs. **2** the shepherd's work of tending the ewes and newborn lambs at this time.

lambkin ('læmkɪn) *n* **1** a small lamb. **2** a term of affection for a small endearing child.

Lamb of God *n* a title given to Christ in the New Testament, probably with reference to his sacrificial death.

lambrequin ('læmbrɪkɪn, 'læmbə-) *n* **1** an ornamental hanging covering the edge of a shelf or the upper part of a window or door. **2** (*often pl*) a scarf worn over a helmet. [C18: from F, from Du. *lamperkin* (unattested), dim. of *lamper* veil]

Lambrusco (læm'bruskəʊ) *n* **1** a red grape grown in Italy. **2** a sparkling red wine made in Italy from this grape. **3** a much less common white variety of this grape or wine.

lambskin ('læm,skɪn) *n* **1** the skin of a lamb, esp. with the wool still on. **2** a material or garment prepared from this skin.

lamb's lettuce *n* another name for **corn salad**.

lamb's tails *pl n* the pendulous catkins of the hazel tree.

lame (leɪm) *adj* **1** disabled or crippled in the legs or feet. **2** painful or weak: *a lame back.* **3** weak; unconvincing: *a lame excuse.* **4** not effective or enthusiastic: *a lame try.* **5** *US sl.* conventional or uninspiring. ◆ *vb* **lames, laming, lamed.** **6** (*tr*) to make lame. [OE *lama*]
  ▸ 'lamely *adv* ▸ 'lameness *n*

lamé ('lɑːmeɪ) *n* a fabric of silk, cotton, or wool interwoven with threads of metal. [C20: from F, from OF *lame* gold or silver thread, thin plate, from L *lāmina* thin plate]

lame duck *n* **1** a person or thing that is disabled or ineffectual. **2** *Stock Exchange.* a speculator who cannot discharge his liabilities. **3** *US.* an elected official or body of officials remaining in office in the interval between the election and inauguration of a successor.

lamella (lə'mɛlə) *n, pl* **lamellae** (-liː) *or* **lamellas.** a thin layer, plate, or membrane, esp. any of the calcified layers of which bone is formed. [C17: NL, from L, dim. of *lāmina* thin plate]
  ▸ la'mellar, **lamellate** ('læmɪ,leɪt, -lɪt), *or* **lamellose** (lə'mɛləʊs, 'læmɪ,ləʊs) *adj*

lamellibranch (lə'mɛlɪ,bræŋk) *n, adj* another word for

bivalve. [C19: from NL *lamellibranchia* plate-gilled (animals)]

lamellicorn (lə'mɛlɪ,kɔːn) *n* **1** any beetle having flattened terminal plates to the antennae, such as the scarabs and stag beetles. ◆ *adj* **2** designating antennae with platelike terminal segments. [C19: from NL *Lamellicornia* plate-horned (animals)]

lament (lə'mɛnt) *vb* **1** to feel or express sorrow, remorse, or regret (for or over). ◆ *n* **2** an expression of sorrow. **3** a poem or song in which a death is lamented. [C16: from L *lāmentum*]
  ▸ la'menter *n* ▸ la'mentingly *adv*

lamentable ('læməntəb³l) *adj* **1** wretched, deplorable, or distressing. **2** an archaic word for **mournful.**
  ▸ 'lamentably *adv*

lamentation (,læmən'teɪʃən) *n* **1** a lament; expression of sorrow. **2** the act of lamenting.

lamented (lə'mɛntɪd) *adj* grieved for or regretted (often in **late lamented**): *our late lamented employer.*
  ▸ la'mentedly *adv*

lamina ('læmɪnə) *n, pl* **laminae** (-,niː) *or* **laminas.** **1** a thin plate, esp. of bone or mineral. **2** *Bot.* the flat blade of a leaf. [C17: NL, from L: thin plate]
  ▸ 'laminar *or* **laminose** ('læmɪ,nəʊs, -,nəʊz) *adj*

laminar flow *n* nonturbulent motion of a fluid in which parallel layers have different velocities relative to each other.

laminate *vb* ('læmɪ,neɪt), **laminates, laminating, laminated.** **1** (*tr*) to make (material in sheet form) by bonding together two or more thin sheets. **2** to split or be split into thin sheets. **3** (*tr*) to beat, form, or press (material, esp. metal) into thin sheets. **4** (*tr*) to cover or overlay with a thin sheet of material. ◆ *n* ('læmɪ,neɪt, -nɪt). **5** a material made by bonding together two or more sheets. ◆ *adj* ('læmɪ,neɪt, -nɪt). **6** having or composed of lamina; laminated. [C17: from NL *lāminātus* plated]
  ▸ 'laminable *adj* ▸ ,lami'nation *n* ▸ 'lami,nator *n*

laminated ('læmɪ,neɪtɪd) *adj* **1** composed of many layers of plastic, wood, etc., bonded together. **2** covered with a thin protective layer of plastic, etc.

lamington ('læmɪŋtən) *n* *Austral. & NZ.* a cube of sponge cake coated in chocolate and dried coconut. [C20: in the earlier sense: a homburg hat): after Lady *Lamington*, wife of Baron Lamington, governor of Queensland (1896–1901)]

Lammas ('læməs) *n* **1** *RC Church.* Aug. 1, held as a feast, commemorating St Peter's miraculous deliverance from prison. **2** Also called: **Lammas Day.** the same day formerly observed in England as a harvest festival. [OE *hlāfmæsse* loaf mass]

lammergeier *or* **lammergeyer** ('læmə,gaɪə) *n* a rare vulture of S Europe, Africa, and Asia, with dark wings, a pale breast, and black feathers around the bill. [C19: from G *Lämmergeier*, from *Lämmer* lambs + *Geier* vulture]

lamp (læmp) *n* **1a** any of a number of devices that produce illumination: *an electric lamp; a gas lamp; an oil lamp.* **1b** (*in combination*): *lampshade.* **2** a device for holding one or more electric light bulbs: *a table lamp.* **3** a vessel in which a liquid fuel is burned to supply illumination. **4** any of a variety of devices that produce radiation, esp. for therapeutic purposes: *an ultraviolet lamp.* [C13 *lampe*, via OF from L *lampas*, from Gk, from *lampein* to shine]

lampblack ('læmp,blæk) *n* a finely divided form of almost pure carbon produced by the incomplete combustion of organic compounds, such as natural gas, used in making carbon electrodes and dynamo brushes and as a pigment.

lamp chimney *n* a glass tube that surrounds the wick in an oil lamp.

Lampedusa¹ ★ (,læmpɪ'djuːzə) *n* an island in the Mediterranean, between Malta and Tunisia. Area: about 21 sq. km (8 sq. miles).

Lampedusa² ★ (,læmpɪ'djuːzə) *n* **Giuseppe Tomasi di.** 1896–1957, Italian novelist: author of the historical novel *The Leopard* (1958).

lamplight ('læmp,laɪt) *n* the light produced by a lamp or lamps.

lamplighter ('læmp,laɪtə) n **1** (formerly) a person who lit and extinguished street lamps, esp. gas ones. **2** *Chiefly US & Canad.* any of various devices used to light lamps.

lampoon (læm'pu:n) n **1** a satire in prose or verse ridiculing a person, literary work, etc. ◆ vb **2** (tr) to attack or satirize in a lampoon. [C17: from F *lampon*, ?from *lampons* let us drink (frequently used as a refrain in poems)]
▸ lam'pooner or lam'poonist n ▸ lam'poonery n

lamppost ('læmp,pəʊst) n a post supporting a lamp, esp. in a street.

lamprey ('læmprɪ) n any eel-like vertebrate having a round sucking mouth for clinging to and feeding on the blood of other animals. Also called: **lamper eel**. [C13: from OF *lamproie*, from LL *lamprēda*, from ?]

Lanai ★ (lɑː'nɑːɪ, lə'naɪ) n an island in central Hawaii, west of Maui Island. Pop.: 2426 (1990). Area: 363 sq. km. (140 sq. miles).

Lanarkshire ★ ('lænək,ʃɪə, -ʃə) n a historic county of S Scotland, now administered by North Lanarkshire, South Lanarkshire, and Glasgow.

Lancashire ★ ('læŋkə,ʃɪə, -ʃə) n **1** a county of NW England, on the Irish Sea: became a county palatine in 1351 and a duchy attached to the Crown; much reduced in size after the 1974 boundary changes, losing the Furness district to Cumbria and much of the south to Greater Manchester, Merseyside, and Cheshire. It was traditionally a cotton textiles manufacturing region. Administrative centre: Preston. Pop.: 1 424 000 (1994 est.). Area: 3063 sq. km (1182 sq. miles). Abbrev.: **Lancs. 2** a mild whitish-coloured cheese with a crumbly texture.

Lancaster[1] ('læŋkəstə, 'læŋ,kæstə) n the English royal house that reigned from 1399 to 1461.

Lancaster[2] ★ ('læŋkəstə) n a city in NW England, former county town of Lancashire, on the River Lune: castle (built on the site of a Roman camp); university (1964). Pop.: 44 497 (1991).

Lancastrian (læŋ'kæstrɪən) n **1** a native or resident of Lancashire or Lancaster. **2** an adherent of the house of Lancaster in the Wars of the Roses. ◆ adj **3** of or relating to Lancashire or Lancaster. **4** of or relating to the house of Lancaster.

lance (lɑːns) n **1** a long weapon with a pointed head used by horsemen. **2** a similar weapon used for hunting, whaling, etc. **3** *Surgery.* another name for **lancet**. ◆ vb **lances, lancing, lanced.** (tr) **4** to pierce (an abscess or boil) with a lancet. **5** to pierce with or as with a lance. [C13 *launce*, from OF *lance*, from L *lancea*]

lance corporal n a noncommissioned army officer of the lowest rank.

lancelet ('lɑːnslɪt) n any of several marine animals closely related to the vertebrates: they burrow in sand. Also called: **amphioxus**. [C19: referring to the slender shape]

Lancelot ★ ('lɑːnslət) n (in Arthurian legend) one of the Knights of the Round Table; the lover of Queen Guinevere.

lanceolate ('lɑːnsɪə,leɪt, -lɪt) adj narrow and tapering to a point at each end: *lanceolate leaves.* [C18: from LL *lanceolātus*, from *lanceola* small LANCE]

lancer ('lɑːnsə) n **1** (formerly) a cavalryman armed with a lance. **2** a member of a regiment retaining such a title.

lancers ('lɑːnsəz) n (functioning as sing) **1** a quadrille for eight or sixteen couples. **2** a piece of music composed for or in the rhythm of this dance.

lancet ('lɑːnsɪt) n **1** Also called: **lance**. a pointed surgical knife with two sharp edges. **2** short for **lancet arch** or **lancet window**. [C15 *lancette*, from OF: small LANCE]

lancet arch n a narrow acutely pointed arch.

lancet window n a narrow window having a lancet arch.

lancewood ('lɑːns,wʊd) n a New Zealand tree with slender leaves showing different configurations in youth and maturity.

Lanchow or **Lan-chou** ★ ('læn'tʃaʊ) n a variant transliteration of the Chinese name for **Lanzhou**.

Lancs (læŋks) abbrev. for Lancashire.

land (lænd) n **1** the solid part of the surface of the earth as distinct from seas, lakes, etc. Related adj: **terrestrial. 2** ground, esp. with reference to its use, quality, etc. **3** rural or agricultural areas as contrasted with urban ones. **4** farming as an occupation or way of life. **5** *Law.* any tract of ground capable of being owned as property. **6a** a country, region, or area. **6b** the people of a country, etc. **7** *Econ.* the factor of production consisting of all natural resources. ◆ vb **8** to transfer (something) or go from a ship or boat to the shore: *land the cargo.* **9** (intr) to come to or touch shore. **10** (intr) (in Canada) to be legally admitted to the country, as an immigrant or **landed immigrant. 11** to come down or bring (something) down to earth after a flight or jump. **12** to come or bring to some point, condition, or state. **13** (tr) *Angling.* to retrieve (a hooked fish) from the water. **14** (tr) *Inf.* to win or obtain: *to land a job.* **15** (tr) *Inf.* to deliver (a blow). ◆ See also **land up.** [OE]
▸ 'landless adj

Land ★ (lænd) n **Edwin Herbert**. 1909–91, US inventor of the Polaroid Land camera.

Land (German lant) n, pl **Länder** ('lɛndər). **1** any of the federal states of Germany. **2** any of the provinces of Austria. [G]

land agent n **1** a person who administers a landed estate and its tenancies. **2** a person who acts as an agent for the sale of land.
▸ **land agency** n

landau ('lændɔː) n a four-wheeled carriage, usually horse-drawn, with two folding hoods over the passenger compartment. [C18: after *Landau* (a town in Germany), where first made]

Landau ★ (Russian lan'dau) n **Lev Davidovich** (ljef da-'vidəvitʃ). 1908–68, Soviet physicist, noted for his researches on quantum theory: Nobel prize for physics 1962.

landaulet (,lændɔː'let) n **1** a small landau. **2** US. an early type of car with a folding hood over the passenger seats.

landed ('lændɪd) adj **1** owning land: *landed gentry.* **2** consisting of or including land: *a landed estate.*

Landes ★ (French lɑ̃d) n **1** a department of SW France, in Aquitaine region. Capital: Mont-de-Marsan. Pop.: 317 828 (1994 est.). Area: 9364 sq. km (3652 sq. miles). **2** a region of SW France, on the Bay of Biscay: occupies most of the Landes department and parts of Gironde and Lot-et-Garonne; consists chiefly of the most extensive forest in France. Area: 14 000 sq. km (5400 sq. miles).

landfall ('lænd,fɔːl) n **1** the act of sighting or nearing land, esp. from the sea. **2** the land sighted or neared.

landfill ('lænd,fɪl) adj of or denoting low-lying sites or tips being filled up with alternate layers of rubbish and earth.

landform ('lænd,fɔːm) n Geol. any natural feature of the earth's surface.

land girl n a girl or woman who does farm work, esp. in wartime.

landgrave ('lænd,greɪv) n German history. **1** (from the 13th century to 1806) a count who ruled over a specified territory. **2** (after 1806) the title of any of various sovereign princes. [C16: via G, from MHG *lantgrāve*, from *lant* land + *grāve* count]

land-holder n a person who owns or occupies land.
▸ **land-,holding** adj, n

landing ('lændɪŋ) n **1a** the act of coming to land, esp. after a flight or a sea voyage. **1b** (as modifier): *landing place.* **2** a place of disembarkation. **3** the floor area at the top of a flight of stairs.

landing craft n Mil. any small vessel designed for the landing of troops and equipment on beaches.

landing field n an area of land on which aircraft land and from which they take off.

landing gear n another name for **undercarriage**.

landing net n Angling. a loose long-handled net for lifting hooked fish from the water.

landing stage *n* a platform used for landing goods and passengers from a vessel.

landing strip *n* another name for **airstrip**.

landlady ('lænd,leɪdɪ) *n*, *pl* **landladies. 1** a woman who owns and leases property. **2** a woman who owns or runs a lodging house, pub, etc.

ländler (*German* 'lɛntlər) *n* **1** an Austrian country dance in which couples spin and clap. **2** a piece of music composed for or in the rhythm of this dance, in three-four time. [G, from dialect *Landl* Upper Austria]

land line *n* a telecommunications wire or cable laid over land.

landlocked ('lænd,lɒkt) *adj* **1** (esp. of lakes) completely surrounded by land. **2** (esp. of certain salmon) living in fresh water that is permanently isolated from the sea.

landlord ('lænd,lɔːd) *n* **1** a man who owns and leases property. **2** a man who owns or runs a lodging house, pub, etc.

landlubber ('lænd,lʌbə) *n* *Naut.* any person having no experience at sea.

landmark ('lænd,mɑːk) *n* **1** a prominent or well-known object or feature of a particular landscape. **2** an important or unique decision, event, fact, discovery, etc. **3** a boundary marker.

landmass ('lænd,mæs) *n* a large continuous area of land, as opposed to seas or islands.

land mine *n* *Mil.* an explosive charge placed in the ground, usually detonated by stepping or driving on it.

land of milk and honey *n* **1** *Old Testament.* the fertile land promised to the Israelites by God (Ezekiel 20:6). **2** any fertile land, state, etc.

land of Nod ★ *n* **1** *Old Testament.* a region to the east of Eden to which Cain went after he had killed Abel (Genesis 4:14). **2** an imaginary land of sleep.

Landor ★ ('lændɔː) *n* **Walter Savage.** 1775–1864, British poet, noted also for his prose works, including *Imaginary Conversations* (1824–29).

landowner ('lænd,əʊnə) *n* a person who owns land.
▸ '**land,owner,ship** *n* ▸ '**land,owning** *n*, *adj*

Landowska ★ (*Polish* lan'dɔfska) *n* **Wanda** ('vanda). 1877–1959, US harpsichordist, born in Poland.

land rail *n* another name for **corncrake.**

land reform *n* the redistributing of large agricultural holdings among the landless.

landscape ('lænd,skeɪp) *n* **1** an extensive area of land regarded as being visually distinct. **2** a painting, drawing, photograph, etc., depicting natural scenery. **3** the genre including such pictures. **4** the distinctive features of a given area of intellectual activity, regarded as an integrated whole. ◆ *adj* **5** *Printing*. **5a** (of an illustration in a book, magazine, etc.) of greater width than depth. Cf. **portrait** (sense 3). **5b** (of a page) carrying an illustration or table printed at right angles to the normal text. ◆ *vb* **landscapes, landscaping, landscaped. 6** (*tr*) to improve the natural features of (a garden, park, etc.), as by creating contoured features and planting trees. **7** (*intr*) to work as a landscape gardener. [C16 *landskip* (orig. a term in painting), from MDu. *lantscap* region]

landscape gardening *n* the art of laying out grounds in imitation of natural scenery. Also called: **landscape architecture.**
▸ **landscape gardener** *n*

landscapist ('lænd,skeɪpɪst) *n* a painter of landscapes.

Landseer ★ ('lænsɪə) *n* Sir **Edwin Henry.** 1802–73, British painter, noted for his studies of animals.

Land's End ★ *n* a granite headland in SW England, on the SW coast of Cornwall: the westernmost point of England.

Landshut ★ (*German* 'lantshuːt) *n* a city in SE Germany, in Bavaria: Trausnitz castle (13th century); manufacturing centre for machinery and chemicals. Pop.: 59 670 (1991).

landside ('lænd,saɪd) *n* **1** the part of an airport farthest from the aircraft, the boundary of which is the security check, customs, passport control, etc. Cf. **airside. 2** the

part of a plough that slides along the face of the furrow wall on the opposite side to the mouldboard.

landslide ('lænd,slaɪd) *n* **1** Also called: **landslip. 1a** the sliding of a large mass of rock material, soil, etc., down the side of a mountain or cliff. **1b** the material dislodged in this way. **2** an overwhelming electoral victory.

landsman ('lændzmən) *n*, *pl* **landsmen.** a person who works or lives on land, as distinguished from a seaman.

Landsteiner ★ (*German* 'lant,ʃtaɪnər) *n* **Karl** (karl). 1868–1943, Austrian immunologist, who discovered (1900) human blood groups and introduced the ABO classification system. He also discovered (1940) the Rhesus (Rh) factor in blood. Nobel prize for physiology or medicine (1930).

land up *vb* (*adv, usually intr*) to arrive or cause to arrive at a final point or condition.

landward ('lændwəd) *adj* **1** lying, facing, or moving towards land. **2** in the direction of the land. ◆ *adv* **3** a variant of **landwards.**

landwards ('lændwədz) *or* **landward** *adv* towards land.

lane (leɪn) *n* **1** a narrow road or way between buildings, hedges, fences, etc. **2a** any of the parallel strips into which the carriageway of a major road or motorway is divided. **2b** any narrow well-defined route or course for ships or aircraft. **3** one of the parallel strips into which a running track or swimming bath is divided for races. **4** the long strip of wooden flooring down which balls are bowled in a bowling alley. [OE *lane, lanu*]

Lanfranc ★ ('lænfræŋk) *n* ?1005–89, Italian ecclesiastic and scholar; archbishop of Canterbury (1070–89) and adviser to William the Conqueror.

Lang ★ (læŋ) *n* **1 Cosmo Gordon,** 1st Baron Lang of Lambeth. 1864–1945, British churchman; archbishop of Canterbury (1928–42). **2 Fritz.** 1890–1976, Austrian film director, later in the US, notable for such silent films as *Metropolis* (1926) and *The Testament of Dr. Mabuse* (1932). **3 Jack** (**John Thomas**). 1876–1975, Australian Labor politician; premier of New South Wales (1925–27; 1930–32): dismissed (1932) by the governor, Sir Philip Game, for acting unconstitutionally.

lang. *abbrev. for* language.

Lange ★ ('lɒŋɪ) *n* **David.** born 1942, New Zealand statesman: Labour prime minister (1984–89).

Langer ★ ('læŋə; *German* 'laŋər) *n* **Bernhard** ('bernhart). born 1957, German professional golfer: won the US Masters Championship (1985, 1993).

Langerhans islets *or* **islands** ('læŋə,hæns) *pl n Anat.* See **islets of Langerhans.**

Langland ★ ('læŋlənd) *n* **William.** ?1332–?1400, English poet. The allegorical religious poem in alliterative verse, *The Vision of William concerning Piers the Plowman*, is attributed to him.

langlauf ('læŋ,laʊf) *n* cross-country skiing. [G, lit.: long run]
▸ **langläufer** ('læŋ,lɔɪfə) *n* ▸ **langläufing** ('læŋ,lɔɪfɪŋ) *n*

Langley ★ ('læŋlɪ) *n* **Samuel Pierpont.** 1834–1906, US astronomer and physicist: invented the bolometer (1878) and pioneered powered flight.

Langmuir ★ ('læŋmjʊə) *n* **Irving.** 1881–1957, US chemist. He developed the gas-filled tungsten lamp and the atomic hydrogen welding process: Nobel prize for chemistry 1932.

langouste ('lɒŋguːst, lɒŋ'guːst) *n* another name for the **spiny lobster.** [F, from OProvençal *langosta*, ? from L *lōcusta* lobster, locust]

langoustine (,lɒŋguːs'tiːn) *n* a large prawn or small lobster. [from F, dim. of LANGOUSTE]

Langres Plateau ★ (*French* lɑ̃grə) *n* a calcareous plateau of E France north of Dijon between the Seine and the Saône, reaching over 580 m (1900 ft): forms a watershed between rivers flowing to the Mediterranean and to the English Channel.

langsam ('læŋzæm) *adj Music.* slow. [G]

langsyne (,læŋ'saɪn) *Scot.* ◆ *adv* **1** long ago; long since.

◆ *n* 2 times long past, esp. those fondly remembered. [C16: Scot.: long since]

Langton ★ ('læntən) *n* Stephen. ?1150–1228, English cardinal; archbishop of Canterbury (1213–28). He was consecrated archbishop by Pope Innocent III in 1207 but was kept out of his see by King John until 1213. He was partly responsible for the Magna Carta (1215).

Langtry ★ ('læntrɪ) *n* Lillie, known as *the Jersey Lily*, real name *Émilie Charlotte le Breton*. 1852–1929, British actress, noted for her friendship with Edward VII.

language ('læŋgwɪdʒ) *n* 1 a system for the expression of thoughts, feelings, etc., by the use of spoken sounds or conventional symbols. 2 the faculty for the use of such systems, which is a distinguishing characteristic of man as compared with other animals. 3 the language of a particular nation or people. 4 any other means of communicating, such as gesture or animal sounds: *the language of love*. 5 the specialized vocabulary used by a particular group: *medical language*. 6 a particular manner or style of verbal expression: *your language is disgusting*. 7 *Computing*. See **programming language**. [C13: from OF *language*, ult. from L *lingua* tongue]

language laboratory *n* a room equipped with tape recorders, etc., for learning foreign languages.

langue (lɑːŋg) *n Linguistics*. language considered as an abstract system or a social institution, being the common possession of a speech community. [C19: from F: language]

Languedoc ★ (*French* lɑ̃gdɔk) *n* 1 a former province of S France, lying between the foothills of the Pyrenees and the River Rhône. It formed around the countship of Toulouse in the 13th century. 2 a wine from this region.

langue d'oc *French*. (lɑ̃g dɔk) *n* the group of medieval French dialects spoken in S France: often regarded as including Provençal. [lit.: language of *oc* (form for the Provençal *yes*), ult. from L *hoc* this]

Languedoc-Roussillon ★ (*French* lɑ̃gdɔkrusijɔ̃) *n* a region of S France, on the Gulf of Lions: consists of the departments of Lozère, Gard, Hérault, Aude, and Pyrénées-Orientales; mainly mountainous with a coastal plain.

langue d'oïl *French*. (lɑ̃g dɔj) *n* the group of medieval French dialects spoken in France north of the Loire; the medieval basis of modern French. [lit.: language of *oïl* (the northern form for *yes*), ult. from L *hoc ille* (*fecit*) this he (did)]

languid ('læŋgwɪd) *adj* 1 without energy or spirit. 2 without interest or enthusiasm. 3 sluggish; inactive. [C16: from L *languidus*, from *languēre* to languish]
▶ 'languidly *adv* ▶ 'languidness *n*

languish ('læŋgwɪʃ) *vb* (*intr*) 1 to lose or diminish in strength or energy. 2 (often foll. by *for*) to be listless with desire; pine. 3 to suffer deprivation, hardship, or neglect: *to languish in prison*. 4 to put on a tender, nostalgic, or melancholic expression. [C14 *languishen*, from OF *languiss-*, stem of *languir*, ult. from L *languēre*]
▶ 'languishing *adj* ▶ 'languishingly *adv* ▶ 'languishment *n*

languor ('læŋgə) *n* 1 physical or mental laziness or weariness. 2 a feeling of dreaminess and relaxation. 3 oppressive silence or stillness. [C14 *langour*, via OF from L *languor*, from *languēre* to languish; the modern spelling is directly from L]
▶ 'languorous *adj*

langur (lʌŋ'gʊə) *n* any of various agile arboreal Old World monkeys of S and SE Asia having a long tail and long hair surrounding the face. [Hindi]

laniard ('lænjəd) *n* a variant spelling of **lanyard**.

laniary ('lænɪərɪ) *adj* 1 (esp. of canine teeth) adapted for tearing. ◆ *n, pl* **laniaries**. 2 a tooth adapted for tearing. [C19: from L *lanius* butcher, from *laniāre* to tear]

laniferous (lə'nɪfərəs) or **lanigerous** (lə'nɪdʒərəs) *adj Biol*. bearing wool or fleecy hairs resembling wool. [C17: from L *lānifer*, from *lāna* wool]

lank (læŋk) *adj* 1 long and limp. 2 thin or gaunt. [OE *hlanc* loose]
▶ 'lankly *adv* ▶ 'lankness *n*

Lankester ★ ('læŋkɪstə) *n* Sir Edwin Ray. 1847–1929, Brit-

ish zoologist, noted particularly for his study of protozoans.

lanky ('læŋkɪ) *adj* **lankier, lankiest**. tall, thin, and loose-jointed.
▶ 'lankily *adv* ▶ 'lankiness *n*

lanner ('lænə) *n* 1 a large falcon of Mediterranean regions, N Africa, and S Asia. 2 *Falconry*. the female of this falcon. The male is called **lanneret**. [C15: from OF (*faucon*) *lanier* cowardly (falcon), from L *lanārius* wool worker, coward; referring to its sluggish flight and timid nature]

lanolin ('lænəlɪn) or **lanoline** ('lænəlɪn, -ˌliːn) *n* a yellowish viscous substance extracted from wool: used in some ointments. [C19: via G from L *lāna* wool + *oleum* oil; see -IN]

Lansbury ★ ('lænzbərɪ) *n* George. 1859–1940, British Labour politician, who led the Labour Party in opposition (1931–35). A committed pacifist, he resigned over the party's reaction to Mussolini's seizure of Ethiopia.

Lansing ★ ('lænsɪŋ) *n* a city in S Michigan, on the Grand River: the state capital. Pop.: 119 590 (1994 est.).

lantern ('læntən) *n* 1 a light with a transparent protective case. 2 a structure on top of a dome or roof having openings or windows to admit light or air. 3 the upper part of a lighthouse that houses the light. [C13: from L *lanterna*, from Gk *lamptēr* lamp, from *lampein* to shine]

lantern jaw *n* (when *pl*, refers to upper and lower jaw; when *sing*, usually to lower jaw) a long hollow jaw that gives the face a drawn appearance.
▶ 'lantern-ˌjawed *adj*

lantern slide *n* (formerly) a photographic slide for projection, used in a magic lantern.

lanthanide ('lænθəˌnaɪd) or **lanthanoid** ('lænθəˌnɔɪd) *n* any of a class of 15 chemically related elements with atomic numbers from 57 (lanthanum) to 71 (lutetium).

lanthanum ('lænθənəm) *n* a silvery-white ductile metallic element of the lanthanide series: used in pyrophoric alloys, electronic devices, and in glass manufacture. Symbol: La; atomic no.: 57; atomic wt.: 138.91. [C19: NL, from Gk *lanthanein* to lie unseen]

lanthorn ('læntˌhɔːn, 'læntən) *n* an archaic word for **lantern**.

lanugo (lə'njuːgəʊ) *n, pl* **lanugos**. a layer of fine hairs, esp. the covering of the human fetus before birth. [C17: from L: down, from *lāna* wool]

Lanús ★ (*Spanish* la'nus) *n* a city in E Argentina: a S suburb of Buenos Aires. Pop.: 466 755 (1991).

lanyard or **laniard** ('lænjəd) *n* 1 a cord, esp. one worn around the neck, to hold a whistle, knife, etc. 2 a cord used in firing certain types of cannon. 3 *Naut*. a line for extending or tightening standing rigging. [C15 *lanyer*, from F *lanière*, from *lasne* strap, prob. of Gmc origin]

Lanzhou, Lanchow, or **Lan-chou** ★ ('læn'dʒəʊ) *n* a city in N China, capital of Gansu province, on the Yellow River: situated on the main route between China and the West. Pop.: 1 510 000 (1991 est.).

Laoag ★ (lɑː'wɑːg) *n* a city in the N Philippines, on NW Luzon: trade centre for an agricultural region. Pop.: 84 000 (1990 est.).

Laocoon ★ (leɪ'ɒkəʊˌɒn) *n Greek myth*. a priest of Apollo at Troy who warned the Trojans against the wooden horse left by the Greeks; killed with his twin sons by two sea serpents.

Laodicea ★ (ˌleɪəʊdɪ'sɪə) *n* the ancient name of several Greek cities in W Asia, notably of Latakia.

laodicean (ˌleɪəʊdɪ'sɪən) *adj* 1 lukewarm and indifferent, esp. in religious matters. ◆ *n* 2 a person having a lukewarm attitude towards religious matters. [C17: referring to the early Christians of Laodicea (Revelation 3:14–16)]

Laoighis ★ ('leɪʃ) *n* a variant spelling of **Laois**.

Laois ★ ('leɪʃ) *n* a county of central Republic of Ireland, in Leinster province: formerly boggy but largely reclaimed for agriculture. County town: Portlaoise. Pop.: 52 314 (1991). Area: 1719 sq. km (664 sq. miles). Also called: **Laoighis, Leix**. Former name: **Queen's County**.

★ people and places

Laomedon ★ (leɪ'ɒmɪˌdɒn) n Greek myth. the founder and ruler of Troy, who cheated Apollo and Poseidon of their wage for constructing the city's walls; the father of Priam.

Laos ★ (lauz, laus) n a republic in SE Asia: first united as the kingdom of Lan Xang ("million elephants") in 1353, after being a province of the Khmer Empire for about four centuries; made part of French Indochina in 1893 and gained independence in 1949; became a republic in 1975. It is generally forested and mountainous, with the Mekong River running almost the whole length of the W border. Official language: Lao. Religion: Buddhist majority, tribal religions. Currency: kip. Capital: Vientiane. Pop.: 5 117 000 (1997). Area: 236 800 sq. km (91 429 sq. miles). Official name: **People's Democratic Republic of Laos.**
▶ **Laotian** ('lauʃɪən) adj, n

Lao Zi ('lau 'zɪə) or **Lao-tzu** ★ ('lau'tsu:) n ?604–?531 B.C., Chinese philosopher, traditionally regarded as the founder of Taoism and the author of the Tao-te Ching.

lap¹ (læp) n **1** the area formed by the upper surface of the thighs of a seated person. **2** Also called: **lapful.** the amount held in one's lap. **3** a protected place or environment: in the lap of luxury. **4** the part of one's clothing that covers the lap. **5 drop in someone's lap.** give someone the responsibility of. [OE læppa flap]

lap² (læp) n **1** one circuit of a racecourse or track. **2** a stage or part of a journey, race, etc. **3a** an overlapping part or projection. **3b** the extent of overlap. **4** the length of material needed to go around an object. **5** a rotating disc coated with fine abrasive for polishing gemstones. ◆ vb **laps, lapping, lapped. 6** (tr) to wrap or fold (around or over): he lapped a bandage around his wrist. **7** (tr) to enclose or envelop in: he lapped his wrist in a bandage. **8** to place or lie partly or completely over or project beyond. **9** (tr; usually passive) to envelop or surround with comfort, love, etc.: lapped in luxury. **10** (intr) to be folded. **11** (tr) to overtake (an opponent) in a race so as to be one or more circuits ahead. **12** (tr) to polish or cut (a workpiece, gemstone, etc.) with a fine abrasive. [C13 (in the sense: to wrap): prob. from LAP¹]
▶ **'lapper** n

lap³ (læp) vb **laps, lapping, lapped. 1** (of small waves) to wash against (a shore, boat, etc.), usually with light splashing sounds. **2** (often foll. by up) (esp. of animals) to scoop (a liquid) into the mouth with the tongue. ◆ n **3** the act or sound of lapping. **4** a thin food for dogs or other animals. ◆ See also **lap up.** [OE lapian]
▶ **'lapper** n

La Palma ★ (Spanish la 'palma) n an island in the N Atlantic, in the NW Canary Islands: administratively part of Spain. Chief town: Santa Cruz de la Palma. Pop.: 77 000 (latest est.). Area: 725 sq. km (280 sq. miles).

laparoscope ('læpərəˌskəup) n a medical instrument consisting of a tube that is inserted through the abdominal wall and illuminated to enable a doctor to view the internal organs. [C19 (applied to various instruments used to examine the abdomen) and C20 (in the specific modern sense): from Gk lapara (see LAPAROTOMY) + -SCOPE]
▶ ˌlapa'roscopy n

laparotomy (ˌlæpə'rɒtəmɪ) n, pl **laparotomies.** surgical incision through the abdominal wall. [C19: from Gk lapara flank, from laparos soft + -TOMY]

La Paz ★ (læ 'pæz; Spanish la 'paθ) n a city in W Bolivia, at an altitude of 3600 m (12 000 ft): seat of government since 1898 (though Sucre is still the official capital); the country's largest city; founded in 1548 by the Spaniards; university (1830). Pop.: 784 976 (1993 est.).

lap dancing n a form of entertainment in which scantily dressed women dance erotically for individual members of the audience.

lap dissolve n Films. the technique of allowing the end of one scene to overlap the beginning of the next scene by fading out the former while fading in the latter.

lapdog ('læpˌdɒg) n a pet dog small and docile enough to be cuddled in the lap.

lapel (lə'pɛl) n the continuation of the turned or folded back collar on a suit, coat, jacket, etc. [C18: from LAP¹]
▶ la'pelled adj

lapheld ('læpˌhɛld) adj (esp. of a personal computer) small enough to be used on one's lap; portable.

lapidary ('læpɪdərɪ) n, pl **lapidaries. 1** a person whose business is to cut, polish, set, or deal in gemstones. ◆ adj **2** of or relating to gemstones or the work of a lapidary. **3** Also: **lapidarian** (ˌlæpɪ'dɛərɪən). engraved, cut, or inscribed in a stone or gemstone. **4** of sufficiently high quality to be engraved on a stone: a lapidary inscription. [C14: from L lapidārius, from lapid-, lapis stone]

lapillus (lə'pɪləs) n, pl **lapilli** (-laɪ). a small piece of lava thrown from a volcano. [C18: L: little stone]

lapis lazuli ('læpɪs 'læzjuˌlaɪ) n **1** a brilliant blue mineral used as a gemstone. **2** the deep blue colour of lapis lazuli. [C14: from L lapis stone + Med. L lazulī, from Ar. lāzaward, from Persian lāzhuward, from ?]

Lapith ★ ('læpɪθ) n, pl **Lapithae** ('læpɪˌθiː) or **Lapiths.** Greek myth. a member of a people in Thessaly who at the wedding of their king, Pirithoüs, fought the drunken centaurs.

lap joint n a joint made by placing one member over another and fastening them together. Also called: **lapped joint.**
▶ 'lap-ˌjointed adj

Laplace ★ (French laplas) n **Pierre Simon** (pjɛr simɔ̃), Marquis de Laplace. 1749–1827, French mathematician, physicist, and astronomer. He formulated the nebular hypothesis (1796). He also developed the theory of probability.

Laplace operator n Maths. the operator $\partial^2/\partial x^2 + \partial^2/\partial y^2 + \partial^2/\partial z^2$, used in differential analysis. Symbol: ∇^2

Lapland ★ ('læpˌlænd) n an extensive region of N Europe, mainly within the Arctic Circle: consists of the N parts of Norway, Sweden, Finland, and the Kola Peninsula of the extreme NW of Russia. Also called (informal): **Land of the Midnight Sun.**
▶ 'Lapˌlander n

La Plata ★ (Spanish la 'plata) n **1** a port in E Argentina, near the Río de la Plata estuary: founded in 1882 and modelled on Washington DC; university (1897). Pop.: 642 979 (1991). **2** See (Río de la) **Plata.**

lap of honour n a ceremonial circuit of a racing track, etc., by the winner of a race.

Lapp (læp) n **1** Also **Laplander.** a member of a nomadic people living chiefly in N Scandinavia and the Kola Peninsula of Russia. **2** the language of this people. ◆ adj **3** of or relating to this people or their language.
▶ 'Lappish adj, n

lappet ('læpɪt) n **1** a small hanging flap or piece of lace, etc. **2** Zool. a lobelike hanging structure, such as the wattle on a bird's head. [C16: from LAP¹ + -ET]

lapse (læps) n **1** a drop in standard of an isolated or temporary nature: a lapse of justice. **2** a break in occurrence, usage, etc.: a lapse of five weeks between letters. **3** a gradual decline or a drop to a lower degree, condition, or state: a lapse from high office. **4** a moral fault. **5** Law. the termination of some right, interest, or privilege, as by neglecting to exercise it or through failure of some contingency. **6** Insurance. the termination of coverage following a failure to pay the premiums. ◆ vb **lapses, lapsing, lapsed.** (intr) **7** to drop in standard or fail to maintain a norm. **8** to decline gradually or fall in status, condition, etc. **9** to be discontinued, esp. through negligence or other failure. **10** (usually foll. by into) to drift or slide (into a condition): to lapse into sleep. **11** (often foll. by from) to turn away (from beliefs or norms). **12** (of time) to slip away. [C15: from L lāpsus error, from lābī to glide]
▶ 'lapsable or 'lapsible adj ▶ lapsed adj ▶ 'lapser n

lapse rate n the rate of change of any meteorological factor with altitude, esp. atmospheric temperature.

Laptev Sea ★ ('læptɪf) n a shallow arm of the Arctic Ocean, along the N coast of Russia between the Taimyr Peninsula and the New Siberian Islands. Former name: **Nordenskjöld Sea.**

laptop ('læpˌtɒp) or **laptop computer** n a personal computer that is small and light enough to be operated on the user's lap. Cf. **palmtop computer.**

lap up vb (tr, adv) **1** to eat or drink. **2** to relish or delight in: *he laps up horror films.* **3** to believe or accept eagerly and uncritically: *he laps up stories.*

lapwing ('læp,wɪŋ) *n* any of several plovers, typically having a crested head, wattles, and spurs. Also called: **green plover, peewit.** [C17: altered form of OE *hlēapewince* plover]

Lara ★ ('lɑːrə) *n* Brian. born 1970, Trinidadian cricketer; holder of records for highest individual score in first-class cricket and for highest Test innings score.

larboard ('lɑːbəd) *n, adj Naut.* a former word for **port**². [C14 *laddeborde* (changed to *larboard* by association with *starboard*), from *laden* to load + *borde* BOARD]

larceny ('lɑːsɪnɪ) *n, pl* **larcenies.** *Law.* (formerly) a technical word for **theft.** [C15: from OF *larcin*, from L *lātrocinium* robbery, from *latrō* robber]
▸ **'larcenist** *or* **'larcener** *n* ▸ **'larcenous** *adj*

larch (lɑːtʃ) *n* **1** any coniferous tree having deciduous needle-like leaves and egg-shaped cones. **2** the wood of any of these trees. [C16: from G *Lärche*, ult. from L *larix*]

lard (lɑːd) *n* **1** the rendered fat from a pig, used in cooking. ◆ *vb* (*tr*) **2** to prepare (lean meat, poultry, etc.) by inserting small strips of bacon or fat before cooking. **3** to cover or smear (foods) with lard. **4** to add extra material to (speech or writing); embellish. [C15: via OF from L *lāridum* bacon fat]
▸ **'lardy** *adj*

larder ('lɑːdə) *n* a room or cupboard, used as a store for food. [C14: from OF *lardier*, from LARD]

Lardner ★ ('lɑːdnə) *n* Ring(old Wilmer). 1885–1933, US short-story writer and journalist, whose best-known works are collected in *How to Write Short Stories* (1924) and *The Love Nest* (1926).

lardon ('lɑːdⁿn) *or* **lardoon** (lɑː'duːn) *n* a strip of fat used in larding meat. [C15: from OF, from LARD]

lardy cake ('lɑːdɪ) *n Brit.* a rich sweet cake made of bread dough, lard, sugar, and dried fruit.

Laredo ★ (lə'reɪdəʊ) *n* a city in the US, in Texas, on the Mexican border: founded by the Spanish in 1755 on the Rio Grande. Pop.: 149 914 (1994 est.).

lares and penates ('lɛəriːz, 'lɑː-) *pl n* **1** *Roman myth.* **1a** household gods. **1b** statues of these gods kept in the home. **2** the valued possessions of a household. [from L]

large (lɑːdʒ) *adj* **1** having a relatively great size, quantity, extent, etc.; big. **2** of wide or broad scope, capacity, or range; comprehensive. **3** having or showing great breadth of understanding. ◆ *n* **4 at large. 4a** (esp. of a dangerous criminal or wild animal) free; not confined. **4b** roaming freely, as in a foreign country. **4c** as a whole; in general. **4d** in full detail; exhaustively. **4e ambassador at large.** See **ambassador** (sense 4). [C12 (orig.: generous): via OF from L *largus* ample]
▸ **'largeness** *n*

large intestine *n* the part of the alimentary canal consisting of the caecum, colon, and rectum.

largely ('lɑːdʒlɪ) *adv* **1** principally; to a great extent. **2** on a large scale or in a large manner.

larger-than-life *adj* exceptionally striking or colourful.

large-scale *adj* **1** wide-ranging or extensive. **2** (of maps and models) constructed or drawn to a big scale.

largesse *or* **largess** (lɑː'dʒɛs) *or* **n** **1** the generous bestowal of gifts, favours, or money. **2** the things so bestowed. **3** generosity of spirit or attitude. [C13: from OF, from LARGE]

larghetto (lɑː'gɛtəʊ) *Music.* ◆ *adj, adv* **1** to be performed moderately slowly. ◆ *n, pl* **larghettos 2** a piece or passage to be performed in this way. [It.: dim. of LARGO]

largish ('lɑːdʒɪʃ) *adj* fairly large.

largo ('lɑːgəʊ) *Music.* ◆ *adj, adv* **1** to be performed slowly and broadly. ◆ *n, pl* **largos 2** a piece or passage to be performed in this way. [C17: from It., from L *largus* large]

Lariam ('læriəm) *n Trademark.* a preparation of the drug mefloquine, used in the treatment and prevention of malaria.

lariat ('lærɪət) *n US & Canad.* **1** another word for **lasso. 2** a rope for tethering animals. [C19: from Sp. *la reata* the LASSO]

Larisa *or* **Larissa** ★ (lə'rɪsə; *Greek* 'larisa) *n* a city in E Greece, in E Thessaly: fortified by Justinian; annexed to Greece in 1881. Pop.: 113 426 (1991).

lark¹ (lɑːk) *n* **1** any brown bird of a predominantly Old World family of songbirds, esp. the skylark: noted for their singing. **2** short for **titlark.** [OE *lāwerce, lǣwerce*, of Gmc origin]

lark² (lɑːk) *Inf.* ◆ *n* **1** a carefree adventure or frolic. **2** a harmless piece of mischief. ◆ *vb* (*intr*) **3** (often foll. by *about*) to have a good time by frolicking. **4** to play a prank. [C19: orig. sl.]
▸ **'larkish** *or* **'larky** *adj*

Larkin ★ ('lɑːkɪn) *n Philip.* 1922–85, British poet: his verse collections include *The Whitsun Weddings* (1964).

larkspur ('lɑːk,spɜː) *n* any of various plants related to the delphinium, with spikes of blue, pink, or white irregular spurred flowers. [C16: LARK¹ + SPUR]

larn (lɑːn) *vb Not standard.* **1** *Facetious.* to learn. **2** (*tr*) to teach (someone) a lesson: *that'll larn you!* [C18: from a dialect form of LEARN]

Larne ★ (lɑːn) *n* a district of E Northern Ireland, on the Irish Sea N of Belfast: harbour services. Administrative centre: Larne. Pop.: 29 419 (1991). Area: 340 sq. km (131 sq. miles).

La Rochefoucauld ★ (*French* la rɔʃfuko) *n* **François** (frɑːswa), Duc de La Rochefoucauld. 1613–80, French writer, best known for his *Réflexions ou sentences et maximes morales* (1665), a collection of cynical epigrams on human nature.

La Rochelle ★ (*French* la rɔʃɛl) *n* a port in W France, on the Bay of Biscay: a Huguenot stronghold until its submission through famine to Richelieu's forces after a long siege (1627–28). Pop.: 71 094 (1990).

Larousse ★ (*French* larus) *n* **Pierre Athanase** (pjɛr atanaz). 1817–75, French grammarian, lexicographer, and encyclopedist. He edited and helped to compile the *Grand Dictionnaire universel du XIX siècle* (1866–76).

larrigan ('lærɪgən) *n* a knee-high oiled leather moccasin boot worn by trappers, etc. [C19: from ?]

larrikin ('lærɪkɪn) *Austral. & NZ sl.* ◆ *n* **1** a mischievous person. **2** a hooligan. ◆ *adj* **3** mischievous: *larrikin wit.* [C19: from E dialect: a mischievous youth]

larrup ('lærəp) *vb* (*tr*) *Dialect.* to beat or flog. [C19: from ?]
▸ **'larruper** *n*

Larry ('lærɪ) *n* **happy as Larry.** *Inf.* very happy.

larva ('lɑːvə) *n, pl* **larvae** (-viː). an immature free-living form of many animals that develops into a different adult form by metamorphosis. [C18: (C17 in the orig. L sense: ghost): NL]
▸ **'larval** *adj*

Larwood ★ ('lɑːwʊd) *n* **Harold.** 1904–95, English cricketer. An outstanding fast bowler, he played 21 times for England between 1926 and 1932.

laryngeal (,lærɪn'dʒiːəl, lə'rɪndʒɪəl) *or* **laryngal** (lə'rɪŋgᵊl) *adj* **1** of or relating to the larynx. **2** *Phonetics.* articulated at the larynx; glottal. [C18: from NL *laryngeus* of the LARYNX]

laryngitis (,lærɪn'dʒaɪtɪs) *n* inflammation of the larynx.
▸ **laryngitic** (,lærɪn'dʒɪtɪk) *adj*

laryngo- *or before a vowel* **laryng-** *combining form.* indicating the larynx: *laryngoscope.*

laryngoscope (lə'rɪŋgə,skəʊp) *n* a medical instrument for examining the larynx.
▸ **laryn'goscopy** *n*

laryngotomy (,lærɪŋ'gɒtəmɪ) *n, pl* **laryngotomies.** surgical incision into the larynx to facilitate breathing.

larynx ('lærɪŋks) *n, pl* **larynges** (lə'rɪndʒiːz) *or* **larynxes.** a cartilaginous and muscular hollow organ forming part of the air passage to the lungs: in higher vertebrates it contains the vocal cords. [C16: from NL, from Gk *larunx*]

lasagne *or* **lasagna** (lə'zænjə, -'sæn-) *n* **1** a form of pasta consisting of wide flat sheets. **2** any of several dishes made from layers of lasagne and meat, cheese, etc. [from It. *lasagna*, from L *lasanum* cooking pot]

La Salle[1] ★ (lə 'sæl) *n* a city in SE Canada, in Quebec: a S suburb of Montreal. Pop.: 73 804 (1991).

La Salle[2] ★ (*French* la sal) *n* Sieur **Robert Cavelier de** (rɔbɛr kavəljə də). 1643–87, French explorer and fur trader in North America; founder of Louisiana (1682).

La Scala ★ (læ 'skɑːlə) *n* the chief opera house in Italy, in Milan (opened 1776).

lascar ('læskə) *n* a sailor from the East Indies. [C17: from Urdu *lashkar* soldier, from Persian: the army]

Lascaux ★ (*French* lasko) *n* site of a cave in SW France, in the Dordogne: contains Palaeolithic wall drawings and paintings.

lascivious (lə'sɪvɪəs) *adj* **1** lustful; lecherous. **2** exciting sexual desire. [C15: from LL *lascīviōsus*, from L *lascīvia* wantonness, from *lascīvus*]
▸ **las'civiously** *adv* ▸ **las'civiousness** *n*

Lasdun ★ ('læzdᵊn) *n* Sir **Denys**. born 1914, British architect. He is best known for the University of East Anglia (1968) and the National Theatre in London (1976).

lase (leɪz) *vb* **lases, lasing, lased**. (*intr*) (of a substance, such as carbon dioxide or ruby) to be capable of acting as a laser.

laser ('leɪzə) *n* **1** a source of high-intensity optical, infrared, or ultraviolet radiation produced as a result of stimulated emission maintained within a solid, liquid, or gaseous medium. The photons involved in the emission process all have the same energy and phase so that the laser beam is monochromatic and coherent, allowing it to be brought to a fine focus. **2** any similar source producing a beam of any electromagnetic radiation, such as infrared or microwave radiation. [C20: from *l*ight *a*mplification by *s*timulated *e*mission of *r*adiation]

laser printer *n* a quiet high-quality computer printer that uses a laser beam shining on a photoconductive drum to produce characters, which are then transferred to paper.

lash[1] (læʃ) *n* **1** a sharp cutting blow from a whip or other flexible object. **2** the flexible end or ends of a whip. **3** a cutting or hurtful blow to the feelings, as one caused by ridicule or scolding. **4** a forceful beating or impact, as of wind, rain, or waves against something. **5 have a lash at.** *Austral. & NZ inf.* to make an attempt at or take part in (something). **6** See **eyelash**. ◆ *vb* (*tr*) **7** to hit (a person or thing) sharply with a whip, rope, etc., esp. as punishment. **8** (of rain, waves, etc.) to beat forcefully against. **9** to attack with words, ridicule, etc. **10** to flick or wave sharply to and fro: *the panther lashed his tail.* **11** to urge or drive as with a whip: *to lash the audience into a violent mood.* ◆ See also **lash out**. [C14: ? imit.]
▸ **'lasher** *n*

lash[2] (læʃ) *vb* (*tr*) to bind or secure with rope, string, etc. [C15: from OF *lachier*, ult. from L *laqueāre* to ensnare, from *laqueus* noose]

-lashed *adj* having eyelashes as specified: *long-lashed.*

lashing[1] ('læʃɪŋ) *n* **1** a whipping; flogging. **2** a scolding. **3** (*pl*; usually foll. by *of*) *Brit. inf.* large amounts; lots.

lashing[2] ('læʃɪŋ) *n* rope, cord, etc., used for binding or securing.

Lashio ★ ('læʃɪˌəʊ) *n* a town in NE central Myanmar: starting point of the Burma Road to Chongqing, China.

Lashkar ★ ('lʌʃkə) *n* a former city in N India, in Madhya Pradesh: capital of the former states of Gwalior and Madhya Bharat; now part of the city of Gwalior.

lash out *vb* (*intr, adv*) **1** to burst into or resort to verbal or physical attack. **2** *Brit. inf.* to be extravagant, as in spending.

lash-up *n* a temporary connection of equipment for experimental or emergency use.

Lasker ★ ('læskə) *n* **Emanuel**. 1868–1941, German chess player: world champion (1894–1921).

Laski ★ ('læskɪ) *n* **Harold (Joseph)**. 1893–1950, British political scientist and socialist leader.

Las Palmas ★ (*Spanish* las 'palmas) *n* a port in the central Canary Islands, on NE Grand Canary: a major fuel-

ling port on the main shipping route between Europe and South America. Pop.: 372 270 (1986).

La Spezia ★ (*Italian* la 'spɛttsia) *n* a port in NW Italy, in Liguria, on the **Gulf of Spezia**: the chief naval base in Italy. Pop.: 100 458 (1992).

lass (læs) *n* **1** a girl or young woman. **2** *Inf.* a familiar form of address for any female. [C13: from ?]

Lassa ★ ('lɑːsə) *n* a variant spelling of **Lhasa**.

Lassa fever ('læsə) *n* a serious viral disease of Central West Africa, characterized by high fever and muscular pains. [from *Lassa*, the Nigerian village where it was first identified]

Lassalle ★ (*German* la'sal) *n* **Ferdinand** ('ferdinant). 1825–64, German socialist and writer: a founder of the first German workers' political party (1863), which later became the Social Democratic Party.

Lassen Peak ★ ('læsᵊn) *n* a volcano in S California, in the S Cascade Range. An area of 416 sq. km (161 sq. miles) was established as **Lassen Volcanic National Park** in 1916. Height: 3187 m (10 457 ft).

lassie ('læsɪ) *n Inf.* a little lass; girl.

lassitude ('læsɪˌtjuːd) *n* physical or mental weariness. [C16: from L *lassitūdō*, from *lassus* tired]

lasso (læ'suː, 'læsəʊ) *n, pl* **lassos** *or* **lassoes**. **1** a long rope or thong with a running noose at one end, used (esp. in America) for roping horses, cattle, etc.; lariat. ◆ *vb* **lassos, lassoing, lassoed**. **2** (*tr*) to catch as with a lasso. [C19: from Sp. *lazo*, ult. from L *laqueus* noose]
▸ **las'soer** *n*

Lassus ★ ('læsəs) *n* **Roland de**. Italian name *Orlando di Lasso*. ?1532–94, Flemish composer.

last[1] (lɑːst) *adj* (*often prenominal*) **1** being, happening, or coming at the end or after all others: *the last horse in the race.* **2** being or occurring just before the present; most recent: *last Thursday.* **3** only remaining: *one's last cigarette.* **4** most extreme; utmost. **5** least suitable, appropriate, or likely: *he was the last person I would have chosen.* **6** (esp. relating to the end of the world) final or ultimate: *last rites.* ◆ *adv* **7** after all others; at or in the end: *he came last.* **8** most recently: *he was last seen in the mountains.* **9** (*sentence modifier*) as the last or latest item. ◆ *n* **10** the last. **10a** a person or thing that is last. **10b** the final moment; end. **11** one's last moments before death. **12** the final appearance, mention, or occurrence: *we've seen the last of him.* **13 at last**. in the end; finally. **14 at long last**. finally, after difficulty, delay, or irritation. [var. of OE *latest, lætest*, sup. of LATE]

> **USAGE NOTE**   Since *last* can mean either *after all others* or *most recent*, it is better to avoid using this word where ambiguity might arise as in *her last novel. Final* or *latest* should be used in such contexts to avoid ambiguity.

last[2] (lɑːst) *vb* **1** (when *intr*, often foll. by *for*) to remain in being (for a length of time); continue: *his hatred lasted for several years.* **2** to be sufficient for the needs of (a person) for (a length of time): *it will last us until Friday.* **3** (when *intr*, often foll. by *for*) to remain fresh, uninjured, or unaltered (for a certain time). ◆ See also **last out**. [OE *læstan*]
▸ **'laster** *n*

last[3] (lɑːst) *n* **1** the wooden or metal form on which a shoe or boot is fashioned or repaired. ◆ *vb* **2** (*tr*) to fit (a shoe or boot) on a last. [OE *læste*, from *lāst* footprint]
▸ **'laster** *n*

last-ditch *n* a last resort or place of last defence. **b** (*as modifier*): *a last-ditch effort.*

last-gasp *n* (*modifier*) done in desperation at the last minute: *a last-gasp attempt to save the talks.*

lasting ('lɑːstɪŋ) *adj* permanent or enduring.
▸ **'lastingly** *adv* ▸ **'lastingness** *n*

Last Judgment *n* **the**. the occasion, after the resurrection of the dead at the end of the world, when, according to biblical tradition, God will decree the final destinies of all men according to the good and evil in their earthly lives. Also called: **the Last Day, Doomsday, Judgment Day.**

lastly ('lɑːstlɪ) *adv* **1** at the end or at the last point. ♦ *sentence connector.* **2** finally.

last name *n* another term for **surname.**

last out *vb (intr, adv)* **1** to be sufficient for one's needs: *how long will our supplies last out?* **2** to endure or survive: *some old people don't last out the winter.*

last post *n* (in the British military services) **1** a bugle call that orders men to retire for sleep. **2** a similar call sounded at military funerals.

last rites *pl n Christianity.* religious rites prescribed for those close to death.

Last Supper *n the.* the meal eaten by Christ with his disciples on the night before his Crucifixion.

Las Vegas ★ (læs 'veɪgəs) *n* a city in SE Nevada: famous for luxury hotels and casinos. Pop.: 368 360 (1995 est.).

lat. *abbrev. for* latitude.

Lat. *abbrev. for* Latin.

latah ('lɑːtə) *n* a psychological condition, observed esp. in Malaysian cultures, in which an individual, after experiencing a shock, becomes anxious and suggestible, often imitating the actions of another person. [C19: from Malay]

Latakia *or* **Lattakia** ★ (,lætə'kiːə) *n* the chief port of Syria, in the northwest: tobacco industry. Pop.: 306 535 (1994 est.). Latin name: **Laodicea ad Mare.**

latch (lætʃ) *n* **1** a fastening for a gate or door that consists of a bar that may be slid or lowered into a groove, hole, etc. **2** a spring-loaded door lock that can be opened by a key from outside. **3** Also called: **latch circuit.** *Electronics.* a logic circuit that transfers the input states to the output states when signalled. ♦ *vb* **4** to fasten, fit, or be fitted as with a latch. [OE *læccan* to seize, of Gmc origin]

latchkey ('lætʃ,kiː) *n* **1** a key for an outside door or gate, esp. one that lifts a latch. **2** a supposed freedom from restrictions.

latchkey child *n* a child who has to let himself in at home on returning from school, as his parents are out at work.

latch on *vb (intr, adv; often foll. by to) Inf.* **1** to attach oneself (to). **2** to understand.

latchstring ('lætʃ,strɪŋ) *n* a length of string fastened to a latch and passed through a hole in the door so that it can be opened from the other side.

late (leɪt) *adj* **1** occurring or arriving after the correct or expected time: *the train was late.* **2** (*prenominal*) occurring at, scheduled for, or being at a relatively advanced time: *a late marriage.* **3** (*prenominal*) towards or near the end: *the late evening.* **4** an advanced time in the evening or at night: *it was late.* **5** (*prenominal*) occurring or being just previous to the present time: *his late remarks on industry.* **6** (*prenominal*) having died, esp. recently: *my late grandfather.* **7** (*prenominal*) just preceding the present or existing person or thing; former: *the late manager of this firm.* **8** **of late.** recently; lately. ♦ *adv* **9** after the correct or expected time: *he arrived late.* **10** at a relatively advanced age: *she married late.* **11** recently; lately: *as late as yesterday he was selling books.* **12 late in the day. 12a** at a late or advanced stage. **12b** too late. [OE *læt*]
▶ **'lateness** *n*

> **USAGE NOTE** Since *late* can mean *deceased*, many people think it is better to avoid using this word to refer to the person who held a post or position before its present holder: *the previous (not the late) editor of The Times.*

lateen (lə'tiːn) *adj Naut.* denoting a rig with a triangular sail (**lateen sail**) bent to a yard hoisted to the head of a low mast, used esp. in the Mediterranean. [C18: from F *voile latine* Latin sail]

Late Greek *n* the Greek language from about the 3rd to the 8th centuries A.D.

Late Latin *n* the form of written Latin used from the 3rd to the 7th centuries A.D.

lately ('leɪtlɪ) *adv* in recent times; of late.

La Tène (læ 'tɛn) *adj* of or relating to a Celtic culture in Europe from about the 5th to the 1st centuries B.C., characterized by a distinctive type of curvilinear decoration. [C20: from *La Tène*, a part of Lake Neuchâtel, Switzerland, where remains of this culture were first discovered]

latent ('leɪt°nt) *adj* **1** potential but not obvious or explicit. **2** (of buds, spores, etc.) not developed. **3** *Pathol.* (esp. of an infectious disease) not yet revealed or manifest. **4** (of a virus) inactive in the host cell. **5** *Psychoanal.* relating to that part of a dream expressive of repressed desires: *latent content.* Cf. **manifest** (sense 2). [C17: from L *latēnt-*, from *latēre* to lie hidden]
▶ **'latency** *n* ▶ **'latently** *adv*

latent heat *n (no longer in technical usage)* the heat evolved or absorbed by unit mass (**specific latent heat**) or unit amount of substance (**molar latent heat**) when it changes phase without change of temperature.

latent image *n Photog.* the invisible image produced by the action of light, etc., on silver halide crystals suspended in the emulsion of a photographic material. It becomes visible after development.

later ('leɪtə) *adj, adv* **1** the comparative of **late.** ♦ *adv* **2** afterwards; subsequently.

lateral ('lætərəl) *adj* **1** of or relating to the side or sides: *a lateral blow.* ♦ *n* **2** a lateral object, part, passage, or movement. [C17: from L *laterālis*, from *latus* side]
▶ **'laterally** *adv*

lateral thinking *n* a way of solving problems by employing unorthodox and apparently illogical means.

laterite ('lætə,raɪt) *n* any of a group of residual insoluble deposits of ferric and aluminium oxides: formed by weathering of rocks in tropical regions. [C19: from L *later* brick]

latest ('leɪtɪst) *adj, adv* **1** the superlative of **late.** ♦ *adj* **2** most recent, modern, or new: *the latest fashions.* ♦ *n* **3 at the latest.** no later than the time specified. **4 the latest.** *Inf.* the most recent fashion or development.

latex ('leɪtɛks) *n, pl* **latexes** *or* **latices** ('leɪtɪ,siːz). **1** a whitish milky fluid containing protein, starch, alkaloids, etc., that is produced by many plants. Latex from the rubber tree is used in the manufacture of rubber. **2** a suspension of synthetic rubber or plastic in water, used in the manufacture of synthetic rubber or plastic products, etc. [C19: NL, from L: liquid]

lath (lɑːθ) *n, pl* **laths** (lɑːðz, lɑːθs). **1** one of several thin narrow strips of wood used to provide a supporting framework for plaster, tiles, etc. **2** expanded sheet metal, wire mesh, etc., used to provide backing for plaster or rendering. **3** any thin strip of wood. ♦ *vb* **4** (*tr*) to attach laths to (a ceiling, roof, floor, etc.). [OE *lætt*]

lathe (leɪð) *n* **1** a machine for shaping or boring metal, wood, etc., in which the workpiece is turned about a horizontal axis against a fixed tool. ♦ *vb* **lathes, lathing, lathed.** **2** (*tr*) to shape or bore a (workpiece) on a lathe. [? C15 *lath* a support, from ON]

lather ('lɑːðə) *n* **1** foam formed by the action of soap or a detergent in water. **2** foam formed by other liquid, such as the sweat of a horse. **3** *Inf.* a state of agitation. ♦ *vb* **4** to coat or become coated with lather. **5** (*intr*) to form a lather. [OE *lēathor* soap]
▶ **'lathery** *adj*

lathi ('lɑːtɪ) *n, pl* **lathis.** a long heavy wooden stick used as a weapon in India, esp. by the police. [Hindi]

Latimer ★ ('lætɪmə) *n* **Hugh.** ?1485–1555, English Protestant bishop: burnt at the stake for refusing to disavow his Protestant beliefs when Mary I assumed the throne.

Latin ('lætɪn) *n* **1** the language of ancient Rome and the Roman Empire and of the educated in medieval Europe. Having originally been the language of Latium in W central Italy, belonging to the Italic branch of the Indo-European family, it later formed the basis of the Romance group. **2** a member of any of those peoples whose languages are derived from Latin. **3** an inhabitant of ancient Latium. ♦ *adj* **4** of or relating to the Latin language, the ancient Latins, or Latium. **5** characteristic of or relating to those peoples in Europe and Latin America whose languages are derived from Latin. **6** of or relating to the Roman Catholic Church. [OE *latin* and *læden* Latin, language, from L *Latīnus* of Latium]

Latina ★ (*Italian* la'ti:na) *n* a city in W central Italy, in Lazio: built as a planned town in 1932 on reclaimed land of the Pontine Marshes. Pop.: 108 819 (1994 est.). Former name (until 1947): **Littoria**.

Latin America ★ *n* those areas of America whose official languages are Spanish and Portuguese, derived from Latin: South America, Central America, Mexico, and certain islands in the Caribbean.
▷ **Latin American** *n, adj*

Latinate ('lætɪ,neɪt) *adj* (of writing, vocabulary, etc.) imitative of or derived from Latin.

Latinism ('lætɪ,nɪzəm) *n* a word, idiom, or phrase borrowed from Latin.

Latinist ('lætɪnɪst) *n* a person who studies or is proficient in Latin.

Latinize *or* **Latinise** ('lætɪ,naɪz) *vb* **Latinizes, Latinizing, Latinized** *or* **Latinises, Latinising, Latinised**. (*tr*) **1** to translate into Latin or Latinisms. **2** to cause to acquire Latin style or customs. **3** to bring Roman Catholic influence to bear upon (the form of religious ceremonies, etc.).
▷ **,Latini'zation** *or* **,Latini'sation** *n* ▷ **'Latin,izer** *or* **'Latin,iser** *n*

Latin Quarter ★ *n* an area of Paris, on the S bank of the River Seine: contains the city's main educational establishments; centre for students and artists.

latish ('leɪtɪʃ) *adj, adv* rather late.

latitude ('lætɪ,tju:d) *n* **1a** an angular distance measured in degrees north or south of the equator (latitude 0°). **1b** (*often pl*) a region considered with regard to its distance from the equator. **2** scope for freedom of action, thought, etc.; freedom from restriction: *his parents gave him a great deal of latitude*. [C14: from L *lātitūdō*, from *lātus* broad]
▷ **,lati'tudinal** *adj* ▷ **,lati'tudinally** *adv*

latitudinarian (,lætɪ,tju:dɪ'neərɪən) *adj* **1** permitting or marked by freedom of attitude or behaviour, esp. in religious matters. ◆ *n* **2** a person with latitudinarian views. [C17: from L *lātitūdō* breadth, infl. in form by TRINITARIAN]
▷ **,lati,tudi'narianism** *n*

Latium ★ ('leɪʃɪəm) *n* an ancient territory in W central Italy, in modern Lazio, on the Tyrrhenian Sea: inhabited by the Latin people from the 10th century B.C. until dominated by Rome (4th century B.C.).

Latona ★ (lə'təʊnə) *n* the Roman name of **Leto**.

Latour ★ (*French* latur) *n* **Maurice Quentin de** (mɔris kɑ̃tē də) 1704–88, French pastelist noted for his portraits.

La Tour ★ (*French* la tur) *n* **Georges de** (ʒɔrʒ də). ?1593–1652, French painter, esp. of candlelit religious scenes.

latria (lə'traɪə) *n RC Church, theol.* the adoration that may be offered to God alone. [C16: via L from Gk *latreia* worship]

latrine (lə'tri:n) *n* a lavatory, as in a barracks, camp, etc. [C17: from F, from L *lātrīna*, shortened form of *lavātrīna* bath, from *lavāre* to wash]

-latry *n combining form.* indicating worship of or excessive veneration of: *idolatry; Mariolatry*. [from Gk *-latria*, from *latreia* worship]
▷ **-latrous** *adj combining form.*

latter ('lætə) *adj* (*prenominal*) **1a** denoting the second or second mentioned of two: distinguished from *former*. **1b** (*as n; functioning as sing or pl*): *the latter is not important.* **2** near or nearer the end: *the latter part of a film*. **3** more advanced in time or sequence; later. [OE *lætra*]

> **USAGE NOTE** *The latter* should only be used to refer to the second of two items: *many people choose to go by hovercraft rather than use the ferry, but I prefer the latter.* The last of three or more items can be referred to as *the last-named.*

latter-day *adj* present-day; modern.

Latter-day Saint *n* a more formal name for a **Mormon**.

latterly ('lætəlɪ) *adv* recently; lately.

lattice ('lætɪs) *n* **1** Also called: **latticework**. an open framework of strips of wood, metal, etc., arranged to form an ornamental pattern. **2a** a gate, screen, etc., formed of such a framework. **2b** (*as modifier*): *a lattice window*. **3** something, such as a decorative or heraldic device, resembling such a framework. **4** an array of objects or points in a periodic pattern in two or three dimensions, esp. an array of atoms, ions, etc., in a crystal or an array of points indicating their positions in space. ◆ *vb* **lattices, latticing, latticed**. **5** to make, adorn, or supply with a lattice or lattices. [C14: from OF *lattis*, from *latte* LATH]
▷ **'latticed** *adj*

Latvia ★ ('lætvɪə) *n* a republic in central Europe, on the Gulf of Riga and the Baltic Sea. It was successively under Teutonic, Polish, Swedish, and Russian rule from the 13th century to 1918, when it became an independent republic: annexed (1940) by the Soviet Union as the Latvian Soviet Socialist Republic: regained independence in 1991. Official language: Latvian. Religion: believers are mostly Christian. Currency: lats. Capital: Riga. Pop.: 2 472 000 (1997). Area: 63 700 sq. km (25 590 sq. miles).

Latvian ('lætvɪən) *adj* **1** of or relating to Latvia, its people, or their language. ◆ *n* **2** Also called: **Lettish**. the official language of Latvia. **3** a native or inhabitant of Latvia.

laud (lɔ:d) *Literary.* ◆ *vb* **1** (*tr*) to praise or glorify. ◆ *n* **2** praise or glorification. [C14: vb from L *laudāre*; n from *laudēs*, pl. of L *laus* praise]

Laud ★ (lɔ:d) *n* **William**. 1573–1645, English prelate; archbishop of Canterbury (1633–45). His persecution of Puritans and his High Church policies in England and Scotland were a cause of the Civil War; he was impeached by the Long Parliament (1640) and executed.
▷ **'Laudian** *adj*

laudable ('lɔ:dəb°l) *adj* deserving or worthy of praise; admirable; commendable.
▷ **'laudableness** *or* **,lauda'bility** *n* ▷ **'laudably** *adv*

laudanum ('lɔ:d°nəm) *n* **1** a tincture of opium. **2** (formerly) any medicine of which opium was the main ingredient. [C16: NL, name chosen by Paracelsus for a preparation prob. containing opium]

laudation (lɔ:'deɪʃən) *n* a formal word for **praise**.

laudatory ('lɔ:dətərɪ, -trɪ) *or* **laudative** *adj* expressing or containing praise; eulogistic.

Lauder ★ ('lɔ:də) *n* **Sir Harry**. real name *Hugh MacLennan*. 1870–1950, Scottish ballad singer and music-hall comedian.

lauds (lɔ:dz) *n* (*functioning as sing or pl*) *Chiefly RC Church.* the traditional morning prayer, constituting with matins the first of the seven canonical hours. [C14: see LAUD]

Laue ★ (*German* 'laʊə) *n* **Max Theodor Felix von** (maks 'te:odo:r 'fe:lɪks fɔn). 1879–1960, German physicist. He pioneered studies of X-ray diffraction by crystals and contributed to the theory of relativity: Nobel prize for physics 1914.

laugh (lɑ:f) *vb* **1** (*intr*) to express or manifest emotion, esp. mirth or amusement, typically by expelling air from the lungs in short bursts to produce an inarticulate voiced noise, with the mouth open. **2** (*intr*) (esp. of certain mammals or birds) to make a noise resembling a laugh. **3** (*tr*) to utter or express with laughter: *he laughed his derision at the play*. **4** (*tr*) to bring or force (someone, esp. oneself) into a certain condition by laughter: *he laughed himself sick*. **5** (*intr; foll. by at*) to make fun (of); jeer (at). **6 laugh up one's sleeve**. to laugh or have grounds for amusement, self-satisfaction, etc., secretly. **7 laugh on the other side of one's face**. to show sudden disappointment or shame after appearing cheerful or confident. ◆ *n* **8** the act or an instance of laughing. **9** a manner of laughter. **10** *Inf.* a person or thing that causes laughter: *that holiday was a laugh*. **11 the last laugh**. the final success in an argument, situation, etc., after previous defeat. ◆ See also **laugh off**. [OE *læhhan, hliehhen*]
▷ **'laugher** *n* ▷ **'laughing** *n, adj* ▷ **'laughingly** *adv*

laughable ('lɑ:fəb°l) *adj* **1** producing scorn; ludicrous: *he* *offered me a laughable sum for the picture.* **2** arousing laughter.

▶ **'laughableness** *n* ▶ **'laughably** *adv*

aughing gas *n* another name for **nitrous oxide.**

aughing jackass *n* another name for the **kookaburra.**

aughing stock *n* an object of humiliating ridicule.

augh off *vb* (*tr, adv*) to treat or dismiss lightly, esp. with stoicism.

aughter ('lɑːftə) *n* **1** the action of or noise produced by laughing. **2** the experience or manifestation of mirth, amusement, scorn, or joy. [OE *hleahtor*]

.aughton ★ ('lɔːt°n) *n* **Charles.** 1899–1962, US actor, born in England: noted esp. for such films as *The Private Life of Henry VIII* (1933) and *Mutiny on the Bounty* (1935).

.aunceston ★ ('lɔːnsəst°n) *n* a city in Australia, the chief port of the island state of Tasmania on the Tamar River, 64 km (40 miles) from Bass Strait. Pop.: 93 347 (1991).

aunch[1] (lɔːntʃ) *vb* **1** to move (a vessel) into the water. **2** to move (a newly built vessel) into the water for the first time. **3** (*tr*) **3a** to start off or set in motion: *to launch a scheme.* **3b** to put (a new product) on the market. **4** (*tr*) to propel with force. **5** to involve (oneself) totally and enthusiastically: *to launch oneself into work.* **6** (*tr*) to set (a missile, spacecraft, etc.) into motion. **7** (*intr*; foll. by *into*) to start talking or writing (about): *he launched into a story.* **8** (*intr*; usually foll. by *out*) to start (out) on a fresh course. ◆ *n* **9** an act or instance of launching. [C14: from Anglo-F *lancher*, from LL *lanceāre* to use a lance, hence, to set in motion. See LANCE]

▶ **'launcher** *n*

aunch[2] (lɔːntʃ) *n* **1** a motor driven boat used chiefly as a transport boat. **2** the largest of the boats of a man-of-war. [C17: via Sp. *lancha* and Port. from Malay *lancharan* boat, from *lanchar* speed]

aunch pad *or* **launching pad** *n* **1** a platform from which a spacecraft, rocket, etc., is launched. **2** an effective starting point for a career, enterprise, or campaign.

aunch window *n* the limited period during which a spacecraft can be launched on a particular mission.

aunder ('lɔːndə) *vb* **1** to wash and often also iron (clothes, linen, etc.). **2** (*intr*) to be capable of being laundered without shrinking, fading, etc. **3** (*tr*) to make (money illegally obtained) appear to be legally gained by passing it through foreign banks or legitimate enterprises. [C14 (n, meaning: a person who washes linen): changed from *lavender* washerwoman, from OF *lavandiere*, ult. from L *lavāre* to wash]

▶ **'launderer** *n*

.Launderette (ˌlɔːndəˈret, lɔːnˈdret) *Brit. & NZ trademark.* a commercial establishment where clothes can be washed and dried, using coin-operated machines. Also called (US, Canad., and NZ): **Laundromat.**

.aundress ('lɔːndrɪs) *n* a woman who launders clothes, sheets, etc., for a living.

.aundry ('lɔːndrɪ) *n, pl* **laundries. 1** a place where clothes and linen are washed and ironed. **2** the clothes or linen washed and ironed. **3** the act of laundering. [C16: changed from C14 *lavendry*; see LAUNDER]

.aundryman ('lɔːndrɪmən) *or* (*fem*) **laundrywoman** *n, pl* **laundrymen** *or* **laundrywomen. 1** a person who collects or delivers laundry. **2** a person who works in a laundry.

Laurasia ★ (lɔːˈreɪʃə) *n* one of the two ancient supercontinents comprising what are now North America, Greenland, Europe, and Asia (excluding India). [C20: from NL *Laur(entia)* (referring to the ancient N American landmass, from *Laurentian* strata of the Canadian Shield) + (*Eur*)*asia*]

laureate ('lɔːrɪt) *adj* (*usually immediately postpositive*) **1** *Literary.* crowned with laurel leaves as a sign of honour. ◆ *n* **2** short for **poet laureate. 3** a person honoured with an award for art or science: *a Nobel laureate.* **4** *Rare.* a person honoured with the laurel crown or wreath. [C14: from L *laureātus*, from *laurea* LAUREL]

▶ **'laureate,ship** *n*

laurel ('lɒrəl) *n* **1** Also called: **bay, bay laurel, sweet bay, true laurel.** a small Mediterranean evergreen tree with glossy aromatic leaves, used for flavouring in cooking, and small blackish berries. **2** a similar and related tree of the Canary Islands and Azores. **3** short for **mountain laurel. 4 spurge laurel.** a European evergreen shrub, *Daphne laureola*, with glossy leaves and small green flowers. **5** (*pl*) a wreath of true laurel, worn on the head as an emblem of victory or honour in classical times. **6** (*pl*) honour, distinction, or fame. **7 look to one's laurels.** to be on guard against one's rivals. **8 rest on one's laurels.** to be satisfied with distinction won by past achievements and cease to strive for further achievements. ◆ *vb* **laurels, laurelling, laurelled** *or US* **laurels, laureling, laureled. 9** (*tr*) to crown with laurel. [C13 *lorer*, from OF *lorier* laurel tree, ult. from L *laurus*]

Laurel and Hardy ★ ('lɒrəl; 'hɑːdɪ) *n* a team of US film comedians, **Stan Laurel,** 1890–1965, born in Britain, the thin one, and his partner, **Oliver Hardy,** 1892–1957, the fat one.

Laurentian (lɔːˈrenʃən) *adj* **1** Also: **Lawrentian.** of or resembling the style of D. H. or T. E. Lawrence. **2** of, relating to, or situated near the St Lawrence River.

Laurentian Mountains ★ *pl n* a range of low mountains in E Canada, in Quebec between the St Lawrence River and Hudson Bay. Highest point: 1191 m (3905 ft). Also called: **Laurentides** ('lɒːrən,taɪdz).

Laurentian Shield *n* another name for the **Canadian Shield.** Also: **Laurentian Plateau.**

Laurier ★ ('lɒːrɪə) *n* Sir **Wilfrid.** 1841–1919, Canadian Liberal statesman; the first French-Canadian prime minister (1896–1911).

laurustinus (ˌlɒːrəˈstaɪnəs) *n* a Mediterranean shrub with glossy evergreen leaves and white or pink fragrant flowers. [C17: from NL, from L *laurus* laurel]

Lausanne ★ (ləʊˈzæn; *French* lozan) *n* a city in W Switzerland, capital of Vaud canton, on Lake Geneva; cultural and commercial centre; university (1537). Pop.: 116 795 (1995 est.).

Lautrec ★ (*French* lotrɛk) *n* See (Henri de) **Toulouse-Lautrec.**

lav (læv) *n Brit. inf.* short for **lavatory.**

lava ('lɑːvə) *n* **1** magma emanating from volcanoes. **2** any extrusive igneous rock formed by the solidification of lava. [C18: from It., from L *lavāre* to wash]

lavabo (ləˈveɪbəʊ) *n, pl* **lavaboes** *or* **lavabos.** *Chiefly RC Church.* **1a** the ritual washing of the celebrant's hands after the offertory at Mass. **1b** (*as modifier*): *lavabo basin; lavabo towel.* **2** another name for **washbasin. 3** a trough for washing in a convent or monastery. [C19: from L: I shall wash, the opening of Psalm 26:6]

lavage ('lævɪdʒ, læˈvɑːʒ) *n Med.* the washing out of a hollow organ by flushing with water. [C19: via F, from L *lavāre* to wash]

Laval[1] **★** (ləˈvæl) *n* a city in SE Canada, in Quebec: a NW suburb of Montreal. Pop.: 314 398 (1991).

Laval[2] **★** (*French* laval) *n* **Pierre** (pjɛr). 1883–1945, French statesman. He was premier of France (1931–32; 1935–36) and premier of the Vichy government (1942–44). He was executed for collaboration with Germany.

lavatorial (ˌlævəˈtɔːrɪəl) *adj* characterized by excessive mention of the excretory functions; vulgar or scatological: *lavatorial humour.*

lavatory ('lævətərɪ, -trɪ) *n, pl* **lavatories. a** a sanitary installation for receiving and disposing of urine and faeces, consisting of a bowl fitted with a water-flushing device and connected to a drain. **b** a room containing such an installation. Also called: **toilet, water closet, WC.** [C14: from LL *lavātōrium*, from L *lavāre* to wash]

lavatory paper *n Brit.* another name for **toilet paper.**

lave (leɪv) *vb* **laves, laving, laved.** an archaic word for **wash.** [OE *lafian*, ?from L *lavāre* to wash]

lavender ('lævəndə) *n* **1** any of various perennial shrubs or herbaceous plants of the labiate family, esp. *Lavandula vera*, cultivated for its mauve or blue flowers and as the source of a fragrant oil (**oil of lavender**). **2** the dried parts of *L. vera*, used to perfume clothes. **3** a pale or light bluish-purple colour. **4** perfume scented with lavender. [C13 *lavendre*, via F from Med. L *lavendula*, from ?]

laver ('leɪvə) *n Old Testament.* a large basin of water used by the priests for ritual ablutions. [C14: from OF *lavoir*, from LL *lavātōrium* washing place]

Laver ★ ('leɪvə) *n* **Rod(ney)**. born 1938, Australian tennis player: Wimbledon champion 1961, 1962, 1968, 1969; US champion 1962, 1969.

lavish ('lævɪʃ) *adj* **1** prolific, abundant, or profuse. **2** generous; unstinting; liberal. **3** extravagant; prodigal; wasteful: *lavish expenditure.* ♦ *vb* **4** (*tr*) to give, expend, or apply abundantly, generously, or in profusion. [C15: adj use of *lavas* profusion, from OF *lavasse* torrent, from L *lavāre* to wash]
▶ 'lavisher *n* ▶ 'lavishly *adv* ▶ 'lavishness *n*

Lavoisier ★ (*French* lavwazje) *n* **Antoine Laurent** (ɑ̃twan lɔrɑ̃). 1743–94, French chemist; one of the founders of modern chemistry. He named oxygen and discovered its importance in respiration and combustion.

law (lɔː) *n* **1** a rule or set of rules, enforceable by the courts regulating the relationship between the state and its subjects, and the conduct of subjects towards one another. **2a** a rule or body of rules made by the legislature. See **statute law**. **2b** a rule or body of rules made by a municipal or other authority. See **bylaw**. **3a** the condition and control enforced by such rules. **3b** (*in combination*): *lawcourt.* **4 law and order. 4a** the policy of strict enforcement of the law, esp. against crime and violence. **4b** (*as modifier*): *law-and-order candidate.* **5** a rule of conduct: *a law of etiquette.* **6** one of a set of rules governing a particular field of activity: *the laws of tennis.* **7 the law. 7a** the legal or judicial system. **7b** the profession or practice of law. **7c** *Inf.* the police or a policeman. **8** Also called: **law of nature.** a generalization based on a recurring fact or event. **9** the science or knowledge of law; jurisprudence. **10** the principles originating and formerly applied only in courts of common law. Cf. **equity** (sense 3). **11** a general principle, formula, or rule describing a phenomenon in mathematics, science, philosophy, etc.: *the laws of thermodynamics.* **12** Also called: **Law of Moses.** (*often cap.*; preceded by *the*) the body of laws contained in the first five books of the Old Testament. **13 go to law.** to resort to legal proceedings on some matter. **14 lay down the law.** to speak in an authoritative or dogmatic manner. ♦ Related adjs.: **judicial, juridical, legal.** [OE *lagu*, from ON]

Law ★ (lɔː) *n* **1 Andrew Bonar** ('bɒnə). 1858–1923, British Conservative statesman, born in Canada; prime minister (1922–23). **2 John.** 1671–1729, Scottish financier. He founded the Mississippi Scheme for the development of Louisiana (1717), which collapsed due to excessive speculation.

law-abiding *adj* adhering more or less strictly to the laws: *a law-abiding citizen.*

law agent *n* (in Scotland) a solicitor entitled to appear for a client in any Sheriff Court.

lawbreaker ('lɔːˌbreɪkə) *n* a person who breaks the law.
▶ 'law,breaking *n, adj*

law centre *n Brit.* an independent service financed by a local authority, which provides free legal advice and information to the general public.

Lawes ★ (lɔːz) *n* **1 Henry.** 1596–1662, English composer, noted for his music for Milton's masque *Comus* (1634) and for his settings of some of Robert Herrick's poems. **2** his brother, **William.** 1602–45, English composer, noted for his instrumental music.

lawful ('lɔːful) *adj* allowed, recognized, or sanctioned by law; legal.
▶ 'lawfully *adv* ▶ 'lawfulness *n*

lawgiver ('lɔːˌgɪvə) *n* **1** the giver of a code of laws. **2** Also called: **lawmaker.** a maker of laws.
▶ 'law,giving *n, adj*

lawks (lɔːks) *interj Brit.* an expression of surprise or dismay. [C18: var. of *Lord!*, prob. infl. in form by ALACK]

lawless ('lɔːlɪs) *adj* **1** without law. **2** disobedient to the law. **3** contrary to or heedless of the law. **4** uncontrolled; unbridled: *lawless rage.*
▶ 'lawlessly *adv* ▶ 'lawlessness *n*

Law Lords *pl n* (in Britain) members of the House of Lords who sit as the highest court of appeal.

lawn[1] (lɔːn) *n* a flat and usually level area of mown and cultivated grass. [C16: changed form of C14 *launde*, from OF *lande*, of Celtic origin]
▶ 'lawny *adj*

lawn[2] (lɔːn) *n* a fine linen or cotton fabric, used for clothing. [C15: prob. from *Laon*, town in France where made]
▶ 'lawny *adj*

lawn mower *n* a hand-operated or power-operated machine for cutting grass on lawns.

lawn tennis *n* **1** tennis played on a grass court. **2** the formal name for **tennis.**

law of averages *n* (popularly) the expectation that a possible event is bound to occur regularly with a frequency approximating to its probability.

law of supply and demand *n* the theory that the price of an article or service is determined by the interaction of supply and demand.

law of the jungle *n* a state of ruthless competition or self-interest.

law of thermodynamics *n* any of three principles governing the relationships between different forms of energy. The **first law** (conservation of energy) states that energy can be transformed but not destroyed. The **second law** states that in any irreversible process entropy always increases. The **third law** states that it is impossible to reduce the temperature of a system to absolute zero in a finite number of steps.

Lawrence ★ ('lɒrəns) *n* **1 D(avid) H(erbert).** 1885–1930, British writer. His novels include *Sons and Lovers* (1913), *Women in Love* (1920), and *Lady Chatterley's Lover* (1928). **2 Ernest Orlando.** 1901–58, US physicist, who invented the cyclotron (1931): Nobel prize for physics 1939. **3 Gertrude.** 1898–1952, British actress, noted esp. for her roles in comedies. **4 Sir Thomas.** 1769–1830, British portrait painter. **5 T(homas) E(dward)**, known as *Lawrence of Arabia.* 1888–1935, British soldier and writer. He took a major part in the Arab revolt against the Turks (1916–18), describing his experiences in *The Seven Pillars of Wisdom* (1926).

lawrencium (lɒ'rensɪəm) *n* an element artificially produced from californium. Symbol: Lr; atomic no.: 103; half-life of most stable isotope, ^{256}Lr: 35 seconds. [C20: after Ernest O. LAWRENCE]

Lawrentian (lɔː'renʃən) *adj* a variant spelling of **Laurentian** (sense 1).

Lawson ★ ('lɔːsən) *n* **Henry Archibald.** 1867–1922, Australian poet and short-story writer, whose work is taken as being most representative of the Australian outback, esp. in *While the Billy Boils* (1896) and *Joe Wilson and his Mates* (1901).

lawsuit ('lɔːˌsuːt) *n* a proceeding in a court of law brought by one party against another, esp. a civil action.

law term *n* **1** an expression or word used in law. **2** any of various periods of time appointed for the sitting of law courts.

lawyer ('lɔːjə, 'lɔɪə) *n* a member of the legal profession, esp. a solicitor. [C14: from LAW]

lax (læks) *adj* **1** lacking firmness; not strict. **2** lacking precision or definition. **3** not taut. **4** *Phonetics.* (of a speech sound) pronounced with little muscular effort. [C14 (orig. used with reference to the bowels): from L *laxus* loose]
▶ 'laxly *adv* ▶ 'laxity or 'laxness *n*

laxative ('læksətɪv) *n* **1** an agent stimulating evacuation of faeces. ♦ *adj* **2** stimulating evacuation of faeces. [C14 (orig.: relaxing): from Med. L *laxātīvus*, from L *laxāre* to loosen]

Laxness ★ (*Icelandic* 'laxsnes) *n* **Halldór (Kiljan)** ('haldɔur). 1902–98, Icelandic novelist, noted for his treatment of rural working life in Iceland. His works include *Salka Valka* (1932) and *Independent People* (1935). Nobel prize for literature 1955.

lay[1] (leɪ) *vb* **lays, laying, laid.** (*mainly tr*) **1** to put in a low or horizontal position; cause to lie: *to lay a cover on a bed.* **2**

★ **people and places**

to place, put, or be in a particular state or position: *he laid his finger on his lips.* **3** (*intr*) *Dialect or not standard.* to be in a horizontal position; lie: *he often lays in bed all the morning.* **4** (sometimes foll. by *down*) to establish as a basis: *to lay a foundation for discussion.* **5** to place or dispose in the proper position: *to lay a carpet.* **6** to arrange (a table) for eating a meal. **7** to prepare (a fire) for lighting by arranging fuel in the grate. **8** (*also intr*) (of birds, esp. the domestic hen) to produce (eggs). **9** to present or put forward: *he laid his case before the magistrate.* **10** to impute or attribute: *all the blame was laid on him.* **11** to arrange, devise, or prepare: *to lay a trap.* **12** to place, set, or locate: *the scene is laid in London.* **13** to make (a bet) with (someone): *I lay you five to one on Prince.* **14** to cause to settle: *to lay the dust.* **15** to allay; suppress: *to lay a rumour.* **16** to bring down forcefully: *to lay a whip on someone's back.* **17** *Taboo sl.* to have sexual intercourse with. **18** to press down or make smooth: *to lay the nap of cloth.* **19** (*intr*) *Naut.* to move or go, esp. into a specified position or direction: *to lay close to the wind.* **20 lay bare.** to reveal or explain: *he laid bare his plans.* **21 lay hold of.** to seize or grasp. **22 lay oneself open.** to make oneself vulnerable (to criticism, attack, etc.). **23 lay open.** to reveal or disclose. ◆ *n* **24** the manner or position in which something lies or is placed. **25** *Taboo sl.* **25a** an act of sexual intercourse. **25b** a sexual partner. ◆ See also **lay aside**, **lay-by**, etc. [OE *lecgan*]

> **USAGE NOTE** In careful English, the verb *lay* is used with an object and *lie* without one: *the soldier laid down his arms; the Queen laid a wreath; the book was lying on the table; he was lying on the floor.* In informal English, *lay* is frequently used for *lie: the book was laying on the table.* All careful writers and speakers observe the distinction even in informal contexts.

lay[2] (ler) *vb* the past tense of **lie**[2].

lay[3] (ler) *adj* **1** of, involving, or belonging to people who are not clergy. **2** nonprofessional or nonspecialist; amateur. [C14: from OF *lai*, from LL *lāicus*, ult. from Gk *laos* people]

lay[4] (ler) *n* **1** a ballad or short narrative poem, esp. one intended to be sung. **2** a song or melody. [C13: from OF *lai*, ? of Gmc origin]

layabout ('leɪəˌbaʊt) *n* a lazy person; loafer.

Layamon ('laɪəmən) *or* **Lawman** ★ ('lɔːmən) *n* 12th-century English poet and priest; author of the *Brut*, a chronicle providing the earliest English version of the Arthurian story.

lay analyst *n* a person without medical qualifications who practises psychoanalysis.

Layard ★ (lɛəd) *n* Sir Austen Henry. 1817–94, British archaeologist, noted for his excavations at Nimrud and Nineveh.

lay aside *vb* (*tr, adv*) **1** to abandon or reject. **2** to store or reserve for future use.

lay brother *or* (*fem*) **lay sister** *n* a person who has taken the vows of a religious order but is not ordained and not bound to divine office.

lay-by *n* **1** *Brit.* a place for drivers to stop at the side of a main road. **2** *Naut.* an anchorage in a narrow waterway, away from the channel. **3** a small railway siding where rolling stock may be stored or parked. **4** *Austral. & NZ.* a system of payment whereby a buyer pays a deposit on an article, which is reserved for him until he has paid the full price. ◆ *vb* **lay by.** (*tr, adv*) **5** to set aside or save for future needs.

lay days *pl n* **1** *Commerce.* the number of days permitted for the loading or unloading of a ship without payment of demurrage. **2** *Naut.* the time during which a ship is kept from sailing because of loading, bad weather, etc.

lay down *vb* (*tr, adv*) **1** to place on the ground, etc. **2** to relinquish or discard: *to lay down one's life.* **3** to formulate (a rule, principle, etc.). **4** to build or begin to build: *the railway was laid down as far as Chester.* **5** to record (plans) on paper. **6** to convert (land) into pasture. **7** to store or

stock: *to lay down wine.* **8** *Inf.* to wager or bet. **9** *Inf.* to record (tracks) in a studio.

layer ('leɪə) *n* **1** a thickness of some relatively substance, such as a stratum or a coating on a surface. **2** a laying hen. **3** *Horticulture.* a shoot or branch rooted during layering. ◆ *vb* **4** to form or make a layer of (something). **5** to take root or cause to take root by layering. [C14 *leyer*, *legger*, from LAY[1] + -ER[1]]

layering ('leɪərɪŋ) *n* **1** *Horticulture.* a method of propagation that induces a shoot to take root while it is still attached to the parent plant. **2** *Geol.* the banded appearance of certain igneous rocks, each band being of a different mineral composition.

layette (leɪ'ɛt) *n* a complete set of articles, including clothing, bedclothes, and other accessories, for a newborn baby. [C19: from F, from OF, from *laie*, from MDu. *laege* box]

lay figure *n* **1** an artist's jointed dummy, used in place of a live model, esp. for studying effects of drapery. **2** a person considered to be subservient or unimportant. [C18: from obs. *layman*, from Du. *leeman*, lit.: joint-man]

lay in *vb* (*tr, adv*) to accumulate and store: *we must lay in food for the party.*

lay into *vb* (*intr, prep*) *Inf.* **1** to attack forcefully. **2** to berate severely.

layman ('leɪmən) *or* (*fem*) **laywoman** *n, pl* **laymen** *or* **laywomen.** **1** a person who is not a clergyman. **2** a person who does not have specialized or professional knowledge of a subject: *science for the layman.*

lay off *vb* **1** (*tr, adv*) to suspend from work with the intention of re-employing later: *the firm had to lay off 100 men.* **2** (*intr*) *Inf.* to leave (a person, thing, or activity) alone: *lay off me, will you!* **3** (*tr, adv*) to mark off the boundaries of. ◆ *n* **lay-off. 4** the act of suspending employees. **5** a period of imposed unemployment.

lay on *vb* (*tr, adv*) **1** to provide or supply: *to lay on entertainment.* **2** *Brit.* to install: *to lay on electricity.* **3 lay it on.** *Sl.* **3a** to exaggerate, esp. when flattering. **3b** to charge an exorbitant price. **3c** to punish or strike harshly.

lay out *vb* (*tr, adv*) **1** to arrange or spread out. **2** to prepare (a corpse) for burial or cremation. **3** to plan or contrive. **4** *Inf.* to spend (money), esp. lavishly. **5** *Inf.* to knock unconscious. ◆ *n* **layout. 6** the arrangement or plan of something, such as a building. **7** the arrangement of written material, photographs, or other artwork on an advertisement or page in a book, newspaper, etc. **8** a preliminary plan indicating this. **9** a drawing showing the relative disposition of parts in a machine, etc. **10** the act of laying out. **11** something laid out.

lay over *US.* ◆ *vb* (*adv*) **1** (*tr*) to postpone for future action. **2** (*intr*) to make a temporary stop in a journey. ◆ *n* **layover. 3** a break in a journey, esp. in waiting for a connection.

lay reader *n* **1** *Church of England.* a person licensed by a bishop to conduct religious services other than the Eucharist. **2** *RC Church.* a layman chosen from among the congregation to read the epistle at Mass.

lay up *vb* (*tr, adv*) **1** to store or reserve for future use. **2** (*usually passive*) *Inf.* to incapacitate or confine through illness.

lazar ('læzə) *n* an archaic word for **leper**. [C14: via OF and Med. L, after LAZARUS]

lazaretto (ˌlæzə'rɛtəʊ), **lazaret**, *or* **lazarette** (ˌlæzə'rɛt) *n, pl* **lazarettos, lazarets,** *or* **lazarettes. 1** Also called: **glory hole.** *Naut.* a small locker at the stern of a boat or a storeroom between decks of a ship. **2** Also called: **lazar house, pesthouse.** (formerly) a hospital for persons with infectious diseases, esp. leprosy. [C16: It., from *lazzaro* LAZAR]

Lazarus ★ ('læzərəs) *n New Testament.* **1** the brother of Mary and Martha, whom Jesus restored to life (John 11–12). **2** the beggar who lay at the gate of the rich man Dives in Jesus' parable (Luke 16:19–31).

laze (leɪz) *vb* **lazes, lazing, lazed. 1** (*intr*) to be indolent or lazy. **2** (*tr*; often foll. by *away*) to spend (time) in indolence. ◆ *n* **3** the act or an instance of idling. [C16: back formation from LAZY]

Lazio ★ ('lattsjo) n **1** a region of W central Italy, on the Tyrrhenian Sea: includes the plain of the lower Tiber, the reclaimed Pontine Marshes, and Campagne. Capital: Rome. Pop.: 5 185 316 (1994 est.). **2** the Italian name for **Latium**.

lazy ('leɪzɪ) adj **lazier, laziest. 1** not inclined to work or exertion. **2** conducive to or causing indolence. **3** moving in a languid or sluggish manner: a lazy river.   [C16: from ?]
▸ **'lazily** adv ▸ **'laziness** n

lazybones ('leɪzɪ,bəʊnz) n Inf. a lazy person.

lazy Susan n a revolving tray, often divided into sections, for holding condiments, etc.

lb abbrev. for: **1** pound (weight).   [L libra] **2** Cricket. leg bye.

LBJ ★ abbrev. for Lyndon Baines Johnson.

LBO abbrev. for leveraged buyout.

lbw Cricket. abbrev. for leg before wicket.

lc abbrev. for: **1** left centre (of a stage, etc.). **2** loco citato. [L: in the place cited] **3** Printing. lower case.

L/C, l/c, or **lc** abbrev. for letter of credit.

LCD abbrev. for: **1** liquid-crystal display. **2** Also: **lcd.** lowest common denominator.

LCJ (in Britain) abbrev. for Lord Chief Justice.

lcm or **LCM** abbrev. for lowest common multiple.

L/Cpl abbrev. for lance corporal.

LD abbrev. for lethal dose (esp. in **LD$_{50}$**). See **median lethal dose**.

LDL abbrev. for low-density lipoprotein.

L-dopa (,ɛl'dəʊpə) n a substance occurring naturally in the body and used to treat Parkinson's disease. Also called: **levodopa**.   [C20: from L-d(ihydr)o(xy)p(henyl)-a(lanine)]

LDS abbrev. for: **1** Latter-day Saints. **2** laus Deo semper. [L: praise be to God forever] **3** (in Britain) Licentiate in Dental Surgery.

lea (liː) n **1** Poetic. a meadow or field. **2** land that has been sown with grass seed.   [OE lēah]

LEA (in Britain) abbrev. for Local Education Authority.

leach (liːtʃ) vb **1** to remove or be removed from a substance by a percolating liquid. **2** to lose or cause to lose soluble substances by the action of a percolating liquid. ◆ n **3** the act or process of leaching. **4** a substance that is leached or the constituents removed by leaching. **5** a porous vessel for leaching.   [C17: var. of obs. letch to wet, ?from OE leccan to water]
▸ **'leacher** n

Leach ★ (liːtʃ) n Bernard (**Howell**). 1887–1979, British potter, born in Hong Kong.

Leacock ★ ('liːˌkɒk) n Stephen Butler. 1869–1944, Canadian humorist and economist: his comic works include Literary Lapses (1910) and Frenzied Fiction (1917).

lead (liːd) vb **leads, leading, led. 1** to show the way to (an individual or a group) by going with or ahead: lead the party into the garden. **2** to guide or be guided by holding, pulling, etc.: he led the horse by its reins. **3** (tr) to cause to act, feel, think, or behave in a certain way; induce; influence: he led me to believe that he would go. **4** (when intr, foll. by to) (of a road, route, etc.) to serve as the means of reaching a place. **5** (tr) to go ahead so as to indicate (esp. in **lead the way**). **6** to guide, control, or direct: to lead an army. **7** (tr) to direct the course of or conduct (water, a rope, or wire, etc.) along or as if along a channel. **8** to initiate the action of (something); have the principal part in (something): to lead a discussion. **9** to go at the head of or have the top position in (something): he leads his class in geography. **10** (intr; foll. by with) to have as the first or principal item: the newspaper led with the naval birth. **11** Music, Brit. to play first violin in (an orchestra). **12** to direct and guide (one's partner) in a dance. **13** (tr) **13a** to pass or spend: I lead a miserable life. **13b** to cause to pass a life of a particular kind: to lead a person a dog's life. **14** (intr; foll. by to) to tend (to) or result (in): this will only lead to misery. **15** to initiate a round of cards by putting down (the first card) or to have the right to do this: she led a diamond. **16** (intr) Boxing. to make an offensive blow, esp. as one's habitual attacking punch. ◆ n **17a** the first, foremost, or most prominent place. **17b** (as modifier): lead singer. **18** example, precedence, or leadership: the class followed the teacher's lead. **19** an advance or advantage held over others: the runner had a lead of twenty yards. **20** anything that guides or directs; indication; clue. **21** another name for **leash**. **22** the act or prerogative of playing the first card in a round of cards or the card so played. **23** the principal role in a play, film, etc., or the person playing such a role. **24a** the principal news story in a newspaper: the scandal was the lead in the papers. **24b** (as modifier): lead story. **25** Music. an important entry assigned to one part. **26** a wire, cable, or other conductor for making an electrical connection. **27** Boxing. **27a** one's habitual attacking punch. **27b** a blow made with this. **28** a deposit of metal or ore; lode. ◆ See also **lead off, lead on**, etc.   [OE lǣdan; rel. to līthan to travel]

lead² (lɛd) n **1** a heavy toxic bluish-white metallic element that is highly malleable: used in alloys, accumulators, cable sheaths, paints, and as a radiation shield. Symbol: Pb; atomic no.: 82; atomic wt.: 207.2. **2** a lead weight suspended on a line used to take soundings of the depth of water. **3** lead weights or shot, as used in cartridges, fishing lines, etc. **4** a thin grooved strip of lead for holding small panes of glass or pieces of stained glass. **5** (pl) **5a** thin sheets or strips of lead used as a roof covering. **5b** a flat or low-pitched roof covered with such sheets. **6** Also called: **leading**. Printing. a thin strip of type metal used for spacing between lines. **7a** graphite used for drawing. **7b** a thin stick of this material, esp. the core of a pencil. **8** (modifier) of, consisting of, relating to, or containing lead. ◆ vb (tr) **9** to fill or treat with lead. **10** to surround, cover, or secure with lead or leads. **11** Printing. to space (type) by use of leads.   [OE]

lead acetate (lɛd) n a white crystalline toxic solid used in dyeing cotton and in making varnishes and enamels. Formula: Pb(CH$_3$COOH)$_2$. Systematic name: **lead ethanoate**.

Leadbelly ★ ('lɛd,bɛlɪ) n, real name Huddie Ledbetter. 1888–1949, US blues singer and guitarist.

lead chromate (lɛd) n Chem. a yellow solid used as a pigment, as in chrome yellow. Formula: PbCrO$_4$.

leaded ('lɛdɪd) adj (of windows) composed of small panes of glass held in place by thin grooved strips of lead: leaded lights.

leaden ('lɛdᵊn) adj **1** heavy and inert. **2** laboured or sluggish: leaden steps. **3** gloomy, spiritless, or lifeless. **4** made partly or wholly of lead. **5** of a dull greyish colour: a leaden sky.
▸ **'leadenly** adv ▸ **'leadenness** n

leader ('liːdə) n **1** a person who rules, guides, or inspires others; head. **2** Music. **2a** Also called (esp. US and Canad.): **concertmaster**. the principal first violinist of an orchestra, who plays solo parts, and acts as the conductor's deputy and spokesman for the orchestra. **2b** US. a conductor or director of an orchestra or chorus. **3a** the leading horse or dog in a team. **3b** the first man on a climbing rope. **4** Chiefly Brit. the leading editorial in a newspaper. Also: **leading article. 5** Angling. another word for **trace²** (sense 2). **6** a strip of blank film or tape used to facilitate threading a projector, developing machine, etc. **7** (pl) Printing. rows of dots or hyphens used to guide the reader's eye across a page, as in a table of contents. **8** Bot. any of the long slender shoots that grow from the stem or branch of a tree. **9** Brit. a member of the Government having primary authority in initiating legislative business (esp. in **Leader of the House of Commons** and **Leader of the House of Lords**).
▸ **'leaderless** adj

leadership ('liːdəʃɪp) n **1** the position or function of a leader. **2** the period during which a person occupies the position of leader: during her leadership very little was achieved. **3a** the ability to lead. **3b** (as modifier): leadership qualities. **4** the leaders as a group of a party, union, etc.: the union leadership is now very reactionary.

lead-free (,lɛd'friː) adj See **unleaded**.

lead glass (lɛd) n glass that contains lead oxide as a flux.

lead-in ('liːd,ɪn) n **1** an introduction to a subject. **2** the connection between a radio transmitter, receiver, etc., and the aerial or transmission line.

leading¹ ('liːdɪŋ) adj **1** guiding, directing, or influencing.

2 (*prenominal*) principal or primary. **3** in the first position.

leading[2] ('lɛdɪŋ) *n Printing.* **1** the spacing between lines of photocomposed or digitized type. **2** another name for **lead**[2] (sense 6). ♦ Also called: **interlinear spacing**.

leading aircraftman ('liːdɪŋ) *n Brit. airforce.* the rank above aircraftman.
▶ **leading aircraftwoman** *fem n*

leading edge ('liːdɪŋ) *n* **1** the forward edge of a propeller blade, wing, or aerofoil. Cf. **trailing edge**. **2** *Electrical engineering.* the part of a pulse signal that has an increasing amplitude. ♦ *modifier.* **leading-edge**. **3** advanced; foremost: *leading-edge technology*.

leading light ('liːdɪŋ) *n* an important or outstanding person, esp. in an organization.

leading note ('liːdɪŋ) *n Music.* **1** another word for **subtonic**. **2** (esp. in cadences) a note that tends most naturally to resolve to the note lying one semitone above it.

leading question ('liːdɪŋ) *n* a question phrased in a manner that tends to suggest the desired answer, such as *What do you think of the horrible effects of pollution?*

leading rating ('liːdɪŋ) *n* a rank in the Royal Navy comparable but junior to that of a corporal in the army.

leading reins or *US & Canad.* **leading strings** ('liːdɪŋ) *pl n* **1** straps or a harness and strap used to assist and control a child who is learning to walk. **2** excessive guidance or restraint.

lead monoxide (lɛd) *n* a poisonous insoluble oxide of lead existing in red and yellow forms: used in making glass, glazes, and cements, and as a pigment. Formula: PbO. Systematic name: **lead(II) oxide**.

lead off (liːd) *vb* (*adv*) **1** to initiate the action of (something); begin. ♦ *n* **lead-off**. **2** an initial move or action.

lead on (liːd) *vb* (*tr, adv*) to lure or entice, esp. into trouble or wrongdoing.

lead pencil (lɛd) *n* a pencil containing a thin stick of a graphite compound.

lead poisoning (lɛd) *n* **1** acute or chronic poisoning by lead, characterized by abdominal pain, vomiting, convulsions, and coma. **2** *US sl.* death or injury resulting from being shot with bullets.

lead screw (liːd) *n* a threaded rod that drives the tool carriage in a lathe.

lead tetraethyl (lɛd) *n* another name for **tetraethyl lead**.

lead time (liːd) *n* **1** *Manufacturing, chiefly US.* the time between the design of a product and its production. **2** *Commerce.* the time from the placing of an order to the delivery of the goods.

lead up to (liːd) *vb* (*intr, adv + prep*) **1** to act as a preliminary or introduction to. **2** to approach (a topic) gradually or cautiously.

leaf (liːf) *n, pl* **leaves** (liːvz). **1** the main organ of photosynthesis and transpiration in higher plants, usually consisting of a flat green blade attached to the stem directly or by a stalk. **2** foliage collectively. **3 in leaf.** (of shrubs, trees, etc.) having a full complement of foliage leaves. **4** one of the sheets of paper in a book. **5** a hinged, sliding, or detachable part, such as an extension to a table. **6** metal in the form of a very thin flexible sheet: *gold leaf.* **7 take a leaf out of** (or **from**) **someone's book.** to imitate someone, esp. in one particular course of action. **8 turn over a new leaf.** to begin a new and improved course of behaviour. ♦ *vb* **9** (when *intr*, usually foll. by *through*) to turn (through pages, sheets, etc.) cursorily. **10** (*intr*) (of plants) to produce leaves. [OE]
▶ '**leafless** *adj* ▶ '**leaf,like** *adj*

leafage ('liːfɪdʒ) *n* a less common word for **foliage**.

leaflet ('liːflɪt) *n* **1** a printed and usually folded sheet of paper for distribution, usually free, esp. for advertising, giving information about a charity, etc. **2** any of the subdivisions of a compound leaf such as a fern leaf. **3** any small leaf or leaflike part. ♦ *vb* **leaflets, leafleting, leafleted.** **4** to distribute leaflets (to).

leaf miner *n* **1** any of various insect larvae that bore into and feed on leaf tissue. **2** the adult insect of any of these larvae.

leaf mould *n* **1** a nitrogen-rich material consisting of decayed leaves, etc., used as a fertilizer. **2** any of various fungus diseases affecting the leaves of certain plants.

leaf spring *n* **1** one of a number of metal strips bracketed together in length to form a spring. **2** the compound spring so formed.

leafstalk ('liːf,stɔːk) *n* the stalk attaching a leaf to a stem or branch. Technical name: **petiole**.

leafy ('liːfɪ) *adj* **leafier, leafiest.** **1** covered with or having leaves. **2** resembling a leaf or leaves.
▶ '**leafiness** *n*

league[1] (liːg) *n* **1** an association or union of persons, nations, etc., formed to promote the interests of its members. **2** an association of sporting clubs that organizes matches between member teams. **3** a class, category, or level: *he is not in the same league.* **4 in league** (**with**). working or planning together with. **5** (*modifier*) of, involving, or belonging to a league: *a league game; a league table.* ♦ *vb* **leagues, leaguing, leagued.** **6** to form or be formed into a league. [C15: from OF *ligue*, from It. *liga*, ult. from L *ligāre* to bind]

league[2] (liːg) *n* an obsolete unit of distance of varying length. It is commonly equal to 3 miles. [C14 *leuge*, from LL *leuga, leuca*, of Celtic origin]

league football *n* **1** Also called: **league.** *Chiefly Austral.* rugby league football. Cf. **rugby union**. **2** *Austral.* an Australian Rules competition conducted within a league.

leaguer ('liːgə) *n Chiefly US & Canad.* a member of a league.

league table *n* **1** a list of sports clubs ranked in order according to their performance. **2** a comparison of performance in any sphere.

Leah ★ ('liːə) *n Old Testament.* the first wife of Jacob and elder sister of Rachel, his second wife (Genesis 29).

leak (liːk) *n* **1a** a crack, hole, etc., that allows the accidental escape or entrance of fluid, light, etc. **1b** such escaping or entering fluid, light, etc. **2 spring a leak.** to develop a leak. **3** something resembling this in effect: *a leak in the defence system.* **4** the loss of current from an electrical conductor because of faulty insulation, etc. **5** a disclosure of secret information. **6** the act or an instance of leaking. **7** a slang word for **urination**. ♦ *vb* **8** to enter or escape or allow to enter or escape through a crack, hole, etc. **9** (when *intr*, often foll. by *out*) to disclose (secret information) or (of secret information) to be disclosed. **10** (*intr*) a slang word for **urinate**. [C15: from ON]
▶ '**leaker** *n*

leakage ('liːkɪdʒ) *n* **1** the act or an instance of leaking. **2** something that escapes or enters by a leak. **3** *Physics.* an undesired flow of electric current, neutrons, etc.

Leakey ★ ('liːkɪ) *n* **1** Louis Seymour Bazett ('bæzɪt). 1903–72, British anthropologist and archaeologist, settled in Kenya; discovered remains of manlike apes. **2** his son, **Richard.** born 1944, Kenyan anthropologist; discovered the remains of primitive man over 2 million years old.

leaky ('liːkɪ) *adj* **leakier, leakiest.** leaking or tending to leak.
▶ '**leakiness** *n*

leal (liːl) *adj Arch. or Scot.* loyal; faithful. [C13: from OF *leial*, from L *lēgālis* LEGAL; rel. to LOYAL]
▶ '**leally** *adv* ▶ **lealty** ('liːltɪ) *n*

Leamington Spa ★ ('lɛmɪŋtən) *n* a town in central England, in central Warwickshire: saline springs. Pop.: 55 396 (1991). Official name: **Royal Leamington Spa**.

lean[1] (liːn) *vb* **leans, leaning, leaned** or **leant**. **1** (foll. by *against, on,* or *upon*) to rest or cause to rest against a support. **2** to incline or cause to incline from a vertical position. **3** (*intr*; foll. by *to* or *towards*) to have or express a tendency or leaning. ♦ *n* **4** the condition of inclining from a vertical position. [OE *hleonian, hlinian*]

lean[2] (liːn) *adj* **1** (esp. of a person or animal) having no surplus flesh or bulk; not fat. **2** not bulky or full. **3** (of meat) having little or no fat. **4** not rich, abundant, or satisfying. **5** (of mixture of fuel and air) containing insufficient fuel and too much air. ♦ *n* **6** the part of meat that contains little or no fat. [OE *hlǣne*, of Gmc origin]
▶ '**leanly** *adv* ▶ '**leanness** *n*

Lean ★ (liːn) *n* Sir **David.** 1908–91, British film director.

His films include *Brief Encounter* (1946), *Oliver Twist* (1948), *The Bridge on the River Kwai* (1957), *Lawrence of Arabia* (1962), *Dr Zhivago* (1965), and *A Passage to India* (1984).

lean-burn *adj* (esp. of an internal-combustion engine) designed to use a lean mixture of fuel and air in order to reduce petrol consumption and exhaust emissions.

Leander ★ (lɪˈændə) *n* (in Greek legend) a youth of Abydos, who drowned in the Hellespont in a storm on one of his nightly visits to Hero, his beloved. See also **Hero**[1].

leaning (ˈliːnɪŋ) *n* a tendency or inclination.

leant (lɛnt) *vb* a past tense and past participle of **lean**[1].

lean-to *n, pl* **lean-tos. 1** a roof that has a single slope adjoining a wall or building. **2** a shed or outbuilding with such a roof.

leap (liːp) *vb* **leaps, leaping, leapt** *or* **leaped. 1** (*intr*) to jump suddenly from one place to another. **2** (*intr;* often foll. by *at*) to move or react quickly. **3** (*tr*) to jump over. **4** to come into prominence rapidly: *the thought leapt into his mind.* **5** (*tr*) to cause (an animal, esp. a horse) to jump a barrier. ◆ *n* **6** the act of jumping. **7** a spot from which a leap was or may be made. **8** an abrupt change or increase. **9 a leap in the dark.** an action performed without knowledge of the consequences. **10 by leaps and bounds.** with unexpectedly rapid progress. [OE *hlēapan*] ▸ **ˈleaper** *n*

leapfrog (ˈliːpˌfrɒg) *n* **1** a children's game in which each player in turn leaps over the others' bent backs. ◆ *vb* **leapfrogs, leapfrogging, leapfrogged. 2a** (*intr*) to play leapfrog. **2b** (*tr*) to leap in this way over (something). **3** to advance or cause to advance by jumps or stages.

leap second *n* a second added to or removed from a scale for reckoning time on one particular occasion, to synchronize it with another scale.

leapt (lɛpt, liːpt) *vb* a past tense and past participle of **leap**.

leap year *n* a calendar year of 366 days, February 29 (**leap day**) being the additional day, that occurs every four years (those whose number is divisible by four) except for century years whose number is not divisible by 400.

Lear ★ (lɪə) *n* Edward. 1812–88, British humorist and painter, noted for his illustrated nonsense poems and limericks.

learn (lɜːn) *vb* **learns, learning, learned** (lɜːnd) *or* **learnt. 1** (when *tr,* may take a clause as object) to gain knowledge of (something) or acquire skill in (some art or practice). **2** (*tr*) to commit to memory. **3** (*tr*) to gain by experience, example, etc. **4** (*intr;* often foll. by *of* or *about*) to become informed; know. **5** *Not standard.* to teach. [OE *leornian*] ▸ **ˈlearnable** *adj* ▸ **ˈlearner** *n*

learned (ˈlɜːnɪd) *adj* **1** having great knowledge or erudition. **2** involving or characterized by scholarship. **3** (*prenominal*) a title applied in referring to a member of the legal profession, esp. to a barrister: *my learned friend.* ▸ **ˈlearnedly** *adv* ▸ **ˈlearnedness** *n*

learning (ˈlɜːnɪŋ) *n* **1** knowledge gained by study; instruction or scholarship. **2** the act of gaining knowledge.

learning curve *n* a graphical representation of progress in learning: *I'm still only halfway up the learning curve.*

learnt (lɜːnt) *vb* a past tense and past participle of **learn**.

lease (liːs) *n* **1** a contract by which property is conveyed to a person for a specified period, usually for rent. **2** the instrument by which such property is conveyed. **3** the period of time for which it is conveyed. **4** a prospect of renewed health, happiness, etc.: *a new lease of life.* ◆ *vb* **leases, leasing, leased.** (*tr*) **5** to grant possession of (land, buildings, etc.) by lease. **6** to take a lease of (property); hold under a lease. [C15: via Anglo-F from OF *lais* (n), from *laissier* to let go, from L *laxāre* to loosen] ▸ **ˈleasable** *adj* ▸ **ˈleaser** *n*

leaseback (ˈliːsˌbæk) *n* a transaction in which the buyer leases the property to the seller.

leasehold (ˈliːsˌhəʊld) *n* **1** land or property held under a lease. **2** the tenure by which such property is held. **3** (*modifier*) held under a lease. ▸ **ˈleaseˌholder** *n*

leash (liːʃ) *n* **1** a line or rope used to walk or control a dog or other animal; lead. **2** something resembling this in function: *he kept a tight leash on his emotions.* **3 straining at the leash.** eagerly impatient to begin something. ◆ *vb* **4** (*tr*) to control or secure as by a leash. [C13: from OF *laisse,* from *laissier* to loose (hence, to let a dog run on a leash), ult. from L *laxus* lax]

least (liːst) *determiner* **1a the.** the superlative of **little:** *you have the least talent of anyone.* **1b** (*as pronoun; functioning as sing*): *least isn't necessarily worst.* **2 at least. 2a** if nothing else: *you should at least try.* **2b** at the least. **3 at least.** Also: **at least.** at the minimum: *at the least you should earn a hundred pounds.* **4 in the least.** (*usually used with a negative*) in the slightest degree; at all: *I don't mind in the least.* ◆ *adv* **5 the least.** superlative of **little:** *they travel the least.* ◆ *adj* **6** of very little importance. [OE *læst,* sup. of *læssa* less]

least common denominator *n* another name for **lowest common denominator.**

least common multiple *n* another name for **lowest common multiple.**

least squares *n* a method for determining the best value of an unknown quantity relating one or more sets of observations or measurements, esp. to find a curve that best fits a set of data.

leastways (ˈliːstˌweɪz) *or* US & Canad. **leastwise** *adv Inf.* at least; anyway; at any rate.

least-worst *adj Inf.* bad but better than any available alternative: *a least-worst scenario.*

leather (ˈlɛðə) *n* **1a** a material consisting of the skin of an animal made smooth and flexible by tanning, removing the hair, etc. **1b** (*as modifier*): *leather goods.* **2** (*pl*) leather clothes, esp. as worn by motorcyclists. ◆ *vb* (*tr*) **3** to cover with leather. **4** to whip as with a leather strap. [OE *lether-* (in compound words)]

Leatherhead ★ (ˈlɛðəˌhɛd) *n* a town in S England, in Surrey. Pop.: 42 903 (1991).

leatherjacket (ˈlɛðəˌdʒækɪt) *n* **1** any of various tropical fishes having a leathery skin. **2** the greyish-brown tough-skinned larva of certain craneflies, which destroy the roots of grasses, etc.

leathern (ˈlɛðən) *adj Arch.* made of or resembling leather.

leatherneck (ˈlɛðəˌnɛk) *n Sl.* a member of the US Marine Corps. [from the custom of facing the neckband of their uniform with leather]

leathery (ˈlɛðərɪ) *adj* having the appearance or texture of leather, esp. in toughness. ▸ **ˈleatheriness** *n*

leave[1] (liːv) *vb* **leaves, leaving, left.** (*mainly tr*) **1** (*also intr*) to go or depart (from a person or place). **2** to cause to remain behind, often by mistake, in or about: *he often leaves his keys in his coat.* **3** to cause to be or remain in a specified state: *paying the bill left him penniless.* **4** to renounce or abandon: *to leave a political movement.* **5** to refrain from consuming or doing something: *the things we have left undone.* **6** to result in; cause: *childhood problems often leave emotional scars.* **7** to entrust or commit: *leave the shopping to her.* **8** to pass in a specified direction: *flying out of the country, we left the cliffs on our left.* **9** to be survived by (members of one's family): *he leaves a wife and two children.* **10** to bequeath: *he left his investments to his children.* **11** (*tr*) to have as a remainder: *37 – 14 leaves 23.* **12** *Not standard.* to permit; let. **13 leave (someone) alone. 13a** Also: **let alone.** See **let**[1] (sense 6). **13b** to permit to stay or be alone. [OE *lǣfan;* rel. to *belīfan* to be left as a remainder] ◆ See also **leave off, leave out.** ▸ **ˈleaver** *n*

leave[2] (liːv) *n* **1** permission to do something: *he was granted leave to speak.* **2 by** or **with your leave.** with your permission. **3** permission to be absent, as from a place of work: *leave of absence.* **4** the duration of such absence: *ten days' leave.* **5** a farewell or departure (esp. in **take (one's) leave**). **6 on leave.** officially excused from work or duty. **7 take leave (of).** to say farewell (to). [OE *lēaf;* rel. to *alȳfan* to permit]

leave[3] (liːv) *vb* **leaves, leaving, leaved.** (*intr*) to produce or grow leaves.

★ people and places

leaved (li:vd) *adj* **a** having a leaf or leaves; leafed. **b** (*in combination*): *a five-leaved stem.*

leaven ('lɛvᵊn) *n also* **leavening.** **1** any substance that produces fermentation in dough or batter, such as yeast, and causes it to rise. **2** a piece of such a substance kept to ferment a new batch of dough. **3** an agency or influence that produces a gradual change. ◆ *vb* (*tr*) **4** to cause fermentation in (dough or batter). **5** to pervade, causing a gradual change, esp. with some moderating or enlivening influence. [C14: via OF ult. from L *levāmen* relief, (hence, raising agent), from *levāre* to raise]

Leavenworth ★ ('lɛvᵊn,wɜːθ, -wəθ) *n* a city in NE Kansas, on the Missouri River: the state's oldest city, founded in 1854 by proslavery settlers from Missouri. Pop.: 38 495 (1990).

leave off *vb* **1** (*intr*) to stop; cease. **2** (*tr, adv*) to stop wearing or using.

leave out *vb* (*tr, adv*) **1** to cause to remain in the open. **2** to omit or exclude.

leaves (li:vz) *n* the plural of **leaf.**

leave-taking *n* the act of departing; a farewell.

leavings ('li:vɪŋz) *pl n* something remaining, such as food on a plate, residue, refuse, etc.

Leavis ★ ('li:vɪs) *n* F(rank) R(aymond). 1895–1978, British literary critic. He edited *Scrutiny* (1932–53) and his books include *The Great Tradition* (1948).
► **'Leavis,ite** *adj, n*

Lebanon ★ ('lɛbənən) *n* (sometimes preceded by *the*) a republic in W Asia, on the Mediterranean: an important centre of the Phoenician civilization in the third millennium B.C.; part of the Ottoman Empire from 1516 until 1919; gained independence in 1941 (effective by 1945). Official language: Arabic; French and English are also widely spoken. Religion: Muslim and Christian. Currency: Lebanese pound. Capital: Beirut. Pop.: 3 112 000 (1997). Area: 10 400 sq. km (4015 sq. miles).
► **Lebanese** (,lɛbə'ni:z) *adj, n*

Lebanon Mountains ★ *pl n* a mountain range in central Lebanon, extending across the whole country parallel with the Mediterranean coast. Highest peak: 3104 m (10 184 ft). Arabic name: **Jebel Liban** ('dʒɛbᵊl 'li:bɑ:n).

Lebensraum ('leɪbənz,raum) *n* territory claimed by a nation or state as necessary for survival or growth. [G, lit.: living space]

Leblanc ★ (*French* ləblɑ̃) *n* **Nicolas** (nikɔla). ?1742–1806, French chemist, who invented a process for the manufacture of soda from common salt.

Lebrun ★ (*French* ləbrœ̃) *n* **1 Albert** (albɛr). 1871–1950, French statesman; president (1932–40). **2** Also: **Le Brun. Charles** (ʃarl). 1619–90, French historical painter.

LEC (lɛk) *n acronym for* Local Enterprise Company. See **Training Agency.**

Le Carré (lə 'kæreɪ) ★ *n* **John,** real name *David John Cornwell.* born 1931, British novelist, esp. of such spy thrillers as *The Spy who came in from the Cold* (1963), *Tinker, Tailor, Soldier, Spy* (1974), and *The Tailor of Panama* (1996).

Lecce ★ (*Italian* 'lɛttʃe) *n* a walled city in SE Italy, in Puglia: Greek and Roman remains. Pop.: 100 474 (1994 est.).

lech (lɛtʃ) *Inf.* ◆ *vb* **1** (*intr;* usually foll. by *after*) to behave lecherously (towards); lust (after). ◆ *n* **2** a lecherous act or indulgence. [C19: back formation from LECHER]

Lech ★ (lɛk; *German* lɛç) *n* a river in central Europe, rising in SW Austria and flowing generally north through S Germany to the River Danube. Length: 285 km (177 miles).

lecher ('lɛtʃə) *n* a promiscuous or lewd man. [C12: from OF *lecheor,* from *lechier* to lick, of Gmc origin]

lecherous ('lɛtʃərəs) *adj* characterized by or inciting lechery.
► **'lecherously** *adv*

lechery ('lɛtʃərɪ) *n, pl* **lecheries.** unrestrained and promiscuous sexuality.

lecithin ('lɛsɪθɪn) *n Biochem.* any of a group of phospholipids that are found in many plant and animal

tissues, esp. egg yolk: used in making candles, cosmetics, and inks, and as an emulsifier and stabilizer (**E322**) in foods. Systematic name: **phosphatidycholine.** [C19: from Gk *lekithos* egg yolk]

lecky ('lɛkɪ) *n Brit. sl.* short for **electricity.**

Lecky ★ ('lɛkɪ) *n* **William Edward Hartpole.** 1838–1903, Irish historian; author of *The History of England in the 18th Century* (1878–90).

Leclanché cell (lə'klɑ:nʃeɪ) *n Electrical engineering.* a primary cell with a carbon anode, surrounded by crushed carbon and manganese dioxide in a porous container in an electrolyte of aqueous ammonium chloride into which a zinc cathode dips. [C19: after Georges *Leclanché* (1839–82), F engineer]

Leconte de Lisle ★ (*French* ləkɔ̃t də lil) *n* **Charles Marie René** (ʃarl mari rəne). 1818–94, French Parnassian poet.

Le Corbusier ★ (*French* lə kɔrbyzje) *n* real name *Charles Édouard Jeanneret.* 1887–1965, French architect and town planner, born in Switzerland. He is noted for his modular system. His works include Unité d'Habitation at Marseilles (1946–52) and the city of Chandigarh, India (1954).

Le Creusot ★ (*French* lə krøzo) *n* a town in E central France: metal, machinery, and armaments industries. Pop.: 33 274 (1983 est.).

lectern ('lɛktən) *n* **1** a reading desk in a church. **2** any similar desk or support. [C14: from OF *lettrun,* from LL *lectrum,* ult. from *legere* to read]

lectionary ('lɛkʃənərɪ) *n, pl* **lectionaries.** a book containing readings appointed to be read at divine services. [C15: from Church L *lectiōnārium,* from *lectio* a reading, from *legere* to read]

lector ('lɛktɔ:) *n* **1** a lecturer or reader in certain universities. **2** *RC Church.* **2a** a person appointed to read lessons at certain services. **2b** (in convents or monastic establishments) a member of the community appointed to read aloud during meals. [C15: from L, from *legere* to read]

lecture ('lɛktʃə) *n* **1** a discourse on a particular subject given or read to an audience. **2** the text of such a discourse. **3** a method of teaching by formal discourse. **4** a lengthy reprimand or scolding. ◆ *vb* **lectures, lecturing, lectured.** **5** to give or read a lecture (to an audience or class). **6** (*tr*) to reprimand at length. [C14: from Med. L *lectūra* reading, from *legere* to read]
► **'lecturer** *n* ► **'lectureship** *n*

led (lɛd) *vb* the past tense and past participle of **lead**¹.

LED *Electronics. abbrev. for* light-emitting diode.

Leda ★ ('li:də) *n* **1** *Greek myth.* a queen of Sparta who was the mother of Helen and Pollux by Zeus, who visited her in the form of a swan.

Lederberg ★ ('leɪdə,bɜ:g) *n* **Joshua.** born 1925, US geneticist, who discovered genetic recombination in bacteria. Nobel prize for physiology or medicine 1958 with George Beadle and Edward Tatum.

lederhosen ('leɪdə,həuzᵊn) *pl n* leather shorts with H-shaped braces, worn by men in Austria, Bavaria, etc. [G]

ledge (lɛdʒ) *n* **1** a narrow horizontal surface resembling a shelf and projecting from a wall, window, etc. **2** a layer of rock that contains an ore; vein. **3** a ridge of rock that lies beneath the surface of the sea. **4** a narrow shelflike projection on a cliff or mountain. [C14 *legge,* ?from *leggen* to LAY¹]
► **'ledgy** or **ledged** *adj*

ledger ('lɛdʒə) *n* **1** *Book-keeping.* the principal book in which the commercial transactions of a company are recorded. **2** *Angling.* a wire trace that allows the weight to rest on the bottom and the bait to float freely. ◆ *vb* **3** (*intr*) *Angling.* to fish using a ledger. [C15 *legger* book retained in a specific place, prob. from *leggen* to LAY¹]

ledger line *n Music.* a short line placed above or below the staff to accommodate notes representing pitches above or below the staff.

lee (li:) *n* **1** a sheltered part or side; the side away from the direction from which the wind is blowing. ◆ *adj* **2** (*prenominal*) *Naut.* on, at, or towards the side or part away from the wind: *on a lee shore.* Cf. **weather** (sense 4). [OE *hlēow* shelter]

Lee[1] ★ (liː) *n* a river in SW Republic of Ireland, flowing east into Cork Harbour. Length: about 80 km (50 miles).

Lee[2] ★ (liː) *n* **1 Laurie** ('lɒrɪ). 1914–97, British writer, best known for the autobiographical novel *Cider with Rosie* (1959) and several volumes of poetry. **2 Richard Henry.** 1732–94, American Revolutionary statesman, who moved the resolution in favour of American independence (1776). **3 Robert E(dward).** 1807–70, American general; commander-in-chief of the Confederate armies in the Civil War. **4 Spike**, real name *Shelton Jackson Lee.* born 1957, US film director: his films include *Malcolm X* (1992) and *He Got Game* (1998). **5 T(sung)-D(ao)** ('tsuːŋ'daʊ). born 1926, US physicist, born in China. With Yang he disproved the principle that parity is always conserved and shared the Nobel prize for physics in 1957.

leech[1] (liːtʃ) *n* **1** an annelid worm which has a sucker at each end of the body and feeds on the blood or tissues of other animals. **2** a person who clings to or preys on another person. **3a** an archaic word for **physician. 3b** (*in combination*): *leechcraft.* ◆ *vb* (*tr*) **4** to use leeches to suck the blood of (a person), as a method of medical treatment. [OE *lǣce, lœce*]

leech[2] (liːtʃ) *n Naut.* the after edge of a fore-and-aft sail or either of the vertical edges of a squaresail. [C15: of Gmc origin]

Leeds ★ (liːdz) *n* **1** a city in N England, in West Yorkshire on the River Aire: linked with Liverpool and Goole by canals; a former centre of the clothing industry; university (1904). Pop.: 424 194 (1991). **2** a unitary authority in N England, in West Yorkshire. Pop.: 724 400 (1994 est.). Area: 562 sq. km (217 sq. miles).

leek (liːk) *n* **1** a vegetable with a slender white bulb, cylindrical stem, and broad flat overlapping leaves. **2** a leek, or a representation of one, as a national emblem of Wales. [OE *lēac*]

leer (lɪə) *vb* **1** (*intr*) to give an oblique, sneering, or suggestive look or grin. ◆ *n* **2** such a look. [C16: ? verbal use of obs. *leer* cheek, from OE *hlēor*]
▸ **'leering** *adj, n* ▸ **'leeringly** *adv*

leery ('lɪərɪ) *adj* **leerier, leeriest. 1** *Now chiefly dialect.* knowing or sly. **2** *Sl.* (foll. by *of*) suspicious or wary. [C18: ?from obs. sense (to look askance) of LEER]
▸ **'leeriness** *n*

lees (liːz) *pl n* the sediment from an alcoholic drink. [C14: pl of obs. *lee,* from OF, prob. from Celtic]

leet (liːt) *n Scot.* a list of candidates for an office. [C15: ?from Anglo-F *litte,* var. of LIST[1]]

Leeuwarden ★ (*Dutch* 'leːwardə) *n* a city in the N Netherlands, capital of Friesland province. Pop.: 87 464 (1994).

Leeuwenhoek ★ ('leɪvˀn,huːk; *Dutch* 'leːwənhuːk) *n* **Anton van** ('ɑntɔn vɑn). 1632–1723, Dutch microscopist, who provided the first accurate description of blood corpuscles, spermatozoa, and microbes.

leeward ('liːwəd; *Naut.* 'luːəd) *Chiefly naut.* ◆ *adj* **1** of, in, or moving to the quarter towards which the wind blows. ◆ *n* **2** the point or quarter towards which the wind blows. **3** the side towards the lee. ◆ *adv* **4** towards the lee. ◆ Cf. **windward.**

Leeward Islands ★ ('liːwəd) *pl n* **1** a group of islands in the Caribbean, in the N Lesser Antilles between Puerto Rico and Martinique. **2** a former British colony in the E West Indies (1871–1956), consisting of Antigua, Barbuda, Redonda, Saint Kitts, Nevis, Anguilla, Montserrat, and the British Virgin Islands. **3** a group of islands in the S Pacific, in French Polynesia in the W Society Archipelago: Huahiné, Raiatéa, Tahaa, Bora-Bora, and Maupiti. Pop.: 22 232 (1988). French name: **Îles sous le Vent.**

lee wave *n Meteorol.* a stationary wave sometimes formed in an air stream on the leeward side of a hill or mountain range.

leeway ('liː,weɪ) *n* **1** room for free movement within limits, as in action or expenditure. **2** sideways drift of a boat or aircraft.

Le Fanu ★ ('lɛfə,njuː) *n* (**Joseph**) **Sheridan**. 1814–73, Irish writer, best known for his stories of mystery and the supernatural, esp. *Uncle Silas* (1864) and the collection *In a Glass Darkly* (1872).

Lefkoşa ★ (lɛf'kɔʃə) *n* the Turkish name for **Nicosia.**

left[1] (lɛft) *adj* **1** (*usually prenominal*) of or designating the side of something or someone that faces west when the front is turned towards the north. **2** (*usually prenominal*) worn on a left hand, foot, etc. **3** (*sometimes cap.*) of or relating to the political left. **4** (*sometimes cap.*) radical or progressive. ◆ *adv* **5** on or in the direction of the left. ◆ *n* **6** a left side, direction, position, area, or part. Related adjs.: **sinister, sinistral. 7** (*often cap.*) the supporters or advocates of varying degrees of social, political, or economic change, reform, or revolution. **8** *Boxing.* **8a** a blow with the left hand. **8b** the left hand. [OE *left* idle, weak, var. of *lyft-* (in *lyftādl* palsy, lit.: left-disease)]

left[2] (lɛft) *vb* the past tense and past participle of **leave**[1].

Left Bank ★ *n* a district of Paris, on the S bank of the River Seine; frequented by artists, students, etc.

left-hand *adj* (*prenominal*) **1** of, relating to, located on, or moving towards the left. **2** for use by the left hand; left-handed.

left-handed *adj* **1** using the left hand with greater ease than the right. **2** performed with the left hand. **3** designed or adapted for use by the left hand. **4** awkward or clumsy. **5** ironically ambiguous: *a left-handed compliment.* **6** turning from right to left; anticlockwise. ◆ *adv* **7** with the left hand.
▸ ,left-'handedly *adv* ▸ ,left-'handedness *n* ▸ ,left-'hander *n*

leftist ('lɛftɪst) *adj* **1** of, tending towards, or relating to the political left or its principles. ◆ *n* **2** a person who supports or belongs to the political left.
▸ **'leftism** *n*

left-luggage office *n Brit.* a place at a railway station, etc., where luggage may be left for a small charge. US and Canad. name: **checkroom.**

leftover ('lɛft,əʊvə) *n* **1** (*often pl*) an unused portion or remnant, as of material or of cooked food. ◆ *adj* **2** left as an unused portion.

leftward ('lɛftwəd) *adj* **1** on or towards the left. ◆ *adv* **2** a variant of **leftwards.**

leftwards ('lɛftwədz) *or* **leftward** *adv* towards or on the left.

left wing *n* **1** (*often cap.*) the leftist faction of an assembly, party, group, etc.; the radical or progressive wing. **2** *Sport.* **2a** the left-hand side of the field of play from the point of view of either team facing its opponents' goal. **2b** a player positioned in this area in certain games. ◆ *adj* **left-wing. 3** of, belonging to, or relating to the political left wing.
▸ ,left-'winger *n*

lefty ('lɛftɪ) *n, pl* **lefties.** *Inf.* **1** a left-winger. **2** *Chiefly US & Canad.* a left-handed person.

leg (lɛg) *n* **1** either of the two lower limbs in humans, or any similar or analogous structure in animals that is used for locomotion or support. **2** this part of an animal, esp. the thigh, used for food: *leg of lamb.* **3** something similar to a leg in appearance or function, such as one of the four supporting members of a chair. **4** a branch, limb, or part of a forked or jointed object. **5** the part of a garment that covers the leg. **6** a section or part of a journey or course. **7** a single stage, lap, length, etc., in a relay race. **8** either the opposite or adjacent side of a right-angled triangle. **9** one of a series of games, matches, or parts of games. **10** *Austral. & NZ.* either one of two races on which a cumulative bet has been placed. **11** *Cricket.* **11a** the side of the field to the left of a right-handed batsman as he faces the bowler. **11b** (*as modifier*): *a leg slip; a leg stump.* **12 not have a leg to stand on.** *Inf.* to have no reasonable or logical basis for an opinion or argument. **13 on his, its,** etc., **last legs.** (of a person or thing) worn out; exhausted. **14 pull** (**someone's**) **leg.** *Inf.* to tease, fool, or make fun of (someone). **15 shake a leg.** *Inf.* to hurry up: usually used in the imperative. **16 stretch one's legs.** to stand up and walk around, esp. after sitting for some time. ◆ *vb* **legs,**

legging, legged. 17 leg it. *Inf.* to walk, run, or hurry. [C13: from ON *leggr*, from ?]

leg. *abbrev. for:* **1** legal. **2** legate. **3** legato. **4** legislation. **5** legislative. **6** legislature.

legacy ('lɛgəsɪ) *n, pl* **legacies. 1** a gift by will, esp. of money or personal property. **2** something handed down or received from an ancestor or predecessor. [C14 (meaning: office of a legate), C15 (meaning: bequest): from Med. L *lēgātia* commission; see LEGATE]

legal ('liːgºl) *adj* **1** established by or founded upon law; lawful. **2** of or relating to law. **3** recognized, enforceable, or having a remedy at law rather than in equity. **4** relating to or characteristic of the profession of law. [C16: from L *lēgālis*, from *lēx* law]
▸ **'legally** *adv*

legal aid *n* financial assistance available to persons unable to meet the full cost of legal proceedings.

legalese (ˌliːgəˈliːz) *n* the conventional language in which legal documents are written.

legalism ('liːgəˌlɪzəm) *n* strict adherence to the law, esp. the letter of the law rather than its spirit.
▸ **'legalist** *n, adj* ▸ **ˌlegal'istic** *adj*

legality (lɪˈgælɪtɪ) *n, pl* **legalities. 1** the state or quality of being legal or lawful. **2** adherence to legal principles.

legalize *or* **legalise** ('liːgəˌlaɪz) *vb* **legalizes, legalizing, legalized** *or* **legalises, legalising, legalised.** (*tr*) to make lawful or legal.
▸ **ˌlegali'zation** *or* **ˌlegali'sation** *n*

legal tender *n* currency that a creditor must by law accept in redemption of a debt.

Legaspi ★ (lɛˈgæspɪ) *n* a port in the Philippines, on SE Luzon on the Gulf of Albay. Pop.: 125 128 (1994 est.).

legate ('lɛgɪt) *n* **1** a messenger, envoy, or delegate. **2** *RC Church.* an emissary representing the Pope. [OE, via OF from L *lēgātus* deputy, from *lēgāre* to delegate; rel. to *lēx* law]
▸ **'legate,ship** *n*

legatee (ˌlɛgəˈtiː) *n* a person to whom a legacy is bequeathed.

legation (lɪˈgeɪʃən) *n* **1** a diplomatic mission headed by a minister. **2** the official residence and office of a diplomatic minister. **3** the act of sending forth a diplomatic envoy. **4** the mission of a diplomatic envoy. **5** the rank or office of a legate. [C15: from L *lēgātiō*, from *lēgātus* LE-GATE]

legato (lɪˈgɑːtəʊ) *Music.* ◆ *adj, adv* **1** to be performed smoothly and connectedly. ◆ *n, pl* **legatos. 2** a style of playing with no perceptible gaps between notes. **2b** (*as modifier*): *a legato passage.* [C19: from It., lit.: bound]

leg before wicket *n Cricket.* a manner of dismissal on the grounds that a batsman would have been struck on the leg by a bowled ball that otherwise would have hit the wicket. Abbrev.: **lbw.**

leg break *n Cricket.* a bowled ball that spins from leg to off on pitching.

legend ('lɛdʒənd) *n* **1** a popular story handed down from earlier times whose truth has not been ascertained. **2** a group of such stories: *the Arthurian legend.* **3** a modern story that has the characteristics of a traditional tale. **4** a person whose fame or notoriety makes him a source of exaggerated or romanticized tales. **5** an inscription or title, as on a coin or beneath a coat of arms. **6** explanatory matter accompanying a table, map, chart, etc. [C14 (in the sense: saint's life): from Med. L *legenda* passages to be read, from L *legere* to read]

legendary ('lɛdʒəndərɪ, -drɪ) *adj* **1** of or relating to legend. **2** celebrated or described in a legend or legends. **3** very famous or notorious.

Legendre ★ (French ləˈʒɑ̃drə) *n* **Adrien Marie** (adriɛ̃ mari). 1752–1833, French mathematician, noted for his work on the theory of numbers, the theory of elliptical functions, and the method of least squares.

Léger ★ (French leˈʒe) *n* **Fernand** (fɛrnɑ̃). 1881–1955, French cubist painter, influenced by industrial technology.

legerdemain (ˌlɛdʒədəˈmeɪn) *n* **1** another name for

sleight of hand. 2 cunning deception or trickery. [C15: from OF: light of hand]

leger line ('lɛdʒə) *n* a variant spelling of **ledger line.**

legged ('lɛgɪd, lɛgd) *adj* **a** having a leg or legs. **b** (*in combination*): *three-legged; long-legged.*

leggiero (lɛdʒˈɛərəʊ) *adj, adv Music.* to be performed lightly and nimbly. [It.]

leggings ('lɛgɪŋz) *pl n* **1** an extra outer covering for the lower legs. **2** children's closefitting trousers, usually with a strap under the instep, worn for warmth in winter. **3** a fashion garment for women consiting of closefitting trousers.

leggy ('lɛgɪ) *adj* **leggier, leggiest. 1** having unusually long legs. **2** (of a woman) having long and shapely legs. **3** (of a plant) having an unusually long and weak stem.
▸ **'legginess** *n*

leghorn ('lɛgˌhɔːn) *n* **1** a type of Italian wheat straw that is woven into hats. **2** any hat made from this straw. [C19: after LEGHORN (Livorno)]

Leghorn ★ *n* **1** (ˌlɛgˈhɔːn). the English name for **Livorno. 2** (lɛˈgɔːn). a breed of domestic fowl.

legible ('lɛdʒəbºl) *adj* (of handwriting, print, etc.) able to be read or deciphered. [C14: from LL *legibilis*, from L *legere* to read]
▸ **ˌlegi'bility** *n* ▸ **'legibly** *adv*

legion ('liːdʒən) *n* **1** a unit in the ancient Roman army of infantry with supporting cavalry of three to six thousand men. **2** any large military force: *the French Foreign Legion.* **3** (*usually cap.*) an association of ex-servicemen: *the British Legion.* **4** (*often pl*) any very large number. ◆ *adj* **5** (*usually postpositive*) very numerous. [C13: from OF, from L *legio*, from *legere* to choose]

legionary ('liːdʒənərɪ) *adj* **1** of a legion. ◆ *n, pl* **legionaries. 2** a soldier belonging to a legion.

legionnaire (ˌliːdʒəˈnɛə) *n* (*often cap.*) a member of certain military forces or associations.

Legionnaire's disease (ˌliːdʒəˈnɛəz) *n* a serious, sometimes fatal, infection, caused by a bacterium (**legionella**), which has symptoms similar to those of pneumonia. [C20: after the outbreak at a meeting of the American Legion in Philadelphia in 1976]

legislate ('lɛdʒɪsˌleɪt) *vb* **legislates, legislating, legislated. 1** (*intr*) to make or pass laws. **2** (*tr*) to bring into effect by legislation. [C18: back formation from LEGISLATOR]

legislation (ˌlɛdʒɪsˈleɪʃən) *n* **1** the act or process of making laws. **2** the laws so made.

legislative ('lɛdʒɪslətɪv) *adj* **1** of or relating to legislation. **2** having the power or function of legislating: *a legislative assembly.* **3** of or relating to a legislature.
▸ **'legislatively** *adv*

legislative assembly *n* (*often caps.*) **1** the bicameral legislature in 28 states of the US. **2** the chamber of the bicameral state legislatures in several Commonwealth countries, such as Australia. **3** the unicameral legislature in most Canadian provinces. **4** any assembly with legislative powers.

legislative council *n* (*often caps.*) **1** the upper chamber of certain bicameral legislatures, such as those of the Indian and Australian states (except Queensland). **2** the unicameral legislature of certain colonies or dependent territories. **3** (in the US) a committee of members of both chambers of a state legislature that discusses problems, constructs a legislative programme, etc.

legislator ('lɛdʒɪsˌleɪtə) *n* **1** a person concerned with the making of laws. **2** a member of a legislature. [C17: from L *lēgis lātor*, from *lēx* law + *lātor* from *lātus*, p.p. of *ferre* to bring]

legislature ('lɛdʒɪsˌleɪtʃə) *n* a body of persons vested with power to make and repeal laws.

legit (lɪˈdʒɪt) *Sl.* ◆ *adj* **1** short for **legitimate.** ◆ *n* **2** legitimate drama.

legitimate *adj* (lɪˈdʒɪtɪmɪt). **1** born in lawful wedlock. **2** conforming to established standards of usage, behaviour, etc. **3** based on correct or acceptable principles of reasoning. **4** authorized by or in accordance with law. **5** of, relating to, or ruling by hereditary right: *a legitimate monarch.* **6** of or relating to a body of famous long-

established plays as distinct from films, television, vaudeville, etc. ◆ *vb* (lɪ'dʒɪtɪ,meɪt), **legitimates, legitimating, legitimated. 7** (*tr*) to make, pronounce, or show to be legitimate. [C15: from Med. L *lēgitimātus* made legal, from *lēx* law]
▶ le'gitimacy *n* ▶ le'gitimately *adv* ▶ le,giti'mation *n*

legitimist (lɪ'dʒɪtɪmɪst) *n* a monarchist who supports the rule of a legitimate dynasty or of its senior branch.
▶ le'gitimism *n*

legitimize, legitimise (lɪ'dʒɪtɪ,maɪz) *or* **legitimatize, legitimatise** (lɪ'dʒɪtɪmə,taɪz) *vb* **legitimizes, legitimizing, legitimized; legitimises, legitimising, legitimised** *or* **legitimatizes, legitimatizing, legitimatized; legitimatises, legitimatising, legitimatised.** (*tr*) to make legitimate; legalize.
▶ le,gitimi'zation, le,gitimi'sation *or* le,gitimati,zation, le,gitimati'sation *n*

legless ('lɛglɪs) *adj* **1** without legs. **2** *Inf.* very drunk.

Legnica ★ (*Polish* lɛg'nitsa) *n* an industrial town in SW Poland. Pop.: 107 800 (1995 est.). German name: **Liegnitz.**

Lego ('lɛgəʊ) *n Trademark.* a construction toy consisting of plastic bricks and other components that fit together. [C20: from Danish *leg godt* play well]

leg-of-mutton *or* **leg-o'-mutton** *n* (*modifier*) (of a sail, sleeve, etc.) tapering sharply.

leg-pull *n Brit. inf.* a practical joke or mild deception.

legroom ('lɛg,ruːm) *n* room to move one's legs comfortably, as in a car.

leg rope *n Austral. & NZ.* a rope used to secure an animal by its hind leg.

leguan ('lɛgjʊ,ɑːn) *n* a large amphibious S African lizard. [C19: Du., from F *l'iguane* the iguana]

legume ('lɛgjuːm, lɪ'gjuːm) *n* **1** the long dry fruit produced by leguminous plants; a pod. **2** any of various table vegetables, esp. beans or peas. **3** any leguminous plant. [C17: from F *légume*, from L *legūmen* bean, from *legere* to pick (a crop)]

leguminous (lɪ'gjuːmɪnəs) *adj* of, relating to, or belonging to any family of flowering plants having pods (or legumes) as fruits and root nodules enabling storage of nitrogen-rich material. [C17: from L *legūmen*; see LEGUME]

legwarmer ('lɛg,wɔːmə) *n* one of a pair of garments resembling stockings without feet, often worn over jeans, tights, etc., or during exercise.

legwork ('lɛg,wɜːk) *n Inf.* work that involves travelling on foot or as if on foot.

Lehár ★ ('leɪhɑː, lɪ'hɑː) *n* **Franz** (frants). 1870–1948, Hungarian composer of operettas, esp. *The Merry Widow* (1905).

Le Havre ★ (lə 'hɑːvrə; *French* lə avrə) *n* a port in N France, on the English Channel at the mouth of the River Seine: transatlantic trade; oil refining. Pop.: 197 219 (1990).

Lehmann ★ ('leɪmən) *n* **1 Lilli** ('lɪlɪ). 1848–1929, German soprano. **2 Lotte** ('lɒtə). 1888–1976, US soprano, born in Germany. **3 Rosamond** (**Nina**). 1903–90, British novelist. Her books include *The Weather in the Streets* (1936) and *The Echoing Grove* (1953).

Lehmbruck ★ (*German* 'leːmbrʊk) *n* **Wilhelm** ('vɪlhɛlm). 1881–1919, German sculptor and graphic artist.

lei (leɪ) *n* (in Hawaii) a garland of flowers, worn around the neck. [from Hawaiian]

Leibnitz *or* **Leibniz** ★ ('laɪbnɪts) *n* **Baron Gottfried Wilhelm von** ('gɔtfriːt 'vɪlhɛlm fɒn). 1646–1716, German rationalist philosopher and mathematician. His works include *Théodicée* (1710) and *Monadologia* (1714). He devised the calculus, independently of Newton.
▶ Leib'nitzian *adj*

Leicester[1] ★ ('lɛstə) *n* **1** a city in central England, on the River Soar: Roman remains and a ruined Norman castle; university (1918); light engineering, hosiery, and footwear industries. Pop.: 293 400 (1994 est.). **2** a unitary authority in central England, in Leicestershire. Pop.: 293 400 (1994 est.). Area: 73 sq. km (28 sq. miles). **3** a fairly mild dark orange whole-milk cheese, similar to Cheddar.

Leicester[2] ★ ('lɛstə) *n* **Earl of.** title of *Robert Dudley.* ?1532–88, English courtier; favourite of Elizabeth I. He led an unsuccessful expedition to the Netherlands (1585–87).

Leicestershire ★ ('lɛstə,ʃɪə, -ʃə) *n* a county of central England, including (since 1974) the former county of Rutland, now a unitary authority, and Leicester city unitary authority: largely agricultural. Administrative centre: Leicester. Pop.: 592 700 (1995 est.). Area: 2553 sq. km (986 sq. miles). Shortened form: **Leicester.** Abbrev.: **Leics.**

Leichhardt ★ ('laɪk,hɑːt; *German* 'laiçhart) *n* **Friedrich Wilhelm Ludwig** ('friːdrɪç 'vɪlhɛlm 'luːtvɪç). 1813–48, Australian explorer, born in Prussia. He disappeared during an attempt to cross Australia from East to West.

Leics *abbrev.* for Leicestershire.

Leiden *or* **Leyden** ★ ('laɪd°n; *Dutch* 'leidə) *n* a city in the W Netherlands, in South Holland province: residence of the Pilgrim Fathers for 11 years before they sailed for America in 1620; university (1575). Pop.: 115 473 (1995 est.).

Leif Ericson ★ ('liːf 'ɛrɪksən) *n* See **Ericson.**

Leigh[1] ★ (liː) *n* a town in NW England, in Wigan, in Greater Manchester: engineering industries. Pop.: 43 150 (1991).

Leigh[2] ★ (liː) *n* **1 Mike.** born 1943, British film director: his films include *Secrets and Lies* (1996). **2 Vivien,** real name *Vivian Hartley.* 1913–67, British stage and film actress. Her films include *Gone with the Wind* (1939) and *A Streetcar Named Desire* (1951).

Leighton ★ ('leɪt°n) *n* **Frederic,** 1st Baron Leighton of Stretton. 1830–96, British painter and sculptor of classical subjects: president of the Royal Academy (1878).

Leinster ★ ('lɛnstə) *n* a province of E and SE Republic of Ireland: it consists of the counties of Carlow, Dublin, Kildare, Kilkenny, Laois, Longford, Louth, Meath, Offaly, Westmeath, Wexford, and Wicklow. Pop.: 1 860 949 (1991). Area: 19 632 sq. km (7580 sq. miles).

Leipzig ★ ('laɪpsɪg; *German* 'laiptsɪç) *n* a city in E central Germany, in Saxony: famous fairs, begun about 1170; publishing and music centre; university (1409); scene of a decisive defeat for Napoleon Bonaparte in 1813. Pop.: 481 121 (1995 est.).

Leiria ★ (*Portuguese* lei'riə) *n* a city in central Portugal: site of the first printing press in Portugal (1466). Pop.: 96 583 (1981).

leishmaniasis (,liːʃmə'naɪəsɪs) *or* **leishmaniosis** (liːʃ,meɪnɪ'əʊsɪs, -,mæn-) *n* any disease, such as kala-azar, caused by protozoa of the genus *Leishmania.* [C20: NL, after Sir W. B. *Leishman* (1865-1926), Scot. bacteriologist]

leister ('liːstə) *n* **1** a spear with three or more prongs for spearing fish, esp. salmon. ◆ *vb* **2** (*tr*) to spear (a fish) with a leister. [C16: from Scand.]

leisure ('lɛʒə) *n* **1a** time or opportunity for ease, relaxation, etc. **1b** (*as modifier*): *leisure activities.* **2** ease or leisureliness. **3 at leisure. 3a** having free time. **3b** not occupied or engaged. **3c** without hurrying. **4 at one's leisure.** when one has free time. [C14: from OF *leisir*; ult. from L *licēre* to be allowed]
▶ 'leisured *adj*

leisure centre *n* a building designed to provide such leisure facilities as a library, sports hall, café, and rooms for meetings.

leisurely ('lɛʒəlɪ) *adj* **1** unhurried; relaxed. ◆ *adv* **2** without haste; in a relaxed way.
▶ 'leisureliness *n*

Leith ★ (liːθ) *n* a port in SE Scotland, on the Firth of Forth: part of Edinburgh since 1920.

leitmotif *or* **leitmotiv** ('laɪtməʊ,tiːf) *n* **1** *Music.* a recurring short melodic phrase used, esp. in Wagnerian music dramas, to suggest a character, thing, etc. **2** an often repeated image or theme in a literary work. [C19: from G: leading motif]

Leitrim ★ ('liːtrɪm) *n* a county of north Republic of Ireland in Connacht province, on Donegal Bay: agricultural. County town: Carrick-on-Shannon. Pop.: 25 301 (1991). Area: 1525 sq. km (589 sq. miles).

★ people and places

Leix ★ (liːʃ) *n* another name for **Laois**.

Leizhou ('lerˈdʒəʊ) *or* **Luichow Peninsula** ★ *n* a peninsula of SE China, in SW Guangdong province, separated from Hainan Island by Hainan Strait.

lek (lɛk) *n* a small area in which birds of certain species, notably the black grouse, gather for sexual display and courtship. [C19: ?from dialect *lake* (vb) from OE *lácan* to frolic, fight, or ?from Swedish *leka* to play]

lekker ('lɛkə) *adj* S. African *sl*. **1** pleasing, enjoyable, or likeable. **2** tasty. [from Afrik., from Du.]

Lely ★ ('liːlɪ) *n* Sir **Peter**, Dutch name *Pieter van der Faes*. 1618–80, Dutch portrait painter in England.

LEM (lɛm) *n acronym for* lunar excursion module.

Lemaître ★ (*French* ləmɛtrə) *n* Abbé **Georges** (**Édouard**) (ʒɔrʒ). 1894–1966, Belgian astronomer and priest, who first proposed the big-bang theory of the universe (1927).

Léman ★ (lemã) *n* Lac. the French name for (Lake) **Geneva**.

Le Mans ★ (*French* lə mã) *n* a city in NW France: scene of the first experiments in motoring and flying; annual motor race. Pop.: 148 465 (1990).

Lemberg ★ ('lɛmbɛrk) *n* the German name for **Lviv**.

lemma ('lɛmə) *n, pl* **lemmas** *or* **lemmata** (-mətə). **1** a subsidiary proposition, assumed to be valid, that is used in the proof of another proposition. **2** an argument or theme, esp. when used as the subject or title of a composition. **3** *Linguistics*. a word considered as its citation form together with all the inflected forms. [C16: (meaning: proposition), C17 (meaning: title, theme): via L from Gk: premise, from *lambanein* to take (for granted)]

lemming ('lɛmɪŋ) *n* **1** any of various volelike rodents of northern and arctic regions of Europe, Asia, and North America. **2** a member of any group following an unthinking course towards destruction. [C17: from Norwegian]
▸ '**lemming-, like** *adj*

Lemnos ★ ('lɛmnɒs) *n* a Greek island in the N Aegean Sea: famous for its medicinal earth (**Lemnian seal**). Chief town: Kastron. Pop.: 16 000 (latest est.). Area: 477 sq. km (184 sq. miles). Modern Greek name: **Límnos**.
▸ **Lemnian** ('lɛmnɪən) *adj, n*

lemon ('lɛmən) *n* **1** a small Asian evergreen tree widely cultivated in warm and tropical regions for its edible fruits. Related adjs.: **citric**, **citrine**, **citrous**. **2a** the yellow oval fruit of this tree, having juicy acidic flesh. **2b** (*as modifier*): *a lemon jelly*. **3** Also called: **lemon yellow**. **3a** a greenish-yellow or pale yellow colour. **3b** (*as adj*): *lemon wallpaper*. **4** a distinctive tart flavour made from or in imitation of the lemon. **5** *Sl*. a person or thing considered to be useless or defective. [C14: from Med. L *lemōn-*, from Ar. *laymūn*]
▸ '**lemony** *adj*

lemonade (ˌlɛməˈneɪd) *n* a drink made from lemon juice, sugar, and water or from carbonated water, citric acid, etc.

lemon balm *n* the full name of **balm**.

lemon cheese *or* **curd** *n* a soft spread made from lemons, sugar, eggs, and butter.

lemon grass *n* a perennial grass with a large flower spike: used in cooking and grown in tropical regions as the source of an aromatic oil (**lemon grass oil**).

lemon sole *n* a European flatfish with a variegated brown body: highly valued as a food fish.

lemon squash *n Brit*. a drink made from a sweetened lemon concentrate and water.

lemur ('liːmə) *n* **1** any of a family of Madagascan prosimian primates such as the ring-tailed lemur. They are typically arboreal, having foxy faces and long tails. **2** any similar or closely related animal, such as a loris or indris. [C18: NL, adapted from L *lemurēs* ghosts; so named for its ghost-like face and nocturnal habits]
▸ **lemuroid** ('lɛmjʊˌrɔɪd) *n, adj*

Lena ★ ('liːnə; *Russian* 'ljɪnə) *n* a river in Russia, rising in S Siberia and flowing generally north through the Sakha Republic to the Laptev Sea by an extensive delta: the longest river in Russia. Length: 4271 km (2653 miles).

lend (lɛnd) *vb* **lends, lending, lent**. **1** (*tr*) to permit the use of (something) with the expectation of its return. **2** to provide (money) temporarily, often at interest. **3** (*intr*) to provide loans, esp. as a profession. **4** (*tr*) to impart or contribute (something, esp. some abstract quality): *her presence lent beauty*. **5 lend an ear**. to listen. **6 lend oneself** *or* **itself**. to possess the right characteristics or qualities for: *the novel lends itself to serialization*. [C15 *lende* (orig. the past tense), from OE *lǣnan*, from *lǣn* loan]
▸ '**lender** *n*

lending library *n* **1** Also called (esp. US): **circulating library**. the department of a public library providing books for use outside the building. **2** a small commercial library.

Lendl ★ ('lɛnd°l) *n* **Ivan** (iːˈvæn, -ˈvɑːn). born 1960, Czech tennis player; US Open champion (1985–87).

lend-lease *n* (during World War II) the system organized by the US in 1941 by which equipment and services were provided for countries fighting Germany.

Lenglen ★ (*French* lãglã) *n* **Suzanne** (syzan). 1899–1938, French tennis player: Wimbledon champion (1919-25).

length (lɛŋθ, lɛŋθ) *n* **1** the linear extent or measurement of something from end to end, usually being the longest dimension. **2** the extent of something from beginning to end, measured in some more or less regular units or intervals: *the book was 600 pages in length*. **3** a specified distance, esp. between two positions: *the length of a race*. **4** a period of time, as between specified limits or moments. **5** a piece or section of something narrow and long: *a length of tubing*. **6** the quality, state, or fact of being long rather than short. **7** (*usually pl*) the amount of trouble taken in pursuing or achieving something (esp. in **to great lengths**). **8** (*often pl*) the extreme or limit of action (esp. in **to any length(s)**). **9** *Prosody, phonetics*. the metrical quantity or temporal duration of a vowel or syllable. **10** the distance from one end of a rectangular swimming bath to the other. **11** *NZ inf*. the general idea; the main purpose. **12 at length**. **12a** in depth; fully. **12b** eventually. **12c** interminably. [OE *lengthu*]

lengthen ('lɛŋkθən, 'lɛŋθən) *vb* to make or become longer.
▸ '**lengthener** *n*

lengthways ('lɛŋkθˌweɪz, 'lɛŋθ-) *or* **lengthwise** *adv, adj* in, according to, or along the direction of length.

lengthy ('lɛŋkθɪ, 'lɛŋθɪ) *adj* **lengthier, lengthiest**. of relatively great or tiresome extent or duration.
▸ '**lengthily** *adv* ▸ '**lengthiness** *n*

lenient ('liːnɪənt) *adj* showing or characterized by mercy or tolerance. [C17: from L *lēnīre* to soothe, from *lēnis* soft]
▸ '**leniency** *or* '**lenience** *n* ▸ '**leniently** *adv*

Lenin ★ ('lɛnɪn) *n* **Vladimir Ilyich** (vlaˈdimir iljˈjitʃ), original surname *Ulyanov*. 1870–1924, Russian statesman; first premier of the Soviet Union. He formed the Bolsheviks (1903) and led them in the October Revolution (1917), which established the Soviet Government. He adopted the New Economic Policy (1921), formed the Comintern (1919), and was the originator of the doctrine of Marxism-Leninism. After the Soviet Union broke up in 1991, many statues of Lenin were demolished.

Leninabad ★ (*Russian* lɪnɪnaˈbat) *n* the former name (1936–91) of **Khojent**.

Leninakan ★ (*Russian* lɪnɪnaˈkan) *n* the former name (1925–91) of **Kumayri**.

Leningrad ★ ('lɛnɪnˌgræd; *Russian* lɪnɪnˈgrat) *n* the former name (1924–91) of **Saint Petersburg**.

Leninism ('lɛnɪˌnɪzəm) *n* the political and economic theories of Lenin.
▸ '**Leninist** *n, adj*

Lenin Peak ★ *n* a mountain in NE Tajikistan; the highest peak in the Trans Alai Range and the second highest in the former Soviet Union. Height: 7134 m (23 406 ft).

lenitive ('lɛnɪtɪv) *adj* **1** soothing or alleviating pain or distress. ◆ *n* **2** a lenitive drug. [C16: from Med. L *lēnītīvus*, from L *lēnīre* to soothe]

lenity ('lɛnɪtɪ) *n, pl* **lenities**. the state or quality of being lenient. [C16: from L *lēnitās* gentleness, from *lēnis* soft]

Lennon ★ ('lɛnən) *n* **John** (**Ono**), original name *John Winston Lennon*. 1940–80, British songwriter, singer, and guitarist: member of the Beatles (1962–70). Subsequent recordings, many in collaboration with his wife Yoko Ono, include *Imagine* (1971) and *Double Fantasy* (1980). He was assassinated.

leno ('liːnəu) *n, pl* **lenos. 1** (in textiles) a weave in which the warp yarns are twisted together in pairs between the weft or filling yarns. **2** a fabric of this weave. [C19: prob. from F *linon* lawn, from *lin* flax, from L *līnum*]

Leno ★ ('liːnəu) *n* **Dan**, original name *George Galvin*. 1860–1904, British music-hall entertainer, noted esp. for his pantomime performances: he died insane.

lens (lɛnz) *n* **1** a piece of glass or other transparent material, used to converge or diverge transmitted light and form optical images. **2** Also called: **compound lens**. a combination of such lenses for forming images or concentrating a beam of light. **3** a device that diverges or converges a beam of electromagnetic radiation, sound, or particles. **4** *Anat.* See **crystalline lens**. [C17: from L *lēns* lentil, referring to the similarity of a lens to the shape of a lentil]

lent (lɛnt) *vb* the past tense and past participle of **lend**.

Lent (lɛnt) *n Christianity*. the period of forty weekdays lasting from Ash Wednesday to Holy Saturday, observed as a time of penance and fasting commemorating Jesus' fasting in the wilderness. [OE *lencten, lengten* spring, lit.: lengthening (of hours of daylight)]

lentamente (ˌlɛntəˈmɛnteɪ) *adv Music*. slowly. [It.]

lenten ('lɛntən) *adj* **1** (*often cap.*) of or relating to Lent. **2** *Arch. or literary*. spare, plain, or meagre: *lenten fare*.

lenticel ('lɛntɪˌsɛl) *n* any of numerous pores in the stem of a woody plant allowing exchange of gases between the plant and the exterior. [C19: from NL *lenticella*, from L *lenticula* dim. of *lēns* lentil]

lenticular (lɛnˈtɪkjʊlə) *adj* **1** shaped like a biconvex lens. **2** of or concerned with a lens or lenses. **3** shaped like a lentil seed. [C17: from L *lenticulāris* like a LENTIL]

lentil ('lɛntɪl) *n* **1** a small annual leguminous plant of the Mediterranean region and W Asia, having edible convex seeds. **2** any of the seeds of this plant, which are cooked and eaten in soups, etc. [C13: from OF *lentille*, from L *lenticula*, dim. of *lēns* lentil]

lentivirus ('lɛntɪˌvaɪrəs) *n* another name for **slow virus**. [C20: NL, from L *lentus* slow + VIRUS]

lent lily *n* another name for the **daffodil**.

lento ('lɛntəu) *Music*. ◆ *adj, adv* **1** to be performed slowly. ◆ *n, pl* **lentos. 2** a movement or passage performed in this way. [C18: It., from L *lentus* slow]

Lent term *n* the spring term at Cambridge University and some other educational establishments.

Lenya ★ ('leɪnjə) *n* **Lotte** ('lɒtə; *German* 'lɔtə), original name *Caroline Blamauer*. 1900–81, Austrian singer and actress, associated esp. with the songs of her husband Kurt Weill.

Leo ('liːəu) *n, Latin genitive* **Leonis** (liːˈəunɪs). **1** *Astron*. a zodiacal constellation in the N hemisphere, lying between Cancer and Virgo. **2** *Astrol*. Also called: **the Lion**. the fifth sign of the zodiac. The sun is in this sign between about July 23 and Aug. 22.

Leo I ★ ('liːəu) *n* **Saint**, known as *Leo the Great*. ?390–461 A.D., pope (440–461). He persuaded Attila not to attack Rome (452). Feast day: Nov. 10 or Feb. 18.

Leo III ★ *n* **Saint**. ?750–816 A.D., pope (795–816). He crowned Charlemagne emperor of the Romans (800). Feast day: June 12.

Leo X ★ *n* original name *Giovanni de' Medici*. 1475–1521, pope (1513–21): noted for his patronage of Renaissance art; excommunicated Luther (1521).

Leo XIII ★ *n* original name *Gioacchino Pecci*. 1810–1903, pope (1878–1903). His encyclicals include *Rerum novarum* (1891) on social problems.

Leoben ★ (*German* leˈoːbən) *n* a city in E central Austria, in Styria on the Mur River: lignite mining. Pop.: 28 504 (1991).

León ★ (*Spanish* leˈɔn) *n* **1** a region and former kingdom

of NW Spain, which united with Castile in 1230. **2** a city of NW Spain: capital of the kingdom of León (10th century). Pop.: 147 311 (1994 est.). **3** a city in central Mexico, in W Guanajuato state: commercial centre of a rich agricultural region. Pop.: 867 920 (1990). Official name **León de los Aldamas** (de los 'aldamas). **4** a city in W Nicaragua: one of the oldest towns of Central America, founded in 1524; capital of Nicaragua until 1855; university (1812). Pop.: 171 375 (1994 est.).

Leonard ★ ('lɛnəd) *n* **Sugar Ray**, real name *Ray Charles Leonard*. born 1956, US boxer: the first man to have won world titles at five officially recognized weights.

Leonardo da Vinci ★ (ˌliːɑːˈnɑːdəu də ˈvɪntʃɪ) *n* 1452–1519, Italian painter, sculptor, architect, and engineer: the most versatile talent of the Italian Renaissance. His paintings include the *Mona Lisa* (or *La Gioconda,* 1503) and the *Last Supper* (?1495–97). His numerous drawings ranged over biology, physiology, hydraulics, and aeronautics. He foresaw the invention of aircraft and submarines.
▸ **Leonardesque** (ˌliːənɑːˈdɛsk) *adj*

Leonardo of Pisa ★ *n* See (Leonardo) **Fibonacci**.

Leoncavallo ★ (*Italian* leoŋkaˈvallo) *n* **Ruggiero** (rudˈdʒɛːro). 1858–1919, Italian composer of operas, notably *I Pagliacci* (1892).

Leonid ('liːənɪd) *n, pl* **Leonids** or **Leonides** (lɪˈɒnɪˌdiːz). any member of a meteor shower appearing to radiate from the constellation Leo. [C19: from NL *Leōnidēs*, from *leō* lion]

Leonidas ★ (lɪˈɒnɪˌdæs) *n* died 480 B.C., king of Sparta (?490–480), hero of the Battle of Thermopylae, in which he was killed by the Persians under Xerxes.

leonine ('liːəˌnaɪn) *adj* of, characteristic of, or resembling a lion. [C14: from L *leōnīnus*, from *leō* lion]

Leonine ('liːəˌnaɪn) *adj* **1** connected with one of the popes called Leo: an epithet applied to a district of Rome fortified by Pope Leo IV (**Leonine City**). **2 Leonine verse. 2a** a type of medieval hexameter or elegiac verse having internal rhyme. **2b** a type of English verse with internal rhyme.

leopard ('lɛpəd) *n* **1** Also called: **panther**. a large feline mammal of forests of Africa and Asia, usually having a tawny yellow coat with black rosette-like spots. **2** any of several similar felines, such as the snow leopard and cheetah. **3** *Heraldry*. a stylized leopard, painted as a lion with the face turned towards the front. [C13: from OF *lepart*, from LL, from LGk *leópardos*, from *leōn* lion + *pardos* PARD (the leopard was thought to be the result of cross-breeding)]
▸ **'leopardess** *fem n*

Leopardi ★ (*Italian* leoˈpardi) *n* **Count Giacomo** ('dʒaːkomo). 1798–1837, Italian poet and philosopher, noted esp. for his lyrics, collected in *I Canti* (1831).

Leopold I ★ ('liːəˌpəuld) *n* **1** 1640–1705, Holy Roman Emperor (1658–1705). His reign was marked by wars with Louis XIV of France and with the Turks. **2** 1790–1865, first king of the Belgians (1831–65).

Leopold II ★ *n* **1** 1747–92, Holy Roman Emperor (1790–92). He formed an alliance with Prussia against France (1792) after the downfall of his brother-in-law Louis XVI. **2** 1835–1909, king of the Belgians (1865–1909); son of Leopold I. He became the first sovereign of the Congo Free State (1885).

Leopold III ★ *n* 1901–83, king of the Belgians (1934–51); son of Albert I. His surrender to the Nazis (1940) forced his abdication in favour of his son, Baudouin.

Léopoldville ★ ('liːəpəuldˌvɪl; *French* leɔpɔlvil) *n* the former name (until 1966) of **Kinshasa**.

leotard ('liːəˌtɑːd) *n* **1** a tight-fitting garment covering the body from the shoulders down to the thighs and worn by acrobats, ballet dancers, etc. **2** (*pl*) *US & Canad*. another name for **tights** (sense 1b). [C19: after Jules *Léotard*, F acrobat]

Lepanto ★ *n* **1** (*Italian* 'lɛːpanto) a port in W Greece, between the Gulfs of Corinth and Patras: scene of a naval battle (1571) in which the Turkish fleet was defeated by the fleets of the Holy League. Pop.: 8200 (latest est.).

★ people and places

Greek name: **Návpaktos. 2** (lɪ'pæntəu). **Gulf of.** another name for the (Gulf of) **Corinth.**

Lepaya ★ (lɪ'pɑːjə) n a variant spelling of **Liepāja.**

leper ('lɛpə) n **1** a person who has leprosy. **2** a person who is ignored or despised. [C14: via LL from Gk *lepra*, n. use of *lepros* scaly, from *lepein* to peel]

lepido- or before a vowel **lepid-** combining form. scale or scaly: *lepidopterous*. [from Gk *lepis* scale; see LEPER]

lepidopteran (ˌlɛpɪ'dɒptərən) n, pl **lepidopterans** or **lepidoptera** (-tərə). **1** any of a large order of insects typically having two pairs of wings covered with fragile scales: comprises the butterflies and moths. ◆ adj also **lepidopterous. 2** of, relating to, or belonging to this order. [C19: from NL, from LEPIDO- + Gk *pteron* wing]

lepidopterist (ˌlɛpɪ'dɒptərɪst) n a person who studies or collects moths and butterflies.

Lepidus ★ ('lɛpɪdəs) n **Marcus Aemilius** ('mɑːkəs iː'mɪlɪəs). died ?13 B.C., Roman statesman: formed the Second Triumvirate with Octavian (later Augustus) and Mark Antony.

Lepontine Alps ★ (lɪ'pɒntaɪn) pl n a range of the S central Alps, in S Switzerland and N Italy. Highest peak: Monte Leone, 3553 m (11 657 ft).

leprechaun ('lɛprəˌkɔːn) n (in Irish folklore) a mischievous elf, often believed to have a treasure hoard. [C17: from Irish Gaelic *leipreachān*, from MIrish *lūchorpān*, from *lū* small + *corp* body, from L *corpus* body]

leprosy ('lɛprəsɪ) n Pathol. a chronic infectious disease occurring mainly in tropical and subtropical regions, characterized by the formation of painful inflamed nodules beneath the skin and disfigurement and wasting of affected parts. [C16: from LEPROUS + -Y[3]]

leprous ('lɛprəs) adj **1** having leprosy. **2** relating to or resembling leprosy. [C13: from OF, from LL *leprosus*, from *lepra* LEPER]

-lepsy or sometimes **-lepsia** n combining form. indicating a seizure: *catalepsy*. [from NL *-lepsia*, from Gk, from *lēpsis* a seizure, from *lambanein* to seize]
▸ **-leptic** adj combining form.

leptodactylous (ˌlɛptəu'dæktɪləs) adj Zool. having slender digits.

lepton[1] ('lɛptɒn) n, pl **lepta** (-tə). **1** a Greek monetary unit worth one hundredth of a drachma. **2** a small coin of ancient Greece. [from Gk *lepton* (*nomisma*) small (coin)]

lepton[2] ('lɛptɒn) n Physics. any of a group of elementary particles and their antiparticles, such as an electron, muon, or neutrino, that participate in electromagnetic and weak interactions. [C20: from Gk *leptos* thin, from *lepein* to peel + -ON]

lepton number n Physics. a quantum number describing the behaviour of elementary particles, equal to the number of leptons present minus the number of antileptons. It is thought to be conserved in all processes.

leptospirosis (ˌlɛptəuspaɪ'rəusɪs) n any of several infectious diseases caused by bacteria, transmitted to man by animals and characterized by jaundice, meningitis, and kidney failure. Also called: **Weil's disease.** [C20: from NL *Leptospira* (from Gk *leptos* thin + *speira* coil + -OSIS)]

Lérida ★ (Spanish 'leriða) n a city in NE Spain, in Catalonia: commercial centre of an agricultural region. Pop.: 114 234 (1994 est.).

Lermontov ★ (Russian 'ljerməntəf) n **Mikhail Yurievich** (mixa'il 'jurjɪvitʃ). 1814–41, Russian novelist and poet: noted for the novel *A Hero of Our Time* (1840).

Lerner ★ ('lɜːnə) n **Alan Jay.** 1914–86, US songwriter and librettist. With Frederick Loewe he wrote *My Fair Lady* (1956) and *Camelot* (1960), as well as a number of film scripts, including *Gigi* (1958).

Lerwick ★ ('lɜːwɪk) n a town in Shetland, administrative centre of the island authority of Shetland, on the island of Mainland: the most northerly town in the British Isles; knitwear, oil refining. Pop.: 7500 (1987 est.).

Le Sage or **Lesage** ★ (French lə saʒ) n **Alain-René** (alɛ̃rəne). 1668–1747, French novelist and dramatist, author of the novel *Gil Blas* (1715–35).

lesbian ('lɛzbɪən) n **1** a female homosexual. ◆ adj **2** of or characteristic of lesbians. [C19: from the homosexuality attributed to SAPPHO]
▸ **'lesbianism** n

Lesbos ★ ('lɛzbɒs) n an island in the E Aegean, off the NW coast of Turkey: a centre of lyric poetry, led by Alcaeus and Sappho (6th century B.C.); annexed to Greece in 1913. Chief town: Mytilene. Pop.: 105 082 (1991). Area: 1630 sq. km (630 sq. miles). Modern Greek name: **Lésvos.** Former name: **Mytilene.**

Les Cayes ★ (leɪ 'keɪ; French le kaj) n a port in SW Haiti, on the S Tiburon Peninsula. Pop.: 45 904 (1992). Also called: **Cayes.** Former name: **Aux Cayes.**

lese-majesty ('liːz'mædʒɪstɪ) n **1** any of various offences committed against the sovereign power in a state; treason. **2** an attack on authority or position. [C16: from F *lèse majesté*, from L *laesa mājestās* wounded majesty]

lesion ('liːʒən) n **1** any structural change in a bodily part resulting from injury or disease. **2** an injury or wound. [C15: via OF from LL *laesiō* injury, from L *laedere* to hurt]

Lesotho ★ (lɪ'suːtu, lə'səutəu) n a kingdom in southern Africa, forming an enclave in the Republic of South Africa: annexed to British Cape Colony in 1871; made a protectorate in 1884; gained independence in 1966; a member of the Commonwealth. It is generally mountainous, with temperate grasslands throughout. Languages: Sesotho and English. Religion: Christian majority. Currency: loti. Capital: Maseru. Pop.: 2 008 000 (1997). Area: 30 344 sq. km (11 716 sq. miles). Former name (1884–1966): **Basutoland.**

less (lɛs) determiner **1a** the comparative of **little** (sense 1): *less sugar; less spirit than before.* **1b** (as pronoun; functioning as sing or pl): *she has less than she needs; the less you eat, the less you want.* **2** (usually preceded by *no*) lower in rank or importance: *no less a man than the president.* **3 less of.** to a smaller extent or degree: *we see less of John these days; less of a success than I'd hoped.* ◆ adv **4** the comparative of *little: she walks less than she should; less quickly; less beautiful.* ◆ prep **5** subtracting; minus: *three weeks less a day.* [OE *lǣssa* (adj), *lǣs* (adv, n)]

> **USAGE NOTE** *Less should not be confused with fewer. Less refers strictly only to quantity and not to number: there is less water than before. Fewer means smaller in number: there are fewer people than before.*

-less suffix forming adjectives. **1** without; lacking: *speechless.* **2** not able to (do something) or not able to be (done, performed, etc.): *countless.* [OE *-lās*, from *lēas* lacking]

lessee (lɛ'siː) n a person to whom a lease is granted; a tenant under a lease. [C15: via Anglo-F from OF *lessé*, from *lesser* to LEASE]

lessen ('lɛsən) vb **1** to make or become less. **2** (tr) to make little of.

Lesseps ★ ('lɛsəps; French lɛsɛps) n **Vicomte Ferdinand Marie de** (ferdinɑ̃ mari də). 1805–94, French diplomat: directed the construction of the Suez Canal (1859–69) and the unsuccessful first attempt to build the Panama Canal (1881–89).

lesser ('lɛsə) adj not as great in quantity, size, or worth.

Lesser Antilles ★ pl n **the.** a group of islands in the Caribbean, including the Leeward Islands, the Windward Islands, Barbados, and the Netherlands Antilles. Also called: **Caribbees.**

lesser celandine n a Eurasian plant, related to the buttercup, having yellow flowers and heart-shaped leaves.

lesser panda n See **panda** (sense 2).

Lesser Sunda Islands ★ pl n the former name of **Nusa Tenggara.**

Lessing ★ ('lɛsɪŋ) n **1 Doris** (**May**). born 1919, British writer, brought up in Rhodesia: her work includes the five-novel sequence *Children of Violence* (1952–69), *The Golden Notebook* (1962), and a series of science-fiction works (1979–83). **2 Gotthold Ephraim** ('gɔthɔlt 'eːfraɪm).

1729–81, German dramatist and critic. His plays include *Miss Sara Sampson* (1755) and *Nathan der Weise* (1779).

lesson ('lɛsᵊn) n **1a** a unit, or single period of instruction in a subject; class: *an hour-long music lesson.* **1b** the content of such a unit. **2** material assigned for individual study. **3** something from which useful knowledge or principles can be learned; example. **4** the principles, knowledge, etc., gained. **5** a reprimand or punishment intended to correct. **6** a portion of Scripture appointed to be read at divine service. [C13: from OF *leçon*, from L *lēctiō*, from *legere* to read]

lessor ('lɛsɔː, lɛ'sɔː) n a person who grants a lease of property.

lest (lest) conj (*subordinating; takes a subjunctive vb*) **1** so as to prevent any possibility that: *keep down lest anyone see us.* **2** (*after vbs. or phrases expressing fear, worry, anxiety, etc.*) for fear that; in case: *he was alarmed lest she should find out.* [OE *the læste*, earlier *thȳ læs the*, lit.: whereby less that]

Lésvos ★ ('lɛzvɔs) n transliteration of the Modern Greek name for **Lesbos.**

let[1] (lɛt) vb **lets, letting, let.** (*tr*; usually takes an infinitive without *to* or an implied infinitive) **1** to permit; allow: *she lets him roam around.* **2** (*imperative or dependent imperative*) **2a** used as an auxiliary to express a request, proposal, or command, or to convey a warning or threat: *let's get on; just let me catch you here again!* **2b** (in mathematical or philosophical discourse) used as an auxiliary to express an assumption or hypothesis: *let "a" equal "b".* **2c** used as an auxiliary to express resigned acceptance of the inevitable: *let the worst happen.* **3a** to allow the occupation of (accommodation) in return for rent. **3b** to assign (a contract for work). **4** to allow or cause the movement of (something) in a specified direction: *to let air out of a tyre.* **5 let alone.** (*conj*) much less; not to mention: *I can't afford wine, let alone champagne.* **6 let** or **leave alone** or **be.** refrain from annoying or interfering with: *let the poor cat alone.* **7 let go.** See **go** (sense 45). **8 let loose. 8a** to set free. **8b** *Inf.* to make (a sound or remark) suddenly: *he let loose a hollow laugh.* **8c** *Inf.* to discharge (rounds) from a gun or guns: *they let loose a couple of rounds of ammunition.* ◆ n **9** *Brit.* the act of letting property or accommodation. ◆ See also **let down, let off,** etc. [OE *lǣtan* to permit]

let[2] (lɛt) n **1** an impediment or obstruction (esp. in **without let or hindrance**). **2** *Tennis, squash, etc.* **2a** a minor infringement or obstruction of the ball, requiring a point to be replayed. **2b** the point so replayed. ◆ vb **lets, letting, letted** or **let. 3** (*tr*) *Arch.* to hinder; impede. [OE *lettan* to hinder, from *læt* late]

-let suffix forming nouns. **1** small or lesser: *booklet.* **2** an article of attire or ornament worn on a specified part of the body: *anklet.* [from OF *-elet*, from L *-āle,* from L *-ellus,* dim. suffix]

Letchworth ★ ('lɛtʃwəθ, -,wɜːθ) n a town in SE England, in N Hertfordshire: the first garden city in Great Britain (founded in 1903). Pop.: 31 418 (1991).

let down vb (*tr, mainly adv*) **1** (*also prep*) to lower. **2** to fail to fulfil the expectations of (a person); disappoint. **3** to undo, shorten, and resew (the hem) so as to lengthen (a dress, skirt, etc.). **4** to untie (long hair that is bound up) and allow to fall loose. **5** to deflate: *to let down a tyre.* ◆ n **letdown. 6** a disappointment.

lethal ('liːθəl) adj **1** able to cause or causing death. **2** of or suggestive of death. [C16: from L *lēthālis,* from *lētum* death]
  ▶ **lethality** (liː'θælɪtɪ) n ▶ **'lethally** adv

lethargy ('lɛθədʒɪ) n, pl **lethargies. 1** sluggishness, slowness, or dullness. **2** an abnormal lack of energy. [C14: from LL *lēthargia,* from Gk *lēthargos* drowsy, from *lēthē* forgetfulness]
  ▶ **lethargic** (lɪ'θɑːdʒɪk) adj ▶ **le'thargically** adv

Lethbridge ★ ('lɛθbrɪdʒ) n a city in Canada, in S Alberta: coal-mining. Pop.: 60 974 (1991).

Lethe ★ ('liːθɪ) n **1** *Greek myth.* a river in Hades that caused forgetfulness in those who drank its waters. **2** forgetfulness. [C16: via L from Gk, from *lēthē* oblivion]
  ▶ **Lethean** (lɪ'θiːən) adj

Leto ★ ('liːtəʊ) n the mother by Zeus of Apollo and Artemis. Roman name: **Latona.**

let off vb (*tr, mainly adv*) **1** (*also prep*) to allow to disembark or leave. **2** to explode or fire (a bomb, gun, etc.). **3** (*also prep*) to excuse from (work or other responsibilities): *I'll let you off for a week.* **4** *Inf.* to allow to get away without the expected punishment, work, etc. **5** to let (accommodation) in portions. **6** to release (liquid, air, etc.).

let on vb (*adv*; when *tr*, takes a clause as object) *Inf.* **1** to allow (something, such as a secret) to be known; reveal: *he never let on that he was married.* **2** (*tr*) to cause or encourage to be believed; pretend.

let out vb (*adv, mainly tr*) **1** to give vent to; emit: *to let out a howl.* **2** to allow to go or run free; release. **3** (*may take a clause as object*) to reveal (a secret). **4** to make available to tenants, hirers, or contractors. **5** to permit to flow out: *to let air out of the tyres.* **6** to make (a garment) larger, as by unpicking (the seams) and sewing nearer the outer edge. ◆ n **let-out. 7** a chance to escape.

let's (lɛts) contraction of let us: used to express a suggestion, command, etc., by the speaker to himself and his hearers.

Lett (lɛt) n a former name for a **Latvian.**

letter ('lɛtə) n **1** any of a set of conventional symbols used in writing or printing a language, each symbol being associated with a group of phonetic values; character of the alphabet. **2** a written or printed communication addressed to a person, company, etc., usually sent by post. **3** (often preceded by *the*) the strict legalistic or pedantic interpretation of the meaning of an agreement, document, etc.; exact wording as distinct from actual intention (esp. in **the letter of the law**). **4 to the letter. 4a** following the literal interpretation or wording exactly. **4b** attending to every detail. ◆ vb **5** to write or mark letters on (a sign, etc.), esp. by hand. **6** (*tr*) to set down or print using letters. [C13: from OF *lettre,* from L *littera* letter of the alphabet]
  ▶ **'letterer** n

letter bomb n an explosive device in an envelope, detonated when the envelope is opened.

letter box n *Chiefly Brit.* **1a** a slot through which letters, etc., are delivered to a building. **1b** a private box into which letters, etc., are delivered. **2** Also: **postbox.** a public box into which letters, etc., are put for collection.

lettered ('lɛtəd) adj **1** well educated in literature, the arts, etc. **2** literate. **3** of or characterized by learning or culture. **4** printed or marked with letters.

letterhead ('lɛtə,hɛd) n a sheet of writing paper printed with one's address, name, etc.

lettering ('lɛtərɪŋ) n **1** the act, art, or technique of inscribing letters on to something. **2** the letters so inscribed.

letter of credit n a letter issued by a bank entitling the bearer to draw funds up to a specified maximum from that bank or its agencies.

letter of intent n a letter indicating that the writer has the serious intention of doing something, such as signing a contract, in the circumstances specified. It does not constitute either a promise or a contract.

letter of marque or **letters of marque** n (formerly) a licence granted by a state to a private citizen to arm a ship and seize merchant vessels of another nation. Also called: **letter of marque and reprisal.**

letter-perfect adj another term (esp. US) for **word-perfect.**

letterpress ('lɛtə,prɛs) n **1a** a method of printing in which ink is transferred from raised surfaces to paper by pressure. **1b** matter so printed. **2** text matter as distinct from illustrations.

letters ('lɛtəz) n (*functioning as sing or pl*) **1** literary knowledge, ability, or learning: *a man of letters.* **2** literary culture in general. **3** an official title, degree, etc., indicated by an abbreviation: *letters after one's name.*

letters patent pl n See **patent** (senses 1, 4).

Lettish ('lɛtɪʃ) n another name for **Latvian** (sense 2).

lettuce ('lɛtɪs) n **1** any of various plants of the composite

---

★ **people and places**

family cultivated in many varieties for their large edible leaves. **2** the leaves of any of these varieties, which are eaten in salads. **3** any of various plants that resemble true lettuce, such as lamb's lettuce. [C13: prob. from OF *laitues*, from L *lactūca*, from *lac-* milk, because of its milky juice]

let up *vb* (*intr, adv*) **1** to diminish, slacken, or stop. **2** (foll. by *on*) *Inf.* to be less harsh (towards someone). ◆ *n* **let-up. 3** *Inf.* a lessening or abatement.

Leucas ★ ('luːkəs) *n* a variant spelling of **Leukas.**

Leucippus ★ (luːˈsɪpəs) *n* 5th century B.C. Greek philosopher, who originated the atomic theory of matter, developed by his disciple, Democritus.

leuco-, leuko- *or before a vowel* **leuc-, leuk-** *combining form.* white or lacking colour: *leucocyte; leukaemia.* [from Gk *leukos* white]

leucoblast *or esp.* US **leukoblast** ('luːkəʊ,blæst) *n* an immature leucocyte.

leucocyte *or esp.* US **leukocyte** ('luːkə,saɪt) *n* any of the various large unpigmented cells in the blood of vertebrates. Also called: **white blood cell, white (blood) corpuscle.**
▸ **leucocytic** *or esp.* US **leukocytic** (,luːkə'sɪtɪk) *adj*

leucoma (luːˈkəʊmə) *n Pathol.* a white opaque scar of the cornea.

leucotomy (luːˈkɒtəmɪ) *n, pl* **leucotomies.** the surgical operation of cutting some of the nerve fibres in the frontal lobes of the brain for treating intractable mental disorders.

Leuctra ★ ('luːktrə) *n* an ancient town in Greece southwest of Thebes in Boeotia: site of a victory of Thebes over Sparta (371 B.C.), which marked the end of Spartan military supremacy in Greece.

leukaemia *or esp.* US **leukemia** (luːˈkiːmɪə) *n* an acute or chronic disease characterized by a gross proliferation of leucocytes, which crowd into the bone marrow, spleen, lymph nodes, etc., and suppress the blood-forming apparatus. [C19: from LEUCO- + Gk *haima* blood]

Leukas *or* **Leucas** ★ ('luːkəs) *n* another name for **Levkás.**

Leuven ★ ('løːvə) *n* the Flemish name for **Louvain.**

Lev. *Bible. abbrev. for* Leviticus.

levant (lɪˈvænt) *n* a type of leather made from the skins of goats, sheep, or seals, having a pattern of irregular creases. [C19: shortened from *Levant morocco* (type of leather)]

Levant ★ (lɪˈvænt) *n the.* a former name for the area of the E Mediterranean now occupied by Lebanon, Syria, and Israel. [C15: from OF, from *lever* to raise (referring to the rising of the sun in the east), from L *levāre*]
▸ **Levantine** ('levən,taɪn) *adj, n*

levanter (lɪˈvæntə) *n* (*sometimes cap.*) **1** an easterly wind in the W Mediterranean area. **2** an inhabitant of the Levant.

levator (lɪˈveɪtə, -tɔː) *n Anat.* any of various muscles that raise a part of the body. [C17: NL, from L *levāre* to raise]

levee[1] ('levɪ) *n US.* **1** an embankment alongside a river, produced naturally by sedimentation or constructed by man to prevent flooding. **2** an embankment that surrounds a field that is to be irrigated. **3** a landing place on a river; quay. [C18: from F, from Med. L *levāta* from L *levāre* to raise]

levee[2] ('levɪ, 'leveɪ) *n* **1** a formal reception held by a sovereign just after rising from bed. **2** (in Britain) a public court reception for men. [C17: from F, var. of *lever* a rising, from L *levāre* to raise]

level ('levᵊl) *adj* **1** on a horizontal plane. **2** having a surface of completely equal height. **3** being of the same height as something else. **4** (of quantities to be measured, as in recipes) even with the top of the cup, spoon, etc. **5** equal to or even with (something or someone else). **6** not having or showing inconsistency or irregularities. **7** Also: **level-headed.** even-tempered; steady. **8** one's level best. the best one can do. ◆ *vb* **levels, levelling, levelled** *or US* **levels, leveling, leveled. 9** (*tr; sometimes foll.* by *off*) to make (a surface) horizontal, level, or even. **10** to make (two or more people or things) equal, as in posi-

tion or status. **11** (*tr*) to raze to the ground. **12** (*tr*) to knock (a person) down as by a blow. **13** (*tr*) to direct (a gaze, criticism, etc.) emphatically at someone. **14** (*intr; often foll.* by *with*) *Inf.* to be straightforward and frank. **15** (*intr; foll.* by *off or out*) to manoeuvre an aircraft into a horizontal flight path after a dive, climb, or glide. **16** (often foll. by *at*) to aim (a weapon) horizontally. ◆ *n* **17** a horizontal datum line or plane. **18** a device, such as a spirit level, for determining whether a surface is horizontal. **19** a surveying instrument used for measuring relative heights of land. **20** position or status in a scale of values. **21** amount or degree of progress; stage. **22** a specified vertical position; altitude. **23** a horizontal line or plane with respect to which measurement of elevation is based: *sea level.* **24** a flat even surface or area of land. **25** *Physics.* the ratio of the magnitude of a physical quantity to an arbitrary magnitude: *sound-pressure level.* **26 on the level.** *Inf.* sincere or genuine. [C14: from OF *livel*, from Vulgar L *lībellum* (unattested), from L *lībella*, dim. of *lībra* scales]
▸ **leveller** *or US* **leveler** *n* ▸ **levelly** *adv* ▸ **levelness** *n*

level crossing *n Brit., Austral., & NZ.* a point at which a railway and a road cross, esp. one with barriers that close the road when a train is due to pass.

level-headed *adj* even-tempered, balanced, and reliable; steady.
▸ **level-'headedly** *adv* ▸ **level-'headedness** *n*

level of attainment *n Brit. education.* one of ten groupings, each with its own attainment criteria based on pupil age and ability, within which a pupil is assessed.

level pegging *Brit. inf.* ◆ *n* **1** equality between two contestants. ◆ *adj* **2** (of two contestants) equal.

level playing field *n* a situation in which none of the competing parties has an advantage at the outset of a competitive activity.

Leven ★ ('liːvᵊn) *n* **Loch. 1** a lake in E central Scotland: one of the shallowest of Scottish lochs, with seven islands, on one of which Mary Queen of Scots was imprisoned (1567–8). Length: 6 km (3·7 miles). Width: 4 km (2·5 miles). **2** a sea loch in W Scotland, extending for about 14 km (9 miles) east from Loch Linnhe.

lever ('liːvə) *n* **1** a rigid bar pivoted about a fulcrum, used to transfer a force to a load and usually to provide a mechanical advantage. **2** any of a number of mechanical devices employing this principle. **3** a means of exerting pressure in order to accomplish something. ◆ *vb* **4** to prise or move (an object) with a lever. [C13: from OF *leveour*, from *lever* to raise, from L *levāre* from *levis* light]

leverage ('liːvərɪdʒ, -vrɪdʒ) *n* **1** the action of a lever. **2** the mechanical advantage gained by employing a lever. **3** strategic advantage. **4** power or influence: *the supermarket chains have greater leverage than single-outlet enterprises.* **5** the US word for **gearing** (sense 3). **6** the use made by a company of its limited assets to guarantee the substantial loans required to finance its business.

leveraged buyout ('liːvərɪdʒd, -vrɪdʒd) *n* a takeover bid in which a small company makes use of its limited assets, and those of the usually larger target company, to raise the loans required to finance the takeover. Abbrev.: **LBO.**

leveret ('levərɪt, -vrɪt) *n* a young hare, esp. one less than one year old. [C15: from Norman F *levrete*, dim. of *levre*, from L *lepus* hare]

Leverhulme ★ ('liːvə,hjuːm) *n* **William Hesketh**, 1st Viscount. 1851–1925, British soap manufacturer and philanthropist, who founded (1881) the model industrial town Port Sunlight.

Leverkusen ★ (*German* 'leːvər,kuːzən) *n* a town in NW Germany, in North Rhine-Westphalia on the Rhine: chemical industries. Pop.: 161 832 (1995 est.).

Leverrier ★ (*French* ləverje) *n* **Urbain Jean Joseph** (yrbɛ̃ ʒɑ̃ ʒozef). 1811–77, French astronomer: calculated the existence and position of the planet Neptune.

Levi[1] ★ ('liːvaɪ) *n* **1** *Old Testament.* **1a** the third son of Jacob and Leah and the ancestor of the tribe of Levi (Genesis 29:34). **1b** the priestly tribe descended from this patriarch (Numbers 18:21–24). **2** *New Testament.* another name for **Matthew** (the apostle).

Levi[2] ★ (*Italian* 'lɛ:vi) *n* **1 Carlo** ('karlo). 1902–75, Italian physician, painter, and writer, best known for his novel *Christ Stopped at Eboli* (1947). **2 Primo** ('pri:mo). 1919–87, Italian novelist. His book *If This is a Man* (1947) relates his experiences in Auschwitz. Other books include *The Drowned and the Saved* (1988), published after his suicide.

leviable ('levɪəbʰl) *adj* **1** (of taxes, etc.) liable to be levied. **2** (of goods, etc.) liable to bear a levy; taxable.

leviathan (lɪ'vaɪəθən) *n* **1** *Bible.* a monstrous beast, esp. a sea monster. **2** any huge or powerful thing. [C14: from LL, ult. from Heb. *liwyāthān*, from ?]

levigate ('levɪˌgeɪt) *vb* **levigates, levigating, levigated.** *Chem.* **1** (*tr*) to grind into a fine powder or a smooth paste. **2** to form or cause to form a homogeneous mixture, as in the production of gels. **3** (*tr*) to suspend (fine particles) by grinding in a liquid, esp. as a method of separating fine from coarse particles. [C17: from L *lēvigāre*, from *lēvis* smooth]
▸ ˌleviˈgation *n*

Levis ('li:vaɪz) *pl n Trademark.* jeans, usually blue and made of denim.

Lévi-Strauss ★ ('levɪ'straus; *French* levistros) *n* **Claude** (klod). born 1908, French anthropologist, leading exponent of structuralism. His books include *The Elementary Structures of Kinship* (1969), *Mythologies* (1964–71), and *Saudades do Brazil* (Memories of Brazil; 1994).

levitate ('levɪˌteɪt) *vb* **levitates, levitating, levitated.** to rise or cause to rise and float in the air, without visible agency, usually attributed, esp. formerly, to supernatural intervention. [C17: from L *levis* light + *-tate*, as in *gravitate*]
▸ ˌleviˈtation *n* ▸ 'leviˌtator *n*

levity ('levɪtɪ) *n, pl* **levities. 1** inappropriate lack of seriousness. **2** fickleness or instability. **3** *Arch.* lightness in weight. [C16: from L *levitās* lightness, from *levis* light]

Levkás (lef'kæs), **Leukas** *or* **Leucas** ★ *n* a Greek island in the Ionian Sea, in the Ionian Islands. Pop.: 22 000 (latest est.). Area: 295 sq. km (114 sq. miles). Italian name: **Santa Maura.**

Levkosia (lef'kəusɪə) *or* **Leukosia** ★ *n* the Greek name for **Nicosia.**

levodopa (ˌli:vəu'dəupə) *n* another name for **L-dopa.**

levy ('levɪ) *vb* **levies, levying, levied.** (*tr*) **1** to impose and collect (a tax, tariff, fine, etc.). **2** to conscript troops for service. **3** to seize or attach (property) in accordance with the judgment of a court. ◆ *n, pl* **levies. 4a** the act of imposing and collecting a tax, tariff, etc. **4b** the money so raised. **5a** the conscription of troops for service. **5b** a person conscripted in this way. [C15: from OF *levée* a raising, from *lever*, from L *levāre* to raise]

Lévy-Bruhl ★ (*French* levibryl) *n* **Lucien** (lysjē). 1857–1939, French anthropologist and philosopher, noted for his study of the psychology of primitive peoples.

lewd (lu:d) *adj* characterized by or intended to excite crude sexual desire; obscene. [C14: from OE *lǣwde* ignorant]
▸ 'lewdly *adv* ▸ 'lewdness *n*

Lewes ★ ('lu:ɪs) *n* a market town in S England, administrative centre of East Sussex, on the River Ouse: site of a battle (1264) in which Henry III was defeated by Simon de Montfort. Pop.: 15 376 (1991).

lewis ('lu:ɪs) *n* a lifting device for heavy stone blocks consisting of a number of curved pieces of metal fitting into a dovetailed recess cut into the stone. [C18: ?from the name of the inventor]

Lewis[1] ★ ('lu:ɪs) *n* the N part of the island of Lewis with Harris, in the Outer Hebrides. Area: 1634 sq. km (631 sq. miles).

Lewis[2] ★ ('lu:ɪs) *n* **1 Carl.** full name *Frederick Carleton Lewis.* born 1961, US athlete: won four gold medals at the Los Angeles Olympics (1984) and single gold medals at the 1988, 1992, and 1996 Olympics, for sprinting, relay, and long jump events. **2** See (Cecil) **Day-Lewis. 3 C(live) S(taples).** 1898–1963, British writer, noted for his theological study *The Screwtape Letters* (1942) and his children's books chronicling the land of Narnia. **4 Matthew Gregory,** known as *Monk Lewis.* 1775–1818, British writer, noted for his Gothic horror story *The Monk* (1796). **5**

Meriwether. 1774–1807, American explorer who led an overland expedition from St Louis to the Pacific Ocean (1804–06). **6 (Harry) Sinclair.** 1885–1951, US writer, whose novels include *Main Street* (1920) and *Babbit* (1922): Nobel prize for literature 1930. **7 (Percy) Wyndham.** 1884–1957, British painter and writer, born in the US. A founder of vorticism, his writings include *The Apes of God* (1930) and the trilogy *The Human Age* (1928–55).

Lewis acid *n* a substance capable of accepting a pair of electrons from a base to form a covalent bond. Cf. **Lewis base.** [C20: after G. N. *Lewis* (1875–1946), US chemist]

Lewis base *n* a substance capable of donating a pair of electrons to an acid to form a covalent bond. Cf. **Lewis acid.** [C20: after G. N. *Lewis;* see LEWIS ACID]

Lewis gun *n* a light air-cooled gas-operated machine gun used chiefly in World Wars I and II. [C20: after I. N. *Lewis* (1858–1931), US soldier]

Lewisham ★ ('lu:ɪʃəm) *n* a borough of S Greater London, on the River Thames. Pop.: 242 400 (1994 est.). Area: 35 sq. km (13 sq. miles).

lewisite ('lu:ɪˌsaɪt) *n* a colourless oily poisonous liquid having a powerful blistering action and used as a war gas. Formula: CICH:CHAsCl$_2$. Systematic name: **1-chloro-2-dichloroarsinoethene.** [C20: after W. L. *Lewis* (1878–1943), US chemist]

Lewis with Harris *or* **Lewis and Harris** ★ *n* an island in the Outer Hebrides, separated from the NW coast of Scotland by the Minch: consists of Lewis in the north and Harris in the south; many lakes and peat moors; economy based chiefly on the Harris tweed industry, with some fishing. Chief town: Stornoway. Pop.: 23 500 (latest est.). Area: 2134 sq. km (824 sq. miles).

lexeme ('leksi:m) *n Linguistics.* a minimal meaningful unit that cannot be understood from the meanings of its component morphemes. [C20: from LEX(ICON) + *-EME*]

lexical ('leksɪkʰl) *adj* **1** of or relating to items of vocabulary in a language. **2** of or relating to a lexicon.
▸ 'lexically *adv*

lexicography (ˌleksɪ'kɒɡrəfɪ) *n* the process or profession of writing or compiling dictionaries.
▸ ˌlexi'cographer *n* ▸ **lexicographic** (ˌleksɪkə'ɡræfɪk) *or* ˌlexico'graphical *adj*

lexicon ('leksɪkən) *n* **1** a dictionary, esp. one of an ancient language such as Greek or Hebrew. **2** a list of terms relating to a particular subject. **3** the vocabulary of a language or of an individual. **4** *Linguistics.* the set of all the morphemes of a language. [C17: NL, from Gk *lexikon*, n use of *lexikos* relating to words, from Gk *lexis* word, from *legein* to speak]

lexigraphy (lek'sɪɡrəfɪ) *n* a system of writing in which each word is represented by a sign. [C19: from Gk *lexis* word + -GRAPHY]

Lexington ★ ('leksɪŋtən) *n* **1** a city in NE central Kentucky, in the bluegrass region: major centre for horse-breeding. Pop.: 237 612 (1995 est.). **2** a city in Massachusetts, northwest of Boston: site of the first action (1775) of the War of American Independence. Pop.: 28 974 (1990).

lexis ('leksɪs) *n* the totality of vocabulary items in a language. [C20: from Gk *lexis* word]

ley (leɪ, li:) *n* **1** arable land temporarily under grass. **2** Also: **ley line.** a line joining two prominent points in the landscape, thought to be the line of a prehistoric track. [C14: var. of LEA]

Leyden[1] ★ ('laɪdʰn; *Dutch* 'leidə) *n* a variant of **Leiden.**

Leyden[2] ★ ('laɪdʰn) *n* See **Lucas van Leyden.**

Leyden jar *n Physics.* an early type of capacitor consisting of a glass jar with the lower part of the inside and outside coated with tin foil. [C18: first made in Leiden]

Leyte ★ ('leɪteɪ) *n* an island in the central Philippines, in the Visayan Islands. Chief town: Tacloban. Pop.: 1 362 050 (1990). Area: 7215 sq. km (2786 sq. miles).

Leyte Gulf ★ *n* an inlet of the Pacific in the E Philippines, east of Leyte and south of Samar: scene of a battle (Oct. 23–26, 1944) during World War II, in which the

★ people and places

Americans defeated almost the entire Japanese navy, thereby ensuring ultimate Allied victory.

If *Printing. abbrev. for* light face.

LF *Radio. abbrev. for* low frequency.

LG *abbrev. for* Low German.

LGV (in Britain) *abbrev. for* large goods vehicle.

lh or **LH** *abbrev. for* left hand.

Lhasa or **Lassa** ★ ('lɑːsə) *n* a city in SW China, capital of Tibet AR, at an altitude of 3606 m (11 830 ft): for centuries the sacred city of Lamaism and residence of the Dalai Lamas from the 17th century until 1950; known as the Forbidden City because it was closed to Westerners until the beginning of the 20th century; annexed by China in 1951. The Dalai Lama fled after an unsuccessful revolt against Chinese rule in 1959. Pop.: 106 885 (1990 est.).

Li *the chemical symbol for* lithium.

LI *abbrev. for:* **1** Long Island. **2** Light Infantry.

liabilities (ˌlaɪə'bɪlɪtɪz) *pl n Accounting.* business obligations not discharged and shown as balanced against assets on the balance sheet.

liability (ˌlaɪə'bɪlɪtɪ) *n, pl* **liabilities. 1** the state of being liable. **2** a financial obligation. **3** a hindrance or disadvantage.

liable ('laɪəb⁰l) *adj (postpositive)* **1** legally obliged or responsible; answerable. **2** susceptible or exposed; subject. **3** probable or likely: *it's liable to happen soon.* [C15: ? via Anglo-F, from OF *lier* to bind, from L *ligāre*]

> **USAGE NOTE** The use of *liable to* to mean *likely to* was formerly considered incorrect, but is now acceptable.

liaise (lɪ'eɪz) *vb* **liaises, liaising, liaised.** *(intr;* usually foll. by *with)* to communicate and maintain contact (with). [C20: back formation from LIAISON]

liaison (lɪ'eɪzɒn) *n* **1** communication and contact between groups or units. **2** a secretive or adulterous sexual relationship. **3** the relationship between military units necessary to ensure unity of purpose. **4** (esp. in French) the pronunciation of a normally silent consonant at the end of a word immediately before another word commencing with a vowel, in such a way that the consonant is taken over as the initial sound of the following word, as in *ils ont* (ilzɔ̃). **5** any thickening for soups, sauces, etc., such as egg yolks or cream. [C17: via F from OF, from *lier* to bind, from L *ligāre*]

Liákoura ★ ('ljakura) *n* transliteration of the Modern Greek name for (Mount) **Parnassus.**

liana (lɪ'ɑːnə) or **liane** (lɪ'ɑːn) *n* any of various woody climbing plants of tropical forests. [C19: changed from earlier *liane* (through infl. of F *lier* to bind) from F, from ?]

Lianyungang ('ljæn'jʊŋ'gæŋ), **Sinhailien,** or **Hsin-hai-lien** ★ *n* a city in E China, near the coast of Jiangsu. Pop.: 354 139 (1990 est.).

Liao ★ (ljau) *n* a river in NE China, rising in SE Inner Mongolia and flowing northeast then southwest to the Gulf of Liaodong. Length: about 1100 km (700 miles).

Liaodong ('ljau'dʊŋ) or **Liaotung** ★ ('ljau'tʊŋ) *n* **1** a peninsula of NE China, in S Manchuria extending south into the Yellow Sea: forms the S part of Liaoning province. **2 Gulf of.** the N part of the Gulf of Chihli, west of the peninsula of Liaodong.

Liaoning ★ ('ljau'nɪŋ) *n* a province of NE China, in S Manchuria. Capital: Shenyang. Pop.: 40 670 000 (1995 est.). Area: 150 000 sq. km (58 500 sq. miles).

Liaoyang ★ ('ljau'jæŋ) *n* a city in NE China, in S Manchuria, in Liaoning province: a regional capital in the early dynasties. Pop.: 492 559 (1990 est.).

liar ('laɪə) *n* a person who tells lies.

Liard ★ ('liːɑːd, liː'ɑːd, -'ɑː) *n* a river in W Canada, rising in the SE Yukon and flowing east and then northwest to the Mackenzie River. Length: 885 km (550 miles).

Lias ('laɪəs) *n* the lowest series of rocks of the Jurassic system. [C15 (referring to a kind of limestone), C19 (geological sense): from OF *liois,* ?from *lie* dregs, so called from its appearance]
> **Liassic** (laɪ'æsɪk) *adj*

lib (lɪb) *n Inf., sometimes derog.* short for **liberation.**

lib. *abbrev. for:* **1** liber. [L: book] **2** librarian. **3** library.

Lib. *abbrev. for* Liberal.

libation (laɪ'beɪʃən) *n* **1a** the pouring-out of wine, etc., in honour of a deity. **1b** the liquid so poured out. **2** *Usually facetious.* an alcoholic drink. [C14: from L *lībātiō,* from *lībāre* to pour an offering of drink]

Libau ★ ('liːbau) *n* the German name for **Liepāja.**

Libava ★ (lɪ'bavə) *n* transliteration of the Russian name for **Liepāja.**

Libby ★ ('lɪbɪ) *n* **Willard Frank.** 1908–80, US chemist, who devised the technique of radiocarbon dating: Nobel prize for chemistry 1960.

libel ('laɪb⁰l) *n* **1** *Law.* **1a** the publication of defamatory matter in permanent form, as by a written or printed statement, picture, etc. **1b** the act of publishing such matter. **2** any defamatory or unflattering representation or statement. **3** *Scots Law.* the formal statement of a charge. ◆ *vb* **libels, libelling, libelled** or *US* **libels, libeling, libeled.** *(tr)* **4** *Law.* to make or publish a defamatory statement or representation about (a person). **5** to misrepresent injuriously. [C13 (in the sense: written statement), hence C14 legal sense: a plaintiff's statement, via OF from L *libellus* a little book]
> **'libeller** or **'libelist** *n* ▸ **'libellous** or **'libelous** *adj*

liberal ('lɪbərəl, 'lɪbrəl) *adj* **1** relating to or having social and political views that favour progress and reform. **2** relating to or having policies or views advocating individual freedom. **3** giving and generous in temperament or behaviour. **4** tolerant of other people. **5** abundant; lavish: *a liberal helping of cream.* **6** not strict; free: *a liberal translation.* **7** of or relating to an education that aims to develop general cultural interests and abilities. ◆ *n* **8** a person who has liberal ideas or opinions. [C14: from L *līberālis* of freedom, from *līber* free]
> **'liberally** *adv* ▸ **'liberalness** *n*

Liberal ('lɪbərəl, 'lɪbrəl) *n* **1** a member or supporter of a Liberal Party or Liberal Democrat party. ◆ *adj* **2** of or relating to a Liberal Party.

liberal arts *pl n* the fine arts, humanities, sociology, languages, and literature. Often shortened to **arts.**

Liberal Democrat *n* a member or supporter of the Liberal Democrats.

Liberal Democrats *pl n* (in Britain) a political party with centrist policies; established in 1988 as the Social and Liberal Democrats when the Liberal Party merged with the Social Democratic Party; renamed Liberal Democrats in 1989.

liberalism ('lɪbərəˌlɪzəm, 'lɪbrə-) *n* liberal opinions, practices, or politics.

liberality (ˌlɪbə'rælɪtɪ) *n, pl* **liberalities. 1** generosity; bounty. **2** the quality or condition of being liberal.

liberalize or **liberalise** ('lɪbərəˌlaɪz, 'lɪbrə-) *vb* **liberalizes, liberalizing, liberalized** or **liberalises, liberalising, liberalised.** to make or become liberal.
> ▸ ˌliberali'zation or ˌliberali'sation *n* ▸ **'liberalˌizer** or **'liberalˌiser** *n*

Liberal Party *n* **1** one of the former major political parties in Britain; in 1988 it merged with the Social Democratic Party to form the Social and Liberal Democrats; renamed the Liberal Democrats in 1989. **2** one of the major political parties in Australia, a conservative party, generally opposed to the Labor Party. **3** any other party supporting liberal policies.

liberal studies *n (functioning as sing) Brit.* a supplementary arts course for those specializing in scientific, technical, or professional studies.

liberate ('lɪbəˌreɪt) *vb* **liberates, liberating, liberated.** *(tr)* **1** to give liberty to; make free. **2** to release (something, esp. a gas) from chemical combination. **3** to release from occupation or subjugation by a foreign power. **4** to free from social prejudices or injustices. **5** *Euphemistic or facetious.* to steal.
> ▸ **'liberˌator** *n*

liberated ('lɪbə,reɪtɪd) *adj* **1** given liberty; freed; released. **2** released from occupation or subjugation by a foreign power. **3** (esp. in feminist theory) not bound by traditional sexual and social roles.

liberation (,lɪbə'reɪʃən) *n* **1** a liberating or being liberated. **2** the seeking of equal status or just treatment for or on behalf of any group believed to be discriminated against: *women's liberation; animal liberation*.
▸ ,liber'ationist *n, adj*

liberation theology *n* the belief that Christianity involves not only faith in the Church but a commitment to change social and political conditions where it is considered exploitation and oppression exist: applied esp. to South America.

Liberec ★ (*Czech* 'lɪbɛrɛts) *n* a city in the NW Czech Republic, on the Neisse River: a centre of the German Sudeten movement in 1938. Pop.: 100 698 (1995 est.). German name: **Reichenberg**.

Liberia ★ (laɪ'bɪərɪə) *n* a republic in W Africa, on the Atlantic: originated in 1822 as a home for freed Afro-American slaves, with land purchased by the American Colonization Society; republic declared in 1847; exports are predominantly rubber and iron ore. Official language: English. Religion: Christian majority, also animist. Currency: dollar. Capital: Monrovia. Pop.: 2 602 000 (1997). Area: 111 400 sq. km (43 000 sq. miles).
▸ Li'berian *adj, n*

libertarian (,lɪbə'tɛərɪən) *n* **1** a believer in freedom of thought, expression, etc. **2** a believer in the doctrine of free will. Cf. **determinism**. ◆ *adj* **3** of, relating to, or characteristic of a libertarian. [C18: from LIBERTY]
▸ ,liber'tarianism *n*

libertine ('lɪbə,tiːn, -,taɪn) *n* **1** a morally dissolute person. ◆ *adj* **2** morally dissolute. [C14 (in the sense: freedman, dissolute person): from L *libertīnus* freedman, from *libertus* freed, from *liber* free]
▸ 'liber,tinage *or* 'libertin,ism *n*

liberty ('lɪbətɪ) *n, pl* **liberties**. **1** the power of choosing, thinking, and acting for oneself; freedom from control or restriction. **2** the right or privilege of access to a particular place; freedom. **3** (*often pl*) a social action regarded as being familiar, forward, or improper. **4** (*often pl*) an action that is unauthorized: *he took liberties with the translation*. **5a** authorized leave granted to a sailor. **5b** (*as modifier*): *liberty man; liberty boat*. **6 at liberty**. free, unoccupied, or unrestricted. **7 take liberties** (**with**). to be overfamiliar or overpresumptuous. [C14: from OF *liberté*, from L *lībertās*, from *līber* free]

liberty bodice *n* a sleeveless vestlike undergarment covering the upper part of the body, formerly worn esp. by young children.

liberty hall *n* (*sometimes caps.*) *Inf.* a place or condition of complete liberty.

Liberty Island ★ *n* a small island in upper New York Bay: site of the Statue of Liberty. Area: 5 hectares (12 acres). Former name (until 1956): **Bedloe's Island**.

Libia ★ ('liːbja) *n* the Italian name for **Libya**.

libidinous (lɪ'bɪdɪnəs) *adj* characterized by excessive sexual desire.
▸ li'bidinously *adv* ▸ li'bidinousness *n*

libido (lɪ'biːdəʊ) *n, pl* **libidos**. **1** *Psychoanal.* psychic energy emanating from the id. **2** sexual urge or desire. [C20 (in psychoanalysis): from L: desire]
▸ libidinal (lɪ'bɪdɪnºl) *adj* ▸ li'bidinally *adv*

libra ('laɪbrə) *n, pl* **librae** (-briː). an ancient Roman unit of weight corresponding to 1 pound. [C14: from L, lit.: scales]

Libra ('liːbrə) *n, Latin genitive* **Librae** ('liːbriː). **1** *Astron.* a small faint zodiacal constellation in the S hemisphere, lying between Virgo and Scorpius. **2** Also called: the **Scales**, the **Balance**. *Astrol.* the seventh sign of the zodiac. The sun is in this sign between about Sept. 23 and Oct. 22.

librarian (laɪ'brɛərɪən) *n* a person in charge of or assisting in a library.
▸ li'brarian,ship *n*

library ('laɪbrərɪ) *n, pl* **libraries**. **1** a room or set of rooms where books and other literary materials are kept. **2** a collection of literary materials, films, CDs, etc., kept for borrowing or reference. **3** the building or institution that houses such a collection: *a public library*. **4** a set of books published as a series, often in a similar format. **5** *Computing*. a collection of standard programs and subroutines, usually stored on disk. **6** a collection of specific items for reference or checking against: *a library of genetic material*. [C14: from OF *librairie*, from Med. L *librāris*, n. use of L *librārius* relating to books, from *liber* book]

libration (laɪ'breɪʃən) *n* **1** the act of oscillating. **2** a real or apparent oscillation of the moon enabling approximately nine per cent of the surface facing away from earth to be seen. [C17: from L, from *librāre* to balance]

librettist (lɪ'brɛtɪst) *n* the author of a libretto.

libretto (lɪ'brɛtəʊ) *n, pl* **librettos** *or* **libretti** (-tiː). a text written for and set to music in an opera, etc. [C18: from It., dim. of *libro* book]

Libreville ★ (*French* librəvil) *n* the capital of Gabon, in the west on the estuary of the Gabon River: founded as a French trading post in 1843 and expanded with the settlement of freed slaves in 1848. Pop.: 362 386 (1993).

Librium ('lɪbrɪəm) *n Trademark*. a preparation of the drug chlordiazepoxide used as a tranquillizer. See also **benzodiazepine**.

Libya ★ ('lɪbɪə) *n* a republic in N Africa, on the Mediterranean: became an Italian colony in 1912; divided after World War II into Tripolitania and Cyrenaica (under British administration) and Fezzan (under French); gained independence in 1951; monarchy overthrown by a military junta in 1969. It consists almost wholly of desert and is a major exporter of oil. Official language: Arabic. Official religion: (Sunni) Muslim. Currency: Libyan dinar. Capital: Tripoli. Pop.: 5 648 000 (1997). Area: 1 760 000 sq. km (680 000 sq. miles). Official name: **Al-Jumhuria al-Arabia allibya** (-,dʒæmə'hɪri:jθ).
▸ 'Libyan *adj, n*

Libyan Desert ★ *n* a desert in N Africa, in E Libya, W Egypt, and the NW Sudan: the NE part of the Sahara.

lice (laɪs) *n* the plural of **louse**.

licence *or US* **license** ('laɪsəns) *n* **1** a certificate, tag, document, etc., giving official permission to do something. **2** formal permission or exemption. **3** liberty of action or thought; freedom. **4** intentional disregard of conventional rules to achieve a certain effect: *poetic licence*. **5** excessive freedom. [C14: via OF and Med. L *licentia* permission, from L: freedom, from *licet* it is allowed]

license ('laɪsəns) *vb* **licenses, licensing, licensed**. (*tr*) **1** to grant or give a licence for (something, such as the sale of alcohol). **2** to give permission to or for.
▸ 'licensable *adj* ▸ 'licenser *or* 'licensor *n*

licensee (,laɪsən'siː) *n* a person who holds a licence, esp. one to sell alcoholic drink.

licentiate (laɪ'sɛnʃɪt) *n* **1** a person who holds a formal attestation of competence to practise a certain profession. **2** a higher degree awarded by certain, chiefly European, universities. **3** a person who holds this degree. **4** *Chiefly Presbyterian Church*. a person holding a licence to preach. [C15: from Med. L *licentiātus*, from *licentiāre* to permit]
▸ li'centiate,ship *n*

licentious (laɪ'sɛnʃəs) *adj* **1** sexually unrestrained or promiscuous. **2** *Now rare*. showing disregard for convention. [C16: from L *licentiōsus* capricious, from *licentia* LICENCE]
▸ li'centiously *adv* ▸ li'centiousness *n*

lichee (,laɪ'tʃiː) *n* a variant spelling of **litchi**.

lichen ('laɪkən, 'lɪtʃən) *n* an organism that is formed by the symbiotic association of a fungus and an alga or cyanobacterium and occurs as crusty patches or bushy growths on tree trunks, bare ground, etc. Lichens are now classified as a phylum of fungi. [C17: via L from Gk *leikhēn*, from *leikhein* to lick]
▸ 'lichened *adj* ▸ 'lichenous *adj*

Lichfield ★ ('lɪtʃ,fiːld) *n* a city in central England, in SE Staffordshire: cathedral with three spires (13th-14th century); birthplace of Samuel Johnson, during whose lifetime the **Lichfield Group** (a literary circle) flourished. Pop.: 28 666 (1991).

lich gate (lɪtʃ) *n* a variant spelling of **lych gate**.

Lichtenstein ★ (ˈlɪktənˌstaɪn) *n* **Roy**. 1923–97, US pop artist.

licit (ˈlɪsɪt) *adj* a less common word for **lawful**. [C15: from L *licitus*, from *licēre* to be permitted] ▶ ˈlicitly *adv* ▶ ˈlicitness *n*

lick (lɪk) *vb* **1** (*tr*) to pass the tongue over, esp. in order to taste or consume. **2** to flicker or move lightly over or round (something): *the flames licked around the door.* **3** (*tr*) *Inf*. **3a** to defeat or vanquish. **3b** to flog or thrash. **3c** to be or do much better than. **4 lick into shape**. to put into a satisfactory condition. **5 lick one's wounds**. to retire after a defeat. ◆ *n* **6** an instance of passing the tongue over something. **7** a small amount: *a lick of paint.* **8** short for **salt lick**. **9** *Inf*. a hit; blow. **10** *Sl*. a short musical phrase, usually on one instrument. **11** *Inf*. rate of movement; speed. **12 a lick and a promise**. something hastily done, esp. a hurried wash. [OE *liccian*]
▶ ˈlicker *n*

lickerish *or* **liquorish** (ˈlɪkərɪʃ) *adj Arch*. **1** lecherous or lustful. **2** greedy; gluttonous. **3** appetizing or tempting. [C16: changed from C13 *lickerous*, from OF *lechereus* lecherous; see LECHER]

lickety-split (ˈlɪkɪtɪˈsplɪt) *adv US & Canad. inf.* very quickly; speedily. [C19: from LICK + SPLIT]

licking (ˈlɪkɪŋ) *n Inf*. **1** a beating. **2** a defeat.

lickspittle (ˈlɪkˌspɪtªl) *n* a flattering or servile person.

licorice (ˈlɪkərɪs) *n* the usual US and Canad. spelling of **liquorice**.

lictor (ˈlɪktə) *n* one of a group of ancient Roman officials, usually bearing fasces, who attended magistrates, etc. [C16 *lictor*, C14 *littour*, from L *ligāre* to bind]

lid (lɪd) *n* **1** a cover, usually removable or hinged, for a receptacle: *a saucepan lid; a desk lid.* **2** short for **eyelid**. **3 put the lid on.** *Inf*. **3a** Brit. to be the final blow to. **3b** to curb, prevent, or discourage. [OE *hlid*]
▶ ˈlidded *adj* ▶ ˈlidless *adj*

Liddell Hart ★ (ˈlɪdªl ˈhɑːt) *n* Sir **Basil Henry**. 1895–1970, British military strategist and advocate of mechanized warfare.

Lidice ★ (Czech ˈlidjtsɛ) *n* a mining village in the Czech Republic: destroyed by the Germans in 1942 in reprisal for the assassination of Reinhard Heydrich; rebuilt as a national memorial.

lido (ˈliːdəʊ) *n, pl* **lidos**. *Brit*. a public place of recreation, including a swimming pool. [C20: after the *Lido*, island bathing beach near Venice, from L *litus* shore]

lie[1] (laɪ) *vb* **lies, lying, lied**. **1** (*intr*) to speak untruthfully with intent to mislead or deceive. **2** (*intr*) to convey a false impression or practise deception: *the camera does not lie.* ◆ *n* **3** an untrue or deceptive statement deliberately used to mislead. **4** something that is deliberately intended to deceive. **5 give the lie to.** **5a** to disprove. **5b** to accuse of lying. ◆ Related adj: **mendacious**. [OE *lyge* (n), *lēogan* (vb)]

lie[2] (laɪ) *vb* **lies, lying, lay, lain**. (*intr*) **1** (often foll. by *down*) to place oneself or be in a prostrate position, horizontal to the ground. **2** to be situated, esp. on a horizontal surface: *the pencil is lying on the desk; India lies to the south of Russia.* **3** to be buried: *here lies Jane Brown.* **4** (*copula*) to be and remain (in a particular state or condition): *to lie dormant.* **5** to stretch or extend: *the city lies before us.* **6** (usually foll. by *on* or *upon*) to rest or weigh: *my sins lie heavily on my mind.* **7** (usually foll. by *in*) to exist or consist inherently: *strength lies in unity.* **8** (foll. by *with*) **8a** to be or rest (with): *the ultimate decision lies with you.* **8b** *Arch*. to have sexual intercourse (with). **9** (of an action, claim, appeal, etc.) to subsist; be maintainable or admissible. **10** *Arch*. to stay temporarily. ◆ *n* **11** the manner, place, or style in which something is situated. **12** the hiding place or lair of an animal. **13 lie of the land**. **13a** the topography of the land. **13b** the way in which a situation is developing. ◆ See also **lie down, lie in**, etc. [OE *licgan* akin to OHG *ligen* to lie, L *lectus* bed]

Lie ★ (liː) *n* **Trygve Halvdan** (ˈtrygvə ˈhaldən). 1896–1968, Norwegian statesman; first secretary-general of the United Nations (1946–52).

Liebig ★ (German ˈliːbɪç) *n* **Justus** (ˈjustus), Baron von Liebig. 1803–73, German chemist, who founded agricultural chemistry and discovered chloroform.

Liebig condenser (ˈliːbɪg) *n Chem*. a laboratory condenser consisting of a glass tube surrounded by a glass envelope through which cooling water flows.

Liebknecht ★ (German ˈliːpknɛçt) *n* **1 Karl** (karl). 1871–1919, German socialist leader: with Rosa Luxemburg he led an unsuccessful Communist revolt (1919) and was assassinated. **2** his father, **Wilhelm** (ˈvɪlhelm). 1826–1900, German socialist leader and founder (1869) of what became (1891) the German Social Democratic Party.

Liechtenstein ★ (ˈlɪktənˌstaɪn; German ˈlɪçtənʃtaɪn) *n* a small mountainous principality in central Europe on the Rhine: formed in 1719 by the uniting of the lordships of Schellenburg and Vaduz, which had been purchased by the Austrian family of Liechtenstein; customs union formed with Switzerland in 1924. Official language: German. Religion: mostly Roman Catholic. Currency: Swiss franc. Capital: Vaduz. Pop.: 31 300 (1997). Area: 160 sq. km (62 sq. miles).

lied (liːd; German liːt) *n, pl* **lieder** (ˈliːdə; German ˈliːdər). *Music*. any of various musical settings for solo voice and piano of a romantic or lyrical poem. [from G: song]

lie detector *n Inf*. a polygraph used esp. by a police interrogator to detect false or devious answers to questions, a sudden change in one or more involuntary physiological responses being considered a manifestation of guilt, fear, etc.

lie down *vb* (*intr, adv*) **1** to place oneself or be in a prostrate position in order to rest. **2** to accept without protest or opposition (esp. in **take something lying down**). ◆ *n* **lie-down**. **3** a rest.

lief (liːf) *adv* **1** *Now rare*. gladly; willingly: *I'd as lief go today as tomorrow.* ◆ *adj* **2** *Arch*. **2a** ready; glad. **2b** dear; beloved. [OE *leof*; rel. to *lufu* love]

liege (liːdʒ) *adj* **1** (of a lord) owed feudal allegiance (esp. in **liege lord**). **2** (of a vassal or servant) owing feudal allegiance: *a liege subject.* **3** faithful; loyal. ◆ *n* **4** a liege lord. **5** a liegeman or true subject. [C13: from OF *lige*, from Med. L *līticus*, from *lītus, laetus* serf, of Gmc origin]

Liège ★ (lɪˈɛːʒ; French ljɛʒ) *n* **1** a province of E Belgium: formerly a principality of the Holy Roman Empire, much larger than the present-day province. Pop.: 1 015 007 (1995 est.). Area: 3877 sq. km (1497 sq. miles). **2** a city in E Belgium, capital of Liège province: the largest French-speaking city in Belgium; river port and industrial centre. Pop.: 192 393 (1995 est.). ◆ Flemish name: **Luik**.

liegeman (ˈliːdʒˌmæn) *n, pl* **liegemen**. **1** (formerly) a vassal. **2** a loyal follower.

Liegnitz ★ (ˈliːgnɪts) *n* the German name for **Legnica**.

lie in *vb* (*intr, adv*) **1** to remain in bed late in the morning. **2** to be confined in childbirth. ◆ *n* **lie-in**. **3** a long stay in bed in the morning.

lien (ˈliːən, liːn) *n Law*. a right to retain possession of another's property pending discharge of a debt. [C16: via OF from L *ligāmen* bond, from *ligāre* to bind]

Liepāja *or* **Lepaya** ★ (lɪˈpɑːjə) *n* a port in Latvia on the Baltic Sea: a naval and industrial centre, with a fishing fleet. Pop.: 100 271 (1995 est.). Russian name: **Libava**. German name: **Libau**.

lierne (lɪˈɜːn) *n Archit*. a short rib that connects the intersections of the primary ribs, esp. in Gothic vaulting. [C19: from F, ? rel. to *lier* to bind]

Liestal ★ (German ˈliːstaːl) *n* a city in NW Switzerland, capital of Basel-Land demicanton. Pop.: 12 161 (1987 est.).

lie to *vb* (*intr, adv*) *Naut*. (of a vessel) to be hove to with little or no swinging.

Lietuva ★ (lɪə'tuːvə) *n* the Lithuanian name for **Lithuania**.

lieu (ljuː, luː) *n* stead; place (esp. in **in lieu, in lieu of**). [C13: from OF, ult. from L *locus* place]

lieutenant (lɛf'tɛnənt; *US* luː'tɛnənt) *n* **1** a military officer holding commissioned rank immediately junior to a captain. **2** a naval officer holding commissioned rank immediately junior to a lieutenant commander. **3** *US*. an officer in a police or fire department ranking immediately junior to a captain. **4** a person who holds an office in subordination to or in place of a superior. [C14: from OF, lit.: place-holding]
▸ **lieu'tenancy** *n*

lieutenant colonel *n* an officer holding commissioned rank immediately junior to a colonel in certain armies, air forces, and marine corps.

lieutenant commander *n* an officer holding commissioned rank in certain navies immediately junior to a commander.

lieutenant general *n* an officer holding commissioned rank in certain armies, air forces, and marine corps immediately junior to a general.

lieutenant governor *n* **1** a deputy governor. **2** (in the US) an elected official who acts as deputy to a state governor. **3** (in Canada) the representative of the Crown in a province: appointed by the federal government.

Lifar ★ (*French* lifar) *n* **Serge** (sɛrʒ). 1905–86, Russian ballet dancer and choreographer: ballet master at the Paris Opera Ballet (1932–58). His ballets include *Prométhée* (1929) and *Phèdre* (1950).

life (laɪf) *n, pl* **lives** (laɪvz). **1** the state or quality that distinguishes living beings or organisms from dead ones and from inorganic matter, characterized chiefly by metabolism, growth, and the ability to reproduce and respond to stimuli. Related adj: **animate**. **2** the period between birth and death. **3** a living person or being: *to save a life*. **4** the time between birth and the present time. **5a** the remainder or extent of one's life. **5b** (*as modifier*): *a life sentence; life membership; life work.* **6** *Inf.* short for **life imprisonment**. **7** the amount of time that something is active or functioning: *the life of a battery.* **8** a present condition, state, or mode of existence: *my life is very dull here.* **9a** a biography. **9b** (*as modifier*): *a life story.* **10** a characteristic state or mode of existence: *town life.* **11** the sum or course of human events and activities. **12** liveliness or high spirits: *full of life.* **13** a source of strength, animation, or vitality: *he was the life of the show.* **14** all living things, taken as a whole: *there is no life on Mars; plant life.* **15** (*modifier*) *Arts.* drawn or taken from a living model: *life drawing.* **16** (in certain games) one of a number of opportunities for participation. **17** a matter of life and death. a matter of extreme urgency. **18** as large as life. *Inf.* real and living. **19** for the life of me (him, her, etc.) though trying desperately. **20** not on your life. *Inf.* certainly not. **21** the life and soul. *Inf.* a person regarded as the main source of merriment and liveliness: *the life and soul of the party.* **22** to the life. (of a copy or image) resembling the original exactly. **23** true to life. faithful to reality. [OE *līf*]

life assurance *n* a form of insurance providing for the payment of a specified sum to a named beneficiary on the death of the policyholder. Also called: **life insurance**.

life belt *n* a buoyant ring used to keep a person afloat when in danger of drowning.

lifeblood ('laɪf,blʌd) *n* **1** the blood, considered as vital to life. **2** the essential or animating force.

lifeboat ('laɪf,bəʊt) *n* **1** a boat used for rescuing people at sea, escaping from a sinking ship, etc. **2** *Inf.* a fund set up by the dealers in a market to rescue any member who may become insolvent as a result of a collapse in market prices.

life buoy *n* any of various kinds of buoyant device for keeping people afloat in an emergency.

life cycle *n* the series of changes occurring in an animal or plant between one stage and the identical stage in the next generation.

life expectancy *n* the statistically determined average number of years of life remaining after a specified age.

lifeguard ('laɪf,gɑːd) *n* a person at a beach or pool to guard people against the risk of drowning.

life imprisonment *n* an indeterminate sentence always given for murder and as a maximum sentence in several other crimes. There is no remission, although the Home Secretary may order the prisoner's release on licence.

life jacket *n* an inflatable sleeveless jacket worn to keep a person afloat when in danger of drowning.

lifeless ('laɪflɪs) *adj* **1** without life; inanimate; dead. **2** not sustaining living organisms. **3** having no vitality or animation. **4** unconscious.
▸ **'lifelessly** *adv* ▸ **'lifelessness** *n*

lifelike ('laɪf,laɪk) *adj* closely resembling or representing life.
▸ **'life,likeness** *n*

lifeline ('laɪf,laɪn) *n* **1** a line thrown or fired aboard a vessel for hauling in a hawser for a breeches buoy. **2** a line by which a deep-sea diver is raised or lowered. **3** a single means of contact, communication, or support on which a person or an area, etc., relies.

lifelong ('laɪf,lɒŋ) *adj* lasting for or as if for a lifetime.

life peer *n* *Brit.* a peer whose title lapses at his death.

life preserver *n* **1** *Brit.* a club or bludgeon, esp. one kept for self-defence. **2** *US & Canad.* a life belt or life jacket.

lifer ('laɪfə) *n* *Inf.* a prisoner sentenced to imprisonment for life.

life raft *n* a raft for emergency use at sea.

life-saver *n* **1** the saver of a person's life. **2** *Austral.* an expert swimmer, esp. a member of a surf life-saving club at a surfing beach, who rescues surfers or swimmers from drowning. **3** *Inf.* a person or thing that gives help in time of need.
▸ **'life-,saving** *adj, n*

life science *n* any one of the branches of science concerned with the structure and behaviour of living organisms, such as biology, botany, zoology, physiology, or biochemistry.

life-size *or* **life-sized** *adj* representing actual size.

life span *n* the period of time during which a human being, animal, machine, etc., may be expected to live or function.

lifestyle ('laɪf,staɪl) *n* **1** a set of attitudes, habits, or possessions associated with a particular person or group. **2** such attitudes, etc., regarded as fashionable or desirable. **3** *NZ.* **3a** a luxurious semirural manner of living. **3b** (*as modifier*): *a lifestyle property.*

lifestyle business *n* a small business in which the owners are more anxious to pursue interests that reflect their lifestyle than to make more than a comfortable living.

life-support *adj* of, providing, or relating to the equipment or treatment necessary to keep a person alive.

lifetime ('laɪf,taɪm) *n* **1a** the length of time a person or animal is alive. **1b** (*as modifier*): *a lifetime supply.* **2** the length of time that something functions, is useful, etc. **3** Also called: **life**. *Physics.* the average time of existence of an unstable or reactive entity.

Liffey ★ ('lɪfɪ) *n* a river in E Republic of Ireland, rising in the Wicklow Mountains and flowing west, then northeast through Dublin into Dublin Bay. Length: 80 km (50 miles).

Lifford ★ ('lɪfəd) *n* the county town of Donegal, Republic of Ireland; market town. Pop.: 1461 (1986).

LIFO ('laɪfəʊ) *n acronym for* last in, first out (as an accounting principle in sorting stock). Cf. **FIFO**.

lift (lɪft) *vb* **1** to rise or cause to rise upwards from the ground or another support to a higher place: *to lift a sack.* **2** to move or cause to move upwards: *to lift one's eyes.* **3** (*tr*) to take hold of in order to carry or remove: *to lift something down from a shelf.* **4** (*tr*) to raise in status, spirituality, estimation, etc.: *his position lifted him from the common crowd.* **5** (*tr*) to revoke or rescind: *to lift tax restrictions.* **6** (*tr*) to take (plants or underground crops) out of the ground for transplanting or harvesting. **7** (*intr*) to disappear or by lifting or as if by lifting: *the fog lifted.* **8** (*tr*) to take unlawfully or dishonourably; steal. **9** (*tr*) *Inf.* to plagiarize. **10** (*tr*) *Sl.* to arrest. **11** (*tr*) to perform a face-lift on. ◆ *n* **12** the act or an instance of lifting. **13** the power or

force available or used for lifting. **14a** *Brit.* a platform, compartment, or cage raised or lowered in a vertical shaft to transport persons or goods in a building. US and Canad. word: **elevator. 14b** See **chairlift, ski lift. 15** the distance or degree to which something is lifted. **16** a ride in a car or other vehicle for part or all of a passenger's journey. **17** a rise in the height of the ground. **18** a rise in morale or feeling of cheerfulness usually caused by some specific thing or event. **19** the force required to lift an object. **20** a layer inserted in the heel of a shoe, etc., to give the wearer added height. **21** aid; help. **22** the component of the aerodynamic forces acting on a wing, etc., at right angles to the airflow and opposing gravity. [C13: from ON]
▶ 'lifter *n*

liftoff ('lɪft,ɒf) *n* **1** the initial movement of a rocket from its launch pad. **2** the instant at which this occurs. ◆ *vb* **lift off. 3** (*intr, adv*) (of a rocket) to leave its launch pad.

lift pump *n* a pump that raises a fluid to a higher level. Cf. **force pump.**

lig (lɪg) *Brit. sl.* ◆ *n* **1** (esp. in the media) a function at which free entertainment and refreshments are available. ◆ *vb* **ligs, ligging, ligged. 2** (*intr*) to attend such a function; freeload. [C20: from ?]
▶ 'ligger *n* ▶ 'ligging *n*

ligament ('lɪgəmənt) *n* **1** *Anat.* any one of the bands of tough fibrous connective tissue that restrict movement in joints, connect various bones or cartilages, support muscles, etc. **2** any physical or abstract bond. [C14: from Med. L *ligāmentum*, from L (in the sense: bandage), from *ligāre* to bind]

ligand ('lɪgənd, 'laɪ-) *n Chem.* an atom, molecule, radical, or ion forming a complex with a central atom. [C20: from L *ligandum*, from *ligāre* to bind]

ligate ('laɪgeɪt) *vb* **ligates, ligating, ligated.** (*tr*) to tie up or constrict (something) with a ligature. [C16: from L *ligātus*, from *ligāre* to bind]
▶ li'gation *n*

ligature ('lɪgətʃə, -,tʃʊə) *n* **1** the act of binding or tying up. **2** something used to bind. **3** a link, bond, or tie. **4** *Surgery.* a thread or wire for tying around a vessel, duct, etc., as for constricting the flow of blood. **5** *Printing.* a character of two or more joined letters, such as ff, fi, fl, ffi. **6** *Music.* a slur or the group of notes connected by it. ◆ *vb* **ligatures, ligaturing, ligatured. 7** (*tr*) to bind with a ligature; ligate. [C14: from LL *ligātūra*, ult. from L *ligāre* to bind]

liger ('laɪgə) *n* the hybrid offspring of a female tiger and a male lion.

Ligeti ★ (*Hungarian* 'lɪgeti) *n* **György** (djørdj). born 1923, Hungarian composer, resident in Vienna. His works include *Atmosphères* (1961), *Volumina* (1962), and a requiem mass (1965).

light[1] (laɪt) *n* **1** the medium of illumination that makes sight possible. **2** Also called: **visible radiation.** electromagnetic radiation that is capable of causing a visual sensation. See also **speed of light. 3** (*not in technical usage*) electromagnetic radiation that has a wavelength outside this range, esp. ultraviolet radiation: *ultraviolet light.* **4** the sensation experienced when electromagnetic radiation within the visible spectrum falls on the retina of the eye. **5** anything that illuminates, such as a lamp or candle. **6** See **traffic light. 7** a particular quality or type of light: *a good light for reading.* **8a** illumination from the sun during the day; daylight. **8b** the time this appears; daybreak; dawn. **9** anything that allows the entrance of light, such as a window or compartment of a window. **10** the condition of being visible or known (esp. in **bring** or **come to light). 11** an aspect or view: *he saw it in a different light.* **12** mental understanding or spiritual insight. **13** a person considered to be an authority or leader. **14** brightness of countenance, esp. a sparkle in the eyes. **15a** the act of igniting or kindling something, such as a cigarette. **15b** something that ignites or kindles, esp. in a specified manner, such as a spark or flame. **15c** something used for igniting or kindling, such as a match. **16** See **lighthouse. 17** in (the) **light of.** in view of; taking into account; considering. **18 see the light.** to acquire insight. **19 see the light (of day).** 19a to come into being. **19b** to come to public notice. **20 strike a light.** 20a (*vb*) to ignite some-

thing, esp. a match, by friction. **20b** (*interj*) *Brit.* an exclamation of surprise. ◆ *adj* **21** full of light; well-lighted. **22** (of a colour) reflecting or transmitting a large amount of light: *light yellow.* ◆ *vb* **lights, lighting, lighted** or **lit. 23** to ignite or cause to ignite. **24** (often foll. by *up*) to illuminate or cause to illuminate. **25** to make or become cheerful or animated. **26** (*tr*) to guide or lead by light. ◆ See also **lights**[1], **light up.** [OE *lēoht*]
▶ 'lightish *adj* ▶ 'lightless *adj*

light[2] (laɪt) *adj* **1** not heavy; weighing relatively little. **2** having relatively low density: *magnesium is a light metal.* **3** lacking sufficient weight; not agreeing with standard or official weights. **4** not great in degree, intensity, or number: *light rain.* **5** without burdens, difficulties, or problems; easily borne or done: *a light heart; light work.* **6** graceful, agile, or deft: *light fingers.* **7** not bulky or clumsy. **8** not serious or profound; entertaining: *light music; light verse.* **9** without importance or consequence; insignificant: *no light matter.* **10** frivolous or capricious. **11** loose in morals. **12** dizzy or unclear: *a light head.* **13** (of bread, cake, etc.) spongy or well leavened. **14** easily digested: *a light meal.* **15** relatively low in alcoholic content: *a light wine.* **16** (of a soil) having a crumbly texture. **17** (of a vessel, lorry, etc.) **17a** designed to carry light loads. **17b** not loaded. **18** carrying light arms or equipment: *light infantry.* **19** (of an industry) engaged in the production of small consumer goods using light machinery. **20** *Aeronautics.* (of an aircraft) having a maximum take-off weight less than 5670 kilograms (12 500 pounds). **21** *Chem.* (of an oil fraction obtained from coal tar) having a boiling range between about 100° and 210°C. **22** (of a railway) having a narrow gauge, or in some cases a standard gauge with speed or load restrictions not applied to a main line. **23** *Phonetics, prosody.* (of a syllable, vowel, etc.) unaccented or weakly stressed; short. **24 light on.** *Inf.* lacking a sufficient quantity of (something). **25 make light of.** to treat as insignificant or trifling. ◆ *adv* **26** a less common word for **lightly. 27** with little equipment, baggage, etc.: *to travel light.* ◆ *vb* **lights, lighting, lighted** or **lit.** (*intr*) **28** (esp. of birds) to settle or land after flight. **29** to get down from a horse, vehicle, etc. **30** (foll. by *on* or *upon*) to come upon unexpectedly. **31** to strike or fall on: *the choice lighted on me.* ◆ See also **light into, light out, lights**[2]. [OE *lēoht*]
▶ 'lightish *adj* ▶ 'lightly *adv* ▶ 'lightness *n*

light air *n* very light air movement of force one (1–3 mph) on the Beaufort scale.

light box *n* a light source contained in a box and covered with a diffuser, used for viewing photographic transparencies, negatives, etc.

light breeze *n* a very light wind of force two (4–7 mph) on the Beaufort scale.

light bulb *n* a glass bulb containing a gas at low pressure and enclosing a thin metal filament that emits light when an electric current is passed through it. Sometimes shortened to **bulb.**

light-emitting diode *n* a semiconductor that emits light when an electric current is applied to it: used in electronic calculators, digital watches, etc.

lighten[1] ('laɪt°n) *vb* **1** to become or make light. **2** (*intr*) to shine; glow. **3** (*intr*) (of lightning) to flash. **4** (*tr*) *Arch.* to cause to flash.

lighten[2] ('laɪt°n) *vb* **1** to make or become less heavy. **2** to make or become less burdensome or oppressive; mitigate. **3** to make or become more cheerful or lively.

lightening ('laɪt°nɪŋ) *n Obstetrics.* the sensation, experienced by many women late in pregnancy when the head of the fetus enters the pelvis, of a reduction in pressure on the diaphragm.

lighter[1] ('laɪtə) *n* **1** a small portable device for providing a naked flame to light cigarettes, etc. **2** a person or thing that ignites something.

lighter[2] ('laɪtə) *n* a flat-bottomed barge used for transporting cargo, esp. in loading or unloading a ship. [C15: prob. from MDu.]

lighterage ('laɪtərɪdʒ) *n* **1** the conveyance or loading and unloading of cargo by means of a lighter. **2** the charge for this service.

light face n 1 *Printing.* a weight of type characterized by light thin lines. ◆ *adj also* **light-faced. 2** (of type) having this weight.

light-fingered *adj* having nimble or agile fingers, esp. for thieving or picking pockets.

light flyweight n 1 an amateur boxer weighing not more than 48 kg (106 pounds). **2** an amateur wrestler weighing not more than 48 kg (106 pounds).

light-footed *adj* having a light or nimble tread.
▸ ,light-'footedly *adv*

light-headed *adj* **1** frivolous. **2** giddy; feeling faint or slightly delirious.
▸ ,light-'headedly *adv* ▸ ,light-'headedness *n*

light-hearted *adj* cheerful or carefree in mood or disposition.
▸ ,light-'heartedly *adv* ▸ ,light-'heartedness *n*

light heavyweight n 1 Also (in Britain): **cruiserweight. 1a** a professional boxer weighing 160–175 pounds (72.5–79.5 kg). **1b** an amateur boxer weighing 75–81 kg (165–179 pounds). **2a** a professional wrestler weighing not more than 198 pounds (90 kg). **2b** an amateur wrestler weighing not more than 90 kg (198 pounds).

lighthouse ('laɪt,haʊs) n a fixed structure in the form of a tower equipped with a light visible to mariners for warning them of obstructions, etc.

lighting ('laɪtɪŋ) n 1 the act or quality of illumination or ignition. **2** the apparatus for supplying artificial light effects to a stage, film, or television set. **3** the distribution of light on an object or figure, as in painting, photography, etc.

lighting cameraman n Films. the person who designs and supervises the lighting of scenes to be filmed.

lighting-up time n the time when vehicles are required by law to have their lights on.

light into vb (tr, prep) Inf. to assail physically or verbally.

light middleweight n an amateur boxer weighing 67–71 kg (148–157 pounds).

lightness ('laɪtnɪs) n the attribute of an object or colour that enables an observer to judge the extent to which the object or colour reflects or transmits incident light.

lightning ('laɪtnɪŋ) n 1 a flash of light in the sky, occurring during a thunderstorm and caused by a discharge of electricity, either between clouds or between a cloud and the earth. **2** (*modifier*) fast and sudden: *a lightning raid.* [C14: var. of *lightening*]

lightning conductor *or* **rod** n a metal strip terminating in sharp points, attached to the highest part of a building, etc., to discharge the electric field before it can reach a dangerous level and cause a lightning strike.

light opera n another term for **operetta.**

light out vb (intr, adv) Inf. to depart quickly, as if being chased.

light pen n Computer technol. **a** a rodlike device which, when applied to the screen of a cathode-ray tube, can detect the time of passage of the illuminated spot across that point thus enabling a computer to determine the position on the screen being pointed at. **b** a penlike device, used to read bar codes, that emits light and determines the intensity of that light as reflected from a small area of an adjacent surface.

light pollution n the glow from street and domestic lighting that obscures the night sky and hinders the observation of faint stars.

light rail n a transport system using small trains or trams, often serving parts of a large metropolitan area.

lights[1] (laɪts) pl n a person's ideas, knowledge, or understanding: *he did it according to his lights.*

lights[2] (laɪts) pl n the lungs, esp. of sheep, bullocks, and pigs, used esp. for feeding pets. [C13: pl n use of LIGHT[2], referring to the light weight of the lungs]

light-sensitive *adj* Physics. (of a surface) having a photoelectric property, such as the ability to generate a current, change its electrical resistance, etc., when exposed to light.

lightship ('laɪt,ʃɪp) n a ship equipped as a lighthouse and

moored where a fixed structure would prove impracticable.

light show n a kaleidoscopic display of moving lights, etc., projected onto a screen, esp. during pop concerts.

lightsome ('laɪtsəm) *adj* Arch. or poetic. **1** light-hearted or gay. **2** airy or buoyant. **3** not serious; frivolous.

lights out n 1 the time when those resident at an institution, such as soldiers in barracks or children at a boarding school, are expected to retire to bed. **2** a signal indicating this.

light table n Printing. a translucent surface of ground glass or a similar substance, illuminated from below and used for the examination of film, pages, etc.

light trap n any mechanical arrangement that allows some form of movement to take place while excluding light, such as a light-proof door or the lips of a film cassette.

light up vb (adv) **1** to light a cigarette, pipe, etc. **2** to illuminate or cause to illuminate. **3** to make or become cheerful or animated.

lightweight ('laɪt,weɪt) *adj* **1** of a relatively light weight. **2** not serious; trivial. ◆ n 3 a person or animal of a relatively light weight. **4a** a professional boxer weighing 130–135 pounds (59–61 kg). **4b** an amateur boxer weighing 57–60 kg (126–132 pounds). **5a** a professional wrestler weighing not more than 154 pounds (70 kg). **5b** an amateur wrestler weighing not more than 68 kg (150 pounds). **6** Inf. a person of little importance or influence.

light welterweight n an amateur boxer weighing 60–63.5 kg (132–140 pounds).

light year n a unit of distance used in astronomy, equal to the distance travelled by light in one year, i.e. 9.4607×10^{12} kilometres or 0.3066 parsecs.

ligneous ('lɪgnɪəs) *adj* of or resembling wood. [C17: from L *ligneus*, from *lignum* wood]

lignin ('lɪgnɪn) n a complex polymer occurring in certain plant cell walls making the plant rigid. [C19: from L *lignum* wood + -IN]

lignite ('lɪgnaɪt) n a brown carbonaceous sedimentary rock with woody texture that consists of accumulated layers of partially decomposed vegetation: used as a fuel. Also called: **brown coal.**
▸ **lignitic** (lɪg'nɪtɪk) *adj*

lignum vitae ('lɪgnəm 'vaɪtɪ) n 1 either of two tropical American trees having blue or purple flowers. **2** the heavy resinous wood of either of these trees. ◆ See also **guaiacum.** [NL, from LL, lit.: wood of life]

ligroin ('lɪgrəʊɪn) n a volatile fraction of petroleum: used as a solvent. [from ?]

Liguria ★ (lɪ'gjʊərɪə) n a region of NW Italy, on the **Ligurian Sea** (an arm of the Mediterranean): the third smallest of the regions of Italy. Pop.: 1 662 658 (1994 est.). Area: 5410 sq. km (2089 sq. miles).
▸ **Li'gurian** *adj, n*

likable *or* **likeable** ('laɪkəb°l) *adj* easy to like; pleasing.
▸ **'likableness** *or* **'likeableness** *n*

Likasi ★ (lɪ'kɑːsɪ) n a city in S Democratic Republic of the Congo, in Shaba province: a centre of copper and cobalt production. Pop.: 299 118 (1994 est.). Former name: **Jadotville.**

like[1] (laɪk) *adj* **1** (*prenominal*) similar; resembling. ◆ *prep* **2** similar to; similarly to; in the manner of: *acting like a maniac; he's so like his father.* **3** used correlatively to express similarity: *like mother, like daughter.* **4** such as: *there are lots of games — like draughts, for instance.* ◆ *adv* **5** a dialect word for **likely.** ◆ *conj* **6** Not standard. as though; as if: *you look like you've just seen a ghost.* **7** in the same way as; in the same way that: *she doesn't dance like you do.* ◆ n 8 the equal or counterpart of a person or thing. **9 the like.** similar things: *dogs, foxes, and the like.* **10 the likes** (*or* **like**) **of.** people or things similar to (someone or something specified): *we don't want the likes of you around here.* [shortened from OE *gelīc*]

USAGE NOTE The use of *like* to mean *such as* was formerly thought to be undesirable in formal writing, but has now become acceptable. It was

---

★ people and places

also thought that *as* rather than *like* should be used to mean *in the same way that*, but now both *as* and *like* are acceptable: *they hunt and catch fish as/like their ancestors used to*. The use of *look like* and *seem like* before a clause, although very common, is thought by many people to be incorrect or non-standard: *it looks as though he won't come* (not *it looks like he won't come*).

like[2] (laɪk) *vb* **likes, liking, liked. 1** (*tr*) to find (something) enjoyable or agreeable or find it enjoyable or agreeable (to do something): *he likes boxing; he likes to hear music.* **2** (*tr*) to be fond of. **3** (*tr*) to prefer or wish (to do something): *we would like you to go.* **4** (*tr*) to feel towards; consider; regard: *how did she like it?* **5** (*intr*) to feel disposed or inclined; choose; wish. ◆ *n* **6** (*usually pl*) a favourable feeling, desire, preference, etc. (esp. in **likes and dislikes**). [OE *lician*]

-like *suffix forming adjectives.* **1** resembling or similar to: *lifelike.* **2** having the characteristics of: *childlike.* [from LIKE[1] (prep)]

likelihood ('laɪklɪ,hʊd) *or* **likeliness** *n* **1** the condition of being likely or probable; probability. **2** something that is probable.

likely ('laɪklɪ) *adj* **1** (usually foll. by an infinitive) tending or inclined; apt: *likely to rain.* **2** probable: *a likely result.* **3** believable or feasible; plausible. **4** appropriate for a purpose or activity. **5** having good possibilities of success: *a likely candidate.* ◆ *adv* **6** probably or presumably. **7** **as likely as not.** very probably. [C14: from ON *líkligr*]

> **USAGE NOTE** *Likely* as an adverb is preceded by another, intensifying adverb, as in *it will very likely rain* or *it will most likely rain*. Its use without an intensifier, as in *it will likely rain* is regarded as unacceptable by most users of British English, though it is common in colloquial US English.

like-minded *adj* agreeing in opinions, goals, etc. ▸ ,like-'mindedly *adv* ▸ ,like-'mindedness *n*

liken ('laɪkən) *vb* (*tr*) to see or represent as the same or similar; compare. [C14: from LIKE[1] (adj)]

likeness ('laɪknɪs) *n* **1** the condition of being alike; similarity. **2** a painted, carved, moulded, or graphic image of a person or thing. **3** an imitative appearance; semblance.

likewise ('laɪk,waɪz) *adv* **1** in addition; moreover; also. **2** in like manner; similarly.

liking ('laɪkɪŋ) *n* **1** the feeling of a person who likes; fondness. **2** a preference, inclination, or pleasure.

lilac ('laɪlək) *n* **1** any of various Eurasian shrubs or small trees of the olive family which have large sprays of purple or white fragrant flowers. **2a** a light or moderate purple colour. **2b** (*as adj*): *a lilac carpet.* [C17: via F from Sp., from Ar. *līlak,* changed from Persian *nīlak* bluish, from *nīl* blue]

Lilburne ★ ('lɪl,bɜːn) *n* **John.** ?1614–57, English Puritan pamphleteer and leader of the Levellers, a radical group prominent during the Civil War.

liliaceous (,lɪlɪ'eɪʃəs) *adj* of, relating to, or belonging to a family of plants having showy flowers and a bulb or bulblike organ: includes the lily, tulip, bluebell, and onion. [C18: from LL *līliāceus,* from *līlium* lily]

Lilienthal ★ (*German* 'liːliəntaːl) *n* **Otto** ('ɔto). 1848–96, German aeronautical engineer, a pioneer of glider design.

Lilith ★ ('lɪlɪθ) *n* **1** (in the Old Testament and in Jewish folklore) a female demon, who attacks children. **2** (in Talmudic literature) Adam's first wife. **3** a witch notorious in medieval demonology.

Liliuokalani ★ (liː,liːʊʊkə'lɑːniː) *n* **Lydia Kamekeha** (,kɑːmeɪ'keɪhə). 1838–1917, queen and last sovereign of the Hawaiian Islands (1891–95).

Lille ★ (*French* lil) *n* an industrial city in N France: the medieval capital of Flanders; forms with Roubaix and Tourcoing one of the largest conurbations in France. Pop.: 178 301 (1990).

Lille Bælt ★ ('lilə 'bɛld) *n* the Danish name for the **Little Belt.**

Lillee ★ ('lɪlɪ) *n* **Dennis (Keith).** born 1949, Australian cricketer who, by the end of the 1982–83 season, had taken a world-record total of 355 wickets in 65 tests.

Lilliputian (,lɪlɪ'pjuːʃən) *n* **1** a tiny person or being. ◆ *adj* **2** tiny; very small. **3** petty or trivial. [C18: from *Lilliput,* an imaginary country of tiny inhabitants in Swift's *Gulliver's Travels* (1726)]

Lilo ('laɪ,ləʊ) *n, pl* **Lilos.** *Trademark.* a type of inflatable plastic or rubber mattress.

Lilongwe ★ (lɪ'lɒŋwɪ) *n* the capital of Malawi, in the central part west of Lake Malawi. Pop.: 395 500 (1994 est.).

lilt (lɪlt) *n* **1** (in music) a jaunty rhythm. **2** a buoyant motion. ◆ *vb* (*intr*) **3** (of a melody) to have a lilt. **4** to move in a buoyant manner. [C14 *lulten,* from ?]
▸ 'lilting *adj*

lily ('lɪlɪ) *n, pl* **lilies. 1** any perennial plant of a N temperate genus, such as the tiger lily, having scaly bulbs and showy typically pendulous flowers. **2** the bulb or flower of any of these plants. **3** any of various similar or related plants, such as the water lily. [OE, from L *līlium*; rel. to Gk *leirion* lily]
▸ 'lily-,like *adj*

lily-livered *adj* cowardly; timid.

lily of the valley *n, pl* **lilies of the valley.** a small liliaceous plant of Eurasia and North America cultivated for its spikes of fragrant white bell-shaped flowers.

lily-white *adj* **1** of a pure white: *lily-white skin.* **2** *Inf.* pure; irreproachable.

Lima ★ ('liːmə) *n* **1** the capital of Peru, near the Pacific coast on the Rímac River: the centre of Spanish colonization in South America; university founded in 1551 (the oldest in South America); an industrial centre with a port at nearby Callao. Pop. (city): 421 570 (1995 est.); (conurbation): 6 022 213 (1995). **2** *Communications.* a code word for the letter L.

lima bean ('laɪmə, 'liː-) *n* **1** any of several varieties of the bean plant native to tropical America, cultivated for its flat pods containing pale green edible seeds. **2** the seed of such a plant. [C19: after LIMA]

Limassol ★ ('lɪmə,sɒl) *n* a port in S Cyprus: trading centre. Pop.: 143 400 (1994 est.). Ancient name: **Lemessus** (lə'mesəs).

Limavady ★ (,lɪmə'vædɪ) *n* a district of N Northern Ireland, on Lough Foyle: mainly agricultural. Administrative centre: Limavady. Pop.: 29 567 (1991). Area: 622 sq. km (240 sq. miles).

limb[1] (lɪm) *n* **1** an arm or leg, or the analogous part on an animal, such as a wing. **2** any of the main branches of a tree. **3** a branching or projecting section or member; extension. **4** a person or thing considered to be a member, part, or agent of a larger group or thing. **5** *Chiefly Brit.* a mischievous child (esp. in **limb of Satan,** etc.). **6 out on a limb. 6a** in a precarious or questionable position. **6b** *Brit.* isolated, esp. because of unpopular opinions. [OE *lim*]
▸ 'limbless *adj*

limb[2] (lɪm) *n* **1** the edge of the apparent disc of the sun, a moon, or a planet. **2** a graduated arc attached to instruments, such as the sextant, used for measuring angles. **3** *Bot.* the expanded part of a leaf, petal, or sepal. **4** Also called: **fold limb.** either of the sides of a geological fold. [C15: from L *limbus* edge]

limbed (lɪmd) *adj* **a** having limbs. **b** (*in combination*): *short-limbed; strong-limbed.*

limber[1] ('lɪmbə) *adj* **1** capable of being easily bent or flexed; pliant. **2** able to move or bend freely; agile. [C16: from ?]
▸ 'limberness *n*

limber[2] ('lɪmbə) *n* **1** part of a gun carriage, consisting of an axle, pole, and two wheels. ◆ *vb* **2** (usually foll. by *up*) to attach the limber (to a gun, etc.). [C15 *lymour* shaft of a gun carriage, from ?]

limber up *vb* (*intr, adv*) (esp. in sports) to exercise in order to be limber and agile.

limbic system ('lɪmbɪk) *n* the part of the brain concerned with basic emotion, hunger, and sex. [C19 *limbic*, from F, from *limbe*, from NL *limbus*, from L: border]

limbo[1] ('lɪmbəʊ) *n, pl* **limbos. 1** (*often cap.*) *Christianity.* the supposed abode of infants dying without baptism and the just who died before Christ. **2** an imaginary place for lost, forgotten, or unwanted persons or things. **3** an unknown intermediate place or condition between two extremes: *in limbo.* [C14: from Med. L *in limbo* on the border (of hell)]

limbo[2] ('lɪmbəʊ) *n, pl* **limbos.** a Caribbean dance in which dancers pass, while leaning backwards, under a bar. [C20: from ?]

Limburg ★ ('lɪmbɜːg; *Dutch* 'lɪmbyrx) *n* **1** a medieval duchy of W Europe: divided between the Netherlands and Belgium in 1839. **2** a province of the SE Netherlands: contains a coalfield and industrial centres. Capital: Maastricht. Pop.: 1 130 050 (1995). Area: 2253 sq. km (809 sq. miles). **3** a province of NE Belgium: contains the industrial regions of the Kempen coalfield. Capital: Hassett. Pop.: 771 613 (1995 est.). Area: 2422 sq. km (935 sq. miles). French name: **Limbourg** (lɛ̃buːr).

Limburger ('lɪm,bɜːgə) *n* a semihard white cheese of very strong smell and flavour. Also called: **Limburg cheese.**

lime[1] (laɪm) *n* **1** short for **quicklime, birdlime, slaked lime. 2** *Agriculture.* any of certain calcium compounds, esp. calcium hydroxide, spread as a dressing on lime-deficient land. ◆ *vb* **limes, liming, limed.** (*tr*) **3** to spread (twigs, etc.) with birdlime. **4** to spread a calcium compound upon (land) to improve plant growth. **5** to catch (animals, esp. birds) as with birdlime. **6** to whitewash (a wall, ceiling, etc.) with a mixture of lime and water (**limewash**). [OE *līm*]

lime[2] (laɪm) *n* **1** a small Asian citrus tree with stiff sharp spines and small round or oval greenish fruits. **2a** the fruit of this tree, having acid fleshy pulp rich in vitamin C. **2b** (*as modifier*): *lime juice.* ◆ *adj* **3** having the flavour of lime fruit. [C17: from F, from Ar. *līmah*]

lime[3] (laɪm) *n* a European linden tree planted in many varieties for ornament. [C17: changed from obs. *line*, from OE *lind* LINDEN]

limeade (,laɪm'eɪd) *n* a drink made from sweetened lime juice and plain or carbonated water.

lime green *n* **a** a moderate greenish-yellow colour. **b** (*as adj*): *a lime-green dress.*

limekiln ('laɪm,kɪln) *n* a kiln in which calcium carbonate is calcined to produce quicklime.

limelight ('laɪm,laɪt) *n* **1** *the.* a position of public attention or notice (esp. in the **limelight**). **2a** a type of lamp, formerly used in stage lighting, in which light is produced by heating lime to white heat. **2b** Also called: **calcium light.** brilliant white light produced in this way.

limerick ('lɪmərɪk) *n* a form of comic verse consisting of five anapaestic lines. [C19: allegedly from *will you come up to Limerick?*, a refrain sung between nonsense verses at a party]

Limerick ★ ('lɪmərɪk) *n* **1** a county of SW Republic of Ireland, in N Munster province: consists chiefly of an undulating plain with rich pasture and mountains in the south. County town: Limerick. Pop.: 161 956 (1991). Area: 2686 sq. km (1037 sq. miles). **2** a port in SW Republic of Ireland, county town of Limerick, at the head of the Shannon estuary. Pop.: 74 900 (1995 est.).

limestone ('laɪm,stəʊn) *n* a sedimentary rock consisting mainly of calcium carbonate: used as a building stone and in making cement, lime, etc.

limewater ('laɪm,wɔːtə) *n* **1** a clear colourless solution of calcium hydroxide in water, sometimes used in medicine as an antacid. **2** water that contains dissolved lime or calcium salts, esp. calcium carbonate or calcium sulphate.

limey ('laɪmɪ) *US, Canad., & Austral. sl.* ◆ *n* **1** a British person. **2** a British sailor or ship. ◆ *adj* **3** British. [abbrev. from C19 *lime-juicer*, because British sailors drank lime juice as a protection against scurvy]

limit ('lɪmɪt) *n* **1** (*sometimes pl*) the ultimate extent, degree, or amount of something: *the limit of endurance.* **2** (*often pl*) the boundary or edge of a specific area: *the city limits.* **3** (*often pl*) the area of premises within specific boundaries. **4** the largest quantity or amount allowed. **5** *Maths.* **5a** a value to which a function approaches as the independent variable approaches a specified value or infinity. **5b** a value to which a sequence a_n approaches as *n* approaches infinity. **5c** the limit of a sequence of partial sums of a convergent infinite series. **6** *Maths.* one of the two specified values between which a definite integral is evaluated. **7 the limit.** *Inf.* a person or thing that is intolerably exasperating. ◆ *vb* **limits, limiting, limited.** (*tr*) **8** to restrict or confine, as to area, extent, time, etc. [C14: from L *līmes* boundary]
▸ **'limitable** *adj* ▸ **'limitless** *adj* ▸ **'limitlessly** *adv* ▸ **'limitlessness** *n*

limitary ('lɪmɪtərɪ, -trɪ) *adj* **1** of, involving, or serving as a limit. **2** restricted or limited.

limitation (,lɪmɪ'teɪʃən) *n* **1** something that limits a quality or achievement. **2** the act of limiting or the condition of being limited. **3** *Law.* a certain period of time, legally defined, within which an action, claim, etc., must be commenced.

limited ('lɪmɪtɪd) *adj* **1** having a limit; restricted; confined. **2** without fullness or scope; narrow. **3** (of governing powers, sovereignty, etc.) restricted or checked, by or as if by a constitution, laws, or an assembly: *limited government.* **4** *Chiefly Brit.* (of a business enterprise) owned by shareholders whose liability for the enterprise's debts is restricted.
▸ **'limitedly** *adv* ▸ **'limitedness** *n*

limited liability *n Brit.* liability restricted to the unpaid portion (if any) of the par value of the shares of a limited company.

limiter ('lɪmɪtə) *n* an electronic circuit that produces an output signal whose positive or negative amplitude, or both, is limited to some predetermined value above which the peaks become flattened. Also called: **clipper.**

limn (lɪm) *vb* (*tr*) **1** to represent in drawing or painting. **2** *Arch.* to describe in words. [C15: from OF *enluminer* to illumine (a manuscript) from L *inlūmināre* to brighten, from *lūmen* light]
▸ **'limner** ('lɪmnə) *n*

limnology (lɪm'nɒlədʒɪ) *n* the study of bodies of fresh water with reference to their plant and animal life, physical properties, geographical features, etc. [C20: from Gk *limnē* lake]
▸ **limnological** (,lɪmnə'lɒdʒɪk'l) *adj* ▸ **lim'nologist** *n*

Límnos ★ ('lɪmnɒs) *n* transliteration of the Modern Greek name for **Lemnos.**

Limoges ★ (lɪ'məʊʒ; *French* limɔʒ) *n* a city in S central France, on the Vienne River: a centre of the porcelain industry since the 18th century. Pop.: 175 646 (1990).

Limousin ★ (*French* limuzɛ̃) *n* a region and former province of W central France, in the W part of the Massif Central.

limousine ('lɪmə,ziːn, ,lɪmə'ziːn) *n* any large and luxurious car, esp. one that has a glass division between the driver and passengers. [C20: from F, lit.: cloak (orig. one worn by shepherds in *Limousin*), hence later applied to the car]

limp[1] (lɪmp) *vb* (*intr*) **1** to walk with an uneven step, esp. with a weak or injured leg. **2** to advance in a labouring or faltering manner. ◆ *n* **3** an uneven walk or progress. [C16: prob. a back formation from obs. *limphalt* lame, from OE *lemphealt*]
▸ **'limper** *n* ▸ **'limping** *adj, n*

limp[2] (lɪmp) *adj* **1** not firm or stiff. **2** not energetic or vital. **3** (of the binding of a book) not stiffened with boards. [C18: prob. of Scand. origin]
▸ **'limply** *adv* ▸ **'limpness** *n*

limpet ('lɪmpɪt) *n* **1** any of numerous marine gastropods, such as the common limpet and keyhole limpet, that have a conical shell and are found clinging to rocks. **2** (*modifier*) relating to or denoting certain weapons that are attached to their targets by magnetic or adhesive properties and resist removal: *limpet mines.* [OE *lempedu*, from L *lepas*, from Gk]

limpid ('lɪmpɪd) *adj* **1** clear or transparent. **2** (esp. of writings, style, etc.) free from obscurity. **3** calm; peaceful. [C17: from F *limpide*, from L *limpidus* clear]
▶ lim'**pidity** *or* '**limpidness** *n* ▶ '**limpidly** *adv*

Limpopo ★ (lɪm'pəʊpəʊ) *n* a river in SE Africa, rising in E South Africa and flowing northeast, then southeast as the border between South Africa and Zimbabwe and through Mozambique to the Indian Ocean. Length: 1770 km (1100 miles).

limp-wristed *adj* ineffectual; effete.

limy[1] ('laɪmɪ) *adj* **limier, limiest.** of, like, or smeared with birdlime.
▶ '**liminess** *n*

limy[2] ('laɪmɪ) *adj* **limier, limiest.** of or tasting of lime (the fruit).

Linacre ★ ('lɪnəkə) *n* **Thomas.** ?1460–1524, English humanist and physician: founded the Royal College of Physicians (1518).

linage ('laɪnɪdʒ) *n* **1** the number of lines in a piece of written or printed matter. **2** payment for written material calculated according to the number of lines.

Linares ★ (*Spanish* li'nares) *n* a city in S Spain: site of Scipio Africanus' defeat of the Carthaginians (208 B.C.); lead mines. Pop.: 57 210 (1991).

Lin Biao ★ ('lɪn 'bjaʊ) *n* See **Lin Piao.**

linchpin *or* **lynchpin** ('lɪntʃ,pɪn) *n* **1** a pin placed transversely through an axle to keep a wheel in position. **2** a person or thing regarded as an essential or coordinating element: *the linchpin of the company.* [C14 *lynspin*, from OE *lynis*]

Lincoln[1] ★ ('lɪŋkən) *n* **1** a city in E central England, administrative centre of Lincolnshire: an important ecclesiastical and commercial centre in the Middle Ages; Roman ruins, a castle (founded by William the Conqueror) and a famous cathedral (begun in 1086). Pop.: 80 281 (1991). Latin name: **Lindum** ('lɪndəm). **2** a city in SE Nebraska: state capital; University of Nebraska (1869). Pop.: 203 076 (1994 est.).

Lincoln[2] ★ ('lɪŋkən) *n* **Abraham.** 1809–65, US Republican statesman; 16th president of the US. He saved the Union in the Civil War (1861–65) and emancipated slaves (1863); assassinated by Booth.

Lincoln green **1** a yellowish-green or brownish-green colour. **1b** (*as adj*): *a Lincoln-green suit.* **2** a cloth of this colour. [C16: after a green fabric formerly made at LINCOLN]

Lincolnshire ★ ('lɪŋkən,ʃɪə, -ʃə) *n* a county of E England, on the North Sea and the Wash; includes the unitary authorities of North Lincolnshire and North East Lincolnshire: mostly low-lying and fertile, with fenland around the Wash and hills (the **Lincoln Wolds**) in the east; one of the main agricultural counties of Great Britain. Administrative centre: Lincoln. Pop.: 922 600 (1996 est.). Area: 7604 sq. km (2936 sq. miles). Abbrev.: **Lincs.**

Lincs (lɪŋks) *abbrev. for* Lincolnshire.

linctus ('lɪŋktəs) *n, pl* **linctuses.** a syrupy medicinal preparation, taken to relieve coughs and sore throats. [C17 (in the sense: medicine to be licked with the tongue): from L, p.p. of *lingere* to lick]

Lind ★ (lɪnd) *n* **Jenny.** Swedish name *Johanna Maria Lind Goldschmidt.* 1820–87, Swedish coloratura soprano.

lindane ('lɪndeɪn) *n* a white poisonous crystalline powder: used as an insecticide and weedkiller. [C20: after T. van der *Linden*, Du. chemist]

Lindbergh ★ ('lɪndbɜːg, 'lɪnbɜːg) *n* **Charles Augustus.** 1902–74, US aviator, who made the first solo nonstop flight across the Atlantic (1927).

Lindemann ★ ('lɪndəmən) *n* **Frederick Alexander,** 1st Viscount Cherwell. 1886–1957, British physicist, born in Germany; Churchill's scientific adviser during World War II.

linden ('lɪndən) *n* any of various deciduous trees of a N temperate genus having heart-shaped leaves and small fragrant yellowish flowers: cultivated for timber and as shade trees. See also **lime**[3]. [C16: n use of obs. adj *linden*, from OE *linde* lime tree]

Lindesnes ★ ('lɪndɪs,nɛs) *n* a cape at the S tip of Norway, projecting into the North Sea. Also called: (the) **Naze.**

Lindisfarne ★ ('lɪndɪs,fɑːn) *n* another name for **Holy Island.**

Lindsay ★ ('lɪndzɪ) *n* **1 Norman Alfred William.** 1879–1969, Australian artist and writer. **2** (**Nicholas**) **Vachel** ('veɪtʃəl). 1879–1931, US poet; best known for *General William Booth Enters into Heaven* (1913) and *The Congo* (1914).

Lindsey ★ ('lɪndzɪ) *n* **Parts of.** an area in E England constituting a former administrative division of Lincolnshire.

Lindwall ★ ('lɪnd,wɔːl) *n* **Ray(mond Russell).** 1921–96, Australian cricketer. A fast bowler, he played for Australia 61 times.

line[1] (laɪn) *n* **1** a narrow continuous mark, as one made by a pencil, pen, or brush across a surface. **2** such a mark cut into or raised from a surface. **3** a thin indented mark or wrinkle. **4** a straight or curved continuous trace having no breadth that is produced by a moving point. **5** *Maths.* **5a** any straight one-dimensional geometrical element whose identity is determined by two points. A **line segment** lies between any two points on a line. **5b** a set of points (x, y) that satisfies the equation $y = mx + c$, where m is the gradient and c is the intercept with the *y*-axis. **6** a border or boundary: *the county line.* **7** *Sport.* **7a** a white or coloured band indicating a boundary or division on a field, track, etc. **7b** a mark or imaginary mark at which a race begins or ends. **8** *American football.* **8a** See **line of scrimmage. 8b** the players arranged in a row on either side of the line of scrimmage at the start of each play. **9** a specified point of change or limit: *the dividing line between sanity and madness.* **10a** the edge or contour of a shape. **10b** the sum or type of such contours, characteristic of a style or design: *the line of a building.* **11** anything long, flexible, and thin, such as a wire or string: *a washing line; a fishing line.* **12** a telephone connection: *a direct line to New York.* **13** a conducting wire, cable, or circuit for making connections between pieces of electrical apparatus, such as a cable for electric-power transmission, telecommunications, etc. **14** a system of travel or transportation, esp. over agreed routes: *a shipping line.* **15** a company operating such a system. **16** a route between two points on a railway. **17** *Chiefly Brit.* a railway track, including the roadbed, sleepers, etc. **18** a course or direction of movement or advance: *the line of flight of a bullet.* **19** a course or method of action, behaviour, etc.: *take a new line with him.* **20** a policy or prescribed course of action or way of thinking (often in **bring** *or* **come into line**). **21** a field of study, interest, occupation, trade, or profession: *this book is in your line.* **22** alignment; true (esp. in **in line, out of line**). **23** one kind of product or article: *a nice line in hats.* **24** a row of persons or things: *a line of cakes on the conveyor belt.* **25** a chronological or ancestral series, esp. of people: *a line of prime ministers.* **26** a row of words printed or written across a page or column. **27** a unit of verse consisting of the number of feet appropriate to the metre being used and written or printed with the words in a single row. **28** a short letter; note: *just a line to say thank you.* **29** a piece of useful information or hint about something: *give me a line on his work.* **30** one of a number of narrow horizontal bands forming a television picture. **31** *Physics.* a narrow band in an electromagnetic spectrum, resulting from a transition in an atom of a gas. **32** *Music.* **32a** any of the five horizontal marks that make up the stave. **32b** the musical part or melody notated on one such set. **32c** a discernible shape formed by sequences of notes or musical sounds: *a meandering melodic line.* **32d** (in polyphonic music) a set of staves that are held together with a bracket or brace. **33** a defensive or fortified position, esp. one that marks the most forward position in war or a national boundary: *the front line.* **34** a formation adopted by a body or a number of military units when drawn up abreast. **35** the combatant forces of certain armies and navies, excluding supporting arms. **36a** the equator (esp. in **crossing the line**). **36b** any circle or arc on the terrestrial or celestial sphere. **37** a US and Canad. word for **queue. 38** *Sl.* a portion of a powdered drug for snorting. **39** *Sl.* something said for effect, esp. to solicit for money, sex, etc. **40 all along the line. 40a** at every stage in a series. **40b** in every detail. **41 draw the line (at).** to object (to) or set a limit (on): *her father draws the line at her*

coming in after midnight. **42 get a line on.** *Inf.* to obtain information about. **43 hold the line. 43a** to keep a telephone line open. **43b** *Football.* to prevent the opponents from taking the ball forward. **43c** (of soldiers) to keep formation, as when under fire. **44 in line for.** in the running for; a candidate for: *he's in line for a directorship.* **45 in line with.** conforming to. **46 lay** *or* **put on the line. 46a** to pay money. **46b** to speak frankly and directly. **46c** to risk (one's career, reputation, etc.) on something. ◆ *vb* **lines, lining, lined. 47** (*tr*) to mark with a line or lines. **48** (*tr*) to draw or represent with a line or lines. **49** (*tr*) to be or put as a border to: *tulips lined the lawns.* **50** to place in or form a row, series, or alignment. ◆ See also **lines, line-up.** [C13: partly from OF *ligne*, ult. from L *līnea*, n. use of *līneus* flaxen, from *līnum* flax; partly from OE *līn*, ult. also from L *līnum* flax]
▶ '**linable** *or* '**lineable** *adj* ▶ '**lined** *adj*

line[2] (laɪn) *vb* **lines, lining, lined.** (*tr*) **1** to attach an inside covering to (a garment, curtain, etc.), as for protection, to hide the seaming, or so that it should hang well. **2** to cover or fit the inside of: *to line the walls with books.* **3** to fill plentifully: *a purse lined with money.* [C14: ult. from L *līnum* flax, since linings were often of linen]

lineage[1] ('lɪnɪɪdʒ) *n* direct descent from an ancestor, esp. a line of descendants from one ancestor. [C14: from OF *lignage*, from L *līnea* LINE[1]]

lineage[2] ('laɪnɪdʒ) *n* a variant spelling of **linage.**

lineal ('lɪnɪəl) *adj* **1** being in a direct line of descent from an ancestor. **2** of, involving, or derived from direct descent. **3** a less common word for **linear.** [C14: via OF from LL *līneālis*, from L *līnea* LINE[1]]
▶ '**lineally** *adv*

lineament ('lɪnɪəmənt) *n* (*often pl*) **1** a facial outline or feature. **2** a distinctive feature. [C15: from L: line, from *līneāre* to draw a line]

linear ('lɪnɪə) *adj* **1** of, in, along, or relating to a line. **2** of or relating to length. **3** resembling, represented by, or consisting of a line or lines. **4** having one dimension. **5** designating a style in the arts, esp. painting, that obtains its effects through line rather than colour or light. **6** *Maths.* of or relating to the first degree: *a linear equation.* **7** narrow and having parallel edges: *a linear leaf.* **8** *Electronics.* **8a** (of a circuit, etc.) having an output that is directly proportional to input: *linear amplifier.* **8b** having components arranged in a line. [C17: from L *līneāris* of lines]
▶ **linearity** (ˌlɪnɪˈærɪtɪ) *n* ▶ '**linearly** *adv*

linear accelerator *n* an accelerator in which charged particles are accelerated along a linear path by potential differences applied to a number of electrodes along their path.

Linear B *n* an ancient system of writing found on clay tablets and jars of the second millennium B.C. excavated in Crete and on the Greek mainland. The script is apparently a modified form of the earlier and hitherto undeciphered **Linear A** and is generally accepted as being an early representation of Mycenaean Greek.

linear measure *n* a unit or system of units for the measurement of length.

linear motor *n* a form of electric motor in which the stator and the rotor are linear and parallel. It can be used to drive a train, one part of the motor being in the locomotive, the other in the track.

linear programming *n* *Maths.* a technique used in economics, etc., for determining the maximum or minimum of a linear function of non-negative variables subject to constraints expressed as linear equalities or inequalities.

lineation (ˌlɪnɪˈeɪʃən) *n* **1** the act of marking with lines. **2** an arrangement of or division into lines.

line dancing *n* a form of dancing performed by rows of people to country and western music.

line drawing *n* a drawing made with lines only.

Line Islands ★ *pl n* a group of coral islands in the central Pacific, including Tabuaeran, Teraina, and Kiritimati: part of Kiribati, with Palmyra and Jarvis administered by the US.

lineman ('laɪnmən) *n, pl* **linemen. 1** another name for **platelayer. 2** a person who does the chaining, taping, or

marking of points for a surveyor. **3** *Austral. & NZ.* (formerly) the member of a beach life-saving team who controlled the line used to help drowning swimmers and surfers. **4** *American football.* a member of the row of players who start each down, positioned on either side of the line of scrimmage. **5** *US & Canad.* another word for **linesman** (sense 2).

line management *n* the managers in charge of specific functions and concerned in the day-to-day operations of a company.

linen ('lɪnɪn) *n* **1a** a hard-wearing fabric woven from the spun fibres of flax. **1b** (*as modifier*): *a linen tablecloth.* **2** yarn or thread spun from flax fibre. **3** clothes, sheets, tablecloths, etc., made from linen cloth or from cotton. [OE *linnen*, ult. from L *līnum* flax]

line of battle *n* a formation adopted by a military or naval force when preparing for action.

line of fire *n* the flight path of a missile discharged or to be discharged from a firearm.

line of force *n* a line in a field of force, such as an electric or magnetic field, for which the tangent at any point is the direction of the force at that point.

line of scrimmage *n* *American football.* an imaginary line, parallel to the goal lines, on which the ball is placed at the start of a down and on either side of which the offense and defense line up.

line-out *n* *Rugby Union.* the method of restarting play when the ball goes into touch, the forwards forming two parallel lines at right angles to the touchline and jumping for the ball when it is thrown in.

line printer *n* an electromechanical device that prints a line of characters at a time: used in printing and in computer systems.

liner[1] ('laɪnə) *n* **1** a passenger ship or aircraft, esp. one that is part of a commercial fleet. **2** See **freightliner. 3** Also called: **eyeliner.** a cosmetic used to outline the eyes. **4** a person or thing that uses lines, esp. in drawing or copying.

liner[2] ('laɪnə) *n* **1** a material used as a lining. **2** a person who supplies or fits linings.

lines (laɪnz) *pl n* **1** general appearance or outline: *a car with fine lines.* **2** a plan of procedure or construction: *built on traditional lines.* **3a** the spoken words of a theatrical presentation. **3b** the words of a particular role: *he forgot his lines.* **4** *Inf., chiefly Brit.* a marriage certificate: *marriage lines.* **5** a defensive position, row of trenches, or other fortification: *we broke through the enemy lines.* **6** a school punishment of writing the same sentence or phrase out a specified number of times. **7 read between the lines.** to understand or find an implicit meaning in addition to the obvious one.

linesman ('laɪnzmən) *n, pl* **linesmen. 1** an official who helps the referee or umpire in various sports, esp. by indicating when the ball has gone out of play. **2** *Chiefly Brit.* a person who installs, maintains, or repairs telephone or electric-power lines. US and Canad. name: **lineman.**

line-up *n* **1** a row or arrangement of people or things assembled for a particular purpose: *the line-up for the football match.* **2** the members of such a row or arrangement. **3** *US.* an identity parade. ◆ *vb* **line up.** (*adv*) **4** to form, put into, or organize a line-up. **5** (*tr*) to produce, organize, and assemble: *they lined up some questions.* **6** (*tr*) to align.

ling[1] (lɪŋ) *n, pl* **ling** *or* **lings. 1** any of several northern coastal food fishes having an elongated body with long fins. **2** another name for **burbot** (a fish). [C13: prob. from Low G]

ling[2] (lɪŋ) *n* another name for **heather.** [C14: from ON *lyng*]

ling. *abbrev.* for linguistics.

-ling[1] *suffix forming nouns.* **1** *Often disparaging.* a person or thing belonging to or associated with a group, activity, or quality specified: *nestling; underling.* **2** used as a diminutive: *duckling.* [OE *-ling,* of Gmc origin]

-ling[2] *suffix forming adverbs.* in a specified condition, manner, or direction: *darkling.* [OE *-ling,* adv. suffix]

★ people and places

lingam ('lɪŋgəm) *or* **linga** ('lɪŋgə) *n* the Hindu phallic image of the god Siva. [C18: from Sansk.]

Lingayen Gulf ★ ('lɪŋgɑːˈjen) *n* a large inlet of the South China Sea in the Philippines, on the NW coast of Luzon: site of Japanese landing in 1941 invasion.

linger ('lɪŋgə) *vb (mainly intr)* **1** to delay or prolong departure. **2** to go in a slow or leisurely manner; saunter. **3** to remain just alive for some time prior to death. **4** to persist or continue, esp. in the mind. **5** to be slow to act; dither. [C13 (northern dialect) *lengeren* to dwell, from *lengen* to prolong, from OE *lengan*]
▶ **'lingerer** *n* ▶ **'lingering** *adj* ▶ **'lingeringly** *adv*

lingerie ('lænʒərɪ) *n* women's underwear and nightwear. [C19: from F, from *linge*, from L *līneus* linen, from *līnum* flax]

lingo ('lɪŋgəʊ) *n, pl* **lingoes**. *Inf.* any foreign or unfamiliar language, jargon, etc. [C17: ?from LINGUA FRANCA]

lingua franca ('lɪŋgwə 'fræŋkə) *n, pl* **lingua francas** *or* **linguae francae** ('lɪŋgwiː 'frænsiː). **1** a language used for communication among people of different mother tongues. **2** a hybrid language containing elements from several different languages used in this way. **3** any system of communication providing mutual understanding. [C17: It., lit.: Frankish tongue]

Lingua Franca *n* a particular lingua franca spoken from the Crusades to the 18th century in the ports of the Mediterranean, based on Italian, Spanish, French, Arabic, Greek, and Turkish.

lingual ('lɪŋgwəl) *adj* **1** *Anat.* of or relating to the tongue. **2a** *Rare.* of or relating to language or languages. **2b** *(in combination)*: polylingual. **3** articulated with the tongue. ◆ *n* **4** a lingual consonant, such as Scots (r).
▶ **'lingually** *adv*

linguiform ('lɪŋgwɪˌfɔːm) *adj* shaped like a tongue.

linguist ('lɪŋgwɪst) *n* **1** a person who is skilled in foreign languages. **2** a person who studies linguistics. [C16: from L *lingua* tongue]

linguistic (lɪŋˈgwɪstɪk) *adj* **1** of or relating to language. **2** of or relating to linguistics.
▶ **lin'guistically** *adv*

linguistic atlas *n* an atlas showing the distribution of distinctive linguistic features.

linguistics (lɪŋˈgwɪstɪks) *n (functioning as sing)* the scientific study of language.

liniment ('lɪnɪmənt) *n* a medicated liquid, usually containing alcohol, camphor, and an oil, applied to the skin to relieve pain, stiffness, etc. [C15: from LL *linīmentum*, from *linere* to smear]

lining ('laɪnɪŋ) *n* **1** material used to line a garment, curtain, etc. **2** any material used as an interior covering.

link[1] (lɪŋk) *n* **1** any of the separate rings, loops, or pieces that connect or make up a chain. **2** something that resembles such a ring, loop, or piece. **3** a road, rail, air, or sea connection, as between two main routes. **4** a connecting part or episode. **5** a connecting piece in a mechanism. **6** Also called: **radio link**. a system of transmitters and receivers that connect two locations by means of radio and television signals. **7** a unit of length equal to one hundredth of a chain. 1 link of a Gunter's chain is equal to 7.92 inches, and of an engineer's chain to 1 foot. ◆ *vb* **8** (often foll. by *up*) to connect or be connected with or as if with links. **9** *(tr)* to connect by association, etc. [C14: from ON]

link[2] (lɪŋk) *n* (formerly) a torch used to light dark streets. [C16: ?from L *lychnus*, from Gk *lukhnos* lamp]

linkage ('lɪŋkɪdʒ) *n* **1** the act of linking or the state of being linked. **2** a system of interconnected levers or rods for transmitting or regulating the motion of a mechanism. **3** *Electronics*. the product of the total number of lines of magnetic flux and the number of turns in a coil or circuit through which they pass. **4** *Genetics*. the occurrence of two genes close together on the same chromosome so that they tend to be inherited as a single unit.

linkman ('lɪŋkmən) *n, pl* **linkmen**. a presenter of a television or radio programme, esp. a sports transmission, consisting of a number of outside broadcasts from different locations.

Linköping ★ (*Swedish* 'lintɕøːpiŋ) *n* a city in S Sweden: a political and ecclesiastical centre in the Middle Ages; engineering industry. Pop.: 131 370 (1996 est.).

links (lɪŋks) *pl n* **1a** short for **golf links**. **1b** *(as modifier): a links course*. See **golf course**. **2** *Chiefly Scot.* undulating sandy ground near the shore. [OE *hlincas* pl. of *hlinc* ridge]

link-up *n* a joining or linking together of two factions, objects, etc.

Linlithgow ★ (lɪnˈlɪθgəʊ) *n* **1** a town in SE Scotland, in West Lothian: ruined palace, residence of Scottish kings and birthplace of Mary, Queen of Scots. Pop.: 11 866 (1991). **2** the former name of **West Lothian**.

linn (lɪn) *n Chiefly Scot.* **1** a waterfall or a pool at the foot of it. **2** a ravine or precipice. [C16: prob. from a confusion of two words, Scot. Gaelic *linne* pool and OE *hlynn* torrent]

Linnaeus ★ (lɪˈniːəs, -ˈneɪ-) *n* **Carolus** ('kærələs), original name *Carl von Linné*. 1707–78, Swedish botanist, who established the binomial system of biological nomenclature.
▶ **Lin'nean** *or* **Lin'naean** *adj*

linnet ('lɪnɪt) *n* a brownish Old World finch: the male has a red breast and forehead. [C16: from OF *linotte*, ult. from L *līnum* flax (because the bird feeds on flaxseeds)]

Linnhe ★ ('lɪnɪ) *n* **Loch**. a sea loch of W Scotland, at the SW end of the Great Glen. Length: about 32 km (20 miles).

lino ('laɪnəʊ) *n* short for **linoleum**.

linocut ('laɪnəʊˌkʌt) *n* **1** a design cut in relief on linoleum mounted on a wooden block. **2** a print made from such a design.

linoleum (lɪˈnəʊlɪəm) *n* a sheet material made of hessian, jute, etc., coated with a mixture of powdered cork, linseed oil, rosin, and pigment, used as a floor covering. Often shortened to **lino**. [C19: from L *līnum* flax + *oleum* oil]

Linotype ('laɪnəʊˌtaɪp) *n* **1** *Trademark*. a typesetting machine, operated by a keyboard, that casts an entire line on one solid slug of metal. **2** type produced by such a machine.

Lin Piao ('lɪn 'pjaʊ) *or* **Lin Biao** ★ *n* 1908–71, Chinese Communist general and statesman. He became minister of defence (1959) and second in rank to Mao Tse-tung (1966). He fell from grace and is reported to have died in an air crash while attempting to flee to the Soviet Union.

linseed ('lɪnˌsiːd) *n* another name for **flaxseed**. [OE *līnsǣd*, from *līn* flax + *sǣd* seed]

linseed oil *n* a yellow oil extracted from seeds of the flax plant. It is used in making oil paints, printer's ink, linoleum, etc.

linsey-woolsey ('lɪnzɪ'wʊlzɪ) *n* **1** a thin rough fabric of linen warp and coarse wool or cotton filling. **2** a strange nonsensical mixture or confusion. [C15: prob. from *Lindsey*, village in Suffolk where first made + WOOL (with rhyming suffix -*sey*)]

lint (lɪnt) *n* **1** an absorbent cotton or linen fabric with the nap raised on one side, used to dress wounds, etc. **2** shreds of fibre, yarn, etc. [C14: prob. from L *linteus* made of linen, from *līnum* flax]
▶ **'linty** *adj*

lintel ('lɪntʲl) *n* a horizontal beam, as over a door or window. [C14: via OF prob. from LL *līmitāris* (unattested) of the boundary, infl. by *līminaris* of the threshold]

linter ('lɪntə) *n* **1** a machine for stripping the short fibres of ginned cotton seeds. **2** *(pl)* the fibres so removed.

Linz ★ (lɪnts) *n* a port in N Austria, capital of Upper Austria, on the River Danube: cultural centre; steelworks. Pop.: 203 044 (1991). Latin name: **Lentia** ('lɛntɪə, 'lɛnsɪə).

lion ('laɪən) *n* **1** a large gregarious predatory feline mammal of open country in parts of Africa and India, having a tawny yellow coat and, in the male, a shaggy mane. Related adj: **leonine**. **2** a conventionalized lion, the principal beast used as an emblem in heraldry. **3** a courageous, strong, or bellicose person. **4** a celebrity or idol who attracts much publicity and a large following. **5** the

lion's share. the largest portion. [OE *līo, lēo* (ME *lioun*, from Anglo-F *liun*), both from L *leo*, Gk *leōn*]
▶ 'lioness *fem n*

Lion ('laɪən) *n* **the.** the constellation Leo, the fifth sign of the zodiac.

lion-hearted *adj* very brave; courageous.

lionize *or* **lionise** ('laɪə,naɪz) *vb* **lionizes, lionizing, lionized** *or* **lionises, lionising, lionised.** (*tr*) to treat as or make into a celebrity.
▶ ,lioni'zation *or* ,lioni'sation *n* ▶ 'lion,izer *or* 'lion,iser *n*

Lions ★ ('laɪənz) *n* **Gulf of.** a wide bay of the Mediterranean off the S coast of France, between the Spanish border and Toulon. French name: **Golfe du Lion** (gɔlf dy ljɔ̃).

lip (lɪp) *n* **1** *Anat.* **1a** either of the two fleshy folds surrounding the mouth. Related adj: **labial. 1b** (*as modifier*): *lip salve.* **2** the corresponding part in animals, esp. mammals. **3** any structure resembling a lip, such as the rim of a crater, the margin of a gastropod shell, etc. **4** a nontechnical word for **labium. 5** *Sl.* impudent talk or backchat. **6 bite one's lip. 6a** to stifle one's feelings. **6b** to be annoyed or irritated. **7 keep a stiff upper lip.** to maintain one's courage or composure during a time of trouble. **8 lick** *or* **smack one's lips.** to anticipate or recall something with glee or relish. ◆ *vb* **lips, lipping, lipped. 9** (*tr*) to touch with the lip or lips. **10** (*tr*) to form or be a lip or lips for. **11** (*tr*) *Rare.* to murmur or whisper. **12** (*intr*) to use the lips in playing a wind instrument. [OE *lippa*]
▶ 'lipless *adj* ▶ 'lip,like *adj*

Lipari Islands ★ ('lɪpərɪ) *pl n* a group of volcanic islands under Italian administration off the N coast of Sicily: remains that form a continuous record from Neolithic times. Chief town: Lipari. Pop.: 10 300 (1987 est.). Area: 114 sq. km (44 sq. miles). Also called: **Aeolian Islands.** Italian name: **Isole Eolie** ('iːzole e'ɔːlje).

lipase ('laɪpeɪs, 'lɪpeɪs) *n* any of a group of fat-digesting enzymes produced in the stomach, pancreas, and liver. [C19: from Gk *lipos* fat + -ASE]

Lipchitz ★ ('lɪpʃɪts) *n* **Jacques** (ʒɑːk). 1891–1973, US sculptor, born in Lithuania: he pioneered cubist sculpture.

Li Peng ★ ('liː 'peŋ) *n* born 1928, Chinese Communist politician: premier of China from 1988.

Lipetsk ★ (*Russian* 'lipitsk) *n* a city in central Russia, on the Voronezh River: steelworks. Pop.: 474 000 (1995 est.).

lip gloss *n* a cosmetic applied to the lips to give a sheen.

lipid *or* **lipide** ('laɪpɪd, 'lɪpɪd) *n Biochem.* any of a large group of organic compounds that are esters of fatty acids or closely related substances. They are important structural materials in living organisms. Former name: **lipoid.** [C20: from F *lipide,* from Gk *lipos* fat]

Lipizzaner *or* **Lippizaner** (,lɪpɪt'sɑːnə) *n* a breed of riding and carriage horse used by the Spanish Riding School in Vienna and nearly always grey in colour. [G, after *Lipizza,* near Trieste, where these horses were bred]

Li Po *or* **Li T'ai-po** ★ ('liː 'taɪ 'pəu) *n* ?700–762 A.D., Chinese poet.

lipo- *or before a vowel* **lip-** *combining form.* fat or fatty: *lipoprotein.* [from Gk *lipos* fat]

lipogram ('lɪpəu,græm) *n* a piece of writing from which all words containing a particular letter have been deliberately omitted.

lipography (lɪ'pɒgrəfɪ) *n* the accidental omission of words or letters in writing. [C19: from Gk *lip-,* stem of *leipein* to omit + -GRAPHY]

lipoid ('lɪpɔɪd, 'laɪ-) *adj also* **lipoidal. 1** resembling fat; fatty. ◆ *n* **2** a fatlike substance, such as wax. **3** *Biochem.* a former name for **lipid.**

lipoprotein (,lɪpəu'prəutiːn, ,laɪ-) *n* any of a group of proteins to which a lipid molecule is attached, important in the transport of lipids in the bloodstream. See also **low-density lipoprotein.**

liposuction ('lɪpəu,sʌkʃən) *n* a cosmetic surgical operation in which subcutaneous fat is removed from the body by suction.

Lippe ★ ('lɪpə) *n* **1** a former state of NW Germany: now part of the German state of North Rhine-Westphalia;

part of West Germany until 1990. **2** a river in NW Germany, flowing west to the Rhine. Length: about 240 km (150 miles).

-lipped *adj* having a lip or lips as specified: *tight-lipped.*

Lippi ★ (*Italian* 'lippi) *n* **1 Filippino** (filip'piːno). ?1457–1504, Italian painter of the Florentine school. **2** his father, **Fra Filippo** (fra fi'lippo). ?1406–69, Italian painter of the Florentine school, noted for his frescoes at Prato Cathedral (1452–64).

Lippizaner (,lɪpɪt'sɑːnə) *n* a variant spelling of **Lipizzaner.**

Lippmann ★ ('lɪpmən; *French* lipman) *n* **Gabriel** (gabriɛl). 1845–1921, French physicist. He devised the earliest process of colour photography: Nobel prize for physics 1908.

lip-read ('lɪp,riːd) *vb* **lip-reads, lip-reading, lip-read** (-'red). to interpret (words) by lip-reading.

lip-reading *n* a method used by the deaf to comprehend spoken words by interpreting movements of the speaker's lips. Also called: **speech-reading.**
▶ 'lip-,reader *n*

lip service *n* insincere support or respect expressed but not practised.

lipstick ('lɪp,stɪk) *n* a cosmetic for colouring the lips, usually in the form of a stick.

lip-synch *or* **lip-sync** ('lɪp,sɪŋk) *vb* to mouth (prerecorded words) on television or film.

liq. *abbrev. for:* **1** liquid. **2** liquor.

liquefacient (,lɪkwɪ'feɪʃənt) *n* **1** a substance that liquefies or that causes liquefaction. ◆ *adj* **2** becoming or causing to become liquid. [C19: from L *liquefacere* to make LIQUID]

liquefied natural gas *n* a mixture of various gases, esp. methane, liquefied under pressure for transportation and used as an engine fuel. Abbrev.: **LNG.**

liquefied petroleum gas *n* a mixture of various petroleum gases, esp. propane and butane, stored as a liquid under pressure and used as an engine fuel. Abbrev.: **LPG** *or* **LP gas.**

liquefy ('lɪkwɪ,faɪ) *vb* **liquefies, liquefying, liquefied.** (esp. of a gas) to become or cause to become liquid. [C15: via OF from L *liquefacere* to make liquid]
▶ liquefaction (,lɪkwɪ'fækʃən) *n* ▶ 'lique,fiable *adj*
▶ 'lique,fier *n*

liquescent (lɪ'kwesənt) *adj* (of a solid or gas) becoming or tending to become liquid. [C18: from L *liquescere*]
▶ li'quescence *or* li'quescency *n*

liqueur (lɪ'kjuə; *French* likœr) *n* **1a** any of several highly flavoured sweetened spirits, such as Kirsch or Cointreau, intended to be drunk after a meal. **1b** (*as modifier*): *liqueur glass.* **2** a small hollow chocolate sweet containing liqueur. [C18: from F; see LIQUOR]

liquid ('lɪkwɪd) *n* **1** a substance in a physical state in which it does not resist change of shape but does resist change of size. Cf. **gas** (sense 1), **solid** (sense 1). **2** a substance that is a liquid at room temperature and atmospheric pressure. **3** *Phonetics.* a frictionless continuant, esp. (l) or (r). ◆ *adj* **4** of, concerned with, or being a liquid or having the characteristic state of liquids: *liquid wax.* **5** shining, transparent, or brilliant. **6** flowing, fluent, or smooth. **7** (of assets) in the form of money or easily convertible into money. [C14: via OF from L *liquidus,* from *liquēre* to be fluid]
▶ li'quidity *or* 'liquidness *n* ▶ 'liquidly *adv*

liquid air *n* air that has been liquefied by cooling: used in the production of pure oxygen, nitrogen, and as a refrigerant.

liquidambar (,lɪkwɪd'æmbə) *n* **1** a deciduous tree of Asia and North and Central America, with star-shaped leaves, and exuding a yellow aromatic balsam. **2** the balsam of this tree, used in medicine. [C16: NL, from L *liquidus* liquid + Med. L *ambar* AMBER]

liquidate ('lɪkwɪ,deɪt) *vb* **liquidates, liquidating, liquidated. 1** to settle or pay off (a debt, claim, etc.). **2a** to terminate the operations of (a commercial firm, bankrupt estate, etc.) by assessment of liabilities and appropriation of assets for their settlement. **2b** (of a commercial firm, etc.)

★ people and places

to terminate operations in this manner. **3** (*tr*) to convert (assets) into cash. **4** (*tr*) to eliminate or kill.
▶ 'liqui‚dator *n*

liquidation (‚lɪkwɪ'deɪʃən) *n* **1a** the process of terminating the affairs of a business firm, etc., by realizing its assets to discharge its liabilities. **1b** the state of a business firm, etc., having its affairs so terminated (esp. in **to go into liquidation**). **2** destruction; elimination.

liquid-crystal display *n* a flat-screen display used, for example, in portable computers, digital watches, and calculators, in which an array of liquid-crystal elements can be selectively activated to generate an image, by means of an electric field, which when applied to an element alters its optical properties.

liquidize *or* **liquidise** ('lɪkwɪ‚daɪz) *vb* **liquidizes, liquidizing, liquidized** *or* **liquidises, liquidising, liquidised.** **1** to make or become liquid; liquefy. **2** (*tr*) to pulverize (food) in a liquidizer so as to produce a fluid.

liquidizer *or* **liquidiser** ('lɪkwɪ‚daɪzə) *n* a kitchen appliance with blades for puréeing vegetables, blending liquids, etc. Also called: **blender.**

liquid measure *n* a unit or system of units for measuring volumes of liquids or their containers.

liquid oxygen *n* the clear pale blue liquid state of oxygen produced by liquefying air and allowing the nitrogen to evaporate: used in rocket fuels. Also called: **lox.**

liquid paraffin *n* an oily liquid obtained by petroleum distillation and used as a laxative. Also called (esp. US and Canad.): **mineral oil.**

liquor ('lɪkə) *n* **1** any alcoholic drink, esp. spirits, or such drinks collectively. **2** any liquid substance, esp. that in which food has been cooked. **3** *Pharmacol.* a solution of a pure substance in water. **4 in liquor.** drunk. [C13: via OF from L, from *liquēre* to be liquid]

liquorice *or* US & Canad. **licorice** ('lɪkərɪs, -ərɪʃ) *n* **1** a perennial Mediterranean leguminous shrub. **2** the dried root of this plant, used as a laxative and in confectionery. **3** a sweet having a liquorice flavour. [C13: via Anglo-Norman and OF from LL *liquiritia*, from L *glycyrrhiza*, from Gk *glukurrhiza*, from *glukus* sweet + *rhiza* root]

lira ('lɪərə; *Italian* 'liːra) *n*, *pl* **lire** ('lɪərɪ; *Italian* 'liːre) *or* **liras.** **1** the standard monetary unit of Italy and San Marino. **2** Also called: **pound.** the standard monetary unit of Turkey. **3** the standard monetary unit of Malta. [It., from L *lībra* pound]

liriodendron (‚lɪrɪəʊ'dɛndrən) *n*, *pl* **liriodendrons** *or* **liriodendra** (-drə). a deciduous tulip tree of North America or a similar Chinese tree. [C18: NL, from Gk *leiron* lily + *dendron* tree]

Lisbon ★ ('lɪzbən) *n* the capital and chief port of Portugal, in the southwest on the Tagus estuary: became capital in 1256; subject to earthquakes and severely damaged in 1755; university (1911). Pop.: 677 790 (1991). Portuguese name: **Lisboa** (liʒ'boa).

Lisburn ★ ('lɪzbɜːn) *n* **1** a town in Northern Ireland in Co. Antrim, noted for its linen industry: headquarters of the British Army in Northern Ireland. Pop.: 42 110 (1991). **2** a district of E Northern Ireland, S of Belfast. Administrative centre: Lisburn. Pop.: 99 458 (1991). Area: 447 sq. km (172 sq. miles).

Lisieux ★ (*French* lizjø) *n* a town in NW France: Roman Catholic pilgrimage centre, for its shrine of St Thérèse, who lived there. Pop.: 24 506 (1990).

lisle (laɪl) *n* **a** a strong fine cotton thread or fabric. **b** (*as modifier*): *lisle stockings.* [C19: after *Lisle* (now Lille), town in France where this thread was orig. manufactured]

lisp (lɪsp) *n* **1** the articulation of *s* and *z* like or nearly like the *th* sounds in English *thin* and *then* respectively. **2** the habit or speech defect of pronouncing *s* and *z* in this manner. **3** the sound of a lisp in pronunciation. ◆ *vb* **4** to use a lisp in the pronunciation of (speech). **5** to speak or pronounce imperfectly or haltingly. [OE *āwlispian*, from *wlisp* lisping (adj), imit.]
▶ 'lisper *n* ▶ 'lisping *adj*, *n* ▶ 'lispingly *adv*

lissom *or* **lissome** ('lɪsəm) *adj* **1** supple in the limbs or

body; lithe; flexible. **2** agile; nimble. [C19: var. of *lithesome*, LITHE + -SOME¹]
▶ 'lissomly *or* 'lissomely *adv* ▶ 'lissomness *or* 'lissomeness *n*

list¹ (lɪst) *n* **1** an item-by-item record of names or things, usually written or printed one under the other. **2** *Computing.* a linearly ordered data structure. ◆ *vb* **3** (*tr*) to make a list of. **4** (*tr*) to include in a list. **5** (*tr*) *Brit.* to declare to be a listed building. **6** (*tr*) *Stock Exchange.* to obtain an official quotation for (a security) so that it may be traded on the recognized market. **7** an archaic word for **enlist.** [C17: from F, ult. rel. to LIST²]
▶ 'listable *adj* ▶ 'listing *n*

list² (lɪst) *n* **1** a border or edging strip, esp. of cloth. **2** a less common word for **selvage.** ◆ *vb* (*tr*) to border with or as if with a list or lists. ◆ See also **lists.** [OE *līst*]

list³ (lɪst) *vb* **1** (esp. of ships) to lean over or cause to lean over to one side. ◆ *n* **2** the act or an instance of leaning to one side. [C17: from ?]

list⁴ (lɪst) *Arch.* ◆ *vb* **1** to be pleasing to (a person). **2** (*tr*) to desire or choose. ◆ *n* **3** a liking or desire. [OE *lystan*]

list⁵ (lɪst) *vb* an archaic or poetic word for **listen.** [OE *hlystan*]

listed building *n* (in Britain) a building officially recognized as having special historical or architectural interest and therefore protected from demolition or alteration.

listed company *n* *Stock Exchange.* a company whose shares are quoted on the main market of the London stock exchange.

listed security *n* *Stock Exchange.* a security that is quoted on the main market of the London stock exchange and appears in its *Official List of Securities.* Cf. **Third Market, Unlisted Securities Market.**

listen ('lɪsⁿn) *vb* (*intr*) **1** to concentrate on hearing something. **2** to take heed; pay attention: *I warned you but you wouldn't listen.* [OE *hlysnan*]
▶ 'listener *n*

listen in *vb* (*intr*, *adv*; often foll. by *to*) **1** to listen to the radio. **2** to intercept radio communications. **3** to listen but not contribute (to a discussion), esp. surreptitiously.

listening post *n* **1** *Mil.* a forward position set up to obtain early warning of enemy movement. **2** any strategic position for obtaining information about another country or area.

lister ('lɪstə) *n* US & Canad. agriculture. a plough with a double mouldboard designed to throw soil to either side of a central furrow. [C19: from LIST²]

Lister ★ ('lɪstə) *n* **Joseph,** 1st Baron Lister. 1827–1912, British surgeon, who introduced the use of antiseptics.

listeriosis (lɪ‚stɪərɪ'əʊsɪs) *n* a serious form of food poisoning, caused by a bacterium (**listeria**). Its symptoms can include meningitis and in pregnant women it may cause damage to the fetus. [after Joseph LISTER]

listless ('lɪstlɪs) *adj* having or showing no interest; lacking vigour or energy. [C15: from *list* desire + -LESS]
▶ 'listlessly *adv* ▶ 'listlessness *n*

Liston ★ ('lɪstən) *n* **Sonny,** real name *Charles.* 1922–70, US boxer; former world heavyweight champion.

list price *n* the selling price of merchandise as quoted in a catalogue or advertisement.

list renting *n* the practice of renting a list of potential customers to a direct-mail seller of goods or to the fundraisers of a charity.

lists (lɪsts) *pl n* **1** *History.* **1a** the enclosed field of combat at a tournament. **1b** the barriers enclosing the field at a tournament. **2** any arena or scene of conflict, controversy, etc. **3 enter the lists.** to engage in a conflict, controversy, etc. [C14: pl of LIST² (border)]

Liszt ★ (lɪst) *n* **Franz** (frants). 1811–86, Hungarian composer and pianist. The greatest piano virtuoso of the 19th century, he originated the symphonic poem, pioneered the one-movement sonata form, and developed new harmonic combinations. His works include the symphonies *Faust* (1861) and *Dante* (1867), piano compositions and transcriptions, songs, and church music.

lit (lɪt) *vb* **1** a past tense and past participle of **light¹** (senses

23–26). **2** a past tense and past participle of **light**[2] (senses 28–31).

lit. *abbrev. for:* **1** literal(ly). **2** literary. **3** literature. **4** litre.

Li T'ai-po ★ ('li: 'taɪ'pəʊ) *n* See **Li Po.**

litany ('lɪtənɪ) *n, pl* **litanies. 1** *Christianity.* **1a** a form of prayer consisting of a series of invocations, each followed by an unvarying response. **1b the Litany.** the general supplication in this form in the Book of Common Prayer. **2** any tedious recital. [C13: via OF from Med. L *litania* from LGk *litaneia* prayer, ult. from Gk *litē* entreaty]

litchi, lichee, *or* **lychee** (ˌlaɪ'tʃiː) *n* **1** a Chinese tree cultivated for its round edible fruits. **2** the fruit of this tree, which has whitish juicy pulp. [C16: from Cantonese *lai chi*]

lite ('laɪt) *adj* **1** (of food and drink) containing few calories or little alcohol or fat. **2** denoting a more restrained or less extreme version of a person or thing: *reggae lite.* [C20: var. spelling of LIGHT[2]]

-lite *n combining form.* (in names of minerals) stone: *chrysolite.* [from F *-lite* or *-lithe,* from Gk *lithos* stone]

liter ('liːtə) *n* the US spelling of **litre.**

literacy ('lɪtərəsɪ) *n* **1** the ability to read and write. **2** the ability to use language proficiently.

literal ('lɪtərəl) *adj* **1** in exact accordance with or limited to the primary or explicit meaning of a word or text. **2** word for word. **3** dull, factual, or prosaic. **4** consisting of, concerning, or indicated by letters. **5** true; actual. ✦ *n* **6** Also called: **literal error.** a misprint or misspelling in a text. [C14: from LL *litterālis* concerning letters, from L *littera* letter]
‣ **'literalness** *or* **literality** (ˌlɪtə'rælɪtɪ) *n*

literalism ('lɪtərəˌlɪzəm) *n* **1** the disposition to take words and statements in their literal sense. **2** literal or realistic portrayal in art or literature.
‣ **'literalist** *n* ‣ **ˌliteral'istic** *adj*

literally ('lɪtərəlɪ) *adv* **1** in a literal manner. **2** (*intensifier*): *there were literally thousands of people.*

> **USAGE NOTE** The use of *literally* as an intensifier is common, esp. in informal contexts. In some cases, it provides emphasis without adding to the meaning: *the house was literally only five minutes walk away.* Often, however, its use results in absurdity: *the news was literally an eye-opener to me.* It is therefore best avoided in formal contexts.

literary ('lɪtərərɪ, 'lɪtrərɪ) *adj* **1** of, relating to, concerned with, or characteristic of literature or scholarly writing: *a literary style.* **2** versed in or knowledgeable about literature. **3** (of a word) formal; not colloquial. [C17: from L *litterārius* concerning reading & writing. See LETTER]
‣ **'literarily** *adv* ‣ **'literariness** *n*

literate ('lɪtərɪt) *adj* **1** able to read and write. **2** educated; learned. ✦ *n* **3** a literate person. [C15: from L *litterātus* learned. See LETTER]
‣ **'literately** *adv*

literati (ˌlɪtə'rɑːtiː) *pl n* literary or scholarly people. [C17: from L]

literature ('lɪtərɪtʃə, 'lɪtrɪ-) *n* **1** written material such as poetry, novels, essays, etc. **2** the body of written work of a particular culture or people: *Scandinavian literature.* **3** written or printed matter of a particular type or genre: *scientific literature.* **4** the art or profession of a writer. **5** *Inf.* printed matter on any subject. [C14: from L *litterātūra* writing; see LETTER]

lith. *abbrev. for:* **1** lithograph. **2** lithography.

Lith. *abbrev. for* Lithuania(n).

-lith *n combining form.* indicating stone or rock: *megalith.* [from Gk *lithos* stone]

litharge ('lɪθɑːdʒ) *n* another name for **lead monoxide.** [C14: via OF from L *lithargyrus,* from Gk, from *lithos* stone + *arguros* silver]

lithe (laɪð) *adj* flexible or supple. [OE (in the sense: gentle; C15: supple)]
‣ **'lithely** *adv* ‣ **'litheness** *n*

lithia ('lɪθɪə) *n* **1** another name for **lithium oxide. 2** lithium present in mineral waters as lithium salts. [C19: NL, ult. from Gk *lithos* stone]

lithic ('lɪθɪk) *adj* **1** of, relating to, or composed of stone. **2** *Pathol.* of or relating to a calculus or calculi. **3** of or containing lithium. [C18: from Gk *lithikos* stony]

-lithic *n and adj combining form.* relating to the use of stone implements in a specified cultural period: *Neolithic.* [from Gk *lithikos,* from *lithos* stone]

lithium ('lɪθɪəm) *n* a soft silvery element of the alkali metal series: the lightest known metal, used as an alloy hardener, as a reducing agent, and in batteries. Symbol: Li; atomic no.: 3; atomic wt.: 6.941. [C19: NL, from LITHO- + -IUM]

lithium carbonate *n* a white crystalline solid used in the treatment of manic-depressive illness and mania. Formula: Li_2CO_3.

lithium oxide *n* a white crystalline compound. It absorbs carbon dioxide and water vapour. Formula: Li_2O.

litho ('laɪθəʊ) *n, pl* **lithos,** *adj, adv* short for **lithography, lithograph, lithographic,** or **lithographically.**

litho- *or before a vowel* **lith-** *combining form.* stone: *lithograph.* [from L, from Gk, from *lithos* stone]

lithograph ('lɪθəˌgrɑːf) *n* **1** a print made by lithography. ✦ *vb* **2** (*tr*) to reproduce (pictures, text, etc.) by lithography. ‣ **lithographic** (ˌlɪθə'græfɪk) *adj* ‣ **ˌlitho'graphically** *adv*

lithography (lɪ'θɒgrəfɪ) *n* a method of printing from a metal or stone surface on which the printing areas are not raised but made ink-receptive as opposed to ink-repellent. [C18: from NL *lithographia*]
‣ **li'thographer** *n*

lithology (lɪ'θɒlədʒɪ) *n* **1** the physical characteristics of a rock, including colour, composition, and texture. **2** the study of rocks.

lithophyte ('lɪθəˌfaɪt) *n* **1** a plant that grows on stony ground. **2** an organism, such as a coral, that is partly composed of stony material.

lithosphere ('lɪθəˌsfɪə) *n* the rigid outer layer of the earth, comprising the earth's crust and the solid upper part of the mantle.

lithotomy (lɪ'θɒtəmɪ) *n, pl* **lithotomies.** the surgical removal of a calculus, esp. one in the urinary bladder. [C18: via LL from Gk]

lithotripsy ('lɪθəʊˌtrɪpsɪ) *n, pl* **-sies.** the use of ultrasound to pulverize kidney stones and gallstones *in situ.* [C20: from LITHO- + Gk *thruptein* to crush]

Lithuania ★ (ˌlɪθjʊ'eɪnɪə) *n* a republic in central Europe, on the Baltic Sea: a grand duchy in medieval times, it came under Russian rule in the 18th century: became an independent republic in 1918: annexed (1940) by the Soviet Union as the Lithuanian Soviet Socialist Republic: declared independence in 1990, which was recognized in 1991. Official language: Lithuanian. Religion: chiefly Roman Catholic. Currency: litas. Capital: Vilnius. Pop.: 3 706 000 (1997). Area: 65 200 sq. km (25 174 sq. miles). Lithuanian name: **Lietuva.**

Lithuanian (ˌlɪθjʊ'eɪnɪən) *adj* **1** of, relating to, or characteristic of Lithuania, its people, or their language. ✦ *n* **2** the official language of Lithuania. **3** a native or inhabitant of Lithuania.

litigable ('lɪtɪgəb°l) *adj Law.* that may be the subject of litigation.

litigant ('lɪtɪgənt) *n* **1** a party to a lawsuit. ✦ *adj* **2** engaged in litigation.

litigate ('lɪtɪˌgeɪt) *vb* **litigates, litigating, litigated. 1** to bring or contest (a claim, action, etc.) in a lawsuit. **2** (*intr*) to engage in legal proceedings. [C17: from L *lītigāre,* from *līt-,* stem of *līs* lawsuit + *agere* to carry on]
‣ **'litiˌgator** *n*

litigation (ˌlɪtɪ'geɪʃən) *n* **1** the act or process of bringing or contesting a lawsuit. **2** a judicial proceeding or contest.

litigious (lɪ'tɪdʒəs) *adj* **1** excessively ready to go to law. **2** of or relating to litigation. **3** inclined to dispute or disagree. [C14: from L *lītigiōsus* quarrelsome, from *lītigium* strife]
‣ **li'tigiously** *adv* ‣ **li'tigiousness** *n*

★ people and places

litmus ('lɪtməs) *n* a soluble powder obtained from certain lichens. It turns red under acid conditions and blue under basic conditions. Absorbent paper treated with it (**litmus paper**) is used as an indicator. [C16: ?from Scand.]

litotes ('laɪtəʊˌtiːz) *n, pl* **litotes.** understatement for rhetorical effect, esp. using negation with a term in place of using an antonym of that term, as in "She was not a little upset" for "She was extremely upset". [C17: from Gk, from *litos* small]

litre *or US* **liter** ('liːtə) *n* **1** one cubic decimetre. **2** (formerly) the volume occupied by 1 kilogram of pure water. This is equivalent to 1.000 028 cubic decimetres or about 1.76 pints. [C19: from F, from Med. L *litra*, from Gk: a unit of weight]

LittD *or* **LitD** *abbrev. for* Doctor of Letters *or* Doctor of Literature. [L: *Litterarum Doctor*]

litter ('lɪtə) *n* **1a** small refuse or waste materials carelessly dropped, esp. in public places. **1b** (*as modifier*): *litter bin.* **2** a disordered or untidy condition or a collection of objects in this condition. **3** a group of offspring produced at one birth by a mammal such as a sow. **4** a layer of partly decomposed leaves, twigs, etc., on the ground in a wood or forest. **5** straw, hay, or similar material used as bedding, protection, etc., by animals or plants. **6** a means of conveying people, esp. sick or wounded people, consisting of a light bed or seat held between parallel sticks. **7** see **cat litter.** ◆ *vb* **8** to make (a place) untidy by strewing (refuse). **9** to scatter (objects, etc.) about or (of objects) to lie around or upon (anything) in an untidy fashion. **10** (of pigs, cats, etc.) to give birth to (offspring). **11** (*tr*) to provide (an animal or plant) with straw or hay for bedding, protection, etc. [C13 (in the sense: bed): via Anglo-F, ult. from L *lectus* bed]

littérateur (ˌlɪtərəˈtɜː; *French* literatœr) *n* an author, esp. a professional writer. [C19: from F from L *litterātor* a grammarian]

litter lout *or US & Canad.* **litterbug** ('lɪtəˌbʌg) *n Sl.* a person who tends to drop refuse in public places.

little ('lɪt²l) *determiner* **1** (often preceded by *a*) **1a** a small quantity, extent, or duration of: *the little hope there is left; very little milk.* **1b** (*as pronoun*): *save a little for me.* **2** not much: *little damage was done.* **3** make little of. to regard or treat as insignificant; dismiss. **4** not a little. **4a** very. **4b** a lot. **5** think little of. to have a low opinion of. ◆ *adj* **6** of small or less than average size. **7** young: *a little boy.* **8** endearingly familiar; dear: *my husband's little ways.* **9** contemptible, mean, or disagreeable: *your filthy little mind.* ◆ *adv* **10** (usually preceded by *a*) a small amount; to a small extent or degree; not a lot: *to laugh a little.* **11** (used preceding a verb) not at all, or hardly: *he little realized his fate.* **12** not much or often: *we go there very little now.* **13** little by little. by small degrees. ◆ See also **less, lesser, least.** [OE *lȳtel*]

Little Bear *n the.* the English name for **Ursa Minor.**

Little Belt ★ *n* a strait in Denmark, between Jutland and Funen Island, linking the Kattegat with the Baltic. Length: about 48 km (30 miles). Width: up to 29 km (18 miles). Danish name: **Lille Bælt.**

Little Bighorn ★ *n* a river in the W central US, rising in N Wyoming and flowing north to the Bighorn River. Its banks were the scene of the defeat (1876) and killing of General Custer and his command by Indians.

Little Diomede ★ *n* the smaller of the two Diomede Islands in the Bering Strait: administered by the US. Area: about 10 sq. km (4 sq. miles).

Little Dipper *n the.* a US name for **Ursa Minor.**

Little John ★ *n* one of Robin Hood's companions, noted for his great size and strength.

little people *pl n Folklore.* small supernatural beings, such as elves or leprechauns.

Little Rock ★ *n* a city in central Arkansas, on the Arkansas River: state capital. Pop.: 178 136 (1994 est.).

Little Russia ★ *n* (formerly) a region of the SW Soviet Union, consisting chiefly of the Ukraine.

little slam *n Bridge, etc.* the winning of all tricks except one. Cf. **grand slam.** Also called: **small slam.**

Little St Bernard Pass ★ *n* a pass over the Savoy Alps, between Bourg-Saint-Maurice, France, and La Thuile, Italy: 11th-century hospice. Height: 2187 m (7177 ft).

Littlewood ★ ('lɪt²lˌwʊd) *n* (**Maud**) **Joan.** born 1914, British theatre director, who founded the Theatre Workshop Company (1945) with the aim of bringing theatre to the working classes: noted esp. for her production of *Oh, What a Lovely War!* (1963).

littoral ('lɪtərəl) *adj* **1** of or relating to the shore of a sea, lake, or ocean. ◆ *n* **2** a coastal or shore region. [C17: from LL *littorālis*, from *lītus* shore]

Littoria ★ (*Italian* litˈtɔːrja) *n* the former name (until 1947) of **Latina.**

liturgical (lɪˈtɜːdʒɪk²l) *adj* **1** of or relating to public worship. **2** of or relating to the liturgy. ▸ **liˈturgically** *adv*

liturgy ('lɪtədʒɪ) *n, pl* **liturgies. 1** the forms of public services officially prescribed by a Church. **2** (*often cap.*) Also called: **Divine Liturgy.** *Chiefly Eastern Churches.* the Eucharistic celebration. **3** a particular order or form of public service laid down by a Church. [C16: via Med. L, from Gk *leitourgia*, from *leitourgos* minister, from *leit-* people + *ergon* work]

Liturgy of the Hours *n Christianity.* another name for **divine office.**

Liu Shao Qi *or* **Liu Shao-ch'i** ★ ('lju: 'ʃaʊ'tʃiː) *n* 1898–1974, Chinese Communist statesman; chairman of the People's Republic of China (1959–68); deposed during the Cultural Revolution.

livable *or* **liveable** ('lɪvəb²l) *adj* **1** (of a room, house, etc.) suitable for living in. **2** worth living; tolerable. **3** (foll. by *with*) pleasant to live (with). ▸ **'livableness, 'liveableness** *or* ˌliva'bility, ˌlivea'bility *n*

live¹ (lɪv) *vb* **lives, living, lived.** (*mainly intr*) **1** to show the characteristics of life; be alive. **2** to remain alive or in existence. **3** to exist in a specified way: *to live poorly.* **4** (usually foll. by *in* or *at*) to reside or dwell: *to live in London.* **5** (often foll. by *on*) to continue or last: *the pain still lives in her memory.* **6** (usually foll. by *by*) to order one's life (according to a certain philosophy, religion, etc.). **7** (foll. by *on, upon,* or *by*) to support one's style of living; subsist: *to live by writing.* **8** (foll. by *with*) to endure the effects of (a crime, mistake, etc.). **9** (foll. by *through*) to experience and survive: *he lived through the war.* **10** (*tr*) to pass or spend (one's life, etc.). **11** to enjoy life to the full: *he knows how to live.* **12** (*tr*) to put into practice in one's daily life; express: *he lives religion every day.* **13** live and let live. to refrain from interfering in others' lives; be tolerant. ◆ See also **live down, live in,** etc. [OE *libban, lifian*]

live² (laɪv) *adj* **1** (*prenominal*) showing the characteristics of life. **2** (*usually prenominal*) of, relating to, or abounding in life: *the live weight of an animal.* **3** (*usually prenominal*) of current interest; controversial: *a live issue.* **4** actual: *a real live cowboy.* **5** *Inf.* full of life and energy. **6** (of a coal, ember, etc.) glowing or burning. **7** (esp. of a volcano) not extinct. **8** loaded or capable of exploding: *a live bomb.* **9** *Radio, television, etc.* transmitted or present at the time of performance, rather than being a recording: *a live show.* **10** (of a record) **10a** recorded in concert. **10b** recorded in one studio take. **11** connected to a source of electric power: *a live circuit.* **12** being in a state of motion or transmitting power. **13** acoustically reverberant. ◆ *adv* **14** during, at, or in the form of a live performance. [C16: from *on live* ALIVE]

-lived (-lɪvd) *adj* having or having had a life as specified: *short-lived.*

lived-in *adj* having a comfortable, natural, or homely appearance.

live down (lɪv) *vb* (*tr, adv*) to withstand the effects of (a crime, mistake, etc.) by waiting until others forget or forgive it.

live in (lɪv) *vb* (*intr, adv*) **1** (of an employee) to dwell at one's place of employment, as in a hotel, etc. ◆ *adj* **live-in. 2** resident: *a live-in nanny; a live-in lover.*

livelihood ('laɪvlɪˌhʊd) *n* occupation or employment.

livelong ('lɪvˌlɒŋ) *adj Chiefly poetic.* **1** (of time) long or seemingly long (esp. in **all the livelong day**). **2** whole; entire.

lively ('laıvlı) *adj* **livelier, liveliest. 1** full of life or vigour. **2** vivacious or animated, esp. when in company. **3** busy; eventful. **4** characterized by mental or emotional intensity; vivid. **5** having a striking effect on the mind or senses. **6** refreshing or invigorating: *a lively breeze.* **7** springy or bouncy or encouraging springiness: *a lively ball.* ◆ *adv* also **livelily. 8** in a brisk or lively manner: *step lively.*
▶ **'liveliness** *n*

liven ('laıvᵊn) *vb* (usually foll. by *up*) to make or become lively; enliven.
▶ **'livener** *n*

live oak (laıv) *n* a hard-wooded evergreen oak of S North America: used for shipbuilding.

live out (lıv) *vb* (*intr, adv*) (of an employee, as in a hospital or hotel) to dwell away from one's place of employment.

liver[1] ('lıvə) *n* **1** a large highly vascular reddish-brown glandular organ in the human abdominal cavity. Its main function is the metabolic transformation of nutrients. It also secretes bile, stores glycogen, and detoxifies certain poisons. Related adj: **hepatic. 2** the corresponding organ in animals. **3** the liver of certain animals used as food. **4** a reddish-brown colour. [OE *lifer*]

liver[2] ('lıvə) *n* a person who lives in a specified way: *a fast liver.*

liveried ('lıvərıd) *adj* (esp. of servants or footmen) wearing livery.

liverish ('lıvərıʃ) *adj* **1** *Inf.* having a disorder of the liver. **2** disagreeable; peevish.
▶ **'liverishness** *n*

liver opal *n* a form of opal having a reddish-brown coloration.

Liverpool[1] ★ ('lıvəˌpuːl) *n* **1** a city in NW England, on the Mersey estuary: second largest seaport in Great Britain; developed chiefly in the 17th century with the industrialization of S Lancashire; university (1881). Pop.: 474 000 (1994 est.). **2** a unitary authority in NW England, in Merseyside. Pop.: 474 000 (1994 est.). Area: 113 sq. km (44 sq. miles).

Liverpool[2] ★ ('lıvəˌpuːl) *n* **Robert Banks Jenkinson,** 2nd Earl of Liverpool. 1770–1828, British Tory statesman; prime minister (1812–27).

Liverpudlian (ˌlıvəˈpʌdlıən) *n* **1** a native or inhabitant of Liverpool. ◆ *adj* **2** of or relating to Liverpool. [C19: from LIVERPOOL, with humorous alteration of *pool* to *puddle*]

liver salts *pl n* a preparation of mineral salts used to treat indigestion.

liver sausage *or esp. US* **liverwurst** ('lıvəˌwɜːst) *n* a sausage containing liver.

liverwort ('lıvəˌwɜːt) *n* any of a class of bryophyte plants growing in wet places and resembling green seaweeds or leafy mosses. [late OE *liferwyrt*]

livery ('lıvərı) *n, pl* **liveries. 1** the identifying uniform, badge, etc., of a member of a guild or one of the servants of a feudal lord. **2** a uniform worn by some menservants. **3** an individual or group that wears such a uniform. **4** distinctive dress or outward appearance. **5a** the stabling, keeping, or hiring out of horses for money. **5b** (*as modifier*): *a livery horse.* **6 at livery.** being kept in a livery stable. [C14: via Anglo-F from OF *livrée* allocation, from *livrer* to hand over, from L *līberāre* to set free]

livery company *n Brit.* one of the chartered companies of the City of London originating from the craft guilds.

liveryman ('lıvərımən) *n, pl* **liverymen. 1** *Brit.* a member of a livery company. **2** a worker in a livery stable.

livery stable *n* a stable where horses are accommodated and from which they may be hired out.

lives (laıvz) *n* the plural of **life.**

livestock ('laıvˌstɒk) *n* (*functioning as sing or pl*) cattle, horses, and similar animals kept for domestic use but not as pets, esp. on a farm.

live together (lıv) *vb* (*intr, adv*) (esp. of an unmarried couple) to dwell in the same house or flat; cohabit.

live up (lıv) *vb* **1** (*intr, adv;* foll. by *to*) to fulfil (an expecta-

tion, obligation, principle, etc.). **2 live it up.** *Inf.* to enjoy oneself, esp. flamboyantly.

live wire (laıv) *n* **1** *Inf.* an energetic or enterprising person. **2** a wire carrying an electric current.

live with (lıv) *vb* (*tr, prep*) to dwell with (a person to whom one is not married).

Livia Drusilla ★ ('lıvıə druːˈsılə) *n* 58 B.C.–29 A.D., Roman noblewoman: wife (from 39 B.C.) of Emperor Augustus and mother of Emperor Tiberius.

livid ('lıvıd) *adj* **1** (of the skin) discoloured, as from a bruise or contusion. **2** of a greyish tinge or colour. **3** *Inf.* angry or furious. [C17: via F from L *līvidus*, from *līvēre* to be black and blue]
▶ **'lividly** *adv* ▶ **'lividness** *or* **li'vidity** *n*

living ('lıvıŋ) *adj* **1a** possessing life; not dead. **1b** (*as collective n* preceded by *the*): *the living.* **2** having the characteristics of life (used esp. to distinguish organisms from nonliving matter). **3** currently in use or valid: *living language.* **4** seeming to be real: *a living image.* **5** (of animals or plants) existing in the present age. **6** presented by actors before a live audience: *living theatre.* **7** (*prenominal*) (intensifier): *the living daylights.* ◆ *n* **8** the condition of being alive. **9** the manner in which one conducts one's life: *fast living.* **10** the means, esp. the financial means, whereby one lives. **11** *Church of England.* another term for **benefice. 12** (*modifier*) of, involving, or characteristic of everyday life: *living area.* **13** (*modifier*) of or involving those now alive (esp. in **living memory**).

living death *n* a life or lengthy experience of constant misery.

living room *n* a room in a private house or flat used for relaxation and entertainment.

Livingston ★ ('lıvıŋstən) *n* a town in SE Scotland, the administrative centre of West Lothian: founded as a new town in 1962. Pop.: 41 647 (1991).

Livingstone ★ ('lıvıŋstən) *n* **David.** 1813–73, Scottish missionary and explorer in Africa, who was the first European to see Lake Ngami (1849), the Zambezi River (1851), the Victoria Falls (1855), and Lake Malawi (1859). Searching for the source of the Nile, he was rescued (1871) by the journalist H. M. Stanley.

living wage *n* a wage adequate to maintain a person and his family in reasonable comfort.

living will *n* a document that states that a person who becomes terminally ill does not wish his or her life to be prolonged by artificial means such as a life-support machine.

Livonia ★ (lıˈvəunıə) *n* **1** a former Russian province on the Baltic, north of Lithuania: became Russian in 1721; divided between Estonia and Latvia in 1918. **2** a city in SE Michigan, west of Detroit. Pop.: 100 415 (1994 est.).
▶ **Li'vonian** *adj, n*

Livorno ★ (*Italian* liˈvorno) *n* a port in W central Italy, in Tuscany on the Ligurian Sea: shipyards; oil-refining. Pop.: 165 536 (1994 est.). English name: **Leghorn.**

Livy ★ ('lıvı) *n* Latin name *Titus Livius.* 59 B.C.–17 A.D., Roman historian, famous for his history of Rome in 142 books of which only 35 survive.

lizard ('lızəd) *n* any of a group of reptiles typically having an elongated body, four limbs, and a long tail: includes the geckos, iguanas, chameleons, monitors, and slowworms. [C14: via OF from L *lacerta*]

Lizard ★ ('lızəd) *n* **the.** a promontory in SW England, in SW Cornwall: the southernmost point in Great Britain. Also called: **Lizard Head, Lizard Peninsula.**

LJ (in Britain) *abbrev. for* Lord Justice.

Ljubljana ★ (luːˈbljɑːnə) *n* the capital of Slovenia: capital of Illyria (1816–49); part of Yugoslavia (1918–92); university (1595). Pop.: 276 119 (1995 est.). German name: **Laibach.**

LL *abbrev. for:* **1** Late Latin. **2** Low Latin. **3** Lord Lieutenant.

ll. *abbrev. for* lines (of written matter).

llama ('lɑːmə) *n* **1** a domesticated South American cudchewing mammal of the camel family, that is used as a beast of burden and is valued for its hair, flesh, and hide. **2** the cloth made from the wool of this animal. [C17: via Sp. from Amerind]

★ people and places

Llandaff ('lændəf, -dæf) *or* **Llandaf** ★ (*Welsh* hlan'dav) *n* a town in SE Wales, now a suburb of Cardiff; the oldest bishopric in Wales (6th century).

Llandudno ★ (læn'dɪdnəʊ; *Welsh* hlan'dɪdnɔ) *n* a town and resort in NW Wales, in Conwy county borough on the Irish Sea. Pop.: 14 576 (1991).

Llanelli *or* **Llanelly** ★ (θlæ'nɛθlɪ; *Welsh* hla'nɛhli:) *n* an industrial town in S Wales, in SE Carmarthenshire on an inlet of Carmarthen Bay. Pop.: 44 953 (1991).

Llanfairpwllgwyngyll (*Welsh* hlan‚vaɪrpʊhl'gwɪn‚gɪhl), **Llanfairpwll,** *or* **Llanfair P. G.** ★ *n* a village in NW Wales, in SE Anglesey: reputed to be the longest place name in Great Britain when unabbreviated; means: St Mary's Church in the hollow of the white hazel near the rapid whirlpool of Llandysilio of the red cave. Full name: **Llanfairpwllgwyngyllgogerychwyrndrobwll-llantysiliogogogoch** (*Welsh* hlan'vaɪrpʊhl'gwɪngɪhlgɔ'gerə-xwɪrn'drɔbʊhl'hlantə'sɪljɔ'gɔgɔ'gɔx).

Llangollen ★ (*Welsh* hlan'gɒhlen) *n* a town in NE Wales, in Denbighshire on the River Dee: International Musical Eisteddfod held annually since 1946. Pop.: 3267 (1991).

llano ('lɑːnəʊ; *Spanish* 'ʎano) *n, pl* **llanos** (-nəʊz; *Spanish* -nɔs). an extensive grassy treeless plain, esp. in South America. [C17: Sp., from L *plānum* level ground]

Llano Estacado ★ ('lɑːnəʊ ‚estə'kɑːdəʊ) *n* the S part of the Great Plains of the US, extending over W Texas and E New Mexico: oil and natural gas resources. Chief towns: Lubbock and Amarillo. Area: 83 700 sq. km (30 000 sq. miles). Also called: **Staked Plain**.

LLB *abbrev. for* Bachelor of Laws. [L: *Legum Baccalaureus*]

LLD *abbrev. for* Doctor of Laws. [L: *Legum Doctor*]

Llewellyn ★ (lʊ'ɛlɪn) *n* Colonel **Harry.** born 1911, Welsh show-jumping rider: on Foxhunter, he was a member of the British team that won the gold medal at the 1952 Olympic Games.

Llewelyn II ★ (hlə'wɛlɪn) *n* See **Llywelyn ap Gruffudd.**

Lleyn Peninsula ★ (*Welsh* hli:n) *n* a peninsula in NW Wales between Cardigan Bay and Caernarvon Bay.

LLM *abbrev. for* Master of Laws. [L: *Legum Magister*]

Lloyd ★ (lɔɪd) *n* **1 Clive (Hubert).** born 1944, West Indian cricketer; captained West Indies (1974–88). **2 Harold (Clayton).** 1893–1971, US comic film actor. **3 Marie,** real name *Matilda Alice Victoria Wood*. 1870–1922, British music-hall entertainer.

Lloyd George ★ *n* **David,** 1st Earl Lloyd George of Dwyfor. 1863–1945, British Liberal statesman: prime minister (1916–22). As chancellor of the exchequer (1908–15) he introduced old age pensions (1908), a radical budget (1909), and an insurance scheme (1911).

Lloyd's (lɔɪdz) *n* an association of London underwriters, set up in the late 17th century. Originally concerned with marine insurance, it now underwrites a variety of insurance policies and publishes a daily list (**Lloyd's List**) of shipping information. [C17: after Edward *Lloyd* (died ?1726) at whose coffee house in London the underwriters orig. carried on their business]

Lloyd Webber ★ ('webə) *n* **Andrew,** Baron. born 1948, British composer. His musicals include *Jesus Christ Superstar* (1970) and *Evita* (1978) (with lyrics by Tim Rice), *Cats* (1981), and *By Jeeves* (1996).

Llywelyn ap Gruffudd ★ (hlə'wɛlɪn æp 'grɪfɪð) *n* died 1282, prince of Wales (1258–82): the only Welsh ruler to be recognized as such by the English.

lm *symbol for* lumen.

LMS (in Britain) *abbrev. for* local management of schools: the system of making each school responsible for controlling its total budget, after the budget has been calculated by the Local Education Authority.

LNG *abbrev. for* liquefied natural gas.

lo (ləʊ) *interj* look! see! (now often in **lo and behold**). [OE *lā*]

loach (ləʊtʃ) *n* a carplike freshwater fish of Eurasia and Africa, having a long narrow body with barbels around the mouth. [C14: from OF *loche*, from ?]

Loach ★ (ləʊtʃ) *n* **Ken(neth).** born 1936, British television

and film director: his films include *Kes* (1970) and *My Name is Joe* (1998).

load (ləʊd) *n* **1** something to be borne or conveyed; weight. **2a** the usual amount borne or conveyed. **2b** (*in combination*): *a carload.* **3** something that weighs down, oppresses, or burdens: *that's a load off my mind.* **4** a single charge of a firearm. **5** the weight that is carried by a structure. **6** *Electrical engineering, electronics.* **6a** a device that receives or dissipates the power from an amplifier, oscillator, generator, or some other source of signals. **6b** the power delivered by a machine, generator, circuit, etc. **7** the resistance overcome by an engine or motor when it is driving a machine, etc. **8** an external force applied to a component or mechanism. **9 a load of.** *Inf.* a quantity of: *a load of nonsense.* **10 get a load of.** *Inf.* pay attention to. **11 have a load on.** *US & Canad. sl.* to be intoxicated. ◆ *vb* (*mainly tr*) **12** (*also intr*) to place or receive (cargo, goods, etc.) upon (a ship, lorry, etc.). **13** to burden or oppress. **14** to supply in abundance: *load with gifts.* **15** to cause to be biased: *to load a question.* **16** (*also intr*) to put an ammunition charge into (a firearm). **17** *Photog.* to position (a film, cartridge, or plate) in (a camera). **18** to weight or bias (a roulette wheel, dice, etc.). **19** *Insurance.* to increase (a premium) to cover expenses, etc. **20** *Computing.* to transfer (a program) to a memory. **21 load the dice. 21a** to add weights to dice in order to bias them. **21b** to arrange to have a favourable or unfavourable position. ◆ See also **loads.** [OE *lād* course; in meaning, infl. by LADE]
▸ **'loader** *n*

loaded ('ləʊdɪd) *adj* **1** carrying a load. **2** (of dice, a roulette wheel, etc.) weighted or otherwise biased. **3** (of a question or statement) containing a hidden trap or implication. **4** charged with ammunition. **5** (of concrete) containing heavy metals, esp. iron or lead, for use in making radiation shields. **6** *Sl.* wealthy. **7** (*postpositive*) *Sl., chiefly US & Canad.* **7a** drunk. **7b** drugged.

loading ('ləʊdɪŋ) *n* **1** a load or burden; weight. **2** the addition of an inductance to electrical equipment, such as a transmission line or aerial, to improve its performance. **3** *Austral. & NZ.* a payment made in addition to a basic wage or salary to reward special skills, compensate for unfavourable conditions, etc.

load line *n* a pattern of lines painted on the hull of a ship, approximately midway between the bow and the stern, indicating the various levels that the water line should reach if the ship is properly loaded in different conditions.

loads (ləʊdz) *Inf.* ◆ *pl n* **1** (often foll. by *of*) a lot. ◆ *adv* **2** (intensifier): *loads better.*

loadstar ('ləʊd‚stɑː) *n* a variant spelling of **lodestar.**

loadstone ('ləʊd‚stəʊn) *n* a variant spelling of **lodestone.**

loaf[1] (ləʊf) *n, pl* **loaves** (ləʊvz). **1** a shaped mass of baked bread. **2** any shaped or moulded mass of food, such as sugar, cooked meat, etc. **3** *Sl.* the head; sense: *use your loaf!* [OE *hlāf*]

loaf[2] (ləʊf) *vb* **1** (*intr*) to loiter or lounge around in an idle way. **2** (*tr*; foll. by *away*) to spend (time) idly: *he loafed away his life.* [C19: ? back formation from LOAFER]

loafer ('ləʊfə) *n* **1** a person who avoids work; idler. **2** *Chiefly US & Canad.* a moccasin-like shoe. [C19: ?from G *Landläufer* vagabond]

loam (ləʊm) *n* **1** rich soil consisting of a mixture of sand, clay, and decaying organic material. **2** a paste of clay and sand used for making moulds in a foundry, plastering walls, etc. ◆ *vb* **3** (*tr*) to cover, treat, or fill with loam. [OE *lām*]
▸ **'loamy** *adj* ▸ **'loaminess** *n*

loan (ləʊn) *n* **1** the act of lending: *the loan of a car.* **2** property lent, esp. money lent at interest for a period of time. **3** the adoption by speakers of one language of a form current in another language. **4** short for **loan word. 5 on loan.** lent out; borrowed. ◆ *vb* **6** to lend (something, esp. money). [C13 *loon, lan,* from ON *lān*]
▸ **'loaner** *n*

loanback ('ləʊn‚bæk) *n* **1** a facility offered by some life-assurance companies in which an individual can borrow from his pension fund. ◆ *vb* **loan back. 2** to make use of this facility.

Loan Council *n* (in Australia) a statutory body that controls borrowing by the states.

Loanda ★ (ləʊˈændə) *n* a variant of **Luanda.**

loan shark *n Inf.* a person who lends funds at illegal or exorbitant rates of interest.

loan translation *n* the adoption by one language of a phrase or compound word whose components are literal translations of the components of a corresponding phrase or compound in a foreign language: *English "superman" from German "Übermensch".* Also called: **calque.**

loan word *n* a word adopted, often in a modified form, from one language into another.

loath *or* **loth** (ləʊθ) *adj* **1** (usually foll. by *to*) reluctant or unwilling. **2 nothing loath.** willing. [OE *lāth* (in the sense: hostile)]

loathe (ləʊð) *vb* **loathes, loathing, loathed.** (*tr*) to feel strong hatred or disgust for. [OE *lāthian,* from LOATH]
► 'loather *n*

loathing (ˈləʊðɪŋ) *n* abhorrence; disgust.

loathly[1] (ˈləʊðlɪ) *adv* with reluctance; unwillingly.

loathly[2] (ˈləʊðlɪ) *adj* an archaic word for **loathsome.**

loathsome (ˈləʊðsəm) *adj* causing loathing; abhorrent.
► 'loathsomely *adv* ► 'loathsomeness *n*

loaves (ləʊvz) *n* the plural of **loaf**[1].

lob (lɒb) *Sport.* ◆ *n* **1** a ball struck in a high arc. **2** *Cricket.* a ball bowled in a slow high arc. ◆ *vb* **lobs, lobbing, lobbed. 3** to hit or kick (a ball) in a high arc. **4** to throw, esp. in a high arc. [C14: prob. from Low G, orig. in the sense: something dangling]

Lobachevsky ★ (*Russian* ləbaˈtʃɛfskɪj) *n* Nikolai Ivanovich (nikaˈlaj iˈvanəvitʃ). 1793–1856, Russian mathematician; a founder of non-Euclidean geometry.

lobar (ˈləʊbə) *adj* of, relating to, or affecting a lobe.

lobate (ˈləʊbeɪt) *adj* **1** having or resembling lobes. **2** (of birds) having separate toes that are each fringed with a weblike lobe.
► 'lobately *adv* ► lo'bation *n*

lobby (ˈlɒbɪ) *n, pl* **lobbies. 1** a room or corridor used as an entrance hall, vestibule, etc. **2** *Chiefly Brit.* a hall in a legislative building used for meetings between the legislators and members of the public. **3** Also called: **division lobby.** *Chiefly Brit.* one of two corridors in a legislative building in which members vote. **4** a group of persons who attempt to influence legislators on behalf of a particular interest. ◆ *vb* **lobbies, lobbying, lobbied. 5** to attempt to influence (legislators, etc.) in the formulation of policy. **6** (*intr*) to act in the manner of a lobbyist. **7** (*tr*) to apply pressure for the passage of (a bill, etc.). [C16: from Med. L *lobia* portico, from OHG *lauba* arbor, from *laub* leaf]
► 'lobbyer *n*

lobbyist (ˈlɒbɪɪst) *n* a person employed by a particular interest to lobby.
► 'lobby,ism *n*

lobe (ləʊb) *n* **1** any rounded projection forming part of a larger structure. **2** any of the subdivisions of a bodily organ or part, delineated by shape or connective tissue. **3** Also called: **ear lobe.** the fleshy lower part of the external ear. **4** any of the parts, not entirely separate from each other, into which a flattened plant part, such as a leaf, is divided. [C16: from LL *lobus,* from Gk *lobos* lobe of the ear or of the liver]

lobectomy (ləʊˈbɛktəmɪ) *n, pl* **lobectomies.** surgical removal of a lobe from any organ or gland in the body.

lobelia (ləʊˈbiːlɪə) *n* any of a genus of plants having red, blue, white, or yellow five-lobed flowers with the three lower lobes forming a lip. [C18: from NL, after Matthias de *Lobel* (1538–1616), Flemish botanist]

Lobengula ★ (ˌləʊbənˈgjuːlə) *n* ?1836–94, last Matabele king (1870–93); his kingdom was destroyed by the British.

Lobito ★ (*Portuguese* luˈβitu) *n* the chief port in Angola, in the west on **Lobito Bay:** terminus of the railway

through Benguela to Mozambique. Pop.: 70 000 (latest est.).

loblolly (ˈlɒbˌlɒlɪ) *n, pl* **loblollies.** a southern US pine tree with bright reddish-brown bark, green needle-like leaves, and reddish-brown cones. [C16: ?from dialect *lob* to boil + obs. dialect *lolly* thick soup]

lobola *or* **lobolo** (lɔːˈbɔːlə, ləˈbəʊ-) *n* (in southern Africa) an African custom by which a bridegroom's family makes a payment in cattle or cash to the bride's family shortly before the marriage. [from Nguni *ukulobola* to give the bride price]

lobotomy (ləʊˈbɒtəmɪ) *n, pl* **lobotomies. 1** surgical incision into a lobe of any organ. **2** Also called: **prefrontal leucotomy.** surgical interruption of one or more nerve tracts in the frontal lobe of the brain: used in the treatment of intractable mental disorders. [C20: from LOBE + -TOMY]

lobscouse (ˈlɒbˌskaʊs) *n* a sailor's stew of meat, vegetables, and hardtack. [C18: ?from dialect *lob* to boil + *scouse* broth]

lobster (ˈlɒbstə) *n, pl* **lobsters** *or* **lobster. 1** any of several large marine decapod crustaceans occurring on rocky shores and having the first pair of limbs modified as large pincers. **2** any of several similar crustaceans, esp. the spiny lobster. **3** the flesh of any of these crustaceans, eaten as a delicacy. [OE *loppestre,* from *loppe* spider]

lobster pot *or* **trap** *n* a round basket or trap made of open slats used to catch lobsters.

lobule (ˈlɒbjuːl) *n* a small lobe or a subdivision of a lobe. [C17: from NL *lobulus,* from LL *lobus* LOBE]
► 'lobular (ˈlɒbjʊlə) *or* **lobulate** (ˈlɒbjʊlɪt) *adj*

lobworm (ˈlɒbˌwɜːm) *n* **1** another name for **lugworm. 2** a large earthworm used as bait in fishing. [C17: from obs. *lob* lump + WORM]

local (ˈləʊkəl) *adj* **1** characteristic of or associated with a particular locality or area. **2** of, concerned with, or relating to a particular place or point in space. **3** *Med.* of, affecting, or confined to a limited area or part. **4** (of a train, bus, etc.) stopping at all stations or stops. ◆ *n* **5** a train, bus, etc., that stops at all stations or stops. **6** an inhabitant of a specified locality. **7** *Brit. inf.* a pub close to one's home or place of work. **8** *Med.* short for **local anaesthetic** (see **anaesthesia**). **9** *US & Canad.* an item of local interest in a newspaper. [C15: via OF from LL *locālis,* from L *locus* place]
► 'locally *adv* ► 'localness *n*

local anaesthetic *n Med.* See **anaesthesia.**

local authority *n Brit. & NZ.* the governing body of a county, district, etc. US equivalent: **local government.**

locale (ləʊˈkɑːl) *n* a place or area, esp. with reference to events connected with it. [C18: from F *local* (n use of adj); see LOCAL]

local government *n* **1** government of the affairs of counties, towns, etc., by locally elected political bodies. **2** the US equivalent of **local authority.**

Local Group *n Astron.* the cluster of galaxies to which the Galaxy and the Andromeda Galaxy belong.

localism (ˈləʊkəˌlɪzəm) *n* **1** a pronunciation, phrase, etc., peculiar to a particular locality. **2** another word for **provincialism.**

locality (ləʊˈkælɪtɪ) *n, pl* **localities. 1** a neighbourhood or area. **2** the site or scene of an event. **3** the fact or condition of having a location or position in space.

localize *or* **localise** (ˈləʊkəˌlaɪz) *vb* **localizes, localizing, localized** *or* **localises, localising, localised. 1** to make or become local in attitude, behaviour, etc. **2** (*tr*) to restrict or confine (something) to a particular area or part. **3** (*tr*) to assign or ascribe to a particular region.
► 'local,izable *or* 'local,isable *adj* ► ˌlocali'zation *or* ˌlocali'sation *n*

local loan *n* (in Britain) a loan issued by a local government authority.

local option *n* (esp. in Scotland, New Zealand, and the US) the privilege of a municipality, county, etc., to determine by referendum whether a particular activity, esp. the sale of liquor, shall be permitted there.

Locarno ★ (*Italian* loˈkarno) *n* a town in S Switzerland, in

★ people and places

Ticino canton at the N end of Lake Maggiore: tourist resort. Pop.: 14 150 (1990 est.).

locate (ləʊˈkeɪt) *vb* **locates, locating, located. 1** (*tr*) to discover the position, situation, or whereabouts of; find. **2** (*tr; often passive*) to situate or place: *located on the edge of the city.* **3** (*intr*) to become established or settled.
▸ lo'cater *n*

location (ləʊˈkeɪʃən) *n* **1** a site or position; situation. **2** the act or process of locating or the state of being located. **3** a place outside a studio where filming is done: *shot on location.* **4** (in South Africa) **4a** a Black African or Coloured township, usually located near a small town. **4b** (formerly) a Black African tribal reserve. **5** *Computing.* a position in a memory capable of holding a unit of information, such as a word, and identified by its address. [C16: from L *locatio*, from *locare* to place]

locative (ˈlɒkətɪv) *Grammar.* ◆ *adj* **1** (of a word or phrase) indicating place or direction. **2** denoting a case of nouns, etc., that refers to the place at which the action described by the verb occurs. ◆ *n* **3a** the locative case. **3b** a word or speech element in this case. [C19: LOCATE + -IVE, on the model of *vocative*]

loc. cit. (in textual annotation) *abbrev. for* loco citato. [L: in the place cited]

loch (lɒx, lɒk) *n* **1** a Scot. word for **lake**[1] (senses 1 and 2). **2** Also: **sea loch.** a long narrow bay or arm of the sea in Scotland. [C14: from Gaelic]

lochia (ˈlɒkɪə) *n* a vaginal discharge of cellular debris, mucus, and blood following childbirth. [C17: NL from Gk *lokhia*, from *lokhos* childbirth]
▸ 'lochial *adj*

loci (ˈləʊsaɪ) *n* the plural of **locus.**

lock[1] (lɒk) *n* **1** a device fitted to a gate, door, drawer, lid, etc., to keep it firmly closed. **2** a similar device attached to a machine, vehicle, etc. **3a** a section of a canal or river that may be closed off by gates to control the water level and the raising and lowering of vessels that pass through it. **3b** (*as modifier*): *a lock gate; a lock keeper.* **4** the jamming, fastening, or locking together of parts. **5** *Brit.* the extent to which a vehicle's front wheels will turn to the right or left: *this car has a good lock.* **6** a mechanism that detonates the charge of a gun. **7 lock, stock, and barrel.** completely; entirely. **8** any wrestling hold in which a wrestler seizes a part of his opponent's body. **9** Also called: **lock forward.** *Rugby.* **9a** a player in the second row of the scrum. **9b** this position. **10** a gas bubble in a hydraulic system or a liquid bubble in a pneumatic system that stops the fluid flow in a pipe, capillary, etc.: *an air lock.* ◆ *vb* **11** to fasten (a door, gate, etc.) or (of a door, etc.) to become fastened with a lock, bolt, etc., so as to prevent entry or exit. **12** (*tr*) to secure (a building) by locking all doors, windows, etc. **13** to fix or become fixed together securely or inextricably. **14** to become or cause to become rigid or immovable: *the front wheels of the car locked.* **15** (when *tr*, *often passive*) to clasp or entangle (someone or each other) in a struggle or embrace. **16** (*tr*) to furnish (a canal) with locks. **17** (*tr*) to move (a vessel) through a system of locks. ◆ See also **lock out, lock up.** [OE *loc*]
▸ 'lockable *adj*

lock[2] (lɒk) *n* **1** a strand, curl, or cluster of hair. **2** a tuft or wisp of wool, cotton, etc. **3** (*pl*) *Chiefly literary.* hair, esp. when curly or fine. [OE *loc*]

Locke ★ (lɒk) *n* **1** John. 1632–1704, English empiricist philosopher; his main works were *An Essay Concerning Human Understanding* (1690) and *Two Treatises on Government* (1690). **2** Matthew. ?1630–77, English composer, esp. of works for the stage.

locked-in syndrome *n* a condition in which a person is conscious but unable to move any part of the body except the eyes: results from damage to the brainstem.

locker (ˈlɒkə) *n* **1a** a small compartment or drawer that may be locked, as one of several in a gymnasium, etc., for clothes and valuables. **1b** (*as modifier*): *a locker room.* **2** a person or thing that locks.

Lockerbie ★ (ˈlɒkəbɪ) *n* a town in SW Scotland, in Dumfries and Galloway: scene (1988) of the UK's worst air disaster when a jumbo jet was brought down by a terror-

ist bomb, killing 270 people, including eleven residents of the town.

locket (ˈlɒkɪt) *n* a small ornamental case, usually on a necklace or chain, that holds a picture, keepsake, etc. [C17: from F *loquet* latch, dim. of *loc* LOCK[1]]

lockjaw (ˈlɒkˌdʒɔː) *n Pathol.* a nontechnical name for **trismus** and (often) **tetanus.**

lock out *vb* (*tr, adv*) **1** to prevent from entering by locking a door. **2** to prevent (employees) from working during an industrial dispute, as by closing a factory. ◆ *n* **lockout. 3** the closing of a place of employment by an employer, in order to bring pressure on employees to agree to terms.

locksmith (ˈlɒkˌsmɪθ) *n* a person who makes or repairs locks.

lock step *n* a method of marching such that the men follow one another as closely as possible.

lock up *vb* (*adv*) **1** (*tr*) Also: **lock in, lock away.** to imprison or confine. **2** to lock or secure the doors, windows, etc., of (a building). **3** (*tr*) to keep or store securely: *secrets locked up in history.* **4** (*tr*) to invest (funds) so that conversion into cash is difficult. ◆ *n* **lockup. 5** the action or time of locking up. **6** a jail or block of cells. **7** *Brit.* a small shop with no attached quarters for the owner. **8** *Brit.* a garage or storage place separate from the main premises. **9** *Stock Exchange.* an investment that is intended to be held for a relatively long period. ◆ *adj* **lock-up. 10** *Brit. & NZ.* (of premises) without living quarters: *a lock-up shop.*

Lockyer ★ (ˈlɒkjə) *n* Sir Joseph Norman. 1836–1920, British astronomer: a pioneer in solar spectroscopy.

loco[1] (ˈləʊkəʊ) *n, pl* **locos.** *Inf.* short for **locomotive.**

loco[2] (ˈləʊkəʊ) *adj* **1** *Sl., chiefly US.* insane. **2** (of an animal) affected with loco disease. ◆ *n, pl* **locos. 3** *US.* short for **locoweed.** ◆ *vb* **locos, locoing, locoed.** (*tr*) **4** to poison with locoweed. **5** *US sl.* to make insane. [C19: via Mexican Sp. from Sp.: crazy]

loco[3] (ˈləʊkəʊ) *adj* denoting a price for goods, esp. goods to be exported, that are in a place specified or known, the buyer being responsible for all transport charges from that place: *loco Bristol; a loco price.* [C20: from L *locō* from a place]

loco disease *n* a disease of cattle, sheep, and horses characterized by paralysis and faulty vision, caused by ingestion of locoweed.

locomotion (ˌləʊkəˈməʊʃən) *n* the act, fact, ability, or power of moving. [C17: from L *locō* from a place, ablative of *locus* place + MOTION]

locomotive (ˌləʊkəˈməʊtɪv) *n* **1a** Also called: **locomotive engine.** a self-propelled engine driven by steam, electricity, or diesel power and used for drawing trains along railway tracks. **1b** (*as modifier*): *a locomotive shed; a locomotive works.* ◆ *adj* **2** of or relating to locomotion. **3** moving or able to move, as by self-propulsion.

locomotor (ˌləʊkəˈməʊtə) *adj* of or relating to locomotion. [C19: from L *locō* from a place + MOTOR (mover)]

locomotor ataxia *n Pathol.* another name for **tabes dorsalis.**

locoweed (ˈləʊkəʊˌwiːd) *n* any of several perennial leguminous plants of W North America that cause loco disease in horses, cattle, and sheep.

Locris *or* **Lokris** ★ (ˈləʊkrɪs, ˈlɒk-) *n* an ancient region of central Greece.
▸ 'Locrian *or* 'Lokrian *adj, n*

loculus (ˈlɒkjʊləs) *n, pl* **loculi** (ˈlɒkjʊˌlaɪ). **1** *Bot.* any of the chambers of an ovary or anther. **2** *Biol.* any small cavity or chamber. [C19: NL, from L: compartment, from *locus* place]
▸ 'locular *adj*

locum tenens (ˈləʊkəm ˈtiːnɛnz) *n, pl* **locum tenentes** (təˈnɛntiːz). *Chiefly Brit.* a person who stands in temporarily for another member of the same profession, esp. for a physician, chemist, or clergyman. Often shortened to **locum.** [C17: Med. L: (someone) holding the place (of another)]

locus (ˈləʊkəs) *n, pl* **loci. 1** (in many legal phrases) a place or area, esp. the place where something occurred. **2** *Maths.* a set of points or lines whose location satisfies or is determined by one or more specified conditions: *the locus of points equidistant from a given point is a circle.* **3** *Genetics.* the position of a particular gene on a chromosome. [C18: L]

locust ('ləukəst) *n* **1** any of numerous insects, related to the grasshopper, of warm and tropical regions of the Old World, which travel in vast swarms, stripping large areas of vegetation. **2** Also called: **locust tree.** a North American leguminous tree having prickly branches, hanging clusters of white fragrant flowers, and reddish-brown seed pods. **3** the yellowish durable wood of this tree. **4** any of several similar trees, such as the honey locust and carob. [C13 (the insect): from L *locusta*; applied to the tree (C17) because the pods resemble locusts]

locution (ləu'kju:ʃən) *n* **1** a word, phrase, or expression. **2** manner or style of speech. [C15: from L *locūtiō* an utterance, from *loquī* to speak]

Lod ★ (lɒd) *n* a town in central Israel, southeast of Tel Aviv: Israel's chief airport. Pop.: 42 000 (1989 est.). Also called: **Lydda.**

lode (ləud) *n* **1** a deposit of valuable ore occurring between definite limits in the surrounding rock; vein. **2** a deposit of metallic ore filling a fissure in the surrounding rock. [OE *lād* course]

loden ('ləud³n) *n* **1** a thick heavy waterproof woollen cloth with a short pile, used for coats. **2** a dark bluish-green colour, in which the cloth is often made. [G, from OHG *lodo* thick cloth]

lodestar *or* **loadstar** ('ləud,sta:) *n* **1** a star, esp. the North Star, used in navigation or astronomy as a point of reference. **2** something that serves as a guide or model. [C14: lit.: guiding star]

lodestone *or* **loadstone** ('ləud,stəun) *n* **1a** magnetite that is naturally magnetic. **1b** a piece of this, which can be used as a magnet. **2** a person or thing regarded as a focus of attraction. [C16: lit.: guiding stone]

lodge (lɒdʒ) *n* **1** *Chiefly Brit.* a small house at the entrance to the grounds of a country mansion, usually occupied by a gatekeeper or gardener. **2** a house or cabin used occasionally, as for some seasonal activity. **3** (*cap. when part of a name*) a large house or hotel. **4** a room for the use of porters in a university, college, etc. **5** a local branch or chapter of certain societies. **6** the building used as the meeting place of such a society. **7** the dwelling place of certain animals, esp. beavers. **8** a hut or tent of certain North American Indian peoples. ◆ *vb* **lodges, lodging, lodged.** **9** to provide or be provided with accommodation or shelter, esp. rented accommodation. **10** (*intr*) to live temporarily, esp. in rented accommodation. **11** to implant, embed, or fix or be implanted, embedded, or fixed. **12** (*tr*) to deposit or leave for safety, storage, etc. **13** (*tr*) to bring (a charge or accusation) against someone. **14** (*tr; often foll. by in or with*) to place (authority, power, etc.) in the control of (someone). [C15: from OF *loge,* ?from OHG *louba* porch]

Lodge ★ (lɒdʒ) *n* **1 David (John).** born 1935, British novelist. His books include *Changing Places* (1975), *Nice Work* (1988), and *Therapy* (1995). **2 Sir Oliver (Joseph).** 1851–1940, British physicist. **3 Thomas.** ?1558–1625, English writer. His romance *Rosalynde* (1590) supplied the plot for Shakespeare's *As You Like It.*

lodger ('lɒdʒə) *n* a person who pays rent in return for accommodation in someone else's house.

lodging ('lɒdʒɪŋ) *n* **1** a temporary residence. **2** (*sometimes pl*) sleeping accommodation.

lodging house *n* a private home providing accommodation and meals for lodgers.

lodgings ('lɒdʒɪŋz) *pl n* a rented room or rooms, esp. in another person's house.

lodgment *or* **lodgement** ('lɒdʒmənt) *n* **1** the act of lodging or the state of being lodged. **2** a blockage or accumulation. **3** a small area gained and held in enemy territory.

Lodi (*Italian* 'lɔ:di) *n* a town in N Italy, in Lombardy: scene of Napoleon's defeat of the Austrians in 1796. Pop.: 42 277 (1993 est.).

Łódź ★ (*Polish* wutʃ) *n* a city in central Poland: the coun-

try's second largest city; major centre of the textile industry; university (1945). Pop.: 828 500 (1995 est.).

loess ('ləuɪs) *n* a light-coloured fine-grained accumulation of clay and silt deposited by the wind. [C19: from G *Löss,* from Swiss G dialect *lösch* loose]
► **loessial** (ləu'esɪəl) *adj*

Loewe ★ *n* **1** (ləu). **Frederick.** 1904–88, US composer of such musicals as *My Fair Lady* (1956) and *Camelot* (1960), with librettos by Alan Jay Lerner. **2** Also: **Löwe** (*German* 'lø:və). **(Johann) Karl (Gottfried).** 1796–1869, German composer, esp. of songs.

Loewi ★ ('ləuɪ) *n* **Otto.** 1873–1961, US pharmacologist, born in Germany. He shared a Nobel prize for physiology or medicine (1936) for work on the transmission of nerve impulses.

Lofoten and Vesterålen ★ (*Norwegian* 'lu:futən; 'vestəro:lən) *pl n* a group of islands off the NW coast of Norway, within the Arctic Circle. Largest island: Hinny. Pop.: 66 600 (1985 est.). Area: about 5130 sq. km (1980 sq. miles).

loft (lɒft) *n* **1** the space inside a roof. **2** a gallery, esp. one for the choir in a church. **3** a room over a stable used to store hay. **4** *US.* an upper storey of a warehouse or factory. **5** a raised house or coop in which pigeons are kept. **6** *Sport.* **6a** (in golf) the angle from the vertical made by the club face to give elevation to a ball. **6b** elevation imparted to a ball. **6c** a lofting stroke or shot. ◆ *vb* (*tr*) **7** *Sport.* to strike or kick (a ball) high in the air. **8** to store or place in a loft. **9** *Golf.* to slant (the face of a golf club). [OE, from ON *lopt* air, ceiling]

lofty ('lɒftɪ) *adj* **loftier, loftiest.** **1** of majestic or imposing height. **2** exalted or noble in character or nature. **3** haughty or supercilious. **4** elevated, eminent, or superior.
► **loftily** *adv* ► **loftiness** *n*

log¹ (lɒg) *n* **1a** a section of the trunk or a main branch of a tree, when stripped of branches. **1b** (*modifier*) constructed out of logs: *a log cabin.* **2a** a detailed record of a voyage of a ship or aircraft. **2b** a record of the hours flown by pilots and aircrews. **2c** a book in which these records are made; logbook. **3** a written record of information about transmissions kept by radio stations, amateur radio operators, etc. **4** Also called: **chip log.** a device consisting of a float with an attached line, formerly used to measure the speed of a ship. **5 like a log.** without stirring or being disturbed (in **sleep like a log**). ◆ *vb* **logs, logging, logged.** **6** (*tr*) to fell the trees of (a forest, area, etc.) for timber. **7** (*tr*) to saw logs from (trees). **8** (*intr*) to work at the felling of timber. **9** (*tr*) to enter (a distance, event, etc.) in a logbook or log. **10** (*tr*) to travel (a specified distance or time) or move at (a specified speed). [C14: of uncertain origin?]

log² (lɒg) *n* short for **logarithm.**

-log *n combining form.* a US variant of **-logue.**

logan ('ləugən) *n* *Canad.* another name for **bogan** (a backwater).

Logan ★ ('ləugən) *n* **Mount.** a mountain in NW Canada, in SW Yukon in the St Elias Range: the highest peak in Canada and the second highest in North America. Height: 6050 m (19 850 ft).

loganberry ('ləugənbərɪ, -brɪ) *n, pl* **loganberries. 1** a trailing prickly hybrid plant of the rose family, cultivated for its edible fruit. **2** the purplish-red acid fruit of this plant. [C19: after James H. *Logan* (1841–1928), American judge and horticulturalist who first grew it (1881)]

logarithm ('lɒgə,rɪðəm) *n* the exponent indicating the power to which a fixed number, the base, must be raised to obtain a given number or variable. It is used esp. to simplify multiplication and division. Often shortened to **log.** [C17: from NL *logarithmus,* coined 1614 by John NAPIER, from Gk *logos* ratio + *arithmos* number]
► **logarithmic** (,lɒgə'rɪðmɪk) *adj*

logarithmic function *n* **a** the mathematical function $y = \log x$. **b** a function that can be expressed in terms of this function.

logbook ('lɒg,buk) *n* **1** a book containing the official record of trips made by a ship or aircraft. **2** *Brit.* a former name for **registration document.**

| ★ people and places |

log chip *n Naut.* the wooden chip or float of a chip log. See **log**[1] (sense 4).

loge (ləʊʒ) *n* a small enclosure or box in a theatre or opera house. [C18: F; see LODGE]

logger ('lɒɡə) *n* another word for **lumberjack**.

loggerhead ('lɒɡə,hɛd) *n* **1** Also called: **loggerhead turtle**. a large-headed turtle occurring in most seas. **2** a tool consisting of a large metal sphere attached to a long handle, used for warming liquids, melting tar, etc. **3** *Arch. or dialect.* a blockhead; dunce. **4** **at loggerheads**. engaged in dispute or confrontation. [C16: prob. from dialect *logger* wooden block + HEAD]

loggia ('lɒdʒə, 'lɒdʒɪə) *n, pl* **loggias** or **loggie** (-dʒɛ). a covered area on the side of a building. [C17: It., from F *loge*. See LODGE]

logging ('lɒɡɪŋ) *n* the work of felling, trimming, and transporting timber.

logic ('lɒdʒɪk) *n* **1** the branch of philosophy concerned with analysing the patterns of reasoning by which a conclusion is properly drawn from a set of premises, without reference to meaning or context. **2** any formal system in which are defined axioms and rules of inference. **3** the system and principles of reasoning used in a specific field of study. **4** a particular method of argument or reasoning. **5** force or effectiveness in argument or dispute. **6** reasoned thought or argument, as distinguished from irrationality. **7** the relationship and interdependence of a series of events, facts, etc. **8** *Electronics, computing.* the principles underlying the units in a computer system that perform arithmetical and logical operations. See also **logic circuit**. [C14: from OF *logique* from Med. L *logica*, from Gk *logikos* concerning speech or reasoning]

logical ('lɒdʒɪk²l) *adj* **1** relating to, used in, or characteristic of logic: *logical connective*. **2** using, according to, or deduced from the principles of logic: *a logical conclusion*. **3** capable of or characterized by clear or valid reasoning. **4** reasonable or necessary because of facts, events, etc.: *the logical candidate*. **5** *Computing.* of, performed by, used in, or relating to the logic circuits in a computer.
▸ **'logi'cality** or **'logicalness** *n* ▸ **'logically** *adv*

logical form *n* the structure of an argument by virtue of which it can be shown to be formally valid.

logical positivism or **empiricism** *n* a philosophical theory holding that the only meaningful statements are those that are analytic or can be tested empirically. It therefore rejects theology, metaphysics, etc., as meaningless.

logic bomb *n Computing.* an unauthorized program that is inserted into a computer system; when activated it interferes with the operation of the computer.

logic circuit *n* an electronic circuit used in computers to perform a logical operation on its two or more input signals.

logician (lɒ'dʒɪʃən) *n* a person who specializes in or is skilled at logic.

logic programming *n* the study or implementation of computer programs capable of discovering or checking proofs of formal expressions or segments.

log in *Computing.* ◆ *vb* **1** Also: **log on**. to enter (an identification number, password, etc.) from a remote terminal to gain access to a multiaccess system. ◆ *n* **2** Also: **login**. the process by which a computer user logs in.

logistics (lɒ'dʒɪstɪks) *n (functioning as sing or pl)* **1** the science of the movement and maintenance of military forces. **2** the management of materials flow through an organization. **3** the detailed planning and organization of any large complex operation. [C19: from F *logistique*, from *loger* to LODGE]
▸ **lo'gistical** *adj*

log jam *n Chiefly US & Canad.* **1** blockage caused by the crowding together of a number of logs floating in a river. **2** a deadlock; standstill.

loglog ('lɒɡlɒɡ) *n* the logarithm of a logarithm (in equations, etc.).

logo ('ləʊɡəʊ, 'lɒɡ-) *n, pl* **logos**. short for **logotype** (sense 2).

logo- *combining form.* indicating word or speech: *logogram.* [from Gk *logos* word, from *legein* to speak]

logogram ('lɒɡə,ɡræm) *n* single symbol representing an entire morpheme, word, or phrase, as for example the symbol (%) meaning *per cent*.

logorrhoea or *esp.* US **logorrhea** (,lɒɡə'rɪə) *n* uncontrollable or incoherent talkativeness.

logos (lɒɡɒs) *n* **1** *Philosophy.* reason, regarded as the controlling principle of the universe. **2** *(cap.)* the divine Word; the second person of the Trinity. [C16: Gk: word, reason]

logotype ('lɒɡəʊ,taɪp) *n* **1** *Printing.* a piece of type with several uncombined characters cast on it. **2** Also called: **logo**. a trademark, company emblem, or similar device.

log out *Computing.* ◆ *vb* **1** Also: **log off**. to disconnect a remote terminal from a multiaccess system by entering (an identification number, password, etc.). ◆ *n* **2** Also: **logout**. the process by which a computer user logs out.

logroll ('lɒɡ,rəʊl) *vb Chiefly US.* to use logrolling in order to procure the passage of (legislation).
▸ **'log,roller** *n*

logrolling ('lɒɡ,rəʊlɪŋ) *n* **1** US. the practice of undemocratic agreements between politicians involving mutual favours, the trading of votes, etc. **2** another name for **birling**. See **birl**.

Logroño ★ *(Spanish* lo'ɣroɲo) *n* a walled city in N Spain, on the Ebro River: trading centre of an agricultural region noted for its wine. Pop.: 124 823 (1994 est.).

-logue or *US* **-log** *n combining form.* indicating speech or discourse of a particular kind: *travelogue; monologue.* [from F, from Gk *-logos*]

logwood ('lɒɡ,wʊd) *n* **1** a leguminous tree of the Caribbean and Central America. **2** the heavy reddish-brown wood of this tree, yielding a dye.

-logy *n combining form.* **1** indicating the science or study of: *musicology.* **2** indicating writing, discourse, or body of writings: *trilogy; phraseology; martyrology.* [from L *-logia*, from Gk, from *logos* word]
▸ **-logical** or **-logic** *adj combining form.* ▸ **-logist** *n combining form.*

Lohengrin ★ ('ləʊɪnɡrɪn) *n* (in German legend) a son of Parzival and knight of the Holy Grail.

loin (lɔɪn) *n* **1** *Anat.* the lower back and sides between the pelvis and the ribs. Related adj: **lumbar**. **2** a cut of meat from this part of an animal. ◆ See also **loins**. [C14: from OF *loigne*, ?from Vulgar L *lumbra* (unattested), from L *lumbus*]

loincloth ('lɔɪn,klɒθ) *n* a piece of cloth worn round the loins. Also called: **breechcloth**.

loins (lɔɪnz) *pl n* **1** the hips and the inner surface of the legs where they join the trunk of the body; crotch. **2** *Euphemistic.* the reproductive organs.

Loire ★ *(French* lwar) *n* **1** a department of E central France, in Rhône-Alpes region. Capital: St Étienne. Pop.: 748 881 (1994 est.). Area: 4799 sq. km (1872 sq. miles). **2** a river in France, rising in the Massif Central and flowing north and west in a wide curve to the Bay of Biscay: the longest river in France. Its valley is famous for its wines and châteaux. Length: 1020 km (634 miles). Ancient name: **Liger**.

Loire-Atlantique ★ *(French* lwaratlãtik) *n* a department of W France, in Pays de la Loire region. Capital: Nantes. Pop.: 1 085 912 (1994 est.). Area: 6980 sq. km (2722 sq. miles).

Loiret ★ *(French* lware) *n* a department of central France, in Centre region. Capital: Orléans. Pop.: 606 652 (1994 est.). Area: 6812 sq. km (2657 sq. miles).

Loir-et-Cher ★ *(French* lwareʃer) *n* a department of N central France, in Centre region. Capital: Blois. Pop.: 311 779 (1994 est.). Area: 6422 sq. km (2505 sq. miles).

loiter ('lɔɪtə) *vb (intr)* to stand or act aimlessly or idly. [C14: ?from MDu. *löteren* to wobble]
▸ **'loiterer** *n* ▸ **'loitering** *n, adj*

Loki ★ ('ləʊkɪ) *n Norse myth.* the god of mischief and destruction.

loll (lɒl) *vb* **1** *(intr)* to lie, lean, or lounge in a lazy or relaxed manner. **2** to hang or allow to hang loosely. ◆ *n* **3** an act or instance of lolling. [C14: ? imit.]
▸ **'loller** *n* ▸ **'lolling** *adj*

★ people and places

Lolland or **Laaland** ★ (Danish 'lɔlan) n an island of Denmark in the Baltic Sea, south of Sjælland. Pop.: 80 500 (1988 est.). Area: 1240 sq. km (480 sq. miles).

Lollard ('lɒləd) n English history. a follower of John Wycliffe during the 14th, 15th, and 16th centuries. [C14: from MDu.; mutterer, from *lollen* to mumble (prayers)]
▶ **'Lollardism** n

lollipop ('lɒlɪˌpɒp) n **1** a boiled sweet or toffee stuck on a small wooden stick. **2** Brit. another word for **ice lolly**. [C18: ?from N. English dialect *lolly* the tongue + POP[1]]

lollipop man or **lady** n Brit. inf. a person who stops traffic by holding up a circular sign on a pole, to enable children to cross the road safely.

lollop ('lɒləp) vb **lollops, lolloping, lolloped.** (intr) Chiefly Brit. **1** to walk or run with a clumsy or relaxed bouncing movement. **2** a less common word for **lounge**. [C18: prob. from LOLL + -op as in GALLOP, to emphasize the contrast in meaning]

lollo rosso ('lɒləʊ 'rɒsəʊ) n a variety of lettuce originating in Italy, having curly red-tipped leaves and a slightly bitter taste.

lolly ('lɒlɪ) n, pl **lollies. 1** an informal word for **lollipop. 2** Brit. short for **ice lolly. 3** Brit., Austral. & NZ. a slang word for **money. 4** Austral. & NZ inf. a sweet, esp. a boiled one. **5 do the** (or **one's**) **lolly.** Austral. inf. to lose one's temper. [shortened from LOLLIPOP]

Lomax ★ ('ləʊmæks) n **Alan.** born 1915, and his father **John Avery** ('eɪvərɪ) (1867–1948), US folklorists.

Lombard[1] ('lɒmbəd, -bɑːd, 'lʌm-) n **1** a native or inhabitant of Lombardy. **2** a member of an ancient Germanic people who settled in N Italy after 568 A.D. ◆ adj also **Lombardic. 3** of or relating to Lombardy or the Lombards.

Lombard[2] ★ ('lɒmbəd, -bɑːd, 'lʌm-) n **Peter.** ?1100–?60, Italian theologian, noted for his *Sententiarum libri quatuor.*

Lombard Street n the British financial and banking world. [C16: from a street in London once occupied by Lombard bankers]

Lombardy ★ ('lɒmbədɪ, 'lʌm-) n a region of N central Italy, bordering on the Alps: dominated by prosperous lordships and city-states during the Middle Ages; later ruled by Spain and then by Austria before becoming part of Italy in 1859; intensively cultivated and in parts highly industrialized. Pop.: 8 901 023 (1994 est.). Area: 23 804 sq. km (9284 sq. miles). Italian name: **Lombardia** (ˌlɔmbarˈdiːa).

Lombardy poplar n an Italian poplar tree with upwardly pointing branches giving it a columnar shape.

Lombok ★ ('lɒmbɒk) n an island of Indonesia, in the Nusa Tenggara Islands east of Java: came under Dutch rule in 1894; important biologically as being transitional between Asian and Australian in flora and fauna, the line of demarcation beginning at **Lombok Strait** (a channel between Lombok and Bali, connecting the Flores Sea with the Indian Ocean). Chief town: Mataram. Pop.: 2 500 000 (1991). Area: 4730 sq. km (1826 sq. miles).

Lomé ★ (French lɔme) n the capital and chief port of Togo, on the Bight of Benin. Pop.: 513 000 (1990 est.).

Lomond ★ ('ləʊmənd) n **1 Loch.** a lake in W Scotland, north of Glasgow: the largest Scottish lake. Length: about 38 km (24 miles). Width: up to 8 km (5 miles). **2** See **Ben Lomond.**

London[1] ★ ('lʌndən) n **1** the capital of the United Kingdom, a port in S England on the River Thames near its estuary on the North Sea: consists of the **City** (the financial quarter), the **West End** (the entertainment and major shopping centre), the **East End** (the industrial and dock area), and extensive suburbs. Latin name: **Londinium.** See also **City. 2 Greater.** the administrative area of London, consisting of the City of London and 32 boroughs (13 Inner London boroughs and 19 Outer London boroughs): formed in 1965 from the City, parts of Surrey, Kent, Essex, and Middlesex. Pop.: 6 964 400 (1994 est.). Area: 1579 sq. km (610 sq. miles). **3** a city in SE Canada, in SE Ontario

on the Thames River: University of Western Ontario (1878). Pop.: 303 165 (1991).
▶ **'Londoner** n

London[2] ★ ('lʌndən) n **Jack,** full name *John Griffith London.* 1876–1916, US writer and adventurer. His works include *Call of the Wild* (1903) and *White Fang* (1906).

Londonderry ★ ('lʌndənˌdɛrɪ) n **1** Also called: **Derry.** a historic county of Northern Ireland, on the Atlantic. Area: 2075 sq. km (801 sq. miles). **2** Also called: **Derry.** a port in N Northern Ireland, second city of Northern Ireland: given to the City of London in 1613 to be colonized by Londoners; besieged by James II's forces (1688–89). Pop.: 72 334 (1991). **3** another name for **Derry** (sense 1).

London pride n a type of saxifrage plant having a basal rosette of leaves and pinkish-white flowers.

Londrina ★ (Portuguese lonˈdrina) n a city in S Brazil, in Paraná: centre of a coffee-growing area. Pop.: 355 062 (1991).

lone (ləʊn) adj (prenominal) **1** unaccompanied; solitary. **2** single or isolated: *a lone house.* **3** a literary word for **lonely. 4** unmarried or widowed. [C14: from the mistaken division of ALONE into *a lone*]
▶ **'loneness** n

lonely ('ləʊnlɪ) adj **lonelier, loneliest. 1** unhappy as a result of being without companions. **2** causing or resulting from the state of being alone. **3** isolated, unfrequented, or desolate. **4** without companions; solitary.
▶ **'loneliness** n

lonely hearts adj (often caps.) of or for people who wish to meet a congenial companion or marriage partner: *a lonely hearts advertisement.*

loner ('ləʊnə) n Inf. a person who avoids the company of others or prefers to be alone.

lonesome ('ləʊnsəm) adj **1** Chiefly US & Canad. another word for **lonely.** ◆ n **2 on** or US **by one's lonesome.** Inf. on one's own.
▶ **'lonesomely** adv ▶ **'lonesomeness** n

long[1] (lɒŋ) adj **1** having relatively great extent in space or duration in time. **2a** (postpositive) of a specified number of units in extent or duration: *three hours long.* **2b** (in combination): *a two-foot-long line.* **3** having or consisting of a relatively large number of items or parts: *a long list.* **4** having greater than the average or expected range, extent, or duration: *a long match.* **5** seeming to occupy a greater time than is really so: *she spent a long afternoon waiting.* **6** (of drinks) containing a large quantity of nonalcoholic beverage. **7** (of a garment) reaching to the wearer's ankles. **8** Inf. (foll. by *on*) plentifully supplied or endowed (with): *long on good ideas.* **9** Phonetics. (of a speech sound, esp. a vowel) **9a** of relatively considerable duration. **9b** (in popular usage) denoting the qualities of the five English vowels in such words as *mate, mete, mite, moat, moot,* and *mute.* **10** from end to end; lengthwise. **11** unlikely to win, happen, succeed, etc.: *a long chance.* **12** Prosody. **12a** denoting a vowel of relatively great duration. **12b** denoting a syllable containing such a vowel. **12c** carrying the emphasis. **13** Finance. having or characterized by large holdings of securities or commodities in anticipation of rising prices. **14** Cricket. (of a fielding position) near the boundary: *long leg.* **15 in the long run.** ultimately; after or over a period of time. ◆ adv **16** for a certain time or period: *how long will it last?* **17** for or during an extensive period of time: *long into the next year.* **18** at a distant time; quite a bit of time: *long before I met you; long ago.* **19** Finance. into a position with more security or commodity holdings than are required by sale contracts and therefore dependent on rising prices for profit: *to go long.* **20 as** (or **so**) **long as. 20a** for or during just the length of time that. **20b** inasmuch as; since. **20c** provided that; if. **21 no longer.** not any more; formerly but not now. ◆ n **22** a long time (esp. in **for long**). **23** a relatively long thing, such as a dash in Morse code. **24** Phonetics. a long vowel or syllable. **25** Finance. a person with large holdings of a security or commodity in expectation of a rise in its price; bull. **26 before long.** soon. **27 the long and the short of it.** the essential points or facts. ◆ See also **longs.** [OE *lang*]

long[2] (lɒŋ) vb (intr; foll. by *for* or an infinitive) to have a strong desire. [OE *langian*]

★ people and places

Long ★ (lɒŋ) n **Crawford Williamson**. 1815–78, US surgeon. He was the first to use ether as an anaesthetic.

long. abbrev. for longitude.

long- adv (in combination) for or lasting a long time: long-awaited; long-established; long-lasting.

long-acting adj (of a drug) slowly effective after initial dosage, but maintaining its effects over a long period of time. Cf. **intermediate-acting**, **short-acting.**

Long Beach ★ n a city in SW California, on San Pedro Bay: resort and naval base; oil-refining. Pop.: 433 852 (1994 est.).

Longbenton ★ (,lɒŋˈbɛntən) n a town in N England, in North Tyneside. Pop.: 34 630 (1991).

longboat (ˈlɒŋˌbəʊt) n the largest boat carried aboard a commercial sailing vessel.

longbow (ˈlɒŋˌbəʊ) n a large powerful hand-drawn bow, esp. as used in medieval England.

longcase clock (ˈlɒŋˌkeɪs) n another name for **grandfather clock.**

longcloth (ˈlɒŋˌklɒθ) n a fine plain-weave cotton cloth made in long strips.

long-dated adj (of a gilt-edged security) having more than 15 years to run before redemption. Cf. **medium-dated**, **short-dated.**

long-day adj (of certain plants) able to mature and flower only if exposed to long periods of daylight. Cf. **short-day.**

long-distance n **1** (modifier) covering relatively long distances: a long-distance driver. **2** (modifier) (of telephone calls, lines, etc.) connecting points a relatively long way apart. **3** Chiefly US & Canad. a long-distance telephone call. **4** a long-distance telephone system or its operator. ◆ adv **5** by a long-distance telephone line: he phoned long-distance.

long-drawn-out adj overprolonged or extended.

Long Eaton ★ (ˈiːtᵊn) n a town in N central England, in SE Derbyshire. Pop.: 44 826 (1991).

longeron (ˈlɒndʒərən) n a main longitudinal structural member of an aircraft. [C20: from F: side support, ult. from L longus LONG¹]

longevity (lɒnˈdʒɛvɪtɪ) n **1** long life. **2** relatively long duration of employment, service, etc. [C17: from LL longaevitās, from L longaevus long-lived, from longus LONG¹ + aevum age]

long face n a disappointed, solemn, or miserable facial expression.
▸ ˌlong-ˈfaced adj

Longfellow ★ (ˈlɒŋˌfɛləʊ) n **Henry Wadsworth**. 1807–82, US poet, noted for his long poems Evangeline (1847) and The Song of Hiawatha (1855).

Longford ★ (ˈlɒŋfəd) n **1** a county of north Republic of Ireland, in Leinster province. County town: Longford. Pop.: 30 296 (1991). Area: 1043 sq. km (403 sq. miles). **2** a town in north Republic of Ireland, county town of Co. Longford. Pop.: 6800 (1995 est.).

longhand (ˈlɒŋˌhænd) n ordinary handwriting in which letters, words, etc., are set down in full, as opposed to typing or to shorthand.

long haul n **1** a journey over a long distance, esp. one involving the transport of goods. **2** a lengthy job.

long-headed adj astute; shrewd; sagacious.
▸ ˌlong-ˈheadedly adv ▸ ˌlong-ˈheadedness n

longhorn (ˈlɒŋˌhɔːn) n **1** a long-horned breed of beef cattle, formerly common in the southwestern US. **2** a British breed of beef cattle with long curved horns.

longing (ˈlɒŋɪŋ) n **1** a prolonged unfulfilled desire or need. ◆ adj **2** having or showing desire or need: a longing look.
▸ ˈlongingly adv

Longinus ★ (lɒnˈdʒaɪnəs) n **Dionysius** (ˌdaɪəˈnɪsɪəs). ?2nd century A.D., supposed author of the famous Greek treatise on literary criticism, On the Sublime.
▸ **Longinean** (lɒnˈdʒɪnɪən) adj

longish (ˈlɒŋɪʃ) adj rather long.

Long Island ★ n an island in SE New York State, separated from the S shore of Connecticut by **Long Island Sound** (an arm of the Atlantic): contains the New York City boroughs of Brooklyn and Queens in the west, many resorts (notably Coney Island), and two large airports (La Guardia and John F. Kennedy). Area: 4462 sq. km (1723 sq. miles).

longitude (ˈlɒndʒɪˌtjuːd, ˈlɒŋgɪ-) n distance in degrees east or west of the prime meridian at 0° measured by the angle between the plane of the prime meridian and that of the meridian through the point in question, or by the time difference. [C14: from L longitūdō length, from longus LONG¹]

longitudinal (ˌlɒndʒɪˈtjuːdɪnᵊl, ˌlɒŋgɪ-) adj **1** of or relating to longitude or length. **2** placed or extended lengthways.
▸ ˌlongiˈtudinally adv

longitudinal wave n a wave that is propagated in the same direction as the displacement of the transmitting medium.

long johns pl n Inf. underpants with long legs.

long jump n an athletic contest in which competitors try to cover the farthest distance possible with a running jump from a fixed board or mark. US and Canad. equivalent: **broad jump.**

long leg n Cricket. **a** a fielding position on the leg side near the boundary almost directly behind the batsman's wicket. **b** a fielder in this position.

long-lived adj having long life, existence, or currency.
▸ ˌlong-ˈlivedness n

long-off n Cricket. **a** a fielding position on the off side near the boundary almost directly behind the bowler. **b** a fielder in this position.

long-on n Cricket. **a** a fielding position on the leg side near the boundary almost directly behind the bowler. **b** a fielder in this position.

long-playing adj of or relating to an LP (long player).

long-range adj **1** of or extending into the future: a long-range weather forecast. **2** (of vehicles, aircraft, etc.) capable of covering great distances without refuelling. **3** (of weapons) made to be fired at a distant target.

longs (lɒŋz) pl n **1** full-length trousers. **2** long-dated gilt-edged securities. **3** unsold securities or commodities held in anticipation of rising prices.

longship (ˈlɒŋˌʃɪp) n a narrow open vessel with oars and a square sail, used esp. by the Vikings.

longshore (ˈlɒŋˌʃɔː) adj situated on, relating to, or along the shore. [C19: short form of alongshore]

longshore drift n the process whereby beach material is gradually shifted laterally.

longshoreman (ˈlɒŋˌʃɔːmən) n, pl **longshoremen.** a US and Canad. word for **docker.**

long shot n **1** a competitor, as in a race, considered to be unlikely to win. **2** a bet against heavy odds. **3** an undertaking, guess, or possibility with little chance of success. **4** Films, television. a shot where the camera is or appears to be distant from the object to be photographed. **5 by a long shot.** by any means: he still hasn't finished by a long shot.

long-sighted adj **1** related to or suffering from hyperopia. **2** able to see distant objects in focus. **3** another term for **far-sighted.**
▸ ˌlong-ˈsightedly adv ▸ ˌlong-ˈsightedness n

Longs Peak ★ n a mountain in N Colorado, in the Front Range of the Rockies: the highest peak in the Rocky Mountain National Park. Height: 4345 m (14 255 ft).

long-standing adj existing for a long time.

long-suffering adj **1** enduring pain, unhappiness, etc., without complaint. ◆ n **2** long and patient endurance.
▸ ˌlong-ˈsufferingly adv

long suit n **1a** the longest suit in a hand of cards. **1b** a holding of four or more cards of a suit. **2** Inf. an outstanding advantage, personal quality, or talent.

long-term adj **1** lasting or extending over a long time: long-term prospects. **2** Finance. maturing after a long period: a long-term bond.

longtime ('lɒŋˌtaɪm) *adj* of long standing.

long ton *n* the full name for **ton**[1] (sense 1).

Longueuil ★ (lɒŋ'geɪl; *French* lɔ̃gœj) *n* a city in SE Canada, in S Quebec: a suburb of Montreal. Pop.: 129 874 (1991).

longueur (*French* lɔ̃gœr) *n* a period of boredom or dullness. [lit.: length]

Longus ★ ('lɒŋɡəs) *n* ?3rd century A.D., Greek author of the prose romance *Daphnis and Chloe*.

long vacation *n* the long period of holiday in the summer during which universities, law courts, etc., are closed.

long wave *n* **a** a radio wave with a wavelength greater than 1000 metres. **b** (*as modifier*): *a long-wave broadcast*.

longways ('lɒŋˌweɪz) *or US & Canad.* **longwise** *adv* another word for **lengthways**.

long weekend *n* a weekend holiday extended by a day or days on either side.

long-winded (ˌlɒŋ'wɪndɪd) *adj* **1** tiresomely long. **2** capable of energetic activity without becoming short of breath. ▸ ˌlong-'windedly *adv* ▸ ˌlong-'windedness *n*

Longyearbyen ★ ('lɒŋjɪəˌbjɛn) *n* a village on Spitsbergen island, administrative centre of the Svalbard archipelago: coal-mining.

lonicera (lɒ'nɪsərə) *n* See **honeysuckle**.

Lons-le-Saunier ★ (*French* lɔ̃ləsonje) *n* a town in E France: saline springs; manufactures sparkling wines. Pop. (urban area): 210 140 (1990).

loo[1] (luː) *n, pl* **loos**. *Brit.* an informal word for **lavatory**. [C20: ?from F *lieux d'aisance* water closet]

loo[2] (luː) *n, pl* **loos**. **1** a gambling card game. **2** a stake used in this game. [C17: shortened from *lanterloo*, via Du. from F *lanterelu*, orig. a nonsense word from the refrain of a popular song]

loofah ('luːfə) *n* the fibrous interior of the fruit of a type of gourd, which is dried and used as a bath sponge or for scrubbing. Also (esp. US): **loofa**, **luffa**. [C19: from NL *luffa*, from Ar. *lūf*]

look (lʊk) *vb* (*mainly intr*) **1** (often foll. by *at*) to direct the eyes (towards): *to look at the sea*. **2** (often foll. by *at*) to direct one's attention (towards): *let's look at the circumstances*. **3** (often foll. by *to*) to turn one's interests or expectations (towards): *to look to the future*. **4** (*copula*) to give the impression of being by appearance to the eye or mind; seem: *that looks interesting*. **5** to face in a particular direction: *the house looks north*. **6** to expect, hope, or plan (to do something): *I look to hear from you soon; he's looking to get rich*. **7** (foll. by *for*) **7a** to search or seek: *I looked for you everywhere*. **7b** to cherish the expectation (of); hope (for): *I look for success*. **8** (foll. by *to*) **8a** to be mindful (of): *to look to the promise one has made*. **8b** to have recourse (to): *look to your swords, men!* **9** (foll. by *into*) to carry out an investigation. **10** (*tr*) to direct a look at (someone) in a specified way: *she looked her rival up and down*. **11** (*tr*) to accord in appearance with (something): *to look one's age*. **12 look alive, lively, sharp,** *or* **smart.** to hurry up; get busy. **13 look here.** an expression used to attract someone's attention, add emphasis to a statement, etc. ◆ *n* **14** the act or an instance of looking: *a look of despair*. **15** a view or sight (of something): *let's have a look*. **16** (*often pl*) appearance to the eye or mind; aspect: *the look of innocence; I don't like the looks of this place*. **17** style; fashion: *the new look for spring*. ◆ *sentence connector*. **18** an expression demanding attention or showing annoyance, determination, etc.: *look, I've had enough of this*. ◆ See also **look after, look back,** etc. [OE *lōcian*]
▸ 'looker *n*

USAGE NOTE See at **like**.

look after *vb* (*intr, prep*) **1** to take care of; be responsible for. **2** to follow with the eyes.

lookalike ('lʊkəˌlaɪk) *n* **a** a person or thing that is the double of another, often well-known, person or thing. **b** (*as modifier*): *a lookalike Minister; a lookalike newspaper*.

look back *vb* (*intr, adv*) **1** to cast one's mind to the past. **2 never look back**: to become increasingly successful: *after his first book was published, he never looked back*.

look down *vb* (*intr, adv;* foll. by *on* or *upon*) to express or show contempt or disdain (for).

look forward to *vb* (*intr, adv + prep*) to wait or hope for, esp. with pleasure.

look-in *Inf.* ◆ *n* **1** a chance to be chosen, participate, etc. **2** a short visit. ◆ *vb* **look in. 3** (*intr, adv;* often foll. by *on*) to pay a short visit.

looking glass *n* a mirror.

look on *vb* (*intr*) **1** (*adv*) to be a spectator at an event or incident. **2** (*prep*) Also: **look upon**. to consider or regard: *she looked on the whole affair as a joke*.
▸ ˌlooker-'on *n*

lookout ('lʊkˌaʊt) *n* **1** the act of keeping watch against danger, etc. **2** a person or persons instructed or employed to keep such a watch, esp. on a ship. **3** a strategic point from which a watch is kept. **4** *Inf.* worry or concern: *that's his lookout*. **5** *Chiefly Brit.* outlook, chances, or view. ◆ *vb* **look out. 6** (*adv, mainly intr*) to heed one's behaviour; be careful. **7** to be on the watch: *look out for my mother at the station*. **8** (*tr*) to search for and find. **9** (foll. by *on* or *over*) to face in a particular direction: *the house looks out over the moor*.

look over *vb* **1** (*intr, prep*) to inspect by making a tour of (a factory, house, etc.). **2** (*tr, adv*) to examine (a document, letter, etc.). ◆ *n* **look-over. 3** an inspection.

look-see *n Sl.* a brief inspection or look.

look up *vb* (*adv*) **1** (*tr*) to discover (something required to be known) by resorting to a work of reference, such as a dictionary. **2** (*intr*) to increase, as in quality or value: *things are looking up*. **3** (*intr;* foll. by *to*) to have respect (for): *I've always wanted a girlfriend I could look up to*. **4** (*tr*) to visit or make contact with (a person): *I'll look you up when I'm in town*.

loom[1] (luːm) *n* an apparatus, worked by hand or mechanically (**power loom**), for weaving yarn into a textile. [C13 (meaning any kind of tool): var. of OE *gelōma* tool]

loom[2] (luːm) *vb* (*intr*) **1** to come into view indistinctly with an enlarged and often threatening aspect. **2** (of an event) to seem ominously close. **3** (often foll. by *over*) (of large objects) to dominate or overhang. ◆ *n* **4** a rising appearance, as of something far away. [C16: ?from East Frisian *lomen* to move slowly]

loon[1] (luːn) *n* the US and Canad. name for **diver** (the bird). [C17: of Scand. origin]

loon[2] (luːn) *n* **1** *Inf.* a simple-minded or stupid person. **2** *Arch.* a person of low rank or occupation. [C15: from ?]

loony *or* **looney** ('luːnɪ) *Sl.* ◆ *adj* **loonier, looniest. 1** lunatic; insane. **2** foolish or ridiculous. ◆ *n, pl* **loonies** *or* **looneys. 3** a foolish or insane person. **4** *Canad.* a Canadian dollar coin with a loon bird on one of its faces.
▸ 'looniness *n*

loony bin *n Sl.* a mental hospital or asylum.

loop (luːp) *n* **1** the round or oval shape formed by a line, string, etc., that curves across to cross itself. **2** any round or oval-shaped thing that is closed or nearly closed. **3** an intrauterine contraceptive device in the shape of a loop. **4** *Electronics*. a closed electric or magnetic circuit through which a signal can circulate, as in a feedback control system. **5** a flight manoeuvre in which an aircraft flies one complete circle in the vertical plane. **6** Also called: **loop line**. *Chiefly Brit.* a railway branch line which leaves the main line and rejoins it after a short distance. **7** *Maths, physics*. a closed curve on a graph: *hysteresis loop*. **8** a continuous strip of cinematographic film. **9** *Computing*. a series of instructions in a program, performed repeatedly until some specified condition is satisfied. **10** a group of people to whom information is circulated (esp. in **in** or **out of the loop**). ◆ *vb* **11** (*tr*) to make a loop in or of (a line, string, etc.). **12** (*tr*) to fasten or encircle with a loop or something like a loop. **13** Also: **loop the loop**. to cause (an aircraft) to perform a loop or (of an aircraft) to perform a loop. **14** (*intr*) to move in loops or in a path like a loop. [C14 *loupe*, from ?]
▸ 'looper *n*

loophole ('lu:p,həʊl) n 1 an ambiguity, omission, etc., as in a law, by which one can avoid a penalty or responsibility. 2 a small gap or hole in a wall, esp. one in a fortified wall. ◆ vb **loopholes, loopholing, loopholed. 3** (tr) to provide with loopholes.

loopy ('lu:pɪ) adj **loopier, loopiest. 1** full of loops; curly or twisted. **2** Inf. slightly mad, crazy.

Loos ★ (German loːs) n **Adolf** ('aːdɔlf). 1870–1933, Austrian architect: a pioneer of modern architecture, noted for his plain austere style in such buildings as Steiner House, Vienna (1910).

loose (luːs) adj **1** free or released from confinement or restraint. **2** not close, compact, or tight in structure or arrangement. **3** not fitted or fitting closely: *loose clothing*. **4** not bundled, packaged, fastened, or put in a container: *loose nails*. **5** inexact; imprecise: *a loose translation*. **6** (of funds, cash, etc.) not allocated or locked away; readily available: *loose change*. **7a** (esp. of women) promiscuous or easy. **7b** (of attitudes, ways of life, etc.) immoral or dissolute. **8a** lacking a sense of responsibility or propriety: *loose talk*. **8b** (*in combination*): *loosetongued*. **9a** (of the bowels) emptying easily, esp. excessively. **9b** (of a cough) accompanied by phlegm, mucus, etc. **10** Inf., *chiefly US & Canad.* very relaxed; easy. ◆ n **11 the loose.** *Rugby.* the part of play when the forwards close round the ball in a ruck or loose scrum. **12 on the loose. 12a** free from confinement or restraint. **12b** Inf. on a spree. ◆ adv **13a** in a loose manner; loosely. **13b** (*in combination*): *loose-fitting*. ◆ vb **looses, loosing, loosed. 14** (tr) to set free or release, as from confinement, restraint, or obligation. **15** (tr) to unfasten or untie. **16** to make or become less strict, tight, firmly attached, compact, etc. **17** (when intr, often foll. by off) to let fly (a bullet, arrow, or other missile). [C13 (in the sense: not bound): from ON *lauss* free]
► **'loosely** adv ► **'looseness** n

loosebox ('luːs,bɒks) n an enclosed stall with a door in which an animal can be confined.

loose cannon n a person or thing that appears to be beyond control and is potentially a source of unintentional damage.

loose cover n a fitted but easily removable cloth cover for a chair, sofa, etc.

loose end n **1** a detail that is left unsettled, unexplained, or incomplete. **2 at a loose end.** without purpose or occupation.

loose head n *Rugby*. the prop on the hooker's left in the front row of a scrum. Cf. **tight head.**

loose-jointed adj **1** supple and easy in movement. **2** loosely built; with ill-fitting joints.
► **,loose-'jointedness** n

loose-leaf adj (of a binder, album, etc.) capable of being opened to allow removal and addition of pages.

loosen ('luːsᵊn) vb **1** to make or become less tight, fixed, etc. **2** (often foll. by up) to make or become less firm, compact, or rigid. **3** (tr) to untie. **4** (tr) to let loose; set free. **5** (often foll. by up) to make or become less strict, severe, etc. **6** (tr) to rid or relieve (the bowels) of constipation. [C14: from LOOSE]
► **'loosener** n

loosestrife ('luːs,straɪf) n **1** any of a genus of plants, esp. the yellow-flowered yellow loosestrife. **2 purple loosestrife.** a purple-flowered marsh plant. [C16: LOOSE + STRIFE, an erroneous translation of L *lysimachia*, as if from Gk *lusimakhos* ending strife, instead of from the name of the supposed discoverer, *Lusimachos*]

loot (luːt) n **1** goods stolen during pillaging, as in wartime, during riots, etc. **2** goods, money, etc., obtained illegally. **3** Inf. money or wealth. ◆ vb **4** to pillage (a city, etc.) during war or riots. **5** to steal (money or goods), esp. during pillaging. [C19: from Hindi *lūt*]
► **'looter** n

lop[1] (lɒp) vb **lops, lopping, lopped.** (tr; usually foll. by off) **1** to sever (parts) from a tree, body, etc., esp. with swift strokes. **2** to cut out or eliminate as excessive. ◆ n **3** a part or parts lopped off, as from a tree. [C15 *loppe* branches cut off]
► **'lopper** n

lop[2] (lɒp) vb **lops, lopping, lopped. 1** to hang or allow to hang loosely. **2** (intr) to slouch about or move awkwardly. [C16: ? rel. to LOP[1]]

lope (ləʊp) vb **lopes, loping, loped. 1** (intr) (of a person) to move or run with a long swinging stride. **2** (intr) (of four-legged animals) to run with a regular bounding movement. **3** to cause (a horse) to canter with a long easy stride or (of a horse) to canter in this manner. ◆ n **4** a long steady gait or stride. [C15: from ON *hlaupa* to LEAP]

lop-eared adj (of animals) having ears that droop.

Lope de Vega ★ (Spanish 'lope ðe 'βeɣa) n full name *Lope Felix de Vega Carpio.* 1562–1635, Spanish dramatist, novelist, and poet. He established the classic form of Spanish drama and was a major influence on European, esp. French, literature. Some 500 of his 1800 plays are extant.

lopsided (,lɒp'saɪdɪd) adj **1** leaning to one side. **2** greater in weight, height, or size on one side.
► **,lop'sidedly** adv ► **,lop'sidedness** n

loquacious (lɒ'kweɪʃəs) adj characterized by or showing a tendency to talk a great deal. [C17: from L *loquāx* from *loquī* to speak]
► **lo'quaciously** adv ► **loquacity** (lɒ'kwæsɪtɪ) or **lo'quaciousness** n

loquat ('ləʊkwɒt, -kwət) n **1** an ornamental evergreen tree of China and Japan, having reddish woolly branches, white flowers, and small yellow edible plumlike fruits. **2** the fruit of this tree. [C19: from Chinese (Cantonese) *lō kwat*, lit.: rush orange]

lor (lɔː) interj Not standard. an exclamation of surprise or dismay. [from LORD (interj.)]

loran ('lɔːrən) n a radio navigation system operating over long distances. Synchronized pulses are transmitted from widely spaced radio stations to aircraft or shipping, the time of arrival of the pulses being used to determine position. [C20: lo(ng-)ra(nge) n(avigation)]

Lorca[1] ★ (Spanish 'lɔrka) n a town in SE Spain, on the Guadalentín River. Pop.: 66 940 (1991).

Lorca[2] ★ (Spanish 'lɔrka) n **Federico García** (feðe'riko gar'θia). 1898–1936, Spanish poet and dramatist. His plays include the trilogy *Bodas de sangre* (1933), *Yerma* (1934), and *La Casa de Bernarda Alba* (1936).

lord (lɔːd) n **1** a person who has power or authority over others, such as a monarch or master. **2** a male member of the nobility, esp. in Britain. **3** (in medieval Europe) a feudal superior, esp. the master of a manor. **4** a husband considered as head of the household (archaic except in the facetious phrase **lord and master**). **5 my lord.** a respectful form of address used to a judge, bishop, or nobleman. ◆ vb **6** (tr) Now rare. to make a lord of (a person). **7** to act in a superior manner towards (esp. in **lord it over**). [OE *hlāford* bread keeper]
► **'lordless** adj ► **'lord,like** adj

Lord (lɔːd) n **1** a title given to God or Jesus Christ. **2** Brit. **2a** a title given to men of high birth, specifically to an earl, marquess, baron, or viscount. **2b** a courtesy title given to the younger sons of a duke or marquess. **2c** the ceremonial title of certain high officials or of a bishop or archbishop: *Lord Mayor.* ◆ interj **3** (sometimes not cap.) an exclamation of dismay, surprise, etc.: *Good Lord!*

Lord Chancellor n Brit. government. the cabinet minister who is head of the judiciary in England and Wales, and Speaker of the House of Lords.

Lord Chief Justice n the judge who is second only to the Lord Chancellor in the English legal hierarchy; president of one division of the High Court of Justice.

Lord High Chancellor n another name for the **Lord Chancellor.**

Lord Howe Island ★ n an island in the Tasman Sea, southeast of Australia; part of New South Wales. Area: 17 sq. km (6 sq. miles). Pop.: 300 (1981 est.).

Lord Lieutenant n **1** (in Britain) the representative of the Crown in a county. **2** (formerly) the British viceroy in Ireland.

lordly ('lɔːdlɪ) adj **lordlier, lordliest. 1** haughty; arrogant;

proud. **2** of or befitting a lord. ◆ *adv* **3** *Arch.* in the manner of a lord.
▶ **'lordliness** *n*

Lord Mayor *n* the mayor in the City of London and in certain other important boroughs and large cities.

Lord of Misrule *n* (formerly, in England) a person appointed master of revels at a Christmas celebration.

Lord of the Flies ★ *n* a name for **Beelzebub**. [translation of Heb.: see BEELZEBUB]

lordosis (lɔː'dəʊsɪs) *n Pathol.* forward curvature of the lumbar spine. [C18: NL from Gk, from *lordos* bent backwards]
▶ **lordotic** (lɔː'dɒtɪk) *adj*

Lord President of the Council *n* (in Britain) the cabinet minister who presides at meetings of the Privy Council.

Lord Privy Seal *n* (in Britain) the senior cabinet minister without official duties.

Lord Protector *n* See **Protector**.

Lord Provost *n* the provost of one of the five major Scottish cities.

Lords (lɔːdz) *n the.* short for **House of Lords**.

Lord's ★ (lɔːdz) *n* a cricket ground in N London; headquarters of the MCC.

lords-and-ladies *n* (*functioning as sing*) another name for **cuckoopint**.

Lord's Day *n the.* the Christian Sabbath; Sunday.

lordship ('lɔːdʃɪp) *n* the position or authority of a lord.

Lordship ('lɔːdʃɪp) *n* (preceded by *Your* or *His*) *Brit.* a title used to address or refer to a bishop, a judge of the high court, or any peer except a duke.

Lord's Prayer *n the.* the prayer taught by Jesus Christ to his disciples, as in Matthew 6:9–13, Luke 11:2–4. Also called: **Our Father, Paternoster** (esp. Latin version).

Lords Spiritual *pl n* the Anglican archbishops and senior bishops of England and Wales who are members of the House of Lords.

Lord's Supper *n the.* another term for **Holy Communion** (I Corinthians 11:20).

Lords Temporal *pl n the.* (in Britain) peers other than bishops in their capacity as members of the House of Lords.

lore (lɔː) *n* **1** collective knowledge or wisdom on a particular subject, esp. of a traditional nature. **2** knowledge or learning. [OE *lār*; rel. to *leornian* to LEARN]

Lorelei ★ ('lɒrə,laɪ) *n* (in German legend) a siren, said to dwell on a rock at the edge of the Rhine south of Koblenz, who lures boatmen to destruction. [C19: from G *Lurlei* name of the rock; from a poem by Clemens Brentano (1778–1842)]

Loren (lə'rɛn, *Italian* 'lɔːren) *n* **Sophia** (səʊ'fiːə, *Italian* so-'fiːa), real name *Sophia Scicolone*. born 1934, Italian film actress. Her films include *The Millionairess* (1961), *The Cassandra Crossing* (1977), and *Prêt à Porter* (1994).

Lorentz ★ (*Dutch* 'lɔːrənts) *n* **Hendrik Antoon** ('hɛndrɪk 'antoːn). 1853–1928, Dutch physicist: shared the Nobel prize for physics (1902) for his work on electromagnetic theory.

Lorenz ★ (*German* 'loːrɛnts) *n* **Konrad Zacharias** ('kɔnraːt tsaxa'riːas) 1903–89, Austrian zoologist, who founded ethology. His works include *On Aggression* (1966): shared the Nobel prize for physiology or medicine 1973.

lorgnette (lɔː'njɛt) *n* a pair of spectacles or opera glasses mounted on a handle. [C19: from F, from *lorgner* to squint, from OF *lorgne* squinting]

Lorient ★ (*French* lɔrjɑ̃) *n* a port in W France, on the Bay of Biscay. Pop.: 59 437 (1990).

lorikeet ('lɒrɪ,kiːt, ,lɒrɪ'kiːt) *n* any of various small lories, such as the varied lorikeet or rainbow lorikeet. [C18: from LORY + *-keet*, as in PARAKEET]

loris ('lɔːrɪs) *n, pl* **loris.** any of several omnivorous nocturnal slow-moving prosimian primates of S and SE Asia, esp. the slow loris and slender loris, having vestigial digits and no tails. [C18: from F; from ?]

lorn (lɔːn) *adj Poetic.* forsaken or wretched. [OE *loren*, p.p. of *-lēosan* to lose]

Lorrain ★ (*French* lɔrɛ̃) *n* See **Claude Lorrain**.

Lorraine ★ (lɒ'reɪn; *French* lɔrɛn) *n* **1** a region and former province of E France; ceded to Germany in 1871 after the Franco-Prussian war and regained by France in 1919; rich iron-ore deposits. German name: **Lothringen**. **2** **Kingdom of.** an early medieval kingdom on the Meuse, Moselle, and Rhine rivers: later a duchy. **3** a former duchy in E France, once the S half of this kingdom.

Lorris ★ (*French* lɔris) *n* See **Guillaume de Lorris**.

lorry ('lɒrɪ) *n, pl* **lorries.** **1** a large motor vehicle designed to carry heavy loads, esp. one with a flat platform. US and Canad. name: **truck. 2 off the back of a lorry.** *Brit. inf.* a phrase used humorously to indicate that something has been dishonestly acquired. **3** any of various vehicles with a flat load-carrying surface, esp. one designed to run on rails. [C19: ? rel. to northern English dialect *lurry* to pull]

lory ('lɔːrɪ), **lowry**, *or* **lowrie** ('laʊrɪ) *n, pl* **lories** *or* **lowries.** any of various small brightly coloured parrots of Australia and Indonesia, having a brush-tipped tongue with which to feed on nectar and pollen. [C17: via Dutch from Malay *lūrī*, var. of *nūrī*]

Los Alamos ★ (lɒs 'æləmɒs) *n* a town in the US, in New Mexico: the first atomic bomb was developed here. Pop.: 11 455 (1990).

Los Angeles ★ (lɒs 'ændʒɪ,liːz) *n* a city in SW California, on the Pacific: the second largest city in the US, having absorbed many adjacent townships; industrial centre and port, with several universities. Pop.: 3 488 613 (1994 est.). Abbrev.: **LA**.

lose (luːz) *vb* **loses, losing, lost.** (*mainly tr*) **1** to part with or come to be without, as through theft, accident, negligence, etc. **2** to fail to keep or maintain: *to lose one's balance.* **3** to suffer the loss or deprivation of: *to lose a parent.* **4** to cease to have or possess. **5** to fail to get or make use of: *to lose a chance.* **6** (*also intr*) to fail to gain or win (a contest, game, etc.): *to lose the match.* **7** to fail to see, hear, perceive, or understand: *I lost the gist of his speech.* **8** to waste: *to lose money gambling.* **9** to wander from so as to be unable to find: *to lose one's way.* **10** to cause the loss of: *his delay lost him the battle.* **11** to allow to go astray or out of sight: *we lost him in the crowd.* **12** (*usually passive*) to absorb or engross: *he was lost in contemplation.* **13** (*usually passive*) to cause the death or destruction of: *two men were lost in the attack.* **14** to outdistance or elude: *he soon lost his pursuers.* **15** (*intr*) to decrease or depreciate in value or effectiveness: *poetry always loses in translation.* **16** (*also intr*) (of a timepiece) to run slow (by a specified amount). **17** (of a woman) to fail to give birth to (a viable baby), esp. as the result of a miscarriage. **18 lose it.** *Sl.* to lose control of oneself or one's temper. [OE *losian* to perish]
▶ **'losable** *adj*

lose out *vb Inf.* **1** (*intr, adv*) to be defeated or unsuccessful. **2 lose out on.** to fail to secure or make use of: *we lost out on the sale.*

loser ('luːzə) *n* **1** a person or thing that loses. **2** *Inf.* a person or thing that seems destined to be taken advantage of, fail, etc.: *a born loser.*

Losey ★ ('ləʊsɪ) *n* **Joseph.** 1909–84, US film director, in Britain from 1952. His films include *The Servant* (1963) and *The Go-Between* (1971).

losing ('luːzɪŋ) *adj* unprofitable; failing: *the business was a losing concern.*

losings ('luːzɪŋz) *pl n* losses, esp. in gambling.

loss (lɒs) *n* **1** the act or an instance of losing. **2** the disadvantage or deprivation resulting from losing: *a loss of reputation.* **3** the person, thing, or amount lost: *a large loss.* **4** (*pl*) military personnel lost by death or capture. **5** (*sometimes pl*) the amount by which the costs of a business transaction or operation exceed its revenue. **6** *Insurance.* **6a** an occurrence of something that has been insured against, thus giving rise to a claim by a policyholder. **6b** the amount of the resulting claim. **7 at a loss. 7a** uncertain what to do; bewildered. **7b** rendered helpless (for lack of something): *at a loss for words.* **7c** with income less than outlay: *the firm was running at a loss.* [C14: n prob.

formed from *lost*, p.p. of *losen* to perish, from OE *lōsian* to be destroyed, from *los* destruction]

loss adjuster *n Insurance.* a person qualified to adjust losses incurred through fire, theft, natural disaster, etc., to agree the loss and the compensation to be paid.

loss leader *n* an article offered below cost to attract customers.

lost (lɒst) *adj* **1** unable to be found or recovered. **2** unable to find one's way or ascertain one's whereabouts. **3** confused, bewildered, or helpless: *he is lost in discussions of theory.* **4** (sometimes foll. by *on*) not utilized, noticed, or taken advantage of (by): *rational arguments are lost on her.* **5** no longer possessed or existing because of defeat, misfortune, or the passage of time: *a lost art.* **6** destroyed physically: *the lost platoon.* **7** (foll. by *to*) no longer available or open (to). **8** (foll. by *to*) insensible or impervious (to a sense of shame, justice, etc.). **9** (foll. by *in*) engrossed (in): *he was lost in his book.* **10** morally fallen: *a lost woman.* **11** damned: *a lost soul.*

Lost Generation *n* (*sometimes not cap.*) **1** the large number of talented young men killed in World War I. **2** the generation of writers, esp. American authors, active after World War I.

lot (lɒt) *pron* **1** (*functioning as sing or pl*; preceded by *a*) a great number or quantity: *a lot to do; a lot of people.* ◆ *n* **2** a collection of objects, items, or people: *a nice lot of youngsters.* **3** portion in life; destiny; fortune: *it falls to my lot to be poor.* **4** any object, such as a straw or slip of paper, drawn from others at random to make a selection or choice (esp. in *draw* or *cast lots*). **5** the use of lots in making a selection or choice (esp. in *by lot*). **6** an assigned or apportioned share. **7** an item or set of items for sale in an auction. **8** *Chiefly US & Canad.* an area of land: *a parking lot.* **9** *Chiefly US & Canad.* a film studio. **10 a bad lot.** an unpleasant or disreputable person. **11 cast** or **throw in one's lot with.** to join with voluntarily and share the fortunes of. **12 the lot.** the entire amount or number. ◆ *adv* (preceded by *a*) *Inf.* **13** to a considerable extent, degree, or amount; very much: *to delay a lot.* **14** a great deal of the time or often: *to sing madrigals a lot.* ◆ *vb* **lots**, **lotting**, **lotted.** **15** to draw lots for (something). **16** (*tr*) to divide (land, etc.) into lots. **17** (*tr*) another word for **allot.** ◆ See also **lots.** [OE *hlot*]

Lot[1] ★ (lɒt) *n* **1** a department of S central France, in Midi-Pyrénées region. Capital: Cahors. Pop.: 156 881 (1994 est.). Area: 5226 sq. km (2038 sq. miles). **2** a river in S France, rising in the Cevennes and flowing west into the Garonne River. Length: about 483 km (300 miles).

Lot[2] ★ (lɒt) *n Old Testament.* Abraham's nephew: he escaped the destruction of Sodom, but his wife was changed into a pillar of salt for looking back as they fled (Genesis 19).

Lot-et-Garonne ★ (*French* lɔtegarɔn) *n* a department of SW France, in Aquitaine. Capital: Agen. Pop.: 303 496 (1994 est.). Area: 5385 sq. km (2100 sq. miles).

loth (ləʊθ) *adj* a variant spelling of **loath.**

Lothair I ★ (ləʊˈθɛə) *n* ?795–855 A.D., Frankish ruler and Holy Roman Emperor (823–30, 833–34, 840–55); son of Louis I.

Lothair II ★ *n* called *the Saxon.* ?1070–1137, German king (1125–37) and Holy Roman Emperor (1133–37).

Lothario (ləʊˈθɑːrɪəʊ,əʊ) *n, pl* **Lotharios.** (*sometimes not cap.*) a rake, libertine, or seducer. [C18: after a seducer in Nicholas Rowe's tragedy *The Fair Penitent* (1703)]

Lothian Region ★ (ˈləʊðɪən) *n* a former local government region in SE central Scotland, replaced in 1996.

Lothians ★ (ˈləʊðɪənz) *pl n* the. three historical counties of SE central Scotland: East Lothian, West Lothian, and Midlothian.

Lothringen ★ (ˈloːtrɪŋən) *n* the German name for **Lorraine.**

lotion (ˈləʊʃən) *n* a liquid preparation having a soothing, cleansing, or antiseptic action, applied to the skin, eyes, etc. [C14: via OF from L *lōtiō* a washing, from *lōtus* p.p. of *lavāre* to wash]

lots (lɒts) *Inf.* ◆ *pl n* **1** (often foll. by *of*) great numbers or quantities: *lots of people; to eat lots.* ◆ *adv* **2** a great deal. **3** (intensifier): *the journey is lots quicker by train.*

lottery (ˈlɒtərɪ) *n, pl* **lotteries.** **1** a game of chance in which tickets are sold, which may later qualify the holder for a prize. **2** an endeavour, the success of which is regarded as a matter of luck. [C16: from OF *loterie*, from MDu. *loterije*]

lotto (ˈlɒtəʊ) *n* **1** Also called: **housey-housey.** a children's game in which numbered discs are drawn at random and called out, while the players cover the corresponding numbers on cards, the winner being the first to cover all the numbers, a particular row, etc. Cf. **bingo.** **2** *Austral.* a lottery with cash prizes based on this principle. [C18: from It., from OF *lot*, from Gmc]

lotus (ˈləʊtəs) *n* **1** (in Greek mythology) a fruit that induces forgetfulness and a dreamy languor in those who eat it. **2** any of several water lilies of tropical Africa and Asia, esp. the **white lotus,** which was regarded as sacred in ancient Egypt. **3** a related plant which is the sacred lotus of India, China, and Tibet. **4** a representation of such a plant, common in Hindu, Buddhist, and ancient Egyptian art. **5** any of a genus of leguminous plants of the legume family of the Old World and North America, having yellow, pink, or white pealike flowers. ◆ Also (rare): **lotos.** [C16: via L from Gk *lōtos*, from Semitic]

lotus-eater *n Greek myth.* one of a people encountered by Odysseus in North Africa who lived in indolent forgetfulness, drugged by the fruit of the legendary lotus.

lotus position *n* a seated cross-legged position used in yoga, meditation, etc.

loud (laʊd) *adj* **1** (of sound) relatively great in volume: *a loud shout.* **2** making or able to make sounds of relatively great volume: *a loud voice.* **3** clamorous, insistent, and emphatic: *loud protests.* **4** (of colours, designs, etc.) offensive or obtrusive to look at. **5** characterized by noisy, vulgar, and offensive behaviour. ◆ *adv* **6** in a loud manner. **7 out loud.** audibly, as distinct from silently. [OE *hlud*] ▸ ˈloudish *adj* ▸ ˈloudly *adv* ▸ ˈloudness *n*

louden (ˈlaʊdⁿn) *vb* to make or become louder.

loud-hailer *n* a portable loudspeaker having a built-in amplifier and microphone. Also (US and Canad.): **bullhorn.**

loudmouth (ˈlaʊdˌmaʊθ) *n Inf.* a person who brags or talks too loudly. ▸ **loudmouthed** (ˈlaʊdˌmaʊðd, -ˌmaʊθt) *adj*

loudspeaker (ˌlaʊdˈspiːkə) *n* a device for converting audio-frequency signals into sound waves. Often shortened to **speaker.**

Lou Gehrig's disease (luː ˈɡɛrɪɡ) *n* another name for **amyotrophic lateral sclerosis.** [C20: named after *Lou Gehrig* (1903–41), US baseball player who suffered from it]

lough (lɒx, lɒk) *n* **1** an Irish word for **lake**[1] (senses 1 and 2). **2** a long narrow bay or arm of the sea in Ireland. [C14: from Irish *loch* lake]

Loughborough ★ (ˈlʌfbərə, -brə) *n* a town in central England, in N Leicestershire: university (1966). Pop.: 46 867 (1991).

Louis ★ (ˈluːɪs) *n* **Joe,** real name *Joseph Louis Barrow,* nicknamed *the Brown Bomber.* 1914–81, US boxer; world heavyweight champion (1937–49).

Louis I ★ (ˈluːɪ; *French* lwi) *n* known as *Louis the Pious* or *Louis the Debonair.* 778–840 A.D., king of France and Holy Roman Emperor (814–23, 830–33, 834–40).

Louis II ★ *n* **1** known as *Louis the German.* ?804–876 A.D., king of Germany (843–76); son of Louis I. **2 de Bourbon.** See (Prince de) **Condé.**

Louis IV ★ *n* known as *Louis the Bavarian.* ?1287–1347, king of Germany (1314–47) and Holy Roman Emperor (1328–47).

Louis V ★ *n* known as *Louis le Fainéant.* ?967–987 A.D., last Carolingian king of France (986–87).

Louis VIII ★ *n* known as *Cœur-de-Lion.* 1187–1226, king of France (1223–26). He was offered the English throne by opponents of King John but his invasion failed (1216).

Louis IX ★ *n* known as *Saint Louis.* 1214–70, king of France (1226–70): led the Sixth Crusade (1248–54) and was held to ransom (1250); died at Tunis while on another crusade.

Louis XI ★ *n* 1423–83, king of France (1461–83); involved in a struggle with his vassals, esp. the duke of Burgundy, in his attempt to unite France.

Louis XII ★ *n* 1462–1515, king of France (1498–1515).

Louis XIII ★ *n* 1601–43, king of France (1610–43). His mother (Marie de Médicis) was regent until 1617.

Louis XIV ★ *n* known as *le roi soleil* (the Sun King). 1638–1715, king of France (1643–1715). Effective ruler from 1661, he failed to establish French supremacy in Europe but his reign was regarded as a golden age of French arts.

Louis XV ★ *n* 1710–74, king of France (1715–74); greatgrandson of Louis XIV. He engaged France in the disastrous Seven Years' War (1756–63).

Louis XVI ★ *n* 1754–93, king of France (1774–92); grandson of Louis XV. He and his wife, Marie Antoinette, were guillotined during the Revolution.

Louis XVII ★ *n* 1785–95, titular king of France (1793–95) during the Revolution; he died in prison.

Louis XVIII ★ *n* 1755–1824, king of France (1814–24). He became titular king after the death of Louis XVII (1795) and ascended the throne at the Bourbon restoration. He was forced to flee during the Hundred Days.

Louisburg *or* **Louisbourg** ★ (ˈluːɪsˌbɜːg) *n* a fortress in Canada, in Nova Scotia on SE Cape Breton Island: founded in 1713 by the French and strongly fortified (1720–40); captured by the British (1758) and demolished; reconstructed as a historic site.

louis d'or (ˌluːɪ ˈdɔː) *n, pl* **louis d'or** (ˌluːɪz ˈdɔː). **1** a former French gold coin worth 20 francs. **2** an old French coin minted in the reign of Louis XIII. ◆ Often shortened to **louis**. [C17: from F: golden louis, after Louis XIII]

Louisiana ★ (luːˌiːzɪˈænə) *n* a state of the southern US, on the Gulf of Mexico: originally a French colony; bought by the US in 1803 as part of the Louisiana Purchase; chiefly low-lying. Capital: Baton Rouge. Pop.: 4 350 579 (1996 est.). Area: 116 368 sq. km (44 930 sq. miles). Abbrevs.: **La.** or (with zip code) **LA**

Louis Napoleon ★ *n* the original name of **Napoleon III**.

Louis Philippe ★ (*French* filip) *n* known as the *Citizen King*. 1773–1850, king of the French (1830–48). His régime became excessively identified with the bourgeoisie and he was forced to abdicate by the revolution of 1848.

Louisville ★ (ˈluːɪˌvɪl) *n* a port in N Kentucky, on the Ohio River: site of the annual Kentucky Derby; university (1837). Pop.: 270 308 (1994 est.).

lounge (laʊndʒ) *vb* **lounges, lounging, lounged. 1** (*intr;* often foll. by *about* or *around*) to sit, lie, walk, or stand in a relaxed manner. **2** to pass (time) lazily or idly. ◆ *n* **3** a communal room in a hotel, ship, etc., used for waiting or relaxing in. **4** *Chiefly Brit.* a living room in a private house. **5** Also called: **lounge bar, saloon.** *Brit.* a more expensive bar in a pub or hotel. **6** a sofa or couch. **7** the act or an instance of lounging. [C16: from ?]

lounger (ˈlaʊndʒə) *n* **1** a comfortable couch or extending chair designed for someone to relax on. **2** a loose comfortable leisure garment. **3** a person who lounges.

lounge suit *n* a man's suit of matching jacket and trousers worn for the normal business day.

loupe (luːp) *n* a small magnifying glass used by jewellers, horologists, etc., worn in the eye socket. [C20: from F (formerly an imperfect precious stone), from OF, from ?]

lour *or* **lower** (ˈlaʊə) *vb* (*intr*) **1** (esp. of the sky, weather, etc.) to be overcast, dark, and menacing. **2** to scowl or frown. ◆ *n* **3** a menacing scowl or appearance. [C13 *louren* to scowl]
  ▸ **ˈlouring** *or* **ˈlowering** *adj*

Lourdes ★ (*French* lurd) *n* a town in SW France: a place of pilgrimage for Roman Catholics after a peasant girl, Bernadette Soubirous, claimed to have seen visions of the Virgin Mary in 1858. Pop.: 17 100 (1995 est.).

Lourenço Marques ★ (lɒˈrɛnsəʊ ˈmɑːk, ˈmɑːks; *Portuguese* loˈrẽsu ˈmarkɪʃ) *n* the former name (until 1975) of **Maputo**.

lourie *or* **loerie** (ˈlaʊrɪ) *n* a type of African bird with bright plumage. [from Malay *luri*]

louse (laʊs) *n, pl* **lice. 1** a wingless bloodsucking insect, such as the head louse, body louse, and crab louse, all of which infest man. **2** biting *or* bird louse. a wingless insect, such as the chicken louse: external parasites of birds and mammals, with biting mouthparts. **3** any of various similar but unrelated insects. **4** (*pl* **louses**) *Sl.* an unpleasant or mean person. ◆ *vb* **louses, lousing, loused.** (*tr*) **5** to remove lice from. **6** (foll. by *up*) *Sl.* to ruin or spoil. [OE *lūs*]

lousewort (ˈlaʊsˌwɜːt) *n* any of various N temperate plants having spikes of white, yellow, or mauve flowers.

lousy (ˈlaʊzɪ) *adj* **lousier, lousiest. 1** *Sl.* very mean or unpleasant. **2** *Sl.* inferior or bad. **3** infested with lice. **4** (foll. by *with*) *Sl.* provided with an excessive amount (of): *he's lousy with money.*
  ▸ **ˈlousily** *adv* ▸ **ˈlousiness** *n*

lout (laʊt) *n* a crude or oafish person; boor. [C16: ? from OE *lūtan* to stoop]
  ▸ **ˈloutish** *adj*

Louth ★ (laʊθ) *n* a county of NE Republic of Ireland, in Leinster province on the Irish Sea: the smallest of the counties. County town: Dundalk. Pop.: 90 724 (1991). Area: 821 sq. km (317 sq. miles).

Louvain ★ (*French* luvɛ̃) *n* a town in central Belgium, in Flemish Brabant province: capital of the duchy of Brabant (11th–15th centuries) and centre of the cloth trade; university (1426). Pop.: 87 165 (1995 est.). Flemish name: **Leuven**.

louvre *or US* **louver** (ˈluːvə) *n* **1a** any of a set of horizontal parallel slats in a door or window, sloping outwards to throw off rain and admit air. **1b** Also called: **louvre boards.** the slats and frame supporting them. **2** *Archit.* a turret that allows smoke to escape. [C14: from OF *lovier*, from ?]
  ▸ **ˈlouvred** *or US* **ˈlouvered** *adj*

Louvre ★ (*French* luvrə) *n* the national museum and art gallery of France, in Paris: formerly a royal palace, begun in 1546; used for its present purpose since 1793.

lovable *or* **loveable** (ˈlʌvəbʳl) *adj* attracting or deserving affection.
  ▸ **ˌlovaˈbility, lov_eaˈbility** *or* **ˈlovableness, ˈloveableness**
  ▸ **ˈlovably** *or* **ˈloveably** *adv*

lovage (ˈlʌvɪdʒ) *n* a European umbelliferous plant with greenish-white flowers and aromatic fruits, which are used for flavouring food. [C14 *loveache*, from OF *luvesche*, from LL *levisticum*, from L *ligusticum*, lit.: Ligurian (plant)]

love (lʌv) *vb* **loves, loving, loved. 1** (*tr*) to have a great attachment to and affection for. **2** (*tr*) to have passionate desire, longing, and feelings for. **3** (*tr*) to like or desire (to do something) very much. **4** (*tr*) to make love to. **5** (*intr*) to be in love. ◆ *n* **6a** an intense emotion of affection, warmth, fondness, and regard towards a person or thing. **6b** (*as modifier*): *love story.* **7** a deep feeling of sexual attraction and desire. **8** wholehearted liking for or pleasure in something. **9** *Christianity.* God's benevolent attitude towards man. **10** Also: **my love.** a beloved person: used esp. as an endearment. **11** *Brit. inf.* a term of address, not necessarily for a person regarded as likable. **12** (in tennis, squash, etc.) a score of zero. **13 fall in love.** to become in love. **14 for love.** without payment. **15 for love or money.** (*used with a negative*) in any circumstances: *I would not eat a snail for love or money.* **16 for the love of.** for the sake of. **17 in love.** in a state of strong emotional attachment and usually sexual attraction. **18 make love (to).** **18a** to have sexual intercourse (with). **18b** *Now arch.* to court. [OE *lufu*]

love affair *n* a romantic or sexual relationship, esp. temporary, between two people.

love apple *n* an archaic name for **tomato**.

lovebird (ˈlʌvˌbɜːd) *n* any of several small African parrots often kept as cagebirds.

lovebite (ˈlʌvˌbaɪt) *n* a temporary red mark left on a person's skin by a partner's biting or sucking it during lovemaking.

love child *n* *Euphemistic.* an illegitimate child; bastard.

love-in-a-mist *n* an erect S European plant, cultivated

★ people and places

as a garden plant, having finely cut leaves and white or pale blue flowers.

Lovelace ★ (ˈlʌvˌleɪs) n 1 **Countess of,** title of *Ada Augusta King.* 1815–52, British mathematician and assistant to Charles Babbage: daughter of Lord Byron. She wrote the first computer program. 2 **Richard.** 1618–58, English Cavalier poet, noted for *To Althea from Prison* (1642) and *Lucasta* (1649).

loveless (ˈlʌvlɪs) adj 1 without love: *a loveless marriage.* 2 receiving or giving no love.
▸ **ˈlovelessly** adv ▸ **ˈlovelessness** n

love-lies-bleeding n any of several plants having drooping spikes of small red flowers.

Lovell ★ (ˈlʌvəl) n Sir **Bernard.** born 1913, British radio astronomer; founder (1951) and director of Jodrell Bank.

lovelock (ˈlʌvˌlɒk) n a long lock of hair worn on the forehead.

lovelorn (ˈlʌvˌlɔːn) adj miserable because of unrequited love or unhappiness in love.

lovely (ˈlʌvlɪ) adj **lovelier, loveliest. 1** very attractive or beautiful. **2** highly pleasing or enjoyable: *a lovely time.* **3** inspiring love; lovable. ◆ n, pl **lovelies. 4** *Sl.* a lovely woman.
▸ **ˈloveliness** n

lovemaking (ˈlʌvˌmeɪkɪŋ) n **1** sexual play and activity between lovers, esp. including sexual intercourse. **2** an archaic word for **courtship.**

love potion n any drink supposed to arouse sexual love in the one who drinks it.

lover (ˈlʌvə) n **1** a person, now esp. a man, who has an extramarital or premarital sexual relationship with another person. **2** *(often pl)* either of the two people involved in a love affair. **3a** someone who loves a specified person or thing: *a lover of music.* **3b** *(in combination):* a music-lover; a cat-lover.

love seat n a small upholstered sofa for two people.

lovesick (ˈlʌvˌsɪk) adj pining or languishing because of love.
▸ **ˈloveˌsickness** n

lovey-dovey (ˌlʌvɪˈdʌvɪ) adj making an excessive or ostentatious display of affection.

loving (ˈlʌvɪŋ) adj feeling or showing love and affection.
▸ **ˈlovingly** adv ▸ **ˈlovingness** n

loving cup n **1** a large vessel, usually two-handled, out of which people drink in turn at a banquet. **2** a similar cup awarded to the winner of a competition.

low[1] (ləʊ) adj **1** having a relatively small distance from base to top; not tall or high: *a low hill; a low building.* **2a** situated at a relatively short distance above the ground, sea level, the horizon, or other reference position: *low cloud.* **2b** *(in combination):* low-lying. **3** of less than usual height, depth, or degree: *low temperature.* **4a** (of numbers) small. **4b** (of measurements) expressed in small numbers. **5a** involving or containing a relatively small amount of something: *a low supply.* **5b** *(in combination):* low-pressure. **6a** having little value or quality. **6b** *(in combination):* low-grade. **7** coarse or vulgar: *a low conversation.* **8a** inferior in culture or status. **8b** *(in combination):* low-class. **9** in a physically or mentally depressed or weakened state. **10** low-necked: *a low dress.* **11** with a hushed tone; quiet or soft: *a low whisper.* **12** of relatively small price or monetary value: *low cost.* **13** *Music.* relating to or characterized by a relatively low pitch. **14** (of latitudes) situated not far north or south of the equator. **15** having little or no money. **16** abject or servile. **17** unfavourable: *a low opinion.* **18** not advanced in evolution: *a low form of plant life.* **19** deep: *a low bow.* **20** *Phonetics.* of, relating to, or denoting a vowel whose articulation is produced by moving the back of the tongue away from the soft palate, such as for the *a* in English *father.* **21** (of a gear) providing a relatively low forward speed for a given engine speed. **22** *(usually cap.)* of or relating to the Low Church. ◆ adv **23** in a low position, level, degree, intensity, etc.: *to bring someone low.* **24** at a low pitch; deep: *to sing low.* **25** at a low price; cheaply: *to buy low.* **26** *lay low.* **26a** to cause to fall by a blow. **26b** to overcome, defeat, or destroy. **27** *lie low.* **27a** to keep to be concealed or quiet. **27b** to wait for a favourable opportunity. ◆ n **28** a low position,

level, or degree: *an all-time low.* **29** an area of relatively low atmospheric pressure, esp. a depression. [C12 *lāh,* from ON *lāgr*]
▸ **ˈlowness** n

low[2] (ləʊ) n also **lowing. 1** the sound uttered by cattle; moo. ◆ vb **2** to make or express by a low or moo. [OE *hlōwan*]

Low ★ (ləʊ) n Sir **David.** 1891–1963, British political cartoonist, born in New Zealand: created Colonel Blimp. See **blimp**[2].

low-alcohol adj (of beer or wine) containing only a small amount of alcohol. Cf. **alcohol-free.**

lowan (ˈləʊən) n another name for **mallee fowl.** [from Abor.]

Low Archipelago ★ n another name for the **Tuamotu Archipelago.**

lowborn (ˌləʊˈbɔːn) or **lowbred** (ˌləʊˈbrɛd) adj Now rare. of ignoble or common parentage.

lowbrow (ˈləʊˌbraʊ) *Disparaging.* ◆ n **1** a person who has uncultivated or nonintellectual tastes. ◆ adj also **lowbrowed. 2** of or characteristic of such a person.

Low Church n **1** the school of thought in the Church of England stressing evangelical beliefs and practices. ◆ adj **Low-Church. 2** of or relating to this school.

low comedy n comedy characterized by slapstick and physical action.

Low Countries ★ pl n the lowland region of W Europe, on the North Sea: consists of Belgium, Luxembourg, and the Netherlands.

low-density lipoprotein n a lipoprotein that is the form in which cholesterol is transported in the bloodstream. High levels in the blood are associated with atheroma. Abbrev.: **LDL.**

low-down *Inf.* ◆ adj **1** mean, underhand, or despicable. ◆ n **2** lowdown. **2** the. information.

Löwe ★ (German ˈløːvə) n See (Karl) **Loewe.**

Lowell ★ (ˈləʊəl) n **1 Amy (Lawrence).** 1874–1925, US imagist poet and critic. **2 James Russell.** 1819–91, US poet, essayist, and diplomat, noted for his poems in Yankee dialect, *Biglow Papers* (1848; 1867). **3 Robert.** 1917–77, US poet. His books include *Lord Weary's Castle* (1946), *Life Studies* (1959), and the verse drama *The Old Glory* (1968).

lower[1] (ˈləʊə) adj **1** being below one or more other things: *the lower shelf.* **2** reduced in amount or value: *a lower price.* **3** *Maths.* (of a limit or bound) less than or equal to one or more numbers or variables. **4** *(sometimes cap.)* denoting the early part of a period, formation, etc.: *Lower Silurian.* ◆ vb **5** (tr) to cause to become low or on a lower level; bring, put, or cause to move down. **6** (tr) to reduce or bring down in estimation, dignity, value, etc.: *to lower oneself.* **7** to reduce or be reduced: *to lower one's confidence.* **8** (tr) to make quieter: *to lower the radio.* **9** (tr) to reduce the pitch of. **10** (intr) to diminish or become less. [C12 (comp. of LOW[1]); C17 (vb)]

lower[2] (ˈlaʊə) vb a variant of **lour.**

Lower Austria ★ n a state of NE Austria: the largest Austrian province, containing most of the Vienna basin. Capital: Sankt Pölten. Pop.: 1 511 555 (1994 est.). Area: 19 170 sq. km (7476 sq. miles). German name: **Niederösterreich.**

Lower California ★ n a mountainous peninsula of NW Mexico, between the Pacific and the Gulf of California: administratively divided into the states of Baja California and Baja California Sur. Spanish name: **Baja California.**

Lower Canada ★ n (from 1791 to 1841) the official name of the S region of the present-day province of Quebec. Cf. **Upper Canada.**

lower case n **1** the bottom half of a compositor's type case, in which the small letters are kept. ◆ adj **lower-case. 2** of or relating to small letters. ◆ vb **lower-case, lower-cases, lower-casing, lower-cased. 3** (tr) to print with lower-case letters.

lower chamber n another name for a **lower house.**

lower class n **1** the social stratum having the lowest position in the social hierarchy. ◆ *adj* **lower-class. 2** of or relating to the lower class. **3** inferior or vulgar.

lowerclassman (ˌləʊˈklɑːsmən) *n, pl* **lowerclassmen.** *US.* a freshman or sophomore. Also called: **underclassman.**

lower deck *n* **1** the deck of a ship situated immediately above the hold. **2** *Inf.* the petty officers and seamen of a ship collectively.

Lower Egypt ★ *n* one of the two main administrative districts of Egypt: consists of the Nile Delta.

lower house *n* one of the houses of a bicameral legislature: usually the larger and more representative. Also called: **lower chamber.**

Lower Hutt ★ (hʌt) *n* an industrial town in New Zealand on the S coast of the North Island. Pop.: 62 900 (1983).

Lower Lakes ★ *pl n Chiefly Canadian.* Lakes Erie and Ontario.

lowermost (ˈləʊəˌməʊst) *adj* lowest.

lower regions *pl n* (usually preceded by *the*) hell.

Lower Saxony ★ *n* a state of N Germany, on the North Sea and including the E Frisian Islands; formerly in West Germany: a leading European producer of petroleum. Capital: Hanover. Pop.: 7 715 400 (1995 est.). Area: 47 408 sq. km (18 489 sq. miles). German name: **Niedersachsen.**

lower world *n* **1** the earth as opposed to heaven. **2** another name for **hell.**

lowest common denominator *n* the smallest integer or polynomial that is exactly divisible by each denominator of a set of fractions. Abbrevs.: **lcd, LCD.** Also called: **least common denominator.**

lowest common multiple *n* the smallest number or quantity that is exactly divisible by each member of a set of numbers or quantities. Abbrevs.: **lcm, LCM.** Also called: **least common multiple.**

Lowestoft ★ (ˈləʊstɒft) *n* a fishing port and resort in E England, in NE Suffolk on the North Sea. Pop.: 62 907 (1991).

low frequency *n* a radio-frequency band or a frequency lying between 300 and 30 kilohertz.

Low German *n* a language of N Germany, spoken esp. in rural areas: more closely related to Dutch than to standard High German. Abbrev.: **LG.** Also called: **Plattdeutsch.**

low-key *or* **low-keyed** *adj* **1** having a low intensity or tone. **2** restrained or subdued. **3** (of a photograph, painting, etc.) having a predominance of dark grey tones or dark colours with few highlights. Cf. **high-key.**

lowland (ˈləʊlənd) *n* **1** relatively low ground. **2** (*often pl*) a low generally flat region. ◆ *adj* **3** of or relating to a lowland or lowlands.
▸ ˈlowlander *n*

Lowland (ˈləʊlənd) *adj* of or relating to the Lowlands of Scotland or the dialects of English spoken there.

Lowlands ★ (ˈləʊləndz) *pl n the.* a low, generally flat region of S central Scotland.
▸ ˈLowlander *n*

Low Latin *n* any form of Latin other than the classical, such as Medieval Latin.

low-level language *n* a computer programming language that is closer to machine language than to human language.

low-level waste *n* waste material contaminated by traces of radioactivity that can be disposed of in steel drums in concrete-lined trenches. Cf. **high-level waste, intermediate-level waste.**

lowlife (ˈləʊˌlaɪf) *n, pl* **lowlifes.** *Sl.* a member or members of the criminal underworld.

low-loader *n* a road or rail vehicle with a low platform for ease of access.

lowly (ˈləʊlɪ) *adj* **lowlier, lowliest. 1** humble or low in position, rank, status, etc. **2** full of humility; meek. **3** simple, unpretentious, or plain. ◆ *adv* **4** in a low or lowly manner.
▸ ˈlowliness *n*

Low Mass *n* a Mass that has a simplified ceremonial form and is spoken rather than sung.

low-minded *adj* having a vulgar or crude mind and character.
▸ ˌlow-ˈmindedly *adv* ▸ ˌlow-ˈmindedness *n*

low-pass filter *n Electronics.* a filter that transmits all frequencies below a specified value, attenuating frequencies above this value.

low-pitched *adj* **1** pitched low in tone. **2** (of a roof) having sides with a shallow slope.

low-pressure *adj* **1** having, using, or involving a pressure below normal: *a low-pressure gas.* **2** relaxed or calm.

low profile *n* **1** a position or attitude characterized by a deliberate avoidance of prominence or publicity. ◆ *adj* **low-profile. 2** (of a tyre) wide in relation to its height.

low-rise *adj* **1** of or relating to a building having only a few storeys. ◆ *n* **2** such a building.

lowry *or* **lowrie** (ˈlaʊrɪ) *n* variant spellings of **lory.**

Lowry ★ (ˈlaʊrɪ) *n* **1** L(awrence) S(tephen). 1887–1976, British painter, noted for his bleak northern industrial scenes. **2** (Clarence) Malcolm. 1909–57. British novelist, best known for his semiautobiographical *Under the Volcano* (1947).

low-spirited *adj* depressed or dejected.
▸ ˌlow-ˈspiritedly *adv* ▸ ˌlow-ˈspiritedness *n*

low tech *n* **1** short for **low technology. 2** a style of interior design using items associated with low technology. ◆ *adj* **low-tech. 3** of or using low technology. **4** of or in the interior design style. ◆ Cf. **hi tech.**

low technology *n* simple unsophisticated technology that is limited to the production of basic necessities.

low-tension *adj* subjected to, carrying, or operating at a low voltage. Abbrev.: **LT.**

low tide *n* **1** the tide when it is at its lowest level or the time at which it reaches this. **2** a lowest point.

Lowveld ★ (ˈləʊˌfelt, -ˌvelt) *n the.* another name for **Bushveld.**

low water *n* **1** another name for **low tide. 2** the state of any stretch of water at its lowest level.

low-water mark *n* **1** the level reached at low tide. **2** the lowest point or level; nadir.

lox[1] (lɒks) *n* a kind of smoked salmon. [C19: from Yiddish *laks*, from MHG *lahs* salmon]

lox[2] (lɒks) *n* short for **liquid oxygen,** esp. when used as an oxidizer for rocket fuels.

loyal (ˈlɔɪəl) *adj* **1** showing allegiance. **2** faithful to one's country, government, etc. **3** of or expressing loyalty. [C16: from OF *loial, leial,* from L *lēgālis* LEGAL]
▸ ˈloyally *adv*

loyalist (ˈlɔɪəlɪst) *n* a patriotic supporter of his sovereign or government.
▸ ˈloyalism *n*

Loyalist (ˈlɔɪəlɪst) *n* **1** (in Northern Ireland) any of the Protestants wishing to retain Ulster's link with Britain. **2** (in North America) an American colonist who supported Britain during the War of American Independence. **3** (in Canada) short for **United Empire Loyalist. 4** (during the Spanish Civil War) a supporter of the republican government.

loyalty (ˈlɔɪəltɪ) *n, pl* **loyalties. 1** the state or quality of being loyal. **2** (*often pl*) allegiance.

loyalty card *n* a swipe card issued by a supermarket or chain store to a customer, used to record credit points awarded for money spent in the store.

Loyang ★ (ˈləʊˈjæŋ) *n* a variant transliteration of the Chinese name for **Luoyang.**

Loyola ★ (lɔɪˈəʊlə) *n* See (Saint) **Ignatius Loyola.**

lozenge (ˈlɒzɪndʒ) *n* **1** *Med.* a medicated tablet held in the mouth until it has dissolved. **2** *Geom.* another name for **rhombus. 3** *Heraldry.* a diamond-shaped charge. [C14: from OF *losange* of Gaulish origin]
▸ ˈlozenged *or* ˈlozengy *adj*

Lozère ★ (*French* lɔzɛr) *n* a department of S central France, in Languedoc-Roussillon region. Capital:

★ people and places

Mende. Pop.: 72 859 (1994 est.). Area: 5180 sq. km (2020 sq. miles).

LP[1] *n* **1a** a long-playing gramophone record, usually 12 inches (30 cm) in diameter, designed to rotate at 33⅓ revolutions per minute. **1b** (*as modifier*): *an LP sleeve.* **2** long play: a slow-recording facility on a VCR which allows twice the length of material to be recorded on a tape from that of standard play.

LP[2] *abbrev. for:* **1** (in Britain) Lord Provost. **2** Also: **lp.** low pressure.

L/P *Printing abbrev. for* letterpress.

LPG *or* **LP gas** *abbrev. for* liquefied petroleum gas.

L-plate *n Brit.* a white rectangle with an "L" sign fixed to the back and front of a motor vehicle; a red "L" sign shows that the driver has not passed the driving test; a green "L" sign may be displayed by new drivers for up to a year after passing the driving test.

Lr *the chemical symbol for* lawrencium.

LSD *n* lysergic acid diethylamide; a crystalline compound prepared from lysergic acid, used in experimental medicine and taken illegally as a hallucinogenic drug. Informal name: **acid**.

L.S.D., £.s.d., *or* **l.s.d.** (in Britain, esp. formerly) *abbrev. for* librae, solidi, denarii. [L: pounds, shillings, pence]

LSE *abbrev. for* London School of Economics.

LSO *abbrev. for* London Symphony Orchestra.

Lt *abbrev. for* Lieutenant.

Ltd *or* **ltd** *abbrev. for* limited (liability). US equivalent: **Inc.**

Lu *the chemical symbol for* lutetium.

Lualaba ★ (ˌluːəˈlɑːbə) *n* a river in SE Democratic Republic of the Congo, rising in Shaba province and flowing north as the W headstream of the River Congo. Length: about 1800 km (1100 miles).

Luanda (lʊˈændə) *or* **Loanda** ★ *n* the capital of Angola, a port in the west, on the Atlantic: founded in 1576, it became a centre of the slave trade to Brazil in the 17th and 18th centuries; oil refining. Pop.: 2 250 000 (1995 est.). Official name: **São Paulo de Loanda**.

Luang Prabang ★ (luːˈæŋ prɑːˈbæŋ) *n* a market town in N Laos, on the Mekong River: residence of the monarch of Laos (1946–75). Pop.: 44 244 (1984 est.).

luau (luːˈaʊ, ˈluːaʊ) *n* a feast of Hawaiian food. [from Hawaiian *luʻau*]

lubber (ˈlʌbə) *n* **1** a big, awkward, or stupid person. **2** short for **landlubber**. [C14 *lobre*, prob. from ON]
► **ʹlubberly** *adj, adv* ► **ʹlubberliness** *n*

lubber line *n* a mark on a ship's compass that designates the fore-and-aft axis of the vessel. Also called: **lubber's line**.

Lubbock ★ (ˈlʌbək) *n* a city in NW Texas: cotton market. Pop.: 194 467 (1994 est.).

Lübeck ★ (*German* ˈlyːbɛk) *n* a port in N Germany, in Schleswig-Holstein: the leading member of the Hanseatic League, and a major European commercial centre until the 15th century. Pop.: 216 854 (1995 est.).

Lublin ★ (*Polish* ˈlublin) *n* an industrial city in E Poland: provisional seat of the government in 1918 and 1944. Pop.: 352 500 (1995 est.). Russian name: **Lyublin**.

lubra (ˈluːbrə) *n Austral.* an Aboriginal woman. [C19: from Abor.]

lubricant (ˈluːbrɪkənt) *n* **1** a lubricating substance, such as oil. ◆ *adj* **2** serving to lubricate. [C19: from L *lūbricāns*, present participle of *lūbricāre*]

lubricate (ˈluːbrɪˌkeɪt) *vb* **lubricates, lubricating, lubricated.** **1** (*tr*) to cover or treat with an oily substance so as to lessen friction. **2** (*tr*) to make greasy, slippery, or smooth. **3** (*intr*) to act as a lubricant. [C17: from L *lūbricāre*, from *lūbricus* slippery]
► ˌlubriʹcation *n* ► ˈlubriˌcative *adj* ► ˈlubriˌcator *n*

lubricity (luːˈbrɪsɪtɪ) *n* **1** *Formal or literary.* lewdness or salaciousness. **2** *Rare.* smoothness or slipperiness. [C15 (lewdness), C17 (slipperiness): from OF *lubricité*, from Med. L *lubricitās*, from L, from *lūbricus* slippery]
► **lubricious** (luːˈbrɪʃəs) *or* **lubricous** (luːˈbrɪkəs) *adj*

Lubumbashi ★ (ˌluːbʊmˈbæʃɪ) *n* a city in S Democratic Republic of the Congo: founded in 1910 as a copper-mining centre; university (1955). Pop.: 851 381 (1994 est.). Former name (until 1966): **Elisabethville**.

Lucan ★ (ˈluːkən) *n* Latin name *Marcus Annaeus Lucanus.* 39–65 A.D., Roman poet. His epic poem *Pharsalia* describes the civil war between Caesar and Pompey.

Lucania ★ (luːˈkeɪnɪə) *n* the Latin name for **Basilicata**.

Lucas ★ (ˈluːkəs) *n* **George.** born 1944, US film director, producer, and writer of screenplays. Films include *American Graffiti* (1973) and *Star Wars* (1977).

Lucas van Leyden ★ (ˈluːkəs væn ˈlaɪdⁿn) *n* ?1494–1533, Dutch painter and engraver.

Lucca ★ (*Italian* ˈlukka) *n* a city in NW Italy, in Tuscany: centre of a rich agricultural region, noted for the production of olive oil. Pop.: 86 676 (1990). Ancient name: **Luca** (ˈluːkə).

luce (luːs) *n* another name for the **pike** (the fish). [C14: from OF *lus*, from LL *lūcius* pike]

lucent (ˈluːsⁿnt) *adj* brilliant, shining, or translucent. [C16: from L *lūcēns*, present participle of *lūcēre* to shine]
► **ʹlucency** *n* ► **ʹlucently** *adv*

lucerne (luːˈsɜːn) *n Brit.* another name for **alfalfa**.

Lucerne ★ (luːˈsɜːn; *French* lysɛrn) *n* **1** a canton in central Switzerland, northwest of Lake Lucerne: joined the Swiss Confederacy in 1332. Pop.: 337 941 (1995 est.). Area: 1494 sq. km (577 sq. miles). **2** a city in central Switzerland, capital of Lucerne canton, on Lake Lucerne: tourist centre. Pop.: 60 600 (1987). **3 Lake.** a lake in central Switzerland: fed and drained chiefly by the River Reuss. Area: 115 sq. km (44 sq. miles). German name: **Vierwaldstättersee**. ◆ German name (for senses 1 and 2): **Luzern**.

Lucian ★ (ˈluːsɪən) *n* 2nd century A.D., Greek writer, noted for his satirical *Dialogues of the Gods* and *Dialogues of the Dead.*

lucid (ˈluːsɪd) *adj* **1** readily understood; clear. **2** shining or glowing. **3** of or relating to a period of normality between periods of insane behaviour. [C16: from L *lūcidus* full of light, from *lūx* light]
► **luʹcidity** *or* **ʹlucidness** *n* ► **ʹlucidly** *adv*

lucifer (ˈluːsɪfə) *n* a friction match: originally a trade name.

Lucifer ★ (ˈluːsɪfə) *n* **1** the leader of the rebellion of the angels; Satan. **2** the planet Venus when it rises as the morning star. [OE, from L *Lūcifer* light-bearer, from *lūx* light + *ferre* to bear]

Lucilius ★ (luːˈsɪlɪəs) *n* **Gaius** (ˈgaɪəs). ?180–102 B.C., Roman satirist, originated poetical satire.

Lucina ★ (luːˈsaɪnə) *n Roman myth.* a title or name given to Juno as goddess of childbirth. [C14: from L *lūcīnus* bringing to the light, from *lūx* light]

luck (lʌk) *n* **1** events that are beyond control and seem subject to chance; fortune. **2** success or good fortune. **3** something considered to bring good luck. **4 down on one's luck.** having little or no good luck to the point of suffering hardships. **5 no such luck.** *Inf.* unfortunately not. **6 try one's luck.** to attempt something that is uncertain. [C15: from MDu. *luc*]

luckless (ˈlʌklɪs) *adj* having no luck; unlucky.
► **ʹlucklessly** *adv* ► **ʹlucklessness** *n*

Lucknow ★ (ˈlʌknaʊ) *n* a city in N India, capital of Uttar Pradesh: capital of Oudh (1775–1856); the British residency was besieged (1857) during the Indian Mutiny. Pop.: 1 619 115 (1991).

lucky (ˈlʌkɪ) *adj* **luckier, luckiest. 1** having or bringing good fortune. **2** happening by chance, esp. as desired.
► **ʹluckily** *adv* ► **ʹluckiness** *n*

lucky dip *n Brit., Austral., & NZ.* **1** a box filled with sawdust containing small prizes for which children search. **2** *Inf.* an undertaking of uncertain outcome.

lucrative (ˈluːkrətɪv) *adj* producing a profit; profitable. [C15: from OF *lucratif*; see LUCRE]
► **ʹlucratively** *adv* ► **ʹlucrativeness** *n*

lucre (ˈluːkə) *n Usually facetious.* money or wealth (esp. in **filthy lucre**). [C14: from L *lūcrum* gain]

Lucretia ★ (luːˈkriːʃɪə) *n* (in Roman legend) a Roman woman who killed herself after being raped by a son of Tarquin the Proud.

Lucretius ★ (luːˈkriːʃɪəs) *n* full name *Titus Lucretius Carus*. ?96–55 B.C., Roman poet and philosopher. In his *De rerum natura*, he expounds Epicurus's atomist theory.
  ▸ **Luˈcretian** *adj*

lucubrate (ˈluːkjʊˌbreɪt) *vb* **lucubrates, lucubrating, lucubrated**. (*intr*) to write or study, esp. at night. [C17: from L *lūcubrāre* to work by lamplight]
  ▸ **ˈlucuˌbrator** *n*

lucubration (ˌluːkjʊˈbreɪʃən) *n* **1** laborious study, esp. at night. **2** (*often pl*) a solemn literary work.

Lucullus ★ (luːˈkʌləs) *n Lucius Licinius* (ˈluːsɪəs lɪˈsɪnɪəs). ?110–56 B.C., Roman general and consul, famous for his banquets.
  ▸ **Luˈcullan, Lucullean** (ˌluːkʌˈlɪən), *or* ˌ**Luculˈlian** *adj*

Lucy ★ (ˈluːsɪ) *n Saint*. died ?303 A.D., a virgin martyred by Diocletian in Syracuse. Feast day: Dec 13.

lud (lʌd) *n Brit*. lord (in **my lud, m'lud**): used when addressing a judge in court.

Lüda (ˈluːˈdɑː) *or* **Lü-ta** ★ *n* a port complex in NE China, in S Liaoning province at the S end of the Liaodong peninsula, comprising the two cities of Lüshun and Dalian: the chief northern port. Pop.: 2 400 000 (1991 est.).

Luddite (ˈlʌdaɪt) *n Brit. history*. **1** any of the textile workers opposed to mechanization, believing that its use led to unemployment, who organized machine-breaking between 1811 and 1816. **2** any opponent of industrial change or innovation. ◆ *adj* **3** of or relating to the Luddites. [C19: alleged to be after Ned *Ludd*, an 18th-century Leicestershire workman, who destroyed industrial machinery]

Ludendorff ★ (German ˈluːdəndɔrf) *n* **Erich Friedrich Wilhelm von** (ˈeːrɪç ˈfriːdrɪç ˈvɪlhɛlm fɔn). 1865–1937, German general, Hindenburg's aide in World War I.

Lüdenscheid ★ (German ˈlyːdənʃait) *n* a city in W Germany, in North Rhine-Westphalia: manufacturing of aluminium and plastics. Pop.: 76 110 (1989 est.).

Lüderitz ★ (German ˈlyːdərɪts) *n* a port in Namibia: diamond-mining centre. Pop.: 6000 (1990).

Ludhiana ★ (ˌlʊdrɪˈɑːnə) *n* a city in N India, in the central Punjab: Punjab Agricultural University (1962). Pop.: 1 042 740 (1991).

ludicrous (ˈluːdɪkrəs) *adj* absurd or incongruous to the point of provoking laughter. [C17: from L *lūdicrus* done in sport, from *lūdus* game]
  ▸ **ˈludicrously** *adv* ▸ **ˈludicrousness** *n*

Ludlow ★ (ˈlʌdləʊ) *n* a market town in W central England, in Shropshire: castle (11th–16th century). Pop.: 9040 (1991).

ludo (ˈluːdəʊ) *n Brit*. a simple board game in which players advance their counters by throwing dice. [C19: from L: I play]

Ludwigsburg ★ (German ˈluːtvɪçsbʊrk) *n* a city in SW Germany, in Baden-Württemberg northeast of Stuttgart: expanded in the 18th century around the palace of the dukes of Württemberg. Pop.: 79 340 (1989 est.).

Ludwigshafen ★ (German ˈluːtvɪçshaːfən) *n* a city in SW Germany, in the Rhineland-Palatinate, on the Rhine: chemical industry. Pop.: 167 883 (1995 est.).

luff (lʌf) *n* **1** *Naut*. the leading edge of a fore-and-aft sail. ◆ *vb* **2** *Naut*. to head (a sailing vessel) into the wind so that her sails flap. **3** (*intr*) *Naut*. (of a sail) to flap when the wind is blowing equally on both sides. **4** to move the jib of (a crane) in order to shift a load. [C13 (in the sense: steering gear): from OF *lof*, ?from MDu. *loef* peg of a tiller]

lug¹ (lʌg) *vb* **lugs, lugging, lugged**. **1** to carry or drag (something heavy) with great effort. **2** (*tr*) to introduce (an irrelevant topic) into a conversation or discussion. ◆ *n* **3** the act or an instance of lugging. [C14: prob. from ON]

lug² (lʌg) *n* **1** a projecting piece by which something is connected, supported, or lifted. **2** a box or basket for vegetables or fruit. **3** *Inf. or Scot*. another word for **ear**¹. **4** *Sl*. a man, esp. a stupid or awkward one. [C15 (Scots dialect) *lugge* ear]

lug³ (lʌg) *n Naut*. short for **lugsail**.

Lugano ★ (luːˈgɑːnəʊ) *n* a town in S Switzerland, on Lake Lugano: a centre for international finance and a tourist resort noted for the beauty of its setting. Pop.: 26 800 (1995).

Lugansk ★ (Russian luˈgansk) *n* an industrial city in the E Ukraine, in the Donbass mining region: established in 1795 as an iron-founding centre. Pop.: 487 000 (1996 est.). Former name (1935–91): **Voroshilovgrad**.

luge (luːʒ) *n* **1** a racing toboggan on which riders lie on their backs, descending feet first. ◆ *vb* **luges, luging, luged**. **2** (*intr*) to ride or race on a luge. [C20: from F]

Luger (ˈluːgə) *n Trademark*. a German 9 mm calibre automatic pistol.

luggage (ˈlʌgɪdʒ) *n* suitcases, trunks, etc. [C16: ? from LUG¹, infl. in form by BAGGAGE]

luggage van *n Brit*. a railway carriage used to transport passengers' luggage, bicycles, etc.

lugger (ˈlʌgə) *n Naut*. a small working boat rigged with a lugsail. [C18: from LUGSAIL]

lughole (ˈlʌgˌhəʊl) *n Brit*. an informal word for **ear**¹. See also **lug**² (sense 3).

Lugo ★ (Spanish ˈluɣo) *n* a city in NW Spain: Roman walls; Romanesque cathedral. Pop.: 86 658 (1991). Latin name: **Lucus Augusti** (ˈluːkəs ɔːˈgʌstɪ; ˈɡasti).

lugsail (ˈlʌgsəl) *n* a four-sided sail bent and hoisted on a yard. [C17: ?from ME (now dialect) *lugge* pole, or from *lugge* ear]

lug screw *n* a small screw without a head.

lugubrious (lʊˈguːbrɪəs) *adj* excessively mournful; doleful. [C17: from L *lūgubris* mournful, from *lūgēre* to grieve]
  ▸ **luˈgubriously** *adv* ▸ **luˈgubriousness** *n*

lugworm (ˈlʌgˌwɜːm) *n* a worm living in burrows on sandy shores and having tufted gills: much used as bait. Sometimes shortened to **lug**. [C17: from ?]

Luichow Peninsula ★ (ˈluːˈtʃaʊ) *n* a variant transliteration of the Chinese name for **Leizhou Peninsula**.

Luik ★ (lœik) *n* the Flemish name for **Liège**.

Lukács ★ (ˈluːkætʃ) *n* **Georg** (ˈgeɪɔːk), original name *György*. 1885–1971, Hungarian Marxist philosopher and literary critic, whose works include *History and Class Consciousness* (1923) and *The Historical Novel* (1955).

Luke ★ (luːk) *n New Testament*. **1 Saint**. a fellow worker of Paul and a physician (Colossians 4:14). Feast day: Oct. 18. **2** the third Gospel, traditionally ascribed to Luke. Related adj: **Lucan**.

lukewarm (ˌluːkˈwɔːm) *adj* **1** (esp. of water) moderately warm; tepid. **2** having or expressing little enthusiasm or conviction. [C14 *luke* prob. from OE *hlēow* warm]
  ▸ **ˌlukeˈwarmly** *adv* ▸ **ˌlukeˈwarmness** *n*

Luleå ★ (Swedish ˈluːlɔː) *n* a port in N Sweden, on the Gulf of Bothnia: industrial and shipbuilding centre; icebound in winter. Pop.: 70 694 (1994).

lull (lʌl) *vb* (*tr*) **1** to soothe (a person or animal) by soft sounds or motions (esp. in **lull to sleep**). **2** to calm (someone or someone's fears, suspicions, etc.), esp. by deception. ◆ *n* **3** a short period of calm or diminished activity. [C14: ? imit. of crooning sounds; rel. to MLow G *lollen* to soothe, MDu. *lollen* to talk drowsily, mumble]

lullaby (ˈlʌləˌbaɪ) *n, pl* **lullabies**. **1** a quiet song to lull a child to sleep. ◆ *vb* **lullabies, lullabying, lullabied**. **2** (*tr*) to quiet or soothe as with a lullaby. [C16: ? a blend of LULL + GOODBYE]

Lully ★ *n* **1** (French lyli). **Jean Baptiste** (ʒɑ̃ batist), Italian name *Giovanni Battista Lulli*. 1632–87, French composer, born in Italy; founder of French opera, writing such operas as *Alceste* (1674) and *Armide* (1686). **2** (ˈlʌlɪ). Also: **Lull** (Spanish lul). **Raymond** *or* **Ramón** (raˈmɔn). ?1235–1315, Spanish philosopher, mystic, and missionary. His chief works are *Ars generalis sive magna* and the Utopian novel *Blaquerna*.

Luluabourg ★ (luːˈluːəˌbʊə) *n* the former name (until 1966) of **Kananga**.

lumbago (lʌmˈbeɪgəʊ) *n* pain in the lower back; backache. [C17: from LL, from L *lumbus* loin]

★ people and places

lumbar ('lʌmbə) *adj* of, near, or relating to the part of the body between the lowest ribs and the hipbones. [C17: from NL *lumbāris*, from L *lumbus* loin]

lumbar puncture *n Med.* insertion of a hollow needle into the lower spinal cord to withdraw cerebrospinal fluid, introduce drugs, etc.

lumber[1] ('lʌmbə) *n* **1** *Chiefly US & Canad.* **1a** logs; sawn timber. **1b** (*as modifier*): *the lumber trade.* **2** *Brit.* **2a** useless household articles that are stored away. **2b** (*as modifier*): *lumber room.* ◆ *vb* **3** (*tr*) to pile together in a disorderly manner. **4** (*tr*) to fill up or encumber with useless household articles. **5** *Chiefly US & Canad.* to convert (the trees) of (a forest) into marketable timber. **6** (*tr*) *Brit. inf.* to burden with something unpleasant, tedious, etc. [C17: ?from a n use of LUMBER[2]]
▸ **'lumberer** *n* ▸ **'lumbering** *n*

lumber[2] ('lʌmbə) *vb* (*intr*) **1** to move or proceed in an awkward heavy manner. **2** an obsolete word for **rumble.** [C14 *lomeren*]
▸ **'lumbering** *adj*

lumberjack ('lʌmbə,dʒæk) *n* (esp. in North America) a person whose work involves felling trees, transporting the timber, etc. [C19: from LUMBER[1] + JACK (man)]

lumberjacket ('lʌmbə,dʒækɪt) *n* a boldly coloured, usually checked jacket in warm cloth.

lumberyard ('lʌmbə,jɑːd) *n* the US and Canad word for **timberyard.**

lumen ('luːmɪn) *n, pl* **lumens** *or* **lumina** (-mɪnə). **1** the derived SI unit of luminous flux; the flux emitted in a solid angle of 1 steradian by a point source having a uniform intensity of 1 candela. Symbol: lm **2** *Anat.* a passage, duct, or cavity in a tubular organ. **3** a cavity within a plant cell. [C19: NL, from L: light, aperture]
▸ **'luminal** *adj*

Lumière ★ (*French* lymjɛr) *n* **Auguste Marie Louis Nicolas** (ogyst mari lwi nikɔlaː). 1862–1954, and his brother, **Louis Jean** (lwi ʒã), 1864–1948, French chemists and cinema pioneers, who invented a cinematograph and a process of colour photography.

luminance ('luːmɪnəns) *n* **1** a state or quality of radiating or reflecting light. **2** a measure (in candelas per square metre) of the brightness of a point on a surface that is radiating or reflecting light. Symbol: *L* [C19: from L *lūmen* light]

luminary ('luːmɪnərɪ) *n, pl* **luminaries. 1** a person who enlightens or influences others. **2** a famous person. **3** *Literary.* something, such as the sun or moon, that gives off light. [C15: via OF, from L *lūmināre* lamp, from *lūmen* light]

luminesce (,luːmɪ'nɛs) *vb* **luminesces, luminescing, luminesced.** (*intr*) to exhibit luminescence. [back formation from LUMINESCENT]

luminescence (,luːmɪ'nɛsəns) *n Physics.* the emission of light at low temperatures by any process other than incandescence. [C19: from L *lūmen* light]
▸ **,lumi'nescent** *adj*

luminous ('luːmɪnəs) *adj* **1** radiating or reflecting light; shining; glowing: *luminous colours.* **2** (*not in technical use*) exhibiting luminescence: *luminous paint.* **3** full of light; well-lit. **4** (of a physical quantity in photometry) evaluated according to the visual sensation produced in an observer rather than by absolute energy measurements: *luminous intensity.* **5** easily understood; lucid; clear. **6** enlightening or wise. [C15: from L *lūminōsus* full of light, from *lūmen* light]
▸ **luminosity** (,luːmɪ'nɒsɪtɪ) *n* ▸ **'luminously** *adv* ▸ **'luminousness** *n*

luminous flux *n* a measure of the rate of flow of luminous energy, evaluated according to its ability to produce a visual sensation. It is measured in lumens.

luminous intensity *n* a measure of the amount of light that a point source radiates in a given direction.

lumme *or* **lummy** ('lʌmɪ) *interj Brit.* an exclamation of surprise or dismay. [C19: alteration of *Lord love me*]

lummox ('lʌməks) *n Inf.* a clumsy or stupid person. [C19: from ?]

lump[1] (lʌmp) *n* **1** a small solid mass without definite shape. **2** *Pathol.* any small swelling or tumour. **3** a collection of things; aggregate. **4** *Inf.* an awkward, heavy, or stupid person. **5 the lump.** *Brit.* self-employed workers in the building trade considered collectively. **6** (*modifier*) in the form of a lump or lumps: *lump sugar.* **7 a lump in one's throat.** a tight dry feeling in one's throat, usually caused by great emotion. **8 in the lump.** collectively; en masse. ◆ *vb* **9** (*tr*; often foll. by *together*) to collect into a mass or group. **10** (*intr*) to grow into lumps or become lumpy. **11** (*tr*) to consider as a single group, often without justification. **12** (*tr*) to make or cause lumps in or on. **13** (*intr*; often foll. by *along*) to move in a heavy manner. [C13: prob. rel. to early Du. *lompe* piece, Scand. dialect *lump* block, MHG *lumpe* rag]

lump[2] (lʌmp) *vb* (*tr*) *Inf.* to tolerate or put up with; endure (in **lump it**). [C16: from ?]

lumpectomy (lʌm'pɛktəmɪ) *n, pl* **lumpectomies.** the surgical removal of a tumour in a breast. [C20: from LUMP[1] + -ECTOMY]

lumpen ('lʌmpˀn) *adj Inf.* stupid or unthinking. [from G *Lump* vagabond, infl. by *Lumpen* rags, as in LUMPENPROLETARIAT]

lumpenproletariat (,lʌmpən,prəʊlɪ'tɛərɪət) *n* (esp. in Marxist theory) the urban social group below the proletariat, consisting of criminals, tramps, etc. [G, lit.: ragged proletariat]

lumpfish ('lʌmp,fɪʃ) *n, pl* **lumpfish** *or* **lumpfishes.** a North Atlantic fish having a globular body covered with tubercles, pelvic fins fused into a sucker, and an edible roe. Also called: **lumpsucker.** [C16 *lump* (now obs.) lumpfish, from MDu. *lompe,* ? rel. to LUMP[1]]

lumpish ('lʌmpɪʃ) *adj* **1** resembling a lump. **2** stupid, clumsy, or heavy.
▸ **'lumpishly** *adv* ▸ **'lumpishness** *n*

lump sum *n* a relatively large sum of money, paid at one time, esp. in cash.

lumpy ('lʌmpɪ) *adj* **lumpier, lumpiest. 1** full of or having lumps. **2** (esp. of the sea) rough. **3** (of a person) heavy or bulky.
▸ **'lumpily** *adv* ▸ **'lumpiness** *n*

Lumumba ★ (lʊ'mʊmbə) *n* **Patrice** (pə'triːs). 1925–61, Congolese statesman; first prime minister of the Democratic Republic of the Congo (1960); assassinated.

Luna ★ ('luːnə) *n* the Roman goddess of the moon. [from L: moon]

lunacy ('luːnəsɪ) *n, pl* **lunacies. 1** (formerly) any severe mental illness. **2** foolishness.

luna moth *n* a large American moth having light green wings with a yellow crescent-shaped marking on each forewing. [C19: from the markings on its wings]

lunar ('luːnə) *adj* **1** of or relating to the moon. **2** occuring on or used on the moon: *lunar module.* **3** relating to, caused by, or measured by the position or orbital motion of the moon. [C17: from L *lūnāris*, from *lūna* moon]

lunar eclipse *n* See **eclipse.**

lunar module *n* the module used to carry astronauts on a spacecraft to the surface of the moon and back to the spacecraft.

lunar month *n* See **month** (sense 6).

lunar year *n* See **year** (sense 6).

lunate ('luːneɪt) *or* **lunated** *adj Anat., bot.* shaped like a crescent. [C18: from L *lūnātus* crescent-shaped, from *lūna* moon]

lunatic ('luːnətɪk) *adj* **1** an archaic word for **insane. 2** foolish; eccentric. ◆ *n* **3** a person who is insane. [C13 (adj): via OF from LL *lūnāticus* crazy, moonstruck, from L *lūna* moon]

lunatic asylum *n Offens.* an institution for the mentally ill.

lunatic fringe *n* the members of a society who adopt views regarded as fanatical.

lunch (lʌntʃ) *n* **1** a meal eaten during the middle of the day. ◆ *vb* **2** (*intr*) to eat lunch. **3** (*tr*) to provide or buy lunch for. [C16: prob. short form of LUNCHEON]
▸ **'luncher** *n*

luncheon ('lʌntʃən) *n* a lunch, esp. a formal one. [C16: prob. var. of *nuncheon*, from ME *noneschench*, from *none* NOON + *schench* drink]

luncheon meat *n* a ground mixture of meat (often pork) and cereal, usually tinned.

luncheon voucher *n* a voucher worth a specified amount issued to employees and redeemable at a restaurant for food. Abbrev.: **LV.**

lunchroom ('lʌntʃˌruːm, -ˌrʊm) *n US & Canad.* a room where lunch is served or where students, employees, etc., may eat lunches they bring.

Lund ★ (lund) *n* a city in SE Sweden, northeast of Malmö: founded in about 1020 by the Danish King Canute; the archbishopric for all Scandinavia in the Middle Ages; university (1668). Pop.: 95 895 (1994).

Lundy ★ ('lʌndɪ) *n* an island in SW England, in Devon, in the Bristol Channel: now a bird sanctuary. Pop.: 52 (1981).

Lüneburg ★ (*German* 'lyːnəburk) *n* a city in N Germany, in Lower Saxony: capital of the duchy of Brunswick-Lüneburg from 1235 to 1369; prominent Hanse town; saline springs. Pop.: 61 000 (1990 est.).

lunette (luːˈnɛt) *n* **1** anything that is shaped like a crescent. **2** an oval or circular opening to admit light in a dome. **3** a semicircular panel containing a window, mural, or sculpture. **4** a type of fortification like a detached bastion. **5** Also called: **lune.** *RC Church.* a case fitted with a bracket to hold the consecrated host. [C16: from F: crescent, from *lune* moon, from L *lūna*]

Lunéville ★ (*French* lynevil) *n* a city in NE France: scene of the signing of the **Peace of Lunéville** between France and Austria (1801). Pop.: 22 393 (1990).

lung (lʌŋ) *n* **1** either one of a pair of spongy saclike respiratory organs within the thorax of higher vertebrates, which oxygenate the blood and remove its carbon dioxide. **2 at the top of one's lungs.** in one's loudest voice; yelling. [OE *lungen*]

lunge[1] (lʌndʒ) *n* **1** a sudden forward motion. **2** *Fencing.* a thrust made by advancing the front foot and straightening the back leg, extending the sword arm forwards. ◆ *vb* **lunges, lunging, lunged. 3** to move or cause to move with a lunge. **4** (*intr*) *Fencing.* to make a lunge. [C18: short form of obs. C17 *allonge*, from F *allonger* to stretch out (one's arm) from LL *ēlongāre* to lengthen]
▶ **'lunger** *n*

lunge[2] (lʌndʒ) *n* **1** a rope used in training or exercising a horse. ◆ *vb* **lunges, lunging, lunged. 2** to exercise or train (a horse) on a lunge. [C17: from OF *longe*, shortened from *allonge*, ult. from L *longus* long]

lungfish ('lʌŋˌfɪʃ) *n, pl* **lungfish** or **lungfishes.** a freshwater bony fish having an air-breathing lung, fleshy paired fins, and an elongated body.

Lungki or **Lung-chi** ★ ('lʊŋ'kiː) *n* the former name of Zhangzhou.

lungwort ('lʌŋˌwɜːt) *n* **1** any of several Eurasian plants which have spotted leaves and clusters of blue or purple flowers: formerly used to treat lung diseases. **2** See **oyster plant.**

lunula ('luːnjʊlə) *n, pl* **lunulae** (-njuˌliː). the white crescent-shaped area at the base of the human fingernail. Nontechnical name: **half-moon.** [C16: from L: small moon, from *lūna*]

Luoyang or **Loyang** ★ ('ləʊˈjæŋ) *n* a city in E China, in N Henan province on the Luo River near its confluence with the Yellow River; an important Buddhist centre in the 5th and 6th centuries; a commercial and industrial centre. Pop.: 1 190 000 (1990 est.).

Lupercalia (ˌluːpɜːˈkeɪlɪə) *n, pl* **Lupercalia** or **Lupercalias.** an ancient Roman festival of fertility, celebrated on Feb. 15. [L, from *Lupercālis* belonging to *Lupercus*, a Roman god of the flocks]
▶ ˌ**Luper'calian** *adj*

lupin or *US* **lupine** ('luːpɪn) *n* a leguminous plant of North America, Europe, and Africa, with large spikes of brightly coloured flowers and flattened pods. [C14: from L *lupīnus* wolfish (see LUPINE); from the belief that the plant ravenously exhausted the soil]

lupine ('luːpaɪn) *adj* of, relating to, or resembling a wolf. [C17: from L *lupīnus*, from *lupus* wolf]

lupus ('luːpəs) *n* any of various ulcerative skin diseases. [C16: via Med. L from L: wolf; so called because it rapidly eats away the affected part]

lupus vulgaris (vʌlˈgɛərɪs) *n* tuberculosis of the skin, esp. of the face. Sometimes shortened to **lupus.**

lurch[1] (lɜːtʃ) *vb* (*intr*) **1** to lean or pitch suddenly to one side. **2** to stagger. ◆ *n* **3** the act or an instance of lurching. [C19: from ?]

lurch[2] (lɜːtʃ) *n* **1 leave (someone) in the lurch.** to desert (someone) in trouble. **2** *Cribbage.* the state of a losing player with less than 30 points at the end of a game. [C16: from F *lourche* a game similar to backgammon, from *lourche* (adj) deceived, prob. of Gmc origin]

lurch[3] (lɜːtʃ) *vb* (*intr*) *Arch. or dialect.* to prowl suspiciously. [C15: ? a var. of LURK]

lurcher ('lɜːtʃə) *n* **1** a crossbred hunting dog, esp. one trained to hunt silently. **2** *Arch.* a person who prowls or lurks. [C16: from LURCH[3]]

lure (lʊə) *vb* **lures, luring, lured.** (*tr*) **1** (sometimes foll. by *away* or *into*) to tempt or attract by the promise of some type of reward. **2** *Falconry.* to entice (a hawk or falcon) from the air to the falconer by a lure. ◆ *n* **3** a person or thing that lures. **4** *Angling.* any of various types of brightly coloured artificial spinning baits. **5** *Falconry.* a feathered decoy to which small pieces of meat can be attached. [C14: from OF *loirre* falconer's lure, from Gmc]
▶ **'lurer** *n*

Lurex ('lʊərɛks) *n* **1** *Trademark.* a thin metallic thread coated with plastic. **2** fabric containing such thread, which makes it glitter.

lurgy ('lɜːgɪ) *n, pl* **lurgies.** *Facetious.* any undetermined illness. [C20: from ?]

lurid ('lʊərɪd) *adj* **1** vivid in shocking detail; sensational. **2** horrible in savagery or violence. **3** pallid in colour; wan. **4** glowing with an unnatural glare. [C17: from L *lūridus* pale yellow]
▶ **'luridly** *adv* ▶ **'luridness** *n*

lurk (lɜːk) *vb* (*intr*) **1** to move stealthily or be concealed, esp. for evil purposes. **2** to be present in an unobtrusive way; be latent. ◆ *n* **3** *Austral. & NZ sl.* a scheme for success. [C13: prob. frequentative of LOUR]
▶ **'lurker** *n*

lurking ('lɜːkɪŋ) *adj* lingering but almost unacknowledged: *a lurking suspicion.*

Lusaka ★ (luːˈzɑːkə, -ˈsɑːkə) *n* the capital of Zambia, in the southeast at an altitude of 1280 m (4200 ft): became capital of Northern Rhodesia in 1932 and of Zambia in 1964; University of Zambia (1966). Pop.: 982 362 (1990).

Lusatia ★ (luːˈseɪʃɪə) *n* a region of central Europe, lying between the upper reaches of the Elbe and Oder Rivers: now mostly in E Germany, extending into SW Poland; inhabited chiefly by Sorbs.
▶ **Lu'satian** *adj, n*

luscious ('lʌʃəs) *adj* **1** extremely pleasurable, esp. to the taste or smell. **2** very attractive. **3** *Arch.* cloying. [C15 *lucius, licius,* ? short for DELICIOUS]
▶ **'lusciously** *adv* ▶ **'lusciousness** *n*

lush[1] (lʌʃ) *adj* **1** (of vegetation) abounding in lavish growth. **2** (esp. of fruits) succulent and fleshy. **3** luxurious, elaborate, or opulent. [C15: prob. from OF *lasche* lazy, from L *laxus* loose]
▶ **'lushly** *adv* ▶ **'lushness** *n*

lush[2] (lʌʃ) *Sl.* ◆ *n* **1** a heavy drinker, esp. an alcoholic. **2** alcoholic drink. ◆ *vb* **3** *US & Canad.* to drink (alcohol) to excess. [C19: from ?]

Lüshun ★ ('luːˈʃʊn) *n* a port in NE China, in S Liaoning province, at the S end of the Liaodong peninsula: together with Dalian it comprises the port complex of Lüda: jointly held by China and the Soviet Union (1945–55). Former name: **Port Arthur.**

Lusitania ★ (ˌluːsɪˈteɪnɪə) *n* an ancient region of the W Iberian Peninsula: a Roman province from 27 B.C. to the late 4th century A.D.; corresponds to most of present-day

lust (lʌst) n **1** a strong desire for sexual gratification. **2** a strong desire or drive. ◆ vb **3** (intr; often foll. by *after* or *for*) to have a lust (for). [OE]
▶ '**lustful** adj ▶ '**lustfully** adv ▶ '**lustfulness** n

lustral ('lʌstrəl) adj of or relating to a ceremony of purification. [C16: from L *lūstrālis* (adj) from LUSTRUM]

lustrate ('lʌstreɪt) vb **lustrates**, **lustrating**, **lustrated**. (tr) to purify by means of religious rituals or ceremonies. [C17: from L *lūstrāre* to brighten]
▶ **lus'tration** n

lustre or US **luster** ('lʌstə) n **1** reflected light; sheen; gloss. **2** radiance or brilliance of light. **3** great splendour of accomplishment, beauty, etc. **4** a dress fabric of cotton and wool with a glossy surface. **5** a vase or chandelier from which hang cut-glass drops. **6** a drop-shaped piece of cut glass or crystal used as such a decoration. **7** a shiny metallic surface on some pottery and porcelain. **8** *Mineralogy.* the way in which light is reflected from the surface of a mineral. ◆ vb **lustres**, **lustring**, **lustred** or US **lusters**, **lustering**, **lustered**. **9** to make, be, or become lustrous. [C16: from OF, from OIt. *lustro*, from L *lustrāre* to make bright]
▶ '**lustreless** or US '**lusterless** adj ▶ '**lustrous** adj

lustreware or US **lusterware** ('lʌstə,wɛə) n pottery with lustre decoration.

lustrum ('lʌstrəm) or **lustre** n, pl **lustrums**, **lustra** (-trə), or **lustres**. *Rare.* a period of five years. [C16: from L: ceremony of purification, from *lustrāre* to brighten, purify]

lusty ('lʌstɪ) adj **lustier**, **lustiest**. **1** having or characterized by robust health. **2** strong or invigorating.
▶ '**lustily** adv ▶ '**lustiness** n

Lü-ta ★ ('luː'tɑː) n a variant transliteration of the Chinese name for **Lüda**.

lute[1] (luːt) n an ancient plucked stringed instrument with a long fretted fingerboard and a body shaped like a sliced pear. [C14: from OF *lut*, from Ar. *al 'ūd*, lit.: the wood]

lute[2] (luːt) n **1** a mixture of cement and clay used to seal the joints between pipes, etc. **2** *Dentistry.* a thin layer of cement used to fix a crown or inlay in place on a tooth. ◆ vb **lutes**, **luting**, **luted**. **3** (tr) to seal (a joint or surface) with lute. [C14: via OF ult. from L *lutum* clay]

lutein ('luːtɪɪn) n a xanthophyll pigment, occurring in plants, that has a light-absorbing function in photosynthesis. [C20: from L *lūteus* yellow + -IN]

luteinizing hormone ('luːtɪɪ,naɪzɪŋ) n a hormone secreted by the anterior lobe of the pituitary gland. In female vertebrates it stimulates ovulation, and in mammals it also induces corpus luteum formation. In male vertebrates it promotes maturation of the interstitial cells of the testes and stimulates androgen secretion. [C19: from L *lūteum* egg yolk, from *lūteus* yellow]

lutenist, lutanist ('luːtənɪst) or US & Canad. (sometimes) **lutist** ('luːtɪst) n a person who plays the lute. [C17: from Med. L *lūtānista*, from *lūtāna*, apparently from OF *lut* LUTE[1]]

Lutetia or **Lutetia Parisiorum** ★ (luː'tiːʃə pə,rɪzɪ-'ɔːrəm) n an ancient name for **Paris**[1].

lutetium or **lutecium** (luː'tiːʃɪəm) n a silvery-white metallic element of the lanthanide series. Symbol: Lu; atomic no.: 71; atomic wt.: 174.97. [C19: NL, from L *Lūtētia* ancient name of Paris, home of G. Urbain (1872–1938), F chemist, who discovered it]

Luther ('luːθə) n **Martin**. 1483–1546, German leader of the Protestant Reformation. He began preaching the doctrine of justification by faith rather than by works, and in 1517 nailed 95 theses to the church door at Wittenberg. He was excommunicated by the Diet of Worms (1521) but he was protected in Wartburg Castle by Frederick III of Saxony (1521–22). He translated the Bible into German (1521–34) and approved Melanchthon's Augsburg Confession (1530), defining the tenets of Lutheranism.
▶ '**Lutherism** n

Lutheran ('luːθərən) n **1** a follower of Luther or a member of a Lutheran Church. ◆ adj **2** of or relating to Luther or his doctrines. **3** of or denoting any of the Churches that follow Luther's doctrines.
▶ '**Lutheranism** n

Luthuli or **Lutuli** ★ (luː'tuːlɪ) n Chief **Albert John**. 1899–1967, South African political leader and president of the African National Congress (1952–60): Nobel peace prize 1961.

Lutine bell ('luːtiːn, luː'tiːn) n a bell, taken from the ship *Lutine*, kept at Lloyd's in London and rung before important announcements, esp. the loss of a vessel.

Luton ★ ('luːt°n) n **1** a town in SE central England, in S Bedfordshire: airport; motor-vehicle industries. Pop.: 171 671 (1991). **2** a unitary authority in SE central England, in Bedfordshire. Pop.: 180 800 (1994 est.). Area: 43 sq. km (17 sq. miles).

Lutyens ★ ('lʌtʃənz) n **1** Sir **Edwin**. 1869–1944, British architect, noted for his neoclassical houses and his planning of New Delhi, India. **2** his daughter, **Elisabeth**. 1906–83, British composer.

Lützen ★ (German 'lytsən) n a town near Leipzig in E Germany, in Saxony: site of a battle (1632) in the Thirty Years' War in which the army of the Holy Roman Empire was defeated by the Swedes.

Lützow-Holm Bay ★ ('lʊtsəʊ'həʊm) n an inlet of the Indian Ocean on the coast of Antarctica, between Enderby Land and Queen Maud Land.

luvvie or **luvvy** ('lʌvɪ) n, pl **luvvies**. *Facetious.* a person who is involved in the acting profession or the theatre, esp. one with a tendency to affectation.

lux (lʌks) n, pl **lux**. the derived SI unit of illumination equal to a luminous flux of 1 lumen per square metre. [C19: from L: light]

Lux. abbrev. for Luxembourg.

luxate ('lʌkseɪt) vb **luxates**, **luxating**, **luxated**. (tr) *Pathol.* to dislocate (a shoulder, knee, etc.). [C17: from L *luxāre* to displace, from *luxus* dislocated]
▶ **lux'ation** n

luxe (lʌks, lʊks; French lyks) n See **de luxe**. [C16: from F from L *luxus* extravagance]

Luxembourg ★ ('lʌksəm,bɜːg; French lyksābur) n **1** a grand duchy in W Europe: formed the Benelux customs union with Belgium and the Netherlands in 1948; a founder member of the Common Market (now the European Union). Official languages: French, German, and Luxembourgian. Religion: mostly Roman Catholic. Currency: Luxembourgian franc; euro; Belgian franc is also used. Capital: Luxembourg. Pop.: 420 000 (1997). **2** the capital of Luxembourg, on the Alzette River: an industrial centre. Pop.: 76 446 (1995 est.). **3** a province in SE Belgium, in the Ardennes. Capital: Arlon. Pop.: 240 281 (1995 est.). Area: 4416 sq. km (1705 sq. miles).

Luxemburg ★ (German 'luksəmburk) n **Rosa** ('rɔːza). 1871–1919, German socialist leader, involved with Karl Liebknecht in an unsuccessful Communist revolt (1919) and assassinated.

Luxor ★ ('lʌksɔː) n a town in S Egypt, on the River Nile: the southern part of the site of ancient Thebes; many ruins and tombs, notably the temple built by Amenhotep III (about 1411–1375 B.C.). Pop.: 155 000 (1994 est.).

luxuriant (lʌg'zjʊərɪənt) adj **1** rich and abundant; lush. **2** very elaborate or ornate. **3** extremely productive or fertile. [C16: from L *luxuriāns*, present participle of *luxuriāre* to abound to excess]
▶ **lux'uriance** n ▶ **lux'uriantly** adv

| **USAGE NOTE** | See at **luxurious**. |

luxuriate (lʌg'zjʊərɪ,eɪt) vb **luxuriates**, **luxuriating**, **luxuriated**. (intr) **1** (foll. by *in*) to take voluptuous pleasure; revel. **2** to flourish profusely. **3** to live in a sumptuous way. [C17: from L *luxuriāre*]
▶ **lux,uri'ation** n

luxurious (lʌg'zjʊərɪəs) adj **1** characterized by luxury. **2**

enjoying or devoted to luxury. [C14: via OF from L *luxuriōsus* excessive]
▸ **lux'uriously** *adv* ▸ **lux'uriousness** *n*

> **USAGE NOTE** *Luxurious* is sometimes wrongly used where *luxuriant* is meant: *he had a luxuriant (not luxurious) moustache; the walls were covered with a luxuriant growth of wisteria.*

luxury ('lʌkʃərɪ) *n*, *pl* **luxuries**. **1** indulgence in and enjoyment of rich and sumptuous living. **2** (*sometimes pl*) something considered an indulgence rather than a necessity. **3** something pleasant and satisfying: *the luxury of independence.* **4** (*modifier*) relating to, indicating, or supplying luxury: *a luxury liner.* [C14 (in the sense: lechery): via OF from L *luxuria* excess, from *luxus* extravagance]

Luzern ★ (luˈtsɛrn) *n* the German name for **Lucerne.**

Luzon ★ (luːˈzɒn) *n* the main and largest island of the Philippines, in the N part of the archipelago, separated from the other islands by the Sibuyan Sea: important agriculturally, producing most of the country's rice, with large forests and rich mineral resources; industrial centres at Manila and Batangas. Capital: Quezon City. Pop.: 32 558 000 (1995 est.). Area: 108 378 sq. km (41 845 sq. miles).

LV *abbrev. for* luncheon voucher.

Lviv ★ (*Ukrainian* lvif) *n* an industrial city in the W Ukraine: it had belonged to Poland (1340–1772; 1819–39), Austria (1772–1918), Germany (1939–45), and the Soviet Union (1945–91); cultural centre, with a university (1661). Pop.: 802 000 (1996 est.). Russian name: **Lvov** (ljvəf). Polish name: **Lwów.** German name: **Lemberg.**

LW *abbrev. for:* **1** *Radio.* long wave. **2** low water.

Lwów ★ (lvuf) *n* the Polish name for **Lviv.**

lx *Physics.* symbol for lux.

LXX *symbol for* Septuagint.

-ly[1] *suffix forming adjectives.* **1** having the nature or qualities of: *godly.* **2** occurring at certain intervals; every: *daily.* [OE *-līc*]

-ly[2] *suffix forming adverbs.* in a certain manner; to a certain degree: *quickly; recently; chiefly.* [OE *-līce*, from *-līc* -LY[1]]

Lyallpur ★ (ˌlaɪəlˈpʊə) *n* the former name (until 1979) of **Faisalabad.**

lyase ('laɪeɪz) *n* any enzyme that catalyses the separation of two parts of a molecule by the formation of a double bond between them. [C20: from Gk *lusis* a loosening + -ASE]

lycanthropy (laɪˈkænθrəpɪ) *n* **1** the supposed magical transformation of a human being into a wolf. **2** *Psychiatry.* a delusion in which a person believes that he is a wolf. [C16: from Gk *lukánthropía*, from *lukos* wolf + *anthrōpos* man]
▸ **lycanthrope** ('laɪkən,θrəʊp) *n* ▸ **lycanthropic** (ˌlaɪkən-'θrɒpɪk) *adj*

Lycaon ★ (laɪˈkeɪɒn) *n Greek myth.* a king of Arcadia said to have offered Zeus a plate of human flesh to learn whether the god was omniscient.

Lycaonia ★ (ˌlaɪkəˈəʊnɪə) *n* an ancient region of S Asia Minor, north of the Taurus Mountains; corresponds to present-day S central Turkey.

lycée ('liːseɪ) *n*, *pl* **lycées** -seɪz). *Chiefly French.* a secondary school. [C19: F, from L: *Lyceum* a school in ancient Athens]

lyceum (laɪˈsɪəm) *n* (now chiefly in the names of buildings) **1** a public building for concerts, lectures, etc. **2** *US.* a cultural organization responsible for presenting concerts, lectures, etc.

lychee (ˌlaɪˈtʃiː) *n* a variant spelling of **litchi.**

lych gate *or* **lich gate** (lɪtʃ) *n* a roofed gate to a churchyard, formerly used as a temporary shelter for the bier. [C15: lich, from OE *līc* corpse]

lychnis ('lɪknɪs) *n* any of a genus of plants having red, pink, or white five-petalled flowers: includes ragged robin. [C17: NL, via L, from Gk *lukhnis* a red flower]

Lycia ★ ('lɪsɪə) *n* an ancient region on the coast of SW Asia Minor: a Persian, Rhodian, and Roman province.
▸ **'Lycian** *adj*, *n*

lycopodium (ˌlaɪkəˈpəʊdɪəm) *n* **1** any of a genus of club moss resembling moss but having woody tissue and spore-bearing cones. **2** a flammable yellow powder from the spores of this plant, used in medicine and in making fireworks. [C18: NL, from Gk, from *lukos* wolf + *pous* foot]

Lycra ('laɪkrə) *n Trademark.* a type of synthetic elastic fabric and fibre used for tight-fitting garments, such as swimming costumes.

Lycurgus ★ (laɪˈkɜːgəs) *n* 9th century B.C., Spartan lawgiver, regarded as the founder of the Spartan constitution.

Lydda ★ ('lɪdə) *n* another name for **Lod.**

lyddite ('lɪdaɪt) *n* an explosive consisting chiefly of fused picric acid. [C19: after *Lydd*, town in Kent near which the first tests were made]

Lydgate ('lɪd,geɪt) *n* **John.** ?1370–?1450, English poet and monk. His devotional works and translations include a version of Boccaccio's *The Fall of Princes* (1430–38).

Lydia ★ ('lɪdɪə) *n* an ancient region on the coast of W Asia Minor: a powerful kingdom in the century and a half before the Persian conquest (546 B.C.). Chief town: Sardis.
▸ **'Lydian** *adj*, *n*

lye (laɪ) *n* **1** any solution obtained by leaching, such as the caustic solution obtained by leaching wood ash. **2** a concentrated solution of sodium hydroxide or potassium hydroxide. [OE *lēag*]

Lyell ★ ('laɪəl) *n* Sir **Charles.** 1797–1875, British geologist.

lying[1] ('laɪɪŋ) *vb* the present participle and gerund of **lie**[1].

lying[2] ('laɪɪŋ) *vb* the present participle and gerund of **lie**[2].

lying-in *n*, *pl* **lyings-in.** confinement in childbirth.

lyke-wake ('laɪk,weɪk) *n Brit.* a watch held over a dead person, often with festivities. [C16: ?from ON]

Lyle ★ (laɪl) *n* **Sandy,** full name *Alexander Walter Barr Lyle.* born 1958, British professional golfer: winner of the British Open Championship (1985) and the US Masters (1988).

Lyly ★ ('lɪlɪ) *n* **John.** ?1554–1606, English dramatist and novelist, noted for his romances, *Euphues, or the Anatomy of Wit* (1578) and *Euphues and his England* (1580). See also **euphuism.**

Lyme disease (laɪm) *n* a disease of domestic animals and humans, caused by a spirochaete and transmitted by ticks, and affecting the joints, heart, and brain. [C20: after *Lyme*, Connecticut, the town where it was first identified in humans]

Lyme Regis ★ ('riːdʒɪs) *n* a resort in S England, in Dorset, on the English Channel: noted for finds of prehistoric fossils. Pop.: 3851 (1991).

Lymington ★ ('lɪmɪŋtən) *n* a market town in S England, in SW Hampshire, on the Solent: yachting centre and holiday resort. Pop.: 13 508 (1991).

lymph (lɪmf) *n* the almost colourless fluid, containing chiefly white blood cells, that is collected from the tissues of the body and transported in the lymphatic system. [C17: from L *lympha* water, from earlier *limpa*, infl. in form by Gk *numphē* nymph]

lymphatic (lɪmˈfætɪk) *adj* **1** of, relating to, or containing lymph. **2** of or relating to the lymphatic system. **3** sluggish or lacking vigour. ◆ *n* **4** a lymphatic vessel. [C17 (meaning: mad): from L *lymphāticus.* Original meaning ?from a confusion between *nymph* and LYMPH]

lymphatic system *n* an extensive network of capillary vessels that transports the interstitial fluid of the body as lymph to the venous blood circulation.

lymphatic tissue *n* tissue, such as the lymph nodes, tonsils, spleen, and thymus, that produces lymphocytes.

lymph gland *n* a former name for **lymph node.**

lymph node *n* any of numerous bean-shaped masses of tissue, situated along the course of lymphatic vessels,

---

★ **people and places**

that help to protect against infection and are a source of lymphocytes.

lympho- *or before a vowel* **lymph-** *combining form.* indicating lymph or the lymphatic system: *lymphocyte.*

lymphocyte ('lɪmfəʊˌsaɪt) *n* a type of white blood cell formed in lymphatic tissue.
► **lymphocytic** (ˌlɪmfəʊ'sɪtɪk) *adj*

lymphoid ('lɪmfɔɪd) *adj* of or resembling lymph, or relating to the lymphatic system.

lymphoma (lɪm'fəʊmə) *n* cancer of the lymph nodes. Also called: **lymphosarcoma** (ˌlɪmfəʊsɑː'kəʊmə).

lynch (lɪntʃ) *vb (tr)* (of a mob) to punish (a person) for some supposed offence by hanging without a trial. [orig. *Lynch's law*; ? after Capt. William *Lynch* (1742–1820) of Virginia, USA]
► **'lyncher** *n* ► **'lynching** *n*

Lynch ★ (lɪntʃ) *n* **John**, known as *Jack Lynch*. born 1917, Irish statesman; prime minister of the Republic of Ireland (1966–73; 1977–79).

lynchet ('lɪntʃɪt) *n* a terrace or ridge formed in prehistoric or medieval times by ploughing a hillside. [OE *hlinc* ridge]

lynch law *n* the practice of punishing a person by mob action without a proper trial.

lynchpin ('lɪntʃˌpɪn) *n* a variant spelling of **linchpin**.

Lynn[1] ★ (lɪn) *n* another name for **King's Lynn**. Also called: **Lynn Regis** ('riːdʒɪs).

Lynn[2] ★ (lɪn) *n* Dame **Vera**, original name *Vera Margaret Lewis*. born 1917, British singer popular during World War II and known as "the forces' sweetheart". Her best-known songs include "We'll Meet Again" and "White Cliffs of Dover".

lynx (lɪŋks) *n, pl* **lynxes** *or* **lynx**. **1** a feline mammal of Europe and North America, with grey-brown mottled fur, tufted ears, and a short tail. **2** the fur of this animal. **3 bay lynx**. another name for **bobcat**. **4 desert lynx**. another name for **caracal**. [C14: via L from Gk *lunx*]
► **'lynx,like** *adj*

lynx-eyed *adj* having keen sight.

Lyon ★ (*French* ljɔ̃) *n* a city in SE central France, capital of Rhône department, at the confluence of the Rivers Rhône and Saône: the third largest city in France; a major industrial centre and river port. Pop.: 422 444 (1990). English name: **Lyons** ('laɪənz). Ancient name: **Lugdunum** (luɡ'duːnəm).

Lyon King of Arms ('laɪən) *n* the chief herald of Scotland. Also called: **Lord Lyon**. [C14: archaic spelling of LION, referring to the figure on the royal shield]

Lyonnais ★ (*French* ljɔnɛ) *n* a former province of E central France, on the Rivers Rhône and Saône: occupied by the present-day departments of Rhône and Loire. Chief town: Lyon.

Lyonnesse ★ (ˌlaɪə'nɛs) *n* (in Arthurian legend) the mythical birthplace of Sir Tristram, situated in SW England and believed to have been submerged by the sea.

Lyons ★ ('laɪənz) *n* **Joseph Aloysius**. 1879–1939, Australian statesman; prime minister of Australia (1931–39).

lyrate ('laɪərɪt) *adj* **1** shaped like a lyre. **2** (of leaves) having a large terminal lobe and smaller lateral lobes. [C18: from NL *lyrātus, from L lyra* LYRE]

lyre ('laɪə) *n* an ancient Greek stringed instrument consisting of a resonating tortoise shell to which a crossbar was attached by two projecting arms. It was plucked

with a plectrum and used for accompanying songs. [C13: via OF from L *lyra, from Gk lura*]

lyrebird ('laɪəˌbɜːd) *n* either of two pheasant-like Australian birds: during courtship displays, the male spreads its tail into the shape of a lyre.

lyric ('lɪrɪk) *adj* **1** (of poetry) **1a** expressing the writer's personal feelings and thoughts. **1b** having the form and manner of a song. **2** of or relating to such poetry. **3** (of music) having songlike qualities. **4** (of a singing voice) having a light quality and tone. **5** intended for singing, esp. (in classical Greece) to the accompaniment of the lyre. ◆ *n* **6** a short poem of songlike quality. **7** (*pl*) the words of a popular song. ◆ Also (for senses 1–4): **lyrical**. [C16: from L *lyricus, from Gk lurikos, from lura lyre*]
► **'lyrically** *adv* ► **'lyricalness** *n*

lyrical ('lɪrɪkᵊl) *adj* **1** another word for **lyric** (senses 1–4). **2** enthusiastic; effusive.

lyricism ('lɪrɪˌsɪzəm) *n* **1** the quality or style of lyric poetry. **2** emotional outpouring.

lyricist ('lɪrɪsɪst) *n* **1** a person who writes the words for a song, opera, or musical play. **2** Also called: **lyrist**. a lyric poet.

Lysander ★ (laɪ'sændə) *n* died 395 B.C., Spartan naval commander of the Peloponnesian War.

lyse (laɪs, laɪz) *vb* **lyses, lysing, lysed**. to undergo or cause to undergo lysis.

Lysenko ★ (lɪ'sɛŋkəʊ; *Russian* li'sjɛnkə) *n* **Trofim Denisovich** (tra'fim dɪ'nisəvɪtʃ). 1898–1976, Soviet biologist and geneticist.

lysergic acid diethylamide (lɪ'sɜːdʒɪk; daɪˌɛθɪl-'eɪmaɪd) *n* See **LSD**.

Lysias ★ ('lɪsɪˌæs) *n* ?450–?380 B.C., Athenian orator.

Lysimachus ★ (laɪ'sɪməkəs) *n* ?360–281 B.C., Macedonian general under Alexander the Great; king of Thrace (323–281); killed in battle.

lysin ('laɪsɪn) *n* any of a group of antibodies that cause dissolution of cells.

Lysippus ★ (laɪ'sɪpəs) *n* 4th century B.C., Greek sculptor.

lysis ('laɪsɪs) *n, pl* **lyses** (-siːz). **1** the destruction of cells by the action of a particular lysin. **2** *Med.* the gradual reduction in the symptoms of a disease. [C19: NL, from Gk, from *luein* to release]

-lysis *n combining form.* indicating a loosening, decomposition, or breaking down: *electrolysis; paralysis.* [from Gk, from *lusis* a loosening; see LYSIS]

Lysol ('laɪsɒl) *n Trademark.* a solution containing a mixture of cresols in water, used as an antiseptic and disinfectant.

-lyte *n combining form.* indicating a substance that can be decomposed or broken down: *electrolyte.* [from Gk *lutos* soluble, from *luein* to loose]

Lytham Saint Anne's ('lɪðəm sənt 'ænz) *n*, *usually abbreviated to* **Lytham St Anne's**. a resort in NW England in Lancashire on the Irish Sea. Pop.: 40 866 (1991).

-lytic *adj combining form.* indicating a loosening or dissolving: *paralytic.* [from Gk, from *lusis; see* -LYSIS]

Lyttelton ★ ('lɪtᵊltən) *n* **Humphrey**. born 1921, British jazz trumpeter and band leader who influenced the British revival of New Orleans jazz.

Lytton ★ ('lɪtᵊn) *n* **1st Baron**, title of *Edward George Earle Lytton Bulwer-Lytton*. 1803–73, British writer and statesman, noted for his historical romances.

Lyublin ★ ('ljʊblɪn) *n* transliteration of the Russian name for **Lublin**.

★ people and places

Mm

m *or* **M** (ɛm) *n, pl* **m's, M's,** *or* **Ms. 1** the 13th letter of the English alphabet. **2** a speech sound represented by this letter, as in *mat*.

m *symbol for:* **1** metre(s). **2** mile(s). **3** milli-. **4** minute(s).

M *symbol for:* **1** mach. **2** *Currency.* mark(s). **3** medium. **4** mega-. **5** million. **6** (in Britain) motorway. ◆ **7** *the Roman numeral for* 1000.

m. *abbrev. for:* **1** *Cricket.* maiden (over). **2** male. **3** mare. **4** married. **5** masculine. **6** meridian. **7** month.

M. *abbrev. for:* **1** Majesty. **2** Manitoba. **3** Master. **4** Medieval. **5** (in titles) Member. **6** million. **7** (*pl* **MM.** *or* **MM**) Also: **M** *French.* Monsieur. [F equivalent of *Mr*]

m- *prefix* short for **meta-** (sense 4).

M'- *prefix* a variant of **Mac-**.

ma (mɑː) *n* an informal word for **mother**.

MA *abbrev. for:* **1** Massachusetts. **2** Master of Arts. **3** Military Academy.

ma'am (mæm, mɑːm; *unstressed* məm) *n* short for **madam**: used as a title of respect, esp. for female royalty.

Maarianhamina ★ (ˌmɑːriɑnhɑminɑ) *n* the Finnish name for **Mariehamn**.

Maas ★ (mɑːs) *n* the Dutch name for the **Meuse**.

Maastricht *or* **Maestricht** ★ (ˈmɑːstrɪxt; *Dutch* mɑːˈstrɪxt) *n* a city in the SE Netherlands near the Belgian and German borders: capital of Limburg province, on the River Maas (Meuse); a European Union treaty (**Maastricht Treaty**) was signed here in 1992. Pop.: 118 341 (1995 est.).

Mab ★ (mæb) *n* (in English and Irish folklore) a fairy queen said to create and control men's dreams.

Mabuse (məˈbjuːz; *French* mabyz) *n* **Jan** (jɑn). original name *Jan Gossaert*. ?1478–?1533, Flemish painter.

mac *or* **mack** (mæk) *n Brit. inf.* short for **mackintosh**.

Mac (mæk) *n Chiefly US & Canad.* an informal term of address to a man. [C20: abstracted from MAC-]

Mac-, Mc-, *or* **M'-** *prefix* (in surnames of Scottish or Irish Gaelic origin) son of: *MacDonald*. [from Goidelic *mac* son of]

macabre (məˈkɑːbə, -brə) *adj* gruesome; ghastly; grim. [C15: from OF *danse macabre* dance of death, prob. from *macabé* relating to the Maccabees, who were associated with death because of the doctrines and prayers for the dead in II Macc. (12:43–46)]

macadam (məˈkædəm) *n* a road surface made of compressed layers of small broken stones, esp. one that is bound together with tar or asphalt. [C19: after John *McAdam* (1756–1836), Scot. engineer, the inventor]

macadamia (ˌmækəˈdeɪmɪə) *n* **1** an Australian tree having clusters of small white flowers and edible nutlike seeds. **2** the seed. [C19: NL, after John *Macadam* (died 1865), Australian chemist]

macadamize *or* **macadamise** (məˈkædəˌmaɪz) *vb* **macadamizes, macadamizing, macadamized** *or* **macadamises, macadamising, macadamised**. (*tr*) to construct or surface (a road) with macadam.
► **mac,adami'zation** *or* **mac,adami'sation** *n* ► **mac'adam,izer** *or* **mac'adam,iser** *n*

Macao ★ (məˈkau) *n* a Portuguese overseas province and city on the coast of S China, across the estuary of the Zhu Jiang from Hong Kong: chief centre of European trade with China in the 18th century; attained partial autonomy in 1976; sovereignty will pass to China in 1999; transit trade with China; tourism. Pop.: 395 304 (1994 est.). Area: 16 sq. km (6 sq. miles). Portuguese name: **Macáu**.

Macapá ★ (*Portuguese* makaˈpa) *n* a town in NE Brazil, capital of the federal territory of Amapá, on the Canal do Norte of the Amazon delta. Pop.: 146 523 (1991).

macaque (məˈkɑːk) *n* any of various Old World monkeys of Asia and Africa. Typically the tail is short or absent and cheek pouches are present. [C17: from F, from Port. *macaco*, from W African *makaku*, from *kaku* monkey]

macaroni *or* **maccaroni** (ˌmækəˈrəʊnɪ) *n, pl* **macaronis, macaronies** *or* **maccaronis, maccaronies. 1** pasta tubes made from wheat flour. **2** (in 18th-century Britain) a dandy who affected foreign manners and style. [C16: from It. (dialect) *maccarone*, prob. from Gk *makaria* food made from barley]

macaroon (ˌmækəˈruːn) *n* a kind of sweet biscuit made of ground almonds, sugar, and egg whites. [C17: via F *macaron* from It. *maccarone* MACARONI]

Macarthur ★ (məˈkɑːθə) *n* **John.** 1767–1834, Australian military officer and entrepreneur, born in England. He established the breeding of merino sheep in Australia.

MacArthur ★ (məˈkɑːθə) *n* **Douglas.** 1880–1964, US general. During World War II he commanded US forces in the Pacific (1944) and accepted the surrender of Japan. He was commander in chief of United Nations forces in Korea (1950–51) until dismissed by President Truman.

Macassar ★ (məˈkæsə) *n* a variant spelling of **Makasar**.

Macassar oil *n* an oily preparation formerly put on the hair to make it smooth and shiny. [C19: from MAKASAR]

Macáu ★ (məˈkau) *n* the Portuguese name for **Macao**.

Macaulay ★ (məˈkɔːlɪ) *n* **1** Dame **Rose.** 1881–1958, British novelist. Her books include *Dangerous Ages* (1921) and *The Towers of Trebizond* (1956). **2 Thomas Babington,** 1st Baron. 1800–59, British historian and statesman, best known for his *History of England from the Accession of James the Second* (1848–61).

macaw (məˈkɔː) *n* a large tropical American parrot having a long tail and brilliant plumage. [C17: from Port. *macau*, from ?]

Macbeth ★ (məkˈbɛθ, mæk-) *n* died 1057, king of Scotland (1040–57): succeeded Duncan, whom he killed in battle; defeated and killed by Duncan's son Malcolm III.

MacBride ★ (məkˈbraɪd) *n* **Sean** (ʃɔːn). 1904–88, Irish statesman; minister for external affairs (1948–51); chairman of Amnesty International (1961–75); Nobel Peace Prize 1974; UN commissioner for Namibia (1974–76).

McBride ★ (məkˈbraɪd) *n* **Willie John.** born 1940, Irish Rugby Union footballer; played for Ireland (1962–75) and the British Lions (1962–74).

Macc. *abbrev. for* Maccabees (books of the Apocrypha).

McCarthy ★ (məˈkɑːθɪ) *n* **1** Joseph **R(aymond).** 1908–57, US Republican senator, who led (1950–54) the notorious investigations of alleged Communist infiltration into the US government. **2 Mary (Therese).** 1912–89, US novelist; her works include *The Group* (1963).

McCarthyism (məˈkɑːθɪˌɪzəm) *n Chiefly US.* **1** the practice of making unsubstantiated accusations of disloyalty or Communist leanings. **2** the use of unsupported accusations for any purpose. [C20: after Senator Joseph MCCARTHY]
► **Mc'Carthyist** *n, adj*

McCartney ★ (məˈkɑːtnɪ) *n* Sir **Paul.** born 1942, British rock musician and songwriter; member of the Beatles (1961–70); leader of Wings (1971–81). His recordings include *Band on the Run* (1973) and "Mull of Kintyre" (1977). See also **Beatles**.

Macclesfield ★ (ˈmækˀlzˌfiːld) *n* a market town in NW England, in Cheshire: silk industry. Pop.: 50 270 (1991).

McCormack ★ (məˈkɔːmæk) *n* **John.** 1884–1945, Irish tenor: became a US citizen 1919.

McCoy (məˈkɔɪ) *n Sl.* the genuine person or thing (esp. in **the real McCoy**). [C20: ? after Kid *McCoy*, professional name of Norman Selby (1873–1940), American boxer,

---

★ people and places

who was called "the real McCoy" to distinguish him from another boxer of that name]

McCullers ★ (mə'kʌləz) *n* Carson. 1917–67, US writer, whose novels include *The Heart is a Lonely Hunter* (1940).

McDiarmid ★ (mək'dɜːmɪd) *n* Hugh, pen name of *Christopher Murray Grieve*. 1892–1978, Scottish poet; a founder of the Scottish National Party. His poems include *A Drunk Man Looks at the Thistle* (1926).

Macdonald ★ (mək'dɒnəld) *n* 1 Flora. 1722–90, Scottish heroine, who helped the Young Pretender to escape to Skye after the battle of Culloden (1746). 2 Sir John Alexander. 1815–91, Canadian statesman, born in Scotland, who was the first prime minister of the Dominion of Canada (1867–73; 1878–91).

MacDonald ★ (mək'dɒnəld) *n* (James) Ramsay. 1866–1937, British statesman, who led the first and second Labour Governments (1924 and 1929–31). He also led a coalition (1931–35).

Macdonnell Ranges ★ (mək'dɒnəl) *pl n* a mountain system of central Australia, in S central Northern Territory, extending about 160 km (100 miles) east and west of Alice Springs. Highest peak: Mount Ziel, 1510 m (4955 ft).

mace[1] (meɪs) *n* 1 a club, usually having a spiked metal head, used esp. in the Middle Ages. 2 a ceremonial staff carried by certain officials. 3 See macebearer. 4 an early form of billiard cue. [C13: from OF, prob. from Vulgar L *mattea* (unattested); apparently rel. to L *mateola* mallet]

mace[2] (meɪs) *n* a spice made from the dried aril round the nutmeg seed. [C14: formed as a singular from OF *macis* (wrongly assumed to be pl), from L *macir* a spice]

macebearer ('meɪs,beərə) *n* a person who carries a mace in processions or ceremonies.

Maced. *abbrev. for* Macedonia(n).

macedoine (,mæsɪ'dwɑːn) *n* 1 a mixture of diced vegetables. 2 a mixture of fruit in a syrup or in jelly. 3 any mixture; medley. [C19: from F, lit.: Macedonian, alluding to the mixture of nationalities in Macedonia]

Macedon ('mæsɪ,dɒn) *or* **Macedonia** ★ *n* a region of the S Balkans, now divided among Greece, Bulgaria, and the Former Yugoslav Republic of Macedonia. As a kingdom in the ancient world it achieved prominence under Philip II (359–336 B.C.) and his son Alexander the Great.

Macedonia ★ (,mæsɪ'dəʊnɪə) *n* 1 a country in SE Europe, comprising part of ancient Macedon: it became part of the kingdom of Serbs, Croats, and Slovenes (subsequently Yugoslavia) in 1913; it declared independence in 1992, but Greece objected to its use of the historical name Macedonia; in 1993 it was recognized by the UN under its current official name. Official language: Macedonian. Religion: Christian majority, Muslim, nonreligious, and Jewish minorities. Currency: denar. Capital: Skopje. Pop.: 1 968 000 (1996). Area: 25 713 sq. km (10 028 sq. miles). Serbian name: ,Makedo'nija. Official name: Former Yugoslav Republic of Macedonia. Abbrev.: FYROM. 2 an area of N Greece, comprising the regions of Macedonia Central, Macedonia West, and part of Macedonia East and Thrace. Modern Greek name: Makedhonia. 3 a district of SW Bulgaria, now occupied by Blagoevgrad province. Area: 6465 sq. km (2496 sq. miles).
▶ ,Mace'donian *adj, n*

Maceió ★ (mase'jɔ) *n* a port in NE Brazil, capital of Alagôas state, on the Atlantic. Pop.: 554 727 (1991).

McEnroe ★ ('mæk°n,rəʊ) *n* John (Patrick Jr). born 1959, US tennis player: US singles champion (1979–81; 1984): Wimbledon singles champion (1981; 1983; 1984).

macerate ('mæsə,reɪt) *vb* macerates, macerating, macerated. 1 to soften or separate or be softened or separated as a result of soaking. 2 to become or cause to become thin. [C16: from L *mācerāre* to soften]
▶ ,macer'ation *n* ▶ 'macer,ator *n*

McEwan ★ (mə'kjuːən) *n* Ian (Russell). born 1948, British writer. His books include *The Child in Time* (1987) and *Amsterdam* (1998).

McGonagall ★ (mə'gɒnəgəl) *n* William. 1830–?1902, Scottish writer of doggerel.

MacGuffin (mə'gʌfɪn) *n* an object or event in a book or

a film that serves as the impetus for the plot. [C20: coined (c. 1935) by Sir Alfred HITCHCOCK]

Mach[1] (mæk) *n* short for Mach number.

Mach[2] ★ (*German* max) *n* Ernst (ɛrnst). 1838–1916, Austrian physicist and philosopher. He devised the Mach number and founded logical positivism.

mach. *abbrev. for:* 1 machine. 2 machinery. 3 machinist.

Machado ★ (*Portuguese* ma'ʃadu) *n* Joaquim Maria (ʒua'kĩ ma'ria). 1839–1908, Brazilian writer, whose novels include *Epitaph of a Small Winner* (1881).

machair ('mæxər) *n Scot.* (in the western Highlands and islands of Scotland) a strip of sandy grassy land just above the shore: used for grazing, etc. [C17: from Scot. Gaelic]

Machel ★ (mə'ʃel) *n* Samora (Moises) (sə'mɔːrə). 1933–86, Mozambique statesman; president of Mozambique (1975–86).

machete (mə'ʃetɪ, -'tʃeɪ-) *n* a broad heavy knife used for cutting or as a weapon, esp. in parts of Central and South America. [C16 *macheto*, from Sp. *machete*, from *macho* club, ?from Vulgar L *mattea* (unattested) club]

Machiavelli ★ (,mækɪə'velɪ) *n* Niccolò (nikko'lɔ). 1469–1527, Florentine statesman and political philosopher; secretary to the war council of the Florentine republic (1498–1512); author of *Il Principe* (*The Prince*, 1532).

Machiavellian (,mækɪə'velɪən) *adj* 1 of or relating to the alleged political principles of Machiavelli; cunning, amoral, and opportunist. ◆ *n* 2 a cunning, amoral, and opportunist person, esp. a politician.
▶ ,Machia'vellian,ism *n*

machicolate (mə'tʃɪkəu,leɪt) *vb* machicolates, machicolating, machicolated. (*tr*) to construct machicolations at the top of (a wall). [C18: from OF *machicoller*, ult. from Provençal *machacol*, from *macar* to crush + *col* neck]

machicolation (mə,tʃɪkəu'leɪʃən) *n* 1 (esp. in medieval castles) a projecting gallery or parapet having openings through which missiles could be dropped. 2 any such opening.

machinate ('mækɪ,neɪt) *vb* machinates, machinating, machinated. (*usually tr*) to contrive, plan, or devise (schemes, plots, etc.). [C17: from L *māchinārī* to plan, from *māchina* MACHINE]
▶ 'machi,nator *n*

machination (,mækɪ'neɪʃən) *n* 1 a plot or scheme. 2 the act of devising plots or schemes.

machine (mə'ʃiːn) *n* 1 an assembly of interconnected components arranged to transmit or modify force in order to perform useful work. 2 a device for altering the magnitude or direction of a force, such as a lever or screw. 3 a mechanically operated device or means of transport, such as a car or aircraft. 4 any mechanical or electrical device that automatically performs tasks or assists in performing tasks. 5 any intricate structure or agency. 6 a mechanically efficient, rigid, or obedient person. 7 an organized body of people that controls activities, policies, etc. ◆ *vb* machines, machining, machined. 8 (*tr*) to shape, cut, or remove (excess material) from (a workpiece) using a machine tool. 9 to use a machine to carry out a process on (something). [C16: via F from L *māchina* machine, from Doric Gk *makhana* pulley]
▶ ma'chinable *or* ma'chineable *adj* ▶ ma,china'bility *n*

machine code *or* **language** *n* instructions for the processing of data in a binary, octal, or hexadecimal code that can be understood and executed by a computer.

machine-down time *n* a period during which a machine, computer, etc., is out of service, because it is out of order or being serviced.

machine gun *n* 1a a rapid-firing automatic gun, using small-arms ammunition. 1b (*as modifier*): *machine-gun fire*. ◆ *vb* machine-gun, machine-guns, machine-gunning, machine-gunned. 2 (*tr*) to shoot or fire at with a machine gun.
▶ machine gunner *n*

machine learning *n* a branch of artificial intelligence in which a computer generates rules underlying or based on raw data that has been fed into it.

machinery (məˈʃiːnərɪ) *n, pl* **machineries. 1** machines, machine parts, or machine systems collectively. **2** a particular machine system or set of machines. **3** a system similar to a machine.

machine shop *n* a workshop in which machine tools are operated.

machine tool *n* a power-driven machine, such as a lathe, for cutting, shaping, and finishing metals, etc. ▸ **maˈchine-ˌtooled** *adj*

machinist (məˈʃiːnɪst) *n* **1** a person who operates machines to cut or process materials. **2** a maker or repairer of machines.

machismo (mæˈkɪzməʊ, -ˈtʃɪz-) *n* strong or exaggerated masculinity. [Mexican Sp., from Sp. *macho* male, from L *masculus* MASCULINE]

Mach number *n* (*often not cap.*) the ratio of the speed of a body in a particular medium to the speed of sound in that medium. Mach number 1 corresponds to the speed of sound. [C19: after Ernst MACH]

macho (ˈmætʃəʊ) *adj* **1** strongly or exaggeratedly masculine. ◆ *n, pl* **machos. 2** a strong virile man. [see MACHISMO]

Machu Picchu ★ (ˈmɑːtʃuː ˈpiːktʃuː) *n* a ruined Incan city in S central Peru.

Macías Nguema ★ (məˈsiːəs ᵊŋˈgweɪmə) *n* the former name (until 1979) of **Bioko**.

mack (mæk) *n Brit. inf.* short for **mackintosh**.

Mackay ★ (məˈkaɪ) *n* a port in E Australia, in Queensland: artificial harbour. Pop.: 55 772 (1993).

McKean ★ (məˈkiːn) *n* Tom. born 1963, Scottish athlete: European 800 metres gold medallist (1990).

Mackellar ★ (məˈkelə) *n* **Dorothea**. 1885–1968, Australian poet, who wrote "My Country".

McKellen ★ (məˈkelən) *n* Sir **Ian** (**Murray**). born 1939, British actor, noted esp. for his Shakespearean roles.

McKenna ★ (məˈkenə) *n* **Siobhán** (ʃəˈvɔːn). 1923–86, Irish actress.

Mackenzie[1] ★ (məˈkenzɪ) *n* a river in NW Canada, in Nunavut and the Northwest Territories, flowing northwest from Great Slave Lake to the Beaufort Sea: the longest river in Canada; navigable in summer. Length: 1770 km (1100 miles).

Mackenzie[2] ★ (məˈkenzɪ) *n* **1** Sir **Alexander**. ?1755–1820, Scottish explorer and fur trader in Canada. He explored the Mackenzie River (1789) and was the first European to cross America north of Mexico (1793). **2** Alexander. 1822–92, Canadian statesman; first Liberal prime minister (1873–78). **3** Sir **Compton**. 1883–1972, British author. His works include *Sinister Street* (1913–14) and the comic novel *Whisky Galore* (1947). **4** Sir **Thomas**. 1854–1930, New Zealand statesman born in Scotland: prime minister of New Zealand (1912).

mackerel (ˈmækrəl) *n, pl* **mackerel** or **mackerels. 1** a spiny-finned food fish occurring in northern coastal regions of the Atlantic and in the Mediterranean. It has a deeply forked tail and a greenish-blue body marked with wavy dark bands on the back. **2** any of various related fishes. [C13: from Anglo-F, from OF *maquerel*, from ?]

mackerel sky *n* a sky patterned with cirrocumulus or small altocumulus clouds. [from similarity to pattern on mackerel's back]

Mackerras ★ (məˈkerəs) *n* **Charles**. born 1925, Australian conductor, esp. of opera; resident in England.

Mackinac ★ (ˈmækɪˌnɔː, -ˌnæk) *n* a wooded island in N Michigan, in the **Straits of Mackinac** (a channel between the lower and upper peninsulas of Michigan): an ancient Indian burial ground; state park. Length: 5 km (3 miles).

McKinley[1] ★ (məˈkɪnlɪ) *n* **Mount**. a mountain in S central Alaska, in the Alaska Range: the highest peak in North America. Height: 6194 m (20 320 ft).

McKinley[2] ★ (məˈkɪnlɪ) *n* **William**. 1843–1901, 25th president of the US (1897–1901): assassinated.

mackintosh or **macintosh** (ˈmækɪnˌtɒʃ) *n* **1** a waterproof raincoat made of rubberized cloth. **2** such cloth. **3** any raincoat. [C19: after Charles *Macintosh* (1760–1843), who invented it]

Mackintosh ★ (ˈmækɪnˌtɒʃ) *n* **Charles Rennie**. 1868–1928, Scottish architect and artist, exponent of the Art Nouveau style.

Maclean ★ (məˈkleɪn) *n* **1** Donald. 1913–83, British civil servant, who spied for the Soviet Union, to which he fled (with Guy Burgess) in 1951. **2 Sorley** (ˈsɔːlɪ). 1911–96, Scottish Gaelic poet. His works include *Spring Tide and Neap Tide* (1977).

Macleod ★ (məˈklaʊd) *n* **John James Rickard**. 1876–1935, Scottish physiologist: shared the Nobel prize for physiology or medicine (1923) with Banting for their part in discovering insulin.

McLuhan ★ (məˈkluːən) *n* (**Herbert**) **Marshall**. 1911–80, Canadian author of works analysing the mass media, including *The Medium is the Message* (1967).

Macmahon ★ (*French* makmaɔ̃) *n* **Marie Edme Patrice Maurice** (mari ɛdmə patris mɔris), Comte de Macmahon. 1808–93, French military commander. He commanded the troops that suppressed the Paris Commune (1871) and was elected president of the Third Republic (1873–79).

McMahon ★ (məkˈmɑːən) *n* Sir **William**. 1908–88, Australian statesman; prime minister of Australia (1971–72).

Macmillan ★ (məkˈmɪlən) *n* (**Maurice**) **Harold**, 1st Earl of Stockton. 1894–1986, British statesman; Conservative prime minister (1957–63).

MacMillan ★ (məkˈmɪlən) *n* Sir **Kenneth**. 1929–92, British ballet dancer and choreographer; director (1970–77) and principal choreographer (1977–92) of the Royal Ballet.

McMillan ★ (məkˈmɪlən) *n* **Edwin M**(**attison**). 1907–91, US physicist; shared Nobel prize for chemistry 1951 for the discovery of transuranic elements.

Mcmurdo Sound ★ (məkˈmɜːdəʊ) *n* an inlet of the Ross Sea in Antarctica, north of Victoria Land.

McNaughten Rules or **McNaghten Rules** (məkˈnɔːtᵊn) *pl n* (in English law) a set of rules established by the case of Regina v. McNaughten (1843) by which legal proof of criminal insanity depends on the accused being shown to be incapable of understanding what he has done.

MacNeice ★ (məkˈniːs) *n* **Louis**. 1907–63, British poet, born in Northern Ireland. His works include the poems in *Autumn Journal* (1939) and *Solstices* (1961).

Macon ★ (ˈmeɪkən) *n* a city in the US, in central Georgia, on the Ocmulgee River. Pop.: 109 191 (1994 est.).

Mâcon ★ (*French* makɔ̃) *n* **1** a city in E central France, in the Saône valley: a centre of the wine-producing region of lower Burgundy. Pop.: 39 700 (1995 est.). **2** a red or white wine from the Mâcon area, heavier than other burgundies.

Maconchy ★ (məˈkɒŋkɪ) *n* Dame **Elizabeth**, married name *Elizabeth LeFanu*. 1907–94, British composer of Irish parentage; noted esp. for her chamber music, which includes 13 string quartets and *Romanza* (1980) for viola and ensemble.

Macpherson ★ (məkˈfɜːsᵊn) *n* **James**. 1736–96, Scottish poet and translator. He published supposed translations of the legendary Gaelic poet Ossian, in reality largely his own work.

Macquarie[1] ★ (məˈkwɒrɪ) *n* **1** an Australian island in the Pacific, southeast of Tasmania: noted for its species of albatross and penguin. Area: about 168 sq. km (65 sq. miles). **2** a river in SE Australia, in E central New South Wales, rising in the Blue Mountains and flowing northwest to the Darling. Length: about 1200 km (750 miles).

Macquarie[2] ★ (məˈkwɒrɪ) *n* **Lachlan**. 1762–1824, Australian colonial administrator; governor of New South Wales (1809–21).

McQueen ★ (məkˈwiːn) *n* **Steve**. 1930–80, US film actor.

macramé (məˈkrɑːmɪ) *n* a type of ornamental work made by knotting and weaving coarse thread. [C19: via F & It. from Turkish *makrama* towel, from Ar. *migramah* striped cloth]

★ people and places

Macready ★ (mə'kriːdɪ) n **William Charles.** 1793–1873, British actor and theatre manager.

macro ('mækrəʊ) n, pl **macros. 1** Photog. a camera lens used for close-up photography. Also called: **macro lens. 2** Computing. a single computer instruction that initiates a set of instructions. Also called: **macro instruction.** [C20: from Gk makros large]

macro- or before a vowel **macr-** combining form. **1** large, long, or great in size or duration: macroscopic. **2** Pathol. indicating abnormal enlargement or overdevelopment: macrocephaly. [from Gk makros large]

macrobiotics (,mækrəʊbaɪ'ɒtɪks) n (functioning as sing) a dietary system which advocates whole grains and vegetables grown without chemical additives. [C20: from MACRO- + Gk biotos life + -ICS]
  ▸ ,macrobi'otic adj

macrocarpa (,mækrəʊ'kɑːpə) n a large Californian coniferous tree, used in New Zealand and elsewhere to form shelter belts on farms and for rough timber. [C19: from NL, from MACRO- + Gk karpos fruit]

macrocephaly (,mækrəʊ'sefəlɪ) n the condition of having an abnormally large head or skull.
  ▸ **macrocephalic** (,mækrəʊsɪ'fælɪk) or ,macro'cephalous adj

macroclimate ('mækrəʊ,klaɪmɪt) n the predominant climate over a large area.

macrocosm ('mækrə,kɒzəm) n a complex structure, such as the universe or society, regarded as an entirety. Cf. microcosm. [C16: via F & L from Gk makros kosmos great world]
  ▸ ,macro'cosmic adj ▸ ,macro'cosmically adv

macroeconomics (,mækrəʊ,iːkə'nɒmɪks, -,ɛk-) n (functioning as sing) the branch of economics concerned with aggregates, such as national income, consumption, and investment.
  ▸ ,macro,eco'nomic adj

macromolecule (,mækrəʊ'mɒlɪ,kjuːl) n any very large molecule, such as a protein or synthetic polymer.

macron ('mækrɒn) n a diacritical mark (‾) placed over a letter to represent a long vowel. [C19: from Gk makron something long, from makros long]

macropod ('mækrəʊ,pɒd) n any member of a family of marsupials consisting of the kangaroos and related animals.

macroscopic (,mækrəʊ'skɒpɪk) adj **1** large enough to be visible to the naked eye. **2** comprehensive; concerned with large units. [C19: see MACRO-, -SCOPIC]
  ▸ ,macro'scopically adv

macula ('mækjʊlə) or **macule** ('mækjuːl) n, pl **maculae** (-jʊ,liː) or **macules.** Anat. **1** a small spot or area of distinct colour, esp. the macula lutea. **2** any small discoloured spot or blemish on the skin, such as a freckle. [C14: from L]
  ▸ 'macular adj ▸ macu'lation n

macula lutea ('luːtɪə) n, pl **maculae luteae** ('luːtɪ,iː). a small yellowish oval-shaped spot on the retina of the eye, where vision is especially sharp. [NL, lit.: yellow spot]

macular degeneration n pathological changes in the macula lutea, resulting in loss of central vision: a common cause of blindness in the elderly.

mad (mæd) adj **madder, maddest. 1** mentally deranged; insane. **2** senseless; foolish. **3** (often foll. by at) Inf. angry; resentful. **4** (foll. by about, on, or over; often postpositive) wildly enthusiastic (about) or fond (of). **5** extremely excited or confused; frantic: a mad rush. **6** temporarily overpowered by violent reactions, emotions, etc.: mad with grief. **7** (of animals) **7a** unusually ferocious: a mad buffalo. **7b** afflicted with rabies. **8 like mad.** Inf. with great energy, enthusiasm, or haste. ◆ vb **mads, madding, madded. 9** US or arch. to make or become mad; act or cause to act as if mad. [OE gemǣded, p.p. of gemǣdan to render insane]

Madag. abbrev. for Madagascar.

Madagascar ★ (,mædə'gæskə) n an island republic in the Indian Ocean, off the E coast of Africa: made a French protectorate in 1895; became autonomous in 1958 and fully independent in 1960; contains unique flora and fauna. Languages: Malagasy and French. Religions: animist and Christian. Currency: franc. Capital: Antananarivo. Pop.: 13 671 000 (1996). Area: 587 041 sq. km (266 657 sq. miles). Official name (since 1975): **Democratic Republic of Madagascar.** Former name (1958–75): **Malagasy Republic.**
  ▸ ,Mada'gascan n, adj

madam ('mædəm) n, pl **madams** or (for sense 1) **mesdames. 1** a polite term of address for a woman, esp. one of relatively high social status. **2** a woman who runs a brothel. **3** Brit. inf. a precocious or pompous little girl. [C13: from OF ma dame my lady]

madame ('mædəm) n, pl **mesdames.** a married Frenchwoman: used as a title equivalent to Mrs, and sometimes extended to older unmarried women to show respect. [C17: from F; see MADAM]

madcap ('mæd,kæp) adj **1** impulsive, reckless, or lively. ◆ n **2** an impulsive, reckless, or lively person.

mad cow disease n an informal name for **BSE.**

madden ('mæd[ə]n) vb to make or become mad or angry.
  ▸ 'maddening adj ▸ 'maddeningly adv

madder ('mædə) n **1** a plant having small yellow flowers and a red fleshy root. **2** this root. **3** a dark reddish-purple dye formerly obtained from this root. **4** a red lake obtained from alizarin and an inorganic base; used as a pigment in inks and paints. [OE mædere]

madding ('mædɪŋ) adj Arch. **1** acting or behaving as if mad: the madding crowd. **2** making mad; maddening.
  ▸ 'maddingly adv

made (meɪd) vb **1** the past tense and past participle of **make.** ◆ adj **2** artificially produced. **3** (in combination) produced or shaped as specified: handmade. **4 get** or **have it made.** Inf. to be assured of success.

Madeira ★ (mə'dɪərə; Portuguese mə'ðəirə) n **1** a group of volcanic islands in the N Atlantic, west of Morocco: constitutes the Portuguese administrative district of Funchal; consists of the chief island, Madeira, Pôrto Santo, and the uninhabited Deserta and Selvagen Islands; gained partial autonomy in 1976. Capital: Funchal. Pop.: 253 800 (1993 est.). Area: 797 sq. km (311 sq. miles). **2** a river in W Brazil, flowing northeast to the Amazon below Manaus. Length: 3241 km (2013 miles). **3** a rich strong fortified white wine made on Madeira.

madeleine ('mædəlɪn, -,leɪn) n a small fancy sponge cake. [C19: ? after Madeleine Paulmier, F pastry cook]

mademoiselle (,mædmwə'zɛl) n, pl **mesdemoiselles. 1** a young unmarried French girl or woman: used as a title equivalent to Miss. **2** a French teacher or governess. [C15: F, from ma my + demoiselle DAMSEL]

made-up adj **1** invented; fictional. **2** wearing make-up. **3** put together. **4** (of a road) surfaced with tarmac, concrete, etc.

madhouse ('mæd,haʊs) n Inf. **1** a mental hospital or asylum. **2** a state of uproar or confusion.

Madhya Bharat ★ ('mʌdjə 'bɑːrət) n a former state of central India: part of Madhya Pradesh since 1956.

Madhya Pradesh ★ ('mʌdjə prɑː'deʃ) n a state of central India, situated on the Deccan Plateau: the largest Indian state; rich in mineral resources, with several industrial cities. Capital: Bhopal. Pop.: 71 950 000 (1994 est.). Area: 443 446 sq. km (171 215 sq. miles).

Madison[1] ★ ('mædɪs[ə]n) n a city in the US in S central Wisconsin, on an isthmus between Lakes Mendota and Monona: the state capital. Pop.: 194 586 (1994 est.).

Madison[2] ★ ('mædɪs[ə]n) n James. 1751–1836, US statesman; 4th president of the US (1809–17). He helped to draft the US Constitution and Bill of Rights.

Madison Avenue ★ n a street in New York City: a centre of American advertising and public-relations firms and a symbol of their attitudes and methods.

madly ('mædlɪ) adv **1** in an insane or foolish manner. **2** with great speed and energy. **3** Inf. extremely or excessively: I love you madly.

madman ('mædmən) or (fem) **madwoman** n, pl **madmen** or **madwomen.** a person who is insane.

madness ('mædnɪs) n **1** insanity; lunacy. **2** extreme anger, excitement, or foolishness. **3** a nontechnical word for **rabies**.

Madonna[1] ★ (mə'dɒnə) *n* **1** *Chiefly RC Church.* a designation of the Virgin Mary. **2** (*sometimes not cap.*) a picture or statue of the Virgin Mary. [C16: It., from *ma* my + *donna* lady]

Madonna[2] ★ (mə'dɒnə) *n* full name *Madonna Louise Veronica Ciccone*. born 1958, US rock singer and actress. Her hits include "Like a Virgin" (1985) and "Vogue" (1990). Her films include *Desperately Seeking Susan* (1985) and *Evita* (1996).

Madonna lily *n* a perennial widely cultivated Mediterranean lily plant with white trumpet-shaped flowers.

madras ('mædrəs, mə'dræs) *n* **1** a strong fine cotton or silk fabric, usually with a woven stripe. **2** a medium-hot curry: *chicken madras*. [from MADRAS]

Madras ★ (mə'drɑːs, -'dræs) *n* **1** a port in SE India, capital of Tamil Nadu, on the Bay of Bengal: founded in 1639 by the English East India Company as **Fort St George**; traditional burial place of St Thomas; university (1857). Pop. (urban area): 5 421 985 (1991). Official name: **Chennai**. **2** the former name (until 1968) for the state of **Tamil Nadu**.

Madre de Dios ★ (*Spanish* 'maðre ðe 'ðiɔs) *n* a river in NE South America, rising in SE Peru and flowing northeast to the Beni River in N Bolivia. Length: about 965 km (600 miles).

madrepore (ˌmædrɪ'pɔː) *n* any coral of the genus *Madrepora*, many of which occur in tropical seas and form large coral reefs. [C18: via F from It. *madrepora* mother-stone]
  ▸ **ˌmadre'poral, madreporic** (ˌmædrɪ'pɒrɪk), *or* **ˌmadre-'porian** *adj*

Madrid ★ (mə'drɪd) *n* the capital of Spain, situated centrally in New Castile: the highest European capital, at an altitude of about 700 m (2300 ft); a Moorish fortress in the 10th century, captured by Castile in 1083 and made capital of Spain in 1561; university (1836). Pop.: 3 041 101 (1994 est.).

madrigal ('mædrɪgˀl) *n* **1** *Music.* a type of 16th- or 17th-century part song for unaccompanied voices, with an amatory or pastoral text. **2** a short love poem. [C16: from It., from Med. L *mātricāle* primitive, apparently from L *mātrīcālis*, from *matrix* womb]
  ▸ **ˌmadri'galˌesque** *adj* ▸ **madrigalian** (ˌmædrɪ'gælɪən, -'geɪ-) *adj* ▸ **'madrigalist** *n*

Madura ★ (mə'dʊərə) *n* an island in Indonesia, off the NE coast of Java: extensive forests and saline springs. Capital: Pamekasan. Area: 5472 sq. km (2113 sq. miles).
  ▸ **Madurese** (ˌmædjʊə'riːz) *adj, n*

Madurai ★ ('mædjuˌraɪ) *n* a city in S India, in S Tamil Nadu: centre of Dravidian culture for over 2000 years; cotton industry. Pop.: 940 989 (1991). Former name: **Madura**.

Maeander ★ (miː'ændə) *n* ancient name of the river Menderes (sense 1). Also spelled: **Meander**.

Maebashi ★ ('mɑːɛ'bɑːʃi) *n* a city in central Japan, on central Honshu: centre of sericulture and silk-spinning; university (1949). Pop.: 284 780 (1995).

Maecenas ★ (miː'siːnæs) *n* **1 Gaius** ('gaɪəs). ?70–8 B.C., Roman statesman; adviser to Augustus and patron of Horace and Virgil. **2** a wealthy patron of the arts.

maelstrom ('meɪlstrəʊm) *n* **1** a large powerful whirlpool. **2** any turbulent confusion. [C17: from obs. Du. *maelstroom*, from *malen* to whirl round + *stroom* STREAM]

Maelstrom ★ ('meɪlstrəʊm) *n* a strong tidal current in a restricted channel in the Lofoten Islands off the NW coast of Norway.

maenad ('miːnæd) *n* **1** *Classical history.* a woman participant in the orgiastic rites of Dionysus, Greek god of wine. **2** a frenzied woman. [C16: from L *Maenas*, from Gk *mainas* madwoman]
  ▸ **mae'nadic** *adj*

maestoso (maɪ'stəʊsəʊ) *Music.* ◆ *adj, adv* **1** to be performed majestically. ◆ *n, pl* **maestosos. 2** a piece or passage directed to be played in this way. [C18: It.: majestic, from L *māiestās* MAJESTY]

Maestricht ★ ('mɑːstrɪxt; *Dutch* ma:'strɪxt) *n* an obsolete spelling of **Maastricht**.

maestro ('maɪstrəʊ) *n, pl* **maestri** (-trɪ) *or* **maestros. 1** a distinguished music teacher, conductor, or musician. **2** any master of an art: often used as a term of address. [C18: It.: master]

Maeterlinck ★ ('meɪtəˌlɪŋk; *French* mɛtɛrlɛ̃k) *n* **Comte Maurice** (mɔris). 1862–1949, Belgian poet and dramatist, noted for such plays as *Pelléas et Mélisande* (1892) and *L'Oiseau bleu* (1909). He won the Nobel prize for literature in 1911.

mae west (meɪ) *n Sl.* an inflatable life jacket, esp. as issued to the US armed forces. [C20: after *Mae* WEST (1892–1980), US actress, renowned for her large bust]

Maewo ★ (mɑː'eɪwəʊ) *n* an almost uninhabited island in Vanuatu. Also called: **Aurora**.

Mafeking ★ ('mæfɪˌkɪŋ) *n* the former name (until 1980) of **Mafikeng**.

MAFF (in Britain) *abbrev.* for Ministry of Agriculture, Fisheries, and Food.

Mafia ('mæfɪə) *n* **1 the**. an international secret criminal organization founded in Sicily, and carried to the US by Italian immigrants. **2** any group considered to resemble the Mafia. [C19: from Sicilian dialect of It., lit.: hostility to the law, ?from Ar. *mahyah* bragging]

Mafikeng ★ ('mæfɪˌkɛŋ) *n* a town in N South Africa: besieged by the Boers for 217 days (1899–1900) during the second Boer War: administrative headquarters of the British protectorate of Bechuanaland until 1965, although outside its borders. Pop.: 7000 (latest est.). Former name (until 1980): **Mafeking**.

mafioso (ˌmæfɪ'əʊsəʊ) *n, pl* **mafiosos** *or* **mafiosi** (-sɪ). a person belonging to the Mafia.

mag. *abbrev. for:* **1** magazine. **2** magnesium. **3** magnetic. **4** magnetism. **5** magnitude.

magainin (mə'geɪnɪn) *n* any of a series of related substances with antibiotic properties, derived from the skins of frogs. [C20: from Heb. *magain* a shield]

Magallanes ★ (*Spanish* maya'ʎanes) *n* the former name of **Punta Arenas**.

magazine (ˌmægə'ziːn) *n* **1** a periodical paperback publication containing articles, fiction, photographs, etc. **2** a metal case holding several cartridges used in some firearms; it is removed and replaced when empty. **3** a building or compartment for storing weapons, explosives, military provisions, etc. **4** a stock of ammunition. **5** *Photog.* another name for **cartridge** (sense 3). **6** a rack for automatically feeding slides through a projector. **7** a TV or radio programme made up of a series of short nonfiction items. [C16: via F *magasin* from It. *magazzino*, from Ar. *makhāzin*, pl. of *makhzan* storehouse, from *khazana* to store away]

magdalen ('mægdəlɪn) *or* **magdalene** ('mægdəˌliːn) *n* **1** *Literary.* a reformed prostitute. **2** *Rare.* a reformatory for prostitutes. [from Mary MAGDALENE]

Magdalena ★ (ˌmægdə'leɪnə, -'liː-; *Spanish* mayða'lena) *n* a river in SW Colombia, rising on the E slopes of the Andes and flowing north to the Caribbean near Barranquilla. Length: 1540 km (956 miles).

Magdalena Bay ★ *n* an inlet of the Pacific on the coast of NW Mexico, in Lower California.

Magdalene ★ ('mægdəˌliːn, ˌmægdə'liːnɪ) *n* See **Mary Magdalene**.

Magdalenian (ˌmægdə'liːnɪən) *adj* **1** of or relating to the latest Palaeolithic culture in Europe, which ended about 10 000 years ago. ◆ *n* **2 the**. the Magdalenian culture. [C19: from F *magdalénien*, after *La Madeleine*, village in Dordogne, France, near which artefacts of the culture were found]

Magdeburg ★ ('mægdəˌbɜːg; *German* 'makdəburk) *n* an industrial city and port in central Germany, on the River Elbe, capital of Saxony-Anhalt: a leading member of the Hanseatic League, whose local laws, the **Magdeburg Laws**, were adopted by many European cities. Pop.: 265 379 (1995 est.).

Magellan[1] ★ (mə'gɛlən) *n* **Strait of.** a strait between the mainland of S South America and Tierra del Fuego, link-

---

★ people and places

ing the S Pacific with the S Atlantic. Length: 600 km (370 miles). Width: up to 32 km (20 miles).

Magellan[2] ★ (mə'gelən) n **Ferdinand**. Portuguese name *Fernão de Magalhães*. ?1480–1521, Portuguese navigator in the service of Spain. He discovered the Strait of Magellan (1520) and crossed the Pacific to the Philippines (1521), where he was killed by natives.

Magellanic cloud (ˌmædʒɪ'lænɪk) n either of two small irregular galaxies near the S celestial pole. Distances: 163 000 light years (Large Magellanic Cloud), 196 000 light years (Small Magellanic Cloud).

magenta (mə'dʒɛntə) n **1a** a deep purplish red. **1b** (*as adj*): *a magenta filter*. **2** another name for **fuchsin**. [C19: after *Magenta*, Italy, alluding to the blood shed in a battle there (1859)]

Maggiore ★ (ˌmædʒɪ'ɔːrɪ; *Italian* mad'dʒore) n **Lake**. a lake in N Italy and S Switzerland, in the S Lepontine Alps.

maggot ('mægət) n **1** the limbless larva of dipterous insects, esp. the housefly and blowfly. **2** *Rare.* a fancy or whim. [C14: from earlier *mathek*; rel. to ON *mathkr* worm, OE *matha*, OHG *mado* grub]

maggoty ('mægətɪ) adj **1** of, like, or ridden with maggots. **2** *Austral. sl.* angry.

Magherafelt ★ (ˌmæxərə'fɛlt) n a district of central Northern Ireland, on the NW shore of Lough Neagh: mainly agricultural. Administrative centre: Magherafelt. Pop.: 36 293 (1991). Area: 635 sq. km (245 sq. miles).

Maghreb or **Maghrib** ★ ('mʌɡrəb) n NW Africa, including Morocco, Algeria, Tunisia, and sometimes Libya. [from Ar., lit.: the West]
▸ '**Maghrebi** or '**Maghribi** adj, n

magi ('meɪdʒaɪ) pl n, sing **magus** ('meɪɡəs). **1** See **magus**. **2 the three Magi**. the wise men from the East who came to do homage to the infant Jesus (Matthew 2:1–12). [see MAGUS]
▸ **magian** ('meɪdʒɪən) adj

magic ('mædʒɪk) n **1** the art that, by use of spells, supposedly invokes supernatural powers to influence events; sorcery. **2** the practice of this art. **3** the practice of illusory tricks to entertain; conjuring. **4** any mysterious or extraordinary quality or power. **5 like magic.** very quickly. ◆ *adj also* **magical. 6** of or relating to magic. **7** possessing or considered to possess mysterious powers. **8** unaccountably enchanting. **9** *Inf.* wonderful; marvellous. ◆ *vb* **magics, magicking, magicked.** (*tr*) **10** to transform or produce by or as if by magic. **11** (foll. by *away*) to cause to disappear as if by magic. [C14: via OF *magique*, from Gk *magikē* witchcraft, from *magos* MAGUS]
▸ '**magically** adv

magic bullet n *Inf.* any therapeutic agent, esp. one in the early stages of development, reputed to be very effective in treating a condition, such as a malignant tumour, by specifically targeting the diseased tissue.

magic eye n a miniature cathode-ray tube in some radio receivers, on the screen of which a pattern is displayed to assist tuning. Also called: **electric eye**.

magician (mə'dʒɪʃən) n **1** another term for **conjuror**. **2** a person who practises magic. **3** a person with extraordinary skill, influence, etc.

magic lantern n an early type of slide projector.

magic mushroom n *Inf.* any of various types of fungi that contain a hallucinogenic substance.

magic realism or **magical realism** n a style of painting or writing that depicts images or scenes of surreal fantasy in a representational or realistic way.
▸ **magic realist** or **magical realist** n

magic square n a square array of rows of integers arranged so that the sum of the integers is the same when taken vertically, horizontally, or diagonally.

Maginot line ('mæʒɪˌnəʊ) n **1** a line of fortifications built by France to defend its border with Germany prior to World War II; it proved ineffective. **2** any line of defence in which blind confidence is placed. [after André *Maginot* (1877–1932), F minister of war when the fortifications were begun in 1929]

magisterial (ˌmædʒɪ'stɪərɪəl) adj **1** commanding; au-

thoritative. **2** domineering; dictatorial. **3** of or relating to a teacher or person of similar status. **4** of or relating to a magistrate. [C17: from LL *magisteriālis*, from *magister* master]
▸ ˌ**magis'terially** adv

magistracy ('mædʒɪstrəsɪ) or **magistrature** ('mædʒɪstrəˌtjʊə) n, pl **magistracies** or **magistratures**. **1** the office or function of a magistrate. **2** magistrates collectively. **3** the district under the jurisdiction of a magistrate.

magistral (mə'dʒɪstrəl) adj **1** *Pharmacol.* made up according to a special prescription. **2** of a master; masterly. [C16: from L *magistrālis*, from *magister* master]
▸ **magistrality** (ˌmædʒɪ'strælɪtɪ) n

magistrate ('mædʒɪˌstreɪt, -strɪt) n **1** a public officer concerned with the administration of law. **2** another name for **justice of the peace**. [C17: from L *magistrātus*, from *magister* master]
▸ '**magis,trateship** n

magistrates' court n (in England) a court held before two or more justices of the peace or a stipendiary magistrate to deal with minor crimes, certain civil actions, and preliminary hearings.

Maglemosian or **Maglemosean** (ˌmæglə'məʊzɪən) n **1** the first Mesolithic culture of N Europe, dating from 8000 B.C. to about 5000 B.C. ◆ *adj* **2** designating or relating to this culture. [C20: after the site at *Maglemose*, Denmark, where the culture was first classified]

magma ('mægmə) n, pl **magmas** or **magmata** (-mətə). **1** a paste or suspension consisting of a finely divided solid dispersed in a liquid. **2** hot molten rock within the earth's crust which sometimes finds its way to the surface where it solidifies to form igneous rock. [C15: from L: dregs (of an ointment), from Gk: salve made by kneading, from *massein* to knead]
▸ **magmatic** (mæg'mætɪk) adj

Magna Carta or **Magna Charta** ('mægnə 'kɑːtə) n *English history*. the charter granted by King John at Runnymede in 1215, recognizing the rights and privileges of the barons, church, and freemen. [Med. L: great charter]

Magna Graecia ★ ('mægnə 'griːʃɪə) n (in the ancient world) S Italy, where numerous colonies were founded by Greek cities. [L: Great Greece]

magnanimity (ˌmægnə'nɪmɪtɪ) n, pl **magnanimities**. generosity. [C14: via OF from L *magnanimitās*, from *magnus* great + *animus* soul]

magnanimous (mæg'nænɪməs) adj generous and noble. [C16: from L *magnanimus* great-souled]
▸ **mag'nanimously** adv

magnate ('mægneɪt, -nɪt) n **1** a person of power and rank, esp. in industry. **2** *History.* a great nobleman. [C15: back formation from earlier *magnates*, from LL: great men, from L *magnus* great]
▸ '**magnate,ship** n

magnesia (mæg'niːʃə) n another name for **magnesium oxide**. [C14: via Med. L from Gk *Magnēsia*, of *Magnēs*, ancient mineral-rich region]
▸ **mag'nesian** or **magnesic** (mæg'niːsɪk) adj

magnesium (mæg'niːzɪəm) n a light silvery-white metallic element of the alkaline earth series that burns with an intense white flame: used in light structural alloys, flashbulbs, flares, and fireworks. Symbol: Mg; atomic no.: 12; atomic wt.: 24.305. [C19: NL, from MAGNESIA]

magnesium oxide n a white tasteless substance used as an antacid and laxative and in refractory materials. Formula: MgO. Also called: **magnesia**.

magnet ('mægnɪt) n **1** a body that can attract certain substances, such as iron or steel, as a result of a magnetic field; a piece of ferromagnetic substance. See also **electromagnet**. **2** a person or thing that exerts a great attraction. [C15: via L from Gk *magnēs*, shortened from *ho Magnēs lithos* the Magnesian stone. See MAGNESIA]

magnetic (mæg'nɛtɪk) adj **1** of, producing, or operated by means of magnetism. **2** of or concerned with a magnet. **3** of or concerned with the magnetism of the earth: *the magnetic equator*. **4** capable of being magnetized. **5** exerting a powerful attraction: *a magnetic personality*.
▸ **mag'netically** adv

magnetic constant *n* the magnetic permeability of free space; it has the value $4\pi \times 10^{-7}$ H m^{-1}.

magnetic declination *n* the angle that a compass needle makes with the direction of the geographical north pole at any given point on the earth's surface.

magnetic dip *or* **inclination** *n* another name for **dip** (sense 24).

magnetic dipole moment *n* a measure of the magnetic strength of a magnet or current-carrying coil, expressed as the torque produced when the magnet or coil is set with its axis perpendicular to unit magnetic field.

magnetic disk *n* another name for **disk** (sense 2).

magnetic equator *n* an imaginary line on the earth's surface, near the equator, at all points on which there is no magnetic dip.

magnetic field *n* a field of force surrounding a permanent magnet or a moving charged particle, in which another permanent magnet or moving charge experiences a force.

magnetic flux *n* a measure of the strength of a magnetic field over a given area, equal to the product of the area and the magnetic flux density through it. Symbol: ϕ

magnetic mine *n* a mine designed to explode when a magnetic field such as that generated by the metal of a ship's hull is detected.

magnetic needle *n* a slender magnetized rod used in certain instruments, such as the magnetic compass, for indicating the direction of a magnetic field.

magnetic north *n* the direction in which a compass needle points, at an angle (the declination) from the direction of true (geographic) north.

magnetic pick-up *n* a type of record-player pick-up in which the stylus moves an iron core in a coil, causing a changing magnetic field that produces the current.

magnetic pole *n* **1** either of two regions in a magnet where the magnetic induction is concentrated. **2** either of two variable points on the earth's surface towards which a magnetic needle points, where the lines of force of the earth's magnetic field are vertical.

magnetic resonance *n* the response by atoms, molecules, or nuclei subjected to a magnetic field to radio waves or other forms of energy: used in medicine for scanning (**magnetic resonance imaging**; abbrev.: **MRI**).

magnetic storm *n* a sudden severe disturbance of the earth's magnetic field, caused by emission of charged particles from the sun.

magnetic stripe *n* (across the back of various types of bank card, credit card, etc.) a dark stripe of magnetic material consisting of several tracks onto which information may be coded and which may be read or written to electronically.

magnetic tape *n* a long narrow plastic or metal strip coated or impregnated with iron oxide, chrome dioxide, etc., used to record sound or video signals or to store information in computing.

magnetism ('mægnɪˌtɪzəm) *n* **1** the property of attraction displayed by magnets. **2** any of a class of phenomena in which a field of force is caused by a moving electric charge. **3** the branch of physics concerned with magnetic phenomena. **4** powerful attraction.

magnetite ('mægnɪˌtaɪt) *n* a black magnetizable mineral that is an important source of iron.

magnetize *or* **magnetise** ('mægnɪˌtaɪz) *vb* **magnetizes, magnetizing, magnetized** *or* **magnetises, magnetising, magnetised.** (*tr*) **1** to make (a substance or object) magnetic. **2** to attract strongly. ▸ **'magnet,izable** *or* **'magnet,isable** *adj* ▸ **,magneti'zation** *or* **,magneti'sation** *n* ▸ **'magnet,izer** *or* **'magnet,iser** *n*

magneto (mæg'ni:təʊ) *n, pl* **magnetos.** a small electric generator in which the magnetic field is produced by a permanent magnet, esp. one for providing the spark in an internal-combustion engine. [C19: short for *magnetoelectric generator*]

magneto- *combining form.* indicating magnetism or magnetic properties: *magnetosphere*.

magnetoelectricity (mægˌni:təʊɪlɛk'trɪsɪtɪ) *n* electricity produced by the action of magnetic fields. ▸ **mag,netoe'lectric** *or* **mag,netoe'lectrical** *adj*

magnetometer (ˌmægnɪ'tɒmɪtə) *n* any instrument for measuring the intensity or direction of a magnetic field, esp. the earth's field. ▸ **ˌmagne'tometry** *n*

magnetomotive (mægˌni:təʊ'məʊtɪv) *adj* causing a magnetic flux.

magnetosphere (mæg'ni:təʊˌsfɪə) *n* the region surrounding a planet, such as the earth, in which the behaviour of charged particles is controlled by the planet's magnetic field.

magnetron ('mægnɪˌtrɒn) *n* a two-electrode electronic valve used with an applied magnetic field to generate high-power microwave oscillations, esp. for use in radar. [C20: from MAGNET + ELECTRON]

magnet school *n* a school that provides a focus on one subject area throughout its curriculum in order to attract, often from an early age, pupils who wish to specialize in this subject.

Magnificat (mæg'nɪfɪˌkæt) *n Christianity.* the hymn of the Virgin Mary (Luke 1:46-55), used as a canticle. [from the opening phrase, *Magnificat anima mea Dominum* (my soul doth magnify the Lord)]

magnification (ˌmægnɪfɪ'keɪʃən) *n* **1** the act of magnifying or the state of being magnified. **2** the degree to which something is magnified. **3** a magnified copy, photograph, drawing, etc., of something. **4** a measure of the ability of a lens or other optical instrument to magnify.

magnificence (mæg'nɪfɪsəns) *n* the quality of being magnificent. [C14: via F from L *magnificentia*]

magnificent (mæg'nɪfɪsˁnt) *adj* **1** splendid or impressive in appearance. **2** superb or very fine. **3** (esp. of ideas) noble or elevated. [C16: from L *magnificentior*, irregular comp. of *magnificus* great in deeds, from *magnus* great + *facere* to do] ▸ **mag'nificently** *adv*

magnifico (mæg'nɪfɪˌkəʊ) *n, pl* **magnificoes.** a magnate; grandee. [C16: It. from L *magnificus*; see MAGNIFICENT]

magnify ('mægnɪˌfaɪ) *vb* **magnifies, magnifying, magnified. 1** to increase, cause to increase, or be increased in apparent size, as through the action of a lens, microscope, etc. **2** to exaggerate or become exaggerated in importance: *don't magnify your troubles.* **3** (*tr*) *Arch.* to glorify. [C14: via OF from L *magnificāre* to praise] ▸ **'magni,fiable** *adj*

magnifying glass *or* **magnifier** *n* a convex lens used to produce an enlarged image of an object.

magniloquent (mæg'nɪləkwənt) *adj* (of speech) lofty in style; grandiloquent. [C17: from L *magnus* great + *loquī* to speak] ▸ **mag'niloquence** *n* ▸ **mag'niloquently** *adv*

Magnitogorsk ★ (*Russian* məgnɪtə'gɔrsk) *n* a city in central Russia, on the Ural River: founded in 1930 to exploit local magnetite ores; site of one of the world's largest (but outdated) metallurgical plants. Pop.: 427 000 (1995 est.).

magnitude ('mægnɪˌtju:d) *n* **1** relative importance or significance: *a problem of the first magnitude.* **2** relative size or extent. **3** *Maths.* a number assigned to a quantity as a basis of comparison for the measurement of similar quantities. **4** Also called: **apparent magnitude.** *Astron.* the apparent brightness of a celestial body expressed on a numerical scale on which bright stars have a low value. **5** Also called: **earthquake magnitude.** *Geol.* a measure of the size of an earthquake based on the quantity of energy released. [C14: from L *magnitūdō* size, from *magnus* great]

magnolia (mæg'nəʊlɪə) *n* **1** any tree or shrub of the genus *Magnolia* of Asia and North America: cultivated for their white, pink, purple, or yellow showy flowers. **2** the flower of any of these plants. **3a** a very pale pinkishwhite colour. **3b** (*as adj*): *magnolia walls.* [C18: NL, after Pierre *Magnol* (1638–1715), F botanist]

magnox ('mægnɒks) *n* an alloy consisting mostly of magnesium with small amounts of aluminium, used in fuel elements of nuclear reactors. [C20: from *mag(nesium) n(o) ox(idation)*]

magnox reactor *n* a nuclear reactor using carbon dioxide as the coolant, graphite as the moderator, and uranium cased in magnox as the fuel.

magnum ('mægnəm) *n, pl* **magnums.** a wine bottle holding the equivalent of two normal bottles (approximately 52 fluid ounces). [C18: from L: a big thing, from *magnus* large]

magnum opus *n* a great work of art or literature, esp. the greatest single work of an artist. [L]

Magog ★ ('meɪgɒg) *n* See **Gog and Magog.**

magpie ('mægˌpaɪ) *n* **1** any of various birds having a black-and-white plumage, long tail, and a chattering call. **2** any of various similar birds of Australia. **3** *Brit.* a person who hoards small objects. **4** a person who chatters. **5a** the outermost ring but one on a target. **5b** a shot that hits this ring. [C17: from *Mag*, dim. of *Margaret*, used to signify a chatterbox + PIE²]

Magritte ★ (*French* magrit) *n* René (rəne). 1898–1967, Belgian surrealist painter.

maguey ('mægweɪ) *n* **1** any of various tropical American agave plants, esp. one that yields a fibre or is used in making an alcoholic beverage. **2** the fibre from any of these plants, used esp. for rope. [C16: Sp., of Amerind origin]

magus ('meɪgəs) *n, pl* **magi. 1** a Zoroastrian priest. **2** an astrologer, sorcerer, or magician of ancient times. [C14: from L, from Gk *magos*, from OPersian *magus* magician]

Magus ★ ('meɪgəs) *n* **Simon.** *New Testament.* a sorcerer who tried to buy spiritual powers from the apostles (Acts 8:9-24).

Magyar ('mægjɑː) *n* **1** (*pl* **Magyars**) a member of the predominant ethnic group of Hungary. **2** the Hungarian language. ◆ *adj* **3** of or relating to the Magyars or their language. **4** *Sewing.* of or relating to a style of sleeve cut in one piece with the bodice.

Magyarország ★ ('mɒdjɔrorsɑːg) *n* the Hungarian name for **Hungary.**

Mahabharata (ˌmɑːhəˈbɑːrətə), **Mahabharatam,** *or* **Mahabharatum** (ˌmɑːhəˈbɑːrətəm) *n* an epic Sanskrit poem of India of which the *Bhagavad-Gita* forms a part. [Sansk., from *mahā* great + *bhārata* story]

Mahajanga ★ (ˌmæhəˈdʒæŋgə) *n* a port in NW Madagascar, on Bombetoka Bay. Pop.: 100 807 (1993). Former name: **Majunga.**

Mahalla el Kubra ★ (məˈhɑːlə ɛl ˈkuːbrə) *n* a city in N Egypt, on the Nile delta: one of the largest diversified textile centres in Egypt. Pop.: 408 000 (1992 est.).

Mahanadi ★ (məˈhɑːnədɪ) *n* a river in E India, rising in S Madhya Pradesh and flowing north, then south and east to the Bay of Bengal. Length: 885 km (550 miles).

maharajah *or* **maharaja** (ˌmɑːhəˈrɑːdʒə) *n* any of various Indian princes, esp. any of the rulers of the former native states. [C17: Hindi, from *mahā* great + RAJAH]

maharani *or* **maharanee** (ˌmɑːhəˈrɑːniː) *n* **1** the wife of a maharajah. **2** a woman holding the rank of maharajah. [C19: from Hindi, from *mahā* great + RANI]

Maharashtra ★ (ˌmɑːhəˈræʃtrə) *n* a state of W central India, formed in 1960 from the Marathi-speaking S and E parts of former Bombay state: lies mainly on the Deccan plateau; mainly agricultural. Capital: Bombay. Pop.: 85 565 000 (1994 est.). Area: 307 690 sq. km (118 800 sq. miles).

maharishi (ˌmɑːhəˈriːʃɪ, məˈhɑːriːʃɪ) *n Hinduism.* a Hindu teacher of religious and mystical knowledge. [from Hindi, from *mahā* great + *rishi* sage]

mahatma (məˈhɑːtmə) *n* (*sometimes cap.*) **1** *Hinduism.* a Brahman sage. **2** *Theosophy.* an adept or sage. [C19: from Sansk. *mahātman*, from *mahā* great + *ātman* soul]

Mahayana (ˌmɑːhəˈjɑːnə) *n* **a** a liberal Buddhist school of Tibet, China, and Japan, whose adherents seek enlightenment for all sentient beings. **b** (*as modifier*): *Mahayana Buddhism.* [from Sansk., from *mahā* great + *yāna* vehicle]

Mahdi ★ ('mɑːdɪ) *n* **1** the title assumed by *Mohammed*

Ahmed. ?1843–85, Sudanese military leader, who led a revolt against Egypt (1881) and captured Khartoum (1885). **2** *Islam.* any of a number of Muslim messiahs expected to forcibly convert all mankind to Islam. [Ar. *mahdīy* one who is guided, from *madā* to guide aright]
▸ '**Mahdism** *n* ▸ '**Mahdist** *n, adj*

Mahé ★ (mɑːˈheɪ) *n* an island in the Indian Ocean, the chief island of the Seychelles. Capital: Victoria. Pop.: 59 500 (1987). Area: 147 sq. km (57 sq. miles).

Mahfouz *or* **Mahfuz** ★ (mɑːˈfuːz) *n* Naguib (nɑːˈgiːb). born 1911, Egyptian writer, known for his novels, including *The Cairo Trilogy* (1956–57) and *Children of Gebelawi* (1959). Nobel prize for literature 1988.

mah jong *or* **mah-jongg** (ˌmɑːˈdʒɒŋ) *n* a game of Chinese origin, usually played by four people, using tiles bearing various designs. [from Chinese, lit.: sparrows]

Mahler ★ ('mɑːlə) *n* **Gustav** ('gustaf). 1860–1911, Austrian composer and conductor. His works include nine symphonies, the symphonic song cycle *Das Lied von der Erde* (1908), and the song cycle *Kindertotenlieder* (1902).

mahlstick ('mɔːlˌstɪk) *n* a variant spelling of **maulstick.**

mahogany (məˈhɒgənɪ) *n, pl* **mahoganies. 1** any of various tropical American trees valued for their hard reddish-brown wood. **2** any of several trees with similar wood, such as African mahogany and Philippine mahogany. **3a** the wood of any of these trees. **3b** (*as modifier*): *a mahogany table.* **4a** a reddish-brown colour. **4b** (*as adj*): *mahogany skin.* [C17: from ?]

Mahomet ★ (məˈhɒmɪt) *n* a variant of **Mohammed.**

Mahometan (məˈhɒmɪt°n) *n, adj* a former word for **Muslim.**

mahonia (məˈhəʊnɪə) *n* any evergreen shrub of the Asian and American genus *Mahonia:* cultivated for their ornamental spiny divided leaves and clusters of small yellow flowers. [C19: NL, after Bernard *McMahon* (died 1816), American botanist]

Mahound ★ (məˈhaʊnd, -ˈhuːnd) *n* an archaic name for **Mohammed.** [C16: from OF *Mahun*]

mahout (məˈhaʊt) *n* (in India and the East Indies) an elephant driver or keeper. [C17: Hindi *mahāut*, from Sansk. *mahāmātra* of great measure, orig. a title]

Mähren ★ ('mɛːrən) *n* the German name for **Moravia**[1].

mahseer ★ ('mɑːsɪə) *n* any of various large freshwater Indian cyprinid fishes. [from Hindi]

Maia ★ ('maɪə) *n Greek myth.* the eldest of the seven Pleiades, mother by Zeus of Hermes.

maid (meɪd) *n* **1** *Arch. or literary.* a young unmarried girl; maiden. **2a** a female servant. **2b** (*in combination*): *a housemaid.* **3** a spinster. [C12: form of MAIDEN]

maiden ('meɪd°n) *n* **1** *Arch. or literary.* **1a** a young unmarried girl, esp. a virgin. **1b** (*as modifier*): *a maiden blush.* **2** *Horse racing.* **2a** a horse that has never won a race. **2b** (*as modifier*) of or relating to an older unmarried woman: *a maiden aunt.* **5** (*modifier*) of or involving an initial experience or attempt: *a maiden voyage.* **6** (*modifier*) (of a person or thing) untried; unused. **7** (*modifier*) (of a place) never trodden, penetrated, or captured. [OE *mægden*]
▸ '**maidenish** *adj* ▸ '**maiden**ˌ**like** *adj*

maidenhair fern *or* **maidenhair** ('meɪd°nˌhɛə) *n* any of various ferns of tropical and warm regions, having delicate fan-shaped fronds with small pale green leaflets. [C15: from the hairlike appearance of its fronds]

maidenhair tree *n* another name for **ginkgo.**

maidenhead ('meɪd°nˌhɛd) *n* **1** a nontechnical word for the **hymen.** **2** virginity; maidenhood. [C13: from *maiden* + *-hed*, var. of -HOOD]

Maidenhead ★ ('meɪd°nˌhɛd) *n* a town in S England, in Berkshire on the River Thames. Pop.: 59 605 (1991).

maidenhood ('meɪd°nˌhʊd) *n* **1** the time during which a woman is a maiden or virgin. **2** the condition of being a maiden or virgin.

maidenly ('meɪd°nlɪ) *adj* of or befitting a maiden.
▸ '**maidenliness** *n*

maiden name *n* a woman's surname before marriage.

★ people and places

maiden over n Cricket. an over in which no runs are scored.

maid of honour n 1 US & Canad. the principal unmarried attendant of a bride. 2 Brit. a small tart with an almond-flavoured filling. 3 an unmarried lady attending a queen or princess.

Maid of Orléans ★ n the. another name for **Joan of Arc**.

maidservant ('meɪd,sɜːvənt) n a female servant.

Maidstone ★ ('meɪdstən, -,stəʊn) n a town in SE England, administrative centre of Kent, on the River Medway. Pop.: 90 878 (1991).

Maiduguri ★ (,maɪdʊ'gʊːrɪ) n a city in NE Nigeria, capital of Bornu State; agricultural trade centre. Pop.: 312 100 (1995 est.). Also called: **Yerwa-Maiduguri.**

maihem ('meɪhɛm) n a variant spelling of **mayhem.**

Maikop ★ (Russian maj'kɔp) n a city in SW Russia, capital of the Adygei Republic: extensive oilfields to the southwest; mineral springs. Pop.: 165 000 (1995 est.).

mail¹ (meɪl) n 1 Also called (esp. Brit.): **post.** letters, packages, etc., that are transported and delivered by the post office. 2 the postal system. 3 a single collection or delivery of mail. 4 a train, ship, or aircraft that carries mail. 5 short for **electronic mail. 6** (modifier) of, involving, or used to convey mail: a mail train. ◆ vb (tr) 7 Chiefly US & Canad. to send by mail. 8 to contact (a person) by electronic mail. 9 to send (a message, document, etc.) by electronic mail. [C13: from OF male bag, prob. from OHG malha wallet]
▶ 'mailable adj

mail² (meɪl) n 1 a type of flexible armour consisting of riveted metal rings or links. 2 the hard protective shell of such animals as the turtle and lobster. ◆ vb 3 (tr) to clothe or arm with mail. [C14: from OF maille mesh, from L macula spot]

mailbag ('meɪl,bæg) or **mailsack** n a large bag for transporting or delivering mail.

mailbox ('meɪl,bɒks) n another name (esp. US and Canad.) for **letter box.**

Mailer ★ ('meɪlə) n **Norman.** born 1923, US author. His works include the war novel The Naked and the Dead (1948), The Armies of the Night (1968), and Harlot's Ghost (1991).

mailing list n a register of names and addresses to which advertising matter, etc., is sent by post or electronic mail.

Maillol ★ (French majɔl) n **Aristide** (aristid). 1861–1944, French sculptor.

maillot (mæ'jəʊ) n 1 tights worn for ballet, gymnastics, etc. 2 a woman's swimsuit. 3 a jersey. [from F]

mailman ('meɪl,mæn) n, pl **mailmen.** Chiefly US & Canad. another name for **postman.**

mail merging n Computing. a software facility that can produce a large number of personalized letters by combining a file containing a list of names and addresses with one containing a single standard document.

mail order n 1 an order for merchandise sent by post. 2a a system of buying and selling merchandise through the post. 2b (as modifier): a mail-order firm.

mailshot ('meɪl,ʃɒt) n a circular, leaflet, or other advertising material sent by post, or the posting of such material to a large group of people at one time.

maim (meɪm) vb (tr) 1 to mutilate, cripple, or disable a part of the body of (a person or animal). 2 to make defective. [C14: from OF mahaignier to wound, prob. of Gmc origin]

mai mai (maɪ maɪ) n NZ. a duck shooter's shelter; hide. [probably from Australian Aboriginal mia-mia shelter]

Maimonides ★ (maɪ'mɒnɪ,diːz) n also called Rabbi Moses ben Maimon. 1135–1204, Jewish philosopher and jurist, born in Spain. He codified Jewish law in Mishneh Torah (1180).
▶ Mai,moni'dean adj, n

main¹ (meɪn) adj (prenominal) 1 chief or principal. 2 sheer or utmost (esp. in by main force). 3 Naut. of, relating to, or denoting any gear, such as a stay or sail, belonging to the mainmast. ◆ n 4 a principal pipe, conduit, duct, or line in a system used to distribute water, electricity, etc. 5 (pl) 5a the main distribution network for water, gas, or electricity. 5b (as modifier): mains voltage. 6 the chief or most important part or consideration. 7 great strength or force (now esp. in might and main). 8 Literary. the open ocean. 9 Arch. short for **Spanish Main. 10** Arch. short for **mainland. 11** in (or for) the main. on the whole; for the most part. [C13: from OE mægen strength]

main² (meɪn) n 1 a throw of the dice in dice games. 2 a cockfighting contest. 3 a match in archery, boxing, etc. [C16: from ?]

Main ★ (meɪn; German main) n a river in central and W Germany, flowing west through Würzburg and Frankfurt to the Rhine. Length: about 515 km (320 miles).

mainbrace ('meɪn,breɪs) n Naut. 1 a brace attached to the main yard. 2 splice the mainbrace. See **splice.**

main clause n Grammar. a clause that can stand alone as a sentence.

Maine ★ (meɪn) n a state of the northeastern US, on the Atlantic: chiefly hilly, with many lakes, rivers, and forests. Capital: Augusta. Pop.: 1 243 316 (1996 est.). Area: 86 156 sq. km (33 265 sq. miles). Abbrev. (with zip code): **ME**

Maine-et-Loire ★ (French mɛnelwar) n a department of W France, in Pays de la Loire region. Capital: Angers. Pop.: 719 172 (1994 est.). Area: 7218 sq. km (2815 sq. miles).

mainframe ('meɪn,freɪm) Computing. ◆ adj 1 denoting a high-speed general-purpose computer, usually with a large store capacity. ◆ n 2 such a computer. 3 the central processing unit of a computer.

mainland ('meɪnlənd) n the main part of a landmass as opposed to an island or peninsula.
▶ 'mainlander n

Mainland ★ ('meɪnlənd) n 1 an island off N Scotland: the largest of the Shetland Islands. Chief town: Lerwick. Pop.: 17 596 (1991). Area: about 583 sq. km (225 sq. miles). 2 Also called: **Pomona.** an island off N Scotland: the largest of the Orkney Islands. Chief town: Kirkwall. Pop.: 15 128 (1991). Area: 492 sq. km (190 sq. miles). 3 the Mainland. NZ. a South Islanders' name for the **South Island.**

main line n 1 Railways. 1a the trunk route between two points, usually fed by branch lines. 1b (as modifier): a main-line station. 2 US. a main road. ◆ vb mainline, mainlines, mainlining, mainlined. 3 (intr) Sl. to inject a drug into a vein. ◆ adj mainline. 4 having an important position.
▶ 'main,liner n

mainly ('meɪnlɪ) adv for the most part; to the greatest extent; principally.

main market n the market for trading in the listed securities of companies on the London stock exchange. Cf. **Third Market, Unlisted Securities Market.**

mainmast ('meɪn,mɑːst) n Naut. the chief mast of a sailing vessel with two or more masts.

mainsail ('meɪn,seɪl; Naut. 'meɪnsˀl) n Naut. the largest and lowermost sail on the mainmast.

mainsheet ('meɪn,ʃiːt) n Naut. the line used to control the angle of the mainsail to the wind.

mainspring ('meɪn,sprɪŋ) n 1 the principal spring of a mechanism, esp. in a watch or clock. 2 the chief cause or motive of something.

mainstay ('meɪn,steɪ) n 1 Naut. the forestay that braces the mainmast. 2 a chief support.

mainstream ('meɪn,striːm) n 1 the main current (of a river, cultural trend, etc.). ◆ adj 2 of or relating to the style of jazz that lies between the traditional and the modern.

mainstream corporation tax n (in Britain) the balance of the corporation tax paid by a company for an accounting period after the advance corporation tax has been deducted.

mainstreeting ('meɪn,striːtɪŋ) n Canad. the practice of a politician walking about the streets of a town or city to gain votes and greet supporters.

maintain (meɪn'teɪn) vb (tr) 1 to continue or retain; keep

★ people and places

in existence. **2** to keep in proper or good condition. **3** to enable (a person) to support a style of living: *the money maintained us for a month.* **4** (*takes a clause as object*) to state or assert. **5** to defend against contradiction; uphold: *she maintained her innocence.* **6** to defend against physical attack. [C13: from OF *maintenir*, ult. from L *manū tenēre* to hold in the hand]
➤ **main'tainable** *adj* ➤ **main'tainer** *n*

maintenance ('meɪntɪnəns) *n* **1** the act of maintaining or the state of being maintained. **2** a means of support; livelihood. **3** (*modifier*) of or relating to the maintaining of buildings, machinery, etc.: *maintenance man.* **4** *Law.* the interference in a legal action by a person having no interest in it, as by providing funds to continue the action. **5** *Law.* a provision ordered to be made by way of periodic payments or a lump sum, as for a spouse after a divorce. [C14: from OF; see MAINTAIN]

Maintenon ★ (*French* mɛ̃tnɔ̃) *n* **Marquise de,** title of *Françoise d'Aubigné.* 1635–1719, the mistress and, from about 1685, second wife of Louis XIV.

maintop ('meɪn,tɒp) *n* a top or platform at the head of the mainmast.

main-topmast *n Naut.* the mast immediately above the mainmast.

maintopsail (,meɪn'tɒpseɪl; *Naut.* ,meɪn'tɒps²l) *n Naut.* a topsail on the mainmast.

main yard *n Naut.* a yard for a square mainsail.

Mainz ★ (*German* maints) *n* a port in W Germany, capital of the Rhineland-Palatinate, at the confluence of the Main and Rhine: an archbishopric from about 780 until 1801; important in the 15th century for the development of printing (by Johann Gutenberg). Pop.: 184 627 (1995 est.). French name: **Mayence.**

maiolica (mə'jɒlɪkə) *n* a variant of **majolica.**

maisonette *or* **maisonnette** (,meɪzə'nɛt) *n* self-contained living accommodation often occupying two floors of a larger house and having its own outside entrance. [C19: from F, dim. of *maison* house]

mai tai ('maɪ ,taɪ) *n* a mixed drink consisting of rum, Curaçao, fruit juice, and grenadine. [C20: from ?]

Maitland[1] ★ ('meɪtlənd) *n* a town in SE Australia, in E New South Wales: industrial centre of an agricultural region. Pop.: 38 863 (1981).

Maitland[2] ★ ('meɪtlənd) *n* **Frederic William.** 1850–1906, British legal historian.

maître d'hôtel (,mɛtrə dəʊ'tɛl) *n, pl* **maîtres d'hôtel. 1** a head waiter or steward. **2** the manager or owner of a hotel. [C16: from F: master of (the) hotel]

maize (meɪz) *n* **1** Also called: **sweet corn, Indian corn. 1a** a tall annual grass cultivated for its yellow edible grains, which develop on a spike. **1b** the grain of this plant, used for food, for fodder, and as a source of oil. **2a** a yellow colour. **2b** (*as adj*): *a maize gown.* [C16: from Sp. *maiz,* from Taino *mahiz*]

Maj. *abbrev. for* Major.

majestic (mə'dʒɛstɪk) *adj* having or displaying majesty or great dignity; grand; lofty.
➤ **ma'jestically** *adv*

majesty ('mædʒɪstɪ) *n* **1** great dignity of bearing; loftiness; grandeur. **2** supreme power or authority. [C13: from OF, from L *mājestās*; rel. to L *major,* comp. of *magnus* great]

Majesty ('mædʒɪstɪ) *n, pl* **Majesties.** (preceded by *Your, His, Her,* or *Their*) a title used to address or refer to a sovereign or the wife or widow of a sovereign.

majolica (mə'dʒɒlɪkə, mə'jɒl-) *or* **maiolica** *n* a type of porous pottery glazed with bright metallic oxides. It was originally imported into Italy via Majorca and was extensively made in Renaissance Italy. [C16: from It., from LL *Mājorica* Majorca]

major ('meɪdʒə) *n* **1** *Mil.* an officer immediately junior to a lieutenant colonel. **2** a person who is superior in a group or class. **3** (often preceded by *the*) *Music.* a major key, chord, mode, or scale. **4** *US, Canad., Austral., & NZ.* **4a** the principal field of study of a student. **4b** a student who is studying a particular subject as his principal field: *a sociology major.* **5** a person who has reached the age of

legal majority. **6** a principal or important record company, film company, etc. **7** *Logic.* a major term or premise. ◆ *adj* **8** larger in extent, number, etc. **9** of greater importance or priority. **10** very serious or significant. **11** main, chief, or principal. **12** of, involving, or making up a majority. **13** *Music.* **13a** (of a scale or mode) having notes separated by a whole tone, except for the third and fourth degrees, and seventh and eighth degrees, which are separated by a semitone. **13b** relating to or employing notes from the major scale: *a major key.* **13c** (*postpositive*) denoting a specified key or scale as being major: *C major.* **13d** denoting a chord or triad having a major third above the root. **13e** (in jazz) denoting a major chord with a major seventh added above the root. **14** *Logic.* constituting the major term or major premise of a syllogism. **15** *Chiefly US, Canad., Austral., & NZ.* of or relating to a student's principal field of study at a university, etc. **16** *Brit.* the elder: used after a schoolboy's surname if he has one or more younger brothers in the same school: *Price major.* **17** of full legal age. ◆ *vb* **18** (*intr;* usually foll. by *in*) *US, Canad., Austral., & NZ.* to do one's principal study (in a particular subject): *to major in English literature.* **19** (*intr;* usually foll. by *on*) to take or deal with as the main area of interest: *the book majors on peasant dishes.* [C15 (adj): from L, comp. of *magnus* great; C17 (n, in military sense): from F, short for SERGEANT MAJOR]
➤ **'majorship** *n*

Major ★ ('meɪdʒə) *n* **John.** born 1943, British Conservative politician: Chancellor of the Exchequer (1989–90); prime minister (1990–97).

Majorca ★ (mə'jɔ:kə, -'dʒɔ:-) *n* an island in the W Mediterranean: the largest of the Balearic Islands; tourism. Capital: Palma. Pop.: 605 512 (1987 est.). Area: 3639 sq. km (1465 sq. miles). Spanish name: **Mallorca.**

major-domo (-'dəʊməʊ) *n, pl* **major-domos. 1** the chief steward or butler of a great household. **2** *Facetious.* a steward or butler. [C16: from Sp. *mayordomo,* from Med. L *mājor domūs* head of the household]

majorette (,meɪdʒə'rɛt) *n* **1** one of a group of girls who practise formation marching and baton twirling. **2** See **drum majorette.**

major general *n Mil.* an officer immediately junior to a lieutenant general.
➤ ,**major-'generalship** *or* **major-'generalcy** *n*

majority (mə'dʒɒrɪtɪ) *n, pl* **majorities. 1** the greater number or part of something. **2** (in an election) the number of votes or seats by which the strongest party or candidate beats the combined opposition or the runner-up. **3** the largest party or group that votes together in a legislative or deliberative assembly. **4** the time of reaching or state of having reached full legal age. **5** the rank, office, or commission of major. **6** *Euphemistic.* the dead (esp. in **join the majority, go** *or* **pass over to the majority**). **7** (*modifier*) of, involving, or being a majority: *a majority decision.* **8** in the majority. forming or part of the greater number of something. [C16: from Med. L *mājoritās,* from MAJOR (adj)]

> **USAGE NOTE** *The majority of* can only refer to a number of things or people. When talking about an amount, *most of* should be used: *most of* (not *the majority of*) *the harvest was saved.*

major league *n US & Canad.* a league of highest classification in baseball, football, hockey, etc.

majorly ('meɪdʒəlɪ) *adv Sl., chiefly US & Canad.* very; extremely: *it was majorly important for us to do that.*

major orders *pl n RC Church.* the three higher degrees of holy orders: bishop, priest, and deacon.

major premise *n Logic.* the premise of a syllogism containing the predicate of its conclusion.

major term *n Logic.* the predicate of the conclusion of a syllogism.

Majunga ★ (*French* maʒɶ̃ga) *n* the former name of **Mahajanga.**

majuscule ('mædʒə,skju:l) *n* **1** a large letter, either capi-

tal or uncial, used in printing or writing. ♦ *adj* **2** relating to, printed, or written in such letters. ♦ Cf. **minuscule**. [C18: via F from L *mājusculus*, dim. of *mājor* bigger]
▸ **majuscular** (mə'dʒʌskjʊlə) *adj*

Makalu ★ ('mʌkə,luː) *n* a massif in NE Nepal, on the border with Tibet in the Himalayas.

Makarios III ★ (mə'kɑːrɪˌɒs) *n* original name *Mikhail Christodoulou Mouskos*. 1913–77, Cypriot archbishop, patriarch, and statesman; first president of the republic of Cyprus (1960–74; 1974–77).

Makasar, Makassar, *or* **Macassar** ★ (mə'kæsə, -'kɑː-) *n* another name for **Ujung Pandang**.

make (meɪk) *vb* **makes, making, made.** (*mainly tr*) **1** to bring into being by shaping, changing, or combining materials, ideas, etc.; form or fashion. **2** to draw up, establish, or form: *to make one's will.* **3** to cause to exist, bring about, or produce: *don't make a noise.* **4** to cause, compel, or induce: *please make him go away.* **5** to appoint or assign: *they made him chairman.* **6** to constitute: *one swallow doesn't make a summer.* **7** (*also intr*) to come or cause to come into a specified state or condition: *to make merry.* **8** (*copula*) to be or become through development: *he will make a good teacher.* **9** to cause or ensure the success of: *your news has made my day.* **10** to amount to: *twelve inches make a foot.* **11** to serve as or be suitable for: *that piece of cloth will make a coat.* **12** to prepare or put into a fit condition for use: *to make a bed.* **13** to be the essential element in or part of: *charm makes a good salesman.* **14** to carry out, effect, or do. **15** (*intr*; foll. by *to, as if to,* or *as though to*) to act with the intention or with a show of doing something: *he made as if to hit her.* **16** to use for a specified purpose: *I will make this town my base.* **17** to deliver or pronounce: *to make a speech.* **18** to give information or an opinion: *what time do you make it?* **19** to cause to seem or represent as being. **20** to earn, acquire, or win for oneself: *to make friends.* **21** to engage in: *to make war.* **22** to traverse or cover (distance) by travelling: *we can make a hundred miles by nightfall.* **23** to arrive in time for: *he didn't make the first act of the play.* **24** *Cards.* **24a** to win a trick with (a specified card). **24b** to shuffle (the cards). **24c** *Bridge.* to fulfil (a contract) by winning the necessary number of tricks. **25** *Cricket.* to score (runs). **26** *Electronics.* to close (a circuit) permitting a flow of current. **27** (*intr*) to increase in depth: *the water in the hold was making a foot a minute.* **28** *Inf.* to gain a place or position on or in: *to make the headlines.* **29** *Inf., chiefly US.* to achieve the rank of. **30** *Taboo sl.* to seduce. **31 make a book.** to take bets on a race or another contest. **32 make a day, night,** etc., **of it.** to cause an activity to last a day, night, etc. **33 make do.** See **do**[1] (sense 32). **34 make eyes at.** to flirt with or ogle. **35 make it. 35a** *Inf.* to be successful in doing something. **35b** (foll. by *with*) *Taboo sl.* to have sexual intercourse. **36 make like.** *Sl., chiefly US & Canad.* **36a** to imitate. **36b** to pretend. ♦ *n* **37** brand, type, or style. **38** the manner or way in which something is made. **39** disposition or character; make-up. **40** the act or process of making. **41** the amount or number made. **42** *Cards.* a player's turn to shuffle. **43 on the make.** *Sl.* **43a** out for profit or conquest. **43b** in search of a sexual partner. ♦ See also **make away, make for,** etc. [OE *macian*]
▸ **'makable** *adj*

make away *vb* (*intr, adv*) **1** to depart in haste. **2 make away with. 2a** to steal or abduct. **2b** to kill, destroy, or get rid of.

make believe *vb* **makes believe, making believe, made believe. 1** to pretend or enact a fantasy. ♦ *n* **make-believe. 2a** a fantasy or pretence. **2b** (*as modifier*): *a make-believe world.*

Makedhonia ★ (ˌmakeðɔ'nia) *n* transliteration of the Modern Greek name for **Macedonia** (sense 1).

make for *vb* (*intr, prep*) **1** to head towards. **2** to prepare to attack. **3** to help bring about.

make of *vb* (*tr, prep*) **1** to interpret as the meaning of. **2** to produce or construct from: *houses made of brick.* **3 make little, much,** etc., **of. 3a** to gain little, much, etc., benefit from. **3b** to attribute little, much, etc., significance to.

make off *vb* **1** (*intr, adv*) to go or run away in haste. **2 make off with.** to steal or abduct.

make out *vb* (*adv*) **1** (*tr*) to discern or perceive. **2** (*tr*) to understand or comprehend. **3** (*tr*) to write out: *he made out a cheque.* **4** (*tr*) to attempt to establish or prove: *he*

made me out to be a liar. **5** (*intr*) to pretend: *he made out that he could cook.* **6** (*intr*) to manage or fare.

make over *vb* (*tr, adv*) **1** to transfer the title or possession of (property, etc.). **2** to renovate or remodel: *she made over the dress to fit her sister.* ♦ *n* **makeover. 3** a complete remodelling. **4** a series of alterations, including beauty treatments and new clothes, intended to make a significant improvement to a person's appearance.

maker ('meɪkə) *n* a person who executes a legal document, esp. one who signs a promissory note.

Maker ('meɪkə) *n* **1** a title given to God (as Creator). **2 (go to) meet one's Maker.** to die.

makeshift ('meɪkˌʃɪft) *adj* **1** serving as a temporary or expedient means. ♦ *n* **2** something serving in this capacity.

make-up *n* **1** cosmetics, such as powder, lipstick, etc., applied to the face. **2a** the cosmetics, false hair, etc., used by an actor to adapt his appearance. **2b** the art or result of applying such cosmetics. **3** the manner of arrangement of the parts or qualities of someone or something. **4** the arrangement of type matter and illustrations on a page or in a book. **5** mental or physical constitution. ♦ *vb* **make up.** (*adv*) **6** (*tr*) to form or constitute: *these arguments make up the case for the defence.* **7** (*tr*) to devise, construct, or compose, sometimes with the intent to deceive: *to make up an excuse.* **8** (*tr*) to supply what is lacking or deficient in; complete: *these extra people will make up our total.* **9** (*tr*) to put in order, arrange, or prepare: *to make up a bed.* **10** (*intr*; foll. by *for*) to compensate or atone (for). **11** to settle (differences) amicably (often in **make it up**). **12** to apply cosmetics to (the face) to enhance one's appearance or for a theatrical role. **13** to assemble (type and illustrations) into (columns or pages). **14** (*tr*) to surface (a road) with tarmac, concrete, etc. **15 make up to.** *Inf.* **15a** to make friendly overtures to. **15b** to flirt with.

makeweight ('meɪkˌweɪt) *n* **1** something put on a scale to make up a required weight. **2** an unimportant person or thing added to make up a lack.

Makeyevka ★ (*Russian* ma'kjejɪfkə) *n* a city in the SE Ukraine: coal-mining centre. Pop.: 409 000 (1996 est.).

Makhachkala ★ (*Russian* məxətʃka'la) *n* a port in SW Russia, capital of the Dagestan Republic, on the Caspian Sea: fishing fleet; oil refining. Pop.: 339 000 (1995 est.). Former name (until 1921): **Petrovsk.**

making ('meɪkɪŋ) *n* **1a** the act of a person or thing that makes or the process of being made. **1b** (*in combination*): *watchmaking.* **2 be the making of.** to cause the success of. **3 in the making.** in the process of becoming or being made. **4** something made or the quantity of something made at one time.

makings ('meɪkɪŋz) *pl n* **1** potentials, qualities, or materials: *he had the makings of a leader.* **2** Also called: **rollings.** *Sl.* the tobacco and cigarette paper used for rolling a cigarette. **3** profits; earnings.

Makkah *or* **Makah** ★ ('mækə, -kɑː) *n* transliteration of the Arabic name for **Mecca.**

mako[1] ('mɑːkəʊ) *n, pl* **makos.** a blue-pointer game shark. [from Maori]

mako[2] ('mɑːkəʊ) *n, pl* **makos.** a small evergreen New Zealand tree. [from Maori]

Makurdi ★ (mə'kɜːdɪ) *n* a port in E central Nigeria, capital of Benue State on the Benue River: agricultural trade centre. Pop.: 120 100 (1995 est.).

Mal. *abbrev. for:* **1** *Bible.* Malachi. **2** Malay(an).

mal- *combining form.* bad or badly; wrong or wrongly; imperfect or defective: *maladjusted; malfunction.* [OF, from L *malus* bad, *male* badly]

Malabar Coast *or* **Malabar** ★ ('mælə,bɑː) *n* a region along the SW coast of India, extending from Goa to Cape Comorin: includes most of Kerala state.

Malabo ★ (mə'lɑːbəʊ) *n* the capital and chief port of Equatorial Guinea, on the island of Bioko in the Gulf of Guinea. Pop.: 58 040 (1991 est.). Former name (until 1973): **Santa Isabel.**

malabsorption (mæləb'sɔːpʃən) *n* a failure of absorption, esp. by the small intestine in coeliac disease, cystic fibrosis, etc.

★ people and places

malacca or **malacca cane** (mə'lækə) n **1** the stem of the rattan palm. **2** a walking stick made from this stem.

Malacca ★ (mə'lækə) n a state of SW Peninsular Malaysia: rubber plantations. Capital: Malacca. Pop.: 583 400 (1993 est.). Area: 1650 sq. km (637 sq. miles).

Malachi ★ ('mælə,kaɪ) n Old Testament. **1** a Hebrew prophet of the 5th century B.C. **2** the book containing his oracles. Douay spelling: **Malachias** (,mælə'kaɪəs).

malachite ('mælə,kaɪt) n a green mineral consisting of hydrated basic copper carbonate: a source of copper, also used for making ornaments. [C16: via OF from L *molochītēs*, from Gk *molokhitis* mallow-green stone, from *molokhē* mallow]

maladjustment (,mælə'dʒʌstmənt) n **1** Psychol. a failure to meet the demands of society, such as coping with problems and social relationships. **2** faulty or bad adjustment.
▶ ,**malad'justed** adj

maladminister (,mæləd'mɪnɪstə) vb (tr) to administer badly, inefficiently, or dishonestly.
▶ ,**malad,minis'tration** n

maladroit (,mælə'drɔɪt) adj **1** clumsy; not dexterous. **2** tactless and insensitive. [C17: from F, from *mal* badly + ADROIT]
▶ ,**mala'droitly** adv ▶ ,**mala'droitness** n

malady ('mælədɪ) n, pl **maladies**. **1** any disease or illness. **2** any unhealthy, morbid, or desperate condition. [C13: from OF, from Vulgar L *male habitus* (unattested) in poor condition, from L *male* badly + *habitus*, from *habēre* to have]

Málaga ★ ('mæləgə; Spanish 'malaɣa) n **1** a port and resort in S Spain, in Andalusia on the Mediterranean. Pop.: 531 443 (1994 est.). **2** a sweet fortified dessert wine from Málaga.

Malagasy (,mælə'gæsɪ) n **1** (pl **Malagasy** or **Malagasies**) a native or inhabitant of Madagascar. **2** the official language of Madagascar. ◆ adj **3** of or relating to Madagascar, its people, or their language.

Malagasy Republic ★ n the former name (1958–75) of **Madagascar**.

malaise (mæ'leɪz) n **1** a feeling of unease or depression. **2** a mild sickness, not symptomatic of any disease or ailment. **3** a complex of problems affecting a country, economy, etc.: *Bulgaria's economic malaise*. [C18: from OF, from *mal* bad + *aise* EASE]

Malamud ★ ('mæləmʌd, -mud) n **Bernard**. 1914–86, US writer. His novels include *The Fixer* (1966) and *Dubin's Lives* (1979).

malamute or **malemute** ('mælə,muːt) n an Alaskan Eskimo dog of the spitz type. [from the name of an Eskimo tribe]

Malang ★ ('mælæŋ) n a city in S Indonesia, on E Java: commercial centre. Pop.: 650 295 (1990).

malapropism ('mæləprɒp,ɪzəm) n **1** the unintentional misuse of a word by confusion with one of similar sound, esp. when creating a ridiculous effect, as in *under the affluence of alcohol*. **2** the habit of misusing words in this manner. [C18: after Mrs *Malaprop* in Sheridan's play *The Rivals* (1775), a character who misused words, from MALAPROPOS]

malapropos (,mæləprə'pəʊ) adj **1** inappropriate or misapplied. ◆ adv **2** in an inappropriate way or manner. ◆ n **3** something inopportune or inappropriate. [C17: from F *mal à propos* not to the purpose]

Mälar ★ ('meɪlə) n **Lake**. a lake in S Sweden, extending 121 km (75 miles) west from Stockholm, where it joins with an inlet of the Baltic Sea (the **Saltsjön**). Area: 1140 sq. km (440 sq. miles). Swedish name: **Mälaren** ('melaren).

malaria (mə'lɛərɪə) n an infectious disease characterized by recurring attacks of chills and fever, caused by the bite of an anopheles mosquito infected with any of certain protozoans. [C18: from It. *mala aria* bad air, from the belief that the disease was caused by the unwholesome air in swampy districts]
▶ ma'larial, ma'larian, or ma'larious adj

malarkey or **malarky** (mə'lɑːkɪ) n Sl. nonsense; rubbish. [C20: from ?]

Malatesta ★ (Italian mala'testa) n an Italian family that ruled Rimini from the 13th to the 16th century.

Malathion (,mælə'θaɪɒn) n Trademark. an insecticide consisting of an organic phosphate. [C20: from (diethyl) MAL(EATE) + THIO- + -ON]

Malatya (,mɑːlɑː'tjɑː) n a city in E central Turkey: nearby is the ruined Roman and medieval city of Melitene (Old Malatya). Pop.: 319 700 (1994 est.).

Malawi ★ (mə'lɑːwɪ) n **1** a republic in E central Africa: established as a British protectorate in 1891; became independent in 1964 and a republic, within the Commonwealth, in 1966; lies along the Great Rift Valley, with Lake Nyasa (Malawi) along the E border, the Nyika Plateau in the northwest, and the Shiré Highlands in the southeast. Official languages: Chichewa; English and Bantu languages are also spoken. Religion: Christian, Muslim, and animist. Currency: kwacha. Capital: Lilongwe. Pop.: 9 453 000 (1996). Area: 118 484 sq. km (45 747 sq. miles). Former name: **Nyasaland**. **2 Lake**. the Malawi name for (Lake) **Nyasa**.

Malay (mə'leɪ) n **1** a member of a people living chiefly in Malaysia and Indonesia. **2** the language of this people. ◆ adj **3** of or relating to the Malays or their language.

Malaya ★ (mə'leɪə) n **1 States of the Federation of**. part of Malaysia, in the S Malay Peninsula, constituting Peninsular Malaysia: consists of the former Federated Malay States, the former Unfederated Malay States, and the former Straits Settlements. Capital: Kuala Lumpur. Pop.: 14 127 556 (1990). Area: 131 587 sq. km (50 806 sq. miles). **2 Federation of**. a federation of the nine Malay States of the Malay Peninsula and two of the Straits Settlements (Malacca and Penang): formed in 1948: became part of the British Commonwealth in 1957 and joined Malaysia in 1963.
▶ **Ma'layan** adj, n

Malayalam or **Malayalaam** (,mælɪ'ɑːləm) n a language of SW India.

Malay Archipelago ★ n a group of islands in the Indian and Pacific Oceans, between SE Asia and Australia: the largest group of islands in the world; includes over 3000 Indonesian islands, about 7000 islands of the Philippines, and, sometimes, New Guinea.

Malayo-Polynesian n **1** Also called: **Austronesian**. a family of languages extending from Madagascar to the central Pacific. ◆ adj **2** of or relating to this family of languages.

Malay Peninsula ★ n a peninsula of SE Asia, extending south from the Isthmus of Kra in Thailand to Cape Tanjong Piai in Malaysia: consists of SW Thailand and the states of Malaya (Peninsular Malaysia). Ancient name: **Chersonesus Aurea** (,kɜːsə'niːsəs 'ɔːrɪə).

Malaysia ★ (mə'leɪzɪə) n a federation in SE Asia (within the Commonwealth), consisting of **Peninsular Malaysia**, on the Malay Peninsula, and **East Malaysia** (Sabah and Sarawak), occupying the N part of the island of Borneo: formed in 1963 as a federation of Malaya, Sarawak, Sabah, and Singapore (the latter seceded in 1965); densely forested and mostly mountainous. Official language: Malay; English, various Chinese and Indian minority languages are also spoken. Official religion: Muslim. Currency: ringgit. Capital: Kuala Lumpur. Pop.: 20 359 000 (1996). Area: 333 403 sq. km (128 727 sq. miles).
▶ **Ma'laysian** adj, n

Malay States ★ pl n the former states of the Malay Peninsula that, together with Penang and Malacca, formed the Union of Malaya (1946) and the Federation of Malaya (1948). Perak, Selangor, Negri Sembilan, and Pahang were established as the **Federated Malay States** by the British in 1895 and Perlis, Kedah, Kelantan, and Trengannu as the **Unfederated Malay States** in 1909 (joined by Johore in 1914).

Malcolm ★ ('mælkəm) n **George**. born 1917, British harpsichordist.

Malcolm III ★ n died 1093, king of Scotland (1057–93). He became king after Macbeth.

Malcolm X ★ (eks) n original name *Malcolm Little*. 1925–65, US Black civil-rights leader: assassinated.

---

malcontent ('mælkən,tɛnt) *adj* **1** disgusted or discontented. ◆ *n* **2** a person who is malcontent. [C16: from OF]

mal de mer *French.* (mal də mɛr) *n* seasickness.

Maldives ★ ('mɔːldaɪvz) *pl n* **Republic of.** a republic occupying an archipelago of 1087 coral islands in the Indian Ocean, southwest of Sri Lanka: came under British protection in 1887; became independent in 1965 and a republic in 1968; a member of the Commonwealth. Official language: Divehi. Official religion: (Sunni) Muslim. Currency: rufiyaa. Capital: Malé. Pop.: 266 000 (1996). Area: 298 sq. km (115 sq. miles). Also called: **Maldive Islands.**
 ▷ **Maldivian** (mɔːl'dɪvɪən) *or* **Maldivan** ('mɔːldaɪvⁿn, -dɪ-) *adj, n*

Maldon ★ ('mɔːldən) *n* a market town in SE England, in Essex; scene of a battle (991) between the East Saxons and the victorious Danes, celebrated in *The Battle of Maldon*, an Old English poem. Pop.: 15 841 (1991).

male (meɪl) *adj* **1** of, relating to, or designating the sex producing gametes (spermatozoa) that can fertilize female gametes (ova). **2** of, relating to, or characteristic of a man. **3** for or composed of men or boys: *a male choir.* **4** (of gametes) capable of fertilizing an egg cell. **5** (of reproductive organs) capable of producing male gametes. **6** (of flowers) bearing stamens but lacking a functional pistil. **7** *Electronics, engineering.* having a projecting part or parts that fit into a female counterpart: *a male plug.* ◆ *n* **8** a male person, animal, or plant. [C14: via OF from L *masculus* MASCULINE]
 ▷ **'maleness** *n*

Malé ★ ('mɑːleɪ) *n* the capital of the Republic of Maldives, on Malé Island in the centre of the island group. Pop.: 62 973 (1995 est.).

maleate ('mælɪ,eɪt) *n* any salt or ester of maleic acid. [C19: from MALE(IC) ACID + -ATE[1]]

Malebranche ★ (*French* malbrɑ̃ʃ) *n* **Nicolas** (nikɔlɑ). 1638–1715, French philosopher, whose works include *De la recherche de la vérité* (1674).

male chauvinism *n* the belief, held or alleged to be held by certain men, that men are superior to women.
 ▷ **male chauvinist** *n, adj*

malediction (,mælɪ'dɪkʃən) *n* **1** the utterance of a curse against someone or something. **2** a slanderous accusation or comment. [C15: from L *maledictiō* a reviling, from *male* ill + *dīcere* to speak]
 ▷ **,male'dictive** *or* **,male'dictory** *adj*

malefactor ('mælɪ,fæktə) *n* a criminal; wrongdoer. [C15: via OF from L, from *malefacere* to do evil]
 ▷ **'male,faction** *n*

maleficent (mə'lɛfɪsənt) *adj* causing evil or mischief; harmful or baleful. [C17: from L, from *maleficus* wicked, from *malum* evil]
 ▷ **ma'lefic** *adj* ▷ **ma'leficence** *n*

maleic acid (mə'leɪɪk) *n* a colourless soluble crystalline substance used to synthesize other compounds, such as polyester resins. Formula: HOOCCH:CHCOOH. Systematic name: **cis-butenedioic acid.** [C19: from F *maléique*, altered form of *malique*; see MALIC ACID]

male menopause *n* a period in a man's later middle age in which he may experience an identity crisis as he feels age overtake his sexual powers.

Malenkov ★ (*Russian* mɐlɪn'kɔf) *n* **Georgi Maksimilianovich** (gɪ'ɔrgij ,mɐksimil'janəvitʃ). 1902–88, Soviet politician; prime minister (1953–55). He was removed from the presidium (1957) for plotting against Khrushchev; expelled from the Communist Party (1961).

Malevich ★ (*Russian* 'malvitʃ) *n* **Kasimir** (kəzi'mir). 1878–1935, Russian painter and founder of Suprematism, an abstract art movement.

malevolent (mə'lɛvələnt) *adj* wishing or appearing to wish evil to others; malicious. [C16: from L *malevolens*, from *male* ill + *volens*, present participle of *velle* to wish]
 ▷ **ma'levolence** *n* ▷ **ma'levolently** *adv*

malfeasance (mæl'fiːz°ns) *n Law.* the doing of a wrongful or illegal act, esp. by a public official. Cf. **misfeasance,**

nonfeasance. [C17: from OF *mal faisant,* from *mal* evil + *faisant,* from *faire* to do, from L *facere*]
 ▷ **mal'feasant** *n, adj*

malformation (,mælfɔː'meɪʃən) *n* **1** the condition of being faulty or abnormal in form or shape. **2** *Pathol.* a deformity, esp. when congenital.
 ▷ **mal'formed** *adj*

malfunction (mæl'fʌŋkʃən) *vb* **1** (*intr*) to function imperfectly or fail to function. ◆ *n* **2** failure to function or defective functioning.

Malherbe ★ (*French* malɛrb) *n* **François de** (frɑ̃swa də). 1555–1628, French poet and critic.

Mali ★ ('mɑːlɪ) *n* a landlocked republic in West Africa: conquered by the French by 1898 and incorporated (as French Sudan) into French West Africa; became independent in 1960; settled chiefly in the basins of the Rivers Senegal and Niger in the south. Official language: French. Religion: Muslim and animist. Currency: franc. Capital: Bamako. Pop.: 9 204 000 (1996). Area: 1 248 574 sq. km (482 077 sq. miles). Former name (1898–1959): **French Sudan.**

malic acid ('mælɪk, 'meɪ-) *n* a colourless crystalline compound occurring in apples and other fruits. [C18 *malic,* via F *malique* from L *mālum* apple]

malice ('mælɪs) *n* **1** the desire to do harm or mischief. **2** evil intent. **3** *Law.* the state of mind with which an act is committed and from which the intent to do wrong may be inferred. [C13: via OF from L *malitia,* from *malus* evil]

malice aforethought *n Law.* **1** the predetermination to do an unlawful act, esp. to kill or seriously injure. **2** the intent with which an unlawful killing is effected, which must be proved for the crime to constitute murder.

malicious (mə'lɪʃəs) *adj* **1** characterized by malice. **2** motivated by wrongful, vicious, or mischievous purposes.
 ▷ **ma'liciously** *adv* ▷ **ma'liciousness** *n*

malign (mə'laɪn) *adj* **1** evil in influence, intention, or effect. ◆ *vb* **2** (*tr*) to slander or defame. [C14: via OF from L *malignus* spiteful, from *malus* evil]
 ▷ **ma'ligner** *n* ▷ **ma'lignly** *adv*

malignancy (mə'lɪgnənsɪ) *n, pl* **malignancies. 1** the state or quality of being malignant. **2** *Pathol.* a cancerous growth.

malignant (mə'lɪgnənt) *adj* **1** having or showing desire to harm others. **2** tending to cause great harm; injurious. **3** *Pathol.* (of a tumour) uncontrollable or resistant to therapy. [C16: from LL *malīgnāre* to behave spitefully, from L *malīgnus* MALIGN]
 ▷ **ma'lignantly** *adv*

malignity (mə'lɪgnɪtɪ) *n, pl* **malignities. 1** the condition or quality of being malign or deadly. **2** (*often pl*) a malign or malicious act or feeling.

malines (mə'liːn) *n* **1** a type of silk net used in dressmaking. **2** another name for **Mechlin lace.** [C19: from F *Malines* (Mechelen), where this lace was traditionally made]

Malines ★ (malin) *n* the French name for **Mechelen.**

malinger (mə'lɪŋgə) *vb* (*intr*) to pretend or exaggerate illness, esp. to avoid work. [C19: from F *malingre* sickly, ?from *mal* badly + OF *haingre* feeble]
 ▷ **ma'lingerer** *n*

Malinowski ★ (,mælɪ'nɒfskɪ) *n* **Bronislaw Kasper** (brɔ'nislaf 'kaspɛr). 1884–1942, Polish anthropologist in Britain and the US.

mall (mɔːl, mæl) *n* **1** a shaded avenue, esp. one open to the public. **2** short for **shopping mall.** [C17: after *the Mall,* in St James's Park, London]

mallard ('mælɑːd) *n, pl* **mallard** *or* **mallards.** a duck common over most of the N hemisphere, the male of which has a dark green head and reddish-brown breast: the ancestor of all domestic breeds of duck. [C14: from OF *mallart,* ?from *maslart* (unattested); see MALE, -ARD]

Mallarmé ★ (*French* malarme) *n* **Stéphane** (stefan). 1842–98, French symbolist poet, whose works include *L'Après-midi d'un Faune* (1876) and *Divagations* (1897).

Malle ★ (*French* mal) *n* **Louis.** 1932–95, French film direc-

---

★ people and places

tor: his films include *Au revoir les enfants* (1987) and *Vanya on 42nd Street* (1994).

malleable ('mælɪəbᵊl) *adj* **1** (esp. of metal) able to be worked, hammered, or shaped under pressure or blows without breaking. **2** able to be influenced; pliable or tractable. [C14: via OF from Med. L *malleābilis*, from L *malleus* hammer]
▶ ˌmallea'bility *or* (*less commonly*) 'malleableness *n*
▶ 'malleably *adv*

mallee ('mælɪ) *n* **1** any of several low shrubby eucalyptus trees in desert regions of Australia. **2** (usually preceded by *the*) *Austral. inf.* another name for the **bush** (sense 4). [C19: Abor.]

Mallee ★ ('mælɪ) *n* a region in NW Victoria, Australia.

mallee fowl *n* an Australian megapode.

malleolus (məˈliːələs) *n, pl* **malleoli** (-ˌlaɪ). either of two rounded bony projections, one on each side of the ankle. [C17: dim. of L *malleus* hammer]

mallet ('mælɪt) *n* **1** a tool resembling a hammer but having a large head of wood, copper, lead, leather, etc., used for driving chisels, beating sheet metal, etc. **2** a long stick with a head like a hammer used to strike the ball in croquet or polo. [C15: from OF *maillet* wooden hammer, dim. of *mail* MAUL (n)]

malleus ('mælɪəs) *n, pl* **mallei** (-lɪˌaɪ). the outermost and largest of the three small bones in the middle ear of mammals. See also **incus, stapes**. [C17: from L: hammer]

mallie ('mɔːlɪ) *n Inf., chiefly US.* a teenage girl who spends most of her spare time loitering in shopping malls.

Mallorca ★ (maˈʎorka) *n* the Spanish name for **Majorca**.

mallow ('mæləʊ) *n* **1** any of several malvaceous plants of Europe, having purple, pink, or white flowers. **2** any of various related plants, such as the marsh mallow. [OE *mealuwe*, from L *malva*]

malm (mɑːm) *n* **1** a soft greyish limestone that crumbles easily. **2** a chalky soil formed from this. **3** an artificial mixture of clay and chalk used to make bricks. [OE *mealm-* (in compound words)]

Malmédy ★ (*French* malmedi) *n* See **Eupen and Malmédy**.

Malmö ★ ('mælməʊ; *Swedish* 'malmœ:) *n* a port in S Sweden, on the Sound: part of Denmark until 1658; industrial centre. Pop.: 248 007 (1997 est.).

malmsey ('mɑːmzɪ) *n* a sweet Madeira wine. [C15: from Med. L *Malmasia*, corruption of Gk *Monembasia*, Gk port from which the wine was shipped]

malnutrition (ˌmælnjuːˈtrɪʃən) *n* lack of adequate nutrition resulting from insufficient food, unbalanced diet, or defective assimilation.

malodorous (mælˈəʊdərəs) *adj* having a bad smell.

Malory ★ ('mælərɪ) *n* Sir **Thomas**. English author of *Le Morte d'Arthur* (?1470), collected Arthurian legends translated from the French.

Malpighi ★ (*Italian* malˈpiːgi) *n* **Marcello** (marˈtʃello). 1628–94, Italian physiologist, who identified the capillary system (1661).
▶ **Malpighian** (mælˈpɪgɪən) *adj*

malpractice (mælˈpræktɪs) *n* **1** immoral, illegal, or unethical professional conduct or neglect of professional duty. **2** any instance of improper professional conduct.

Malraux ★ (*French* malro) *n* **André** (ɑ̃dre). 1901–76, French writer and statesman. His novels include *La Condition humaine* (1933) and *L'Espoir* (1937).

malt (mɔːlt) *n* **1** cereal grain, such as barley, that is kiln-dried after it has germinated by soaking in water. **2** See **malt liquor, malt whisky**. ◆ *vb* **3** to make into or become malt. **4** to make (something, esp. liquor) with malt. [OE *mealt*]
▶ 'malty *adj*

Malta ★ ('mɔːltə) *n* a republic occupying the islands of Malta, Gozo, and Comino, in the Mediterranean south of Sicily: governed by the Knights Hospitallers from 1530 until Napoleon's conquest in 1798; French driven out, with British help, 1800; became British dependency 1814; suffered severely in World War II; became independent in 1964 and a republic in 1974; a member of the Commonwealth. Official languages: Maltese and

English. Official religion: Roman Catholic. Currency: Maltese lira. Capital: Valletta. Pop.: 372 000 (1996). Area: 316 sq. km (122 sq. miles).

malted milk *n* **1** a soluble powder made from dehydrated milk and malted cereals. **2** a drink made from this powder.

Maltese (mɔːlˈtiːz) *adj* **1**. of or relating to Malta, its inhabitants, or their language. ◆ *n* **2** (*pl* **Maltese**) a native or inhabitant of Malta or a descendant of one. **3** the official language of Malta, a form of Arabic with borrowings from Italian, etc.

Maltese cross *n* a cross with triangular arms that taper towards the centre, sometimes having indented outer sides.

malt extract *n* a sticky substance obtained from an infusion of malt.

Malthus ★ ('mælθəs) *n* **Thomas Robert**. 1766–1834, British economist, noted for his population theory in *An Essay on the Principle of Population* (1798).

Malthusian (mælˈθjuːzɪən) *adj* **1**. of or relating to the theory of Malthus stating that increases in population tend to exceed increases in the means of subsistence and that therefore sexual restraint should be exercised. ◆ *n* **2** a supporter of this theory.
▶ **Mal'thusianism** *n*

malting ('mɔːltɪŋ) *n* a building in which malt is made or stored. Also called: **malt house**.

malt liquor *n* any alcoholic drink brewed from malt.

maltose ('mɔːltəʊz) *n* a sugar formed by the enzymic hydrolysis of starch. [C19: from MALT + -OSE²]

maltreat (mælˈtriːt) *vb* (*tr*) to treat badly, cruelly, or inconsiderately. [C18: from F *maltraiter*]
▶ **mal'treater** *n* ▶ **mal'treatment** *n*

maltster ('mɔːltstə) *n* a person who makes or deals in malt.

malt whisky *n* whisky made from malted barley.

Maluku ★ (mɑːˈluːkuː) *n* the Indonesian name for the **Moluccas**.

malvaceous (mælˈveɪʃəs) *adj* of, relating to, or belonging to a family of plants that includes mallow, cotton, okra, althaea, and abutilon. [C17: from L *malvāceus*, from *malva* MALLOW]

Malvern ★ ('mɔːlvən) *n* a town and resort in W England, in Hereford and Worcester on the E slopes of the **Malvern Hills**: annual dramatic festival; mineral springs. Pop.: 31 537 (1991).

malversation (ˌmælvɜːˈseɪʃən) *n Rare*. professional or public misconduct. [C16: from F, from *malverser* to behave badly, from L *male versārī*]

Malvinas ★ (*Spanish* malˈβinas) *pl n* **Islas** ('izlas). the Argentine name for the **Falkland Islands**.

mam (mæm) *n Inf. or dialect*. another word for **mother**.

mama *or esp. US* **mamma** (məˈmɑː) *n Old-fashioned*. an informal word for **mother**¹. [C16: reduplication of childish syllable *ma*]

mamba ('mæmbə) *n* any of various partly arboreal tropical African venomous snakes, esp. the **green** and **black mambas**. [From Zulu *im-amba*]

mambo ('mæmbəʊ) *n, pl* **mambos**. **1** a modern Latin American dance, resembling the rumba. ◆ *vb* **2** (*intr*) to perform this dance. [American Sp., prob. from Haitian Creole: voodoo priestess]

Mameluke *or* **Mamaluke** ('mæmɪˌluːk) *n* **1** a member of a military class, originally of Turkish slaves, ruling in Egypt from 1250 to 1517 and remaining powerful until 1811. **2** (in Muslim countries) a slave. [C16: via F, ult. from Ar. *mamlūk* slave, from *malaka* to possess]

Mamet ★ ('mæmɪt) *n* **David**. born 1947, US dramatist and film director. His plays include *Oleanna* (1992) and his films include *House of Games* (1986) and *The Spanish Prisoner* (1998).

mamilla *or US* **mammilla** (mæˈmɪlə) *n, pl* **mamillae** (-liː) *or US* **mammillae**. **1** a nipple or teat. **2** any nipple-shaped prominence. [C17: from L, dim. of *mamma* breast]
▶ **'mamillary** *or US* **'mammillary** *adj*

mamma ('mæmə) *n, pl* **mammae** (-miː). the milk-secreting

organ of female mammals: the breast in women, the udder in cows, sheep, etc. [C17: from L: breast]
▸ 'mammary adj

mammal ('mæməl) n any animal of the Mammalia, a large class of warm-blooded vertebrates having mammary glands in the female. [C19: via NL from L mamma breast]
▸ mammalian (mæ'meılıən) adj, n

mammary gland n any of the milk-producing glands in mammals.

mammogram ('mæməʊˌgræm) n an X-ray photograph of the breast.

mammography (mæ'mɒgrəfı) n examination of the breasts by X-ray, esp. to detect early signs of cancer.

mammon ('mæmən) n riches or wealth regarded as a source of evil and corruption. [C14: via LL from New Testament Gk mammōnas, from Aramaic māmōnā wealth]
▸ 'mammonish adj ▸ 'mammonism n ▸ 'mammonist or 'mammonite n

Mammon ('mæmən) n Bible. the personification of riches and greed in the form of a false god.

mammoth ('mæməθ) n 1 any large extinct elephant of the Pleistocene epoch, such as the **woolly mammoth**, having a hairy coat and long curved tusks. ♦ adj 2 of gigantic size or importance. [C18: from Russian mamot, from Tartar mamont, ?from mamma earth, because of a belief that the animal made burrows]

mammy or **mammie** ('mæmı) n, pl **mammies. 1** a child's word for **mother**[1] (senses 1–3). **2** Chiefly southern US. a Black woman employed as a nurse or servant to a White family.

Mamoré ★ (Spanish mamo're) n a river in central Bolivia, flowing north to the Beni River to form the Madeira River. Length: about 1500 km (930 miles).

man (mæn) n, pl **men. 1** an adult male human being, as distinguished from a woman. **2** (modifier) male; masculine: a man child. **3** a human being, considered as representative of mankind. **4** human beings collectively; mankind. **5** Also called: **modern man. 5a** a member of any of the living races of Homo sapiens, characterized by erect bipedal posture, a highly developed brain, and powers of articulate speech, abstract reasoning, and imagination. **5b** any extinct member of the species Homo sapiens, such as Cro-Magnon man. **6** a member of any of the extinct species of the genus Homo, such as Java man. **7** an adult male human being with qualities associated with the male, such as courage or virility: be a man. **8** manly qualities or virtues: the man in him was outraged. **9a** a subordinate, servant, or employee. **9b** (in combination): the man-days required to complete a job. **10** (usually pl) a member of the armed forces who does not hold commissioned, warrant, or noncommissioned rank (as in **officers and men**). **11** a member of a group, team, etc. **12** a husband, boyfriend, etc. **13** an expression used parenthetically to indicate an informal relationship between speaker and hearer. **14** a movable piece in various games, such as draughts. **15** a vassal of a feudal lord. **16** S. African sl. any person: used as a term of address. **17 as one man.** with unanimous action or response. **18 be one's own man.** to be independent or free. **19 he's your man.** he's the person needed. **20 man and boy.** from childhood. **21 sort out** or **separate the men from the boys.** to separate the experienced from the inexperienced. **22 to a man.** without exception. ♦ interj **23** Inf. an exclamation or expletive, often indicating surprise or pleasure. ♦ vb **mans, manning, manned.** (tr) **24** to provide with sufficient men for operation, defence, etc. **25** to take one's place at or near in readiness for action. [OE mann]

Man (mæn) n **Isle of.** an island in the British Isles, in the Irish Sea between Cumbria and Northern Ireland: a Crown possession with its own parliament, the Court of Tynwald; a dependency of Norway until 1266, when it came under Scottish rule; its own language, Manx, is now almost extinct. Capital: Douglas. Pop.: 69 788 (1991). Area: 588 sq. km (227 sq. miles).

Man. abbrev. for: **1** Manila paper. **2** Manitoba.

-man n combining form. indicating a person who has a

role, works in a place, or operates equipment as specified: salesman; barman; cameraman.

mana ('mɑːnə) n Anthropol. **1** (in Polynesia, Melanesia, etc.) a concept of a life force associated with high social status and ritual power. **2** any power achieved by ritual means; prestige; authority. [of Polynesian origin]

man about town n a fashionable sophisticate, esp. one in a big city.

manacle ('mænəkªl) n **1** (usually pl) a shackle, handcuff, or fetter, used to secure the hands of a prisoner, convict, etc. ♦ vb **manacles, manacling, manacled.** (tr) **2** to put manacles on. **3** to confine or constrain. [C14: via OF from L manicula, dim. of manus hand]

Manado ★ (mə'nɑːdəʊ) n a variant of **Menado.**

manage ('mænɪdʒ) vb **manages, managing, managed.** (mainly tr) **1** (also intr) to be in charge (of); administer: to manage a shop. **2** to succeed in being able (to do something); contrive. **3** to have room, time, etc., for: can you manage dinner tomorrow? **4** to exercise control or domination over. **5** (intr) to contrive to carry on despite difficulties, esp. financial ones. **6** to wield or handle (a weapon). [C16: from It. maneggiare to train (esp. horses), ult. from L manus hand]

manageable ('mænɪdʒəbªl) adj able to be managed or controlled.
▸ ˌmanageaˈbility or 'manageableness n ▸ 'manageably adv

managed currency n a currency subject to governmental control with respect to the amount in circulation and rate of exchange.

managed fund n an investment managed by an insurance company to provide low-risk investments for the small investor.

management ('mænɪdʒmənt) n **1** the members of the executive or administration of an organization or business. **2** managers or employers collectively. **3** the technique, practice, or science of managing or controlling. **4** the skilful or resourceful use of materials, time, etc. **5** the specific treatment of a disease, etc.

management buyout n the purchase of a company by its managers, usually with outside backing from a bank or other institution.

management company n a company that manages a unit trust.

manager ('mænɪdʒə) n **1** a person who directs or manages an organization, industry, shop, etc. **2** a person who controls the business affairs of an actor, entertainer, etc. **3** a person who controls the training of a sportsman or team. **4** a person who has a talent for managing efficiently. **5** (in Britain) a member of either House of Parliament appointed to arrange a matter in which both Houses are concerned. **6** Computing. a computer program that organizes a resource, such as a set of files or a database.
▸ 'managership n

manageress (ˌmænɪdʒə'res) n a woman who is in charge of a shop, department, etc.

managerial (ˌmænɪ'dʒɪərɪəl) adj of or relating to a manager or management.
▸ ˌmana'gerially adv

managing ('mænɪdʒɪŋ) adj having administrative control or authority: a managing director.

Managua ★ (mə'nægwə; Spanish ma'naɣwa) n **1** the capital of Nicaragua, on the S shore of Lake Managua: chosen as capital in 1857. Pop.: 1 195 000 (1995 est.). **2 Lake.** a lake in W Nicaragua: drains into Lake Nicaragua by the Tipitapa River. Length: 61 km (38 miles). Width: about 26 km (16 miles).

Manama ★ (məˈnɑːmə) *n* the capital of Bahrain, at the N end of Bahrain Island: transit port. Pop.: 140 401 (1992 est.).

mañana *Spanish.* (məˈnjɑːnə) *n, adv* **a** tomorrow. **b** some other and later time.

Manáos ★ (*Portuguese* məˈnaus) *n* a variant spelling of **Manaus.**

Manassas ★ (məˈnæsəs) *n* a town in NE Virginia, west of Alexandria: site of the victory of Confederate forces in the Battles of Bull Run, or First and Second Manassas (1861; 1862), during the American Civil War. Pop.: 27 957 (1990).

Manasseh ★ (məˈnæsɪ) *n Old Testament.* **1** the elder son of Joseph (Genesis 41:51). **2** the Israelite tribe descended from him. **3** the territory of this tribe, in the upper Jordan valley. Douay spelling: **Manases** (məˈnæsiːz).

man-at-arms *n, pl* **men-at-arms.** a soldier, esp. a heavily armed mounted soldier in medieval times.

manatee (ˌmænəˈtiː) *n* a sirenian mammal occurring in tropical coastal waters of America, the Caribbean, and Africa, having a prehensile upper lip and a broad flattened tail. [C16: via Sp. from Carib *Manattouï*]

Manaus *or* **Manáos** ★ (*Portuguese* məˈnaus) *n* a port in N Brazil, capital of Amazonas state, on the Rio Negro 19 km (12 miles) above its confluence with the Amazon: chief commercial centre of the Amazon basin. Pop. (urban area): 1 189 000 (1995).

Manche ★ (*French* mɑ̃ʃ) *n* **1** a department of NW France, in Basse-Normandie region. Capital: St Lô. Pop.: 483 352 (1994 est.). Area: 6412 sq. km (2501 sq. miles). **2 La.** the French name for the **English Channel.**

manchester (ˈmæntʃɪstə) *n Austral. & NZ.* **1** goods, such as sheets and pillowcases, which are, or were originally, made of cotton. **2 manchester department.** a section of a store which sells such goods. [from MANCHESTER, England]

Manchester ★ (ˈmæntʃɪstə) *n* **1** a city in NW England, linked to the Mersey estuary by the **Manchester Ship Canal:** commercial and industrial centre, esp. of the cotton and textile trades; university (1846). Pop.: 402 889 (1991). Latin name: **Man'cunium.** **2** a unitary authority in NW England, in Greater Manchester. Pop.: 431 100 (1994 est.). Area: 116 sq. km (45 sq. miles).

manchineel (ˌmæntʃɪˈniːl) *n* a tropical American tree having fruit and milky highly caustic poisonous sap, which causes skin blisters. [C17: via F from Sp. MANZANILLA]

Manchu (mænˈtʃuː) *n* **1** (*pl* **Manchus** *or* **Manchu**) a member of a Mongoloid people of Manchuria, a region of NE China, who conquered China in the 17th century, establishing a dynasty that lasted until 1912. **2** the language of this people. ◆ *adj* **3** Also: **Ching.** of or relating to the dynasty of the Manchus. [from Manchu, lit.: pure]

Manchukuo *or* **Manchoukuo** ★ (ˈmænˈtʃuːˈkwəu) *n* a former state of E Asia (1932–45), consisting of the three provinces of old Manchuria and Jehol.

Manchuria ★ (mænˈtʃuərɪə) *n* a region of NE China, historically the home of the Manchus, rulers of China from 1644 to 1912: includes part of the Inner Mongolian AR and the provinces of Heilongjiang, Jilin, and Liaoning. Area: about 1 300 000 sq. km (502 000 sq. miles).
▶ **Man'churian** *adj, n*

manciple (ˈmænsɪpˈl) *n* a steward who buys provisions, esp. in an Inn of Court. [C13: via OF from L *mancipium* purchase, from *manceps* purchaser, from *manus* hand + *capere* to take]

Mancunian (mænˈkjuːnɪən) *n* **1.** a native or inhabitant of Manchester. ◆ *adj* **2** of or relating to Manchester. [from Med. L *Mancunium* Manchester]

-mancy *n combining form.* indicating divination of a particular kind: *chiromancy.* [from OF *-mancie*, from L *-mantia*, from Gk *manteia* soothsaying]
▶ **-mantic** *adj combining form.*

mandala (ˈmændələ, mænˈdɑːlə) *n Hindu & Buddhist art.* any of various designs symbolizing the universe, usually circular. [Sansk.: circle]

Mandalay ★ (ˌmændəˈleɪ) *n* a city in central Myanmar,

on the Irrawaddy River: the second largest city in the country and former capital of Burma and of Upper Burma; Buddhist religious centre. Pop.: 677 000 (1995 est.).

mandamus (mænˈdeɪməs) *n, pl* **mandamuses.** *Law.* (formerly) a writ from (now an order of) a superior court commanding an inferior tribunal, public official, etc., to carry out a public duty. [C16: L, lit.: we command, from *mandāre*]

mandarin (ˈmændərɪn) *n* **1** (in the Chinese Empire) a member of a senior grade of the bureaucracy. **2** a high-ranking official whose powers are extensive and thought to be outside political control. **3** a person of standing and influence, as in literary or intellectual circles, esp. one regarded as conservative or reactionary. **4a** a small citrus tree cultivated for its edible fruit. **4b** the fruit, resembling the tangerine. [C16: from Port. via Malay from Sansk. *mantrin* counsellor, from *mantra* counsel]
▶ **'mandarinate** *n*

Mandarin Chinese *or* **Mandarin** *n* the official language of China since 1917.

Mandarin collar *n* a high stiff round collar.

mandarin duck *n* an Asian duck, the male of which has a distinctive brightly coloured and patterned plumage and crest.

mandate *n* (ˈmændeɪt, -dɪt). **1** an official or authoritative instruction or command. **2** *Politics.* the support or commission given to a government and its policies or an elected representative and his policies through an electoral victory. **3** (*often cap.*) Also called: **mandated territory.** (formerly) any of the territories under the trusteeship of the League of Nations administered by one of its member states. **4a** *Roman law.* a contract by which one person commissions another to act for him gratuitously. **4b** *Contract law.* a contract under which a party entrusted with goods undertakes to perform gratuitously some service in respect of such goods. **4c** *Scots Law.* a contract by which a person is engaged to act in the management of the affairs of another. ◆ *vb* (ˈmændeɪt), **mandates, mandating, mandated.** (*tr*) **5** to assign (territory) to a nation under a mandate. **6** to delegate authority to. [C16: from L *mandātum* something commanded, from *mandāre* to command, ?from *manus* hand + *dāre* to give]
▶ **'mandator** *n*

mandatory (ˈmændətərɪ, -trɪ) *adj* **1** having the nature or powers of a mandate. **2** obligatory; compulsory. **3** (of a state) having received a mandate over some territory. ◆ *n, pl* **mandatories.** *also* **mandatary.** **4** a person or state holding a mandate.
▶ **'mandatorily** *adv*

Mandela ★ (mænˈdɛlə) *n* **1** Nelson (**Rolihlahla**). born 1918, South African statesman: first Black president of South Africa (1994–99); jailed for life (1964), but released (1990) after an international campaign; instrumental in ending apartheid; awarded the Nobel peace prize (1993) jointly with F. W. de Klerk. **2** (**Numzano**) Winnie. born 1934, South African politician and political activist: married to Nelson Mandela from 1958 until 1996, campaigned for his release from prison.

Mandelstam *or* **Mandelshtam** ★ (ˈmænd'lˌʃtɑːm) *n* **Osip** (**Emilyevich**) (ˈɒsɪːp). 1891–?1938, Soviet poet and writer, born in Warsaw; persecuted by Stalin, he died in a labour camp. His works include *Tristia* (1922) and the autobiographical *Journey to Armenia* (1933).

Mandeville ★ (ˈmændəvɪl) *n* **1** Bernard de. ?1670–1733, English author, born in Holland, noted for his satire *The Fable of the Bees* (1723). **2** Sir **John.** 14th century, English author of *The Travels of Sir John Mandeville.*

mandible (ˈmændɪbˈl) *n* **1** the lower jawbone in vertebrates. **2** either of a pair of mouthparts in insects and other arthropods that are usually used for biting and crushing food. **3** *Ornithol.* either part of the bill, esp. the lower part. [C16: via OF from LL *mandibula* jaw, from *mandere* to chew]
▶ **mandibular** (mænˈdɪbjulə) *adj* ▶ **mandibulate** (mænˈdɪbjulɪt, -ˌleɪt) *n, adj*

mandolin *or* **mandoline** (ˌmændəˈlɪn) *n* a plucked stringed instrument having four pairs of strings stretched over a small light body with a fretted finger-

board: usually played with a plectrum. [C18: via F from It. *mandolino*, dim. of *mandora* lute, ult. from Gk *pandoura* musical instrument with three strings]
▶ ˌmandoˈlinist *n*

mandrake ('mændreɪk) *or* **mandragora** (mæn-'drægərə) *n* **1** a Eurasian plant with purplish flowers and a forked root. It was formerly thought to have magic powers and a narcotic was prepared from its root. **2** another name for the **May apple**. [C14: prob. via MDu. from L *mandragoras*, from Gk. The form *mandrake* was prob. adopted through folk etymology, because of the allegedly human appearance of the root and because *drake* (dragon) suggested magical powers]

mandrel *or* **mandril** ('mændrəl) *n* **1** a spindle on which a workpiece is supported during machining operations. **2** a shaft or arbor on which a machining tool is mounted. [C16: ? rel. to F *mandrin* lathe]

mandrill ('mændrɪl) *n* an Old World monkey of W Africa. It has a short tail and brown hair, and the ridged muzzle, nose, and hindquarters are red and blue. [C18: from MAN + DRILL⁴]

mane (meɪn) *n* **1** the long coarse hair that grows from the crest of the neck in such mammals as the lion and horse. **2** long thick human hair. [OE *manu*]
▶ **maned** *adj*

manège *or* **manege** (mæ'neɪʒ) *n* **1** the art of training horses and riders. **2** a riding school. [C17: via F from It. *maneggio*, from *maneggiare* to MANAGE]

manes ('mɑːneɪz) *pl n* (*sometimes cap.*) (in Roman legend) **1** the spirits of the dead, often revered as minor deities. **2** (*functioning as sing*) the shade of a dead person. [C14: from L, prob.: the good ones, from OL *mānus* good]

Manes ★ ('meɪniːz) *n* See **Mani**.

Manet ★ (*French* mane) *n* **Édouard** (edwar). 1832–83, French painter. His painting *Le Déjeuner sur l'herbe* (1863), which was condemned by the Parisian establishment, was acclaimed by the impressionists, whom he decisively influenced.

maneuver (mə'nuːvə) *n, vb* the usual US spelling of **manoeuvre**.

man Friday *n* **1** a loyal male servant or assistant. **2** Also: **girl Friday, person Friday**. any factotum, esp. in an office. [after the native in Daniel Defoe's novel *Robinson Crusoe* (1719)]

manful ('mænful) *adj* resolute, strong; manly.
▶ **'manfully** *adv* ▶ **'manfulness** *n*

mangabey ('mæŋgəˌbeɪ) *n* any of several large agile arboreal Old World monkeys of central Africa, having long limbs and tail. [C18: after a region in Madagascar]

Mangalore ★ (ˌmæŋgə'lɔː) *n* a port in S India, in Karnataka on the Malabar Coast. Pop.: 273 304 (1991).

manganese ('mæŋgəˌniːz) *n* a brittle greyish-white metallic element: used in making steel and ferromagnetic alloys. Symbol: Mn; atomic no.: 25; atomic wt.: 54.938. [C17: via F from It., prob. altered form of Med. L MAGNESIA]

mange (meɪndʒ) *n* an infectious disorder mainly affecting domestic animals, characterized by itching and loss of hair: caused by parasitic mites. [C14: from OF *mangeue* itch, from *mangier* to eat]

mangelwurzel ('mæŋgəlˌwɜːzəl) *or* **mangoldwurzel** ('mæŋgəʊldˌwɜːzəl) *n* a Eurasian variety of beet, cultivated as a cattle food, having a large yellowish root. [C18: from G *Mangoldwurzel*, from *Mangold* beet + *Wurzel* root]

manger ('meɪndʒə) *n* a trough or box in a stable, barn, etc., from which horses or cattle feed. [C14: from OF *maingeure* food trough, from *mangier* to eat, ult. from L *mandūcāre* to chew]

mangetout (ˌmɒnʒ'tuː) *n* a variety of garden pea in which the pod is also edible. Also called: **sugar pea**. [C20: from F lit.: eat all]

mangey ('meɪndʒɪ) *adj* mangier, mangiest. a variant spelling of **mangy**.

mangle¹ ('mæŋgəl) *vb* mangles, mangling, mangled. (*tr*) **1** to mutilate, disfigure, or destroy by cutting, crushing, or

tearing. **2** to ruin, spoil, or mar. [C14: from Norman F *mangler*, prob. from OF *mahaignier* to maim]
▶ **'mangled** *adj* ▶ **'mangler** *n*

mangle² ('mæŋgəl) *n* **1** Also called: **wringer**. a machine for pressing or drying textiles, clothes, etc., consisting of two heavy rollers between which the cloth is passed. ◆ *vb* mangles, mangling, mangled. (*tr*) **2** to press or dry in a mangle. [C18: from Du. *mangel*, ult. from LL *manganum*. See MANGONEL]

mango ('mæŋgəʊ) *n, pl* mangoes *or* mangos. **1** a tropical Asian evergreen tree, cultivated in the tropics for its fruit. **2** the ovoid edible fruit of this tree, having a smooth rind and sweet juicy flesh. [C16: via Port. from Malay *mangā*, from Tamil *mānkāy*, from *mān* mango tree + *kāy* fruit]

mangonel ('mæŋgəˌnɛl) *n History*. a war engine for hurling stones. [C13: via OF from Med. L *manganellus*, ult. from Gk *manganon*]

mangrove ('mæŋgrəʊv, 'mæn-) *n* any of various tropical evergreen trees or shrubs, having stiltlike intertwining aerial roots and forming dense thickets along coasts. [C17 *mangrow* (changed through infl. of *grove*), from Port. *mangue*, ult. from Taino]

mangy *or* **mangey** ('meɪndʒɪ) *adj* mangier, mangiest. **1** having or caused by mange. **2** scruffy or shabby.
▶ **'mangily** *adv* ▶ **'manginess** *n*

manhandle ('mænˌhændəl, ˌmæn'hændəl) *vb* manhandles, manhandling, manhandled. (*tr*) **1** to handle or push (someone) about roughly. **2** to move or do by manpower rather than by machinery.

Manhattan ★ (mæn'hætən, mən-) *n* **1** an island at the N end of New York Bay, between the Hudson, East, and Harlem Rivers: administratively with (adjacent islets) a borough of New York City; a major financial, commercial, and cultural centre. Pop.: 1 487 536 (1990). Area: 47 sq. km (22 sq. miles). **2** a mixed drink consisting of four parts whisky, one part vermouth, and a dash of bitters.

manhole ('mænˌhəʊl) *n* **1** Also called: **inspection chamber**. a shaft with a removable cover that leads down to a sewer or drain. **2** a hole, usually with a detachable cover, through which a man can enter a boiler, tank, etc.

manhood ('mænhʊd) *n* **1** the state or quality of being a man or being manly. **2** men collectively. **3** the state of being human.

man-hour *n* a unit of work in industry, equal to the work done by one man in one hour.

manhunt ('mænˌhʌnt) *n* an organized search, usually by police, for a wanted man or fugitive.

Mani ★ ('mɑːnɪ) *n* ?216–?276 A.D., Persian prophet who founded Manichaeism. Also called: **Manes, Manichaeus**.

mania ('meɪnɪə) *n* **1** a mental disorder characterized by great excitement and occasionally violent behaviour. **2** obsessional enthusiasm or partiality. [C14: via LL from Gk: madness]

-mania *n combining form*. indicating extreme desire or pleasure of a specified kind or an abnormal excitement aroused by something: *kleptomania; nymphomania; pyromania*. [from MANIA]
▶ **-maniac** *n and adj combining form*.

maniac ('meɪnɪˌæk) *n* **1** a wild disorderly person. **2** a person who has a great craving or enthusiasm for something. **3** *Psychiatry, obs*. a person afflicted with mania. [C17: from LL *maniacus* belonging to madness, from Gk]

maniacal (mə'naɪəkəl) *or* **maniac** *adj* **1** affected with or characteristic of mania. **2** characteristic of or befitting a maniac: *maniacal laughter*.
▶ **ma'niacally** *adv*

manic ('mænɪk) *adj* **1** characterizing, denoting, or affected by mania. ◆ *n* **2** a person afflicted with mania. [C19: from Gk, from MANIA]

manic-depressive *Psychiatry*. ◆ *adj* **1** denoting a mental disorder characterized by an alternation between extreme euphoria and deep depression. ◆ *n* **2** a person afflicted with this disorder.

Manichaeism *or* **Manicheism** ('mænɪkiːˌɪzəm) *n* the system of religious doctrines taught by the Persian prophet Mani about the 3rd century A.D. It was based on

a supposed primordial conflict between light and darkness or goodness and evil. [C14: from LL *Manichaeus*, from LGk *Manikhaios* of Mani]
▷ ˌMani'chaean *or* ˌMani'chean *adj, n* ▷ 'Manichee *n*

Manichaeus *or* **Manicheus** ★ (ˌmænɪ'kiːəs) *n* See Mani.

manicure ('mænɪˌkjʊə) *n* **1** care of the hands and fingernails, involving shaping the nails, removing cuticles, etc. **2** Also called: **manicurist**. a person who gives manicures, esp. as a profession. ◆ *vb* **manicures, manicuring, manicured. 3** to care for (the hands and fingernails) in this way. [C19: from F, from L *manus* hand + *cūra* care]

manifest ('mænɪˌfest) *adj* **1** easily noticed or perceived; obvious. **2** *Psychoanalysis.* of or relating to the ostensible elements of a dream: *manifest content.* Cf. **latent** (sense 5).
◆ *vb* **3** (*tr*) to show plainly; reveal or display. **4** (*tr*) to prove beyond doubt. **5** (*intr*) (of a disembodied spirit) to appear in visible form. ◆ *n* **6** a customs document containing particulars of a ship, its cargo, and its destination. **7a** a list of cargo, passengers, etc., on an aeroplane. **7b** a list of railway trucks or their cargo. [C14: from L *manifestus* plain, lit.: struck with the hand]
▷ 'mani,festable *adj* ▷ 'mani,festly *adv*

manifestation (ˌmænɪfe'steɪʃən) *n* **1** the act of demonstrating; display. **2** the state of being manifested. **3** an indication or sign. **4** a public demonstration of feeling. **5** the materialization of a disembodied spirit.
▷ ˌmani'festative *adj*

manifesto (ˌmænɪ'festəʊ) *n, pl* **manifestos** *or* **manifestoes**. a public declaration of intent, policy, aims, etc., as issued by a political party, government, or movement. [C17: from It., from *manifestare* to MANIFEST]

manifold ('mænɪˌfəʊld) *adj Formal.* **1** of several different kinds; multiple. **2** having many different forms, features, or elements. ◆ *n* **3** something having many varied parts, forms, or features. **4** a chamber or pipe with a number of inlets or outlets used to collect or distribute a fluid. In an internal-combustion engine the **inlet manifold** carries the vaporized fuel from the carburettor to the inlet ports and the **exhaust manifold** carries the exhaust gases away.
◆ *vb* (*tr*) **5** to duplicate (a page, book, etc.). **6** to make manifold; multiply. [OE *manigfeald*. See MANY, -FOLD]
▷ 'mani,foldly *adv* ▷ 'mani,foldness *n*

manikin *or* **mannikin** ('mænɪkɪn) *n* **1** a little man; dwarf or child. **2** an anatomical model of the body or a part of the body, esp. for use in medical or art instruction. **3** a variant of **mannequin**. [C17: from Du. *manneken*, dim. of MAN]

Manila ★ (mə'nɪlə) *n* **1** the chief port of the Philippines, on S Luzon on Manila Bay: capital of the republic until 1948 and from 1976; seat of the Far Eastern University and the University of Santo Tomas (1611). Pop. (urban area): 8 594 150 (1994 est.). **2** a type of cigar made in this city. **3** (*often not cap.*) short for **Manila hemp, Manila paper**.

Manila Bay ★ *n* an almost landlocked inlet of the South China Sea in the Philippines, in W Luzon: mostly forms Manila harbour. Area: 1994 sq. km (770 sq. miles).

Manila hemp *or* **Manilla hemp** *n* a fibre obtained from the abaca plant, used for rope, paper, etc.

Manila paper *or* **Manilla paper** *n* a strong usually brown paper made from Manila hemp or similar fibres.

manilla (mə'nɪlə) *n* an early form of currency in W Africa in the pattern of a small bracelet. [from Sp.: bracelet, dim. of *mano* hand, from L *manus*]

man in the street *n* the typical or ordinary person.

manioc ('mænɪˌɒk) *or* **manioca** (ˌmænɪ'əʊkə) *n* another name for **cassava** (sense 1). [C16: from Tupi *mandioca*]

manipulate (mə'nɪpjʊˌleɪt) *vb* **manipulates, manipulating, manipulated. 1** (*tr*) to handle or use, esp. with some skill. **2** to control or influence (something or someone) cleverly, deviously, or skilfully. **3** to falsify (a bill, accounts, etc.) for one's own advantage. **4** (in physiotherapy) to examine or treat manually, as in loosening a joint. [C19: back formation from *manipulation*, from L *manipulus* handful]
▷ **manipulability** (mə,nɪpjʊlə'bɪlɪtɪ) *n* ▷ **ma'nipu,latable** *or* **ma'nipulable** *adj* ▷ **ma,nipu'lation** *n* ▷ **ma'nipulative** *adj* ▷ **ma'nipu,lator** *n* ▷ **ma'nipulatory** *adj*

Manipur ★ (ˌmʌnɪ'pʊə) *n* a state in NE India: largely densely forested mountains. Capital: Imphal. Pop.: 2 010 000 (1994 est.). Area: 22 327 sq. km (8621 sq. miles).

Manisa ★ ('mɑːnɪˌsɑː) *n* a city in W Turkey: the Byzantine seat of government (1204–1313). Pop.: 187 500 (1994 est.).

Manitoba ★ (ˌmænɪ'təʊbə) *n* **1** a province of W Canada: consists of prairie in the southwest, with extensive forests in the north and tundra near Hudson Bay in the northeast. Capital: Winnipeg. Pop.: 1 137 500 (1995 est.). Area: 650 090 sq. km (251 000 sq. miles). Abbrev.: **MB. 2** Lake. a lake in W Canada, in S Manitoba: fed by the outflow from Lake Winnipegosis; drains into Lake Winnipeg. Area: 4706 sq. km (1817 sq. miles).
▷ ˌMani'toban *n, adj*

manitou, manitu ('mænɪˌtuː), *or* **manito** ('mænɪˌtəʊ) *n, pl* **manitous, manitus, manitos** *or* **manitou, manitu, manito**. (among the Algonquian Indians) a deified spirit or force. [C17: of Amerind origin]

Manitoulin Island ★ (ˌmænɪ'tuːlɪn) *n* an island in N Lake Huron in Ontario: the largest freshwater island in the world. Length: 129 km (80 miles). Width: up to 48 km (30 miles).

Manizales ★ (ˌmænɪ'zɑːles; *Spanish* mani'θales) *n* a city in W Colombia, in the Cordillera Central of the Andes at an altitude of 2100 m (7000 ft): commercial centre of a rich coffee-growing area. Pop.: 358 194 (1997 est.).

man jack *n Inf.* a single individual (in **every man jack, no man jack**).

mankind (ˌmæn'kaɪnd) *n* **1** human beings collectively; humanity. **2** men collectively, as opposed to womankind.

> **USAGE NOTE** Some people object to the use of *mankind* to refer to all human beings and prefer the term *humankind*.

Manley ★ ('mænlɪ) *n* **Michael Norman**. 1924–97, Jamaican statesman; prime minister of Jamaica (1972–80; 1989–92).

manlike ('mænˌlaɪk) *adj* resembling or befitting a man.

manly ('mænlɪ) *adj* **manlier, manliest. 1** possessing qualities, such as vigour or courage, generally regarded as appropriate to or typical of a man; masculine. **2** characteristic of or befitting a man.
▷ 'manliness *n*

man-made *adj* made by man; artificial.

Mann ★ (*German* man) *n* **1** **Heinrich** ('hainrɪç). 1871–1950, German novelist: works include *Professor Unrat* (1905), filmed as *The Blue Angel* (1928), and *Man of Straw* (1918). **2** his brother, **Thomas** ('toːmas). 1875–1955, German novelist, in the US after 1937. His works include the short story *Death in Venice* (1913) and the novels *The Magic Mountain* (1924) and *Doctor Faustus* (1947): Nobel prize for literature 1929.

manna ('mænə) *n* **1** *Old Testament.* the miraculous food which sustained the Israelites in the wilderness (Exodus 16:14–36). **2** any spiritual or divine nourishment. **3** a windfall (esp. in **manna from heaven**). **4** a sweet substance obtained from various plants, esp. from the **manna** or **flowering ash** of S Europe, used as a mild laxative. [OE via LL from Gk, from Heb. *mān*]

Mannar ★ (mə'nɑː) *n Gulf of.* the part of the Indian Ocean between SE India and the island of Sri Lanka: pearl fishing.

manned (mænd) *adj* **1** supplied or equipped with men, esp. soldiers. **2** (of spacecraft, etc.) having a human crew.

mannequin ('mænɪkɪn) *n* **1** a woman who wears the clothes displayed in a fashion show; model. **2** a life-size dummy of the human body used to fit or display clothes. [C18: via F from Du. *manneken* MANIKIN]

manner ('mænə) *n* **1** a way of doing or being. **2** a person's bearing and behaviour. **3** the style or customary way of doing or accomplishing something. **4** type or kind. **5** mannered style, as in art; mannerism. **6** in a manner of

speaking. in a way; so to speak. **7 to the manner born.** naturally fitted to a specified role or activity. [C12: via Norman F from OF *maniere*, from Vulgar L *manuāria* (unattested) a way of handling something, noun use of L *manuārius* belonging to the hand, from *manus* hand]

mannered ('mænəd) *adj* **1** having idiosyncrasies or mannerisms; affected. **2** (*in combination*) having manners as specified: *ill-mannered.*

Mannerheim ★ ('mænə,heɪm) *n* Baron **Carl Gustaf Emil.** 1867–1951, Finnish soldier and statesman; president of Finland (1944–46).

mannerism ('mænə,rɪzəm) *n* **1** a distinctive and individual gesture or trait. **2** (*often cap.*) a principally Italian movement in art and architecture between the High Renaissance and Baroque periods (1520–1600), using distortion and exaggeration of human proportions, perspective, etc. **3** adherence to a distinctive or affected manner, esp. in art or literature.
▶ **'mannerist** *n, adj* ▶ ,**manner'istic** *adj* ▶ ,**manner'istically** *adv*

mannerless ('mænəlɪs) *adj* having bad manners; boorish.
▶ **'mannerlessness** *n*

mannerly ('mænəlɪ) *adj* **1** well-mannered; polite. ◆ *adv* **2** *Now rare.* with good manners; politely.
▶ **'mannerliness** *n*

manners ('mænəz) *pl n* **1** social conduct. **2** a socially acceptable way of behaving.

Mannheim ★ ('mænhaɪm; *German* 'manhaɪm) *n* a city in SW Germany, in Baden-Württemberg at the confluence of the Rhine and Neckar: one of Europe's largest inland harbours; a cultural and musical centre. Pop.: 316 223 (1995 est.).

mannikin ('mænɪkɪn) *n* a variant spelling of **manikin.**

Manning ★ ('mænɪŋ) *n* **1 Henry Edward.** 1808–92, British churchman. An Anglican who converted to Roman Catholicism (1851), he became archbishop of Westminster (1865) and cardinal (1875). **2 Olivia.** 1908–80, British writer, best known for her novel sequence *Fortunes of War*, comprising the *Balkan Trilogy* (1960–65) and the *Levant Trilogy* (1977–80).

mannish ('mænɪʃ) *adj* **1** (of a woman) displaying qualities regarded as typical of a man. **2** of or resembling a man.
▶ **'mannishly** *adv* ▶ **'mannishness** *n*

manoeuvre *or US* **maneuver** (mə'nuːvə) *n* **1** a contrived, complicated, and possibly deceptive plan or action. **2** a movement or action requiring dexterity and skill. **3a** a tactic or movement of a military or naval unit. **3b** (*pl*) tactical exercises, usually on a large scale. **4** a planned movement of an aircraft in flight. **5** any change from the straight steady course of a ship. ◆ *vb* **manoeuvres, manoeuvring, manoeuvred** *or US* **manoeuvers, manoeuvering, manoeuvered. 6** (*tr*) to contrive or accomplish with skill or cunning. **7** (*intr*) to manipulate situations, etc., in order to gain some end. **8** (*intr*) to perform a manoeuvre or manoeuvres. **9** to move or deploy or be moved or deployed, as military units, etc. [C15: from F, from Med. L *manuopera* manual work, from L *manū operāre* to work with the hand]
▶ ma'**noeuvrable** *or US* ma'**neuverable** *adj* ▶ ma,**noeuvra-'bility** *or US* ma,**neuvera'bility** *n* ▶ ma'**noeuvrer** *or US* ma-'**neuverer** *n* ▶ ma'**noeuvring** *or US* ma'**neuvering** *n*

man of God *n* **1** a saint or prophet. **2** a clergyman.

man of straw *n* **1** a man who cannot be relied upon to honour his financial commitments, esp. because of his limited resources. **2** any weak or vulnerable man.

man-of-war *or* **man o' war** *n, pl* **men-of-war** *or* **men o' war. 1** a warship. **2** See **Portuguese man-of-war.**

man-of-war bird *or* **man-o'-war bird** *n* another name for **frigate bird.**

Manolete ★ (*Spanish* mano'lete) *n* original name *Manuel Rodríguez y Sánchez.* 1917–47, Spanish bullfighter.

manometer (mə'nɒmɪtə) *n* an instrument for comparing pressures. [C18: from F *manomètre*, from Gk *manos* sparse + *metron* measure]
▶ **manometric** (,mænəʊ'mɛtrɪk) *or* ,**mano'metrical** *adj*

manor ('mænə) *n* **1** (in medieval Europe) the manor house of a lord and the lands attached to it. **2** a manor house. **3** a landed estate. **4** *Brit. sl.* a geographical area of operation, esp. of a local police force. [C13: from OF *manoir* dwelling, from *maneir* to dwell, from L *manēre* to remain]
▶ **manorial** (mə'nɔːrɪəl) *adj*

manor house *n* (esp. formerly) the house of the lord of a manor.

manpower ('mæn,paʊə) *n* **1** power supplied by men. **2** a unit of power based on the rate at which a man can work; roughly 75 watts. **3** the number of people needed or available for a job.

manqué *French.* ('mɒŋkeɪ) *adj* (*postpositive*) unfulfilled; potential; would-be: *the manager is an actor manqué.* [C19: lit.: having missed]

Manresa (*Spanish* man'resa) *n* a city in NE Spain: contains a cave used as the spiritual retreat of St Ignatius Loyola. Pop.: 65 607 (1988 est.).

mansard ('mænsɑːd, -səd) *n* a roof having two slopes on both sides and both ends, the lower slopes being steeper than the upper. Also called: **mansard roof.** [C18: from F *mansarde,* after François MANSART]

Mansart ★ (*French* mãsar) *n* **1 François** (frãswa). 1598–1666, French architect, who established the French classical style. **2** his great-nephew, **Jules Hardouin.** 1646–1708, French architect and town planner, who completed the Palace of Versailles.

manse (mæns) *n* (in certain religious denominations) the house provided for a minister. [C15: from Med. L *mansus* dwelling, from p.p. of L *manēre* to stay]

Mansell ★ ('mænsᵊl) *n* **Nigel.** born 1953, British motor-racing driver; world champion in 1992.

manservant ('mæn,sɜːvənt) *n, pl* **menservants.** a male servant, esp. a valet.

Mansfield[1] ★ ('mæns,fiːld) *n* a town in central England, in W Nottinghamshire: former coal-mining and cotton-textiles industries. Pop.: 71 858 (1991).

Mansfield[2] ★ ('mæns,fiːld) *n* **Katherine,** real name *Kathleen Mansfield Beauchamp.* 1888–1923, British writer, born in New Zealand, noted for such short-story collections as *Bliss* (1920) and *The Garden Party* (1922).

Mansholt ★ (*Dutch* 'mɑnshɔlt) *n* **Sicco Leendert** ('siko 'leːndərt). 1908–95, Dutch economist and politician; vice president (1958–72) and president (1972–73) of the EC Commission.

mansion ('mænʃən) *n* **1** Also called: **mansion house.** a large and imposing house. **2** a less common word for **manor house. 3** (*pl*) *Brit.* a block of flats. [C14: via OF from L *mansio* a remaining, from *mansus*; see MANSE]

Mansion House ★ *n* **the. 1** the residence of the Lord Mayor of London. **2** the residence of the Lord Mayor of Dublin.

man-sized *adj* **1** of a size appropriate for or convenient for a man. **2** *Inf.* big; large.

manslaughter ('mæn,slɔːtə) *n* **1** *Law.* the unlawful killing of one human being by another without malice aforethought. Cf. **murder. 2** (loosely) the killing of a human being.

Mansûra ★ (mæn'sʊərə) *n* See **El Mansûra.**

manta ('mæntə) *n* **1** Also called: **manta ray, devilfish, devil ray.** any large ray (fish), having very wide winglike pectoral fins and feeding on plankton. **2** a rough cotton cloth made in Spain and Spanish America. **3** a piece of this used as a blanket or shawl. [Sp.: cloak, from Vulgar L; see MANTLE]

manteau ('mæntəʊ) *n, pl* **manteaus** (-təʊz) *or* **manteaux** (-təʊ). a cloak or mantle. [C17: via F from L *mantellum* MANTLE]

Mantegna ★ (*Italian* man'teɲɲa) *n* **Andrea** (an'drɛːa). 1431–1506, Italian painter and engraver.

mantel ('mæntᵊl) *n* **1** a wooden, stone, or iron frame around the opening of a fireplace, together with its decorative facing. **2** Also called: **mantel shelf.** a shelf above this frame. [C15: from F, var. of MANTLE]

mantelet ('mæntᵊ,lɛt) *or* **mantlet** *n* **1** a woman's short mantle, worn in the mid-19th century. **2** a portable bul-

★ people and places

letproof screen or shelter. [C14: from OF, dim. of *mantel* MANTLE]

mantelpiece ('mænt³l,pi:s) *n* 1 Also called: **mantel shelf, chimneypiece.** a shelf above a fireplace often forming part of the mantel. 2 another word for **mantel** (sense 1).

mantic ('mæntɪk) *adj* 1 of or relating to divination and prophecy. 2 having divining or prophetic powers. [C19: from Gk *mantikos* prophetic, from *mantis* seer]
▶ '**mantically** *adv*

-mantic *adj combining form.* forming adjectives from nouns ending in **-mancy.**

mantilla (mæn'tɪlə) *n* a woman's lace or silk scarf covering the shoulders and head, worn esp. in Spain. [C18: Sp., dim. of *manta* cloak]

Mantinea *or* **Mantineia** ★ (,mæntɪ'neɪə) *n* (in ancient Greece) a city in E Arcadia; site of several battles.

mantis ('mæntɪs) *n, pl* **mantises** *or* **mantes** (-ti:z). any carnivorous typically green insect of warm and tropical regions, having a long body and large eyes and resting with the first pair of legs raised as if in prayer. Also called: **praying mantis.** [C17: NL, from Gk: prophet, alluding to its praying posture]

mantissa (mæn'tɪsə) *n* the fractional part of a common logarithm representing the digits of the associated number but not its magnitude: *the mantissa of 2.4771 is .4771.* [C17: from L: something added]

mantle ('mænt³l) *n* 1 *Arch.* a loose wrap or cloak. 2 such a garment regarded as a symbol of someone's power or authority. 3 anything that covers completely or envelops. 4 a small dome-shaped or cylindrical mesh, used to increase illumination in a gas or oil lamp by becoming incandescent. 5 *Zool.* a protective layer of epidermis in molluscs and brachiopods that secretes a substance forming the shell. 6 *Ornithol.* the feathers of the folded wings and back, esp. when of a different colour from the remaining feathers. 7 *Geol.* the part of the earth between the crust and the core. 8 a less common spelling of **mantel.** ◆ *vb* **mantles, mantling, mantled.** 9 (*tr*) to envelop or supply with a mantle. 10 (*tr*) to spread over or become spread over. 11 (*intr*) to blush; flush. [C13: via OF from L *mantellum,* dim. of *mantum* cloak]

mantle rock *n* the loose rock material, including glacial drift, soils, etc., that covers the bedrock and forms the land surface.

Mantova ★ ('mantova) *n* the Italian name for **Mantua.**

mantra ('mæntrə, 'mʌn-) *n* 1 *Hinduism.* any of those parts of the Vedic literature which consist of the metrical psalms of praise. 2 *Hinduism, Buddhism.* any sacred word or syllable used as an object of concentration. [C19: from Sansk., lit.: speech, instrument of thought, from *man* to think]

mantua ('mæntjʊə) *n* a woman's loose gown of the 17th and 18th centuries. [C17: changed from MANTEAU, through the infl. of MANTUA]

Mantua ★ ('mæntjʊə) *n* a city in N Italy, in E Lombardy, surrounded by lakes: birthplace of Virgil. Pop.: 54 808 (1990). Italian name: **Mantova.**

manual ('mænjʊəl) *adj* 1 of or relating to a hand or hands. 2 operated or done by hand. 3 physical, as opposed to mental or mechanical: *manual labour.* 4 by human labour rather than automatic or computer-aided means. ◆ *n* 5 a book, esp. of instructions or information. 6 *Music.* one of the keyboards played by hand on an organ. 7 *Mil.* the prescribed drill with small arms. [C15: via OF from L *manuālis,* from *manus* hand]
▶ '**manually** *adv*

manufactory (,mænjʊ'fæktərɪ, -trɪ) *n, pl* **manufactories.** an obsolete word for **factory.** [C17: from obs. *manufact;* see MANUFACTURE]

manufacture (,mænjʊ'fæktʃə) *vb* **manufactures, manufacturing, manufactured.** 1 to process or make (a product) from a raw material, esp. as a large-scale operation using machinery. 2 (*tr*) to invent or concoct. ◆ *n* 3 the production of goods, esp. by industrial processes. 4 a manufactured product. 5 the creation or production of anything. [C16: from obs. *manufact* handmade, from LL *manūfactus,* from L *manus* hand + *facere* to make]
▶ ,**manu'facturing** *n, adj*

manufacturer (,mænjʊ'fæktʃərə) *n* a person or business concern that manufactures goods or owns a factory.

manuka ('mɑ:nʊkə) *n* a New Zealand tree with strong elastic wood and aromatic leaves. Also called: **tea tree.** [from Maori]

Manukau ★ ('mɑ:nʊ,kaʊ) *n* a city in New Zealand, on **Manukau Harbour** (an inlet of the Tasman Sea) near Auckland on NW North Island. Pop.: 254 577 (1996).

manumit (,mænjʊ'mɪt) *vb* **manumits, manumitting, manumitted.** (*tr*) to free from slavery, servitude, etc.; emancipate. [C15: from L *manūmittere* to release, from *manū* from one's hand + *ēmittere* to send away]
▶ **manumission** (,mænjʊ'mɪʃən) *n*

manure (mə'njʊə) *n* 1 animal excreta, usually with straw, etc., used to fertilize land. 2 *Chiefly Brit.* any material, esp. chemical fertilizer, used to fertilize land. ◆ *vb* **manures, manuring, manured.** 3 (*tr*) to spread manure upon (fields or soil). [C14: from Med. L *manuopera* manual work; see MANOEUVRE]
▶ **ma'nurer** *n*

manus ('meɪnəs) *n, pl* **manus. 1** *Anat.* the wrist and hand. 2 the corresponding part in other vertebrates. [C19: L: hand]

manuscript ('mænjʊ,skrɪpt) *n* 1 a book or other document written by hand. 2 the original handwritten or typed version of a book, article, etc., as submitted by an author for publication. 3 handwriting, as opposed to printing. [C16: from Med. L *manūscriptus,* from L *manus* hand + *scribere* to write]

Manutius ★ (mə'nju:ʃəs) *n* See **Aldus Manutius.**

Manx (mæŋks) *adj* 1 of or relating to the Isle of Man (an island in the Irish Sea), its inhabitants, their language, or their dialect of English. ◆ *n* 2 an almost extinct language of the Isle of Man, closely related to Scottish Gaelic. 3 **the Manx.** (*functioning as pl*) the people of the Isle of Man. [C16: earlier *Maniske,* of Scand. origin, from *Mana* Isle of Man + *-iske* -ISH]

Manx cat *n* a short-haired tailless variety of cat, believed to originate on the Isle of Man.

Manxman ('mæŋksmən) *or* (*fem*) **Manxwoman** ('mæŋks,wʊmən) *n, pl* **Manxmen** *or* **Manxwomen.** a native or inhabitant of the Isle of Man.

many ('mɛnɪ) *determiner* 1 (sometimes preceded by *a great* or *a good*) 1a a large number of: *many times.* 1b (*as pron; functioning as pl*): *many are seated already.* 2 (foll. by *a, an,* or *another,* and a sing noun) each of a considerable number of: *many a man.* 3 (preceded by *as, too, that,* etc.) 3a a great number of: *as many apples as you like.* 3b (*as pron; functioning as pl*): *I have as many as you.* ◆ *n* 4 **the many.** the majority of mankind, esp. the common people. [OE *manig*]

many-sided *adj* having many sides, aspects, etc.
▶ ,**many-'sidedness** *n*

many-valued logic *n* any of various logics in which the truth-values that a proposition may have are not restricted to truth and falsity.

manzanilla (,mænzə'nɪlə) *n* a very dry pale sherry. [C19: from Sp.: camomile (referring to its bouquet)]

Manzoni ★ (*Italian* man'dzo:ni) *n* **Alessandro** (ales-'sandro). 1785–1873, Italian romantic novelist and poet, famous for his historical novel *I Promessi sposi* (1825–27).

Maoism ('maʊɪzəm) *n* 1 Marxism-Leninism as interpreted by Mao Tse-tung: distinguished by its theory of guerrilla warfare and its emphasis on the revolutionary potential of the peasantry. 2 adherence to or reverence for Mao Tse-tung and his teachings.
▶ '**Maoist** *n, adj*

Maori ('maʊrɪ) *n* 1 (*pl* **Maoris** *or* **Maori**) a member of the people of Polynesian origin living in New Zealand and the Cook Islands since before the arrival of European settlers. 2 the language of this people, belonging to the Malayo-Polynesian family. ◆ *adj* 3 of or relating to this people or their language.

Maoriland ★ ('maʊrɪ,lænd) *n* an obsolete name for **New Zealand.**
▶ '**Maori,lander** *n*

Mao Tse-tung ('maʊ tseɪ'tʊŋ) *or* **Mao Ze Dong** ★ *n*

map 898 **marble**

1893–1976, Chinese Marxist and statesman, who helped to found the Chinese Communist Party (1921) and established a soviet republic in SE China (1931–34). He led the retreat of Communist forces to NW China known as the Long March (1935–36), emerging as leader of the party. He united with the Kuomintang regime in World War II, but defeated them in the ensuing civil war. He founded the People's Republic of China (1949), of which he was chairman until 1959, and as party chairman instigated the Cultural Revolution in 1966.

map (mæp) *n* **1** a diagrammatic representation of the earth's surface or part of it, showing the geographical distributions, positions, etc., of features such as roads, towns, relief, rainfall, etc. **2** a diagrammatic representation of the stars or of the surface of a celestial body. **3** a maplike drawing of anything. **4** *Maths.* another name for **function** (sense 5). **5** a slang word for **face** (sense 1). **6 off the map.** no longer important; out of existence (esp. in **wipe off the map**). **7 put on the map.** to make (a town, company, etc.) well-known. ◆ *vb* **maps, mapping, mapped.** (*tr*) **8** to make a map of. **9** *Maths.* to represent or transform (a function, figure, set, etc.). ◆ See also **map out.** [C16: from Med. L *mappa* (*mundi*) map (of the world), from L *mappa* cloth]

Map (mæp) *or* **Mapes** ★ (mæps, 'merpi:z) *n* Walter. ?1140–?1209, Welsh ecclesiastic and satirical writer. His chief work is the miscellany *De Nugis curialium.*

maple ('merp^al) *n* **1** any tree or shrub of a N temperate genus, having winged seeds borne in pairs and lobed leaves. **2** the hard wood of any of these trees, used for furniture and flooring. **3** the flavour of the sap of the sugar maple. ◆ See also **sugar maple.** [C14: from OE *mapel-*, as in *mapeltrēow* maple tree]

maple leaf *n* the leaf of the maple tree, the national emblem of Canada.

maple sugar *n US & Canad.* sugar made from the sap of the sugar maple.

maple syrup *n Chiefly US & Canad.* a very sweet syrup made from the sap of the sugar maple.

map out *vb* (*tr, adv*) to plan or design.

mapping ('mæpɪŋ) *n Maths.* another name for **function** (sense 5).

map projection *n* a means of representing or a representation of a globe or celestial sphere or part of it on a flat map.

Maputo ★ (mə'pu:təʊ) *n* the capital and chief port of Mozambique, in the south on Delagoa Bay: became capital in 1907; the nearest port to the Rand gold-mining and industrial region of South Africa. Pop.: 931 591 (1991 est.). Former name (until 1975): **Lourenço Marques.**

maquette (mæ'kɛt) *n* a sculptor's small preliminary model or sketch. [C20: from F, from It. *macchietta* a little sketch, from *macchiare,* from L *macula* blemish]

maquis (mɑ:'ki:) *n, pl* **maquis** (-'ki:). **1** shrubby, mostly evergreen, vegetation found in coastal regions of the Mediterranean. **2** (*often cap.*) **2a** the French underground movement that fought against the German occupying forces in World War II. **2b** a member of this movement. [C20: from F, from It. *macchia* thicket, from L *macula* spot]

mar (mɑ:) *vb* **mars, marring, marred.** (*tr*) to cause harm to; spoil or impair. [OE *merran*]
▶ **'marrer** *n*

mar. *abbrev. for:* **1** maritime. **2** married.

Mar. *abbrev. for* March.

marabou ('mærə,bu:) *n* **1** a large black-and-white African carrion-eating stork. **2** a down feather of this bird, used to trim garments. [C19: from F, from Ar. *murābit* MARABOUT: the stork is considered a holy bird in Islam]

marabout ('mærə,bu:) *n* **1** a Muslim holy man or hermit of North Africa. **2** a shrine of the grave of a marabout. [C17: via F & Port. *marabuto,* from Ar. *murābit*]

maraca (mə'rækə) *n* a percussion instrument, usually one of a pair, consisting of a gourd or plastic shell filled with dried seeds, pebbles, etc. [C20: Brazilian Port., Amerind origin]

Maracaibo ★ (,mærə'kaɪbəʊ; *Spanish* mara'kaiβo) *n* **1** a

port in NW Venezuela, on the channel from Lake Maracaibo to the Gulf of Venezuela: the second largest city in the country; University of Zulia (1891); major oil centre. Pop.: 1 249 670 (1990). **2 Lake.** a lake in NW Venezuela, linked with the Gulf of Venezuela by a dredged channel: centre of the Venezuelan and South American oil industry. Area: about 13 000 sq. km (500 sq. miles).

Maracanda ★ (,mærə'kændə) *n* the ancient name for **Samarkand.**

Maracay ★ (*Spanish* mara'kai) *n* a city in N central Venezuela: developed greatly as the headquarters of Juan Vicente Gómez during his dictatorship; textile industries. Pop.: 354 196 (1990).

Maradona ★ (,mærə'dɒnə) *n* **Diego Armando** (dɪ'eɪgəʊ). born 1960, Argentinian footballer.

marae (mə'raɪ) *n* **1** *NZ.* a traditional Maori tribal meeting place, originally one in the open air, now frequently a purpose-built building. **2** (in Polynesia) an open-air place of worship. [from Maori]

Marajó ★ (*Portuguese* mara'ʒɔ) *n* an island in N Brazil, at the mouth of the Amazon. Area: 38 610 sq. km (15 444 sq. miles).

Maranhão ★ (*Portuguese* marə'ɲəu) *n* a state of NE Brazil, on the Atlantic: forested and humid in the northwest, with high plateaus in the east and south. Capital: São Luís. Pop.: 5 231 300 (1995 est.). Area: 328 666 sq. km (128 179 sq. miles).

Marañón ★ (*Spanish* mara'ɲon) *n* a river in NE Peru, rising in the Andes and flowing northwest into the Ucayali River, forming the Amazon. Length: about 1450 km (900 miles).

maranta (mɑ:'ræntə) *n* any of various tropical monocotyledons with ornamental leaves. [C19: after B. *Maranta* 16th-century Venetian botanist]

Maraş ★ (*Turkish* 'marɑʃ) *n* a town in S Turkey: noted formerly for the manufacture of weapons but now for carpets and embroidery. Pop.: 228 129 (1985).

marasca (mə'ræskə) *n* a European cherry tree with red acid-tasting fruit. [C19: from It., var. of *amarasca,* ult. from L *amārus* bitter]

maraschino (,mærə'ski:nəʊ, -'ʃi:nəʊ) *n* a liqueur made from marasca cherries, having a taste like bitter almonds. [C18: from It.; see MARASCA]

maraschino cherry *n* a cherry preserved in maraschino or an imitation of this liqueur.

marasmus (mə'ræzməs) *n Pathol.* general emaciation, esp. of infants, thought to be associated with severe malnutrition or impaired utilization of nutrients. [C17: from NL, from Gk *marasmos,* from *marainein* to waste]
▶ **ma'rasmic** *adj*

Marat ★ (*French* mara) *n* **Jean Paul** (ʒɑ̃ pɔl). 1743–93, French revolutionary leader and founder of the newspaper *L'Ami du peuple.* Instrumental in overthrowing the Girondists (1793), he was assassinated by Charlotte Corday.

marathon ('mærəθən) *n* **1** a race on foot of 26 miles 385 yards (42.195 kilometres). **2a** any long or arduous task, etc. **2b** (*as modifier*): *a marathon effort.* [referring to the feat of the messenger who ran more than 20 miles from Marathon to Athens to bring the news of victory in 490 B.C.]

Marathon ★ ('mærəθən) *n* a plain in Attica northeast of Athens: site of a victory of the Athenians and Plataeans over the Persians (490 B.C.).

marathon group *n* (in psychotherapy) an encounter group that lasts for many hours or days.

maraud (mə'rɔːd) *vb* to wander or raid in search of plunder. [C18: from F *marauder* to prowl, from *maraud* vagabond]
▶ **ma'rauder** *n* ▶ **ma'rauding** *adj*

marble ('mɑːb^al) *n* **1a** a hard crystalline metamorphic rock resulting from the recrystallization of a limestone. **1b** (*as modifier*): *a marble bust.* **2** a block or work of art of marble. **3** a small round glass or stone ball used in playing marbles. ◆ *vb* **marbles, marbling, marbled. 4** (*tr*) to mottle with variegated streaks in imitation of marble. [C12:

★ people and places

via OF from L *marmor*, from Gk *marmaros*, rel. to Gk *marmairein* to gleam]
▶ **'marbled** *adj*

marbles ('mɑːbᵊlz) *n* **1** (*functioning as sing*) a game in which marbles are rolled at one another, similar to bowls. **2** (*functioning as pl*) *Inf.* wits: *to lose one's marbles*.

marbling ('mɑːblɪŋ) *n* **1** a mottled effect or pattern resembling marble. **2** such an effect obtained by transferring floating colours from a gum solution. **3** the streaks of fat in lean meat.

Marburg ★ ('mɑːˌbɜːg; *German* 'maːrburk) *n* **1** a city in W central Germany, in Hesse: famous for the religious debate between Luther and Zwingli in 1529; Europe's first Protestant university (1527). Pop.: 75 400 (1995 est.). **2** the German name for **Maribor**.

Marburg disease *n* a severe, sometimes fatal, viral disease of vervet (green) monkeys, which may be transmitted to humans. Also called: **green monkey disease**. [C20: after MARBURG, in which the first human cases were recorded]

marc (mɑːk) *n* **1** the remains of grapes or other fruit that have been pressed for wine-making. **2** a brandy distilled from these. [C17: from F, from OF *marchier* to trample (grapes)]

Marc ★ (*German* mark) *n* **Franz** (frants). 1880–1916, German expressionist painter; cofounder with Kandinsky of the *Blaue Reiter* group (1911). He is noted for his symbolic compositions of animals.

marcasite ('mɑːkəˌsaɪt) *n* **1** a metallic pale yellow mineral consisting of iron pyrites in crystalline form used in jewellery. **2** a cut and polished form of steel or any white metal used for making jewellery. [C15: from Med. L *marcasīta*, from Ar. *marqashītā*, ?from Persian]

marcato (mɑːˈkɑːtəʊ) *adj, adv Music.* with each note heavily accented. [from It.: marked]

Marceau ★ (*French* marso) *n* **Marcel** (marsɛl). born 1923, French mime artist.

Marcellus ★ (mɑːˈsɛləs) *n* **Marcus Claudius** ('mɑːkəs 'klɔːdɪəs). ?268–208 B.C., Roman general and consul, who captured Syracuse (212) in the Second Punic War.

march[1] (mɑːtʃ) *vb* **1** (*intr*) to walk or proceed with stately or regular steps, usually in a procession or military formation. **2** (*tr*) to make (a person or group) proceed. **3** (*tr*) to traverse or cover by marching. ◆ *n* **4** the act or an instance of marching. **5** a regular stride. **6** a long or exhausting walk. **7** advance; progression (of time, etc.). **8** a distance or route covered by marching. **9** a piece of music, as for a march. **10 steal a march on**. to gain an advantage over, esp. by a secret enterprise or trick. [C16: from OF *marchier* to tread, prob. of Gmc origin]
▶ **'marcher** *n*

march[2] (mɑːtʃ) *n* **1** a frontier, border, or boundary or the land lying along it, often of disputed ownership. ◆ *vb* **2** (*intr*; often foll. by *upon* or *with*) to share a common border (with). [C13: from OF *marche*, of Gmc origin]

March[1] (mɑːtʃ) *n* the third month of the year, consisting of 31 days. [from OF, from L *Martius* (month) of Mars]

March[2] ★ (març) *n* the German name for the **Morava** (sense 1).

Marche ★ (*French* marʃ) *n* a former province of central France.

Marches ★ ('mɑːtʃɪz) *n* **the. 1** the border area between England and Wales or Scotland, both characterized by continual feuding (13th–16th centuries). **2** a region of central Italy. Capital: Ancona. Pop.: 1 438 223 (1994 est.). Area: 9692 sq. km (3780 sq. miles). Italian name: **Le Marche** (le 'marke). **3** any of various other border regions.

March hare *n* a hare during its breeding season in March, noted for its wild and excitable behaviour (esp. in **mad as a March hare**).

marching orders *pl n* **1** military orders, esp. to infantry, giving instructions about a march, its destination, etc. **2** *Inf.* any dismissal, esp. notice of dismissal from employment.

marchioness ('mɑːʃənɪs, ˌmɑːʃəˈnɛs) *n* **1** the wife or widow of a marquis. **2** a woman who holds the rank of

marquis. [C16: from Med. L *marchionissa*, fem. of *marchiō* MARQUIS]

marchpane ('mɑːtʃˌpeɪn) *n* an archaic word for **marzipan**. [C15: from F]

Marciano ★ (ˌmɑːsɪˈænəʊ, -ˈɑːnəʊ) *n* **Rocky**. original name *Rocco Francis Marchegiano*. 1923–69, US boxer; world heavyweight champion, 1952–56.

Marconi ★ (mɑːˈkəʊnɪ) *n* **Guglielmo** (guʎˈʎɛlmo). 1874–1937, Italian physicist, who transmitted radio signals across the Atlantic (1901), making wireless telegraphy a reality: Nobel prize for physics 1909.

Marco Polo ★ ('mɑːkəʊ 'pəʊləʊ) *n* See (Marco) **Polo**.

Marcos ★ ('mɑːkɒs) *n* **Ferdinand** (Edralin). 1917–89, Filipino statesman; president of the Philippines 1965–86: deposed and exiled.

Marcus Aurelius Antoninus ★ ('mɑːkəs ɔːˈriːlɪəs ˌæntəˈnaɪnəs) *n* original name *Marcus Annius Verus*. 121–180 A.D., Roman emperor (161–180) noted particularly for his *Meditations*.

Marcuse ★ (mɑːˈkuːzə) *n* **Herbert**. 1898–1979, US philosopher, born in Germany. His works include *Eros and Civilization* (1958) and *One Dimensional Man* (1964).

Mar del Plata ★ (*Spanish* 'mar ðel 'plata) *n* a city and resort in E Argentina, on the Atlantic: fishing port. Pop.: 512 880 (1991).

Mardi Gras ('mɑːdɪ 'grɑː) *n* the festival of Shrove Tuesday, celebrated in some cities with great revelry. [F: fat Tuesday]

Marduk ★ ('mɑːduk) *n* the chief god of the Babylonian pantheon.

mare[1] (mɛə) *n* the adult female of a horse or zebra. [C12: from OE, of Gmc origin]

mare[2] ('mɑːreɪ, -rɪ) *n, pl* **maria. 1** (*cap. when part of a name*) any of a large number of huge dry plains on the surface of the moon, visible as dark markings and once thought to be seas. **2** a similar area on the surface of Mars. [from L: sea]

Marengo ★ (məˈrɛŋgəʊ; *Italian* maˈreŋgo) *n* a village in NW Italy: site of a major battle in which Napoleon decisively defeated the Austrians (1800).

Marenzio ★ (*Italian* maˈrɛntsjo) *n* **Luca** ('luːka). 1553–99, Italian composer of madrigals.

mare's-nest ('mɛəzˌnɛst) *n* **1** a discovery imagined to be important but proving worthless. **2** a disordered situation.

mare's-tail ('mɛəzˌteɪl) *n* **1** a wisp of trailing cirrus cloud, indicating strong winds at high levels. **2** an erect pond plant with minute flowers and crowded whorls of narrow leaves.

Margaret ★ ('mɑːgrət) *n* **1** called the *Maid of Norway*. ?1282–90, queen of Scotland (1286–90); daughter of Eric II of Norway. Her death while sailing to England to marry the future Edward II led Edward I to declare dominion over Scotland. **2 Princess**. born 1930, younger sister of Queen Elizabeth II.

Margaret of Anjou ★ *n* 1430–82, queen of England. She married the mentally unstable Henry VI of England in 1445 to confirm the truce with France during the Hundred Years' War. She became a leader of the Lancastrians in the Wars of the Roses and was defeated at Tewkesbury (1471) by Edward IV.

Margaret of Navarre ★ *n* 1492–1549, queen of Navarre (1544–49) by marriage to Henry II of Navarre; sister of Francis I of France. She was a poet, a patron of humanism, and author of the *Heptaméron* (1558). Also called: **Margaret of Angoulême**.

Margaret of Scotland ★ *n* Saint. 1045–93, queen consort of Malcolm III of Scotland. Her piety led to her canonization (1250). Feast days: June 10, Nov. 16.

Margaret of Valois ★ *n* 1553–1615, daughter of Henry II of France and Catherine de' Medici; queen of Navarre (1572) by marriage to Henry of Navarre. The marriage was dissolved (1599) after his accession as Henry IV of France: noted for her *Mémoires*.

margaric (mɑːˈgærɪk) *or* **margaritic** *adj* of or resembling pearl. [C19: from Gk *margaron* pearl]

margarine (ˌmɑːdʒəˈriːn, ˌmɑːgə-) *n* a substitute for butter, prepared from vegetable and animal fats with added small amounts of milk, salt, vitamins, colouring matter, etc. [C19: from MARGARIC]

Margarita ★ (ˌmɑːgəˈriːtə) *n* an island in the Caribbean, off the NE coast of Venezuela: pearl fishing. Capital: La Asunción.

Margate ★ (ˈmɑːgeɪt) *n* a town and resort in SE England, in E Kent on the Isle of Thanet. Pop.: 56 734 (1991).

marge[1] (mɑːdʒ) *n Brit. inf.* short for **margarine**.

marge[2] (mɑːdʒ) *n Arch.* a margin. [C16: from F]

margin (ˈmɑːdʒɪn) *n* **1** an edge or rim, and the area immediately adjacent to it; border. **2** the blank space surrounding the text on a page. **3** a vertical line on a page delineating this space. **4** an additional amount or one beyond the minimum necessary: *a margin of error.* **5** *Chiefly Austral.* a payment made in addition to a basic wage, esp. for special skill or responsibility. **6** a bound or limit. **7** the amount by which one thing differs from another. **8** *Commerce.* the profit on a transaction. **9** *Econ.* the minimum return below which an enterprise becomes unprofitable. **10** *Finance.* collateral deposited by a client with a broker as security. ◆ Also (archaic): **margent** (ˈmɑːdʒənt). ◆ *vb (tr)* **11** to provide with a margin; border. **12** *Finance.* to deposit a margin upon. [C14: from L *margō* border]

marginal (ˈmɑːdʒɪnᵊl) *adj* **1** of, in, on, or constituting a margin. **2** close to a limit, esp. a lower limit: *marginal legal ability.* **3** not considered central or important; insignificant. **4** *Econ.* relating to goods or services produced and sold at the margin of profitability: *marginal cost.* **5** *Politics, chiefly Brit. & NZ.* of or designating a constituency in which elections tend to be won by small margins: *a marginal seat.* **6** designating agricultural land on the margin of cultivated zones. ◆ *n* **7** *Politics, chiefly Brit. & NZ.* a marginal constituency.
► **marginality** (ˌmɑːdʒɪˈnælɪtɪ) *n* ► ˈmarginally *adv*

marginalia (ˌmɑːdʒɪˈneɪlɪə) *pl n* notes in the margin of a book, manuscript, or letter. [C19: NL, noun (neuter pl) from *marginālis* marginal]

marginate (ˈmɑːdʒɪˌneɪt) *vb* **marginates, marginating, marginated.** **1** *(tr)* to provide with a margin or margins. ◆ *adj* **2** *Biol.* having a margin of a distinct colour or form. [C18: from L *margināre*]
► ˌmarginˈation *n*

margrave (ˈmɑːˌgreɪv) *n* a German nobleman ranking above a count. Margraves were originally counts appointed to govern frontier provinces, but all eventually became princes of the Holy Roman Empire. [C16: from MDu. *markgrave*, lit.: count of the MARCH[2]]
► **margravate** (ˈmɑːgrəvɪt) *n*

margravine (ˈmɑːgrəˌviːn) *n* **1** the wife or widow of a margrave. **2** a woman who holds the rank of margrave. [C17: from MDu., fem of MARGRAVE]

Margrethe II ★ (Danish marˈgreːdə) *n* born 1940, queen of Denmark from 1972.

marguerite (ˌmɑːgəˈriːt) *n* **1** a cultivated garden plant whose flower heads have white or pale yellow rays around a yellow disc. **2** any of various related plants with daisy-like flowers. [C19: from F: daisy, pearl, from L, from Gk, from *margaron*]

maria (ˈmɑːrɪə) *n* the plural of **mare**[2].

mariachi (ˌmɑːrɪˈɑːtʃɪ) *n* a small ensemble of street musicians in Mexico. [C20: from Mexican Sp.]

Maria de' Medici ★ (Italian maˈriːa de ˈmɛːditʃi) *n* French name *Marie de Médicis*. 1573–1642, queen of France (1600–10) by marriage to Henry IV of France. She became regent for her son (later Louis XIII) but was finally exiled from France in 1631 after plotting to undermine Richelieu's influence.

Mariana Islands ★ (ˌmærɪˈɑːnə) *pl n* a chain of volcanic and coral islands in the W Pacific, east of the Philippines and north of New Guinea: administered by the US and divided politically into Guam and the islands north of Guam constituting the Commonwealth of the Northern Mariana Islands. Pop.: 187 400 (1995 est.). Area: 958 sq. km (370 sq. miles). Former name (1521–1668): **Ladrone Islands.**

Marianao ★ (*Spanish* marjaˈnao) *n* a city in NW Cuba, adjacent to W Havana city: the chief Cuban military base. Pop.: 133 016 (1989 est.).

Mariánské Lázně ★ (*Czech* ˈmarjanskɛ ˈlaːznjɛ) *n* a town in the W Czech Republic: a fashionable spa in the 18th and 19th centuries. Pop.: 15 380 (1991). German name: **Marienbad.**

Maria Theresa ★ (məˈriːə təˈreɪzə) *n* 1717–80, archduchess of Austria and queen of Hungary and Bohemia (1740–80); the daughter and heiress of Emperor Charles VI of Austria and wife of Emperor Francis I. In the War of the Austrian Succession (1740–48) she was confirmed in all her possessions except Silesia, which she attempted unsuccessfully to regain in the Seven Years' War (1756–63).

Mari El Republic ★ (ˈmɑːrɪ) *n* a constituent republic of W central Russia, in the middle Volga basin. Capital: Yoshkar-Ola. Pop.: 766 000 (1995 est.). Area: 23 200 sq. km (8955 sq. miles).

Maribor ★ (ˈmærɪbɔː) *n* an industrial city in N Slovenia, on the Drava River: a flourishing Hapsburg trading centre in the 13th century; resort. Pop.: 134 979 (1995 est.). German name: **Marburg.**

Marie Antoinette ★ (*French* mari ɑ̃twanɛt) *n* 1755–93, queen of France (1774–93) by marriage to Louis XVI of France. Her opposition to reform during the Revolution contributed to the overthrow of the monarchy; guillotined.

Marie Byrd Land ★ (ˈmɑːrɪ ˈbɜːd) *n* the former name of **Byrd Land.**

Marie Galante ★ (*French* mari galɑ̃t) *n* an island in the E Caribbean southeast of Guadeloupe, of which it is a dependency. Chief town: Grand Bourg. Pop.: 13 463 (1990). Area: 155 sq. km (60 sq. miles).

Mariehamn ★ (mariəˈhamn) *n* a city in SW Finland, chief port of the Åland Islands. Pop.: 10 260 (1990). Finnish name: **Maarianhamina.**

Marie Louise ★ (*French* mari lwiz) *n* 1791–1847, empress of France (1811–15) as the second wife of Napoleon I; daughter of Francis I of Austria. On Napoleon's abdication (1815) she became Duchess of Parma.

Marienbad ★ (ˈmærɪənˌbæd; *German* maˈriːənbaːt) *n* the German name for **Mariánské Lázně.**

marigold (ˈmærɪˌgəʊld) *n* **1** any of various tropical American plants cultivated for their yellow or orange flower heads and strongly scented foliage. **2** any of various similar or related plants, such as the marsh marigold. [C14: from *Mary* (the Virgin) + GOLD]

marijuana *or* **marihuana** (ˌmærɪˈhwɑːnə) *n* **1** the dried leaves and flowers of the hemp plant, used for its euphoric effects, esp. in cigarettes. See also **cannabis**. **2** another name for **hemp** (the plant). [C19: from Mexican Sp.]

marimba (məˈrɪmbə) *n* a Latin American percussion instrument consisting of a set of hardwood plates placed over tuned metal resonators, played with two softheaded sticks in each hand. [C18: of West African origin]

Marin ★ (ˈmɑːrɪn) *n* **John.** 1870–1953, US watercolour painter.

marina (məˈriːnə) *n* an elaborate docking facility for yachts and other pleasure boats. [C19: via It. & Sp. from L: MARINE]

marinade *n* (ˌmærɪˈneɪd). **1** a spiced liquid mixture of oil, wine, vinegar, etc., in which meat or fish is soaked before cooking. **2** meat or fish soaked in this. ◆ *vb* (ˈmærɪˌneɪd). **marinades, marinading, marinaded. 3** a variant of **marinate.** [C17: from F, from Sp., from *marinar* to MARINATE]

marinate (ˈmærɪˌneɪt) *vb* **marinates, marinating, marinated.** to soak in marinade. [C17: prob. from It. *marinato*, from *marinare* to pickle, ult. from L *marīnus* MARINE]
► ˌmariˈnation *n*

Marinduque ★ (ˌmɑːrɪnˈduːkeɪ) *n* an island of the central Philippines, east of Mindoro: forms, with offshore is-

★ people and places

lets, a province of the Philippines. Capital: Boac. Pop.: 173 715 (1980). Area: 960 sq. km (370 sq. miles).

marine (mə'ri:n) *adj* (*usually prenominal*) **1** of, found in, or relating to the sea. **2** of or relating to shipping, navigation, etc. **3** of or relating to a body of seagoing troops: *marine corps.* **4** of or relating to a government department concerned with maritime affairs. **5** used or adapted for use at sea. ◆ *n* **6** shipping and navigation in general. **7** (*cap. when part of a name*) a member of a marine corps or similar body. **8** a picture of a ship, seascape, etc. **9 tell it to the marines.** *Inf.* an expression of disbelief. [C15: from OF *marin*, from L *marīnus*, from *mare* sea]

mariner ('mærɪnə) *n* a formal or literary word for **seaman.** [C13: from Anglo-F, ult. from L *marīnus* MARINE]

Marinetti ★ (*Italian* mari'netti) *n* **Filippo Tommaso** (fi-'lippo tom'ma:zo). 1876–1944, Italian poet; founder of futurism (1909).

Mariolatry (,mɛərɪ'ɒlətrɪ) *n Derog.* devotion to the Virgin Mary, considered as excessive.
▸ ,Mari'olater *n* ▸ ,Mari'olatrous *adj*

marionette (,mærɪə'nɛt) *n* a puppet or doll whose jointed limbs are moved by strings. [C17: from F, from *Marion*, dim. of *Marie* Mary + -ETTE]

Marist ('mɛərɪst) *n RC Church.* a member of the Society of Mary, a religious congregation founded in 1824. [C19: from F *Mariste*, from *Marie* Mary (the Virgin)]

Maritain ★ (*French* maritɛ̃) *n* **Jacques** (ʒak). 1882–1973, French neo-Thomist Roman Catholic philosopher.

marital ('mærɪt³l) *adj* **1** of or relating to marriage. **2** of or relating to a husband. [C17: from L *marītālis*, from *marītus* married (adj), husband (n)]
▸ 'maritally *adv*

maritime ('mærɪ,taɪm) *adj* **1** of or relating to navigation, shipping, etc. **2** of, relating to, near, or living near the sea. **3** (of a climate) having small temperature differences between summer and winter. [C16: from L *maritimus*, from *mare* sea]

Maritime Alps ★ *pl n* a range of the W Alps in SE France and NW Italy. Highest peak: Argentera, 3297 m (10 817 ft).

Maritime Provinces *or* **Maritimes** ★ *pl n* the. another name for the **Atlantic Provinces,** but often excluding Newfoundland.

Maritimer ('mærɪ,taɪmə) *n* a native or inhabitant of the Maritime Provinces of Canada.

Maritsa ★ (*Bulgarian* ma'ritsa) *n* a river in S Europe, rising in S Bulgaria and flowing east into Turkey, then south from Edirne as part of the border between Turkey and Greece to the Aegean. Length: 483 km (300 miles). Turkish name: **Meriç.** Greek name: **Évros.**

Mariupol ★ (*Russian* məri'upəlj) *n* a port in the SE Ukraine, near the Sea of Azov: industrial centre. Pop.: 529 000 (1987). Former name (1948–91): **Zhdanov.**

Marius ★ ('mɛərɪəs, 'mærɪəs) *n* **Gaius** ('gaɪəs). ?155–86 B.C., Roman general and consul. He defeated Jugurtha, the Cimbri, and the Teutons (107–101), but his rivalry with Sulla caused civil war (88). He was exiled but returned (87) and took Rome.

Marivaux ★ (*French* marivo) *n* **Pierre Carlet de Chamblain de** (pjɛr karlə də ʃɑ̃blɛ̃ də). 1688–1763, French dramatist and novelist, noted for such comedies as *La Vie de Marianne* (1731–41).

marjoram ('ma:dʒərəm) *n* **1** Also called: **sweet marjoram.** an aromatic Mediterranean plant with sweet-scented leaves, used for seasoning food and in salads. **2** Also called: **wild marjoram, pot marjoram, origan.** a similar and related European plant. See also **oregano.** [C14: via OF *majorane*, from Med. L *marjorana*]

mark¹ (ma:k) *n* **1** a visible impression, stain, etc., on a surface, such as a spot or scratch. **2** a sign, symbol, or other indication that distinguishes something. **3** a cross or other symbol made instead of a signature. **4** a written or printed sign or symbol, as for punctuation. **5** a letter, number, or percentage used to grade academic work. **6** a thing that indicates position or directs; marker. **7** a desired or recognized standard: *up to the mark.* **8** an indication of some quality, feature, or prowess. **9** quality or

importance: *a person of little mark.* **10** a target or goal. **11** impression or influence. **12** one of the temperature settings on a gas oven: *gas mark 5.* **13** *Sl.* a suitable victim, esp. for swindling. **14** (*often cap.*) (in trade names) a model, brand, or type. **15** *Naut.* one of the intervals distinctively marked on a sounding lead. **16** *Rugby.* an action in which a player within his own 22 m line catches a forward kick by an opponent and shouts "mark", which entitles him to a free kick. **17** *Australian Rules football.* **17a** a catch of the ball from a kick of at least 10 yards, after a free kick is taken. **17b** the spot where this occurs. **18** (in medieval England and Germany) a piece of land held in common by the free men of a community. **19** the mark. *Boxing.* the middle of the stomach. **20 make one's mark.** to succeed or achieve recognition. **21 on your mark** *or* **marks.** a command given to runners in a race to prepare themselves at the starting line. ◆ *vb* **22** to make or receive (a visible impression, trace, or stain) on (a surface). **23** (*tr*) to characterize or distinguish. **24** (often foll. by *off* or *out*) to set boundaries or limits (on). **25** (*tr*) to select, designate, or doom by or as if by a mark: *a marked man.* **26** (*tr*) to put identifying or designating labels, stamps, etc., on, esp. to indicate price. **27** (*tr*) to pay heed or attention to: *mark my words.* **28** to observe; notice. **29** to grade or evaluate (scholastic work). **30** *Football, etc.* to stay close to (an opponent) to hamper his play. **31** to keep (score) in some games. **32 mark time. 32a** to move the feet alternately as in marching but without advancing. **32b** to act in a mechanical and routine way. **32c** to halt progress temporarily. ◆ See also **markdown, mark-up.** [OE *mearc* mark]
▸ 'marker *n*

mark² (ma:k) *n* **1** See **Deutschmark, markka, Reichsmark, Ostmark. 2** a former monetary unit and coin in England and Scotland worth two thirds of a pound sterling. **3** a silver coin of Germany until 1924. [OE *marc* unit of weight of precious metal, ?from the marks on metal bars; apparently of Gmc origin and rel. to MARK¹]

Mark ★ (ma:k) *n New Testament.* **1** one of the four Evangelists. Feast day: April 25. **2** the second Gospel, traditionally ascribed to him.

Mark Antony ★ *n* See (Mark) **Antony.**

markdown ('ma:k,daun) *n* **1** a price reduction. ◆ *vb* **mark down. 2** (*tr, adv*) to reduce in price.

marked ('ma:kt) *adj* **1** obvious, evident, or noticeable. **2** singled out, esp. as the target of attack: *a marked man.* **3** *Linguistics.* distinguished by a specific feature, as in phonology. For example, of the two phonemes /t/ and /d/, the /d/ is marked because it exhibits the feature of voice.
▸ **markedly** ('ma:kɪdlɪ) *adv* ▸ 'markedness *n*

market ('ma:kɪt) *n* **1a** an event or occasion, usually held at regular intervals, at which people meet to buy and sell merchandise. **1b** (*as modifier*): *market day.* **2** a place at which a market is held. **3** a shop that sells a particular merchandise: *an antique market.* **4** the trading or selling opportunities provided by a particular group of people: *the foreign market.* **5** demand for a particular product or commodity. **6** See **stock market. 7** See **market price, market value. 8** be in the market for. to wish to buy or acquire. **9 on the market.** available for purchase. **10 seller's** (*or* **buyer's**) **market.** a market characterized by excess demand (or supply) and thus favourable to sellers (or buyers). **11 the market.** business or trade in a commodity as specified: *the sugar market.* ◆ *vb* **markets, marketing, marketed. 12** (*tr*) to offer or produce for sale. **13** (*intr*) to buy or deal in a market. [C12: from L *mercātus*, from *mercāri* to trade, from *merx* merchandise]
▸ 'marketable *adj* ▸ 'marketer *n*

marketeer (,ma:kɪ'tɪə) *n* **1** *Brit.* a supporter of the EU and of Britain's membership of it. **2** a marketer.

market forces *pl n* the effect of supply and demand on trading within a free market.

market garden *n Chiefly Brit.* an establishment where fruit and vegetables are grown for sale.
▸ **market gardener** *n* ▸ **market gardening** *n*

marketing ('ma:kɪtɪŋ) *n* the provision of goods or services to meet consumer needs.

market maker *n* a dealer in securities on the London

stock exchange, who buys and sells as a principal and since 1986 can also deal directly with the public.

marketplace ('mɑːkɪt‚pleɪs) n **1** a place where a public market is held. **2** any centre where ideas, etc., are exchanged. **3** the commercial world of buying and selling.

market price n the prevailing price, as determined by supply and demand, at which goods, services, etc., may be bought or sold.

market research n the study of influences upon customer behaviour and the analysis of market characteristics and trends.

market-test vb (tr) to put (a section of a public-sector enterprise) out to tender, often as a prelude to full-scale privatization.

market town n Chiefly Brit. a town that holds a market, esp. an agricultural centre.

market value n the amount obtainable on the open market for the sale of property, financial assets, or goods and services.

Markham ★ ('mɑːkəm) n Mount. a mountain in Antarctica, in Victoria Land. Height: 4350 m (14 272 ft).

markhor ('mɑːkɔː) or **markhoor** ('mɑːkuə) n, pl **markhors, markhor** or **markhoors, markhoor.** a large wild Himalayan goat with large spiralled horns. [C19: from Persian, lit.: snake-eater]

Markiewicz ★ (mɑːˈkjɛrvɪtʃ) n Constance, Countess, original name Constance Gore-Booth. 1868–1927, Irish nationalist, married to a Polish count. She fought in the Easter Rising (1916) and was sentenced to death but reprieved. The first woman elected to the British parliament (1918), she refused to take her seat.

marking ('mɑːkɪŋ) n **1** a mark or series of marks. **2** the arrangement of colours on an animal, plant, etc. **3** assessment and correction of pupils' or students' written work by teachers.

markka ('mɑːkɑː, -kə) n, pl **markkaa** (-kɑː). the standard monetary unit of Finland. [Finnish; see MARK²]

Markova ★ (mɑːˈkəʊvə) n Dame Alicia, real name Lilian Alicia Marks. born 1910, British ballerina.

marksman ('mɑːksmən) n, pl **marksmen. 1** a person skilled in shooting. **2** a serviceman selected for his skill in shooting.
▸ **'marksmanship** n

mark-up n **1** an amount added to the cost of a commodity to provide the seller with a profit. **2a** an increase in the price of a commodity. **2b** the amount of this. ◆ vb **mark up.** (tr, adv) **3** to add a percentage for profit, etc., to the cost of (a commodity). **4** to increase the price of.

marl (mɑːl) n **1** a fine-grained sedimentary rock consisting of clay minerals, calcium carbonate, and silt: used as a fertilizer. ◆ vb **2** (tr) to fertilize (land) with marl. [C14: via OF, from LL margila, dim. of L marga]
▸ **'marly** adj

Marlborough¹ ★ ('mɔːlbərə, -brə, 'mɔːl-) n a town in S England, in Wiltshire: besieged and captured by Royalists in the Civil War (1642); site of Marlborough College, a public school founded in 1843. Pop.: 6429 (1991).

Marlborough² ★ ('mɔːlbərə, -brə, 'mɔːl-) n 1st Duke of, title of John Churchill. 1650–1722, English general; commander of British forces in the War of the Spanish Succession (1701-14).

Marley ★ ('mɑːlɪ) n Bob, full name Robert Nesta Marley. 1945–81, Jamaican reggae singer, guitarist, and songwriter.

marlin ('mɑːlɪn) n, pl **marlin** or **marlins.** any of several large food and game fishes of warm and tropical seas, having a very long upper jaw. [C20: from MARLINESPIKE, from shape of the beak]

marline or **marlin** ('mɑːlɪn) n Naut. a light rope, usually tarred, made of two strands laid left-handed. [C15: from Du. marlijn, from marren to tie + lijn line]

marlinespike or **marlinspike** ('mɑːlɪn‚spaɪk) n Naut. a pointed metal tool used in separating strands of rope, etc.

marlite ('mɑːlaɪt) or **marlstone** ('mɑːl‚stəʊn) n a type of marl that is resistant to the decomposing action of air.

Marlowe ★ ('mɑːləʊ) n Christopher. 1564–93, English dramatist. His plays include Tamburlaine the Great (1590) and Dr Faustus (1604). He was killed in a tavern brawl.

marmalade ('mɑːmə‚leɪd) n a preserve made by boiling the pulp and rind of citrus fruits, esp. oranges, with sugar. [C16: via F from Port. marmelada, from marmelo quince, from L, from Gk melimēlon, from meli honey + mēlon apple]

Marmara or **Marmora** ★ ('mɑːmərə) n Sea of. a deep inland sea in NW Turkey, linked with the Black Sea by the Bosporus and with the Aegean by the Dardanelles: separates Turkey in Europe from Turkey in Asia. Area: 11 471 sq. km (4429 sq. miles). Ancient name: Propontis.

marmite ('mɑːmaɪt) n a large cooking pot. [from F: pot]

Marmite ('mɑːmaɪt) n Trademark. a yeast and vegetable extract used as a spread, flavouring, etc.

Marmolada ★ (Italian marmoˈlaːda) n a mountain in NE Italy: highest peak in the Dolomites. Height: 3342 m (10 965 ft).

marmoreal (mɑːˈmɔːrɪəl) adj of, relating to, or resembling marble. [C18: from L marmoreus, from marmor marble]

marmoset ('mɑːmə‚zɛt) n **1** any of various small South American monkeys having long hairy tails. **2** pygmy marmoset. a related form: the smallest monkey, inhabiting tropical forests of the Amazon. [C14: from OF marmouset grotesque figure, from ?]

marmot ('mɑːmət) n **1** any of various burrowing rodents of Europe, Asia, and North America. They are heavily built and have coarse fur. **2** prairie marmot. another name for prairie dog. [C17: from F marmotte, ? ult. from L mūr- (stem of mūs) mouse + montis of the mountain]

Marne ★ (French marn) n **1** a department of NE France, in Champagne-Ardenne region. Capital: Châlons-sur-Marne. Pop.: 566 222 (1994 est.). Area: 8205 sq. km (3200 sq. miles). **2** a river in NE France, rising on the plateau of Langres and flowing north, then west to the River Seine, north of Paris: linked by canal with the Rivers Saône, Rhine, and Aisne; scene of two unsuccessful German offensives (1914, 1918) during World War I. Length: 525 km (326 miles).

Maroc ★ (marɔk) n the French name for Morocco.

marocain ('mærə‚keɪn) n **1** a fabric of ribbed crepe. **2** a garment made from this fabric. [C20: from F maroquin Moroccan]

maroon¹ (məˈruːn) vb (tr) **1** to abandon ashore, esp. on an island. **2** to isolate without resources. ◆ n **3** a descendant of a group of runaway slaves living in the remoter areas of the Caribbean or Guyana. [C17 (applied to fugitive slaves): from American Sp. cimarrón wild, lit.: dwelling on peaks, from Sp. cima summit]

maroon² (məˈruːn) n **1a** a dark red to purplish-red colour. **1b** (as adj): a maroon carpet. **2** an exploding firework, esp. one used as a warning signal. [C18: from F, lit.: chestnut]

Maros ★ ('mɔrɔʃ) n the Hungarian name for the Mureş.

Marprelate ★ ('mɑː‚prɛlɪt) n Martin, the pen name of the anonymous author of a series of Puritan tracts (1588–89) attacking the bishops of the Church of England.

Marq. abbrev. for: **1** Marquess. **2** Marquis.

Marquand ★ (mɑːˈkwɒnd) n J(ohn) P(hillips). 1893–1960, US novelist, noted for his fictional Japanese detective Mr Moto and for his comedies, such as The Late George Apley (1937).

marque (mɑːk) n **1** a brand of product, esp. of a car. **2** See letter of marque. [from F, from marquer to MARK¹]

marquee (mɑːˈkiː) n **1** a large tent used for entertainment, exhibition, etc. **2** Also called: marquise. Chiefly US & Canad. a canopy over the entrance to a theatre, hotel, etc. [C17 (orig. an officer's tent): invented sing form of MARQUISE, erroneously taken to be pl]

Marquesas Islands ★ (mɑːˈkeɪsæs) pl n a group of volcanic islands in the S Pacific, in French Polynesia. Pop.: 7538 (1988). Area: 1287 sq. km (497 sq. miles). French name: Îles Marquises (il markiz).

marquess ('mɑːkwɪs) n **1** (in the British Isles) a nobleman ranking between a duke and an earl. **2** See marquis.

★ people and places

marquetry or **marqueterie** ('mɑːkɪtrɪ) n, pl **marquetries** or **marqueteries**. a pattern of inlaid veneers of wood, brass, ivory, etc., used chiefly as ornamentation in furniture. [C16: from OF, from *marqueter* to inlay, from *marque* MARK[1]]

Marquette ★ (mɑː'kɛt) n **Jacques** (ʒak), known as *Père Marquette*. 1637–75, French Jesuit missionary and explorer of the Mississippi river.

Márquez ★ (*Spanish* 'markɛθ) n **Gabriel García**. See (Gabriel) **García Márquez**.

marquis ('mɑːkwɪs, mɑː'kiː) n, pl **marquises** or **marquis**. (in various countries) a nobleman ranking above a count, corresponding to a British marquess. The title of marquis is often used in place of that of marquess. [C14: from OF *marchis*, lit.: count of the march, from *marche* MARCH[2]]

Marquis ★ ('mɑːkwɪs) n **Don(ald Robert Perry)**. 1878–1937, US humorist; author of *archy and mehitabel* (1927).

marquise (mɑː'kiːz) n **1** (in various countries) another word for **marchioness**. **2a** a gemstone, esp. a diamond, cut in a pointed oval shape and usually faceted. **2b** a piece of jewellery, esp. a ring, set with such a stone or with an oval cluster of stones. **3** another name for **marquee** (sense 2). [C18: from F, fem of MARQUIS]

marquisette (ˌmɑːkɪ'zɛt, -kwɪ-) n a leno-weave fabric of cotton, silk, etc. [C20: from F, dim. of MARQUISE]

Marrakech or **Marrakesh** (mə'rækɛʃ, ˌmærə'kɛʃ) n a city in W central Morocco: several times capital of Morocco; tourist centre. Pop.: 602 000 (1993 est.).

marram grass ('mærəm) n any of several grasses that grow on sandy shores: often planted to stabilize sand dunes. [C17 *marram*, from ON *marálmr*, from *marr* sea + *hálmr* HAULM]

marri ('mærɪ) n a species of eucalyptus of Western Australia, widely cultivated for its coloured flowers. [C19: from Abor.]

marriage ('mærɪdʒ) n **1** the state or relationship of being husband and wife. **2a** the legal union or contract made by a man and woman to live as husband and wife. **2b** (*as modifier*): *marriage certificate*. **3** the ceremony formalizing this union; wedding. **4** a close or intimate union, relationship, etc. [C13: from OF; see MARRY[1], -AGE]

marriageable ('mærɪdʒəb°l) adj (esp. of women) suitable for marriage, usually with reference to age.
▸ ˌmarriageaˈbility n

marriage guidance n advice given to couples who have problems in their married life.

married ('mærɪd) adj **1** having a husband or wife. **2** joined in marriage. **3** of or involving marriage or married persons. **4** closely or intimately united. ◆ n **5** (usually pl) a married person (esp. in **young marrieds**).

Marriner ★ ('mærɪnə) n **Sir Neville**. born 1924, British conductor and violinist; founder (1956) and director of the Academy of St Martin in the Fields.

marrons glacés *French*. (marɔ̃ glase) pl n chestnuts cooked in syrup and glazed.

marrow ('mærəʊ) n **1** the fatty network of connective tissue that fills the cavities of bones. **2** the vital part; essence. **3** *Brit*. short for **vegetable marrow**. [OE *mærg*]
▸ 'marrowy adj

marrowbone ('mærəʊˌbəʊn) n **a** a bone containing edible marrow. **b** (*as modifier*): *marrowbone jelly*.

marrowfat ('mærəʊˌfæt) or **marrow pea** n **1** any of several varieties of pea plant that have large seeds. **2** the seed of such a plant.

marry[1] ('mærɪ) vb **marries, marrying, married**. **1** to take (someone as one's husband or wife) in marriage. **2** (*tr*) to join or give in marriage. **3** to unite closely or intimately. **4** (*tr*; sometimes foll. by *up*) to fit together or align (two things); join. **5** (*tr*) *Naut*. to match up (the strands of ropes) before splicing. [C13: from OF *marier*, from L *maritāre*, from *maritus* married (man), ?from *mās* male]

marry[2] ('mærɪ) interj *Arch*. an exclamation of surprise, anger, etc. [C14: euphemistic for the Virgin *Mary*]

Marryat ★ ('mærɪət) n **Frederick**, known as *Captain Marryat*. 1792–1848, British novelist and naval officer; author of novels of sea life, such as *Mr Midshipman Easy*

(1836), and children's stories, such as *The Children of the New Forest* (1847).

marry off vb (*tr, adv*) to find a husband or wife for (a person, esp. one's son or daughter).

Mars[1] ★ (mɑːz) n the Roman god of war.

Mars[2] (mɑːz) n the fourth planet from the sun.

Marsala ★ (mɑː'sɑːlə) n **1** a port in W Sicily: landing place of Garibaldi at the start of his Sicilian campaign (1860). Pop.: 80 760 (1990). **2** (*sometimes not caps.*) a dark sweet dessert wine made in Sicily.

Marsalis ★ (mɑː'sɑːlɪs) n **Wynton**. born 1962, US jazz and classical trumpeter.

Marseillaise (ˌmɑːseɪ'jeɪz, -sə'leɪz) n **the**. the French national anthem. [C18: from F (*chanson*) *marseillaise* song of Marseilles (first sung in Paris by the battalion of Marseilles)]

marseille (mɑː'seɪl) or **marseilles** (mɑː'seɪlz) n a strong cotton fabric with a raised pattern, used for bedspreads, etc. [C18: from *Marseille quilting*, made in Marseilles]

Marseille ★ (*French* marsɛj) n a port in SE France, on the Gulf of Lions: second largest city in the country and a major port; founded in about 600 B.C. by Greeks from Phocaea; oil refining. Pop.: 807 726 (1990). Ancient name: **Mas'silia**. English name: **Marseilles** (mɑː'seɪ, -'seɪlz).

marsh (mɑːʃ) n low poorly drained land that is sometimes flooded and often lies at the edge of lakes, etc. Cf. **swamp** (sense 1). [OE *merisc*]

Marsh ★ (mɑːʃ) n **1** Dame (**Edith**) **Ngaio** ('naɪəʊ). 1899–1981, New Zealand crime writer, living in Britain from 1928. Her novels include *Final Curtain* (1947) and *Last Ditch* (1977). **2** **Rodney** (**William**). born 1947, Australian cricketer.

marshal ('mɑːʃəl) n **1** (in some armies and air forces) an officer of the highest rank. **2** (in England) an officer who accompanies a judge on circuit and performs secretarial duties. **3** (in the US) **3a** a Federal court officer assigned to a judicial district whose functions are similar to those of a sheriff. **3b** (in some states) the chief police or fire officer. **4** an officer who organizes or conducts ceremonies, parades, etc. **5** Also called: **knight marshal**. (formerly in England) an officer of the royal family or court, esp. one in charge of protocol. ◆ vb **marshals, marshalling, marshalled** or US **marshals, marshaling, marshaled**. (*tr*) **6** to arrange in order: *to marshal the facts*. **7** to assemble and organize (troops, vehicles, etc.) prior to onward movement. **8** to guide or lead, esp. in a ceremonious way. **9** to combine (coats of arms) on one shield. [C13: from OF *mareschal*; rel. to OHG *marahscalc*, from *marah* horse + *scalc* servant]
▸ 'marshalcy or 'marshalship n

Marshall ★ ('mɑːʃəl) n **1 Alfred**. 1842–1924, British economist, author of *Principles of Economics* (1890). **2 George Catlett**. 1880–1959, US general and statesman; chief of staff of the US army (1939–45); as secretary of state (1947–49), he proposed the Marshall Plan (1947): Nobel peace prize 1953. **3 John**. 1755–1835, US jurist and statesman; chief justice of the Supreme Court (1801–35). **4 Sir John Ross**. 1912–88, New Zealand politician; prime minister (1972).

marshalling yard n *Railways*. a place or depot where railway wagons are shunted and made up into trains.

Marshall Islands ★ pl n a republic consisting of a group of 34 coral islands in the W central Pacific, in E Micronesia: formerly part of the Trust Territory of the Pacific Islands (1947–87); status of free association with the US from 1986; consists of two parallel chains, Ralik and Ratak. Official languages: Marshallese and English. Religion: Roman Catholic majority. Currency: US dollar. Capital: Majuro. Pop.: 58 500 (1996). Area: (land) 181 sq. km (70 sq. miles); (lagoon) 11 655 sq. km (4500 sq. miles).

Marshal of the Royal Air Force n a rank in the Royal Air Force comparable to that of a field marshal in the army.

marsh fever n another name for **malaria**.

marsh gas n a hydrocarbon gas largely composed of

methane formed when organic material decays in the absence of air.

marshmallow (ˌmɑːʃˈmæləʊ) *n* **1** a spongy sweet containing gum arabic or gelatine, sugar, etc. **2** a sweetened paste or confection made from the root of the marsh mallow.

marsh mallow *n* a malvaceous plant that grows in salt marshes and has pale pink flowers. The roots yield a mucilage formerly used to make marshmallows.

marsh marigold *n* a yellow-flowered plant that grows in swampy places.

marshy (ˈmɑːʃɪ) *adj* **marshier, marshiest**. of, involving, or like a marsh.
► ˈmarshiness *n*

Marsilius of Padua ★ (mɑːˈsɪlɪəs) *n* Italian name *Marsiglio dei Mainardini*. ?1290–?1343, Italian political philosopher, best known as the author of the *Defensor pacis* (1324), which upheld the power of the temporal ruler over that of the church.

Marston ★ (ˈmɑːstən) *n* **John**. ?1576–1634, English dramatist and satirist. His works include the revenge tragedies *Antonio and Mellida* (1602) and *Antonio's Revenge* (1602) and the satirical comedy *The Malcontent* (1604).

Marston Moor ★ *n* a flat low-lying area in NE England, west of York: scene of a battle (1644) in which the Parliamentarians defeated the Royalists.

marsupial (mɑːˈsjuːpɪəl, -ˈsuː-) *n* **1** any mammal of an order in which the young are born in an immature state and continue development in the marsupium. The order occurs mainly in Australia and South and Central America and includes the opossums and kangaroos. ♦ *adj* **2** of, relating to, or belonging to marsupials. **3** of or relating to a marsupium. [C17: see MARSUPIUM]

marsupium (mɑːˈsjuːpɪəm, -ˈsuː-) *n, pl* **marsupia** (-pɪə). an external pouch in most female marsupials within which the newly born offspring complete their development. [C17: NL, from L: purse, from Gk, dim. of *marsipos*]

mart (mɑːt) *n* a market or trading centre. [C15: from MDu.: MARKET]

Martaban ★ (ˌmɑːtɑːˈbɑːn) *n* **Gulf of**. an inlet of the Bay of Bengal in Myanmar.

martagon *or* **martagon lily** (ˈmɑːtəgən) *n* a Eurasian lily plant cultivated for its mottled purplish-red flowers with reflexed petals. [C15: from F, from Turkish *martagān* a type of turban]

Martel ★ (mɑːˈtɛl) *n* See **Charles Martel**.

Martello tower (mɑːˈtɛləʊ) *n* a small circular tower for coastal defence. [C18: after Cape *Mortella* in Corsica, where the British navy captured a tower of this type in 1794]

marten (ˈmɑːtɪn) *n, pl* **martens** *or* **marten**. **1** any of several agile arboreal mammals of Europe, Asia, and North America, having bushy tails and golden-brown to blackish fur. See also **pine marten. 2** the highly valued fur of these animals. ♦ See also **sable** (sense 1). [C15: from MDu. *martren*, from OF *(peau) martrine* skin of a marten, from *martre*, prob. of Gmc origin]

Martha ★ (ˈmɑːθə) *n* **Saint**. *New Testament*. a sister of Mary and Lazarus, who lived at Bethany and ministered to Jesus (Luke 10:38–42). Feast day: July 29 or June 4.

martial (ˈmɑːʃəl) *adj* of, relating to, or characteristic of war, soldiers, or the military life. [C14: from L *martiālis* of MARS[1]]
► ˈmartialism *n* ► ˈmartialist *n* ► ˈmartially *adv*

Martial ★ (ˈmɑːʃəl) *n* full name *Marcus Valerius Martialis*. ?40–?104 A.D., Latin epigrammatist and poet, born in Spain.

martial art *n* any of various philosophies of self-defence and techniques of single combat, such as judo or karate, originating in the Far East.

martial law *n* rule of law maintained by the military in the absence of civil law.

Martian (ˈmɑːʃən) *adj* **1** of, occurring on, or relating to the planet Mars. ♦ *n* **2** an inhabitant of Mars, esp. in science fiction.

martin (ˈmɑːtɪn) *n* any of various birds of the swallow family, having a square or slightly forked tail. See also **house martin**. [C15: ?from St MARTIN, because the birds were believed to migrate at the time of Martinmas]

Martin ★ (ˈmɑːtɪn) *n* **1 Archer John Porter**. 1910–94, British biochemist; Nobel prize for chemistry 1952 for developing paper chromatography (1944). He subsequently developed gas chromatography (1953). **2** (*French* martɛ̃) **Frank** (frɑ̃k). 1890–1974, Swiss composer. Works include *Petite Symphonie Concertante* (1946) and the oratorio *Golgotha* (1949). **3 John**. 1789–1854, British painter. **4 Saint**, called *Saint Martin of Tours*. ?316–?397 A.D., bishop of Tours (?371–?397); a patron saint of France. Feast day: Nov. 11 or 12.

Martin du Gard ★ (*French* martɛ̃ dy gar) *n* **Roger** (rɔʒe). 1881–1958, French novelist, noted for his series of novels, *Les Thibault* (1922–40): Nobel prize for literature 1937.

martinet (ˌmɑːtɪˈnɛt) *n* a person who maintains strict discipline, esp. in a military force. [C17: from F, from General *Martinet*, drillmaster under Louis XIV]

martingale (ˈmɑːtɪnˌgeɪl) *n* **1** a strap from the reins to the girth of a horse, preventing it from carrying its head too high. **2** any gambling system in which the stakes are raised, usually doubled, after each loss. **3** *Naut.* a chain or cable running from a jib boom to the stern or stem. [C16: from F, from ?]

martini (mɑːˈtiːnɪ) *n* **1** (*often cap.*) *Trademark*. an Italian vermouth. **2** a cocktail of gin and vermouth. [C19 (sense 2): ?from the name of the inventor]

Martini ★ (*Italian* marˈtiːni) *n* **Simone** (siˈmoːne). ?1284–1344, Sienese painter.

Martinique ★ (ˌmɑːtɪˈniːk) *n* an island in the E Caribbean, in the Windward Islands of the Lesser Antilles: administratively an overseas region of France. Capital: Fort-de-France. Pop.: 394 000 (1996). Area: 1090 sq. km (420 sq. miles).
► ˌMartiˈnican *n, adj*

Martinmas (ˈmɑːtɪnməs) *n* the feast of St Martin on Nov. 11; a quarter day in Scotland.

Martinů ★ (ˈmɑːtɪˌnuː; *Czech* ˈmartjinuː) *n* **Bohuslav** (ˈbɔhuslaf). 1890–1959, Czech composer.

martyr (ˈmɑːtə) *n* **1** a person who suffers death rather than renounce his religious beliefs. **2** a person who suffers greatly or dies for a cause, belief, etc. **3** a person who suffers from poor health, misfortune, etc.: *a martyr to rheumatism*. ♦ *vb also* ˈmartyrize *or* martyrise. (*tr*) **4** to kill as a martyr. **5** to make a martyr of. [OE *martir*, from Church L *martyr*, from LGk *martur-, martus* witness]
► ˈmartyrdom *n* ► ˌmartyriˈzation *or* ˌmartyriˈsation *n*

martyrology (ˌmɑːtəˈrɒlədʒɪ) *n, pl* **martyrologies. 1** an official list of martyrs. **2** *Christianity*. the study of the lives of the martyrs. **3** a historical account of the lives of martyrs.
► ˌmartyˈrologist *n*

marvel (ˈmɑːvᵊl) *vb* **marvels, marvelling, marvelled** *or US* **marvels, marveling, marveled. 1** (when *intr*, often foll. by *at* or *about;* when *tr*, *takes a clause as object*) to be filled with surprise or wonder. ♦ *n* **2** something that causes wonder. **3** *Arch.* astonishment. [C13: from OF *merveille*, from LL *mīrābilia*, from L *mīrābilis* from *mīrārī* to wonder at]

Marvell ★ (ˈmɑːvᵊl) *n* **Andrew**. 1621–78, English poet, noted for his lyrical poems and satires attacking the government after the Restoration.

marvellous *or US* **marvelous** (ˈmɑːvᵊləs) *adj* **1** causing great wonder, surprise, etc.; extraordinary. **2** improbable or incredible. **3** excellent; splendid.
► ˈmarvellously *or US* ˈmarvelously *adv* ► ˈmarvellousness *or US* ˈmarvelousness *n*

marvel-of-Peru *n, pl* **marvels-of-Peru**. another name for **four-o'clock** (the plant). [C16: first found in Peru]

Marx ★ (mɑːks) *n* **Karl** (karl). 1818–83, German founder of modern communism, in Britain from 1849. With Engels, he wrote *The Communist Manifesto* (1848). Other works include *Das Kapital* (1867; 1885; 1895). He was a founder of the International Workingmen's Association (First International) (1864).
► ˈMarxian *adj*

★ people and places

Marx Brothers ★ (mɑːks) *n the.* a US family of film co-medians, **Arthur Marx**, known as *Harpo* (1888–1964), **Herbert Marx**, known as *Zeppo* (1901–79), **Julius Marx**, known as *Groucho* (1890–1977), and **Leonard Marx**, known as *Chico* (1886–1961). Their films include *Animal Crackers* (1930), *Duck Soup* (1933), and *A Day at the Races* (1937).

Marxism ('mɑːksɪzəm) *n* the economic and political theory originated by Karl Marx and Friedrich Engels, holding that human institutions are economically determined, the class struggle is the agency of historical change, and communism will ultimately replace capitalism.
▷ **'Marxist** *n, adj*

Marxism-Leninism *n* the modification of Marxism by Lenin stressing that imperialism is the highest form of capitalism.
▷ **'Marxist-'Leninist** *n, adj*

Mary ★ ('mɛərɪ) *n* **1** *New Testament.* **1a** *Saint.* Also called: **the Virgin Mary.** the mother of Jesus, believed to have conceived and borne him while still a virgin; she was married to Joseph (Matthew 1:18–25). Major feast days: Feb. 2, Mar. 25, May 31, Aug. 15, Sept. 8. **1b** the sister of Martha and Lazarus (Luke 10:38–42; John 11:1–2). **2** original name *Princess Mary of Teck.* 1867–1953, queen of Great Britain and Northern Ireland (1910–36) by marriage to George V. **3** (*pl* **Maries**) *Austral. derog. sl.* an Aboriginal woman or girl.

Mary I ★ *n* family name *Tudor,* known as *Bloody Mary.* 1516–58, queen of England (1553–58). The daughter of Henry VIII and Catherine of Aragon, she married Philip II of Spain in 1554. She restored Roman Catholicism to England and about 300 Protestants were burnt at the stake.

Mary II ★ *n* 1662–94, queen of England, Scotland, and Ireland (1689–94), ruling jointly with her husband William III. They were offered the crown by parliament, which objected to the arbitrary rule of her father James II.

Maryland ★ ('mɛərɪˌlænd, 'mɛrɪlənd) *n* a state of the eastern US, on the Atlantic: divided into two unequal parts by Chesapeake Bay: mostly low-lying, with the Alleghenies in the northwest. Capital: Annapolis. Pop.: 5 071 604 (1996 est.). Area: 31 864 sq. km (12 303 sq. miles). Abbrevs.: **Md.** or (with zip code) **MD**

Mary Magdalene ★ *n New Testament.* **Saint.** a woman of Magdala ('mægdələ) in Galilee whom Jesus cured of evil spirits (Luke 8:2) and who is often identified with the sinful woman of Luke 7:36–50. In Christian tradition she is usually taken to have been a prostitute. See **magdalen.** Feast day: July 22.

Mary, Queen of Scots ★ *n* family name *Stuart.* 1542–87, queen of Scotland (1542–67); daughter of James V of Scotland and Mary of Guise. She was married to Francis II of France (1558–60), her cousin Lord Darnley (1565–67), and the Earl of Bothwell (1567–71). Forced to abdicate in favour of her son (later James VI of Scotland), she fled to England. Imprisoned by Elizabeth I until 1587, she was beheaded for plotting against the English crown.

marzipan ('mɑːzɪˌpæn) *n* **1** a paste made from ground almonds, sugar, and egg whites, used to coat fruit cakes or moulded into sweets. **2** (*modifier*) *Inf.* of or relating to the stratum of middle managers in a financial institution or other business: *marzipan layer job losses.* [C19: via G from It. *marzapane*]

-mas *n combining form.* indicating a Christian festival: *Christmas; Michaelmas.* [from MASS]

Masaccio ★ (*Italian* maˈzattʃo) *n* original name *Tommaso Guidi.* 1401–28, Florentine painter, who first applied the laws of perspective discovered by Brunelleschi.

Masada ★ (məˈsɑːdə) *n* an ancient mountaintop fortress in Israel, 400 m (1300 ft) above the W shore of the Dead Sea: the last Jewish stronghold during a revolt in Judaea (66–73 A.D.). Besieged by the Romans for a year, almost all the inhabitants killed themselves rather than surrender. The site is an Israeli national monument.

Masai ★ ('mɑːsaɪ, mɑːˈsaɪ) *n* **1** (*pl* **Masais** or **Masai**) a member of a Nilotic people, formerly noted as warriors, living chiefly in Kenya and Tanzania. **2** the language of this people.

Masan ★ ('mɑːˌsɑːn) *n* a port in SE South Korea, on an inlet of the Korea Strait: first opened to foreign trade in 1899. Pop.: 441 358 (1995).

Masaryk ★ (*Italian; Czech* 'masarik) *n* **1 Jan** (jan). 1886–1948, Czech statesman; foreign minister (1941–48). He died in mysterious circumstances after the Communist coup. **2** his father, **Tomáš Garrigue** ('tɔmaːʃ 'garik). 1850–1937, Czech statesman; a founder of Czechoslovakia (1918) and its first president (1918–35).

Masbate ★ (mæsˈbɑːtɪ) *n* **1** an island in the central Philippines, between Negros and SE Luzon: agricultural, with resources of gold, copper, and manganese. Pop.: 599 355 (1990). Area: 4045 sq. km (1562 sq. miles). **2** the capital of this island, a port in the northeast. Pop.: 54 000 (latest est.).

masc. *abbrev. for* masculine.

Mascagni ★ (*Italian* masˈkaɲɲi) *n* **Pietro** ('pjɛːtro). 1863–1945, Italian composer of operas, including *Cavalleria rusticana* (1890).

mascara (mæˈskɑːrə) *n* a cosmetic for darkening the eyelashes. [C20: from Sp.: mask]

Mascarene Islands ★ (ˌmæskəˈriːn) *pl n* a group of volcanic islands in the W Indian Ocean, east of Madagascar: consists of the islands of Réunion, Mauritius, and Rodrigues. French name: **Îles Mascareignes.**

mascarpone (ˌmæskəˈpəʊnɪ) *n* an Italian soft cream cheese. [from It. from dialect *mascherpa* ricotta]

mascon ('mæskɒn) *n* any of several lunar regions of high gravity. [C20: from MAS(S) + CON(CENTRATION)]

mascot ('mæskət) *n* a person, animal, or thing considered to bring good luck. [C19: from F *mascotte,* from Provençal *mascotto* charm, from *masco* witch]

masculine ('mæskjʊlɪn) *adj* **1** possessing qualities or characteristics considered typical of or appropriate to a man; manly. **2** unwomanly. **3** *Grammar.* denoting a gender of nouns that includes all kinds of referents as well as some male animate referents. **4** *Prosody.* denoting an ending consisting of a single stressed syllable. **5** *Prosody.* denoting a rhyme between pairs of single final stressed syllables. [C14: via F from L *masculīnus,* from *masculus* male, from *mās* a male]
▷ **'masculinely** *adv* ▷ **mascu'linity** *n*

masculinize *or* **masculinise** ('mæskjʊlɪnˌaɪz) *vb* **masculinizes, masculinizing, masculinized** *or* **masculinises, masculinising, masculinised.** to make or become masculine, esp. to cause (a woman) to show male secondary characteristics as a result of taking steroids.
▷ ˌmasculini'zation *or* ˌmasculini'sation *n*

Masefield ★ ('meɪsˌfiːld) *n* **John.** 1878–1967, British poet, novelist, and critic; poet laureate (1930–67).

maser ('meɪzə) *n* a device for amplifying microwaves, working on the same principle as a laser. [C20: m(icrowave) a(mplification by) s(timulated) e(mission of) r(adiation)]

Maseru ★ (məˈsɛəruː) *n* the capital of Lesotho, in the northwest near the W border with South Africa; established as capital of Basutoland in 1869. Pop.: 170 000 (1990 est.).

mash (mæʃ) *n* **1** a soft pulpy mass or consistency. **2** *Agriculture.* a feed of bran, meal, or malt mixed with water and fed to horses, cattle, or poultry. **3** (esp. in brewing) a mixture of mashed malt grains and hot water, from which malt is extracted. **4** *Brit. inf.* mashed potatoes. ◆ *vb* (*tr*) **5** to beat or crush into a mash. **6** to steep (malt grains) in hot water in order to extract malt. **7** *Scot. & N English dialect.* to brew (tea). [OE *mæsc-* (in compound words)]
▷ **mashed** *adj* ▷ **'masher** *n*

Masharbrum *or* **Masherbrum** ★ ('mʌʃəˌbrʊm) *n* a mountain in N India, in N Kashmir in the Karakoram Range of the Himalayas. Height: 7822 m (25 660 ft).

Mashhad (mæʃˈhæd) *or* **Meshed** ★ *n* a city in NE Iran: the holy city of Shi'ite Muslims; carpet manufacturing. Pop.: 1 759 155 (1991).

mashie *or* **mashy** ('mæʃɪ) *n, pl* **mashies.** *Golf.* (formerly) an iron for lofting shots, usually No. 5. [C19: ?from F *massue* club, ult. from L *mateola* mallet]

Masinissa *or* **Massinissa** ★ (ˌmæsɪˈnɪsə) *n* ?238–?149 B.C., king of Numidia (?210–149), who fought as an ally of Rome against Carthage in the Second Punic War.

mask (mɑːsk) *n* **1** any covering for the whole or a part of the face worn for amusement, protection, disguise, etc. **2** a fact, action, etc., that conceals something. **3** another name for **masquerade. 4** a likeness of a face or head, either sculpted or moulded, such as a death mask. **5** an image of a face worn by an actor, esp. in classical drama, in order to symbolize a character. **6** a variant spelling of **masque. 7** *Surgery.* a sterile gauze covering for the nose and mouth worn to minimize the spread of germs. **8** *Sport.* a protective covering for the face worn for fencing, ice hockey, etc. **9** a carving in the form of a face or head, used as an ornament. **10** a device placed over the nose and mouth to facilitate or prevent inhalation of a gas. **11** *Photog.* a shield of paper, paint, etc., placed over an area of unexposed photographic surface to stop light falling on it. **12** the face or head of an animal, such as a fox. **13** *Rare.* a person wearing a mask. ◆ *vb* **14** to cover with or put on a mask. **15** (*tr*) to conceal; disguise: *to mask an odour.* **16** (*tr*) to cover; protect. **17** (*tr*) *Photog.* to shield a particular area of (an unexposed photographic surface) to prevent or reduce the action of light there. [C16: from It. *maschera,* ult. from Ar. *maskharah* clown, from *sakhira* mockery]
► **masked** *adj* ► ˈ**masker** *n*

masked ball *n* a ball at which masks are worn.

masking tape *n* an adhesive tape used to protect surfaces surrounding an area to be painted.

maskinonge (ˈmæskəˌnɒndʒ) *n* another name for **muskellunge.**

masochism (ˈmæsəˌkɪzəm) *n* **1** *Psychiatry.* an abnormal condition in which pleasure, esp. sexual pleasure, is derived from pain or from humiliation, domination, etc., by another person. **2** a tendency to take pleasure from one's own suffering. Cf. **sadism.** [C19: after Leopold von Sacher *Masoch* (1836–95), Austrian novelist, who described it]
► ˈ**masochist** *n, adj* ► ˌmasoˈchistic *adj* ► ˌmasoˈchistically *adv*

mason (ˈmeɪsən) *n* **1** a person skilled in building with stone. **2** a person who dresses stone. ◆ *vb* **3** (*tr*) to construct or strengthen with masonry. [C13: from OF *masson,* of Frankish origin; ? rel. to OE *macian* to make]

Mason (ˈmeɪsən) *n* short for **Freemason.**

Mason-Dixon Line (-ˈdɪksən) *n* in the US, the state boundary between Maryland and Pennsylvania: surveyed between 1763 and 1767 by Charles Mason and Jeremiah Dixon; popularly regarded as the dividing line between North and South.

masonic (məˈsɒnɪk) *adj* **1** (*often cap.*) of or relating to Freemasons or Freemasonry. **2** of or relating to masons or masonry.
► maˈsonically *adv*

Masonite (ˈmeɪsənaɪt) *n Austral. trademark.* a kind of dark brown hardboard.

masonry (ˈmeɪsənrɪ) *n, pl* **masonries. 1** the craft of a mason. **2** work that is built by a mason; stonework or brickwork. **3** (*often cap.*) short for **Freemasonry.**

Masqat ★ (ˈmʌskæt, -kæt) *n* a transliteration of the Arabic name for **Muscat.**

masque *or* **mask** (mɑːsk) *n* **1** a dramatic entertainment of the 16th to 17th centuries, consisting of pantomime, dancing, dialogue, and song. **2** the words and music for this. **3** short for **masquerade.** [C16: var. of MASK]

masquerade (ˌmæskəˈreɪd) *n* **1** a party or other gathering at which the guests wear masks and costumes. **2** the disguise worn at such a function. **3** a pretence or disguise. ◆ *vb* **masquerades, masquerading, masqueraded.** (*intr*) **4** to participate in a masquerade; disguise oneself. **5** to dissemble. [C16: from Sp. *mascarada,* from *mascara* MASK]
► ˌmasquerˈader *n*

mass (mæs) *n* **1** a large coherent body of matter without a definite shape. **2** a collection of the component parts

of something. **3** a large amount or number, as of people. **4** the main part or majority. **5 in the mass.** in the main; collectively. **6** the size of a body; bulk. **7** *Physics.* a physical quantity expressing the amount of matter in a body. It is a measure of a body's resistance to changes in velocity (**inertial mass**) and also of the force experienced in a gravitational field (**gravitational mass**). **8** (in painting, drawing, etc.) an area of unified colour, shade, or intensity, usually denoting a solid form or plane. ◆ (*modifier*) **9** done or occurring on a large scale: *mass hysteria.* **10** consisting of a mass or large number, esp. of people: *a mass meeting.* ◆ *vb* **11** to form (people or things) or (of people or things) to join together into a mass. ◆ See also **masses.** [C14: from OF *masse,* from L *massa* that which forms a lump, from Gk *maza* barley cake]

Mass (mæs, mɑːs) *n* **1** (in the Roman Catholic Church and certain Protestant Churches) the celebration of the Eucharist. See also **High Mass, Low Mass. 2** a musical setting of those parts of the Eucharistic service sung by choir or congregation. [OE *mæsse,* from Church L *missa,* ult. from L *mittere* to send away; ?from the concluding dismissal in the Roman Mass, *Ite, missa est* Go, it is the dismissal]

Mass. *abbrev. for* Massachusetts.

Massa ★ (*Italian* ˈmassa) *n* a town in W Italy, in NW Tuscany. Pop.: 67 780 (1990).

Massachusetts ★ (ˌmæsəˈtʃuːsɪts) *n* a state of the northeastern US, on the Atlantic: a centre of resistance to English colonial policy during the War of American Independence; consists of a coastal plain rising to mountains in the west. Capital: Boston. Pop.: 6 092 352 (1996 est.). Area: 20 269 sq. km (7826 sq. miles). Abbrevs.: **Mass.** or (with zip code) **MA**

Massachusetts Bay ★ *n* an inlet of the Atlantic on the E coast of Massachusetts.

massacre (ˈmæsəkə) *n* **1** the wanton or savage killing of large numbers of people, as in battle. **2** *Inf.* an overwhelming defeat, as in a game. ◆ *vb* **massacres, massacring, massacred.** (*tr*) **3** to kill indiscriminately or in large numbers. **4** *Inf.* to defeat overwhelmingly. [C16: from OF]

massage (ˈmæsɑːʒ, -sɑːdʒ) *n* **1** the act of kneading, rubbing, etc., parts of the body to promote circulation, suppleness, or relaxation. ◆ *vb* **massages, massaging, massaged.** (*tr*) **2** to give a massage to. **3** to treat (stiffness, etc.) by a massage. **4** to manipulate (statistics, etc.) to produce a desired result; doctor. **5 massage (someone's) ego.** to boost (someone's) sense of self-esteem by flattery. [C19: from F, from *masser* to rub]

massasauga (ˌmæsəˈsɔːgə) *n* a North American venomous snake that has a horny rattle at the end of the tail. [C19: after the *Missisauga* River, Ontario, Canada, where it was first found]

Massasoit ★ (ˈmæsəˌsɔɪt) *n* died 1661, Wampanoag Indian chief, who negotiated peace with the Pilgrim Fathers (1621).

Massawa *or* **Massaua** ★ (məˈsɑːwə) *n* a port in E central Eritrea, on the Red Sea: capital of the Italian colony of Eritrea from 1885 until 1900. Pop.: 40 000 (1992).

mass defect *n Physics.* the amount by which the mass of a particular nucleus is less than the total mass of its constituent particles.

massé *or* **massé shot** (ˈmæsɪ) *n Billiards.* a stroke made by hitting the cue ball off centre with the cue held nearly vertically, esp. so as to make the ball move in a curve. [C19: from F, from *masser,* from *masse* sledgehammer, from OF *mace* MACE¹]

Masséna ★ (*French* masena) *n* **André** (ɑ̃dre), Prince d'Essling. 1758–1817, French marshal under Napoleon I: victories at Saorgio (1794), Loano (1795), Rivoli (1797), Zürich (1799), and Caldiero (1805): defeated by Wellington in the Peninsular War (1810–11).

Massenet ★ (ˈmæsəˌneɪ; *French* masnɛ) *n* **Jules Émile Frédéric** (ʒyl emil frederik). 1842–1912, French composer of operas, including *Manon* (1884), *Werther* (1892), and *Thaïs* (1894).

masses (ˈmæsɪz) *pl n* **1** (preceded by *the*) the body of

★ people and places

common people. **2** (often foll. by *of*) *Inf., chiefly Brit.* great numbers or quantities: *masses of food.*

masseur (mæˈsɜː) *or (fem)* **masseuse** (mæˈsɜːz) *n* a person who gives massages, esp. as a profession. [C19: from F *masser* to MASSAGE]

Massey ★ (ˈmæsɪ) *n* **1** Raymond. 1896–1983, Canadian stage and film actor. **2** Vincent. 1887–1967, Canadian statesman: first Canadian governor general of Canada (1952–59). **3** William Ferguson. 1856–1925, New Zealand statesman, born in Ireland: prime minister of New Zealand (1912–25).

massif (ˈmæsiːf) *n* a mass of rock or a series of connected masses forming a mountain range. [C19: from F, noun use of *massif* MASSIVE]

Massif Central ★ (*French* masif sɑ̃tral) *n* a mountainous plateau region of S central France, occupying about one sixth of the country: contains several extinct volcanic cones, notably Puy de Dôme, 1465 m (4806 ft). Highest point: Puy de Sancy, 1886 m (6188 ft). Area: about 85 000 sq. km (33 000 sq. miles).

Massine ★ (mɑːˈsiːn) *n* **Léonide** (leɔnid). 1896–1979, US ballet dancer and choreographer, born in Russia.

Massinger ★ (ˈmæsɪndʒə) *n* **Philip.** 1583–?1640, English dramatist, noted esp. for his comedy *A New Way to pay Old Debts* (1633).

Massinissa ★ (ˌmæsɪˈnɪsə) *n* a variant spelling of **Masinissa.**

massive (ˈmæsɪv) *adj* **1** (of objects) large in mass; bulky, heavy, and usually solid. **2** impressive or imposing. **3** relatively intensive or large; considerable: *a massive dose.* **4** *Geol.* **4a** (of igneous rocks) having no stratification, cleavage, etc.; homogeneous. **4b** (of sedimentary rocks) arranged in thick poorly defined strata. **5** *Mineralogy.* without obvious crystalline structure. [C15: from F *massif*, from *masse* MASS]
  ▶ ˈmassively *adv* ▶ ˈmassiveness *n*

mass-market *adj* of, for, or appealing to a large number of people; popular: *mass-market paperbacks.*

mass media *pl n* the means of communication that reach large numbers of people, such as television, newspapers, magazines, and radio.

mass noun *n* a noun that refers to an extended substance rather than to each of a set of objects, e.g., *water* as opposed to *lake.* In English when used indefinitely they are characteristically preceded by *some* rather than *a* or *an;* they do not have normal plural forms. Cf. **count noun.**

mass number *n* the total number of neutrons and protons in the nucleus of a particular atom.

mass observation *n* (*sometimes cap.*) *Chiefly Brit.* the study of the social habits of people through observation, interviews, etc.

mass-produce *vb* **mass-produces, mass-producing, mass-produced.** (*tr*) to manufacture (goods) to a standardized pattern on a large scale by means of extensive mechanization and division of labour.
  ▶ ˌmass-proˈduced *adj* ▶ ˌmass-proˈducer *n* ▶ mass production *n*

mass spectrometer *or* **spectroscope** *n* an instrument in which ions, produced from a sample, are separated by electric or magnetic fields according to their ratios of charge to mass. A record is produced (**mass spectrum**) of the types of ion present and their amounts.

mast¹ (mɑːst) *n* **1** *Naut.* any vertical spar for supporting sails, rigging, flags, etc., above the deck of a vessel. **2** any sturdy upright pole used as a support. **3** before the mast. *Naut.* as an apprentice seaman. ◆ *vb* **4** (*tr*) *Naut.* to equip with a mast or masts. [OE *mæst*; rel. to MDu. *mast* & L *mālus* pole]

mast² (mɑːst) *n* the fruit of forest trees, such as beech, oak, etc., used as food for pigs. [OE *mæst*; rel. to OHG *mast* food]

mastaba *or* **mastabah** (ˈmæstəbə) *n* a mudbrick superstructure above tombs in ancient Egypt. [from Ar.: bench]

mast cell *n* any of a number of cells in connective tissue that release heparin, histamine, and serotonin during inflammation and allergic reactions.

mastectomy (mæˈstɛktəmɪ) *n, pl* **mastectomies.** the surgical removal of a breast.

master (ˈmɑːstə) *n* **1** the man in authority, such as the head of a household, the employer of servants, or the owner of slaves or animals. **2a** a person with exceptional skill at a certain thing. **2b** (*as modifier): a master thief.* **3** (*often cap.*) a great artist, esp. an anonymous but influential one. **4a** a person who has complete control of a situation, etc. **4b** an abstract thing regarded as having power or influence: *they regarded fate as the master of their lives.* **5a** a workman or craftsman fully qualified to practise his trade and to train others. **5b** (*as modifier): master carpenter.* **6a** an original copy, stencil, tape, etc., from which duplicates are made. **6b** (*as modifier): master copy.* **7** a player of a game, esp. chess or bridge, who has won a specified number of tournament games. **8** the principal of some colleges. **9** a highly regarded teacher or leader. **10** a graduate holding a master's degree. **11** the chief executive officer aboard a merchant ship. **12** a person presiding over a function, organization, or institution. **13** *Chiefly Brit.* a male teacher. **14** an officer of the Supreme Court of Judicature subordinate to a judge. **15** the superior person or side in a contest. **16** (*often cap.*) the heir apparent of a Scottish viscount or baron. ◆ (*modifier*) **17** overall or controlling: *master plan.* **18** designating a device or mechanism that controls others: *master switch.* **19** main; principal: *master bedroom.* ◆ *vb* (*tr*) **20** to become thoroughly proficient in. **21** to overcome; defeat. **22** to rule or control as master. [OE *magister* teacher, from L]

Master (ˈmɑːstə) *n* **1** a title of address for a boy. **2** a term of address, esp. as used by disciples addressing or referring to a religious teacher. **3** an archaic equivalent of **Mr.**

master aircrew *n* a warrant rank in the Royal Air Force, equal to but before a warrant officer.

master-at-arms *n, pl* **masters-at-arms.** the senior rating in a naval unit responsible for discipline and police duties.

master builder *n* **1** a person skilled in the design and construction of buildings, esp. before the foundation of the profession of architecture. **2** a self-employed builder who employs labour.

masterclass (ˈmɑːstəˌklɑːs) *n* a session of tuition by an expert, esp. a musician, for exceptional students, usually given in public or on television.

masterful (ˈmɑːstəfʊl) *adj* **1** having or showing mastery. **2** fond of playing the master; imperious.
  ▶ ˈmasterfully *adv* ▶ ˈmasterfulness *n*

> **USAGE NOTE** The use of *masterful* to mean *masterly* as in *a masterful performance*, although common, is considered incorrect by many people.

master key *n* a key that opens all the locks of a set. Also called: **passkey.**

masterly (ˈmɑːstəlɪ) *adj* of the skill befitting a master.
  ▶ ˈmasterliness *n*

master mason *n* **1** see master (sense 5a). **2** a Freemason who has reached the rank of third degree.

mastermind (ˈmɑːstəˌmaɪnd) *vb* **1** (*tr*) to plan and direct (a complex undertaking). ◆ *n* **2** a person of great intelligence or executive talent, esp. one who directs an undertaking.

Master of Arts *n* a degree, usually postgraduate and in a nonscientific subject, or the holder of this degree. Abbrev.: **MA.**

master of ceremonies *n* a person who presides over a public ceremony, formal dinner, or entertainment, introducing the events, performers, etc.

Master of Science *n* a postgraduate degree, usually in science, or the holder of this degree. Abbrev.: **MSc.**

Master of the Rolls *n* (in England) a judge of the court of appeal: the senior civil judge in the country and the Keeper of the Records at the Public Record Office.

masterpiece (ˈmɑːstəˌpiːs) *or* (*less commonly*) **masterwork** (ˈmɑːstəˌwɜːk) *n* **1** an outstanding work or performance. **2** the most outstanding piece of work of a creative artist, craftsman, etc. [C17: cf. Du. *meesterstuk*, G *Meisterstück*, a sample of work submitted to a guild by a craftsman in order to qualify for the rank of master]

masterstroke ('mɑːstəˌstrəʊk) *n* an outstanding piece of strategy, skill, talent, etc.

mastery ('mɑːstərɪ) *n, pl* **masteries. 1** full command or understanding of a subject. **2** outstanding skill; expertise. **3** the power of command; control. **4** victory or superiority.

masthead ('mɑːstˌhɛd) *n* **1** *Naut.* the head of a mast. **2** the name of a newspaper or periodical, its proprietors, staff, etc., printed at the top of the front page. ◆ *vb* (*tr*) **3** to send (a sailor) to the masthead as a punishment. **4** to raise (a sail) to the masthead.

mastic ('mæstɪk) *n* **1** an aromatic resin obtained from the mastic tree and used as an astringent and to make varnishes and lacquers. **2 mastic tree.** a small Mediterranean evergreen tree that yields the resin mastic. **3** any of several putty-like substances used as a filler, adhesive, or seal in wood, plaster, or masonry. **4** a liquor flavoured with mastic gum. [C14: via OF from LL *mastichum*, from L from Gk *mastikhē* resin used as chewing gum]

masticate ('mæstɪˌkeɪt) *vb* **masticates, masticating, masticated. 1** to chew (food). **2** to reduce (materials such as rubber) to a pulp by crushing, grinding, or kneading. [C17: from LL *masticāre*, from Gk *mastikhan* to grind the teeth]
▶ ˌmasti'cation *n* ▶ 'masti,cator *n*

masticatory ('mæstɪkətərɪ, -trɪ) *adj* **1** of, relating to, or adapted to chewing. ◆ *n, pl* **masticatories. 2** a medicinal substance chewed to increase the secretion of saliva.

mastiff ('mæstɪf) *n* a breed of large powerful shorthaired dog, usually fawn or brindled. [C14: from OF, ult. from L *mansuētus* tame]

mastitis (mæ'staɪtɪs) *n* inflammation of a breast or an udder.

masto- *or before a vowel* **mast-** *combining form.* indicating the breast, mammary glands, or something resembling a breast or nipple: *mastodon; mastoid.* [from Gk *mastos* breast]

mastodon ('mæstəˌdɒn) *n* an extinct elephant-like mammal common in Pliocene times. [C19: from NL, lit.: breast-tooth, referring to the nipple-shaped projections on the teeth]

mastoid ('mæstɔɪd) *adj* **1** shaped like a nipple or breast. **2** designating or relating to a nipple-like process of the temporal bone behind the ear. ◆ *n* **3** the mastoid process. **4** *Inf.* mastoiditis.

mastoiditis (ˌmæstɔɪ'daɪtɪs) *n* inflammation of the mastoid process.

Mastroianni ★ (ˌmæstrɔɪ'jɑːnɪ) *n* **Marcello** (mɑː'tʃɛləʊ). 1924–96, Italian film actor; his films include *Le Notti Bianche* (1957), *La Dolce Vita* (1960), and *Prêt à Porter* (1995).

masturbate ('mæstəˌbeɪt) *vb* **masturbates, masturbating, masturbated.** to stimulate the genital organs of (oneself or another) to achieve sexual pleasure. [C19: from L *masturbārī*, from ?; formerly thought to be derived from *manus* hand + *stuprāre* to defile]
▶ ˌmastur'bation *n* ▶ 'mastur,bator *n* ▶ masturbatory ('mæstəˌbeɪtərɪ) *adj*

Masuria ★ (mə'sjʊərɪə) *n* a region of NE Poland: until 1945 part of East Prussia: includes the **Masurian Lakes**, scene of Russian defeats by the Germans (1914, 1915) during World War I.
▶ Ma'surian *adj, n*

mat[1] (mæt) *n* **1** a thick flat piece of fabric used as a floor covering, a place to wipe one's shoes, etc. **2** a smaller pad of material used to protect a surface from the heat, scratches, etc., of an object placed upon it. **3** a large piece of thick padded material put on the floor as a surface for wrestling, judo, etc. **4** any surface or mass that is densely interwoven or tangled: *a mat of weeds.* ◆ *vb* **mats, matting, matted. 5** to tangle or weave or become tangled or woven into a dense mass. **6** (*tr*) to cover with a mat or mats. [OE *matte*]

mat[2] (mæt) *n* **1** a border of cardboard, cloth, etc., placed around a picture as a frame or between picture and frame. ◆ *adj* **2** having a dull, lustreless, or roughened surface. ◆ *vb* **mats, matting, matted.** (*tr*) to furnish (a picture) with a mat. **4** to give (a surface) a mat finish. ◆ Also (for senses 2 & 4): **matt.** [C17: from F, lit.: dead]

mat[3] (mæt) *n Printing, inf.* short for **matrix** (senses 4 and 5).

mat. *abbrev. for* matinée.

Matabeleland ★ (ˌmætə'biːlɪˌlænd, -'bɛlɪ-) *n* a region of W Zimbabwe, between the Rivers Limpopo and Zambezi: rich gold deposits. Chief town: Bulawayo. Area: 181 605 sq. km (70 118 sq. miles).

Matadi ★ (mə'tɑːdɪ) *n* the chief port of the Democratic Republic of the Congo, in the west at the mouth of the River Congo. Pop.: 172 730 (1994 est.).

matador ('mætəˌdɔː) *n* **1** the principal bullfighter who kills the bull. **2** (in some card games) one of the highest cards. **3** a game played with dominoes in which the dots on adjacent halves must total seven. [C17: from Sp., from *matar* to kill]

matagouri (ˌmætə'gʊːrɪ) *n* a New Zealand thorny bush which forms thickets in open country. Also called: **wild Irishman.** [from Maori *tumatakuru*]

Mata Hari ★ ('mɑːtə 'hɑːrɪ) *n* real name *Gertrud Margarete Zelle*. 1876–1917, Dutch dancer in France; executed as a German spy in World War I.

matai ('mɑːtaɪ) *n* a New Zealand tree, the black pine, the wood of which is used as building timber. Also called: **black pine.** [from Maori]

Matamoros ★ (ˌmætə'mɔːrəs; *Spanish* mata'moros) *n* a port in NE Mexico, on the Río Grande: scene of bitter fighting during the US-Mexican War; centre of a cotton-growing area. Pop.: 266 055 (1990).

Matanzas ★ (mə'tænzəs; *Spanish* ma'tanθas) *n* a port in W central Cuba: founded in 1693 and developed into the second city of Cuba in the mid-19th century; exports chiefly sugar. Pop.: 123 843 (1994 est.).

Matapan ★ ('mætəˌpæn, ˌmætə'pæn) *n* **Cape.** a cape in S Greece, at the S central tip of the Peloponnese: the southern point of the mainland of Greece. Modern Greek name: **Taínaron.**

match[1] (mætʃ) *n* **1** a formal game or sports event in which people, teams, etc., compete. **2** a person or thing able to provide competition for another: *she's met her match.* **3** a person or thing that resembles, harmonizes with, or is equivalent to another in a specified respect. **4** a person or thing that is an exact copy or equal of another. **5a** a partnership between a man and a woman, as in marriage. **5b** an arrangement for such a partnership. **6** a person regarded as a possible partner, as in marriage. ◆ *vb* (*mainly tr*) **7** to fit (parts) together. **8** (*also intr; sometimes foll. by up*) to resemble, harmonize with, or equal (one another or something else). **9** (*sometimes foll. by with or against*) to compare in order to determine which is the superior. **10** (*often foll. by to or with*) to adapt so as to correspond with: *to match hope with reality.* **11** (*often foll. by with or against*) to arrange a competition between. **12** to find a match for. **13** *Electronics.* to connect (two circuits) so that their impedances are equal, to produce a maximum transfer of energy. [OE *gemæcca* spouse]
▶ 'matchable *adj* ▶ 'matching *adj*

match[2] (mætʃ) *n* **1** a thin strip of wood or cardboard tipped with a chemical that ignites by friction on a rough surface or a surface coated with a suitable chemical (see **safety match**). **2** a length of cord or wick impregnated with a chemical so that it burns slowly. It is used to fire cannons, explosives, etc. [C14: from OF *meiche*, ?from L *myxa* wick, from Gk *muxa* lamp nozzle]

matchboard ('mætʃˌbɔːd) *n* a long flimsy board tongued and grooved for lining work.

matchbox ('mætʃˌbɒks) *n* a small box for holding matches.

match-fit *adj Sport.* in good physical condition for competing in a match.

matchless ('mætʃlɪs) *adj* unequalled; incomparable; peerless.
▶ 'matchlessly *adv*

matchlock ('mætʃ,lɒk) n **1** an obsolete type of gunlock igniting the powder by means of a slow match. **2** a gun having such a lock.

matchmaker ('mætʃ,meɪkə) n **1** a person who brings together suitable partners for marriage. **2** a person who arranges competitive matches.
▸ 'match,making n, adj

match play n Golf. scoring according to the number of holes won and lost. Cf. **Stableford, stroke play.**
▸ match player n

match point n **1** Tennis, squash, etc. the final point needed to win a match. **2** Bridge. the unit used for scoring in tournaments.

matchstick ('mætʃ,stɪk) n **1** the wooden part of a match. ◆ adj **2** made with or as if with matchsticks. **3** (esp. of drawn figures) thin and straight: matchstick men.

matchwood ('mætʃ,wʊd) n **1** wood suitable for making matches. **2** splinters or fragments.

mate[1] (meɪt) n **1** the sexual partner of an animal. **2** a marriage partner. **3a** Inf., chiefly Brit., Austral. & NZ. a friend, usually of the same sex: often used to any male in direct address. **3b** (in combination) an associate, colleague, fellow sharer, etc.: a classmate. **4** one of a pair of matching items. **5** Naut. **5a** short for **first mate. 5b** any officer below the master on a commercial ship. **6** (in some trades) an assistant: a plumber's mate. ◆ vb **mates, mating, mated. 7** to pair (a male and female animal) or (of animals) to pair for reproduction. **8** to marry or join in marriage. **9** (tr) to join as a pair. [C14: from MLow G; rel. to OE gemetta table-guest, from mete MEAT]

mate[2] (meɪt) n, vb **mates, mating, mated.** Chess. See **checkmate.**

maté or **mate** ('mɑːteɪ) n **1** an evergreen tree cultivated in South America for its leaves, which contain caffeine. **2** a stimulating milky beverage made from the dried leaves of this tree. ◆ Also called: **Paraguay tea, yerba, yerba maté.** [C18: from American Sp. (orig. referring to the vessel in which the drink was brewed), from Quechua máti gourd]

matelot, matlo, or **matlow** ('mætləʊ) n Sl., chiefly Brit. a sailor. [C20: from F]

mater ('meɪtə) n Brit. sl. a word for **mother**[1]: often used facetiously. [C16: from L]

material (mə'tɪərɪəl) n **1** the substance of which a thing is made or composed; component or constituent matter. **2** facts, notes, etc., that a finished work may be based on or derived from. **3** cloth or fabric. **4** a person who has qualities suitable for a given occupation, training, etc.: that boy is university material. ◆ adj **5** of, relating to, or composed of physical substance: material possessions. **6** of, relating to, or affecting economic or physical wellbeing: material ease. **7** of or concerned with physical rather than spiritual interests. **8** of great import or consequence: material benefit. **9** (often foll. by to) relevant. **10** Philosophy. of or relating to matter as opposed to form. ◆ See also **materials.** [C14: via F from LL māteriālis, from L māteria MATTER]
▸ ma,teri'ality n

material implication n Logic. a form of implication in which the proposition "if A then B" is true except when A is true and B is false.

materialism (mə'tɪərɪə,lɪzəm) n **1** interest in and desire for money, possessions, etc., rather than spiritual or ethical values. **2** Philosophy. the doctrine that matter is the only reality and that the mind, the emotions, etc., are merely functions of it. Cf. **idealism, dualism. 3** Ethics. the rejection of any religious or supernatural account of things.
▸ ma'terialist n ▸ ma,terial'istic adj ▸ ma,terial'istically adv

materialize or **materialise** (mə'tɪərɪə,laɪz) vb **materializes, materializing, materialized** or **materialises, materialising, materialised. 1** (intr) to become fact; actually happen. **2** to invest or become invested with a physical shape or form. **3** to cause (a spirit, as of a dead person) to appear in material form or (of a spirit) to appear in such form. **4** (intr) to take shape; become tangible.
▸ ma,teriali'zation or ma,teriali'sation n ▸ ma'terial,izer or ma'terial,iser n

materially (mə'tɪərɪəlɪ) adv **1** to a significant extent; considerably. **2** with respect to material objects. **3** Philosophy. with respect to substance as distinct from form.

materials (mə'tɪərɪəlz) pl n the equipment necessary for a particular activity.

materia medica (mə'tɪərɪə 'mɛdɪkə) n **1** the branch of medical science concerned with the study of drugs used in the treatment of disease. **2** the drugs used in the treatment of disease. [C17: from Med. L: medical matter]

materiel or **matériel** (mə,tɪərɪ'ɛl) n the materials and equipment of an organization, esp. of a military force. [C19: from F: MATERIAL]

maternal (mə'tɜːnˀl) adj **1** of, relating to, or characteristic of a mother. **2** related through the mother's side of the family: his maternal uncle. [C15: from Med. L māternālis, from L māternus, from māter mother]
▸ ma'ternalism n ▸ ma,ternal'istic adj ▸ ma'ternally adv

maternity (mə'tɜːnɪtɪ) n **1** motherhood. **2** the characteristics associated with motherhood; motherliness. **3** (modifier) relating to pregnant women or women at the time of childbirth: a maternity ward.

mateship ('meɪtʃɪp) n Austral. friendly egalitarian comradeship.

mate's rates pl n NZ inf. discounted or preferential rates of payment offered to a friend or colleague: he got the job done cheaply by a plumber friend at mate's rates.

matey or **maty** ('meɪtɪ) Brit. inf. ◆ adj **1** friendly or intimate. ◆ n **2** friend or fellow: usually used in direct address.
▸ 'mateyness or 'matiness n

math (mæθ) n US & Canad. inf. short for **mathematics.** Brit. equivalent: **maths.**

mathematical (,mæθə'mætɪkˀl) or **mathematic** adj **1** of, used in, or relating to mathematics. **2** characterized by or using the precision of mathematics. **3** using, determined by, or in accordance with the principles of mathematics.
▸ ,mathe'matically adv

mathematical logic n symbolic logic, esp. when concerned with the foundations of mathematics.

mathematician (,mæθəmə'tɪʃən) n an expert or specialist in mathematics.

mathematics (,mæθə'mætɪks) n **1** (functioning as sing) a group of related sciences, including algebra, geometry, and calculus, concerned with the study of number, quantity, shape, and space and their interrelationships by using a specialized notation. **2** (functioning as sing or pl) mathematical operations and processes involved in the solution of a problem or study of some scientific field. [C14 mathematik (n), via L from Gk (adj), from mathēma a science; rel. to manthanein to learn]

maths (mæθs) n (functioning as sing) Brit. inf. short for **mathematics.** US and Canad. equivalent: **math.**

Mathura ★ ('mʌtʊərə, mʌ'θʊərə) n a city in N India, in W Uttar Pradesh on the Jumna River: a place of Hindu pilgrimage, revered as the birthplace of Krishna. Pop.: 226 691 (1991). Former name: **Muttra.**

Matilda[1] (mə'tɪldə) n Austral. inf. **1** a bushman's swag. **2** waltz Matilda. to travel as a bushman carrying one's swag. [C20: from the Christian name]

Matilda[2] ★ (mə'tɪldə) n known as the Empress Maud. 1102–67, wife of Geoffrey of Anjou. After the death (1135) of her father, Henry I of England, she unsuccessfully waged war with Stephen for the English throne; her son succeeded as Henry II.

matin, mattin ('mætɪn), or **matinal** adj of or relating to matins. [C14: see MATINS]

matinée ('mætɪ,neɪ) n a daytime, esp. afternoon, performance of a play, concert, etc. [C19: from F; see MATINS]

matinée coat or **jacket** n a short coat for a baby.

matins or **mattins** ('mætɪnz) n (functioning as sing or pl) **1a** Chiefly RC Church. the first of the seven canonical hours of prayer. **1b** the service of morning prayer in the Church of England. **2** Literary. a morning song, esp. of birds. [C13: from OF, ult. from L mātūtīnus of the morning, from Mātūta goddess of dawn]

☆ **★ people and places**

Matisse ★ (*French* matis) *n* **Henri** (ãri). 1869–1954, French painter and sculptor; leader of Fauvism.

matlo *or* **matlow** ('mætləu) *n* variant spellings of **matelot**.

Matlock ★ ('mæt,lɒk) *n* a town in N England, on the River Derwent, administrative centre of Derbyshire: mineral springs. Pop.: 14 680 (1991).

Mato Grosso *or* **Matto Grosso** ★ ('mætəu 'grɒsəu; *Portuguese* 'matu 'grosu) *n* **1** a high plateau of SW Brazil: forms the watershed separating the Amazon and Plata river systems. **2** a state of W central Brazil: mostly on the Mato Grosso Plateau, with the Amazon basin to the north; valuable mineral resources. Capital: Cuiabá. Pop.: 2 313 600 (1995 est.). Area: 881 001 sq. km (340 083 sq. miles).

Mato Grosso do Sul ★ ('du: sul) *n* a state of W central Brazil: formed in 1979 from part of Mato Grosso state. Capital: Campo Grande. Pop.: 1 912 800 (1995 est.). Area: 350 548 sq. km (135 318 sq. miles).

Matopo Hills (mə'təupə) *or* **Matopos** ★ *pl n* the granite hills south of Bulawayo, Zimbabwe, where Cecil Rhodes chose to be buried.

Matozinhos ★ (*Portuguese* mətu'ziɲuʃ) *n* a port in N Portugal, on the estuary of the Leça River north of Oporto: fishing industry. Pop.: 26 500 (latest est.).

matrass ('mætrəs) *n Chem., obs.* a long-necked glass flask, used for distilling, dissolving substances, etc. [C17: from F, ? rel. to L *mētiri* to measure]

matri- *combining form.* mother or motherhood: *matriarchy.* [from L *māter* mother]

matriarch ('meɪtrɪ,ɑ:k) *n* **1** a woman who dominates an organization, community, etc. **2** the female head of a tribe or family. **3** a very old or venerable woman. [C17: from MATRI- + -ARCH, by false analogy with PATRIARCH]
▶ ˌmatriˈarchal *or* ˌmatriˈarchic *adj*

matriarchy ('meɪtrɪ,ɑ:kɪ) *n, pl* **matriarchies. 1** a form of social organization in which a female is head of the family or society, and descent and kinship are traced through the female line. **2** any society dominated by women.

matric (mə'trɪk) *n Brit.* short for **matriculation** (see **matriculate**).

matrices ('meɪtrɪ,si:z, 'mæ-) *n* a plural of **matrix**.

matricide ('mætrɪ,saɪd, 'meɪ-) *n* **1** the act of killing one's own mother. **2** a person who kills his mother. [C16: from L *mātrīcīdium* (the act), *mātrīcīda* (the agent). See MATRI-, -CIDE]
▶ ˌmatriˈcidal *adj*

matriculate (mə'trɪkju,leɪt) *vb* **matriculates, matriculating, matriculated. 1** to enrol or be enrolled in an institution, esp. a college or university. **2** (*intr*) to attain the academic standard required for a course at such an institution. [C16: from Med. L *mātrīculāre* to register, from *mātrīcula,* dim. of *matrix* list]
▶ maˌtricuˈlation *n*

matrilineal (,mætrɪ'lɪnɪəl, ,meɪ-) *adj* relating to descent or kinship through the female line.

matrimony ('mætrɪmənɪ) *n, pl* **matrimonies. 1** the state or condition of being married. **2** the ceremony of marriage. **3a** a card game in which the king and queen together are a winning combination. **3b** such a combination. [C14: via Norman F from L *mātrimōnium* wedlock, from *māter* mother]
▶ ˌmatriˈmonial *adj*

matrix ('meɪtrɪks, 'mæ-) *n, pl* **matrices** *or* **matrixes. 1** a substance, situation, or environment in which something has its origin, takes form, or is enclosed. **2** the intercellular substance of bone, cartilage, connective tissue, etc. **3** the rock in which fossils, pebbles, etc., are embedded. **4** *Printing.* **4a** a metal mould for casting type. **4b** a papier-mâché or plastic mould impressed from the forme and used for stereotyping. **5** a mould used in the production of gramophone records. **6** a bed of perforated material placed beneath a workpiece in a press or stamping machine against which the punch operates. **7** *Maths.* a rectangular array of elements set out in rows and columns, used to facilitate the solution of problems, such as transformation of coordinates. **8** *Obs.* the womb.

[C16: from L: womb, female animal used for breeding, from *māter* mother]

matron ('meɪtrən) *n* **1** a married woman regarded as staid or dignified. **2** a woman in charge of the domestic or medical arrangements in an institution. **3** *US.* a wardress in a prison. **4** *Brit.* the administrative head of the nursing staff in a hospital. Official name: **nursing officer.** [C14: via OF from L *mātrōna,* from *māter* mother]
▶ 'matronal *or* 'matronly *adj* ▶ 'matron,hood *or* 'matronship *n*

matron of honour *n, pl* **matrons of honour.** a married woman serving as chief attendant to a bride.

Matsu *or* **Mazu** ★ (mæt'su:) *n* an island group in Formosa Strait, off the SE coast of mainland China: belongs to Taiwan. Pop.: 3145 (1990 est.). Area: 44 sq. km (17 sq. miles).

Matsuo Basho ★ (mɑ:'tsu:əu bɑ:'ʃɔ:) *n* See **Basho.**

Matsuyama ★ (,mætsu'jɑ:mə) *n* a port in SW Japan, on NW Shikoku: textile and chemical industries; Ehime University (1949). Pop.: 460 870 (1995).

matt *or* **matte** (mæt) *adj, vb* **matts, matting, matted** *or* **mattes, matting, matted.** variant spellings of **mat**[2] (senses 2 & 4).

Matt. *Bible. abbrev.* for Matthew.

mattamore ('mætə,mɔ:) *n* a subterranean storehouse or dwelling. [C17: from F, from Ar. *matmurā,* from *tamara* to store, bury]

matted ('mætɪd) *adj* **1** tangled into a thick mass. **2** covered with or formed of matting.

matter ('mætə) *n* **1** that which makes up something, esp. a physical object; material. **2** substance that occupies space and has mass, as distinguished from substance that is mental, spiritual, etc. **3** substance of a specified type: *vegetable matter.* **4** (sometimes foll. by *of* or *for*) thing; affair; concern; question: *a matter of taste.* **5** a quantity or amount: *a matter of a few pence.* **6** the content of written or verbal material as distinct from its style or form. **7** (*used with a negative*) importance; consequence. **8** *Philosophy.* (in the writings of Aristotle and the Scholastics) that which is itself formless but can receive form and become substance. **9** *Philosophy.* (in the Cartesian tradition) one of two basic modes of existence, the other being mind. **10** *Printing.* **10a** type set up. **10b** copy to be set in type. **11** a secretion or discharge, such as pus. **12** *Law.* **12a** something to be proved. **12b** statements or allegations to be considered by a court. **13 for that matter.** as regards that. **14 no matter. 14a** regardless of; irrespective of: *no matter what the excuse, you must not be late.* **14b** (*sentence substitute*) it is unimportant. **15 the matter.** wrong; the trouble: *there's nothing the matter.* ◆ *vb* (*intr*) **16** to be of consequence or importance. **17** to form and discharge pus. [C13 (n), C16 (vb): from L *māteria* cause, substance, esp. wood, or a substance that produces something else]

Matterhorn ★ ('mætə,hɔ:n) *n* a mountain on the border between Italy and Switzerland, in the Pennine Alps. Height: 4477 m (14 688 ft). French name: **Mont Cervin.** Italian name: **Monte Cervino** ('monte tʃer'vi:no).

matter of course *n* **1** an event or result that is natural or inevitable. ◆ *adj* **matter-of-course. 2** (*usually postpositive*) occurring as a matter of course. **3** accepting things as inevitable or natural: *a matter-of-course attitude.*

matter of fact *n* **1** a fact that is undeniably true. **2** *Law.* a statement of facts the truth of which the court must determine on the basis of the evidence before it. **3 as a matter of fact.** actually; in fact. ◆ *adj* **matter-of-fact. 4** unimaginative or emotionless: *he gave a matter-of-fact account of the murder.*

Matthew ★ ('mæθju:) *n New Testament.* **1** Also called: **Levi.** a tax collector of Capernaum called by Christ to be one of the 12 apostles (Matthew 9:9–13; 10:3). Feast day: Sept. 12 or Nov. 16. **2** the first Gospel, traditionally ascribed to him.

Matthew Paris ★ *n* See (Matthew) **Paris**[2] (sense 2).

Matthews ★ ('mæθju:z) *n* Sir **Stanley.** born 1915, English footballer.

Matthias ★ (mə'θaɪəs) *n New Testament.* the disciple chosen by lot to replace Judas as one of the 12 apostles (Acts 1:15–26).

Matthias I Corvinus ★ (kɔːˈvaɪnəs) n ?1440–90, king of Hungary (1458–90): a patron of Renaissance art, he founded the Corvina library. Hungarian name: **Mátyás Hollós** (ˈmɑːtjɑːʃ ˈhɔlɔʃ).

matting[1] (ˈmætɪŋ) n **1** a coarsely woven fabric, usually made of a natural fibre such as straw or hemp and used as a floor covering, packing material, etc. **2** the act or process of making mats. **3** material for mats.

matting[2] (ˈmætɪŋ) n **1** another word for **mat**[2] (sense 1). **2** the process of producing a mat finish.

mattins (ˈmætɪnz) n a variant spelling of **matins**.

mattock (ˈmætək) n a type of large pick that has one end of its blade shaped like an adze, used for loosening soil, cutting roots, etc. [OE *mattuc*, from ?; rel. to L *mateola* club, mallet]

Matto Grosso ★ (ˈmætəʊ ˈɡrɒsəʊ) n a variant spelling of **Mato Grosso**.

mattress (ˈmætrɪs) n **1** a large flat pad with a strong cover, filled with straw, foam rubber, etc., and often incorporating coiled springs, used as a bed or as part of a bed. **2** a woven mat of brushwood, poles, etc., used to protect an embankment, dyke, etc., from scour. **3** a concrete or steel raft or slab used as a foundation or footing. [C13: via OF from It. *materasso*, from Ar. *almatrah* place where something is thrown]

maturate (ˈmætjʊˌreɪt, ˈmætʃʊ-) vb **maturates, maturating, maturated. 1** to mature or bring to maturity. **2** a less common word for **suppurate**.
▸ ˌmatuˈration n ▸ **maturative** (məˈtjʊərətɪv, məˈtʃʊə-) adj

mature (məˈtjʊə, -ˈtʃʊə) adj **1** relatively advanced physically, mentally, etc.; grown-up. **2** (of plans, theories, etc.) fully considered; perfected. **3** due or payable: *a mature debenture*. **4** *Biol.* **4a** fully developed or differentiated: *a mature cell*. **4b** fully grown; adult: *a mature animal*. **5** (of fruit, wine, cheese, etc.) ripe or fully aged. ◆ vb **matures, maturing, matured. 6** to make or become mature. **7** (intr) (of notes, bonds, etc.) to become due for payment or repayment. [C15: from L *mātūrus* early, developed]
▸ maˈturely adv ▸ maˈtureness n

mature student n a student at a college or university who has passed the usual age for formal education.

maturity (məˈtjʊərɪtɪ, -ˈtʃʊə-) n **1** the state or quality of being mature; full development. **2** *Finance.* **2a** the date upon which a bond, note, etc., becomes due for repayment. **2b** the state of a bill, note, etc., when due.

matutinal (ˌmætjʊˈtaɪnᵊl) adj of, occurring in, or during the morning. [C17: from LL *mātūtīnālis*, from L, from *Mātūta* goddess of the dawn]

matzo, matzoh (ˈmætsəʊ) or **matza, matzah** (ˈmætsə) n, pl **matzos, matzohs, matzas, matzahs,** or **matzoth** (*Hebrew* maˈtsɔt). a large very thin biscuit of unleavened bread, traditionally eaten during Passover. [from Heb. *matsāh*]

Maubeuge ★ (*French* mobøʒ) n an industrial town in N France, near the border with Belgium. Pop.: 35 225 (1990).

maudlin (ˈmɔːdlɪn) adj foolishly tearful or sentimental, as when drunk. [C17: from ME *Maudelen* Mary Magdalene, typically portrayed as a tearful penitent]

Maugham ★ (ˈmɔːm) n W(illiam) **Somerset.** 1874–1965, British writer. His works include the novels *Of Human Bondage* (1915) and *Cakes and Ale* (1930), short stories, and comedies.

maugre or **mauger** (ˈmɔːɡə) prep *Obs.* in spite of. [C13 (meaning: ill will): from OF *maugre*, lit.: bad pleasure]

Maui ★ (ˈmaʊɪ) n a volcanic island in S central Hawaii: the second largest of the Hawaiian Islands. Pop.: 91 361 (1990). Area: 1885 sq. km (728 sq. miles).

maul (mɔːl) vb (tr) **1** to handle clumsily; paw. **2** to batter or lacerate. ◆ n **3** a heavy two-handed hammer. **4** *Rugby.* a loose scrum. [C13: from OF *mail*, from L *malleus* hammer]
▸ ˈmauler n

Maulmain ★ (maʊlˈmeɪn) n a variant spelling of **Moulmein.**

maulstick or **mahlstick** (ˈmɔːlˌstɪk) n a long stick used by artists to steady the hand holding the brush. [C17:

partial translation of Du. *maalstok*, from obs. *malen* to paint + *stok* STICK[1]]

Mauna Kea ★ (ˈmaʊnɑː ˈkeɪɑː) n an extinct volcano in Hawaii, on N central Hawaii Island: the highest island mountain in the world. Height: 4206 m (13 799 ft).

Mauna Loa ★ (ˈmaʊnɑː ˈləʊɑː) n an active volcano in Hawaii, on S central Hawaii Island. Height: 4171 m (13 684 ft).

maunder (ˈmɔːndə) vb (intr) to move, talk, or act aimlessly or idly. [C17: ?from obs. *maunder* to beg, from L *mendīcāre*]

maundy (ˈmɔːndɪ) n, pl **maundies**. *Christianity.* the ceremonial washing of the feet of poor persons in commemoration of Jesus' washing of his disciples' feet. [C13: from OF *mandé* something commanded, from L, ult. from Christ's words: *Mandātum novum dō vōbīs* A new commandment give I unto you]

Maundy money n specially minted coins distributed by the British sovereign on the Thursday before Easter (**Maundy Thursday**).

Maupassant ★ (*French* mopasɑ̃) n (Henri René Albert) **Guy de** (gi də). 1850–93, French writer, noted esp. for his short stories, such as *Boule de suif* (1880) and *Mademoiselle Fifi* (1883). His novels include *Bel Ami* (1885).

Maupertuis ★ (*French* mopɛrtɥi) n Pierre Louis Moreau de (pjɛr lwi mɔrɔ də). 1698–1759, French mathematician, who originated the principle of least action (or Maupertuis principle).

Mauretania ★ (ˌmɒrɪˈteɪnɪə) n an ancient region of N Africa, corresponding approximately to the N parts of modern Algeria and Morocco.
▸ ˌMaureˈtanian adj, n

Mauriac ★ (*French* mɔrjak) n **François** (frɑ̃swa). 1885–1970, French novelist. His works include *Le Désert de l'amour* (1925) and *Le Nœud de vipères* (1932): Nobel prize for literature 1952.

Maurice ★ (ˈmɒrɪs) n **1** 1521–53, duke of Saxony (1541–53) and elector of Saxony (1547–53); promoted Protestantism in Germany. **2** known as *Maurice of Nassau*. 1567–1625, prince of Orange and count of Nassau; the son of William the Silent, after whose death he led the United Provinces of the Netherlands in their struggle for independence. **3** **Frederick Denison.** 1805–72, British Anglican theologian who pioneered Christian socialism.

Mauritania ★ (ˌmɒrɪˈteɪnɪə) n a republic in NW Africa, on the Atlantic: established as a French protectorate in 1903 and a colony in 1920; gained full independence in 1960; lies mostly in the Sahara; contains rich resources of iron ore. Official language: Arabic; African languages and French are also spoken. Official religion: Muslim. Currency: ouguiya. Capital: Nouakchott. Pop.: 2 333 000 (1996). Area: 1 030 700 sq. km (398 000 sq. miles). Official name: **Islamic Republic of Mauritania.**
▸ ˌMauriˈtanian adj, n

Mauritius ★ (məˈrɪʃəs) n an island and state in the Indian Ocean, east of Madagascar: originally uninhabited, it was settled by the Dutch (1638–1710) then abandoned; taken by the French in 1715 and the British in 1810; became an independent member of the Commonwealth in 1968. It is economically dependent on sugar. Official language: English; a French creole is widely spoken. Religion: mostly Hindu and Christian. Currency: rupee. Capital: Port Louis. Pop.: 1 141 000 (1996). Area: 1865 sq. km (720 sq. miles). Former name (1715–1810): **Île-de-France.**
▸ Mauˈritian adj, n

Maurois ★ (*French* mɔrwa) n **André** (ɑ̃dre), pen name of *Émile Herzog*. 1885–1967, French writer, known for his biographies of Shelley, Byron, and Proust.

Maury ★ (ˈmɔːrɪ) n **Matthew Fontaine.** 1806–73, US pioneer hydrographer and oceanographer.

mausoleum (ˌmɔːsəˈlɪəm) n, pl **mausoleums** or **mausolea** (-ˈlɪə). a large stately tomb. [C16: via L from Gk *mausōleion*, the tomb of *Mausolus*, king of Caria; built at Halicarnassus in the 4th cent. B.C.]

mauve (məʊv) n **1a** any of various pale to moderate pinkish-purple or bluish-purple colours. **1b** (as adj): a *mauve flower*. **2** a reddish-purple aniline dye. [C19: from F, from L *malva* MALLOW]

maven *or* **mavin** ('meɪvən) *n US*. an expert or connoisseur. [C20: from Yiddish, from Heb. *mevin* understanding]

maverick ('mævərɪk) *n* **1** (in the US and Canada) an unbranded animal, esp. a stray calf. **2a** a person of independent or unorthodox views. **2b** (*as modifier*): *a maverick politician*. [C19: after Samuel A. *Maverick* (1803–70), Texas rancher, who did not brand his cattle]

mavis ('meɪvɪs) *n* a popular name for the **song thrush**. [C14: from OF *mauvis* thrush; from ?]

maw (mɔː) *n* **1** the mouth, throat, crop, or stomach of an animal, esp. of a voracious animal. **2** *Inf*. the mouth or stomach of a greedy person. [OE *maga*]

mawkish ('mɔːkɪʃ) *adj* **1** falsely sentimental, esp. in a weak or maudlin way. **2** nauseating or insipid. [C17: from obs. *mawk* MAGGOT + -ISH]
▸ **'mawkishly** *adv* ▸ **'mawkishness** *n*

Mawson ★ ('mɔːsən) *n* Sir **Douglas**. 1882–1958, Australian Antarctic explorer, born in England.

max (mæks) *n Inf*. **1** the most significant, highest, furthest, or greatest thing. **2 to the max**. to the ultimate extent.

max. *abbrev. for* maximum.

maxi ('mæksɪ) *adj* **1a** (of a garment) reaching the ankle. **1b** (*as n*): *she wore a maxi*. **1c** (*in combination*): *a maxidress*. **2** large or considerable. [C20: from MAXIMUM]

maxilla (mæk'sɪlə) *n*, *pl* **maxillae** (-liː). **1** the upper jawbone in vertebrates. **2** any member of one or two pairs of mouthparts in insects and other arthropods. [C17: NL, from L: jaw]
▸ **max'illary** *adj*

maxim ('mæksɪm) *n* a brief expression of a general truth, principle, or rule of conduct. [C15: via F from Med. L, from *maxima*, in the phrase *maxima prōpositio* basic axiom (lit.: greatest proposition)]

Maxim ★ ('mæksɪm) *n* Sir **Hiram Stevens**. 1840–1916, British inventor of the first automatic machine gun (1884), born in the US.

maxima ('mæksɪmə) *n* a plural of **maximum**.

maximal ('mæksɪməl) *adj* of, relating to, or achieving a maximum; being the greatest or best possible.
▸ **'maximally** *adv*

Maximilian ★ (ˌmæksɪ'mɪlɪən) *n* full name *Ferdinand Maximilian Joseph*. 1832–67, archduke of Austria and emperor of Mexico (1864–67). After the French had partially conquered Mexico, he was offered the throne but was defeated and shot by the Mexicans under Juárez.

Maximilian I ★ *n* 1459–1519, king of Germany (1486–1519) and Holy Roman Emperor (1493–1519).

maximin ('mæksɪˌmɪn) *n* **1** *Maths*. the highest of a set of minimum values. **2** (in game theory, etc.) the procedure of choosing the strategy that most benefits the least advantaged member of a group. Cf. **minimax**. [C20: from MAXI(MUM) + MIN(IMUM)]

maximize *or* **maximise** ('mæksɪˌmaɪz) *vb* **maximizes, maximizing, maximized** *or* **maximises, maximising, maximised**. (*tr*) to make as high or great as possible; increase to a maximum.
▸ ˌmaximi'zation *or* ˌmaximi'sation *n* ▸ 'maxiˌmizer *or* 'maxiˌmiser *n*

maximum ('mæksɪməm) *n*, *pl* **maximums** *or* **maxima**. **1** the greatest possible amount, degree, etc. **2** the highest value of a variable quantity. ◆ *adj* **3** of, being, or showing a maximum or maximums. ◆ Abbrev.: **max**. [C18: from L: greatest (neuter form used as noun), from *magnus* great]

Max Müller ★ (*German* maks 'mylər) *n* See (Friedrich Max) **Müller**.

maxwell ('mækswəl) *n* the cgs unit of magnetic flux equal to the flux through one square centimetre normal to a field of one gauss. It is equivalent to 10^{-8} weber. Symbol: Mx [C20: after J. C. MAXWELL]

Maxwell ★ ('mækswəl) *n* **1 James Clerk**. 1831–79, Scottish physicist. He developed the equations (**Maxwell equa-**

tions) upon which classical electromagnetic theory is based and also contributed to the kinetic theory of gases. **2** (**Ian**) **Robert**, original name *Jan Ludvik Hoch*. 1923–91, British publisher, born in Czechoslovakia; chairman (1984–91) of Mirror Group Newspapers Ltd; posthumously disgraced for fraud and theft.

may[1] (meɪ) *vb past* **might**. (takes an infinitive without *to* or an implied infinitive) used as an auxiliary: **1** to indicate that permission is requested by or granted to someone: *he may go*. **2** (often foll. by *well*) to indicate possibility: *the rope may break*. **3** to indicate ability or capacity, esp. in questions: *may I help you?* **4** to express a strong wish: *long may she reign*. **5** to indicate result or purpose: used only in clauses introduced by *that* or *so that*: *he writes so that the average reader may understand*. **6** another word for **might**[1]. **7** to express courtesy in a question: *whose child may this little girl be?* **8 be that as it may**. in spite of that: a sentence connector conceding the possible truth of a previous statement and introducing an adversative clause: *be that as it may, I still think he should come*. **9 come what may**. whatever happens. **10 that's as may be**. (foll. by a clause introduced by *but*) that may be so. [OE *mæg*, from *magan*]

USAGE NOTE It was formerly considered correct to use *may* rather than *can* when referring to permission, as in: *you may use the laboratory for your experiments*, but this use of *may* is now almost entirely restricted to polite questions such as: *may I open the window?* The use of *may* with *if* in constructions such as *your analysis may have been more credible if...* is generally regarded as incorrect, *might* being preferred: *your analysis might have been more credible if...*

may[2] *or* **may tree** (meɪ) *n* a Brit. name for **hawthorn**. [C16: from MAY]

May[1] (meɪ) *n* the fifth month of the year, consisting of 31 days. [from OF, from L *Maius* (month) of *Maia*, Roman goddess]

May[2] ★ (meɪ) *n* Sir **Robert McCredie**. born 1936, Australian biologist and ecologist.

Maya[1] ('maɪə) *n* **1** (*pl* **Maya** *or* **Mayas**) Also called: **Mayan**. a member of an American Indian people of Yucatán, Belize, and N Guatemala, once having an advanced civilization. **2** the language of this people.

Maya[2] ★ ('maɪə, 'mɑːjə, 'mɑːjɑː) *n* the Hindu goddess of illusion, the personification of the idea that the material world is illusory.
▸ **'Mayan** *adj*

Mayagüez ★ (*Spanish* majaˈɣweθ) *n* a port in W Puerto Rico; needlework industry. Pop.: 101 684 (1995 est.).

Mayakovski *or* **Mayakovsky** ★ (*Russian* məjɪˈkɔfskij) *n* **Vladimir Vladimirovich** (vlaˈdimir vlaˈdimirəvitʃ). 1893–1930, Russian Futurist poet and dramatist. His poems include *At the Top of my Voice* (1930); his plays include *The Bedbug* (1929).

May apple *n* **1** an American plant with edible yellowish egg-shaped fruit. **2** the fruit.

maybe ('meɪˌbiː) *adv* **1** perhaps. ◆ *sentence substitute*. **2** possibly; neither yes nor no.

May beetle *or* **bug** *n* another name for **cockchafer**.

Mayday ('meɪˌdeɪ) *n* the international radiotelephone distress signal. [C20: phonetic spelling of F *m'aidez* help me]

May Day *n* the first day of May, traditionally a celebration of the coming of spring: in some countries now observed as a holiday in honour of workers.

Mayence ★ (majɑ̃s) *n* the French name for **Mainz**.

Mayenne ★ (*French* majɛn) *n* a department of NW France, in Pays de la Loire region. Capital: Laval. Pop.: 281 301 (1994 est.). Area: 5212 sq. km (2033 sq. miles).

Mayer ★ (*German* 'maɪər) *n* **Julius Robert von** ('juːlɪus 'roːbɛrt fɔn). 1814–78, German physicist who contributed to the discovery of the law of conservation of energy.

mayest ('meɪɪst) *vb* a variant of **mayst**.

Mayfair ★ ('meɪˌfɛə) n a fashionable district of London.

mayflower ('meɪˌflaʊə) n **1** any of various plants that bloom in May. **2** Brit. another name for **hawthorn, cowslip,** or **marsh marigold.**

Mayflower ('meɪˌflaʊə) n the. the ship in which the Pilgrim Fathers sailed from Plymouth to America in 1620.

mayfly ('meɪˌflaɪ) n, pl **mayflies.** any of an order of short-lived insects having large transparent wings.

mayhap ('meɪˌhæp) adv an archaic word for **perhaps.** [C16: shortened from it may hap]

mayhem or **maihem** ('meɪhem) n **1** Law. the wilful and unlawful infliction of injury upon a person, esp. (formerly) the injuring or removing of a limb rendering him less capable of defending himself against attack. **2** any violent destruction or confusion. [C15: from Anglo-F mahem injury, of Gmc origin]

Mayhew ★ ('meɪhjuː) n **Henry.** 1812–87, British journalist, and writer; a founder of Punch (1841): best known for London Labour and the London Poor (1851–62).

Maying ('meɪɪŋ) n the traditional celebration of May Day.

mayn't ('meɪənt, meɪnt) contraction of may not.

Mayo ★ ('meɪəʊ) n a county of NW Republic of Ireland, in NW Connacht province, on the Atlantic: has many offshore islands and several large lakes. County town: Castlebar. Pop.: 110 713 (1991). Area: 5397 sq. km (2084 sq. miles).

Mayon ★ (mɑːˈjɔːn) n a volcano in the Philippines, on SE Luzon: Height: 2421 m (7943 ft).

mayonnaise (ˌmeɪəˈneɪz) n a thick creamy sauce made from egg yolks, oil, and vinegar or lemon juice. [C19: from F, ? from mahonnais of Mahón, a port in Minorca]

mayor (mɛə) n the civic head of a municipal corporation in many countries. Scot. equivalent: **provost.** [C13: from OF maire, from L maior greater]
► 'mayoral adj ► 'mayorship n

mayoralty ('mɛərəltɪ) n, pl **mayoralties.** the office or term of office of a mayor. [C14: from OF mairalté]

mayoress ('mɛərɪs) n **1** Chiefly Brit. the wife of a mayor. **2** a female mayor.

Mayotte ★ (French majɔt) n an island in the Indian Ocean, northwest of Madagascar; administered by France. Pop.: 109 600 (1994 est.). Area: 374 sq. km (146 sq. miles).

maypole ('meɪˌpəʊl) n a tall pole around which people dance during May-Day celebrations.

May queen n a girl chosen, esp. for her beauty, to preside over May-Day celebrations.

mayst (meɪst) or **mayest** vb Arch. (used with thou or its relative equivalent) a singular form of the present tense of may[1].

mayweed ('meɪˌwiːd) n **1** Also called: **dog fennel, stinking mayweed.** a widespread Eurasian weedy plant having evil-smelling leaves and daisy-like flower heads. **2** scentless mayweed. a similar and related plant, with scentless leaves. [C16: changed from OE mægtha mayweed + WEED]

Mazarin ★ ('mæzərɪn; French mazarɛ̃) n **Jules** (ʒyl), original name Giulio Mazarini. 1602–61, French cardinal and statesman, born in Italy. He succeeded Richelieu (1642) as chief minister to Louis XIII.

Mazatlán ★ (Spanish maθaˈtlan) n a port in W Mexico, in S Sinaloa on the Pacific: situated opposite the tip of the peninsula of Lower California, for which it is the chief link with the mainland. Pop.: 262 705 (1990).

maze (meɪz) n **1** a complex network of paths or passages, esp. one with high hedges in a garden, designed to puzzle those walking through it. **2** a similar system represented diagrammatically as a pattern of lines. **3** any confusing network of streets, paths, etc. **4** a state of confusion. ◆ vb **mazes, mazing, mazed. 5** an archaic or dialect word for **amaze.** [C13: see AMAZE]
► 'mazement n ► 'mazy adj

Mazu ★ ('mæ'zu:) n the Pinyin transliteration of the Chinese name for **Matsu.**

mazurka or **mazourka** (məˈzɜːkə) n **1** a Polish national dance in triple time. **2** a piece of music composed for this

dance. [C19: from Polish: (dance) of Mazur (Mazovia) province in Poland]

Mazzini ★ (Italian matˈtsiːni) n **Giuseppe** (dʒuˈzɛppe). 1805–72, Italian nationalist. In 1831, in exile, he established the Young Italy association which sought to unite Italy. In 1849 he was one of the triumvirate that ruled the short-lived Roman republic.

Mb Computing. abbrev. for megabyte.

MB abbrev. for Bachelor of Medicine.

MBA abbrev. for Master of Business Administration.

Mbabane ★ (ᵊmbɑːˈbɑːnɪ) n the capital of Swaziland, in the northwest: administrative and financial centre, with a large iron mine nearby. Pop.: 47 000 (1990 est.).

mbaqanga (ᵊmbɑːˈkæŋɡə) n a style of Black popular music of urban South Africa. [C20: ? from Zulu umbaqanga mixture]

MBE abbrev. for Member of the Order of the British Empire (a Brit. title).

Mbeki ★ (ᵊmˈbɛkɪ) n **Thabo** ('tɑːbəʊ). born 1942, South African politician: deputy president of South Africa from 1994.

mbira (ᵊmˈbiːrə) n an African musical instrument consisting of tuned metal strips attached to a resonating box, which are plucked with the thumbs. Also called: **thumb piano.** [Bantu]

Mbujimayi ★ (ᵊmˈbuːdʒɪˌmaɪɪ) n a city in S Democratic Republic of the Congo: diamond mining. Pop.: 806 475 (1994 est.).

MC abbrev. for: **1** Master of Ceremonies. **2** (in the US) Member of Congress. **3** (in Britain) Military Cross.

Mc- prefix a variant of **Mac-.** For entries beginning with this prefix, see under **Mac-.**

MCC (in Britain) abbrev. for Marylebone Cricket Club.

MCh abbrev. for Master of Surgery. [L Magister Chirurgiae]

MCP Inf. abbrev. for male chauvinist pig.

Md the chemical symbol for mendelevium.

MD abbrev. for: **1** Doctor of Medicine. [from L Medicinae Doctor] **2** Managing Director. **3** mentally deficient.

Md. abbrev. for Maryland.

MDMA abbrev. for 3,4-methylenedioxymethamphetamine. See **ecstasy** (sense 4).

MDS See **MMDS.**

MDT (in the US and Canada) abbrev. for Mountain Daylight Time.

me[1] (miː; unstressed mɪ) pron (objective) **1** refers to the speaker or writer: that shocks me. ◆ n **2** Inf. the personality of the speaker or writer or something that expresses it: the real me. [OE mē (dative)]

me[2] (miː) n a variant spelling of **mi** (sense 2).

ME abbrev. for: **1** Marine Engineer. **2** Mechanical Engineer. **3** Methodist Episcopal. **4** Middle English. **5** Mining Engineer. **6** (in titles) Most Excellent. **7** myalgic encephalomyelitis.

Me. abbrev. for: **1** Maine. **2** Maître.

mea culpa Latin. ('meɪɑː 'kʊlpɑː) an acknowledgment of guilt. [lit.: my fault]

mead[1] (miːd) n an alcoholic drink made by fermenting a solution of honey, often with spices added. [OE meodu]

mead[2] (miːd) n an archaic or poetic word for **meadow.** [OE mæd]

Mead[1] ★ (miːd) n Lake. a reservoir in NW Arizona and SE

Nevada, formed by the Hoover Dam across the Colorado River: one of the largest man-made lakes in the world. Area: 588 sq. km (227 sq. miles).

Mead[2] ★ (miːd) *n* **Margaret**. 1901–78, US anthropologist. Her works include *Male and Female* (1949).

Meade ★ (miːd) *n* **George Gordon**. 1815–72, Union general in the American Civil War. He defeated the Confederates at Gettysburg (1863).

meadow ('mɛdəʊ) *n* **1** an area of grassland, often used for hay or for grazing of animals. **2** a low-lying piece of grassland, often boggy and near a river. [OE *mædwe*, from *mæd* MEAD[2]]
  ▸ **'meadowy** *adj*

meadow grass *n* a perennial grass that grows in meadows and similar places in N temperate regions.

meadow saffron *n* another name for **autumn crocus**.

meadowsweet ('mɛdəʊˌswiːt) *n* **1** a Eurasian plant with dense heads of small fragrant cream-coloured flowers. **2** any of several related North American plants. See also **spiraea**.

meagre *or US* **meager** ('miːgə) *adj* **1** deficient in amount, quality, or extent. **2** thin or emaciated. **3** lacking in richness or strength. [C14: from OF *maigre*, from L *macer* lean, poor]
  ▸ **'meagrely** *adv* ▸ **'meagreness** *n*

meal[1] (miːl) *n* **1a** any of the regular occasions, such as breakfast, lunch, dinner, etc., when food is served and eaten. **1b** (*in combination*): *mealtime*. **2** the food served and eaten. **3 make a meal of**. *Inf*. to perform (a task) with unnecessarily great effort. [OE *mæl* measure, set time, meal]

meal[2] (miːl) *n* **1** the edible parts of a grain or pulse (excluding wheat) ground to a coarse powder. **2** *Scot*. oatmeal. **3** *Chiefly US*. maize flour. [OE *melu*]

mealie *or* **mielie** ('miːlɪ) *n* (*often pl*) a S. African word for **maize**. [C19: from Afrik. *milie*, from Port. *milho*, from L *milium* millet]

mealie-meal *n* S. *African*. meal made from finely ground maize.

meals-on-wheels *n* (*functioning as sing*) a service taking hot meals to the elderly, infirm, etc., in their own homes.

meal ticket *n* Sl. a person, situation, etc., providing a source of livelihood or income. [from orig. US sense of ticket entitling holder to a meal]

mealworm ('miːlˌwɜːm) *n* the larva of various beetles feeding on stored foods, esp. meal and flour.

mealy ('miːlɪ) *adj* **mealier, mealiest**. **1** resembling meal; powdery. **2** containing or consisting of meal or grain. **3** sprinkled or covered with meal or similar granules. **4** (esp. of horses) spotted; mottled. **5** pale in complexion. **6** short for **mealy-mouthed**.
  ▸ **'mealiness** *n*

mealy bug *n* any of various plant-eating insects coated with a powdery waxy secretion: some species are pests of citrus fruits and greenhouse plants.

mealy-mouthed *adj* hesitant or afraid to speak plainly; not outspoken. [C16: from MEALY (in the sense: soft, soft-spoken)]

mean[1] (miːn) *vb* **means, meaning, meant**. (*mainly tr*) **1** (*may take a clause as object or an infinitive*) to intend to convey or express. **2** (*may take a clause as object or an infinitive*) to intend: *she didn't mean to hurt it*. **3** (*may take a clause as object*) to say or do in all seriousness: *the boss means what he says*. **4** (*often passive; often foll. by for*) to destine or design (for a certain person or purpose): *she was meant for greater things*. **5** (*may take a clause as object*) to denote or connote; signify; represent. **6** (*may take a clause as object*) to produce; cause: *the weather will mean long traffic delays*. **7** (*may take a clause as object*) to foretell; portend: *those dark clouds mean rain*. **8** to have the importance of: *money means nothing to him*. **9** (*intr*) to have the intention of behaving or acting (esp. in **mean well** *or* **mean ill**). [OE *mænan*]

USAGE NOTE In standard English, *mean* should not be followed by *for* when expressing intention: *I didn't mean this to happen* (not *I didn't mean for this to happen*).

mean[2] (miːn) *adj* **1** *Chiefly Brit*. miserly, ungenerous, or petty. **2** despicable, ignoble, or callous: *a mean action*. **3** poor or shabby: *a mean abode*. **4** *Inf.*, chiefly *US & Canad*. bad-tempered; vicious. **5** *Sl*. ashamed: *he felt mean about not letting the children stay out late*. **6** *Sl*. excellent; skilful: *he plays a mean trombone*. **7 no mean**. **7a** of high quality: *no mean performer*. **7b** difficult: *no mean feat*. [C12: from OE *gemǣne* common]
  ▸ **'meanly** *adv* ▸ **'meanness** *n*

mean[3] (miːn) *n* **1** the middle point, state, or course between limits or extremes. **2** moderation. **3** *Maths*. **3a** the second and third terms of a proportion, as *b* and *c* in $a/b = c/d$. **3b** another name for **average** (sense 2). **4** *Statistics*. a statistic obtained by multiplying each possible value of a variable by its probability and then taking the sum or integral over the range of the variable. ◆ *adj* **5** intermediate or medium in size, quantity, etc. **6** occurring halfway between extremes or limits; average. [C14: via Anglo-Norman from OF *moien*, from LL *mediānus* MEDIAN]

meander (mɪ'ændə) *vb* (*intr*) **1** to follow a winding course. **2** to wander without definite aim or direction. ◆ *n* **3** (*often pl*) a curve or bend, as in a river. **4** (*often pl*) a winding course or movement. **5** an ornamental pattern, esp. as used in ancient Greek architecture. [C16: from L *maeander*, from Gk *Maiandros* the River Maeander; see MENDERES (sense 1)]
  ▸ **me'andering** *adj*

Meander ★ (miː'ændə) *n* a variant spelling of **Maeander**.

mean deviation *n* *Statistics*. **1** the difference between an observed value of a variable and its mean. **2** Also called: **mean deviation from the mean** (*or* **median**), **average deviation**. a measure of dispersion derived by computing the mean of the absolute values of the differences between observed values of a variable and the variable's mean.

meanie *or* **meany** ('miːnɪ) *n* *Inf.* **1** *Chiefly Brit*. a miserly or stingy person. **2** *Chiefly US*. a nasty ill-tempered person.

meaning ('miːnɪŋ) *n* **1** the sense or significance of a word, sentence, symbol, etc.; import. **2** the purpose behind speech, action, etc. **3** the inner, symbolic, or true interpretation, value, or message. **4** valid content; efficacy. ◆ *adj* **5** expressive of some sense, intention, criticism, etc.: *a meaning look*. ◆ See also **well-meaning**.

meaningful ('miːnɪŋfʊl) *adj* **1** having great meaning or validity. **2** eloquent; expressive: *a meaningful silence*.
  ▸ **'meaningfully** *adv* ▸ **'meaningfulness** *n*

meaningless ('miːnɪŋlɪs) *adj* futile or empty of meaning.
  ▸ **'meaninglessly** *adv* ▸ **'meaninglessness** *n*

mean lethal dose *n* another term for **median lethal dose**.

mean life *n* *Physics*. the average time of existence of an unstable or reactive entity, such as a nucleus, elementary particle, etc.

means (miːnz) *n* **1** (*functioning as sing or pl*) the medium, method, or instrument used to obtain a result or achieve an end: *a means of communication*. **2** (*functioning as pl*) resources or income. **3** (*functioning as pl*) considerable wealth or income: *a man of means*. **4 by all means**. without hesitation or doubt; certainly. **5 by means of**. with the use or help of. **6 by no manner of means**. definitely not. **7 by no** (*or* **not by any**) **means**. on no account; in no way.

means test *n* the checking of a person's income to determine whether he qualifies for financial or social aid from a government.

mean sun *n* an imaginary sun moving along the celestial equator at a constant speed and completing its annual course in the same time as the sun takes to move round the ecliptic at a varying speed. It is used in the measurement of mean solar time.

meant (mɛnt) *vb* the past tense and past participle of **mean**[1].

meantime ('miːnˌtaɪm) *or* **meanwhile** ('miːnˌwaɪl) *n* **1** the intervening time or period (esp. in **in the meantime**). ◆ *adv* **2** during the intervening time or period. **3** at the same time, esp. in another place.

mean time *or* **mean solar time** *n* the times, at a particular place, measured in terms of the passage of the mean sun, giving 24-hour days (mean solar days) throughout a year.

meany ('miːnɪ) *n, pl* **meanies.** a variant of **meanie.**

Mearns ★ (mɛənz) *n* **the.** another name for **Kincardineshire.**

measles ('miːzəlz) *n (functioning as sing)* **1** a highly contagious viral disease common in children, characterized by fever, profuse nasal discharge of mucus, conjunctivitis, and a rash of small red spots. See also **German measles.** **2** a disease of cattle, sheep, and pigs, caused by infestation with tapeworm larvae. [C14: from MLow G *masele* spot on the skin; infl. by ME *mesel* leper, from L *misellus*, dim. of *miser* wretched]

measly ('miːzlɪ) *adj* **measlier, measliest. 1** *Inf.* meagre in quality or quantity. **2** (of meat) infested with tapeworm larvae. **3** having or relating to measles. [C17: see MEASLES]

measurable ('mɛʒərəb³l) *adj* able to be measured; perceptible or significant.
▸ '**measurably** *adv*

measure ('mɛʒə) *n* **1** the extent, quantity, amount, or degree of something, as determined by measurement or calculation. **2** a device for measuring distance, volume, etc., such as a graduated scale or container. **3** a system of measurement: *metric measure.* **4** a standard used in a system of measurements. **5** a specific or standard amount of something: *a measure of grain; full measure.* **6** a basis or standard for comparison. **7** reasonable or permissible limit or bounds: *within measure.* **8** degree or extent (often in **in some measure, in a measure,** etc.): *a measure of freedom.* **9** (*often pl*) a particular action intended to achieve an effect. **10** a legislative bill, act, or resolution. **11** *Music.* another word for **bar**[1] (sense 15). **12** *Prosody.* poetic rhythm or cadence; metre. **13** a metrical foot. **14** *Poetic.* a melody or tune. **15** the act of measuring; measurement. **16** *Arch.* a dance. **17** *Printing.* the width of a page or column of type. **18 for good measure.** as an extra precaution or beyond requirements. **19 made to measure.** (of clothes) made to fit an individual purchaser. ♦ *vb* **measures, measuring, measured. 20** (*tr*; often foll. by *up*) to determine the size, amount, etc., of by measurement. **21** (*intr*) to make a measurement. **22** (*tr*) to estimate or determine. **23** (*tr*) to function as a measurement of: *the ohm measures electrical resistance.* **24** (*tr*) to bring into competition or conflict with: *he measured his strength against that of his opponent.* **25** (*intr*) to be as specified in extent, amount, etc.: *the room measures six feet.* **26** (*tr*) to travel or move over as if measuring. ♦ See also **measure up.** [C13: from OF, from L *mēnsūra*, from *mēnsus*, p.p. of *mētīrī* to measure]

measured ('mɛʒəd) *adj* **1** determined by measurement. **2** slow or stately. **3** carefully considered; deliberate.
▸ '**measuredly** *adv*

measureless ('mɛʒəlɪs) *adj* limitless, vast, or infinite.
▸ '**measurelessly** *adv*

measurement ('mɛʒəmənt) *n* **1** the act or process of measuring. **2** an amount, extent, or size determined by measuring. **3** a system of measures based on a particular standard.

measures ('mɛʒəz) *pl n* rock strata that are characterized by a particular type of sediment or deposit: *coal measures.*

measure up *vb* **1** (*adv*) to determine the size of (something) by measurement. **2 measure up to.** to fulfil (expectations, standards, etc.).

measuring jug *n* a graduated jug used in cooking to measure ingredients.

measuring worm *n* the larva of a geometrid moth: it moves in a series of loops. Also called: **inchworm.**

meat (miːt) *n* **1** the flesh of mammals used as food. **2** anything edible, esp. flesh with the texture of meat: *crab meat.* **3** food, as opposed to drink. **4** the essence or gist of. **5** an archaic word for **meal**[1] (senses 1 and 2). **6 meat and drink.** a source of pleasure. [OE *mete*]
▸ '**meatless** *adj*

meatball ('miːt,bɔːl) *n* **1** minced beef, shaped into a ball before cooking. **2** *US & Canad. sl.* a stupid or boring person.

Meath ★ (miːð, miːθ) *n* a county of E Republic of Ireland,

in Leinster province on the Irish Sea: formerly a kingdom much larger than the present county; livestock farming. County town: Trim. Pop.: 105 370 (1991). Area: 2338 sq. km (903 sq. miles).

meatus (mɪ'eɪtəs) *n, pl* **meatuses** *or* **meatus.** *Anat.* a natural opening or channel, such as the canal leading from the outer ear to the eardrum. [C17: from L: passage, from *meāre* to pass]

meaty ('miːtɪ) *adj* **meatier, meatiest. 1** of, relating to, or full of meat. **2** heavily built; fleshy or brawny. **3** full of import or interest: *a meaty discussion.*
▸ '**meatily** *adv* ▸ '**meatiness** *n*

Mecca *or* **Mekka** ★ ('mɛkə) *n* **1** a city in W Saudi Arabia, joint capital (with Riyadh) of Saudi Arabia: birthplace of Mohammed; the holiest city of Islam, containing the Kaaba. Pop.: 630 000 (1991 est.). Arabic name: **Makkah. 2** (*sometimes not cap.*) a place that attracts many visitors: *Athens is a Mecca for tourists.*

Meccano (mɪ'kɑːnəʊ) *n Trademark.* a construction set of miniature metal parts from which mechanical models can be made.

mech. *abbrev. for:* **1** mechanical. **2** mechanics. **3** mechanism.

mechanic (mɪ'kænɪk) *n* a person skilled in maintaining or operating machinery, motors, etc. [C14: from L *mēchanicus*, from Gk, from *mēkhanē* MACHINE]

mechanical (mɪ'kænɪk³l) *adj* **1** made, performed, or operated by or as if by a machine or machinery. **2** concerned with machines or machinery. **3** relating to or controlled or operated by physical forces. **4** of or concerned with mechanics. **5** (of a gesture, etc.) automatic; lacking thought, feeling, etc. **6** *Philosophy.* accounting for phenomena by physically determining forces.
▸ me'**chanicalism** *n* ▸ me'**chanically** *adv* ▸ me'**chanicalness** *n*

mechanical advantage *n* the ratio of the working force exerted by a mechanism to the applied effort.

mechanical drawing *n* a drawing to scale of a machine, machine component, architectural plan, etc., from which dimensions can be taken.

mechanical engineering *n* the branch of engineering concerned with the design, construction, and operation of machines.

mechanical equivalent of heat *n Physics.* a factor for converting units of energy into heat units.

mechanician (,mɛkə'nɪʃən) *or* **mechanist** *n* a person skilled in making machinery and tools; technician.

mechanics (mɪ'kænɪks) *n* **1** (*functioning as sing*) the branch of science, divided into statics, dynamics, and kinematics, concerned with the equilibrium or motion of bodies in a particular frame of reference. **2** (*functioning as sing*) the science of designing, constructing, and operating machines. **3** the working parts of a machine. **4** the technical aspects of something.

mechanism ('mɛkə,nɪzəm) *n* **1** a system or structure of moving parts that performs some function, esp. in a machine. **2** something resembling a machine in the arrangement and working of its parts. **3** any mechanical device or part of such a device. **4** a process or technique: *the mechanism of novel writing.* **5** *Philosophy.* the doctrine that human action can be explained in purely physical terms. **6** *Psychoanal.* **6a** the ways in which psychological forces interact and operate. **6b** a structure having an influence on the behaviour of a person, such as a defence mechanism.

mechanistic (,mɛkə'nɪstɪk) *adj* **1** *Philosophy.* of or relating to the theory of mechanism. **2** *Maths.* of or relating to mechanics.
▸ '**mechanist** *n* ▸ ,mecha'**nistically** *adv*

mechanize *or* **mechanise** ('mɛkə,naɪz) *vb* **mechanizes, mechanizing, mechanized** *or* **mechanises, mechanising, mechanised.** (*tr*) **1** to equip (a factory, industry, etc.) with machinery. **2** to make mechanical, automatic, or monotonous. **3** to equip (an army, etc.) with motorized or armoured vehicles.
▸ ,mechani'**zation** *or* ,mechani'**sation** *n* ▸ '**mecha,nizer** *or* '**mecha,niser** *n*

mechanoreceptor (ˌmɛkənəʊrɪˈsɛptə) n Physiol. a sensory receptor, as in the skin, that is sensitive to a mechanical stimulus, such as pressure.

mechanotherapy (ˌmɛkənəʊˈθɛrəpɪ) n the treatment of disorders or injuries by means of mechanical devices, esp. devices that provide exercise for bodily parts.

Mechelen ★ (ˈmɛxələn) n a city in N Belgium, in Antwerp province: capital of the Netherlands from 1507 to 1530; formerly famous for lace-making; now has an important vegetable market. Pop.: 75 718 (1995 est.). French name: **Malines**. English name: **Mechlin**.

Mechlin ★ (ˈmɛklɪn) n the English name for **Mechelen**.

Mechlin lace n bobbin lace made at Mechelin, characterized by patterns outlined by a heavier flat thread. Also called: **malines**.

Mecklenburg ★ (ˈmɛklənˌbɜːɡ; German ˈmeːklənburk) n a historic region and former state of NE Germany, along the Baltic coast: now part of Mecklenburg-West Pomerania: formerly in East Germany.

Mecklenburg-West Pomerania ★ n a state of NE Germany, along the Baltic coast: consists of the former state of Mecklenburg and those parts of W Pomerania not incorporated into Poland after World War II: part of East Germany until 1990. Pop.: 1 832 300 (1995 est.).

meconium (mɪˈkəʊnɪəm) n the first faeces of a newborn infant. [C17: from NL, from L: poppy juice, from Gk, from mēkōn poppy]

meconopsis (ˌmiːkənˈɒpsɪs) n any of various mainly Asiatic poppies. [C19: from Gk mēkōn poppy + -OPSIS]

Med (mɛd) n Inf. the Mediterranean region.

MEd abbrev. for Master of Education.

med. abbrev. for: **1** medical. **2** medicine. **3** medieval. **4** medium.

médaillons (French medajɔ̃) pl n Cookery. small round pieces of meat, fish, vegetables, etc. Also called: **medallions**.

medal (ˈmɛdᵊl) n a small flat piece of metal bearing an inscription or image, given as an award or commemoration of some outstanding event, etc. [C16: from F médaille, prob. from It. medaglia, ult. from L metallum METAL]

medallion (mɪˈdæljən) n **1** a large medal. **2** an oval or circular decorative device resembling a medal, usually bearing a portrait or relief moulding, used in architecture and textile design. [C17: from F, from It., from medaglia MEDAL]

medallist or US **medalist** (ˈmɛdˀlɪst) n **1** a designer, maker, or collector of medals. **2** Chiefly sport. a recipient of a medal or medals.

medal play n Golf. another name for **stroke play**.

Medan ★ (ˈmɛdɑːn) n a city in Indonesia, in NE Sumatra: seat of the University of North Sumatra (1952) and the Indonesian Islam University (1952). Pop.: 1 685 972 (1990).

Medawar ★ (ˈmɛdəwə) n Sir **Peter Brian**. 1915–87, British zoologist, who shared the Nobel prize for physiology or medicine (1960) for work on immunology.

meddle (ˈmɛdᵊl) vb **meddles, meddling, meddled. (intr) 1** (usually foll. by with) to interfere officiously or annoyingly. **2** (usually foll. by in) to involve oneself unwarrantedly. [C14: from OF medler, ult. from L miscēre to mix]
► ˈmeddler n ► ˈmeddling adj

meddlesome (ˈmɛdᵊlsəm) adj intrusive or meddling.
► ˈmeddlesomely adv ► ˈmeddlesomeness n

Mede (miːd) n a member of an Indo-European people who established an empire in SW Asia in the 7th and 6th centuries B.C.
► ˈMedian n, adj

Medea ★ (mɪˈdɪə) n Greek myth. a princess of Colchis, who assisted Jason in obtaining the Golden Fleece from her father.

Medellín ★ (Spanish meðeˈʎin) n a city in W Colombia, at an altitude of 1554 m (5100 ft): the second largest city in the country, with three universities; important coffee centre, with large textile mills; dominated by drug cartels in recent years. Pop.: 1 970 691 (1997 est.).

media (ˈmiːdɪə) n **1** a plural of **medium**. **2** the means of communication that reach large numbers of people, such as television, newspapers, and radio. ♦ adj **3** of or relating to the mass media: media hype.

USAGE NOTE When media refers to the mass media, it is sometimes treated as a singular form, as in: the media has shown great interest in these events. Many people think this use is incorrect and that media should always be treated as a plural form: the media have shown great interest in these events.

Media ★ (ˈmiːdɪə) n an ancient country of SW Asia, south of the Caspian Sea: inhabited by the Medes; overthrew the Assyrian Empire in 612 B.C. in alliance with Babylonia; conquered by Cyrus the Great in 550 B.C.; corresponds to present-day NW Iran.

mediaeval (ˌmɛdɪˈiːvᵊl) adj a variant spelling of **medieval**.

media event n an event that is staged for or exploited by the mass media.

medial (ˈmiːdɪəl) adj **1** of or situated in the middle. **2** ordinary or average in size. **3** Maths. relating to an average. **4** another word for **median** (senses 1, 2). [C16: from LL mediālis, from medius middle]
► ˈmedially adv

median (ˈmiːdɪən) adj **1** of, relating to, situated in, or directed towards the middle. **2** Statistics. of or relating to the median. ♦ n **3** a middle point, plane, or part. **4** Geom. **4a** a straight line joining one vertex of a triangle to the midpoint of the opposite side. **4b** a straight line joining the midpoints of the nonparallel sides of a trapezium. **5** Statistics. the middle value in a frequency distribution, below and above which lie values with equal total frequencies. **6** Statistics. the middle number or average of the two middle numbers in an ordered sequence of numbers. [C16: from L mediānus, from medius middle]
► ˈmedianly adv

median lethal dose or **mean lethal dose** n **1** the amount of a drug or other substance that, when administered to a group of experimental animals, will kill 50 per cent of the group in a specified time. **2** the amount of ionizing radiation that will kill 50 per cent of a population in a specified time. ♦ Abbrev.: LD_{50}.

mediant (ˈmiːdɪənt) n Music. **a** the third degree of a major or minor scale. **b** (as modifier): a mediant chord. [C18: from It. mediante, from LL mediāre to be in the middle]

mediastinum (ˌmiːdɪəˈstaɪnəm) n, pl **mediastina** (-nə). Anat. **1** a membrane between two parts of an organ or cavity such as the pleural tissue between the two lungs. **2** the part of the thoracic cavity that lies between the lungs, containing the heart, trachea, etc. [C16: from Medical L, neuter of Med. L mediastīnus median, from L: low grade of servant, from medius mean]
► ˌmediasˈtinal adj

mediate vb (ˈmiːdɪˌeɪt), **mediates, mediating, mediated. 1** (intr; usually foll. by between or in) to intervene (between parties or in a dispute) in order to bring about agreement. **2** to bring about (an agreement) between parties in a dispute. **3** to resolve (differences) by mediation. **4** (intr) to be in an intermediate position. **5** (tr) to serve as a medium for causing (a result) or transferring (objects, information, etc.). ♦ adj (ˈmiːdɪɪt). **6** occurring as a result of or dependent upon mediation. [C16: from LL mediāre to be in the middle]
► ˈmediately adv ► ˈmediˌator n

mediation (ˌmiːdɪˈeɪʃən) n the act of mediating; intercession between people, states, etc. in an attempt to reconcile disputed matters.

Medibank (ˈmɛdɪbæŋk) n (in Australia), a government-run health insurance scheme.

medic[1] (ˈmɛdɪk) n Inf. a doctor, medical orderly, or medical student. [C17: from MEDICAL]

medic[2] ('mɛdɪk) *n* the usual US spelling of **medick**.

medicable ('mɛdɪkəb²l) *adj* potentially able to be treated or cured medically.

medical ('mɛdɪk²l) *adj* **1** of or relating to the science of medicine or to the treatment of patients by drugs, etc., as opposed to surgery. ◆ *n* **2** *Inf*. a medical examination. [C17: from Med. L *medicālis*, from L *medicus* physician, surgeon, from *medērī* to heal]
▶ '**medically** *adv*

medical certificate *n* **1** a document stating the result of a satisfactory medical examination. **2** a doctor's certificate giving evidence of a person's unfitness for work.

medical jurisprudence *n* another name for **forensic medicine**.

medicament (mɪ'dɪkəmənt, 'mɛdɪ-) *n* a medicine or remedy. [C16: via F from L *medicāmentum*, from *medicāre* to cure]

medicate ('mɛdɪ,keɪt) *vb* **medicates, medicating, medicated**. (*tr*) **1** to cover or impregnate (a wound, etc.) with an ointment, etc. **2** to treat (a patient) with a medicine. **3** to add a medication to (a bandage, shampoo, etc.). [C17: from L *medicāre* to heal]
▶ '**medicative** *adj*

medication (,mɛdɪ'keɪʃən) *n* **1** treatment with drugs or remedies. **2** a drug or remedy.

Medici ★ ('mɛdɪtʃɪ, mə'diːtʃɪ; *Italian* 'mɛːditʃi) *n* **1** an Italian family of bankers, art patrons, and rulers of Florence and Tuscany, prominent in the 15th, 16th, and 17th centuries, including: **Catherine de'** (ka'triːn de). See **Catherine de' Medici**. **3 Cosimo I** ('kɔːzimo), known as *Cosimo the Great*. 1519–74, duke of Florence and first grand duke of Tuscany (1569–74). **4 Cosimo de'**, known as *Cosimo the Elder*. 1389–1464, who established the political power of the family in Florence (1434). **5 Giovanni de'**, (dʒo'vanni de). See **Leo X**. **6 Giulio de'** ('dʒuːljo de). See **Clement VII**. **7 Lorenzo de'** (lo'rɛntso de), known as *Lorenzo the Magnificent*. 1449–92, ruler of Florence (1469–92) and first patron of Michelangelo. **8 Maria de'** (ma'riːa de). See **Maria de' Medici**. ◆ French name: **Médicis** (medisis).
▶ **Medicean** (,mɛdɪ'siːən, -'tʃiː-) *adj*

medicinal (mɛ'dɪsɪn²l) *adj* **1** relating to or having therapeutic properties. ◆ *n* **2** a medicinal substance.
▶ me'**dicinally** *adv*

medicine ('mɛdsɪn, 'mɛdsɪn) *n* **1** any drug or remedy for use in treating, preventing, or alleviating the symptoms of disease. **2** the science of preventing, diagnosing, alleviating, or curing disease. **3** any nonsurgical branch of medical science. **4** the practice or profession of medicine. **5** something regarded by primitive people as having magical or remedial properties. **6 a taste** (or **dose**) **of one's own medicine**. an unpleasant experience in retaliation for a similar unkind or aggressive act. **7 take one's medicine**. to accept a deserved punishment. [C13: via OF from L *medicīna* (*ars*) (art) of healing, from *medicus* doctor, from *medērī* to heal]

medicine ball *n* a heavy ball used for physical training.

medicine man *n* (among certain peoples, esp. North American Indians) a person believed to have supernatural powers of healing; a magician or sorcerer.

medick or *US* **medic** ('mɛdɪk) *n* any of various small plants having yellow or purple flowers and trifoliate leaves. [C15: from L *mēdica*, from Gk *mēdikē* (*poa*) Median (grass), a type of clover]

medico ('mɛdɪ,kəu) *n, pl* **medicos**. *Inf*. a doctor or medical student. [C17: via It. from L *medicus*]

medieval or **mediaeval** (,mɛdɪ'iːv²l) *adj* **1** of, relating to, or in the style of the Middle Ages. **2** *Inf*. old-fashioned; primitive. [C19: from NL *medium aevum* middle age]

Medieval Greek *n* the Greek language from the 7th century A.D. to shortly after the sacking of Constantinople in 1204. Also called: **Middle Greek, Byzantine Greek**.

medievalism or **mediaevalism** (,mɛdɪ'iːvə,lɪzəm) *n* **1** the beliefs, life, or style of the Middle Ages or devotion to those. **2** a belief, custom, or point of style copied or surviving from the Middle Ages.

medievalist or **mediaevalist** (,mɛdɪ'iːvəlɪst) *n* a student or devotee of the Middle Ages.

Medieval Latin *n* the Latin language as used throughout Europe in the Middle Ages.

Medina ★ (mɛ'diːnə) *n* a city in W Saudi Arabia: the second most holy city of Islam (after Mecca), with the tomb of Mohammed; university (1960). Pop.: 400 000 (1991 est.). Arabic name: **Al Madinah**. Ancient Arabic name: **Yathrib**.

mediocre (,miːdɪ'əukə) *adj* Often *derog*. average or ordinary in quality. [C16: via F from L *mediocris* moderate, lit.: halfway up the mountain, from *medius* middle + *ocris* stony mountain]

mediocrity (,miːdɪ'ɒkrɪtɪ, ,mɛd-) *n, pl* **mediocrities**. **1** the state or quality of being mediocre. **2** a mediocre person or thing.

Medit. *abbrev*. for Mediterranean.

meditate ('mɛdɪ,teɪt) *vb* **meditates, meditating meditated**. **1** (*intr*; foll. by *on* or *upon*) to think about something deeply. **2** (*intr*) to reflect deeply on spiritual matters, esp. as a religious act. **3** (*tr*) to plan, consider, or think of doing (something). [C16: from L *meditārī* to reflect upon]
▶ '**meditative** *adj* ▶ '**meditatively** *adv* ▶ '**medi,tator** *n*

meditation (,mɛdɪ'teɪʃən) *n* **1** the act of meditating; reflection. **2** contemplation of spiritual matters, esp. as a religious practice.

Mediterranean ★ (,mɛdɪtə'reɪnɪən) *n* **1** short for the **Mediterranean Sea**. **2** a native or inhabitant of a Mediterranean country. ◆ *adj* **3** of, relating to, situated or dwelling near the Mediterranean Sea. **4** denoting a postulated subdivision of the Caucasoid race, characterized by slender build and dark complexion. **5** *Meteorol*. (of a climate) characterized by hot summers and relatively warm winters when most of the annual rainfall occurs. **6** (*often not cap*.) *Obs*. situated in the middle of a landmass; inland. [C16: from L *mediterrāneus*, from *medius* middle + -*terrāneus*, from *terra* land]

Mediterranean Sea ★ *n* a large inland sea between S Europe, N Africa, and SW Asia: linked with the Atlantic by the Strait of Gibraltar, with the Red Sea by the Suez Canal, and with the Black Sea by the Dardanelles, Sea of Marmara, and Bosporus; many ancient civilizations developed around its shores. Greatest depth: 4770 m (15 900 ft). Length: (west to east) over 3700 km (2300 miles). Greatest width: about 1368 km (850 miles). Area: (excluding the Black Sea) 2 512 300 sq. km (970 000 sq. miles). Ancient name: **Mare Internum** ('mɑːreɪ ɪn'tɜːnəm).

medium ('miːdɪəm) *adj* **1** midway between extremes; average. ◆ *n, pl* **media** or **mediums**. **2** an intermediate or middle state, degree, or condition; mean: *the happy medium*. **3** an intervening substance or agency for transmitting or producing an effect; vehicle. **4** a means or agency for communicating or diffusing information, news, etc., to the public. **5** a person supposedly used as a spiritual intermediary between the dead and the living. **6** the substance in which specimens of animals and plants are preserved or displayed. **7** *Biol*. Also called: **culture medium**. a nutritive substance in which cultures of bacteria or fungi are grown. **8** the substance or surroundings in which an organism naturally lives or grows. **9** *Art*. **9a** the category of a work of art, as determined by its materials and methods of production. **9b** the materials used in a work of art. **10** any solvent in which pigments are mixed and thinned. [C16: from L: neuter sing of *medius* middle]

| USAGE NOTE | See at **media**. |

medium-dated *adj* (of a gilt-edged security) having between five and fifteen years to run before redemption. Cf. **long-dated, short-dated**.

medium frequency *n* a radio-frequency band or radio frequency lying between 3000 and 300 kilohertz. Abbrev: **MF**.

medium wave *n* **a** a radio wave with a wavelength between 100 and 1000 metres. **b** (*as modifier*): *a medium-wave broadcast*.

medlar ('mɛdlə) n **1** a small Eurasian tree. **2** its fruit, which resembles the crab apple and is not edible until it has begun to decay. [C14: from OF *medlier*, from L *mespilum* medlar fruit, from Gk *mespilon*]

medley ('mɛdlɪ) n **1** a mixture of various types or elements. **2** a musical composition consisting of various tunes arranged as a continuous whole. **3** Also called: **medley relay. 3a** *Swimming.* a race in which a different stroke is used for each length. **3b** *Athletics.* a relay race in which each leg has a different distance. [C14: from OF *medlee*, from *medler* to mix, quarrel]

Médoc ★ (mer'dɔk, 'mɛdɔk; *French* medɔk) n **1** a district of SW France, on the left bank of the Gironde estuary: famous vineyards. **2** a fine red wine from this district.

medulla (mɪ'dʌlə) n, pl **medullas** or **medullae** (-liː). **1** *Anat.* **1a** the innermost part of an organ or structure. **1b** short for **medulla oblongata. 2** *Bot.* another name for **pith** (sense 4). [C17: from L: marrow, prob. from *medius* middle]
▶ **me'dullary** or **me'dullar** adj

medulla oblongata (,ɒblɒŋ'gɑːtə) n, pl **medulla oblongatas** or **medullae oblongatae** (mɪ'dʌliː ,ɒblɒŋ'gɑːtiː). the lower stalklike section of the brain, continuous with the spinal cord, containing control centres for the heart and lungs. [C17: NL: oblong-shaped medulla]

medusa (mɪ'djuːzə) n, pl **medusas** or **medusae** (-ziː). another name for **jellyfish** (sense 1). [C18: from the likeness of its tentacles to the snaky locks of MEDUSA]
▶ **me'dusoid** adj, n

Medusa ★ (mɪ'djuːzə) n *Greek myth.* a mortal woman who was transformed by Athena into one of the three Gorgons. She became so hideous that those who looked at her were turned to stone. Perseus eventually slew her. See also **Pegasus.**
▶ **Me'dusan** adj

Medway ★ ('mɛd,weɪ) n **1** a river in SE England, flowing through Kent and the **Medway towns** (Rochester, Chatham, and Gillingham) to the Thames estuary. Length: 110 km (70 miles). **2** a unitary authority in SE England, in Kent. Pop.: 239 500 (1996 est.).

meed (miːd) n *Arch.* a recompense; reward. [OE: wages]

meek (miːk) adj **1** patient, long-suffering, or submissive; humble. **2** spineless or spiritless; compliant. [C12: rel. to ON *mjūkr* amenable]
▶ **'meekly** adv ▶ **'meekness** n

meerkat ('mɪə,kæt) n any of several South African mongooses, esp. the slender-tailed meerkat or suricate, which has a lemur-like face and four-toed feet. [C19: from Du.: sea-cat]

meerschaum ('mɪəʃəm) n **1** a white, yellowish, or pink compact earthy mineral consisting of hydrated magnesium silicate: used to make tobacco pipes and as a building stone. **2** a tobacco pipe having a bowl made of this mineral. [C18: from G *Meerschaum* lit.: sea foam]

Meerut ★ ('mɪərət) n an industrial city in N India, in W Uttar Pradesh: founded as a military base by the British in 1806 and scene of the first uprising (1857) of the Indian Mutiny. Pop.: 753 778 (1991).

meet[1] (miːt) vb **meets, meeting, met. 1** (sometimes foll. by *up* or (US) *with*) to come together (with), either by design or by accident; encounter. **2** to come into or be in conjunction or contact with (something or each other). **3** (*tr*) to come to or be at the place of arrival of: *to meet a train.* **4** to make the acquaintance of or be introduced to (someone or each other). **5** to gather in the company of (someone or each other). **6** to come into the presence of (someone or each other) as opponents. **7** (*tr*) to cope with effectively; satisfy: *to meet someone's demands.* **8** (*tr*) to be apparent in (esp. in **meet the eye**). **9** (*tr*) to return or counter: *to meet a blow with another.* **10** to agree with (someone or each other): *we met him on the price he suggested.* **11** (*tr*; sometimes foll. by *with*) to experience; suffer: *he met his death in a road accident.* **12** (*intr*) to occur together: *courage and kindliness met in him.* ◆ n **13** the assembly of hounds, huntsmen, etc., prior to a hunt. **14** a meeting, esp. a sports meeting. [OE *mētan*]
▶ **'meeter** n

meet[2] (miːt) adj *Arch.* proper, fitting, or correct. [C13: from var. of OE *gemǣte*]
▶ **'meetly** adv

meeting ('miːtɪŋ) n **1** an act of coming together; encounter. **2** an assembly or gathering. **3** a conjunction or union. **4** a sporting competition, as of athletes, or of horse racing.

meeting house n the place in which certain religious groups, esp. Quakers, hold their meetings for worship.

mefloquine ('mɛfləʊ,kwiːn) n a synthetic drug administered orally to prevent or treat malaria. [C20]

mega ('mɛgə) adj *Sl.* extremely good, great, or successful. [C20: prob. independent use of MEGA-]

mega- *combining form.* **1** denoting 10^6: *megawatt.* Symbol: M **2** (in computer technology) denoting 2^{20} (1 048 576): *megabyte.* **3** large or great: *megalith.* **4** *Inf.* greatest: *megastar.* [from Gk *megas* huge, powerful]

megabit ('mɛgə,bɪt) n *Computing.* **1** one million bits. **2** 2^{20} bits.

megabuck ('mɛgə,bʌk) n *US & Canad. sl.* a million dollars.

megacephaly (,mɛgə'sɛfəlɪ) or **megalocephaly** n the condition of having an unusually large head or cranial capacity.
▶ **megacephalic** (,mɛgəsɪ'fælɪk), **mega'cephalous,** ,**megaloce'phalic,** or ,**megalo'cephalous** adj

megacycle ('mɛgə,saɪkˀl) n a former unit of frequency equal to one million cycles per second; megahertz.

megadeath ('mɛgə,dɛθ) n the death of a million people, esp. in a nuclear war or attack.

Megaera ★ (mɪ'dʒɪərə) n *Greek myth.* one of the three Furies; the others are Alecto and Tisiphone.

megafauna ('mɛgə,fɔːnə) n the component of the fauna of a region or period that comprises the larger terrestrial animals.

megaflop ('mɛgə,flɒp) n *Computing.* a measure of processing speed, consisting of a million floating-point operations a second. [C20: from MEGA- + *flo(ating)* *p(oint)*]

megahertz ('mɛgə,hɜːts) n, pl **megahertz.** one million hertz. Former name: **megacycle.**

megalith ('mɛgəlɪθ) n a stone of great size, esp. one forming part of a prehistoric monument.
▶ ,**mega'lithic** adj

megalo- *or before a vowel* **megal-** *combining form.* indicating greatness or abnormal size: *megalopolis.* [from Gk *megas* great]

megalomania (,mɛgələʊ'meɪnɪə) n **1** a mental illness characterized by delusions of grandeur, power, wealth, etc. **2** *Inf.* a lust or craving for power.
▶ ,**megalo'maniac** adj, n ▶ **megalomaniacal** (,mɛgələʊmə'naɪəkˀl) adj

megalopolis (,mɛgə'lɒpəlɪs) n an urban complex, usually comprising several large towns. [C20: MEGALO- + Gk *polis* city]
▶ **megalopolitan** (,mɛgələ'pɒlɪtˀn) adj, n

megalosaur ('mɛgələʊ,sɔː) n any very large Jurassic or Cretaceous bipedal carnivorous dinosaur. [C19: from NL *megalosaurus*, from MEGALO- + Gk *sauros* lizard]

megaphone ('mɛgə,fəʊn) n a funnel-shaped instrument used to amplify the voice. See also **loud-hailer.**
▶ **megaphonic** (,mɛgə'fɒnɪk) adj

megapode ('mɛgə,pəʊd) n any of various ground-living gallinaceous birds of Australia, New Guinea, and adjacent islands. Their eggs incubate in mounds of sand, rotting vegetation, etc., by natural heat.

Megara ★ ('mɛgərə) n a town in E central Greece: an ancient trading city, founding many colonies in the 7th and 8th centuries B.C. Pop.: 26 562 (1991 est.).

megathere ('mɛgə,θɪə) n any of various gigantic extinct American sloths, common in late Cenozoic times. [C19: from NL *megathērium*, from MEGA- + *-there*, from Gk *thērion* wild beast]

megaton ('mɛgə,tʌn) n **1** one million tons. **2** an explosive power, esp. of a nuclear weapon, equal to the power of one million tons of TNT.

Me generation n the. the generation, originally in the

1970s, characterized by self-absorption; in the 1980s, characterized by material greed.

Megger ('mɛgə) *n Trademark.* an instrument that generates a high voltage in order to test the resistance of insulation, etc.

Meghalaya ★ (ˌmeɪgə'leɪə) *n* a state of NE India, created in 1969 from part of Assam. Capital: Shillong. Pop.: 1 960 000 (1994 est.). Area: 22 429 sq. km (7800 sq. miles).

Megiddo ★ (mə'gɪdəʊ) *n* an ancient town in N Palestine, strategically located on a route linking Egypt to Mesopotamia: site of many battles, including an important Egyptian victory over rebel chieftains in 1469 or 1468 B.C. See also **Armageddon**.

megilp *or* **magilp** (mə'gɪlp) *n* an oil-painting medium of linseed oil mixed with mastic varnish or turpentine. [C18: from ?]

megohm ('mɛgˌəʊm) *n* one million ohms.

megrim ('miːgrɪm) *n Arch.* **1** a caprice. **2** a migraine. **3** (*pl*) *Rare.* a fit of depression. **4** (*pl*) a disease of horses and cattle; staggers. [C14: see MIGRAINE]

Mehemet Ali (mɪ'hɛmɪt 'ɑːlɪ) *or* **Mohammed Ali** ★ *n* 1769–1849, Albanian commander in the service of Turkey. He was made viceroy of Egypt (1805) and its hereditary ruler (1841), founding a dynasty that ruled until 1952.

meibomian gland (maɪ'bəʊmɪən) *n* any of the small sebaceous glands in the eyelid, beneath the conjunctiva. [C19: after H. *Meibom* (1638–1700), G anatomist]

meiosis (maɪ'əʊsɪs) *n, pl* **meioses** (-ˌsiːz). **1** a type of cell division in which a nucleus divides into four daughter nuclei, each containing half the chromosome number of the parent nucleus. **2** *Rhetoric.* another word for **litotes**. [C16: via NL from Gk, from *meioun* to diminish, from *meiōn* less]
▸ **meiotic** (maɪ'ɒtɪk) *adj* ▸ **mei'otically** *adv*

Meir ★ (meɪ'ɪə) *n* **Golda** ('gəʊldə) 1898–1978, Israeli stateswoman, born in Russia; prime minister (1969–74).

Meissen ★ (German 'maɪsən) *n* a town in E Germany, in Saxony, in Dresden district on the River Elbe: famous for its porcelain (Dresden china), first made here in 1710. Pop.: 38 100 (1989 est.).

Meistersinger ('maɪstəˌsɪŋə) *n, pl* **Meistersinger** *or* **Meistersingers.** a member of one of the German guilds organized to compose and perform poetry and music, esp. in the 15th and 16th centuries. [C19: from G *Meistersinger* master singer]

Meitner ★ (German 'maɪtnər) *n* **Lise** ('liːzə). 1878–1968, Austrian physicist. With Hahn, she discovered protactinium (1918), and demonstrated the fission of uranium.

meitnerium (ˌmaɪt'nɛərɪəm) *n* a synthetic element produced in small quantities by high-energy ion bombardment. Symbol: Mt; atomic no.: 109. [C20: from Lise MEITNER]

Méjico ★ ('mɛxiko) *n* the Spanish name for **Mexico**.

Mekka ★ ('mɛkə) *n* a variant spelling of **Mecca**.

Meknès ★ (mɛk'nɛs) *n* a city in N central Morocco, in the Middle Atlas Mountains: noted for the making of carpets. Pop.: 401 000 (1993 est.).

Mekong ★ (ˌmiː'kɒŋ) *n* a river in SE Asia, rising in SW China in Qinghai province: flows southeast forming the border between Laos and Myanmar, and part of the border between Laos and Thailand, then continues south across Cambodia and Vietnam to the South China Sea by an extensive delta, one of the greatest rice-growing areas in Asia. Length: about 4025 km (2500 miles).

melaleuca (ˌmɛlə'luːkə) *n* any shrub or tree of the mostly Australian genus *Melaleuca*, found in sandy or swampy regions. [C19: NL from Gk *melas* black + *leukos* white, from its black trunk and white branches]

melamine ('mɛləˌmiːn) *n* **1** a colourless crystalline compound used in making synthetic resins. Formula: $C_3N_6H_6$. **2** a resin produced from melamine (**melamine resin**) or a material made from this resin. [C19: from G *Melamin*, from *Melam* distillate of ammonium thiocyanate, with *-am* representing *ammonia*]

melancholia (ˌmɛlən'kəʊlɪə) *n* a former name for **depression** (sense 3).
▸ ˌmelan'choliˌac *adj, n*

melancholy ('mɛlənkəlɪ) *n, pl* **melancholies**. **1** a tendency to gloominess or depression. **2** a sad thoughtful state of mind. **3** *Arch.* **3a** a gloomy character. **3b** one of the four bodily humours; black bile. ◆ *adj* **4** characterized by, causing, or expressing sadness, dejection, etc. [C14: via OF from LL *melancholia*, from Gk, from *melas* black + *kholē* bile]
▸ 'melanˌcholic *adj, n*

Melanchthon ★ (mə'læŋkθən; German me'lançtən) *n* **Philipp** ('fiːlɪp). original surname *Schwarzerd.* 1497–1560, German Protestant reformer. His *Loci Communes* (1521) was the first presentation of Protestant theology. In the Augsburg Confession (1530) he stated the Lutheran faith.

Melanesia ★ (ˌmɛlə'niːzɪə) *n* one of the three divisions of islands in the Pacific (the others being Micronesia and Polynesia); the SW division of Oceania: includes Fiji, New Caledonia, Vanuatu, the Bismarck Archipelago, and the Louisiade, Solomon, Santa Cruz, and Loyalty Islands, which all lie northeast of Australia. [C19: from Gk *melas* black + *nēsos* island; with reference to the dark skins of the inhabitants; on the model of *Polynesia*]

Melanesian (ˌmɛlə'niːʒən, -ʒɪən) *adj* **1** of or relating to Melanesia, its people, or their languages. ◆ *n* **2** a native or inhabitant of Melanesia: generally Negroid with frizzy hair and small stature. **3** a group or branch of languages spoken in Melanesia.

melange *or* **mélange** (meɪ'lɑːnʒ) *n* a mixture; confusion. [C17: from F *mêler* to mix]

melanin ('mɛlənɪn) *n* any of a group of black or dark brown pigments present in the hair, skin, and eyes of man and animals: produced in excess in certain skin diseases and in melanomas.

melanism ('mɛləˌnɪzəm) *n* **1** the condition in man and animals of having dark-coloured or black skin, feathers, etc. **2** another name for **melanosis**.
▸ ˌmela'nistic *adj*

melano- *or before a vowel* **melan-** *combining form.* black or dark: *melanin; melanism; melanoma*. [from Gk *melas* black]

melanoma (ˌmɛlə'nəʊmə) *n, pl* **melanomas** *or* **melanomata** (-mətə). *Pathol.* a malignant tumour composed of melanin-containing cells, occurring esp. in the skin, often as a result of excessive exposure to sunlight.

melanosis (ˌmɛlə'nəʊsɪs) *or* **melanism** ('mɛləˌnɪzəm) *n Pathol.* a skin condition characterized by excessive deposits of melanin.
▸ **melanotic** (ˌmɛlə'nɒtɪk) *adj*

Melba ★ ('mɛlbə) *n* **1** Dame **Nellie**, stage name of *Helen Porter Mitchell*. 1861–1931, Australian soprano. **2 do a Melba.** *Austral. sl.* to make repeated farewell appearances.

Melba toast *n* very thin crisp toast. [C20: after Dame Nellie MELBA]

Melbourne[1] ★ ('mɛlbən) *n* a port in SE Australia, capital of Victoria, on Port Phillip Bay: the second largest city in the country; settled in 1835 and developed rapidly with the discovery of rich goldfields in 1851; three universities. Pop.: 3 218 100 (1996 est.).
▸ **Melburnian** (mɛl'bɜːnɪən) *n, adj*

Melbourne[2] ★ ('mɛlbən) *n* **William Lamb**, 2nd Viscount. 1779–1848; Whig prime minister (1834; 1835–41) and chief political adviser to the young Queen Victoria.

Melchior ★ ('mɛlkɪˌɔː) *n* **1** (in Christian tradition) one of the Magi, the others being Balthazar and Caspar. **2 Lauritz** ('laʊrɪts). 1890–1973, US operatic tenor, born in Denmark.

Melchizedek ★ (mɛl'kɪzəˌdɛk) *n Old Testament.* the priest-king of Salem who blessed Abraham (Genesis 14:18-19) and was taken as a prototype of Christ's priesthood (Hebrews 7). Douay spelling: **Melchisedech**.

meld[1] (mɛld) *vb* to blend or become blended; combine. [C20: blend of MELT + WELD[1]]

meld[2] (mɛld) *vb* **1** (in some card games) to declare or lay down (cards), which then score points. ◆ *n* **2** the act of melding. **3** a set of cards for melding. [C19: from G *melden* to announce]

Meleager ★ (ˌmɛlɪˈeɪgə) *n Greek myth.* one of the Argonauts, slayer of the Calydonian boar.

melee *or* **mêlée** (ˈmɛleɪ) *n* a noisy riotous fight or brawl. [C17: from F *mêlée*, from *mêler* to mix]

Méliès ★ (*French* meljɛs) *n* **Georges** (ʒɔrʒ). 1861–1938, French film director.

Melilla ★ (*French* melija) *n* the chief town of a Spanish enclave in Morocco, on the Mediterranean coast: founded by the Phoenicians; exports iron ore. Pop.: 58 052 (1994 est.).

meliorate (ˈmiːlɪəˌreɪt) *vb* **meliorates, meliorating, meliorated.** a variant of **ameliorate.**
▶ ˌmelioˈration *n* ▶ **meliorative** (ˈmiːlɪərətɪv) *adj, n*

melisma (mɪˈlɪzmə) *n, pl* **melismata** (-mətə) *or* **melismas.** *Music.* an expressive vocal phrase or passage consisting of several notes sung to one syllable. [C19: from Gk: melody]

Melitopol ★ (*Russian* mɪliˈtɔpəlj) *n* a city in the SE Ukraine. Pop.: 174 000 (1996 est.).

Melk ★ (mɛlk) *n* a town in N Austria, on the River Danube: noted for its baroque Benedictine abbey. Pop.: 5163 (1991).

melliferous (mɪˈlɪfərəs) *or* **mellific** (mɪˈlɪfɪk) *adj* forming or producing honey. [C17: from L *mellifer*, from *mel* honey + *ferre* to bear]

mellifluous (mɪˈlɪflʊəs) *or* **mellifluent** *adj* (of sounds or utterances) smooth or honeyed; sweet. [C15: from LL *mellifluus*, from L *mel* honey + *fluere* to flow]
▶ melˈlifluously *adv* ▶ melˈlifluousness *or* melˈlifluence *n*

mellow (ˈmɛləʊ) *adj* **1** (esp. of fruits) full-flavoured; sweet; ripe. **2** (esp. of wines) well-matured. **3** (esp. of colours or sounds) soft or rich. **4** kind-hearted, esp. through maturity or old age. **5** genial, as through the effects of alcohol. **6** (of soil) soft and loamy. ◆ *vb* **7** to make or become mellow. **8** (foll. by *out*) to become calm and relaxed or (esp. of a drug) to have a calming and relaxing effect on (someone). [C15: ?from OE *meru* soft (as through ripeness)]
▶ ˈmellowness *n*

melodeon *or* **melodion** (mɪˈləʊdɪən) *n Music.* **1** a type of small accordion. **2** a type of keyboard instrument similar to the harmonium. [C19: from G, from *Melodie* melody]

melodic (mɪˈlɒdɪk) *adj* **1** of or relating to melody. **2** of or relating to a part in a piece of music. **3** melodious.
▶ meˈlodically *adv*

melodic minor scale *n Music.* a minor scale modified from the natural by the sharpening of the sixth and seventh when taken in ascending order and the restoration of their original pitches when taken in descending order.

melodious (mɪˈləʊdɪəs) *adj* **1** having a tune that is pleasant to the ear. **2** of or relating to melody; melodic.
▶ meˈlodiously *adv* ▶ meˈlodiousness *n*

melodist (ˈmɛlədɪst) *n* **1** a composer of melodies. **2** a singer.

melodize *or* **melodise** (ˈmɛləˌdaɪz) *vb* **melodizes, melodizing, melodized** *or* **melodises, melodising, melodised. 1** (*tr*) to provide with a melody. **2** (*tr*) to make melodious. **3** (*intr*) to sing or play melodies.
▶ ˈmeloˌdizer *or* ˈmeloˌdiser *n*

melodrama (ˈmɛləˌdrɑːmə) *n* **1** a play, film, etc., characterized by extravagant action and emotion. **2** (formerly) a romantic drama characterized by sensational incident, music, and song. **3** overdramatic emotion or behaviour. [C19: from F *mélodrame*, from Gk *melos* song + *drame* DRAMA]
▶ melodramatist (ˌmɛləˈdræmətɪst) *n* ▶ melodramatic (ˌmɛlədrəˈmætɪk) *adj* ▶ ˌmelodraˈmatics *pl n* ▶ ˌmelodraˈmatically *adv*

melody (ˈmɛlədɪ) *n, pl* **melodies. 1** *Music.* **1a** a succession of notes forming a distinctive sequence; tune. **1b** the horizontally represented aspect of the structure of a piece of music. Cf. **harmony** (sense 4b). **2** sounds that are pleasant because of tone or arrangement, esp. words of

poetry. [C13: from OF, from LL *melōdia*, from Gk *melōidía*, from *melos* song + *aoidein* to sing]

melon (ˈmɛlən) *n* **1** any of several varieties of trailing plants (see **muskmelon, watermelon**), cultivated for their edible fruit. **2** the fruit of any of these plants, which has a hard rind and juicy flesh. [C14: via OF from LL *mēlo*, form of *mēlopepō*, from Gk, from *mēlon* apple + *pepōn* gourd]

Melos ★ (ˈmiːlɒs) *n* an island in the SW Aegean Sea, in the Cyclades: of volcanic origin, with hot springs; centre of early Aegean civilization, where the Venus de Milo was found. Pop.: 5000 (latest est.). Area: 132 sq. km (51 sq. miles). Modern Greek name: **Mílos.**

Melpomene ★ (mɛlˈpɒmɪnɪ) *n Greek myth.* the Muse of tragedy.

melt (mɛlt) *vb* **melts, melting, melted; melted** *or* **molten. 1** to liquefy (a solid) or (of a solid) to become liquefied, as a result of the action of heat. **2** to become or make liquid; dissolve. **3** (often foll. by *away*) to disappear; fade. **4** (foll. by *down*) to melt (metal scrap) for reuse. **5** (often foll. by *into*) to blend or cause to blend gradually. **6** to make or become emotional or sentimental; soften. ◆ *n* **7** the act or process of melting. **8** something melted or an amount melted. [OE *meltan* to digest]
▶ ˈmeltable *adj* ▶ ˈmelter *n* ▶ ˈmeltingly *adv*

meltdown (ˈmɛltˌdaʊn) *n* **1** (in a nuclear reactor) the melting of the fuel rods as a result of a defect in the cooling system, with the possible escape of radiation. **2** *Inf.* a sudden disastrous failure with potential for widespread harm, as a stock-exchange crash. **3** *Inf.* the process or state of irreversible breakdown or decline: *the community is slowly going into meltdown.*

melting point *n* the temperature at which a solid turns into a liquid.

melting pot *n* **1** a pot in which metals or other substances are melted, esp. in order to mix them. **2** an area in which many races, ideas, etc., are mixed.

melton (ˈmɛltən) *n* a heavy smooth woollen fabric with a short nap. Also called: **melton cloth.** [C19: from MELTON MOWBRAY, a former centre for making this]

Melton Mowbray ★ (ˈmɛltən ˈməʊbrɪ) *n* a town in central England, in Leicestershire: pork pies and Stilton cheese. Pop.: 24 348 (1991).

meltwater (ˈmɛltˌwɔːtə) *n* melted snow or ice.

Melville ★ (ˈmɛlvɪl) *n* **Herman.** 1819–91, US writer. His works include *Moby Dick* (1851) and *Billy Budd* (written 1891, published 1924).

Melville Island ★ *n* **1** an island in the Arctic Ocean, north of Victoria Island: administratively part of the Northwest Territories of Canada. Area: 41 865 sq. km (16 164 sq. miles). **2** an island in the Arafura Sea, off the N central coast of Australia, separated from the mainland by Clarence Strait. Area: 6216 sq. km (2400 sq. miles).

Melville Peninsula ★ *n* a peninsula of N Canada, in the Northwest Territories, between the Gulf of Boothia and Foxe Basin.

mem. *abbrev. for:* **1** member. **2** memoir. **3** memorandum. **4** memorial.

member (ˈmɛmbə) *n* **1** a person who belongs to a club, political party, etc. **2** any individual plant or animal in a taxonomic group. **3** any part of an animal body, such as a limb. **4** any part of a plant, such as a petal, root, etc. **5** *Maths, logic.* any individual object belonging to a set or logical class. **6** a component part of a building or construction. [C13: from L *membrum* limb, part]
▶ ˈmemberless *adj*

Member (ˈmɛmbə) *n* (*sometimes not cap.*) **1** short for **Member of Parliament. 2** short for **Member of Congress. 3** a member of some other legislative body.

Member of Congress *n* a member of the US Congress, esp. of the House of Representatives.

Member of Parliament *n* a member of the House of Commons or similar legislative body, as in many Commonwealth countries.

membership (ˈmɛmbəˌʃɪp) *n* **1** the members of an organization collectively. **2** the state of being a member.

membrane ('mɛmbreɪn) *n* **1** any thin pliable sheet of material. **2** a pliable sheetlike usually fibrous tissue that covers, lines, or connects plant and animal organs or cells. [C16: from L *membrāna* skin covering a part of the body, from *membrum* MEMBER]
▸ **membranous** ('mɛmbrənəs) *or* **membraneous** (mɛm-'breɪnɪəs) *adj*

Memel ★ ('meːməl) *n* **1** the German name for **Klaipeda**. **2** the lower course of the Neman River.

memento (mɪ'mɛntəʊ) *n, pl* **mementos** *or* **mementoes**. something that reminds one of past events; a souvenir. [C15: from L, imperative of *meminisse* to remember]

memento mori ('mɔːriː) *n, pl* **memento mori**. an object, such as a skull, intended to remind people of death. [C16: L: remember you must die]

Memling ('mɛmlɪŋ) *or* **Memlinc** ★ ('mɛmlɪŋk) *n* Hans (hɑns). ?1430–94, Flemish painter.

Memnon ★ ('mɛmnɒn) *n* **1** *Greek myth.* a king of Ethiopia, son of Eos: slain by Achilles in the Trojan War. **2** a colossal statue of Amenhotep III at Thebes in ancient Egypt, which emitted a sound thought by the Greeks to be the voice of Memnon.
▸ **Memnonian** (mɛm'nəʊnɪən) *adj*

memo ('mɛməʊ, 'miːməʊ) *n, pl* **memos**. short for **memorandum**.

memoir ('mɛmwɑː) *n* **1** a biography or historical account, esp. one based on personal knowledge. **2** an essay, as on a specialized topic. [C16: from F, from L *memoria* MEMORY]
▸ **'memoirist** *n*

memoirs ('mɛmwɑːz) *pl n* **1** a collection of reminiscences about a period, series of events, etc., written from personal experience or special sources. **2** an autobiographical record. **3** a record, as of transactions of a society, etc.

memorabilia (ˌmɛmərə'bɪlɪə) *pl n, sing* **memorabile** (-'ræbɪlɪ). **1** memorable events or things. **2** objects connected with famous people or events. [C17: from L, from *memorābilis* MEMORABLE]

memorable ('mɛmərəb°l) *adj* worth remembering or easily remembered. [C15: from L *memorābilis*, from *memorāre* to recall, from *memor* mindful]
▸ **ˌmemoraˈbility** *n* ▸ **'memorably** *adv*

memorandum (ˌmɛmə'rændəm) *n, pl* **memorandums** *or* **memoranda** (-də). **1** a written statement, record, or communication. **2** a note of things to be remembered. **3** an informal diplomatic communication. **4** *Law.* a short written summary of the terms of a transaction. ◆ Often (esp. for senses 1, 2) shortened to **memo**. [C15: from L: (something) to be remembered]

memorial (mɪ'mɔːrɪəl) *adj* **1** serving to preserve the memory of the dead or a past event. **2** of or involving memory. ◆ *n* **3** something serving as a remembrance. **4** a written statement of facts submitted to a government, authority, etc., in conjunction with a petition. **5** an informal diplomatic paper. [C14: from LL *memoriāle* a reminder, neuter of *memoriālis*]
▸ **me'morially** *adv*

memorialize *or* **memorialise** (mɪ'mɔːrɪəˌlaɪz) *vb* **memorializes, memorializing, memorialized** *or* **memorialises, memorialising, memorialised**. (*tr*) **1** to honour or commemorate. **2** to present or address a memorial to.

memorize *or* **memorise** ('mɛməˌraɪz) *vb* **memorizes, memorizing, memorized** *or* **memorises, memorising, memorised**. (*tr*) to commit to memory; learn so as to remember.

memory ('mɛmərɪ) *n, pl* **memories**. **1a** the ability of the mind to store and recall past sensations, thoughts, knowledge, etc.: *he can do it from memory.* **1b** the part of the brain that appears to have this function. **2** the sum of everything retained by the mind. **3** a particular recollection of an event, person, etc. **4** the time over which recollection extends: *within his memory.* **5** commemoration or remembrance: *in memory of our leader.* **6** the state of being remembered, as after death. **7** a part of a computer in which information is stored for immediate use by the central processing unit. Cf. **RAM**[1]. [C14: from OF *memorie*, from L *memoria*, from *memor* mindful]

Memphis ★ ('mɛmfɪs) *n* **1** a port in SW Tennessee, on the Mississippi River: the largest city in the state; a major cotton and timber market; Memphis State University (1909). Pop.: 614 289 (1994 est.). **2** a ruined city in N Egypt, the ancient centre of Lower Egypt, on the Nile: administrative and artistic centre, sacred to the worship of Ptah.
▸ **'Memphian** *adj, n*

Memphremagog ★ (ˌmɛmfriː'meɪgɒg) *n* **Lake.** a lake on the border between the US and Canada, in N Vermont and S Quebec. Length: about 43 km (27 miles). Width: up to 6 km (4 miles).

memsahib ('mɛmˌsɑːɪb, -hɪb) *n* (formerly, in India) a term of respect used for a European married woman. [C19: from MA'AM + SAHIB]

men (mɛn) *n* the plural form of **man**.

menace ('mɛnɪs) *vb* **menaces, menacing, menaced**. **1** to threaten with violence, danger, etc. ◆ *n* **2** *Literary.* a threat. **3** something menacing; a source of danger. **4** *Inf.* a nuisance. [C13: ult. rel. to L *minax* threatening, from *mināri* to threaten]
▸ **'menacer** *n* ▸ **'menacing** *adj* ▸ **'menacingly** *adv*

menad ('miːnæd) *n* a variant spelling of **maenad**.

Menado (mɛ'nɑːdəʊ) *or* **Manado** ★ *n* a port in NE Indonesia, on NE Sulawesi: founded by the Dutch in 1657. Pop.: 275 374 (1990).

ménage (meɪ'nɑːʒ) *n* the persons of a household. [C17: from F, from Vulgar L (unattested) *mansiōnāticum* household]

ménage à trois *French.* (menaʒ a trwa) *n, pl* **ménages à trois** (menaʒ a trwa). a sexual arrangement involving a married couple and the lover of one of them. [lit.: household of three]

menagerie (mɪ'nædʒərɪ) *n* **1** a collection of wild animals kept for exhibition. **2** the place where such animals are housed. [C18: from F: household management, which formerly included care of domestic animals]

Menai Strait ★ ('mɛnaɪ) *n* a channel of the Irish Sea between the island of Anglesey and the mainland of NW Wales: famous suspension bridge (1819–26) designed by Thomas Telford and tubular bridge (1846–50) designed by Robert Stephenson. Length: 24 km (15 miles). Width: up to 3 km (2 miles).

Menander ★ (mə'nændə) *n* ?342–?292 B.C., Greek comic dramatist. The *Dyskolos* is his only complete extant comedy but others survive in adaptations by Terence and Plautus.

Mencius ★ ('mɛnʃɪəs, -ʃəs) *n* Chinese name *Mengzi* or *Meng-tze*. ?372–?289 B.C., Chinese philosopher, who propounded the ethical system of Confucius.

Mencken ★ ('mɛŋkən) *n* **H(enry) L(ouis)**. 1880–1956, US journalist and critic, noted for *The American Language* (1919): editor of the *American Mercury*, which he founded (1924).

mend (mɛnd) *vb* **1** (*tr*) to repair (something broken or unserviceable). **2** to improve or undergo improvement; reform (often in **mend one's ways**). **3** (*intr*) to heal or recover. **4** (*intr*) (of conditions) to improve; become better. ◆ *n* **5** the act of repairing. **6** a mended area, esp. on a garment. **7 on the mend**. becoming better, esp. in health. [C12: from AMEND]
▸ **'mendable** *adj* ▸ **'mender** *n*

mendacity (mɛn'dæsɪtɪ) *n, pl* **mendacities**. **1** the tendency to be untruthful. **2** a falsehood. [C17: from LL *mendācitās*, from L *mendāx* untruthful]
▸ **mendacious** (mɛn'deɪʃəs) *adj* ▸ **men'daciously** *adv*

Mendel ★ ('mɛnd°l) *n* **Gregor Johann** ('greːgɔr jo'han). 1822–84, Austrian monk and botanist; founder of genetics, with his experiments on the hybridization of green peas. His findings were published (1865) but unrecognized until 1900. See **Mendel's laws**.

mendelevium (ˌmɛndɪ'liːvɪəm) *n* a transuranic element artificially produced by bombardment of einsteinium. Symbol: Md; atomic no.: 101; half-life of most stable isotope, ^{258}Md: 60 days (approx.). [C20: after D. I. MENDELEYEV]

Mendeleyev *or* **Mendeleev** ★ (*Russian* mɪndɪ'ljejɪf) *n* **Dmitri Ivanovich** ('dmitrij i'vanəvitʃ). 1834–1907, Russian chemist. He devised the first form of the periodic table (1869).

Mendelian (mɛn'diːlɪən) *adj* of or relating to Mendel's laws.

Mendel's laws *pl n* the principles of heredity proposed by Gregor Mendel. The **Law of Segregation** states that each hereditary character is determined by a pair of units in the reproductive cells: the pairs separate during meiosis so that each gamete carries only one unit of each pair. The **Law of Independent Assortment** states that the separation of the units of each pair is not influenced by that of any other pair.

Mendelssohn ★ ('mɛndˀlsən; *German* 'mɛndəlzoːn) *n* **1** Felix ('feːlɪks), full name *Jacob Ludwig Felix Mendelssohn-Bartholdy*. 1809–47, German composer. His works include the overtures *A Midsummer Night's Dream* (1826) and *Fingal's Cave* (1832), five symphonies, the oratorio *Elijah* (1846), a violin concerto, and many songs. **2** his grandfather, **Moses** ('moːzəs). 1729–86, German Jewish philosopher, noted for his book *Jerusalem* (1783).

Menderes ★ (ˌmɛndɛ'rɛs) *n* **1** a river in SW Turkey flowing southwest, then west to the Aegean. Length: about 386 km (240 miles). Ancient name: **Maeander. 2** a river in NW Turkey flowing west and northwest to the Dardanelles. Length: 104 km (65 miles). Ancient name: **Scamander.**

Mendès-France ★ (*French* mɛ̃dɛsfrɑ̃s) *n* **Pierre** (pjɛr). 1907–82, French statesman; prime minister (1954–55).

mendicant ('mɛndɪkənt) *adj* **1** begging. **2** (of a member of a religious order) dependent on alms for sustenance. ◆ *n* **3** a mendicant friar. **4** a less common word for **beggar.** [C16: from L *mendīcāre*, from *mendīcus* beggar, from *mendus* flaw]
  ▸ 'mendicancy *or* mendicity (mɛn'dɪsɪtɪ) *n*

Mendips ★ ('mɛndɪps) *pl n* a range of limestone hills in SW England, in N Somerset: includes the Cheddar Gorge and numerous caves. Highest point: 325 m (1068 ft). Also called: **Mendip Hills.**

Mendoza[1] ★ (mɛn'dəuzə; *Spanish* men'doθa) *n* a city in W central Argentina, in the foothills of the Sierra de los Paramillos: largely destroyed by an earthquake in 1861; commercial centre of an intensively cultivated irrigated region; University of Cuyo (1939). Pop.: 773 113 (1991).

Mendoza[2] ★ (*Spanish* men'doθa) *n* **Pedro de** ('peðro de). died 1537, Spanish soldier and explorer; founder of Buenos Aires (1536).

meneer (mə'nɪə) *n* a S. African title of address equivalent to *sir* when used alone or *Mr* when placed before a name. [Afrik.]

Menelaus ★ (ˌmɛnɪ'leɪəs) *n* *Greek myth.* a king of Sparta and the brother of Agamemnon. He was the husband of Helen, whose abduction led to the Trojan War.

Menelik II ★ ('mɛnɪlɪk) *n* 1844–1913, emperor of Abyssinia (1889–1910). He defeated the Italians at Aduwa (1896), maintaining the independence of Abyssinia.

Menes ★ ('miːniːz) *n* the first king of the first dynasty of Egypt (?3100 B.C.). He is said to have united Upper and Lower Egypt and founded Memphis.

menfolk ('mɛnˌfəuk) *pl n* men collectively, esp. the men of a particular family.

Mengelberg ★ ('mɛŋˀlˌbɜːg; *Dutch* 'mɛŋəlbɛrx) *n* (**Josef**) **Willem** ('wɪləm). 1871–1951, Dutch conductor.

Mengistu Haile Mariam ★ (mɛŋ'gɪstuː 'haɪlɪ 'mɑːrɪəm) *n* born 1937, Ethiopian soldier and statesman; head of state from 1977 until overthrown and forced into exile in 1991.

Mengzi *or* **Meng-tze** ★ ('mɛŋ'tseɪ) *n* the Chinese name for **Mencius.**

menhaden (mɛn'heɪdˀn) *n, pl* **menhaden.** a marine North American fish: source of fishmeal, fertilizer, and oil. [C18: from Algonquian; prob. rel. to another Amerind word, *munnawhatteaúg* fertilizer]

menhir ('mɛnhɪə) *n* a single standing stone, dating from prehistoric times. [C19: from Breton *men* stone + *hir* long]

menial ('miːnɪəl) *adj* **1** consisting of or occupied with work requiring little skill, esp. domestic duties. **2** of, in-

volving, or befitting servants. **3** servile. ◆ *n* **4** a domestic servant. **5** a servile person. [C14: from Anglo-Norman *meignial*, from OF *meinie* household]

Meninga ★ (mɪn'ɪŋgə) *n* Mal. born 1960, Australian rugby league player.

meninges (mɪ'nɪndʒiːz) *pl n, sing* **meninx** ('miːnɪŋks). the three membranes (**dura mater, arachnoid, pia mater**) that envelop the brain and spinal cord. [C17: from Gk, pl of *meninx* membrane]
  ▸ **meningeal** (mɪ'nɪndʒɪəl) *adj*

meningitis (ˌmɛnɪn'dʒaɪtɪs) *n* inflammation of the membranes that surround the brain or spinal cord, caused by infection.
  ▸ **meningitic** (ˌmɛnɪn'dʒɪtɪk) *adj*

meningococcus (mɛˌnɪŋgəu'kɒkəs) *n, pl* **meningococci** (-'kɒksaɪ). the bacterium that causes cerebrospinal meningitis.
  ▸ me,ningo'coccal *adj*

meniscus (mɪ'nɪskəs) *n, pl* **menisci** (-'nɪsaɪ) *or* **meniscuses. 1** the curved upper surface of a liquid standing in a tube, produced by the surface tension. **2** a crescent-shaped lens; a concavo-convex or convexo-concave lens. [C17: from NL, from Gk *mēniskos* crescent, dim. of *mēnē* moon]
  ▸ me'niscoid *adj*

Mennonite ('mɛnəˌnaɪt) *n* a member of a Protestant sect that rejects infant baptism and Church organization, and in most cases refuses military service, public office, and the taking of oaths. [C16: from G *Mennonit*, after *Menno* Simons (1496–1561), Frisian religious leader]
  ▸ 'Mennonitism *n*

meno ('mɛnəu) *adv Music.* to be played less quickly, less softly, etc. [from It., from L *minus* less]

meno- *combining form.* menstruation. [from Gk *mēn* month]

Menon ★ ('mɛnən) *n* Vengalil Krishnan Krishna ('vɛŋgəlɪl 'kriːʃnən 'krɪʃnə). 1897–1974, Indian diplomat and close associate of Nehru.

menopause ('mɛnəuˌpɔːz) *n* the period during which a woman's menstrual cycle ceases, normally at an age of 45 to 50. [C19: from F, from Gk *mēn* month + *pausis* halt]
  ▸ ,meno'pausal *adj*

menorah (mɪ'nɔːrə) *n Judaism.* **1** a seven-branched candelabrum used in the Temple and now an emblem of Judaism and the badge of the state of Israel. **2** a similar lamp lit during the Chanukah festival. [from Heb.: candlestick]

Menorca ★ (me'nɔrka) *n* the Spanish name for **Minorca.**

menorrhagia (ˌmɛnɔ'reɪdʒɪə) *n* excessive bleeding during menstruation.

menorrhoea (ˌmɛnə'rɪə) *n* normal bleeding in menstruation.

Menotti ★ (mə'nɒtɪ; *Italian* me'nɔtti) *n* Gian Carlo (dʒan 'karlo). born 1911, Italian composer, in the US from 1928. His operas include *The Consul* (1950) and *Amahl and the Night Visitors* (1951).

menses ('mɛnsiːz) *n* (*functioning as sing or pl*) **1** another name for **menstruation. 2** the period of time during which one menstruation occurs. **3** the matter discharged during menstruation. [C16: from L, pl of *mensis* month]

Menshevik ('mɛnʃɪvɪk) *or* **Menshevist** *n* a member of the moderate wing of the Russian Social Democratic Party. Cf. **Bolshevik.** [C20: from Russian, lit.: minority, from *menshe* less, from *malo* few]
  ▸ 'Menshe,vism *n*

menstruate ('mɛnstrʊˌeɪt) *vb* **menstruates, menstruating, menstruated.** (*intr*) to undergo menstruation. [C17: from L *menstruāre*, from *mensis* month]

menstruation (ˌmɛnstrʊ'eɪʃən) *n* the approximately monthly discharge of blood and cellular debris from the uterus by nonpregnant women from puberty to the menopause.
  ▸ 'menstrual *or* 'menstruous *adj*

menstruum ('mɛnstrʊəm) *n, pl* **menstruums** *or* **menstrua** (-strʊə). a solvent, esp. one used in the preparation of a drug. [C17 (meaning: solvent), C14 (menstrual discharge): from Med. L, from L *mēnstruus* monthly, from *mēnsis* month; from alchemical comparison between a

★ people and places

base metal being transmuted into gold and the supposed action of the menses]

mensurable ('mɛnsjʊrəbᵊl, -ʃə-) *adj* a less common word for **measurable**. [C17: from LL *mēnsūrābilis*, from *mēnsūra* MEASURE]
▶ ,mensura'bility *n*

mensural ('mɛnʃərəl) *adj* 1 of or involving measure. 2 *Music.* of or relating to music in which notes have fixed values. [C17: from LL *mēnsūrālis*, from *mēnsūra* MEASURE]

mensuration (,mɛnʃə'reɪʃən) *n* 1 the study of the measurement of geometric magnitudes such as length. 2 the act or process of measuring.
▶ **mensurative** ('mɛnʃərətɪv) *adj*

-ment *suffix forming nouns, esp. from verbs.* 1 indicating state, condition, or quality: *enjoyment.* 2 indicating the result or product of an action: *embankment.* 3 indicating process or action: *management.* [from F, from L *-mentum*]

mental ('mɛntᵊl) *adj* 1 of or involving the mind. 2 occurring only in the mind: *mental arithmetic.* 3 affected by mental illness: *a mental patient.* 4 concerned with mental illness: *a mental hospital.* 5 *Sl.* insane. [C15: from LL *mentālis*, from L *mēns* mind]
▶ 'mentally *adv*

mental deficiency *n Psychiatry.* a less common term for **mental retardation.**

mental handicap *n* any intellectual disability resulting from injury to the brain or from abnormal neurological development.
▶ **mentally handicapped** *adj*

mental healing *n* the healing of a disorder by mental concentration or suggestion.

mental illness *n* any of various disorders in which a person's thoughts, emotions, or behaviour are so abnormal as to cause suffering to himself, herself, or other people.

mentalism ('mɛntᵊ,lɪzəm) *n Philosophy.* the doctrine that mind is the fundamental reality and that objects of knowledge exist only as aspects of the subject's consciousness.
▶ ,mental'istic *adj*

mentality (mɛn'tælɪtɪ) *n, pl* **mentalities.** 1 the state or quality of mental or intellectual ability. 2 a way of thinking; mental inclination or character.

mental lexicon *n* the store of words in a person's mind.

mental reservation *n* a tacit withholding of full assent or an unexpressed qualification made when taking an oath, making a statement, etc.

mental retardation *n Psychiatry.* the condition of having a low intelligence quotient (below 70).

menthol ('mɛnθɒl) *n* an organic compound found in peppermint oil and used as an antiseptic, in inhalants, and as an analgesic. Formula: $C_{10}H_{19}OH$. [C19: from G, from L *mentha* MINT[1]]

mentholated ('mɛnθə,leɪtɪd) *adj* containing, treated with, or impregnated with menthol.

mention ('mɛnʃən) *vb* (*tr*) 1 to refer to or speak about briefly or incidentally. 2 to acknowledge or honour. 3 **not to mention (something).** to say nothing of (something too obvious to mention). ◆ *n* 4 a recognition or acknowledgment. 5 a slight reference or allusion. 6 the act of mentioning. [C14: via OF from L *mentiō* a calling to mind, from *mēns* mind]
▶ 'mentionable *adj*

Menton ★ (mɛn'tɒn; *French* mɑ̃tɔ̃) *n* a town and resort in SE France, on the Mediterranean: belonged to Monaco from the 14th century until 1848, then an independent republic until purchased by France in 1860. Pop.: 25 500 (latest est.).

mentor ('mɛntɔ:) *n* a wise or trusted adviser or guide. [C18: from MENTOR]

Mentor ★ ('mɛntɔ:) *n* the friend whom Odysseus put in charge of his household when he left for Troy. He was the adviser of the young Telemachus.

mentoring ('mɛntərɪŋ) *n* (in business) the practice of as-

signing a junior member of staff to the care of a more experienced person who assists him in his career.

menu ('mɛnju:) *n* 1 a list of dishes served at a meal or that can be ordered in a restaurant. 2 a list of options displayed on a visual display unit from which the operator selects an action to be carried out. [C19: from F *menu* small, detailed (list), from L *minūtus* MINUTE[2]]

menuetto (mɛnju'ɛtəʊ) *n, pl* **menuettos.** *Music.* another term for **minuet.** [from It.]

Menuhin ★ ('mɛnjuɪn) *n* **Yehudi,** Baron. (jɛ'hu:dɪ) 1916–99, British violinist, born in the US.

Menzies ★ ('mɛnzɪz) *n* Sir **Robert Gordon.** 1894–1978, Australian statesman; prime minister (1939–41; 1949–66).

meow, miaou, miaow (mɪ'aʊ, mjaʊ), *or* **miaul** (mɪ'aʊl, mjaʊl) *vb* 1 (*intr*) (of a cat) to make a characteristic crying sound. ◆ *interj* 2 an imitation of this sound.

MEP (in Britain) *abbrev. for* Member of the European Parliament.

mepacrine ('mɛpəkrɪn) *n Brit.* a drug formerly widely used to treat malaria. [C20: from ME(THYL) + PA(LUDISM + A)CR(ID)INE]

meperidine (mə'pɛrɪ,di:n, -dɪn) *n* the US name for **pethidine.** [C20: from METHYL + PIPERIDINE]

Mephistopheles (,mɛfɪ'stɒfɪ,li:z) *or* **Mephisto** ★ (mə'fɪstəʊ) *n* a devil in medieval mythology and the one to whom Faust sold his soul in German legend.
▶ **Mephistophelean** *or* **Mephistophelian** (,mɛfɪstə'fi:lɪən) *adj*

mephitic (mɪ'fɪtɪk) *or* **mephitical** *adj* 1 poisonous; foul. 2 foul-smelling; putrid. [C17: from LL *mephīticus* pestilential]

meprobamate (mə'prəʊbə,meɪt, ,mɛprəʊ'bæmeɪt) *n* a white bitter powder used as a tranquillizer. [C20: from ME(THYL) + PRO(PYL + *car*)bamate a salt or ester of an amide of carbonic acid]

-mer *suffix forming nouns. Chem.* denoting a substance of a particular class: *monomer; polymer.* [from Gk *meros* part]

Merano ★ (mə'rɑ:nəʊ; *Italian* me'ra:no) *n* a town and resort in NE Italy, in the foothills of the central Alps: capital of the Tyrol (12th–15th century); under Austrian rule until 1919. Pop.: 33 638 (1993 est.). German name: **Meran** (me'ra:n).

Merca ★ ('mɛəkə) *n* a port in S Somalia on the Indian Ocean. Pop.: 100 000 (1987 est.).

mercantile ('mɜ:kən,taɪl) *adj* 1 of, relating to, or characteristic of trade or traders; commercial. 2 of or relating to mercantilism. [C17: from F, from It., from *mercante* MERCHANT]

mercantilism ('mɜ:kəntɪ,lɪzəm) *n Econ.* a theory prevalent in Europe during the 17th and 18th centuries asserting that the wealth of a nation depends on possession of precious metals and therefore that a government must maximize foreign trade surplus and foster national commercial interests, a merchant marine, the establishment of colonies, etc.
▶ 'mercantilist *n, adj*

mercaptan (mɜ:'kæptæn) *n* another name (not in technical use) for **thiol.** [C19: from G, from Med. L *mercurium captans,* lit.: seizing quicksilver]

Mercator ★ (mɜ:'keɪtə) *n* **Gerardus** (dʒə'rɑ:dəs). Latinized name of *Gerhard Kremer.* 1512–94, Flemish cartographer and mathematician.

Mercator projection *n* a conformal map projection on which parallels and meridians form a rectangular grid, scale being exaggerated with increasing distance from the equator. Also called: **Mercator's projection.** [C17: after G. MERCATOR]

mercenary ('mɜ:sɪnərɪ, -sɪnrɪ) *adj* 1 influenced by greed or desire for gain. 2 of or relating to a mercenary or mercenaries. ◆ *n, pl* **mercenaries.** 3 a man hired to fight for a foreign army, etc. 4 *Rare.* any person who works solely for pay. [C16: from L *mercēnārius,* from *mercēs* wages]

mercer ('mɜ:sə) *n Brit.* a dealer in textile fabrics and fine cloth. [C13: from OF *mercier* dealer, from Vulgar L, from L *merx* wares]
▶ 'mercery *n*

mercerize or **mercerise** ('mɜːsə,raɪz) *vb* **mercerizes, mercerizing, mercerized** or **mercerises, mercerising, mercerised.** (*tr*) to treat (cotton yarn) with an alkali to increase its strength and reception to dye and impart a lustrous silky appearance. [C19: after John *Mercer* (1791–1866), E maker of textiles]

merchandise *n* ('mɜːtʃən,daɪs, -,daɪz). **1** commercial goods; commodities. ◆ *vb* ('mɜːtʃən,daɪz), **merchandises, merchandising, merchandised. 2** to engage in the commercial purchase and sale of (goods or services); trade. [C13: from OF; see MERCHANT]

merchandising ('mɜːtʃən,daɪzɪŋ) *n* **1** the selection and display of goods in a retail outlet. **2** commercial goods, esp. ones issued to exploit the popularity of a pop group, sporting event, etc.

merchant ('mɜːtʃənt) *n* **1** a person engaged in the purchase and sale of commodities for profit; trader. **2** *Chiefly Scot., US, & Canad.* a person engaged in retail trade. **3** (esp. in historical contexts) any trader. **4** *Derog.* a person dealing or involved in something undesirable: *a gossip merchant.* **5** (*modifier*) **5a** of the merchant navy: *a merchant sailor.* **5b** of or concerned with trade: *a merchant ship.* ◆ *vb* **6** (*tr*) to conduct trade in; deal in. [C13: from OF, prob. from Vulgar L, from L *mercārī* to trade, from *merx* wares]

Merchant ★ ('mɜːtʃənt) *n* Ismail ('ɪzmeɪəl). born 1936, Indian film producer, noted for his collaboration with James Ivory on such films as *Shakespeare Wallah* (1965), *A Room with a View* (1986), and *A Soldier's Daughter Never Cries* (1998).

merchantable ('mɜːtʃəntəbəl) *adj* suitable for trading.

merchant bank *n Brit.* a financial institution engaged primarily in accepting foreign bills, advising companies on flotations and takeovers, underwriting new issues, hire-purchase finance, making long-term loans to companies, and managing investment portfolios, funds, and trusts.
▸ **merchant banker** *n*

merchantman ('mɜːtʃəntmən) *n, pl* **merchantmen.** a merchant ship.

merchant navy or **marine** *n* the ships or crew engaged in a nation's commercial shipping.

Mercia ★ ('mɜːʃɪə) *n* a kingdom and earldom of central and S England during the Anglo-Saxon period that reached its height under King Offa (757–96).

Mercian ('mɜːʃən) *adj* **1** of or relating to Mercia, or its dialect. ◆ *n* **2** the dialect of Old and Middle English spoken in Mercia. **3** a native or inhabitant of Mercia.

merciful ('mɜːsɪfʊl) *adj* showing or giving mercy; compassionate.
▸ **mercifully** *adv* ▸ **mercifulness** *n*

merciless ('mɜːsɪlɪs) *adj* without mercy; pitiless, cruel, or heartless.
▸ **mercilessly** *adv* ▸ **mercilessness** *n*

Merckx ★ ('mɜːks) *n* Eddy. born 1945, Belgian professional cyclist: five times winner of the Tour de France.

Mercouri ★ (mɜː'kuːrɪ) *n* Melina (mə'liːnə). 1925–94, Greek actress and politician: her films include *Never on Sunday* (1960); minister of culture and science (1981–85), minister of culture (1985–89; 1993–94).

mercurial (mɜː'kjʊərɪəl) *adj* **1** of, like, containing, or relating to mercury. **2** volatile; lively: *a mercurial temperament.* **3** (*sometimes cap.*) of, like, or relating to the god or the planet Mercury. ◆ *n* **4** *Med.* any salt of mercury for use as a medicine. [C14: from L *mercuriālis*]
▸ **mer,curi'ality** *n* ▸ **mer'curially** *adv*

mercuric (mɜː'kjʊərɪk) *adj* of or containing mercury in the divalent state; denoting a mercury(II) compound.

mercuric chloride *n* a white poisonous crystalline substance used as a pesticide, antiseptic, and preservative for wood. Formula: $HgCl_2$. Systematic name: **mercury(II) chloride.**

Mercurochrome (mə'kjʊərə,krəʊm) *n Trademark.* a solution of a crystalline compound, used as a tropical antibacterial agent.

mercurous ('mɜːkjʊrəs) *adj* of or containing mercury in

the monovalent state; denoting a mercury(I) compound.

mercury ('mɜːkjʊrɪ) *n, pl* **mercuries. 1** Also called: **quicksilver.** a heavy silvery-white toxic liquid metallic element: used in thermometers, barometers, mercury-vapour lamps, and dental amalgams. Symbol: Hg; atomic no.: 80; atomic wt.: 200.59. **2** any plant of the genus *Mercurialis.* **3** *Arch.* a messenger or courier. [C14: from L *Mercurius,* messenger of Jupiter, god of commerce; rel. to *merx* merchandise]

Mercury[1] ★ ('mɜːkjʊrɪ) *n Roman myth.* the messenger of the gods.

Mercury[2] ('mɜːkjʊrɪ) *n* the second smallest planet and the nearest to the sun.

mercury-vapour lamp *n* a lamp in which an electric discharge through mercury vapour is used to produce a greenish-blue light.

mercy ('mɜːsɪ) *n, pl* **mercies. 1** compassionate treatment of or attitude towards an offender, adversary, etc., who is in one's power or care; clemency; pity. **2** the power to show mercy. **3** a relieving or welcome occurrence or state of affairs. **4 at the mercy of.** in the power of. [C12: from OF, from L *mercēs* recompense, from *merx* goods]

mercy flight *n* an aircraft flight to bring a seriously ill or injured person to hospital from an isolated community.

mercy killing *n* another term for **euthanasia.**

mere[1] (mɪə) *adj* being nothing more than something specified: *a mere child.* [C15: from L *merus* pure]
▸ **'merely** *adv*

mere[2] (mɪə) *n* **1** *Dialect or arch.* a lake or marsh. **2** *Obs.* the sea or an inlet of it. [OE *mere* sea, lake]

mere[3] ('mɛrɪ) *n* a short flat Maori striking weapon. [from Maori]

-mere *n combining form.* indicating a part or division. [from Gk *meros* part]
▸ **meric** *adj combining form.*

Meredith ★ ('mɛrɪdɪθ) *n* George. 1828–1909, British novelist and poet. His works include the novels *Beauchamp's Career* (1876) and *The Egoist* (1879) and the poem *Modern Love* (1862).

meretricious (,mɛrɪ'trɪʃəs) *adj* **1** superficially or garishly attractive. **2** insincere. **3** *Arch.* of, like, or relating to a prostitute. [C17: from L *merētrīcius,* from *merētrix* prostitute, from *merēre* to earn money]
▸ **,mere'triciously** *adv* ▸ **,mere'triciousness** *n*

merganser (mɜː'gænsə) *n, pl* **mergansers** or **merganser.** any of several typically crested large marine diving ducks, having a long slender hooked bill with serrated edges. [C18: from NL, from L *mergus* waterfowl, from *mergere* to plunge + *anser* goose]

merge (mɜːdʒ) *vb* **merges, merging, merged. 1** to meet and join or cause to meet and join. **2** to blend or cause to blend; fuse. [C17: from L *mergere* to plunge]
▸ **'mergence** *n*

merger ('mɜːdʒə) *n* **1** *Commerce.* the combination of two or more companies. **2** *Law.* the absorption of an estate, interest, offence, etc., into a greater one. **3** the act of merging or the state of being merged.

Mergui Archipelago ★ (mɜː'gwiː) *n* a group of over 200 islands in the Andaman Sea, off the Tenasserim coast of S Myanmar: mountainous and forested.

Meriç ★ (mə'riːtʃ) *n* the Turkish name for the **Maritsa.**

Mérida ★ (*Spanish* 'meriða) *n* **1** a city in SE Mexico, capital of Yucatán state: founded in 1542 on the site of the ancient Mayan city of T'ho; centre of the henequen industry; university. Pop.: 523 422 (1990). **2** a city in W Venezuela: founded in 1558 by Spanish conquistadores; University of Los Andes (1785). Pop.: 167 990 (1991). **3** a market town in W Spain, in Estremadura, on the Guadiana River: founded in 25 B.C.; became the capital of Lusitania and one of the chief cities of Iberia. Pop.: 49 830 (1991). Latin name: **Au'gusta E'merita.**

meridian (mə'rɪdɪən) *n* **1a** one of the imaginary lines joining the north and south poles at right angles to the equator, designated by degrees of longitude from 0° at Greenwich to 180°. **1b** the great circle running through

★ people and places

both poles. **2** *Astron.* the great circle on the celestial sphere passing through the north and south celestial poles and the zenith and nadir of the observer. **3** the peak; zenith: *the meridian of his achievements.* **4** (in acupuncture, etc.) any of the channels through which vital energy is believed to circulate round the body. **5** *Obs.* noon. ♦ *adj* **6** along or relating to a meridian. **7** of or happening at noon. **8** relating to the peak of something. [C14: from L *merīdiānus* of midday, from *merīdiēs* midday, from *medius* MID¹ + *diēs* day]

meridional (mə'rɪdɪənᵉl) *adj* **1** along, relating to, or resembling a meridian. **2** characteristic of or located in the south, esp. of Europe. ♦ *n* **3** an inhabitant of the south, esp. of France. [C14: from LL *merīdiōnālis* southern; see MERIDIAN]

Mérimée ★ (*French* merime) *n* Prosper (prɔsper). 1803–70, French writer, noted for his short novel *Carmen* (1845), on which Bizet's opera was based.

meringue (mə'ræŋ) *n* **1** stiffly beaten egg whites mixed with sugar and baked. **2** a small cake or shell of this mixture, often filled with cream. [C18: from F, from ?]

merino (mə'riːnəʊ) *n, pl* **merinos. 1** a breed of sheep originating in Spain. **2** the long fine wool of this sheep. **3** the yarn made from this wool, often mixed with cotton. ♦ *adj* **4** made from merino wool. [C18: from Sp., from ?]

Merionethshire ★ (ˌmɛrɪ'ɒnɪθˌʃɪə, -ʃə) *n* (until 1974) a county of N Wales, now part of Gwynedd.

meristem ('mɛrɪˌstɛm) *n* a plant tissue responsible for growth, whose cells divide and differentiate to form the tissues and organs of the plant. [C19: from Gk *meristos* divided, from *merizein*, from *meris* portion]
  ▶ **meristematic** (ˌmɛrɪstɪ'mætɪk) *adj*

merit ('mɛrɪt) *n* **1** worth or superior quality; excellence. **2** (*often pl*) a deserving or commendable quality or act. **3** *Christianity.* spiritual credit granted or received for good works. **4** the fact or state of deserving; desert. ♦ *vb* **merits, meriting, merited. 5** (*tr*) to be worthy of; deserve. [C13: via OF from L *meritum* reward, from *merēre* to deserve]
  ▶ **'merited** *adj* ▶ **'meritless** *adj*

meritocracy (ˌmɛrɪ'tɒkrəsɪ) *n, pl* **meritocracies. 1** rule by persons chosen for their superior talents or intellect. **2** the persons constituting such a group. **3** a social system formed on such a basis.
  ▶ **meritocratic** (ˌmɛrɪtə'krætɪk) *adj*

meritorious (ˌmɛrɪ'tɔːrɪəs) *adj* praiseworthy; showing merit. [C15: from L *meritōrius* earning money]
  ▶ **ˌmeri'toriously** *adv* ▶ **ˌmeri'toriousness** *n*

merits ('mɛrɪts) *pl n* **1** the actual and intrinsic rights and wrongs of an issue, esp. in a law case. **2 on its** (**his, her,** etc.) **merits.** on the intrinsic qualities or virtues.

merle *or* **merl** (mɜːl) *n Scot.* another name for the (European) **blackbird.** [C15: via OF from L *merula*]

merlin ('mɜːlɪn) *n* a small falcon that has a dark plumage with a black-barred tail. [C14: from OF *esmerillon*, from *esmeril*, of Gmc origin]

Merlin ★ ('mɜːlɪn) *n* (in Arthurian legend) a wizard and counsellor to King Arthur eternally imprisoned in a tree by a woman to whom he revealed his secret craft.

mermaid ('mɜːˌmeɪd) *n* an imaginary sea creature fabled to have a woman's head and upper body and a fish's tail. [C14: from MERE² + MAID]

merman ('mɜːˌmæn) *n, pl* **mermen.** a male counterpart of the mermaid. [C17: see MERMAID]

Meroë ('mɛrəʊˌiː) *n* an ancient city in N Sudan, on the Nile; capital of a kingdom that flourished from about 700 B.C. to about 350 A.D.

-merous *adj combining form.* (in biology) having a certain number or kind of parts. [from Gk *meros* part]

Merovingian (ˌmɛrəʊ'vɪndʒɪən) *adj* **1** of or relating to a Frankish dynasty which ruled Gaul and W Germany from about 500 to 751 A.D. ♦ *n* **2** a member or supporter of this dynasty. [C17: from F, from Med. L *Merovingi* offspring of *Merovaeus*, L form of *Merowig*, traditional founder of the line]

merriment ('mɛrɪmənt) *n* gaiety, fun, or mirth.

merry ('mɛrɪ) *adj* **merrier, merriest. 1** cheerful; jolly. **2** very funny; hilarious. **3** *Brit. inf.* slightly drunk. **4 make merry.**

to revel; be festive. **5 play merry hell with.** *Inf.* to disturb greatly; disrupt. [OE *merige* agreeable]
  ▶ **'merrily** *adv* ▶ **'merriness** *n*

merry-andrew (-'ændruː) *n* a joker, clown, or buffoon. [C17: from ?]

merry-go-round *n* **1** another name for **roundabout** (sense 1). **2** a whirl of activity.

merrymaking ('mɛrɪˌmeɪkɪŋ) *n* fun, revelry, or festivity.
  ▶ **'merryˌmaker** *n*

merrythought ('mɛrɪˌθɔːt) *n Brit.* a less common word for **wishbone.**

Merse ★ (mɜːs; *Scot.* mɛrs) *n* **the.** a fertile lowland area of SE Scotland, in the Scottish Borders, north of the Tweed.

Merseburg ★ (*German* 'mɛrzəburk) *n* a city in E Germany, on the Saale River, in Saxony-Anhalt: residence of the dukes of Saxe-Merseburg (1656–1738); chemical industry. Pop.: 46 250 (1989 est.).

Mersey ★ ('mɜːzɪ) *n* a river in W England, rising in N Derbyshire and flowing northwest and west to the Irish Sea through a large estuary on which is situated the port of Liverpool. Length: about 112 km (70 miles).

Merseyside ★ ('mɜːzɪˌsaɪd) *n* a metropolitan county of NW England, administered by the unitary authorities of Sefton, Liverpool, St Helens, Knowsley, and Wirral. Area: 652 sq. km (252 sq. miles).

Mersin ★ (mɛə'siːn) *n* a port in S Turkey, on the Mediterranean: oil refinery. Pop.: 523 00 (1994 est.). Also called: **İçel.**

Merthyr Tydfil ★ ('mɜːθə 'tɪdvɪl) *n* **1** a town in SE Wales, a former mining town. Pop.: 39 482 (1991). **2** a county borough in SE Wales. Pop.: 59 500 (1996 est.). Area: 111 sq. km (43 sq. miles).

Merton¹ ★ ('mɜːtᵉn) *n* a borough in SW Greater London. Pop.: 177 200 (1994 est.). Area: 38 sq. km (15 sq. miles).

Merton² ★ ('mɜːtᵉn) *n* Thomas (Feverel). 1915–68, US monk and mystic; noted for his autobiography *The Seven Storey Mountain* (1948).

mesa ('meɪsə) *n* a flat tableland with steep edges, common in the southwestern US. [from Sp.: table]

mésalliance (me'zælɪəns) *n* a marriage with a person of lower social status. [C18: from F: MISALLIANCE]

Mesa Verde ★ ('meɪsə 'vɜːd) *n* a high plateau in SW Colorado: remains of numerous prehistoric cliff dwellings, inhabited by the Pueblo Indians.

mescal (me'skæl) *n* **1** Also called: **peyote.** a spineless globe-shaped cactus of Mexico and the southwestern US. Its button-like tubercles (**mescal buttons**) are chewed by certain Indian tribes for their hallucinogenic effects. **2** a colourless alcoholic spirit distilled from the fermented juice of certain agave plants. [C19: from American Sp., from Nahuatl *mexcalli* the liquor, from *metl* MAGUEY + *ixcalli* stew]

mescaline *or* **mescalin** ('mɛskəˌliːn, -lɪn) *n* a hallucinogenic drug derived from mescal buttons.

mesdames ('meɪˌdæm) *n* the plural of **madame** and **madam** (sense 1).

mesdemoiselles (ˌmeɪdmwɑ'zɛl) *n* the plural of **mademoiselle.**

meseems (mɪ'siːmz) *vb* (*tr; takes a clause as object*) *Arch.* it seems to me.

mesembryanthemum (mɪzˌɛmbrɪ'ænθɪməm) *n* any of a genus of plants with succulent leaves and bright flowers with rayed petals which typically open at midday. [C18: NL, from Gk *mesēmbria* noon + *anthemon* flower]

mesencephalon (ˌmɛsɛn'sɛfəˌlɒn) *n* the part of the brain that develops from the middle portion of the embryonic neural tube. Nontechnical name: **midbrain.**

mesentery ('mɛsəntərɪ, 'mɛz-) *n, pl* **mesenteries.** the double layer of peritoneum that is attached to the back wall of the abdominal cavity and supports most of the small intestine. [C16: from NL *mesenterium, from* MESO- + Gk *enteron* intestine]
  ▶ **ˌmesen'teric** *adj* ▶ **mesenteritis** (mɛsˌɛntə'raɪtɪs) *n*

mesh (mɛʃ) *n* **1** a network; net. **2** an open space between the strands of a network. **3** (*often pl*) the strands surrounding these spaces. **4** anything that ensnares, or holds like a net. **5** the engagement of teeth on interacting gearwheels: *the gears are in mesh.* ◆ *vb* **6** to entangle or become entangled. **7** (of gear teeth) to engage or cause to engage. **8** (*intr;* often foll. by *with*) to coordinate (with). **9** to work or cause to work in harmony. [C16: prob. from Du. *maesche*]

Meshach ★ ('miːʃæk) *n Old Testament.* one of Daniel's three companions who, together with Shadrach and Abednego, was miraculously saved from destruction in Nebuchadnezzar's fiery furnace (Daniel 3:12-30).

Meshed ★ (mɛ'ʃed) *n* a variant of **Mashhad**.

mesial ('miːzɪəl) *adj Anat.* another word for **medial** (sense 1). [C19: from MESO- + -IAL]

mesmerism ('mɛzmə,rɪzəm) *n Psychol.* **1** a hypnotic state induced by the operator's imposition of his will on that of the patient. **2** an early doctrine concerning this. [C19: after F. A. *Mesmer* (1734–1815), Austrian physician] ▶ **mesmeric** (mɛz'mɛrɪk) *adj* ▶ **'mesmerist** *n*

mesmerize *or* **mesmerise** ('mɛzmə,raɪz) *vb* **mesmerizes, mesmerizing, mesmerized** *or* **mesmerises, mesmerising, mesmerised.** (*tr*) **1** to hold (someone) as if spellbound. **2** a former word for **hypnotize**. ▶ ,mesmeri'zation *or* ,mesmeri'sation *n* ▶ 'mesmer,izer *or* 'mesmer,iser *n*

mesne (miːn) *adj Law.* **1** intermediate or intervening: *a mesne assignment of property.* **2 mesne profits.** rents or profits accruing during the rightful owner's exclusion from his land. [C15: from legal F *meien* in the middle]

meso- *or before a vowel* **mes-** *combining form.* middle or intermediate: *mesomorph.* [from Gk *misos* middle]

mesoblast ('mɛsəʊ,blæst) *n* another name for **mesoderm**. ▶ ,meso'blastic *adj*

mesocarp ('mɛsəʊ,kɑːp) *n* the middle layer of the pericarp of a fruit, such as the flesh of a peach.

mesocephalic (,mɛsəʊsɪ'fælɪk) *Anat.* ◆ *adj* **1** having a medium-sized head. ◆ *n* **2** an individual with such a head. ▶ mesocephaly (,mɛsəʊ'sɛfəlɪ) *n*

mesoderm ('mɛsəʊ,dɜːm) *n* the middle germ layer of an animal embryo, giving rise to muscle, blood, bone, connective tissue, etc. ▶ ,meso'dermal *or* ,meso'dermic *adj*

Mesolithic (,mɛsəʊ'lɪθɪk) *n* **1** the period between the Palaeolithic and the Neolithic, in Europe from about 12 000 to 3000 B.C. ◆ *adj* **2** of or relating to the Mesolithic.

Mesolonghi ★ (,mɛsə'lɔːŋgɪ) *n* a variant of **Missolonghi**.

Mesolóngion ★ (,mɛsə'lɒŋgɪ,ɒn) *n* transliteration of the Modern Greek name for **Missolonghi**.

mesomorph ('mɛsəʊ,mɔːf) *n* a type of person having a muscular body build with a relatively prominent underlying bone structure.

mesomorphic (,mɛsəʊ'mɔːfɪk) *adj* **1** *Chem.* existing in or concerned with an intermediate state of matter between a true liquid and a true solid. **2** relating to or being a mesomorph. ◆ Also: **mesomorphous**. ▶ ,meso'morphism *n*

meson ('miːzɒn) *n* any of a group of elementary particles that have a rest mass between those of an electron and a proton, and an integral spin. [C20: from MESO- + -ON] ▶ me'sonic *or* 'mesic *adj*

mesophyte ('mɛsəʊ,faɪt) *n* any plant that grows in surroundings receiving an average supply of water.

Mesopotamia ★ (,mɛsəpə'teɪmɪə) *n* a region of SW Asia between the lower and middle reaches of the Tigris and Euphrates rivers: site of several ancient civilizations. [L, from Gk *mesopotamia (khora)* (the land) between rivers] ▶ ,Mesopo'tamian *n, adj*

mesosphere ('mɛsəʊ,sfɪə) *n* the atmospheric layer lying between the stratosphere and the thermosphere.

Mesozoic (,mɛsəʊ'zəʊɪk) *adj* **1** of, denoting, or relating to an era of geological time that began 225 000 000 years ago and lasted about 155 000 000 years. ◆ *n* **2 the.** the Mesozoic era.

mesquite *or* **mesquit** (mɛ'skiːt, 'mɛskiːt) *n* any of vari-

ous small trees, esp. a tropical American variety, whose sugary pods (**mesquite beans**) are used as animal fodder. [C19: from Mexican Sp., from Nahautl *mizquitl*]

mess (mɛs) *n* **1** a state of confusion or untidiness, esp. if dirty or unpleasant. **2** a chaotic or troublesome state of affairs; muddle. **3** *Inf.* a dirty or untidy person or thing. **4** *Arch.* a portion of food, esp. soft or semiliquid food. **5** a place where service personnel eat or take recreation. **6** a group of people, usually servicemen, who eat together. **7** the meal so taken. ◆ *vb* **8** (*tr;* often foll. by *up*) to muddle or dirty. **9** (*intr*) to make a mess. **10** (*intr;* often foll. by *with*) to interfere; meddle. **11** (*intr;* often foll. by *with* or *together*) *Mil.* to group together, esp. for eating. [C13: from OF *mes* dish of food, from LL *missus* course (at table), from L *mittere* to send forth]

mess about *or* **around** *vb* (*adv*) **1** (*intr*) to occupy oneself trivially; potter. **2** (when *intr,* often foll. by *with*) to interfere or meddle (with). **3** (*intr;* sometimes foll. by *with*) *Chiefly US.* to engage in adultery.

message ('mɛsɪdʒ) *n* **1** a communication, usually brief, from one person or group to another. **2** an implicit meaning, as in a work of art. **3** a formal communiqué. **4** an inspired communication of a prophet or religious leader. **5** a mission; errand. **6 get the message.** *Inf.* to understand. ◆ *vb* **messages, messaging, messaged. 7** (*tr*) to send as a message. [C13: from OF, from Vulgar L *missāticum* (unattested) something sent, from L *missus,* p.p. of *mittere*]

Messager ★ (*French* mɛsaʒe) *n* André **(Charles Prosper)** (ãdre). 1853–1929, French composer and conductor.

messages ('mɛsɪdʒɪz) *pl n Scot. & NE English dialect.* household shopping.

message stick *n* a stick bearing carved symbols, carried by a native Australian as identification.

Messalina ★ (,mɛsə'liːnə) *n* **Valeria** (və'lɪərɪə). died 48 A.D., wife of the Roman emperor Claudius, notorious for her debauchery.

Messene ★ (mɛ'siːnɪ) *n* an ancient Greek city in the SW Peloponnese: founded in 369 B.C. as the capital of Messenia.

messenger ('mɛsɪndʒə) *n* **1** a person who takes messages from one person or group to another. **2** a person who runs errands. **3** a carrier of official dispatches; courier. [C13: from OF *messagier,* from MESSAGE]

messenger RNA *n Biochem.* a form of RNA, transcribed from a single strand of DNA, that carries genetic information required for protein synthesis from DNA to the ribosomes.

Messenia ★ (mə'siːnɪə) *n* the southwestern area of the Peloponnese in S Greece.

Messerschmitt ★ (*German* 'mɛsərʃmɪt) *n* **Willy** ('vɪli). 1898–1978, German aeronautical engineer. His planes figured in World War II, including the Me-262, the first jet fighter.

mess hall *n* a military dining room.

Messiaen ★ (*French* mɛsjã) *n* **Olivier** (ɔlivje). 1908–92, French composer and organist. His music is distinguished by its rhythmic intricacy; he was influenced by Hindu and Greek rhythms and bird song.

Messiah (mɪ'saɪə) *n* **1** *Judaism.* the awaited king of the Jews, to be sent by God to free them. **2** Jesus Christ, when regarded in this role. **3** an exceptional or hoped-for liberator of a country or people. [C14: from OF *Messie,* ult. from Heb. *māshīah* anointed] ▶ Mes'siahship *n* ▶ Messianic *or* messianic (,mɛsɪ'ænɪk) *adj*

Messier catalogue ('mɛsɪ,eɪ) *n Astronomy.* a catalogue of 103 nonstellar objects, such as nebulae and galaxies, prepared in 1781–86. An object is referred to by its number in this catalogue, for example the Andromeda Galaxy is referred to as *M31.* [C18: after Charles *Messier* (1730–1817), F astronomer]

messieurs ('mɛsəz) *n* the plural of **monsieur**.

Messina ★ (mɛ'siːnə) *n* a port in NE Sicily, on the **Strait of Messina:** colonized by Greeks around 730 B.C.; under Spanish rule (1282–1676 and 1678–1713); university (1549). Pop.: 233 845 (1994 est.).

★ people and places

mess jacket *n* a waist-length jacket, worn by officers in the mess for formal dinners.

mess kit *n Mil.* **1** *Brit.* formal evening wear for officers. **2** Also called: **mess gear.** eating utensils used esp. in the field.

messmate ('mɛs,meɪt) *n* a person with whom one shares meals in a mess, esp. in the army.

Messrs ('mɛsəz) *n* the plural of **Mr.** [C18: abbrev. from F *messieurs*, pl. of MONSIEUR]

messy ('mɛsɪ) *adj* **messier, messiest.** dirty, confused, or untidy.
▶ '**messily** *adv* ▶ '**messiness** *n*

mestizo (mɛ'stiːzəʊ, mɪ-) *n, pl* **mestizos** *or* **mestizoes.** a person of mixed parentage, esp. the offspring of a Spanish American and an American Indian. [C16: from Sp., ult. from L *miscēre* to mix]
▶ **mestiza** (mɛ'stiːzə) *fem n*

mestranol ('mɛstrə,nɒl, -,nəʊl) *n* a synthetic oestrogen used in combination with progesterones as an oral contraceptive. [C20: from M(ETHYL) + (O)ESTR(OGEN) + (*pregn*)*an*(*e*) + -OL]

Meštrović ★ (*Serbo-Croat* 'mɛʃtrɔvitʃ) *n* **Ivan** ('ivan). 1883–1962, US sculptor, born in Austria.

met (mɛt) *vb* the past tense and past participle of **meet**[1].

met. *abbrev. for:* **1** meteorological. **2** meteorology. **3** metropolitan.

Meta ★ ('meɪtə; *Spanish* 'meta) *n* a river in Colombia, rising in the Andes and flowing northeast and east, forming part of the border between Colombia and Venezuela, to join the Orinoco River. Length: about 1000 km (620 miles).

meta- *or sometimes before a vowel* **met-** *prefix* **1** indicating change or alternation: *metabolism; metamorphosis.* **2** (of an academic discipline) concerned with the concepts and results of that discipline: *metamathematics.* **3** occurring or situated behind or after: *metaphysics.* **4** (*often in italics*) denoting that an organic compound contains a benzene ring with substituents in the 1,3-positions: *meta*-cresol. Abbrev.: *m-.* **5** denoting an isomer, polymer, or compound related to a specified compound: *metaldehyde.* **6** denoting an oxyacid that is the least hydrated form of the anhydride or a salt of such an acid: *metaphosphoric acid.* [from Gk (prep)]

metabolism (mɪ'tæbə,lɪzəm) *n* **1** the sum total of the chemical processes that occur in living organisms, resulting in growth, production of energy, elimination of waste, etc. **2** the sum total of the chemical processes affecting a particular substance in the body: *carbohydrate metabolism.* [C19: from Gk *metabolē* change, from *metaballein*, from META- + *ballein* to throw]
▶ **metabolic** (,mɛtə'bɒlɪk) *adj* ▶ ,**meta'bolically** *adv*

metabolize *or* **metabolise** (mɪ'tæbə,laɪz) *vb* **metabolizes, metabolizing, metabolized** *or* **metabolises, metabolising, metabolised.** to produce or be produced by metabolism.

metacarpus (,mɛtə'kɑːpəs) *n, pl* **metacarpi** (-paɪ). **1** the skeleton of the hand between the wrist and the fingers, consisting of five long bones. **2** the corresponding bones in other vertebrates.
▶ ,**meta'carpal** *adj, n*

metacentre *or US* **metacenter** ('mɛtə,sɛntə) *n* the intersection of a vertical line through the centre of buoyancy of a floating body at equilibrium with a vertical line through the centre of buoyancy when the body is tilted.
▶ ,**meta'centric** *adj*

metage ('miːtɪdʒ) *n* **1** the official measuring of weight or contents. **2** a charge for this. [C16: from METE[1]]

metal ('mɛtᵊl) *n* **1a** any of a number of chemical elements, such as iron or copper, that are often lustrous ductile solids, have basic oxides, form positive ions, and are good conductors of heat and electricity. **1b** an alloy, such as brass or steel, containing one or more of these elements. **2** the substance of glass in a molten state or as the finished product. **3** short for **road metal. 4** *Inf.* short for **heavy metal. 5** *Heraldry.* gold or silver. **6** the basic quality of a person or thing; stuff. **7** (*pl*) the rails of a railway. ◆ *adj* **8** made of metal. ◆ *vb* **metals, metalling, metalled** *or US* **met-**

als, metaling, metaled. (*tr*) **9** to fit or cover with metal. **10** to make or mend (a road) with road metal. [C13: from L *metallum* mine, product of a mine, from Gk *metallon*]
▶ '**metalled** *adj*

metal. *or* **metall.** *abbrev. for:* **1** metallurgical. **2** metallurgy.

metalanguage ('mɛtə,læŋwɪdʒ) *n* a language or system of symbols used to discuss another language or system. Cf. **object language.**

metal detector *n* a device that gives an audible or visual signal when its search head comes close to a metallic object embedded in food, buried in the ground, etc.

metallic (mɪ'tælɪk) *adj* **1** of, concerned with, or consisting of metal or a metal. **2** suggestive of a metal: *a metallic click; metallic lustre.* **3** *Chem.* (of a metal element) existing in the free state rather than in combination: *metallic copper.*

metallic soap *n* any one of a number of salts or esters containing a metal, such as aluminium, calcium, magnesium, iron, and zinc. They are used as bases for ointments, fungicides, fireproofing and waterproofing agents, and dryers for paints and varnishes.

metalliferous (,mɛtᵊ'lɪfərəs) *adj* containing a metallic element. [C17: from L *metallifer* yielding metal, from *metallum* metal + *ferre* to bear]

metallize, metallise, *or US* **metalize** ('mɛtə,laɪz) *vb* **metallizes, metallizing, metallized; metallises, metallising, metallised** *or US* **metalizes, metalizing, metalized.** (*tr*) to make metallic or to coat or treat with metal.
▶ ,**metalli'zation, metalli'sation,** *or US* ,**metali'zation** *n*

metallography (,mɛtə'lɒɡrəfɪ) *n* the branch of metallurgy concerned with the composition and structure of metals and alloys.
▶ **metallographic** (mɪ,tælə'ɡræfɪk) *adj*

metalloid ('mɛtə,lɔɪd) *n* **1** a nonmetallic element, such as arsenic or silicon, that has some of the properties of a metal. ◆ *adj also* ,**metal'loidal. 2** of or being a metalloid. **3** resembling a metal.

metallurgy (mɛ'tælədʒɪ) *n* the scientific study of the extraction, refining, alloying, and fabrication of metals and of their structure and properties.
▶ **metallurgic** (,mɛtə'lɜːdʒɪk) *or* ,**metal'lurgical** *adj* ▶ **metallurgist** (mɛ'tælədʒɪst, 'mɛtə,lɜːdʒɪst) *n*

metal tape *n* a magnetic recording tape coated with pure iron: it gives enhanced recording quality.

metalwork ('mɛtᵊl,wɜːk) *n* **1** the craft of working in metal. **2** work in metal or articles made from metal.

metalworking ('mɛtᵊl,wɜːkɪŋ) *n* the processing of metal to change its shape, size, etc.
▶ '**metal,worker** *n*

metamere ('mɛtə,mɪə) *n* one of the similar body segments into which earthworms, crayfish, and similar animals are divided longitudinally.
▶ **metameral** (mɪ'tæmərəl) *adj*

metamerism (mɪ'tæmə,rɪzəm) *n* **1** Also called: (**metameric) segmentation.** the division of an animal into metameres. **2** *Chem.* a type of isomerism in which molecular structures differ by the attachment of different groups to the same atom.
▶ **metameric** (,mɛtə'mɛrɪk) *adj*

metamict ('mɛtə,mɪkt) *adj* of or denoting the amorphous state of a substance that has lost its crystalline structure as a result of the radioactivity of uranium or thorium within it.
▶ ,**meta,micti'zation** *or* ,**meta,micti'sation** *n*

metamorphic (,mɛtə'mɔːfɪk) *or* **metamorphous** *adj* **1** relating to or resulting from metamorphosis or metamorphism. **2** (of rocks) altered considerably from the original structure and composition by pressure and heat.

metamorphism (,mɛtə'mɔːfɪzəm) *n* **1** the process by which metamorphic rocks are formed. **2** a variant of **metamorphosis.**

metamorphose (,mɛtə'mɔːfəʊz) *vb* **metamorphoses, metamorphosing, metamorphosed.** to undergo or cause to undergo metamorphosis or metamorphism.

metamorphosis (,mɛtə'mɔːfəsɪs) *n, pl* **metamorphoses** (-,siːz). **1** a complete change of physical form or substance. **2** a complete change of character, appearance, etc. **3** a person or thing that has undergone metamorphosis. **4** *Zool.* the rapid transformation of a larva into an adult that occurs in certain animals, for example the stage between chrysalis and butterfly. [C16: via L from Gk: transformation, from META- + *morphē* form]

metaphor ('mɛtəfə, -ˌfɔː) *n* a figure of speech in which a word or phrase is applied to an object or action that it does not literally denote in order to imply a resemblance, for example *he is a lion in battle*. Cf. **simile**. [C16: from L, from Gk *metaphora*, from *metapherein* to transfer, from META- + *pherein* to bear]
▸ **metaphoric** (ˌmɛtə'fɒrɪk) *or* ˌmeta'**phorical** *adj* ▸ ˌmeta-'**phorically** *adv*

metaphrase ('mɛtəˌfreɪz) *n* **1** a literal translation. ♦ *vb* **metaphrases, metaphrasing, metaphrased.** (*tr*) **2** to alter or manipulate the wording of. **3** to translate literally. [C17: from Gk *metaphrazein* to translate]

metaphrast ('mɛtəˌfræst) *n* a person who metaphrases, esp. one who changes the form of a text, as by rendering verse into prose. [C17: from Med. Gk *metaphrastēs* translator]
▸ ˌmeta'**phrastic** *or* ˌmeta'**phrastical** *adj* ▸ ˌmeta-'**phrastically** *adv*

metaphysic (ˌmɛtə'fɪzɪk) *n* the system of first principles and assumptions underlying an inquiry or philosophical theory.

metaphysical (ˌmɛtə'fɪzɪkˑl) *adj* **1** of or relating to metaphysics. **2** (of a statement or theory) having an empirical form but in fact immune from empirical testing. **3** (popularly) abstract, abstruse, or unduly theoretical. **4** incorporeal; supernatural.
▸ ˌmeta'**physically** *adv*

Metaphysical (ˌmɛtə'fɪzɪkˑl) *adj* **1** denoting or relating to certain 17th-century poets who combined intense feeling with elaborate imagery. ♦ *n* **2** a poet of this group.

metaphysics (ˌmɛtə'fɪzɪks) *n* (*functioning as sing*) **1** the branch of philosophy that deals with first principles, esp. of being and knowing. **2** the philosophical study of the nature of reality. **3** (popularly) abstract or subtle discussion or reasoning. [C16: from Med. L, from Gk *ta meta ta phusika* the things after the physics, from the arrangement of subjects treated in the works of Aristotle]
▸ **metaphysician** (ˌmɛtəfɪ'zɪʃən) *or* **metaphysicist** (ˌmɛtə'fɪzɪsɪst) *n*

metapsychology (ˌmɛtəsaɪ'kɒlədʒɪ) *n Psychol.* **1** the study of philosophical questions, such as the relation between mind and body, that go beyond the laws of experimental psychology. **2** any attempt to state the general laws of psychology. **3** another word for **parapsychology.**
▸ ˌmetapsy**chological** (ˌmɛtəˌsaɪkə'lɒdʒɪkˑl) *adj*

metastable (ˌmɛtə'steɪbˑl) *adj Physics.* (of a body or system) having a state of apparent equilibrium although capable of changing to a more stable state.
▸ ˌmetasta'**bility** *n*

metastasis (mɪ'tæstəsɪs) *n, pl* **metastases** (-ˌsiːz). *Pathol.* the spreading of a disease organism, esp. cancer cells, from one part of the body to another. [C16: via L from Gk: transition]
▸ **metastatic** (ˌmɛtə'stætɪk) *adj* ▸ ˌmeta'**statically** *adv*

metastasize *or* **metastasise** (mɪ'tæstəˌsaɪz) *vb* **metastasizes, metastasizing, metastasized** *or* **metastasises, metastasising, metastasised.** (*intr*) *Pathol.* (esp. of cancer cells) to spread to a new site in the body via blood or lymph vessels.

metatarsus (ˌmɛtə'tɑːsəs) *n, pl* **metatarsi** (-saɪ). **1** the skeleton of the human foot between the toes and the tarsus, consisting of five long bones. **2** the corresponding skeletal part in other vertebrates.
▸ ˌmeta'**tarsal** *adj, n*

metathesis (mɪ'tæθəsɪs) *n, pl* **metatheses** (-ˌsiːz). the transposition of two sounds or letters in a word. [C16: from LL, from Gk, from *metatithenai* to transpose]
▸ **metathetic** (ˌmɛtə'θɛtɪk) *adj* ▸ ˌmeta'**thetical** *adj*

metazoan (ˌmɛtə'zəʊən) *n* **1** any multicellular animal: includes all animals except sponges. ♦ *adj also* **metazoic.**

2 of or relating to the metazoans. [C19: from NL *Metazoa*; see META-, -ZOA]

Metchnikoff ★ (*French* mɛtʃnikɔf; *Russian* 'mjɛtʃnikəf) *n* **Élie** (eli). 1845–1916, Russian bacteriologist in France. He shared the Nobel prize for physiology or medicine (1908) for his theory of phagocytosis.

mete[1] (miːt) *vb* **metes, meting, meted.** (*tr*) (usually foll. by *out*) *Formal.* to distribute or allot (something, often unpleasant). **2** *Poetic, dialect.* to measure. [OE *metan*]

mete[2] (miːt) *n Rare.* a mark, limit, or boundary (esp. in **metes and bounds**). [C15: from OF, from L *mēta* goal, turning post (in race)]

metempsychosis (ˌmɛtəmsaɪ'kəʊsɪs) *n, pl* **metempsychoses** (-siːz). the migration of a soul from one body to another. [C16: via LL from Gk, from *metempsukhousthai*, from META- + *-em-* in + *psukhē* soul]
▸ ˌmetempsy'**chosist** *n*

meteor ('miːtɪə) *n* **1** a very small meteoroid that has entered the earth's atmosphere. **2** Also called: **shooting star, falling star.** the bright streak of light appearing in the sky due to the incandescence of such a body heated by friction at its surface. [C15: from Med. L *meteōrum*, from Gk *meteōron*, from *meteōros* lofty, from *meta-* (intensifier) + *aeirein* to raise]

meteoric (ˌmiːtɪ'ɒrɪk) *adj* **1** of, formed by, or relating to meteors. **2** like a meteor in brilliance, speed, or transience. **3** *Rare.* of weather; meteorological.
▸ ˌmete'**orically** *adv*

meteorism ('miːtɪəˌrɪzəm) *n Med.* another name for **tympanites.**

meteorite ('miːtɪəˌraɪt) *n* a rocklike object consisting of the remains of a meteoroid that has fallen on earth.
▸ **meteoritic** (ˌmiːtɪə'rɪtɪk) *adj*

meteoroid ('miːtɪəˌrɔɪd) *n* any of the small celestial bodies that are thought to orbit the sun. When they enter the earth's atmosphere, they become visible as meteors.
▸ ˌmeteor'**oidal** *adj*

meteorol. *or* **meteor.** *abbrev for:* **1** meteorological. **2** meteorology.

meteorology (ˌmiːtɪə'rɒlədʒɪ) *n* the study of the earth's atmosphere, esp. of weather-forming processes and weather forecasting. [C17: from Gk; see METEOR, -LOGY]
▸ **meteorological** (ˌmiːtɪərə'lɒdʒɪkˑl) *or* ˌmeteoro'**logic** *adj*
▸ ˌmeteoro'**logically** *adv* ▸ ˌmeteor'**ologist** *n*

meteor shower *n* a transient rain of meteors occurring at regular intervals and coming from a particular region in the sky.

meter[1] ('miːtə) *n* **1** any device that measures and records a quantity, such as of gas, current, voltage, etc., that has passed through it during a specified period. **2** See **parking meter.** ♦ *vb* (*tr*) **3** to measure (a rate of flow) with a meter. [C19: see METE[1]]

meter[2] ('miːtə) *n* the US spelling of **metre**[1].

meter[3] ('miːtə) *n* the US spelling of **metre**[2].

-meter *n combining form.* **1** indicating an instrument for measuring: *barometer.* **2** *Prosody.* indicating a verse having a specified number of feet: *pentameter.* [from Gk *metron* measure]

Meth. *abbrev. for* Methodist.

meth- *combining form.* indicating a chemical compound derived from methane or containing methyl groups: *methacrylic acid.*

methacrylic acid (ˌmɛθə'krɪlɪk) *n* a colourless crystalline water-soluble substance used in the manufacture of acrylic resins.

methadone ('mɛθəˌdəʊn) *or* **methadon** ('mɛθəˌdɒn) *n* a narcotic analgesic drug similar to morphine and formerly thought to be less habit-forming. [C20: from (*di*)*meth*(*yl*) + A(MINO) + *d*(*iphenyl*) + -ONE]

methamphetamine (ˌmɛθæm'fɛtəmiːn, -mɪn) *n* a variety of amphetamine used for its stimulant action. [C20: from METH- + AMPHETAMINE]

methanal ('mɛθəˌnæl) *n* the systematic name for **formaldehyde.**

methane ('miːθeɪn) *n* a colourless odourless flammable

gas, the main constituent of natural gas: used as a fuel. Formula: CH_4.

methane series *n* another name for **alkane series.**

methanoic acid ('mɛθə,nəʊɪk) *n* the systematic name for **formic acid.**

methanol ('mɛθə,nɒl) *n* a colourless volatile poisonous liquid compound used as a solvent and fuel. Formula: CH_3OH. Also called: **methyl alcohol, wood alcohol.** [C20: from METHANE + -OL[1]]

methinks (mɪ'θɪŋks) *vb past* **methought.** (*tr; takes a clause as object*) *Arch.* it seems to me.

metho ('mɛθəʊ) *n Austral. inf.* **1** another name for **methylated spirits. 2** (*pl* **methos**) a drinker of methylated spirits.

method ('mɛθəd) *n* **1** a way of proceeding or doing something, esp. a systematic or regular one. **2** orderliness of thought, action, etc. **3** (*often pl*) the techniques or arrangement of work for a particular field or subject. [C16: via F from L, from Gk *methodos*, lit.: a going after, from *meta-* after + *hodos* way]

Method ('mɛθəd) *n* (*sometimes not cap.*) **a** a technique of acting in which the actor bases his role on the inner motivation of the character played. **b** (*as modifier*): *a Method actor.*

methodical (mɪ'θɒdɪk°l) *or* (*less commonly*) **methodic** *adj* characterized by method or orderliness; systematic.
▶ **me'thodically** *adv*

Methodism ('mɛθə,dɪzəm) *n* the system and practices of the Methodist Church.

Methodist ('mɛθədɪst) *n* **1** a member of any of the Nonconformist denominations that derive from the system of faith initiated by John Wesley and his followers. ◆ *adj also* ,**Method'istic** *or* ,**Method'istical. 2** of or relating to Methodism or the Church embodying it (the **Methodist Church**).

Methodius ★ (mɛ'θəʊdɪəs) *n* **Saint,** with his younger brother Saint Cyril called *the Apostles of the Slavs.* 815–885 A.D., Greek theologian sent as a missionary to the Moravians. Feast day: Feb. 14 or May 11.

methodize *or* **methodise** ('mɛθə,daɪz) *vb* **methodizes, methodizing, methodized** *or* **methodises, methodising, methodised.** (*tr*) to organize according to a method; systematize
▶ **'method,izer** *or* **'methodiser** *n*

methodology (,mɛθə'dɒlədʒɪ) *n, pl* **methodologies. 1** the system of methods and principles used in a particular discipline. **2** the branch of philosophy concerned with the science of method.
▶ **methodological** (,mɛθədə'lɒdʒɪk°l) *adj* ▶ ,**methodo'logically** *adv* ▶ ,**method'ologist** *n*

methought (mɪ'θɔːt) *vb Arch.* the past tense of **methinks.**

meths (mɛθs) *n Chiefly Brit., Austral., & NZ.* an informal name for **methylated spirits.**

Methuselah ★ (mɪ'θjuːzələ) *n Old Testament.* a patriarch reputed to have lived 969 years (Genesis 5:21–27), regarded as epitomizing longevity. Douay spelling: **Mathusala.**

methyl ('miːθaɪl, 'mɛθɪl) *n* **1** (*modifier*) of, consisting of, or containing the monovalent group of atoms CH_3. **2** a compound in which methyl groups are bound directly to a metal atom. [C19: from F *méthyle*, back formation from METHYLENE]
▶ **methylic** (mə'θɪlɪk) *adj*

methyl acetate *n* a colourless volatile flammable liquid ester used as a solvent, esp. in paint removers. Formula: CH_3COOCH_3. Systematic name: **methyl ethanoate.**

methyl alcohol *n* another name for **methanol.**

methylate ('mɛθɪ,leɪt) *vb* **methylates, methylating, methylated.** (*tr*) to mix with methanol.

methylated spirits *n* (*functioning as sing or pl*) alcohol that has been denatured by the addition of methanol and pyridine and a violet dye. Also: **methylated spirit.**

methyl chloride *n* a colourless gas with an ether-like odour, used as a refrigerant and anaesthetic. Formula: CH_3Cl. Systematic name: **chloromethane.**

methylene ('mɛθɪ,liːn) *n* (*modifier*) of, consisting of, or containing the divalent group of atoms $=CH_2$: *a methylene group or radical.* [C19: from F *méthylène*, from Gk

methu wine + *hulē* wood + -ENE: orig. referring to a substance distilled from wood]

methylene dichloride *n* the traditional name for **dichloromethane.**

methylphenol (,miːθaɪl'fiːnɒl) *n* the systematic name for **cresol.**

meticulous (mɪ'tɪkjʊləs) *adj* very precise about details; painstaking. [C16 (meaning: timid): from L *meticulōsus* fearful, from *metus* fear]
▶ **me'ticulously** *adv* ▶ **me'ticulousness** *n*

métier ('mɛtɪeɪ) *n* **1** a profession or trade. **2** a person's strong point or speciality. [C18: from F, ult. from L *ministerium* service]

Métis (meɪ'tiːs) *n, pl* **Métis** (-'tiːs, -'tiːz). a person of mixed parentage, esp. the offspring of a French Canadian and a North American Indian. [C19: from F, from Vulgar L *mixtīcius* (unattested) of mixed race]
▶ **Métisse** (meɪ'tiːs) *fem n*

metol ('miːtɒl) *n* a colourless soluble organic substance used, in the form of its sulphate, as a photographic developer. [C20: from G, arbitrary coinage]

Metonic cycle (mɪ'tɒnɪk) *n* a cycle of 235 synodic months after which the phases of the moon recur on the same day of the month. [C17: after *Meton*, 5th-cent. B.C. Athenian astronomer]

metonymy (mɪ'tɒnɪmɪ) *n, pl* **metonymies.** the substitution of a word referring to an attribute for the thing that is meant, e.g. *the crown*, used to refer to a monarch. Cf. **synecdoche.** [C16: from LL, from Gk, from *meta-* (indicating change) + *onoma* name]
▶ **metonymical** (,mɛtə'nɪmɪk°l) *or* ,**meto'nymic** *adj*

metope ('mɛtəʊp, 'mɛtəpɪ) *n Archit.* a square space between triglyphs in a Doric frieze. [C16: via L from Gk, from *meta* between + *opē* one of the holes for the beam-ends]

metre[1] *or US* **meter** ('miːtə) *n* **1** a metric unit of length equal to approximately 1.094 yards. **2** the basic SI unit of length; the length of the path travelled by light in free space during a time interval of 1/299 792 458 of a second. Symbol: m [C18: from F; see METRE[2]]

metre[2] *or US* **meter** ('miːtə) *n* **1** *Prosody.* the rhythmic arrangement of syllables in verse, usually according to the number and kind of feet in a line. **2** *Music.* another word (esp. US) for **time** (sense 22). [C14: from L *metrum*, from Gk *metron* measure]

metre-kilogram-second *n* See **mks units.**

metric ('mɛtrɪk) *adj* of or relating to the metre or metric system.

metrical ('mɛtrɪk°l) *or* **metric** *adj* **1** of or relating to measurement. **2** of or in poetic metre.
▶ **'metrically** *adv*

metricate ('mɛtrɪ,keɪt) *vb* **metricates, metricating, metricated.** to convert (a measuring system, instrument, etc.) from nonmetric to metric units.
▶ ,**metri'cation** *n*

metric system *n* any decimal system of units based on the metre. For scientific purposes SI units are used.

metric ton *n* another name (not in technical use) for **tonne.**

metro ('mɛtrəʊ) *or* **métro** *French.* (metro) *n, pl* **metros.** an underground, or largely underground, railway system in certain cities, such as that in Paris. [C20: from F, *chemin de fer métropolitain* metropolitan railway]

Metro ('mɛtrəʊ) *n Canad.* a metropolitan city administration, esp. Metropolitan Toronto.

metronome ('mɛtrə,nəʊm) *n* a device which indicates the tempo of music by producing a clicking sound from a pendulum with an adjustable period of swing. [C19: from Gk *metron* measure + *nomos* law]
▶ **metronomic** (,mɛtrə'nɒmɪk) *adj*

metronymic (,mɛtrəʊ'nɪmɪk) *adj* **1** (of a name) derived from the name of the mother or other female ancestor. ◆ *n* **2** a metronymic name. [C19: from Gk *mētronumikos*, from *mētēr* mother + *onoma* name]

metropolis (mɪ'trɒpəlɪs) *n, pl* **metropolises. 1** the main city, esp. of a country or region. **2** a centre of activity. **3**

the chief see in an ecclesiastical province. [C16: from LL from Gk, from *mētēr* mother + *polis* city]

metropolitan (ˌmɛtrəˈpɒlɪtən) *adj* **1** of or characteristic of a metropolis. **2** constituting a city and its suburbs. **3** of, relating to, or designating an ecclesiastical metropolis. **4** of or belonging to the home territories of a country, as opposed to overseas territories: *metropolitan France.* ◆ *n* **5a** *Eastern Churches.* the head of an ecclesiastical province, ranking between archbishop and patriarch. **5b** *Church of England.* an archbishop. **5c** *RC Church.* an archbishop or bishop having authority over the dioceses in his province.
▸ ˌmetroˈpolitanism *n*

metropolitan county *n* (in England) any of the six conurbations established as units in the new local government system in 1974; the metropolitan county councils were abolished in 1986.

metropolitan district *n* (in England since 1974) any of the districts that make up the metropolitan counties of England: since 1986 they have functioned as unitary authorities.

Metropolitan Museum of Art ★ *n* the principal museum in New York City: founded in 1870 and housed in its present premises on the edge of Central Park since 1880.

metrorrhagia (ˌmiːtrɔːˈreɪdʒɪə, ˌmɛt-) *n* abnormal bleeding from the uterus. [C19: NL, from Gk *mētra* womb + *-rrhagia* a breaking forth]

-metry *n combining form.* indicating the process or science of measuring: *geometry.* [from OF *-metrie*, from L, ult. from Gk *metron* measure]
▸ **-metric** *adj combining form.*

Metternich ★ (German ˈmɛtərnɪç) *n* **Klemens** (ˈkleːməns). 1773–1859, Austrian statesman. Foreign minister (1809–48) and chancellor of Austria (1821–48).

mettle (ˈmɛt°l) *n* **1** courage; spirit. **2** character. **3 on one's mettle.** roused to making one's best efforts. [C16: orig. var. of METAL]

mettled (ˈmɛt°ld) *or* **mettlesome** (ˈmɛt°lsəm) *adj* courageous, spirited, or valiant.

Metz ★ (mets; *French* mes) *n* a city in NE France on the River Moselle: a free imperial city in the 13th century; annexed by France in 1552; part of Germany (1871–1918); centre of the Lorraine iron-mining region. Pop.: 123 920 (1990).

Meung ★ (*French* mœ) *n* See **Jean de Meung.**

Meurthe-et-Moselle ★ (*French* mœrtemozɛl) *n* a department of NE France, in Lorraine region. Capital: Nancy. Pop.: 715 907 (1994 est.). Area: 5280 sq. km (2059 sq. miles).

Meuse ★ (mɜːz; *French* møz) *n* **1** a department of N France, in Lorraine region: heavy fighting occurred here in World War I. Capital: Bar-le-Duc. Pop.: 194 384 (1994 est.). Area: 6241 sq. km (2434 sq. miles). **2** a river in W Europe, rising in NE France and flowing north across E Belgium and the S Netherlands to join the Waal River before entering the North Sea. Length: 926 km (575 miles). Dutch name: **Maas.**

MeV *symbol for* million electronvolts (10^6 electronvolts).

mevrou (məˈfrəʊ) *n* a S. African title of address equivalent to *Mrs* when placed before a surname or *madam* when used alone. [Afrik.]

mew[1] (mjuː) *vb* **1** (*intr*) (esp. of a cat) to make a characteristic high-pitched cry. ◆ *n* **2** such a sound. [C14: imit.]

mew[2] (mjuː) *n* any seagull, esp. the common gull. [OE *mǣw*]

mew[3] (mjuː) *n* **1** a room or cage for hawks, esp. while moulting. ◆ *vb* (*tr*) **2** (often foll. by *up*) to confine (hawks or falcons) in a shelter, cage, etc. **3** to confine; conceal. [C14: from OF *mue*, from *muer* to moult, from L *mūtāre* to change]

Mewar ★ (meˈwɑː) *n* another name for **Udaipur** (sense 1).

mewl (mjuːl) *vb* **1** (*intr*) (esp. of a baby) to cry weakly; whimper. ◆ *n* **2** such a cry. [C17: imit.]

mews (mjuːz) *n* (*functioning as sing or pl*) *Chiefly Brit.* **1** a yard or street lined by buildings originally used as stables but now often converted into dwellings. **2** the build-

ings around a mews. [C14: pl of MEW[3], orig. referring to royal stables built on the site of hawks' mews at Charing Cross in London]

Mex. *abbrev. for:* **1** Mexican. **2** Mexico.

Mexicali ★ (ˌmɛksɪˈkɑːlɪ; *Spanish* mɛxiˈkali) *n* a city in NW Mexico, capital of Baja California Norte state, on the border with the US adjoining Calexico, California: centre of a rich irrigated agricultural region. Pop.: 438 377 (1990).

Mexican wave *n* the rippling effect produced when the spectators in successive sections of a sports stadium stand up while raising their arms and then sit down. [C20: first seen at the World Cup in Mexico in 1986]

Mexico ★ (ˈmɛksɪˌkəʊ) *n* **1** a republic in North America, on the Gulf of Mexico and the Pacific: early Mexican history includes the Maya, Toltec, and Aztec civilizations; conquered by the Spanish between 1519 and 1525 and achieved independence in 1821; lost Texas to the US in 1836 and California and New Mexico in 1848. It is generally mountainous with three ranges of the Sierra Madre (east, west, and south) and a large central plateau. Official language: Spanish. Religion: chiefly Roman Catholic. Currency: peso. Capital: Mexico City. Pop.: 92 711 000 (1996). Area: 1 967 183 sq. km (761 530 sq. miles). Official name: **United Mexican States.** Spanish name: **Méjico. 2** a state of Mexico, on the central plateau surrounding Mexico City, which is not administratively part of the state. Capital: Toluca. Pop.: 11 704 934 (1995 est.). Area: 21 460 sq. km (8287 sq. miles). **3 Gulf of.** an arm of the Atlantic, bordered by the US, Cuba, and Mexico: linked with the Atlantic by the Straits of Florida and with the Caribbean by the Yucatán Channel. Area: about 1 600 000 sq. km (618 000 sq. miles).
▸ **Mexican** (ˈmɛksɪkən) *adj, n*

Mexico City ★ *n* the capital of Mexico, on the central plateau at an altitude of 2240 m (7350 ft): founded as the Aztec capital (Tenochtitlán) in about 1300; conquered and rebuilt by the Spanish in 1521; forms, with its suburbs, the federal district of Mexico; the largest industrial complex in the country. Pop.: 9 815 795 (1990).

Meyerbeer ★ (German ˈmaɪərbeːr) *n* **Giacomo** (ˈdʒaːkomo), real name *Jakob Liebmann Beer.* 1791–1864, German composer, esp. of operas, such as *Les Huguenots* (1836) and *L'Africaine* (1864).

Meyerhof ★ (German ˈmaɪərhoːf) *n* **Otto** (Fritz) (ˈɔto). 1884–1951, German physiologist, noted for his work on the metabolism of muscles. He shared the Nobel prize for physiology or medicine 1922.

Meyerhold ★ (ˈmiːəˌhəʊlt) *n* **Vsevolod** (Emilievich) (ˈfsjevələt), original name *Karl Theodor Kasimir.* 1874–?1940, Russian theatre director; died in custody.

MEZ *abbrev. for* Central European Time. [from G *Mitteleuropäische Zeit*]

mezcal (mɛˈskæl) *n* a variant spelling of **mescal.**

mezcaline (ˈmɛskəˌliːn) *n* a variant spelling of **mescaline.**

Mézières ★ (*French* mezjɛr) *n* a town in NE France, on the River Meuse opposite Charleville. See **Charleville-Mézières.**

mezuzah (məˈzuzə) *n, pl* **mezuzahs** *or* **mezuzoth** (Hebrew məzuˈzɔt). *Judaism.* **1** a piece of parchment inscribed with biblical passages and fixed to the doorpost of a Jewish house. **2** a metal case for such a parchment, sometimes worn as an ornament. [from Heb., lit.: doorpost]

mezzanine (ˈmɛzəˌniːn, ˈmɛtsəˌniːn) *n* **1** Also called: **mezzanine floor.** an intermediate storey, esp. a low one between the ground and first floor of a building. **2** *Theatre, US & Canad.* the first balcony. **3** *Theatre, Brit.* a room or floor beneath the stage. ◆ *adj* **4** often shortened to **mezz.** of or relating to an intermediate stage in a financial process: *mezzanine funding.* [C18: from F, from It., dim. of *mezzano* middle, from L *mediānus* MEDIAN]

mezzo (ˈmɛtsəʊ) *adv Music.* moderately; quite: *mezzo piano.* [C19: from It., lit.: half, from L *medius* middle]

mezzo-soprano *n, pl* **mezzo-sopranos. 1** a female voice intermediate between a soprano and contralto. **2** a singer with such a voice.

mezzotint (ˈmɛtsəʊˌtɪnt) *n* **1** a method of engraving a copper plate by scraping and burnishing the roughened surface. **2** a print made from a plate so treated. ◆ *vb* **3** (*tr*) to engrave (a copper plate) in this fashion. [C18: from It. *mezzotinto* half tint]

mf *Music. symbol for* mezzo forte. [It.: moderately loud]

MF *abbrev. for:* **1** *Radio.* medium frequency. **2** Middle French.

mfd *abbrev. for* manufactured.

mfg *abbrev. for* manufacturing.

MFH *Hunting. abbrev. for* Master of Foxhounds.

mfr *abbrev. for:* **1** manufacture. **2** manufacturer.

mg *symbol for* milligram.

Mg *the chemical symbol for* magnesium.

M. Glam *abbrev. for* Mid Glamorgan.

Mgr *abbrev. for:* **1** manager. **2** Monseigneur. **3** Monsignor.

MHA (in Australia) *abbrev. for* Member of the House of Assembly.

MHG *abbrev. for* Middle High German.

mho (məʊ) *n, pl* **mhos.** the former name for **siemens.** [C19: formed by reversing the letters of OHM (first used by Lord Kelvin)]

MHR (in the US and Australia) *abbrev. for* Member of the House of Representatives.

MHz *symbol for* megahertz.

mi (miː) *n Music.* **1** the syllable used in the fixed system of solmization for the note E. **2** Also: **me.** (in tonic sol-fa) the third degree of any major scale; a mediant. [C14: see GAMUT]

MI *abbrev. for:* **1** Michigan. **2** Military Intelligence.

mi. *abbrev. for* mile.

MI5 *abbrev. for* Military Intelligence, section five; a former official and current popular name for the counter-intelligence agency of the British Government.

MI6 *abbrev. for* Military Intelligence, section six; a former official and current popular name for the intelligence and espionage agency of the British Government.

Miami ★ (maɪˈæmɪ) *n* a city and resort in SE Florida, on Biscayne Bay: developed chiefly after 1896, esp. with the Florida land boom of the 1920s; centre of an extensive tourist area. Pop.: 373 024 (1994 est.).

Miami Beach ★ *n* a resort in SE Florida, on an island separated from Miami by Biscayne Bay. Pop.: 90 153 (1994 est.).

miaou *or* **miaow** (mɪˈaʊ, mjaʊ) *vb, interj* variant spellings of **meow.**

miasma (mɪˈæzmə) *n, pl* **miasmata** (-mətə) *or* **miasmas.** **1** an unwholesome or foreboding atmosphere. **2** pollution in the atmosphere, esp. noxious vapours from decomposing organic matter. [C17: NL, from Gk: defilement, from *miainein* to defile]
▸ **mi·asmal** *or* **miasmatic** (ˌmiːəzˈmætɪk) *adj*

Mic. *Bible. abbrev. for* Micah.

mica (ˈmaɪkə) *n* any of a group of minerals consisting of hydrous silicates of aluminium, potassium, etc., in monoclinic crystalline form, occurring in igneous and metamorphic rock. Because of their resistance to electricity and heat they are used as dielectrics, in heating elements, etc. Also called: **isinglass.** [C18: from L: crumb]
▸ **micaceous** (maɪˈkeɪʃəs) *adj*

Micah ★ (ˈmaɪkə) *n Old Testament.* **1** a Hebrew prophet of the late 8th century B.C. **2** the book containing his prophecies. Douay spelling: **Micheas** (maɪˈkiːəs).

mice (maɪs) *n* the plural of **mouse.**

micelle, micell (mɪˈsɛl), *or* **micella** (mɪˈsɛlə) *n Chem.* **a** a charged aggregate of molecules of colloidal size in a solution. **b** any molecular aggregate of colloidal size. [C19: from NL *micella*, dim. of L *mīca* crumb]

Mich. *abbrev. for:* **1** Michaelmas. **2** Michigan.

Michael ★ (ˈmaɪkəl) *n* **1** 1596–1645, tsar of Russia (1613–45); founder of the Romanov dynasty. **2** born 1921, king of Romania (1927–30 as part of a three-part regency, 1940–47), who relinquished the throne (1930–40) in favour of his father, Carol II. He led the coup d'état that overthrew Antonescu (1944) but was forced to abdicate

(1947) by the Communists. **3 Saint.** *Bible.* one of the archangels. Feast day: Sept. 29 or Nov. 8.

Michaelmas (ˈmɪkəlməs) *n* Sept. 29, the feast of St Michael the archangel; in England, Ireland, and Wales, one of the four quarter days.

Michaelmas daisy *n Brit.* any of various composite plants that have small autumn-blooming purple, pink, or white flowers.

Michaelmas term *n* the autumn term at Oxford and Cambridge Universities, the Inns of Court, and some other educational establishments.

Michelangelo ★ (ˌmaɪkəlˈændʒɪˌləʊ) *n* full name *Michelangelo Buonarroti.* 1475–1564, Florentine sculptor, architect, and painter. His works include the sculptures of *David* (1504) and of *Moses,* the painted ceiling of the Sistine Chapel (1508–12), the painting *The Last Judgment* (1533–41), the design of the Laurentian Library (1523–29) and of the dome of St Peter's, Rome.

Michelet ★ (*French* miʃlɛ) *n* **Jules** (ʒyl). 1798–1874, French historian, noted for his *Histoire de France* (1833–67).

Michelin ★ (*French* miʃlɛ̃) *n* **André** (ɑ̃dre). 1853–1931, French industrialist; founder, with his brother **Édouard Michelin** (1859–1940), of the Michelin Tyre Company (1888).

Michelozzo ★ (*Italian* mikeˈlɔttso) *n* full name *Michelozzo di Bartolommeo.* 1396–1472, Italian architect and sculptor.

Michelson ★ (ˈmaɪkəlsən) *n* **Albert Abraham.** 1852–1931, US physicist, born in Germany: noted for his part in the Michelson-Morley experiment: Nobel prize for physics 1907.

Michigan ★ (ˈmɪʃɪɡən) *n* **1** a state of the N central US, occupying two peninsulas between Lakes Superior, Huron, Michigan, and Erie: generally low-lying. Capital: Lansing. Pop.: 9 594 350 (1996 est.). Area: 147 156 sq. km (56 817 sq. miles). Abbrevs.: **Mich.** or (with zip code) **MI 2 Lake.** a lake in the N central US between Wisconsin and Michigan: the third largest of the five Great Lakes and the only one wholly in the US; linked with Lake Huron by the Straits of Mackinac. Area: 58 000 sq. km (22 400 sq. miles).
▸ **Michigander** (ˌmɪʃɪˈɡændə) *n* ▸ **'Michiganˌite** *adj, n*

Michoacán ★ (*Spanish* mitʃoaˈkan) *n* a state of SW Mexico, on the Pacific: rich mineral resources. Capital: Morelia. Pop.: 3 869 133 (1995 est.). Area: 59 864 sq. km (23 114 sq. miles).

Mick (mɪk) *n* (*sometimes not cap.*) **1** Also: **Mickey.** *Derog.* a slang name for an **Irishman** or a **Roman Catholic. 2** *Austral.* the tails side of a coin. [C19: from nickname for *Michael*]

mickey *or* **micky** (ˈmɪkɪ) *n Inf.* **take the mickey (out of).** to tease. [C20: from ?]

Mickey Finn *n Sl.* **a** a drink containing a drug to make the drinker unconscious. **b** the drug itself. ◆ Often shortened to **Mickey.** [C20: from ?]

Mickiewicz ★ (*Polish* mitsˈkjevitʃ) *n* **Adam** (ˈadam). 1798–1855, Polish poet, whose epic *Thaddeus* (1834) is highly regarded.

mickle (ˈmɪkəl) *or* **muckle** (ˈmʌkəl) *Arch. or Scot. & N English dialect.* ◆ *adj* **1** great or abundant. ◆ *adv* **2** much; greatly. ◆ *n* **3** a great amount, esp. in the proverb, *many a little makes a mickle.* **4** *Scot.* a small amount, esp. in the proverb *mony a mickle makes a muckle.* [C13 *mikel,* from ON *mikill,* replacing OE *micel* MUCH]

micro (ˈmaɪkrəʊ) *adj* **1** very small. ◆ *n, pl* **micros. 2** short for **microcomputer, microprocessor, microwave oven.**

micro- *or* **micr-** *combining form.* **1** small or minute: *microdot.* **2** involving the use of a microscope: *microscopy.* **3** indicating a method or instrument for dealing with small quantities: *micrometer.* **4** (in pathology) indicating abnormal smallness or underdevelopment: *microcephaly.* **5** denoting 10^{-6}: *microsecond.* Symbol: μ [from Gk *mikros* small]

microbe (ˈmaɪkrəʊb) *n* any microscopic organism, esp. a disease-causing bacterium. [C19: from F, from MICRO- + Gk *bios* life]
▸ **mi·crobial** *or* **mi·crobic** *adj*

microbiology (ˌmaɪkrəʊbaɪˈɒlədʒɪ) *n* the branch of biology involving the study of microorganisms. ▸ **microbiological** (ˌmaɪkrəʊˌbaɪəˈlɒdʒɪkªl) *or* ˌmicroˌbioˈlogic *adj* ▸ ˌmicroˌbioˈlogically *adv* ▸ ˌmicrobiˈologist *n*

microcephaly (ˌmaɪkrəʊˈsɛfəlɪ) *n* the condition of having an abnormally small head or cranial capacity. ▸ **microcephalic** (ˌmaɪkrəʊsɪˈfælɪk) *adj, n* ▸ ˌmicroˈcephalous *adj*

microchemistry (ˌmaɪkrəʊˈkɛmɪstrɪ) *n* chemical experimentation with minute quantities of material. ▸ ˌmicroˈchemical *adj*

microchip (ˈmaɪkrəʊˌtʃɪp) *n* another word for **chip** (sense 7).

microcircuit (ˈmaɪkrəʊˌsɜːkɪt) *n* a miniature electronic circuit, esp. one in which a number of permanently connected components are contained in one small chip of semiconducting material. See **integrated circuit**. ▸ ˌmicroˈcircuitry *n*

microclimate (ˈmaɪkrəʊˌklaɪmɪt) *n Ecology.* the atmospheric conditions affecting an individual or a small group of organisms, esp. when they differ from the climate of the rest of the community. ▸ **microclimatic** (ˌmaɪkrəʊklaɪˈmætɪk) *adj* ▸ ˌmicroˌclimaˈtology *n*

microcomputer (ˌmaɪkrəʊkəmˈpjuːtə) *n* a computer in which the central processing unit is contained in one or more silicon chips.

microcosm (ˈmaɪkrəʊˌkɒzəm) *or* **microcosmos** (ˌmaɪkrəʊˈkɒzmɒs) *n* **1** a miniature representation of something. **2** man regarded as epitomizing the universe. ◆ Cf. **macrocosm**. [C15: via Med. L from Gk *mikros kosmos* little world] ▸ ˌmicroˈcosmic *or* ˌmicroˈcosmical *adj*

microdot (ˈmaɪkrəʊˌdɒt) *n* **1** a greatly reduced photographic copy (about the size of a pinhead) of a document, etc., used esp. in espionage. **2** a tiny tablet containing LSD.

microeconomics (ˌmaɪkrəʊˌiːkəˈnɒmɪks, -ˌɛkə-) *n (functioning as sing)* the branch of economics concerned with particular commodities, firms, or individuals and the economic relationships between them. ▸ ˌmicroˌecoˈnomic *adj*

microelectronics (ˌmaɪkrəʊɪlɛkˈtrɒnɪks) *n (functioning as sing)* the branch of electronics concerned with microcircuits.

microfiche (ˈmaɪkrəʊˌfiːʃ) *n* a sheet of film, usually the size of a filing card, on which books, newspapers, documents, etc., can be recorded in miniaturized form. [C20: from F, from MICRO- + *fiche* small card]

microfilm (ˈmaɪkrəʊˌfɪlm) *n* **1** a strip of film on which books, documents, etc., can be recorded in miniaturized form. ◆ *vb* **2** to photograph (a page, document, etc.) on microfilm.

microgravity (ˈmaɪkrəʊˌɡrævɪtɪ) *n* gravitational effects operating, or apparently operating, in a localized region, as in a spacecraft under conditions of weightlessness.

microhabitat (ˌmaɪkrəʊˈhæbɪtæt) *n Ecology.* the smallest part of the environment that supports a distinct flora and fauna, such as a fallen log in a forest.

microlight *or* **microlite** (ˈmaɪkrəʊˌlaɪt) *n* a small private aircraft carrying no more than two people, with a wing area not less than 10 square metres: used in pleasure flying and racing.

microlith (ˈmaɪkrəʊˌlɪθ) *n Archaeol.* a small Mesolithic flint tool which formed part of a hafted tool. ▸ ˌmicroˈlithic *adj*

micrometer (maɪˈkrɒmɪtə) *n* **1** any of various instruments or devices for the accurate measurement of distances or angles. **2** Also called: **micrometer gauge, micrometer calliper.** a type of gauge for the accurate measurement of small distances, thicknesses, etc. The gap between its measuring faces is adjusted by a fine screw (**micrometer screw**). ▸ **micrometric** (ˌmaɪkrəʊˈmɛtrɪk) *or* ˌmicroˈmetrical *adj* ▸ miˈcrometry *n*

microminiaturization *or* **microminiaturisation** (ˌmaɪkrəʊˌmɪnɪtʃəraɪˈzeɪʃən) *n* the production and appli-

cation of very small components and the circuits and equipment in which they are used.

micron (ˈmaɪkrɒn) *n, pl* **microns** *or* **micra** (-krə). a unit of length equal to 10^{-6} metre. It is being replaced by the micrometre, the equivalent SI unit. [C19: NL, from Gk *mikros* small]

Micronesia ★ (ˌmaɪkrəʊˈniːzɪə) *n* **1** one of the three divisions of islands in the Pacific (the others being Melanesia and Polynesia); the NW division of Oceania: includes the Mariana, Caroline, Marshall, and Kiribati island groups, and Nauru Island. **2 Federated States of.** an island group in the W Pacific, formerly within the United States Trust Territory of the Pacific Islands: comprises the islands of Truk, Yap, Ponape, and Kosrae: formed in 1979 when the islands became self-governing: status of free association with the US from 1982. Languages: English and Micronesian languages. Religion: Christian majority. Currency: US dollar. Capital: Palikir. Pop.: 106 000 (1996). [C19: from MICRO- + Greek *nēsos* island; so called from the small size of many of the islands; on the model of *Polynesia*]

Micronesian (ˌmaɪkrəʊˈniːʒən, -ʒɪən) *adj* **1.** of or relating to Micronesia, its inhabitants, or their languages. ◆ *n* **2** a native or inhabitant of Micronesia or a descendant of one. **3** a group of languages spoken in Micronesia.

microorganism (ˌmaɪkrəʊˈɔːɡəˌnɪzəm) *n* any organism, such as a bacterium, of microscopic size.

microphone (ˈmaɪkrəˌfəʊn) *n* a device used in sound-reproduction systems for converting sound into electrical energy. ▸ **microphonic** (ˌmaɪkrəˈfɒnɪk) *adj*

microprint (ˈmaɪkrəʊˌprɪnt) *n* a greatly reduced photographic copy of print, read by a magnifying device. It is used in order to reduce the size of large books, etc.

microprocessor (ˌmaɪkrəʊˈprəʊsɛsə) *n Computing.* a single integrated circuit performing the basic functions of the central processing unit in a small computer.

microscope (ˈmaɪkrəˌskəʊp) *n* **1** an optical instrument that uses a lens or combination of lenses to produce a magnified image of a small, close object. **2** any instrument, such as the electron microscope, for producing a magnified visual image of a small object.

microscopic (ˌmaɪkrəˈskɒpɪk) *or* (*less commonly*) **microscopical** *adj* **1** not large enough to be seen with the naked eye but visible under a microscope. **2** very small; minute. **3** of, concerned with, or using a microscope. ▸ ˌmicroˈscopically *adv*

microscopy (maɪˈkrɒskəpɪ) *n* **1** the study, design, and manufacture of microscopes. **2** investigation by use of a microscope. ▸ **microscopist** (maɪˈkrɒskəpɪst) *n*

microsecond (ˈmaɪkrəʊˌsɛkənd) *n* one millionth of a second.

microstructure (ˈmaɪkrəʊˌstrʌktʃə) *n* structure on a microscopic scale, esp. the structure of an alloy as observed by etching, polishing, and observation under a microscope.

microsurgery (ˌmaɪkrəʊˈsɜːdʒərɪ) *n* intricate surgery performed on cells, tissues, etc., using a specially designed operating microscope and miniature precision instruments.

microswitch (ˈmaɪkrəʊˌswɪtʃ) *n Electrical engineering.* a switch that operates by small movements of a lever.

microtome (ˈmaɪkrəʊˌtəʊm) *n* an instrument used for cutting thin sections for microscopical examination. ▸ **microtomy** (maɪˈkrɒtəmɪ) *n*

microwave (ˈmaɪkrəʊˌweɪv) *n* **1a** electromagnetic radiation in the wavelength range 0.3 to 0.001 metres: used in radar, cooking, etc. **1b** (*as modifier*): *microwave oven.* **2** short for **microwave oven.** ◆ *vb* **microwaves, microwaving, microwaved.** (*tr*) **3** to cook in a microwave oven.

microwave background *n* a background of microwave electromagnetic radiation discovered in space in 1965, believed to have emanated from the big bang with which the universe began.

microwave detector *n* NZ. a device for recording the speed of a motorist.

microwave oven *n* an oven in which food is cooked by microwaves. Often shortened to **micro, microwave**.

microwave spectroscopy *n* a type of spectroscopy in which information is obtained on the structure and chemical bonding of molecules and crystals by measurements of the wavelengths of microwaves emitted or absorbed by the sample.
▶ **microwave spectroscope** *n*

micturate ('mɪktjʊˌreɪt) *vb* **micturates, micturating, micturated**. (*intr*) a less common word for **urinate**. [C19: from L *micturīre* to desire to urinate, from *mingere* to urinate]
▶ **micturition** (ˌmɪktjʊ'rɪʃən) *n*

mid[1] (mɪd) *adj* **1** *Phonetics*. of, relating to, or denoting a vowel whose articulation lies approximately halfway between high and low, such as *e* in English *bet*. ◆ *n* **2** an archaic word for **middle**. [C12 *midre* (inflected form of *midd*, unattested)]

mid[2] *or* **'mid** (mɪd) *prep* a poetic word for **amid**.

mid- *combining form*. indicating a middle part, point, time, or position: *midday; mid-April; mid-Victorian*. [OE; see MIDDLE, MID[1]]

midair (ˌmɪd'ɛə) *n* **a** some point above ground level, in the air. **b** (*as modifier*): *a midair collision of aircraft*.

Midas ★ ('maɪdəs) *n* **1** *Greek legend*. a king of Phrygia given the power by Dionysus of turning everything he touched into gold. **2 the Midas touch**. ability to make money.

mid-Atlantic *adj* characterized by a blend of British and American styles, elements, etc.: *a mid-Atlantic accent*.

midbrain ('mɪdˌbreɪn) *n* the nontechnical name for **mesencephalon**.

midday ('mɪd'deɪ) *n* **a** the middle of the day; noon. **b** (*as modifier*): *a midday meal*.

Middelburg ★ ('mɪd^əlˌbɜːg; *Dutch* 'mɪdəlbyrx) *n* a city in the SW Netherlands, capital of Zeeland province, on Walcheren Island: an important trading centre in the Middle Ages and member of the Hanseatic League; 12th-century abbey; market town. Pop.: 40 118 (1994).

middelskot ('mɪd^əlˌskɒt) *n* (in South Africa) an intermediate payment to a farmers' cooperative for a crop or wool clip. [from Afrik. *middel* middle + *skot* payment]

midden ('mɪd^ən) *n* **1a** *Arch*. or dialect. a dunghill or pile of refuse. **1b** *Dialect*. a dustbin. **2** See **kitchen midden**. [C14: from ON]

middle ('mɪd^əl) *adj* **1** equally distant from the ends or periphery of something; central. **2** intermediate in status, situation, etc. **3** located between the early and late parts of a series, time sequence, etc. **4** not extreme, esp. in size; medium. **5** (esp. in Greek and Sanskrit grammar) denoting a voice of verbs expressing reciprocal or reflexive action. **6** (*usually cap.*) (of a language) intermediate between the earliest and the modern forms. ◆ *n* **7** an area or point equal in distance from the ends or periphery or in time between the early and late parts. **8** an intermediate part or section, such as the waist. **9** *Grammar*. the middle voice. **10** *Logic*. See **middle term**. **11** *Cricket*. a position on the batting crease in alignment with the middle stumps on which a batsman may take guard. ◆ *vb* **middles, middling, middled**. (*tr*) **12** to place in the middle. **13** *Naut*. to fold in two. **14** *Cricket*. to hit (the ball) with the middle of the bat. [OE *middel*]

middle age *n* the period of life between youth and old age, usually (in man) considered to occur approximately between the ages of 40 and 60.
▶ ˌmiddle-'aged *adj*

Middle Ages *n* the. *European history*. **1** (broadly) the period from the deposition of the last W Roman emperor in 476 A.D. to the Italian Renaissance (or the fall of Constantinople in 1453). **2** (narrowly) the period from about 1000 A.D. to the 15th century. Cf. **Dark Ages**.

Middle America ★ *n* **1** the territories between the US and South America: Mexico, Central America, and the Antilles. **2** the US middle class, central. those groups that are politically conservative.
▶ **Middle American** *adj, n*

middle-and-leg *n* *Cricket*. a position on the batting crease in alignment with the middle and leg stumps on which a batsman may take guard.

middle-and-off *n* *Cricket*. a position on the batting crease in alignment with the middle and off stumps on which a batsman may take guard.

Middle Atlantic States *or* **Middle States** ★ *pl n* the states of New York, Pennsylvania, and New Jersey.

middlebrow ('mɪd^əlˌbraʊ) *Disparaging*. ◆ *n* **1** a person with conventional tastes and limited cultural appreciation. ◆ *adj also* **middlebrowed**. **2** of or appealing to middlebrows.

middle C *n* *Music*. the note written on the first ledger line below the treble staff or the first ledger line above the bass staff.

middle class *n* **1** Also called: **bourgeoisie**. a social stratum between the lower and upper classes. It consists of businessmen, professional people, etc., along with their families, and is marked by bourgeois values. ◆ *adj* **middle-class**. **2** of, relating to, or characteristic of the middle class.

Middle Congo ★ *n* one of the four territories of former French Equatorial Africa, in W central Africa: became an autonomous member of the French Community, as the Republic of the Congo, in 1958.

middle ear *n* the sound-conducting part of the ear, containing the malleus, incus, and stapes.

Middle East ★ *n* **1** (loosely) the area around the E Mediterranean, esp. Israel and the Arab countries from Turkey to North Africa and eastwards to Iran. **2** (formerly) the area extending from the Tigris and Euphrates to Myanmar.
▶ **Middle Eastern** *adj*

Middle England *n* a characterization of a predominantly middle-class, middle-income section of British society living mainly in suburban and rural England.

Middle English *n* the English language from about 1100 to about 1450.

middle game *n* *Chess*. the central phase between the opening and the endgame.

Middle High German *n* High German from about 1200 to about 1500.

Middle Low German *n* Low German from about 1200 to about 1500.

middleman ('mɪd^əlˌmæn) *n, pl* **middlemen**. **1** a trader engaged in the distribution of goods from producer to consumer. **2** an intermediary.

middlemost ('mɪd^əlˌməʊst) *adj* another word for **midmost**.

middle name *n* **1** a name between a person's first name and surname. **2** a characteristic quality for which a person is known: *caution is my middle name*.

middle-of-the-road *adj* **1** not extreme, esp. in political views; moderate. **2** of, denoting, or relating to popular music having a wide general appeal.

middle passage *n* the. *History*. the journey across the Atlantic Ocean from the W coast of Africa to the Caribbean: the longest part of the journey of the slave ships.

Middlesbrough ★ ('mɪd^əlzbrə) *n* **1** an industrial town in NE England, on the Tees estuary, administrative centre of Cleveland. Pop.: 145 800 (1994 est.). **2** a unitary authority in NE England, in North Yorkshire. Pop.: 146 000 (1996 est.). Area: 54 sq. km (21 sq. miles).

middle school *n* (in England and Wales) a school for children aged between 8 or 9 and 12 or 13.

Middlesex ★ ('mɪd^əlˌsɛks) *n* a former county of SE England: became mostly part of N and W Greater London in 1965. Abbrev.: **Middx**.

Middle States ★ *pl n* another name for the **Middle Atlantic States**.

middle term *n* *Logic*. the term that appears in both minor and major premises but not in the conclusion of a syllogism.

Middleton[1] ★ ('mɪd^əltən) *n* a town in NW England, in Oldham unitary authority, in Greater Manchester. Pop.: 45 621 (1991).

★ people and places

Middleton[2] ★ ('mɪdəltən) n **Thomas**. ?1570–1627, English dramatist. His plays include *Women beware Women* (1621) and the satire *A Game at Chess* (1624).

middle watch n *Naut*. the watch between midnight and 4 a.m.

middleweight ('mɪdəlˌweɪt) n **1a** a professional boxer weighing 154–160 pounds (70–72.5 kg). **1b** an amateur boxer weighing 71–75 kg (157–165 pounds). **2a** a professional wrestler weighing 166–176 pounds (76–80 kg). **2b** an amateur wrestler weighing 75–82 kg (162–180 pounds).

Middle West ★ n another name for the **Midwest**.
  ▸ **Middle Western** adj ▸ **Middle Westerner** n

middling ('mɪdlɪŋ) adj **1** mediocre in quality, size, etc.; neither good nor bad, esp. in health (often in **fair to middling**). ◆ adv **2** *Inf*. moderately: *middling well*. [C15 (N English & Scot.): from MID[1] + -LING[2]]
  ▸ **'middlingly** adv

Middx. abbrev. for Middlesex.

middy ('mɪdɪ) n, pl **middies**. **1** *Inf*. short for **midshipman**. **2** *Austral*. **2a** a glass of middling size, used for beer. **2b** the measure of beer it contains.

Mideast ★ (ˌmɪd'iːst) n *Chiefly US*. another name for **Middle East**.

midfield (ˌmɪd'fiːld) n *Soccer*. **a** the general area between the two opposing defences. **b** (*as modifier*): *a midfield player*.

Midgard ('mɪdgɑːd), **Midgarth** ('mɪdgɑːθ), or **Mithgarthr** ★ ('mɪðgɑːðə) n *Norse myth*. the dwelling place of mankind, formed from the body of the giant Ymir and linked by the bridge Bifrost to Asgard, home of the gods. [C19: from Old Norse *mithgarthr*; see MID[1], YARD[2]]

midge (mɪdʒ) n **1** a mosquito-like dipterous insect occurring in dancing swarms, esp. near water. **2** a small or diminutive person or animal. [OE *mycge*]
  ▸ **'midgy** adj

midget ('mɪdʒɪt) n **1** a dwarf whose skeleton and features are of normal proportions. **2a** something small of its kind. **2b** (*as modifier*): *a midget car*. [C19: from MIDGE + -ET]

Mid Glamorgan ★ n (from 1974 to 1996) a county of S Wales, formed from three historic counties and replaced by four county boroughs. Abbrev.: M Glam.

midgut ('mɪdˌgʌt) n **1** the middle part of the digestive tract of vertebrates, including the small intestine. **2** the middle part of the digestive tract of arthropods.

mid-heavyweight n **a** a professional wrestler weighing 199–209 pounds (91–95 kg). **b** an amateur wrestler weighing 91–100 kg (199–220 pounds).

midi ('mɪdɪ) adj (formerly) **a** (of a skirt, coat, etc.) reaching to below the knee or midcalf. **b** (*as n*): *she wore her new midi*. [C20: from MID-, on the model of MINI]

Midi ★ (*French* midi) n **1** the south of France. **2 Canal du.** a canal in S France, extending from the River Garonne at Toulouse to the Mediterranean at Sète and providing a link between the Mediterranean and Atlantic coasts: built between 1666 and 1681. Length: 181 km (150 miles).

MIDI ('mɪdɪ) n (*modifier*) a generally accepted specification for the external control of electronic musical instruments: *a MIDI synthesizer; a MIDI system*. [C20: from m(usical) i(nstrument) d(igital) i(nterface)]

midi- *combining form*. of medium or middle size, length, etc.: *midibus; midi system*.

Midian ★ ('mɪdɪən) n *Old Testament*. **1** a son of Abraham (Genesis 25:1–2). **2** a nomadic nation claiming descent from him.
  ▸ **'Midian,ite** n, adj ▸ **'Midian,itish** adj

midinette (ˌmɪdɪ'nɛt) n a Parisian seamstress or salesgirl in a clothes shop. [C20: from F, from *midi* noon + *dinette* light meal; the girls had time for only a snack at midday]

Midi-Pyrénées ★ (*French* midipirene) n a region of SW France: consists of N slopes of the Pyrenees in the south, a fertile lowland area in the west crossed by the River Garonne, and the edge of the Massif Central in the north and east.

midiron ('mɪdˌaɪən) n *Golf*. a club, usually a No. 5, 6, or 7 iron, used for medium-length approach shots.

midi system n a complete set of hi-fi sound equipment designed as a single unit that is more compact than the standard equipment.

midland ('mɪdlənd) n **a** the central or inland part of a country. **b** (*as modifier*): *a midland region*.

Midlands ★ ('mɪdləndz) n (*functioning as pl or sing*) **the.** the central counties of England: characterized by manufacturing industries.
  ▸ **'Midlander** n

midlife crisis n a crisis that may be experienced in middle age involving frustration, panic, and feelings of pointlessness, sometimes resulting in radical and often ill-advised changes of lifestyle.

Midlothian ★ (mɪd'ləʊðɪən) n a council area of SE central Scotland, roughly corresponding to the historic county of Midlothian. Administrative centre: Dalkeith. Pop.: 79 910 (1996 est.). Area: 356 sq. km (137 sq. miles).

midmost ('mɪdˌməʊst) adj, adv in the middle or midst.

midnight ('mɪdˌnaɪt) n **1a** the middle of the night; 12 o'clock at night. **1b** (*as modifier*): *the midnight hour*. **2 burn the midnight oil**. to work or study late into the night.

midnight sun n the sun visible at midnight during the summer inside the Arctic and Antarctic circles.

mid-off n *Cricket*. the fielding position on the off side closest to the bowler.

mid-on n *Cricket*. the fielding position on the on side closest to the bowler.

midpoint ('mɪdˌpɔɪnt) n **1** the point on a line that is at an equal distance from either end. **2** a point in time halfway between the beginning and end of an event.

midrib ('mɪdˌrɪb) n the main vein of a leaf, running down the centre of the blade.

midriff ('mɪdrɪf) n **1a** the middle part of the human body, esp. between waist and bust. **1b** (*as modifier*): *midriff bulge*. **2** *Anat*. another name for the **diaphragm** (sense 1). **3** the part of a woman's garment covering the midriff. [OE *midhrif*, from MID[1] + *hrif* belly]

midship ('mɪdˌʃɪp) *Naut*. ◆ adj **1** in, of, or relating to the middle of a vessel. ◆ n **2** the middle of a vessel.

midshipman ('mɪdˌʃɪpmən) n, pl **midshipmen**. a probationary rank held by young naval officers under training, or an officer holding such a rank.

midships ('mɪdˌʃɪps) adv, adj *Naut*. See **amidships**.

midst[1] (mɪdst) n **1 in our midst**. among us. **2 in the midst of**. surrounded or enveloped by; at a point during. [C14: back formation from *amiddes* AMID]

midst[2] (mɪdst) prep *Poetic*. See **amid**.

midsummer ('mɪd'sʌmə) n **1a** the middle or height of the summer. **1b** (*as modifier*): *a midsummer carnival*. **2** another name for **summer solstice**.

Midsummer's Day or **Midsummer Day** n June 24, the feast of St John the Baptist; in England, Ireland, and Wales, one of the four quarter days. See also **summer solstice**.

midterm ('mɪdˈtɜːm) n **1a** the middle of a term in a school, university, etc. **1b** (*as modifier*): *midterm exam*. **2** *US politics*. **2a** the middle of a term of office, esp. of a presidential term, when congressional and local elections are held. **2b** (*as modifier*): *midterm elections*. **3a** the middle of the gestation period. **3b** (*as modifier*): *midterm pregnancy*. See **term** (sense 6).

mid-Victorian adj **1** *Brit. history*. of or relating to the middle period of the reign of Queen Victoria (1837–1901). ◆ n **2** a person of the mid-Victorian era.

midway ('mɪdˌweɪ or, for adv, n ˌmɪd'weɪ) adj **1** in or at the middle of the distance; halfway. ◆ adv **2** to the middle of the distance. ◆ n **3** *Obs*. a middle place, way, etc.

Midway Islands ★ pl n an atoll in the central Pacific, about 2100 km (1300 miles) northwest of Honolulu: annexed by the US in 1867: scene of a decisive battle (June, 1942), in which the US combined fleets destroyed Japan's carrier fleet. Pop.: 450 (1995 est.). Area: 5 sq. km (2 sq. miles).

★ people and places

midweek ('mɪd'wiːk) *n* **a** the middle of the week. **b** (*as modifier*): *a midweek holiday.*

Midwest ('mɪd'west) *or* **Middle West** ★ *n* the N central part of the US; the states from Ohio westwards that border on the Great Lakes, and often the upper Mississippi and Missouri valleys.
▶ 'Mid'western *adj* ▶ 'Mid'westerner *n*

mid-wicket *n Cricket.* the fielding position on the on side, midway between square leg and mid-on.

midwife ('mɪd,waɪf) *n, pl* **midwives** (-,waɪvz). a person qualified to deliver babies and to care for women before, during, and after childbirth. [C14: from OE *mid* with + *wif* woman]

midwifery ('mɪd,wɪfərɪ) *n* the training, art, or practice of a midwife; obstetrics.

midwinter ('mɪd'wɪntə) *n* **1a** the middle or depth of the winter. **1b** (*as modifier*): *a midwinter festival.* **2** another name for **winter solstice.**

midyear ('mɪd'jɪə) *n* the middle of the year.

mien (miːn) *n Literary.* a person's manner, bearing, or appearance. [C16: prob. var. of obs. *demean* appearance; rel. to F *mine* aspect]

Mieres ★ (*Spanish* 'mjeres) *n* a city in N Spain, south of Oviedo: steel and chemical industries; iron and coal mines. Pop.: 26 500 (1987 est.).

Mies van der Rohe ★ ('miːz væn də 'rəuə) *n* **Ludwig.** 1886–1969, US architect, born in Germany, who directed the Bauhaus (1929–33); his works include the Seagram building, New York (1958).

mifepristone (mɪ'feprɪ,stəun) *n* See **abortion pill.**

miff (mɪf) *Inf.* ◆ *vb* **1** to take offence or to offend. ◆ *n* **2** a petulant mood. **3** a petty quarrel. [C17: ? an imitative expression of bad temper]
▶ 'miffy *adj*

might[1] (maɪt) *vb* (takes an implied infinitive or an infinitive without *to*) used as an auxiliary. **1** making the past tense or subjunctive mood of **may**[1]: *he might have come.* **2** (*often foll. by* well) expressing possibility: *he might well come.* In this sense *might* looks to the future and functions as a weak form of *may.* See **may**[1] (sense 2). [OE *miht*]

USAGE NOTE See at **may**[1].

might[2] (maɪt) *n* **1** power, force, or vigour, esp. of a great or supreme kind. **2** physical strength. **3** (**with**) **might and main.** See **main**[1] (sense 7). [OE *miht*]

mighty ('maɪtɪ) *adj* **mightier, mightiest. 1a** having or indicating might; powerful or strong. **1b** (*as collective n*; *preceded by the*): *the mighty.* **2** very large; vast. **3** very great in extent, importance, etc. ◆ *adv* **4** *Inf.*, chiefly *US & Canad.* (*intensifier*): *mighty tired.*
▶ 'mightily *adv* ▶ 'mightiness *n*

mignon ('mɪnjɒn) *adj* small and pretty; dainty. [C16: from F, from OF *mignot* dainty]
▶ **mignonne** ('mɪnjɒn) *fem n*

mignonette (,mɪnjə'net) *n* **1** any of various mainly Mediterranean plants, such as **garden mignonette,** that have spikes of small greenish-white flowers. **2** a type of fine pillow lace. **3a** a greyish-green colour. **3b** (*as adj*): *mignonette ribbons.* [C18: from F, dim. of MIGNON]

migraine ('miːɡreɪn, 'maɪ-) *n* a throbbing headache usually affecting only one side of the head and commonly accompanied by nausea and visual disturbances. [C18: (earlier form, C14 *mygrame* MEGRIM): from F, from LL *hēmicrānia* pain in half of the head, from Gk, from HEMI- + *kranion* CRANIUM]
▶ 'migrainous *adj*

migrant ('maɪɡrənt) *n* **1** a person or animal that moves from one region, place, or country to another. **2** an itinerant agricultural worker. ◆ *adj* **3** moving from one region, place, or country to another; migratory.

migrate (maɪ'ɡreɪt) *vb* **migrates, migrating, migrated.** (*intr*) **1** to go from one place to settle in another, esp. in a foreign country. **2** (of birds, fishes, etc.) to journey between

different habitats at specific times of the year. [C17: from L *migrāre* to change one's abode]
▶ mi'grator *n*

migration (maɪ'ɡreɪʃən) *n* **1** the act or an instance of migrating. **2** a group of people, birds, etc., migrating in a body. **3** *Chem.* a movement of atoms, ions, or molecules, such as the motion of ions in solution under the influence of electric fields.
▶ mi'grational *adj*

migratory ('maɪɡrətərɪ, -trɪ) *adj* **1** of or characterized by migration. **2** nomadic; itinerant.

mihrab ('miːræb, -rəb) *n Islam.* the niche in a mosque showing the direction of Mecca. [from Ar.]

mikado (mɪ'kɑːdəu) *n, pl* **mikados.** (*often cap.*) *Arch.* the Japanese emperor. [C18: from Japanese, from *mi-* honourable + *kado* gate]

mike (maɪk) *n Inf.* short for **microphone.**

Míkonos ★ ('mikɔnɔs) *n* transliteration of the Modern Greek name for **Mykonos.**

mil (mɪl) *n* **1** a unit of length equal to one thousandth of an inch. **2** a unit of angular measure, used in gunnery, equal to one six-thousand-four-hundredth of a circumference. **3** *Photog.* short for millimetre: *35-mil film.* [C18: from L *millēsimus* thousandth]

mil. *abbrev. for:* **1** military. **2** militia.

milady *or* **miladi** (mɪ'leɪdɪ) *n, pl* **miladies.** (formerly) a continental title used for an English gentlewoman.

Milan ★ (mɪ'læn) *n* a city in N Italy, in central Lombardy: Italy's second largest city and chief financial and industrial centre; a centre of the Renaissance under the Visconti and Sforza families. Pop.: 1 334 171 (1994 est.). Italian name: **Milano** (mi'laːno).
▶ ,Mila'nese *adj, n*

Milazzo ★ (*Italian* mi'lattso) *n* a port in NE Sicily: founded in the 8th century B.C.; scene of a battle (1860), in which Garibaldi defeated the Bourbon forces. Pop.: 32 000 (1987 est.). Ancient name: **Mylae** (maɪ,liː).

milch (mɪltʃ) *n* **1** (*modifier*) (esp. of cattle) yielding milk. **2 milch cow.** *Inf.* a source of easy income, esp. a person. [C13: from OE *-milce* (in compounds); rel. to OE *melcan* to milk]

mild (maɪld) *adj* **1** (of a taste, sensation, etc.) not powerful or strong; bland. **2** gentle or temperate in character, climate, behaviour, etc. **3** not extreme; moderate. **4** feeble; unassertive. ◆ *n* **5** *Brit.* draught beer, of darker colour than bitter and flavoured with fewer hops. [OE *milde*]
▶ 'mildly *adv* ▶ 'mildness *n*

mildew ('mɪl,djuː) *n* **1** any of various diseases of plants that affect mainly the leaves and are caused by parasitic fungi. **2** any fungus causing this. **3** another name for **mould**[2]. ◆ *vb* **4** to affect or become affected with mildew. [OE *mildēaw*, from *mil-* honey + *dēaw* DEW]
▶ 'mil,dewy *adj*

mild steel *n* any of a class of strong tough steels that contain a low quantity of carbon.

mile (maɪl) *n* **1** Also called: **statute mile.** a unit of length used in the UK, the US, and certain other countries, equal to 1760 yards. 1 mile is equivalent to 1.60934 kilometres. **2** See **nautical mile. 3** the Roman mile, equivalent to 1620 yards. **4** (*often pl*) *Inf.* a great distance; great deal: *he missed by a mile.* **5** a race extending over a mile. ◆ *adv* **6 miles.** (*intensifier*): *that's miles better.* [OE *mīl*, from L *mīlia* (*passuum*) a thousand (paces)]

mileage *or* **milage** ('maɪlɪdʒ) *n* **1** a distance expressed in miles. **2** the total number of miles that a motor vehicle has travelled. **3** allowance for travelling expenses, esp. as a fixed rate per mile. **4** the number of miles a motor vehicle will travel on one gallon of fuel. **5** *Inf.* use, benefit, or service provided by something. **6** *Inf.* grounds, substance, or weight: *some mileage in their arguments.*

mileometer *or* **milometer** (maɪ'lɒmɪtə) *n* a device that records the number of miles that a bicycle or motor vehicle has travelled.

milepost ('maɪl,pəust) *n* **1** *Horse racing.* a marking post on a racecourse a mile before the finishing line. **2** *Chiefly*

US & Canad. a signpost that shows the distance in miles to or from a place.

miler ('maɪlə) n an athlete, horse, etc., that runs or specializes in races of one mile.

Miles ★ (maɪlz) n **Bernard**, Baron Miles of Blackfriars. 1907–91, British actor and theatre manager. He founded the Mermaid Theatre in Blackfriars, London, and was known as a character actor.

milestone ('maɪl,stəun) n **1** a stone pillar that shows the distance in miles to or from a place. **2** a significant event in life, history, etc.

Miletus ★ (mɪ'li:təs) n an ancient city on the W coast of Asia Minor: a major Ionian centre of trade and learning in the ancient world.
▷ **Mi'lesian** adj, n

milfoil ('mɪl,fɔɪl) n **1** another name for **yarrow. 2** See **water milfoil**. [C13: from OF, from L milifolium, from mille thousand + folium leaf]

Milford Haven ★ ('mɪlfəd) n a port in SW Wales, in Pembrokeshire, on **Milford Haven** (a large inlet of St George's Channel): major oil port. Pop.: 13 194 (1991).

Milhaud ★ (French mijo) n **Darius** (darjys). 1892–1974, French composer; member of Les Six. His works include operas, symphonies, ballets, string quartets, and songs.

miliaria (,mɪlɪ'ɛərɪə) n an acute itching eruption of the skin, caused by blockage of the sweat glands. [C19: from NL, from L miliārius MILIARY]

miliary ('mɪljərɪ) adj **1** resembling or relating to millet seeds. **2** (of a disease or skin eruption) characterized by small lesions resembling millet seeds: miliary fever. [C17: from L miliārius, from milium MILLET]

milieu ('mi:ljɜ:; French miljø) n, pl **milieux** (-ljɜ:, -ljɜ:z; French -ljø) or **milieus**. (miljø). surroundings, location, or setting. [C19: from F, from mi- MID[1] + lieu place]

militant ('mɪlɪtənt) adj **1** aggressive or vigorous, esp. in the support of a cause. **2** warring; engaged in warfare. ◆ n **3** a militant person. [C15: from L mīlitāre to be a soldier, from mīles soldier]
▷ **'militancy** n ▷ **'militantly** adv

militarism ('mɪlɪtə,rɪzəm) n **1** military spirit; pursuit of military ideals. **2** domination by the military, esp. on a political level. **3** a policy of maintaining a strong military organization in aggressive preparedness for war.
▷ **'militarist** n

militarize or **militarise** ('mɪlɪtə,raɪz) vb **militarizes, militarizing, militarized** or **militarises, militarising, militarised**. (tr) **1** to convert to military use. **2** to imbue with militarism.
▷ **,militari'zation** or **,militari'sation** n

military ('mɪlɪtərɪ, -trɪ) adj **1** of or relating to the armed forces, warlike matters, etc. **2** of or characteristic of soldiers. ◆ n, pl **militaries** or **military. 3** (preceded by the) the armed services, esp. the army. [C16: via F from L mīlitāris, from mīles soldier]
▷ **mili'tarily** adv

military police n a corps within an army that performs police and disciplinary duties.
▷ **military policeman** n

militate ('mɪlɪ,teɪt) vb **militates, militating, militated**. (intr; usually foll. by against or for) (of facts, etc.) to have influence or effect: the evidence militated against his release. [C17: from L mīlitātus, from mīlitāre to be a soldier]

USAGE NOTE See at **mitigate.**

---

militia (mɪ'lɪʃə) n **1** a body of citizen (as opposed to professional) soldiers. **2** an organization containing men enlisted for service in emergency only. [C16: from L: soldiery, from mīles soldier]
▷ **mi'litiaman** n

milk (mɪlk) n **1a** a whitish fluid secreted by the mammary glands of mature female mammals and used for feeding their young until weaned. **1b** the milk of cows, goats, etc., used by man as a food or in the production of butter, cheese, etc. **2** any similar fluid in plants, such as the juice of a coconut. **3** a milklike pharmaceutical preparation, such as milk of magnesia. **4** cry over spilt milk. to la-

ment something that cannot be altered. ◆ vb **5** to draw milk from the udder of (an animal). **6** (intr) (of animals) to yield milk. **7** (tr) to draw off or tap in small quantities: to milk the petty cash. **8** (tr) to extract as much money, help, etc., as possible from: to milk a situation of its news value. **9** (tr) to extract venom, sap, etc., from. [OE milc]
▷ **'milker** n

milk-and-water adj (**milk and water** when postpositive). weak, feeble, or insipid.

milk bar n **1** a snack bar at which milk drinks and light refreshments are served. **2** (in Australia) a shop selling, in addition to milk, basic provisions and other items.

milk chocolate n chocolate that has been made with milk, having a creamy taste.

milk float n Brit. a small motor vehicle used to deliver milk to houses.

milk leg n inflammation and thrombosis of the femoral vein following childbirth, characterized by painful swelling of the leg.

milkmaid ('mɪlk,meɪd) n a girl or woman who milks cows.

milkman ('mɪlkmən) n, pl **milkmen**. a man who delivers or sells milk.

milk of magnesia n a suspension of magnesium hydroxide in water, used as an antacid and laxative.

milk pudding n Chiefly Brit. a pudding made by boiling or baking milk with a grain, esp. rice.

milk round n Brit. **1** a route along which a milkman regularly delivers milk. **2** a regular series of visits, esp. as made by recruitment officers from industry to universities.

milk run n Aeronautics, inf. a routine and uneventful flight. [C20: from a milkman's safe and regular routine]

milk shake n a cold frothy drink made of milk, flavouring, and sometimes ice cream, whisked or beaten together.

milksop ('mɪlk,sɒp) n a feeble or ineffectual man or youth.

milk sugar n another name for **lactose.**

milk tooth n any of the first teeth to erupt; a deciduous tooth. Also called: **baby tooth.**

milkwort ('mɪlk,wɜ:t) n any of several plants having small blue, pink, or white flowers. They were formerly believed to increase milk production in nursing women.

milky ('mɪlkɪ) adj **milkier, milkiest. 1** resembling milk, esp. in colour or cloudiness. **2** of or containing milk. **3** spiritless or spineless.
▷ **'milkily** adv ▷ **'milkiness** n

Milky Way n the. the diffuse band of light stretching across the night sky that consists of millions of faint stars, nebulae, etc., and forms part of the Galaxy. [C14: translation of L via lactea]

mill (mɪl) n **1** a building in which grain is crushed and ground to make flour. **2** a building fitted with machinery for processing materials, manufacturing goods, etc.; factory. **3** a machine that processes materials, manufactures goods, etc., by performing a continuous or repetitive operation, such as a machine to grind flour, pulverize solids, or press fruit. **4** a machine that tools or polishes metal. **5** a small machine for grinding solids: a pepper mill. **6** a system, institution, etc., that influences people or things in the manner of a factory: the educational mill. **7** an unpleasant experience; ordeal (esp. in **go** or **be put through the mill**). **8** a fist fight. ◆ vb **9** (tr) to grind, press, or pulverize in or as if in a mill. **10** (tr) to process or produce in or with a mill. **11** to cut or roll (metal) with or as if with a milling machine. **12** (tr) to groove or flute the edge of (a coin). **13** (intr; often foll. by about or around) to move about in a confused manner. **14** Arch. sl. to fight, esp. with the fists. [OE mylen from LL molīna a mill, from L mola mill, from molere to grind]
▷ **'millable** adj ▷ **'milled** adj

Mill ★ (mɪl) n **1 James.** 1773–1836, Scottish philosopher, historian, and economist. He expounded Bentham's utilitarian philosophy in Elements of Political Economy (1821) and Analysis of the Phenomena of the Human Mind (1829) and also wrote a History of British India (1817–18).

★ people and places

2 his son, **John Stuart.** 1806–73, British philosopher and economist. He modified Bentham's utilitarian philosophy in *Utilitarianism* (1861) and in his treatise *On Liberty* (1859) he defended the rights and freedom of the individual. Other works include *A System of Logic* (1843) and *Principles of Political Economy* (1848).

Millais ★ ('mɪleɪ) *n* Sir **John Everett.** 1829–96, British painter, who was a founder of the Pre-Raphaelite Brotherhood. His works include *The Order of Release* (1853) and *The Blind Girl* (1856).

Millay ★ (mɪ'leɪ) *n* **Edna St Vincent.** 1892–1950, US poet, noted esp. for her sonnets; her collections include *The Buck in the Snow* (1928) and *Fatal Interview* (1931).

millboard ('mɪl,bɔːd) *n* strong pasteboard, used esp. in book covers. [C18: from *milled board*]

milldam ('mɪl,dæm) *n* a dam built in a stream to raise the water level sufficiently for it to turn a millwheel.

millefeuille *French.* (milfœj) *n Brit.* a small iced cake made of puff pastry filled with jam and cream. [lit.: thousand leaves]

millefleurs ('miːl,flɜː) *n* (*functioning as sing*) a design of stylized floral patterns, used in textiles, paperweights, etc. [F: thousand flowers]

millenarian (,mɪlɪ'neərɪən) *adj* **1** of or relating to a thousand or to a thousand years. **2** of or relating to the millennium or millenarianism. ♦ *n* **3** an adherent of millenarianism.

millenarianism (,mɪlɪ'neərɪə,nɪzəm) *n* **1** *Christianity.* the belief in a future millennium during which Christ will reign on earth: based on Revelation 20:1–5. **2** any belief in a future period of ideal peace and happiness.

millenary (mɪ'lenərɪ) *n, pl* **millenaries. 1** a sum or aggregate of one thousand. **2** another word for a **millennium**. ♦ *adj, n* **3** another word for **millenarian**. [C16: from LL *millēnārius* containing a thousand, from L *mille* thousand]

millennium (mɪ'lenɪəm) *n, pl* **millennia** (-nɪə) *or* **millenniums. 1** the. *Christianity.* the period of a thousand years of Christ's awaited reign upon earth. **2** a period or cycle of one thousand years. **3** a time of peace and happiness, esp. in the distant future. [C17: from NL, from L *mille* thousand + *annus* year] ▸ mil'**lennial** *adj* ▸ mil'**lennialist** *n*

millennium bug *n Computing.* any software problem arising from the change in date at the start of the 21st century.

millepede ('mɪlɪ,piːd) *or* **milleped** *n* variants of **millipede.**

millepore ('mɪlɪ,pɔː) *n* any of a genus of tropical colonial coral-like hydrozoans, having a calcareous skeleton. [C18: from NL, from L *mille* thousand + *porus* hole]

miller ('mɪlə) *n* **1** a person who keeps, operates, or works in a mill, esp. a corn mill. **2** another name for **milling machine. 3** a person who operates a milling machine.

Miller ★ ('mɪlə) *n* **1 Arthur.** born 1915, US dramatist. His plays include *Death of a Salesman* (1949), *The Crucible* (1953), *A View from the Bridge* (1955), and *Mr Peters' Connections* (1998). **2 Glenn.** 1904–44, US band leader. His compositions include "Moonlight Serenade". He died when his aeroplane disappeared on a flight between England and France. **3 Henry.** 1891–1980, US novelist, author of *Tropic of Cancer* (1934) and *Tropic of Capricorn* (1938). **4 Jonathan** (**Wolfe**). born 1934, British doctor, theatre director, and television broadcaster.

miller's thumb *n* any of several small freshwater European fishes having a flattened body. [C15: from the alleged likeness of the fish's head to a thumb]

millesimal (mɪ'lesɪməl) *adj* **1a** denoting a thousandth. **1b** (*as n*): *a millesimal.* **2** of, consisting of, or relating to a thousandth. [C18: from L *millēsimus*]

millet ('mɪlɪt) *n* **1** a cereal grass cultivated for grain and animal fodder. **2a** an Indian annual grass cultivated for grain and forage, having pale round shiny seeds. **2b** the seed of this plant. **3** any of various similar or related grasses. [C14: via OF from L *milium*]

Millet ★ (*French* mile) *n* **Jean François** (ʒɑ̃ frɑ̃swa). 1814–75, French painter of the Barbizon school.

milli- *prefix* denoting 10⁻³: *millimetre.* Symbol: m [from F, from L *mille* thousand]

milliard ('mɪlɪ,ɑːd, 'mɪljɑːd) *n Brit.* (no longer in technical use) a thousand million. US & Canad. equivalent: **billion.** [C19: from F]

millibar ('mɪlɪ,bɑː) *n* a cgs unit of atmospheric pressure equal to 10⁻³ bar, 100 newtons per square metre or 0.7500617 millimetre of mercury.

Milligan ★ ('mɪlɪgən) *n* **Spike.** real name *Terence Alan Milligan.* born 1918, British comedian and author, born in India, who appeared in *The Goon Show* (1952–60): noted also for the wartime memoir *Adolf Hitler, My Part in his Downfall* (1971) and its sequels.

milligram *or* **milligramme** ('mɪlɪ,græm) *n* one thousandth of a gram. [C19: from F]

Millikan ★ ('mɪlɪkən) *n* **Robert Andrews.** 1868–1953, US physicist. He measured electronic charge (1910) and studied cosmic rays; Nobel prize for physics 1923.

millilitre *or US* **milliliter** ('mɪlɪ,liːtə) *n* one thousandth of a litre.

millimetre *or US* **millimeter** ('mɪlɪ,miːtə) *n* one thousandth of a metre.

millimicron ('mɪlɪ,maɪkrɒn) *n Obs.* one thousand-millionth of a metre; nanometre.

milliner ('mɪlɪnə) *n* a person who makes or sells women's hats. [C16: orig. *Milaner,* a native of *Milan,* at that time famous for its fancy goods]

millinery ('mɪlɪnərɪ, -ɪnrɪ) *n* **1** hats, trimmings, etc., sold by a milliner. **2** the business or shop of a milliner.

milling ('mɪlɪŋ) *n* **1** the act or process of grinding, pressing, or crushing in a mill. **2** the grooves or fluting on the edge of a coin, etc.

milling machine *n* a machine tool in which a horizontal arbor or vertical spindle rotates a cutting tool above a horizontal table.

million ('mɪljən) *n, pl* **millions** *or* **million. 1** the cardinal number that is the product of 1000 multiplied by 1000. **2** a numeral, 1 000 000, 10⁶, M̄, etc., representing this number. **3** (*often pl*) *Inf.* an extremely large but unspecified number or amount: *I have millions of things to do.* ♦ *determiner* **4** (preceded by *a* or by a numeral) **4a** amounting to a million: *a million light years.* **4b** (*as pron*): *I can see a million.* [C17: via OF from early It. *millione,* from *mille* thousand, from L]

millionaire (,mɪljə'neə) *n* a person whose assets are worth at least a million of the standard monetary units of his or her country. ▸ ,**million'airess** *fem n*

millionth ('mɪljənθ) *n* **1a** one of 1 000 000 equal parts of something. **1b** (*as modifier*): *a millionth part.* **2** one of 1 000 000 equal divisions of a scientific quantity. **3** the fraction one divided by 1 000 000. ♦ *adj* **4** (*usually prenominal*) **4a** being the ordinal number of 1 000 000 in numbering or counting order, etc. **4b** (*as n*): *the millionth to be manufactured.*

millipede, millepede ('mɪlɪ,piːd), *or* **milleped** ('mɪlɪ,pɛd) *n* any of various terrestrial herbivorous arthropods, having a cylindrical segmented body, each segment of which bears two pairs of legs. [C17: from L, from *mille* thousand + *pēs* foot]

millisecond ('mɪlɪ,sɛkənd) *n* one thousandth of a second.

millpond ('mɪl,pɒnd) *n* **1** a pool formed by damming a stream to provide water to turn a mill-wheel. **2** any expanse of calm water.

millrace ('mɪl,reɪs) *or* **millrun** *n* **1** the current of water that turns a millwheel. **2** the channel for this water.

Mills ★ (mɪlz) *n* **1 Hayley.** born 1946, British actress. Her films include *Pollyanna* (1960). **2** her father, Sir **John.** born 1908, British actor. His films include *This Happy Breed* (1944) and *Ryan's Daughter* (1971).

Mills bomb (mɪlz) *n* a type of high-explosive hand grenade. [C20: after Sir William *Mills* (1856–1932), Brit. inventor]

millstone ('mɪl,stəun) *n* **1** one of a pair of heavy flat disc-shaped stones that are rotated one against the other to grind grain. **2** a heavy burden, such as a responsibility or obligation.

millstream ('mɪl,striːm) *n* a stream of water used to turn a millwheel.

millwheel ('mɪl,wiːl) *n* a wheel, esp. a waterwheel, that drives a mill.

millwork ('mɪl,wɜːk) *n* work done in a mill.

millwright ('mɪl,raɪt) *n* a person who designs, builds, or repairs grain mills or mill machinery.

Milne ★ (mɪln) *n* **A(lan) A(lexander)**. 1882–1956, British writer, noted for his children's books, including *When We Were Very Young* (1924) and *Winnie the Pooh* (1926).

milometer (maɪˈlɒmɪtə) *n* a variant spelling of **mileometer**.

milord (mɪˈlɔːd) *n* (formerly) a continental title used for an English gentleman. [C19: via F from E *my lord*]

Mílos ★ ('milɒs) *n* transliteration of the Modern Greek name for **Melos**.

Miłosz ★ ('miːlɒʃ; *Polish* 'miwoʃ) *n* **Czeslaw** ('tʃɛslɔ:; 'tʃeswaf). born 1911, US poet and writer, born in Lithuania, writing in Polish; author of *The Captive Mind* (1953). Nobel prize for literature 1980.

milt (mɪlt) *n* **1** the testis of a fish. **2** the spermatozoa and seminal fluid produced by a fish. **3** *Rare.* the spleen, esp. of fowls and pigs. ◆ *vb* **4** to fertilize (fish roe) with milt, esp. artificially. [OE *milte* spleen; in the sense: fish sperm, prob. from MDu. *milte*]
▸ 'milter *n*

Miltiades ★ (mɪlˈtaɪəˌdiːz) *n* ?540–?489 B.C., Athenian general, who defeated the Persians at Marathon (490).

Milton ★ ('mɪltən) *n* **John**. 1608–74, English poet. His early works include *L'Allegro* and *Il Penseroso* (1632), the masque *Comus* (1634), and the elegy *Lycidas* (1637). He also published pamphlets during the Civil War, including *Areopagitica* (1644). His later works included the poems *Paradise Lost* (1667; 1674) and *Paradise Regained* (1671).
▸ **Mil'tonic** *or* **Mil'tonian** *adj*

Milton Keynes ★ ('mɪltən 'kiːnz) *n* **1** a new town in N Buckinghamshire, founded in 1967: electronics, clothing, machinery. Pop.: 156 148 (1991). **2** a unitary authority in central England, Buckinghamshire. Pop.: 188 400 (1994 est). Area: 310 sq. km (119 sq. miles).

Milwaukee ★ (mɪlˈwɔːkiː) *n* a port in SE Wisconsin, on Lake Michigan: the largest city in the state; established as a trading post in the 18th century; an important industrial centre. Pop.: 617 044 (1994 est.).
▸ **Mil'waukeean** *adj, n*

mim (mɪm) *adj Dialect.* prim, modest, or demure. [C17: ? imit. of lip-pursing]

mime (maɪm) *n* **1** the theatrical technique of expressing an idea or mood or portraying a character entirely by gesture and bodily movement without the use of words. **2** Also called: **mime artist.** a performer specializing in this. **3** a dramatic presentation using such a technique. **4** (in the classical theatre) **4a** a comic performance with exaggerated gesture and physical action. **4b** an actor in such a performance. ◆ *vb* **mimes, miming, mimed. 5** to express (an idea, etc.) in actions or gestures without speech. **6** (of singers or musicians) to perform as if singing a song or playing a piece of music that is actually prerecorded. [OE *mīma*, from L *mīmus* mimic actor, from Gk *mimos* imitator]
▸ 'mimer *n*

Mimeograph ('mɪmɪəˌgrɑːf) *n* **1** *Trademark.* an office machine for printing multiple copies of text or line drawings from a stencil. **2** a copy produced by this. ◆ *vb* **3** to print copies from (a prepared stencil) using this machine.

mimesis (mɪˈmiːsɪs) *n* **1** *Art, literature.* the imitative representation of nature or human behaviour. **2** *Biol.* another name for **mimicry** (sense 2). **3** *Rhetoric.* representation of another person's alleged words in a speech. [C16: from Gk, from *mimeisthai* to imitate]

mimetic (mɪˈmɛtɪk) *adj* **1** of, resembling, or relating to mimesis or imitation, as in art, etc. **2** *Biol.* of or exhibiting mimicry.
▸ mi'metically *adv*

mimic ('mɪmɪk) *vb* **mimics, mimicking, mimicked.** (*tr*) **1** to imitate (a person, a manner, etc.), esp. for satirical effect; ape. **2** to take on the appearance of: *certain flies mimic wasps.* **3** to copy closely or in a servile manner. ◆ *n* **4** a person or an animal, such as a parrot, that is clever at mimicking. **5** an animal that displays mimicry. ◆ *adj* **6** of, relating to, or using mimicry. **7** simulated, makebelieve, or mock. [C16: from L *mīmicus*, from Gk *mimikos*, from *mimos* MIME]
▸ 'mimicker *n*

mimicry ('mɪmɪkrɪ) *n, pl* **mimicries. 1** the act or art of copying or imitating closely; mimicking. **2** the resemblance shown by one animal species to another, which protects it from predators.

MIMinE *abbrev. for* Member of the Institute of Mining Engineers.

Mimir ★ ('miːmɪə) *n Norse myth.* a giant who guarded the well of wisdom near the roots of Yggdrasil.

mimosa (mɪˈməʊsə, -zə) *n* any of various tropical shrubs or trees having ball-like clusters of typically yellow flowers and leaves that are often sensitive to touch or light. See also **sensitive plant.** [C18: from NL, prob. from L *mīmus* MIME, because the plant's sensitivity to touch imitates the similar reaction of animals]

mimulus ('mɪmjʊləs) *n* any of a genus of flowering plants of temperate regions. See **monkey flower.** [C19: Med. L, from L *mimus* MIME, alluding to masklike flowers]

min. *abbrev. for:* **1** mineralogy. **2** minimum. **3** mining. **4** minute or minutes.

Min. *abbrev. for:* **1** Minister. **2** Ministry.

Mina Hassan Tani ★ ('miːnə hɑːˈsɑːn 'tɑːnɪ) *n* a port in NW Morocco, on the Sebou River 16 km (10 miles) from the Atlantic. Pop.: 234 000 (1993 est.). Also called: **Kénitra.** Former name (1932–56): **Port Lyautey.**

minaret (ˌmɪnəˈrɛt, 'mɪnəˌrɛt) *n* a slender tower of a mosque having one or more balconies. [C17: from F, from Turkish, from Ar. *manārat* lamp, from *nār* fire]
▸ ˌmina'reted *adj*

Minas Basin ★ ('maɪnəs) *n* a bay in E Canada, in central Nova Scotia: the NE arm of the Bay of Fundy, with which it is linked by **Minas Channel.**

Minas Gerais ★ (*Portuguese* 'minaʒ ʒəˈrais) *n* an inland state of E Brazil: situated on the high plateau of the Brazilian Highlands; large reserves of iron ore and manganese. Capital: Belo Horizonte. Pop.: 16 505 300 (1995 est.). Area: 587 172 sq. km (226 707 sq. miles).

minatory ('mɪnətərɪ, -trɪ) *or* **minatorial** *adj* threatening or menacing. [C16: from LL *minātōrius*, from L *mināri* to threaten]

mince (mɪns) *vb* **minces, mincing, minced. 1** (*tr*) to chop, grind, or cut into very small pieces. **2** (*tr*) to soften or moderate: *I didn't mince my words.* **3** (*intr*) to walk or speak in an affected dainty manner. ◆ *n* **4** *Chiefly Brit.* minced meat. [C14: from OF *mincier*, ult. from LL *minūtia*; see MINUTIAE]
▸ 'mincer *n*

mincemeat ('mɪns,miːt) *n* **1** a mixture of dried fruit, spices, etc., used esp. for filling pies. **2 make mincemeat of.** *Inf.* to defeat completely.

mince pie *n* a small round pastry tart filled with mincemeat.

Minch ★ (mɪntʃ) *n* **the.** a channel of the Atlantic divided into the **North Minch**, between the mainland of Scotland and the Isle of Lewis, and the **Little Minch**, between the Isle of Skye and Harris and North Uist.

mincing ('mɪnsɪŋ) *adj* (of a person) affectedly elegant in gait, manner, or speech.
▸ 'mincingly *adv*

mind (maɪnd) *n* **1** the human faculty to which are ascribed thought, feelings, intention, etc. **2** intelligence or the intellect, esp. as opposed to feelings or wishes. **3** recollection or remembrance: *it comes to mind.* **4** the faculty of original or creative thought; imagination: *it's all in the mind.* **5** a person considered as an intellectual being: *great minds.* **6** condition, state, or manner of feeling or thought: *his state of mind.* **7** an inclination, desire, or purpose: *I have a mind to go.* **8** attention or thoughts: *keep your*

★ people and places

mind on your work. **9** a sound mental state; sanity (esp. in **out of one's mind**). **10** (in Cartesian philosophy) one of two basic modes of existence, the other being matter. **11 blow someone's mind.** *Sl.* **11a** (of a drug) to alter someone's mental state. **11b** to astound or surprise someone. **12 change one's mind.** to alter one's decision or opinion. **13 in** *or* **of two minds.** undecided; wavering. **14 give (someone) a piece of one's mind.** to criticize or censure (someone) frankly or vehemently. **15 make up one's mind.** to decide (something or to do something). **16 on one's mind.** in one's thoughts. ◆ *vb* **17** (when *tr, may take a clause as object*) to take offence at: *do you mind if I smoke?* **18** to pay attention to (something); heed; notice: *to mind one's own business.* **19** (*tr; takes a clause as object*) to make certain; ensure: *mind you tell her.* **20** (*tr*) to take care of; have charge of: *to mind the shop.* **21** (when *tr, may take a clause as object*) to be cautious or careful about (something): *mind how you go.* **22** (*tr*) to obey (someone or something); heed: *mind your father!* **23** to be concerned (about); be troubled (about): *never mind about your hat.* **24** (*tr; passive; takes an infinitive*) to be intending or inclined (to do something): *clearly he was not minded to finish the story.* **25 mind you.** an expression qualifying a previous statement: *Dogs are nice. Mind you, I don't like all dogs.* ◆ Related adj: **mental.** ◆ See also **mind out.** [OE *gemynd* mind]

Mindanao ★ (ˌmɪndəˈnaʊ) *n* the second largest island of the Philippines, in the S part of the archipelago: mountainous and volcanic. Chief towns: Davao, Zamboanga. Pop.: 14 298 000 (1990). Area: (including offshore islands) 94 631 sq. km (36 537 sq. miles).

mind-bending *adj Inf.* **1** Also: **mind-blowing.** altering one's state of consciousness, esp. as a result of taking drugs. **2** reaching the limit of credibility: *they offered a mind-bending salary.* ◆ *n* **3** the process of brainwashing.

mind-boggling *adj Inf.* astonishing; bewildering.

minded (ˈmaɪndɪd) *adj* **1** having a mind, inclination, intention, etc., as specified: *politically minded.* **2** (*in combination*): *money-minded.*

minder (ˈmaɪndə) *n* **1** someone who looks after someone or something. **2** short for **childminder.** **3** *Sl.* an aide to someone in public life who keeps control of press and public relations. **4** *Sl.* someone acting as a bodyguard or assistant, esp. in the criminal underworld.

mindful (ˈmaɪndfʊl) *adj* (usually *postpositive* and foll. by *of*) keeping aware; heedful: *mindful of your duty.*
▸ ˈ**mindfully** *adv* ▸ ˈ**mindfulness** *n*

mindless (ˈmaɪndlɪs) *adj* **1** stupid or careless. **2** requiring little or no intellectual effort.
▸ ˈ**mindlessly** *adv* ▸ ˈ**mindlessness** *n*

mind-numbing *adj* extremely boring and uninspiring.
▸ ˈmind-ˌ**numbingly** *adv*

Mindoro ★ (mɪnˈdɔːrəʊ) *n* a mountainous island in the central Philippines, south of Luzon. Pop.: 912 000 (1995 est.). Area: 9736 sq. km (3759 sq. miles).

mind out *vb* (*intr, adv*) *Brit.* to be careful or pay attention.

mind-reader *n* a person seemingly able to discern the thoughts of another.
▸ ˈmind-ˌ**reading** *n*

mind-set *n* the ideas and attitudes with which a person approaches a situation, esp. when these are seen as being difficult to alter.

mind's eye *n* the visual memory or the imagination.

Mindszenty ★ (ˈmɪndsɛntɪ) *n* **Joseph.** 1892–1975, Hungarian cardinal. Sentenced to life imprisonment for treason (1949), he was released during the 1956 Revolution.

mine[1] (maɪn) *pron* **1** something or someone belonging to or associated with me: *mine is best.* **2 of mine.** belonging to or associated with me. ◆ *determiner* **3** (*preceding a vowel*) an archaic word for **my:** *mine eyes; mine host.* [OE *mīn*]

mine[2] (maɪn) *n* **1** a system of excavations made for the extraction of minerals, esp. coal, ores, or precious stones. **2** any deposit of ore or minerals. **3** a lucrative source or abundant supply: *a mine of information.* **4** a device containing explosive designed to destroy ships, vehicles, or personnel, usually laid beneath the ground or in water. **5** a tunnel dug to undermine a fortification, etc. ◆ *vb* **mines, mining, mined.** **6** to dig into (the earth) for (minerals). **7** to make (a hole, tunnel, etc.) by digging or boring.

8 to place explosive mines in position below the surface of (the sea or land). **9** to undermine (a fortification, etc.) by digging mines. **10** another word for **undermine.** [C13: from OF, prob. of Celtic origin]

mine detector *n* an instrument designed to detect explosive mines.
▸ **mine detection** *n*

mine dump *n S. African.* a large mound of residue esp. from gold-mining operations.

minefield (ˈmaɪnˌfiːld) *n* **1** an area of ground or water containing explosive mines. **2** a subject, situation, etc., beset with hidden problems.

minelayer (ˈmaɪnˌleɪə) *n* a warship or aircraft designed for the carrying and laying of mines.

miner (ˈmaɪnə) *n* **1** a person who works in a mine. **2** any of various insects or insect larvae that bore into and feed on plant tissues. See also **leaf miner.** **3** *Austral.* any of several honeyeaters.

mineral (ˈmɪnərəl, ˈmɪnrəl) *n* **1** any of a class of naturally occurring solid inorganic substances with a characteristic crystalline form and a homogeneous chemical composition. **2** any inorganic matter. **3** any substance obtained by mining, esp. a metal ore. **4** (*often pl*) *Brit.* short for **mineral water. 5** *Brit.* a soft drink containing carbonated water and flavourings. ◆ *adj* **6** of, relating to, containing, or resembling minerals. [C15: from Med. L *minerāle* (n), from *minerālis* (adj); rel. to *minera* mine, ore, from ?]

mineral. *abbrev.* for mineralogy or mineralogical.

mineralize *or* **mineralise** (ˈmɪnərəˌlaɪz) *vb* **mineralizes, mineralizing, mineralized** *or* **mineralises, mineralising, mineralised.** (*tr*) **1a** to impregnate (organic matter, water, etc.) with a mineral substance. **1b** to convert (such matter) into a mineral; petrify. **2** (of gases, vapours, etc., in magma) to transform (a metal) into an ore.
▸ ˌmineraliˈzation *or* ˌmineraliˈsation *n* ▸ ˈmineralˌizer *or* ˈmineralˌiser *n*

mineralogy (ˌmɪnəˈrælədʒɪ) *n* the branch of geology concerned with the study of minerals.
▸ **mineralogical** (ˌmɪnərəˈlɒdʒɪkˀl) *or* ˌmineraˈlogic *adj* ▸ ˌminerˈalogist *n*

mineral oil *n Brit.* any oil of mineral origin, esp. petroleum.

mineral water *n* water containing dissolved mineral salts or gases, usually having medicinal properties.

mineral wool *n* a fibrous material made by blowing steam or air through molten slag and used for packing and insulation.

miner's right *n Austral.* a licence to prospect for and mine gold, etc.

Minerva ★ (mɪˈnɜːvə) *n* the Roman goddess of wisdom. Greek counterpart: **Athena.**

minestrone (ˌmɪnɪˈstrəʊnɪ) *n* a soup made from a variety of vegetables and pasta. [from It., from *minestrare* to serve]

minesweeper (ˈmaɪnˌswiːpə) *n* a naval vessel equipped to clear mines.
▸ ˈmineˌsweeping *n*

Ming (mɪŋ) *n* **1** the imperial dynasty of China from 1368 to 1644. ◆ *adj* **2** of or relating to Chinese porcelain from the Ming dynasty.

mingle (ˈmɪŋɡˀl) *vb* **mingles, mingling, mingled.** **1** to mix or cause to mix. **2** (*intr; often foll. by with*) to come into close association. [C15: from OE *mengan* to mix]
▸ ˈ**mingler** *n*

Mingus ★ (ˈmɪŋɡəs) *n* **Charles,** known as *Charlie Mingus.* 1922–79, US jazz bass player, composer, and band leader.

mingy (ˈmɪndʒɪ) *adj* **mingier, mingiest.** *Brit. inf.* miserly, stingy, or niggardly. [C20: prob. a blend of MEAN[2] + STINGY[1]]

Minho ★ (ˈmiːɲu) *n* the Portuguese name for the **Miño.**

mini (ˈmɪnɪ) *adj* **1** (of a woman's dress, skirt, etc.) very short; thigh-length. **2** (*prenominal*) small; miniature. ◆ *n, pl* **minis.** **3** something very small of its kind, esp. a small car or a miniskirt.

mini- *combining form.* smaller or shorter than the standard size: *minibus; miniskirt.* [C20: from MINIATURE & MINIMUM]

miniature ('mɪnɪtʃə) *n* **1** a model, copy, or representation on a very small scale. **2** anything that is very small of its kind. **3** a very small painting, esp. a portrait. **4** an illuminated decoration in a manuscript. **5 in miniature.** on a small scale. ◆ *adj* **6** greatly reduced in size, etc. **7** on a small scale; minute. [C16: from It., from Med. L, from *miniāre* to paint red (in illuminating manuscripts), from *minium* red lead]
▸ 'miniaturist *n*

miniaturize or **miniaturise** ('mɪnɪtʃə,raɪz) *vb* **miniaturizes, miniaturizing, miniaturized** or **miniaturises, miniaturising, miniaturised.** (*tr*) to make or construct (something, esp. electronic equipment) on a very small scale; reduce in size.
▸ ,miniaturi'zation or ,miniaturi'sation *n*

minibar ('mɪnɪ,bɑː) *n* a selection of drinks and confectionery provided in a hotel room and charged to the guest's bill if used.

minibus ('mɪnɪ,bʌs) *n* a small bus able to carry approximately ten passengers.

minicab ('mɪnɪ,kæb) *n Brit.* a small saloon car used as a taxi.

minicomputer (,mɪnɪkəm'pjuːtə) *n* a small comparatively cheap digital computer.

minim ('mɪnɪm) *n* **1** a unit of fluid measure equal to one sixtieth of a drachm. It is approximately equal to one drop. Symbol: **M** **2** *Music.* a note having the time value of half a semibreve. **3** a small or insignificant thing. **4** a downward stroke in calligraphy. [C15 (*Music.*): from L *minimus* smallest]

minimal art *n* abstract painting or sculpture in which expressiveness and illusion are minimized by the use of simple geometric shapes, flat colour, and arrangements of ordinary objects.
▸ **minimal artist** *n*

minimalism ('mɪnɪmə,lɪzəm) *n* **1** another name for **minimal art. 2** a type of music based on simple elements and avoiding elaboration or embellishment. **3** design or style in which the simplest and fewest elements are used to create the maximum effect.
▸ 'minimalist *adj, n*

minimax ('mɪnɪ,mæks) *n* **1** *Maths.* the lowest of a set of maximum values. **2** (in game theory, etc.) the procedure of choosing the strategy that least benefits the most disadvantaged member of a group. Cf. **maximin.** [C20: from MINI(MUM) + MAX(IMUM)]

minimize or **minimise** ('mɪnɪ,maɪz) *vb* **minimizes, minimizing, minimized** or **minimises, minimising, minimised.** (*tr*) **1** to reduce to or estimate at the least possible degree or amount. **2** to rank or treat at less than the true worth; belittle.
▸ ,minimi'zation or ,minimi'sation *n* ▸ 'mini,mizer or 'mini,miser *n*

minimum ('mɪnɪməm) *n, pl* **minimums** or **minima** (-mə). **1** the least possible amount, degree, or quantity. **2** the least amount recorded, allowed, or reached. **3** (*modifier*) being the least possible, recorded, allowed, etc.: *minimum age.* ◆ *adj* **4** of or relating to a minimum or minimums. [C17: from L: smallest thing, from *minimus* least]
▸ 'minimal *adj* ▸ 'minimally *adv*

minimum lending rate *n* (in Britain) the minimum rate at which the Bank of England would lend to discount houses between 1971 and 1981, after which it was replaced by the less formal base rate.

minimum wage *n* the lowest wage that an employer is permitted to pay by law or union contract.

mining ('maɪnɪŋ) *n* **1** the act, process, or industry of extracting coal, ores, etc., from the earth. **2** *Mil.* the process of laying mines.

minion ('mɪnjən) *n* **1** a favourite or dependant, esp. a servile or fawning one. **2** a servile agent. [C16: from F *mignon*, from OF *mignot*, of Gaulish origin]

minipill ('mɪnɪ,pɪl) *n* a low-dose oral contraceptive containing progesterone only.

miniseries ('mɪnɪ,sɪərɪːz) *n, pl* **miniseries.** a television programme in several parts that is shown on consecutive days for a short period.

miniskirt ('mɪnɪ,skɜːt) *n* a very short skirt, originally in the 1960s, one at least four inches above the knee. Often shortened to **mini.**

minister ('mɪnɪstə) *n* **1** (esp. in Presbyterian and some Nonconformist Churches) a member of the clergy. **2** a head of a government department. **3** any diplomatic agent accredited to a foreign government or head of state. **4** Also called: **minister plenipotentiary.** another term for **envoy**[1] (sense 1). **5** Also called: **minister resident.** a diplomat ranking after an envoy. **6** a person who attends to the needs of others, esp. in religious matters. **7** a person who acts as the agent or servant of a person or thing; take care (of). **9** (*tr*) *Arch.* to provide; supply. [C13: via OF from L: servant; rel. to *minus* less] ◆ *vb* **8** (*intr*; often foll. by *to*) to attend to the needs (of);

ministerial (,mɪnɪ'stɪərɪəl) *adj* **1** of or relating to a minister of religion or his office. **2** of or relating to a government minister or ministry. **3** (*often cap.*) of or supporting the ministry against the opposition. **4** *Law.* relating to or possessing delegated executive authority. **5** acting as an agent or cause; instrumental.
▸ ,minis'terially *adv*

minister of state *n* **1** (in the British Parliament) a minister, usually below cabinet rank, appointed to assist a senior minister. **2** any government minister.

Minister of the Crown *n Brit.* any Government minister of cabinet rank.

minister plenipotentiary *n, pl* **ministers plenipotentiary.** another term for **envoy**[1] (sense 1).

ministrant ('mɪnɪstrənt) *adj* **1** ministering or serving as a minister. ◆ *n* **2** a person who ministers. [C17: from L *ministrans*, from *ministrāre* to wait upon]

ministration (,mɪnɪ'streɪʃən) *n* **1** the act or an instance of serving or giving aid. **2** the act or an instance of ministering religiously. [C14: from L *ministrātiō*, from *ministrāre* to wait upon]
▸ **ministrative** ('mɪnɪstrətɪv) *adj*

ministry ('mɪnɪstrɪ) *n, pl* **ministries. 1a** the profession or duties of a minister of religion. **1b** the performance of these duties. **2** ministers of religion or government ministers considered collectively. **3** the tenure of a minister. **4a** a government department headed by a minister. **4b** the buildings of such a department. [C14: from L *ministerium* service; see MINISTER]

miniver ('mɪnɪvə) *n* white fur, used in ceremonial costumes. [C13: from OF *menu vair*, from *menu* small + *vair* variegated fur]

mink (mɪŋk) *n, pl* **mink** or **minks. 1** any of several mammals of Europe, Asia, and North America, having slightly webbed feet. **2** their highly valued fur, esp. that of the American mink. **3** a garment made of this, esp. a woman's coat or stole. [C15: from ON]

Minkowski ★ (mɪŋ'kɒfskɪ) *n* **Hermann** ('hɜːmən). 1864–1909, German mathematician, born in Russia. His four-dimensional space-time continuum (1907) was used by Einstein in his general theory of relativity.

Minn. *abbrev.* for Minnesota.

Minna ★ ('mɪnə) *n* a city in W central Nigeria, capital of Niger state. Pop.: 133 600 (1995 est.).

Minneapolis ★ (,mɪnɪ'æpəlɪs) *n* a city in SE Minnesota, on the Mississippi River adjacent to St Paul: the largest city in the state; important centre for the grain trade. Pop.: 354 590 (1994 est.).

Minnelli ★ (mɪ'nɛlɪ) *n* **Liza** ('laɪzə). born 1946, US actress, daughter of Judy Garland. Her films include *Cabaret* (1972).

minneola (,mɪnɪ'əʊlə) *n* a juicy citrus fruit that is a cross between a tangerine and a grapefruit. [C20: ?from *Mineola*, Texas]

minnesinger ('mɪnɪ,sɪŋə) *n* one of the German lyric poets and musicians of the 12th to 14th centuries. [C19: from G *Minnesinger* love-singer]

★ people and places

Minnesota ★ (ˌmɪnɪˈsəʊtə) n 1 a state of the N central US: chief US producer of iron ore. Capital: St Paul. Pop.: 4 657 758 (1996 est.). Area: 218 600 sq. km (84 402 sq. miles). Abbrevs.: **Minn.** or (with zip code) **MN** 2 a river in S Minnesota, flowing southeast and northeast to the Mississippi River near St Paul. Length: 534 km (332 miles).
▶ ˌMinne'sotan adj, n

minnow (ˈmɪnəʊ) n, pl **minnows** or **minnow**. 1 a small slender European freshwater cyprinid fish. 2 a small or insignificant person. [C15: rel. to OE myne minnow]

Miño ★ (Spanish ˈmiɲo) n a river in SW Europe, rising in NW Spain and flowing southwest (as part of the border between Spain and Portugal) to the Atlantic. Length: 338 km (210 miles). Portuguese name: **Minho**.

Minoan (mɪˈnəʊən) adj 1 of or denoting the Bronze Age culture of Crete from about 3000 B.C. to about 1100 B.C. ◆ n 2 a Cretan belonging to the Minoan culture. [C19: after MINOS from the excavations at his supposed palace at Knossos]

minor (ˈmaɪnə) adj 1 lesser or secondary in amount, importance, etc. 2 of or relating to the minority. 3 below the age of legal majority. 4 Music. 4a (of a scale) having a semitone between the second and third and fifth and sixth degrees (**natural minor**). 4b (of a key) based on the minor scale. 4c (postpositive) denoting a specified key based on the minor scale: C minor. 4d (of an interval) reduced by a semitone from the major. 4e (of a chord, esp. a triad) having a minor third above the root. 4f (esp. in jazz) of or relating to a chord built upon a minor triad and containing a minor seventh: a minor ninth. 5 Logic. (of a term or premise) having less generality or scope than another term or proposition. 6 US education. of or relating to an additional secondary subject taken by a student. 7 (immediately postpositive) Brit. the younger or junior: sometimes used after the surname of a schoolboy if he has an older brother in the same school. ◆ n 8 a person or thing that is lesser or secondary. 9 a person below the age of legal majority. 10 US & Canad. education. a subsidiary subject. 11 Music. a minor key, chord, mode, or scale. 12 Logic. a minor term or premise. ◆ vb 13 (intr; usually foll. by in) US education. to take a minor. [C13: from L: less, smaller]

minor axis n the shorter or shortest axis of an ellipse or ellipsoid.

Minorca ★ (mɪˈnɔːkə) n an island in the W Mediterranean, northeast of Majorca: the second largest of the Balearic Islands. Chief town: Mahón. Pop.: 55 500 (1985). Area: 702 sq. km (271 sq. miles). Spanish name: **Menorca**.
▶ Mi'norcan adj, n

minority (maɪˈnɒrɪtɪ, mɪ-) n, pl **minorities**. 1 the smaller of two parts, factions, or groups. 2 a group that is different racially, politically, etc., from a larger group of which it is a part. 3a the state of being a minor. 3b the period during which a person is below legal age. 4 (modifier) relating to or being a minority: a minority opinion. [C16: from Med. L minōritās, from L MINOR]

minor league n US & Canad. any professional league in baseball other than a major league.

minor orders pl n RC Church. the four lower degrees of holy orders, namely porter, exorcist, lector, and acolyte.

minor premise n Logic. the premise of a syllogism containing the subject of its conclusion.

minor term n Logic. the subject of the conclusion of a syllogism.

Minos ★ (ˈmaɪnɒs) n Greek myth. a king of Crete for whom Daedalus built the Labyrinth to contain the Minotaur.

Minotaur ★ (ˈmaɪnətɔː) n Greek myth. a monster with the head of a bull and the body of a man. It was kept in the Labyrinth in Crete, feeding on human flesh, until destroyed by Theseus. [C14: via L from Gk Minōtauros, from MINOS + tauros bull]

Minsk ★ (mɪnsk) n the capital of Belarus: an industrial city and an educational and cultural centre, with a university (1921). Pop.: 1 700 000 (1996 est.).

minster (ˈmɪnstə) n Brit. any of certain cathedrals and large churches, usually originally connected to a monastery. [OE mynster, prob. from Vulgar L monisterium (unattested), var. of Church L monastērium MONASTERY]

minstrel (ˈmɪnstrəl) n 1 a medieval musician who performed songs or recited poetry with instrumental accompaniment. 2 a performer in a minstrel show. 3 Arch. or poetic. any poet, musician, or singer. [C13: from OF menestral, from LL ministeriālis an official, from L MINISTER]

minstrel show n a theatrical entertainment consisting of songs, dances, etc., performed by actors wearing black face make-up.

minstrelsy (ˈmɪnstrəlsɪ) n, pl **minstrelsies**. 1 the art of a minstrel. 2 the poems, music, or songs of a minstrel. 3 a troupe of minstrels.

mint[1] (mɪnt) n 1 any N temperate plant of a genus having aromatic leaves. The leaves of some species are used for seasoning and flavouring. See also **peppermint**, **spearmint**. 2 a sweet flavoured with mint. [OE minte, from L mentha, from Gk minthē]
▶ 'minty adj

mint[2] (mɪnt) n 1 a place where money is coined by governmental authority. 2 a very large amount of money. ◆ adj 3 (of coins, postage stamps, etc.) in perfect condition as issued. 4 **in mint condition**. in perfect condition; as if new. ◆ vb 5 to make (coins) by stamping metal. 6 (tr) to invent (esp. phrases or words). [OE mynet coin, from L monēta money, mint, from the temple of Juno Monēta, used as a mint in ancient Rome]
▶ 'minter n

mintage (ˈmɪntɪdʒ) n 1 the process of minting. 2 the money minted. 3 a fee paid for minting a coin. 4 an official impression stamped on a coin.

mint julep n Chiefly US. a long drink consisting of bourbon whiskey, crushed ice, sugar, and sprigs of mint.

minuend (ˈmɪnjʊˌɛnd) n the number from which another number, the **subtrahend**, is to be subtracted. [C18: from L minuendus (numerus) (the number) to be diminished]

minuet (ˌmɪnjʊˈɛt) n 1 a stately court dance of the 17th and 18th centuries in triple time. 2 a piece of music composed for or in the rhythm of this dance. [C17: from F menuet dainty, from menu small]

minus (ˈmaɪnəs) prep 1 reduced by the subtraction of: four minus two (written 4 − 2). 2 Inf. deprived of; lacking: minus the trimmings. ◆ adj 3a indicating or involving subtraction: a minus sign. 3b Also: **negative**. having a value or designating a quantity less than zero: a minus number. 4 involving a disadvantage, harm, etc.: a minus factor. 5 (postpositive) Education. slightly below the standard of a particular grade: a B minus. 6 denoting a negative electric charge. ◆ n 7 short for **minus sign**. 8 a negative quantity. 9 a disadvantage, loss, or deficit. 10 Inf. something detrimental or negative. ◆ Mathematical symbol: − [C15: from L, neuter of MINOR]

minuscule (ˈmɪnəˌskjuːl) n 1 a lower-case letter. 2 writing using such letters. 3 a small cursive 7th-century style of lettering. ◆ adj 4 relating to, printed in, or written in small letters. Cf. **majuscule**. 5 very small. 6 (of letters) lower-case. [C18: from F, from L (littera) minuscula very small (letter), dim. of MINOR]
▶ minuscular (mɪˈnʌskjʊlə) adj

minus sign n the symbol −, indicating subtraction or a negative quantity.

minute[1] (ˈmɪnɪt) n 1 a period of time equal to 60 seconds; one sixtieth of an hour. 2 Also called: **minute of arc**. a unit of angular measure equal to one sixtieth of a degree. Symbol: ′. 3 any very short period of time; moment. 4 a short note or memorandum. 5 the distance that can be travelled in a minute: it's only two minutes away. 6 **up to the minute** (up-to-the-minute when prenominal). the very latest or newest. ◆ vb **minutes**, **minuting**, **minuted**. (tr) 7 to record in minutes: to minute a meeting. 8 to time in terms of minutes. ◆ See also **minutes**. [C14: from OF, from Med. L minūta, n. use of L minūtus MINUTE[2]]
▶ minutely (ˈmɪnɪtlɪ) adv

minute[2] (maɪˈnjuːt) adj 1 very small; diminutive; tiny. 2

unimportant; petty. **3** precise or detailed. [C15: from L *minūtus*, p.p. of *minuere* to diminish]
▸ mi'nuteness *n* ▸ mi'nutely *adv*

minute gun ('mɪnɪt) *n* a gun fired at one-minute intervals as a sign of distress or mourning.

minute hand ('mɪnɪt) *n* the pointer on a timepiece that indicates minutes.

Minuteman ('mɪnɪt,mæn) *n, pl* **Minutemen. 1** (*sometimes not cap.*) (in the War of American Independence) a colonial militiaman who promised to be ready to fight at one minute's notice. **2** a US three-stage intercontinental ballistic missile.

minutes ('mɪnɪts) *pl n* an official record of the proceedings of a meeting, conference, etc.

minute steak ('mɪnɪt) *n* a small piece of steak that can be cooked quickly.

minutiae (mɪ'njuːʃɪˌiː) *pl n, sing* **minutia** (-ʃɪə). small, precise, or trifling details. [C18: pl of LL *minūtia* smallness, from L *minūtus* MINUTE²]

minx (mɪŋks) *n* a bold, flirtatious, or scheming woman. [C16: from ?]

Minya ★ ('mɪnjə) *n* See **El Minya.**

Miocene ('maɪə,siːn) *adj* **1** of or denoting the fourth epoch of the Tertiary period. ◆ *n* **2** the. this epoch or rock series. [C19: Gk *meiōn* less + -CENE]

miosis *or* **myosis** (maɪ'əʊsɪs) *n, pl* **mioses** (-siːz) *or* **myoses. 1** excessive contraction of the pupil of the eye. **2** a variant spelling of **meiosis** (sense 1). [C20: from Gk *muein* to shut the eyes + -OSIS]
▸ **miotic** *or* **myotic** (maɪ'ɒtɪk) *adj, n*

MIP *abbrev. for:* **1** monthly investment plan. **2** maximum investment plan: an endowment assurance policy designed to produce maximum profits.

Miquelon ★ ('miːkə,lɒn; *French* miklɔ̃) *n* a group of islands in the French territory of **Saint Pierre and Miquelon.**

Mir (mɪə) *n* the Russian (formerly Soviet) orbiting space station. [Russian]

Mirabeau ★ (*French* mirabo) *n* **Comte de,** title of *Honoré-Gabriel Riqueti.* 1749–91, French Revolutionary politician.

miracle ('mɪrək³l) *n* **1** an event contrary to the laws of nature and attributed to a supernatural cause. **2** any amazing or wonderful event. **3** a marvellous example of something: *a miracle of engineering.* **4** short for **miracle play. 5** (*modifier*) being or seeming a miracle: *a miracle cure.* [C12: from L *mīrāculum,* from *mīrārī* to wonder at]

miracle play *n* a medieval play based on a biblical story or the life of a saint. Cf. **mystery play.**

miraculous (mɪ'rækjʊləs) *adj* **1** of, like, or caused by a miracle; marvellous. **2** surprising. **3** having the power to work miracles.
▸ mi'raculously *adv* ▸ mi'raculousness *n*

Miraflores ★ (ˌmɪrə'flɔːrəs; *Spanish* mira'flores) *n* **Lake.** an artificial lake in Panama, in the S Canal Zone of the Panama Canal.

mirage (mɪ'rɑːʒ) *n* **1** an image of a distant object or sheet of water, often inverted or distorted, caused by atmospheric refraction by hot air. **2** something illusory. [C19: from F, from (*se*) *mirer* to be reflected]

mire ('maɪə) *n* **1** a boggy or marshy area. **2** mud, muck, or dirt. ◆ *vb* **mires, miring, mired. 3** to sink or cause to sink in a mire. **4** (*tr*) to make dirty or muddy. **5** (*tr*) to involve, esp. in difficulties. [C14: from ON *mȳrr*]

mirepoix (mɪə'pwɑː) *n* a mixture of sautéed root vegetables used as a base for braising meat or for various sauces. [F, prob. after Duke of *Mirepoix,* 18th-cent. F general]

Miriam ★ ('mɪrɪəm) *n Old Testament.* the sister of Moses and Aaron. (Numbers 12:1–15). Douay name: **Mary.**

mirk (mɜːk) *n* a variant spelling of **murk.**
▸ 'mirky *adj* ▸ 'mirkily *adv* ▸ 'mirkiness *n*

Miró ★ (*Spanish* mi'ro) *n* **Joan** (xwan). 1893–1983, Spanish surrealist painter.

mirror ('mɪrə) *n* **1** a surface, such as polished metal or glass coated with a metal film, that reflects an image of an object placed in front of it. **2** such a reflecting surface mounted in a frame. **3** any reflecting surface. **4** a thing that reflects or depicts something else. ◆ *vb* **5** (*tr*) to reflect, represent, or depict faithfully: *he mirrors his teacher's ideals.* [C13: from OF from *mirer* to look at, from L *mīrārī* to wonder at]

mirror ball *n* a large revolving ball covered with small pieces of mirror glass so that it reflects light in changing patterns: used in discos and ballrooms.

mirror carp *n* a variety of carp with a smooth shiny body surface.

mirror image *n* **1** an image as observed in a mirror. **2** an object that corresponds to another but has left and right reversed as if seen in a mirror.

mirror writing *n* backward writing that forms a mirror image of normal writing.

mirth (mɜːθ) *n* laughter, gaiety, or merriment. [OE *myrgth*]
▸ 'mirthful *adj* ▸ 'mirthfulness *n* ▸ 'mirthless *adj* ▸ 'mirthlessness *n*

MIRV (mɜːv) *n acronym for* multiple independently targeted re-entry vehicle: a missile that has several warheads, each one being directed to a different enemy target.

mis- *prefix* **1** wrong or bad; wrongly or badly: *misunderstanding; misfortune; mistreat; mislead.* **2** lack of; not: *mistrust.* [OE *mis(se)*-]

misadventure (ˌmɪsəd'vɛntʃə) *n* **1** an unlucky event; misfortune. **2** *Law.* accidental death not due to crime or negligence.

misalliance (ˌmɪsə'laɪəns) *n* an unsuitable alliance or marriage.
▸ ˌmisal'ly *vb*

misanthrope ('mɪzən,θrəʊp) *or* **misanthropist** (mɪ'zænθrəpɪst) *n* a person who dislikes or distrusts other people or mankind in general. [C17: from Gk *mīsanthrōpos,* from *mīsos* hatred + *anthrōpos* man]
▸ **misanthropic** (ˌmɪzən'θrɒpɪk) *or* ˌmisan'thropical *adj* ▸ mi'santhropy (mɪ'zænθrəpɪ) *n*

misapply (ˌmɪsə'plaɪ) *vb* **misapplies, misapplying, misapplied.** (*tr*) **1** to apply wrongly or badly. **2** another word for **misappropriate.**
▸ **misapplication** (ˌmɪsæplɪ'keɪʃən) *n*

misapprehend (ˌmɪsæprɪ'hɛnd) *vb* (*tr*) to misunderstand.
▸ **misapprehension** (ˌmɪsæprɪ'hɛnʃən) *n* ▸ ˌmisappre'hensive *adj* ▸ ˌmisappre'hensiveness *n*

misappropriate (ˌmɪsə'prəʊprɪ,eɪt) *vb* **misappropriates, misappropriating, misappropriated.** (*tr*) to appropriate for a wrong or dishonest use; embezzle or steal.
▸ ˌmisap,propri'ation *n*

misbecome (ˌmɪsbɪ'kʌm) *vb* **misbecomes, misbecoming, misbecame, misbecome.** (*tr*) to be unbecoming to or unsuitable for.

misbegotten (ˌmɪsbɪ'gɒt³n) *adj* **1** unlawfully obtained. **2** badly conceived, planned, or designed. **3** *Literary and dialect.* illegitimate; bastard.

misbehave (ˌmɪsbɪ'heɪv) *vb* **misbehaves, misbehaving, misbehaved.** to behave (oneself) badly.
▸ ˌmisbe'haver *n* ▸ misbehaviour *or US* **misbehavior** (ˌmɪsbɪ'heɪvjə) *n*

misbelief (ˌmɪsbɪ'liːf) *n* a false or unorthodox belief.
▸ ˌmisbe'liever *n*

misc. *abbrev. for:* **1** miscellaneous. **2** miscellany.

miscalculate (ˌmɪs'kælkjʊ,leɪt) *vb* **miscalculates, miscalculating, miscalculated.** (*tr*) to calculate wrongly.
▸ ˌmiscalcu'lation *n*

miscall (ˌmɪs'kɔːl) *vb* (*tr*) **1** to call by the wrong name. **2** *Dialect.* to abuse or malign.
▸ ˌmis'caller *n*

miscarriage (mɪs'kærɪdʒ) *n* **1** (*also* 'mɪskær-). spontaneous expulsion of a fetus from the womb, esp. prior to the 20th week of pregnancy. **2** an act of mismanagement or failure: *a miscarriage of justice.* **3** *Brit.* the failure of freight to reach its destination.

miscarry (mɪs'kærɪ) *vb* **miscarries, miscarrying, miscarried.** (*intr*) **1** to expel a fetus prematurely from the womb;

abort. **2** to fail. **3** *Brit.* (of freight, mail, etc.) to fail to reach a destination.

miscast (ˌmɪsˈkɑːst) *vb* **miscasts, miscasting, miscast.** (*tr*) **1** to cast badly. **2** (*often passive*) **2a** to cast (a role) in (a play, film, etc.) inappropriately: *Falstaff was miscast.* **2b** to assign an inappropriate role to: *he was miscast as Othello.*

miscegenation (ˌmɪsɪdʒɪˈneɪʃən) *n* interbreeding of races, esp. where differences of pigmentation are involved. [C19: from L *miscēre* to mingle + *genus* race]

miscellanea (ˌmɪsəˈleɪnɪə) *pl n* a collection of miscellaneous items, esp. literary works. [C16: from L: neuter pl of *miscellāneus* MISCELLANEOUS]

miscellaneous (ˌmɪsəˈleɪnɪəs) *adj* **1** composed of or containing a variety of things; mixed. **2** having varied capabilities, sides, etc. [C17: from L *miscellāneus*, from *miscellus* mixed, from *miscēre* to mix]
  ▶ ˌmiscelˈlaneously *adv* ▶ ˌmiscelˈlaneousness *n*

miscellany (mɪˈsɛlənɪ; *US* ˈmɪsəˌleɪnɪ) *n, pl* **miscellanies. 1** a mixed assortment of items. **2** (*sometimes pl*) a miscellaneous collection of items, esp. essays, poems, etc. [C16: from F *miscellanées* (pl) MISCELLANEA]
  ▶ **miscellanist** (mɪˈsɛlənɪst) *n*

mischance (mɪsˈtʃɑːns) *n* **1** bad luck. **2** a stroke of bad luck.

mischief (ˈmɪstʃɪf) *n* **1** wayward but not malicious behaviour, usually of children, that causes trouble, irritation, etc. **2** a playful inclination to behave in this way or to tease or disturb. **3** injury or harm caused by a person or thing. **4** a person, esp. a child, who is mischievous. **5** a source of trouble, difficulty, etc. [C13: from OF *meschief*, from *meschever* to meet with calamity; from *mes-* MIS- + *chever*, from *chef* end]

mischievous (ˈmɪstʃɪvəs) *adj* **1** inclined to acts of mischief. **2** teasing; slightly malicious. **3** causing or intended to cause harm.
  ▶ ˈmischievously *adv* ▶ ˈmischievousness *n*

miscible (ˈmɪsɪbʲl) *adj* capable of mixing: *miscible with water.* [C16: from Med. L *miscibilis*, from L *miscēre* to mix]
  ▶ ˌmisciˈbility *n*

misconceive (ˌmɪskənˈsiːv) *vb* **misconceives, misconceiving, misconceived.** to have the wrong idea; fail to understand.
  ▶ ˌmisconˈceiver *n*

misconception (ˌmɪskənˈsɛpʃən) *n* a false or mistaken view, opinion, or attitude.

misconduct *n* (mɪsˈkɒndʌkt). **1** behaviour, such as adultery or professional negligence, that is regarded as immoral or unethical. ♦ *vb* (ˌmɪskənˈdʌkt). (*tr*) **2** to conduct (oneself) in such a way. **3** to manage (something) badly.

misconstrue (ˌmɪskənˈstruː) *vb* **misconstrues, misconstruing, misconstrued.** (*tr*) to interpret mistakenly.
  ▶ ˌmisconˈstruction *n*

miscreant (ˈmɪskrɪənt) *n* **1** a wrongdoer or villain. **2** *Arch.* an unbeliever or heretic. ♦ *adj* **3** evil or villainous. **4** *Arch.* unbelieving or heretical. [C14: from OF *mescreant* unbelieving, from *mes-* MIS- + *creant*, ult. from L *credere* to believe]

miscue (ˌmɪsˈkjuː) *n* **1** *Billiards, etc.* a faulty stroke in which the cue tip slips off the cue ball or misses it. **2** *Inf.* a blunder or mistake. ♦ *vb* **miscues, miscuing, miscued.** (*intr*) **3** *Billiards.* to make a miscue. **4** *Theatre.* to fail to answer one's cue.

miscue analysis *n Brit. education.* analysis of the errors a pupil makes while reading.

misdate (mɪsˈdeɪt) *vb* **misdates, misdating, misdated.** (*tr*) to date (a letter, event, etc.) wrongly.

misdeal (ˌmɪsˈdiːl) *vb* **misdeals, misdealing, misdealt. 1** (*intr*) to deal out cards incorrectly. ♦ *n* **2** a faulty deal.
  ▶ ˌmisˈdealer *n*

misdeed (ˌmɪsˈdiːd) *n* an evil or illegal action.

misdemean (ˌmɪsdɪˈmiːn) *vb* a rare word for **misbehave.**

misdemeanour *or US* **misdemeanor** (ˌmɪsdɪˈmiːnə) *n* **1** *Criminal law.* (formerly) an offence generally less heinous than a felony. **2** any minor offence or transgression.

misdirect (ˌmɪsdɪˈrɛkt) *vb* (*tr*) **1** to give (a person) wrong directions or instructions. **2** to address (a letter, parcel, etc.) wrongly.
  ▶ ˌmisdiˈrection *n*

misdoubt (mɪsˈdaʊt) *vb* an archaic word for **doubt** or **suspect.**

mise en scène *French.* (miz ɑ̃ sɛn) *n* **1a** the arrangement of properties, scenery, etc., in a play. **1b** the objects so arranged; stage setting. **2** the environment of an event.

Miseno ★ (*Italian* miˈzɛːno) *n* a cape in SW Italy, on the N shore of the Bay of Naples: remains of the town of **Misenum,** a naval base constructed by Agrippa in 31 B.C.

miser (ˈmaɪzə) *n* **1** a person who hoards money or possessions, often living miserably. **2** a selfish person. [C16: from L: wretched]

miserable (ˈmɪzərəbʲl) *adj* **1** unhappy or depressed; wretched. **2** causing misery, discomfort, etc.: *a miserable life.* **3** contemptible: *a miserable villain.* **4** sordid or squalid: *miserable living conditions.* **5** mean; stingy. [C16: from OF, from L *miserābilis*, from *miserārī* to pity, from *miser* wretched]
  ▶ ˈmiserableness *n* ▶ ˈmiserably *adv*

misère (mɪˈzɛə) *n* **1** a call in solo whist, etc. declaring a hand that will win no tricks. **2** a hand that will win no tricks. [C19: from F: misery]

Miserere (ˌmɪzəˈrɛərɪ, -ˈrɪərɪ) *n* the 51st psalm, the Latin version of which begins "Miserere mei, Deus" ("Have mercy on me, O God").

misericord *or* **misericorde** (mɪˈzɛrɪˌkɔːd) *n* **1** a ledge projecting from the underside of the hinged seat of a choir stall in a church, on which the occupant can support himself while standing. **2** *Christianity.* **2a** a relaxation of certain monastic rules for infirm or aged monks or nuns. **2b** a monastery or room where this can be enjoyed. **3** a medieval dagger used to give the death stroke to a wounded foe. [C14: from OF, from L *misericordia* compassion, from *miserēre* to pity + *cor* heart]

miserly (ˈmaɪzəlɪ) *adj* of or resembling a miser; avaricious.
  ▶ ˈmiserliness *n*

misery (ˈmɪzərɪ) *n, pl* **miseries. 1** intense unhappiness, suffering, etc. **2** a cause of such unhappiness, etc. **3** squalid or poverty-stricken conditions. **4** *Brit. inf.* a person who is habitually depressed: *he is such a misery.* [C14: via Anglo-Norman from L *miseria*, from *miser* wretched]

misfeasance (mɪsˈfiːzəns) *n Law.* the improper performance of an act that is lawful in itself. Cf. **malfeasance, nonfeasance.** [C16: from OF *mesfaisance*, from *mesfaire* to perform misdeeds]

misfile (ˌmɪsˈfaɪl) *vb* **misfiles, misfiling, misfiled.** to file (papers, records, etc.) wrongly.

misfire (ˌmɪsˈfaɪə) *vb* **misfires, misfiring, misfired.** (*intr*) **1** (of a firearm or its projectile) to fail to fire or explode as expected. **2** (of a motor engine or vehicle, etc.) to fail to fire at the correct time. **3** to fail to operate or occur as intended. ♦ *n* **4** the act or an instance of misfiring.

misfit *n* (ˈmɪsˌfɪt). **1** a person not suited to a particular social environment. **2** something that does not fit or fits badly. ♦ *vb* (ˌmɪsˈfɪt). **misfits, misfitting, misfitted.** (*intr*) **3** to fail to fit or be fitted.

misfortune (mɪsˈfɔːtʃən) *n* **1** evil fortune; bad luck. **2** an unfortunate or disastrous event.

misgive (mɪsˈgɪv) *vb* **misgives, misgiving, misgave, misgiven.** to make or be apprehensive or suspicious.

misgiving (mɪsˈgɪvɪŋ) *n* (*often pl*) a feeling of uncertainty, apprehension, or doubt.

misguide (ˌmɪsˈgaɪd) *vb* **misguides, misguiding, misguided.** (*tr*) to guide or direct wrongly or badly.

misguided (ˌmɪsˈgaɪdɪd) *adj* foolish or unreasonable, esp. in action or behaviour.
  ▶ ˌmisˈguidedly *adv*

mishandle (ˌmɪsˈhændʲl) *vb* **mishandles, mishandling, mishandled.** (*tr*) to handle or treat badly or inefficiently.

mishap (ˈmɪshæp) *n* **1** an unfortunate accident. **2** bad luck.

Mishima ★ ('mɪʃɪmə) n Yukio ('juːkɪəu). 1925–70, Japanese writer. He committed harakiri in protest at the decline of traditional Japanese values.

mishit Sport. ◆ n ('mɪs,hɪt). **1** a faulty shot or stroke. ◆ vb (,mɪs'hɪt), **mishits, mishitting, mishit. 2** to hit (a ball) with a faulty stroke.

mishmash ('mɪʃ,mæʃ) n a confused collection or mixture. [C15: reduplication of MASH]

Mishna ('mɪʃnə) n, pl **Mishnayoth** (mɪʃ'nɑːjəut). Judaism. a compilation of precepts collected in the late second century A.D. It forms the earlier part of the Talmud. [C17: from Heb., from shānāh to repeat]
▶ **Mishnaic** (mɪʃ'neɪɪk) or **'Mishnic** adj

misinform (,mɪsɪn'fɔːm) vb (tr) to give incorrect information to.
▶ **misinformation** (,mɪsɪnfə'meɪʃən) n

misinterpret (,mɪsɪn'tɜːprɪt) vb (tr) to interpret badly, misleadingly, or incorrectly.
▶ ,misin'terpre'tation n ▶ ,misin'terpreter n

misjudge (mɪs'dʒʌdʒ) vb **misjudges, misjudging, misjudged.** to judge (a person or persons) wrongly or unfairly.
▶ **mis'judger** n ▶ **mis'judgment** or **mis'judgement** n

Miskolc ★ (Hungarian 'mɪʃkolts) n a city in NE Hungary: the second most important industrial centre in Hungary; iron and steel industries. Pop.: 178 000 (1997 est.).

mislay (mɪs'leɪ) vb **mislays, mislaying, mislaid.** (tr) **1** to lose (something) temporarily, esp. by forgetting where it is. **2** to lay (something) badly.

mislead (mɪs'liːd) vb **misleads, misleading, misled.** (tr) **1** to give false or confusing information to. **2** to lead or guide in the wrong direction.
▶ **mis'leader** n ▶ **mis'leading** adj

mismarriage (mɪs'mærɪdʒ) n a marriage to an unsuitable partner.

mismatch (,mɪs'mætʃ) vb **1** to match badly, esp. in marriage. ◆ n **2** a bad match.

misname (mɪs'neɪm) vb **misnames, misnaming, misnamed.** (tr) to call by a wrong or inappropriate name.

misnomer (,mɪs'nəumə) n **1** an incorrect or unsuitable name for a person or thing. **2** the act of referring to a person by the wrong name. [C15: via Anglo-Norman from OF mesnommer to misname, from L nōmināre to call by name]

miso- or before a vowel **mis-** combining form. indicating hatred: misogyny. [from Gk misos hatred]

misogamy (mɪ'sɒɡəmɪ, maɪ-) n hatred of marriage.
▶ mi'sogamist n

misogyny (mɪ'sɒdʒɪnɪ, maɪ-) n hatred of women. [C17: from Gk, from MISO- + gunē woman]
▶ mi'sogynist n ▶ mi'sogynous or mi,sogy'nistic adj

misplace (,mɪs'pleɪs) vb **misplaces, misplacing, misplaced.** (tr) **1** to put (something) in the wrong place, esp. to lose (something) temporarily by forgetting where it was placed. **2** (often passive) to bestow (trust, affection, etc.) unadvisedly.
▶ ,mis'placement n

misplaced modifier n Grammar. a participle intended to modify a noun but having the wrong grammatical relationship to it, for example having left in the sentence Having left Europe for good, Peter's future seemed bleak.

misplay (,mɪs'pleɪ) vb **1** (tr) to play badly or wrongly in games or sports. ◆ n **2** a wrong or unskilful play.

misprint n ('mɪs,prɪnt). **1** an error in printing, made through damaged type, careless reading, etc. ◆ vb (,mɪs'prɪnt). **2** (tr) to print (a letter) incorrectly.

misprision[1] (mɪs'prɪʒən) n **a** a failure to inform the authorities of the commission of an act of treason. **b** the deliberate concealment of the commission of a felony. [C15: via Anglo-F from OF mesprision error, from mesprendre to mistake, from mes- MIS- + prendre to take]

misprision[2] (mɪs'prɪʒən) n Arch. **1** contempt. **2** failure to appreciate the value of something. [C16: from MISPRIZE]

misprize or **misprise** (mɪs'praɪz) vb **misprizes, misprizing, misprized** or **misprises, misprising, misprised.** to fail to appreciate the value of; disparage. [C15: from OF mesprisier, from mes- MIS- + prisier to PRIZE[2]]

mispronounce (,mɪsprə'nauns) vb **mispronounces, mispronouncing, mispronounced.** to pronounce (a word) wrongly.
▶ **mispronunciation** (,mɪsprə,nʌnsɪ'eɪʃən) n

misproportion (,mɪsprə'pɔːʃən) n a lack of due proportion.

misquote (,mɪs'kwəut) vb **misquotes, misquoting, misquoted.** to quote (a text, speech, etc.) inaccurately.
▶ ,misquo'tation n

misread (,mɪs'riːd) vb **misreads, misreading, misread** (-'rɛd). (tr) **1** to read incorrectly. **2** to misinterpret.

misrepresent (,mɪsrɛprɪ'zɛnt) vb (tr) to represent wrongly or inaccurately.
▶ ,misrepresen'tation n ▶ ,misrepre'sentative adj

misrule (,mɪs'ruːl) vb **misrules, misruling, misruled. 1** (tr) to govern inefficiently or without justice. ◆ n **2** inefficient or unjust government. **3** disorder.

miss[1] (mɪs) vb **1** to fail to reach, hit, meet, find, or attain (some aim, target, etc.). **2** (tr) to fail to attend or be present for: to miss an appointment. **3** (tr) to fail to see, hear, understand, or perceive. **4** (tr) to lose, overlook, or fail to take advantage of: to miss an opportunity. **5** (tr) to leave out; omit: to miss an entry in a list. **6** (tr) to discover or regret the loss or absence of: she missed him. **7** (tr) to escape or avoid (something, esp. a danger), usually narrowly: he missed death by inches. ◆ n **8** a failure to reach, hit, etc. **9 give (something) a miss.** Inf. to avoid (something): give the pudding a miss. ◆ See also **miss out.** [OE missan (meaning: to fail to hit)]

miss[2] (mɪs) n Inf. an unmarried woman or girl. [C17: from MISTRESS]

Miss (mɪs) n a title of an unmarried woman or girl, usually used before the surname or sometimes alone in direct address. [C17: shortened from MISTRESS]

Miss. abbrev. for Mississippi.

missal ('mɪsˀl) n RC Church. a book containing the prayers, rites, etc., of the Masses for a complete year. [C14: from Church L missale (n), from missālis concerning the MASS]

misshape vb (,mɪs'ʃeɪp), **misshapes, misshaping, misshaped; misshaped** or **misshapen. 1** (tr) to shape badly; deform. ◆ n ('mɪs,ʃeɪp). **2** something that is badly shaped.

misshapen (,mɪs'ʃeɪpˀn) adj badly shaped; deformed.
▶ ,mis'shapenness n

missile ('mɪsaɪl) n **1** any object or weapon that is thrown at a target or shot from an engine, gun, etc. **2** a rocket-propelled weapon that flies either in a fixed trajectory (**ballistic missile**) or in a trajectory controlled during flight (**guided missile**). [C17: from L missilis, from mittere to send]

missilery or **missilry** ('mɪsaɪlrɪ) n **1** missiles collectively. **2** the design, operation, or study of missiles.

missing ('mɪsɪŋ) adj **1** not present; absent or lost. **2** not able to be traced and not known to be dead: nine men were missing after the attack. **3 go missing.** to become lost or disappear.

missing link n **1** (sometimes cap.; usually preceded by the) a hypothetical extinct animal, formerly thought to be intermediate between the anthropoid apes and man. **2** any missing section or part in a series.

mission ('mɪʃən) n **1** a specific task or duty assigned to a person or group of people. **2** a person's vocation (often in **mission in life**). **3** a group of persons representing or working for a particular country, business, etc., in a foreign country. **4** a special embassy sent to a foreign country for a specific purpose. **5a** a group of people sent by a religious body, esp. a Christian church, to a foreign country to do religious and social work. **5b** the campaign undertaken by such a group. **6a** a building in which missionary work is performed. **6b** the area assigned to a particular missionary. **7** the dispatch of aircraft or spacecraft to achieve a particular task. **8** a charitable centre that offers shelter or aid to the destitute or underprivileged. **9** (modifier) of or relating to an ecclesiastical mission: a mission station. ◆ vb **10** (tr) to direct a mission to or establish a mission in (a given region). [C16: from L missiō, from mittere to send]

missionary ('mɪʃənərɪ) *n, pl* **missionaries. 1** a member of a religious mission. ◆ *adj* **2** of or relating to missionaries: *missionary work.* **3** resulting from a desire to convert people to one's own beliefs: *missionary zeal.*

missionary position *n Inf.* a position for sexual intercourse in which the man lies on top of the woman and they are face to face. [C20: from the belief that missionaries advocated this as the proper position to primitive peoples among whom it was unknown]

Missionary Ridge ★ *n* a ridge in NW Georgia and SE Tennessee: site of a battle (1863) during the Civil War: Northern victory leading to the campaign in Georgia.

mission statement *n* an official statement of the aims and objectives of a business or other organization.

Mississauga ★ (ˌmɪsə'sɔːgə) *n* a town in SE Ontario: a SW suburb of Toronto. Pop.: 463 388 (1991).

Mississippi ★ (ˌmɪsɪ'sɪpɪ) *n* **1** a state of the southeastern US, on the Gulf of Mexico: consists of a largely forested undulating plain, with swampy regions in the northwest and on the coast, the Mississippi river forming the W border; cotton, rice, and oil. Capital: Jackson. Pop.: 2 716 115 (1996 est.). Area: 122 496 sq. km (47 296 sq. miles). Abbrevs.: **Miss.** or (with zip code) **MS 2.** a river in the central US, rising in NW Minnesota and flowing generally south to the Gulf of Mexico through several mouths, known as the Passes: the second longest river in North America (after its tributary, the Missouri), with the third largest drainage basin in the world (after the Amazon and the Congo). Length: 3780 km (2348 miles).

Mississippian (ˌmɪsɪ'sɪpɪən) *adj* **1.** of or relating to the state of Mississippi, or the Mississippi river. **2** (in North America) of or denoting the lower of two subdivisions of the Carboniferous period (see also **Pennsylvanian** (sense 2)). ◆ *n* **3** an inhabitant or native of the state of Mississippi. **4 the.** the Mississippian period or rock system.

missive ('mɪsɪv) *n* **1** a formal or official letter. **2** a formal word for **letter.** [C15: from Med. L *missivus*, from *mittere* to send]

Missolonghi (ˌmɪsə'lɒŋgɪ) or **Mesolonghi** ★ *n* a town in W Greece, near the Gulf of Patras: famous for its defence against the Turks in 1822–23 and 1825–26 and for its association with Lord Byron, who died here in 1824. Pop.: 11 275 (1981). Modern Greek name: **Mesolóngion.**

Missouri ★ (mɪ'zuərɪ) *n* **1** a state of the central US: consists of rolling prairies in the north, the Ozark Mountains in the southeast, and part of the Mississippi flood plain in the southeast, with the Mississippi forming the E border; chief US producer of lead and barytes. Capital: Jefferson City. Pop.: 5 358 692 (1996 est.). Area: 178 699 sq. km (68 995 sq. miles). Abbrevs.: **Mo.** or (with zip code) **MO 2.** a river in the W and central US, rising in SW Montana: flows north, east, and southeast to join the Mississippi above St Louis; the longest river in North America; chief tributary of the Mississippi. Length: 3970 km (2466 miles).

▶ **Mis'sourian** *n, adj*

miss out *vb* (adv) **1** (*tr*) to leave out; overlook. **2** (*intr*; often foll. by *on*) to fail to experience: *you missed out on the celebrations.*

misspell (ˌmɪs'spel) *vb* **misspells, misspelling, misspelt** or **misspelled.** to spell (a word or words) wrongly.

misspelling (ˌmɪs'spelɪŋ) *n* a wrong spelling.

misspend (ˌmɪs'spend) *vb* **misspends, misspending, misspent.** to spend thoughtlessly or wastefully.

misstep (ˌmɪs'step) *n* **1** a false step. **2** an error.

missus or **missis** ('mɪsɪz, -ɪs) *n* **1** (usually preceded by *the*) *Inf.* one's wife or the wife of the person addressed or referred to. **2** an informal term of address for a woman. [C19: spoken version of MISTRESS]

missy ('mɪsɪ) *n, pl* **missies.** *Inf.* an affectionate or disparaging form of address to a young girl.

mist (mɪst) *n* **1** a thin fog resulting from condensation in the air near the earth's surface. **2** *Meteorol.* such an atmospheric condition with a horizontal visibility of 1–2 kilometres. **3** a fine spray of liquid, such as that produced by an aerosol container. **4** condensed water vapour on a surface. **5** something that causes haziness or

lack of clarity, such as a film of tears. ◆ *vb* **6** to cover or be covered with or as if with mist. [OE]

mistake (mɪ'steɪk) *n* **1** an error or blunder in action, opinion, or judgment. **2** a misconception or misunderstanding. ◆ *vb* **mistakes, mistaking, mistook, mistaken. 3** (*tr*) to misunderstand; misinterpret: *she mistook his meaning.* **4** (*tr;* foll. by *for*) to take (for), interpret (as), or confuse (with): *she mistook his directness for honesty.* **5** (*tr*) to choose badly or incorrectly: *he mistook his path.* **6** (*intr*) to make a mistake. [C13 (meaning: to do wrong, err): from ON *mistaka* to take erroneously]

▶ **mis'takable** *adj*

mistaken (mɪ'steɪkən) *adj* **1** (*usually predicative*) wrong in opinion, judgment, etc.: *a mistaken viewpoint.* **2** arising from error in opinion, judgment, etc.

▶ **mis'takenly** *adv* ▶ **mis'takenness** *n*

Mistassini ★ (ˌmɪstə'siːnɪ) *n* **Lake.** a lake in E Canada, in N Quebec: the largest lake in the province; drains through the Rupert River into James Bay. Area: 2175 sq. km (840 sq. miles). Length: about 160 km (100 miles).

mister ('mɪstə) (*sometimes cap.*) ◆ *n* **1** an informal form of address for a man. **2** *Mil.* the official form of address for subordinate or senior warrant officers. **3** *Naval.* the official form of address for all officers in a merchant ship, other than the captain. **4** *Brit.* the form of address for a surgeon. **5** the form of address for officials holding certain positions: *mister chairman.* ◆ *vb* **6** (*tr*) *Inf.* to call (someone) mister. [C16: var. of MASTER]

Mister ('mɪstə) *n* the full form of **Mr.**

misterioso (mɪˌstɛrɪ'əʊsəʊ) *adv Music.* in a mysterious manner; mysteriously. [It.]

Misti ★ (*Spanish* 'misti) *n* See **El Misti.**

mistigris ('mɪstɪgriː) *n* **1** the joker or a blank card used as a wild card in a variety of draw poker. **2** the game. [C19: from F: jack of clubs, game in which this card was wild]

mistime (ˌmɪs'taɪm) *vb* **mistimes, mistiming, mistimed.** (*tr*) to time (an action, utterance, etc.) wrongly.

mistle thrush or **missel thrush** ('mɪsᵊl) *n* a large European thrush with a brown back and spotted breast, noted for feeding on mistletoe berries. [C18: from OE *mistel* MISTLETOE]

mistletoe ('mɪsᵊlˌtəʊ) *n* **1** a Eurasian evergreen shrub with waxy white berries: grows as a partial parasite on various trees: used as a Christmas decoration. **2** any of several similar and related American plants. [OE *misteltān*, from *mistel* mistletoe + *tān* twig; rel. to ON *mistilteinn*]

mistook (mɪ'stʊk) *vb* the past tense of **mistake.**

mistral ('mɪstrəl, mɪ'strɑːl) *n* a strong cold dry wind that blows through the Rhône valley and S France to the Mediterranean coast, mainly in the winter. [C17: via F from Provençal, from L *magistrālis* MAGISTRAL]

Mistral ★ *n* **1** (*French* mistral). **Frédéric** (frederik). 1830–1914, French Provençal poet, who shared the Nobel prize for literature 1904. **2** (*Spanish* mis'tral). **Gabriela** (ga'βrjela), pen name of *Lucila Godoy de Alcayaga.* 1889–1957, Chilean poet, educationalist, and diplomatist. Her poetry includes the collection *Desolación* (1922): Nobel prize for literature 1945.

mistreat (ˌmɪs'triːt) *vb* (*tr*) to treat badly.

▶ **mis'treatment** *n*

mistress ('mɪstrɪs) *n* **1** a woman who has a continuing extramarital sexual relationship with a man, esp. a married man. **2** a woman in a position of authority, ownership, or control. **3** a woman having control over something specified: *mistress of her own destiny.* **4** *Chiefly Brit.* short for **schoolmistress. 5** an archaic or dialect word for **sweetheart.** [C14: from OF; see MASTER, -ESS]

Mistress ('mɪstrɪs) *n* an archaic or dialect title equivalent to **Mrs.**

Mistress of the Robes *n* (in Britain) a lady of high rank in charge of the Queen's wardrobe.

mistrial (mɪs'traɪəl) *n* **1** a trial made void because of some error. **2** *US.* an inconclusive trial, as when a jury cannot agree on a verdict.

mistrust (ˌmɪs'trʌst) vb **1** to have doubts or suspicions about (someone or something). ♦ n **2** distrust.
▸ ˌmis'trustful adj ▸ ˌmis'trustfully adv ▸ ˌmis'trustfulness n

misty ('mɪstɪ) adj **mistier, mistiest. 1** consisting of or resembling mist. **2** obscured as by mist. **3** indistinct; blurred.
▸ 'mistily adv ▸ 'mistiness n

misunderstand (ˌmɪsʌndə'stænd) vb **misunderstands, misunderstanding, misunderstood.** to fail to understand properly.

misunderstanding (ˌmɪsʌndə'stændɪŋ) n **1** a failure to understand properly. **2** a disagreement.

misunderstood (ˌmɪsʌndə'stʊd) adj not properly or sympathetically understood: *a misunderstood adolescent.*

misuse n (ˌmɪs'juːs), *also* **misusage. 1** erroneous, improper, or unorthodox use: *misuse of words.* **2** cruel or inhumane treatment. ♦ vb (ˌmɪs'juːz), **misuses, misusing, misused.** (tr) **3** to use wrongly. **4** to treat badly or harshly.
▸ ˌmis'user n

Mitchell ★ ('mɪtʃəl) n **1 Joni,** original name *Roberta Joan Anderson.* born 1943, Canadian singer and songwriter. Her albums include *Blue* (1971) and *Turbulent Indigo* (1994). **2 Margaret.** 1900–49, US novelist; author of *Gone with the Wind* (1936). **3 Reginald Joseph.** 1895–1937, British aeronautical engineer; designer of the Spitfire fighter. **4** Sir **Thomas Livingstone,** known as *Major Mitchell.* 1792–1855, Australian explorer born in Scotland.

Mitchum ★ ('mɪtʃəm) n **Robert.** 1917–97, US film actor. His films include *Night of the Hunter* (1955) and *Farewell my Lovely* (1975).

mite[1] (maɪt) n any of numerous small terrestrial or aquatic free-living or parasitic arachnids. [OE *mīte*]

mite[2] (maɪt) n **1** a very small particle, creature, or object. **2** a very small contribution or sum of money. See also **widow's mite. 3** a former Flemish coin of small value. **4 a mite.** *Inf.* somewhat: *he's a mite foolish.* [C14: from MLowG, MDu. *mīte*]

Mithgarthr ★ ('mɪðˌɡaːðə) n a variant of **Midgard.**

Mithraism ('mɪθreɪˌɪzəm) *or* **Mithraicism** (mɪθ'reɪɪˌsɪzəm) n the ancient religion of Mithras.
▸ **Mithraic** (mɪθ'reɪɪk) adj ▸ 'Mithraist n, adj

Mithras ('mɪθræs) *or* **Mithra** ★ ('mɪθrə) n *Persian myth.* the god of light, identified with the sun, who slew a primordial bull and fertilized the world with its blood.

Mithridates VI *or* **Mithradates VI** ★ (ˌmɪθrɪ'deɪtiːz) n called *the Great.* ?132–63 B.C., king of Pontus (?120–63). He waged three wars against Rome (88–84; 83–81; 74–64) and was finally defeated by Pompey: committed suicide.

mithridatism ('mɪθrɪˌdeɪtɪzəm) n immunity to large doses of poison by prior ingestion of gradually increased doses.
▸ **mithridatic** (ˌmɪθrɪ'dætɪk, -'deɪ-) adj

mitigate ('mɪtɪˌɡeɪt) vb **mitigates, mitigating, mitigated.** to make or become less severe or harsh; moderate. [C15: from L *mītigāre,* from *mītis* mild + *agere* to make]
▸ 'mitigable adj ▸ ˌmiti'gation n ▸ 'miti,gative *or* 'miti,gatory adj ▸ 'miti,gator n

> **USAGE NOTE** *Mitigate* is sometimes wrongly used where *militate* is meant: *his behaviour militates (not mitigates) against his chances of promotion.*

Mitilíni ★ (miti'lini) n transliteration of the Modern Greek name for **Mytilene** (sense 1).

mitochondrion (ˌmaɪtəʊ'kɒndrɪən) n, pl **mitochondria** (-drɪə). a small spherical or rodlike body, in the cytoplasm of most cells: contains enzymes responsible for energy production. [C19: NL, from Gk *mitos* thread + *khondrion* small grain]

mitosis (maɪ'təʊsɪs, mɪ-) n a method of cell division, in which the nucleus divides into daughter nuclei, each containing the same number of chromosomes as the parent nucleus. [C19: from NL, from Gk *mitos* thread]
▸ **mitotic** (maɪ'tɒtɪk, mɪ-) adj

mitral ('maɪtrəl) adj **1** of or like a mitre. **2** *Anat.* of or relating to the mitral valve.

mitral valve n the valve between the left atrium and the left ventricle of the heart.

mitre *or US* **miter** ('maɪtə) n **1** *Christianity.* the liturgical headdress of a bishop or abbot, consisting of a tall pointed cleft cap with two bands hanging down at the back. **2** Also called: **mitre joint.** a corner joint formed by cutting bevels of equal angles at the ends of each piece of material. **3** a bevelled surface of a mitre joint. ♦ **mitres, mitring, mitred** *or US* **miters, mitering, mitered.** (tr) **4** to make a mitre joint between (two pieces of material). **5** to confer a mitre upon: *a mitred abbot.* [C14: from OF, from L *mitra,* from Gk: turban]

mitre box n an open-ended box with sides slotted to guide a saw in cutting mitre joints.

mitt (mɪt) n **1** any of various glovelike hand coverings, such as one that does not cover the fingers. **2** short for **mitten** (sense 1). **3** *Baseball.* a large round thickly padded leather mitten worn by the catcher. **4** (*often pl*) a slang word for **hand. 5** *Sl.* a boxing glove. [C18: from MITTEN]

Mittelland Canal ★ (*German* 'mɪtəllant) n a canal in Germany, linking the Rivers Rhine and Elbe. Length: 325 km (202 miles).

mitten ('mɪt°n) n **1** a glove having one section for the thumb and a single section for the other fingers. Sometimes shortened to **mitt. 2** *Sl.* a boxing glove. [C14: from OF *mitaine,* from ?]

Mitterrand ★ (*French* miterɑ̃) n **François Maurice Marie** (frɑ̃swa mɔris mari). 1916–96, French statesman; first secretary of the socialist party (1971–81); president of France (1981–95).

mittimus ('mɪtɪməs) n, pl **mittimuses.** *Law.* a warrant of commitment to prison or a command to a jailer to hold someone in prison. [C15: from L: we send, the first word of such a command]

mix (mɪks) vb **1** (tr) to combine or blend (ingredients, liquids, objects, etc.) together into one mass. **2** (intr) to become or have the capacity to become combined, joined, etc.: *some chemicals do not mix.* **3** (tr) to form (something) by combining constituents: *to mix cement.* **4** (tr; often foll. by *in* or *into*) to add as an additional element to a mass or compound: *to mix flour into a batter.* **5** (tr) to do at the same time: *to mix study and pleasure.* **6** (tr) to consume (different alcoholic drinks) in close succession. **7** to come or cause to come into association socially: *Pauline mixed well.* **8** (intr; often foll. by *with*) to go together; complement. **9** (tr) to crossbreed (differing strains of plants or breeds of livestock), esp. more or less at random. **10** *Music.* to balance and adjust (individual performers' parts) to make an overall sound by electronic means. **11 mix it.** *Inf.* to cause mischief or trouble, often for a person named: *she tried to mix it for John.* ♦ n **12** the act or an instance of mixing. **13** the result of mixing; mixture. **14** a mixture of ingredients, esp. one commercially prepared for making a cake, bread, etc. **15** *Inf.* a state of confusion. **16** *Music.* the sound produced by mixing. ♦ See also **mix-up.** [C15: back formation from *mixt* mixed, via OF from L *mixtus,* from *miscēre* to mix]
▸ 'mixable adj

mixed (mɪkst) adj **1** formed or blended together by mixing. **2** composed of different elements, races, sexes, etc.: *a mixed school.* **3** consisting of conflicting elements, thoughts, attitudes, etc.: *mixed feelings.* **4** *Maths.* (of a number) consisting of the sum of an integer and a fraction or a decimal fraction, as 5½ or 17.43.
▸ **mixedness** ('mɪksɪdnɪs) n

mixed bag n *Inf.* something composed of diverse elements, characteristics, people, etc.

mixed blessing n an event, situation, etc., having both advantages and disadvantages.

mixed doubles pl n *Tennis.* a doubles game with a man and a woman as partners on each side.

mixed economy n an economic system in which the public and private sectors coexist.

mixed farming n combined arable and livestock farming (on **mixed farms**).

★ people and places

mixed marriage *n* a marriage between persons of different races or religions.

mixed metaphor *n* a combination of incongruous metaphors, as *when the Nazi jackboots sing their swan song.*

mixed-up *adj* in a state of mental confusion.

mixer ('mɪksə) *n* **1** a person or thing that mixes. **2** *Inf.* **2a** a person considered in relation to his ability to mix socially. **2b** a person who creates trouble for others. **3** a kitchen appliance, usually electrical, used for mixing foods, etc. **4** a drink such as ginger ale, fruit juice, etc., used in preparing cocktails. **5** *Electronics.* a device in which two or more input signals are combined to give a single output signal.

mixer tap *n* a tap in which hot and cold water supplies have a joint outlet but are controlled separately.

mixture ('mɪkstʃə) *n* **1** the act of mixing or state of being mixed. **2** something mixed; a result of mixing. **3** *Chem.* a substance consisting of two or more substances mixed together without any chemical bonding between them. **4** *Pharmacol.* a liquid medicine in which an insoluble compound is suspended in the liquid. **5** *Music.* an organ stop that controls several ranks of pipes. **6** the mixture of petrol vapour and air in an internal-combustion engine. [C16: from L *mixtūra*, from *mixtus*, p.p. of *miscere* to mix]

mix-up *n* **1** a confused condition or situation. **2** *Inf.* a fight. ◆ *vb* **mix up**. (*tr, adv*) **3** to make into a mixture. **4** to confuse or confound: *Tom mixes John up with Bill.* **5** (*often passive*) to put (someone) into a state of confusion: *I'm all mixed up.* **6** (foll. by *in* or *with*; *usually passive*) to involve (in an activity or group, esp. one that is illegal): *mixed up in the drugs racket.*

Mizoguchi ★ (ˌmiːtsəˈguːtʃɪ) *n* Kenji ('kɛndʒɪ). 1898–1956, Japanese film director. His films include *A Paper Doll's Whisper of Spring* (1925) and *Ugetsu Monogatari* (1952).

Mizoram ★ (mɪˈzɔːrəm) *n* a state (since 1986) in NE India, created in 1972 from the former Mizo Hills District of Assam. Capital: Aijal. Pop.: 775 000 (1994 est.). Area: about 21 081 sq. km (8140 sq. miles).

mizzen or **mizen** ('mɪzᵊn) *Naut.* ◆ *n* **1** a sail set on a mizzenmast. **2** short for **mizzenmast**. ◆ *adj* **3** of or relating to a mizzenmast: *a mizzen staysail.* [C15: from F *misaine*, from It. *mezzana, mezzano* middle]

mizzenmast or **mizenmast** ('mɪzᵊn,mɑːst; *Naut.* 'mɪzᵊnməst) *n Naut.* (on a vessel with three or more masts) the third mast from the bow.

mizzle¹ ('mɪzᵊl) *vb* mizzles, mizzling, mizzled, *n* a dialect word for **drizzle**. [C15: ?from Low G *miseln* to drizzle]
▶ 'mizzly *adj*

mizzle² ('mɪzᵊl) *vb* mizzles, mizzling, mizzled. (*intr*) *Brit. sl.* to decamp. [C18: from ?]

mk *Currency. symbol for:* **1** mark. **2** markka.

mks units *pl n* a metric system of units based on the metre, kilogram, and second as the units of length, mass, and time; it forms the basis of the SI units.

mkt *abbrev. for* market.

ml *symbol for:* **1** mile. **2** millilitre.

ML *abbrev. for* Medieval Latin.

MLA *abbrev. for:* **1** Member of the Legislative Assembly. **2** Modern Language Association (of America).

MLC (in Australia and India) *abbrev. for* Member of the Legislative Council.

MLitt *abbrev. for* Master of Letters. [L *Magister Litterarum*]

Mlle or **Mlle.** *pl* **Mlles** or **Mlles.** the French equivalent of **Miss**. [from F *Mademoiselle*]

MLR *abbrev. for* minimum lending rate.

mm *symbol for* millimetre.

MM **1** the French equivalent of **Messrs**. [from F *Messieurs*] **2** *abbrev. for* Military Medal.

MMC (in Britain) *abbrev. for* Monopolies and Mergers Commission.

MMDS *abbrev. for* multipoint microwave distribution system: a radio alternative to cable television. Sometimes shortened to **MDS**.

Mme *pl* **Mmes** the French equivalent of **Mrs**. [from F *Madame, Mesdames*]

MMP *abbrev. for* mixed member proportional: a system of proportional representation, used in Germany and New Zealand.

MMR *n* a combined vaccine against measles, mumps, and rubella, given to very young children.

MMus *abbrev. for* Master of Music.

Mn *the chemical symbol for* manganese.

MN *abbrev. for:* **1** (in Britain) Merchant Navy. **2** Minnesota.

MNA (in Canada) *abbrev. for* Member of the National Assembly (of Quebec).

mnemonic (nɪˈmɒnɪk) *adj* **1** aiding or meant to aid one's memory. **2** of or relating to memory or mnemonics. ◆ *n* **3** something, such as a verse, to assist memory. [C18: from Gk *mnēmonikos*, from *mnēmōn* mindful, from *mnasthai* to remember!]
▶ mne'monically *adv*

mnemonics (nɪˈmɒnɪks) *n* (*usually functioning as sing*) **1** the art or practice of improving or of aiding the memory. **2** a system of rules to aid the memory.

Mnemosyne ★ (niːˈmɒzɪ,niː, -ˈmɒs-) *n Greek myth.* the goddess of memory and mother by Zeus of the Muses.

mo (məʊ) *n Inf.* **1** *Chiefly Brit.* short for **moment** (sense 1) (esp. in **half a mo**). **2** *Austral.* short for **moustache** (sense 1).

Mo *the chemical symbol for* molybdenum.

MO *abbrev. for:* **1** Missouri. **2** Medical Officer.

Mo. *abbrev. for* Missouri.

m.o. or **MO** *abbrev. for:* **1** mail order. **2** money order.

-mo *suffix forming nouns.* (in bookbinding) indicating book size by specifying the number of leaves formed by folding one sheet of paper: *16mo* or *sixteenmo*. [abstracted from DUODECIMO]

moa ('məʊə) *n* any of various recently extinct large flightless birds of New Zealand (see **ratite**). [C19: from Maori]

Moab ★ ('məʊæb) *n Old Testament.* an ancient kingdom east of the Dead Sea, in what is now the SW part of Jordan: flourished mainly from the 9th to the 6th centuries B.C.
▶ **Moabite** ('məʊə,baɪt) *adj, n*

moa hunter *n NZ.* an anthropologists' term for an early Maori.

moan (məʊn) *n* **1** a low prolonged mournful sound expressive of suffering or pleading. **2** any similar mournful sound, esp. that made by the wind. **3** *Inf.* a grumble or complaint. ◆ *vb* **4** to utter (words, etc.) in a low mournful manner. **5** (*intr*) to make a sound like a moan. **6** (*usually intr*) *Inf.* to grumble or complain. [C13: rel. to OE *mǣnan* to grieve over]
▶ 'moaner *n* ▶ 'moanful *adj* ▶ 'moaning *n, adj*

moat (məʊt) *n* **1** a wide water-filled ditch surrounding a fortified place, such as a castle. ◆ *vb* **2** (*tr*) to surround with or as if with a moat. [C14: from OF *motte* mound]

mob (mɒb) *n* **1a** a riotous or disorderly crowd of people; rabble. **1b** (as modifier): *mob law.* **2** *Often derog.* a group or class of people, animals, or things. **3** *Often derog.* the masses. **4** *Sl.* a gang of criminals. **5** *Austral. & NZ.* a large number of anything. **6** *Austral. & NZ.* a flock or herd of animals. **7** *mobs of. Austral. & NZ inf.* lots of. ◆ *vb* **mobs, mobbing, mobbed.** (*tr*) **8** to attack in a group resembling a mob. **9** (of a group of animals of a prey species) to harass (a predator). **10** to surround, esp. in order to acclaim. **11** to crowd into (a building, etc.). [C17: shortened from L *mōbile vulgus* the fickle populace]

mobcap ('mɒb,kæp) *n* a woman's large cotton cap with a pouched crown, worn esp. during the 18th century. [C18: from obs. *mob* woman, esp. loose-living, + CAP]

mobile ('məʊbaɪl) *adj* **1** having freedom of movement; movable. **2** changing quickly in expression: *a mobile face.* **3** *Sociol.* (of individuals or social groups) moving within and between classes, occupations, and localities. **4** (of military forces) able to move freely and quickly. **5** (*postpositive*) *Inf.* having transport available: *are you mobile?* ◆ *n* **6a** a sculpture suspended in midair with delicately balanced parts that are set in motion by air

currents. **6b** (*as modifier*): *mobile sculpture.* **7** short for **mobile phone.** [C15: via OF from L *mōbilis*, from *movēre* to move]
▸ **mobility** (məʊˈbɪlɪtɪ) *n*

Mobile ★ (ˈməʊbiːl, məʊˈbiːl) *n* a port in SW Alabama, on **Mobile Bay** (an inlet of the Gulf of Mexico): the state's only port and its first permanent settlement, made by French colonists in 1711. Pop.: 204 490 (1994 est.).

-mobile (məʊˌbiːl) *suffix forming nouns.* indicating a vehicle designed for a particular person or purpose: *Popemobile.*

mobile home *n* living quarters mounted on wheels and capable of being towed by a motor vehicle.

mobile phone *n* a portable telephone that works by means of a cellular radio system.

mobilize *or* **mobilise** (ˈməʊbɪˌlaɪz) *vb* **mobilizes, mobilizing, mobilized** *or* **mobilises, mobilising, mobilised. 1** to prepare for war or another emergency by organizing (national resources, the armed services, etc.). **2** (*tr*) to organize for a purpose. **3** (*tr*) to put into motion or use.
▸ ˈmobiˌlizable *or* ˈmobiˌlisable *adj* ▸ ˌmobiliˈzation *or* ˌmobiliˈsation *n*

Möbius strip (ˈmɜːbɪəs) *n Maths.* a one-sided continuous surface, formed by twisting a long narrow rectangular strip of material through 180° and joining the ends. [C19: after August *Möbius* (1790–1868), G mathematician]

mobocracy (mɒˈbɒkrəsɪ) *n, pl* **mobocracies. 1** rule or domination by a mob. **2** the mob that rules.

mobster (ˈmɒbstə) *n* a US slang word for **gangster.**

Mobutu[1] ★ (məˈbuːtuː) *n Lake.* a lake in E Africa, between the Democratic Republic of the Congo and Uganda in the Great Rift Valley, 660 m (2200 ft) above sea level: a source of the Nile, fed by the Victoria Nile, which leaves as the Albert Nile. Area: 5345 sq. km (2064 sq. miles). Former name: **Lake Albert.**

Mobutu[2] ★ (məˈbuːtuː) *n* **Sese Seko** (ˈsɛsɛ ˈsɛkəʊ), original name *Joseph.* 1930–97, Zaïrese statesman; president of Zaïre (1970–97): accused of corruption and overthrown by rebels who renamed Zaïre the Democratic Republic of the Congo: died in exile.

Moçambique ★ (musəmˈbikə) *n* the Portuguese name for **Mozambique.**

moccasin (ˈmɒkəsɪn) *n* **1** a shoe of soft leather, esp. deerskin, worn by North American Indians. **2** any soft shoe resembling this. **3** short for **water moccasin.** [C17: of Amerind origin]

moccasin flower *n* any of several North American orchids with a pink solitary flower. See also **lady's-slipper, cypripedium.**

mocha (ˈmɒkə) *n* **1** a dark brown coffee originally imported from the port of Mocha in Arabia. **2** a flavouring made from coffee and chocolate. **3** a soft glove leather, made from goatskin or sheepskin. **4a** a dark brown colour. **4b** (*as adj*): *mocha shoes.*

Mocha *or* **Mokha** ★ (ˈmɒkə) *n* a port in Yemen, on the Red Sea; in North Yemen until 1990: formerly important for the export of Arabian coffee. Pop.: 2000 (1990 est.).

mock (mɒk) *vb* **1** (when *intr*, often foll. by *at*) to behave with scorn or contempt (towards); show ridicule (for). **2** (*tr*) to imitate, esp. in fun; mimic. **3** (*tr*) to deceive, disappoint, or delude. **4** (*tr*) to defy or frustrate. ◆ *n* **5** the act of mocking. **6** a person or thing mocked. **7** a counterfeit; imitation. **8** (*often pl*) *Inf.* (in England and Wales) school examinations taken as practice before public exams. ◆ *adj* (*prenominal*) **9** sham or counterfeit. **10** serving as an imitation or substitute, esp. for practice purposes: *a mock battle.* ◆ See also **mock-up.** [C15: from OF *mocquer*]
▸ ˈmocker *n* ▸ ˈmocking *n, adj* ▸ ˈmockingly *adv*

mockers (ˈmɒkəz) *pl n Inf.* **put the mockers on.** to ruin the chances of success of. [C20: ?from MOCK]

mockery (ˈmɒkərɪ) *n, pl* **mockeries. 1** ridicule, contempt, or derision. **2** a derisive action or comment. **3** an imitation or pretence, esp. a derisive one. **4** a person or thing that is mocked. **5** a person, thing, or action that is inadequate.

mock-heroic *adj* **1** (of a literary work, esp. a poem) imitating the style of heroic poetry in order to satirize an unheroic subject. ◆ *n* **2** burlesque imitation of the heroic style.

mockingbird (ˈmɒkɪŋˌbɜːd) *n* any of various American songbirds, noted for their ability to mimic the song of other birds.

mock orange *n* **1** Also called: **syringa, philadelphus.** a shrub with white fragrant flowers resembling those of the orange. **2** an Australian shrub with white flowers and dark shiny leaves.

mock turtle soup *n* an imitation turtle soup made from a calf's head.

mock-up *n* **1** a working full-scale model of a machine, apparatus, etc., for testing, research, etc. **2** a layout of printed matter. ◆ *vb* **mock up. 3** (*tr, adv*) to build or make a mock-up of.

mod[1] (mɒd) *n Brit.* **a** a member of a group of teenagers, originally in the mid-1960s, noted for their clothes-consciousness. **b** a member of a revived group of this type in the late 1970s and early 1980s. [C20: from MODERNIST]

mod[2] (mɒd) *n* an annual Highland Gaelic meeting with musical and literary competitions. [C19: from Gaelic *mōd* assembly, from ON]

MOD (in Britain) *abbrev. for* Ministry of Defence.

mod. *abbrev. for:* **1** moderate. **2** moderato. **3** modern.

modal (ˈməʊdˀl) *adj* **1** of or relating to mode or manner. **2** *Grammar.* (of a verb form or auxiliary verb) expressing a distinction of mood, such as that between possibility and actuality. **3** qualifying, or expressing a qualification of, the truth of some statement. **4** *Metaphysics.* of or relating to the form of a thing as opposed to its attributes, substance, etc. **5** *Music.* of or relating to a mode. **6** of or relating to a statistical mode.
▸ moˈdality *n* ▸ ˈmodally *adv*

modal logic *n* **1** the logical study of such philosophical concepts as necessity, possibility, contingency, etc. **2** the logical study of concepts whose formal properties resemble certain moral, epistemological, and psychological concepts.

mod cons *pl n Inf.* modern conveniences; the usual installations of a modern house, such as hot water, heating, etc.

mode (məʊd) *n* **1** a manner or way of doing, acting, or existing. **2** the current fashion or style. **3** *Music.* **3a** any of the various scales of notes within one octave, esp. any of the twelve natural diatonic scales taken in ascending order used in plainsong, folk song, and art music until 1600. **3b** (in the music of classical Greece) any of the descending diatonic scales from which the liturgical modes evolved. **3c** either of the two main scale systems in music since 1600: *major mode; minor mode.* **4** *Logic, linguistics.* another name for **mood**[2]. **5** *Philosophy.* a complex combination of ideas which is not simply the sum of its component ideas. **6** that one of a range of values that has the highest frequency as determined statistically. [C14: from L *modus* manner]

model (ˈmɒdˀl) *n* **1a** a representation, usually on a smaller scale, of a device, structure, etc. **1b** (*as modifier*): *a model train.* **2a** a standard to be imitated. **2b** (*as modifier*): *a model wife.* **3** a representative form, style, or pattern. **4** a person who poses for a sculptor, painter, or photographer. **5** a person who wears clothes to display them to prospective buyers; mannequin. **6** a preparatory sculpture in clay, wax, etc., from which the finished work is copied. **7** a design or style of a particular product. ◆ *vb* **models, modelling, modelled** *or US* **models, modeling, modeled. 8** to make a model of (something or someone). **9** to form in clay, wax, etc.; mould. **10** to display (clothing and accessories) as a mannequin. **11** to plan or create according to a model or pattern. [C16: from OF *modelle*, from It., from L *modulus*, dim. of *modus* MODE]
▸ ˈmodeller *or US* ˈmodeler *n*

modelling *or US* **modeling** (ˈmɒdˀlɪŋ) *n* **1** the act or an instance of making a model. **2** the practice or occupation of a person who models clothes. **3** a technique in psychotherapy in which the therapist encourages the patient to model his behaviour on his own.

★ people and places

modem ('məʊdɛm) *n Computing.* a device for connecting two computers by a telephone line, consisting of a modulator that converts computer signals into audio signals and a corresponding demodulator. [C20: from *mo(dulator) dem(odulator)*]

Modena ★ (*Italian* 'mɔːdena) *n* a city in N Italy, in Emilia-Romagna: ruled by the Este family (18th–19th century); university (1678). Pop.: 176 588 (1994 est.). Ancient name: **Mutina.**

moderate *adj* ('mɒdərɪt). **1** not extreme or excessive. **2** not violent; mild or temperate. **3** of average quality or extent: *moderate success.* ◆ *n* ('mɒdərɪt). **4** a person who holds moderate views, esp. in politics. ◆ *vb* ('mɒdə,reɪt). **moderates, moderating, moderated. 5** to become or cause to become less extreme or violent. **6** (when *intr,* often foll. by *over*) to preside over a meeting, discussion, etc. **7** *Physics.* to slow down (neutrons), esp. by using a moderator. [C14: from L *moderātus,* from *moderārī* to restrain]

moderate breeze *n* a wind of force 4 on the Beaufort scale, reaching speeds of 13 to 18 mph.

moderation (,mɒdə'reɪʃən) *n* **1** the state or an instance of being moderate. **2** the act of moderating. **3 in moderation.** within moderate or reasonable limits.

moderato (,mɒdə'rɑːtəʊ) *adv Music.* **1** at a moderate tempo. **2** a direction indicating that the tempo specified is to be used with restraint: *allegro moderato.* [It.]

moderator ('mɒdə,reɪtə) *n* **1** a person or thing that moderates. **2** *Presbyterian Church.* a minister appointed to preside over a Church court, synod, or general assembly. **3** a presiding officer at a public or legislative assembly. **4** a material, such as heavy water, used for slowing down neutrons in nuclear reactors. **5** an examiner at Oxford or Cambridge Universities in first public examinations. **6** (in Britain and New Zealand) one who is responsible for consistency of standards in the grading of some public examinations. ▸ '**moder,atorship** *n*

modern ('mɒdən) *adj* **1** of, involving, or befitting the present or a recent time; contemporary. **2** of, relating to, or characteristic of contemporary styles or schools of art, literature, music, etc., esp. those of an experimental kind. **3** belonging or relating to the period in history from the end of the Middle Ages to the present. ◆ *n* **4** a contemporary person. [C16: from OF, from LL *modernus,* from *modō* (adv) just recently, from *modus* MODE] ▸ mo'**dernity** *or* '**modernness** *n*

modern apprenticeship *n* an arrangement that allows a school-leaver to gain vocational qualifications while being trained in a job.

Modern English *n* the English language since about 1450.

Modern Hebrew *n* the official language of Israel; a revived form of ancient Hebrew.

modernism ('mɒdə,nɪzəm) *n* **1** modern tendencies, thoughts, etc., or the support of these. **2** something typical of contemporary life or thought. **3** a 20th-century divergence in the arts from previous traditions, esp. in architecture. See **International Style. 4** (*cap.*) *RC Church.* the movement at the end of the 19th and beginning of the 20th centuries that sought to adapt doctrine to modern thought. ▸ '**modernist** *n, adj* ▸ ,**modern'istic** *adj* ▸ ,**modern'istically** *adv*

modernize *or* **modernise** ('mɒdə,naɪz) *vb* **modernizes, modernizing, modernized** *or* **modernises, modernising, modernised. 1** (*tr*) to make modern in appearance or style. **2** (*intr*) to adopt modern ways, ideas, etc. ▸ ,**moderni'zation** *or* ,**moderni'sation** *n* ▸ '**modern,izer** *or* '**modern,iser** *n*

modern pentathlon *n* an athletic contest consisting of five different events: horse riding with jumps, fencing with electric épée, freestyle swimming, pistol shooting, and cross-country running.

modest ('mɒdɪst) *adj* **1** having or expressing a humble opinion of oneself or one's accomplishments or abilities. **2** reserved or shy. **3** not ostentatious or pretentious.

4 not extreme or excessive. **5** decorous or decent. [C16: via OF from L *modestus* moderate, from *modus* MODE] ▸ '**modestly** *adv*

modesty ('mɒdɪstɪ) *n, pl* **modesties.** the quality or condition of being modest.

modicum ('mɒdɪkəm) *n* a small amount or portion. [C15: from L: a little way, from *modicus* moderate]

modification (,mɒdɪfɪ'keɪʃən) *n* **1** the act of modifying or the condition of being modified. **2** something modified. **3** a small change or adjustment. **4** *Grammar.* the relation between a modifier and the word or phrase that it modifies. ▸ '**modifi,catory** *or* '**modifi,cative** *adj*

modifier ('mɒdɪ,faɪə) *n* **1** Also called: **qualifier.** *Grammar.* a word or phrase that qualifies the sense of another word; for example, the noun *alarm* is a modifier of *clock* in *alarm clock* and the phrase *every day* is an adverbial modifier of *walks* in *he walks every day.* **2** a person or thing that modifies.

modify ('mɒdɪ,faɪ) *vb* **modifies, modifying, modified.** (*mainly tr*) **1** to change the structure, character, intent, etc., of. **2** to make less extreme or uncompromising. **3** *Grammar.* (of a word or phrase) to bear the relation of modifier to (another word or phrase). **4** *Linguistics.* to change (a vowel) by umlaut. **5** (*intr*) to be or become modified. [C14: from OF *modifier,* from L *modificāre* to limit, from *modus* measure + *facere* to make] ▸ '**modi,fiable** *adj*

Modigliani ★ (*Italian* modiʎ'ʎaːni) *n* **Amedeo** (ame'dɛːo). 1884–1920, Italian painter and sculptor, noted for the elongated forms of his portraits.

modish ('məʊdɪʃ) *adj* in the current fashion or style. ▸ '**modishly** *adv* ▸ '**modishness** *n*

modiste (məʊ'diːst) *n* a fashionable dressmaker or milliner. [C19: from F, from *mode* fashion]

Modred ('məʊdrɪd) *or* **Mordred** ★ *n* (in Arthurian legend) a knight of the Round Table who rebelled against and killed his uncle King Arthur.

modular ('mɒdjʊlə) *adj* of, consisting of, or resembling a module or modulus.

modulate ('mɒdjʊ,leɪt) *vb* **modulates, modulating, modulated. 1** (*tr*) to change the tone, pitch, or volume of. **2** (*tr*) to adjust or regulate the degree of. **3** *Music.* **3a** to change or cause to change from one key to another. **3b** (often foll. by *to*) to make or become in tune (with a pitch, key, etc.). **4** *Physics, electronics.* to superimpose the amplitude, frequency, phase, etc., of a wave or signal onto another wave or signal or onto an electron beam. [C16: from L *modulātus* in due measure, melodious, from *modulārī,* from *modus* measure] ▸ ,**modu'lation** *n* ▸ '**modu,lator** *n*

module ('mɒdjuːl) *n* **1** a standard unit of measure, esp. one used to coordinate the dimensions of buildings and components. **2** a standard self-contained unit or item, such as an assembly of electronic components, or a standardized piece of furniture, that can be used in combination with other units. **3** *Astronautics.* any of several self-contained separable units making up a spacecraft or launch vehicle, each of which has one or more specified tasks. **4** *Education.* a short course of study that together with other such courses counts towards a qualification. [C16: from L *modulus,* dim. of *modus* MODE]

modulus ('mɒdjʊləs) *n, pl* **moduli** (-,laɪ). **1** *Physics.* a coefficient expressing a specified property of a specified substance. See **modulus of elasticity. 2** *Maths.* another name for the **absolute value** of a complex number. **3** *Maths.* the number by which a logarithm to one base is multiplied to give the corresponding logarithm to another base. **4** *Maths.* an integer that can be divided exactly into the difference between two other integers: *7 is a modulus of 25 and 11.* [C16: from L, dim. of *modus* measure]

modulus of elasticity *n* the ratio of the stress applied to a body or substance to the resulting strain within the elastic limit. Also called: **elastic modulus.**

modus operandi ('məʊdəs ,ɒpə'rændiː, -'rændaɪ) *n, pl* **modi operandi** ('məʊdiː ,ɒpə'rændiː, 'məʊdaɪ ,ɒpə'rændaɪ). procedure; method of operating. [C17: from L]

modus vivendi ('məʊdəs vɪ'vɛndiː, -'vɛndaɪ) *n, pl* **modi**

vivendi ('məʊdiː vɪ'vɛndiː, 'məʊdaɪ vɪ'vɛndaɪ). a working arrangement between conflicting interests; practical compromise. [C19: from L: way of living]

Moers ★ (*German* møːrs) *n* a city in W Germany, in North Rhine-Westphalia: coalmining centre. Pop.: 107 011 (1995 est.).

mog (mɒg) *or* **moggy** *n, pl* **mogs** *or* **moggies**. *Brit.* a slang name for **cat**[1]. [C20: dialect, orig. a pet name for a cow]

Mogadishu (,mɒgə'dɪʃuː) *or* **Mogadiscio** ★ (,mɒgə'dɪʃɪ,əʊ, -'dɪʃəʊ) *n* the capital and chief port of Somalia, on the Indian Ocean: founded by Arabs around the 10th century; taken by the Sultan of Zanzibar in 1871 and sold to Italy in 1905. Pop.: 900 000 (1995 est.).

Mogadon ('mɒgə,dɒn) *n Trademark.* a minor tranquilizer used to treat insomnia.

Mogador ★ (,mɒgə'dɔː; *French* mɔgadɔr) *n* the former name (until 1956) of **Essaouira**.

Mogilev (*Russian* məgi'ljɔf) *or* **Mohilev** ★ *n* an industrial city in E Belarus, on the Dnieper River: passed to Russia in 1772 after Polish rule. Pop.: 367 000 (1996 est.).

mogul ('məʊgʌl, məʊ'gʌl) *n* an important or powerful person. [C18: from MOGUL]

Mogul ('məʊgʌl, məʊ'gʌl) *n* **1** a member of the Muslim dynasty of Indian emperors established in 1526. **2** a Muslim Indian, Mongol, or Mongolian. ◆ *adj* **3** of or relating to the Moguls or their empire. [C16: from Persian *mughul* Mongolian]

mogul skiing *n* an event in which skiers descend a slope covered in mounds of snow, making two jumps during their descent. [C20: *mogul* ? from G dialect *Mugl* hillock or hummock]

MOH (in Britain) *abbrev. for* Medical Officer of Health.

mohair ('məʊ,hɛə) *n* **1** Also called: **angora**. the long soft silky hair of the Angora goat. **2a** a fabric made from the yarn of this hair and cotton or wool. **2b** (*as modifier*): *a mohair suit*. [C16: (infl. by *hair*), ult. from Ar. *mukhayyar*, lit.: choice]

Moham. *abbrev. for* Mohammedan.

Mohammed (məʊ'hæmɪd) *or* **Muhammad** ★ *n* ?570–632 A.D., the prophet and founder of Islam. He began to teach in Mecca in 610 but persecution forced him to flee with his followers to Medina in 622. After several battles, he conquered Mecca (630), establishing the principles of Islam (embodied in the Koran) over all Arabia. Other names: **Mahomet, Mahound,** (*archaic*) **Mahound.**

Mohammed II ★ *n* ?1430–81, Ottoman sultan of Turkey (1451–81). He captured Constantinople (1453) and conquered large areas of the Balkans.

Mohammed Ahmed ★ (məʊ'hæmɪd 'ɑːmɛd) *n* the original name of the **Mahdi**.

Mohammed Ali ★ *n* **1** See **Mehemet Ali. 2** See **Muhammad Ali.**

Mohammedan (məʊ'hæmɪdᵊn) *n, adj* another word (not in Muslim use) for **Muslim.**

Mohammedanism (məʊ'hæmɪdᵊ,nɪzəm) *n* another word (not in Muslim use) for **Islam.**

Mohammed Reza Pahlavi ★ (məʊ'hæmɪd 'riːzə) *n* See **Pahlavi** (sense 1).

Mohave Desert *or* **Mojave Desert** ★ *n* a desert in S California, south of the Sierra Nevada: part of the Great Basin. Area: 38 850 sq. km (15 000 sq. miles).

Mohawk[1] ('məʊhɔːk) *n* **1** (*pl* **Mohawks** *or* **Mohawk**) a member of a North American Indian people formerly living along the Mohawk River. **2** the Iroquoian language of this people.

Mohawk[2] ★ ('məʊhɔːk) *n* a river in E central New York State, flowing south and east to the Hudson River at Cohoes: the largest tributary of the Hudson. Length: 238 km (148 miles).

Mohenjo-Daro ★ (mə'hɛndʒəʊ'dɑːrəʊ) *n* an excavated city in SE Pakistan, southwest of Sukkur near the River Indus: flourished during the third millennium B.C.

mohican (məʊ'hiːkən) *n* a punk hairstyle in which the head is shaved at the sides and the remaining strip of

hair is worn stiffly erect and sometimes brightly coloured.

Moholy-Nagy ★ (mə'həʊlɪ'nɒdʒ) *n* Laszlo ('læzləʊ) *or* **Ladislaus** ('lɑːdɪs,laʊs). 1895–1946, US painter and teacher, born in Hungary. He worked at the Bauhaus (1923–29).

moidore ('mɔɪdɔː) *n* a former Portuguese gold coin. [C18: from Port. *moeda de ouro* money of gold]

moiety ('mɔɪɪtɪ) *n, pl* **moieties. 1** a half. **2** one of two parts or divisions of something. [C15: from OF *moitié*, from L *mediētās* middle, from *medius*]

moil (mɔɪl) *Arch. or dialect.* ◆ *vb* **1** to moisten or soil or become moist, soiled, etc. **2** (*intr*) to toil or drudge (esp. in **toil and moil**). ◆ *n* **3** toil; drudgery. **4** confusion. [C14 (to moisten; later: to work hard in unpleasantly wet conditions) from OF *moillier*, ult. from L *mollis* soft]

Moirai ★ ('mɔɪriː) *pl n, sing* **Moira** ('mɔɪrə), **the.** the Greek goddesses of fate. Roman counterparts: the **Parcae**. See **Fates.**

moire (mwɑː) *n* a fabric, usually silk, having a watered effect. [C17: from F, earlier *mouaire*, from MOHAIR]

moiré ('mwɑːreɪ) *adj* **1** having a watered or wavelike pattern. ◆ *n* **2** such a pattern, impressed on fabrics by means of engraved rollers. **3** any fabric having such a pattern; moire. **4** Also: **moiré pattern.** a pattern seen when two geometrical patterns, such as grids, are visually superimposed. [C17: from F, from *moire* MOHAIR]

Moism ('məʊ,ɪzəm) *n* the religious and ethical teaching of Mo-Zi (?470–?391 B.C.), Chinese philosopher, and his followers, emphasizing universal love, ascetic self-discipline, and obedience to the will of Heaven.

moist (mɔɪst) *adj* **1** slightly damp or wet. **2** saturated with or suggestive of moisture. [C14: from OF, ult. rel. to L *mūcidus* musty]
▶ **'moistly** *adv* ▶ **'moistness** *n*

moisten ('mɔɪsᵊn) *vb* to make or become moist.

moisture ('mɔɪstʃə) *n* water or other liquid diffused as vapour or condensed on or in objects.

moisturize *or* **moisturise** ('mɔɪstʃə,raɪz) *vb* **moisturizes, moisturizing, moisturized** *or* **moisturises, moisturising, moisturised.** (*tr*) to add moisture to (the air, the skin, etc.).
▶ **'moistur,izer** *or* **'moistur,iser** *n*

mojo ('məʊdʒəʊ) *n, pl* **mojos** *or* **mojoes.** *US sl.* **1** an amulet, charm, or magic spell. **2** the art of casting magic spells. [C20: of W African origin]

moke (məʊk) *n Brit. sl.* a donkey. [C19: from ?]

Mokha ★ ('məʊkə, 'mɒk-) *n* a variant of **Mocha.**

Mokpo ★ (,məʊk'pəʊ) *n* a port in SW South Korea, on the Yellow Sea. Pop.: 247 524 (1995).

mol *Chem. symbol for* mole[3].

mol. *abbrev. for:* **1** molecular. **2** molecule.

molal ('məʊləl) *adj Chem.* of or consisting of a solution containing one mole of solute per thousand grams of solvent. [C20: from MOLE[3] + -AL[1]]

molar[1] ('məʊlə) *n* **1** any of the 12 grinding teeth in man. **2** a corresponding tooth in other mammals. ◆ *adj* **3** of or relating to any of these teeth. **4** used for or capable of grinding. [C16: from L *molāris*, from *mola* millstone]

molar[2] ('məʊlə) *adj* **1** (of a physical quantity) per unit amount of substance: *molar volume.* **2** (not recommended in technical usage) (of a solution) containing one mole of solute per litre of solution. [C19: from L *mōlēs* a mass]

molasses (mə'læsɪz) *n* (*functioning as sing*) **1** the thick brown uncrystallized bitter syrup obtained from sugar during refining. **2** the US and Canad. name for **treacle** (sense 1). [C16: from Port. *melaço*, from LL *mellāceum* must, from L *mel* honey]

mold (məʊld) *n, vb* the US spelling of **mould.**

Moldau ★ ('mɒldaʊ) *n* **1** the German name for **Moldavia.** **2** the German name for the **Vltava.**

Moldavia ★ (mɒl'deɪvɪə) *n* **1** another name for **Moldova. 2** a former principality of E Europe, consisting of the basins of the Rivers Prut and Dniester: the E part (Bessarabia) formed part of the Soviet Union from 1940 until 1991, when it became the republic of Moldavia;

★ people and places

the W part remains a province of Romania. Romanian name: **Moldova** (mol'dovə). German name: **Moldau**.
▶ **Mol'davian** *adj, n*

moldboard ('məʊld,bɔːd) *n* the US spelling of **mouldboard**.

molder ('məʊldə) *vb* the US spelling of **moulder**.

molding ('məʊldɪŋ) *n* the US spelling of **moulding**.

Moldova ★ (mɒl'dəʊvə) *n* a republic in SE Europe, comprising part of the former principality of Moldavia: as the Moldavian Soviet Socialist Republic, it was part of the Soviet Union from 1940 until gaining independence in 1991; an agricultural region. Official language: Romanian. Religion: nonreligious and Christian. Currency: leu. Capital: Kishinev. Pop.: 4 372 000 (1996). Area: 37 670 sq. km (13 000 sq. miles). Also called: **Moldavia**.
▶ **Mol'dovan** *adj, n*

moldy ('məʊldɪ) *adj* the US spelling of **mouldy**.

mole[1] (məʊl) *n Pathol.* a nontechnical name for **naevus**. [OE *māl*]

mole[2] (məʊl) *n* **1** any small burrowing mammal of a family of Europe, Asia, and North and Central America. They have velvety, typically dark fur and forearms specialized for digging. **2** *Inf.* a spy who has infiltrated an organization and become a trusted member of it. [C14: from MDu. *mol*, of Gmc origin]

mole[3] (məʊl) *n* the basic SI unit of amount of substance; the amount that contains as many elementary entities as there are atoms in 0.012 kilogram of carbon-12. The entity may be an atom, a molecule, an ion, a radical, etc. Symbol: mol. See also **gram molecule**. [C20: from G *Mol*, short for *Molekül* MOLECULE]

mole[4] (məʊl) *n* **1** a breakwater. **2** a harbour protected by a breakwater. [C16: from F *môle*, from L *mōlēs* mass]

Molech ★ ('məʊlɛk) *n Old Testament.* a variant of **Moloch**.

molecular (məʊ'lɛkjʊlə, mə-) *adj* of or relating to molecules.
▶ **mo'lecularly** *adv*

molecular biology *n* the study of the structure and function of biological molecules, esp. nucleic acids and proteins.

molecular formula *n* a chemical formula indicating the numbers and types of atoms in a molecule: H_2SO_4 is the molecular formula of sulphuric acid.

molecular genetics *n* (*functioning as sing*) the study of the molecular constitution of genes and chromosomes.

molecular weight *n* the former name for **relative molecular mass**.

molecule ('mɒlɪ,kjuːl) *n* **1** the simplest unit of a chemical compound that can exist, consisting of two or more atoms held together by chemical bonds. **2** a very small particle. [C18: via F from NL *mōlēcula*, dim. of L *mōlēs* mass]

molehill ('məʊl,hɪl) *n* **1** the small mound of earth thrown up by a burrowing mole. **2 make a mountain out of a molehill.** to exaggerate an unimportant matter out of all proportion.

moleskin ('məʊl,skɪn) *n* **1** the dark grey dense velvety pelt of a mole, used as a fur. **2** a hard-wearing cotton fabric of twill weave. **3** (*modifier*): *a moleskin waistcoat*.

molest (mə'lɛst) *vb* (*tr*) **1** to disturb or annoy by malevolent interference. **2** to accost or attack, esp. with the intention of assaulting sexually. [C14: from L *molestāre* to annoy, from *molestus* troublesome, from *mōlēs* mass]
▶ **molestation** (,məʊlɛ'steɪʃən) *n* ▶ **mo'lester** *n*

Molière ★ (*French* mɔljɛr) *n* real name *Jean-Baptiste Poquelin*. 1622–73, French dramatist. His works include *Tartuffe* (1664), *Le Misanthrope* (1666), *L'Avare* (1668), and *Le Malade imaginaire* (1673).

Molise ★ (*Italian* mo'liːze) *n* a region of S central Italy, the second smallest of the regions: separated from **Abruzzi e Molise** in 1965. Capital: Campobasso. Pop.: 331 990 (1994 est.). Area: 4438 sq. km (1731 sq. miles).

moll (mɒl) *n Sl.* **1** the female accomplice of a gangster. **2** a prostitute. [C17: from *Moll,* familiar form of *Mary*]

mollify ('mɒlɪ,faɪ) *vb* **mollifies, mollifying, mollified.** (*tr*) **1** to pacify; soothe. **2** to lessen the harshness or severity of.

[C15: from OF *mollifier*, via LL, from L *mollis* soft + *facere* to make]
▶ **'molli,fiable** *adj* ▶ **,mollifi'cation** *n* ▶ **'molli,fier** *n*

mollusc *or US* **mollusk** ('mɒləsk) *n* any of various invertebrates having a soft unsegmented body and often a shell, secreted by a fold of skin (the mantle). The group includes the gastropods (snails, slugs, etc.), bivalves (clams, mussels, etc.), and cephalopods (squid, octopuses, etc.). [C18: via NL from L *molluscus*, from *mollis* soft]
▶ **molluscan** *or US* **molluskan** (mɒ'lʌskən) *adj, n* ▶ **mollusc-like** *or US* **mollusk-like** *adj*

molly[1] ('mɒlɪ) *n, pl* **mollies.** any of various brightly coloured tropical or subtropical American freshwater fishes. [C19: from NL *Mollienisia*, from Comte F. N. *Mollien* (1758–1850), F statesman]

molly[2] ('mɒlɪ) *n, pl* **mollies.** *Irish inf.* an effeminate, weak, or cowardly boy or man. [C18: perhaps from *Molly*, pet name for *Mary*]

mollycoddle ('mɒlɪ,kɒd°l) *vb* **mollycoddles, mollycoddling, mollycoddled.** **1** (*tr*) to treat with indulgent care; pamper.
♦ *n* **2** a pampered person. [C19: from MOLLY[2] + CODDLE]

Molnár ★ (*Hungarian* 'molnaːr) *n* **Ferenc** ('fɛrɛnts). 1878–1952, Hungarian dramatist and novelist. His works include the play *Liliom* (1909).

Moloch ('məʊlɒk) *or* **Molech** ★ ('məʊlɛk) *n Old Testament.* a Semitic deity to whom parents sacrificed their children.

Molokai ★ (,mɒləʊ'kɑːɪ) *n* an island in central Hawaii. Pop.: 6717 (1990). Area: 676 sq. km (261 sq. miles).

Molopo ★ (mə'ləʊpəʊ) *n* a seasonal river rising in N central South Africa and flowing west and southwest to the Orange river. Length: about 1000 km (600 miles).

Molotov[1] ★ ('mɒlə,tɒf; *Russian* 'mɔlətəf) *n* the former name (1940–62) for **Perm**.

Molotov[2] ★ ('mɒlə,tɒf; *Russian* 'mɔlətəf) *n* **Vyacheslav Mikhailovich** (vɪtʃɪ'slaf mi'xajləvitʃ), original surname *Skriabin*. 1890–1986, Soviet statesman. As commissar and later minister for foreign affairs (1939–49; 1953–56) he negotiated the nonaggression pact with Nazi Germany.

Molotov cocktail *n* an elementary incendiary weapon, usually a bottle of petrol with a short delay fuse or wick; petrol bomb. [C20: after V. M. MOLOTOV]

molt (məʊlt) *vb, n* the usual US spelling of **moult**.
▶ **'molter** *n*

molten ('məʊltən) *adj* **1** liquefied; melted. **2** made by having been melted: *molten casts*. ♦ *vb* **3** the past participle of **melt**.

Moltke ★ (*German* 'mɔltkə) *n* **1** Count **Helmuth Johannes Ludwig von** ('hɛlmuːt jo'hanəs 'luːtvɪç fɔn). 1848–1916, German general; chief of the German general staff (1906–14). **2** his uncle Count **Helmuth Karl Bernhard von** ('hɛlmuːt karl 'bɛrnhart fɔn). 1800–91, German field marshal; chief of the Prussian general staff (1858–88).

molto ('mɒltəʊ) *adv Music.* very: *allegro molto; molto adagio*. [from It., from L *multum* (adv) much]

Moluccas (məʊ'lʌkəz, mə-) *or* **Molucca Islands** ★ *pl n* a group of islands in the Malay Archipelago, between Sulawesi (Celebes) and New Guinea. Capital: Amboina. Pop.: 2 094 700 (1995 est.). Area: about 74 505 sq. km (28 766 sq. miles). Indonesian name: **Maluku**. Former name: **Spice Islands**.

mol. wt. *abbrev. for* molecular weight.

moly ('məʊlɪ) *n, pl* **molies. 1** *Greek myth.* a magic herb given by Hermes to Odysseus to nullify the spells of Circe. **2** a variety of wild garlic of S Europe having yellow flowers. [C16: from L *mōly*, from Gk *mōlu*]

molybdenite (mɒ'lɪbdɪ,naɪt) *n* a soft grey mineral consisting of molybdenum sulphide in hexagonal crystalline form with rhenium as an impurity. Formula: MoS_2.

molybdenum (mɒ'lɪbdɪnəm) *n* a very hard silvery-white metallic element occurring principally in molybdenite: used in alloys, esp. to harden and strengthen steels. Symbol: Mo; atomic no.: 42; atomic wt.: 95.94. [C19: from NL, from L *molybdaena* galena, from Gk, from *molubdos* lead]

mom (mɒm) *n Chiefly US & Canad.* an informal word for **mother**[1].

Mombasa ★ (mɒm'bæsə) *n* a port in S Kenya, on a coral island in a bay of the Indian Ocean: the chief port for Kenya, Uganda, and NE Tanzania; became British in 1887, capital of the East African Protectorate until 1907. Pop.: 600 000 (1991 est.).

moment ('məumənt) *n* **1** a short indefinite period of time. **2** a specific instant or point in time: *at that moment the phone rang.* **3 the moment.** the present point of time: *at the moment it's fine.* **4** import, significance, or value: *a man of moment.* **5** *Physics.* **5a** a tendency to produce motion, esp. rotation about a point or axis. **5b** the product of a physical quantity, such as force or mass, and its distance from a fixed reference point. See also **moment of inertia.** [C14: from OF, from L *mōmentum*, from *movēre* to move]

momentarily ('məuməntərɪlɪ, -trɪlɪ, ˌməumən'tærɪlɪ) *adv* **1** for an instant; temporarily. **2** from moment to moment; every instant. **3** *US & Canad.* very soon. ◆ Also (for senses 1, 2): **momently.**

momentary ('məuməntərɪ, -trɪ) *adj* **1** lasting for only a moment; temporary. **2** *Rare.* occurring or present at each moment.
▸ **'momentariness** *n*

moment of inertia *n* the tendency of a body to resist angular acceleration, expressed as the sum of the products of the mass of each particle in the body and the square of its perpendicular distance from the axis of rotation.

moment of truth *n* **1** a moment when a person or thing is put to the test. **2** the point in a bullfight when the matador is about to kill the bull.

momentous (məu'mentəs) *adj* of great significance.
▸ **mo'mentously** *adv* ▸ **mo'mentousness** *n*

momentum (məu'mentəm) *n, pl* **momenta** (-tə) *or* **momentums. 1** *Physics.* the product of a body's mass and its velocity. **2** the impetus of a body resulting from its motion. **3** driving power or strength. [C17: from L: movement; see MOMENT]

momma ('mɒmə) *n Chiefly US.* **1** an informal or childish word for **mother**[1]. **2** *Inf.* a buxom and voluptuous woman.

Mommsen ★ (*German* 'mɔmzən) *n* **Theodor** ('te:odo:r). 1817–1903, German historian, noted esp. for *The History of Rome* (1854–56): Nobel prize for literature 1902.

Momus ★ ('məuməs) *n, pl* **Momuses** *or* **Momi** (-maɪ). **1** *Greek myth.* the god of blame and mockery. **2** a cavilling critic.

mon. *abbrev. for* monetary.

Mon. *abbrev. for* Monday.

mon- *combining form.* a variant of **mono-** before a vowel.

Monaco ★ ('mɒnəˌkəu, məˈnɑːkəu; *French* mɔnako) *n* a principality in SW Europe, on the Mediterranean and forming an enclave in SE France: the second smallest sovereign state in the world (after the Vatican); consists of **Monaco-Ville** (the capital) on a rocky headland, **La Condamine** (a business area and port), **Monte Carlo** (the resort centre), and **Fontvieille,** a light industrial area. Language: French. Religion: Roman Catholic. Currency: franc. Pop.: 31 900 (1997 est.). Area: 189 hectares (476 acres). Related adj: **Monegasque.**
▸ **Monacan** ('mɒnəkən, məˈnɑː-) *n, adj*

monad ('mɒnæd, 'məu-) *n* **1** (*pl* **monads** *or* **monades** (-əˌdiːz)). *Philosophy.* any fundamental singular metaphysical entity, esp. if autonomous. **2** a single-celled organism. **3** an atom, ion, or radical with a valency of one. ◆ Also (for senses 1, 2): **monas.** [C17: from LL *monas*, from Gk: unit, from *monos* alone]
▸ **monadic** (mɒ'nædɪk) *adj*

monadelphous (ˌmɒnə'dɛlfəs) *adj* **1** (of stamens) having united filaments forming a tube around the style. **2** (of flowers) having monadelphous stamens. [C19: from MONO- + Gk *adelphos* brother]

monadnock (mə'nædnɒk) *n* a residual hill of hard rock in an otherwise eroded area. [C19: after Mount *Monadnock,* New Hampshire, US]

Monaghan ★ ('mɒnəhən) *n* **1** a county of NE Republic of Ireland, in Ulster province: many small lakes. County

town: Monaghan. Pop.: 51 293 (1991). Area: 1292 sq. km (499 sq. miles). **2** a town in NE Republic of Ireland, county town of Co. Monaghan. Pop.: 6200 (1995 est.).

monandrous (mɒ'nændrəs) *adj* **1** having only one male sexual partner over a period of time. **2** (of plants) having flowers with only one stamen. **3** (of flowers) having only one stamen. [C19: from MONO- + -ANDROUS]
▸ **mo'nandry** *n*

Mona Passage ★ ('məunə) *n* a strait between Puerto Rico and the Dominican Republic, linking the Atlantic with the Caribbean.

monarch ('mɒnək) *n* **1** a sovereign head of state, esp. a king, queen, or emperor, who rules usually by hereditary right. **2** a supremely powerful or pre-eminent person or thing. **3** Also called: **milkweed.** a large migratory orange-and-black butterfly that feeds on the milkweed plant. [C15: from LL *monarcha,* from Gk; see MONO-, -ARCH]
▸ **monarchal** (mɒ'nɑːk'l) *or* **mo'narchial** *adj* ▸ **mo'narchical** *or* **mo'narchic** *adj* ▸ **'monarchism** *n* ▸ **'monarchist** *n, adj* ▸ ˌmonar'chistic *adj*

monarchy ('mɒnəkɪ) *n, pl* **monarchies. 1** a form of government in which supreme authority is vested in a single and usually hereditary figure, such as a king. **2** a country reigned over by a monarch.

monarda (mɒ'nɑːdə) *n* any of various mintlike North American plants. [C19: from NL, after N. *Monardés* (1493–1588), Sp. botanist]

monastery ('mɒnəstərɪ) *n, pl* **monasteries.** the residence of a religious community, esp. of monks, living in seclusion from secular society and bound by religious vows. [C15: from Church L *monastērium,* ult. from Gk *monazein* to live alone, from *monos* alone]
▸ **monasterial** (ˌmɒnə'stɪərɪəl) *adj*

monastic (mə'næstɪk) *adj* **1** of or relating to monasteries or monks, nuns, etc. **2** resembling this sort of life. ◆ *n* **3** a person committed to this way of life, esp. a monk.

monasticism (mə'næstɪˌsɪzəm) *n* the monastic system, movement, or way of life.

monatomic (ˌmɒnə'tɒmɪk) *or* **monoatomic** (ˌmɒnəuə'tɒmɪk) *adj Chem.* **1** (of an element) having or consisting of single atoms. **2** (of a compound or molecule) having only one atom or group that can be replaced in a chemical reaction.

monaural (mɒ'nɔːrəl) *adj* **1** relating to, having, or hearing with only one ear. **2** another word for **monophonic.**
▸ **mon'aurally** *adv*

monazite ('mɒnəˌzaɪt) *n* a yellow to reddish-brown mineral consisting of a phosphate of thorium, cerium, and lanthanum in monoclinic crystalline form. [C19: from G, from Gk *monazein* to live alone, so called because of its rarity]

Mönchengladbach ★ (*German* mœnçən'glatbax) *n* a city in W Germany, in W North Rhine-Westphalia: headquarters of NATO forces in N central Europe; textile industry. Pop.: 266 073 (1995 est.). Former name: **München-Gladbach.**

Monck ★ (mʌŋk) *n* **George.** 1st Duke of Albemarle. 1608–70, English general. A Royalist until captured (1644) in the Civil War and persuaded to support the Commonwealth. After Cromwell's death he was instrumental in the restoration of Charles II (1660).

Moncton ★ ('mɒŋktən) *n* a city in E Canada, in SE New Brunswick. Pop.: 80 744 (1991).

Monday ('mʌndɪ) *n* the second day of the week; first day of the working week. [OE *mōnandæg* moon's day, translation of LL *lūnae diēs*]

Mondrian ★ (*Dutch* 'mɔndriːaːn) *n* **Piet** (piːt). 1872–1944, Dutch painter, noted as an exponent of De Stijl.

monecious (mɒ'niːʃəs) *adj* a variant spelling of **monoecious.**

Monel metal *or* **Monell metal** (mɒ'nɛl) *n Trademark.* any of various silvery corrosion-resistant alloys. [C20: after A. *Monell* (died 1921), president of the International Nickel Co., New York, which introduced the alloys]

Monet ★ (*French* mɔne) *n* **Claude** (klod). 1840–1926, French impressionist painter, whose works include the

★ people and places

series *Haystacks* (1889–93), *Rouen Cathedral* (1892–94), and the *Thames* (1899–1904).

monetarism ('mʌnɪtə,rɪzəm) *n* **1** the theory that inflation is caused by an excess quantity of money in an economy. **2** an economic policy based on this theory and on a belief in the efficiency of free market forces.
▸ 'monetarist *n, adj*

monetary ('mʌnɪtərɪ, -trɪ) *adj* **1** of or relating to money or currency. **2** of or relating to monetarism. [C19: from LL *monētārius*, from L *monēta* MONEY]
▸ 'monetarily *adv*

monetize *or* **monetise** ('mʌnɪ,taɪz) *vb* **monetizes, monetizing, monetized** *or* **monetises, monetising, monetised.** (*tr*) **1** to establish as legal tender. **2** to give a legal value to (a coin).
▸ ,moneti'zation *or* ,moneti'sation *n*

money ('mʌnɪ) *n* **1** a medium of exchange that functions as legal tender. **2** the official currency, in the form of banknotes, coins, etc., issued by a government or other authority. **3** a particular denomination or form of currency: *silver money.* **4** (*Law or arch. pl* **moneys** *or* **monies**) a pecuniary sum or income. **5** an unspecified amount of paper currency or coins: *money to lend.* **6 for one's money.** in one's opinion. **7 in the money.** *Inf.* well-off; rich. **8 one's money's worth.** full value for the money one has paid for something. **9 put money on.** to place a bet on. ♦ Related adj: **pecuniary.** [C13: from OF *moneie*, from L *monēta*; see MINT²]

moneybags ('mʌnɪ,bægz) *n* (*functioning as sing*) *Inf.* a very rich person.

moneychanger ('mʌnɪ,tʃeɪndʒə) *n* **1** a person engaged in the business of exchanging currencies or money. **2** *Chiefly US.* a machine for dispensing coins.

moneyed *or* **monied** ('mʌnɪd) *adj* **1** having a great deal of money; rich. **2** arising from or characterized by money.

money-grubbing *adj Inf.* seeking greedily to obtain money.
▸ 'money-,grubber *n*

moneylender ('mʌnɪ,lendə) *n* a person who lends money at interest as a living.
▸ 'money,lending *adj, n*

moneymaker ('mʌnɪ,meɪkə) *n* **1** a person who is intent on accumulating money. **2** a person or thing that is or might be profitable.
▸ 'money,making *adj, n*

money of account *n* another name (esp. US and Canad.) for **unit of account.**

money-spinner *n Inf.* an enterprise, idea, person, or thing that is a source of wealth.

money supply *n* the total amount of money in a country's economy at a given time, which can be calculated in various ways.

monger ('mʌŋgə) *n* **1** (*in combination except in archaic use*) a trader or dealer: *ironmonger.* **2** (*in combination*) a promoter of something: *warmonger.* [OE *mangere*, ult. from L *mangō* dealer]
▸ 'mongering *n, adj*

mongol ('mɒŋgəl) *n* (not in technical use) a person affected by Down's syndrome.

Mongol ★ ('mɒŋgɒl, -gəl) *n* another word for **Mongolian.**

Mongolia ★ (mɒŋ'gəʊlɪə) *n* **1** a republic in E central Asia: made a Chinese province in 1691; became autonomous in 1911 and a republic in 1924; multiparty democracy introduced in 1990. It consists chiefly of a high plateau, with the Gobi Desert in the south, a large lake district in the northwest, and the Altai and Khangai Mountains in the west. Official language: Khalkha. Religion: nonreligious majority. Currency: tugrik. Capital: Ulan Bator. Pop.: 2 334 000 (1996). Area: 1 565 000 sq. km (604 095 sq. miles). Former names: **Outer Mongolia** (until 1924), **Mongolian People's Republic** (1924–92). **2** a vast region of central Asia, inhabited chiefly by Mongols: now divided into Mongolia, the Inner Mongolian Autonomous Region of China, and the Tuva Autonomous Republic of Russia; at its height during the 13th century under Genghis Khan.

mongolian (mɒŋ'gəʊlɪən) *adj* (not in technical use) of, relating to, or affected by Down's syndrome.

Mongolian (mɒŋ'gəʊlɪən) *adj* **1.** of or relating to Mongolia, its people, or their language. ♦ *n* **2** a native or inhabitant of Mongolia. **3** the language of Mongolia.

Mongolic (mɒŋ'gɒlɪk) *n* **1** a branch or subfamily of the Altaic family of languages, including Mongolian and Kalmuck. **2** another word for **Mongoloid.**

mongolism ('mɒŋgə,lɪzəm) *n Pathol.* a former name (not in technical use) for **Down's syndrome.** [C20: the condition produces facial features similar to those of the Mongoloid peoples]

mongoloid ('mɒŋgə,lɔɪd) *adj* (not in technical use) **1** relating to or characterized by Down's syndrome. ♦ *n* **2** a person affected by Down's syndrome.

Mongoloid ('mɒŋgə,lɔɪd) *adj* **1** of or relating to a major racial group of mankind, characterized by yellowish complexion, straight black hair, slanting eyes, short nose, and scanty facial hair, including most of the peoples of Asia, the Eskimos, and the North American Indians. ♦ *n* **2** a member of this group.

mongoose ('mɒŋ,guːs) *n, pl* **mongooses.** any of various small predatory mammals occurring in Africa and from S Europe to SE Asia, typically having a long tail and brindled coat. [C17: from Marathi (a language of India) *mangūs*]

mongrel ('mʌŋgrəl) *n* **1** a plant or animal, esp. a dog, of mixed or unknown breeding. **2** *Derog.* a person of mixed race. ♦ *adj* **3** of mixed origin, breeding, character, etc. [C15: from obs. *mong* mixture]
▸ 'mongrelism *n* ▸ 'mongre,lize *or* 'mongre,lise *vb*
▸ ,mongreli'zation *or* ,mongreli'sation *n* ▸ 'mongrelly *adj*

'mongst (mʌŋst) *prep Poetic.* short for **amongst.**

monied ('mʌnɪd) *adj* a less common spelling of **moneyed.**

monies ('mʌnɪz) *n Law, arch.* a plural of **money.**

moniker *or* **monicker** ('mɒnɪkə) *n Sl.* a person's name or nickname. [C19: from Shelta *munnik*, altered from Irish Gaelic *ainm* name]

monism ('mɒnɪzəm) *n* **1** *Philosophy.* the doctrine that reality consists of only one basic substance or element, such as mind or matter. Cf. **dualism** (sense 2), **pluralism** (sense 4). **2** the attempt to explain anything in terms of one principle only.
▸ 'monist *n, adj* ▸ mo'nistic *adj*

monition (məʊ'nɪʃən) *n* **1** a warning or caution; admonition. **2** *Christianity.* a formal notice from a bishop or ecclesiastical court requiring a person to refrain from committing a specific offence. [C14: via OF from L *monitiō*, from *monēre* to warn]

monitor ('mɒnɪtə) *n* **1** a person or piece of equipment that warns, checks, controls, or keeps a continuous record of something. **2** *Education.* **2a** a senior pupil with various supervisory duties, etc. **2b** a pupil assisting a teacher in classroom organization, etc. **3** a television set used to display certain kinds of information in a television studio, airport, etc. **4a** a loudspeaker used in a recording studio to determine quality or balance. **4b** a loudspeaker used on stage to enable musicians to hear themselves. **5** any of various large predatory lizards inhabiting warm regions of Africa, Asia, and Australia. **6** (formerly) a small heavily armoured warship used for coastal assault. ♦ *vb* **7** to act as a monitor of. **8** (*tr*) to observe or record (the activity or performance of) (an engine or other device). **9** (*tr*) to check (the technical quality of) (a radio or television broadcast). [C16: from L, from *monēre* to advise]
▸ monitorial (,mɒnɪ'tɔːrɪəl) *adj* ▸ 'monitorship *n*
▸ 'monitress *fem n*

monitory ('mɒnɪtərɪ, -trɪ) *adj also* **monitorial. 1** warning or admonishing. ♦ *n, pl* **monitories. 2** *Rare.* a letter containing a monition.

monk (mʌŋk) *n* a male member of a religious community bound by vows of poverty, chastity, and obedience. Related adj: **monastic.** [OE *munuc*, from LL *monachus*, from LGk: solitary (man), from Gk *monos* alone]
▸ 'monkish *adj*

Monk ★ (mʌŋk) *n* **1 Thelonious (Sphere)** (θəˈləʊnɪəs). 1920–

82, US jazz pianist and composer. **2** a variant spelling of (George) **Monck**.

monkey ('mʌŋkɪ) n **1** any of numerous long-tailed primates excluding lemurs, tarsiers, etc.: see **Old World monkey**, **New World monkey**. **2** any primate except man. **3** a naughty or mischievous person, esp. a child. **4** the head of a pile-driver (**monkey engine**) or of some similar mechanical device. **5** *US & Canad. sl.* an addict's dependence on a drug (esp. in **have a monkey on one's back**). **6** *Sl.* a butt of derision; someone made to look a fool (esp. in **make a monkey of**). **7** *Sl.* (esp. in bookmaking) £500. **8** *US & Canad. sl.* $500. ◆ vb **9** (*intr*; usually foll. by *around*, *with*, etc.) to meddle, fool, or tinker. **10** (*tr*) *Rare.* to imitate; ape. [C16: ?from Low G; cf. MLow G *Moneke*, name of the ape's son in the tale of Reynard the Fox]

monkey business n *Inf.* mischievous, suspect, or dishonest behaviour or acts.

monkey flower n any of various plants of the genus *Mimulus*, cultivated for their yellow or red flowers.

monkey jacket n a short close-fitting jacket, esp. a waist-length jacket similar to a mess jacket.

monkey nut n *Brit.* another name for a **peanut**.

monkey puzzle n a South American coniferous tree having branches shaped like a candelabrum and stiff sharp leaves. Also called: **Chile pine**.

monkey's wedding n *S. African inf.* a combination of rain and sunshine. [from ?]

monkey tricks or *US* **monkey shines** pl n *Inf.* mischievous behaviour or acts.

monkey wrench n a wrench with adjustable jaws.

monkfish ('mʌŋk,fɪʃ) n, pl **monkfish** or **monkfishes**. **1** any of various angler fishes. **2** another name for **angelfish** (sense 3).

monk's cloth n a heavy cotton fabric of basket weave, used mainly for bedspreads.

monkshood ('mʌŋks,hʊd) n any of several poisonous N temperate plants that have hooded blue-purple flowers.

Monmouth[1] ★ ('mɒnməθ) n a market town in E Wales, in Monmouthshire: Norman castle, where Henry V was born in 1387. Pop.: 7246 (1991).

Monmouth[2] ★ ('mɒnməθ) n **James Scott**, Duke of Monmouth. 1649–85, the illegitimate son of Charles II of England, he led a rebellion against James II in support of his own claim to the Crown; captured and beheaded.

Monmouthshire ★ ('mɒnməθˌʃɪə, -ʃə) n a county of E Wales: administratively part of England for three centuries (until 1830): mainly absorbed into Gwent in 1974; reinstated with reduced boundaries in 1996. Administrative centre: Cwmbran. Pop.: 85 600 (1996 est.). Area: 851 sq. km (329 sq. miles).

Monnet ★ (*French* mɔnɛ) n **Jean** (ʒɑ̃). 1888–1979, French economist, regarded as founding father of the European Economic Community. He was first president (1952–55) of the European Coal and Steel Community.

mono ('mɒnəʊ) adj **1** short for **monophonic**. ◆ n **2** monophonic sound.

mono- or before a vowel **mon-** combining form. **1** one; single: *monorail*. **2** indicating that a chemical compound contains a single specified atom or group: *monoxide*. [from Gk *monos*]

monoacid (ˌmɒnəʊ'æsɪd), **monacid**, **monoacidic** (ˌmɒnəʊə'sɪdɪk), or **monacidic** adj *Chem.* (of a base) capable of reacting with only one molecule of a monobasic acid; having only one hydroxide ion per molecule.

monobasic (ˌmɒnəʊ'beɪsɪk) adj *Chem.* (of an acid, such as hydrogen chloride) having only one replaceable hydrogen atom per molecule.

monocarpic (ˌmɒnəʊ'kɑːpɪk) or **monocarpous** adj (of some flowering plants) producing fruit only once before dying.

monochromatic (ˌmɒnəʊkrəʊ'mætɪk) or **mono-chroic** (ˌmɒnəʊ'krəʊɪk) adj (of light or other electromagnetic radiation) having only one wavelength.

monochromator (ˌmɒnəʊ'krəʊmˌeɪtə) n *Physics.* a device that isolates a single wavelength of radiation.

monochrome ('mɒnə,krəʊm) n **1** a black-and-white

photograph or transparency. **2** *Photog.* black-and-white. **3a** a painting, drawing, etc., done in a range of tones of a single colour. **3b** the technique or art of this. **4** (*modifier*) executed in or resembling monochrome: *a monochrome print*. ◆ adj **5** devoid of any distinctive or stimulating characteristics. ◆ Also called (for senses 3, 4): **monotint**. [C17: via Med. L from Gk *monokhrōmos* of one colour] ▶ ˌmono'chromic adj ▶ 'mono,chromist n

monocle ('mɒnəkᵊl) n a lens for correcting defective vision of one eye, held in position by the facial muscles. [C19: from F, from LL, from MONO- + *oculus* eye] ▶ 'monocled adj

monocline ('mɒnəʊ,klaɪn) n a fold in stratified rocks in which the strata are inclined in the same direction from the horizontal. [C19: from MONO- + Gk *klīnein* to lean] ▶ ˌmono'clinal adj, n

monoclinic (ˌmɒnəʊ'klɪnɪk) adj *Crystallog.* relating to or belonging to the crystal system characterized by three unequal axes, one pair of which are not at right angles to each other. [C19: from MONO- + Gk *klīnein* to lean]

monoclinous (ˌmɒnəʊ'klaɪnəs, 'mɒnəʊˌklaɪnəs) adj (of flowering plants) having the male and female reproductive organs on the same flower. Cf. **diclinous**. [C19: from MONO- + Gk *klīne* bed] ▶ 'mono,clinism n

monoclonal antibody (ˌmɒnəʊ'kləʊnᵊl) n an antibody, produced by a single clone of cells grown in culture, that is both pure and specific and capable of proliferating indefinitely: used in diagnosis, therapy, and biotechnology.

monocotyledon (ˌmɒnəʊ,kɒtɪ'liːdᵊn) n any of various flowering plants having a single embryonic seed leaf, leaves with parallel veins, and flowers with parts in threes: includes grasses, lilies, palms, and orchids. Cf. **dicotyledon**. ▶ ˌmono,coty'ledonous adj

monocracy (mə'nɒkrəsɪ) n, pl **monocracies**. government by one person. ▶ **monocrat** ('mɒnə,kræt) n ▶ ˌmono'cratic adj

monocular (mə'nɒkjʊlə) adj having or intended for the use of only one eye. [C17: from LL *monoculus* one-eyed] ▶ mo'nocularly adv

monoculture ('mɒnəʊ,kʌltʃə) n the continuous growing of one type of crop.

monocycle ('mɒnə,saɪkᵊl) n another name for **unicycle**.

monocyte ('mɒnə,saɪt) n the largest type of white blood cell that acts as part of the immune system by engulfing particles, such as invading microorganisms.

monody ('mɒnədɪ) n, pl **monodies**. **1** (in Greek tragedy) an ode sung by a single actor. **2** any poem of lament for someone's death. **3** *Music.* a style of composition consisting of a single vocal part, usually with accompaniment. [C17: via LL from Gk *monōidia*, from MONO- + *aeidein* to sing] ▶ **monodic** (mə'nɒdɪk) adj ▶ 'monodist n

monoecious (mɒ'niːʃəs) adj **1** (of some flowering plants) having the male and female reproductive organs in separate flowers on the same plant. **2** (of some animals and lower plants) hermaphrodite. [C18: from NL *monoecia*, from MONO- + Gk *oikos* house]

monofilament (ˌmɒnə'fɪləmənt) or **monofil** ('mɒnə-fɪl) n synthetic thread or yarn composed of a single strand rather than twisted fibres.

monogamy (mɒ'nɒgəmɪ) n **1** the state or practice of having only one husband or wife over a period of time. **2** *Zool.* the practice of having only one mate. [C17: via F from LL *monogamia*; see MONO- + -GAMY] ▶ mo'nogamist n ▶ mo'nogamous adj

monogenesis (ˌmɒnə'dʒɛnɪsɪs) or **monogeny** (mɒ-'nɒdʒɪnɪ) n **1** the hypothetical descent of all organisms from a single cell. **2** asexual reproduction in animals. **3** the direct development of an ovum into an organism resembling the adult. **4** the hypothetical descent of all human beings from a single pair of ancestors.

monogram ('mɒnə,græm) n a design of one or more let-

★ people and places

ters, esp. initials, on clothing, stationery, etc. [C17: from LL *monogramma*, from Gk; see MONO-, -GRAM]
▶ **monogrammatic** (ˌmɒnəgrəˈmætɪk) *adj*

monograph ('mɒnəˌgrɑːf) *n* **1** a paper, book, or other work concerned with a single subject or aspect of a subject. ◆ *vb* **monographs, monographing, monographed.** (*tr*) **2** to write a monograph on.
▶ **monographer** (mɒˈnɒgrəfə) *or* **moˈnographist** *n* ▶ ˌmono-'graphic *adj*

monogyny (mɒˈnɒdʒɪnɪ) *n* the custom of having only one female sexual partner over a period of time.
▶ **mo'nogynous** *adj*

monohull ('mɒnəʊˌhʌl) *n* a sailing vessel with a single hull.

monokini ('mɒnəʊˌkiːnɪ) *n* a woman's one-piece bathing garment usually equivalent to the bottom half of a bikini. [C20: from MONO- + BIKINI (as if *bikini* were from BI-)]

monolayer ('mɒnəʊˌleɪə) *n* a single layer of atoms or molecules adsorbed on a surface. Also called: **molecular film.**

monolingual (ˌmɒnəʊˈlɪŋɡwəl) *adj* knowing or expressed in only one language.

monolith ('mɒnəlɪθ) *n* **1** a large block of stone or anything that resembles one in appearance, intractability, etc. **2** a statue, obelisk, column, etc., cut from one block of stone. **3** a large hollow foundation piece sunk as a caisson and filled with concrete. [C19: via F from Gk *monolithos* made from a single stone]
▶ ˌmono'lithic *adj*

monologue ('mɒnəˌlɒɡ) *n* **1** a long speech made by one actor in a play, film, etc., esp. when alone. **2** a dramatic piece for a single performer. **3** any long speech by one person, esp. when interfering with conversation. [C17: via F from Gk *monologos* speaking alone]
▶ **monologic** (ˌmɒnəˈlɒdʒɪk) *or* ˌmono'logical *adj* ▶ **monologist** ('mɒnəˌlɒɡɪst) *n* ▶ **monologize** *or* **monologise** (mɒˈnɒlədʒaɪz) *vb*

USAGE NOTE See at **soliloquy.**

monomania (ˌmɒnəʊˈmeɪnɪə) *n* an excessive mental preoccupation with one thing, idea, etc.
▶ ˌmono'maniˌac *n, adj* ▶ **monomaniacal** (ˌmɒnəʊmə'naɪəkᵊl) *adj*

monomark ('mɒnəmɑːk) *n Brit.* a series of letters or figures to identify goods, personal articles, etc.

monomer ('mɒnəmə) *n Chem.* a compound whose molecules can join together to form a polymer.
▶ **monomeric** (ˌmɒnə'mɛrɪk) *adj*

monometallism (ˌmɒnəʊˈmetᵊˌlɪzəm) *n* **1** the use of one metal, e.g. gold or silver, as the sole standard of value and currency. **2** the economic policies supporting a monometallic standard.
▶ **monometallic** (ˌmɒnəʊmɪ'tælɪk) *adj* ▶ ˌmono'metallist *n*

monomial (mɒˈnəʊmɪəl) *n* **1** *Maths.* an expression consisting of a single term, such as *5ax*. ◆ *adj* **2** consisting of a single algebraic term. [C18: MONO- + (BIN)OMIAL]

monomorphic (ˌmɒnəʊˈmɔːfɪk) *or* **monomorphous** *adj* **1** (of an individual organism) showing little or no change in structure during the entire life history. **2** (of a species) existing or having parts that exist in only one form. **3** (of a chemical compound) having only one crystalline form.

Monongahela ★ (məˌnɒŋɡəˈhiːlə) *n* a river in the northeastern US, flowing generally north to the Allegheny River at Pittsburgh, Pennsylvania, forming the Ohio River. Length: 206 km (128 miles).

mononucleosis (ˌmɒnəʊˌnjuːklɪ'əʊsɪs) *n* **1** *Pathol.* the presence of a large number of monocytes in the blood. **2** See **infectious mononucleosis.**

monophonic (ˌmɒnəʊˈfɒnɪk) *adj* **1** Also: **monaural.** (of a system of broadcasting, recording, or reproducing sound) using only one channel between source and loudspeaker. Sometimes shortened to **mono.** Cf. **stereo-**

phonic. 2 *Music.* of or relating to a style of musical composition consisting of a single melodic line.

monophthong ('mɒnəfˌθɒŋ) *n* a simple or pure vowel. [C17: from Gk *monophthongos*, from MONO- + *thongos* sound]

Monophysite (mɒˈnɒfɪˌsaɪt) *n Christianity.* a person who holds that there is only one nature in the person of Christ, which is primarily divine with human attributes. [C17: via Church L from LGk, from MONO- + *phusis* nature]
▶ **Monophysitic** (ˌmɒnəʊfɪ'sɪtɪk) *adj*

monoplane ('mɒnəʊˌpleɪn) *n* an aeroplane with only one pair of wings. Cf. **biplane.**

monopole ('mɒnəˌpəʊl) *n Physics.* **1** an electric charge or magnetic pole considered in isolation. **2** Also called: **magnetic monopole.** a hypothetical elementary particle postulated in certain theories of particle physics to exist as an isolated north or south magnetic pole.

monopolize *or* **monopolise** (mə'nɒpəˌlaɪz) *vb* **monopolizes, monopolizing, monopolized** *or* **monopolises, monopolising, monopolised.** (*tr*) **1** to have, control, or make use of fully, excluding others. **2** to obtain, maintain, or exploit a monopoly of (a market, commodity, etc.).
▶ **mo,nopoli'zation** *or* **mo,nopoli'sation** *n* ▶ **mo'nopo,lizer** *or* **mo'nopo,liser** *n*

monopoly (mə'nɒpəlɪ) *n, pl* **monopolies. 1** exclusive control of the market supply of a product or service. **2a** an enterprise exercising this control. **2b** the product or service so controlled. **3** *Law.* the exclusive right granted to a person, company, etc., by the state to purchase, manufacture, use, or sell some commodity or to trade in a specified area. **4** exclusive control, possession, or use of something. [C16: from LL, from Gk *monopōlion*, from MONO- + *pōlein* to sell]
▶ **mo'nopolist** *n* ▶ **mo,nopo'listic** *adj*

Monopoly (mə'nɒpəlɪ) *n Trademark.* a board game for two to six players who throw dice to advance their tokens, the object being to acquire the property on which their tokens land.

monorail ('mɒnəʊˌreɪl) *n* a single-rail railway, often elevated and with suspended cars.

monosaccharide (ˌmɒnəʊ'sækəˌraɪd) *n* a simple sugar, such as glucose or fructose, that does not hydrolyse to yield other sugars.

monoski ('mɒnəʊˌskiː) *n* a wide ski on which the skier stands with both feet.
▶ 'mono,skier *n* ▶ 'mono,skiing *n*

monosodium glutamate (ˌmɒnəʊ'səʊdɪəm 'gluːtəˌmeɪt) *n* a white crystalline substance that has little flavour itself but enhances protein flavours: used as a food additive.

monostable (ˌmɒnəʊ'steɪbᵊl) *adj Physics.* (of an electronic circuit) having only one stable state but able to pass into a second state in response to an input pulse.

monosyllabic (ˌmɒnəsɪ'læbɪk) *adj* **1** (of a word) containing only one syllable. **2** characterized by monosyllables; curt.
▶ ˌmonosyl'labically *adv*

monosyllable ('mɒnəˌsɪləbᵊl) *n* a word of one syllable, esp. one used as a sentence.

monoterpene ('mɒnəˌtɜːpiːn) *n Chem.* an isoprene unit, C_5H_8, forming a terpene.

monotheism ('mɒnəʊθɪˌɪzəm) *n* the belief or doctrine that there is only one God.
▶ 'mono,theist *n, adj* ▶ ˌmonothe'istic *adj* ▶ ˌmonothe'istically *adv*

monotint ('mɒnəˌtɪnt) *n* another word for **monochrome** (senses 3, 4).

monotone ('mɒnəˌtəʊn) *n* **1** a single unvaried pitch level in speech, sound, etc. **2** utterance, etc., without change of pitch. **3** lack of variety in style, expression, etc. ◆ *adj* **4** unvarying.

monotonous (mə'nɒtənəs) *adj* **1** tedious, esp. because of repetition. **2** in unvarying tone.
▶ **mo'notonously** *adv* ▶ **mo'notonousness** *n*

monotony (mə'nɒtənɪ) *n, pl* **monotonies. 1** wearisome routine; dullness. **2** lack of variety in pitch or cadence.

★ people and places

monotreme ('mɒnəu,triːm) *n* any mammal of a primitive order of Australia and New Guinea, having a single opening (cloaca) for the passage of eggs or sperm, faeces, and urine. The group contains only the echidnas and the platypus. [C19: via NL from MONO- + Gk *trēma* hole]
▶ **monotrematous** (,mɒnəu'triːmətəs) *adj*

monotype ('mɒnə,taɪp) *n* **1** a single print made from a metal or glass plate on which a picture has been painted. **2** *Biol*. a monotypic genus or species.

Monotype ('mɒnə,taɪp) *n* **1** *Trademark*. any of various typesetting systems, esp. originally one in which each character was cast individually from hot metal. **2** type produced by such a system.

monotypic (,mɒnəu'tɪpɪk) *adj* **1** (of a genus or species) consisting of only one type of animal or plant. **2** of or relating to a monotype.

monounsaturated (,mɒnəuʌn'sætʃə,reɪtɪd) *adj* of or relating to a class of vegetable oils, such as olive oil, the molecules of which have long chains of carbon atoms containing only one double bond. See also **polyunsaturated**.

monovalent (,mɒnəu'veɪlənt) *adj Chem*. **a** having a valency of one. **b** having only one valency. ◆ Also: **univalent**.
▶ ,mono'valence *or* ,mono'valency *n*

monoxide (mɒ'nɒksaɪd) *n* an oxide that contains one oxygen atom per molecule.

Monroe ★ (mən'rəu) *n* **1** James. 1758–1831, US statesman; fifth president of the US (1817–25). He promulgated the Monroe Doctrine (1823). **2 Marilyn**, real name *Norma Jean Baker or Mortenson*. 1926–62, US actress, whose films include *Gentlemen Prefer Blondes* (1953) and *Some Like It Hot* (1959).

Monrovia ★ (mɒn'rəuvɪə) *n* the capital and chief port of Liberia, on the Atlantic: founded in 1822 as a home for freed American slaves; University of Liberia (1862). Pop.: 668 000 (1990 est.).

Mons ★ (French mɔ̃s) *n* a town in SW Belgium, capital of Hainaut province: scene of the first battle (1914) of the British Expeditionary Force during World War I. Pop.: 92 666 (1995 est.). Flemish name: **Bergen**.

Monseigneur *French*. (mɔ̃seɲœr) *n*, *pl* **Messeigneurs** (meseɲœr). a title given to French bishops, prelates, and princes. [lit.: my lord]

monsieur (məs'jɜː) *n*, *pl* **messieurs**. a French title of address equivalent to *sir* when used alone or *Mr* before a name. [lit.: my lord]

Monsignor (mɒn'siːnjə) *n*, *pl* **Monsignors** *or* **Monsignori** (*Italian* monsiɲˈɲoːri). *RC Church*. an ecclesiastical title attached to certain offices. [C17: from It., from F MONSEIGNEUR]

monsoon (mɒn'suːn) *n* **1** a seasonal wind of S Asia from the southwest in summer and from the northeast in winter. **2** the rainy season when the SW monsoon blows, from about April to October. **3** any wind that changes direction with the seasons. [C16: from obs. Du. *monssoen*, from Port., from Ar. *mawsim* season]
▶ **mon'soonal** *adj*

mons pubis ('mɒnz 'pjuːbɪs) *n*, *pl* **montes pubis** ('mɒntiːz). the fatty flesh in human males over the junction of the pubic bones. Cf. **mons veneris**. [C17: NL: hill of the pubes]

monster ('mɒnstə) *n* **1** an imaginary beast, usually made up of various animal or human parts. **2** a person, animal, or plant with a marked deformity. **3** a cruel, wicked, or inhuman person. **4a** a very large person, animal, or thing. **4b** (*as modifier*): *a monster cake*. [C13: from OF *monstre*, from L *monstrum* portent, from *monēre* to warn]

monstera (mɒn'stɪərə) *n* any of various tropical evergreen climbing plants. [from ?]

monstrance ('mɒnstrəns) *n RC Church*. a receptacle in which the consecrated Host is exposed for adoration. [C16: from Med. L *mōnstrantia*, from L *mōnstrāre* to show]

monstrosity (mɒn'strɒsɪtɪ) *n*, *pl* **monstrosities**. **1** an outrageous or ugly person or thing; monster. **2** the state or quality of being monstrous.

monstrous ('mɒnstrəs) *adj* **1** abnormal, hideous, or

unnatural in size, character, etc. **2** (of plants and animals) abnormal in structure. **3** outrageous, atrocious, or shocking. **4** huge. **5** of, relating to, or resembling a monster.
▶ 'monstrously *adv* ▶ 'monstrousness *n*

mons veneris ('mɒnz 'venərɪs) *n*, *pl* **montes veneris** ('mɒntiːz). the fatty flesh in human females over the junction of the pubic bones. Cf. **mons pubis**. [C17: NL: hill of Venus]

Mont. *abbrev. for* Montana.

montage (mɒn'tɑːʒ) *n* **1** the art or process of composing pictures of miscellaneous elements, such as other pictures or photographs. **2** such a composition. **3** a method of film editing by juxtaposition or partial superimposition of several shots to form a single image. **4** a film sequence of this kind. [C20: from F, from *monter* to MOUNT[1]]

Montagu ★ ('mɒntə,gjuː) *n* **1 Charles**. See (Earl of) **Halifax**. **2** Lady **Mary Wortley**. 1689–1762, British writer, noted for her *Letters from the East* (1763).

Montaigne ★ (*French* mɔ̃tɛɲ) *n* Michel Eyquem de (miʃel ikɛm də). 1533–92, French writer. His *Essays* (begun in 1571), established the essay as a literary genre.

Montale ★ (*Italian* mon'taːle) *n* **Eugenio** (eu'dʒɛːnjo). 1896–1981, Italian poet: Nobel prize for literature 1975.

Montana[1] ★ (mɒn'tænə) *n* a state of the western US: consists of the Great Plains in the east and the Rocky Mountains in the west. Capital: Helena. Pop.: 879 372 (1996 est.). Area: 377 070 sq. km (145 587 sq. miles). Abbrevs.: **Mont.** or (with zip code) **MT**
▶ **Mon'tanan** *adj*, *n*

Montana[2] ★ (mɒn'tænə) *n* **Joe**. born 1958, American footballer.

montane ('mɒnteɪn) *adj* of or inhabiting mountainous regions. [C19: from L *montānus*, from *mons* MOUNTAIN]

Montauban ★ (*French* mɔ̃tobɑ̃) *n* a city in SW France: a Huguenot stronghold in the 16th and 17th centuries, taken by Richelieu in 1629. Pop.: 53 280 (1990).

Montbéliard ★ (*French* mɔ̃beljar) *n* an industrial town in E France: former capital of the duchy of Burgundy. Pop.: 30 639 (1990).

Mont Blanc ★ (*French* mɔ̃ blɑ̃) *n* a massif in SW Europe, mainly between France and Italy: the highest mountain in the Alps; beneath it is **Mont Blanc Tunnel**, 12 km (7.5 miles) long. Highest peak (in France): 4807 m (15 771 ft). Italian name: **Monte Bianco** ('monte 'bjaŋko).

montbretia (mɒn'briːʃə) *n* any plant of an African genus related to the iris with ornamental orange or yellow flowers. [C19: NL, after A. F. E. Coquebert de *Montbret* (1780–1801), F botanist]

Montcalm ★ (mɒnt'kɑːm; *French* mɔ̃kalm) *n* **Louis Joseph** (lwi ʒozɛf), Marquis de Montcalm de Saint-Véran. 1712–59, French general in Canada (1756); killed in Quebec by British forces under General Wolfe.

Mont Cenis ★ (*French* mɔ̃səni) *n* See (Mont) **Cenis**.

Mont Cervin ★ (mɔ̃ sɛrvɛ̃) *n* the French name for the **Matterhorn**.

monte ('mɒntɪ) *n* a gambling card game of Spanish origin. [C19: from Sp.: mountain, hence pile of cards]

Monte Carlo ★ ('mɒntɪ 'kɑːləu; *French* mɔ̃te karlo) *n* a town and resort forming part of the principality of Monaco, on the Riviera: famous casino and the destination of an annual car rally (the **Monte Carlo Rally**). Pop.: 12 000 (1985).

Monte Cassino ★ ('mɒntɪ kə'siːnəu; *Italian* 'monte kas-'siːno) *n* a hill above Cassino in central Italy: site of Benedictine monastery (530 A.D.); in 1944 mistaken for German observation post and destroyed by the Allies.

Monte Corno ★ (*Italian* 'monte 'korno) *n* See (Monte) **Corno**.

Montego Bay ★ (mɒn'tiːgəu) *n* a port and resort in NW Jamaica. Pop.: 83 446 (1991).

Montenegro ★ (,mɒntɪ'niːgrəu) *n* a constituent republic of Yugoslavia, bordering on the Adriatic: declared a kingdom in 1910 and united with Serbia, Croatia, and other territories in 1918 to form Yugoslavia; remained

---

★ people and places

united with Serbia as the Federal Republic of Yugoslavia when the other former Yugoslav republics became independent in 1991–92. Capital: Podgorica. Pop.: 635 000 (1995 est.). Area: 13 812 sq. km (5387 sq. miles).
▶ ˌMonte'negrin *adj, n*

Monterey ★ (ˌmɒntə'reɪ) *n* a city in W California: capital of Spain's Pacific empire from 1774 to 1825; taken by the US (1846). Pop.: 31 954 (1990).

Monterrey ★ (ˌmɒntə'reɪ; *Spanish* mɒnte'rrei) *n* a city in NE Mexico, capital of Nuevo Léon state: a major industrial centre, esp. for metals. Pop.: 1 068 996 (1990).

Montespan ★ (*French* mɔ̃tɛspɑ̃) *n* **Marquise de,** title of *Françoise Athénaïs de Rochechouart.* 1641–1707, French noblewoman; mistress of Louis XIV of France.

Montesquieu ★ (*French* mɔ̃tɛskjø) *n* **Baron de la Brède et de** (barɔ̃ də la brɛd e də), title of *Charles Louis de Secondat.* 1689–1755, French political philosopher. His chief works are the satirical *Lettres persanes* (1721) and *L'Esprit des lois* (1748).

Montessori ★ (ˌmɒntɪ'sɔːrɪ; *Italian* montes'sɔːri) *n* **Maria** (ma'riːa). 1870–1952, Italian educational reformer, who evolved the **Montessori method** of teaching children, providing them with facilities for practical play and allowing them to develop at their own pace.

Monteux ★ (*French* mɔ̃tø) *n* **Pierre** (pjɛr). 1875–1964, US conductor, born in France.

Monteverdi ★ (ˌmɒntɪ'vɛədɪ) *n* **Claudio** ('klaʊdɪˌəʊ). ?1567–1643, Italian composer. His operas include *Orfeo* (1607) and he also wrote many motets and madrigals.

Montevideo ★ (ˌmɒntɪvɪ'deɪəʊ; *Spanish* mɔnteβi'ðeo) *n* the capital and chief port of Uruguay, in the south on the Río de la Plata estuary: the largest city in the country: University of the Republic (1849); resort. Pop.: 1 378 707 (1996).

Montezuma II ★ (ˌmɒntɪ'zuːmə) *n* 1466–1520, Aztec emperor of Mexico (?1502–20). He was overthrown and killed by the Spanish conquistador Cortés.

Montfort ★ ('mɒntfət) *n* **Simon de,** Earl of Leicester. ?1208–65, English soldier, born in Normandy. He led the baronial rebellion against Henry III and ruled England from 1264 to 1265; he was killed at Evesham.

Montgolfier ★ (*French* mɔ̃gɔlfje) *n* **Jacques Étienne** (ʒak etjɛn), 1745–99, and his brother **Joseph Michel** (ʒozɛf miʃɛl), 1740–1810, French inventors, who made the first hot-air balloon ascent (1783).

Montgomery[1] ★ (mənt'gʌmərɪ) *n* a city in central Alabama, on the Alabama River: state capital; capital of the Confederacy (1861). Pop.: 195 471 (1994 est.).

Montgomery[2] ★ (mənt'gʌmərɪ) *n* **Bernard Law,** 1st Viscount Montgomery of Alamein, nicknamed *Monty.* 1887–1976, British field marshal. As commander of the 8th Army in North Africa, he launched the offensive that drove Rommel's forces back to Tunis. He also commanded the ground forces in Normandy (1944) and accepted Germany's surrender (May 7, 1945).

Montgomeryshire ★ (mənt'gʌmərɪˌʃɪə, -ʃə) *n* (until 1974) a county of central Wales, now part of Powys.

month (mʌnθ) *n* **1** one of the twelve divisions (**calendar months**) of the calendar year. **2** a period of time extending from one date to a corresponding date in the next calendar month. **3** a period of four weeks or of 30 days. **4** the period of time (**solar month**) taken by the moon to return to the same longitude after one complete revolution around the earth; 27.321 58 days (approximately 27 days, 7 hours, 43 minutes, 4.5 seconds). **5** the period of time (**sidereal month**) taken by the moon to make one complete revolution around the earth, measured between two successive conjunctions with a particular star; 27.321 66 days (approximately 27 days, 7 hours, 43 minutes, 11 seconds). **6** Also called: **lunation**. the period of time (**lunar** or **synodic month**) taken by the moon to make one complete revolution around the earth, measured between two successive new moons; 29.530 59 days (approximately 29 days, 12 hours, 44 minutes, 3 seconds). [OE *mōnath*]

Montherlant ★ (*French* mɔ̃tɛrlɑ̃) *n* **Henri (Millon) de** (ɑ̃ri də). 1896–1972, French novelist and dramatist: his nov-

els include *Les Jeunes Filles* (1935–39) and *Le Chaos et la nuit* (1963).

monthly ('mʌnθlɪ) *adj* **1** occurring, done, appearing, payable, etc., once every month. **2** lasting or valid for a month. ◆ *adv* **3** once a month. ◆ *n, pl* **monthlies**. **4** a book, periodical, magazine, etc., published once a month. **5** *Inf.* a menstrual period.

Montluçon ★ (*French* mɔ̃lysɔ̃) *n* an industrial city in central France, on the Cher River. Pop.: 56 434 (1983 est.).

Montmartre ★ (*French* mɔ̃martrə) *n* a district of N Paris: the highest point in the city and famous for its association with artists.

Montparnasse ★ (*French* mɔ̃parnas) *n* a district of S Paris, on the left bank of the Seine, frequented by artists, writers, and students.

Montpelier ★ (mɒnt'piːljə) *n* a city in N central Vermont, on the Winooski River: the state capital. Pop.: 8254 (1990).

Montpellier ★ (*French* mɔ̃pəlje) *n* a city in S France, the chief town of Languedoc: its university was founded by Pope Nicholas IV in 1289; wine trade. Pop.: 210 866 (1990).

Montreal ★ (ˌmɒntrɪ'ɔːl) *n* a city and major port in central Canada, in S Quebec on **Montreal Island** at the junction of the Ottawa and St Lawrence Rivers. Pop.: 1 017 666 (1991), with a conurbation of 3 127 242 (1991). French name: **Montréal** (mɔ̃real).

Montreuil ★ (*French* mɔ̃trœj) *n* an E suburb of Paris: formerly famous for peaches, but now increasingly industrialized. Pop.: 94 754 (1990).

Montreux ★ (*French* mɔ̃trø) *n* a town and resort in W Switzerland, in Vaud canton on Lake Geneva: annual television festival. Pop.: 19 850 (1990).

Montrose ★ (mɒn'trəʊz) *n* **James Graham,** 1st Marquess and 5th Earl of Montrose. 1612–50, Scottish general, noted for his victories in Scotland for Charles I in the Civil War. He was later captured and hanged.

Mont-Saint-Michel ★ (*French* mɔ̃sɛ̃miʃɛl) *n* a rocky islet off the coast of NW France, accessible at low tide by a causeway: Benedictine abbey (966), used as a prison from the Revolution until 1863; reoccupied by Benedictine monks since 1966. Area: 1 hectare (3 acres).

Montserrat ★ *n* **1** (ˌmɒntsə'ræt). a volcanic island in the Caribbean, in the Leeward Islands of the West Indies: a UK overseas territory: devastated by volcanic eruptions in 1997. Capital: Plymouth. Pop.: 11 957 (1991). Area: 103 sq. km (40 sq. miles). **2** (*Spanish* mɒnse'rrat). a mountain in NE Spain, northwest of Barcelona: famous Benedictine monastery. Height: 1235 m (4054 ft). Ancient name: **Mons Serratus** (mɒnz sə'rætəs).

monument ('mɒnjʊmənt) *n* **1** an obelisk, statue, building, etc., erected in commemoration of a person or event. **2** a notable building or site, esp. one preserved as public property. **3** a tomb or tombstone. **4** a literary or artistic work regarded as commemorative of its creator or a particular period. **5** *US.* a boundary marker. **6** an exceptional example: *his lecture was a monument of tedium.* [C13: from L *monumentum,* from *monēre* to remind]

Monument ★ ('mɒnjʊmənt) *n* **the.** a tall columnar building designed (1671) by Sir Christopher Wren to commemorate the Fire of London (1666), which destroyed a large part of the medieval city.

monumental (ˌmɒnjʊ'mɛntl̩) *adj* **1** like a monument, esp. in large size, endurance, or importance. **2** of, relating to, or being a monument. **3** *Inf.* (intensifier): *monumental stupidity.*
▶ ˌmonu'mentally *adv*

Monza ★ (*Italian* 'montsa) *n* a city in N Italy, northeast of Milan: the ancient capital of Lombardy; scene of the assassination of King Umberto I in 1900; motor-racing circuit. Pop.: 120 882 (1994 est.).

moo (muː) *vb* **1** (*intr*) (of a cow, bull, etc.) to make a characteristic deep long sound; low. ◆ *interj* **2** an instance or imitation of this sound.

mooch (muːtʃ) *vb Sl.* **1** (*intr*; often with *around*) to loiter or walk aimlessly. **2** (*intr*) to lurk; skulk. **3** (*tr*) to cadge. **4** (*tr*)

Chiefly *US & Canad.* to steal. [C17: ?from OF *muchier* to skulk]
▸ **'moocher** *n*

mood[1] (muːd) *n* **1** a temporary state of mind or temper: *a cheerful mood.* **2** a sullen or gloomy state of mind, esp. when temporary: *she's in a mood.* **3** a prevailing atmosphere or feeling. **4 in the mood.** in a favourable state of mind. [OE *mōd* mind, feeling]

mood[2] (muːd) *n* **1** *Grammar.* a category of the verb or verbal inflections that expresses semantic and grammatical differences, including such forms as the indicative, subjunctive, and imperative. **2** *Logic.* one of the possible arrangements of the syllogism, classified by whether the component propositions are universal or particular and affirmative or negative. ◆ Also called: **mode.** [C16: from MOOD[1], infl. in meaning by MODE]

moody ('muːdɪ) *adj* **moodier, moodiest. 1** sullen, sulky, or gloomy. **2** temperamental or changeable.
▸ **'moodily** *adv* ▸ **'moodiness** *n*

Moody ★ ('muːdɪ) *n* **Dwight Lyman.** 1837–99, US evangelist and hymnodist, noted for his revivalist campaigns in Britain and the US with I. D. Sankey.

Moog (muːg, məʊg) *n Music, trademark.* a type of synthesizer. [C20: after Robert *Moog* (born 1934), US engineer]

mooi (mɔɪ) *adj S. African sl.* pleasing; nice. [from Afrik.]

mooli ('muːlɪ) *n* a type of large white radish. [E African native name]

moolvie *or* **moolvi** ('muːlvɪ) *n* (esp. in India) a Muslim doctor of the law, teacher, or learned man: also used as a title of respect. [C17: from Urdu, from Ar. *mawlawīy;* cf. MULLAH]

Moomba ('muːmbə) *n* an annual carnival that takes place in Melbourne, Australia, in March. [from Abor. *moom* buttocks, anus; *moomba* orig. thought to be Abor. word meaning "Let's get together and have fun"]

moon (muːn) *n* **1** the natural satellite of the earth. **2** the face of the moon as it is seen during its revolution around the earth, esp. at one of its phases: *new moon; full moon.* **3** any natural satellite of a planet. **4** moonlight. **5** something resembling a moon. **6** a month, esp. a lunar one. **7 over the moon.** *Inf.* extremely happy; ecstatic. ◆ *vb* **8** (when *tr,* often foll. by *away;* when *intr,* often foll. by *around*) to be idle in a listless way, as if in love, or to idle (time) away. **9** (*intr*) *Sl.* to expose one's buttocks to passers-by. [OE *mōna*]
▸ **'moonless** *adj*

Moon ★ (muːn) *n* **William.** 1818–94, blind British inventor of the Moon writing system (1847) for blind children.

moonbeam ('muːn,biːm) *n* a ray of moonlight.

mooncalf ('muːn,kɑːf) *n, pl* **mooncalves** (-,kɑːvz). **1** a born fool; dolt. **2** a person who idles time away.

moon-faced *adj* having a round face.

moonlight ('muːn,laɪt) *n* **1** light from the sun received on earth after reflection by the moon. **2** (*modifier*) illuminated by the moon: *a moonlight walk.* ◆ *vb* **moonlights, moonlighting, moonlighted. 3** (*intr*) *Inf.* to work at a secondary job, esp. at night and illegally.
▸ **'moon,lighter** *n*

moonlight flit *n Brit. inf.* a hurried departure at night, esp. from rented accommodation to avoid payments of rent owed. Often shortened to **moonlight.**

moonlit ('muːn,lɪt) *adj* illuminated by the moon.

moonquake ('muːn,kweɪk) *n* a light tremor of the moon, detected on the moon's surface.

moonscape ('muːn,skeɪp) *n* the general surface of the moon or a representation of it.

moonshine ('muːn,ʃaɪn) *n* **1** another word for **moonlight** (sense 1). **2** *US & Canad.* illegally distilled or smuggled whisky. **3** foolish talk or thought.

moonshot ('muːn,ʃɒt) *n* the launching of a spacecraft, rocket, etc., to the moon.

moonstone ('muːn,stəʊn) *n* a gem variety of orthoclase or albite that is white and translucent.

moonstruck ('muːn,strʌk) *or* **moonstricken** ('muːn,strɪkən) *adj* deranged or mad.

moony ('muːnɪ) *adj* **moonier, mooniest. 1** *Inf.* dreamy or listless. **2** of or like the moon.

moor[1] (mʊə, mɔː) *n* a tract of unenclosed ground, usually covered with heather, coarse grass, bracken, and moss. [OE *mōr*]

moor[2] (mʊə, mɔː) *vb* **1** to secure (a ship, boat, etc.) with cables or ropes. **2** (of a ship, boat, etc.) to be secured in this way. **3** (not in technical usage) a less common word for **anchor** (senses 7 and 8). [C15: of Gmc origin; rel. to OE *mǣrelsrāp* rope for mooring]
▸ **moorage** ('mʊərɪdʒ) *n*

Moor (mʊə, mɔː) *n* a member of a Muslim people of North Africa, of mixed Arab and Berber descent. [C14: via OF from L *Maurus,* from Gk *Mauros,* ?from Berber]
▸ **'Moorish** *adj*

moorcock ('mʊə,kɒk, 'mɔː-) *n* the male of the red grouse.

Moore ★ (mʊə, mɔː) *n* **1 Bobby,** full name *Robert Frederick Moore.* 1941–93, British footballer: captain of England team that won the World Cup in 1966. **2 George.** 1852–1933, Irish novelist. His works include *Esther Waters* (1894). **3 G(eorge) E(dward).** 1873–1958, British philosopher, noted esp. for his *Principia Ethica* (1903). **4 Henry.** 1898–1986, British sculptor. His many works include the *Madonna and Child* (1943) at St Matthew's Church, Northampton. **5** Sir **John.** 1761–1809, British general; commander of the British army (1808–09) in the Peninsular War: killed at Corunna. **6 Marianne.** 1887–1972, US poet. **7 Thomas.** 1779–1852, Irish poet, best known for *Irish Melodies* (1807–34).

moorhen ('mʊə,hen, 'mɔː-) *n* **1** a bird of the rail family, inhabiting ponds, lakes, etc., having a black plumage, red bill, and a red shield above the bill. **2** the female of the red grouse.

mooring ('mʊərɪŋ, 'mɔː-) *n* **1** a place for mooring a vessel. **2** a permanent anchor with a floating buoy, to which vessels can moor.

moorings ('mʊərɪŋz, 'mɔː-) *pl n* **1** *Naut.* the ropes, anchors, etc., used in mooring a vessel. **2** (*sometimes sing*) something that provides security or stability.

Moorish idol *n* a tropical marine spiny-finned fish that is common around coral reefs. It has a deeply compressed body with yellow and black stripes.

moorland ('mʊələnd) *n Brit.* an area of moor.

moose (muːs) *n, pl* **moose.** a large North American deer having large flattened palmate antlers: also occurs in Europe and Asia where it is called an elk. [C17: of Amerind origin]

Moose Jaw ★ *n* a city in W Canada, in S Saskatchewan. Pop.: 33 593 (1991).

moot (muːt) *adj* **1** subject or open to debate: *a moot point.* ◆ *vb* **2** (*tr*) to suggest or bring up for debate. **3** (*intr*) to plead or argue hypothetical cases, as an academic exercise or as training for law students. ◆ *n* **4** a discussion or debate of a hypothetical case or point, held as an academic activity. **5** (in Anglo-Saxon England) an assembly dealing with local legal and administrative affairs. [OE *gemōt*]

moot court *n* a mock court trying hypothetical legal cases.

mop (mɒp) *n* **1** an implement with a wooden handle and a head made of twists of cotton or a piece of synthetic sponge, used for polishing or washing floors, or washing dishes. **2** something resembling this, such as a tangle of hair. ◆ *vb* **mops, mopping, mopped.** (*tr*) **3** (often foll. by *up*) to clean or soak up as with a mop. ◆ See also **mop up.** [C15 *mappe,* ult. from L *mappa* napkin]

mopani *or* **mopane** (mɒ'pɑːnɪ) *n* **1** a leguminous tree, native to southern Africa, that is highly resistant to drought and produces very hard wood. **2** Also called: **mopani worm.** an edible caterpillar that feeds on mopani leaves. [C19: from Bantu]

mope (məʊp) *vb* **mopes, moping, moped.** (*intr*) **1** to be gloomy or apathetic. **2** to move or act in an aimless way. ◆ *n* **3** a gloomy person. [C16: ?from obs. *mope* fool & rel. to *mop* grimace]
▸ **'moper** *n* ▸ **'mopy** *adj*

★ people and places

moped ('məʊpɛd) *n* a light motorcycle not over 50cc. [C20: from MOTOR + PEDAL¹]

mopes (məʊps) *pl n* **the.** low spirits.

mopoke ('məʊˌpəʊk) *n* **1** a small spotted owl of Australia and New Zealand. In Australia the tawny frogmouth is often wrongly identified as the mopoke. **2** *Austral. & NZ sl.* a slow or lugubrious person. ◆ Also called: **morepork**. [C19: imit. of the bird's cry]

moppet ('mɒpɪt) *n* a less common word for **poppet** (sense 1). [C17: from obs. *mop* rag doll; from ?]

mop up *vb* (*tr, adv*) **1** to clean with a mop. **2** *Inf.* to complete (a task, etc.). **3** *Mil.* to clear (remaining enemy forces) after a battle, as by killing, taking prisoner, etc.

moquette (mɒ'kɛt) *n* a thick velvety fabric used for carpets, upholstery, etc. [C18: from F; from ?]

MOR *abbrev. for* middle-of-the-road: used esp. in radio programming.

Mor. *abbrev. for* Morocco.

mora *or* **morra** ('mɔːrə) *n* a guessing game played with the fingers, esp. in Italy and China. [C18: from It. *mora*]

Moradabad ★ (ˌmɒːrədə'bæd) *n* a city in N India, in N Uttar Pradesh. Pop.: 429 214 (1991).

moraine (mɒ'reɪn) *n* a mass of debris, carried by glaciers and forming ridges and mounds when deposited. [C18: from F, from Savoy dialect *morena*, from ?]
▶ **mo'rainal** *or* **mo'rainic** *adj*

moral ('mɒrəl) *adj* **1** concerned with or relating to human behaviour, esp. the distinction between good and bad or right and wrong behaviour: *moral sense.* **2** adhering to conventionally accepted standards of conduct. **3** based on a sense of right and wrong according to conscience: *moral courage; moral law.* **4** having psychological rather than tangible effects: *moral support.* **5** having the effects but not the appearance of (victory or defeat): *a moral victory.* **6** having a strong probability: *a moral certainty.* ◆ *n* **7** the lesson to be obtained from a fable or event. **8** a concise truth; maxim. **9** (*pl*) principles of behaviour in accordance with standards of right and wrong. **10** *Austral. sl.* a certainty: *a moral to win.* [C14: from L *mōrālis* relating to morals or customs, from *mōs* custom]
▶ **'morally** *adv*

morale (mɒ'rɑːl) *n* the degree of mental or moral confidence of a person or group. [C18: morals, from F, n use OF MORAL (adj)]

moralist ('mɒrəlɪst) *n* **1** a person who seeks to regulate the morals of others. **2** a person who lives in accordance with moral principles.
▶ ˌmoral'istic *adj* ▶ ˌmoral'istically *adv*

morality (mə'rælɪtɪ) *n, pl* **moralities. 1** the quality of being moral. **2** conformity, or degree of conformity, to conventional standards of moral conduct. **3** a system of moral principles. **4** an instruction or lesson in morals. **5** short for **morality play**.

morality play *n* a type of drama between the 14th and 16th centuries concerned with the conflict between personified virtues and vices.

moralize *or* **moralise** ('mɒrəˌlaɪz) *vb* **moralizes, moralizing, moralized** *or* **moralises, moralising, moralised. 1** (*intr*) to make moral pronouncements. **2** (*tr*) to interpret or explain in a moral sense. **3** (*tr*) to improve the morals of.
▶ ˌmorali'zation *or* ˌmorali'sation *n* ▶ 'moral,izer *or* 'moral,iser *n*

moral majority *n* a presumed majority of people believed to be in favour of a stricter code of public morals. [C20: after *Moral Majority*, a right-wing US religious organization, based on SILENT MAJORITY]

moral philosophy *n* the branch of philosophy dealing with ethics.

Moral Rearmament *n* a worldwide movement for moral and spiritual renewal founded by Frank Buchman in 1938. Also called: **Buchmanism**. Former name: **Oxford Group**.

moral theology *n* the branch of theology dealing with ethics.

Morar ★ ('mɔːrə) *n* **Loch.** a lake in W Scotland, in the SW Highlands: the deepest in Scotland. Length: 18 km (11 miles). Depth: 296 m (987 ft).

morass (mə'ræs) *n* **1** a tract of swampy low-lying land. **2** a disordered or muddled situation or circumstance, esp. one that impedes progress. [C17: from Du. *moeras*, ult. from OF *marais* MARSH]

moratorium (ˌmɒrə'tɔːrɪəm) *n, pl* **moratoria** (-rɪə) *or* **moratoriums. 1** a legally authorized postponement of the fulfilment of an obligation. **2** an agreed suspension of activity. [C19: NL, from LL *morātōrius* dilatory, from *mora* delay]

Morava ★ (mə'rɑːvə) *n* **1** a river in central Europe, rising in the Sudeten Mountains, in the Czech Republic, and flowing south to the Danube: forms part of the border between the Czech Republic, Slovakia, and Austria. Length: 370 km (230 miles). German name: **March. 2** a river in E Yugoslavia, formed by the confluence of the Southern Morava and the Western Morava near Stalac: flows north to the Danube. Length: 209 km (130 miles). **3** ('mɒrava). the Czech name for **Moravia**¹.

Moravia¹ ★ (mə'reɪvɪə, mɒ-) *n* a region of the Czech Republic, around the Morava River, bounded by the Bohemian-Moravian Highlands, the Sudeten Mountains, and the W Carpathians: became a separate Austrian crownland in 1848; part of Czechoslovakia (1918–92); valuable mineral resources. Czech name: **Morava**. German name: **Mähren**.

Moravia² ★ (*Italian* mo'ra:vja) *n* **Alberto** (al'bɛrto), pen name of *Alberto Pincherle*. 1907–90, Italian writer: his works include *The Woman of Rome* (1949) and *Erotic Tales* (1985).

Moravian (mə'reɪvɪən, mɒ-) *adj* **1** of or relating to Moravia, its people, or their dialect of Czech. **2** of or relating to the Moravian Church. ◆ *n* **3** the Moravian dialect. **4** a native or inhabitant of Moravia. **5** a member of the Moravian Church.
▶ **Mo'ravianism** *n*

moray (mɒ'reɪ) *n, pl* **morays.** a voracious marine coastal eel marked with brilliant colours. [C17: from Port. *moréia*, from L *mūrēna*, from Gk *muraina*]

Moray¹ ★ ('mʌrɪ) *n* **1** a council area of NE Scotland. Administrative centre: Elgin. Pop.: 86 250 (1996 est.). Area: 2238 sq. km (874 sq miles). **2** another name for **Morayshire**.

Moray² *or* **Murray** ★ ('mʌrɪ) *n* **1st Earl of,** title of *James Stuart*. ?1531–70, regent of Scotland (1567–70) following the abdication of Mary, Queen of Scots, his half-sister. He defeated Mary and Bothwell at Langside (1568); assassinated by a follower of Mary.

Moray Firth ★ *n* an inlet of the North Sea on the NE coast of Scotland. Length: about 56 km (35 miles).

Morayshire ★ ('mʌrɪˌ∫ɪə, -∫ə) *n* a historic county of NE Scotland. Former name: **Elgin**.

morbid ('mɔːbɪd) *adj* **1** having an unusual interest in death or unpleasant events. **2** gruesome. **3** relating to or characterized by disease. [C17: from L *morbidus* sickly, from *morbus* illness]
▶ **mor'bidity** *n* ▶ 'morbidly *adv* ▶ 'morbidness *n*

morbid anatomy *n* the branch of medical science concerned with the study of the structure of diseased organs and tissues.

morbific (mɔː'bɪfɪk) *adj* causing disease.

Morbihan ★ (*French* mɔrbiã) *n* a department of NW France, in S Brittany. Capital: Vannes. Pop.: 631 290 (1994 est.). Area: 7092 sq. km (2766 sq. miles).

mordant ('mɔːdᵊnt) *adj* **1** sarcastic or caustic. **2** having the properties of a mordant. **3** pungent. ◆ *n* **4** a substance used before the application of a dye, possessing the ability to fix colours. **5** an acid or other corrosive fluid used to etch lines on a printing plate. [C15: from OF: biting, from *mordre* to bite, from L *mordēre*]
▶ 'mordancy *n* ▶ 'mordantly *adv*

Mordecai ★ (ˌmɔːdɪ'keɪ, 'mɔːdəˌkaɪ) *n Old Testament.* the cousin of Esther who averted a threatened massacre of the Jews (Esther 2–9).

mordent ('mɔːdᵊnt) *n Music.* a melodic ornament consisting of the rapid alternation of a note with a note one degree lower than it. [C19: from G, from It. *mordente*, from *mordere* to bite]

★ people and places

Mordred ★ (ˈmɔːdrɪd) *n* a variant of **Modred**.

Mordvinian Republic ★ (mɔːˈdvɪnɪən) *n* a constituent republic of W central Russia, in the middle Volga basin. Capital: Saransk. Pop.: 960 000 (1995 est.). Area: 26 200 sq. km (10 110 sq. miles). Also called: **Mordovian Republic** (mɔːˈdəʊvɪən), **Mordovia** (mɔːˈdəʊvɪə).

more (mɔː) *determiner* **1a** the comparative of **much** or **many**: *more joy than you know*; *more sausages*. **1b** (*as pron; functioning as sing or pl*): *he has more than she has*; *even more are dying*. **2a** additional; further: *no more bananas*. **2b** (*as pron; functioning as sing or pl*): *I can't take any more*; *more than expected*. **3 more of**. to a greater extent or degree: *we see more of Sue*; *more of a nuisance*. ◆ *adv* **4** used to form the comparative of some adjectives and adverbs: *a more believable story*; *more quickly*. **5** the comparative of **much**: *people listen to the radio more now*. **6 more or less**. **6a** as an estimate; approximately. **6b** to an unspecified extent or degree: *the party was ruined, more or less*. [OE *māra*]

> **USAGE NOTE** See at **most**.

More ★ (mɔː) *n* **1 Hannah**. 1745–1833, British writer, noted for her religious tracts, esp. *The Shepherd of Salisbury Plain*. **2** Sir **Thomas**. 1478–1535, English statesman and Roman Catholic Saint; Lord Chancellor (1529–32) to Henry VIII. He opposed the annulment of Henry's marriage to Catherine of Aragon and refused to recognize the Act of Supremacy; executed on a charge of treason. In *Utopia* (1516), he set forth his concept of the ideal state. Feast day: June 22 or July 6.

Morea ★ (mɔːˈrɪə) *n* the medieval name for the **Peloponnese**.

Moreau ★ (*French* mɔro) *n* **1 Gustave** (gystav) 1826–98, French symbolist painter. **2 Jeanne** (ʒan). born 1928, French actress. Her films include *Jules et Jim* (1961) and *Viva Maria* (1965). **3 Jean Victor** (ʒɑ̃ viktɔr). 1763–1813, French general in the Revolutionary and Napoleonic Wars.

Morecambe ★ (ˈmɔːkəm) *n* a port and resort in NW England, in NW Lancashire on **Morecambe Bay** (an inlet of the Irish Sea). Pop. (with Heysham): 46 657 (1991).

Morecambe and Wise ★ (ˈmɔːkəm; waɪz) *n* a team of British comedians, **Eric Morecambe**, real name *John Eric Bartholomew*, 1926–84, and **Ernie Wise**, real name *Ernest Wiseman*, 1925–99.

moreish *or* **morish** (ˈmɔːrɪʃ) *adj Inf.* (of food) causing a desire for more.

morel (mɒˈrɛl) *n* an edible fungus in which the mushroom has a pitted cap. [C17: from F *morille*, prob. of Gmc origin]

Morelia ★ (*Spanish* moˈrelia) *n* a city in central Mexico, capital of Michoacán state: a cultural centre during colonial times; two universities. Pop.: 428 486 (1990). Former name (until 1828): **Valladolid**.

morello (mɒˈrɛləʊ) *n, pl* **morellos**. a variety of small very dark sour cherry. [C17: ?from Med. L *amārellum*, dim. of L *amārus* bitter, but also infl. by It. *morello* blackish]

Morelos ★ (*Spanish* moˈrelɔs) *n* an inland state of S central Mexico, on the S slope of the great plateau. Capital: Cuernavaca. Pop.: 1 442 587 (1995 est.). Area: 4988 sq. km (1926 sq. miles).

morendo (mɒˈrɛndəʊ) *adv Music.* gradually dying away. [It.: dying]

moreover (mɔːˈrəʊvə) *sentence connector.* in addition to what has already been said.

morepork (ˈmɔːˌpɔːk) *n* another name, esp. in New Zealand, for **mopoke**.

mores (ˈmɔːreɪz) *pl n* the customs and conventions embodying the fundamental values of a group or society. [C20: from L, pl of *mōs* custom]

Morgan ★ (ˈmɔːgən) *n* **1** Sir **Henry**. 1635–88, Welsh buccaneer, who raided Spanish colonies in the West Indies. **2 John Pierpont**. 1837–1913, US financier, philanthropist, and art collector. **3 Thomas Hunt**. 1866–1945, US biologist, who formulated the chromosome theory of heredity. Nobel prize for physiology or medicine 1933.

morganatic (ˌmɔːgəˈnætɪk) *adj* of or designating a marriage between a person of high rank and a person of low rank, by which the latter is not elevated to the higher rank and any issue have no rights to the succession of the higher party's titles, property, etc. [C18: from Med. L *mātrimōnium ad morganāticum* marriage based on the morning-gift (a token present after consummation representing the husband's only liability); *morganātica*, ult. from OHG *morgan* morning]
> ▸ ˌmorga'natically *adv*

Morgan le Fay (ˈmɔːgən lə ˈfeɪ) *or* **Morgain le Fay** ★ (ˈmɔːgaɪn, -gən) *n* a wicked sorceress of Arthurian legend, the half-sister of King Arthur.

morgen (ˈmɔːgən) *n* **1** a South African unit of area, equal to about two acres or 0.8 hectare. **2** a unit of area, formerly used in Prussia and Scandinavia, equal to about two thirds of an acre. [C17: from Du.: morning, a morning's ploughing]

morgue (mɔːg) *n* **1** another word for **mortuary**. **2** *Inf.* a room or file containing clippings, etc., used for reference in a newspaper. [C19: from F *le Morgue*, a Paris mortuary]

moribund (ˈmɒrɪˌbʌnd) *adj* **1** near death. **2** without force or vitality. [C18: from L, from *morī* to die]
> ▸ ˌmori'bundity *n* ▸ 'mori,bundly *adv*

Mörike ★ (*German* ˈmøːrɪkə) *n* **Eduard** (ˈeːduart). 1804–75, German poet, noted for his lyrics, such as *On a Winter's Morning before Sunrise* and *At Midnight*.

Morisco (məˈrɪskəʊ) *or* **Moresco** (məˈreskəʊ) *n, pl* **Moriscos** *or* **Moriscoes**. **1** a Spanish Moor. **2** a morris dance. ◆ *adj* **3** another word for **Moorish**; see **Moor**. [C16: from Sp., from *Moro* MOOR]

morish (ˈmɔːrɪʃ) *adj* a variant spelling of **moreish**.

Morisot ★ (*French* mɔrizo) *n* **Berthe** (bert). 1841–95, French impressionist painter.

Morley[1] ★ (ˈmɔːlɪ) *n* an industrial town in N England, in Leeds unitary authority West Yorkshire. Pop.: 47 579 (1991).

Morley[2] ★ (ˈmɔːlɪ) *n* **1 Edward Williams**. 1838–1923, US chemist who collaborated with A. A. Michelson in the Michelson-Morley experiment. **2 John**, Viscount Morley of Blackburn. 1838–1923, British Liberal statesman and writer; secretary of state for India (1905–10). **3 Robert**. 1908–92, British actor. His many films include *Oscar Wilde* (1960) and *The Blue Bird* (1976). **4 Thomas**. ?1557–?1603, English composer, noted for his madrigals and his textbook on music.

Mormon (ˈmɔːmən) *n* **1** a member of the Church of Jesus Christ of Latter-day Saints, founded in 1830 in New York by Joseph Smith. **2** a prophet whose supposed revelations were recorded by Joseph Smith in the Book of Mormon. ◆ *adj* **3** of or relating to the Mormons, their Church, or their beliefs.
> ▸ 'Mormonism *n*

morn (mɔːn) *n* a poetic word for **morning**. [OE *morgen*]

mornay (ˈmɔːneɪ) *adj* (*often immediately postpositive*) denoting a cheese sauce: *eggs mornay*. [? after Philippe de MORNAY]

Mornay ★ (*French* mɔrne) *n* **Philippe de** (filip də), Seigneur du Plessis-Marly. 1549–1623, French Huguenot leader. Also called: **Duplessis-Mornay** (dyplesimɔrne).

morning (ˈmɔːnɪŋ) *n* **1** the first part of the day, ending at noon. **2** sunrise; daybreak; dawn. **3** the beginning or early period. **4 the morning after**. *Inf.* the aftereffects of excess, esp. a hangover. **5** (*modifier*) of, used in, or occurring in the morning: *morning coffee*. [C13 *morwening*, from MORN, on the model of EVENING]

morning-after pill *n* an oral contraceptive that is effective if taken some hours after intercourse.

morning dress *n* formal day dress for men, comprising a cutaway frock coat (**morning coat**), usually with grey trousers and top hat.

morning-glory *n, pl* **morning-glories**. any of various mainly tropical plants of the convolvulus family, with trumpet-shaped blue, pink, or white flowers, which close in late afternoon.

> ★ people and places

mornings ('mɔːnɪŋz) *adv Inf.* in the morning, esp. regularly, or during every morning.

morning sickness *n* nausea occurring shortly after rising: a symptom of pregnancy.

morning star *n* a planet, usually Venus, seen just before sunrise. Also called: **daystar.**

Moro[1] ('mɔːrəʊ) *n* **1** (*pl* **Moros** or **Moro**) a member of a group of predominantly Muslim peoples of the S Philippines. **2** the language of these peoples. [C19: via Sp. from L *Maurus* MOOR]

Moro[2] ★ (*Italian* 'mɔːro) *n* **Aldo** ('aldo). 1916–78, Italian Christian Democrat statesman; prime minister of Italy (1963–68; 1974–76) and minister of foreign affairs (1965–66; 1969–72; 1973–74); kidnapped by the Red Brigades in 1978 and murdered.

morocco (mə'rɒkəʊ) *n* a fine soft leather made from goatskins, used for bookbinding, shoes, etc. [C17: after MOROCCO, where it was orig. made]

Morocco ★ (mə'rɒkəʊ) *n* a kingdom in NW Africa, on the Mediterranean and the Atlantic: conquered by the Arabs in about 683, who introduced Islam; at its height under Berber dynasties (11th–13th centuries); became a French protectorate in 1912 and gained independence in 1956. It is mostly mountainous, with the Atlas Mountains in the centre and the Rif range along the Mediterranean coast, with the Sahara in the south and southeast; an important exporter of phosphates. Official languages: Arabic; Berber and French are also widely spoken. Official religion: (Sunni) Muslim. Currency: dirham. Capital: Rabat. Pop.: 26 736 000 (1996). Area: 458 730 sq. km (177 117 sq. miles). French name: **Maroc.**
▶ **Moroccan** (mə'rɒkən) *adj, n*

moron ('mɔːrɒn) *n* **1** a foolish or stupid person. **2** a person having an intelligence quotient of between 50 and 70. [C20: from Gk *mōros* foolish]
▶ **moronic** (mə'rɒnɪk) *adj* ▶ **mo'ronically** *adv*
▶ **'moronism** or **mo'ronity** *n*

Moroni ★ (mə'rəʊnɪ; *French* mɔrɔni) *n* the capital of Comoros, on the island of Njazídja (Grande Comore). Pop.: 30 000 (1991).

morose (mə'rəʊs) *adj* ill-tempered or gloomy. [C16: from L *mōrōsus* peevish, from *mōs* custom, will]
▶ **mo'rosely** *adv* ▶ **mo'roseness** *n*

-morph *n combining form.* indicating shape, form, or structure of a specified kind: *ectomorph.* [from Gk *-morphos*, from *morphē* shape]
▶ **-morphic** or **-morphous** *adj combining form.* ▶ **-morphy** *n combining form.*

morpheme ('mɔːfiːm) *n Linguistics.* a speech element having a meaning or grammatical function that cannot be subdivided into further such elements. [C20: from F, from Gk *morphē* form, on the model of PHONEME]
▶ **mor'phemic** *adj* ▶ **mor'phemically** *adv*

Morpheus ★ ('mɔːfɪəs, -fjuːs) *n Greek myth.* the god of sleep and dreams.
▶ **'Morphean** *adj*

morphine ('mɔːfiːn) or **morphia** ('mɔːfɪə) *n* an alkaloid extracted from opium: used in medicine as an anaesthetic and sedative. [C19: from F, from MORPHEUS]

morphing ('mɔːfɪŋ) *n* a computer technique used for graphics and in films, in which one image is gradually transformed into another. [C20: from METAMORPHOSIS]

morphogenesis (ˌmɔːfəʊ'dʒɛnɪsɪs) *n* **1** the development of form in an organism during its growth. **2** the evolutionary development of form in an organism or part of an organism.
▶ **morphogenetic** (ˌmɔːfəʊdʒɪ'nɛtɪk) *adj*

morphology (mɔː'fɒlədʒɪ) *n* **1** the branch of biology concerned with the form and structure of organisms. **2** the form and structure of words in a language. **3** the form and structure of anything.
▶ **morphologic** (ˌmɔːfə'lɒdʒɪk) or **ˌmorpho'logical** *adj*
▶ **ˌmorpho'logically** *adv* ▶ **mor'phologist** *n*

Morphy ★ ('mɔːfɪ) *n* **Paul.** 1837–84, US chess player, widely considered to have been the world's greatest player.

Morris ★ ('mɒrɪs) *n* **William.** 1834–96, British Pre-Raphaelite painter, craftsman, and writer.

Morris chair *n* an armchair with an adjustable back. [C19: after William MORRIS]

morris dance *n* any of various old English folk dances usually performed by men (**morris men**) adorned with bells and often representing characters from folk tales. Often shortened to **morris.** [C15 *moreys daunce* Moorish dance]
▶ **morris dancing** *n*

Morrison ★ ('mɒrɪsªn) *n* **1 Herbert Stanley,** Baron Morrison of Lambeth. 1888–1965, British Labour statesman, Home Secretary and Minister for Home Security (1942–45). **2 Jim,** full name *James Douglas Morrison.* 1943–71, US rock singer and songwriter, lead vocalist with the Doors. **3 Toni.** full name *Chloe Anthony Morrison.* born 1931, US novelist: her works include *Sula* (1974) and *Jazz* (1992): Nobel prize for literature 1993. **4 Van,** full name *George Ivan Morrison.* born 1945, Northern Irish rock singer and songwriter: his albums include *Moondance* (1970) and *Too Long in Exile* (1993).

morro ('mɒrəʊ) *n, pl* **morros** (-rəʊz). a rounded hill or promontory. [from Sp.]

morrow ('mɒrəʊ) *n* (usually preceded by *the*) *Arch.* or *poetic.* **1** the next day. **2** the period following a specified event. **3** the morning. [C13 *morwe*, from OE *morgen* morning]

Mors ★ (mɔːz) *n* the Roman god of death. Greek counterpart: **Thanatos.**

Morse ★ (mɔːs) *n* **Samuel Finley Breese** ('fɪnlɪ briːz). 1791–1872, US inventor and painter. He invented the first electric telegraph and the Morse code.

Morse code *n* a telegraph code used internationally for transmitting messages. Letters, numbers, etc., are represented by groups of shorter dots and longer dashes, or by groups of the corresponding sounds.

morsel ('mɔːsªl) *n* **1** a small slice or mouthful of food. **2** a small piece; bit. **3** *Irish inf.* a term of endearment for a child. [C13: from OF, from *mors* a bite, from L *morsus*, from *mordēre* to bite]

mortal ('mɔːtªl) *adj* **1** (of living beings, esp. human beings) subject to death. **2** of or involving life or the world. **3** ending in or causing death; fatal: *a mortal blow.* **4** deadly or unrelenting: *a mortal enemy.* **5** of or like the fear of death: *mortal terror.* **6** great or very intense: *mortal pain.* **7** conceivable or possible: *there was no mortal reason to go.* **8** *Sl.* long and tedious: *for three mortal hours.* ♦ *n* **9** a mortal being. **10** *Inf.* a person: *a mean mortal.* [C14: from L *mortālis*, from *mors* death]
▶ **'mortally** *adv*

mortality (mɔː'tælɪtɪ) *n, pl* **mortalities. 1** the condition of being mortal. **2** great loss of life, as in war or disaster. **3** the number of deaths in a given period. **4** mankind; humanity.

mortal sin *n Christianity.* a sin regarded as involving total loss of grace.

mortar ('mɔːtə) *n* **1** a mixture of cement or lime or both with sand and water, used as a bond between bricks or stones or as a covering on a wall. **2** a cannon having a short barrel and relatively wide bore that fires low-velocity shells in high trajectories. **3** a vessel, usually bowl-shaped, in which substances are pulverized with a pestle. ♦ *vb* (*tr*) **4** to join (bricks or stones) or cover (a wall) with mortar. **5** to fire on with mortars. [C13: from L *mortārium* basin in which mortar is mixed; in some senses, via OF *mortier* substance mixed inside such a vessel]

mortarboard ('mɔːtəˌbɔːd) *n* **1** a black tasselled academic cap with a flat square top. **2** a small square board with a handle on the underside for carrying mortar.

mortgage ('mɔːgɪdʒ) *n* **1** an agreement under which a person borrows money to buy property, esp. a house, and the lender may take possession of the property if the borrower fails to repay the money. **2** the deed affecting such an agreement. **3** the loan obtained under such an agreement: *a mortgage of £48000.* **4** a regular payment of money borrowed under such an agreement: *a mortgage of £347 per month.* ♦ *vb* **mortgages, mortgaging, mortgaged.** (*tr*)

4 to convey (property) by mortgage. **5** *Inf.* to pledge. [C14: from OF, lit.: dead pledge]
▸ 'mortgageable *adj*

mortgagee (ˌmɔːgɪˈdʒiː) *n Law.* the party to a mortgage who makes the loan.

mortgagor (ˌmɔːgɪˈdʒɔː) or **mortgager** *n Property law.* a person who borrows money by mortgaging his property to the lender as security.

mortician (mɔːˈtɪʃən) *n Chiefly US.* another word for **undertaker.** [C19: from MORTUARY + -*ician*, as in *physician*]

mortification (ˌmɔːtɪfɪˈkeɪʃən) *n* **1** a feeling of humiliation. **2** something causing this. **3** *Christianity.* the practice of mortifying the senses. **4** another word for **gangrene.**

mortify ('mɔːtɪˌfaɪ) *vb* **mortifies, mortifying, mortified. 1** (*tr*) to humiliate or cause to feel shame. **2** (*tr*) *Christianity.* to subdue and bring under control by self-denial, disciplinary exercises, etc. **3** (*intr*) to undergo tissue death or become gangrenous. [C14: via OF from Church L *mortificāre* to put to death, from L *mors* death + *facere* to do]
▸ 'morti,fier *n* ▸ 'morti,fying *adj*

Mortimer ★ ('mɔːtɪmə) *n* **1** Sir **John** (**Clifford**). born 1923, British barrister and writer. His works include *The Dock Brief* (1958) and *The Sound of Trumpets* (1998); best known for the television series featuring the barrister Horace Rumpole. **2 Roger de,** 8th Baron of Wigmore and 1st Earl of March. 1287–1330, lover of Isabella, the wife of Edward II of England: they invaded England in 1326 and compelled the king to abdicate in favour of his son, Edward III; executed.

mortise or **mortice** ('mɔːtɪs) *n* **1** a slot or recess cut into a piece of wood, stone, etc., to receive a matching projection (tenon) of another piece, or a mortise lock. ◆ *vb* **mortises, mortising, mortised** or **mortices, morticing, morticed.** (*tr*) **2** to cut a slot or recess in (a piece of wood, stone, etc.). **3** to join (two pieces of wood, stone, etc.) by means of a mortise and tenon. [C14: from OF *mortoise*, ?from Ar. *murtazza* fastened in position]

mortise lock *n* a lock set into a mortise in a door so that the mechanism of the lock is enclosed by the door.

mortmain ('mɔːt,meɪn) *n Law.* the state or condition of lands, buildings, etc., held inalienably, as by an ecclesiastical or other corporation. [C15: from OF *mortemain,* from Med. L *mortua manus* dead hand, inalienable ownership]

Morton ★ ('mɔːtⁿn) *n* **Jelly Roll,** real name *Ferdinand Joseph La Menthe Morton.* 1885–1941, US jazz pianist and songwriter; one of the creators of New Orleans jazz.

mortuary ('mɔːtʃʊərɪ) *n, pl* **mortuaries. 1** Also called: **morgue.** a building where dead bodies are kept before cremation or burial. ◆ *adj* **2** of or relating to death or burial. [C14 (as n, a funeral gift to a parish priest): via Med. L *mortuārium* (n) from L *mortuārius* of the dead]

morwong ('mɔː,wɒŋ) *n* a food fish of Australasian coastal waters. [from Abor.]

moryah (mɒrˈjæ) *interj Irish.* an exclamation of annoyance, disbelief, etc. [from Irish Gaelic *Mar dhea* forsooth]

mosaic (məˈzeɪɪk) *n* **1** a design or decoration made up of small pieces of coloured glass, stone, etc. **2** the process of making a mosaic. **3a** a mottled yellowing that occurs in the leaves of plants affected with any of various virus diseases. **3b** Also called: **mosaic disease.** any of the diseases, such as **tobacco mosaic,** that produce this discoloration. **4** a light-sensitive surface on a television camera tube, consisting of a large number of granules of photoemissive material. [C16: via F & It. from Med. L, from LGk: mosaic work, from Gk: of the Muses, from *mousa* MUSE]
▸ mosaicist (məˈzeɪɪsɪst) *n*

Mosaic (məʊˈzeɪɪk) *adj* of or relating to Moses or the laws and traditions ascribed to him.

Mosaic law *n Bible.* the laws ascribed to Moses and contained in the Pentateuch.

moschatel (ˌmɒskəˈtɛl) *n* a small N temperate plant with greenish-white musk-scented flowers. Also called:

townhall clock, five-faced bishop. [C18: via F from It. *moscatella,* dim. of *moscato* MUSK]

Moscow ★ ('mɒskəʊ) *n* the capital of Russia, on the Moskva River: dates from the 11th century; capital of the grand duchy of Russia from 1547 to 1712; capital of the Soviet Union (1918–91); centres on the medieval Kremlin; chief political, cultural, and industrial centre of Russia, with two universities. Pop.: 8 717 000 (1995 est.). Russian name: *Moskva.*

Moseley ★ ('məʊzlɪ) *n* Henry Gwyn-Jeffreys. 1887–1915, British physicist. He showed that the wavelengths of X-rays emitted from the elements are related to their atomic numbers.

Moselle ★ (məʊˈzɛl) *n* **1** a department of NE France, in Lorraine region. Capital: Metz. Pop.: 1 015 593 (1994 est.). Area: 6253 sq. km (2439 sq. miles). **2** a river in W Europe, rising in NE France and flowing northwest, forming part of the border between Luxembourg and Germany, then northeast to the Rhine: many vineyards along its lower course. Length: 547 km (340 miles). German name: **Mosel** ('moːzᵊl). **3** (*sometimes not cap.*) a German white wine from the Moselle valley.

Moses ★ ('məʊzɪz) *n* **1** *Old Testament.* the Hebrew prophet who led the Israelites out of Egypt to the Promised Land and gave them divinely revealed laws. **2 Ed.** born 1956, US hurdler; winner of the 400 m hurdles in the 1976 and 1984 Olympic Games. **3 Grandma,** real name *Anna Mary Robertson Moses.* 1860–1961, US painter of primitives, who began to paint at the age of 75.

mosey ('məʊzɪ) *vb* (*intr*) *Inf.* (often foll. by *along* or *on*) to amble. [C19: from ?]

Moshesh (mɒˈʃɛʃ) or **Moshoeshoe** ★ (mɒˈʃuːʃu) *n* died 1870, African chief, who founded the Basotho nation, now Lesotho.

Moskva ★ (*Russian* masˈkva) *n* **1** transliteration of the Russian name for **Moscow. 2** a river in W central Russia, rising in the Smolensk-Moscow upland, and flowing southeast through Moscow to the Oka River: linked with the River Volga by the Moscow Canal. Length: about 500 km (310 miles).

Moslem ('mɒzləm) *n, pl* **Moslems** or **Moslem.** *adj* a variant of **Muslim.**
▸ **Moslemic** (mɒzˈlɛmɪk) *adj* ▸ 'Moslemism *n*

Mosley ★ ('məʊzlɪ) *n* Sir **Oswald Ernald.** 1896–1980, British politician; founder of the British Union of Fascists (1932).

mosque (mɒsk) *n* a Muslim place of worship. [C14: earlier *mosquee,* from OF via It. *moschea,* ult. from Ar. *masjid* temple]

mosquito (məˈskiːtəʊ) *n, pl* **mosquitoes** or **mosquitos.** any dipterous insect of the family Culicidae: the females have a long proboscis adapted for piercing the skin of man and animals to suck their blood. See also **aedes, anopheles, culex.** [C16: from Sp., dim. of *mosca* fly, from L *musca*]

mosquito net or **netting** *n* a fine curtain or net to keep mosquitoes out.

moss (mɒs) *n* **1** any of a class of plants, typically growing in dense mats on trees, rocks, moist ground, etc. **2** a clump or growth of any of these plants. **3** any of various similar but unrelated plants, such as Spanish moss and reindeer moss. **4** *Scot. & N English.* a peat bog or marsh. [OE *mos* swamp]
▸ 'moss,like *adj* ▸ 'mossy *adj* ▸ 'mossiness *n*

Moss ★ (mɒs) *n* **Stirling.** born 1929, British racing driver.

moss agate *n* a variety of chalcedony with dark greenish mossy markings.

mossie ('mɒsɪ) *n* another name for the **Cape sparrow.** [Afrik.]

mosso ('mɒsəʊ) *adv Music.* to be performed with rapidity. [It., p.p. of *muovere* to MOVE]

moss rose *n* a variety of rose that has a mossy stem and calyx and fragrant pink flowers.

moss stitch *n* a knitting stitch made up of alternate plain and purl stitches.

mosstrooper ('mɒs,truːpə) *n* a raider in the Borders of

★ people and places

England and Scotland in the mid-17th century. [C17 *moss*, in dialect sense: bog]

most (məʊst) *determiner* **1a** a great majority of; nearly all: *most people like eggs.* **1b** (*as pron; functioning as sing or pl*): *most of them don't know; most of it is finished.* **2 the most. 2a** the superlative of **many** and **much**: *you have the most money; the most apples.* **2b** (*as pron*): *the most he can afford is two pounds.* **3 at** (**the**) **most.** at the maximum: *that girl is four at the most.* **4 make the most of.** to use to the best advantage: *she makes the most of her accent.* ◆ *adv* **5 the most.** used to form the superlative of some adjectives and adverbs: *he suffered the most terribly of all.* **6** the superlative of **much**: *people welcome a drink most after work.* **7** (intensifier): *a most absurd story.* [OE *māst* or *mǣst*, whence ME *moste*, *mēst*]

-most *suffix. forming the superlative degree of some adjectives and adverbs: hindmost; uppermost.* [OE *-mǣst, -mest*, orig. a sup. suffix, later mistakenly taken as from *mǣst* (adv) *most*]

Mostaganem ★ (mə,stægə'nem) *n* a port in NW Algeria, on the Mediterranean Sea: exports wine, fruit, and vegetables. Pop.: 107 000 (1987 est.).

mostly ('məʊstlɪ) *adv* **1** almost entirely; chiefly. **2** on many or most occasions; usually.

Most Reverend *n* (in Britain) a courtesy title applied to Anglican and Roman Catholic archbishops.

Mosul ★ ('məʊs°l) *n* a city in N Iraq, on the River Tigris opposite the ruins of Nineveh: an important commercial centre with nearby Ayn Zalah oilfield; university. Pop.: 664 221 (1987).

mot (məʊ) *n* short for **bon mot.** [C16: via F from Vulgar L *mottum* (unattested) utterance, from L *muttum*, from *muttīre* to mutter]

MOT (in Britain and New Zealand) *abbrev. for:* **1** Ministry of Transport (*Brit.*, now Department of Transport). **2** *Brit.* MOT test: a compulsory annual test for all road vehicles over a certain age, which require a valid **MOT certificate.**

mote (məʊt) *n* a tiny speck. [OE *mot*]

motel (məʊ'tɛl) *n* a roadside hotel for motorists. [C20: from *motor* + *hotel*]

motet (məʊ'tɛt) *n* a polyphonic choral composition used as an anthem in the Roman Catholic service. [C14: from OF, dim. of *mot* word; see MOT]

moth (mɒθ) *n* any of numerous insects that typically have stout bodies with antennae of various shapes (but not clubbed), including large brightly coloured species, such as hawk moths, and small inconspicuous types, such as the clothes moths. Cf. **butterfly** (sense 1). [OE *moththe*]

mothball ('mɒθ,bɔːl) *n* **1** a small ball of camphor or naphthalene used to repel clothes moths in stored clothing, etc. **2 put in mothballs.** to postpone work on (a project, activity, etc.). ◆ *vb* (*tr*) **3** to prepare (a ship) for a long period of storage by sealing with plastic. **4** to take (a factory, etc.) out of operation but maintain it for future use. **5** to postpone work on (a project, activity, etc.).

moth-eaten *adj* **1** decayed, decrepit, or outdated. **2** eaten away by or as if by moths.

mother[1] ('mʌðə) *n* **1a** a female who has given birth to offspring. **1b** (*as modifier*): *a mother bird.* **2** (*often cap., esp. as a term of address*) a person's own mother. **3** a female substituting in the function of a mother. **4** (*often cap.*) *Chiefly arch.* a term of address for an old woman. **5a** motherly qualities, such as maternal affection: *it appealed to the mother in her.* **5b** (*as modifier*): *mother love.* **5c** (*in combination*): *mothercraft.* **6a** a female or thing that creates, nurtures, protects, etc., something. **6b** (*as modifier*): *mother church; mother earth.* **7** a title given to certain

members of female religious orders. **8** (*modifier*) native or innate: *mother wit.* **9 the mother of all...** *Inf.* the greatest example of its kind: *the mother of all parties.* ◆ *vb* (*tr*) **10** to give birth to or produce. **11** to nurture, protect, etc. as a mother. [OE *mōdor*]
▸ **'motherless** *adj*

mother[2] ('mʌðə) *n* a stringy slime containing various bacteria that forms on the surface of liquids undergoing fermentation. Also called: **mother of vinegar.** [C16: ?from MOTHER[1], but cf. Sp. *madre* scum, Du. *modder* dregs, MLow G *modder* decaying object, *mudde* sludge]

Mother Carey's chicken ('kɛərɪz) *n* another name for **stormy petrel.** [from ?]

mother country *n* **1** the original country of colonists or settlers. **2** a person's native country.

Mother Goose *n* the imaginary author of a collection of nursery rhymes. [C18: translated from F *Contes de ma mère l'Oye* (1697), a collection of tales by Charles PERRAULT]

motherhood ('mʌðə,hʊd) *n* **1** the state of being a mother. **2** the qualities characteristic of a mother.

Mothering Sunday ('mʌðərɪŋ) *n Brit.* the fourth Sunday in Lent, when mothers traditionally receive presents from their children. Also called: **Mother's Day.**

mother-in-law *n, pl* **mothers-in-law.** the mother of one's wife or husband.

motherland ('mʌðə,lænd) *n* a person's native country.

mother lode *n Mining.* the principal lode in a system.

motherly ('mʌðəlɪ) *adj* of or resembling a mother, esp. in warmth or protectiveness.
▸ **'motherliness** *n*

mother-of-pearl *n* a hard iridescent substance that forms the inner layer of the shells of certain molluscs, such as the oyster. It is used to make buttons, etc. Also called: **nacre.**

Mother's Day *n* **1** *US & Canad.* the second Sunday in May, observed as a day in honour of mothers. **2** See **Mothering Sunday.**

mother ship *n* a ship providing facilities and supplies for a number of small vessels.

mother superior *n, pl* **mother superiors** *or* **mothers superior.** the head of a community of nuns.

mother tongue *n* **1** the language first learned by a child. **2** a language from which another has evolved.

Motherwell ★ ('mʌðəwəl) *n* a town in S central Scotland, the administrative centre of North Lanarkshire on the River Clyde: industrial centre. Pop.: 30 717 (1991).

mother wit *n* native practical intelligence; common sense.

mothproof ('mɒθ,pruːf) *adj* **1** (esp. of clothes) chemically treated so as to repel clothes moths. ◆ *vb* **2** (*tr*) to make (clothes, etc.) mothproof.

mothy ('mɒθɪ) *adj* **mothier, mothiest. 1** moth-eaten. **2** containing moths; full of moths.

motif (məʊ'tiːf) *n* **1** a distinctive idea, esp. a theme elaborated on in a piece of music, literature, etc. **2** Also called: **motive.** a recurring shape in a design. **3** a single decoration, such as a symbol or name on a jumper, sweatshirt, etc. [C19: from F; see MOTIVE]

motile ('məʊtaɪl) *adj* capable of moving spontaneously and independently. [C19: from L *mōtus* moved, from *movēre* to move]
▸ **motility** (məʊ'tɪlɪtɪ) *n*

motion ('məʊʃən) *n* **1** the process of continual change in the physical position of an object; movement. **2** a movement or action, esp. of part of the human body; a gesture. **3a** the capacity for movement. **3b** a manner of movement, esp. walking; gait. **4** a mental impulse. **5** a formal proposal to be discussed and voted on in a debate, meeting, etc. **6** *Law.* an application made to a judge or court for an order or ruling necessary to the conduct of legal proceedings. **7** *Brit.* **7a** the evacuation of the bowels. **7b** excrement. **8a** part of a moving mechanism. **8b** the action of such a part. **9 go through the motions. 9a** to act or perform the task (of doing something) mechanically or without sincerity. **9b** to mimic the action (of some-

thing) by gesture. **10 in motion.** operational or functioning (often in **set in motion, set the wheels in motion**). ◆ *vb* **11** (when *tr, may take a clause as object or an infinitive*) to signal or direct (a person) by a movement or gesture. [C15: from L *mōtiō* a moving, from *movēre* to move]
▸ **'motionless** *adj*

motion picture *n* a US and Canad. term for **film** (sense 1).

motivate ('məʊtɪˌveɪt) *vb* **motivates, motivating, motivated.** (*tr*) to give incentive to.
▸ ˌmoti'vation *n*

motivational research (ˌməʊtɪ'veɪʃənᵊl) *n* the application of psychology to the study of consumer behaviour, esp. the planning of advertising and sales campaigns. Also called: **motivation research.**

motive ('məʊtɪv) *n* **1** the reason for a certain course of action, whether conscious or unconscious. **2** a variant of **motif** (sense 2). ◆ *adj* **3** of or causing motion: *a motive force.* **4** of or acting as a motive; motivating. ◆ *vb* **motives, motiving, motived.** (*tr*) **5** to motivate. [C14: from OF *motif*, from LL *mōtīvus* (adj) moving, from L *mōtus*, p.p. of *movēre* to move]
▸ **'motiveless** *adj*

motive power *n* **1** any source of energy used to produce motion. **2** the means of supplying power to an engine, vehicle, etc.

mot juste *French.* (mo ʒyst) *n, pl* **mots justes** (mo ʒyst). the appropriate word or expression.

motley ('mɒtlɪ) *adj* **1** made up of elements of varying type, quality, etc. **2** multicoloured. ◆ *n* **3** a motley collection. **4** the particoloured attire of a jester. [C14: ?from *mot* speck]

moto ('məʊtəʊ) *n Music.* movement. [It.]

motocross ('məʊtəˌkrɒs) *n* **1** cross-country motorcycle racing across rough ground. **2** another name for **rallycross.** [C20: from MOTO(R) + CROSS(-COUNTRY)]

motor ('məʊtə) *n* **1a** the engine, esp. an internal-combustion engine, of a vehicle. **1b** (*as modifier*): *a motor scooter.* **2** Also called: **electric motor.** a machine that converts electrical energy into mechanical energy. **3** any device that converts another form of energy into mechanical energy to produce motion. **4a** *Chiefly Brit.* a car. **4b** (*as modifier*): *motor spares.* ◆ *adj* **5** producing or causing motion. **6** *Physiol.* **6a** of or relating to nerves or neurons that carry impulses that cause muscles to contract. **6b** of or relating to movement or to muscles that induce movement. ◆ *vb* **7** (*intr*) to travel by car. **8** (*tr*) *Brit.* to transport by car. **9** (*intr*) *Inf.* to move fast; make good progress. [C16: from L *mōtor* a mover, from *movēre* to move]

motorbicycle ('məʊtəˌbaɪsɪkᵊl) *n* **1** a motorcycle. **2** a moped.

motorbike ('məʊtəˌbaɪk) *n* a less formal name for **motorcycle.**

motorboat ('məʊtəˌbəʊt) *n* any boat powered by a motor.

motorbus ('məʊtəˌbʌs) *n* a bus driven by an internal-combustion engine.

motorcade ('məʊtəˌkeɪd) *n* a parade of cars. [C20: from MOTOR + CAVALCADE]

motorcar ('məʊtəˌkɑː) *n* **1** a more formal word for **car. 2** a self-propelled electric railway car.

motorcycle ('məʊtəˌsaɪkᵊl) *n* **1** Also called: **motorbike.** a two-wheeled vehicle that is driven by a petrol engine. ◆ *vb* **motorcycles, motorcycling, motorcycled.** (*intr*) **2** to ride on a motorcycle.
▸ **'motorˌcyclist** *n*

motorist ('məʊtərɪst) *n* a driver of a car.

motorize or **motorise** ('məʊtəˌraɪz) *vb* **motorizes, motorizing, motorized** or **motorises, motorising, motorised.** (*tr*) **1** to equip with a motor. **2** to provide (military units) with motor vehicles.
▸ ˌmotori'zation or ˌmotori'sation *n*

motorman ('məʊtəmən) *n, pl* **motormen. 1** the driver of an electric train. **2** the operator of a motor.

motormouth ('məʊtəˌmaʊθ) *n Sl.* a garrulous person.

motor scooter *n* a light motorcycle with small wheels and an enclosed engine. Often shortened to **scooter.**

motor vehicle *n* a road vehicle driven esp. by an internal-combustion engine.

motorway ('məʊtəˌweɪ) *n Brit., Austral., & NZ.* a main road for fast-moving traffic, having separate carriageways for vehicles travelling in opposite directions.

Motown ('məʊˌtaʊn) *n Trademark.* music combining rhythm and blues and pop, or gospel rhythms and modern ballad harmony. [C20: from *Motown Records* of Detroit, from *Mo(tor) Town*, nickname for Detroit, centre of the US car industry]

motte (mɒt) *n History.* a mound on which a castle was erected. [C14: see MOAT]

MOT test *n* (in Britain) See **MOT** (sense 2).

mottle ('mɒtᵊl) *vb* **mottles, mottling, mottled. 1** (*tr*) to colour with streaks or blotches of different shades. ◆ *n* **2** a mottled appearance, as of the surface of marble. [C17: back formation from MOTLEY]
▸ **'mottled** *adj*

motto ('mɒtəʊ) *n, pl* **mottoes** or **mottos. 1** a short saying expressing the guiding maxim or ideal of a family, organization, etc., esp. when part of a coat of arms. **2** a verse or maxim contained in a paper cracker. **3** a quotation prefacing a book or chapter of a book. [C16: via It. from L *muttum* utterance]

moue *French.* (mu) *n* a pouting look.

moufflon ('muːflɒn) *n* a wild short-fleeced mountain sheep of Corsica and Sardinia. [C18: via F from Romance *mufrone*, from LL *mufrō*]

mouillé ('mwiːeɪ) *adj Phonetics.* palatalized, as in the sounds represented by Spanish *ll* or *ñ*, (pronounced as (ʎ) and (ɲ)), or French *ll* (representing a (j) sound). [C19: from F, p.p. of *mouiller* to moisten, from L *mollis* soft]

moujik ('muːʒɪk) *n* a variant spelling of **muzhik.**

mould¹ or US **mold** (məʊld) *n* **1** a shaped cavity used to give a definite form to fluid or plastic material. **2** a frame on which something may be constructed. **3** something shaped in or made on a mould. **4** shape, form, design, or pattern. **5** specific nature, character, or type. ◆ *vb* (*tr*) **6** to make in a mould. **7** to shape or form, as by using a mould. **8** to influence or direct: *to mould opinion.* **9** to cling to: *the skirt moulds her figure.* **10** *Metallurgy.* to make (a material) into a mould used in casting. [C13 (n): from OF *modle*, from L *modulus* a small measure]
▸ **'mouldable** or US **'moldable** *adj* ▸ **'moulder** or US **'molder** *n*

mould² or US **mold** (məʊld) *n* **1** a coating or discoloration caused by various fungi that develop in a damp atmosphere on the surface of food, fabrics, etc. **2** any of the fungi that cause this growth. ◆ *vb* **3** to become or cause to become covered with this growth. ◆ Also called: **mildew.** [C15: dialect (N English) *mowlde* mouldy, from p.p. of *moulen* to become mouldy, prob. from ON]

mould³ or US **mold** (məʊld) *n* loose soil, esp. when rich in organic matter. [OE *molde*]

mouldboard or US **moldboard** ('məʊldˌbɔːd) *n* the curved blade of a plough, which turns over the furrow.

moulder or US **molder** ('məʊldə) *vb* (often foll. by *away*) to crumble or cause to crumble, as through decay. [C16: verbal use of MOULD³]

moulding or US **molding** ('məʊldɪŋ) *n* **1** *Archit.* **1a** a shaped outline, esp. one used on cornices, etc. **1b** a shaped strip made of wood, stone, etc. **2** something moulded.

mouldy or US **moldy** ('məʊldɪ) *adj* **mouldier, mouldiest** or US **moldier, moldiest. 1** covered with mould. **2** stale or musty, esp. from age or lack of use. **3** *Sl.* boring; dull.
▸ **'mouldiness** or US **'moldiness** *n*

Moulin ★ (*French* mulɛ̃) *n* Jean (ʒɑ̃). 1899–1943, French lawyer and Resistance hero; Chairman of the National Council of the Resistance (1943): tortured to death by the Nazis.

Moulins ★ (*French* mulɛ̃) *n* a market town in central France, on the Allier River. Pop.: 25 548 (1982).

Moulmein or **Maulmain ★** (maʊl'meɪn) *n* a port in S

Myanmar, near the mouth of the Salween River: exports teak and rice. Pop.: 23 350 (1990).

moult *or US* **molt** (məʊlt) *vb* **1** (of birds, mammals, arthropods, etc.) to shed (feathers, hair, or cuticle) in order that new growth can take place. ◆ *n* **2** the periodic process of moulting. [C14 *mouten*, from OE *mūtian*, as in *bimūtian* to exchange for, from L *mūtāre* to change] ▸ '**moulter** *or US* '**molter** *n*

mound (maʊnd) *n* **1** a raised mass of earth, debris, etc. **2** any heap or pile. **3** a small natural hill. **4** an artificial ridge of earth, stone, etc., as used for defence. ◆ *vb* **5** (often foll. by *up*) to gather into a mound; heap. **6** (*tr*) to cover or surround with a mound: *to mound a grave*. [C16: earthwork, ?from OE *mund* hand, hence defence]

Mound Builder *n* a member of a group of prehistoric inhabitants of the Mississippi region of the US, who built altar mounds, barrows, etc.

mound-builder *n* another name for **megapode**.

mount[1] (maʊnt) *vb* **1** to go up (a hill, stairs, etc.); climb. **2** to get up on (a horse, a platform, etc.). **3** (*intr*; often foll. by *up*) to increase; accumulate: *excitement mounted*. **4** (*tr*) to fix onto a backing, setting, or support: *to mount a photograph; to mount a slide*. **5** (*tr*) to provide with a horse for riding, or to place on a horse. **6** (of male animals) to climb onto (a female animal) for copulation. **7** (*tr*) to prepare (a play, etc.) for production. **8** (*tr*) to plan and organize (a campaign, etc.). **9** (*tr*) to prepare (a skeleton, etc.) for exhibition as a specimen. **10** (*tr*) to place or carry (weapons) in such a position that they can be fired. **11 mount guard.** See **guard.** ◆ *n* **12** a backing, setting, or support onto which something is fixed. **13** the act or manner of mounting. **14** a horse for riding. **15** a slide used in microscopy. [C16: from OF *munter*, from Vulgar L *montāre* (unattested) from L *mons* MOUNT²] ▸ '**mountable** *adj* ▸ '**mounter** *n*

mount[2] (maʊnt) *n* a mountain or hill: used in literature and (when cap.) in proper names: *Mount Everest*. [OE *munt*, from L *mons* mountain, but infl. in ME by OF *mont*]

mountain ('maʊntɪn) *n* **1a** a natural upward projection of the earth's surface, higher and steeper than a hill. **1b** (*as modifier*): *mountain scenery*. **1c** (*in combination*): *a mountaintop*. **2** a huge heap or mass: *a mountain of papers*. **3** anything of great quantity or size. **4** a surplus of a commodity, esp. in the European Union: *a butter mountain*. [C13: from OF *montaigne*, ult. from L *montānus*, from *mons* mountain]

mountain ash *n* **1** any of various trees, such as the European mountain ash or rowan, having clusters of small white flowers and bright red berries. **2** any of several Australian eucalyptus trees, such as *Eucalyptus regnans*.

mountain avens *n* See **avens** (sense 2).

mountain bike *n* a type of sturdy bicycle with at least 16 gears, straight handlebars, and heavy-duty tyres.

mountain cat *n* any of various wild feline mammals, such as the bobcat, lynx, or puma.

mountaineer (,maʊntɪ'nɪə) *n* **1** a person who climbs mountains. **2** a person living in a mountainous area. ◆ *vb* **3** (*intr*) to climb mountains. ▸ ,**mountain'eering** *n*

mountain goat *n* any wild goat inhabiting mountainous regions.

mountain laurel *n* any of various ericaceous shrubs or trees of E North America having leathery poisonous leaves and clusters of pink or white flowers. Also called: **calico bush**.

mountain lion *n* another name for **puma**.

mountainous ('maʊntɪnəs) *adj* **1** of or relating to mountains: *a mountainous region*. **2** like a mountain, esp. in size or impressiveness.

mountain sickness *n* nausea, headache, and shortness of breath caused by climbing to high altitudes. Also called: **altitude sickness**.

Mountbatten ★ (maʊnt'bæt°n) *n* Louis (**Francis Albert Victor Nicholas**), 1st Earl Mountbatten of Burma. 1900–79, British naval commander; great-grandson of Queen Victoria. During World War II he was supreme allied commander in SE Asia (1943–46). He was the last vice-

roy of India (1947) and governor general (1947–48); killed by an IRA bomb.

Mount Desert Island ★ *n* an island off the coast of Maine: lakes and granite peaks. Area: 279 sq. km (108 sq. miles).

mountebank ('maʊntɪ,bæŋk) *n* **1** (formerly) a person who sold quack medicines in public places. **2** a charlatan; fake. ◆ *vb* **3** (*intr*) to play the mountebank. [C16: from It. *montambanco* a climber on a bench, from *montare* to MOUNT¹ + *banco* BENCH] ▸ ,**mounte'bankery** *n*

mounted ('maʊntɪd) *adj* **1** riding horses: *mounted police*. **2** provided with a support, backing, etc.

Mountie *or* **Mounty** ('maʊntɪ) *n, pl* **Mounties**. *Inf.* a member of the Royal Canadian Mounted Police. [from MOUNTED]

mounting ('maʊntɪŋ) *n* another word for **mount**¹ (sense 12).

mounting-block *n* a block of stone formerly used to aid a person when mounting a horse.

Mount Isa ★ ('aɪzə) *n* a city in NE Australia in NW Queensland: mining of copper and other minerals. Pop.: 24 104 (1988 est.).

Mount McKinley National Park ★ *n* a national park in S central Alaska: contains part of the Alaska Range. Area: 7847 sq. km (3030 sq. miles).

Mount Rainier National Park ★ *n* a national park in W Washington, in the Cascade Range. Area: 976 sq. km (377 sq. miles).

mourn (mɔːn) *vb* **1** to feel or express sadness for the death or loss of (someone or something). **2** (*intr*) to observe the customs of mourning, as by wearing black. [OE *murnan*] ▸ '**mourner** *n*

mournful ('mɔːnful) *adj* **1** evoking grief; sorrowful. **2** gloomy; sad. ▸ '**mournfully** *adv* ▸ '**mournfulness** *n*

mourning ('mɔːnɪŋ) *n* **1** the act or feelings of one who mourns; grief. **2** the conventional symbols of grief, such as the wearing of black. **3** the period of time during which a death is officially mourned. ◆ *adj* **4** of or relating to mourning. ▸ '**mourningly** *adv*

mourning band *n* a piece of black material, esp. an armband, worn to indicate mourning.

mourning dove *n* a brown North American dove with a plaintive song.

mouse *n* (maʊs), *pl* **mice** (maɪs). **1** any of numerous small long-tailed rodents that are similar to but smaller than rats. See also **fieldmouse, harvest mouse, house mouse**. **2** any of various related rodents, such as the jumping mouse. **3** a quiet, timid, or cowardly person. **4** *Computing.* a handheld device used to control cursor movements and computing functions without keying. **5** *Sl.* a black eye. ◆ *vb* (maʊz), **mouses, mousing, moused**. **6** to stalk and catch (mice, etc.). **7** (*intr*) to go about stealthily. [OE *mūs*] ▸ '**mouse,like** *adj*

mouser ('maʊzə, 'maʊsə) *n* a cat or other animal that is used to catch mice.

mousetrap ('maʊs,træp) *n* **1** any trap for catching mice, esp. one with a spring-loaded metal bar that is released by the taking of the bait. **2** *Brit. inf.* cheese of indifferent quality.

moussaka *or* **mousaka** (muˈsɑːkə) *n* a dish originating in the Balkan States, consisting of meat, aubergines, and tomatoes, topped with cheese sauce. [C20: from Mod. Gk]

mousse (muːs) *n* **1** a light creamy dessert made with eggs, cream, fruit, etc., set with gelatine. **2** a similar dish made from fish or meat. **3** short for **styling mousse**. [C19: from F: froth]

mousseline (*French* muslin) *n* **1** a fine fabric made of rayon or silk. **2** a type of fine glass. [C17: F: MUSLIN]

Moussorgsky ★ (muˈsɔːgskɪ; *Russian* ˈmusərkskij) *n* a variant spelling of (Modest Petrovich) **Mussorgsky**.

moustache *or US* **mustache** (məˈstɑːʃ) *n* **1** the

unshaved growth of hair on the upper lip. **2** a similar growth of hair or bristles (in animals). **3** a mark like a moustache. [C16: via F from It. *mostaccio*, ult. from Doric Gk *mustax* upper lip]
▶ **mous'tached** or US **mus'tached** adj

moustache cup n a cup with a partial cover to protect a drinker's moustache.

Mousterian (muːˈstɪərɪən) n **1** a culture characterized by flint flake tools and associated with Neanderthal man, dating from before 70 000–32 000 B.C. ◆ adj **2** of or relating to this culture. [C20: from F *moustérien*, from archaeological finds of the same period in the cave of *Le Moustier*, Dordogne, France]

mousy or **mousey** (ˈmaʊsɪ) adj **mousier, mousiest. 1** resembling a mouse, esp. in hair colour. **2** shy or ineffectual. **3** infested with mice.
▶ **'mousily** adv ▶ **'mousiness** n

mouth n (maʊθ), pl **mouths** (maʊðz). **1** the opening through which many animals take in food and issue vocal sounds. **2** the system of organs surrounding this opening, including the lips, tongue, teeth, etc. **3** the visible part of the lips on the face. **4** a person regarded as a consumer of food: *four mouths to feed*. **5** a particular manner of speaking: *a foul mouth*. **6** *Inf.* boastful, rude, or excessive talk: *he is all mouth*. **7** the point where a river issues into a sea or lake. **8** the opening of a container, such as a jar. **9** the opening of a cave, tunnel, volcano, etc. **10** that part of the inner lip of a horse on which the bit acts. **11** a pout; grimace. **12 down in** or **at the mouth.** in low spirits. ◆ vb (maʊð). **13** to speak or say (something) insincerely, esp. in public. **14** (tr) to form (words) with movements of the lips but without speaking. **15** (tr) to take (something) into the mouth or to move (something) around inside the mouth. **16** (intr; usually foll. by at) to make a grimace. [OE *mūth*]
▶ **mouther** (ˈmaʊðə) n

mouthful (ˈmaʊθˌfʊl) n, pl **mouthfuls. 1** as much as is held in the mouth at one time. **2** a small quantity, as of food. **3** a long word or phrase that is difficult to say. **4** *Brit. inf.* an abusive response.

mouth organ n another name for **harmonica.**

mouthpart (ˈmaʊθˌpɑːt) n any of the paired appendages in arthropods that surround the mouth and are specialized for feeding.

mouthpiece (ˈmaʊθˌpiːs) n **1** the part of a wind instrument into which the player blows. **2** the part of a telephone receiver into which a person speaks. **3** the part of a container forming its mouth. **4** a person who acts as a spokesman, as for an organization. **5** a publication expressing the official views of an organization.

mouthwash (ˈmaʊθˌwɒʃ) n a medicated solution for gargling and cleansing the mouth.

mouthy (ˈmaʊðɪ) adj **mouthier, mouthiest.** bombastic; excessively talkative.

mouton (ˈmuːtɒn) n sheepskin processed to resemble the fur of another animal, esp. beaver or seal. [from F: sheep]

movable or **moveable** (ˈmuːvəb²l) adj **1** able to be moved; not fixed. **2** (esp. of Easter) varying in date from year to year. **3** (usually spelt **moveable**) *Law.* denoting or relating to personal property as opposed to realty. ◆ n **4** (often pl) a movable article, esp. a piece of furniture.
▶ **ˌmova'bility** or **'movableness** n ▶ **'movably** adv

move (muːv) vb **moves, moving, moved. 1** to go or take from one place to another; change in position. **2** (usually intr) to change (one's dwelling, place of business, etc.). **3** to be or cause to be in motion; stir. **4** (intr) (of machines, etc.) to work or operate. **5** (tr) to cause (to do something); prompt. **6** (intr) to begin to act: *move soon or we'll lose the order.* **7** (intr) to associate oneself with a specified social circle: *to move in exalted spheres.* **8** (intr) to make progress. **9** (tr) to arouse affection, pity, or compassion in; touch. **10** (in board games) to change the position of (a piece) or (of a piece) to change position. **11** (intr) (of merchandise) to be disposed of by being bought. **12** (when tr, often takes a clause as object; when intr, often foll. by for) to suggest (a proposal) formally, as in debating or parliamentary procedure. **13** (intr; usually foll. by on or along) to go away or

to another place; leave. **14** to cause (the bowels) to evacuate or (of the bowels) to be evacuated. ◆ n **15** the act of moving; movement. **16** one of a sequence of actions, usually part of a plan; manoeuvre. **17** the act of moving one's residence, place of business, etc. **18** (in board games) **18a** a player's turn to move his piece. **18b** a manoeuvre of a piece. **19 get a move on.** *Inf.* **19a** to get started. **19b** to hurry up. **20 on the move. 20a** travelling from place to place. **20b** advancing; succeeding. **20c** very active; busy. [C13: from Anglo-F *mover*, from L *movēre*]

move in vb (mainly adv) **1** (also prep) Also (when prep): **move into.** to occupy or take possession of (a new residence, place of business, etc.). **2** (intr; often foll. by on) *Inf.* to creep close (to), as in preparing to capture. **3** (intr; often foll. by on) *Inf.* to try to gain power or influence (over).

movement (ˈmuːvmənt) n **1a** the act, process, or result of moving. **1b** an instance of moving. **2** the manner of moving. **3a** a group of people with a common ideology. **3b** the organized action of such a group. **4** a trend or tendency. **5** the driving and regulating mechanism of a watch or clock. **6** (often pl) a person's location and activities during a specific time. **7a** the evacuation of the bowels. **7b** the matter evacuated. **8** *Music.* a principal self-contained section of a symphony, sonata, etc. **9** tempo or pace, as in music or literature. **10** *Fine arts.* the appearance of motion in painting, sculpture, etc. **11** *Prosody.* the rhythmic structure of verse. **12** a positional change by one or a number of military units. **13** a change in the market price of a security or commodity.

mover (ˈmuːvə) n **1** *Inf.* a person, business, idea, etc., that is advancing or progressing. **2** a person or thing that moves. **3** a person who moves a proposal, as in a debate. **4** *US & Canad.* a removal firm or a person who works for one.

movers and shakers pl n *Inf.* the people with power and influence in a particular field of activity. [C20: ? from the line "We are the movers and shakers of the world for ever" in 'Ode' by Arthur O'Shaughnessy (1844–81), Brit. poet]

movie (ˈmuːvɪ) n **a** an informal word for **film** (sense 1). **b** (as modifier): *movie ticket.*

moving (ˈmuːvɪŋ) adj **1** arousing or touching the emotions. **2** changing or capable of changing position. **3** causing motion.
▶ **'movingly** adv

moving staircase or **stairway** n less common terms for **escalator** (sense 1).

mow (məʊ) vb **mows, mowing, mowed; mowed** or **mown. 1** to cut down (grass, crops, etc.), with a hand implement or machine. **2** (tr) to cut the growing vegetation of (a field, lawn, etc.). [OE *māwan*]
▶ **'mower** n

mow down vb (tr, adv) to kill in large numbers, esp. by gunfire.

Mowlam ★ (ˈməʊlæm) n **Mo,** full name *Marjorie Mowlam.* born 1949, British Labour politician; secretary of state for Northern Ireland from 1997.

mown (məʊn) vb the past participle of **mow.**

Moya ★ (ˈmɔɪjə) n **(John)** Hidalgo. 1920–94, British architect.

Moyle ★ (mɔɪl) n a district of N Northern Ireland, on the North Channel and including Rathlin Island: tourism, agriculture. Administrative centre: Ballycastle. Pop.: 14 789 (1991). Area: 494 sq. km (191 sq. miles).

Mozambique ★ (ˌməʊzæmˈbiːk) n a republic in SE Africa: colonized by the Portuguese from 1505 onwards and a slave-trade centre until 1878; made an overseas province of Portugal in 1951; became an independent republic in 1975; joined the Commonwealth in 1995. Official language: Portuguese. Religion: animist majority. Currency: metical. Capital: Maputo. Pop.: 17 878 000 (1996). Area: 812 379 sq. km (313 661 sq. miles). Portuguese name: **Moçambique.** Also called (until 1975): **Portuguese East Africa.**

Mozambique Channel ★ n a strait between Mozambique and Madagascar. Length: about 1600 km (1000 miles). Width: 400 km (250 miles).

★ people and places

Mozart ★ ('məʊtsɑːt) n **Wolfgang Amadeus** ('vɔlfgaŋ ama-'deːʊs). 1756–91, composer born in Salzburg. A child prodigy, his works include operas, such as *The Marriage of Figaro* (1786) and *The Magic Flute* (1791), symphonies, concertos, chamber music, sonatas, songs, and Masses, such as the unfinished *Requiem* (1791).
▸ **Mo'zartean** or **Mo'zartian** adj

mozzarella (ˌmɒtsə'relə) n a moist white curd cheese originally made in Italy from buffalo milk. [from It., dim. of *mozza* a type of cheese, from *mozzare* to cut off]

mp 1 abbrev. for melting point. 2 *Music.* symbol for mezzo piano. [It.: moderately soft]

MP abbrev. for: 1 (in Britain, Canada, etc.) Member of Parliament. 2 (in Britain) Metropolitan Police. 3 Military Police. 4 Mounted Police.

mpg abbrev. for miles per gallon.

mph abbrev. for miles per hour.

MPhil or **MPh** abbrev. for Master of Philosophy.

MPP (in Canada) abbrev. for Member of Provincial Parliament.

Mpumalanga ★ (ᵊm'pʌmɑːˌlɑːŋgə) n a province of E South Africa. Capital: Nelspruit. Pop.: 3 007 100 (1995 est.). Area: 78 370 sq. km (30 259 sq. miles).

MPV abbrev. for multipurpose vehicle.

Mr ('mɪstə) n, pl **Messrs.** a title used before a man's name or before some office that he holds: *Mr Jones; Mr President.* [C17: abbrev. of MISTER]

MR abbrev. for: 1 (in Britain) Master of the Rolls. 2 motivation(al) research.

MRC (in Britain) abbrev. for Medical Research Council.

MRI abbrev. for magnetic resonance imaging.

m-RNA abbrev. for messenger RNA.

MRP abbrev. for manufacturers' recommended price.

Mrs ('mɪsɪz) n, pl **Mrs** or **Mesdames**. a title used before the name or names of a married woman. [C17: orig. abbrev. of MISTRESS]

MRSA abbrev. for methicillin-resistant *Staphylococcus aureus*: a bacterium that enters the skin through open wounds to cause septicaemia and is extremely resistant to most antibiotics. It has been responsible for outbreaks of untreatable infections among patients in hospitals.

Ms (mɪz, məs) n a title substituted for **Mrs** or **Miss** to avoid making a distinction between married and unmarried women.

MS abbrev. for: 1 Master of Surgery. 2 (on gravestones, etc.) memoriae sacrum. [L: sacred to the memory of] 3 multiple sclerosis.

MS. or **ms.** pl **MSS.** or **mss.** abbrev. for manuscript.

MSc abbrev. for Master of Science.

MS-DOS (ɛm'ɛs'dɒs) n *Trademark, computing.* a type of disk operating system. [C20: from M(icro)s(oft), the company that developed it, + DOS]

MSF (in Britain) abbrev. for Manufacturing, Science, and Finance Union.

MSG abbrev. for monosodium glutamate.

Msgr abbrev. for Monsignor.

MST abbrev. for Mountain Standard Time.

Mt or **mt** abbrev. for: 1 mount: *Mt Everest.* 2 Also: **mtn.** mountain.

MT abbrev. for Montana.

MTech abbrev. for Master of Technology.

mtg abbrev. for: 1 meeting. 2 Also: **mtge.** mortgage.

MTV abbrev. for music television: a US music channel that operates 24 hours a day.

mu (mjuː) n the 12th letter in the Greek alphabet (M, μ).

Mubarak ★ (mʊ'bɑːrək) n (**Muhammad**) **Hosni** ('hʊsnɪ). born 1928, Egyptian statesman; president of Egypt from 1981.

much (mʌtʃ) determiner **1a** (*usually used with a negative*) a great quantity or degree of: *there isn't much honey left.* **1b** (*as pron*): *much has been learned from this.* **2 a bit much.** *Inf.* rather excessive. **3 make much of. 3a** (*used with a negative*)

to make sense of: *he couldn't make much of her babble.* **3b** to give importance to: *she made much of this fact.* **3c** to pay flattering attention to: *the reporters made much of the film star.* **4 not much of.** not to any appreciable degree or extent: *he's not much of an actor really.* **5 not up to much.** *Inf.* of a low standard: *this beer is not up to much.* ◆ adv **6** considerably: *they're much better now.* **7** practically; nearly (esp. in **much the same**). **8** (*usually used with a negative*) often; a great deal: *it doesn't happen much in this country.* **9** (as) **much as.** even though; although: *much as I'd like to, I can't come.* ◆ See also **more, most.** [OE *mycel*]

muchness ('mʌtʃnɪs) n **1** *Arch.* or *inf.* magnitude. **2 much of a muchness.** *Brit.* very similar.

mucilage ('mjuːsɪlɪdʒ) n **1** a sticky preparation, such as gum or glue, used as an adhesive. **2** a complex glutinous carbohydrate secreted by certain plants. [C14: via OF from LL *mūcilāgo* mouldy juice, from L, from *mucēre* to be mouldy]
▸ **mucilaginous** (ˌmjuːsɪ'lædʒɪnəs) adj

muck (mʌk) n **1** farmyard dung or decaying vegetable matter. **2** an organic soil rich in humus and used as a fertilizer. **3** dirt or filth. **4** *Sl., chiefly Brit.* rubbish. **5 make a muck of.** *Sl., chiefly Brit.* to ruin or spoil. ◆ vb (tr) **6** to spread manure upon (fields, etc.). **7** to soil or pollute. **8** (*usually foll. by up*) *Brit. sl.* to ruin or spoil. **9** (often foll. by *out*) to clear muck from. [C13: prob. from ON]
▸ **'mucky** adj

muck about vb *Brit. sl.* **1** (intr) to waste time; misbehave. **2** (when intr, foll. by *with*) to interfere (with), annoy, or waste the time (of).

mucker ('mʌkə) n *Brit. sl.* **a** a friend; mate. **b** a coarse person.
▸ **'muckerish** adj

muck in vb (intr, adv) *Brit. sl.* to share duties, work, etc. (with other people).

muckrake ('mʌkˌreɪk) vb **muckrakes, muckraking, muckraked.** (intr) to seek out and expose scandal, esp. concerning public figures.
▸ **'muck,raker** n ▸ **'muck,raking** n

mucksweat ('mʌkˌswɛt) n *Brit. inf.* profuse sweat or a state of profuse sweating.

mucous ('mjuːkəs) adj of, resembling, or secreting mucus. [C17: from L *mūcōsus* slimy, from MUCUS]
▸ **mucosity** (mjuː'kɒsɪtɪ) n

> **USAGE NOTE** The noun *mucus* is often misspelled as *mucous*. *Mucous* can only be correctly used as an adjective.

mucous membrane n a mucus-secreting membrane that lines body cavities or passages that are open to the external environment.

mucus ('mjuːkəs) n the slimy protective secretion of the mucous membranes. [C17: from L: nasal secretions; cf. *mungere* to blow the nose]

> **USAGE NOTE** See at **mucous.**

mud (mʌd) n **1** a fine-grained soft wet deposit that occurs on the ground after rain, at the bottom of ponds, etc. **2** *Inf.* slander or defamation. **3 clear as mud.** *Inf.* not at all clear. **4 here's mud in your eye.** *Inf.* a humorous drinking toast. **5** (someone's) **name is mud.** *Inf.* (someone) is disgraced. **6 throw** (*or* sling) **mud at.** *Inf.* to slander; vilify. ◆ vb **muds, mudding, mudded. 7** (tr) to soil or cover with mud. [C14: prob. from MLow G *mudde*]

mud bath n **1** a medicinal bath in heated mud. **2** a dirty or muddy occasion, state, etc.

mudbrick ('mʌdˌbrɪk) n a brick made with mud.

muddle ('mʌdᵊl) vb **muddles, muddling, muddled.** (tr) **1** (often foll. by *up*) to mix up (objects, items, etc.). **2** to confuse. **3** *US.* to mix or stir (alcoholic drinks, etc.). ◆ n **4** a state of physical or mental confusion. [C16: ?from MDu. *moddelen* to make muddy]
▸ **'muddled** adj ▸ **'muddler** n ▸ **'muddling** adj, n

muddleheaded (ˌmʌdºl'hɛdɪd) *adj* mentally confused or vague.
> ˌmuddle'headedness *n*

muddle through *vb* (*intr, adv*) *Chiefly Brit.* to succeed in spite of lack of organization.

muddy ('mʌdɪ) *adj* **muddier, muddiest. 1** covered or filled with mud. **2** not clear or bright: *muddy colours*. **3** cloudy: *a muddy liquid*. **4** (esp. of thoughts) confused or vague. ◆ *vb* **muddies, muddying, muddied. 5** to become or cause to become muddy.
> 'muddily *adv* > 'muddiness *n*

mudfish ('mʌdˌfɪʃ) *n, pl* **mudfish** or **mudfishes.** any of various fishes, such as the bowfin, that live in the muddy bottoms of rivers, lakes, etc.

mud flat *n* a tract of low muddy land that is covered at high tide and exposed at low tide.

mudflow ('mʌdˌfləʊ) *n Geol.* a flow of soil mixed with water down a steep unstable slope.

mudguard ('mʌdˌgɑːd) *n* a curved part of a motorcycle, bicycle, etc., attached above the wheels to reduce the amount of water or mud thrown up by them. US and Canad. name: **fender.**

mud hen *n* any of various birds that frequent marshes, esp. the coots, rails, etc.

mudlark ('mʌdˌlɑːk) *n* **1** (formerly) a person who made a living by picking up odds and ends in the mud of tidal rivers. **2** *Sl., now rare.* a street urchin. **3** *Austral. sl.* a racehorse that runs well on a wet or muddy course.

mud map *n Austral.* **1** a rough map drawn on the ground with a stick. **2** any rough sketch map.

mudpack ('mʌdˌpæk) *n* a cosmetic astringent paste containing fuller's earth.

mud puppy *n* an aquatic North American salamander having persistent larval features.

mudskipper ('mʌdˌskɪpə) *n* any of various gobies that occur in tropical coastal regions of Africa and Asia and can move on land by means of their strong pectoral fins.

mudslinging ('mʌdˌslɪŋɪŋ) *n* casting malicious slurs on an opponent, esp. in politics.
> 'mudˌslinger *n*

mudstone ('mʌdˌstəʊn) *n* a dark grey clay rock similar to shale.

mud turtle *n* any of various small turtles that inhabit muddy rivers in North and Central America.

muesli ('mjuːzlɪ) *n* a mixture of rolled oats, nuts, fruit, etc., usually eaten with milk. [Swiss G, from G *Mus* mush, purée + *-li*, dim. suffix]

muezzin (muː'ɛzɪn) *n Islam.* the official of a mosque who calls the faithful to prayer from the minaret. [C16: from Ar. *mu'adhdhin*]

muff[1] (mʌf) *n* an open-ended cylinder of fur or cloth into which the hands are placed for warmth. [C16: prob. from Du. *mof*, ult. from F *mouffle* MUFFLE[1]]

muff[2] (mʌf) *vb* **1** to perform (an action) awkwardly. **2** (*tr*) to bungle (a shot, catch, etc.). ◆ *n* **3** any unskilful play, esp. a dropped catch. **4** any bungled action. **5** a bungler. [C19: from ?]

muffin ('mʌfɪn) *n* **1** *Brit.* a thick round baked yeast roll, usually toasted and served with butter. **2** *US & Canad.* a small cup-shaped sweet bread roll, usually eaten hot with butter. [C18: ?from Low G *muffen* cakes]

muffin man *n Brit.* (formerly) an itinerant seller of muffins.

muffle[1] ('mʌfºl) *vb* **muffles, muffling, muffled.** (*mainly tr*) **1** (*also intr*; often foll. by *up*) to wrap up (the head) in a scarf, cloak, etc., esp. for warmth. **2** (*also intr*) to deaden (a sound or noise), esp. by wrapping. **3** to prevent (the expression of something) by (someone). ◆ *n* **4** something that muffles. **5** a kiln with an inner chamber for firing porcelain, enamel, etc. [C15: prob. from OF; cf. OF *moufle* mitten, *emmouflé* wrapped up]

muffle[2] ('mʌfºl) *n* the fleshy hairless part of the upper lip and nose in ruminants and some rodents. [C17: from F *mufle*, from ?]

muffler ('mʌflə) *n* **1** a thick scarf, collar, etc. **2** the US and Canad. name for **silencer** (sense 1).

mufti[1] ('mʌftɪ) *n* civilian dress, esp. as worn by a person who normally wears a military uniform. [C19: ?from MUFTI]

Mufti[2] ('mʌftɪ) *n, pl* **Muftis.** a Muslim legal expert and adviser on the law of the Koran. [C16: from Ar. *muftī*, from *aftā* to give a (legal) decision]

Mufulira ★ (ˌmuːfuː'lɪərə) *n* a mining town in the Copper Belt of Zambia. Pop.: 152 944 (1990).

mug[1] (mʌg) *n* **1** a drinking vessel with a handle, usually cylindrical and made of earthenware. **2** Also called: **mugful.** the quantity held by a mug or its contents. [C16: prob. of Scand. origin]

mug[2] (mʌg) *n* **1** *Sl.* a person's face or mouth. **2** *Brit. sl.* a gullible person, esp. one who is swindled easily. **3 a mug's game.** a worthless activity. ◆ *vb* **mugs, mugging, mugged. 4** (*tr*) *Inf.* to attack or rob (someone) violently. [C18: ?from MUG[1], since drinking vessels were sometimes modelled into the likeness of a face]
> 'mugger *n*

Mugabe ★ (muˈgɑːbɪ) *n* Robert. born 1925, Zimbabwean politician; leader of one wing of the Patriotic Front and the Zanu party; prime minister (1980–87); president from 1988.

muggins ('mʌgɪnz) *n* (*functioning as sing*) **1** *Brit. sl.* **1a** a simpleton. **1b** a title used humorously to refer to oneself as a dupe or victim. **2** a card game. [C19: prob. from the surname *Muggins*]

muggy ('mʌgɪ) *adj* **muggier, muggiest.** (of weather, air, etc.) unpleasantly warm and humid. [C18: dialect *mug* drizzle, prob. of Scand. origin]
> 'mugginess *n*

mug shot *n Inf.* a photograph of a person's face, esp. one resembling a police-file picture.

mug up *vb* (*adv*) *Brit. sl.* to study (a subject) hard, esp. for an exam. [C19: from ?]

Muhammad ★ (muˈhæməd) *n* a variant of **Mohammed.**

Muhammad Ali or **Mohammad Ali** ★ ('ɑːlɪ, ɑːˈliː, ˈælɪ) *n* original name *Cassius (Marcellus) Clay.* born 1942, US boxer; world heavyweight champion (1964–67; 1974–78; 1978).

Muhammadan or **Muhammedan** (muˈhæmədºn) *n, adj* another word (not in Muslim use) for **Muslim.**

Mühlhausen ★ (myːl'haʊzən) *n* the German name for **Mulhouse.**

Muir ★ (mjʊə) *n* Edwin. 1887–1959, Scottish poet and novelist.

Muir Glacier ★ *n* a glacier in SE Alaska, in the St Elias Mountains, flowing southeast from Mount Fairweather. Area: about 900 sq. km (350 sq. miles).

mujaheddin or **mujahedeen** (ˌmuːdʒəhəˈdiːn) *pl n* (preceded by *the; sometimes cap.*) (in Afghanistan and Iran) fundamentalist Muslim guerrillas. In Afghanistan in 1992 the mujaheddin overthrew the government but were unable to agree on a new constitution and were themselves overthrown by the Taliban militia in 1996. [C20: from Ar. *mujāhidīn* fighters, ult. from JIHAD]

Mukden ★ ('mukdən) *n* a former name of **Shenyang.**

mukluk ('mʌklʌk) *n* a soft boot, usually of sealskin, worn by Eskimos. [from Eskimo *muklok* large seal]

mulatto (mjuːˈlætəʊ) *n, pl* **mulattos** or **mulattoes. 1** a person having one Black and one White parent. ◆ *adj* **2** of a light brown colour; tawny. [C16: from Sp. *mulato* young mule, var. of *mulo* MULE[1]]

mulberry ('mʌlbərɪ, -brɪ) *n, pl* **mulberries. 1** a tree having edible blackberry-like fruit, such as the white mulberry, the leaves of which are used to feed silkworms. **2** the fruit of any of these trees. **3** any of several similar or related trees. **4a** a dark purple colour. **4b** (*as adj*): *a mulberry dress.* [C14: from L *mōrum*, from Gk *moron*; rel. to OE *mōrberie*]

mulch (mʌltʃ) *n* **1** half-rotten vegetable matter, peat, etc., used to prevent soil erosion or enrich the soil. ◆ *vb* **2** (*tr*) to cover (the surface of land) with mulch. [C17: from obs. *mulch* soft; rel. to OE *mylisc* mellow]

Mulciber ★ ('mʌlsɪbə) *n* another name for **Vulcan.**

mulct (mʌlkt) *vb* (*tr*) **1** to cheat or defraud. **2** to fine (a person). ◆ *n* **3** a fine or penalty. [C15: via F from L *multa* a fine]

Muldoon ★ (mʌl'duːn) *n* Sir **Robert David**. 1921–92, New Zealand statesman; prime minister (1975–84).

mule[1] (mjuːl) *n* **1** the sterile offspring of a male donkey and a female horse, used as a beast of burden. **2** any hybrid animal: *a mule canary*. **3** Also called: **spinning mule**. a machine that spins cotton into yarn and winds the yarn on spindles. **4** *Inf.* an obstinate or stubborn person. [C13: from OF *mul*, from L *mūlus* ass, mule]

mule[2] (mjuːl) *n* a backless shoe or slipper. [C16: from OF from L *mulleus* a magistrate's shoe]

muleta (mjuː'lɛtə) *n* the small cape attached to a stick used by the matador during a bullfight. [Sp.: small mule, crutch, from *mula* MULE[1]]

muleteer (ˌmjuːlɪ'tɪə) *n* a person who drives mules.

mulga ('mʌlgə) *n Austral.* **1** any of various Australian acacia shrubs. **2** scrub comprised of a dense growth of acacia. **3** *Inf.* the outback; bush. [from Abor.]

Mulhacén ★ (*Spanish* mula'θen) *n* a mountain in S Spain, in the Sierra Nevada: the highest peak in Spain. Height: 3478 m (11 410 ft).

Mülheim an der Ruhr (*German* 'myːlhaim an der 'ruːr) *or* **Mülheim** ★ *n* an industrial city in W Germany, in North Rhine-Westphalia on the River Ruhr: river port. Pop.: 176 513 (1995 est.).

Mulhouse ★ (*French* myluz) *n* a city in E France, on the Rhône–Rhine canal: under German rule (1871–1918); textiles. Pop.: 109 905 (1990). German name: **Mühlhausen.**

muliebrity (ˌmjuːlɪ'ɛbrɪtɪ) *n* **1** the condition of being a woman. **2** femininity. [C16: via LL from L *muliēbris* womanly, from *mulier* woman]

mulish ('mjuːlɪʃ) *adj* stubborn; obstinate.
▶ 'mulishly *adv* ▶ 'mulishness *n*

mull[1] (mʌl) *vb* (*tr*) (often foll. by *over*) to study or ponder. [C19: prob. from MUDDLE]

mull[2] (mʌl) *vb* (*tr*) to heat (wine, ale, etc.) with sugar and spices. [C17: from ?]
▶ mulled *adj*

mull[3] (mʌl) *n* a light muslin fabric of soft texture. [C18: earlier *mulmull*, from Hindi *malmal*]

mull[4] (mʌl) *n Scot.* a promontory. [C14: rel. to Gaelic *maol*, Icelandic *múli*]

Mull ★ (mʌl) *n* a mountainous island off the west coast of Scotland, in the Inner Hebrides, separated from the mainland by the **Sound of Mull**. Chief town: Tobermory. Pop.: 2605 (latest est.). Area: 909 sq. km (351 sq. miles).

mullah *or* **mulla** ('mʌlə, 'mʊlə) *n* (formerly) a Muslim scholar, teacher, or religious leader: also used as a title of respect. [C17: from Turkish *molla*, Persian & Hindi *mulla*, from Ar. *mawlā* master]

mullein ('mʌlɪn) *n* any of various Mediterranean herbaceous plants such as the common mullein or Aaron's rod, typically having tall spikes of yellow flowers and broad hairy leaves. [C15: from OF *moleine*, prob. from OF *mol* soft, from L *mollis*]

muller ('mʌlə) *n* a flat heavy implement of stone or iron used to grind material against a slab of stone, etc. [C15: prob. from *mullen* to grind to powder]

Muller ★ ('mʌlə) *n* **Hermann Joseph**. 1890–1967, US geneticist, noted for his work on the transmutation of genes by X-rays: Nobel prize for physiology or medicine 1946.

Müller ★ (*German* 'mylər) *n* **1** Friedrich Max ('friːdrɪç maks). 1823–1900, British Sanskrit scholar born in Germany. **2 Johann** (jo'han). See **Regiomontanus. 3 Johannes Peter** (jo'hanəs 'peːtər). 1801–58, German physiologist, anatomist, and experimental psychologist. **4 Paul Hermann** (paul 'herman). 1899–1965, Swiss chemist. He synthesized DDT (1939) and discovered its use as an insecticide: Nobel prize for physiology or medicine 1948.

mullet ('mʌlɪt) *n* any of various teleost food fishes such as the grey mullet or red mullet. [C15: via OF from L *mullus*, from Gk *mullos*]

mulligatawny (ˌmʌlɪgə'tɔːnɪ) *n* a curry-flavoured soup of Anglo-Indian origin, made with meat stock. [C18:

from Tamil *milakutanni*, from *milaku* pepper + *tanni* water]

Mulliken ★ ('mʌlɪkən) *n* **Robert Sanderson**. 1896–1986, US physicist and chemist; Nobel prize for chemistry (1966) for his work on chemical bonding.

Mullingar ★ (ˌmʌlɪŋ'gɑː) *n* a town in N central Republic of Ireland, the county town of Co. Westmeath; site of cathedral; cattle raised. Pop.: 11 800 (1995 est.).

mullion ('mʌlɪən) *n* **1** a vertical member between the casements or panes of a window. ◆ *vb* (*tr*) to furnish (a window, screen, etc.) with mullions. [C16: var. of ME *munial*, from OF *moinel*, from ?]

mullock ('mʌlək) *n Austral.* **1** waste material from a mine. **2** poke mullock at. *Inf.* to ridicule. [C14: rel. to OE *myl* dust, ON *mylja* to crush]

mulloway ('mʌlə,weɪ) *n* a large Australian marine food fish. [C19: from ?]

Mulroney ★ (mʌl'rəʊnɪ) *n* (**Martin**) **Brian**. born 1939, Canadian statesman; Conservative prime minister (1984–93).

Multan ★ (ˌmʊl'tɑːn) *n* a city in central Pakistan, near the Chenab River. Pop.: 1 257 000 (1995 est.).

multangular (mʌl'tæŋgjʊlə) *or* **multiangular** *adj* having many angles.

multi- *combining form.* **1** many or much: *multimillion.* **2** more than one: *multistorey.* [from L *multus* much, many]

multicultural (ˌmʌltɪ'kʌltʃərəl) *adj* consisting of, relating to, or designed for the cultures of several different races.
▶ ˌmulti'cultural,ism *n*

multifactorial (ˌmʌltɪfæk'tɔːrɪəl) *adj* having many separate factors, causes, components, etc.: *multifactorial disease; multifactorial inheritance.*

multifarious (ˌmʌltɪ'fɛərɪəs) *adj* having many parts of great variety. [C16: from LL *multifārius* manifold, from L *multifāriam* on many sides]
▶ ˌmulti'fariously *adv* ▶ ˌmulti'fariousness *n*

multiflora rose (ˌmʌltɪ'flɔːrə) *n* an Asian climbing shrubby rose having clusters of small fragrant flowers.

multiform ('mʌltɪ,fɔːm) *adj* having many forms.
▶ ˌmulti'formity *n*

multigym ('mʌltɪ,dʒɪm) *n* an exercise apparatus incorporating a variety of weights, used for toning the muscles.

multilateral (ˌmʌltɪ'lætərəl, -'lætrəl) *adj* **1** of or involving more than two nations or parties: *a multilateral pact.* **2** having many sides.
▶ ˌmulti'laterally *adv*

multilingual (ˌmʌltɪ'lɪŋgwəl) *adj* **1** able to speak more than two languages. **2** written or expressed in more than two languages.

multimedia (ˌmʌltɪ'miːdɪə) *adj* **1** of or relating to the combined use of such media as television, slides, etc. **2** *Computing.* of or relating to any of various systems that can manipulate data in a variety of forms, such as sound, graphics, or text.

multimillionaire (ˌmʌltɪ,mɪljə'nɛə) *n* a person with a fortune of several million pounds, dollars, etc.

multinational (ˌmʌltɪ'næʃənəl) *adj* **1** (of a large business company) operating in several countries. ◆ *n* **2** such a company.

multipack ('mʌltɪ,pæk) *n* a form of packaging of foodstuffs, etc., that contains several units and is offered at a price below that of the equivalent number of units.

multiparous (mʌl'tɪpərəs) *adj* (of certain species of mammal) producing many offspring at one birth. [C17: from NL *multiparus*]

multipartite (ˌmʌltɪ'pɑːtaɪt) *adj* **1** divided into many parts or sections. **2** *Government.* a less common word for **multilateral.**

multiparty (ˌmʌltɪ'pɑːtɪ) *adj* of or relating to a state, political system, etc., in which more than one political party is permitted: *multiparty democracy.*

multiple ('mʌltɪp'l) *adj* **1** having or involving more than one part, individual, etc. **2** *Electronics, US & Canad.* (of a circuit) having a number of conductors in parallel. ◆ *n* **3** the product of a given number or polynomial and any other one: *6 is a multiple of 2*. **4** short for **multiple store**. [C17: via F from LL *multiplus*, from L MULTIPLEX] ▸ **'multiply** *adv*

multiple-choice *adj* having a number of possible given answers out of which the correct one must be chosen.

multiple personality *n* Psychiatry. a mental disorder in which an individual's personality appears to have become separated into two or more distinct personalities. Nontechnical name: **split personality**.

multiple sclerosis *n* a chronic progressive disease of the central nervous system, resulting in speech and visual disorders, tremor, muscular incoordination, partial paralysis, etc.

multiple store *n* one of several retail enterprises under the same ownership and management. Also called: **multiple shop**.

multiplex ('mʌltɪˌplɛks) *n* **1** Telecomm. **1a** the use of a common communications channel for sending two or more messages or signals. **1b** (*as modifier*): *a multiplex transmitter*. **2a** a purpose-built complex containing a number of cinemas and usually a restaurant or bar. **2b** (*as modifier*): *a multiplex cinema*. ◆ *adj* **3** a less common word for **multiple**. ◆ *vb* **4** to send (messages or signals) or (of messages and signals) to be sent by multiplex. [C16: from L: having many folds, from MULTI- + *plicāre* to fold]

multiplicand (ˌmʌltɪplɪˈkænd) *n* a number to be multiplied by another number, the **multiplier**. [C16: from L *multiplicandus*, gerund of *multiplicāre* to MULTIPLY]

multiplication (ˌmʌltɪplɪˈkeɪʃən) *n* **1** a mathematical operation, the inverse of division, in which the product of two or more numbers or quantities is calculated. Usually written $a \times b$, *a.b*, *ab*. **2** the act of multiplying or state of being multiplied. **3** the act or process in animals, plants, or people, of reproducing or breeding.

multiplication sign *n* the symbol ×, placed between numbers to be multiplied.

multiplication table *n* one of a group of tables giving the results of multiplying two numbers together.

multiplicity (ˌmʌltɪˈplɪsɪtɪ) *n, pl* **multiplicities**. **1** a large number or great variety. **2** the state of being multiple.

multiplier ('mʌltɪˌplaɪə) *n* **1** a person or thing that multiplies. **2** the number by which another number, the **multiplicand**, is multiplied. **3** Physics. any instrument, such as a photomultiplier, for increasing an effect. **4** Econ. the ratio of the total change in income (resulting from successive rounds of spending) to an initial autonomous change in expenditure.

multiply ('mʌltɪˌplaɪ) *vb* **multiplies, multiplying, multiplied**. **1** to increase or cause to increase in number, quantity, or degree. **2** (*tr*) to combine (two numbers or quantities) by multiplication. **3** (*intr*) to increase in number by reproduction. [C13: from OF *multiplier*, from L *multiplicāre* to multiply, from *multus* much, many + *plicāre* to fold] ▸ **'multi,pliable** *or* **multiplicable** ('mʌltɪˌplɪkəbˀl) *adj*

multiprocessor (ˌmʌltɪˈprəʊsɛsə) *n* Computing. a number of central processing units linked together to enable parallel processing to take place.

multipurpose vehicle *n* a large car, similar to a van, designed to carry up to eight passengers. Abbrev.: **MPV**.

multiskilling ('mʌltɪˌskɪlɪŋ) *n* the practice of training employees to do a number of different tasks.

multistage ('mʌltɪˌsteɪdʒ) *adj* **1** (of a rocket or missile) having several stages, each of which can be jettisoned after it has burnt out. **2** (of a turbine, compressor, or supercharger) having more than one rotor. **3** (of any process or device) having more than one stage.

multistorey (ˌmʌltɪˈstɔːrɪ) *adj* **1** (of a building) having many storeys. ◆ *n* **2** a multistorey car park.

multitrack ('mʌltɪˌtræk) *adj* (in sound recording) using tape containing two or more tracks, usually four to twenty-four.

multitude ('mʌltɪˌtjuːd) *n* **1** a large gathering of people. **2** the. the common people. **3** a large number. **4** the state or quality of being numerous. [C14: via OF from L *multitūdō*]

multitudinous (ˌmʌltɪˈtjuːdɪnəs) *adj* **1** very numerous. **2** Rare. great in extent, variety, etc. **3** Poetic. crowded. ▸ ˌmulti'tudinously *adv* ▸ ˌmulti'tudinousness *n*

multi-user *adj* (of a computer) capable of being used by several people at once.

multivalent (ˌmʌltɪˈveɪlənt) *adj* another word for **polyvalent**. ▸ ˌmulti'valency *n*

mum[1] (mʌm) *n* Chiefly Brit. an informal word for **mother**. [C19: a child's word]

mum[2] (mʌm) *adj* **1** keeping information, etc., to oneself; silent. ◆ *n* **2** mum's the word. (*interj*) silence or secrecy is to be observed. [C14: suggestive of closed lips]

mum[3] (mʌm) *vb* **mums, mumming, mummed**. (*intr*) to act in a mummer's play. [C16: verbal use of MUM[2]]

Mumbai ★ (mʊmˈbaɪ) *n* the Hindi name for **Bombay**.

mumble ('mʌmbˀl) *vb* **mumbles, mumbling, mumbled**. **1** to utter indistinctly, as with the mouth partly closed. **2** Rare. to chew (food) ineffectually. ◆ *n* **3** an indistinct or low utterance or sound. [C14 *momelen*, from MUM[2]] ▸ **'mumbler** *n* ▸ **'mumbling** *adj* ▸ **'mumblingly** *adv*

mumbo jumbo ('mʌmbəʊ) *n, pl* **mumbo jumbos**. **1** foolish religious reverence, ritual, or incantation. **2** meaningless or unnecessarily complicated language. **3** an object of superstitious awe or reverence. [C18: prob. from W African *mama dyumbo*, name of a tribal god]

mu meson (mjuː) *n* a former name for **muon**.

Mumford ★ ('mʌmfəd) *n* Lewis. 1895–1990, US sociologist, whose works include *The City in History* (1962) and *Roots of Contemporary Architecture* (1972).

mummer ('mʌmə) *n* **1** one of a group of masked performers in a folk play or mime. **2** Humorous or derog. an actor. [C15: from OF *momeur*, from *momer* to mime]

Mummerset ('mʌməsɪt, -ˌsɛt) *n* an imitation West Country accent used in drama. [C20: from MUMMER + (SOMER)SET]

mummery ('mʌmərɪ) *n, pl* **mummeries**. **1** a performance by mummers. **2** hypocritical or ostentatious ceremony.

mummify ('mʌmɪˌfaɪ) *vb* **mummifies, mummifying, mummified**. **1** (*tr*) to preserve (a body) as a mummy. **2** (*intr*) to dry up; shrivel. ▸ ˌmummifi'cation *n*

mummy[1] ('mʌmɪ) *n, pl* **mummies**. **1** an embalmed or preserved body, esp. as prepared for burial in ancient Egypt. **2** a mass of pulp. **3** a dark brown pigment. [C14: from OF *momie*, from Med. L, from Ar.: asphalt, from Persian *mūm* wax]

mummy[2] ('mʌmɪ) *n, pl* **mummies**. Chiefly Brit. a child's word for **mother**[1] (senses 1–3). [C19: var. of MUM[1]]

mumps (mʌmps) *n* (*functioning as sing or pl*) **1** an acute contagious viral disease of the parotid salivary glands, characterized by swelling of the affected parts, fever, and pain beneath the ear. **2** sulks. [C16: from *mump* to grimace] ▸ **'mumpish** *adj*

mumsy ('mʌmzɪ) *adj* **mumsier, mumsiest**. homely or drab. ▸ **'mumsiness** *n*

mun. *abbrev. for* municipal.

munch (mʌntʃ) *vb* to chew (food) steadily, esp. with a crunching noise. [C14 *monche*, imit.]

Munch ★ (mʊŋk) *n* Edvard ('ɛdvard). 1863–1944, Norwegian painter and engraver, whose works include *The Cry* (1893).

München ★ ('mʏnçən) *n* the German name for **Munich**.

München-Gladbach ★ (ˌmʏnçənˈglatbax) *n* the former name of **Mönchengladbach**.

mundane (mʌnˈdeɪn, ˈmʌndeɪn) *adj* **1** everyday, ordinary, or banal. **2** relating to the world or worldly matters. [C15: from F *mondain*, via LL, from L *mundus* world] ▸ **mun'danely** *adv* ▸ **mun'daneness** *n*

mung bean (mʌŋ) *n* **1** an E Asian bean plant grown for forage and as the source of bean sprouts for cookery. **2** the seed of this plant. [C20: from *mung*, changed from *mungo*, from Tamil *mūngu*, from Sansk. *mudga*]

Munich ★ ('mjuːnɪk) *n* a city in SW Germany, capital of

★ people and places

the state of Bavaria, on the Isar River: became capital of Bavaria in 1508; headquarters of the Nazi movement in the 1920s; a major financial, commercial, and manufacturing centre. Pop.: 1 244 676 (1995 est.). German name: **München**.

municipal (mjuːˈnɪsɪpᵊl) adj of or relating to a town, city, or borough or its local government. [C16: from L *mūnicipium* a free town, from *mūniceps* citizen, from *mūnia* responsibilities + *capere* to take]
▶ mu'nicipally adv

municipality (mjuːˌnɪsɪˈpælɪtɪ) n, pl **municipalities**. 1 a city, town, or district enjoying local self-government. 2 the governing body of such a unit.

municipalize or **municipalise** (mjuːˈnɪsɪpəˌlaɪz) vb **municipalizes, municipalizing, municipalized** or **municipalises, municipalising, municipalised**. (tr) 1 to bring under municipal ownership or control. 2 to make a municipality of.
▶ mu,nicipali'zation or mu,nicipali'sation n

munificent (mjuːˈnɪfɪsənt) adj 1 (of a person) generous; bountiful. 2 (of a gift) liberal. [C16: back formation from L *mūnificentia* liberality, from *mūnificus*, from *mūnus* gift + *facere* to make]
▶ mu'nificence n ▶ mu'nificently adv

muniments (ˈmjuːnɪmənts) pl n Law. the title deeds and other documentary evidence relating to the title to land. [C15: via OF from L *munire* to defend]

munition (mjuːˈnɪʃən) vb (tr) to supply with munitions. [C16: via F from L *mūnītiō* fortification, from *mūnīre* to fortify]

munitions (mjuːˈnɪʃənz) pl n (sometimes sing) military equipment and stores, esp. ammunition.

Munro[1] (mʌnˈrəʊ) n, pl **Munros**. Mountaineering. any separate mountain peak over 3000 feet high: originally used of Scotland only but now sometimes extended to other parts of the British Isles. [C20: after Hugh Thomas Munro (1856–1919), who listed these in 1891]

Munro[2] (mʌnˈrəʊ) n **H**(ector) **H**(ugh), pen name Saki. 1870–1916, Scottish author, born in Burma, noted for his satirical short stories.

Munster ★ (ˈmʌnstə) n a province of SW Republic of Ireland: the largest of the four provinces and historically a kingdom; consists of the counties of Clare, Cork, Kerry, Limerick, Tipperary, and Waterford. Capital: Cork. Pop.: 1 009 533 (1991). Area: 24 125 sq. km (9315 sq. miles).

Münster ★ (German) n a city in NW Germany in North Rhine-Westphalia, on the Dortmund–Ems Canal: one of the treaties comprising the Peace of Westphalia (1648) was signed here; became capital of Prussian Westphalia in 1815. Pop.: 264 887 (1995 est.).

muntjac or **muntjak** (ˈmʌntˌdʒæk) n any small Asian deer typically having a chestnut-brown coat and small antlers. [C18: prob. from Javanese *mindjangan* deer]

Müntzer ★ (ˈmʊntsə; German ˈmʏntsər) n **Thomas**. ?1490–1525, German religious and political reformer; executed for organizing the Peasants' War (1524–25).

muon (ˈmjuːɒn) n a positive or negative elementary particle with a mass 207 times that of an electron. It was originally called the **mu meson**. [C20: short for MU MESON]
▶ mu'onic adj

mural (ˈmjʊərəl) n 1 a large painting on a wall. ◆ adj 2 of or relating to a wall. [C15: from L *mūrālis*, from *mūrus* wall]
▶ 'muralist n

Murasaki Shikibu ★ (ˌmjʊərəˈsɑːkɪ ˈʃiːkiːˌbuː) n 11th-century Japanese court lady, author of The Tale of Genji, perhaps the world's first novel.

Murat ★ (French myra) n **Joachim** (ʒɔaʃɛ̃). 1767?–1815, French marshal, during the Napoleonic Wars; king of Naples (1808–15).

Murchison ★ (ˈmɜːtʃɪsᵊn) n Sir **Roderick Impey**. 1792–1871, Scottish geologist: established parts of the geological time scale.

Murcia ★ (Spanish ˈmurθja) n 1 a region and ancient kingdom of SE Spain, on the Mediterranean: taken by the Moors in the 8th century; an independent Muslim kingdom in the 11th and 12th centuries. 2 a city in SE Spain, capital of Murcia province: trading centre for a

rich agricultural region; silk industry; university (1915). Pop.: 341 531 (1994 est.).

murder (ˈmɜːdə) n 1 the unlawful premeditated killing of one human being by another. Cf. **manslaughter**. 2 Inf. something dangerous, difficult, or unpleasant: driving around London is murder. 3 cry blue murder. Inf. to make an outcry. 4 get away with murder. Inf. to escape censure; do as one pleases. ◆ vb (mainly tr) 5 (also intr) to kill (someone) unlawfully with premeditation or during the commission of a crime. 6 to kill brutally. 7 Inf. to destroy; ruin. 8 Inf. to defeat completely; beat decisively: the home team murdered their opponents. [OE morthor]
▶ 'murderer n ▶ 'murderess fem n

murderous (ˈmɜːdərəs) adj 1 intending, capable of, or guilty of murder. 2 Inf. very dangerous or difficult: a murderous road.
▶ 'murderously adv ▶ 'murderousness n

Murdoch ★ (ˈmɜːdɒk) n 1 Dame (**Jean**) Iris. 1919–99, British novelist and philosopher. Her novels include The Bell (1958), The Sea, The Sea (1978), and Jackson's Dilemma (1995). 2 (**Keith**) Rupert. born 1931, US entrepreneur, born in Australia; chairman of News International Ltd and Times Newspapers Ltd.

Mureş ★ (ˈmʊəreʃ) n a river in SE central Europe, rising in central Romania in the Carpathian Mountains and flowing west to the Tisza River at Szeged, Hungary. Length: 885 km (550 miles). Hungarian name: **Maros**.

murex (ˈmjʊəreks) n, pl **murices** (ˈmjʊərɪˌsiːz). any of a genus of spiny-shelled marine gastropods: formerly used as a source of the dye Tyrian purple. [C16: from L *mūrex* purple fish]

muriatic acid (ˌmjʊərɪˈætɪk) n a former name for **hydrochloric acid**. [C17: from L *muriāticus* pickled, from *muria* brine]

Murillo ★ (mjʊəˈrɪləʊ; Spanish muˈriʎo) n **Bartolomé Esteban** (bartoloˈme esˈteβan). 1618–82, Spanish painter.

murk or **mirk** (mɜːk) n 1 gloomy darkness. ◆ adj 2 an archaic variant of **murky**. [C13: prob. from ON *myrkr* darkness]

murky or **mirky** (ˈmɜːkɪ) adj **murkier, murkiest** or **mirkier, mirkiest**. 1 gloomy or dark. 2 cloudy or impenetrable, as with smoke or fog. 3 Inf. obscure and suspicious; shady: she had a murky past.
▶ 'murkily or 'mirkily adv ▶ 'murkiness or 'mirkiness n

Murman Coast (ˈmʊəmən) or **Murmansk Coast** ★ n a coastal region of NW Russia, in the north of the Kola Peninsula: within the Arctic Circle, but ice-free.

Murmansk ★ (Russian ˈmurmənsk) n a port in NW Russia, on the Kola Inlet of the Barents Sea: founded in 1915; the world's largest town north of the Arctic Circle, with a large fishing fleet. Pop.: 407 000 (1995 est.).

murmur (ˈmɜːmə) n 1 a continuous low indistinct sound, as of distant voices. 2 an indistinct utterance: a murmur of satisfaction. 3 a complaint; grumble: he made no murmur at my suggestion. 4 Med. any abnormal soft blowing sound heard usually over the chest (heart murmur). ◆ vb murmurs, murmuring, murmured. 5 to utter (something) in a murmur. 6 (intr) to complain. [C14: as n, from L *murmur*; vb. via OF *murmurer* from L *murmurāre* to rumble]
▶ 'murmurer n ▶ 'murmuring n, adj ▶ 'murmuringly adv
▶ 'murmurous adj

murphy (ˈmɜːfɪ) n, pl **murphies**. a dialect or informal word for **potato**. [C19: from the common Irish surname Murphy]

murrain (ˈmʌrɪn) n 1 any plaguelike disease in cattle. 2 Arch. a plague. [C14: from OF *morine*, from *morir* to die, from L *morī*]

Murray[1] ★ (ˈmʌrɪ) n a river in SE Australia, rising in New South Wales and flowing northwest into SE South Australia, then south into the sea at Encounter Bay: the main river of Australia, important for irrigation and power. Length: 2590 km (1609 miles).

Murray[2] ★ (ˈmʌrɪ) n 1 **1st Earl of**. See (1st Earl of) **Moray**. 2 Sir (**George**) **Gilbert** (**Aimé**). 1866–1957, British classical scholar, born in Australia. 3 Sir **James Augustus Henry**. 1837–1915, British lexicographer; one of the original editors (1879–1915) of what became the Oxford English Dictionary.

★ people and places

Murray cod *n* a large greenish Australian freshwater food fish. [after MURRAY River]

Murrumbidgee ★ (ˌmʌrəm'bɪdʒɪ) *n* a river in SE Australia, rising in S New South Wales and flowing north and west to the Murray River: important for irrigation. Length: 1690 km (1050 miles).

murther ('mɜːðə) *n, vb* an archaic word for **murder**.
▸ 'murtherer *n*

mus. *abbrev. for:* **1** museum. **2** music. **3** musical.

MusB *or* **MusBac** *abbrev. for* Bachelor of Music.

muscadine ('mʌskədɪn, -ˌdaɪn) *n* **1** a woody climbing plant of the southeastern US. **2** the musk-scented purple grape produced by this plant: used to make wine. [C16: from MUSCATEL]

muscae volitantes ('mʌsi: vɒlɪ'tænti:z) *pl n Pathol.* moving black specks or threads seen before the eyes, caused by opaque fragments floating in the vitreous humour or a defect in the lens. [C18: NL: flying flies]

muscat ('mʌskət, -kæt) *n* **1** any of various grapevines that produce sweet white grapes used for making wine or raisins. **2** another name for **muscatel** (sense 1). [C16: via OF from Provençal, from *musc* MUSK]

Muscat ★ ('mʌskət, -kæt) *n* the capital of the Sultanate of Oman, a port on the Gulf of Oman: a Portuguese port from the early 16th century; controlled by Persia (1650–1741). Pop.: 51 969 (1993). Arabic name: **Masqat.**

Muscat and Oman ★ *n* the former name (until 1970) of (the Sultanate of) **Oman.**

muscatel (ˌmʌskə'tɛl) *or* **muscadel** *n* **1** Also called: **muscat.** a rich sweet wine made from muscat grapes. **2** the grape or raisin from a muscat vine. [C14: from OF *muscadel,* from OProvençal, from *moscadel,* from *muscat* musky]

muscle ('mʌs⁰l) *n* **1** a tissue composed of bundles of elongated cells capable of contraction and relaxation to produce movement in an organ or part. **2** an organ composed of muscle tissue. **3** strength or force. ◆ *vb* **muscles, muscling, muscled. 4** (*intr;* often foll. by *in, on,* etc.) *Inf.* to force one's way (in). [C16: from Medical L *musculus* little mouse, from the imagined resemblance of some muscles to mice]
▸ 'muscly *adj*

muscle-bound *adj* **1** having overdeveloped and inelastic muscles. **2** lacking flexibility.

muscleman ('mʌs⁰lˌmæn) *n, pl* **musclemen. 1** a man with highly developed muscles. **2** a henchman employed by a gangster to intimidate or use violence upon victims.

Muscovite ('mʌskəˌvaɪt) *n* **1** a native or inhabitant of Moscow. ◆ *adj* **2** an archaic word for **Russian.**

Muscovy ('mʌskəvɪ) *n* **1** a Russian principality (13th to 16th centuries), of which Moscow was the capital. **2** an archaic name for **Russia** and **Moscow.**

Muscovy duck *or* **musk duck** *n* a large crested widely domesticated South American duck, having a greenish-black plumage with white markings and a large red caruncle on the bill. [C17: orig. *musk duck,* a name later mistakenly associated with MUSCOVY]

muscular ('mʌskjʊlə) *adj* **1** having well-developed muscles; brawny. **2** of, relating to, or consisting of muscle. [C17: from NL *muscularis,* from *musculus* MUSCLE]
▸ **muscularity** (ˌmʌskjʊ'lærɪtɪ) *n* ▸ 'muscularly *adv*

muscular dystrophy *n* a genetic disease characterized by progressive deterioration and wasting of muscle fibres.

musculature ('mʌskjʊlətʃə) *n* **1** the arrangement of muscles in an organ or part. **2** the total muscular system of an organism.

MusD *or* **MusDoc** *abbrev. for* Doctor of Music.

muse[1] (mjuːz) *vb* **muses, musing, mused. 1** (when *intr,* often foll. by *on* or *about*) to reflect (about) or ponder (on), usually in silence. **2** (*intr*) to gaze thoughtfully. ◆ *n* **3** a state of abstraction. [C14: from OF *muser,* ?from *mus* snout, from Med. L *mūsus*]

muse[2] (mjuːz) *n* (often preceded by *the*) a goddess that inspires a creative artist, esp. a poet. [C14: from OF, from L *Mūsa,* from Gk *Mousa* a Muse]

Muse (mjuːz) *n Greek myth.* any of nine sister goddesses, each of whom was regarded as the protectress of a different art or science.

musette (mjuː'zɛt) *n* **1** a type of bagpipe popular in France during the 17th and 18th centuries. **2** a dance, originally accompanied by a musette. [C14: from OF, dim. of *muse* bagpipe]

museum (mjuː'zɪəm) *n* a building where objects of historical, artistic, or scientific interest are exhibited and preserved. [C17: via L from Gk *Mouseion* home of the Muses, from *Mousa* MUSE]

museum piece *n* **1** an object of sufficient age or interest to be kept in a museum. **2** *Inf.* a person or thing regarded as antiquated.

Museveni ★ (musə'veɪnɪ) *n* Yoweri. born 1944, Ugandan politician; president of Uganda from 1986.

mush[1] (mʌʃ) *n* **1** a soft pulpy mass or consistency. **2** *US.* a thick porridge made from corn meal. **3** *Inf.* cloying sentimentality. [C17: from obs. *moose* porridge; prob. rel. to MASH]

mush[2] (mʌʃ) *Canad.* ◆ *interj* **1** an order to dogs in a sled team to start up or go faster. ◆ *vb* **2** to travel by or drive a dogsled. ◆ *n* **3** a journey with a dogsled. [C19: ?from imperative of F *marcher* to advance]

mushroom ('mʌʃruːm, -rʊm) *n* **1a** the fleshy spore-producing body of any of various fungi, typically consisting of a cap at the end of a stem. Some species, such as the field mushroom, are edible. Cf. **toadstool. 1b** (*as modifier*): *mushroom soup.* **2a** something resembling a mushroom in shape or rapid growth. **2b** (*as modifier*): *mushroom expansion.* ◆ *vb* (*intr*) **3** to grow rapidly: *demand mushroomed overnight.* **4** to assume a mushroom-like shape. [C15: from OF *mousseron,* from LL *mussiriō,* from ?]

mushroom cloud *n* the large mushroom-shaped cloud produced by a nuclear explosion.

mushy ('mʌʃɪ) *adj* **mushier, mushiest. 1** soft and pulpy. **2** *Inf.* excessively sentimental or emotional.
▸ 'mushily *adv* ▸ 'mushiness *n*

music ('mjuːzɪk) *n* **1** an art form consisting of sequences of sounds in time, esp. tones of definite pitch organized melodically, harmonically and rhythmically. **2** the sounds so produced, esp. by singing or musical instruments. **3** written or printed music, such as a score or set of parts. **4** any sequence of sounds perceived as pleasing or harmonious. **5 face the music.** *Inf.* to confront the consequences of one's actions. [C13: via OF from L *mūsica,* from Gk *mousikē* (*tekhnē*) (art) belonging to the Muses, from *Mousa* MUSE]

musical ('mjuːzɪk⁰l) *adj* **1** of, relating to, or used in music. **2** harmonious; melodious: *musical laughter.* **3** talented in or fond of music. **4** involving or set to music. ◆ *n* **5** Also called: **musical comedy.** a light romantic play or film having dialogue interspersed with songs and dances.
▸ ˌmusi'cality *n* ▸ 'musically *adv*

musical box *or* **music box** *n* a mechanical instrument that plays tunes by means of pins on a revolving cylinder striking the tuned teeth of a comblike metal plate, contained in a box.

musical chairs *n* (*functioning as sing*) **1** a party game in which players walk around chairs while music is played, there being one more player than chairs. Whenever the music stops, the player who fails to find a chair is eliminated. **2** any situation involving several people in a series of interrelated changes.

music centre *n* a single hi-fi unit containing a turntable, amplifier, radio, cassette player, and compact disc player.

music drama *n* **1** an opera in which the musical and dramatic elements are of equal importance and strongly interfused. **2** the genre of such operas. [C19: from G *Musikdrama,* coined by Wagner to describe his later operas]

music hall *n Chiefly Brit.* **1** a variety entertainment consisting of songs, comic turns, etc. US and Canad. name: **vaudeville. 2** a theatre at which such entertainments are staged.

★ people and places

musician (mjuːˈzɪʃən) *n* a person who plays or composes music, esp. as a profession.
▸ **muˈsicianly** *adj* ▸ **muˈsicianship** *n*
musicology (ˌmjuːzɪˈkɒlədʒɪ) *n* the scholarly study of music.
▸ **musicological** (ˌmjuːzɪkəˈlɒdʒɪkˀl) *adj* ▸ ˌmusiˈcologist *n*
music paper *n* paper ruled or printed with a stave for writing music.
Musil ★ (*German* ˈmuːzɪl) *n* **Robert** (ˈroːbɛrt). 1880–1942, Austrian novelist, best known for *The Man Without Qualities* (1930–42).
musique concrète *French.* (myzik kɔ̃krɛt) *n* another term for **concrete music.**
musk (mʌsk) *n* **1** a strong-smelling glandular secretion of the male musk deer, used in perfumery. **2** a similar substance produced by certain other animals, such as the civet and otter, or manufactured synthetically. **3** a North American plant which has yellow flowers and was formerly cultivated for its musky scent. **4** the smell of musk or a similar heady smell. **5** (*modifier*) containing or resembling musk: *musk oil*. [C14: from LL *muscus*, from Gk, from Persian, prob. from Sansk. *mushká* scrotum (from the appearance of the musk deer's musk bag), dim. of *mūsh* MOUSE]
musk deer *n* a small central Asian mountain deer. The male secretes musk.
musk duck *n* **1** another name for **Muscovy duck. 2** a duck inhabiting swamps, lakes, and streams in Australia. The male emits a musky odour.
muskeg (ˈmʌsˌkeɡ) *n Chiefly Canad.* **1** undrained boggy land. **2** a bog or swamp of this nature. [C19: of Amerind origin: grassy swamp]
muskellunge (ˈmʌskəˌlʌndʒ) *or* **maskinonge** (ˈmæskɪˌnɒndʒ) *n, pl* **muskellunges** *or* **muskellunge, maskinonges** *or* **maskinonge.** a large North American freshwater game fish, related to the pike. Often shortened (informally) to **musky** *or* **muskie.** [C18 *maskinunga*, of Amerind origin]
musket (ˈmʌskɪt) *n* a long-barrelled muzzle-loading shoulder gun used between the 16th and 18th centuries by infantry soldiers. [C16: from F *mousquet*, from It. *moschetto* arrow, earlier: sparrow hawk, from *moscha* a fly, from L *musca*]
musketeer (ˌmʌskɪˈtɪə) *n* (formerly) a soldier armed with a musket.
musketry (ˈmʌskɪtrɪ) *n* **1** muskets or musketeers collectively. **2** the technique of using small arms.
Muskie ★ (ˈmʌskɪ) *n* **Edmund** (**Sixtus**). 1914–96, US Democratic politician: Governor of Maine (1955–59): senator for Maine (1959–80): Secretary of State (1980–81).
muskmelon (ˈmʌskˌmɛlən) *n* **1** any of several varieties of the melon, such as the cantaloupe and honeydew. **2** the fruit of any of these melons, having ribbed or warty rind and sweet yellow, white, orange, or green flesh with a musky aroma.
musk ox *n* a large bovid mammal, which has a dark shaggy coat, short legs, and widely spaced downward-curving horns, and emits a musky smell: now confined to the tundras of Canada and Greenland.
muskrat (ˈmʌskˌræt) *n, pl* **muskrats** *or* **muskrat. 1** a North American beaver-like amphibious rodent, closely related to but larger than the voles. **2** the brown fur of this animal. ◆ Also called: **musquash.**
musk rose *n* a Mediterranean rose, cultivated for its white musk-scented flowers.
musky (ˈmʌskɪ) *adj* **muskier, muskiest.** resembling the smell of musk; having a heady or pungent sweet aroma.
▸ ˈmuskiness *n*
Muslim (ˈmʊzlɪm, ˈmʌz-) *or* **Moslem** *n, pl* **Muslims** *or* **Muslim, Moslems** *or* **Moslem. 1** a follower of the religion of Islam. ◆ *adj* **2** of or relating to Islam, its doctrines, culture, etc. ◆ Also (but not in Muslim use): **Mohammedan, Muhammadan.** [C17: from Ar., lit.: one who surrenders]
▸ ˈMuslimism *or* ˈMoslemism *n*
muslin (ˈmʌzlɪn) *n* a fine plain-weave cotton fabric. [C17: from F *mousseline*, from It., from Ar. *mawṣilīy* of Mosul (Iraq), where it was first produced]

muso (ˈmjuːzəʊ) *n, pl* **musos.** *Sl.* **1** *Brit. derog.* a musician, esp. a pop musician, regarded as being overconcerned with technique rather than musical content or expression. **2** *Austral.* any musician, esp. a professional one.
musquash (ˈmʌskwɒʃ) *n* another name for **muskrat,** esp. the fur. [C17: of Amerind origin]
muss (mʌs) *US & Canad. inf.* ◆ *vb* **1** (*tr;* often foll. by *up*) to make untidy; rumple. ◆ *n* **2** a state of disorder; muddle. [C19: prob. a blend of MESS + FUSS]
▸ ˈmussy *adj*
mussel (ˈmʌsˀl) *n* **1** any of various marine bivalves, esp. the edible mussel, having a dark slightly elongated shell and living attached to rocks, etc. **2** any of various freshwater bivalves, attached to rocks, sand, etc., having a flattened oval shell (a source of mother-of-pearl). [OE *muscle*, from Vulgar L *muscula* (unattested), from L *musculus*, dim. of *mūs* mouse]
Musset ★ (*French* mysɛ) *n* **Alfred de** (alfrɛd də). 1810–57, French romantic poet and dramatist: his works include the play *Lorenzaccio* (1834) and the lyrics *Les Nuits* (1835–37).
Mussolini ★ (ˌmʊsəˈliːnɪ; *Italian* mussoˈliːni) *n* **Benito** (beˈniːto) known as *il Duce.* 1883–1945, Italian Fascist dictator. He was appointed prime minister by King Victor Emmanuel III (1922) and assumed dictatorial powers. He annexed Abyssinia and allied Italy with Germany (1936), entering World War II in 1940. Forced to resign following the Allied invasion of Sicily (1943), he was shot by Italian partisans.
Mussorgsky *or* **Moussorgsky** ★ (mʊˈsɔːɡskɪ; *Russian* ˈmusərkskij) *n* **Modest Petrovich** (maˈdɛst pɪˈtrɔvitʃ). 1839–81, Russian composer. His works include the song cycle *Songs and Dances of Death* (1875–77), the opera *Boris Godunov* (1874), and *Pictures at an Exhibition* (1874) for piano.
Mussulman (ˈmʌsˀlmən) *n pl* **Mussulmans.** an archaic word for **Muslim.** [C16: from Persian *Musulmān* (pl) from Ar. *Muslimūn,* pl. of MUSLIM]
must[1] (mʌst; *unstressed* məst, məs) *vb* (takes an infinitive without *to* or an implied infinitive) used as an auxiliary: **1** to express obligation or compulsion: *you must pay your dues.* In this sense, *must* does not form a negative. If used with a negative infinitive it indicates obligatory prohibition. **2** to indicate necessity: *I must go to the bank tomorrow.* **3** to indicate the probable correctness of a statement: *he must be there by now.* **4** to indicate inevitability: *all good things must come to an end.* **5** to express resolution: **5a** on the part of the speaker: *I must finish this.* **5b** on the part of another or others: *let him get drunk if he must.* **6** (used emphatically) to express conviction or certainty on the part of the speaker: *you must be joking.* **7** (foll. by *away*) used with an implied verb of motion to express compelling haste: *I must away.* ◆ *n* **8** an essential or necessary thing: *strong shoes are a must for hill walking.* [OE *mōste,* p.t. of *mōtan* to be allowed, be obliged to]
must[2] (mʌst) *n* the pressed juice of grapes or other fruit ready for fermentation. [OE, from L *mustum* new wine, from *mustus* newborn]
must[3] (mʌst) *n* mustiness or mould. [C17: back formation from MUSTY]
mustache (məˈstɑːʃ) *n* the US spelling of **moustache.**
▸ musˈtached *adj*
mustachio (məˈstɑːʃɪˌəʊ) *n, pl* **mustachios.** (*often pl*) *Often humorous.* a moustache, esp. when bushy or elaborately shaped. [C16: from Sp. *mostacho* & It. *mostaccio*]
▸ musˈtachioed *adj*
Mustafa Kemal ★ (ˈmʊstəfə kəˈmɑːl) *n* See (Kemal) Atatürk.
mustang (ˈmʌstæŋ) *n* a small breed of horse, often wild or half wild, found in the southwestern US. [C19: from Mexican Sp. *mestengo,* from *mesta* a group of stray animals]
mustard (ˈmʌstəd) *n* **1** any of several Eurasian plants, esp. black mustard and white mustard, having yellow flowers and slender pods: cultivated for their pungent seeds. **2** a paste made from the powdered seeds of any of these plants and used as a condiment. **3a** a brownish-yellow colour. **3b** (*as adj*): *a mustard carpet.* **4** *Sl., chiefly US.*

zest or enthusiasm. [C13: from OF *moustarde*, from L *mustum* MUST², since the original was made by adding must]

mustard and cress *n* seedlings of white mustard and garden cress, used in salads, etc.

mustard gas *n* an oily liquid vesicant compound used in chemical warfare. Its vapour causes blindness and burns.

mustard plaster *n Med.* a mixture of powdered black mustard seeds applied to the skin for its counterirritant effects.

musteline ('mʌstɪˌlaɪn, -lɪn) *adj* of or belonging to a family of typically predatory mammals, including weasels, ferrets, badgers, skunks, and otters. [C17: from L *mustēlinus*, from *mustēla* weasel]

muster ('mʌstə) *vb* **1** to call together (numbers of men) for duty, inspection, etc., or (of men) to assemble in this way. **2 muster in** *or* **out.** *US.* to enlist into or discharge from military service. **3** (*tr;* sometimes foll. by *up*) to summon or gather: *to muster one's arguments; to muster up courage.* **4** (*tr*) *Austral. & NZ.* to round up (stock). ◆ *n* **5** an assembly of military personnel for duty, etc. **6** a collection, assembly, or gathering. **7** *Austral. & NZ.* the act of rounding up stock. **8 pass muster.** to be acceptable. [C14: from OF *moustrer*, from L *monstrāre* to show, from *monstrum* portent]

musth *or* **must** (mʌst) *n* (often preceded by *in*) a state of frenzied sexual excitement in the males of certain large mammals, esp. elephants. [C19: from Urdu *mast,* from Persian: drunk]

musty ('mʌstɪ) *adj* **mustier, mustiest. 1** smelling or tasting old, stale, or mouldy. **2** old-fashioned, dull, or hackneyed: *musty ideas.* [C16: ? var. of obs. *moisty*]
► 'mustily *adv* ► 'mustiness *n*

mutable ('mju:təbəl) *adj* able to or tending to change. [C14: from L *mūtābilis* fickle, from *mūtāre* to change]
► ˌmuta'bility *or* (*less commonly*) 'mutableness *n* ► 'mutably *adv*

mutagen ('mju:tədʒən) *n* a substance that can induce genetic mutation. [C20: from MUTATION + -GEN]
► mutagenic (ˌmju:tə'dʒɛnɪk) *adj*

mutagenesis (ˌmju:tə'dʒɛnɪsɪs) *n Genetics.* the origin and development of a mutation. [C20: from MUTA(TION) + -GENESIS]

mutant ('mju:tⁿnt) *n* **1** Also called: **mutation.** an animal, organism, or gene that has undergone mutation. ◆ *adj* **2** of, undergoing, or resulting from mutation. [C20: from L *mutāre* to change]

Mutare ★ (mu:'tɑ:rɪ) *n* a city in E Zimbabwe, near the Mozambique border: rail and trade centre in a mining and tobacco-growing region. Pop.: 131 808 (1992). Former name (until 1982): **Umtali.**

mutate (mju:'teɪt) *vb* **mutates, mutating, mutated.** to undergo or cause to undergo mutation. [C19: from L *mūtātus,* p.p. of *mūtāre* to change]

mutation (mju:'teɪʃən) *n* **1** the act or process of mutating; change; alteration. **2** a change or alteration. **3** a change in the chromosomes or genes of a cell which may affect the structure and development of the resultant offspring. **4** another word for **mutant** (sense 1). **5** a physical characteristic of an individual resulting from this type of chromosomal change. **6** *Phonetics.* **6a** (in Germanic languages) another name for **umlaut. 6b** (in Celtic languages) a phonetic change in certain initial consonants caused by a preceding word.
► mu'tational *adj* ► mu'tationally *adv*

mutatis mutandis *Latin.* (mu:'tɑ:tɪs mu:'tændɪs) the necessary changes having been made.

mutch (mʌtʃ) *n* a close-fitting linen cap formerly worn by women and children in Scotland. [C15: from MDu. *mutse* cap, from Med. L *almucia* AMICE]

mute (mju:t) *adj* **1** not giving out sound or speech; silent. **2** unable to speak; dumb. **3** unspoken or unexpressed. **4** *Law.* (of a person arraigned on indictment) refusing to answer a charge. **5** *Phonetics.* another word for **plosive. 6** (of a letter in a word) silent. ◆ *n* **7** a person who is unable to speak. **8** *Law.* a person who refuses to plead. **9** any of various devices used to soften the tone of stringed or

brass instruments. **10** *Phonetics.* a plosive consonant. **11** a silent letter. **12** an actor in a dumb show. **13** a hired mourner. ◆ *vb* **mutes, muting, muted.** (*tr*) **14** to reduce the volume of (a musical instrument) by means of a mute, soft pedal, etc. **15** to subdue the strength of (a colour, tone, lighting, etc.). [C14: *muwet* from OF *mu,* from L *mūtus* silent]
► 'mutely *adv* ► 'muteness *n*

mute swan *n* a Eurasian swan with a pure white plumage and an orange-red bill.

muti ('mu:tɪ) *n S. African inf.* medicine, esp. herbal. [from Zulu *umuthi* tree, medicine]

mutilate ('mju:tɪˌleɪt) *vb* **mutilates, mutilating, mutilated.** (*tr*) **1** to deprive of a limb, essential part, etc.; maim. **2** to expurgate, damage, etc. (a text, book, etc.). [C16: from L *mutilāre* to cut off; rel. to *mutilus* maimed]
► ˌmuti'lation *n* ► 'muti,lative *adj* ► 'muti,lator *n*

mutineer (ˌmju:tɪ'nɪə) *n* a person who mutinies.

mutinous ('mju:tɪnəs) *adj* **1** openly rebellious. **2** characteristic or indicative of mutiny.
► 'mutinously *adv* ► 'mutinousness *n*

mutiny ('mju:tɪnɪ) *n, pl* **mutinies. 1** open rebellion against constituted authority, esp. by seamen or soldiers against their officers. ◆ *vb* **mutinies, mutinying, mutinied. 2** (*intr*) to engage in mutiny. [C16: from obs. *mutine,* from OF *mutin* rebellious, from *meute* mutiny, ult. from L *movēre* to move]

mutism ('mju:ˌtɪzəm) *n* **1** the state of being mute. **2** *Psychiatry.* **2a** a refusal to speak. **2b** the lack of development of speech.

mutt (mʌt) *n Sl.* **1** an inept, ignorant, or stupid person. **2** a mongrel dog; cur. [C20: from MUTTONHEAD]

mutter ('mʌtə) *vb* **1** to utter (something) in a low and indistinct tone. **2** (*intr*) to grumble or complain. **3** (*intr*) to make a low continuous murmuring sound. ◆ *n* **4** a muttered sound or complaint. [C14 *moteren*]
► 'muttering *n, adj*

Mutter ★ ('mutə) *n* **Anne-Sophie.** born 1963, German violinist.

mutton ('mʌtⁿn) *n* **1** the flesh of sheep, esp. of mature sheep, used as food. **2 mutton dressed as lamb.** an older woman dressed up to look young. [C13 *moton* sheep, from OF, from Med. L *multō,* of Celtic origin]
► 'muttony *adj*

mutton bird *n* any of several shearwaters, having a dark plumage with greyish underparts. In New Zealand, applied to one collected for food, esp. by Maoris. [C19: from the taste of its flesh]

mutton chop *n* a piece of mutton from the loin.

muttonchops ('mʌtⁿnˌtʃɒps) *pl n* side whiskers trimmed in the shape of chops.

muttonhead ('mʌtⁿnˌhɛd) *n Sl.* a stupid or ignorant person; fool.
► 'mutton,headed *adj*

Muttra ★ ('mʌtrə) *n* the former name of **Mathura.**

mutual ('mju:tʃuəl) *adj* **1** experienced or expressed by each of two or more people about the other; reciprocal: *mutual distrust.* **2** *Inf.* common to or shared by both: *a mutual friend.* **3** denoting an insurance company, etc., in which the policyholders share the profits and expenses and there are no shareholders. See also **mutual insurance.** [C15: from OF *mutuel,* from L *mūtuus* reciprocal (orig.: borrowed); rel. to *mūtāre* to change]
► mutuality (ˌmju:tʃu'ælɪtɪ) *n* ► 'mutually *adv*

USAGE NOTE The use of *mutual* to mean *common to or shared by two or more parties* was formerly considered incorrect, but is now acceptable. Tautologous use of *mutual* should be avoided: *cooperation* (not *mutual cooperation*) *between the two countries.*

---

mutual induction *n* the production of an electromotive force in a circuit by a current change in a second circuit magnetically linked to the first.

---

mutual insurance *n* a system of insurance by which all policyholders become company members under contract to pay premiums into a common fund out of which claims are paid. See also **mutual** (sense 3).

mutuel ('mju:tʃuəl) *n* short for **pari-mutuel**.

muu-muu ('mu:,mu:) *n* a loose brightly coloured dress worn by women in Hawaii. [from Hawaiian]

Muzak ('mju:zæk) *n Trademark.* recorded light music played in shops, restaurants, factories, etc.

muzhik *or* **moujik** ('mu:ʒɪk) *n* a Russian peasant, esp. under the tsars. [C16: from Russian: peasant]

Muzorewa ★ (,muzə'reɪwə) *n* **Abel (Tendekayi)** ('eɪbʰl). born 1925, Zimbabwean Methodist bishop and politician; president of the African National Council (1971–85); prime minister of Rhodesia (1979).

muzzle ('mʌzʰl) *n* **1** the projecting part of the face, usually the jaws and nose, of animals such as the dog and horse. **2** a guard or strap fitted over an animal's nose and jaws to prevent it biting or eating. **3** the front end of a gun barrel. ◆ *vb* **muzzles, muzzling, muzzled.** (*tr*) **4** to prevent from being heard or noticed. **5** to put a muzzle on (an animal). [C15 *mosel*, from OF *musel*, dim. of *muse* snout, from Med. L *mūsus*, from ?]
► '**muzzler** *n*

muzzle-loader *n* a firearm receiving its ammunition through the muzzle.
► '**muzzle-,loading** *adj*

muzzle velocity *n* the velocity of a projectile as it leaves a firearm's muzzle.

muzzy ('mʌzɪ) *adj* **muzzier, muzziest. 1** blurred or hazy. **2** confused or befuddled. [C18: from ?]
► '**muzzily** *adv* ► '**muzziness** *n*

MVO (in Britain) *abbrev. for* Member of the Royal Victorian Order.

MW 1 *symbol for* megawatt. **2** *Radio. abbrev. for* medium wave.

Mweru ★ ('mweəru:) *n* a lake in central Africa, on the border between Zambia and the Democratic Republic of the Congo. Area: 4196 sq. km (1620 sq. miles).

Mx *Physics. symbol for* maxwell.

my (maɪ) *determiner* **1** of, belonging to, or associated with the speaker or writer (me): *my own ideas*. **2** used in various forms of address: *my lord.* ◆ *interj* **3** an exclamation of surprise, awe, etc.: *my, how you've grown!* [C12 *mī*, var. of OE *mīn* when preceding a word beginning with a consonant]

USAGE NOTE   See at **me**[1].

myalgia (maɪ'ældʒɪə) *n* pain in a muscle or a group of muscles. [C19: from MYO- + -ALGIA]

myalgic encephalomyelitis (maɪ'ældʒɪk ɛn,sefələʊ-,maɪɪ'laɪtɪs) *n* a former name for **chronic fatigue syndrome.** Abbrev.: **ME**.

myalism ('maɪə,lɪzəm) *n* a kind of witchcraft practised esp. in the Caribbean. [C19: from *myal*, prob. West African]

myall ('maɪəl) *n* **1** any of several Australian acacias having hard scented wood. **2** a native Australian living independently of society. [C19: Abor. name]

Myanmar *or* **Myanma** ★ ('maɪæn,mɑ:; 'mjænmɑ:) *n* a republic in SE Asia, on the Bay of Bengal and the Andaman Sea: unified from small states in 1752; annexed by Britain (1823–85) and made a province of India in 1886; became independent in 1948. It is generally mountainous, with the basins of the Chindwin and Irrawaddy Rivers in the central part and the Irrawaddy delta in the south. Official language: Burmese. Religion: chiefly Buddhist. Currency: kyat. Capital: Yangon. Pop.: 45 976 000 (1996). Area: 676 577 sq. km (261 228 sq. miles). Official name: **the Union of Myanmar.** Former name (until 1989): **Burma.**

mycelium (maɪ'si:lɪəm) *n, pl* **mycelia** (-lɪə). the vegetative body of fungi: a mass of branching filaments (hyphae). [C19 (lit.: nail of fungus): from MYCO- + Gk *hēlos* nail]
► **my'celial** *adj*

Mycenae ★ (maɪ'si:ni:) *n* an ancient Greek city in the NE Peloponnesus on the plain of Argos.

Mycenaean (,maɪsɪ'ni:ən) *adj* **1**. of or relating to ancient Mycenae, or its inhabitants. **2** of or relating to the Aegean civilization of Mycenae (1400 to 1100 B.C.).

-mycete *n combining form.* indicating a member of a class of fungi: *myxomycete.* [from NL *-mycetes*, from Gk *mukētes*, pl. of *mukēs* fungus]

myco- *or before a vowel* **myc-** *combining form.* indicating fungus: *mycology.* [from Gk *mukēs* fungus]

mycology (maɪ'kɒlədʒɪ) *n* the branch of biology concerned with the study of fungi.
► **mycological** (,maɪkə'lɒdʒɪkʰl) *or* ,**myco'logic** *adj* ► **my'cologist** *n*

mycoplasma (,maɪkəʊ'plæzmə) *n* any one of a genus of prokaryotic microorganisms some species of which cause disease (**mycoplasmosis**) in animals and humans.

mycorrhiza *or* **mycorhiza** (,maɪkə'raɪzə) *n, pl* **mycorrhizae** (-zi:) *or* **mycorrhizas, mycorhizae** *or* **mycorhizas.** an association of a fungus and a plant in which the fungus lives within or on the outside of the plant's roots forming a symbiotic or parasitic relationship. [C19: from MYCO- + Gk *rhiza* root]
► ,**mycor'rhizal** *or* ,**myco'rhizal** *adj*

mycosis (maɪ'kəʊsɪs) *n* any infection or disease caused by fungus.
► **mycotic** (maɪ'kɒtɪk) *adj*

mycotoxin (,maɪkə'tɒksɪn) *n* any of various toxic substances produced by fungi, some of which may affect food.
► ,**mycotox'ology** *n*

mycotrophic (,maɪkəʊ'trɒfɪk) *adj Bot.* (of a plant) symbiotic with a fungus, esp. a mycorrhizal fungus.
► **mycotrophy** (maɪ'kɒtrəfɪ) *n*

myelin ('maɪɪlɪn) *or* **myeline** ('maɪɪ,li:n) *n* a white tissue forming an insulating sheath (**myelin sheath**) around certain nerve fibres. Damage to the myelin sheath causes neurological disease, as in multiple sclerosis.

myelitis (,maɪɪ'laɪtɪs) *n* inflammation of the spinal cord or of the bone marrow.

myeloma (,maɪə'ləʊmə) *n, pl* **myelomas** *or* **myelomata** (-mətə). a usually malignant tumour of the bone marrow.

Myers ★ ('maɪəz) *n* **L(eopold) H(amilton).** 1881–1944, British novelist, best known for his novel sequence *The Near and the Far* (1929–40).

Mykonos ★ ('mɪkənɒs, -nəʊs, 'mi:kə-) *n* a Greek island in the S Aegean Sea, one of the Cyclades: a popular tourist resort with many churches. Pop.: 5500 (latest est.). Greek name: **Míkonos.**

My Lai ★ ('maɪ 'laɪ, 'mi:) *n* a village in S Vietnam where in 1968 US troops massacred over 400 civilians.

mynah *or* **myna** ('maɪnə) *n* any of various tropical Asian starlings, some of which can mimic human speech. [C18: from Hindi *mainā*, from Sansk. *madana*]

Mynheer (mə'nɪə) *n* a Dutch title of address equivalent to *Sir* when used alone or to *Mr* before a name. [C17: from Du. *mijnheer* my lord]

myo- *or before a vowel* **my-** *combining form.* muscle: *myocardium.* [from Gk *mus* MUSCLE]

myocardium (,maɪəʊ'kɑ:dɪəm) *n, pl* **myocardia** (-dɪə). the muscular tissue of the heart. [C19: *myo-* + *cardium*, from Gk *kardia* heart]
► ,**myo'cardial** *adj*

myology (maɪ'ɒlədʒɪ) *n* the branch of medical science concerned with muscles.

myope ('maɪəʊp) *n* any person afflicted with myopia. [C18: via F from Gk *muōps*; see MYOPIA]

myopia (maɪ'əʊpɪə) *n* inability to see distant objects clearly because the images are focused in front of the retina; short-sightedness. [C18: via NL from Gk *muōps* short-sighted, from *mūein* to close (the eyes), + *ōps* eye]
► **myopic** (maɪ'ɒpɪk) *adj* ► **my'opically** *adv*

myosin ('maɪəsɪn) *n* the chief protein of muscle. [C19: from MYO- + -OSE[2] + -IN]

myosotis (,maɪə'səʊtɪs) *n* any plant of the genus *Myoso-*

myriad

tis. See **forget-me-not**. [C18: NL from Gk *muosōtis* mouse-ear (referring to its furry leaves), from *mus* mouse + *ous* ear]

myriad ('mɪrɪəd) *adj* **1** innumerable. ◆ *n (also used in pl)* **2** a large indefinite number. **3** *Arch*. ten thousand. [C16: via LL from Gk *murias* ten thousand]

myriapod ('mɪrɪəˌpɒd) *n* **1** any of a group of terrestrial arthropods having a long segmented body and many walking limbs, such as the centipedes and millipedes. ◆ *adj* **2** of, relating to, or belonging to this group. [C19: from NL *Myriapoda*. See MYRIAD, -POD]

Myrmidon ('mɜːmɪˌdɒn, -dən) *n* **1** *Greek myth*. one of a race of people who were led against Troy by Achilles. **2** (*often not cap*.) a follower or henchman.

myrobalan (maɪ'rɒbələn, mɪ-) *n* **1** the dried plumlike fruit of various tropical trees used in dyeing, tanning, ink, and medicine. **2** a dye extracted from this fruit. [C16: via L from Gk *murobalanos*, from *muron* ointment + *balanos* acorn]

Myron ★ ('maɪərən) *n* 5th century B.C., Greek sculptor.

myrrh (mɜː) *n* **1** any of several trees and shrubs of Africa and S Asia that exude an aromatic resin. **2** the resin obtained from such a plant, used in perfume, incense, and medicine. [OE *myrre*, via L from Gk *murrha*, ult. from Akkadian *murrū*]

myrtle ('mɜːt°l) *n* an evergreen shrub or tree, esp. a S European shrub with pink or white flowers and aromatic blue-black berries. [C16: from Med. L *myrtilla*, from L *myrtus*, from Gk *murtos*]

myself (maɪ'sɛlf) *pron* **1a** the reflexive form of *I* or *me*. **1b** (intensifier): *I myself know of no answer*. **2** (*preceded by a copula*) my usual self: *I'm not myself today*. **3** *Not standard*. used instead of *I* or *me* in compound noun phrases: *John and myself are voting together*.

Mysia ★ ('mɪsɪə) *n* an ancient region in the NW corner of Asia Minor. ▸ '**Mysian** *adj, n*

Mysore ★ (maɪ'sɔː) *n* **1** a city in S India, in S Karnataka state: former capital of the state of Mysore; manufacturing and trading centre; university (1916). Pop.: 480 692 (1991). **2** the former name (until 1973) of **Karnataka**.

mysterious (mɪ'stɪərɪəs) *adj* **1** characterized by or indicative of mystery. **2** puzzling, curious. ▸ **mys'teriously** *adv* ▸ **mys'teriousness** *n*

mystery[1] ('mɪstərɪ, -trɪ) *n, pl* **mysteries**. **1** an unexplained or inexplicable event, phenomenon, etc. **2** a person or thing that arouses curiosity or suspense because of an unknown, obscure, or enigmatic quality. **3** the state or quality of being obscure, inexplicable, or enigmatic. **4** a story, film, etc., which arouses suspense and curiosity because of facts concealed. **5** *Christianity*. any truth that is divinely revealed but otherwise unknowable. **6** *Christianity*. a sacramental rite, such as the Eucharist, or (*when pl*) the consecrated elements of the Eucharist. **7** (*often pl*) any rites of certain ancient Mediterranean religions. **8** short for **mystery play**. [C14: via L from Gk *mustērion* secret rites]

mystery[2] ('mɪstərɪ) *n, pl* **mysteries**. *Arch*. **1** a trade, occupation, or craft. **2** a guild of craftsmen. [C14: from Med. L *mistērium*, from L *ministerium* occupation, from *minister* official]

mystery play *n* (in the Middle Ages) a type of drama based on the life of Christ. Cf. **miracle play**.

mystery tour *n* an excursion to an unspecified destination.

mystic ('mɪstɪk) *n* **1** a person who achieves mystical experience or an apprehension of divine mysteries. ◆ *adj* **2** another word for **mystical**. [C14: via L from Gk *mustikos*, from *mustēs* mystery initiate; rel. to *muein* to initiate into sacred rites]

mystical ('mɪstɪk°l) *adj* **1** relating to or characteristic of mysticism. **2** *Christianity*. having a divine or sacred significance that surpasses human apprehension. **3** having occult or metaphysical significance. ▸ '**mystically** *adv*

mysticism ('mɪstɪˌsɪzəm) *n* **1** belief in or experience of a reality surpassing normal human understanding or experience. **2** a system of contemplative prayer and spirituality aimed at achieving direct intuitive experience of the divine. **3** obscure or confused belief or thought.

mystify ('mɪstɪˌfaɪ) *vb* **mystifies, mystifying, mystified**. (*tr*) **1** to confuse, bewilder, or puzzle. **2** to make obscure. [C19: from F *mystifier*, from *mystère* MYSTERY[1] or *mystique* MYSTIC] ▸ ˌmystifi'cation *n* ▸ 'mystiˌfying *adj*

mystique (mɪ'stiːk) *n* an aura of mystery, power, and awe that surrounds a person or thing. [C20: from F (adj): MYSTIC]

myth (mɪθ) *n* **1a** a story about superhuman beings of an earlier age, usually of how natural phenomena, social customs, etc., came into existence. **1b** another word for **mythology** (senses 1, 3). **2** a person or thing whose existence is fictional or unproven. [C19: via LL from Gk *muthos* fable]

myth. *abbrev. for:* **1** mythological. **2** mythology.

mythical ('mɪθɪk°l) or **mythic** *adj* **1** of or relating to myth. **2** imaginary or fictitious. ▸ '**mythically** *adv*

mythicize or **mythicise** ('mɪθɪˌsaɪz) *vb* **mythicizes, mythicizing, mythicized** or **mythicises, mythicising, mythicised**. (*tr*) to make into or treat as a myth. ▸ '**mythicist** *n*

mytho- *combining form*. myth: *mythopoeia*.

mythologize or **mythologise** (mɪ'θɒləˌdʒaɪz) *vb* **mythologizes, mythologizing, mythologized** or **mythologises, mythologising, mythologised**. **1** to tell, study, or explain (myths). **2** (*intr*) to create or make up myths. **3** (*tr*) to convert into a myth. ▸ my'tholoˌgizer or my'tholoˌgiser *n*

mythology (mɪ'θɒlədʒɪ) *n, pl* **mythologies**. **1** a body of myths, esp. one associated with a particular culture, person, etc. **2** a body of stories about a person, institution, etc. **3** myths collectively. **4** the study of myths. ▸ **mythological** (ˌmɪθə'lɒdʒɪk°l) *adj* ▸ my'thologist *n*

mythomania (ˌmɪθəʊ'meɪnɪə) *n Psychiatry*. the tendency to lie or exaggerate, occurring in some mental disorders. ▸ ˌmytho'maniˌac *n, adj*

mythopoeia (ˌmɪθəʊ'piːə) *n* the composition or making of myths. [C19: from Gk, ult. from *muthos* myth + *poiein* to make] ▸ ˌmytho'poeic *adj*

mythos ('maɪθɒs, 'mɪθɒs) *n, pl* **mythoi** (-θɔɪ). **1** the complex of beliefs, values, attitudes, etc., characteristic of a specific group or society. **2** another word for **myth** or **mythology**.

Mytilene ★ (ˌmɪtɪ'liːnɪ) *n* **1** a port on the Greek island of Lesbos: Roman remains; Byzantine fortress. Pop.: 25 000 (latest est.). Modern Greek name: **Mitilíni**. **2** a former name for **Lesbos**.

myxo ('mɪksəʊ) *n Austral. sl*. myxomatosis.

myxo- or *before a vowel* **myx-** *combining form*. mucus or slime: *myxomatosis*. [from Gk *muxa*]

myxoedema or *US* **myxedema** (ˌmɪksɪ'diːmə) *n* a disease resulting from underactivity of the thyroid gland characterized by puffy eyes, face, and hands and mental sluggishness. See also **cretinism**.

myxoma (mɪk'səʊmə) *n, pl* **myxomas** or **myxomata** (-mətə). a tumour composed of mucous connective tissue, usually situated in subcutaneous tissue. ▸ **myxomatous** (mɪk'sɒmətəs) *adj*

myxomatosis (ˌmɪksəmə'təʊsɪs) *n* an infectious and usually fatal viral disease of rabbits characterized by swelling of the mucous membranes and formation of skin tumours.

myxomycete (ˌmɪksəʊmaɪ'siːt) *n* a slime mould, esp. a slime mould of the phylum *Myxomycota* (division *Myxomycetes* in traditional classifications).

myxovirus ('mɪksəʊˌvaɪrəs) *n* any of a group of viruses that cause influenza, mumps, etc.

Nn

n *or* **N** (ɛn) *n, pl* **n's, N's,** *or* **Ns. 1** the 14th letter of the English alphabet. **2** a speech sound represented by this letter.

n[1] *symbol for:* **1** neutron. **2** *Optics.* index of refraction. **3** nano-.

n[2] (ɛn) *determiner* an indefinite number (of): *there are n objects in a box.*

N *symbol for:* **1** Also: **kt.** *Chess.* knight. **2** newton(s). **3** *Chem.* nitrogen. **4** North. **5** noun. **6** (*in combination*) nuclear: *N-power; N-plant.*

n. *abbrev. for:* **1** neuter. **2** new. **3** nominative. **4** noon. **5** note. **6** noun. **7** number.

N. *abbrev. for:* **1** National(ist). **2** Navy. **3** New. **4** Norse.

Na *the chemical symbol for* sodium. [L *natrium*]

NA *abbrev. for* North America.

NAAFI *or* **Naafi** ('næfɪ) *n* **1** *acronym for* Navy, Army, and Air Force Institutes: an organization providing canteens, shops, etc., for British military personnel at home or overseas. **2** a canteen, shop, etc., run by this organization.

naartjie ('nɑːtʃɪ) *n S. African.* a tangerine. [from Afrik., from Tamil]

nab (næb) *vb* **nabs, nabbing, nabbed.** (*tr*) *Inf.* **1** to arrest (a criminal, etc.). **2** to seize suddenly; snatch. [C17: ? of Scand. origin]

nabla ('næblə) *n Maths.* another name for **del.** [C19: from Gk: stringed instrument, because it is shaped like a harp]

Nablus ★ ('nɑːbləs) *n* a town west of the River Jordan: near the site of ancient Shechem. Pop.: 98 000 (1989 est.).

nabob ('neɪbɒb) *n* **1** *Inf.* a rich or important man. **2** (formerly) a European who made a fortune in India. **3** another name for a **nawab.** [C17: from Port. *nababo,* from Hindi *nawwāb;* see NAWAB]

Nabokov ★ (nə'bɒkɒf, 'næbə,kɒf) *n* **Vladimir Vladimirovich** (vla'dimir vla'dimirəvitʃ). 1899–1977, US novelist, born in Russia. His works include *Lolita* (1955), *Pnin* (1957), and *Ada* (1969).
▶ **Nabokovian** (,næbə'kəuvɪən) *adj*

Naboth ★ ('neɪbɒθ) *n Old Testament.* an inhabitant of Jezreel, murdered by King Ahab at the instigation of his wife Jezebel for refusing to sell his vineyard (I Kings 21).

NAC *abbrev. for* National Advisory Council.

nacelle (nə'sɛl) *n* a streamlined enclosure on an aircraft, not part of the fuselage, to accommodate an engine, passengers, crew, etc. [C20: from F: small boat, from LL *nāvicella,* a dim. of L *nāvis* ship]

nacho ('nɑːtʃəu) *n, pl* **nachos.** a Mexican snack consisting of a piece of tortilla topped with melted cheese.

NACODS ('neɪkɒdz) *n* (in Britain) *acronym for* National Association of Colliery Overmen, Deputies, and Shotfirers.

nacre ('neɪkə) *n* the technical name for **mother-of-pearl.** [C16: via F from Olt. *naccara,* from Ar. *naqqārah* shell, drum]
▶ **'nacred** *adj*

nacreous ('neɪkrɪəs) *adj* relating to, consisting of, or having the lustre of mother-of-pearl.

NACRO *or* **Nacro** ('nækrəu) *n* (in Britain) *acronym for* National Association for the Care and Resettlement of Offenders.

Nader ★ ('neɪdə) *n* **Ralph.** born 1934, US lawyer and campaigner for consumer rights.

nadir ('neɪdɪə, 'næ-) *n* **1** the point on the celestial sphere directly below an observer and diametrically opposite the zenith. **2** the lowest point; depths. [C14: from OF, from Ar. *nazīr as-samt,* lit.: opposite the zenith]

nae (neɪ) *or* **na** (nɑː) a Scot. word for **no**[2] *or* **not.**

naevus *or US* **nevus** ('niːvəs) *n, pl* **naevi** *or US* **nevi** (-vaɪ). any pigmented blemish on the skin; birthmark or mole. [C19: from L; rel. to (*g*)*natus* born, produced by nature]
▶ **'naevoid** *or US* **'nevoid** *adj*

naff (næf) *adj Brit. sl.* inferior; in poor taste. [C19: ?from back slang on *fan,* short for FANNY]
▶ **'naffness** *n*

naff off *sentence substitute. Brit sl.* a forceful expression of dismissal or contempt.

nag[1] (næg) *vb* **nags, nagging, nagged. 1** to scold or annoy constantly. **2** (when *intr,* often foll. by *at*) to be a constant source of discomfort or worry (to). ◆ *n* **3** a person, esp. a woman, who nags. [C19: of Scand. origin]
▶ **'nagger** *n*

nag[2] (næg) *n* **1** *Often derog.* a horse. **2** a small riding horse. [C14: of Gmc origin]

Nagaland ★ ('nɑːgə,lænd) *n* a state of NE India: formed in 1962 from parts of Assam and the North-East Frontier Agency; inhabited chiefly by Naga tribes; consists of almost inaccessible forested hills and mountains (the **Naga Hills**); shifting cultivation predominates. Capital: Kohima. Pop.: 1 410 000 (1994 est.). Area: 16 579 sq. km (6401 sq. miles).

nagana (nə'gɑːnə) *n* a disease of hoofed animals of central and southern Africa, transmitted by tsetse flies. [from Zulu *u-nakane*]

Nagano ★ (nə'gɑːnəu) *n* a city in central Japan, on central Honshu: Buddhist shrine; two universities. Pop.: 358 512 (1995).

Nagasaki ★ (,nɑːgə'sɑːkɪ) *n* a port in SW Japan, on W Kyushu: almost completely destroyed in 1945 by the second atomic bomb dropped on Japan by the US; shipbuilding industry. Pop.: 438 724 (1995).

Nagorno-Karabakh Autonomous Region ★ (nə'gɔːnəukərʌ'bɑːk) *n* an administrative division of S Azerbaijan: acquired by Russia in 1813. In 1991 Armenian claims to the region culminated in its unilateral declaration as an independent Armenian republic and armed conflict broke out. Capital: Stepanakert. Pop.: 193 300 (1991 est.). Area: 4400 sq. km (1700 sq. miles).

Nagoya ★ ('nɑːgəujə) *n* a city in central Japan, on S Honshu on Ise Bay: a major industrial centre. Pop.: 2 152 258 (1995).

Nagpur ★ (næg'puə) *n* a city in central India, in NE Maharashtra state: became capital of the kingdom of Nagpur (1743); capital of the Central Provinces (later Madhya Pradesh) from 1861 to 1956. Pop.: 1 624 752 (1991).

Nagy ★ (*Hungarian* nɔdj) *n* **Imre** ('imrɛ). 1896–1958, Hungarian statesman; prime minister (1953–55; 1956): removed from office when Soviet forces suppressed the revolution of 1956: executed; reburied with honours in 1989.

Nagyszeben ★ ('nɔdjsɛ:,bɛn) *n* the Hungarian name for Sibiu.

Nagyvárad ★ ('nɔdjvɑːrɔd) *n* the Hungarian name for Oradea.

Nah. *Bible. abbrev. for* Nahum.

Naha ★ ('nɑːhə) *n* a port in S Japan, on the SW coast of Okinawa Island: chief city of the Ryukyu Islands. Pop.: 301 928 (1995).

NAHT (in Britain) *abbrev. for* National Association of Head Teachers.

Nahuatl ('nɑːwɑːt°l, nɑː'wɑːt°l) *n* (*pl* **Nahuatl** *or* **Nahuatls**) a member of one of a group of Central American and Mexican Indian peoples including the Aztecs. **2** the language of these peoples.

Nahum ★ ('neɪhəm) *n Old Testament.* **1** a Hebrew prophet of the 7th century B.C. **2** the book containing his oracles.

naiad ('naɪæd) n, pl **naiads** or **naiades** (-ə,diːz). 1 Greek myth. a nymph dwelling in a lake, river, or spring. 2 the aquatic larva of the dragonfly, mayfly, and related insects. 3 Also called: **water nymph**. a submerged aquatic plant, having narrow leaves and small flowers. [C17: via L from Gk nāias water nymph; rel. to náein to flow]

naïf (nɑːˈiːf) adj, n a less common word for **naive**.

nail (neɪl) n 1 a fastening device, usually made of metal, having a point at one end and a head at the other. 2 anything resembling such a device in function or shape. 3 the horny plate covering part of the dorsal surface of the fingers or toes. Related adj: **ungual**. 4 the claw of a mammal, bird, or reptile. 5 a unit of length, formerly used for measuring cloth, equal to two and a quarter inches. 6 **hit the nail on the head**. to do or say something correct or telling. 7 **on the nail**. (of payments) at once. ◆ vb (tr) 8 to attach with or as if with nails. 9 Inf. to arrest, catch, or seize. 10 Inf. to hit or bring down, as with a shot. 11 Inf. to expose or detect (a lie or liar). 12 to fix (one's eyes, attention, etc.) on. 13 to stud with nails. [OE nægl]
▸ 'nailer n

nail-biting n 1 the act or habit of biting one's fingernails. 2a anxiety or tension. 2b (as modifier): nail-biting suspense.

nail bomb n an explosive device containing nails, used by terrorists to cause serious injuries in crowded situations.

nailbrush ('neɪl,brʌʃ) n a small stiff-bristled brush for cleaning the fingernails.

nailfile ('neɪl,faɪl) n a small file of metal or of board coated with emery, used to trim the nails.

nail polish or **varnish** or esp. US **enamel** n a quick-drying cosmetic lacquer applied to colour the nails or make them shiny or esp. both.

nail set or **punch** n a punch for driving the head of a nail below or flush with the surrounding surface.

nainsook ('neɪnsuk, 'næn-) n a light soft plain-weave cotton fabric. [C19: from Hindi, from nain eye + sukh delight]

Naipaul ★ (naɪ'pɔːl) n Sir **V(idiadhar) S(urajprasad)**. born 1932, Trinidadian novelist of Indian descent, living in Britain. His novels include A House for Mr Biswas (1961) and A Way in the World (1994).

naira ('naɪrə) n the standard monetary unit of Nigeria. [C20: altered from Nigeria]

Nairnshire ★ ('neən,ʃɪə, -ʃə) n a historic county of NE Scotland, now part of Highland.

Nairobi ★ (naɪ'rəʊbɪ) n the capital of Kenya, in the southwest at an altitude of 1650 m (5500 ft): founded in 1899; became capital in 1905; commercial and industrial centre; the **Nairobi National Park** (a game reserve) is nearby. Pop.: 2 000 000 (1991 est.).

naive, naïve (nɑːˈiːv, naɪ'iːv), or **naïf** adj 1 having or expressing innocence and credulity; ingenuous. 2 lacking developed powers of reasoning or criticism: a naive argument. 3 another word for **primitive** (sense 5). ◆ n 4 a person who is naive, esp. in artistic style. See **primitive** (sense 10). [C17: from F fem of naïf, from OF: native, spontaneous, from L nātīvus NATIVE]
▸ na'ively, na'ïvely, or na'ïfly adv ▸ na'iveness, na'ïveness, or na'ïfness n

naivety (naɪ'iːvtɪ), **naiveté**, or **naïveté** (,nɑːiːv'teɪ) n, pl **naivetes, naivetés** or **naïvetés**. 1 the state or quality of being naive. 2 a naive act or statement.

naked ('neɪkɪd) adj 1 having the body unclothed; undressed. 2 having no covering; exposed: a naked flame. 3 with no qualification or concealment: the naked facts. 4 unaided by any optical instrument (esp. in **the naked eye**). 5 (usually foll. by of) destitute: naked of weapons. 6 (of animals) lacking hair, feathers, scales, etc. 7 Law. 7a unsupported by authority: a naked contract. 7b lacking some essential condition to render valid; incomplete. [OE nacod]
▸ 'nakedly adv ▸ 'nakedness n

naked ladies n (functioning as sing) another name for **autumn crocus**.

naked lady n a pink orchid found in Australia and New Zealand.

Nakhichevan ★ (Russian nəxitʃı'vanj) n a city in W Azerbaijan, capital of the Nakhichevan Autonomous Republic: an ancient trading town. Pop.: 66 800 (1994). Ancient name: **Naxuana** (,næk'swɑːnə).

Nakhichevan Autonomous Republic ★ (nə,kıtʃe'vɑːn) n an administrative division of Azerbaijan, from which it is separated by part of Armenia; annexed by Russia in 1828; unilaterally declared secession from the Soviet Union in 1990. Capital: Nakhichevan. Pop.: 315 000 (1994). Area: 5500 sq. km (2120 sq. miles).

Nakuru ★ (nə'kuːruː) n a town in W Kenya, on Lake Nakuru: commercial centre of an agricultural region. Pop.: 124 200 (1991 est.).

Nalchik ★ (Russian 'naljtʃik) n a city in SW Russia, capital of the Kabardino-Balkar Autonomous Republic, in a valley of the Caucasus: health resort. Pop.: 239 000 (1995 est.).

NALGO ('nælgəʊ) n (formerly, in Britain) acronym for National and Local Government Officers' Association.

Nam or **'Nam** (næm) n US inf. short for Vietnam (referring to the Vietnam War).

Namangan ★ (Russian nəman'gan) n a city in E Uzbekistan. Pop.: 341 000 (1996).

Namaqualand ★ (nə'mɑːkwə,lænd) n a semiarid coastal region of SW Africa, extending from near Windhoek, in Namibia, into W South Africa: divided by the Orange River into **Little Namaqualand** in South Africa, and **Great Namaqualand** in Namibia; rich mineral resources. Area: 47 961 sq. km (18 518 sq. miles). Also called: **Namaland** ('nɑːmə,lænd).

namby-pamby (,næmbɪ'pæmbɪ) adj 1 sentimental or prim in a weak insipid way. 2 clinging, feeble, or spineless. ◆ n, pl **namby-pambies**. 3 a person who is namby-pamby. [C18: a nickname of Ambrose Phillips (died 1749), whose pastoral verse was ridiculed for being insipid]

Nam Co ('nɑːm 'kɔː) or **Nam Tso** ★ n a salt lake in SW China, in SE Tibet at an altitude of 4629 m (15 186 ft). Area: about 1800 sq. km (700 sq. miles). Also called: **Tengri Nor.**

name (neɪm) n 1 a word or term by which a person or thing is commonly and distinctively known. 2 mere outward appearance as opposed to fact: he was ruler in name only. 3 a word or phrase descriptive of character, usually abusive: to call a person names. 4 reputation, esp., if unspecified, good reputation: he's made quite a name for himself. 5a a famous person or thing: a name in the advertising world. 5b Chiefly US & Canad. (as modifier): a name product. 6 a member of Lloyd's who provides part of the capital of a syndicate and shares in its profits or losses but does not arrange its business. 7 **in the name of**. 7a for the sake of. 7b by the authority of. 8 **name of the game**. 8a anything that is significant or important. 8b normal conditions, circumstances, etc.: in gambling, losing money's the name of the game. 9 **to one's name**. belonging to one: I haven't a penny to my name. ◆ vb **names, naming, named**. (tr) 10 to give a name to. 11 to refer to by name; cite: he named three French poets. 12 to fix or specify: they have named a date for the meeting. 13 to appoint or nominate: he was named Journalist of the Year. 14 (tr) to ban (an MP) from the House of Commons by mentioning him formally by name as being guilty of disorderly conduct. 15 **name names**. to cite people, esp. in order to blame or accuse them. 16 **name the day**. to choose the day for an event, esp. one's wedding. [OE nama, rel. to L nomen, Gk noma]
▸ 'namable or 'nameable adj

name-calling n verbal abuse.

namecheck ('neɪm,tʃɛk) vb (tr) 1 to mention (someone) specifically by name. ◆ n 2 a specific mention of someone's name, for example on a radio programme.

name day n 1 RC Church. the feast day of a saint whose name one bears. 2 another name for **ticket day**.

name-dropping n Inf. the practice of referring fre-

quently to famous people, esp. as though they were intimate friends, in order to impress others.
▸ **'name-,dropper** *n*

nameless ('neɪmlɪs) *adj* **1** without a name. **2** indescribable: *a nameless horror seized him.* **3** too unpleasant or disturbing to be mentioned: *nameless atrocities.*
▸ **'namelessness** *n*

namely ('neɪmlɪ) *adv* that is to say.

Namen ★ ('nɑːmə) *n* the Flemish name for **Namur**.

nameplate ('neɪm,pleɪt) *n* a small panel on or next to the door of a room or building, bearing the occupant's name and profession.

namesake ('neɪm,seɪk) *n* a person or thing named after another, or with the same name as another. [C17: prob. describing people connected *for the name's sake*]

nametape ('neɪm,teɪp) *n* a tape bearing the owner's name and attached to an article.

Namhoi ★ ('nɑːm'hɔɪ) *n* another name for **Foshan**.

Namibe ★ (nə'miːb) *n* a port in SW Angola: fishing industry. Pop.: 77 000 (1987).

Namibia ★ (nə'mɪbɪə) *n* a country in southern Africa bordering on South Africa: annexed by Germany in 1884 and mandated by the League of Nations to South Africa in 1920. The mandate was terminated by the UN in 1966 but this was ignored by South Africa; achieved independence in 1990 and joined the Commonwealth. Official language: English; Afrikaans and German also spoken. Religion: mostly animist, with some Christians. Currency: dollar. Capital: Windhoek. Pop.: 1 709 000 (1996). Area: 823 328 sq. km (317 887 sq. miles). Also called: **South West Africa**. Former name (1885–1919): **German Southwest Africa**.
▸ **Na'mibian** *adj, n*

Namier ★ ('neɪmɪə) *n* Sir **Lewis Bernstein**, original name *Ludwik Bernsztajn vel Niemirowski*. 1888–1960, British political historian, born in Poland.

Nam Tso ★ ('nɑːm 'tsɔː) *n* a variant transliteration of the Chinese name for **Nam Co**.

Namur ★ (næ'mʊə; *French* namyr) *n* **1** a province of S Belgium. Capital: Namur. Pop.: 434 446 (1995 est.). Area: 3660 sq. km (1413 sq. miles). **2** a town in S Belgium, capital of Namur province: strategically situated on a promontory between the Sambre and Meuse Rivers, besieged and captured many times. Pop.: 105 014 (1995 est.). Flemish name: **Namen**.

nan (næn), **nana**, *or* **nanna** ('nænə) *n* a child's word for grandmother.

nana ('nɑːnə) *n* **1** *Sl.* a fool. **2 do one's nana.** *Austral. sl.* to become very angry. **3 off one's nana.** *Austral. sl.* mad; insane. [C19: prob. from BANANA]

nan bread *or* **naan** (nɑːn) *n* (in Indian cookery) a slightly leavened bread in a large flat leaf shape. [from Hindi]

Nanchang *or* **Nan-ch'ang** ★ ('næn'tʃæŋ) *n* a walled city in SE China, capital of Jiangxi province, on the Kan River: largest city in the Poyang basin. Pop.: 1 350 000 (1991 est.).

Nan-ching ★ ('næn'tʃɪŋ) *n* a variant spelling of **Nanjing**.

nancy ('nænsɪ) *n, pl* **nancies.** an effeminate or homosexual boy or man. Also called: **nance, nancy boy**. [C20: from the girl's name *Nancy*]

Nancy ★ ('nænsɪ; *French* nɑ̃si) *n* a city in NE France: became the capital of the dukes of Lorraine in the 12th century, becoming French in 1766; administrative and financial centre. Pop.: 102 410 (1990).

Nanda Devi ★ ('nʌndə 'diːvɪ) *n* a mountain in N India, in N Uttar Pradesh in the Himalayas. Height: 7817 m (25 645 ft).

NAND circuit *or* **gate** (nænd) *n Electronics.* a computer logic circuit having two or more input wires and one output wire that has an output signal if one or more of the input signals are at a low voltage. Cf. **OR circuit.** [C20: from *not* + AND; see NOT CIRCUIT, AND CIRCUIT]

Nanga Parbat ★ ('nʌŋgə 'pɑːbʌt) *n* a mountain in N India, in NW Kashmir in the W Himalayas. Height: 8126 m (26 660 ft).

Nanhai ★ ('nɑː'nhaɪ) *n* the Chinese name for the **South China Sea.**

Nanjing ('næn'dʒɪŋ), **Nanking** ('næn'kɪŋ) *or* **Nan-ching** ★ *n* a port in E central China, capital of Jiangsu province, on the Yangtze River: capital of the Chinese empire and a literary centre from the 14th to 17th centuries; capital of Nationalist China (1928–37); site of a massacre of about 300 000 civilians by the invading Japanese army in 1937; university (1928). Pop.: 2 500 000 (1991 est.).

nankeen (næŋ'kiːn) *or* **nankin** ('nænkɪn) *n* **1** a hardwearing buff-coloured cotton fabric. **2a** a pale greyish-yellow colour. **2b** (*as adj*): *a nankeen carpet.* [C18: after *Nanking*, China, where it originated]

Nanning *or* **Nan-ning** ★ ('næn'nɪŋ) *n* a port in S China, capital of Guanxi Zhuang AR, on the Xiang River: rail links with North Vietnam. Pop.: 1 070 000 (1991 est.).

nanny ('nænɪ) *n, pl* **nannies. 1** a nurse or nursemaid for children. **2a** any person or thing regarded as treating people like children, esp. by being overprotective. **2b** (*as modifier*): *the nanny state.* **3** a child's word for **grandmother**. ♦ *vb* **nannies, nannying, nannied. 4** (*intr*) to nurse or look after someone else's children. **5** (*tr*) to be overprotective towards. [C19: child's name for a nurse]

nannygai ('nænɪ,gaɪ) *n, pl* **nannygais.** an edible red Australian sea fish. [from Abor.]

nanny goat *n* a female goat.

nano- *combining form.* denoting 10⁻⁹: *nanometre; nanosecond.* Symbol: n [from L *nānus* dwarf, from Gk *nanos*]

nanotechnology (,nænəʊtɛk'nɒlədʒɪ) *n* a branch of technology dealing with the manufacture of objects with dimensions of less than 100 thousand-millionths of a metre and the manipulation of individual molecules and atoms.

Nansen ★ ('nænsən) *n* **Fridtjof** ('fridjɔf). 1861–1930, Norwegian arctic explorer. He attempted to reach the North Pole (1893–96), and became League of Nations' high commissioner for refugees (1920–22): Nobel peace prize 1922.

Nansen bottle *n* an instrument used by oceanographers for obtaining samples of sea water from a desired depth. [C19: after F. NANSEN]

Nan Shan ★ ('næn 'ʃæn) *pl n* a mountain range in N central China, mainly in Qinghai province, with peaks over 6000 m (20 000 ft).

Nanterre ★ (*French* nɑ̃tɛr) *n* a town in N France, on the Seine: an industrial suburb of Paris. Pop.: 84 565 (1990).

Nantes ★ (*French* nɑ̃t) *n* a port in W France, at the head of the Loire estuary: scene of the signing of the Edict of Nantes and of the Noyades (drownings) during the French Revolution; extensive shipyards, and large metallurgical and food processing industries. Pop.: 264 857 (1990).

Nantong *or* **Nantung** ★ ('næn'tʌŋ) *n* a city in E China, in Jiangsu province on the Yangtze estuary. Pop.: 343 341 (1990 est.).

Nantucket ★ (næn'tʌkɪt) *n* an island off SE Massachusetts: formerly a centre of the whaling industry; now a resort. Length: nearly 24 km (15 miles). Width: 5 km (3 miles). Pop.: 6012 (1990).

Naoise ★ ('niːʃə) *n Irish myth.* the husband of Deirdre, killed by his uncle Conchobar. See also **Deirdre.**

Naomi ★ ('neɪəmɪ) *n Old Testament.* the mother-in-law of Ruth (Ruth 1:2). Douay spelling: **Noemi.**

nap¹ (næp) *vb* **naps, napping, napped.** (*intr*) **1** to sleep for a short while; doze. **2** to be inattentive or off guard (esp. in **catch someone napping**). ♦ *n* **3** a short light sleep; doze. [OE *hnappian*]

nap² (næp) *n* **1a** the raised fibres of velvet or similar cloth. **1b** the direction in which these fibres lie. **2** any similar downy coating. **3** *Austral. inf.* blankets; bedding. ♦ *vb* **naps, napping, napped. 4** (*tr*) to raise the nap of (velvet, etc.) by brushing. [C15: prob. from MDu. *noppe*]

nap³ (næp) *n* **1** Also called: **napoleon.** a card game similar to whist, usually played for stakes. **2** a call in this game, undertaking to win all five tricks. **3** *Horse racing.* a tipster's choice for a certain winner. **4 nap hand.** a position in which there is a very good chance of success if a risk is taken. ◆ *vb* **naps, napping, napped.** (*tr*) **5** *Horse racing.* to name (a horse) as likely to win a race. [C19: from NAPOLEON, the card game]

napalm ('neɪpɑːm, 'næ-) *n* **1** a thick and highly incendiary liquid, usually consisting of petrol gelled with aluminium soaps, used in firebombs, flame-throwers, etc. ◆ *vb* **2** (*tr*) to attack with napalm. [C20: from NA(PHTHENE) + *palm*(*itate*) salt of PALMITIC ACID]

nape (neɪp) *n* the back of the neck. [C13: from ?]

napery ('neɪpərɪ) *n Scot. & Arch.* household linen, esp. table linen. [C14: from OF *naperie*, from *nape* tablecloth, from L *mappa*]

Naphtali ★ ('næftə,laɪ) *n Old Testament.* **1** Jacob's sixth son, whose mother was Rachel's handmaid (Genesis 30:7–8). **2** the tribe descended from him. **3** the territory of this tribe, between the Sea of Galilee and the mountains of central Galilee. Douay spelling: **Nephtali.**

naphtha ('næfθə, 'næp-) *n* a distillation product from coal tar or petroleum: used as a solvent and in petrol. [C16: via L from Gk, from Iranian]

naphthalene ('næfθə,liːn, 'næp-) *n* a white crystalline hydrocarbon with a characteristic penetrating odour, used in mothballs and in dyes, explosives, etc. Formula: $C_{10}H_8$. [C19: from NAPHTHA + ALCOHOL + -ENE]
▶ **naphthalic** (næf'θælɪk, næp-) *adj*

naphthene ('næfθiːn, 'næp-) *n* any of various cyclic methylene hydrocarbons found in petroleum. [C20: from NAPHTHA + -ENE]

naphthol ('næfθɒl, 'næp-) *n* a white crystalline solid having two isomeric forms, used in dyes and as an antioxidant. Formula: $C_{10}H_7OH$. [C19: from NAPHTHA + -OL[1]]

Napier[1] ★ ('neɪpɪə) *n* a port in New Zealand, on E North Island on Hawke Bay: wool trade centre. Pop.: 53 500 (1995 est.).

Napier[2] ★ ('neɪpɪə) *n* **1** Sir **Charles James.** 1782–1853, British general: conquered Sind (1843): governor of Sind (1843–47). **2 John.** 1550–1617, Scottish mathematician: invented logarithms and pioneered the decimal notation.

Napierian logarithm (nə'pɪərɪən, neɪ-) *n* another name for **natural logarithm.**

Napier's bones *pl n* a set of graduated rods formerly used for multiplication and division. [C17: based on a method invented by John NAPIER]

napkin ('næpkɪn) *n* **1** Also called: **table napkin.** a usually square piece of cloth or paper used while eating to protect the clothes, wipe the mouth, etc.; serviette. **2** *Rare.* a small piece of cloth. **3** a more formal name for **nappy**[1]. **4** a less common term for **sanitary towel.** [C15: from OF, from *nape* tablecloth, from L *mappa* cloth]

Naples ★ ('neɪp°lz) *n* **1** a port in SW Italy, capital of Campania region, on the Bay of Naples: the third largest city in the country; founded by Greeks in the 6th century B.C.; incorporated into the Kingdom of the Two Sicilies in 1140 and its capital (1282–1503); university (1224). Pop.: 1 061 583 (1994 est.). Ancient name: **Ne'apolis.** Italian name: **Napoli.** Related adj: **Neapolitan. 2 Bay of.** an inlet of the Tyrrhenian Sea in the SW coast of Italy.

napoleon (nə'pəʊlɪən) *n* **1** a former French gold coin worth 20 francs. **2** *Cards.* the full name for **nap**[3] (sense 1). [C19: from F *napoléon*, after NAPOLEON I]

Napoleon I ★ (nə'pəʊlɪən) *n* full name *Napoleon Bonaparte.* 1769–1821, Emperor of the French (1804–15). Coming to power after a coup in 1799, he defeated every European coalition against him until, weakened by the Peninsular War and the Russian campaign (1812), he was defeated at Leipzig (1813) and, finally, at Waterloo (1815). The *Code Napoléon* remains the basis of French law.

Napoleon II ★ *n* Duke of Reichstadt. 1811–32, son of Napoleon Bonaparte and Marie Louise. Known as the *King of Rome* during the first French empire, he was entitled Napoleon II by Bonapartists after his father's death (1821).

Napoleon III ★ *n* full name *Charles Louis Napoleon Bonaparte,* known as *Louis-Napoleon.* 1808–73, Emperor

of the French (1852–70); nephew of Napoleon I. He was elected president of the Second Republic (1848), establishing the Second Empire in 1852. He was deposed after the disastrous Franco-Prussian War.

Napoleonic (nə,pəʊlɪ'ɒnɪk) *adj* relating to or characteristic of Napoleon I or his era.

Napoli ★ ('naːpoli) *n* the Italian name for **Naples.**

nappe (næp) *n* **1** a large sheet or mass of rock, originally a recumbent fold, that has been thrust from its original position by earth movements. **2** the sheet of water that flows over a dam or weir. **3** *Geom.* either of the two parts into which a cone is divided by the vertex. [C20: from F: tablecloth]

nappy[1] ('næpɪ) *n, pl* **nappies.** *Brit.* a piece of soft towelling or a disposable material wrapped around a baby in order to absorb its urine or excrement. Also called: **napkin.** US and Canad. name: **diaper.** [C20: changed from NAPKIN]

nappy[2] ('næpɪ) *adj* **nappier, nappiest. 1** having a nap; downy; fuzzy. **2** (of beer) **2a** having a head; frothy. **2b** strong or heady.

nappy rash *n Brit.* (in babies) any irritation to the skin around the genitals, anus, or buttocks, usually caused by contact with urine or excrement. Formal name: **napkin rash.** US and Canad. name: **diaper rash.**

Nara ★ ('nɑːrə) *n* a city in central Japan, on S Honshu: the first permanent capital of Japan (710–784). Pop.: 359 234 (1995).

Narayan ★ (nə'raɪjən) *n* **R**(**asipuram**) **K**(**rishnaswamy**). born 1906, Indian novelist writing in English. His books include *Swami and Friends* (1938) and *Under the Banyan Tree* (1985).

Narayanganj ★ (nə'rɑː,jən,gʌndʒ) *n* a city in central Bangladesh, on the Ganges delta just southeast of Dhaka. Pop.: 296 000 (1991).

Narbada ★ (nə'bʌdə) *n* another name for the **Narmada.**

Narbonne ★ (*French* narbɔn) *n* a city in S France: capital of the Roman province of **Gallia Narbonensis**; harbour silted up in the 14th century. Pop.: 47 090 (1990).

narc (nɑːk) *n US sl.* a narcotics agent.

narcissism ('nɑːsɪ,sɪzəm) *or* **narcism** ('nɑːsɪzəm) *n* **1** an exceptional interest in or admiration for oneself, esp. one's physical appearance. **2** sexual satisfaction derived from contemplation of one's own physical endowments. [C19: after NARCISSUS]
▶ **'narcissist** *n* ▶ **,narcis'sistic** *adj*

narcissus (nɑː'sɪsəs) *n, pl* **narcissuses** *or* **narcissi** (-'sɪsaɪ). a plant of a Eurasian genus whose yellow, orange, or white flowers have a crown surrounded by spreading segments. [C16: via L from Gk *nárkissos*, ?from *narkē* numbness, because of narcotic properties attributed to the plant]

Narcissus ★ (nɑː'sɪsəs) *n Greek myth.* a beautiful youth who fell in love with his reflection in a pool and pined away, becoming the flower that bears his name.

narco- *or sometimes before a vowel* **narc-** *combining form.* **1** indicating numbness or torpor: *narcolepsy.* **2** connected with or derived from illicit drug production: *narcoeconomies.* [from Gk *narkē* numbness]

narcoanalysis (,nɑːkəʊə'nælɪsɪs) *n* psychoanalysis of a patient in a trance induced by a narcotic drug.

narcolepsy ('nɑːkə,lepsɪ) *n Pathol.* a rare condition characterized by sudden episodes of deep sleep.
▶ **,narco'leptic** *adj*

narcosis (nɑː'kəʊsɪs) *n* unconsciousness induced by narcotics or general anaesthetics.

narcosynthesis (,nɑːkəʊ'sɪnθɪsɪs) *n* a method of treating severe personality disorders by working with the patient while he is under the influence of a barbiturate drug.

narcotic (nɑː'kɒtɪk) *n* **1** any of a group of drugs, such as opium and morphine, that produce numbness and stupor. **2** anything that relieves pain or induces sleep, mental numbness, etc. **3** any illegal drug. ◆ *adj* **4** of or relating to narcotics or narcotics addicts. **5** of or relating to narcosis. [C14: via Med. L from Gk *narkōtikós*, from *narkoûn* to numb, from *narkē* numbness]
▶ **nar'cotically** *adv*

narcotism ('nɑːkə,tɪzəm) *n* stupor or addiction induced by narcotic drugs.

narcotize *or* **narcotise** ('nɑːkə,taɪz) *vb* **narcotizes, narcotizing, narcotized** *or* **narcotises, narcotising, narcotised.** (*tr*) to place under the influence of a narcotic drug.
▶ ,narcoti'zation *or* ,narcoti'sation *n*

nard (nɑːd) *n* **1** another name for **spikenard. 2** any of several plants whose aromatic roots were formerly used in medicine. [C14: via L from Gk *nárdos*, ? ult. from Sansk. *nalada* Indian spikenard]

nardoo ('nɑːduː) *n* (in Australia) **1** any of certain cloverlike ferns that grow in swampy areas. **2** the spores of such a plant, used as food. [C19: from Abor.]

nares ('nɛəriːz) *pl n, sing* **naris** ('nɛərɪs). *Anat.* the technical name for the nostrils. [C17: from L; rel. to OE *nasu*, L *nāsus* nose]
▶ 'narial *adj*

narghile, nargile, *or* **nargileh** ('nɑːgɪlɪ, -,leɪ) *n* another name for **hookah.** [C19: from F *narguilé*, from Persian *nārğīleh* a pipe having a bowl made of coconut shell, from *nārğīl* coconut]

nark (nɑːk) *Sl.* ◆ *n* **1** *Brit., Austral., & NZ.* an informer or spy: *copper's nark.* **2** *Brit.* someone who complains in an irritating or whining manner. ◆ *vb* **3** *Brit., Austral., & NZ.* to annoy, upset, or irritate. **4** (*intr*) *Brit., Austral., & NZ.* to inform or spy, esp. for the police. **5** (*intr*) *Brit.* to complain irritatingly. [C19: prob. from Romany *nāk* nose]

narky ('nɑːkɪ) *adj* **narkier, narkiest.** *Sl.* irritable, complaining, or sarcastic.

Narmada (nə'mʌdə) *or* **Narbada** ★ *n* a river in central India, rising in Madhya Pradesh and flowing generally west to the Gulf of Cambay in a wide estuary: the second most sacred river in India. Length: 1290 km (801 miles).

Narraganset (,nærə'gænsɪt) *n* **1** (*pl* **Narraganset** *or* **Narragansets**) a member of a North American Indian people formerly living in Rhode Island. **2** the language of this people, belonging to the Algonquian family.

Narragansett Bay ★ *n* an inlet of the Atlantic in SE Rhode Island: contains several islands, including Rhode Island, Prudence Island, and Conanicut Island.

narrate (nə'reɪt) *vb* **narrates, narrating, narrated. 1** to tell (a story); relate. **2** to speak in accompaniment of (a film, etc.). [C17: from L *narrāre* to recount, from *gnārus* knowing]
▶ nar'ratable *adj* ▶ nar'rator *n*

narration (nə'reɪʃən) *n* **1** the act or process of narrating. **2** a narrated account or story.

narrative ('nærətɪv) *n* **1** an account or story, as of events, experiences, etc. **2** the part of a literary work, etc., that relates events. **3** the process or technique of narrating. ◆ *adj* **4** telling a story: *a narrative poem.* **5** of or relating to narration: *narrative art.*

narrow ('nærəʊ) *adj* **1** small in breadth, esp. in comparison to length. **2** limited in range or extent. **3** limited in outlook. **4** limited in means or resources. **5** barely adequate or successful (esp. in **a narrow escape**). **6** painstakingly thorough: *a narrow scrutiny.* **7** *Finance.* denoting an assessment of liquidity as including notes and coins in circulation with the public, banks' till money, and banks' balances: *narrow money.* Cf. **broad** (sense 12). **8** *Phonetics.* another word for **tense**[1] (sense 4). ◆ *vb* **9** to make or become narrow. **10** (often foll. by *down*) to limit or restrict. ◆ *n* **11** a narrow place, esp. a pass or strait. ◆ See also **narrows.** [OE *nearu*]
▶ 'narrowly *adv* ▶ 'narrowness *n*

narrowboat ('nærəʊ,bəʊt) *n* a long bargelike boat with a beam of 2.1 metres (7 feet), used on canals.

narrow gauge *n* **1** a railway track with a smaller distance between the lines than the standard gauge of 56½ inches. ◆ *adj* **narrow-gauge. 2** of or denoting a railway with a narrow gauge.

narrow-minded *adj* having a biased or illiberal viewpoint; bigoted, intolerant, or prejudiced.
▶ ,narrow-'mindedness *n*

narrows ('nærəʊz) *pl n* a narrow part of a strait, river, current, etc.

narthex ('nɑːθɛks) *n* **1** a portico at the west end of a church, esp. one at right angles to the nave. **2** a rectangular entrance hall between the porch and nave of a church. [C17: via L from Med. Gk: enclosed porch (earlier: box), from Gk *narthēx* giant fennel, the stems of which were used to make boxes]

Narva ★ (*Russian* 'narvə) *n* a port in Estonia on the Narva River near the Gulf of Finland: developed around a Danish fortress in the 13th century; textile centre. Pop.: 77 770 (1995).

Narvik ★ ('nɑːvɪk; *Norwegian* 'narvik) *n* a port in N Norway: scene of two naval battles in 1940; exports iron ore from Kiruna and Gällivare (Sweden). Pop.: 18 500 (1990).

narwhal, narwal ('nɑːwəl), *or* **narwhale** ('nɑː,weɪl) *n* an arctic toothed whale having a black-spotted whitish skin and, in the male, a long spiral tusk. [C17: of Scand. origin; cf. Danish, Norwegian *narhval*, from ON *nāhvalr*, from *nār* corpse + *hvalr* whale]

nary ('nɛərɪ) *adv Dialect or inf.* not; never: *nary a man was left.* [C19: var. of *ne'er a* never a]

NASA ('næsə) *n* (in the US) *acronym for* National Aeronautics and Space Administration.

nasal ('neɪzᵊl) *adj* **1** of the nose. **2** *Phonetics.* pronounced with the soft palate lowered allowing air to escape via the nasal cavity. ◆ *n* **3** a nasal speech sound, such as English *m, n,* or *ng.* [C17: from F from LL *nāsālis*, from L *nāsus* nose]
▶ nasality (neɪ'zælɪtɪ) *n* ▶ 'nasally *adv*

nasalize *or* **nasalise** ('neɪzᵊ,laɪz) *vb* **nasalizes, nasalizing, nasalized** *or* **nasalises, nasalising, nasalised.** (*tr*) to pronounce nasally.
▶ ,nasali'zation *or* ,nasali'sation *n*

nascent ('næsᵊnt, 'neɪ-) *adj* starting to grow or develop; being born. [C17: from L *nascēns*, present participle of *nāscī* to be born]
▶ 'nascency *n*

nascent hydrogen *n Chem.* hydrogen produced in a reactive form within the reaction mixture.

Naseby ★ ('neɪzbɪ) *n* a village in Northamptonshire: site of a major Parliamentarian victory (1645) in the Civil War.

Nash ★ (næʃ) *n* **1 John.** 1752–1835, British town planner and architect. He designed Regent's Park, Regent Street, and the Marble Arch in London. **2 Ogden.** 1902–71, US humorous poet. **3 Paul.** 1889–1946, British painter, noted as a war artist in both World Wars. **4 Richard,** known as *Beau Nash.* 1674–1762, English dandy. **5 Thomas.** See (Thomas) **Nashe. 6** Sir **Walter.** 1882–1968, New Zealand Labour statesman, born in England: prime minister (1957–60).

Nashe *or* **Nash** ★ (næʃ) *n* **Thomas.** 1567–1601, English pamphleteer and novelist.

Nashville ★ ('næʃvɪl) *n* a city in central Tennessee, the state capital, on the Cumberland River: an industrial and commercial centre, noted for its recording industry. Pop.: 504 505 (1994 est.).

Nasik ★ ('nɑːsɪk) *n* a city in W India, in Maharashtra: a centre for Hindu pilgrims. Pop.: 656 925 (1991).

naso- *combining form.* nose: *nasopharynx.* [from L *nāsus* nose]

nasogastric (,neɪzəʊ'gæstrɪk) *adj Anat.* of or relating to the nose and stomach: *a nasogastric tube.*

Nassau ★ *n* **1** (*German* 'nasaʊ). a region of W central Germany: formerly a duchy (1816–66), from which a branch of the House of Orange arose (represented by the present rulers of the Netherlands and Luxembourg); annexed to the Prussian province of Hesse-Nassau in 1866; corresponds to present-day W Hesse and NE Rhineland-Palatinate states; formerly (1949–90) part of West Germany. **2** ('næsɔː). the capital and chief port of the Bahamas, on the NE coast of New Providence Island: resort. Pop.: 172 196 (1990).

Nasser ★ ('nɑːsə, 'næsə) *n* **Gamal Abdel** (gə'mɑːl 'æbdɛl). 1918–70, Egyptian soldier and statesman; president (1956–70). A leader of the coup that deposed King Farouk (1952), he became premier (1954). His nationalization of the Suez Canal (1956) led to an international crisis.

nastic movement ('næstɪk) *n* a response of plant parts that is independent of the direction of the external stimulus, such as the opening of buds caused by an alteration in light intensity.   [C19 *nastic*, from Gk *nastos* close-packed, from *nassein* to press down]

nasturtium (nə'stɜːʃəm) *n* a plant having round leaves and yellow, red, or orange trumpet-shaped spurred flowers.   [C17: from L: kind of cress, from *nāsus* nose + *tortus* twisted; because the pungent smell causes one to wrinkle one's nose]

nasty ('nɑːstɪ) *adj* **nastier, nastiest. 1** unpleasant or repugnant. **2** dangerous or painful: *a nasty wound.* **3** spiteful or ill-natured. **4** obscene or indecent. ♦ *n, pl* **nasties. 5** an offensive or unpleasant person or thing: *a video nasty.* [C14: from ?; prob. rel. to Swedish dialect *nasket* & Du. *nestig* dirty]
▶ '**nastily** *adv* ▶ '**nastiness** *n*

NAS/UWT (in Britain) *abbrev. for* National Association of Schoolmasters/Union of Women Teachers.

nat. *abbrev. for:* **1** national. **2** native. **3** natural.

natal ('neɪtᵊl) *adj* of or relating to birth.   [C14: from L *nātālis* of one's birth, from *nātus*, from *nascī* to be born]

Natal ★ *n* **1** (nə'tæl). a former province of E South Africa, in 1994 it was replaced by the Kwazulu/Natal region. **2** (*Portuguese* na'tal). a port in NE Brazil, capital of Rio Grande do Norte state, near the mouth of the Potengi River. Pop.: 459 827 (1991).

natant ('neɪtᵊnt) *adj* floating or swimming.   [C18: from L *natāns*, present participle of *natāre* to swim]

natation (nə'teɪʃən) *n* a literary word for **swimming.** [C16: from L *natātiō* a swimming, from *natāre* to swim]

natatory (nə'teɪtərɪ) *or* **natatorial** (ˌnætə'tɔːrɪəl) *adj* of or relating to swimming.   [C18: from LL *natātōrius*, from L *natāre* to swim]

natch (nætʃ) *sentence substitute. Inf.* short for **naturally.**

nates ('neɪtiːz) *pl n, sing* **natis** (-tɪs). a technical word for the **buttocks.** [C17: from L]

NATFHE (in Britain) *abbrev. for* National Association of Teachers in Further and Higher Education.

Nathan ★ ('neɪθən) *n Old Testament.* a prophet at David's court (II Samuel 7:1–17; 12:1–15).

Nathanael ★ (nə'θænjəl) *n New Testament.* a Galilean who is perhaps to be identified with Bartholomew among the apostles (John 1:45–51; 21:1).

natheless ('neɪθlɪs) *or* **nathless** ('næθlɪs) *Arch. sentence connector.* nonetheless.   [OE *nāthylæs*, from *nā* never + *thȳ* for that + *læs* less]

nation ('neɪʃən) *n* **1** an aggregation of people or peoples of one or more cultures, races, etc., organized into a single state: *the Australian nation.* **2** a community of persons not constituting a state but bound by common descent, language, history, etc.: *the French-Canadian nation.* [C13: via OF from L *nātiō* birth, tribe, from *nascī* to be born]
▶ '**nation,hood** *n*

national ('næʃənᵊl) *adj* **1** of or relating to a nation as a whole. **2** characteristic of a particular nation: *the national dress of Poland.* ♦ *n* **3** a citizen or subject. **4** a national newspaper.
▶ '**nationally** *adv*

national anthem *n* a patriotic song adopted by a nation for use on public occasions.

national assistance *n* (formerly, in Britain) a weekly allowance paid to individuals of various groups by the state to bring their incomes up to minimum levels established by law. Now replaced by income support.

national bank *n* **1** (in the US) a commercial bank incorporated under a Federal charter and legally required to be a member of the Federal Reserve System. **2** a bank operated by a government.

national call *n Brit.* a telephone call made to a number within the country but outside the local area.

National Curriculum *n* (in England and Wales) the curriculum of subjects taught in state schools from 1989. The ten foundation subjects are: English, maths,

and science (the core subjects); art, design and technology, geography, history, music, physical education, and a foreign language. Pupils are assessed at four stages. Abbrev.: **NC.**

national debt *n* the total outstanding borrowings of a nation's central government.

National Economic Development Council *n* a former advisory body on economic policy in Britain, composed of representatives of government, management, and trade unions: abolished in 1992. Abbrevs.: **NEDC,** (inf.) **Neddy.**

National Enterprise Board *n* a public corporation established in 1975 to help the economy of the UK. In 1981 it merged with the National Research and Development Council to form the British Technology Group. Abbrev.: **NEB.**

National Football *n* (in Australia) another name for **Australian Rules.**

National Front *n* an extreme right-wing British political party founded in 1967.

National Gallery ★ *n* a major art gallery in London, in Trafalgar Square. Founded in 1824, it contains the largest collection of paintings in Britain.

national grid *n Brit.* **1** a network of high-voltage electric power lines linking major electric power stations. **2** the metric coordinate system used in ordnance survey maps.

National Guard *n* **1** (*sometimes not cap.*) the armed force that was established in France in 1789 and existed intermittently until 1871. **2** (in the US) a state military force that can be called into federal service by the president.

National Health Service *n* (in Britain) the system of national medical services since 1948, financed mainly by taxation. Abbrev.: **NHS.**

national hunt *n Brit.* (*often caps.*) **a** the racing of horses on racecourses with jumps. **b** (*as modifier*): *a National Hunt jockey.*

national income *n Econ.* the total of all incomes accruing over a specified period to residents of a country.

national insurance *n* (in Britain) state insurance based on weekly contributions from employees and employers and providing payments to the unemployed, the sick, the retired, etc., as well as medical services.

nationalism ('næʃənəˌlɪzəm) *n* **1** a sentiment based on common cultural characteristics that binds a population and often produces a policy of national independence. **2** loyalty to one's country; patriotism. **3** exaggerated or fanatical devotion to a national community.
▶ '**nationalist** *n, adj* ▶ ˌ**national'istic** *adj*

nationality (ˌnæʃə'nælɪtɪ) *n, pl* **nationalities. 1** the fact of being a citizen of a particular nation. **2** a body of people sharing common descent, history, language, etc.; a nation. **3** a national group: *30 different nationalities are found in this city.* **4** national character. **5** the fact of being a nation; national status.

nationalize *or* **nationalise** ('næʃənəˌlaɪz) *vb* **nationalizes, nationalizing, nationalized** *or* **nationalises, nationalising, nationalised. (tr) 1** to put (an industry, resources, etc.) under state control. **2** to make national in character or status. **3** a less common word for **naturalize.**
▶ ˌ**nationali'zation** *or* ˌ**nationali'sation** *n*

national park *n* an area of countryside for public use designated by a national government as being of notable scenic, environmental, or historical importance.

National Park ★ *n NZ.* a mountainous volcanic region in the North Island.

National Party *n* **1** (in New Zealand) the more conservative of the two main political parties. **2** (in Australia) a political party drawing its main support from rural areas. Former name: **National Country Party. 3** (in South Africa) a political party composed mainly of centre-to-right-wing Afrikaners. It ruled from 1948 until 1994, when South Africa's first multiracial elections were won by the African National Congress.

National Savings Bank *n* (in Britain) a government savings bank, run through the Post Office.

★ people and places

national service *n Chiefly Brit.* compulsory military service.

National Socialism *n German history.* the doctrines and practices of the Nazis, involving the supremacy of Hitler as Führer, anti-Semitism, state control of the economy, and national expansion.
▸ **National Socialist** *n, adj*

national superannuation *n NZ.* a government pension given on the attainment of a specified age; old age pension.

National Theatre ★ *n* the former name of the **Royal National Theatre.**

National Trust *n* **1** (in Britain) an organization concerned with the preservation of historic buildings and areas of the countryside of great beauty. **2** (in Australia) a similar organization in each of the states.

nationwide ('neɪʃən‚waɪd) *adj* covering or available to the whole of a nation; national.

native ('neɪtɪv) *adj* **1** relating or belonging to a person by virtue of conditions existing at birth: *a native language.* **2** natural or innate: *a native strength.* **3** born in a specified place: *a native Indian.* **4** (when *postpositive,* foll. by *to*) originating in: *kangaroos are native to Australia.* **5** relating to the indigenous inhabitants of a country: *the native art of the New Guinea Highlands.* **6** (of metals) found naturally in the elemental form; not chemically combined as in an ore. **7** unadulterated by civilization, artifice, or adornment; natural. **8** *Arch.* related by birth or race. **9 go native.** (of a settler) to adopt the lifestyle of the local population, esp. when it appears less civilized. ♦ *n* **10** (usually foll. by *of*) a person born in a particular place: *a native of Geneva.* **11** (usually foll. by *of*) a species of animal or plant originating in a particular place. **12** a member of an indigenous people of a country, esp. a non-White people, as opposed to colonial immigrants. [C14: from L *nātīvus* innate, natural, from *nascī* to be born]
▸ 'natively *adv* ▸ 'nativeness *n*

Native American *n* another name for an **American Indian.**

native bear *n* an Australian name for **koala.**

native-born *adj* born in the country or area indicated.

native companion *n* (in Australia) another name for **brolga.**

native dog *n Austral.* a dingo.

Native States ★ *pl n* the former 562 semi-independent states of India, ruled by Indians but subject to varying degrees of British authority: merged with provinces by 1948; largest states were Hyderabad, Gwalior, Baroda, Mysore, Cochin, Jammu and Kashmir, Travancore, Sikkim, and Indore. Also called: **Indian States and Agencies.**

nativity (nə'tɪvɪtɪ) *n, pl* **nativities.** birth or origin. [C14: from LL *nātīvitas* birth; see NATIVE]

Nativity (nə'tɪvɪtɪ) *n* **1** the birth of Christ. **2** the feast of Christmas as a commemoration of this. **3a** an artistic representation of the circumstances of the birth of Christ. **3b** (*as modifier*): *a Nativity play.*

NATO *or* **Nato** ('neɪtəʊ) *n acronym for* North Atlantic Treaty Organization: an international organization established (1949) for purposes of collective security.

natron ('neɪtrən) *n* a whitish or yellow mineral that consists of hydrated sodium carbonate and occurs in saline deposits and salt lakes. [C17: via F & Sp. from Ar. *natrūn,* from Gk *nitron* NITRE]

NATSOPA (næt'səʊpə) *n* (formerly, in Britain) *acronym for* National Society of Operative Printers, Graphical and Media Personnel.

natter ('nætə) *Chiefly Brit. inf.* ♦ *vb* **1** (*intr*) to talk idly and at length; chatter. ♦ *n* **2** prolonged idle chatter. [C19: from *gnatter* to grumble, imit.]

natterjack ('nætə‚dʒæk) *n* a European toad having a greyish-brown body marked with reddish warty processes. [C18: from ?]

natty ('nætɪ) *adj* **nattier, nattiest.** *Inf.* smart; spruce; dapper. [C18: from obs. *netty,* from *net* NEAT¹]
▸ 'nattily *adv* ▸ 'nattiness *n*

natural ('nætʃrəl) *adj* **1** of, existing in, or produced by nature: *natural science; natural cliffs.* **2** in accordance with human nature. **3** as is normal or to be expected: *the natural course of events.* **4** not acquired; innate: *a natural gift for sport.* **5** being so through innate qualities: *a natural leader.* **6** not supernatural or strange: *natural phenomena.* **7** genuine or spontaneous. **8** lifelike: *she looked more natural without make-up.* **9** not affected by man; wild: *in the natural state this animal is not ferocious.* **10** being or made from organic material; not synthetic: *a natural fibre like cotton.* **11** born out of wedlock. **12** not adopted but rather related by blood: *her natural parents.* **13** *Music.* **13a** not sharp or flat. **13b** (*postpositive*) denoting a note that is neither sharp nor flat. **13c** (of a key or scale) containing no sharps or flats. **14** based on the principles and findings of human reason rather than on revelation: *natural religion.* ♦ *n* **15** *Inf.* a person or thing regarded as certain to qualify for success, selection, etc.: *the horse was a natural for first place.* **16** *Music.* **16a** Also called (US): **cancel.** an accidental cancelling a previous sharp or flat. Usual symbol: ♮ **16b** a note affected by this accidental. **17** *Obs.* an imbecile; idiot.
▸ 'naturalness *n*

natural childbirth *n* a method of childbirth characterized by the absence of anaesthetics, in which the expectant mother is given special breathing and relaxing exercises.

natural gas *n* a gaseous mixture, consisting mainly of methane, trapped below ground; used extensively as a fuel.

natural history *n* **1** the study of animals and plants in the wild state. **2** the sum of these phenomena in a given place or at a given time.
▸ **natural historian** *n*

natural immunity *n* immunity with which an individual is born, which has a genetic basis.

naturalism ('nætʃrə‚lɪzəm) *n* **1** a movement, esp. in art and literature, advocating detailed realistic and factual description. **2** the belief that all religious truth is based not on revelation but rather on the study of natural causes and processes. **3** *Philosophy.* a scientific account of the world in terms of causes and natural forces. **4** action or thought caused by natural instincts.

naturalist ('nætʃrəlɪst) *n* **1** a person who is versed in or interested in botany or zoology. **2** a person who advocates or practises naturalism.

naturalistic (‚nætʃrə'lɪstɪk) *adj* **1** of or reproducing nature in effect or characteristics. **2** of or characteristic of naturalism. **3** of naturalists.
▸ ‚natural'istically *adv*

naturalize *or* **naturalise** ('nætʃrə‚laɪz) *vb* **naturalizes, naturalizing, naturalized** *or* **naturalises, naturalising, naturalised.** **1** (*tr*) to give citizenship to (a person of foreign birth). **2** to be or cause to be adopted in another place, as a word, custom, etc. **3** (*tr*) to introduce (a plant or animal from another region) and cause it to adapt to local conditions. **4** (*intr*) (of a plant or animal) to adapt successfully to a foreign environment. **5** (*tr*) to make natural or more lifelike.
▸ ‚naturali'zation *or* ‚naturali'sation *n*

natural language *n* a language that has evolved naturally as a means of communication among people, as opposed to an invented language or a code.

natural logarithm *n* a logarithm to the base e. Usually written $\log_e$ or ln. Also called: **Napierian logarithm.**

naturally ('nætʃrəlɪ) *adv* **1** in a natural way. **2** instinctively. ♦ *adv, sentence substitute.* **3** of course; surely.

natural number *n* any of the numbers 0, 1, 2, 3, 4,... that can be used to count the members of a set; the nonnegative integers.

natural philosophy *n* physical science, esp. physics.
▸ **natural philosopher** *n*

natural resources *pl n* naturally occurring materials such as coal, fertile land, etc.

natural science *n* the sciences that are involved in the study of the physical world and its phenomena, including biology, physics, chemistry, and geology.

natural selection *n* a process resulting in the survival of those individuals from a population of animals or plants that are best adapted to the prevailing environmental conditions.

natural theology *n* the attempt to derive theological truth, and esp. the existence of God, from empirical facts by reasoned argument. Cf. **revealed religion**.

natural wastage *n* the loss of employees, etc., through not replacing those who retire or resign rather than dismissal or redundancy.

nature ('neɪtʃə) *n* **1** fundamental qualities; identity or essential character. **2** (*often cap.*) the whole system of the existence, forces, and events of all physical life that are not controlled by man. **3** plant and animal life, as distinct from man. **4** a wild primitive state untouched by man. **5** natural unspoilt countryside. **6** disposition or temperament. **7** desires or instincts governing behaviour. **8** the normal biological needs of the body. **9** sort; character. **10 against nature.** unnatural or immoral. **11 by nature.** essentially or innately. **12 call of nature.** *Inf.* the need to urinate or defecate. **13 from nature.** using natural models in drawing, painting, etc. **14 in** (or **of**) **the nature of.** essentially the same as; by way of. [C13: via OF from L *nātūra*, from *nātus*, p.p. of *nascī* to be born]

nature reserve *n* an area of land that is protected and managed in order to preserve its flora and fauna.

nature study *n* the study of the natural world, esp. animals and plants, by direct observation at an elementary level.

nature trail *n* a path through countryside designed and usually signposted to draw attention to natural features of interest.

naturism ('neɪtʃə,rɪzəm) *n* another name for **nudism**.
▸ **'naturist** *n, adj*

naturopathy (,nætʃə'rɒpəθɪ) *n* the treatment of illness by stimulating natural healing, esp. by herbal remedies, manipulation, etc.
▸ **'naturo,path** *n* ▸ **,naturo'pathic** *adj*

Naucratis ★ ('nɔːkrətɪs) *n* an ancient Greek city in N Egypt, in the Nile delta: founded in the 7th century B.C.

naught (nɔːt) *n* **1** *Arch. or literary.* nothing; ruin or failure. **2** a variant spelling (esp. US) of **nought**. **3 set at naught.** to disregard or scorn; disdain. ◆ *adv* **4** *Arch. or literary.* not at all: *it matters naught.* ◆ *adj* **5** *Obs.* worthless, ruined, or wicked. [OE *nāwiht*, from *nā* NO¹ + *wiht* thing, person]

naughty ('nɔːtɪ) *adj* **naughtier, naughtiest. 1** (esp. of children) mischievous or disobedient. **2** mildly indecent; titillating. [C14: (orig.: needy, poor): from NAUGHT]
▸ **'naughtily** *adv* ▸ **'naughtiness** *n*

nauplius ('nɔːplɪəs) *n, pl* **nauplii** (-plɪ,aɪ). the larva of many crustaceans, having a rounded unsegmented body with three pairs of limbs. [C19: from L: type of shellfish, from Gk *Nauplios*, one of the sons of the Greek god Poseidon]

Nauru ★ (nɑː'uːruː) *n* an island republic in the SW Pacific, west of Kiribati: administered jointly by Australia, New Zealand, and Britain as a UN trust territory before becoming independent and a special member of the Commonwealth in 1968. The economy is based on export of phosphates. Languages: Nauruan (a Malayo-Polynesian language) and English. Religion: Christian. Currency: Australian dollar. Pop.: 8100 (1990). Area: 2130 hectares (5263 acres). Former name: **Pleasant Island**.
▸ **Na'uruan** *adj, n*

nausea ('nɔːzɪə, -sɪə) *n* **1** the sensation that precedes vomiting. **2** a feeling of revulsion. [C16: via L from Gk: seasickness, from *naus* ship]

nauseate ('nɔːzɪ,eɪt, -sɪ-) *vb* **nauseates, nauseating, nauseated. 1** (*tr*) to arouse feelings of disgust or revulsion in. **2** to feel or cause to feel sick.
▸ **'nause,ating** *adv*

nauseous ('nɔːzɪəs, -sɪəs) *adj* **1** causing nausea. **2** distasteful; repulsive.
▸ **'nauseously** *adv* ▸ **'nauseousness** *n*

Nausicaä ★ (nɔː'sɪkɪə) *n* in Greek myth. a daughter of Alcinous, king of the Phaeacians, who assisted the shipwrecked Odysseus after discovering him on a beach.

nautch *or* **nauch** (nɔːtʃ) *n* an intricate traditional Indian dance performed by professional dancing girls. [C18:

from Hindi *nāc*, from Sansk., from *nrtyati* he acts or dances]

nautical ('nɔːtɪkᵊl) *adj* of or involving ships, navigation, or seamen. [C16: from L *nauticus*, from Gk *nautikos*, from *naus* ship]
▸ **'nautically** *adv*

nautical mile *n* **1** Also called **international nautical mile, air mile.** a unit of length, used esp. in navigation, equivalent to the average length of a minute of latitude, and corresponding to a latitude of 45°, i.e. 1852 m (6076.12 ft). **2** a former British unit of length equal to 1853.18 m (6080 ft), which was replaced by the international nautical mile in 1970. Former name: **geographical mile**. Cf. **sea mile**.

nautilus ('nɔːtɪləs) *n, pl* **nautiluses** *or* **nautili** (-,laɪ). **1** any of a genus of cephalopod molluscs, esp. the pearly nautilus. **2** short for **paper nautilus**. [C17: via L from Gk *nautilos* sailor, from *naus* ship]

NAV *abbrev. for* net asset value.

Navaho *or* **Navajo** ('nævə,həʊ) *n* **1** (*pl* **Navaho, Navahos, Navahoes** *or* **Navajo, Navajos, Navajoes**) a member of a North American Indian people of Arizona, New Mexico, and Utah. **2** the language of this people. [C18: from Sp. *Navajó* pueblo, from Tena *Navahu* large planted field]

naval ('neɪvᵊl) *adj* **1** of, characteristic of, or having a navy. **2** of or relating to ships; nautical. [C16: from L *nāvālis*, from *nāvis* ship]

naval architecture *n* the designing of ships.
▸ **naval architect** *n*

Navaratri (,nævə'rɑːtrɪ) *n* an annual Hindu festival celebrated over nine days in September–October. It commemorates the slaying of demons by Rama and the goddess Durga. Also called: **Durga Puja**. [from Sansk. *navaratri* nine nights]

navarin ('nævərɪn) *n* a stew of mutton or lamb with root vegetables. [from F]

Navarino ★ (nava'riːno) *n* the Italian name for **Pylos**.

Navarre ★ (nə'vɑː) *n* a former kingdom of SW Europe: established in the 9th century by the Basques; the parts south of the Pyrenees joined Spain in 1515 and the N parts passed to France in 1589. Capital: Pamplona. Spanish name: **Navarra** (na'βarra).

nave¹ (neɪv) *n* the central space in a church, extending from the narthex to the chancel and often flanked by aisles. [C17: via Med. L from L *nāvis* ship, from the similarity of shape]

nave² (neɪv) *n* the central block or hub of a wheel. [OE *nafu, nafa*]

navel ('neɪvᵊl) *n* **1** the scar in the centre of the abdomen, usually forming a slight depression, where the umbilical cord was attached. Technical name: **umbilicus**. Related adj: **umbilical**. **2** a central part or point. [OE *nafela*]

navel orange *n* a sweet orange that has at its apex a navel-like depression enclosing an underdeveloped secondary fruit.

navelwort ('neɪvᵊl,wɜːt) *n* another name for **pennywort** (sense 1).

navicular (nə'vɪkjʊlə) *Anat.* ◆ *adj* **1** shaped like a boat. ◆ *n* **2** a small boat-shaped bone of the wrist or foot. [C16: from LL *nāviculāris*, from L *nāvicula*, dim. of *nāvis* ship]

navigable ('nævɪgəbᵊl) *adj* **1** wide, deep, or safe enough to be sailed through: *a navigable channel.* **2** capable of being steered: *a navigable raft.*
▸ **,naviga'bility** *n* ▸ **'navigably** *adv*

navigate ('nævɪ,geɪt) *vb* **navigates, navigating, navigated. 1** to direct or plot the path or position of (a ship, an aircraft, etc.). **2** (*tr*) to travel over, through, or on in a boat, aircraft, etc. **3** *Inf.* to direct (oneself) carefully or safely: *he navigated his way to the bar.* **4** (*intr*) (of a passenger in a motor vehicle) to give directions to the driver; point out the route. [C16: from L *nāvigāre* to sail, from *nāvis* ship + *agere* to drive]

navigation (,nævɪ'geɪʃən) *n* **1** the skill or process of plotting a route and directing a ship, aircraft, etc., along it. **2** the act or practice of navigating: *dredging made navigation of the river possible.*
▸ **,navi'gational** *adj*

navigator ('nævɪˌgeɪtə) n 1 a person who performs navigation. 2 (esp. formerly) a person who explores by ship. 3 an instrument for assisting a pilot to navigate an aircraft.

Návpaktos ★ (Greek 'nafpaktos) n the Greek name for **Lepanto**.

Navratilova ★ (næˌvrætɪ'ləuvə) n **Martina**. born 1956, Czech-born US tennis player: Wimbledon champion 1978–79, 1982–87, 1990; US Open champion 1983, 1984, 1986, 1987; world champion 1980.

navvy ('nævɪ) n, pl **navvies**. Brit. inf. a labourer on a building site, etc. [C19: from navigator builder of a navigation (in the sense: canal)]

navy ('neɪvɪ) n, pl **navies**. 1 the warships and auxiliary vessels of a nation or ruler. 2 (often cap.) the branch of a country's armed services comprising such ships, their crews, and all their supporting services. 3 short for **navy blue**. 4 Arch. or literary. a fleet of ships. [C14: via OF from Vulgar L nāvia (unattested) ship, from L nāvis ship]

navy blue n a a dark greyish-blue colour. b (as adj): a navy-blue suit. [C19: from the colour of the British naval uniform]

Navy List n (in Britain) an official list of all commissioned officers of the Royal Navy.

navy yard n a naval shipyard, esp. in the US.

nawab (nə'wɑːb) n (formerly) a Muslim ruling prince or powerful landowner in India. [C18: from Hindi nawwāb, from Ar. nuwwāb, pl. of na'ib viceroy]

Naxos ★ ('næksɒs) n a Greek island in the S Aegean, the largest of the Cyclades: ancient centre of the worship of Dionysius. Pop.: 14 000 (latest est.). Area: 438 sq. km (169 sq. miles).

nay (neɪ) sentence substitute. 1 a word for **no**¹: archaic or dialectal except in voting by voice. ◆ n 2 a person who votes in the negative. ◆ adv 3 (sentence modifier) Arch. an emphatic form of **no**¹. [C12: from ON nei, from ne not + ei ever]

Nayarit ★ (Spanish naja'rit) n a state of W Mexico, on the Pacific: includes the offshore Tres Marías Islands. Capital: Tepic. Pop.: 895 975 (1995 est.). Area: 27 621 sq. km (10 772 sq. miles).

Nazarene (ˌnæzə'riːn) n 1 an early name for a **Christian** (Acts 24:5) or (when preceded by the) for **Jesus Christ**. 2 a member of one of several groups of Jewish-Christians found principally in Syria. ◆ adj 3 of Nazareth in N Israel, or the Nazarenes.

Nazareth ★ ('næzərɪθ) n a town in N Israel, in Lower Galilee: the home of Jesus in his youth. Pop.: 51 000 (1989).

Nazarite ('næzəˌraɪt) or **Nazirite** n a religious ascetic of ancient Israel. [C16: from L Nazaraeus, from Heb. nāzar to consecrate + -ITE¹]

Naze (neɪz) n **the**. 1 a flat marshy headland in SE England, in Essex on the North Sea coast. 2 another name for **Lindesnes**.

Nazi ('nɑːtsɪ) n, pl **Nazis**. 1 a member of the fascist National Socialist German Workers' Party, which seized political control in Germany in 1933. ◆ adj 2 characteristic of or relating to the Nazis. [C20: from G, phonetic spelling of the first two syllables of Nationalsozialist National Socialist]
▶ **Nazism** ('nɑːtsɪzəm) or **Naziism** ('nɑːtsɪˌɪzəm) n

Nb the chemical symbol for niobium.

NB abbrev. for New Brunswick.

NB, N.B., nb, or **n.b.** abbrev. for nota bene. [L: note well]

NBA abbrev. for Net Book Agreement.

NC or **N.C.** abbrev. for: 1 North Carolina. 2 Brit. education. National Curriculum.

NCB (in Britain) abbrev. for National Coal Board: now British Coal.

NCC (in Britain) abbrev. for: 1 Nature Conservancy Council. 2 Brit. education. National Curriculum Council: a statutory organization responsible for the content of the National Curriculum.

NCO abbrev. for noncommissioned officer.

NCU (in Britain) abbrev. for National Communications Union.

nd abbrev. for no date.

Nd the chemical symbol for neodymium.

ND, N.D., or **N. Dak.** abbrev. for North Dakota.

Ndjamena or **N'djamena** ★ (°ndʒɑː'meɪnə) n the capital of Chad, in the southwest, at the confluence of the Shari and Logone Rivers: trading centre for livestock. Pop.: 530 965 (1993). Former name (until 1973): **Fort Lamy**.

Ndola ★ (°n'dəulə) n a city in N Zambia: copper, cobalt, and sugar refineries. Pop.: 376 311 (1990).

NDP abbrev. for: 1 net domestic product. 2 (in Canada) New Democratic Party.

NDT (in Canada) abbrev. for Newfoundland Daylight Time.

Ne the chemical symbol for neon.

NE 1 symbol for northeast(ern). 2 abbrev. for Nebraska. 3 Also: **N.E.** abbrev. for New England.

ne- combining form. a variant of **neo-**, esp. before a vowel: Nearctic.

Neagh ★ (neɪ) n **Lough**. a lake in Northern Ireland, in SW Co. Antrim: the largest lake in the British Isles. Area: 388 sq. km (150 sq. miles).

Neanderthal man (nɪ'ændəˌtɑːl) n a type of primitive man occurring throughout much of Europe in late Palaeolithic times. They are not thought to be ancestors of modern humans. [C19: from the anthropological findings (1857) in the Neandertal, a valley near Düsseldorf, Germany]

neap (niːp) adj 1 of, relating to, or constituting a neap tide. ◆ n 2 short for **neap tide**. [OE, as in nēpflōd neap tide, from ?]

Neapolitan (ˌnɪə'pɒlɪt°n) n 1 a native or inhabitant of Naples. ◆ adj 2 of or relating to Naples. [C15: from L Neāpolītānus, ult. from Gk Neapolis new town]

Neapolitan ice cream n ice cream with several layers of different colours and flavours.

neap tide n either of the tides that occur at the first or last quarter of the moon when the tide-generating forces of the sun and moon oppose each other and produce the smallest rise and fall in tidal level. Cf. spring tide (sense 1).

near (nɪə) prep 1 at or to a place or time not far away from; close to. ◆ adv 2 at or to a place or time not far away; close by. 3 short for **nearly** (sense 1): I was nearly killed. ◆ adj 4 (postpositive) at or in a place not far away. 5 (prenominal) only just successful or only just failing: a near thing. 6 (postpositive) Inf. miserly, mean. 7 (prenominal) closely connected or intimate: a near relation. ◆ vb 8 to come or draw close (to). ◆ n 9 Also called: **nearside**. 9a the left side of a horse, vehicle, etc. 9b (as modifier): the near foreleg. [OE nēar (adv), comp. of nēah close]
▶ 'nearness n

nearby adj ('nɪəˌbaɪ), adv (ˌnɪə'baɪ). not far away; close at hand.

Nearctic (nɪ'ɑːktɪk) adj of a zoogeographical region consisting of North America, north of the tropic of Cancer, and Greenland.

Near East ★ n 1 another term for the **Middle East**. 2 (formerly) the Balkan States and the area of the Ottoman Empire.

near gale n Meteorol. a wind of force seven on the Beaufort scale or from 32-38 mph.

nearly ('nɪəlɪ) adv 1 almost. 2 not nearly. nowhere near: not nearly enough. 3 closely: the person most nearly concerned.

near-market n (modifier) (of scientific research, etc.) very close to being commercially exploitable.

near miss n 1 a bomb, shell, etc., that does not exactly hit the target. 2 any attempt or shot that just fails to be successful. 3 an incident in which two aircraft, etc., narrowly avoid collision.

near point n Optics. the nearest point to the eye at which an object remains in focus.

nearside ('nɪəˌsaɪd) n 1 (usually preceded by the) Chiefly

Brit. **1a** the side of a vehicle, etc., nearer the kerb. **1b** (*as modifier*): *the nearside door.* **2a** the left side of an animal, etc. **2b** (*as modifier*): *the nearside flank.*

near-sighted (ˌnɪəˈsaɪtɪd) *adj* relating to or suffering from myopia.
▶ ˌnear-ˈsightedly *adv*

near thing *n Inf.* an event or action whose outcome is nearly a failure, success, disaster, etc.

neat[1] (niːt) *adj* **1** clean, tidy, and orderly. **2** liking or insisting on order and cleanliness. **3** smoothly or competently done; efficient: *a neat job.* **4** pat or slick: *his excuse was suspiciously neat.* **5** (of alcoholic drinks, etc.) undiluted. **6** (of language) concise and well-phrased. **7** *Sl., chiefly US & Canad.* pleasing; admirable; excellent. [C16: from OF *net*, from L *nitidus* clean, from *nitēre* to shine]
▶ ˈneatly *adv* ▶ ˈneatness *n*

neat[2] (niːt) *n, pl* **neat.** *Arch. or dialect.* a domestic bovine animal. [OE *neat*]

neaten (ˈniːtᵊn) *vb* (*tr*) to make neat; tidy.

neath *or* **'neath** (niːθ) *prep Arch.* short for **beneath.**

Neath Port Talbot ★ (ˈniːθ ˈpɔːt ˈtɔːlbət, ˈtæl-) *n* a county borough in S Wales. Administrative centre: Port Talbot. Pop.: 106 307 (1996 est.). Area: 439 sq. km (169 sq. miles).

neat's-foot oil *n* a yellow oil obtained by boiling the feet and shinbones of cattle.

neb (nɛb) *n Arch. or dialect.* **1** the peak of a cap. **2** the beak of a bird or the nose or snout of an animal. **3** the projecting end of anything. [OE *nebb*]

NEB *abbrev. for:* **1** New English Bible. **2** National Enterprise Board.

Nebo ★ (ˈniːbəʊ) *n Mount.* a mountain in Jordan, northeast of the Dead Sea: the highest point of a ridge known as Pisgah, from which Moses viewed the Promised Land just before his death (Deuteronomy 34:1). Height: 802 m (2631 ft).

Nebr. *abbrev. for* Nebraska.

Nebraska ★ (nɪˈbræskə) *n* a state of the western US: consists of an undulating plain. Capital: Lincoln. Pop.: 1 652 093 (1996 est.). Area: 197 974 sq. km (76 483 sq. miles). Abbrevs.: **Nebr.** or (with zip code) **NE**
▶ Neˈbraskan *adj, n*

Nebuchadnezzar *or* **Nebuchadrezzar** ★ (ˌnɛbjʊkədˈnɛzə, -ˈdrɛzə) *n Old Testament.* a king of Babylon, 605–562 B.C., who conquered and destroyed Jerusalem and exiled the Jews to Babylon (II Kings 24–25).

nebula (ˈnɛbjʊlə) *n, pl* **nebulae** (-ˌliː) *or* **nebulas.** **1** *Astron.* a diffuse cloud of particles and gases visible either as a hazy patch of light (either an **emission** or **reflection nebula**) or an irregular dark region (**dark nebula**). **2** *Pathol.* opacity of the cornea. [C17: from L: mist, cloud]
▶ ˈnebular *adj*

nebular hypothesis *n* the theory that the solar system evolved from nebular matter.

nebulize *or* **nebulise** (ˈnɛbjʊˌlaɪz) *vb* **nebulizes, nebulizing, nebulized** *or* **nebulises, nebulising, nebulized.** (*tr*) to convert (a liquid) into a fine mist or spray; atomize.
▶ ˌnebuliˈzation *or* ˌnebuliˈsation *n*

nebulizer *or* **nebuliser** (ˈnɛbjʊˌlaɪzə) *n* a device for converting a drug in liquid form into a mist or fine spray which is inhaled through a mask to provide medication for the respiratory system.

nebulosity (ˌnɛbjʊˈlɒsɪtɪ) *n, pl* **nebulosities.** **1** the state of being nebulous. **2** *Astron.* a nebula.

nebulous (ˈnɛbjʊləs) *adj* **1** lacking definite form, shape, or content; vague or amorphous. **2** of a nebula. **3** *Rare.* misty or hazy.
▶ ˈnebulousness *n*

NEC *abbrev. for* National Executive Committee.

necessaries (ˈnɛsɪsərɪz) *pl n* (*sometimes sing*) what is needed; essential items: *the necessaries of life.*

necessarily (ˈnɛsɪsərɪlɪ, ˌnɛsɪˈsɛrɪlɪ) *adv* **1** as an inevitable or natural consequence; as a certainty: *he won't necessarily come.* **2** as a certainty: *he won't necessarily come.*

necessary (ˈnɛsɪsərɪ) *adj* **1** needed to achieve a certain desired result; required. **2** inevitable: *the necessary conse-*

quences of your action. **3** *Logic.* **3a** (of a statement, formula, etc.) true under all interpretations. **3b** (of a proposition) determined to be true by its meaning, so that its denial would be self-contradictory. Cf. **sufficient** (sense 2). **4** *Rare.* compelled, as by necessity or law; not free. ◆ *n* **5** (preceded by *the*) *Inf.* the money required for a particular purpose. **6 do the necessary.** *Inf.* to do something that is necessary in a particular situation. ◆ See also **necessaries.** [C14: from L *necessārius* indispensable, from *necesse* unavoidable]

necessitarianism (nɪˌsɛsɪˈtɛərɪəˌnɪzəm) *n Philosophy.* another word for **determinism.**
▶ neˌcessiˈtarian *n, adj*

necessitate (nɪˈsɛsɪˌteɪt) *vb* **necessitates, necessitating, necessitated.** (*tr*) **1** to cause as an unavoidable result. **2** (*usually passive*) to compel or require (someone to do something).

necessitous (nɪˈsɛsɪtəs) *adj* very needy; destitute; poverty-stricken.

necessity (nɪˈsɛsɪtɪ) *n, pl* **necessities.** **1** (*sometimes pl*) something needed; prerequisite: *necessities of life.* **2** a condition or set of circumstances that inevitably requires a certain result: *it is a matter of necessity to wear formal clothes when meeting the Queen.* **3** the state or quality of being obligatory or unavoidable. **4** urgent requirement, as in an emergency. **5** poverty or want. **6** *Rare.* compulsion through laws of nature; fate. **7** *Logic.* the property of being necessary. **8 of necessity.** inevitably.

neck (nɛk) *n* **1** the part of an organism connecting the head with the body. **2** the part of a garment around the neck. **3** something resembling a neck in shape or position: *the neck of a bottle.* **4** *Anat.* a constricted portion of an organ or part. **5** a narrow strip of land; peninsula or isthmus. **6** a strait or channel. **7** the part of a violin, cello, etc., that extends from the body to the tuning pegs and supports the fingerboard. **8** a solid block of lava from an extinct volcano, exposed after erosion of the surrounding rock. **9** the length of a horse's head and neck taken as an approximate distance by which one horse beats another in a race: *to win by a neck.* **10** *Archit.* the narrow band at the top of the shaft of a column. **11** *Inf.* impudence or cheek. **12 get it in the neck.** *Inf.* to be reprimanded or punished severely. **13 neck and neck.** absolutely level in a race or competition. **14 neck of the woods.** *Inf.* a particular area: *what brings you to this neck of the woods?* **15 neck or nothing.** at any cost. **16 save one's** *or* **someone's neck.** *Inf.* to escape from or help someone else to escape from a difficult or dangerous situation. **17 stick one's neck out.** *Inf.* to risk criticism, ridicule, etc., by speaking one's mind. ◆ *vb* **18** (*intr*) *Inf.* to kiss or fondle someone or one another passionately. [OE *hnecca*]

Neckar ★ (ˈnɛkɑː) *n* a river in SW Germany, rising in the Black Forest and flowing generally north into the Rhine at Mannheim. Length: 394 km (245 miles).

neckband (ˈnɛkˌbænd) *n* a band around the neck of a garment as finishing, decoration, or a base for a collar.

neckcloth (ˈnɛkˌklɒθ) *n* a large ornamental usually white cravat worn formerly by men.

neckerchief (ˈnɛkətʃɪf, -ˌtʃiːf) *n* a piece of ornamental cloth, often square, worn round the neck. [C14: from NECK + KERCHIEF]

necking (ˈnɛkɪŋ) *n Inf.* the activity of kissing and embracing lovingly.

necklace (ˈnɛklɪs) *n* **1** a chain, band, or cord, often bearing beads, pearls, jewels, etc., worn around the neck as an ornament, esp. by women. **2** (in South Africa) **2a** a tyre soaked in petrol, placed round a person's neck, and set on fire in order to burn the person to death. **2b** (*as modifier*): *necklace victims.* ◆ *vb* **necklaces, necklacing, necklaced.** (*tr*) **3** (in South Africa) to kill (a person) by means of a necklace.

neckline (ˈnɛkˌlaɪn) *n* the shape or position of the upper edge of a dress, blouse, etc.

necktie (ˈnɛkˌtaɪ) *n* the US name for **tie** (sense 10).

neckwear (ˈnɛkˌwɛə) *n* articles of clothing, such as ties, scarves, etc., worn round the neck.

necro- *or before a vowel* **necr-** *combining form.* indicating

---

★ people and places

death, a dead body, or dead tissue: *necrosis.* [from Gk *nekros* corpse]

necrobiosis (ˌnɛkrəʊbaɪˈəʊsɪs) *n Physiol.* the normal degeneration and death of cells.

necrolatry (nɛˈkrɒlətrɪ) *n* the worship of the dead.

necrology (nɛˈkrɒlədʒɪ) *n, pl* **necrologies. 1** a list of people recently dead. **2** a less common word for **obituary.**
▶ **necrological** (ˌnɛkrəˈlɒdʒɪkˀl) *adj*

necromancy (ˈnɛkrəʊˌmænsɪ) *n* **1** the art of supposedly conjuring up the dead, esp. in order to obtain from them knowledge of the future. **2** black magic; sorcery. [C13: (sense 1) ult. from Gk *nekromanteia,* from *nekros* corpse; (sense 2) from Med. L *nigromantia,* from L *niger* black, which replaced *necro-* through folk etymology]
▶ **ˈnecroˌmancer** *n* ▶ ˌ**necroˈmantic** *adj*

necrophilia (ˌnɛkrəʊˈfɪlɪə) *n* sexual attraction for or sexual intercourse with dead bodies. Also called: **necromania, necrophilism.**
▶ **necrophile** (ˈnɛkrəʊˌfaɪl) *n* ▶ ˌ**necroˈphilic** *adj*

necropolis (nɛˈkrɒpəlɪs) *n, pl* **necropolises** or **necropoleis** (-ˌleɪs). a burial site or cemetery. [C19: from Gk, from *nekros* dead + *polis* city]

necropsy (ˈnɛkrɒpsɪ) or **necroscopy** (nɛˈkrɒskəpɪ) *n, pl* **necropsies** or **necroscopies.** another name for **autopsy.** [C19: from Gk *nekros* dead body + *opsis* sight]

necrosis (nɛˈkrəʊsɪs) *n* **1** the death of one or more cells in the body, usually within a localized area, as from an interruption of the blood supply. **2** death of plant tissue due to disease, frost, etc. [C17: NL, from Gk *nekrōsis,* from *nekroun* to kill, from *nekros* corpse]
▶ **necrotic** (nɛˈkrɒtɪk) *adj*

nectar (ˈnɛktə) *n* **1** a sugary fluid produced in the nectaries of flowers and collected by bees. **2** *Classical myth.* the drink of the gods. Cf. **ambrosia** (sense 1). **3** any delicious drink. [C16: via L from Gk *néktar*]
▶ **ˈnectarous** *adj*

nectarine (ˈnɛktərɪn) *n* **1** a variety of peach tree. **2** the smooth-skinned fruit of this tree. [C17: apparently from NECTAR]

nectary (ˈnɛktərɪ) *n, pl* **nectaries.** any of various structures secreting nectar that occur in the flowers, leaves, stipules, etc., of a plant. [C18: from NL *nectarium,* from NECTAR]

ned (nɛd) *n Scot. sl.* a hooligan. [from ?]

NEDC *abbrev.* for National Economic Development Council. Also (inf.): **Neddy** (ˈnɛdɪ).

neddy (ˈnɛdɪ) *n, pl* **neddies.** a child's word for a **donkey.** [C18: from *Ned,* pet form of *Edward*]

Nederland ★ (ˈneːdərlɑnt) *n* the Dutch name for the **Netherlands.**

née or **nee** (neɪ) *adj* indicating the maiden name of a married woman: *Mrs Bloggs née Blandish.* [C19: from F: p.p. (fem) of *naître* to be born, from L *nascī*]

need (niːd) *vb* **1** (*tr*) to be in want of: *to need money.* **2** (*tr*) to be obliged: *to need to do more work.* **3** (takes an infinitive without *to*) used as an auxiliary to express necessity or obligation and does not add *-s* when used with *he, she, it,* and singular nouns: *need he go?* **4** (*intr*) *Arch.* to be essential to: *there needs no reason for this.* ♦ *n* **5** the fact or an instance of feeling the lack of something: *he has need of a new coat.* **6** a requirement: *the need for vengeance.* **7** necessity or obligation: *no need to be frightened.* **8** distress: *a friend in need.* **9** poverty or destitution. ♦ See also **needs.** [OE *nēad, nied*]

needful (ˈniːdfʊl) *adj* **1** necessary; required. **2** *Arch.* poverty-stricken. ♦ *n* **3 the needful.** *Inf.* what is necessary, esp. money.
▶ **ˈneedfulness** *n*

needle (ˈniːdˀl) *n* **1** a pointed slender piece of metal with a hole in it through which thread is passed for sewing. **2** a somewhat larger rod with a point at one end, used in knitting. **3** a similar instrument with a hook at one end for crocheting. **4** a small thin pointed device, esp. one made of stainless steel, used to transmit the vibrations from a gramophone record to the pick-up. Cf. **stylus** (sense 3). **5** *Med.* the long hollow pointed part of a hypodermic syringe, which is inserted into the body. **6** *Sur-*

gery. a pointed instrument, often curved, for suturing, puncturing, or ligating. **7** a long narrow stiff leaf in which water loss is greatly reduced: *pine needles.* **8** any slender sharp spine. **9** a pointer on the scale of a measuring instrument. **10** short for **magnetic needle. 11** a sharp pointed instrument used in engraving. **12** anything long and pointed, such as an obelisk. **13** *Inf.* **13a** anger or intense rivalry, esp. in a sporting encounter. **13b** (*as modifier*): *a needle match.* **14 have** or **get the needle.** *Brit. inf.* to feel dislike, nervousness, or annoyance: *she got the needle after he had refused her invitation.* ♦ *vb* **needles, needling, needled.** (*tr*) **15** *Inf.* to goad or provoke, esp. by constant criticism. **16** to sew, embroider, or prick (fabric) with a needle. [OE *nǣdl*]

needlecord (ˈniːdˀlˌkɔːd) *n* a corduroy fabric with narrow ribs.

needlepoint (ˈniːdˀlˌpɔɪnt) *n* **1** embroidery done on canvas with various stitches so as to resemble tapestry. **2** another name for **point lace.**

needless (ˈniːdlɪs) *adj* not required; unnecessary.
▶ **ˈneedlessly** *adv* ▶ **ˈneedlessness** *n*

needle time *n* the limited time allocated by a radio channel to the broadcasting of music from records.

needlewoman (ˈniːdˀlˌwʊmən) *n, pl* **needlewomen.** a woman who does needlework; seamstress.

needlework (ˈniːdˀlˌwɜːk) *n* sewing and embroidery.

needs (niːdz) *adv* **1** (preceded by or foll. by *must*) of necessity: *we must needs go.* ♦ *pl n* **2** what is required; necessities: *his needs are modest.*

needy (ˈniːdɪ) *adj* **needier, neediest. a** in need of practical or emotional support; distressed. **b** (*as collective n;* preceded by *the*): *the needy.*

Néel ★ (*French* neɛl) *n* **Louis** (lwi). born 1904, French physicist, noted for his research on magnetism; shared the Nobel prize for physics in 1970.

ne'er (nɛə) *adv* a poetic contraction of **never.**

ne'er-do-well *n* **1** an improvident, irresponsible, or lazy person. ♦ *adj* **2** useless; worthless: *your ne'er-do-well schemes.*

nefarious (nɪˈfɛərɪəs) *adj* evil; wicked; sinful. [C17: from L *nefarius,* from *nefās* unlawful deed, from *nē* not + *fās* divine law]
▶ **neˈfariously** *adv* ▶ **neˈfariousness** *n*

Nefertiti (ˌnɛfəˈtiːtɪ) or **Nofretete** ★ *n* 14th century B.C., Egyptian queen; wife of Akhenaton.

neg. *abbrev.* for negative(ly).

negate (nɪˈgeɪt) *vb* **negates, negating, negated.** (*tr*) **1** to nullify; invalidate. **2** to contradict. [C17: from L *negāre,* from *neg-,* var. of *nec* not + *aio* I say]
▶ **neˈgator** or **neˈgater** *n*

negation (nɪˈgeɪʃən) *n* **1** the opposite or absence of something. **2** a negative thing or condition. **3** the act of negating. **4** *Logic.* a proposition that is the denial of another proposition and is true only if the original proposition is false.

negative (ˈnɛgətɪv) *adj* **1** expressing a refusal or denial: *a negative answer.* **2** lacking positive qualities, such as enthusiasm or optimism. **3** showing opposition or resistance. **4** measured in a direction opposite to that regarded as positive. **5** *Biol.* indicating movement or growth away from a stimulus: *negative geotropism.* **6** *Med.* indicating absence of the disease or condition for which a test was made. **7** another word for **minus** (senses 3b, 4). **8** *Physics.* **8a** (of an electric charge) having the same polarity as the charge of an electron. **8b** (of a body, system, ion, etc.) having a negative electric charge; having an excess of electrons. **9** short for **electronegative. 10** of or relating to a photographic negative. **11** *Logic.* (of a categorial proposition) denying the satisfaction by the subject of the predicate, as in *some men are irrational; no pigs have wings.* ♦ *n* **12** a statement or act of denial or refusal. **13** a negative thing. **14** *Photog.* a piece of photographic film or a plate, previously exposed and developed, showing an image that, in black-and-white photography, has a reversal of tones. **15** *Physics.* a negative object, such as a terminal or a plate in a voltaic cell. **16** a sentence or other linguistic element with a negative

meaning, as the English word *not*. **17** a quantity less than zero. **18** *Logic*. a negative proposition. **19 in the negative**. indicating denial or refusal. ◆ *vb* **negatives, negativing, negatived**. *(tr)* **20** to deny; negate. **21** to show to be false; disprove. **22** to refuse consent to or approval of: *the proposal was negatived*.
▸ **'negatively** *adv* ▸ **'negativeness** *or* **,nega'tivity** *n*

negative equity *n* the state of holding a property the value of which is less than the amount of mortgage still unpaid.

negative feedback *n* See **feedback**.

negative resistance *n* a characteristic of certain electronic components in which an increase in the applied voltage increases the resistance, producing a proportional decrease in current.

negative sign *n* the symbol (–) used to indicate a negative quantity or a subtraction.

negativism ('nɛgətɪv,ɪzəm) *n* **1** a tendency to be unconstructively critical. **2** any sceptical or derisive system of thought.
▸ **'negativist** *n, adj*

Negev ('nɛgɛv) *or* **Negeb** ★ ('nɛgɛb) *n* the S part of Israel, on the Gulf of Aqaba: a triangular-shaped semidesert region, with large areas under irrigation; scene of fighting between Israeli and Egyptian forces in 1948. Chief town: Beersheba. Area: 12 820 sq. km (4950 sq. miles).

neglect (nɪ'glɛkt) *vb* *(tr)* **1** to fail to give due care, attention, or time to: *to neglect a child*. **2** to fail (to do something) through carelessness: *he neglected to tell her*. **3** to disregard. ◆ *n* **4** lack of due care or attention; negligence: *the child starved through neglect*. **5** the act or an instance of neglecting or the state of being neglected. [C16: from L *neglegere*, from *nec* not + *legere* to select]

neglectful (nɪ'glɛktfʊl) *adj* (when *postpositive*, foll. by *of*) careless; heedless.

negligee *or* **negligée** ('nɛglɪ,ʒeɪ) *n* **1** a woman's light dressing gown, esp. one that is lace-trimmed. **2** a thin and revealing woman's nightdress. **3** (formerly) any informal women's attire. [C18: from F *négligée*, p.p. (fem) of *négliger* to NEGLECT]

negligence ('nɛglɪdʒəns) *n* **1** the state of being negligent. **2** a negligent act. **3** *Law*. a civil wrong whereby the defendant is in breach of a legal duty of care, resulting in injury to the plaintiff.

negligent ('nɛglɪdʒənt) *adj* **1** lacking attention, care, or concern; neglectful. **2** careless or nonchalant.
▸ **'negligently** *adv*

negligible ('nɛglɪdʒəbᵊl) *adj* so small, unimportant, etc., as to be not worth considering.
▸ **'negligibly** *adv*

negotiable (nɪ'gəʊʃəbᵊl) *adj* **1** able to be negotiated. **2** (of a bill of exchange, promissory note, etc.) legally transferable in title from one party to another.
▸ **ne,gotia'bility** *n*

negotiable instrument *n* a legal document, such as a cheque or bill of exchange, that is freely negotiable.

negotiate (nɪ'gəʊʃɪ,eɪt) *vb* **negotiates, negotiating, negotiated**. **1** to talk (with others) to achieve (an agreement, etc.). **2** *(tr)* to succeed in passing round or over. **3** *(tr)* *Finance*. **3a** to transfer (a negotiable commercial paper) to another in return for value received. **3b** to sell (financial assets). **3c** to arrange for (a loan). [C16: from L *negōtiārī* to do business, from *negōtium* business, from *nec* not + *ōtium* leisure]
▸ **ne,goti'ation** *n* ▸ **ne'goti,ator** *n*

Negress ('niːgrɪs) *n* a female Black person.

Negrillo (nɪ'grɪləʊ) *n, pl* **Negrillos** *or* **Negrilloes**. a member of a dwarfish Negroid race of central and southern Africa. [C19: from Sp., dim. of *negro* black]

Negri Sembilan ★ ('nɛgrɪ sɛm'biːlən) *n* a state of S Peninsular Malaysia: mostly mountainous, with large areas under paddy and rubber. Capital: Seremban. Pop.: 723 900 (1993 est.). Area: 6643 sq. km (2565 sq. miles).

Negrito (nɪ'griːtəʊ) *n, pl* **Negritos** *or* **Negritoes**. a member of any of various dwarfish Negroid peoples of SE Asia and Melanesia. [C19: from Sp., dim. of *negro* black]

negritude ('niːgrɪ,tjuːd, 'nɛg-) *n* **1** the fact of being a Negro. **2** awareness and cultivation of the Negro heritage, values, and culture. [C20: from F, from *nègre* NEGRO[1]]

Negro[1] ('niːgrəʊ) *Old-fashioned*. ◆ *n, pl* **Negroes**. **1** a member of any of the dark-skinned indigenous peoples of Africa and their descendants elsewhere. ◆ *adj* **2** relating to or characteristic of Negroes. [C16: from Sp. or Port.: black, from L *niger*]
▸ **'Negro,ism** *n*

Negro[2] ★ ('neɪgrəʊ, 'nɛg-) *n* **Río**. **1** a river in NW South America, rising in E Colombia (as the Guainía) and flowing east, then south as part of the border between Colombia and Venezuela, entering Brazil and continuing southeast to join the Amazon at Manáus. Length: about 2250 km (1400 miles). **2** a river in S central Argentina, formed by the confluence of the Neuquén and Limay Rivers and flowing east and southeast to the Atlantic. Length: about 1014 km (630 miles). **3** a river in central Uruguay, rising in S Brazil and flowing southwest into the Uruguay River. Length: about 467 km (290 miles).

Negroid ('niːgrɔɪd) *adj* **1** denoting, relating to, or belonging to one of the major racial groups of mankind, characterized by brown-black skin, tightly curled hair, a short nose, and full lips. ◆ *n* **2** a member of this racial group.

Negropont ★ ('nɛgrəʊ,pɒnt) *n* **1** the former English name for **Euboea**. **2** the medieval English name for **Chalcis**.

Negros ★ ('neɪgrəʊs; *Spanish* 'neɣrɒs) *n* an island of the central Philippines, one of the Visayan Islands. Capital: Bacolod. Pop.: 3 168 000 (1990 est.). Area: 13 670 sq. km (5278 sq. miles).

negus ('niːgəs) *n, pl* **neguses**. a hot drink of port and lemon juice, usually spiced and sweetened. [C18: after Col. Francis *Negus* (died 1732), its E inventor]

Negus ('niːgəs) *n, pl* **Neguses**. *History*. a title of the emperor of Ethiopia. [from Amharic: king]

Neh. *Bible*. *abbrev. for* Nehemiah.

Nehemiah ★ (,niːɪ'maɪə) *n Old Testament*. **1** a Jewish official at the court of Artaxerxes, king of Persia, who in 444 B.C. became a leader in the rebuilding of Jerusalem after the Babylonian captivity. **2** the book recounting the acts of Nehemiah.

Nehru ★ ('neəruː) *n* **1 Jawaharlal** (dʒəwəhə'laːl). 1889–1964, Indian statesman and first premier of the republic; imprisoned several times (1921–45) for noncooperation with Britain. **2** his father, **Motilal** (məʊtɪ'laːl), known as *Pandit Nehru*. 1861–1931, Indian nationalist; first president of the reconstructed Indian National Congress.

neigh (neɪ) *n* **1** the high-pitched cry of a horse. ◆ *vb* **2** to make a neigh or utter with a sound like a neigh. [OE *hnǣgan*]

neighbour *or US* **neighbor** ('neɪbə) *n* **1** a person who lives near or next to another. **2a** a person or thing near or next to another. **2b** (*as modifier*): *neighbour states*. ◆ *vb* **3** (when *intr*, often foll. by *on*) to be or live close to. [OE *nēahbūr*, from *nēah* NIGH + *būr*, *gebūr* dweller; see BOOR]
▸ **'neighbouring** *or US* **'neighboring** *adj*

neighbourhood *or US* **neighborhood** ('neɪbə,hʊd) *n* **1** the immediate environment; surroundings. **2** a district where people live. **3** the people in a particular area. **4** *Maths*. the set of all points whose distance from a given point is less than a specified value. **5** (*modifier*) living or situated in and serving the needs of a local area: *a neighbourhood community worker*. **6 in the neighbourhood of**. approximately.

neighbourhood watch *n* a scheme in which members of a community agree to take joint responsibility for keeping a watch on each other's property, as a way of preventing crime.

neighbourly *or US* **neighborly** ('neɪbəlɪ) *adj* kind, friendly, or sociable, as befits a neighbour.
▸ **'neighbourliness** *or US* **'neighborliness** *n*

Neill ★ (niːl) *n* **A(lexander) S(utherland)**. 1883–1973, Scottish progressive educationalist; founder (1921) of Summerhill school.

★ people and places

Neisse ★ ('naɪsə) n 1 Also called: Glatzer Neisse ('glɑːtsə). Polish name: Nysa. a river in SW Poland, rising on the northern Czech border and flowing northeast to join the Oder near Brzeg. Length: about 193 km (120 miles). 2 Also called: Lusatian Neisse. a river in E Europe, rising near Liberec, in the Czech Republic, and flowing north to join the Oder: forms part of the German-Polish border. Length: 225 km (140 miles).

neither ('naɪðə, 'niːðə) determiner 1a not one nor the other (of two). 1b (as pronoun): neither can win. ◆ conj 2 (coordinating) 2a (used preceding alternatives joined by nor) not: neither John nor Mary nor Joe went. 2b another word for nor (sense 2). ◆ adv (sentence modifier) 3 Not standard. another word for either (sense 4). [C13 (lit.: ne either not either): changed from OE nāwther, from nāhwæther, from nā not + hwæther which of two]

USAGE NOTE A verb following a compound subject that uses neither...(nor) should be in the singular if both subjects are in the singular: neither Jack nor John has done the work.

Nejd ★ (nɛʒd, neɪd) n a region of central Saudi Arabia: formerly an independent sultanate of Arabia; it was united with Hejaz to form the kingdom of Saudi Arabia (1932).

nekton ('nɛktɒn) n the population of free-swimming animals that inhabits the middle depths of a sea or lake. [C19: via G from Gk nēkton a swimming thing, from nēkhein to swim]

nelly ('nɛlɪ) n not on your nelly. (sentence substitute). Brit. sl. certainly not.

nelson ('nɛlsən) n any wrestling hold in which a wrestler places his arm or arms under his opponent's arm or arms from behind and exerts pressure with the palms of his hands on the back of his opponent's neck. [C19: from a proper name]

Nelson[1] ★ ('nɛlsən) n 1 a town in NW England, in E Lancashire: textile industry. Pop.: 29 120 (1991). 2 a port in New Zealand, on South Island on Tasman Bay. Pop.: 51 200 (1995 est.). 3 River. a river in central Canada, in N central Manitoba, flowing from Lake Winnipeg northeast to Hudson Bay. Length: about 650 km (400 miles).

Nelson[2] ★ ('nɛlsən) n Horatio, Viscount Nelson. 1758–1805, British naval commander during the Revolutionary and Napoleonic Wars. He destroyed French naval power at the battle of the Nile (1798); killed at Trafalgar (1805) after defeating Villeneuve's fleet.

Neman or **Nyeman** ★ (Russian 'njɛmən) n a river in central Europe, rising in Belarus and flowing generally northwest through Lithuania to the Baltic. Length: 937 km (582 miles). Polish name: Niemen.

nematic (nɪ'mætɪk) adj Chem. (of a substance) existing in or having a mesomorphic state in which a linear orientation of the molecules causes anisotropic properties. [C20: NEMAT(O)- (referring to the threadlike chains of molecules in liquid) + -IC]

nemato- or before a vowel **nemat-** combining form. indicating a threadlike form: nematocyst. [from Gk nēma thread]

nematocyst ('nɛmətə,sɪst, nɪ'mætə-) n a structure in coelenterates, such as jellyfish, consisting of a capsule containing a hollow coiled thread that can sting or paralyse.

nematode ('nɛmə,təʊd) n any of a class of unsegmented worms having a tough outer cuticle, including the hookworm and filaria. Also called: nematode worm, roundworm.

Nembutal ('nɛmbjʊ,tɑːl) n a trademark for pentobarbitone sodium.

Nemea ★ (nɪ'miːə) n (in ancient Greece) a valley in N Argolis in the NE Peloponnese; site of the Nemean Games, a Panhellenic festival and athletic competition held every other year.
▸ **Ne'mean** adj

Nemean lion n Greek myth. an enormous lion that was strangled by Hercules as his first labour.

nemertean (nɪ'mɜːtɪən) or **nemertine** ('nɛmə,taɪn) n 1 any of a class of soft flattened ribbon-like marine worms having an eversible threadlike proboscis. ◆ adj 2 of or belonging to the Nemertea. [C19: via NL from Gk Nēmertēs a NEREID]

nemesia (nɪ'miːzə) n any plant of a southern African genus cultivated for their brightly coloured flowers. [C19: NL, from Gk nemesion, name of a plant resembling this]

Nemesis ★ ('nɛmɪsɪs) n 1 Greek myth. the goddess of retribution and vengeance. 2 (pl Nemeses (-,siːz)). (sometimes not cap.) any agency of retribution and vengeance. [C16: via L from Gk: righteous wrath, from nemein to distribute what is due]

nemophila (nɛ'mɒfɪlə) n an annual trailing plant with blue flowers. [from Gk nemos grove + philos loving]

neo- or sometimes before a vowel **ne-** combining form. 1 (sometimes cap.) new, recent, or a modern form: neoclassicism; neocolonialism. 2 (usually cap.) the most recent subdivision of a geological period: Neogene. [from Gk neos new]

neoclassicism (,niːəʊ'klæsɪ,sɪzəm) n 1 a late 18th- and early 19th-century style in architecture and art, based on classical models. 2 Music. a movement of the 1920s that sought to avoid the emotionalism of late romantic music.
▸ **neoclassical** (,niːəʊ'klæsɪkˀl) or **neo'classic** adj

neocolonialism (,niːəʊkə'ləʊnɪə,lɪzəm) n (in the modern world) political control by an outside power of a country that is in theory independent, esp. through the domination of its economy.
▸ **,neoco'lonialist** n, adj

Neo-Darwinism (,niːəʊ'dɑːwɪn,ɪzəm) n a modern theory of evolution that relates Darwinism to the occurrence of inheritable variation by genetic mutation.

neodymium (,niːəʊ'dɪmɪəm) n a toxic silvery-white metallic element of the lanthanide series. Symbol: Nd; atomic no.: 60; atomic wt.: 144.24. [C19: NL; see NEO- + DIDYMIUM]

neogothic (,niːəʊ'gɒθɪk) n another name for Gothic Revival.

Neolithic (,niːə'lɪθɪk) n 1 the cultural period that was characterized by primitive farming and the use of polished stone and flint tools and weapons. ◆ adj 2 relating to this period.

neologism (nɪ'ɒlə,dʒɪzəm) or **neology** n, pl neologisms or neologies. 1 a newly coined word, or a phrase or familiar word used in a new sense. 2 the practice of using or introducing neologisms. [C18: via F from NEO- + -logism, from Gk logos word]
▸ **ne'ologist** n

neologize or **neologise** (nɪ'ɒlə,dʒaɪz) vb neologizes, neologizing, neologized or neologises, neologising, neologised. (intr) to invent or use neologisms.

neomycin (,niːəʊ'maɪsɪn) n an antibiotic obtained from the bacterium Streptomyces fradiae, administered in the treatment of skin and eye infections. [C20: from NEO- + Gk mukēs fungus + -IN]

neon ('niːɒn) n 1 a colourless odourless rare gaseous element occurring in trace amounts in the atmosphere: used in illuminated signs and lights. Symbol: Ne; atomic no.: 10; atomic wt.: 20.179. 2 (modifier) of or illuminated by neon: neon sign. [C19: via NL from Gk neon new]

neonatal (,niːəʊ'neɪtˀl) adj occurring in or relating to the first few weeks of life in human babies.
▸ **'neo,nate** n

neon light n a glass bulb or tube containing neon at low pressure that gives a pink or red glow when a voltage is applied.

neophyte ('niːəʊ,faɪt) n 1 a person newly converted to a religious faith. 2 a novice in a religious order. 3 a beginner. [C16: via Church L from New Testament Gk neophutos recently planted, from neos new + phuton a plant]

★ people and places

neoplasm ('niːəʊˌplæzəm) *n Pathol.* any abnormal new growth of tissue; tumour.

Neo-Platonism (ˌniːəʊ'pleɪtəˌnɪzəm) *n* a philosophical system which was developed in the 3rd century A.D. as a synthesis of Platonic, Pythagorean, and Aristotelian elements.
▶ **Neo-Platonic** (ˌniːəʊplə'tɒnɪk) *adj* ▶ ˌNeo-'Platonist *n, adj*

neoprene ('niːəʊˌpriːn) *n* a synthetic rubber obtained by the polymerization of chloroprene, a colourless liquid derivative of butadiene, resistant to oil and ageing and used in waterproof products. [C20: from NEO- + PR(OPYL) + -ENE]

Neoptolemus (ˌniːɒp'tɒləməs) ★ *n Greek myth.* a son of Achilles and slayer of King Priam of Troy. Also called: **Pyrrhus.**

neoteny (nɪ'ɒtənɪ) *n* the persistence of larval or fetal features in the adult form of an animal. [C19: from NL *neotenia*, from Gk NEO- + *teinein* to stretch]

neoteric (ˌniːəʊ'terɪk) *Rare.* ◆ *adj* **1** belonging to a new fashion or trend; modern. ◆ *n* **2** a new writer or philosopher. [C16: via LL from Gk *neōterikos* young, fresh, from *neoteros* younger, more recent, from *neos* new, recent]

Nepal ★ (nɪ'pɔːl) *n* a kingdom in S Asia: the world's only Hindu kingdom; united in 1768 by the Gurkhas; consists of swampy jungle in the south and great massifs, valleys, and gorges of the Himalayas over the rest of the country, with many peaks over 8000 m (26 000 ft) (notably Everest and Kangchenjunga). A multiparty democracy was instituted in 1990. Official language: Nepali. Official religion: Hindu and Mahayana Buddhist. Currency: rupee. Capital: Katmandu. Pop.: 20 892 000 (1996). Area: 147 181 sq. km (56 815 sq. miles).
▶ **Nepalese** (ˌnepə'liːz) *adj, n*

Nepali (nɪ'pɔːlɪ) *n* **1** the official language of Nepal, also spoken in Sikkim and parts of India. **2** (*pl* **Nepali** or **Nepalis**) a native or inhabitant of Nepal; a Nepalese. ◆ *adj* **3** of or relating to Nepal, its inhabitants, or their language; Nepalese.

nepenthe (nɪ'penθɪ) or **nepenthes** (nɪ'penθiːz) *n* a drug that ancient writers referred to as a means of forgetting grief or trouble. [C16: via L from Gk *nēpenthes* sedative made from a herb, from *nē-* not + *penthos* grief]

nepeta ('nepɪtə, nə'piːtə) *n* any of a genus of plants found in N temperate regions. It includes catmint. [from L]

nephew ('nevjuː, 'nef-) *n* a son of one's sister or brother. [C13: from OF *neveu*, from L *nepōs*]

nephology (nɪ'fɒlədʒɪ) *n* the study of clouds. [C19: from Gk *nephos* cloud + -LOGY]

nephridium (nɪ'frɪdɪəm) *n, pl* **nephridia** (-ɪə). a simple excretory organ of many invertebrates, consisting of a tube through which waste products pass to the exterior. [C19: NL: little kidney]

nephrite ('nefraɪt) *n* a tough fibrous mineral: a variety of jade. Also called: **kidney stone.** [C18: via G from Gk *nephros* kidney; it was thought to help in kidney disorders]

nephritic (nɪ'frɪtɪk) *adj* **1** of or relating to the kidneys. **2** relating to or affected with nephritis.

nephritis (nɪ'fraɪtɪs) *n* inflammation of a kidney.

nephro- or before a vowel **nephr-** combining form. kidney or kidneys: *nephritis*. [from Gk *nephros*]

nephrology (nɪ'frɒlədʒɪ) *n* the branch of medicine concerned with diseases of the kidney.
▶ **ne'phrologist** *n*

nephron ('nefrɒn) *n* one of the units of the kidney that secretes urine, via ducts, into the ureter.

nephroscope ('nefrəˌskəʊp) *n* a tubular medical instrument inserted through an incision in the skin to enable examination of a kidney.
▶ **nephroscopy** (nɪ'frɒskəpɪ) *n*

ne plus ultra *Latin.* ('neɪ 'plʊs 'ʊltrɑː) *n* the extreme or perfect point or state. [lit.: not more beyond (that is, go no further), allegedly a warning to sailors inscribed on the Pillars of Hercules at Gibraltar]

nepotism ('nepəˌtɪzəm) *n* favouritism shown to relatives or close friends by those with power. [C17: from It. *nepotismo*, from *nepote* NEPHEW, from the former papal practice of granting favours to nephews or other relatives]
▶ **'nepotist** *n*

Neptune[1] ('neptjuːn) *n* the Roman god of the sea. Greek counterpart: **Poseidon.**

Neptune[2] ('neptjuːn) *n* the eighth planet from the sun, having two satellites, Triton and Nereid.

neptunium (nep'tjuːnɪəm) *n* a silvery metallic element synthesized in the production of plutonium and occurring in trace amounts in uranium ores. Symbol: Np; atomic no.: 93; half-life of most stable isotope, [237]Np: 2.14×10^6 years. [C20: from NEPTUNE[2], the planet beyond Uranus, because neptunium is beyond uranium in the periodic table]

NERC *abbrev. for* Natural Environment Research Council.

nerd or **nurd** (nɜːd) *n Sl.* **1** a boring or unpopular person, esp. one obsessed with something specified: *computer nerd.* **2** a stupid and feeble person. [C20: from ?]
▶ **'nerdish** or **'nurdish** *adj* ▶ **'nerdy** or **'nurdy** *adj*

Nereid ('nɪərɪɪd) *n, pl* **Nereides** (nə'riːədiːz). *Greek myth.* any of 50 sea nymphs who were the daughters of the sea god Nereus. [C17: via L from Gk]

Nereus ★ ('nɪərɪˌuːs) *n Greek myth.* a sea god who lived in the depths of the sea with his wife Doris and their daughters the Nereides.

Neri ★ ('nɪərɪ) *n* **Saint Philip.** Italian name *Filippo de' Neri.* 1515–95, Italian priest; founder of the Congregation of the Oratory (1564). Feast day: May 26.

nerine (nɪ'raɪnɪ; *S. African* nə'riːn) *n* any of a genus of bulbous plants native to South Africa and grown elsewhere as greenhouse plants for their pink, red, or orange flowers: includes the Guernsey lily. [after the water nymph *Nerine* in Roman myth]

Nernst ★ (*German* nernst) *n* **Walther Hermann** ('valtər 'herman). 1864–1941, German physical chemist who formulated the third law of thermodynamics: Nobel prize for chemistry 1920.

Nero ★ ('nɪərəʊ) *n* full name *Nero Claudius Caesar Drusus Germanicus;* original name *Lucius Domitius Ahenobarbus.* 37–68 A.D., Roman emperor (54–68). Notorious for his cruelty, he was alleged to have started the fire (64) that largely destroyed Rome.

neroli oil or **neroli** ('nɪərəlɪ) *n* a brown oil distilled from the flowers of various orange trees: used in perfumery. [C17: after Anne Marie de la Tremoïlle of *Neroli,* French-born It. princess believed to have discovered it]

Neruda ★ (*Spanish* ne'ruða) *n* **Pablo** ('paβlo), real name *Neftalí Ricardo Reyes.* 1904–73, Chilean poet. His works include *Canto general* (1950): Nobel prize for literature 1971.

Nerva ★ ('nɜːvə) *n* full name *Marcus Cocceius Nerva.* ?30–98 A.D., Roman emperor (96–98); adopted Trajan as his son and successor.

Nerval ★ (*French* nɛrval) *n* **Gérard de** (ʒerar də), real name *Gérard Labrunie.* 1808–55, French poet.

nervate ('nɜːveɪt) *adj* (of leaves) having veins.

nervation (nɜː'veɪʃən) or **nervature** ('nɜːvətʃə) *n* a less common word for **venation.**

nerve (nɜːv) *n* **1** any of the cordlike bundles of fibres that conduct impulses between the brain or spinal cord and another part of the body. **2** bravery or steadfastness. **3** **lose one's nerve.** to become timid, esp. failing to perform some audacious act. **4** *Inf.* effrontery; impudence. **5** muscle or sinew (often in **strain every nerve**). **6** a vein in a leaf or an insect's wing. ◆ *vb* **nerves, nerving, nerved.** (*tr*) **7** to give courage to (oneself); steel (oneself). **8** to provide with nerve or nerves. ◆ See also **nerves.** [C16: from L *nervus;* rel. to Gk *neuron*]

nerve block *n* induction of anaesthesia in a specific part of the body by injecting a local anaesthetic close to the sensory nerves that supply it.

nerve cell *n* another name for **neurone.**

nerve centre *n* **1** a group of nerve cells associated with a specific function. **2** a principal source of control over any complex activity.

★ people and places

nerve fibre *n* a threadlike extension of a nerve cell; axon.

nerve gas *n* any of various poisonous gases that have a paralysing effect on the central nervous system that can be fatal.

nerve impulse *n* the electrical wave transmitted along a nerve fibre, usually following stimulation of the nerve-cell body.

nerveless ('nɜːvlɪs) *adj* 1 calm and collected. 2 listless or feeble.
▸ **'nervelessly** *adv*

nerve-racking *or* **nerve-wracking** *adj* very distressing, exhausting, or harrowing.

nerves (nɜːvz) *pl n Inf.* 1 the imagined source of emotional control: *my nerves won't stand it.* 2 anxiety, tension, or imbalance: *she's all nerves.* 3 **get on one's nerves.** to irritate or upset one.

nervine ('nɜːviːn) *adj* 1 having a soothing effect upon the nerves. ◆ *n* 2 a nervine agent. [C17: from NL *nervīnus*, from L *nervus* NERVE]

nervous ('nɜːvəs) *adj* 1 very excitable or sensitive; highly strung. 2 (*often foll. by of*) apprehensive or worried. 3 of or containing nerves: *nervous tissue.* 4 affecting the nerves or nervous tissue: *a nervous disease.* 5 *Arch.* vigorous or forceful.
▸ **'nervously** *adv* ▸ **'nervousness** *n*

nervous breakdown *n* any mental illness not primarily of organic origin, in which the patient ceases to function properly, often accompanied by severely impaired concentration, anxiety, insomnia, and lack of self-esteem.

nervous system *n* the sensory and control apparatus of animals, consisting of a network of neurones.

nervure ('nɜːvjʊə) *n* 1 *Entomol.* any of the chitinous rods that form the framework of an insect's wing; vein. 2 *Bot.* any of the veins of a leaf. [C19: from F; see NERVE, -URE]

nervy ('nɜːvɪ) *adj* **nervier, nerviest.** 1 *Brit. inf.* tense or apprehensive. 2 having or needing bravery or endurance. 3 *US & Canad. inf.* brash or cheeky. 4 *Arch.* muscular; sinewy.

nescience ('nɛsɪəns) *n* a formal or literary word for **ignorance.** [C17: from LL *nescientia*, from L *nescīre* to be ignorant of, from *ne* not + *scīre* to know]
▸ **'nescient** *adj*

ness (nɛs) *n Arch.* a promontory or headland. [OE *næs* headland]

Ness (nɛs) ★ *n* **Loch.** a lake in NW Scotland, in the Great Glen: said to be inhabited by a legendary aquatic monster. Length: 36 km (22.5 miles). Depth: 229 m (754 ft).

-ness *suffix forming nouns chiefly from adjectives and participles.* indicating state, condition, or quality: *greatness; selfishness.* [OE *-nes*, of Gmc origin]

Nessus ('nɛsəs) ★ *n Greek myth.* a centaur that killed Hercules. A garment dipped in its blood fatally poisoned Hercules, who had been given it by Deianira who thought it was a love charm.

nest (nɛst) *n* 1 a place or structure in which birds, fishes, etc., lay eggs or give birth to young. 2 a number of animals of the same species occupying a common habitat: *an ants' nest.* 3 a place fostering something undesirable: *a nest of thievery.* 4 a cosy or secluded place. 5 a set of things, usually of graduated sizes, designed to fit together: *a nest of tables.* ◆ *vb* 6 (*intr*) to make or inhabit a nest. 7 (*intr*) to hunt for birds' nests. 8 (*tr*) to place in a nest. 9 *Computing.* to position data within other data at different ranks or levels so that the different levels of data can be used or accessed recursively. [OE]

nest egg *n* 1 a fund of money kept in reserve; savings. 2 a natural or artificial egg left in a nest to induce hens to lay their eggs in it.

nestle ('nɛsəl) *vb* **nestles, nestling, nestled.** 1 (*intr; often foll. by up or down*) to snuggle, settle, or cuddle closely. 2 (*intr*) to be in a sheltered position; lie snugly. 3 (*tr*) to shelter or place snugly or partly concealed, as in a nest. [OE *nestlian*]

nestling ('nɛstlɪŋ, 'nɛslɪŋ) *n* **a** a young bird not yet fledged. **b** (*as modifier*): *a nestling thrush.* [C14: from NEST + -LING¹]

Nestor ('nɛstɔː) ★ ('nɛstɔː) *n Greek myth.* the oldest and wisest of the Greeks in the Trojan War.

Nestorius (nɛ'stɔːrɪəs) ★ *n* died ?451 A.D., Syrian patriarch of Constantinople (428–431); deposed by the Council of Ephesus.

net¹ (nɛt) *n* 1 an openwork fabric of string, wire, etc.; mesh. 2 a device made of net, used to protect or enclose things or to trap animals. 3 a thin light mesh fabric used for curtains, etc. 4 a plan, strategy, etc., intended to trap or ensnare: *the murderer slipped through the police net.* 5 *Tennis, badminton, etc.* 5a a strip of net that divides the playing area into two equal parts. 5b a shot that hits the net. 6 the goal in soccer, hockey, etc. 7 (*often pl*) *Cricket.* 7a a pitch surrounded by netting, used for practice. 7b a practice session in a net. 8 *Inf.* short for **Internet.** 9 another word for **network** (sense 2). ◆ *vb* **nets, netting, netted.** 10 (*tr*) to ensnare. 11 (*tr*) to shelter or surround with a net. 12 (*intr*) *Tennis, badminton, etc.* to hit a shot into the net. 13 to make a net out of (rope, string, etc.). [OE *net*; rel. to Gothic *nati*, Du. *net*]

net² *or* **nett** (nɛt) *adj* 1 remaining after all deductions, as for taxes, expenses, losses, etc.: *net profit.* Cf. **gross** (sense 2). 2 (of weight) after deducting tare. 3 final; conclusive (esp. in **net result**). ◆ *n* 4 net income, profits, weight, etc. ◆ *vb* **nets, netting, netted.** 5 (*tr*) to yield or earn as clear profit. [C14: clean, neat, from F *net* NEAT¹]

Netaji ('neɪtɑːdʒɪ) ★ *n* the title for (Subhash Chandra) **Bose.** [Hindi, from *neta* leader + *-ji*, suffix denoting respect]

Netanyahu (nɛtⁿjɑːhuː) ★ *n* **Benjamin** ('bɪnjæˌmiːn). born 1949, Israeli politician: prime minister from 1996.

net asset value *n* the total value of the assets of an organization less its liabilities and capital charges. Abbrev.: **NAV.**

netball ('nɛtˌbɔːl) *n* a game for two teams of seven players (usually women) played on a hard court. Points are scored by shooting the ball through a net hanging from a ring at the top of a pole.

Net Book Agreement *n* a former (until 1995) agreement between UK publishers and booksellers that prohibited booksellers from reducing the price of books. Abbrev.: **NBA.**

net domestic product *n Econ.* the gross domestic product minus an allowance for the depreciation of capital goods. Abbrev.: **NDP.**

Neth. *abbrev. for* Netherlands.

nether ('nɛðə) *adj* below, beneath, or underground: *nether regions.* [OE *niothera, nithera,* lit.: further down, from *nither* down]

Netherlands ('nɛðələndz) ★ *n* (*functioning as sing or pl*) **the. 1** Also called: **Holland.** a kingdom in NW Europe, on the North Sea: declared independence from Spain in 1581 as the United Provinces; became a major maritime and commercial power in the 17th century, gaining many overseas possessions; a member of the European Union. It is mostly flat and low-lying, with about 40 per cent of the land being below sea level, much of it on polders protected by dykes. Official language: Dutch. Religion: Christian majority with both Protestant and Roman Catholic Churches. Currency: guilder and euro. Capital: Amsterdam, with the seat of government at The Hague. Pop.: 15 589 000 (1996). Area: 41 526 sq. km (16 033 sq. miles). Dutch name: **Nederland. 2** the kingdom of the Netherlands together with the Flemish-speaking part of Belgium, esp. as ruled by Spain and Austria before 1581; the Low Countries.
▸ **Netherlander** ('nɛðəˌlændə) *n*

Netherlands Antilles ★ *pl n* **the.** two groups of islands in the Caribbean, in the Lesser Antilles: overseas division of the Netherlands, consisting of the S group of Curaçao, Aruba, and Bonaire, and the N group of St Eustatius, Saba, and the S part of St Martin; economy based on refining oil from Venezuela. Capital: Willemstad (on Curaçao). Pop.: 202 244 (1994 est.). Area: 996 sq. km (390 sq. miles). Former name: **Curaçao** (until 1949), **Dutch West Indies, Netherlands West Indies.**

Netherlands East Indies ★ *pl n* **the.** a former name (1798–1945) for **Indonesia.**

Netherlands Guiana ★ *n* a former name for **Surinam.**

Netherlands West Indies ★ *pl n the.* a former name for the **Netherlands Antilles.**

nethermost ('nɛðə,məʊst) *adj the.* farthest down; lowest.

nether world *n* **1** the underworld. **2** hell. ◆ Also called: **nether regions.**

netiquette ('nɛtɪ,kɛt) *n* the informal code of behaviour on the Internet. [C20: from NET(WORK) + (ET)IQUETTE]

net national product *n* gross national product minus an allowance for the depreciation of capital goods. Abbrev.: **NNP.**

net present value *n Accounting.* an assessment of the long-term profitability of a project made by adding together all the revenue it can be expected to achieve over its whole life and deducting all the costs involved. Abbrev.: **NPV.**

net profit *n* gross profit minus all operating costs not included in the calculation of gross profit, esp. wages, overheads, and depreciation.

net realizable value *n* the net value of an asset if it were to be sold. Abbrev.: **NRV.**

net statutory income *n* (in Britain) the total taxable income of a person for the tax assessment year, after the deduction of personal allowances.

netsuke ('nɛtsʊki) *n* (in Japan) a carved toggle, esp. of wood or ivory, originally used to tether a medicine box, purse, etc., worn dangling from the waist. [C19: from Japanese]

nett (nɛt) *adj, n, vb* a variant spelling of **net**².

netting ('nɛtɪŋ) *n* any netted fabric or structure.

nettle ('nɛtᵊl) *n* **1** a plant having serrated leaves with stinging hairs and greenish flowers. **2** any of various other plants with stinging hairs or spines. **3** any of various plants that resemble nettles, such as the dead-nettle. **4 grasp the nettle.** to attempt something with boldness and courage. ◆ *vb* **nettles, nettling, nettled.** (*tr*) **5** to bother; irritate. **6** to sting as a nettle does. [OE *netele*]

nettle rash *n* a nontechnical name for **urticaria.**

network ('nɛt,wɜːk) *n* **1** an interconnected group or system: *a network of shops.* **2** a system of intersecting lines, roads, veins, etc. **3** another name for **net**¹ (sense 1) or **netting. 4** *Radio & TV.* a group of broadcasting stations that all transmit the same programme simultaneously. **5** *Computing.* a system of interconnected computer systems, terminals, and other equipment. **6** *Electronics.* a system of interconnected components or circuits. ◆ *vb* **7** *Radio & TV.* to broadcast over a network. **8** (of computers, terminals, etc.) to connect or be connected. **9** (*intr*) to form business contacts through informal social meetings.

Neubrandenburg ★ (*German* nɔy'brandənburk) *n* a city in NE Germany, in Mecklenburg-West Pomerania: 14th-century city walls. Pop.: 87 880 (1991).

Neuchâtel ★ (*French* nøʃatɛl) *n* **1** a canton in the Jura Mountains of W Switzerland. Capital: Neuchâtel. Pop.: 164 176 (1995 est.). Area: 798 sq. km (308 sq. miles). **2** a town in W Switzerland, capital of Neuchâtel canton, on Lake Neuchâtel: until 1848 the seat of the last hereditary rulers in Switzerland. Pop.: 158 569 (1990). **3** *Lake.* a lake in W Switzerland: the largest lake wholly in Switzerland. Area: 216 sq. km (83 sq. miles). ◆ German name (for senses 1, 2): **Neuenburg** ('nɔyənburk).

Neuilly-sur-Seine ★ (*French* nœjisyrsɛn) *n* a town in N France, on the Seine: a suburb of NW Paris. Pop.: 61 768 (1990).

Neumann ★ *n* **1** (*German* 'nɔyman). **Johann Balthasar** (jo-'han 'baltazar). 1687–1753, German rococo architect. **2** ('njuːmən). See (John) **von Neumann.**

neume *or* **neum** (njuːm) *n Music.* one of a series of notational symbols used before the 14th century. [C15: from Med. L *neuma* group of notes sung on one breath, from Gk *pneuma* breath]

Neumünster ★ (*German* nɔy'mynstər) *n* a town in N Germany, in Schleswig-Holstein: manufacturing of textiles and machinery. Pop.: 81 175 (1991).

neural ('njʊərəl) *adj* of or relating to a nerve or the nervous system.
▸ **'neurally** *adv*

neural chip *n* another name for **neurochip.**

neural computer *n* another name for **neurocomputer.**

neuralgia (njuˈrældʒə) *n* severe spasmodic pain caused by damage to or malfunctioning of a nerve and often following the course of the nerve.
▸ **neuˈralgic** *adj*

neural tube *n* the embryonic brain and spinal cord in mammals. Incomplete development results in **neural-tube defects,** such as spina bifida, in a newborn baby.

neurasthenia (,njʊərəsˈθiːnɪə) *n* (no longer in technical use) a neurosis characterized by extreme lassitude and inability to cope with any but the most trivial tasks.

neuritis (njuˈraɪtɪs) *n* inflammation of a nerve or nerves, often accompanied by pain and loss of function in the affected part.
▸ **neuritic** (njuˈrɪtɪk) *adj*

neuro- *or before a vowel* **neur-** *combining form.* indicating a nerve or the nervous system: *neurology.* [from Gk *neuron* nerve; rel. to L *nervus*]

neurobiology (,njʊərəʊbaɪˈɒlədʒɪ) *n* the study of the anatomy, physiology, and biochemistry of the nervous system.
▸ **,neurobiˈologist** *n*

neurochip ('njʊərəʊ,tʃɪp) *n Computing.* a semiconductor chip designed for use in an electronic neural network. Also called: **neural chip.**

neurocomputer ('njʊərəʊkəm,pjuːtə) *n* a type of computer designed to mimic the action of the human brain by use of an electronic neural network. Also called: **neural computer.**

neuroendocrine (,njʊərəʊˈɛndəʊ,kraɪn) *adj* of, relating to, or denoting the dual control of certain body functions by both nervous and hormonal stimulation: *neuroendocrine system.*

neuroglia (njuˈrɒglɪə) *n* another name for **glia.**

neurohormone ('njʊərəʊ,hɔːməʊn) *n* a hormone, such as noradrenaline, that is produced by specialized nervous tissue rather than by endocrine glands.

neurolemma (,njʊərəʊˈlɛmə) *n* the thin membrane that forms a sheath around nerve fibres. [C19: NL, from NEURO- + Gk *eilēma* covering]

neurology (njuˈrɒlədʒɪ) *n* the study of the anatomy, physiology, and diseases of the nervous system.
▸ **neurological** (,njʊərəˈlɒdʒɪkˈl) *adj*

neuromuscular (,njʊərəʊˈmʌskjʊlə) *adj* of, relating to, or affecting nerves and muscles.

neurone ('njʊərəʊn) *or* **neuron** ('njʊərɒn) *n* a cell specialized to conduct nerve impulses: consists of a cell body, axon, and dendrites. Also called: **nerve cell.**
▸ **neuˈronal** *adj* ▸ **neuronic** (njuˈrɒnɪk) *adj*

neuropathology (,njʊərəʊpəˈθɒlədʒɪ) *n* the study of diseases of the nervous system.

neuropathy (njuˈrɒpəθɪ) *n* any disease of the nervous system.
▸ **neuropathic** (,njʊərəʊˈpæθɪk) *adj* ▸ **,neuroˈpathically** *adv*

neurophysiology (,njʊərəʊ,fɪzɪˈɒlədʒɪ) *n* the study of the functions of the nervous system.
▸ **neurophysiological** (,njʊərəʊ,fɪzɪəˈlɒdʒɪkˈl) *adj*

neuropterous (njuˈrɒptərəs) *or* **neuropteran** *adj* of or belonging to an order of insects having two pairs of large much-veined wings and biting mouthparts. [C18: from NL *Neuroptera,* from NEURO- + Gk *pteron* wing]

neuroscience ('njʊərəʊsaɪəns) *n* the study of the anatomy, physiology, and biochemistry of the nervous system.

neurosis (njuˈrəʊsɪs) *n, pl* **neuroses** (-siːz). a relatively mild mental disorder, characterized by hysteria, anxiety, depression, or obsessive behaviour.

neurosurgery (,njʊərəʊˈsɜːdʒərɪ) *n* the branch of surgery concerned with the nervous system.
▸ **,neuroˈsurgical** *adj*

neurotic (njuˈrɒtɪk) *adj* **1** of or afflicted by neurosis. ◆

★ **people and places**

2 a person who is afflicted with a neurosis or who tends to be emotionally unstable. ▶ **neu'rotically** *adv* ▶ **neu'roti,cism** *n*

neurotomy (njuˈrɒtəmɪ) *n, pl* **neurotomies**. the surgical cutting of a nerve.

neurotransmitter (,njuərəʊtrænzˈmɪtə) *n* a chemical by which a nerve cell communicates with another nerve cell or with a muscle.

Neusatz ★ (ˈnɔyzats) *n* the German name for **Novi Sad**.

Neuss ★ (*German* nɔys) *n* an industrial city in W Germany, in North Rhine-Westphalia west of Düsseldorf: founded as a Roman fortress in the 1st century A.D. Pop.: 148 870 (1995 est.). Latin name: **Noˈvaesium**.

Neustria ★ (ˈnjuːstrɪə) *n* the western part of the kingdom of the Merovingian Franks formed in 561 A.D. in what is now N France. ▶ ˈ**Neustrian** *adj*

neuter (ˈnjuːtə) *adj* **1** *Grammar*. **1a** denoting or belonging to a gender of nouns which do not specify the sex of their referents. **1b** (*as n*): *German "Mädchen" (meaning "girl") is a neuter*. **2** (of animals and plants) having nonfunctional, underdeveloped, or absent reproductive organs. **3** giving no indication of sex. ◆ *n* **4** a sexually underdeveloped female insect, such as a worker bee. **5** a castrated animal. ◆ *vb* **6** (*tr*) to castrate (an animal). [C14: from L, from *ne* not + *uter* either (of two)]

neutral (ˈnjuːtrəl) *adj* **1** not siding with any party to a war or dispute. **2** of or belonging to a neutral party, country, etc. **3** of no distinctive quality or type. **4** (of a colour) **4a** having no hue; achromatic. **4b** dull, but harmonizing with most other colours. **5** a less common term for **neuter** (sense 2). **6** *Chem*. neither acidic nor alkaline. **7** *Physics*. having zero charge or potential. **8** *Phonetics*. (of a vowel) articulated with the tongue relaxed in mid-central position: *"about" begins with a neutral vowel*. ◆ *n* **9** a neutral person, nation, etc. **10** a citizen of a neutral state. **11** the position of the controls of a gearbox that leaves the transmission disengaged. [C16: from L *neutrālis*; see NEUTER] ▶ ˈ**neutrally** *adv*

neutralism (ˈnjuːtrə,lɪzəm) *n* (in international affairs) the policy of noninvolvement or nonalignment with power blocs. ▶ ˈ**neutralist** *n*

neutrality (njuːˈtrælɪtɪ) *n* **1** the state of being neutral. **2** the condition of being chemically or electrically neutral.

neutralize *or* **neutralise** (ˈnjuːtrə,laɪz) *vb* **neutralizes, neutralizing, neutralized** *or* **neutralises, neutralising, neutralised**. (*mainly tr*) **1** (*also intr*) to render or become neutral by counteracting, mixing, etc. **2** (*also intr*) to make or become electrically or chemically neutral. **3** to exclude (a country) from warfare or alliances by international agreement: *the great powers neutralized Belgium in the 19th century*. ▶ ,**neutraliˈzation** *or* ,**neutraliˈsation** *n* ▶ ˈ**neutral,izer** *or* ˈ**neutral,iser** *n*

neutretto (njuːˈtrɛtəʊ) *n, pl* **neutrettos**. *Physics*. **1** the neutrino associated with the muon. **2** (formerly) any of various hypothetical neutral particles. [C20: from NEUTR(INO) + diminutive suffix *-etto*]

neutrino (njuːˈtriːnəʊ) *n, pl* **neutrinos**. *Physics*. a stable elementary particle with zero rest mass and spin ½ that travels at the speed of light. [C20: from It., dim. of *neutrone* NEUTRON]

neutron (ˈnjuːtrɒn) *n Physics*. a neutral elementary particle with approximately the same mass as a proton. In the nucleus of an atom it is stable but when free it decays. [C20: from NEUTRAL, on the model of ELECTRON]

neutron bomb *n* a type of nuclear weapon designed to cause little blast or long-lived radioactive contamination. The neutrons destroy all life in the target area. Technical name: **enhanced radiation weapon**.

neutron gun *n Physics*. a device used for producing a beam of fast neutrons.

neutron number *n* the number of neutrons in the nucleus of an atom. Symbol: *N*

neutron star *n* a star, composed solely of neutrons, that has collapsed under its own gravity.

Nev. *abbrev. for* Nevada.

Neva ★ (ˈniːvə; *Russian* nɪˈva) *n* a river in NW Russia, flowing west to the Gulf of Finland by the delta on which Saint Petersburg stands. Length: 74 km (46 miles).

Nevada ★ (nɪˈvɑːdə) *n* a state of the western US: lies almost wholly within the Great Basin, a vast desert plateau; noted for production of gold and copper. Capital: Carson City. Pop.: 1 603 163 (1996 est.). Area: 284 612 sq. km (109 889 sq. miles). Abbrevs.: **Nev.** or (with zip code) **NV**

névé (ˈnɛveɪ) *n* a mass of porous ice, formed from snow, that has not yet been frozen into glacier ice. [C19: from Swiss F *névé* glacier, from LL *nivātus* snow-cooled, from *nix* snow]

never (ˈnɛvə) *adv, sentence substitute*. **1** at no time; not ever. **2** certainly not; by no means; in no case. ◆ *sentence substitute*. **3** Also: **well I never!** surely not! [OE *næfre*, from *ne* not + *æfre* EVER]

> **USAGE NOTE** In informal speech and writing, *never* can be used instead of *not* with the simple past tenses of certain verbs, for emphasis (*I never said that; I never realized how clever he was*), but this usage should be avoided in serious writing.

nevermore (,nɛvəˈmɔː) *adv Literary*. never again.

never-never *Inf.* ◆ *n* **1** *Brit*. the hire-purchase system of buying. **2** *Austral*. remote desert country. ◆ *adj* **3** imaginary; idyllic (esp. in **never-never land**).

Nevers ★ (*French* nəvɛr) *n* a city in central France: capital of the former duchy of Nivernais; engineering industry. Pop.: 43 890 (1990).

nevertheless (,nɛvəðəˈlɛs) *sentence connector*. in spite of that; however; yet.

Nevis ★ *n* **1** (ˈniːvɪs, ˈnɛvɪs). an island in the Caribbean: part of St Kitts-Nevis; the volcanic cone of **Nevis Peak**, which rises to 1002 m (3287 ft), lies in the centre of the island. Capital: Charlestown. Pop.: 8794 (1991). Area: 129 sq. km (50 sq. miles). **2** (ˈnɛvɪs). See **Ben Nevis**.

Nevski ★ (ˈnɛfskɪ; *Russian* ˈnjefskij) *n* See **Alexander Nevski**.

new (njuː) *adj* **1a** recently made or brought into being. **1b** (*as collective n; preceded by the*): *the new*. **2** of a kind never before existing; novel: *a new concept in marketing*. **3** recently discovered: *a new comet*. **4** markedly different from what was before: *the new liberalism*. **5** (often foll. by *to* or *at*) recently introduced (to); inexperienced (in) or unaccustomed (to): *new to this neighbourhood*. **6** (*cap. in names or titles*) more or most recent of things with the same name: *the New Testament*. **7** (*prenominal*) fresh; additional: *send some new troops*. **8** (often foll. by *to*) unknown: *this is new to me*. **9** (of a cycle) beginning or occurring again: *a new year*. **10** (*prenominal*) (of crops) harvested early. **11** changed, esp. for the better: *she returned a new woman*. **12** up-to-date; fashionable. ◆ *adv* (*usually in combination*) **13** recently, freshly: *new-laid eggs*. **14** anew; again. ◆ See also **news**. [OE *nīowe*] ▶ ˈ**newness** *n*

New Age *n* **1a** a philosophy, originating in the late 1980s, characterized by a belief in alternative medicine, astrology, spiritualism, etc. **1b** (*as modifier*): *New Age therapies*. **2** short form for **New Age music**.

New Age music *or* **New Age** *n* a type of gentle melodic popular music originating in the US in the late 1980s, which takes in elements of jazz, folk, and classical music and is played largely on synthesizers and acoustic instruments.

New Amsterdam ★ *n* the Dutch settlement established on Manhattan (1624–26); capital of New Netherlands; captured by the English and renamed New York in 1664.

Newark ★ (ˈnjuːək) *n* **1** a town in N central England, in Nottinghamshire. Pop.: 35 129 (1991). Official name:

Newark-on-Trent. 2 a port in NE New Jersey, just west of New York City, on Newark Bay and the Passaic River: the largest city in the state; founded in 1666 by Puritans from Connecticut; industrial and commercial centre. Pop.: 258 751 (1994 est.).

New Australia ★ *n* the colony on socialist principles founded by William Lane in Paraguay in 1893.

New Australian *n* an Australian name for a recent immigrant, esp. one from Europe.

New Bedford ★ *n* a port and resort in SE Massachusetts, near Buzzards Bay: settled by Plymouth colonists in 1652; a leading whaling port (18th–19th centuries). Pop.: 94 623 (1994 est.).

newborn ('nju:ˌbɔːn) *adj* **1** recently or just born. **2** (of hope, faith, etc.) reborn.

New Britain ★ *n* an island in the S Pacific, northeast of New Guinea: the largest island of the Bismarck Archipelago; part of Papua New Guinea; mountainous, with several active volcanoes. Capital: Rabaul. Pop.: 312 955 (1990). Area: 36 519 sq. km (14 100 sq. miles).

New Brunswick ★ *n* a province of SE Canada on the Gulf of St Lawrence and the Bay of Fundy: extensively forested. Capital: Fredericton. Pop.: 760 100 (1995 est.). Area: 72 092 sq. km (27 835 sq. miles). Abbrev.: **NB**.

▶ **New Brunswicker** ('brʌnzwɪkə) *n*

new brutalism *n* another name for **brutalism**.

Newbury ★ ('nju:bərɪ) *n* a market town in S England, in Berkshire: scene of a Parliamentarian victory (1643) and a Royalist victory (1644) during the Civil War; racecourse. Pop.: 33 273 (1991).

New Caledonia ★ *n* an island in the SW Pacific, east of Australia: forms, with its dependencies, an overseas territory of France; discovered by Captain Cook in 1774; rich mineral resources. Capital: Nouméa. Pop.: 183 200 (1994 est.). Area: 19 103 sq. km (7374 miles). French name: **Nouvelle-Calédonie**.

New Canadian *n Canad.* a recent immigrant to Canada.

New Castile ★ *n* a region and former province of central Spain. Chief town: Toledo.

Newcastle[1] ★ ('nju:ˌkɑːsᵊl) *n* a port in SE Australia, in E New South Wales near the mouth of the Hunter River: important industrial centre, with extensive steel, metalworking, engineering, shipbuilding, and chemical industries: site of Australia's first fatal earthquake (1989). Pop.: 466 000 (1995 est.).

Newcastle[2] ★ ('nju:ˌkɑːsᵊl) *n* **Duke of,** the title of *Thomas Pelham Holles.* 1693–1768, English Whig prime minister (1754–56; 1757–62).

Newcastle-under-Lyme ★ *n* a town in W central England, in Staffordshire. Pop.: 73 731 (1991). Often shortened to **Newcastle**.

Newcastle upon Tyne ★ *n* **1** a port in NE England, in Tyne and Wear, near the mouth of the River Tyne opposite Gateshead: Roman remains; engineering industries; university (1937). Pop.: 189 150 (1991). Often shortened to **Newcastle**. **2** a unitary authority in NE England, in Tyne and Wear. Pop.: 283 600 (1994 est.). Area: 112 sq. km (43 sq. miles).

new chum *n* **1** *Austral.* a novice in any activity. **2** *Austral. & NZ inf.* (formerly) a recent British immigrant.

Newcomen ★ ('nju:ˌkʌmən) *n* **Thomas.** 1663–1729, English engineer who invented a steam engine.

newcomer ('nju:ˌkʌmə) *n* a person who has recently arrived or started to participate in something.

New Country *n* a style of country music of the late 1980s characterized by down-to-earth lyrics.

New Delhi ★ *n* See **Delhi**.

newel ('nju:əl) *n* **1** the central pillar of a winding staircase, esp. one that is made of stone. **2** Also called: **newel post**. the post at the top or bottom of a flight of stairs that supports the handrail. [C14: from OF *nouel* knob, from Med. L *nōdellus,* dim. of *nōdus* NODE]

New England ★ *n* **1** the NE part of the US, consisting of the states of Maine, New Hampshire, Vermont, Massachusetts, Rhode Island, and Connecticut: settled originally chiefly by Puritans in the mid-17th century. **2** a region in SE Australia, in the northern tablelands of New South Wales.

▶ **New Englander** *n*

New England Range ★ *n* a mountain range in SE Australia, in NE New South Wales: part of the Great Dividing Range. Highest peak: Ben Lomond, 1520 m (4986 ft).

New English Bible *n* a new translation of the Bible made between 1962 and 1970.

newfangled ('nju:'fæŋgᵊld) *adj* newly come into existence or fashion, esp. excessively modern. [C14 *newfangel* liking new things, from *new* + *-fangel,* from OE *fōn* to take]

New Forest ★ *n* a region of woodland and heath in S England, in SW Hampshire: a hunting ground of the West Saxon kings; tourist area, noted for its ponies. Area: 336 sq. km (130 sq. miles).

new-found *adj* newly or recently discovered: *new-found confidence.*

Newfoundland ★ ('nju:fəndlənd, -fənlənd, -ˌlænd; nju:'faʊndlənd) *n* **1** an island of E Canada, separated from the mainland by the Strait of Belle Isle: with the Coast of Labrador forms the province of Newfoundland; consists of a rugged plateau with the Long Range Mountains in the west. Area: 110 681 sq. km (42 734 sq. miles). **2** a province of E Canada, consisting of the island of Newfoundland and the Coast of Labrador. Capital: St John's. Pop.: 575 400 (1995 est.). Area: 404 519 sq. km (156 185 sq. miles). Abbrevs.: **Nfld** or **NF. 3** a large heavy breed of dog with a flat coarse usually black coat.

▶ **New'foundlander** *n*

New France ★ *n* the former French colonies and possessions in North America, most of which were lost to England and Spain by 1763: often restricted to the French possessions in Canada.

Newgate ★ ('nju:gɪt, -ˌgeɪt) *n* a famous London prison, demolished in 1902.

New Georgia ★ *n* **1** a group of islands in the SW Pacific, in the Solomon Islands. **2** the largest island in this group. Area: about 1300 sq. km (500 sq. miles).

New Granada ★ *n* **1** a former Spanish presidency and later viceroyalty in South America. At its greatest extent it consisted of present-day Panama, Colombia, Venezuela, and Ecuador. **2** the name of Colombia when it formed, with Panama, part of Great Colombia (1819–30).

New Guinea ★ *n* **1** an island in the W Pacific, north of Australia: divided politically into Irian Jaya (a province of Indonesia) in the west and Papua New Guinea in the east. There is a central chain of mountains and a lowland area of swamps in the south and along the Sepik River in the north. Area: 775 213 sq. km (299 310 sq. miles). **2 Trust Territory of.** (until 1975) an administrative division of the former Territory of Papua and New Guinea, consisting of the NE part of the island of New Guinea together with the Bismarck Archipelago; now part of Papua New Guinea.

Newham ★ ('nju:əm) *n* a borough of E Greater London, on the River Thames: established in 1965. Pop.: 226 800 (1994 est.). Area: 36 sq. km (14 sq. miles).

New Hampshire ★ *n* a state of the northeastern US: generally hilly. Capital: Concord. Pop.: 1 162 481 (1996 est.). Area: 23 379 sq. km (9027 sq. miles). Abbrevs.: **N.H.** or (with zip code) **NH**

New Harmony ★ *n* a village in SW Indiana, on the Wabash River: scene of two experimental cooperative communities, the first founded in 1815 by George Rapp, a German religious leader, and the second by Robert Owen in 1825.

Newhaven ★ ('nju:ˌheɪvᵊn) *n* a ferry port and resort on the S coast of England, in East Sussex. Pop.: 11 208 (1991).

New Haven ★ *n* an industrial city and port in S Connecticut, on Long Island Sound: settled in 1638 by English Puritans, who established it as a colony in 1643; seat of Yale University (1701). Pop.: 119 604 (1994 est.).

★ people and places

New Hebrides ★ *pl n* the former name (until 1980) of **Vanuatu.**

Ne Win ★ ('neɪ 'wɪn) *n* **U** (uː). born 1911, Burmese statesman; prime minister (1958–60) and president (1974–81).

New Ireland ★ *n* an island in the S Pacific, in the Bismarck Archipelago, separated from New Britain by St George's Channel: part of Papua New Guinea. Chief town and port: Kavieng. Pop.: 87 194 (1990). Area (including adjacent islands): 9850 sq. km (3800 sq. miles).

newish ('njuːɪʃ) *adj* fairly new.

new issue *n Stock Exchange.* an issue of shares being offered to the public for the first time.

New Jersey ★ *n* a state of the eastern US, on the Atlantic and Delaware Bay: mostly low-lying, with a heavy industrial area in the northeast and many coastal resorts. Capital: Trenton. Pop.: 7 987 933 (1996 est.). Area: 19 479 sq. km (7521 sq. miles). Abbrevs.: **N.J.** or (with zip code) **NJ**

New Jerusalem *n Christianity.* heaven.

New Journalism *n* a style of journalism using techniques borrowed from fiction to portray a situation or event as vividly as possible.

Newlands ★ ('njuːləndz) *n* **John Alexander.** 1838–98, British chemist: discovered the law of octaves.

New Latin *n* the form of Latin used since the Renaissance, esp. for scientific nomenclature.

New Look *n* **the.** a fashion in women's clothes introduced in 1947, characterized by long full skirts.

newly ('njuːlɪ) *adv* **1** recently. **2** again; anew: *newly raised hopes.* **3** in a new manner; differently: *a newly arranged hairdo.*

newlywed ('njuːlɪ,wɛd) *n* (*often pl*) a recently married person.

Newman ★ ('njuːmən) *n* **1** **John Henry.** 1801–90, British theologian. Originally an Anglican minister, he was prominent in the Oxford Movement before becoming a Roman Catholic priest (1847) and a cardinal (1879). **2** **Paul.** born 1925, US actor, whose films include *Butch Cassidy and the Sundance Kid* (1969), *The Sting* (1973), and *Twilight* (1998).

New Man *n* **the.** a type of modern man who allows the caring side of his nature to show by being supportive and by sharing child care and housework.

Newmarket ★ ('njuː,mɑːkɪt) *n* a town in SE England, in W Suffolk: a famous horse-racing centre since the reign of James I. Pop.: 18 430 (1991).

new maths *n* (*functioning as sing*) *Brit.* an approach to mathematics in which the basic principles of set theory are introduced at an elementary level.

New Mexico ★ *n* a state of the southwestern US: consists of high semiarid plateaus and mountains, crossed by the Rio Grande and the Pecos River; large Spanish-American and Indian populations; contains over two-thirds of US uranium reserves. Capital: Santa Fé. Pop.: 1 713 407 (1996 est.). Area: 314 451 sq. km (121 412 sq. miles). Abbrevs.: **N. Mex, N.M.,** or (with zip code) **NM** ▶ **New Mexican** *adj, n*

new moon *n* the moon when it appears as a narrow waxing crescent.

New Netherland ★ ('nɛðələnd) *n* a Dutch North American colony of the early 17th century, centred on the Hudson valley. Captured by the English in 1664, it was divided into New York and New Jersey.

New Orleans ★ ('ɔːliːənz, -lənz; ɔːˈliːnz) *n* a port in SE Louisiana, on the Mississippi River about 172 km (107 miles) from the sea: the largest city in the state and the second most important port in the US; founded by the French in 1718; belonged to Spain (1763–1803). It is largely below sea level, built around the Vieux Carré (French quarter); famous for its annual Mardi Gras festival and for its part in the history of jazz; a major commercial, industrial, and transportation centre. Pop.: 484 149 (1994 est.).

New Plymouth ★ *n* a port in New Zealand, on W North Island: founded in 1841. Pop.: 49 800 (1995 est.).

Newport ★ ('njuː,pɔːt) *n* **1** a port in SE Wales on the River Usk. Pop.: 129 900 (1991). **2** a county borough in SE Wales. Pop.: 133 318 (1996 est.). Area: 190 sq. km (73 sq. miles). **3** a port in SE Rhode Island: founded in 1639, it became one of the richest towns of colonial America; centre of a large number of US naval establishments. Pop.: 28 227 (1990). **4** a town in S England, administrative centre of the Isle of Wight. Pop.: 20 574 (1991).

Newport News ★ *n* (*functioning as sing*) a port in SE Virginia, at the mouth of the James River: an industrial centre, with one of the world's largest shipyards. Pop.: 179 127 (1994 est.).

New Providence ★ *n* an island in the Atlantic, in the Bahamas. Chief town: Nassau. Pop.: 172 196 (1990). Area: 150 sq. km (58 sq. miles).

New Quebec ★ *n* a region of E Canada, formerly the Ungava district of Northwest Territories (1895–1912), extending from the line of the Eastmain and Hamilton Rivers north between Hudson Bay and Labrador: absorbed by Quebec in 1912: contains extensive iron deposits. Area: about 777 000 sq. km (300 000 sq. miles).

New Romney ★ *n* a market town in SE England, in Kent on Romney Marsh: of early importance as one of the Cinque Ports, but is now over 1.6 km (1 mile) inland. Pop.: 5000 (latest est.). Former name (until 1563): **Romney.**

Newry ★ ('njuərɪ) *n* a port in Northern Ireland, in Co. Down: close to the border with the Republic of Ireland, it has been the scene of sectarian violence. Pop.: 22 975 (1991).

Newry and Mourne ★ (mɔːn) *n* a district of SE Northern Ireland, on the Irish Sea and bordering the Irish Republic: agriculture, textiles. Administrative centre: Newry. Pop.: 82 943 (1991). Area: 890 sq. km (344 sq. miles).

news (njuːz) *n* (*functioning as sing*) **1** important or interesting recent happenings. **2** information about such events, as in the mass media. **3 the news.** a presentation, such as a radio broadcast, of information of this type. **4** interesting or important information not previously known. **5** a person, fashion, etc., widely reported in the mass media: *she is news in the film world.* [C15: from ME *newes*, pl. of *newe* new (adj), a model of OF *noveles* or Med. L *nova* new things] ▶ **'newsless** *adj*

news agency *n* an organization that collects news reports for newspapers, etc. Also called: **press agency.**

newsagent ('njuːz,eɪdʒənt) *or US* **newsdealer** *n* a shopkeeper who sells newspapers, stationery, etc.

newscast ('njuːz,kɑːst) *n* a radio or television broadcast of the news. [C20: from NEWS + (BROAD)CAST] ▶ **'news,caster** *n*

news conference *n* another term for **press conference.**

newsflash ('njuːz,flæʃ) *n* a brief item of important news, often interrupting a radio or television programme.

newsgroup ('njuːz,gruːp) *n Computing.* a forum where subscribers exchange information about a specific subject by electronic mail.

New Siberian Islands ★ *pl n* an archipelago in the Arctic Ocean, off the N mainland of Russia, in the Sakha Republic. Area: about 37 555 sq. km (14 500 sq. miles).

newsletter ('njuːz,lɛtə) *n* **1** Also called: **news-sheet.** a printed periodical bulletin circulated to members of a group. **2** *History.* a written or printed account of the news.

newsmonger ('njuːz,mʌŋgə) *n Old-fashioned.* a gossip.

New South ★ *n Austral. inf.* short for **New South Wales.**

New South Wales ★ *n* a state of SE Australia: originally contained over half the continent, but was reduced by the formation of other states (1825–1911); consists of a narrow coastal plain, separated from extensive inland plains by the Great Dividing Range; the most populous state; mineral resources. Capital: Sydney. Pop.: 6 173 000 (1996 est.). Area: 801 428 sq. km (309 433 sq. miles).

New Spain ★ *n* a Spanish viceroyalty of the 16th to 19th centuries, composed of Mexico, Central America north of Panama, the Spanish West Indies, the south-western US, and the Philippines.

newspaper ('nju:z,peɪpə) n a weekly or daily publication consisting of folded sheets and containing articles on the news, features, reviews, and advertisements. Often shortened to **paper.**

newspaperman ('nju:z,peɪpə,mæn) n, pl **newspapermen.** 1 a person who works for a newspaper as a reporter or editor. 2 the owner or proprietor of a newspaper. 3 a person who sells newspapers in the street.

newspeak ('nju:,spi:k) n the language of bureaucrats and politicians, regarded as deliberately ambiguous and misleading. [C20: from *1984*, a novel by George Orwell]

newsprint ('nju:z,prɪnt) n an inexpensive wood-pulp paper used for newspapers.

newsreader ('nju:z,ri:də) n a news announcer on radio or television.

newsreel ('nju:z,ri:l) n a short film with a commentary presenting current events.

newsroom ('nju:z,ru:m, -,rum) n a room in a newspaper office, television station, etc., where news is received and prepared for publication or broadcasting.

newsstand ('nju:z,stænd) n a portable stand or stall from which newspapers are sold.

New Style n the present method of reckoning dates using the Gregorian calendar.

news vendor n a person who sells newspapers.

newsworthy ('nju:z,wɜ:ðɪ) adj sufficiently interesting to be reported in a news bulletin, etc.

newsy ('nju:zɪ) adj **newsier, newsiest.** full of news, esp. gossipy or personal news.

newt (nju:t) n any of various small semiaquatic amphibians having a long slender body and tail and short feeble legs. [C15: from *a newt*, a mistaken division of *an ewt; ewt*, from OE *eveta* EFT]

New Testament n a collection of writings composed soon after Christ's death and added to the Jewish writings of the Old Testament to make up the Christian Bible.

newton ('nju:tⁿn) n the derived SI unit of force that imparts an acceleration of 1 metre per second per second to a mass of 1 kilogram. Symbol: N [C20: after Sir Isaac NEWTON]

Newton ★ ('nju:tⁿn) n Sir **Isaac.** 1642–1727, English mathematician and physicist, noted for his law of gravitation, laws of motion, and theory of light and for developing calculus independently of Leibnitz. His works include *Principia Mathematica* (1687) and *Opticks* (1704).
▸ **Newtonian** (nju:'təʊnɪən) adj

Newtonian telescope n a type of astronomical reflecting telescope in which light is reflected from a large concave mirror onto a plane mirror, and through a hole in the side of the body of the telescope to form an image.

Newton's law of gravitation n the principle that two particles attract each other with forces directly proportional to the product of their masses divided by the square of the distance between them.

Newton's laws of motion pl n three laws of mechanics describing the motion of a body. **The first law** states that a body remains at rest or in uniform motion unless acted upon by a force. **The second law** states that a body's rate of change of momentum is proportional to the force causing it. **The third law** states that when a force acts on a body an equal and opposite force acts simultaneously on another body.

new town n (in Britain) a town planned as a complete unit and built with government sponsorship, esp. to accommodate overspill population.

Newtown ★ (,nju:taʊn) n a new town in central Wales, in Powys. Pop.: 10 548 (1991).

Newtownabbey ★ (,nju:tⁿn'æbɪ) n 1 a town in Northern Ireland, in Co. Antrim on Belfast Lough: the third largest town in Northern Ireland, formed in 1958 by the amalgamation of seven villages; light industrial centre, esp. for textiles. Pop.: 57 103 (1991). 2 a district of E Northern Ireland, on Belfast Lough: residential area for

Belfast, light industry. Administrative centre: Ballyclare. Pop.: 74 035 (1991). Area: 150 sq. km (58 sq. miles).

Newtown St Boswells ★ ('nju:taʊn sənt 'bɒzwəlz) n a village in SE Scotland, administrative centre of Scottish Borders: agricultural centre. Pop.: 1108 (1991).

new wave n a movement in art, politics, etc., that consciously breaks with traditional ideas, esp. **the New Wave,** a movement in the French cinema of the 1960s, characterized by a fluid use of the camera.

New Windsor ★ n the official name of **Windsor**[1] (sense 1).

New World ★ n **the.** the Americas; the western hemisphere.

New World monkey n any of a family of monkeys of Central and South America, many of which are arboreal and have a prehensile tail.

New Year n the first day or days of the year in various calendars, usually a holiday.

New Year's Day n January 1, celebrated as a holiday in many countries. Often shortened to (US and Canad. inf.) **New Year's.**

New Year's Eve n the evening of Dec. 31. See also **Hogmanay.**

New York ★ n 1 Also called: **New York City.** a city in SE New York State, at the mouth of the Hudson River: largest city and chief port of the US; settled by the Dutch as New Amsterdam in 1624 and captured by the British in 1664; the country's leading commercial and industrial city. Pop.: 7 333 253 (1994 est.). Abbrevs.: **N.Y.C., NYC.** 2 a state of the northeastern US: consists chiefly of a plateau with the Finger Lakes in the centre, the Adirondack Mountains in the northeast, the Catskill Mountains in the southeast, and Niagara Falls in the west. Capital: Albany. Pop.: 18 184 774 (1996 est.). Area: 123 882 sq. km (47 831 sq. miles). Abbrevs.: **N.Y.** or (with zip code) **NY**
▸ **New Yorker** n

New York Bay ★ n an inlet of the Atlantic at the mouth of the Hudson River: forms the harbour of the port of New York.

New York State Barge Canal ★ n a system of inland waterways in New York State, connecting the Hudson River with Lakes Erie and Ontario and, via Lake Champlain, with the St Lawrence. Length: 845 km (525 miles).

New Zealand ★ ('zi:lənd) n an independent dominion within the Commonwealth, occupying two main islands (the North Island and the South Island), Stewart Island, the Chatham Islands, and a number of minor islands in the SE Pacific: original Maori inhabitants surrendered sovereignty in 1840 and were finally subdued by 1870; became a dominion in 1907; a major world exporter of dairy products, wool, and meat. Official languages: English and Maori. Religion: Christian majority, nonreligious and Maori minorities. Currency: New Zealand dollar. Capital: Wellington. Pop.: 3 619 000 (1996). Area: 270 550 sq. km (104 454 sq. miles).
▸ **New Zealander** n

Nexø ★ (Danish 'negsø:) n Martin Andersen ('marten). 1869–1954, Danish novelist. His chief works are the novels *Pelle the Conqueror* (1906–10), which deals with the labour movement, and *Ditte, Daughter of Man* (1917–21).

next (nekst) adj 1 immediately following: *the next patient to be examined.* 2 immediately adjoining: *the next room.* 3 closest to in degree: *the next-best thing.* 4 the next (**Sunday**) **but one.** the (Sunday) after the next. ◆ adv 5 at a time immediately to follow: *the patient to be examined next.* 6 **next to.** 6a adjacent to: *the house next to ours.* 6b following in degree: *next to your mother, who do you love most?* 6c almost: *next to impossible.* ◆ prep 7 Arch. next to. [OE *nēhst*, sup. of *nēah* NIGH]

next door adj (**next-door** when prenominal), adv at or to the adjacent house, flat, etc.

next of kin n a person's closest relative.

nexus ('neksəs) n, pl **nexus.** 1 a means of connection; link;

★ people and places

bond. **2** a connected group or series. [C17: from L, from *nectere* to bind]

Ney ★ (neɪ; *French* nɛ) *n* **Michel** (miʃɛl), Duc d'Elchingen. 1769–1815, French marshal, who earned the epithet *Bravest of the Brave* at the battle of Borodino (1812); executed for treason (1815).

Nez Percé (ˈnɛz ˈpɜːs) *n* **1** (*pl* **Nez Percés** (ˈpɜːsɪz) or **Nez Percé**) a member of a North American Indian people of the Pacific coast. **2** the language of this people. [F, lit. pierced nose]

NF (in Britain) *abbrev. for* National Front.

Nfld. *or* **NF.** *abbrev. for* Newfoundland.

NFU (in Britain) *abbrev. for* National Farmers' Union.

NG *abbrev. for:* **1** (in the US) National Guard. **2** New Guinea. **3** Also: **ng.** no good.

NGA (formerly, in Britain) *abbrev. for* National Graphical Association.

ngaio (ˈnaɪəʊ) *n, pl* **ngaios.** a small evergreen New Zealand tree. [from Maori]

Ngaliema Mountain ★ (ˀŋɡɑːˈljeɪmə) *n* the Congolese name for (Mount) **Stanley.**

ngati (ˈnɑːtiː) *n, pl* **ngati.** NZ. a tribe or clan. [from Maori]

Nguyen Kao Ky ★ (ˀŋˈɡuːjɛn ˈkaʊ ˈkiː) *n* See (Nguyen Kao) **Ky.**

Nha Trang ★ (njɑː ˈtræŋ) *n* a port in SE Vietnam, on the South China Sea: nearby temples of the Cham civilization; fishing industry. Pop.: 221 331 (1992 est.).

NHI (in Britain) *abbrev. for* National Health Insurance.

NHS (in Britain) *abbrev. for* National Health Service.

Ni *the chemical symbol for* nickel.

NI *abbrev. for:* **1** (in Britain) National Insurance. **2** Northern Ireland. **3** (in New Zealand) North Island.

niacin (ˈnaɪəsɪn) *n* another name for **nicotinic acid.** [C20: from NI(COTINIC) AC(ID) + -IN]

Niagara ★ (naɪˈæɡrə, -ˈæɡərə) *n* **1** a river in NE North America, on the border between W New York State and Ontario, Canada, flowing from Lake Erie to Lake Ontario. Length: 45 km (28 miles). **2** a torrent.

Niagara Falls ★ *n* **1** (*functioning as pl*) the falls of the Niagara River, on the border between the US and Canada: divided by Goat Island into the American Falls, 50 m (167 ft) high, and the Horseshoe or Canadian Falls, 47 m (158 ft) high. **2** (*functioning as sing*) a city in W New York State, situated at the falls of the Niagara River. Pop.: 61 840 (1990). **3** (*functioning as sing*) a city in S Canada, in SE Ontario on the Niagara River just below the falls: linked to the city of Niagara Falls in the US by three bridges. Pop.: 75 399 (1991).

Niamey ★ (njɑːˈmeɪ) *n* the capital of Niger, in the southwest on the River Niger: became capital in 1926; airport and land route centre. Pop.: 495 000 (1995 est.).

Niarchos ★ (nɪˈɑːkɒs) *n* **Stavros Spyro** (ˈstævrɒs ˈspɪərəʊ). 1909–96, Greek shipowner.

nib (nɪb) *n* **1** the writing point of a pen, esp. an insertable tapered metal part. **2** a point, tip, or beak. **3** (*pl*) crushed cocoa beans. ◆ *vb* **nibs, nibbing, nibbed.** (*tr*) **4** to provide with a nib. **5** to sharpen the nib of. [C16 (in the sense: beak): from ?]

nibble (ˈnɪbᵊl) *vb* **nibbles, nibbling, nibbled.** (when *intr*, often foll. by *at*) **1** (esp. of animals) to take small repeated bites (of). **2** to take dainty or tentative bites: *to nibble at a cake.* **3** to bite (at) gently. ◆ *n* **4** a small mouthful. **5** an instance of nibbling. [C15: rel. to Low G *nibbelen*]
▸ **'nibbler** *n*

Nibelung ★ (ˈniːbəˌlʊŋ) *n, pl* **Nibelungs** or **Nibelungen** (-ˌlʊŋən). *German myth.* **1** any of the race of dwarfs who possessed a treasure hoard subsequently stolen by Siegfried. **2** one of Siegfried's companions or followers. **3** (in the *Nibelungenlied*) a member of the family of Gunther, king of Burgundy.

niblick (ˈnɪblɪk) *n Golf.* (formerly) a club giving a great deal of lift. [C19: from ?]

nibs (nɪbz) *pl n* **his nibs.** *Sl.* a mock title used of someone in authority. [C19: from ?]

Nicaea ★ (naɪˈsiːə) *n* an ancient city in NW Asia Minor, in Bithynia: site of the **first council of Nicaea** (325 A.D.), which composed the Nicene Creed. Modern Turkish name: **Iznik.**
▸ **Nicene** (ˈnaɪsiːn) *or* **Ni'caean** *adj*

NICAM (ˈnaɪkæm) *n acronym for* near-instantaneous companded audio multiplex: a technique for coding audio signals into digital form.

Nicaragua ★ (ˌnɪkəˈræɡjʊə, -ɡwə; *Spanish* nikaˈraɣwa) *n* **1** a republic in Central America, on the Caribbean and the Pacific: colonized by the Spanish from the 1520s; gained independence in 1821 and was annexed by Mexico, becoming a republic in 1838. Official language: Spanish. Religion: Roman Catholic. Currency: córdoba. Capital: Managua. Pop.: 4 272 000 (1996). Area: 131 812 sq. km (50 893 sq. miles). **2 Lake.** a lake in SW Nicaragua, separated from the Pacific by an isthmus 19 km (12 miles) wide: the largest lake in Central America. Area: 8264 sq. km (3191 sq. miles).
▸ **Nica'raguan** *adj, n*

nice (naɪs) *adj* **1** pleasant: *a nice day.* **2** kind or friendly: *a nice gesture of help.* **3** good or satisfactory: *they made a nice job of it.* **4** subtle or discriminating: *a nice point in the argument.* **5** precise; skilful: *a nice fit.* **6** *Now rare.* fastidious; respectable: *he was not too nice about his methods.* **7** *Obs.* **7a** foolish or ignorant. **7b** delicate. **7c** shy; modest. **7d** wanton. [C13 (orig.: foolish): from OF *nice* simple, silly, from L *nescius*, from *nescire* to be ignorant]
▸ **'nicely** *adv* ▸ **'niceness** *n* ▸ **'nicish** *adj*

Nice ★ (*French* nis) *n* a city in SE France, on the Mediterranean: a leading resort of the French Riviera; founded by Phocaeans from Marseille in about the 3rd century B.C. Pop.: 345 674 (1990).

nice-looking *adj Inf.* attractive in appearance; pretty or handsome.

nicety (ˈnaɪsɪtɪ) *n, pl* **niceties. 1** a subtle point: *a nicety of etiquette.* **2** (*usually pl*) a refinement or delicacy: *the niceties of first-class travel.* **3** subtlety, delicacy, or precision. **4 to a nicety.** with precision.

niche (nɪtʃ, niːʃ) *n* **1** a recess in a wall, esp. one that contains a statue, etc. **2** a position particularly suitable for the person occupying it: *he found his niche in politics.* **3** (*modifier*) relating to or aimed at a small specialized group or market: *shampoo shops and other niche retailing ventures.* **4** *Ecology.* the status of a plant or animal within its community, which determines its activities, relationships with other organisms, etc. ◆ *vb* **niches, niching, niched. 5** (*tr*) to place (a statue) in a niche; ensconce (oneself). [C17: from F, from OF *nichier* to nest, from Vulgar L *nīdicāre* (unattested), from L *nīdus* NEST]

Nicholas ★ (ˈnɪkələs) *n* **Saint.** 4th-century A.D. bishop of Myra, in Asia Minor; patron saint of Russia and of children. Feast day: Dec. 6. See also **Santa Claus.**

Nicholas I ★ *n* **1 Saint,** called *the Great.* died 867 A.D., Italian ecclesiastic; pope (858–867). Feast day: Nov. 13. **2** 1796–1855, tsar of Russia (1825–55): notorious for his autocracy.

Nicholas II ★ *n* 1868–1918, tsar of Russia (1894–1917). His autocracy precipitated the Russian Revolution (1917): he abdicated and was shot.

Nicholas V ★ *n* original name *Tommaso Parentucelli.* 1397–1455, Italian ecclesiastic; pope (1447–55).

Nicholas of Cusa ★ (ˈkjuːzə) *n* 1401–64, German cardinal and mathematician: asserted that the earth revolves around the sun.

Nicholson ★ (ˈnɪkᵊlsən) *n* **1 Ben.** 1894–1982, British abstract painter. **2 Jack.** born 1937, US actor. His films include *Easy Rider* (1969), *One Flew Over the Cuckoo's Nest* (1974), and *As Good As It Gets* (1998).

Nichrome (ˈnaɪkrəʊm) *n Trademark.* any of various alloys containing nickel, iron, and chromium, used in electrical heating elements, furnaces, etc.

Nicias ★ (ˈnɪsɪəs) *n* died 414 B.C., Athenian statesman and general. Made peace with Sparta (421), ending the first part of the Peloponnesian War.

nick (nɪk) *n* **1** a small notch or indentation. **2** *Brit. sl.* a prison or police station. **3 in good nick.** *Inf.* in good condition. **4 in the nick of time.** just in time. ◆ *vb* **5** (*tr*) to chip or cut. **6** *Sl., chiefly Brit.* **6a** to steal. **6b** to arrest. **7** (*intr; often* foll. by *off*) *Inf.* to depart rapidly. **8 nick (someone) for.** *US & Canad. sl.* to defraud (someone) to the extent of. **9** to divide and reset (the tail muscles of a horse) to give the tail a high carriage. **10** (*tr*) to guess, catch, etc., exactly. [C15: ? changed from C14 *nocke* NOCK]

nickel ('nɪkᵊl) *n* **1** a malleable silvery-white metallic element that is corrosion-resistant: used in alloys, in electroplating, and as a catalyst in organic synthesis. Symbol: Ni; atomic no.: 28; atomic wt.: 58.71. **2** a US or Canadian coin worth five cents. ◆ *vb* **nickels, nickelling, nickelled** *or US* **nickels, nickeling, nickeled. 3** (*tr*) to plate with nickel. [C18: from G *Kupfernickel* niccolite, lit.: copper demon; it was mistakenly thought to contain copper]

nickelodeon (ˌnɪkə'ləʊdɪən) *n US.* **1** an early form of jukebox. **2** (formerly) a Pianola, esp. one operated by inserting a five-cent piece. [C20: from NICKEL + (MEL)ODEON]

nickel plate *n* a thin layer of nickel deposited on a surface, usually by electrolysis.

nickel silver *n* any of various white alloys containing copper, zinc, and nickel: used in making tableware, etc. Also called: **German silver.**

nickel steel *n Engineering.* steel containing between 0.5 and 6.0 per cent nickel to increase its strength.

nicker[1] ('nɪkə) *vb* (*intr*) **1** (of a horse) to neigh softly. **2** to snigger. [C18: ?from NEIGH]

nicker[2] ('nɪkə) *n, pl* **nicker.** *Brit. sl.* a pound sterling. [C20: from ?]

Nicklaus ★ ('nɪklaʊs) *n* **Jack.** born 1940, US golfer: won the British Open Championship (1966; 1970; 1978) and the US Open Championship (1962; 1967; 1972; 1980).

nick-nack ('nɪkˌnæk) *n* a variant spelling of **knick-knack.**

nickname ('nɪkˌneɪm) *n* **1** a familiar, pet, or derisory name given to a person, animal, or place. **2** a shortened or familiar form of a person's name: *Joe is a nickname for Joseph.* ◆ *vb* **nicknames, nicknaming, nicknamed. 3** (*tr*) to call by a nickname. [C15 *a nekename,* mistaken division of *an ekename* an additional name]

Nicobar Islands ★ ('nɪkəˌbɑː) *pl n* a group of 19 islands in the Indian Ocean, south of the Andaman Islands, with which they form a territory of India. Area: 1645 sq. km (635 sq. miles).

Nicodemus ★ (ˌnɪkə'diːməs) *n New Testament.* a Pharisee and a member of the Sanhedrin, who supported Jesus against the other Pharisees (John 8:50–52).

Nicolai ★ (*German* niko'laɪ) *n* **Carl Otto Ehrenfried** (karl 'ɔto 'eːrənfriːt). 1810–49, German composer: noted for his opera *The Merry Wives of Windsor* (1849).

Nicol prism ('nɪkᵊl) *n* two prisms of Iceland spar or calcite cut at specified angles and cemented together, to produce plane-polarized light. [C19: after William *Nicol* (?1768–1851), Scot. physicist, its inventor]

Nicosia ★ (ˌnɪkə'siːə, -'sɪə) *n* the capital of Cyprus, in the central part on the Pedieos River: capital since the 10th century. Pop.: 228 215 (1994 est.). Greek name: **Levkosia** *or* **Leukosia.** Turkish name: **Lefkoşa.**

nicotiana (nɪˌkəʊʃɪ'ɑːnə) *n* a plant of an American and Australian genus, having white, yellow, or purple fragrant flowers. Also called: **tobacco plant.** [C16: see NICOTINE]

nicotinamide (ˌnɪkə'tɪnəˌmaɪd) *n* the amide of nicotinic acid: a component of the vitamin B complex. Formula: $C_6H_6ON_2$.

nicotine ('nɪkəˌtiːn) *n* a colourless oily acrid toxic liquid that turns yellowish-brown in air and light: the principal alkaloid in tobacco. [C19: from F, from NL *herba nicotiana* Nicot's plant, after J. *Nicot* (1530-1600), F diplomat who introduced tobacco into France]
▸ **'nicoˌtined** *adj* ▸ **nicotinic** (ˌnɪkə'tɪnɪk) *adj*

nicotinic acid *n* a vitamin of the B complex that occurs in milk, liver, yeast, etc. Lack of it in the diet leads to the disease pellagra.

nicotinism ('nɪkətiːˌnɪzəm) *n Pathol.* a toxic condition of the body caused by nicotine.

Nictheroy ★ (*Portuguese* nite'rɔi) *n* another name for **Niterói.**

nictitate ('nɪktɪˌteɪt) *or* **nictate** ('nɪkteɪt) *vb* **nictitates, nictitating, nictitated** *or* **nictates, nictating, nictated.** a technical word for **blink.** [C19: from Med. L *nictitāre* to wink repeatedly, from L *nictāre* to blink]
▸ **ˌnicti'tation** *or* **nic'tation** *n*

nictitating membrane *n* (in reptiles, birds, and some mammals) a thin fold of skin beneath the eyelid that can be drawn across the eye.

Nidaros ★ (*Norwegian* 'niːdaroːs) *n* the former name (1930–31) of **Trondheim.**

nidicolous (nɪ'dɪkələs) *adj* (of young birds) remaining in the nest some time after hatching. [C19: from L *nīdus* nest + *colere* to inhabit]

nidifugous (nɪ'dɪfjʊgəs) *adj* (of young birds) leaving the nest very soon after hatching. [C19: from L *nīdus* nest + *fugere* to flee]

nidify ('nɪdɪˌfaɪ) *or* **nidificate** ('nɪdɪfɪˌkeɪt) *vb* **nidifies, nidifying, nidified** *or* **nidificates, nidificating, nidificated.** (*intr*) (of birds) to make or build a nest. [C17: from L *nīdificāre,* from *nīdus* a nest + *facere* to make]
▸ **ˌnidifi'cation** *n*

niece (niːs) *n* a daughter of one's sister or brother. [C13: from OF: niece, granddaughter, ult. from L *neptis* granddaughter]

Niederösterreich ★ ('niːdərøːstəraɪç) *n* the German name for **Lower Austria.**

Niedersachsen ★ ('niːdərzaksən) *n* the German name for **Lower Saxony.**

niello (nɪ'ɛləʊ) *n, pl* **nielli** (-lɪ) *or* **niellos. 1** a black compound of sulphur and silver, lead, or copper used to incise a design on a metal surface. **2** this process. **3** an object decorated with niello. [C19: from It. from L *nigellus* blackish, from *niger* black]

Nielsen ★ ('niːlsən; *Danish* 'nelsən) *n* **Carl (August)** (karl). 1865–1931, Danish composer. His works include six symphonies and the opera *Masquerade* (1906).

Niemen ★ ('njɛmɛn) *n* the Polish name for the **Neman.**

Niemeyer ★ ('niːˌmaɪə) *n* **Oscar.** born 1907, Brazilian architect. His work includes many buildings in Brasília.

Niemöller ★ (*German* 'niːmœlər) *n* **Martin** ('martiːn). 1892–1984, German Protestant theologian; imprisoned (1938–45) for opposing Hitler.

Niepce ★ (*French* njɛps) *n* **Joseph-Nicéphore** (ʒozɛfnisefɔr). 1765–1833, French inventor. He produced the first permanent camera photograph (1826).

Nietzsche ★ ('niːtʃə) *n* **Friedrich Wilhelm** ('friːdrɪç 'vɪlhɛlm). 1844–1900, German philosopher. His works include *Thus Spake Zarathustra* (1883–91) and *Beyond Good and Evil* (1886).
▸ **Nietzschean** ('niːtʃɪən) *n, adj* ▸ **'Nietzscheˌism** *or* **'Nietzscheanˌism** *n*

Nièvre ★ (*French* njɛvrə) *n* a department of central France, in Burgundy region. Capital: Nevers. Pop.: 230 529 (1994 est.). Area: 6888 sq. km (2686 sq. miles).

niff (nɪf) *Brit. sl.* ◆ *n* **1** a bad smell. ◆ *vb* (*intr*) **2** to stink. [C20: ?from SNIFF]
▸ **'niffy** *adj*

Niflheim ★ ('nɪvᵊlˌheɪm) *n Norse myth.* the abode of the dead. [ON, lit.: mist home]

nifty ('nɪftɪ) *adj* **niftier, niftiest.** *Inf.* **1** pleasing, apt, or stylish. **2** quick; agile. [C19: from ?]
▸ **'niftily** *adv* ▸ **'niftiness** *n*

nigella (naɪ'dʒɛlə) *n* another name for **love-in-a-mist.**

Niger ★ *n* **1** (niː'ʒɛə, 'naɪdʒə) a landlocked republic in West Africa: important since earliest times for its trans-Saharan trade routes; made a French colony in 1922 and became fully independent in 1960; exports peanuts and livestock. Official language: French. Religion: mostly Muslim. Currency: franc. Capital: Niamey. Pop.: 9 465 000 (1996). Area: 1 267 000 sq. km (489 000 sq. miles). **2** ('naɪdʒə) a river in West Africa, rising in S Guinea and flowing in a great northward curve through Mali, then southwest through Niger and Nigeria to the Gulf of Guinea: the third longest river in Africa, with the largest delta, covering an area of 36 260 sq. km (14 000 sq. miles). Length: 4184 km (2600 miles). **3** ('naɪdʒə) a state of W central Nigeria, formed in 1976 from part of

North-Western State. Capital: Minna. Pop.: 2 556 838 (1992 est.). Area: 65 037 sq. km (25 105 sq. miles).

Nigeria ★ (naɪˈdʒɪərɪə) *n* a republic in West Africa, on the Gulf of Guinea: Lagos annexed by the British in 1861; protectorates of Northern and Southern Nigeria formed in 1900 and united as a colony in 1914; gained independence as a member of the Commonwealth in 1960 (membership suspended in 1995 following human rights violations); Eastern Region seceded as the Republic of Biafra for the duration of the severe civil war (1967–70); ruled by military governments from 1966; in 1993 the annulment of democratic elections by the military government precipitated a political and social crisis. It consists of a belt of tropical rain forest in the south, with semidesert in the extreme north and highlands in the east; the main export is petroleum. Official language: English; Hausa, Ibo, and Yoruba are the chief regional languages. Religion: animist, Muslim, and Christian. Currency: naira. Capital: Abuja. Pop.: 103 912 000 (1996). Area: 923 773 sq. km (356 669 sq. miles).
▶ Niˈgerian *adj, n*

niggard (ˈnɪgəd) *n* **1** a stingy person. ◆ *adj* **2** *Arch.* miserly. [C14: ?from ON]

niggardly (ˈnɪgədlɪ) *adj* **1** stingy. **2** meagre: *a niggardly salary*. ◆ *adv* **3** stingily; grudgingly.
▶ ˈniggardliness *n*

nigger (ˈnɪgə) *n Derog.* **1** another name for a Negro. **2** a member of any dark-skinned race. **3 nigger in the woodpile.** a hidden cause of trouble. [C18: from C16 dialect *neeger*, from F *nègre*, from Sp. NEGRO[1]]

niggle (ˈnɪgəl) *vb* **niggles, niggling, niggled. 1** (*intr*) to find fault continually. **2** (*intr*) to be preoccupied with details; fuss. **3** (*tr*) to irritate; worry. ◆ *n* **4** a trivial objection or complaint. **5** a slight feeling as of misgiving, uncertainty, etc. [C16: from Scand.]
▶ ˈniggler *n* ▶ ˈniggly *adj*

niggling (ˈnɪglɪŋ) *adj* **1** petty. **2** fussy. **3** irritating. **4** requiring painstaking work. **5** persistently troubling.

nigh (naɪ) *adj, adv, prep* an archaic, poetic, or dialect word for **near**. [OE *nēah, nēh*]

night (naɪt) *n* **1** the period of darkness that occurs each 24 hours, as distinct from day. **2** (*modifier*) of, occurring, working, etc., at night: *a night nurse*. **3** this period considered as a unit: *four nights later they left.* **4** the period between sunset and retiring to bed; evening. **5** the time between bedtime and morning. **6** the weather at night: *a clear night.* **7** the activity or experience of a person during a night. **8** (*sometimes cap.*) any evening designated for a special observance or function. **9** nightfall or dusk. **10** a state or period of gloom, ignorance, etc. **11 make a night of it.** to celebrate for most of the night. ◆ Related adj: **nocturnal.** ◆ See also **nights.** [OE *niht*]

night blindness *n Pathol.* a nontechnical term for **nyctalopia.**
▶ ˈnight-ˌblind *adj*

nightcap (ˈnaɪtˌkæp) *n* **1** a bedtime drink. **2** a soft cap formerly worn in bed.

nightclothes (ˈnaɪtˌkləʊðz) *pl n* clothes worn in bed.

nightclub (ˈnaɪtˌklʌb) *n* a place of entertainment open until late at night, usually offering food, drink, a floor show, dancing, etc.

nightdress (ˈnaɪtˌdrɛs) *n Brit.* a loose dress worn in bed by women. Also called: **nightgown, nightie.**

nightfall (ˈnaɪtˌfɔːl) *n* the approach of darkness; dusk.

night fighter *n* an interceptor aircraft used for operations at night.

nightgown (ˈnaɪtˌgaʊn) *n* **1** another name for **nightdress. 2** a man's nightshirt.

nighthawk (ˈnaɪtˌhɔːk) *n* **1** any of various nocturnal American birds. **2** *Inf.* another name for **night owl.**

nightie *or* **nighty** (ˈnaɪtɪ) *n, pl* **nighties.** *Inf.* short for **nightdress.**

nightingale (ˈnaɪtɪŋˌgeɪl) *n* a brownish European songbird with a broad reddish-brown tail: well known for its musical song, usually heard at night. [OE *nihtegale*, from NIGHT + *galan* to sing]

Nightingale ★ (ˈnaɪtɪŋˌgeɪl) *n* **Florence,** known as *the Lady with the Lamp.* 1820–1910, British nurse, noted for her work during the Crimean War.

nightjar (ˈnaɪtˌdʒɑː) *n* any of a family of nocturnal birds which have large eyes and feed on insects. [C17: NIGHT + JAR[2], so called from its discordant cry]

night latch *n* a door lock operated by means of a knob on the inside and a key on the outside.

nightlife (ˈnaɪtˌlaɪf) *n* social life or entertainment taking place at night.

night-light *n* a dim light burning at night, esp. for children.

nightlong (ˈnaɪtˌlɒŋ) *adj, adv* throughout the night.

nightly (ˈnaɪtlɪ) *adj* **1** happening or relating to each night. **2** happening at night. ◆ *adv* **3** at night or each night.

nightmare (ˈnaɪtˌmɛə) *n* **1** a terrifying or deeply distressing dream. **2a** an event or condition resembling a terrifying dream. **2b** (*as modifier*): *a nightmare drive.* **3** a thing that is feared. **4** (formerly) an evil spirit supposed to suffocate sleeping people. [C13: (meaning: incubus; C16: bad dream): from NIGHT + OE *mare, mære* evil spirit, from Gmc]
▶ ˈnightˌmarish *adj*

night owl *or* **nighthawk** *n Inf.* a person who is or prefers to be up and about late at night.

nights (naɪts) *adv Inf.* at night, esp. regularly: *he works nights.*

night safe *n* a safe built into the outside wall of a bank, in which customers can deposit money at times when the bank is closed.

night school *n* an educational institution that holds classes in the evening.

nightshade (ˈnaɪtˌʃeɪd) *n* any of various solanaceous plants, such as deadly nightshade and black nightshade. [OE *nihtscada*, apparently NIGHT + SHADE, referring to the poisonous or soporific qualities of these plants]

night shift *n* **1** a group of workers who work a shift during the night. **2** the period worked.

nightshirt (ˈnaɪtˌʃɜːt) *n* a loose knee-length or longer shirtlike garment worn in bed.

nightspot (ˈnaɪtˌspɒt) *n* an informal word for **nightclub.**

night-time *n* the time from sunset to sunrise; night as distinct from day.

night watch *n* **1** a watch or guard kept at night, esp. for security. **2** the period of time the watch is kept. **3** a night watchman.

night watchman *n* **1** Also called: **night watch.** a person who keeps guard at night on a factory, public building, etc. **2** *Cricket.* a batsman sent in to bat to play out time when a wicket has fallen near the end of a day's play.

nightwear (ˈnaɪtˌwɛə) *n* apparel worn in bed or before retiring to bed; pyjamas, etc.

nigrescent (naɪˈgrɛsənt) *adj* blackish; dark. [C18: from L *nigrescere* to grow black, from *niger* black]
▶ niˈgrescence *n*

nihilism (ˈnaɪɪˌlɪzəm) *n* **1** a complete denial of all established authority and institutions. **2** *Philosophy.* an extreme form of scepticism that systematically rejects all values, belief in existence, etc. **3** a revolutionary doctrine of destruction for its own sake. **4** the practice of terrorism. [C19: from L *nihil* nothing]
▶ ˈnihilist *n, adj* ▶ ˌnihilˈistic *adj* ▶ nihility (naɪˈhɪlɪtɪ) *n*

nihil obstat (ˈnaɪhɪl ˈɒbstæt) the phrase used by a Roman Catholic censor to declare publication inoffensive to faith or morals. [L, lit.: nothing hinders]

Nihon ★ (ˈniːˈhɒn) *n* transliteration of a Japanese name for **Japan.**

Niigata ★ (ˈniːˌgɑːtə) *n* a port in central Japan, on NW Honshu at the mouth of the Shinano River: the chief port on the Sea of Japan. Pop.: 494 785 (1995).

Nijinsky ★ (nɪˈdʒɪnskɪ) *n* **Waslaw** *or* **Vaslaw** (*Russian* vatsˈlaf). 1890–1950, Russian ballet dancer and choreographer.

Nijmegen ★ (ˈnaɪˌmeɪgən; *Dutch* ˈnɛimeːxə) *n* an industrial town in the E Netherlands, in Gelderland province on the Waal River: the oldest town in the country; scene of the signing (1678) of the peace treaty between Louis XIV, the Netherlands, Spain, and the Holy Roman Empire. Pop.: 147 018 (1994). Latin name: ˌNovio'magus. German name: Nimwegen.

-nik *suffix forming nouns.* denoting a person associated with a specified state or quality: *beatnik*. [C20: from Russian *-nik*, as in Sputnik, and infl. by Yiddish *-nik* (agent suffix)]

Nikaria ★ (nɪˈkɛərɪə, naɪ-) *n* another name for **Icaria.**

Nike ★ ('naɪkiː) *n Greek myth.* the winged goddess of victory. Roman counterpart: **Victoria.** [from Gk: victory]

Nikkei Stock Average ('nɪkeɪ) *n* an index of share prices based on an average of 225 equities quoted on the Tokyo Stock Exchange. [C20: from *Nik(on) Kei(zai Shimbun)*, a Japanese newspaper group]

Nikko ★ ('niːkəʊ) *n* a town in central Japan, on NE Honshu: a major pilgrimage centre, with a 4th-century Shinto shrine, a Buddhist temple (767), and the shrines and mausoleums of the Tokugawa shoguns. Pop.: 20 128 (1990).

Nikolainkaupunki ★ (*Finnish* ˌnikəlaɪnˈkaʊpʊŋki) *n* the former name of **Vaasa.**

Nikolayev ★ (*Russian* nikaˈlajɪf) *n* a city in the S Ukraine, on the Southern Bug about 64 km (40 miles) from the Black Sea: founded as a naval base in 1788; one of the leading Black Sea ports. Pop.: 508 000 (1996 est.). Former name: **Vernoleninsk.**

nil (nɪl) *n* nothing: used esp. in the scoring of certain games. [C19: from L]

Nile ★ (naɪl) *n* a river in Africa, rising in S central Burundi in its remotest headstream, the **Luvironza:** flows into Lake Victoria and leaves the lake as the **Victoria Nile,** flowing to Lake Albert, which is drained by the **Albert Nile,** becoming the White Nile on the border between Uganda and the Sudan; joined by its chief tributary, the **Blue Nile** (which rises near Lake Tana, Ethiopia) at Khartoum, and flows north to its delta on the Mediterranean; the longest river in the world. Length: (from the source of the Luvironza to the Mediterranean) 6741 km (4187 miles).

Nile green *n* **a** a pale bluish-green colour. **b** (*as adj*): *a Nile-green dress.*

nilgai ('nɪlgaɪ) *or* **nilghau** ('nɪlgɔː) *n, pl* **nilgai, nilgais** *or* **nilghau, nilghaus.** a large Indian antelope, the male of which has small horns. [C19: from Hindi *nīlgāw*, from Sansk. *nīla* blue + *go* bull]

Nilgiri Hills ('nɪlgɪrɪ) *or* **Nilgiris** ★ *pl n* a plateau in S India, in Tamil Nadu. Average height: 2000 m (6500 ft), reaching 2635 m (8647 ft) in Doda Betta.

Nilotic (naɪˈlɒtɪk) *adj* **1** of the Nile. **2** of or belonging to a Negroid pastoral people inhabiting the S Sudan, parts of Kenya and Uganda, and neighbouring countries. **3** relating to the group of languages spoken by the Nilotic peoples. [C17: via L from Gk *Nilotikós*, from *Neilos* the Nile]

Nilsson ★ (*Swedish* 'nilsɔn) *n* **Birgit** ('birgit). born 1918, Swedish soprano.

nimble ('nɪmbʰl) *adj* **1** agile, quick, and neat in movement. **2** alert; acute. [OE *nǣmel* quick to grasp, & *numol* quick at seizing, both from *niman* to take]
▸ 'nimbleness *n* ▸ 'nimbly *adv*

nimbostratus (ˌnɪmbəʊˈstreɪtəs, -ˈstrɑːtəs) *n, pl* **nimbostrati** (-taɪ). a dark rain-bearing stratus cloud.

nimbus ('nɪmbəs) *n, pl* **nimbi** (-baɪ) *or* **nimbuses. 1a** a dark grey rain-bearing cloud. **1b** (*in combination*): *cumulonimbus clouds.* **2a** an emanation of light surrounding a saint or deity. **2b** a representation of this emanation. **3** a surrounding aura. [C17: from L: cloud]

NIMBY ('nɪmbɪ) *n acronym for* not in my back yard: a person who objects to the occurrence of something if it will affect them or take place in their locality.

Nîmes ★ (*French* nim) *n* a city in S France: Roman remains including an amphitheatre and the Pont du Gard aqueduct. Pop.: 133 607 (1990).

Nimrod ★ ('nɪmrɒd) *n* **1** a hunter famous for his prowess (Genesis 10:8–9). **2** a person dedicated to or skilled in hunting.

Nimrud ★ (nɪmˈruːd) *n* an ancient city in Assyria, near the present-day city of Mosul (Iraq): founded in about 1250 B.C. and destroyed by the Medes in 612 B.C.; excavated by Sir Austen Henry Layard.

Nimwegen ★ ('nɪmveːgən) *n* the German name for **Nijmegen.**

nincompoop ('nɪnkəmˌpuːp, 'nɪŋ-) *n* a stupid person; fool; idiot. [C17: from ?]

nine (naɪn) *n* **1** the cardinal number that is the sum of one and eight. **2** a numeral, 9, IX, etc., representing this number. **3** something representing, represented by, or consisting of nine units, such as a playing card with nine symbols on it. **4** Also: **nine o'clock.** nine hours after noon or midnight: *the play starts at nine.* **5** dressed (up) to the **nines.** *Inf.* elaborately dressed. **6 999** (in Britain) the telephone number of the emergency services. **7 nine to five.** normal office hours: *a nine-to-five job.* ◆ *determiner* **8a** amounting to nine: *nine days.* **8b** (*as pronoun*): *nine are ready.* [OE *nigon*]

nine-days wonder *n* something that arouses great interest but only for a short period.

ninefold ('naɪnˌfəʊld) *adj* **1** equal to or having nine times as many or as much. **2** composed of nine parts. ◆ *adv* **3** by nine times as much.

ninepins ('naɪnˌpɪnz) *n* **1** (*functioning as sing*) another name for **skittles. 2** (*sing*) one of the pins used in this game.

nineteen ('naɪnˈtiːn) *n* **1** the cardinal number that is the sum of ten and nine. **2** a numeral, 19, XIX, etc., representing this number. **3** something represented by, representing, or consisting of 19 units. **4 talk nineteen to the dozen.** to talk incessantly. ◆ *determiner* **5a** amounting to nineteen: *nineteen pictures.* **5b** (*as pronoun*): *only nineteen voted.* [OE *nigontīne*]

nineteenth (ˌnaɪnˈtiːnθ) *adj* **1** (*usually prenominal*) **1a** coming after the eighteenth in numbering, position, etc.; being the ordinal number of *nineteen.* Often written: 19th. **1b** (*as n*): *the nineteenth was rainy.* ◆ *n* **2a** one of 19 equal parts of something. **2b** (*as modifier*): *a nineteenth part.* **3** the fraction equal to one divided by 19 (1/19).

nineteenth hole *n Golf, sl.* the bar in a golf clubhouse. [C20: from its being the next objective after a standard 18-hole round]

ninetieth ('naɪntɪɪθ) *adj* **1** (*usually prenominal*) **1a** being the ordinal number of *ninety* in numbering, position, etc. Often written: 90th. **1b** (*as n*): *ninetieth in succession.* ◆ *n* **2a** one of 90 equal parts of something. **2b** (*as modifier*): *a ninetieth part.* **3** the fraction one divided by 90 (1/90).

ninety ('naɪntɪ) *n, pl* **nineties. 1** the cardinal number that is the product of ten and nine. **2** a numeral, 90, XC, etc., representing this number. **3** something represented by, representing, or consisting of 90 units. ◆ *determiner* **4a** amounting to ninety: *ninety times.* **4b** (*as pronoun*): *at least ninety are missing.* [OE *nigontig*]
▸ 'ninetieth *adj, n*

Nineveh ★ ('nɪnɪvə) *n* the ancient capital of Assyria, on the River Tigris opposite the present-day city of Mosul (N Iraq): at its height in the 8th and 7th centuries B.C., destroyed in 612 B.C. by the Medes and Babylonians.
▸ 'Ninevite *n*

Ningbo *or* **Ningpo** ★ ('nɪŋ'pəʊ) *n* a port in E China, in NE Zhejiang, on the Yung River, about 20 km (12 miles) from its mouth at Hangzhou Bay: one of the first sites of European settlement in China. Pop.: 1 090 000 (1991 est.).

Ningsia *or* **Ninghsia** ★ ('nɪŋ'ʃjɑː) *n* **1** a former province of NW China: mostly included in the Inner Mongolian AR in 1956, with the smaller part constituted as the Ningxia Hui AR in 1958. **2** the former name of **Yinchuan.**

Ningxia Hui Autonomous Region ★ ('nɪŋ'ʃjɑː 'huːɪ) *n* an administrative division of NW China, south of the Inner Mongolian AR. Capital: Yinchuan. Pop.: 5 040 000 (1995 est.). Area: 66 400 sq. km (25 896 sq. miles).

Ninian ★ ('nɪnjən) *n* **Saint.** ?360–?432 A.D., the first apostle of Scotland; built a stone church at his native Whithorn. Feast day: Sept. 16.

★ people and places

ninja ('nɪndʒə) *n, pl* **ninja** *or* **ninjas**. (*sometimes cap.*) a person skilled in **ninjutsu**, a Japanese martial art characterized by stealthy movement and camouflage. [Japanese]

ninny ('nɪnɪ) *n, pl* **ninnies**. a dull-witted person. [C16: ?from *an innocent* simpleton]

ninth (naɪnθ) *adj* **1** (*usually prenominal*) **1a** coming after the eighth in order, position, etc.; being the ordinal number of *nine*. Often written: 9th. **1b** (*as n*): *ninth in line.* ♦ *n* **2a** one of nine equal parts. **2b** (*as modifier*): *a ninth part.* **3** the fraction one divided by nine (1/9). **4** *Music.* an interval of one octave plus a second. ♦ *adv* **5** Also: **ninthly**. after the eighth person, position, event, etc. [OE *nigotha*]

Ninus ★ ('naɪnəs) *n* a king of Assyria and the legendary founder of Nineveh, husband of Semiramis.

Niobe ★ ('naɪəbɪ) *n Greek myth.* a daughter of Tantalus, whose children were slain after she boasted of them: although turned into stone, she continued to weep.
▸ **Niobean** (naɪ'əʊbɪən) *adj*

niobium (naɪ'əʊbɪəm) *n* a ductile white superconductive metallic element that occurs principally in the black mineral columbite and tantalite. Symbol: Nb; atomic no.: 41; atomic wt.: 92.906. Former name: **columbium**. [C19: from NL, from NIOBE; because it occurred in TANTALITE]

nip¹ (nɪp) *vb* **nips, nipping, nipped.** (*mainly tr*) **1** to compress, as between a finger and the thumb; pinch. **2** (often foll. by *off*) to remove by clipping, biting, etc. **3** (when *intr*, often foll. by *at*) to give a small sharp bite (to): *the dog nipped at his heels.* **4** (esp. of the cold) to affect with a stinging sensation. **5** to harm through cold: *the frost nipped the young plants.* **6** to check or destroy the growth of (esp. in **nip in the bud**). **7** (*intr;* foll. by *along, up, out,* etc.) *Brit. inf.* to hurry; dart. **8** *Sl., chiefly US & Canad.* to snatch. ♦ *n* **9** a pinch, snip, etc. **10** severe frost or cold: *the first nip of winter.* **11** **put the nips in.** *Austral. & NZ sl.* to exert pressure on someone, esp. in order to extort money. **12** *Arch.* a taunting remark. **13** **nip and tuck.** *US & Canad.* neck and neck. [C14: from ON]

nip² (nɪp) *n* **1** a small drink of spirits; dram. ♦ *vb* **nips, nipping, nipped. 2** to drink spirits, esp. habitually in small amounts. [C18: from *nipperkin* a vessel holding a half-pint or less, from ?]

Nipigon ★ ('nɪpəgɒn) *n* **Lake.** a lake in central Canada, in NW Ontario, draining into Lake Superior via the **Nipigon River.** Area: 4843 sq. km (1870 sq. miles).

Nipissing ★ ('nɪpɪsɪŋ) *n* **Lake.** a lake in central Canada, in E Ontario between the Ottawa River and Georgian Bay. Area: 855 sq. km (330 sq. miles).

nipper ('nɪpə) *n* **1** a person or thing that nips. **2** the large pincer-like claw of a lobster, crab, etc. **3** *Inf., chiefly Brit. & Austral.* a small child. **4** *Austral.* a type of small prawn used as bait.

nippers ('nɪpəz) *pl n* an instrument or tool, such as a pair of pliers, for snipping or squeezing.

nipple ('nɪpˀl) *n* **1** the small conical projection in the centre of each breast, which in women contains the outlet of the milk ducts. **2** something resembling a nipple in shape or function. **3** Also called: **grease nipple.** a small drilled bush, usually screwed into a bearing, through which grease is introduced. [C16: from earlier *neble, nible,* ?from NEB, NIB]

nipplewort ('nɪpˀl,wɜːt) *n* an annual Eurasian plant with pointed oval leaves and small yellow flower heads.

Nippon ★ ('nɪpɒn) *n* transliteration of a Japanese name for **Japan.**
▸ **Nipponese** (,nɪpə'niːz) *adj, n*

Nippur ★ (nɪ'pʊə) *n* an ancient Sumerian and Babylonian city, the excavated site of which is in SE Iraq: an important religious centre, abandoned in the 12th or 13th century.

nippy ('nɪpɪ) *adj* **nippier, nippiest. 1** (of weather) frosty or chilly. **2** *Brit. inf.* **2a** quick; nimble; active. **2b** (of a motor vehicle) small and relatively powerful. **3** (of dogs) inclined to bite.
▸ **'nippily** *adv*

Nirenberg ★ ('naɪrən,bɜːg) *n* Marshall Warren. born 1927,

US biochemist; shared the Nobel prize for physiology or medicine (1968) for helping to decipher the genetic code.

NIREX ('naɪreks) *n acronym for* Nuclear Industry Radioactive Waste Executive.

nirvana (nɪə'vɑːnə, nɜː-) *n Buddhism & Hinduism.* final release from the cycle of reincarnation attained by extinction of all desires and individual existence, culminating (in Buddhism) in absolute blessedness, or (in Hinduism) in absorption into Brahman. [C19: from Sansk.: extinction, from *nir-* out + *vāti* it blows]

Niš *or* **Nish** ★ (niːʃ) *n* an industrial town in E Yugoslavia, in SE Serbia: situated on routes between central Europe and the Aegean. Pop.: 175 391 (1991).

Nisei ('niːseɪ) *n* a native-born citizen of the United States or Canada whose parents were Japanese immigrants. [Japanese, lit.: second generation]

Nishapur ★ (,niːʃɑː'pʊə) *n* a town in NE Iran, at an altitude of 1195 m (3920 ft): birthplace and burial place of Omar Khayyám. Pop.: 135 681 (1991).

Nishinomiya ★ (,niːʃɪ'nɒmɪjə) *n* an industrial city in central Japan, on S Honshu, northwest of Osaka. Pop.: 390 388 (1995).

nisi ('naɪsaɪ) *adj* (*postpositive*) *Law.* (of a court order) coming into effect on a specified date unless cause is shown why it should not: *a decree nisi.* [C19: from: unless, if not]

Nissen hut ('nɪsˀn) *n* a military shelter of semicircular cross section, made of corrugated steel sheet. [C20: after Lt Col. Peter Nissen (1871–1930), British mining engineer, its inventor]

nit¹ (nɪt) *n* **1** the egg of a louse, esp. adhering to human hair. **2** the larva of a louse. [OE *hnitu*]

nit² (nɪt) *n* a unit of luminance equal to 1 candela per square metre. [C20: from L *nitor* brightness]

nit³ (nɪt) *n Inf., chiefly Brit.* short for **nitwit.**

nit⁴ (nɪt) *n* a unit of information equal to 1.44 bits. Also called: **nepit.** [C20: from N(*apierian dig*)*it*]

nit⁵ (nɪt) *n* **keep nit.** *Austral. inf.* to keep watch, esp. during illegal activity. [C19: from *nix!* a shout of warning]
▸ **'nit-,keeper** *n*

Niterói ★ (*Portuguese* nite'rɔi) *n* a port in SE Brazil, on Guanabara Bay opposite Rio de Janeiro: contains Brazil's chief shipyards. Pop.: 400 586 (1991). Also called: **Nictheroy.**

nit-picking *Inf.* ♦ *n* **1** a concern with insignificant details, esp. with the intention of finding fault. ♦ *adj* **2** showing such a concern; fussy. [C20: from NIT¹ + PICK¹]
▸ **'nit-,picker** *n*

nitrate ('naɪtreɪt) *n* **1** any salt or ester of nitric acid. **2** a fertilizer containing nitrate salts. ♦ *vb* **nitrates, nitrating, nitrated. 3** (*tr*) to treat with nitric acid or a nitrate. **4** to convert or be converted into a nitrate.
▸ **ni'tration** *n*

nitre *or US* **niter** ('naɪtə) *n* another name for **potassium nitrate** or **sodium nitrate.** [C14: via OF from L *nitrum,* prob. from Gk *nitron*]

nitric ('naɪtrɪk) *adj* of or containing nitrogen.

nitric acid *n* a colourless corrosive liquid important in the manufacture of fertilizers, explosives, and many other chemicals. Formula: HNO_3. Former name: **aqua fortis.**

nitric oxide *n* a colourless reactive gas. Formula: NO. Systematic name: **nitrogen monoxide.**

nitride ('naɪtraɪd) *n* a compound of nitrogen with a more electropositive element.

nitrification (,naɪtrɪfɪ'keɪʃən) *n* **1** the oxidation of the ammonium compounds in dead organic material into nitrites and nitrates by soil nitrobacteria, making nitrogen available to plants. **2** the addition of a nitro group to an organic compound.

nitrify ('naɪtrɪ,faɪ) *vb* **nitrifies, nitrifying, nitrified.** (*tr*) **1** to treat or cause to react with nitrogen. **2** to treat (soil) with nitrates. **3** (of nitrobacteria) to convert (ammonium compounds) into nitrates by oxidation.
▸ **'nitri,fiable** *adj*

nitrite ('naɪtraɪt) *n* any salt or ester of nitrous acid.

nitro- *or before a vowel* **nitr-** *combining form.* **1** indicating that a chemical compound contains a nitro group, -NO₂: *nitrobenzene.* **2** indicating that a chemical compound is a nitrate ester: *nitrocellulose.* [from Gk *nitron* NATRON]

nitrobacteria (ˌnaɪtrəʊbæk'tɪərɪə) *pl n, sing* **nitrobacterium** (-'tɪərɪəm). soil bacteria that are involved in nitrification.

nitrobenzene (ˌnaɪtrəʊ'bɛnziːn) *n* a yellow oily liquid compound, used as a solvent and in the manufacture of aniline. Formula: C₆H₅NO₂.

nitrocellulose (ˌnaɪtrəʊ'sɛljʊˌləʊs) *n* another name (not in chemical usage) for **cellulose nitrate.**

nitrogen ('naɪtrədʒən) *n* a colourless odourless relatively unreactive gaseous element that forms 78 per cent of the air and is an essential constituent of proteins and nucleic acids. Symbol: N; atomic no.: 7; atomic wt.: 14.0067.

nitrogen cycle *n* the natural circulation of nitrogen by living organisms. Nitrates in the soil, derived from dead organic matter by bacterial action, are absorbed and synthesized into complex organic compounds by plants and reduced to nitrates again when the plants and the animals feeding on them die and decay.

nitrogen dioxide *n* a red-brown poisonous gas that is an intermediate in the manufacture of nitric acid, a nitrating agent, and an oxidizer for rocket fuels. Formula: NO₂.

nitrogen fixation *n* **1** the conversion of atmospheric nitrogen into nitrogen compounds by certain bacteria in the root nodules of legumes. **2** a process in which atmospheric nitrogen is converted into a nitrogen compound, used esp. for fertilizer.

nitrogenize *or* **nitrogenise** (naɪ'trɒdʒɪˌnaɪz) *vb* **nitrogenizing, nitrogenizing, nitrogenized** *or* **nitrogenises, nitrogenising, nitrogenised.** to combine or treat with nitrogen or a nitrogen compound.
> niˌtrogeni'zation *or* niˌtrogeni'sation *n*

nitrogen monoxide *n* the systematic name for **nitric oxide.**

nitrogen mustard *n* any of a class of organic compounds resembling mustard gas in their molecular structure: important in the treatment of cancer.

nitrogenous (naɪ'trɒdʒɪnəs) *adj* containing nitrogen or a nitrogen compound.

nitroglycerine (ˌnaɪtrəʊ'glɪsəriːn) *or* **nitroglycerin** (ˌnaɪtrəʊ'glɪsəˌrɪn) *n* a pale yellow viscous explosive liquid made from glycerol and nitric and sulphuric acids. Formula: CH₂NO₃CHNO₃CH₂NO₃. Also called: **trinitroglycerine.**

nitromethane (ˌnaɪtrəʊ'miːθeɪn) *n* an oily colourless liquid obtained from methane and used as a solvent and rocket fuel.

nitrous ('naɪtrəs) *adj* of, derived from, or containing nitrogen, esp. in a low valency state. [C17: from L *nitrōsus* full of natron]

nitrous acid *n* a weak monobasic acid known only in solution and in the form of nitrite salts. Formula: HNO₂. Systematic name: **dioxonitric(III) acid.**

nitrous oxide *n* a colourless gas with a sweet smell: used as an anaesthetic in dentistry. Formula: N₂O. Also called: **laughing gas.** Systematic name: **dinitrogen oxide.**

nitty ('nɪtɪ) *adj* **nittier, nittiest.** infested with nits.

nitty-gritty ('nɪtɪ'grɪtɪ) *n* **the.** *Inf.* the basic facts of a matter, situation, etc.; the core. [C20: ? rhyming compound from GRIT]

nitwit ('nɪtˌwɪt) *n Inf.* a foolish or dull person. [C20: ? from NIT¹ + WIT¹]

Niue ★ ('njuːeɪ) *n* an island in the S Pacific, between Tonga and the Cook Islands: annexed by New Zealand (1901); achieved full internal self-government in 1974. Chief town and port: Alofi. Pop.: 1977 (1993 est.). Area: 260 sq. km (100 sq. miles). Also called: **Savage Island.**
> **Niuean** (njuː'ɪən) *n, adj*

Niven ★ ('nɪvᵊn) *n* David. 1909–83, British film actor. His films include *The Prisoner of Zenda* (1937), *Around the*

World in 80 Days (1956), and *Paper Tiger* (1975). His autobiographical books include *The Moon's a Balloon* (1972).

Nivernais ★ (*French* nivɛrnɛ) *n* a former province of central France, around Nevers.

nix¹ (nɪks) *Inf.* ◆ *sentence substitute.* **1** another word for **no**¹. ◆ *n* **2** a refusal. **3** nothing. [C18: from G, inf. form of *nichts* nothing]

nix² (nɪks) *or (fem)* **nixie** ('nɪksɪ) *n Germanic myth.* a water sprite, usually unfriendly to humans. [C19: from G *Nixe*, from OHG *nihhus*]

Nixon ★ ('nɪksən) *n* Richard M(ilhous). 1913–94, US Republican politician; 37th president from 1969 until he resigned in 1974.

Nizam ★ (nɪ'zɑːm) *n* the title of the ruler of Hyderabad, India, from 1724 to 1948.

Nizhni Novgorod ★ (*Russian* 'nɪʒnij 'nɔvgərət) *n* industrial city and port in central Russia, at the confluence of the Volga and Oka Rivers: situated on the Volga route from the Baltic to central Asia; birthplace of Maxim Gorki. Pop.: 1 383 000 (1995 est.). Former name (1932–91): **Gorki.**

Nizhni Tagil ★ (*Russian* 'nɪʒnij ta'gil) *n* a city in central Russia, on the E slopes of the Ural Mountains: a major metallurgical centre. Pop.: 409 000 (1995 est.).

NJ *or* **N.J.** *abbrev. for* New Jersey.

Njord (njɔːd) *or* **Njorth** ★ (njɔːθ) *n Norse myth.* the god of the sea, fishing, and prosperity.

Nkomo ★ (ᵊŋ'kəʊməʊ) *n* Joshua. born 1917, Zimbabwean politician; coleader, with Robert Mugabe, of the Patriotic Front (1976–80); vice-president of Zimbabwe from 1990.

Nkrumah ★ (ᵊŋ'kruːmə) *n* Kwame ('kwɑːmɪ). 1909–72, Ghanaian statesman; prime minister (1957–60) and president (1960–66).

NM *or* **N. Mex.** *abbrev. for* New Mexico.

NMR *abbrev. for* nuclear magnetic resonance.

NNE *symbol for* north-northeast.

NNP *abbrev. for* net national product.

NNW *symbol for* north-northwest.

no¹ (nəʊ) *sentence substitute.* **1** used to express denial, disagreement, refusal, etc. ◆ *n, pl* **noes** *or* **nos. 2** an answer or vote of no. **3 not take no for an answer.** to continue in a course of action, etc., despite refusals. **4** (*often pl*) a person who votes in the negative. **5 the noes have it.** there is a majority of votes in the negative. [OE *nā*, from *ne* not, no + *ā* ever]

no² (nəʊ) *determiner* **1** not any, not a, or not one: *there's no money left; no card in the file.* **2** not at all: *she's no youngster.* **3** (foll. by comparative adjectives and adverbs): *not: no less than forty; no taller than a child.* [OE *nā*, from *nān* NONE]

No¹ *or* **Noh** (nəʊ) *n, pl* **No** *or* **Noh.** the stylized classic drama of Japan, developed in the 15th century or earlier, using music, dancing, and themes from religious stories or myths. [from Japanese *nō* talent, from Chinese *neng*]

No² *the chemical symbol for* nobelium.

No³ ★ (nəʊ) *n* Lake. a lake in the S central Sudan, where the Bahr el Jebel (White Nile) is joined by the Bahr el Ghazal. Area: about 103 sq. km (40 sq. miles).

no' (no, nəʊ) *adv Scot.* not.

No. *abbrev. for:* **1** north(ern). **2** Also: **no.** (*pl* **Nos.** *or* **nos.**) number. [from L *numero* the ablative of *numerus* number]

n.o. *Cricket. abbrev. for* not out.

no-account *adj* **1** worthless; good-for-nothing. ◆ *n* **2** a worthless person.

Noah ★ ('nəʊə) *n Old Testament.* a Hebrew patriarch, who saved himself, his family, and a pair of each species of animal and bird from the Flood by building a ship (**Noah's Ark**) in which they all survived (Genesis 6–8).

nob¹ (nɒb) *n Cribbage.* **1** the jack of the suit turned up. **2 one for his nob.** the call made with this jack, scoring one point. [C19: from ?]

nob² (nɒb) *n Sl., chiefly Brit.* a person of wealth or social distinction. [C19: from ?]

★ people and places

no-ball *n* **1** *Cricket.* an illegal ball, as for overstepping the crease, for which the batting side scores a run, and from which the batsman can only be out by being run out. **2** *Rounders.* an illegal ball, esp. one bowled too high or too low. ◆ *interj* **3** *Cricket, rounders.* a call by the umpire indicating a no-ball.

nobble ('nɒbªl) *vb* **nobbles, nobbling, nobbled.** (*tr*) *Brit. sl.* **1** to disable (a racehorse), esp. with drugs. **2** to win over or outwit (a person) by underhand means. **3** to suborn (a person, esp. a juror) by threats, bribery, etc. **4** to steal. **5** to grab. **6** to kidnap. [C19: from *nobbler*, from a false division of *an hobbler* (one who hobbles horses) as *a nobbler*]

Nobel ★ (nəʊˈbɛl) *n* **Alfred Bernhard** ('alfreːd 'bæːrnhard). 1833–96, Swedish chemist and philanthropist, noted for his invention of dynamite (1866) and his bequest for the Nobel prizes.

nobelium (nəʊˈbiːlɪəm) *n* a transuranic element produced artificially from curium. Symbol: No; atomic no.: 102; half-life of most stable isotope, ^{255}No: 180 seconds (approx.). [C20: NL, after *Nobel* Institute, Stockholm, where it was discovered]

Nobel prize *n* a prize for outstanding contributions to chemistry, physics, physiology or medicine, literature, economics, and peace that may be awarded annually; established 1901. [C20: after Alfred NOBEL]

nobility (nəʊˈbɪlɪtɪ) *n, pl* **nobilities. 1** a privileged class whose titles are conferred by descent or royal decree. **2** the quality of being good; dignity: *nobility of mind.* **3** (in the British Isles) the class of people holding the title of dukes, marquesses, earls, viscounts, or barons and their feminine equivalents; peerage.

nobilmente (ˌnəʊbɪlˈmentɛɪ) *adj, adv Music.* to be performed in a noble manner. [It.]

noble ('nəʊbªl) *adj* **1** of or relating to a hereditary class with special status, often derived from a feudal period. **2** of or characterized by high moral qualities; magnanimous: *a noble deed.* **3** having dignity or eminence; illustrious. **4** imposing; magnificent: *a noble avenue of trees.* **5** superior; excellent: *a noble strain of horses.* **6** *Chem.* **6a** (of certain elements) chemically unreactive. **6b** (of certain metals, esp. copper, silver, and gold) resisting oxidation. ◆ *n* **7** a person belonging to a privileged class whose status is usually indicated by a title. **8** (in the British Isles) a person holding the title of duke, marquess, earl, viscount, or baron, or a feminine equivalent. **9** a former British gold coin having the value of one third of a pound. [C13: via OF from L *nōbilis*, orig., capable of being known, hence well-known, from *noscere* to know]
▶ 'nobleness *n* ▶ 'nobly *adv*

nobleman ('nəʊbªlmən) *or* (*fem*) **noblewoman** *n, pl* **noblemen** *or* **noblewomen.** a person of noble rank, title, or status; peer; aristocrat.

noble savage *n* (in romanticism) an idealized view of primitive man.

noblesse oblige (nəʊˈblɛs əʊˈbliːʒ) *n Often ironic.* the supposed obligation of nobility to be honourable and generous. [F, lit.: nobility obliges]

nobody ('nəʊbədɪ) *pron* **1** no person; no-one. ◆ *n, pl* **nobodies. 2** an insignificant person.

USAGE NOTE See at **everyone.**

nock (nɒk) *n* **1** a notch on an arrow that fits on the bowstring. **2** either of the grooves at each end of a bow that hold the bowstring. ◆ *vb* (*tr*) **3** to fit (an arrow) on a bowstring. [C14: rel. to Swedish *nock* tip]

no-claims bonus *n* a reduction on an insurance premium, esp. one covering a motor vehicle, if no claims have been made within a specified period. Also called: **no-claim bonus.**

noctambulism (nɒkˈtæmbjʊˌlɪzəm) *or* **noctambulation** *n* another word for **somnambulism.** [C19: from L *nox* night + *ambulāre* to walk]

noctilucent (ˌnɒktɪˈluːsªnt) *adj* shining at night, usually of very thin high altitude clouds observable in the summer twilight sky. [from L, from *nox* night + *lūcēre* to shine]

noctuid ('nɒktjʊɪd) *n* any of a large family of nocturnal moths that includes the underwings. [C19: via NL from L *noctua* night owl, from *nox* night]

noctule ('nɒktjuːl) *n* any of several large Old World insectivorous bats. [C18: prob. from LL *noctula* small owl, from L *noctua* night owl]

nocturnal (nɒkˈtɜːnªl) *adj* **1** of, used during, occurring in, or relating to the night. **2** (of animals) active at night. **3** (of plants) having flowers that open at night and close by day. [C15: from LL *nocturnālis*, from L *nox* night]
▶ ˌnoctur'nality *n* ▶ noc'turnally *adv*

nocturne ('nɒktɜːn) *n* **1** a short, dreamy, and melodic piece of music, esp. one for the piano. **2** a painting of a night scene.

nod (nɒd) *vb* **nods, nodding, nodded. 1** to lower and raise (the head) briefly, as to indicate agreement, etc. **2** (*tr*) to express by nodding: *she nodded approval.* **3** (*intr*) (of flowers, trees, etc.) to sway or bend forwards and back. **4** (*intr*) to let the head fall forwards through drowsiness; be almost asleep. **5** (*intr*) to be momentarily careless: *even Homer sometimes nods.* **6 nodding acquaintance.** a slight, casual, or superficial knowledge (of a subject or person). ◆ *n* **7** a quick down-and-up movement of the head, as in assent, command, etc. **8 on the nod.** *Inf.* agreed, as in committee, without formal procedure. **9** See **land of Nod.** ◆ See also **nod off.** [C14 *nodde*, from ?]
▶ 'nodding *adj, n*

noddle[1] ('nɒdªl) *n Inf., chiefly Brit.* the head or brains: *use your noddle!* [C15: from ?]

noddle[2] ('nɒdªl) *vb* **noddles, noddling, noddled.** *Inf., chiefly Brit.* to nod (the head), as through drowsiness. [C18: from NOD]

noddy[1] ('nɒdɪ) *n, pl* **noddies. 1** any of several tropical terns, typically having a dark plumage. **2** a fool or dunce. [C16: ? n use of obs. *noddy* foolish, drowsy, ?from NOD (vb); the bird is so called because it allows itself to be caught by hand]

noddy[2] ('nɒdɪ) *n, pl* **noddies.** (*usually pl*) *Television.* film footage of an interviewer's reactions to comments made by an interviewee, used in editing the interview after it has been recorded. [C20: from NOD]

node (nəʊd) *n* **1** a knot, swelling, or knob. **2** the point on a plant stem from which the leaves or lateral branches grow. **3** *Physics.* a point at which the amplitude of one of the two kinds of displacement in a standing wave has zero or minimum value. **4** Also called: **crunode.** *Maths.* a point at which two branches of a curve intersect. **5** *Maths., linguistics.* one of the objects of which a graph or a tree consists. **6** *Astron.* either of the two points at which the orbit of a body intersects the plane of the ecliptic. **7** *Anat.* any natural bulge or swelling, such as those along the course of a lymphatic vessel (**lymph node**). **8** *Computing.* an interconnection point on a computer network. [C16: from L *nōdus* knot]
▶ 'nodal *adj*

nod off *vb* (*intr, adv*) *Inf.* to fall asleep.

nodule ('nɒdjuːl) *n* **1** a small knot, lump, or node. **2** any of the knoblike outgrowths on the roots of clover and other legumes that contain bacteria involved in nitrogen fixation. **3** a small rounded lump of rock or mineral substance, esp. in a matrix of different rock material. [C17: from L *nōdulus*, from *nōdus* knot]
▶ 'nodular, 'nodulose, *or* 'nodulous *adj*

Noel *or* **Noël** (nəʊˈɛl) *n* (in carols, etc.) another word for **Christmas.** [C19: from F, from L *nātālis* a birthday]

noetic (nəʊˈɛtɪk) *adj* of or relating to the mind. [C17: from Gk *noētikos*, from *noein* to think]

Nofretete ★ (ˌnɒfreˈtiːtɪ) *n* a variant of **Nefertiti.**

nog *or* **nogg** (nɒg) *n* **1** Also called: **flip.** a drink, esp. an alcoholic one, containing beaten egg. **2** *East Anglian dialect.* strong local beer. [C17 (orig.: a strong beer): from ?]

noggin ('nɒgɪn) *n* **1** a small quantity of spirits. **2** a small mug. **3** *Inf.* the head. [C17: from ?]

no-go area *n* a district in a town that is barricaded off, usually by a paramilitary organization, which the police, army, etc., can only enter by force.

Noh (nəʊ) *n* a variant spelling of **No**[1].

noir (nwɑː) *adj* (of a film) showing characteristics of a *film noir*, in plot or style. [C20: from French, lit.: black]

noise (nɔɪz) *n* **1** a sound, esp. one that is loud or disturbing. **2** loud shouting; clamour; din. **3** any undesired electrical disturbance in a circuit, etc. **4** undesired or irrelevant elements in a visual image: *removing noise from pictures*. **5** (*pl*) conventional comments or sounds conveying a reaction: *sympathetic noises*. **6 make a noise.** to talk a great deal or complain (about). ♦ *vb* **noises, noising, noised. 7** (*tr*; usually foll. by *abroad* or *about*) to spread (news, gossip, etc.). [C13: from OF, from L: NAUSEA]

noiseless ('nɔɪzlɪs) *adj* making little or no sound.
▶ **'noiselessly** *adv* ▶ **'noiselessness** *n*

noise pollution *n* annoying or harmful noise in an environment.

noisette (nwɑː'zɛt) *adj* **1** flavoured with hazelnuts. **2** nutbrown, as butter browned over heat. ♦ *n* **3** a small round or oval piece of meat. **4** a hazelnut chocolate. [from F: hazelnut]

noisome ('nɔɪsəm) *adj* **1** (esp. of smells) offensive. **2** harmful or noxious. [C14: from obs. *noy*, var. of ANNOY + -SOME[1]]
▶ **'noisomeness** *n*

noisy ('nɔɪzɪ) *adj* **noisier, noisiest. 1** making a loud or constant noise. **2** full of or characterized by noise.
▶ **'noisily** *adv* ▶ **'noisiness** *n*

Nolan ★ ('nəʊlən) *n* Sir **Sidney.** 1917–92, Australian painter.

nolens volens *Latin.* ('nəʊlɛnz 'vəʊlɛnz) *adv* whether willing or unwilling.

nolle prosequi ('nɒlɪ 'prɒsɪ,kwaɪ) *n Law.* an entry made on the court record when the plaintiff or prosecutor undertakes not to continue the action or prosecution. [L: do not pursue]

nomad ('nəʊmæd) *n* **1** a member of a people or tribe who move from place to place to find pasture and food. **2** a wanderer. [C16: via F from L *nomas* wandering shepherd, from Gk]
▶ **no'madic** *adj* ▶ **'nomadism** *n*

no-man's-land *n* **1** land between boundaries, esp. an unoccupied zone between opposing forces. **2** an unowned or unclaimed piece of land. **3** an ambiguous area of activity.

nom de guerre ('nɒm də 'gɛə) *n, pl* **noms de guerre** ('nɒm də 'gɛə). an assumed name. [F, lit.: war name]

nom de plume ('nɒm də 'pluːm) *n, pl* **noms de plume** ('nɒm də 'pluːm). another term for **pen name.** [F]

nomenclature (nəʊ'mɛnklətʃə; *US.* 'nəʊmən,kleɪtʃər) *n* the terminology used in a particular science, art, activity, etc. [C17: from L *nōmenclātūra* list of names]

nominal ('nɒmɪn°l) *adj* **1** in name only; theoretical: *the nominal leader.* **2** minimal in comparison with real worth; token: *a nominal fee.* **3** of, constituting, or giving a name. **4** *Grammar.* of or relating to a noun or noun phrase. ♦ *n* **5** *Grammar.* a noun, noun phrase, or syntactically similar structure. [C15: from L *nōminālis*, from *nōmen* name]
▶ **'nominally** *adv*

nominalism ('nɒmɪn°l,ɪzəm) *n* the philosophical theory that the variety of objects to which a single general name, such as *dog*, applies have nothing in common other than that name.
▶ **'nominalist** *n*

nominal value *n* another name for **par value.**

nominate ('nɒmɪ,neɪt) *vb* **nominates, nominating, nominated.** (*mainly tr*) **1** to propose as a candidate, esp. for an elective office. **2** to appoint to an office or position. **3** to name (someone) to act on one's behalf, esp. to conceal one's identity. **4** (*intr*) *Austral.* to stand as a candidate in an election. [C16: from L *nōmināre* to call by name, from *nōmen* name]
▶ **,nomi'nation** *n* ▶ **'nomi,nator** *n*

nominative ('nɒmɪnətɪv) *adj* **1** *Grammar.* denoting a case of nouns and pronouns in inflected languages that is used esp. to indicate the subject of a finite verb. **2** appointed rather than elected to a position, office, etc. ♦ *n*

3 *Grammar.* **3a** the nominative case. **3b** a word or speech element in the nominative case. [C14: from L *nōminātīvus* belonging to naming, from *nōmen* name]
▶ **nominatival** (,nɒmɪnə'taɪv°l) *adj*

nominee (,nɒmɪ'niː) *n* **1** a person who is nominated to an office or as a candidate. **2a** a person or organization named to act on behalf of someone else, esp. to conceal the identity of the nominator. **2b** (*as modifier*): *nominee shareholder.* [C17: from NOMINATE + -EE]

nomogram ('nɒmə,græm, 'nəʊmə-) or **nomograph** an arrangement of two linear or logarithmic scales such that an intersecting straight line enables intermediate values or values on a third scale to be read off. [C20: from Gk *nomos* law + -GRAM]

-nomy *n combining form.* indicating a science or the laws governing a certain field of knowledge: *agronomy; economy.* [from Gk *-nomia* law]
▶ **-nomic** *adj combining form.*

non- *prefix* **1** indicating negation: *nonexistent.* **2** indicating refusal or failure: *noncooperation.* **3** indicating exclusion from a specified class: *nonfiction.* **4** indicating lack or absence: *nonobjective; nonevent.* [from L *nōn* not]

nonaddictive (,nɒnə'dɪktɪv) *adj* (of a drug, etc.) not causing addiction.

nonage ('nəʊnɪdʒ) *n* **1** *Law.* the state of being under any of various ages at which a person may legally enter into certain transactions, such as marrying, etc. **2** any period of immaturity.

nonagenarian (,nəʊnədʒɪ'nɛərɪən) *n* **1** a person who is from 90 to 99 years old. ♦ *adj* **2** of, relating to, or denoting a nonagenarian. [C19: from L *nōnāgēnārius*, from *nōnāginta* ninety]

nonaggression (,nɒnə'grɛʃən) *n* **a** restraint of aggression, esp. between states. **b** (*as modifier*): *a nonaggression pact.*

nonagon ('nɒnə,gɒn) *n* a polygon having nine sides.
▶ **nonagonal** (nɒn'æɡən°l) *adj*

nonalcoholic (,nɒn,ælkə'hɒl'ɪk) *adj* (of a drink, etc.) not containing alcohol.

nonaligned (,nɒnə'laɪnd) *adj* (of states, etc.) not part of a major alliance or power bloc.
▶ **,nona'lignment** *n*

non-A, non-B hepatitis *n* a form of viral hepatitis, not caused by the agents responsible for hepatitis A and hepatitis B, that is commonly transmitted by infected blood transfusions. The causative virus has been isolated. Also called: **hepatitis C.**

nonce (nɒns) *n* the present time or occasion (now only in **for the nonce**). [C12: from *for the nonce*, a mistaken division of *for then anes*, from *then* dative singular of *the* + *anes* ONCE]

nonce word *n* a word coined for a single occasion.

nonchalant ('nɒnʃələnt) *adj* casually unconcerned or indifferent; uninvolved. [C18: from F, from *nonchaloir* to lack warmth, from NON- + *chaloir* from L *calēre* to be warm]
▶ **'nonchalance** *n*

non-com ('nɒn,kɒm) *n* short for **noncommissioned officer.**

noncombatant (nɒn'kɒmbətənt) *n* **1** a civilian in time of war. **2** a member of the armed forces whose duties do not include fighting, such as a chaplain or surgeon.

noncommissioned officer (,nɒnkə'mɪʃənd) *n* (in the armed forces) a person, such as a sergeant or corporal, who is appointed from the ranks as a subordinate officer.

noncommittal (,nɒnkə'mɪt°l) *adj* not involving or revealing commitment to any particular opinion or action.

non compos mentis *Latin.* ('nɒn 'kɒmpəs 'mɛntɪs) *adj* mentally incapable of managing one's own affairs; of unsound mind. [L: not in control of one's mind]

nonconformist (,nɒnkən'fɔːmɪst) *n* **1** a person who does not conform to generally accepted patterns of behaviour or thought. ♦ *adj* **2** of or characterized by behaviour that does not conform to accepted patterns.
▶ **,noncon'formity** or **,noncon'formism** *n*

★ people and places

Nonconformist (ˌnɒnkən'fɔːmɪst) n **1** a member of a Protestant denomination that dissents from an Established Church, esp. the Church of England. ♦ adj **2** of, relating to, or denoting Nonconformists.
▶ ˌNoncon'formity or ˌNoncon'formism n

noncontributory (ˌnɒnkən'trɪbjʊtərɪ) adj **1** denoting an insurance or pension scheme for employees, the premiums of which are paid by the employer. **2** (of a state benefit) not dependent on national insurance contributions.

nondenominational (ˌnɒndɪˌnɒmɪ'neɪʃənˀl) adj not restricted with regard to religious denomination.

nondescript ('nɒndɪˌskrɪpt) adj **1** having no outstanding features. ♦ n **2** a nondescript person or thing. [C17: from NON- + L dēscriptus, p.p. of dēscrībere to copy]

nondomiciled (nɒn'dɒmɪˌsaɪld) adj of, relating to, or denoting a person who is not domiciled in his country of origin.

none[1] (nʌn) pron **1** not any of a particular class: none of my letters has arrived. **2** no-one; nobody: there was none to tell the tale. **3** not any (of): none of it looks edible. **4** none other. no other person: none other than the Queen herself. **5** none the. (foll. by a comparative adj) in no degree: she was none the worse for her ordeal. **6** none too. not very: he was none too pleased. [OE nān, lit.: not one]

> **USAGE NOTE** None is a singular pronoun and should be used with a singular form of a verb: none of the students has (not have) a car.

none[2] (nəʊn) n another word for **nones**.

nonentity (nɒn'entɪtɪ) n, pl **nonentities**. **1** an insignificant person or thing. **2** a nonexistent thing. **3** the state of not existing; nonexistence.

nones (nəʊnz) n (functioning as sing or pl) **1** (in the Roman calendar) the ninth day before the ides of each month: the seventh day of March, May, July, and October, and the fifth of each other month. **2** Chiefly RC Church. the fifth of the seven canonical hours of the divine office, originally fixed at the ninth hour of the day, about 3 p.m. [OE nōn, from L nōna hora ninth hour, from nōnus ninth]

nonesuch or **nonsuch** ('nʌnˌsʌtʃ) n Arch. a matchless person or thing; nonpareil.

nonet (nəʊ'nɛt) n **1** a piece of music for nine instruments or voices. **2** a group of nine singers or instrumentalists.

nonetheless (ˌnʌnðə'lɛs) sentence connector. despite that; however; nevertheless.

non-Euclidean geometry n the branch of modern geometry in which certain axioms of Euclidean geometry are denied.

nonevent (ˌnɒnɪ'vɛnt) n a disappointing or insignificant occurrence, esp. one predicted to be important.

nonexecutive director (ˌnɒnɪg'zɛkjʊtɪv) n a director of a commercial company who is not a full-time employee of the company.

nonexistent (ˌnɒnɪg'zɪstənt) adj **1** not having being or reality. **2** not present under specified conditions or in a specified place.
▶ nonex'istence n

nonfeasance (nɒn'fiːzˀns) n Law. a failure to act when under an obligation to do so. Cf. **malfeasance, misfeasance**. [C16: from NON- + feasance (obs.) doing, from F faisance, from faire to do, L facere]

nonferrous (nɒn'fɛrəs) adj **1** denoting any metal other than iron. **2** not containing iron.

nonflammable (nɒn'flæməbˀl) adj incapable of burning or not easily set on fire.

nonfunctional (nɒn'fʌŋkʃənˀl) adj not having a function.

nong (nɒŋ) n Austral. sl. a stupid or incompetent person. [C19: ?from obs. E dialect nigmenog silly fellow, from ?]

non-Hodgkin's Lymphoma n any form of lymphoma other than Hodgkin's disease.

nonillion (nəʊ'nɪljən) n **1** (in Britain, France, and Germany) the number represented as one followed by 54 zeros (10^{54}). **2** (in the US and Canada) the number represented as one followed by 30 zeros (10^{30}). Brit. word: **quintillion**. [C17: from F, from L nōnus ninth, on the model of MILLION]

nonintervention (ˌnɒnɪntə'vɛnʃən) n refusal to intervene, esp. the abstention by a state from intervening in the affairs of other states or in its own internal disputes.

noninvasive (ˌnɒnɪn'veɪsɪv) adj (of medical treatment) not involving the making of a relatively large incision in the body or the insertion of instruments, etc., into the patient.

nonjudgmental (ˌnɒndʒʌdʒ'mɛntˀl) adj avoiding moral judgments, esp. relating to the conduct of others.

nonjuror (nɒn'dʒʊərə) n a person who refuses to take an oath, as of allegiance.

Nonjuror (nɒn'dʒʊərə) n any of a group of clergy in England and Scotland who declined to take the oath of allegiance to William and Mary in 1689.

nonlinear (ˌnɒn'lɪnɪə) adj not linear, esp. with regard to dimension.

nonmetal (nɒn'mɛtˀl) n any of a number of chemical elements that have acidic oxides and are poor conductors of heat and electricity.
▶ ˌnonme'tallic adj

nonmoral (nɒn'mɒrəl) adj not involving morality or ethics; neither moral nor immoral.

Nono ★ (Italian 'nɔːno) n **Luigi** (lu'iːdʒi). 1924–90, Italian composer of 12-tone music.

nonobjective (ˌnɒnəb'dʒɛktɪv) adj of or designating an art movement in which things are depicted in an abstract or purely formalized way.

no-nonsense (ˌnəʊ'nɒnsəns) adj sensible, practical, and straightforward: a severe no-nonsense look.

nonpareil ('nɒnpərəl, ˌnɒnpə'reɪl) n a person or thing that is unsurpassed; peerless example. [C15: from F, from NON- + pareil similar]

nonpersistent (ˌnɒnpə'sɪstənt) adj (of pesticides) breaking down rapidly after application; not persisting in the environment.

non-person n a person regarded as nonexistent or unimportant; a nonentity.

nonplus (nɒn'plʌs) vb **nonplusses, nonplussing, nonplussed** or US **nonpluses, nonplusing, nonplused**. **1** (tr) to put at a loss; confound. ♦ n, pl **nonpluses**. **2** a state of utter perplexity prohibiting action or speech. [C16: from L nōn plūs no further]

nonprofessional (ˌnɒnprə'fɛʃənˀl) adj **1** not professional in status. ♦ n **2** a person who is not a professional.

non-profit-making adj not yielding a profit, esp. because organized or established for some other reason: a non-profit-making organization.

nonproliferation (ˌnɒnprəˌlɪfər'eɪʃən) n a limitation of the production or spread of something, esp. nuclear or chemical weapons. **b** (as modifier): a nonproliferation treaty.

non-pros (ˌnɒn'prɒs) n **1** short for **non prosequitur**. ♦ vb **non-prosses, non-prossing, non-prossed**. **2** (tr) to enter a judgment of non prosequitur against (a plaintiff).

non prosequitur ('nɒn prəʊ'sɛkwɪtə) n Law. (formerly) a judgment in favour of a defendant when the plaintiff failed to take the necessary steps in an action within the time allowed. [L, lit.: he does not prosecute]

nonracial (ˌnɒn'reɪʃəl) adj not involving race or racial factors.

nonrepresentational (ˌnɒnrɛprɪzɛn'teɪʃənˀl) adj Art. another word for **abstract**.

nonresident (nɒn'rɛzɪdənt) n **1** a person who is not residing in the place implied or specified. **2** a British person employed abroad for a minimum of one year, who is exempt from UK income tax provided that he does not spend more than 90 days in the UK during that tax year. ♦ adj **3** not residing in the place specified.
▶ non'residence or non'residency n ▶ ˌnonresi'dential adj

★ people and places

nonresistant (ˌnɒnrɪˈzɪstənt) *adj* **1** incapable of resisting something, such as a disease; susceptible. **2** *History.* (esp. in 17th-century England) practising passive obedience to royal authority even when its commands were unjust.

nonrestrictive (ˌnɒnrɪˈstrɪktɪv) *adj* **1** not limiting. **2** *Grammar.* denoting a relative clause that is not restrictive. Cf. **restrictive** (sense 2).

nonsense (ˈnɒnsəns) *n* **1** something that has or makes no sense; unintelligible language; drivel. **2** conduct or action that is absurd. **3** foolish behaviour: *she'll stand no nonsense.* **4** things of little or no value; trash. ◆ *interj* **5** an exclamation of disagreement.
▸ **nonsensical** (nɒnˈsɛnsɪkˀl) *adj* ▸ **non'sensically** *adv* ▸ **non'sensicalness** *or* **non,sensi'cality** *n*

nonsense verse *n* verse in which the sense is nonexistent or absurd.

non sequitur (ˈnɒn ˈsɛkwɪtə) *n* **1** a statement having little or no relevance to what preceded it. **2** *Logic.* a conclusion that does not follow from the premises. [L, lit.: it does not follow]

nonsmoker (nɒnˈsməʊkə) *n* **1** a person who does not smoke. **2** a train compartment in which smoking is forbidden.
▸ **non'smoking** *adj*

nonspecific urethritis *n* inflammation of the urethra as a result of a sexually transmitted infection that cannot be traced to a specific cause. Abbrev.: **NSU.**

nonstandard (nɒnˈstændəd) *adj* **1** denoting or characterized by idiom, vocabulary, etc., that is not regarded as correct and acceptable by educated native speakers of a language; not standard. **2** deviating from a given standard.

nonstarter (nɒnˈstɑːtə) *n* **1** a horse that fails to run in a race for which it has been entered. **2** a person or thing that has little chance of success.

nonstick (ˈnɒnˈstɪk) *adj* (of saucepans, etc.) coated with a substance that prevents food sticking to them.

nonstop (ˈnɒnˈstɒp) *adj, adv* done without pause or interruption: *a nonstop flight.*

nonsuch (ˈnʌnˌsʌtʃ) *n* a variant spelling of **nonesuch.**

nonsuit (nɒnˈsuːt) *Law.* ◆ *n* **1** an order of a judge dismissing a suit when the plaintiff fails to show he has a good cause of action or fails to produce any evidence. ◆ *vb* **2** (*tr*) to order the dismissal of the suit of (a person).

nontechnical (ˌnɒnˈtɛknɪkˀl) *adj* **1** not technical in nature. **2** (of a person) not having technical knowledge or aptitude.

non troppo (ˈnɒn ˈtrɒpəʊ) *adv Music.* (preceded by a direction, esp. a tempo marking) not to be observed too strictly (esp. in **allegro ma non troppo, adagio ma non troppo**). [It.]

non-U (nɒnˈjuː) *adj Brit. inf.* (esp. of language) not characteristic of or used by the upper class.

nonunion (nɒnˈjuːnjən) *adj* **1** not belonging or related to a trade union: *nonunion workers.* **2** not favouring or employing union labour: *a nonunion shop.* **3** not produced by union labour.

nonvoter (nɒnˈvəʊtə) *n* **1** a person who does not vote. **2** a person not eligible to vote.

nonvoting (nɒnˈvəʊtɪŋ) *adj* **1** of or relating to a nonvoter. **2** *Finance.* (of shares, etc.) not entitling the holder to vote at company meetings.

noodle[1] (ˈnuːdˀl) *n* (*often pl*) pasta in the form of ribbons or fine strands. [C18: from G *Nudel* from ?]

noodle[2] (ˈnuːdˀl) *n* **1** *US & Canad. sl.* the head. **2** a simpleton. [C18: ? a blend of NOODLE[1] & NOODLE[1]]

nook (nʊk) *n* **1** a corner or narrow recess. **2** a secluded or sheltered place. [C13: from ?]

nooky *or* **nookie** (ˈnʊkɪ) *n Sl.* lovemaking.

noon (nuːn) *n* **1** the middle of the day; 12 o'clock. **2** *Poetic.* the most important part; culmination. [OE *nōn*, from L *nōna* (*hōra*) ninth hour (orig. 3 p.m., the ninth hour from sunrise)]

noonday (ˈnuːnˌdeɪ) *n* the middle of the day; noon.

no-one *or* **no one** *pron* no person; nobody.

USAGE NOTE   See at **everyone.**

noontime (ˈnuːnˌtaɪm) *or* **noontide** *n* the middle of the day; noon.

Noordbrabant ★ (noːrdˈbrɑːbɑnt) *n* the Dutch name for **North Brabant.**

Noordholland ★ (noːrtˈhɔlɑnt) *n* the Dutch name for **North Holland.**

noose (nuːs) *n* **1** a loop in the end of a rope, such as a lasso or hangman's halter, usually tied with a slipknot. **2** something that restrains or traps. **3 put one's head in a noose.** to bring about one's own downfall. ◆ *vb* **nooses, noosing, noosed.** (*tr*) **4** to secure as in a noose. **5** to make a noose of or in. [C15: ?from Provençal *nous*, from L *nōdus* NODE]

no-par *adj* (of securities) without a par value.

nor (nɔː; *unstressed* nə) *conj* (*coordinating*) **1** (used to join alternatives, the first of which is preceded by *neither*) and not: *neither measles nor mumps.* **2** (foll. by a verb) (and) not…either: *they weren't talented – nor were they particularly funny.* **3** *Poetic.* neither: *nor wind nor rain.* [C13: contraction of OE *nōther*, from *nāhwæther* NEITHER]

Nor. *abbrev. for:* **1** Norman. **2** north. **3** Norway. **4** Norwegian.

noradrenaline (ˌnɔːrəˈdrɛnəlɪn, -liːn) *or* **noradrenalin** *n* a hormone secreted by the adrenal medulla, increasing blood pressure and heart rate. US name: **norepinephrine.**

NOR circuit *or* **gate** (nɔː) *n Computing.* a logic circuit having two or more input wires and one output wire that has a high-voltage output signal only if all input signals are at a low voltage. Cf. **AND circuit.** [C20: from NOR; the action performed is similar to the operation of the conjunction *nor* in logic]

Nord ★ (French nɔr) *n* a department of N France, in Nord-Pas-de-Calais region. Capital: Lille. Pop.: 2 553 939 (1994 est.). Area: 5774 sq. km (2252 sq. miles).

Nordenskjöld ★ (Swedish ˈnuːrdənˌɧœld) *n* Baron **Nils Adolf Erik** (nils ˈɑːdɔlf ˈeːrik). 1832–1901, Swedish Arctic explorer and geologist, born in Finland. He was the first to navigate the Northeast Passage (1878–79).

Nordenskjöld Sea ★ *n* the former name of the **Laptev Sea.** [named after N. A. E. NORDENSKJÖLD]

nordic (ˈnɔːdɪk) *adj Skiing.* of competitions in cross-country racing and ski-jumping. Cf. **alpine** (sense 4).

Nordic (ˈnɔːdɪk) *adj* of or belonging to a subdivision of the Caucasoid race typified by the tall blond blue-eyed long-headed inhabitants of Scandinavia. [C19: from F *nordique*, from *nord* NORTH]

Nordkyn Cape ★ (Norwegian ˈnuːrçyːn) *n* a cape in N Norway: the northernmost point of the European mainland.

Nord-Pas-de-Calais ★ (French nɔrpɑdəkalɛ) *n* a region of N France, on the Straits of Dover (the **Pas de Calais**): coal-mining, textile, and metallurgical industries.

Nordrhein-Westfalen ★ (ˈnɔrtraɪnvɛstˈfaːlən) *n* the German name for **North Rhine-Westphalia.**

norepinephrine (ˌnɔːrɛpɪˈnɛfrɪn, -riːn) *n* the US name for **noradrenaline.**

Norfolk ★ (ˈnɔːfək) *n* **1** a county of E England, on the North Sea and the Wash: low-lying, with large areas of fens in the west and the Broads in the east; rich agriculturally. Administrative centre: Norwich. Pop.: 768 500 (1994 est.). Area: 5368 sq. km (2072 sq. miles). **2** a port in SE Virginia, on the Elizabeth River and Hampton Roads: headquarters of the US Atlantic fleet; shipbuilding. Pop.: 241 426 (1994 est.).

Norfolk Island ★ *n* an island in the S Pacific, between New Caledonia and N New Zealand: an Australian external territory; discovered by Captain Cook in 1774; a penal settlement in early years. Pop.: 2665 (1993). Area: 36 sq. km (14 sq. miles).

Norfolk jacket *n* a man's single-breasted belted jacket

★ people and places

with one or two chest pockets and a box pleat down the back. [C19: worn in NORFOLK for duck shooting]

Norge ★ ('nɔrgə) *n* the Norwegian name for **Norway**.

noria ('nɔːrɪə) *n* a water wheel with buckets attached to its rim for raising water from a stream into irrigation canals, etc. [C18: via Sp. from Ar. *nā'ūra*, from *na'ara* to creak]

Noricum ★ ('nɒrɪkəm) *n* an Alpine kingdom of the Celts, south of the Danube: comprises present-day central Austria and parts of Bavaria; a Roman province from about 16 B.C.

nork (nɔːk) *n* (*usually pl*) *Austral. taboo sl.* a female breast. [C20: from ?]

norm (nɔːm) *n* 1 an average level of achievement or performance, as of a group. 2 a standard of achievement or behaviour that is required, desired, or designated as normal. [C19: from L *norma* carpenter's square]

normal ('nɔːm²l) *adj* 1 usual; regular; common; typical: *the normal level.* 2 constituting a standard: *if we take this as normal.* 3 *Psychol.* 3a being within certain limits of intelligence, ability, etc. 3b conforming to the conventions of one's group. 4 (of laboratory animals) maintained in a natural state for purposes of comparison with animals treated with drugs, etc. 5 *Chem.* (of a solution) containing a number of grams equal to the equivalent weight of the solute in each litre of solvent. 6 *Geom.* another word for **perpendicular** (sense 1). ◆ *n* 7 the usual, average, or typical state, degree, form, etc. 8 anything that is normal. 9 *Geom.* a perpendicular line or plane. [C16: from L *normālis* conforming to the carpenter's square, from *norma* NORM]

▸ **normality** (nɔːˈmælɪtɪ) *or esp. US* **normalcy** *n*

normal curve *n Statistics.* a symmetrical bell-shaped curve representing the probability density function of a normal distribution.

normal distribution *n Statistics.* a continuous distribution of a random variable with its mean, median, and mode equal.

normalize *or* **normalise** ('nɔːməˌlaɪz) *vb* **normalizes, normalizing, normalized** *or* **normalises, normalising, normalised.** (*tr*) 1 to bring or make into the normal state. 2 to bring into conformity with a standard. 3 to heat (steel) above a critical temperature and allow it to cool in air to relieve internal stresses; anneal.

▸ ˌnormaliˈzation *or* ˌnormaliˈsation *n*

normally ('nɔːməlɪ) *adv* 1 as a rule; usually; ordinarily. 2 in a normal manner.

Norman[1] ('nɔːmən) *n* 1 (in the Middle Ages) a member of the people of Normandy in N France, descended from the 10th-century Scandinavian conquerors of the country and the native French. 2 a native or inhabitant of Normandy. 3 another name for **Norman French**. ◆ *adj* 4 of or characteristic of the Normans, esp. the Norman kings of England and the Norman people living in England, or their dialect of French. 5 of or characteristic of Normandy. 6 denoting or having the style of Romanesque architecture used in Britain from the Norman Conquest until the 12th century, characterized by the rounded arch, massive masonry walls, etc.

Norman[2] ★ ('nɔːmən) *n* 1 *Greg.* born 1955, Australian golfer. 2 *Jessye* ('dʒɛsɪ). born 1945, US Black soprano.

Norman Conquest *n* the invasion and settlement of England by the Normans, following the Battle of Hastings (1066).

Normandy ★ ('nɔːməndɪ) *n* a former province of N France, on the English Channel: settled by Vikings under Rollo in the 10th century; scene of the Allied landings in 1944. Chief town: Rouen. French name: **Normandie** (nɔrmɑ̃di).

Norman French *n* the medieval Norman and English dialect of Old French.

normative ('nɔːmətɪv) *adj* 1 implying, creating, or prescribing a norm or standard, as in language: *normative grammar.* 2 expressing value judgments as contrasted with stating facts.

Norn[1] ★ (nɔːn) *n Norse myth.* any of the three virgin goddesses of fate. [C18: ON]

Norn[2] (nɔːn) *n* the medieval Norse language of the Orkneys, Shetlands, and parts of N Scotland. [C17: from ON *norrǽna* Norwegian, from *northr* north]

Norodom Sihanouk ★ (ˌnɒrəˈdɒm ˈsiːənuk) *n* See (Norodom) **Sihanouk.**

Norrköping ★ (*Swedish* 'nɔrtçøːpiŋ) *n* a port in SE Sweden, near the Baltic. Pop.: 123 795 (1996 est.).

Norse (nɔːs) *adj* 1 of ancient and medieval Scandinavia or its inhabitants. 2 of or characteristic of Norway. ◆ *n* 3a the N group of Germanic languages, spoken in Scandinavia. 3b any one of these languages, esp. in their ancient or medieval forms. 4 **the Norse.** (*functioning as pl*) 4a the Norwegians. 4b the Vikings.

Norseman ('nɔːsmən) *n, pl* **Norsemen.** another name for a **Viking.**

north (nɔːθ) *n* 1 one of the four cardinal points of the compass, at 0° or 360°, that is 90° from east and west and 180° from south. 2 the direction along a meridian towards the North Pole. 3 the direction in which a compass needle points; magnetic north. 4 **the north.** (*often cap.*) any area lying in or towards the north. 5 (*usually cap.*) *Cards.* the player or position at the table corresponding to north on the compass. ◆ *adj* 6 in, towards, or facing the north. 7 (esp. of the wind) from the north. ◆ *adv* 8 in, to, or towards the north. [OE]

North[1] (nɔːθ) *n* **the.** 1 the northern area of England, generally regarded as reaching the southern boundaries of Yorkshire, Derbyshire, and Cheshire. 2 (in the US) the states north of the Mason-Dixon Line that were known as the Free States during the Civil War. 3 the northern part of North America, esp. Alaska, the Yukon and the Northwest Territories. 4 the countries of the world that are economically and technically advanced. ◆ *adj* 5 of or denoting the northern part of a specified country, area, etc.

North[2] ★ (nɔːθ) *n* 1 *Frederick,* 2nd Earl of Guildford, called *Lord North.* 1732–92, British statesman; prime minister (1770–82), dominated by George III. He was held responsible for the loss of the American colonies. 2 *Sir Thomas.* ?1535–?1601, English translator of Plutarch's *Lives* (1579), which was the chief source of Shakespeare's Roman plays.

North Africa ★ *n* the part of Africa between the Mediterranean and the Sahara: consists chiefly of Morocco, Algeria, Tunisia, Libya, and N Egypt.

▸ **North African** *adj, n*

Northallerton ★ (nɔːˈθælətˀn) *n* a market town in N England, administrative centre of North Yorkshire. Pop.: 13 774 (1991).

North America ★ *n* the third largest continent, linked with South America by the Isthmus of Panama and bordering on the Arctic Ocean, the N Pacific, the N Atlantic, the Gulf of Mexico, and the Caribbean. It consists generally of a great mountain system (the Western Cordillera) extending along the entire W coast, actively volcanic in the extreme north and south, with the Great Plains to the east and the Appalachians still further east, separated from the Canadian Shield by an arc of large lakes (Great Bear, Great Slave, Winnipeg, Superior, Michigan, Huron, Erie, Ontario); reaches its greatest height of 6194 m (20 320 ft) in Mount McKinley, Alaska, and its lowest point of 85 m (280 ft) below sea level in Death Valley, California, and ranges from snowfields, tundra, and taiga in the north to deserts in the southwest and tropical forests in the extreme south. Pop.: 421 006 000 (1996 est.). Area: over 24 000 000 sq. km (9 500 000 sq. miles).

▸ **North American** *adj, n*

Northampton ★ (nɔːˈθæmptən, nɔːθ'hæmp-) *n* 1 a town in central England, administrative centre of Northamptonshire, on the River Nene: footwear and engineering industries. Pop.: 179 596 (1991). 2 short for **Northamptonshire.**

Northamptonshire ★ (nɔːˈθæmptən,ʃɪə, -ʃə, nɔːθ'hæmp-) *n* a county of central England: agriculture, food processing, engineering. Administrative centre: Northampton. Pop.: 570 300 (1988 est.). Area: 2367 sq. km (914 sq. miles). Abbrev.: **Northants.**

Northants (nɔː'θænts) *abbrev. for* Northamptonshire.

North Atlantic Drift *or* **Current** *n* the warm ocean current flowing northeast, under the influence of prevailing winds, from the Gulf of Mexico towards NW Europe and warming its climate. Also called: **Gulf Stream.**

North Ayrshire ★ *n* a council area of W central Scotland, on the Firth of Clyde. Administrative centre: Irvine. Pop.: 139 020 (1996 est.). Area: 884 sq. km (341 sq. miles).

North Borneo ★ *n* the former name (until 1963) of **Sabah.**

northbound ('nɔːθ,baʊnd) *adj* going or leading towards the north.

North Brabant ★ *n* a province of the S Netherlands: formed part of the medieval duchy of Brabant. Capital: 's Hertogenbosch. Pop.: 2 276 207 (1995). Area: 4965 sq. km (1917 sq. miles). Dutch name: **Noordbrabant.**

north by east *n* one point on the compass east of north.

north by west *n* one point on the compass west of north.

North Cape ★ *n* 1 a cape on N Magerøy Island, in the Arctic Ocean off the N coast of Norway. 2 a cape on N North Island, New Zealand.

North Carolina ★ *n* a state of the southeastern US, on the Atlantic: consists of a coastal plain rising to the Piedmont Plateau and the Appalachian Mountains in the west. Capital: Raleigh. Pop.: 7 322 870 (1996 est.). Area: 126 387 sq. km (48 798 sq. miles). Abbrevs.: **N.C.** or (with zip code) **NC**
▸ **North Carolinian** *adj, n*

North Channel ★ *n* a strait between NE Ireland and SW Scotland, linking the North Atlantic with the Irish Sea.

Northcliffe ★ ('nɔːθklɪf) *n* **Viscount.** title of *Alfred Charles William Harmsworth.* 1865–1922, British newspaper proprietor. With his brother, 1st Viscount Rothermere, he built up a chain of newspapers.

North Country *n* (usually preceded by *the*) 1 another name for **North**[1] (sense 1). 2 another name for **North**[1] (sense 3).

Northd *abbrev. for* Northumberland.

North Dakota ★ *n* a state of the western US: mostly undulating prairies and plains, rising from the Red River valley in the east to the Missouri plateau in the west, with the infertile Bad Lands in the extreme west. Capital: Bismarck. Pop.: 643 539 (1996 est.). Area: 183 019 sq. km (70 664 sq. miles). Abbrevs.: **N.Dak., N.D.,** or (with zip code) **ND**
▸ **North Dakotan** *adj, n*

North Down ★ *n* a district of E Northern Ireland, on Belfast Lough E of Belfast: residential area for Belfast, tourism. Administrative centre: Bangor. Area: 74 sq. km (28 sq. miles). Pop.: 71 832 (1991).

northeast (,nɔːθ'iːst; *Naut.* ,nɔːr'iːst) *n* 1 the point of the compass or direction midway between north and east. 2 (*often cap.;* usually preceded by *the*) any area lying in or towards this direction. ◆ *adj also* **northeastern.** 3 (*sometimes cap.*) of or denoting the northeastern part of a specified country, area, etc.: *northeast Lincolnshire.* 4 in, towards, or facing the northeast. 5 (esp. of the wind) from the northeast. ◆ *adv* 6 in, to, or towards the northeast.
▸ ,**north'easternmost** *adj*

Northeast (,nɔːθ'iːst) *n* (usually preceded by *the*) the northeastern part of England, esp. Northumberland, Durham, and the Tyneside area.

northeast by east *n* one point on the compass east of northeast.

northeast by north *n* one point on the compass north of northeast.

northeaster (,nɔːθ'iːstə; *Naut.* ,nɔːr'iːstə) *n* a strong wind or storm from the northeast.

northeasterly (,nɔːθ'iːstəlɪ; *Naut.* ,nɔːr'iːstəlɪ) *adj, adv* 1 in, towards, or (esp. of a wind) from the northeast. ◆ *n, pl* **northeasterlies.** 2 a wind or storm from the northeast.

North East Frontier Agency ★ *n* the former name (until 1972) of **Arunachal Pradesh.**

North East Lincolnshire ★ *n* a unitary authority in E England, in Lincolnshire. Pop.: 164 000 (1996 est.). Area: 192 sq. km (74 sq. miles).

Northeast Passage ★ *n* a shipping route along the Arctic coasts of Europe and Asia, between the Atlantic and Pacific: first navigated by Nordenskjöld (1878–79).

northeastward (,nɔːθ'iːstwəd; *Naut.* ,nɔːr'iːstwəd) *adj* 1 towards or (esp. of a wind) from the northeast. ◆ *n* 2 a direction towards or area in the northeast.
▸ ,**north'eastwardly** *adj, adv*

norther ('nɔːðə) *n Chiefly southern US.* a wind or storm from the north.

northerly ('nɔːðəlɪ) *adj* 1 of or situated in the north. ◆ *adv, adj* 2 towards the north. 3 from the north: *a northerly wind.* ◆ *n, pl* **northerlies.** 4 a wind from the north.
▸ '**northerliness** *n*

northern ('nɔːðən) *adj* 1 in or towards the north. 2 (esp. of winds) proceeding from the north. 3 (*sometimes cap.*) of or characteristic of the north or North.

Northern Dvina ★ *n* See **Dvina** (sense 1).

Northerner ('nɔːðənə) *n* (*sometimes not cap.*) a native or inhabitant of the north of any specified region, esp. England, the US, or the far north of Canada.

northern hemisphere *n* (*often caps.*) that half of the globe lying north of the equator.

Northern Ireland ★ *n* that part of the United Kingdom occupying the NE part of Ireland: separated from the rest of Ireland, which became officially independent in 1920, remaining part of the United Kingdom, with a separate Parliament (Stormont), which was inaugurated in 1921, and limited self-government: scene of severe conflict between Catholics and Protestants, including terrorist bombing from 1969; peace agreement reached in 1998: direct administration from Westminster from 1972; separate Northern Irish assembly established in 1998. Capital: Belfast. Pop.: 1 641 700 (1994 est.). Area: 14 121 sq. km (5452 sq. miles).

Northern Isles ★ *pl n* the Orkneys and Shetland.

northern lights *pl n* another name for **aurora borealis.**

northernmost ('nɔːðən,məʊst) *adj* situated or occurring farthest north.

Northern Rhodesia ★ *n* the former name (until 1964) of **Zambia.**

Northern Territories ★ *pl n* a former British protectorate in W Africa, established in 1897; attached to the Gold Coast in 1901; now constitutes the Northern Region of Ghana (since 1957).

Northern Territory ★ *n* an administrative division of N central Australia, on the Timor and Arafura Seas: includes Ashmore and Cartier Islands; the Arunta Desert lies in the east, the Macdonnell Ranges in the south, and Arnhem Land in the north (containing Australia's largest Aboriginal reservation). Capital: Darwin. Pop.: 177 500 (1996 est.). Area: 1 347 525 sq. km (520 280 sq. miles).

North Holland ★ *n* a province of the NW Netherlands, on the peninsula between the North Sea and IJsselmeer: includes the West Frisian Island of Texel. Capital: Haarlem. Pop.: 2 463 611 (1995). Area: 2663 sq. km (1029 sq. miles). Dutch name: **Noordholland.**

northing ('nɔːθɪŋ, -ðɪŋ) *n* 1 *Navigation.* movement or distance covered in a northerly direction, esp. as expressed in the resulting difference in latitude. 2 *Astron.* a north or positive declination.

North Island ★ *n* **the.** the northernmost of the two main islands of New Zealand. Pop.: 2 733 083 (1996). Area: 114 729 sq. km (44 297 sq. miles).

North Korea ★ *n* a republic in NE Asia, on the Sea of Japan and the Yellow Sea: established in 1948 as a people's republic; invaded South Korea in 1950 but division remained unchanged at the end of the war (1953): mostly rugged and mountainous, with fertile lowlands in the west. Language: Korean. Currency: won. Capital: Pyongyang. Pop.: 21 890 000 (1988 est.). Area: 122 313

★ people and places

sq. km (47 225 sq. miles). Official name: **Democratic People's Republic of Korea.** Korean name: **Chosŏn.**

▸ **North Korean** *adj, n*

North Lanarkshire ★ *n* a council area of central Scotland. Administrative centre: Motherwell. Pop.: 307 100 (1996 est.). Area: 1771 sq. km (684 sq. miles).

Northland ★ ('nɔːθlənd) *n* **1** the peninsula containing Norway and Sweden. **2** (in Canada) the far north.

▸ **'Northlander** *n*

North Lincolnshire ★ *n* a unitary authority of E England, in Lincolnshire. Pop.: 153 000 (1996 est.). Area: 1497 sq. km (578 sq. miles).

Northman ('nɔːθmən) *n, pl* **Northmen.** another name for a **Viking.**

north-northeast *n* **1** the point on the compass or the direction midway between north and northeast. ◆ *adj, adv* **2** in, from, or towards this direction.

north-northwest *n* **1** the point on the compass or the direction midway between northwest and north. ◆ *adj, adv* **2** in, from, or towards this direction.

North Ossetian Republic ★ (əˈsiːʃən) *n* a constituent republic of S Russia, on the N slopes of the central Caucasus Mountains. Capital: Vladikavkaz. Pop.: 658 000 (1995 est.). Area: 8000 sq. km (3088 sq. miles). Also called: **North Ossetia** (əˈsiːʃə), **Alania.**

North Pole ★ *n* **1** the northernmost point on the earth's axis, at a latitude of 90°N, characterized by very low temperatures. **2** Also called: **north celestial pole.** *Astron.* the point of intersection of the earth's extended axis and the northern half of the celestial sphere. **3** (*usually not cap.*) the pole of a freely suspended magnet, which is attracted to the earth's magnetic North Pole.

North Rhine-Westphalia ★ *n* a state of W Germany: formed in 1946 by the amalgamation of the Prussian province of Westphalia with the N part of the Prussian Rhine province and later with the state of Lippe; part of West Germany until 1990: highly industrialized. Capital: Düsseldorf. Pop.: 17 816 100 (1995 est.). Area: 34 039 sq. km (13 142 sq. miles). German name: **Nordrhein-Westfalen.**

North Riding ★ *n* (until 1974) an administrative division of Yorkshire, now constituting most of North Yorkshire.

North Saskatchewan ★ *n* a river in W Canada, rising in W Alberta and flowing northeast, east, and southeast to join the South Saskatchewan River and form the Saskatchewan River. Length: 1223 km (760 miles).

North Sea ★ *n* an arm of the Atlantic between Great Britain and the N European mainland. Area: about 569 800 sq. km (220 000 sq. miles). Former name: **German Ocean.**

North-Sea gas *n* (in Britain) natural gas obtained from deposits below the North Sea.

North Somerset ★ *n* a unitary authority of SW England, in Somerset. Pop.: 177 000 (1996 est.). Area: 375 sq. km (145 sq. miles).

North Star *n* the. another name for **Polaris.**

North Tyneside ★ *n* a unitary authority of NE England, in Tyne and Wear. Pop.: 194 000 (1996 est.). Area: 84 sq. km (32 sq. miles).

Northumberland[1] ★ (nɔːˈθʌmbələnd) *n* the northernmost county of England, on the North Sea: hilly in the north (the Cheviots) and west (the Pennines), with many Roman remains, notably Hadrian's Wall; shipbuilding, coal-mining. Administrative centre: Morpeth. Pop.: 307 700 (1994 est.). Area: 5032 sq. km (1943 sq. miles). Also called: **Northumbria.** Abbrev.: **Northd.**

Northumberland[2] ★ (nɔːˈθʌmbələnd) *n* **1st Duke of,** title of *John Dudley.* 1502–53, English statesman and soldier, who governed England (1549–53) during the minority of Edward VI. His attempt (1553) to gain the throne for his daughter-in-law, Lady Jane Grey, led to his execution.

Northumbria ★ (nɔːˈθʌmbrɪə) *n* **1** (in Anglo-Saxon Britain) a region that stretched from the Humber to the Firth of Forth: formed in the 7th century A.D., it became

an important intellectual centre; a separate kingdom until 876 A.D. **2** another name for **Northumberland**[1].

▸ **Nor'thumbrian** *adj*

North Vietnam ★ *n* a region of N Vietnam, on the Gulf of Tonkin: an independent Communist state from 1954 until 1976. Area: 164 061 sq. km (63 344 sq. miles).

northward ('nɔːθwəd; *Naut.* 'nɔːðəd) *adj* **1** moving, facing, or situated towards the north. ◆ *n* **2** the northward part, direction, etc. ◆ *adv also* **northwards. 3** towards the north.

northwest (ˌnɔːθˈwest; *Naut.* ˌnɔːˈwest) *n* **1** the point of the compass or direction midway between north and west. **2** (*often cap.*; usually preceded by *the*) any area lying in or towards this direction. ◆ *adj also* **northwestern. 3** (*sometimes cap.*) of or denoting the northwestern part of a specified country, area, etc.: *northwest Greenland.* ◆ *adj, adv* **4** in, to, or towards the northwest.

▸ **ˌnorth'westernmost** *adj*

Northwest (ˌnɔːθˈwest) *n* (usually preceded by *the*) the northwestern part of England, esp. Lancashire and the Lake District.

northwest by north *n* one point on the compass north of northwest.

northwest by west *n* one point on the compass south of northwest.

northwester (ˌnɔːθˈwestə; *Naut.* ˌnɔːˈwestə) *n* a strong wind or storm from the northwest.

northwesterly (ˌnɔːθˈwestəlɪ; *Naut.* ˌnɔːˈwestəlɪ) *adj, adv* **1** in, towards, or (esp. of a wind) from the northwest. ◆ *n, pl* **northwesterlies. 2** a wind or storm from the northwest.

North-West Frontier Province ★ *n* a province in N Pakistan between Afghanistan and Jammu and Kashmir: part of British India (1901–47); of strategic importance, esp. for the Khyber Pass. Capital: Peshawar. Pop.: 12 287 000 (1985 est.). Area: 74 522 sq. km (28 773 sq. miles).

Northwest Passage ★ *n* the passage by sea from the Atlantic to the Pacific along the N coast of America: attempted for over 300 years by Europeans seeking a short route to the Far East, before being successfully navigated by Amundsen (1903–06).

Northwest Territories ★ *pl n* the part of Canada north of the provinces and east of the Yukon Territory, including the islands of the Arctic, Hudson Bay, James Bay, and Ungava Bay; comprised over a third of Canada's total area until Nunavut became a separate territory in 1999: rich mineral resources. Pop.: 41 800 (1999 est.). Area: 2 011 204 sq. km (438 431 sq. miles). Abbrev.: **NWT.**

Northwest Territory ★ *n* See **Old Northwest.**

northwestward (ˌnɔːθˈwestwəd; *Naut.* ˌnɔːˈwestwəd) *adj* **1** towards or (esp. of a wind) from the northwest. ◆ *n* **2** a direction towards or area in the northwest.

▸ **ˌnorth'westwardly** *adj, adv*

Northwich ★ ('nɔːθwɪtʃ) *n* a town in NW England, in Cheshire: salt and chemical industries. Pop.: 34 520 (1991).

North Yemen ★ *n* a former republic (1962–90) in SW Arabia, on the Red Sea; now part of Yemen. Official name: **Yemen Arab Republic.** See also **Yemen, South Yemen.**

North Yorkshire ★ *n* a county in N England, formed in 1974 from most of the North Riding of Yorkshire and parts of the East and West Ridings; includes four unitary authorities. Administrative centre: Northallerton. Pop.: 1 016 000 (1996 est.). Area: 8603 sq. km (3322 sq. miles).

Norw. *abbrev. for:* **1** Norway. **2** Norwegian.

Norway ★ ('nɔː,weɪ) *n* a kingdom in NW Europe, occupying the W part of the Scandinavian peninsula: first united in the Viking age (800–1050); under the rule of Denmark (1523–1814) and Sweden (1814–1905); became an independent monarchy in 1905. Its coastline is deeply indented by fjords and fringed with islands, rising inland to plateaus and mountains. Norway has a large fishing fleet and its merchant navy is among the world's largest. Official language: Norwegian. Official religion: Lutheran. Currency: krone. Capital: Oslo. Pop.:

4 382 000 (1996). Area: 323 878 sq. km (125 050 sq. miles). Norwegian name: **Norge.**

Norway lobster *n* a European lobster fished for food.

Norway maple *n* a large Eurasian maple tree.

Norway spruce *n* a European spruce tree having drooping branches and dark green needle-like leaves.

Norwegian (nɔːˈwiːdʒən) *adj* **1** of or characteristic of Norway, its language, or its people. ♦ *n* **2** any of the various North Germanic languages of Norway. **3** a native or inhabitant of Norway.

Norwegian Sea ★ *n* part of the Arctic Ocean between Greenland and Norway.

Norwich ★ (ˈnɒrɪdʒ) *n* a city in E England, administrative centre of Norfolk: cathedral (founded 1096); University of East Anglia (1963); footwear industry. Pop.: 171 304 (1991).

Nos. *or* **nos.** *abbrev. for* numbers.

nose (nəʊz) *n* **1** the organ of smell and entrance to the respiratory tract, consisting of a prominent structure divided into two hair-lined air passages. Related adj: **nasal. 2** the sense of smell itself: in animals, the ability to follow trails by scent (esp. in **a good nose**). **3** the scent, aroma, bouquet of something, esp. wine. **4** instinctive skill in discovering things (sometimes in **follow one's nose**): *he had a nose for good news stories.* **5** any part resembling a nose in form or function, such as a nozzle or spout. **6** the forward part of a vehicle, aircraft, etc. **7** narrow margin of victory (in (**win**) **by a nose**). **8 cut off one's nose to spite one's face.** to carry out a vengeful action that hurts oneself more than another. **9 get up (someone's) nose.** *Inf.* to annoy or irritate (someone). **10 keep one's nose clean.** to stay out of trouble. **11 lead by the nose.** to make (someone) do unquestioningly all one wishes; dominate. **12 look down one's nose at.** *Inf.* to be disdainful of. **13 nose to tail.** (of vehicles) moving or standing very close behind one another. **14 on the nose.** *Sl.* **14a** (in horserace betting) to win only: *I bet twenty pounds on the nose on that horse.* **14b** *Chiefly US & Canad.* precisely; exactly. **14c** *Austral.* bad or bad-smelling. **15 pay through the nose.** *Inf.* to pay an exorbitant price. **16 put someone's nose out of joint.** *Inf.* to thwart or offend someone. **17 rub someone's nose in it.** *Inf.* to remind someone unkindly of a failing or error. **18 turn up one's nose (at).** *Inf.* to behave disdainfully (towards). **19 with one's nose in the air.** haughtily. ♦ *vb* **noses, nosing, nosed. 20** (*tr*) (esp. of horses, dogs, etc.) to rub, touch, or sniff with the nose; nuzzle. **21** to smell or sniff (wine, etc.). **22** (*intr*; usually foll. by *after* or *for*) to search (for) by or as if by scent. **23** to move or cause to move forwards slowly and carefully: *we nosed the car into the garage.* **24** (*intr*; foll. by *into, around, about,* etc.) to pry or snoop (into) or meddle (in). [OE *nosu*]
▶ **'noseless** *adj* ▶ **'nose,like** *adj*

nosebag (ˈnəʊzˌbæg) *n* a bag, fastened around the head of a horse and covering the nose, in which feed is placed.

noseband (ˈnəʊzˌbænd) *n* the detachable part of a horse's bridle that goes around the nose.

nosebleed (ˈnəʊzˌbliːd) *n* bleeding from the nose as the result of injury, etc.

nose cone *n* the conical forward section of a missile, spacecraft, etc., designed to withstand high temperatures, esp. during re-entry into the earth's atmosphere.

nose dive *n* **1** a sudden plunge with the nose or front pointing downwards, esp. of an aircraft. **2** *Inf.* a sudden drop or sharp decline: *prices took a nose dive.* ♦ *vb* **nose-dive, nose-dives, nose-diving, nose-dived.** (*intr*) **3** to perform a nose dive.

nose flute *n* (esp. in the South Sea Islands) a type of flute blown through the nose.

nosegay (ˈnəʊzˌgeɪ) *n* a small bunch of flowers; posy. [C15: from NOSE + *gay* (arch.) toy]

nose job *n Sl.* a surgical remodelling of the nose for cosmetic reasons.

nosepiece (ˈnəʊzˌpiːs) *n* **1** a piece of armour to protect the nose. **2** the connecting part of a pair of spectacles that rests on the nose; bridge. **3** the part of a microscope to which one or more objective lenses are attached. **4** a less common word for **noseband.**

nose rag *n Sl.* a handkerchief.

nose ring *n* a ring fixed through the nose, as for leading a bull.

nose wheel *n* a wheel fitted to the forward end of a vehicle, esp. the landing wheel under the nose of an aircraft.

nosey (ˈnəʊzɪ) *adj* a variant spelling of **nosy.**

nosh (nɒʃ) *Sl.* ♦ *n* **1** food or a meal. ♦ *vb* **2** to eat. [C20: from Yiddish; cf. G *naschen* to nibble]

no-show *n* a person who fails to take up a reserved seat, place, etc., without having cancelled it.

nosh-up *n Brit. sl.* a large and satisfying meal.

no-side *n Rugby.* the end of a match, signalled by the referee's whistle.

nosocomial (ˌnɒsəˈkəʊmɪəl) *adj* of or denoting an infection that originates in a hospital. [C19: from Gk *nosokomos* one that tends the sick, from *nosos* disease + *komein* to tend]

nosology (nɒˈsɒlədʒɪ) *n* the branch of medicine concerned with the classification of diseases. [C18: from Gk *nosos* disease]
▶ **nosological** (ˌnɒsəˈlɒdʒɪkᵊl) *adj*

nostalgia (nɒˈstældʒə, -dʒɪə) *n* **1** a yearning for past circumstances, events, etc. **2** the evocation of this emotion, as in a book, film, etc. **3** homesickness. [C18: NL, from Gk *nostos* a return home + -ALGIA]
▶ **nos'talgic** *adj* ▶ **nos'talgically** *adv*

nostoc (ˈnɒstɒk) *n* a gelatinous cyanobacterium occurring in moist places. [C17: NL, coined by Paracelsus (1493–1541) Swiss physician]

Nostradamus ★ (ˌnɒstrəˈdɑːməs) *n* Latinized name of *Michel de Notredame.* 1503–66, French physician and astrologer; author of a book of prophecies in rhymed quatrains, *Centuries* (1555).

nostril (ˈnɒstrɪl) *n* either of the two external openings of the nose. See **nares.** [OE *nosthyrl*, from *nosu* NOSE + *thyrel* hole]

nostro account (ˈnɒstrəʊ) *n* a bank account conducted by a British bank with a foreign bank, usually in the foreign currency. Cf. **vostro account.**

nostrum (ˈnɒstrəm) *n* **1** a patent or quack medicine. **2** a favourite remedy. [C17: from L: our own (make), from *noster* our]

nosy *or* **nosey** (ˈnəʊzɪ) *adj* **nosier, nosiest.** *Inf.* prying or inquisitive.
▶ **'nosily** *adv* ▶ **'nosiness** *n*

nosy parker *n Inf.* a prying person. [C20: arbitrary use of surname *Parker*]

not (nɒt) *adv* **1a** used to negate the sentence, phrase, or word that it modifies: *I will not stand for it.* **1b** (*in combination*): *they cannot go.* **2 not that.** (*conj*) Also (arch.): **not but what.** which is not to say or suppose that: *I expect to lose the game – not that I mind.* ♦ *sentence substitute.* **3** used to indicate denial or refusal: *certainly not.* [C14 *not,* var. of *nought* nothing, from OE *nāwiht,* from *nā* no + *wiht* creature, thing]

nota bene *Latin.* (ˈnəʊtə ˈbiːnɪ) note well; take note. Abbrevs.: **NB, N.B., nb, n.b.**

notability (ˌnəʊtəˈbɪlɪtɪ) *n, pl* **notabilities. 1** the quality of being notable. **2** a distinguished person.

notable (ˈnəʊtəbᵊl) *adj* **1** worthy of being noted or remembered; remarkable; distinguished. ♦ *n* **2** a notable person. [C14: via OF from L *notābilis,* from *notāre* to NOTE]
▶ **'notably** *adv*

notarize *or* **notarise** (ˈnəʊtəˌraɪz) *vb* **notarizes, notarizing, notarized** *or* **notarises, notarising, notarised.** (*tr*) *US.* to attest to (a document, entry, etc.), as a notary.

notary (ˈnəʊtərɪ) *n, pl* **notaries. 1** a notary public. **2** (formerly) a clerk licensed to prepare legal documents. **3** *Arch.* a clerk or secretary. [C14: from L *notārius* clerk, from *nota* a mark, note]
▶ **notarial** (nəʊˈtɛərɪəl) *adj* ▶ **'notaryship** *n*

notary public *n, pl* **notaries public.** a public official, usually a solicitor, who is legally authorized to administer oaths, attest and certify certain documents, etc.

notation (nəʊ'teɪʃən) *n* **1** any series of signs or symbols used to represent quantities or elements in a specialized system, such as music or mathematics. **2** the act or process of notating. **3** a note or record. [C16: from L *notātiō*, from *notāre* to NOTE]
▸ no'**tational** *adj*

notch (nɒtʃ) *n* **1** a V-shaped cut or indentation; nick. **2** a nick made in a tally stick. **3** *US & Canad.* a narrow gorge. **4** *Inf.* a step or level (esp. in **a notch above**). ◆ *vb* (*tr*) **5** to cut or make a notch in. **6** to record with or as if with a notch. **7** (usually foll. by *up*) *Inf.* to score or achieve: *the team notched up its fourth win.* [C16: from incorrect division of *an otch* (as *a notch*), from OF *oche* notch, from L *obsecāre*, from *secāre* to cut]

NOT circuit or **gate** (nɒt) *n Computing.* a logic circuit that has a high-voltage output signal if the input signal is low, and vice versa: used extensively in computing. Also called: **inverter, negator.** [C20: the action performed on electrical signals is similar to the operation of *not* in logical constructions]

note (nəʊt) *n* **1** a brief record in writing, esp. a jotting for future reference. **2** a brief informal letter. **3** a formal written communication, esp. from one government to another. **4** a short written statement giving any kind of information. **5** a critical comment, explanatory statement, or reference in a book. **6** short for **banknote.** **7** a characteristic atmosphere: *a note of sarcasm.* **8** a distinctive vocal sound, as of a species of bird or animal. **9** any of a series of graphic signs representing the pitch and duration of a musical sound. **10** Also called (esp. US and Canad.): **tone.** a musical sound of definite fundamental frequency or pitch. **11** a key on a piano, organ, etc. **12** a sound used as a signal or warning: *the note to retreat was sounded.* **13** short for **promissory note.** **14** *Arch.* or *poetic.* a melody. **15 of note. 15a** distinguished or famous. **15b** important: *nothing of note.* **16 strike the right** (*or* **a false**) **note.** to behave appropriately (or inappropriately). **17 take note.** (often foll. by *of*) to pay attention (to). ◆ *vb* **notes, noting, noted.** (*tr; may take a clause as object*) **18** to notice; perceive. **19** to pay close attention to: *they noted every movement.* **20** to make a written note of: *she noted the date in her diary.* **21** to remark upon: *I note that you do not wear shoes.* **22** to write down (music, a melody, etc.) in notes. **23** to take (an unpaid or dishonoured bill of exchange) to a notary public to re-present the bill and if it is still unaccepted or unpaid to note the circumstances in a register. See **protest** (sense 9). **24** a less common word for **annotate.** [C13: via OF from L *nota* sign]
▸ '**noteless** *adj*

notebook ('nəʊt,bʊk) *n* a book for recording notes or memoranda.

notebook computer *n* a portable computer smaller than a laptop model, often approximately the size of a sheet of A4 paper.

notecase ('nəʊt,keɪs) *n* a less common word for **wallet** (sense 1).

noted ('nəʊtɪd) *adj* **1** celebrated; famous. **2** of special significance; noticeable.
▸ '**notedly** *adv*

notelet ('nəʊtlɪt) *n* a folded card with a printed design on the front, for writing a short letter.

notepaper ('nəʊt,peɪpə) *n* paper for writing letters; writing paper.

noteworthy ('nəʊt,wɜːðɪ) *adj* worthy of notice; notable.
▸ '**note,worthiness** *n*

nothing ('nʌθɪŋ) *pron* **1** (*indefinite*) no thing; not anything: *I can give you nothing.* **2** no part or share: *to have nothing to do with this crime.* **3** a matter of no importance: *it doesn't matter, it's nothing.* **4** indicating the absence of anything perceptible; nothingness. **5** indicating the absence of meaning, value, worth, etc.: *to amount to nothing.* **6** zero quantity; nought. **7 be nothing to. 7a** not to concern or be significant to (someone). **7b** to be not nearly as good, etc., as. **8 have** *or* **be nothing to do with.** to have no connection with. **9 nothing but.** not something other than; only. **10 nothing doing.** *Inf.* an expression of dismissal, refusal, etc. **11 nothing if not.** at the very least; certainly. **12 nothing less than** *or* **nothing short of.** downright; truly. **13 there's nothing to it.** it is very simple, easy, etc. **14**

think nothing of. 14a to regard as easy or natural. **14b** to have no compunction about. **14c** to have a very low opinion of. ◆ *adv* **15** in no way; not at all: *he looked nothing like his brother.* ◆ *n* **16** *Inf.* a person or thing of no importance or significance. **17 sweet nothings.** words of endearment or affection. [OE *nāthing, nān thing*, from *nān* NONE[1] + THING]

> **USAGE NOTE** *Nothing* normally takes a singular verb, but when *nothing but* is followed by a plural form of a noun, a plural verb is usually used: *it was a large room where nothing but souvenirs were sold.*

nothingness ('nʌθɪŋnɪs) *n* **1** the state of being nothing; nonexistence. **2** absence of consciousness or life. **3** complete insignificance. **4** something that is worthless.

notice ('nəʊtɪs) *n* **1** observation; attention: *to escape notice.* **2 take notice.** to pay attention. **3 take no notice of.** to ignore or disregard. **4** a warning; announcement. **5** a displayed placard or announcement giving information. **6** advance notification of intention to end an arrangement, contract, etc., as of employment (esp. in **give notice**). **7 at short notice.** with notification only a little in advance. **8** *Chiefly Brit.* dismissal from employment. **9** favourable, interested, or polite attention: *she was beneath his notice.* **10** a theatrical or literary review: *the play received very good notices.* ◆ *vb* **notices, noticing, noticed. 11** to become aware (of); perceive; note. **12** (*tr*) to point out or remark upon. **13** (*tr*) to pay polite or interested attention to. **14** (*tr*) to acknowledge (an acquaintance, etc.). [C15: via OF from L *notitia* fame, from *nōtus* known]

noticeable ('nəʊtɪsəb'l) *adj* easily seen or detected; perceptible.
▸ '**noticeably** *adv*

notice board *n* a board on which notices, advertisements, bulletins, etc., are displayed. US and Canad. name: **bulletin board.**

notifiable ('nəʊtɪ,faɪəb'l) *adj* **1** denoting certain infectious diseases of humans, such as tuberculosis, outbreaks of which must be reported to the public health authorities. **2** denoting certain infectious diseases of animals, such as BSE and rabies, outbreaks of which must be reported to the appropriate veterinary authority.

notification (,nəʊtɪfɪ'keɪʃən) *n* **1** the act of notifying. **2** a formal announcement. **3** something that notifies; a notice.

notify ('nəʊtɪ,faɪ) *vb* **notifies, notifying, notified.** (*tr*) **1** to tell. **2** *Chiefly Brit.* to make known; announce. [C14: from OF *notifier*, from L *notificāre*, from *nōtus* known + *facere* to make]
▸ '**noti,fier** *n*

notion ('nəʊʃən) *n* **1** a vague idea; impression. **2** an idea, concept, or opinion. **3** an inclination or whim. ◆ See also **notions.** [C16: from L *nōtiō* a becoming acquainted (with), examination (of), from *noscere* to know]

notional ('nəʊʃən'l) *adj* **1** expressing or consisting of ideas. **2** not evident in reality; hypothetical or imaginary: *a notional tax credit.* **3** characteristic of a notion, esp. in being speculative or abstract. **4** *Grammar.* **4a** (of a word) having lexical meaning. **4b** another word for **semantic.**
▸ '**notionally** *adv*

notions ('nəʊʃənz) *pl n Chiefly US & Canad.* pins, cotton, ribbon, etc., used for sewing; haberdashery.

notochord ('nəʊtə,kɔːd) *n* a fibrous longitudinal rod in all embryo and some adult chordate animals, immediately above the gut, that supports the body. [C19: from Gk *nōton* the back + CHORD[1]]

notorious (nəʊ'tɔːrɪəs) *adj* **1** well-known for some bad or unfavourable quality, deed, etc.; infamous. **2** *Rare.* generally known or widely acknowledged. [C16: from Med. L *notōrius* well-known, from *nōtus* known]
▸ **notoriety** (,nəʊtə'raɪɪtɪ) *n* ▸ no'**toriously** *adv*

notornis (nəʊ'tɔːnɪs) *n* a rare flightless rail of New Zealand. [C19: NL, from Gk *notos* south + *ornis* bird]

not proven ('prəʊv'n) *adj* (*postpositive*) a third verdict available to Scottish courts, returned when there is insufficient evidence against the accused to convict.

Notre Dame ★ (ˈnəʊtrə ˈdɑːm, ˈnɒtrə; *French* nɔtrə dam) *n* the early Gothic cathedral of Paris, on the Île de la Cité: built between 1163 and 1257.

no-trump *Cards.* ◆ *n also* **no-trumps. 1** a bid or contract to play without trumps. ◆ *adj also* **no-trumper. 2** (of a hand) suitable for playing without trumps.

Nottingham ★ (ˈnɒtɪŋəm) *n* a city and unitary authority in N central England, administrative centre of Nottinghamshire, on the River Trent: scene of the outbreak of the Civil War (1642); famous for its associations with the Robin Hood legend; university (1881). Pop.: 270 222 (1991).

Nottinghamshire ★ (ˈnɒtɪŋəmˌʃɪə, -ʃə) *n* an inland county of central England: generally low-lying, with part of the S Pennines and the remnant of Sherwood Forest in the east. Administrative centre: Nottingham. Pop.: 1 030 900 (1994 est.). Area: 2164 sq. km (835 sq. miles). Abbrev.: **Notts.**

Nottm *abbrev. for* Nottingham.

Notts (nɒts) *abbrev. for* Nottinghamshire.

Notus ★ (ˈnəʊtəs) *n Classical myth.* a personification of the south or southwest wind.

notwithstanding (ˌnɒtwɪθˈstændɪŋ) *prep* **1** (*often immediately postpositive*) in spite of; despite. ◆ *conj* **2** (*subordinating*) although. ◆ *sentence connector.* **3** nevertheless.

Nouakchott ★ (*French* nwakʃɔt) *n* the capital of Mauritania, near the Atlantic coast: replaced St Louis as capital in 1957; situated on important caravan routes. Pop.: 480 395 (1992 est.).

nougat (ˈnuːgɑː) *n* a hard chewy pink or white sweet containing chopped nuts, cherries, etc. [C19: via F from Provençal *nogat*, from *noga* nut, from L *nux* nut]

nought (nɔːt) *n also* **naught, ought, aught. 1** another name for **zero**: used esp. in numbering. ◆ *n, adj, adv* **2** a variant spelling of **naught.** [OE *nōwiht*, from *ne* not, no + *ōwiht* something]

noughts and crosses *n* (*functioning as sing*) a game in which two players, one using a nought, "O", the other a cross, "X", alternately mark squares formed by two pairs of crossed lines, the winner being the first to get three of his symbols in a row. US and Canad. term: **tick-tack-toe,** (US) **crisscross.**

Nouméa ★ (ˌnuːˈmeɪə; *French* numea) *n* the capital and chief port of the French Overseas Territory of New Caledonia. Pop.: 65 000 (1994 est.).

noun (naʊn) *n* **a** a word or group of words that refers to a person, place, or thing. **b** (*as modifier*): *a noun phrase.* Abbrev.: **N, n.** Related adj: **nominal.** [C14: via Anglo-F from L *nōmen* NAME]
▶ **ˈnounal** *adj*

nourish (ˈnʌrɪʃ) *vb* (*tr*) **1** to provide with the materials necessary for life and growth. **2** to encourage (an idea, etc.); foster: *to nourish resentment.* [C14: from OF *norir,* from L *nūtrīre* to feed]
▶ **ˈnourisher** *n* ▶ **ˈnourishing** *adj*

nourishment (ˈnʌrɪʃmənt) *n* **1** the act or state of nourishing. **2** a substance that nourishes; food.

nous (naʊs) *n* **1** *Metaphysics.* mind or reason, esp. regarded as the principle governing all things. **2** *Brit. sl.* common sense. [C17: from Gk: mind]

nouveau *or before a plural noun* **nouveaux** (ˈnuːvəʊ) *adj* (*prenominal*) *Facetious or derog.* having recently become the thing specified: *a nouveau hippy.* [C20: F, lit.: new; on the model of NOUVEAU RICHE]

nouveau riche (riːʃ) *n, pl* **nouveaux riches** (riːʃ). (*often preceded by the*) a person who has acquired wealth recently and is regarded as vulgarly ostentatious or lacking in social graces. [C19: from F lit.: new rich]

Nouvelle-Calédonie ★ (*French* nuvɛlkaledɔni) *n* the French name for **New Caledonia.**

nouvelle cuisine (ˈnuːvɛl kwiˈziːn; *French* nuvɛl kɥizin) *n* a style of cooking based on presenting small attractively arranged helpings of lightly cooked fresh ingredients. [C20: F, lit.: new cookery]

Nov. *abbrev. for* November.

nova (ˈnəʊvə) *n, pl* **novae** (-viː) *or* **novas.** a variable star that undergoes a cataclysmic eruption, observed as a sudden large increase in brightness with a subsequent decline over months or years; it is a close binary system with one component a white dwarf. [C19: NL *nova* (*stella*) new (star), from L *novus* new]

Novalis ★ (*German* noˈvaːlɪs) *n* real name *Friedrich von Hardenberg.* 1772–1801, German romantic poet. His works include the mystical *Hymnen an die Nacht* (1797; published 1800) and *Geistliche Lieder* (1799).

Nova Lisboa ★ (*Portuguese* ˈnɒvə liʒˈβɔə) *n* the former name (1928–73) of **Huambo.**

Novara ★ (*Italian* noˈvaːra) *n* a city in NW Italy, in NE Piedmont: scene of the Austrian defeat of the Piedmontese in 1849. Pop.: 102 768 (1994 est.).

Nova Scotia ★ (ˈnəʊvə ˈskəʊʃə) *n* **1** a peninsula in E Canada, between the Gulf of St Lawrence and the Bay of Fundy. **2** a province of E Canada, consisting of the Nova Scotia peninsula and Cape Breton Island: first settled by the French as Acadia. Capital: Halifax. Pop.: 937 800 (1995 est.). Area: 52 841 sq. km (20 402 sq. miles). Abbrev.: **NS.**
▶ **Nova ˈScotian** *n, adj*

Novaya Zemlya ★ (*Russian* ˈnɒvəjə zɪmˈlja) *n* an archipelago in the Arctic Ocean, off the NE coast of Russia: consists of two large islands and many islets. Area: about 81 279 sq. km (31 382 sq. miles).

novel[1] (ˈnɒvəl) *n* **1** an extended fictional work in prose dealing with character, action, thought, etc., esp. in the form of a story. **2 the novel.** the literary genre represented by novels. [C15: from OF *novelle,* from L *novella* (*narrātiō*) new (story); see NOVEL[2]]

novel[2] (ˈnɒvəl) *adj* of a kind not seen before; fresh; new; original: *a novel suggestion.* [C15: from L *novellus,* dim. of *novus* new]

novelette (ˌnɒvəˈlɛt) *n* **1** an extended prose narrative or short novel. **2** a novel that is regarded as slight, trivial, or sentimental. **3** a short piece of lyrical music, esp. for piano.

novelettish (ˌnɒvəˈlɛtɪʃ) *adj* characteristic of a novelette; trite or sentimental.

novelist (ˈnɒvəlɪst) *n* a writer of novels.

novelistic (ˌnɒvəˈlɪstɪk) *adj* of or characteristic of novels, esp. in style or method of treatment.

novella (nəʊˈvɛlə) *n, pl* **novellas** *or* **novelle** (-leɪ). **1** a short narrative tale, esp. one having a satirical point, such as those in Boccaccio's *Decameron.* **2** a short novel. [C20: from It.; see NOVEL[1]]

Novello ★ (nəˈvɛləʊ) *n* **Ivor,** real name *Ivor Novello Davies.* 1893–1951, Welsh actor and composer of musicals.

novelty (ˈnɒvəltɪ) *n, pl* **novelties. 1a** the quality of being new and interesting. **1b** (*as modifier*): *novelty value.* **2** a new or unusual experience. **3** (*often pl*) a small usually cheap new ornament or trinket. [C14: from OF *novelté;* see NOVEL[2]]

November (nəʊˈvɛmbə) *n* the eleventh month of the year, consisting of 30 days. [C13: via OF from L: ninth month (the Roman year orig. began in March), from *novem* nine]

novena (nəʊˈviːnə) *n, pl* **novenas** *or* **novenae** (-niː). *RC Church.* a devotion consisting of prayers or services on nine consecutive days. [C19: from Med. L, from L *novem* nine]

Novgorod ★ (*Russian* ˈnɔvɡərət) *n* a city in NW Russia, on the Volkhov River. Novgorod became a principality in 862 under Rurik, an event regarded as the founding of the Russian state; a major trading centre in the Middle Ages; destroyed by Ivan the Terrible in 1570. Pop.: 233 000 (1995 est.).

novice (ˈnɒvɪs) *n* **1a** a person who is new to or inexperienced in a certain task, situation, etc.; beginner; tyro. **1b** (*as modifier*): *novice driver.* **2** a probationer in a religious order. **3** a racehorse that has not won a specified number of races. [C14: via OF from L *novīcius,* from *novus* new]

Novi Sad ★ (*Serbo-Croat* ˈnɔviː ˈsaːd) *n* a port in NE Yugoslavia, in Serbia, on the River Danube: founded in 1690 as the seat of the Serbian patriarch; university (1960). Pop.: 179 626 (1991). German name: **Neusatz.**

novitiate *or* **noviciate** (nəʊ'vɪʃɪɪt, -,eɪt) *n* **1** the state of being a novice, esp. in a religious order, or the period for which this lasts. **2** the part of a religious house where the novices live. [C17: from F *noviciat,* from L *novīcius* NOV-ICE]

Novocaine ('nəʊvə,keɪn) *n* a trademark for **procaine hydrochloride.** See **procaine.**

Novokuznetsk ★ (*Russian* nɔvəkuz'njetsk) *n* a city in S central Russia: iron and steel works. Pop.: 572 000 (1995 est.). Former name (1932–61): **Stalinsk.**

Novosibirsk ★ (*Russian* nəvəsi'birsk) *n* a city in W central Russia, on the River Ob: the largest town in Siberia; developed with the coming of the Trans-Siberian railway in 1893. Pop.: 1 369 000 (1995 est.).

now (naʊ) *adv* **1** at or for the present time. **2** immediately. **3** in these times; nowadays. **4** given the present circumstances: *now we'll have to stay to the end.* **5** (preceded by *just*) very recently: *he left just now.* **6** (often preceded by *just*) very soon: *he is leaving just now.* **7** (**every**) **now and again** *or* **then.** occasionally; on and off. **8** **now now!** an exclamation used to rebuke or pacify someone. ◆ *conj* **9** (*subordinating;* often foll. by *that*) seeing that: *now you're in charge, things will be better.* ◆ *sentence connector.* **10a** used as a hesitation word: *now, I can't really say.* **10b** used for emphasis: *now listen to this.* **10c** used at the end of a command: *run along, now.* ◆ *n* **11** the present time: *now is the time to go.* ◆ *adj* **12** *Inf.* of the moment; fashionable: *the now look.* [OE *nū*]

nowadays ('naʊə,deɪz) *adv* in these times. [C14: from NOW + *adays* from OE *a* on + *daeges* genitive of DAY]

noway ('nəʊ,weɪ) *adv* **1** not at all. ◆ *sentence substitute.* **no way. 2** used to make an emphatic refusal, denial, etc.

Nowel *or* **Nowell** (nəʊ'el) *n* archaic spellings of **Noel.**

nowhere ('nəʊweə) *adv* **1** in, at, or to no place; not anywhere. **2** **get nowhere (fast).** *Inf.* to fail completely to make any progress. **3 nowhere near.** far from; not nearly. ◆ *n* **4** a nonexistent or insignificant place. **5 middle of nowhere.** a completely isolated place.

no-win *adj* offering no possibility of a favourable outcome (esp. in a **no-win situation**).

nowise ('nəʊ,waɪz) *adv* in no manner; not at all.

nowt (naʊt) *n N English.* a dialect word for **nothing.** [from NAUGHT]

Nox ★ (nɒks) *n* the Roman goddess of the night. Greek counterpart: **Nyx.**

noxious ('nɒkʃəs) *adj* poisonous or harmful. [C17: from L *noxius* harmful, from *noxa* injury]
  ▶ '**noxiously** *adv* ▶ '**noxiousness** *n*

Noyon ★ (*French* nwajɔ̃) *n* a town in N France: scene of the coronations of Charlemagne (768) and Hugh Capet (987); birthplace of John Calvin. Pop.: 14 426 (1990).

nozzle ('nɒzᵊl) *n* a projecting pipe or spout from which fluid is discharged. [C17 *nosle, nosel,* dim. of NOSE]

Np *the chemical symbol for* neptunium.

NP *or* **np.** *abbrev. for* Notary Public.

NPA *abbrev. for* Newspaper Publishers' Association.

NPD *Commerce. abbrev. for* new product development.

NPL *abbrev. for* National Physical Laboratory.

NPV *abbrev. for:* **1** net present value. **2** no par value.

NRV *abbrev. for* net realizable value.

NS *abbrev. for:* **1** New Style (method of reckoning dates). **2** Nova Scotia. **3** Nuclear Ship.

NSAID *abbrev. for* nonsteroidal anti-inflammatory drug: any of a class of drugs, including aspirin and ibuprofen, used for treating rheumatic diseases.

NSB (in Britain) *abbrev. for* National Savings Bank.

NSC (in Britain) *abbrev. for* National Safety Council.

NSG *Brit. education. abbrev. for* nonstatutory guidelines: practical nonmandatory advice and information on the implementation of the National Curriculum.

NSPCC (in Britain) *abbrev. for* National Society for the Prevention of Cruelty to Children.

NST (in Canada) *abbrev. for* Newfoundland Standard Time.

NSU *abbrev. for* nonspecific urethritis.

NSW *abbrev. for* New South Wales.

NT *abbrev. for:* **1** (in Britain) National Trust. **2** New Testament. **3** Northern Territory. **4** no-trump.

-n't *contraction of* not: used as an enclitic after *be* and *have* when they function as main verbs and after auxiliary verbs or verbs operating syntactically as auxiliaries: *can't; don't; isn't.*

nth (enθ) *adj* **1** *Maths.* of or representing an unspecified ordinal number, usually the greatest in a series: *the nth power.* **2** *Inf.* being the last or most extreme of a long series: *for the nth time.* **3 to the nth degree.** *Inf.* to the utmost extreme.

NTP *abbrev. for* normal temperature and pressure. Also: STP.

nt. wt. *or* **nt wt** *abbrev. for* net weight.

n-type *adj* **1** (of a semiconductor) having more conduction electrons than mobile holes. **2** associated with or resulting from the movement of electrons in a semiconductor.

nu (njuː) *n* the 13th letter in the Greek alphabet (N, ν), a consonant. [from Gk, of Semitic origin]

Nu ★ (njuː) *n* **U** (uː), original name *Thakin Nu.* 1907–95, Burmese statesman; prime minister (1948–56, 1957–58, 1960–62).

nuance (njuː'ɑːns, 'njuːɑːns) *n* a subtle difference in colour, meaning, tone, etc. [C18: from F, from *nuer* to show light and shade, ult. from L *nūbēs* a cloud]

nub (nʌb) *n* **1** a small lump or protuberance. **2** a small piece or chunk. **3** the point or gist: *the nub of a story.* [C16: var. of *knub,* from MLow G *knubbe* KNOB]
  ▶ '**nubbly** *or* '**nubby** *adj*

nubble ('nʌbᵊl) *n* a small lump. [C19: dim. of NUB]

Nubia ★ ('njuːbɪə) *n* an ancient region of NE Africa, on the Nile, extending from Aswan to Khartoum.
  ▶ '**Nubian** *n, adj*

Nubian Desert ★ *n* a desert in the NE Sudan, between the Nile valley and the Red Sea: mainly a sandstone plateau.

nubile ('njuːbaɪl) *adj* (of a girl) **1** ready or suitable for marriage by virtue of age or maturity. **2** sexually attractive. [C17: from L *nūbilis,* from *nūbere* to marry]
  ▶ **nubility** (njuː'bɪlɪtɪ) *n*

nucha ('njuːkə) *n, pl* **nuchae** (-kiː). *Zool., anat.* the back or nape of the neck. [C14: from Med. L, from Ar.: spinal marrow]
  ▶ '**nuchal** *adj*

nuclear ('njuːklɪə) *adj* **1** of or involving the nucleus of an atom: *nuclear fission.* **2** *Biol.* of, relating to, or contained within the nucleus of a cell: *a nuclear membrane.* **3** of, forming, or resembling any other kind of nucleus. **4** of or operated by energy from fission or fusion of atomic nuclei: *a nuclear weapon.* **5** involving or possessing nuclear weapons: *nuclear war.*

nuclear bomb *n* a bomb whose force is due to uncontrolled nuclear fusion or nuclear fission.

nuclear chemistry *n* the branch of chemistry concerned with nuclear reactions.

nuclear energy *n* energy released during a nuclear reaction as a result of fission or fusion. Also called: **atomic energy.**

nuclear family *n Sociol., anthropol.* a primary social unit consisting of parents and their offspring.

nuclear fission *n* the splitting of an atomic nucleus into approximately equal parts, either spontaneously or as a result of the impact of a particle usually with an associated release of energy. Sometimes shortened to **fission.**

nuclear fuel *n* a fuel that provides nuclear energy, used in nuclear submarines, etc.

nuclear fusion *n* a reaction in which two nuclei combine to form a nucleus with the release of energy. Sometimes shortened to **fusion.**

★ people and places

nuclear magnetic resonance *n* a technique for determining the magnetic moments of nuclei by subjecting a substance to high-frequency radiation and a large magnetic field. It is used for determining structure, esp. in body scanning. Abbrev.: **NMR.**

nuclear medicine *n* the branch of medicine concerned with the use of radionuclides in the diagnosis and treatment of disease.

nuclear physics *n* (*functioning as sing*) the branch of physics concerned with the structure and behaviour of the nucleus and the particles of which it consists.

nuclear power *n* power, esp. electrical or motive, produced by a nuclear reactor. Also called: **atomic power.**

nuclear reaction *n* a process in which the structure and energy content of an atomic nucleus is changed by interaction with another nucleus or particle.

nuclear reactor *n* a device in which a nuclear reaction is maintained and controlled for the production of nuclear energy. Sometimes shortened to **reactor.**

nuclear waste *n* another name for **radioactive waste.**

nuclear winter *n* a period of low temperatures and little light that has been suggested would occur after a nuclear war.

nuclease ('nju:klı‚eız) *n* any of a group of enzymes that hydrolyse nucleic acids to simple nucleotides.

nucleate *adj* ('nju:klɪt, -‚eɪt). **1** having a nucleus. ♦ *vb* ('nju:klɪ‚eɪt), **nucleates, nucleating, nucleated.** (*intr*) **2** to form a nucleus.

nuclei ('nju:klɪ‚aɪ) *n* a plural of **nucleus.**

nucleic acid (nju:'kli:ɪk, -'kleɪ-) *n Biochem.* any of a group of complex compounds with a high molecular weight that are vital constituents of all living cells. See also **RNA, DNA.**

nucleo- *or before a vowel* **nucle-** *combining form.* **1** nucleus or nuclear. **2** nucleic acid. [from Latin *nucleus* kernel, from *nux* nut]

nucleolus (‚nju:klɪ'əuləs) *n, pl* **nucleoli** (-laɪ). a small rounded body within a resting cell nucleus that contains RNA and proteins and is involved in protein synthesis. Also called: **nucleole.** [C19: from L, dim. of NUCLEUS]
  ▸ ‚nucle'olar *adj*

nucleon ('nju:klɪ‚ɒn) *n* a proton or neutron, esp. one present in an atomic nucleus.

nucleonics (‚nju:klɪ'ɒnɪks) *n* (*functioning as sing*) the branch of physics concerned with the applications of nuclear energy.
  ▸ ‚nucle'onic *adj* ▸ ‚nucle'onically *adv*

nucleon number *n* the number of nucleons in an atomic nucleus; mass number.

nucleophile ('nju:klɪ‚əu‚faɪl) *n* a molecule or ion that can donate electrons.
  ▸ nucleophilic (‚nju:klɪə'fɪlɪk) *adj*

nucleoside ('nju:klɪə‚saɪd) *n Biochem.* a compound containing a purine or pyrimidine base linked to a sugar (usually ribose or deoxyribose).

nucleotide ('nju:klɪə‚taɪd) *n Biochem.* a compound consisting of a nucleoside linked to phosphoric acid.

nucleus ('nju:klɪəs) *n, pl* **nuclei** *or* **nucleuses. 1** a central or fundamental thing around which others are grouped; core. **2** a centre of growth or development; basis: *the nucleus of an idea.* **3** *Biol.* the spherical or ovoid compartment of a cell that contains the chromosomes and associated molecules that control the characteristics and growth of the cell. **4** *Astron.* the central portion in the head of a comet, consisting of small solid particles of ice and frozen gases. **5** *Physics.* the positively charged dense region at the centre of an atom, composed of protons and neutrons, about which electrons orbit. **6** *Chem.* a fundamental group of atoms in a molecule serving as the base structure for related compounds. [C18: from L: kernel, from *nux* nut]

nuclide ('nju:klaɪd) *n* a species of atom characterized by its atomic number and its mass number. [C20: from NUCLEO- + -*ide*, from Gk *eidos* shape]

nude (nju:d) *adj* **1** completely undressed. **2** having no covering; bare; exposed. **3** *Law.* **3a** lacking some essential legal requirement. **3b** (of a contract, etc.) made without consideration and void unless under seal. ♦ *n* **4** the state of being naked (esp. in **in the nude**). **5** a naked figure, esp. in painting, sculpture, etc. [C16: from L *nūdus*]
  ▸ '**nudely** *adv*

nudge (nʌdʒ) *vb* **nudges, nudging, nudged.** (*tr*) **1** to push (someone) gently, esp. with the elbow, to get attention; jog. **2** to push slowly or lightly: *as I drove out, I just nudged the gatepost.* ♦ *n* **3** a gentle poke or push. [C17: ?from Scand.]
  ▸ '**nudger** *n*

nudibranch ('nju:dɪ‚bræŋk) *n* a marine gastropod of an order characterized by a shell-less, often beautifully coloured, body bearing external gills. Also called: **sea slug.** [C19: from L *nudus* naked + *branche*, from L *branchia* gills]

nudism ('nju:dɪzəm) *n* the practice of nudity, esp. for reasons of health, etc.
  ▸ '**nudist** *n, adj*

nudity ('nju:dɪtɪ) *n, pl* **nudities.** the state or fact of being nude; nakedness.

Nuevo Laredo ★ (*Spanish* 'nweβo la'reðo) *n* a city and port of entry in NE Mexico, in Tamaulipas state on the Rio Grande opposite Laredo, Texas: oil industries. Pop.: 218 413 (1990).

Nuevo León ★ ('nweɪvəu leɪ'əun, nu:'eɪ-; *Spanish* 'nweβo le'on) *n* a state of NE Mexico: the first centre of heavy industry in Latin America. Capital: Monterrey. Pop.: 3 549 273 (1995 est.). Area: 64 555 sq. km (24 925 sq. miles).

Nuffield ★ ('nʌfi:ld) *n* **William Richard Morris,** 1st Viscount Nuffield. 1877–1963, British car manufacturer and philanthropist. He endowed Nuffield College at Oxford (1937) and the Nuffield Foundation (1943).

nugatory ('nju:gətərɪ, -trɪ) *adj* **1** of little value; trifling. **2** not valid: *a nugatory law.* [C17: from L *nūgātōrius*, from *nūgārī* to jest, from *nūgae* trifles]

nugget ('nʌgɪt) *n* **1** a small piece or lump, esp. of gold in its natural state. **2** something small but valuable or excellent. [C19: from ?]

nuggety ('nʌgɪtɪ) *adj* **1** of or resembling a nugget. **2** *Austral. & NZ inf.* (of a person) thickset; stocky.

nuisance ('nju:səns) *n* **1a** a person or thing that causes annoyance or bother. **1b** (*as modifier*): *nuisance calls.* **2** *Law.* something unauthorized that is obnoxious or injurious to the community at large or to an individual, esp. in relation to his ownership of property. **3 nuisance value.** the usefulness of a person's or thing's capacity to cause difficulties or irritation. [C15: via OF from *nuire* to injure, from L *nocēre*]

NUJ (in Britain) *abbrev. for* National Union of Journalists.

Nu Jiang ★ ('nu: 'dʒjæŋ) *n* the Chinese name for the **Salween.**

nuke (nju:k) *Sl., chiefly US.* ♦ *vb* **nukes, nuking, nuked.** (*tr*) **1** to attack or destroy with nuclear weapons. ♦ *n* **2** a nuclear bomb.

Nuku'alofa ★ (‚nu:ku:ə'lɔ:fə) *n* the capital of Tonga, a port on the N coast of Tongatapu Island. Pop.: 34 000 (1990 est.).

Nukus ★ (*Russian* nu'kus) *n* a city in Uzbekistan, capital of the Kara-Kalpak Autonomous Republic, on the Amu Darya River. Pop.: 185 000 (1993 est.).

null (nʌl) *adj* **1** without legal force; invalid; (esp. in **null and void**). **2** without value or consequence; useless. **3** lacking distinction; characterless. **4** nonexistent; amounting to nothing. **5** *Maths.* **5a** quantitatively zero. **5b** relating to zero. **5c** (of a set) having no members. **6** *Physics.* involving measurement in which conditions are adjusted so that an instrument has a zero reading, as with a Wheatstone bridge. [C16: from L *nullus* none, from *ne* not + *ullus* any]

nullah ('nʌlɑ:) *n* a stream or drain. [C18: from Hindi *nālā*]

Nullarbor Plain ★ ('nʌlə‚bɔ:) *n* a vast low plateau of S Australia: extends north from the Great Australian Bight to the Great Victoria Desert; has no surface water or trees. Area: 260 000 sq. km (100 000 sq. miles).

null hypothesis *n Statistics.* the residual hypothesis if

★ people and places

the alternative hypothesis tested against it fails to achieve a predetermined significance level.

nullify ('nʌlɪˌfaɪ) vb **nullifies, nullifying, nullified.** (tr) **1** to render legally void or of no effect. **2** to render ineffective or useless; cancel out. [C16: from LL *nullificāre* to despise, from L *nullus* of no account + *facere* to make]
▸ ˌnullifiˈcation n

nullity ('nʌlɪtɪ) n, pl **nullities. 1** the state of being null. **2** a null or legally invalid act or instrument. **3** something null, ineffective, characterless, etc. [C16: from Med. L *nullitās*, from L *nullus* no, not any]

NUM (in Britain) abbrev. for National Union of Mineworkers.

num. abbrev. for: **1** number. **2** numeral.

Num. Bible. abbrev. for Numbers.

Numantia ★ (nju:'mæntɪə) n an ancient city in N Spain: a centre of Celtic resistance to Rome in N Spain: captured by Scipio the Younger in 133 B.C.
▸ **Nuˈmantian** adj, n

Numa Pompilius ★ ('nju:mə pɒm'pɪlɪəs) n the legendary second king of Rome (?715–?673 B.C.).

numb (nʌm) adj **1** deprived of feeling through cold, shock, etc. **2** unable to move; paralysed. ◆ vb **3** (tr) to make numb; deaden, shock, or paralyse. [C15 *nomen*, lit.: taken (with paralysis), from OE *niman* to take]
▸ 'numbly adv ▸ 'numbness n

numbat ('nʌm,bæt) n a small Australian marsupial having a long snout and tongue and strong claws for hunting and feeding on termites. [C20: from Abor.]

number ('nʌmbə) n **1** a concept of quantity that is or can be derived from a single unit, the sum of a collection of units, or zero. Every number occupies a unique position in a sequence, enabling it to be used in counting. See also **cardinal number, ordinal number. 2** the symbol used to represent a number; numeral. **3** a numeral or string of numerals used to identify a person or thing: *a telephone number.* **4** the person or thing so identified or designated: *she was number seven in the race.* **5** sum or quantity: *a large number of people.* **6** one of a series, of a magazine; issue. **7a** a self-contained piece of pop or jazz music. **7b** a self-contained part of an opera or other musical score. **8** a group of people, esp. an exclusive group: *he was not one of our number.* **9** Sl. a person, esp. a sexually attractive girl: *who's that nice little number?* **10** Inf. an admired article: *that little number is by Dior.* **11** a grammatical category for the variation in form of nouns, pronouns, and any words agreeing with them, depending on how many persons or things are referred to. **12** any number of. several or many. **13** by numbers. Mil. (of a drill procedure, etc.) performed step by step, each move being made on the call of a number. **14** get or have someone's number. Inf. to discover a person's true character or intentions. **15** one's number is up. Brit. inf. one is finished; one is ruined or about to die. **16** without or beyond number. innumerable. ◆ vb (mainly tr) **17** to assign a number to. **18** to add up to; total. **19** (also intr) to list (items) one by one; enumerate. **20** (also intr) to put or be put into a group, category, etc.: *they were numbered among the worst hit.* **21** to limit the number of: *his days were numbered.* [C13: from OF *nombre*, from L *numerus*]

number crunching n Computing. the large-scale processing of numerical data.

numbered account n Banking. an account identified only by a number, esp. one in a Swiss bank that could contain funds illegally obtained.

numberless ('nʌmbəlɪs) adj **1** too many to be counted; countless. **2** not containing numbers.

number one n **1** the first in a series or sequence. **2** an informal phrase for **oneself, myself,** etc.: *to look after number one.* **3** Inf. the most important person; chief: *he's number one in the organization.* **4** Inf. the bestselling pop record in any one week. ◆ adj **5** first in importance, urgency, quality, etc.: *number one priority.*

numberplate ('nʌmbə,pleɪt) n a plate mounted on the front and back of a motor vehicle bearing the registration number. Usual US term: **license plate,** (Canad.) **licence plate.**

numbers game or **racket** n US. an illegal lottery in which money is wagered on a certain combination of

digits appearing at the beginning of a series of numbers published in a newspaper, as in share prices or sports results. Often shortened to **numbers.**

Number Ten n 10 Downing Street, the British prime minister's official London residence.

number theory n the study of integers, their properties, and the relationship between integers.

numbfish ('nʌm,fɪʃ) n, pl **numbfish** or **numbfishes.** any of several electric rays. [C18: so called because it numbs its victims]

numbles ('nʌmb³lz) pl n Arch. the heart, lungs, liver, etc., of a deer or other animal. [C14: from OF *nombles*, pl. of *nomble* thigh muscle of a deer, changed from L *lumbulus*, dim. of *lumbus* loin]

numbskull or **numskull** ('nʌm,skʌl) n a stupid person; dolt; blockhead.

numen ('nju:mɛn) n, pl **numina** (-mɪnə). **1** (esp. in ancient Roman religion) a deity or spirit presiding over a thing or place. **2** a guiding principle, force, or spirit. [C17: from L: a nod (indicating a command), divine power]

numerable ('nju:mərəb³l) adj able to be numbered or counted.
▸ 'numerably adv

numeral ('nju:mərəl) n **1** a symbol or group of symbols used to express a number: for example, 6 (*Arabic*), VI (*Roman*), 110 (*binary*). ◆ adj **2** of, consisting of, or denoting a number. [C16: from LL *numerālis* belonging to number, from L *numerus*]

numerate adj ('nju:mərɪt). **1** able to use numbers, esp. in arithmetical operations. ◆ vb ('nju:mə,reɪt), **numerates, numerating, numerated.** (tr) **2** to read (a numerical expression). **3** a less common word for **enumerate.** [C18 (vb): from L *numerus* number + -ATE[1], by analogy with *literate*]
▸ 'numeracy ('nju:mərəsɪ) n

numeration (ˌnju:mə'reɪʃən) n **1** the writing, reading, or naming of numbers. **2** a system of numbering.
▸ 'numerative adj

numerator ('nju:mə,reɪtə) n **1** Maths. the dividend of a fraction: the numerator of 7/8 is 7. Cf. **denominator. 2** a person or thing that numbers; enumerator.

numerical (nju:'mɛrɪk³l) or **numeric** adj **1** of, relating to, or denoting a number or numbers. **2** measured or expressed in numbers: *numerical value.*
▸ nuˈmerically adv

numerology (ˌnju:mə'rɒlədʒɪ) n the study of numbers, such as the figures in a birth date, and of their supposed influence on human affairs.
▸ **numerological** (ˌnju:mərə'lɒdʒɪk³l) adj

numerous ('nju:mərəs) adj **1** being many. **2** consisting of many parts: *a numerous collection.*
▸ 'numerously adv ▸ 'numerousness n

Numidia ★ (nju:'mɪdɪə) n an ancient country of N Africa, corresponding roughly to present-day Algeria: flourished until its invasion by Vandals in 429; chief towns were Cirta and Hippo Regius.
▸ **Nuˈmidian** n, adj

numinous ('nju:mɪnəs) adj **1** denoting, being, or relating to a numen; divine. **2** arousing spiritual or religious emotions. **3** mysterious or awe-inspiring. [C17: from L *numin-*, NUMEN + -OUS]

numismatics (ˌnju:mɪz'mætɪks) n (functioning as sing) the study or collection of coins, medals, etc. Also called: ˌnumisma'tology. [C18: from F *numismatique*, from L *nomisma*, from Gk: piece of currency, from *nomizein* to have in use, from *nómos* use]
▸ ˌnumis'matic adj ▸ ˌnumis'matically adv

nummulite ('nʌmju,laɪt) n any of a family of large fossil protozoans common in Tertiary times. [C19: from NL, from L *nummulus*, from *nummus* coin]

numpty ('nʌmptɪ) n, pl **numpties.** Scot. inf. a foolish or ignorant person.

numskull ('nʌm,skʌl) n a variant spelling of **numbskull.**

nun (nʌn) n a female member of a religious order. [OE *nunne,* from Church L *nonna,* from LL: form of address used for an elderly woman]
▸ 'nunhood n ▸ 'nunlike adj

★ people and places

Nunavut ★ ('nuːnəvʊt) *n* a territory of N Canada, created in 1999 from part of Northwest Territories as an autonomous region for the Inuit people. Pop.: 24 000 (1999 est.). Area: 1 235 200 sq. km (772 000 sq. miles).

nun buoy *n Naut.* a buoy, conical at the top, marking the right side of a channel leading into a harbour: green in British waters but red in US waters. [C18: from obs. *nun* child's spinning top + BUOY]

Nunc Dimittis ('nʌŋk dɪ'mɪtɪs, 'nʊŋk) *n* **1** the Latin name for the Canticle of Simeon (Luke 2:29–32). **2** a musical setting of this. [from the opening words (Vulgate): now let depart]

nunciature ('nʌnsɪətʃə) *n* the office or term of office of a nuncio. [C17: from It. *nunziatura;* see NUNCIO]

nuncio ('nʌnʃɪˌəʊ, -sɪ-) *n, pl* **nuncios.** *RC Church.* a diplomatic representative of the Holy See. [C16: via It. from L *nuntius* messenger]

Nuneaton ★ (nʌn'iːtʰn) *n* a town in central England, in Warwickshire. Pop.: 66 715 (1991).

Nunn ★ (nʌn) *n* **Trevor (Robert).** born 1940, British theatre director; chief executive (1978–86) of the Royal Shakespeare Company; artistic director of the Royal National Theatre from 1997.

nunnery ('nʌnərɪ) *n, pl* **nunneries.** the convent or religious house of a community of nuns.

NUPE ('njuːpɪ) *n* (formerly, in Britain) *acronym for* National Union of Public Employees.

nuptial ('nʌpʃəl, -tʃəl) *adj* **1** relating to marriage; conjugal: *nuptial vows.* **2** *Zool.* of or relating to mating: *the nuptial flight of a queen bee.* [C15: from L *nuptiālis,* from *nuptiae* marriage, from *nubere* to marry]
▸ **'nuptially** *adv*

nuptials ('nʌpʃəlz, -tʃəlz) *pl n* (*sometimes sing*) a marriage ceremony; wedding.

NUR (formerly, in Britain) *abbrev. for* National Union of Railwaymen.

nurd a variant spelling of **nerd.**

Nuremberg ★ ('njʊərəmˌbɜːɡ) *n* a city in S Germany, in N Bavaria: scene of annual Nazi rallies (1933–38), the anti-Semitic Nuremberg decrees (1935), and the trials of Nazi leaders for their war crimes (1945–46); important metalworking and electrical industries. Pop.: 495 845 (1995 est.). German name: **Nürnberg.**

Nureyev ★ ('njʊərɪɛf, njuː'reɪ-) *n* **Rudolf.** 1938–93, Austrian ballet dancer, born in the Soviet Union: joined the Royal Ballet in 1962; artistic director of the Paris Opéra Ballet (1983–89).

Nuristan ★ (ˌnʊərɪ'stɑːn) *n* a region of E Afghanistan: consists mainly of high mountains (including part of the Hindu Kush), steep narrow valleys, and extensive forests. Area: about 13 000 sq. km (5000 sq. miles). Former name: **Kafiristan.**

Nürnberg ★ ('nyrnberk) *n* the German name for **Nuremberg.**

nurse (nɜːs) *n* **1** a person, often a woman, who is trained to tend the sick and infirm, assist doctors, etc. **2** short for **nursemaid. 3** a woman employed to breast-feed another woman's child; wet nurse. **4** a worker in a colony of social insects that takes care of the larvae. ◆ *vb* **nurses, nursing, nursed.** (*mainly tr*) **5** (*also intr*) to tend (the sick). **6** (*also intr*) to feed (a baby) at the breast. **7** to try to cure (an ailment). **8** to clasp fondly: *she nursed the child in her arms.* **9** to look after (a child) as one's employment. **10** to harbour; preserve: *to nurse a grudge.* **11** to give special attention to, esp. in order to promote goodwill: *to nurse a difficult constituency.* **12** Billiards. to keep (the balls) together for a series of cannons. [C16: from earlier *norice,* OF *nourice,* from LL *nūtrīcia,* from L *nūtrīcius* nourishing, from *nūtrīre* to nourish]

nursemaid ('nɜːsˌmeɪd) *or* **nurserymaid** *n* a woman employed to look after someone else's children. Often shortened to **nurse.**

nursery ('nɜːsrɪ) *n, pl* **nurseries. 1** a room in a house set apart for children. **2** a place where plants, young trees, etc., are grown commercially. **3** an establishment providing daycare for babies and young children; crèche. **4** anywhere serving to foster or nourish new ideas, etc. **5**

Also called: **nursery cannon.** *Billiards.* **5a** a series of cannons with the three balls adjacent to a cushion, esp. near a corner pocket. **5b** a cannon in such a series.

nurseryman ('nɜːsrɪmən) *n, pl* **nurserymen.** a person who owns or works in a nursery in which plants are grown.

nursery rhyme *n* a short traditional verse or song for children, such as *Little Jack Horner.*

nursery school *n* a school for young children, usually from three to five years old.

nursery slopes *pl n* gentle slopes used by beginners in skiing.

nursery stakes *pl n* a race for two-year-old horses.

nurse shark *n* any of various sharks having an external groove on each side of the head between the mouth and nostril. [C15 *nusse fisshe* (later infl. in spelling by NURSE), ?from a division of obs. *an huss* shark, dogfish (from ?) as *a nuss*]

nursing ('nɜːsɪŋ) *n* **1a** the practice or profession of caring for the sick and injured. **1b** (*as modifier*): *a nursing home.*

nursing home *n* a private hospital or residence for aged or infirm persons.

nursing officer *n* (in Britain) the official name for **matron** (sense 4).

nursling *or* **nurseling** ('nɜːslɪŋ) *n* a child or young animal that is being suckled, nursed, or fostered.

nurture ('nɜːtʃə) *n* **1** the act or process of promoting development, etc., of a child. **2** something that nourishes. ◆ *vb* **nurtures, nurturing, nurtured.** (*tr*) **3** to feed or support. **4** to educate or train. [C14: from OF *norriture,* from L *nūtrīre* to nourish]
▸ **'nurtural** *adj* ▸ **'nurturer** *n*

NUS (in Britain) *abbrev. for:* **1** (formerly) National Union of Seamen. **2** National Union of Students.

Nusa Tenggara ★ ('nuːsə tɛŋ'ɡɑːrə) *n* an island chain of Indonesia, east of Java: the main islands are Bali, Lombok, Sumbawa, Sumba, Flores, Alor, and Timor. Pop.: 7 237 600 (1995 est.). Area: 73 144 sq. km (28 241 sq. miles). Former name: **Lesser Sunda Islands.**

nut (nʌt) *n* **1** a dry one-seeded indehiscent fruit that usually possesses a woody wall. **2** (*not in technical use*) any similar fruit, such as the walnut, having a hard shell and an edible kernel. **3** the edible kernel of such a fruit. **4** *Sl.* an eccentric or mad person. **5** *Sl.* the head. **6 do one's nut.** *Brit. sl.* to be extremely angry. **7 off one's nut.** *Sl.* mad or foolish. **8** a person or thing that presents difficulties (esp. in **a tough nut to crack**). **9** a small square hexagonal block, usually metal, with a threaded hole through the middle for screwing on the end of a bolt. **10** Also called (US and Canad.): **frog.** *Music.* **10a** the ridge at the upper end of the fingerboard of a violin, cello, etc., over which the strings pass to the tuning pegs. **10b** the end of a violin bow that is held by the player. **11** a small usually gingery biscuit. **12** *Brit.* a small piece of coal. ◆ *vb* **nuts, nutting, nutted. 13** (*intr*) to gather nuts. ◆ See also **nuts.** [OE *hnutu*]

NUT (in Britain) *abbrev. for* National Union of Teachers.

nutant ('njuːtʰnt) *adj Bot.* having the apex hanging down. [C18: from L *nūtāre* to nod]

nutation (njuː'teɪʃən) *n* **1** *Astron.* a periodic variation in the precession of the earth's axis causing the earth's poles to oscillate about their mean position. **2** the spiral growth of a shoot or similar plant organ, caused by variation in the growth rate in different parts. **3** the act of nodding. [C17: from L *nūtātiō,* from *nūtāre* to nod]

nutbrown (nʌt'braʊn) *adj* reddish-brown.

nutcase ('nʌtˌkeɪs) *n Sl.* an insane or very foolish person.

nutcracker ('nʌtˌkrækə) *n* **1** (*often pl*) a device for cracking the shells of nuts. **2** either an Old World bird or a North American bird (**Clark's nutcracker**) having speckled plumage and feeding on nuts, seeds, etc.

nutgall ('nʌtˌɡɔːl) *n* a nut-shaped gall caused by gall wasps on the oak and other trees.

nuthatch ('nʌtˌhætʃ) *n* a songbird having strong feet and bill, and feeding on insects, seeds, and nuts. [C14 *notehache,* from *note* nut + *hache* hatchet, from its habit of splitting nuts]

★ people and places

nuthouse ('nʌt,haʊs) *n Sl.* a mental hospital.

nutmeg ('nʌt,mɛg) *n* **1** an East Indian evergreen tree cultivated in the tropics for its hard aromatic seed. See also **mace**[2]. **2** the seed of this tree, used as a spice. ◆ *vb* **nutmegs, nutmegging, nutmegged.** (*tr*) **3** *Brit. sport inf.* to kick or hit the ball between the legs of (an opposing player). [C13: from OF *nois muguede*, from OProvençal *noz muscada* musk-scented nut, from L *nux* NUT + *muscus* MUSK]

nutria ('nju:trɪə) *n* another name for **coypu,** esp. the fur. [C19: from Sp., var. of *lutria,* ult. from L *lūtra* otter]

nutrient ('nju:trɪənt) *n* **1** any of the mineral substances that are absorbed by the roots of plants. **2** any substance that nourishes an animal. ◆ *adj* **3** providing or contributing to nourishment. [C17: from L *nūtrīre* to nourish]

nutriment ('nju:trɪmənt) *n* any material providing nourishment. [C16: from L *nūtrīmentum,* from *nūtrīre* to nourish]
▸ **nutrimental** (,nju:trɪ'ment°l) *adj*

nutrition (nju:'trɪʃən) *n* **1** a process in animals and plants involving the intake and assimilation of nutrient materials. **2** the act or process of nourishing. **3** the study of nutrition, esp. in humans. [C16: from LL *nūtrītiō,* from *nūtrīre* to nourish]
▸ **nu'tritional** *adj* ▸ **nu'tritionist** *n*

nutritious (nju:'trɪʃəs) *adj* nourishing. [C17: from L *nūtrīcius,* from *nūtrix* NURSE]
▸ **nu'tritiously** *adv* ▸ **nu'tritiousness** *n*

nutritive ('nju:trɪtɪv) *adj* **1** providing nourishment. **2** of, concerning, or promoting nutrition. ◆ *n* **3** a nutritious food.

nuts (nʌts) *adj* **1** a slang word for **insane. 2** (foll. by *about* or *on*) *Sl.* extremely fond (of) or enthusiastic (about). ◆ *interj* **3** *Sl.* an expression of contempt, refusal, or defiance.

nuts and bolts *pl n Inf.* the essential or practical details.

nutshell ('nʌt,ʃɛl) *n* **1** the shell around the kernel of a nut. **2 in a nutshell.** in essence; briefly.

nutter ('nʌtə) *n Brit. sl.* a mad or eccentric person.

nutty ('nʌtɪ) *adj* **nuttier, nuttiest. 1** containing nuts. **2** resembling nuts. **3** a slang word for **insane. 4** (foll. by *over* or *about*) *Inf.* extremely enthusiastic (about).
▸ **'nuttiness** *n*

Nuuk ★ (nu:k) *n* the capital of Greenland, in the southwest: the oldest Danish settlement in Greenland, founded in 1721. Pop.: 12 181 (1993). Former name (until 1979): **Godthaab.**

nux vomica ('nʌks 'vɒmɪkə) *n* **1** an Indian tree with orange-red berries containing poisonous seeds. **2** any of the seeds of this tree, which contain strychnine and other poisonous alkaloids. **3** a medicine manufactured from the seeds of this tree, formerly used as a heart stimulant. [C16: from Med. L: vomiting nut]

nuzzle ('nʌz°l) *vb* **nuzzles, nuzzling, nuzzled. 1** to push or rub gently with the nose or snout. **2** (*intr*) to nestle; lie close. **3** (*tr*) to dig out with the snout. [C15 *nosele,* from NOSE (n)]

NV *abbrev. for* Nevada.

NVQ *abbrev. for* National Vocational Qualification.

NW *symbol for* northwest(ern).

NWMP (in Canada) *abbrev. for* North West Mounted Police.

NWT *abbrev. for* Northwest Territories (of Canada).

NY *or* **N.Y.** *abbrev. for* New York (city or state).

nyala ('njɑ:lə) *n, pl* **nyala** *or* **nyalas. 1** a spiral-horned southern African antelope with a fringe of white hairs along the length of the back and neck. **2 mountain nyala.** a similar Ethiopian animal lacking the white crest. [from Zulu]

Nyasa *or* **Nyassa** ★ (nɪ'æsə, naɪ'æsə) *n* **Lake.** a lake in central Africa at the S end of the Great Rift Valley: the third largest lake in Africa, drained by the Shiré River into the Zambezi. Area: about 28 500 sq. km (11 000 sq. miles). Malawi name: **Lake Malawi.**

Nyasaland ★ (nɪ'æsə,lænd, naɪ'æsə-) *n* the former name (until 1964) of **Malawi.**

NYC *abbrev. for* New York City.

nyctalopia (,nɪktə'ləʊpɪə) *n* inability to see normally in dim light. Nontechnical name: **night blindness.** [C17: via LL from Gk *nuktálōps,* from *nux* night + *alaos* blind + *ōps* eye]

nyctitropism (nɪk'tɪtrə,pɪzəm) *n* a tendency of some plant parts to assume positions at night that are different from their daytime positions. [C19: *nyct-,* from Gk *nukt-, nux* night + -TROPISM]

nye (naɪ) *n* a flock of pheasants. Also called: **nide, eye.** [C15: from OF *ni,* from L *nīdus* nest]

Nyeman ★ (*Russian* 'njemən) *n* a variant spelling of **Neman.**

Nyerere ★ (njə'rɛrɪ, nɪ-) *n* **Julius Kambarage** (kæm-'baːraːgə). born 1922, Tanzanian statesman; president (1964–85). He became prime minister of Tanganyika (1961) and president (1962), negotiating the union of Tanganyika and Zanzibar to form Tanzania (1964).

Nyíregyháza ★ (*Hungarian* 'njiːretjhaːzɒ) *n* a market town in NE Hungary. Pop.: 113 000 (1997 est.).

Nykøbing ★ (*Danish* 'nykøːbeŋ) *n* a port in Denmark, on the W coast of Falster Island. Pop.: 64 428 (1987).

nylon ('naɪlɒn) *n* **1** a class of synthetic polyamide materials of which monofilaments are used for bristles, etc., and fibres can be spun into yarn. **2** yarn or cloth made of nylon, used for clothing, stockings, etc. [C20: orig. a trademark]

nylons ('naɪlɒnz) *pl n* stockings made of nylon.

nymph (nɪmf) *n* **1** *Myth.* a spirit of nature envisaged as a beautiful maiden. **2** *Chiefly poetic.* a beautiful young woman. **3** the larva of insects such as the dragonfly. It resembles the adult, apart from having underdeveloped wings, and develops without a pupal stage. [C14: via OF from L, from Gk *numphē*]
▸ **'nymphal** *or* **nymphean** ('nɪmfɪən) *adj* ▸ **'nymphlike** *adj*

nympha ('nɪmfə) *n, pl* **nymphae** (-fiː). *Anat.* either one of the labia minora. [C17: from L: bride]

nymphet ('nɪmfɪt) *n* a young girl who is sexually precocious and desirable. [C17 (meaning: a young nymph): dim. of NYMPH]

nympho ('nɪmfəʊ) *n, pl* **nymphos.** *Inf.* short for **nymphomaniac.**

nympholepsy ('nɪmfə,lɛpsɪ) *n, pl* **nympholepsies.** a state of violent emotion, esp. when associated with a desire for something that one cannot have. [C18: from Gk *numpholēptos* caught by nymphs, from *numphē* nymph + *lambanein* to seize]
▸ **'nympho,lept** *n* ▸ **,nympho'leptic** *adj*

nymphomania (,nɪmfə'meɪnɪə) *n* a neurotic compulsion in women to have sexual intercourse with many men without being able to have lasting relationships with them. [C18: NL, from Gk *numphē* nymph + -MANIA]
▸ **,nympho'maniac** *n, adj*

Nysa ★ ('naɪsə) *n* the Polish name for the **Neisse** (sense 1).

nystagmus (nɪ'stægməs) *n* involuntary movement of the eye comprising a smooth drift followed by a flick back. [C19: NL, from Gk *nustagmos*]
▸ **nys'tagmic** *adj*

Nyx ★ (nɪks) *n Greek myth.* the goddess of the night, daughter of Chaos. Roman counterpart: **Nox.**

NZ *or* **N. Zeal.** *abbrev. for* New Zealand.

NZBC (formerly) *abbrev. for* New Zealand Broadcasting Commission.

NZEF (in New Zealand) *abbrev. for* New Zealand Expeditionary Force, the New Zealand army that served 1914-18. **2NZEF** refers to the Second New Zealand Expeditionary Force, in World War II.

Oo

o or **O** (əʊ) n, pl **o's**, **O's**, or **Os**. **1** the 15th letter and fourth vowel of the English alphabet. **2** any of several speech sounds represented by this letter, as in *code, pot, cow,* or *form.* **3** another name for **nought**.

O[1] symbol for: **1** *Chem.* oxygen. **2** a human blood type of the ABO group. **3** Old.

O[2] (əʊ) interj **1** a variant of **oh**. **2** an exclamation introducing an invocation, entreaty, wish, etc.: *O God! O for the wings of a dove!*

o. abbrev. for: **1** octavo. **2** old. **3** only. **4** order. **5** *Pharmacol.* pint. [from L *octarius*]

O. abbrev. for: **1** Ocean. **2** octavo. **3** old.

o' (ə) prep Inf. or arch. shortened form of **of**: *a cup o' tea.*

O'- prefix (in surnames of Irish Gaelic origin) descendant of: *O'Corrigan.* [from Irish Gaelic *ó, ua* descendant]

-o suffix forming nouns. indicating a diminutive or slang abbreviation: *wino.*

oaf (əʊf) n a stupid or loutish person. [C17: var. of OE *ælf* ELF]
▸ **'oafish** adj ▸ **'oafishness** n

Oahu ★ (əʊˈɑːhuː) n an island in central Hawaii: the third largest of the Hawaiian Islands. Chief town: Honolulu. Pop.: 836 231 (1990). Area: 1574 sq. km (608 sq. miles).

oak (əʊk) n **1** any deciduous or evergreen tree or shrub having acorns as fruits and lobed leaves. **2a** the wood of any of these trees, used esp. as building timber and for making furniture. **2b** (as modifier): *an oak table.* **3** any of various trees that resemble the oak, such as the poison oak. **4** the leaves of an oak tree, worn as a garland. [OE *āc*]

oak apple or **gall** n any of various brownish round galls on oak trees, containing the larvae of certain wasps.

oaken (ˈəʊkən) adj made of the wood of the oak.

Oakham ★ (ˈəʊkəm) n a market town in E central England, in Rutland. Pop.: 8691 (1991).

Oakland ★ (ˈəʊklənd) n a port and industrial centre in W California, on San Francisco Bay; damaged by earthquake in 1989. Pop.: 366 926 (1994 est.).

Oakley ★ (ˈəʊklɪ) n *Annie,* real name *Phoebe Anne Oakley Mozee.* 1860–1926, US markswoman.

Oaks (əʊks) n (functioning as sing) **the**. a horse race for fillies held annually at Epsom since 1779: one of the classics of English flat racing. [named after an estate near Epsom]

oakum (ˈəʊkəm) n loose fibre obtained by unravelling old rope, used esp. for caulking seams in wooden ships. [OE *ācuma*, var. of *ācumba*, lit.: off-combings, from *ā-* off + *-cumba*, from *cemban* to COMB]

Oakville ★ (ˈəʊkvɪl) n a city in SE Canada, in SE Ontario on Lake Ontario southwest of Toronto: motor-vehicle industry. Pop.: 114 670 (1991).

O & M abbrev. for organization and method (in studies of working methods).

OAP (in Britain) abbrev. for old age pension or pensioner.

oar (ɔː) n **1** a long shaft of wood for propelling a boat by rowing, having a broad blade that is dipped into and pulled against the water. **2** short for **oarsman**. **3 stick** or **put one's oar in**. to interfere or interrupt. ◆ vb **4** to row or propel with or as if with oars. [OE *ār*, of Gmc origin]
▸ **'oarless** adj ▸ **'oar,like** adj

oarfish (ˈɔːˌfɪʃ) n, pl **oarfish** or **oarfishes**. a very long ribbonfish with long slender ventral fins. [C19: referring to the flattened oarlike body]

oarlock (ˈɔːˌlɒk) n the usual US and Canad. word for **rowlock**.

oarsman (ˈɔːzmən) n, pl **oarsmen**. a man who rows, esp. one who rows in a racing boat.
▸ **'oarsmanship** n

OAS abbrev. for: **1** *Organisation de l'Armée Secrète;* an organization which opposed Algerian independence by acts of terrorism. **2** Organization of American States.

oasis (əʊˈeɪsɪs) n, pl **oases** (-iːz). **1** a fertile patch in a desert occurring where the water table approaches or reaches the ground surface. **2** a place of peace, safety, or happiness. [C17: via L from Gk, prob. from Egyptian]

oast (əʊst) n *Chiefly Brit.* **1** a kiln for drying hops. **2** Also called: **oast house**. a building containing such kilns, usually having a conical or pyramidal roof. [OE *āst*]

oat (əʊt) n **1** an erect annual grass grown in temperate regions for its edible seed. **2** (usually pl) the seeds or fruits of this grass. **3** any of various other grasses such as the wild oat. **4** *Poetic.* a flute made from an oat straw. **5 feel one's oats**. *US & Canad. inf.* **5a** to feel exuberant. **5b** to feel self-important. **6 sow one's (wild) oats**. to indulge in adventure or promiscuity during youth. [OE *āte*, from ?]

oatcake (ˈəʊtˌkeɪk) n a crisp brittle unleavened biscuit made of oatmeal.

oaten (ˈəʊtᵊn) adj made of oats or oat straw.

Oates ★ (əʊts) n **1** Captain **Lawrence Edward Grace**. 1880–1912, British explorer; died on Scott's second Antarctic expedition. **2** *Titus* (ˈtaɪtəs). 1649–1705, English conspirator. He fabricated the Popish Plot (1678), a supposed Catholic conspiracy to kill Charles II.

oath (əʊθ) n, pl **oaths** (əʊðz). **1** a solemn pronouncement to affirm the truth of a statement or to pledge a person to some course of action. **2** the form of such a pronouncement. **3** an irreverent or blasphemous expression, esp. one involving the name of a deity; curse. **4 my oath**. *Austral. sl.* certainly; yes indeed. **5 on, upon,** or **under oath. 5a** under the obligation of an oath. **5b** *Law.* having sworn to tell the truth, usually with one's hand on the Bible. **6 take an oath**. to declare formally with a pledge, esp. before giving evidence. [OE *āth*]

oatmeal (ˈəʊtˌmiːl) n **1** meal ground from oats, used for making porridge, oatcakes, etc. **2a** a greyish-yellow colour. **2b** (as adj): *an oatmeal coat.*

OAU abbrev. for Organization of African Unity.

Oaxaca ★ (wəˈhɑːkə; *Spanish* oaˈxaka) n **1** a state of S Mexico, on the Pacific: includes most of the Isthmus of Tehuantepec; inhabited chiefly by Indians. Capital: Oaxaca de Juárez. Pop.: 3 224 270 (1995 est.). Area: 95 363 sq. km (36 820 sq. miles). **2** a city in S Mexico, capital of Oaxaca state; founded in 1486 by the Aztecs and conquered by Spain in 1521. Pop.: 212 818 (1990). Official name: **Oaxaca de Juárez** (de ˈxwareθ).

Ob ★ (Russian ɔpj) n a river in N central Russia, formed by Bisk by the confluence of the Biya and Katun Rivers and flowing generally north to the **Gulf of Ob** (an inlet of the Arctic Ocean): one of the largest rivers in the world, with a drainage basin of about 2 930 000 sq. km (1 131 000 sq. miles). Length: 3682 km (2287 miles).

OB Brit. abbrev. for: **1** Old Boy. **2** outside broadcast.

ob. abbrev. for: **1** (on tombstones, etc.) obiit. [L: he (or she) died] **2** obiter. [L: incidentally; in passing] **3** oboe.

ob- prefix inverse or inversely: *obovate.* [from OF, from L *ob*. In compound words from L, *ob-* (and *oc-, of-, op-*) indicates: to, towards (object); against (oppose); away from (obsolete); before (obstetric); and is used as an intensifier (oblong)]

Obad. Bible. abbrev. for Obadiah.

Obadiah ★ (ˌəʊbəˈdaɪə) n Old Testament. **1** a Hebrew prophet. **2** the book containing his oracles, chiefly directed against Edom. Douay spelling: **Abdias** (æbˈdaɪəs).

Oban ★ (ˈəʊbᵊn) n a small port and resort in W Scotland, in Argyll and Bute on the Firth of Lorne. Pop.: 8203 (1991).

obbligato or **obligato** (ˌɒblɪˈɡɑːtəʊ) *Music.* ◆ adj **1** not to be omitted in performance ◆ *n, pl* **obbligatos, obbligati** (-ti:) *or* **obligatos, obligati** (-ti:). **2** an essential part in a score: *with oboe obbligato.* [C18: from It., from *obbligare* to OBLIGE]

obconic (ɒb'kɒnɪk) *or* **obconical** *adj Bot.* (of a fruit) shaped like a cone and attached at the pointed end.

obcordate (ɒb'kɔːdeɪt) *adj Bot.* heart-shaped and attached at the pointed end: *obcordate leaves.*

obdurate ('ɒbdjʊrɪt) *adj* **1** not easily moved by feelings or supplication; hardhearted. **2** impervious to persuasion. [C15: from L *obdūrāre* to make hard, from *ob-* (intensive) + *dūrus* hard]
▶ **'obduracy** *or* **'obdurateness** *n* ▶ **'obdurately** *adv*

OBE *abbrev. for* Officer of the Order of the British Empire (a Brit. title).

obeah ('əʊbɪə) *n* **1** a kind of witchcraft practised by some West Indians. **2** a charm used in this. [of W African origin]

obedience (ə'biːdɪəns) *n* **1** the condition or quality of being obedient. **2** the act or an instance of obeying; dutiful or submissive behaviour. **3** the authority vested in a Church or similar body. **4** the collective group of persons submitting to this authority.

obedient (ə'biːdɪənt) *adj* obeying or willing to obey. [C13: from OF, from L *oboediens*, present participle of *oboedīre* to OBEY]
▶ **o'bediently** *adv*

obeisance (əʊ'beɪsəns) *n* **1** an attitude of deference or homage. **2** a gesture expressing obeisance. [C14: from OF *obéissant*, present participle of *obéir* to OBEY]
▶ **o'beisant** *adj*

obelisk ('ɒbɪlɪsk) *n* **1** a stone pillar having a square or rectangular cross section and sides that taper towards a pyramidal top. **2** *Printing.* another name for **dagger** (sense 2). [C16: via L from Gk *obeliskos* a little spit, from *obelos* spit]
▶ **,obe'liscal** *adj* ▶ **,obe'liskoid** *adj*

obelus ('ɒbɪləs) *n, pl* **obeli** (-laɪ). **1** a mark (— or ÷) used in ancient documents to indicate spurious words or passages. **2** another name for **dagger** (sense 2). [C14: via LL from Gk *obelos* spit]

Oberammergau ★ (German oːbər'amərgau) *n* a village in S Germany, in Bavaria in the foothills of the Alps: famous for its Passion Play, performed by the villagers every ten years (except during the World Wars) since 1634, in thanksgiving for the end of the Black Death. Pop.: 4740 (1989 est.).

Oberhausen ★ (German 'oːbərhauzən) *n* an industrial city in W Germany, in North Rhine-Westphalia on the Rhine-Herne Canal: site of the first ironworks in the Ruhr. Pop.: 225 443 (1995 est.).

Oberland ★ ('əʊbə,lænd) *n* the lower parts of the Bernese Alps in central Switzerland, mostly in S Bern canton.

Oberon ★ ('əʊbə,rɒn) *n* (in medieval folklore) the king of the fairies, husband of Titania.

Oberösterreich ★ ('oːbər,øːstəraɪç) *n* the German name for **Upper Austria.**

obese (əʊ'biːs) *adj* excessively fat or fleshy; corpulent. [C17: from L *obēsus*, from *ob-* (intensive) + *edere* to eat]
▶ **o'besity** *or* **o'beseness** *n*

obey (ə'beɪ) *vb* **1** to carry out (instructions or orders); comply with (demands). **2** to behave or act in accordance with (one's feelings, whims, etc.). [C13: from OF *obéir*, from L *oboedīre*, from *ob-* towards + *audīre* to hear]
▶ **o'beyer** *n*

obfuscate ('ɒbfʌs,keɪt) *vb* **obfuscates, obfuscating, obfuscated.** *(tr)* **1** to obscure or darken. **2** to perplex or bewilder. [C16: from L *ob-* (intensive) + *fuscāre* to blacken, from *fuscus* dark]
▶ **,obfus'cation** *n* ▶ **obfus,catory** *adj*

obi ('əʊbɪ) *n, pl* **obis** *or* **obi.** a broad sash tied in a large flat bow at the back, worn as part of the Japanese national costume. [C19: from Japanese]

obit ('ɒbɪt, 'əʊbɪt) *n Inf.* **1** short for **obituary.** **2** a memorial service.

obiter dictum ('ɒbɪtə 'dɪktəm, 'əʊ-) *n, pl* **obiter dicta** ('dɪktə). **1** *Law.* an observation by a judge on some point of law not directly in issue in the case before him. **2** any comment or remark made in passing. [L: something said in passing]

obituary (ə'bɪtjʊərɪ) *n, pl* **obituaries.** a published announcement of a death, often accompanied by a short biography of the dead person. [C18: from Med. L *obituārius*, from L *obīre* to fall]
▶ **o'bituarist** *n*

obj. *abbrev. for:* **1** objection. **2** *Grammar.* object(ive).

object[1] ('ɒbdʒɪkt) *n* **1** a tangible and visible thing. **2** a person or thing seen as a focus for feelings, thought, etc. **3** an aim or objective. **4** *Inf.* a ridiculous or pitiable person, spectacle, etc. **5** *Philosophy.* that towards which cognition is directed as contrasted with the thinking subject. **6** *Grammar.* a noun, pronoun, or noun phrase whose referent is the recipient of the action of a verb. See also **direct object, indirect object. 7** *Grammar.* a noun, pronoun, or noun phrase that is governed by a preposition. **8** *Computing.* a self-contained identifiable component of a software system or design. **9 no object.** not a hindrance or obstacle: *money is no object.* [C14: from LL *objectus* something thrown before (the mind), from L *obicere*; see OBJECT[2]]

object[2] (əb'dʒɛkt) *vb* **1** *(tr; takes a clause as object)* to state as an objection. **2** *(intr; often foll. by to)* to raise or state an objection (to); present an argument (against). [C15: from L *obicere*, from *ob-* against + *jacere* to throw]
▶ **ob'jector** *n*

object glass *n Optics.* another name for **objective** (sense 10).

objectify (əb'dʒɛktɪ,faɪ) *vb* **objectifies, objectifying, objectified.** *(tr)* to represent concretely; present as an object.
▶ **ob,jectifi'cation** *n*

objection (əb'dʒɛkʃən) *n* **1** an expression or feeling of opposition or dislike. **2** a cause for such an expression or feeling. **3** the act of objecting.

objectionable (əb'dʒɛkʃənəb°l) *adj* unpleasant, offensive, or repugnant.
▶ **ob,jectiona'bility** *or* **ob'jectionableness** *n* ▶ **ob'jectionably** *adv*

objective (əb'dʒɛktɪv) *adj* **1** existing independently of perception or an individual's conceptions. **2** undistorted by emotion or personal bias. **3** of or relating to actual and external phenomena as opposed to thoughts, feelings, etc. **4** *Med.* (of disease symptoms) perceptible to persons other than the individual affected. **5** *Grammar.* denoting a case of nouns and pronouns, esp. in languages having only two cases, that is used to identify the direct object of a finite verb or preposition. See also **accusative. 6** of or relating to a goal or aim. ◆ *n* **7** the object of one's endeavours; goal; aim. **8** an actual phenomenon; reality. **9** *Grammar.* the objective case. **10** Also called: **object glass.** *Optics.* the lens or combination of lenses nearest to the object in an optical instrument. ◆ Abbrev.: **obj.** Cf. **subjective.**
▶ **objectival** (,ɒbdʒɛk'taɪvəl) *adj* ▶ **ob'jectively** *adv* ▶ **,objec'tivity** *or* (*less commonly*) **ob'jectiveness** *n*

objectivism (əb'dʒɛktɪ,vɪzəm) *n* **1** the tendency to stress what is objective. **2** the philosophical doctrine that reality is objective, and that sense data correspond with it.
▶ **ob'jectivist** *n, adj* ▶ **ob,jectiv'istic** *adj*

object language *n* a language described by another language. Cf. **metalanguage.**

object lesson *n* a convincing demonstration of some principle or ideal.

object program *n* a computer program translated from the equivalent source program into machine language by the compiler or assembler.

object relations theory *n* a form of psychoanalytic theory postulating that people relate to others in order to develop themselves.

objet d'art *French.* (ɔbʒɛ dar) *n, pl* **objets d'art** (ɔbʒɛ dar). a small object considered to be of artistic worth. [F: object of art]

objurgate ('ɒbdʒə,geɪt) vb **objurgates, objurgating, objurgated.** (tr) to scold or reprimand. [C17: from L *objurgāre*, from *ob*- against + *jurgāre* to scold]
▸ ,objur'gation n ▸ 'objur,gator n ▸ **objurgatory** (ɒb'dʒɜ:ɡətərɪ, -trɪ) adj

obl. abbrev. for: **1** oblique. **2** oblong.

oblate[1] ('ɒbleɪt) adj having an equatorial diameter of greater length than the polar diameter: *the earth is an oblate sphere.* Cf. **prolate.** [C18: from NL *oblātus* lengthened, from L *ob*- towards + *lātus*, p.p. of *ferre* to bring]

oblate[2] ('ɒbleɪt) n a person dedicated to a monastic or religious life. [C19: from F *oblat*, from Med. L *oblātus*, from L *offerre* to OFFER]

oblation (ɒ'bleɪʃən) n **1** Christianity. the offering of the Eucharist to God. **2** any offering made for religious or charitable purposes. [C15: from Church L *oblātiō*; see OB-LATE[2]]
▸ **oblatory** ('ɒblətərɪ, -trɪ) or **ob'lational** adj

obligate ('ɒblɪ,ɡeɪt) vb **obligates, obligating, obligated. 1** to compel, constrain, or oblige morally or legally. **2** (in the US) to bind (property, funds, etc.) as security. ◆ adj **3** compelled, bound, or restricted. **4** Biol. able to exist under only one set of environmental conditions. [C16: from L *obligāre* to OBLIGE]
▸ **'obligable** adj ▸ **ob'ligative** adj ▸ **'obli,gator** n

obligation (,ɒblɪ'ɡeɪʃən) n **1** a moral or legal requirement; duty. **2** the act of obligating or the state of being obligated. **3** Law. **3a** a written contract containing a penalty. **3b** an instrument acknowledging indebtedness to secure the repayment of money borrowed. **4** a person or thing to which one is bound morally or legally. **5** a service or favour for which one is indebted.

obligato (,ɒblɪ'ɡɑːtəʊ) adj, n Music. a variant spelling of **obbligato.**

obligatory (ɒ'blɪɡətərɪ, -trɪ) adj **1** required to be done, obtained, possessed, etc. **2** of the nature of or constituting an obligation.
▸ **ob'ligatorily** adv

oblige (ə'blaɪdʒ) vb **obliges, obliging, obliged. 1** (tr; often passive) to bind or constrain (someone to do something) by legal, moral, or physical means. **2** (tr; usually passive) to make indebted or grateful (to someone) by doing a favour. **3** to do a service or favour to (someone): *she obliged the guests with a song.* [C13: from OF *obliger*, from L *obligāre*, from *ob*- towards + *ligāre* to bind]
▸ **o'bliger** n

obligee (,ɒblɪ'dʒiː) n a person in whose favour an obligation, contract, or bond is created; creditor.

obliging (ə'blaɪdʒɪŋ) adj ready to do favours; agreeable; kindly.
▸ **o'bligingly** adv ▸ **o'bligingness** n

obligor (,ɒblɪ'ɡɔː) n a person who binds himself by contract to perform some obligation; debtor.

oblique (ə'bliːk) adj **1** at an angle; slanting; sloping. **2** Geom. **2a** (of lines, planes, etc.) neither perpendicular nor parallel to one another or to another line, plane, etc. **2b** not related to or containing a right angle. **3** indirect or evasive. **4** Grammar. denoting any case of nouns, pronouns, etc., other than the nominative and vocative. **5** Biol. having asymmetrical sides or planes: *an oblique leaf.* ◆ n **6** something oblique, esp. a line. **7** another name for **solidus** (sense 1). ◆ vb **obliques, obliquing, obliqued.** (intr) **8** to take or have an oblique direction. **9** (of a military formation) to move forward at an angle. [C15: from OF, from L *oblīquus*, from ?]
▸ **o'bliquely** adv ▸ **o'bliqueness** n ▸ **obliquity** (ə'blɪkwɪtɪ) n

oblique angle n an angle that is not a right angle or any multiple of a right angle.

obliterate (ə'blɪtə,reɪt) vb **obliterates, obliterating, obliterated.** (tr) to destroy every trace of; wipe out completely. [C16: from L *oblitterāre* to erase, from *ob*- out + *littera* letter]
▸ o,blite'ration n ▸ **o'bliterative** adj ▸ **o'bliter,ator** n

oblivion (ə'blɪvɪən) n **1** the condition of being forgotten

or disregarded. **2** Law. amnesty; pardon. [C14: via OF from L *oblīviō* forgetfulness, from *oblīvīscī* to forget]

oblivious (ə'blɪvɪəs) adj (foll. by *of* or *to*) unaware or forgetful.
▸ **ob'liviously** adv ▸ **ob'liviousness** n

> **USAGE NOTE** It was formerly considered incorrect to use *oblivious* to mean *unaware*, but this use is now acceptable.

oblong ('ɒb,lɒŋ) adj **1** having an elongated, esp. rectangular, shape. ◆ n **2** a figure or object having this shape. [C15: from L *oblongus*, from *ob*- (intensive) + *longus* LONG[1]]

obloquy ('ɒbləkwɪ) n, pl **obloquies. 1** defamatory or censorious statements, esp. when directed against one person. **2** disgrace brought about by public abuse. [C15: from L *obloquium* contradiction, from *ob*- against + *loquī* to speak]

obnoxious (əb'nɒkʃəs) adj **1** extremely unpleasant. **2** Obs. exposed to harm, injury, etc. [C16: from L *obnoxius*, from *ob*- to + *noxa* injury, from *nocēre* to harm]
▸ **ob'noxiously** adv ▸ **ob'noxiousness** n

oboe ('əʊbəʊ) n **1** a woodwind instrument consisting of a conical tube fitted with a mouthpiece having a double reed. It has a penetrating nasal tone. **2** a person who plays this instrument in an orchestra. ◆ Arch. form: **hautboy.** [C18: via It. *oboe*, phonetic approximation to F *haut bois*, lit.: high wood (referring to its pitch)]
▸ **'oboist** n

oboe d'amore (dɑː'mɔːreɪ) n a type of oboe pitched a minor third lower than the oboe itself: used chiefly in baroque music.

Obote ★ (ɒ'bəʊteɪ, -tɪ) n (Apollo) Milton. born 1924, Ugandan politician; prime minister of Uganda (1962–66) and president (1966–71; 1980–85). He was deposed by Amin in 1971 and remained in exile until 1980; deposed again in 1985.

O'Brien ★ (ə'braɪən) n **1** Edna. born 1936, Irish writer. Her novels include *The Country Girls* (1960) and *Down by the River* (1997). **2** Flann, real name *Brian O'Nolan.* 1911–66, Irish novelist. His novels include *At Swim-Two-Birds* (1939).

obs. abbrev. for: **1** observation. **2** obsolete.

obscene (əb'siːn) adj **1** offensive or outrageous to accepted standards of decency or modesty. **2** Law. (of publications, etc.) having a tendency to deprave or corrupt. **3** disgusting; repellent. [C16: from L *obscēnus* inauspicious]
▸ **ob'scenely** adv

obscenity (əb'sɛnɪtɪ) n, pl **obscenities. 1** the state or quality of being obscene. **2** an obscene act, statement, work, etc.

obscurant (əb'skjʊərənt) n an opposer of reform and enlightenment.
▸ **obscurantism** (,ɒbskjʊə'ræn,tɪzəm) n ▸ ,obscu'rantist n, adj

obscure (əb'skjʊə) adj **1** unclear. **2** indistinct, vague, or indefinite. **3** inconspicuous or unimportant. **4** hidden, secret, or remote. **5** (of a vowel) reduced to a neutral vowel (ə). **6** gloomy, dark, clouded, or dim. ◆ vb **obscures, obscuring, obscured.** (tr) **7** to make unclear, vague, or hidden. **8** to cover or cloud over. **9** Phonetics. to pronounce (a vowel) so that it becomes a neutral sound represented by (ə). [C14: via OF from L *obscūrus* dark]
▸ **obscuration** (,ɒbskjʊ'reɪʃən) n ▸ **ob'scurely** adv ▸ **ob'scureness** n

obscurity (əb'skjʊərɪtɪ) n, pl **obscurities. 1** the state or quality of being obscure. **2** an obscure person or thing.

obsequies ('ɒbsɪkwɪz) pl n, sing **obsequy.** funeral rites. [C14: via Anglo-Norman from Med. L *obsequiae* (infl. by L *exsequiae*), from *obsequium* compliance]

obsequious (əb'siːkwɪəs) adj **1** obedient or attentive in an ingratiating or servile manner. **2** Now rare. submissive or compliant. [C15: from L *obsequiōsus* compliant, from *obsequi* to follow]
▸ **ob'sequiously** adv ▸ **ob'sequiousness** n

observance (əb'zɜːvəns) n 1 recognition of or compliance with a law, custom, practice, etc. 2 a ritual, ceremony, or practice, esp. of a religion. 3 observation or attention. 4 the degree of strictness of a religious order in following its rule. 5 Arch. respectful or deferential attention.

observant (əb'zɜːvənt) adj 1 paying close attention to detail; watchful or heedful. 2 adhering strictly to rituals, ceremonies, laws, etc.
▸ ob'servantly adv

observation (ˌɒbzɜ'veɪʃən) n 1 the act of observing or the state of being observed. 2 a comment or remark. 3 detailed examination of phenomena prior to analysis, diagnosis, or interpretation: the patient was under observation. 4 the facts learned from observing. 5 Navigation. 5a a sight taken with an instrument to determine the position of an observer relative to that of a given heavenly body. 5b the data so taken.
▸ ˌobser'vational adj ▸ ˌobser'vationally adv

observatory (əb'zɜːvətərɪ, -trɪ) n, pl observatories. 1 an institution or building specially designed and equipped for observing meteorological and astronomical phenomena. 2 any building or structure providing an extensive view of its surroundings.

observe (əb'zɜːv) vb observes, observing, observed. 1 (tr; may take a clause as object) to see; perceive; notice: we have observed that you steal. 2 (when tr, may take a clause as object) to watch (something) carefully; pay attention to (something). 3 to make observations of (something), esp. scientific ones. 4 (when intr, usually foll. by on or upon; when tr, may take a clause as object) to make a comment or remark: the speaker observed that times had changed. 5 (tr) to abide by, keep, or follow (a custom, tradition, etc.). [C14: via OF from L observāre, from ob- to + servāre to watch]
▸ ob'servable adj ▸ ob'server n

obsess (əb'sɛs) vb 1 (tr; when passive, foll. by with or by) to preoccupy completely; haunt. 2 (intr, usually foll. by on or over) to brood obsessively. [C16: from L obsessus besieged, p.p. of obsidēre, from ob- in front of + sedēre to sit]
▸ ob'sessive adj, n ▸ ob'sessively adv ▸ ob'sessiveness n

obsession (əb'sɛʃən) n 1 Psychiatry. a persistent idea or impulse, often associated with anxiety and mental illness. 2 a persistent preoccupation, idea, or feeling. 3 the act of obsessing or the state of being obsessed.
▸ ob'sessional adj ▸ ob'sessionally adv

obsidian (ɒb'sɪdɪən) n a dark glassy volcanic rock formed by very rapid solidification of lava. Also called: Iceland agate. [C17: from L obsidiānus, erroneous transcription of obsiānus (lapis) (stone of) Obsius, (in Pliny) the discoverer of a stone resembling obsidian]

obsolesce (ˌɒbsə'lɛs) vb obsolesces, obsolescing, obsolesced. (intr) to become obsolete.

obsolescent (ˌɒbsə'lɛsˁnt) adj becoming obsolete or out of date. [C18: from L obsolescere; see OBSOLETE]
▸ ˌobso'lescence n

obsolete (ˈɒbsəˌliːt, ˌɒbsə'liːt) adj 1 out of use or practice; not current. 2 out of date; unfashionable or outmoded. 3 Biol. (of parts, organs, etc.) vestigial; rudimentary. [C16: from L obsolētus worn out, p.p. of obsolēre (unattested), from ob- opposite to + solēre to be used]
▸ 'obso,letely adv ▸ 'obso,leteness n

> **USAGE NOTE** The word obsoleteness is hardly ever used, obsolescence standing as the noun form for both obsolete and obsolescent.

obstacle ('ɒbstəkˁl) n 1 a person or thing that opposes or hinders something. 2 Brit. a fence or hedge used in showjumping. [C14: via OF from L obstāculum, from obstāre, from ob- against + stāre to stand]

obstacle race n a race in which competitors have to negotiate various obstacles.

obstetric (ɒb'stɛtrɪk) or **obstetrical** adj of or relating to childbirth or obstetrics. [C18: via NL from L obstetrīcius, from obstetrix a midwife, lit.: woman who stands opposite, from obstāre to stand in front of; see OBSTACLE]
▸ ob'stetrically adv

obstetrician (ˌɒbstɪ'trɪʃən) n a physician who specializes in obstetrics.

obstetrics (ɒb'stɛtrɪks) n (functioning as sing) the branch of medicine concerned with childbirth and the treatment of women before and after childbirth.

obstinacy ('ɒbstɪnəsɪ) n, pl obstinacies. 1 the state or quality of being obstinate. 2 an obstinate act, attitude, etc.

obstinate ('ɒbstɪnɪt) adj 1 adhering fixedly to a particular opinion, attitude, course of action, etc. 2 self-willed or headstrong. 3 difficult to subdue or alleviate; persistent: an obstinate fever. [C14: from L obstinātus, p.p. of obstināre to persist in, from ob- (intensive) + stin-, var. of stare to stand]
▸ 'obstinately adv

obstreperous (əb'strɛpərəs) adj noisy or rough, esp. in resisting restraint or control. [C16: from L, from obstrepere, from ob- against + strepere to roar]
▸ ob'streperously adv ▸ ob'streperousness n

obstruct (əb'strʌkt) vb (tr) 1 to block (a road, passageway, etc.) with an obstacle. 2 to make (progress or activity) difficult. 3 to impede or block a clear view of. [C17: L obstructus built against, p.p. of obstruere, from ob- against + struere to build]
▸ ob'structive adj, n ▸ ob'structively adv ▸ ob'structiveness n ▸ ob'structor n

obstruction (əb'strʌkʃən) n 1 a person or thing that obstructs. 2 the act or an instance of obstructing. 3 delay of business, esp. in a legislature by means of procedural devices. 4 Sport. the act of unfairly impeding an opposing player.
▸ ob'structional adj

obstructionist (əb'strʌkʃənɪst) n a person who deliberately obstructs business, etc., esp. in a legislature.
▸ ob'structionism n

obtain (əb'teɪn) vb 1 (tr) to gain possession of; acquire; get. 2 (intr) to be customary, valid, or accepted: a new law obtains in this case. [C15: via OF from L obtinēre to take hold of]
▸ ob'tainable adj ▸ ob,taina'bility n ▸ ob'tainer n ▸ ob'tainment n

obtrude (əb'truːd) vb obtrudes, obtruding, obtruded. 1 to push (oneself, one's opinions, etc.) on others in an unwelcome way. 2 (tr) to push out or forward. [C16: from L obtrūdere, from ob- against + trūdere to push forward]
▸ ob'truder n ▸ obtrusion (əb'truːʒən) n

obtrusive (əb'truːsɪv) adj 1 obtruding or tending to obtrude. 2 sticking out; protruding; noticeable.
▸ ob'trusively adv ▸ ob'trusiveness n

obtuse (əb'tjuːs) adj 1 mentally slow or emotionally insensitive. 2 Maths. (of an angle) lying between 90° and 180°. 3 not sharp or pointed. 4 indistinctly felt, heard, etc.; dull: obtuse pain. 5 (of a leaf or similar flat part) having a rounded or blunt tip. [C16: from L obtūsus dulled, p.p. of obtundere to beat down]
▸ ob'tusely adv ▸ ob'tuseness n

obverse ('ɒbvɜːs) adj 1 facing or turned towards the observer. 2 forming or serving as a counterpart. 3 (of leaves) narrower at the base than at the top. ♦ n 4 a counterpart or complement. 5 Logic. a proposition derived from another by replacing the original predicate by its negation and changing the proposition from affirmative to negative or vice versa, as no sum is correct from every sum is incorrect. 6 the side of a coin that bears the main design or device. [C17: from L obversus turned towards, p.p. of obvertere]
▸ ob'versely adv

obvert (ɒb'vɜːt) vb (tr) 1 Logic. to deduce the obverse of (a proposition). 2 Rare. to turn so as to show the main or other side. [C17: from L obvertere to turn towards]
▸ ob'version n

obviate ('ɒbvɪˌeɪt) vb obviates, obviating, obviated. (tr) to avoid or prevent (a need or difficulty). [C16: from LL *obviātus* prevented, p.p. of *obviāre*; see OBVIOUS]

▶ ˌobviˈation *n*

USAGE NOTE Only things which have not yet occurred can be *obviated*. For example, one can *obviate* a possible future difficulty, but not one which already exists.

---

obvious ('ɒbvɪəs) *adj* **1** easy to see or understand; evident. **2** exhibiting motives, feelings, intentions, etc., clearly or without subtlety. **3** naive or unsubtle: *the play was rather obvious.* [C16: from L *obvius*, from *obviam* in the way]

▶ ˈobviously *adv* ▶ ˈobviousness *n*

OC *abbrev. for* Officer Commanding.

Oc. *abbrev. for* Ocean.

o/c *abbrev. for* overcharge.

ocarina (ˌɒkəˈriːnə) *n* an egg-shaped wind instrument with a protruding mouthpiece and six to eight finger holes, producing an almost pure tone. [C19: from It.: little goose, from *oca* goose, ult. from L *avis* bird]

O'Casey ★ (əʊˈkeɪsɪ) *n* **Sean** (ʃɔːn). 1880–1964, Irish dramatist. His plays include *Juno and the Paycock* (1924).

Occam ★ ('ɒkəm) *n* a variant spelling of (William of) **Ockham.**

Occam's razor *n* a variant spelling of **Ockham's razor.**

occas. *abbrev. for* occasional(ly).

occasion (əˈkeɪʒən) *n* **1** (sometimes foll. by *of*) the time of a particular happening or event. **2** (sometimes foll. by *for*) a reason or cause (to do or be something); grounds: *there was no occasion to complain.* **3** an opportunity (to do something); chance. **4** a special event, time, or celebration: *the party was quite an occasion.* **5 on occasion.** every so often. **6 rise to the occasion.** to have the courage, wit, etc., to meet the special demands of a situation. **7 take occasion.** to avail oneself of an opportunity (to do something). ◆ *vb* **8** (*tr*) to bring about, esp. incidentally or by chance. [C14: from L *occāsiō* a falling down, from *occidere* to fall]

occasional (əˈkeɪʒənᵊl) *adj* **1** taking place from time to time; not frequent or regular. **2** of, for, or happening on special occasions. **3** serving as an occasion (for something).

▶ ocˈcasionally *adv*

occasional table *n* a small table with no regular use.

occident ('ɒksɪdənt) *n* a literary or formal word for **west.** Cf. **orient.** [C14: via OF from L *occidere* to fall (with reference to the setting sun)]

▶ ˌocciˈdental *adj*

Occident ('ɒksɪdənt) *n* (usually preceded by *the*) **1** the countries of Europe and America. **2** the western hemisphere.

▶ ˌOcciˈdental *adj, n*

occipital (ɒkˈsɪpɪtᵊl) *adj* **1** of or relating to the back of the head or skull. ◆ *n* **2** short for **occipital bone.** [See OCCIPUT]

occipital bone *n* the bone that forms the back part of the skull and part of its base.

occipital lobe *n* the posterior portion of each cerebral hemisphere, concerned with the interpretation of visual sensory impulses.

occiput ('ɒksɪˌpʌt) *n, pl* **occiputs** or **occipita** (ɒkˈsɪpɪtə). the back part of the head or skull. [C14: from L, from *ob-* at the back of + *caput* head]

occlude (əˈkluːd) *vb* **occludes, occluding, occluded. 1** (*tr*) to block or stop up (a passage or opening); obstruct. **2** (*tr*) to prevent the passage of. **3** *Chem.* (of a solid) to incorporate (a substance) by absorption or adsorption. **4** *Meteorol.* to form or cause to form an occluded front. **5** *Dentistry.* to produce or cause to produce occlusion, as in chewing. [C16: from L *occlūdere*, from *ob-* (intensive) + *claudere* to close]

▶ ocˈcludent *adj*

occluded front *n Meteorol.* the line or plane occurring where the cold front of a depression has overtaken the warm front, raising the warm sector from ground level. Also called: **occlusion.**

occlusion (əˈkluːʒən) *n* **1** the act of occluding or the state of being occluded. **2** *Meteorol.* another term for **occluded front. 3** *Dentistry.* the normal position of the teeth when the jaws are closed.

▶ ocˈclusive *adj*

occult *adj* (ɒˈkʌlt, 'ɒkʌlt). **1a** of or characteristic of mystical or supernatural phenomena or influences. **1b** (*as n*): *the occult.* **2** beyond ordinary human understanding. **3** secret or esoteric. ◆ *vb* (ɒˈkʌlt). **4** *Astron.* (of a celestial body) to hide (another celestial body) from view by occultation or (of a celestial body) to become hidden by occultation. **5** to hide or become hidden or shut off from view. **6** (*intr*) (of lights, esp. in lighthouses) to shut off at regular intervals. [C16: from L *occultus*, p.p. of *occulere*, from *ob-* over, up + *-culere*, rel. to *celāre* to conceal]

▶ ˈocculˌtism *n* ▶ ˈoccultist *n* ▶ ocˈcultness *n*

occultation (ˌɒkʌlˈteɪʃən) *n* the temporary disappearance of one celestial body as it moves out of sight behind another body.

occupancy ('ɒkjʊpənsɪ) *n, pl* **occupancies. 1** the act of occupying; possession of a property. **2** *Law.* the possession and use of property by or without agreement and without any claim to ownership. **3** *Law.* the act of taking possession of unowned property, esp. land, with the intent of thus acquiring ownership. **4** the condition or fact of being an occupant, esp. a tenant. **5** the period of time during which one is an occupant, esp. of property.

occupant ('ɒkjʊpənt) *n* **1** a person, thing, etc., holding a position or place. **2** *Law.* a person who has possession of something, esp. an estate, house, etc.; tenant. **3** *Law.* a person who acquires by occupancy the title to something previously without an owner.

occupation (ˌɒkjʊˈpeɪʃən) *n* **1** a person's regular work or profession; job. **2** any activity on which time is spent by a person. **3** the act of occupying or the state of being occupied. **4** the control of a country by a foreign military power. **5** the period of time that a nation, place, or position is occupied. **6** (*modifier*) for the use of the occupier of a particular property: *occupation road.*

▶ ˌoccuˈpational *adj*

occupational psychology *n* the scientific study of mental or emotional problems associated with the working environment.

occupational therapy *n Med.* treatment of people with physical, emotional, or social problems, using purposeful activity to help them overcome or learn to deal with their problems.

occupation groupings *pl n* a system of classifying people according to occupation, based originally on information obtained by government census and subsequently developed by market research. The classifications are used by the advertising industry to identify potential markets. The groups are **A, B, C1, C2, D,** and **E.**

occupier ('ɒkjʊˌpaɪə) *n* **1** *Brit.* a person who is in possession or occupation of a house or land. **2** a person or thing that occupies.

occupy ('ɒkjʊˌpaɪ) *vb* **occupies, occupying, occupied.** (*tr*) **1** to live or be established in (a house, flat, office, etc.). **2** (*often passive*) to keep (a person) busy or engrossed. **3** (*often passive*) to take up (time or space). **4** to take and hold possession of, esp. as a demonstration: *students occupied the college buildings.* **5** to fill or hold (a position or rank). [C14: from OF *occuper*, from L *occupāre* to seize hold of]

occur (əˈkɜː) *vb* **occurs, occurring, occurred.** (*intr*) **1** to happen; take place; come about. **2** to be found or be present; exist. **3** (foll. by *to*) to be realized or thought of (by); suggest itself (to). [C16: from L *occurrere* to run up to]

USAGE NOTE It is usually regarded as incorrect to talk of pre-arranged events *occurring* or *happening*: *the wedding took place* (not *occurred* or *happened*) *in the afternoon.*

★ people and places

occurrence (ə'kʌrəns) *n* **1** something that occurs; a happening; event. **2** the act or an instance of occurring: *a crime of frequent occurrence.*
▸ oc'current *adj*

ocean ('əʊʃən) *n* **1** a very large stretch of sea, esp. one of the five oceans of the world, the Atlantic, Pacific, Indian, Arctic, and Antarctic. **2** the body of salt water covering approximately 70 per cent of the earth's surface. **3** a huge quantity or expanse: *an ocean of replies.* **4** *Literary.* the sea. [C13: via OF from L *ōceanus*, from OCEANUS]

oceanarium (ˌəʊʃə'nɛərɪəm) *n, pl* **oceanariums** *or* **oceanaria** (-ɪə). a large saltwater aquarium for marine life.

ocean-going *adj* (of a ship, boat, etc.) suited for travel on the open ocean.

Oceania ★ (ˌəʊʃɪ'ɑːnɪə) *n* the islands of the central and S Pacific, including Melanesia, Micronesia, and Polynesia: sometimes also including Australasia and the Malay Archipelago.
▸ ˌOce'anian *adj, n*

oceanic (ˌəʊʃɪ'ænɪk) *adj* **1** of or relating to the ocean. **2** living in the depths of the ocean beyond the continental shelf at a depth exceeding 200 metres: *oceanic fauna.* **3** huge or overwhelming.

Oceanid (əʊ'sɪənɪd) *n, pl* **Oceanids** *or* **Oceanides** (ˌəʊsɪ'ænɪˌdiːz). *Greek myth.* an ocean nymph.

oceanography (ˌəʊʃə'nɒɡrəfɪ, ˌəʊʃɪə-) *n* the branch of science dealing with the physical, chemical, geological, and biological features of the oceans.
▸ ˌocean'ographer *n* ▸ **oceanographic** (ˌəʊʃənə'ɡræfɪk, ˌəʊʃɪə-) *or* ˌoceano'graphical *adj*

oceanology (ˌəʊʃə'nɒlədʒɪ, ˌəʊʃɪə-) *n* the study of the sea, esp. of its economic geography.

Oceanus ★ (əʊ'sɪənəs) *n Greek myth.* a Titan, divinity of the stream believed to flow around the earth.

ocellus (ʊ'sɛləs) *n, pl* **ocelli** (-laɪ). **1** the simple eye of insects and some other invertebrates, consisting basically of light-sensitive cells. **2** any eyelike marking in animals, such as the eyespot on the tail feather of a peacock. [C19: via NL from L: small eye, from *oculus* eye]
▸ o'cellar *adj* ▸ **ocellate** ('ɒsɪˌleɪt) *or* 'ocelˌlated *adj* ▸ ˌocel'lation *n*

ocelot ('ɒsɪˌlɒt, 'əʊ-) *n* a feline mammal inhabiting Central and South America and having a dark-spotted buff-brown coat. [C18: via F from Nahuatl *ocelotl* jaguar]

och (ɒx) *interj Scot. & Irish.* an expression of surprise, contempt, disagreement, etc.

oche ('ɒkɪ) *n Darts.* the mark or ridge on the floor behind which a player must stand to throw. [from ?]

ochlocracy (ɒk'lɒkrəsɪ) *n, pl* **ochlocracies.** rule by the mob; mobocracy. [C16: via F, from Gk *okhlokratia*, from *okhlos* mob + *kratos* power]
▸ **ochlocrat** ('ɒklə,kræt) *n* ▸ ˌochlo'cratic *adj*

ochone (ɒ'xəʊn) *interj Scot. & Irish.* an expression of sorrow or regret. [from Gaelic *ochóin*]

ochre *or US* **ocher** ('əʊkə) *n* **1** any of various natural earths containing ferric oxide, silica, and alumina: used as yellow or red pigments. **2a** a moderate yellow-orange to orange colour. **2b** (*as adj*): *an ochre dress.* ◆ *vb* **ochres, ochring, ochred** *or US* **ochers, ochering, ochered.** **3** (*tr*) to colour with ochre. [C15: from OF *ocre*, from L *ōchra*, from Gk *ōkhros* pale yellow]
▸ **ochreous** ('əʊkrɪəs, 'əʊkərəs), **ochrous** ('əʊkrəs), **ochry** ('əʊkərɪ, 'əʊkrɪ) *or US* 'ocherous, 'ochery *adj*

-ock *suffix forming nouns.* indicating smallness: *hillock.* [OE *-oc, -uc*]

ocker ('ɒkə) *Austral. sl.* ◆ *n* **1** (*often cap.*) an uncultivated or boorish Australian. ◆ *adj* **2** typical of such a person. [C20: after an Australian TV character]

Ockham *or* **Occam** ★ ('ɒkəm) *n* **William of.** died ?1349, English philosopher. See **Ockham's razor.**

Ockham's razor *or* **Occam's razor** *n* a maxim, attributed to William of Ockham, stating that in explaining something assumptions must not be needlessly multiplied. Also called: **the principle of economy.**

o'clock (ə'klɒk) *adv* **1** used after a number from one to twelve to indicate the hour of the day or night. **2** used after a number to indicate direction or position relative

to the observer, twelve o'clock being directly ahead and other positions being obtained by comparisons with a clock face. [C18: abbrev. for *of the clock*]

O'Connell ★ (əʊ'kɒnʳl) *n* **Daniel.** 1775–1847, Irish nationalist leader; his election to the British House of Commons (1828) forced the acceptance of Catholic emancipation (1829).

OCR *abbrev.* for optical character reader *or* recognition.

oct. *abbrev.* for octavo.

Oct. *abbrev.* for October.

oct- *combining form.* a variant of **octo-** before a vowel.

octa- *combining form.* a variant of **octo-**.

octad ('ɒktæd) *n* **1** a group or series of eight. **2** *Chem.* an element with a valency of eight. [C19: from Gk *oktás*, from *oktō* eight]
▸ oc'tadic *adj*

octagon ('ɒktəɡən) *n* a polygon having eight sides. [C17: from L from Gk *oktagōnos* having eight angles]
▸ **octagonal** (ɒk'tæɡənʳl) *adj*

octahedron (ˌɒktə'hiːdrən) *n, pl* **octahedrons** *or* **octahedra** (-drə). a solid figure having eight plane faces.

octal notation *or* **octal** ('ɒktʰl) *n Computing.* a number system having a base 8, one octal digit being equivalent to a group of three bits.

octane ('ɒkteɪn) *n* a liquid hydrocarbon found in petroleum. Formula: C_8H_{18}.

octane number *or* **rating** *n* a measure of the antiknock quality of a petrol expressed as a percentage.

octant ('ɒktənt) *n* **1** *Maths.* **1a** any of the eight parts into which the three planes containing the Cartesian coordinate axes divide space. **1b** an eighth part of a circle. **2** *Astron.* the position of a celestial body when it is at an angular distance of 45° from another body. **3** an instrument used for measuring angles, similar to a sextant but having a graduated arc of 45°. [C17: from L *octans* half quadrant, from *octo* eight]

octavalent (ˌɒktə'veɪlənt) *adj Chem.* having a valency of eight.

octave ('ɒktɪv) *n* **1a** the interval between two musical notes one of which has twice the pitch of the other and lies eight notes away from it counting inclusively along the diatonic scale. **1b** one of these two notes, esp. the one of higher pitch. **1c** (*as modifier*): *an octave leap.* **2** *Prosody.* a rhythmic group of eight lines of verse. **3** ('ɒktɪv). **3a** a feast day and the seven days following. **3b** the final day of this period. **4** the eighth of eight basic positions in fencing. **5** any set or series of eight. ◆ *adj* **6** consisting of eight parts. [C14: (orig.: eighth day) via OF from Med. L *octāva diēs* eighth day (after a festival), from L *octo* eight]

Octavian ★ (ɒk'teɪvɪən) *n* the name of **Augustus** before he became emperor (27 B.C.).

octavo (ɒk'teɪvəʊ) *n, pl* **octavos.** **1** a book size resulting from folding a sheet of paper of a specified size to form eight leaves: *demi-octavo.* Often written: **8vo, 8°. 2** a book of this size. [C16: from NL *in octavo* in an eighth (of a sheet)]

octennial (ɒk'tɛnɪəl) *adj* **1** occurring every eight years. **2** lasting for eight years. [C17: from L *octennium*, from *octo* eight + *annus* year]
▸ oc'tennially *adv*

octet (ɒk'tɛt) *n* **1** any group of eight, esp. singers or musicians. **2** a piece of music composed for such a group. **3** *Prosody.* another word for **octave** (sense 2). **4** *Chem.* a stable group of eight electrons. ◆ Also (for senses 1, 2, 3): **octette.** [C19: from L *octo* eight, on the model of DUET]

octillion (ɒk'tɪljən) *n* **1** (in Britain and Germany) the number represented as one followed by 48 zeros (10^{48}). **2** (in the US, Canada, and France) the number represented as one followed by 27 zeros (10^{27}). [C17: from F, on the model of MILLION]
▸ oc'tillionth *adj, n*

octo-, octa- *or before a vowel* **oct-** *combining form.* eight: *octosyllabic; octagon.* [from L *octo*, Gk *oktō*]

October (ɒk'təʊbə) *n* the tenth month of the year, consisting of 31 days. [OE, from L, from *octo* eight, since it was orig. the eighth month in Roman reckoning]

Octobrist (ɒkˈtəʊbrɪst) *n* a member of a Russian political party favouring the constitutional reforms granted in a manifesto issued by Nicholas II in Oct. 1905.

octocentenary (ˌɒktəʊsenˈtiːnərɪ) *n, pl* **octocentenaries.** an 800th anniversary.

octogenarian (ˌɒktəʊdʒɪˈnɛərɪən) *n* **1** a person who is from 80 to 89 years old. ◆ *adj* **2** of or relating to an octogenarian. [C19: from L *octōgēnārius* containing eighty, from *octōgēnī* eighty each]

octopus (ˈɒktəpəs) *n, pl* **octopuses. 1** a cephalopod mollusc having a soft oval body with eight long suckered tentacles and occurring at the sea bottom. **2** a powerful influential organization, etc., with far-reaching effects, esp. harmful ones. [C18: via NL from Gk *oktṓpous* having eight feet]

octoroon *or* **octaroon** (ˌɒktəˈruːn) *n* a person having one quadroon and one White parent and therefore having one-eighth Black blood. Cf. **quadroon.** [C19: OCTO- + *-roon* as in QUADROON]

octosyllable (ˈɒktəˌsɪləbᵊl) *n* **1** a line of verse composed of eight syllables. **2** a word of eight syllables.
▸ **octosyllabic** (ˌɒktəʊsɪˈlæbɪk) *adj*

octroi (ˈɒktrwɑː) *n* **1** (in some European countries, esp. France) a duty on goods brought into certain towns. **2** the place where it is collected. **3** the officers responsible for its collection. [C17: from F *octroyer* to concede, from Med. L *auctorizāre* to AUTHORIZE]

octuple (ˈɒktjʊpᵊl) *n* **1** a quantity or number eight times as great as another. ◆ *adj* **2** eight times as much or as many. **3** consisting of eight parts. ◆ *vb* **octuples, octupling, octupled. 4** (*tr*) to multiply by eight. [C17: from L *octuplus*, from *octo* eight + *-plus* as in *duplus* double]

ocular (ˈɒkjʊlə) *adj* **1** of or relating to the eye. ◆ *n* **2** another name for **eyepiece.** [C16: from L *oculāris* from *oculus* eye]
▸ **ˈocularly** *adv*

ocularist (ˈɒkjʊlərɪst) *n* a person who makes artificial eyes.

oculate (ˈɒkjʊlɪt) *adj Zool.* **1** having eyes. **2** relating to or resembling eyes: *oculate markings.*

oculist (ˈɒkjʊlɪst) *n Med.* a former term for **ophthalmologist.** [C17: via F from L *oculus* eye]

od (ɒd, əʊd), **odyl,** *or* **odyle** (ˈɒdɪl) *n Arch.* a hypothetical force formerly thought to be responsible for many natural phenomena, such as magnetism, light, and hypnotism. [C19: coined by Baron Karl von Reichenbach (1788–1869), G scientist]
▸ **ˈodic** *adj*

OD[1] (ˌəʊˈdiː) *Inf.* ◆ *n* **1** an overdose of a drug. ◆ *vb* **OD's, OD'ing, OD'd.** (*intr*) **2** to take an overdose of a drug. [C20: from *o(ver)d(ose)*]

OD[2] *abbrev. for:* **1** Officer of the Day. **2** Also: **o.d.** *Mil.* olive drab. **3** Also: **O/D** *Banking.* **3a** on demand. **3b** overdrawn. **4** ordnance datum. **5** outside diameter.

ODA (in Britain) *abbrev. for* Overseas Development Administration.

odalisque *or* **odalisk** (ˈəʊdəlɪsk) *n* a female slave or concubine. [C17: via F, changed from Turkish *ōdalik,* from *ōdah* room + *-lik,* n. suffix]

odd (ɒd) *adj* **1** unusual or peculiar in appearance, character, etc. **2** occasional, incidental, or random: *odd jobs.* **3** leftover or additional: *odd bits of wool.* **4a** not divisible by two. **4b** represented or indicated by a number that is not divisible by two: *graphs are on odd pages.* Cf. **even**[1] (sense 7). **5** being part of a matched pair or set when the other or others are missing: *an odd sock.* **6** (*in combination*) used to designate an indefinite quantity more than the quantity specified in round numbers: *fifty-odd pounds.* **7** out-of-the-way or secluded: *odd corners.* **8 odd man out.** a person or thing excluded from others forming a group, unit, etc. ◆ *n* **9** *Golf.* **9a** one stroke more than the score of one's opponent. **9b** a handicap of one stroke. **10** a thing or person that is odd in sequence or number. ◆ See also **odds.** [from ON *oddi* triangle, point]
▸ **ˈoddly** *adv* ▸ **ˈoddness** *n*

oddball (ˈɒdˌbɔːl) *Inf.* ◆ *n* **1** Also: **odd bod, odd fish.** a

strange or eccentric person or thing. ◆ *adj* **2** strange or peculiar.

Oddfellow (ˈɒdˌfɛləʊ) *n* a member of a secret benevolent and fraternal association founded in England in the 18th century.

oddity (ˈɒdɪtɪ) *n, pl* **oddities. 1** an odd person or thing. **2** an odd quality or characteristic. **3** the condition of being odd.

odd-jobman *or* **odd-jobber** *n* a person who does casual work, esp. domestic repairs.

oddment (ˈɒdmənt) *n* **1** (*often pl*) an odd piece or thing; leftover. **2** *Printing.* **2a** pages that do not make a complete signature. **2b** any individual part of a book excluding the main text.

odd pricing *n* pricing goods in such a way as to imply that a bargain is being offered, as £5.99 instead of £6.

odds (ɒdz) *pl n* **1** (foll. by *on* or *against*) the probability, expressed as a ratio, that a certain event will take place: *the odds against the outsider are a hundred to one.* **2** the amount, expressed as a ratio, by which the wager of one better is greater than that of another: *he was offering odds of five to one.* **3** the likelihood that a certain state of affairs will be so: *the odds are that he is drunk.* **4** an equalizing allowance, esp. one given to a weaker side in a contest. **5** the advantage that one contender is judged to have over another. **6** *Brit.* a significant difference (esp. in **it makes no odds**). **7 at odds.** on bad terms. **8 give** *or* **lay odds.** to offer a bet with favourable odds. **9 over the odds. 9a** more than is expected, necessary, etc. **9b** unfair or excessive. **10 take odds.** to accept a bet with favourable odds. **11 what's the odds?** *Brit. inf.* what difference does it make?

odds and ends *pl n* miscellaneous items or articles.

odds-on *adj* **1** (of a horse, etc.) rated at even money or less to win. **2** regarded as more or most likely to win, succeed, happen, etc.

ode (əʊd) *n* **1** a lyric poem, typically addressed to a particular subject, with lines of varying lengths and complex rhythms. **2** (formerly) a poem meant to be sung. [C16: via F from LL *ōda,* from Gk *ōidē,* from *aeidein* to sing]

-ode[1] *n combining form.* denoting resemblance: *nematode.* [from Gk *-ōdēs,* from *eidos* shape]

-ode[2] *n combining form.* denoting a path or way: *electrode.* [from Gk *-odos,* from *hodos* a way]

Odense ★ (*Danish* ˈoːðənsə) *n* a port in S Denmark, on Funen Island: cathedral founded by King Canute in the 11th century. Pop.: 182 617 (1995 est.).

Oder ★ (ˈəʊdə) *n* a river in central Europe, rising in the N Czech Republic and flowing north and west, forming part of the border between Germany and Poland to the Baltic. Length: 913 km (567 miles). Czech and Polish name: **Odra.**

Oder-Neisse Line ★ (-ˈnaɪsə) *n* the present-day boundary between Germany and Poland along the Rivers Oder and Neisse. Established in 1945, it originally separated the Soviet Zone of Germany from the regions of Germany under Polish administration.

Odessa ★ (əʊˈdɛsə; *Russian* aˈdjɛsə) *n* a port in the S Ukraine, on the Black Sea: the chief Russian grain port in the 19th century; university (1865); industrial centre, major port, and naval base. Pop.: 1 046 000 (1996 est.).

odeum (ˈəʊdɪəm) *n, pl* **odea** (ˈəʊdɪə). (esp. in ancient Greece and Rome) a building for musical performances. Also called: **odeon.** [C17: from L, from Gk *ōideion,* from *ōidē* ODE]

Odin (ˈəʊdɪn) *or* **Othin** ★ *n Norse myth.* the supreme creator; the divinity of wisdom, culture, war, and the dead. Germanic counterpart: **Wotan, Woden.**

odious (ˈəʊdɪəs) *adj* offensive; repugnant. [C17: from L; see ODIUM]
▸ **ˈodiousness** *n*

odium (ˈəʊdɪəm) *n* **1** the dislike accorded to a hated person or thing. **2** hatred; repugnance. [C17: from L; rel. to *ōdī* I hate, Gk *odussasthai* to be angry]

Odoacer (ˌɒdəˈeɪsə) *or* **Odovacar** ★ (ˌəʊdəˈvɑːkə) *n* ?434–493 A.D., barbarian ruler of Italy (476–493); assassinated by Theodoric.

odometer (ɒˈdɒmɪtə, əʊ-) *n* the usual US and Canad.

★ people and places

name for **mileometer**. [C18 *hodometer*, from Gk *hodos* way + -METER]
▶ o'**dometry** *n*

-odont *adj and n combining form.* -toothed: *acrodont*. [from Gk *odón* tooth]

odonto- *or before a vowel* **odont-** *combining form.* indicating a tooth or teeth: *odontology*. [from Gk *odón* tooth]

odontoglossum (ˌɒdɒntə'glɒsəm) *n* a tropical American epiphytic orchid having clusters of brightly coloured flowers.

odontology (ˌɒdɒn'tɒlədʒɪ) *n* the branch of science concerned with the anatomy, development, and diseases of teeth.
▶ **odontological** (ɒˌdɒntə'lɒdʒɪk'l) *adj* ▶ ˌ**odon'tologist** *n*

odoriferous (ˌəʊdə'rɪfərəs) *adj* having or emitting an odour, esp. a fragrant one.
▶ ˌodor'iferously *adv* ▶ ˌodor'iferousness *n*

odoriphore (əʊ'dɒrɪˌfɔː) *n Chem.* the group of atoms in an odorous molecule responsible for its odour.

odorous ('əʊdərəs) *adj* having or emitting a characteristic smell or odour.
▶ 'odorously *adv* ▶ 'odorousness *n*

odour *or US* **odor** ('əʊdə) *n* **1** the property of a substance that gives it a characteristic scent or smell. **2** a pervasive quality about something: *an odour of dishonesty.* **3** repute or regard (in **in good odour, in bad odour**). **4** *Arch.* a sweet-smelling fragrance. [C13: from OF *odur*, from L *odor*]
▶ 'odourless *or US* 'odorless *adj*

Odovacar ★ (ˌəʊdə'vɑːkə) *n* a variant of **Odoacer**.

Odra ★ ('ɒdrə) *n* the Czech and Polish name for the **Oder**.

Odysseus ★ (ə'diːsɪəs) *n Greek myth.* one of the foremost of the Greek heroes at the siege of Troy, noted for his courage and ingenuity. His return to his kingdom of Ithaca was fraught with adventures in which he lost all his companions. Roman name: **Ulysses**.

Odyssey ('ɒdɪsɪ) *n* **1** a Greek epic poem, attributed to Homer, describing the ten-year homeward wanderings of Odysseus after the fall of Troy. **2** (*often not cap.*) any long eventful journey.
▶ **Odyssean** (ˌɒdɪ'siːən) *adj*

Oe *symbol for* oersted.

OE *abbrev. for* Old English (language).

OECD *abbrev. for* Organization for Economic Cooperation and Development.

OED *abbrev. for* Oxford English Dictionary.

oedema *or* **edema** (ɪ'diːmə) *n, pl* **oedemata** *or* **edemata** (-mətə). **1** *Pathol.* an excessive accumulation of serous fluid in the intercellular spaces of tissue. **2** *Bot.* an abnormal swelling in a plant caused by parenchyma or an accumulation of water in the tissues. [C16: via NL from Gk *oidēma*, from *oidein* to swell]
▶ **oedematose, edematous** (ɪ'dɛmətəs) *or* **oe'dema,tose, e'dema,tose** *adj*

Oedipus ★ ('iːdɪpəs) *n Greek myth.* the son of Laius and Jocasta. He killed his father, unaware of his identity, and unwittingly married his mother. When the truth was revealed, he put out his eyes and Jocasta killed herself.

Oedipus complex *n Psychoanal.* the repressed sexual feeling of a child, esp. a male child, for its parent of the opposite sex combined with a rivalry with the parent of the same sex.
▶ 'oedipal *or* ˌoedi'pean *adj*

OEEC *abbrev. for* Organization for European Economic Cooperation. It was superseded by the OECD in 1961.

Oehlenschläger *or* **Öhlenschläger** ★ (*Danish* 'øːlənsleˌgər) *n* **Adam Gottlob** ('adam 'gɔtlɔp). 1779–1850, Danish romantic poet and dramatist.

OEM *abbrev. for* original equipment manufacturer: a computer company whose products are made by combining basic parts supplied by others to meet a customer's needs.

oenology *or* **enology** (iː'nɒlədʒɪ) *n* the study of wine. [C19: from Gk *oinos* wine + -LOGY]
▶ **oenological** *or* **enological** (ˌiːnə'lɒdʒɪk'l) *adj* ▶ **oe'nologist** *or* **e'nologist** *n*

Oenone ★ (iː'nəʊnɪ) *n Greek myth.* a nymph of Mount Ida, whose lover Paris left her for Helen.

oenothera (iː'nɒθərə) *n* any of various hardy biennial or herbaceous perennial plants having yellow flowers. Also called: **evening primrose**. [from Gk *oinothēras*, ?from *onothēras* a plant whose roots smell of wine]

o'er (ɔː, əʊə) *prep, adv* a poetic contraction of **over**.

oersted ('ɜːsted) *n* the cgs unit of magnetic field strength: the field strength that would cause a unit magnetic pole to experience a force of 1 dyne in free space. It is equivalent to 79.58 amperes per metre. Symbol. Oe [C20: after H. C. *Oersted* (1777–1851), Danish physicist who discovered electromagnetism]

oesophagus *or US* **esophagus** (iː'sɒfəgəs) *n, pl* **oesophagi** *or US* **esophagi** (-ˌgaɪ). the part of the alimentary canal between the pharynx and the stomach; gullet. [C16: via NL from Gk *oisophagos*, from *oisein*, future infinitive of *pherein* to carry + -*phagos*, from *phagein* to eat]
▶ **oesophageal** *or US* **esophageal** (iːˌsɒfə'dʒiːəl) *adj*

oestradiol (ˌiːstrə'daɪɒl, ˌestrə-) *or US* **estradiol** *n* the most potent oestrogenic horome secreted by the mammalian ovary: synthesized and used to treat oestrogen deficiency and cancer of the breast. [C20: from NL, from OESTRIN + DI-[1] + -OL[1]]

oestrin ('iːstrɪn) *n* an obsolete term for **oestrogen**. [C20: from OESTRUS) + -IN]

oestrogen ('iːstrədʒən, 'estrə-) *or US* **estrogen** *n* any of several hormones that induce oestrus, stimulate changes in the female reproductive organs, and promote development of female secondary sexual characteristics. [C20: from OESTRUS + -GEN]
▶ **oestrogenic** (ˌiːstrə'dʒenɪk, ˌestrə-) *or US* **estrogenic** (ˌestrə'dʒenɪk, ˌiːstrə-) *adj* ▶ ˌoestro'genically *or US* ˌestro-'genically *adv*

oestrous cycle ('iːstrəs) *n* a hormonally controlled cycle of activity of the reproductive organs in many female mammals.

oestrus ('iːstrəs, 'estrəs) *or US* **estrus, estrum** ('estrəm, 'iːstrəm) *n* a regularly occurring period of sexual receptivity in most female mammals, except humans, during which ovulation occurs and copulation can take place; heat. [C17: from L *oestrus* gadfly, hence frenzy, from Gk *oistros*]
▶ 'oestrous, 'oestral *or US* 'estrous, 'estral *adj*

oeuvre *French.* (œvrə) *n* **1** a work of art, literature, music, etc. **2** the total output of a writer, painter, etc. [ult. from L *opera*, pl. of *opus* work]

of (ɒv; *unstressed* əv) *prep* **1** used with a verbal noun or gerund to link it with a following noun that is either the subject or the object of the verb embedded in the gerund: *the breathing of a fine swimmer* (subject); *the breathing of clean air* (object). **2** used to indicate possession, origin, or association: *the house of my sister; to die of hunger.* **3** used after words or phrases expressing quantities: *a pint of milk.* **4** constituted by, containing, or characterized by: *a family of idiots; a rod of iron; a man of some depth.* **5** used to indicate separation, as in time or space: *within a mile of the town; within ten minutes of the beginning of the concert.* **6** used to mark apposition: *the city of Naples; a speech on the subject of archaeology.* **7** about; concerning: *speak to me of love.* **8** used in passive constructions to indicate the agent: *he was beloved of all.* **9** *Inf.* used to indicate a day or part of a period of time when some activity habitually occurs: *I go to the pub of an evening.* **10** *US.* before the hour of: *a quarter of nine.* [OE (as prep & adv); rel. to L *ab*]

USAGE NOTE   See at **off**.

OF *abbrev. for* Old French (language).

off (ɒf) *prep* **1** used to indicate actions in which contact is absent, as between an object and a surface: *to lift a cup off the table.* **2** used to indicate the removal of something that is appended to or in association with something else: *to take the tax off potatoes.* **3** out of alignment with: *we are off course.* **4** situated near to or leading away from: *just off the High Street.* **5** not inclined towards: *I've gone off you.* ◆ *adv* **6** (*particle*) so as to be deactivated or disengaged: *turn off the radio.* **7** (*particle*) **7a** so as to get rid of: *sleep off a hangover.* **7b** so as to be removed from, esp. as a reduction: *he took ten per cent off.* **8** spent away from work or other duties: *take the afternoon off.* **9a** on a trip, journey, or race: *I saw her off at the station.* **9b** (*particle*) so as to be completely absent, used up, or exhausted: *this stuff kills off all vermin.* **10** out from the shore or land: *the ship stood off.* **11a** out of contact; at a distance: *the ship was 10 miles off.* **11b** out of the present location: *the girl ran off.* **12** away in the future: *August is less than a week off.* **13** (*particle*) so as to be no longer taking place: *the match has been rained off.* **14** (*particle*) removed from contact with something, as clothing from the body: *the girl took all her clothes off.* **15** offstage: *noises off.* **16 off and on.** intermittently; from time to time: *he comes here off and on.* **17 off with.** (*interj*) a command or an exhortation to remove or cut off (something specified): *off with his head; off with that coat.* ◆ *adj* **18** not on; no longer operative: *the off position on the dial.* **19** (*postpositive*) not taking place; cancelled or postponed: *the meeting is off.* **20** in a specified condition regarding money, provisions, etc.: *well off; how are you off for bread?* **21** unsatisfactory or disappointing: *his performance was rather off; an off year for good tennis.* **22** (*postpositive*) in a condition as specified: *I'd be better off without this job.* **23** (*postpositive*) no longer on the menu: *haddock is off.* **24** (*postpositive*) (of food or drink) having gone bad, sour, etc.: *this milk is off.* ◆ *n* **25** *Cricket.* **25a** the part of the field on that side of the pitch to which the batsman presents his bat when taking strike. **25b** (*in combination*) a fielding position in this part of the field: *mid-off.* **25c** (*as modifier*): *the off stump.* [orig. var. of OF; fully distinguished from it in the 17th cent.]

USAGE NOTE In standard English, *off* is not followed by *of: he stepped off* (not *off of*) *the platform.*

---

off. *abbrev. for:* **1** offer. **2** office. **3** officer. **4** official.

Offa ★ (ˈɒfə) *n* died 796 A.D., king of Mercia (757–796), who constructed an earthwork (**Offa's Dyke**) between Wales and Mercia.

offal (ˈɒfᵊl) *n* **1** the edible internal parts of an animal, such as the heart, liver, and tongue. **2** dead or decomposing organic matter. **3** refuse; rubbish. [C14: from OFF + FALL, referring to parts fallen or cut off]

Offaly ★ (ˈɒfəlɪ) *n* an inland county of E central Republic of Ireland, in Leinster province: formerly an ancient kingdom, which also included parts of Tipperary, Leix, and Kildare. County town: Tullamore. Pop.: 58 494 (1991). Area: 2000 sq. km (770 sq. miles).

off-balance-sheet reserve *n Accounting.* a sum of money or an asset that should appear on a company's balance but does not; hidden reserve.

offbeat (ˈɒfˌbiːt) *n* **1** *Music.* any of the normally unaccented beats in a bar, such as the second and fourth beats in a bar of four-four time. ◆ *adj* **2a** unusual, unconventional, or eccentric. **2b** (*as n*): *he liked the offbeat in fashion.*

off break *n Cricket.* a bowled ball that spins from off to leg on pitching.

off-Broadway *adj* **1** designating the kind of experimental, low-budget, or noncommercial productions associated with theatre outside the Broadway area in New York. **2** (of theatres) not located on Broadway.

off colour *adj* (**off-colour** when prenominal). **1** *Chiefly Brit.* slightly ill; unwell. **2** indecent or indelicate; risqué.

offcut (ˈɒfˌkʌt) *n* a piece of paper, wood, fabric, etc., remaining after the main pieces have been cut; remnant.

Offenbach¹ ★ (*German* ˈɔfənbax) *n* a city in central Germany, on the River Main in Hesse opposite Frankfurt am Main: leather-goods industry. Pop.: 116 482 (1995 est.).

Offenbach² ★ (ˈɒfənˌbaːk; *French* ɔfɛnbak) *n* **Jacques** (ʒak). 1819–80, German-born French composer of operettas, including *Orpheus in the Underworld* (1858), and the opera *The Tales of Hoffmann* (1881).

offence *or US* **offense** (əˈfɛns) *n* **1** a violation or breach of a law, rule, etc. **2** any public wrong or crime. **3** annoyance, displeasure, or resentment. **4 give offence (to).** to

cause annoyance or displeasure (to). **5 take offence.** to feel injured, humiliated, or offended. **6** a source of annoyance, displeasure, or anger. **7** attack; assault. **8** *Arch.* injury or harm.

offend (əˈfɛnd) *vb* **1** to hurt the feelings, sense of dignity, etc., of (a person, etc.). **2** (*tr*) to be disagreeable to; disgust: *the smell offended him.* **3** (*intr except in archaic uses*) to break (a law). [C14: via OF *offendre* to strike against, from L *offendere*]
▸ of'fender *n* ▸ of'fending *adj*

offensive (əˈfɛnsɪv) *adj* **1** unpleasant or disgusting, as to the senses. **2** causing anger or annoyance; insulting. **3** for the purpose of attack rather than defence. ◆ *n* **4** (usually preceded by *the*) an attitude or position of aggression. **5** an assault, attack, or military initiative, esp. a strategic one.
▸ of'fensively *adv* ▸ of'fensiveness *n*

offer (ˈɒfə) *vb* **1** to present (something, someone, oneself, etc.) for acceptance or rejection. **2** (*tr*) to present as part of a requirement: *she offered English as a second subject.* **3** (*tr*) to provide or make accessible: *this stream offers the best fishing.* **4** (*intr*) to present itself: *if an opportunity should offer.* **5** (*tr*) to show or express willingness or the intention (to do something). **6** (*tr*) to put forward (a proposal, opinion, etc.) for consideration. **7** (*tr*) to present for sale. **8** (*tr*) to propose as payment; bid or tender. **9** (when *tr,* often foll. by *up*) to present (a prayer, sacrifice, etc.) as or during an act of worship. **10** (*tr*) to show readiness for: *to offer battle.* **11** (*intr*) *Arch.* to make a proposal of marriage. ◆ *n* **12** something, such as a proposal or bid, that is offered. **13** the act of offering or the condition of being offered. **14** a proposal of marriage. **15 on offer.** for sale at a reduced price. [OE, from L *offerre* to present, from *ob-* to + *ferre* to bring]

offer document *n* a document sent by a person or firm making a takeover bid to the shareholders of the target company, giving details of the offer that has been made and, usually, reasons for accepting it.

offering (ˈɒfərɪŋ) *n* **1** something that is offered. **2** a contribution to the funds of a religious organization. **3** a sacrifice, as of an animal, to a deity.

offertory (ˈɒfətərɪ) *n, pl* **offertories.** *Christianity.* **1** the oblation of the bread and wine at the Eucharist. **2** the offerings of the worshippers at this service. **3** the prayers said or sung while the worshippers' offerings are being brought to the altar during the **offertory procession.** [C14: from Church L *offertōrium* place appointed for offerings, from L *offerre* to OFFER]

offhand (ˌɒfˈhænd) *adj also* **offhanded,** *adv* **1** without care, thought, attention, or consideration; sometimes; brusque or ungracious: *an offhand manner.* **2** without preparation or warning; impromptu.
▸ ˌoff'handedly *adv* ▸ ˌoff'handedness *n*

office (ˈɒfɪs) *n* **1a** a room or rooms in which business, professional duties, clerical work, etc., are carried out. **1b** (*as modifier*): *office furniture; an office boy.* **2** (*often pl*) the building or buildings in which the work of an organization, such as a business, is carried out. **3** a commercial or professional business: *the architect's office approved the plans.* **4** the group of persons working in an office: *it was a happy office until she came.* **5** (*cap. when part of a name*) a department of the national government: *the Home Office.* **6** (*cap. when part of a name*) **6a** a governmental agency, esp. of the Federal government in the US. **6b** a subdivision of such an agency: *Office of Science and Technology.* **7a** a position of trust, responsibility, or duty, esp. in a government or organization: *to seek office.* **7b** (*in combination*): *an office-holder.* **8** duty or function: *the office of an administrator.* **9** (*often pl*) a minor task or service: *domestic offices.* **10** (*often pl*) an action performed for another, usually a beneficial action: *through his good offices.* **11** a place where tickets, information, etc., can be obtained: *a ticket office.* **12** *Christianity.* **12a** (*often pl*) a ceremony or service, prescribed by ecclesiastical authorities, esp. one for the dead. **12b** *RC Church.* the official daily service. **12c** short for **divine office. 13** (*pl*) the parts of a house or estate where work is done, goods are stored, etc. **14** (*usually pl*) *Brit., euphemistic.* a lavatory (esp. in **usual offices**). **15 in** (*or* **out of**) **office.** (of a government) in (*or* out of) power. **16** the

---

★ people and places

office. a hint or signal. [C13: via OF from L *officium* service, duty, from *opus* work, service + *facere* to do]

office block *n* a large building designed to provide office accommodation.

office boy *n* a male office junior.

office junior *n* a young person, esp. a school-leaver, employed in an office for running errands and doing other minor jobs.

officer ('ɒfɪsə) *n* **1** a person in the armed services who holds a position of responsibility, authority, and duty. **2** See **police officer**. **3** (on a non-naval ship) any person, including the captain and mate, who holds a position of authority and responsibility: *radio officer; engineer officer*. **4** a person appointed or elected to a position of responsibility or authority in a government, society, etc. **5** a government official: *a customs officer*. **6** (in the Order of the British Empire) a member of the grade below commander. ◆ *vb* (*tr*) **7** to furnish with officers. **8** to act as an officer over (some section, group, organization, etc.).

officer of the day *n* a military officer whose duty is to take charge of the security of the unit or camp for a day. Also called: **orderly officer**.

official (ə'fɪʃəl) *adj* **1** of or relating to an office, its administration, or its duration. **2** sanctioned by, recognized by, or derived from authority: *an official statement*. **3** having a formal ceremonial character: *an official dinner*. ◆ *n* **4** a person who holds a position in an organization, government department, etc., esp. a subordinate position.
▸ **of'ficially** *adv*

officialdom (ə'fɪʃəldəm) *n* **1** the outlook or behaviour of officials, esp. those rigidly adhering to regulations; bureaucracy. **2** officials or bureaucrats collectively.

officialese (ə,fɪʃə'liːz) *n* language characteristic of official documents, esp. when verbose or pedantic.

Official Receiver *n* an officer appointed by the Department of Trade and Industry to receive the income and manage the estate of a bankrupt. See also **receiver** (sense 2).

officiant (ə'fɪʃɪənt) *n* a person who presides and officiates at a religious ceremony.

officiate (ə'fɪʃɪ,eɪt) *vb* **officiates, officiating, officiated.** (*intr*) **1** to hold the position, responsibility, or function of an official. **2** to conduct a religious or other ceremony. [C17: from Med. L *officiāre*, from L *officium*; see OFFICE]
▸ **of,fici'ation** *n* ▸ **of'fici,ator** *n*

officious (ə'fɪʃəs) *adj* **1** unnecessarily or obtrusively ready to offer advice or services. **2** *Diplomacy.* informal or unofficial. [C16: from L *officiōsus* kindly, from *officium* service; see OFFICE]
▸ **of'ficiously** *adv* ▸ **of'ficiousness** *n*

offing ('ɒfɪŋ) *n* **1** the part of the sea that can be seen from the shore. **2 in the offing.** likely to occur soon.

offish ('ɒfɪʃ) *adj Inf.* aloof or distant in manner.
▸ **'offishly** *adv* ▸ **'offishness** *n*

off key *adj* (off-key *when prenominal*), *adv* **1** *Music.* **1a** not in the correct key. **1b** out of tune. **2** out of keeping; discordant.

off-licence *n Brit.* **1** a shop or a counter in a pub or hotel where alcoholic drinks are sold for consumption elsewhere. US equivalents: **package store, liquor store**. **2** a licence permitting such sales.

off limits *adj* (off-limits *when prenominal*). **1** *US, chiefly mil.* not to be entered; out of bounds. ◆ *adv* **2** in or into an area forbidden by regulations.

off line *adj* (off-line *when prenominal*). **1** of or concerned with a part of a computer system not connected to the central processing unit but controlled by a computer storage device. Cf. **on line**. **2** disconnected from a computer; switched off.

off-load *vb* (*tr*) to get rid of (something unpleasant), as by delegation to another.

off message *adj* (off-message *when prenominal*) (esp. of a politician) not following the official line of his or her party.

off-peak *adj* of or relating to services as used outside periods of intensive use.

off-piste *adj* of or relating to skiing on virgin snow off the regular runs.

off-putting *adj Brit. inf.* arousing reluctance or aversion.

off-road *adj* **1** denoting the use of a vehicle away from public roads, esp. on rough terrain: *off-road motorcycling*. **2** (of a vehicle) designed or built for off-road use.

off-roader *n* a motor vehicle designed for use away from public roads, esp. on rough terrain.

off-sales *pl n Brit.* sales of alcoholic drink for consumption off the premises by a pub or an off-licence attached to a pub.

off season *adj* (off-season *when prenominal*). **1** denoting or occurring during a period of little activity in a trade or business. ◆ *n* **2** such a period. ◆ *adv* **3** in an off-season period.

offset *n* ('ɒf,sɛt). **1** something that counterbalances or compensates for something else. **2a** a printing method in which the impression is made onto an intermediate surface, such as a rubber blanket, which transfers it to the paper. **2b** (*modifier*) relating to, involving, or printed by offset: *offset letterpress*. **3** another name for **set off**. **4** *Bot.* a short runner in certain plants that produces roots and shoots at the tip. **5** a ridge projecting from a range of hills or mountains. **6** a narrow horizontal or sloping surface formed where a wall is reduced in thickness towards the top. **7** *Surveying.* a measurement of distance to a point at right angles to a survey line. ◆ *vb* (,ɒf'sɛt), **offsets, offsetting, offset. 8** (*tr*) to counterbalance or compensate for. **9** (*tr*) to print (text, etc.) using the offset process. **10** (*tr*) to construct an offset in (a wall). **11** (*intr*) to project or develop as an offset.

offshoot ('ɒf,ʃuːt) *n* **1** a shoot or branch growing from the main stem of a plant. **2** something that develops or derives from a principal source or origin.

offshore (,ɒf'ʃɔː) *adj, adv* **1** from, away from, or at some distance from the shore. ◆ *adj* **2** sited or conducted at sea: *offshore industries*. **3** based or operating abroad: *offshore banking; offshore fund*.

offside *adj, adv* (,ɒf'saɪd). **1** *Sport.* (in football, etc.) in a position illegally ahead of the ball when it is played. Cf. **onside**. ◆ *n* ('ɒf,saɪd). **2** (usually preceded by *the*) *Chiefly Brit.* **2a** the side of a vehicle, etc., nearest the centre of the road. **2b** (as *modifier*): *the offside passenger door*.

off-sider (,ɒf'saɪdə) *n Austral. & NZ.* a partner or assistant.

offspring ('ɒf,sprɪŋ) *n* **1** the immediate descendant or descendants of a person, animal, etc.; progeny. **2** a product, outcome, or result.

offstage ('ɒf'steɪdʒ) *adj, adv* out of the view of the audience; off the stage.

off-the-peg *adj* (of clothing) ready to wear; not produced especially for the person buying.

off the shelf *adv* **1** from stock and readily available: *you can have this model off the shelf*. ◆ *adj* (off-the-shelf *when prenominal*). **2** of or relating to a product that is readily available: *an off-the-shelf model*. **3** of or denoting a company that has been registered with the Registrar of Companies for the sole purpose of being sold.

off-the-wall *adj* (off the wall *when postpositive*). *Sl.* new or unexpected in an unconventional or eccentric way. [C20: ?from the use of the phrase in handball and squash to describe a shot that is unexpected]

off-white *n* **1** a colour consisting of white with a tinge of grey or yellow. ◆ *adj* **2** of such a colour: *an off-white coat*.

OFS *abbrev.* for Orange Free State.

oft (ɒft) *adv* short for **often** (archaic or poetic except in combinations such as **oft-repeated** and **oft-recurring**). [OE *oft*; rel. to OHG *ofto*]

OFT (in Britain) *abbrev.* for Office of Fair Trading.

Oftel ('ɒf,tɛl) *n* (in Britain) *acronym for* Office of Telecommunications: a government body set up in 1984 to supervise telecommunications activities in the UK, and to protect the interests of the consumers.

often ('ɒfªn) *adv* **1** frequently or repeatedly; much of the time. Arch. equivalents: **'often,times, 'oft,times. 2 as often as not.** quite frequently. **3 every so often.** at intervals. **4 more often than not.** in more than half the instances. ◆ *adj* **5**

Arch. repeated; frequent. [C14: var. of OFT before vowels and *h*]

Ogaden ★ (ˌɒɡəˈdɛn) *n* **the.** an autonomous region of SE Ethiopia, bordering on Somalia: consists of a desert plateau, inhabited by Somali nomads; a secessionist movement, supported by Somalia, has existed within the region since the early 1960s and led to bitter fighting between Ethiopia and Somalia (1977–78).

Ogasawara Gunto ★ (ˌɒɡəsəˈwɑːrə ˈɡuːntəʊ) *n* transliteration of the Japanese name for the **Bonin Islands.**

Ogbomosho ★ (ˌɒɡbəˈməʊʃəʊ) *n* a city in SW Nigeria: the third largest town in Nigeria; trading centre for an agricultural region. Pop.: 711 900 (1995 est.).

Ogden ★ (ˈɒɡdən) *n* C(**harles**) K(**ay**). 1889–1957, British linguist, who, with I. A. Richards, devised Basic English.

ogee (ˈəʊdʒiː) *n Archit.* **1** Also called: **talon.** a moulding having a cross section in the form of a letter S. **2** short for **ogee arch.** [C15: prob. var. of OGIVE]

ogee arch *n Archit.* a pointed arch having an S-shaped curve on both sides. Sometimes shortened to **ogee.**

Ogen melon (ˈəʊɡen) *n* a variety of small melon with sweet pale orange flesh. [C20: after a kibbutz in Israel where it was first developed]

ogham *or* **ogam** (ˈɒɡəm) *n* an ancient alphabetical writing system used by the Celts in Britain, consisting of straight lines drawn or carved perpendicular to or at an angle to another long straight line. [C17: from OIrish *ogom,* from ?, but associated with the name *Ogma,* legendary inventor of this alphabet]

ogive (ˈəʊdʒaɪv, əʊˈdʒaɪv) *n* **1** a diagonal rib or groin of a Gothic vault. **2** another name for **lancet arch.** [C17: from OF, from ?]
▸ o'**gival** *adj*

ogle (ˈəʊɡ°l) *vb* **ogles, ogling, ogled. 1** to look at (someone) amorously or lustfully. **2** (*tr*) to stare or gape at. ◆ *n* **3** a flirtatious or lewd look. [C17: prob. from Low G *oegeln,* from *oegen* to look at]
▸ '**ogler** *n*

Oglethorpe ★ (ˈəʊɡ°l,θɔːp) *n* James Edward. 1696–1785, British general; founder of the colony of Georgia (1733).

Ogooué *or* **Ogowe** ★ (ɒˈɡəʊweɪ) *n* a river in W central Africa, rising in the SW Congo Republic and flowing generally northwest and north through Gabon to the Atlantic. Length: about 970 km (683 miles).

O grade *n* (formerly, in Scotland). **1a** the basic level of the Scottish Certificate of Education, now replaced by **Standard Grade. 1b** (*as modifier*): *O-grade history.* **2** a pass in a subject at O grade: *she has ten O grades.*

ogre (ˈəʊɡə) *n* **1** (in folklore) a giant, usually given to eating human flesh. **2** any monstrous or cruel person. [C18: from F, ?from L *Orcus,* god of the infernal regions]
▸ '**ogreish** *adj* ▸ '**ogress** *fem n*

Ogun ★ (əʊˈɡuːn) *n* a state of SW Nigeria, formed in 1976 from part of Western State. Capital: Abeokuta. Pop.: 2 408 727 (1992 est.). Area: 16 762 sq. km (6472 sq. miles).

oh (əʊ) *interj* an exclamation expressive of surprise, pain, pleasure, etc.

OH *abbrev. for* Ohio.

OHG *abbrev. for* Old High German.

O'Higgins ★ (əʊˈhɪɡɪnz; *Spanish* oˈiɣins) *n* **1 Ambrosio** (æmˈbrəʊzɪˌəʊ). ?1720–1801, Irish soldier, who became viceroy of Chile (1789–96) and of Peru (1796–1801). **2** his son, **Bernardo** (berˈnarðo). 1778–1842, Chilean revolutionary; became Chile's first president (1817–23).

Ohio ★ (əʊˈhaɪəʊ) *n* **1** a state of the central US, in the Midwest on Lake Erie: consists of prairies in the W and the Allegheny plateau in the E, the Ohio River forming the S and most of the E borders. Capital: Columbus. Pop.: 11 172 782 (1996 est.). Area: 107 044 sq. km (41 330 sq. miles). Abbrev. (with zip code): **OH 2** a river in the eastern US, formed by the confluence of the Allegheny and Monongahela Rivers at Pittsburgh: flows generally W and SW to join the Mississippi at Cairo, Illinois, as its chief E tributary. Length: 1570 km (975 miles).

Öhlenschläger *Danish.* ★ (ˈøːləns‚lɛːɣər) *n* a variant spelling of **Oehlenschläger.**

ohm (əʊm) *n* the derived SI unit of electrical resistance the resistance between two points on a conductor when a constant potential difference of 1 volt between them produces a current of 1 ampere. Symbol: Ω [C19: after Georg Simon OHM]
▸ '**ohmage** *n*

Ohm ★ (əʊm) *n* Georg Simon (ˈɡeːɔrk ˈziːmɔn). 1787–1854 German physicist. See **Ohm's law.**

ohmmeter (ˈəʊm‚miːtə) *n* an instrument for measuring electrical resistance.

OHMS (in Britain and the Commonwealth) *abbrev. fo* On Her (*or* His) Majesty's Service.

Ohm's law *n* the principle that the electric current pass ing through a conductor is directly proportional to the potential difference across it. The constant of propor tionality is the resistance of the conductor.

oho (əʊˈhəʊ) *interj* an exclamation expressing surprise, ex ultation, or derision.

-oic *suffix forming adjectives.* indicating that a chemical compound is a carboxylic acid: *ethanoic acid.*

-oid *suffix forming adjectives and associated nouns.* indicat ing likeness, resemblance, or similarity: *anthropoid* [from Gk *-oeidēs* resembling, from *eidos* form]

-oidea *suffix forming plural proper nouns.* forming the names of zoological classes or superfamilies: *Canoidea* [from NL, from L *-oīdēs* -OID]

oil (ɔɪl) *n* **1** any of a number of viscous liquids with a smooth sticky feel. They are usually flammable, insol uble in water, soluble in organic solvents, and are ob tained from plants and animals, from mineral deposits and by synthesis. See also **essential oil.** *ethanoic acid.* for **petroleum. 2b** (*as modifier*): *an oil engine; an oil rig.* **3** any of a number of substances usually derived from pe troleum and used for lubrication. **3b** (*in combination*): *an oilcan.* **3c** (*as modifier*): *an oil pump.* **4** Also called: **fuel oil.** a petroleum product used as a fuel in domestic heating marine engines, etc. **5** *Brit.* **5a** paraffin, esp. when used a a domestic fuel. **5b** (*as modifier*): *an oil lamp.* **6** any sub stance of a consistency resembling that of oil: *oil of vit riol.* **7** the solvent, usually linseed oil, with whic pigments are mixed to make artists' paints. **8a** (*often p* oil colour or paint. **8b** (*as modifier*): *an oil painting.* **9** an oi painting. **10** *Austral. & NZ sl.* facts or news. **11** **strike oi 11a** to discover petroleum while drilling for it. **11b** *Inf.* t become very rich or successful. ◆ *vb* (*tr*) **12** to lubricate smear, polish, etc., with oil or an oily substance. **13** oi **one's tongue.** *Inf.* to speak flatteringly or glibly. **14** oil **some one's palm.** *Inf.* to bribe someone. **15** **oil the wheels.** to mak things run smoothly. [C12: from OF *oile,* from L *oleum* (olive) oil, from *olea* olive tree, from Gk *elaia* OLIVE]
▸ '**oiler** *n* ▸ '**oil-‚like** *adj*

oil cake *n* stock feed consisting of compressed cube made from the residue of the crushed seeds of oil bearing crops such as linseed.

oilcan (ˈɔɪl‚kæn) *n* a container with a long nozzle for ap plying lubricating oil to machinery.

oilcloth (ˈɔɪl‚klɒθ) *n* **1** waterproof material made by treat ing one side of a cotton fabric with a drying oil or a syn thetic resin. **2** another name for **linoleum.**

oil drum *n* a metal drum used to contain or transport oil

oilfield (ˈɔɪl‚fiːld) *n* an area containing reserves of petro leum, esp. one that is already being exploited.

oilfired (ˈɔɪl‚faɪəd) *adj* (of central heating, etc.) using oi as fuel.

oilgas (ˈɔɪl‚ɡæs) *n* a gaseous mixture of hydrocarbon used as a fuel, obtained by the destructive distillation o mineral oils.

oilman (ˈɔɪlmən) *n, pl* **oilmen. 1** a person who owns or op erates oil wells. **2** a person who sells oil.

oil minister *n* a government official in charge of or rep resenting the interests of an oil-producing country.

oil of cloves *n* another name for **clove oil.**

oil of vitriol *n* another name for **sulphuric acid.**

oil paint *n* paint made of pigment ground in oil, usually linseed oil.

oil painting *n* **1** a picture painted with oil paints. **2** th art or process of painting with oil paints. **3 he's** or **she's no oil painting.** *Inf.* he or she is not good-looking.

oil palm *n* a tropical African palm tree, the fruits of which yield palm oil.

oil rig *n* See **rig** (sense 6).

Oil Rivers ★ *pl n* the delta of the Niger River in S Nigeria.

oil sand *n* a sandstone impregnated with hydrocarbons, esp. such deposits in Alberta, Canada.

oil-seed rape *n* another name for **rape**².

oil shale *n* a carbonaceous rock from which oil can be extracted.

oilskin ('ɔɪlˌskɪn) *n* **1a** a cotton fabric treated with oil and pigment to make it waterproof. **1b** (*as modifier*): *an oilskin hat.* **2** (*often pl*) a protective outer garment of this fabric.

oil slick *n* a mass of floating oil covering an area of water.

oilstone ('ɔɪlˌstəʊn) *n* a stone with a fine grain lubricated with oil and used for sharpening cutting tools. See also **whetstone.**

oil well *n* a boring into the earth or sea bed for the extraction of petroleum.

oily ('ɔɪlɪ) *adj* **oilier, oiliest. 1** soaked in or smeared with oil or grease. **2** consisting of, containing, or resembling oil. **3** flatteringly servile or obsequious.
▸ **'oilily** *adv* ▸ **'oiliness** *n*

oink (ɔɪŋk) *interj* an imitation or representation of the grunt of a pig.

ointment ('ɔɪntmənt) *n* **1** a fatty or oily medicated preparation applied to the skin to heal or protect. **2** a similar substance used as a cosmetic. [C14: from OF *oignement,* from L *unguentum* UNGUENT]

Oireachtas ('ɛrəkθəs) *n* the parliament of the Republic of Ireland. [Irish Gaelic: assembly, from OIrish *airech* nobleman]

Oise ★ (*French* waz) *n* **1** a department of N France, in Picardy region. Capital: Beauvais. Pop.: 760 070 (1994 est.). Area: 5887 sq. km (2296 sq. miles). **2** a river in N France, rising in Belgium, in the Ardennes, and flowing southwest to join the Seine at Conflans. Length: 302 km (188 miles).

Oistrakh ★ ('ɔɪstrɑːk; *Russian* 'ɔjstrəx) *n* **1** David (də'vit). 1908–74, Russian violinist. **2** his son, **Igor** ('igərj). born 1931, Russian violinist.

Oita ★ ('ɔɪtə) *n* an industrial city in SW Japan, on NE Kyushu: dominated most of Kyushu in the 16th century. Pop.: 426 981 (1995).

Ojibwa (əʊ'dʒɪbwə) *n* **1** (*pl* **Ojibwas** or **Ojibwa**) a member of a North American Indian people living west of Lake Superior. **2** the language of this people.

OK *abbrev. for* Oklahoma.

O.K. (ˌəʊ'keɪ) *Inf.* ◆ *sentence substitute.* **1** an expression of approval or agreement. ◆ *adj* (*usually postpositive*), *adv* **2** in good or satisfactory condition. ◆ *vb* **O.K.s, O.K.ing** (ˌəʊ'keɪɪŋ), **O.K.ed** (ˌəʊ'keɪd). **3** (*tr*) to approve or endorse. ◆ *n, pl* **O.K.s. 4** approval or agreement. ◆ Also: **okay.** [C19: ?from *o(ll) k(orrect),* jocular alteration of *all correct*]

Okanagan ★ (ˌəʊkə'nɑːgən) *n* a river in North America that flows south from Okanagan Lake in Canada into the Columbia River in NE Washington, US. Length: about 483 km (300 miles). Also (US): **ˌOka'nogan.**

Okanagan Lake ★ *n* a lake in SW Canada, in S British Columbia: drained by the Okanagan River into the Columbia River. Length: about 111 km (69 miles). Width: from 3.2–6.4 km (2–4 miles).

okapi (əʊ'kɑːpɪ) *n, pl* **okapis** or **okapi.** a ruminant mammal of the forests of central Africa, having a reddish-brown coat with horizontal white stripes on the legs, and small horns. [C20: from a Central African word]

Okavango or **Okovango** ★ (ˌəʊkə'væŋgəʊ) *n* a river in SW central Africa, rising in central Angola and flowing southeast, then east as part of the border between Angola and Namibia, then southeast across the Caprivi Strip into Botswana to form a great marsh known as the **Okavango Basin.** Length: about 1600 km (1000 miles).

okay (ˌəʊ'keɪ) *sentence substitute, adj, adv, vb, n* a variant spelling of **O.K.**

Okayama ★ (ˌɒkə'jɑːmə) *n* a city in SW Japan, on W Honshu on the Inland Sea. Pop.: 616 056 (1995).

Okeechobee ★ (ˌəʊkɪ'tʃəʊbɪ) *n* **Lake.** a lake in S Florida, in the Everglades: second largest freshwater lake wholly within the US. Area: 1813 sq. km (700 sq. miles).

O'Keeffe ★ (əʊ'kiːf) *n* **Georgia.** 1887–1986, US painter, best known for her semiabstract still lifes.

Okefenokee Swamp ★ (ˌəʊkɪfɪ'nəʊkɪ) *n* a swamp in the US, in SE Georgia and N Florida: protected flora and fauna. Area: 1554 sq. km (600 sq. miles).

Okhotsk ★ ('əʊkɒtsk; *Russian* ɐ'xɔtsk) *n* **Sea of.** part of the NW Pacific, surrounded by the Kamchatka Peninsula, the Kurile Islands, Sakhalin Island, and the E coast of Siberia. Area: 1 589 840 sq. km (613 838 sq. miles).

Okinawa ★ (ˌəʊkɪ'nɑːwə) *n* a coral island of SW Japan, the largest of the Ryukyu Islands in the N Pacific: scene of heavy fighting in World War II; administered by the US (1945–72); agricultural. Chief town: Naha City. Pop.: 1 273 508 (1995). Area: 1176 sq. km (454 sq. miles).

Okla. *abbrev. for* Oklahoma.

Oklahoma ★ (ˌəʊklə'həʊmə) *n* a state in the S central US: consists of plains in the west, rising to mountains in the southwest and east; important for oil. Capital: Oklahoma City. Pop.: 3 300 902 (1996 est.). Area: 181 185 sq. km (69 956 sq. miles). Abbrevs.: **Okla.** or (with zip code) **OK**
▸ **ˌOkla'homan** *adj, n*

Oklahoma City ★ *n* a city in central Oklahoma: the state capital and a major agricultural and industrial centre. Pop.: 463 201 (1994 est.).

Okovango ★ (ˌəʊkə'væŋgəʊ) *n* a variant spelling of **Okavango.**

okra ('əʊkrə) *n* **1** an annual plant of the Old World tropics, with yellow-and-red flowers and edible oblong green pods. **2** the pod of this plant, eaten in soups, stews, etc. See also **gumbo** (sense 1). [C18: of West African origin]

-ol¹ *suffix forming nouns.* denoting a chemical compound containing a hydroxyl group, esp. alcohols and phenols: *ethanol; quinol.* [from ALCOHOL]

-ol² *n combining form.* (not used systematically) a variant of **-ole**¹.

Olaf I ('əʊləf) or **Olav I** ★ ('əʊləv) *n* known as *Olaf Tryggvesson.* ?965–?1000 A.D., king of Norway (995–?1000). He began the conversion of Norway to Christianity.

Olaf II or **Olav II** ★ *n* Saint. 995–1030 A.D., king of Norway (1015–28); deposed by Canute: patron saint of Norway. Feast day: July 29.

Olaf V or **Olav V** ★ *n* 1903–91, king of Norway (1957–91).

Öland ★ (*Swedish* 'øːland) *n* an island in the Baltic Sea, separated from the mainland of SE Sweden by Kalmar Sound: the second largest Swedish island. Chief town: Borgholm. Pop.: 24 100 (1988 est.). Area: 1347 sq. km (520 sq. miles).

old (əʊld) *adj* **1** having lived or existed for a relatively long time: *an old man; an old tradition; an old house.* **2a** of or relating to advanced years or a long life: *old age.* **2b** (*as collective n;* preceded by *the*): *the old.* **2c old and young.** people of all ages. **3** decrepit or senile. **4** worn with age or use: *old clothes; an old car.* **5a** (*postpositive*) having lived or existed for a specified period: *a child who is six years old.* **5b** (*in combination*): *a six-year-old child.* **5c** (*as n in combination*): *a six-year-old.* **6** (*cap. when part of a name or title*) earlier or earliest of two or more things with the same name: *the old edition; the Old Testament.* **7** (*cap. when part of a name*) designating the form of a language in which the earliest known records are written: *Old English.* **8** (*prenominal*) familiar through long acquaintance or repetition: *an old friend; an old excuse.* **9** practised; hardened: *old in cunning.* **10** (*prenominal; often preceded by good*) cherished; dear: used as a term of affection or familiarity: *good old George.* **11** *Inf.* (with any of several nouns) used as a familiar form of address to a person: *old thing; old bean; old stick.* **12** skilled through long experience (esp. in **an old hand**). **13** out of date; unfashionable. **14** remote or distant in origin or time of origin: *an old culture.* **15**

(*prenominal*) former; previous: *my old house was small*. **16a** (*prenominal*) established for a relatively long time: *an old member*. **16b** (*in combination*): *old-established*. **17** sensible, wise, or mature: *old beyond one's years*. **18** (intensifier) (esp. in **a high old time, any old thing, any old how,** etc.). **19 good old days.** an earlier period of time regarded as better than the present. **20 little old.** *Inf.* indicating affection, esp. humorous affection. **21 the old one** (*or* **gentleman**). *Inf.* a jocular name for **Satan**. ◆ *n* **22** an earlier or past time: *in days of old*. [OE *eald*]
▶ ¹**oldish** *adj* ▶ ¹**oldness** *n*

old age pension *n* a former name for **retirement pension**.
▶ **old age pensioner** *n*

Old Bailey ★ ('beɪlɪ) *n* the Central Criminal Court of England.

Old Bill (bɪl) *n* (*functioning as pl*, preceded by *the*) *Brit. sl.* policemen collectively. [C20: ?from the World War I cartoon of a soldier with a drooping moustache]

old boy *n* **1** (*sometimes caps.*) *Brit.* a male ex-pupil of a school. **2** *Inf., chiefly Brit.* **2a** a familiar name used to refer to a man. **2b** an old man.

old boy network *n* *Brit. inf.* the appointment to power of former pupils of the same small group of public schools or universities.

Old Castile ★ *n* a region of N Spain, on the Bay of Biscay: formerly a province. Spanish name: **Castilla la Vieja.**

Oldcastle ★ ('əʊld,kɑːsᵊl) *n* Sir **John,** Baron Cobham. ?1378–1417, Lollard leader; hanged as a heretic. He is thought to have been a model for Shakespeare's Falstaff.

Old Contemptibles *pl n* the British expeditionary force to France in 1914. [from the Kaiser's alleged reference to them as a "contemptible little army"]

old country *n* the country of origin of an immigrant or an immigrant's ancestors.

Old Dart ★ *n* the. *Austral. sl.* Britain, esp. England. [C19: from ?]

Old Delhi ★ *n* See **Delhi.**

olden ('əʊldᵊn) *adj* an archaic or poetic word for **old** (often in **in olden days** and **in olden times**).

Oldenbarneveldt ★ (*Dutch* ɔldən'bɑrnəvɛlt) *n* **Johan van** (joː'han van). 1547–1619, Dutch statesman, regarded as a founder of Dutch independence: executed by Maurice of Nassau.

Oldenburg¹ ★ ('əʊldᵊn,bɜːg; *German* 'ɔldənburk) *n* **1** a city in NW Germany, in Lower Saxony: former capital of Oldenburg state. Pop.: 149 691 (1995 est.). **2** a former state of NW Germany: became part of Lower Saxony in 1946.

Oldenburg² ★ ('əʊldᵊn,bɜːg) *n* **Claes** (klɔːs). born 1929, US pop sculptor and artist, born in Sweden.

Old English *n* **1** Also called: **Anglo-Saxon.** the English language from the time of the earliest Saxon settlements in the fifth century A.D. to about 1100. Abbrev.: **OE.** **2** *Printing.* a Gothic typeface commonly used in England up to the 18th century.

Old English sheepdog *n* a breed of large bobtailed sheepdog with a profuse shaggy coat.

older ('əʊldə) *adj* **1** the comparative of **old. 2** Also (of people): **elder.** of greater age.

old-fashioned *adj* **1** belonging to, characteristic of, or favoured by former times; outdated: *old-fashioned ideas*. **2** favouring or adopting the dress, manners, fashions, etc., of a former time. **3** *Scot. & N English dialect*. old for one's age: *an old-fashioned child*. ◆ *n* **4** a cocktail containing spirit, bitters, fruit, etc.

Old French *n* the French language in its earliest forms, from about the 9th century up to about 1400. Abbrev.: **OF.**

old girl *n* **1** (*sometimes caps.*) *Brit.* a female ex-pupil of a school. **2** *Inf., chiefly Brit.* **2a** a familiar name used to refer to a woman. **2b** an old woman.

Old Glory *n* a nickname for the flag of the United States of America.

old gold *n* **a** a dark yellow colour, sometimes with a brownish tinge. **b** (*as adj*): *an old-gold carpet*.

old guard *n* **1** a group that works for a long-established or old-fashioned cause or principle. **2** the conservative element in a political party or other group. [C19: after Napoleon's imperial guard]

Oldham ★ ('əʊldəm) *n* **1** a town in NW England, in Greater Manchester. Pop.: 103 931 (1991). **2** a unitary authority in NW England, in Greater Manchester. Pop.: 220 400 (1996 est.). Area: 141 sq. km (54 sq. miles).

old hat *adj* (*postpositive*) old-fashioned or trite.

Old High German *n* a group of West Germanic dialects that eventually developed into modern German; High German up to about 1200. Abbrev.: **OHG.**

oldie ('əʊldɪ) *n* *Inf.* an old joke, song, film, person, etc.

Old Irish *n* the Celtic language of Ireland up to about 900 A.D.

old lady *n* an informal term for **mother** or **wife.**

Old Latin *n* the Latin language before the classical period, up to about 100 B.C.

Old Low German *n* the Saxon and Low Franconian dialects of German up to about 1200; the old form of modern Low German and Dutch. Abbrev.: **OLG.**

old maid *n* **1** a woman regarded as unlikely ever to marry; spinster. **2** *Inf.* a prim, fastidious, or excessively cautious person. **3** a card game in which players try to avoid holding the unpaired card at the end of the game.
▶ ,old-'maidish *adj*

old man *n* **1** an informal term for **father** or **husband. 2** (*sometimes caps.*) *Inf.* a man in command, such as an employer, foreman, or captain of a ship. **3** *Sometimes facetious.* an affectionate term used in addressing a man. **4** Also called: **southernwood.** an aromatic shrubby wormwood of S Europe, having drooping yellow flowers. **5** *Christianity.* the unregenerate aspect of human nature.

old man's beard *n* any of various plants having white feathery seed heads, esp. traveller's joy and Spanish moss.

old master *n* **1** one of the great European painters of the period 1500 to 1800. **2** a painting by one of these.

old moon *n* a phase of the moon lying between last quarter and new moon, when it appears as a waning crescent.

Old Nick *n* *Inf.* a jocular name for **Satan.**

Old Norse *n* the language or group of dialects of medieval Scandinavia and Iceland from about 700 to about 1350. Abbrev.: **ON.**

Old Northwest ★ *n* (in the early US) the land between the Great Lakes, the Mississippi, and the Ohio River. Awarded to the US in 1783, it was organized into the **Northwest Territory** in 1787 and now forms the states of Ohio, Indiana, Illinois, Wisconsin, Michigan, and part of Minnesota.

Old Pretender ★ *n* See (James Francis Edward) **Stuart.**

Old Prussian *n* the former language of the non-German Prussians, belonging to the Baltic branch of the Indo-European family: extinct by 1700.

old rose *n* **a** a greyish-pink colour. **b** (*as adj*): *old-rose gloves*.

Old Saxon *n* the Saxon dialect of Low German up to about 1200, from which modern Low German is derived. Abbrev.: **OS.**

old school *n* **1** *Chiefly Brit.* one's former school. **2** a group of people favouring traditional ideas or conservative practices.

old school tie *n* **1** *Brit.* a distinctive tie that indicates which school the wearer attended. **2** the attitudes, loyalties, values, etc., associated with British public schools.

Old South *n* the American South before the Civil War.

oldster ('əʊldstə) *n* *Inf.* an older person.

old style *n* *Printing.* a type style reviving the characteristics of **old face**, a type style that originated in the 18th century and was characterized by having little contrast between thick and thin strokes.

Old Style *n* the former method of reckoning dates using the Julian calendar. Cf. **New Style.**

Old Testament *n* the collection of books comprising

★ people and places

the sacred Scriptures of the Hebrews; the first part of the Christian Bible.

old-time *adj* (*prenominal*) of or relating to a former time; old-fashioned: *old-time dancing.*

old-timer *n* **1** a person who has been in a certain place, occupation, etc., for a long time. **2** *US.* an old man.

Olduvai Gorge ★ ('ɒldu,vaɪ) *n* a gorge in N Tanzania, north of the Ngorongoro Crater: fossil evidence of early man and other closely related species, together with artefacts.

old wives' tale *n* a belief, usually superstitious or erroneous, passed on by word of mouth as a piece of traditional wisdom.

old woman *n* **1** an informal term for **mother** or **wife. 2** a timid, fussy, or cautious person.
► ,old-'womanish *adj*

Old World *n* that part of the world that was known before the discovery of the Americas; the eastern hemisphere.

old-world *adj* of or characteristic of former times, esp., in Europe, quaint or traditional.

Old World monkey *n* any monkey such as a macaque, baboon, or mandrill, which has nostrils that are close together and a nonprehensile tail.

-ole[1] *or* **-ol** *n combining form.* **1** denoting an organic unsaturated compound containing a 5-membered ring: *thiazole.* **2** denoting an aromatic organic ether: *anisole.* [from L *oleum* oil, from Gk *elaion*, from *elaia* olive]

-ole[2] *suffix of nouns.* indicating something small: *arteriole.* [from L *-olus*, dim. suffix]

oleaceous (,əʊlɪ'eɪʃəs) *adj* of, relating to, or belonging to a family of trees and shrubs which includes the ash, jasmine, privet, lilac, and olive. [C19: via NL from L *olea* OLIVE; see also OIL]

oleaginous (,əʊlɪ'ædʒɪnəs) *adj* **1** resembling or having the properties of oil. **2** containing or producing oil. [C17: from L *oleāginus*, from *olea* OLIVE; see also OIL]

oleander (,əʊlɪ'ændə) *n* a poisonous evergreen Mediterranean shrub or tree with fragrant white, pink, or purple flowers. Also called: **rosebay.** [C16: from Med. L, var. of *arodandrum*, ?from L RHODODENDRON]

oleate ('əʊlɪ,eɪt) *n* any salt or ester of oleic acid.

oleic acid (əʊ'li:ɪk) *n* a colourless oily liquid unsaturated acid occurring, as the glyceride, in almost all natural fats; used in making soaps, ointments, cosmetics, and lubricating oils. Formula: $CH_3(CH_2)_7CH:CH(CH_2)_7COOH$. Systematic name: **cis-9-octadecenoic acid.** [C19 *oleic*, from L *oleum* oil + -IC]

olein ('əʊlɪɪn) *n* another name for **triolein.** [C19: from F *oléine*, from L *oleum* oil + -IN]

oleo- *combining form.* oil: *oleomargarine.* [from L *oleum* OIL]

oleomargarine (,əʊlɪəʊ,mɑːdʒə'riːn) *or* **oleomargarin** (,əʊlɪəʊ'mɑːdʒərɪn) *n* another name (esp. US) for **margarine.**

oleoresin (,əʊlɪəʊ'rezɪn) *n* **1** a semisolid mixture of a resin and essential oil, obtained from certain plants. **2** *Pharmacol.* a liquid preparation of resins and oils, obtained by extraction from plants.
► ,oleo'resinous *adj*

oleum ('əʊlɪəm) *n, pl* **olea** ('əʊlɪə) *or* **oleums.** another name for **fuming sulphuric acid.** [from L: oil, referring to its oily consistency]

O level *n Brit.* **1a** the former basic (ordinary) level of the General Certificate of Education. **1b** (*as modifier*): *O-level maths.* **2** a pass in a particular subject at O level: *he has eight O levels.*

olfaction (ɒl'fækʃən) *n* **1** the sense of smell. **2** the act or function of smelling.

olfactory (ɒl'fæktərɪ, -trɪ) *adj* **1** of or relating to the sense of smell. ◆ *n, pl* **olfactories. 2** (*usually pl*) an organ or nerve concerned with the sense of smell. [C17: from L *olfactus*, p.p. of *olfacere*, from *olere* to smell + *facere* to make]

OLG *abbrev.* for Old Low German.

oligarch ('ɒlɪ,gɑːk) *n* a member of an oligarchy.

oligarchy ('ɒlɪ,gɑːkɪ) *n, pl* **oligarchies. 1** government by a small group of people. **2** a state or organization so governed. **3** a small body of individuals ruling such a state. **4** *Chiefly US.* a small clique of private citizens who exert a strong influence on government. [C16: via Med. L from Gk *oligarkhia*, from *oligos* few + -ARCHY]
► ,oli'garchic *or* ,oli'garchical *adj*

oligo- *or before a vowel* **olig-** *combining form.* indicating a few or little: *oligopoly.* [from Gk *oligos* little, few]

Oligocene ('ɒlɪgəʊ,siːn, ɒ'lɪg-) *adj* **1** of, denoting, or formed in the third epoch of the Tertiary period. ◆ *n* **2 the.** the Oligocene epoch or rock series. [C19: OLIGO- + -CENE]

oligochaete ('ɒlɪgəʊ,kiːt) *n* **1** any freshwater or terrestrial annelid worm having bristles borne singly along the length of the body: includes the earthworms. ◆ *adj* **2** of or relating to this type of worm. [C19: from NL from OLIGO- + Gk *khaitē* long hair]

oligopoly (ɒlɪ'gɒpəlɪ) *n, pl* **oligopolies.** *Econ.* a market situation in which control over the supply of a commodity is held by a small number of producers. [C20: from OLIGO- + Gk *pōlein* to sell]
► ,oli,gopo'listic *adj*

oligospermia (,ɒlɪgəʊ'spɜːmɪə) *n* the condition of having less than the normal number of spermatozoa in the semen: a cause of infertility in men.

oligotrophic (,ɒlɪgəʊ'trɒfɪk) *adj* (of lakes and similar habitats) poor in nutrients and plant life and rich in oxygen. [C20: from OLIGO- + Gk *trophein* to nourish + -IC]
► **oligotrophy** (,ɒlɪ'gɒtrəfɪ) *n*

Ólimbos ★ ('ɔlimbɒs) *n* transliteration of the Modern Greek name for (Mount) **Olympus** (sense 1).

olio ('əʊlɪ,əʊ) *n, pl* **olios. 1** a dish of many different ingredients. **2** a miscellany or potpourri. [C17: from Sp. *olla* stew, from L: jar]

Oliphant ★ ('ɒlɪfənt) *n* Sir **Marcus Laurence Elwin.** born 1901, British nuclear physicist, born in Australia.

olivaceous (,ɒlɪ'veɪʃəs) *adj* of an olive colour.

olive ('ɒlɪv) *n* **1** an evergreen oleaceous tree of the Mediterranean region having white fragrant flowers and edible fruits that are black when ripe. **2** the fruit of this plant, eaten as a relish and used as a source of olive oil. **3** the wood of the olive tree, used for ornamental work. **4a** a yellow-green colour like that of an unripe olive. **4b** (*as adj*): *an olive coat.* ◆ *adj* **5** of, relating to, or made of the olive tree, its wood, or its fruit. [C13: via OF from L *oliva*, rel. to Gk *elaia* olive tree]

olive branch *n* **1** a branch of an olive tree used to symbolize peace. **2** any offering of peace or conciliation.

olive crown *n* (esp. in ancient Greece and Rome) a garland of olive leaves awarded as a token of victory.

olive drab *n US.* **1a** a dull but fairly strong greyish-olive colour. **1b** (*as adj*): *an olive-drab jacket.* **2** cloth or clothes in this colour, esp. the uniform of the US Army.

olive green *n* **a** a colour that is greener, stronger, and brighter than olive; deep yellowish-green. **b** (*as adj*): *an olive-green coat.*

olive oil *n* a yellow to yellowish-green oil pressed from ripe olive fruits and used in cooking, medicines, etc.

Oliver ★ ('ɒlɪvə) *n* **1** one of Charlemagne's 12 paladins. See also **Roland. 2 Joseph,** known as *King Oliver.* 1885–1938, US jazz cornettist.

Olives ★ ('ɒlɪvz) *n* **Mount of.** a hill to the east of Jerusalem: in New Testament times the village Bethany (Mark 11:11) was on its eastern slope and Gethsemane on its western slope.

Olivier ★ (ə'lɪvɪ,eɪ) *n* **Laurence (Kerr),** Baron Olivier of Brighton. 1907–89, British actor: his films include *Henry V* (1944) and *Richard III* (1956); director National Theatre Company (1961–73).

olivine ('ɒlɪ,viːn, ,ɒlɪ'viːn) *n* any of a group of hard glassy olive-green minerals consisting of magnesium iron silicate in crystalline form. [C18: from G, after its colour]

olla ('ɒlə) *n* **1** a cooking pot. **2** short for **olla podrida.** [Sp., from L *olla*, var. of *aulla* pot]

olla podrida ('ɒlə pɒ'driːdə) *n* **1** a Spanish dish, consisting of a stew with beans, sausages, etc. **2** an assortment; miscellany. [Sp., lit.: rotten pot]

Olmec ('ɒlmɛk) *n*, *pl* **Olmecs** or **Olmec**. **1** a member of an ancient Central American Indian people who inhabited the S Gulf Coast of Mexico. ◆ *adj* **2** of or relating to this people.

Olmütz ★ ('ɒlmyts) *n* the German name for **Olomouc**.

ology ('ɒlədʒɪ) *n*, *pl* **ologies**. *Inf.* a science or other branch of knowledge. [C19: abstracted from words such as *theology, biology*, etc.; see -LOGY]

-ology *n combining form*. See **-logy**.

Olomouc ★ (*Czech* 'ɔlɔmouts) *n* a city in the Czech Republic, in North Moravia on the Morava River: capital of Moravia until 1640; university (1576). Pop.: 106 278 (1995 est.). German name: **Olmütz**.

oloroso (ˌɒlə'rəʊsəʊ) *n*, *pl* **olorosos**. a full-bodied golden-coloured sweet sherry. [from Sp.: fragrant]

Olsztyn ★ (*Polish* 'ɔlʃtin) *n* a town in NE Poland: founded in 1334 by the Teutonic Knights; communications centre. Pop.: 167 000 (1995 est.).

Olympia ★ (ə'lɪmpɪə) *n* **1** a plain in Greece, in the NW Peloponnese: in ancient times a major sanctuary of Zeus and site of the original Olympic Games. **2** a port in W Washington, the state capital, on Puget Sound. Pop.: 33 840 (1990).

Olympiad (ə'lɪmpɪˌæd) *n* **1** a staging of the modern Olympic Games. **2** the four-year period between consecutive celebrations of the Olympic Games; a unit of ancient Greek chronology dating back to 776 B.C. **3** an international contest in chess, bridge, etc.

Olympian (ə'lɪmpɪən) *adj* **1** of or relating to Mount Olympus or to the classical Greek gods. **2** majestic or godlike in manner or bearing. **3** of or relating to ancient Olympia, a plain in Greece, or its inhabitants. ◆ *n* **4** a god of Mount Olympus. **5** an inhabitant of ancient Olympia. **6** *Chiefly US.* a competitor in the Olympic Games.

Olympic (ə'lɪmpɪk) *adj* **1** of or relating to the Olympic Games. **2** of or relating to ancient Olympia.

Olympic Games *n* (*functioning as sing or pl*) **1** the greatest Panhellenic festival, held every fourth year in honour of Zeus at ancient Olympia, consisting of games and festivities. **2** Also called: **the Olympics**. the modern revival of these games, consisting of international athletic and sporting contests held every four years in a selected country.

Olympic Mountains ★ *pl n* a mountain range in NW Washington: part of the Coast Range. Highest peak: Mount Olympus, 2427 m (7965 ft).

Olympic Peninsula ★ *n* a large peninsula of W Washington.

Olympus ★ (əʊ'lɪmpəs) *n* **1** **Mount**. a mountain in NE Greece: the highest mountain in Greece, believed in Greek mythology to be the dwelling place of the greater gods. Height: 2911 m (9550 ft). Modern Greek name: **Ólimbos**. **2** **Mount**. a mountain in NW Washington: highest peak of the Olympic Mountains. Height: 2427 m (7965 ft).

Olynthus ★ (əʊ'lɪnθəs) *n* an ancient city in N Greece: the centre of Chalcidice.

OM *abbrev. for* Order of Merit (a Brit. title).

-oma *n combining form*. indicating a tumour: *carcinoma*. [from Gk *-ōma*]

Omagh ★ (əʊ'mɑː, 'əʊmə) *n* **1** a market town in Northern Ireland. Pop.: 17 280 (1991). **2** a district of W central Northern Ireland: cattle and sheep. Administrative centre: Omagh. Pop.: 45 809 (1991). Area: 1125 sq. km (434 sq. miles).

Omaha ('əʊməˌhɑː) *n* a city in E Nebraska, on the Missouri River opposite Council Bluffs, Iowa: the largest city in the state; the country's largest livestock market and meat-packing centre. Pop.: 345 033 (1994 est.).

Oman ★ (əʊ'mɑːn) *n* a sultanate in SE Arabia, on the **Gulf of Oman** and the Arabian Sea: the most powerful state in Arabia in the 19th century, ruling Zanzibar, much of the Persian coast, and part of Pakistan. Official language: Arabic. Official religion: Muslim. Currency: rial. Capital:

Muscat. Pop.: 2 265 000 (1997). Area: 306 000 sq. km (118 150 sq. miles). Former name (until 1970): **Muscat and Oman**.
▸ **O'mani** *adj*, *n*

Omar ('əʊmɑː) or **Umar** ★ *n* died 644 A.D., the second caliph of Islam (634–44).

Omar Khayyám ★ ('əʊmɑː kaɪ'ɑːm) *n* ?1050–?1123, Persian poet and astronomer, noted for the *Rubáiyát*, a collection of quatrains.

omasum (əʊ'meɪsəm) *n*, *pl* **omasa** (-sə). another name for **psalterium**. [C18: from L: bullock's tripe]

Omayyad or **Ommiad** ★ (əʊ'maɪæd) *n*, *pl* **Omayyads, Omayyades** (-əˌdiːz) or **Ommiads, Ommiades** (-əˌdiːz). **1** a caliph of the dynasty ruling (661–750 A.D.) from its capital at Damascus. **2** an emir (756–929 A.D.) or caliph (929–1031 A.D.) of the Omayyad dynasty in Spain.

ombre or *US* **omber** ('ɒmbə) *n* an 18th-century card game. [C17: from Sp. *hombre* man, referring to the player who attempts to win the stakes]

ombudsman ('ɒmbʊdzmən) *n*, *pl* **ombudsmen**. an official who investigates citizens' complaints against the government or its servants. Also called (Brit.): **Parliamentary Commissioner**. See also **Financial Ombudsman**. [C20: from Swedish: commissioner]

Omdurman ★ (ˌɒmdɜː'mɑːn) *n* a city in the central Sudan, on the White Nile, opposite Khartoum: the largest town in the Sudan; scene of the **Battle of Omdurman** (1898), in which the Mahdi's successor was defeated by Lord Kitchener's forces. Pop.: 1 267 077 (1993).

-ome *n combining form*. denoting a mass or part of a specified kind: *rhizome*. [var. of -OMA]

omega ('əʊmɪgə) *n* **1** the 24th and last letter of the Greek alphabet (Ω, ω). **2** the ending or last of a series. [C16: from Gk *ō mega* big o]

omega minus *n* an unstable negatively charged elementary particle, classified as a baryon, that has a mass 3276 times that of the electron.

omelette or *esp. US* **omelet** ('ɒmlɪt) *n* a savoury or sweet dish of beaten eggs cooked in fat. [C17: from F *omelette*, changed from *alumette*, from *alumelle* sword blade, changed by mistaken division from *la lemelle*, from L (see LAMELLA); apparently from the flat shape of the omelette]

omen ('əʊmən) *n* **1** a phenomenon or occurrence regarded as a sign of future happiness or disaster. **2** prophetic significance. ◆ *vb* **3** (*tr*) to portend. [C16: from L]

omentum (əʊ'mɛntəm) *n*, *pl* **omenta** (-tə). *Anat.* a double fold of peritoneum connecting the stomach with other abdominal organs. [C16: from L: membrane, esp. a caul, from ?]

omertà *Italian*. (omer'ta) *n* a conspiracy of silence.

omicron (əʊ'maɪkrɒn, 'ɒmɪkrɒn) *n* the 15th letter in the Greek alphabet (O, o). [from Gk *ō mikron* small o]

ominous ('ɒmɪnəs) *adj* **1** foreboding evil. **2** serving as or having significance as an omen. [C16: from L *ōminōsus*, from OMEN]
▸ **'ominously** *adv* ▸ **'ominousness** *n*

omission (əʊ'mɪʃən) *n* **1** something that has been omitted or neglected. **2** the act of omitting or the state of having been omitted. [C14: from L *omissiō*, from *omittere* to OMIT]
▸ **o'missive** *adj*

omit (əʊ'mɪt) *vb* **omits, omitting, omitted**. (*tr*) **1** to neglect to do or include. **2** to fail (to do something). [C15: from L *omittere*, from *ob-* away + *mittere* to send]
▸ **omissible** (əʊ'mɪsɪbᵊl) *adj* ▸ **o'mitter** *n*

omni- *combining form*. all or everywhere: *omnipresent*. [from L *omnis* all]

omnibus ('ɒmnɪˌbʌs, -bəs) *n*, *pl* **omnibuses**. **1** a formal word for **bus** (sense 1). **2** Also called: **omnibus volume**. a collection of works by one author or several works on a similar topic, reprinted in one volume. **3** Also called: **omnibus edition**. a television or radio programme consisting of two or more episodes of a serial broadcast earlier in the week. ◆ *adj* **4** (*prenominal*) of, dealing with, or providing

★ **people and places**

for many different things or cases. [C19: from L, lit.: for all, dative pl of *omnis* all]

omnicompetent (ˌɒmnɪˈkɒmpɪtənt) *adj* able to judge or deal with all matters.
➤ ˌomniˈcompetence *n*

omnidirectional (ˌɒmnɪdɪˈrekʃənəl, -daɪ-) *adj* (of an antenna) capable of transmitting and receiving radio signals equally in any direction of the horizontal plane.

omnifarious (ˌɒmnɪˈfɛərɪəs) *adj* of many or all varieties or forms. [C17: from LL *omnifārius*, from L *omnis* all + *-farius* doing]
➤ ˌomniˈfariously *adv* ➤ ˌomniˈfariousness *n*

omnific (ɒmˈnɪfɪk) or **omnificent** (ɒmˈnɪfɪsənt) *adj Rare.* creating all things. [C17: via Med. L from L *omni-* + *-ficus*, from *facere* to do]
➤ omˈnificence *n*

omnipotent (ɒmˈnɪpətənt) *adj* 1 having very great or unlimited power. ◆ *n* 2 **the Omnipotent.** an epithet for God. [C14: via OF from L *omnipotens* all-powerful, from OMNI- + *potens*, from *posse* to be able]
➤ omˈnipotence *n* ➤ omˈnipotently *adv*

omnipresent (ˌɒmnɪˈprezᵊnt) *adj* (esp. of a deity) present in all places at the same time.
➤ ˌomniˈpresence *n*

omniscient (ɒmˈnɪsɪənt) *adj* 1 having infinite knowledge or understanding. 2 having very great or seemingly unlimited knowledge. [C17: from Med. L *omnisciens*, from L OMNI- + *scīre* to know]
➤ omˈniscience *n* ➤ omˈnisciently *adv*

omnium-gatherum (ˈɒmnɪəmˈgæðərəm) *n Often facetious.* a miscellaneous collection. [C16: from L *omnium* of all, + Latinized form of E *gather*]

omnivorous (ɒmˈnɪvərəs) *adj* 1 eating any type of food indiscriminately. 2 taking in or assimilating everything, esp. with the mind. [C17: from L *omnivorus* all-devouring, from OMNI- + *vorāre* to eat greedily]
➤ ˈomniˌvore *n* ➤ omˈnivorously *adv* ➤ omˈnivorousness *n*

Omphale (ˈɒmfəˌliː) *n Greek myth.* a queen of Lydia, whom Hercules was required to serve as a slave to atone for the murder of Iphitus.

omphalos (ˈɒmfəˌlɒs) *n* 1 (in the ancient world) a sacred conical object, esp. a stone. The famous omphalos at Delphi was assumed to mark the centre of the earth. 2 the central point. 3 *Literary.* another word for **navel.** [Gk: navel]

Omsk ★ (ɒmsk) *n* a city in W central Russia, at the confluence of the Irtysh and Om Rivers: a major industrial centre, with pipelines from the second Baku oilfield. Pop.: 1 163 000 (1995 est.).

Omuta ★ (ˈəʊmuːˌtɑː) *n* a city in SW Japan, on W Kyushu on Ariake Bay: chemical industries. Pop.: 146 691 (1996).

on (ɒn) *prep* 1 in contact or connection with the surface of; at the upper surface of: *an apple on the ground; a mark on the tablecloth.* 2 attached to: *a puppet on a string.* 3 carried with: *I've no money on me.* 4 in the immediate vicinity of; close to or along the side of: *a house on the sea.* 5 within the time limits of (a day or date): *he arrived on Thursday.* 6 being performed upon or relayed through the medium of: *what's on the television?* 7 at the occasion of: *on his retirement.* 8 used to indicate support, subsistence, contingency, etc.: *he lives on bread.* 9a regularly taking (a drug): *she's on the pill.* 9b addicted to: *he's on heroin.* 10 by means of (something considered as a mode of transport) (esp. in **on foot, on horseback,** etc.). 11 in the process or course of: *on a journey; on strike.* 12 concerned with or relating to: *a programme on archaeology.* 13 used to indicate the basis or grounds, as of a statement or action: *I have it on good authority.* 14 against: used to indicate opposition: *they marched on the city at dawn.* 15 used to indicate a meeting or encounter: *he crept up on her.* 16 (used with any preceded by *the*) indicating the manner or way in which an action is carried out: *on the sly; on the cheap.* 17 staked or wagered as a bet upon: *ten pounds on that horse.* 18 *Inf.* charged to: *the drinks are on me.* ◆ *adv* (*often used as a particle*) 19 in the position or state required for the commencement or sustained continuation, as of a mechanical operation: *the radio's been on all*

night. 20 attached to, surrounding, or placed in contact with something: *the child had nothing on.* 21 arranged: *we've nothing on for tonight.* 22 in a manner indicating continuity, persistence, etc.: *don't keep on about it; the play went on all afternoon.* 23 in a direction towards something, esp. forward: *we drove on towards London; march on!* 24 **on and off.** intermittently; from time to time. 25 **on and on.** without ceasing; continually. ◆ *adj* 26 functioning; operating: *the on position on a radio.* 27 (*postpositive*) *Inf.* performing, as on stage, etc.: *I'm on in five minutes.* 28 definitely taking place: *the match is on for Friday.* 29 tolerable or practicable, acceptable, etc.: *your plan just isn't on.* 30 *Cricket.* (of a bowler) bowling. 31 **on at.** *Inf.* nagging: *she was always on at her husband.* ◆ *n* 32 *Cricket.* 32a (*modifier*) relating to or denoting the leg side of a cricket field or pitch: *an on drive.* 32b (*in combination*) used to designate certain fielding positions on the leg side: *mid-on.* [OE *an, on*]

On ★ (ɒn) *n* the ancient Egyptian and biblical name for **Heliopolis.**

ON *abbrev. for:* 1 Old Norse. 2 Ontario.

-on *suffix forming nouns.* 1 indicating a chemical substance: *interferon.* 2 (in physics) indicating an elementary particle or quantum: *electron; photon.* 3 (in chemistry) indicating an inert gas: *neon; radon.* 4 (in biochemistry) a molecular unit: *codon; operon.* [from ION]

onager (ˈɒnədʒə) *n, pl* **onagri** (-ˌgraɪ) or **onagers.** 1 a Persian variety of the wild ass. 2 an ancient war engine for hurling stones, etc. [C14: from LL: military engine for stone throwing, from L: wild ass, from Gk *onagros*, from *onos* ass + *agros* field]

onanism (ˈəʊnəˌnɪzəm) *n* 1 the withdrawal of the penis from the vagina before ejaculation. 2 masturbation. [C18: after *Onan*, son of Judah; see Genesis 38:9]
➤ ˈonanist *n, adj* ➤ ˌonanˈistic *adj*

Onassis ★ (əʊˈnæsɪs) *n* **Aristotle (Socrates).** 1906–75, Argentinian (formerly Greek) shipowner, born in Turkey.

ONC (in Britain) *abbrev. for* Ordinary National Certificate.

once (wʌns) *adv* 1 one time; on one occasion or in one case. 2 at some past time: *I could speak French once.* 3 by one step or degree (of relationship): *a cousin once removed.* 4 (*in conditional clauses, negatives, etc.*): *if you once forget it.* 5 multiplied by one. 6 **once and away.** 6a conclusively. 6b occasionally. 7 **once and for all.** conclusively; for the last time. 8 **once in a while.** occasionally; now and then. 9 **once or twice** or **once and again.** a few times. 10 **once upon a time.** used to begin fairy tales and children's stories. ◆ *conj* 11 (*subordinating*) as soon as; if ever: *once you begin, you'll enjoy it.* ◆ *n* 12 one occasion or case: *you may do it, this once.* 13 **all at once.** 13a suddenly. 13b simultaneously. 14 **at once.** 14a immediately. 14b simultaneously. 15 **for once.** this time, if (or but) at no other time. [C12 *ones, anes,* adverbial genitive of *on, an* ONE]

once-over *n Inf.* 1 a quick examination or appraisal. 2 a quick but comprehensive piece of work. 3 a violent beating or thrashing (esp. in **give (a person** or **thing) the** (or **a) once-over).**

oncer (ˈwʌnsə) *n* 1 *Brit. sl.* (formerly) a one-pound note. 2 *Austral. sl.* a person elected to Parliament who can only expect to serve one term. 3 *Austral. & NZ.* something which happens only once. [C20: from ONCE]

oncogene (ˈɒŋkəʊˌdʒiːn) *n* any of several genes, present in all cells, that when abnormally activated can cause cancer. [C20: from Gk *onkos* mass, tumour + GENE]
➤ **oncogenic** (ˌɒŋkəʊˈdʒenɪk) *adj*

oncoming (ˈɒnˌkʌmɪŋ) *adj* 1 coming nearer in space or time; approaching. ◆ *n* 2 the approach or onset: *the oncoming of winter.*

oncost (ˈɒnˌkɒst) *n Brit.* 1 another word for **overhead** (sense 5). 2 (*sometimes pl*) another word for **overheads.**

OND (in Britain) *abbrev. for* Ordinary National Diploma.

Ondaatje ★ (ɒnˈdɑːtjə) *n* **Michael.** born 1943, Sri Lankan-born Canadian writer: his novels include *The English Patient* (1992).

on dit *French* (ɔ̃ di) *n, pl* **on dits** (ɔ̃ di). a rumour; piece of gossip. [lit.: it is said, they say]

★ people and places

Ondo ★ ('ɒndəʊ) *n* a state of SW Nigeria, on the Bight of Benin: formed in 1976 from part of Western State. Capital: Akure. Pop.: 4 001 020 (1992 est.). Area: 20 959 sq. km (8092 sq. miles).

one (wʌn) *determiner* **1a** single; lone; not two or more. **1b** (*as pron*): *one is enough for now; one at a time.* **1c** (*in combination*): *one-eyed.* **2a** distinct from all others; only; unique: *one girl in a million.* **2b** (*as pron*): *one of a kind.* **3a** a specified (person, item, etc.) as distinct from another or others of its kind: *raise one hand and then the other.* **3b** (*as pron*): *which one is correct?* **4** a certain, indefinite, or unspecified (time); some: *one day you'll be sorry.* **5** *Inf.* an emphatic word for **a** or **an**[1]: *it was one hell of a fight.* **6** a certain (person): *one Miss Jones was named.* **7** (**all**) in **one**. combined; united. **8** at **one**. **8a** all the same. **8b** of no consequence: *it's all one to me.* **9** at **one**. (often foll. by *with*) in a state of agreement or harmony. **10** be made **one**. to become married. **11** many a **one**. many people. **12** neither one thing nor the other. indefinite, undecided, or mixed. **13** never a **one**. none. **14** one and all. everyone, without exception. **15** one by **one**. one at a time; individually. **16** one or two. a few. **17** one way and another. on balance. **18** one with another. on average. ◆ *pron* **19** an indefinite person regarded as typical of every person: *one can't say any more than that.* **20** any indefinite person: used as the subject of a sentence to form an alternative grammatical construction to that of the passive voice: *one can catch fine trout in this stream.* **21** *Arch.* an unspecified person: *one came to him.* ◆ *n* **22** the smallest natural number and the first cardinal number; unity. **23** a numeral (1, I, i, etc.) representing this number. **24** *Inf.* a joke or story (esp. in **the one about**). **25** something representing, represented by, or consisting of one unit. **26** Also: **one o'clock**. one hour after noon or midnight. **27** a blow or setback (esp. in **one in the eye for**). **28** the Evil one. Satan. **29** the Holy One *or* the One above. God. ◆ *Related prefixes*: **mono-**, **uni-**. [OE *ān*]

-one *suffix forming nouns.* indicating that a chemical compound is a ketone: *acetone.* [arbitrarily from Gk *-ōnē*, fem. patronymic suffix, but ? infl. by *-one* in OZONE]

one another *pron* the reflexive form of plural pronouns when the action, attribution, etc., is reciprocal: *they kissed one another; knowing one another.* Also: **each other.**

one-armed bandit *n Inf.* a fruit machine operated by pulling down a lever at one side.

Onega ★ (*Russian* a'njega) *n* a lake in NW Russia, mostly in the Karelian Republic: the second largest lake in Europe and fourth largest in the former Soviet Union. Area: 9891 sq. km (3819 sq. miles).

one-horse *adj* **1** drawn by or using one horse. **2** (*prenominal*) *Inf.* small or obscure: *a one-horse town.*

Oneida ★ (əʊ'naɪdə) *n* **Lake**. a lake in central New York State: part of the New York State Barge Canal system. Length: about 35 km (22 miles). Greatest width: 9 km (6 miles).

O'Neill ★ (əʊ'niːl) *n* Eugene (**Gladstone**). 1888–1953, US dramatist. His works include *Desire under the Elms* (1924), *Mourning Becomes Elektra* (1931), and *The Iceman Cometh* (1946): Nobel prize for literature 1936.

one-liner *n Inf.* a short joke or witty remark.

one-man *adj* consisting of or done by or for one man: *a one-man band; a one-man show.*

oneness ('wʌnnɪs) *n* **1** the state or quality of being one; singleness. **2** the state of being united; agreement. **3** uniqueness. **4** sameness.

one-night stand *n* **1** a performance given only once at any one place. **2** *Inf.* a sexual encounter lasting only one evening or night.

one-off *n Brit.* **a** something that is carried out or made only once. **b** (*as modifier*): *a one-off job.*

one-on-one *adj* another term for **one-to-one** (sense 2).

one-parent family *n* another term for **single-parent family.**

one-piece *adj* **1** (of a garment, esp. a bathing costume) consisting of one piece. ◆ *n* **2** a garment, esp. a bathing costume, consisting of one piece.

onerous ('ɒnərəs, 'əʊ-) *adj* **1** laborious or oppressive. **2** *Law.* (of a contract, etc.) having or involving burdens or obligations. [C14: from L *onerōsus* burdensome, from *onus* load]
> ▸ **'onerously** *adv* ▸ **'onerousness** *n*

oneself (wʌn'sɛlf) *pron* **1a** the reflexive form of *one.* **1b** (intensifier): *one doesn't do that oneself.* **2** (*preceded by a copula*) one's normal or usual self: *one doesn't feel oneself after such an experience.*

one-sided *adj* **1** considering or favouring only one side of a matter, problem, etc. **2** having all the advantage on one side: *a one-sided boxing match.* **3** larger or more developed on one side. **4** having, existing on, or occurring on one side only.
> ▸ **,one-'sidedly** *adv* ▸ **,one-'sidedness** *n*

one-step *n* an early 20th-century ballroom dance with long quick steps, the precursor of the foxtrot.

one-stop *adj* having or providing a range of related services or goods in one place: *a one-stop shop.*

One Thousand Guineas *n* See **Thousand Guineas.**

one-time *adj* (*prenominal*) at some time in the past; former.

one-to-one *adj* **1** (of two or more things) corresponding exactly. **2** denoting a relationship or encounter in which someone is involved with only one other person: *one-to-one tuition.* **3** *Maths.* involving the pairing of each member of one set with only one member of another set, without remainder.

one-track *adj* **1** *Inf.* obsessed with one idea, subject, etc. **2** having or consisting of a single track.

one-up *adj Inf.* having an advantage or lead over someone or something.
> ▸ **,one-'upmanship** *n*

one-way *adj* **1** moving or allowing travel in one direction only: *one-way traffic; a one-way bus ticket.* **2** entailing no reciprocal obligation, action, etc.: *a one-way agreement.*

ongoing ('ɒn,gəʊɪŋ) *adj* **1** actually in progress: *ongoing projects.* **2** continually moving forward; developing. **3** remaining in existence; continuing.

onion ('ʌnjən) *n* **1** an alliaceous plant having greenish-white flowers: cultivated for its rounded edible bulb. **2** the bulb of this plant, consisting of concentric layers of white succulent leaf bases with a pungent odour and taste. **3** know one's onions. *Brit. sl.* to be fully acquainted with a subject. [C14: via Anglo-Norman from OF *oignon*, from L *unio* onion]
> ▸ **'oniony** *adj*

onionskin ('ʌnjən,skɪn) *n* a glazed translucent paper.

Onitsha ★ (ə'nɪtʃə) *n* a port in S Nigeria, in Anambra State on the Niger River: industrial centre. Pop.: 362 700 (1995 est.).

on line *adj* (**on-line** *when prenominal*). of or concerned with a peripheral device that is directly connected to and controlled by the central processing unit of a computer. Cf. **off line.**

onlooker ('ɒn,lʊkə) *n* a person who observes without taking part.
> ▸ **'on,looking** *adj*

only ('əʊnlɪ) *adj* (*prenominal*) **1** the. being single or very few in number: *the only men left in town were too old to bear arms.* **2** (of a child) having no siblings. **3** unique by virtue of being superior to anything else; peerless. **4** one and only. **4a** (*adj*) incomparable; unique. **4b** (*as n*) the object of all one's love: *you are my one and only.* ◆ *adv* **5** without anyone or anything else being included; alone: *you have one choice only; only a genius can do that.* **6** merely or just: *it's only Henry.* **7** no more or no greater than: *we met only an hour ago.* **8** used in conditional clauses introduced by *if* to emphasize the impossibility of the condition ever being fulfilled: *if I had only known, this would never have happened.* **9** not earlier than; not…until: *I found out yesterday.* **10** if only *or* if…only. an expression used to introduce a wish, esp. one felt to be unrealizable. **11** only if. never…except when. **12** only too. **12a** (intensifier): *he was only too pleased to help.* **12b** most regrettably (esp. in **only too true**). ◆ *sentence connector.* **13** but; however: used to introduce an exception or condition: *you may* *play outside: only don't go into the street.* [OE *ānlīc*, from *ān* ONE + *-līc* -LY[1]]

> **USAGE NOTE** In informal English, *only* is often used as a sentence connector: *I would have phoned you, only I didn't know your number.* This use should be avoided in formal writing: *I would have phoned you if I'd known your number.* In formal speech and writing, *only* is placed directly before the word or words that it modifies: *she could interview only three applicants in the morning.* In all but the most formal contexts, however, it is generally regarded as acceptable to put *only* before the verb: *she could only interview three applicants in the morning.* Care must be taken not to create ambiguity, esp. in written English, in which intonation will not, as it does in speech, help to show to which item in the sentence *only* applies. A sentence such as *she only drinks tea in the afternoon* is capable of two interpretations and is therefore better rephrased either as *she drinks only tea in the afternoon* (i.e. no other drink) or *she drinks tea only in the afternoon* (i.e. at no other time).

o.n.o. *abbrev. for* or near(est) offer.

onomastics (ˌɒnəˈmæstɪks) *n* (*functioning as sing*) the study of proper names, esp. of their origins. [from Gk *onomastikos*, from *onomazein* to name, from *onoma* NAME]

onomatopoeia (ˌɒnəˌmætəˈpiːə) *n* 1 the formation of words whose sound is imitative of the sound of the noise or action designated, such as *hiss.* 2 the use of such words for poetic or rhetorical effect. [C16: via LL from Gk *onoma* name + *poiein* to make]
> **ono**maˈtoˈpoeic *or* onomatopoetic (ˌɒnəˌmætəpəʊˈɛtɪk) *adj* > **ono**ˌmatoˈpoeically *or* ˌono**ˌ**matopoˈetically *adv*

Onondaga ★ (ˌɒnənˈdɑːɡə) *n Lake.* a salt lake in central New York State. Area: about 13 sq. km (5 sq. miles).

onrush (ˈɒnˌrʌʃ) *n* a forceful forward rush or flow.

onset (ˈɒnˌsɛt) *n* 1 an attack; assault. 2 a start; beginning.

onshore (ˈɒnˈʃɔː) *adj, adv* 1 towards the land: *an onshore gale.* 2 on land; not at sea.

onside (ˌɒnˈsaɪd) *adj, adv* 1 *Football, etc.* (of a player) in a legal position, as when behind the ball or with a required number of opponents between oneself and the opposing team's goal line. Cf. **offside.** ◆ *adj* 2 taking one's part or side; working towards the same goal (esp. in **get someone onside**).

onslaught (ˈɒnˌslɔːt) *n* a violent attack. [C17: from MDu. *aenslag*, from *aan* ON + *slag* a blow]

Ont. *abbrev. for* Ontario.

Ontario ★ (ɒnˈtɛərɪəʊ) *n* 1 a province of central Canada: lies mostly on the Canadian Shield and contains the fertile plain of the lower Great Lakes and the St Lawrence River, one of the world's leading industrial areas; the second largest and the most populous province. Capital: Toronto. Pop.: 11 100 300 (1995 est.). Area: 891 198 sq. km (344 092 sq. miles). Abbrevs.: **Ont.** *or* **ON.** 2 *Lake.* a lake between the US and Canada, bordering on New York State and Ontario province: the smallest of the Great Lakes; linked with Lake Erie by the Niagara River and Welland Canal; drained by the St Lawrence. Area: 19 684 sq. km (7600 sq. miles).
> **On**ˈtarian *or* Ontarioan (ɒnˈtɛərɪˌəʊən) *n, adj*

onto *or* **on to** 'ɒntʊ; *unstressed* 'ɒntə) *prep* 1 to a position that is on: *step onto the train.* 2 having become aware of (something illicit or secret): *the police are onto us.* 3 into contact with: *get onto the factory.*

> **USAGE NOTE** *Onto* is now generally accepted as a word in its own right. *On to* is still used, however, where *on* is considered to be part of the verb: *he moved on to a different town* as contrasted with *he jumped onto the stage.*

onto- *combining form.* existence or being: *ontogeny; ontol-*

ogy. [from LGk, from *ōn* (stem *ont-*) being, present participle of *einai* to be]

ontogeny (ɒnˈtɒdʒənɪ) *or* **ontogenesis** (ˌɒntəˈdʒɛnɪsɪs) *n* the entire sequence of events involved in the development of an individual organism. Cf. **phylogeny.**
> **ontogenic** (ˌɒntəˈdʒɛnɪk) *or* **ontogenetic** (ˌɒntədʒɪˈnɛtɪk) *adj* > **onto**ˈgenically *or* ˌontoge**ˈ**netically *adv*

ontology (ɒnˈtɒlədʒɪ) *n* 1 *Philosophy.* the branch of metaphysics that deals with the nature of being. 2 *Logic.* the set of entities presupposed by a theory.
> ˌonto**ˈ**logical *adj* > ˌonto**ˈ**logically *adv*

onus (ˈəʊnəs) *n, pl* **onuses.** a responsibility, task, or burden. [C17: L: burden]

onward (ˈɒnwəd) *adj* 1 directed or moving forwards, onwards, etc. ◆ *adv* 2 a variant of **onwards.**

onwards (ˈɒnwədz) *or* **onward** *adv* at or towards a point or position ahead, in advance, etc.

onychophoran (ˌɒnɪˈkɒfərən) *n* a wormlike invertebrate having a segmented body and short unjointed limbs, and breathing by means of tracheae. [from NL *Onychophora,* from Gk *onukh-* claw + -PHORE]

-onym *n combining form.* indicating a name or word: *pseudonym.* [from Gk *-onumon,* from var. of *onoma* name]

onyx (ˈɒnɪks) *n* 1 a variety of chalcedony with alternating black-and-white parallel bands, used as a gemstone. 2 a variety of calcite used as an ornamental stone; onyx marble. [C13: from L, from Gk: fingernail (so called from its veined appearance)]

ONZ *abbrev. for* Order of New Zealand.

oo- *or* **oö-** *combining form.* egg or ovum: *oosperm.* [from Gk *ōion* EGG[1]]

oocyte (ˈəʊəˌsaɪt) *n* an immature female germ cell that gives rise to an ovum after two meiotic divisions.

oodles (ˈuːdªlz) *pl n Inf.* great quantities: *oodles of money.* [C20: from ?]

oogamy (əʊˈɒɡəmɪ) *n* sexual reproduction involving a small motile male gamete and a large much less motile female gamete.
> o**ˈ**ogamous *adj*

Ookpik (ˈuːkpɪk) *n Canad.* trademark. a sealskin doll resembling an owl, first made in 1963 by an Inuit and used abroad as a symbol of Canadian handicrafts. [from Eskimo *ukpik* a snowy owl]

oolite (ˈəʊəˌlaɪt) *n* any sedimentary rock, esp. limestone, consisting of tiny spherical concentric grains within a fine matrix. [C18: from F, from NL *oolītēs,* lit.: egg stone; prob. a translation of G *Rogenstein* roe stone]
> **oolitic** (ˌəʊəˈlɪtɪk) *adj*

oolith (ˈəʊəˌlɪθ) *n* any of the tiny spherical grains of sedimentary rock of which oolite is composed.

oology (əʊˈɒlədʒɪ) *n* the branch of ornithology concerned with the study of birds' eggs.
> **oological** (ˌəʊəˈlɒdʒɪkˈl) *adj* > o**ˈ**ologist *n*

oolong (ˈuːˌlɒŋ) *n* a kind of dark tea, grown in China, that is partly fermented before being dried. [C19: from Chinese *wu lung,* from *wu* black + *lung* dragon]

oomiak *or* **oomiac** (ˈuːmɪˌæk) *n* a variant of **umiak.**

oompah (ˈuːmˌpɑː) *n* a representation of the sound made by a deep brass instrument, esp. in military band music.

oomph (ʊmf) *n Inf.* 1 enthusiasm, vigour, or energy. 2 sex appeal. [C20: from ?]

oops (ʊps, uːps) *interj* an exclamation of surprise or of apology as when someone drops something or makes a mistake.

Oostende ★ (oːstˈɛndə) *n* the Flemish name for **Ostend.**

ooze[1] (uːz) *vb* **oozes, oozing, oozed.** 1 (*intr*) to flow or leak out slowly, as through small holes. 2 to emit (moisture, etc.). 3 (*tr*) to overflow with: *to ooze charm.* 4 (*intr;* often foll. by *away*) to disappear or escape gradually. ◆ *n* 5 a slow flowing or leaking. 6 an infusion of vegetable matter, such as oak bark, used in tanning. [OE *wōs* juice]

ooze[2] (uːz) *n* 1 a soft wet mud found at the bottom of lakes and rivers. 2 a fine-grained marine deposit consisting of the hard parts of planktonic organisms. 3 muddy ground, esp. of bogs. [OE *wāse* mud]

★ people and places

oozy[1] ('u:zɪ) adj **oozier, ooziest.** moist or dripping.

oozy[2] ('u:zɪ) adj **oozier, ooziest.** of, resembling, or containing mud; slimy.
▸ **'oozily** adv ▸ **'ooziness** n

OP abbrev. for: **1** Ordo Praedictatorum (the Dominicans). [L: Order of Preachers] **2** organophosphate.

op. abbrev. for: **1** opera. **2** operation. **3** operator. **4** optical. **5** opposite. **6** opus.

o.p. or **O.P.** abbrev. for out of print.

opacity (əʊˈpæsɪtɪ) n, pl **opacities. 1** the state or quality of being opaque. **2** the degree to which something is opaque. **3** an opaque object or substance. **4** obscurity of meaning; unintelligibility.

opah ('əʊpə) n a large soft-finned deep-sea teleost fish having a deep, brilliantly coloured body. Also called: **moonfish, kingfish.** [C18: of West African origin]

opal ('əʊp°l) n an amorphous form of hydrated silicon dioxide that can be of almost any colour. It is used as a gemstone. [C16: from L opalus, from Gk opallios, from Sansk. upala precious stone]
▸ **'opal-, like** adj

opalescent (ˌəʊpəˈlɛs°nt) adj having or emitting an iridescence like that of an opal.
▸ **ˌopa'lesce** vb (intr) ▸ **ˌopal'escence** n

opal glass n glass that is opalescent or white, made by the addition of fluorides.

opaline ('əʊpəˌlaɪn) adj **1** opalescent. ◆ n **2** an opaque or semiopaque whitish glass.

opaque (əʊˈpeɪk) adj **1** not transmitting light; not transparent or translucent. **2** not reflecting light; lacking lustre or shine; dull. **3** hard to understand; unintelligible. **4** unintelligent; dense. ◆ n **5** Photog. an opaque pigment used to block out areas on a negative. ◆ vb **opaques, opaquing, opaqued.** (tr) **6** to make opaque. **7** Photog. to block out areas on (a negative), using an opaque. [C15: from L opācus shady]
▸ **o'paquely** adv ▸ **o'paqueness** n

op art (op) n a style of abstract art chiefly concerned with the exploitation of optical effects such as the illusion of movement. [C20 op, short for optical]

op. cit. (in textual annotations) abbrev. for opere citato. [L: in the work cited]

ope (əʊp) vb **opes, oping, oped,** adj an archaic or poetic word for **open.**

OPEC ('əʊpɛk) n acronym for Organization of Petroleum-Exporting Countries.

open ('əʊp°n) adj **1** not closed or barred. **2** affording free passage, access, view, etc.; not blocked or obstructed. **3** not sealed, fastened, or wrapped. **4** having the interior part accessible: an open drawer. **5** extended, expanded, or unfolded: an open flower. **6** ready for business. **7** able to be obtained; available: the position is no longer open. **8** unobstructed by buildings, trees, etc.: open countryside. **9** free to all to join, enter, use, visit, etc.: an open competition. **10** unengaged or unoccupied: the doctor has an hour open for you to call. **11** See open season. **12** not decided or finalized: an open question. **13** ready to entertain new ideas; not biased or prejudiced. **14** unreserved or candid. **15** liberal or generous: an open hand. **16** extended or eager to receive (esp. in with open arms). **17** exposed to view; blatant: open disregard of the law. **18** liable or susceptible: you will leave yourself open to attack. **19** (of climate or seasons) free from frost; mild. **20** free from navigational hazards, such as ice, sunken ships, etc. **21** having large or numerous spacing or apertures: open cells. **22** full of small openings or gaps; porous: an open texture. **23** Music. **23a** (of a string) not stopped with the finger. **23b** (of a pipe, such as an organ pipe) not closed at either end. **23c** (of a note) played on such a string or pipe. **24** Commerce. **24a** in operation; active: an open account. **24b** unrestricted; unlimited: open credit; open insurance cover. **25** See open cheque. **26** (of a return ticket) not specifying a date for travel. **27** Sport. (of a goal, court, etc.) unguarded or relatively unprotected. **28** (of a wound) exposed to the air. **29** (esp. of the large intestine) free from obstruction. **30** undefended and of no military significance: an open city. **31** Phonetics. **31a** denoting a vowel pronounced with the lips relatively wide apart. **31b** denoting a syllable that does not end in a consonant, as in pa. **32** Maths. (of a set) containing points whose neighbourhood consists of other points of the same set. **33** Computing. designed to an internationally agreed standard in order to allow communication between computers, irrespective of size, manufacturer, etc. ◆ vb **34** to move from a closed or fastened position: to open a window. **35** (when intr, foll. by on or onto) to render, be, or become accessible or unobstructed: to open a road; to open a parcel. **36** (intr) to come into or appear in view: the lake opened before us. **37** to extend or unfold or cause to extend or unfold: to open a newspaper. **38** to disclose or uncover or be disclosed or uncovered: to open one's heart. **39** to cause (the mind) to become receptive or (of the mind) to become receptive. **40** to operate or cause to operate: to open a shop. **41** (when intr, sometimes foll. by out) to make or become less compact or dense in structure: to open ranks. **42** to set or be set in action; start: to open the batting. **43** (tr) to arrange for (a bank account, etc.), usually by making an initial deposit. **44** to turn to a specified point in (a book, etc.): open at page one. **45** Law. to make the opening statement in (a case before a court of law). **46** (intr) Cards. to bet, bid, or lead first on a hand. ◆ n **47** (often preceded by the) any wide or unobstructed space or expanse, esp. of land or water. **48** See open air. **49** Sport. a competition which anyone may enter. **50** bring (or come) into the open. to make (or become) evident or public. ◆ See also open up. [OE]
▸ **'openable** adj ▸ **'opener** n ▸ **'openly** adv ▸ **'openness** n

open air n **a** the place or space where the air is unenclosed; the outdoors. **b** (as modifier): an open-air concert.

open-and-shut adj easily decided or solved; obvious: an open-and-shut case.

opencast mining ('əʊp°n,kɑ:st) n Brit. mining by excavating from the surface. Also called: (esp. US) **strip mining,** (Austral. and NZ) **open cut mining.** [C18: from OPEN + arch. cast ditch, cutting]

open chain n a chain of atoms in a molecule that is not joined at its ends into the form of a ring.

open cheque n an uncrossed cheque that can be cashed at the drawee bank.

open circuit n an incomplete electrical circuit in which no current flows.

Open College n the. (in Britain) a college of art founded in 1987 for mature students studying foundation courses in arts and crafts by television programmes, written material, and tutorials.

open day n an occasion on which an institution, such as a school, is open for inspection by the public.

open door n **1** a policy or practice by which a nation grants opportunities for trade to all other nations equally. **2** free and unrestricted admission. ◆ adj **open-door. 3** open to all; accessible.

open-ended adj **1** without definite limits, as of duration or amount: an open-ended contract. **2** denoting a question, esp. one on a questionnaire, that cannot be answered "yes", "no", or "don't know".

open-eyed adj **1** with the eyes wide open, as in amazement. **2** watchful; alert.

open-faced adj **1** having an ingenuous expression. **2** (of a watch) having no lid or cover other than the glass.

open-handed adj generous.
▸ **ˌopen-'handedly** adv ▸ **ˌopen-'handedness** n

open-hearted adj **1** kindly and warm. **2** disclosing intentions and thoughts clearly; candid.
▸ **ˌopen-'heartedness** n

open-hearth furnace n (esp. formerly) a steel-making reverbatory furnace in which pig iron and scrap are contained in a shallow hearth and heated by producer gas.

open-heart surgery n surgical repair of the heart during which the blood circulation is often maintained mechanically.

open house n **1** a US and Canad. name for **at-home. 2 keep open house.** to be always ready to receive guests.

opening ('əʊpənɪŋ) n **1** the act of making or becoming open. **2** a vacant or unobstructed space, esp. one that will serve as a passageway; gap. **3** Chiefly US. a tract in a forest in which trees are scattered or absent. **4** the first part or stage of something. **5a** the first performance of something, esp. a theatrical production. **5b** (as modifier): the opening night. **6** a specific or formal sequence of moves at the start of any of certain games, esp. chess or draughts. **7** an opportunity or chance. **8** Law. the preliminary statement made by counsel to the court or jury.

opening batsman n Cricket. one of the two batsmen beginning an innings.

opening time n Brit. the time at which public houses can legally start selling alcoholic drinks.

open learning n a system of further education on a flexible part-time basis.

open letter n a letter, esp. one of protest, addressed to a person but also made public, as through the press.

open market n a a market in which prices are determined by supply and demand, there are no barriers to entry, and trading is not restricted to a specific area. **b** (as modifier): open-market value.

open marriage n a marriage in which the partners agree to pursue separate social and sexual lives.

open-minded adj having a mind receptive to new ideas, arguments, etc.; unprejudiced.
▶ ,open-'mindedness n

open-mouthed adj **1** having an open mouth, esp. in surprise. **2** greedy or ravenous. **3** clamorous or vociferous.

open-plan adj having no or few dividing walls between areas: an open-plan office floor.

open position n Commerce. a situation in which a dealer in commodities, securities, or currencies has either unsold stock or uncovered sales.

open prison n a penal establishment in which the prisoners are trusted to serve their sentences and so do not need to be locked up.

open punctuation n punctuation which has relatively few semicolons, commas, etc. Cf. **close punctuation**.

open question n **1** a matter which is undecided. **2** a question that cannot be answered with "yes" or "no" but requires a developed answer.

open-reel adj another term for **reel-to-reel**.

open season n a specified period of time in the year when it is legal to hunt or kill game or fish protected at other times by law.

open secret n something that is supposed to be secret but is widely known.

open sesame n a very successful means of achieving a result. [from the magical words used in the Arabian Nights' Entertainments to open the robbers' den]

open shop n an establishment in which persons are employed irrespective of their membership or nonmembership of a trade union.

open slather n See **slather**.

Open University n the. (in Britain) a university founded in 1969 for mature students studying by television and radio lectures, correspondence courses, local counselling, and summer schools.

open up vb (adv) **1** (intr) to start firing a gun or guns. **2** (intr) to speak freely or without restraint. **3** (intr) Inf. (of a motor vehicle) to accelerate. **4** (tr) to render accessible: the road opened up the remoter areas. **5** (intr) to make or become more exciting: the game opened up after half-time.

open verdict n a finding by a coroner's jury of death without stating the cause.

openwork ('əʊpˈn,wɜːk) n ornamental work, as of metal or embroidery, having a pattern of openings or holes.

opera[1] ('ɒpərə, 'ɒprə) n **1** an extended dramatic work in which music constitutes a dominating feature. **2** the branch of music or drama represented by such works. **3** the score, libretto, etc., of an opera. **4** a theatre where opera is performed. [C17: via It. from L: work, a work, pl of opus work]

opera[2] ('ɒpərə) n a plural of **opus**.

operable ('ɒpərəbˈl, 'ɒprə-) adj **1** capable of being treated by a surgical operation. **2** capable of being operated. **3** capable of being put into practice.
▶ ,opera'bility n ▶ 'operably adv

opéra bouffe ('ɒpərə 'buːf) n, pl opéras bouffes ('ɒpərə 'buːf). a type of light or satirical opera common in France during the 19th century. [F: comic opera]

opera buffa ('buːfə) n, pl opera buffas. comic opera, esp. that originating in Italy during the 18th century. [It.: comic opera]

opéra comique (kɒ'miːk) n, pl opéras comiques. ('ɒpərə kɒ'miːk). a type of opera current in France during the 19th century and characterized by spoken dialogue. [F: comic opera: it originated in satirical parodies of grand opera]

opera glasses pl n small low-powered binoculars used by audiences in theatres, etc.

opera hat n a collapsible top hat operated by a spring.

opera house n a theatre designed for opera.

operand ('ɒpə,rænd) n a quantity or function upon which a mathematical or logical operation is performed. [C19: from L operandum (something) to be worked upon, from operārī to work]

operant ('ɒpərənt) adj **1** producing effects; operating.
♦ n **2** a person or thing that operates. **3** Psychol. any response by an organism that is not directly caused by stimulus.

opera seria ('sɪərɪə) n, pl opera serias. a type of opera current in 18th-century Italy based on a serious plot, esp. a mythological tale. [It.: serious opera]

operate ('ɒpə,reɪt) vb operates, operating, operated. **1** to function or cause to function. **2** (tr) to control the functioning of. **3** to manage, direct, run, or pursue (a business, system, etc.). **4** (intr) to perform a surgical operation (upon a person or animal). **5** (intr) to produce a desired effect. **6** (tr; usually foll. by on) to treat or process in a particular or specific way. **7** (intr) to conduct military or naval operations. **8** (intr) to deal in securities on a stock exchange. [C17: from L operārī to work]

operatic (,ɒpə'rætɪk) adj **1** of or relating to opera. **2** histrionic or exaggerated.
▶ ,oper'atically adv

operating budget n Accounting. a forecast of the sales revenue, production costs, overheads, cash flow, etc., of an organization, used to monitor its trading activities, usually for one year.

operating cycle n the time taken by a firm to convert its raw materials into finished goods and thereafter sell them and collect payment.

operating system n the set of software controlling a computer.

operating theatre n a room in which surgical operations are performed.

operation (,ɒpə'reɪʃən) n **1** the act, process, or manner of operating. **2** the state of being in effect, in action, or operative (esp. in **in** or **into operation**). **3** a process, method, or series of acts, esp. of a practical or mechanical nature. **4** Surgery. any manipulation of the body or one of its organs or parts to repair damage, arrest the progress of a disease, remove foreign matter, etc. **5a** a military or naval action, such as a campaign, manoeuvre, etc. **5b** (cap. and prenominal when part of a name): Operation Crossbow. **6** Maths. any procedure, such as addition, in which one or more numbers or quantities are operated upon according to specific rules. **7** a commercial or financial transaction.

operational (,ɒpə'reɪʃənˀl) adj **1** of or relating to an operation. **2** in working order and ready for use. **3** Mil. capable of, needed in, or actually involved in operations.
▶ ,oper'ationally adv

operationalism (,ɒpə'reɪʃənə,lɪzəm) or **operationism** (,ɒpə'reɪʃə,nɪzəm) n Philosophy. the theory that scientific terms are defined by the experimental operations which determine their applicability.
▶ ,oper,ational'istic adj

operations research n the analysis of problems in business and industry involving quantitative techniques. Also called: **operational research**.

operative ('ɒpərətɪv) adj **1** in force, effect, or operation. **2** exerting force or influence. **3** producing a desired effect; significant: the operative word. **4** of or relating to a

surgical procedure. ◆ *n* **5** a worker, esp. one with a special skill. **6** *US*. a private detective.
> ▶ '**operatively** *adv* ▶ '**operativeness** or ₁**opera'tivity** *n*

operator ('ɒpəˌreɪtə) *n* **1** a person who operates a machine, instrument, etc., esp. a telephone switchboard. **2** a person who owns or operates an industrial or commercial establishment. **3** a speculator, esp. one who operates on currency or stock markets. **4** *Inf*. a person who manipulates affairs and other people. **5** *Maths*. any symbol, term, letter, etc., used to indicate or express a specific operation or process, such as ʃ (the integral operator).

operculum (əʊ'pɜːkjʊləm) *n*, *pl* **opercula** (-lə) or **operculums**. **1** *Zool*. **1a** the hard bony flap covering the gill slits in fishes. **1b** the bony plate in certain gastropods covering the opening of the shell when the body is withdrawn. **2** *Biol*. & *Bot*. any other covering or lid in various organisms. [C18: via NL from L: lid, from *operīre* to cover]
> ▶ o'**percular** or **operculate** (əʊ'pɜːkjʊlɪt, -ˌleɪt) *adj*

operetta (ˌɒpə'rɛtə) *n* a type of comic or light-hearted opera. [C18: from It.: a small OPERA[1]]
> ▶ ˌoper'**ettist** *n*

ophicleide ('ɒfɪˌklaɪd) *n Music*. an obsolete keyed wind instrument of bass pitch. [C19: from F *ophicléide*, from Gk *ophis* snake + *kleis* key]

ophidian (əʊ'fɪdɪən) *adj* **1** snakelike. **2** of, relating to, or belonging to the suborder of reptiles that comprises the snakes. ◆ *n* **3** any reptile of this suborder; a snake. [C19: from NL *Ophidia*, name of suborder, from Gk *ophidion*, from *ophis* snake]

Ophir ★ ('əʊfə) *n Bible*. a region, probably situated on the SW coast of Arabia on the Red Sea, renowned, esp. in King Solomon's reign, for its gold and precious stones (I Kings 9:28; 10:10).

ophthalmia (ɒf'θælmɪə) *n* inflammation of the eye, often including the conjunctiva. [C16: via LL from Gk, from *ophthalmos* eye; see OPTIC]

ophthalmic (ɒf'θælmɪk) *adj* of or relating to the eye.

ophthalmic optician *n* See **optician**.

ophthalmo- or before a vowel **ophthalm-** *combining form*. indicating the eye or the eyeball. [from Gk *ophthalmos* EYE]

ophthalmology (ˌɒfθæl'mɒlədʒɪ) *n* the branch of medicine concerned with the eye and its diseases.
> ▶ **ophthalmological** (ɒfˌθælmə'lɒdʒɪk*ə*l) *adj* ▶ ˌophthal'**mologist** *n*

ophthalmoscope (ɒf'θælməˌskəʊp) *n* an instrument for examining the interior of the eye.
> ▶ **ophthalmoscopic** (ɒfˌθælmə'skɒpɪk) *adj*

-opia *n combining form*. indicating a visual defect or condition: *myopia*. [from Gk, from *ōps* eye]
> ▶ **-opic** *adj combining form*.

opiate *n* ('əʊpɪɪt). **1** any of various narcotic drugs containing opium. **2** any other narcotic or sedative drug. **3** something that soothes, deadens, or induces sleep. ◆ *adj* ('əʊpɪɪt). **4** containing or consisting of opium. **5** inducing relaxation; soporific. ◆ *vb* ('əʊpɪˌeɪt), **opiates, opiating, opiated**. (*tr*) *Rare*. **6** to treat with an opiate. **7** to dull or deaden. [C16: from Med. L *opiātus*, from L *opium* OPIUM]

opine (əʊ'paɪn) *vb* **opines, opining, opined**. (when *tr*, usually takes a clause as object) to hold or express an opinion: *he opined that it was a mistake*. [C16: from L *opīnārī*]

opinion (ə'pɪnjən) *n* **1** judgment or belief not founded on certainty or proof. **2** the prevailing or popular feeling or view: *public opinion*. **3** evaluation, impression, or estimation of the value or worth of a person or thing. **4** an evaluation or judgment given by an expert: *a medical opinion*. **5** the advice given by counsel on a case submitted to him for his view on the legal points involved. **6 a matter of opinion**. a point open to question. **7 be of the opinion (that)**. to believe (that). [C13: via OF from L *opīniō* belief, from *opīnārī* to think]

opinionated (ə'pɪnjəˌneɪtɪd) *adj* holding obstinately and unreasonably to one's own opinions; dogmatic.
> ▶ o'**pinion**ˌatedly *adv* ▶ o'**pinion**ˌatedness *n*

opinionative (ə'pɪnjənətɪv) *adj Rare*. **1** of or relating to opinion. **2** another word for **opinionated**.
> ▶ o'**pinionatively** *adv* ▶ o'**pinionativeness** *n*

opinion poll *n* another term for a **poll** (sense 3).

opioid ('əʊpɪˌɔɪd) *n* any of a group of substances that resemble morphine in their physiological or pharmacological effects, esp. in their pain-relieving properties.

opium ('əʊpɪəm) *n* **1** an addictive narcotic drug extracted from the seed capsules of the opium poppy: used in medicine as an analgesic and hypnotic. **2** something having a tranquillizing or stupefying effect. [C14: from L: poppy juice, from Gk *opion*, dim. of *opos*, juice of a plant]

opium poppy *n* a poppy of SW Asia, with greyish-green leaves and typically white or reddish flowers: widely cultivated as a source of opium.

Oporto ★ (ə'pɔːtəʊ) *n* a port in NW Portugal, near the mouth of the Douro River: the second largest city in Portugal, famous for port wine (begun in 1678). Pop.: 309 485 (1991). Portuguese name: **Pôrto**.

opossum (ə'pɒsəm) *n*, *pl* **opossums** or **opossum**. **1** a thick-furred marsupial, esp. the **common opossum** of North and South America, having an elongated snout and a hairless prehensile tail. **2** *Austral*. & *NZ*. any of various similar animals, esp. a phalanger. ◆ Often shortened to **possum**. [C17: from Algonquian *aposoum*]

opp. *abbrev. for*: **1** opposed. **2** opposite.

Oppenheimer ★ ('ɒpənˌhaɪmə) *n* **J(ulius) Robert**. 1904–67, US nuclear physicist. Director of the Los Alamos laboratory (1943–45), which produced the first atomic bomb, he opposed the development of the hydrogen bomb (1949); declared a security risk (1953), he was later exonerated.

opponent (ə'pəʊnənt) *n* **1** a person who opposes another in a contest, battle, etc. **2** *Anat*. an opponent muscle. ◆ *adj* **3** opposite, as in position. **4** *Anat*. (of a muscle) bringing two parts into opposition. **5** opposing; contrary. [C16: from L *oppōnere* to oppose]
> ▶ op'**ponency** *n*

opportune ('ɒpəˌtjuːn) *adj* **1** occurring at a time that is suitable or advantageous. **2** fit or suitable for a particular purpose or occurrence. [C15: via OF from L *opportūnus*, from *ob-* to + *portus* harbour (orig.: coming to the harbour, obtaining timely protection)]
> ▶ '**opportunely** *adv* ▶ '**opportuneness** *n*

opportunist (ˌɒpə'tjuːnɪst) *n* **1** a person who adapts his actions, responses, etc., to take advantage of opportunities, circumstances, etc. ◆ *adj* **2** taking advantage of opportunities and circumstances in this way.
> ▶ ˌoppor'**tunism** *n*

opportunistic (ˌɒpətjuː'nɪstɪk) *adj* **1** of or characterized by opportunism. **2** *Med*. (of an infection) caused by any microorganism that is harmless to a healthy person but debilitates a person whose immune system has been weakened.

opportunity (ˌɒpə'tjuːnɪtɪ) *n*, *pl* **opportunities**. **1** a favourable, appropriate, or advantageous combination of circumstances. **2** a chance or prospect.

opportunity shop *n Austral*. & *NZ*. a shop selling used goods for charitable funds.

opposable (ə'pəʊzəb*ə*l) *adj* **1** capable of being opposed. **2** Also: **apposable**. (of the thumb of primates, esp. man) capable of being moved into a position facing the other digits so as to be able to touch the ends of each. **3** capable of being placed opposite something else.
> ▶ opˌposa'**bility** *n* ▶ op'**posably** *adv*

oppose (ə'pəʊz) *vb* **opposes, opposing, opposed**. **1** (*tr*) to fight against, counter, or resist strongly. **2** (*tr*) to be hostile or antagonistic to; be against. **3** (*tr*) to place or set in opposition; contrast or counterbalance. **4** (*tr*) to place opposite or facing. **5** (*intr*) to be or act in opposition. [C14: via OF from L *oppōnere*, from *ob-* against + *pōnere* to place]
> ▶ op'**poser** *n* ▶ op'**posing** *adj* ▶ **oppositive** (ə'pɒzɪtɪv)

opposite ('ɒpəzɪt, -sɪt) *adj* **1** situated or being on the other side or at each side of something between. **2** facing or going in contrary directions: *opposite ways*. **3** diametri-

cally different in character, tendency, belief, etc. **4** *Bot.*
4a (of leaves) arranged in pairs on either side of the stem.
4b (of parts of a flower) arranged opposite the middle of
another part. **5** *Maths.* (of a side in a triangle) facing a
specified angle. Abbrev.: **opp.** ◆ *n* **6** a person or thing
that is opposite; antithesis. ◆ *prep* **7** Also: **opposite to.** facing; corresponding to (something on the other side of a
division). **8** as a co-star with: *she played opposite Olivier.*
◆ *adv* **9** on opposite sides: *she lives opposite.*
▶ **'oppositely** *adv* ▶ **'oppositeness** *n*

pposite number *n* a person holding an equivalent
and corresponding position on another side or situation.

pposition (ˌɒpəˈzɪʃən) *n* **1** the act of opposing or the
state of being opposed. **2** hostility, unfriendliness, or antagonism. **3** a person or group antagonistic or opposite
in aims to another. **4a** (usually preceded by *the*) a political party or group opposed to the ruling party or government. **4b** (*cap. as part of a name, esp. in Britain and
Commonwealth countries*): *Her Majesty's Loyal Opposition.*
4c in opposition. (of a political party) opposing the government. **5** a position facing or opposite another. **6** something that acts as an obstacle to some course or progress.
7 *Astron.* the position of an outer planet or the moon
when it is in line with the earth as seen from the sun and
is approximately at its nearest to the earth. **8** *Astrol.* an
exact aspect of 180° between two planets, etc., an orb of
8° being allowed. **9** *Logic.* the relation between propositions having the same subject and predicate but differing in quality, quantity, or both, as with *all men are
wicked; no men are wicked; some men are not wicked.*
▶ ˌoppoˈsitional *adj* ▶ ˌoppoˈsitionist *n* ▶ ˌoppoˈsitionless
adj

ppress (əˈprɛs) *vb* (*tr*) **1** to subjugate by cruelty, force,
etc. **2** to afflict or torment. **3** to lie heavy on (the mind,
etc.). [C14: via OF from Med. L *oppressāre*, from L
opprimere, from *ob-* against + *premere* to press]
▶ opˈpressing *adj* ▶ opˈpression *n* ▶ opˈpressor *n*

ppressive (əˈprɛsɪv) *adj* **1** cruel, harsh, or tyrannical. **2**
heavy, constricting, or depressing.
▶ opˈpressively *adv* ▶ opˈpressiveness *n*

pprobrious (əˈprəʊbrɪəs) *adj* **1** expressing scorn, disgrace, or contempt. **2** shameful or infamous.
▶ opˈprobriously *adv* ▶ opˈprobriousness *n*

pprobrium (əˈprəʊbrɪəm) *n* **1** the state of being abused
or scornfully criticized. **2** reproach or censure. **3** a cause
of disgrace or ignominy. [C17: from L *ob-* against +
probrum a shameful act]

ppugn (əˈpjuːn) *vb* (*tr*) to call into question; dispute.
[C15: from L *oppugnāre*, from *ob-* against + *pugnāre* to
fight, from *pugnus* clenched fist]
▶ opˈpugner *n*

ps ★ (ɒps) *n* the Roman goddess of abundance and fertility, wife of Saturn. Greek counterpart: **Rhea.**

psin (ˈɒpsɪn) *n* the protein that together with retinene
makes up the purple visual pigment rhodopsin. [C20:
back formation from RHODOPSIN]

opsis *n combining form.* indicating a specified appearance or resemblance: *meconopsis.* [from Gk *opsis* sight]

psonin (ˈɒpsənɪn) *n* a constituent of blood serum that
renders bacteria more susceptible to ingestion by
phagocytes. [C20: from Gk *opsōnion* victuals]
▶ opsonic (ɒpˈsɒnɪk) *adj*

pt (ɒpt) *vb* (when *intr*, foll. by *for*) to show preference
(for) or choose (to do something). See also **opt in, opt out.**
[C19: from F *opter*, from L *optāre* to choose]

pt. *abbrev. for:* **1** *Grammar.* optative. **2** optical. **3** optician.
4 optimum. **5** optional.

ptative (ˈɒptətɪv) *adj* **1** indicating or expressing choice
or wish. **2** *Grammar.* denoting a mood of verbs in Greek
and Sanskrit expressing a wish. ◆ *n* **3** *Grammar.* **3a** the
optative mood. **3b** a verb in this mood. [C16: via F
optatif, from LL *optātīvus*, from L *optāre* to desire]

ptic (ˈɒptɪk) *adj* **1** of or relating to the eye or vision. **2** a
less common word for **optical.** ◆ *n* **3** an informal word
for **eye**[1]. **4** *Brit.*, *trademark.* a device attached to an inverted bottle for dispensing measured quantities of liq-

uid. [C16: from Med. L *opticus*, from Gk *optikos*, from
optos visible; rel. to *ōps* eye]

optical (ˈɒptɪkˀl) *adj* **1** of, relating to, producing, or involving light. **2** of or relating to the eye or to the sense of
sight; optic. **3** (esp. of a lens) aiding vision or correcting a
visual disorder.
▶ **'optically** *adv*

optical activity *n* the ability of substances that are optical isomers to rotate the plane of polarization of a
transmitted beam of plane-polarized light.

optical character reader *n* a computer peripheral
device enabling letters, numbers, or other characters
usually printed on paper to be optically scanned and
input to a storage device, such as magnetic tape. The device uses the process of **optical character recognition.**
Abbrev. (for both *reader* and *recognition*): **OCR.**

optical crown *n* an optical glass of low dispersion and
relatively low refractive index.

optical disc *n* *Computing.* an inflexible disc on which
information is stored in digital form by laser technology. Also called: **video disc.**

optical fibre *n* a communications cable consisting of a
thin glass fibre in a protective sheath. Light transmitted
along the fibre may be modulated with vision, sound, or
data signals. See also **fibre optics.**

optical flint *n* an optical glass of high dispersion and
high refractive index containing lead oxide, used in the
manufacture of lenses, artificial gems, and cut glass.

optical glass *n* any of several types of clear homogeneous glass of known refractive index used in the construction of lenses, etc.

optical isomerism *n* isomerism of chemical compounds in which the two isomers differ only in that
their molecules are mirror images of each other.
▶ **optical isomer** *n*

optical scanner *n* a computer peripheral device enabling printed material, including characters and diagrams, to be scanned and converted into a form that can
be stored in a computer. See also **optical character reader.**

optician (ɒpˈtɪʃən) *n* a general name used to refer to: **a** an
ophthalmic optician. one qualified to examine the eyes and
prescribe and supply spectacles and contact lenses. **b** a
dispensing optician. one who supplies and fits spectacle
frames and lenses, but is not qualified to prescribe
lenses.

optics (ˈɒptɪks) *n* (*functioning as sing*) the branch of science concerned with vision and the generation, nature,
propagation, and behaviour of electromagnetic light.

optimal (ˈɒptɪməl) *adj* another word for **optimum** (sense
2).

optimism (ˈɒptɪˌmɪzəm) *n* **1** the tendency to expect the
best in all things. **2** hopefulness; confidence. **3** the doctrine of the ultimate triumph of good over evil. **4** the
philosophical doctrine that this is the best of all possible
worlds. ◆ Cf. **pessimism.** [C18: from F *optimisme,* from L
optimus best, sup. of *bonus* good]
▶ **'optimist** *n* ▶ ˌoptiˈmistic *adj* ▶ ˌoptiˈmistically *adv*

optimize *or* **optimise** (ˈɒptɪˌmaɪz) *vb* **optimizes, optimiz-
ing, optimized** *or* **optimises, optimising, optimised. 1** (*tr*) to take
full advantage of. **2** (*tr*) to plan or carry out (an economic
activity) with maximum efficiency. **3** (*intr*) to be optimistic. **4** (*tr*) to write or modify (a computer program) to
achieve maximum efficiency.
▶ ˌoptimiˈzation *or* ˌoptimiˈsation *n*

optimum (ˈɒptɪməm) *n, pl* **optima** (-mə) *or* **optimums. 1** a
condition, degree, amount, or compromise that pro-
duces the best possible result. ◆ *adj* **2** most favourable or
advantageous; best: *optimum conditions.* [C19: from L:
the best (thing), from *optimus*; see OPTIMISM]

optimum population *n Econ.* a population that is sufficiently large to provide an adequate workforce with
minimal unemployment.

opt in *vb* (*intr, adv*) to choose to be involved in or part of a
scheme, etc.

option (ˈɒpʃən) *n* **1** the act or an instance of choosing or
deciding. **2** the power or liberty to choose. **3** an exclusive
opportunity, usually for a limited period, to buy some-

thing at a future date: *a six-month option on the Canadian rights to this book.* **4** *Commerce.* the right to buy (**call option**) or sell (**put option**) a fixed quantity of a commodity, security, foreign exchange, etc., at a fixed price at a specified date in the future. See also **traded option. 5** something chosen; choice. **6 keep** (*or* **leave**) **one's options open.** not to commit oneself. **7 soft option.** an easy alternative. ◆ *vb* **8** (*tr*) to obtain or grant an option on: *the BBC have optioned her latest novel.* [C17: from L *optiō* free choice, from *optāre* to choose]

optional ('ɒpʃənəl) *adj* possible but not compulsory; left to personal choice.
▸ **'optionally** *adv*

option money *n Commerce.* the price paid for buying an option.

optometrist (ɒp'tɒmɪtrɪst) *n* a person who is qualified to examine the eyes and prescribe and supply spectacles and contact lenses. Also called (esp. Brit.): **ophthalmic optician.**

optometry (ɒp'tɒmɪtrɪ) *n* the science or practice of testing visual acuity and prescribing corrective lenses.
▸ **optometric** (ˌɒptə'mɛtrɪk) *adj*

optophone ('ɒptəˌfəʊn) *n* a device for blind people that converts printed words into sounds.

opt out *vb* **1** (*intr, adv;* often foll. by *of*) to choose not to be involved (in) or part (of). ◆ *n* **opt-out. 2** the act of opting out, esp. of a local-authority administration: *opt-outs by hospitals and schools.*

opulent ('ɒpjʊlənt) *adj* **1** having or indicating wealth. **2** abundant or plentiful. [C17: from L *opulens,* from *opēs* (pl) wealth]
▸ **'opulence** *or* (*less commonly*) **'opulency** *n* ▸ **'opulently** *adv*

opuntia (ɒ'pʌnʃɪə) *n* a cactus, esp. the prickly pear, having fleshy branched stems and green, red, or yellow flowers. [C17: NL, from L *Opuntia* (*herba*) the Opuntian (plant), from *Opus,* ancient town of Locris, Greece]

opus ('əʊpəs) *n, pl* **opuses** *or* **opera. 1** an artistic composition, esp. a musical work. **2** (*often cap.*) (usually followed by a number) a musical composition by a particular composer, generally catalogued in order of publication: *Beethoven's opus 61.* Abbrev.: **op.** [C18: from L: a work]

Opus Dei ('əʊpəs 'deɪiː) *n* **1** another name for **divine office. 2** an international Roman Catholic organization founded in Spain in 1928 by Josemaria Escrivá de Balaguer (1902–75), to spread Christian principles.

or[1] (ɔː; *unstressed* ə) *conj* (*coordinating*) **1** used to join alternatives. **2** used to join rephrasings of the same thing: *twelve, or a dozen.* **3** used to join two alternatives when the first is preceded by *either* or *whether: either yes or no.* **4 one or two, four or five,** etc. a few. **5** a poetic word for **either** or **whether,** as the first element in correlatives, with *or* also preceding the second alternative. [C13: contraction of *other,* changed (through infl. of EITHER) from OE *oththe*]

or[2] (ɔː) *adj* (*usually postpositive*) *Heraldry.* of the metal gold. [C16: via F from L *aurum* gold]

OR *abbrev. for:* **1** operational research. **2** Oregon. **3** *Mil.* other ranks.

-or[1] *suffix forming nouns from verbs.* a person or thing that does what is expressed by the verb: *actor; conductor; generator; sailor.* [via OF -*eur,* -*eor,* from L -*or* or -*ātor*]

-or[2] *suffix forming nouns.* **1** indicating state, condition, or activity: *terror; error.* **2** the US spelling of **-our.**

ora ('ɔːrə) *n* the plural of **os**[2].

orache *or esp.* US **orach** ('ɒrɪtʃ) *n* any of several herbaceous plants or small shrubs of the goosefoot family, esp. **garden orache,** which is cultivated as a vegetable. They have typically greyish-green lobed leaves and inconspicuous flowers. [C15: from OF *arache,* from L *atriplex,* from Gk *atraphaxus,* from ?]

oracle ('ɒrəkˀl) *n* **1** a prophecy revealed through the medium of a priest or priestess at the shrine of a god. **2** a shrine at which an oracular god is consulted. **3** an agency through which a prophecy is transmitted. **4** any person or thing believed to indicate future action with

infallible authority. [C14: via OF from L *ōrāculum,* from *ōrāre* to request]

Oracle ('ɒrəkˀl) *n Trademark.* the Teletext system operated by ITV. See **Teletext.** [C20: acronym of *o(ptiona)r(eception of) a(nnouncements by) c(oded) l(ine) e(lectronics)*]

oracular (ɒ'rækjʊlə) *adj* **1** of or relating to an oracle. **2** wise and prophetic. **3** mysterious or ambiguous.
▸ **o'racularly** *adv*

oracy ('ɔːrəsɪ) *n* the capacity to express oneself in an understand speech. [C20: from L *or-, os* mouth, by analogy with *literacy*]

Oradea ★ (*Romanian* o'radea) *n* an industrial city in NW Romania, in Transylvania: ceded by Hungary (1919) Pop.: 221 559 (1993 est.). German name: **Grosswardein** Hungarian name: **Nagyvárad.**

oral ('ɔːrəl, 'ɒrəl) *adj* **1** spoken or verbal. **2** relating to, affecting, or for use in the mouth: *an oral thermometer.* **3** denoting a drug to be taken by mouth: *an oral contraceptive.* **4** of, relating to, or using spoken words. **5** *Psychoanal.* relating to a stage of psychosexual development during which the child's interest is concentrated on the mouth. ◆ *n* **6** an examination in which the questions and answers are spoken rather than written. [C17: from L *ōrālis,* from L *ōs* face]
▸ **'orally** *adv*

oral history *n* the memories of living people about events or social conditions in their earlier lives taped and preserved as historical evidence.

oral hygiene *n* the maintenance of healthy teeth and gums by brushing, etc. Also called: **dental hygiene.**

oral society *n* a society that has not developed literacy

Oran ★ (ə'ræn, ə'rɑːn; *French* ɔrɑ̃) *n* a port in NW Algeria the second largest city in the country; scene of the destruction by the British of most of the French fleet in the harbour in 1940 to prevent its capture by the Germans. Pop.: 609 823 (1987).

orange ('ɒrɪndʒ) *n* **1** any of several citrus trees, esp. **sweet orange** and the Seville orange, cultivated in warm regions for their round edible fruit. **2a** the fruit of any of these trees, having a yellowish-red bitter rind and segmented juicy flesh. **2b** (*as modifier*): *orange peel.* **3** the hard wood of any of these trees. **4** any of a group of colours, such as that of the skin of an orange, that lie between red and yellow in the visible spectrum. **5** a dye or pigment producing these colours. **6** orange cloth or clothing: *dressed in orange.* **7** any of several trees or herbaceous plants that resemble the orange, such as mock orange. ◆ *adj* **8** of the colour orange. [C14: via OF *auranja,* from Ar. *nāranj,* from Persian, from Sansk. *nāranga*]

Orange[1] ★ *n* **1** ('ɒrɪndʒ) a river in S Africa, rising in NE Lesotho and flowing generally west across the South African plateau to the Atlantic: the longest river in South Africa. Length: 2093 km (1300 miles). **2** (*French* ɔrɑ̃ʒ). town in SE France: a small principality in the Middle Ages, the descendants of which formed the House of Orange. Pop.: 28 136 (1990). Ancient name: **Arausio** (ə'rɔːsɪəʊ).

Orange[2] ★ ('ɒrɪndʒ) *n* **1** a princely family of Europe. Its possessions, originally centred in S France, passed in 1544 to the count of Nassau, who became William I of Orange and helped to found the United Provinces of the Netherlands. Since 1815 it has been the name of the reigning house of the Netherlands. It was the ruling house of Great Britain and Ireland under William III and Mary (1689–94) and under William III as sole monarch (1694–1702). **2** (*modifier*) of or relating to the Orangemen. **3** (*modifier*) of or relating to the royal dynasty of Orange.

orangeade (ˌɒrɪndʒ'eɪd) *n* an effervescent or still orange-flavoured drink.

orange blossom *n* the flowers of the orange tree, traditionally worn by brides.

Orange Free State ★ *n* a former province of central South Africa, between the Orange and Vaal rivers: settled by Boers in 1836 after the Great Trek; annexed by Britain in 1848; became a province of South Africa in 1910; in 1994 it was replaced by Free State region. Capi-

★ people and places

tal: Bloemfontein. Area: 29 152 sq. km (49 866 sq. miles).

Orangeman ('ɒrɪndʒmən) n, pl **Orangemen**. a member of a society founded in Ireland (1795) to uphold Protestantism. [C18: after William, prince of *Orange*, later William III]

Orangeman's Day n the 12th of July, celebrated by Protestants in Northern Ireland and elsewhere, to commemorate the anniversary of the Battle of the Boyne (1690).

orange pekoe n a superior grade of black tea growing in India and Sri Lanka.

orange roughy ('rʌfɪ) n a marine food fish of S Pacific waters.

orangery ('ɒrɪndʒərɪ, -dʒrɪ) n, pl **orangeries**. a building, such as a greenhouse, in which orange trees are grown.

orange stick n a small stick used to clean the fingernails and cuticles.

orangewood ('ɒrɪndʒˌwʊd) n **a** the hard fine-grained yellowish wood of the orange tree. **b** (*as modifier*): *an orangewood table.*

orang-utan (ˌɔːˌræŋuːˈtæn, ˌɔːˈræŋˈuːtæn) *or* **orang-utang** (ˌɔːˌræŋuːˈtæŋ, ˌɔːˈræŋˈuːtæŋ) n a large anthropoid ape of the forests of Sumatra and Borneo, with shaggy reddish-brown hair and strong arms. Sometimes shortened to **orang**. [C17: from Malay *orang hutan*, from *ōrang* man + *hūtan* forest]

orate (ɔːˈreɪt) vb **orates, orating, orated.** (*intr*) **1** to make or give an oration. **2** to speak pompously and lengthily.

oration (ɔːˈreɪʃən) n **1** a formal public declaration or speech. **2** any rhetorical, lengthy, or pompous speech. [C14: from L *ōrātiō* speech, harangue, from *ōrāre* to plead, pray]

orator ('ɒrətə) n **1** a public speaker, esp. one versed in rhetoric. **2** a person given to lengthy or pompous speeches. **3** *Obs.* the plaintiff in a cause of action in chancery.

oratorio (ˌɒrəˈtɔːrɪəʊ) n, pl **oratorios**. a dramatic but unstaged musical composition for soloists, chorus, and orchestra, based on a religious theme. [C18: from It., lit.: ORATORY², referring to the Church of the Oratory at Rome where musical services were held]

oratory¹ ('ɒrətərɪ, -trɪ) n **1** the art of public speaking. **2** rhetorical skill or style. [C16: from L (*ars*) *ōrātōria* (the art of) public speaking]
▶ ˌora'torical adj ▶ ˌora'torically adv

oratory² ('ɒrətərɪ, -trɪ) n, pl **oratories**. a small room or secluded place, set apart for private prayer. [C14: from Anglo-Norman, from Church L *ōrātōrium* place of prayer, from *ōrāre* to plead, pray]

orb (ɔːb) n **1** (in regalia) an ornamental sphere surmounted by a cross. **2** a sphere; globe. **3** *Poetic*. another word for **eye¹** (sense 1). **4** *Obs. or poetic*. **4a** a celestial body, esp. the earth or sun. **4b** the orbit of a celestial body. ♦ vb **5** to make or become circular or spherical. **6** (*tr*) an archaic word for **encircle**. [C16: from L *orbis* circle, disc]

orbicular (ɔːˈbɪkjʊlə), **orbiculate**, *or* **orbiculated** adj **1** circular or spherical. **2** (of a leaf or similar flat part) nearly or nearly circular.
▶ **orbicularity** (ɔːˌbɪkjuːˈlærɪtɪ) n ▶ or'bicularly adv

orbit ('ɔːbɪt) n **1** *Astron*. the curved path followed by a planet, satellite, etc., in its motion around another celestial body. **2** a range or field of action or influence; sphere. **3** the bony cavity containing the eyeball; eye socket. **4** *Zool*. **4a** the skin surrounding the eye of a bird. **4b** the hollow in which lies the eye or eyestalk of an insect. **5** *Physics*. the path of an electron around the nucleus of an atom. **6 go into orbit**. *Inf*. to reach an extreme and often uncontrolled state: *when he realized the price he nearly went into orbit.* ♦ vb **7** to move around (a body) in a curved path. **8** (*tr*) to send (a satellite, spacecraft, etc.) into orbit. **9** (*intr*) to move in or as if in an orbit. [C16: from L *orbita* course, from *orbis* circle]
▶ 'orbitally adv

orbital ('ɔːbɪtəl) adj **1** of or denoting an orbit. **2** (of a motorway or major road) circling a large city. ♦ n **3** the

region around an atomic nucleus, or around two nuclei in a molecule, within which an electron moves. **4** an orbital road.

orbital velocity n the velocity required by a spacecraft to enter and maintain a given orbit.

orc (ɔːk) n **1** any of various whales, such as the killer and grampus. **2** a mythical monster. [C16: via L *orca*, ?from Gk *orux* whale]

Orcadian (ɔːˈkeɪdɪən) n **1** a native or inhabitant of the Orkneys. ♦ adj **2** of or relating to the Orkneys. [from L *Orcades* the Orkney Islands]

Orcagna ★ (*Italian* orˈcaɲɲa) n **Andrea** (anˈdrɛːa), original name *Andrea di Cione.* ?1308–68, Florentine painter, sculptor, and architect.

orchard ('ɔːtʃəd) n **1** an area of land devoted to the cultivation of fruit trees. **2** a collection of fruit trees especially cultivated. [OE *orceard, ortigeard,* from *ort-,* from L *hortus* garden + *geard* YARD²]

orchestra ('ɔːkɪstrə) n **1** a large group of musicians, esp. one whose members play a variety of different instruments. **2** a group of musicians, each playing the same type of instrument. **3** Also called: **orchestra pit**. the space reserved for musicians in a theatre, immediately in front of or under the stage. **4** *Chiefly US & Canad.* the stalls in a theatre. **5** (in ancient Greek theatre) the semicircular space in front of the stage. [C17: via L from Gk: the space in the theatre for the chorus, from *orkheisthai* to dance]
▶ **orchestral** (ɔːˈkɛstrəl) adj ▶ or'chestrally adv

orchestrate ('ɔːkɪˌstreɪt) vb **orchestrates, orchestrating, orchestrated.** (*tr*) **1** to score or arrange (a piece of music) for orchestra. **2** to arrange, organize, or build up for special or maximum effect. ♦
▶ ˌorches'tration n ▶ 'orches,trator n

orchid ('ɔːkɪd) n a terrestrial or epiphytic plant having flowers of unusual shapes and beautiful colours, usually with one petal larger than the other two. The flowers are specialized for pollination by certain insects. [C19: from NL *Orchideae*; see ORCHIS]

orchidectomy (ˌɔːkɪˈdɛktəmɪ) n, pl **orchidectomies**. the surgical removal of one or both testes. [C19: from Gk *orkhis* testicle + -ECTOMY]

orchil ('ɔːkɪl, -tʃɪl) *or* **archil** n **1** a purplish dye obtained by treating various lichens with aqueous ammonia. **2** the lichens yielding this dye. [C15: from OF *orcheil,* from ?]

orchis ('ɔːkɪs) n **1** a N temperate terrestrial orchid having fleshy tubers and spikes of typically pink flowers. **2** any of various temperate or tropical orchids such as the fringed orchis. [C16: via L from Gk *orkhis* testicle; so called from the shape of its roots]

OR circuit *or* **gate** (ɔː) n *Computing*. a logic circuit having two or more input wires and one output wire that gives a high-voltage output signal if one or more input signals are at a high voltage: used extensively as a basic circuit in computing. [C20: from its similarity to the function of *or* in logical constructions]

Orcus ★ ('ɔːkəs) n another name for Dis (sense 1).

Orczy ★ ('ɔːtsɪ) n **Baroness Emmuska** ('ɛmuʃkə). 1865–1947, British novelist, born in Hungary; author of *The Scarlet Pimpernel* (1905).

Ord ★ (ɔːd) n a river in NE Western Australia, rising on the Kimberley Plateau and flowing generally north to the Timor Sea: subject of a major irrigation scheme. Length: about 500 km (300 miles).

ord. *abbrev. for:* **1** order. **2** ordinal. **3** ordinance. **4** ordinary.

ordain (ɔːˈdeɪn) vb (*tr*) **1** to consecrate (someone) as a priest; confer holy orders upon. **2** (*may take a clause as object*) to decree, appoint, or predestine irrevocably. **3** (*may take a clause as object*) to order, establish, or enact with authority. [C16: from Anglo-Norman *ordeiner,* from LL *ordināre,* from L *ordo* ORDER]
▶ or'dainer n ▶ or'dainment n

ordeal (ɔːˈdiːl) n **1** a severe or trying experience. **2** *History*. a method of trial in which the innocence of an accused person was determined by subjecting him to physical danger, esp. by fire or water. [OE *ordāl*, *ordēl* verdict]

order ('ɔːdə) *n* **1** a state in which all components or elements are arranged logically, comprehensibly, or naturally. **2** an arrangement or disposition of things in succession; sequence: *alphabetical order*. **3** an established or customary method or state, esp. of society. **4** a peaceful or harmonious condition of society: *order reigned in the streets*. **5** (*often pl*) a class, rank, or hierarchy: *the lower orders*. **6** *Biol.* any of the taxonomic groups into which a class is divided and which contains one or more families. **7** an instruction that must be obeyed; command. **8a** a commission or instruction to produce or supply something in return for payment. **8b** the commodity produced or supplied. **8c** (*as modifier*): *order form*. **9** a procedure followed by an assembly, meeting, etc. **10** (*cap. when part of a name*) a body of people united in a particular aim or purpose. **11** (*usually cap.*) Also called: **religious order**. a group of persons who bind themselves by vows in order to devote themselves to the pursuit of religious aims. **12** (*often pl*) another name for **holy orders, major orders**, or **minor orders**. **13** *History*. a society of knights constituted as a fraternity, such as the Knights Templars. **14a** a group of people holding a specific honour for service or merit, conferred on them by a sovereign or state. **14b** the insignia of such a group. **15a** any of the five major classical styles of architecture classified by the style of columns and entablatures used. **15b** any style of architecture. **16** *Christianity*. **16a** the sacrament by which bishops, priests, etc., have their offices conferred upon them. **16b** any of the degrees into which the ministry is divided. **16c** the office of an ordained Christian minister. **17** *Maths*. **17a** the number of times a function must be differentiated to obtain a given derivative. **17b** the order of the highest derivative in a differential equation. **17c** the number of rows or columns in a determinant or square matrix. **17d** the number of members of a finite group. **18** *Mil.* (often preceded by *the*) the dress, equipment, or formation directed for a particular purpose or undertaking: *battle order*. **19** a tall order. something difficult, demanding, or exacting. **20** in order. **20a** in sequence. **20b** properly arranged. **20c** appropriate or fitting. **21** in order that. (*conj*) with the purpose that; so that. **22** in order to. (*prep*; foll. by an infinitive) so that it is possible to: *to eat in order to live*. **23** keep order. to maintain or enforce order. **24** of or in the order of. having an approximately specified size or quantity. **25** on order. having been ordered but not having been delivered. **26** out of order. **26a** not in sequence. **26b** not working. **26c** not following the rules or customary procedure. **27** to order. **27a** according to a buyer's specifications. **27b** on request or demand. ◆ *vb* **28** (*tr*) to give a command to (a person or animal to do or be something). **29** to request (something) to be supplied or made, esp. in return for payment. **30** (*tr*) to instruct or command to move, go, etc. (to a specified place): *they ordered her into the house*. **31** (*tr*; may take a clause as object) to authorize; prescribe: *the doctor ordered a strict diet*. **32** (*tr*) to arrange, regulate, or dispose (articles, etc.) in their proper places. **33** (*tr*) (of fate) to will; ordain. ◆ *interj* **34** an exclamation demanding that orderly behaviour be restored. [C13: from OF *ordre*, from L *ordō*]
► 'orderer *n*

order-driven *adj* denoting an electronic market system, esp. for stock exchanges, in which prices are determined by the publication of orders to buy or sell. Cf. **quote-driven**.

order in council *n* (in Britain) a decree of the Cabinet, usually made under the authority of a statute: in theory a decree of the sovereign and Privy Council.

orderly ('ɔːdəlɪ) *adj* **1** in order, properly arranged, or tidy. **2** obeying or appreciating method, system, and arrangement. **3** *Mil.* of or relating to orders: *an orderly book*. ◆ *n*, *pl* **orderlies**. **4** *Med.* a male hospital attendant. **5** *Mil.* a junior rank detailed to carry orders or perform minor tasks for a more senior officer.
► 'orderliness *n*

orderly room *n Mil.* a room in the barracks of a battalion or company used for general administrative purposes.

order of magnitude *n* a numerical value expressed to the nearest power of ten.

Order of Merit *n Brit.* an order conferred on civilian and servicemen for eminence in any field.

order of the day *n* **1** the general directive of a commander in chief or the specific instructions of a commanding officer. **2** *Inf.* the prescribed or only thing offered or available. **3** (in Parliament) any item of public business ordered to be considered on a specific day. **4** an agenda or programme.

Order of the Garter *n* See **Garter**.

order paper *n* a list indicating the order in which business is to be conducted, esp. in Parliament.

ordinal ('ɔːdɪnᵊl) *adj* **1** denoting a certain position in a sequence of numbers. **2** of, relating to, or characteristic of an order in biological classification. ◆ *n* **3** short for **ordinal number**. **4** a book containing the forms of services for the ordination of ministers. **5** *RC Church*. a service book.

ordinal number *n* a number denoting relative position in a sequence, such as *first, second, third*. Sometimes shortened to **ordinal**.

ordinance ('ɔːdɪnəns) *n* an authoritative regulation, decree, law, or practice. [C14: from OF *ordenance*, from L *ordināre* to set in order]

ordinarily ('ɔːdᵊnrɪlɪ) *adv* in ordinary, normal, or usual practice; usually; normally.

ordinary ('ɔːdᵊnrɪ) *adj* **1** of common or established type or occurrence. **2** familiar, everyday, or unexceptional. **3** uninteresting or commonplace. **4** having regular or ex officio jurisdiction: *an ordinary judge*. **5** *Maths*. (of a differential equation) containing two variables only and derivatives of one of the variables with respect to the other. ◆ *n*, *pl* **ordinaries**. **6** a common or average situation, amount, or degree (esp. in **out of the ordinary**). **7** a normal or commonplace person or thing. **8** *Civil law*. a judge who exercises jurisdiction in his own right. **9** (*usually cap.*) an ecclesiastic, esp. a bishop, holding an office to which certain jurisdictional powers are attached. **10** *RC Church*. **10a** the parts of the Mass that do not vary from day to day. **10b** a prescribed form of divine service, esp. the Mass. **11** the US name for **penny-farthing**. **12** *Heraldry*. any of several conventional figures, such as the bend and the cross, commonly charged upon shields. **13** *History*. a clergyman who visited condemned prisoners. **14** *Brit. obs.* a meal provided regularly at a fixed price. **14b** the inn, etc., providing such meals. **15** in ordinary. *Brit.* (used esp. in titles) in regular service or attendance: *physician in ordinary to the sovereign*. [C16 (adj) & C13 (some n senses): ult. from L *ordinārius* orderly, from *ordō* order]

Ordinary level *n* a formal name for **O level**.

ordinary rating *n* a rank in the Royal Navy comparable to that of a private in the army.

ordinary seaman *n* a seaman of the lowest rank, being insufficiently experienced to be an able-bodied seaman.

ordinary shares *pl n Brit.* shares representing part of the capital issued by a company, entitling their holders to a share in the profits and the net assets. US equivalent: **common stock**. Cf. **preference shares**.

ordinate ('ɔːdɪnɪt) *n* the vertical or *y*-coordinate of a point in a two-dimensional system of Cartesian coordinates. Cf. **abscissa**. [C16: from NL (*linea*) *ordināta* (*applicāta*) (line applied) in an orderly manner, from *ordināre* to arrange in order]

ordination (ˌɔːdɪ'neɪʃən) *n* **1a** the act of conferring holy orders. **1b** the reception of holy orders. **2** the condition of being ordained or regulated. **3** an arrangement of order.

ordnance ('ɔːdnəns) *n* **1** cannon or artillery. **2** military supplies; munitions. **3** the. a department of an army or government dealing with military supplies. [C14: variant of ORDINANCE]

ordnance datum *n* mean sea level calculated from observation taken at Newlyn, Cornwall, and used as the official basis for height calculation on British maps. Abbrev.: **OD**.

★ people and places

Ordnance Survey *n* the official map-making body of the British or Irish government.

Ordovician (ˌɔːdəʊˈvɪʃɪən) *adj* **1** of, denoting, or formed in the second period of the Palaeozoic era, between the Cambrian and Silurian periods. ◆ *n* **2** the. the Ordovician period or rock system. [C19: from L *Ordovices*, ancient Celtic tribe in N Wales]

ordure (ˈɔːdjʊə) *n* excrement; dung. [C14: via OF, from *ord* dirty, from L *horridus* shaggy]

Ordzhonikidze or **Orjonikidze** ★ (*Russian* ardʒəniˈkidzɪ) *n* the former name (1944–91) of **Vladikavkaz.**

ore (ɔː) *n* any naturally occurring mineral or aggregate of minerals from which economically important constituents, esp. metals, can be extracted. [OE *ār*, *ōra*]

öre (ˈøːrə) *n*, *pl* **öre**. a Scandinavian monetary unit worth one hundredth of a Swedish krona or (**øre**) one hundredth of a Danish and Norwegian krone.

oread (ˈɔːrɪˌæd) *n Greek myth.* a mountain nymph. [C16: via L from Gk *Oreias*, from *oros* mountain]

Örebro ★ (*Swedish* œːrəˈbruː) *n* a town in S Sweden: one of Sweden's oldest towns. Pop.: 120 774 (1997 est.).

Oreg. *abbrev. for* Oregon.

oregano (ˌɒrɪˈɡɑːnəʊ) *n* **1** a Mediterranean variety of wild marjoram (*Origanum vulgare*), with pungent leaves. **2** the dried powdered leaves of this plant, used to season food. [C18: American Sp., from Sp., from L *orīganum*, from Gk *origanon* an aromatic herb, ? marjoram]

Oregon ★ (ˈɒrɪɡən) *n* a state of the northwestern US, on the Pacific: consists of the Coast and Cascade Ranges in the west and a plateau in the east; important timber production. Capital: Salem. Pop.: 3 203 735 (1996 est.). Area: 251 418 sq. km (97 073 sq. miles). Abbrevs.: **Oreg.** or (with zip code) **OR**

Oregon trail ★ *n* an early pioneering route across the central US, from Independence, W Missouri, to the Columbia River country of N Oregon: used chiefly between 1804 and 1860. Length: about 3220 km (2000 miles).

Orel or **Oryol** ★ (*Russian* aˈrjɔl) *n* a city in W Russia. Pop.: 348 000 (1995 est.).

Ore Mountains ★ (ɔː) *pl n* another name for the **Erzgebirge.**

Orenburg ★ (ˈɒrənˌbɜːɡ; *Russian* arɪnˈburk) *n* a city in W Russia, on the Ural River. Pop.: 532 000 (1995 est.). Former name (1938–57): **Chkalov.**

Orense ★ (*Spanish* oˈrense) *n* a city in NW Spain, in Galicia on the Miño River: warm springs. Pop.: 108 547 (1994 est.).

Orestes ★ (ɒˈrestiːz) *n Greek myth.* the son of Agamemnon and Clytemnestra, who killed his mother and her lover Aegisthus in revenge for their murder of his father.

Øresund ★ (œːrəˈsund) *n* the Swedish and Danish name for the **Sound.**

orfe (ɔːf) *n* a small slender European cyprinoid fish, occurring in two colour varieties, namely the **silver orfe** and the **golden orfe**, popular aquarium fishes. [C17: from G; rel. to L *orphus*, Gk *orphos* the sea perch]

Orff ★ (ɔːf; *German* ɔrf) *n* Carl (karl). 1895–1982, German composer. His works include the oratorio *Carmina Burana* (1937).

organ (ˈɔːɡən) *n* **1a** Also called: **pipe organ**. a large complex musical keyboard instrument in which sound is produced by means of a number of pipes arranged in sets or stops, supplied with air from a bellows. **1b** (*as modifier*): *organ stop; organ loft.* **2** any instrument, such as a harmonium, in which sound is produced in this way. **3** a fully differentiated structural and functional unit, such as a kidney or a root, in an animal or plant. **4** an agency or medium of communication, esp. a periodical issued by a specialist group or party. **5** an instrument with which something is done or accomplished. **6** a euphemistic word for **penis**. [C13: from OF *organe*, from L *organum* implement, from Gk *organon* tool]

organdie or *esp. US* **organdy** (ˈɔːɡəndɪ) *n*, *pl* **organdies**. a fine and slightly stiff cotton fabric used for dresses, etc. [C19: from F *organdi*, from ?]

organelle (ˌɔːɡəˈnɛl) *n* a structural and functional unit in a cell or unicellular organism. [C20: from NL *organella*, from L *organum*; see ORGAN]

organ-grinder *n* a street musician playing a hand organ for money.

organic (ɔːˈɡænɪk) *adj* **1** of, relating to, or derived from living plants and animals. **2** of or relating to animal or plant constituents or products having a carbon basis. **3** of or relating to one or more organs of an animal or plant. **4** of, relating to, or belonging to the class of chemical compounds that are formed from carbon: *an organic compound.* **5** constitutional in the structure of something; fundamental; integral. **6** of or characterized by the coordination of integral parts; organized. **7** of or relating to the essential constitutional laws regulating the government of a state: *organic law.* **8** of, relating to, or grown with the use of fertilizers or pesticides deriving from animal or vegetable matter, rather than from chemicals. ◆ *n* **9** any substance, such as a fertilizer or pesticide, that is derived from animal or vegetable matter rather than from chemicals.
▸ or'ganically *adv*

organic chemistry *n* the branch of chemistry concerned with the compounds of carbon.

organism (ˈɔːɡəˌnɪzəm) *n* **1** any living animal or plant, including any bacterium or virus. **2** anything resembling a living creature in structure, behaviour, etc.
▸ ˌorgan'ismal or ˌorgan'ismic *adj* ▸ ˌorgan'ismally *adv*

organist (ˈɔːɡənɪst) *n* a person who plays the organ.

organization or **organisation** (ˌɔːɡənaɪˈzeɪʃən) *n* **1** the act of organizing or the state of being organized. **2** an organized structure or whole. **3** a business or administrative concern united and constructed for a particular end. **4** a body of administrative officials, as of a government department, etc. **5** order, tidiness, or system; method.
▸ ˌorgani'zational or ˌorgani'sational *adj*

organizational psychology *n* the study of the structure of an organization and of the ways in which the people in it interact, usually undertaken in order to improve the organization.

organize or **organise** (ˈɔːɡəˌnaɪz) *vb* **organizes, organizing, organized** or **organises, organising, organised. 1** to form (parts or elements of something) into a structured whole; coordinate. **2** (*tr*) to arrange methodically or in order. **3** (*tr*) to provide with an organic structure. **4** (*tr*) to enlist (the workers) of (a factory, etc.) in a trade union. **5** (*intr*) to join or form an organization or trade union. **6** (*tr*) *Inf.* to put (oneself) in an alert and responsible frame of mind. [C15: from Med. L *organizare*, from L *organum* ORGAN]
▸ 'organ,izer or 'organ,iser *n*

organometallic (ɔːˌɡænəʊmɪˈtælɪk) *adj* of, concerned with, or being an organic compound with one or more metal atoms in its molecules.

organon (ˈɔːɡəˌnɒn) or **organum** *n*, *pl* **organa** (-nə), **organons** or **organa, organums. 1** *Epistemology.* a system of logical or scientific rules, esp. that of Aristotle. **2** *Arch.* a sense organ, regarded as an instrument for acquiring knowledge. [C16: from Gk: implement; see ORGAN]

organophosphate (ɔːˌɡænəʊˈfɒsfeɪt) *n* any of a group of organic compounds containing phosphorus and used as a pesticide.

organotin (ɔːˈɡænəʊˌtɪn) *adj* **1** of, concerned with, or being an organic compound with one or more tin atoms in its molecules. ◆ *n* **2** such a compound used as a pesticide, formerly believed to decompose safely, now found to be toxic in the food chain.

organza (ɔːˈɡænzə) *n* a thin stiff fabric of silk, cotton, nylon, rayon, etc. [C20: from ?]

orgasm (ˈɔːɡæzəm) *n* **1** the most intense point during sexual excitement. **2** *Rare.* intense or violent excitement. [C17: from NL *orgasmus*, from Gk *orgasmos*, from *organ* to mature, swell]
▸ or'gasmic or or'gastic *adj*

orgeat (ˈɔːʒɑː) *n* a drink made from barley or almonds, and orangeflower water. [C18: via F, from *orge* barley, from L *hordeum*]

orgy (ˈɔːdʒɪ) *n*, *pl* **orgies. 1** a wild gathering marked by pro-

miscuous sexual activity, excessive drinking, etc. **2** an act of immoderate or frenzied indulgence. **3** (*often pl*) secret religious rites of Dionysus, Bacchus, etc., marked by drinking, dancing, and songs. [C16: from F *orgies*, from L *orgia*, from Gk: nocturnal festival]
▸ **orgi'astic** *adj*

oribi ('ɒrɪbɪ) *n, pl* **oribi** *or* **oribis.** a small African antelope of the grasslands and bush south of the Sahara, with fawn-coloured coat and, in the male, ridged spikelike horns. [C18: from Afrik., prob. from Khoikhoi *arab*]

oriel window ('ɔːrɪəl) *n* a bay window, esp. one that is supported by one or more brackets or corbels. Sometimes shortened to **oriel.** [C14: from OF *oriol* gallery, ?from Med. L *auleolum* niche]

orient *n* ('ɔːrɪənt). **1** *Poetic.* another word for **east.** Cf. **occident. 2** *Arch.* the eastern sky or the dawn. **3a** the iridescent lustre of a pearl. **3b** (*as modifier*): *orient pearls.* **4** a pearl of high quality. ◆ *adj* ('ɔːrɪənt). **5** *Now chiefly poetic.* oriental. **6** *Arch.* (of the sun, stars, etc.) rising. ◆ *vb* ('ɔːrɪ,ɛnt). **7** to adjust or align (oneself or something else) according to surroundings or circumstances. **8** (*tr*) to position or set (a map, etc.) with reference to the compass or other specific directions. **9** (*tr*) to build (a church) with the chancel end facing in an easterly direction. [C18: via F from L *oriēns* rising (sun), from *orīrī* to rise]

Orient ('ɔːrɪənt) *n* (usually preceded by *the*) **1** the countries east of the Mediterranean. **2** the eastern hemisphere.

oriental (,ɔːrɪ'ɛntˀl) *adj* another word for **eastern.**

Oriental (,ɔːrɪ'ɛntˀl) *adj* **1** (*sometimes not cap.*) of or relating to the Orient. **2** of or denoting a region consisting of southeastern Asia from India to Borneo, Java, and the Philippines. ◆ *n* **3** (*sometimes not cap.*) an inhabitant, esp. a native, of the Orient.

Orientalism (,ɔːrɪ'ɛntə,lɪzəm) *n* **1** knowledge of or devotion to the Orient. **2** an Oriental quality, style, or trait.
▸ **Ori'entalist** *n* ▸ **Ori,ental'istic** *adj*

orientate ('ɔːrɪɛn,teɪt) *vb* **orientates, orientating, orientated.** another word for **orient** (senses 7, 8, 9).

orientation (,ɔːrɪɛn'teɪʃən) *n* **1** the act or process of orienting or the state of being oriented. **2** positioning with relation to the compass or other specific directions. **3** the adjustment or alignment of oneself or one's ideas to surroundings or circumstances. **4** Also called: **orientation course.** *Chiefly US & Canad.* **4a** a course, lecture, etc., introducing a new situation or environment. **4b** (*as modifier*): *an orientation talk.* **5** *Psychol.* the knowledge of one's own temporal, social, and practical circumstances. **6** the siting of a church on an east-west axis.
▸ **,orien'tational** *adj*

-oriented *suffix forming adjectives.* geared or directed towards: *sports-oriented.*

orienteer (,ɔːrɪən'tɪə) *vb* (*intr*) **1** to take part in orienteering. ◆ *n* **2** a person who takes part in orienteering.

orienteering (,ɔːrɪən'tɪərɪŋ) *n* a sport in which contestants race on foot over a course consisting of checkpoints found with the aid of a map and a compass. [C20: from Swedish *orientering*]

orifice ('ɒrɪfɪs) *n Chiefly technical.* an opening or mouth into a cavity; vent; aperture. [C16: via F from LL *ōrificium*, from L *ōs* mouth + *facere* to make]

oriflamme ('ɒrɪ,flæm) *n* a scarlet flag adopted as the national banner of France in the Middle Ages. [C15: via OF, from L *aurum* gold + *flamma* flame]

orig. *abbrev. for:* **1** origin. **2** original(ly).

origami (,ɒrɪ'gɑːmɪ) *n* the art or process, originally Japanese, of paper folding. [from Japanese, from *ori* a fold + *kami* paper]

origan ('ɒrɪgən) *n* another name for **marjoram** (sense 2). [C16: from L *orīganum*, from Gk *origanon* an aromatic herb]

origanum (,ɒrɪ'gɑːnəm) *n* See **oregano.**

Origen ★ ('ɒrɪ,dʒɛn) *n* ?185–?254 A.D., Christian theologian, born in Alexandria. His writings include *Contra Celsum* and *De principiis.*

origin ('ɒrɪdʒɪn) *n* **1** a primary source; derivation. **2** the beginning of something; first part. **3** (*often pl*) ancestry or

parentage; birth; extraction. **4** *Anat.* **4a** the end of a muscle, opposite its point of insertion. **4b** the beginning of a nerve or blood vessel or the site where it first starts to branch out. **5** *Maths.* **5a** the point of intersection of coordinate axes or planes. **5b** the point whose coordinates are all zero. **6** *Commerce.* the country from which a commodity or product originates: *shipment from origin.* [C16: from F *origine*, from L *orīgō* beginning, from *orīrī* to spring from]

original (ə'rɪdʒɪnˀl) *adj* **1** of or relating to an origin or beginning. **2** fresh and unusual; novel. **3** able to think of or carry out new ideas or concepts. **4** being that from which a copy, translation, etc., is made. ◆ *n* **5** the first and genuine form of something, from which others are derived. **6** a person or thing used as a model in art or literature. **7** a person whose way of thinking is unusual or creative. **8** the first form or occurrence of something.
▸ **o'riginally** *adv*

originality (ə,rɪdʒɪ'nælɪtɪ) *n, pl* **originalities. 1** the quality or condition of being original. **2** the ability to create or innovate.

original sin *n* a state of sin held to be innate in mankind as the descendants of Adam.

originate (ə'rɪdʒɪ,neɪt) *vb* **originates, originating, originated. 1** to come or bring into being. **2** (*intr*) *US & Canad.* (of a bus, train, etc.) to begin its journey at a specified point.
▸ **o,rigi'nation** *n* ▸ **o'rigi,nator** *n*

O-ring *n* a rubber ring used in machinery as a seal against oil, air, etc.

Orinoco ★ (,ɒrɪ'nəʊkəʊ) *n* a river in N South America, rising in S Venezuela and flowing west, then north as part of the border between Colombia and Venezuela, then east to the Atlantic by a great delta: the third largest river system in South America, draining an area of 945 000 sq. km (365 000 sq. miles); reaches a width of 22 km (14 miles) during the rainy season. Length: about 2575 km (1600 miles).

oriole ('ɔːrɪ,əʊl) *n* **1** a tropical Old World songbird, such as the **golden oriole,** having a long pointed bill and a mostly yellow-and-black plumage. **2** an American songbird, esp. the Baltimore oriole, with a typical male plumage of black with either orange or yellow. [C18: from Med. L *oryolus,* from L *aureolus,* dim. of *aureus,* from *aurum* gold]

Orion[1] (ə'raɪən) *n Greek myth.* a Boeotian giant famed as a great hunter, who figures in several tales.

Orion[2] (ə'raɪən) *n* a conspicuous constellation containing two first-magnitude stars (Betelgeuse and Rigel) and a distant bright emission nebula (the **Orion Nebula**).

orison ('ɒrɪzˀn) *n Literary.* another word for **prayer** (senses 1 and 2). [C12: from OF *oreison,* from LL *ōrātiō,* from L: speech, from *ōrāre* to speak]

Orissa ★ (ɒ'rɪsə) *n* a state of E India, on the Bay of Bengal: part of the province of Bihar and Orissa (1912–36); enlarged by the addition of 25 native states in 1949. Capital: Bhubaneswar. Pop.: 33 795 000 (1994 est.). Area: 155 707 sq. km (60 119 sq. miles).

Oriya (ɒ'rɪə) *n* **1** (*pl* **Oriya**) a member of a people of India living chiefly in Orissa. **2** the state language of Orissa, belonging to the Indo-European family.

Orizaba ★ (,ɔːrɪ'zɑːbə; *Spanish* ori'θaβa) *n* **1** a city and resort in SE Mexico, in Veracruz state. Pop.: 114 216 (1990). **2** Pico de. the Spanish name for **Citlaltépetl.**

Orjonikidze ★ (*Russian* ardʒəni'kidzɪ) *n* a variant spelling of **Ordzhonikidze.**

Orkneys ★ ('ɔːknɪz), **Orkney** ('ɔːknɪ), *or* **Orkney Islands** ★ *pl n* a group of over 70 islands off the N coast of Scotland, separated from the mainland by the Pentland Firth: constitutes an island authority of Scotland; low-lying and treeless; prehistoric remains. Administrative centre: Kirkwall. Pop.: 19 800 (1996 est.). Area: 974 sq. km (376 sq. miles). Related adj: **Orcadian.**
▸ **'Orkneyman** *n*

Orlando ★ (ɔː'lændəʊ) *n* a city in the US, in Florida: site of Walt Disney World. Pop.: 176 948 (1994 est.).

Orléans[1] (ɔː'lɪənz; *French* ɔrleɑ̃) *n* a city in N central France, on the River Loire: famous for its deliverance by

★ people and places

Joan of Arc from the long English siege in 1429; university (1305); an important rail and road junction. Pop.: 107 965 (1990).

Orléans[2] ★ (*French* ɔrleɑ̃) *n* **Louis Philippe Joseph** (lwi filip ʒozɛf), Duc d'Orléans, known as *Philippe Égalité*. 1747–93, French nobleman, who supported the French Revolution; executed after his son, the future king Louis-Philippe, defected to the Austrians.

Orlon ('ɔːlɒn) *n Trademark.* a crease-resistant acrylic fibre or fabric used for clothing, etc.

orlop *or* **orlop deck** ('ɔːlɒp) *n Naut.* (in a vessel with four or more decks) the lowest deck. [C15: from Du. *overloop* to spill]

Orly ★ ('ɔːliː; *French* ɔrli) *n* a suburb of SE Paris, France, with an international airport.

Ormandy ★ ('ɔːməndɪ) *n* **Eugene.** 1899–1985, US conductor, born in Hungary.

Ormazd ★ ('ɔːmæzd) *n Zoroastrianism.* the creative deity, embodiment of good and opponent of Ahriman. Also called: **Ahura Mazda.** [from Persian]

ormer ('ɔːmə) *n* **1** Also called: **sea-ear.** an edible marine gastropod mollusc that has an ear-shaped shell perforated with holes and occurs near the Channel Islands. **2** any other abalone. [C17: from F, apparently from L *auris* ear + *mare* sea]

ormolu ('ɔːməˌluː) *n* **1a** a gold-coloured alloy of copper, tin, or zinc used to decorate furniture, etc. **1b** (*as modifier*): *an ormolu clock.* **2** gold prepared for gilding. [C18: from F *or moulu* ground gold]

Ormuz ★ ('ɔːmʌz) *n* a variant spelling of **Hormuz.**

ornament *n* ('ɔːnəmənt). **1** anything that enhances the appearance of a person or thing. **2** decorations collectively: *she was totally without ornament.* **3** a small decorative object. **4** something regarded as a source of pride or beauty. **5** *Music.* any of several decorations, such as the trill, etc. ◆ *vb* ('ɔːnəˌmɛnt). (*tr*) **6** to decorate with or as if with ornaments. **7** to serve as an ornament to. [C14: from L *ornāmentum*, from *ornāre* to adorn]
 ▸ ˌornamen'tation *n*

ornamental (ˌɔːnə'mɛntˀl) *adj* **1** of value as an ornament; decorative. **2** (of a plant) used to decorate houses, gardens, etc. ◆ *n* **3** a plant cultivated for show or decoration.
 ▸ ˌorna'mentally *adv*

ornate (ɔː'neɪt) *adj* **1** heavily or elaborately decorated. **2** (of style in writing, etc.) over-embellished; flowery. [C15: from L *ornāre* to decorate]
 ▸ or'nately *adv* ▸ or'nateness *n*

Orne ★ (*French* ɔrn) *n* a department of NW France, in Basse-Normandie. Capital: Alençon. Pop.: 294 596 (1994 est.). Area: 6144 sq. km (2396 sq. miles).

ornery ('ɔːnərɪ) *adj US & Canad. dialect or inf.* **1** stubborn or vile-tempered. **2** low; treacherous: *an ornery trick.* **3** ordinary. [C19: alteration of ORDINARY]
 ▸ 'orneriness *n*

ornitho- *or before a vowel* **ornith-** *combining form.* bird or birds. [from Gk *ornis, ornith-* bird]

ornithology (ˌɔːnɪ'θɒlədʒɪ) *n* the study of birds.
 ▸ ornithological (ˌɔːnɪθə'lɒdʒɪkˀl) *adj* ▸ ˌornitho'logically *adv* ▸ ˌorni'thologist *n*

ornithorhynchus (ˌɔːnɪθəʊ'rɪŋkəs) *n* the technical name for **duck-billed platypus.** [C19: NL, from ORNITHO- + Gk *rhunkhos* bill]

oro-[1] *combining form.* mountain: *orogeny.* [from Gk *oros*]

oro-[2] *combining form.* oral; mouth: *oromaxillary.* [from L, from *ōs*]

orogeny (ɒ'rɒdʒɪnɪ) *or* **orogenesis** (ˌɒrəʊ'dʒɛnɪsɪs) *n* the formation of mountain ranges.
 ▸ orogenic (ˌɒrəʊ'dʒɛnɪk) *or* orogenetic (ˌɒrəʊdʒɪ'nɛtɪk) *adj*

Orontes ★ (ɒ'rɒntiːz) *n* a river in SW Asia, rising in Lebanon and flowing north through Syria into Turkey, where it turns west to the Mediterranean. Length: 571 km (355 miles). Arabic name: **'Asi.**

orotund ('ɒrəʊˌtʌnd) *adj* **1** (of the voice) resonant; boom-

ing. **2** (of speech or writing) bombastic; pompous. [C18: from L *ore rotundo* with rounded mouth]

Orozco ★ (*Spanish* o'rɔθko) *n* **José Clemente** (xo'se kle'mente). 1883–1949, Mexican mural painter.

orphan ('ɔːfən) *n* **1a** a child, one or both of whose parents are dead. **1b** (*as modifier*): *an orphan child.* ◆ *vb* **2** (*tr*) to deprive of one or both parents. [C15: from LL *orphanus*, from Gk *orphanos*]

orphanage ('ɔːfənɪdʒ) *n* **1** an institution for orphans and abandoned children. **2** the state of being an orphan.

Orphean ('ɔːfɪən) *adj* **1** of or relating to Orpheus. **2** melodious or enchanting.

Orpheus ★ ('ɔːfɪəs, -fjuːs) *n Greek myth.* a poet and lyre-player credited with the authorship of the poems forming the basis of Orphism. He married Eurydice and sought her in Hades after her death. He failed to win her back and was killed by a band of bacchantes.

Orphic ('ɔːfɪk) *adj* **1** of or relating to Orpheus or Orphism, a mystery religion of ancient Greece. **2** (*sometimes not cap.*) mystical or occult.
 ▸ 'Orphically *adv*

orpine ('ɔːpaɪn) *or* **orpin** ('ɔːpɪn) *n* a succulent perennial N temperate plant with toothed leaves and heads of small purplish-white flowers. [C14: from OF, apparently from *orpiment*, a yellow mineral (? referring to the yellow flowers of a related species)]

Orpington ★ ('ɔːpɪŋtən) *n* a district of SE London, part of the Greater London borough of Bromley from 1965.

orrery ('ɒrərɪ) *n, pl* **orreries.** a mechanical model of the solar system in which the planets can be moved at the correct relative velocities around the sun. [C18: orig. made for Charles Boyle, Earl of *Orrery*]

orris[1] *or* **orrice** ('ɒrɪs) *n* **1** any of various irises that have fragrant rhizomes. **2** Also: **orrisroot.** the rhizome of such a plant, prepared and used as perfume. [C16: var. of IRIS]

orris[2] ('ɒrɪs) *n* a kind of lace made of gold or silver, used esp. in the 18th century. [from Old French *orfreis*, from L *auriphrygium* Phrygian gold]

Orsini ★ (*Italian* or'siːni) *n* an Italian aristocratic family that was prominent in Rome from the 12th to the 18th century.

Orsk ★ (*Russian* ɔrsk) *n* a city in W Russia, on the Ural River: a major railway and industrial centre, with an oil refinery linked by pipeline with the Emba field (on the Caspian). Pop.: 275 000 (1995 est.).

Ortega ★ (ɔː'teɪgə) *n* **Daniel,** full surname *Ortega Saavedra.* born 1945, Nicaraguan politician and former guerrilla leader; president of Nicaragua (1985–90).

Ortegal ★ (*Spanish* ɔrte'yal) *n* **Cape.** a cape in NW Spain, projecting into the Bay of Biscay.

Ortega y Gasset ★ (*Spanish* ɔr'teɣa i ga'set) *n* **José** (xo'se). 1883–1955, Spanish philosopher, noted for his *The Revolt of the Masses* (1930).

orthicon ('ɔːθɪˌkɒn) *n* a television camera tube in which an optical image produces a corresponding electrical charge pattern on a mosaic surface that is scanned from behind by an electron beam. The resulting discharge of the mosaic provides the output signal current. See also **image orthicon.** [C20: from ORTHO- + ICON(OSCOPE)]

ortho- *or before a vowel* **orth-** *combining form.* **1** straight or upright: *orthorhombic.* **2** perpendicular or at right angles: *orthogonal.* **3** correct or right: *orthodontics.* **4** (*often in italics*) denoting an organic compound containing a benzene ring with substituents attached to adjacent carbon atoms (the 1,2- positions). **5** denoting an oxyacid regarded as the highest hydrated form of the anhydride or a salt of such an acid: *orthophosphoric acid.* **6** denoting a diatomic substance in which the spins of the two atoms are parallel: *orthohydrogen.* [from Gk *orthos* straight, upright]

orthochromatic (ˌɔːθəʊkrəʊ'mætɪk) *adj Photog.* of or relating to an emulsion giving a rendering of relative light intensities of different colours that corresponds approximately to the colour sensitivity of the eye, esp. one that is insensitive to red light. Sometimes shortened to **ortho.**
 ▸ orthochromatism (ˌɔːθəʊ'krəʊməˌtɪzəm) *n*

orthoclase ('ɔːθəʊˌkleɪs, -ˌkleɪz) *n* a white or coloured feldspar mineral consisting of an aluminium silicate of potassium in monoclinic crystalline form.

orthodontics (ˌɔːθəʊˈdɒntɪks) *or* **orthodontia** (ˌɔːθəʊˈdɒntɪə) *n* (*functioning as sing*) the branch of dentistry concerned with preventing or correcting irregularities of the teeth.
  ▸ **ortho'dontic** *adj* ▸ **ortho'dontist** *n*

orthodox (ˈɔːθəˌdɒks) *adj* **1** conforming with established standards, as in religion, behaviour, or attitudes. **2** conforming to the Christian faith as established by the early Church. [C16: via Church L from Gk *orthodoxos*, from *orthos* correct + *doxa* belief]
  ▸ **'ortho,doxy** *n*

Orthodox (ˈɔːθəˌdɒks) *adj* **1** of or relating to the Orthodox Church of the East. **2** (*sometimes not cap.*) of or relating to Orthodox Judaism.

Orthodox Church *n* **1** the collective body of those Eastern Churches that were separated from the western Church in the 11th century and are in communion with the Greek patriarch of Constantinople. **2** any of these Churches.

Orthodox Judaism *n* a form of Judaism characterized by traditional interpretation and strict observance of the Mosaic Law.

orthoepy (ˈɔːθəʊˌɛpɪ) *n* the study of correct or standard pronunciation. [C17: from Gk *orthoepeia*, from ORTHO- straight + *epos* word]
  ▸ **orthoepic** (ˌɔːθəʊˈɛpɪk) *adj* ▸ **ortho'epically** *adv*

orthogenesis (ˌɔːθəʊˈdʒɛnɪsɪs) *n* **1** *Biol.* **1a** evolution of a group of organisms in a particular direction, which is generally predetermined. **1b** the theory that proposes such a development. **2** the theory that there is a series of stages through which all cultures pass in the same order.
  ▸ **orthogenetic** (ˌɔːθəʊdʒɪˈnɛtɪk) *adj* ▸ **,orthoge'netically** *adv*

orthogonal (ɔːˈθɒɡənᵊl) *adj* relating to, consisting of, or involving right angles; perpendicular.
  ▸ **or'thogonally** *adv*

orthographic (ˌɔːθəˈɡræfɪk) *or* **orthographical** *adj* of or relating to spelling.
  ▸ **,ortho'graphically** *adv*

orthography (ɔːˈθɒɡrəfɪ) *n, pl* **orthographies. 1** a writing system. **2a** spelling considered to be correct. **2b** the principles underlying spelling. **3** the study of spelling.
  ▸ **or'thographer** *or* **or'thographist** *n*

orthopaedics *or US* **orthopedics** (ˌɔːθəʊˈpiːdɪks) *n* (*functioning as sing*) **1** the branch of surgery concerned with disorders of the spine and joints and the repair of deformities of these parts. **2** dental orthopaedics. another name for **orthodontics**.
  ▸ **,ortho'paedic** *or US* **,ortho'pedic** *adj* ▸ **,ortho'paedist** *or US* **,ortho'pedist** *n*

orthopteran (ɔːˈθɒptərən) *n, pl* **orthoptera** (-tərə). **1** Also: **orthopteron** (*pl* **orthoptera**). any orthopterous insect. ♦ *adj* **2** another word for **orthopterous**.

orthopterous (ɔːˈθɒptərəs) *adj* of, relating to, or belonging to a large order of insects, including crickets, locusts, and grasshoppers, having leathery forewings and membranous hind wings.

orthoptic (ɔːˈθɒptɪk) *adj* relating to normal binocular vision.

orthoptics (ɔːˈθɒptɪks) *n* (*functioning as sing*) the science or practice of correcting defective vision, as by exercises to strengthen weak eye muscles.
  ▸ **or'thoptist** *n*

orthorhombic (ˌɔːθəʊˈrɒmbɪk) *adj Crystallog.* relating to the crystal system characterized by three mutually perpendicular unequal axes.

Ortles ★ (*Italian* ˈɔːtles) *pl n* a range of the Alps in N Italy. Highest peak: 3899 m (12 792 ft). Also called: **Ortler** (ˈɔːtlə).

ortolan (ˈɔːtələn) *n* **1** a brownish Old World bunting regarded as a delicacy. **2** any of various other small birds eaten as delicacies, esp. the bobolink. [C17: via F from L *hortulānus*, from *hortulus*, dim. of *hortus* garden]

Orton ★ (ˈɔːtən) *n* Joe. 1933–67, British dramatist, his

black comedies include *Loot* (1965) and *What the Butler Saw* (1969).

Oruro ★ (*Spanish* oˈruro) *n* a city in W Bolivia: a former silver-mining centre; university (1892); tin, copper, and tungsten. Pop.: 201 831 (1993 est.).

Orvieto ★ (*Italian* orˈvjɛːto) *n* **1** a market town in central Italy, in Umbria: Etruscan remains. Pop.: 21 575 (1990). Latin name: **Urbs Vetus** (ʊəbz ˈviːtəs). **2** a light white wine from this region.

Orwell ★ (ˈɔːwəl, -wɛl) *n* George, real name *Eric Arthur Blair*. 1903–50, British novelist, born in India. His works include *The Road to Wigan Pier* (1932), *Animal Farm* (1945), and *1984* (1949).
  ▸ **Orwellian** (ɔːˈwɛlɪən) *adj*

-ory[1] *suffix forming nouns.* **1** indicating a place for: *observatory*. **2** something having a specified use: *directory*. [via OF *-orie*, from L *-ōrium, -ōria*]

-ory[2] *suffix forming adjectives.* of or relating to; characterized by; having the effect of: *contributory*. [via OF *-orie*, from L *-ōrius*]

Oryol ★ (*Russian* aˈrjol) *n* a variant spelling of **Orel**.

oryx (ˈɒrɪks) *n, pl* **oryxes** *or* **oryx.** any large African antelope of the genus *Oryx*, typically having long straight nearly upright horns. [C14: via L from Gk *orux* stonemason's axe, used also of the pointed horns of an antelope]

os[1] (ɒs) *n, pl* **ossa** (ˈɒsə). *Anat.* the technical name for **bone**. [C16: from L: bone]

os[2] (ɒs) *n, pl* **ora**. *Anat., zool.* a mouth or mouthlike part or opening. [C18: from L]

Os *the chemical symbol for* osmium.

OS *abbrev. for:* **1** Old Saxon (language). **2** Old Style. **3** Ordinary Seaman. **4** (in Britain) Ordnance Survey. **5** outsize.

Osage orange (əʊˈseɪdʒ) *n* **1** a North American thorny tree, grown for hedges and ornament. **2** the warty orange-like fruit of this plant. [from *Osage* Amerind tribe]

Osaka ★ (əʊˈsɑːkə) *n* a port in S Japan, on S Honshu on **Osaka Bay** (an inlet of the Pacific): the third largest city in Japan (the chief commercial city during feudal times); university (1931); an industrial and commercial centre. Pop.: 2 602 352 (1995).

Osborne ★ (ˈɒzbən, -ˌbɔːn) *n* John (James). 1929–94, British dramatist. His plays include *Look Back in Anger* (1956), *The Entertainer* (1957), *Luther* (1960), and *Déjà Vu* (1992).

Oscar (ˈɒskə) *n* any of several small gold statuettes awarded annually in the US for outstanding achievements in films. Official name: **Academy Award.** [C20: said to have been named after a remark made by a secretary that it reminded her of her uncle Oscar]

Oscar II ★ *n* 1829–1907, king of Sweden (1872–1907) and of Norway (1872–1905).

oscillate (ˈɒsɪˌleɪt) *vb* **oscillates, oscillating, oscillated. 1** (*intr*) to move or swing from side to side regularly. **2** (*intr*) to waver between opinions, courses of action, etc. **3** *Physics.* to undergo or produce or cause to undergo or produce oscillation. [C18: from L *oscillāre* to swing]

oscillating universe theory *n* the theory that the universe is oscillating between periods of expansion and contraction.

oscillation (ˌɒsɪˈleɪʃən) *n* **1** *Statistics, physics.* **1a** regular fluctuation in value, position, or state about a mean value, such as the variation in an alternating current. **1b** a single cycle of such a fluctuation. **2** the act or process of oscillating.
  ▸ **oscillatory** (ˈɒsɪlətərɪ, -trɪ) *adj*

oscillator (ˈɒsɪˌleɪtə) *n* **1** a circuit or instrument for producing an alternating current or voltage of a required frequency. **2** any instrument for producing oscillations. **3** a person or thing that oscillates.

oscillogram (ɒˈsɪləˌɡræm) *n* the recording obtained from an oscillograph or the trace on an oscilloscope screen.

oscillograph (ɒˈsɪləˌɡrɑːf) *n* a device for producing a graphical record of the variation of an oscillating quantity, such as an electric current.
  ▸ **oscillographic** (ɒˌsɪləˈɡræfɪk) *adj* ▸ **oscillography** (ˌɒsɪˈlɒɡrəfɪ) *n*

★ people and places

oscilloscope (ɒ'sɪlə,skəʊp) *n* an instrument for producing a representation of a rapidly changing quantity on the screen of a cathode-ray tube.

oscine ('ɒsaɪn, 'ɒsɪn) *adj* of, relating to, or belonging to the suborder of passerine birds that includes most of the songbirds.   [C17: via NL from L *oscen* singing bird]

oscitancy ('ɒsɪtənsɪ) *or* **oscitance** *n*, *pl* **oscitancies** *or* **oscitances.** **1** the state of being drowsy, lazy, or inattentive. **2** the act of yawning.   ◆ Also called: **oscitation.**   [C17: from L *oscitāre* to yawn]
  ▶ 'oscitant *adj*

oscular ('ɒskjʊlə) *adj* **1** *Zool.* of or relating to a mouthlike aperture, esp. of a sponge. **2** of or relating to the mouth or to kissing.

osculate ('ɒskjʊ,leɪt) *vb* **osculates, osculating, osculated.** **1** *Usually humorous.* to kiss. **2** (*intr*) (of an organism) to be intermediate between two taxonomic groups. **3** *Geom.* to touch in osculation.   [C17: from L *ōsculārī* to kiss]

osculation (,ɒskjʊ'leɪʃən) *n* **1** *Maths.* Also called: **tacnode.** a point at which two branches of a curve have a common tangent, each branch extending in both directions of the tangent. **2** *Rare.* the act of kissing.
  ▶ **osculatory** ('ɒskjʊlətərɪ, -trɪ) *adj*

-ose[1] *suffix forming adjectives.* possessing; resembling: *grandiose.*   [from L *-ōsus*; see -OUS]

-ose[2] *suffix forming nouns.* **1** indicating a carbohydrate, esp. a sugar: *lactose.* **2** indicating a decomposition product of protein: *albumose.*   [from GLUCOSE]

Oshawa ★ ('ɒʃəwə) *n* a city in central Canada, in SE Ontario on Lake Ontario: motor-vehicle industry. Pop.: 129 344 (1991).

Oshogbo ★ (ə'ʃɒgbəʊ) *n* a city in SW Nigeria: trade centre. Pop.: 465 000 (1995 est.).

osier ('əʊzɪə) *n* **1** any of various willow trees, whose flexible branches or twigs are used for making baskets, etc. **2** a twig or branch from such a tree. **3** any of several North American dogwoods, esp. the red osier.   [C14: from OF, prob. from Med. L *ausēria*, ? of Gaulish origin]

Osijek ★ (*Serbo-Croat* 'ɒsijɛk) *n* a town in NE Croatia, on the Drava River: under Turkish rule from 1526 to 1687. Pop.: 129 792 (1991). Ancient name: **Mursa** ('mʊəsə).

Osiris ★ (əʊ'saɪrɪs) *n* an ancient Egyptian god, ruler of the underworld and judge of the dead.
  ▶ O'sirian *adj*

-osis *suffix forming nouns.* **1** indicating a process or state: *metamorphosis.* **2** indicating a diseased condition: *tuberculosis.* Cf. **-iasis.** **3** indicating the formation or development of something: *fibrosis.*   [from Gk, suffix used to form nouns from verbs with infinitives in *-oein* or *-oun*]

Oslo ★ ('ɒzləʊ; *Norwegian* 'uslu) *n* the capital and chief port of Norway, in the southeast at the head of **Oslo Fjord** (an inlet of the Skagerrak): founded in about 1050; university (1811); a major commercial and industrial centre, producing about a quarter of Norway's total output. Pop.: 493 973 (1997 est.). Former names: **Christiania** (1624–1877), **Kristi'ania** (1877–1924).

Osman I ('ɒzmən, ɒz'mɑːn) *or* **Othman I** ★ *n* 1259–1326, Turkish sultan; founder of the Ottoman Empire.

Osmanli (ɒz'mænlɪ) *adj* **1** of or relating to the Ottoman Empire.   ◆ *n* **2** (formerly) a subject of the Ottoman Empire.   [C19: from Turkish, from OSMAN I]

osmiridium (,ɒzmɪ'rɪdɪəm) *n* a very hard corrosion-resistant white or grey natural alloy of osmium and iridium: used in pen nibs, etc.   [C19: from OSM(IUM) + IRIDIUM]

osmium ('ɒzmɪəm) *n* a very hard brittle bluish-white metal, the heaviest known element, occurring with platinum and alloyed with iridium in osmiridium. Symbol: Os; atomic no.: 76; atomic wt.: 190.2.   [C19: from Gk *osmē* smell, from its penetrating odour]

osmoregulation (,ɒzməʊ,rɛgjʊ'leɪʃən) *n* *Zool.* the adjustment of the osmotic pressure of a cell or organism in relation to the surrounding fluid.

osmose ('ɒzməʊs, -məʊz, 'ɒs-) *vb* **osmoses, osmosing, osmosed.** to undergo or cause to undergo osmosis.   [C19 (*n*): abstracted from the earlier terms *endosmose* and *exosmose*; rel. to Gk *ōsmos* push]

osmosis (ɒz'məʊsɪs, ɒs-) *n* **1** the tendency of the solvent of a less concentrated solution of dissolved molecules to pass through a semipermeable membrane into a more concentrated solution until both solutions are of the same concentration. **2** diffusion through any membrane or porous barrier, as in dialysis. **3** gradual or unconscious assimilation or adoption, as of ideas.   [C19: Latinized form from OSMOSE, from Gk *ōsmos* push]
  ▶ **osmotic** (ɒz'mɒtɪk, ɒs-) *adj* ▶ **os'motically** *adv*

osmotic pressure *n* the pressure necessary to prevent osmosis into a given solution when the solution is separated from the pure solvent by a semipermeable membrane.

osmunda (ɒz'mʌndə) *or* **osmund** ('ɒzmənd) *n* any of a genus of ferns having large spreading fronds.   [C13: from OF *osmonde*, from ?]

Osnabrück ★ (*German* ɔsna'brʏk) *n* an industrial city in NW Germany, in Lower Saxony: a member of the Hanseatic League in the Middle Ages. Pop.: 168 050 (1995 est.).

osprey ('ɒsprɪ, -preɪ) *n* **1** a large broad-winged fish-eating diurnal bird of prey, with a dark back and whitish head and underparts. Often called (US and Canad.): **fish hawk. 2** any of the feathers of various other birds, used esp. as trimming for hats.   [C15: from OF *ospres*, apparently from L *ossifraga*, lit.: bone-breaker, from *os* bone + *frangere* to break]

Ossa ★ ('ɒsə) *n* a mountain in NE Greece, in E Thessaly: famous in mythology for the attempt of the twin giants, Otus and Ephialtes, to reach heaven by piling Ossa on Olympus and Pelion on Ossa. Height: 1978 m (6489 ft).

ossein ('ɒsɪɪn) *n* a protein that forms the organic matrix of bone.   [C19: from L *osseus* bony, from *os* bone]

osseous ('ɒsɪəs) *adj* consisting of or containing bone, bony.   [C17: from L *osseus*, from *os* bone]
  ▶ 'osseously *adv*

Ossetia ★ (ɒ'siːʃə) *n* a region of central Asia, in the Caucasus: consists administratively of the North Ossetian Republic of Russia and the South Ossetian Autonomous Region of Georgia.
  ▶ Os'setic *or* Os'setian *adj*

Ossian ★ ('ɒsɪən) *n* a legendary Irish hero and bard of the 3rd century A.D. See also (James) **Macpherson.**
  ▶ ,Ossi'anic *adj*

Ossietzky ★ (,ɒsɪ'ɛtskɪ) *n* **Carl von** (karl fɒn). 1889–1938, German pacifist; imprisoned for revealing Germany's secret rearmament (1931–32) and again under Hitler (1933–36): Nobel peace prize 1935.

ossify ('ɒsɪ,faɪ) *vb* **ossifies, ossifying, ossified. 1** to convert or be converted into bone. **2** (*intr*) (of habits, attitudes, etc.) to become inflexible.   [C18: from F *ossifier*, from L *os* bone + *facere* to make]
  ▶ ,ossifi'cation *n* ▶ 'ossi,fier *n*

ossuary ('ɒsjʊərɪ) *n*, *pl* **ossuaries.** any container for the burial of human bones, such as an urn or vault.   [C17: from LL *ossuārium*, from L *os* bone]

osteal ('ɒstɪəl) *adj* **1** of or relating to bone or to the skeleton. **2** composed of bone; osseous.   [C19: from Gk *osteon* bone]

osteitis (,ɒstɪ'aɪtɪs) *n* inflammation of a bone.
  ▶ osteitic (,ɒstɪ'ɪtɪk) *adj*

Ostend ★ (ɒs'tɛnd) *n* a port and resort in NW Belgium, in West Flanders on the North Sea. Pop.: 68 858 (1995 est.). French name: **Ostende** (ɔstɑ̃d). Flemish name: **Oostende.**

ostensible (ɒ'stɛnsɪb'l) *adj* **1** apparent; seeming. **2** pretended.   [C18: via F from Med. L *ostensibilis*, from L *ostendere* to show, from *ob-* before + *tendere* to extend]
  ▶ os,tensi'bility *n* ▶ os'tensibly *adv*

ostensive (ɒ'stɛnsɪv) *adj* **1** obviously or manifestly demonstrative. **2** (of a definition) giving examples of objects to which a word or phrase is properly applied. **3** a less common word for **ostensible.**   [C17: from LL *ostentīvus*, from L *ostendere* to show; see OSTENSIBLE]
  ▶ os'tensively *adv*

ostentation (,ɒstɛn'teɪʃən) *n* pretentious, showy, or vulgar display.
  ▶ ,osten'tatious *adj* ▶ ,osten'tatiously *adv* ▶ ,osten-'tatiousness *n*

★ **people and places**

osteo- *or before a vowel* **oste-** *combining form.* indicating bone or bones. [from Gk *osteon*]

osteoarthritis (ˌɒstɪəʊɑːˈθraɪtɪs) *n* chronic inflammation of the joints, esp. those that bear weight, with pain and stiffness.
▶ **osteoarthritic** (ˌɒstɪəʊɑːˈθrɪtɪk) *adj, n*

osteology (ˌɒstɪˈɒlədʒɪ) *n* the study of the structure and function of bones.
▶ **osteological** (ˌɒstɪəˈlɒdʒɪkˈl) *adj* ▶ ˌosteoˈlogically *adv*
▶ ˌosteˈologist *n*

osteoma (ˌɒstɪˈəʊmə) *n, pl* **osteomata** (-mətə) *or* **osteomas**. a benign tumour composed of bone or bonelike tissue.

osteomalacia (ˌɒstɪəʊməˈleɪʃɪə) *n* a disease characterized by softening of the bones, resulting from a deficiency of vitamin D and of calcium and phosphorus. [C19: from NL, from OSTEO- + Gk *malakia* softness]
▶ ˌosteomaˈlacial *or* **osteomalacic** (ˌɒstɪəʊməˈlæsɪk) *adj*

osteomyelitis (ˌɒstɪəʊˌmaɪɪˈlaɪtɪs) *n* inflammation of bone marrow, caused by infection.

osteopathy (ˌɒstɪˈɒpəθɪ) *n* a system of healing based on the manipulation of bones or other parts of the body.
▶ ˈosteoˌpath *n* ▶ **osteopathic** (ˌɒstɪəˈpæθɪk) *adj* ▶ ˌosteoˈpathically *adv*

osteoplasty (ˈɒstɪəˌplæstɪ) *n, pl* **osteoplasties**. the branch of surgery concerned with bone repair or bone grafting.

osteoporosis (ˌɒstɪəʊpɔːˈrəʊsɪs) *n* porosity and brittleness of the bones caused by loss of calcium from the bone matrix. [C19: from OSTEO- + PORE² + -OSIS]
▶ **osteoporotic** (ˌɒstɪəʊpɔːˈrɒtɪk) *adj*

Österreich ★ (ˈøːstəraiç) *n* the German name for **Austria**.

Ostia ★ (ˈɒstɪə) *n* an ancient town in W central Italy, originally at the mouth of the Tiber but now about 6 km (4 miles) inland: served as the port of ancient Rome; harbours built by Claudius and Trajan; ruins excavated since 1854.

ostinato (ˌɒstɪˈnɑːtəʊ) *n, pl* **ostinatos**. a a continuously reiterated musical phrase. b (*as modifier*): *an ostinato passage*. [It.: from L *obstinātus* OBSTINATE]

ostler *or* **hostler** (ˈɒslə) *n Arch.* a stableman, esp. one at an inn. [C15: var. of *hostler*, from HOSTEL]

Ostmark (ˈɒstmɑːk; *German* ˈɔstmark) *n* (formerly) the standard monetary unit of East Germany, divided into 100 pfennigs. [G, lit.: east mark]

Ostpreussen ★ (ˈɔstprɔʏsən) *n* the German name for **East Prussia**.

ostracize *or* **ostracise** (ˈɒstrəˌsaɪz) *vb* **ostracizes, ostracizing, ostracized** *or* **ostracises, ostracising, ostracised**. (*tr*) **1** to exclude or banish (a person) from a particular group, society, etc. **2** (in ancient Greece) to punish by temporary exile. [C17: from Gk *ostrakizein* to select someone for banishment by voting on potsherds, from *ostrakon* potsherd]
▶ ˈostracism *n* ▶ ˈostraˌcizable *or* ˈostraˌcisable *adj*
▶ ˈostra,cizer *or* ˈostra,ciser *n*

Ostrava ★ (*Czech* ˈɔstrava) *n* an industrial city in the E Czech Republic, on the River Oder: the chief coal-mining area in the Czech Republic, in Upper Silesia. Pop.: 325 827 (1995 est.).

ostrich (ˈɒstrɪtʃ) *n, pl* **ostriches** *or* **ostrich**. **1** a fast-running flightless African bird that is the largest living bird with stout two-toed feet and dark feathers, except on the naked head, neck, and legs. **2** *American ostrich*. another name for **rhea**. **3** a person who refuses to recognize the truth, reality, etc. [C13: from OF *ostrice*, from L *avis* bird + LL *struthio* ostrich, from Gk *strouthiōn*]

Ostwald ★ (*German* ˈɔstvalt) *n* **Wilhelm** (ˈvɪlhelm). 1853–1932, German chemist, noted for his pioneering work in catalysis: Nobel prize for chemistry 1909.

Osun ★ (əʊˈsʌn) *n* a state of SW Nigeria. Capital: Oshogbo. Pop.: 2 269 107 (1992 est.). Area: 9251 sq. km (3572 sq. miles).

Oswald ★ (ˈɒzwəld) *n* **1 Saint**. ?605–41 A.D., king of Northumbria (634–41); with St Aidan he restored Christianity to the region. Feast day: Aug. 5. **2 Lee Harvey**. 1939–63, presumed assassin (1963) of US president John F. Kennedy; murdered by Jack Ruby two days later.

Oświęcim ★ (*Polish* ɔʃˈfjɛntʃim) *n* the Polish name for **Auschwitz**.

OT *abbrev. for:* **1** occupational therapy. **2** Old Testament. **3** overtime.

Otago ★ (ɒˈtɑːgəʊ) *n* a council region of New Zealand, formerly a province, founded by Scottish settlers in the south of South Island. The University of Otago (1869) in Dunedin is the oldest university in New Zealand. Chief town: Dunedin. Pop.: 191 684 (1996).

otalgia (əʊˈtældʒɪə, -dʒə) *n* the technical name for **earache**.

OTC (in Britain) *abbrev. for:* **1** Officers' Training Corps. **2** over-the-counter.

OTE *abbrev. for* on target earnings: referring to the salary a salesman should be able to achieve.

other (ˈʌðə) *determiner* **1a** (when used before a singular noun, usually preceded by *the*) the remaining (one or ones in a group of which one or some have been specified): *I'll read the other sections of the paper later*. **1b the other**. (*as pron; functioning as sing*): *one walks while the other rides*. **2** (a) different (one or ones from that or those already specified or understood): *no other man but you*. **3** additional; further: *there are no other possibilities*. **4** (preceded by *every*) alternate; two: *it buzzes every other minute*. **5 other than**. **5a** apart from; besides: *a lady other than his wife*. **5b** different from: *he couldn't be other than what he is*. Archaic form: **other from. 6 no other**. *Arch.* nothing else: *I can do no other*. **7 or other**. (preceded by a phrase or word with *some*) used to add vagueness to the preceding pronoun, noun, or noun phrase: *he's somewhere or other*. **8 other things being equal**. conditions being the same or unchanged. **9 the other day, night**, etc. a few days, nights, etc., ago. **10 the other thing**. an unexpressed alternative. ◆ *pron* **11** another: *show me one other*. **12** (*pl*) additional or further ones. **13** (*pl*) other people or things. **14 the others**. the remaining ones (of a group). ◆ *adv* **15** (usually used with a negative and foll. by *than*) otherwise; differently: *they couldn't behave other than they do*. [OE *ōther*]
▶ ˈotherness *n*

> USAGE NOTE   See at **otherwise**.

other-directed *adj* guided by values derived from external influences.

other ranks *pl n* (*rarely sing*) *Chiefly Brit.* (in the armed forces) all those who do not hold a commissioned rank.

otherwise (ˈʌðəˌwaɪz) *sentence connector*. **1** or else; if not, then: *go home — otherwise your mother will worry*. ◆ *adv* **2** differently: *I wouldn't have thought otherwise*. **3** in other respects: *an otherwise hopeless situation*. ◆ *adj* **4** (*predicative*) of an unexpected nature; different: *the facts are otherwise*. ◆ *pron* **5** something different in outcome: *success or otherwise*. [C14: from OE *on ōthre wīsan* in other manner]

> USAGE NOTE   The expression *otherwise than* means *in any other way than* and should not be followed by an adjective: *no-one taught by this method can be other than* (not *otherwise than*) *successful; you are not allowed to use the building otherwise than as a private dwelling*.

other world *n* the spirit world or afterlife.

otherworldly (ˌʌðəˈwɜːldlɪ) *adj* **1** of or relating to the spiritual or imaginative world. **2** impractical or unworldly.
▶ ˌotherˈworldliness *n*

Othin ★ (ˈəʊðɪn) *n* a variant of **Odin**.

Othman (ˈɒθmən, ɒθˈmɑːn) *adj, n* a variant of **Ottoman**.

Othman I ★ *n* a variant of **Osman I**.

Otho I ★ (ˈəʊθəʊ) *n* a variant of **Otto I**.

otic (ˈəʊtɪk, ˈɒtɪk) *adj* of or relating to the ear. [C17: from Gk *ōtikos*, from *ous* ear]

-otic *suffix forming adjectives.* **1** relating to or affected by: *sclerotic*. **2** causing: *narcotic*. [from Gk *-ōtikos*]

★ people and places

otiose ('əʊtɪ,əʊs, -,əʊz) *adj* **1** serving no useful purpose: *otiose language.* **2** *Rare.* indolent; lazy. [C18: from L *ōtiōsus* leisured, from *ōtium* leisure]
▸ otiosity (,əʊtɪ'ɒsɪtɪ) *or* 'oti,oseness *n*

otitis (əʊ'taɪtɪs) *n* inflammation of the ear.

oto- *or before a vowel* **ot-** *combining form.* indicating the ear. [from Gk *ous*, *ōt-* ear]

otolaryngology (,əʊtəʊ,lærɪŋ'ɡɒlədʒɪ) *n* another name for **otorhinolaryngology**.
▸ otolaryngological (,əʊtəʊlə,rɪŋɡə'lɒdʒɪkˀl) *adj* ▸ ,oto-,laryn'gologist *n*

otolith ('əʊtəʊ,lɪθ) *n* any of the granules of calcium carbonate in the inner ear of vertebrates. Movement of otoliths, caused by a change in the animal's position, stimulates sensory hair cells, which convey information to the brain.
▸ ,oto'lithic *adj*

otology (əʊ'tɒlədʒɪ) *n* the branch of medicine concerned with the ear.
▸ otological (,əʊtə'lɒdʒɪkˀl) *adj* ▸ o'tologist *n*

O'Toole (əʊ'tuːl) *n* (**Seamus**) ('ʃeɪməs) **Peter**. born 1932, British actor, born in Ireland. His films include *Lawrence of Arabia* (1962), *The Lion in Winter* (1968), and *Fairytale* (1998).

otorhinolaryngology (,əʊtəʊ,raɪnəʊ,lærɪŋ'ɡɒlədʒɪ) *n* the branch of medicine concerned with the ear, nose, and throat. Sometimes called **otolaryngology**.

otoscope ('əʊtəʊ,skəʊp) *n* a medical instrument for examining the external ear.
▸ otoscopic (,əʊtəʊ'skɒpɪk) *adj*

Otranto ★ (*Italian* 'ɔːtranto) *n* a small port in SE Italy, in Apulia on the **Strait of Otranto**: the most easterly town in Italy; an important Roman port. Pop.: 5075 (1987 est.).

OTT *Sl. abbrev. for* over the top: see **top**[1] (sense 16b).

ottava rima (əʊ'tɑːvə 'riːmə) *n Prosody.* a stanza form consisting of eight iambic pentameter lines, rhyming a b a b a b c c. [It.: eighth rhyme]

Ottawa ★ ('ɒtəwə) *n* **1** the capital of Canada, in E Ontario on the Ottawa River: name changed from Bytown to Ottawa in 1854. Pop.: 313 987 (1991). **2** a river in central Canada, rising in W Quebec and flowing west, then southeast to join the St Lawrence River as its chief tributary at Montreal; forms the border between Quebec and Ontario for most of its length. Length: 1120 km (696 miles).

otter ('ɒtə) *n, pl* **otters** *or* **otter**. **1** a freshwater carnivorous mammal, esp. the **Eurasian otter**, typically having smooth fur, a streamlined body, and webbed feet. **2** the fur of this animal. **3** a type of fishing tackle consisting of a weighted board to which hooked and baited lines are attached. [OE *otor*]

Otterburn ★ ('ɒtə,bɜːn) *n* a village in NE England, in central Northumberland: scene of a battle (1388) in which the Scots, led by the Earl of Douglas, defeated the English, led by Hotspur.

otter hound *n* a large rough-coated dog of a breed formerly used for otter hunting.

Otto ★ ('ɒtəʊ) *n* **Nikolaus August**. 1832–91, German engineer; invented the four-stroke engine.

Otto I ('ɒtəʊ) *or* **Otho I** ★ *n* called *the Great*. 912–73 A.D., king of Germany (936–73); Holy Roman Emperor (962–73).

ottoman ('ɒtəmən) *n, pl* **ottomans**. **1a** a low padded seat, usually armless, sometimes in the form of a chest. **1b** a cushioned footstool. **2** a corded fabric. [C17: from F *ottomane*, fem. of OTTOMAN]

Ottoman ('ɒtəmən) *or* **Othman** ('ɒθmən) *adj* **1** *History.* of or relating to the Ottomans or the Ottoman Empire. **2** denoting or relating to the Turkish language. ◆ *n, pl* **Ottomans** *or* **Othmans**. **3** a member of a Turkish people who invaded the Near East in the late 13th century. [C17: from F, via Med. L, from Ar. *Othmānī* Turkish, from Turkish *Othman* OSMAN I]

Ottoman Empire *n* the former Turkish empire in Europe, Asia, and Africa, which lasted from the late 13th century until the end of World War I.

Otway ★ ('ɒtweɪ) *n* **Thomas**. 1652–85, English dramatist, noted for *Venice Preserv'd* (1682).

ou (əʊ) *n S. African. sl.* a man, bloke, or chap. [from Afrik., ?from Du.]

OU *abbrev. for:* **1** the Open University. **2** Oxford University.

Ouachita *or* **Washita** ★ ('wɒʃɪ,tɔː) *n* a river in the S central US, rising in the **Ouachita Mountains** and flowing east, south, and southeast into the Red River in E Louisiana. Length: 974 km (605 miles).

Ouagadougou ★ (,wɑːɡə'duːɡuː) *n* the capital of Burkina-Faso, on the central plateau: terminus of the railway from Abidjan (Côte d'Ivoire). Pop.: 690 000 (1993 est.).

ouananiche (,wɑːnə'niːʃ) *n* a landlocked variety of the Atlantic salmon found in lakes in SE Canada. [from Canad. F, of Amerind origin, from *wananish*, dim. of *wanans* salmon]

oubaas ('əʊ,bɑːs) *n S. African.* a man in authority. [from Afrik., from Du. *oud* old + *baas* boss]

Oubangui ★ (uː'bɑːŋɡiː, juː'bæŋɡɪ) *n* the French name for **Ubangi**.

oubliette (,uːblɪ'et) *n* a dungeon, the only entrance to which is through the top. [C19: from F, from *oublier* to forget]

ouch (aʊtʃ) *interj* an exclamation of sharp sudden pain.

Oudh ★ (aʊd) *n* **1** a region of N India, in central Uttar Pradesh: annexed by Britain in 1856 and a centre of the Indian Mutiny (1857–58); joined with Agra in 1877, becoming the United Provinces of Agra and Oudh in 1902, which were renamed Uttar Pradesh in 1950. **2** another name for **Ayodha**.

Ouessant ★ (wesɑ̃) *n* the French name for **Ushant**.

ought[1] (ɔːt) *vb* (foll. by *to; takes an infinitive or implied infinitive*) used as an auxiliary: **1** to indicate duty or obligation: *you ought to pay.* **2** to express prudent expediency: *you ought to be more careful with your money.* **3** (usually with reference to future time) to express probability or expectation: *you ought to finish this by Friday.* **4** to express a desire or wish on the part of the speaker: *you ought to come next week.* [OE *āhte*, p.t. of *āgan* to OWE]

> **USAGE NOTE** In correct English, *ought* is not used with *did* or *had*. *I ought not to do it*, not *I didn't ought to do it*; *I ought not to have done it*, not *I hadn't ought to have done it*.

ought[2] (ɔːt) *pron, adv* a variant spelling of **aught**.

ought[3] (ɔːt) *n* a less common word for **nought** (zero). [C19: mistaken division of *a nought* as *an ought*; see NOUGHT]

Ouija board ('wiːdʒə) *n Trademark.* a board on which are marked the letters of the alphabet. Answers to questions are spelt out by a pointer and are supposedly formed by spirits. [C19: from F *oui* yes + G *ja* yes]

Oujda ★ (uːdʒ'dɑː) *n* a city in NE Morocco, near the border with Algeria: frontier post. Pop.: 331 000 (1993 est.).

Oulu ★ ('ɒulu) *n* an industrial city and port in W Finland, on the Gulf of Bothnia: university (1959). Pop.: 111 556 (1997 est.). Swedish name: **Uleåborg**.

ouma ('əʊmɑː) *n S. African.* **1** grandmother, esp. in titular use with her surname. **2** *Sl.* any elderly woman. [from Afrik., from Du. *oma* grandmother]

ounce[1] (aʊns) *n* **1** a unit of weight equal to one sixteenth of a pound (avoirdupois). Abbrev.: **oz. 2** a unit of weight equal to one twelfth of a Troy or Apothecaries' pound; 1 ounce is equal to 480 grains. **3** short for **fluid ounce**. **4** a small portion or amount. [C14: from OF *unce*, from L *uncia* a twelfth]

ounce[2] (aʊns) *n* another name for **snow leopard**. [C18: from OF *once*, by mistaken division of *lonce* as if *l'once*, from L LYNX]

oupa ('əʊpɑː) *n S. African.* **1** grandfather, esp. in titular use with surname. **2** *Sl.* any elderly man. [Afrik.]

our ('aʊə) *determiner* **1** of, belonging to, or associated in some way with us: *our best vodka; our parents are good to us.* **2** belonging to or associated with all people or people in general: *our nearest planet is Venus.* **3** a formal word for *my* used by editors or other writers, and monarchs. [OE *ūre* (genitive pl), from US]

-our *suffix forming nouns.* indicating state, condition, or activity: *behaviour; labour.* [in OF *-eur,* from L *-or,* n. suffix]

Our Father *n* another name for the **Lord's Prayer,** taken from its opening words.

ours ('aʊəz) *pron* **1** something or someone belonging to or associated with us: *ours have blue tags.* **2 of ours.** belonging to or associated with us.

ourself (aʊə'sɛlf) *pron Arch.* a variant of **myself,** formerly used by monarchs or editors.

ourselves (aʊə'sɛlvz) *pron* **1a** the reflexive form of *we* or *us: we ourselves will finish it.* **2** (*preceded by a copula*) our usual selves: *we are ourselves when we're together.* **3** *Not standard.* used instead of *we* or *us* in compound noun phrases: *other people and ourselves.*

-ous *suffix forming adjectives.* **1** having or full of: *dangerous; spacious.* **2** (in chemistry) indicating that an element is chemically combined in the lower of two possible valency states: *ferrous.* Cf. **-ic** (sense 2). [from OF, from L *-sus* or *-us,* Gk *-os,* adj. suffixes]

Ouse ★ (uːz) *n* **1** Also called: **Great Ouse.** a river in E England, rising in Northamptonshire and flowing northeast to the Wash near King's Lynn; for the last 56 km (35 miles) follows mainly artificial channels. Length: 257 km (160 miles). **2** a river in NE England, in Yorkshire, formed by the confluence of the Swale and Ure Rivers; flows southeast to the Humber. Length: 92 km (57 miles). **3** a river in S England, rising in Sussex and flowing south to the English Channel. Length: 48 km (30 miles).

ousel ('uːzəl) *n* a variant spelling of **ouzel.**

oust (aʊst) *vb* (*tr*) **1** to force out of a position or place; supplant or expel. **2** *Property law.* to deprive (a person) of the possession of land, etc. [C16: from Anglo-Norman *ouster,* from L *obstāre* to withstand]

ouster ('aʊstə) *n Property law.* the act of dispossessing of freehold property; eviction.

out (aʊt) *adv* (*when predicative, can in some senses be regarded as adj*) **1** (*often used as a particle*) at or to a point beyond the limits of some location; outside: *get out at once.* **2** (*particle*) used to indicate exhaustion or extinction: *the sugar's run out; put the light out.* **3** not in a particular place, esp., not at home. **4** public; revealed: *the secret is out.* **5** on sale or on view to the public: *the book is being brought out next May.* **6** (of the sun, stars, etc.) visible. **7** in flower: *the roses are out now.* **8** not in fashion, favour, or current usage. **9** not or not any longer worth considering: *that plan is out.* **10** not allowed: *smoking on duty is out.* **11** (of a fire or light) no longer burning or providing illumination. **12** not working: *the radio's out.* **13** Also: **out on strike.** on strike. **14** (of a jury) withdrawn to consider a verdict in private. **15** (*particle*) out of consciousness: *she passed out.* **16** (*particle*) used to indicate a burst of activity as indicated by the verb: *fever broke out.* **17** (*particle*) used to indicate obliteration of an object: *the graffiti was painted out.* **18** (*particle*) used to indicate an approximate drawing or description: *chalk out.* **19** at or to the fullest length or extent: *spread out.* **20** loudly; clearly: *calling out.* **21** desirous of or intent on (something or doing something): *I'm out for as much money as I can get.* **22** (*particle*) used to indicate a goal or object achieved at the end of the action specified by the verb: *he worked it out.* **23** (*preceded by a superlative*) existing: *the friendliest dog out.* **24** an expression in signalling, radio, etc., to indicate the end of a transmission. **25** used up; exhausted: *our supplies are completely out.* **26** worn into holes: *out at the elbows.* **27** inaccurate, deficient, or discrepant: *out by six pence.* **28** not in office or authority. **29** completed or concluded, as of time: *before the year is out.* **30** *Obs.* (of a young woman) in or into society: *Lucinda had a large party when she came out.* **31** *Sport.* denoting the state in which a player is caused to discontinue active participation, esp. in some specified role. **32 out of. 32a** at or to a point outside: *out of his reach.* **32b** away from; not in: *stepping out of line; out of*

focus. **32c** because of; motivated by: *out of jealousy.* **32d** from (a material or source): *made out of plastic.* **32e** not or no longer having any of (a substance, material, etc.): *we're out of sugar.* **32f** no longer in a specified state or condition: *out of work; out of practice.* **32g** (of a horse) born of. ◆ *adj* **33** directed or indicating direction outwards: *the out tray.* **34** (of an island) remote from the mainland. **35** *Inf.* not concealing one's homosexuality. ◆ *prep* **36** *Nonstandard or US.* out of; out through: *he ran out the door.* ◆ *interj* **37a** an exclamation of dismissal, reproach, etc. **37b** (in wireless telegraphy) an expression used to signal that the speaker is signing off. **38 out with it.** a command to make something known immediately, without missing any details. ◆ *n* **39** *Chiefly US.* a method of escape from a place, difficult situation, etc. **40** *Baseball.* an instance of causing a batter to be out by fielding. ◆ *vb* **41** (*tr*) to put or throw out. **42** (*intr*) to be made known or effective despite efforts to the contrary (esp. **in the truth will out**). **43** (*tr*) *Inf.* (of homosexuals) to expose (a public figure) as being a fellow homosexual. **44** *Inf.* to expose something secret, embarrassing, or unknown about (a person): *he was eventually outed as a talented goal scorer.* [OE *ūt*]

> **USAGE NOTE** The use of *out* as a preposition, though common in American English, is regarded as incorrect in British English: *he climbed out of* (not *out*) *a window; he went out through the door.*

out- *prefix* **1** excelling or surpassing in a particular action: *outlast; outlive.* **2** indicating an external location or situation away from the centre: *outpost; outpatient.* **3** indicating emergence, an issuing forth, etc.: *outcrop; outgrowth.* **4** indicating the result of an action: *outcome.*

outage ('aʊtɪdʒ) *n* **1** a quantity of goods missing or lost after storage or shipment. **2** a period of power failure, machine stoppage, etc.

out and away *adv* by far.

out-and-out *adj* (*prenominal*) thoroughgoing; complete.

outback ('aʊt,bæk) *n* **a** the remote bush country of Australia. **b** (*as modifier*): *outback life.*

outbalance (,aʊt'bæləns) *vb* **outbalances, outbalancing, outbalanced.** another word for **outweigh.**

outboard ('aʊt,bɔːd) *adj* **1** (of a boat's engine) portable, with its own propeller, and designed to be attached externally to the stern. **2** in a position away from, or further away from, the centre line of a vessel or aircraft, esp. outside the hull or fuselage. ◆ *adv* **3** away from the centre line of a vessel or aircraft, esp. outside the hull or fuselage. ◆ *n* **4** an outboard motor.

outbound ('aʊt,baʊnd) *adj* going out; outward bound.

outbrave (,aʊt'breɪv) *vb* **outbraves, outbraving, outbraved.** (*tr*) **1** to surpass in bravery. **2** to confront defiantly.

outbreak ('aʊt,breɪk) *n* a sudden, violent, or spontaneous occurrence, esp. of disease or strife.

outbuilding ('aʊt,bɪldɪŋ) *n* a building separate from a main building; outhouse.

outburst ('aʊt,bɜːst) *n* **1** a sudden and violent expression of emotion. **2** an explosion or eruption.

outcast ('aʊt,kɑːst) *n* **1** a person who is rejected or excluded from a social group. **2** a vagabond or wanderer. **3** anything thrown out or rejected. ◆ *adj* **4** rejected, abandoned, or discarded; cast out.

outcaste ('aʊt,kɑːst) *n* **1** a person who has been expelled from a caste. **2** a person having no caste. ◆ *vb* **outcastes, outcasting, outcasted.** **3** (*tr*) to cause (someone) to lose his caste.

outclass (,aʊt'klɑːs) *vb* (*tr*) **1** to surpass in class, quality, etc. **2** to defeat easily.

outcome ('aʊt,kʌm) *n* something that follows from an action or situation; result; consequence.

outcrop *n* ('aʊt,krɒp). **1** part of a rock formation or mineral vein that appears at the surface of the earth. **2** an emergence; appearance. ◆ *vb* (,aʊt'krɒp), **outcrops, out-**

★ **people and places**

cropping, outcropped. **3** (*intr*) (of rock strata, mineral veins, etc.) to protrude through the surface of the earth.

outcry *n* ('aut,krai), *pl* **outcries. 1** a widespread or vehement protest. **2** clamour; uproar. **3** *Commerce.* a method of trading in which dealers shout out bids and offers at a prearranged meeting: *sale by open outcry.* ◆ *vb* (,aut'krai), **outcries, outcrying, outcried.** (*tr*) **4** to cry louder or make more noise than (someone or something).

outdated (,aut'deitid) *adj* old-fashioned or obsolete.

outdo (,aut'du:) *vb* **outdoes, outdoing, outdid, outdone.** (*tr*) to surpass or exceed in performance.

outdoor ('aut'dɔː) *adj* (*prenominal*) taking place, existing, or intended for use in the open air: *outdoor games; outdoor clothes.* Also: **out-of-door.**

outdoors (,aut'dɔːz) *adv* **1** Also: **out-of-doors.** in the open air; outside. ◆ *n* **2** the world outside or far away from human habitation.

outer ('autə) *adj* (*prenominal*) **1** being or located on the outside; external. **2** further from the middle or central part. ◆ *n* **3** *Archery.* **3a** the white outermost ring on a target. **3b** a shot that hits this ring. **4** *Austral. & NZ.* the unsheltered part of the spectator area at a sports ground. **5 on the outer.** *Austral. & NZ.* excluded or neglected.

outer bar *n* (in England) a collective name for junior barristers who plead from outside the bar of the court.

Outer Hebrides ★ *pl n* See **Hebrides.**

Outer Mongolia ★ *n* the former name (until 1924) of (the republic of) **Mongolia.**

outermost ('autə,məust) *adj* furthest from the centre or middle; outmost.

outer space *n* any region of space beyond the atmosphere of the earth.

outfall ('aut,fɔːl) *n* the end of a river, sewer, drain, etc., from which it discharges.

outfield ('aut,fiːld) *n* **1** *Cricket.* the area of the field relatively far from the pitch; the deep. Cf. **infield** (sense 1). **2** *Baseball.* **2a** the area of the playing field beyond the lines connecting first, second, and third bases. **2b** the positions of the left fielder, centre fielder, and right fielder taken collectively. **3** *Agriculture.* farmland most distant from the farmstead.
▶ **'out,fielder** *n*

outfit ('aut,fit) *n* **1** a set of articles or equipment for a particular task, etc. **2** a set of clothes, esp. a carefully selected one. **3** *Inf.* any group or association regarded as a cohesive unit, such as a military company, etc. ◆ *vb* **outfits, outfitting, outfitted. 4** to furnish or be furnished with an outfit, equipment, etc.
▶ **'out,fitter** *n*

outflank (,aut'flæŋk) *vb* (*tr*) **1** to go around the flank of (an opposing army, etc.). **2** to get the better of.

outflow ('aut,fləu) *n* **1** anything that flows out, such as liquid, money, etc. **2** the amount that flows out. **3** the act or process of flowing out.

outfox (,aut'foks) *vb* (*tr*) to surpass in guile or cunning.

outgeneral (,aut'dʒenərəl) *vb* **outgenerals, outgeneralling, outgeneralled** or *US* **outgenerals, outgeneraling, outgeneraled.** (*tr*) to surpass in generalship.

outgo *vb* (,aut'gəu), **outgoes, outgoing, outwent, outgone. 1** (*tr*) to exceed or outstrip. ◆ *n* ('aut,gəu). **2** cost; outgoings; outlay. **3** something that goes out; outflow.

outgoing ('aut,gəuiŋ) *adj* **1** departing; leaving. **2** retiring from office. **3** friendly and sociable. ◆ *n* **4** the act of going out.

outgoings ('aut,gəuiŋz) *pl n* expenditure.

outgrow (,aut'grəu) *vb* **outgrows, outgrowing, outgrew, outgrown.** (*tr*) **1** to grow too large for (clothes, shoes, etc.). **2** to lose (a habit, idea, reputation, etc.) in the course of development or time. **3** to grow larger or faster than.

outgrowth ('aut,grəuθ) *n* **1** a thing growing out of a main body. **2** a development, result, or consequence. **3** the act of growing out.

outgun (,aut'gʌn) *vb* **outguns, outgunning, outgunned.** (*tr*) **1** to surpass in fire power. **2** to surpass in shooting. **3** *Inf.* to surpass or excel.

outhouse ('aut,haus) *n* a building near to, but separate from, a main building; outbuilding.

outing ('autiŋ) *n* **1** a short outward and return journey; trip; excursion. **2** *Inf.* the naming by homosexuals of other prominent homosexuals, often against their will.

outjockey (,aut'dʒɒki) *vb* (*tr*) to outwit by deception.

outlandish (aut'lændiʃ) *adj* **1** grotesquely unconventional in appearance, habits, etc. **2** *Arch.* foreign.
▶ **out'landishly** *adv* ▶ **out'landishness** *n*

outlast (,aut'lɑːst) *vb* (*tr*) to last longer than.

outlaw ('aut,lɔː) *n* **1** (formerly) a person excluded from the law and deprived of its protection. **2** any fugitive from the law, esp. a habitual transgressor. ◆ *vb* (*tr*) **3** to put (a person) outside the law and deprive of its protection. **4** to ban.
▶ **'out,lawry** *n*

outlay *n* ('aut,lei). **1** an expenditure of money, effort, etc. ◆ *vb* (,aut'lei), **outlays, outlaying, outlaid. 2** (*tr*) to spend (money, etc.).

outlet ('autlet, -lit) *n* **1** an opening or vent permitting escape or release. **2a** a market for a product or service. **2b** a commercial establishment retailing the goods of a particular producer or wholesaler. **3** a channel that drains a body of water. **4** a point in a wiring system from which current can be taken to supply electrical devices.

outlier ('aut,laiə) *n* **1** an outcrop of rocks that is entirely surrounded by older rocks. **2** a person, thing, or part situated away from a main or related body. **3** a person who lives away from his place of work, duty, etc.

outline ('aut,lain) *n* **1** a preliminary or schematic plan, draft, etc. **2** (*usually pl*) the important features of a theory, work, etc. **3** the line by which an object or figure is or appears to be bounded. **4a** a drawing or manner of drawing consisting only of external lines. **4b** (*as modifier*): *an outline map.* ◆ *vb* **outlines, outlining, outlined.** (*tr*) **5** to draw or display the outline of. **6** to give the main features or general idea of.

outlive (,aut'liv) *vb* **outlives, outliving, outlived.** (*tr*) **1** to live longer than (someone). **2** to live beyond (a date or period): *he outlived the century.* **3** to live through (an experience).

outlook ('aut,luk) *n* **1** a mental attitude or point of view. **2** the probable or expected condition or outcome of something: *the weather outlook.* **3** the view from a place. **4** view or prospect. **5** the act or state of looking out.

outlying ('aut,laiiŋ) *adj* distant or remote from the main body or centre, as of a town or region.

outmanoeuvre or *US* **outmaneuver** (,autmə'nuːvə) *vb* **outmanoeuvres, outmanoeuvring, outmanoeuvred** or *US* **outmaneuvers, outmaneuvering, outmaneuvered.** (*tr*) to secure a strategic advantage over by skilful manoeuvre.

outmoded (,aut'məudid) *adj* no longer fashionable or widely accepted.
▶ **,out'modedly** *adv* ▶ **,out'modedness** *n*

outmost ('aut,məust) *adj* another word for **outermost.**

out of bounds *adj* (*postpositive*), *adv* **1** (often foll. by *to*) not to be entered (by); barred (to). **2** outside specified or prescribed limits.

out of date *adj* (**out-of-date** when *prenominal*), *adv* no longer valid, current, or fashionable; outmoded.

out-of-door *adj* (*prenominal*) another term for **outdoor.**

out-of-doors *adv*, *adj* (*postpositive*) in the open air; outside. Also: **outdoors.**

out of pocket *adj* (**out-of-pocket** when *prenominal*). **1** (*postpositive*) having lost money, as in a commercial enterprise. **2** without money to spend. **3** (*prenominal*) (of expenses) unbudgeted and paid for in cash.

out of the way *adj* (**out-of-the-way** when *prenominal*). **1** distant from more populous areas. **2** uncommon or unusual.

outpace (,aut'peis) *vb* **outpaces, outpacing, outpaced.** (*tr*) **1** to go faster than (someone). **2** to surpass or outdo (something or someone) in growth, development. etc.

outpatient ('aut,peiʃənt) *n* a nonresident hospital patient. Cf. **inpatient.**

outperform (ˌaʊtpəˈfɔːm) *vb* (*tr*) to outdo or surpass in a specified field or activity.

outplacement (ˈaʊtˌpleɪsmənt) *n* a service that offers counselling and careers advice, esp. to redundant executives, which is paid for by their previous employer.

outpoint (aʊtˈpɔɪnt) *vb* (*tr*) to score more points than.

outport (ˈaʊtˌpɔːt) *n* **1** *Chiefly Brit.* a subsidiary port built in deeper water than the original port. **2** *Canad.* a small fishing village of Newfoundland.

outpost (ˈaʊtˌpəʊst) *n* **1** *Mil.* **1a** a position stationed at a distance from the area occupied by a major formation. **1b** the troops assigned to such a position. **2** an outlying settlement or position.

outpour *n* (ˈaʊtˌpɔː). **1** the act of flowing or pouring out. **2** something that pours out. ◆ *vb* (ˌaʊtˈpɔː). **3** to pour or cause to pour out freely or rapidly.

outpouring (ˈaʊtˌpɔːrɪŋ) *n* **1** a passionate or exaggerated outburst; effusion. **2** another word for **outpour** (senses 1, 2).

output (ˈaʊtˌpʊt) *n* **1** the act of production or manufacture. **2** the amount produced, as in a given period: *a weekly output.* **3** the material produced, manufactured, etc. **4** *Electronics.* **4a** the power, voltage, or current delivered by a circuit or component. **4b** the point at which the signal is delivered. **5** the power, energy, or work produced by an engine or a system. **6** *Computing.* **6a** the information produced by a computer. **6b** the operations and devices involved in producing this information. **7** (*modifier*) of or relating to electronic or computer output: *output signal.* ◆ *vb* **outputs, outputting, outputted** *or* **output.** **8** (*tr*) *Computing.* to cause (data) to be emitted as output.

outrage (ˈaʊtˌreɪdʒ) *n* **1** a wantonly vicious or cruel act. **2** a gross violation of decency, morality, honour, etc. **3** profound indignation, anger, or hurt, caused by such an act. ◆ *vb* **outrages, outraging, outraged.** (*tr*) **4** to cause profound indignation, anger, or resentment in. **5** to offend grossly. **6** to commit an act of wanton viciousness, cruelty, or indecency on. **7** a euphemistic word for **rape**[1]. [C13 (meaning: excess): via F from *outré* beyond, from L *ultrā*]

outrageous (aʊtˈreɪdʒəs) *adj* **1** being or having the nature of an outrage. **2** grossly offensive to decency, authority, etc. **3** violent or unrestrained in behaviour or temperament. **4** extravagant or immoderate.
▸ **out'rageously** *adv* ▸ **out'rageousness** *n*

outrank (ˌaʊtˈræŋk) *vb* (*tr*) **1** to be of higher rank than. **2** to take priority over.

outré (ˈuːtreɪ) *adj* deviating from what is usual or proper. [C18: from F, p.p. of *outrer* to pass beyond]

outride (ˌaʊtˈraɪd) *vb* **outrides, outriding, outrode, outridden.** (*tr*) **1** to outdo by riding faster, farther, or better than. **2** (of a vessel) to ride out (a storm).

outrider (ˈaʊtˌraɪdə) *n* **1** a person who goes in advance to investigate, discover a way, etc.; scout. **2** a person who rides in front of or beside a carriage, esp. as an attendant or guard. **3** *US.* a mounted herdsman.

outrigger (ˈaʊtˌrɪɡə) *n* **1** a framework for supporting a pontoon outside and parallel to the hull of a boat to provide stability. **2** a boat equipped with such a framework, esp. one of the canoes of the South Pacific. **3** any projecting framework attached to a boat, aircraft, building, etc., to act as a support. **4** *Rowing.* another name for **rigger** (sense 2). [C18: from OUT- + RIG + -ER[1]]

outright *adj* (ˈaʊtˌraɪt). (*prenominal*) **1** without qualifications or limitations: *outright ownership.* **2** complete; total. **3** straightforward; direct. ◆ *adv* (ˌaʊtˈraɪt). **4** without restrictions. **5** without reservation or concealment: *ask outright.* **6** instantly: *he was killed outright.*

outrush (ˈaʊtˌrʌʃ) *n* a flowing or rushing out.

outset (ˈaʊtˌset) *n* a start; beginning (esp. in **from** (*or* **at**) **the outset**).

outside *prep* (ˌaʊtˈsaɪd). **1** (sometimes foll. by *of*) on or to the exterior of: *outside the house.* **2** beyond the limits of. **3** apart from; other than: *no-one knows outside you.* ◆ *adj* (ˈaʊtˌsaɪd). **4** (*prenominal*) situated on the exterior: *an outside lavatory.* **5** remote; unlikely. **6** not a member of. **7** the greatest possible or probable (prices, odds, etc.). **8** (of a

road lane, esp. in a dual carriageway or motorway) situated nearer or nearest to the central reservation, for use by faster or overtaking vehicles. ◆ *adv* (ˌaʊtˈsaɪd). **9** outside a specified thing or place; out of doors. **10** *Sl.* not in prison. ◆ *n* (ˈaʊtˌsaɪd). **11** the external side or surface. **12** the external appearance or aspect. **13** (of a pavement etc.) the side nearest the road or away from a wall. **14** *Sport.* an outside player, as in football. **15** (*pl*) the outer sheets of a ream of paper. **16** *Canad.* (in the north) the settled parts of Canada. **17 at the outside.** *Inf.* at the most or at the greatest extent: *two days at the outside.*

outside broadcast *n Radio, television.* a broadcast not made from a studio.

outside director *n* a director of a company who is not employed by that company but is often employed by a holding or associated company.

outsider (ˌaʊtˈsaɪdə) *n* **1** a person or thing excluded from or not a member of a set, group, etc. **2** a contestant, esp. a horse, thought unlikely to win in a race. **3** *Canad.* a person who does not live in the Arctic regions.

outsize (ˈaʊtˌsaɪz) *adj* **1** Also: **outsized.** very large or larger than normal. ◆ *n* **2** something outsize, such as a garment or person. **3** (*modifier*) relating to or dealing in outsize clothes: *an outsize shop.*

outskirts (ˈaʊtˌskɜːts) *pl n* (*sometimes sing*) outlying or bordering areas, districts, etc., as of a city.

outsmart (ˌaʊtˈsmɑːt) *vb* (*tr*) *Inf.* to get the better of; outwit.

outspan *S. African.* ◆ *n* (ˈaʊtˌspæn). **1** an area on a farm kept available for travellers to rest and refresh animals etc. **2** the act of unharnessing or unyoking. ◆ *vb* (ˌaʊtˈspæn), **outspans, outspanning, outspanned.** **3** to unharness or unyoke (animals). [C19: partial translation of Afrik. *uitspan,* from *uit* out + *spannen* to stretch]

outspoken (ˌaʊtˈspəʊkən) *adj* **1** candid or bold in speech. **2** said or expressed with candour or boldness.

outspread *vb* (ˌaʊtˈspred), **outspreads, outspreading, outspread.** **1** to spread out. ◆ *adj* (ˈaʊtˌspred). **2** spread or stretched out. **3** scattered or diffused widely. ◆ *n* (ˈaʊtˌspred). **4** a spreading out.

outstanding (ˌaʊtˈstændɪŋ) *adj* **1** superior; excellent. **2** prominent, remarkable, or striking. **3** unsettled, unpaid, or unresolved. **4** (of shares, bonds, etc.) issued and sold. **5** projecting or jutting upwards or outwards.
▸ **'out'standingly** *adv*

outstare (ˌaʊtˈsteə) *vb* **outstares, outstaring, outstared.** (*tr*) **1** to outdo in staring. **2** to disconcert by staring.

outstation (ˈaʊtˌsteɪʃən) *n* a station or post at a distance from the base station or in a remote region.

outstay (ˌaʊtˈsteɪ) *vb* (*tr*) **1** to stay longer than. **2** to stay beyond (a limit). **3 outstay one's welcome.** See **overstay** (sense 2).

outstretch (ˌaʊtˈstretʃ) *vb* (*tr*) **1** to extend or expand; stretch out. **2** to stretch or extend beyond.

outstrip (ˌaʊtˈstrɪp) *vb* **outstrips, outstripping, outstripped.** (*tr*) **1** to surpass in a sphere of activity, competition, etc. **2** to be or grow greater than. **3** to go faster than and leave behind.

outtake (ˈaʊtˌteɪk) *n* an unreleased take from a recording session, film, or television programme.

out-tray *n* (in an office, etc.) a tray for outgoing correspondence, documents, etc.

outturn (ˈaʊtˌtɜːn) *n* another word for **output** (sense 2).

outvote (ˌaʊtˈvəʊt) *vb* **outvotes, outvoting, outvoted.** (*tr*) to defeat by a majority of votes.

outward (ˈaʊtwəd) *adj* **1** of or relating to what is apparent or superficial. **2** of or relating to the outside of the body. **3** belonging or relating to the external, as opposed to the mental, spiritual, or inherent. **4** of, relating to, or on

directed towards the outside or exterior. **5 the outward man. 5a** *Theol.* the body as opposed to the soul. **5b** *Facetious.* clothing. ◆ *adv* **6** (of a ship) away from port. **7** a variant of **outwards.** ◆ *n* **8** the outward part; exterior.
▶ **'outwardness** *n*

Outward Bound movement *n Trademark.* (in Britain) a scheme to provide adventure training for young people.

outwardly ('autwədlɪ) *adv* **1** in outward appearance. **2** with reference to the outside or outer surface; externally.

outwards ('autwədz) *or* **outward** *adv* towards the outside; out.

outwear (,aut'wɛə) *vb* **outwears, outwearing, outwore, outworn.** (*tr*) **1** to use up or destroy by wearing. **2** to last or wear longer than. **3** to outlive, outgrow, or develop beyond. **4** to deplete or exhaust in strength, determination, etc.

outweigh (,aut'weɪ) *vb* (*tr*) **1** to prevail over; overcome. **2** to be more important or significant than. **3** to be heavier than.

outwit (,aut'wɪt) *vb* **outwits, outwitting, outwitted.** (*tr*) to get the better of by cunning or ingenuity.

outwith (,aut'wɪθ) *prep Scot.* outside; beyond.

outwork *n* (,aut'wɜːk). **1** (*often pl*) defences which lie outside main defensive works. **2** work done away from the factory, etc., by which it has been commissioned. ◆ *vb* (,aut'wɜːk). (*tr*) **3** to work better, harder, etc., than. **4** to work out to completion.
▶ **'out,worker** *n*

ouzel *or* **ousel** ('uːz°l) *n* **1** short for **water ouzel.** See **dipper** (sense 2). **2** an archaic name for the (European) **blackbird.** [OE *ōsle*]

ouzo ('uːzəu) *n, pl* **ouzos.** a strong aniseed-flavoured spirit from Greece. [Mod. Gk *ouzon*, from ?]

ova ('əuvə) *n* the plural of **ovum.**

oval ('əuv°l) *adj* **1** having the shape of an ellipse or ellipsoid. ◆ *n* **2** anything that is oval in shape, such as a sports ground. **3** *Austral.* **3a** an Australian Rules ground. **3b** any sports field. [C16: from Med. L *ōvālis*, from L *ōvum* egg]
▶ **'ovally** *adv* ▶ **'ovalness** *or* **ovality** (əu'vælɪtɪ) *n*

Oval ★ ('əuv°l) *n* **the.** a cricket ground in the S London borough of Lambeth.

ovariectomy (əu,vɛərɪ'ɛktəmɪ) *n, pl* **ovariectomies.** *Surgery.* surgical removal of an ovary or ovarian tumour.

ovary ('əuvərɪ) *n, pl* **ovaries. 1** either of the two female reproductive organs, which produce ova and secrete oestrogen hormones. **2** the corresponding organ in vertebrate and invertebrate animals. **3** *Bot.* the hollow basal region of a carpel containing one or more ovules. [C17: from NL *ōvārium*, from L *ōvum* egg]
▶ **ovarian** (əu'vɛərɪən) *adj*

ovate ('əuveɪt) *adj* **1** shaped like an egg. **2** (esp. of a leaf) shaped like the longitudinal section of an egg, with the broader end at the base. [C18: from L *ōvātus* egg-shaped]
▶ **'ovately** *adv*

ovation (əu'veɪʃən) *n* **1** an enthusiastic reception, esp. one of prolonged applause. **2** a victory procession less glorious than a triumph awarded to a Roman general. [C16: from L *ovātiō* rejoicing, from *ovāre* to exult]
▶ **o'vational** *adj*

oven ('ʌv°n) *n* **1** an enclosed heated compartment or receptacle for baking or roasting food. **2** a similar device, usually lined with a refractory material, used for drying substances, firing ceramics, heat-treating, etc. ◆ *vb* **3** (*tr*) to cook in an oven. [OE *ofen*]
▶ **'oven-,like** *adj*

ovenable ('ʌv°nəb°l) *adj* suitable for cooking in or using in an oven.

ovenbird ('ʌv°n,bɜːd) *n* **1** any of numerous small brownish South American passerine birds that build oven-shaped clay nests. **2** a common North American warbler that has an olive-brown striped plumage with an orange crown and builds a cup-shaped nest on the ground.

oven-ready *adj* (of various foods) bought already prepared so that they are ready to be cooked in the oven.

ovenware ('ʌv°n,wɛə) *n* heat-resistant dishes in which food can be both cooked and served.

over ('əuvə) *prep* **1** directly above; on the top of; via the top or upper surface of: *over one's head.* **2** on or to the other side of: *over the river.* **3** during; through or throughout (a period of time). **4** in or throughout all parts of: *to travel over England.* **5** throughout the whole extent of: *over the racecourse.* **6** above; in preference to. **7** by the agency of (an instrument of telecommunication): *over the radio.* **8** more than: *over a century ago.* **9** on the subject of; about: *an argument over nothing.* **10** while occupied in: *discussing business over golf.* **11** having recovered from the effects of. **12 over and above.** added to; in addition to. ◆ *adv* **13** in a state, condition, situation, or position that is placed or put over something: *to climb over.* **14** (*particle*) so as to cause to fall: *knocking over a policeman.* **15** at or to a point across intervening space, water, etc. **16** throughout a whole area: *the world over.* **17** (*particle*) from beginning to end, usually cursorily: *to read a document over.* **18** throughout a period of time: *stay over for this week.* **19** (esp. in signalling and radio) it is now your turn to speak, act, etc. **20** more than is expected or usual: *not over well.* **21 over again.** once more. **22 over against. 22a** opposite to. **22b** contrasting with. **23 over and over.** (often foll. by *again*) repeatedly. ◆ *adj* **24** (*postpositive*) finished; no longer in progress. ◆ *adv, adj* **25** remaining; surplus (often in **left over**). ◆ *n* **26** *Cricket.* **26a** a series of six balls bowled by a bowler from the same end of the pitch. **26b** the play during this. [OE *ofer*]

over- *prefix* **1** excessive or excessively; beyond an agreed or desirable limit: *overcharge; overdue.* **2** indicating superior rank: *overseer.* **3** indicating location or movement above: *overhang.* **4** indicating movement downwards: *overthrow.*

overage (,əuvər'eɪdʒ) *adj* beyond a specified age.

overall *adj* ('əuvər,ɔːl). (*prenominal*) **1** from one end to the other. **2** including or covering everything: *the overall cost.* ◆ *adv* (,əuvər'ɔːl). **3** in general; on the whole. ◆ *n* ('əuvər,ɔːl). **4** *Brit.* a protective work garment usually worn over ordinary clothes. **5** (*pl*) hard-wearing work trousers with a bib and shoulder straps or jacket attached.

overarch (,əuvər'ɑːtʃ) *vb* (*tr*) to form an arch over.

overarching (,əuvər'ɑːtʃɪŋ) *adj* overall; all-encompassing: *an overarching concept.*

overarm ('əuvər,ɑːm) *adj* **1** *Sport, esp. cricket.* bowled, thrown, or performed with the arm raised above the shoulder. ◆ *adv* **2** with the arm raised above the shoulder.

overawe (,əuvər'ɔː) *vb* **overawes, overawing, overawed.** (*tr*) to subdue, restrain, or overcome by affecting with a feeling of awe.

overbalance *vb* (,əuvə'bæləns), **overbalances, overbalancing, overbalanced. 1** to lose or cause to lose balance. **2** (*tr*) another word for **outweigh.** ◆ *n* ('əuvə,bæləns). **3** excess of weight, value, etc.

overbear (,əuvə'bɛə) *vb* **overbears, overbearing, overbore, overborne. 1** (*tr*) to dominate or overcome. **2** (*tr*) to press or bear down with weight or physical force. **3** to produce (fruit, etc.) excessively.

overbearing (,əuvə'bɛərɪŋ) *adj* **1** domineering or dictatorial in manner or action. **2** of particular or overriding importance or significance.
▶ **,over'bearingly** *adv*

overblown (,əuvə'bləun) *adj* **1** overdone or excessive. **2** bombastic; turgid: *overblown prose.* **3** (of flowers) past the stage of full bloom.

overboard ('əuvə,bɔːd) *adv* **1** from on board a vessel into the water. **2 go overboard.** *Inf.* **2a** to be extremely enthusiastic. **2b** to go to extremes. **3 throw overboard.** to reject or abandon.

overbook (,əuvə'buk) *vb* (*tr, also absol.*) to make more reservations than there are places, tickets, etc., available.

overbuild (,əuvə'bɪld) *vb* **overbuilds, overbuilding, overbuilt.** (*tr*) **1** to build over or on top of. **2** to erect too many buildings in (an area). **3** to build too large or elaborately.

overburden *vb* (,əuvə'bɜːd°n). **1** (*tr*) to load with excessive weight, work, etc. ◆ *n* ('əuvə,bɜːd°n). **2** an excessive

burden or load. **3** *Geol.* the sedimentary rock material that covers coal seams, mineral veins, etc.
▸ ˌover'**burdensome** *adj*

overcast *adj* (ˈəʊvəˌkɑːst). **1** covered over or obscured, esp. by clouds. **2** *Meteorol.* (of the sky) cloud-covered. **3** gloomy or melancholy. **4** sewn over by overcasting. ◆ *vb* (ˌəʊvəˈkɑːst), **overcasts, overcasting, overcast. 5** to sew (an edge, as of a hem) with long stitches passing successively over the edge. ◆ *n* (ˈəʊvəˌkɑːst). **6** *Meteorol.* the state of the sky when it is cloud-covered.

overcharge *vb* (ˌəʊvəˈtʃɑːdʒ), **overcharges, overcharging, overcharged. 1** to charge too much. **2** (*tr*) to fill or load beyond capacity. **3** *Literary.* another word for **exaggerate**. ◆ *n* (ˈəʊvəˌtʃɑːdʒ). **4** an excessive price or charge. **5** an excessive load.

overcloud (ˌəʊvəˈklaʊd) *vb* **1** to make or become covered with clouds. **2** to make or become dark or dim.

overcoat (ˈəʊvəˌkəʊt) *n* a warm heavy coat worn over the outer clothes in cold weather.

overcome (ˌəʊvəˈkʌm) *vb* **overcomes, overcoming, overcame, overcome. 1** (*tr*) to get the better of in a conflict. **2** (*tr; often passive*) to render incapable or powerless by laughter, sorrow, exhaustion, etc. **3** (*tr*) to surmount obstacles, objections, etc. **4** (*intr*) to be victorious.

overcrop (ˌəʊvəˈkrɒp) *vb* **overcrops, overcropping, overcropped.** (*tr*) to exhaust (land) by excessive cultivation.

overdo (ˌəʊvəˈduː) *vb* **overdoes, overdoing, overdid, overdone.** (*tr*) **1** to take or carry too far; do to excess. **2** to exaggerate, overelaborate, or overplay. **3** to cook or bake too long. **4 overdo it** *or* **things.** to overtax one's strength, capacity, etc.

overdose *n* (ˈəʊvəˌdəʊs). **1** (esp. of drugs) an excessive dose. ◆ *vb* (ˌəʊvəˈdəʊs), **overdoses, overdosing, overdosed. 2** to take an excessive dose or give an excessive dose to.
▸ ˌover'**dosage** *n*

overdraft (ˈəʊvəˌdrɑːft) *n* **1** a deficit in a bank or building-society cheque account caused by withdrawing more money than is credited to it. **2** the amount of this deficit.

overdraw (ˌəʊvəˈdrɔː) *vb* **overdraws, overdrawing, overdrew, overdrawn. 1** to draw on (a bank account) in excess of the credit balance. **2** (*tr*) to exaggerate in describing or telling.

overdress *vb* (ˌəʊvəˈdrɛs). **1** to dress (oneself or another) too elaborately or finely. ◆ *n* (ˈəʊvəˌdrɛs). **2** a dress that may be worn over a jumper, blouse, etc.

overdrive *n* (ˈəʊvəˌdraɪv). **1** a very high gear in a motor vehicle used at high speeds to reduce wear. ◆ *vb* (ˌəʊvəˈdraɪv), **overdrives, overdriving, overdrove, overdriven. 2** (*tr*) to drive too hard or too far; overwork or overuse.

overdub (in multitrack recording) ◆ *vb* (ˌəʊvəˈdʌb), **overdubs, overdubbing, overdubbed. 1** to add (new sound) on a spare track or tracks. ◆ *n* (ˈəʊvəˌdʌb). **2** the blending of various layers of sound in one recording by this method.

overdue (ˌəʊvəˈdjuː) *adj* past the time specified, required, or preferred for arrival, occurrence, payment, etc.

overestimate *vb* (ˌəʊvərˈɛstɪˌmeɪt), **overestimates, overestimating, overestimated. 1** (*tr*) to estimate too highly. ◆ *n* (ˌəʊvərˈɛstɪmɪt). **2** an estimate that is too high.
▸ ˌover,esti'**mation** *n*

overexpose (ˌəʊvərɪksˈpəʊz) *vb* **overexposes, overexposing, overexposed.** (*tr*) **1** to expose too much or for too long. **2** *Photog.* to expose (a film, etc.) for too long or with too bright a light.
▸ ˌover,ex'**posure** *n*

overflow *vb* (ˌəʊvəˈfləʊ), **overflows, overflowing, overflowed** *or* (*formerly*) **overflown. 1** to flow or run over (a limit, brim, etc.). **2** to fill or be filled beyond capacity so as to spill or run over. **3** (*intr; usually foll. by with*) to be filled with happiness, tears, etc. **4** (*tr*) to spread or cover over; flood or inundate. ◆ *n* (ˈəʊvəˌfləʊ). **5** overflowing matter, esp. liquid. **6** any outlet that enables surplus liquid to be discharged or drained off. **7** the amount by which a limit, capacity, etc., is exceeded.

overfold (ˈəʊvəˌfəʊld) *n Geol.* a fold in the form of an anticline in which one limb is more steeply inclined than the other.

overfunding (ˈəʊvəˌfʌndɪŋ) *n* (in Britain) a government policy in which it sells more of its securities than would be required to finance public spending, with the object of absorbing surplus funds to curb inflation.

overgrow (ˌəʊvəˈɡrəʊ) *vb* **overgrows, overgrowing, overgrew, overgrown. 1** (*tr*) to grow over or across (an area, path, etc.). **2** (*tr*) to choke or supplant by a stronger growth. **3** (*tr*) to grow too large for. **4** (*intr*) to grow beyond normal size.
▸ '**over,growth** *n*

overhand (ˈəʊvəˌhænd) *adj* **1** thrown or performed with the hand raised above the shoulder. **2** sewn with thread passing over two edges in one direction. ◆ *adv* **3** with the hand above the shoulder; overarm. **4** with shallow stitches passing over two edges. ◆ *vb* **5** to sew (two edges) overhand.

overhang *vb* (ˌəʊvəˈhæŋ), **overhangs, overhanging, overhung. 1** to project or extend beyond (a surface, building, etc.). **2** (*tr*) to hang or be suspended over. **3** (*tr*) to menace, threaten, or dominate. ◆ *n* (ˈəʊvəˌhæŋ). **4** a formation, object, etc., that extends beyond or hangs over something, such as an outcrop of rock overhanging a mountain face. **5** the amount or extent of projection.

overhaul *vb* (ˌəʊvəˈhɔːl). (*tr*) **1** to examine carefully for faults, necessary repairs, etc. **2** to make repairs or adjustments to (a car, machine, etc.). **3** to overtake. ◆ *n* (ˈəʊvəˌhɔːl). **4** a thorough examination and repair.

overhead *adj* (ˈəʊvəˌhɛd). **1** situated or operating above head height or some other reference level. **2** (*prenominal*) inclusive: *the overhead price included meals.* ◆ *adv* (ˌəʊvəˈhɛd). **3** over or above head height, esp. in the sky. ◆ *n* (ˈəʊvəˌhɛd). **4a** a stroke in racket games played from above head height. **4b** (*as modifier*): *an overhead smash.* **5** (*modifier*) of, concerned with, or resulting from overheads: *overhead costs.*

overhead camshaft *n* a type of camshaft situated above the cylinder head in an internal-combustion engine.

overhead projector *n* a projector that throws an enlarged image of a transparency onto a surface above and behind the person using it.

overheads (ˈəʊvəˌhɛdz) *pl n* business expenses, such as rent, that are not directly attributable to any department or product and can therefore be assigned only arbitrarily.

overhead-valve engine *n* a type of internal-combustion engine in which the inlet and exhaust valves are in the cylinder head above the pistons. US name: **valve-in-head engine.**

overhear (ˌəʊvəˈhɪə) *vb* **overhears, overhearing, overheard.** (*tr*) to hear (a person, remark, etc.) without the knowledge of the speaker.

overheat (ˌəʊvəˈhiːt) *vb* **1** to make or become excessively hot. **2** (*tr; often passive*) to make very agitated, irritated, etc. **3** (*intr*) (of an economy) to tend towards inflation, often as a result of excessive growth in demand. **4** (*tr*) to cause (an economy) to tend towards inflation. ◆ *n* **5** the condition of being overheated.

Overijssel ★ (*Dutch* oːvərˈeisəl) *n* a province of the E Netherlands: generally low-lying. Capital: Zwolle. Pop.: 1 050 389 (1995). Area: 3929 sq. km (1517 sq. miles).

overjoy (ˌəʊvəˈdʒɔɪ) *vb* (*tr*) to give great delight to.
▸ ˌover'**joyed** *adj*

overkill (ˈəʊvəˌkɪl) *n* **1** the capability to deploy more weapons, esp. nuclear weapons, than is necessary to ensure military advantage. **2** any capacity or treatment that is greater than that required or appropriate.

overland (ˈəʊvəˌlænd) *adj* (*prenominal*), *adv* **1** over or across land. ◆ *vb* **2** *Austral.* (formerly) to drive (cattle or sheep) overland.
▸ '**over,lander** *n*

overlap *vb* (ˌəʊvəˈlæp), **overlaps, overlapping, overlapped. 1** (of two things) to extend or lie partly over (each other). **2** to cover and extend beyond (something). **3** (*intr*) to coincide partly in time, subject, etc. ◆ *n* (ˈəʊvəˌlæp). **4** a part that overlaps or is overlapped. **5** the amount, length, etc., overlapping. **6** *Geol.* the horizontal extension of the lower beds in a series of rock strata beyond the upper beds.

overlay vb (,əʊvə'leɪ), **overlays, overlaying, overlaid.** (tr) **1** to lay or place over or upon (something else). **2** (often foll. by with) to cover, overspread, or conceal (with). **3** (foll. by with) to cover (a surface) with an applied decoration: *ebony overlaid with silver.* **4** to achieve the correct printing pressure all over (a forme or plate) by adding to the appropriate areas of the packing. ◆ n ('əʊvə,leɪ). **5** something that is laid over something else; covering. **6** an applied decoration or layer, as of gold leaf. **7** a transparent sheet giving extra details to a map or diagram over which it is designed to be placed. **8** *Printing.* material, such as paper, used to overlay a forme or plate.

overleaf (,əʊvə'liːf) adv on the other side of the page.

overlie (,əʊvə'laɪ) vb **overlies, overlying, overlay, overlain.** (tr) **1** to lie or rest upon. Cf. **overlay. 2** to kill (a baby or newborn animal) by lying upon it.

overlong (,əʊvə'lɒŋ) adj, adv too or excessively long.

overlook vb (,əʊvə'lʊk). (tr) **1** to fail to notice or take into account. **2** to disregard deliberately or indulgently. **3** to afford a view of from above: *the house overlooks the bay.* **4** to rise above. **5** to look at carefully. **6** to cast the evil eye upon (someone). ◆ n ('əʊvə,lʊk). *US.* **7** a high place affording a view. **8** an act of overlooking.

overlord ('əʊvə,lɔːd) n a supreme lord or master.
▸ 'over,lordship n

overly ('əʊvəlɪ) adv too; excessively.

overman vb (,əʊvə'mæn), **overmans, overmanning, overmanned.** **1** (tr) to supply with an excessive number of men. ◆ n ('əʊvə,mæn), pl **overmen. 2** a man who oversees others. **3** a superman.

overmaster (,əʊvə'mɑːstə) vb (tr) to overpower.

overmatch *Chiefly US.* ◆ vb (,əʊvə'mætʃ). (tr) **1** to be more than a match for. **2** to match with a superior opponent. ◆ n ('əʊvə,mætʃ). **3** a person superior in ability. **4** a match in which one contestant is superior.

overmuch (,əʊvə'mʌtʃ) adv, adj **1** too much; very much. ◆ n **2** an excessive amount.

overnice (,əʊvə'naɪs) adj too fastidious, precise, etc.

overnight adv (,əʊvə'naɪt). **1** for the duration of the night. **2** in or as if in the course of one night; suddenly: *the situation changed overnight.* ◆ adj ('əʊvə,naɪt). (usually prenominal) **3** done in, occurring in, or lasting the night: *an overnight stop.* **4** staying for one night. **5** for use during a single night. **6** occurring in or as if in the course of one night; sudden: *an overnight victory.*

overpass n ('əʊvə,pɑːs). **1** another name for **flyover** (sense 1). ◆ vb ('əʊvə'pɑːs). (tr) *Now rare.* **2** to pass over, through, or across. **3** to exceed. **4** to ignore.

overplay (,əʊvə'pleɪ) vb **1** (tr) to exaggerate the importance of. **2** to act or behave in an exaggerated manner. **3 overplay one's hand.** to overestimate the worth or strength of one's position.

overpower (,əʊvə'paʊə) vb (tr) **1** to conquer or subdue by superior force. **2** to have such a strong effect on as to make helpless or ineffective. **3** to supply with more power than necessary.
▸ ,over'powering adj

overprice (,əʊvə'praɪs) vb **overprices, overpricing, overpriced.** (tr) to ask too high a price for.

overprint vb (,əʊvə'prɪnt). **1** (tr) to print (additional matter or another colour) on a sheet of paper. ◆ n ('əʊvə,prɪnt). **2** additional matter or another colour printed onto a previously printed sheet. **3** additional matter applied to a finished postage stamp by printing, stamping, etc.

overqualified (,əʊvə'kwɒlɪfaɪd) adj having more managerial experience or academic qualifications than required for a particular job.

overrate (,əʊvə'reɪt) vb **overrates, overrating, overrated.** (tr) to assess too highly.

overreach (,əʊvə'riːtʃ) vb **1** (tr) to defeat or thwart (oneself) by attempting to do or gain too much. **2** (tr) to aim for but miss by going too far. **3** to get the better of (a person) by trickery. **4** (tr) to reach beyond or over. **5** (intr) to reach or go too far. **6** (intr) (of a horse) to strike the back of a forefoot with the edge of the opposite hind foot.

overreact (,əʊvərɪ'ækt) vb (intr) to react excessively to something.
▸ ,overre'action n

override vb (,əʊvə'raɪd), **overrides, overriding, overrode, overridden.** (tr) **1** to set aside or disregard with superior authority or power. **2** to supersede or annul. **3** to dominate or vanquish by or as if by trampling down. **4** to take manual control of (a system that is usually under automatic control). **5** to extend or pass over, esp. to overlap. **6** to ride (a horse, etc.) too hard. **7** to ride over. ◆ n ('əʊvə,raɪd). **8** a device that can override an automatic control.

overrider ('əʊvə,raɪdə) n either of two attachments fitted to the bumper of a motor vehicle to prevent it interlocking with that of another vehicle.

overriding (,əʊvə'raɪdɪŋ) adj taking precedence.

overrule (,əʊvə'ruːl) vb **overrules, overruling, overruled.** (tr) **1** to disallow the arguments of (a person) by the use of authority. **2** to rule or decide against (an argument, decision, etc.). **3** to prevail over, dominate, or influence. **4** to exercise rule over.

overrun vb (,əʊvə'rʌn), **overruns, overrunning, overran, overrun.** **1** (tr) to swarm or spread over rapidly. **2** to run over (something); overflow. **3** to extend or run beyond a limit. **4** (intr) (of an engine) to run with a closed throttle at a speed dictated by that of the vehicle it drives. **5** (tr) to print (a book, journal, etc.) in a greater quantity than ordered. **6** (tr) *Printing.* to transfer (set type) from one column, line, or page, to another. **7** (tr) *Arch.* to run faster than. ◆ n ('əʊvə,rʌn). **8** the act or an instance of overrunning. **9** the amount or extent of overrunning. **10** the number of copies of a publication in excess of the quantity ordered.

overseas adv (,əʊvə'siːz). **1** beyond the sea; abroad. ◆ adj ('əʊvə'siːz). **2** of, to, in, from, or situated in countries beyond the sea. **3** Also: **oversea.** of or relating to passage over the sea. ◆ n (,əʊvə'siːz). **4** (functioning as sing) *Inf.* a foreign country or foreign countries collectively.

overseas territory n See **United Kingdom overseas territory.**

oversee (,əʊvə'siː) vb **oversees, overseeing, oversaw, overseen.** (tr) **1** to watch over and direct; supervise. **2** to watch secretly or accidentally. **3** *Arch.* to scrutinize; inspect.

overseer ('əʊvə,siːə) n **1** a person who oversees others, esp. workmen. **2** *Brit. history.* a minor official of a parish attached to the poorhouse.

oversell (,əʊvə'sɛl) vb **oversells, overselling, oversold. 1** (tr) to sell more of (a commodity, etc.) than can be supplied. **2** to use excessively aggressive methods in selling (commodities). **3** (tr) to exaggerate the merits of.

overset (,əʊvə'sɛt) vb **oversets, oversetting, overset.** (tr) **1** to disturb or upset. **2** *Printing.* to set (type or copy) in excess of the space available.

oversew ('əʊvə,səʊ, ,əʊvə'səʊ) vb **oversews, oversewing, oversewed; oversewn,** or **oversewed.** to sew (two edges) with close stitches that pass over them both.

oversexed (,əʊvə'sɛkst) adj having an excessive preoccupation with sexual activity.

overshadow (,əʊvə'ʃædəʊ) vb (tr) **1** to render insignificant or less important in comparison. **2** to cast a shadow or gloom over.

overshoe ('əʊvə,ʃuː) n a protective shoe worn over an ordinary shoe.

overshoot vb (,əʊvə'ʃuːt), **overshoots, overshooting, overshot. 1** to shoot or go beyond (a mark or target). **2** (of an aircraft) to fly or taxi too far along a runway. **3** (tr) to pass swiftly over or down over, as water over a wheel. ◆ n ('əʊvə,ʃuːt). **4** an act or instance of overshooting. **5** the extent of such overshooting.

overshot ('əʊvə,ʃɒt) adj **1** having or designating an upper jaw that projects beyond the lower jaw. **2** (of a water wheel) driven by a flow of water that passes over the wheel.

oversight ('əʊvə,saɪt) n **1** an omission or mistake, esp. one made through failure to notice something. **2** supervision.

oversize adj (,əʊvə'saɪz). **1** Also: **oversized.** larger than the usual size. ◆ *n* ('əʊvəˌsaɪz). **2** a size larger than the usual or proper size. **3** something that is oversize.

overskirt ('əʊvəˌskɜːt) *n* an outer skirt, esp. one that reveals a decorative underskirt.

overspend *vb* (ˌəʊvə'spɛnd), **overspends, overspending, overspent. 1** to spend in excess of (one's desires or what one can afford or is allocated). **2** (*tr; usually passive*) to wear out; exhaust. ◆ *n* ('əʊvəˌspɛnd). **3** the amount by which someone or something is overspent.

overspill *n* ('əʊvəˌspɪl). **1a** something that spills over or is in excess. **1b** (*as modifier*): *overspill population.* ◆ *vb* (ˌəʊvə'spɪl), **overspills, overspilling, overspilt** *or* **overspilled. 2** (*intr*) to overflow.

overspread (ˌəʊvə'sprɛd) *vb* (*tr*) **overspreads, overspreading, overspread.** to extend or spread over.

overstate (ˌəʊvə'steɪt) *vb* **overstates, overstating, overstated.** (*tr*) to state too strongly; exaggerate or overemphasize.
▶ **over'statement** *n*

overstay (ˌəʊvə'steɪ) *vb* (*tr*) **1** to stay beyond the time, limit, or duration of. **2 overstay** *or* **outstay one's welcome.** to stay (at a party, etc.), longer than pleases the host or hostess.

overstep (ˌəʊvə'stɛp) *vb* **oversteps, overstepping, overstepped.** (*tr*) to go beyond (a certain or proper limit).

overstrung (ˌəʊvə'strʌŋ) *adj* **1** too highly strung; tense. **2** (of a piano) having two sets of strings crossing each other at an oblique angle.

overstuff (ˌəʊvə'stʌf) *vb* (*tr*) **1** to force too much into. **2** to cover (furniture, etc.) entirely with upholstery.

oversubscribe (ˌəʊvəsəb'skraɪb) *vb* **oversubscribes, oversubscribing, oversubscribed.** (*tr; often passive*) to subscribe or apply for in excess of available supply.
▶ **oversub'scription** *n*

overt ('əʊvɜːt, əʊ'vɜːt) *adj* **1** open to view; observable. **2** *Law.* open; deliberate. [C14: via OF, from *ovrir* to open, from L *aperīre*]
▶ **'overtly** *adv*

overtake (ˌəʊvə'teɪk) *vb* **overtakes, overtaking, overtook, overtaken. 1** *Chiefly Brit.* to move past (another vehicle or person) travelling in the same direction. **2** (*tr*) to pass or do better than, after catching up with. **3** (*tr*) to come upon suddenly or unexpectedly: *night overtook him.* **4** (*tr*) to catch up with; draw level with.

overtax (ˌəʊvə'tæks) *vb* (*tr*) **1** to tax too heavily. **2** to impose too great a strain on.

over-the-counter *adj* **1** (of a stock exchange dealing) conducted between brokers in areas for which no official market prices are quoted. **2** (of a medicinal drug) able to be sold without prescription. Cf. **POM.** ◆ Abbrev.: **OTC.**

overthrow *vb* (ˌəʊvə'θrəʊ), **overthrows, overthrowing, overthrew, overthrown. 1** (*tr*) to effect the downfall or destruction of (a ruler, institution, etc.), esp. by force. **2** (*tr*) to throw or turn over. **3** to throw (something, esp. a ball) too far. ◆ *n* ('əʊvəˌθrəʊ). **4** downfall; destruction. **5** *Cricket.* **5a** a ball thrown back too far by a fielder. **5b** a run scored because of this.

overthrust ('əʊvəˌθrʌst) *n Geol.* a reverse fault in which the rocks on the upper surface of a fault plane have moved over the rocks on the lower surface.

overtime *n* ('əʊvəˌtaɪm). **1a** work at a regular job done in addition to regular working hours. **1b** (*as modifier*): *overtime pay.* **2** the rate of pay established for such work. **3** time in excess of a set period. **4** *Sport, US & Canad.* extra time. ◆ *adv* ('əʊvəˌtaɪm). **5** beyond the regular or stipulated time. ◆ *vb* (ˌəʊvə'taɪm), **overtimes, overtiming, overtimed. 6** (*tr*) to exceed the required time for (a photographic exposure, etc.).

overtone ('əʊvəˌtəʊn) *n* **1** (*often pl*) additional meaning or nuance: *overtones of despair.* **2** *Music, acoustics.* any of the tones, with the exception of the fundamental, that constitute a musical sound and contribute to its quality.

overture ('əʊvəˌtjʊə) *n* **1** *Music.* **1a** a piece of orchestral music that is played at the beginning of an opera or oratorio, often containing the main musical themes of the work. **1b** a one-movement orchestral piece, usually having a descriptive or evocative title. **2** (*often pl*) a proposal, act, or gesture initiating a relationship, negotiation, etc.

3 something that introduces what follows. ◆ *vb* **overtures, overturing, overtured.** (*tr*) **4** to make or present an overture to. **5** to introduce with an overture. [C14: via OF from LL *apertūra* opening, from L *aperīre* to open]

overturn *vb* (ˌəʊvə'tɜːn). **1** to turn or cause to turn from an upright or normal position. **2** (*tr*) to overthrow or destroy. **3** (*tr*) to invalidate; reverse. ◆ *n* ('əʊvəˌtɜːn). **4** the act of overturning or the state of being overturned.

overuse *vb* (ˌəʊvə'juːz), **overuses, overusing, overused. 1** (*tr*) to use excessively. ◆ *n* (ˌəʊvə'juːs) **2** excessive use.

overview ('əʊvəˌvjuː) *n* a general survey.

overweening (ˌəʊvə'wiːnɪŋ) *adj* **1** (of a person) excessively arrogant or presumptuous. **2** (of opinions, appetites, etc.) excessive; immoderate. [C14: from OVER + *weening* from OE *wēnan* WEEN]
▶ **over'weeningness** *n*

overweight *adj* (ˌəʊvə'weɪt). **1** weighing more than is usual, allowed, or healthy. ◆ *n* ('əʊvəˌweɪt). **2** extra or excess weight. ◆ *vb* (ˌəʊvə'weɪt). (*tr*) **3** to give too much emphasis or consideration to. **4** to add too much weight to. **5** to weigh down.

overwhelm (ˌəʊvə'wɛlm) *vb* (*tr*) **1** to overpower the thoughts, emotions, or senses of. **2** to overcome with irresistible force. **3** to cover over or bury completely. **4** to weigh or rest upon overpoweringly.
▶ **over'whelming** *adj*

overwind (ˌəʊvə'waɪnd) *vb* **overwinds, overwinding, overwound.** (*tr*) to wind (a watch, etc.) beyond the proper limit.

overwork *vb* (ˌəʊvə'wɜːk). (*mainly tr*) **1** (*also intr*) to work too hard or too long. **2** to use too much: *to overwork an excuse.* **3** to decorate the surface of. ◆ *n* ('əʊvəˌwɜːk). **4** excessive or excessively tiring work.

overwrite (ˌəʊvə'raɪt) *vb* **overwrites, overwriting, overwrote, overwritten. 1** to write (something) in an excessively ornate style. **2** to write too much about (someone or something). **3** to write on top of (other writing). **4** to record on a storage medium, such as a magnetic disk, thus destroying what was originally recorded there.

overwrought (ˌəʊvə'rɔːt) *adj* **1** full of nervous tension; agitated. **2** too elaborate; fussy: *an overwrought style.* **3** (*often postpositive* and foll. by *with*) with the surface decorated or adorned.

Ovett ★ ('əʊvɛt) *n* **Steve.** born 1955, British middle-distance runner.

ovi- *or* **ovo-** *combining form.* egg or ovum: *oviform; ovoviviparous.* [from L *ōvum*]

Ovid ★ ('ɒvɪd) *n* Latin name *Publius Ovidius Naso.* 43 B.C.–?17 A.D., Roman poet.
▶ **Ovidian** (ɒ'vɪdɪən) *adj*

oviduct ('ɒvɪˌdʌkt, 'əʊ-) *n* the tube through which ova are conveyed from an ovary. Also called (in mammals): **Fallopian tube.**
▶ **oviducal** (ˌɒvɪ'djuːk°l, ˌəʊ-) *or* **ovi'ductal** *adj*

Oviedo ★ (*Spanish* o'βjeðo) *n* a city in NW Spain: capital of Asturias from 810 until 1002; centre of a coal- and iron-mining area. Pop.: 201 712 (1994 est.).

oviform ('əʊvɪˌfɔːm) *adj Biol.* shaped like an egg.

ovine ('əʊvaɪn) *adj* of, relating to, or resembling a sheep. [C19: from LL *ovīnus*, from L *ovis* sheep]

oviparous (əʊ'vɪpərəs) *adj* (of fishes, reptiles, birds, etc.) producing eggs that hatch outside the body of the mother. Cf. **ovoviviparous, viviparous** (sense 1).
▶ **oviparity** (ˌəʊvɪ'pærɪtɪ) *n* ▶ **o'viparously** *adv*

ovipositor (ˌəʊvɪ'pɒzɪtə) *n* **1** the egg-laying organ of most female insects, consisting of a pair of specialized appendages at the end of the abdomen. **2** a similar organ in certain female fishes, formed by an extension of the edges of the genital opening. [C19: from OVI- + L *positor*, from *ponere* to place]
▶ **ovi'posit** *vb* (*intr*)

ovoid ('əʊvɔɪd) *adj* **1** egg-shaped. ◆ *n* **2** something that is ovoid.

ovoviviparous (ˌəʊvəʊvaɪ'vɪpərəs) *adj* (of certain reptiles, fishes, etc.) producing eggs that hatch within the body of the mother. Cf. **oviparous, viviparous** (sense 1).
▶ **ovoviviparity** (ˌəʊvəʊˌvaɪvɪ'pærɪtɪ) *n*

ovulate ('ɒvjʊˌleɪt) *vb* **ovulates, ovulating, ovulated.** (*intr*) to produce or discharge eggs from an ovary. [C19: from OVULE]
▶ ˌovu'lation *n*

ovulation method *n* another name for **Billings method.**

ovule ('ɒvjuːl) *n* **1** a small body in seed-bearing plants that contains the egg cell and develops into the seed after fertilization. **2** *Zool.* an immature ovum. [C19: via F from Med. L *ōvulum* a little egg, from L *ōvum* egg]
▶ 'ovular *adj*

ovum ('əʊvəm) *n, pl* **ova.** an unfertilized female gamete; egg cell. [from L: egg]

ow (aʊ) *interj* an exclamation of pain.

owe (əʊ) *vb* **owes, owing, owed.** (*mainly tr*) **1** to be under an obligation to pay (someone) to the amount of. **2** (*intr*) to be in debt: *he still owes for his house.* **3** (often foll. by *to*) to have as a result (of). **4** to feel the need or obligation to do, give, etc. **5** to hold or maintain in the mind or heart (esp. in **owe a grudge**). [OE *āgan* to have (C12: to have to)]

Owen ★ ('əʊɪn) *n* **1 David (Anthony Llewellyn)** Baron. born 1938, British politician: Labour foreign secretary (1977–79); cofounder (1981) and leader (1983–87) of the Social Democratic Party; peace envoy to Bosnia-Herzegovina (1992–94). **2 Sir Richard.** 1804–92, British comparative anatomist and palaeontologist. **3 Robert.** 1771–1858, Welsh industrialist and social reformer. He formed a model industrial community at New Lanark, Scotland. **4 Wilfred.** 1893–1918, British poet of World War I; killed in action.

Owen gun *n* a type of simple recoil-operated submachine-gun first used by Australian forces in World War II. [after E. E. *Owen* (1915–49), its Austral. inventor]

Owens ★ ('əʊɪnz) *n* **Jesse,** real name *John Cleveland Owens.* 1913–80, US Black athlete: won four gold medals at the Berlin Olympics (1936).

Owen Stanley Range ★ *n* a mountain range in SE New Guinea. Highest peak: Mount Victoria, 4073 m (13 363 ft).

Owerri ★ (ə'werɪ) *n* a market town in S Nigeria, capital of Imo state. Pop.: 35 010 (latest est.).

owing ('əʊɪŋ) *adj* **1** (*postpositive*) owed; due. **2 owing to.** because of or on account of.

owl (aʊl) *n* **1** a nocturnal bird of prey having large front-facing eyes, a small hooked bill, soft feathers, and a short neck. **2** any of various breeds of owl-like fancy domestic pigeon. **3** a person who looks or behaves like an owl, esp. in having a solemn manner. [OE *ūle*]
▶ 'owlish *adj* ▶ 'owl-ˌlike *adj*

owlet ('aʊlɪt) *n* a young or nestling owl.

own (əʊn) *determiner* (*preceded by a possessive*) **1a** (intensifier): *John's own idea.* **1b** (*as pron*): *I'll use my own.* **2** on behalf of oneself or in relation to oneself: *he is his own worst enemy.* **3 come into one's own. 3a** to become fulfilled: *she really came into her own when she got divorced.* **3b** to receive what is due to one. **4 hold one's own.** to maintain one's situation or position, esp. in spite of opposition or difficulty. **5 on one's own. 5a** without help. **5b** by oneself; alone. ♦ *vb* **6** (*tr*) to have as one's possession. **7** (when *intr*, often foll. by *up, to,* or *up to*) to confess or admit; acknowledge. **8** (*tr; takes a clause as object*) Now rare. to concede: *I own that you are right.* See OWE]
▶ 'owner *n* ▶ 'ownership *n*

own brand *n* a product which displays the name of the retailer rather than the producer.

owner-occupier *n* someone who has bought or is buying the house in which he lives.

own goal *n* **1** *Soccer.* a goal scored by a player accidentally playing the ball into his own team's net. **2** *Inf.* any action that results in disadvantage to the person who took it or to his associates.

ox (ɒks) *n, pl* **oxen. 1** an adult castrated male of any domesticated species of cattle used for draught work and meat. **2** any bovine mammal, esp. any of the domestic cattle. [OE *oxa*]

oxalic acid (ɒk'sælɪk) *n* a colourless poisonous crystalline acid found in many plants: used as a bleach and a cleansing agent for metals. Formula: $(COOH)_2$. Recommended name: **ethanedioic acid.** [C18: from F *oxalique,* from L *oxalis* garden sorrel; see OXALIS]

oxalis ('ɒksəlɪs, ɒk'sælɪs) *n* a plant having clover-like leaves which contain oxalic acid and white, pink, red, or yellow flowers. See also **wood sorrel.** [C18: via L from Gk: sorrel, sour wine, from *oxus* acid, sharp]

oxblood ('ɒksˌblʌd) *or* **oxblood red** *adj* of a dark reddish-brown colour.

oxbow ('ɒksˌbəʊ) *n* **1** a U-shaped piece of wood fitted under and around the neck of a harnessed ox and attached to the yoke. **2** Also called: **oxbow lake.** a small curved lake lying on the flood plain of a river and constituting the remnant of a former meander.

Oxbridge ('ɒksˌbrɪdʒ) *n* **a** the British universities of Oxford and Cambridge, esp. considered as ancient and prestigious academic institutions, bastions of privilege and superiority, etc. **b** (*as modifier*): *Oxbridge graduates.*

oxen ('ɒksən) *n* the plural of **ox.**

oxeye ('ɒksˌaɪ) *n* **1** a Eurasian composite plant having daisy-like flower heads with yellow rays and dark centres. **2** of various North American plants having daisy-like flowers. **3 oxeye daisy.** a type of hardy perennial chrysanthemum.

ox-eyed *adj* having large round eyes, like those of an ox.

Oxfam ('ɒksˌfæm) *n acronym for* Oxford Committee for Famine Relief.

Oxford[1] ★ ('ɒksfəd) *n* **1** a city in S England, administrative centre of Oxfordshire, at the confluence of the Rivers Thames and Cherwell: Royalist headquarters during the Civil War; university, consisting of 40 separate colleges, the oldest being University College (1249). Pop.: 118 795 (1991). **2** a type of stout laced shoe with a low heel. **3** a lightweight fabric of plain or twill weave used esp. for men's shirts.

Oxford[2] ★ ('ɒksfəd) *n* **1st Earl of.** title of (Robert) **Harley.**

Oxford bags *pl n* trousers with very wide baggy legs.

Oxford blue *n* **1a** a dark blue colour. **1b** (*as adj*): *an Oxford-blue scarf.* **2** a person who has been awarded a blue from Oxford University.

Oxford Movement *n* a movement within the Church of England that began at Oxford in 1833. It affirmed the continuity of the Church with early Christianity and strove to restore the High-Church ideals of the 17th century. Also called: **Tractarianism.**

Oxfordshire ★ ('ɒksfədˌʃɪə, -ʃə) *n* an inland county of S central England: situated mostly in the basin of the Upper Thames, with the Cotswolds in the west and the Chilterns in the southeast. Administrative centre: Oxford. Pop.: 590 200 (1994 est.). Area: 2608 sq. km (1007 sq. miles). Abbrev.: **Oxon.**

oxidant ('ɒksɪdənt) *n* a substance that acts or is used as an oxidizing agent. Also called (esp. in rocketry): **oxidizer.**

oxidation (ˌɒksɪ'deɪʃən) *n* **a** the act or process of oxidizing. **b** (*as modifier*): *an oxidation state.*
▶ 'oxiˌdate *vb* ▶ ˌoxi'dational *adj* ▶ 'oxiˌdative *adj*

oxidation-reduction *n* **a** a reversible chemical process usually involving the transfer of electrons, in which one reaction is an oxidation and the reverse reaction is a reduction. **b** (*as modifier*): *an oxidation-reduction reaction.*
♦ Also: **redox.**

oxide ('ɒksaɪd) *n* **1** any compound of oxygen with another element. **2** any organic compound in which an oxygen atom is bound to two alkyl groups; an ether. [C18: from F, from *ox(ygène)* + *(ac)ide*]

oxidize *or* **oxidise** ('ɒksɪˌdaɪz) *vb* **oxidizes, oxidizing, oxidized** *or* **oxidises, oxidising, oxidised. 1** to undergo or cause to undergo a chemical reaction with oxygen, as in formation of an oxide. **2** to form or cause to form a layer of metal oxide, as in rusting. **3** to lose or cause to lose hydrogen atoms. **4** to undergo or cause to undergo a decrease in the number of electrons.
▶ ˌoxidi'zation *or* ˌoxidi'sation *n*

oxidizing agent *n Chem.* a substance that oxidizes another substance, being itself reduced in the process.

oxlip ('ɒksˌlɪp) *n* **1** a Eurasian woodland plant, with small drooping pale yellow flowers. **2** a similar and related plant that is a natural hybrid between the cowslip and primrose. [OE *oxanslyppe*, lit.: ox's slippery dropping; see SLIP³]

oxo acid ('ɒksəʊ) *n* another name for **oxyacid**.

Oxon *abbrev. for* Oxfordshire. [from L *Oxonia*]

Oxon. *abbrev. for* (in degree titles, etc.) of Oxford. [from L *Oxoniensis*]

Oxonian (ɒk'səʊnɪən) *adj* **1** of or relating to Oxford or Oxford University. ◆ *n* **2** a member of Oxford University. **3** an inhabitant or native of Oxford.

oxpecker ('ɒks,pɛkə) *n* either of two African starlings, having flattened bills with which they obtain food from the hides of cattle. Also called: **tick-bird**.

oxtail ('ɒks,teɪl) *n* the skinned tail of an ox, used esp. in soups and stews.

oxter ('ʌukstə) *n Scot., Irish, & N English dialect.* the armpit. [C16: from OE *oxta*]

oxtongue ('ɒks,tʌŋ) *n* **1** any of various Eurasian composite plants having oblong bristly leaves and clusters of dandelion-like flowers. **2** any of various other plants having bristly tongue-shaped leaves. **3** the tongue of an ox, braised or boiled as food.

Oxus ★ ('ɒksəs) *n* the ancient name for the **Amu Darya**.

oxy-¹ *combining form.* denoting something sharp; acute: *oxytone*. [from Gk, from *oxus*]

oxy-² *combining form.* containing or using oxygen: *oxyacetylene*.

oxyacetylene (,ɒksɪə'sɛtɪ,liːn) *n* **a** a mixture of oxygen and acetylene; used in torches for cutting or welding metals at high temperatures. **b** (*as modifier*): *an oxyacetylene burner*.

oxyacid (,ɒksɪ'æsɪd) *n* any acid that contains oxygen with the acidic hydrogen atoms bound to oxygen atoms. Also called: **oxo acid**.

oxygen ('ɒksɪdʒən) *n* **a** a colourless odourless highly reactive gaseous element: the most abundant element in the earth's crust. Symbol: O; atomic no.: 8; atomic wt.: 15.9994. **b** (*as modifier*): *an oxygen mask*.
▸ **oxygenic** (,ɒksɪ'dʒɛnɪk) *or* **oxygenous** (ɒk'sɪdʒɪnəs) *adj*

oxygenate ('ɒksɪdʒɪ,neɪt) *or* **oxygenize, oxygenise** *vb* **oxygenates, oxygenating, oxygenated** *or* **oxygenizes, oxygenizing, oxygenized; oxygenises, oxygenising, oxygenised.** to enrich or be enriched with oxygen: *to oxygenate blood*.
▸ ,**oxygen'ation** *n* ▸ '**oxygen,izer** *or* '**oxygen,iser** *n*

oxygen tent *n Med.* a transparent enclosure covering a bedridden patient, into which oxygen is released to help maintain respiration.

oxyhaemoglobin (,ɒksɪ,hiːməʊ'gləʊbɪn) *n Biochem.* the bright red product formed when oxygen from the lungs combines with haemoglobin in the blood.

oxyhydrogen (,ɒksɪ'haɪdrɪdʒən) *n* **a** a mixture of hydrogen and oxygen used to provide an intense flame for welding. **b** (*as modifier*): *an oxyhydrogen blowpipe*.

oxymoron (,ɒksɪ'mɔːrɒn) *n, pl* **oxymora** (-'mɔːrə). *Rhetoric.* an epigrammatic effect, by which contradictory terms are used in conjunction: *living death*. [C17: via NL from Gk *oxumōron*, from *oxus* sharp + *mōros* stupid]

oxytetracycline (,ɒksɪ,tɛtrə'saɪklɪn) *n* a broad-spectrum antibiotic obtained from *Streptomyces rimosus*.

oyer and terminer ('ɔɪə; 'tɜːmɪnə) *n* **1** *English law.* (formerly) a commission issued to judges to try cases on assize. **2** the court in which such a hearing was held. [C15: from Anglo-Norman, from *oyer* to hear + *terminer* to judge]

oyez *or* **oyes** ('əʊ'jɛs, -'jɛz) *sentence substitute.* **1** a cry, usually uttered three times, by a public crier or court official for silence and attention before making a proclamation.

◆ *n* **2** such a cry. [C15: via Anglo-Norman from OF *oiez* hear!]

-oyl *suffix of nouns* (in chemistry) indicating an acyl group or radical: *ethanoyl, methanoyl*. [C20: from O(XYGEN) -YL]

Oyo ★ ('əʊjəʊ) *n* a state of SW Nigeria, formed in 197 from part of Western State. Capital: Ibadan. Pop 3 593 453 (1992 est.). Area: 28 454 sq. km (10 986 sc miles).

oyster ('ɔɪstə) *n* **1a** an edible marine bivalve mollusc ha ing a rough irregularly shaped shell and occurring o the sea bed, mostly in coastal waters. **1b** (*as modifier*): *oys ter farm; oyster knife*. **2** any of various similar and relate molluscs, such as the pearl oyster and the saddle oyste **3** the oyster-shaped piece of dark meat in the hollow c the pelvic bone of a fowl. **4** something from which ac vantage, delight, profit, etc., may be derived: *the world i his oyster*. **5** *Inf.* a very uncommunicative person. ◆ *vb* (*intr*) to dredge for, gather, or raise oysters. [C14 *oistr* from OF *uistre*, from L *ostrea*, from Gk *ostreon*; rel. to G *osteon* bone, *ostrakon* shell]

oyster bed *n* a place, esp. on the sea bed, where oyste breed and grow naturally or are cultivated for food c pearls. Also called: **oyster bank, oyster park**.

oystercatcher ('ɔɪstə,kætʃə) *n* a shore bird having black or black-and-white plumage and a long stout late ally compressed red bill.

oyster crab *n* any of several small soft-bodied crabs tha live as commensals in the mantles of oysters.

oyster plant *n* **1** another name for **salsify** (sense 1). Also called: **sea lungwort**. a prostrate coastal plant wit clusters of blue flowers.

oz *or* **oz.** *abbrev. for* ounce. [from It. *onza*]

Oz (ɒz) *n Austral. sl.* Australia.

Özal ★ (əʊ'zɑːl) *n* Turgut ('tɜːgʊt). 1927–93, Turkish states man: prime minister (1983–89); president (1989–93).

Ozalid ('ɒzəlɪd) *n* **1** *Trademark.* a method of duplicatin type matter, illustrations, etc., when printed on translu cent paper. **2** a reproduction produced by this method

Ozark Plateau ★ ('əʊzɑːk) *n*, **Ozark Mountains**, *c* **Ozarks** *pl n* an eroded plateau in S Missouri, N Arkan sas, and NE Oklahoma. Area: about 130 000 sq. kr (50 000 sq. miles).

ozocerite *or* **ozokerite** (əʊ'zəʊkə,raɪt) *n* a brown c greyish wax that occurs associated with petroleum an is used for making candles and waxed paper. [C19: fron G *Ozokerit*, from Gk *ozein* odour + *kēros* beeswax]

ozone ('əʊzəʊn, əʊ'zəʊn) *n* **1** a colourless gas with chlorine-like odour, formed by an electric discharge ii oxygen: a strong oxidizing agent, used in bleaching sterilizing water, purifying air, etc. Formula: O_3. Techni cal name: **trioxygen**. **2** *Inf.* clean bracing air, as found a the seaside. [C19: from G *Ozon*, from Gk: smell]
▸ **ozonic** (əʊ'zɒnɪk) *or* **ozonous** *adj*

ozone-friendly *adj* not harmful to the ozone laye using substances that do not produce gases harmful t the ozone layer: *an ozone-friendly refrigerator*.

ozone layer *n* the region of the stratosphere with th highest concentration of ozone molecules, which by ab sorbing high-energy solar ultraviolet radiation protect organisms on earth. Also called: **ozonosphere**.

ozonize *or* **ozonise** ('əʊzəʊ,naɪz) *vb* **ozonizes, ozonizing ozonized** *or* **ozonises, ozonising, ozonised.** (*tr*) **1** to conver (oxygen) into ozone. **2** to treat (a substance) with ozone
▸ ,**ozoni'zation** *n* ▸ ,**ozoni'sation** *n* ▸ '**ozo,nizer** *or* '**ozo,nise** *n*

ozonosphere (əʊ'zəʊnə,sfɪə, -'zɒnə-) *n* another nam for **ozone layer**.

Pp

p *or* **P** (piː) *n, pl* **p's, P's,** *or* **Ps. 1** the 16th letter of the English alphabet. **2** a speech sound represented by this letter. **3 mind one's p's and q's.** to be careful to behave correctly and use polite or suitable language.

p *symbol for:* **1** (in Britain) penny *or* pence. **2** *Music.* piano: an instruction to play quietly. **3** pico-. **4** *Physics.* **4a** momentum. **4b** proton. **4c** pressure.

P *symbol for:* **1** *Chem.* phosphorus. **2** *Physics.* **2a** parity. **2b** poise. **2c** power. **2d** pressure. **3** (on road signs) parking. **4** *Chess.* pawn. **5** *Currency.* **5a** peseta. **5b** peso. **6** (of a medicine or drug) available only from a chemist's shop, but not requiring a prescription to obtain it.

p. *abbrev. for:* **1** (*pl* **pp.**) page. **2** part. **3** participle. **4** past. **5** per. **6** pint. **7** pipe. **8** population. **9** post. [L: after] **10** pro. [L: in favour of; for]

p- *prefix* short for **para-**¹ (sense 6).

pa (pɑː) *n* an informal word for **father.**

Pa 1 *the chemical symbol for* protactinium. **2** *symbol for* pascal.

PA *abbrev. for:* **1** personal assistant. **2** *Mil.* Post Adjutant. **3** power of attorney. **4** press agent. **5** Press Association. **6** private account. **7** public-address system. **8** publicity agent. **9** Publishers Association. **10** purchasing agent. **11** *Insurance.* particular average.

Pa. *abbrev. for* Pennsylvania.

p.a. *abbrev. for* per annum. [L: yearly]

Pabst ★ (*German* paːpst) *n* **G(eorge) W(ilhelm)**. 1885–1967, German film director, whose films include *Joyless Street* (1925), *Pandora's Box* (1929), and *The Last Act* (1954).

pabulum ('pæbjuləm) *n Rare.* **1** food. **2** food for thought, esp. when bland or dull. [C17: from L, from *pascere* to feed]

PABX (in Britain) *abbrev. for* private automatic branch exchange. See also **PBX.**

Pac. *abbrev. for* Pacific.

paca ('pɑːkə, 'pækə) *n* a large burrowing rodent of Central and South America, having white-spotted brown fur. [C17: from Sp., from Amerind]

pace¹ (peɪs) *n* **1a** a single step in walking. **1b** the distance covered by a step. **2** a measure of length equal to the average length of a stride, approximately 3 feet. **3** speed of movement, esp. of walking or running. **4** rate or style of proceeding at some activity: *to live at a fast pace.* **5** manner or action of stepping, walking, etc.; gait. **6** any of the manners in which a horse or other quadruped walks or runs. **7** a manner of moving, sometimes developed in the horse, in which the two legs on the same side are moved at the same time. **8 keep pace with.** to proceed at the same speed as. **9 put (someone) through his paces.** to test the ability of (someone). **10 set the pace.** to determine the rate at which a group runs or walks or proceeds at some other activity. ◆ *vb* **paces, pacing, paced. 11** (*tr*) to set or determine the pace for, as in a race. **12** (often foll. by *about, up and down,* etc.) to walk with regular slow or fast paces, as in boredom, agitation, etc.: *to pace the room.* **13** (*tr;* often foll. by *out*) to measure by paces: *to pace out the distance.* **14** (*intr*) to walk with slow regular strides. **15** (*intr*) (of a horse) to move at the pace (the specially developed gait). [C13: via OF from L *passūs* step, from *pandere* to extend (the legs as in walking)]

pace² ('peɪsɪ; *Latin* 'pɑːke) *prep* with due deference to: used to acknowledge politely someone who disagrees. [C19: from L, from *pāx* peace]

PACE (peɪs) *n* (in England and Wales) *acronym for* Police and Criminal Evidence Act.

pace bowler *n Cricket.* a bowler who characteristically delivers the ball rapidly.

pacemaker ('peɪs,meɪkə) *n* **1** a person, horse, vehicle, etc., used in a race or speed trial to set the pace. **2** a per-

son, organization, etc., regarded as being the leader in a particular activity. **3** Also called: **cardiac pacemaker.** a small area of specialized tissue within the wall of the heart whose spontaneous electrical activity initiates and controls the heartbeat. **4** Also called: **artificial pacemaker.** an electronic device to assume the functions of the natural cardiac pacemaker.

pacer ('peɪsə) *n* **1** a horse trained to move at a special gait. **2** another word for **pacemaker** (sense 1).

pacesetter ('peɪs,sɛtə) *n* another word for **pacemaker** (senses 1, 2).

paceway ('peɪs,weɪ) *n Austral.* a racecourse for trotting and pacing.

Pachelbel ★ (*German* 'paxɛlbəl) *n* **Johann** ('joːhan). 1653–1706, German organist and composer, noted esp. for his popular *Canon in D Major.*

pachisi (pə'tʃiːzɪ) *n* an Indian game somewhat resembling backgammon, played on a cruciform board using six cowries as dice. [C18: from Hindi, from *pacīs* twenty-five (the highest throw)]

Pachuca ★ (*Spanish* pa'tʃuka) *n* a city in central Mexico, capital of Hidalgo state, in the Sierra Madre Oriental: silver mines; university (1961). Pop.: 174 013 (1990).

pachyderm ('pækɪ,dɜːm) *n* any very large thick-skinned mammal, such as an elephant, rhinoceros, or hippopotamus. [C19: from F *pachyderme,* from Gk *pakhudermos,* from *pakhus* thick + *derma* skin]
► ,pachy'dermatous *adj*

pacific (pə'sɪfɪk) *adj* **1** tending or conducive to peace; conciliatory. **2** not aggressive. **3** free from conflict; peaceful. [C16: from OF, from L *pācificus,* from *pāx* peace + *facere* to make]
► pa'cifically *adv*

Pacific ★ (pə'sɪfɪk) *n* **1** *the.* short for **Pacific Ocean.** ◆ *adj* **2** of or relating to the Pacific Ocean or its islands.

Pacific Islands ★ *pl n* a former Trust Territory; an island group in the W Pacific Ocean, mandated to Japan after World War I and assigned to the US by the United Nations in 1947: comprised 2141 islands (96 inhabited) of the Caroline, Marshall, and Mariana groups (excluding Guam). In 1978 the Northern Marianas became a commonwealth in union with the US. The three remaining entities consisting of the Marshall Islands, the Republic of Belau (formerly Palau), and the Federated States of Micronesia became self-governing during the period 1979–80. In 1982 they signed agreements of free association with the US. Administrative centre: Saipan (Mariana Islands). Land area: about 1800 sq. km (700 sq. miles), scattered over about 7 500 000 sq. km (3 000 000 sq. miles) of ocean.

Pacific Northwest ★ *n* the region of North America lying north of the Columbia River and west of the Rockies.

Pacific Ocean ★ *n* the world's largest and deepest ocean, lying between Asia and Australia and North and South America. Area: about 165 760 000 sq. km (64 000 000 sq. miles). Average depth: 4215 m (14 050 ft). Greatest depth: Challenger Deep (in the Marianas Trench), 11 033 m (37 073 ft). Greatest width: (between Panama and Mindanao, Philippines) 17 066 km (10 600 miles).

Pacific rim *n* the regions, countries, etc. that lie on the western shores of the Pacific Ocean, esp. in the context of their developing manufacturing capacity and consumer markets.

pacifier ('pæsɪ,faɪə) *n* **1** a person or thing that pacifies. **2** *US & Canad.* a baby's dummy or teething ring.

pacifism ('pæsɪ,fɪzəm) *n* **1** the belief that violence of any kind is unjustifiable and that one should not participate

in war, etc. **2** the belief that international disputes can be settled by arbitration rather than war.
▸ **'pacifist** *n, adj*

pacify ('pæsɪˌfaɪ) *vb* **pacifies, pacifying, pacified.** (*tr*) **1** to calm the anger or agitation of; mollify. **2** to restore to peace or order. [C15: from OF *pacifier*; see PACIFIC]
▸ **paci,fiable** *adj* ▸ **pacification** (ˌpæsɪfɪ'keɪʃən) *n*

Pacino ★ (pə'tʃiːnəʊ) *n* **Al,** full name *Alfredo James Pacino.* born 1940, US film actor; his films include *The Godfather* (1972), *Scent of a Woman* (1992), and *Heat* (1995).

pack[1] (pæk) *n* **1a** a bundle or load, esp. one carried on the back. **1b** (*as modifier*): *a pack animal.* **2** a collected amount of anything. **3** a complete set of similar things, esp. a set of 52 playing cards. **4** a group of animals of the same kind, esp. hunting animals: *a pack of hounds.* **5** any group or band that associates together, esp. for criminal purposes. **6** any group or set regarded dismissively: *a pack of fools; a pack of lies.* **7** *Rugby.* the forwards of a team. **8** the basic organizational unit of Cub Scouts and Brownie Guides. **9** *US & Canad.* same as **packet** (sense 1). **10** short for **pack ice. 11** the quantity of something, such as food, packaged for preservation. **12** *Med.* a sheet or blanket, either damp or dry, for wrapping about the body, esp. for its soothing effect. **13** another name for **rucksack** or **backpack. 14** Also called: **face pack.** a cream treatment that cleanses and tones the skin. **15** a parachute folded and ready for use. **16 go to the pack.** *Austral. & NZ inf.* to fall into a worse state or condition. **17** *Computing.* another name for **deck** (sense 4). ◆ *vb* **18** to place or arrange (articles) in (a container), such as clothes in a suitcase. **19** (*tr*) to roll up into a bundle. **20** (when *passive,* often foll. by *out*) to press tightly together; cram: *the audience packed into the foyer; the hall was packed out.* **21** to form (snow, ice, etc.) into a hard compact mass or (of snow, etc.) to become compacted. **22** (*tr*) to press in or cover tightly. **23** (*tr*) to load (a horse, donkey, etc.) with a burden. **24** (often foll. by *off* or *away*) to send away or go away, esp. hastily. **25** (*tr*) to seal (a joint) by inserting a layer of compressible material between the faces. **26** (*tr*) *Med.* to treat with a pack. **27** (*tr*) *Sl.* to be capable of inflicting (a blow, etc.): *he packs a mean punch.* **28** (*tr*) *US inf.* to carry or wear habitually: *he packs a gun.* **29** (*tr*; often foll. by *in, into, to,* etc.) *US, Canad., & NZ.* to carry (goods, etc.), esp. on the back. **30 send packing.** *Inf.* to dismiss peremptorily. ◆ See also **pack in, pack up.** [C13: from ?]
▸ **'packable** *adj*

pack[2] (pæk) *vb* (*tr*) to fill (a legislative body, committee, etc.) with one's own supporters: *to pack a jury.* [C16: ? changed from PACT]

package ('pækɪdʒ) *n* **1** any wrapped or boxed object or group of objects. **2a** a proposition, offer, or thing for sale in which separate items are offered together as a unit. **2b** (*as modifier*): *a package holiday; a package deal.* **3** the act or process of packing or packaging. **4** *Computing.* a set of programs designed for a specific type of problem. **5** the usual US and Canad. word for **packet** (sense 1). ◆ *vb* **packages, packaging, packaged.** (*tr*) **6** to wrap in or put into a package. **7** to design and produce a package for (retail goods). **8** to group (separate items) together as a single unit. **9** to compile (complete books) for a publisher to market.
▸ **'packager** *n*

packaging ('pækɪdʒɪŋ) *n* **1** the box or wrapping in which a product is offered for sale. **2** the presentation of a person, product, etc., to the public in a way designed to build up a favourable image.

pack drill *n* a military punishment of marching about carrying a full pack of equipment.

packer ('pækə) *n* **1** a person or company whose business is to pack goods, esp. food: *a meat packer.* **2** a person or machine that packs.

packet ('pækɪt) *n* **1** a small or medium-sized container of cardboard, paper, etc., often together with its contents: *a packet of biscuits.* Usual US and Canad. word: **package, pack. 2** a small package; parcel. **3** Also called: **packet boat.** a boat that transports mail, passengers, goods, etc., on a fixed short route. **4** *Sl.* a large sum of money: *to cost a packet.* **5** *Computing.* a unit into which a larger piece of data is broken down for more efficient transmission.

◆ *vb* **6** (*tr*) to wrap up in a packet or as a packet. [C16: from OF *pacquet,* from *pacquer* to pack, from ODu. *pak* a pack]

packhorse ('pækˌhɔːs) *n* a horse used to transport goods, equipment, etc.

pack ice *n* a large area of floating ice, consisting of pieces that have become massed together.

pack in *vb* (*tr, adv*) *Brit. & NZ inf.* to stop doing (something) (esp. in **pack it in**).

packing ('pækɪŋ) *n* **1a** material used to cushion packed goods. **1b** (*as modifier*): *a packing needle.* **2** the packaging of foodstuffs. **3** any substance or material used to make joints watertight or gastight.

pack rat *n* a rat of W North America, having a long tail that is furry in some species.

packsaddle ('pækˌsædˀl) *n* a saddle hung with packs, equipment, etc., used on a pack animal.

packthread ('pækˌθrɛd) *n* a strong twine for sewing or tying up packages.

pack up *vb* (*adv*) **1** to put (things) away in a proper or suitable place. **2** *Inf.* to give up (an attempt) or stop doing (something). **3** (*intr*) (of an engine, etc.) to fail to operate; break down.

pact (pækt) *n* an agreement or compact between two or more parties, nations, etc. [C15: from OF *pacte,* from L *pactum,* from *pacīscī* to agree]

pad[1] (pæd) *n* **1** a thick piece of soft material used to make something comfortable, give it shape, or protect it. **2** Also called: **stamp pad, ink pad.** a block of firm absorbent material soaked with ink for transferring to a rubber stamp. **3** Also called: **notepad, writing pad.** a number of sheets of paper fastened together along one edge. **4** a flat piece of stiff material used to back a piece of blotting paper. **5a** the fleshy cushion-like underpart of the foot of a cat, dog, etc. **5b** any of the parts constituting such a structure. **6** any of various level surfaces or flat-topped structures, such as a launch pad. **7** the large flat floating leaf of the water lily. **8** *Sl.* a person's residence. ◆ *vb* **pads, padding, padded.** (*tr*) **9** to line, stuff, or fill out with soft material, esp. in order to protect or shape. **10** (often foll. by *out*) to inflate with irrelevant or false information: *to pad out a story.* [C16: from ?]

pad[2] (pæd) *vb* **pads, padding, padded. 1** (*intr*; often foll. by *along, up,* etc.) to walk with a soft or muffled tread. **2** (when *intr,* often foll. by *around*) to travel (a route, etc.) on foot, esp. at a slow pace; tramp: *to pad around the country.* ◆ *n* **3** a dull soft sound, esp. of footsteps. [C16: ?from MDu. *paden,* from *pad* PATH]

Padang ★ ('pɑːdɑːŋ) *n* a port in W Indonesia, in W Sumatra at the foot of the **Padang Highlands** on the Indian Ocean. Pop.: 477 344 (1990).

padded cell *n* a room, esp. one in a mental hospital, with padded surfaces in which violent inmates are placed.

padding ('pædɪŋ) *n* **1** any soft material used to pad clothes, etc. **2** superfluous material put into a speech or written work to pad it out; waffle. **3** inflated or false entries in a financial account, esp. an expense account.

paddle[1] ('pædˀl) *n* **1** a short light oar with a flat blade at one or both ends, used without a rowlock. **2** Also called: **float.** a blade of a water wheel or paddle wheel. **3** a period of paddling: *to go for a paddle upstream.* **4a** a paddle wheel used to propel a boat. **4b** (*as modifier*): *a paddle steamer.* **5** any of various instruments shaped like a paddle and used for beating, mixing, etc. **6** a table-tennis bat. **7** the flattened limb of a seal, turtle, etc., specialized for swimming. ◆ *vb* **paddles, paddling, paddled. 8** to propel (a canoe, etc.) with a paddle. **9 paddle one's own canoe. 9a** to be self-sufficient. **9b** to mind one's own business. **10** (*tr*) to stir or mix with or as if with a paddle. **11** to row (a boat) steadily, but not at full pressure. **12** (*intr*) to swim with short rapid strokes, like a dog. **13** (*tr*) *US & Canad. inf.* to spank. [C15: from ?]
▸ **'paddler** *n*

paddle[2] ('pædˀl) *vb* **paddles, paddling, paddled.** (*mainly intr*) **1** to walk or play barefoot in shallow water, mud, etc. **2** to dabble the fingers, hands, or feet in water. **3** to walk

unsteadily, like a baby. **4** (*tr*) *Arch.* to fondle with the fingers. ◆ *n* **5** the act of paddling in water. [C16: from ?]
▶ **'paddler** *n*

paddle wheel *n* a large wheel fitted with paddles, turned by an engine to propel a vessel.

paddock ('pædək) *n* **1** a small enclosed field, often for grazing or training horses. **2** (in horse racing) the enclosure in which horses are paraded and mounted before a race. **3** *Austral. & NZ.* any area of fenced land. [C17: var. of dialect *parrock*, from OE *pearruc* enclosure, of Gmc origin. See PARK]

paddy[1] ('pædɪ) *n, pl* **paddies. 1** Also called: **paddy field.** a field planted with rice. **2** rice as a growing crop or when harvested but not yet milled. [from Malay *pādī*]

paddy[2] ('pædɪ) *n, pl* **paddies.** *Brit. inf.* a fit of temper. [C19: from *Paddy* inf. name for an Irishman]

pademelon *or* **paddymelon** ('pædɪ,mɛlən) *n* a small wallaby of coastal scrubby regions of Australia. [C19: of Abor. origin]

Paderborn ★ (*German* pɑːdər'bɔrn) *n* a market town in NW Germany in North Rhine-Westphalia: scene of the meeting between Charlemagne and Pope Leo III (799 A.D.) that led to the foundation of the Holy Roman Empire. Pop.: 131 513 (1995 est.).

Paderewski ★ (*Polish* padɛ'rɛfski) *n* **Ignace Jan** (iɲas jan). 1860–1941, Polish pianist, composer, and statesman; prime minister (1919).

padlock ('pæd,lɒk) *n* **1** a detachable lock having a hinged or sliding shackle, which can be used to secure a door, lid, etc., by passing the shackle through rings or staples. ◆ *vb* **2** (*tr*) to fasten as with a padlock. [C15 *pad*, from ?]

Padova ★ ('pɑːdova) *n* the Italian name for **Padua.**

padre ('pɑːdrɪ) *n Inf.* (*sometimes cap.*) **1** father: used to address or refer to a priest. **2** a chaplain to the armed forces. [via Sp. or It. from L *pater* father]

padsaw ('pæd,sɔː) *n* a small narrow saw used for cutting curves. [C19: from PAD[1] (in the sense: a handle that can be fitted to various tools) + SAW[1]]

Padua ★ ('pædjʊə, 'pædjʊə) *n* a city in NE Italy, in Veneto: important in Roman and Renaissance times; university (1222); botanical garden (1545). Pop.: 212 589 (1994 est.). Latin name: **Patavium** (pə'teɪvɪəm). Italian name: **Padova.**

Padus ★ ('peɪdəs) *n* the Latin name for the **Po**[2].

paean *or US* (*sometimes*) **pean** ('piːən) *n* **1** a hymn sung in ancient Greece in thanksgiving to a deity. **2** any song of praise. **3** enthusiastic praise: *the film received a paean from the critics.* [C16: via L from Gk *paiān* hymn to Apollo, from his title *Paiān*, the physician of the gods]

paediatrician *or esp. US* **pediatrician** (,piːdɪə'trɪʃən) *n* a medical practitioner who specializes in paediatrics.

paediatrics *or esp. US* **pediatrics** (,piːdɪ'ætrɪks) *n* (*functioning as sing*) the branch of medical science concerned with children and their diseases.
▶ ,**paedi'atric** *or esp. US* ,**pedi'atric** *adj*

paedo-, *before a vowel* **paed-,** *or esp. US* **pedo-, ped-** *combining form.* indicating a child or children: *paedophilia.* [from Gk *pais, paid-* child]

paedomorphosis (,piːdəʊ'mɔːfəsɪs) *n* the resemblance of adult animals to the young of their ancestors.

paedophilia *or esp. US* **pedophilia** (,piːdəʊ'fɪlɪə) *n* the condition of being sexually attracted to children.
▶ **paedophile** *or esp. US* **pedophile** ('piːdəʊ,faɪl) *or* ,**paedo-'phili,ac** *or esp. US* ,**pedo'phili,ac** *n, adj*

paella (paɪ'ɛlə) *n, pl* **paellas** (-ləz). **1** a Spanish dish made from rice, shellfish, chicken, and vegetables. **2** the pan in which a paella is cooked. [from Catalan, from OF *paelle*, from L *patella* small pan]

paeony ('piːənɪ) *n, pl* **paeonies.** a variant spelling of **peony.**

Paestum ★ ('pɛstəm) *n* an ancient Greek colony on the coast of Lucania in S Italy.

pagan ('peɪgən) *n* **1** a member of a group professing any religion other than Christianity, Judaism, or Islam. **2** a person without any religion; heathen. ◆ *adj* **3** of or relating to pagans. **4** heathen; irreligious. [C14: from

Church L *pāgānus* civilian (hence, not a soldier of Christ), from L: villager, from *pāgus* village]
▶ **'pagandom** *n* ▶ **'paganish** *adj* ▶ **'paganism** *n*

Paganini ★ (*Italian* paga'niːni) *n* **Niccolò** (nikko'lɔ). 1782–1840, Italian violinist and composer.

paganize *or* **paganise** ('peɪgə,naɪz) *vb* **paganizes, paganizing, paganized** *or* **paganises, paganising, paganised.** to become pagan or convert to paganism.

page[1] (peɪdʒ) *n* **1** one side of one of the leaves of a book, newspaper, etc., or the written or printed matter it bears. **2** such a leaf considered as a unit. **3** an episode, phase, or period: *a glorious page in the revolution.* **4** a screenful of information from a website, teletext service, etc., displayed on a television monitor or visual display unit. ◆ *vb* **pages, paging, paged. 5** another word for **paginate.** [C15: via OF from L *pāgina*]

page[2] (peɪdʒ) *n* **1** a boy employed to run errands, carry messages, etc., for the guests in a hotel, club, etc. **2** a youth in attendance at official functions or ceremonies, esp. weddings. **3** *Medieval history.* **3a** a boy in training for knighthood in personal attendance on a knight. **3b** a youth in the personal service of a person of rank. ◆ *vb* **pages, paging, paged.** (*tr*) **4** to call out the name of (a person), esp. by a loudspeaker system, so as to give him a message. **5** to call (a person) by an electronic device, such as a bleeper. **6** to act as a page to or attend as a page. [C13: via OF from It. *paggio*, prob. from Gk *paidion* boy, from *pais* child]

Page ★ (peɪdʒ) *n* **1** Sir **Earle** (**Christman Grafton**). 1880–1961, Australian statesman; co-leader, with S. M. Bruce, of the federal government of Australia (1923–29). **2** Sir **Frederick Handley.** 1885–1962, British pioneer in the design and manufacture of aircraft.

pageant ('pædʒənt) *n* **1** an elaborate colourful display portraying scenes from history, etc. **2** any magnificent or showy display, procession, etc. [C14: from Med. L *pāgina* scene of a play, from L: PAGE[1]]

pageantry ('pædʒəntrɪ) *n, pl* **pageantries. 1** spectacular display or ceremony. **2** *Arch.* pageants collectively.

pageboy ('peɪdʒ,bɔɪ) *n* **1** a smooth medium-length hairstyle with the ends of the hair curled under. **2** a less common word for **page**[2].

pager ('peɪdʒə) *n* an electronic device, capable of receiving short messages, used by people who need to be contacted urgently.

page-three *n modifier Brit.* denoting a scantily dressed attractive girl, as photographed on page three of some tabloid newspapers.

page-turner *n* a very exciting or interesting book. [C20: from the notion that a reader cannot stop turning the pages]

paginate ('pædʒɪ,neɪt) *vb* **paginates, paginating, paginated.** (*tr*) to number the pages of (a book, manuscript, etc.) in sequence. Cf. **foliate.**
▶ ,**pagi'nation** *n*

Pagnol ★ (*French* paɲɔl) *n* **Marcel** (**Paul**) (marsɛl). 1895–1974, French dramatist, film director, and novelist, noted for his depiction of Provençal life in such films as *Manon des Sources* (1952; remade 1986).

pagoda (pə'gəʊdə) *n* an Indian or Far Eastern temple, esp. a tower, usually pyramidal and having many storeys. [C17: from Port. *pagode*, ult. from Sansk. *bhagavatī* divine]

pagoda tree *n* a Chinese leguminous tree with ornamental white flowers.

Pago Pago ★ ('pɑːŋgəʊ 'pɑːŋgəʊ) *n* a port in American Samoa, on SE Tutuila Island. Pop.: 4000 (1990). Former name: **Pango Pango.**

Pahang ★ (pə'hʌŋ) *n* a state of Peninsular Malaysia, on the South China Sea: the largest Malayan state; mountainous and heavily forested. Capital: Kuala Lipis. Pop.: 1 056 100 (1993 est.). Area: 35 964 sq. km (13 886 sq. miles).

Pahlavi ★ ('pɑːləvɪ) *n* **1** Mohammed Reza ('riːzə). 1919–80, shah of Iran (1941–79); forced into exile (1979). **2** his father, **Reza.** 1877–1944, shah of Iran (1925–41). Originally an army officer, he gained power by a coup d'état (1921) and was chosen shah by the National Assembly.

Pahsien ★ ('pɑː'fjen) *n* another name for **Chongqing**.

paid (peɪd) *vb* **1** the past tense and past participle of **pay**[1]. **2 put paid to.** *Chiefly Brit. & NZ.* to end or destroy: *breaking his leg put paid to his hopes of running in the Olympics.*

paid-up *adj* **1** having paid the required fee to be a member of an organization, etc. **2** denoting a security in which all the instalments have been paid; fully paid: *a paid-up share.* **3** denoting all the money that a company has received from its shareholders: *the paid-up capital.* **4** denoting an endowment assurance policy on which the payment of premiums has stopped and the surrender value has been used to purchase a new single-premium policy.

Paignton ★ ('peɪntən) *n* a town and resort in SW England, in Devon: administratively part of Torbay since 1968.

pail (peɪl) *n* **1** a bucket, esp. one made of wood or metal. **2** Also called: **pailful.** the quantity that fills a pail. [OE *pægel*]

paillasse ('pælɪˌæs, ˌpælɪ'æs) *n* a variant spelling (esp. US) of **palliasse**.

pain (peɪn) *n* **1** the sensation of acute physical hurt or discomfort caused by injury, illness, etc. **2** emotional suffering or mental distress. **3 on pain of.** subject to the penalty of. **4** Also called: **pain in the neck.** *Inf.* a person or thing that is a nuisance. ◆ *vb* (*tr*) **5** to cause (a person) hurt, grief, anxiety, etc. **6** *Inf.* to annoy; irritate. ◆ See also **pains**. [C13: from OF *peine*, from L *poena* punishment, grief, from Gk *poinē* penalty]
▶ 'painless *adj*

Paine ★ (peɪn) *n* **Thomas.** 1737–1809, US political pamphleteer, born in England. His works include *Common Sense* (1776), supporting the American colonists' fight for independence; and *The Rights of Man* (1791–92), a justification of the French Revolution.

pained (peɪnd) *adj* having or expressing pain or distress, esp. mental or emotional distress.

painful ('peɪnfʊl) *adj* **1** causing pain; distressing: *a painful duty.* **2** affected with pain. **3** tedious or difficult. **4** *Inf.* extremely bad.
▶ 'painfully *adv* ▶ 'painfulness *n*

painkiller ('peɪnˌkɪlə) *n* **1** an analgesic drug or agent. **2** anything that relieves pain.

pains (peɪnz) *pl n* **1** care or trouble (esp. in **take pains, be at pains to**). **2** painful sensations experienced during contractions in childbirth; labour pains.

painstaking ('peɪnzˌteɪkɪŋ) *adj* extremely careful, esp. as to fine detail.
▶ 'pains,takingly *adv* ▶ 'pains,takingness *n*

paint (peɪnt) *n* **1** a substance used for decorating or protecting a surface, esp. a mixture consisting of a solid pigment suspended in a liquid that dries to form a hard coating. **2** a dry film of paint on a surface. **3** *Inf.* face make-up, such as rouge. **4** short for **greasepaint**. ◆ *vb* **5** to make (a picture) of (a figure, landscape, etc.) with paint applied to a surface such as canvas. **6** to coat (a surface, etc.) with paint, as in decorating. **7** (*tr*) to apply (liquid, etc.) onto (a surface): *she painted the cut with antiseptic.* **8** (*tr*) to apply make-up onto (the face, lips, etc.). **9** (*tr*) to describe vividly in words. **10 paint the town red.** *Inf.* to celebrate uninhibitedly. [C13: from OF *peint* painted, from *peindre* to paint, from L *pingere* to paint]
▶ 'painty *adj*

paintball game ('peɪntˌbɔːl) *n* a game in which teams of players simulate a military skirmish, shooting each other with paint pellets that explode on impact.

paintbox ('peɪntˌbɒks) *n* a box containing a tray of dry watercolour paints.

paintbrush ('peɪntˌbrʌʃ) *n* a brush used to apply paint.

Painted Desert ★ *n* a section of high plateau country of N central Arizona, along the N side of the Little Colorado River Valley: brilliant-coloured rocks; occupied largely by Navaho and Hopi Indians. Area: about 20 000 sq. km (7500 sq. miles).

painted lady *n* a migratory butterfly with pale brownish-red mottled wings.

painter[1] ('peɪntə) *n* **1** a person who paints surfaces as a trade. **2** an artist who paints pictures.
▶ 'painterly *adj*

painter[2] ('peɪntə) *n* a line attached to the bow of a boat for tying it up. [C15: prob. from OF *penteur* strong rope]

painting ('peɪntɪŋ) *n* **1** the art of applying paints to canvas, etc. **2** a picture made in this way. **3** the act of applying paint to a surface.

paint stripper *or* **remover** *n* a liquid, often caustic, used to remove paint from a surface.

paintwork ('peɪntˌwɜːk) *n* a surface, such as wood or a car body, that is painted.

pair (peə) *n, pl* **pairs** *or* (*functioning as sing or pl*) **pair. 1** two identical or similar things matched for use together: *a pair of socks.* **2** two persons, animals, things, etc., used or grouped together: *a pair of horses; a pair of scoundrels.* **3** an object considered to be two identical or similar things joined together: *a pair of trousers.* **4** two people joined in love or marriage. **5** a male and a female animal of the same species kept for breeding purposes. **6** *Parliament.* **6a** two opposed members who both agree not to vote on a specified motion. **6b** the agreement so made. **7** two playing cards of the same rank or denomination. **8** one member of a matching pair: *I can't find the pair to this glove.* ◆ *vb* **9** (often foll. by *off*) to arrange or fall into groups of twos. **10** to group or be grouped in matching pairs. **11** to join or be joined in marriage; mate or couple. **12** (when *tr*, *usually passive*) *Parliament.* to form or cause to form a pair. [C13: from OF *paire*, from L *paria* equal (things), from *pār* equal]

> **USAGE NOTE** Like other collective nouns, *pair* takes a singular or a plural verb according to whether it is seen as a unit or as a collection of two things: *the pair are said to dislike each other; a pair of good shoes is essential.*

paisley ('peɪzlɪ) *n* **1** a pattern of small curving shapes with intricate detailing. **2** a soft fine wool fabric traditionally printed with this pattern. **3** a shawl made of this fabric, popular in the late 19th century. **4** (*modifier*) of or decorated with this pattern: *a paisley scarf.* [C19: after PAISLEY[1]]

Paisley[1] ★ ('peɪzlɪ) *n* an industrial town in SW Scotland, the administrative centre of Renfrewshire: one of the world's chief centres for the manufacture of thread, linen, and gauze in the 19th century. Pop.: 75 526 (1991).

Paisley[2] ★ ('peɪzlɪ) *n* **Ian (Richard Kyle).** born 1926, Northern Ireland politician and Presbyterian minister; cofounder and leader of the Ulster Democratic Unionist Party.
▶ 'Paisley,ite *n*

pajamas (pə'dʒɑːməz) *pl n* the US spelling of **pyjamas**.

pakeha ('pɑːkɪˌhɑː) *n NZ.* a European, as distinct from a Maori: *Maori and pakeha.* [from Maori]

Paki ('pækɪ) *Brit. sl., offens.* ◆ *n, pl* **Pakis. 1** a Pakistani or person of Pakistani descent. ◆ *adj* **2** Pakistani or of Pakistani descent.

Pakistan ★ (ˌpɑːkɪ'stɑːn) *n* **1** a republic in S Asia, on the Arabian Sea: the Union of Pakistan, formed in 1947, comprised West and East Pakistan; East Pakistan gained independence as Bangladesh in 1971 and West Pakistan became Pakistan; a member of the Commonwealth from 1947, it withdrew from 1972 until 1989: contains the fertile plains of the Indus valley rising to mountains in the north and west. Official language: Urdu. Official religion: Muslim. Currency: rupee. Capital: Islamabad. Pop.: 136 183 000 (1997). Area: 801 508 sq. km (309 463 sq. miles). **2** a former republic in S Asia consisting of the provinces of West Pakistan and East Pakistan (now Bangladesh), 1500 km (900 miles) apart: formed in 1947 from the predominantly Muslim parts of India.
▶ ,Paki'stani *n, adj*

pakora (pə'kɔːrə) *n* an Indian dish consisting of pieces of

★ people and places

vegetable, chicken, etc., dipped in spiced batter and deep-fried. [C20: from Hindi]

pal (pæl) *Inf.* ◆ *n* **1** a close friend; comrade. ◆ *vb* **pals, palling, palled. 2** (*intr;* usually foll. by *with*) to associate as friends. [C17: from E Gypsy: brother, ult. from Sansk. *bhrātar* BROTHER]

PAL (pæl) *n acronym for* phase alternation line: a colour-television broadcasting system used generally in Europe.

Pal. *abbrev. for* Palestine.

palace ('pælɪs) *n* (*cap. when part of a name*) **1** the official residence of a reigning monarch. **2** the official residence of various high-ranking people, as of an archbishop. **3** a large and richly furnished building resembling a royal palace. [C13: from OF *palais*, from L *Palātium* PALATINE]

Palacio Valdés ★ (*Spanish* pa'laθjo bal'des) *n* **Armando** (ar'mando). 1853–1938, Spanish novelist and critic.

paladin ('pælədɪn) *n* **1** one of the legendary twelve peers of Charlemagne's court. **2** a knightly champion. [C16: via F from It. *paladino*, from L *palātīnus* imperial official]

palaeo-, *before a vowel* **palae-** *or esp. US* **paleo-, pale-** *combining form.* old, ancient, or prehistoric: *palaeography.* [from Gk *palaios* old]

palaeobotany *or US* **paleobotany** (,pælɪəʊ'bɒtənɪ) *n* the study of fossil plants.
▸ ,palaeo'botanist *or US* ,paleo'botanist *n*

Palaeocene *or US* **Paleocene** ('pælɪəʊ,siːn) *adj* **1** of, denoting, or formed in the first epoch of the Tertiary period. ◆ *n* **2** the. the Palaeocene epoch or rock series. [C19: from F, from *paléo* PALAEO- + Gk *kainos* new]

palaeoclimatology *or US* **paleoclimatology** (,pælɪəʊ,klaɪmə'tɒlədʒɪ) *n* the study of climates of the geological past.
▸ ,palaeo,clima'tologist *or US* ,paleo,clima'tologist *n*

palaeoecology *or US* **paleoecology** (,pælɪəʊɪ-'kɒlədʒɪ) *n* the study of fossil animals and plants in order to deduce their ecology and the environment conditions in which they lived.
▸ ,palaeo,eco'logical *or US* ,paleo,eco'logical *adj*
▸ ,palaeo'cologist *or US* ,paleo'cologist *n*

palaeography *or US* **paleography** (,pælɪ'ɒɡrəfɪ) *n* **1** the study of the handwritings of the past, and often the manuscripts, etc., so that they may be dated, read, etc. **2** a handwriting of the past.
▸ ,palae'ographer *or US* ,pale'ographer *n* ▸ **palaeographic** (,pælɪəʊ'ɡræfɪk), ,palaeo'graphical *or US* ,paleo'graphic, ,paleo'graphical *adj*

Palaeolithic *or US* **Paleolithic** (,pælɪəʊ'lɪθɪk) *n* **1** the period of the emergence of primitive man and the manufacture of unpolished chipped stone tools, about 2.5 million to 3 million years ago. ◆ *adj* **2** (*sometimes not cap.*) of or relating to this period.

palaeomagnetism *or* US **paleomagnetism** (,pælɪəʊ'mæɡnɪtɪzəm) *n* the study of the fossil magnetism in rocks, used to determine the past configuration of the earth's constituents.

palaeontology *or US* **paleontology** (,pælɪɒn-'tɒlədʒɪ) *n* the study of fossils to determine the structure and evolution of extinct animals and plants and the age and conditions of deposition of the rock strata in which they are found. [C19: from PALAEO- + ONTO- + -LOGY]
▸ **palaeontological** *or US* **paleontological** (,pælɪ,ɒntə-'lɒdʒɪk'l) *adj* ▸ ,palaeon'tologist *or US* ,paleon'tologist *n*

Palaeozoic (,pælɪəʊ'zəʊɪk) *adj* **1** of, denoting, or relating to an era of geological time that began 600 million years ago with the Cambrian period and lasted about 375 million years until the end of the Permian period. ◆ *n* **2** the. the Palaeozoic era. [C19: from PALAEO- + Gk *zōē* life + -IC]

palanquin *or* **palankeen** (,pælən'kiːn) *n* a covered litter, formerly used in the Orient, carried on the shoulders of four men. [C16: from Port. *palanquim*, from Prakrit *pallanka*, from Sansk. *paryanka* couch]

palatable ('pælətəb'l) *adj* **1** pleasant to taste. **2** acceptable or satisfactory.
▸ ,palata'bility *or* 'palatableness *n* ▸ 'palatably *adv*

palatal ('pælət'l) *adj* **1** Also: **palatine.** of or relating to the palate. **2** *Phonetics.* of, relating to, or denoting a speech

sound articulated with the blade of the tongue touching the hard palate. ◆ *n* **3** Also called: **palatine.** the bony plate that forms the palate. **4** *Phonetics.* a palatal speech sound, such as (j).
▸ 'palatally *adv*

palatalize *or* **palatalise** ('pælətə,laɪz) *vb* **palatalizes, palatalizing, palatalized** *or* **palatalises, palatalising, palatalised.** (*tr*) to pronounce (a speech sound) with the blade of the tongue touching the palate.
▸ ,palatali'zation *or* ,palatali'sation *n*

palate ('pælɪt) *n* **1** the roof of the mouth, separating the oral and nasal cavities. See **hard palate, soft palate. 2** the sense of taste: *she had no palate for the wine.* **3** relish or enjoyment. [C14: from L *palātum,* ? of Etruscan origin]

> **USAGE NOTE** Avoid confusion with **palette** or **pallet.**

palatial (pə'leɪʃəl) *adj* of, resembling, or suitable for a palace; sumptuous.
▸ pa'latially *adv*

palatinate (pə'lætɪnɪt) *n* a territory ruled by a palatine prince or noble or count palatine.

Palatinate (pə'lætɪnɪt) *n* **1 the.** either of two territories in SW Germany, once ruled by the counts palatine. **Upper Palatinate** is now in Bavaria; **Lower** or **Rhine Palatinate** is now in Rhineland-Palatinate, Baden-Württemberg, and Hesse. German name: **Pfalz. 2** a native or inhabitant of the Palatinate.
▸ 'Pala,tine *adj, n*

palatine[1] ('pælə,taɪn) *adj* **1** (of an individual) possessing royal prerogatives in a territory. **2** of or relating to a count palatine, county palatine, palatinate, or palatine. **3** of or relating to a palace. ◆ *n* **4** *Feudal history.* the lord of a palatinate. **5** any of various important officials at the late Roman, Merovingian, or Carolingian courts. [C15: via F from L *palātīnus* belonging to the palace, from *palātium*; see PALACE]

palatine[2] ('pælə,taɪn) *adj* **1** of the palate. ◆ *n* **2** either of two bones forming the hard palate. [C17: from F *palatin,* from L *palātum* palate]

Palatine ★ ('pælə,taɪn) *n* **1** one of the Seven Hills of Rome: traditionally the site of the first settlement of Rome. ◆ *adj* **2** of, relating to, or designating this hill.

Palau Islands ★ (pɑː'laʊ) *pl n* a former name (until 1981) of th (of the Republic of) **Belau.**

palaver (pə'lɑːvə) *n* **1** tedious or time-consuming business, esp. when of a formal nature: *all the palaver of filling in forms.* **2** confused talk and activity; hubbub. **3** (often used humorously) a conference. **4** *Now rare.* an intended to flatter or persuade. ◆ *vb* **5** (*intr*) (often used humorously) to have a conference. **6** (*intr*) to talk confusedly. **7** (*tr*) to flatter or cajole. [C18: from Port. *palavra* talk, from L *parabola* PARABLE]

Palawan ★ (*Spanish* pa'lavan) *n* an island of the SW Philippines between the South China Sea and the Sulu Sea: the westernmost island in the country; mountainous and forested. Capital: Puerto Princesa. Pop.: 311 548 (1980). Area: 11 785 sq. km (4550 sq. miles).

palazzo pants (pə'lætsəʊ) *pl n* women's trousers with very wide legs. [C20: *palazzo* from It., lit.: PALACE]

pale[1] (peɪl) *adj* **1** lacking brightness or colour: *pale morning light.* **2** (of a colour) whitish. **3** dim or wan: *the pale stars.* **4** feeble: *a pale effort.* ◆ *vb* **pales, paling, paled. 5** to make or become pale or paler; blanch. **6** (*intr;* often foll. by *before*) to lose superiority (in comparison to): *her beauty paled before that of her hostess.* [C13: from OF *palle,* from L *pallidus,* from *pallēre* to look wan]
▸ 'palely *adv* ▸ 'paleness *n* ▸ 'palish *adj*

pale[2] (peɪl) *n* **1** a wooden post or strip used as an upright member in a fence. **2** an enclosing barrier, esp. a fence made of pales. **3** an area enclosed by a pale. **4** *Heraldry.* a vertical stripe, usually in the centre of a shield. **5 beyond the pale.** outside the limits of social convention. [C14: from OF *pal,* from L *pālus* stake]

paleface ('peɪlˌfeɪs) *n* a derogatory term for a White person, said to have been used by North American Indians.

Palembang ★ (pɑːˈlɛmbɑːŋ) *n* a port in W Indonesia, in S Sumatra; oil refineries; university (1955). Pop.: 1 084 483 (1990).

Palencia ★ (*Spanish* paˈlenθia) *n* a city in N central Spain: earliest university in Spain (1208); seat of Castilian kings (12th–13th centuries); communications centre. Pop.: 77 752 (1991).

Palenque ★ (*Spanish* paˈleŋke) *n* the site of an ancient Mayan city in S Mexico famous for its architectural ruins.

paleo- *or before a vowel* **pale-** *combining form.* variants (esp. US) of **palaeo-**.

Palermo ★ (pəˈlɛəməu, -ˈlɜː-; *Italian* paˈlɛrmo) *n* the capital of Sicily, on the NW coast: founded by the Phoenicians in the 8th century B.C. Pop.: 694 749 (1994 est.).

Palestine ★ ('pælɪˌstaɪn) *n* 1 Also called: the **Holy Land**, **Canaan**. the area between the Jordan River and the Mediterranean Sea in which most of the biblical narrative is located. 2 the province of the Roman Empire in this region. 3 the former British mandatory territory created by the League of Nations in 1922 (but effective from 1920), and including all of the present territories of Israel, which was created following the British withdrawal in 1948. In 1993 Israel offered Palestinians autonomy in the Gaza Strip and Jericho (implemented in 1994).

Palestine Liberation Organization *n* an organization founded in 1964 with the aim of creating a state for Palestinian Arabs. In 1993 it signed a peace agreement with Israel, which granted Palestinian autonomy in the Gaza Strip and West Bank. Abbrev.: **PLO**.

Palestinian (ˌpælɪˈstɪnɪən) *adj* 1 of or relating to Palestine, its native Arab population, or their descendants. ◆ *n* 2 a Palestinian Arab, esp. one now living in the Palestinian Administered Territories, Israel, Jordan, Lebanon, or as a refugee from Israeli-occupied territory.

Palestinian Administered Territories ★ *n* the Gaza Strip and the West Bank in Israel: these areas were granted autonomous status under the control of the Palestinian National Authority following the 1993 peace agreement between Israel and the Palestine Liberation Organization. Also called: **Palestinian Autonomous Areas**.

Palestinian National Authority *n* the authority formed in 1994 to govern the Palestinian Administered Territories. Abbrev.: **PNA**.

Palestrina ★ (ˌpælɛˈstriːnə) *n* **Giovanni Pierluigi da** (dʒoˈvanni pierˈluiːdʒi da). ?1525–94, Italian composer and master of counterpoint. His works, nearly all for unaccompanied choir and religious in nature, include the *Missa Papae Marcelli* (1555).

palette ('pælɪt) *n* 1 Also: **pallet**. a flat piece of wood, plastic, etc., used by artists as a surface on which to mix their paints. 2 the range of colours characteristic of a particular artist, painting, or school of painting: *a restricted palette*. 3 the available range of colours or patterns that can be displayed by a computer on a visual display unit. [C17: from F, dim. of *pale* shovel, from L *pala* spade]

> **USAGE NOTE** Avoid confusion with **palate** or **pallet**.

palette *or* **pallet knife** *n* a spatula with a thin flexible blade used in painting and cookery.

Paley ★ ('peɪlɪ) *n* **William**. 1743–1805, British theologian and utilitarian philosopher. His works include *Horae Paulinae* (1790) and *Natural Theology* (1802).

palfrey ('pɔːlfrɪ) *n Arch.* a light saddle horse, esp. ridden by women. [C12: from OF *palefrei*, from Med. L, from LL *paraverēdus*, from Gk *para* beside + L *verēdus* light fleet horse, of Celtic origin]

Pali ('pɑːlɪ) *n* an ancient language of India derived from Sanskrit; the language of the Buddhist scriptures. [C19: from Sansk. *pāli-bhāsa*, from *pāli* canon + *bhāsa* language, of Dravidian origin]

palimony ('pælɪmənɪ) *n US.* alimony awarded to a nonmarried partner after the break-up of a long-term relationship. [C20: from PAL + ALIMONY]

palimpsest ('pælɪmpˌsɛst) *n* 1 a manuscript on which two or more texts have been written, each one being erased to make room for the next. ◆ *adj* 2 (of a text) written on a palimpsest. 3 (of a document, etc.) used as a palimpsest. [C17: from L *palimpsestus*, from Gk *palimpsēstos*, from *palin* again + *psēstos* rubbed smooth]

palindrome ('pælɪnˌdrəʊm) *n* a word or phrase the letters of which, when taken in reverse order, read the same: *able was I ere I saw Elba*. [C17: from Gk *palindromos* running back again]
> **palindromic** (ˌpælɪnˈdrɒmɪk) *adj*

paling ('peɪlɪŋ) *n* 1 a fence made of pales. 2 pales collectively. 3 a single pale. 4 the act of erecting pales.

palisade (ˌpælɪˈseɪd) *n* 1 a strong fence made of stakes driven into the ground, esp. for defence. 2 one of the stakes used in such a fence. ◆ *vb* **palisades, palisading, palisaded**. 3 (*tr*) to enclose with a palisade. [C17: via F from OProvençal *palissada*, ult. from L *pālus* stake]

Palk Strait ★ (pɔːk, pɔːlk) *n* a channel between SE India and N Ceylon. Width: about 64 km (40 miles).

pall[1] (pɔːl) *n* 1 a cloth covering, usually black, spread over a coffin or tomb. 2 a coffin, esp. during the funeral ceremony. 3 a dark heavy covering; shroud: *the clouds formed a pall over the sky*. 4 a depressing or oppressive atmosphere: *her bereavement cast a pall on the party*. 5 *Heraldry*. a Y-shaped bearing. 6 *Christianity*. a small square linen cloth with which the chalice is covered at the Eucharist. ◆ *vb* 7 (*tr*) to cover or depress with a pall. [OE *pæll*, from L *pallium* cloak]

pall[2] (pɔːl) *vb* 1 (*intr*; often foll. by *on*) to become boring, insipid, or tiresome (to): *history classes palled on me*. 2 to cloy or satiate, or become cloyed or satiated. [C14: var. of APPAL]

Palladian (pəˈleɪdɪən) *adj* denoting, relating to, or having the style of architecture created by Andrea Palladio. [C18: after Andrea PALLADIO]
> **Pal'ladian,ism** *n*

Palladio ★ (*Italian* palˈlaːdio) *n* **Andrea** (anˈdrɛːa). 1508–80, Italian architect who revived and developed classical architecture, esp. the ancient Roman ideals of symmetrical planning and harmonic proportions. His treatise *Four Books on Architecture* (1570) and his designs for villas and palaces influenced architecture in England and the US.

palladium[1] (pəˈleɪdɪəm) *n* a ductile malleable silvery-white element of the platinum metal group: used as a catalyst and, alloyed with gold, in jewellery, etc. Symbol: Pd; atomic no.: 46; atomic wt.: 106.4. [C19: after the asteroid *Pallas*, at the time (1803) a recent discovery]

palladium[2] (pəˈleɪdɪəm) *n* something believed to ensure protection; safeguard. [C17: after the *Palladium*, a statue of Pallas Athena, Gk goddess of wisdom]

Pallas Athena *or* **Pallas** ★ *n* another name for **Athena**.

pallbearer ('pɔːlˌbeərə) *n* a person who carries or escorts the coffin at a funeral.

pallet[1] ('pælɪt) *n* a straw-filled mattress or bed. [C14: from Anglo-Norman *paillet*, from OF *paille* straw, from L *palea* straw]

> **USAGE NOTE** Avoid confusion with **palate** or **palette**.

pallet[2] ('pælɪt) *n* 1 an instrument with a handle and a flat, sometimes flexible, blade used by potters for shaping. 2 a portable platform for storing and moving goods. 3 *Horology*. the locking lever that engages and disengages to give impulses to the balance. 4 a variant spelling of **palette** (sense 1). 5 *Music*. a flap valve that opens to allow air from the wind chest to enter an organ pipe, causing it to sound. [C16: from OF *palette* a little shovel, from L *pala* spade]

palletize *or* **palletise** ('pælətaɪz) *vb* **palletizes, palletizing, palletized** *or* **palletises, palletising, palletised**. (*tr*) to store or transport (goods) on pallets.
> **,palleti'zation** *or* **,palleti'sation** *n*

★ people and places

palliasse *or esp.* US **paillasse** ('pælɪˌæs, ˌpælɪ'æs) *n* a straw-filled mattress; pallet. [C18: from F *paillasse*, from It. *pagliaccio*, ult. from L *palea* PALLET[1]]

palliate ('pælɪˌeɪt) *vb* **palliates, palliating, palliated.** (*tr*) **1** to lessen the severity of (pain, disease, etc.) without curing; alleviate. **2** to cause (an offence, etc.) to seem less serious; extenuate. [C16: from LL *palliāre* to cover up, from L *pallium* a cloak]
▸ ˌpalliˈation *n*

palliative ('pælɪətɪv) *adj* **1** relieving without curing. ♦ *n* **2** something that palliates, such as a sedative drug.
▸ 'palliatively *adv*

pallid ('pælɪd) *adj* lacking colour, brightness, or vigour: *a pallid complexion; a pallid performance.* [C17: from L *pallidus*, from *pallēre* to be PALE[1]]
▸ 'pallidly *adv* ▸ pal'lidity *n*

pall-mall ('pæl'mæl) *n Obs.* **1** a game in which a ball is driven by a mallet along an alley and through an iron ring. **2** the alley itself. [C17: from obs. F, from It. *pallamaglio*, from *palla* ball + *maglio* mallet]

Pall Mall ★ ('pæl 'mæl) *n* a street in London, noted for its many clubs.

pallor ('pælə) *n* a pale condition, esp. when unnatural: *fear gave his face a deathly pallor.* [C17: from L: whiteness (of the skin), from *pallēre* to be PALE[1]]

pally ('pælɪ) *adj* **pallier, palliest.** *Inf.* on friendly terms.

palm[1] (pɑːm) *n* **1** the inner part of the hand from the wrist to the base of the fingers. **2** a linear measure based on the breadth or length of a hand, equal to three to four inches (7.5 to 10 centimetres) or seven to ten inches (17.5 to 25 centimetres) respectively. **3** the part of a glove that covers the palm. **4a** one side of the blade of an oar. **4b** the face of the fluke of an anchor. **5** a flattened part of the antlers of certain deer. **6 in the palm of one's hand.** at one's mercy or command. ♦ *vb* (*tr*) **7** to conceal in or about the hand, as in sleight-of-hand tricks, etc. ♦ See also **palm off.** [C14 *paume*, via OF from L *palma*]
▸ palmar ('pælmə) *adj*

palm[2] (pɑːm) *n* **1** any treelike plant of a tropical and subtropical family having a straight unbranched trunk crowned with large pinnate or palmate leaves. **2** a leaf or branch of any of these trees, a symbol of victory, success, etc. **3** merit or victory. [OE, from L *palma*, from the likeness of its spreading fronds to a hand; see PALM[1]]
▸ palmaceous (pæl'meɪʃəs) *adj*

Palma[1] ★ (*Spanish* 'palma) *n* the capital of the Balearic Islands, on the SW coast of Majorca: a tourist centre. Pop.: 296 754 (1991). Official name: **Palma de Mallorca.**

Palma[2] ★ (*Italian* 'palma) *n* **Jacopo** ('jaːkopo), known as *Palma Vecchio*, original name *Jacopo Negretti*. ?1480–1528, Venetian painter, noted esp. for his portraits of women.

palmate ('pælmeɪt, -mɪt) *or* **palmated** *adj* **1** shaped like an open hand: *palmate antlers.* **2** *Bot.* having five lobes that spread out from a common point: *palmate leaves.* **3** (of most water birds) having three toes connected by a web.

Palm Beach ★ *n* a town in SE Florida, on an island between Lake Worth (a lagoon) and the Atlantic: major resort and tourist centre. Pop.: 9814 (1990).

Palme ★ (*Swedish* 'palmə) *n* (**Sven**) **Olof** (**Joachim**) ('uːlɔf). 1927–86, Swedish Social Democratic statesman; prime minister (1969–76, 1982–86); assassinated.

palmer ('pɑːmə) *n* (in medieval Europe) **1** a pilgrim bearing a palm branch as a sign of his visit to the Holy Land. **2** any pilgrim. [C13: from OF *palmier*, from Med. L, from L *palma* PALM[2]]

Palmer ★ ('pɑːmə) *n* **1 Arnold.** born 1929, US professional golfer: won the US Open Championship (1960) and the British Open Championship (1961; 1962). **2 Samuel.** 1805–81, British painter of visionary landscapes, influenced by William Blake.

Palmer Archipelago ★ *n* a group of islands between South America and Antarctica: part of the British colony of Falkland Islands and Dependencies. Former name: **Antarctic Archipelago.**

Palmer Land ★ *n* the S part of the Antarctic Peninsula.

Palmer Peninsula ★ *n* the former name (until 1964) for the **Antarctic Peninsula.**

Palmerston[1] ★ ('pɑːməstən) *n* the former name (1869–1911) of **Darwin[1].**

Palmerston[2] ★ ('pɑːməstən) *n* **Henry John Temple**, 3rd Viscount Palmerston. 1784–1865, British statesman; foreign secretary (1830–34; 1835–41; 1846–51); prime minister (1855–58; 1859–65). His talent was for foreign affairs, in which he earned a reputation as a British nationalist and for high-handedness and gunboat diplomacy.

Palmerston North ★ *n* a city in New Zealand, in the S North Island on the Manawatu River. Pop. (urban area): 76 300 (1995 est.).

palmetto (pæl'metəʊ) *n, pl* **palmettos** *or* **palmettoes.** any of several small chiefly tropical palms with fan-shaped leaves. [C16: from Sp. *palmito* a little PALM[2]]

Palmira ★ (*Spanish* pal'mira) *n* a city in W Colombia: agricultural trading centre. Pop.: 256 823 (1995 est.).

palmistry ('pɑːmɪstrɪ) *n* the process or art of telling fortunes, etc., by the configuration of lines and bumps on a person's hand. Also called: **chiromancy.** [C15 *pawmestry*, from *paume* PALM[1]; the second element is unexplained]
▸ 'palmist *n*

palmitic acid (pæl'mɪtɪk) *n* a white crystalline solid that is a saturated fatty acid: used in the manufacture of soap and candles. Formula: $C_{15}H_{31}COOH$. Systematic name: **hexadecanoic acid.** [C19: from F]

palm off *vb* (*tr, adv*; often foll. by *on*) **1** to offer, sell, or spend fraudulently: *to palm off a counterfeit coin.* **2** to divert in order to be rid of: *I palmed the unwelcome visitor off on John.*

palm oil *n* an oil obtained from the fruit of certain palms, used as an edible fat and in soap, etc.

Palm Springs ★ *n* a city in the US, in California: a popular tourist resort. Pop.: 40 181 (1990).

Palm Sunday *n* the Sunday before Easter commemorating Christ's triumphal entry into Jerusalem.

palmtop computer ('pɑːmˌtɒp) *n* a computer that is small enough to be held in the hand. Often shortened to **palmtop.** Cf. **laptop computer.**

palmy ('pɑːmɪ) *adj* **palmier, palmiest. 1** prosperous, flourishing, or luxurious: *a palmy life.* **2** covered with, relating to, or resembling palms.

palmyra (pæl'maɪrə) *n* a tall tropical Asian palm with large fan-shaped leaves used for thatching and weaving. [C17: from Port. *palmeira* palm tree; ? infl. by PALMYRA, in Syria]

Palmyra ★ (pæl'maɪrə) *n* **1** an ancient city in central Syria: said to have been built by Solomon. Biblical name: **Tadmor. 2** an island in the central Pacific, in the Line Islands: under US administration.

Palo Alto ★ *n* **1** ('pæləʊ 'æltəʊ). a city in W California, southeast of San Francisco: founded in 1891 as the seat of Stanford University. Pop.: 55 900 (1990). **2** (*Spanish* 'palo 'alto). a battlefield in E Mexico, northwest of Monterrey, where the first battle (1846) of the Mexican War took place, in which the Mexicans under General Mariano Arista were defeated by the Americans under General Zachary Taylor.

Palomar ★ ('pæləˌmɑː) *n* **Mount.** a mountain in S California, northeast of San Diego: site of **Mount Palomar Observatory,** which has a large (200-inch) reflecting telescope. Height: 1871 m (6140 ft).

palomino (ˌpælə'miːnəʊ) *n, pl* **palominos.** a golden horse with a white mane and tail. [American Sp., from Sp.: dovelike, from L, from *palumbēs* ring dove]

Palos ★ (*Spanish* 'palɒs) *n* a village and former port in SW Spain: starting point of Columbus' voyage of discovery to America (1492).

palp (pælp) *or* **palpus** ('pælpəs) *n, pl* **palps** *or* **palpi** ('pælpaɪ). either of a pair of sensory appendages that arise from the mouthparts of crustaceans and insects. [C19: from F, from L *palpus* a touching]

palpable ('pælpəb[ə]l) *adj* **1** (*usually prenominal*) easily perceived by the senses or the mind; obvious: *a palpable lie.*

2 capable of being touched; tangible. [C14: from LL *palpābilis* that may be touched, from L *palpāre* to touch]
► ˌpalpaˈbility *n* ► ˈpalpably *adv*

palpate (ˈpælpeɪt) *vb* palpates, palpating, palpated. (*tr*) *Med.* to examine (an area of the body) by the sense of touch. [C19: from L *palpāre* to stroke]
► palˈpation *n*

palpebral (ˈpælpɪbrəl) *adj* of or relating to the eyelid. [C19: from LL, from L *palpebra* eyelid]

palpitate (ˈpælpɪˌteɪt) *vb* palpitates, palpitating, palpitated. (*intr*) **1** (of the heart) to beat rapidly. **2** to flutter or tremble. [C17: from L *palpitāre* to throb, from *palpāre* to stroke]
► ˈpalpitant *adj* ► ˌpalpiˈtation *n*

palsy (ˈpɔːlzɪ) *Pathol.* ♦ *n, pl* palsies. **1** paralysis, esp. of a specified type: *cerebral palsy.* ♦ *vb* palsies, palsying, palsied. (*tr*) **2** to paralyse. [C13 *palesi*, from OF *paralisie*, from L PARALYSIS]
► ˈpalsied *adj*

palter (ˈpɔːltə) *vb* (*intr*) **1** to act or talk insincerely. **2** to haggle. [C16: from ?]

paltry (ˈpɔːltrɪ) *adj* paltrier, paltriest. **1** insignificant; meagre. **2** worthless or petty. [C16: from Low Gmc *palter*, *paltrig* ragged]
► ˈpaltrily *adv* ► ˈpaltriness *n*

paludal (pəˈljuːdəl) *adj Rare.* **1** of or relating to marshes. **2** malarial. [C19: from L *palus* marsh]

paludism (ˈpæljuˌdɪzəm) *n* a less common word for **malaria**. [C19: from L *palus* marsh]

palynology (ˌpælɪˈnɒlədʒɪ) *n* the study of living and fossil pollen grains and plant spores. [C20: from Gk *palunein* to scatter + -LOGY]
► palynological (ˌpælɪnəˈlɒdʒɪkˀl) *adj* ► ˌpalyˈnologist *n*

Pamirs ★ (pəˈmɪəz) *pl n* the. a mountainous area of central Asia, mainly in Tajikistan and partly in Kyrgyzstan, extending into China and Afghanistan: consists of a complex of high ranges, from which the Tian Shan projects to the north, the Kunlun and Karakoram to the east, and the Hindu Kush to the west. Highest peak: Kongur Shan, 7719 m (25 326 ft). Also called: **Paˈmir**.

Pamlico Sound ★ (ˈpæmlɪkəʊ) *n* an inlet of the Atlantic between the E coast of North Carolina and its chain of offshore islands. Length: 130 km (80 miles).

pampas (ˈpæmpəz) *n* (*functioning as sing or more often pl*) **a** the extensive grassy plains of temperate South America, esp. in Argentina. **b** (*as modifier*): *pampas dwellers.* [C18: from American Sp. *pampa* (sing), from Amerind *bamba* plain]
► pampean (ˈpæmpɪən, pæmˈpiːən) *adj*

pampas grass (ˈpæmpəs, -pəz) *n* any of various large South American grasses, widely cultivated for their large feathery silver-coloured flower branches.

Pampeluna ★ (ˌpæmpəˈluːnə) *n* the former name of **Pamplona**.

pamper (ˈpæmpə) *vb* (*tr*) **1** to treat with affectionate and usually excessive indulgence; coddle; spoil. **2** *Arch.* to feed to excess. [C14: of Gmc origin]
► ˈpamperer *n*

pamphlet (ˈpæmflɪt) *n* **1** a brief publication generally having a paper cover; booklet. **2** a brief treatise, often on a subject of current interest, in pamphlet form. [C14 *pamflet*, from Med. L *Pamphilus* title of a 12th-century amatory poem from Gk *Pamphilos* proper name]

pamphleteer (ˌpæmflɪˈtɪə) *n* **1** a person who writes or issues pamphlets. ♦ *vb* **2** (*intr*) to write or issue pamphlets.

Pamphylia ★ (pæmˈfɪlɪə) *n* an area on the S coast of ancient Asia Minor.

Pamplona ★ (pæmˈpləʊnə; *Spanish* pamˈplona) *n* a city in N Spain in the foothills of the Pyrenees: capital of the kingdom of Navarre from the 11th century until 1841. Pop.: 182 465 (1994 est.). Former name: **Pampeluna**.

pan[1] (pæn) *n* **1a** a wide metal vessel used in cooking. **1b** (*in combination*): *saucepan.* **2** Also called: **panful.** the amount such a vessel will hold. **3** any of various similar vessels used in industry, etc. **4** a dish used esp. by gold prospectors for separating gold from gravel by washing and agitating. **5** either of the two dishlike receptacles on

a balance. **6** Also called: **lavatory pan.** *Brit.* the bowl of a lavatory. **7a** a natural or artificial depression in the ground where salt can be obtained by the evaporation of brine. **7b** a natural depression containing water or mud. **8** See **hardpan, brainpan. 9** a small cavity containing priming powder in the locks of old guns. **10** a hard substratum of soil. ♦ *vb* pans, panning, panned. **11** (when *tr*, often foll. by *off* or *out*) to wash (gravel) in a pan to separate particles of (valuable minerals) from it. **12** (*intr*; often foll. by *out*) (of gravel, etc.) to yield valuable minerals by this process. **13** (*tr*) *Inf.* to criticize harshly: *the critics panned his new play.* ♦ See also **pan out.** [OE *panne*]

pan[2] (pæn) *vb* pans, panning, panned. **1** to move (a film camera) or (of a film camera) to be moved so as to follow a moving object or obtain a panoramic effect. ♦ *n* **2** the act of panning. [C20: shortened from PANORAMIC]

Pan ★ (pæn) *n Greek myth.* the god of fields, woods, shepherds, and flocks, represented as a man with a goat's legs, horns, and ears. Related adjs.: **Pandean, Panic.**

Pan. *abbrev. for* Panama.

pan- *combining form.* **1** all or every: *panchromatic.* **2** including or relating to all parts or members: *Pan-American; pantheistic.* [from Gk *pan*, neuter of *pas* all]

panacea (ˌpænəˈsɪə) *n* a remedy for all diseases or ills. [C16: via L from Gk *panakeia*, from *pan* all + *akēs* remedy]
► ˌpanaˈcean *adj*

panache (pəˈnæʃ, -ˈnɑːʃ) *n* **1** a dashing manner; swagger: *he rides with panache.* **2** a plume on a helmet. [C16: via F from OIt. *pennacchio*, from LL *pinnāculum* feather, from L *pinna* feather]

panada (pəˈnɑːdə) *n* a mixture of flour, water, etc., or of breadcrumbs soaked in milk, used as a thickening. [C16: from Sp., from *pan* bread, from L *pānis*]

Panaji ★ (pɑːˈnɑːdʒiː) *n* a variant of **Panjim.**

Panama ★ (ˌpænəˈmɑː, ˈpænəˌmɑː) *n* **1** a republic in Central America, occupying the Isthmus of Panama: gained independence from Spain in 1821 and joined Greater Colombia; became independent in 1903, with the immediate area around the canal forming the Canal Zone under US jurisdiction; in 1979 Panama assumed sovereignty over the Canal Zone. Official language: Spanish; English is also widely spoken. Religion: chiefly Roman Catholic. Currency: balboa. Capital: Panama City. Pop.: 2 719 000 (1997). Area: 75 650 sq. km (29 201 sq. miles). **2 Isthmus of.** an isthmus linking North and South America, between the Pacific and the Caribbean. Length: 676 km (420 miles). Width (at its narrowest point): 50 km (31 miles). Former name: (Isthmus of) **Darien. 3 Gulf of.** a wide inlet of the Pacific in Panama.
► Panamanian (ˌpænəˈmeɪnɪən) *adj, n*

Panama Canal ★ *n* a canal across the Isthmus of Panama, linking the Atlantic and Pacific Oceans: extends from Colón on the Caribbean Sea southeast to Balboa on the Gulf of Panama; built by the US (1904–14), after an unsuccessful previous attempt (1880–89) by the French under de Lesseps. Length: 64 km (40 miles).

Panama Canal Zone ★ *n* See **Canal Zone.**

Panama City ★ *n* the capital of Panama, near the Pacific entrance of the Panama Canal: developed rapidly with the building of the Panama Canal; seat of the University of Panama (1935). Pop.: 445 902 (1994 est.).

Panama hat *n* (*sometimes not cap.*) a hat made of the plaited leaves of a palmlike plant of Central and South America. Often shortened to **panama** or **Panama.**

Pan-American *adj* of, relating to, or concerning North, South, and Central America collectively or the advocacy of political or economic unity among American countries.
► ˈPan-Aˈmericanˌism *n*

panatella (ˌpænəˈtɛlə) *n* a long slender cigar. [American Sp. *panetela* long slim biscuit, from It. *panatella* small loaf, from *pane* bread, from L *pānis*]

Panay ★ (pɑːˈnaɪ) *n* an island in the central Philippines, the westernmost of the Visayan Islands. Pop.: 2 595 314 (1980). Area: 12 300 sq. km (4750 sq. miles).

pancake (ˈpænˌkeɪk) *n* **1** a thin flat cake made from batter and fried on both sides. **2** a stick or flat cake of compressed make-up. **3** Also called: **pancake landing.** an aircraft landing made by levelling out a few feet from the ground and then dropping onto it. ◆ *vb* **pancakes, pancaking, pancaked. 4** to cause (an aircraft) to make a pancake landing or (of an aircraft) to make a pancake landing.

Pancake Day *n* another name for **Shrove Tuesday.** See **Shrovetide.**

panchromatic (ˌpænkrəʊˈmætɪk) *adj Photog.* (of an emulsion or film) made sensitive to all colours.
▶ **panchromatism** (pænˈkrəʊmə,tɪzəm) *n*

pancosmism (pænˈkɒz,mɪzəm) *n* the philosophical doctrine that the material universe is all that exists.

pancreas (ˈpæŋkrɪəs) *n* a large elongated glandular organ, situated behind the stomach, that secretes insulin and pancreatic juice. [C16: via NL from Gk *pankreas,* from PAN- + *kreas* flesh]
▶ **pancreatic** (ˌpæŋkrɪˈætɪk) *adj*

pancreatic juice *n* the clear alkaline secretion of the pancreas that is released into the duodenum and contains digestive enzymes.

pancreatin (ˈpæŋkrɪətɪn) *n* the powdered extract of the pancreas of certain animals, used in medicine as an aid to the digestion.

panda (ˈpændə) *n* **1** Also called: **giant panda.** a large black-and-white herbivorous bearlike mammal, related to the raccoons and inhabiting the high mountain bamboo forests of China. **2** lesser *or* red panda. a closely related smaller animal resembling a raccoon, of the mountain forests of S Asia, having a reddish-brown coat and ringed tail. [C19: via F from a native Nepalese word]

panda car *n Brit.* a police patrol car. [C20: so called because its blue-and-white markings resemble the black-and-white markings of the giant panda]

pandanus (pænˈdeɪnəs) *n, pl* **pandanuses.** any of various Old World tropical palmlike plants having leaves and roots yielding a fibre used for making mats, etc. [C19: via NL from Malay *pandan*]

Pandarus ★ (ˈpændərəs) *n* **1** *Greek myth.* the leader of the Lycians, allies of the Trojans in their war with the Greeks. He broke the truce by shooting Menelaus with an arrow and was killed in the ensuing battle by Diomedes. **2** (in medieval legend) the procurer of Cressida on behalf of Troilus.

Pandean (pænˈdiːən) *adj* of or relating to the god Pan.

pandect (ˈpændɛkt) *n* **1** a treatise covering all aspects of a particular subject. **2** (*often pl*) the complete body of laws of a country; legal code, esp. the digest of Roman civil law made in the 6th century by order of Justinian. [C16: via LL from Gk *pandektēs* containing everything, from PAN- + *dektēs* receiver]

pandemic (pænˈdɛmɪk) *adj* **1** (of a disease) affecting persons over a wide geographical area; extensively epidemic. ◆ *n* **2** a pandemic disease. [C17: from LL *pandēmus,* from Gk *pandēmos* general, from PAN- + *demos* the people]

pandemonium (ˌpændɪˈməʊnɪəm) *n* **1** wild confusion; uproar. **2** a place of uproar and chaos. [C17: coined by Milton for the capital of hell in *Paradise Lost,* from PAN- + Gk *daimōn* DEMON]

pander (ˈpændə) *vb* **1** (*intr;* foll. by *to*) to give gratification (to weaknesses or desires). **2** (*arch.* when tr) to act as a go-between in a sexual intrigue (for). ◆ *n also* **panderer. 3** a person who caters for vulgar desires. **4** a person who procures a sexual partner for another; pimp. [C16 (n): from *Pandare* Pandarus, in legend, the procurer of Cressida for Troilus]

pandit (ˈpʌndɪt; *spelling pron* ˈpændɪt) *n Hinduism.* a variant of **pundit** (sense 3).

P & L *abbrev. for* profit and loss.

P & O *abbrev. for* the Peninsular and Oriental Steam Navigation Company.

Pandora (pænˈdɔːrə) *or* **Pandore** ★ (pænˈdɔː, ˈpændɔː) *n Greek myth.* the first woman, made out of earth as the gods' revenge on man for obtaining fire from Prometheus. Given a box (**Pandora's box**) that she was forbidden to open, she disobeyed out of curiosity and released

from it all the ills that beset man, leaving only hope within. [from Gk, lit.: all-gifted]

p & p *Brit. abbrev. for* postage and packing.

pane (peɪn) *n* **1** a sheet of glass in a window or door. **2** a panel of a window, wall, etc. **3** a flat section or face, as of a cut diamond. [C13: from OF *pan* portion, from L *pannus* rag]

panegyric (ˌpænɪˈdʒɪrɪk) *n* a formal public commendation; eulogy. [C17: via F & L from Gk, from *panēguris* public gathering]
▶ **pane'gyrical** *adj* ▶ **pane'gyrically** *adv* ▶ **pane'gyrist** *n*
▶ **panegyrize** *or* **panegyrise** (ˈpænɪdʒɪ,raɪz) *vb*

panel (ˈpæn³l) *n* **1** a flat section of a wall, door, etc. **2** any distinct section of something formed from a sheet of material, esp. of a car body. **3** a piece of material inserted in a skirt, etc. **4a** a group of persons selected to act as a team in a quiz, to discuss a topic before an audience, etc. **4b** (*as modifier*): *a panel game.* **5** *Law.* **5a** a list of persons summoned for jury service. **5b** the persons on a jury. **6** *Scots Law.* a person accused of a crime. **7a** a thin board used as a surface or backing for an oil painting. **7b** a painting done on such a surface. **8** any picture with a length much greater than its breadth. **9** See **instrument panel.** **10** *Brit.* (formerly) **10a** a list of patients insured under the National Health Insurance Scheme. **10b** a list of medical practitioners available for consultation by these patients. ◆ *vb* **panels, panelling, panelled** *or US* **panels, paneling, paneled.** (*tr*) **11** to furnish or decorate with panels. **12** *Law.* **12a** to empanel (a jury). **12b** (in Scotland) to bring (a person) to trial; indict. [C13: from OF: portion, from *pan* piece of cloth, from L *pannus*]

panel beater *n* a person who beats out the bodywork of motor vehicles, etc.

panelling *or US* **paneling** (ˈpæn³lɪŋ) *n* **1** panels collectively, as on a wall or ceiling. **2** material used for making panels.

panellist *or US* **panelist** (ˈpæn³lɪst) *n* a member of a panel, esp. on radio or television.

panel pin *n* a slender nail with a narrow head.

panel saw *n* a saw with a long narrow blade for cutting thin wood.

panel van *n Austral. & NZ.* a small van.

Pan-European *adj* of or relating to all European countries or the advocacy of political or economic unity among European countries.

pang (pæŋ) *n* a sudden brief sharp feeling, as of loneliness, physical pain, or hunger. [C16: var. of earlier *prange,* of Gmc origin]

panga (ˈpæŋgə) *n* a broad heavy knife of E Africa. [from a native E African word]

Pangaea *or* **Pangea** ★ (pænˈdʒiːə) *n* the ancient supercontinent, comprising all the present continents joined together, which began to break up about 200 million years ago. See also **Laurasia, Gondwanaland.** [C20: from Gk, lit.: all-earth]

Pang-fou ★ (ˈpæŋˈfuː) *n* a variant transliteration of the Chinese name for Bengbu.

pangolin (pæŋˈgəʊlɪn) *n* a mammal of tropical Africa, S Asia, and Indonesia, having a scaly body and a long snout for feeding on ants and termites. Also called: **scaly anteater.** [C18: from Malay *peng-gōling,* from *gōling* to roll over; from its ability to roll into a ball]

Pango Pango ★ (ˈpɑːŋgəʊ ˈpɑːŋgəʊ) *n* the former name of **Pago Pago.**

panhandle[1] (ˈpæn,hænd³l) *n* (*sometimes cap.*) (in the US) a narrow strip of land that projects from one state into another.

panhandle[2] (ˈpæn,hænd³l) *vb* **panhandles, panhandling, panhandled.** *US inf.* to beg from (passers-by). [C19: prob. a back formation from *panhandler* a person who begs with a pan]
▶ **'pan,handler** *n*

Panhellenic (ˌpænhɛˈliːnɪk) *adj* of or relating to all the Greeks or all Greece.

panic (ˈpænɪk) *n* **1** a sudden overwhelming feeling of terror or anxiety, esp. one affecting a whole group of people. **2** (*modifier*) of or resulting from such terror: *panic*

measures. **3** (*modifier*) for use in an emergency: *panic stations; panic button.* ◆ *vb* **panics, panicking, panicked. 4** to feel or cause to feel panic. [C17: from F *panique*, from NL, from Gk *panikos* emanating from PAN, considered as the source of irrational fear]
▸ **'panicky** *adj*

Panic ('pænɪk) *adj* of or relating to the god Pan.

panic attack *n* an episode of acute and disabling anxiety associated with such physical symptoms as hyperventilation and sweating.

panic button *n* a button or switch that operates a safety device or alarm, for use in an emergency.

panic disorder *n Psychiatry.* a condition in which a person experiences recurrent panic attacks.

panic grass *n* any of various grasses, such as millet, grown in warm and tropical regions for fodder and grain. [C15 *panic*, from L *pānicum*, prob. a back formation from *pānicula* PANICLE]

panicle ('pænɪk°l) *n* a compound raceme, as in the oat. [C16: from L *pānicula* tuft, dim. of *panus* thread, ult. from Gk *penos* web]
▸ **'panicled** *adj* ▸ **paniculate** (pə'nɪkjuˌleɪt, -lɪt) *adj*

panic-stricken *or* **panic-struck** *adj* affected by panic.

panjandrum (pæn'dʒændrəm) *n* a pompous self-important official or person of rank. [C18: after a character in a nonsense work (1755) by S. Foote, E playwright]

Panjim ('pɑːnˌdʒɪm) *or* **Panaji** ★ *n* the capital of the Indian union territory of Goa, Daman, and Diu: a port on the Arabian Sea on the coast of Goa. Pop.: 85 515 (1991).

Pankhurst ★ ('pæŋkhɜːst) *n* **1** Dame **Christabel**. 1880–1958, British suffragette. **2** her mother, **Emmeline**. 1858–1928, British suffragette leader, who founded the militant Women's Social and Political Union (1903). **3** Sylvia, daughter of Emmeline Pankhurst. 1882–1960, British suffragette and pacifist.

pan loaf *n Scot.* a loaf of bread with a light crust all the way round. Often shortened to **pan.**

Panmunjom ★ ('pɑːn'mun'dʒɒm) *n* a village in the demilitarized zone of Korea: site of truce talks leading to the end of the Korean War (1950–53).

pannage ('pænɪdʒ) *n Arch.* **1** the right to pasture pigs in a forest. **2** payment for this. **3** acorns, beech mast, etc., on which pigs feed. [C13: from OF *pasnage*, ult. from L *pastion-, pastiō* feeding, from *pascere* to feed]

pannier ('pæniə) *n* **1** a large basket, esp. one of a pair slung over a beast of burden. **2** one of a pair of bags slung either side of the back wheel of a motorcycle, etc. **3** (esp. in the 18th century) **3a** a hooped framework to distend a woman's skirt. **3b** one of two puffed-out loops of material worn drawn back onto the hips. [C13: from OF *panier*, from L *pānārium* basket for bread, from *pānis* bread]

pannikin ('pænɪkɪn) *n Chiefly Brit.* a small metal cup or pan. [C19: from PAN[1] + -KIN]

pannikin boss *n Austral. sl.* a minor overseer.

Pannonia ★ (pə'nəʊnɪə) *n* a region of the ancient world south and west of the Danube: made a Roman province in 6 A.D.

panoply ('pænəplɪ) *n, pl* **panoplies. 1** a complete or magnificent array. **2** the entire equipment of a warrior. [C17: via F from Gk, from PAN- + *hopla* armour]
▸ **'panoplied** *adj*

panoptic (pæn'ɒptɪk) *adj* taking in all parts, aspects, etc., in a single view; all-embracing. [C19: from Gk *panoptēs* seeing everything]

panorama (ˌpænə'rɑːmə) *n* **1** an extensive unbroken view in all directions. **2** a wide or comprehensive survey of a subject. **3** a large extended picture of a scene, unrolled before spectators a part at a time so as to appear continuous. **4** another name for **cyclorama**. [C18: from PAN- + Gk *horāma* view]
▸ **panoramic** (ˌpænə'ræmɪk) *adj* ▸ **pano'ramically** *adv*

pan out *vb* (*intr, adv*) *Inf.* to work out; result.

panpipes ('pænˌpaɪps) *pl n* (*often sing; often cap.*) a number of reeds or whistles of graduated lengths bound together to form a musical wind instrument. Also called: **pipes of Pan, syrinx.**

pansy ('pænzɪ) *n, pl* **pansies. 1** a garden plant having flowers with rounded velvety petals, white, yellow, or purple in colour. See also **wild pansy. 2** *Sl.* an effeminate or homosexual man or boy. [C15: from OF *pensée* thought, from *penser* to think, from L *pensāre*]

pant (pænt) *vb* **1** to breathe with noisy deep gasps, as when out of breath from exertion. **2** to say (something) while breathing thus. **3** (*intr; often foll. by for*) to have a frantic desire (for). **4** (*intr*) to throb rapidly. ◆ *n* **5** the act or an instance of panting. **6** a short deep gasping noise. [C15: from OF *pantaisier*, from Gk *phantasioun* to have visions, from *phantasia* FANTASY]

pantalets *or* **pantalettes** (ˌpæntə'lets) *pl n* **1** long drawers extending below the skirts: worn during the 19th century. **2** ruffles for the ends of such drawers. [C19: dim. of PANTALOONS]

pantaloon (ˌpæntə'luːn) *n* **1** (in pantomime) an absurd old man, the butt of the clown's tricks. **2** (*usually cap.*) in commedia dell'arte) a lecherous old merchant dressed in pantaloons. [C16: from F *Pantalon*, from It. *Pantalone*, prob. from *San Pantaleone*, a fourth-century Venetian saint]

pantaloons (ˌpæntə'luːnz) *pl n* **1** *History.* **1a** men's tight-fitting trousers fastened below the calf or under the shoe. **1b** children's trousers resembling these. **2** *Inf.* any trousers, esp. baggy ones.

pantechnicon (pæn'teknɪkən) *n Brit.* **1** a large van, esp. one used for furniture removals. **2** a warehouse where furniture is stored. [C19: from PAN- + Gk *tekhnikon* relating to the arts, from *tekhnē* art; orig. a London bazaar, later used as a furniture warehouse]

Pantelleria ★ (*Italian* pantelle'riːa) *n* an Italian island in the Mediterranean, between Sicily and Tunisia: of volcanic origin; used by the Romans as a place of banishment. Pop.: 7316 (1991 est.). Area: 83 sq. km (32 sq. miles). Ancient name: **Cossyra** (kə'saɪrə).

pantheism ('pænθɪˌɪzəm) *n* **1** the doctrine that regards God as identical with the material universe or the forces of nature. **2** readiness to worship all gods.
▸ **'pantheist** *n* ▸ **panthe'istic** *or* **panthe'istical** *adj* ▸ **panthe'istically** *adv*

pantheon ('pænθɪən) *n* **1** (esp. in ancient Greece or Rome) a temple to all the gods. **2** all the gods of a religion. **3** a building commemorating a nation's dead heroes. [C14: via L from Gk *Pantheion*, from PAN- + -*theios* divine, from *theos* god]

Pantheon ★ (pæn'θiːən, 'pænθɪən) *n* a circular temple in Rome dedicated to all the gods, built by Agrippa in 27 B.C., rebuilt by Hadrian 120–24 A.D., and used since 609 A.D. as a Christian church.

panther ('pænθə) *n, pl* **panthers** *or* **panther. 1** another name for **leopard** (sense 1), esp. the black variety (**black panther**). **2** *US & Canad.* any of various related animals, esp. the puma. [C14: from OF *pantère*, from L *panthēra*, from Gk *panthēr*]

panties ('pæntɪz) *pl n* a pair of women's or children's underpants.

pantihose ('pæntɪˌhəʊz) *pl n* See **panty hose.**

pantile ('pænˌtaɪl) *n* a roofing tile, with an S-shaped cross section, so that the downward curve of one tile overlaps the upward curve of the next. [C17: from PAN[1] + TILE]

pantisocracy (ˌpæntɪ'sɒkrəsɪ) *n, pl* **pantisocracies. 1** a community, social group, etc., in which all have rule and everyone is equal. [C18: (coined by Robert SOUTHEY) from Gk, from PANTO- + *isos* equal + -CRACY]

panto ('pæntəʊ) *n, pl* **pantos.** *Brit. inf.* short for **pantomime** (sense 1).

panto- *or before a vowel* **pant-** *combining form.* all: *pantisocracy; pantograph; pantomime.* [from Gk *pant-, pas*]

pantograph ('pæntəˌɡrɑːf) *n* **1** an instrument consisting of pivoted levers for copying drawings, maps, etc., to any scale. **2** a sliding type of current collector, esp. a diamond-shaped frame mounted on a train roof in con-

---

★ people and places

tact with an overhead wire. **3** a device used to suspend a studio lamp so that its height can be adjusted.
▸ **pantographic** (ˌpæntəˈɡræfɪk) *adj*

antomime (ˈpæntəˌmaɪm) *n* **1** (in Britain) a kind of play performed at Christmas time characterized by farce, music, lavish sets, stock roles, and topical jokes. **2** a theatrical entertainment in which words are replaced by gestures and bodily actions. **3** action without words as a means of expression. **4** *Inf., chiefly Brit.* a confused or farcical situation. ♦ *vb* **pantomimes, pantomiming, pantomimed. 5** another word for **mime**. [C17: via L from Gk *pantomīmos*]
▸ **pantomimic** (ˌpæntəˈmɪmɪk) *adj* ▸ **pantomimist** (ˈpæntəˌmaɪmɪst) *n*

antothenic acid (ˌpæntəˈθɛnɪk) *n* an oily acid that is a vitamin of the B complex: occurs widely in animal and vegetable foods. [C20: from Gk *pantothen* from every side]

antry (ˈpæntrɪ) *n, pl* **pantries.** a small room in which provisions, cooking utensils, etc., are kept; larder. [C13: via Anglo-Norman from OF *paneterie* store for bread, ult. from L *pānis* bread]

ants (pænts) *pl n* **1** *Brit.* an undergarment covering the body from the waist to the thighs or knees. **2** the usual US and Canad. name for **trousers. 3** bore, scare, etc., **the pants off.** *Inf.* to bore, scare, etc., extremely. [C19: shortened from *pantaloons*]

anty girdle (ˈpæntɪ) *n* a foundation garment with a crotch, often of lighter material than a girdle.

anty hose *pl n* the US name for **tights** (sense 1). Also (Canad. and NZ) **pantyhose,** (Austral.) **pantihose.**

anufnik ★ (pæˈnuːfnɪk) *n* Sir **Andrzej** (ˈændreɪ). 1914–91, British composer and conductor, born in Poland. His works include ten symphonies, the cantata *Winter Solstice* (1972), and ballet music.

anzer (ˈpænzə; *German* ˈpantsər) *n* **1** (*modifier*) of or relating to the fast mechanized armoured units employed by the German army in World War II: *a panzer attack.* **2** a vehicle belonging to a panzer unit, esp. a tank. **3** (*pl*) armoured troops. [C20: from G, from MHG, from OF *panciere* coat of mail, from L *pantex* PAUNCH]

ão de Açúcar ★ (pãun di aˈsukar) *n* the Portuguese name for the **Sugar Loaf Mountain.**

aolozzi ★ (pauˈlɒtsɪ) *n* Sir **Eduardo** (**Luigi**) (ɛdˈwɑːdəu). born 1924, British sculptor and designer, noted esp. for his semiabstract metal figures.

aoting *or* **Pao-ting** ★ (ˈpauˈtɪŋ) *n* a variant transliteration of the Chinese name for **Baoding.**

aotow ★ (ˈpauˈtau) *n* a variant transliteration of the Chinese name for **Baotou.**

ap[1] (pæp) *n* **1** any soft or semiliquid food, esp. for babies or invalids; mash. **2** worthless or oversimplified ideas, etc.; drivel. **3** *S. African.* maize porridge. [C15: from MLow G *pappe,* via Med. L from L *pappāre* to eat]

ap[2] (pæp) *n* **1** *Arch. or Scot. & N English dialect.* a nipple or teat. **2** something resembling a breast, such as one of a pair of rounded hilltops. [C12: from ON, imit. of a sucking sound]

apa (pəˈpɑː) *n Old-fashioned.* an informal word for **father.** [C17: from F, a children's word for father]

apacy (ˈpeɪpəsɪ) *n, pl* **papacies. 1** the office or term of office of a pope. **2** the system of government in the Roman Catholic Church that has the pope as its head. [C14: from Med. L *pāpātia,* from *pāpa* POPE]

apadopoulos ★ (ˌpæpəˈdɒpələs; *Greek* papaˈðopulos) *n* **Georgios.** born 1919, Greek army officer and statesman; prime minister (1967–73) and president (1973) in Greece's military government.

apain (pəˈpeɪɪn, -ˈpaɪɪn) *n* an enzyme occurring in the unripe fruit of the papaya tree: used as a meat tenderizer and in medicine as an aid to protein digestion. [C19: from PAPAYA]

apal (ˈpeɪpˀl) *adj* of or relating to the pope or the papacy.
▸ **'papally** *adv*

apal States ★ *pl n* the temporal domain of the popes

in central Italy from 756 A.D. until the unification of Italy in 1870. Also called: **States of the Church.**

Papandreou ★ (ˌpæpənˈdreɪuː; *Greek* papanˈðreu) *n* **Andreas** (**George**) (anˈdreas). 1919–96, Greek socialist politician; prime minister (1981–89; 1993–96).

paparazzo (ˌpæpəˈrætsəu) *n, pl* **paparazzi** (-ˈrætsiː). a freelance photographer who specializes in candid camera shots of famous people. [C20: from It.]

papaver (pæˈpɑːvə) *n* any of a genus of hardy annual or perennial plants with showy flowers; poppy. [L: poppy]

papaveraceous (pəˌpeɪvəˈreɪʃəs) *adj* of or relating to a family of plants having large showy flowers and a cylindrical seed capsule with pores beneath the lid: includes the poppies and greater celandine. [C19: from NL, from L *papāver* poppy]

papaverine (pəˈpeɪvəˌriːn, -rɪn) *n* a white crystalline alkaloid found in opium and used to treat coronary spasms and certain types of colic. [C19: from L *papāver* poppy]

papaw (pəˈpɔː) *or* **pawpaw** *n* **1** Also called: **custard apple. 1a** a bush or small tree of Central North America, having small fleshy edible fruit. **1b** the fruit of this tree. **2** another name for **papaya.** [C16: from Sp. PAPAYA]

papaya (pəˈpaɪə) *n* **1** a Caribbean evergreen tree with a crown of large dissected leaves and large green hanging fruit. **2** the fruit of this tree, having a yellow sweet edible pulp and small black seeds. ♦ Also called: **papaw, pawpaw.** [C15 *papaye,* from Sp. *papaya,* of Amerind origin]

Papeete ★ (ˌpɑːpɪˈiːtɪ) *n* the capital of French Polynesia, on the NW coast of Tahiti: one of the largest towns in the S Pacific. Pop.: 78 814 (1988).

Papen ★ (*German* ˈpaːpən) *n* **Franz von** (frants fɒn). 1879–1969, German statesman; chancellor (1932) and vice chancellor (1933–34) under Hitler, whom he was instrumental in bringing to power.

paper (ˈpeɪpə) *n* **1** a substance made from cellulose fibres derived from rags, wood, etc., and formed into flat thin sheets suitable for writing on, decorating walls, wrapping, etc. **2** a single piece of such material, esp. if written or printed on. **3** (*usually pl*) documents for establishing the identity of the bearer. **4** (*pl*) Also called: **ship's papers.** official documents relating to a ship. **5** (*pl*) collected diaries, letters, etc. **6** See **newspaper, wallpaper. 7** *Government.* See **white paper, green paper. 8** a lecture or treatise on a specific subject. **9** a short essay. **10a** a set of examination questions. **10b** the student's answers. **11** *Commerce.* See **commercial paper. 12** *Theatre sl.* a free ticket. **13 on paper.** in theory, as opposed to fact. ♦ *adj* **14** made of paper: *paper cups do not last long.* **15** thin like paper: *paper walls.* **16** (*prenominal*) existing only as recorded on paper but not yet in practice: *paper expenditure.* **17** taking place in writing: *paper battles.* ♦ *vb* **18** to cover (walls) with wallpaper. **19** (*tr*) to cover or furnish with paper. **20** (*tr*) *Theatre sl.* to fill (a performance, etc.) by giving away free tickets (esp. in **paper the house**). ♦ See also **paper over.** [C14: from L PAPYRUS]
▸ **'paperer** *n* ▸ **'papery** *adj*

paperback (ˈpeɪpəˌbæk) *n* **1** a book or edition with covers made of flexible card. ♦ *adj* **2** of or denoting a paperback or publication of paperbacks. ♦ *vb* **3** (*tr*) to publish a paperback edition of a book.

paperbark (ˈpeɪpəˌbɑːk) *n* any of several Australian trees of swampy regions, having papery bark that can be peeled off in thin layers.

paperboy (ˈpeɪpəˌbɔɪ) *n* a boy employed to deliver newspapers, etc.
▸ **'paper,girl** *fem n*

paper chase *n* a former type of cross-country run in which a runner laid a trail of paper for others to follow.

paperclip (ˈpeɪpəˌklɪp) *n* a clip for holding sheets of paper together, esp. one of bent wire.

paper-cutter *n* a machine for cutting paper, usually a blade mounted over a table.

paperhanger (ˈpeɪpəˌhæŋə) *n* a person who hangs wallpaper as an occupation.

paperknife ('peɪpə,naɪf) *n*, *pl* **paperknives.** a knife with a comparatively blunt blade for opening sealed envelopes, etc.

paper money *n* paper currency issued by the government or the central bank as legal tender and which circulates as a substitute for specie.

paper mulberry *n* a small E Asian tree, the inner bark of which was formerly used for making paper in Japan. See also **tapa.**

paper nautilus *n* a cephalopod mollusc of warm and tropical seas, having a papery external spiral shell. Also called: **argonaut.**

paper over *vb* (*tr*, *adv*) to conceal (something controversial or unpleasant) (esp. in **paper over the cracks**).

paper tape *n* a strip of paper for recording information in the form of rows of either six or eight holes, some or all of which are punched to produce a combination used as a discrete code symbol, formerly used in computers, telex machines, etc. US equivalent: **perforated tape.**

paper tiger *n* a nation, institution, etc., that appears powerful but is in fact weak or insignificant. [C20: translation of a Chinese phrase first applied to the US]

paperweight ('peɪpə,weɪt) *n* a small heavy object to prevent loose papers from scattering.

paperwork ('peɪpə,wɜːk) *n* clerical work, such as the writing of reports or letters.

Paphian ('peɪfɪən) *adj* **1** of or relating to Paphos. **2** of or relating to Aphrodite. **3** *Literary.* of sexual love.

Paphlagonia ★ (,pæflə'gəʊnɪə) *n* an ancient country and Roman province in N Asia Minor, on the Black Sea.

Paphos[1] ★ ('peɪfɒs) *n* a town in SW Cyprus, near the sites of two ancient cities: famous as the centre of Aphrodite worship and traditionally the place at which she landed after her birth among the waves. Pop.: 32 575 (1992 est.).

Paphos[2] or **Paphus** ★ ('peɪfəs) *n* Greek myth. the son of Pygmalion and Galatea, who succeeded his father on the throne of Cyprus.

papier-mâché (,pæpjeɪ'mæʃeɪ) *n* **1** a hard strong substance made of paper pulp or layers of paper mixed with paste, size, etc., and moulded when moist. ◆ *adj* **2** made of papier-mâché. [C18: from F, lit.: chewed paper]

papilionaceous (pə,pɪlɪə'neɪʃəs) *adj* of, relating to, or belonging to a family of leguminous plants having irregular flowers: includes peas, beans, clover, alfalfa, gorse, and broom. [C17: from NL, from L *pāpiliō* butterfly]

papilla (pə'pɪlə) *n*, *pl* **papillae** (-liː). **1** the small projection of tissue at the base of a hair, tooth, or feather. **2** any similar protuberance. [C18: from L: nipple]
▸ pa'pillary *or* 'papillate *adj*

papilloma (,pæpɪ'ləʊmə) *n*, *pl* **papillomata** (-mətə) *or* **papillomas.** *Pathol.* a benign tumour forming a rounded mass. [C19: from PAPILLA + -OMA]

papillon ('pæpɪ,lɒn) *n* a breed of toy dog with large ears. [F: butterfly, from L *pāpiliō*]

papillote ('pæpɪ,ləʊt) *n* **1** a paper frill around cutlets, etc. **2 en papillote** (ã papijɔt). (of food) cooked in oiled greaseproof paper or foil. [C18: from F PAPILLON]

papist ('peɪpɪst) *n*, *adj* (*often cap.*) *Usually disparaging.* another term for **Roman Catholic.** [C16: from F *papiste*, from Church L *pāpa* POPE]
▸ pa'pistical *or* pa'pistic *adj* ▸ 'papistry *n*

papoose (pə'puːs) *n* **1** an American Indian baby. **2** a pouchlike bag used for carrying a baby, worn on the back. [C17: from Algonquian *papoos*]

pappus ('pæpəs) *n*, *pl* **pappi** ('pæpaɪ). a ring of fine feathery hairs surrounding the fruit in composite plants, such as the thistle. [C18: via NL from Gk *pappos* old man, old man's beard, hence: pappus, down]
▸ 'pappose *or* 'pappous *adj*

paprika ('pæprɪkə, pæ'priː-) *n* **1** a mild powdered seasoning made from a sweet variety of red pepper. **2** the fruit or plant from which this seasoning is obtained. [C19: via Hungarian from Serbian, from *papar* PEPPER]

Pap test *or* **smear** (pæp) *n* Med. **1** another name for **cervical smear. 2** a similar test for precancerous cells in organs other than the cervix. ◆ Also called: **Papanicolaou smear.** [C20: after George *Papanicolaou* (1883–1962), U anatomist, who devised it]

Papua ★ ('pæpjʊə) *n* **1 Territory of.** a former territory o Australia, consisting of SE New Guinea and adjacent is lands: now part of Papua New Guinea. Former name (1888–1906): **British New Guinea. 2 Gulf of.** an inlet of the Coral Sea in the SE coast of New Guinea.
▸ 'Papuan *adj*, *n*

Papua New Guinea ★ *n* a country in the SW Pacific consists of the E half of New Guinea, the Bismarck Ar chipelago, the W Solomon Islands, Trobriand Islands D'Entrecasteaux Islands, Woodlark Island, and the Louisiade Archipelago; administered by Australia from 1949 until 1975, when it became an independent mem ber of the Commonwealth. Official language: English Tok Pisin (English Creole) and Motu are widely spoken Religion: Christian majority. Currency: kina. Capita Port Moresby. Pop.: 4 496 000 (1997). Area: 461 693 sq km (178 260 sq. miles).

papule ('pæpjuːl) *or* **papula** ('pæpjʊlə) *n*, *pl* **papules** *o* **papulae** (-ju,liː). *Pathol.* a small solid usually round eleva tion of the skin. [C19: from L *papula* pustule]
▸ 'papular *adj*

papyrology (,pæpɪ'rɒlədʒɪ) *n* the study of ancient pa pyri.
▸ ,papy'rologist *n*

papyrus (pə'paɪrəs) *n*, *pl* **papyri** (-raɪ) *or* **papyruses. 1** a tal aquatic plant of S Europe and N and central Africa. **2** a kind of paper made from the stem pith of this plant used by the ancient Egyptians, Greeks, and Romans. ∴ an ancient document written on this paper. [C14: via] from Gk *papūros* reed used in making paper]

par (pɑː) *n* **1** an accepted standard, such as an averag (esp. in **up to par**). **2** a state of equality (esp. in **on a pa with**). **3** *Finance.* the established value of the unit of on national currency in terms of the unit of another. **4** *Com merce.* **4a** See **par value. 4b** equality between the curren market value of a share, bond, etc., and its face value, in dicated by **at par; above** (*or* **below**) **par** indicates that th market value is above (or below) face value. **5** *Golf.* standard score for a hole or course that a good playe should make: *par for the course was 72.* ◆ *adj* **6** average o normal. **7** (*usually prenominal*) of or relating to par: *pa value.* [C17: from L *pār* equal]

par. *abbrev. for:* **1** paragraph. **2** parallel. **3** parenthesis. parish.

Par. *abbrev. for* Paraguay.

para ('pærə) *n Inf.* **1a** a soldier in an airborne unit. **1b** a airborne unit. **2** a paragraph.

Pará ★ (*Portuguese* pa'ra) *n* **1** a state of N Brazil, on the At lantic: mostly dense tropical rainforest. Capital: Belém Pop.: 5 448 600 (1995 est.). Area: 1 248 042 sq. km (474 896 sq. miles). **2** another name for **Belém. 3** an estu ary in N Brazil into which flow the Tocantins River and ∴ branch of the Amazon. Length: about 320 km (20) miles).

para-[1] *or before a vowel* **par-** *prefix* **1** beside; near: *parame ter.* **2** beyond: *parapsychology.* **3** resembling: *paratyphoi fever.* **4** defective; abnormal: *paranoia.* **5** (*usually in italics*) denoting that an organic compound contains a benzen ring with substituents attached to atoms that are di rectly opposite (the 1,4- positions): *paracresol.* **6** denot ing an isomer, polymer, or compound related to specified compound: *paraldehyde.* **7** denoting the form o a diatomic substance in which the spins of the two con stituent atoms are antiparallel: *parahydrogen.* [from G *para* (prep) alongside, beyond]

para-[2] *combining form.* indicating an object that acts as protection against something: *parachute; parasol.* [via] from It. *para-*, from *parare* to defend, ult. from L *parāre* t prepare]

para-aminobenzoic acid (ə,maɪnəʊben'zəʊɪk, -,mɪ *n Biochem.* an acid present in yeast and liver: used in th manufacture of dyes and pharmaceuticals.

parabasis (pə'ræbəsɪs) *n*, *pl* **parabases** (-,siːz). (in classica Greek comedy) an address by the chorus. [C19: from Gk, from *parabanein* to step forward]

★ people and places

parabiosis (ˌpærəbaɪˈəʊsɪs) *n* **1** the natural union of two individuals, such as Siamese twins. **2** a similar union induced for experimental or therapeutic purposes. [C20: from PARA-[1] + Gk *biōsis* manner of life, from *bios* life]
▸ **parabiotic** (ˌpærəbaɪˈɒtɪk) *adj*

parable (ˈpærəbʰl) *n* **1** a short story that uses familiar events to illustrate a religious or ethical point. **2** any of the stories of this kind told by Jesus Christ. [C14: from OF *parabole*, from L *parabola* comparison, from Gk *parabolē* analogy, from *paraballein* to throw alongside]

parabola (pəˈræbələ) *n* a conic section formed by the intersection of a cone by a plane parallel to its side. [C16: via NL from Gk *parabolē* a setting alongside; see PARABLE]

parabolic[1] (ˌpærəˈbɒlɪk) *adj* **1** of, relating to, or shaped like a parabola. **2** shaped like a paraboloid: *a parabolic mirror.*

parabolic[2] (ˌpærəˈbɒlɪk) *or* **parabolical** *adj* of or like a parable.
▸ **parabolically** *adv*

parabolic aerial *n* a formal name for **dish aerial.**

paraboloid (pəˈræbəˌlɔɪd) *n* a geometric surface whose sections parallel to two coordinate planes are parabolic and whose sections parallel to the third plane are either elliptical or hyperbolic.
▸ **paraboloidal** *adj*

Paracelsus ★ (ˌpærəˈsɛlsəs) *n* **Philippus Aureolus** (ˈfɪlɪpəs ˌɔːrɪˈəʊləs), real name *Theophrastus Bombastus von Hohenheim.* 1493–1541, Swiss physician and alchemist, who pioneered the use of specific treatment, based on observation and experience, to remedy particular diseases.

paracetamol (ˌpærəˈsiːtəˌmɒl, -ˈsɛtə-) *n* a mild analgesic drug. [C20: from *para-acetamidophenol*]

parachronism (pəˈrækrəˌnɪzəm) *n* an error in dating, esp. by giving too late a date. [C17: from PARA-[1] + -*chronism*, as in ANACHRONISM]

parachute (ˈpærəˌʃuːt) *n* **1** a device used to retard the fall of a person or package from an aircraft, consisting of a large fabric canopy connected to a harness. ◆ *vb* **parachutes, parachuting, parachuted.** **2** (of troops, supplies, etc.) to land or cause to land by parachute from an aircraft. [C18: from F, from PARA-[2] + *chute* fall]
▸ **ˈparaˌchutist** *n*

Paraclete (ˈpærəˌkliːt) *n Christianity.* the Holy Ghost as comforter or advocate. [C15: via OF from Church L *Paraclētus*, from LGk *Paraklētos* advocate, from Gk *parakalein* to summon help]

parade (pəˈreɪd) *n* **1** an ordered, esp. ceremonial, march or procession, as of troops being reviewed. **2** Also called: **parade ground.** a place where military formations regularly assemble. **3** a visible show or display: *to make a parade of one's grief.* **4** a public promenade or street of shops. **5** a successive display of things or people. **6 on parade. 6a** on display. **6b** showing oneself off. ◆ *vb* **parades, parading, paraded. 7** (when *intr*, often foll. by *through* or *along*) to walk or march, esp. in a procession. **8** (*tr*) to exhibit or flaunt: *he was parading his medals.* **9** (*tr*) to cause to assemble in formation, as for a military parade. **10** (*intr*) to walk about in a public place. [C17: from F: a making ready, a boasting display]
▸ **paˈrader** *n*

paradiddle (ˈpærəˌdɪdʰl) *n* a group of four drumbeats played with alternate sticks in the pattern right-left-right-right or left-right-left-left. [C20: imit.]

paradigm (ˈpærəˌdaɪm) *n* **1** the set of all the inflected forms of a word. **2** a pattern or model. **3** (in the philosophy of science) a general conception of the nature of scientific endeavour within which a given enquiry is undertaken. [C15: via F & L from Gk *paradeigma* pattern, from *paradeiknunai* to compare]
▸ **paradigmatic** (ˌpærədɪgˈmætɪk) *adj*

paradisal (ˌpærəˈdaɪsʰl), **paradisiacal** (ˌpærədɪˈsaɪəkʰl), *or* **paradisiac** (ˌpærəˈdɪsɪˌæk) *adj* of, relating to, or resembling paradise.

paradise (ˈpærəˌdaɪs) *n* **1** heaven as the ultimate abode or state of the righteous. **2** *Islam.* the sensual garden of delights that the Koran promises the faithful after death. **3** Also called: **limbo.** (according to some theologians) the

intermediate abode or state of the just prior to the Resurrection of Jesus. **4** the Garden of Eden. **5** any place or condition that fulfils all one's desires or aspirations. **6** a park in which foreign animals are kept. [OE, from Church L *paradīsus*, from Gk *paradeisos* garden, of Persian origin]

paradise duck *n* a New Zealand duck with bright plumage.

paradox (ˈpærəˌdɒks) *n* **1** a seemingly absurd or self-contradictory statement that is or may be true: *religious truths are often expressed in paradox.* **2** a self-contradictory proposition, such as *I always tell lies.* **3** a person or thing exhibiting apparently contradictory characteristics. **4** an opinion that conflicts with common belief. [C16: from LL *paradoxum*, from Gk *paradoxos* opposed to existing notions]
▸ **paraˈdoxical** *adj* ▸ **paraˈdoxically** *adv*

paradoxical sleep *n Physiol.* sleep that appears deep but is characterized by a brain wave pattern similar to that of wakefulness, rapid eye movements, and heavier breathing.

paraffin (ˈpærəfɪn) *n* **1** Also called: **paraffin oil,** (esp. US, Canad., Austral., & NZ) **kerosene.** a liquid mixture consisting mainly of alkane hydrocarbons, used as an aircraft fuel, in domestic heaters, and as a solvent. **2** another name for **alkane. 3** See **paraffin wax.** **4** See **liquid paraffin.** ◆ *vb* (*tr*) **5** to treat with paraffin. [C19: from G, from L *parum* too little + *affinis* adjacent; so called from its chemical inertia]

paraffin wax *n* a white insoluble odourless waxlike solid consisting mainly of alkane hydrocarbons, used in candles, waterproof paper, and as a sealant. Also called: **paraffin.**

paragliding (ˈpærəˌglaɪdɪŋ) *n* the sport of cross-country gliding using a specially designed parachute shaped like flexible wings. The parachutist glides from an aeroplane to a predetermined landing area.

paragon (ˈpærəgən) *n* a model of excellence; pattern: *a paragon of virtue.* [C16: via F from OIt. *paragone* comparison, from Med. Gk *parakonē*, from PARA-[1] + *akonē* whetstone]

paragraph (ˈpærəˌgrɑːf) *n* **1** (in a piece of writing) one of a series of subsections each usually devoted to one idea and each marked by the beginning of a new line, indention, etc. **2** *Printing.* the character ¶, used to indicate the beginning of a new paragraph. **3** a short article, etc., in a newspaper. ◆ *vb* (*tr*) **4** to form into paragraphs. **5** to express or report in a paragraph. [C16: from Med. L *paragraphus*, from Gk *paragraphos* line drawing attention to part of a text, from *paragraphein* to write beside]
▸ **paragraphic** (ˌpærəˈgræfɪk) *adj*

paragraphia (ˌpærəˈgrɑːfɪə) *n Psychiatry.* the habitual writing of a different word or letter from the one intended, often the result of a mental disorder. [C20: from NL; see PARA-[1], -GRAPH]

Paraguay ★ (ˈpærəˌgwaɪ) *n* **1** an inland republic in South America: colonized by the Spanish from 1537, gaining independence in 1811; lost 142 500 sq. km (55 000 sq. miles) of territory and over half its population after its defeat in the war against Argentina, Brazil, and Uruguay (1865–70). It is divided by the Paraguay River into a sparsely inhabited semiarid region (Chaco) in the west, and a central region of wooded hills, tropical forests, and rich grasslands, rising to the Paraná plateau in the east. Official languages: Spanish and Guarani. Religion: Roman Catholic majority. Currency: guarani. Capital: Asunción. Pop.: 5 089 000 (1997). Area: 406 750 sq. km (157 047 sq. miles). **2** a river in South America flowing south through Brazil and Paraguay to the Paraná River. Length: about 2400 km (1500 miles).
▸ **ˌParaˈguayan** *adj*, *n*

Paraguay tea *n* another name for **maté.**

parahydrogen (ˌpærəˈhaɪdrədʒən) *n Chem.* the form of molecular hydrogen in which the nuclei of the two atoms in each molecule spin in opposite directions.

Paraíba ★ (*Portuguese* paraˈiba) *n* **1** a state of NE Brazil, on the Atlantic: consists of a coastal strip, with hills and plains inland; irrigated agriculture. Capital: João Pessoa.

Pop.: 3 340 000 (1995 est.). Area: 56 371 sq. km (21 765 sq. miles). **2** Also called: **Paraíba do Sul** ('du: 'sul). a river in SE Brazil, flowing southwest and then northeast to the Atlantic near Campos. Length: 1060 km (660 miles). **3** Also called: **Paraíba do Norte** ('du: 'nɔrtə). a river in NE Brazil, in Paraíba state, flowing northeast and east to the Atlantic. Length: 386 km (240 miles). **4** the former name (until 1930) of **João Pessoa**.

parakeet or **parrakeet** ('pærə,ki:t) n any of numerous small long-tailed parrots. [C16: from Sp. *periquito* & OF *paroquet* parrot, from ?]

paraldehyde (pə'rældɪ,haɪd) n a colourless liquid that is a cyclic trimer of acetaldehyde: used as a hypnotic.

paralipsis (,paerə'lɪpsɪs) or **paraleipsis** (,pærə'laɪpsɪs) n, pl **paralipses** or **paraleipses** (-si:z). a rhetorical device in which an idea is emphasized by the pretence that it is too obvious to discuss, as in *there are many practical drawbacks, not to mention the cost*. [C16: via LL from Gk: neglect, from *paraleipein* to leave aside]

parallax ('pærə,læks) n **1** an apparent change in the position of an object resulting from a change in position of the observer. **2** *Astron.* the angle subtended at a celestial body, esp. a star, by the radius of the earth's orbit. [C17: via F from NL *parallaxis*, from Gk: change, from *parallassein* to change]
▸ **parallactic** (,pærə'læktɪk) adj

parallel ('pærə,lɛl) adj (when postpositive, usually foll. by to) **1** separated by an equal distance at every point; never touching or intersecting: *parallel walls*. **2** corresponding; similar: *parallel situations*. **3** *Music.* Also: **consecutive.** (of two or more parts or melodies) moving in similar motion but keeping the same interval apart throughout: *parallel fifths*. **4** *Grammar.* denoting syntactic constructions in which the constituents of one construction correspond to those of the other. **5** *Computing.* operating on several items of information, instructions, etc., simultaneously. ◆ n **6** *Maths.* one of a set of parallel lines, planes, etc. **7** an exact likeness. **8** a comparison. **9** Also called: **parallel of latitude.** any of the imaginary lines around the earth parallel to the equator, designated by degrees of latitude. **10** *Electronics.* **10a** an arrangement of two or more electrical components connected between two points in a circuit so that the same voltage is applied to each (esp. in **in parallel**). Cf. **series** (sense 6). **10b** (as modifier): *a parallel circuit.* **11** *Printing.* the character (‖) used as a reference mark. ◆ vb **parallels, paralleling, paralleled.** (tr) **12** to make parallel. **13** to supply a parallel to. **14** to be a parallel to or correspond with: *your experience parallels mine*. [C16: via F & L from Gk *parallēlos* alongside one another, from PARA-[1] + *allēlos* one another]

parallel bars pl n *Gymnastics*. a pair of wooden bars on uprights used for various exercises.

parallelepiped (,pærə,lɛlɪ'paɪpɛd) or **parallelepipedon** (,pærə,lɛlɪ'paɪpɪdən) n a geometric solid whose six faces are parallelograms. [C16: from Gk, from *parallēlos* PARALLEL + *epipedon* plane surface, from EPI- + *pedon* ground]

parallel importing n the importing of certain goods, esp. pharmaceutical drugs, by dealers who undersell local manufacturers.

paralleling ('pærə,lɛlɪŋ) n a form of trading in which companies buy highly priced goods in a market in which the prices are low in order to be able to sell them in a market in which the prices are higher.

parallelism ('pærə,lɛlɪzəm) n **1** the state of being parallel. **2** *Grammar*. the repetition of a syntactic construction in successive sentences for rhetorical effect. **3** *Philosophy*. the doctrine that mental and physical processes are regularly correlated but are not casually connected, so that, for example, pain always accompanies, but is not caused by, a pinprick.

parallelogram (,pærə'lɛlə,græm) n a quadrilateral whose opposite sides are parallel and equal in length. [C16: via F from LL, from Gk *parallēlogrammon*, from *parallēlos* PARALLEL + *grammē* line]

parallelogram rule n *Maths, physics*. a rule for finding the resultant of two vectors by constructing a parallelogram with two adjacent sides representing the magnitudes and directions of the vectors, the diagonal

through the point of intersection of the vectors representing their resultant.

parallel processing n the performance by a computer system of two or more simultaneous operations.

parallel ruler n *Engineering*. a drawing instrument in which two parallel edges are connected so that they remain parallel, although the distance between them can be varied.

paralogism (pə'rælə,dʒɪzəm) n **1** *Logic, psychol.* an argument that is unintentionally invalid. Cf. **sophism. 2** any invalid argument or conclusion. [C16: via LL from Gk *paralogismos*, from *paralogizesthai* to argue fallaciously, from PARA-[1] + *-logizesthai*, ult. from *logos* word]
▸ **pa'ralogist** n

Paralympian (,pærə'lɪmpɪən) n a competitor in the Paralympics.

Paralympics (,pærə'lɪmpɪks) n the. (functioning as sing or pl) a sporting event, modelled on the Olympic Games, held solely for disabled competitors. Also called: **the Parallel Olympics.** [C20: from PARALLEL + OLYMPICS]

paralyse or US **paralyze** ('pærə,laɪz) vb **paralyses, paralysing, paralysed** or US **paralyzes, paralyzing, paralyzed.** (tr) **1** *Pathol.* to affect with paralysis. **2** *Med.* to render (a part of the body) insensitive to pain, touch, etc. **3** to make immobile; transfix. [C19: from F *paralyser*, from *paralysie* PARALYSIS]
▸ **,paraly'sation** or US **,paraly'zation** n ▸ **'para,lyser** or US **'para,lyzer** n

paralysis (pə'rælɪsɪs) n, pl **paralyses** (-,si:z). **1** *Pathol.* **1a** impairment or loss of voluntary muscle function or of sensation (**sensory paralysis**) in a part or area of the body. **1b** a disease characterized by such impairment or loss; palsy. **2** cessation or impairment of activity: *paralysis of industry by strikes*. [C16: via L from Gk *paralusis*; see PARA-[1], -LYSIS]

paralytic (,pærə'lɪtɪk) adj **1** of, relating to, or of the nature of paralysis. **2** afflicted with or subject to paralysis. **3** *Brit. inf.* very drunk. ◆ n **4** a person afflicted with paralysis.

paramagnetism (,pærə'mægnɪ,tɪzəm) n *Physics*. a weakly magnetic condition of substances with a relative permeability just greater than unity: used in some special low temperature techniques.
▸ **paramagnetic** (,pærəmæg'nɛtɪk) adj

Paramaribo ★ (,pærə'mærɪ,bəʊ; Dutch pa:ra:'ma:ri:bo:) n the capital and chief port of Surinam, 27 km (17 miles) from the Atlantic on the Surinam River: the only large town in the country. Pop.: 200 970 (1993 est.).

paramatta or **parramatta** (,pærə'mætə) n a lightweight twill-weave dress fabric of wool with silk or cotton, now used esp. for rubber-proofed garments. [C19: after *Parramatta*, New South Wales, Australia, where orig. produced]

paramecium (,pærə'mi:sɪəm) n, pl **paramecia** (-sɪə) any of a genus of freshwater protozoa having an oval body covered with cilia and a ventral groove for feeding. [C18: NL, from Gk *paramēkēs* elongated, from PARA-[1] + *mēkos* length]

paramedic (,pærə'mɛdɪk) n **1** a person, such as a laboratory technician, who supplements the work of the medical profession. **2** a member of an ambulance crew trained in a number of life-saving skills, including vision and cardiac care.
▸ **,para'medical** adj

parameter (pə'ræmɪtə) n **1** an arbitrary constant that determines the specific form of a mathematical expression, such as a and b in $y = ax^2 + b$. **2** a characteristic constant of a statistical population, such as its variance or mean. **3** *Inf.* any constant or limiting factor: *a designer must work within the parameters of budget and practicality*. [C17: from NL; see PARA-[1], -METER]
▸ **parametric** (,pærə'mɛtrɪk) adj

parametric amplifier n a type of high-frequency amplifier in which energy is transferred to the input signal through a circuit with a varying reactance.

paramilitary (,pærə'mɪlɪtərɪ, -trɪ) adj **1** denoting or relating to a group of personnel with military structure functioning either as a civil force or in support of military forces. **2** denoting or relating to a force with military structure conducting armed operations against a ruling power.

paramount ('pærə,maunt) *adj* of the greatest importance or significance. [C16: via Anglo-Norman from OF *paramont*, from *par* by + *-amont* above, from L *ad montem* to the mountain]
▸ **'para,mountcy** *n* ▸ **'para,mountly** *adv*

paramour ('pærə,muə) *n* **1** *Now usually derog.* a lover, esp. adulterous. **2** an archaic word for **beloved**. [C13: from OF, lit.: through love]

Paraná ★ *n* **1** (*Portuguese* parə'na). a state of S Brazil, on the Atlantic: consists of a coastal plain and a large rolling plateau with extensive forests. Capital: Curitiba. Pop.: 8 712 800 (1995 est.). Area: 199 555 sq. km (77 048 sq. miles). **2** (*Portuguese* para'na). a city in E Argentina, on the Paraná River opposite Santa Fe: capital of Argentina (1853–1862). Pop.: 211 936 (1991). **3** (*Portuguese* parə'na; *Spanish* para'na). a river in central South America, formed by the confluence of the Rio Grande and the Paranaíba River and flowing generally south to the Atlantic through the Río de la Plata estuary. Length: 2900 km (1800 miles).

parang ('pɑːræŋ) *n* a Malay short stout straight-edged knife used in Borneo. [C19: from Malay]

paranoia (,pærə'nɔɪə) *n* **1** a mental disorder characterized by any of several types of delusions, as of grandeur or persecution. **2** *Inf.* intense fear or suspicion, esp. when unfounded. [C19: via NL from Gk: frenzy, from *paranoos* distraught, from PARA-[1] + *noos* mind]
▸ **'para,noid**, **paranoiac** (,pærə'nɔɪɪk) *or* **paranoic** (,pærə'nəʊɪk) *adj, n*

paranormal (,pærə'nɔːməl) *adj* **1** beyond normal explanation. ♦ *n* **2** the. paranormal happenings generally.

parapente ('pærə,pɒnt) *n* **1** another name for **paraskiing**. **2** the form of parachute used in this sport. [C20: from PARA(CHUTE) + F *pente* slope]

parapet ('pærəpɪt, -,pet) *n* **1** a low wall or railing along the edge of a balcony, roof, etc. **2** *Mil.* a rampart, mound of sandbags, etc., in front of a trench giving protection from fire. [C16: from It. *parapetto*, lit.: chest-high wall, from L *pectus* breast]

paraph ('pæræf) *n* a flourish after a signature, originally to prevent forgery. [C14: via F from Med. L *paraphus*, var. of *paragraphus* PARAGRAPH]

paraphernalia (,pærəfə'neɪlɪə) *pl n* (*sometimes functioning as sing*) **1** miscellaneous articles or equipment. **2** *Law.* (formerly) articles of personal property given to a married woman by her husband and regarded in law as her possessions. [C17: via Med. L from L *parapherna* personal property of a married woman, apart from her dowry, from Gk, from PARA-[1] + *phernē* dowry, from *pherein* to carry]

paraphrase ('pærə,freɪz) *n* **1** an expression of a statement or text in other words. ♦ *vb* **paraphrases, paraphrasing, paraphrased. 2** to put into other words; restate. [C16: via F from L *paraphrasis*, from Gk, from *paraphrazein* to recount]
▸ **paraphrastic** (,pærə'fræstɪk) *adj*

paraplegia (,pærə'pliːdʒə) *n Pathol.* paralysis of the lower half of the body, usually as the result of disease or injury of the spine. [C17: via NL from Gk: a blow on one side, from PARA-[1] + *plēssein* to strike]
▸ **para'plegic** *adj, n*

parapraxis (,pærə'præksɪs) *n, pl* **parapraxes** (-'præksiːz) *Psychoanal.* a minor error in action, such as a slip of the tongue. [C20: from PARA-[1] + Gk *praxis* a deed]

parapsychology (,pærəsaɪ'kɒlədʒɪ) *n* the study of mental phenomena, such as telepathy, which are beyond the scope of normal physical explanation.
▸ **,parapsy'chologist** *n*

Paraquat ('pærə,kwɒt) *n Trademark.* a yellow extremely poisonous weedkiller.

parascending ('pærə,sendɪŋ) *n* a sport in which a parachutist, starting from ground level, is towed by a vehicle until he is airborne and then descends in the normal way.

paraselene (,pærəsɪ'liːnɪ) *n, pl* **paraselenae** (-niː). a bright image of the moon on a lunar halo. Also called: **mock moon**. [C17: NL, from PARA-[1] + Gk *selēnē* moon]

parasite ('pærə,saɪt) *n* **1** an animal or plant that lives in or on another (the host) from which it obtains nourishment. **2** a person who habitually lives at the expense of others; sponger. [C16: via L from Gk *parasitos* one who lives at another's expense, from PARA-[1] + *sitos* grain]
▸ **parasitic** (,pærə'sɪtɪk) *or* **,para'sitical** *adj* ▸ **,para'sitically** *adv* ▸ **'parasi,tism** *n*

parasitize *or* **parasitise** ('pærəsɪ,taɪz) *vb* **parasitizes, parasitizing, parasitized** *or* **parasitises, parasitising, parasitised.** (*tr*) **1** to infest with parasites. **2** to live on (another organism) as a parasite.
▸ **,parasiti'zation** *or* **,parasiti'sation** *n*

parasitoid ('pærəsɪ,tɔɪd) *n Zool.* an animal, esp. an insect, that is parasitic as a larva but becomes free-living when adult.

parasitology (,pærəsə'tɒlədʒɪ) *n* the branch of biology that is concerned with the study of parasites.
▸ **,parasit'ologist** *n*

paraskiing ('pærə,skiːɪŋ) *n* the sport of jumping off high mountains wearing skis and a light parachute composed of inflatable fabric tubes that form a semirigid wing. Also called: **parapente**.

parasol ('pærə,sɒl) *n* an umbrella used for protection against the sun; sunshade. [C17: via F from It. *parasole*, from PARA-[2] + *sole* sun, from L *sōl*]

parasuicide (,pærə'suːɪ,saɪd) *n* an attempt to inflict an injury on oneself, not motivated by a desire to die.

parasympathetic (,pærə,sɪmpə'θetɪk) *adj Anat., Physiol.* of or relating to the division of the autonomic nervous system that acts by slowing the heartbeat, constricting the bronchi of the lungs, stimulating the smooth muscles of the digestive tract, etc. Cf. **sympathetic** (sense 4).

parasynthesis (,pærə'sɪnθɪsɪs) *n* formation of words by compounding a phrase and adding an affix, as *light-headed, light + head* with the affix *-ed*.
▸ **parasynthetic** (,pærəsɪn'θetɪk) *adj*

parataxis (,pærə'tæksɪs) *n* the juxtaposition of clauses without the use of a conjunction, as *None of my friends stayed—they all left early*. [C19: NL, from Gk, from *paratassein*, lit.: to arrange side by side]
▸ **paratactic** (,pærə'tæktɪk) *adj*

parathion (,pærə'θaɪɒn) *n* a toxic oil used as an insecticide. [from PARA-[1] + Gk *theion* sulphur]

parathyroid gland (,pærə'θaɪrɔɪd) *n* any one of the small egg-shaped endocrine glands situated near or embedded within the thyroid gland.

paratroops ('pærə,truːps) *pl n* troops trained and equipped to be dropped by parachute into a battle area. Also called: **paratroopers**.

paratyphoid fever (,pærə'taɪfɔɪd) *n* a disease resembling but less severe than typhoid fever, caused by bacteria of the genus *Salmonella*.

paravane ('pærə,veɪn) *n* a torpedo-shaped device towed from the bow of a vessel so that the cables will cut the anchors of any moored mines. [C20: from PARA-[2] + VANE]

par avion *French.* (par avjõ) *adv* by aeroplane: used in labelling mail sent by air.

parazoan (,pærə'zəʊən) *n, pl* **parazoa** (-'zəʊə). any multicellular invertebrate of a division of the animal kingdom, the sponges. [C19: from *parazoa*, on the model of *protozoa* & *metazoa*, from PARA-[1] + Gk *zōon* animal]

parboil ('pɑː,bɔɪl) *vb* (*tr*) **1** to boil until partially cooked. **2** to subject to uncomfortable heat. [C15: from OF *parboillir*, from LL *perbullīre* to boil thoroughly (see PER-, BOIL[1]); modern meaning due to confusion of *par-* with *part*]

parbuckle ('pɑː,bʌkᵊl) *n* **1** a rope sling for lifting or lowering a heavy cylindrical object, such as a cask. ♦ *vb* **parbuckles, parbuckling, parbuckled. 2** (*tr*) to raise or lower (an object) with such a sling. [C17 *parbunkel*: from ?]

Parcae ★ ('pɑːsiː) *pl n, sing* **Parca** ('pɑːkə). **the.** the Roman goddesses of fate. Greek counterparts: The **Moirai**.

parcel ('pɑːs°l) n 1 something wrapped up; package. 2 a group of people or things having some common characteristic. 3 a quantity of some commodity offered for sale; lot. 4 a distinct portion of land. ◆ vb parcels, parcelling, parcelled or US parcels, parceling, parceled. (tr) 5 (often foll. by up) to make a parcel of; wrap up. 6 (often foll. by out) to divide (up) into portions. [C14: from OF parcelle, from L particula PARTICLE]

parch (pɑːtʃ) vb 1 to deprive or be deprived of water; dry up: the sun parches the fields. 2 (tr; usually passive) to make very thirsty. 3 (tr) to roast (corn, etc.) lightly. [C14: from ?]

Parcheesi (pɑːˈtʃiːzɪ) n Trademark. a board game derived from the ancient game of pachisi.

parchment ('pɑːtʃmənt) n 1 the skin of certain animals, such as sheep, treated to form a durable material, as for manuscripts. 2 a manuscript, etc., made of this material. 3 a type of stiff yellowish paper resembling parchment. [C13: from OF parchemin, via L from Gk pergamēnē, from Pergamēnos of Pergamum (where parchment was made); OF parchemin was infl. by parche leather, from L Parthica (pellis) Parthian (leather)]

pard (pɑːd) n Arch. a leopard or panther. [C13: via OF from L pardus, from Gk pardos]

pardon ('pɑːd°n) vb (tr) 1 to excuse or forgive (a person) for (an offence, mistake, etc.): to pardon someone; to pardon a fault. ◆ n 2 forgiveness. 3a release from punishment for an offence. 3b the warrant granting such release. 4 a Roman Catholic indulgence. ◆ sentence substitute. 5 Also: pardon me, I beg your pardon. 5a sorry; excuse me. 5b what did you say? [C13: from OF, from Med. L perdōnum, from perdōnāre to forgive freely, from L per (intensive) + dōnāre to grant]
▸ 'pardonable adj ▸ 'pardonably adv

pardoner ('pɑːd°nə) n (before the Reformation) a person licensed to sell ecclesiastical indulgences.

Pardubice ★ (Czech 'pardubitsɛ) n a city in the central Czech Republic, on the Elbe River: 13th-century cathedral; oil refinery. Pop.: 163 000 (1993).

pare (pɛə) vb pares, paring, pared. (tr) 1 to peel (the outer layer) from (something). 2 to cut the edges from (the nails). 3 to decrease bit by bit. [C13: from OF parer to adorn, from L parāre to make ready]
▸ 'parer n

Paré ★ (French pare) n Ambroise (ãbrwaz). 1510–90, French surgeon. He reintroduced ligature of arteries following amputation instead of cauterization.

paregoric (ˌpærəˈgɒrɪk) n a medicine consisting of opium, benzoic acid, and camphor, formerly widely used to relieve diarrhoea and coughing. [C17 (meaning: relieving pain): via LL from Gk parēgoros relating to soothing speech, from PARA-[1] (beside) + agora assembly]

pareira (pəˈrɛərə) n the root of a South American climbing plant, used as a diuretic, tonic, and as a source of curare. [C18: from Port. pareira brava, lit.: wild vine]

parenchyma (pəˈrɛŋkɪmə) n 1 a soft plant tissue consisting of simple thin-walled cells: constitutes the greater part of fruits, stems, roots, etc. 2 animal tissue that constitutes the essential part of an organ as distinct from the blood vessels, connective tissue, etc. [C17: via NL from Gk parenkhuma something poured in beside, from PARA-[1] + enkhuma infusion]
▸ parenchymatous (ˌpærɛŋˈkɪmətəs) adj

parent ('pɛərənt) n 1 a father or mother. 2 a person acting as a father or mother; guardian. 3 Rare. an ancestor. 4 a source or cause. 5 an organism or organization that has produced one or more organisms similar to itself. 6 Physics, chem. a precursor, such as a nucleus or compound, of a derived entity. [C15: via OF from L parens parent, from parere to bring forth]
▸ pa'rental adj ▸ 'parenthood n

parentage ('pɛərəntɪdʒ) n 1 ancestry. 2 derivation from a particular origin. 3 the state or condition of being a parent.

parent company n a company that owns a number of subsidiary companies.

parenteral (pæˈrɛntərəl) adj Med. 1 (esp. of the route by which a drug is administered) by means other than

through the digestive tract, esp. by injection. 2 designating a drug to be injected. [C20: from PARA-[1] + ENTERO- + -AL[1]]

parenthesis (pəˈrɛnθɪsɪs) n, pl parentheses (-ˌsiːz). 1 a phrase, often explanatory or qualifying, inserted into a passage with which it is not grammatically connected, and marked off by brackets, dashes, etc. 2 Also called: bracket. either of a pair of characters, ( ), used to enclose such a phrase or as a sign of aggregation in mathematical or logical expressions. 3 an interlude; interval. 4 in parenthesis. inserted as a parenthesis. [C16: via L from Gk: something placed in besides, from parentithenai, from PARA-[1] + EN-[2] + tithenai to put]
▸ parenthetic (ˌpærənˈθɛtɪk) or ˌparenˈthetical adj
▸ ˌparenˈthetically adv

parenthesize or **parenthesise** (pəˈrɛnθɪˌsaɪz) vb parenthesizes, parenthesizing, parenthesized or parenthesises, parenthesising, parenthesised. (tr) 1 to place in parentheses. 2 to insert as a parenthesis. 3 to intersperse (a speech, writing, etc.) with parentheses.

parenting ('pɛərəntɪŋ) n all the skills and experience of bringing up children.

parent teacher association n a social group of the parents of children at a school and their teachers formed in order to foster better understanding between them and to organize fund-raising activities on behalf of the school.

parergon (pəˈrɛːgɒn) n, pl parerga (-gə). work that is not one's main employment. [C17: from L, from Gk, from PARA-[1] + ergon work]

paresis (pəˈriːsɪs, ˈpærɪsɪs) n, pl pareses (-ˌsiːz). Pathol. incomplete or slight paralysis of motor functions. [C17: via NL from Gk: a relaxation, from parienai to let go]
▸ paretic (pəˈrɛtɪk) adj

Pareto ★ (Italian paˈrɛːto) n Vilfredo (vilˈfreːdo). 1848–1923, Italian sociologist and economist. He anticipated Fascist principles of government in his Mind and Society (1916).

par excellence French. (par ɛksɛlɑ̃s; English pɑːr ˈɛksələns) adv to a degree of excellence; beyond comparison. [F, lit.: by (way of) excellence]

parfait (pɑːˈfeɪ) n a rich frozen dessert made from eggs and cream, fruit, etc. [from F: PERFECT]

parget ('pɑːdʒɪt) n 1 Also called: pargeting. 1a plaster, mortar, etc., used to line chimney flues or cover walls. 1b plasterwork that has incised ornamental patterns. ◆ vb (tr). 2 to cover or decorate with parget. [C14: from OF pargeter to throw over, from par PER- + geter to throw]

parhelic circle n Meteorol. a luminous band at the same altitude as the sun, parallel to the horizon, caused by reflection of the sun's rays by ice crystals in the atmosphere.

parhelion (pɑːˈhiːlɪən) n, pl parhelia (-lɪə). one of several bright spots on the parhelic circle or solar halo, caused by the diffraction of light by ice crystals in the atmosphere. Also called: mock sun. [C17: via L from Gk parēlion, from PARA-[1] (beside) + hēlios sun]
▸ parˈhelic or parheliacal (ˌpɑːhɪˈlaɪək°l) adj

pariah (pəˈraɪə, ˈpærɪə) n 1 a social outcast. 2 (formerly) a member of a low caste in South India. [C17: from Tamil paraiyan drummer, from parai drum: members were drummers at festivals]

pariah dog n another term for pye-dog.

Paricutín ★ (Spanish parikuˈtin) n a volcano in W central Mexico, in Michoacán state, formed in 1943 after a week of earth tremors; grew to a height of 2500 m (8200 ft) in a year and buried the village of Paricutín.

parietal (pəˈraɪɪt°l) adj 1 Anat., biol. of or forming the walls of a bodily cavity: the parietal bones of the skull. 2 of or relating to the side of the skull. 3 (of plant ovaries) having ovules attached to the walls. 4 US. living or having authority within a college. ◆ n 5 a parietal bone. [C16: from LL parietālis, from L pariēs wall]

parietal lobe n the portion of each cerebral hemisphere concerned with the perception of sensations of touch, temperature, and taste and with muscular movements.

pari-mutuel (ˌpærɪˈmjuːtʃʊəl) n, pl pari-mutuels or paris-

mutuels (ˌpærɪ'mjuːtʃʊəlz). a system of betting in which those who have bet on the winners of a race share in the total amount wagered less a percentage for the management. [C19: from F, lit.: mutual wager]

paring ('peərɪŋ) n (often pl) something pared or cut off.

pari passu Latin. (ˌpærɪ 'pæsuː, 'pɑːrɪ) adv Usually legal. with equal speed or progress.

Paris[1] ★ ('pærɪs; French pari) n the capital of France, in the north on the River Seine: constitutes a department; dates from the 3rd century B.C., becoming capital of France in 987; centre of the French Revolution; centres around its original site on an island in the Seine, the Île de la Cité, containing Notre Dame; university (1150). Pop.: 2 175 200 (1990). Ancient name: **Lutetia**. [via F and OF, from LL (Lūtētia) Parisiōrum (marshes) of the Parisii, a tribe of Celtic Gaul]
▶ **Parisian** (pə'rɪzɪən) n, adj

Paris[2] ★ ('pærɪs) n 1 Greek myth. a prince of Troy, whose abduction of Helen from her husband Menelaus started the Trojan War. 2 **Matthew**. ?1200–59, English chronicler, whose principal work is the Chronica Majora.

Paris Club n another name for **Group of Ten**.

Paris Commune n French history. the council established in Paris in the spring of 1871 in opposition to the National Assembly and esp. to the peace negotiated with Prussia following the Franco-Prussian War.

Paris green n an emerald-green poisonous substance used as a pigment and insecticide.

parish ('pærɪʃ) n 1 a subdivision of a diocese, having its own church and a clergyman. 2 the churchgoers of such a subdivision. 3 (in England and, formerly, Wales) the smallest unit of local government. 4 (in Louisiana) a county. 5 (in Quebec and New Brunswick, Canada) a subdivision of a county. 6 the people living in a parish. 7 **on the parish**. History. receiving parochial relief. [C13: from OF paroisse, from Church L, from LGk, from paroikos Christian, sojourner, from Gk: neighbour, from PARA-[1] (beside) + oikos house]

parish clerk n a person designated to assist in various church functions.

parish council n (in England and, formerly, Wales) the administrative body of a parish. See **parish** (sense 3).

parishioner (pə'rɪʃənə) n a member of a particular parish.

parish pump adj of only local interest; parochial.

parish register n a book in which the births, baptisms, marriages, and deaths in a parish are recorded.

parity ('pærɪtɪ) n, pl **parities**. 1 equality of rank, pay, etc. 2 close or exact analogy or equivalence. 3 Finance. the amount of a foreign currency equivalent to a specific sum of domestic currency. 4 equality between prices of commodities or securities in two separate markets. 5 Physics. 5a a property of a physical system characterized by the behaviour of the sign of its wave function when reflected in space. The wave function either remains unchanged (**even parity**) or changes in sign (**odd parity**). 5b a quantum number describing this property, equal to +1 for even parity systems and –1 for odd parity systems. Symbol: P 6 Maths. a relationship between two integers. If both are odd or both even they have the same parity; if one is odd and one even they have different parity. [C16: from LL pāritās; see PAR]

parity check n a check made of computer data to ensure that the total number of bits of value 1 (or 0) in each unit of information remains odd or even after transfer between a peripheral device and the memory or vice versa.

park (pɑːk) n 1 a large area of land preserved in a natural state for recreational use by the public. 2 a piece of open land for public recreation in a town. 3 a large area of land forming a private estate. 4 an area designed to accommodate a number of related enterprises: a business park. 5 US & Canad. a playing field or sports stadium. 6 **the park**. Brit. inf. a soccer pitch. 7 a gear selector position on the automatic transmission of a motor vehicle that acts as a parking brake. 8 the area in which the equipment and supplies of a military formation are assembled. ◆ vb 9 to stop and leave (a vehicle) temporarily. 10 to

manoeuvre (a motor vehicle) into a space for it to be left: try to park without hitting the kerb. 11 Stock Exchange. to register (securities) in the name of another or of nominees in order to conceal their real ownership. 12 (tr) Inf. to leave or put somewhere: park yourself in front of the fire. 13 (intr) Mil. to arrange equipment in a park. 14 (tr) to enclose in or as a park. [C13: from OF parc, from Med. L parricus enclosure, from Gmc]

Park ★ (pɑːk) n 1 **Mungo** ('mʌŋgəʊ). 1771–1806, Scottish explorer. He led two expeditions (1795–97; 1805–06) to trace the course of the Niger in Africa. He was drowned during the second expedition. 2 **Chung Hee** ('tʃʊŋ 'hiː). 1917–79, South Korean politician; president of the Republic of Korea (1963–79); assassinated.

parka ('pɑːkə) n a warm weatherproof coat with a hood, originally worn by Eskimos. [C19: from Aleutian: skin]

Parker ★ ('pɑːkə) n 1 **Charlie**. nickname Bird or Yardbird. 1920–55, US jazz alto saxophonist and composer; the leading exponent of early bop. 2 **Dorothy** (**Rothschild**). 1893–1967, US writer, noted esp. for the ironical humour of her short stories. 3 **Matthew**. 1504–75, English prelate. As archbishop of Canterbury (1559–75), he supervised Elizabeth I's religious settlement.

Parkes ★ (pɑːks) n Sir Henry. 1815–96, Australian journalist and politician born in England, five times premier of New South Wales.

parkin ('pɑːkɪn) n (in Britain and New Zealand) moist spicy ginger cake usually containing oatmeal. [C19: from ?]

parking lot n the US and Canad. term for **car park**.

parking meter n a timing device, usually coin-operated, that indicates how long a vehicle may be left parked.

parking orbit n an orbit around the earth or moon in which a spacecraft can be placed temporarily in order to prepare for the next step in its programme.

parking ticket n a summons served for a parking offence.

Parkinson's disease ('pɑːkɪnsənz) n a progressive chronic disorder of the central nervous system characterized by impaired muscular coordination and tremor. Often shortened to **Parkinson's**. Also called: **Parkinsonism**. [C19: after James Parkinson (1755–1824), Brit. surgeon, who first described it]

Parkinson's law n the notion, expressed facetiously as a law of economics, that work expands to fill the time available for its completion. [C20: after C. N. Parkinson (1909–93), Brit. historian and writer, who formulated it]

park keeper n (in Britain) an official who patrols and supervises a public park.

parkland ('pɑːkˌlænd) n grassland with scattered trees.

parky ('pɑːkɪ) adj **parkier**, **parkiest**. (usually postpositive) Brit. inf. (of the weather) chilly; cold. [C19: ?from PERKY]

Parl. abbrev. for: 1 Parliament. 2 Also: **parl.** parliamentary.

parlance ('pɑːləns) n a particular manner of speaking, esp. when specialized; idiom: political parlance. [C16: from OF, from parler to talk, via Med. L from LL parabola speech]

parlando (pɑː'lændəʊ) adj, adv Music. to be performed as though speaking. [It.: speaking]

parley ('pɑːlɪ) n 1 a discussion, esp. between enemies under a truce to decide terms of surrender, etc. ◆ vb 2 (intr) to discuss, esp. with an enemy. [C16: from F, from parler to talk, from Med. L parabolāre, from LL parabola speech]

parliament ('pɑːləmənt) n 1 an assembly of the representatives of a political nation or people, often the supreme legislative authority. 2 any legislative or deliberative assembly, conference, etc. [C13: from Anglo-L parliamentum, from OF parlement, from parler to speak; see PARLEY]

Parliament ('pɑːləmənt) n 1 the highest legislative authority in Britain, consisting of the House of Commons, which exercises effective power, the House of Lords, and the sovereign. 2 a similar legislature in another country or state. 3 any of the assemblies of such a body created by a general election and royal summons and dissolved before the next election.

parliamentarian (ˌpɑːləmɛnˈtɛərɪən) n 1 an expert in parliamentary procedures. ◆ adj 2 of or relating to a parliament.

parliamentary (ˌpɑːləˈmɛntərɪ) adj (sometimes cap.) 1 of or proceeding from a parliament or Parliament: a parliamentary decree. 2 conforming to the procedures of a parliament or Parliament: parliamentary conduct. 3 having a parliament or Parliament.

Parliamentary Commissioner or in full **Parliamentary Commissioner for Administration** n (in Britain) the official name for **ombudsman** (sense 2).

parliamentary private secretary n (in Britain) a backbencher in Parliament who assists a minister. Abbrev.: **PPS**.

parliamentary secretary n a member of Parliament appointed to assist a minister of the Crown with his departmental responsibilities.

parlour or US **parlor** (ˈpɑːlə) n 1 Old-fashioned. a living room, esp. one kept tidy for the reception of visitors. 2 a small room for guests away from the public rooms in an inn, club, etc. 3 Chiefly US, Canad., & NZ. a room or shop equipped as a place of business: a billiard parlour. 4 a building equipped for the milking of cows. [C13: from Anglo-Norman parlur, from OF parleur room in convent for receiving guests, from parler to speak; see PARLEY]

parlous (ˈpɑːləs) Arch. or humorous. ◆ adj 1 dangerous or difficult. 2 cunning. ◆ adv 3 extremely. [C14 perlous, var. of PERILOUS]
▸ **'parlously** adv

Parma ★ n 1 (Italian ˈparma). a city in N Italy, in Emilia-Romagna: capital of the duchy of Parma and Piacenza from 1545 until it became part of Italy in 1860; important food industry (esp. Parmesan cheese). Pop.: 169 299 (1994 est.). 2 (ˈpɑːmə). a city in NE Ohio, south of Cleveland. Pop.: 85 792 (1994 est.).
▸ **Parmesan** (ˌpɑːmɪˈzæn, ˈpɑːmɪˌzæn) adj, n

Parmenides ★ (pɑːˈmɛnɪˌdiːz) n 5th century B.C., Greek philosopher, born in Italy. He held that the universe is single and unchanging and denied the existence of change and motion. His doctrines are expounded in his poem On Nature, of which only fragments are extant.

Parmesan cheese n a hard dry cheese used grated, esp. on pasta dishes and soups.

Parmigianino ★ (Italian parmidʒaˈnino) n real name Girolamo Francesco Maria Mazzola. 1503–40, Italian painter, one of the originators of mannerism. Also called: **Parmigiano** (parmiˈdʒano).

Parnaíba or **Parnahiba** ★ (Portuguese parnaˈiba) n a river in NE Brazil, rising in the Serra das Mangabeiras and flowing generally northeast, to the Atlantic. Length: about 1450 km (900 miles).

Parnassus ★ (pɑːˈnæsəs) n 1 Mount. a mountain in central Greece: in ancient times sacred to Apollo and the Muses. 2a the world of poetry. 2b a centre of poetic or other creative activity.
▸ **Par'nassian** adj

Parnell ★ (ˈpɑːnᵊl, pɑːˈnɛl) n Charles Stewart. 1846–91, Irish nationalist, who led the Irish Home Rule movement in Parliament (1880–90) with a calculated policy of obstruction. Although Gladstone was converted to Home Rule (1886), Parnell's career was ruined by the scandal over his adultery with Mrs Katherine O'Shea.
▸ **'Parnel,lism** n ▸ **'Parnellite** n, adj

parochial (pəˈrəʊkɪəl) adj 1 narrow in outlook or scope; provincial. 2 of or relating to a parish. [C14: via OF from Church L parochiālis; see PARISH]
▸ **pa'rochial,ism** n ▸ **pa'rochially** adv

parody (ˈpærədɪ) n, pl **parodies**. 1 a musical, literary, or other composition that mimics the style of another composer, author, etc., in a humorous or satirical way. 2 something so badly done as to seem an intentional mockery; travesty. ◆ vb **parodies, parodying, parodied**. 3 (tr) to make a parody of. [C16: via L from Gk paroidiā satirical poem, from PARA-¹ + ōidē song]
▸ **parodic** (pəˈrɒdɪk) or **pa'rodical** adj ▸ **'parodist** n

parol (ˈpærəl, pəˈrəʊl) Law. ◆ n 1 an oral statement; word of mouth (now only in **by parol**). ◆ adj 2a (of a contract, lease, etc.) made orally or in writing but not under seal. 2b expressed or given by word of mouth: parol evidence. [C15: from OF parole speech; see PAROLE]

parole (pəˈrəʊl) n 1a the freeing of a prisoner before his sentence has expired, on the condition that he is of good behaviour. 1b the duration of such conditional release. 2 a promise given by a prisoner, as to be of good behaviour if granted liberty or partial liberty. 3 Linguistics. language as manifested in the individual speech acts of particular speakers. 4 **on parole**. conditionally released from detention. ◆ vb **paroles, paroling, paroled**. (tr) 5 to place (a person) on parole. [C17: from OF, from parole d'honneur word of honour; parole from LL parabola speech]
▸ **parolee** (pəˌrəʊˈliː) n

paronomasia (ˌpærənəʊˈmeɪzɪə) n Rhetoric. a play on words, esp. a pun. [C16: via L from Gk, from paronomazein to make a change in naming, from PARA-¹ (besides) + onomazein to name, from onoma a name]

Páros ★ (ˈpærɒs) n a Greek island in the S Aegean Sea, in the Cyclades: site of the discovery (1627) of the Parian Chronicle, a marble tablet outlining Greek history from before 1000 B.C. to about 354 B.C. (now at Oxford University). Pop.: 8000 (latest est.). Area: 166 sq. km (64 sq. miles).
▸ **'Parian** adj, n

parotid (pəˈrɒtɪd) adj 1 relating to or situated near the parotid gland. ◆ n 2 See **parotid gland**. [C17: via F, via L from Gk parōtis, from PARA-¹ (near) + -ōtis, from ous ear]

parotid gland n a large salivary gland, in man situated in front of and below each ear.

parotitis (ˌpærəˈtaɪtɪs) n inflammation of the parotid gland. See also **mumps**.

-parous adj combining form. giving birth to: oviparous. [from L -parus, from parere to bring forth]

paroxysm (ˈpærəkˌsɪzəm) n 1 an uncontrollable outburst: a paroxysm of giggling. 2 Pathol. 2a a sudden attack or recurrence of a disease. 2b any fit or convulsion. [C17: via F from Med. L paroxysmus annoyance, from Gk, from paroxunein to goad, from PARA-¹ (intensifier) + oxunein to sharpen, from oxus sharp]
▸ **parox'ysmal** adj

parquet (ˈpɑːkeɪ, -kɪ) n 1 a floor covering of pieces of hardwood fitted in a decorative pattern; parquetry. 2 Also called: **parquet floor**. a floor so covered. 3 US. the stalls of a theatre. ◆ vb (tr) 4 to cover a floor with parquet. [C19: from OF: small enclosure, from parc enclosure; see PARK]

parquetry (ˈpɑːkɪtrɪ) n a geometric pattern of inlaid pieces of wood, esp. as used to cover a floor.

parr (pɑː) n, pl **parrs** or **parr**. a salmon up to two years of age. [C18: from ?]

Parr ★ (pɑː) n Catherine. 1512–48, sixth wife of Henry VIII of England.

parrakeet (ˈpærəˌkiːt) n a variant spelling of **parakeet**.

parramatta (ˌpærəˈmætə) n a variant spelling of **paramatta**.

parricide (ˈpærɪˌsaɪd) n 1 the act of killing either of one's parents. 2 a person who kills his or her parent. [C16: from L parricīdium murder of a parent or relative, & from parricīda one who murders a relative, from parri- (rel. to Gk péos kinsman) + -CIDE]
▸ **parri'cidal** adj

parrot (ˈpærət) n 1 any of several related tropical and subtropical birds having a short hooked bill, bright plumage, and an ability to mimic sounds. 2 a person who repeats or imitates the words or actions of another. 3 **sick as a parrot**. Usually facetious. extremely disappointed. ◆ vb **parrots, parroting, parroted**. 4 (tr) to repeat or imitate without understanding. [C16: prob. from F paroquet, from ?]

parrot-fashion adv Inf. without regard for meaning; by rote: she learned it parrot-fashion.

parrot fever or **disease** n another name for **psittacosis**.

parrotfish (ˈpærətˌfɪʃ) n, pl **parrotfish** or **parrotfishes**.

★ people and places

brightly coloured tropical marine percoid fish having parrot-like jaws.

Parrott ★ ('pærət) *n* **John.** born 1964, British snooker player.

parry ('pærɪ) *vb* **parries, parrying, parried. 1** to ward off (an attack, etc.) by blocking or deflecting, as in fencing. **2** (*tr*) to evade (questions, etc.), esp. adroitly. ◆ *n, pl* **parries. 3** an act of parrying. **4** a skilful evasion, as of a question. [C17: from F *parer* to ward off, from L *parāre* to prepare]

Parry ★ ('pærɪ) *n* **1** Sir **(Charles) Hubert (Hastings).** 1848–1918, British composer, noted esp. for his choral works. **2** Sir **William Edward.** 1790–1855, British arctic explorer, who searched for the Northwest Passage (1819–25) and attempted to reach the North Pole (1827).

parse (pɑːz) *vb* **parses, parsing, parsed.** *Grammar.* to assign constituent structure to (a sentence or the words in a sentence). [C16: from L *pars (orātiōnis)* part (of speech)]

parsec ('pɑːˌsek) *n* a unit of astronomical distance equivalent to 3.0857×10^{16} metres or 3.262 light years. [C20: from PARALLAX + SECOND[2]]

Parsee or **Parsi** (ˌpɑːˈsiː, ˈpɑːˌsiː) *n* an adherent of a Zoroastrian religion, the practitioners of which were driven out of Persia by the Muslims in the eighth century A.D. It is now found chiefly in western India. [C17: from Persian *Pārsī* a Persian, from OPersian *Pārsa* PERSIA]
▶ **'Parsee,ism** or **'Parsi,ism** *n*

parser ('pɑːzə) *n Computing.* a program that interprets ordinary language typed into a computer by recognizing key words or analysing sentence structure and then translating it into the appropriate machine language.

Parsifal or **Parzival** ★ ('pɑːsɪfˀl, -ˌfɑːl) *n German myth.* the hero of a medieval cycle of legends about the Holy Grail. English equivalent: **Percival.**

parsimony ('pɑːsɪmənɪ) *n* extreme care in spending; niggardliness. [C15: from L *parcimōnia*, from *parcere* to spare]
▶ **parsimonious** (ˌpɑːsɪˈməʊnɪəs) *adj* ▶ **ˌparsiˈmoniously** *adv*

parsley ('pɑːslɪ) *n* **1** a S European umbelliferous plant, widely cultivated for its curled aromatic leaves, which are used in cooking. **2** any of various similar and related plants, such as fool's-parsley and cow parsley. [C14 *persely*, from OE *petersilie* + OF *persil, peresil*, both ult. from L *petroselīnum* rock parsley, from Gk, from *petra* rock + *selinon* parsley]

parsnip ('pɑːsnɪp) *n* **1** an umbelliferous plant cultivated for its long whitish root. **2** the root of this plant, eaten as a vegetable. [C14: from OF *pasnaie*, from L *pastināca*, from *pastināre* to dig, from *pastinum* two-pronged tool for digging]

parson ('pɑːsˀn) *n* **1** a parish priest in the Church of England. **2** any clergyman. [C13: from Med. L *persōna* parish priest, from L: personage; see PERSON]

parsonage ('pɑːsˀnɪdʒ) *n* the residence of a parson, as provided by the parish.

parson bird *n* another name for **tui.**

Parsons ★ ('pɑːsənz) *n* Sir **Charles Algernon.** 1854–1931, British engineer, who developed the steam turbine.

parson's nose *n* the fatty extreme end portion of the tail of a fowl when cooked.

part (pɑːt) *n* **1** a piece or portion of a whole. **2** an integral constituent of something: *dancing is part of what we teach.* **3** an amount less than the whole; bit: *they only recovered part of the money.* **4** one of several equal divisions: *mix two parts flour to one part water.* **5** an actor's role in a play. **6** a person's proper role or duty: *everyone must do his part.* **7** (*often pl*) region; area: *you're well known in these parts.* **8** *Anat.* any portion of a larger structure. **9** a component that can be replaced in a machine, etc. **10** the US, Canad., and Austral. word for **parting** (sense 1). **11** *Music.* one of a number of separate melodic lines which is assigned to one or more instrumentalists or singers. **12 for one's part.** as far as one is concerned. **13 for the most part.** generally. **14 in part.** to some degree; partly. **15 of many parts.** having many different abilities. **16 on the part of.** on behalf of. **17 part and parcel.** an essential ingredient. **18 play a part. 18a** to pretend to be what one is not. **18b** to

have something to do with; be instrumental. **19 take in good part.** to respond to (teasing, etc.) with good humour. **20 take part in.** to participate in. **21 take someone's part.** to support one person in an argument, etc. ◆ *vb* **22** to divide or separate from one another; take or come apart: *to part the curtains; the seams parted when I washed the dress.* **23** to go away or cause to go away from one another: *the couple parted amicably.* **24** (*intr*; foll. by *from*) to leave; say goodbye to. **25** (*intr*; foll. by *with*) to relinquish, esp. reluctantly: *I couldn't part with my teddy bear.* **26** (*tr*; foll. by *from*) to cause to relinquish, esp. reluctantly: *he's not easily parted from his cash.* **27** (*intr*) to split; separate: *the path parts here.* **28** (*tr*) to arrange (the hair) in such a way that a line of scalp is left showing. **29** (*intr*) *Euphemistic.* to die. **30** (*intr*) *Arch.* to depart. ◆ *adv* **31** to some extent; partly. ◆ See also **parts.** [C13: via OF from L *partīre* to divide, from *pars* part]

part. *abbrev. for:* **1** participle. **2** particular.

partake (pɑːˈteɪk) *vb* **partakes, partaking, partook, partaken.** (*mainly intr*) **1** (foll. by *in*) to have a share; participate. **2** (foll. by *of*) to take or receive a portion, esp. of food or drink. **3** (foll. by *of*) to suggest or have some of the quality (of): *music partaking of sadness.* [C16: back formation from *partaker*, earlier *part taker*, based on L *particeps* participant]
▶ **par'taker** *n*

> **USAGE NOTE** *Partake of* is sometimes wrongly used as if it were a synonym for *eat* or *drink*. Correctly, one can only *partake of* food or drink which is available for several people to share.

parterre (pɑːˈtɛə) *n* **1** a formally patterned flower garden. **2** the pit of a theatre. [C17: from F, from *par* along + *terre* ground]

parthenogenesis (ˌpɑːθɪnəʊˈdʒɛnɪsɪs) *n* a type of reproduction, occurring in some insects and flowers, in which the unfertilized ovum develops directly into a new individual. [C19: from Gk *parthenos* virgin + *genesis* birth]
▶ **parthenogenetic** (ˌpɑːθɪˌnəʊdʒɪˈnɛtɪk) *adj*

Parthenon ★ ('pɑːθəˌnɒn, -nən) *n* the temple on the Acropolis in Athens built in the 5th century B.C. and regarded as the finest example of the Greek Doric order.

Parthenopaeus ★ (ˌpɑːθənəʊˈpiːəs) *n Greek myth.* one of the Seven against Thebes, son of Atalanta.

Parthenope ★ (pɑːˈθɛnəpɪ) *n Greek myth.* a siren, who drowned herself when Odysseus evaded the lure of the sirens' singing. Her body was said to have been cast ashore at what became Naples.

Parthia ★ ('pɑːθɪə) *n* a country in ancient Asia, southeast of the Caspian Sea, that expanded into a great empire dominating SW Asia in the 2nd century B.C. It was destroyed by the Seleucids in the 3rd century A.D.
▶ **'Parthian** *n, adj*

Parthian shot *n* a hostile remark or gesture delivered while departing. [alluding to the custom of Parthian archers who shot their arrows backwards while retreating]

partial ('pɑːʃəl) *adj* **1** relating to only a part; not general or complete: *a partial eclipse.* **2** biased: *a partial judge.* **3** (*postpositive;* foll. by *to*) having a particular liking (for). **4** *Maths.* designating or relating to an operation in which only one of a set of independent variables is considered at a time. ◆ *n* **5** Also called: **partial tone.** *Music, acoustics.* any of the component tones of a single musical sound. **6** *Maths.* a partial derivative. [C15: from OF *parcial*, from LL *partiālis* incomplete, from L *pars* part]
▶ **'partially** *adv* ▶ **'partialness** *n*

> **USAGE NOTE** See at **partly.**

partial derivative *n* the derivative of a function of two or more variables with respect to one of the variables, the other or others being considered constant. Written $\partial f / \partial x$.

partiality (ˌpɑːʃɪˈælɪtɪ) *n, pl* **partialities. 1** favourable bias.

2 (usually foll. by *for*) liking or fondness. **3** the state of being partial.

partible ('pɑːtəbʰl) *adj* (esp. of property or an inheritance) divisible; separable. [C16: from LL *partibilis*, from *part-*, *pars* part]

participate (pɑː'tɪsɪ,peɪt) *vb* **participates, participating, participated.** (*intr;* often foll. by *in*) to take part, be or become actively involved, or share (in). [C16: from L *participāre*, from *pars* part + *capere* to take]
▸ par'ticipant *adj, n* ▸ par,tici'pation *n* ▸ par'tici,pator *n*
▸ par'ticipatory *adj*

participle ('pɑːtɪsɪpʰl) *n* a nonfinite form of verbs, in English and other languages, used adjectivally and in the formation of certain compound tenses. See also **present participle, past participle.** [C14: via OF from L *participium*, from *participes*, from *pars* part + *capere* to take]
▸ participial (,pɑːtɪ'sɪpɪəl) *adj* ▸ ,parti'cipially *adv*

particle ('pɑːtɪkʰl) *n* **1** an extremely small piece of matter; speck. **2** a very tiny amount; iota: *it doesn't make a particle of difference.* **3** a function word, esp. (in certain languages) a word belonging to an uninflected class having grammatical function: *"up" is sometimes regarded as an adverbial particle.* **4** a common affix, such as *re-, un-,* or *-ness.* **5** *Physics.* a body with finite mass that can be treated as having negligible size, and internal structure. **6** See **elementary particle.** [C14: from L *particula* a small part, from *pars* part]

particle accelerator *n* a machine for accelerating charged elementary particles to very high energies, used in nuclear physics.

particle physics *n* the study of fundamental particles and their properties. Also called: **high-energy physics.**

parti-coloured ('pɑːtɪ,kʌləd) *adj* having different colours in different parts; variegated. [C16 *parti*, from (obs.) *party* of more than one colour, from OF: striped, from L *partīre* to divide]

particular (pə'tɪkjulə) *adj* **1** (*prenominal*) of or belonging to a single or specific person, thing, category, etc.; specific; special: *the particular demands of the job.* **2** (*prenominal*) exceptional or marked: *a matter of particular importance.* **3** (*prenominal*) relating to or providing specific details or circumstances: *a particular account.* **4** exacting or difficult to please, esp. in details; fussy. **5** (of the solution of a differential equation) obtained by giving specific values to the arbitrary constants in a general equation. **6** *Logic.* (of a proposition) affirming or denying something about only some members of a class of objects, as in *some men are not wicked.* Cf. **universal** (sense 9). ◆ *n* **7** a separate distinct item that helps to form a generalization: opposed to *general.* **8** (*often pl*) an item of information; detail: *complete in every particular.* **9 in particular.** especially or exactly. [C14: from OF *particuler,* from LL *particulāris* concerning a part, from L *particula* PARTICLE]
▸ par'ticularly *adv*

particular average *n Insurance.* partial damage to or loss of a ship or its cargo affecting only the shipowner or one cargo owner. Abbrev.: **PA.** Cf. **general average.**

particularism (pə'tɪkjulə,rɪzəm) *n* **1** exclusive attachment to the interests of one group, class, sect, etc. **2** the principle of permitting each state in a federation the right to further its own interests. **3** *Christian theol.* the doctrine that divine grace is restricted to the elect.
▸ par'ticularist *n, adj*

particularity (pə,tɪkju'lærɪtɪ) *n, pl* **particularities.** **1** (*often pl*) a specific circumstance: *the particularities of the affair.* **2** great attentiveness to detail; fastidiousness. **3** the quality of being precise: *a description of great particularity.* **4** the state or quality of being particular as opposed to general; individuality.

particularize *or* **particularise** (pə'tɪkjulə,raɪz) *vb* **particularizes, particularizing, particularized** *or* **particularises, particularising, particularised.** **1** to treat in detail; give details (about). **2** (*intr*) to go into detail.
▸ par,ticulari'zation *or* par,ticulari'sation *n*

particulate (pɑː'tɪkjulɪt, -,leɪt) *n* **1** a substance consisting of separate particles. ◆ *adj* **2** of or made up of separate particles.

parting ('pɑːtɪŋ) *n* **1** *Brit.* the line of scalp showing when sections of hair are combed in opposite directions. US, Canad., and Austral. equivalent: **part. 2** the act of separating or the state of being separated. **3a** a departure or leave-taking, esp. one causing a final separation. **3b** (*as modifier*): *a parting embrace.* **4** a place or line of separation or division. **5** a euphemism for **death.** ◆ *adj* (*prenominal*) **6** *Literary.* departing: *the parting day.* **7** serving to divide or separate.

partisan *or* **partizan** (,pɑːtɪ'zæn, 'pɑːtɪ,zæn) *n* **1** an adherent or devotee of a cause, party, etc. **2** a member of an armed resistance group within occupied territory. ◆ *adj* **3** of, relating to, or characteristic of a partisan. **4** excessively devoted to one party, faction, etc.; one-sided. [C16: via F from OIt. *partigiano,* from *parte* faction, from L *pars* part]
▸ ,parti'sanship *or* ,parti'zanship *n*

partita (pɑː'tiːtə) *n, pl* **partite** (-teɪ) *or* **partitas** *Music.* a type of suite. [It.: divided (piece), from L *partīre* to divide]

partite ('pɑːtaɪt) *adj* **1** (*in combination*) composed of or divided into a specified number of parts: *bipartite.* **2** (esp. of plant leaves) divided almost to the base to form two or more parts. [C16: from L *partīre* to divide]

partition (pɑː'tɪʃən) *n* **1** a division into parts; separation. **2** something that separates, such as a large screen dividing a room in two. **3** a part or share. **4** *Property law.* a division of property, esp. realty, among joint owners. ◆ *vb* (*tr*) **5** (often foll. by *off*) to separate or apportion into sections: *to partition a room off with a large screen.* **6** *Property law.* to divide (property, esp. realty) among joint owners. [C15: via OF from L *partītiō,* from *partīre* to divide]
▸ par'titioner *or* par'titionist *n*

partitive ('pɑːtɪtɪv) *adj* **1** *Grammar.* indicating that a noun involved in a construction refers only to a part of what it otherwise refers to. The phrase *some of the butter* is a partitive construction. **2** serving to separate or divide into parts. ◆ *n* **3** *Grammar.* a partitive linguistic element or feature. [C16: from Med. L *partītīvus* serving to divide, from L *partīre* to divide]
▸ 'partitively *adv*

partly ('pɑːtlɪ) *adv* not completely.

USAGE NOTE *Partly* and *partially* are to some extent interchangeable, but *partly* should be used when referring to a part or parts of something: *the building is partly* (not *partially*) *of stone,* while *partially* is preferred for the meaning *to some extent: his mother is partially* (not *partly*) *sighted.*

partner ('pɑːtnə) *n* **1** an ally or companion: *a partner in crime.* **2** a member of a partnership. **3** one of a pair of dancers or players on the same side in a game: *my bridge partner.* **4** either member of a couple in a relationship. ◆ *vb* **5** to be or cause to be a partner (of). [C14: var. (infl. by PART) of *parcener* one who shares equally with another, from OF *parçonier,* ult. from L *partīre* to divide]

partnership ('pɑːtnəʃɪp) *n* **1a** a contractual relationship between two or more persons carrying on a joint business venture. **1b** the deed creating such a relationship. **1c** the persons associated in such a relationship. **2** the state or condition of being a partner.

part of speech *n* a class of words sharing important syntactic or semantic features; a group of words in a language that may occur in similar positions or fulfil similar functions in a sentence. The chief parts of speech in English are noun, pronoun, adjective, determiner, adverb, verb, preposition, conjunction, and interjection.

parton ('pɑː,tɒn) *n Physics.* a hypothetical elementary particle postulated as a constituent of neutrons and protons. [from PART + -ON]

Parton ★ ('pɑːtən) *n* **Dolly.** born 1946, US country and pop singer and songwriter.

partook (pɑː'tʊk) *vb* the past tense of **partake.**

partridge ('pɑːtrɪdʒ) *n, pl* **partridges** *or* **partridge.** any of various small Old World game birds of the pheasant family, esp. the common or European partridge. [C13: from OF *perdriz,* from L *perdix,* from Gk]

parts (pɑːts) *pl n* **1** personal abilities or talents: *a man of many parts.* **2** short for **private parts.**

Parts of Holland ★ *n* See **Holland**[1] (sense 3).

Parts of Kesteven ★ *n* See (Parts of) **Kesteven.**

Parts of Lindsey ★ *n* See (Parts of) **Lindsey.**

part song *n* **1** a song composed in harmonized parts. **2** (*in more technical usage*) a piece of homophonic choral music in which the topmost part carries the melody.

part-time *adj* **1** occupying less than the full time normally associated with an activity: *a part-time job.* ◆ *adv* **part time. 2** on a part-time basis: *he works part time.* ◆ Cf. **full-time.**
  ▶ ˌpart-ˈtimer *n*

parturient (pɑːˈtjʊərɪənt) *adj* **1** of or relating to childbirth. **2** giving birth. **3** producing a new idea, etc. [C16: via L *parturīre*, from *parere* to bring forth]
  ▶ par'turiency *n*

parturition (ˌpɑːtjʊˈrɪʃən) *n* the act or process of giving birth. [C17: from LL *parturītiō*, from *parturīre* to be in labour]

part work *n Brit.* a series of magazines issued weekly or monthly, which are designed to be bound together to form a complete book.

party (ˈpɑːtɪ) *n, pl* **parties. 1a** a social gathering for pleasure, often held as a celebration. **1b** (*as modifier*): *party spirit.* **1c** (*in combination*): *partygoer.* **2** a group of people associated in some activity: *a rescue party.* **3a** (*often cap.*) a group of people organized together to further a common political aim, etc. **3b** (*as modifier*): *party politics.* **4** a person, esp. one entering into a contract. **5** the person or persons taking part in legal proceedings: *a party to the action.* **6** *Inf.*, *humorous.* a person. ◆ *vb* **parties, partying, partied.** (*intr*) **7** *Inf.* to celebrate; revel. ◆ *adj* **8** *Heraldry.* (of a shield) divided vertically into two colours, metals, or furs. [C13: from OF *partie* part, from L *partīre* to divide; see PART]

party line *n* **1** a telephone line serving two or more subscribers. **2** the policies or dogma of a political party, etc.

party list *n* (*modifier*) of or relating to a system of voting in which people vote for a party rather than for a candidate. Parties are assigned the number of seats that reflects their share of the vote. See **proportional representation.**

party pooper (ˈpuːpə) *n Inf.* a person whose behaviour or personality spoils other people's enjoyment. [C20: orig. US]

party wall *n Property law.* a wall separating two properties or pieces of land and over which each of the adjoining owners has certain rights.

par value *n* the value imprinted on the face of a share certificate or bond and used to assess dividend, capital ownership, or interest.

parvenu *or* (*fem*) **parvenue** (ˈpɑːvəˌnjuː) *n* **1** a person who, having risen socially or economically, is considered to be an upstart. ◆ *adj* **2** of or characteristic of a parvenu. [C19: from F, from *parvenir* to attain, from L *pervenīre*, from *per* through + *venīre* to come]

parvovirus (ˈpɑːvəʊˌvaɪrəs) *n* any of a group of viruses characterized by their very small size, each of which is specific to a particular species, as for example canine parvovirus. [C20: NL, from L *parvus* little + VIRUS]

Parzival ★ (*German* ˈpartsifal) *n* a variant of **Parsifal.**

pas (pɑː) *n, pl* **pas.** a dance step or movement, esp. in ballet. [C18: from F, lit.: step]

Pasadena ★ (ˌpæsəˈdiːnə) *n* a city in SW California, east of Los Angeles. Pop.: 134 170 (1994 est.).

Pasargadae ★ (pæˈsɑːgəˌdiː) *n* an ancient city in Persia, northeast of Persepolis in present-day Iran: built by Cyrus the Great.

Pasay ★ (ˈpɑːsaɪ) *n* a city in the Philippines, on central Luzon just south of Manila, on Manila Bay. Pop.: 374 000 (1990). Also called: **Rizal.**

pascal (ˈpæskəl) *n* the derived SI unit of pressure; the pressure exerted on an area of 1 square metre by a force of 1 newton; equivalent to 10 dynes per square centi-

metre or 1.45×10^{-4} pound per square inch. Symbol: Pa [C20: after B. PASCAL]

Pascal ★ (*French* paskal) *n* **Blaise** (blɛz). 1623–62, French philosopher, mathematician, and physicist. As a scientist, he made important contributions to hydraulics and the study of atmospheric pressure and, with Fermat, developed the theory of probability. His chief philosophical works are *Lettres provinciales* (1656–57), written in defence of Jansenism and against the Jesuits, and *Pensées* (1670), fragments of a Christian apologia.

PASCAL (ˈpæsˌkæl) *n* a high-level computer-programming language developed as a teaching language.

Pascal's triangle *n* a triangle consisting of rows of numbers; the apex is 1 and each row starts and ends with 1, other numbers being obtained by adding together the two numbers on either side in the row above: used to calculate probabilities. [C17: after B. PASCAL]

paschal (ˈpæskəl) *adj* **1** of or relating to **Passover** (sense 1). **2** of or relating to **Easter.** [C15: from OF *pascal*, via Church L from Heb. *pesakh* Passover]

Paschal Lamb *n* **1** (*sometimes not caps.*) *Old Testament.* the lamb killed and eaten on the first day of the Passover. **2** Christ regarded as this sacrifice.

pas de basque (ˌpɑː də ˈbɑː) *n, pl* **pas de basque.** a dance step performed usually on the spot and used esp. in reels and jigs. [from F, lit.: Basque step]

Pas-de-Calais ★ (*French* pɑdkalɛ) *n* a department of N France, in Nord-Pas-de-Calais region, on the Straits of Dover (the **Pas de Calais**): the part of France closest to the British Isles. Capital: Arras. Pop.: 1 437 555 (1994 est.). Area: 6752 sq. km (2633 sq. miles).

pas de deux (*French* paddø) *n, pl* **pas de deux.** *Ballet.* a sequence for two dancers. [F: step for two]

pash (pæʃ) *n Sl.* infatuation. [C20: from PASSION]

pasha *or* **pacha** (ˈpɑːʃə, ˈpæʃə) *n* (formerly) a high official of the Ottoman Empire or the modern Egyptian kingdom: placed after a name when used as a title. [C17: from Turkish *paşa*]

pashm (ˈpæʃəm) *n* the underfur of various Tibetan animals, esp. goats, used for Cashmere shawls. [from Persian, lit.: wool]

Pashto, Pushto (ˈpʌʃtəʊ), *or* **Pushtu** (ˈpʌʃtuː) *n* **1** a language of Afghanistan and NW Pakistan. **2** (*pl* **Pashto** *or* **Pashtos, Pashtu** *or* **Pashtus; Pushto** *or* **Pushtos, Pushtu** *or* **Pushtus**) a speaker of the Pashto language; a Pathan. ◆ *adj* **3** denoting or relating to this language or a speaker of it.

Pasionaria ★ (*Spanish* pasjoˈnarja) *n* **La** (la), real name *Dolores Ibarruri.* 1895–1989, Spanish Communist leader, who lived in exile in the Soviet Union (1939–75).

Pasiphaë ★ (pəˈsɪfiː) *n Greek myth.* the wife of Minos and mother (by a bull) of the Minotaur.

Pasmore ★ (ˈpæsˌmɔː) *n* **Victor.** 1908–98, British artist. Originally influenced by cubism, he devoted himself to abstract paintings and reliefs after 1947.

paso doble (ˈpæsəʊ ˈdəʊbleɪ) *n, pl* **paso dobles** *or* **pasos dobles. 1** a modern ballroom dance in fast duple time. **2** a piece of music composed for or in the rhythm of this dance. [Sp.: double step]

Pasolini ★ (*Italian* pazoˈlini) *n* **Pier Paolo** (pjɛr ˈpɑːolo). 1922–75, Italian film director. His films include *The Gospel according to St Matthew* (1964), *Oedipus Rex* (1967), *Theorem* (1968), *Pigsty* (1969), and *Decameron* (1970).

pas op (ˈpɑːs ˌɒp) *interj S. African.* beware. [Afrik.]

pasqueflower (ˈpɑːskˌflaʊə) *n* **1** a small purple-flowered plant of N and Central Europe and W Asia. **2** any of several related North American plants. [C16: from F *passefleur*, from *passer* to excel + *fleur* flower; changed to *pasqueflower* Easter flower, because it blooms at Easter]

pasquinade (ˌpæskwɪˈneɪd) *n* an abusive lampoon or satire, esp. one posted in a public place. [C17: from It. *Pasquino* name given to an ancient Roman statue disinterred in 1501, which was annually posted with satirical verses]

pass (pɑːs) *vb* **1** to go onwards or move by or past (a person, thing, etc.). **2** to run, extend, or lead through, over, or across (a place): *the route passes through the city.* **3** to go through or cause to go through (an obstacle or barrier): *to pass a needle through cloth.* **4** to move or cause to move onwards or over: *he passed his hand over her face.* **5** (*tr*) to go beyond or exceed: *this victory passes all expectation.* **6** to gain or cause to gain an adequate mark or grade in (an examination, course, etc.). **7** (often foll. by *away* or *by*) to elapse or allow to elapse: *we passed the time talking.* **8** (*intr*) to take place or happen: *what passed at the meeting?* **9** to speak or exchange or be spoken or exchanged: *angry words passed between them.* **10** to spread or cause to spread: *we passed the news round the class.* **11** to transfer or exchange or be transferred or exchanged: *the bomb passed from hand to hand.* **12** (*intr*) to undergo change or transition: *to pass from joy to despair.* **13** (when *tr*, often foll. by *down*) to transfer or be transferred by inheritance: *the house passed to the younger son.* **14** to agree to or be agreed to by a legislative body, etc.: *the assembly passed 10 resolutions.* **15** (*tr*) (of a legislative measure) to undergo (a procedural stage) and be agreed: *the bill passed the committee stage.* **16** (when *tr*, often foll. by *on* or *upon*) to pronounce (judgment, findings, etc.): *the court passed sentence.* **17** to go or allow to go without comment or censure: *the insult passed unnoticed.* **18** (*intr*) to opt not to exercise a right, as by not answering a question or not making a bid or a play in card games. **19** to discharge (urine, etc.) from the body. **20** (*intr*) to come to an end or disappear: *his anger soon passed.* **21** (*intr*; usually foll. by *for* or *as*) to be likely to be mistaken for (someone or something else): *you could easily pass for your sister.* **22** (*intr*; foll. by *away*, *on*, or *over*) *Euphemistic.* to die. **23** *Sport.* to hit, kick, or throw (the ball, etc.) to another player. **24 bring to pass.** *Arch.* to cause to happen. **25 come to pass.** *Arch.* to happen. ◆ *n* **26** the act of passing. **27** a route through a range of mountains where there is a gap between peaks. **28** a permit, licence, or authorization to do something without restriction. **29a** a document allowing entry to and exit from a military installation. **29b** a document authorizing leave of absence. **30** *Brit.* **30a** the passing of a college or university examination to a satisfactory standard but not as high as honours. **30b** (*as modifier*): *a pass degree.* **31** a dive, sweep, or bombing or landing run by an aircraft. **32** a motion of the hand or of a wand as part of a conjuring trick. **33** *Inf.* an attempt to invite sexual intimacy (esp. in **make a pass at**). **34** a state of affairs, esp. a bad one (esp. in **a pretty pass**). **35** *Sport.* the transfer of a ball, etc., from one player to another. **36** *Fencing.* a thrust or lunge. **37** *Bridge, etc.* the act of passing (making no bid). ◆ *sentence substitute.* **38** *Bridge, etc.* a call indicating that a player has no bid to make. ◆ See also **pass off, pass out,** etc. [C13: from OF *passer* to pass, surpass, from L *passūs* step]

pass. *abbrev. for:* **1** passive. **2** passenger. **3** passage.

passable (ˈpɑːsəbᵊl) *adj* **1** adequate, fair, or acceptable. **2** (of an obstacle) capable of being crossed. **3** (of currency) valid for circulation. **4** (of a proposed law) able to be enacted.
▷ ˈ**passableness** *n* ▷ ˈ**passably** *adv*

passacaglia (ˌpæsəˈkɑːljə) *n* **1** an old Spanish dance in slow triple time. **2** a slow instrumental piece characterized by a series of variations on a particular theme played over a repeated bass part. [C17: earlier *passacalle*, from Sp. *pasacalle* street dance, from *paso* step + *calle* street]

passage (ˈpæsɪdʒ) *n* **1** a channel, opening, etc., through or by which a person or thing may pass. **2** *Music.* a section or division of a piece, movement, etc. **3** a way, as in a hall or lobby. **4** a section of a written work, speech, etc. **5** a journey, esp. by ship. **6** the act or process of passing from one place, condition, etc., to another: *passage of a gas through a liquid.* **7** the permission, right, or freedom to pass: *to be denied passage through a country.* **8** the enactment of a law by a legislative body. **9** *Rare.* an exchange, as of blows, words, etc. [C13: from OF from *passer* to PASS]

passageway (ˈpæsɪdʒˌweɪ) *n* a way, esp. one in or between buildings; passage.

Passamaquoddy Bay ★ (ˌpæsəməˈkwɒdɪ) *n* an inlet of the Bay of Fundy between the province of New Brunswick, in Canada, and the state of Maine, in the US, at the mouth of the St Croix River.

pass band *n* the band of frequencies that is transmitted with maximum efficiency through a circuit, filter, etc.

passbook (ˈpɑːsˌbʊk) *n* **1** a book for keeping a record of withdrawals from and payments into a building society. **2** another name for **bankbook**. **3** *S. African.* an official document to identify the bearer, his race, residence, and employment.

Passchendaele ★ (ˈpæfᵊnˌdeɪ'l) *n* a village in NW Belgium, in West Flanders province: the scene of heavy fighting during the third battle of Ypres in World War I during which 245 000 British troops were lost.

passé (ˈpɑːseɪ, ˈpæseɪ) *adj* **1** out-of-date: *passé ideas.* **2** past the prime; faded: *a passé society beauty.* [C18: from F, p.p. of *passer* to PASS]

passenger (ˈpæsɪndʒə) *n* **1a** a person travelling in a car, train, boat, etc., not driven by him. **1b** (*as modifier*): *a passenger seat.* **2** *Chiefly Brit.* a member of a group or team who is not participating fully in the work. [C14: from OF *passager* passing, from PASSAGE]

passenger pigeon *n* a gregarious North American pigeon, now extinct.

passe-partout (ˌpæspɑːˈtuː) *n* **1** a mounting for a picture in which strips of gummed paper bind together the glass, picture, and backing. **2** the gummed paper used for this. **3** a mat on which a photograph, etc., is mounted. **4** something that secures entry everywhere, esp. a master key. [C17: from F, lit.: pass everywhere]

passepied (pɑːˈspjeɪ) *n, pl* **passepieds** (-ˈpjeɪ). **1** a lively minuet in triple time, popular in the 17th century. **2** a piece of music composed for or in the rhythm of this dance. [C17: from F: pass foot]

passer-by *n, pl* **passers-by.** a person who is passing or going by, esp. on foot.

passerine (ˈpæsəˌraɪn, -ˌriːn) *adj* **1** of, relating to, or belonging to an order of birds characterized by the perching habit: includes the larks, finches, starlings, etc. ◆ *n* **2** any bird belonging to this order. [C18: from L *passer* sparrow]

passim *Latin.* (ˈpæsɪm) *adv* here and there; throughout: used to indicate that what is referred to occurs frequently in the work cited.

passing (ˈpɑːsɪŋ) *adj* **1** transitory or momentary: *a passing fancy.* **2** cursory or casual in action or manner: *a passing reference.* ◆ *adv, adj* **3** *Arch.* to an extreme degree: *the events were passing strange.* ◆ *n* **4** a place where or means by which one may pass, cross, ford, etc. **5** a euphemistic word for **death. 6 in passing.** by the way; incidentally.

passing bell *n* a bell rung to announce a death or a funeral. Also called: **death knell.**

passing note *or US* **passing tone** *n* a nonharmonic note through which a melody passes from one harmonic note to the next.

passion (ˈpæʃən) *n* **1** ardent love or affection. **2** intense sexual love. **3** a strong affection or enthusiasm for an object, concept, etc.: *a passion for poetry.* **4** any strongly felt emotion, such as love, hate, envy, etc. **5** an outburst of anger: *he flew into a passion.* **6** the object of an intense desire, ardent affection, or enthusiasm. **7** an outburst expressing intense emotion: *he burst into a passion of sobs.* **8** the sufferings and death of a Christian martyr. [C12: via F from Church L *passiō* suffering, from L *patī* to suffer]
▷ ˈ**passional** *adj* ▷ ˈ**passionless** *adj*

Passion (ˈpæʃən) *n* **1** the sufferings of Christ from the Last Supper to his death on the cross. **2** any of the four Gospel accounts of this. **3** a musical setting of this: *the St Matthew Passion.*

passionate (ˈpæʃənɪt) *adj* **1** manifesting or exhibiting intense sexual feeling or desire. **2** capable of, revealing, or characterized by intense emotion. **3** easily roused to anger; quick-tempered.
▷ ˈ**passionately** *adv*

passionflower (ˈpæʃənˌflaʊə) *n* any plant of a tropical American genus cultivated for their red, yellow, greenish, or purple showy flowers: some species have edible fruit. [C17: from alleged resemblance betweeen parts of the flower and the instruments of the Crucifixion]

★ people and places

passion fruit n the edible fruit of any of various passionflowers, esp. granadilla.

passion play n a play depicting the Passion of Christ.

passive ('pæsɪv) adj **1** not active or not participating perceptibly in an activity, organization, etc. **2** unresisting and receptive to external forces; submissive. **3** affected or acted upon by an external object or force. **4** Grammar. denoting a voice of verbs in sentences in which the grammatical subject is the recipient of the action described by the verb, as was broken in the sentence The glass was broken by a boy. **5** Chem. (of a substance, esp. a metal) apparently chemically unreactive. **6** Electronics, telecomm. **6a** capable only of attenuating a signal: a passive network. **6b** not capable of amplifying a signal or controlling a function: a passive communications satellite. **7** Finance. (of a bond, share, debt, etc.) yielding no interest. ◆ n **8** Grammar. **8a** the passive voice. **8b** a passive verb. [C14: from L passīvus susceptible of suffering, from patī to undergo]
▸ '**passively** adv ▸ **pas'sivity** or '**passiveness** n

passive resistance n resistance to a government, law, etc., without violence, as by fasting, demonstrating, or refusing to cooperate.

passive smoking n the inhalation of smoke from other people's cigarettes by a nonsmoker.

passkey ('pɑːsˌkiː) n **1** any of various keys, esp. a latchkey. **2** another term for **master key** or **skeleton key**.

pass law n (formerly, in South Africa) a law restricting the movement of Black Africans.

pass off vb (adv) **1** to be or cause to be accepted in a false character: he passed the fake diamonds off as real. **2** (intr) to come to a gradual end; disappear: eventually the pain passed off. **3** (intr) to take place: the meeting passed off without disturbance. **4** (tr) to set aside or disregard: I managed to pass off his insult.

pass out vb (adv) **1** (intr) Inf. to become unconscious; faint. **2** (intr) Brit. (esp. of an officer cadet) to qualify for a military commission, etc. **3** (tr) to distribute.

pass over vb **1** (tr, adv) to take no notice of; disregard: they passed me over in the last round of promotions. **2** (intr, prep) to disregard (something bad or embarrassing).

Passover ('pɑːsˌəʊvə) n **1** an eight-day Jewish festival celebrated in commemoration of the passing over or sparing of the Israelites in Egypt (Exodus 12). **2** another term for the **Paschal Lamb**. [C16: from pass over, translation of Heb. pesah, from pāsah to pass over]

passport ('pɑːspɔːt) n **1** an official document issued by a government, identifying an individual, granting him permission to travel abroad, and requesting the protection of other governments for him. **2** a quality, asset, etc., that gains a person admission or acceptance. [C15: from F passeport, from passer to PASS + PORT¹]

pass up vb (tr, adv) Inf. to let go by; ignore: I won't pass up this opportunity.

password ('pɑːsˌwɜːd) n **1** a secret word, phrase, etc., that ensures admission by proving identity, membership, etc. **2** an action, quality, etc., that gains admission or acceptance. **3** Computing. a sequence of characters used to gain access to a computer system.

past (pɑːst) adj **1** completed, finished, and no longer in existence: past happiness. **2** denoting or belonging to the time that has elapsed at the present moment: the past history of the world. **3** denoting a specific unit of time that immediately precedes the present one: the past month. **4** (prenominal) denoting a person who has held an office or position; former: a past president. **5** Grammar. denoting any of various tenses of verbs that are used in describing actions, events, or states that have been begun or completed at the time of utterance. ◆ n **6** the past. the period of time that has elapsed: forget the past. **7** the history, experience, or background of a nation, person, etc. **8** an earlier period of someone's life, esp. one regarded as disreputable. **9** Grammar. **9a** a past tense. **9b** a verb in a past tense. ◆ adv **10** at a time before the present; ago: three years past. **11** on or onwards: I greeted him but he just walked past. ◆ prep **12** beyond in time: it's past midnight. **13** beyond in place or position: the library is past the church. **14** moving beyond: he walked past me. **15** beyond

or above the reach, limit, or scope of: his foolishness is past comprehension. **16** past it. Inf. unable to perform the tasks one could do when one was younger. **17** not put it past someone. to consider someone capable of (the action specified). [C14: from passed, p.p. of PASS]

> **USAGE NOTE** The past participle of pass is sometimes wrongly spelt past: the time for recrimination has passed (not past).

pasta ('pæstə) n any of several variously shaped edible preparations made from a flour and water dough, such as spaghetti. [It., from LL: PASTE]

paste (peɪst) n **1** a mixture of a soft or malleable consistency, such as toothpaste. **2** an adhesive made from water and flour or starch, used for joining pieces of paper, etc. **3** a preparation of food, such as meat, that has been pounded to a creamy mass, for spreading on bread, etc. **4** any of various sweet doughy confections: almond paste. **5** dough, esp. for making pastry. **6a** a hard shiny glass used for making imitation gems. **6b** an imitation gem made of this glass. **7** the combined ingredients of porcelain. See also **hard paste, soft paste.** ◆ vb **pastes, pasting, pasted.** (tr) **8** (usually foll. by on or onto) to attach as by using paste: he pasted posters onto the wall. **9** (usually foll. by with) to cover (a surface) with paper, etc.: he pasted the wall with posters. **10** Sl. to thrash or beat; defeat. [C14: via OF from LL pasta dough, from Gk pastē barley porridge, from passein to sprinkle]

pasteboard ('peɪstˌbɔːd) n **1** a stiff board formed from layers of paper or pulp pasted together. ◆ adj **2** flimsy or fake.

pastel ('pæstᵊl, pæ'stel) n **1a** a substance made of ground pigment bound with gum. **1b** a crayon of this. **1c** a drawing done in such crayons. **2** the medium or technique of pastel drawing. **3** a pale delicate colour. ◆ adj **4** (of a colour) pale; delicate: pastel blue. [C17: via F from It. pastello, from LL pastellus woad, dim. of pasta PASTE]
▸ '**pastelist** or '**pastellist** n

pastern ('pæstən) n the part of a horse's foot between the fetlock and the hoof. [C14: from OF pasturon, from pasture a hobble, from L pāstōrius of a shepherd, from PASTOR]

Pasternak ★ ('pæstəˌnæk; Russian pəstɪr'nak) n Boris Leonidovich (ba'ris lɪə'nidəvɪtʃ). 1890–1960, Russian poet, novelist, and translator, noted esp. for his novel Dr. Zhivago (1957). He was awarded the Nobel prize for literature in 1958, but was forced to decline it.

paste-up n Printing. a sheet of paper or board on which are pasted artwork, proofs, etc., for photographing prior to making a plate.

Pasteur ★ (French pastœr) n **Louis** (lwi). 1822–95, French chemist and bacteriologist. His discovery that the fermentation of milk and alcohol was caused by microorganisms resulted in the process of pasteurization. He also devised methods of immunization against anthrax and rabies and pioneered stereochemistry.

pasteurism ('pæstəˌrɪzəm, -stjə-, 'pɑː-) n Med. a method of securing immunity from rabies or of treating patients with other viral infections by the serial injection of progressively more virulent suspensions of the causative virus. Also called: **Pasteur treatment.**

pasteurization or **pasteurisation** (ˌpæstəraɪ'zeɪʃən, -stjə-, ˌpɑː-) n the process of heating beverages, such as milk, beer, wine, or cider, or solid foods, such as cheese or crab meat, to destroy harmful microorganisms.

pasteurize or **pasteurise** ('pæstəˌraɪz, -stjə-, 'pɑː-) vb **pasteurizes, pasteurizing, pasteurized** or **pasteurises, pasteurising, pasteurised.** (tr) to subject (milk, beer, etc.) to pasteurization.
▸ '**pasteurˌizer** or '**pasteurˌiser** n

pastiche (pæ'stiːʃ) or **pasticcio** (pæ'stɪtʃəʊ) n, pl **pastiches** or **pasticcios. 1** a work of art that mixes styles, materials, etc. **2** a work of art that imitates the style of another artist or period. [C19: F pastiche, It. pasticcio, lit.: piecrust (hence, something blended) from LL pasta PASTE]

pastille or **pastil** ('pæstɪl) n **1** a small flavoured or medicated lozenge. **2** an aromatic substance burnt to fumigate the air. [C17: via F from L *pastillus* small loaf, from *pānis* bread]

pastime ('pɑːs,taɪm) *n* an activity or entertainment which makes time pass pleasantly.

past master *n* **1** a person with talent for, or experience in, a particular activity. **2** a person who has held the office of master in a guild, etc.

Pasto ★ (*Spanish* 'pasto) *n* a city in SE Colombia, at an altitude of 2590 m (8500 ft). Pop.: 362 227 (1997 est.).

pastor ('pɑːstə) *n* **1** a clergyman or priest in charge of a congregation. **2** a person who exercises spiritual guidance over a number of people. **3** a S Asian starling having a black head and wings and a pale pink body. [C14: from L: shepherd, from *pascere* to feed]
▸ **'pastorship** *n*

pastoral ('pɑːstərəl) *adj* **1** of, characterized by, or depicting rural life, scenery, etc. **2** (of a literary work) dealing with an idealized form of rural existence. **3** (of land) used for pasture. **4** of or relating to a clergyman or priest in charge of a congregation or his duties as such. **5** of or relating to shepherds, their work, etc. **6** of or relating to a teacher's responsibility for the personal, as distinct from the educational, development of pupils. ◆ *n* **7** a literary work or picture portraying rural life, esp. in an idealizing way. **8** *Music.* a variant spelling of **pastorale**. **9a** a letter from a clergyman to the people under his charge. **9b** the letter of a bishop to the clergy or people of his diocese. **9c** Also called: **pastoral staff.** the crosier carried by a bishop. [C15: from L, from PASTOR]
▸ **'pastoralism** *n* ▸ **'pastorally** *adv*

pastorale (,pæstə'rɑːl) *n, pl* **pastorales.** *Music.* **1** a composition evocative of rural life, sometimes with a droning accompaniment. **2** a musical play based on a rustic story. [C18: It., from L: PASTORAL]

pastoralist ('pɑːstərəlɪst) *n Austral.* a grazier raising sheep, cattle, etc., on a large scale.

pastorate ('pɑːstərɪt) *n* **1** the office or term of office of a pastor. **2** a body of pastors.

pastourelle (,pɑːstuː'rɛl) *n Music.* **1** a pastoral piece of music. **2** one of the figures in a quadrille. [C19: from F: little shepherdess]

past participle *n* a participial form of verbs used to modify a noun that is logically the object of a verb, also used in certain compound tenses and passive forms of the verb.

past perfect *Grammar.* ◆ *adj* **1** denoting a tense of verbs used in relating past events where the action had already occurred at the time of the action of a main verb that is itself in a past tense. In English this is a compound tense formed with *had* plus the past participle. ◆ *n* **2a** the past perfect tense. **2b** a verb in this tense.

pastrami (pə'strɑːmɪ) *n* highly seasoned smoked beef. [from Yiddish, from Romanian *pastramă*, from *păstra* to preserve]

pastry ('peɪstrɪ) *n, pl* **pastries.** **1** a dough of flour, water, and fat. **2** baked foods, such as tarts, made with this dough. **3** an individual cake or pastry pie. [C16: from PASTE]

pasturage ('pɑːstʃərɪdʒ) *n* **1** the business of grazing cattle. **2** another word for **pasture**.

pasture ('pɑːstʃə) *n* **1** land covered with grass or herbage and grazed by or suitable for grazing by livestock. **2** the grass or herbage growing on it. ◆ *vb* **pastures, pasturing, pastured.** **3** (*tr*) to cause (livestock) to graze or (of livestock) to graze (a pasture). [C13: via OF from LL *pāstūra,* from *pascere* to feed]

pasty[1] ('peɪstɪ) *adj* **pastier, pastiest. 1** of or like the colour, texture, etc., of paste. **2** (esp. of the complexion) pale or unhealthy-looking.
▸ **'pastily** *adv* ▸ **'pastiness** *n*

pasty[2] ('pæstɪ) *n, pl* **pasties.** a round of pastry folded over a filling of meat, vegetables, etc. [C13: from OF *pastée,* from LL *pasta* dough]

PA system *n* See **public-address system.**

pat[1] (pæt) *vb* **pats, patting, patted. 1** to hit (something) lightly with the palm of the hand or some other flat sur-

face: *to pat a ball.* **2** to slap (a person or animal) gently, esp. on the back, as an expression of affection, congratulation, etc. **3** (*tr*) to shape, smooth, etc., with a flat instrument or the palm. **4** (*intr*) to walk or run with light footsteps. **5 pat (someone) on the back.** *Inf.* to congratulate. **10 pat on the back.** *Inf.* a gesture or word indicating approval. ◆ *n* **6** a light blow with something flat. **7** a gentle slap. **8** a small mass of something: *a pat of butter.* **9** the sound of patting. **10 pat on the back.** *Inf.* a gesture or word indicating approval. [C14: ? imit.]

pat[2] (pæt) *adv* **1** Also: **off pat.** exactly or fluently memorized: *he recited it pat.* **2** opportunely or aptly. **3 stand pat. 3a** *Chiefly US & Canad.* to refuse to abandon a belief, decision, etc. **3b** (in poker, etc.) to play without adding new cards to the hand dealt. ◆ *adj* **4** exactly right; apt: *a pat reply.* **5** too exactly fitting; glib: *a pat answer to a difficult problem.* **6** exactly right: *a pat hand in poker.* [C17: ? adv use ("with a light stroke") of PAT[1]]

pat[3] (pæt) *n* **on one's pat.** *Austral. inf.* alone. [C20: rhyming slang, from *Pat Malone*]

pat. *abbrev. for* patent(ed).

patagium (pə'teɪdʒɪəm) *n, pl* **patagia** (-dʒɪə). **1** a web of skin in bats and gliding mammals that functions as a wing. **2** a membranous fold of skin connecting a bird's wing to the shoulder. [C19: NL, from L, from Gk *patageion* gold border on a tunic]

Patagonia ★ (,pætə'gəʊnɪə) *n* **1** the southernmost region of South America, in Argentina and Chile extending from the Andes to the Atlantic. **2** an arid tableland in the southernmost part of Argentina, rising towards the Andes in the west.
▸ **,Pata'gonian** *adj*

patch (pætʃ) *n* **1** a piece of material used to mend a garment, etc., or to make patchwork, a sewn-on pocket, etc. **2a** a small plot of land. **2b** its produce: *a patch of cabbages.* **3** *Med.* **3a** a protective covering for an injured eye. **3b** any protective dressing. **4** an imitation beauty spot made of black silk, etc., worn esp. in the 18th century. **5** an identifying piece of fabric worn on the shoulder of a uniform. **6** a small contrasting section: *a patch of cloud in the blue sky.* **7** a scrap; remnant. **8 a bad patch.** a difficult or troubled time. **9 not a patch on.** not nearly as good as. ◆ *vb* (*tr*) **10** to mend or supply (a garment, etc.) with a patch or patches. **11** to put together or produce with patches. **12** (of material) to serve as a patch to. **13** (often foll. by *up*) to mend hurriedly or in a makeshift way. **14** (often foll. by *up*) to make (up) or settle (a quarrel, etc.). **15** to connect (electric circuits) together temporarily by means of a patch board. [C16 *pacche,* ? from F *pieche* PIECE]
▸ **'patcher** *n*

patch board *or* **panel** *n* a device with a large number of sockets into which electrical plugs can be inserted to form many different temporary circuits: used in telephone exchanges, computer systems, etc. Also called: **plugboard.**

patchouli *or* **patchouly** ('pætʃʊlɪ, pə'tʃuːlɪ) *n, pl* **patchoulis** *or* **patchoulies. 1** any of several Asiatic trees, the leaves of which yield a heavy fragrant oil. **2** the perfume made from this oil. [C19: from Tamil *paccilai,* from *paccu* green + *ilai* leaf]

patch pocket *n* a pocket on the outside of a garment.

patch test *n Med.* a test to detect an allergic reaction by applying small amounts of a suspected substance to the skin.

patchwork ('pætʃ,wɜːk) *n* **1** needlework done by sewing pieces of different materials together. **2** something made up of various parts.

patchy ('pætʃɪ) *adj* **patchier, patchiest. 1** irregular in quality, occurrence, intensity, etc.: *a patchy essay.* **2** having or forming patches.
▸ **'patchily** *adv* ▸ **'patchiness** *n*

pate (peɪt) *n* the head, esp. with reference to baldness or (in facetious use) intelligence. [C14: from ?]

pâté ('pæteɪ) *n* **1** a spread of finely minced liver, poultry, etc., served usually as an hors d'oeuvre. **2** a savoury pie. [C18: from F: PASTE]

pâté de foie gras (pɑte də fwɑ grɑ) *n, pl* **pâtés de foie gras** (pɑte). a smooth rich paste made from the liver of a specially fattened goose. [F: pâté of fat liver]

patella (pə'tɛlə) n, pl **patellae** (-liː). Anat. a small flat triangular bone in front of and protecting the knee joint. Nontechnical name: **kneecap**. [C17: from L, from patina shallow pan]
▶ pa'**tellar** adj

paten ('pætᵊn) n a plate, usually made of silver or gold, esp. for the bread in the Eucharist. [C13: from OF patene, from Med. L, from L patina pan]

patency ('peɪtᵊnsɪ) n the condition of being obvious.

patent ('peɪtᵊnt, 'pætᵊnt) n **1a** a government grant to an inventor assuring him the sole right to make, use, and sell his invention for a limited period. **1b** a document conveying such a grant. **2** an invention, privilege, etc., protected by a patent. **3a** an official document granting a right. **3b** any right granted by such a document. ◆ adj **4** open or available for inspection (esp. in **letters patent**, **patent writ**). **5** ('peɪtᵊnt). obvious: their scorn was patent to everyone. **6** concerning protection, appointment, etc., of or by a patent or patents. **7** proprietary. **8** (esp. of a bodily passage or duct) being open or unobstructed. ◆ vb (tr) **9** to obtain a patent for. **10** to grant by a patent. [C14: via OF from L patēre to lie open; n use, short for letters patent, from Med. L litterae patentes letters lying open (to public inspection)]
▶ '**patentable** adj ▶ ,**paten'tee** n ▶ ,**paten'tor** n

> **USAGE NOTE** The pronunciation "'pætᵊnt" is heard in *letters patent* and *Patent Office* and is the usual US pronunciation for all senses. In Britain "'pætᵊnt" is sometimes heard for senses 1, 2, and 3, but "'peɪtᵊnt" is commoner and is regularly used in collocations like *patent leather*.

patent leather ('peɪtᵊnt) n leather processed with lacquer to give a hard glossy surface.

patently ('peɪtᵊntlɪ) adv obviously.

patent medicine ('peɪtᵊnt) n a medicine with a patent, available without a prescription.

Patent Office ('pætᵊnt) n a government department that issues patents.

Patent Rolls ('pætᵊnt) pl n (in Britain) the register of patents issued.

pater ('peɪtə) n Brit. sl. another word for **father**: now chiefly used facetiously. [from L]

Pater ★ ('peɪtə) n **Walter (Horatio)**. 1839–94, British essayist and critic, noted for his prose style and his advocation of the "love of art for its own sake". His works include the philosophical romance *Marius the Epicurean* (1885), *Studies in the History of the Renaissance* (1873), and *Imaginary Portraits* (1887).

paterfamilias (,peɪtəfə'mɪlɪˌæs) n, pl **patresfamilias** (,pɑːtreɪzfə'mɪlɪˌæs). the male head of a household. [L: father of the family]

paternal (pə'tɜːnᵊl) adj **1** relating to or characteristic of a father; fatherly. **2** (prenominal) related through the father: his paternal grandfather. **3** inherited or derived from the male parent. [C17: from LL paternālis, from L pater father]
▶ pa'**ternally** adv

paternalism (pə'tɜːnəˌlɪzəm) n the attitude or policy of a government or other authority that manages the affairs of a country, company, etc., in the manner of a father, esp. in usurping individual responsibility.
▶ pa'**ternalist** n, adj ▶ pa,**ternal'istic** adj ▶ pa,**ternal-'istically** adv

paternity (pə'tɜːnɪtɪ) n **1a** the fact or state of being a father. **1b** (as modifier): a paternity suit; paternity leave. **2** descent or derivation from a father. **3** authorship or origin. [C15: from LL paternitās, from L pater father]

paternoster (,pætə'nɒstə) n **1** RC Church. the beads at the ends of each decade of the rosary at which the Paternoster is recited. **2** a type of fishing tackle in which short lines and hooks are attached at intervals to the main line. **3** a type of lift in which platforms are attached to continuous chains: passengers enter while it is moving.

[L, lit.: our father (from the opening of the Lord's Prayer)]

Paternoster (,pætə'nɒstə) n (sometimes not cap.) RC Church. **1** the Lord's Prayer, esp. in Latin. **2** the recital of this as an act of devotion.

Paterson[1] ★ ('pætəsᵊn) n a city in NE New Jersey: settled by the Dutch in the late 17th century. Pop.: 138 290 (1994 est.).

Paterson[2] ★ ('pætəsᵊn) n **Andrew Barton**, known as Banjo Paterson. 1864–1941, Australian poet. His works include "Waltzing Matilda" and "The Man from Snowy River".

Paterson's curse n an Australian name for **viper's bugloss**.

path (pɑːθ) n, pl **paths** (pɑːðz). **1** a road or way, esp. a narrow trodden track. **2** a surfaced walk, as through a garden. **3** the course or direction in which something moves: the path of a whirlwind. **4** a course of conduct: the path of virtue. [OE pæth]
▶ '**pathless** adj

path. abbrev. for: **1** pathological. **2** pathology.

-path n combining form. **1** denoting a person suffering from a specified disease or disorder: neuropath. **2** denoting a practitioner of a particular method of treatment: osteopath. [back formation from -PATHY]

Pathan (pə'tɑːn) n a member of the Pashto-speaking people of Afghanistan, NW Pakistan, and elsewhere. [C17: from Hindi]

pathetic (pə'θɛtɪk) adj **1** evoking or expressing pity, sympathy, etc. **2** distressingly inadequate: the old man sat huddled before a pathetic fire. **3** Brit. sl. ludicrously or contemptibly uninteresting or worthless. **4** Obs. of or affecting the feelings. [C16: from F pathétique, via LL from Gk pathetikos sensitive, from pathos suffering]
▶ pa'**thetically** adv

pathetic fallacy n (in literature) the presentation of inanimate objects in nature as possessing human feelings.

pathfinder ('pɑːθˌfaɪndə) n **1** a person who makes or finds a way, esp. through unexplored areas or fields of knowledge. **2** an aircraft or parachutist that indicates a target area by dropping flares, etc. **3** a radar device used for navigation or homing onto a target.

pathfinder prospectus n a prospectus regarding the flotation of a new company that contains only sufficient details to test the market reaction.

patho- or before a vowel **path-** combining form. disease: pathology. [from Gk pathos suffering]

pathogen ('pæθəˌdʒɛn) n any agent that can cause disease.
▶ ,**patho'genic** adj

pathogenesis (,pæθə'dʒɛnɪsɪs) or **pathogeny** (pə-'θɒdʒɪnɪ) n the development of a disease.
▶ ,**pathogenetic** (,pæθəʊdʒɪ'nɛtɪk) adj

pathological (,pæθə'lɒdʒɪkᵊl) or (less commonly) **pathologic** adj **1** of or relating to pathology. **2** relating to, involving, or caused by disease. **3** Inf. compulsively motivated: a pathological liar.
▶ ,**patho'logically** adv

pathology (pə'θɒlədʒɪ) n, pl **pathologies**. **1** the branch of medicine concerned with the cause, origin, and nature of disease, including the changes occurring as a result of disease. **2** the manifestations of disease, esp. changes occurring in tissues or organs.
▶ pa'**thologist** n

pathos ('peɪθɒs) n **1** the quality or power, esp. in literature or speech, of arousing feelings of pity, sorrow, etc. **2** a feeling of sympathy or pity. [C17: from Gk: suffering]

pathway ('pɑːθˌweɪ) n **1** a path. **2** Biochem. a chain of reactions associated with a particular metabolic process.

-pathy n combining form. **1** indicating feeling or perception: telepathy. **2** indicating disease: psychopathy. **3** indicating a method of treating disease: osteopathy. [from Gk patheia suffering; see PATHOS]
▶ -**pathic** adj combining form.

Patiala ★ (,pʌtɪ'ɑːlə) n a city in N India, in E Punjab: seat of the Punjabi University (1962). Pop.: 238 368 (1991).

patience ('peɪʃəns) n **1** tolerant and even-tempered perseverance. **2** the capacity for calmly enduring pain, trying situations, etc. **3** *Chiefly Brit.* any of various card games for one player only. US word: **solitaire.** [C13: via OF from L *patientia* endurance, from *patī* to suffer]

patient ('peɪʃənt) adj **1** enduring trying circumstances with even temper. **2** tolerant; understanding. **3** capable of accepting delay with equanimity. **4** persevering or diligent: *a patient worker.* ♦ n **5** a person who is receiving medical care. [C14: see PATIENCE]
▸ 'patiently adv

patina[1] ('pætɪnə) n, pl **patinas. 1** a film formed on the surface of a metal, esp. the green oxidation of bronze or copper. **2** any fine layer on a surface: *a patina of frost.* **3** the sheen on a surface caused by much handling. [C18: from It.: coating, from L: PATINA[2]]

patina[2] ('pætɪnə) n, pl **patinae** (-ˌniː). a broad shallow dish used in ancient Rome. [from L, from Gk *patanē* platter]

patio ('pætɪˌəʊ) n, pl **patios. 1** an open inner courtyard, esp. one in a Spanish or Spanish-American house. **2** an area adjoining a house, esp. one that is paved. [C19: from Sp.: courtyard]

patisserie (pəˈtiːsərɪ) n **1** a shop where fancy pastries are sold. **2** such pastries. [C18: F, from *pâtissier* pastry cook, ult. from LL *pasta* PASTE]

Patmore ★ ('pætmɔː) n Coventry (Kersey Dighton). 1823–96, British poet. His works, celebrating both conjugal and divine love, include *The Angel in the House* (1854–62) and *The Unknown Eros* (1877).

Patmos ★ ('pætmɒs) n a Greek island in the Aegean, in the NW Dodecanese: St John's place of exile (about 95 A.D.), where he wrote the Apocalypse. Pop.: 2650 (1995 est.). Area: 34 sq. km (13 sq. miles).

Patna ★ ('pætnə) n a city in NE India, capital of Bihar state, on the River Ganges: founded in the 5th century B.C.; university (1917); centre of a rice-growing region. Pop.: 917 243 (1991).

Patna rice n a variety of long-grain rice, used for savoury dishes.

patois ('pætwɑː) n, pl **patois** ('pætwɑːz). **1** a regional dialect of a language, usually considered substandard. **2** the jargon of a particular group. [C17: from OF: rustic speech, ?from *patoier* to handle awkwardly, from *patte* paw]

Paton ★ ('peɪt'n) n Alan (Stewart). 1903–88, South African writer, noted esp. for his novel dealing with racism and apartheid in South Africa, *Cry, the Beloved Country* (1965).

pat. pend. *abbrev.* for patent pending.

Patras ★ (pəˈtræs, ˈpætrəs) n a port in W Greece, in the NW Peloponnese on the Gulf of Patras (an inlet of the Ionian Sea): one of the richest cities in Greece until the 3rd century B.C.; under Turkish rule from 1458 to 1687 and from 1715 until the War of Greek Independence, which began here in 1821. Pop.: 155 180 (1991). Modern Greek name: Pátrai ('patrɛ).

patri- *combining form.* father: *patricide; patriarch.* [from L *pater,* Gk *patēr* father]

patrial ('peɪtrɪəl) n (in Britain, formerly) a person having by statute the right of abode in the United Kingdom. [C20: from L *patria* native land]

patriarch ('peɪtrɪˌɑːk) n **1** the male head of a tribe or family. **2** a very old or venerable man. **3** *Bible.* **3a** any of a number of persons regarded as the fathers of the human race. **3b** any of the three ancestors of the Hebrew people: Abraham, Isaac, or Jacob. **3c** any of Jacob's twelve sons, regarded as the ancestors of the twelve tribes of Israel. **4** *Early Christian Church.* the bishop of one of several principal sees, esp. those of Rome, Antioch, and Alexandria. **5** *Eastern Orthodox Church.* the bishops of the four ancient principal sees of Constantinople, Antioch, Alexandria, and Jerusalem, and also of Russia, Rumania, and Serbia. **6** *RC Church.* **6a** a title given to the pope. **6b** a title given to a number of bishops, esp. of the Uniat Churches, indicating their rank as immediately below that of the pope. **7** the oldest or most venerable member of a group, community, etc. **8** a person regarded as the founder of a community, tradition, etc. [C12: via OF from Church L *patriarcha*]
▸ ˌpatriˈarchal adj

patriarchate ('peɪtrɪˌɑːkɪt) n the office, jurisdiction, province, or residence of a patriarch.

patriarchy ('peɪtrɪˌɑːkɪ) n, pl **patriarchies. 1** a form of social organization in which a male is the head of the family and descent, kinship, and title are traced through the male line. **2** any society governed by such a system.

patrician (pəˈtrɪʃən) n **1** a member of the hereditary aristocracy of ancient Rome. **2** (in medieval Europe) a member of the upper class in numerous Italian republics and German free cities. **3** an aristocrat. **4** a person of refined conduct, tastes, etc. ♦ adj **5** (esp. in ancient Rome) of, relating to, or composed of patricians. **6** aristocratic. [C15: from OF *patricien,* from L *patricius* noble, from *pater* father]

patricide ('pætrɪˌsaɪd) n **1** the act of killing one's father. **2** a person who kills his father.
▸ ˌpatriˈcidal adj

Patrick ★ ('pætrɪk) n Saint. 5th century A.D., Christian missionary in Ireland, probably born in Britain; patron saint of Ireland. Feast day: March 17.

patrilineal (ˌpætrɪˈlɪnɪəl) adj tracing descent, kinship, or title through the male line.

patrimony ('pætrɪmənɪ) n, pl **patrimonies. 1** an inheritance from one's father or other ancestor. **2** the endowment of a church. [C14 *patrimoyne,* from OF, from L *patrimonium* paternal inheritance]
▸ **patrimonial** (ˌpætrɪˈməʊnɪəl) adj

patriot ('peɪtrɪət, 'pæt-) n a person who vigorously supports his country and its way of life. [C16: via F from LL *patriōta,* from Gk *patriotēs,* from *patris* native land; rel. to Gk *patēr* father; cf. L *pater* father, *patria* fatherland]
▸ **patriotic** (ˌpætrɪˈɒtɪk) adj ▸ ˌpatriˈotically adv

Patriot ('peɪtrɪət) n a US surface-to-air missile system with multiple launch stations and the capability to track multiple targets by radar.

patriotism ('pætrɪəˌtɪzəm) n devotion to one's own country and concern for its defence.

patristic (pəˈtrɪstɪk) or **patristical** adj of or relating to the Fathers of the Church, their writings, or the study of these.
▸ paˈtristics n (*functioning as sing*)

Patroclus ★ (pəˈtrɒkləs) n *Greek myth.* a friend of Achilles, killed in the Trojan War by Hector. His death made Achilles return to the fight after his quarrel with Agamemnon.

patrol (pəˈtrəʊl) n **1** the action of going round a town, etc., at regular intervals for purposes of security or observation. **2** a person or group that carries out such an action. **3** a military detachment with the mission of security or combat with enemy forces. **4** a division of a troop of Scouts or Guides. ♦ vb **patrols, patrolling, patrolled. 5** to engage in a patrol of (a place). [C17: from F *patrouiller,* from *patouiller* to flounder in mud, from *patte* paw]
▸ paˈtroller n

patrol car n a police car used for patrolling streets and motorways.

patrology (pəˈtrɒlədʒɪ) n **1** the study of the writings of the Fathers of the Church. **2** a collection of such writings. [C17: from Gk *patr-, patēr* father + -LOGY]
▸ paˈtrologist n

patrol wagon n the usual US, Austral., and NZ term for Black Maria.

patron[1] ('peɪtrən) n **1** a person who sponsors or aids artists, charities, etc.; protector or benefactor. **2** a customer of a shop, hotel, etc., esp. a regular one. **3** See patron saint. [C14: via OF from L *patrōnus* protector, from *pater* father]
▸ 'patroness *fem* n

patron[2] ('pætrɔ̃) n the owner of a restaurant, hotel, etc., esp. a French one. [F]

patronage ('pætrənɪdʒ) n **1a** the support given or custom brought by a patron. **1b** the position of a patron. **2** (in politics) **2a** the practice of making appointments to office, granting contracts, etc. **2b** the favours, etc., so distributed. **3a** a condescending manner. **3b** any kindness done in a condescending way.

patronize or **patronise** ('pætrəˌnaɪz) vb **patronizes,**

patronizing, patronized or **patronises, patronising, patronised. 1** to behave or treat in a condescending way. **2** (tr) to act as a patron by sponsoring or bringing trade to.
▶ **'patron,izer** or **'patron,iser** n ▶ **'patron,izing** or **'patron,ising** adj ▶ **'patron,izingly** or **'patron,isingly** adv

patron saint n a saint regarded as the particular guardian of a country, person, etc.

patronymic (ˌpætrəˈnɪmɪk) adj **1** (of a name) derived from the name of its bearer's father or ancestor. ♦ n **2** a patronymic name. [C17: via LL from Gk patronumikos, from patēr father + onoma NAME]

patroon (pəˈtruːn) n US. a Dutch land holder in New Netherland and New York with manorial rights in the colonial era. [C18: from Du.: PATRON[1]]

patsy (ˈpætsɪ) n, pl **patsies**. Sl., chiefly US & Canad. **1** a person who is easily cheated, victimized, etc. **2** a scapegoat. [C20: from ?]

patten (ˈpætˀn) n a wooden clog or sandal on a raised wooden platform or metal ring. [C14: from OF patin, prob. from patte paw]

patter[1] (ˈpætə) vb **1** (intr) to walk or move with quick soft steps. **2** to strike with or make a quick succession of light tapping sounds. ♦ n **3** a quick succession of light tapping sounds, as of feet: the patter of mice. [C17: from PAT[1]]

patter[2] (ˈpætə) n **1** the glib rapid speech of comedians, etc. **2** quick idle talk; chatter. **3** the jargon of a particular group, etc.; lingo. ♦ vb **4** (intr) to speak glibly and rapidly. **5** to repeat (prayers, etc.) in a mechanical or perfunctory manner. [C14: from L pater in Pater Noster Our Father]

pattern (ˈpætˀn) n **1** an arrangement of repeated or corresponding parts, decorative motifs, etc. **2** a decorative design: a paisley pattern. **3** a style: various patterns of cutlery. **4** a plan or diagram used as a guide in making something: a paper pattern for a dress. **5** a standard way of moving, acting, etc.: traffic patterns. **6** a model worthy of imitation: a pattern of kindness. **7** a representative sample. **8** a wooden or metal shape or model used in a foundry to make a mould. ♦ vb (tr) **9** (often foll. by after or on) to model. **10** to arrange as or decorate with a pattern. [C14: patron, from Med. L patrōnus example, from L: PATRON[1]]

Patti ★ (ˈpætɪ) n **Adelina** (adeˈliːna). 1843–1919, Italian operatic coloratura soprano, born in Spain.

Patton ★ (ˈpætˀn) n **George Smith**. 1885–1945, US general, who successfully developed tank warfare as an extension of cavalry tactics in World War II: captured Palermo, Sicily (1942) and much of France (1944).

patty (ˈpætɪ) n, pl **patties. 1** a small cake of minced food. **2** a small pie. [C18: from F PÂTÉ]

patu (ˈpɑːtuː) n, pl **patus**. NZ. a short Maori club, now ceremonial only. [from Maori]

patulous (ˈpætjʊləs) adj Bot. spreading widely or expanded: patulous branches. [C17: from L patulus open, from patēre to lie open]

Pau ★ (French po) n a city in SW France: residence of the French kings of Navarre; tourist centre for the Pyrenees. Pop.: 82 157 (1990).

paua (ˈpɑːvɑ) n an edible abalone of New Zealand, having an iridescent shell used for jewellery, etc. [from Maori]

paucity (ˈpɔːsɪtɪ) n **1** insufficiency; dearth. **2** smallness of number; fewness. [C15: from L paucitās scarcity, from paucus few]

Paul ★ (pɔːl) n **1** Saint. Also called: **Paul the Apostle, Saul of Tarsus**. original name Saul. died ?67 A.D., one of the first Christian missionaries to the Gentiles, who died a martyr in Rome. Until his revelatory conversion he had assisted in persecuting the Christians. He wrote many of the Epistles in the New Testament. Feast day: June 29. **2 Jean**. See **Jean Paul**. **3 Les**, real name Lester Polfuss. born 1915, US guitarist: creator of the solid-body electric guitar and pioneer in multitrack recording.

Paul III ★ n original name Alessandro Farnese. 1468–1549, Italian ecclesiastic; pope (1534–49). He excommunicated Henry VIII of England (1538) and inaugurated the Counter-Reformation by approving the establishment of the Jesuits (1540), instituting the Inquisition in Italy, and convening the Council of Trent (1545).

Paul VI ★ n original name Giovanni Battista Montini. 1897–1978, Italian ecclesiastic; pope (1963–1978).

Pauli ★ (ˈpɔːlɪ, ˈpaʊlɪ) n **Wolfgang** (ˈvɒlf,gæŋ). 1900–58, US physicist, born in Austria. He formulated the exclusion principle (1924) and postulated the existence of the neutrino (1931), later confirmed by Fermi: Nobel prize for physics 1945.

Pauli exclusion principle n Physics. the principle that two identical fermions cannot occupy the same quantum state in a body, such as an atom; sometimes shortened to **exclusion principle**.

Pauline (ˈpɔːlaɪn) adj relating to Saint Paul or his doctrines.

Pauling ★ (ˈpɔːlɪŋ) n **Linus Carl** (ˈlaɪnəs). 1901–94, US chemist, noted particularly for his work on the nature of the chemical bond and his opposition to nuclear tests: Nobel prize for chemistry 1954; Nobel peace prize 1962.

Paulinus ★ (pɔːˈlaɪnəs) n Saint. died 644 A.D., Roman missionary to England; first bishop of York and archbishop of Rochester. Feast day: Oct. 10.

Paul Jones n an old-time dance in which partners are exchanged. [C19: after John Paul JONES]

paulownia (pɔːˈləʊnɪə) n a tree of a Japanese genus, esp. one having large heart-shaped leaves and clusters of purplish or white flowers. [C19: NL, after Anna Paulovna, daughter of Paul I of Russia]

Paumotu Archipelago ★ (paʊˈməʊtuː) n another name for the **Tuamotu Archipelago**.

paunch (pɔːntʃ) n **1** the belly or abdomen, esp. when protruding. **2** another name for **rumen**. ♦ vb (tr) **3** to stab in the stomach; disembowel. [C14: from Anglo-Norman paunche, from OF pance, from L panticēs (pl) bowels]
▶ **'paunchy** adj ▶ **'paunchiness** n

pauper (ˈpɔːpə) n **1** a person who is extremely poor. **2** (formerly) a person supported by public charity. [C16: from L: poor]
▶ **'pauper,ism** n

pauperize or **pauperise** (ˈpɔːpəˌraɪz) vb **pauperizes, pauperizing, pauperized** or **pauperises, pauperising, pauperised**. (tr) to make a pauper of; impoverish.

Pausanias ★ (pɔːˈseɪnɪəs) n 2nd century A.D. Greek geographer and historian. His Description of Greece gives a valuable account of the topography of ancient Greece.

pause (pɔːz) vb **pauses, pausing, paused**. (intr) **1** to cease an action temporarily. **2** to hesitate; delay: she replied without pausing. ♦ n **3** a temporary stop or rest, esp. in speech or action; short break. **4** Prosody. another word for **caesura. 5** Also called: **fermata**. Music. a continuation of a note or rest beyond its normal length. Usual symbol: ⌒ **6 give pause to**. to cause to hesitate. [C15: from L pausa pause, from Gk pausis, from pauein to halt]

pav (pæv) n Austral. & NZ inf. short for **pavlova**.

pavane or **pavan** (pəˈvɑːn, ˈpævˀn) n **1** a slow and stately dance of the 16th and 17th centuries. **2** a piece of music composed for or in the rhythm of this dance. [C16 pavan, via F from Sp. pavana, from OIt. padovana Paduan (dance), from Padova Padua]

Pavarotti ★ (ˌpævəˈrɒtɪ, Italian pavaˈrɔtti) n **Luciano** (luˈtʃaːno). born 1935, Italian operatic tenor.

pave (peɪv) vb **paves, paving, paved**. (tr) **1** to cover (a road, etc.) with a firm surface suitable for travel, as with paving stones or concrete. **2** to serve as the material for a pavement or other hard layer: bricks paved the causeway. **3** (often foll. by with) to cover with a hard layer (of): shelves paved with marble. **4** to prepare or make easier (esp. in **pave the way**). [C14: from OF paver, from L pavīre to ram down]
▶ **'paver** n

pavement (ˈpeɪvmənt) n **1** a hard-surfaced path for pedestrians alongside and a little higher than a road. US and Canad. word: **sidewalk. 2** the material used in paving. [C13: from L pavīmentum hard floor, from pavīre to beat hard]

Pavese ★ (Italian paˈveːse) n **Cesare** (ˈtʃeːzare). 1908–50, Italian writer and translator. His works include collections of poems, such as Verrà la morte e avra i tuoi occhi

(1953), short stories, such as the collection *Notte di festa* (1953), and the novel *La Luna e i falò* (1950).

Pavia ★ (pə'viːə) *n* a town in N Italy, in Lombardy: noted for its Roman and medieval remains, including the tomb of St Augustine. Pop.: 80 650 (1990). Latin name: **Ticinum**.

pavilion (pə'vɪljən) *n* **1** *Brit.* a building at a sports ground, esp. a cricket pitch, in which players change, etc. **2** a summerhouse or other decorative shelter. **3** a building or temporary structure, esp. one that is open and ornamental, for housing exhibitions, etc. **4** a large ornate tent, esp. one with a peaked top, as used by medieval armies. **5** one of a set of buildings that together form a hospital or other large institution. ◆ *vb* (*tr*) *Literary.* **6** to place as in a pavilion: *pavilioned in splendour.* **7** to provide with a pavilion or pavilions. [C13: from OF *pavillon* canopied structure, from L *pāpiliō* butterfly, tent]

paving ('peɪvɪŋ) *n* **1** a paved surface; pavement. **2** material used for a pavement.

Pavlodar ★ (*Russian* pəvlə'dar) *n* a port in NE Kazakhstan, on the Irtysh River: major industrial centre with an oil refinery. Pop.: 340 700 (1995 est.).

Pavlov ★ ('pævlɒv; *Russian* 'pavləf) *n* **Ivan Petrovich** (i'van pɪ'trɔvɪtʃ). 1849–1936, Russian physiologist. His study of conditioned reflexes in dogs influenced behaviourism. He also made important contributions to the study of digestion: Nobel prize for physiology or medicine 1904.
▸ **Pav'lovian** *adj*

pavlova (pæv'ləʊvə) *n* a meringue cake topped with whipped cream and fruit. [C20: after Anna Pavlova]

Pavlova ★ (pæv'ləʊvə; *Russian* 'pavləvə) *n* **Anna** ('annə). 1885–1931, Russian ballerina.

paw (pɔː) *n* **1** any of the feet of a four-legged mammal, bearing claws or nails. **2** *Inf.* a hand, esp. one that is large, clumsy, etc. ◆ *vb* **3** to scrape or contaminate with the paws or feet. **4** (*tr*) *Inf.* to touch or caress in a clumsy, rough, or overfamiliar manner. [C13: via OF from Gmc]

pawky ('pɔːkɪ) *adj* **pawkier**, **pawkiest**. *Dialect or Scot.* having a dry wit. [C17: from Scot. *pawk* trick, from ?]
▸ **'pawkily** *adv* ▸ **'pawkiness** *n*

pawl (pɔːl) *n* a pivoted lever shaped to engage with a ratchet to prevent motion in a particular direction. [C17: ?from Du. *pal* pawl]

pawn[1] (pɔːn) *vb* (*tr*) **1** to deposit (an article) as security for the repayment of a loan, esp. from a pawnbroker. **2** to stake: *to pawn one's honour.* ◆ *n* **3** an article deposited as security. **4** the condition of being so deposited (esp. in **in pawn**). **5** a person or thing that is held as a security. **6** the act of pawning. [C15: from OF *pan* security, from L *pannus* cloth, apparently because clothing was often left as a surety]
▸ **'pawnage** *n*

pawn[2] (pɔːn) *n* **1** a chess man of the lowest theoretical value. **2** a person, group, etc., manipulated by another. [C14: from Anglo-Norman *poun*, from OF, from Med. L *pedō* infantryman, from L *pēs* foot]

pawnbroker ('pɔːn,brəʊkə) *n* a dealer licensed to lend money at a specified rate of interest on the security of movable personal property, which can be sold if the loan is not repaid within a specified period.
▸ **'pawn,broking** *n*

pawnshop ('pɔːn,ʃɒp) *n* the premises of a pawnbroker.

pawn ticket *n* a receipt for goods pawned.

pawpaw ('pɔː,pɔː) *n* another name for **papaw** or **papaya**.

pax (pæks) *n* **1** *Chiefly RC Church.* **1a** the kiss of peace. **1b** a small metal or ivory plate, formerly used to convey the kiss of peace from the celebrant at Mass to those attending it. ◆ *interj* **2** *Brit. school sl.* a call signalling an end to hostilities or claiming immunity from the rules of a game. [L: peace]

Pax ★ (pæks) *n* the Roman goddess of peace. Greek counterpart: **Irene**. [L: peace]

PAX (in Britain) *abbrev. for* private automatic exchange.

Paxton ★ ('pækstən) *n* **Sir Joseph**. 1801–65, British architect, who designed the Crystal Palace (1851), the first large structure of prefabricated glass and iron parts.

pay[1] (peɪ) *vb* **pays**, **paying**, **paid**. **1** to discharge (a debt, obli-

gation, etc.) by giving or doing something: *he paid his creditors.* **2** (when *intr*, often foll. by *for*) to give (money, etc.) to (a person) in return for goods or services: *they pay their workers well; they pay by the hour.* **3** to give or afford (a person, etc.) a profit or benefit: *it pays one to be honest.* **4** (*tr*) to give or bestow (a compliment, regards, attention, etc.). **5** (*tr*) to make (a visit or call). **6** (*intr*; often foll. by *for*) to give compensation or make amends. **7** (*tr*) to yield a return of: *the shares pay 15 per cent.* **8** *Austral. inf.* to acknowledge or accept (something) as true, just, etc. **9 pay one's way. 9a** to contribute one's share of expenses. **9b** to remain solvent without outside help. ◆ *n* **10a** money given in return for work or services; a salary or wage. **10b** (*as modifier*): *a pay slip; a pay claim.* **11** paid employment (esp. in **in the pay of**). **12** (*modifier*) requiring the insertion of money before or during use: *a pay phone.* **13** (*modifier*) rich enough in minerals to be profitably worked: *pay gravel.* ◆ See also **pay back, pay for,** etc. [C12: from OF *payer*, from L *pācāre* to appease (a creditor), from *pāx* peace]
▸ **'payer** *n*

pay[2] (peɪ) *vb* **pays**, **paying**, **payed**. (*tr*) *Naut.* to caulk (the seams of a wooden vessel) with pitch or tar. [C17: from OF *peier*, from L *picāre*, from *pix* pitch]

payable ('peɪəbᵊl) *adj* **1** (often foll. by *on*) to be paid: *payable on the third of each month.* **2** that is capable of being paid. **3** capable of being profitable. **4** (of a debt, etc.) imposing an obligation on the debtor to pay, esp. at once.

pay-and-display *adj* denoting a car-parking system in which a motorist buys a permit to park for a specified period, usually from a coin-operated machine, and displays the permit on or near the windscreen of his or her car so that it can be seen by a parking attendant.

pay back *vb* (*tr, adv*) **1** to retaliate against: *to pay someone back for an insult.* **2** to give or do (something equivalent) in return for a favour, insult, etc. **3** to repay (a loan, etc.).

pay bed *n* an informal name for **private pay bed**.

payday ('peɪ,deɪ) *n* the day on which wages or salaries are paid.

pay dirt *n Chiefly US.* **1** soil, gravel, ore, etc. that contains sufficient minerals to make it worthwhile mining. **2 hit** (*or* **strike**) **pay dirt.** *Inf.* to become wealthy, successful, etc.

PAYE (in Britain and New Zealand) *abbrev. for* pay as you earn; a system by which income tax levied on wage and salary earners is paid by employers directly to the government.

payee (peɪ'iː) *n* the person to whom a cheque, money order, etc., is made out.

pay for *vb* (*prep*) **1** to make payment for. **2** (*intr*) to suffer or be punished, as for a mistake, wrong decision, etc.

paying guest *n* a euphemism for **lodger**.

payload ('peɪ,ləʊd) *n* **1** that part of a cargo earning revenue. **2a** the passengers, cargo, or bombs carried by an aircraft. **2b** the equipment carried by a rocket, satellite, or spacecraft. **3** the explosive power of a warhead, bomb, etc., carried by a missile or aircraft.

paymaster ('peɪ,mɑːstə) *n* an official of a government, business, etc., responsible for the payment of wages and salaries.

payment ('peɪmənt) *n* **1** the act of paying. **2** a sum of money paid. **3** something given in return; punishment or reward.

paynim ('peɪnɪm) *n Arch.* **1** a heathen or pagan. **2** a Muslim. [C13: from OF *paienime*, from LL *pāgānismus* paganism, from *pāgānus* PAGAN]

pay off *vb* **1** (*tr, adv*) to pay all that is due in wages, etc., and discharge from employment. **2** (*tr, adv*) to pay the complete amount of (a debt, bill, etc.). **3** (*intr, adv*) to turn out to be profitable, effective, etc.: *the gamble paid off.* **4** (*tr, adv or intr, prep*) to take revenge on (a person) or for (a wrong done): *to pay someone off for an insult.* **5** (*tr, adv*) *Inf.* to give a bribe to. ◆ *n* **payoff. 6** the final settlement, esp. in retribution. **7** *Inf.* the climax, consequence, or outcome of events, a story, etc. **8** the final payment of a debt, salary, etc. **9** the time of such a payment. **10** *Inf.* a bribe.

payola (peɪ'əʊlə) *n Inf.* **1** a bribe given to secure special treatment, esp. to a disc jockey to promote a commercial product. **2** the practice of paying or receiving such bribes. [C20: from PAY¹ + *-ola*, as in PIANOLA]

pay out *vb* (*adv*) **1** to distribute (money, etc.); disburse. **2** (*tr*) to release (a rope) gradually, hand over hand. ◆ *n* **payout**. **3** a sum of money paid out.

pay-per-view *n* **a** a system of television broadcasting by which subscribers pay for each programme they wish to receive. **b** (*as modifier*): *a pay-per-view channel.*

payphone ('peɪ,fəʊn) *n* a public telephone operated by coins or a phonecard.

payroll ('peɪ,rəʊl) *n* **1** a list of employees, specifying the salary or wage of each. **2a** the total of these amounts or the actual money equivalent. **2b** (*as modifier*): *a payroll tax.*

Paysandú ★ (*Spanish* paisan'du) *n* a port in W Uruguay, on the Uruguay River: the third largest city in the country. Pop.: 75 200 (1985).

Pays de la Loire ★ (*French* pei də la lwar) *n* a region of W France, on the Bay of Biscay: generally low-lying, drained by the River Loire and its tributaries; agricultural.

payt *abbrev. for* payment.

pay up *vb* (*adv*) to pay (money) promptly, in full, or on demand.

Paz ★ (*Spanish* pas) *n* **Octavio** (ɔk'taβo). 1914–98, Mexican poet and essayist. His poems include the cycle *Piedra de Sol* (1957) and *Blanco* (1967). Nobel prize for literature 1990.

Pb *the chemical symbol for* lead. [from NL *plumbum*]

PB *Athletics abbrev. for* personal best.

PBS *US abbrev. for* Public Broadcasting Service.

PBX (in Britain) *abbrev. for* private branch exchange; a telephone system that handles the internal and external calls of a building, firm, etc.

pc *abbrev. for:* **1** per cent. **2** postcard. **3** (in prescriptions) post cibum. [L: *after meals*]

PC *abbrev. for:* **1** personal computer. **2** Parish Council(lor). **3** (in Britain) Police Constable. **4** politically correct. **5** (in Britain) Privy Council(lor). **6** (in Canada) Progressive Conservative.

pc. *abbrev. for:* **1** (*pl* **pcs.**) piece. **2** price.

PCB *abbrev. for* polychlorinated biphenyl; any of a group of compounds in which chlorine atoms replace the hydrogen atoms in biphenyl: used in electrical insulators and in the manufacture of plastics; a toxic pollutant.

PCC (in Britain) *abbrev. for* Press Complaints Commission.

PCP *n Trademark.* phencyclidine; a depressant drug used illegally as a hallucinogen.

PCV (in Britain) *abbrev. for* passenger carrying vehicle.

pd *abbrev. for:* **1** paid. **2** Also: **PD.** per diem. **3** potential difference.

Pd *the chemical symbol for* palladium.

PDR *abbrev. for* price-dividend ratio.

P-D ratio *n* short for **price-dividend ratio.**

PDSA (in Britain) *abbrev. for* People's Dispensary for Sick Animals.

PDT (in the US and Canada) *abbrev. for* Pacific Daylight Time.

PE *abbrev. for:* **1** physical education. **2** potential energy. **3** Presiding Elder. **4** Also: **p.e.** printer's error. **5** *Statistics.* probable error. **6** Protestant Episcopal.

pea (pi:) *n* **1** an annual climbing plant with small white flowers and long green pods containing edible green seeds: cultivated in temperate regions. **2** the seed of this plant, eaten as a vegetable. **3** any of several other leguminous plants, such as the sweet pea. [C17: from PEASE (incorrectly assumed to be a pl)]

Peabody ★ ('pi:,bɒdɪ) *n* **George.** 1795–1869, US merchant, banker, and philanthropist in the US and England.

peace (pi:s) *n* **1a** the state existing during the absence of war. **1b** (*as modifier*): *peace negotiations.* **2** (*often cap.*) a treaty marking the end of a war. **3** a state of harmony between people or groups. **4** law and order within a state: *a breach of the peace.* **5** absence of mental anxiety (often in **peace of mind**). **6** a state of stillness, silence, or serenity. **7** at peace. **7a** in a state of harmony or friendship. **7b** in a state of serenity. **7c** dead: *the old lady is at peace now.* **8 hold** or **keep one's peace.** to keep silent. **9 keep the peace.** to maintain law and order. ◆ *vb* **peaces, peacing, peaced.** **10** (*intr*) *Obs.* except as an imperative. to be or become silent or still. ◆ *modifier* **11** denoting a person or thing symbolizing support for international peace: *peace women.* [C12: from OF *pais*, from L *pāx*]

peaceable ('pi:səb°l) *adj* **1** inclined towards peace. **2** tranquil; calm.
▶ **'peaceableness** *n* ▶ **'peaceably** *adv*

Peace Corps *n* an agency of the US government that sends volunteers to developing countries to work on educational projects, etc.

peace dividend *n* additional money available to a government from cuts in defence expenditure because of the end of a period of hostilities.

peaceful ('pi:sfʊl) *adj* **1** not in a state of war or disagreement. **2** calm; tranquil. **3** not involving violence: *peaceful picketing.* **4** of, relating to, or in accord with a time of peace. **5** inclined towards peace.
▶ **'peacefully** *adv* ▶ **'peacefulness** *n*

peacekeeping ('pi:s,ki:pɪŋ) *n* **a** the maintenance of peace, esp. the prevention of further fighting between hostile forces. **b** (*as modifier*): *a UN peacekeeping force.*

peacemaker ('pi:s,meɪkə) *n* a person who establishes peace, esp. between others.
▶ **'peace,making** *n*

peace offering *n* **1** something given to an adversary in the hope of procuring or maintaining peace. **2** *Judaism.* a sacrificial meal shared between the offerer and Jehovah.

peace pipe *n* a long decorated pipe smoked by North American Indians, esp. as a token of peace. Also called: **calumet.**

Peace River ★ *n* a river in W Canada, rising in British Columbia as the Finlay River and flowing northeast into the Slave River. Length: 1715 km (1065 miles).

peace sign *n* a gesture made with the palm of the hand outwards and the index and middle fingers raised in a V.

peacetime ('pi:s,taɪm) *n* **a** a period without war; time of peace. **b** (*as modifier*): *a peacetime agreement.*

peach¹ (pi:tʃ) *n* **1** a small tree with pink flowers and rounded edible fruit: cultivated in temperate regions. **2** the soft juicy fruit of this tree, which has a downy reddish-yellow skin, yellowish-orange sweet flesh, and a single stone. **3a** a pinkish-yellow to orange colour. **3b** (*as adj*): *a peach dress.* **4** *Inf.* a person or thing that is especially pleasing. [C14: from OF, from Med. L *persica*, from L *Persicum mālum* Persian apple]

peach² (pi:tʃ) *vb* (*intr*) *Sl.* to inform against an accomplice. [C15: var. of earlier *apeche*, from F, from LL *impedicāre* to entangle; see IMPEACH]

peach brandy *n* (esp. in S. Africa) a coarse brandy made from fermented peaches.

peach Melba *n* a dessert made of halved peaches, vanilla ice cream, and raspberries. [C20: after Dame Nellie MELBA]

peachy ('pi:tʃɪ) *adj* **peachier, peachiest. 1** of or like a peach, esp. in colour or texture. **2** *Inf.* excellent; fine.
▶ **'peachiness** *n*

peacock ('pi:,kɒk) *n, pl* **peacocks** or **peacock. 1** a male peafowl, having a crested head and a very large fanlike tail marked with blue and green eyelike spots. **2** another name for **peafowl. 3** a vain strutting person. ◆ *vb* **4** to display (oneself) proudly. [C14 *pecok, pe-* from OE *pāwa* (from L *pāvō* peacock) + COCK¹]
▶ **'pea,cockish** *adj* ▶ **'pea,hen** *fem n*

Peacock ★ ('pi:,kɒk) *n* **Thomas Love.** 1785–1866, British novelist and poet, noted for his satirical romances, including *Headlong Hall* (1816) and *Nightmare Abbey* (1818).

peacock blue *n* **a** a greenish-blue colour. **b** (*as adj*): *a peacock-blue car.*

peafowl ('pi:,faʊl) *n, pl* **peafowls** or **peafowl.** either of two large pheasants of India and Ceylon and of SE Asia. The males (see **peacock** (sense 1)) have a characteristic bright plumage.

pea green *n* a a yellowish-green colour. **b** (*as adj*): *a pea-green teapot.*

pea jacket *or* **peacoat** ('pi:ˌkəʊt) *n* a sailor's short heavy woollen overcoat. [C18: from Du. *pijjekker*, from *pij* coat of coarse cloth + *jekker* jacket]

peak[1] (pi:k) *n* **1** a pointed end, edge, or projection: *the peak of a roof.* **2** the pointed summit of a mountain. **3** a mountain with a pointed summit. **4** the point of greatest development, strength, etc.: *the peak of his career.* **5a** a sharp increase followed by a sharp decrease: *a voltage peak.* **5b** the maximum value of this quantity. **5c** (*as modifier*): *peak voltage.* **6** Also called: **visor.** a projecting piece on the front of some caps. **7** *Naut.* **7a** the extreme forward (**forepeak**) or aft (**afterpeak**) part of the hull. **7b** (of a fore-and-aft quadrilateral sail) the after uppermost corner. **7c** the after end of a gaff. ◆ *vb* **8** to form or reach or cause to form or reach a peak. **9** (*tr*) *Naut.* to set (a gaff) or tilt (oars) vertically. ◆ *adj* **10** of or relating to a period of greatest use or demand: *peak viewing hours.* [C16: ?from PIKE[2], infl. by BEAK[1]]

peak[2] (pi:k) *vb* (*intr*) to become wan, emaciated, or sickly. [C16: from ?]
▸ **'peaky** *or* **'peakish** *adj*

Peak District ★ *n* a region of N central England, mainly in N Derbyshire at the S end of the Pennines: consists of moors in the north and a central limestone plateau; many caves. Highest point: 727 m (2088 ft).

Peake ★ (pi:k) *n* **Mervyn.** 1911–68, British novelist, poet, and illustrator. In his trilogy *Gormenghast* (1946–59), he creates, with vivid imagination, a grotesque Gothic world.

peaked (pi:kt) *adj* having a peak; pointed.

peak load *n* the maximum load on an electrical power-supply system.

peal (pi:l) *n* **1** a loud prolonged usually reverberating sound, as of bells, thunder, or laughter. **2** *Bell-ringing.* a series of changes rung in accordance with specific rules. **3** (*not in technical usage*) the set of bells in a belfry. ◆ *vb* **4** (*intr*) to sound with a peal or peals. **5** (*tr*) to give forth loudly and sonorously. **6** (*tr*) to ring (bells) in peals. [C14 *pele*, var. of *apele* APPEAL]

peanut ('pi:ˌnʌt) *n* **a** a leguminous plant widely cultivated for its edible seeds. **b** the edible nutlike seed of this plant, used for food and as a source of oil. Also called: **groundnut, monkey nut.** ◆ See also **peanuts.**

peanut butter *n* a brownish oily paste made from peanuts.

peanuts ('pi:ˌnʌts) *n Sl.* a trifling amount of money.

pear (peə) *n* **1** a widely cultivated tree, having white flowers and edible fruits. **2** the sweet gritty-textured juicy fruit of this tree, which has a globular base and tapers towards the apex. **3** the wood of this tree, used for making furniture. **4 go pear-shaped.** *Inf.* to go wrong: *the plan started to go pear-shaped.* [OE *pere*, ult. from L *pirum*]

pearl[1] (pɜːl) *n* **1** a hard smooth lustrous typically rounded structure occurring on the inner surface of the shell of a clam or oyster around an invading particle such as a sand grain; much valued as a gem. **2** any artificial gem resembling this. **3** See **mother-of-pearl. 4** a person or thing that is like a pearl, esp. in beauty or value. **5** a pale grey-ish-white colour, often with a bluish tinge. ◆ *adj* **6** of, made of, or set with pearl or mother-of-pearl. **7** having the shape or colour of a pearl. ◆ *vb* **8** (*tr*) to set with or as if with pearls. **9** to shape into or assume a pearl-like form or colour. **10** (*intr*) to dive or search for pearls. [C14: from OF, from Vulgar L *pernula* (unattested), from L *perna* sea mussel]

pearl[2] (pɜːl) *n, vb* a variant spelling of **purl**[1] (senses 2, 3, 5).

pearl ash *n* the granular crystalline form of potassium carbonate.

pearl barley *n* barley ground into small round grains, used esp. in soups and stews.

Pearl Harbor ★ *n* an almost landlocked inlet of the Pa-

cific on the S coast of the island of Oahu, Hawaii: site of a US naval base attacked by the Japanese in 1941, resulting in the US entry into World War II.

Pearl River ★ *n* **1** a river in central Mississippi, flowing southwest and south to the Gulf of Mexico. Length: 789 km (490 miles). **2** the English name for the **Zhu Jiang.**

pearly ('pɜːlɪ) *adj* **pearlier, pearliest. 1** resembling a pearl, esp. in lustre. **2** decorated with pearls or mother-of-pearl. ◆ *n, pl* **pearlies.** *Brit.* **3** a London costermonger or his wife who wear on ceremonial occasions a traditional dress of dark clothes covered with pearl buttons. **4** (*pl*) the clothes or the buttons themselves.
▸ **'pearliness** *n*

Pearly Gates *pl n Inf.* the entrance to heaven.

pearly king *or* (*fem*) **pearly queen** *n* the London costermonger whose ceremonial clothes display the most lavish collection of pearl buttons.

pearly nautilus *n* any of several cephalopod molluscs of warm and tropical seas, having a partitioned pale pearly external shell with brown stripes. Also called: **chambered nautilus.**

pearmain ('peəˌmeɪn) *n* any of several varieties of apple having a red skin. [C15: from OF *permain* a type of pear, ?from L *Parmēnsis* of Parma]

Pears ★ (pɪəz) *n* Sir **Peter.** 1910–86, British operatic tenor.

Pearse ★ (pɪəs) *n* **Patrick** (**Henry**), Irish name *Pádraic.* 1879–1916, Irish nationalist, who planned and led the Easter Rising (1916): executed by the British.

Pearson ★ ('pɪəs°n) *n* **1 Karl.** 1857–1936, British mathematician, noted for his work in statistics, esp. as applied to biological problems. **2 Lester B**(**owles**). 1897–1972, Canadian Liberal statesman; prime minister (1963–68): Nobel peace prize 1957 for helping to resolve the Suez crisis (1956).

peart (pɪət) *adj Dialect.* lively; spirited; brisk. [C15: var. of PERT]
▸ **'peartly** *adv*

Peary ★ ('pɪərɪ) *n* **Robert Edwin.** 1856–1920, US arctic explorer, generally regarded as the first man to reach the North Pole (1909).

peasant ('pez°nt) *n* **1** a member of a class of low social status that depends on either cottage industry or agricultural labour as a means of subsistence. **2** *Inf.* a person who lives in the country; rustic. **3** *Inf.* an uncouth or uncultured person. [C15: from Anglo-F, from OF *païsant*, from *païs* country, from L *pāgus* rural area]

peasantry ('pez°ntrɪ) *n* peasants as a class.

pease (pi:z) *n, pl* **pease.** *Arch.* or *dialect.* another word for **pea.** [OE *peose*, via LL from L *pisa* peas, pl of *pisum*, from Gk *pison*]

peasecod *or* **peascod** ('pi:zˌkɒd) *n Arch.* the pod of a pea plant. [C14: from PEASE + COD[2]]

pease pudding *n* (esp. in Britain) a dish of split peas that have been soaked and boiled.

peashooter ('pi:ˌʃuːtə) *n* a tube through which dried peas are blown, used as a toy weapon.

peasouper (ˌpi:'su:pə) *n* **1** *Inf., chiefly Brit.* dense dirty yellowish fog. **2** *Canad.* a disparaging name for a **French Canadian.**

peat (pi:t) *n* **a** a compact brownish deposit of partially decomposed vegetable matter saturated with water: found in uplands and bogs and used as a fuel (when dried) and as a fertilizer. **b** (*as modifier*): *peat bog.* [C14: from Anglo-L *peta*, ?from Celtic]
▸ **'peaty** *adj*

peat moss *n* any of various mosses, esp. sphagnum, that grow in wet places and decay to form peat. See also **sphagnum.**

pebble ('peb°l) *n* **1** a small smooth rounded stone, esp. one worn by the action of water. **2a** a transparent colourless variety of rock crystal, used for making certain lenses. **2b** such a lens. **3** (*modifier*) *Inf.* (of a lens or of spectacles) thick, with a high degree of magnification or distortion. **4a** a grainy irregular surface, esp. on leather. **4b** leather having such a surface. ◆ *vb* **pebbles, pebbling, pebbled.** (*tr*) **5** to cover with pebbles. **6** to impart a grainy

surface to (leather). [OE *papolstān,* from *papol-* (? imit.) + *stān* stone]
► **'pebbly** *adj*

pebble dash *n Brit.* a finish for external walls consisting of small stones embedded in plaster.

pec (pɛk) *n* (*usually pl*) *Inf.* short for **pectoral muscle.**

pecan (prˈkæn, ˈpiːkən) *n* **1** a hickory tree of the southern US having deeply furrowed bark and edible nuts. **2** the smooth oval nut of this tree, which has a sweet oily kernel. [C18: from Algonquian *paccan*]

peccable (ˈpɛkəbᵊl) *adj* liable to sin. [C17: via F from Med. L *peccābilis,* from L *peccāre* to sin]

peccadillo (ˌpɛkəˈdɪləʊ) *n, pl* **peccadilloes** *or* **peccadillos.** a petty sin or fault. [C16: from Sp., from *pecado* sin, from L *peccātum,* from *peccāre* to transgress]

peccant (ˈpɛkənt) *adj Rare.* **1** guilty of an offence; corrupt. **2** violating or disregarding a rule; faulty. **3** producing disease; morbid. [C17: from L *peccans,* from *peccāre* to sin]
► **'peccancy** *n*

peccary (ˈpɛkərɪ) *n, pl* **peccaries** *or* **peccary.** either of two piglike mammals of forests of southern North America, Central and South America. [C17: from Carib]

Pechora ★ (*Russian* prˈtʃɔrə) *n* a river in N Russia, rising in the Ural Mountains and flowing north in a great arc to the **Pechora Sea** (the SE part of the Barents Sea). Length: 1814 km (1127 miles).

peck[1] (pɛk) *n* **1** a unit of dry measure equal to 8 quarts or one quarter of a bushel. **2** a container used for measuring this quantity. **3** a large quantity or number. [C13: from Anglo-Norman, from ?]

peck[2] (pɛk) *vb* **1** (when *intr,* sometimes foll. by *at*) to strike with the beak or with a pointed instrument. **2** (*tr;* sometimes foll. by *out*) to dig (a hole, etc.) by pecking. **3** (*tr*) (of birds) to pick up (corn, worms, etc.) by pecking. **4** (*intr;* often foll. by *at*) to nibble or pick (at one's food). **5** *Inf.* to kiss (a person) quickly and lightly. **6** (*intr;* foll. by *at*) to nag. ◆ *n* **7** a quick light blow, esp. from a bird's beak. **8** a mark made by such a blow. **9** *Inf.* a quick light kiss. [C14: from ?]

Peck ★ (pɛk) *n* **Gregory.** born 1916, US film actor; his films include *The Gunfighter* (1950), *The Big Country* (1958), *The Omen* (1976), and *Other People's Money* (1991).

pecker (ˈpɛkə) *n Brit. sl.* spirits (esp. in **keep one's pecker up**).

pecking order *n* **1** Also called: **peck order.** a natural hierarchy in a group of gregarious birds, such as domestic fowl. **2** any hierarchical order, as among people in a particular group.

Peckinpah ★ (ˈpɛkɪnˌpɑː) *n* **Sam(uel David).** 1926–84, US film director, esp. of Westerns, such as *The Wild Bunch* (1969). Among his other films are *Straw Dogs* (1971).

peckish (ˈpɛkɪʃ) *adj Inf., chiefly Brit.* feeling slightly hungry. [from PECK[2]]

Pecos ★ (ˈpeɪkəs; *Spanish* ˈpekɔs) *n* a river in the southwestern US, rising in N central New Mexico and flowing southeast to the Rio Grande. Length: about 1180 km (735 miles).

Pécs ★ (*Hungarian* peːtʃ) *n* an industrial city in SW Hungary: university (1367). Pop.: 161 000 (1997 est.).

pecten (ˈpɛktɪn) *n, pl* **pectens** *or* **pectines** (-tɪˌniːz). **1** a comblike structure in the eye of birds and reptiles, consisting of a network of blood vessels projecting inwards from the retina. **2** any other comblike part or organ. [C18: from L: a comb, from *pectere* to comb]

pectin (ˈpɛktɪn) *n Biochem.* any of the acidic polysaccharides that occur in ripe fruit and vegetables: used in the manufacture of jams because of their ability to solidify to a gel. [C19: from Gk *pēktos* congealed, from *pegnuein* to set]
► **'pectic** *or* **'pectinous** *adj*

pectoral (ˈpɛktərəl) *adj* **1** of or relating to the chest, breast, or thorax: *pectoral fins.* **2** worn on the breast or chest: *a pectoral medallion.* ◆ *n* **3** a pectoral organ or part, esp. a muscle or fin. **4** a medicine for disorders of the chest or lungs. **5** anything worn on the chest or breast for decoration or protection. [C15: from L *pectorālis,* from *pectus* breast]
► **'pectorally** *adv*

pectoral fin *n* either of a pair of fins, situated just behind the head in fishes, that help to control the direction of movement during locomotion.

pectoral muscle *n* either of two large chest muscles (**pectoralis major** and **pectoralis minor**), that assist in movements of the shoulder and upper arm.

peculate (ˈpɛkjʊˌleɪt) *vb* **peculates, peculating, peculated.** to appropriate or embezzle (public money, etc.). [C18: from L *pecūlārī,* from *pecūlium* private property (orig., cattle); see PECULIAR]
► **ˌpecu'lation** *n* ► **'pecuˌlator** *n*

peculiar (prˈkjuːlɪə) *adj* **1** strange or unusual; odd: *a peculiar idea.* **2** distinct from others; special. **3** (*postpositive;* foll. by *to*) belonging characteristically or exclusively (to): *peculiar to North America.* [C15: from L *pecūliāris* concerning private property, from *pecūlium,* lit.: property in cattle, from *pecus* cattle]
► **pe'culiarly** *adv*

peculiarity (prˌkjuːlɪˈærɪtɪ) *n, pl* **peculiarities. 1** a strange or unusual habit or characteristic. **2** a distinguishing trait, etc., that is characteristic of a particular person; idiosyncrasy. **3** the state or quality of being peculiar.

pecuniary (prˈkjuːnɪərɪ) *adj* **1** of or relating to money. **2** *Law.* (of an offence) involving a monetary penalty. [C16: from L *pecūniāris,* from *pecūnia* money]
► **pe'cuniarily** *adv*

pecuniary advantage *n Law.* financial advantage that is dishonestly obtained by deception and that constitutes a criminal offence.

-ped *or* **-pede** *n combining form.* foot or feet: *quadruped; centipede.* [from L *pēs,* *ped-* foot]

pedagogue *or US* (*sometimes*) **pedagog** (ˈpɛdəˌgɒg) *n* **1** a teacher or educator. **2** a pedantic or dogmatic teacher. [C14: from L *paedagōgus,* from Gk *paidagōgos* slave who looked after his master's son, from *pais* boy + *agōgos* leader]
► **ˌpeda'gogic** *or* **ˌpeda'gogical** *adj* ► **ˌpeda'gogically** *adv*

pedagogy (ˈpɛdəˌgɒgɪ, -ˌgɒdʒɪ, -ˌgɒʊdʒɪ) *n* the principles, practice, or profession of teaching.

pedal[1] (ˈpɛdᵊl) *n* **1a** any foot-operated lever, esp. one of the two levers that drive the chainwheel of a bicycle, the foot brake, clutch control, or accelerator of a car, one of the levers on an organ controlling deep bass notes, or one of the levers on a piano used to mute or sustain tone. **1b** (*as modifier*): *a pedal cycle.* ◆ *vb* **pedals, pedalling, pedalled** *or US* **pedals, pedaling, pedaled. 2** to propel (a bicycle, etc.) by operating the pedals. **3** (*intr*) to operate the pedals of an organ, piano, etc. **4** to work (pedals of any kind). [C17: from L *pedālis;* see PEDAL[2]]

pedal[2] (ˈpiːdᵊl) *adj* of or relating to the foot or feet. [C17: from L *pedālis,* from *pēs* foot]

pedal point (ˈpɛdᵊl) *n Music.* a sustained bass note, over which the other parts move bringing changing harmonies. Often shortened to **pedal.**

pedal steel guitar (ˈpɛdᵊl) *n* a floor-mounted multineck steel guitar with each set of strings tuned to a different open chord and foot pedals to raise or lower the pitch.

pedant (ˈpɛdᵊnt) *n* **1** a person who relies too much on academic learning or who is concerned chiefly with insignificant detail. **2** *Arch.* a schoolmaster or teacher. [C16: via OF from It. *pedante* teacher]
► **pedantic** (prˈdæntɪk) *adj* ► **pe'dantically** *adv*

pedantry (ˈpɛdᵊntrɪ) *n, pl* **pedantries.** the habit or an instance of being a pedant, esp. in the display of useless knowledge or minute observance of petty rules or details.

pedate (ˈpɛdeɪt) *adj* **1** (of a plant leaf) deeply divided into several lobes. **2** *Zool.* having or resembling a foot: *a pedate appendage.* [C18: from L *pedātus* equipped with feet, from *pēs* foot]

peddle (ˈpɛdᵊl) *vb* **peddles, peddling, peddled. 1** to go from place to place selling (goods, esp. small articles). **2** (*tr*) to sell (illegal drugs, esp. narcotics). **3** (*tr*) to advocate (ideas, etc.) persistently: *to peddle a new philosophy.* [C16: back formation from PEDLAR]

peddler ('pɛdlə) *n* **1** a person who sells illegal drugs, esp. narcotics. **2** the usual US spelling of **pedlar**.

pederasty *or* **paederasty** ('pɛdə,ræstɪ) *n* homosexual relations between men and boys. [C17: from NL *paederastia*, from Gk, from *pais* boy + *erastēs* lover, from *eran* to love]
▶ 'peder,ast *or* 'paeder,ast *n* ,peder'astic *or* ,paeder'astic *adj*

pedestal ('pɛdɪst°l) *n* **1** a base that supports a column, statue, etc. **2** a position of eminence or supposed superiority (esp. in **place, put,** *or* **set on a pedestal**). [C16: from F *piédestal*, from OIt. *piedestallo*, from *pie* foot + *di* of + *stallo* a stall]

pedestrian (pɪ'dɛstrɪən) *n* **1a** a person travelling on foot; walker. **1b** (*as modifier*): *a pedestrian precinct.* ◆ *adj* **2** dull; commonplace: *a pedestrian style of writing.* [C18: from L *pedester*, from *pēs* foot]

pedestrian crossing *n Brit.* a path across a road marked as a crossing for pedestrians.

pedestrianize *or* **pedestrianise** (pɪ'dɛstrɪə,naɪz) *vb* **pedestrianizes**, **pedestrianizing**, **pedestrianized** *or* **pedestrianises**, **pedestrianising**, **pedestrianised**. (*tr*) to convert (a street, etc.) into an area for the use of pedestrians only.
▶ pe,destriani'zation *or* pe,destriani'sation *n*

pedi- *combining form.* indicating the foot: *pedicure.* [from L *pēs*, *ped-* foot]

pedicab ('pɛdɪ,kæb) *n* a pedal-operated tricycle, available for hire in some Asian countries, with an attached seat for one or two passengers.

pedicel ('pɛdɪ,sɛl) *n* **1** the stalk bearing a single flower of an inflorescence. **2** Also called: **peduncle**. *Biol.* any short stalk bearing an organ or organism. ◆ Also called: **pedicle**. [C17: from NL *pedicellus*, from L *pedīculus*, from *pēs* foot]
▶ 'pedicellate (pɪ'dɪsɪ,leɪt) *adj*

pediculosis (pɪ,dɪkjʊ'ləʊsɪs) *n Pathol.* the state of being infested with lice. [C19: via NL from L *pedīculus* louse]
▶ **pediculous** (pɪ'dɪkjʊləs) *adj*

pedicure ('pɛdɪ,kjʊə) *n* treatment of the feet, either by a medical expert or a cosmetician. [C19: via F from L *pēs* foot + *curāre* to care for]

pedigree ('pɛdɪ,griː) *n* **1a** the line of descent of a pure-bred animal. **1b** (*as modifier*): *a pedigree bull.* **2** a document recording this. **3** a genealogical table, esp. one indicating pure ancestry. [C15: from OF *pie de grue* crane's foot, alluding to the spreading lines used in a genealogical chart]
▶ 'pedi,greed *adj*

pediment ('pɛdɪmənt) *n* a low-pitched gable, esp. one that is triangular as used in classical architecture. [C16: from obs. *periment*, ? workman's corruption of PYRAMID]
▶ ,pedi'mental *adj*

pedipalp ('pɛdɪ,pælp) *n* either member of the second pair of head appendages of arachnids: specialized for feeding, locomotion, etc. [C19: from NL *pedipalpi*, from L *pēs* foot + *palpus* palp]

pedlar *or esp. US* **peddler** ('pɛdlə) *n* a person who peddles; hawker. [C14: changed from *peder*, from *ped, pedde* basket, from ?]

pedo- *or before a vowel* **ped-** a variant (esp. US) of **paedo-**.

pedology (pɪ'dɒlədʒɪ) *n* the study of soils. [C20: from Gk *pedon* ground, earth + -OLOGY]

pedometer (pɪ'dɒmɪtə) *n* a device that records the number of steps taken in walking and hence the distance travelled.

peduncle (pɪ'dʌŋk°l) *n* **1** the stalk of a plant bearing an inflorescence or solitary flower. **2** *Anat., pathol.* any stalklike structure. **3** *Biol.* another name for **pedicel** (sense 2). [C18: from NL *pedunculus*, from L *pedīculus* little foot]
▶ **peduncular** (pɪ'dʌŋkjʊlə) *or* **pedunculate** (pɪ'dʌŋkjʊlɪt, -,leɪt) *adj*

pee (piː) *Inf.* ◆ *vb* **pees, peeing, peed. 1** (*intr*) to urinate. ◆ *n* **2** urine. **3** the act of urinating. [C18: euphemistic for PISS, based on the initial letter]

Peebles ★ ('piːb°lz) *n* a town in SE Scotland, in Scottish Borders. Pop.: 7065 (1991).

Peeblesshire ★ ('piːb°lz,ʃɪə, -ʃə) *n* a historic county of SE Scotland, now part of Scottish Borders. Also called: **Tweeddale.**

peek (piːk) *vb* **1** (*intr*) to glance quickly or furtively. ◆ *n* **2** such a glance. [C14 *pike*, rel. to M Du *kiken* to peek]

peekaboo ('piːkə,buː) *n* **1** a game for young children, in which one person hides his face and suddenly reveals it and cries "peekaboo". ◆ *adj* **2** (of a garment) made of fabric that is sheer or patterned with small holes. [C16: from PEEK + BOO]

peel[1] (piːl) *vb* **1** (*tr*) to remove (the skin, rind, etc.) of (a fruit, egg, etc.). **2** (*intr*) (of paint, etc.) to be removed from a surface, esp. by weathering. **3** (*intr*) (of a surface) to lose its outer covering of paint, etc., esp. by weathering. **4** (*intr*) (of a person or part of the body) to shed skin in flakes or (of skin) to be shed in flakes, esp. as a result of sunburn. ◆ *n* **5** the skin or rind of a fruit, etc. ◆ See also **peel off.** [OE *pilian* to strip off the outer layer, from L *pilāre* to make bald, from *pilus* a hair]
▶ 'peeler *n*

peel[2] (piːl) *n* a long-handled shovel used by bakers for moving bread in an oven. [C14 *pele*, from OF, from L *pāla* spade, from *pangere* to drive in]

peel[3] (piːl) *n Brit.* a fortified tower of the 16th century on the borders of Scotland. [C14 (fence made of stakes): from OF *piel* stake, from L *pālus*]

Peel ★ (piːl) *n* Sir **Robert.** 1788–1850, British statesman; Conservative prime minister (1834–35; 1841–46). As Home Secretary (1828–30) he founded the Metropolitan Police and in his second ministry carried through a series of free-trade budgets culminating in the repeal of the Corn Laws (1846), which split the Tory party.
▶ 'Peelite *n*

Peele ★ (piːl) *n* **George.** ?1556–?96, English dramatist and poet. His works include the pastoral drama *The Arraignment of Paris* (1584) and the comedy *The Old Wives' Tale* (1595).

peeler ('piːlə) *n Irish & obs. Brit. sl.* another word for **policeman.** [C19: from the founder of the police force, Sir Robert PEEL]

peeling ('piːlɪŋ) *n* a strip of skin, rind, bark, etc., that has been peeled off: *a potato peeling.*

peel off *vb* (*adv*) **1** to remove or be removed by peeling. **2** (*intr*) *Sl.* to undress. **3** (*intr*) (of an aircraft) to turn away as by banking, and leave a formation.

peen (piːn) *n* **1** the end of a hammer head opposite the striking face, often rounded or wedge-shaped. ◆ *vb* **2** (*tr*) to strike with the peen of a hammer or a stream of metal shot. [C17: var. of *pane*, ?from F *panne*, ult. from L *pinna* point]

Peenemünde ★ (*German* peːnə'myndə) *n* a village in N Germany, on the Baltic coast: site of a German rocket-development centre in World War II.

peep[1] (piːp) *vb* (*intr*) **1** to look furtively or secretly, as through a small aperture or from a hidden place. **2** to appear partially or briefly: *the sun peeped through the clouds.* ◆ *n* **3** a quick or furtive look. **4** the first appearance: *the peep of dawn.* [C15: var. of PEEK]

peep[2] (piːp) *vb* (*intr*) **1** (esp. of young birds) to utter shrill small noises. **2** to speak in a weak voice. ◆ *n* **3** a peeping sound. [C15: imit.]

peeper ('piːpə) *n* **1** a person who peeps. **2** (*often pl*) a slang word for **eye**[1] (sense 1).

peephole ('piːp,həʊl) *n* a small aperture, as in a door, for observing callers before opening.

Peeping Tom *n* a man who furtively observes women undressing; voyeur. [C19: after the tailor who, according to legend, peeped at Lady Godiva when she rode naked through Coventry]

peepshow ('piːp,ʃəʊ) *n* **1** Also called: **raree show.** a box with a peephole through which a series of pictures can be seen. **2** a booth from which a viewer can see a live nude model for a fee.

peepul ('piːp°l) *or* **pipal** *n* an Indian tree resembling the banyan: regarded as sacred by Buddhists. Also called: **bo tree.** [C18: from Hindi *pīpal*, from Sansk. *pippala*]

peer[1] (pɪə) *n* **1** a member of a nobility; nobleman. **2** a per-

son who holds any of the five grades of the British nobility: duke, marquess, earl, viscount, and baron. See also **life peer. 3** a person who is an equal in social standing, rank, age, etc.: *to be tried by one's peers.* [C14 (in sense 3): from OF *per*, from L *pār* equal]

peer[2] (pɪə) *vb* (*intr*) **1** to look intently with or as if with difficulty: *to peer into the distance.* **2** to appear partially or dimly: *the sun peered through the fog.* [C16: from Flemish *pieren* to look with narrowed eyes]

peerage ('pɪərɪdʒ) *n* **1** the whole body of peers; aristocracy. **2** the position, rank, or title of a peer. **3** (esp. in the British Isles) a book listing the peers and giving their genealogy.

peeress ('pɪərɪs) *n* **1** the wife or widow of a peer. **2** a woman holding the rank of a peer in her own right.

peer group *n* a social group composed of individuals of approximately the same age.

peerless ('pɪəlɪs) *adj* having no equals; matchless.

peeve (piːv) *Inf.* ◆ *vb* **peeves, peeving, peeved. 1** (*tr*) to irritate; vex; annoy. ◆ *n* **2** something that irritates; vexation. [C20: back formation from PEEVISH]
▶ **peeved** *adj*

peevish ('piːvɪʃ) *adj* fretful or irritable. [C14: from ?]
▶ **'peevishly** *adv* ▶ **'peevishness** *n*

peewee ('piːwiː) *n* a small black-and-white Australian bird with long thin legs. [imit.]

peewit *or* **pewit** ('piːwɪt) *n* another name for **lapwing.** [C16: imit. of its call]

peg (pɛg) *n* **1** a small cylindrical pin or dowel used to join two parts together. **2** a pin pushed or driven into a surface: used to mark scores, define limits, support coats, etc. **3** any of several pins on a violin, etc., which can be turned so as to tune strings wound around them. **4** Also called: **clothes peg.** *Brit., Austral., & NZ.* a split or hinged pin for fastening wet clothes to a line to dry. US and Canad. equivalent: **clothespin. 5** *Brit.* a small drink of wine or spirits. **6** an opportunity or pretext for doing something: *a peg on which to hang a theory.* **7** *Inf.* a level of self-esteem, importance, etc. (esp. in **bring** *or* **take down a peg). 8** *Inf.* See **peg leg. 9 off the peg.** *Chiefly Brit.* (of clothes) ready-to-wear, as opposed to tailor-made. ◆ *vb* **pegs, pegging, pegged. 10** (*tr*) to knock or insert a peg into. **11** (*tr*) to secure with pegs: *to peg a tent.* **12** (*tr*) to mark (a score) with pegs, as in some card games. **13** (*tr*) *Inf.* to throw (stones, etc.) at a target. **14** (*intr*; foll. by *away, along*, etc.) *Chiefly Brit.* to work steadily: *he pegged away at his job for years.* **15** (*tr*) to stabilize (the price of a commodity, an exchange rate, etc.). [C15: from Low Gmc *pegge*]

Pegasus ★ ('pɛgəsəs) *n Greek myth.* an immortal winged horse, which sprang from the blood of the slain Medusa and enabled Bellerophon to achieve many great deeds as his rider.

pegboard ('pɛg,bɔːd) *n* **1** a board having a pattern of holes into which small pegs can be fitted, used for playing certain games or keeping a score. **2** another name for **solitaire** (sense 1). **3** hardboard perforated by a pattern of holes in which articles may be hung, as for display.

peg leg *n Inf.* **1** an artificial leg, esp. one made of wood. **2** a person with an artificial leg.

pegmatite ('pɛgmə,taɪt) *n* any of a class of coarse-grained intrusive igneous rocks consisting chiefly of quartz and feldspar. [C19: from Gk *pegma* something joined together]

peg out *vb* (*adv*) **1** (*intr*) *Inf.* to collapse or die. **2** (*intr*) *Cribbage.* to score the point that wins the game. **3** (*tr*) to mark or secure with pegs: *to peg out one's claims to a piece of land.*

peg top *n* a child's spinning top, usually made of wood with a metal centre pin.

peg-top *adj* (of skirts, trousers, etc.) wide at the hips then tapering off towards the ankle.

Pegu ★ (pɛ'guː) *n* a city in S Myanmar: capital of a united Burma (16th century). Pop.: 150 447 (latest est.).

Péguy ★ (*French* pegi) *n* **Charles** (ʃarl). 1873–1914, French poet and essayist, whose works include *Le Mystère de la charité de Jeanne d'Arc* (1910): killed in World War I.

Pei ★ (peɪ) *n* **I(eoh) M(ing).** born 1917, US architect, born in China. His buildings include the E wing of the National Museum of Art, Washington DC (1978), a glass and steel pyramid at the Louvre, Paris (1989), and the Rock and Roll Hall of Fame, Cleveland, in the US (1995).

PEI *abbrev. for* Prince Edward Island.

peignoir ('peɪnwɑː) *n* a woman's dressing gown. [C19: from F, from *peigner* to comb, since the garment was worn while the hair was combed]

Peipus ★ ('paɪpəs) *n* a lake in NE Europe, on the boundary between Russia and Estonia: drains into the Gulf of Finland. Area: 3512 sq. km (1356 sq. miles). Russian name: **Chudskoye Ozero.**

Peiraeus ★ (paɪ'riːəs, pɪ'reɪ-) *n* a variant spelling of **Piraeus.**

Peirce ★ (pɪəs) *n* **Charles Sanders.** 1839–1914, US logician, philosopher, and mathematician; pioneer of pragmatism.

pejoration (ˌpiːdʒə'reɪʃən) *n* **1** semantic change whereby a word acquires unfavourable connotations. **2** the process of worsening.

pejorative (prɪ'dʒɒrətɪv, 'piːdʒər-) *adj* **1** (of words, expressions, etc.) having an unpleasant or disparaging connotation. ◆ *n* **2** a pejorative word, etc. [C19: from F *péjoratif*, from LL *pējōrātus*, p.p. of *pējōrāre* to make worse, from L *pēior* worse]
▶ **pe'joratively** *adv*

pekan ('pɛkən) *n* another name for **fisher** (the animal). [C18: from Canad. F *pékan*, from Amerind]

peke (piːk) *n Inf.* a Pekingese dog.

Peking ★ ('piː'kɪŋ) *n* the former English name of **Beijing.**

Pekingese (ˌpiːkɪŋ'iːz) *or* **Pekinese** (ˌpiːkə'niːz) *n* **1** (*pl* **Pekingese** *or* **Pekinese**) a small breed of pet dog with a profuse straight coat, curled plumed tail, and short wrinkled muzzle. **2** the dialect of Mandarin Chinese spoken in Beijing (formerly Peking). **3** (*pl* **Pekingese** *or* **Pekinese**) a native or inhabitant of Beijing (formerly Peking). ◆ *adj* **4** of Beijing (formerly Peking) or its inhabitants.

Peking man (piː'kɪŋ) *n* an early type of man, of the Lower Palaeolithic age, remains of which were found in a cave near Beijing (formerly Peking).

pekoe ('piːkəʊ) *n* a high-quality tea made from the downy tips of the young buds of the tea plant. [C18: from Chinese *peh ho*, from *peh* white + *ho* down]

pelage ('pɛlɪdʒ) *n* the coat of a mammal, consisting of hair, wool, fur, etc. [C19: via F from OF *pel* animal's coat, from L *pilus* hair]

Pelagian Islands ★ (pe'leɪdʒɪən) *pl n* a group of Italian islands (Lampedusa, Linosa, and Lampione) in the Mediterranean, between Tunisia and Malta. Pop.: 4500 (latest est.). Area: about 27 sq. km (11 sq. miles). Italian name: **Isole Pelagie** ('iːzole pe'ladʒe).

Pelagianism (pe'leɪdʒɪə,nɪzəm) *n Christianity.* a heretical doctrine, first formulated by Pelagius, that rejected the concept of original sin.
▶ **Pe'lagian** *n, adj*

pelagic (pe'lædʒɪk) *adj* **1** of or relating to the open sea: *pelagic whaling.* **2** (of marine life) occurring in the upper waters of open sea. [C17: from L *pelagicus*, from *pelagus*, from Gk *pelagos* sea]

Pelagius ★ (pe'leɪdʒɪəs) *n* ?360–?420 A.D., British monk, who originated the body of doctrines known as Pelagianism and was condemned for heresy (417).

pelargonium (ˌpɛlə'gəʊnɪəm) *n* any plant of a chiefly southern African genus having circular or lobed leaves and red, pink, or white aromatic flowers: includes many cultivated geraniums. [C19: via NL from Gk *pelargos* stork, on the model of GERANIUM; from the likeness of the seed vessels to a stork's bill]

Pelé ★ ('peleɪ) *n* real name *Edson Arantes do Nascimento.* born 1940, Brazilian footballer: awarded an honorary knighthood in 1997.

Pelée ★ (pə'leɪ) *n* **Mount.** a volcano in the Caribbean, in N Martinique: erupted in 1902, killing every person but one in the town of St Pierre. Height: 1463 m (4800 ft).

Peleus ★ ('peliəs, 'piːliəs) *n Greek myth.* a king of the Myrmidons; father of Achilles.

★ people and places

Pelew Islands ★ (piː'luː) *pl n* a former name of (the Republic of) **Belau.**

pelf (pɛlf) *n Contemptuous.* money or wealth; lucre. [C14: from OF *pelfre* booty]

pelham ('pɛləm) *n* a horse's bit for a double bridle, less severe than a curb but more severe than a snaffle. [prob. from the name *Pelham*]

Pelham ★ ('pɛləm) *n* **Henry.** 1696–1754, British statesman: prime minister (1743–54); brother of Thomas Pelham Holles, 1st Duke of Newcastle.

Pelham Holles ★ ('hɒlɪs) *n* **Thomas.** See (1st Duke of) **Newcastle.**

Pelias ★ ('piːlɪˌæs) *n Greek myth.* a son of Poseidon and Tyro. He feared his nephew Jason and sent him to recover the Golden Fleece, hoping he would not return.

pelican ('pɛlɪkən) *n* any aquatic bird of a tropical and warm water family. They have a long straight flattened bill, with a distensible pouch for engulfing fish. [OE *pellican*, from LL *pelicānus*, from Gk *pelekān*]

pelican crossing *n* a type of road crossing with a pedestrian-operated traffic-light system. [C20: from *pe(destrian) li(ght) con(trolled) crossing*, with -*con* adapted to -*can* of *pelican*]

Pelion ★ ('piːlɪən) *n* a mountain in NE Greece, in E Thessaly. In Greek mythology it was the home of the centaurs. Height: 1548 m (5079 ft). Modern Greek name: **Pílion.**

pelisse (pe'liːs) *n* **1** a fur-trimmed cloak. **2** a loose coat, usually fur-trimmed, worn esp. by women in the early 19th century. [C18: via OF from Med. L *pellicia* cloak, from L *pellis* skin]

Pella ★ ('pɛlə) *n* an ancient city in N Greece: the capital of Macedonia under Philip II.

pellagra (pə'leɪɡrə, -'læ-) *n Pathol.* a disease caused by a dietary deficiency of nicotinic acid, characterized by scaling of the skin, inflammation of the mouth, diarrhoea, mental impairment, etc. [C19: via It. from *pelle* skin + -*agra*, from Gk *agra* paroxysm]
▶ **pel'lagrous** *adj*

pellet ('pɛlɪt) *n* **1** a small round ball, esp. of compressed matter. **2a** an imitation bullet used in toy guns. **2b** a piece of small shot. **3** a stone ball formerly used in a catapult. **4** *Ornithol.* a mass of undigested food that is regurgitated by birds of prey. **5** a small pill. ◆ *vb* (*tr*) **6** to strike with pellets. **7** to make or form into pellets. [C14: from OF *pelote*, from Vulgar L *pilota* (unattested), from L *pila* ball]

Pelletier ★ (*French* pɛltje) *n* **Pierre Joseph** (pjɛr ʒozɛf). 1788–1842, French chemist, who isolated quinine, chlorophyll, and other chemical substances.

pellitory ('pɛlɪtərɪ, -trɪ) *n, pl* **pellitories. 1** any of various plants of a S and W European genus, esp. wall pellitory, that grow in crevices and have long narrow leaves and small pink flowers. **2 pellitory of Spain.** a small Mediterranean plant, the root of which contains an oil formerly used to relieve toothache. [C16 *peletre*, from OF *piretre*, from L, from Gk *purethron*, from *pur* fire, from the hot pungent taste of the root]

pell-mell ('pɛl'mɛl) *adv* **1** in a confused headlong rush: *the hounds ran pell-mell into the yard.* **2** in a disorderly manner: *the things were piled pell-mell in the room.* ◆ *adj* **3** disordered; tumultuous: *a pell-mell rush for the exit.* ◆ *n* **4** disorder; confusion. [C16: from OF *pesle-mesle*, jingle based on *mesler* to MEDDLE]

pellucid (pe'luːsɪd) *adj* **1** transparent or translucent. **2** extremely clear in style and meaning. [C17: from L *pellūcidus*, var. of *perlūcidus*, from *perlūcēre* to shine through]
▶ ,**pellu'cidity** *or* **pel'lucidness** *n* ▶ **pel'lucidly** *adv*

pelmet ('pɛlmɪt) *n* an ornamental drapery or board fixed above a window to conceal the curtain rail. [C19: prob. from F *palmette* palm-leaf decoration on cornice moulding]

Peloponnese ★ (,pɛləpə'niːs) *n* **the.** the S peninsula of Greece, joined to central Greece by the Isthmus of Corinth: chief cities in ancient times were Sparta and Corinth, now Patras. Pop.: 607 428 (1991). Area: 21 439 sq.

km (8361 sq. miles). Medieval name: **Morea.** Modern Greek name: **Peloponnesos.** Also called: **Peloponnesus.**
▶ **Peloponnesian** (,pɛləpə'niːʃən) *adj*

Pelops ★ ('piːlɒps) *n Greek myth.* the son of Tantalus, who as a child was killed by his father and served up as a meal for the gods.

pelota (pə'lɒtə) *n* any of various games played in Spain, Spanish America, SW France, etc., by two players who use a basket strapped to their wrists or a wooden racket to propel a ball against a specially marked wall. [C19: from Sp.: ball, from OF *pelote*; see PELLET]

Pelotas ★ (*Portuguese* pe'lɒtas) *n* a port in S Brazil, in Rio Grande do Sul on the Canal de São Gonçalo. Pop.: 260 510 (1991).

peloton ('pɛləˌtɒn) *n* the main field of riders in a cycling race. [C20: F, lit.: pack]

pelt[1] (pɛlt) *vb* **1** (*tr*) to throw (missiles, etc.) at (a person, etc.). **2** (*tr*) to hurl (insults, etc.) at (a person, etc.). **3** (*intr*; foll. by *along*, etc.) to hurry. **4** (*intr*) to rain heavily. ◆ *n* **5** a blow. **6** speed (esp. in **at full pelt**). [C15: from ?]

pelt[2] (pɛlt) *n* **1** the skin of a fur-bearing animal, esp. when it has been removed from the carcass. **2** the hide of an animal, stripped of hair. [C15: ? back formation from PELTRY]

peltate ('pɛlteɪt) *adj* (of leaves) having the stalk attached to the centre of the lower surface. [C18: from L *peltātus* equipped with a *pelta* small shield]

peltry ('pɛltrɪ) *n, pl* **peltries.** the pelts of animals collectively. [C15: from OF *peleterie* collection of pelts, from L *pilus* hair]

pelvic fin *n* either of a pair of fins attached to the pelvic girdle of fishes that help to control the direction of movement during locomotion.

pelvic inflammatory disease *n* inflammation of a woman's womb, Fallopian tubes, or ovaries as a result of infection. Abbrev.: **PID.**

pelvimetry (pɛl'vɪmɪtrɪ) *n Obstetrics.* measurement of the dimensions of the female pelvis.

pelvis ('pɛlvɪs) *n, pl* **pelvises** *or* **pelves** (-viːz). **1** the large funnel-shaped structure at the lower end of the trunk of most vertebrates. **2** Also called: **pelvic girdle.** the bones that form this structure. **3** any anatomical cavity or structure shaped like a funnel or cup. [C17: from L: basin]
▶ **'pelvic** *adj*

Pemba ★ ('pɛmbə) *n* an island in the Indian Ocean, off the E coast of Africa north of Zanzibar: part of Tanzania; produces most of the world's cloves. Chief town: Chake Chake. Pop.: 265 039 (1988). Area: 984 sq. km (380 sq. miles).

Pembroke ★ ('pɛmbrʊk) *n* a town in SW Wales, in Pembrokeshire on Milford Haven: 11th-century castle where Henry VII was born. Pop.: 15 424 (1991).

Pembrokeshire ★ ('pɛmbrʊkˌʃɪə, -ʃə) *n* a county of SW Wales, on the Irish Sea and the Bristol Channel; formerly (1974–96) part of Dyfed: hilly with an indented coast. Administrative centre: Haverfordwest. Pop.: 113 500 (1996 est.). Area: 1589 sq. km (614 sq. miles).

pemmican *or* **pemican** ('pɛmɪkən) *n* a small pressed cake of shredded dried meat, pounded into paste, used originally by Native Americans and now chiefly for emergency rations. [C19: from Amerind *pimikân*, from *pimii* grease]

pemphigus ('pɛmfɪɡəs, pɛm'faɪ-) *n Pathol.* any of a group of blistering skin diseases. [C18: via NL from Gk *pemphix* blister]

pen[1] (pɛn) *n* **1** an implement for writing or drawing using ink, formerly consisting of a sharpened and split quill, and now of a metal nib attached to a holder. See also **ballpoint, fountain pen. 2** the writing end of such an implement; nib. **3** style of writing. **4 the pen.** writing as an occupation. ◆ *vb* **pens, penning, penned. 5** (*tr*) to write or compose. [OE *pinne*, from LL *penna* (quill) pen, from L: feather]

pen[2] (pɛn) *n* **1** an enclosure in which domestic animals are kept. **2** any place of confinement. **3** a dock for servicing submarines, esp. having a bombproof roof. ◆ *vb*

pens, penning, penned or **pent. 4** (*tr*) to enclose in a pen. [OE *penn*]

pen³ (pɛn) *n US & Canad. inf.* short for **penitentiary** (sense 1).

pen⁴ (pɛn) *n* a female swan. [C16: from ?]

PEN (pɛn) *n acronym for* International Association of Poets, Playwrights, Editors, Essayists, and Novelists.

Pen. *abbrev. for* Peninsula.

penal ('piːnᵊl) *adj* **1** of, relating to, constituting, or prescribing punishment. **2** used or designated as a place of punishment: *a penal institution.* [C15: from LL *poenālis* concerning punishment, from L *poena* penalty]
▸ **'penally** *adv*

penal code *n* the codified body of the laws that relate to crime and its punishment.

penalize or **penalise** ('piːnə,laɪz) *vb* **penalizes, penalizing, penalized** or **penalises, penalising, penalised.** (*tr*) **1** to impose a penalty on (someone), as for breaking a law or rule. **2** to inflict a disadvantage on. **3** *Sport.* to award a free stroke, point, or penalty against (a player or team). **4** to declare (an act) legally punishable.
▸ **,penali'zation** or **,penali'sation** *n*

penalty ('pɛnᵊltɪ) *n, pl* **penalties. 1** a legal or official punishment, such as a term of imprisonment. **2** some other form of punishment, such as a fine or forfeit for not fulfilling a contract. **3** loss, suffering, or other misfortune occurring as a result of one's own action, error, etc. **4** *Sport, games, etc.* a handicap awarded against a player or team for illegal play, such as a free shot at goal by the opposing team. [C16: from Med. L *poenālitās* penalty; see PENAL]

penalty area *n* another name for **penalty box** (sense 1).

penalty box *n* **1** *Soccer.* a rectangular area in front of the goal, within which a penalty is awarded for a serious foul by the defending team. **2** *Ice hockey.* a bench for players serving time penalties.

penalty corner *n Hockey.* a free hit from the goal line taken by the attacking side. Also called: **short corner.**

penalty rates *pl n Austral. & NZ.* rates of pay for employees working outside normal hours.

penalty shoot-out *n* **1** *Soccer.* a method of deciding the winner of a drawn match, in which players from each team attempt to score with a penalty kick. **2** a similar method of resolving a tie in hockey, ice hockey, polo, etc.

penance ('pɛnəns) *n* **1** voluntary self-punishment to atone for a sin, crime, etc. **2** a feeling of regret for one's wrongdoings. **3** *Christianity.* a punishment usually consisting of prayer, fasting, etc., imposed by church authority as a condition of absolution. **4** *RC Church.* a sacrament in which repentant sinners are absolved on condition of confession of their sins to a priest and of performing a penance. ◆ *vb* **penances, penancing, penanced. 5** (*tr*) (of ecclesiastical authorities) to impose a penance upon (a sinner). [C13: via OF from L *paenitentia* repentance]

Penang ★ (pɪ'næŋ) *n* **1** a state of Peninsular Malaysia: consists of the island of Penang and the province Wellesley on the mainland, which first united administratively in 1798 as a British colony. Capital: George Town. Pop.: 1 141 500 (1993 est). Area: 1031 sq. km (398 sq. miles). Also called: **Pulau Pinang. 2** a forested island off the NW coast of Malaya, in the Strait of Malacca. Area: 293 sq. km (113 sq. miles). Former name (until about 1867): **Prince of Wales Island. 3** another name for **George Town.**

penates (pə'nɑːtiːz) *pl n* See **lares and penates.**

pence (pɛns) *n* a plural of **penny.**

> **USAGE NOTE** Since the decimalization of British currency and the introduction of the abbreviation **p,** as in *10p, 85p,* etc., the abbreviation has tended to replace *pence* in speech, as in *4p* (,fɔː'piː), *12p* (,twelv'piː), etc.

penchant ('pɒŋʃɒn) *n* strong inclination or liking; bent

or taste. [C17: from F, from *pencher* to incline, from L *pendēre* to be suspended]

Penchi ★ ('pɛn'tʃiː) *n* a variant transliteration of the Chinese name for **Benxi.**

pencil ('pɛnsᵊl) *n* **1** a thin cylindrical instrument used for writing, drawing, etc., consisting of a rod of graphite or other marking substance usually encased in wood and sharpened. **2** something similar in shape or function: *a styptic pencil.* **3** a narrow set of lines or rays, such as light rays, diverging from or converging to a point. **4** *Rare.* an artist's individual style. **5** a type of artist's brush. ◆ *vb* **pencils, pencilling, pencilled** or *US* **pencils, penciling, penciled.** (*tr*) **6** to draw, colour, or write with a pencil. **7** to mark with a pencil. [C14: from OF *pincel*, from L *pēnicillus* painter's brush, from *pēniculus* a little tail]
▸ **'penciller** or *US* **'penciler** *n*

pend (pɛnd) *vb* (*intr*) to await judgment or settlement. [C15: from L *pendēre* to hang]

pendant ('pɛndənt) *n* **1a** an ornament that hangs from a piece of jewellery. **1b** a necklace with such an ornament. **2** a hanging light, esp. a chandelier. **3** a carved ornament that is suspended from a ceiling or roof. ◆ *adj* **4** a variant spelling of **pendent.** [C14: from OF, from *pendre* to hang, from L *pendēre* to hang down]

pendent ('pɛndənt) *adj* **1** dangling. **2** jutting. **3** (of a grammatical construction) incomplete. **4** a less common word for **pending.** ◆ *n* **5** a variant spelling of **pendant.** [C15: from OF *pendant*, from *pendre* to hang; see PENDANT]
▸ **'pendency** *n*

pendentive (pɛn'dɛntɪv) *n* any of four triangular sections of vaulting with concave sides, positioned at a corner of a rectangular space to support a dome. [C18: from F *pendentif*, from L *pendens* hanging, from *pendere* to hang]

Penderecki ★ (*Polish* pɛndɛ'rɛtski) *n* **Krzysztof** ('kʃɪʃtɔf). born 1933, Polish composer. His works include *Threnody for the Victims of Hiroshima* for strings (1960), *Polish Requiem* (1983–84), and the opera *Ubu Rex* (1991).

pending ('pɛndɪŋ) *prep* **1** while waiting for. ◆ *adj* (*postpositive*) **2** not yet decided, confirmed, or finished. **3** imminent: *these developments have been pending for some time.*

pendragon (pɛn'drægən) *n* a supreme war chief or leader of the ancient Britons. [Welsh, lit.: head dragon]

pendulous ('pɛndjʊləs) *adj* hanging downwards, esp. so as to swing from side to side. [C17: from L *pendulus*, from *pendēre* to hang down]
▸ **'pendulously** *adv* ▸ **'pendulousness** *n*

pendulum ('pɛndjʊləm) *n* **1** a body mounted so that it can swing freely under the influence of gravity. **2** such a device used to regulate a clock mechanism. **3** something that changes fairly regularly: *the pendulum of public opinion.* [C17: from L *pendulus* PENDULOUS]

Penelope ★ (pə'nɛləpɪ) *n Greek myth.* the wife of Odysseus, who remained true to him during his long absence despite the importunities of many suitors.

peneplain or **peneplane** ('piːnɪ,pleɪn) *n* a relatively flat land surface produced by erosion. [C19: from L *paene* almost + PLAIN¹]

penetrant ('pɛnɪtrənt) *adj* **1** sharp; penetrating. ◆ *n* **2** *Chem.* a substance that lowers the surface tension of a liquid and thus causes it to penetrate or be absorbed more easily. **3** a person or thing that penetrates.

penetrate ('pɛnɪ,treɪt) *vb* **penetrates, penetrating, penetrated. 1** to find or force a way into or through (something); pierce; enter. **2** to diffuse through (a substance), etc.); permeate. **3** (*tr*) to see through: *their eyes could not penetrate the fog.* **4** (*tr*) (of a man) to insert the penis into the vagina of (a woman). **5** (*tr*) to grasp the meaning of (a principle, etc.). **6** (*intr*) to be understood: *his face lit up as the new idea penetrated.* [C16: from L *penetrāre*]
▸ **'penetrable** *adj* ▸ **,penetra'bility** *n* ▸ **'pene,trator** *n*

penetrating ('pɛnɪ,treɪtɪŋ) *adj* tending to or able to penetrate: *a penetrating mind; a penetrating voice.*
▸ **'pene,tratingly** *adv*

penetration (,pɛnɪ'treɪʃən) *n* **1** the act or an instance of penetrating. **2** the ability or power to penetrate. **3** keen insight or perception. **4** *Mil.* an offensive manoeuvre that breaks through an enemy's defensive position. **5** Also called: **market penetration.** the proportion of the total number of potential purchasers of a product or service who either are aware of its existence or actually buy it.

Peneus ★ (pɪˈniːəs) *n* the ancient name for the **Salambria.**

pen friend *n* a person with whom one exchanges letters, often a person in another country whom one has not met. Also called: **pen pal.**

Penghu *or* **P'eng-hu** ★ (ˈpɛŋˈhuː) *n* transliteration of the Chinese name for the **Pescadores.**

Pengpu ★ (ˈpɛŋˈpuː) *n* a variant transliteration of the Chinese name for **Bengbu.**

penguin (ˈpɛŋgwɪn) *n* a flightless marine bird of cool southern, esp. Antarctic, regions: they have wings modified as flippers, webbed feet, and feathers lacking barbs. [C16: ?from Welsh *pen gwyn*, from *pen* head + *gwyn* white]

penicillin (ˌpɛnɪˈsɪlɪn) *n* any of a group of antibiotics with powerful action against bacteria: originally obtained from the fungus *Penicillium.* [C20: from PENICILLIUM]

penicillium (ˌpɛnɪˈsɪlɪəm) *n, pl* **penicilliums** *or* **penicillia** (-ˈsɪlɪə). any saprophytic fungus of the genus *Penicillium*, which commonly grow as a green or blue mould on stale food. [C19: NL, from L *pēnicillus* tuft of hairs; from the appearance of the sporangia of this fungus]

penillion *or* **pennillion** (pɪˈnɪlɪən) *pl n, sing* **penill** (pɪˈnɪl). the Welsh art or practice of singing poetry in counterpoint to a traditional melody played on the harp. [from Welsh: verses]

peninsula (pɪˈnɪnsjʊlə) *n* a narrow strip of land projecting into a sea or lake from the mainland. [C16: from L, lit.: almost an island, from *paene* almost + *insula* island]
▶ **penˈinsular** *adj*

> **USAGE NOTE** The noun *peninsula* is sometimes confused with the adjective *peninsular: the Iberian peninsula* (not *peninsular*).

Peninsula ★ (pɪˈnɪnsjʊlə) *n* the. short for the **Iberian Peninsula.**

penis (ˈpiːnɪs) *n, pl* **penises** *or* **penes** (-niːz). the male organ of copulation in higher vertebrates, also used for urine excretion in many mammals. [C17: from L: penis]
▶ **penile** (ˈpiːnaɪl) *adj*

penitent (ˈpɛnɪtənt) *adj* **1** feeling regret for one's sins; repentant. ◆ *n* **2** a person who is penitent. **3** *Christianity.* **3a** a person who repents his sins and seeks forgiveness for them. **3b** *RC Church.* a person who confesses his sins and submits to a penance. [C14: from Church L *paenitēns* regretting, from *paenitēre* to repent, from ?]
▶ **ˈpenitence** *n* ▶ **ˈpenitently** *adv*

penitential (ˌpɛnɪˈtɛnʃəl) *adj* **1** of, showing, or constituting penance. ◆ *n* **2** *Chiefly RC Church.* a book or compilation of instructions for confessors. **3** a less common word for **penitent** (senses 2, 3).
▶ **ˌpeniˈtentially** *adv*

penitentiary (ˌpɛnɪˈtɛnʃərɪ) *n, pl* **penitentiaries.** **1** (in the US and Canada) a state or federal prison. Also (US and Canad. inf.): **pen.** **2** *RC Church.* **2a** a cardinal who presides over a tribunal that decides all matters affecting the sacrament of penance. **2b** this tribunal itself. ◆ *adj* **3** another word for **penitential** (sense 1). **4** *US & Canad.* (of an offence) punishable by imprisonment in a penitentiary. [C15 (meaning also: an officer dealing with penances): from Med. L *poenitentiārius*, from L *paenitēns* PENITENT]

Penki ★ (ˈpɛnˈtʃiː) *n* a variant transliteration of the Chinese name for **Benxi.**

penknife (ˈpɛnˌnaɪf) *n, pl* **penknives.** a small knife with one or more blades that fold into the handle; pocketknife.

penman (ˈpɛnmən) *n, pl* **penmen.** **1** a person skilled in handwriting. **2** a person who writes by hand in a specified way: *a bad penman.* **3** an author. **4** *Rare.* a scribe.

penmanship (ˈpɛnmənʃɪp) *n* style or technique of writing by hand.

Penn ★ (pɛn) *n* **William.** 1644–1718, English Quaker and founder of Pennsylvania.

Penn. *abbrev. for* Pennsylvania.

penna (ˈpɛnə) *n, pl* **pennae** (-niː). *Ornithol.* any large feather that has a vane and forms part of the main plumage of a bird. [L: feather]

pen name *n* an author's pseudonym. Also called: **nom de plume.**

pennant (ˈpɛnənt) *n* **1** a type of pennon, esp. one flown from vessels as identification or for signalling. **2** *Chiefly US, Canad., & Austral.* **2a** a flag serving as an emblem of championship in certain sports. **2b** (*as modifier*): *pennant cricket.* [C17: prob. a blend of PENDANT & PENNON]

pennate (ˈpɛneɪt) *adj Biol.* **1** having feathers, wings, or winglike structures. **2** another word for **pinnate.** [C19: from L *pennātus*, from *penna* wing]

Penney ★ (ˈpɛnɪ) *n* **William George,** Baron Penney of East Hendred. 1909–91, British mathematician. He worked on the first atomic bomb and became chairman of the UK Atomic Energy Authority (1964–67).

penni (ˈpɛnɪ) *n, pl* **penniä** (-nɪə) *or* **pennis.** a Finnish monetary unit worth one hundredth of a markka. [Finnish, from Low G *pennig* PENNY]

penniless (ˈpɛnɪlɪs) *adj* very poor; almost totally without money.
▶ **ˈpennilessly** *adv* ▶ **ˈpennilessness** *n*

Pennine Alps ★ (ˈpɛnaɪn) *pl n* a range of the Alps between Switzerland and Italy. Highest peak: Monte Rosa, 4634 m (15 204 ft).

Pennines ★ (ˈpɛnaɪnz) *pl n* a system of hills in England, extending from the Cheviot Hills in the north to the River Trent in the south: forms the watershed for the main rivers of N England. Highest peak: Cross Fell, 893 m (2930 ft). Also called: (the) **Pennine Chain.**

Pennine Way ★ *n* a long-distance footpath extending from Edale, Derbyshire, for 402 km (250 miles) to Kirk Yetholm, Scottish Borders.

pennon (ˈpɛnən) *n* **1** a long flag, often tapering and divided at the end, originally a knight's personal flag. **2** a small tapering or triangular flag borne on a ship or boat. **3** a poetic word for **wing.** [C14: via OF ult. from L *penna* feather]

Pennsylvania ★ (ˌpɛnsɪlˈveɪnɪə) *n* a state of the northeastern US: almost wholly in the Appalachians, with the Allegheny Plateau to the west and a plain in the southeast; the second most important US state for manufacturing. Capital: Harrisburg. Pop.: 12 056 112 (1996 est.). Area: 116 462 sq. km (44 956 sq. miles). Abbrevs.: **Pa., Penn., Penna.,** or (with zip code) **PA**

Pennsylvania Dutch *n* **1** a dialect of German spoken in E Pennsylvania. **2** (preceded by *the;* functioning as *pl*) a group of German-speaking people in E Pennsylvania, descended from 18th-century settlers from SW Germany and Switzerland.

Pennsylvanian (ˌpɛnsɪlˈveɪnɪən) *adj* **1.** of the state of Pennsylvania. **2** (in North America) of, denoting, or formed in the upper of two divisions of the Carboniferous period. ◆ *n* **3** an inhabitant or native of the state of Pennsylvania. **4** (preceded by *the*) the Pennsylvanian period or rock system.

penny (ˈpɛnɪ) *n, pl* **pennies** *or* **pence** (pɛns). **1** Also called: **new penny.** *Brit.* a bronze coin having a value equal to one hundredth of a pound. Abbrev.: **p. 2** *Brit.* (before 1971) a bronze or copper coin having a value equal to one twelfth of a shilling. Abbrev.: **d. 3** a monetary unit of the Republic of Ireland worth one hundredth of a pound. **4** (*pl* **pennies**) *US & Canad.* a cent. **5** a coin of similar value, as used in several other countries. **6** (*used with a negative*) *Inf., chiefly Brit.* the least amount of money: *I don't have a penny.* **7 a pretty penny.** *Inf.* a considerable sum of money. **8 spend a penny.** *Brit. inf.* to urinate. **9 the penny dropped.** *Inf., chiefly Brit.* the explanation of something was finally realized. [OE *penig, pening*]

penny arcade *n Chiefly US.* a public place with various coin-operated machines for entertainment.

Penny Black *n* the first adhesive postage stamp, issued in Britain in 1840.

penny-dreadful *n, pl* **penny-dreadfuls**. *Brit. inf.* a cheap, often lurid book or magazine.

penny-farthing *n Brit.* an early type of bicycle with a large front wheel and a small rear wheel, the pedals being on the front wheel.

penny-pinching *adj* **1** excessively careful with money; miserly. ♦ *n* **2** miserliness.
▶ **'penny-,pincher** *n*

pennyroyal (,penɪ'rɔɪəl) *n* **1** a Eurasian plant with hairy leaves and small mauve flowers, yielding an aromatic oil used in medicine. **2** a similar and related plant of E North America. **[C16:** var. of Anglo-Norman *puliol real*, from OF *pouliol* (from L *pūleium* pennyroyal) + *real* ROYAL]

penny shares *pl n Stock Exchange.* securities with a low market price, esp. less than 20p, enabling small investors to purchase a large number for a relatively small outlay.

pennyweight ('penɪ,weɪt) *n* a unit of weight equal to 24 grains or one twentieth of an ounce (Troy).

penny whistle *n* a type of flageolet with six finger holes, esp. a cheap metal one. Also called: **tin whistle**.

penny-wise *adj* **1** greatly concerned with saving small sums of money. **2 penny-wise and pound-foolish.** careful about trifles but wasteful in large ventures.

pennywort ('penɪ,wɜːt) *n* **1** a Eurasian rock plant with whitish-green tubular flowers and rounded leaves. **2** a marsh plant of Europe and North Africa, having circular leaves and greenish-pink flowers. **3** any of various other plants with rounded penny-like leaves.

pennyworth ('penɪ,wɜːθ) *n* **1** the amount that can be bought for a penny. **2** a small amount: *he hasn't got a pennyworth of sense*.

penology (piː'nɒlədʒɪ) *n* **1** the branch of the social sciences concerned with the punishment of crime. **2** the science of prison management. **[C19:** from Gk *poinē* punishment]
▶ **penological** (,piːnə'lɒdʒɪk'l) *adj* ▶ **pe'nologist** *n*

pen pal *n* another name for **pen friend**.

penpusher ('pen,pʊʃə) *n* a person who writes a lot, esp. a clerk involved with boring paperwork.
▶ **'pen,pushing** *adj, n*

Penrith ★ (pen'rɪθ) *n* a market town in NW England, in Cumbria. Pop.: 12 049 (1991).

Penrose ★ ('pen,rəʊz) *n* Sir **Roger.** born 1931, British mathematician and theoretical physicist, noted for his investigation of black holes.

pension[1] ('penʃən) *n* **1** a regular payment made by the state to people over a certain age to enable them to subsist without having to work. **2** a regular payment made by an employer to former employees after they retire. **3** any regular payment made by way of patronage, or in recognition of merit, service, etc.: *a pension paid to a disabled soldier*. ♦ *vb* **4** (*tr*) to grant a pension to. **[C14:** via OF from L *pēnsiō* a payment, from *pendere* to pay]
▶ **'pensionable** *adj* ▶ **'pensionary** *adj* ▶ **'pensioner** *n*

pension[2] *French.* (pɑ̃sjɔ̃) *n* (in France and some other countries) a relatively cheap boarding house. **[C17:** from F; extended meaning of *pension* grant; see PENSION[1]]

pensioneer trustee (,penʃə'nɪə) *n* (in Britain) a person authorized by the Inland Revenue to oversee the management of a pension fund.

pension off *vb* (*tr, adv*) **1** to cause to retire from a job and pay a pension to. **2** to discard, because of age: *to pension off submarines*.

pensive ('pensɪv) *adj* **1** deeply or seriously thoughtful, often with a tinge of sadness. **2** expressing or suggesting pensiveness. **[C14:** from OF *pensif*, from *penser* to think, from L *pensāre* to consider]
▶ **'pensively** *adv* ▶ **'pensiveness** *n*

penstemon (pen'stiːmən) *n* a variant (esp. US) of **penstemon**.

penstock ('pen,stɒk) *n* **1** a conduit that supplies water to a hydroelectric power plant. **2** a channel bringing water from the head gates to a water wheel. **3** a sluice for controlling water flow. **[C17:** from PEN[2] + STOCK]

pent (pent) *vb* a past tense and past participle of **pen**[2] (sense 4).

penta- *or before a vowel* **pent-** *combining form.* five: *pentagon; pentode*. **[from Gk *pente*]**

pentacle ('pentək'l) *n* another name for **pentagram**. **[C16:** from It. *pentacolo* something having five corners]

pentad ('pentæd) *n* **1** a group or series of five. **2** the number or sum of five. **3** a period of five years. **4** *Chem.* a pentavalent element, atom, or radical. **5** *Meteorol.* a period of five days. **[C17:** from Gk *pentas* group of five]

pentadactyl (,pentə'dæktɪl) *adj* (of the limbs of amphibians, reptiles, birds, and mammals) having a hand or foot bearing five digits.

pentagon ('pentə,gon) *n* a polygon having five sides.
▶ **pentagonal** (pen'tæg'n'l) *adj*

Pentagon ★ ('pentə,gon) *n* **1** the five-sided building in Arlington, Virginia, that houses the headquarters of the US Department of Defense. **2** the military leadership of the US.

pentagram ('pentə,græm) *n* **1** a star-shaped figure with five points. **2** such a figure used by the Pythagoreans, black magicians, etc. ♦ Also called: **pentacle, pentangle.**

pentahedron (,pentə'hiːdrən) *n, pl* **pentahedrons** *or* **pentahedra** (-drə). a solid figure having five plane faces.
▶ **,penta'hedral** *adj*

pentamerous (pen'tæmərəs) *adj* consisting of five parts, esp. (of flowers) having the petals, sepals, and other parts arranged in groups of five.

pentameter (pen'tæmɪtə) *n* **1** a verse line consisting of five metrical feet. **2** (in classical prosody) a verse line consisting of two dactyls, one stressed syllable, two dactyls, and a final stressed syllable. ♦ *adj* **3** designating a verse line consisting of five metrical feet.

pentamidine (pen'tæmɪ,diːn, -dɪn) *n* a drug used to treat protozoal infections, esp. pneumonia caused by *Pneumocystis carinii* in AIDS patients.

pentane ('penteɪn) *n* an alkane hydrocarbon having three isomers, esp. the isomer with a straight chain of carbon atoms (*n*-pentane) which is a colourless flammable liquid used as a solvent.

pentangle ('pen,tæŋg'l) *n* another name for **pentagram**.

pentanoic acid (,pentə'nəʊɪk) *n* a colourless liquid carboxylic acid used in making perfumes, flavourings, and pharmaceuticals. Formula: $CH_3(CH_2)_3COOH$. Former name: **valeric acid.**

Pentateuch ('pentə,tjuːk) *n* the first five books of the Old Testament. **[C16:** from Church L *pentateuchus*, from Gk PENTA- + *teukhos* tool (in LGk: scroll)]
▶ **,Penta'teuchal** *adj*

pentathlon (pen'tæθlən) *n* an athletic contest consisting of five different events. **[C18:** from Gk *pentathlon*, from PENTA- + *athlon* contest]

pentatomic (,pentə'tomɪk) *adj Chem.* having five atoms in the molecule.

pentatonic scale (,pentə'tonɪk) *n Music.* any of several scales consisting of five notes.

pentavalent (,pentə'veɪlənt) *adj Chem.* having a valency of five. Also: **quinquevalent.**

pentazocine (pen'tæzəʊ,siːn) *n* a powerful synthetic opiate used in medical practice as an analgesic.

Pentecost ('pentɪ,kɒst) *n* **1** a Christian festival occurring on Whit Sunday commemorating the descent of the Holy Ghost on the apostles. **2** *Judaism.* the harvest festival, celebrated on the fiftieth day after the second day of Passover. Hebrew name: **Shavuot.** **[OE,** from Church L, from Gk *pentēkostē* fiftieth]

Pentecostal (,pentɪ'kɒst'l) *adj* **1** (*usually prenominal*) of or relating to any of various Christian groups that emphasize the charismatic aspects of Christianity and adopt a fundamental attitude to the Bible. **2** of or relating to Pentecost or the influence of the Holy Spirit. ♦ *n* **3** a member of a Pentecostal Church.
▶ **,Pente'costalist** *n, adj*

Pentelikon ★ (pen'telɪkon) *n* a mountain in SE Greece, near Athens: famous for its white marble, worked regularly from the 6th century B.C., from which the chief buildings and sculptures in Athens are made. Height: 1109 m (3638 ft). Latin name: **Pen'telicus.**

Penthesileia *or* **Penthesilea** ★ (ˌpɛnθəsɪˈleɪə) *n Greek myth.* the daughter of Ares and queen of the Amazons, whom she led to the aid of Troy. She was slain by Achilles.

Pentheus ★ ('pɛnθɪəs) *n Greek myth.* the grandson of Cadmus and his successor as king of Thebes, who resisted the introduction of the cult of Dionysus. In revenge the god drove him mad and he was torn to pieces by a group of bacchantes, one of whom was his mother.

penthouse ('pɛntˌhaʊs) *n* **1** a flat or maisonette built onto the top floor or roof of a block of flats. **2** a construction on the roof of a building, esp. one used to house machinery, etc. **3** a shed built against a building, esp. one that has a sloping roof. [C14 *pentis* (later *penthouse*), from OF *apentis*, from LL *appendicium* appendage, from L *appendere* to hang from; see APPEND]

Pentland Firth ★ ('pɛntlənd) *n* a channel between the mainland of N Scotland and the Orkney Islands: notorious for rough seas. Length: 32 km (20 miles). Width: up to 13 km (8 miles).

pentobarbitone sodium (ˌpɛntəˈbɑːbɪˌtəʊn) *n* a barbiturate drug used in medicine as a sedative and hypnotic.

pentode ('pɛntəʊd) *n* **1** an electronic valve having five electrodes: a cathode, anode, and three grids. **2** (*modifier*) (of a transistor) having three terminals at the base or gate. [C20: from PENTA- + Gk *hodos* way]

Pentothal sodium ('pɛntəˌθæl) *n* a trademark for thiopentone sodium.

pentstemon (pɛnt'stiːmən) *n esp. US* **penstemon** *n* any plant of a North American genus having white, pink, red, blue, or purple flowers with five stamens, one of which is sterile. [C18: NL, from PENTA- + Gk *stēmōn* thread (here: stamen)]

pent-up *adj* not released; repressed: *pent-up emotions.*

pentyl acetate ('pɛntaɪl, -tɪl) *n* a colourless combustible liquid used as a solvent for paints, in the extraction of penicillin, in photographic film, and as a flavouring. Formula: $C_2H_5OOCCH_3$. Also called: **amyl acetate.**

penult ('pɛnʌlt, pɪ'nʌlt) *n* the last syllable but one in a word. [C16: L *paenultima syllaba*, from *paene ultima* almost the last]

penultimate (pɪ'nʌltɪmɪt) *adj* **1** next to the last. ◆ *n* **2** anything next to last, esp. a penult.

penumbra (pɪ'nʌmbrə) *n, pl* **penumbrae** (-briː) *or* **penumbras. 1** a fringe region of half shadow resulting from the partial obstruction of light by an opaque object. **2** *Astron.* the lighter and outer region of a sunspot. **3** *Painting.* the area in which light and shade blend. [C17: via NL from L *paene* almost + *umbra* shadow]
▶ pe'numbral *adj*

penurious (pɪ'njʊərɪəs) *adj* **1** niggardly with money. **2** lacking money or means. **3** scanty.
▶ pe'nuriously *adv* ▶ pe'nuriousness *n*

penury ('pɛnjʊrɪ) *n* **1** extreme poverty. **2** extreme scarcity. [C15: from L *pēnūria* dearth, from ?]

Penza ★ (*Russian* 'pjɛnzə) *n* a city in W Russia: manufacturing centre. Pop.: 534 000 (1995 est.).

Penzance ★ (pɛn'zæns) *n* a town in SW England, in SW Cornwall: the westernmost town in England; resort and fishing port. Pop.: 19 709 (1991).

Penzias ★ ('pɛntsɪəs, 'pɛnz-) *n* **Arno Allan.** born 1933, US astrophysicist, who shared the Nobel prize for physics (1978) with Robert W. Wilson for their discovery of cosmic microwave background radiation.

peon[1] ('piːən, 'piːɒn) *n* **1** a Spanish-American farm labourer or unskilled worker. **2** (formerly, in Spanish America) a debtor compelled to work off his debts. **3** any very poor person. [C19: from Sp. *peón* peasant, from Med. L *pedō* man who goes on foot, from L *pēs* foot]
▶ 'peonage *n*

peon[2] (pjuːn, 'piːən, 'piːɒn) *n* (in India, Sri Lanka, etc., esp. formerly) **1** a messenger or attendant, esp. in an office. **2** a native policeman. **3** a foot soldier. [C17: from Port. *peão* orderly; see PEON[1]]

peony *or* **paeony** ('piːənɪ) *n, pl* **peonies** *or* **paeonies. 1** any of a genus of shrubs and plants of Eurasia and North America, having large pink, red, white, or yellow flowers. **2** the flower of any of these plants. [OE *peonie*, from L *paeōnia*, from Gk *paiōnia*; rel. to *paiōnios* healing, from *paiōn* physician]

people ('piːpˀl) *n* (*usually functioning as pl*) **1** persons collectively or in general. **2** a group of persons considered together: *blind people.* **3** (*pl* **peoples**) the persons living in a country and sharing the same nationality: *the French people.* **4** one's family: *he took her home to meet his people.* **5** persons loyal to someone powerful: *the king's people accompanied him in exile.* **6 the people. 6a** the mass of persons without special distinction, privileges, etc. **6b** the body of persons in a country, etc., esp. those entitled to vote.
◆ *vb* **peoples, peopling, peopled. 7** (*tr*) to provide with or as if with people or inhabitants. [C13: from OF *pople,* from L *populus*]

▨ **USAGE NOTE**   See at **person.**

people carrier *n* another name for **multipurpose vehicle.**

people mover *n* **1** any of various automated forms of transport for large numbers of passengers over short distances, such as a moving pavement, driverless cars, etc. **2** another name for **multipurpose vehicle.**

people's democracy *n* (in Communist ideology) a country or government in transition from bourgeois democracy to socialism.

people's front *n* a less common term for **popular front.**

Peoria ★ (piːˈɔːrɪə) *n* a port in N central Illinois, on the Illinois River. Pop.: 112 875 (1994 est.).

pep (pɛp) *n* **1** high spirits, energy, or vitality. ◆ *vb* **peps, pepping, pepped. 2** (*tr;* usually foll. by *up*) to liven by imbuing with new vigour. [C20: short for PEPPER]

PEP (pɛp) *n acronym for* **1** personal equity plan: a method of saving in the UK with certain tax advantages, in which investments up to a fixed annual value can be purchased. ◆ *abbrev. for* **2** political and economic planning.

peperomia (ˌpɛpərˈəʊmɪə) *n* any of a genus of tropical plants cultivated for their ornamental foliage. [C19: NL from Gk *peperi* pepper + *omoros* similar]

Pepin the Short ★ ('pɛpɪn) *n* died 768 A.D., king of the Franks (751–768); son of Charles Martel and father of Charlemagne. He deposed the Merovingian king (751) and founded the Carolingian dynasty.

peplum ('pɛpləm) *n, pl* **peplums** *or* **pepla** (-lə). a flared ruffle attached to the waist of a jacket, bodice, etc. [C17: from L: full upper garment, from Gk *peplos* shawl]

pepo ('piːpəʊ) *n, pl* **pepos.** the fruit of any of various plants, such as the melon, cucumber, and pumpkin, having a firm rind, fleshy watery pulp, and numerous seeds. [C19: from L: pumpkin, from Gk *pepōn* edible gourd, from *peptein* to ripen]

pepper ('pɛpə) *n* **1** a woody climbing plant, *Piper nigrum,* of the East Indies, having small black berry-like fruits. **2** the dried fruit of this plant, which is ground to produce a sharp hot condiment. See also **black pepper, white pepper. 3** any of various other plants of the genus *Piper.* **4** Also called: **capsicum.** any of various tropical plants, the fruits of which are used as a vegetable and a condiment. See also **sweet pepper, red pepper, cayenne pepper. 5** the fruit of any of these capsicums, which has a mild or pungent taste. **6** the condiment made from the fruits of any of these plants. ◆ *vb* (*tr*) **7** to season with pepper. **8** to sprinkle liberally; dot: *his prose was peppered with alliteration.* **9** to pelt with small missiles. [OE *piper,* from L, from Gk *peperi*]

pepper-and-salt *adj* **1** (of cloth, etc.) marked with a fine mixture of black and white. **2** (of hair) streaked with grey.

peppercorn ('pɛpəˌkɔːn) *n* **1** the small dried berry of the pepper plant. **2** something trifling.

peppercorn rent *n* a rent that is very low or nominal.

pepper mill *n* a small hand mill used to grind pepper-corns.

peppermint ('pepə,mınt) *n* **1** a temperate mint plant with purple or white flowers and downy leaves, which yield a pungent oil. **2** the oil from this plant, which is used as a flavouring. **3** a sweet flavoured with pepper-mint.

pepperoni (,pepə'rəʊnı) *n* a highly seasoned dry sausage of pork and beef spiced with pepper, used esp. on pizza. [C20: from It. *peperoni*, pl of *peperone* cayenne pepper]

pepper pot *n* **1** a small container with perforations in the top for sprinkling pepper. **2** a West Indian stew of meat, etc., highly seasoned with an extract of bitter cas-sava.

pepper tree *n* any of several evergreen trees of a chiefly South American genus having yellowish-white flowers and bright red ornamental fruits.

peppery ('pepərı) *adj* **1** flavoured with or tasting of pep-per. **2** quick-tempered; irritable. **3** full of bite and sharp-ness: *a peppery speech.*
▶ '**pepperiness** *n*

pep pill *n Inf.* a tablet containing a stimulant drug.

peppy ('pepı) *adj* **peppier, peppiest.** *Inf.* full of vitality; bouncy or energetic.
▶ '**peppily** *adv* ▶ '**peppiness** *n*

pepsin ('pepsın) *n* an enzyme produced in the stomach, which, when activated by acid, splits proteins into peptones. [C19: via G from Gk *pepsis*, from *peptein* to di-gest]

pep talk *n Inf.* an enthusiastic talk designed to increase confidence, production, cooperation, etc.

peptic ('peptık) *adj* **1** of, relating to, or promoting diges-tion. **2** of, relating to, or caused by pepsin or the action of the digestive juices. [C17: from Gk *peptikos* capable of digesting, from *peptein* to digest]

peptic ulcer *n Pathol.* an ulcer of the mucous mem-brane lining those parts of the alimentary tract exposed to digestive juices. It can occur in the oesophagus, the stomach, the duodenum, the jejunum, or in the ileum.

peptide ('peptaɪd) *n* any of a group of compounds con-sisting of two or more amino acids linked by chemical bonding between their respective carboxyl and amino groups.

peptide bond *n Biochem.* a chemical amide linkage, -NH-CO-, formed by the condensation of the amino group of one amino acid with the carboxyl group of another.

peptone ('peptəʊn) *n Biochem.* any of a group of com-pounds that form an intermediary group in the diges-tion of proteins to amino acids. [C19: from G *Pepton*, from Gk *pepton* something digested, from *peptein* to di-gest]
▶ **peptonic** (pep'tɒnık) *adj*

Pepys ★ (pi:ps) *n* **Samuel.** 1633–1703, English diarist and naval administrator. His diary, which covers the period 1660–69, is a vivid account of London life through such disasters as the Great Plague and the Fire of London.

per (pɜ:; *unstressed* pə) *determiner* **1** for every: *three pence per pound.* ◆ *prep* **2** (esp. in some Latin phrases) by; through. **3** as per. according to: *as per specifications.* **4** as per usual. *Inf.* as usual. [C15: from L: by, for each]

per. *abbrev. for:* **1** period. **2** person.

per- *prefix* **1** through: *pervade.* **2** throughout: *perennial.* **3** away, beyond: *perfidy.* **4** (*intensifier*): *perfervid.* **5** indicat-ing that a chemical compound contains a high propor-tion of a specified element: *peroxide.* **6** indicating that a chemical element is in a higher than usual state of oxi-dation: *permanganate.* [from L *per* through]

Pera ★ ('pɪərə) *n* the former name of **Beyoğlu.**

peracid (pɜ:r'æsıd) *n* an acid, such as perchloric acid ($HClO_4$), in which the element forming the acid radical exhibits its highest valency.

peradventure (pərəd'ventʃə, ,pɜ:r-) *Arch.* ◆ *adv* **1** by chance; perhaps. ◆ *n* **2** chance or doubt. [C13: from OF *par aventure* by chance]

Peraea *or* **Perea** ★ (pə'ri:ə) *n* a region of ancient Pales-tine, east of the River Jordan and the Dead Sea.

Perak ★ ('peərə, 'pɪərə, pı'ræk) *n* a state of NW Peninsular Malaysia, on the Strait of Malacca: tin mining. Capital: Ipoh. Pop.: 2 222 400 (1993 est.). Area: 20 680 sq. km (8030 sq. miles).

perambulate (pə'ræmbju,leɪt) *vb* **perambulates, perambu-lating, perambulated. 1** to walk about (a place). **2** (*tr*) to walk round in order to inspect. [C16: from L *perambulāre* to traverse, from *per-* through + *ambulāre* to walk]
▶ **per,ambu'lation** *n* ▶ **perambulatory** (pə'ræmbjulətərı, -trı) *adj*

perambulator (pə'ræmbju,leɪtə) *n* a formal word for **pram**[1].

per annum (pər 'ænəm) *adv* every year or by the year. [L]

P-E ratio *abbrev. for* price-earnings ratio.

percale (pə'keɪl, -'kɑ:l) *n* a close-textured woven cotton fabric, used esp. for sheets. [C17: via F from Persian *pargālah* piece of cloth]

per capita (pə 'kæpɪtə) *adj, adv* of or for each person. [L, lit.: according to heads]

perceive (pə'si:v) *vb* **perceives, perceiving, perceived. 1** to become aware of (something) through the senses; recog-nize or observe. **2** (*tr; may take a clause as object*) to come to comprehend; grasp. [C13: from OF *perçoivre*, from L *percipere* to seize entirely]
▶ **per'ceivable** *adj* ▶ **per'ceivably** *adv*

per cent (pə 'sent) *adv* **1** Also: **per centum.** in or for every hundred. Symbol: % ◆ *n* also **percent. 2** a percentage or proportion. **3** (*often pl*) securities yielding a rate of inter-est as specified: *he bought three percents.* [C16: from Med. L *per centum* out of every hundred]

percentage (pə'sentɪdʒ) *n* **1** proportion or rate per hun-dred parts. **2** *Commerce.* the interest, tax, commission, or allowance on a hundred items. **3** any proportion in rela-tion to the whole. **4** *Inf.* profit or advantage.

percentile (pə'sentaɪl) *n* one of 99 actual or notional values of a variable dividing its distribution into 100 groups with equal frequencies. Also called: **centile.**

percept ('pɜ:sept) *n* **1** a concept that depends on recogni-tion by the senses, such as sight, of some external object or phenomenon. **2** an object or phenomenon that is perceived. [C19: from L *perceptum*, from *percipere* to PER-CEIVE]

perceptible (pə'septəb³l) *adj* able to be perceived; no-ticeable or recognizable.
▶ **per,cepti'bility** *n* ▶ **per'ceptibly** *adv*

perception (pə'sepʃən) *n* **1** the act or the effect of per-ceiving. **2** insight or intuition gained by perceiving. **3** the ability or capacity to perceive. **4** way of perceiving; view. **5** the process by which an organism detects and in-terprets the external world by means of the sensory re-ceptors. [C15: from L *perceptiō* comprehension; see PERCEIVE]
▶ **per'ceptional** *adj* ▶ **perceptual** (pə'septjʊəl) *adj*

perceptive (pə'septɪv) *adj* **1** quick at perceiving; obser-vant. **2** perceptual. **3** able to perceive.
▶ **per'ceptively** *adv* ▶ **per'ceptiveness** *or* ,**percep'tivity** *n*

Perceval ★ ('pɜ:sɪv³l) *n* **Spencer.** 1762–1812, British statesman; prime minister (1809–12); assassinated.

perch[1] (pɜ:tʃ) *n* **1** a pole, branch, or other resting place above ground on which a bird roosts. **2** a similar resting place for a person or thing. **3** another name for **rod** (sense 7). ◆ *vb* **4** (usually foll. by *on*) to alight, rest, or cause to rest on or as if on a perch: *the bird perched on the branch; the cap was perched on his head.* [C13 *perche* stake, from OF, from L *pertica* long staff]

perch[2] (pɜ:tʃ) *n*, *pl* **perch** *or* **perches. 1** any of a family of freshwater spiny-finned teleost fishes of Europe and North America: valued as food and game fishes. **2** any of various similar or related fishes. [C13: from OF *perche*, from L *perca*, from Gk *perkē*]

perchance (pə'tʃɑ:ns) *adv Arch. or poetic.* **1** perhaps; pos-sibly. **2** by chance; accidentally. [C14: from Anglo-F *par chance*]

★ people and places

Percheron ('pɜːʃə,rɒn) *n* a compact heavy breed of carthorse. [C19: from F, from *le Perche*, region of NW France, where the breed originated]

perchloric acid (pə'klɔːrɪk) *n* a colourless syrupy oxyacid of chlorine containing a greater proportion of oxygen than chloric acid. It is a powerful oxidizing agent. Formula: HClO₄. Systematic name: **chloric(VII) acid**.

percipient (pə'sɪpɪənt) *adj* **1** able to perceive. **2** perceptive. ◆ *n* **3** a person who perceives. [C17: from L *percipiens* observing, from *percipere* to grasp]
▸ **per'cipience** *n* ▸ **per'cipiently** *adv*

Percival *or* **Perceval** ★ ('pɜːsɪvºl) *n* (in Arthurian legend) a knight in King Arthur's court. German equivalent: **Parzival**.

percolate *vb* ('pɜːkə,leɪt), **percolates, percolating, percolated**. **1** to cause (a liquid) to pass through a fine mesh, porous substance, etc., or (of a liquid) to pass through a fine mesh, etc.; trickle: *rain percolated through the roof*. **2** to permeate; penetrate gradually: *water percolated the road*. **3** to make (coffee) or (of coffee) to be made in a percolator. ◆ *n* ('pɜːkəlɪt, -,leɪt). **4** a product of percolation. [C17: from L *percolāre*, from PER- + *cōlāre* to strain, from *cōlum* a strainer; see COLANDER]
▸ **percolable** ('pɜːkələbºl) *adj* ▸ **,perco'lation** *n*

percolator ('pɜːkə,leɪtə) *n* a kind of coffeepot in which boiling water is forced up through a tube and filters down through the coffee grounds into a container.

per contra ('pɜː 'kɒntrə) *adv* on the contrary. [from L]

percuss (pə'kʌs) *vb* (*tr*) **1** to strike sharply or suddenly. **2** *Med.* to tap on (a body surface) with the fingertips or a special hammer to aid diagnosis. [C16: from L *percutere*, from *per-* through + *quatere* to shake]
▸ **per'cussor** *n*

percussion (pə'kʌʃən) *n* **1** the act, an instance, or an effect of percussing. **2** *Music.* the family of instruments in which sound arises from the striking of materials with sticks or hammers. **3** *Music.* instruments of this family constituting a section of an orchestra, etc. **4** *Med.* the act of percussing a body surface. **5** the act of exploding a percussion cap. [C16: from L *percussiō*, from *percutere* to hit; see PERCUSS]
▸ **per'cussive** *adj* ▸ **per'cussively** *adv* ▸ **per'cussiveness** *n*

percussion cap *n* a detonator consisting of a paper or thin metal cap containing material that explodes when struck.

percussion instrument *n* any of various musical instruments that produce a sound when their resonating surfaces are struck directly, as with a stick or mallet, or by leverage action.

percussionist (pə'kʌʃənɪst) *n Music.* a person who plays any of several percussion instruments.

percutaneous (,pɜːkju'teɪnɪəs) *adj Med.* effected through the skin, as in the absorption of an ointment.

Percy ★ ('pɜːsɪ) *n* **1** Sir **Henry**, known as *Harry Hotspur*. 1364–1403, English rebel, who was killed leading an army against Henry IV. **2 Thomas.** 1729–1811, British bishop and antiquary. His *Reliques of Ancient English Poetry* (1765) stimulated the interest of Romantic writers in old English and Scottish ballads.

Perdido ★ (*Spanish* per'ðiðo) *n* **Monte** ('mɒnte). a mountain in NE Spain, in the central Pyrenees. Height: 3352 m (10 997 ft). French name: (Mont) **Perdu**.

per diem ('pɜː 'daɪem, 'diːem) *adv* **1** every day or by the day. ◆ *n* **2** an allowance for daily expenses. [from L]

perdition (pə'dɪʃən) *n* **1** *Christianity.* **1a** final and irrevocable spiritual ruin. **1b** this state as one that the wicked are said to be destined to endure forever. **2** another word for **hell**. **3** *Arch.* utter ruin or destruction. [C14: from LL *perditiō* ruin, from L *perdere* to lose, from PER- (away) + *dāre* to give]

Perdu ★ (perdy) *n* **Mont**. the French name for (Monte) **Perdido**.

perdurable (pə'djuərəbºl) *adj Rare.* extremely durable. [C13: from LL *perdūrābilis*, from L *per-* (intensive) + *dūrābilis* long-lasting, from *dūrus* hard]

père *French*. (pɛr; *English* peə) *n* an addition to a French surname to specify the father rather than the son of the same name: *Dumas père*.

Perea ★ (pə'riːə) *n* a variant spelling of **Peraea**.

Père David's deer *n* a large grey deer, surviving only in captivity. [C20: after Father A. *David* (died 1900), F missionary]

peregrinate ('pɛrɪgrɪ,neɪt) *vb* **peregrinates, peregrinating, peregrinated**. **1** (*intr*) to travel or wander about from place to place; voyage. **2** (*tr*) to travel through (a place). [C16: from L, from *peregrīnārī* to travel; see PEREGRINE]
▸ **,peregri'nation** *n* ▸ **'peregri,nator** *n*

peregrine ('pɛrɪgrɪn) *adj Arch.* **1** coming from abroad. **2** travelling. [C14: from L *peregrīnus* foreign, from *pereger* being abroad, from *per* through + *ager* land (that is, beyond one's own land)]

peregrine falcon *n* a falcon occurring in most parts of the world, having a dark plumage on the back and wings and lighter underparts.

Pereira ★ (*Spanish* pe'reira) *n* a town in W central Colombia: cattle trading and coffee processing. Pop.: 434 267 (1997 est.).

Perelman ★ ('pɛrəlmən, 'pɜːl-) *n* **S(idney) J(oseph)**. 1904–79, US humorous writer. After scriptwriting for the Marx Brothers, he published many collections of articles, including *Crazy Like a Fox* (1944).

peremptory (pə'rɛmptərɪ) *adj* **1** urgent or commanding: *a peremptory ring on the bell*. **2** not able to be remitted or debated; decisive. **3** dogmatic. **4** *Law.* **4a** admitting of no denial or contradiction; precluding debate. **4b** obligatory rather than permissive. [C16: from Anglo-Norman *peremptorie*, from L *peremptōrius* decisive, from *perimere* to take away completely]
▸ **per'emptorily** *adv* ▸ **per'emptoriness** *n*

perennial (pə'rɛnɪəl) *adj* **1** lasting throughout the year or through many years. **2** everlasting; perpetual. ◆ *n* **3** a woody or herbaceous plant that continues its growth for at least three years. [C17: from L *perennis* continual, from *per* through + *annus* year]
▸ **per'ennially** *adv*

Peres ★ ('pɛrɛs) *n* **Shimon** (ji:'məun). born 1923, Israeli statesman, born in Poland: prime minister (1984–86; 1995–96); foreign minister (1986–88 and from 1992); shared Nobel peace prize 1994.

perestroika (,pɛrə'strɔɪkə) *n* the policy of reconstructing the economy, etc., of the former Soviet Union under the leadership of Mikhail Gorbachov. [C20: Russian, lit.: reconstruction]

Pérez de Cuéllar ★ ('pɛrɛs də 'kweɪjɑː) *n* **Javier** ('hævɪ,eɪ). born 1920, Peruvian diplomat; UN secretary-general (1982–91).

Pérez Galdós ★ ('pɛrɛs gɑː'lðəus) *n* **Benito**. 1843–1920, Spanish novelist. His works include the *Episodios nacionales* (1873–1912), a series of historical novels, and *Fortunata y Jacinta* (1886–87).

perfect *adj* ('pɜːfɪkt). **1** having all essential elements. **2** unblemished; faultless: *a perfect gemstone*. **3** correct or precise: *perfect timing*. **4** utter or absolute: *a perfect stranger*. **5** excellent in all respects: *a perfect day*. **6** *Maths.* exactly divisible into equal integral or polynomial roots: *36 is a perfect square*. **7** *Bot.* **7a** (of flowers) having functional stamens and pistils. **7b** (of plants) having all parts present. **8** *Grammar.* denoting a tense of verbs used in describing an action that has been completed. In English this is formed with *have* or *has* plus the past participle. **9** *Music.* **9a** of or relating to the intervals of the unison, fourth, fifth, and octave. **9b** (of a cadence) ending on the tonic chord, giving a feeling of conclusion. Also: **final**. ◆ *n* ('pɜːfɪkt). **10** *Grammar.* **10a** the perfect tense. **10b** a verb in this tense. ◆ *vb* (pə'fɛkt). (*tr*) **11** to make perfect; improve to one's satisfaction: *he is in Paris to perfect his French*. **12** to make fully accomplished. [C13: from L *perfectus*, from *perficere* to perform, from *per-* through + *facere* to do]

★ people and places

that cannot be qualified; thus something is either *perfect* or *not perfect*, and cannot be *more perfect*. However when *perfect* means excellent in all respects, a comparative can be used with it without absurdity: *the next day the weather was even more perfect.*

perfect gas *n* another name for **ideal gas**.

perfectible (pə'fɛktəb°l) *adj* capable of becoming or being made perfect.
▶ per,fecti'bility *n*

perfection (pə'fɛkʃən) *n* 1 the act of perfecting or the state or quality of being perfect. 2 the highest degree of a quality, etc. 3 an embodiment of perfection. [C13: from L *perfectiō* a completing, from *perficere* to finish]

perfectionism (pə'fɛkʃə,nɪzəm) *n* 1 *Philosophy.* the doctrine that man can attain perfection in this life. 2 the demand for the highest standard of excellence.
▶ per'fectionist *n, adj*

perfective (pə'fɛktɪv) *adj* 1 tending to perfect. 2 *Grammar.* denoting an aspect of verbs used to express that the action or event described by the verb is or was completed: *I lived in London for ten years* is perfective; *I have lived in London for ten years* is imperfective, since the implication is that I still live in London.

perfectly ('pɜːfɪktlɪ) *adv* 1 completely, utterly, or absolutely. 2 in a perfect way.

perfect number *n* an integer, such as 28, that is equal to the sum of all its possible factors, excluding itself.

perfect participle *n* another name for **past participle**.

perfect pitch *n* another name (not in technical usage) for **absolute pitch** (sense 1).

perfervid (pɜː'fɜːvɪd) *adj Literary.* extremely ardent or zealous. [C19: from NL *perfervidus*]

perfidious (pə'fɪdɪəs) *adj* guilty, treacherous, or faithless; deceitful. [C18: from L, from *perfidus* faithless]
▶ per'fidiously *adv* ▶ per'fidiousness *n* ▶ 'perfidy *n*

perfoliate (pə'fəʊlɪt, -ˌeɪt) *adj* (of a leaf) having a base that completely encloses the stem, so that the stem appears to pass through it. [C17: from NL *perfoliātus*, from L *per-* through + *folium* leaf]
▶ per,foli'ation *n*

perforate *vb* ('pɜːfə,reɪt), **perforates, perforating, perforated.** 1 to make a hole or holes in (something). 2 (*tr*) to punch rows of holes between (stamps, etc.) for ease of separation. ◆ *adj* ('pɜːfərɪt). 3 *Biol.* pierced by small holes: *perforate shells.* 4 *Philately.* another word for **perforated.** [C16: from L *perforāre*, from *per-* through + *forāre* to pierce]
▶ 'perforable *adj* ▶ 'perfo,rator *n*

perforated ('pɜːfə,reɪtɪd) *adj* 1 pierced with holes. 2 (esp. of stamps) having perforations.

perforation (,pɜːfə'reɪʃən) *n* 1 the act of perforating or the state of being perforated. 2 a hole or holes made in something. 3a a method of making individual stamps, etc. easily separable by punching holes along their margins. 3b the holes punched in this way. Abbrev.: **perf.**

perforce (pə'fɔːs) *adv* by necessity; unavoidably. [C14: from OF *par force*]

perform (pə'fɔːm) *vb* 1 to carry out (an action). 2 (*tr*) to fulfil: *to perform someone's request.* 3 to present or enact (a play, concert, etc.): *the group performed Hamlet.* [C14: from Anglo-Norman *performer* (infl. by *forme* FORM), from OF *parfournir*, from *par-* PER- + *fournir* to provide]
▶ per'formable *adj* ▶ per'former *n*

performance (pə'fɔːməns) *n* 1 the act, process, or art of performing. 2 an artistic or dramatic production: *last night's performance was terrible.* 3 manner or quality of functioning: *a machine's performance.* 4 *Inf.* mode of conduct or behaviour, esp. when distasteful: *what did you mean by that performance at the restaurant?* 5 *Inf.* any tiresome procedure: *the performance of preparing to go out in the snow.*

performance art *n* a theatrical presentation that incorporates various art forms, such as dance, sculpture, etc.

performative (pə'fɔːmətɪv) *adj Linguistics, philosophy.* 1a denoting an utterance that itself constitutes the act de-

scribed by the verb. For example, the sentence *I confess that I was there* is itself a confession. 1b (*as n*): *that sentence is a performative.* 2a denoting a verb that may be used as the main verb in such an utterance. 2b (*as n*): *"promise" is a performative.*

performing arts the arts, such as a music and drama, that require a public performance.

perfume *n* ('pɜːfjuːm). 1 a mixture of alcohol and fragrant essential oils extracted from flowers, etc., or made synthetically. 2 a scent or odour, esp. a fragrant one. ◆ *vb* (pə'fjuːm), **perfumes, perfuming, perfumed.** 3 (*tr*) to impart a perfume to. [C16: from F *parfum*, prob. from OProvençal *perfum*, from *perfumar* to make scented, from *per* through (from L) + *fumar* to smoke, from L *fumāre* to smoke]

perfumer (pə'fjuːmə) or **perfumier** (pə'fjuːmjeɪ) *n* a person who makes or sells perfume.

perfumery (pə'fjuːmərɪ) *n, pl* **perfumeries.** 1 a place where perfumes are sold. 2 a factory where perfumes are made. 3 the process of making perfumes. 4 perfumes in general.

perfunctory (pə'fʌŋktərɪ) *adj* 1 done superficially, only as a matter of routine. 2 dull or indifferent. [C16: from LL *perfunctōrius* negligent, from *perfunctus* dispatched, from *perfungī* to fulfil]
▶ per'functorily *adv* ▶ per'functoriness *n*

perfuse (pə'fjuːz) *vb* **perfuses, perfusing, perfused.** (*tr*) 1 to suffuse or permeate (a liquid, colour, etc.) through or over (something). 2 *Surgery.* to pass (a fluid) through (tissue). [C16: from L *perfūsus* wetted, from *perfundere* to pour over]
▶ per'fused *adj*

perfusionist (pə'fjuːʒənɪst) *n Surgery.* the person in a surgical team who is responsible for the perfusion of blood through the patient's lung tissue to ensure adequate exchange of oxygen and carbon dioxide.

Pergamum ★ ('pɜːgəməm) *n* an ancient city in NW Asia Minor, in Mysia: capital of a major Hellenistic monarchy of the same name that later became a Roman province.

pergola ('pɜːgələ) *n* a horizontal trellis or framework, supported on posts, that carries climbing plants. [C17: via It. from L *pergula* projection from a roof, from *pergere* to go forward]

Pergolesi ★ (*Italian* pergo'leːsi) *n* **Giovanni Battista** (dʒo-'vanni bat'tista). 1710–36, Italian composer: his works include the *Stabat Mater* (1736) for women's voices.

perhaps (pə'hæps; *informal* præps) *adv* 1a possibly; maybe. 1b (*as sentence modifier*): *he'll arrive tomorrow, perhaps.* ◆ *sentence substitute.* 2 it may happen, be so, etc.; maybe. [C16 *perhappes*, from *per* by + *happes* chance]

peri ('pɪərɪ) *n, pl* **peris.** 1 (in Persian folklore) one of a race of beautiful supernatural beings. 2 any beautiful fairy-like creature. [C18: from Persian: fairy, from Avestan *pairikā* witch]

peri- *prefix* 1 enclosing, encircling, or around: *pericardium; pericarp.* 2 near or adjacent: *perihelion.* [from Gk *peri* around]

perianth ('pɛrɪˌænθ) *n* the outer part of a flower, consisting of the calyx and corolla. [C18: from F *périanthe*, from NL, from *peri-* + Gk *anthos* flower]

periapt ('pɛrɪˌæpt) *n Rare.* a charm or amulet. [C16: via F from Gk *periapton*, from PERI- + *haptos* clasped, from *haptein* to fasten]

pericarditis (,pɛrɪkɑː'daɪtɪs) *n* inflammation of the pericardium.

pericardium (,pɛrɪ'kɑːdɪəm) *n, pl* **pericardia** (-dɪə). the membranous sac enclosing the heart. [C16: via NL from Gk *perikardion*, from PERI- + *kardia* heart]
▶ ,peri'cardial or ,peri'cardiˌac *adj*

pericarp ('pɛrɪˌkɑːp) *n* the part of a fruit enclosing the seeds that develops from the wall of the ovary. [C18: via F from NL *pericarpium*]
▶ ,peri'carpial *adj*

perichondrium (,pɛrɪ'kɒndrɪəm) *n, pl* **perichondria** (-drɪə). the fibrous membrane that covers the cartilage. [C18: NL, from PERI- + Gk *chondros* cartilage]

periclase ('pɛrɪ,kleɪs) *n* a mineral consisting of magnesium oxide. [C19: from NL *periclasia*, from Gk *peri* very + *klasis* a breaking, referring to its perfect cleavage]

Pericles ★ ('perɪ,kliːz) *n* ?495–429 B.C., Athenian statesman, who contributed greatly to Athens' political and cultural supremacy in Greece. In power from about 460 B.C., he was responsible for the construction of the Parthenon. He conducted the Peloponnesian War (431–404 B.C.) successfully until his death.
▸ ,Peri'clean *adj*

pericline ('perɪ,klaɪn) *n* **1** a white translucent variety of albite in the form of elongated crystals. **2** Also called: **dome.** a dome-shaped formation of stratified rock with its slopes following the direction of folding. [C19: from Gk *periklinēs* sloping on all sides]
▸ ,peri'clinal *adj*

pericranium (,perɪ'kreɪnɪəm) *n*, *pl* **pericrania** (-nɪə). the fibrous membrane covering the external surface of the skull. [C16: NL, from Gk *perikranion*]

peridot ('perɪ,dɒt) *n* a pale green transparent variety of the olivine chrysolite, used as a gemstone. [C14: from OF *peritot*, from ?]

perigee ('perɪ,dʒiː) *n* the point in its orbit around the earth when the moon or a satellite is nearest the earth. [C16: via F from Gk *perigeion*, from PERI- + *gea* earth]
▸ ,peri'gean *adj*

periglacial (,perɪ'gleɪʃəl) *adj* relating to a region bordering a glacier: *periglacial climate*.

Périgueux ★ (,perɪ'gɜː; *French* perigø) *n* a town in SW France, capital of the Dordogne: noted for its Roman remains, medieval cathedral, and pâté de foie gras. Pop.: 32 850 (1990).

perihelion (,perɪ'hiːlɪən) *n*, *pl* **perihelia** (-lɪə). the point in its orbit when a planet or comet is nearest the sun. [C17: from NL *perihēlium*, from PERI- + Gk *hēlios* sun]

peril ('perɪl) *n* exposure to risk or harm; danger or jeopardy. [C13: via OF from L *perīculum*]

perilous ('perɪləs) *adj* very hazardous or dangerous: *a perilous journey*.
▸ 'perilously *adv* ▸ 'perilousness *n*

perilune ('perɪ,luːn) *n* the point in a lunar orbit when a spacecraft is nearest the moon. [C20: from PERI- + *-lune*, from L *lūna* moon]

perimeter (pə'rɪmɪtə) *n* Maths. **1a** the curve or line enclosing a plane area. **1b** the length of this curve or line. **2a** any boundary around something. **2b** (*as modifier*): *a perimeter fence*. **3** a medical instrument for measuring the field of vision. [C16: from F *périmètre*, from L *perimetros*]
▸ perimetric (,perɪ'metrɪk) *adj*

perinatal (,perɪ'neɪt°l) *adj* of or occurring in the period from about three months before to one month after birth.

perineum (,perɪ'niːəm) *n*, *pl* **perinea** (-'niːə). **1** the region of the body between the anus and the genital organs. **2** the surface of the human trunk between the thighs. [C17: from NL, from Gk *perinaion*, from PERI- + *inein* to empty]
▸ ,peri'neal *adj*

period ('pɪərɪəd) *n* **1** a portion of time of indefinable length: *he spent a period away from home*. **2a** a portion of time specified in some way: *Picasso's blue period*. **2b** (*as modifier*): *period costume*. **3** a nontechnical name for an occurence of menstruation. **4** Geol. a unit of geological time during which a system of rocks is formed: *the Jurassic period*. **5** a division of time, esp. of the academic day. **6** Physics, maths. the time taken to complete one cycle of a regularly recurring phenomenon; the reciprocal of frequency. Symbol: *T* **7** Astron. **7a** the time required by a body to make one complete rotation on its axis. **7b** the time interval between two successive maxima or minima of light variation of a variable star. **8** Chem. one of the horizontal rows of elements in the periodic table. Each period starts with an alkali metal and ends with a rare gas. **9** another term (esp. US and Canad.) for **full stop. 10** a complete sentence, esp. one with several clauses. **11** a completion or end. [C14 *peryod*, from L *periodus*, from Gk *periodos* circuit, from PERI- + *hodos* way]

periodic (,pɪərɪ'ɒdɪk) *adj* **1** happening or recurring at intervals; intermittent. **2** of, relating to, or resembling a

period. **3** having or occurring in a series of repeated periods or cycles.
▸ ,peri'odically *adv* ▸ **periodicity** (,pɪərɪə'dɪsɪtɪ) *n*

periodical (,pɪərɪ'ɒdɪk°l) *n* **1** a publication issued at regular intervals, usually monthly or weekly. ◆ *adj* **2** of or relating to such publications. **3** published at regular intervals. **4** periodic or occasional.

periodic function *n* Maths. a function whose value is repeated at constant intervals.

periodic law *n* the principle that the chemical properties of the elements are periodic functions of their atomic weights or, more accurately, of their atomic numbers.

periodic sentence *n* Rhetoric. a sentence in which the completion of the main clause is left to the end, thus creating an effect of suspense.

periodic table *n* a table of the elements, arranged in order of increasing atomic number, based on the periodic law.

periodontal ('perɪə'dɒnt°l) *adj* of, denoting, or affecting the gums and other tissues surrounding the teeth: *periodontal disease*.

periodontics (,perɪə'dɒntɪks) *n* (*functioning as sing*) the branch of dentistry concerned with diseases affecting the tissues and structures that surround teeth. Also called: **periodontology**. [C19: from PERI- + *-odontics*, from Gk *odōn* tooth]
▸ ,perio'dontical *adj*

periosteum (,perɪ'ɒstɪəm) *n*, *pl* **periostea** (-tɪə). a thick fibrous two-layered membrane covering the surface of bones. [C16: NL, from Gk *periosteon*, from PERI- + *osteon* bone]
▸ ,peri'osteal *adj*

peripatetic (,perɪpə'tetɪk) *adj* **1** itinerant. **2** Brit. employed in two or more educational establishments and travelling from one to another: *a peripatetic football coach*. ◆ *n* **3** a peripatetic person. [C16: from L *peripatēticus*, from Gk, from *peripatein* to pace to and fro]
▸ ,peripa'tetically *adv*

Peripatetic (,perɪpə'tetɪk) *adj* **1** of or relating to the teachings of Aristotle, who used to teach philosophy while walking about the Lyceum in ancient Athens. ◆ *n* **2** a student of Aristotelianism.

peripeteia (,perɪpɪ'taɪə, -'tɪə) *n* (esp. in drama) an abrupt turn of events or reversal of circumstances. [C16: from Gk, from PERI- + *piptein* to fall (to change suddenly, lit.: to fall around)]

peripheral (pə'rɪfərəl) *adj* **1** not relating to the most important part of something; incidental. **2** of or relating to a periphery. **3** Anat. of, relating to, or situated near the surface of the body: *a peripheral nerve*.
▸ pe'ripherally *adv*

peripheral device or **unit** *n* Computing. any device, such as a disk, printer, modem, or screen, concerned with input/output, storage, etc. Often shortened to **peripheral**.

periphery (pə'rɪfərɪ) *n*, *pl* **peripheries**. **1** the outermost boundary of an area. **2** the outside surface of something. [C16: from LL *peripherīa*, from Gk, from PERI- + *pherein* to bear]

periphrasis (pə'rɪfrəsɪs) *n*, *pl* **periphrases** (-rə,siːz). **1** a roundabout way of expressing something; circumlocution. **2** an expression of this kind. [C16: via L from Gk, from PERI- + *phrazein* to declare]

periphrastic (,perɪ'fræstɪk) *adj* **1** employing or involving periphrasis. **2** expressed in two or more words rather than by an inflected form of one: used esp. of a tense of a verb where the alternative word is an auxiliary verb, as in *He does go*.
▸ ,peri'phrastically *adv*

perisarc ('perɪ,saːk) *n* the outer chitinous layer secreted by colonial hydrozoan coelenterates. [C19: from PERI- + *-sarc*, from Gk *sarx* flesh]

periscope ('perɪ,skəup) *n* any of a number of optical instruments that enable the user to view objects that are not in the direct line of vision, such as one in a submarine for looking above the surface of the water. They

have a system of mirrors or prisms to reflect the light. [C19: from Gk *periskopein* to look around]
> **periscopic** (ˌperɪˈskɒpɪk) *adj*

perish (ˈperɪʃ) *vb* **1** (*intr*) to be destroyed or die, esp. in an untimely way. **2** (*tr* sometimes foll. by *with* or *from*) to cause to suffer: *we were perished with cold.* **3** to rot or cause to rot: *leather perishes if exposed to bad weather.* ◆ *n* **4 do a perish.** *Austral. inf.* to die or come near to dying of thirst or starvation. [C13: from OF *périr*, from L *perīre* to pass away entirely]

perishable (ˈperɪʃəbᵊl) *adj* **1** liable to rot. ◆ *n* **2** (*often pl*) a perishable article, esp. food.
> ˌperisha'bility *or* 'perishableness *n*

perishing (ˈperɪʃɪŋ) *adj* **1** *Inf.* (of weather, etc.) extremely cold. **2** *Sl.* (intensifier qualifying something undesirable): *it's a perishing nuisance!*
> 'perishingly *adv*

perisperm (ˈperɪˌspɜːm) *n* the nutritive tissue surrounding the embryo in certain seeds.

perissodactyl (pəˌrɪsəʊˈdæktɪl) *n* **1** any of an order of placental mammals having hooves with an odd number of toes: includes horses, tapirs, and rhinoceroses. ◆ *adj* **2** of, relating to, or belonging to this order. [C19: from NL *perissodactylus*, from Gk *perissos* uneven + *daktulos* digit]

peristalsis (ˌperɪˈstælsɪs) *n, pl* **peristalses** (-siːz). *Physiol.* the succession of waves of involuntary muscular contraction of various bodily tubes, esp. of the alimentary tract, where it effects transport of food and waste products. [C19: from NL, from PERI- + Gk *stalsis* compression, from *stellein* to press together]
> ˌperi'staltic *adj*

peristome (ˈperɪˌstəʊm) *n* **1** a fringe of pointed teeth surrounding the opening of a moss capsule. **2** any of various parts surrounding the mouth of invertebrates, such as echinoderms and earthworms, and of protozoans. [C18: from NL *peristoma*, from PERI- + Gk *stoma* mouth]

peristyle (ˈperɪˌstaɪl) *n* **1** a colonnade round a court or building. **2** an area surrounded by a colonnade. [C17: via F from L *peristȳlum*, from Gk *peristulon*, from PERI- + *stulos* column]

peritoneum (ˌperɪtəˈniːəm) *n, pl* **peritonea** (-ˈniːə) *or* **peritoneums.** a serous sac that lines the walls of the abdominal cavity and covers the viscera. [C16: via LL from Gk *peritonaion*, from *peritonos* stretched around]
> ˌperito'neal *adj*

peritonitis (ˌperɪtəˈnaɪtɪs) *n* inflammation of the peritoneum.

periwig (ˈperɪˌwɪg) *n* a wig, such as a peruke. [C16 *perwyke*, changed from F *perruque* wig, PERUKE]

periwinkle[1] (ˈperɪˌwɪŋkᵊl) *n* any of various edible marine gastropods having a spirally coiled shell. Often shortened to **winkle.** [C16: from ?]

periwinkle[2] (ˈperɪˌwɪŋkᵊl) *n* any of several Eurasian evergreen plants having trailing stems and blue flowers. [C14 *pervenke*, from OE *perwince*, from LL *pervinca*]

perjure (ˈpɜːdʒə) *vb* **perjures, perjuring, perjured.** (*tr*) *Criminal law.* to render (oneself) guilty of perjury. [C15: from OF *parjurer*, from L *perjūrāre*, from PER- + *jūrāre* to make an oath, from *jūs* law]
> 'perjurer *n*

perjured (ˈpɜːdʒəd) *adj Criminal law.* **1a** having sworn falsely. **1b** having committed perjury. **2** involving or characterized by perjury: *perjured evidence.*

perjury (ˈpɜːdʒərɪ) *n, pl* **perjuries.** *Criminal law.* the offence committed by a witness in judicial proceedings who, having been lawfully sworn, wilfully gives false evidence. [C14: from Anglo-F *parjurie*, from L *perjūrium* a false oath; see PERJURE]
> **perjurious** (pɜːˈdʒʊərɪəs) *adj*

perk[1] (pɜːk) *adj* **1** pert; brisk; lively. ◆ *vb* **2** See **perk up.** [C16: see PERK UP]

perk[2] (pɜːk) *vb Inf.* short for **percolate** (sense 3).

perk[3] (pɜːk) *n Brit. inf.* short for **perquisite.**

perk up *vb* (*adv*) **1** to make or become more cheerful, hopeful, or lively. **2** to rise or cause to rise briskly: *the dog's ears perked up.* **3** (*tr*) to make smarter in appearance:

she perked up her outfit with a bright scarf. [C14 *perk*, ?from Norman F *perquer*; see PERCH[1]]

perky (ˈpɜːkɪ) *adj* **perkier, perkiest. 1** jaunty; lively. **2** confident; spirited.
> 'perkily *adv* > 'perkiness *n*

Perl (pɜːl) *n* a computer language that is used for text manipulation, esp. on the World Wide Web. [C20: *p(ractical) e(xtraction) and r(eport) l(anguage)*]

Perlis ★ (ˈpɛəlɪs, ˈpɜː-) *n* a state of NW Peninsular Malaysia, on the Andaman Sea: a dependency of Thailand until 1909. Capital: Kangar. Pop.: 187 600 (1993 est.). Area: 803 sq. km (310 sq. miles).

perlite (ˈpɜːlaɪt) *n* a variety of obsidian consisting of masses of globules. [C19: from F, from *perle* PEARL[1]]

Perlman ★ (ˈpɜːlmən) *n* **Itzhak** (ˈɪtzæk). born 1945, Israeli violinist; polio victim.

perm[1] (pɜːm) *n* **1** a hairstyle produced by treatment with heat, chemicals, etc. which gives long-lasting waves or curls. Also called (esp. formerly): **permanent wave.** ◆ *vb* **2** (*tr*) to give a perm to (hair).

perm[2] (pɜːm) *vb, n Inf.* short for **permutate, permutation** (sense 4).

Perm ★ (*Russian* pjermj) *n* a port in W Russia, on the Kama River: oil refinery; university (1916). Pop.: 1 032 000 (1995 est.). Former name (1940–62): **Molotov.**

permafrost (ˈpɜːməˌfrɒst) *n* ground that is permanently frozen. [C20: from PERMA(NENT) + FROST]

permalloy (pɜːˈmælɔɪ) *n* any of various alloys containing iron and nickel and sometimes smaller amounts of chromium and molybdenum.

permanence (ˈpɜːmənəns) *n* the state or quality of being permanent.

permanency (ˈpɜːmənənsɪ) *n, pl* **permanencies. 1** a person or thing that is permanent. **2** another word for **permanence.**

permanent (ˈpɜːmənənt) *adj* **1** existing or intended to exist for an indefinite period: *a permanent structure.* **2** not expected to change; not temporary: *a permanent condition.* [C15: from L *permanens* continuing, from *permanēre* to stay to the end]
> 'permanently *adv*

permanent health insurance *n* a form of insurance that provides up to 75 per cent of a person's salary, until retirement, in case of prolonged illness or disability.

permanent magnet *n* a magnet, often of steel, that retains its magnetization after the magnetic field producing it has been removed.

permanent press *n* a chemical treatment for clothing that makes the fabric crease-resistant and sometimes provides a garment with a permanent crease or pleats.

permanent wave *n* another name (esp. formerly) for **perm**[1] (sense 1).

permanent way *n Chiefly Brit.* the track of a railway, including the sleepers, rails, etc.

permanganate (pəˈmæŋɡəˌneɪt, -nɪt) *n* a salt of permanganic acid.

permanganic acid (ˌpɜːmæŋˈɡænɪk) *n* a monobasic acid known only in solution and in the form of permanganate salts. Formula: $HMnO_4$. Systematic name: **manganic(VII) acid.**

permeability (ˌpɜːmɪəˈbɪlɪtɪ) *n* **1** the state or quality of being permeable. **2** a measure of the ability of a medium to modify a magnetic field, expressed as the ratio of the magnetic flux density in the medium to the field strength; measured in henries per metre. Symbol: μ

permeable (ˈpɜːmɪəbᵊl) *adj* capable of being permeated, esp. by liquids. [C15: from LL *permeābilis*, from L *permeāre* to pervade; see PERMEATE]
> 'permeably *adv*

permeance (ˈpɜːmɪəns) *n* **1** the act of permeating. **2** the reciprocal of the reluctance of a magnetic circuit.
> 'permeant *adj, n*

permeate (ˈpɜːmɪˌeɪt) *vb* **permeates, permeating, permeated. 1** to penetrate or pervade (a substance, area, etc.): *a lovely smell permeated the room.* **2** to pass through or cause to

pass through by osmosis or diffusion: *to permeate a membrane.* [C17: from L *permeāre*, from *per-* through + *meāre* to pass]
▸ ˌperme'ation *n* ▸ 'permeative *adj*

Permian ('pɜːmɪən) *adj* **1** of, denoting, or formed in the last period of the Palaeozoic era, between the Carboniferous and Triassic periods. ◆ *n* **2 the.** the Permian period or rock system. [C19: after PERM]

permissible (pə'mɪsəb³l) *adj* permitted; allowable.
▸ perˌmissi'bility *n* ▸ per'missibly *adv*

permission (pə'mɪʃən) *n* authorization to do something.

permissive (pə'mɪsɪv) *adj* **1** tolerant; lenient: *permissive parents.* **2** indulgent in matters of sex: *a permissive society.* **3** granting permission.
▸ per'missively *adv* ▸ per'missiveness *n*

permit *vb* (pə'mɪt), **permits, permitting, permitted. 1** (*tr*) to grant permission to do something: *you are permitted to smoke.* **2** (*tr*) to consent to or tolerate: *she will not permit him to come.* **3** (when *intr*, often foll. by *of*; when *tr*, often foll. by an infinitive) to allow the possibility (of): *the passage permits of two interpretations; his work permits him to relax nowadays.* ◆ *n* ('pɜːmɪt). **4** an official document granting authorization; licence. **5** permission. [C15: from L *permittere*, from *per-* through + *mittere* to send]
▸ per'mitter *n*

permittivity (ˌpɜːmɪ'tɪvɪtɪ) *n, pl* **permittivities.** a measure of the ability of a substance to transmit an electric field.

permutate ('pɜːmjuˌteɪt) *vb* **permutates, permutating, permutated.** to alter the sequence or arrangement (of): *endlessly permutating three basic designs.*

permutation (ˌpɜːmju'teɪʃən) *n* **1** *Maths.* **1a** an ordered arrangement of the numbers, terms, etc., of a set into specified groups: *the permutations of a, b, and c, taken two at a time, are ab, ba, ac, ca, bc, cb.* **1b** a group formed in this way. **2** a combination of items, etc., made by reordering. **3** an alteration; transformation. **4** a fixed combination for selections of results on football pools. Usually shortened to **perm.** [C14: from L *permūtātiō*, from *permūtāre* to change thoroughly]
▸ ˌpermu'tational *adj*

permute (pə'mjuːt) *vb* **permutes, permuting, permuted.** (*tr*) **1** to change the sequence of. **2** *Maths.* to subject to permutation. [C14: from L *permūtāre*, from PER- + *mūtāre* to change]

Pernambuco ★ (ˌpɜːnəm'bjuːkəʊ; *Portuguese* pernəm'buku) *n* **1** a state of NE Brazil, on the Atlantic: consists of a humid coastal plain rising to a high inland plateau. Capital: Recife. Pop.: 7 445 200 (1995 est.). Area: 98 280 sq. km (37 946 sq. miles). **2** the former name of **Recife.**

pernicious (pə'nɪʃəs) *adj* **1** wicked or malicious: *pernicious lies.* **2** causing grave harm; deadly. [C16: from L *perniciōsus*, from *perniciēs* ruin, from PER- (intensive) + *nex* death]
▸ per'niciously *adv* ▸ per'niciousness *n*

pernicious anaemia *n* a form of anaemia characterized by lesions of the spinal cord, weakness, sore tongue, diarrhoea, etc.: associated with inadequate absorption of vitamin B$_{12}$.

pernickety (pə'nɪkɪtɪ) *adj Inf.* **1** excessively precise; fussy. **2** (of a task) requiring close attention. [C19: orig. Scot. from ?]

Pernik ★ (*Bulgarian* 'pɛrnik) *n* an industrial town in W Bulgaria, on the Struma River. Pop.: 99 643 (1990). Former name (1962–92): **Dimitrovo** (di'mitrovo).

Perón ★ (*Spanish* pe'rɔn) *n* **1 Juan Domingo** (xwan do-'mɪŋɡo). 1895–1974, Argentine soldier and statesman; dictator (1946–55). He was deposed in 1955, remaining in exile until 1973, when he was elected president (1973–74). **2** his third wife, **María Estella** (ma'ria es'teʎa), known as *Isabel.* born 1931, president of Argentina (1974–76); deposed. **3 (María) Eva (Duarte) de Perón** ('eβa), known as *Evita,* second wife of Juan Domingo Perón. 1919–52, Argentine film actress: active in politics and social welfare (1946–52).
▸ Pe'ronist *n, adj*

peroneal (ˌpɛrə'niːəl) *adj Anat.* of or relating to the fibula. [C19: from NL *peronē,* from Gk: fibula]

perorate ('pɛrəˌreɪt) *vb* **perorates, perorating, perorated.** (*intr*) **1** to speak at length, esp. in a formal manner. **2** to conclude a speech or sum up.

peroration (ˌpɛrə'reɪʃən) *n* the conclusion of a speech or discourse, in which points made previously are summed up. [C15: from L *perōrātiō,* from PER- (thoroughly) + *orāre* to speak]

perovskite (pɛ'rɒvskaɪt) *n* a yellow, brown, or greyish-black mineral. [C19: after *Perovski,* Russian mineralogist]

peroxide (pə'rɒksaɪd) *n* **1** short for **hydrogen peroxide,** esp. when used for bleaching hair. **2** any of a class of metallic oxides, such as sodium peroxide, Na$_2$O$_2$. **3** (*not in technical usage*) any of certain dioxides, such as manganese(VI) oxide, MnO$_2$, that resemble peroxides in their formula. **4** any of a class of organic compounds whose molecules contain two oxygen atoms bound together. **5** (*modifier*) of, relating to, bleached with, or resembling peroxide: *a peroxide blonde.* ◆ *vb* **peroxides, peroxiding, peroxided. 6** (*tr*) to bleach (the hair) with peroxide.

perpendicular (ˌpɜːpən'dɪkjʊlə) *adj* **1** at right angles to a horizontal plane. **2** denoting, relating to, or having the style of Gothic architecture used in England during the 14th and 15th centuries, characterized by tracery having vertical lines. **3** upright; vertical. ◆ *n* **4** *Geom.* a line or plane perpendicular to another. **5** any instrument used for indicating the vertical line through a given point. [C14: from L *perpendiculāris,* from *perpendiculum* a plumb line, from *per-* through + *pendēre* to hang]
▸ perpendicularity (ˌpɜːpənˌdɪkju'lærɪtɪ) *n* ▸ ˌperpen'dicularly *adv*

perpetrate ('pɜːpɪˌtreɪt) *vb* **perpetrates, perpetrating, perpetrated.** (*tr*) to perform or be responsible for (a deception, crime, etc.). [C16: from L *perpetrāre,* from *per-* (thoroughly) + *patrāre* to perform]
▸ ˌperpe'tration *n* ▸ 'perpeˌtrator *n*

> **USAGE NOTE** *Perpetrate* and *perpetuate* are sometimes confused: *he must answer for the crimes he has perpetrated* (not *perpetuated*); *the book helped to perpetuate* (not *perpetrate*) *some of the myths surrounding his early life.*

perpetual (pə'pɛtjʊəl) *adj* **1** (*usually prenominal*) eternal; permanent. **2** (*usually prenominal*) seemingly ceaseless because often repeated: *your perpetual complaints.* [C14: via OF from L *perpetuālis* universal, from *perpes* continuous, from *per-* (thoroughly) + *petere* to go towards]
▸ per'petually *adv*

perpetual debenture *n* a bond or debenture that can either never be redeemed or cannot be redeemed on demand.

perpetual motion *n* motion of a hypothetical mechanism that continues indefinitely without any external source of energy. It is impossible in practice because of friction.

perpetuate (pə'pɛtjuˌeɪt) *vb* **perpetuates, perpetuating, perpetuated.** (*tr*) to cause to continue: *to perpetuate misconceptions.* [C16: from L *perpetuāre* to continue without interruption, from *perpetuus* PERPETUAL]
▸ perˌpetu'ation *n*

> **USAGE NOTE** See at **perpetrate.**

perpetuity (ˌpɜːpɪ'tjuːɪtɪ) *n, pl* **perpetuities. 1** eternity. **2** the state of being perpetual. **3** *Property law.* a limitation preventing the absolute disposal of an estate for longer than the period allowed by law. **4** an annuity that is payable indefinitely. **5 in perpetuity.** forever. [C15: from OF *perpetuite,* from L *perpetuitās* continuity; see PERPETUAL]

Perpignan ★ (*French* pɛrpiɲã) *n* a town in S France: historic capital of Roussillon. Pop.: 108 049 (1990).

perplex (pə'plɛks) vb (tr) **1** to puzzle; bewilder; confuse. **2** to complicate: *to perplex an issue*. [C15: from obs. *perplex* (adj) intricate, from L *perplexus* entangled, from *per-* (thoroughly) + *plectere* to entwine] ▸ **perplexedly** (pə'plɛksɪdlɪ, -'plɛkstlɪ) *adv* ▸ **per'plexingly** *adv*

perplexity (pə'plɛksɪtɪ) *n, pl* **perplexities. 1** the state of being perplexed. **2** the state of being intricate or complicated. **3** something that perplexes.

per pro ('pɜː 'prəʊ) *prep* by delegation to: through the agency of: used when signing documents on behalf of someone else. [L: abbrev. of *per prōcūratiōnem*]

USAGE NOTE See at **pp.**

perquisite ('pɜːkwɪzɪt) *n* **1** an incidental benefit gained from a certain type of employment, such as the use of a company car. **2** a customary benefit received in addition to a regular income. **3** a customary tip. **4** something expected or regarded as an exclusive right. ◆ Often shortened (informal) to **perk**. [C15: from Med. L *perquīsītum*, from L *perquīrere* to seek earnestly for something]

Perrault ★ (French pɛro) *n* **Charles** (ʃarl). 1628–1703, French author, noted for his *Contes de ma mère l'oye* (1697), which contains the fairy tales *Little Red Riding Hood*, *Cinderella*, and *The Sleeping Beauty*.

Perrier water or **Perrier** ('pɛrɪeɪ) *n Trademark.* a sparkling mineral water from the south of France. [C20: after a spring, *Source Perrier*, at Vergèze, France]

Perrin ★ (French pɛrɛ̃) *n* **Jean Baptiste** (ʒɑ̃ batist). 1870–1942, French physicist. His researches on the distribution and diffusion of particles in colloids (1911) gave evidence for the physical reality of molecules, confirmed the explanation of Brownian movement in terms of kinetic theory, and determined the magnitude of the Avogadro constant. He also studied cathode rays: Nobel prize for physics 1926.

perron ('pɛrən) *n* an external flight of steps, esp. one at the front entrance of a building. [C14: from OF, from *pierre* stone, from L *petra*]

perry ('pɛrɪ) *n, pl* **perries.** wine made of pears, similar in taste to cider. [C14 *pereye*, from OF *peré*, ult. from L *pirum* pear]

Perry ★ ('pɛrɪ) *n* **1 Fred(erick John).** 1909–95, British tennis and table-tennis player; world singles table-tennis champion (1929); Wimbledon singles champion (1934–36). **2 Matthew Calbraith.** 1794–1858, US naval officer, who led a naval expedition to Japan that obtained a treaty (1854) opening up Japan to western trade. **3** his brother, **Oliver Hazard.** 1785–1819, US naval officer. His defeat of a British squadron on Lake Erie (1813) was the turning point in the War of 1812, leading to the recapture of Detroit.

pers. *abbrev. for:* **1** person. **2** personal.

Pers. *abbrev. for* Persia(n).

perse (pɜːs) *n* **a** a dark greyish-blue colour. **b** (*as adj*): *perse cloth*. [C14: from OF, from Med. L *persus*, ? changed from L *Persicus* Persian]

Perse ★ (pɜːs; French pɛrs) *n* **Saint-John** ('sɪndʒən), real name *Alexis Saint-Léger*. 1887–1975, French poet, born in Guadeloupe. His works include *Anabase* (1922). Nobel prize for literature 1960.

per se ('pɜː 'seɪ) *adv* by or in itself; intrinsically. [L]

persecute ('pɜːsɪˌkjuːt) *vb* **persecutes, persecuting, persecuted.** (tr) **1** to oppress, harass, or maltreat, esp. because of race, religion, etc. **2** to bother persistently. [C15: from OF, from *persecuteur*, from LL *persecūtor* pursuer, from L *persequī* to take vengeance upon] ▸ ˌperse'cution *n* ▸ 'perse,cutive *adj* ▸ 'perse,cutor *n*

persecution complex *n Psychol.* an acute irrational fear that other people are plotting one's downfall.

Persephone ★ (pə'sɛfənɪ) *n Greek myth.* a daughter of Zeus and Demeter, abducted by Hades and made his wife and queen of the underworld, but allowed part of each year to leave it. Roman counterpart: **Proserpina.**

Persepolis ★ (pə'sɛpəlɪs) *n* the capital of ancient Persia

in the Persian Empire and under the Seleucids: founded by Darius; sacked by Alexander the Great in 330 B.C.

Perseus ★ ('pɜːsɪəs) *n Greek myth.* a son of Zeus and Danaë, who with Athena's help slew the Gorgon Medusa and rescued Andromeda from a sea monster.

perseverance (ˌpɜːsɪ'vɪərəns) *n* **1** continued steady belief or efforts; persistence. **2** *Christian theol.* continuance in a state of grace.

perseveration (pɜːˌsɛvə'reɪʃən) *n Psychol.* the tendency for an impression, idea, or feeling to dissipate only slowly and to recur during subsequent experiences.

persevere (ˌpɜːsɪ'vɪə) *vb* **perseveres, persevering, persevered.** (intr; often foll. by *in*) to show perseverance. [C14: from OF *perseverer*, from L, from *perseverus* very strict; see SEVERE]

Pershing ★ ('pɜːʃɪŋ) *n* **John Joseph,** nickname *Black Jack.* 1860–1948, US general. He was commander in chief of the American Expeditionary Force in Europe (1917–19).

Persia ★ ('pɜːʃə) *n* **1** the former name (until 1935) of **Iran. 2** another name for **Persian Empire.**

Persian ('pɜːʃən) *adj* **1** of or relating to ancient Persia or modern Iran, their inhabitants, or their languages. ◆ *n* **2** a native, citizen, or inhabitant of modern Iran; an Iranian. **3** the language of Iran or Persia in any of its ancient or modern forms.

Persian carpet or **rug** *n* a carpet or rug made in Persia or the Near East by knotting silk or wool yarn by hand onto a woven backing in rich colours and flowing or geometric designs.

Persian cat *n* a long-haired variety of domestic cat.

Persian Empire ★ *n* the S Asian empire established by Cyrus the Great in the 6th century B.C. and overthrown by Alexander the Great in the 4th century B.C. At its height it extended from India to Europe.

Persian Gulf ★ *n* a shallow arm of the Arabian Sea between SW Iran and Arabia: linked with the Arabian Sea by the Strait of Hormuz and the Gulf of Oman; important for the oilfields on its shores. Area: 233 000 sq. km (90 000 sq. miles).

Persian lamb *n* **1** a black loosely curled fur from the karakul lamb. **2** a karakul lamb.

persiennes (ˌpɜːsɪ'ɛnz) *pl n* outside window shutters having louvres. [C19: from F, from *persien* Persian]

persiflage ('pɜːsɪˌflɑːʒ) *n* light frivolous conversation, style, or treatment; friendly teasing. [C18: via F from *persifler* to tease, from *per-* (intensive) + *siffler* to whistle, from L *sībilāre* to whistle]

persimmon (pɜː'sɪmən) *n* **1** any of several tropical trees, typically having hard wood and large orange-red fruit. **2** Also called: **sharon fruit.** the sweet fruit of any of these trees, which is edible when completely ripe. [C17: from Amerind]

Persis ★ ('pɜːsɪs) *n* an ancient region of SW Iran: homeland of the Achaemenid dynasty.

persist (pə'sɪst) *vb* (intr) **1** (often foll. by *in*) to continue steadfastly or obstinately despite opposition. **2** to continue without interruption: *the rain persisted throughout the night.* [C16: from L *persistere*, from *per-* (intensive) + *sistere* to stand steadfast] ▸ per'sister *n*

persistence (pə'sɪstəns) or **persistency** *n* **1** the quality of persisting; tenacity. **2** the act of persisting; continued effort or existence.

persistent (pə'sɪstənt) *adj* **1** showing persistence. **2** incessantly repeated; unrelenting: *your persistent questioning.* **3** (of plant parts) remaining attached to the plant after the normal time of withering. **4** *Zool.* (of parts normally present only in young stages) present in the adult. **5** (of a chemical, esp. when used as a insecticide) slow to break down. ▸ per'sistently *adv*

persistent vegetative state *n Med.* an irreversible condition, resulting from brain damage, characterized by lack of consciousness, thought, and feeling, although reflex activities (such as breathing) continue. Abbrev.: **PVS.**

person ('pɜːsən) *n, pl* **persons. 1** an individual human being. **2** the body of a human being: *guns hidden on his* *person.* **3** a grammatical category into which pronouns and forms of verbs are subdivided depending on whether they refer to the speaker, the person addressed, or some other individual, thing, etc. **4** a human being or a corporation recognized in law as having certain rights and obligations. **5 in person.** actually present: *the author will be there in person.* [C13: from OF *persone,* from L *persōna* mask, ?from Etruscan *phersu* mask]

> **USAGE NOTE** *People* is the word usually used to refer to more than one individual: *there were a hundred people at the reception. Persons* is rarely used, except in official English: *several persons were interviewed.*

-person *n combining form.* sometimes used instead of *-man* and *-woman* or *-lady: chairperson.*

> **USAGE NOTE** See at **-man.**

persona (pɜːˈsəʊnə) *n, pl* **personae** (-niː). **1** (*often pl*) a character in a play, novel, etc. **2** (in Jungian psychology) the mechanism that conceals a person's true thoughts and feelings, esp. in adaptation to the outside world. [L: mask]

personable (ˈpɜːsənəbʰl) *adj* pleasant in appearance and personality.
> ▶ ˈ**personableness** *n* ▶ ˈ**personably** *adv*

personage (ˈpɜːsənɪdʒ) *n* **1** an important or distinguished person. **2** another word for **person** (sense 1). **3** *Rare.* a figure in literature, history, etc.

persona grata *Latin.* (pɜːˈsəʊnə ˈɡrɑːtə) *n, pl* **personae gratae** (pɜːˈsəʊniː ˈɡrɑːtiː). an acceptable person, esp. a diplomat.

personal (ˈpɜːsənʰl) *adj* **1** of or relating to the private aspects of a person's life: *personal letters.* **2** (*prenominal*) of or relating to a person's body, its care, or its appearance: *personal hygiene.* **3** belonging to or intended for a particular person and no-one else: *for your personal use.* **4** (*prenominal*) undertaken by an individual: *a personal appearance by a celebrity.* **5** referring to or involving a person's individual personality, intimate affairs, etc., esp. in an offensive way: *personal remarks; don't be so personal.* **6** having the attributes of an individual conscious being: *a personal God.* **7** of, relating to, or denoting grammatical person. **8** *Law.* of or relating to movable property, as money, etc.

personal column *n* a newspaper column containing personal messages and advertisements.

personal computer *n* a small inexpensive computer used in word processing, computer games, etc.

personal equity plan *n* the full name for **PEP.**

personality (ˌpɜːsəˈnælɪtɪ) *n, pl* **personalities. 1** *Psychol.* the sum total of all the behavioural and mental characteristics by means of which an individual is recognized as being unique. **2** the distinctive character of a person that makes him socially attractive: *a salesman needs a lot of personality.* **3** a well-known person in a certain field, such as entertainment. **4** a remarkable person. **5** (*often pl*) a personal remark.

personalize *or* **personalise** (ˈpɜːsənəˌlaɪz) *vb* **personalizes, personalizing, personalized** *or* **personalises, personalising, personalised.** (*tr*) **1** to endow with personal or individual qualities. **2** to mark (stationery, clothing, etc.) with a person's initials, name, etc. **3** to take (a remark, etc.) personally. **4** another word for **personify.**
> ▶ ˌ**personaliˈzation** *or* ˌ**personaliˈsation** *n*

personally (ˈpɜːsənəlɪ) *adv* **1** without the help or intervention of others: *I'll attend to it personally.* **2** (*sentence modifier*) in one's own opinion or as regards oneself: *personally, I hate onions.* **3** as if referring to oneself: *to take the insults personally.* **4** as a person: *we like him personally, but professionally he's incompetent.*

personal organizer *n* **1** a diary that stores personal

records, appointments, notes, etc. **2** a pocket-sized electronic device that performs the same functions.

personal pronoun *n* a pronoun having a definite person or thing as an antecedent and functioning grammatically in the same way as the noun that it replaces. The personal pronouns include *I, you, he, she, it, we,* and *they.*

personal property *n Law.* movable property, such as furniture or money. Also called: **personalty.** Cf. **real property.**

personal stereo *n* a small audio cassette player worn attached to a belt and used with lightweight headphones.

persona non grata *Latin.* (pɜːˈsəʊnə nɒn ˈɡrɑːtə) *n, pl* **personae non gratae** (pɜːˈsəʊniː nɒn ˈɡrɑːtiː). **1** an unacceptable or unwelcome person. **2** a diplomat who is not acceptable to the government to whom he or she is accredited.

personate (ˈpɜːsəˌneɪt) *vb* **personates, personating, personated.** (*tr*) **1** to act the part of (a character in a play); portray. **2** *Criminal law.* to assume the identity of (another person) with intent to deceive.
> ▶ ˌ**personˈation** *n* ▶ ˈ**personative** *adj* ▶ ˈ**personˌator** *n*

personification (pɜːˌsɒnɪfɪˈkeɪʃən) *n* **1** the attribution of human characteristics to things, abstract ideas, etc. **2** the representation of an abstract quality or idea in the form of a person, creature, etc., as in art and literature. **3** a person or thing that personifies. **4** a person or thing regarded as an embodiment of a quality: *he is the personification of optimism.*

personify (pɜːˈsɒnɪˌfaɪ) *vb* **personifies, personifying, personified.** (*tr*) **1** to attribute human characteristics to (a thing or abstraction). **2** to represent (an abstract quality) in human or animal form. **3** (of a person or thing) to represent (an abstract quality), as in art. **4** to be the embodiment of.
> ▶ **perˈsoniˌfier** *n*

personnel (ˌpɜːsəˈnɛl) *n* **1** the people employed in an organization or for a service. **2a** the department that interviews, appoints, or keeps records of employees. **2b** (*as modifier*): *a personnel officer.* [C19: from F, ult. from LL *personālis* personal (adj); see PERSON]

perspective (pəˈspɛktɪv) *n* **1** a way of regarding situations, facts, etc., and judging their relative importance. **2** the proper or accurate point of view or the ability to see it; objectivity: *try to get some perspective on your troubles.* **3** a view over some distance in space or time; prospect. **4** the theory or art of suggesting three dimensions on a two-dimensional surface, in order to recreate the appearance and spatial relationships that objects or a scene in recession present to the eye. **5** the appearance of objects, buildings, etc., relative to each other, as determined by their distance from the viewer, or the effects of this distance on their appearance. [C14: from Med. L *perspectīva ars* the science of optics, from L *perspicere* to inspect carefully]
> ▶ **perˈspectively** *adv*

Perspex (ˈpɜːspɛks) *n Trademark.* any of various clear acrylic resins.

perspicacious (ˌpɜːspɪˈkeɪʃəs) *adj* acutely perceptive or discerning. [C17: from L *perspicax,* from *perspicere* to look at closely]
> ▶ ˌ**perspiˈcaciously** *adv* ▶ **perspicacity** (ˌpɜːspɪˈkæsɪtɪ) *or* ˌ**perspiˈcaciousness** *n*

perspicuous (pəˈspɪkjʊəs) *adj* (of speech or writing) easily understood; lucid. [C15: from L *perspicuus* transparent, from *perspicere* to explore thoroughly]
> ▶ **perˈspicuously** *adv* ▶ **perˈspicuousness** *or* **perspicuity** (ˌpɜːspɪˈkjuːɪtɪ) *n*

perspiration (ˌpɜːspəˈreɪʃən) *n* **1** the salty fluid secreted by the sweat glands of the skin. **2** the act of secreting this fluid.
> ▶ **perspiratory** (pəˈspaɪrətərɪ) *adj*

perspire (pəˈspaɪə) *vb* **perspires, perspiring, perspired.** to secrete or exude (perspiration) through the pores of the skin. [C17: from L *perspīrāre* to blow, from *per-* (through) + *spīrāre* to breathe]
> ▶ **perˈspiringly** *adv*

persuade (pəˈsweɪd) *vb* **persuades, persuading, persuaded.** (*tr; may take a clause as object or an infinitive*) **1** to induce,

★ people and places

urge, or prevail upon successfully: *he finally persuaded them to buy it.* **2** to cause to believe; convince: *even with the evidence, the police were not persuaded.* [C16: from L *persuādēre,* from *per-* (intensive) + *suādēre* to urge, advise]
▶ **per'suadable** *or* **per'suasible** *adj* ▶ **per,suada'bility** *or* **per,suasi'bility** *n* ▶ **per'suader** *n*

persuasion (pə'sweɪʒən) *n* **1** the act of persuading or of trying to persuade. **2** the power to persuade. **3** a strong belief. **4** an established creed or belief, esp. a religious one. **5** a sect, party, or faction. [C14: from L *persuāsiō*]

persuasive (pə'sweɪsɪv) *adj* having the power or tending to persuade: *a persuasive salesman.*
▶ **per'suasively** *adv* ▶ **per'suasiveness** *n*

pert (pɜːt) *adj* **1** saucy, impudent, or forward. **2** jaunty: *a pert little hat.* **3** *Obs.* clever or brisk. [C13: var. of earlier *apert,* from L *apertus* open, from *aperīre* to open]
▶ **'pertly** *adv* ▶ **'pertness** *n*

pert. *abbrev. for* pertaining.

pertain (pə'teɪn) *vb* (*intr; often foll. by to*) **1** to have reference or relevance: *issues pertaining to women.* **2** to be appropriate: *the product pertains to real user needs.* **3** to belong (to) or be a part (of). [C14: from L *pertinēre,* from *per-* (intensive) + *tenēre* to hold]

Perth ★ (pɜːθ) *n* **1** a city in central Scotland, in Perth and Kinross on the River Tay: capital of Scotland from the 12th century until the assassination of James I there in 1437. Pop.: 41 453 (1991). **2** a city in SW Australia, capital of Western Australia, on the Swan River: major industrial centre; University of Western Australia (1911). Pop.: 1 262 600 (1995 est.).

Perth and Kinross ★ (kɪn'rɒs) *n* a council area of N central Scotland, formed in 1996: mountainous. Administrative centre: Perth. Pop.: 132 570 (1996 est.). Area: 5321 sq. km (2019 sq. miles).

Perthshire ★ ('pɜːθ,ʃɪə, -ʃə) *n* (until 1975) a county of central Scotland, now part of Perth and Kinross council area.

pertinacious (,pɜːtɪ'neɪʃəs) *adj* **1** doggedly resolute in purpose or belief; unyielding. **2** stubbornly persistent. [C17: from L *pertināx,* from *per-* (intensive) + *tenāx* clinging, from *tenēre* to hold]
▶ **,perti'naciously** *adv* ▶ **pertinacity** (,pɜːtɪ'næsɪtɪ) *or* **,perti'naciousness** *n*

pertinent ('pɜːtɪnənt) *adj* relating to the matter at hand; relevant. [C14: from L *pertinēns,* from *pertinēre* to PERTAIN]
▶ **'pertinence** *or* **'pertinency** *n* ▶ **'pertinently** *adv*

perturb (pə'tɜːb) *vb* (*tr; often passive*) **1** to disturb the composure of; trouble. **2** to throw into disorder. **3** *Physics, astron.* to cause (a planet, electron, etc.) to undergo a perturbation. [C14: from OF *pertourber,* from L *perturbāre* to confuse, from *per-* (intensive) + *turbāre* to agitate]
▶ **per'turbable** *adj* ▶ **per'turbing** *adj*

perturbation (,pɜːtə'beɪʃən) *n* **1** the act of perturbing or the state of being perturbed. **2** a cause of disturbance. **3** *Physics.* a secondary influence on a system that modifies simple behaviour, such as the effect of the other electrons on one electron in an atom. **4** *Astron.* a small continuous deviation in the orbit of a planet or comet, due to the attraction of neighbouring planets.

pertussis (pə'tʌsɪs) *n* the technical name for **whooping cough.** [C18: NL, from L *per-* (intensive) + *tussis* cough]
▶ **per'tussal** *adj*

Peru (pə'ruː) *n* a republic in W South America, on the Pacific: the centre of the great Inca Empire when conquered by the Spanish in 1532; gained independence in 1824 by defeating Spanish forces with armies led by San Martín and Bolívar; consists of a coastal desert, rising to the Andes; an important exporter of minerals and a major fishing nation. Official languages: Spanish, Quechua, and Aymara. Official religion: Roman Catholic. Currency: nuevo sol. Capital: Lima. Pop.: 24 371 000 (1997). Area: 1 285 215 sq. km (496 222 sq. miles).
▶ **Peru'vian** ('ruːvɪən) *adj, n*

Peru Current *n* a cold ocean current flowing northwards off the Pacific coast of South America. Also called: **Humboldt Current.**

Perugia ★ (pə'ruːdʒə; *Italian* pe'ruːdʒa) *n* **1** a city in cen-

tral Italy, in Umbria: centre of the Umbrian school of painting (15th century); university (1308); Etruscan and Roman remains. Pop.: 147 489 (1994 est.). Ancient name: **Pe'rusia. 2 Lake.** another name for (Lake) **Trasimene.**

Perugino ★ (*Italian* peru'dʒino) *n* **Il** (il), real name *Pietro Vannucci.* 1446–1523, Italian painter. His works include the fresco *Christ giving the Keys to Peter* in the Sistine Chapel, Rome.

peruke (pə'ruːk) *n* a wig for men in the 17th and 18th centuries. Also called: **periwig.** [C16: from F *perruque,* from It. *perrucca* wig, from ?]

peruse (pə'ruːz) *vb* **peruses, perusing, perused.** (*tr*) **1** to read or examine with care; study. **2** to browse or read in a leisurely way. [C15 (meaning: to use up): from PER- (intensive) + USE]
▶ **pe'rusal** *n* ▶ **pe'ruser** *n*

Perutz ★ (pə'ruts) *n* **Max Ferdinand.** born 1914, British biochemist, born in Austria. With J. C. Kendrew, he worked on the structure of haemoglobin and shared the Nobel prize for chemistry 1962.

Peruzzi ★ (*Italian* pe'ruttsi) *n* **Baldassare Tommaso** (baldas-'saːre tom'maːzo). 1481–1536, Italian architect and painter of the High Renaissance. The design of the Palazzo Massimo, Rome, is attributed to him.

perv (pɜːv) *Sl.* ◆ *n* **1** a pervert. **2** *Austral.* a lascivious look. ◆ *vb also* **perve.** (*intr*) *Austral.* to behave like a voyeur.

pervade (pɜː'veɪd) *vb* **pervades, pervading, pervaded.** (*tr*) to spread through or throughout, esp. subtly or gradually; permeate. [C17: from L *pervādere,* from *per-* through + *vādere* to go]
▶ **pervasion** (pɜː'veɪʒən) *n* ▶ **pervasive** (pɜː'veɪsɪv) *adj* ▶ **per'vasively** *adv* ▶ **per'vasiveness** *n*

perverse (pə'vɜːs) *adj* **1** deliberately deviating from what is regarded as normal, good, or proper. **2** persistently holding to what is wrong. **3** wayward or contrary; obstinate. [C14: from OF *pervers,* from L *perversus* turned the wrong way]
▶ **per'versely** *adv* ▶ **per'verseness** *or* **per'versity** *n*

perversion (pə'vɜːʃən) *n* **1** any abnormal means of obtaining sexual satisfaction. **2** the act of perverting or the state of being perverted. **3** a perverted form or usage.

pervert *vb* (pə'vɜːt). (*tr*) **1** to use wrongly or badly. **2** to interpret wrongly or badly; distort. **3** to lead into deviant or perverted beliefs or behaviour; corrupt. **4** to debase. ◆ *n* ('pɜːvɜːt). **5** a person who practises sexual perversion. [C14: from OF *pervertir,* from L *pervertere* to turn the wrong way]
▶ **per'verted** *adj* ▶ **per'verter** *n* ▶ **per'vertible** *adj* ▶ **per'versive** *adj*

pervious ('pɜːvɪəs) *adj* **1** able to be penetrated; permeable. **2** receptive to new ideas, etc.; open-minded. [C17: from L *pervius,* from *per-* (through) + *via* a way]
▶ **'perviously** *adv* ▶ **'perviousness** *n*

pes (peɪz, piːz) *n, pl* **pedes** ('pediːz). the technical name for the human **foot.** [C19: NL: foot]

Pesaro ★ (*Italian* 'peːzaro) *n* a port and resort in E central Italy, in the Marches on the Adriatic. Pop.: 90 340 (1990). Ancient name: **Pisaurum** (pɪ'saʊrəm).

Pescadores ★ (,peskə'dɔːrɪz) *pl n* a group of 64 islands in Formosa Strait, separated from Taiwan (to which it belongs) by the **Pescadores Channel.** Pop.: 91 263 (1995). Area: 127 sq. km (49 sq. miles). Chinese names: **Penghu, P'eng-hu.**

Pescara ★ (*Italian* pes'kaːra) *n* a city and resort in E central Italy, on the Adriatic. Pop.: 120 613 (1994 est.).

peseta (pə'seɪtə; *Spanish* pe'seta) *n* the standard monetary unit of Spain, divided into 100 céntimos. [C19: from Sp., dim. of PESO]

Peshawar (pə'ʃɔːə) *n* a city in N Pakistan, at the E end of the Khyber Pass: one of the oldest cities in Pakistan and capital of the ancient kingdom of Gandhara; university (1950). Pop.: 1 676 000 (1995 est.).

pesky ('peskɪ) *adj* **peskier, peskiest.** *US & Canad. inf.* troublesome. [C19: prob. changed from *pesty;* see PEST]
▶ **'peskily** *adv* ▶ **'peskiness** *n*

peso ('peɪsəʊ; *Spanish* 'peso) *n, pl* **pesos** (-səʊz; *Spanish* -sos). the standard monetary unit of Argentina, Chile,

Colombia, Cuba, the Dominican Republic, Guinea-Bissau, Mexico, the Philippines, and Uruguay. [C16: from Sp.: weight, from L *pēnsum* something weighed out, from *pendere* to weigh]

pessary ('pesərɪ) *n, pl* **pessaries.** *Med.* **1** a device for inserting into the vagina, either as a support for the uterus or (**diaphragm pessary**) as a contraceptive. **2** a vaginal suppository. [C14: from LL *pessārium*, from L *pessum*, from Gk *pessos* plug]

pessimism ('pesɪ,mɪzəm) *n* **1** the tendency to expect the worst in all things. **2** the doctrine of the ultimate triumph of evil over good. **3** the doctrine that this world is corrupt and that man's sojourn in it is a preparation for some other existence. [C18: from L *pessimus* worst, sup. of *malus* bad]
▸ **'pessimist** *n* ▸ ,**pessi'mistic** *adj* ▸ ,**pessi'mistically** *adv*

Pessoa ★ (*Portuguese* pə'soə) *n* **Fernando** (fər'nəndu). 1888–1935, Portuguese poet, who ascribed much of his work to three imaginary poets, Alvaro de Campos, Alberto Caeiro, and Ricardo Reis.

pest (pest) *n* **1** a person or thing that annoys, esp. by imposing itself when it is not wanted; nuisance. **2** any organism that damages crops, or injures or irritates livestock or man. **3** *Rare.* an epidemic disease. [C16: from L *pestis* plague, from ?]

Pestalozzi ★ (,pestə'lɒtsɪ) *n* **Johann Heinrich** (jo'han 'haɪnrɪç). 1746–1827, Swiss educational reformer, who emphasized learning by observation.

pester ('pestə) *vb* (*tr*) to annoy or nag continually. [C16: from OF *empestrer* to hobble (a horse), from Vulgar L *impāstōriāre* (unattested) to use a hobble, ult. from L *pastor* herdsman]

pesticide ('pestɪ,saɪd) *n* a chemical used for killing pests, esp. insects.
▸ ,**pesti'cidal** *adj*

pestiferous (pe'stɪfərəs) *adj* **1** *Inf.* troublesome; irritating. **2** breeding, carrying, or spreading infectious disease. **3** corrupting; pernicious. [C16: from L *pestifer*, from *pestis* contagion + *ferre* to bring]

pestilence ('pestɪləns) *n* **1a** any epidemic of a deadly infectious disease, such as the plague. **1b** such a disease. **2** an evil influence.

pestilent ('pestɪlənt) *adj* **1** annoying; irritating. **2** highly destructive morally or physically; pernicious. **3** likely to cause epidemic or infectious disease. [C15: from L *pestilens* unwholesome, from *pestis* plague]
▸ **'pestilently** *adv* ▸ **pestilential** (,pestɪ'lenʃəl) *adj*
▸ ,**pesti'lentially** *adv*

pestle ('pesəl) *n* **1** a club-shaped instrument for mixing or grinding substances in a mortar. **2** a tool for pounding or stamping. ◆ *vb* **pestles, pestling, pestled. 3** to pound (a substance or object) with or as if with a pestle. [C14: from OF *pestel*, from L *pistillum*]

pesto ('pestəʊ) *n* a sauce for pasta, consisting of basil leaves, nuts, garlic, oil, and Parmesan cheese, all crushed together. [It., shortened form of *pestato*, p.p. of *pestare* to pound, crush]

pet[1] (pet) *n* **1** a tame animal kept for companionship, amusement, etc. **2** a person who is fondly indulged; favourite: *teacher's pet.* ◆ *adj* **3** kept as a pet: *a pet dog.* **4** of or for pet animals: *pet food.* **5** particularly cherished: *a pet hatred.* **6** familiar or affectionate: *a pet name.* ◆ *vb* **pets, petting, petted. 7** (*tr*) to treat (a person, animal, etc.) as a pet; pamper. **8** (*tr*) to pat or fondle (an animal, child, etc.). **9** (*intr*) *Inf.* (of two people) to caress each other in an erotic manner. [C16: from ?]
▸ **'petter** *n*

pet[2] (pet) *n* a fit of sulkiness, esp. at what is felt to be a slight; pique. [C16: from ?]

PET (pet) *n acronym for* positron emission tomography.

Pet. *Bible. abbrev. for* Peter.

peta- *prefix denoting* 10[15]: *petametres.* Symbol: P [C20: so named because it is the SI prefix after TERA-; on the model of PENTA-, the prefix after TETRA-]

Pétain ★ (*French* petɛ̃) *n* **Henri Philippe Omer** (ɑ̃ri filip ɔmɛr). 1856–1951, French marshal, noted for his victory at Verdun (1916) in World War I and his leadership of the

pro-Nazi government of unoccupied France at Vichy (1940–44); imprisoned for treason (1945).

petal ('petəl) *n* any of the separate parts of the corolla of a flower: often brightly coloured. [C18: from NL *petalum*, from Gk *petalon* leaf]
▸ **'petaline** *adj* ▸ **'petalled** *adj* ▸ **'petal-,like** *adj*

-petal *adj combining form.* seeking: *centripetal.* [from NL *-petus*, from L *petere* to seek]

petard (pɪ'tɑːd) *n* **1** (formerly) a device containing explosives used to breach a wall, doors, etc. **2** hoist with one's own petard. being the victim of one's own schemes, etc. [C16: from F: firework, from *péter* to break wind, from L *pēdere*]

petaurist (pə'tɔːrɪst) *n* another name for **flying phalanger**. [C19: from L, from Gk *petauristēs* performer on the springboard]

petcock ('pet,kɒk) *n* a small valve for checking the water content of a steam boiler or draining waste from the cylinder of a steam engine. [C19: from PET[1] or ? F *pet*, from *péter* to break wind + COCK[1]]

petechia (pɪ'tiːkɪə) *n, pl* **petechiae** (-kɪ,iː). a minute discoloured spot on the surface of the skin. [C18: via NL from It. *petecchia* freckle, from ?]
▸ **pe'techial** *adj*

peter[1] ('piːtə) *vb* (*intr*; foll. by *out* or *away*) to fall (off) in volume, intensity, etc., and finally cease. [C19: from ?]

peter[2] ('piːtə) *n Sl.* **1** a safe, till, or cashbox. **2** a prison cell. [C17 (meaning a case): from the name *Peter*]

Peter ★ ('piːtə) *n New Testament.* **Saint.** Also called: **Simon Peter.** died ?67 A.D., a fisherman of Bethsaida, who became leader of the apostles and is regarded by Roman Catholics as the first pope; probably martyred at Rome.

Peter I ★ *n* known as *Peter the Great.* 1672–1725, tsar of Russia (1682–1725), who assumed sole power in 1689. He introduced many reforms in government and technology, acquired new territories for Russia in the Baltic, and founded the new capital of St Petersburg (1703).

Peter III ★ *n* 1728–62, grandson of Peter I and tsar of Russia (1762): deposed in a coup d'état led by his wife (later Catherine II); assassinated.

Peterborough ★ ('piːtəbərə, -brə) *n* **1** a city and unitary authority in central England, in N Cambridgeshire on the River Nene: industrial centre; under development as a new town since 1968. Pop.: 134 788 (1991). **2** Soke of. a former administrative area in E central England: absorbed into Cambridgeshire in 1974. **3** a city in SE Canada, in SE Ontario: manufacturing centre. Pop.: 62 500 (1990).

Peterlee ★ ('piːtə,liː) *n* a new town in Co. Durham, founded in 1948. Pop.: 23 500 (1990).

peterman ('piːtəmən) *n, pl* **petermen.** *Sl.* a burglar skilled in safe-breaking. [C19: from PETER[2]]

Petermann Peak ★ ('piːtəmən) *n* a mountain in E Greenland. Height: 2932 m (9645 ft).

Peter Pan *n* a youthful, boyish, or immature man. [C20: after the main character in *Peter Pan* (1904), a play by J. M. BARRIE]

Peter Principle *n* the. the theory, usually taken facetiously, that all members in a hierarchy rise to their own level of incompetence. [C20: from the book *The Peter Principle* (1969) by Dr Lawrence J. *Peter* and Raymond Hull]

Petersburg ★ ('piːtəz,bɜːg) *n* a city in SE Virginia, on the Appomattox River: scene of prolonged fighting (1864–65) during the final months of the American Civil War. Pop.: 38 386 (1990).

petersham ('piːtəʃəm) *n* **1** a thick corded ribbon used to stiffen belts, etc. **2** a heavy woollen fabric used for coats, etc. **3** a kind of overcoat made of such fabric. [C19: after Viscount *Petersham* (died 1851), E army officer]

Peterson ★ ('piːtəsᵊn) *n* **Oscar** (**Emmanuel**). born 1925, Black Canadian jazz pianist and singer.

Peter's pence *or* **Peter pence** *n* **1** an annual tax, originally of one penny, formerly levied for the maintenance of the Papal See: abolished by Henry VIII in 1534. **2** a voluntary contribution made by Roman Catholics in

★ people and places

many countries for the same purpose. [C13: referring to St PETER, considered as the first pope]

Peters' projection *n* a form of modified Mercator's map projection that gives prominence to Third World countries. [C20: after Arno *Peters*, G historian]

Peter the Hermit ★ *n* ?1050–1115, French monk and preacher of the First Crusade.

pethidine ('pεθɪ,di:n) *n* a white crystalline water-soluble drug used as an analgesic. [C20: ? a blend of PIPERIDINE + ETHYL]

petiole ('pεtɪ,əʊl) *n* **1** the stalk by which a leaf is attached to the plant. **2** *Zool.* a slender stalk or stem, as between the thorax and abdomen of ants. [C18: via F from L *petiolus* little foot, from *pēs* foot]
▸ **petiolate** ('pεtɪə,leɪt) *adj*

petit ('pεtɪ) *adj* (*prenominal*) *Chiefly law.* of lesser importance; small. [C14: from OF: little, from ?]

Petit ★ (*French* pəti) *n* **Roland** (rɔlɑ̃). born 1924, French ballet dancer and choreographer. His innovative ballets include *Carmen* (1949) and *Kraanerg* (1969).

petit bourgeois ('bʊəʒwɑ:) *n, pl* **petits bourgeois** ('bʊəʒwɑ:z). **1** Also called: **petite bourgeoisie, petty bourgeoisie.** the section of the middle class with the lowest social status, as shopkeepers, lower clerical staff, etc. **2** a member of this stratum. ◆ *adj* **3** of, relating to, or characteristic of the petit bourgeois, esp. indicating a sense of self-righteousness and conformity to established standards of behaviour.

petite (pə'ti:t) *adj* (of a woman) small, delicate, and dainty. [C18: from F, fem of *petit* small]

petit four (fɔ:) *n, pl* **petits fours** (fɔ:z). any of various very small fancy cakes and biscuits. [F, lit.: little oven]

petition (pɪ'tɪʃən) *n* **1** a written document signed by a large number of people demanding some form of action from a government or other authority. **2** any formal request to a higher authority; entreaty. **3** *Law.* a formal application in writing made to a court asking for some specific judicial action: *a petition for divorce.* **4** the action of petitioning. ◆ *vb* **5** (*tr*) to address or present a petition to (a person in authority, government, etc.): *to petition Parliament.* **6** (*intr;* foll. by *for*) to seek by petition: *to petition for a change in the law.* [C14: from L *petītiō*, from *petere* to seek]
▸ **pe'titionary** *adj*

petitioner (pɪ'tɪʃənə) *n* **1** a person who presents a petition. **2** *Chiefly Brit.* the plaintiff in a divorce suit.

petitio principii (pɪ'tɪʃɪ,əʊ prɪn'kɪpɪ,aɪ) *n Logic.* a form of fallacious reasoning in which the conclusion has been assumed in the premises; begging the question. [C16: L, translation of Gk *to en arkhei aiteisthai* an assumption at the beginning]

petit jury *n* a jury of 12 persons empanelled to determine the facts of a case and decide the issue pursuant to the direction of the court on points of law. Also called: **petty jury.**
▸ **petit juror** *n*

petit larceny *n* (formerly, in England) the stealing of property valued at 12 pence or under. Abolished 1827. Also called: **petty larceny.**

petit mal (mæl) *n* a mild form of epilepsy characterized by periods of impairment or loss of consciousness for up to 30 seconds. Cf. **grand mal.** [C19: F: little illness]

petit point ('pεtɪ 'pɔɪnt; *French* pəti pwε̃) *n* **1** a small diagonal needlepoint stitch used for fine detail. **2** work done with such stitches. [F: small point]

Petőfi ★ (*Hungarian* 'pεtø:fi) *n* **Sándor** ('ʃɑːndor). 1823–49, Hungarian lyric poet and patriot.

Petra ★ ('pεtrə, 'pi:trə) *n* an ancient city in the south of present-day Jordan; capital of the Nabataean kingdom.

Petrarch ★ ('pεtrɑːk) *n* Italian name *Francesco Petrarca.* 1304–74, Italian lyric poet and scholar, who greatly influenced the values of the Renaissance. His collection of poems *Canzoniere,* inspired by his ideal love for Laura, was written in the Tuscan dialect. He also wrote much in Latin.
▸ **Pe'trarchan** *adj*

Petrarchan sonnet *n* a sonnet form associated with

the poet Petrarch, having an octave rhyming a b b a a b b a and a sestet rhyming either c d e c d e or c d c d c d.

petrel ('pεtrəl) *n* any of a family of oceanic birds having a hooked bill and tubular nostrils: includes albatrosses, storm petrels, and shearwaters. [C17: var. of earlier *pitteral,* associated by folk etymology with St *Peter,* because the bird appears to walk on water]

Petri dish ('pεtrɪ) *n* a shallow dish, often with a cover, used in laboratories, esp. for producing cultures of microorganisms. [C19: after J. R. *Petri* (1852–1921), G bacteriologist]

Petrie ★ ('pεtrɪ) *n* Sir (**William Matthew**) **Flinders.** 1853–1942, British Egyptologist and archaeologist.

petrifaction (,pεtrɪ'fækʃən) *or* **petrification** (,pεtrɪfɪ-'keɪʃən) *n* **1** the act or process of forming petrified organic material. **2** the state of being petrified.

Petrified Forest ★ *n* a national park in E Arizona, containing petrified coniferous trees about 170 000 000 years old.

petrify ('pεtrɪ,faɪ) *vb* **petrifies, petrifying, petrified. 1** (*tr; often passive*) to convert (organic material) into a fossilized form by impregnation with dissolved minerals so that the original appearance is preserved. **2** to make or become dull, unresponsive, etc.; deaden. **3** (*tr; often passive*) to stun or daze with horror, fear, etc. [C16: from F *pétrifier,* ult. from Gk *petra* stone]
▸ **'petri,fier** *n*

petro- *or before a vowel* **petr-** *combining form.* **1** indicating stone or rock: *petrology.* **2** indicating petroleum, its products, etc.: *petrochemical.* **3** of or relating to the production, export, or sale of petroleum: *petrostate.* [from Gk *petra* rock *or petros* stone]

petrochemical (,pεtrəʊ'kεmɪkᵊl) *n* **1** any substance, such as acetone or ethanol, obtained from petroleum. ◆ *adj* **2** of, concerned with, or obtained from petrochemicals or related to petrochemistry.
▸ **,petro'chemistry** *n*

petrodollar ('pεtrəʊ,dɒlə) *n* money earned by a country by the exporting of petroleum.

petroglyph ('pεtrə,glɪf) *n* a drawing or carving on rock, esp. a prehistoric one. [C19: via F from Gk *petra* stone + *gluphē* carving]

Petrograd ★ ('pεtrəʊ,græd; *Russian* pɪtra'grat) *n* a former name (1914–24) of **Saint Petersburg** (sense 1).

petrography (pε'trɒgrəfɪ) *n* the branch of petrology concerned with the description and classification of rocks.
▸ **pe'trographer** *n* ▸ **petrographic** (,pεtrə'græfɪk) *or* **,petro-'graphical** *adj*

petrol ('pεtrəl) *n* any one of various volatile flammable liquid mixtures of hydrocarbons, obtained from petroleum and used as a solvent and a fuel for internal-combustion engines. US and Canad. name: **gasoline.** [C16: via F from Med. L PETROLEUM]

petrolatum (,pεtrə'leɪtəm) *n* a translucent gelatinous substance obtained from petroleum; used as a lubricant and in medicine as an ointment base. Also called: **petroleum jelly.**

petrol bomb *n* **1** a device filled with petrol that bursts into flames on impact. ◆ *vb* **petrol-bomb.** (*tr*) **2** to attack with petrol bombs.

petrol engine *n* an internal-combustion engine that uses petrol as fuel.

petroleum (pə'trəʊlɪəm) *n* a dark-coloured thick flammable crude oil occurring in sedimentary rocks, consisting mainly of hydrocarbons. Fractional distillation separates the crude oil into petrol, paraffin, diesel oil, lubricating oil, etc. Fuel oil, paraffin wax, asphalt, and carbon black are extracted from the residue. [C16: from Med. L, from L *petra* stone + *oleum* oil]

petroleum jelly *n* another name for **petrolatum.**

petrology (pε'trɒlədʒɪ) *n, pl* **petrologies.** the study of the composition, origin, structure, and formation of rocks.
▸ **petrological** (,pεtrə'lɒdʒɪkᵊl) *adj* ▸ **pe'trologist** *n*

petrol station *n Brit.* another term for **filling station.**

Petronius ★ (pɪ'trəʊnɪəs) *n* **Gaius** ('gaɪəs), known as *Petronius Arbiter.* died 66 A.D., Roman satirist, supposed author of the *Satyricon,* a picaresque account of the licentiousness of contemporary society.

Petropavlovsk ★ (*Russian* pɪtra'pavləfsk) *n* a city in N Kazakhstan, on the Ishim River. Pop.: 239 000 (1995 est.).

Petrópolis ★ (*Portuguese* pe'trɔpulis) *n* a city in SE Brazil, north of Rio de Janeiro: resort. Pop.: 164 849 (1991).

petrous ('pɛtrəs, 'piː-) *adj Anat.* denoting the dense part of the temporal bone that surrounds the inner ear. [C16: from L *petrōsus* full of rocks]
▸ **petrosal** (pe'trəus'l) *adj*

Petrovsk ★ (*Russian* pɪ'trɔfsk) *n* the former name (until 1921) of **Makhachkala**.

Petrozavodsk ★ (*Russian* pɪtrəza'vɔtsk) *n* a city in NW Russia, capital of the Karelian Autonomous Republic, on Lake Onega: developed around ironworks established by Peter the Great in 1703; university (1940). Pop.: 280 000 (1995 est.).

Petsamo ★ (*Finnish* 'pɛtsamɔ) *n* a former territory of N Finland ceded by the Soviet Union to Finland in 1920 and taken back in 1940; now in NW Russia.

petticoat ('pɛtɪˌkəut) *n* 1 a woman's underskirt. 2 *Inf.* 2a a humorous or mildly disparaging name for a woman. 2b (*as modifier*): *petticoat politics.* [C15: see PETTY, COAT]

pettifogger ('pɛtɪˌfɒgə) *n* 1 a lawyer who conducts unimportant cases, esp. one who resorts to trickery. 2 any person who quibbles. [C16: from PETTY + *fogger,* from ?, perhaps from *Fugger,* a family (C15–16) of G financiers]
▸ **'petti,foggery** *n* ▸ **'petti,fog** *vb* **'petti,fogs, 'petti,fogging, 'petti,fogged.** (*intr*) ▸ **'petti,fogging** *adj*

pettish ('pɛtɪʃ) *adj* peevish; petulant. [C16: from PET²]
▸ **'pettishly** *adv* ▸ **'pettishness** *n*

petty ('pɛtɪ) *adj* **pettier, pettiest.** 1 trivial; trifling: *petty details.* 2 narrow-minded, mean: *petty spite.* 3 minor or subordinate in rank: *petty officialdom.* 4 *Law.* a variant of **petit.** [C14: from OF PETIT]
▸ **'pettily** *adv* ▸ **'pettiness** *n*

petty cash *n* a small cash fund for minor incidental expenses.

petty jury *n* a variant of **petit jury.**

petty larceny *n* a variant of **petit larceny.**

petty officer *n* a noncommissioned officer in a naval service comparable in rank to a sergeant in an army or marine corps.

petty sessions *n* (*functioning as sing or pl*) another term for **magistrates' court.**

petulant ('pɛtjʊlənt) *adj* irritable, impatient, or sullen in a peevish or capricious way. [C16: via OF from L *petulāns* bold, from *petulāre* (unattested) to attack playfully, from *petere* to assail]
▸ **'petulance** *or* **'petulancy** *n* ▸ **'petulantly** *adv*

petunia (pɪ'tjuːnɪə) *n* any plant of a tropical American genus cultivated for their colourful funnel-shaped flowers. [C19: via NL from obs. F *petun* variety of tobacco, from Tupi *petyn*]

petuntse (pɪ'tʌntsɪ, -'tʊn-) *n* a fusible mineral used in hard-paste porcelain. [C18: from Chinese, from *pe* white + *tun* heap + *tzu* offspring]

Pevsner ★ ('pɛvznə) *n* 1 **Antoine** (ātwan). 1886–1962, French constructivist sculptor and painter, born in Russia; brother of Naum Gabo. 2 Sir **Nikolaus** ('nɪkəlaus). 1902–83, British architectural historian, born in Germany: his monumental series *Buildings of England* (1951–74) describes every structure of account in the country.

pew (pjuː) *n* 1 (in a church) 1a one of several long benchlike seats with backs, used by the congregation. 1b an enclosed compartment reserved for the use of a family or other small group. 2 *Brit. inf.* a seat (esp. in **take a pew**). [C14 *pywe,* from OF, from L *podium* a balcony, from Gk *podion* supporting structure, from *pous* foot]

pewit *or* **peewit** ('piːwɪt) *n* other names for **lapwing.** [C13: imit. of the bird's cry]

pewter ('pjuːtə) *n* 1a any of various alloys containing tin, lead, and sometimes copper and antimony. 1b (*as modifier*): *pewter ware; a pewter tankard.* 2 plate or kitchen utensils made from pewter. [C14: from OF *peaultre,* from ?]
▸ **'pewterer** *n*

peyote (peɪ'əʊtɪ, pɪ-) *n* another name for **mescal** (the plant). [Mexican Sp., from Nahuatl *peyotl*]

pF *abbrev. for* picofarad.

pf. *abbrev for:* 1 perfect. 2 Also: **pfg.** pfennig. 3 preferred.

Pfalz ★ (pfalts) *n* the German name for the **Palatinate.**

pfennig ('fɛnɪg; *German* 'pfɛnɪç) *n, pl* **pfennigs** *or* **pfennige** (*German* -nɪgə). a German monetary unit worth one hundredth of a Deutschmark. [G: PENNY]

PFI (in Britain) *abbrev. for* Private Finance Initiative.

Pforzheim ★ (*German* 'pfɔrtshaim) *n* a city in Germany, in W Baden-Württemberg: centre of the German watch and jewellery industry. Pop.: 117 960 (1995 est.).

PG *symbol for* a film certified for viewing by anyone, but which contains scenes that may be unsuitable for children, for whom parental guidance is necessary. [C20: from abbrev. of *parental guidance*]

pg. *abbrev. for* page.

Pg. *abbrev. for:* 1 Portugal. 2 Portuguese.

PGR *abbrev. for* psychogalvanic response.

pH *n* potential of hydrogen; a measure of the acidity or alkalinity of a solution. Pure water has a pH of 7, acid solutions have a pH less than 7, and alkaline solutions a pH greater than 7.

phacelia (fæ'siːlɪə) *n* any of a genus of N American plants having clusters of blue flowers. [NL from Gk *phakelos* a cluster]

Phaeacian ★ (fiː'eɪʃən) *n Greek myth.* one of a race of people inhabiting the island of Scheria visited by Odysseus on his way home from the Trojan War.

Phaedra ★ ('fiːdrə) *n Greek myth.* the wife of Theseus, who falsely accused her stepson Hippolytus of raping her because he spurned her amorous advances.

Phaedrus ★ ('fiːdrəs) *n* ?15 B.C.–?50 A.D., Roman author of five books of Latin verse fables, based chiefly on Aesop.

Phaëthon ★ ('feɪəθən) *n Greek myth.* the son of Helios (the sun god) who borrowed his father's chariot and nearly set the earth on fire by approaching too close to it. Zeus averted the catastrophe by striking him down with a thunderbolt.

phaeton ('feɪt'n) *n* a light four-wheeled horse-drawn carriage with or without a top. [C18: from PHAËTHON]

-phage *n combining form.* indicating something that eats or consumes something specified: *bacteriophage.* [from Gk *-phagos;* see PHAGO-]
▸ **-phagous** *adj combining form.*

phago- *or before a vowel* **phag-** *combining form.* eating, consuming, or destroying: *phagocyte.* [from Gk *phagein* to consume]

phagocyte ('fægəˌsaɪt) *n* a cell or protozoan that engulfs particles, such as microorganisms.
▸ **phagocytic** (ˌfægə'sɪtɪk) *adj*

phagocytosis (ˌfægəsaɪ'təʊsɪs) *n* the process by which a cell, such as a white blood cell, ingests microorganisms, other cells, etc.

-phagy *or* **-phagia** *n combining form.* indicating an eating or devouring: *anthropophagy.* [from Gk *-phagia;* see PHAGO-]

phalange ('fælændʒ) *n, pl* **phalanges** (fæ'lændʒiːz). *Anat.* another name for **phalanx** (sense 4). [C16: via F, ult. from Gk PHALANX]

phalangeal (fə'lændʒɪəl) *adj Anat.* of or relating to a phalanx or phalanges.

phalanger (fə'lændʒə) *n* any of various Australasian arboreal marsupials having dense fur and a long tail. Also called (Austral. and NZ): **possum.** See also **flying phalanger.** [C18: via NL from Gk *phalaggion* spider's web, referring to its webbed hind toes]

phalanx ('fælæŋks) *n, pl* **phalanxes** *or* **phalanges** (fæ'lændʒiːz). 1 an ancient Greek and Macedonian battle formation of hoplites presenting long spears from behind a wall of overlapping shields. 2 any closely ranked unit or mass of people: *the police formed a phalanx to pro-*

tect the embassy. **3** a number of people united for a common purpose. **4** *Anat.* any of the bones of the fingers or toes. **5** *Bot.* a bundle of stamens. [C16: via L from Gk: infantry formation in close ranks, bone of finger or toe]

phalarope ('fælə,rəup) *n* any of a family of aquatic shore birds of northern oceans and lakes, having a long slender bill and lobed toes. [C18: via F from NL *Phalaropus*, from Gk *phalaris* coot + *pous* foot]

phallic ('fælɪk) *adj* **1** of, relating to, or resembling a phallus: *a phallic symbol.* **2** *Psychoanal.* relating to a stage of psychosexual development during which a male child's interest is concentrated on the genital organs. **3** of or relating to phallicism.

phallicism ('fælɪ,sɪzəm) *or* **phallism** *n* the worship or veneration of the phallus.

phallus ('fæləs) *n, pl* **phalluses** *or* **phalli** (-laɪ). **1** another word for **penis**. **2** an image of the male sexual organ, esp. as a symbol of reproductive power. [C17: via LL from Gk *phallos*]

-phane *n combining form.* indicating something resembling a specified substance: *cellophane.* [from Gk *phainein* to shine, appear]

phanerogam ('fænərəu,gæm) *n* any plant of a former major division which included all seed-bearing plants; a former name for **spermatophyte**. [C19: from NL *phanerogamus*, from Gk *phaneros* visible + *gamos* marriage]
▸ **phanero'gamic** *or* **phanerogamous** (,fænə'rɒgəməs) *adj*

phantasm ('fæntæzəm) *n* **1** a phantom. **2** an illusory perception of an object, person, etc. [C13: from OF *fantasme*, from L *phantasma*, from Gk]
▸ **phan'tasmal** *or* **phan'tasmic** *adj*

phantasmagoria (,fæntæzmə'gɔːrɪə) *or* **phantasmagory** (fæn'tæzmǝgəri) *n* **1** *Psychol.* a shifting medley of real or imagined figures, as in a dream. **2** *Films.* a sequence of pictures made to vary in size rapidly. **3** a shifting scene composed of different elements. [C19: prob. from F, from PHANTASM + *-agorie*, ?from Gk *ageirein* to gather together]
▸ **phantasmagoric** (,fæntæzmə'gɒrɪk) *or* **phantasma-'gorical** *adj*

phantasy ('fæntəsɪ) *n, pl* **phantasies.** an archaic spelling of **fantasy**.

phantom ('fæntəm) *n* **1a** an apparition or spectre. **1b** (*as modifier*): *a phantom army marching through the sky.* **2** the visible representation of something abstract, esp. as in a dream or hallucination: *phantoms of evil haunted his sleep.* **3** something apparently unpleasant or horrific that has no material form. [C13: from OF *fantosme*, from L *phantasma*]

phantom limb *n* the illusion that a limb still exists following its amputation, sometimes with the sensation of pain (**phantom limb pain**).

phantom pregnancy *n* the occurrence of signs of pregnancy, such as enlarged abdomen and absence of menstruation, when no embryo is present, due to hormonal imbalance. Also called: **false pregnancy**.

-phany *n combining form.* indicating a manifestation: *theophany.* [from Gk *-phania*, from *phainein* to show]
▸ **-phanous** *adj combining form.*

phar., Phar., pharm., *or* **Pharm.** *abbrev. for:* **1** pharmaceutical. **2** pharmacist. **3** pharmacopoeia. **4** pharmacy.

Pharaoh ('feǝrəu) *n* the title of the ancient Egyptian kings. [OE *Pharaon*, via L, Gk, & Heb., ult. from Egyptian *pr-'o* great house]
▸ **Pharaonic** (feǝ'rɒnɪk) *adj*

Pharisaic (,færɪ'seɪɪk) *or* **Pharisaical** *adj* **1** *Judaism.* of, relating to, or characteristic of the Pharisees or Pharisaism. **2** (*often not cap.*) righteously hypocritical.
▸ **Phari'saically** *adv*

Pharisaism ('færɪseɪ,ɪzəm) *or* **Phariseeism** ('færɪsiː,ɪzəm) *n* **1** *Judaism.* the tenets and customs of the Pharisees. **2** (*often not cap.*) observance of the external forms of religion without genuine belief; hypocrisy.

Pharisee ('færɪ,siː) *n* **1** a member of an ancient Jewish sect teaching strict observance of Jewish traditions. **2** (*often not cap.*) a self-righteous or hypocritical person.

[OE *Farīsēus*, ult. from Aramaic *perīshāiyā*, pl. of *perīsh* separated]

pharmaceutical (,fɑːmə'sjuːtɪk'l) *or* (*less commonly*) **pharmaceutic** *adj* of or relating to drugs or pharmacy. [C17: from LL *pharmaceuticus*, from Gk *pharmakeus* purveyor of drugs; see PHARMACY]
▸ **,pharma'ceutically** *adv*

pharmaceutics (,fɑːmə'sjuːtɪks) *n* **1** (*functioning as sing*) another term for **pharmacy** (sense 1). **2** pharmaceutical remedies.

pharmacist ('fɑːməsɪst) *n* a person qualified to prepare and dispense drugs.

pharmaco- *combining form.* indicating drugs: *pharmacology.* [from Gk *pharmakon* drug]

pharmacognosy (,fɑːmə'kɒgnəsɪ) *n* the study of crude drugs of plant and animal origin. [C19: from PHARMACO- + *gnosy*, from Gk *gnosis* knowledge]
▸ **,pharma'cognosist** *n*

pharmacology (,fɑːmə'kɒlədʒɪ) *n* the science or study of drugs, including their characteristics, action, and uses.
▸ **pharmacological** (,fɑːməkə'lɒdʒɪk'l) *adj* ▸ **,pharmaco-'logically** *adv* ▸ **,pharma'cologist** *n*

pharmacopoeia *or US* (*sometimes*) **pharmacopeia** (,fɑːmǝkǝ'piːǝ) *n* an authoritative book containing a list of medicinal drugs with their uses, preparation, dosages, formulas, etc. [C17: via NL from Gk *pharmakopoiia* art of preparing drugs, from PHARMACO- + *-poiia*, from *poiein* to make]
▸ **,pharmaco'poeial** *adj*

pharmacy ('fɑːməsɪ) *n, pl* **pharmacies. 1** Also: **pharmaceutics.** the practice or art of preparing and dispensing drugs. **2** a dispensary. [C14: from Med. L *pharmacia*, from Gk *pharmakeia* making of drugs, from *pharmakon* drug]

pharos ('feǝrɒs) *n* any marine lighthouse or beacon. [C16: after a large Hellenistic lighthouse on an island off Alexandria in Egypt]

Pharsalus ★ (fɑː'seɪləs) *n* an ancient town in Thessaly in N Greece. Several major battles were fought nearby, including Caesar's victory over Pompey (48 B.C.).

pharyngeal (,færɪn'dʒiːǝl) *or* **pharyngal** (fǝ'rɪŋg'l) *adj* **1** of, relating to, or situated in or near the pharynx. **2** *Phonetics.* pronounced with an articulation in or constriction of the pharynx. [C19: from NL *pharyngeus*; see PHARYNX]

pharyngitis (,færɪn'dʒaɪtɪs) *n* inflammation of the pharynx.

pharynx ('færɪŋks) *n, pl* **pharynges** (fæ'rɪndʒiːz) *or* **pharynxes.** the part of the alimentary canal between the mouth and the oesophagus. [C17: via NL from Gk *pharunx* throat]

phase (feɪz) *n* **1** any distinct or characteristic period or stage in a sequence of events: *there were two phases to the resolution.* **2** *Astron.* one of the recurring shapes of the portion of the moon or an inferior planet illuminated by the sun. **3** *Physics.* the fraction of a cycle of a periodic quantity that has been completed at a specific reference time, expressed as an angle. **4** *Physics.* a particular stage in a periodic process or phenomenon. **5 in phase.** (of two waveforms) reaching corresponding phases at the same time. **6 out of phase.** (of two waveforms) not in phase. **7** *Chem.* a distinct state of matter characterized by homogeneous composition and properties and the possession of a clearly defined boundary. **8** *Zool.* a variation in the normal form of an animal, esp. a colour variation, brought about by seasonal or geographical change. ◆ *vb* **phases, phasing, phased.** (*tr*) **9** (*often passive*) to execute, arrange, or introduce gradually or in stages: *the withdrawal was phased over several months.* **10** (*sometimes foll. by with*) to cause (a part, process, etc.) to function or coincide with (another part, etc.): *he tried to phase the intake and output of the machine; he phased the intake with the output.* **11** *Chiefly US.* to arrange (processes, goods, etc.) to be supplied or executed when required. [C19: from NL *phases*, pl. of *phasis*, from Gk: aspect]
▸ **'phasic** *adj*

★ people and places

phase in vb (tr, adv) to introduce in a gradual or cautious manner: *the legislation was phased in over two years.*

phase modulation n a type of modulation in which the phase of a radio carrier wave is varied by an amount proportional to the instantaneous amplitude of the modulating signal.

phase out vb (tr, adv) **1** to discontinue or withdraw gradually. ◆ n **phase-out.** **2** *Chiefly US.* the action or an instance of phasing out: *a phase-out of conventional forces.*

phase rule n the principle that in any system in equilibrium the number of degrees of freedom is equal to the number of components less the number of phases plus two.

-phasia n combining form. indicating speech disorder of a specified kind: *aphasia.* [from Gk, from *phanai* to speak]
▸ **-phasic** adj and n combining form.

phatic ('fætɪk) adj (of speech) used to establish social contact and to express sociability rather than specific meaning. [C20: from Gk *phat(os)* spoken + -IC]

PhD abbrev. for Doctor of Philosophy. Also: **DPhil.**

pheasant ('fɛzᵊnt) n **1** any of various long-tailed gallinaceous birds, having a brightly-coloured plumage in the male: native to Asia but introduced elsewhere. **2** any of various other related birds, including the quails and partridges. **3** *US & Canad.* any of several other gallinaceous birds, esp. the ruffed grouse. [C13: from OF *fesan*, from L *phāsiānus*, from Gk *phasianos ornis* Phasian bird, after the River *Phasis*, in Colchis]

Phebe ★ ('fiːbɪ) n a variant spelling of **Phoebe.**

Pheidippides or **Phidippides ★** (faɪ'dɪpɪˌdiːz) n Athenian athlete, who ran to Sparta to seek help against the Persians before the Battle of Marathon (490 B.C.).

phellem ('fɛləm) n Bot. the technical name for **cork** (sense 4). [C20: from Gk *phellos* cork + PHLOEM]

phenacetin (fɪ'næsɪtɪn) n a white crystalline solid used in medicine to relieve pain and fever. Also called: **acetophenetidin.** [C19: from PHENO- + ACETYL + -IN]

phenix ('fiːnɪks) n a US spelling of **phoenix.**

pheno- or before a vowel **phen-** combining form. **1** showing or manifesting: *phenotype.* **2** indicating that a molecule contains benzene rings: *phenobarbitone.* [from Gk *phaino-* shining, from *phainein* to show; its use in a chemical sense is exemplified in *phenol,* so called because orig. prepared from illuminating gas]

phenobarbitone (ˌfiːnəʊ'bɑːbɪˌtəʊn) or **phenobarbital** (ˌfiːnəʊ'bɑːbɪtᵊl) n a white crystalline derivative of barbituric acid used as a sedative for treating insomnia and epilepsy.

phenocryst ('fiːnəˌkrɪst, 'fɛn-) n any of several large crystals in igneous rocks such as porphyry. [C19: from PHENO- (shining) + CRYSTAL]

phenol ('fiːnɒl) n **1** Also called: **carbolic acid.** a white crystalline derivative of benzene, used as an antiseptic and disinfectant and in the manufacture of resins, explosives, and pharmaceuticals. Formula: C_6H_5OH. **2** *Chem.* any of a class of organic compounds whose molecules contain one or more hydroxyl groups bound directly to a carbon atom in an aromatic ring.
▸ **phe'nolic** adj

phenolic resin n any one of a class of resins derived from phenol, used in paints, adhesives, and as thermosetting plastics.

phenology (fɪ'nɒlədʒɪ) n the study of recurring phenomena, such as animal migration, esp. as influenced by climatic conditions. [C19: from PHENO(MENON) + -LOGY]
▸ **phenological** (ˌfiːnə'lɒdʒɪkᵊl) adj ▸ **phe'nologist** n

phenolphthalein (ˌfiːnɒl'θeɪliːn, -lɪɪn, -'θæl-) n a colourless crystalline compound used in medicine as a laxative and in chemistry as an indicator. [from PHENO- + *phthal-,* short form of NAPHTHALENE + -IN]

phenomena (fɪ'nɒmɪnə) n a plural of **phenomenon.**

phenomenal (fɪ'nɒmɪnᵊl) adj **1** of or relating to a phenomenon. **2** extraordinary; outstanding; remarkable: *a phenomenal achievement.* **3** *Philosophy.* known or perceived by the senses rather than the mind.
▸ **phe'nomenally** adv

phenomenalism (fɪ'nɒmɪnəˌlɪzəm) n *Philosophy.* the doctrine that statements about physical objects and the external world can be analysed in terms of possible or actual experiences, and that entities, such as physical objects, are only mental constructions out of phenomenal appearances.
▸ **phe'nomenalist** n, adj

phenomenology (fɪˌnɒmɪ'nɒlədʒɪ) n *Philosophy.* **1** the movement that concentrates on the detailed description of conscious experience. **2** the science of phenomena as opposed to the science of being.
▸ **phenomenological** (fɪˌnɒmɪnə'lɒdʒɪkᵊl) adj

phenomenon (fɪ'nɒmɪnən) n, pl **phenomena** (-ɪnə) or **phenomenons.** **1** anything that can be perceived as an occurrence or fact by the senses. **2** any remarkable occurrence or person. **3** *Philosophy.* **3a** the object of perception, experience, etc. **3b** (in the writings of Kant) a thing as it appears, as distinguished from its real nature as a thing-in-itself. [C16: via LL from Gk *phainomenon,* from *phainesthai* to appear, from *phainein* to show]

> **USAGE NOTE** Although *phenomena* is often treated as if it were singular, correct usage is to employ *phenomenon* with a singular construction and *phenomena* with a plural: *that is an interesting phenomenon* (not *phenomena*); *several new phenomena were recorded in his notes.*

phenotype ('fiːnəʊˌtaɪp) n the physical constitution of an organism as determined by the interaction of its genetic constitution and the environment.
▸ **phenotypic** (ˌfiːnəʊ'tɪpɪk) or **pheno'typical** adj ▸ **pheno-'typically** adv

phenyl ('fiːnaɪl, 'fɛnɪl) n (*modifier*) of, containing, or consisting of the monovalent group C_6H_5, derived from benzene: *a phenyl group.*

phenylalanine (ˌfiːnaɪl'æləˌniːn) n an essential amino acid; a component of proteins.

phenylbutazone (ˌfiːnaɪl'bjuːtəˌzəʊn) n an anti-inflammatory drug used in the treatment of rheumatic diseases. [C20: from (*dioxodi*)*phenylbut*(*ylpr*)*azo*(*lidi*)*ne*]

phenylketonuria (ˌfiːnaɪlˌkiːtə'njʊərɪə) n a congenital metabolic disorder characterized by the abnormal accumulation of phenylalanine in the body fluids, resulting in mental deficiency. [C20: NL; see PHENYL, KETONE, -URIA]

pheromone ('fɛrəˌməʊn) n a chemical substance, secreted externally by certain animals, such as insects, affecting the behaviour of other animals of the same species. [C20 *phero-,* from Gk *pherein* to bear + (HOR)MONE]

phew (fjuː) interj an exclamation of relief, surprise, disbelief, weariness, etc.

phi (faɪ) n, pl **phis.** the 21st letter in the Greek alphabet, Φ, φ.

phial ('faɪəl) n a small bottle for liquids, etc.; vial. [C14: from OF *fiole,* from L *phiola* saucer, from Gk *phialē* wide shallow vessel]

Phi Beta Kappa ('faɪ 'beɪtə 'kæpə, 'biːtə) n (in the US) **1** a national honorary society, founded in 1776, membership of which is based on high academic ability. **2** a member of this society. [from the initials of the Gk motto *philosophia biou kubernētēs* philosophy the guide of life]

Phidias ★ ('fɪdɪˌæs) n 5th century B.C., Greek sculptor, regarded as one of the greatest of sculptors. He executed the sculptures of the Parthenon and the colossal statue of Zeus at Olympia, one of the Seven Wonders of the World: neither survives in the original.
▸ **'Phidian** adj

Phidippides ★ (faɪ'dɪpɪˌdiːz) n a variant spelling of **Pheidippides.**

phil. abbrev. for: **1** philharmonic. **2** philosophy.

Phil. abbrev. for: **1** Philadelphia. **2** Bible. Philippians. **3** Philippines. **4** Philharmonic.

Philadelphia ★ (ˌfɪlə'dɛlfɪə) n a city and port in SE Pennsylvania, at the confluence of the Delaware and

> ★ people and places

hiladelphus

Schuylkill Rivers: the fourth largest city in the US;
(1790–1800); scene of the Continental Congresses
(1774–83) and the signing of the Declaration of Inde-

hiladelphus (ˌfɪləˈdɛlfəs) *n* any of a N temperate genus
Gk *philadelphon* mock orange, lit.: loving one's brother]

hilae ★ (ˈfaɪliː) *n* an island in Upper Egypt, in the Nile

hilander (fɪˈlændə) *vb* (*intr*; often foll. by *with*) (of a
fond of men, used as a name for a lover in literary works]
▸ phiˈlanderer *n*

hilanthropic (ˌfɪlənˈθrɒpɪk) *or* **philanthropical** *adj*
▸ ˌphilanˈthropically *adv*

hilanthropy (fɪˈlænθrəpɪ) *n*, *pl* **philanthropies**. **1** the
2 love of mankind in general. [C17: from LL
philanthrōpia, from Gk: love of mankind, from *philos* lov-
▸ phiˈlanthropist *or* philanthrope (ˈfɪlənˌθrəup) *n*

hilately (fɪˈlætəlɪ) *n* the collection and study of postage
▸ **philatelic** (ˌfɪləˈtɛlɪk) *adj* ▸ ˌphilaˈtelically *adv* ▸ phi-
ˈlatelist *n*

Philby ★ (ˈfɪlbɪ) *n* **Harold**, known as *Kim*. 1912–88, British
double agent; defected to the Soviet Union (1963).

-phile *or* **-phil** *n combining form*. indicating a person or

Philem. *Bible*. *abbrev*. for Philemon.

Philemon[1] ★ (faɪˈliːmɒn) *n New Testament*. **1** a Christian
the book (in full **The Epistle of Paul the Apostle to Philemon**),

Philemon[2] ★ (faɪˈliːmɒn) *n Greek myth*. a poor Phrygian,

philharmonic (ˌfɪlhɑːˈmɒnɪk, ˌfɪlə-) *adj* **1** fond of music.
2 (*cap. when part of a name*) denoting an orchestra, choir,
society, etc., devoted to music. ◆ *n* **3** (*cap. when part of a

philhellene (fɪlˈhɛliːn) *n* **1** a lover of Greece and Greek
Greek national independence.
▸ **philhellenic** (ˌfɪlheˈliːnɪk) *adj*

-philia *n combining form*. **1** indicating a tendency towards:
haemophilia. **2** indicating an abnormal liking for:
necrophilia. [from Gk *philos* loving]
▸ **-philiac** *n combining form*. ▸ **-philous** *or* **-philic** *adj com-

philibeg (ˈfɪlɪˌbɛg) *n* a variant spelling of filibeg.

Philip ★ (ˈfɪlɪp) *n* **1** *New Testament*. **1a** an apostle from
Bethsaida (John 1:43–51; 6:5–7; 12:21; 14:8). **1b** Also
pointed by the early Church. **1c** Also called: **Philip the Tetrarch**. one of the sons of Herod the Great, who was ruler
of part of former Judaea (4 B.C.–34 A.D.) (Luke 3:1). **2 King**,
American Indian name *Metacomet*. died 1676, American
Indian chief, the son of Massasoit. He waged King
Philip's War against the colonists of New England
(1675–76) and was killed in battle. **3 Prince**. another

Philip II ★ *n* **1** 382–336 B.C., king of Macedonia (359–
336); the father of Alexander the Great. **2** known as
Philip Augustus. 1165–1223, Capetian king of France
(1180–1223); set out on the Third Crusade with Richard

I of England (1190). **3** 1527–98, king of Spain (1556–98)
Counter-Reformation, sending the Armada against Eng-

Philip IV ★ *n* known as *Philip the Fair*. 1268–1314, king

Philip V ★ *n* 1683–1746, king of Spain (1700–46) and

Philip VI ★ *n* 1293–1350, first Valois king of France
(1328–50). Edward III of England claimed his throne,
Hundred Years' War (1337).

Philippeville ★ (ˈfɪlɪpˌvɪl) *n* the former name of **Skikda**.

Philippi ★ (fɪˈlɪpaɪ, ˈfɪlɪ-) *n* an ancient city in NE Macedo-
Brutus and Cassius (42 B.C.).
▸ Phiˈlippian *adj*

philippic (fɪˈlɪpɪk) *n* a bitter or impassioned speech of
Demosthenes, against PHILIP of Macedon]

Philippine (ˈfɪlɪˌpiːn) *n*, *adj* another word for **Filipino**.

Philippines ★ (ˈfɪlɪˌpiːnz, ˌfɪlɪˈpiːnz) *n* (*functioning as
sing*) **Republic of the**. a republic in SE Asia, occupying an
Mindanao, Samar, and Negros): became a Spanish col-
ony in 1571 but ceded to the US in 1898 after the
Spanish-American War; gained independence in 1946.
The islands are generally mountainous and volcanic. Of-
Religion: chiefly Roman Catholic. Currency: peso. Capi-
tal: Manila. Pop.: 71 539 000 (1997). Area: 300 076 sq.

Philippine Sea ★ *n* part of the NW Pacific Ocean, east
and north of the Philippines.

Philippopolis ★ (ˌfɪlɪˈpɒpəlɪs) *n* transliteration of the
Greek name for **Plovdiv**.

Philip the Good ★ *n* 1396–1467, duke of Burgundy
(1419–67), under whose rule Burgundy was one of the

Philistia ★ (fɪˈlɪstɪə) *n* an ancient country on the coast of
SW Palestine.
▸ Phiˈlistian *adj*

Philistine (ˈfɪlɪˌstaɪn) *n* **1** a person who is hostile towards
culture, the arts, etc.; a smug boorish person. **2** a mem-
Philistia. ◆ *adj* **3** (*sometimes not cap.*) boorishly uncul-
▸ **Philistinism** (ˈfɪlɪstɪˌnɪzəm) *n*

Phillip ★ (ˈfɪlɪp) *n* **Arthur**. 1738–1814, British naval commander: founded New South Wales.

Phillips ★ (ˈfɪlɪps) *n* Captain **Mark**. born 1948, British

phillumenist (fɪˈljuːməˌnɪst, -ˈluː-) *n* a person who col-
+ -IST]

philo- *or before a vowel* **phil-** *combining form*. indicating a
love of: *philology; philanthropic*. [from Gk *philos* loving]

Philoctetes ★ (ˌfɪlɒkˈtiːtiːz, fɪˈlɒktɪˌtiːz) *n Greek myth*. a
hero of the Trojan War, in which he killed Paris with the

philodendron (ˌfɪləˈdendrən) *n*, *pl* **philodendrons** *or*
philodendra (-drə). an evergreen climbing plant of a tropi-
NL from Gk: lover of trees]

philogyny (fɪˈlɒdʒɪnɪ) *n Rare*. fondness for women.
[C17: from Gk *philogunia*, from PHILO- + *gunē* woman]
▸ phiˈlogynist *n*

Philo Judaeus ★ (ˈfaɪləu dʒuːˈdiːəs) *n* ?20 B.C.–?50 A.D.,
Jewish philosopher, born in Alexandria. He sought to

★ people and places

philology (fɪˈlɒlədʒɪ) *n* **1** comparative and historical linguistics. **2** the scientific analysis of written records and literary texts. **3** (no longer in scholarly use) the study of literature. [C17: from L *philologia*, from Gk: love of language]
▸ **philological** (ˌfɪləˈlɒdʒɪkəl) *adj* ▸ ˌ**philoˈlogically** *adv*
▸ **phiˈlologist** or (less commonly) **phiˈlologer** *n*

philomel (ˈfɪləˌmɛl) or **philomela** (ˌfɪləˈmiːlə) *n poetic* names for a **nightingale**. [C14 *philomene*, via Med. L from L *philomēla*, from Gk]

Philomela ★ (ˌfɪləʊˈmiːlə) *n Greek myth*. an Athenian princess, who was raped and had her tongue cut out by her brother-in-law Tereus, and subsequently was transformed into a nightingale. See **Procne**.

philoprogenitive (ˌfɪləʊprəʊˈdʒɛnɪtɪv) *adj Rare*. **1** fond of children. **2** producing many offspring.

philos. *abbrev. for:* **1** philosopher. **2** philosophical.

philosopher (fɪˈlɒsəfə) *n* **1** a student, teacher, or devotee of philosophy. **2** a person of philosophical temperament, esp. one who is patient, wise, and stoical. **3** (formerly) an alchemist or devotee of occult science.

philosopher's stone *n* a stone or substance thought by alchemists to be capable of transmuting base metals into gold.

philosophical (ˌfɪləˈsɒfɪkəl) or **philosophic** *adj* **1** of or relating to philosophy or philosophers. **2** reasonable, wise, or learned. **3** calm and stoical, esp. in the face of difficulties or disappointments.
▸ ˌ**philoˈsophically** *adv*

philosophical analysis *n* a philosophical method in which language and experience are analysed in an attempt to provide new insights into various philosophical problems.

philosophize or **philosophise** (fɪˈlɒsəˌfaɪz) *vb* **philosophizes, philosophizing, philosophized** or **philosophises, philosophising, philosophised**. **1** (*intr*) to make philosophical pronouncements and speculations. **2** (*tr*) to explain philosophically.
▸ **phiˈlosoˌphizer** or **phiˈlosoˌphiser** *n*

philosophy (fɪˈlɒsəfɪ) *n, pl* **philosophies**. **1** the academic discipline concerned with making explicit the nature and significance of ordinary and scientific beliefs and investigating the intelligibility of concepts by means of rational argument concerning their presuppositions, implications, and interrelationships. **2** the particular doctrines relating to these issues of a specific individual or school: *the philosophy of Descartes*. **3** the basic principles of a discipline: *the philosophy of law*. **4** any system of belief, values, or tenets. **5** a personal outlook or viewpoint. **6** serenity of temper. [C13: from OF *filosofie*, from L *philosophia*, from Gk, from *philosophos* lover of wisdom]

-philous or **-philic** *adj combining form*. indicating love of or fondness for: *heliophilous*. [from L *-philus*, from Gk *-philos*]

philtre or *US* **philter** (ˈfɪltə) *n* a drink supposed to arouse desire. [C16: from L *philtrum*, from Gk *philtron* love potion, from *philos* loving]

phimosis (faɪˈməʊsɪs) *n* abnormal tightness of the foreskin, preventing its being retracted. [C17: via NL from Gk: a muzzling]

phiz (fɪz) *n Sl., chiefly Brit*. the face or a facial expression. Also called: **phizog** (fɪˈzɒɡ). [C17: colloquial shortening of PHYSIOGNOMY]

Phiz ★ (fɪz) *n* real name *Hablot Knight Browne*. 1815–82, British painter, noted for his illustrations for Dickens' novels.

phlebitis (flɪˈbaɪtɪs) *n* inflammation of a vein. [C19: via NL from Gk]
▸ **phlebitic** (flɪˈbɪtɪk) *adj*

phlebo- or before a vowel **phleb-** *combining form*. indicating a vein: *phlebotomy*. [from Gk *phleps, phleb-* vein]

phlebotomy (flɪˈbɒtəmɪ) *n, pl* **phlebotomies**. surgical incision into a vein. [C14: from OF *flebothomie*, from LL *phlebotomia*, from Gk]

Phlegethon ★ (ˈflɛɡɪˌθɒn) *n Greek myth*. a river of fire in Hades. [C14: from Gk, lit.: blazing, from *phlegethein* to flame, blaze]

phlegm (flɛm) *n* **1** the viscid mucus secreted by the walls of the respiratory tract. **2** *Arch*. one of the four bodily humours. **3** apathy; stolidity. **4** imperturbability; coolness. [C14: from OF *fleume*, from LL *phlegma*, from Gk: inflammation, from *phlegein* to burn]
▸ **ˈphlegmy** *adj*

phlegmatic (flɛɡˈmætɪk) or **phlegmatical** *adj* **1** having a stolid or unemotional disposition. **2** not easily excited.
▸ **phlegˈmatically** *adv*

phloem (ˈfləʊɛm) *n* tissue in higher plants that conducts synthesized food substances to all parts of the plant. [C19: via G from Gk *phloos* bark]

phlogiston (flɒˈdʒɪstɒn, -tən) *n Chem*. a hypothetical substance formerly thought to be present in all combustible materials. [C18: via NL from Gk, from *phlogizein* to set alight]

phlox (flɒks) *n, pl* **phlox** or **phloxes**. any of a chiefly North American genus of plants cultivated for their clusters of white, red, or purple flowers. [C18: via L from Gk: a plant of glowing colour, lit.: flame]

phlyctena (flɪkˈtiːnə) *n, pl* **phlyctenae** (-niː). *Pathol*. a small blister, vesicle, or pustule. [C17: via NL from Gk *phluktaina*, from *phluzein* to swell]

Phnom Penh or **Pnom Penh** ★ (ˌnɒm ˈpɛn) *n* the capital of Cambodia, a port in the south at the confluence of the Mekong and Tonle Sap Rivers: capital of the country since 1865; university (1960). Pop.: 920 000 (1994 est.).

-phobe *n combining form*. indicating one that fears or hates: *xenophobe*. [from Gk *-phobos* fearing]
▸ **-phobic** *adj combining form*.

phobia (ˈfəʊbɪə) *n Psychiatry*. an abnormal intense and irrational fear of a given situation, organism, or object. [C19: from Gk *phobos* fear]
▸ **ˈphobic** *adj, n*

-phobia *n combining form*. indicating an extreme abnormal fear of or aversion to: *acrophobia; claustrophobia*. [via L from Gk, from *phobos* fear]
▸ **-phobic** *adj combining form*.

Phocaea ★ (fəʊˈsiːə) *n* an ancient port in Asia Minor, the northernmost of Ionian cities on the W coast of Asia Minor: an important maritime state (about 1000–600 B.C.).

Phocis ★ (ˈfəʊsɪs) *n* an ancient district of central Greece, on the Gulf of Corinth: site of the Delphic oracle.

phocomelia (ˌfəʊkəʊˈmiːlɪə) *n* a congenital deformity characterized esp. by short stubby hands or feet attached close to the body. [C19: via NL from Gk *phōkē* a seal + *melos* a limb]

phoebe (ˈfiːbɪ) *n* any of several greyish-brown North American flycatchers. [C19: imit.]

Phoebe or **Phebe** ★ (ˈfiːbɪ) *n* **1** *Classical myth*. a Titaness, who later became identified with Artemis (Diana) as goddess of the moon. **2** *Poetic*. a personification of the moon.

Phoebus ★ (ˈfiːbəs) *n* **1** Also called: **Phoebus Apollo**. *Greek myth*. Apollo as the sun god. **2** *Poetic*. a personification of the sun. [C14: via L from Gk *Phoibos* bright; related to *phaos* light]

Phoenicia ★ (fəˈnɪʃɪə, -ˈniː-) *n* an ancient maritime country extending from the Mediterranean Sea to the Lebanon Mountains, now occupied by the coastal regions of Lebanon and parts of Syria and Israel: consisted of a group of city-states, at their height between about 1200 and 1000 B.C., that were leading traders of the ancient world.

Phoenician (fəˈnɪʃən, -ˈniːʃən) *n* **1** a member of an ancient Semitic people of NW Syria. **2** the extinct language of this people. ◆ *adj* **3** of Phoenicia, the Phoenicians, or their language.

phoenix or *US* **phenix** (ˈfiːnɪks) *n* **1** a legendary Arabian bird said to set fire to itself and rise anew from the ashes every 500 years. **2** a person or thing of surpassing beauty or quality. [OE *fenix*, via L from Gk *phoinix*]

Phoenix ★ (ˈfiːnɪks) *n* a city in central Arizona, capital

★ people and places

city of the state, on the Salt River. Pop.: 1 048 949 (1994 est.).

Phoenix Islands ★ *pl n* a group of eight coral islands in the central Pacific: administratively part of Kiribati. Area: 28 sq. km (11 sq. miles).

Phomvihane ★ (ˈpɒmvɪhɑːn) *n* **Kaysone** (ˈkaɪsɒn). 1920–92, Laotian Communist statesman; prime minister of Laos (1975–91); president (1991–92).

phon (fɒn) *n* a unit of loudness that measures the intensity of a sound by the number of decibels it is above a reference tone. [C20: via G from Gk *phōnē* sound]

phonate (fəʊˈneɪt) *vb* **phonates, phonating, phonated.** (*intr*) to articulate speech sounds, esp. voiced speech sounds. [C19: from Gk *phōnē* voice]
▸ pho'nation *n*

phone[1] (fəʊn) *n, vb* **phones, phoning, phoned.** short for **telephone.**

phone[2] (fəʊn) *n Phonetics.* a single speech sound. [C19: from Gk *phōnē* sound, voice]

-phone *combining form.* **1** (*forming nouns*) indicating a device giving off sound: *telephone.* **2** (*forming nouns and adjectives*) (a person) speaking a particular language: *Francophone.* [from Gk *phōnē* voice, sound]
▸ -phonic *adj combining form.*

phonecard (ˈfəʊnˌkɑːd) *n* a card used instead of coins to operate certain public telephones.

phone-in *n* **a** a radio or television programme in which listeners' or viewers' questions, comments, etc., are telephoned to the studio and broadcast live as part of a discussion. **b** (*as modifier*): *a phone-in programme.*

phoneme (ˈfəʊniːm) *n Linguistics.* one of the set of speech sounds in any given language that serve to distinguish one word from another. [C20: via F from Gk *phōnēma* sound, speech]
▸ phonemic (fəˈniːmɪk) *adj*

phonemics (fəˈniːmɪks) *n* (*functioning as sing*) that aspect of linguistics concerned with the classification and analysis of the phonemes of a language.
▸ pho'nemicist *n*

phonetic (fəˈnɛtɪk) *adj* **1** of or relating to phonetics. **2** denoting any perceptible distinction between one speech sound and another. **3** conforming to pronunciation: *phonetic spelling.* [C19: from NL *phōnēticus*, from Gk, from *phōnein* to make sounds, speak]
▸ pho'netically *adv*

phonetics (fəˈnɛtɪks) *n* (*functioning as sing*) the science concerned with the study of speech processes, including the production, perception, and analysis of speech sounds.
▸ phonetician (ˌfəʊnɪˈtɪʃən) *or* phonetist (ˈfəʊnɪtɪst) *n*

phoney *or esp. US* **phony** (ˈfəʊnɪ) *Inf.* ◆ *adj* **phonier, phoniest.** **1** not genuine; fake. **2** (of a person) insincere or pretentious. ◆ *n, pl* **phoneys** *or esp. US* **phonies.** **3** an insincere or pretentious person. **4** something that is not genuine; a fake. [C20: from ?]
▸ 'phoneyness *or esp. US* 'phoniness *n*

phonics (ˈfɒnɪks) *n* (*functioning as sing*) **1** an obsolete name for **acoustics** (sense 1). **2** a method of teaching people to read by training them to associate letters with their phonetic values.
▸ 'phonic *adj* ▸ 'phonically *adv*

phono- *or before a vowel* **phon-** *combining form.* indicating a sound or voice: *phonograph; phonology.* [from Gk *phōnē* voice, sound]

phonogram (ˈfəʊnəˌgræm) *n* any written symbol standing for a sound, syllable, morpheme, or word.
▸ ˌphono'gramic *or* ˌphono'grammic *adj*

phonograph (ˈfəʊnəˌgrɑːf) *n* **1** an early form of gramophone capable of recording and reproducing sound on wax cylinders. **2** an obsolete US and Canad. word for **gramophone** or **record player.**

phonography (fəʊˈnɒgrəfɪ) *n* **1** a writing system that represents sounds by individual symbols. **2** the employment of such a writing system.
▸ phonographic (ˌfəʊnəˈgræfɪk) *adj*

phonology (fəˈnɒlədʒɪ) *n, pl* **phonologies.** **1** the study of

the sound system of a language or of languages in general. **2** such a sound system.
▸ phonological (ˌfəʊnəˈlɒdʒɪkˈl, ˌfɒn-) *adj* ▸ ˌphono'logically *adv* ▸ pho'nologist *n*

phonon (ˈfəʊnɒn) *n Physics.* a quantum of vibrational energy in the acoustic vibrations of a crystal lattice. [C20: from PHONO- + -ON]

-phony *n combining form.* indicating a specified type of sound: *cacophony; euphony.* [from Gk *-phōnia*, from *phōnē* sound]
▸ -phonic *adj combining form.*

phooey (ˈfuːɪ) *interj Inf.* an exclamation of scorn, contempt, etc. [C20: prob. var. of PHEW]

-phore *n combining form.* indicating one that bears or produces: *semaphore.* [from NL *-phorus*, from Gk *-phoros* bearing, from *pherein* to bear]
▸ -phorous *adj combining form.*

-phoresis *n combining form.* indicating a transmission: *electrophoresis.* [from Gk *phorēsis* being carried, from *pherein* to bear]

phormium (ˈfɔːmɪəm) *n* any of a genus of plants of the lily family with tough leathery evergreen leaves. Also called: **New Zealand flax, flax lily.** [C19: NL from Gk *phormos* basket]

phosgene (ˈfɒzdʒiːn) *n* a colourless poisonous gas: used in chemical warfare and in the manufacture of pesticides, dyes, and polyurethane resins. [C19: from Gk *phōs* light + *-gene*, var. of -GEN]

phosphate (ˈfɒsfeɪt) *n* **1** any salt or ester of any phosphoric acid. **2** (*often pl*) any of several chemical fertilizers containing phosphorous compounds. [C18: from F *phosphat*; see PHOSPHORUS, -ATE[1]]
▸ phosphatic (fɒsˈfætɪk) *adj*

phosphatide (ˈfɒsfəˌtaɪd) *n* another name for **phospholipid.**

phosphatidylcholine (ˌfɒsfæˌtaɪdaɪlˈkəʊliːn) *n* the systematic name for **lecithin.**

phosphene (ˈfɒsfiːn) *n* the sensation of light caused by pressure on the eyelid of a closed eye. [C19: from Gk *phōs* light + *phainein* to show]
▸ phos'phenic *adj*

phosphide (ˈfɒsfaɪd) *n* any compound of phosphorus with another element, esp. a more electropositive element.

phosphine (ˈfɒsfiːn) *n* a colourless flammable gas that is slightly soluble in water and has a strong fishy odour: used as a pesticide. Formula: PH_3.

phosphite (ˈfɒsfaɪt) *n* any salt or ester of phosphorous acid.

phospho- *or before a vowel* **phosph-** *combining form.* containing phosphorus: *phosphoric.* [from F, from *phosphore* PHOSPHORUS]

phospholipid (ˌfɒsfəˈlɪpɪd) *n* any of a group of fatty compounds: important constituents of all membranes. Also called: **phosphatide.**

phosphonic acid (fɒsˈfɒnɪk) *n* the systematic name for **phosphorous acid.**

phosphor (ˈfɒsfə) *n* a substance capable of emitting light when irradiated with particles of electromagnetic radiation. [C17: from F, ult. from Gk *phōsphoros* PHOSPHORUS]

phosphorate (ˈfɒsfəˌreɪt) *vb* **phosphorates, phosphorating, phosphorated.** to treat or combine with phosphorus.

phosphor bronze *n* any of various hard corrosion-resistant alloys containing phosphorus: used in gears, bearings, cylinder casings, etc.

phosphoresce (ˌfɒsfəˈrɛs) *vb* **phosphoresces, phosphorescing, phosphoresced.** (*intr*) to exhibit phosphorescence.

phosphorescence (ˌfɒsfəˈrɛsəns) *n* **1** *Physics.* a fluorescence that persists after the bombarding radiation producing it has stopped. **2** the light emitted in phosphorescence. **3** the emission of light in which insufficient heat is evolved to cause fluorescence. Cf. **fluorescence.**
▸ ˌphospho'rescent *adj*

phosphoric (fɒsˈfɒrɪk) *adj* of or containing phosphorus in the pentavalent state.

phosphoric acid *n* **1** a colourless solid tribasic acid used in the manufacture of fertilizers and soap. Formula: H_3PO_4. Systematic name: **phosphoric(V) acid**. Also called: **orthophosphoric acid**. **2** any oxyacid of phosphorus produced by reaction between phosphorus pentoxide and water.

phosphorous ('fosfərəs) *adj* of or containing phosphorus in the trivalent state.

phosphorous acid *n* **1** a white or yellowish hygroscopic crystalline dibasic acid. Formula: H_3PO_3. Systematic name: **phosphonic acid**. Also called: **orthophosphorous acid**. **2** any oxyacid of phosphorus containing less oxygen than the corresponding phosphoric acid.

phosphorus ('fosfərəs) *n* **1** an allotropic nonmetallic element occurring in phosphates and living matter. Ordinary phosphorus is a toxic flammable phosphorescent white solid; the red form is less reactive and nontoxic: used in matches, pesticides, and alloys. The radioisotope **phosphorus-32** (**radiophosphorus**), with a half-life of 14.3 days, is used in radiotherapy and as a tracer. Symbol: P; atomic no.: 15; atomic wt.: 30.974. **2** a less common name for a **phosphor**. [C17: via L from Gk *phōsphoros* light-bringing, from *phōs* light + *pherein* to bring]

Phosphorus ('fosfərəs) *n* a morning star, esp. Venus.

phossy jaw ('fosɪ) *n* a gangrenous condition of the lower jawbone caused by prolonged exposure to phosphorus fumes. [C19: *phossy*, colloquial shortening of PHOSPHORUS]

phot (fot, fəut) *n* a unit of illumination equal to one lumen per square centimetre. 1 phot is equal to 10 000 lux. [C20: from Gk *phōs* light]

phot. *abbrev. for:* **1** photograph. **2** photographic. **3** photography.

photic ('fəutɪk) *adj* **1** of or concerned with light. **2** designating the zone of the sea where photosynthesis takes place.

photo ('fəutəu) *n, pl* **photos.** short for **photograph**.

photo- *combining form.* **1** of, relating to, or produced by light: *photosynthesis.* **2** indicating a photographic process: *photolithography.* [from Gk *phōs, phōt-* light]

photo call *n* a time arranged for photographers, esp. press photographers, to take pictures of a celebrity.

photocell ('fəutəu,sɛl) *n* a device in which the photoelectric or photovoltaic effect or photoconductivity is used to produce a current or voltage when exposed to light or other electromagnetic radiation. They are used in exposure meters, burglar alarms, etc. Also called: **photoelectric cell, electric eye.**

photochemistry (,fəutəu'kɛmɪstrɪ) *n* the branch of chemistry concerned with the chemical effects of light and other electromagnetic radiations.
▸ **photochemical** (,fəutəu'kɛmɪkʰl) *adj*

photochromic (,fəutəu'krəumɪk) *adj* (of glass) changing colour with the intensity of incident light, used, for example, in sunglasses that darken as the sunlight becomes brighter.

photocomposition (,fəutəu,kɒmpə'zɪʃən) *n* another name (esp. US and Canad.) for **filmsetting**.

photoconductivity (,fəutəu,kɒndʌk'tɪvɪtɪ) *n* the change in the electrical conductivity of certain substances, such as selenium, as a result of the absorption of electromagnetic radiation.
▸ **photoconductive** (,fəutəukən'dʌktɪv) *adj* ▸ **photoconductor** *n*

photocopier ('fəutəu,kɒpɪə) *n* an instrument using light-sensitive photographic materials to reproduce written, printed, or graphic work.

photocopy ('fəutəu,kɒpɪ) *n, pl* **photocopies. 1** a photographic reproduction of written, printed, or graphic work. ◆ *vb* **photocopies, photocopying, photocopied. 2** to reproduce (written, printed, or graphic work) on photographic material.

photodegradable (,fəutəudɪ'greɪdəbʰl) *adj* (of plastic) capable of being decomposed by prolonged exposure to light.

photoelectric (,fəutəuɪ'lɛktrɪk) *adj* of or concerned with electric or electronic effects caused by light or other electromagnetic radiation.
▸ **photoelectricity** (,fəutəuɪlɛk'trɪsɪtɪ) *n*

photoelectric cell *n* another name for **photocell**.

photoelectric effect *n* **1** the ejection of electrons from a solid by an incident beam of sufficiently energetic electromagnetic radiation. **2** any phenomenon involving electric current and electromagnetic radiation, such as photoemission.

photoelectron (,fəutəuɪ'lɛktrɒn) *n* an electron ejected from an atom, molecule, or solid by an incident photon.

photoemission (,fəutəuɪ'mɪʃən) *n* the emission of electrons due to the impact of electromagnetic radiation.

photoengraving (,fəutəuɪn'greɪvɪŋ) *n* **1** a photomechanical process for producing letterpress printing plates. **2** a plate made by this process. **3** a print made from such a plate.
▸ **photoen'grave** *vb (tr)*

photo finish *n* **1** a finish of a race in which contestants are so close that a photograph is needed to decide the result. **2** any race or competition in which the winners are separated by a very small margin.

Photofit ('fəutəu,fɪt) *n Trademark.* **a** a method of combining photographs of facial features, hair, etc., into a composite picture of a face: used by the police to trace suspects, criminals, etc. **b** (*as modifier*): *a Photofit picture.*

photoflash ('fəutəu,flæʃ) *n* another name for **flashbulb**.

photoflood ('fəutəu,flʌd) *n* a highly incandescent tungsten lamp used for indoor photography, television, etc.

photog. *abbrev. for:* **1** photograph. **2** photographer. **3** photographic. **4** photography.

photogenic (,fəutə'dʒɛnɪk) *adj* **1** (esp. of a person) having a general facial appearance that looks attractive in photographs. **2** *Biol.* producing or emitting light.
▸ **photo'genically** *adv*

photogram ('fəutə,græm) *n* **1** a picture, usually abstract, produced on a photographic material without the use of a camera. **2** *Obs.* a photograph.

photogrammetry (,fəutə'græmɪtrɪ) *n* the process of making measurements from photographs, used esp. in the construction of maps from aerial photographs.

photograph ('fəutə,grɑːf) *n* **1** an image of an object, person, scene, etc., in the form of a print or slide recorded by a camera. Often shortened to **photo.** ◆ *vb* **2** to take a photograph of (an object, person, scene, etc.).

photographic (,fəutə'græfɪk) *adj* **1** of or relating to photography. **2** like a photograph in accuracy or detail. **3** (of a person's memory) able to retain facts, appearances, etc., in precise detail.
▸ **photo'graphically** *adv*

photography (fə'tɒgrəfɪ) *n* **1** the process of recording images on sensitized material by the action of light, X-rays, etc. **2** the art, practice, or occupation of taking photographs.
▸ **pho'tographer** *n*

photogravure (,fəutəugrə'vjuə) *n* **1** any of various methods in which an intaglio plate for printing is produced by the use of photography. **2** matter printed from such a plate. [C19: from PHOTO- + F *gravure* engraving]

photojournalism (,fəutəu'dʒɜːnəˌlɪzəm) *n* journalism in which photographs are the predominant feature.
▸ **photo'journalist** *n*

photokinesis (,fəutəukɪ'niːsɪs, -kaɪ-) *n Biol.* the movement of an organism in response to the stimulus of light.

photolithography (,fəutəulɪ'θɒgrəfɪ) *n* **1** a lithographic printing process using photographically made plates. Often shortened to **photolitho**. **2** *Electronics.* a process used in the manufacture of semiconductor devices and printed circuits in which a particular pattern is transferred from a photograph onto a substrate.
▸ **photoli'thographer** *n*

photoluminescence (,fəutəu,luːmɪ'nɛsəns) *n* luminescence resulting from the absorption of light or infrared or ultraviolet radiation.

★ people and places

photolysis (fəʊˈtɒlɪsɪs) *n* chemical decomposition caused by light or other electromagnetic radiation.
▶ **photolytic** (ˌfəʊtəʊˈlɪtɪk) *adj*

photomechanical (ˌfəʊtəʊmɪˈkænɪkᵊl) *adj* of or relating to any of various methods by which printing plates are made using photography.
▶ ˌ**photomeˈchanically** *adv*

photometer (fəʊˈtɒmɪtə) *n* an instrument used in photometry, usually one that compares the illumination produced by a particular light source with that produced by a standard source.

photometry (fəʊˈtɒmɪtrɪ) *n* **1** the measurement of the intensity of light. **2** the branch of physics concerned with such measurements.
▶ **phoˈtometrist** *n*

photomicrograph (ˌfəʊtəʊˈmaɪkrəˌgrɑːf) *n* a photograph of a microscope image.
▶ **photomicrography** (ˌfəʊtəʊmaɪˈkrɒɡrəfɪ) *n*

photomontage (ˌfəʊtəʊmɒnˈtɑːʒ) *n* **1** the technique of producing a composite picture by combining several photographs. **2** the composite picture so produced.

photomultiplier (ˌfəʊtəʊˈmʌltɪˌplaɪə) *n* a device sensitive to electromagnetic radiation which produces a detectable pulse of current.

photon (ˈfəʊtɒn) *n* a quantum of electromagnetic radiation with energy equal to the product of the frequency of the radiation and the Planck constant.

photo-offset *n Printing.* an offset process in which the plates are produced photomechanically.

photo opportunity *n* an opportunity, either preplanned or accidental, for the press to photograph a politician, celebrity, or event.

photoperiodism (ˌfəʊtəʊˈpɪərɪəˌdɪzəm) *n* the response of plants and animals by behaviour, growth, etc., to the period of daylight in every 24 hours (**photoperiod**).
▶ ˌ**photoˌperiˈodic** *adj*

photophobia (ˌfəʊtəʊˈfəʊbɪə) *n* **1** *Pathol.* abnormal sensitivity of the eyes to light. **2** *Psychiatry.* abnormal fear of sunlight or well-lit places.
▶ ˌ**photoˈphobic** *adj*

photopolymer (ˌfəʊtəʊˈpɒlɪmə) *n* a polymeric material that is sensitive to light: used in printing plates, microfilms, etc.

photoreceptor (ˌfəʊtəʊrɪˈsɛptə) *n Zool., physiol.* a light-sensitive cell or organ that conveys impulses through the sensory neuron connected to it.

photosensitive (ˌfəʊtəʊˈsɛnsɪtɪv) *adj* sensitive to electromagnetic radiation, esp. light.
▶ ˌ**photoˌsensiˈtivity** *n* ▶ ˌ**photoˈsensiˌtize** or ˌ**photoˈsensiˌtise** *vb* (*tr*)

photoset (ˈfəʊtəʊˌsɛt) *vb* **photosets, photosetting, photoset.** another word for **filmset.**
▶ ˈ**photoˌsetter** *n*

photosphere (ˈfəʊtəʊˌsfɪə) *n* the visible surface of the sun.
▶ **photospheric** (ˌfəʊtəʊˈsfɛrɪk) *adj*

photostat (ˈfəʊtəʊˌstæt) *n* **1** a machine or process used to make photographic copies of written, printed, or graphic matter. **2** any copy made by such a machine. ◆ *vb* **photostats, photostatting** or **photostating, photostatted** or **photostated. 3** to make a photostat copy (of).

photosynthesis (ˌfəʊtəʊˈsɪnθɪsɪs) *n* (in plants) the synthesis of organic compounds from carbon dioxide and water using light energy absorbed by chlorophyll.
▶ ˌ**photoˈsynthesize** or ˌ**photoˈsynthesise** *vb* ▶ **photosynthetic** (ˌfəʊtəʊsɪnˈθɛtɪk) *adj* ▶ ˌ**photosynˈthetically** *adv*

phototaxis (ˌfəʊtəʊˈtæksɪs) *n* the movement of an entire organism in response to light.

phototropism (ˌfəʊtəʊˈtrəʊpɪzəm) *n* the growth response of plant parts to the stimulus of light, producing a bending towards the light source.
▶ ˈ**photoˈtropic** *adj*

photovoltaic effect (ˌfəʊtəʊvɒlˈteɪɪk) *n* the effect when electromagnetic radiation falls on a thin film of one solid deposited on the surface of a dissimilar solid producing a difference in potential between the two materials.

phrasal verb *n* a phrase that consists of a verb plus an adverbial or prepositional particle, esp. one the meaning of which cannot be deduced from the constituents: "*take in*" *meaning* "*deceive*" *is a phrasal verb.*

phrase (freɪz) *n* **1** a group of words forming a syntactic constituent of a sentence. Cf. **clause** (sense 1). **2** an idiomatic or original expression. **3** manner or style of speech or expression. **4** *Music.* a small group of notes forming a coherent unit of melody. ◆ *vb* **phrases, phrasing, phrased.** (*tr*) **5** *Music.* to divide (a melodic line, part, etc.) into musical phrases, esp. in performance. **6** to express orally or in a phrase. [C16: from L *phrasis*, from Gk: speech, from *phrazein* to tell]
▶ ˈ**phrasal** *adj*

phrase book *n* a book containing frequently used expressions and their equivalents in a foreign language.

phrase marker *n Linguistics.* a representation, esp. a tree diagram, of the constituent structure of a sentence.

phraseogram (ˈfreɪzɪəˌgræm) *n* a symbol representing a phrase, as in shorthand.

phraseology (ˌfreɪzɪˈɒlədʒɪ) *n, pl* **phraseologies. 1** the manner in which words or phrases are used. **2** a set of phrases used by a particular group of people.
▶ **phraseological** (ˌfreɪzɪəˈlɒdʒɪkᵊl) *adj*

phrasing (ˈfreɪzɪŋ) *n* **1** the way in which something is expressed, esp. in writing; wording. **2** *Music.* the division of a melodic line, part, etc., into musical phrases.

phrenetic (frɪˈnɛtɪk) *adj* an obsolete spelling of **frenetic.**
▶ **phreˈnetically** *adv*

phrenic (ˈfrɛnɪk) *adj* **1a** of or relating to the diaphragm. **1b** (*as n*): *the phrenic.* **2** *Obs.* of or relating to the mind. [C18: from NL *phrenicus*, from Gk *phrēn* mind, diaphragm]

phrenology (frɪˈnɒlədʒɪ) *n* (formerly) the branch of science concerned with determination of the strength of the faculties by the shape and size of the skull overlying the parts of the brain thought to be responsible for them.
▶ **phrenological** (ˌfrɛnəˈlɒdʒɪkᵊl) *adj* ▶ **phreˈnologist** *n*

phrensy (ˈfrɛnzɪ) *n, pl* **phrensies** an obsolete spelling of **frenzy.**

Phrixus ★ (ˈfrɪksəs) *n Greek myth.* the son of Athamas and Nephele who escaped the wrath of his father's mistress, Ino, by flying to Colchis on a winged ram with a golden fleece. See also **Helle, Golden Fleece.**

Phrygia ★ (ˈfrɪdʒɪə) *n* an ancient country of W central Asia Minor.

Phrygian (ˈfrɪdʒɪən) *adj* **1.** of or relating to ancient Phrygia, its inhabitants, or their extinct language. **2** *Music.* of or relating to an authentic mode represented by the natural diatonic scale from E to E. ◆ *n* **3** a native or inhabitant of ancient Phrygia. **4** an ancient language of Phrygia.

Phrygian cap *n* a conical cap of soft material worn during ancient times, that became a symbol of liberty during the French Revolution.

Phryne ★ (ˈfraɪnɪ) *n* real name *Muesarete.* 4th century B.C., Greek courtesan; lover of Praxiteles and model for Apelles' painting *Aphrodite Rising from the Waves.*

phthisis (ˈθaɪsɪs, ˈfθaɪ-, ˈtaɪ-) *n* any disease that causes wasting of the body, esp. pulmonary tuberculosis. [C16: via L from Gk, from *phthinein* to waste away]

Phuket ★ (ˌpuːˈkɛt) *n* an island and province of S Thailand, in the Andaman Sea. Area: 534 sq. km (206 sq. miles).

phut (fʌt) *Inf.* ◆ *n* **1** a representation of a muffled explosive sound. ◆ *adv* **2 go phut.** to break down or collapse. [C19: imit.]

phycomycete (ˌfaɪkəʊˈmaɪsiːt) *n* any of a primitive group of fungi formerly included in the class *Phycomycetes,* but now classified in different phyla: includes certain mildews and moulds. [from Gk *phukos* seaweed + -MYCETE]

Phyfe or **Fife** ★ (faɪf) *n* **Duncan.** ?1768–1854, US cabinetmaker, born in Scotland.

★ people and places

phyla ('faɪlə) *n* the plural of **phylum**.

phylactery (fɪ'læktərɪ) *n, pl* **phylacteries. 1** *Judaism.* either of the pair of blackened square cases containing parchments inscribed with biblical passages, bound by leather thongs to the head and left arm, and worn by Jewish men during weekday morning prayers. **2** a reminder. **3** *Arch.* an amulet or charm. [C14: from LL *phylactērium*, from Gk *phulaktērion* outpost, from *phulax* a guard]

phyletic (faɪ'lɛtɪk) *adj* of or relating to the evolutionary development of organisms. [C19: from Gk *phuletikos* tribal]

-phyll *or* **-phyl** *n combining form.* leaf: *chlorophyll*. [from Gk *phullon*]

phyllo- *or before a vowel* **phyll-** *combining form.* leaf: *phyllopod*. [from Gk *phullon* leaf]

phyllode ('fɪləʊd) *n* a flattened leafstalk that resembles and functions as a leaf. [C19: from NL *phyllodium*, from Gk *phullōdēs* leaflike]

phylloquinone (ˌfɪləʊkwɪ'nəʊn) *n* a viscous fat-soluble liquid occurring in plants: essential for the production of prothrombin, required in blood clotting. Also called: **vitamin K₁**.

phyllotaxis (ˌfɪlə'tæksɪs) *or* **phyllotaxy** *n, pl* **phyllotaxes** (-'tæksiːz) *or* **phyllotaxies. 1** the arrangement of the leaves on a stem. **2** the study of this arrangement.
▸ ˌphyllo'tactic *adj*

-phyllous *adj combining form.* having leaves of a specified number or type: *monophyllous*. [from Gk *-phullos* of a leaf]

phylloxera (ˌfɪlɒk'sɪərə, fɪ'lɒksərə) *n, pl* **phylloxerae** (-riː) *or* **phylloxeras.** any of a genus of homopterous insects, such as vine phylloxera, typically feeding on plant juices. [C19: NL, from PHYLLO- + *xēros* dry]

phylo- *or before a vowel* **phyl-** *combining form.* tribe; race; phylum: *phylogeny*. [from Gk *phulon* race]

phylogeny (faɪ'lɒdʒɪnɪ) *or* **phylogenesis** (ˌfaɪləʊ'dʒɛnɪsɪs) *n, pl* **phylogenies** *or* **phylogeneses** (-'dʒɛnɪˌsiːz) *Biol.* the sequence of events involved in the evolution of a species, genus, etc. Cf. **ontogeny.** [C19: from PHYLO- + -GENY]
▸ **phylogenic** (ˌfaɪləʊ'dʒɛnɪk) *or* **phylogenetic** (ˌfaɪləʊdʒɪ'nɛtɪk) *adj*

phylum ('faɪləm) *n, pl* **phyla. 1** a major taxonomic division of living organisms that contain one or more classes. **2** a group of related language families or linguistic stocks. [C19: NL, from Gk *phulon* race]

phys. *abbrev. for:* **1** physical. **2** physician. **3** physics. **4** physiological. **5** physiology.

physalis (faɪ'seɪlɪs) *n* any of a genus of plants producing inflated orange seed vessels. See **Chinese lantern.** [NL from Gk *physallis* bladder]

physic ('fɪzɪk) *n* **1** *Rare.* a medicine, esp. a cathartic. **2** *Arch.* the art or skill of healing. ◆ *vb* **physics, physicking, physicked. 3** (*tr*) *Arch.* to treat (a patient) with medicine. [C13: from OF *fisique*, via L, from Gk *phusikē*, from *phusis* nature]

physical ('fɪzɪk°l) *adj* **1** of or relating to the body, as distinguished from the mind or spirit. **2** of, relating to, or resembling material things or nature: *the physical universe*. **3** involving or requiring bodily contact: *rugby is a physical sport*. **4** of or concerned with matter and energy. **5** of or relating to physics. **6** perceptible to the senses; apparent: *a physical manifestation.* ◆ See also **physicals.**
▸ **'physically** *adv*

physical anthropology *n* the branch of anthropology dealing with the genetic aspect of human development and its physical variations.

physical chemistry *n* the branch of chemistry concerned with the way in which the physical properties of substances depend on their chemical structure, properties, and reactions.

physical education *n* training and practice in sports, gymnastics, etc. Abbrev.: **PE.**

physical geography *n* the branch of geography that deals with the natural features of the earth's surface.

physical jerks *pl n Brit. inf.* See **jerk**[1] (sense 6).

physicals ('fɪzɪk°lz) *pl n Commerce.* commodities that can be purchased and used, as opposed to those bought and sold in a futures market. Also called: **actuals.**

physical science *n* any of the sciences concerned with nonliving matter, such as physics, chemistry, astronomy, and geology.

physical therapy *n Chiefly US.* another term for **physiotherapy.**

physician (fɪ'zɪʃən) *n* **1** a person legally qualified to practise medicine, esp. other than surgery; doctor of medicine. **2** *Arch.* any person who treats diseases; healer. [C13: from OF *fisicien*, from *fisique* PHYSIC]

physicist ('fɪzɪsɪst) *n* a person versed in or studying physics.

physics ('fɪzɪks) *n (functioning as sing)* **1** the branch of science concerned with the properties of matter and energy and the relationships between them. It is based on mathematics and traditionally includes mechanics, optics, electricity and magnetism, acoustics, and heat. Modern physics, based on quantum theory, includes atomic, nuclear, particle, and solid-state studies. **2** physical properties of behaviour: *the physics of the electron*. **3** *Arch.* natural science. [C16: from L *physica*, translation of Gk *ta phusika* natural things, from *phusis* nature]

physio ('fɪzɪəʊ) *n Inf.* **1** short for **physiotherapy. 2** (*pl* **physios**) short for **physiotherapist.**

physio- *or before a vowel* **phys-** *combining form.* **1** of or relating to nature or natural functions: *physiology*. **2** physical: *physiotherapy*. [from Gk *phusio*, ult. from *phuein* to make grow]

physiocrat ('fɪzɪəʊˌkræt) *n* a believer in the 18th-century French economic theory that the inherent natural order governing society was based on land and its natural products as the only true form of wealth. [C18: from F *physiocrate*; see PHYSIO-, -CRAT]
▸ **physiocracy** (ˌfɪzɪ'ɒkrəsɪ) *n*

physiognomy (ˌfɪzɪ'ɒnəmɪ) *n* **1** a person's features considered as an indication of personality. **2** the art or practice of judging character from facial features. **3** the outward appearance of something. [C14: from OF *phisonomie*, via Med. L, from LGk *phusiognōmia*, from *phusis* nature + *gnōmōn* judge]
▸ **physiognomic** (ˌfɪzɪəʊ'nɒmɪk) *or* **physiog'nomical** *adj*
▸ **ˌphysiog'nomically** *adv* ▸ **ˌphysi'ognomist** *n*

physiography (ˌfɪzɪ'ɒgrəfɪ) *n* another name for **geomorphology** *or* **physical geography.**
▸ **ˌphysi'ographer** *n* ▸ **physiographic** (ˌfɪzɪə'græfɪk) *or* **ˌphysio'graphical** *adj*

physiol. *abbrev. for:* **1** physiological. **2** physiology.

physiology (ˌfɪzɪ'ɒlədʒɪ) *n* **1** the branch of science concerned with the functioning of organisms. **2** the processes and functions of all or part of an organism. [C16: from L *physiologia*, from Gk]
▸ **ˌphysi'ologist** *n* ▸ **physiological** (ˌfɪzɪə'lɒdʒɪk°l) *adj*
▸ **ˌphysio'logically** *adv*

physiotherapy (ˌfɪzɪəʊ'θɛrəpɪ) *n* the treatment of disease, injury, etc., by physical means, such as massage or exercises, rather than by drugs.
▸ **ˌphysio'therapist** *n*

physique (fɪ'ziːk) *n* the general appearance of the body with regard to size, shape, muscular development, etc. [C19: via F from *physique* (adj) natural, from L *physicus* physical]

-phyte *n combining form.* indicating a plant of a specified type or habitat: *lithophyte*. [from Gk *phuton* plant]
▸ **-phytic** *adj combining form.*

phyto- *or before a vowel* **phyt-** *combining form.* indicating a plant or vegetation: *phytogenesis*. [from Gk *phuton* plant, from *phuein* to make grow]

phytochrome ('faɪtəʊˌkrəʊm) *n Bot.* a blue-green pigment, present in most plants, that mediates many light-dependent processes, including photoperiodism and the greening of leaves.

phytogenesis (ˌfaɪtəʊ'dʒɛnɪsɪs) *or* **phytogeny** (faɪ'tɒdʒənɪ) *n* the branch of botany concerned with the origin and evolution of plants.

phyton ('faɪtɒn) *n* a unit of plant structure, usually considered as the smallest part of the plant that is capable of growth when detached from the parent plant. [C20: from Gk; see -PHYTE]

phytopathology (ˌfaɪtəʊpə'θɒlədʒɪ) n the branch of botany concerned with diseases of plants.

phytoplankton (ˌfaɪtə'plæŋktən) n the photosynthesizing constituent of plankton, mainly unicellular algae.

phytotoxin (ˌfaɪtə'tɒksɪn) n a toxin, such as strychnine, that is produced by a plant.
▸ ˌphyto'toxic adj

pi[1] (paɪ) n, pl **pis. 1** the 16th letter in the Greek alphabet (Π, π). **2** *Maths.* a transcendental number, fundamental to mathematics, that is the ratio of the circumference of a circle to its diameter. Approximate value: 3.141 592... ; symbol: π [C18 (mathematical use): representing the first letter of Gk *periphereia* PERIPHERY]

pi[2] *or* **pie** (paɪ) n, pl **pies. 1** a jumbled pile of printer's type. **2** a jumbled mixture. ◆ vb **pies, piing, pied** *or* **pies, pieing, pied.** (tr) **3** to spill and mix (set type) indiscriminately. **4** to mix up. [C17: from ?]

pi[3] (paɪ) adj Brit. sl. short for **pious** (sense 3).

PI abbrev. for: **1** Phillipine Islands. **2** private investigator.

Piacenza ★ (Italian pja'tʃentsa) n a town in N Italy, in Emilia-Romagna on the River Po. Pop.: 101 692 (1994 est.). Latin name: **Placentia** (plə'sentʃɪə).

piacevole (pi:ætʃ'eɪvəʊleɪ) adv Music. in an agreeable, pleasant manner. [It.]

piacular (paɪ'ækjʊlə) adj **1** making expiation. **2** requiring expiation. [C17: from L *piāculum* propitiatory sacrifice, from *piāre* to appease]

Piaf ★ (French pjaf) n **Edith** (edit), real name *Edith Giovanna Gassion,* nicknamed *the Little Sparrow.* 1915–63, French singer.

piaffe (pɪ'æf) n Dressage. a slow trot done on the spot. [C18: from F, from *piaffer* to strut]

Piaget ★ (French pjaʒe) n **Jean** (ʒɑ̃). 1896–1980, Swiss psychologist, noted for his work on the development of the cognitive functions in children.

pia mater ('paɪə 'meɪtə) n the innermost of the three membranes (see **meninges**) that cover the brain and spinal cord. [C16: from Med. L, lit.: pious mother]

pianism ('pi:ə,nɪzəm) n technique, skill, or artistry in playing the piano.
▸ ˌpia'nistic adj

pianissimo (pɪə'nɪsɪ,məʊ) adj, adv Music. to be performed very quietly. Symbol: *pp* [C18: from It., sup. of *piano* soft]

pianist ('pɪənɪst) n a person who plays the piano.

piano[1] (pɪ'ænəʊ) n, pl **pianos.** a musical stringed instrument played by depressing keys that cause hammers to strike the strings and produce audible vibrations. [C19: short for PIANOFORTE]

piano[2] ('pjɑ:nəʊ) adj, adv Music. to be performed softly. [C17: from It., from L *plānus* flat]

piano accordion (pɪ'ænəʊ) n an accordion in which the right hand plays a piano-like keyboard. See **accordion.**
▸ **piano accordionist** n

pianoforte (pɪ,ænəʊ'fɔːtɪ) n the full name for **piano**[1]. [C18: from It., orig. (*gravecembalo col) piano e forte* (harpsichord with) soft & loud; see PIANO[2], FORTE[2]]

Pianola (pɪə'nəʊlə) n Trademark. a type of mechanical piano in which the keys are depressed by air pressure, this air flow being regulated by perforations in a paper roll.

piano roll (pɪ'ænəʊ) n a perforated roll of paper for a Pianola.

piastre *or* **piaster** (pɪ'æstə) n **1** (formerly) the standard monetary unit of South Vietnam. **2a** a fractional monetary unit of Egypt, Lebanon, and Syria worth one hundredth of a pound: also used in the Sudan but its use is being phased out. **2b** Also called: **kurus.** a Turkish monetary unit worth one hundredth of a lira. **2c** a Libyan monetary unit worth one hundredth of a dinar. [C17: from F *piastre,* from It. *piastra d'argento* silver plate]

Piauí ★ (Portuguese pja'ui) n a state of NE Brazil, on the At-

lantic: rises to a semiarid plateau, with the more humid Paranaíba valley in the west. Capital: Teresina. Pop.: 2 725 900 (1995 est.). Area: 250 934 sq. km (96 886 sq. miles).

Piave ★ (Italian 'pja:ve) n a river in NE Italy, rising near the border with Austria and flowing south and southeast to the Adriatic: the main line of Italian defence during World War I. Length: 220 km (137 miles).

piazza (pɪ'ætsə; Italian 'pjattsa) n **1** a large open square in an Italian town. **2** Chiefly Brit. a covered passageway or gallery. [C16: from It.: marketplace, from L *platēa* courtyard, from Gk *plateia;* see PLACE]

pibroch ('pi:brɒk; Gaelic 'pi:brɒx) n a form of music for Scottish bagpipes, consisting of a theme and variations. [C18: from Gaelic *piobaireachd,* from *piobair* piper]

pic (pɪk) n, pl **pics** *or* **pix.** Inf. a photograph or illustration. [C20: shortened from PICTURE]

pica[1] ('paɪkə) n **1** another word for **em. 2** (formerly) a size of printer's type equal to 12 point. **3** a typewriter type size having 10 characters to the inch. [C15: from Anglo-L *pīca* list of ecclesiastical regulations, apparently from L *pīca* magpie, with reference to its habit of collecting things; the connection between the orig. sense & the typography meanings is obscure]

pica[2] ('paɪkə) n Pathol. an abnormal craving to ingest substances such as clay, dirt, or hair. [C16: from Medical L, from L: magpie, an allusion to its omnivorous feeding habits]

Picabia ★ (pɪ'kɑːbɪə; French pikabja) n **Francis.** 1879–1953, French painter, designer, and writer, associated with the cubist, Dadaist, and surrealist movements.

picador ('pɪkə,dɔː) n Bullfighting. a horseman who pricks the bull with a lance to weaken it. [C18: from Sp., lit.: pricker, from *picar* to prick]

Picard ★ (French pikar) n **Jean** (ʒɑ̃). 1620–82, French astronomer. He was the first to make a precise measurement of a longitude line, enabling him to estimate the earth's radius.

Picardy ★ ('pɪkədɪ) n a region of N France: mostly lowlying; scene of heavy fighting in World War I. French name: **Picardie** (pikardi).

picaresque (ˌpɪkə'resk) adj of or relating to a type of fiction in which the hero, a rogue, goes through a series of episodic adventures. [C19: via F from Sp. *picaresco,* from *pícaro* a rogue]

picaroon (ˌpɪkə'ruːn) n Arch. an adventurer or rogue. [C17: from Sp. *picarón,* from *pícaro*]

Picasso ★ (pɪ'kæsəʊ) n **Pablo** ('pæbləʊ). 1881–1973, Spanish painter and sculptor, resident in France: a highly influential figure in 20th-century art and a founder, with Braque, of cubism. A prolific artist, his works include *Les Demoiselles d'Avignon* (1907) and *Guernica* (1937), inspired by an event in the Spanish Civil War.

picayune (ˌpɪkə'juːn) adj also **picayunish.** US & Canad. inf. **1** of small value or importance. **2** mean; petty. ◆ n **3** any coin of little value, esp. a five-cent piece. **4** an unimportant person or thing. [C19: from F *picaillon* coin from Piedmont, from Provençal *picaioun,* from ?]

Piccadilly ★ (ˌpɪkə'dɪlɪ) n one of the main streets of London, running from Piccadilly Circus to Hyde Park Corner.

piccalilli ('pɪkə,lɪlɪ) n a pickle of mixed vegetables in a mustard sauce. [C18 *piccalillo,* ? based on PICKLE]

piccanin ('pɪkə,nɪn) n S. African offens. a Black African child. [var. of PICCANINNY]

piccaninny *or esp. US* **pickaninny** (ˌpɪkə'nɪnɪ) n, pl **piccaninnies** *or esp. US* **pickaninnies.** Offens. a small Black child. [C17: ?from Port. *pequenino* tiny one, from *pequeno* small]

Piccard ★ (French pikar) n **1 Auguste** (ogyst). 1884–1962, Swiss physicist, whose study of cosmic rays led to his pioneer balloon ascents in the stratosphere (1931–32). **2** his twin brother, **Jean Félix** (ʒɑ̃ feliks). 1884–1963, US chemist and aeronautical engineer, born in Switzerland, noted for his balloon ascent into the stratosphere (1934).

★ people and places

piccolo ('pɪkə,ləʊ) *n, pl* **piccolos.** a woodwind instrument an octave higher than the flute. [C19: from It.: small]

pick[1] (pɪk) *vb* **1** to choose (something) deliberately or carefully, as from a number; select. **2** to pluck or gather (fruit, berries, or crops) from (a tree, bush, field, etc.). **3** (*tr*) to remove loose particles from (the teeth, the nose, etc.). **4** (esp. of birds) to nibble or gather (corn, etc.). **5** (*tr*) to pierce, dig, or break up (a hard surface) with a pick. **6** (*tr*) to form (a hole, etc.) in this way. **7** (when *intr*, foll. by *at*) to nibble (at) fussily or without appetite. **8** to separate (strands, fibres, etc.), as in weaving. **9** (*tr*) to provoke (an argument, fight, etc.) deliberately. **10** (*tr*) to steal (money or valuables) from (a person's pocket). **11** (*tr*) to open (a lock) with an instrument other than a key. **12** to pluck the strings of (a guitar, banjo, etc.). **13** (*tr*) to make (one's way) carefully on foot: *they picked their way through the rubble*. **14 pick and choose.** to select fastidiously, fussily, etc. **15 pick someone's brains.** to obtain information or ideas from someone. ♦ *n* **16** freedom or right of selection (esp. in **take one's pick**). **17** a person, thing, etc., that is chosen first or preferred: *the pick of the bunch*. **18** the act of picking. **19** the amount of a crop picked at one period or from one area. ♦ See also **pick at, pick off,** etc. [C15: from earlier *piken* to pick, infl. by F *piquer* to pierce]
▸ **'picker** *n*

pick[2] (pɪk) *n* **1** a tool with a handle carrying a long steel head curved and tapering to a point at one or both ends, used for loosening soil, breaking rocks, etc. **2** any of various tools used for picking, such as an ice pick or tooth-pick. **3** a plectrum. [C14: ? a var. of PIKE[2]]

pickaback ('pɪkə,bæk) *n, adv* another word for **piggyback.**

pick at *vb* (*intr, prep*) to make criticisms of in a niggling or petty manner.

pickaxe *or US* **pickax** ('pɪk,æks) *n* **1** a large pick or mattock. ♦ *vb* **pickaxes, pickaxing, pickaxed. 2** to use a pickaxe on (earth, rocks, etc.). [C15: from earlier *pikois* (but infl. also by AXE), from OF, from *pic* PICK[2]]

pickerel ('pɪkərəl, 'pɪkrəl) *n, pl* **pickerel** *or* **pickerels. 1** a small pike. **2** any of several North American freshwater game fishes of the pike family. [C14: dim. of PIKE[1]]

Pickering ★ ('pɪkərɪŋ) *n* **1 Edward Charles.** 1846–1919, US astronomer, who invented the meridian photometer. **2** his brother, **William Henry.** 1858–1938, US astronomer, who discovered Phoebe, the ninth satellite of Saturn, and predicted (1919) the existence and position of Pluto.

picket ('pɪkɪt) *n* **1** a pointed stake that is driven into the ground to support a fence, etc. **2** an individual or group standing outside an establishment to make a protest, to dissuade or prevent employees or clients from entering, etc. **3** a small detachment of troops positioned to give early warning of attack. ♦ *vb* **4** to post or serve as pickets at (a factory, embassy, etc.). **5** to guard (a main body or place) by using or acting as a picket. **6** (*tr*) to fasten (a horse or other animal) to a picket. **7** (*tr*) to fence (an area, etc.) with pickets. [C18: from F *piquet*, from OF *piquer* to prick; see PIKE[2]]
▸ **'picketer** *n*

picket fence *n* a fence consisting of pickets driven into the ground.

picket line *n* a line of people acting as pickets.

Pickford ★ ('pɪkfəd) *n* **Mary,** real name *Gladys Mary Smith.* 1893–1979, US actress in silent films, born in Canada.

pickings ('pɪkɪŋz) *pl n* (*sometimes sing*) money, profits, etc., acquired easily; spoils.

pickle ('pɪk³l) *n* **1** (*often pl*) vegetables, such as onions, etc., preserved in vinegar, brine, etc. **2** any food preserved in this way. **3** a liquid or marinade, such as spiced vinegar, for preserving vegetables, meat, fish, etc. **4** *Chiefly US & Canad.* a cucumber that has been preserved and flavoured in a pickling solution, as brine or vinegar. **5** *Inf.* an awkward or difficult situation: *to be in a pickle.* **6** *Brit. inf.* a mischievous child. ♦ *vb* **pickles, pickling, pickled.** (*tr*) **7** to preserve in a pickling liquid. **8** to immerse (a metallic object) in a liquid, such as an acid, to remove surface scale. [C14: ?from MDu. *pekel*]
▸ **'pickler** *n*

pickled ('pɪk³ld) *adj* **1** preserved in a pickling liquid. **2** *Inf.* intoxicated; drunk.

picklock ('pɪk,lɒk) *n* **1** a person who picks locks. **2** an instrument for picking locks.

pick-me-up *n Inf.* a tonic or restorative, esp. a special drink taken as a stimulant.

pick off *vb* (*tr, adv*) to aim at and shoot one by one.

pick on *vb* (*intr, prep*) to select for something unpleasant, esp. in order to bully or blame.

pick out *vb* (*tr, adv*) **1** to select for use or special consideration, etc., as from a group. **2** to distinguish (an object from its surroundings), as in painting: *she picked out the woodwork in white.* **3** to recognize (a person or thing): *we picked out his face among the crowd.* **4** to distinguish (sense or meaning) as from a mass of detail or complication. **5** to play (a tune) tentatively, as by ear.

pickpocket ('pɪk,pɒkɪt) *n* a person who steals from the pockets of others in public places.

pick-up *n* **1** the light balanced arm of a record player that carries the wires from the cartridge to the preamplifier. **2** an electromagnetic transducer that converts vibrations into electrical signals. **3** another name for **cartridge** (sense 2). **4** Also called: **pick-up truck.** a small truck with an open body used for light deliveries. **5** *Inf., chiefly US.* an ability to accelerate rapidly: *this car has good pick-up.* **6** *Inf.* a casual acquaintance, usually one made with sexual intentions. **7** *Inf.* **7a** a stop to collect passengers, goods, etc. **7b** the people or things collected. **8** *Inf.* an improvement. **9** *Sl.* a pick-me-up. ♦ *adj* **10** *US & Canad.* organized or assembled hastily and without planning: *a pick-up game.* ♦ *vb* **pick up.** (*adv*) **11** (*tr*) to gather up in the hand or hands. **12** (*reflexive*) to raise (oneself) after a fall or setback. **13** (*tr*) to obtain casually, incidentally, etc. **14** (*intr*) to improve in health, condition, activity, etc.: *the market began to pick up.* **15** (*tr*) to learn gradually or as one goes along. **16** to resume; return to. **17** (*tr*) to accept the responsibility for paying (a bill). **18** (*tr*) to collect or give a lift to (passengers, goods, etc.). **19** (*tr*) *Inf.* to become acquainted with, esp. with a view to having sexual relations. **20** (*tr*) *Inf.* to arrest. **21** to increase (speed). **22** (*tr*) to receive (electrical signals, a radio signal, sounds, etc.).

Pickwickian (pɪk'wɪkɪən) *adj* **1** of, relating to, or resembling Mr Pickwick in Charles Dickens' *The Pickwick Papers,* esp. in being naive or benevolent. **2** (of the use or meaning of a word) odd or unusual.

picky ('pɪkɪ) *adj* **pickier, pickiest.** *Inf.* fussy; finicky.
▸ **'pickily** *adv* ▸ **'pickiness** *n*

picnic ('pɪknɪk) *n* **1** a trip or excursion on which people bring food to be eaten in the open air. **2a** any informal meal eaten outside. **2b** (*as modifier*): *a picnic lunch.* **3** *Inf.* an easy or agreeable task. ♦ *vb* **picnics, picnicking, picnicked. 4** (*intr*) to eat or take part in a picnic. [C18: from F *piquenique,* from ?]
▸ **'picnicker** *n*

picnic races *pl n Austral.* horse races for amateur riders held in rural areas.

pico- *prefix* denoting 10^{-12}: *picofarad.* Symbol: **p** [from Sp. *pico* small quantity, odd number, peak]

Pico de Aneto ★ (*Spanish* 'piko de a'neto) *n* See **Aneto.**

Pico della Mirandola ★ (*Italian* 'pi:ko ,della mi-'randola) *n* Count **Giovanni.** 1463–94, Italian Platonist philosopher. His attempt to reconcile the ideas of classical, Christian, and Arabic writers in a collection of theses was condemned by the pope.

Pico de Teide ★ (*Spanish* 'piko de 'teiðe) *n* See **Teide.**

picot ('pi:kəʊ) *n* any of a pattern of small loops, as on lace. [C19: from F: small point, from *pic* point]

picotee (,pɪkə'ti:) *n* a type of carnation having pale petals edged with a darker colour. [C18: from F *picoté* marked with points, from *picot* PICOT]

picric acid ('pɪkrɪk) *n* a toxic sparingly soluble crystalline yellow acid used as a dye, antiseptic, and explosive. Formula: $C_6H_3(NO_2)_3$. Systematic name: **2,4,6-trinitrophenol.** [C19: from Gk *pikros* bitter + -IC]

Pict (pɪkt) *n* a member of any of the peoples who lived in N Britain in the first to the fourth centuries A.D. [OE

★ **people and places**

Peohtas; later forms from LL *Pictī* painted men, from *pingere* to paint]
▸ **'Pictish** *adj*

pictograph ('pɪktə,grɑːf) *n* **1** a picture or symbol standing for a word or group of words, as in written Chinese. **2** a chart on which symbols are used to represent values. ◆ Also called: **pictogram**. [C19: from L *pictus*, from *pingere* to paint]
▸ **pictographic** (,pɪktə'græfɪk) *adj* ▸ **pictography** (pɪk-'tɒgrəfɪ) *n*

pictorial (pɪk'tɔːrɪəl) *adj* **1** relating to, consisting of, or expressed by pictures. **2** (of language, style, etc.) suggesting a picture; vivid; graphic. ◆ *n* **3** a magazine, newspaper, etc., containing many pictures. [C17: from LL *pictōrius,* from L *pictor* painter, from *pingere* to paint]
▸ **pic'torially** *adv*

picture ('pɪktʃə) *n* **1a** a visual representation of something, such as a person or scene, produced on a surface, as in a photograph, painting, etc. **1b** (*as modifier*): *picture gallery; picture postcard.* **2** a mental image: *a clear picture of events.* **3** a verbal description, esp. one that is vivid. **4** a situation considered as an observable scene: *the political picture.* **5** a person or thing resembling another: *he was the picture of his father.* **6** a person, scene, etc., typifying a particular state: *the picture of despair.* **7** the image on a television screen. **8** a motion picture; film. **9 the pictures.** *Chiefly Brit.* a cinema or film show. **10** another name for **tableau vivant. 11 in the picture.** informed about a situation. ◆ *vb* **pictures, picturing, pictured.** (*tr*) **12** to visualize or imagine. **13** to describe or depict, esp. vividly. **14** (*often passive*) to put in a picture or make a picture of: *they were pictured sitting on the rocks.* [C15: from L *pictūra* painting, from *pingere* to paint]

picture card *n* another name for **court card.**

picture hat *n* a hat with a very wide brim.

picture moulding *n* **1** the edge around a framed picture. **2** Also called: **picture rail.** the moulding or rail near the top of a wall from which pictures are hung.

picture palace *or* **house** *n* Brit., old-fashioned. another name for **cinema.**

picturesque (,pɪktʃə'rɛsk) *adj* **1** visually pleasing, esp. in being striking or quaint: *a picturesque view.* **2** (of language) graphic; vivid. [C18: from F *pittoresque* (but also infl. by PICTURE), from It., from *pittore* painter, from L *pictor*]
▸ ,**pictur'esquely** *adv* ▸ ,**pictur'esqueness** *n*

picture tube *n* another name for **television tube.**

picture window *n* a large window having a single pane of glass, usually facing a view.

picture writing *n* **1** any writing system that uses pictographs. **2** a system of artistic expression and communication using pictures.

PID *abbrev. for* pelvic inflammatory disease.

piddle ('pɪd°l) *vb* **piddles, piddling, piddled. 1** (*intr*) Inf. to urinate. **2** (when *tr*, often foll. by *away*) to spend (one's time) aimlessly; fritter. [C16: from ?]
▸ **'piddler** *n*

piddling ('pɪdlɪŋ) *adj* Inf. petty; trifling; trivial.

piddock ('pɪdək) *n* a marine bivalve boring into rock, clay, or wood by means of sawlike shell valves. [C19: from ?]

pidgin ('pɪdʒɪn) *n* a language made up of elements of two or more other languages and used for contacts, esp. trading contacts, between the speakers of other languages. [C19: ?from Chinese pronunciation of E *business*]

pidgin English *n* a pidgin in which one of the languages involved is English.

pie[1] (paɪ) *n* **1** a baked sweet or savoury filling in a pastry-lined dish, often covered with a pastry crust. **2 pie in the sky.** illusory hope or promise of some future good. [C14: from ?]

pie[2] (paɪ) *n* an archaic or dialect name for **magpie.** [C13: via OF from L *pīca* magpie]

pie[3] (paɪ) *n, vb* **pies, pieing, pied.** *Printing.* a variant spelling of **pi**[2].

piebald ('paɪ,bɔːld) *adj* **1** marked in two colours, esp.

black and white. ◆ *n* **2** a black-and-white horse. [C16: PIE[2] + BALD; see also PIED]

pie cart *n* NZ. a mobile van selling warmed-up food and drinks.

piece (piːs) *n* **1** an amount or portion forming a separate mass or structure; bit: *a piece of wood.* **2** a small part, item, or amount forming part of a whole, esp. when broken off or separated: *a piece of bread.* **3** a length by which a commodity is sold, esp. cloth, wallpaper, etc. **4** an instance or occurrence: *a piece of luck.* **5** an example or specimen of a style or type: *a beautiful piece of Dresden.* **6** Inf. an opinion or point of view: *to state one's piece.* **7** a literary, musical, or artistic composition. **8** a coin: *a fifty-pence piece.* **9** a small object used in playing certain games: *chess pieces.* **10** a firearm or cannon. **11** any chessman other than a pawn. **12** Brit. dialect. a packed lunch taken to work. **13** NZ. fragments of fleece wool. **14 go to pieces. 14a** (of a person) to lose control of oneself; have a breakdown. **14b** (of a building, organization, etc.) to disintegrate. **15 nasty piece of work.** Brit. inf. a cruel or mean person. **16 of a piece.** of the same kind; alike. ◆ *vb* **pieces, piecing, pieced.** (*tr*) **17** (often foll. by *together*) to fit or assemble piece by piece. **18** (often foll. by *up*) to patch or make up (a garment, etc.) by adding pieces. [C13 *pece,* from OF, of Gaulish origin]

pièce de résistance *French.* (pjɛs də rezistɑ̃s) *n* **1** the principal or most outstanding item in a series. **2** the main dish of a meal. [lit.: piece of resistance]

piece goods *pl n* goods, esp. fabrics, made in standard widths and lengths.

piecemeal ('piːs,miːl) *adv* **1** by degrees; bit by bit; gradually. **2** in or into pieces. ◆ *adj* **3** fragmentary or unsystematic: *a piecemeal approach.* [C13 *pecemele,* from PIECE + *-mele,* from OE *mælum* quantity taken at one time]

piece of eight *n, pl* **pieces of eight.** a former Spanish coin worth eight reals; peso.

piecework ('piːs,wɜːk) *n* work paid for according to the quantity produced.

pie chart *n* a circular graph divided into sectors proportional to the magnitudes of the quantities represented.

piecrust table ('paɪ,krʌst) *n* a round table, edged with moulding suggestive of a pie crust.

pied (paɪd) *adj* having markings of two or more colours. [C14: from PIE[2]; an allusion to the magpie's colouring]

pied-à-terre (,pjeɪtɑː'tɛə) *n, pl* **pieds-à-terre** (,pjeɪtɑː'tɛə). a flat or other lodging for occasional use. [from F, lit.: foot on (the) ground]

piedmont ('piːdmɒnt) *adj* (*prenominal*) (of glaciers, plains, etc.) formed or situated at the foot of a mountain. [via F from It. *piémonte,* from *pié,* var. of *piede* foot + *mont* mountain]

Piedmont ★ ('piːdmɒnt) *n* **1** a region of NW Italy: consists of the upper Po Valley; mainly agricultural. Chief town: Turin. Pop.: 4 306 565 (1994 est.). Area: 25 399 sq. km (9807 sq. miles). Italian name: **Piemonte. 2** a low plateau of the eastern US, between the coastal plain and the Appalachian Mountains.

Pied Piper ★ *n* **1** Also called: **the Pied Piper of Hamelin.** (in German legend) a piper who rid the town of Hamelin of rats by luring them away with his music and then, when he was not paid for his services, lured away its children. **2** (*sometimes not caps.*) a person who entices others to follow him.

pied wagtail *n* a British songbird with a black throat and back, long black tail, and white underparts and face.

pie-eyed *adj* Sl. drunk.

Piemonte ★ (*Italian* pje'monte) *n* the Italian name for **Piedmont** (sense 1).

pier (pɪə) *n* **1** a structure with a deck that is built out over water, and used as a landing place, promenade, etc. **2** a pillar that bears heavy loads. **3** the part of a wall between two adjacent openings. **4** another name for **buttress** (sense 1). [C12 *per,* from Anglo-L *pera* pier supporting a bridge]

pierce (pɪəs) *vb* **pierces, piercing, pierced.** (*mainly tr*) **1** to form or cut (a hole) in (something) as with a sharp instrument. **2** to thrust into sharply or violently: *the thorn*

pierced his heel. **3** to force (a way, route, etc.) through (something). **4** (of light, etc.) to shine through or penetrate (darkness). **5** (*also intr*) to discover or realize (something) suddenly or (of an idea, etc.) to become suddenly apparent. **6** (of sounds or cries) to sound sharply through (the silence, etc.). **7** to move or affect deeply or sharply: *the cold pierced their bones.* **8** (*intr*) to penetrate: *piercing cold.* [C13 *percen,* from OF *percer,* ult. from L *pertundere,* from *per* through + *tundere* to strike]
▸ ˈpiercing *adj* ▸ ˈpiercingly *adv*

Pierce ★ (pɪəs) *n* **Franklin.** 1804–69, US statesman; 14th president of the US (1853–57).

pier glass *n* a tall narrow mirror, designed to hang on the wall between windows.

Pieria ★ (paɪˈɪərɪə) *n* a region of ancient Macedonia, west of the Gulf of Salonika: site of the Pierian Spring.

Pierian Spring ★ (paɪˈɪərɪən) *n* a sacred fountain in Pieria, in Greece, fabled to inspire those who drank from it.

Pierides ★ (paɪˈɪərɪˌdiːz) *pl n Greek myth.* **1** another name for the Muses (see **Muse**). **2** nine maidens of Thessaly, who were defeated in a singing contest by the Muses and turned into magpies for their effrontery.

pieris (ˈpaɪrɪs) *n* an evergreen shrub with white flowers like lily of the valley in spring. [C19: from L, from Gk *Pieris,* a Muse]

Piero della Francesca ★ (*Italian* ˈpjɛːro ˌdɛlla franˈtʃeska) *n* ?1420–92, Italian painter, noted particularly for his frescoes of the *Legend of the True Cross* in San Francisco, Arezzo.

Piero di Cosimo ★ (*Italian* ˈpjɛːro di ˈkɔːzimo) *n* 1462–1521, Italian painter, noted for his mythological works.

Pierre ★ (pɪə) *n* a city in central South Dakota, capital of the state, on the Missouri River. Pop.: 12 906 (1990).

Pierrot (ˈpɪərəʊ; *French* pjɛro) *n* **1** a male character from French pantomime with a whitened face, white costume, and pointed hat. **2** (*usually not cap.*) a clown so made up.

pier table *n* a side table designed to stand against a wall between windows.

pietà (pɪeˈtɑː) *n* a sculpture, painting, or drawing of the dead Christ, supported by the Virgin Mary. [It.: pity, from L *pietās* PIETY]

Pietermaritzburg ★ (ˌpiːtəˈmærɪtsˌbɜːg) *n* a city in E South Africa: founded in 1839 by the Boers: gateway to mountain resorts; major industrial centre. Pop.: 156 473 (1991).

pietism (ˈpaɪɪˌtɪzəm) *n* exaggerated or affected piety.
▸ ˈpietist *n* ▸ ˌpieˈtistic *or* ˌpieˈtistical *adj*

piet-my-vrou (ˈpɪtˌmeɪˈfrəʊ) *n S. African.* a red-breasted cuckoo. [imit.]

Pietro da Cortona ★ (*Italian* ˈpjɛːtro da korˈtoːna) *n* real name *Pietro Berrettini.* 1596–1669, Italian baroque painter and architect.

piety (ˈpaɪɪtɪ) *n, pl* **pieties. 1** dutiful devotion to God and observance of religious principles. **2** the quality of being pious. **3** a pious action, saying, etc. **4** *Now rare.* devotion and obedience to parents or superiors. [C13 *piete,* from OF, from L *pietās* piety, dutifulness, from *pius* pious]

piezoelectric effect (paɪˌiːzəʊɪˈlɛktrɪk) *or* **piezo-electricity** (paɪˌiːzəʊɪlɛkˈtrɪsɪtɪ) *n Physics.* **a** the production of electricity or electric polarity by applying a mechanical stress to certain crystals. **b** the converse effect in which stress is produced in a crystal as a result of an applied potential difference. [C19: from Gk *piezein* to press]
▸ piˌezoeˈlectrically *adv*

piffle (ˈpɪfˀl) *Inf.* ◆ *n* **1** nonsense. ◆ *vb* **piffles, piffling, piffled. 2** (*intr*) to talk or behave feebly. [C19: from ?]

piffling (ˈpɪflɪŋ) *adj Inf.* worthless; trivial.

pig (pɪg) *n* **1** any artiodactyl mammal of an African and Eurasian family, esp. the domestic pig, typically having a long head with a movable snout and a thick bristle-covered skin. Related adj: **porcine. 2** *Inf.* a dirty, greedy, or bad-mannered person. **3** the meat of swine; pork. **4** *Derog.* a slang word for **policeman. 5a** a mass of metal cast into a simple shape. **5b** the mould used. **6** *Brit. inf.* some-

thing that is difficult or unpleasant. **7 a pig in a poke.** something bought or received without prior sight or knowledge. **8 make a pig of oneself.** *Inf.* to overindulge oneself. ◆ *vb* **pigs, pigging, pigged. 9** (*intr*) (of a sow) to give birth. **10** (*intr*) Also: **pig it.** *Inf.* to live in squalor. **11** (*tr*) *Inf.* to devour (food) greedily. [C13 *pigge,* from ?]

pigeon[1] (ˈpɪdʒɪn) *n* **1** any of numerous related birds having a heavy body, small head, short legs, and long pointed wings. **2** *Sl.* a victim or dupe. [C14: from OF *pijon* young dove, from LL *pīpiō* young bird, from *pīpīre* to chirp]

pigeon[2] (ˈpɪdʒɪn) *n Brit. inf.* concern or responsibility (often in **it's his, her,** etc., **pigeon**). [C19: altered from PIDGIN]

pigeon breast *n* a deformity of the chest characterized by an abnormal protrusion of the breastbone, caused by rickets.

pigeonhole (ˈpɪdʒɪnˌhəʊl) *n* **1** a small compartment for papers, letters, etc., as in a bureau. **2** a hole or recess in a dovecote for pigeons to nest in. ◆ *vb* **pigeonholes, pigeon-holing, pigeonholed.** (*tr*) **3** to put aside or defer. **4** to classify or categorize.

pigeon-toed *adj* having the toes turned inwards.

pigface (ˈpɪgˌfeɪs) *n Austral.* a creeping succulent plant having bright-coloured flowers and red fruits and often grown for ornament.

piggery (ˈpɪgərɪ) *n, pl* **piggeries. 1** a place where pigs are kept. **2** great greediness.

piggish (ˈpɪgɪʃ) *adj* **1** like a pig, esp. in appetite or manners. **2** *Inf.,* chiefly *Brit.* obstinate or mean.
▸ ˈpiggishly *adv* ▸ ˈpiggishness *n*

Piggott ★ (ˈpɪgət) *n* **Lester (Keith).** born 1935, British flat-racing jockey: he won the Derby nine times.

piggy (ˈpɪgɪ) *n, pl* **piggies. 1** a child's word for a **pig. 2** a child's word for a **toe.** ◆ *adj* **piggier, piggiest. 3** another word for **piggish.**

piggyback (ˈpɪgɪˌbæk) *or* **pickaback** *n* **1** a ride on the back and shoulders of another person. **2** a system whereby a vehicle, aircraft, etc., is transported for part of its journey on another vehicle. ◆ *adv* **3** on the back and shoulders of another person. **4** on or as an addition. ◆ *adj* **5** of or for a piggyback: *a piggyback ride; piggyback lorry trains.* **6** of or relating to a type of heart transplant in which the transplanted heart functions in conjunction with the patient's own heart.

piggy bank *n* a child's coin bank shaped like a pig with a slot for coins.

pig-headed *adj* stupidly stubborn.
▸ ˌpig-ˈheadedly *adv* ▸ ˌpig-ˈheadedness *n*

pig iron *n* crude iron produced in a blast furnace and poured into moulds.

Pig Island ★ *n NZ inf.* New Zealand.
▸ **Pig Islander** *n*

piglet (ˈpɪglɪt) *n* a young pig.

pigmeat (ˈpɪgˌmiːt) *n* a less common name for pork, ham, or bacon.

pigment (ˈpɪgmənt) *n* **1** a substance occurring in plant or animal tissue and producing a characteristic colour. **2** any substance used to impart colour. **3** a powder that is mixed with a liquid to give a paint, ink, etc. [C14: from L *pigmentum,* from *pingere* to paint]
▸ ˈpigmentary *adj*

pigmentation (ˌpɪgmənˈteɪʃən) *n* **1** coloration in plants, animals, or man caused by the presence of pigments. **2** the deposition of pigment in animals, plants, or man.

Pigmy (ˈpɪgmɪ) *n, pl* **Pigmies.** a variant spelling of **Pygmy.**

pignut (ˈpɪgˌnʌt) *n* **1** Also called: **hognut. 1a** the bitter nut of any of several North American hickory trees. **1b** any of the trees bearing such a nut. **2** another name for **earthnut.**

pig-root *vb* (*intr*) *Austral. & NZ sl.* (of a horse) to buck slightly.

pigs (pɪgz) *interj Austral. sl.* an expression of derision or disagreement. Also: **pig's arse, pig's bum.**

Pigs ★ (pɪgz) *n* **Bay of.** See **Bay of Pigs.**

pigskin (ˈpɪgˌskɪn) *n* **1** the skin of the domestic pig. **2**

★ people and places

leather made of this skin. **3** *US & Canad. inf.* a football. ◆ *adj* **4** made of pigskin.

pigsticking ('pɪg,stɪkɪŋ) *n* the sport of hunting wild boar.
▸ **'pig,sticker** *n*

pigsty ('pɪg,staɪ) *or US & Canad.* **pigpen** *n, pl* **pigsties** *or US & Canad.* **pigpens. 1** a pen for pigs; sty. **2** *Brit.* an untidy place.

pigswill ('pɪg,swɪl) *n* waste food or other edible matter fed to pigs. Also called: **pig's wash.**

pigtail ('pɪg,teɪl) *n* **1** a plait of hair or one of two plaits on either side of the face. **2** a twisted roll of tobacco.

pika ('paɪkə) *n* a burrowing mammal of mountainous regions of North America and Asia, having short rounded ears, a rounded body, and rudimentary tail. [C19: from E Siberian *piika*]

pikau ('pi:kau) *n NZ.* a pack, knapsack, or rucksack. [Maori]

pike[1] (paɪk) *n, pl* **pike** *or* **pikes. 1** any of several large predatory freshwater teleost fishes having a broad flat snout, strong teeth, and an elongated body covered with small scales. **2** any of various similar fishes. [C14: short for *pikefish*, from OE *pīc* point, with reference to the shape of its jaw]

pike[2] (paɪk) *n* **1** a medieval weapon consisting of a metal spearhead joined to a long pole. **2** a point or spike. ◆ *vb* **pikes, piking, piked. 3** (*tr*) to pierce using a pike. [OE *pīc* point, from ?]
▸ **'pikeman** *n*

pike[3] (paɪk) *n* short for **turnpike** (sense 1).

pike[4] (paɪk) *n Northern English dialect.* a pointed or conical hill. [OE *pīc*]

pike[5] (paɪk) *or* **piked** (paɪkt) *adj* (of the body position of a diver) bent at the hips but with the legs straight.

pike[6] (paɪk) *vb* **pikes, piking, piked.** (*intr;* foll. by *out*) *Austral. sl.* to shirk. [from PIKER]

pikeperch ('paɪk,pɜːtʃ) *n, pl* **pikeperch** *or* **pikeperches.** any of various pikelike freshwater teleost fishes of the perch family of Europe.

piker ('paɪkə) *n US, Austral., & NZ sl.* **1** a person who will not accept a challenge; shirker. **2** a mean person. [C19: from *Pike* county, Missouri, US]

Pikes Peak ★ *n* a mountain in central Colorado, in the Rockies. Height: 4300 m (14 109 ft).

pikestaff ('paɪk,stɑːf) *n* the wooden handle of a pike.

pilaster (pɪ'læstə) *n* a shallow rectangular column attached to the face of a wall. [C16: from F *pilastre*, from L *pīla* pillar]
▸ **pi'lastered** *adj*

Pilate ★ ('paɪlət) *n* **Pontius** ('pɒnʃəs, 'pɒntɪəs). Roman procurator of Judaea (?26–?36 A.D.), who ordered the crucifixion of Jesus, allegedly reluctantly against his better judgment.

Pilatus ★ (*German* pi'laːtus) *n* a mountain in central Switzerland, in Unterwalden canton: derives its name from the legend that the body of Pontius Pilate lay in a former lake on the mountain. Height: 2122 m (6962 ft).

pilau (pɪ'lau), **pilaf, pilaff,** *or* **pilaw** (pɪ'lɔː) *n* a dish originating from the East, consisting of rice flavoured with spices and cooked in stock, to which meat, poultry, or fish may be added. [C17: from Turkish *pilāw*, from Persian]

pilchard ('pɪltʃəd) *n* a European food fish of the herring family, with a rounded body covered with large scales. [C16 *pylcher*, from ?]

Pilcomayo ★ (*Spanish* pilko'majo) *n* a river in S central South America, rising in W central Bolivia and flowing southeast, forming the border between Argentina and Paraguay, to the Paraguay River at Asunción. Length: about 1600 km (1000 miles).

pile[1] (paɪl) *n* **1** a collection of objects laid on top of one another; heap; mound. **2** *Inf.* a large amount of money (esp. in **make a pile**). **3** (*often pl*) *Inf.* a large amount: *a pile of work.* **4** a less common word for **pyre. 5** a large building or group of buildings. **6** *Physics.* a structure of uranium and a moderator used for producing atomic energy; nu-

clear reactor. ◆ *vb* **piles, piling, piled. 7** (often foll. by *up*) to collect or be collected into or as if into a pile: *snow piled up in the drive.* **8** (*intr;* foll. by *in, into, off, out,* etc.) to move in a group, esp. in a hurried or disorganized manner: *to pile off the bus.* **9 pile it on.** *Inf.* to exaggerate. ◆ See also **pile up.** [C15: via OF from L *pīla* stone pier]

pile[2] (paɪl) *n* **1** a long column of timber, concrete, or steel, driven into the ground as a foundation for a structure. ◆ *vb* **piles, piling, piled.** (*tr*) **2** to drive (piles) into the ground. **3** to support (a structure) with piles. [OE *pīl,* from L *pīlum*]

pile[3] (paɪl) *n* **1** the yarns in a fabric that stand up or out from the weave, as in carpeting, velvet, etc. **2** soft fine hair, fur, wool, etc. [C15: from Anglo-Norman *pyle,* from L *pilus* hair]

pileate ('paɪlɪt, -,eɪt, 'pɪl-) *or* **pileated** ('paɪlɪ,eɪtɪd, 'pɪl-) *adj* **1** (of birds) having a crest. **2** *Bot.* having a pileus. [C18: from L *pīleātus* wearing a felt cap, from PILEUS]

pile-driver *n* a machine that drives piles into the ground.

pileous ('paɪlɪəs, 'pɪl-) *adj Biol.* **1** hairy. **2** of or relating to hair. [C19: ult. from L *pilus* a hair]

piles (paɪlz) *pl n* a nontechnical name for **haemorrhoids.** [C15: from L *pilae* balls (referring to the external piles)]

pileum ('paɪlɪəm, 'pɪl-) *n, pl* **pilea** (-lɪə). the top of a bird's head from the base of the bill to the occiput. [C19: NL, from L PILEUS]

pile up *vb* (*adv*) **1** to gather or be gathered in a pile. **2** *Inf.* to crash or cause to crash. ◆ *n* **pile-up. 3** *Inf.* a multiple collision of vehicles.

pileus ('paɪlɪəs) *n, pl* **pilei** (-lɪ,aɪ). the upper cap-shaped part of a mushroom. [C18: (botanical use): NL, from L: felt cap]

pilewort ('paɪl,wɜːt) *n* any of several plants, such as lesser celandine, thought to be effective in treating piles.

pilfer ('pɪlfə) *vb* to steal (minor items), esp. in small quantities. [C14 *pylfre* (n) from OF *pelfre* booty]
▸ **'pilferage** *n* ▸ **'pilferer** *n*

pilgrim ('pɪlgrɪm) *n* **1** a person who undertakes a journey to a sacred place. **2** any wayfarer. [C12: from Provençal *pelegrin,* from L *peregrīnus* foreign, from *per* through + *ager* land]

pilgrimage ('pɪlgrɪmɪdʒ) *n* **1** a journey to a shrine or other sacred place. **2** a journey or long search made for exalted or sentimental reasons. ◆ *vb* **pilgrimages, pilgrimaging, pilgrimaged. 3** (*intr*) to make a pilgrimage.

Pilgrim Fathers *or* **Pilgrims** *pl n the.* the English Puritans who sailed on the Mayflower to New England, where they founded Plymouth Colony in SE Massachusetts (1620).

piliferous (paɪ'lɪfərəs) *adj* (esp. of plants) bearing or ending in a hair or hairs. [C19: from L *pilus* hair + -FEROUS]
▸ **'pili,form** *adj*

piling ('paɪlɪŋ) *n* **1** the act of driving piles. **2** a number of piles. **3** a structure formed of piles.

Pílion ★ ('piljɒn) *n* transliteration of the Modern Greek name for **Pelion.**

pill[1] (pɪl) *n* **1** a small spherical or ovoid mass of a medicinal substance, intended to be swallowed whole. **2 the pill.** (*sometimes cap.*) *Inf.* an oral contraceptive. **3** something unpleasant that must be endured (esp. in **bitter pill to swallow). 4** *Sl.* a ball or disc. **5** *Sl.* an unpleasant or boring person. ◆ *vb* **6** (*tr*) to give pills to. [C15: from MFlemish *pille,* from L *pilula* a little ball, from *pila* ball]

pill[2] (pɪl) *vb* **1** *Arch. or dialect.* to peel or skin (something). **2** *Arch.* to pillage or plunder (a place, etc.). [OE *pilian,* from L *pilāre* to strip]

pillage ('pɪlɪdʒ) *vb* **pillages, pillaging, pillaged. 1** to rob (a town, village, etc.) of (booty or spoils). ◆ *n* **2** the act of pillaging. **3** something obtained by pillaging; booty. [C14: via OF from *piller* to despoil, prob. from *peille* rag, from L *pīleus* felt cap]
▸ **'pillager** *n*

pillar ('pɪlə) *n* **1** an upright structure of stone, brick, metal, etc. that supports a superstructure. **2** something resembling this in shape or function: *a pillar of smoke.* **3** a prominent supporter: *a pillar of the Church.* **4 from pillar to**

post. from one place to another. [C13: from OF *pilier*, from L *pīla*]

pillar box *n* (in Britain) a red pillar-shaped public letter box situated on a pavement.

Pillars of Hercules ★ *pl n* the two promontories at the E end of the Strait of Gibraltar: the Rock of Gibraltar on the European side and the Jebel Musa on the African side; according to legend, formed by Hercules.

pillbox ('pɪl,bɒks) *n* **1** a box for pills. **2** a small enclosed fortified emplacement, made of reinforced concrete. **3** a small round hat.

pillion ('pɪljən) *n* **1** a seat or place behind the rider of a motorcycle, scooter, horse, etc. ◆ *adv* **2** on a pillion: *to ride pillion.* [C16: from Gaelic; cf. Scot. *pillean*, Irish *pillín* couch]

pilliwinks ('pɪlɪ,wɪŋks) *pl n* a medieval instrument of torture for the fingers. [C14: from ?]

pillock ('pɪlək) *n Brit. sl.* a stupid or annoying person. [C14: from Scand. dialect *pillicock* penis]

pillory ('pɪlərɪ) *n, pl* **pillories. 1** a wooden framework into which offenders were formerly locked by the neck and wrists and exposed to public abuse and ridicule. **2** exposure to public scorn or abuse. ◆ *vb* **pillories, pillorying, pilloried.** (*tr*) **3** to expose to public scorn or ridicule. **4** to punish by putting in a pillory. [C13: from Anglo-L *pillorium*, from OF *pilori*, from ?]

pillow ('pɪləʊ) *n* **1** a cloth case stuffed with feathers, foam rubber, etc., used to support the head, esp. during sleep. **2** Also called: **cushion.** a padded cushion or board on which pillow lace is made. **3** anything like a pillow in shape or function. ◆ *vb* (*tr*) **4** to rest (one's head) on or as if on a pillow. **5** to serve as a pillow for. [OE *pylwe*, from L *pulvīnus* cushion]

pillowcase ('pɪləʊ,keɪs) *or* **pillowslip** ('pɪləʊ,slɪp) *n* a removable washable cover of cotton, linen, nylon, etc., for a pillow.

pillow fight *n* a mock fight in which participants thump each other with pillows.

pillow lace *n* lace made by winding thread around bobbins on a padded cushion or board. Cf. **point lace.**

pillow talk *n* confidential talk between sexual partners in bed.

Pílos ★ ('pilɒs) *n* transliteration of the Modern Greek name for **Pylos.**

pilose ('paɪləʊz) *adj Biol.* covered with fine soft hairs: *pilose leaves.* [C18: from L *pilōsus*, from *pilus* hair]
▶ **pilosity** (paɪˈlɒsɪtɪ) *n*

pilot ('paɪlət) *n* **1** a person who is qualified to operate an aircraft or spacecraft in flight. **2a** a person who is qualified to steer or guide a ship into or out of a port, river mouth, etc. **2b** (*as modifier*): *a pilot ship.* **3** a person who steers a ship. **4** a person who acts as a leader or guide. **5** *Machinery.* a guide used to assist in joining two mating parts together. **6** an experimental programme on radio or television. **7** (*modifier*) serving as a test or trial: *a pilot project.* **8** (*modifier*) serving as a guide: *a pilot beacon.* ◆ *vb* (*tr*) **9** to act as pilot of. **10** to control the course of. **11** to guide or lead (a project, people, etc.). [C16: from F *pilote*, from Med. L *pilotus*, ult. from Gk *pēdon* oar]

pilotage ('paɪlətɪdʒ) *n* **1** the act of piloting an aircraft or ship. **2** a pilot's fee.

pilot balloon *n* a meteorological balloon used to observe air currents.

pilot fish *n* a small fish of tropical and subtropical seas, marked with dark vertical bands: often accompanies sharks.

pilot house *n Naut.* an enclosed structure on the bridge of a vessel from which it can be navigated; a wheelhouse.

pilot lamp *n* a small light in an electric circuit or device that lights when the current is on.

pilot light *n* **1** a small auxiliary flame that ignites the main burner of a gas appliance. **2** a small electric light used as an indicator.

pilot officer *n* the most junior commissioned rank in the British Royal Air Force and in certain other air forces.

pilot study *n* a small-scale experiment undertaken to decide whether and how to launch a full-scale project.

Pils (pɪlz, pɪls) *n* a type of lager-like beer. [C20: abbrev. of PILSNER]

Pilsen ★ ('pɪlzən) *n* the German name for **Plzeň.**

Pilsner ('pɪlznə) *or* **Pilsener** *n* a type of pale beer with a strong flavour of hops. [after PILSEN, where it was orig. brewed]

Pilsudski ★ (*Polish* piwˈsutski) *n* Józef ('juzɛf). 1867–1935, Polish nationalist leader and statesman; president (1918–21) and premier (1926–28; 1930).

pilule ('pɪljuːl) *n* a small pill. [C16: via F from L *pilula* little ball, from *pila* ball]
▶ **'pilular** *adj*

pimento (pɪˈmɛntəʊ) *n, pl* **pimentos.** another name for **allspice** or **pimiento.** [C17: from Sp. *pimiento* pepper plant, from Med. L *pigmenta* spiced drink, from L *pigmentum* PIGMENT]

pi meson *n* another name for **pion.**

pimiento (pɪˈmjɛntəʊ, -ˈmɛn-) *n, pl* **pimientos.** a Spanish pepper with a red fruit used as a vegetable. Also called: **pimento.** [var. of PIMENTO]

pimp[1] (pɪmp) *n* **1** a man who solicits for a prostitute or brothel. **2** a man who procures sexual gratification for another; procurer; pander. ◆ *vb* **3** (*intr*) to act as a pimp. [C17: from ?]

pimp[2] (pɪmp) *Sl., chiefly Austral. & NZ.* ◆ *n* **1** a spy or informer. ◆ *vb* **2** (*intr;* often foll. by *on*) to inform (on). [from ?]

pimpernel ('pɪmpə,nɛl, -n°l) *n* any of several plants, such as the scarlet pimpernel, typically having small star-shaped flowers. [C15: from OF *pimpernelle*, ult. from L *piper* PEPPER]

pimple ('pɪmp°l) *n* a small round usually inflamed swelling of the skin. [C14: rel. to OE *pipilian* to break out in spots]
▶ **'pimpled** *adj* ▶ **'pimply** *adj* ▶ **'pimpliness** *n*

pin (pɪn) *n* **1** a short stiff straight piece of wire pointed at one end and either rounded or having a flattened head at the other: used mainly for fastening pieces of cloth, paper, etc. **2** short for **cotter pin, hairpin, panel pin, rolling pin,** or **safety pin. 3** an ornamental brooch, esp. a narrow one. **4** a badge worn fastened to the clothing by a pin. **5** something of little or no importance (esp. in **not care** *or* **give a pin (for).)** **6** a peg or dowel. **7** anything resembling a pin in shape, function, etc. **8** (in various bowling games) a usually club-shaped wooden object set up in groups as a target. **9** Also called: **safety pin.** a clip on a hand grenade that prevents its detonation until removed or released. **10** *Naut.* **10a** See **belaying pin. 10b** the sliding closure for a shackle. **11** *Music.* a metal tuning peg on a piano. **12** *Surgery.* a metal rod, esp. of stainless steel, for holding together adjacent ends of fractured bones during healing. **13** *Chess.* a position in which a piece is pinned against a more valuable piece or the king. **14** *Golf.* the flagpole marking the hole on a green. **15** (*usually pl*) *Inf.* a leg. ◆ *vb* **pins, pinning, pinned.** (*tr*) **16** to attach, hold, or fasten with or as if with a pin or pins. **17** to transfix with a pin, spear, etc. **18** (foll. by *on*) *Inf.* to place (the blame for something): *he pinned the charge on his accomplice.* **19** *Chess.* to cause (an enemy piece) to be effectively immobilized since moving it would reveal a check or expose a more valuable piece to capture. ◆ See also **pin down.** [OE *pinn*]

PIN (pɪn) *n acronym for* personal identification number: a number used by a holder of a cash card or credit card used in EFTPOS.

pinaceous (paɪˈneɪfəs) *adj* of, relating to, or belonging to a family of conifers with needle-like leaves: includes pine, spruce, fir, larch, and cedar. [C19: via NL from L *pīnus* a pine]

pinafore ('pɪnə,fɔː) *n* **1** *Chiefly Brit.* an apron, esp. one with a bib. **2** Also called: **pinafore dress.** a dress with a sleeveless bodice or bib top, worn over a jumper or blouse. [C18: from PIN + AFORE]

Pinar del Río ★ (*Spanish* piˈnar ðel ˈrrio) *n* a city in W Cuba: tobacco industry. Pop.: 128 570 (1994 est.).

pinaster (paɪˈnæstə) *n* a Mediterranean pine tree with paired needles and prickly cones. Also called: **maritime** (*or* **cluster**) **pinaster**. [C16: from L: wild pine, from *pīnus* pine]

pinball (ˈpɪnˌbɔːl) *n* **a** a game in which the player shoots a small ball through several hazards on a table, electrically operated machine, etc. **b** (*as modifier*): *a pinball machine*.

pince-nez (ˈpæns‚neɪ, ˈpɪns-; *French* pɛ̃sne) *n, pl* **pince-nez.** eyeglasses that are held in place only by means of a clip over the bridge of the nose. [C19: F, lit.: pinch-nose]

pincers (ˈpɪnsəz) *pl n* **1** Also called: **pair of pincers.** a gripping tool consisting of two hinged arms with handles at one end and, at the other, curved bevelled jaws that close on the workpiece. **2** The pair or pairs of jointed grasping appendages in lobsters and certain other arthropods. [C14: from OF *pinceour*, from OF *pincier* to pinch]

pinch (pɪntʃ) *vb* **1** to press (something, esp. flesh) tightly between two surfaces, esp. between a finger and thumb. **2** to confine, squeeze, or painfully press (toes, fingers, etc.) because of lack of space: *these shoes pinch.* **3** (*tr*) to cause stinging pain to: *the cold pinched his face.* **4** (*tr*) to make thin or drawn-looking, as from grief, lack of food, etc. **5** (usually foll. by *on*) to provide (oneself or another person) with meagre allowances, amounts, etc. **6 pinch pennies.** to live frugally because of meanness or to economize. **7** (usually foll. by *off, out,* or *back*) to remove the tips of (buds, shoots, etc.) to correct or encourage growth. **8** (*tr*) *Inf.* to steal or take without asking. **9** (*tr*) *Inf.* to arrest. ◆ *n* **10** a squeeze or sustained nip. **11** the quantity of a substance, such as salt, that can be taken between a thumb and finger. **12** a very small quantity. **13** (usually preceded by *the*) sharp, painful, or extreme stress, need, etc.: *feeling the pinch of poverty.* **14** *Sl.* a robbery. **15** *Sl.* a police raid or arrest. **16 at a pinch.** if absolutely necessary. [C16: prob. from OF *pinchier* (unattested)]

pinchbeck (ˈpɪntʃˌbek) *n* **1** an alloy of copper and zinc, used as imitation gold. **2** a spurious or cheap imitation. ◆ *adj* **3** made of pinchbeck. **4** sham or cheap. [C18 (the alloy), C19 (something spurious): after C. *Pinchbeck* (?1670–1732), E watchmaker who invented it]

pinchpenny (ˈpɪntʃˌpenɪ) *adj* **1** niggardly; miserly. ◆ *n, pl* **pinchpennies.** **2** a miserly person.

Pinckney ★ (ˈpɪŋknɪ) *n* **Charles Cotesworth.** 1746–1825, US statesman, who was a member of the convention that framed the US Constitution (1787).

Pincus ★ (ˈpɪŋkəs) *n* **Gregory Goodwin.** 1903–67, US physiologist, whose work on steroid hormones led to the development of the first contraceptive pill.

pincushion (ˈpɪnˌkuʃən) *n* a small well-padded cushion in which pins are stuck ready for use.

Pindar ★ (ˈpɪndə) *n* ?518–?438 B.C., Greek lyric poet, noted for his *Epinikia,* odes commemorating victories in the Greek games.
▸ **Pindaric** (pɪnˈdærɪk) *adj*

pin down *vb* (*tr, adv*) **1** to force (someone) to make a decision or carry out a promise. **2** to define clearly: *he had a vague suspicion that he couldn't quite pin down.* **3** to confine to a place.

Pindus ★ (ˈpɪndəs) *n* a mountain range in central Greece between Epirus and Thessaly. Highest peak: Mount Smólikas, 2633 m (8639 ft). Modern Greek name: **Píndhos** (ˈpɪndɔs).

pine[1] (paɪn) *n* **1** any of a genus of evergreen resinous coniferous trees of the N hemisphere, with long needle-shaped leaves (**pine needles**) and brown cones. **2** the wood of any of these trees. [OE *pīn,* from L *pīnus* pine]

pine[2] (paɪn) *vb* **pines, pining, pined.** **1** (*intr;* often foll. by *for* or an infinitive) to feel great longing or desire; yearn. **2** (*intr;* often foll. by *away*) to become ill or thin through worry, longing, etc. [OE *pīnian* to torture, from *pīn* pain, from Med. L *pēna,* from L *poena* PAIN]

pineal eye (ˈpɪnɪəl) *n* an outgrowth of the pineal gland that forms an eyelike structure on the top of the head in certain cold-blooded vertebrates. [C19: from F, from L *pīnea* pine cone]

pineal gland *or* **body** *n* a pea-sized organ situated at the base of the brain that secretes a hormone, melatonin, into the bloodstream. Technical names: **epiphysis, epiphysis cerebri.**

pineapple (ˈpaɪnˌæpəl) *n* **1** a tropical American plant cultivated for its large fleshy edible fruit. **2** the fruit of this plant, consisting of an inflorescence clustered around a fleshy axis and surmounted by a tuft of leaves. **3** *Mil. sl.* a hand grenade. [C14 *pinappel* pine cone; C17: applied to the fruit because of its appearance]

pine cone *n* the seed-producing structure of a pine tree. See **cone** (sense 3a).

pine marten *n* a marten of N European and Asian coniferous woods, having dark brown fur with a creamy-yellow patch on the throat.

pinene (ˈpaɪniːn) *n* either of two isomeric terpenes, found in many essential oils and constituting the main part of oil of turpentine. [C20: from PINE[1] + -ENE]

pine nut *or* **kernel** *n* the edible seed of certain pine trees.

Pinero ★ (pɪˈnɪərəʊ) *n* **Sir Arthur Wing.** 1855–1934, British dramatist. His works include the farce *Dandy Dick* (1887) and the problem play *The Second Mrs Tanqueray* (1893).

Pines ★ (paɪnz) *n* **Isle of.** the former name of the (Isle of) **Youth.**

pine tar *n* a brown or black semisolid, produced by the destructive distillation of pine wood, used in roofing compositions, paints, medicines, etc.

pinfeather (ˈpɪnˌfeðə) *n* **Ornithol.** a feather emerging from the skin and still enclosed in its horny sheath.

pinfold (ˈpɪnˌfəʊld) *n* **1** a pound for stray cattle. ◆ *vb* **2** (*tr*) to gather or confine in or as if in a pinfold. [OE *pundfald*]

ping (pɪŋ) *n* **1** a short high-pitched resonant sound, as of a bullet striking metal or a sonar echo. ◆ *vb* **2** (*intr*) to make such a noise. [C19: imit.]

pinger (ˈpɪŋə) *n* a device that makes a pinging sound, esp. one that can be preset to ring at a particular time.

Ping-Pong (ˈpɪŋˌpɒŋ) *n* **Trademark.** another name for **table tennis.** Also: **ping pong.**

pinhead (ˈpɪnˌhed) *n* **1** the head of a pin. **2** something very small. **3** *Inf.* a stupid person.
▸ **ˈpinˌheaded** *adj* ▸ **ˈpinˌheadedness** *n*

pinhole (ˈpɪnˌhəʊl) *n* a small hole made with or as if with a pin.

pinion[1] (ˈpɪnjən) *n* **1** *Chiefly poetic.* a bird's wing. **2** the part of a bird's wing including the flight feathers. ◆ *vb* (*tr*) **3** to hold or bind (the arms) of (a person) so as to restrain or immobilize him. **4** to confine or shackle. **5** to make (a bird) incapable of flight by removing the flight feathers. [C15: from OF *pignon* wing, from L *pinna* wing]

pinion[2] (ˈpɪnjən) *n* a cogwheel that engages with a larger wheel or rack. [C17: from F *pignon* cogwheel, from OF *peigne* comb, from L *pecten*]

Piniós ★ (piˈnjɔs) *n* transliteration of the Modern Greek name for the **Salambria.**

pink[1] (pɪŋk) *n* **1** a pale reddish colour. **2** pink cloth or clothing: *dressed in pink.* **3** any of various Old World plants, such as the garden pink, cultivated for their fragrant flowers. See also **carnation** (sense 1). **4** the flower of any of these plants. **5** the highest or best degree, condition, etc. (esp. in **in the pink**). **6a** a huntsman's scarlet coat. **6b** a huntsman who wears a scarlet coat. ◆ *adj* **7** of the colour pink. **8** *Brit.* left-wing. **9** *Inf.* of or relating to homosexuals or homosexuality: *the pink vote.* **10** (of a huntsman's coat) scarlet or red. ◆ *vb* **11** (*intr*) another word for **knock** (sense 7). [C16 (the flower), C18 (the colour): ? short for PINKEYE]
▸ **ˈpinkish** *or* **ˈpinky** *adj* ▸ **ˈpinkness** *n*

pink[2] (pɪŋk) *vb* (*tr*) **1** to prick lightly with a sword, etc. **2** to decorate (leather, etc.) with a perforated or punched pattern. **3** to cut with pinking shears. [C14: ? of Low G origin]

pink[3] (pɪŋk) *n* a sailing vessel with a narrow overhanging transom. [C15: from MDu. *pinke,* from ?]

Pinkerton ★ (ˈpɪŋkətən) *n* **Allan.** 1819–84, US private detective, born in Scotland. He founded the first detective agency in the US (1850) and organized an intelligence system for the Federal States of America (1861).

pinkeye ('pɪŋk,aɪ) *n* **1** Also called: **acute conjunctivitis**. an acute contagious inflammation of the conjunctiva of the eye, characterized by redness, discharge, etc. **2** Also called: **infectious keratitis**. a similar condition affecting the cornea of horses and cattle. [C16: partial translation of obs. Du. *pinck oogen* small eyes]

pinkie *or* **pinky** ('pɪŋkɪ) *n, pl* **pinkies**. *Scot., US, & Canad.* the little finger. [C19: from Du. *pinkje*]

pinking shears *pl n* scissors with a serrated edge on one or both blades, producing a wavy edge to material cut, thus preventing fraying.

pink salmon *n* **1** any salmon having pale pink flesh. **2** the flesh of such a fish.

pin money *n* **1** an allowance by a husband to his wife for personal expenditure. **2** money saved or earned for incidental expenses.

pinna ('pɪnə) *n, pl* **pinnae** (-niː) *or* **pinnas**. **1** any leaflet of a pinnate compound leaf. **2** *Zool.* a feather, wing, fin, etc. **3** another name for **auricle** (sense 2). [C18: via NL from L: wing]

pinnace ('pɪnɪs, -əs) *n* any of various kinds of ship's tender. [C16: from F *pinace*, ?from OSp. *pinaza*, lit.: something made of pine, ult. from L *pīnus* pine]

pinnacle ('pɪnəkəl) *n* **1** the highest point, esp. of fame, success, etc. **2** a towering peak, as of a mountain. **3** a slender upright structure in the form of a spire on the top of a buttress, gable, or tower. ◆ *vb* **pinnacles, pinnacling, pinnacled**. (*tr*) **4** to set as on a pinnacle. **5** to furnish with a pinnacle or pinnacles. **6** to crown with a pinnacle. [C14: via OF from LL *pinnāculum* a peak, from L *pinna* wing]

pinnate ('pɪneɪt, 'pɪnɪt) *adj* **1** like a feather in appearance. **2** (of compound leaves) having the leaflets growing opposite each other in pairs on either side of the stem. [C18: from L *pinnātus*, from *pinna* feather] ▸ **'pinnately** *adv* ▸ **pin'nation** *n*

pinniped ('pɪnɪ,pɛd) *adj* **1** of, relating to, or belonging to an order of aquatic placental mammals having a streamlined body and limbs specialized as flippers: includes seals, sea lions, and the walrus. ◆ *n* **2** any pinniped animal. [C19: from NL *pinnipēs*, from L *pinna* fin + *pēs* foot]

pinnule ('pɪnjuːl) *n* **1** any of the lobes of a leaflet of a pinnate compound leaf, which is itself pinnately divided. **2** *Zool.* any feather-like part, such as any of the arms of a sea lily. [C16: from L *pinnula*, dim. of *pinna* feather] ▸ **'pinnular** *adj*

pinny ('pɪnɪ) *n, pl* **pinnies**. a child's or informal name for **pinafore** (sense 1).

Pinochet ★ ('piːnə,ʃeɪ) *n* **Augusto** (**Ugarte**) (au'gusto). born 1915, Chilean general and statesman; president of Chile (1974–90), following his overthrow of Allende (1973).

pinochle *or* **pinocle** ('piːnʌkəl) *n* **1** a card game for two to four players similar to bezique. **2** the combination of queen of spades and jack of diamonds in this game. [C19: from ?]

pinpoint ('pɪn,pɔɪnt) *vb* (*tr*) **1** to locate or identify exactly: *to pinpoint a problem; to pinpoint a place on a map.* ◆ *n* **2** an insignificant or trifling thing. **3** the point of a pin. **4** (*modifier*) exact: *a pinpoint aim.*

pinprick ('pɪn,prɪk) *n* **1** a slight puncture made by or as if by a pin. **2** a small irritation. ◆ *vb* **3** (*tr*) to puncture with or as if with a pin.

pins and needles *n* (*functioning as sing*) *Inf.* **1** a tingling sensation in the fingers, toes, legs, etc., caused by the return of normal blood circulation after its temporary impairment. **2 on pins and needles**. in a state of anxious suspense.

Pinsk ★ (*Russian* pinsk) *n* a city in SW Belarus: capital of a principality (13th–14th centuries). Pop.: 130 000 (1996 est.).

pinstripe ('pɪn,straɪp) *n* (in textiles) a very narrow stripe in fabric or the fabric itself.

pint (paɪnt) *n* **1** a unit of liquid measure of capacity equal to one eighth of a gallon. 1 Brit. pint is equal to 0.568

litre, 1 US pint to 0.473 litre. **2** a unit of dry measure of capacity equal to one half of a quart. 1 US dry pint is equal to one sixty-fourth of a US bushel or 0.5506 litre. **3** a measure having such a capacity. **4** *Brit. inf.* **4a** a pint of beer. **4b** a drink of beer: *he's gone out for a pint.* [C14: from OF *pinte*, from ?; ?from Med. L *pincta* marks used in measuring liquids, ult. from L *pingere* to paint]

pinta ('paɪntə) *n Inf.* a pint of milk. [C20: phonetic rendering of *pint of*]

pintail ('pɪn,teɪl) *n, pl* **pintails** *or* **pintail**. a greyish-brown duck with a pointed tail.

Pinter ★ ('pɪntə) *n* **Harold.** born 1930, British dramatist. His plays, such as *The Caretaker* (1960), *The Homecoming* (1965), and *Ashes to Ashes* (1996), are noted for their equivocal and halting dialogue.

pintle ('pɪntəl) *n* **1** a pin or bolt forming the pivot of a hinge. **2** the link bolt, hook, or pin on a vehicle's towing bracket. **3** the needle or plunger of the injection valve of an oil engine. [OE *pintel* penis]

pinto ('pɪntəʊ) *US & Canad.* ◆ *adj* **1** marked with patches of white; piebald. ◆ *n, pl* **pintos**. **2** a pinto horse. [C19: from American Sp. (orig.: painted, spotted), ult. from L *pingere* to paint]

pint-size *or* **pint-sized** *adj Inf.* very small.

pin tuck *n* a narrow, ornamental fold, esp. used on shirt fronts and dress bodices.

Pinturicchio (*Italian* pintu'rikkjo) *or* **Pintoricchio** ★ (*Italian* pinto'rikkjo) *n* real name *Bernardino di Betto*. ?1454–1513, Italian painter of the Umbrian school.

pin-up *n* **1** *Inf.* **1a** a picture of a sexually attractive person, esp. when partially or totally undressed. **1b** (*as modifier*): *a pin-up magazine.* **2** *Sl.* a person who has appeared in such a picture. **3** a photograph of a famous personality.

pinus radiata ('paɪnəs ˌreɪdɪ'ɑːtə) *n* a pine tree grown in New Zealand and Australia to produce building timber.

pinwheel ('pɪn,wiːl) *n* another name for a **Catherine wheel** (sense 1).

pinworm ('pɪn,wɜːm) *n* a parasitic nematode worm, infecting the colon, rectum, and anus of humans. Also called: **threadworm**.

piny ('paɪnɪ) *adj* **pinier, piniest**. of, resembling, or covered with pine trees.

Pinyin ('pɪn'jɪn) *n* a system of spelling used to transliterate Chinese characters into the Roman alphabet.

Pinzón ★ (*Spanish* pin'θon) *n* **1 Martín Alonzo** (mar'tin a'lɔnθo). ?1440–93, Spanish navigator, who commanded the *Pinta* on Columbus' first expedition (1492–93). **2** his brother, **Vicente Yáñez** (bi'θente 'jaɲɛθ). ?1460–?1524, Spanish navigator, who commanded the *Niña* on Columbus' first expedition (1492–93).

pion ('paɪɒn) *or* **pi meson** *n Physics.* a meson having a positive or negative charge and a rest mass 273 times that of the electron, or no charge and a rest mass 264 times that of the electron. [C20: from Gk letter PI + -ON]

pioneer (ˌpaɪə'nɪə) *n* **1a** a colonist, explorer, or settler of a new land, region, etc. **1b** (*as modifier*): *a pioneer wagon.* **2** an innovator or developer of something new. **3** *Mil.* a member of an infantry group that digs entrenchments, makes roads, etc. ◆ *vb* **4** to be a pioneer (in or of). **5** (*tr*) to initiate, prepare, or open up: *to pioneer a medical programme.* [C16: from OF *paonier* infantryman, from *paon* PAWN²]

pious ('paɪəs) *adj* **1** having or expressing reverence for a god or gods; religious; devout. **2** marked by reverence. **3** marked by false reverence; sanctimonious. **4** sacred; not secular. [C17: from L *pius*] ▸ **'piously** *adv* ▸ **'piousness** *n*

pip¹ (pɪp) *n* **1** the seed of a fleshy fruit, such as an apple or pear. **2** any of the segments marking the surface of a pineapple. [C18: short for PIPPIN]

pip² (pɪp) *n* **1** a short high-pitched sound, a sequence of which can act as a time signal, esp. on radio. **2** a radar blip. **3a** a device, such as a spade, diamond, heart, or club on a playing card. **3b** any of the spots on dice or dominoes. **4** *Inf.* the emblem worn on the shoulder by junior officers in the British Army, indicating their rank. ◆ *vb* **pips, pipping, pipped**. **5** (of a young bird) **5a** (*intr*) to chirp; peep. **5b** to pierce (the shell of its egg) while hatching. **6** (*intr*) to make a short high-pitched sound. [C16 (in the sense: spot); C17 (vb); C20 (in the sense: short high-pitched sound): ? imit.]

pip³ (pɪp) *n* **1** a contagious disease of poultry characterized by the secretion of thick mucus in the mouth and throat. **2** *Facetious sl.* a minor human ailment. **3** *Brit. sl.* a bad temper or depression (esp. in **give (someone) the pip**). ♦ *vb* **pips, pipping, pipped. 4** *Brit. sl.* to cause to be annoyed or depressed. [C15: from MDu. *pippe*, ult. from L *pituita* phlegm]

pip⁴ (pɪp) *vb* **pips, pipping, pipped.** (*tr*) *Brit. sl.* **1** to wound, esp. with a gun. **2** to defeat (a person), esp. when his success seems certain (often in **pip at the post**). **3** to blackball or ostracize. [C19 (orig. in the sense: to blackball): prob. from PIP²]

pipal ('piːpəl) *n* a variant of **peepul**.

pipe¹ (paɪp) *n* **1** a long tube of metal, plastic, etc., used to convey water, oil, gas, etc. **2** a long tube or case. **3** an object made in various shapes and sizes, consisting of a small bowl with an attached tubular stem, in which tobacco or other substances are smoked. **4** Also called: **pipeful.** the amount of tobacco that fills the bowl of a pipe. **5 put that in your pipe and smoke it.** *Inf.* accept that fact if you can. **6** *Zool., bot.* any of various hollow organs, such as the respiratory passage of certain animals. **7a** any musical instrument whose sound production results from the vibration of an air column in a simple tube. **7b** any of the tubular devices on an organ. **8 the pipes.** See **bagpipes. 9** a shrill voice or sound, as of a bird. **10a** a boatswain's pipe. **10b** the sound it makes. **11** (*pl*) *Inf.* the respiratory tract or vocal cords. **12** *Metallurgy.* a conical hole in the head of an ingot. **13** a cylindrical vein of rich ore. **14** Also called: **volcanic pipe.** a vertical cylindrical passage in a volcano through which molten lava is forced during eruption. ♦ *vb* **pipes, piping, piped. 15** to play (music) on a pipe. **16** (*tr*) to summon or lead by a pipe: *to pipe the dancers.* **17** to utter (something) shrilly. **18a** to signal orders to (the crew) by a boatswain's pipe. **18b** (*tr*) to signal the arrival or departure of: *to pipe the admiral aboard.* **19** (*tr*) to convey (water, gas, etc.) by a pipe or pipes. **20** (*tr*) to provide with pipes. **21** (*tr*) to trim (an article, esp. of clothing) with piping. **22** to force cream or icing, etc., through a shaped nozzle to decorate food. ♦ See also **pipe down, pipe up.** [OE *pīpe* (n), *pīpian* (vb), ult. from L *pīpāre* to chirp]

pipe² (paɪp) *n* **1** a large cask for wine, oil, etc. **2** a measure of capacity for wine equal to four barrels or 105 Brit. gallons. **3** a cask holding this quantity with its contents. [C14: via OF (in the sense: tube), ult. from L *pīpāre* to chirp]

pipe bomb *n* a small explosive device hidden in a pipe or drain, detonated by means of a timer.

pipeclay ('paɪp,kleɪ) *n* **1** a fine white pure clay, used in the manufacture of tobacco pipes and pottery and for whitening leather and similar materials. ♦ *vb* **2** (*tr*) to whiten with pipeclay.

pipe cleaner *n* a short length of thin wires twisted so as to hold tiny tufts of yarn: used to clean the stem of a tobacco pipe.

piped music *n* light popular music prerecorded and played through amplifiers in a shop, restaurant, factory, etc., as background music.

pipe down *vb* (*intr, adv*) *Inf.* to stop talking, making noise, etc.

pipe dream *n* a fanciful or impossible plan or hope. [alluding to dreams produced by smoking an opium pipe]

pipefish ('paɪp,fɪʃ) *n, pl* **pipefish** or **pipefishes.** any of various teleost fishes having a long tubelike snout and an elongated body covered with bony plates. Also called: **needlefish.**

pipefitting ('paɪp,fɪtɪŋ) *n* **a** the act or process of bending and joining pipes. **b** the branch of plumbing involving this. ▶ '**pipe,fitter** *n*

pipeline ('paɪp,laɪn) *n* **1** a long pipe used to transport oil, natural gas, etc. **2** a medium of communication, esp. a private one. **3 in the pipeline.** in the process of being completed, delivered, or produced. ♦ *vb* **pipelines, pipelining, pipelined.** (*tr*) **4** to convey by pipeline. **5** to supply with a pipeline.

pipe major *n* the noncommissioned officer responsible for the training of a pipe band.

pipe organ *n* another name for **organ** (the musical instrument).

piper ('paɪpə) *n* **1** a person who plays a pipe or bagpipes. **2 pay the piper and call the tune.** to bear the cost of an undertaking and control it.

Piper ★ ('paɪpə) *n* John. 1903–92, British artist. An official war artist in World War II, he is known also for his stained glass in Coventry Cathedral.

piperidine (pɪ'perɪ,diːn) *n* a liquid compound with a peppery ammoniacal odour: used in making rubbers and curing epoxy resins.

piperine ('pɪpə,raɪn) *n* an alkaloid that is the active ingredient of pepper, used as a flavouring and as an insecticide. [C19: from L *piper* PEPPER]

piperonal ('pɪpərəʊ,næl) *n* a white fragrant aldehyde used in flavourings, perfumery, and suntan lotions.

pipette (pɪ'pet) *n* a calibrated glass tube drawn to a fine bore at one end, filled by sucking liquid into the bulb, and used to transfer or measure known volumes of liquid. [C19: via F: little pipe]

pipe up *vb* (*intr, adv*) **1** to commence singing or playing a musical instrument: *the band piped up.* **2** to speak up, esp. in a shrill voice.

pipi ('pɪpiː) *n, pl* **pipi** or **pipis. 1** an edible shellfish of New Zealand. **2** an Australian mollusc of sandy beaches, widely used as bait. [from Maori]

piping ('paɪpɪŋ) *n* **1** pipes collectively, as in the plumbing of a house. **2** a cord of icing, whipped cream, etc., often used to decorate desserts and cakes. **3** a thin strip of covered cord or material, used to edge hems, etc. **4** the sound of a pipe or bagpipes. **5** the art or technique of playing a pipe or bagpipes. **6** a shrill voice or sound, esp. a whistling sound. ♦ *adj* **7** making a shrill sound. **8 piping hot.** extremely hot.

pipistrelle (,pɪpɪ'strel) *n* any of a genus of numerous small brownish insectivorous bats, occurring in most parts of the world. [C18: via F from It. *pipistrello*, from L *vespertīliō* a bat, from *vesper* evening, because of its nocturnal habits]

pipit ('pɪpɪt) *n* any of various songbirds, esp. the **meadow pipit**, having brownish speckled plumage and a long tail. [C18: prob. imit.]

pipkin ('pɪpkɪn) *n* a small earthenware vessel. [C16: ? dim. of PIPE²; see -KIN]

pippin ('pɪpɪn) *n* any of several varieties of eating apple. [C13: from OF *pepin*, from ?]

pipsissewa (pɪp'sɪsəwə) *n* any of several ericaceous plants of an Asian and American genus, having jagged evergreen leaves and white or pinkish flowers. Also called: **wintergreen.** [C19: from Algonquian *pipisisikweu*, lit.: it breaks it into pieces, so called because believed to be efficacious in treating bladder stones]

pipsqueak ('pɪp,skwiːk) *n Inf.* a person or thing that is insignificant or contemptible.

piquant ('piːkənt, -kɑːnt) *adj* **1** having an agreeably pungent or tart taste. **2** lively or stimulating to the mind. [C16: from F (lit.: prickling), from *piquer* to prick, goad] ▶ '**piquancy** *n* ▶ '**piquantly** *adv*

pique (piːk) *n* **1** a feeling of resentment or irritation, as from having one's pride wounded. ♦ *vb* **piques, piquing, piqued.** (*tr*) **2** to cause to feel resentment or irritation. **3** to excite or arouse. **4** (foll. by *on* or *upon*) to pride or congratulate (oneself). [C16: from F, from *piquer* to prick]

piqué ('piːkeɪ) *n* a close-textured fabric of cotton, silk, or spun rayon woven with lengthwise ribs. [C19: from F *piqué* pricked, from *piquer* to prick]

piquet (pɪ'ket, -'keɪ) *n* a card game for two people played with a reduced pack. [C17: from F, from ?]

piracy ('paɪrəsɪ) *n, pl* **piracies. 1** *Brit.* robbery on the seas. **2** a felony, such as robbery or hijacking, committed aboard a ship or aircraft. **3** the unauthorized use or appropriation of patented or copyrighted material, ideas, etc. [C16: from Anglo-L *pirātia*, from LGk *peirāteia;* see PIRATE]

Piraeus or **Peiraeus** ★ (paɪˈriːəs, pɪˈreɪ-) *n* a port in SE Greece, adjoining Athens: the country's chief port; founded in the 5th century B.C. as the port of Athens. Pop.: 169 622 (1991). Modern Greek name: **Piraiévs** (ˌpɪreˈɛfs).

Pirandello ★ (*Italian* piranˈdɛllo) *n* **Luigi** (luˈiːdʒi). 1867–1936, Italian dramatist and writer. His plays include *Six Characters in Search of an Author* (1921) and *Henry IV* (1922): Nobel prize for literature 1934.

Piranesi ★ (*Italian* piraˈneːsi) *n* **Giambattista** (dʒambatˈtista). 1720–78, Italian etcher and architect: etchings include *Imaginary Prisons* and *Views of Rome.*

piranha or **piraña** (pɪˈrɑːnjə) *n* any of various small freshwater voracious fishes of tropical America, having strong jaws and sharp teeth. [C19: via Port. from Tupi: fish with teeth, from *pirá* fish + *sainha* tooth]

pirate (ˈpaɪrɪt) *n* **1** a person who commits piracy. **2a** a vessel used by pirates. **2b** (*as modifier*): *a pirate ship.* **3** a person who illicitly uses or appropriates someone else's literary, artistic, or other work. **4a** a person or group of people who broadcast illegally. **4b** (*as modifier*): *a pirate radio station.* ♦ *vb* **pirates, pirating, pirated. 5** (*tr*) to use, appropriate, or reproduce (artistic work, ideas, etc.) illicitly. [C15: from L *pīrāta*, from Gk *peirātēs* one who attacks, from *peira* an attack]
  ▸ **pi'ratical** or **piratic** (paɪˈrætɪk) *adj* ▸ **pi'ratically** *adv*

Pirithoüs ★ (paɪˈrɪθəʊəs) *n Greek myth.* a prince of the Lapiths, who accomplished many great deeds with his friend Theseus.

pirogue (pɪˈrəʊg) or **piragua** (pɪˈrɑːgwə, -ˈræg-) *n* any of various kinds of dugout canoes. [C17: via F from Sp., of Amerind origin]

pirouette (ˌpɪruˈɛt) *n* **1** a body spin, esp. in dancing, on the toes or the ball of the foot. ♦ *vb* **pirouettes, pirouetting, pirouetted. 2** (*intr*) to perform a pirouette. [C18: from F, from OF *pirouet* spinning top]

Pisa (ˈpiːzə; *Italian* ˈpiːsa) *n* a city in Tuscany, NW Italy, near the mouth of the River Arno: flourishing maritime republic (11th–12th centuries), contains a university (1343), a cathedral (1063), and the Leaning Tower (begun in 1174 and about 5 m (17 ft) from perpendicular); tourism. Pop.: 102 150 (1990).

Pisanello ★ (*Italian* pisaˈnɛllo) *n* **Antonio** (anˈtɔːnjo). ?1395–?1455, Italian painter and medallist in the International Gothic style: best known for his portrait medals and drawings of animals.

Pisano ★ (*Italian* pisaˈnɔːno) *n* **1 Giovanni** (dʒoˈvanni). ?1250–?1320, Italian sculptor, noted for his pulpit at St Andrea, Pistoia. **2** his father, **Nicola** (niˈkɔːla). ?1220–?84, Italian sculptor, who pioneered the classical style: noted esp. for his pulpit in the baptistry of Pisa Cathedral.

piscatorial (ˌpɪskəˈtɔːrɪəl) or **piscatory** (ˈpɪskətərɪ, -trɪ) *adj* **1** of or relating to fish, fishing, or fishermen. **2** devoted to fishing. [C19: from L *piscātōrius*, from *piscātor* fisherman]
  ▸ **ˌpiscaˈtorially** *adv*

Pisces (ˈpaɪsiːz, ˈpɪ-) *n, Latin genitive* **Piscium** (ˈpaɪsɪəm). **1** *Astron.* a faint extensive zodiacal constellation lying between Aquarius and Aries on the ecliptic. **2** *Astrol.* Also called: the **Fishes.** the twelfth sign of the zodiac. The sun is in this sign between about Feb. 19 and March 20. **3a** a taxonomic group that comprises all fishes. See **fish** (sense 1). **3b** a taxonomic group that comprises the bony fishes only. See **teleost.** [C14: L: the fish (pl)]

pisci- *combining form.* fish: *pisciculture.* [from L *piscis*]

pisciculture (ˈpɪsɪˌkʌltʃə) *n* the rearing and breeding of fish under controlled conditions.
  ▸ **ˌpisciˈcultural** *adj* ▸ **ˌpisciˈculturist** *n, adj*

piscina (pɪˈsiːnə) *n, pl* **piscinae** (-niː) or **piscinas.** *RC Church.* a stone basin, with a drain, in a church or sacristy where water used at Mass is poured away. [C16: from L: fish pond, from *piscis* a fish]

piscine (ˈpɪsaɪn) *adj* of, relating to, or resembling a fish.

piscivorous (pɪˈsɪvərəs) *adj* feeding on fish.

Pisgah ★ (ˈpɪzgə) *n* **Mount.** *Old Testament.* the mountain slopes to the northeast of the Dead Sea, from one of which, Mount Nebo, Moses viewed Canaan.

pish (pʃ, pɪʃ) *interj* **1** an exclamation of impatience or contempt. ♦ *vb* **2** to make this exclamation at (someone or something).

Pishpek ★ (pɪʃˈpɛk) *n* a variant transliteration of the Kyrgyz name for **Bishkek.**

pisiform (ˈpɪsɪˌfɔːm) *adj* **1** *Zool., bot.* resembling a pea. ♦ *n* **2** a small pealike bone on the ulnar side of the carpus. [C18: via NL from L *pīsum* pea + *forma* shape]

Pisistratus ★ (paɪˈsɪstrətəs) *n* ?600–527 B.C., tyrant of Athens: he established himself in firm control of the city following his defeat of his aristocratic rivals at Pallene (546).

pismire (ˈpɪsˌmaɪə) *n* an archaic or dialect word for an **ant.** [C14: lit.: urinating ant, from the odour of formic acid): from PISS + obs. *mire* ant, from ON]

piss (pɪs) *Sl.* ♦ *vb* **1** (*intr*) *Taboo.* to urinate. **2** (*tr*) *Taboo.* to discharge as or in one's urine: *to piss blood.* ♦ *n* **3** *Taboo.* an act of urinating. **4** *Taboo.* urine. **5 take the piss.** to tease or make fun of someone or something. [C13: from OF *pisser*, prob. imit.]

Pissarro ★ (pɪˈsɑːrəʊ; *French* pisaro) *n* **Camille** (kamij). 1830–1903, French impressionist painter, esp. of landscapes.

piss artist *n Sl.* **1** a boastful or incompetent person. **2** a person who drinks heavily and gets drunk frequently.

pissed (pɪst) *adj Sl.* **1** *Brit. taboo.* drunk. **2** *US.* annoyed, irritated, or disappointed.

piss off *vb* (*adv*) *Taboo sl.* **1** (*tr; often passive*) to annoy, irritate, or disappoint. **2** (*intr*) *Chiefly Brit.* to go away; depart: often used to dismiss a person.

piss-up *n Sl.* a party involving a considerable amount of drinking.

pistachio (pɪˈstɑːʃɪˌəʊ) *n, pl* **pistachios. 1** a tree of the Mediterranean region and W Asia, with small hard-shelled nuts. **2** Also called: **pistachio nut.** the nut of this tree, having an edible green kernel. **3** the sweet flavour of the pistachio nut, used in ice creams, etc. ♦ *adj* **4** of a yellowish-green colour. [C16: via It. & L from Gk *pistakion* pistachio nut, from *pistakē* pistachio tree, from Persian *pistah*]

piste (piːst) *n* a slope or course for skiing. [C18: via OF from OIt. *pista*, from *pistare* to tread down]

pistil (ˈpɪstɪl) *n* the female reproductive part of a flower, consisting of one or more separate or fused carpels. [C18: from L *pistillum* pestle]

pistillate (ˈpɪstɪlɪt, -ˌleɪt) *adj* (of plants) **1** having pistils but no anthers. **2** having or producing pistils.

Pistoia ★ (*Italian* pisˈtoːja) *n* a city in N Italy, in N Tuscany: scene of the defeat and death of Catiline in 62 B.C. Pop.: 89 972 (1990).

pistol (ˈpɪstəl) *n* **1** a short-barrelled handgun. **2 hold a pistol to a person's head.** to threaten a person in order to force him to do what one wants. ♦ *vb* **pistols, pistolling, pistolled** or *US* **pistols, pistoling, pistoled. 3** (*tr*) to shoot with a pistol. [C16: from F *pistole*, from G, from Czech *pišťala* pistol, pipe]

pistole (pɪsˈtəʊl) *n* any of various gold coins of varying value, formerly used in Europe. [C16: from OF, shortened from *pistolet*, lit.: little PISTOL]

pistol grip *n* **a** a handle shaped like the butt of a pistol. **b** (*as modifier*): *a pistol-grip camera.*

pistol-whip *vb* **pistol-whips, pistol-whipping, pistol-whipped.** (*tr*) *US.* to beat or strike with a pistol barrel.

piston (ˈpɪstən) *n* a disc or cylindrical part that slides to and fro in a hollow cylinder. In an internal-combustion engine it is attached by a pivoted connecting rod to a crankshaft or flywheel, thus converting reciprocating motion into rotation. [C18: via F from OIt. *pistone*, from *pistare* to grind, from L *pinsere* to beat]

piston ring *n* a split ring that fits into a groove on the rim of a piston to provide a spring-loaded seal against the cylinder wall.

piston rod n 1 the rod that connects the piston of a reciprocating steam engine to the crosshead. 2 a less common name for a **connecting rod**.

pit[1] (pɪt) n 1 a large, usually deep opening in the ground. 2a a mine or excavation, esp. for coal. 2b the shaft in a mine. 2c (as modifier): pit pony; pit prop. 3 a concealed danger or difficulty. 4 the pit. hell. 5 Also called: orchestra pit. the area that is occupied by the orchestra in a theatre, located in front of the stage. 6 an enclosure for fighting animals or birds. 7 Anat. 7a a small natural depression on the surface of a body, organ, or part. 7b the floor of any natural bodily cavity: the pit of the stomach. 8 Pathol. a small indented scar at the site of a former pustule; pockmark. 9 a working area at the side of a motor-racing track for servicing or refuelling vehicles. 10 a section on the floor of a commodity exchange devoted to a special line of trading. 11 the ground floor of the auditorium of a theatre. 12 another word for **pitfall** (sense 2). ◆ vb **pits, pitting, pitted.** 13 (tr; often foll. by against) to match in opposition, esp. as antagonists. 14 to mark or become marked with pits. 15 (tr) to place or bury in a pit. [OE pytt, from L puteus]

pit[2] (pɪt) Chiefly US & Canad. ◆ n 1 the stone of a cherry, etc. ◆ vb **pits, pitting, pitted.** (tr) 2 to extract the stone from (a fruit). [C19: from Du.: kernel]

pitapat (ˈpɪtəˌpæt) adv 1 with quick light taps. ◆ vb **pitapats, pitapatting, pitapatted.** 2 (intr) to make quick light taps. ◆ n 3 such taps. [C16: imit.]

pit bull terrier n a dog resembling the Staffordshire bull terrier but somewhat larger: originally developed for dogfighting.

Pitcairn Island ★ (pɪtˈkɛən, ˈpɪtkɛən) n an island in the S Pacific: forms with other islands a UK overseas territory; uninhabited until the landing in 1790 of the mutineers of H.M.S. Bounty and their Tahitian companions. Pop.: 54 (1995). Area: 4.6 sq. km (1.75 sq. miles).

pitch[1] (pɪtʃ) vb 1 to hurl or throw (something); cast; fling. 2 (usually tr) to set up (a camp, tent, etc.). 3 (tr) to aim or fix (something) at a particular level, position, style, etc.: if you advertise privately you may pitch the price too low. 4 (tr) to aim to sell (a product) to a specified market or on a specified basis. 5 (intr) to slope downwards. 6 (intr) to fall forwards or downwards. 7 (intr) (of a vessel) to dip and raise its bow and stern alternately. 8 Cricket. to bowl (a ball) so that it bounces on a certain part of the wicket, or (of a ball) to bounce on a certain part of the wicket. 9 (intr) (of a missile, aircraft, etc.) to deviate from a stable flight attitude by movement of the longitudinal axis about the lateral axis. 10 (tr) (in golf, etc.) to hit (a ball) steeply into the air. 11 (tr) Music. 11a to sing or play accurately (a note, interval, etc.). 11b (usually passive) (of a wind instrument) to specify or indicate its basic key or harmonic series by its size, manufacture, etc. 12 Baseball, softball. 12a (tr) to throw (a ball) to a batter. 12b (intr) to act as a pitcher in a game. ◆ n 13 the degree of elevation or depression. 14a the angle of descent of a downward slope. 14b such a slope. 15 the extreme height or depth. 16 Mountaineering. a section of a route between two belay points. 17 the degree of slope of a roof. 18 the distance between corresponding points on adjacent members of a body of regular form, esp. the distance between teeth on a gearwheel or between threads on a screw thread. 19 the pitching motion of a ship, missile, etc. 20 Music. 20a the height or depth of a note as determined by its frequency relative to that of other notes: high pitch; low pitch. 20b an absolute frequency assigned to a specific note, fixing the relative frequencies of all other notes. 21 Cricket. the rectangular area between the stumps, 22 yards long and 10 feet wide; the wicket. 22 the act or manner of pitching a ball, as in cricket, etc. 23 Chiefly Brit. a vendor's station, esp. on a pavement. 24 Sl. a persuasive sales talk, esp. one routinely repeated. 25 Chiefly Brit. (in many sports) the field of play. 26 Golf. Also called: **pitch shot.** an approach shot in which the ball is struck in a high arc. 27 **queer someone's pitch.** Brit. inf. to upset someone's plans. ◆ See also **pitch in, pitch into.** [C13 picchen]

pitch[2] (pɪtʃ) n 1 any of various heavy dark viscid substances obtained as a residue from the distillation of tars. 2 any of various similar substances, such as asphalt, oc-

curring as natural deposits. 3 crude turpentine obtained as sap from pine trees. ◆ vb 4 (tr) to apply pitch to (something). [OE pic, from L pix]

pitch-black adj 1 extremely dark; unlit: the room was pitch-black. 2 of a deep black colour.

pitchblende (ˈpɪtʃˌblɛnd) n a blackish mineral that occurs in veins, frequently associated with silver: the principal source of uranium and radium. [C18: partial translation of G Pechblende, from Pech PITCH[2] (from its black colour) + BLENDE]

pitch-dark adj extremely or completely dark.

pitched battle n 1 a battle ensuing from the deliberate choice of time and place. 2 any fierce encounter, esp. one with large numbers.

pitcher[1] (ˈpɪtʃə) n a large jug, usually rounded with a narrow neck and often of earthenware, used mainly for holding water. [C13: from OF pichier, from Med. L picārium, var. of bicārium BEAKER]

pitcher[2] (ˈpɪtʃə) n Baseball. the player on the fielding team who throws the ball to the batter.

pitcher plant n any of various insectivorous plants, having leaves modified to form pitcher-like organs that attract and trap insects, which are then digested.

pitchfork (ˈpɪtʃˌfɔːk) n 1 a long-handled fork with two or three long curved tines for tossing hay. ◆ vb (tr) 2 to use a pitchfork on (something). 3 to thrust (someone) unwillingly into a position.

pitch in vb (intr, adv) 1 to cooperate or contribute. 2 to begin energetically.

pitch into vb (intr, prep) Inf. 1 to assail physically or verbally. 2 to get on with doing (something).

pitch pine n 1 any of various coniferous trees of North America: valued as a source of turpentine and pitch. 2 the wood of any of these trees.

pitch pipe n a small pipe that sounds a note or notes of standard frequency. It is used for establishing the correct starting note for unaccompanied singing.

pitchy (ˈpɪtʃɪ) adj **pitchier, pitchiest.** 1 full of or covered with pitch. 2 resembling pitch.
▶ ˈpitchiness n

piteous (ˈpɪtɪəs) adj exciting or deserving pity.
▶ ˈpiteously adv ▶ ˈpiteousness n

pitfall (ˈpɪtˌfɔːl) n 1 an unsuspected difficulty or danger. 2 a trap in the form of a concealed pit, designed to catch men or wild animals. [OE pytt PIT[1] + fealle trap]

pith (pɪθ) n 1 the soft fibrous tissue lining the inside of the rind in fruits such as the orange. 2 the essential or important part, point, etc. 3 weight; substance. 4 Bot. the central core of unspecialized cells surrounded by conducting tissue in stems. 5 the soft central part of a bone, feather, etc. ◆ vb (tr) 6 to kill (animals) by severing the spinal cord. 7 to remove the pith from (a plant). [OE pitha]

pithead (ˈpɪtˌhɛd) n the top of a mine shaft and the buildings, hoisting gear, etc., around it.

pithecanthropus (ˌpɪθɪkænˈθrəʊpəs) n, pl **pithecanthropi** (-ˌpaɪ). any primitive apelike man of the former genus Pithecanthropus, now included in the genus Homo. See **Java man.** [C19: NL, from Gk pithēkos ape + anthrōpos man]

pith helmet n a lightweight hat made of the pith of the sola, an E Indian swamp plant, that protects the wearer from the sun. Also called: **topee, topi.**

pithos (ˈpɪθɒs, ˈpaɪ-) n, pl **pithoi** (-ɔɪ). a large ceramic container for oil or grain. [from Gk]

pithy (ˈpɪθɪ) adj **pithier, pithiest.** 1 terse and full of meaning or substance. 2 of, resembling, or full of pith.
▶ ˈpithily adv ▶ ˈpithiness n

pitiable (ˈpɪtɪəbəl) adj exciting or deserving pity or contempt.
▶ ˈpitiableness n ▶ ˈpitiably adv

pitiful (ˈpɪtɪfʊl) adj 1 arousing or deserving pity. 2 arousing or deserving contempt. 3 Arch. full of pity or compassion.
▶ ˈpitifully adv ▶ ˈpitifulness n

pitiless (ˈpɪtɪlɪs) adj having or showing little or no pity or mercy.
▶ ˈpitilessly adv ▶ ˈpitilessness n

pitman ('pɪtmən) *n, pl* **pitmen**. *Chiefly Scot. & N English.* a person who works in a pit, esp. a coal miner.

Pitman ★ ('pɪtmən) *n* Sir **Isaac**. 1813–97, British inventor of a system of phonetic shorthand (1837).

piton ('pi:tɒn) *n Mountaineering.* a metal spike that may be driven into a crevice and used to secure a rope, etc. [C20: from F: ringbolt]

pits (pɪts) *pl n* **the**. *Sl.* the worst possible person, place, or thing. [C20: from ? *armpits*]

pit stop *n* 1 *Motor racing.* a brief stop made at a pit by a racing car for repairs, refuelling, etc. 2 *Inf.* any stop made during a car journey for refreshment, rest, or refuelling.

Pitt ★ (pɪt) *n* 1 **William**, known as *Pitt the Elder*, 1st Earl of Chatham. 1708–78, British statesman. He was first minister (1756–57; 1757–61; 1766–68) and achieved British victory in the Seven Years' War (1756–63). 2 his son **William**, known as *Pitt the Younger*. 1759–1806, British statesman. As prime minister (1783–1801; 1804–06), he carried through important fiscal and tariff reforms. From 1793, his attention was focused on the wars with revolutionary and Napoleonic France.

pitta bread *or* **pitta** ('pɪtə) *n* a flat rounded slightly leavened bread, originally from the Middle East. [from Mod. Gk: a cake]

pittance ('pɪt°ns) *n* a small amount or portion, esp. a meagre allowance of money. [C16: from OF *pietance* ration, ult. from L *pietās* duty]

pitter-patter ('pɪtəˌpætə) *n* 1 the sound of light rapid taps or pats, as of raindrops. ◆ *vb* 2 (*intr*) to make such a sound. ◆ *adv* 3 with such a sound.

Pittsburgh ★ ('pɪtsbɜːg) *n* a port in SW Pennsylvania, at the confluence of the Allegheny and Monongahela Rivers, which form the Ohio River: settled around Fort Pitt in 1758; developed rapidly with the discovery of iron deposits and one of the world's richest coalfields; the largest river port in the US and an important industrial centre, formerly with large steel mills. Pop.: 358 883 (1994 est.).

pituitary (pɪ'tjuːɪtərɪ) *n, pl* **pituitaries**. 1 See **pituitary gland**. ◆ *adj* 2 of or relating to the pituitary gland. [C17: from LL *pītuītārius* slimy, from *pītuīta* phlegm]

pituitary gland *or* **body** *n* the master endocrine gland, attached by a stalk to the base of the brain. Its two lobes secrete hormones affecting skeletal growth, development of the sex glands, and the functioning of the other endocrine glands.

pit viper *n* any venomous snake of a New World family, having a heat-sensitive organ in a pit on each side of the head: includes the rattlesnakes.

pity ('pɪtɪ) *n, pl* **pities**. 1 sympathy or sorrow felt for the sufferings of another. 2 **have** (*or* **take**) **pity on**. to have sympathy or show mercy for. 3 something that causes regret. 4 an unfortunate chance: *what a pity you can't come.* ◆ *vb* **pities, pitying, pitied.** (*tr*) 5 to feel pity for. [C13: from OF *pité*, from L *pietās* duty]
▸ **'pitying** *adj* ▸ **'pityingly** *adv*

pityriasis (ˌpɪtə'raɪəsɪs) *n* any of a group of skin diseases characterized by the shedding of dry flakes of skin. [C17: via NL from Gk *pituriasis* scurfiness, from *pituron* bran]

più (pjuː) *adv* (in combination) *Music.* more (quickly, etc.): *più allegro.* [It., from L *plus* more]

piupiu ('piːuːˌpiːuː) *n* a skirt made from leaves of the New Zealand flax, worn by Maoris on ceremonial occasions. [from Maori]

Piura ★ (Spanish 'pjura) *n* a city in NW Peru: the oldest colonial city in Peru, founded by Pizarro in 1532; commercial centre of an agricultural district. Pop.: 277 964 (1993).

Pius II ★ ('paɪəs) *n* pen name *Aeneas Silvius*, original name *Enea Silvio de' Piccolomini*. 1405–64, Italian ecclesiastic, humanist, poet, and historian; pope (1458–64).

Pius IV ★ *n* original name *Giovanni Angelo de' Medici*. 1499–1565, pope (1559–65). He reconvened the Council of Trent (1562), confirming its final decrees.

Pius V ★ *n* Saint. original name *Michele Ghislieri*. 1504–72,

pope (1566–72). He attempted to enforce the reforms decreed by the Council of Trent, excommunicated Elizabeth I of England (1570), and organized the alliance that defeated the Turks at Lepanto (1571). Feast day: Apr. 30.

Pius VII ★ *n* original name *Luigi Barnaba Chiaramonti*. 1740–1823, Italian ecclesiastic; pope (1800–23). He concluded a concordat with Napoleon (1801) but resisted his annexation of the Papal States (1809).

Pius IX ★ *n* original name *Giovanni Maria Mastai-Ferretti*. 1792–1878, Italian ecclesiastic; pope (1846–78). He decreed the dogma of the Immaculate Conception (1854) and convened the Vatican Council, which laid down the doctrine of papal infallibility (1870).

Pius X ★ *n* Saint. original name *Giuseppe Sarto*. 1835–1914, Italian ecclesiastic; pope (1903–14). He condemned Modernism (1907) and initiated a new codification of canon law. Feast day: Aug. 21.

Pius XI ★ *n* original name *Achille Ratti*. 1857–1939, Italian ecclesiastic; pope (1922–39). He signed the Lateran Treaty (1929), by which the Vatican City was recognized as an independent state.

Pius XII ★ *n* original name *Eugenio Pacelli*. 1876–1958, Italian ecclesiastic; pope (1939–58): his attitude towards Nazi German anti-Semitism has been a matter of controversy.

pivot ('pɪvət) *n* 1 a short shaft or pin supporting something that turns; fulcrum. 2 the end of a shaft or arbor that terminates in a bearing. 3 a person or thing upon which progress, success, etc., depends. 4 the person or position from which a military formation takes its reference when altering position, etc. ◆ *vb* 5 (*tr*) to mount on or provide with a pivot or pivots. 6 (*intr*) to turn on or as if on a pivot. [C17: from OF]

pivotal ('pɪvət°l) *adj* 1 of, involving, or acting as a pivot. 2 of crucial importance.

pix[1] (pɪks) *n* a plural of **pic**.

pix[2] (pɪks) *n* a less common spelling of **pyx**.

pixel ('pɪksəl) *n* any of a number of very small picture elements that make up a picture, as on a visual display unit. [C20: from *pix* pictures + *el(ement)*]

pixie *or* **pixy** ('pɪksɪ) *n, pl* **pixies**. (in folklore) a fairy or elf. [C17: from ?]

pixilated *or* **pixillated** ('pɪksɪˌleɪtɪd) *adj Chiefly US.* 1 eccentric or whimsical. 2 *Sl.* drunk. [C20: from PIXIE + -*lated*, as in *stimulated, titillated,* etc.]

Pizarro ★ (pɪ'zɑːrəʊ; *Spanish* pi'θarrɔ) *n* **Francisco** (fran'θisko). ?1475–1541, Spanish conqueror of Peru. He landed in Peru (1532), murdered the Inca King Atahualpa (1533), and founded Lima as the new capital of Peru (1535). He was murdered by his own followers.

pizza ('piːtsə) *n* a dish of Italian origin consisting of a baked disc of dough covered with cheese and tomato, plus ham, mushrooms, etc. [C20: from It., ?from Vulgar L *picea* (unattested), ? rel. to Mod. Gk *pitta* cake]

pizzazz *or* **pizazz** (pə'zæz) *n Inf.* an attractive combination of energy and style; sparkle. Also: **bezazz**. [C20: ?]

pizzeria (ˌpiːtsə'riːə) *n* a place where pizzas are made, sold, or eaten.

pizzicato (ˌpɪtsɪ'kɑːtəʊ) *Music.* ◆ *adj, adv* 1 (in music for the violin family) to be plucked with the finger. ◆ *n* 2 this style or technique of playing. [C19: from It.: pinched, from *pizzicare* to twist]

pizzle ('pɪz°l) *n Arch. or dialect.* the penis of an animal, esp. a bull. [C16: of Gmc origin]

pk *pl* **pks** *abbrev. for:* 1 pack. 2 park. 3 peak.

pkg. *pl* **pkgs.** *abbrev. for* package.

pl *abbrev. for:* 1 place. 2 plate. 3 plural.

Pl. (in street names) *abbrev. for* Place.

PLA *abbrev. for* Port of London Authority.

plaas (plɑːs) *n S. African.* a farm. [from Afrik., from Du.]

placable ('plækəb°l) *adj* easily placated or appeased. [C15: via OF from L *plācābilis*, from *plācāre* to appease]
▸ ˌplaca'bility *n*

placard ('plækɑːd) *n* 1 a notice for public display; poster.

2 a small plaque or card. ◆ *vb* (*tr*) **3** to post placards on or in. **4** to advertise by placards. **5** to display as a placard. [C15: from OF *plaquart*, from *plaquier* to plate, lay flat; see PLAQUE]

placate (pləˈkeɪt) *vb* **placates, placating, placated.** (*tr*) to pacify or appease. [C17: from L *plācāre*]
▶ **plaˈcation** *n* ▶ **plaˈcatory** *adj*

place (pleɪs) *n* **1** a particular point or part of space or of a surface, esp. that occupied by a person or thing. **2** a geographical point, such as a town, city, etc. **3** a position or rank in a sequence or order. **4** an open square lined with houses in a city or town. **5** space or room. **6** a house or living quarters. **7** a country house with grounds. **8** any building or area set aside for a specific purpose. **9** a passage in a book, play, film, etc.: *to lose one's place.* **10** proper, right, or customary surroundings (esp. in **out of place, in place**). **11** right, prerogative, or duty: *it is your place to give a speech.* **12** appointment, position, or job: *a place at college.* **13** position, condition, or state: *if I were in your place.* **14a** a space or seat, as at a dining table. **14b** (*as modifier*): *place mat.* **15** *Maths.* the relative position of a digit in a number. **16** any of the best times in a race. **17** *Horse racing.* **17a** *Brit., Austral., & NZ.* the first, second, or third position at the finish. **17b** *US & Canad.* usually the second position at the finish. **17c** (*as modifier*): *a place bet.* **18 all over the place.** in disorder or disarray. **19 give place** (*to*). to make room (for) or be superseded (by). **20 go places.** *Inf.* **20a** to travel. **20b** to become successful. **21 in place of.** **21a** instead of; in lieu of: *go in place of my sister.* **21b** in exchange for: *he gave her it in place of her ring.* **22 know one's place.** to be aware of one's inferior position. **23 put someone in his** (*or* **her**) **place.** to humble someone who is arrogant, conceited, forward, etc. **24 take one's place.** to take up one's usual or specified position. **25 take place.** to happen or occur. **26 take the place of.** to be a substitute for. ◆ *vb* **places, placing, placed.** (*mainly tr*) **27** to put or set in a particular or appropriate place. **28** to find or indicate the place of. **29** to identify or classify by linking with an appropriate context: *to place a face.* **30** to regard or view as being: *to place prosperity above sincerity.* **31** to make (an order, bet, etc.). **32** to find a home or job for (someone). **33** to appoint to an office or position. **34** (often foll. by *with*) to put under the care (of). **35** to direct or aim carefully. **36** (*passive*) *Brit.* to cause (a racehorse, greyhound, athlete, etc.) to arrive in first, second, third, or sometimes fourth place. **37** *US & Canad.* (*intr*) (of a racehorse, greyhound, etc.) to finish among the first three in a contest, esp. in second position. **38** to invest (funds). **39** (*tr*) to insert (an advertisement) in a newspaper, journal, etc. [C13: via OF from L *platēa* courtyard, from Gk *plateia,* from *platus* broad]

placebo (pləˈsiːbəʊ) *n, pl* **placebos** *or* **placeboes. 1** *Med.* an inactive substance administered to a patient usually to compare its effects with those of a real drug but sometimes for the psychological benefit to the patient through his believing he is receiving treatment. **2** something said or done to please or humour another. **3** *RC Church.* a traditional name for the vespers of the office for the dead. [C13 (in the ecclesiastical sense): from L *Placebo Domino* I shall please the Lord; C19 (in the medical sense)]

placebo effect *n Med.* a positive therapeutic effect claimed by a patient after receiving a placebo believed by him to be an active drug.

place card *n* a card placed on a dinner table before a seat, indicating who is to sit there.

place kick *Football, etc.* ◆ *n* **1** a kick in which the ball is placed in position before it is kicked. ◆ *vb* **place-kick. 2** to kick (a ball) in this way.

placement (ˈpleɪsmənt) *n* **1** the act of placing or the state of being placed. **2** arrangement or position. **3** the process of finding employment.

placenta (pləˈsɛntə) *n, pl* **placentas** *or* **placentae** (-tiː). **1** the vascular organ formed in the uterus of most mammals during pregnancy, consisting of both maternal and embryonic tissues and providing oxygen and nutrients for the fetus. **2** *Bot.* the part of the ovary of flowering plants to which the ovules are attached. [C17: via L from Gk *plakoeis* flat cake, from *plax* flat]
▶ **plaˈcental** *adj*

placer (ˈplæsə) *n* a surface sediment containing particles of gold or some other valuable mineral. **b** (*in combination*): *placer-mining.* [C19: from American Sp.: deposit, from Sp. *plaza* PLACE]

place setting *n* the cutlery, crockery, and glassware laid for one person at a dining table.

placet (ˈpleɪsɛt) *n* a vote or expression of assent by saying *placet.* [C16: from L, lit.: it pleases]

placid (ˈplæsɪd) *adj* having a calm appearance or nature. [C17: from L *placidus* peaceful]
▶ **placidity** (pləˈsɪdɪtɪ) *or* **ˈplacidness** *n* ▶ **ˈplacidly** *adv*

placing (ˈpleɪsɪŋ) *n Stock Exchange.* a method of issuing securities to the public using an intermediary, such as a stockbroking firm.

placket (ˈplækɪt) *n Dressmaking.* **1** a piece of cloth sewn in under a closure with buttons, zips, etc. **2** the closure itself. [C16: ?from MDu. *plackaet* breastplate, from Med. L *placca* metal plate]

placoid (ˈplækɔɪd) *adj* **1** platelike or flattened. **2** (of the scales of sharks) toothlike; composed of dentine with an enamel tip and basal pulp cavity. [C19: from Gk *plac-,* *plax* flat]

plafond (pləˈfɒn; *French* plafɔ̃) *n* a ceiling, esp. one having ornamentation. [C17: from F, from *plat* flat + *fond* bottom, from L *fundus*]

plagal (ˈpleɪɡəl) *adj* **1** (of a cadence) progressing from the subdominant to the tonic chord, as in the *Amen* of a hymn. **2** (of a mode) commencing upon the dominant of an authentic mode, but sharing the same final as the authentic mode. ◆ Cf. **authentic** (sense 5). [C16: from Med. L *plagālis,* from *plaga,* ?from Gk *plagos* side]

plage (plɑːʒ) *n Astron.* a bright patch in the sun's chromosphere. [F, lit.: beach]

plagiarism (ˈpleɪdʒəˌrɪzəm) *n* **1** the act of plagiarizing. **2** something plagiarized. [C17: from L *plagiārus* plunderer, from *plagium* kidnapping]
▶ **ˈplagiarist** *n* ▶ **ˌplagiaˈristic** *adj*

plagiarize *or* **plagiarise** (ˈpleɪdʒəˌraɪz) *vb* **plagiarizes, plagiarizing, plagiarized** *or* **plagiarises, plagiarising, plagiarised.** to appropriate (ideas, passages, etc.) from (another work or author).
▶ **ˈplagiaˌrizer** *or* **ˈplagiaˌriser** *n*

plagioclase (ˈpleɪdʒɪəʊˌkleɪz) *n* a series of feldspar minerals consisting of a mixture of sodium and calcium aluminium silicates in triclinic crystalline form. [C19: from Gk, from *plagos* side + -CLASE]
▶ **plagioclastic** (ˌpleɪdʒɪəʊˈklæstɪk) *adj*

plague (pleɪɡ) *n* **1** any widespread and usually highly contagious disease with a high fatality rate. **2** an infectious disease of rodents, esp. rats, transmitted to man by the bite of the rat flea. **3** See **bubonic plague. 4** something that afflicts or harasses. **5** *Inf.* an annoyance or nuisance. **6** a pestilence, affliction, or calamity on a large scale, esp. when regarded as sent by God. ◆ *vb* **plagues, plaguing, plagued.** (*tr*) **7** to afflict or harass. **8** to bring down a plague upon. **9** *Inf.* to annoy. [C14: from LL *plāga* pestilence, from L: a blow]

plaguy *or* **plaguey** (ˈpleɪɡɪ) *Arch., inf.* ◆ *adj* **1** disagreeable or vexing. ◆ *adv* **2** disagreeably or annoyingly.
▶ **ˈplaguily** *adv*

plaice (pleɪs) *n, pl* **plaice** *or* **plaices. 1** a European flatfish having an oval brown body marked with red or orange spots and valued as a food fish. **2** *US & Canad.* any of various other related fishes. [C13: from OF *plaïz,* from LL *platessa* flatfish, from Gk *platus* flat]

plaid (plæd, pleɪd) *n* **1** a long piece of cloth of a tartan pattern, worn over the shoulder as part of Highland costume. **2a** a crisscross weave or cloth. **2b** (*as modifier*): *a plaid scarf.* [C16: from Scot. Gaelic *plaide,* from ?]

Plaid Cymru (ˌplaɪd ˈkʌmrɪ) *n* the Welsh nationalist party. [Welsh]

plain[1] (pleɪn) *adj* **1** flat or smooth; level. **2** not complicated; clear: *the plain truth.* **3** not difficult; simple or easy: *a plain task.* **4** honest or straightforward. **5** lowly, esp. in social rank or education. **6** without adornment or show: *a plain coat.* **7** (of fabric) without pattern or of simple untwilled weave. **8** not attractive. **9** not mixed; simple:

plain vodka. **10** (of knitting) done in plain stitch. ◆ *n* **11** a level or almost level tract of country. **12** a simple stitch in knitting made by passing the wool round the front of the needle. ◆ *adv* **13** (intensifier): *just plain tired.* [C13: from OF: simple, from L *plānus* level, clear]
▸ 'plainly *adv* ▸ 'plainness *n*

plain[2] (pleɪn) *vb* a dialect or poetic word for **complain**. [C14 *pleignen*, from OF *plaindre* to lament, from L *plangere* to beat]

plainchant ('pleɪnˌtʃɑːnt) *n* another name for **plainsong**. [C18: from F, for Med. L *cantus plānus*]

plain chocolate *n* chocolate with a slightly bitter flavour and dark colour.

plain clothes *pl n* **a** ordinary clothes, as distinguished from uniform, as worn by a police detective on duty. **b** (*as modifier*): *a plain-clothes policeman.*

plain flour *n* flour to which no raising agent has been added.

plain sailing *n* **1** *Inf.* smooth or easy progress. **2** *Naut.* sailing in a body of water that is unobstructed; clear sailing.

plainsman ('pleɪnzmən) *n, pl* **plainsmen.** a person who lives in a plains region, esp. in the Great Plains of North America.

Plains of Abraham ★ *n* (*functioning as sing*) a field in E Canada between Quebec City and the St Lawrence River: site of an important British victory (1759) in the Seven Years' War, which cost the French their possession of Canada.

plainsong ('pleɪnˌsɒŋ) *n* the style of unison unaccompanied vocal music used in the medieval Church, esp. in Gregorian chant. [C16: translation of Med. L *cantus plānus*]

plain-spoken *adj* candid; frank; blunt.

plaint (pleɪnt) *n* **1** *Arch.* a complaint or lamentation. **2** *Law.* a statement in writing of grounds of complaint made to a court of law. [C13: from OF *plainte*, from L *planctus* lamentation, from *plangere* to beat]

plaintiff ('pleɪntɪf) *n* a person who brings a civil action in a court of law. [C14: from legal F *plaintif*, from OF *plaintif* (adj) complaining, from *plainte* PLAINT]

plaintive ('pleɪntɪv) *adj* expressing melancholy; mournful. [C14: from OF *plaintif* grieving, from PLAINT]
▸ 'plaintively *adv* ▸ 'plaintiveness *n*

plait (plæt) *n* **1** a length of hair, etc., that has been plaited. **2** a rare spelling of **pleat.** ◆ *vb* **3** (*tr*) to intertwine (strands or strips) in a pattern. [C15 *pleyt*, from OF *pleit*, from L *plicāre* to fold]

plan (plæn) *n* **1** a detailed scheme, method, etc., for attaining an objective. **2** (*sometimes pl*) a proposed, usually tentative idea for doing something. **3** a drawing to scale of a horizontal section through a building taken at a given level. **4** an outline, sketch, etc. ◆ *vb* **plans, planning, planned. 5** to form a plan (for) or make plans (for). **6** (*tr*) to make a plan of (a building). **7** (*tr; takes a clause as object or an infinitive*) to have in mind as a purpose; intend. [C18: via F from L *plānus* flat]

planar ('pleɪnə) *adj* **1** of or relating to a plane. **2** lying in one plane; flat. [C19: from LL *plānāris* on level ground, from L *plānus* flat]

planarian (pləˈnɛərɪən) *n* any of various free-living mostly aquatic flatworms, having a three-branched intestine. [C19: from NL *Plānāria* type genus, from LL *plānārius* flat; see PLANE[1]]

planar process *n* a method of producing diffused junctions in semiconductor devices. A pattern of holes is etched into an oxide layer formed on a silicon substrate, into which impurities are diffused through the holes.

planchet ('plɑːntʃɪt) *n* a piece of metal ready to be stamped as a coin, medal, etc.; flan. [C17: from F: little board, from *planche* PLANK]

planchette (plɑːnˈʃɛt) *n* a heart-shaped board on wheels, on which messages are written under supposed spirit guidance. [C19: from F: little board, from *planche* PLANK]

Planck ★ (plæŋk; *German* plaŋk) *n* **Max (Karl Ernst Ludwig)** (maks). 1858–1947, German physicist who first formulated the quantum theory (1900): Nobel prize for physics 1918.

Planck constant *or* **Planck's constant** *n* a fundamental constant equal to the energy of any quantum of radiation divided by its frequency.

plane[1] (pleɪn) *n* **1** *Maths.* a flat surface in which a straight line joining any two of its points lies entirely on that surface. **2** a level surface. **3** a level of existence, attainment, etc. **4a** short for **aeroplane. 4b** a wing or supporting surface of an aircraft. ◆ *adj* **5** level or flat. **6** *Maths.* lying entirely in one plane. ◆ *vb* **planes, planing, planed.** (*intr*) **7** to glide. **8** (of a boat) to rise partly and skim over the water when moving at a certain speed. [C17: from L *plānum* level surface]

plane[2] (pleɪn) *n* **1** a tool with a steel blade set obliquely in a wooden or iron body, for smoothing timber surfaces, cutting grooves, etc. **2** a flat tool, usually metal, for smoothing the surface of clay or plaster in a mould. ◆ *vb* **planes, planing, planed.** (*tr*) **3** to smooth or cut (timber etc.) using a plane. **4** (often foll. by *off*) to remove using a plane. [C14: via OF from LL *plāna* plane, from *plānāre* to level]

plane[3] (pleɪn) *n* See **plane tree**.

plane geometry *n* the study of the properties of plane curves, figures, etc.

plane polarization *n* a type of polarization in which waves of light or other radiation are restricted to vibration in a single plane.

planet ('plænɪt) *n* **1** Also called: **major planet**. any of the nine celestial bodies, Mercury, Venus, Earth, Mars, Jupiter, Saturn, Uranus, Neptune, or Pluto, that revolve around the sun in elliptical orbits. **2** any celestial body revolving around a star. **3** *Astrol.* any of the planets of the solar system, excluding the earth but including the sun and moon, each thought to rule one or sometimes two signs of the zodiac. [C12: via OF from LL *planēta*, from Gk *planētēs* wanderer, from *planaein* to wander]

plane table *n* a surveying instrument consisting of a drawing board mounted on adjustable legs.

planetarium (ˌplænɪˈtɛərɪəm) *n, pl* **planetariums** *or* **planetaria** (-rə). **1** an instrument for simulating the apparent motions of the sun, moon, and planets by projecting images of these bodies onto a domed ceiling. **2** a building in which such an instrument is housed. **3** a model of the solar system.

planetary ('plænɪtərɪ, -trɪ) *adj* **1** of a planet. **2** mundane; terrestrial. **3** wandering or erratic. **4** *Astrol.* under the influence of one of the planets. **5** (of a gear) having an axis that rotates around that of another gear.

planetesimal hypothesis (ˌplænɪˈtɛsɪməl) *n* the discredited theory that the close passage of a star to the sun caused many small bodies (**planetesimals**) to be drawn from the sun, eventually coalescing to form the planets. [C20: *planetesimal*, from PLANET + INFINITESIMAL]

planetoid ('plænɪˌtɔɪd) *n* another name for **asteroid** (sense 1).
▸ ˌplaneˈtoidal *adj*

plane tree *or* **plane** *n* a tree with ball-shaped heads of fruit and leaves with pointed lobes. [C14: *plane*, from OF, from L *platanus*, from Gk, from *platos* wide, referring to the leaves]

plangent ('plændʒənt) *adj* **1** having a loud deep sound. **2** resonant and mournful. [C19: from L *plangere* to beat (esp. the breast, in grief)]

planimeter (plæˈnɪmɪtə) *n* a mechanical instrument for measuring the area of an irregular plane figure by moving a point attached to an arm.
▸ plaˈnimetry *n*

planish ('plænɪʃ) *vb* (*tr*) to give a final finish to (metal etc.) by hammering or rolling. [C16: from OF *planir* to smooth out, from L *plānus* flat]

planisphere ('plænɪˌsfɪə) *n* a projection or representation of all or part of a sphere on a plane surface. [C14 from Med. L *plānisphaerium*, from L *plānus* flat + Gk *sphaira* globe]

plank (plæŋk) *n* **1** a stout length of sawn timber. **2** something that supports or sustains. **3** one of the policies in a political party's programme. **4 walk the plank.** to be forced by pirates, etc., to walk to one's death off the end of a plank jutting out from the side of a ship. ♦ *vb* **5** (*tr*) to cover or provide with planks. [C13: from OF *planke*, from LL *planca* board, from *plancus* flat-footed]

planking ('plæŋkɪŋ) *n* a number of planks.

plankton ('plæŋktən) *n* the organisms inhabiting the surface layer of a sea or lake, consisting of small drifting plants and animals. [C19: via G from Gk *planktos* wandering, from *plazesthai* to roam]

planned economy *n* another name for **command economy.**

planned obsolescence *n* the policy of deliberately limiting the life of a product in order to encourage the purchaser to replace it. Also called: **built-in obsolescence.**

planner ('plænə) *n* **1** a person who makes plans, esp. for the development of a town, building, etc. **2** a chart for recording future appointments, tasks, goals, etc.

planning permission *n* (in Britain) formal permission granted by a local authority for the development or changed use of land or buildings.

plano- *or sometimes before a vowel* **plan-** *combining form.* indicating flatness or planeness: *plano-concave.* [from L *plānus* flat]

plano-concave (ˌpleɪnəʊˈkɒnkeɪv) *adj* (of a lens) having one side concave and the other plane.

plano-convex (ˌpleɪnəʊˈkɒnvɛks) *adj* (of a lens) having one side convex and the other plane.

plant[1] (plɑːnt) *n* **1** any living organism that typically synthesizes its food from inorganic substances, lacks specialized sense organs, and has no powers of locomotion. **2** such an organism that is smaller than a shrub or tree; a herb. **3** a cutting, seedling, or similar structure, esp. when ready for transplantation. **4** *Inf.* a thing positioned secretly for discovery by another, esp. in order to incriminate an innocent person. **5** *Inf.* a person, placed in an audience, whose rehearsed responses, etc., seem spontaneous to the rest of the audience. **6** *Inf.* a person placed secretly in a group or organization to obtain information, etc. ♦ *vb* (*tr*) **7** (often foll. by *out*) to set (seeds, crops, etc.) into (ground) to grow. **8** to place firmly in position. **9** to establish; found. **10** (foll. by *with*) to stock or furnish. **11** to implant in the mind. **12** *Sl.* to deliver (a blow). **13** *Inf.* to position or hide, esp. in order to deceive or observe. **14** *Inf.* to hide or secrete, esp. for some illegal purpose or in order to incriminate someone. [OE, from *planta* a shoot]
▸ **'plantable** *adj*

plant[2] (plɑːnt) *n* **1** the land, buildings, and equipment used in carrying on an industry or business. **2** a factory or workshop. **3** mobile mechanical equipment for construction, road-making, etc. [C20: special use of PLANT[1]]

Plantagenet ★ (plænˈtædʒɪnɪt) *n* a line of English kings, ruling from the ascent of Henry II (1154) to the death of Richard III (1485). [C12: from OF, lit.: sprig of broom, with reference to the crest of the Angevin kings, from L *planta* sprig + *genista* broom]

plantain[1] ('plæntɪn) *n* any of various N temperate plants, esp. the great plantain, which has a rosette of broad leaves and a slender spike of small greenish flowers. See also **ribwort.** [C14 *plauntein*, from OF, from L *plantāgō*, from *planta* sole of the foot]

plantain[2] ('plæntɪn) *n* a large tropical plant with a green-skinned banana-like fruit which is eaten as a staple food in many tropical regions. [C16: Sp. *platano* plantain, PLANE TREE]

plantain lily *n* any of several Asian plants of the genus *Hosta*, having broad ribbed leaves.

plantar ('plæntə) *adj* of or on the sole of the foot. [C18: from L *plantāris*, from *planta* sole of the foot]

plantation (plænˈteɪʃən) *n* **1** an estate, esp. in tropical countries, where cash crops such as rubber, oil palm, etc., are grown on a large scale. **2** a group of cultivated trees or plants. **3** (formerly) a colony or group of settlers.

planter ('plɑːntə) *n* **1** the owner or manager of a plantation. **2** a machine designed for rapid and efficient plant-

ing of seeds. **3** a colonizer or settler. **4** a decorative pot for house plants.

plantigrade ('plæntɪˌɡreɪd) *adj* **1** walking with the entire sole of the foot touching the ground, as man and bears. ♦ *n* **2** a plantigrade animal. [C19: via F from NL *plantigradus*, from L *planta* sole of the foot + *gradus* a step]

plant louse *n* another name for an **aphid.**

plaque (plæk, plɑːk) *n* **1** an ornamental or commemorative inscribed tablet. **2** a small flat brooch or badge. **3** *Pathol.* any small abnormal patch on or within the body. **4** short for **dental plaque.** [C19: from F, from *plaquier* to plate, from MDu. *placken* to beat into a thin plate]

plash (plæʃ) *vb, n* a less common word for **splash.** [OE *plæsc*, prob. imit.]
▸ **'plashy** *adj*

-plasia *or* **-plasy** *n combining form.* indicating growth, development, or change. [from NL, from Gk *plasis* a moulding, from *plassein* to mould]

plasm ('plæzəm) *n* **1** protoplasm of a specified type: *germ plasm.* **2** a variant of **plasma.**

-plasm *n combining form.* (in biology) indicating the material forming cells: *protoplasm; cytoplasm.* [from Gk *plasma* something moulded; see PLASMA]
▸ **-plasmic** *adj combining form.*

plasma ('plæzmə) *or* **plasm** *n* **1** the clear yellowish fluid portion of blood or lymph in which the corpuscles and cells are suspended. **2** Also called: **blood plasma.** a sterilized preparation of such fluid, taken from the blood, for use in transfusions. **3** a former name for **protoplasm** or **cytoplasm.** **4** *Physics.* a hot ionized gas containing positive ions and electrons. **5** a green variety of chalcedony. [C18: from LL: something moulded, from Gk, from *plassein* to mould]
▸ **plasmatic** (plæzˈmætɪk) *or* **'plasmic** *adj*

plasma torch *n* an electrical device for converting a gas into a plasma, used for melting metal, etc.

plasmid ('plæzmɪd) *n* a small circle of bacterial DNA that is independent of the main bacterial chromosome. Plasmids often contain genes for drug resistances and can be transmitted between bacteria of the same and different species: used in genetic engineering. [C20: from PLASM + -ID[1]]

plasmodium (plæzˈməʊdɪəm) *n, pl* **plasmodia** (-dɪə). **1** an amoeboid mass of protoplasm, containing many nuclei: a stage in the life cycle of certain organisms. **2** a parasitic protozoan which causes malaria. [C19: NL; see PLASMA, -ODE[1]]
▸ **plas'modial** *adj*

plasmolysis (plæzˈmɒlɪsɪs) *n* the shrinkage of protoplasm away from cell walls that occurs as a result of excessive water loss, esp. in plant cells.

Plassey ★ ('plæsɪ) *n* a village in NE India, in W Bengal: scene of Clive's victory (1757) over Siraj-ud-daula, which established British supremacy over India.

-plast *n combining form.* indicating a living cell or particle of living matter: *protoplast.* [from Gk *plastos* formed, from *plassein* to form]

plaster ('plɑːstə) *n* **1** a mixture of lime, sand, and water that is applied to a wall or ceiling as a soft paste that hardens when dry. **2** *Brit., Austral., & NZ.* an adhesive strip of material for dressing a cut, wound, etc. **3** short for **mustard plaster** or **plaster of Paris.** ♦ *vb* **4** to coat (a wall, ceiling, etc.) with plaster. **5** (*tr*) to apply like plaster: *she plastered make-up on her face.* **6** (*tr*) to cause to lie flat or to adhere. **7** (*tr*) to apply a plaster cast to. **8** (*tr*) *Sl.* to strike or defeat with great force. [OE, from Med. L *plastrum* medicinal salve, building plaster, via L from Gk *emplastron* curative dressing]
▸ **'plasterer** *n*

plasterboard ('plɑːstəˌbɔːd) *n* a thin rigid board, in the form of a layer of plaster compressed between two layers of fibreboard, used to form or cover walls, etc.

plastered ('plɑːstəd) *adj Sl.* intoxicated; drunk.

plaster of Paris *n* **1** a white powder that sets to a hard solid when mixed with water, used for making sculptures and casts, as an additive for lime plasters, and for making casts for setting broken limbs. **2** the hard plaster produced when this powder is mixed with water. [C15: from Med. L *plastrum parisiense*, orig. made from the gypsum of *Paris*]

plastic ('plæstɪk) *n* **1** any one of a large number of synthetic materials that have a polymeric structure and can be moulded when soft and then set. Plastics are used in the manufacture of many articles and in coatings, artificial fibres, etc. ♦ *adj* **2** made of plastic. **3** easily influenced; impressionable. **4** capable of being moulded or formed. **5a** of moulding or modelling: *the plastic arts*. **5b** produced or apparently produced by moulding: *the plastic draperies of Giotto's figures*. **6** having the power to form or influence: *the plastic forces of the imagination*. **7** *Biol.* able to change, develop, or grow: *plastic tissues*. **8** *Sl.* superficially attractive yet unoriginal or artificial: *plastic food*. [C17: from L *plasticus* relating to moulding, from Gk *plastikos*, from *plassein* to form]
▸ 'plastically *adv* ▸ plasticity (plæ'stɪsɪtɪ) *n*

-plastic *adj combining form.* growing or forming. [from Gk *plastikos*; see PLASTIC]

plastic bomb *n* a bomb consisting of plastic explosive fitted around a detonator.

plastic bullet *n* a bullet consisting of a cylinder of plastic about four inches long, generally causing less severe injuries than an ordinary bullet, and used esp. for riot control. Also called: **baton round.**

plastic explosive *n* an adhesive jelly-like explosive substance.

Plasticine ('plæstɪˌsiːn) *n Trademark.* a soft coloured material used, esp. by children, for modelling.

plasticize *or* **plasticise** ('plæstɪˌsaɪz) *vb* **plasticizes, plasticizing, plasticized** *or* **plasticises, plasticising, plasticised.** to make or become plastic, as by the addition of a plasticizer.
▸ ,plastici'zation *or* ,plastici'sation *n*

plasticizer *or* **plasticiser** ('plæstɪˌsaɪzə) *n* any of a number of substances added to materials. Their uses include softening and improving the flexibility of plastics and preventing dried paint coatings from becoming too brittle.

plastic money *n* credit cards as opposed to cash.

plastic surgery *n* the branch of surgery concerned with therapeutic or cosmetic repair or re-formation of missing, injured, or malformed tissues or parts.
▸ plastic surgeon *n*

plastid ('plæstɪd) *n* any of various small particles in the cells of plants and some animals which contain starch, oil, protein, etc. [C19: via G from Gk *plastēs* sculptor, from *plassein* to form]

plastron ('plæstrən) *n* the bony plate forming the ventral part of the shell of a tortoise or turtle. [C16: via F from It. *piastrone*, from *piastra* breastplate, from L *emplastrum* PLASTER]
▸ 'plastral *adj*

-plasty *n combining form.* indicating plastic surgery: *rhinoplasty*. [from Gk *-plastia*; see -PLAST]

plat¹ (plæt) *n* a small area of ground; plot. [C16 (also in ME place names): orig. a var. of PLOT²]

plat² (plæt) *vb* **plats, platting, platted,** *n* a dialect variant spelling of **plait.** [C16]

Plata ★ (*Spanish* 'plata) *n* Río de la ('rio de la). an estuary on the SE coast of South America, between Argentina and Uruguay, formed by the Uruguay and Paraná Rivers. Length: 275 km (171 miles). Width: (at its mouth) 225 km (140 miles). Also called: **La Plata.** English name: (River) **Plate.**

Plataea ★ (plə'tiːə) *n* an ancient city in S Boeotia, traditionally an ally of Athens: scene of the defeat of a great Persian army by the Greeks in 479 B.C.

platan ('plætᵊn) *n* another name for **plane tree.** [C14: see PLANE TREE]

plat du jour ('plɑː də 'ʒuə; *French* pla dy zur) *n, pl* **plats du jour** ('plɑːz də 'ʒuə; *French* pla dy zur). the specially prepared or recommended dish of the day on a restaurant's menu. [F, lit.: dish of the day]

plate (pleɪt) *n* **1a** a shallow usually circular dish made of porcelain, earthenware, glass, etc., on which food is served. **1b** (*as modifier*): *a plate rack*. **2a** Also called: **plateful.** the contents of a plate. **2b** *Austral. & NZ.* a plate of cakes, sandwiches, etc., brought by a guest to a party: *everyone was asked to bring a plate*. **3** an entire course of a meal: *a cold plate*. **4** any shallow receptacle, esp. for receiving a collection in church. **5** flat metal of uniform thickness obtained by rolling, usually having a thickness greater than about three millimetres. **6** a thin coating of metal usually on another metal, as produced by electrodeposition. **7** metal or metalware that has been coated in this way: *Sheffield plate*. **8** dishes, cutlery, etc., made of gold or silver. **9** a sheet of metal, plastic, rubber, etc., having a printing surface produced by a process such as stereotyping. **10** a print taken from such a sheet or from a woodcut. **11** a thin flat sheet of a substance, such as metal or glass. **12** a small piece of metal, plastic, etc., designed to bear an inscription and to be fixed to another surface. **13** armour made of overlapping or articulated pieces of thin metal. **14** *Photog.* a sheet of glass, or sometimes metal, coated with photographic emulsion on which an image can be formed by exposure to light. **15** a device for straightening teeth. **16** an informal word for **denture** (sense 1). **17** *Anat.* any flat platelike structure. **18a** a cup awarded to the winner of a sporting contest, esp. a horse race. **18b** a race or contest for such a prize. **19** any of the rigid layers of the earth's lithosphere. **20** *Electronics, chiefly US.* the anode in an electronic valve. **21** a horizontal timber joist that supports rafters. **22** a light horseshoe for flat racing. **23** *RC Church.* Also called: **Communion plate.** a flat plate held under the chin of a communicant in order to catch any fragments of the consecrated Host. **24 on a plate.** acquired without trouble: *he was handed the job on a plate*. **25 on one's plate.** waiting to be done or dealt with. ♦ *vb* **plates, plating, plated.** (*tr*) **26** to coat (a surface, usually metal) with a thin layer of other metal by electrolysis, etc. **27** to cover with metal plates, as for protection. **28** *Printing.* to make a stereotype or electrotype from (type or another plate). **29** to form (metal) into plate, esp. by rolling. [C13: from OF: thin metal sheet, something flat, from Vulgar L *plattus* (unattested)]

Plate ★ (pleɪt) *n* **River.** the English name for the (Río de la) **Plata.**

plateau ('plætəʊ) *n, pl* **plateaus** *or* **plateaux** (-əʊz). **1** a wide mainly level area of elevated land. **2** a relatively long period of stability; levelling off: *the rising prices reached a plateau*. ♦ *vb* (*intr*) **3** to remain at a stable level for a relatively long period. [C18: from F, from OF *platel* something flat, from *plat* flat]

Plateau ★ ('plætəʊ) *n* a state of central Nigeria, formed in 1976 from part of Benue-Plateau State: tin mining. Capital: Jos. Pop.: 3 283 704 (1991). Area: 58 030 sq. km (22 405 sq. miles).

plated ('pleɪtɪd) *adj* **a** coated with a layer of metal. **b** (*in combination*): *gold-plated*.

plate glass *n* glass formed into a sheet by rolling, used for windows, etc.

platelayer ('pleɪtˌleɪə) *n Brit.* a workman who lays and maintains railway track. US equivalent: **trackman.**

platelet ('pleɪtlɪt) *n* a minute particle occurring in the blood of vertebrates and involved in the clotting of the blood. [C19: a small PLATE]

platen ('plætᵊn) *n* **1** a flat plate in a printing press that presses the paper against the type. **2** the roller on a typewriter, against which the keys strike. [C15: from OF *platine*, from *plat* flat]

plater ('pleɪtə) *n* **1** a person or thing that plates. **2** *Horse racing.* a mediocre horse entered chiefly for minor races.

plate tectonics *n* (*functioning as sing*) *Geol.* the study of the earth's crust with reference to the theory that the lithosphere is divided into rigid blocks (plates) that float on semimolten rock and are thus able to interact with each other at their boundaries.

platform ('plætfɔːm) *n* **1** a raised floor or other horizontal surface. **2** a raised area at a railway station, from which passengers have access to the trains. **3** See **drilling platform. 4** the declared principles, aims, etc., of a political party, etc. **5a** the thick raised sole of some shoes. **5b** (*as modifier*): *platform shoes*. **6** a vehicle or level place on which weapons are mounted and fired. **7** a specific type of computer hardware or computer operating system. [C16: from F *plateforme*, from *plat* flat + *forme* layout]

platform ticket *n* a ticket for admission to railway platforms but not for travel.

Plath ★ (plæθ) *n* **Sylvia**. 1932–63, US poet living in England. She wrote two volumes of verse, *The Colossus* (1960) and *Ariel* (1965), and a novel, *The Bell Jar* (1963).

plating ('pleɪtɪŋ) *n* **1** a coating or layer of material, esp. metal. **2** a layer or covering of metal plates.

platiniridium (,plætɪnɪ'rɪdɪəm) *n* any alloy of platinum and iridium.

platinize *or* **platinise** ('plætɪ,naɪz) *vb* **platinizes, platinizing, platinized** *or* **platinises, platinising, platinised**. (*tr*) to coat with platinum.
▶ ,platini'zation *or* ,platini'sation *n*

platinum ('plætɪnəm) *n* a ductile malleable silvery-white metallic element, very resistant to heat and chemicals: used in jewellery, laboratory apparatus, electrical contacts, dentistry, electroplating, and as a catalyst. Symbol: Pt; atomic no.: 78; atomic wt.: 195.08. [C19: NL, from Sp. *platina* silvery element, from *plata* silver, from Provençal: silver plate + the suffix -*um*]

platinum black *n Chem.* a black powder consisting of very finely divided platinum metal.

platinum-blond *or* (*fem*) **platinum-blonde** *adj* **1** (of hair) of a pale silver-blond colour. **2a** having hair of this colour. **2b** (*as n*): *she was a platinum blonde*.

platinum disc *n* **1** (in Britain) an LP record certified to have sold 300 000 copies or a single certified to have sold 600 000 copies. **2** (in the US) an LP record or single certified to have sold one million copies.

platinum metal *n* any of the group of precious metallic elements consisting of ruthenium, rhodium, palladium, osmium, iridium, and platinum.

platitude ('plætɪ,tjuːd) *n* **1** a trite, dull, or obvious remark. **2** staleness or insipidity of thought or language; triteness. [C19: from F, lit.: flatness, from *plat* flat]
▶ ,plati'tudinous *adj*

platitudinize *or* **platitudinise** (,plætɪ'tjuːdɪ,naɪz) *vb* **platitudinizes, platitudinizing, platitudinized** *or* **platitudinises, platitudinising, platitudinised**. (*intr*) to speak or write in platitudes.

Plato ★ ('pleɪtəʊ) *n* ?427–?347 B.C., Greek philosopher: with his teacher Socrates and his pupil Aristotle, he is regarded as the initiator of western philosophy. His distinction between objects of sense perception and the universal Ideas or Forms of which they are an expression is formulated in such dialogues as *Phaedo*, *Symposium*, and *The Republic*.

Platonic (plə'tɒnɪk) *adj* **1** of or relating to Plato or his teachings. **2** (*often not cap.*) free from physical desire: *Platonic love*.
▶ Pla'tonically *adv*

Platonic solid *n* any of the five possible regular polyhedrons: cube, tetrahedron, octahedron, icosahedron, and dodecahedron.

Platonism ('pleɪtə,nɪzəm) *n* the teachings of Plato and his followers; esp. the philosophical theory that the meanings of general words are real entities (Forms) and that particular objects have properties in common by virtue of their relationship with these Forms.
▶ 'Platonist *n*

platoon (plə'tuːn) *n* **1** *Mil.* a subunit of a company, usually comprising three sections of ten to twelve men. **2** a group of people sharing a common activity, etc. [C17: from F *peloton* little ball, group of men, from *pelote* ball; see PELLET]

Plattdeutsch (*German* 'platdɔytʃ) *n* another name for **Low German**. [lit.: flat German]

Platte ★ (plæt) *n* a river system of the central US, formed by the confluence of the **North Platte** and **South Platte** at North Platte, Nebraska: flows generally east to the Missouri River. Length: 499 km (310 miles).

platteland ('platə,lant) *n* **the**. (in South Africa) the country districts or rural areas. [C20: from Afrik., from Du. *plat* flat + *land* country]

platter ('plætə) *n* **1** a large shallow usually oval dish or plate. **2** a course of a meal, usually consisting of several different foods served on the same plate: *a seafood platter*. [C14: from Anglo-Norman *plater*, from *plat* dish, from OF *plat* flat; see PLATE]

platy- *combining form*. indicating something flat, as **platyhelminth**, the flatworm. [from Gk *platus* flat]

platypus ('plætɪpəs) *n, pl* **platypuses**. See **duck-billed platypus**. [C18: NL, from PLATY- + -*pus*, from Gk *pous* foot]

platyrrhine ('plætɪ,raɪn) *or* **platyrrhinian** (,plætɪ-'rɪnɪən) *adj* **1** (esp. of New World monkeys) having widely separated nostrils opening to the side of the face. **2** (of a human) having an unusually short wide nose. [C19: from NL *platyrrhinus*, from PLATY- + -*rrhinus*, from Gk *rhis* nose]

plaudit ('plɔːdɪt) *n* (*usually pl*) **1** an expression of enthusiastic approval. **2** a round of applause. [C17: from earlier *plaudite*, from L: applaud!, from *plaudere* to APPLAUD]

Plauen ★ (*German* 'plauən) *n* a city in E central Germany, in Saxony: textile centre. Pop.: 70 860 (1991).

plausible ('plɔːzɪbᵊl) *adj* **1** apparently reasonable, valid, truthful, etc.: *a plausible excuse*. **2** apparently trustworthy or believable: *a plausible speaker*. [C16: from L *plausibilis* worthy of applause, from *plaudere* to APPLAUD]
▶ ,plausi'bility *or* 'plausibleness *n* ▶ 'plausibly *adv*

Plautus ★ ('plɔːtəs) *n* **Titus Maccius**. ?254–?184 B.C., Roman comic dramatist. His 21 extant works, adapted from Greek plays, esp. those by Menander, include *Menaechmi* (the basis of Shakespeare's *The Comedy of Errors*), *Miles Gloriosus*, *Rudens*, and *Captivi*.

play (pleɪ) *vb* **1** to occupy oneself in (a sport or diversion). **2** (*tr*) to contend against (an opponent) in a sport or game: *Ed played Tony at chess and lost*. **3** to fulfil or cause to fulfil (a particular role) in a team game: *he plays in the defence*. **4** (*intr*; often foll. by *about* or *around*) to behave carelessly, esp. in a way that is unconsciously cruel or hurtful: *to play about with a young girl's affections*. **5** (when *intr*, often foll. by *at*) to perform or act the part (of) in or as in a dramatic production. **6** to perform (a dramatic production). **7a** to have the ability to perform on (a musical instrument): *David plays the harp*. **7b** to perform as specified: *he plays out of tune*. **8** (*tr*) **8a** to reproduce (a piece of music, note, etc.) on an instrument. **8b** to perform works by: *to play Brahms*. **9** to discharge or cause to discharge: *he played the water from the hose onto the garden*. **10** to cause (a radio, etc.) to emit sound. **11** to move freely, quickly, or irregularly: *lights played on the scenery*. **12** (*tr*) *Stock Exchange.* to speculate or operate aggressively for gain in (a market). **13** (*tr*) *Angling.* to attempt to tire (a hooked fish) by alternately letting out and reeling in line. **14** to put (a card, counter, piece, etc.) into play. **15** to gamble. **16 play fair** (*or* **false**). (often foll. by *with*) to prove oneself fair (or unfair) in one's dealings. **17 play for time**. to delay the outcome of some activity so as to gain time to one's own advantage. **18 play into the hands of**. to act directly to the advantage of (an opponent). ♦ *n* **19** a dramatic composition written for performance by actors on a stage, etc.; drama. **20** the performance of a dramatic composition. **21a** games, exercise, or other activity undertaken for pleasure, esp. by children. **21b** (*in combination*): *playroom*. **22** conduct: *fair play*. **23** the playing of a game or the period during which a game is in progress: *rain stopped play*. **24** *US*. a manoeuvre in a game: *a brilliant play*. **25** the situation of a ball, etc., that is within the defined area and being played according to the rules (in **in play, out of play**). **26** gambling. **27** activity or operation: *the play of the imagination*. **28** freedom of movement: *too much play in the rope*. **29** light, free, and rapidly shifting motion: *the play of light on the water*. **30** fun, jest, or joking: *I only did it in play*. **31 call into play**. to bring into operation. **32 make a play for**. *Inf.* to make an obvious attempt to gain. ♦ See also **play along, playback**, etc. [OE *plega* (n), *plegan* (vb)]
▶ 'playable *adj*

play-act *vb* **1** (*intr*) to pretend or make believe. **2** (*intr*) to behave in an overdramatic or affected manner. **3** to act in or as in (a play).
▶ 'play-,acting *n* ▶ 'play-,actor *n*

play along vb (adv) **1** (intr; usually foll. by with) to cooperate (with), esp. as a temporary measure. **2** (tr) to manipulate as if in a game, esp. for one's own advantage: he played the widow along until she gave him her money.

playback ('pleɪ,bæk) n **1** the act or process of reproducing a recording, esp. on magnetic tape. **2** the part of a tape recorder serving to reproduce or used for reproducing recorded material. ◆ vb **play back**. (adv) **3** to reproduce (recorded material) on (a magnetic tape) by means of a tape recorder.

playbill ('pleɪ,bɪl) n **1** a poster or bill advertising a play. **2** the programme of a play.

playboy ('pleɪ,bɔɪ) n a man, esp. one of private means, who devotes himself to the pleasures of nightclubs, female company, etc.

play down vb (tr, adv) to make little or light of; minimize the importance of.

player ('pleɪə) n **1** a person who participates in or is skilled at some game or sport. **2** a person who plays a game or sport professionally. **3** a person who plays a musical instrument. **4** an actor. **5** Inf. a participant, esp. a powerful one, in a particular field of activity: a leading city player.

Player ★ ('pleɪə) n **Gary** ('gærɪ). born 1935, South African professional golfer: won the British Open Championship (1959; 1968; 1974) and the US Open Championship (1965).

player piano n a mechanical piano; Pianola.

playful ('pleɪfʊl) adj **1** full of high spirits and fun: a playful kitten. **2** good-natured and humorous: a playful remark. ▸ 'playfully adv

playgoer ('pleɪ,gəʊə) n a person who goes to theatre performances, esp. frequently.

playground ('pleɪ,graʊnd) n **1** an outdoor area for children's play, esp. one having swings, slides, etc., or adjoining a school. **2** a place popular as a sports or holiday resort.

playgroup ('pleɪ,gru:p) n a regular meeting of small children for supervised creative play.

playhouse ('pleɪ,haʊs) n **1** a theatre. **2** US. a small house for children to play in.

playing card n one of a pack of 52 rectangular pieces of stiff card, used for playing a wide variety of games, each card having one or more symbols of the same kind on the face, but an identical design on the reverse.

playing field n Chiefly Brit. a field or open space used for sport.

playlet ('pleɪlɪt) n a short play.

playlist ('pleɪ,lɪst) n **1** a list of records chosen for playing, as on a radio station. ◆ vb **2** (tr) to put (a song or record) on a playlist.

playmaker ('pleɪ,meɪkə) n Sport. a player whose role is to create scoring opportunities for his or her teammates.

playmate ('pleɪ,meɪt) or **playfellow** n a friend or partner in play or recreation.

play off vb (adv) **1** (tr; usually foll. by against) to manipulate as if in playing a game: to play one person off against another. **2** (intr) to take part in a play-off. ◆ n **play-off**. **3** Sport. an extra contest to decide the winner when competitors are tied. **4** Chiefly US & Canad. a contest or series of games to determine a championship.

play on vb (intr) **1** (adv) to continue to play. **2** (prep) Also: **play upon**. to exploit or impose upon (the feelings or weakness of another).

play on words n another term for pun[1].

playpen ('pleɪ,pen) n a small enclosure, usually portable, in which a young child can be left to play in safety.

playschool ('pleɪ,sku:l) n an informal nursery group for preschool children.

plaything ('pleɪ,θɪŋ) n **1** a toy. **2** a person regarded or treated as a toy.

playtime ('pleɪ,taɪm) n a time for play or recreation, esp. the school break.

play up vb (adv) **1** (tr) to highlight: to play up one's best fea-

tures. **2** Brit. inf. to behave irritatingly (towards). **3** (intr) Brit. inf. (of a machine, etc.) to function erratically: the car is playing up again. **4** to hurt; give (one) trouble: my back's playing up again. **5 play up to. 5a** to support (another actor) in a performance. **5b** to try to gain favour with by flattery.

playwright ('pleɪ,raɪt) n a person who writes plays.

plaza ('plɑːzə) n **1** an open space or square, esp. in Spain. **2** Chiefly US & Canad. a modern complex of shops, buildings, and parking areas. [C17: from Sp., from L platēa courtyard; see PLACE]

plc or **PLC** abbrev. for public limited company.

plea (pliː) n **1** an earnest entreaty or request. **2a** Law. something alleged by or on behalf of a party to legal proceedings in support of his claim or defence. **2b** Criminal law. the answer made by an accused to the charge: a plea of guilty. **2c** (in Scotland and formerly in England) a suit or action at law. **3** an excuse, justification, or pretext: he gave the plea of a previous engagement. [C13: from Anglo-Norman plai, from OF plaid lawsuit, from Med. L placitum court order (lit.: what is pleasing), from L placēre to please]

plea bargaining n an agreement between the prosecution and defence, sometimes including the judge, in which the accused agrees to plead guilty to a lesser charge in return for more serious charges being dropped.

plead (pliːd) vb **pleads, pleading; pleaded, plead** (pled), or esp. Scot. & US. **pled. 1** (when intr, often foll. by with) to appeal earnestly or humbly (to). **2** (tr; may take a clause as object) to give as an excuse: to plead ignorance. **3** Law. to declare oneself to be (guilty or not guilty) in answer to the charge. **4** Law. to advocate (a case) in a court of law. **5** (intr) Law. **5a** to file pleadings. **5b** to address a court as an advocate. [C13: from OF plaidier, from Med. L placitāre to have a lawsuit, from L placēre to please] ▸ 'pleadable adj ▸ 'pleader n

pleadings ('pliːdɪŋz) pl n Law. the formal written statements presented alternately by the plaintiff and defendant in a lawsuit.

pleasance ('plezəns) n **1** a secluded part of a garden laid out with trees, walks, etc. **2** Arch. enjoyment or pleasure. [C14 plesaunce, from OF plaisance, ult. from plaisir to PLEASE]

pleasant ('plezᵊnt) adj **1** giving or affording pleasure; enjoyable. **2** having pleasing or agreeable manners, appearance, habits, etc. **3** Obs. merry and lively. [C14: from OF plaisant, from plaisir to PLEASE] ▸ 'pleasantly adv

Pleasant Island ★ n the former name of **Nauru**.

pleasantry ('plezᵊntrɪ) n, pl **pleasantries. 1** (often pl) an agreeable or amusing remark, etc., often one made in order to be polite: they exchanged pleasantries. **2** an agreeably humorous manner or style. [C17: from F plaisanterie, from plaisant PLEASANT]

please (pliːz) vb **pleases, pleasing, pleased. 1** to give satisfaction, pleasure, or contentment to (a person). **2** to be the will of or have the will (to): if it pleases you; the court pleases. **3 if you please.** if you wish or, sometimes used in ironic exclamation. **4 pleased with.** happy because of. **5 please oneself.** to do as one likes. ◆ adv **6** (sentence modifier) used in making polite requests, pleading, etc. **7 yes please.** a polite formula for accepting an offer, invitation, etc. [C14 plese, from OF plaisir, from L placēre] ▸ **pleased** adj ▸ **pleasedly** ('pliːzɪdlɪ) adv

Pleasence ★ ('plezəns) n **Donald.** 1919–95, British actor. His films include Dr Crippen (1962) and Cul de Sac (1966).

pleasing ('pliːzɪŋ) adj giving pleasure; likable or gratifying. ▸ 'pleasingly adv

pleasurable ('pleʒərəbᵊl) adj enjoyable, agreeable, or gratifying. ▸ 'pleasurably adv

pleasure ('pleʒə) n **1** an agreeable or enjoyable sensation or emotion: the pleasure of hearing good music. **2** something that gives enjoyment: his garden was his only pleasure. **3a** amusement, recreation, or enjoyment. **3b** (as modifier): a pleasure ground. **4** Euphemistic. sexual gratification: he took his pleasure of her. **5** a person's preference.

★ people and places

♦ *vb* **pleasures, pleasuring, pleasured. 6** (when *intr*, often foll. by *in*) *Arch.* to give pleasure to or take pleasure (in). [C14 *plesir*, from OF]

pleat (pliːt) *n* **1** any of various types of fold formed by doubling back fabric, etc., and pressing, stitching, or steaming into place. **2** (*tr*) to arrange (material, part of a garment, etc.) in pleats. [C16: var. of PLAIT]

pleb (plɛb) *n* **1** short for **plebeian. 2** *Brit. inf., often derog.* a common vulgar person.

plebeian (plə'biːən) *adj* **1** of or characteristic of the common people, esp. those of ancient Rome. **2** lacking refinement; philistine or vulgar: *plebeian tastes.* ♦ *n* **3** one of the common people, esp. one of the Roman plebs. **4** a person who is coarse, vulgar, etc. [C16: from L *plēbēius* of the people, from *plēbs* the common people of ancient Rome]
▸ **ple'beian,ism** *n*

plebiscite ('plɛbɪ,saɪt, -sɪt) *n* **1** a direct vote by the electorate of a state, region, etc., on some question, usually of national importance. **2** any expression of public opinion on some matter. ♦ See also **referendum**. [C16: from OF *plébiscite*, from L *plēbiscītum* decree of the people, from *plēbs* the populace + *scīscere* to decree, from *scīre* to know]
▸ **plebiscitary** (plə'bɪsɪtərɪ, -trɪ) *adj*

plectrum ('plɛktrəm) *n, pl* **-trums** or **-tra** (-trə) any implement for plucking a string, such as a small piece of plastic, wood, etc., used to strum a guitar. [C17: from L, from Gk *plektron*, from *plessein* to strike]

pled (plɛd) *vb US or* (*esp. in legal usage*) *Scot.* a past tense and past participle of **plead**.

pledge (plɛdʒ) *n* **1** a formal or solemn promise or agreement. **2a** collateral for the payment of a debt or the performance of an obligation. **2b** the condition of being collateral (esp. **in pledge). 3** a token: *the gift is a pledge of their sincerity.* **4** an assurance of support or goodwill, conveyed by drinking a toast: *we drank a pledge to their success.* **5** a person who binds himself, as by becoming bail or surety for another. **6 take** *or* **sign the pledge.** to make a vow to abstain from alcoholic drink. ♦ *vb* **pledges, pledging, pledged. 7** to promise formally or solemnly. **8** (*tr*) to bind by or as if by a pledge: *they were pledged to secrecy.* **9** to give or offer (one's word, freedom, property, etc.) as a guarantee, as for the repayment of a loan. **10** to drink a toast to (a person, cause, etc.). [C14: from OF *plege*, from LL *plebium* security, from *plebīre* to pledge, of Gmc origin]
▸ **pledgable** *adj* ▸ **pledger** *or* **pledgor** *n*

pledgee (plɛdʒ'iː) *n* **1** a person to whom a pledge is given. **2** a person to whom property is delivered as a pledge.

pledget ('plɛdʒɪt) *n* a small flattened pad of wool, cotton, etc., esp. for use as a pressure bandage to be applied to wounds. [C16: from ?]

-plegia *n combining form.* indicating a specified type of paralysis: *paraplegia.* [from Gk, from *plēgē* stroke, from *plēssein* to strike]
▸ **-plegic** *adj and n combining form.*

pleiad ('plaɪəd) *n* a brilliant or talented group, esp. one with seven members. [C16: orig. F *Pléiade*, name given by Ronsard to himself and six other poets, ult. after the PLEIADES]

Pleiades ★ ('plaɪə,diːz) *pl n Greek myth.* the seven daughters of Atlas, placed as stars in the sky either to save them from the pursuit of Orion or, in another account, after they had killed themselves for grief over the death of their half-sisters the Hyades.

Pleiocene ('plaɪəʊ,siːn) *adj, n* a variant spelling of **Pliocene.**

Pleistocene ('plaɪstə,siːn) *adj* **1** of, denoting, or formed in the first epoch of the Quaternary period. It was characterized by extensive glaciations of the N hemisphere and the evolutionary development of man. ♦ *n* **2** the. the Pleistocene epoch or rock series. [C19: from Gk *pleistos* most + *kainos* recent]

plenary ('pliːnərɪ, 'plɛn-) *adj* **1** full, unqualified, or complete: *plenary powers; plenary indulgence.* **2** (of assemblies,

councils, etc.) attended by all the members. [C15: from LL *plēnārius*, from L *plēnus* full]
▸ **'plenarily** *adv*

plenipotentiary (,plɛnɪpə'tɛnʃərɪ) *adj* **1** (esp. of a diplomatic envoy) invested with or possessing full authority. **2** conferring full authority. **3** (of power or authority) full; absolute. ♦ *n, pl* **plenipotentiaries. 4** a person invested with full authority to transact business, esp. a diplomat authorized to represent a country. See also **envoy**[1] (sense 1). [C17: from Med. L *plēnipotentiārius*, from L *plēnus* full + *potentia* POWER]

plenitude ('plɛnɪ,tjuːd) *n* **1** abundance. **2** the condition of being full or complete. [C15: via OF from L *plēnitūdō*, from *plēnus* full]

plenteous ('plɛntɪəs) *adj* **1** ample; abundant: *a plenteous supply of food.* **2** producing or yielding abundantly: *a plenteous grape harvest.* [C13 *plenteus*, from OF, from *plentif*, from *plenté* PLENTY]
▸ **'plenteously** *adv* ▸ **'plenteousness** *n*

plentiful ('plɛntɪful) *adj* **1** ample; abundant. **2** having or yielding an abundance: *a plentiful year.*
▸ **'plentifully** *adv* ▸ **'plentifulness** *n*

plenty ('plɛntɪ) *n, pl* **plenties. 1** (often foll. by *of*) a great number, amount, or quantity; lots: *plenty of time; there are plenty of cars on display here.* **2** ample supplies or resources: *the age of plenty.* **3 in plenty.** existing in abundance: *food in plenty.* ♦ *determiner* **4a** very many; ample: *plenty of people believe in ghosts.* **4b** (*as pron*): *that's plenty, thanks.* ♦ *adv* **5** *Inf.* fully or abundantly: *the coat was plenty big enough.* [C13: from OF *plenté*, from LL *plēnitās* fullness, from L *plēnus* full]

Plenty ★ ('plɛntɪ) *n* **Bay of.** a large bay of the Pacific on the NE coast of the North Island, New Zealand.

plenum ('pliːnəm) *n, pl* **plenums** or **plena** (-nə). **1** an enclosure containing gas at a higher pressure than the surrounding environment. **2** a fully attended meeting. **3** (esp. in the philosophy of the Stoics) space regarded as filled with matter. [C17: from L: space filled with matter, from *plēnus* full]

pleochroism (plɪ'ɒkrəʊ,ɪzəm) *n* a property of certain crystals of absorbing light waves selectively and therefore of showing different colours when looked at from different directions. [C19: from Gk *pleiōn* more, from *polus* many + *-chroism* from *khrōs* skin colour]
▸ **pleochroic** (,plɪə'krəʊɪk) *adj*

pleomorphism (,plɪə'mɔːfɪzəm) *or* **pleomorphy** ('plɪə,mɔːfɪ) *n* **1** the occurrence of more than one different form in the life cycle of a plant or animal. **2** another word for **polymorphism** (sense 2).
▸ **,pleo'morphic** *adj*

pleonasm ('plɪə,næzəm) *n Rhetoric.* **1** the use of more words than necessary or an instance of this, such as *a tiny little child.* **2** a word or phrase that is superfluous. [C16: from L *pleonasmus*, from Gk *pleonasmos* excess, from *pleonazein* to be redundant]
▸ **,pleo'nastic** *adj*

plesiosaur ('plɪːsɪə,sɔː) *n* any of various marine reptiles of Jurassic and Cretaceous times, having a long neck, short tail, and paddle-like limbs. [C19: from NL *plēsiosaurus*, from Gk *plēsios* near + *sauros* a lizard]

plethora ('plɛθərə) *n* **1** superfluity or excess; overabundance. **2** *Pathol., obs.* a condition caused by dilation of superficial blood vessels, characterized esp. by a reddish face. [C16: via Med. L from Gk *plēthōrē* fullness, from *plēthein* to grow full]
▸ **plethoric** (plɛ'θɒrɪk) *adj*

pleura ('plʊərə) *n, pl* **pleurae** ('plʊəriː). the thin transparent membrane enveloping the lungs and lining the walls of the thoracic cavity. [C17: via Med. L from Gk: side, rib]
▸ **'pleural** *adj*

pleurisy ('plʊərɪsɪ) *n* inflammation of the pleura, characterized by pain that is aggravated by deep breathing or coughing. [C14: from OF *pleurisie*, from LL, from Gk *pleuritis*, from *pleura* side]
▸ **pleuritic** (plʊ'rɪtɪk) *adj, n*

pleuro- *or before a vowel* **pleur-** *combining form.* **1** of or relating to the side. **2** indicating the pleura. [from Gk *pleura* side]

pleuropneumonia (ˌplʊərəʊnjuːˈməʊnɪə) *n* the combined disorder of pleurisy and pneumonia.

Pleven (*Bulgarian* ˈplɛvɛn) *or* **Plevna** ★ (*Bulgarian* ˈplɛvna) *n* a town in N Bulgaria: taken by Russia from the Turks in 1877 after a siege of 143 days. Pop.: 125 029 (1996 est.).

Plexiglas (ˈplɛksɪˌglɑːs) *n US. trademark.* a transparent plastic, polymethylmethacrylate, used for combs, plastic sheeting, etc.

plexor (ˈplɛksə) *or* **plessor** *n Med.* a small hammer with a rubber head for use in percussion of the chest and testing reflexes. [C19: from Gk *plēxis* a stroke, from *plēssein* to strike]

plexus (ˈplɛksəs) *n, pl* **plexuses** *or* **plexus. 1** any complex network of nerves, blood vessels, or lymphatic vessels. **2** an intricate network or arrangement. [C17: NL, from L *plectere* to braid]

pliable (ˈplaɪəb°l) *adj* easily moulded, bent, influenced, or altered.
▶ ˌpliaˈbility *or* ˈpliableness *n* ▶ ˈpliably *adv*

pliant (ˈplaɪənt) *adj* **1** easily bent; supple: *a pliant young tree.* **2** adaptable; yielding readily to influence; compliant. [C14: from OF, from *plier* to fold; see PLY[2]]
▶ ˈpliancy *n* ▶ ˈpliantly *adv*

plicate (ˈplaɪkeɪt) *or* **plicated** *adj* having or arranged in parallel folds or ridges; pleated: *a plicate leaf; plicate rock strata.* [C18: from L *plicātus* folded, from *plicāre* to fold]
▶ pliˈcation *n*

plié (ˈpliːeɪ) *n* a classic ballet practice posture with back erect and knees bent. [F: bent]

plier (ˈplaɪə) *n* a person who plies a trade.

pliers (ˈplaɪəz) *pl n* a gripping tool consisting of two hinged arms usually with serrated jaws. [C16: from PLY[1]]

plight[1] (plaɪt) *n* a condition of extreme hardship, danger, etc. [C14 *plit*, from OF *pleit* fold; prob. infl. by OE *pliht* PLIGHT[2]]

plight[2] (plaɪt) *vb* (*tr*) **1** to promise formally or pledge (allegiance, support, etc.). **2 plight one's troth.** to make a promise, esp. of marriage. ◆ *n* **3** *Arch. or dialect.* a solemn promise, esp. of engagement; pledge. [OE *pliht* peril]
▶ ˈplighter *n*

plimsoll *or* **plimsole** (ˈplɪmsəl) *n Brit.* a light rubbersoled canvas shoe worn for various sports. Also called: **gym shoe, sandshoe.** [C20: from the resemblance of the sole to a Plimsoll line]

Plimsoll line (ˈplɪmsəl) *n* another name for **load line.** [C19: after Samuel *Plimsoll* (1824–98), Brit. politician who advocated its adoption]

plinth (plɪnθ) *n* **1** the rectangular slab or block that forms the lowest part of the base of a column, statue, pedestal, or pier. **2** Also called: **plinth course.** the lowest part of the wall of a building, esp. one that is formed of a course of stone or brick. **3** a flat block on either side of a doorframe, where the architrave meets the skirting. [C17: from L *plinthus*, from Gk *plinthos* brick]

Pliny ★ (ˈplɪnɪ) *n* **1** known as *Pliny the Elder.* Latin name *Gaius Plinius Secundus.* 23–79 A.D., Roman writer, the author of the encyclopedic *Natural History* (77). **2** his nephew, known as *Pliny the Younger.* Latin name *Gaius Plinius Caecilius Secundus.* ?62–?113 A.D., Roman writer and administrator, noted for his letters.

Pliocene *or* **Pleiocene** (ˈplaɪəʊˌsiːn) *adj* **1** of, denoting, or formed in the last epoch of the Tertiary period, during which many modern mammals appeared. ◆ *n* **2 the.** the Pliocene epoch or rock series. [C19: from Gk *pleiōn* more, from *polus* many + -*cene* from *kainos* recent]

plissé (ˈpliːseɪ, ˈplɪs-) *n* **1** fabric with a wrinkled finish, achieved by treatment involving caustic soda: *cotton plissé.* **2** such a finish on a fabric. [F: pleated]

PLO *abbrev.* for Palestine Liberation Organization.

Płock ★ (plɒk; *Polish* pwɔtsk) *n* a town in central Poland, on the River Vistula: several Polish kings are buried in the cathedral: oil refining, petrochemical works. Pop.: 126 500 (1995 est.).

plod (plɒd) *vb* **plods, plodding, plodded. 1** to make (one's way) or walk along (a path, etc.) with heavy usually slow steps. **2** (*intr*) to work slowly and perseveringly. ◆ *n* **3** the act of plodding. **4** *Brit.* a slang word for **policeman.** [C16: imit.]
▶ ˈplodder *n* ▶ ˈplodding *adj* ▶ ˈploddingly *adv*

Ploeşti ★ (*Romanian* ploˈjeʃtj) *n* a city in SE central Romania: centre of the Romanian petroleum industry. Pop.: 254 304 (1993 est.).

-ploid *adj and n combining form.* indicating a specific multiple of a single set of chromosomes: *diploid.* [from Gk -*pl(oos)* -fold + -OID]
▶ -**ploidy** *n combining form.*

plonk[1] (plɒŋk) *vb* **1** (often foll. by *down*) to drop or be dropped heavily: *he plonked the money on the table.* ◆ *n* **2** the act or sound of plonking. [var. of PLUNK]

plonk[2] (plɒŋk) *n Inf.* alcoholic drink, usually wine, esp. of inferior quality. [C20: ?from F *blanc* white, as in *vin blanc* white wine]

plonker (ˈplɒŋkə) *n Sl.* a stupid person. [C20: from PLONK[1]]

plop (plɒp) *n* **1** the characteristic sound made by an object dropping into water without a splash. ◆ *vb* **plops, plopping, plopped. 2** to fall or cause to fall with the sound of a plop: *the stone plopped into the water.* ◆ *interj* **3** an exclamation imitative of this sound: *to go plop.* [C19: imit.]

plosion (ˈpləʊʒən) *n Phonetics.* the sound of an abrupt break or closure, esp. the audible release of a stop. Also called: **explosion.**

plosive (ˈpləʊsɪv) *Phonetics.* ◆ *adj* **1** accompanied by plosion. ◆ *n* **2** a plosive consonant; stop. [C20: from F, from *explosif* EXPLOSIVE]

plot[1] (plɒt) *n* **1** a secret plan to achieve some purpose, esp. one that is illegal or underhand. **2** the story or plan of a play, novel, etc. **3** *Mil.* a graphic representation of an individual or tactical setting that pinpoints an artillery target. **4** *Chiefly US.* a diagram or plan. **5 lose the plot.** *Inf.* to lose one's ability or judgment in a given situation. ◆ *vb* **plots, plotting, plotted. 6** to plan secretly (something illegal, revolutionary, etc.); conspire. **7** (*tr*) to mark (a course, as of a ship or aircraft) on a map. **8** (*tr*) to make a plan or map of. **9a** to locate and mark (points) on a graph by means of coordinates. **9b** to draw (a curve) through these points. **10** (*tr*) to construct the plot of (a literary work, etc.). [C16: from PLOT[2], infl. by obs. *complot* conspiracy, from OF, from ?]
▶ ˈplotter *n*

plot[2] (plɒt) *n* a small piece of land: *a vegetable plot.* [OE]

Plotinus ★ (plɒˈtaɪnəs) *n* ?205–?270 A.D., Roman Neo-Platonist philosopher, born in Egypt.

plough *or esp. US* **plow** (plaʊ) *n* **1** an agricultural implement with sharp blades for cutting or turning over the earth. **2** any of various similar implements, such as a device for clearing snow. **3** ploughed land. **4 put one's hand to the plough.** to begin or undertake a task. ◆ *vb* **5** to till (the soil, etc.) with a plough. **6** to make (furrows or grooves) in (something) with or as if with a plough. **7** (when *intr*, usually foll. by *through*) to move (through something) in the manner of a plough. **8** (*intr*, foll. by *through*) to work at slowly or perseveringly. **9** (*intr*; foll. by *into* or *through*) (of a vehicle) to run uncontrollably into something in its path. **10** (*intr*) *Brit. sl.* to fail an examination. [OE *plōg* plough land]
▶ ˈplougher *or esp. US* ˈplower *n*

Plough (plaʊ) *n* **the.** the group of the seven brightest stars in the constellation Ursa Major. Also called: **Charles's Wain.** Usual US name: the **Big Dipper.**

plough back *vb* (*tr, adv*) to reinvest (the profits of a business) in the same business.

ploughman *or esp. US* **plowman** (ˈplaʊmən) *n, pl* **ploughmen** *or esp. US* **plowmen.** a man who ploughs, esp. using horses.

ploughman's lunch *n* a snack lunch, served esp. in a pub, consisting of bread and cheese with pickle.

ploughshare *or esp. US* **plowshare** (ˈplaʊˌʃɛə)

★ people and places

horizontal pointed cutting blade of a mouldboard plough.

Plovdiv ★ (Bulgarian 'plɔvdif) n a city in S Bulgaria on the Maritsa River: the second largest town in Bulgaria; conquered by Philip II of Macedonia in 341 B.C.; capital of Roman Thracia; commercial centre of a rich agricultural region. Pop.: 344 326 (1996 est.). Greek name: **Philippopolis**.

plover ('plʌvə) n 1 any of a family of shore birds, typically having a round head, straight bill, and large pointed wings. 2 **green plover**. another name for **lapwing**. [C14: from OF plovier rainbird, from L pluvia rain]

plow (plaʊ) n, vb the usual US spelling of **plough**.

Plowright ★ ('plaʊˌraɪt) n **Joan**. born 1929, British actress, married (1961–89) to Laurence Olivier.

ploy (plɔɪ) n 1 a manoeuvre or tactic in a game, conversation, etc. 2 any business, job, hobby, etc., with which one is occupied: angling is his latest ploy. 3 Chiefly Brit. a frolic, escapade, or practical joke. [C18: orig. Scot. & N English, obs. n sense of EMPLOY meaning an occupation]

PLP (in Britain) abbrev. for Parliamentary Labour Party.

PLR abbrev. for Public Lending Right.

pluck (plʌk) vb 1 (tr) to pull off (feathers, fruit, etc.) from (a fowl, tree, etc.). 2 (when intr, foll. by at) to pull or tug. 3 (tr; foll. by off, away, etc.) Arch. to pull (something) forcibly or violently (from something or someone). 4 (tr) to sound (the strings) of (a musical instrument) with the fingers, a plectrum, etc. 5 (tr) Sl. to swindle or swindle. ◆ n 6 courage, usually in the face of difficulties or hardship. 7 a sudden pull or tug. 8 the heart, liver, and lungs, esp. of an animal used for food. [OE pluccian, plyccan]
▸ **'plucker** n

pluck up vb (tr, adv) 1 to pull out; uproot. 2 to muster (courage, one's spirits, etc.).

plucky ('plʌkɪ) adj **pluckier**, **pluckiest**. having or showing courage in the face of difficulties, danger, etc.
▸ **'pluckily** adv ▸ **'pluckiness** n

plug (plʌg) n 1 a piece of wood, cork, or other material, used to stop up holes or waste pipes or as a wedge for taking a screw or nail. 2 a device having one or more pins to which an electric cable is attached: used to make an electrical connection when inserted into a socket. 3 Also called: **volcanic plug**. a mass of solidified magma filling the neck of an extinct volcano. 4 See **sparking plug**. 5a a cake of pressed or twisted tobacco, esp. for chewing. 5b a small piece of such a cake. 6 Inf. a favourable mention of a product, show, etc., as on television. ◆ vb **plugs**, **plugging**, **plugged**. 7 (tr) to stop up or secure (a hole, gap, etc.) with or as if with a plug. 8 (tr) to insert or use (something) as a plug: to plug a finger into one's ear. 9 (tr) Inf. to make favourable and often-repeated mentions of (a song, product, show, etc.), as on television. 10 (tr) Sl. to shoot: he plugged six rabbits. 11 (tr) Sl. to punch. 12 (intr; foll. by along, away, etc.) Inf. to work steadily or persistently. [C17: from MDu. plugge]
▸ **'plugger** n

plug-and-play adj Computing. capable of detecting the addition of a new input or output device and automatically activating the appropriate control software.

plughole ('plʌgˌhəʊl) n a hole in a sink, etc., through which waste water drains and which can be closed with a plug.

plug in vb (tr, adv) to connect (an electrical appliance, etc.) with a power source by means of an electrical plug.

plug-ugly adj 1 Inf. extremely ugly. ◆ n, pl **plug-uglies**. 2 US sl. a city tough; ruffian. [C19: from ?]

plum (plʌm) n 1 a small rosaceous tree with an edible oval fruit that is purple, yellow, or green and contains an oval stone. 2 the fruit of this tree. 3 a raisin, as used in a cake or pudding. 4a a dark reddish-purple colour. 4b (as adj): a plum carpet. 5 Inf. **5a** something of a superior or desirable kind, such as a financial bonus. **5b** (as modifier): a plum job. [OE plūme]

plumage ('pluːmɪdʒ) n the layer of feathers covering the body of a bird. [C15: from OF, from plume feather, from L plūma down]

plumate ('pluːmeɪt, -mɪt) or **plumose** adj Zool., bot. 1 of

or possessing feathers or plumes. 2 covered with small hairs: a plumate seed. [C19: from L plumātus covered with feathers; see PLUME]

plumb (plʌm) n 1 a weight, usually of lead, suspended at the end of a line and used to determine water depth or verticality. 2 the perpendicular position of a freely suspended plumb line (esp. in **out of plumb**, **off plumb**). ◆ adv also **plum**. 3 vertical or perpendicular. 4 Inf., chiefly US. (intensifier): plumb stupid. 5 Inf. exactly; precisely. ◆ vb 6 (tr; often foll. by up) to test the alignment of or adjust to the vertical with a plumb line. 7 (tr) to experience (the worst extremes of): to plumb the depths of despair. 8 (tr) to understand or master (something obscure): to plumb a mystery. 9 to connect or join (a device such as a tap) to a water pipe or drainage system. [C13: from OF plomb (unattested) lead line, from plon lead, from L plumbum]
▸ **'plumbable** adj

plumbago (plʌmˈbeɪgəʊ) n, pl **plumbagos**. 1 a plant of warm regions, having clusters of blue, white, or red flowers. 2 another name for **graphite**. [C17: from L: lead ore, translation of Gk polubdaina, from polubdos lead]

plumber ('plʌmə) n a person who installs and repairs pipes, fixtures, etc., for water, drainage, and gas. [C14: from OF plommier worker in lead, from LL plumbārius, from L plumbum lead]

plumbing ('plʌmɪŋ) n 1 the trade or work of a plumber. 2 the pipes, fixtures, etc., used in a water, drainage, or gas installation. 3 the act or procedure of using a plumb.

plumbism ('plʌmˌbɪzəm) n chronic lead poisoning. [C19: from L plumbum lead]

plumb line n a string with a metal weight, or **plumb bob**, at one end that, when suspended, points directly towards the earth's centre of gravity and so is used to determine verticality, depth, etc.

plumb rule n a plumb line attached to a narrow board, used by builders, surveyors, etc.

plume (pluːm) n 1 a feather, esp. one that is large or ornamental. 2 a feather or cluster of feathers worn esp. formerly as a badge or ornament in a headband, hat, etc. 3 Biol. any feathery part. 4 something that resembles a plume: a plume of smoke. 5 a token or decoration of honour; prize. ◆ vb **plumes**, **pluming**, **plumed**. (tr) 6 to adorn with feathers or plumes. 7 (of a bird) to clean or preen (itself or its feathers). 8 (foll. by on or upon) to pride or congratulate (oneself). [C14: from OF, from L plūma downy feather]

plummet ('plʌmɪt) vb **plummets**, **plummeting**, **plummeted**. 1 (intr) to drop down; plunge. ◆ n 2 the weight on a plumb line; plumb bob. 3 a lead plumb used by anglers. [C14: from OF plommet ball of lead, from plomb lead, from L plumbum]

plummy ('plʌmɪ) adj **plummier**, **plummiest**. 1 of, full of, or resembling plums. 2 Brit. inf. (of speech) deep, refined, and somewhat drawling. 3 Brit. inf. choice; desirable.

plumose ('pluːməʊs, -məʊz) adj another word for **plumate**. [C17: from L plūmōsus feathery]

plump¹ (plʌmp) adj 1 well filled out or rounded; chubby: a plump turkey. 2 bulging; full: a plump wallet. ◆ vb 3 (often foll. by up or out) to make or become plump: to plump up a pillow. [C15 (meaning: dull, rude), C16 (in current senses): ?from MDu. plomp blunt]
▸ **'plumply** adv ▸ **'plumpness** n

plump² (plʌmp) vb 1 (often foll. by down, into, etc.) to drop or fall suddenly and heavily. 2 (intr; foll. by for) to give support (to) or make a choice (of) one out of a group or number. ◆ n 3 a heavy abrupt fall or the sound of this. ◆ adv 4 suddenly or heavily. 5 straight down; directly: the helicopter landed plump in the middle of the field. ◆ adj, adv 6 in a blunt, direct, or decisive manner. [C14: prob. imit.]

plum pudding n Brit. a boiled or steamed pudding made with flour, suet, sugar, and dried fruit.

plumule ('pluːmjuːl) n 1 the embryonic shoot of seed-bearing plants. 2 a down feather of young birds. [C18: from LL plūmula a little feather]

plumy ('pluːmɪ) adj **plumier**, **plumiest**. 1 plumelike; feathery. 2 consisting of, covered with, or adorned with feathers.

plunder ('plʌndə) vb **1** to steal (valuables, goods, sacred items, etc.) from (a town, church, etc.) by force, esp. in time of war; loot. **2** (tr) to rob or steal (choice or desirable things) from (a place): to plunder an orchard. ◆ n **3** anything taken by plundering; booty. **4** the act of plundering; pillage. [C17: prob. from Du. plunderen (orig.: to plunder household goods)]
▶ 'plunderer n

plunge (plʌndʒ) vb **plunges, plunging, plunged. 1** (usually foll. by into) to thrust or throw (something, oneself, etc.): they plunged into the sea. **2** to throw or be thrown into a certain condition: the room was plunged into darkness. **3** (usually foll. by into) to involve or become involved deeply (in). **4** (intr) to move or dash violently or with great speed or impetuosity. **5** (intr) to descend very suddenly or steeply: the ship plunged in heavy seas; a plunging neckline. **6** (intr) Inf. to speculate or gamble recklessly, for high stakes, etc. ◆ n **7** a leap or dive. **8** Inf. a swim; dip. **9** a pitching or tossing motion. **10 take the plunge.** Inf. to resolve to do something dangerous or irrevocable. [C14: from OF plongier, from Vulgar L plumbicāre (unattested) to sound with a plummet, from L plumbum lead]

plunger ('plʌndʒə) n **1** a rubber suction cup used to clear blocked drains, etc. **2** a device or part of a machine that has a plunging or thrusting motion; piston. **3** Inf. a reckless gambler.

plunk (plʌŋk) vb **1** to pluck (the strings) of (a banjo, etc.) or (of such an instrument) to give forth a sound when plucked. **2** (often foll. by down) to drop or be dropped, esp. heavily or suddenly. ◆ n **3** the act or sound of plunking. [C20: imit.]

Plunket or **Plunkett** ★ ('plʌŋkɪt) n **Saint Oliver.** 1629–81, Irish Roman Catholic churchman and martyr; wrongly executed as a supposed conspirator in the Popish Plot (1678). Feast day: July 11.

pluperfect (pluː'pɜːfɪkt) adj, n Grammar. another term for **past perfect.** [C16: from L plūs quam perfectum more than perfect]

plural ('plʊərəl) adj **1** containing, involving, or composed of more than one. **2** denoting a word indicating that more than one referent is being referred to or described. ◆ n **3** Grammar. **3a** the plural number. **3b** a plural form. [C14: from OF plurel, from LL plūrālis concerning many, from L plūs more]
▶ 'plurally adv

pluralism ('plʊərə,lɪzəm) n **1** the holding by a single person of more than one ecclesiastical benefice or office; plurality. **2** Sociol. a theory of society as several autonomous but interdependent groups. **3** the existence in a society of groups having distinctive ethnic origin, cultural forms, religions, etc. **4** Philosophy. **4a** the metaphysical doctrine that reality consists of more than two basic types of substance. Cf. **monism** (sense 1), **dualism** (sense 2). **4b** the metaphysical doctrine that reality consists of independent entities rather than one unchanging whole.
▶ 'pluralist n, adj ▶ ,plural'istic adj

plurality (plʊə'rælɪtɪ) n, pl **pluralities. 1** the state of being plural. **2** Maths. a number greater than one. **3** the US term for **relative majority. 4** a large number. **5** the greater number; majority. **6** another word for **pluralism** (sense 1).

pluralize or **pluralise** ('plʊərə,laɪz) vb **pluralizes, pluralizing, pluralized** or **pluralises, pluralising, pluralised. 1** (intr) to hold more than one ecclesiastical benefice or office at the same time. **2** to make or become plural.

pluri- combining form. denoting several. [from L plur-, plus more, plures several]

plus (plʌs) prep **1** increased by the addition of: four plus two. **2** with or with the addition of: a good job, plus a new car. ◆ adj **3** (prenominal) indicating or involving addition: a plus sign. **4** another word for **positive** (senses 7, 8). **5** on the positive part of a scale or coordinate axis: a value of +x. **6** indicating the positive side of an electrical circuit. **7** involving advantage: a plus factor. **8** (postpositive) Inf. having a value above that which is stated: she had charm plus. **9** (postpositive) slightly above a specified standard: he received a B+ grade for his essay. ◆ n **10** short for **plus sign. 11** a positive quantity. **12** Inf. something positive or to the good. **13** a gain, surplus, or advantage. ◆ Mathematical symbol: + [C17: from L: more]

plus fours pl n men's baggy knickerbockers reaching below the knee, now only worn for golf, etc. [C20: because made with four inches of material to hang over at the knee]

plush (plʌʃ) n **1** a fabric with a cut pile that is longer and softer than velvet. ◆ adj **2** Also: **plushy.** Inf. lavishly appointed; rich; costly. [C16: from F pluche, from OF peluchier to pluck, ult. from L pilus a hair]
▶ 'plushly adv

plus sign n the symbol +, indicating addition or positive quantity.

Plutarch ★ ('pluːtɑːk) n ?46–?120 A.D., Greek biographer and philosopher, noted for his Parallel Lives of distinguished Greeks and Romans.

Pluto[1] ★ ('pluːtəʊ) n Gk myth. the god of the underworld; Hades.
▶ Plu'tonian adj

Pluto[2] ('pluːtəʊ) n the smallest planet and the farthest known from the sun. [L, from Gk Ploutōn, lit.: the rich one]

plutocracy (pluː'tɒkrəsɪ) n, pl **plutocracies. 1** the rule of society by the wealthy. **2** a state or government characterized by the rule of the wealthy. **3** a class that exercises power by virtue of its wealth. [C17: from Gk ploutokratia, from ploutos wealth + -kratia rule]
▶ plutocratic (,pluːtə'krætɪk) adj ▶ ,pluto'cratically adv

plutocrat ('pluːtə,kræt) n a member of a plutocracy.

pluton ('pluːtɒn) n any mass of igneous rock that has solidified below the surface of the earth. [C20: back formation from PLUTONIC]

plutonic (pluː'tɒnɪk) adj (of igneous rocks) derived from magma that has cooled and solidified below the surface of the earth. [C20: after PLUTO[1]]

plutonium (pluː'təʊnɪəm) n a highly toxic metallic transuranic element. It occurs in trace amounts in uranium ores and is produced in a nuclear reactor by neutron bombardment of uranium-238. The most stable isotope, **plutonium-239**, readily undergoes fission and is used as a reactor fuel. Symbol: Pu; atomic no.: 94; half-life of ^{239}Pu: 24 360 years. [C20: after PLUTO[2] because Pluto lies beyond Neptune and plutonium was discovered soon after NEPTUNIUM]

Plutus ★ ('pluːtus) n the Greek god of wealth. [from Gk ploutos wealth]

pluvial ('pluːvɪəl) adj **1** of, characterized by, or due to the action of rain; rainy. ◆ n **2** Geol. a period of persistent rainfall. [C17: from L pluviālis rainy, from pluvia rain]

pluviometer (,pluːvɪ'ɒmɪtə) n another name for **rain gauge.**
▶ pluviometric (,pluːvɪə'metrɪk) adj ▶ ,pluvio'metrically adv

ply[1] (plaɪ) vb **plies, plying, plied.** (mainly tr) **1** to carry on, pursue, or work at (a job, trade, etc.). **2** to manipulate or wield (a tool, etc.). **3** to sell (goods, wares, etc.), esp. at a regular place. **4** (usually foll. by with) to provide (with) or subject (to) repeatedly or persistently: he plied us with drink; he plied the speaker with questions. **5** (intr) to work steadily or diligently. **6** (also intr) (esp. of a ship, etc.) to travel regularly along (a route) or in (an area): to ply the trade routes. [C14 plye, short for aplye to APPLY]

ply[2] (plaɪ) n, pl **plies. 1a** a layer, fold, or thickness, as of yarn. **1b** (in combination): four-ply. **2** a thin sheet of wood glued to other similar sheets to form plywood. **3** one of the strands twisted together to make rope, yarn, etc. [C15: from OF pli fold, from plier to fold, from L plicāre]

Plymouth ★ ('plɪməθ) n **1** a port and unitary authority in SW England, in SW Devon on **Plymouth Sound** (an inlet of the English Channel): Britain's chief port in Elizabethan times; the last port visited by the Pilgrim Fathers in the *Mayflower* before sailing to America; naval base. Pop.: 245 295 (1991). **2** a city in SE Massachusetts, on **Plymouth Bay**: the first permanent European settlement in New England; founded by the Pilgrim Fathers. Pop.: 45 608 (1990).

Plymouth Brethren *pl n* a religious sect founded about 1827, strongly Puritanical in outlook and having no organized ministry.

plywood ('plaɪˌwʊd) *n* a structural board consisting of thin layers of wood glued together under pressure, with the grain of one layer at right angles to the grain of the adjoining layer.

Plzeň ★ (*Czech* 'plzɛnj) *n* an industrial city in the W Czech Republic. Pop.: 171 908 (1995 est.). German name: **Pilsen**.

pm *abbrev. for* premium.

Pm *the chemical symbol for* promethium.

PM *abbrev. for:* **1** Past Master (of a fraternity). **2** Paymaster. **3** Postmaster. **4** Prime Minister. **5** *Mil.* Provost Marshal.

p.m., P.M., pm, *or* **PM** *abbrev. for:* **1** (indicating the time from midday to midnight) post meridiem. [L: after noon] **2** postmortem (examination).

PMG *abbrev. for:* **1** Paymaster General. **2** Postmaster General.

PMS *abbrev. for* premenstrual syndrome.

PMT *abbrev. for* premenstrual tension.

PNdB *abbrev. for* perceived noise decibel.

pneumatic (njuː'mætɪk) *adj* **1** of or concerned with air, gases, or wind. **2** (of a machine or device) operated by compressed air or by a vacuum. **3** containing compressed air: *a pneumatic tyre.* **4** (of the bones of birds) containing air spaces which reduce their weight as an adaptation to flying. ✦ *n* **5** a pneumatic tyre. [C17: from LL *pneumaticus* of air or wind, from Gk, from *pneuma* breath, wind]
▸ **pneu'matically** *adv*

pneumatics (njuː'mætɪks) *n* (*functioning as sing*) the branch of physics concerned with the mechanical properties of gases, esp. air.

pneumatology (ˌnjuːmə'tɒlədʒɪ) *n* **1** the branch of theology concerned with the Holy Ghost and other spiritual beings. **2** an obsolete name for **psychology** (the science).

pneumatophore (njuː'mætəʊˌfɔː) *n* **1** a specialized root of certain swamp plants, such as the mangrove, that branches upwards and undergoes gaseous exchange with the atmosphere. **2** a polyp such as the Portuguese man-of-war, that is specialized as a float.

pneumococcus (ˌnjuːməʊ'kɒkəs) *n, pl* **pneumococci** (-'kɒksaɪ). a bacterium that causes pneumonia.

pneumoconiosis (ˌnjuːməʊˌkəʊnɪ'əʊsɪs) *or* **pneumonoconiosis** (ˌnjuːməʊˌkəʊnɪ'əʊsɪs) *n* any disease of the lungs or bronchi caused by the inhalation of metallic or mineral particles. [C19: shortened from *pneumonoconiosis*, from Gk *pneumōn* lung + *-coniosis*, from *konis* dust]

pneumoencephalogram (ˌnjuːməʊɛn'sɛfələˌgræm) *n* See **encephalogram**.

pneumogastric (ˌnjuːməʊ'gæstrɪk) *adj Anat.* **1** of or relating to the lungs and stomach. **2** a former term for **vagus**.

pneumonectomy (ˌnjuːməʊ'nɛktəmɪ) *or* **pneumectomy** *n, pl* **pneumonectomies** *or* **pneumectomies.** the surgical removal of a lung or part of a lung. [C20: from Gk *pneumōn* lung + -ECTOMY]

pneumonia (njuː'məʊnɪə) *n* inflammation of one or both lungs, in which the air sacs (alveoli) become filled with liquid. [C17: NL from Gk from *pneumōn* lung]
▸ **pneumonic** (njuː'mɒnɪk) *adj*

pneumothorax (ˌnjuːməʊ'θɔːræks) *n* the abnormal presence of air between the lung and the wall of the chest (pleural cavity), resulting in collapse of the lung.

PNI *abbrev. for* psychoneuroimmunology.

p-n junction *n Electronics.* a boundary between a p-type

and n-type semiconductor that functions as a rectifier and is used in diodes and junction transistors.

Pnom Penh ★ ('nɒm 'pɛn) *n* a variant spelling of **Phnom Penh**.

po (pəʊ) *n, pl* **pos.** *Brit.* an informal word for **chamber pot.** [C19: from POT[1]]

Po[1] *the chemical symbol for* polonium.

Po[2] ★ (pəʊ) *n* a river in N Italy, rising in the Cottian Alps and flowing northeast to Turin, then east to the Adriatic: the longest river in Italy. Length: 652 km (405 miles). Latin name: **Padus**.

PO *abbrev. for:* **1** Personnel Officer. **2** petty officer. **3** Pilot Officer. **4** Also: **p.o.** postal order. **5** Post Office.

poach[1] (pəʊtʃ) *vb* **1** to catch (game, fish, etc.) illegally by trespassing on private property. **2** to encroach on or usurp (another person's rights, duties, etc.) or steal (an idea, employee, etc.). **3** *Tennis, badminton, etc.* to take or play (shots that should belong to one's partner). **4** to break up (land) into wet muddy patches, as by riding over it. [C17: from OF *pocher*, of Gmc origin]
▸ **'poacher** *n*

poach[2] (pəʊtʃ) *vb* to simmer (eggs, fish, etc.) very gently in water, milk, stock, etc. [C15: from OF *pochier* to enclose in a bag (as the yolks are enclosed by the whites)]
▸ **'poacher** *n*

Pocahontas ★ (ˌpɒkə'hɒntəs) *n* original name *Matoaka*; married name *Rebecca Rolfe*. ?1595–1617, American Indian, who allegedly saved the colonist Captain John Smith from being killed.

pochard ('pəʊtʃəd) *n, pl* **pochards** *or* **pochard.** any of various diving ducks, esp. a European variety, the male of which has a grey-and-black body and a reddish head. [C16: from ?]

pock (pɒk) *n* **1** any pustule resulting from an eruptive disease, esp. from smallpox. **2** another word for **pockmark** (sense 1). [OE *pocc*]
▸ **'pocky** *adj*

pocket ('pɒkɪt) *n* **1** a small bag or pouch in a garment for carrying small articles, money, etc. **2** any bag or pouch or anything resembling this. **3** *S. African.* a bag or sack of vegetables or fruit. **4** a cavity in the earth, etc., such as one containing ore. **5** a small enclosed or isolated area: *a pocket of resistance.* **6** any of the six holes with pouches or nets let into the corners and sides of a billiard table. **7 in one's pocket.** under one's control. **8 in** *or* **out of pocket.** having made a profit or loss. **9 line one's pockets.** to make money, esp. by dishonesty when in a position of trust. **10** (*modifier*) small: *a pocket edition.* ✦ *vb* **pockets, pocketing, pocketed.** **11** (*tr*) to put into one's pocket. **12** to take surreptitiously or unlawfully; steal. **13** (*usually passive*) to confine in or as if in a pocket. **14** to conceal or keep back: *he pocketed his pride and asked for help.* **15** *Billiards, etc.* to drive (a ball) into a pocket. [C15: from Anglo-Norman *poket* a little bag, from *poque* bag, from MDu. *poke* bag]
▸ **'pocketless** *adj*

pocket battleship *n* a small heavily armed battle cruiser specially built to conform with treaty limitations on tonnage and armament.

pocket billiards *n* (*functioning as sing*) *Billiards.* **1** another name for **pool**[2] (sense 5). **2** any game played on a table in which the object is to pocket the balls, esp. snooker and pool.

pocketbook ('pɒkɪtˌbʊk) *n* **1** *Chiefly US.* a small bag or case for money, papers, etc. **2** a pocket-sized notebook.

pocket borough *n* (before the Reform Act of 1832) an English borough constituency controlled by one person or family who owned the land.

pocketful ('pɒkɪtfʊl) *n, pl* **pocketfuls.** as much as a pocket will hold.

pocketknife ('pɒkɪtˌnaɪf) *n, pl* **pocketknives.** a small knife with one or more blades that fold into the handle; penknife.

pocket money *n* **1** *Brit.* a small weekly sum of money given to children by parents as an allowance. **2** money for day-to-day spending, incidental expenses, etc.

pockmark ('pɒkˌmɑːk) *n* **1** Also called: **pock.** a pitted scar left on the skin after the healing of a smallpox or similar pustule. **2** any pitting of a surface that resembles such scars. ◆ *vb* **3** (*tr*) to scar or pit with pockmarks.

poco ('pəʊkəʊ; *Italian* 'pɔːko) *or* **un poco** *adj, adv* (*in combination*) *Music.* a little; to a small degree. [from It.: little, from L *paucus* few]

poco a poco *adv* (*in combination*) *Music.* little by little: *poco a poco rall.* [It.]

pod (pɒd) *n* **1a** the fruit of any leguminous plant, consisting of a long two-valved case that contains seeds. **1b** the seedcase as distinct from the seeds. **2** any similar fruit. **3** a streamlined structure attached to an aircraft and used to house a jet engine, fuel tank, armament, etc. ◆ *vb* **pods, podding, podded. 4** (*tr*) to remove the pod from. [C17: ? back formation from earlier *podware* bagged vegetables]

-pod *or* **-pode** *n combining form.* indicating a certain type or number of feet: *arthropod; tripod.* [from Gk *-podos* footed, from *pous* foot]

podagra (pə'dægrə) *n* gout of the foot or big toe. [C15: via L from Gk, from *pous* foot + *agra* a trap]

poddy ('pɒdɪ) *n, pl* **poddies.** *Austral.* a handfed calf or lamb. [?from *poddy* (adj) fat]

Podgorica *or* **Podgoritsa** ★ (*Russian* 'pɒdgɔ,riːtsa) *n* a city in Yugoslavia, the capital of Montenegro. Pop.: 117 875 (1991). Former name (1946–91): **Titograd.**

podgy ('pɒdʒɪ) *adj* **podgier, podgiest. 1** short and fat; chubby. **2** (of the face, arms, etc.) unpleasantly chubby and pasty-looking. [C19: from *podge* a short plump person]
▸ **'podgily** *adv* ▸ **'podginess** *n*

podium ('pəʊdɪəm) *n, pl* **podiums** *or* **podia** (-dɪə). **1** a small raised platform used by lecturers, conductors, etc. **2** a plinth that supports a colonnade or wall. **3** a low wall surrounding the arena of an ancient amphitheatre. **4** *Zool.* any footlike organ, such as the tube foot of a starfish. [C18: from L: platform, from Gk *podion* little foot, from *pous* foot]

-podium *n combining form.* a part resembling a foot: *pseudopodium.* [from NL: footlike; see PODIUM]

Podolsk ★ (*Russian* pa'dɒljsk) *n* an industrial city in W Russia, near Moscow. Pop.: 202 000 (1995 est.).

podophyllin (,pɒdəʊ'fɪlɪn) *n* a bitter yellow resin obtained from the dried underground stems of the May apple and mandrake: used as a cathartic. [C19: from NL *Podophyllum*, genus of herbs, from *podo-*, from Gk *pous* foot + *phullon* leaf]

-podous *adj combining form.* having feet of a certain kind or number: *cephalopodous.*

podzol ('pɒdzɒl) *or* **podsol** ('pɒdsɒl) *n* a type of soil characteristic of coniferous forest regions having a greyish-white colour in its upper layers from which certain minerals have leached. [C20: from Russian: ash ground]

Poe ★ (pəʊ) *n* **Edgar Allan.** 1809–49, US short-story writer, poet, and critic. Most of his short stories, such as *The Fall of the House of Usher* (1839) and the *Tales of the Grotesque and Arabesque* (1840), are about death and madness.

poem ('pəʊɪm) *n* **1** a composition in verse, usually characterized by words chosen for their sound and suggestive power as well as for their sense, and using such techniques as metre, rhyme, and alliteration. **2** a literary composition that is not in verse but exhibits the intensity of imagination and language common to it: *a prose poem.* **3** anything resembling a poem in beauty, effect, etc. [C16: from L *poēma*, from Gk, var. of *poiēma* something created, from *poiein* to make]

poesy ('pəʊɪzɪ) *n, pl* **poesies. 1** an archaic word for **poetry. 2** *Poetic.* the art of writing poetry. [C14: via OF from L *poēsis*, from Gk, from *poiēsis* poetic art, from *poiein* to make]

poet ('pəʊɪt) *or* (*sometimes when fem*) **poetess** *n* **1** a person who writes poetry. **2** a person with great imagination and creativity. [C13: from L *poēta*, from Gk *poiētēs* maker, poet]

poetaster (,pəʊɪ'tæstə, -'teɪ-) *n* a writer of inferior verse. [C16: from Med. L; see POET, -ASTER]

poetic (pəʊ'etɪk) *or* **poetical** *adj* **1** of poetry. **2** charac-

teristic of poetry, as in being elevated, sublime, etc. **3** characteristic of a poet. **4** recounted in verse.
▸ **po'etically** *adv*

poeticize, poeticise (pəʊ'etɪ,saɪz) *or* **poetize, poetise** ('pəʊɪ,taɪz) *vb* **poeticizes, poeticizing, poeticized; poeticises, poeticising, poeticised** *or* **poetizes, poetizing, poetized; poetises, poetising, poetised. 1** (*tr*) to put into poetry or make poetic. **2** (*intr*) to speak or write poetically.

poetic justice *n* fitting retribution.

poetic licence *n* justifiable departure from conventional rules of form, fact, etc., as in poetry.

poetics (pəʊ'etɪks) *n* (*usually functioning as sing*) **1** the principles and forms of poetry or the study of these. **2** a treatise on poetry.

poet laureate *n, pl* **poets laureate.** *Brit.* the poet appointed as court poet of Britain who is given a lifetime post in the Royal Household.

poetry ('pəʊɪtrɪ) *n* **1** literature in metrical form; verse. **2** the art or craft of writing verse. **3** poetic qualities, spirit, or feeling in anything. **4** anything resembling poetry in rhythm, beauty, etc. [C14: from Med. L *poētria*, from L *poēta* POET]

po-faced *adj* **1** wearing a disapproving stern expression. **2** narrow-minded; strait-laced. [C20: from PO + POKER-FACED]

pogo stick ('pəʊgəʊ) *n* a stout pole with a handle at the top, steps for the feet and a spring at the bottom, so that the user can spring up, down, and along on it. [C20: from ?]

pogrom ('pɒgrəm) *n* an organized persecution or extermination of an ethnic group, esp. of Jews. [C20: via Yiddish from Russian: destruction, from *po-* like + *grom* thunder]

Pohai ★ (,pəʊ'haɪ) *n* a variant transliteration of the Chinese name for **Bohai.**

pohutukawa (pə,huːtuː'kɑːwə) *n* a New Zealand tree which grows on the coast and produces red flowers in the summer. Also called: **Christmas tree.**

poi (pɔɪ) *n NZ.* a ball of woven New Zealand flax swung rhythmically by Maori women while performing poi dances.

poi dance *n NZ.* a women's formation dance that involves singing and manipulating a poi.

-poiesis *n combining form.* indicating the act of making or producing something specified. [from Gk, from *poiēsis* a making; see POESY]
▸ **-poietic** *adj combining form.*

poignant ('pɔɪnjənt, -nənt) *adj* **1** sharply distressing or painful to the feelings. **2** to the point; cutting or piercing: *poignant wit.* **3** keen or pertinent in mental appeal: *a poignant subject.* **4** pungent in smell. [C14: from OF, from L *pungens* pricking, from *pungere* to sting]
▸ **'poignancy** *or* **'poignance** *n* ▸ **'poignantly** *adv*

poikilothermic (,pɔɪkɪləʊ'θɜːmɪk) *or* **poikilothermal** (,pɔɪkɪləʊ'θɜːməl) *adj* (of all animals except birds and mammals) having a body temperature that varies with the temperature of the surroundings. [C19: from Gk *poikilos* various + THERMAL]
▸ **,poikilo'thermy** *n*

Poincaré ★ (*French* pwɛ̃kare) *n* **1 Jules Henri** (ʒyl ɑ̃ri). 1854–1912, French mathematician, physicist, and philosopher. He made important contributions to the theory of functions and to astronomy and electromagnetic theory. **2** his cousin, **Raymond** (rɛmɔ̃). 1860–1934, French statesman; premier of France (1912–13; 1922–24; 1926–29); president (1913–20).

poinciana (,pɔɪnsɪ'ɑːnə) *n* a tree of a tropical genus having large orange or red flowers. [C17: NL, after M. de *Poinci*, 17th-cent. governor of the French Antilles]

poind (pɔɪnd) *vb* (*tr*) *Scots Law.* **1** to take (property of a debtor, etc.) in execution of distress; distrain. **2** to impound (stray cattle, etc.). [C15: from Scot., var. of OE *pyndan* to impound]

poinsettia (pɔɪn'setɪə) *n* a shrub of Mexico and Central America, widely cultivated for its showy scarlet bracts, which resemble petals. [C19: NL, after J. P. *Poinsett* (1799–1851), US Minister to Mexico]

★ people and places

point ('pɔɪnt) *n* **1** a dot or tiny mark. **2** a location, spot, or position. **3** any dot used in writing or printing, such as a decimal point or a full stop. **4** the sharp tapered end of a pin, knife, etc. **5** *Maths.* **5a** a geometric element having no dimensions whose position is located by means of its coordinates. **5b** a location: *point of inflection.* **6** a small promontory. **7** a specific condition or degree. **8** a moment: *at that point he left the room.* **9** a reason, aim, etc.: *the point of this exercise is to train new teachers.* **10** an essential element in an argument: *I take your point.* **11** a suggestion or tip. **12** a detail or item. **13** a characteristic, physical attribute, etc.: *he has his good points.* **14** a distinctive characteristic or quality of an animal, esp. one used as a standard in judging livestock. **15** (*often pl*) any of the extremities, such as the tail, ears, or feet, of a domestic animal. **16** (*often pl*) *Ballet.* the tip of the toes. **17** a single unit for measuring or counting, as in the scoring of a game. **18** *Printing.* a unit of measurement equal to one twelfth of a pica. There are approximately 72 points to the inch. **19** *Finance.* a unit of value used to quote security and commodity prices and their fluctuations. **20** *Navigation.* **20a** one of the 32 marks on the compass indicating direction. **20b** the angle of 11°15' between two adjacent marks. **21** *Cricket.* a fielding position at right angles to the batsman on the off side and relatively near the pitch. **22** either of the two electrical contacts that make or break the current flow in the distributor of an internal-combustion engine. **23** *Brit., Austral., & NZ.* (*often pl*) a junction of railway tracks in which a pair of rails can be moved so that a train can be directed onto either of two lines. US and Canad. equivalent: **switch. 24** (*often pl*) a piece of ribbon, cord, etc., with metal tags at the end: used during the 16th and 17th centuries to fasten clothing. **25** *Brit.* short for **power point. 26** the position of the body of a pointer or setter when it discovers game. **27** *Boxing.* a mark awarded for a scoring blow, knockdown, etc. **28** any diacritic used in a writing system, esp. in a phonetic transcription, to indicate modifications of vowels or consonants. **29** *Jewellery.* a unit of weight equal to 0.01 carat. **30** the act of pointing. **31 beside the point.** irrelevant. **32 case in point.** a specific or relevant instance. **33 make a point of. 33a** to make (something) one's regular habit. **33b** to do (something) because one thinks it important. **34 not to put too fine a point on it.** to speak plainly and bluntly. **35 on** (*or* **at**) **the point of.** at the moment immediately before: *on the point of leaving the room.* **36 score points off.** to gain an advantage at someone else's expense. **37 to the point.** relevant. **38 up to a point.** not completely. ◆ *vb* **39** (usually foll. by *at* or *to*) to indicate the location or direction of by or as by extending (a finger or other pointed object) towards it: *he pointed to the front door; don't point that gun at me.* **40** (*intr;* usually foll. by *at* or *to*) to indicate or identify a specific person or thing among several: *all evidence pointed to Donald as the murderer.* **41** (*tr*) to direct or face in a specific direction: *point me in the right direction.* **42** (*tr*) to sharpen or taper. **43** (*intr*) (of gun dogs) to indicate the place where game is lying by standing rigidly with the muzzle turned in its direction. **44** (*tr*) to finish or repair the joints of (brickwork, masonry, etc.) with mortar or cement. **45** (*tr*) *Music.* to mark (a psalm text) with vertical lines to indicate the points at which the music changes during chanting. **46** (*tr*) *Phonetics.* to provide (a letter or letters) with diacritics. **47** (*tr*) to provide (a Hebrew or similar text) with vowel points. ◆ See also **point off, point out, point up.** [C13: from OF: spot, from L *punctum* a point, from *pungere* to pierce]

point after *n American football.* a score given for a successful kick between the goalposts and above the crossbar, following a touchdown.

point-blank *adj* **1a** aimed or fired at a target so close that it is unnecessary to make allowance for the drop in the course of the projectile. **1b** permitting such aim or fire without loss of accuracy: *at point-blank range.* **2** aimed or fired at nearly zero range. **3** plain or blunt: *a point-blank question.* ◆ *adv* **4** directly or straight. **5** plainly or bluntly. [C16: from POINT + BLANK (in the sense: centre spot of an archery target)]

Point de Galle ★ (pɔɪnt də 'gɑːlə) *n* a former name of **Galle.**

point duty *n* **1** the stationing of a policeman or traffic

warden at a road junction to control and direct traffic. **2** the position at the head of a military control, regarded as being the most dangerous.

pointe ('pɔɪnt) *n Ballet.* the tip of the toe (esp. in **on pointes**). [from F: point]

Pointe-à-Pitre ★ (*French* pwɛ̃tapitrə) *n* the chief port of Guadeloupe, on SW Grande Terre Island in the Caribbean. Pop.: 26 029 (1990).

pointed ('pɔɪntɪd) *adj* **1** having a point. **2** cutting or incisive: *a pointed wit.* **3** obviously directed at a particular person or aspect: *pointed criticism.* **4** emphasized or made conspicuous: *pointed ignorance.* **5** (of an arch or style of architecture) Gothic. **6** *Music.* (of a psalm text) marked to show changes in chanting. **7** (of Hebrew text) with vowel points marked.
▸ '**pointedly** *adv*

Pointe-Noire ★ (*French* pwɛ̃tnwar) *n* a port in the S Congo Republic, on the Atlantic: the country's chief port and former capital (1950–58). Pop.: 576 206 (1995 est.).

pointer ('pɔɪntə) *n* **1** a person or thing that points. **2** an indicator on a measuring instrument. **3** a long rod or cane used by a lecturer to point to parts of a map, blackboard, etc. **4** one of a breed of large smooth-coated gun dogs, usually white with black, liver, or lemon markings. **5** a helpful piece of information.

pointillism ('pwæntɪ,lɪzəm) *n* the technique of painting elaborated from impressionism, in which dots of unmixed colour are juxtaposed on a white ground so that from a distance they fuse in the viewer's eye into appropriate intermediate tones. [C19: from F, from *pointiller* to mark with tiny dots, from *pointille* little point, from It., from *punto* POINT]
▸ '**pointillist** *n, adj*

pointing ('pɔɪntɪŋ) *n* the act or process of repairing or finishing joints in brickwork, masonry, etc., with mortar.

point lace *n* lace made by a needle with buttonhole stitch on a paper pattern. Also called: **needlepoint.** Cf. pillow lace.

pointless ('pɔɪntlɪs) *adj* **1** without a point. **2** without meaning, relevance, or force. **3** *Sport.* without a point scored.
▸ '**pointlessly** *adv*

point off *vb* (*tr, adv*) to mark off from the right-hand side (a number of decimal places) in a whole number to create a mixed decimal: *point off three decimal places in 12345 and you get 12.345.*

point of honour *n, pl* **points of honour.** a circumstance, event, etc., that involves the defence of one's principles, social honour, etc.

point of no return *n* **1** a point at which an irreversible commitment must be made to an action, progression, etc. **2** a point in a journey at which, if one continues, supplies will be insufficient for a return to the starting place.

point of order *n, pl* **points of order.** a question raised in a meeting as to whether the rules governing procedures are being breached.

point of sale *n* (in retail distribution) **a** the place at which a sale is made. Abbrev.: **POS. b** (*as modifier*): *a point-of-sale display.*

point of view *n, pl* **points of view. 1** a position from which someone or something is observed. **2** a mental viewpoint or attitude.

point out *vb* (*tr, adv*) to indicate or specify.

pointsman ('pɔɪnts,mæn, -mən) *n, pl* **pointsmen. 1** a person who operates railway points. **2** a policeman or traffic warden on point duty.

point source *n Optics.* a source of light or other radiation that can be considered to have negligible dimensions.

points system *n Brit.* a system used to assess applicants' eligibility for local authority housing, based on (points awarded for) such factors as the length of time the applicant has lived in the area, how many children are in the family, etc.

point-to-point *n Brit.* a steeplechase organized by a recognized hunt or other body, usually restricted to amateurs riding horses that have been regularly used in hunting.

point up *vb (tr, adv)* to emphasize, esp. by identifying: *he pointed up the difficulties.*

poise[1] (pɔɪz) *n* **1** composure or dignity of manner. **2** physical balance. **3** equilibrium; stability. **4** the position of hovering. ◆ *vb* **poises, poising, poised. 5** to be or cause to be balanced or suspended. **6** (*tr*) to hold, as in readiness: *to poise a lance.* [C16: from OF *pois* weight, from L *pēnsum*, from *pendere* to weigh]

poise[2] (pwɑːz, pɔɪz) *n* the cgs unit of viscosity; the viscosity of a fluid in which a tangential force of 1 dyne per square centimetre maintains a difference in velocity of 1 centimetre per second between two parallel planes 1 centimetre apart. Symbol: P [C20: after Jean Louis Marie *Poiseuille* (1799–1869), F physician]

poised (pɔɪzd) *adj* **1** self-possessed; dignified. **2** balanced and prepared for action.

poison ('pɔɪz°n) *n* **1** any substance that can impair function or otherwise injure the body. **2** something that destroys, corrupts, etc. **3** a substance that retards a chemical reaction or the activity of a catalyst. **4** a substance that absorbs neutrons in a nuclear reactor and thus slows down the reaction. ◆ *vb* (*tr*) **5** to give poison to (a person or animal), esp. with intent to kill. **6** to add poison to. **7** to taint or infect with or as if with poison. **8** (foll. by *against*) to turn (a person's mind) against: *he poisoned her mind against me.* **9** to retard or stop (a chemical or nuclear reaction) by the action of a poison. [C13: from OF *puison* potion, from L *pōtiō* a drink, esp. a poisonous one, from *pōtāre* to drink]
▸ **'poisoner** *n*

poison ivy *n* any of several North American shrubs or climbing plants that cause an itching rash on contact.

poisonous ('pɔɪzənəs) *adj* **1** having the effects or qualities of a poison. **2** capable of killing or inflicting injury. **3** corruptive or malicious.
▸ **'poisonously** *adv* ▸ **'poisonousness** *n*

poison-pen letter *n* a letter written in malice, usually anonymously, and intended to abuse, frighten, or insult the recipient.

poison pill *n Finance.* a tactic used by a company fearing an unwelcome takeover bid, in which the value of the company is automatically reduced, as by the sale of an issue of shares having an option unfavourable to the bidders, if the bid is successful.

poison sumach *n* a swamp shrub of the southeastern US that causes an itching rash on contact with the skin.

Poisson distribution ('pwɑːs°n) *n Statistics.* a distribution that represents the number of events occurring randomly in a fixed time at an average rate λ. [C19: after S. D. *Poisson* (1781–1840), F mathematician]

Poitiers ★ (*French* pwatje) *n* a city in S central France: capital of the former province of Poitou until 1790; scene of the battle (1356) in which the English under the Black Prince defeated the French; university (1432). Pop.: 78 894 (1990).

Poitou ★ (*French* pwatu) *n* a former province of W central France, on the Atlantic. Chief town: Poitiers.

Poitou-Charentes ★ (*French* pwatuʃarɑ̃t) *n* a region of W central France, on the Bay of Biscay: mainly low-lying.

poke[1] (pəʊk) *vb* **pokes, poking, poked. 1** (*tr*) to jab or prod, as with the elbow, a stick, etc. **2** (*tr*) to make (a hole) by or as by poking. **3** (when *intr*, often foll. by *at*) to thrust (at). **4** (*tr*) *Inf.* to hit with the fist; punch. **5** (usually foll. by *in, through*, etc.) to protrude or cause to protrude: *don't poke your arm out of the window.* **6** (*tr*) to stir (a fire, etc.) by poking. **7** (*intr*) to meddle or intrude. **8** (*intr*; often foll. by *about* or *around*) to search or pry. **9 poke one's nose into.** to interfere with or meddle in. ◆ *n* **10** a jab or prod. **11** *Inf.* a blow with one's fist; punch. [C14: from Low G & MDu. *poken* to prod]

poke[2] (pəʊk) *n* **1** *Dialect.* a pocket or bag. **2 a pig in a poke.** See **pig**. [C13: from OF *poque*, of Gmc origin]

poke[3] (pəʊk) *n* **1** Also called: **poke bonnet.** a bonnet with a brim that projects at the front, popular in the 18th and 19th centuries. **2** the brim itself. [C18: from POKE[1] (in the sense: to project)]

poker[1] ('pəʊkə) *n* a metal rod, usually with a handle, for stirring a fire.

poker[2] ('pəʊkə) *n* a card game of bluff and skill in which bets are made on the hands dealt, the highest-ranking hand winning the pool. [C19: prob. from F *poque* similar card game]

poker face *n Inf.* a face without expression, as that of a poker player attempting to conceal the value of his cards.
▸ **'poker-,faced** *adj*

poker machine *n Austral. & NZ.* a fruit machine.

pokerwork ('pəʊkə,wɜːk) *n* the art of producing pictures or designs on wood by charring it with a heated tool.

pokeweed ('pəʊk,wiːd), **pokeberry,** *or* **pokeroot** *n* a tall North American plant that has a poisonous purple root used medicinally. [C18: *poke,* from Algonquian *puccoon* plant used in dyeing, from *pak* blood]

pokie ('pəʊkɪ) *n Austral. inf.* short for **poker machine.**

poky *or* **pokey** ('pəʊkɪ) *adj* **pokier, pokiest. 1** (esp. of rooms) small and cramped. **2** *Inf., chiefly US.* without speed or energy; slow. [C19: from POKE[1] (in sl. sense: to confine)]
▸ **'pokily** *adv* ▸ **'pokiness** *n*

pol. *abbrev. for:* **1** political. **2** politics.

Pol. *abbrev. for:* **1** Poland. **2** Polish.

Pola ★ ('pɔːla) *n* the Italian name for **Pula.**

Poland ★ ('pəʊlənd) *n* a republic in central Europe, on the Baltic: first united in the 10th century; dissolved after the third partition effected by Austria, Russia, and Prussia in 1795; re-established independence in 1918; invaded by Germany in 1939; ruled by a Communist government from 1947 to 1989, when a multiparty system was introduced. It consists chiefly of a low undulating plain in the north, rising to a low plateau in the south, with the Sudeten and Carpathian Mountains along the S border. Official language: Polish. Religion: Roman Catholic majority. Currency: zloty. Capital: Warsaw. Pop.: 38 802 000 (1997). Area: 311 730 sq. km (120 359 sq. miles). Polish name: **Polska.**

Polanski ★ (pəˈlænskɪ) *n Roman.* born 1933, Polish film director with a taste for the macabre, as in *Repulsion* (1965) and *Rosemary's Baby* (1968): later films include *Tess* (1980) and *Death and the Maiden* (1995).

polar ('pəʊlə) *adj* **1** at, near, or relating to either of the earth's poles or the area inside the Arctic or Antarctic Circles: *polar regions.* **2** having or relating to a pole or poles. **3** pivotal or guiding in the manner of the Pole Star. **4** directly opposite, as in tendency or character. **5** *Chem.* (of a molecule) having an uneven distribution of electrons and thus a permanent dipole moment: *water has polar molecules.*

polar bear *n* a white carnivorous bear of coastal regions of the North Pole.

polar circle *n* a term for either the **Arctic Circle** or **Antarctic Circle.**

polar coordinates *pl n* a pair of coordinates for locating a point in a plane by means of the length of a radius vector, *r*, which pivots about the origin to establish the angle, θ, that the position of the point makes with a fixed line. Usually written (*r*, θ).

polar distance *n* the angular distance of a star, planet, etc., from the celestial pole; the complement of the declination.

polar front *n Meteorol.* a front dividing cold polar air from warmer temperate or tropical air.

Polari (pəˈlɑːrɪ) *n* an English slang derived from the Lingua Franca of Mediterranean ports; brought to England by sailors from the 16th century onwards. [C19: from It. *parlare* to speak]

polarimeter (,pəʊləˈrɪmɪtə) *n* an instrument for measuring the polarization of light.
▸ **polarimetric** (,pəʊlərɪˈmɛtrɪk) *adj*

★ people and places

Polaris (pə'lɑːrɪs) n 1 Also called: the **Pole Star**, the **North Star**. the brightest star in the constellation Ursa Minor, situated slightly less than 1° from the north celestial pole. 2 a type of US two-stage intermediate-range ballistic missile, usually fired by a submerged submarine. [from Med. L *stella polāris* polar star]

polariscope (pəʊ'lærɪˌskəʊp) n an instrument for detecting polarized light or for observing objects under polarized light, esp. for detecting strain in transparent materials.

polarity (pəʊ'lærɪtɪ) n, pl **polarities**. 1 the condition of having poles. 2 the condition of a body or system in which it has opposing physical properties, esp. magnetic poles or electric charge. 3 the particular state of a part that has polarity: *an electrode with positive polarity*. 4 the state of having or expressing two directly opposite tendencies, opinions, etc.

polarization or **polarisation** (ˌpəʊlərɑɪ'zeɪʃən) n 1 the condition of having or giving polarity. 2 *Physics.* the phenomenon in which waves of light or other radiation are restricted to certain directions of vibration.

polarize or **polarise** ('pəʊləˌrɑɪz) vb **polarizes, polarizing, polarized** or **polarises, polarising, polarised**. 1 to acquire or cause to acquire polarity or polarization. 2 (*tr*) to cause (people) to adopt extreme opposing positions: *to polarize opinion*.
▸ 'polarˌizer or 'polarˌiser n

polar lights pl n the aurora borealis in the N hemisphere or the aurora australis in the S hemisphere.

polarography (ˌpəʊlə'rɒgrəfɪ) n a technique for analysing and studying ions in solution by using an electrolytic cell with a very small cathode and obtaining a graph (**polarogram**) of the current against the potential to determine the concentration and nature of the ions.

Polaroid ('pəʊləˌrɔɪd) n *Trademark.* 1 a type of plastic sheet that can polarize a transmitted beam of normal light because it is composed of long parallel molecules. It only transmits plane-polarized light if these molecules are parallel to the plane of polarization. 2 **Polaroid Land Camera.** any of several types of camera yielding a finished print by means of a special developing and processing technique that occurs inside the camera and takes only a few seconds. 3 (*pl*) sunglasses with lenses made from Polaroid plastic.

polder ('pəʊldə, 'pɒl-) n a stretch of land reclaimed from the sea or a lake, esp. in the Netherlands. [C17: from MDu. *polre*]

pole[1] (pəʊl) n 1 a long slender usually round piece of wood, metal, or other material. 2 the piece of timber on each side of which a pair of carriage horses are hitched. 3 another name for **rod** (sense 7). 4 **up the pole**. *Brit., Austral., & NZ inf.* 4a slightly mad. 4b mistaken; on the wrong track. ◆ vb **poles, poling, poled.** 5 (*tr*) to strike or push with a pole. 6 (*tr*) 6a to set out (an area of land or garden) with poles. 6b to support (a crop, such as hops) on poles. 7 to punt (a boat). [OE *pāl*, from L *pālus* a stake]

pole[2] (pəʊl) n 1 either of the two antipodal points where the earth's axis of rotation meets the earth's surface. See also **North Pole, South Pole.** 2 *Physics.* 2a either of the two regions at the extremities of a magnet to which the lines of force converge. 2b either of two points at which there are opposite electric charges, as at the terminals of a battery. 3 *Biol.* either end of the axis of a cell, spore, ovum, or similar body. 4 either of two mutually exclusive or opposite actions, opinions, etc. 5 **poles apart** (*or* **asunder**). having widely divergent opinions, tastes, etc. [C14: from L *polus* end of an axis, from Gk *polos* pivot]

Pole[1] (pəʊl) n a native, inhabitant, or citizen of Poland or a speaker of Polish.

Pole[2] (pəʊl) ★ n **Reginald**. 1500–58, English cardinal; last Roman Catholic archbishop of Canterbury (1556–58).

poleaxe or US **poleax** ('pəʊlˌæks) n 1 another term for a battle-axe or a butcher's axe. ◆ vb **poleaxes, poleaxing, poleaxed.** 2 (*tr*) to hit or fell with or as if with a poleaxe. [C14 *pollax* battle-axe, from POLL + AXE]

polecat ('pəʊlˌkæt) n, pl **polecats** or **polecat.** 1 a dark brown musteline mammal of Europe, Asia, and N Africa, that is closely related to but larger than the weasel and gives off an unpleasant smell. 2 *US.* a nontechnical name for **skunk** (sense 1). [C14 *polcat*, ?from OF *pol* cock, from L *pullus*, + CAT; from its preying on poultry]

polemic (pə'lemɪk) adj also **polemical.** 1 of or involving dispute or controversy. ◆ n 2 an argument or controversy, esp. over a doctrine, belief, etc. 3 a person engaged in such controversy. [C17: from Med. L *polemicus*, from Gk *polemikos* relating to war, from *polemos* war]
▸ po'lemically adv ▸ polemicist (pə'lemɪsɪst) n

polemics (pə'lemɪks) n (*functioning as sing*) the art or practice of dispute or argument, as in attacking or defending a doctrine or belief.

pole position n 1 (in motor racing) the starting position on the inside of the front row, generally considered the best one. 2 an advantageous starting position.

pole star n a guiding principle, rule, etc.

Pole Star n the. the star closest to the N celestial pole at any particular time. At present this is Polaris, but it will eventually be replaced owing to precession of the earth's axis.

pole vault n 1 the. a field event in which competitors attempt to clear a high bar with the aid of an extremely flexible long pole. ◆ vb **pole-vault.** 2 (*intr*) to perform a pole vault or compete in the pole vault.
▸ 'pole-ˌvaulter n

poley ('pəʊlɪ) adj *Austral.* (of cattle) hornless or polled.

police (pə'liːs) n 1 (often preceded by *the*) the organized civil force of a state, concerned with maintenance of law and order. 2 (*functioning as pl*) the members of such a force collectively. 3 any organized body with a similar function: *security police*. ◆ vb **polices, policing, policed.** (*tr*) 4 to regulate, control, or keep in order by means of a police or similar force. 5 to observe or record the activity or enforcement of: *a committee was set up to police the new agreement on picketing.* [C16: via F from L *polītīa* administration; see POLITY]

police dog n a dog, often an Alsatian, trained to help the police, as in tracking.

policeman (pə'liːsmən) or (*fem*) **policewoman** n, pl **policemen** or **policewomen.** a member of a police force, esp. one holding the rank of constable.

police officer n a member of a police force, esp. a constable; policeman.

police procedural n a novel, film, or television drama that deals realistically with police work.

police state n a state or country in which a repressive government maintains control through the police.

police station n the office or headquarters of the police force of a district.

policing (pə'liːsɪŋ) n the policies, techniques, and practice of a police force in keeping order, preventing crime, etc.

policy[1] ('pɒlɪsɪ) n, pl **policies.** 1 a plan of action adopted or pursued by an individual, government, party, business, etc. 2 wisdom, shrewdness, or sagacity. 3 (*often pl*) *Scot.* the improved grounds surrounding a country house. [C14: from OF *policie*, from L *polītīa* administration, POLITY]

policy[2] ('pɒlɪsɪ) n, pl **policies.** a document containing a contract of insurance. [C16: from OF *police* certificate, from OIt. from L *apodixis* proof, from Gk *apodeixis*]
▸ 'policyˌholder n

Polignac ★ (French pɔliɲak) n **Prince de**, title of *Auguste Jules Armand Marie de Polignac.* 1780–1847, French statesman; prime minister (1829–30) to Charles X.

polio ('pəʊlɪəʊ) n short for **poliomyelitis.**

poliomyelitis (ˌpəʊlɪəʊˌmɑɪə'lɑɪtɪs) n an acute infectious viral disease, esp. affecting children. In its paralytic form the brain and spinal cord are involved, causing paralysis and wasting of muscle. Also called: **infantile paralysis.** [C19: NL, from Gk *polios* grey + *muelos* marrow]

polish ('pɒlɪʃ) vb 1 to make or become smooth and shiny by rubbing, esp. with wax or an abrasive. 2 (*tr*) to make perfect or complete. 3 to make or become elegant or refined. ◆ n 4 a finish or gloss. 5 the act of polishing. 6 a substance used to produce a shiny, often protective sur-

face. **7** elegance or refinement, esp. in style, manner, etc. [C13 *polis*, from OF *polir*, from L *polīre* to polish]
▶ **'polisher** *n*

Polish ('pəʊlɪʃ) *adj* **1** of, relating to, or characteristic of Poland, its people, or their language. ♦ *n* **2** the official language of Poland.

Polish Corridor ★ *n* the strip of land through E Pomerania providing Poland with access to the sea (1919–39), given to her in 1919 in the Treaty of Versailles, and separating East Prussia from the rest of Germany. It is now part of Poland.

polished ('pɒlɪʃt) *adj* **1** accomplished: *a polished actor.* **2** impeccably or professionally done: *a polished performance.* **3** (of rice) milled to remove the outer husk.

polish off *vb* (*tr, adv*) *Inf.* **1** to finish or process completely. **2** to dispose of or kill.

polish up *vb* (*adv*) **1** to make or become smooth and shiny by polishing. **2** (when *intr*, foll. by *on*) to study or practise until adept (at): *he's polishing up on his German.*

Politburo ('pɒlɪtˌbjʊərəʊ) *n* **1** the executive and policy-making committee of a Communist Party. **2** the supreme policy-making authority in most Communist countries. [C20: from Russian: contraction of *Politicheskoe Buro* political bureau]

polite (pə'laɪt) *adj* **1** showing a great regard for others, as in manners, etc.; courteous. **2** cultivated or refined: *polite society.* **3** elegant or polished: *polite letters.* [C15: from L *polītus* polished]
▶ **po'litely** *adv* ▶ **po'liteness** *n*

politesse (ˌpɒlɪ'tɛs) *n* formal or genteel politeness. [C18: via F from It. *politezza*, ult. from L *polīre* to polish]

Politian ★ (pəʊ'lɪʃən, pɒ-) *n* Italian name *Angelo Polliziano*; original name *Angelo Ambrogini.* 1454–94, Florentine humanist and poet.

politic ('pɒlɪtɪk) *adj* **1** artful or shrewd; ingenious. **2** crafty or unscrupulous; cunning. **3** wise or prudent, esp. in statesmanship: *a politic choice.* **4** an archaic word for **political.** ♦ See also **body politic.** [C15: from OF *politique*, from L *polīticus* concerning civil administration, from Gk, from *polītēs* citizen, from *polis* city]
▶ **'politicly** *adv*

political (pə'lɪtɪkᵊl) *adj* **1** of or relating to the state, government, public administration, etc. **2a** of or relating to government policy-making as distinguished from administration or law. **2b** of or relating to the civil aspects of government as distinguished from the military. **3** of, dealing with, or relating to politics: *a political person.* **4** of or relating to the parties and the partisan aspects of politics. **5** organized with respect to government: *a political unit.*
▶ **po'litically** *adv*

political economy *n* the former name for **economics** (sense 1).

politically correct *adj* demonstrating progressive ideals, esp. by avoiding vocabulary that is considered offensive, discriminatory, or judgmental, esp. concerning race, gender, and sexuality. Abbrev.: **PC.**
▶ **political correctness** *n*

political prisoner *n* a person imprisoned for holding or expressing particular political beliefs.

political science *n* the study of the state, government, and politics: one of the social sciences.
▶ **political scientist** *n*

politician (ˌpɒlɪ'tɪʃən) *n* **1** a person actively engaged in politics, esp. a full-time professional member of a deliberative assembly. **2** a person who is experienced or skilled in government or administration; statesman. **3** *Disparaging, chiefly US.* a person who engages in politics out of a wish for personal gain.

politicize *or* **politicise** (pə'lɪtɪˌsaɪz) *vb* **politicizes, politicizing, politicized** *or* **politicises, politicising, politicised.** **1** (*tr*) to render political in tone, interest, or awareness. **2** (*intr*) to participate in political discussion or activity.
▶ **po,litici'zation** *or* **po,litici'sation** *n*

politicking ('pɒlɪtɪkɪŋ) *n* political activity, esp. seeking votes.

politico (pə'lɪtɪˌkəʊ) *n, pl* **politicos.** *Chiefly US.* an informal word for a **politician** (senses 1, 3). [C17: from It. or Sp.]

politics ('pɒlɪtɪks) *n* **1** (*functioning as sing*) the art and science of directing and administrating states and other political units; government. **2** (*functioning as sing*) the complex or aggregate of relationships of people in society, esp. those relationships involving authority or power. **3** (*functioning as pl*) political activities or affairs: *party politics.* **4** (*functioning as sing*) the business or profession of politics. **5** (*functioning as sing or pl*) any activity concerned with the acquisition of power, etc.: *company politics are frequently vicious.* **6** manoeuvres or factors leading up to or influencing (something): *the politics of the decision.* **7** (*functioning as pl*) opinions, sympathies, etc., with respect to politics: *his conservative politics.*

polity ('pɒlɪtɪ) *n, pl* **polities. 1** a form of government or organization of a society, etc.; constitution. **2** a politically organized society, etc. **3** the management of public affairs. **4** political organization. [C16: from L *polītīa*, from Gk *politeia* citizenship, civil administration, from *polītēs* citizen, from *polis* city]

Polk ★ (pəʊk) *n* **James Knox.** 1795–1849, US statesman; 11th president of the US (1845–49). During his administration, Texas and territory now included in New Mexico, Colorado, Utah, Nevada, Arizona, Oregon, and California were added to the Union.

polka ('pɒlkə) *n* **1** a 19th-century Bohemian dance with three steps and a hop, in fast duple time. **2** a piece of music composed for or in the rhythm of this dance. ♦ *vb* **polkas, polkaing, polkaed. 3** (*intr*) to dance a polka. [C19: via F from Czech *pulka* half-step]

polka dot *n* one of a pattern of small circular regularly spaced spots on a fabric.

poll (pəʊl) *n* **1** the casting, recording, or counting of votes in an election; a voting. **2** the result of such a voting: *a heavy poll.* **3** Also called: **opinion poll. 3a** a canvassing of a representative sample of people on some question in order to determine the general opinion. **3b** the results of such a canvassing. **4** any counting or enumeration, esp. for taxation or voting purposes. **5** the back part of the head of an animal. ♦ *vb* (*mainly tr*) **6** to receive (a vote or quantity of votes): *he polled 10 000 votes.* **7** to receive, take, or record the votes of: *he polled the whole town.* **8** to canvass (a person, group, area, etc.) as part of a survey of opinion. **9** (*sometimes intr*) to cast (a vote) in an election. **10** to clip or shear. **11** to remove or cut short the horns of (cattle). [C13 (in the sense: a human head) & C17 (in the sense: votes): from MLow G *polle* hair of the head, head, top of a tree]

pollack *or* **pollock** ('pɒlək) *n, pl* **pollacks, pollack** *or* **pollocks, pollock.** a gadoid food fish that has a projecting lower jaw and occurs in northern seas. [C17: from earlier Scot. *podlok*, from ?]

Pollack ★ ('pɒlək) *n* **Sydney.** born 1934, US film director. His films include *Tootsie* (1982), *Out of Africa* (1986), and *The Firm* (1993).

Pollaiuolo ★ (*Italian* pollaj'wɔːlo) *n* **1 Antonio** (an'tɔːnjo), ?1432–98, Florentine painter, sculptor, goldsmith, and engraver: his paintings include the *Martyrdom of St Sebastian.* **2** his brother **Piero** ('pjɛːro). ?1443–96, Florentine painter and sculptor.

pollan ('pɒlən) *n* any of several varieties of whitefish that occur in lakes in Northern Ireland. [C18: prob. from Irish *poll* lake]

pollard ('pɒləd) *n* **1** an animal, such as a sheep or deer, that has either shed its horns or antlers or has had them removed. **2** a tree that has had its branches cut back to encourage a more bushy growth. ♦ *vb* **3** (*tr*) to convert into a pollard; poll. [C16: hornless animal; see POLL]

pollen ('pɒlən) *n* a substance produced by the anthers of seed-bearing plants, consisting of numerous fine grains containing the male gametes. [C16: from L: powder]
▶ **pollinic** (pə'lɪnɪk) *adj*

Pollen ★ ('pɒlən) *n* **Daniel.** 1813–96, New Zealand statesman, born in Ireland: prime minister of New Zealand (1876).

pollen analysis *n* another name for **palynology.**

pollen count *n* a measure of the pollen present in the

★ people and places

air over a 24-hour period, often published to enable sufferers from hay fever to predict the severity of their attacks.

pollex ('pɒlɛks) n, pl **pollices** (-lɪˌsiːz). the first digit of the forelimb of amphibians, reptiles, birds, and mammals, such as the thumb of man. [C19: from L: thumb, big toe]
▶ **pollical** ('pɒlɪkˀl) adj

pollinate ('pɒlɪˌneɪt) vb **pollinates, pollinating, pollinated.** (tr) to transfer pollen from the anthers to the stigma of (a flower).
▶ ˌpolli'nation n ▶ 'polliˌnator n

polling booth n a semienclosed space in which a voter stands to mark a ballot paper during an election.

polling station n a building, such as a school, designated as the place to which voters go during an election in order to cast their votes.

polliwog or **pollywog** ('pɒlɪˌwɒg) n Dialect, US, & Canad. a tadpole. [C15 polwygle]

Pollock ★ ('pɒlək) n 1 Sir **Frederick.** 1845–1937, British legal scholar: with Maitland, he wrote History of English Law before the Time of Edward I (1895). 2 **Jackson.** 1912–56, US abstract expressionist painter; chief exponent of action painting in the US.

pollster ('pəʊlstə) n a person who conducts opinion polls.

poll tax n 1 a tax levied per head of adult population. 2 an informal name for **community charge.**

pollutant (pə'luːt°nt) n a substance that pollutes, esp. a chemical produced as a waste product of an industrial process.

pollute (pə'luːt) vb **pollutes, polluting, polluted.** (tr) 1 to contaminate, as with poisonous or harmful substances. 2 to make morally corrupt. 3 to desecrate. [C14 polute, from L polluere to defile]
▶ **pol'luter** n ▶ **pol'lution** n

Pollux ★ ('pɒləks) n Classical myth. See **Castor and Pollux.**

Pollyanna (ˌpɒlɪ'ænə) n a person who is optimistic. [C20: after the chief character in Pollyanna (1913), a novel by Eleanor Porter (1868–1920), US writer]

polo ('pəʊləʊ) n 1 a game similar to hockey played on horseback using long-handled mallets (**polo sticks**) and a wooden ball. 2 short for **water polo. 3** Also called: **polo neck. 3a** a collar on a garment, worn rolled over to fit closely round the neck. **3b** a garment, esp. a sweater, with such a collar. [C19: from Balti (dialect of Kashmir): ball, from Tibetan pulu]

Polo ★ ('pəʊləʊ) n **Marco** ('mɑːkəʊ). 1254–1324, Venetian merchant, famous for his account of his travels in Asia. After travelling overland to China (1271–75), he spent 17 years serving Kublai Khan before returning to Venice by sea (1292–95).

polonaise (ˌpɒlə'neɪz) n 1 a ceremonial marchlike dance in three-four time from Poland. 2 a piece of music composed for or in the rhythm of this dance. 3 a woman's costume with a tight bodice and an overskirt drawn back to show a decorative underskirt. [C18: from F danse polonaise Polish dance]

polonium (pə'ləʊnɪəm) n a very rare radioactive element that occurs in trace amounts in uranium ores. Symbol: Po; atomic no.: 84; half-life of most stable isotope, ^{209}Po: 103 years. [C19: NL, from Med. L Polōnia Poland; in honour of the nationality of its discoverer, Marie Curie]

polony (pə'ləʊnɪ) n, pl **polonies.** Brit. another name for **bologna sausage.**

polo shirt n a knitted cotton short-sleeved shirt with a collar and three-button opening at the neck.

Pol Pot ★ ('pɒl 'pɒt) n original name Kompong Thom. 1925–98, Cambodian Communist leader; prime minister of Kampuchea (1976; 1977–79); his policies led to the deaths of thousands in labour camps: overthrown by Vietnamese forces.

Polska ★ ('pɒlska) n the Polish name for **Poland.**

Poltava ★ (Russian pal'tavə) n a city in the E Ukraine: scene of the victory (1709) of the Russians under Peter the Great over the Swedes under Charles XII. Pop.: 321 000 (1996 est.).

poltergeist ('pɒltəˌgaɪst) n a spirit believed to manifest its presence by noises and acts of mischief, such as throwing furniture about. [C19: from G, from poltern to be noisy + Geist GHOST]

poltroon (pɒl'truːn) n an abject or contemptible coward. [C16: from OF poultron, from OIt. poltrone lazy good-fornothing, apparently from poltrīre to lie indolently in bed]

poly ('pɒlɪ) n, pl **polys.** Inf. short for **polytechnic.**

poly- combining form. 1 more than one; many or much: polyhedron. 2 having an excessive or abnormal number or amount: polyphagia. [from Gk polus much, many]

polyamide (ˌpɒlɪ'æmaɪd, -mɪd) n any of a class of synthetic polymeric materials, including nylon.

polyandry ('pɒlɪˌændrɪ) n 1 the practice or condition of being married to more than one husband at the same time. 2 the practice in animals of a female mating with more than one male during one breeding season. 3 the condition in flowers of having a large indefinite number of stamens. [C18: from Gk poluandria, from POLY- + -andria from anēr man]
▶ ˌpoly'androus adj

polyanthus (ˌpɒlɪ'ænθəs) n, pl **polyanthuses.** any of several hybrid garden primroses with brightly coloured flowers. [C18: NL, from Gk: having many flowers]

polyatomic (ˌpɒlɪə'tɒmɪk) adj (of a molecule) containing more than two atoms.

poly bag ('pɒlɪ) n Brit. inf. a polythene bag, esp. one used to store or protect food or household articles.

polybasic (ˌpɒlɪ'beɪsɪk) adj (of an acid) having two or more replaceable hydrogen atoms per molecule.

Polybius ★ (pəʊ'lɪbɪəs) n ?205–?123 B.C., Greek historian, who wrote in 40 books a history of Rome from 264 B.C. to 146 B.C.

polycarboxylate (ˌpɒlɪkɑː'bɒksɪˌleɪt) n a salt or ester of a polycarboxylic acid. Polycarboxylate esters are used in certain detergents.

polycarboxylic acid ('pɒlɪˌkɑːbɒk'sɪlɪk) n a type of carboxylic acid containing two or more carboxyl groups.

Polycarp ★ ('pɒlɪˌkɑːp) n Saint. ?69–?155 A.D., Christian martyr and bishop of Smyrna, noted for his letter to the church at Philippi. Feast day: Feb. 23.

polycarpic (ˌpɒlɪ'kɑːpɪk) or **polycarpous** adj (of a plant) able to produce flowers and fruit several times in succession.
▶ 'polyˌcarpy n

polycentrism (ˌpɒlɪ'sentrɪzəm) n (formerly) the fact or advocacy of the existence of more than one predominant ideological or political centre in a political system, alliance, etc., in the Communist world.

polychaete ('pɒlɪˌkiːt) n 1 a marine annelid worm having a distinct head and paired fleshy appendages (parapodia) that bear bristles and are used in swimming.
◆ adj also **polychaetous.** 2 of or denoting such a creature. [C19: from NL, from Gk polukhaitēs having much hair]

polychromatic (ˌpɒlɪkrəʊ'mætɪk), **polychromic** (ˌpɒlɪ'krəʊmɪk), or **polychromous** adj 1 having various or changing colours. 2 (of light or other radiation) containing radiation with more than one wavelength.
▶ ˌpoly'chromaˌtizəm n)

polyclinic (ˌpɒlɪ'klɪnɪk) n a hospital or clinic able to treat a wide variety of diseases.

Polyclitus, Polycleitus (ˌpɒlɪ'klaɪtəs), or **Polycletus** ★ (ˌpɒlɪ'kliːtəs) n 5th-century B.C. Greek sculptor, noted particularly for his idealized bronze sculptures of the male nude, such as the Doryphoros.

polycotton ('pɒlɪkɒt°n) n a fabric made from a mixture of polyester and cotton.

polycotyledon (ˌpɒlɪˌkɒtɪ'liːd°n) n any of various plants, esp. gymnosperms, that have or appear to have more than two cotyledons.
▶ ˌpolyˌcoty'ledonous adj

Polycrates ★ (pə'lɪkrəˌtiːz) n died ?522 B.C., Greek tyrant of Samos, who was crucified by a Persian satrap.

polycyclic (ˌpɒlɪ'saɪklɪk) adj 1 (of a molecule or compound) having molecules that contain two or more closed rings of atoms. **2** *Biol.* having two or more rings or whorls: *polycyclic shells.* ◆ *n* **3** a polycyclic compound.

polycystic (ˌpɒlɪ'sɪstɪk) *adj Med.* containing many cysts: *a polycystic ovary.*

polydactyl (ˌpɒlɪ'dæktɪl) *adj also* **polydactylous. 1** (of man and other vertebrates) having more than the normal number of digits. ◆ *n* **2** a human or other vertebrate having more than the normal number of digits.

Polydeuces ★ (ˌpɒlɪ'dju:si:z) *n* the Greek name of **Pollux.** See **Castor and Pollux.**

polyester (ˌpɒlɪ'ɛstə) *n* any of a large class of synthetic materials that are polymers containing recurring -COO- groups: used as plastics, textile fibres, and adhesives.

polyethene (ˌpɒlɪ'ɛθi:n) *n* the systematic name for **polythene.**

polyethylene (ˌpɒlɪ'ɛθɪˌli:n) *n* another name for **polythene.**

polygamy (pə'lɪgəmɪ) *n* **1** the practice of having more than one wife or husband at the same time. **2** the condition of having male, female, and hermaphrodite flowers on the same plant or on separate plants of the same species. **3** the practice in male animals of having more than one mate during one breeding season. [C16: via F from Gk *polugamia*]
▸ po'lygamist *n* ▸ po'lygamous *adj* ▸ po'lygamously *adv*

polygene ('pɒlɪˌdʒi:n) *n* any of a group of genes that each produce a small quantitative effect on a particular characteristic, such as height.

polygenesis (ˌpɒlɪ'dʒɛnɪsɪs) *n* **1** *Biol.* evolution of organisms from different ancestral groups. **2** the hypothetical descent of different races from different ultimate ancestors.
▸ polygenetic (ˌpɒlɪdʒɪ'nɛtɪk) *adj*

polyglot ('pɒlɪˌglɒt) *adj* **1** having a command of many languages. **2** written in or containing many languages. ◆ *n* **3** a person with a command of many languages. **4** a book, esp. a Bible, containing several versions of the same text written in various languages. **5** a mixture of languages. [C17: from Gk *poluglōttos*, lit.: many-tongued]

Polygnotus ★ (ˌpɒlɪg'nəʊtəs) *n* 5th century B.C., Greek painter: associated with Cimon in rebuilding Athens.

polygon ('pɒlɪˌgɒn) *n* a closed plane figure bounded by three or more straight sides that meet in pairs in the same number of vertices and do not intersect other than at these vertices. Specific polygons are named according to the number of sides, such as triangle, pentagon, etc. [C16: via L from Gk *polugōnon* figure with many angles]
▸ polygonal (pə'lɪgən'l) *adj* ▸ po'lygonally *adv*

polygonum (pə'lɪgənəm) *n* a plant having stems with knotlike joints and spikes of small white, green, or pink flowers. [C18: NL, from Gk *polugonon* knotgrass, from *polu-* POLY- + *-gonon*, from *gonu* knee]

polygraph ('pɒlɪˌgrɑ:f) *n* **1** an instrument for the simultaneous recording of several involuntary physiological activities, including pulse rate and perspiration, used esp. as a lie detector. **2** a device for producing copies of written matter. [C18: from Gk *polugraphos* writing copiously]

polygyny (pə'lɪdʒɪnɪ) *n* **1** the practice or condition of being married to more than one wife at the same time. **2** the practice in animals of a male mating with more than one female during one breeding season. **3** the condition in flowers of having many styles. [C18: from POLY- + *-gyny*, from Gk *gunē* a woman]
▸ po'lygynous *adj*

polyhedron (ˌpɒlɪ'hi:drən) *n, pl* **polyhedrons** or **polyhedra** (-drə). a solid figure consisting of four or more plane faces (all polygons), pairs of which meet along an edge, three or more edges meeting at a vertex. Specific polyhedrons are named according to the number of faces, such as tetrahedron, icosahedron, etc. [C16: from Gk *poluedron*, from POLY- + *hedron* side]
▸ ˌpoly'hedral *adj*

Polyhymnia ★ (ˌpɒlɪ'hɪmnɪə) *n Greek myth.* the Muse of

singing, mime, and sacred dance. [L, from Gk *Polumnia* full of songs]

polymath ('pɒlɪˌmæθ) *n* a person of great and varied learning. [C17: from Gk *polumathēs* having much knowledge]
▸ **polymathy** (pə'lɪməθɪ) *n*

polymer ('pɒlɪmə) *n* a naturally occurring or synthetic compound, such as starch or Perspex, that has large molecules made up of many relatively simple repeated units.
▸ **polymerism** (pə'lɪməˌrɪzəm, 'pɒlɪmə-) *n*

polymerase ('pɒlɪməˌreɪs, -ˌreɪz) *n* any enzyme that catalyses the synthesis of a polymer, esp. the synthesis of DNA or RNA.

polymeric (ˌpɒlɪ'mɛrɪk) *adj* of, concerned with, or being a polymer: *a polymeric compound.* [C19: from Gk *polumerēs* having many parts]

polymerization or **polymerisation** (pəˌlɪmərai'zeɪʃən, ˌpɒlɪmərai-) *n* the act or process of forming a polymer or copolymer.

polymerize or **polymerise** ('pɒlɪməˌraiz, pə'lɪmə-) *vb* **polymerizes, polymerizing, polymerized** or **polymerises, polymerising, polymerised.** to react or cause to react to form a polymer.

polymerous (pə'lɪmərəs) *adj Biol.* having or being composed of many parts.

polymorph ('pɒlɪˌmɔ:f) *n* a species of animal or plant, or a crystalline form of a chemical compound, that exhibits polymorphism. [C19: from Gk *polumorphos* having many forms]

polymorphic function *n Computing.* a function in a computer program that can deal with a number of different types of data.

polymorphism (ˌpɒlɪ'mɔ:fɪzəm) *n* **1** the occurrence of more than one form of individual in a single species within an interbreeding population. **2** the existence or formation of different types of crystal of the same chemical compound.

polymorphous (ˌpɒlɪ'mɔ:fəs) or **polymorphic** *adj* **1** having, taking, or passing through many different forms or stages. **2** exhibiting or undergoing polymorphism.

Polynesia ★ (ˌpɒlɪ'ni:ʒə, -ʒɪə) *n* one of the three divisions of islands in the Pacific, the others being Melanesia and Micronesia: includes Samoa, Society, Marquesas, Mangareva, Tuamotu, Cook, and Tubuai Islands, and Tonga. [C18: via F from Gk *nēsos* island]

Polynesian (ˌpɒlɪ'ni:ʒən, -ʒɪən) *adj* **1.** of or relating to Polynesia, its people, or any of their languages. ◆ *n* **2** a member of the people that inhabit Polynesia, generally of Caucasoid features with light skin and wavy hair. **3** a branch of the Malayo-Polynesian family of languages, including Maori and Hawaiian.

polyneuritis (ˌpɒlɪnju'raitɪs) *n* inflammation of many nerves at the same time.

Polynices ★ (ˌpɒlɪ'naisi:z) *n Greek myth.* a son of Oedipus and Jocasta, for whom the Seven Against Thebes sought to regain Thebes. He and his brother Eteocles killed each other in single combat before its walls.

polynomial (ˌpɒlɪ'nəʊmɪəl) *adj* **1** of, consisting of, or referring to two or more names or terms. ◆ *n* **2a** a mathematical expression consisting of a sum of terms each of which is the product of a constant and one or more variables raised to a positive or zero integral power. **2b** Also called: **multinomial.** any mathematical expression consisting of the sum of a number of terms. **3** *Biol.* a taxonomic name consisting of more than two terms, such as *Parus major minor* in which *minor* designates the subspecies.

polynucleotide (ˌpɒlɪ'nju:klɪəˌtaid) *n Biochem.* a molecular chain of nucleotides chemically bonded by a series of ester linkages between the phosphoryl group of one nucleotide and the hydroxyl group of the sugar in the adjacent nucleotide.

polynya ('pɒlənˌjɑ:) *n* a stretch of open water surrounded by ice, esp. near the mouths of large rivers, in arctic seas. [C19: from Russian, from *poly* open]

polyp ('pɒlɪp) *n* **1** *Zool.* one of the two forms of individual that occur in coelenterates. It usually has a hollow cylin-

★ people and places

drical body with a ring of tentacles around the mouth. **2** Also called: **polypus**. *Pathol*. a small growth arising from the surface of a mucous membrane. [C16 *polip*, from F *polype* nasal polyp, from L *pōlypus*, from Gk *polypous* having many feet]
► **'polypous** *or* **'polypoid** *adj*

polypeptide (ˌpɒlɪ'pɛptaɪd) *n* any of a group of natural or synthetic polymers made up of amino acids chemically linked together; includes the proteins.

polypetalous (ˌpɒlɪ'pɛtələs) *adj* (of flowers) having many distinct or separate petals.

polyphagia (ˌpɒlɪ'feɪdʒə) *n* **1** an abnormal desire to consume excessive amounts of food. **2** the habit of certain animals, esp. certain insects, of feeding on many different types of food. [C17: NL, from Gk, from *poluphagos* eating much]
► **polyphagous** (pə'lɪfəgəs) *adj*

polyphase ('pɒlɪˌfeɪz) *adj* **1** (of an electrical system, circuit, or device) having or using alternating voltages of the same frequency, the phases of which are cyclically displaced by fractions of a period. **2** having more than one phase.

Polyphemus ★ (ˌpɒlɪ'fiːməs) *n Greek myth*. a cyclops who imprisoned Odysseus and his companions in his cave. To effect his escape, Odysseus blinded him.

polyphone ('pɒlɪˌfəʊn) *n* a letter or character having more than one phonetic value, such as *c* in English.

polyphonic (ˌpɒlɪ'fɒnɪk) *adj* **1** *Music*. composed of relatively independent parts; contrapuntal. **2** many-voiced. **3** *Phonetics*. denoting a polyphone.
► **poly'phonically** *adv*

polyphony (pə'lɪfənɪ) *n, pl* **polyphonies**. **1** polyphonic style of composition or a piece of music utilizing it. **2** the use of polyphones in a writing system. [C19: from Gk *poluphōnia* diversity of tones]
► **po'lyphonous** *adj* ► **po'lyphonously** *adv*

polyploid ('pɒlɪˌplɔɪd) *adj* (of cells, organisms, etc.) having more than twice the basic (haploid) number of chromosomes.
► **poly'ploidal** *adj* ► **'poly,ploidy** *n*

polypod ('pɒlɪˌpɒd) *adj* **1** (esp. of insect larvae) having many legs or similar appendages. ◆ *n* **2** an animal of this type.

polypody ('pɒlɪˌpəʊdɪ) *n, pl* **polypodies**. any of various ferns having deeply divided leaves and round naked sporangia. [C15: from L *polypodium*, from Gk, from POLY- + *pous* foot]

polypropylene (ˌpɒlɪ'prəʊpɪˌliːn) *n* any of various tough flexible synthetic thermoplastic materials made by polymerizing propylene. Systematic name: **polypropene** (ˌpɒlɪ'prəʊpiːn).

polypus ('pɒlɪpəs) *n, pl* **polypi** (-paɪ). *Pathol*. another word for **polyp** (sense 2). [C16: via L from Gk: POLYP]

polysaccharide (ˌpɒlɪ'sækəˌraɪd, -rɪd) *or* **polysaccharose** (ˌpɒlɪ'sækəˌrəʊz, -ˌrəʊs) *n* any one of a class of carbohydrates whose molecules contain linked monosaccharide units: includes starch, inulin, and cellulose.

polysemy (ˌpɒlɪ'siːmɪ, pə'lɪsəmɪ) *n* the existence of several meanings in a single word. [C20: from NL *polysēmia*, from Gk *polusēmos* having many meanings]
► **poly'semous** *adj*

polysomic (ˌpɒlɪ'səʊmɪk) *adj* of, relating to, or designating a basically diploid chromosome complement, in which some but not all the chromosomes are represented more than twice.

polystyrene (ˌpɒlɪ'staɪriːn) *n* a synthetic thermoplastic material obtained by polymerizing styrene; used as a white rigid foam (**expanded polystyrene**) for insulating and packing and as a glasslike material in light fittings.

polysyllable ('pɒlɪˌsɪləbˀl) *n* a word consisting of more than two syllables.
► **polysyllabic** (ˌpɒlɪsɪ'læbɪk) *adj* ► **polysyl'labically** *adv*

polysyndeton (ˌpɒlɪ'sɪndɪtən) *n Rhetoric*. the use of several conjunctions in close succession, esp. where some might be omitted, as in *he ran and jumped and laughed for*

joy. [C16: POLY- + *-syndeton*, from Gk *sundetos* bound together]

polytechnic (ˌpɒlɪ'tɛknɪk) *n* **1** *Brit*. (formerly) a college offering advanced courses in many fields at and below degree standard. ◆ *adj* **2** of or relating to technical instruction and training. [C19: via F from Gk *polutekhnos* skilled in many arts]

polytetrafluoroethylene (ˌpɒlɪˌtɛtrəˌfluərəʊ'ɛθɪˌliːn) *n* a white thermoplastic material with a waxy texture, made by polymerizing tetrafluoroethylene. It is used for making gaskets, hoses, insulators, bearings, and for coating metal surfaces. Abbrev.: **PTFE**. Also called (trademark): **Teflon**.

polytheism ('pɒlɪˌθiːˌɪzəm, ˌpɒlɪ'θiːɪzəm) *n* the worship of or belief in more than one god.
► **polythe'istic** *adj* ► **polythe'istically** *adv*

polythene ('pɒlɪˌθiːn) *n* any one of various light thermoplastic materials made from ethylene with properties depending on the molecular weight of the polymer. Systematic name: **polyethene**. Also called: **polyethylene**.

polytonality (ˌpɒlɪtəʊ'nælɪtɪ) *or* **polytonalism** *n Music*. the simultaneous use of more than two different keys or tonalities.
► **poly'tonal** *adj* ► **poly'tonally** *adv*

polyunsaturated (ˌpɒlɪʌn'sætʃəˌreɪtɪd) *adj* of or relating to a class of animal and vegetable fats, the molecules of which consist of long carbon chains with many double bonds. Polyunsaturated compounds are less likely to be converted into cholesterol in the body. See also **monounsaturated**.

polyurethane (ˌpɒlɪ'juərəˌθeɪn) *n* a class of synthetic materials commonly used as a foam for insulation and packing.

polyvalent (ˌpɒlɪ'veɪlənt, pə'lɪvələnt) *adj* **1** *Chem*. having more than one valency. **2** (of a vaccine) effective against several strains of the same disease-producing microorganism, antigen, or toxin.
► **poly'valency** *n*

polyvinyl (ˌpɒlɪ'vaɪnɪl, -'vaɪnˀl) *n* (*modifier*) designating a plastic or resin formed by polymerization of a vinyl derivative.

polyvinyl acetate *n* a colourless odourless tasteless resin used in emulsion paints, adhesives, sealers, a substitute for chicle in chewing gum, and for sealing porous surfaces.

polyvinyl chloride *n* the full name of **PVC**.

polyvinyl resin *n* any of a class of thermoplastic resins made by polymerizing a vinyl compound. The commonest type is PVC.

Polyxena ★ (pɒ'lɪksɪnə) *n Greek myth*. a daughter of King Priam of Troy, who was sacrificed on the command of Achilles' ghost.

polyzoan (ˌpɒlɪ'zəʊən) *n, adj* another word for **bryozoan**. [C19: from NL, *Polyzoa* class name, from POLY- + -*zoan*, from Gk *zoion* an animal]

pom (pɒm) *n Austral*. & *NZ sl*. short for **pommy**.

POM *abbrev*. for prescription only medicine (*or* medication). Cf. **OTC**.

pomace ('pʌmɪs) *n* **1** the pulpy residue of apples or similar fruit after crushing and pressing, as in cider-making. **2** any pulpy substance left after crushing, mashing, etc. [C16: from Med. L *pōmācium* cider, from L *pōmum* apple]

pomaceous (pɒ'meɪʃəs) *adj* of, relating to, or bearing pomes, such as the apple and quince trees. [C18: from NL *pōmāceus*, from L *pōmum* apple]

pomade (pə'mɑːd) *n* **1** a perfumed oil or ointment put on the hair, as to make it smooth and shiny. ◆ *vb* **pomades, pomading, pomaded**. **2** (*tr*) to put pomade on. ◆ Also: **pomatum**. [C16: from F *pommade*, from It. *pomato* (orig. made partly from apples), from L *pōmum* apple]

pomander (pəʊ'mændə) *n* **1** a mixture of aromatic substances in a sachet or an orange, formerly carried as scent or as a protection against disease. **2** a container for such a mixture. [C15: from OF *pome d'ambre*, from Med. L *pōmum ambrae* apple of amber]

Pombal ★ (*Portuguese* pom'bal) *n* **Marquês de** (mərkeɪ 'dɔː). title of *Sebastiâo José de Carvalho e Mello*. 1699–1782, Portuguese statesman, who dominated Portuguese government from 1750 to 1777 and instituted many administrative and economic reforms.

pome (pəʊm) *n* the fleshy fruit of the apple and related plants, consisting of an enlarged receptacle enclosing the ovary and seeds. [C15: from OF, from LL *pōma*, pl. of L *pōmum* apple]

pomegranate ('pɒmɪ,grænɪt, 'pɒm,grænɪt) *n* **1** an Asian shrub or small tree cultivated in semitropical regions for its edible fruit. **2** the many-chambered globular fruit of this tree, which has tough reddish rind, juicy red pulp, and many seeds. [C14: from OF *pome grenate*, from L *pōmum* apple + *grenate*, from *grānātus* full of seeds]

pomelo ('pɒmɪ,ləʊ) *n, pl* **pomelos. 1** Also called: **shaddock.** the edible yellow fruit, resembling a grapefruit, of a tropical tree widely grown in oriental regions. **2** *US.* another name for **grapefruit.** [C19: from Du. *pompelmoes*]

Pomerania ★ (,pɒmə'reɪnɪə) *n* a region of N central Europe, extending along the S coast of the Baltic Sea from Stralsund to the Vistula River: now chiefly in Poland, with a small area in NE Germany. German name: **Pommern.** Polish name: **Pomorze.**

Pomeranian (,pɒmə'reɪnɪən) *adj* **1.** of or relating to Pomerania. ◆ *n* **2** a breed of toy dog of the spitz type with a long thick straight coat.

pomfret ('pʌmfrɪt, 'pɒm-) *or* **pomfret-cake** *n* a small black liquorice confection of liquorice. Also called: **Pontefract cake.** [C19: from *Pomfret*, earlier form of PONTEFRACT, where orig. made]

pomiculture ('pɒmɪ,kʌltʃə) *n* the cultivation of fruit. [C19: from L *pōmum* fruit + CULTURE]

pommel ('pʌməl, 'pɒm-) *n* **1** the raised part on the front of a saddle. **2** a knob at the top of a sword or similar weapon. ◆ *vb* **pommels, pommelling, pommelled** *or US* **pommels, pommeling, pommeled. 3** a less common word for **pummel.** [C14: from OF *pomel* knob, from Vulgar L *pōmellum* (unattested) little apple, from L *pōmum* apple]

Pommern ★ ('pɔmərn) *n* the German name for **Pomerania.**

pommy ('pɒmɪ) *n, pl* **pommies.** (*sometimes cap.*) *Sl.* a mildly offensive word used by Australians and New Zealanders for a British person. Sometimes shortened to **pom.** [C20: from ?, ? a blend of IMMIGRANT & POMEGRANATE (alluding to the red cheeks of British immigrants)]

pomology (pə'mɒlədʒɪ) *n* the branch of horticulture concerned with the study and cultivation of fruit. [C19: from NL *pōmologia*, from L *pōmum* fruit]
▶ **pomological** (,pɒmə'lɒdʒɪk²l) *adj*

Pomona[1] ★ (pə'məʊnə) *n* another name for **Mainland** (in the Orkneys).

Pomona[2] ★ (pə'məʊnə) *n* the Roman goddess of fruit trees.

Pomorze ★ (pɔ'mɔʒɛ) *n* the Polish name for **Pomerania.**

pomp (pɒmp) *n* **1** stately or magnificent display; ceremonial splendour. **2** vain display, esp. of dignity or importance. **3** *Obs.* a procession or pageant. [C14: from OF *pompe*, from L *pompa* procession, from Gk *pompē*]

pompadour ('pɒmpə,dʊə) *n* an early 18th-century hairstyle for women, having the front hair arranged over a pad to give it greater height and bulk. [C18: after the Marquise de POMPADOUR, who originated it]

Pompadour ★ (*French* pɔ̃padur) *n* **Marquise de,** title of *Jeanne Antoinette Poisson.* 1721–64, mistress of Louis XV of France (1745–64), whom she greatly influenced.

pompano ('pɒmpə,nəʊ) *n, pl* **pompano** *or* **pompanos. 1** any of several food fishes of American coastal regions of the Atlantic. **2** a spiny-finned food fish of North American coastal regions of the Pacific. [C19: from Sp. *pámpano*, from ?]

Pompeii ★ (pɒm'peɪiː) *n* an ancient city in Italy, southeast of Naples: buried by an eruption of Vesuvius (79 A.D.); excavation of the site, which is extremely well preserved, began in 1748.
▶ **Pompeiian** (pɒm'peɪən, -'piː-) *adj, n*

Pompey[1] ★ ('pɒmpɪ) *n* an informal name for **Portsmouth.**

Pompey[2] ★ ('pɒmpɪ) *n* called *Pompey the Great;* Latin name *Gnaeus Pompeius Magnus.* 106–48 B.C., Roman gen-

eral and statesman; a member with Caesar and Crassus of the first triumvirate (60). He later quarrelled with Caesar, who defeated him at Pharsalus (48). He fled to Egypt and was murdered.

Pompidou ★ (*French* pɔ̃pidu) *n* **Georges** (ʒɔrʒ). 1911–74, French statesman; president of France (1969–74).

pompom ('pɒmpɒm) *or* **pompon** *n* **1** a ball of tufted silk, wool, feathers, etc., worn on a hat for decoration. **2a** the small globelike flower head of certain varieties of dahlia and chrysanthemum. **2b** (*as modifier*): *pompom dahlia.* [C18: from F, from OF *pompe* knot of ribbons, from ?]

pom-pom ('pɒmpɒm) *n* an automatic rapid-firing small-calibre cannon, esp. a type of anti-aircraft cannon used in World War II. Also called: **pompom.** [C19: imit.]

pomposo (pɒm'pəʊsəʊ) *adv Music.* in a pompous manner. [It.]

pompous ('pɒmpəs) *adj* **1** exaggeratedly or ostentatiously dignified or self-important. **2** ostentatiously lofty in style: *a pompous speech.* **3** *Rare.* characterized by ceremonial pomp or splendour.
▶ **pomposity** (pɒm'pɒsɪtɪ) *or* **pompousness** *n* ▶ **'pompously** *adv*

'pon (pɒn) *Poetic or arch.* contraction of **upon.**

ponce (pɒns) *Derog. sl., chiefly Brit.* ◆ *n* **1** a man given to ostentatious or effeminate display. **2** another word for **pimp**[1]. ◆ *vb* **ponces, poncing, ponced. 3** (*intr;* often foll. by *around* or *about*) to act like a ponce. [C19: from Polari, from Sp. *pu(n)to* male prostitute or F *pront* prostitute]
▶ **'poncy** *or* **'poncey** *adj*

Ponce ★ (*Spanish* 'pɒnθe) *n* a port in S Puerto Rico, on the Caribbean: the second largest town on the island; settled in the 16th century. Pop.: 159 151 (1990).

Ponce de León ★ ('pɒns də 'liːən; *Spanish* 'pɒnθe ðe leˈɔn) *n* **Juan** (xwan). ?1460–1521, Spanish explorer. He settled (1509) and governed (1510–12) Puerto Rico and discovered (1513) Florida.

poncho ('pɒntʃəʊ) *n, pl* **ponchos.** a cloak of a kind originally worn in South America, made of a rectangular or circular piece of cloth with a hole in the middle for the head. [C18: from American Sp., of Amerind origin, from *pantho* woollen material]

pond (pɒnd) *n* a pool of still water, often artificially created. [C13 *ponde* enclosure]

ponder ('pɒndə) *vb* (when *intr,* sometimes foll. by *on* or *over*) to give thorough or deep consideration (to); meditate (upon). [C14: from OF *ponderer,* from L *ponderāre* to weigh, consider, from *pondus* weight]
▶ **'ponderable** *adj*

ponderous ('pɒndərəs) *adj* **1** heavy; huge. **2** (esp. of movement) lacking ease or lightness; lumbering or graceless. **3** dull or laborious: *a ponderous oration.* [C14: from L *ponderōsus* of great weight, from *pondus* weight]
▶ **'ponderously** *adv* ▶ **'ponderousness** *or* **ponderosity** (,pɒndə'rɒsɪtɪ) *n*

Pondicherry ★ (,pɒndɪ'tʃɛrɪ) *n* **1** a Union Territory of SE India: transferred from French to Indian administration in 1954 and made a Union Territory in 1962. Capital: Pondicherry. Pop.: 894 000 (1994 est.). Area: 479 sq. km (185 sq. miles). **2** a port in SE India, capital of the Union Territory of Pondicherry, on the Coromandel Coast. Pop.: 203 065 (1991).

pond lily *n* another name for **water lily.**

pondok ('pɒndɒk) *or* **pondokkie** (in southern Africa) a crudely made house built of tin sheet, reeds, etc. [C20: from Malay *pondók* leaf house]

Pondoland ★ ('pɒndəʊ,lænd) *n* an area of SE South Africa, inhabited chiefly by the Pondo people.

pond scum *n* a greenish layer floating on the surface of stagnant waters, consisting of algae.

pondweed ('pɒnd,wiːd) *n* **1** any of various water plants of the genus *Potamogeton,* which grow in ponds and slow streams. **2** Also called: **waterweed.** *Brit.* any of various water plants, such as mare's-tail, that have thin or much-divided leaves.

pone[1] (pəʊn, 'pəʊnɪ) *n Cards.* the player to the right of the dealer, or the nondealer in two-handed games. [C19: from L: put!, that is, play, from *ponere* to put]

pone[2] (pəʊn) *n Southern US.* bread made of maize. Also called: **pone bread, corn pone.** [C17: of Amerind origin]

pong (pɒŋ) *Brit. inf.* ◆ *n* **1** a disagreeable or offensive smell; stink. ◆ *vb* **2** (*intr*) to stink. [C20: ?from Romany *pan* to stink]
▶ **'pongy** *adj*

ponga ('pɒŋə) *n* a tall New Zealand tree fern with large leathery leaves.

pongee (pɒn'dʒiː, 'pɒndʒiː) *n* **1** a thin plain-weave silk fabric from China or India, left in its natural colour. **2** a cotton or rayon fabric similar to this. [C18: from Mandarin Chinese (Peking) *pen-chī* woven at home, from *pen* own + *chi* loom]

pongid ('pɒŋgɪd, 'pɒndʒɪd) *n* **1** any primate of the family Pongidae, which includes the gibbons and the great apes. ◆ *adj* **2** of this family. [from NL *Pongo* type genus, from Congolese *mpongo* ape]

pongo ('pɒŋgəʊ) *n, pl* **pongos.** an anthropoid ape, esp. an orang-utan or (formerly) a gorilla. [C17: from Congolese *mpongo*]

poniard ('pɒnjəd) *n* **1** a small dagger with a slender blade. ◆ *vb* **2** (*tr*) to stab with a poniard. [C16: from OF *poignard*, from *poing* fist, from L *pugnus*]

pons Varolii (pɒnz və'rəʊlɪ,aɪ) *n, pl* **pontes Varolii** ('pɒntiːz). a broad white band of connecting nerve fibres that bridges the hemispheres of the cerebellum in mammals. Sometimes shortened to **pons.** [C16: NL, lit.: bridge of Varoli, after Costanzo *Varoli* (?1543–75), It. anatomist]

Ponta Delgada ★ (*Portuguese* 'pontə ðɛl'gaðə) *n* a port in the E Azores, on S São Miguel Island: chief commercial centre of the archipelago. Pop.: 21 091 (1991 est.).

Pontchartrain ★ ('pɒntʃə,treɪn) *n* **Lake.** a shallow lagoon in SE Louisiana, linked with the Gulf of Mexico by a narrow channel, the **Rigolets:** resort and fishing centre. Area: 1620 sq. km (625 sq. miles).

Pontefract ★ ('pɒntɪ,frækt) *n* an industrial town in N England, in Wakefield, in West Yorkshire: castle (1069), in which Richard II was imprisoned and murdered (1400). Pop.: 28 358 (1991).

Pontevedra ★ (*Spanish* pɒnte'βeðra) *n* a port in NW Spain: takes its name from a 12-arched Roman bridge, the Pons Vetus. Pop.: 74 850 (1991).

Pontiac ★ ('pɒntɪ,æk) *n* died 1769, chief of the Ottawa Indians, who led a rebellion against the British (1763–66).

Pontianak ★ (,pɒntɪ'ɑːnæk) *n* a port in Indonesia, on W coast of Borneo almost exactly on the equator. Pop.: 387 112 (1990).

Pontic ('pɒntɪk) *adj* denoting or relating to the Black Sea. [C15: from L *Ponticus*, from Gk, from *Pontos* PONTUS]

pontifex ('pɒntɪ,fɛks) *n, pl* **pontifices** (pɒn'tɪfɪ,siːz). (in ancient Rome) any of the senior members of the Pontifical College, presided over by the **Pontifex Maximus.** [C16: from L, ?from Etruscan but infl. by folk etymology as if meaning lit.: bridge-maker]

pontiff ('pɒntɪf) *n* a former title of the pagan high priest at Rome, later used of popes and occasionally of other bishops, and now confined to the pope. [C17: from F *pontife*, from L PONTIFEX]

pontifical (pɒn'tɪfɪk°l) *adj* **1** of, relating to, or characteristic of a pontiff. **2** having an excessively authoritative manner; pompous. ◆ *n* **3** *RC Church, Church of England.* a book containing the prayers and ritual instructions for ceremonies restricted to a bishop.
▶ **pon'tifically** *adv*

pontificals (pɒn'tɪfɪk°lz) *pl n Chiefly RC Church.* the insignia and special vestments worn by a bishop, esp. when celebrating High Mass.

pontificate *vb* (pɒn'tɪfɪ,keɪt), **pontificates, pontificating, pontificated.** (*intr*) **1** to speak or behave in a pompous or dogmatic manner. **2** to serve or officiate at a Pontifical Mass. ◆ *n* (pɒn'tɪfɪkɪt). **3** the office or term of office of a pope.

Pontine Marshes ★ ('pɒntaɪn) *pl n* an area of W Italy,

southeast of Rome: formerly malarial swamps, drained in 1932–34 after numerous attempts since 160 B.C. had failed. Italian name: **Agro Pontino** ('ɑːgro pon'tiːno)

Pontius Pilate ★ ('pɒnʃəs, 'pɒntəs 'paɪlət) *n* See **Pilate.**

pontoon[1] (pɒn'tuːn) *n* **a** a watertight float or vessel used where buoyancy is required in water, as in supporting a bridge, in salvage work, or where a temporary or mobile structure is required in military operations. **b** (*as modifier*): *a pontoon bridge.* [C17: from F *ponton*, from L *pontō* punt, from *pōns* bridge]

pontoon[2] (pɒn'tuːn) *n* a gambling game in which players try to obtain card combinations worth 21 points. Also called: **twenty-one** (esp. US), **vingt-et-un.** [C20: prob. an alteration of F *vingt-et-un*, lit.: twenty-one]

Pontoppidan ★ (*Danish* pon'tobidan) *n* **Henrik** ('hɛnrək). 1857–1943, Danish novelist and short-story writer, author of the novel sequences *The Promised Land* (1891–95), *Lykke-Per* (1898–1904), and *The Empire of Death* (1912–16). Nobel prize for literature 1917.

Pontormo ★ (*Italian* pon'tormo) *n* **Jacopo da** ('jaːkopo da). original name *Jacopo Carrucci*. 1494–1556, Italian mannerist painter.

Pontus ★ ('pɒntəs) *n* an ancient region of NE Asia Minor, on the Black Sea: became a kingdom in the 4th century B.C.; at its height under Mithridates VI (about 115–63 B.C.), when it controlled all Asia Minor; defeated by the Romans in the mid-1st century B.C.

Pontus Euxinus ★ (juːk'saɪnəs) *n* the Latin name of the Black Sea.

Pontypool ★ (,pɒntɪ'puːl) *n* an industrial town in E Wales, in Torfaen: famous for lacquered ironware in the 18th century. Pop.: 35 564 (1991).

Pontypridd ★ (,pɒntɪ'priːð) *n* an industrial town in S Wales, in Rhondda, Cynon, Taff. Pop.: 28 487 (1991).

pony ('pəʊnɪ) *n, pl* **ponies. 1** any of various breeds of small horse, usually under 14.2 hands. **2** a small drinking glass, esp. for liqueurs. **3** anything small of its kind. **4** *Brit. sl.* a sum of £25, esp. in bookmaking. **5** Also called: **trot.** *US sl.* a translation used by students, often illicitly; crib. [C17: from Scot. *powney*, ?from obs. F *poulenet* a little colt, from L *pullus* young animal, foal]

ponytail ('pəʊnɪ,teɪl) *n* a hairstyle in which the hair is gathered together tightly by a band into a bunch at the back of the head.

pony trekking *n* the act of riding ponies cross-country, esp. as a pastime.

pooch (puːtʃ) *n Chiefly US & Canad.* a slang word for **dog.** [from ?]

poodle ('puːd°l) *n* **1** a breed of dog with curly hair, which is generally clipped from ribs to tail. **2** a servile person; lackey. [C19: from G *Pudel*, short for *Pudelhund*, from *pudeln* to splash + *Hund* dog; formerly trained as water dogs]

poof (puf, puːf), **poove** (puːv), or **poofter** ('puːftə) *n Brit. & Austral. derog. sl.* a male homosexual. [C20: from F *pouffe* puff]
▶ **'poofy** *adj*

pooh (puː) *interj* an exclamation of disdain, contempt, or disgust.

Pooh-Bah ('puː'bɑː) *n* a pompous self-important official holding several offices at once and fulfilling none of them. [C19: after the character, the Lord-High-Everything-Else, in *The Mikado* (1885), by Gilbert & Sullivan]

pooh-pooh ('puː'puː) *vb* (*tr*) to express disdain or scorn for; dismiss or belittle.

pool[1] (puːl) *n* **1** a small body of still water, usually fresh; small pond. **2** a small isolated collection of spilt liquid; puddle: *a pool of blood.* **3** a deep part of a stream or river where the water runs very slowly. **4** an underground accumulation of oil or gas. **5** See **swimming pool.** [OE *pōl*]

pool[2] (puːl) *n* **1** any communal combination of resources, funds, etc.: *a typing pool.* **2** the combined stakes of the betters in many gambling games; kitty. **3** *Commerce.* a group of producers who agree to establish and maintain output levels and high prices, each member of the group being allocated a maximum quota. **4** *Finance, chiefly US.* a joint fund organized by security-holders for speculative or manipulative purposes on financial markets. **5** any of various billiard games in which the object is to pot all the balls with the cue ball, esp. that played with 15 coloured and numbered balls, popular in the US. Also called: **pocket billiards.** ◆ *vb* (*tr*) **6** to combine (investments, money, interests, etc.) into a common fund, as for a joint enterprise. **7** *Commerce.* to organize a pool of (enterprises). [C17: from F *poule*, lit.: hen used to signify stakes in a card game, from Med. L *pulla* hen, from L *pullus* young animal]

Poole ★ (puːl) *n* **1** a port and resort in S England, in Dorset on **Poole Harbour.** Pop.: 138 479 (1991). **2** a unitary authority in S England, in Dorset. Pop.: 138 100 (1994 est.). Area: 37 sq. km (14 sq. miles).

Pool Malebo ★ ('puːl mə'liːbəʊ) *n* the Congolese name for **Stanley Pool.**

pools (puːlz) *pl n* **the** *Brit.* an organized nationwide principally postal gambling pool betting on the result of football matches. Also called: **football pools.**

Poona *or* **Pune** ★ ('puːnə) *n* a city in W India, in W Maharashtra: under British rule served as the seasonal capital of the Bombay Presidency. Pop.: 1 566 651 (1991).

poop[1] (puːp) *Naut.* ◆ *n* **1** a raised structure at the stern of a vessel, esp. a sailing ship. **2** Also called: **poop deck.** a raised deck at the stern of a ship. ◆ *vb* **3** (*tr*) (of a wave or sea) to break over the stern of (a vessel). **4** (*intr*) (of a vessel) to ship a wave or sea over the stern, esp. repeatedly. [C15: from OF *pupe*, from L *puppis*]

poop[2] (puːp) *vb US & Canad. sl.* **1** (*tr; usually passive*) to cause to become exhausted; tire: *he was pooped after the race.* **2** (*intr*; usually foll. by *out*) to give up or fail: *he pooped out of the race.* [C14 *poupen* to blow, ? imit.]

poop[3] (puːp) *Inf.* ◆ *vb* (*intr*) **1** to defecate. ◆ *n* **2** faeces; excrement. [perhaps related to POOP[2]]

pooper-scooper *n* a device used to remove dogs' excrement from public areas. [C20: POOP[3] + -ER[1] + SCOOP]

Poopó ★ (*Spanish* poo'po) *n* **Lake.** a lake in SW Bolivia, at an altitude of 3688 m (12 100 ft): fed by the Desaguadero River. Area: 2540 sq. km (980 sq. miles).

poor (pʊə, pɔː) *adj* **1** lacking financial or other means of subsistence; needy. **2** characterized by or indicating poverty: *the country had a poor economy.* **3** scanty or inadequate: *a poor salary.* **4** (when *postpositive*, usually foll. by *in*) badly supplied (with resources, etc.): *a region poor in wild flowers.* **5** inferior. **6** contemptible or despicable. **7** disappointing or disagreeable: *a poor play.* **8** (*prenominal*) deserving of pity; unlucky: *poor John is ill again.* [C13: from OF *povre*, from L *pauper*]
▸ **'poorness** *n*

poor box *n* a box, esp. one in a church, used for the collection of alms or money for the poor.

poorhouse ('pʊəˌhaʊs, 'pɔː-) *n* another name for **workhouse** (sense 1).

poor law *n English history.* a law providing for the relief or support of the poor from parish funds.

poorly ('pʊəlɪ, 'pɔː-) *adv* **1** badly. ◆ *adj* **2** (*usually postpositive*) *Inf.* in poor health; rather ill.

poort (pʊət) *n* (in South Africa) a steep narrow mountain pass, usually following a river or stream. [C19: from Afrik., from Du.: gateway]

poor White *n Often offens.* **a** a poverty-stricken and underprivileged White person, esp. in the southern US and South Africa. **b** (*as modifier*): *poor White trash.*

pop[1] (pɒp) *vb* **pops, popping, popped.** **1** to make or cause to make a light sharp explosive sound. **2** to burst open with such a sound. **3** (*intr*; often foll. by *in, out,* etc.) *Inf.* to come (to) or go (from) rapidly or suddenly. **4** (*intr*) (esp. of the eyes) to protrude: *her eyes popped with amazement.* **5** to shoot at (a target) with a firearm. **6** (*tr*) to place with a sudden movement: *she popped some tablets into her mouth.* **7** (*tr*) *Inf.* to pawn: *he popped his watch yesterday.* **8** (*tr*) *Sl.* to take (a drug) in pill form or as an injection. **9 pop the question.** *Inf.* to propose marriage. ◆ *n* **10** a light sharp explosive sound; crack. **11** *Inf.* a flavoured nonalcoholic carbonated beverage. ◆ *adv* **12** with a popping sound. ◆ See also **pop off.** [C14: imit.]

pop[2] (pɒp) *n* **1a** music of general appeal, esp. among young people, that originated as a distinctive genre in the 1950s. It is generally characterized by a heavy rhythmic element and the use of electrical amplification. **1b** (*as modifier*): *a pop group.* **2** *Inf.* a piece of popular or light classical music. ◆ *adj* **3** *Inf.* short for **popular.**

pop[3] (pɒp) *n* **1** an informal word for **father.** **2** *Inf.* a name used in addressing an old man.

POP *abbrev. for* Post Office Preferred (size of envelopes, etc.).

pop. *abbrev. for:* **1** popular(ly). **2** population.

pop art *n* a movement in modern art that imitates the methods, styles, and themes of popular culture and mass media, such as comic strips, advertising, and science fiction.

popcorn ('pɒpˌkɔːn) *n* **1** a variety of maize having hard pointed kernels that puff up and burst when heated. **2** the puffed edible kernels of this plant.

pope (pəʊp) *n* **1** (*often cap.*) the bishop of Rome as head of the Roman Catholic Church. **2** *Eastern Orthodox Churches.* a title sometimes given to a parish priest or to the Greek Orthodox patriarch of Alexandria. [OE *papa*, from Church L: bishop, esp. of Rome, from LGk *papas* father-in-God, from Gk *pappas* father]
▸ **'popedom** *n*

Pope ★ (pəʊp) *n* **Alexander.** 1688–1744, British poet, regarded as the most brilliant satirist of the Augustan period. His works include *The Rape of the Lock* (1712–14), *The Dunciad* (1728; 1742), *An Essay on Man* (1733–34), and *Imitations of Horace* (1733–38).

popery ('pəʊpərɪ) *n* a derogatory name for **Roman Catholicism.**

popeyed ('pɒpˌaɪd) *adj* **1** having bulging prominent eyes. **2** staring in astonishment.

popgun ('pɒpˌgʌn) *n* a toy gun that fires a pellet or cork by means of compressed air.

popinjay ('pɒpɪnˌdʒeɪ) *n* **1** a conceited, foppish, or excessively talkative person. **2** an archaic word for **parrot. 3** the figure of a parrot used as a target. [C13 *papeniai*, from OF *papegay* a parrot, from Sp., from Ar. *babaghā*]

popish ('pəʊpɪʃ) *adj Derog.* belonging to or characteristic of Roman Catholicism.

poplar ('pɒplə) *n* **1** a tree of N temperate regions, having triangular leaves, flowers borne in catkins, and light soft wood. **2** *US.* the tulip tree. [C14: from OF *poplier*, from L *pōpulus*]

poplin ('pɒplɪn) *n* a strong fabric, usually of cotton, in plain weave with fine ribbing. [C18: from F *papeline*, ?from *Poperinge*, a centre of textile manufacture in Flanders]

popliteal (pɒp'lɪtɪəl, ˌpɒplɪ'tiːəl) *adj* of, relating to, or near the part of the leg behind the knee. [C18: from NL *popliteus* the muscle behind the knee joint, from L *poples* the ham of the knee]

popmobility (ˌpɒpməʊ'bɪlɪtɪ) *n* a form of exercise that combines aerobics in a continuous dance routine, performed to pop music. [C20: POP[2] + MOBILITY]

Popocatépetl ★ (ˌpɒpə'kætəpet°l, -ˌkætə'pet°l; *Spanish* popoka'tepetl) *n* a volcano in SE central Mexico, southeast of Mexico City. Height: 5452 m (17 887 ft).

pop off *vb* (*intr, adv*) *Inf.* **1** to depart suddenly or unexpectedly. **2** to die, esp. suddenly.

Popov ★ (*Russian* pa'pɔf) *n* **Alexander Stepanovich** (alɪk-'sandˤr stɪ'panəvitʃ). 1859–1906, Russian physicist, the first to use an aerial in experiments with radio waves.

poppadom *or* **poppadum** ('pɒpədəm) *n* a thin round crisp Indian bread, fried or roasted and served with curry. [from Hindi]

popper ('pɒpə) *n* **1** a person or thing that pops. **2** *Brit.* an informal name for **press stud. 3** *Chiefly US & Canad.* a container for cooking popcorn in. **4** *Sl.* an amyl nitrite capsule, crushed and inhaled by drug users.

Popper ★ ('pɒpə) *n* **Sir Karl.** 1902–94, British philosopher, born in Vienna. His works include *The Logic of Scientific Discovery* (1934), *The Open Society and its Enemies* (1945), and *Objective Knowledge* (1972).
▸ **Popperian** (pɒ'pɪərɪən) *n, adj*

★ people and places

poppet ('pɒpɪt) n 1 a term of affection for a small child or sweetheart. 2 Also called: **poppet valve**. a mushroom-shaped valve that is lifted from its seating by applying an axial force to its stem. 3 *Naut.* a temporary supporting brace for a vessel hauled on land. [C14: early var. of PUPPET]

popping crease n *Cricket.* a line four feet in front of and parallel with the bowling crease, at or behind which the batsman stands. [C18: from POP¹ (in the obs. sense: to hit) + CREASE]

popple ('pɒp°l) vb **popples, poppling, poppled.** (intr) 1 (of boiling water or a choppy sea) to heave or toss; bubble. 2 (often foll. by *along*) (of a stream or river) to move with an irregular tumbling motion. [C14: imit.]

poppy ('pɒpɪ) n, pl **poppies.** 1 any of numerous papaveraceous plants having red, orange, or white flowers and a milky sap. 2 any of several similar or related plants, such as the California poppy and Welsh poppy. 3 any of the drugs, such as opium, that are obtained from these plants. 4a a strong red to reddish-orange colour. 4b (as adj): *a poppy dress*. 5 an artificial red poppy flower worn to mark Remembrance Sunday. [OE *popæg*, ult. from L *papāver*]

poppycock ('pɒpɪ,kɒk) n *Inf.* nonsense. [C19: from Du. dialect *pappekak*, lit.: soft excrement]

Poppy Day n an informal name for **Remembrance Sunday.**

poppyhead ('pɒpɪ,hɛd) n 1 the hard dry seed-containing capsule of a poppy. 2 a carved ornament, esp. one used on the top of the end of a pew or bench in Gothic church architecture.

poppy seed n the small grey seeds of the opium poppy, used esp. on loaves.

pop socks pl n knee-length nylon stockings.

popsy ('pɒpsɪ) n, pl **popsies.** Old-fashioned Brit. sl. an attractive young woman. [C19: dim. from *pop*, shortened from POPPET; orig. a nursery term]

populace ('pɒpjʊləs) n (sometimes functioning as pl) 1 local inhabitants. 2 the common people; masses. [C16: via F from It. *popolaccio* the common herd, from *popolo* people, from L *populus*]

popular ('pɒpjʊlə) adj 1 widely favoured or admired. 2 favoured by an individual or limited group: *I'm not very popular with her.* 3 prevailing among the general public; common: *popular discontent.* 4 appealing to or comprehensible to the layman: *a popular lecture on physics.* ◆ 5 (usually pl) a cheap newspaper with a mass circulation. [C15: from L *populāris* of the people, democratic]
► **popularity** (,pɒpjʊ'lærɪtɪ) n ► **popularly** adv

popular front n (often cap.) any of the left-wing groups or parties that were organized from 1935 onwards to oppose the spread of fascism.

popularize or **popularise** ('pɒpjʊlə,raɪz) vb **popularizes, popularizing, popularized** or **popularises, popularising, popularised.** (tr) 1 to make popular. 2 to make or cause to become easily understandable or acceptable.
► **,populari'zation** or **,populari'sation** n ► **'popular,izer** or **'popular,iser** n

populate ('pɒpjʊ,leɪt) vb **populates, populating, populated.** (tr) 1 (often passive) to live in; inhabit. 2 to provide a population for; colonize or people. [C16: from Med. L *populāre*, from L *populus* people]

population (,pɒpjʊ'leɪʃən) n 1 (sometimes functioning as pl) all the persons inhabiting a specified place. 2 the number of such inhabitants. 3 (sometimes functioning as pl) all the people of a particular class in a specific area: *the Chinese population of San Francisco.* 4 the act or process of providing a place with inhabitants; colonization. 5 Ecology. a group of individuals of the same species inhabiting a given area. 6 Astron. either of two main groups of stars classified according to age and location. 7 Statistics. the entire aggregate of individuals or items from which samples are drawn.

population explosion n a rapid increase in the size of a population caused by such factors as a sudden decline in infant mortality or an increase in life expectancy.

population pyramid n a pyramid-shaped diagram illustrating the age distribution of a population: the youngest are represented by a rectangle at the base, the oldest by one at the apex.

populism ('pɒpjʊ,lɪzəm) or **popularism** n the practice, esp. by a politician of making a calculated appeal to the interests, tastes, or prejudices of ordinary people.

populist ('pɒpjʊlɪst) adj appealing to the interests or prejudices of ordinary people. ◆ n 2 a person, esp. a politician, who appeals to the interests or prejudices of ordinary people.

Populist ('pɒpjʊlɪst) n 1 US history. a member of the People's Party, formed largely by agrarian interests to contest the 1892 presidential election. ◆ adj 2 of or relating to the People's Party or any individual or movement with similar aims. Also: **Populistic.**
► **'Popu,lism** n

populous ('pɒpjʊləs) adj containing many inhabitants. [C15: from LL *populōsus*]
► **'populously** adv ► **'populousness** n

porangi ('pɔːræŋɪ) adj NZ inf. crazy; mad. [from Maori]

porbeagle ('pɔː,biːg°l) n any of several voracious sharks of northern seas. Also called: **mackerel shark.** [C18: from Cornish *porgh-bugel*, from ?]

porcelain ('pɔːslɪn) n 1 a more or less translucent ceramic material, the principal ingredients being kaolin and petuntse (hard paste) or other clays, bone ash, etc. 2 an object made of this or such objects collectively. 3 (modifier) of, relating to, or made from this material: *a porcelain cup.* [C16: from F *porcelaine*, from It. *porcellana* cowrie shell, lit.: relating to a sow, from *porcella* little sow, from *porca* sow, from L; see PORK]
► **porcellaneous** (,pɔːsə'leɪnɪəs) adj

porch (pɔːtʃ) n 1 a low structure projecting from the doorway of a house and forming a covered entrance. 2 US & Canad. a veranda. [C13: from F *porche*, from L *porticus* portico]

porcine ('pɔːsaɪn) adj of or characteristic of pigs. [C17: from L *porcīnus*, from *porcus* a pig]

porcupine ('pɔːkjʊ,paɪn) n any of various large rodents that have a body covering of protective spines or quills. [C14 *porc despyne* pig with spines, from OF *porc espin*; see PORK, SPINE]
► **'porcu,pinish** adj ► **'porcu,piny** adj

porcupine fish n any of various fishes of temperate and tropical seas having a body that is covered with sharp spines and can be inflated into a globe. Also called: **globefish.**

porcupine grass n Austral. another name for **spinifex.**

porcupine provisions pl n Finance. provisions, such as poison pills or staggered directorships, made in the bylaws of a company to deter takeover bids. Also called: **shark repellents.**

pore¹ (pɔː) vb **pores, poring, pored.** (intr) 1 (foll. by *over*) to make a close intent examination or study (of): *he pored over the documents for several hours.* 2 (foll. by *over, on,* or *upon*) to think deeply (about). 3 (foll. by *over, on,* or *upon*) Rare. to gaze fixedly (upon). [C13 *pouren*]

USAGE NOTE See at **pour.**

---

pore² (pɔː) n 1 any small opening in the skin or outer surface of an animal. 2 Bot. any small aperture, esp. that of a stoma, through which water vapour and gases pass. 3 any other small hole, such as a space in a rock, etc. [C14: from LL *porus*, from Gk *poros* passage, pore]

porgy ('pɔːgɪ) n, pl **porgy** or **porgies.** any of various perchlike fishes, many of which occur in American Atlantic waters. [C18: from Sp. *pargo*, from L *phager*, from Gk *phagros* sea bream]

Pori ★ (Finnish 'pori) n a port in SW Finland, on the Gulf of Bothnia. Pop.: 76 561 (1994). Swedish name: **Björneborg.**

poriferan (pɔː'rɪfərən) n any invertebrate of the phylum Porifera, which comprises the sponges. [C19: from NL *porifer* bearing pores]

Porirua ★ (,pɔːrɪ'ruːə) n a city in New Zealand, on the North Island, north of Wellington. Pop.: 46 601 (1991).

pork (pɔːk) *n* the flesh of pigs used as food. [C13: from OF *porc*, from L *porcus* pig]

porker ('pɔːkə) *n* a pig, esp. a young one, fattened to provide meat.

pork pie *n* **1** a pie filled with minced seasoned pork. **2** See **porky**[2].

porkpie hat ('pɔːk,paɪ) *n* a hat with a round flat crown and a brim that can be turned up or down.

porky[1] ('pɔːkɪ) *adj* **porkier, porkiest**. **1** characteristic of pork. **2** *Inf.* fat; obese.

porky[2] ('pɔːkɪ) *n, pl* **porkies**. *Brit. sl.* a lie. Also called: **pork pie**. [from rhyming slang *pork pie* lie]

porn (pɔːn) *or* **porno** ('pɔːnəʊ) *n, adj Inf.* short for **pornography** *or* **pornographic**.

pornography (pɔː'nɒɡrəfɪ) *n* **1** writings, pictures, films, etc., designed to stimulate sexual excitement. **2** the production of such material. ♦ Sometimes (informal) shortened to **porn** or **porno**. [C19: from Gk *pornographos* writing of harlots]
▸ **por'nographer** *n* ▸ **pornographic** (,pɔːnə'ɡræfɪk) *adj*
▸ **,porno'graphically** *adv*

poromeric (,pɔːrə'merɪk) *adj* **1** (of a plastic) permeable to water vapour. ♦ *n* **2** a substance having this characteristic, esp. one used in place of leather in making shoe uppers. [C20: from PORO(SITY) + (POLY)MER + -IC]

porous ('pɔːrəs) *adj* **1** permeable to water, air, or other fluids. **2** *Biol. & geol.* having pores. [C14: from Med. L *porōsus*, from LL *porus* PORE[2]]
▸ **'porously** *adv* ▸ **'porosity** (pɔː'rɒsɪtɪ) *or* **'porousness** *n*

porphyria (pɔː'fɪrɪə) *n* a hereditary disease of body metabolism, producing abdominal pain, mental confusion, etc. [C19: from NL, from *porphyrin* a purple substance excreted by patients suffering from this condition, from Gk *porphura* purple]

porphyry ('pɔːfɪrɪ) *n, pl* **porphyries**. **1** a reddish-purple rock consisting of large crystals of feldspar in a finer groundmass of feldspar, hornblende, etc. **2** any igneous rock with large crystals embedded in a finer groundmass of minerals. [C14 *porfurie*, from LL, from Gk *porphuritēs* (*lithos*) purple (stone), from *porphuros* purple]
▸ **,porphy'ritic** *adj*

Porphyry ★ ('pɔːfɪrɪ) *n* original name *Malchus*. 232–305 A.D., Greek Neo-Platonist philosopher, born in Syria; disciple and biographer of Plotinus.

porpoise ('pɔːpəs) *n, pl* **porpoises** *or* **porpoise**. any of various small cetacean mammals having a blunt snout and many teeth. [C14: from F *pourpois*, from Med. L *porcopiscus*, from L *porcus* pig + *piscis* fish]

porridge ('pɒrɪdʒ) *n* **1** a dish made from oatmeal or another cereal, cooked in water or milk to a thick consistency. **2** *Sl.* a term of imprisonment. [C16: var. (infl. by ME *porray* pottage) of POTTAGE]

porringer ('pɒrɪndʒə) *n* a small dish, often with a handle, for soup, porridge, etc. [C16: changed from ME *potinger, poteger*, from OF, from *potage* soup; see POTTAGE]

Porsena ('pɔːsɪnə) *or* **Porsenna** ★ (pɔː'senə) *n* **Lars** (lɑːz). 6th century B.C., a legendary Etruscan king, alleged to have besieged Rome in a vain attempt to reinstate Tarquinius Superbus on the throne.

port[1] (pɔːt) *n* **1** a town or place alongside navigable water with facilities for the loading and unloading of ships. **2** See **port of entry**. [OE, from L *portus*]

port[2] (pɔːt) *n* **1** Also called (formerly): **larboard**. the left side of an aircraft or vessel when facing the nose or bow. Cf. **starboard** (sense 1). ♦ *vb* **2** to turn or be turned towards the port. [C17: from ?]

port[3] (pɔːt) *n* a sweet fortified dessert wine. [C17: after *Oporto*, Portugal, from where it came orig.]

port[4] (pɔːt) *n* **1** *Naut.* **1a** an opening in the side of a ship, fitted with a watertight door, for access to the holds. **1b** See **porthole** (sense 1). **2** a small opening in a wall, armoured vehicle, etc., for firing through. **3** an aperture by which fluid enters or leaves the cylinder head of an engine, compressor, etc. **4** *Electronics.* a logical circuit for the input and ouput of data. **5** *Chiefly Scot.* a gate in a town or fortress. [OE, from L *porta* gate]

port[5] (pɔːt) *vb* (*tr*) *Mil.* to carry (a rifle, etc.) in a position

diagonally across the body with the muzzle near the left shoulder. [C14: from OF, from *porter* to carry, from L *portāre*]

port[6] (pɔːt) *n Austral.* (esp. in Queensland) a suitcase or school case. [C20: shortened from PORTMANTEAU]

Port. *abbrev. for:* **1** Portugal. **2** Portuguese.

portable ('pɔːtəbᵊl) *adj* **1** able to be carried or moved easily, esp. by hand. **2** (of computer software, files, etc.) able to be transferred from one type of computer system to another. ♦ *n* **3** an article designed to be readily carried by hand, such as a television, typewriter, etc. [C14: from LL *portābilis*, from L *portāre* to carry]
▸ **,porta'bility** *n* ▸ **'portably** *adv*

Port Adelaide ★ *n* the chief port of South Australia, near Adelaide on St Vincent Gulf. Pop.: 39 000 (latest est.).

Portadown ★ (,pɔːtə'daʊn) *n* a town in S Northern Ireland, in the district of Armagh. Pop.: 21 299 (1991).

portage ('pɔːtɪdʒ) *n* **1** the act of carrying; transport. **2** the cost of carrying or transporting. **3** the transporting of boats, supplies, etc., overland between navigable waterways. **4** the route used for such transport. ♦ *vb* **portages, portaging, portaged**. **5** to transport (boats, supplies, etc.) thus. [C15: from F, from OF *porter* to carry]

Portakabin ('pɔːtə,kæbɪn) *n Trademark.* a portable building quickly set up for use as a temporary office, etc.

portal ('pɔːtᵊl) *n* **1** an entrance, gateway, or doorway, esp. one that is large and impressive. **2** *Anat.* of or relating to a portal vein: *hepatic portal system*. [C14: via OF from Med. L *portāle*, from L *porta* gate]

portal vein *n* any vein connecting two capillary networks, esp. in the liver.

portamento (,pɔːtə'mentəʊ) *n, pl* **portamenti** (-tɪ). *Music.* a smooth slide from one note to another in which intervening notes are not separately discernible. [C18: from It.: a carrying, from L *portāre* to carry]

Port Arthur ★ *n* **1** a former penal settlement (1833–70) in Australia, on the S coast of the Tasman Peninsula, Tasmania. **2** the former name of **Lüshun**.

portative ('pɔːtətɪv) *adj* **1** a less common word for **portable**. **2** concerned with the act of carrying. [C14: from F, from L *portāre* to carry]

Port-au-Prince ★ ('pɔːtəʊ'prɪns; *French* pɔrtoprɛ̃s) *n* the capital and chief port of Haiti, in the south on the Gulf of Gonaïves: founded in 1749 by the French; university (1944). Pop.: 846 247 (1995 est.).

Port Blair ★ (bleə) *n* the capital of the Indian Union Territory of the Andaman and Nicobar Islands, a port on the SE coast of South Andaman Island: a former penal colony. Pop.: 74 955 (1991).

portcullis (pɔːt'kʌlɪs) *n* an iron or wooden grating suspended vertically in grooves in the gateway of a castle or town and able to be lowered so as to bar the entrance. [C14 *port colice*, from OF *porte coleïce* sliding gate, from *porte* door + *coleïce*, from *couler* to slide, from LL *cōlāre* to filter]

Porte (pɔːt) *n* short for Sublime Porte; the court or government of the Ottoman Empire. [C17: shortened from F *Sublime Porte* High Gate, rendering the Turkish title *Babi Ali*, the imperial gate, regarded as the seat of government]

porte-cochere (,pɔːtkɒ'ʃeə) *n* **1** a large covered entrance for vehicles leading into a courtyard. **2** a large roof projecting over a drive to shelter travellers entering or leaving vehicles. [C17: from F: carriage entrance]

Port Elizabeth ★ *n* a port in S South Africa, on Algoa Bay: motor-vehicle manufacture and fruit canning; resort. Pop.: 303 353 (1991).

portend (pɔː'tend) *vb* (*tr*) to give warning of; foreshadow. [C15: from L *portendere* to indicate]

portent ('pɔːtent) *n* **1** a sign of a future event; omen. **2** momentous or ominous significance: *a cry of dire portent*. **3** a marvel. [C16: from L *portentum* sign, from *portendere* to portend]

portentous (pɔː'tentəs) *adj* **1** of momentous or ominous significance. **2** miraculous, amazing, or awe-inspiring. **3** self-important or pompous.

★ people and places

orter[1] ('pɔːtə) n 1 a person employed to carry luggage, parcels, supplies, etc., at a railway station or hotel. 2 (in hospitals) a person employed to move patients from place to place. 3 US & Canad. a railway employee who waits on passengers, esp. in a sleeper. [C14: from OF portour, from LL portātōr, from L portāre to carry]
▶ 'porterage n

orter[2] ('pɔːtə) n 1 Chiefly Brit. a person in charge of a gate or door; doorman or gatekeeper. 2 a person employed as a caretaker and doorkeeper who also answers inquiries. 3 a person in charge of the maintenance of a building, esp. a block of flats. [C13: from OF portier, from LL portārius, from L porta door]

orter[3] ('pɔːtə) n Brit. a dark sweet ale brewed from black malt. [C18: from porter's ale, apparently because it was a favourite beverage of porters]

orter ★ ('pɔːtə) n 1 **Cole.** 1893–1964, US composer and lyricist of musical comedies. His most popular songs include Night and Day and Let's Do It. 2 **George**, 1st Baron. born 1920, British chemist, who shared a Nobel prize for chemistry in 1967 for his work on flash photolysis. 3 **Katherine Anne**. 1894–1980, US short-story writer and novelist. Her collections of stories include Flowering Judas (1930) and Pale Horse, Pale Rider (1939). 4 **Peter**. born 1929, Australian poet, living in Britain. 5 **Rodney Robert**. 1917–85, British biochemist: shared the Nobel prize for physiology or medicine (1972) for determining the structure of an antibody.

orterhouse ('pɔːtə,haus) n 1 Also called: **porterhouse steak**. a thick choice steak of beef cut from the middle ribs or sirloin. 2 (formerly) a place in which porter, beer, etc., and sometimes chops and steaks, were served. [C19 (sense 1): said to be after a porterhouse in New York]

ortfire ('pɔːt,faɪə) n a slow-burning fuse used for firing rockets and fireworks and, in mining, for igniting explosives. [C17: from F porte-feu, from porter to carry + feu fire]

ortfolio (pɔːt'fəʊlɪəʊ) n, pl **portfolios**. 1 a flat case, esp. of leather, used for carrying maps, drawings, etc. 2 the contents of such a case, such as drawings or photographs, that demonstrate recent work. 3 such a case used for carrying ministerial or state papers. 4 the responsibilities or role of the head of a government department: the portfolio for foreign affairs. 5 **Minister without portfolio**. a cabinet minister who is not responsible for any government department. 6 the complete investments held by an individual investor or a financial organization. [C18: from It. portafoglio, from portāre to carry + foglio leaf, from L folium]

ortfolio management n the service provided by an investment adviser who manages a financial portfolio on behalf of the investor.

ort-Gentil ★ (French pɔrʒãti) n the chief port of Gabon, in the west near the mouth of the Ogooué River: oil refinery. Pop.: 80 841 (1993).

ort Harcourt ★ ('hɑːkət, -kɔːt) n a port in S Nigeria, capital of Rivers state on the Niger delta: the nation's second largest port; industrial centre. Pop.: 399 700 (1995 est.).

orthole ('pɔːt,həʊl) n 1 a small aperture in the side of a vessel to admit light and air, fitted with a watertight cover. Sometimes shortened to **port**. 2 an opening in a wall or parapet through which a gun can be fired.

ortico ('pɔːtɪkəʊ) n, pl **porticoes** or **porticos**. 1 a covered entrance to a building; porch. 2 a covered walkway in the form of a roof supported by columns or pillars, esp. one built on to the exterior of a building. [C17: via It. from L porticus]

ortière (,pɔːtɪ'ɛə; French pɔrtjɛr) n a curtain hung in a doorway. [C19: via F from Med. L portāria, from L porta door]
▶ ,porti'èred adj

Orţile de Fier ★ (pɔr'tsiːlɛ dɛ 'fjɛr) n the Romanian name for the **Iron Gate**.

ortion ('pɔːʃən) n 1 a part of a whole. 2 a part allotted or belonging to a person or group. 3 an amount of food served to one person; helping. 4 Law. 4a a share of prop-

erty, esp. one coming to a child from the estate of his parents. 4b a dowry. 5 a person's lot or destiny. ◆ vb (tr) 6 to divide up; share out. 7 to give a share to (a person). [C13: via OF from L portiō]
▶ 'portionless adj

Port Jackson ★ n an inlet of the Pacific on the coast of SE Australia, forming a fine natural harbour: site of the city of Sydney, spanned by Sydney Harbour Bridge.

Portland[1] ★ ('pɔːtlənd) n 1 **Isle of**. a rugged limestone peninsula in SW England, in Dorset, connected to the mainland by a narrow isthmus and by Chesil Bank: the lighthouse at the S tip; famous for the quarrying of **Portland stone**, a fine building material. Pop.: 13 000 (latest est.). 2 an inland port in NW Oregon, on the Willamette River: the largest city in the state; shipbuilding and chemical industries. Pop.: 450 777 (1994 est.). 3 a port in SW Maine, on Casco Bay: the largest city in the state; settled by Englishmen in 1632, destroyed successively by French, Indian, and British attacks, and rebuilt; capital of Maine (1820–32). Pop.: 62 466 (1992 est.).

Portland[2] ★ ('pɔːtlənd) n 3rd Duke of. title of William Henry Cavendish Bentinck. 1738–1809, British statesman; prime minister (1783; 1807–09); father of Lord William Cavendish Bentinck.

Portland cement n a cement that hardens under water and is made by heating clay and crushed chalk or limestone. [C19: after the Isle of PORTLAND, because its colour resembles that of the stone quarried there]

Portlaoise ★ (,pɔːt'liːʃə) n a town in central Republic of Ireland, county town of Laois: site of a top-security prison. Pop.: 9500 (1990 est.).

Port Louis ★ ('luːɪs, 'luːɪ) n the capital and chief port of Mauritius, on the NW coast on the Indian Ocean. Pop.: 144 776 (1994 est.).

portly ('pɔːtlɪ) adj **portlier**, **portliest**. 1 stout or corpulent. 2 Arch. stately; impressive. [C16: from PORT[5] (in the sense: deportment)]
▶ 'portliness n

Port Lyautey ★ (ljəʊ'teɪ) n the former name (1932–56) of **Mina Hassan Tani**.

portmanteau (pɔːt'mæntəʊ) n, pl **portmanteaus** or **portmanteaux** (-təʊz). 1 (formerly) a large travelling case made of stiff leather, esp. one hinged at the back so as to open out into two compartments. 2 (modifier) embodying several uses or qualities: the heroine is a portmanteau figure of all the virtues. [C16: from F: cloak carrier]

portmanteau word n another name for **blend** (sense 7). [C19: from the idea that two meanings are packed into one word]

Port Moresby ★ ('mɔːzbɪ) n the capital and chief port of Papua New Guinea, on the SE coast on the Gulf of Papua: important Allied base in World War II. Pop.: 193 242 (1990).

Port Nicholson ★ n 1 the first British settlement in New Zealand, established on Wellington Harbour in 1840: grew into Wellington. 2 the former name for Wellington Harbour.

Pôrto ★ ('portu) n the Portuguese name for **Oporto**.

Pôrto Alegre ★ (Portuguese 'portu a'legri) n a port in S Brazil, capital of the Rio Grande do Sul state: the country's chief inland port; the chief commercial centre of S Brazil, with two universities (1936 and 1948). Pop. (city): 1 237 223 (1991); (urban area): 3 349 000 (1995).

Portobello ★ (,pɔːtəʊ'bɛləʊ) n a small port in Panama, on the Caribbean northeast of Colón: the most important port in South America in colonial times; declined with the opening of the. Panama Canal. Pop.: 3026 (1990 est.).

port of call n 1 a port where a ship stops. 2 any place visited on a traveller's itinerary.

port of entry n Law. an airport, harbour, etc., where customs officials are stationed to supervise the entry into and exit from a country of persons and merchandise.

Port of Spain ★ n the capital and chief port of Trinidad and Tobago, on the W coast of Trinidad. Pop.: 52 451 (1992 est.).

Porto Novo ★ ('pɔːtəu 'nəuvəu) *n* the capital of Benin, in the southwest on a coastal lagoon: formerly a centre of Portuguese settlement and the slave trade. Pop.: 177 660 (1992).

Porto Rico ★ ('pɔːtə 'riːkəu) *n* the former name (until 1932) of **Puerto Rico**.
▶ **Porto Rican** *adj, n*

Pôrto Velho ★ (*Portuguese* 'portu 'vɛʎu) *n* a city in W Brazil, capital of the federal territory of Rondônia on the Madeira River. Pop.: 226 198 (1991).

Port Phillip Bay *or* **Port Phillip** ★ *n* a bay in SE Australia, which forms the harbour of Melbourne.

portrait ('pɔːtrɪt, -treɪt) *n* **1** a painting or other likeness of an individual, esp. of the face. **2** a verbal description, esp. of a person's character. ♦ *adj* **3** *Printing.* (of an illustration in a book, magazine, etc.) of greater height than width. Cf. **landscape** (sense 5a). [C16: from F, from *portraire* to PORTRAY]
▶ **'portraitist** *n*

portraiture ('pɔːtrɪtʃə) *n* **1** the practice or art of making portraits. **2a** a portrait. **2b** portraits collectively. **3** a verbal description.

portray (pɔː'treɪ) *vb* (*tr*) **1** to make a portrait of. **2** to depict in words. **3** to play the part of (a character) in a play or film. [C14: from OF *portraire* to depict, from L *prōtrahere* to drag forth]
▶ **por'trayal** *n* ▶ **por'trayer** *n*

Port Royal ★ *n* **1** a fortified town in SE Jamaica, at the entrance to Kingston harbour: capital of Jamaica in colonial times. **2** the former name (until 1710) of **Annapolis Royal.**

Port Said ★ ('sɑːiːd, saɪd) *n* a port in NE Egypt, at the N end of the Suez Canal: founded in 1859 when the Suez Canal was begun; became the largest coaling station in the world and later an oil-bunkering port; damaged in the Arab–Israeli wars of 1967 and 1973. Pop.: 460 000 (1994 est.).

Port-Salut ('pɔː sə'luː; *French* pɔrsaly) *n* a mild semihard whole-milk cheese of a round flat shape. Also called: **Port du Salut.** [C19: named after the Trappist monastery at *Port du Salut* in NW France where it was first made]

Portsmouth ★ ('pɔːtsməθ) *n* **1** a port in S England, in Hampshire on the English Channel: Britain's chief naval base. Pop.: 174 690 (1991). Informal name: **Pompey. 2** a unitary authority in S England, in Hampshire. Pop.: 189 300 (1994 est.). Area: 37 sq. km (14 sq. miles). **3** a port in SE Virginia, on the Elizabeth River: naval base; shipyards. Pop.: 103 464 (1994 est.).

Port Sudan ★ *n* the chief port of the Sudan, in the NE on the Red Sea. Pop.: 305 385 (1993).

Port Talbot ★ ('tɔːlbət, 'tæl-) *n* a port in SE Wales, on Swansea Bay: established as a coal port in the mid-19th century. Pop.: 37 647 (1991).

Portugal ★ ('pɔːtjugʰl) *n* a republic in SW Europe, on the Atlantic: became an independent monarchy in 1139 and expelled the Moors in 1249 after more than four centuries of Muslim rule; became a republic in 1910; under the dictatorship of Salazar from 1932 until 1968, when he was succeeded by Dr Caetano, who was overthrown by a junta in 1974: constitutional government was restored in 1976; a member of the European Union. Official language: Portuguese. Religion: Roman Catholic. Currency: escudo and euro. Capital: Lisbon. Pop.: 9 943 000 (1997). Area: 91 231 sq. km (35 456 sq. miles).

Portuguese (ˌpɔːtjuˈɡiːz) *n* **1** the official language of Portugal and Brazil; it belongs to the Romance group of the Indo-European family. **2** (*pl* **Portuguese**) a native, citizen, or inhabitant of Portugal. ♦ *adj* **3** of Portugal, its inhabitants, or their language.

Portuguese East Africa ★ *n* a former name (until 1975) of **Mozambique.**

Portuguese Guinea ★ *n* the former name (until 1974) of **Guinea-Bissau.**
▶ **Portuguese Guinean** *adj, n*

Portuguese India ★ *n* a former Portuguese overseas province on the W coast of India, consisting of Goa, Daman, and Diu: established between 1505 and 1510; annexed by India in 1961.

Portuguese man-of-war *n* any of several large hydrozoans having an aerial float and long stinging tentacles. Sometimes shortened to **man-of-war.**

Portuguese Timor ★ *n* a former Portuguese overseas province in the Malay Archipelago, consisting of the east of the island of Timor, an enclave on the NW coast, and the islands of Ataúro and Jaco: annexed by Indonesia (1975).

Portuguese West Africa ★ *n* a former name (until 1975) of **Angola.**

portulaca (ˌpɔːtjuˈlækə, -ˈleɪkə) *n* any of a genus of plants of tropical and subtropical America, having yellow, pink, or purple showy flowers. [C16: from L: PURSLANE]

POS *abbrev. for* point of sale.

pose[1] (pəuz) *vb* **poses, posing, posed. 1** to assume or cause to assume a physical attitude, as for a photograph or painting. **2** (*intr;* often foll. by *as*) to present oneself (as something one is not). **3** (*intr*) to affect an attitude in order to impress others. **4** (*tr*) to put forward or ask: *to pose a question.* **5** (*intr*) *Sl.* to adopt a particular style of appearance and stand or strut around, esp. in bars, discotheques, etc., in order to attract attention. ♦ *n* **6** a physical attitude, esp. one deliberately adopted for an artist or photographer. **7** a mode of behaviour that is adopted for effect. [C14: from OF *poser* to set in place, from LL *pausāre* to cease, put down (infl. by L *pōnere* to place)]

pose[2] (pəuz) *vb* **poses, posing, posed.** (*tr*) *Rare.* to puzzle or baffle. [C16: from obs. *appose*, from L *appōnere* to put to]

Poseidon ★ (pɒ'saɪdʰn) *n Greek myth.* the god of the sea and of earthquakes; brother of Zeus, Hades, and Hera. He is generally depicted in art wielding a trident. Roman counterpart: **Neptune.**

Posen ★ ('pɔːzən) *n* the German name for **Poznań.**

poser[1] ('pəuzə) *n* **1** a person who poses. **2** *Inf.* a person who likes to be seen in trendsetting clothes in fashionable bars, discos, etc.

poser[2] ('pəuzə) *n* a baffling or insoluble question.

poseur (pəu'zɜː) *n* a person who strikes an attitude or assumes a pose in order to impress others. [C19: from F, from *poser* to POSE[1]]

posh (pɒʃ) *adj Inf., chiefly Brit.* **1** smart, elegant, or fashionable. **2** upper-class or genteel. [C19: often said to be an acronym of *port out, starboard home*, the most desirable location for a cabin in British ships sailing to & from the East, being the shaded side; but more likely from obs. sl. *posh* (n) a dandy]

posit ('pɒzɪt) *vb* (*tr*) **1** to assume or put forward as fact or the factual basis for an argument; postulate. **2** to put in position. [C17: from L *pōnere* to place]

position (pə'zɪʃən) *n* **1** place, situation, or location: *he took up a position to the rear.* **2** the appropriate or customary location: *the telescope is in position for use.* **3** the manner in which a person or thing is placed; arrangement. **4** *Mil.* an area or point occupied for tactical reasons. **5** point of view; stand: *what's your position on this issue?* **6** social status, esp. high social standing. **7** a post of employment; job. **8** the act of positing a fact or viewpoint. **9** something posited, such as an idea. **10** *Sport.* the part of a field or playing area where a player is placed or where he generally operates. **11** *Music.* the vertical spacing or layout of the written notes in a chord. **12** (in classical prosody) the situation in which a short vowel may be regarded as long, that is, when it occurs before two or more consonants. **13** *Finance.* the market commitment of a dealer in securities, currencies, or commodities: *a short position.* **14** **in a position.** (foll. by an infinitive) able (to). ♦ *vb* (*tr*) **15** to put in the proper or appropriate place; locate. **16** *Sport.* to place (oneself or another player) in a particular part of the field or playing area. [C15: from LL *positiō* a positioning, affirmation, from *pōnere* to place]
▶ **po'sitional** *adj*

positional notation *n* the method of denoting numbers by the use of a finite number of digits, each digit having its value multiplied by its place value, as in $936 = (9 \times 100) + (3 \times 10) + 6$.

osition audit *n Commerce.* a systematic assessment of the current strengths and weaknesses of an organization as a prerequisite for future strategic planning.

ositive ('pozɪtɪv) *adj* **1** expressing certainty or affirmation: *a positive answer.* **2** possessing actual or specific qualities; real: *a positive benefit.* **3** tending to emphasize what is good or laudable; constructive: *he takes a very positive attitude when correcting pupils' mistakes.* **4** tending towards progress or improvement. **5** *Philosophy.* constructive rather than sceptical. **6** (*prenominal*) *Inf.* (intensifier): *a positive delight.* **7** *Maths.* having a value greater than zero: *a positive number.* **8** *Maths.* **8a** measured in a direction opposite to that regarded as negative. **8b** having the same magnitude as but opposite sense to an equivalent negative quantity. **9** *Grammar.* denoting the usual form of an adjective as opposed to its comparative or superlative form. **10** *Physics.* **10a** (of an electric charge) having an opposite polarity to the charge of an electron and the same polarity as the charge of a proton. **10b** (of a body, system, ion, etc.) having a positive electric charge. **11** short for **electropositive.** **12** *Med.* (of the results of an examination or test) indicating the presence of a suspected disorder or organism. **13** *Economics.* of or denoting an analysis that is free of ethical, political, or value judgments. ♦ *n* **14** something that is positive. **15** *Maths.* a quantity greater than zero. **16** *Photog.* a print or slide showing a photographic image whose colours or tones correspond to those of the original subject. **17** *Grammar.* the positive degree of an adjective or adverb. **18** a positive object, such as a terminal or plate in a voltaic cell. [C13: from LL *positīvus*, from *pōnere* to place]
▶ 'positiveness *or* ˌposi'tivity *n*

ositive discrimination *n* the provision of special opportunities for a disadvantaged group.

ositive feedback *n* See **feedback** (sense 2).

ositively ('pozɪtɪvlɪ) *adv* **1** in a positive manner. **2** (intensifier): *he disliked her; in fact, he positively hated her.*

ositive vetting *n* the checking of a person's background, to assess his suitability for a position that may involve national security.

ositivism ('pozɪtɪˌvɪzəm) *n* **1** a form of empiricism, esp. as established by Auguste Comte, that rejects metaphysics and theology and holds that experimental investigation and observation are the only sources of substantial knowledge. See also **logical positivism.** **2** the quality of being definite, certain, etc.
▶ 'positivist *n, adj*

ositron ('pozɪˌtron) *n Physics.* the antiparticle of the electron, having the same mass but an equal and opposite charge. [C20: from *posi(tive + elec)tron*]

ositron emission tomography *n* a technique for assessing brain activity and function by recording the emission of positrons when radioactively labelled glucose, introduced into the brain, is metabolized.

ositronium (ˌpozɪ'trəʊnɪəm) *n Physics.* a short-lived entity consisting of a positron and an electron bound together.

osology (pə'solədʒɪ) *n* the branch of medicine concerned with the determination of appropriate doses of drugs or agents. [C19: from F *posologie,* from Gk *posos* how much]

oss. *abbrev. for:* **1** possession. **2** possessive. **3** possible. **4** possibly.

osse ('posɪ) *n* **1** *US.* short for **posse comitatus,** the ablebodied men of a district forming a group upon whom the sheriff may call for assistance in maintaining law and order. **2** *Sl.* a Jamaican street gang in the US. **3** *Inf.* a group of friends or associates. **4** (in W Canada) a troop of trained horses and riders who perform at stampedes. **5** *Law.* possibility (esp. in **in posse**). [C16: from Med. L (n): power, from L (vb): to be able]

osse comitatus (ˌkomɪ'tɑːtəs) *n* the formal legal term for **posse** (sense 1). [Med. L: strength (manpower) of the county]

ossess (pə'zɛs) *vb* (*tr*) **1** to have as one's property; own. **2** to have as a quality, characteristic, etc.: *to possess good*

eyesight. **3** to have knowledge of: *to possess a little French.* **4** to gain control over or dominate: *whatever possessed you to act so foolishly?* **5** (foll. by *of*) to cause to be the owner or possessor: *I am possessed of the necessary information.* **6** to have sexual intercourse with. **7** *Now rare.* to maintain (oneself or one's feelings) in a certain state or condition: *possess yourself in patience until I tell you the news.* [C15: from OF *possesser,* from L *possidēre*]
▶ pos'sessor *n* ▶ pos'sessory *adj*

possessed (pə'zɛst) *adj* **1** (foll. by *of*) owning or having. **2** (*usually postpositive*) under the influence of a powerful force, such as a spirit or strong emotion. **3** a less common term for **self-possessed.**

possession (pə'zɛʃən) *n* **1** the act of possessing or state of being possessed: *in possession of the crown.* **2** anything that is owned or possessed. **3** (*pl*) wealth or property. **4** the state of being controlled by or as if by evil spirits. **5** the occupancy of land, property, etc., whether or not accompanied by ownership: *to take possession of a house.* **6** a territory subject to a foreign state: *colonial possessions.* **7** *Sport.* control of the ball, puck, etc., as exercised by a player or team: *he got possession in his own half.*

possessive (pə'zɛsɪv) *adj* **1** of or relating to possession. **2** having or showing an excessive desire to possess or dominate: *a possessive husband.* **3** *Grammar.* **3a** another word for **genitive. 3b** denoting an inflected form of a noun or pronoun used to convey the idea of possession, association, etc., as *my* or *Harry's.* ♦ *n* **4** *Grammar.* **4a** the possessive case. **4b** a word or speech element in the possessive case.
▶ pos'sessively *adv* ▶ pos'sessiveness *n*

posset ('posɪt) *n* a drink of hot milk curdled with ale, beer, etc., flavoured with spices, formerly used as a remedy for colds. [C15 *poshoote,* from ?]

possibility (ˌposɪ'bɪlɪtɪ) *n, pl* **possibilities. 1** the state or condition of being possible. **2** anything that is possible. **3** a competitor, candidate, etc., who has a moderately good chance of winning, being chosen, etc. **4** (*often pl*) a future prospect or potential: *my new house has great possibilities.*

possible ('posɪb⁸l) *adj* **1** capable of existing, taking place, or proving true without contravention of any natural law. **2** capable of being achieved: *it is not possible to finish in three weeks.* **3** having potential: *the idea is a possible money-spinner.* **4** feasible but less than probable: *it is possible that man will live on Mars.* **5** *Logic.* (of a statement, formula, etc.) capable of being true under some interpretation or in some circumstances. ♦ *n* **6** another word for **possibility** (sense 3). [C14: from L *possibilis* that may be, from *posse* to be able]

> **USAGE NOTE** Although it is very common to talk about something being *very possible* or *more possible,* these uses are generally thought to be incorrect, since *possible* describes an absolute state, and therefore something can only be *possible* or *not possible: it is very likely* (not *very possible*) *that he will resign; it has now become easier* (not *more possible*) *to obtain an entry visa.*

possibly ('posɪblɪ) *sentence substitute, adv* **1a** perhaps or maybe. **1b** (*as sentence modifier*): *possibly he'll come.* ♦ *adv* **2** by any chance; at all: *he can't possibly come.*

possum ('posəm) *n* **1** an informal name for **opossum. 2** an Australian and New Zealand name for **phalanger. 3 play possum.** to pretend to be dead, ignorant, asleep, etc., in order to deceive an opponent. **4 stir the possum** *Austral. sl.* to cause trouble.

post¹ (pəʊst) *n* **1** a length of wood, metal, etc., fixed upright to serve as a support, marker, point of attachment, etc. **2** *Horse racing.* **2a** either of two upright poles marking the beginning (**starting post**) and end (**winning post**) of a racecourse. **2b** the finish of a horse race. ♦ *vb* (*tr*) **3** (sometimes foll. by *up*) to fasten or put up (a notice) in a public place. **4** to announce by or as if by means of a poster: *to post banns.* **5** to publish (a name) on a list. **6** to denounce publicly; brand. [OE, from L *postis*]

post² (pəʊst) *n* **1** a position to which a person is appointed or elected; appointment; job. **2** a position to which a person, such as a sentry, is assigned for duty. **3** a permanent military establishment. **4** *Brit.* either of two military bugle calls (**first post** and **last post**) giving notice of the time to retire for the night. **5** See **trading post.** ◆ *vb* **6** (*tr*) to assign to or station at a particular place or position. **7** *Chiefly Brit.* to transfer to a different unit or ship on taking up a new appointment, etc. [C16: from F *poste*, from It. *posto*, ult. from L *pōnere* to place]

post[3] (pəʊst) *n* **1** *Chiefly Brit.* letters, packages, etc., that are transported and delivered by the Post Office; mail. **2** *Chiefly Brit.* a single collection or delivery of mail. **3** *Brit.* an official system of mail delivery. **4** (formerly) any of a series of stations furnishing relays of men and horses to deliver mail over a fixed route. **5** a rider who carried mail between such stations. **6** *Brit.* a postbox or post office: *take this to the post.* **7** any of various book sizes, esp. 5¼ by 8¼ inches (**post octavo**). **8 by return of post.** *Brit.* by the next mail in the opposite direction. ◆ *vb* **9** (*tr*) *Chiefly Brit.* to send by post. US and Canad. word: **mail. 10** (*tr*) *Book-keeping.* **10a** to enter (an item) in a ledger. **10b** (often foll. by *up*) to compile or enter all paper items in (a ledger). **11** (*tr*) to inform of the latest news. **12** (*intr*) (formerly) to travel with relays of post horses. **13** *Arch.* to travel or dispatch with speed; hasten. ◆ *adv* **14** with speed; rapidly. **15** (formerly) by means of post horses. [C16: via F from It. *poste*, from L *posita* something placed, from *pōnere* to put]

post- *prefix* **1** after in time or sequence; following; subsequent: *postgraduate.* **2** behind; posterior to: *postorbital.* [from L, from *post* after, behind]

postage ('pəʊstɪdʒ) *n* **a** the charge for delivering a piece of mail. **b** (*as modifier*): *postage charges.*

postage meter *n Chiefly US & Canad.* a postal franking machine. Also called: **postal meter.**

postage stamp *n* **1** a printed paper label with a gummed back for attaching to mail as an official indication that the required postage has been paid. **2** a mark printed on an envelope, etc., serving the same function.

postal ('pəʊst°l) *adj* of or relating to a Post Office or to the mail-delivery service.
▸ **'postally** *adv*

postal note *n Austral. & NZ.* the usual name for **postal order.**

postal order *n* a written order for the payment of a sum of money, to a named payee, obtainable and payable at a post office.

postbag ('pəʊst,bæg) *n* **1** *Chiefly Brit.* another name for **mailbag. 2** the mail received by a magazine, radio programme, public figure, etc.

postbox ('pəʊst,bɒks) *n* another name for **letter box** (sense 2).

postcard ('pəʊst,kɑːd) *n* a card, often bearing a photograph, picture, etc., on one side (**picture postcard**), for sending a message by post without an envelope. Also called (US): **postal card.**

post chaise *n* a closed four-wheeled horse-drawn coach used as a rapid means for transporting mail and passengers in the 18th and 19th centuries. [C18: from POST[3] + CHAISE]

postclassical (pəʊst'klæsɪk°l) *adj* (esp. of Greek or Roman literature) later than the classical period.

postcode ('pəʊst,kəʊd) *n* a code of letters and digits used as part of a postal address to aid the sorting of mail. Also called: **postal code.** US name: **zip code.**

postconsonantal (pəʊst,kɒnsə'nænt°l) *adj* (of a speech sound) immediately following a consonant.

postdate (pəʊst'deɪt) *vb* **postdates, postdating, postdated.** (*tr*) **1** to write a future date on (a document, etc.), as on a cheque to prevent it being paid until then. **2** to assign a date to (an event, period, etc.) that is later than its previously assigned date of occurrence. **3** to be or occur at a later date than.

postdoctoral (pəʊst'dɒktərəl) *adj* of, relating to, or designating studies, research, or professional work above the level of a doctorate.

poster ('pəʊstə) *n* **1** a large printed picture, used for deco-

ration. **2** a placard or bill posted in a public place as an advertisement. **3** a person who posts bills.

poste restante ('pəʊst rɪ'stænt) *n* **1** an address on mail indicating that it should be kept at a specified post office until collected by the addressee. **2** the mail-delivery service or post-office department that handles mail having this address. ◆ US and Canad. equivalent: **general delivery.** [F, lit.: mail remaining]

posterior (pɒ'stɪərɪə) *adj* **1** situated at the back of or behind something. **2** coming after or following another in a series. **3** coming after in time. ◆ *n* **4** the buttocks; rump. [C16: from L: latter, from *posterius* coming next, from *post* after]
▸ **pos'teriorly** *adv*

posterity (pɒ'stɛrɪtɪ) *n* **1** future or succeeding generations. **2** all of one's descendants. [C14: from F *postérité*, from L *posteritās*, from *posterus* coming after, from *post* after]

postern ('pɒstən) *n* a back door or gate, esp. one that is for private use. [C13: from OF *posterne*, from LL *posterula* (*jānua*) a back (entrance), from *posterus* coming behind]

poster paint or **colour** *n* a gum-based opaque watercolour paint used for writing posters, etc.

postfeminist (pəʊst'fɛmɪnɪst) *adj* **1** resulting from or including the beliefs and ideas of feminism. **2** differing from or showing moderation of these beliefs and ideas. ◆ *n* **3** a person who believes in or advocates any of the ideas that have developed from the feminist movement.

post-Fordism (pəʊst'fɔːd,ɪzəm) *n* the idea that modern industrial production has moved away from mass production in huge factories, as pioneered by Henry Ford, towards specialized markets based on small flexible manufacturing units.
▸ **post-'Fordist** *adj*

post-free *adv, adj* **1** *Brit.* with the postage prepaid; postpaid. **2** free of postal charge.

postglacial (pəʊst'gleɪsɪəl, -ʃəl) *adj* formed or occurring after a glacial period.

postgraduate (pəʊst'grædjʊɪt) *n* **1** a student who has obtained a degree from a university, etc., and is pursuing studies for a more advanced qualification. **2** (*modifier*) of or relating to such a student or his studies. ◆ Also (US and Canad.): **graduate.**

posthaste (pəʊst'heɪst) *adv* **1** with great haste. ◆ *n* **2** *Arch.* great haste.

post horn *n* a simple valveless natural horn consisting of a long tube of brass or copper.

post horse *n* (formerly) a horse kept at an inn or post house for use by postriders or for hire to travellers.

post house *n* (formerly) a house or inn where horses were kept for postriders or for hire to travellers.

posthumous ('pɒstjʊməs) *adj* **1** happening or continuing after one's death. **2** (of a book, etc.) published after the author's death. **3** (of a child) born after the father's death. [C17: from L *postumus* the last, but modified as though from L *post* after + *humus* earth, that is, after the burial]
▸ **'posthumously** *adv*

posthypnotic suggestion (,pəʊsthɪp'nɒtɪk) *n* a suggestion made to the subject while he is in a hypnotic trance, to be acted upon at some time after emerging from the trance.

postiche (pɒ'stiːʃ) *adj* **1** (of architectural ornament) inappropriately applied; sham. **2** false or artificial; spurious. ◆ *n* **3** another term for **hairpiece** (sense 2). **4** anything that is false; sham or pretence. [C19: from F, from It. *apposticcio* (n), from LL *appositīcius* (adj); see APPOSITE]

postilion or **postillion** (pɒ'stɪljən) *n* a person who rides the near horse of the leaders in order to guide a team of horses drawing a coach. [C16: from F *postillon*, from It. *postiglione*, from *posta* POST[3]]

postimpressionism (,pəʊstɪm'prɛʃə,nɪzəm) *n* a movement in painting in France at the end of the 19th century which rejected the naturalism and momentary

★ people and places

effects of impressionism but adapted its use of pure colour to paint subjects with greater subjective emotion.
▶ ˌpostimˈpressionist *n, adj*

post-industrial (ˌpəʊstɪnˈdʌstrɪəl) *adj* denoting work or a society that is no longer based on heavy industry.

posting (ˈpəʊstɪŋ) *n* **1** an appointment to a position or post, usually in another town or country. **2** *Computing.* an electronic message sent to a bulletin board, website, etc., and intended for access by every user.

postliminy (pəʊstˈlɪmɪnɪ) *or* **postliminium** (ˌpəʊstlɪˈmɪnɪəm) *n, pl* **postliminies** *or* **postliminia** (-ɪə). *International law.* the right by which persons and property seized in war are restored to their former status on recovery. [C17: from L *post* behind + *limen, liminis* threshold]

postlude (ˈpəʊstluːd) *n Music.* a final or concluding piece or movement. [C19: from POST- + *-lude*, from L *lūdus* game; cf. PRELUDE]

postman (ˈpəʊstmən) *or* *(fem)* **postwoman** *n, pl* **postmen** *or* **postwomen**. a person who carries and delivers mail as a profession.

postman's knock *n* a children's party game in which a kiss is exchanged for a pretend letter.

postmark (ˈpəʊstˌmɑːk) *n* **1** any mark stamped on mail by postal officials, usually showing the date and place of posting. ◆ *vb* **2** *(tr)* to put such a mark on (mail).

postmaster (ˈpəʊstˌmɑːstə) *n* **1** Also *(fem)* **postmistress**. an official in charge of a local post office. **2** the person responsible for managing the electronic mail at a site.

postmaster general *n, pl* **postmasters general**. the executive head of the postal service in certain countries.

postmeridian (ˌpəʊstməˈrɪdɪən) *adj* after noon; in the afternoon or evening. [C17: from L *postmerīdiānus* in the afternoon]

post meridiem (ˈpəʊst məˈrɪdɪəm) the full form of **p.m.** [C17: L: after noon]

post mill *n* a windmill built around a central post on which the whole mill can be turned so that the sails catch the wind.

postmillennialism (ˌpəʊstmɪˈlenɪəˌlɪzəm) *n Christian theol.* the doctrine or belief that the Second Coming of Christ will be preceded by the millennium.
▶ ˌpostmilˈlennialist *n*

postmodernism (pəʊstˈmɒdəˌnɪzəm) *n* (in the arts, architecture, etc.) a style and school of thought that rejects the dogma and practices of any form of modernism; in architecture it contrasts with international modernism and features elements from several periods, esp. the Classical, often with ironic use of decoration.
▶ postˈmodernist *n, adj*

postmortem (pəʊstˈmɔːtəm) *adj* **1** *(prenominal)* occurring after death. ◆ *n* **2** analysis or study of a recent event: *a postmortem on a game of chess.* **3** See **postmortem examination**. [C18: from L, lit.: after death]

postmortem examination *n* dissection and examination of a dead body to determine the cause of death. Also called: **autopsy, necropsy**.

postnatal (pəʊstˈneɪtᵊl) *adj* of or relating to the period after childbirth.

post-obit (pəʊstˈəʊbɪt, -ˈɒbɪt) *Chiefly law.* ◆ *n* **1** a bond given by a borrower, payable after the death of a specified person, esp. one given to a moneylender by an expectant heir promising to repay when his interest falls into possession. ◆ *adj* **2** taking effect after death. [C18: from L *post obitum* after death]

post office *n* a building or room where postage stamps are sold and other postal business is conducted.

Post Office *n* a government department or authority in many countries responsible for postal services and often telecommunications.

post office box *n* a private numbered place in a post office, in which letters received are kept until called for.

postoperative (pəʊstˈɒpərətɪv) *adj* of or occurring in the period following a surgical operation.

post-paid *adv, adj* with the postage prepaid.

postpone (pəʊstˈpəʊn, pəˈspəʊn) *vb* **postpones, postponing,**

postponed. *(tr)* **1** to put off or delay until a future time. **2** to put behind in order of importance; defer. [C16: from L *postpōnere* to put after]
▶ postˈponement *n*

postpositive (pəʊstˈpɒzɪtɪv) *adj* **1** (of an adjective or other modifier) placed after the word modified, either immediately after, as in *two men abreast*, or as part of a complement, as in *those men are bad*. ◆ *n* **2** a postpositive modifier.

postprandial (pəʊstˈprændɪəl) *adj usually humorous.* after a meal.

postrider (ˈpəʊstˌraɪdə) *n* (formerly) a person who delivered post on horseback.

postscript (ˈpəʊsˌskrɪpt, ˈpəʊst-) *n* **1** a message added at the end of a letter, after the signature. **2** any supplement, as to a document or book. [C16: from LL *postscribere* to write after]

poststructuralism (pəʊstˈstrʌktʃərəˌlɪzəm) *n* an approach to literature that, proceeding from the tenets of structuralism, maintains that, as words have no absolute meaning, any text is open to an unlimited range of interpretations.
▶ postˈstructuralist *n, adj*

post-traumatic stress disorder *n* a psychological condition, characterized by anxiety, withdrawal, and a proneness to physical illness, that may follow a traumatic experience.

postulant (ˈpɒstjʊlənt) *n* a person who makes a request or application, esp. a candidate for admission to a religious order. [C18: from L *postulāns* asking, from *postulāre* to ask]

postulate *vb* (ˈpɒstjʊˌleɪt), **postulates, postulating, postulated**. *(tr; may take a clause as object)* **1** to assume to be true or existent; take for granted. **2** to ask, demand, or claim. **3** to nominate (a person) to a post or office subject to approval by a higher authority. ◆ *n* (ˈpɒstjʊlɪt). **4** something taken as self-evident or assumed as the basis of an argument. **5** a prerequisite. **6** a fundamental principle. **7** *Logic, maths.* an unproved statement that should be taken for granted: used as an initial premise in a process of reasoning. [C16: from L *postulāre* to ask for]
▶ ˌpostuˈlation *n*

postulator (ˈpɒstjʊˌleɪtə) *n RC Church.* a person who presents a plea for the beatification or canonization of some deceased person.

posture (ˈpɒstʃə) *n* **1** a position or attitude of the limbs or body. **2** a characteristic manner of bearing the body: *good posture.* **3** the disposition of the parts of a visible object. **4** a mental attitude. **5** a state or condition. **6** a false or affected attitude; pose. ◆ *vb* **postures, posturing, postured**. **7** to assume or cause to assume a bodily attitude. **8** *(intr)* to assume an affected posture; pose. [C17: via F from It. *postura*, from L *positūra*, from *pōnere* to place]
▶ ˈpostural *adj* ▶ ˈposturer *n*

postviral syndrome (ˌpəʊstˈvaɪrəl) *n* another name for **chronic fatigue syndrome**. Abbrev.: **PVS**.

postwar (pəʊstˈwɔː) *adj* happening or existing after a war.

posy (ˈpəʊzɪ) *n, pl* **posies**. **1** a small bunch of flowers. **2** *Arch.* a brief motto or inscription, esp. one on a trinket or a ring. [C16: var. of POESY]

pot[1] (pɒt) *n* **1** a container, usually round and deep and often having a handle and lid, used for cooking and other domestic purposes. **2** the amount that a pot will hold; potful. **3** a large mug or tankard. **4** *Austral.* any of various measures used for serving beer. **5** the money or stakes in the pool in gambling games. **6** a wicker trap for catching fish, esp. crustaceans: *a lobster pot.* **7** *Billiards, etc.* a shot by which a ball is pocketed. **8** a chamber pot, esp. a small one designed for a baby or toddler. **9** *(often pl)* *Inf.* a large amount (esp. of money). **10** *Inf.* a prize or trophy. **11** *Chiefly Brit.* short for **chimneypot**. **12** short for **flowerpot, teapot**. **13** See **potbelly**. **14** **go to pot**. to go to ruin. ◆ *vb* **pots, potting, potted**. *(mainly tr)* **15** to put or preserve (meat, etc.) in a pot. **16** to plant (a cutting, seedling, etc.) in soil in a flowerpot. **17** to cause (a baby or toddler) to use or sit on a pot. **18** to shoot (game) for food rather than for sport. **19** *(also intr)* to shoot casually or without careful aim. **20** (*also intr*) to shape clay as a potter. **21** *Billiards, etc.* to pocket (a ball). **22** *Inf.* to capture or win. [LOE *pott*, from Med. L *pottus* (unattested), ?from L *pōtus* a drink]

pot[2] (pɒt) *n Sl.* cannabis used as a drug in any form. [C20: ? shortened from Mexican Indian *potiguaya*]

potable ('pəʊtəb³l) *adj* drinkable. [C16: from LL *pōtābilis* drinkable, from L *pōtāre* to drink]
▸ ˌpota'bility *n*

potae ('pɒtaɪ) *n NZ.* a hat. [Maori]

potage *French.* (pɒtaʒ; *English* pəʊ'tɑːʒ) *n* any thick soup. [C16: from OF; see POTTAGE]

potamic (pə'tæmɪk) *adj* of or relating to rivers. [C19: from Gk *potamos* river]

potash ('pɒt,æʃ) *n* **1** another name for **potassium carbonate** or **potassium hydroxide. 2** potassium chemically combined in certain compounds: *chloride of potash.* [C17 *pot ashes*, translation of obs. Du. *potaschen;* because orig. obtained by evaporating the lye of wood ashes in pots]

potassium (pə'tæsɪəm) *n* a light silvery element of the alkali metal group that is highly reactive and rapidly oxidizes in air. Symbol: K; atomic no.: 19; atomic wt.: 39.098. [C19: NL *potassa* potash]
▸ po'tassic *adj*

potassium-argon dating *n* a technique for determining the age of minerals based on the occurrence in natural potassium of a small fixed amount of radioisotope ^{40}K that decays to the stable argon isotope ^{40}Ar with a half-life of 1.28×10^9 years. Measurement of the ratio of these isotopes thus gives the age of the mineral.

potassium bromide *n* a white crystalline soluble substance with a bitter saline taste used in making photographic papers and plates and in medicine as a sedative. Formula: KBr.

potassium carbonate *n* a white odourless substance used in making glass and soft soap and as an alkaline cleansing agent. Formula: K_2CO_3.

potassium chlorate *n* a white crystalline soluble substance used in explosives and as a disinfectant and bleaching agent. Formula: $KClO_3$.

potassium cyanide *n* a white poisonous granular soluble solid substance used in photography. Formula: KCN.

potassium hydrogen tartrate *n* a white soluble crystalline salt used in baking powders, soldering fluxes, and laxatives. Formula: $KHC_4H_4O_6$. Also called: **cream of tartar.**

potassium hydroxide *n* a white deliquescent alkaline solid used in the manufacture of soap, liquid shampoos, and detergents. Formula: KOH.

potassium nitrate *n* a colourless or white crystalline compound·used in gunpowders, pyrotechnics, fertilizers, and as a preservative for foods (**E 252**). Formula: KNO_3. Also called: **saltpetre, nitre.**

potassium permanganate *n* a dark purple poisonous odourless soluble crystalline solid, used as a bleach, disinfectant, and antiseptic. Formula: $KMnO_4$. Systematic name: **potassium manganate(V).**

potation (pəʊ'teɪʃən) *n* **1** the act of drinking. **2** a drink or draught, esp. of alcoholic drink. [C15: from L *pōtātiō*, from *pōtāre* to drink]

potato (pə'teɪtəʊ) *n, pl* **potatoes. 1a** a plant of South America widely cultivated for its edible tubers. **1b** the starchy oval tuber of this plant, which has a brown or red skin and is cooked and eaten as a vegetable. **2** any of various similar plants, esp. the sweet potato. [C16: from Sp. *patata* white potato, from Taino *batata* sweet potato]

potato beetle *n* another name for the **Colorado beetle.**

potato chip *n* (*usually pl*) **1** another name for **chip** (sense 4). **2** the US, Canad., Austral., and NZ term for **crisp** (sense 10).

potato crisp *n* (*usually pl*) another name for **crisp** (sense 10).

potbelly ('pɒt,belɪ) *n, pl* **potbellies. 1** a protruding or distended belly. **2** a person having such a belly.
▸ 'pot,bellied *adj*

potboiler ('pɒt,bɔɪlə) *n Inf.* an artistic work of little merit produced quickly to make money.

pot-bound *adj* (of a pot plant) having grown to fill all the available root space and therefore lacking room for continued growth.

potboy ('pɒt,bɔɪ) *or* **potman** ('pɒtmən) *n, pl* **potboys** *or* **potmen.** *Chiefly Brit.* (esp. formerly) a man employed at a public house to serve beer, etc.

potch (pɒtʃ) *n Chiefly Austral., sl.* inferior quality opal. [C20: from ?]

poteen (pɒ'tiːn) *or* **poitín** (pɒ'tʃiːn) *n* (in Ireland) illicit spirit, often distilled from potatoes. [C19: from Irish *poitín* little pot, from *pota* pot]

Potemkin *or* **Potyomkin** ★ (pɒ'temkɪn; *Russian* pa'tjomkɪn) *n* **Grigori Aleksandrovich** (gri'gɔrij alɪk'sandrəvitʃ). 1739–91, Russian soldier and statesman; lover of Catherine II, whose favourite he remained until his death.

potent[1] ('pəʊt³nt) *adj* **1** possessing great strength; powerful. **2** (of arguments, etc.) persuasive or forceful. **3** influential or authoritative. **4** tending to produce violent physical or chemical effects: *a potent poison.* **5** (of a male) capable of having sexual intercourse. [C15: from L *posse* to be able, from *posse* to be able]
▸ 'potency *or* 'potence *n* ▸ 'potently *adv*

potent[2] ('pəʊt³nt) *adj Heraldry.* (of a cross) having flat bars across the ends of the arms. [C17: from obs. *potent* a crutch, from L *potentia* power]

potentate ('pəʊt³n,teɪt) *n* a ruler or monarch. [C14: from LL *potentātus*, from L: rule, from *potens* powerful, from *posse* to be able]

potential (pə'tenʃəl) *adj* **1a** possible but not yet actual. **1b** (*prenominal*) capable of being or becoming; latent. **2** *Grammar.* (of a verb) expressing possibility, as English *may* and *might.* ◆ *n* **3** latent but unrealized ability: *Jones has great potential as a sales manager.* **4** *Grammar.* a potential verb or verb form. **5** short for **electric potential.** [C14: from OF *potencial,* from LL *potentiālis,* from L *potentia* power]
▸ po'tentially *adv*

potential difference *n* the difference in electric potential between two points in an electric field; the work that has to be done in transferring unit positive charge from one point to the other, measured in volts. Abbrev.: **pd.**

potential energy *n* the energy of a body or system as a result of its position in an electric, magnetic, or gravitational field. Abbrev.: **PE.**

potentiality (pə,tenʃɪ'ælɪtɪ) *n, pl* **potentialities. 1** latent or inherent capacity for growth, fulfilment, etc. **2** a person or thing that possesses this.

potentiate (pə'tenʃɪ,eɪt) *vb* **potentiates, potentiating, potentiated.** (*tr*) **1** to cause to be potent. **2** *Med.* to increase (the individual action or effectiveness) of two drugs by administering them in combination.

potentilla (,pəʊt³n'tɪlə) *n* any rosaceous plant or shrub of the N temperate genus *Potentilla,* having five-petalled flowers. [C16: NL, from Med. L: garden valerian, from L *potēns* powerful]

potentiometer (pə,tenʃɪ'ɒmɪtə) *n* **1** an instrument for determining a potential difference of electromotive force. **2** a device used in electronic circuits, esp. as a volume control. Sometimes shortened to **pot.**
▸ po,tenti'ometry *n*

potful ('pɒtful) *n* the amount held by a pot.

pother ('pɒðə) *n* **1** a commotion, fuss, or disturbance. **2** a choking cloud of smoke, dust, etc. ◆ *vb* **3** to make or be troubled or upset. [C16: from ?]

potherb ('pɒt,hɜːb) *n* any plant having leaves, flowers, stems, etc., that are used in cooking.

pothole ('pɒt,həʊl) *n* **1** *Geog.* **1a** a deep hole in limestone areas resulting from action by running water. **1b** a circular hole in the bed of a river produced by abrasion. **2** a deep hole produced in a road surface by wear or weathering.

potholing ('pɒt,həʊlɪŋ) *n Brit.* a sport in which participants explore underground caves.
▸ 'pot,holer *n*

★ people and places

pothook ('pɒt,hʊk) n **1** a curved or S-shaped hook used for suspending a pot over a fire. **2** a long hook used for lifting hot pots, lids, etc. **3** an S-shaped mark, often made by children when learning to write.

pothouse ('pɒt,haʊs) n Brit. (formerly) a small tavern or pub.

pothunter ('pɒt,hʌntə) n **1** a person who hunts for profit without regard to the rules of sport. **2** Inf. a person who enters competitions for the sole purpose of winning prizes.

potion ('pəʊʃən) n a drink, esp. of medicine, poison, or some supposedly magic beverage. [C13: via OF from L pōtiō a drink, esp. a poisonous one, from pōtāre to drink]

Potiphar ★ ('pɒtɪfə) n Old Testament. one of Pharaoh's officers, who bought Joseph as a slave (Genesis 37:36).

potlatch ('pɒt,lætʃ) n Anthropol. a competitive ceremonial activity among certain North American Indians, involving a lavish distribution of gifts to emphasize the wealth and status of the chief or clan. [C19: of Amerind origin, from patshatl a present]

pot luck n Inf. **1** whatever food happens to be available without special preparation. **2** whatever is available (esp. in **take pot luck**).

pot marigold n a Central European and Mediterranean plant grown for its rayed orange-and-yellow showy flowers.

Potomac ★ (pə'təʊmək) n a river in the E central US, rising in the Appalachian Mountains of West Virginia: flows northeast, then generally southeast to Chesapeake Bay. Length (from the confluence of headstreams): 462 km (287 miles).

potometer (pə'tɒmɪtə) n an apparatus that measures the rate of water uptake by a plant or plant part. [from L pōtāre to drink + -METER]

potoroo (,pɒtə'ruː) n another name for **kangaroo rat**. [from Abor.]

Potosí ★ (Spanish poto'si) n a city in S Bolivia, at an altitude of 4066 m (13 340 ft): one of the highest cities in the world; developed with the discovery of local silver in 1545; tin mining; university (1571). Pop.: 123 327 (1993 est.).

potpourri (,pəʊ'pʊərɪ) n, pl **potpourris**. **1** a collection of mixed flower petals dried and preserved in a pot to scent the air. **2** a collection of unrelated items; miscellany. **3** a medley of popular tunes. [C18: from F, lit.: rotten pot, translation of Sp. olla podrida miscellany]

pot roast n meat cooked slowly in a covered pot with very little water.

Potsdam ★ ('pɒtsdæm; German 'pɔtsdam) n a city in Germany, the capital of Brandenburg on the Havel River: residence of Prussian kings and German emperors and scene of the **Potsdam Conference** of 1945. Pop.: 138 268 (1995 est.).

potsherd ('pɒt,ʃɜːd) or **potshard** ('pɒt,ʃɑːd) n a broken fragment of pottery. [C14: from POT[1] + schoord piece of broken crockery; see SHARD]

pot shot n **1** a chance shot taken casually, hastily, or without careful aim. **2** a shot fired to kill game in disregard of the rules of sport. **3** a shot fired at quarry within easy range.

pot still n a type of still in which heat is applied directly to the pot in which the wash is contained: used in distilling whisky.

pottage ('pɒtɪdʒ) n a thick soup. [C13: from OF potage contents of a pot, from pot POT[1]]

potted ('pɒtɪd) adj **1** placed or grown in a pot. **2** cooked or preserved in a pot: potted shrimps. **3** Inf. abridged: a potted version of a novel.

potter[1] ('pɒtə) n a person who makes pottery.

potter[2] ('pɒtə) or esp. US & Canad. **putter** vb **1** (intr; often foll. by about or around) to busy oneself in a desultory though agreeable manner. **2** (intr; often foll. by along or about) to move with little energy or direction: to potter about town. **3** (tr; usually foll. by away) to waste (time): to potter the day away. [C16 (in the sense: to poke repeatedly): from OE potian to thrust]
▶ 'potterer or esp. US 'putterer n

Potter ★ ('pɒtə) n **1 (Helen) Beatrix**. 1866–1943, British author and illustrator of children's animal stories, such as The Tale of Peter Rabbit (1902). **2 Dennis (Christopher George)**. 1935–94, British playwright. His TV successes include Pennies from Heaven (1978) and The Singing Detective (1986). **3 Paulus**. 1625–54, Dutch painter, esp. of animals.

Potteries ★ ('pɒtərɪz) pl n **the**. (sometimes functioning as sing) a region of W central England, in Staffordshire, in which the china industries are concentrated.

potter's field n **1** New Testament. the land bought by the Sanhedrin with the money paid for the betrayal of Jesus, to be used as a burial place for strangers (Acts 1:19; Matthew 27:7). **2** US. a cemetery where the poor or unidentified are buried at the public's expense.

potter's wheel n a device with a horizontal rotating disc, on which clay is shaped by hand.

pottery ('pɒtərɪ) n, pl **potteries**. **1** articles made from earthenware and baked in a kiln. **2** a place where such articles are made. **3** the craft or business of making such articles. [C15: from OF poterie, from potier potter, from pot POT[1]]

potting shed n a building in which plants are set in flowerpots and in which empty pots, potting compost, etc., are stored.

pottle ('pɒt°l) n Arch. a liquid measure equal to half a gallon. [C14 potel, from OF: a small POT[1]]

potto ('pɒtəʊ) n, pl **pottos**. a short-tailed prosimian primate having vertebral spines protruding through the skin in the neck region. Also called: **kinkajou**. [C18: of W African origin]

Pott's disease (pɒts) n a disease of the spine, characterized by weakening and gradual disintegration of the vertebrae. [C18: after Percivall Pott (1714–88), Brit. surgeon]

Pott's fracture n a fracture of the lower part of the fibula, usually with the dislocation of the ankle. [C18: see POTT'S DISEASE]

potty[1] ('pɒtɪ) adj **pottier, pottiest**. Brit. inf. **1** foolish or slightly crazy. **2** trivial or insignificant. **3** (foll. by about) very keen (on). [C19: ?from POT[1]]
▶ 'pottiness n

potty[2] ('pɒtɪ) n, pl **potties**. a child's word for **chamber pot**.

Potyomkin ★ (Russian pa'tjomkin) n a variant spelling of **Potemkin**.

pouch (paʊtʃ) n **1** a small flexible baglike container: a tobacco pouch. **2** a saclike structure in any of various animals, such as the cheek fold in rodents. **3** Anat. any sac, pocket, or pouchlike cavity. **4** a Scot. word for **pocket**. ◆ vb **5** (tr) to place in or as if in a pouch. **6** to arrange or become arranged in a pouchlike form. **7** (tr) (of certain birds and fishes) to swallow. [C14: from OF pouche, from OF poche bag]
▶ 'pouchy adj

pouf or **pouffe** (puːf) n **1** a large solid cushion used as a seat. **2a** a woman's hairstyle, fashionable esp. in the 18th century, in which the hair is piled up in rolled puffs. **2b** a pad set in the hair to make such puffs. **3** (also puf). Brit. derog. sl. less common spellings of **poof**. [C19: from F]

poulard or **poularde** ('puːlɑːd) n a hen that has been spayed for fattening. Cf. **capon**. [C18: from OF pollarde, from polle hen]

Poulenc ★ (French pulɛ̃k) n **Francis** (frɑ̃sis). 1899–1963, French composer; a member of Les Six. His works include the operas Les Mamelles de Tirésias (1947) and Dialogues des Carmélites (1957), and the ballet Les Biches (1924).

poult (pəʊlt) n the young of a gallinaceous bird, esp. of domestic fowl. [C15: var. of poulet PULLET]

poulterer ('pəʊltərə) n Brit. another word for a **poultryman**. [C17: from obs. poulter, from OF pouletier, from poulet PULLET]

poultice ('pəʊltɪs) n Med. a local moist and often heated application to the skin used to improve the circulation, treat inflamed areas, etc. [C16: from earlier pultes, from L puls a thick porridge]

poultry ('pəʊltrɪ) *n* domestic fowls collectively. [C14: from OF *pouletrie*, from *pouletier* poultry dealer]

poultryman ('pəʊltrɪmən) *or* **poulterer** *n, pl* **poultrymen** *or* **poulterers. 1** Also called: **chicken farmer.** a person who rears domestic fowls for their eggs or meat. **2** a dealer in poultry.

pounce[1] (paʊns) *vb* **pounces, pouncing, pounced. 1** (*intr;* often foll. by *on* or *upon*) to spring or swoop, as in capturing prey. ◆ *n* **2** the act of pouncing; a spring or swoop. **3** the claw of a bird of prey. [C17: apparently from ME *punson* pointed tool]
▸ **'pouncer** *n*

pounce[2] (paʊns) *n* **1** a very fine resinous powder, esp. of cuttlefish bone, formerly used to dry ink. **2** a fine powder, esp. of charcoal, that is tapped through perforations in paper in order to transfer the design to another surface. ◆ *vb* **pounces, pouncing, pounced.** (*tr*) **3** to dust (paper) with pounce. **4** to transfer (a design) by means of pounce. [C18: from OF *ponce,* from L *pūmex* pumice]

pouncet box ('paʊnsɪt) *n* a box with a perforated top used for perfume. [C16 *pouncet,* ? alteration of *pounced* perforated]

pound[1] (paʊnd) *vb* **1** (when *intr,* often foll. by *on* or *at*) to strike heavily and often. **2** (*tr*) to beat to a pulp; pulverize. **3** (*tr;* foll. by *out*) to produce, as by typing heavily. **4** to walk or move with heavy steps or thuds. **5** (*intr*) to throb heavily. ◆ *n* **6** the act of pounding. [OE *pūnian*]
▸ **'pounder** *n*

pound[2] (paʊnd) *n* **1** an avoirdupois unit of weight that is divided into 16 ounces and is equal to 0.453 592 kilograms. Abbrev.: **lb. 2** a troy unit of weight divided into 12 ounces equal to 0.373 242 kilograms. **3a** the standard monetary unit of the United Kingdom, divided into 100 pence. Official name: **pound sterling. 3b** (*as modifier*): *a pound coin.* **4** the standard monetary unit of various other countries, including Cyprus, Egypt, Israel, and Syria. **5** Also called: **pound Scots.** a former Scottish monetary unit originally worth an English pound but later declining in value to 1 shilling 8 pence. [OE *pund,* from L *pondō*]

pound[3] (paʊnd) *n* **1** an enclosure for keeping officially removed vehicles or distrained goods or animals, esp. stray dogs. **2** a place where people are confined. **3** a trap for animals. ◆ *vb* **4** (*tr*) to confine in or as if in a pound; impound, imprison, or restrain. [C14: from LOE *pund-,* as in *pundfeald* PINFOLD]

Pound ★ (paʊnd) *n* **Ezra** (**Loomis**). 1885–1972, US poet, translator, and critic, living in Europe. Indicted for treason by the US government (1945) for pro-Fascist broadcasts during World War II, he was committed to a mental hospital until 1958. His life work, the *Cantos* (1925–70), is an unfinished sequence of poems, which incorporates mythological and historical materials in several languages as well as political, economic, and autobiographical elements.

poundage ('paʊndɪdʒ) *n* **1** a charge of so much per pound of weight. **2** a charge of so much per pound sterling. **3** a weight expressed in pounds.

poundal ('paʊnd²l) *n* the fps unit of force; the force that imparts an acceleration of 1 foot per second per second to a mass of 1 pound. Abbrev.: **pdl.** [C19: from POUND[2] + QUINTAL]

pound cost averaging *n Stock Exchange.* a method of accumulating capital by investing a fixed sum in a particular security at regular intervals, in order to achieve an average purchase price below the arithmetic average of the market prices on the purchase dates.

-pounder ('paʊndə) *n* (*in combination*) **1** something weighing a specified number of pounds: *a 200-pounder.* **2** something worth a specified number of pounds: *a ten-pounder.* **3** a gun that discharges a shell weighing a specified number of pounds: *a two-pounder.*

pound sterling *n* See **pound**[2] (sense 3).

pour (pɔː) *vb* **1** to flow or cause to flow in a stream. **2** (*tr*) to emit in a profuse way. **3** (*intr;* often foll. by *down*) Also: **pour with rain.** to rain heavily. **4** (*intr*) to move together in large numbers; swarm. **5** (*intr*) to serve tea, coffee, etc.: *shall I pour?* **6 it never rains but it pours.** events, esp. unfortunate ones, come in rapid succession. **7 pour oil on troubled waters.** to calm a quarrel, etc. ◆ *n* **8** a pouring, downpour, etc. [C13: from ?]
▸ **'pourer** *n*

pourboire *French.* (purbwar) *n* a tip; gratuity. [lit.: for drinking]

poussin (*French* pusɛ̃) *n* a young chicken reared for eating. [from F]

Poussin ★ (*French* pusɛ̃) *n* **Nicolas** (nikɔla). 1594–1665, French painter, regarded as a leader of French classical painting. He is best known for the austere historical and biblical paintings and landscapes of his later years.

pout[1] (paʊt) *vb* **1** to thrust out (the lips), as when sullen or (of the lips) to be thrust out. **2** (*intr*) to swell out; protrude. **3** (*tr*) to utter with a pout. ◆ *n* **4** Also: **the pouts.** a fit of sullenness. **5** the act or state of pouting. [C14: from ?]
▸ **'poutingly** *adv*

pout[2] (paʊt) *n, pl* **pout** *or* **pouts. 1** short for **eelpout. 2** Also called: **horned pout.** a N American catfish with barbels round the mouth. **3** any of various gadoid food fishes. [OE *-pūte,* as in *ælepūte* eelpout]

pouter ('paʊtə) *n* **1** a person or thing that pouts. **2** a breed of domestic pigeon with a large crop capable of being greatly puffed out.

poverty ('pɒvətɪ) *n* **1** the condition of being without adequate food, money, etc. **2** scarcity: *a poverty of wit.* **3** a lack of elements conducive to fertility in soil. [C12: from OF *poverté,* from L *paupertās* restricted means, from *pauper* poor]

poverty-stricken *adj* suffering from extreme poverty.

poverty trap *n* the situation of being unable to raise one's living standard because one is dependent on state benefits which are reduced or withdrawn if one gains any extra income.

pow (paʊ) *interj* an exclamation imitative of a collision, explosion, etc.

POW *abbrev. for* prisoner of war.

powan ('paʊən) *n* a freshwater whitefish occurring in some Scottish lakes. [C17: Scot. var. of POLLAN]

powder ('paʊdə) *n* **1** a substance in the form of tiny loose particles. **2** any of various preparations in this form, such as gunpowder, face powder, or soap powder. ◆ *vb* **3** to turn into powder; pulverize. **4** (*tr*) to cover or sprinkle with or as if with powder. [C13: from OF *poldre,* from L *pulvis* dust]
▸ **'powderer** *n* ▸ **'powdery** *adj*

powder blue *n* a dusty pale blue colour.

powder burn *n* a superficial burn of the skin caused by a momentary intense explosion.

powder flask *n* a small flask or case formerly used to carry gunpowder.

powder horn *n* a powder flask consisting of the hollow horn of an animal.

powder keg *n* **1** a small barrel to hold gunpowder. **2** a potential source of violence, disaster, etc.

powder metallurgy *n* the science and technology of producing solid metal components from metal powder by compaction and sintering.

powder monkey *n* (formerly) a boy who carried powder from the magazine to the guns on warships.

powder puff *n* a soft pad of fluffy material used for applying cosmetic powder to the skin.

powder room *n* a ladies' cloakroom.

powdery mildew *n* a plant disease characterized by a white powdery growth on stems and leaves, caused by parasitic fungi.

Powell ★ ('paʊəl) *n* **1** ('pəʊəl). **Anthony** (**Dymoke**). born 1905, British novelist, best known for his sequence of novels *A Dance to the Music of Time* (1951–75). **2 Cecil**

Frank. 1903–69, British physicist, who was awarded the Nobel prize for physics (1950) for his discovery of the pi-meson. **3 Earl,** known as *Bud Powell*. 1924–1966, US modern-jazz pianist. **4 (John) Enoch.** 1912–98, British politician. An opponent of Commonwealth immigration, he resigned from the Conservative Party, returning to Parliament as a United Ulster Unionist Council member (1974–87). **5 Michael.** 1905–90, British film writer, producer, and director, best known for his collaboration (1942–57) with Emeric Pressburger. Films include *The Life and Death of Colonel Blimp* (1943), *A Matter of Life and Death* (1946), and *Peeping Tom* (1960).

power ('pauə) *n* **1** ability to do something. **2** (*often pl*) a specific ability, capacity, or faculty. **3** political, financial, social, etc., force or influence. **4** control or dominion or a position of control, dominion, or authority. **5** a state or other political entity with political, industrial, or military strength. **6** a person or group that exercises control, influence, or authority: *he's a power in the state.* **7** a prerogative, privilege, or liberty. **8** legal authority to act for another. **9a** a military force. **9b** military potential. **10** *Maths.* **10a** the value of a number or quantity raised to some exponent. **10b** another name for **exponent** (sense 4). **11** *Physics, engineering.* a measure of the rate of doing work expressed as the work done per unit time. It is measured in watts, horsepower, etc. **12a** the rate at which electrical energy is fed into or taken from a device or system. It is measured in watts. **12b** (*as modifier*): *a power amplifier.* **13** the ability to perform work. **14a** mechanical energy as opposed to manual labour. **14b** (*as modifier*): *a power tool.* **15** a particular form of energy: *nuclear power.* **16a** a measure of the ability of a lens or optical system to magnify an object. **16b** another word for **magnification. 17** *Inf.* a large amount: *a power of good.* **18** in one's **power.** (*often foll. by an infinitive*) able or allowed (to). **19 in (someone's) power.** under the control of (someone). **20 the powers that be.** established authority. ♦ *vb* **21** (*tr*) to give or provide power to. **22** (*tr*) to fit (a machine) with a motor or engine. **23** *Inf.* to move or cause to move by the exercise of physical power. [C13: from Anglo-Norman *poer*, from Vulgar L *potēre* (unattested), from L *posse* to be able]

power amplifier *n Electronics.* an amplifier that is usually the final amplification stage in a device and is designed to give the required power output.

powerboat ('pauə,bəut) *n* a boat, esp. a fast one, propelled by an inboard or outboard motor.

powerboating ('pauə,bəutɪŋ) *n* the sport of driving powerboats in racing competitions.

power cut *n* a temporary interruption or reduction in the supply of electrical power.

power dive *n* **1** a steep dive by an aircraft with its engines at high power. ♦ *vb* **power-dive, power-dives, power-diving, power-dived. 2** to cause (an aircraft) to perform a power dive or (of an aircraft) to perform a power dive.

power dressing *n* a style of dressing in severely tailored suits, adopted by some women executives to project an image of efficiency.

powerful ('pauəful) *adj* **1** having great power. **2** extremely effective or efficient: *a powerful drug.* ♦ *adv* **3** *Dialect.* very: *he ran powerful fast.*
▶ **'powerfully** *adv* ▶ **'powerfulness** *n*

powerhouse ('pauə,haus) *n* **1** an electrical generating station or plant. **2** *Inf.* a forceful or powerful person or thing.

powerless ('pauəlɪs) *adj* without power or authority.
▶ **'powerlessly** *adv* ▶ **'powerlessness** *n*

power lunch *n* a high-powered business meeting conducted over lunch.

power of attorney *n* **1** legal authority to act for another person in certain specified matters. **2** the document conferring such authority.

power pack *n* a device for converting the current from a supply into direct or alternating current at the voltage required by a particular electrical or electronic device.

power plant *n* **1** the complex, including machinery, associated equipment, and the structure housing it, that is used in the generation of power, esp. electrical power. **2** the equipment supplying power to a particular machine.

power point *n* an electrical socket mounted on or recessed into a wall.

power-sharing *n* a political arrangement in which opposing groups in a society participate in government.

power station *n* an electrical generating station.

power steering *n* a form of steering used on vehicles, where the torque applied to the steering wheel is augmented by engine power. Also called: **power-assisted steering.**

power structure *n* the structure or distribution of power and authority in a community.

Powhatan ★ (,pauhə'tæn, pau'hæt'n) *n* American Indian name *Wahunsonacock*. died 1618, American Indian chief of a confederacy of tribes; father of Pocahontas.

powwow ('pau,wau) *n* **1** a talk, conference, or meeting. **2** a magical ceremony of certain North American Indians. **3** (among certain North American Indians) a medicine man. **4** a meeting of North American Indians. ♦ *vb* **5** (*intr*) to hold a powwow. [C17: of Amerind origin]

Powys[1] ★ ('pauɪs) *n* a county in E Wales, formed in 1974 from most of Breconshire, Montgomeryshire, and Radnorshire. Administrative centre: Llandrindod Wells. Pop.: 122 000 (1995 est.). Area: 5077 sq. km (1960 sq. miles).

Powys[2] ★ ('pauɪs) *n* **1 John Cowper** ('ku:pə). 1872–1963, British novelist, essayist, and poet, who spent much of his life in the US. His novels include *Wolf Solent* (1929) and *A Glastonbury Romance* (1932). **2** his brother, **T(heodore) F(rancis).** 1875–1953, British writer, noted for such religious fables as *Mr Weston's Good Wine* (1927).

pox (pɒks) *n* **1** any disease characterized by the formation of pustules on the skin that often leave pockmarks when healed. **2** (usually preceded by *the*) an informal name for **syphilis. 3 a pox on (someone or something).** (*interj*) *Arch.* an expression of intense disgust or aversion. [C15: changed from *pocks,* pl. of POCK]

Poyang *or* **P'o-yang** ★ ('pɔ:'jæŋ) *n* a lake in E China, in N Jiangxi province, connected by canal with the Yangtze River: the second largest lake in China. Area (at its greatest): 2780 sq. km (1073 sq. miles).

Poznań ★ (*Polish* 'poznajn) *n* a city in W Poland, on the Warta River: the centre of Polish resistance to German rule (1815–1918, 1939–45). Pop.: 582 300 (1995 est.). German name: **Posen.**

Pozsony ★ ('poʒonj) *n* the Hungarian name for **Bratislava.**

pozzuolana (,pɒtswə'lɑːnə) *or* **pozzolana** (,pɒtsə-'lɑːnə) *n* **1** a type of porous volcanic ash used in making hydraulic cements. **2** any of various artificial substitutes for this ash used in cements. [C18: from It.: of POZZUOLI]

Pozzuoli ★ (*Italian* pot'tswɔːli) *n* a port in SW Italy, in Campania on the **Gulf of Pozzuoli** (an inlet of the Bay of Naples): in a region of great volcanic activity; founded in the 6th century B.C. by the Greeks. Pop.: 65 025 (1987 est.).

pp *abbrev. for:* **1** past participle. **2** (in formal correspondence) per pro. [L: *per procurationem:* by delegation to] ♦ **3** *Music. symbol for* pianissimo.

> **USAGE NOTE** In formal correspondence, when Brenda Smith is signing on behalf of Peter Jones, she should write *Peter Jones pp* (or *per pro*) *Brenda Smith,* not the other way about.

pp *or* **PP** *abbrev. for:* **1** parcel post. **2** post-paid. **3** (in prescriptions) post prandium. [L: after a meal] **4** prepaid.

PP *abbrev. for:* **1** Parish Priest. **2** past President.

pp. *abbrev. for* pages.

ppd *abbrev. for:* **1** post-paid. **2** prepaid.

PPE *abbrev. for* philosophy, politics, and economics: a university course.

ppm *Chem. abbrev. for* parts per million.

PPP *abbrev. for* purchasing power parity: a rate of exchange between two currencies that gives them equal purchasing powers in their own economies.

ppr *or* **p.pr.** *abbrev. for* present participle.

PPS *abbrev. for:* **1** parliamentary private secretary. **2** Also: **pps** post postscriptum. [L: after postscript; additional postscript]

PQ *abbrev. for:* **1** (in Canada) Parti Québecois. **2** Province of Quebec.

pr *abbrev. for:* **1** (*pl* **prs**) pair. **2** paper. **3** power.

Pr *the chemical symbol for* praseodymium.

PR *abbrev. for:* **1** proportional representation. **2** public relations. **3** Puerto Rico.

pr. *abbrev. for:* **1** price. **2** pronoun.

practicable ('præktɪkəbªl) *adj* **1** capable of being done; feasible. **2** usable. [C17: from F *praticable*, from *pratiquer* to practise; see PRACTICAL]
▶ ,practica'bility *or* 'practicableness *n* ▶ 'practicably *adv*

> **USAGE NOTE** See at **practical.**

practical ('præktɪkªl) *adj* **1** of or concerned with experience or actual use; not theoretical. **2** of or concerned with ordinary affairs, work, etc. **3** adapted or adaptable for use. **4** of, involving, or trained by practice. **5** being such for all general purposes; virtual. ♦ *n* **6** an examination or lesson in a practical subject. [C17: from earlier *practic*, from F *pratique*, via LL from Gk *praktikos*, from *prassein* to experience]
▶ ,practi'cality *or* 'practicalness *n*

> **USAGE NOTE** A distinction is usually made between *practical* and *practicable*. *Practical* refers to a person, idea, project, etc., as being more concerned with or relevant to practice than theory: *he is a very practical person; the idea had no practical application*. *Practicable* refers to a project or idea as being capable of being done or put into effect: *the plan was expensive, yet practicable*.

practical joke *n* a prank or trick usually intended to make the victim appear foolish.
▶ **practical joker** *n*

practically ('præktɪkəlɪ, -klɪ) *adv* **1** virtually; almost: *it rained practically every day*. **2** in actuality rather than in theory: *what can we do practically to help?*

practice ('præktɪs) *n* **1** a usual or customary action: *it was his practice to rise at six*. **2** repetition of an activity in order to achieve mastery and fluency: *they had one last practice the day before the show*. **3** the condition of having mastery of a skill or activity through repetition (esp. in **in practice, out of practice**). **4** the exercise of a profession: *he set up practice as a lawyer*. **5** the act of doing something: *he put his plans into practice*. **6** the established method of conducting proceedings in a court of law. ♦ *vb* **practices, practicing, practiced**. **7** the US spelling of **practise**. [C16: from Med. L *practicāre* to practise, from Gk *praktikē* practical work, from *prattein* to do]

practise *or US* **practice** ('præktɪs) *vb* **practises, practising, practised** *or US* **practices, practicing, practiced**. **1** to do or cause to do repeatedly in order to gain skill. **2** (*tr*) to do (something) habitually or frequently: *they practise ritual murder*. **3** to observe or pursue (something): *to practise Christianity*. **4** to work at (a profession, etc.): *he practises medicine*. [C15: see PRACTICE]

practised *or US* **practiced** ('præktɪst) *adj* **1** expert; skilled; proficient. **2** acquired or perfected by practice.

practitioner (præk'tɪʃənə) *n* **1** a person who practises a profession or art. **2** *Christian Science*. a person authorized to practise spiritual healing. [C16: from *practician*, from OF, from *pratiquer* to PRACTISE]

Prader-Willi syndrome (,prɑːdə'vɪlɪ) *n* a congenital condition characterized by obsessive eating, obesity, mental retardation, and small genitalia. [C20: after Andrea *Prader* (b. 1919) and H. *Willi* (b. 1900), Swiss paediatricians]

Prado ★ ('prɑːdəʊ) *n* an art gallery in Madrid housing an important collection of Spanish paintings.

prae- *prefix* an archaic variant of **pre-**.

praedial *or* **predial** ('priːdɪəl) *adj* **1** of or relating to land, farming, etc. **2** attached to or occupying land. [C16: from Med. L *praediālis*, from L *praedium* farm, estate]

praesidium (prɪ'sɪdɪəm) *n* a variant of **presidium**.

praetor *or esp. US* **pretor** ('priːtə, -tɔː) *n* (in ancient Rome) any of several senior magistrates ranking just below the consuls. [C15: from L: one who leads the way, prob. from *praeīre*, from *prae-* before + *īre* to go]
▶ **prae'torian** *or* **pre'torian** *adj, n* ▶ **'praetorship** *or* **'pretorship** *n*

Praetorius ★ (*German* prɛ'toːriʊs) *n* **Michael** ('mɪçaeːl). 1571–1621, German composer and musicologist, noted esp. for his description of contemporary musical practices and instruments, *Syntagma musicum* (1615–19).

pragmatic (præg'mætɪk) *adj* **1** advocating behaviour dictated more by practical consequences than by theory. **2** *Philosophy*. of pragmatism. **3** involving everyday or practical business. **4** of or concerned with the affairs of a state or community. **5** *Rare*. meddlesome; officious. Also (for senses 3, 5): **pragmatical**. [C17: from LL *prāgmaticus*, from Gk *prāgmatikos*, from *pragma* act, from *prattein* to do]
▶ **prag,mati'cality** *n* ▶ **prag'matically** *adv*

pragmatic sanction *n* an edict, decree, or ordinance issued with the force of fundamental law by a sovereign.

pragmatism ('prægmə,tɪzəm) *n* **1** action or policy dictated by consideration of the practical consequences rather than by theory. **2** *Philosophy*. the doctrine that the content of a concept consists only in its practical applicability.
▶ **'pragmatist** *n, adj*

Prague ★ (prɑːg) *n* the capital and largest city of the Czech Republic, on the Vltava River: a rich commercial centre during the Middle Ages; site of Charles University (1348) and a technical university (1707); scene of defenestrations (1419 and 1618) that contributed to the outbreak of the Hussite Wars and the Thirty Years' War respectively. Pop.: 1 213 299 (1995 est.). Czech name: **Praha**.

Praha ★ ('praha) *n* the Czech name for **Prague**.

prairie ('preərɪ) *n* (*often pl*) a treeless grassy plain of the central US and S Canada. [C18: from F, from OF *prairie*, from L *prātum* meadow]

prairie chicken, fowl, grouse, *or* **hen** *n* either of two mottled brown-and-white grouse of North America.

prairie dog *n* any of several rodents that live in large complex burrows in the prairies of North America. Also called: **prairie marmot.**

prairie oyster *n* a drink consisting of raw unbeaten egg, vinegar or Worcester sauce, salt, and pepper: a supposed cure for a hangover.

Prairie Provinces ★ *pl n* the Canadian provinces of Manitoba, Saskatchewan, and Alberta, which lie in the N Great Plains region of North America: the chief wheat and petroleum producing area of Canada.

prairie schooner *n Chiefly US*. a horse-drawn covered wagon used in the 19th century to cross the prairies of North America.

prairie wolf *n* another name for **coyote**.

praise (preɪz) *n* **1** the act of expressing commendation, admiration, etc. **2** the rendering of homage and gratitude to a deity. **3** sing someone's praises. to commend someone highly. ♦ *vb* **praises, praising, praised**. (*tr*) **4** to express commendation, admiration, etc., for. **5** to proclaim the glorious attributes of (a deity) with homage and thanksgiving. [C13: from OF *preisier*, from LL *pretiāre* to esteem highly, from L *pretium* prize]

praiseworthy ('preɪz,wɜːðɪ) *adj* deserving of praise; commendable.
▶ **'praise,worthily** *adv* ▶ **'praise,worthiness** *n*

Prakrit ('prɑːkrɪt) *n* any of the vernacular Indic languages as distinguished from Sanskrit: spoken from about 300 B.C. to the Middle Ages. [C18: from Sansk. *prākrta* original]
▶ **Pra'kritic** *adj*

> ★ **people and places**

praline ('prɑːliːn) *n* **1** a confection of nuts with caramelized sugar. **2** Also called: **sugared almond.** a sweet consisting of an almond encased in sugar. [C18: from F, after César de Choiseul, comte de Plessis-*Praslin* (1598–1675), F field marshal whose chef first concocted it]

pralltriller ('prɑːl,trɪlə) *n* an ornament used in 18th-century music consisting of an inverted mordent with an added initial upper note. [G: bouncing trill]

pram[1] (præm) *n Brit.* a cotlike four-wheeled carriage for a baby. US term: **baby carriage.** [C19: shortened & altered from PERAMBULATOR]

pram[2] (prɑːm) *n Naut.* a light tender with a flat bottom and a bow formed from the ends of the side and bottom planks meeting in a small raised transom. [C16: from MDu. *prame*]

prance (prɑːns) *vb* **prances, prancing, pranced.** **1** (*intr*) to swagger or strut. **2** (*intr*) to caper, gambol, or dance about. **3** (*intr*) (of a horse) to move with high lively springing steps. **4** (*tr*) to cause to prance. ◆ *n* **5** the act or an instance of prancing. [C14 *prauncen,* from ?]
▶ 'prancer *n* ▶ 'prancing *adj*

prandial ('prændɪəl) *adj Facetious.* of or relating to a meal. [C19: from L *prandium* meal, luncheon]

prang (præŋ) *Chiefly Brit. sl.* ◆ *n* **1** an accident or crash in an aircraft, car, etc. **2** an aircraft bombing raid. ◆ *vb* **3** to crash or damage (an aircraft, car, etc.). **4** to damage (a town, etc.) by bombing. [C20: ? imit.]

prank[1] (præŋk) *n* a mischievous trick or joke. [C16: from ?]
▶ 'prankish *adj* ▶ 'prankster *n*

prank[2] (præŋk) *vb* **1** (*tr*) to dress or decorate showily or gaudily. **2** (*intr*) to make an ostentatious display. [C16: from MDu. *pronken*]

prase (preɪz) *n* a light green translucent variety of chalcedony. [C14: from F, from L *prasius* a leek-green stone, from Gk *prasios,* from *prason* a leek]

praseodymium (,preɪzɪəʊ'dɪmɪəm) *n* a malleable ductile silvery-white element of the lanthanide series of metals. Symbol: Pr; atomic no.: 59; atomic wt.: 140.91. [C20: NL, from Gk *prasios* of a leek-green colour + DIDYMIUM]

prate (preɪt) *vb* **prates, prating, prated.** **1** (*intr*) to talk idly and at length; chatter. **2** (*tr*) to utter in an idle or empty way. ◆ *n* **3** idle or trivial talk; chatter. [C15: of Gmc origin]
▶ 'prater *n* ▶ 'prating *adj*

pratfall ('præt,fɔːl) *n US & Canad. sl.* a fall upon one's buttocks. [C20: from C16 *prat* buttocks (from ?) + FALL]

pratincole ('prætɪŋ,kəʊl, 'preɪ-) *n* any of various swallow-like shore birds of the Old World, having long pointed wings, short legs, and a short bill. [C18: from NL *pratincola* field-dwelling, from L *prātum* meadow + *incola* inhabitant]

Prato ★ (*Italian* 'prɑːto) *n* a walled city in central Italy, in Tuscany: woollen industry. Pop.: 166 305 (1994 est.). Official name: **Prato in Toscana** (in tos'kɑːna).

prattle ('præt⁰l) *vb* **prattles, prattling, prattled. 1** (*intr*) to talk in a foolish or childish way; babble. **2** (*tr*) to utter in a foolish or childish way. ◆ *n* **3** foolish or childish talk. [C16: from MLow G *pratelen* to chatter]
▶ 'prattler *n* ▶ 'prattling *adj*

prau (prau) *n* a variant of **proa.**

prawn (prɔːn) *n* **1** any of various small edible marine decapod crustaceans having a slender flattened body with a long tail and two pairs of pincers. **2 come the raw prawn with.** *Austral. inf.* to attempt to deceive. [C15: from ?]

praxis ('præksɪs) *n, pl* **praxes** ('præksiːz) *or* **praxises. 1** the practice of a field of study, as opposed to the theory. **2** a practical exercise. **3** accepted practice or custom. [C16: via Med. L from Gk: deed, action, from *prassein* to do]

Praxiteles ★ (præk'sɪtɪ,liːz) *n* 4th-century B.C. Greek sculptor: his works include statues of Hermes at Olympia, which survives, and of Aphrodite at Cnidus.

pray (preɪ) *vb* **1** (when *intr,* often foll. by *for;* when *tr,* usually takes a clause as object) to utter prayers (to God or other object of worship). **2** (when *tr,* usually takes a clause as object or an infinitive) to beg or implore: *she prayed to be allowed to go.* ◆ *sentence substitute.* **3** *Arch.* I beg you; please: *pray, leave us alone.* [C13: from OF *preier,* from L *precārī* to implore, from *prex* an entreaty]

prayer[1] (preə) *n* **1** a personal communication or petition addressed to a deity, esp. in the form of supplication, adoration, praise, contrition, or thanksgiving. **2** a similar personal communication that does not involve adoration, addressed to beings closely associated with a deity, such as saints. **3** the practice of praying: *prayer is our solution to human problems.* **4** (*often pl*) a form of devotion spent mainly or wholly praying: *morning prayers.* **5** (*cap. when part of a recognized name*) a form of words used in praying: *the Lord's Prayer.* **6** an object or benefit prayed for. **7** an earnest request or entreaty. [C13 *preiere,* from OF, from Med. L, from L *precārius* obtained by begging, from *prex* prayer]
▶ 'prayerful *adj*

prayer[2] ('preɪə) *n* a person who prays.

prayer book (preə) *n* a book containing the prayers used at church services or recommended for private devotions.

prayer rug (preə) *n* the small carpet on which a Muslim kneels and prostrates himself while saying his prayers. Also called: **prayer mat.**

prayer wheel (preə) *n Buddhism.* (esp. in Tibet) a wheel or cylinder inscribed with or containing prayers, each revolution of which is counted as an uttered prayer, so that such prayers can be repeated by turning it.

praying mantis *or* **mantid** *n* another name for **mantis.**

PRB *abbrev. for* Pre-Raphaelite Brotherhood.

pre- *prefix* before in time, position, etc.: *predate; pre-eminent.* [from L *prae* before]

preach (priːtʃ) *vb* **1** to make known (religious truth) or give religious or moral instruction or exhortation in (sermons). **2** to advocate (a virtue, action, etc.), esp. in a moralizing way. [C13: from OF *prechier,* from Church L *praedicāre,* from L: to proclaim in public; see PREDICATE]

preacher ('priːtʃə) *n* a person who preaches, esp. a Protestant clergyman.

preachify ('priːtʃɪ,faɪ) *vb* **preachifies, preachifying, preachified.** (*intr*) *Inf.* to preach or moralize in a tedious manner.
▶ ,preachifi'cation *n*

preachment ('priːtʃmənt) *n* **1** the act of preaching. **2** a tedious or pompous sermon.

preachy ('priːtʃɪ) *adj* **preachier, preachiest.** *Inf.* inclined to or marked by preaching.

preacquisition profit (,priːækwɪ'zɪʃən) *n* the retained profit of a company earned before a takeover and therefore not eligible for distribution as a dividend to the shareholders of the acquiring company.

preamble (priː'æmb⁰l) *n* **1** a preliminary or introductory statement, esp. attached to a statute setting forth its purpose. **2** a preliminary event, fact, etc. [C14: from OF *préambule,* from LL *praeambulum,* from L *prae-* before + *ambulāre* to walk]

preamplifier (priː'æmplɪ,faɪə) *n* an electronic amplifier used to improve the signal-to-noise ratio of an electronic device. It boosts a low-level signal to an intermediate level before it is transmitted to the main amplifier.

prebend ('prebənd) *n* **1** the stipend assigned by a cathedral or collegiate church to a canon or member of the chapter. **2** the land, tithe, or other source of such a stipend. **3** a less common word for **prebendary. 4** *Church of England.* the office of a prebendary. [C15: from OF *prébende,* from Med. L *praebenda* stipend, from L *praebēre* to offer, from *prae* forth + *habēre* to have]
▶ **prebendal** (prɪ'bend⁰l) *adj*

prebendary ('prebəndərɪ, -drɪ) *n, pl* **prebendaries. 1** a canon or member of the chapter of a cathedral or collegiate church who holds a prebend. **2** *Church of England.* an honorary canon with the title of prebendary.

Precambrian *or* **Pre-Cambrian** (priː'kæmbrɪən) *adj* **1** of, denoting, or formed in the earliest geological era, which lasted for about 4 000 000 000 years before the Cambrian period. ◆ *n* **2 the.** the Precambrian era.

precancel (priːˈkænsᵊl) vb **precancels, precancelling, precancelled** or US **precancels, precancelling, precanceled**. (tr) to cancel (postage stamps) before placing them on mail.

precancerous adj (esp. of cells) displaying characteristics that may develop into cancer.

precarious (prɪˈkɛərɪəs) adj **1** liable to failure or catastrophe; insecure; perilous. **2** Arch. dependent on another's will. [C17: from L precārius obtained by begging, from prex PRAYER¹]
▶ **preˈcariously** adv ▶ **preˈcariousness** n

precast (ˈpriːˌkɑːst) adj (esp. of concrete when employed as a structural element in building) cast in a particular form before being used.

precaution (prɪˈkɔːʃən) n **1** an action taken to avoid a dangerous or undesirable event. **2** caution practised beforehand; circumspection. [C17: from F, from LL praecautiō, from L, from prae before + cavēre to beware]
▶ **preˈcautionary** adj

precede (prɪˈsiːd) vb **precedes, preceding, preceded. 1** to go or be before (someone or something) in time, place, rank, etc. **2** (tr) to preface or introduce. [C14: via OF from L praecēdere to go before]

precedence (ˈprɛsɪdəns) or **precedency** n **1** the act of preceding or the condition of being precedent. **2** the ceremonial order or priority to be observed on formal occasions: the officers are seated according to precedence. **3** a right to preferential treatment: I take precedence over you.

precedent n (ˈprɛsɪdənt). **1** Law. a judicial decision that serves as an authority for deciding a later case. **2** an example or instance used to justify later similar occurrences. ◆ adj (prɪˈsiːdᵊnt, ˈprɛsɪdənt). **3** preceding.

precedented (ˈprɛsɪˌdɛntɪd) adj (of a decision, etc.) supported by having a precedent.

precedential (ˌprɛsɪˈdɛnʃəl) adj **1** of or serving as a precedent. **2** having precedence.

preceding (prɪˈsiːdɪŋ) adj (prenominal) going or coming before; former.

precentor (prɪˈsɛntə) n **1** a cleric who directs the choral services in a cathedral. **2** a person who leads a congregation or choir in the sung parts of church services. [C17: from LL praecentor, from prae before + canere to sing]
▶ **precentorial** (ˌpriːsɛnˈtɔːrɪəl) adj ▶ **preˈcentorˌship** n

precept (ˈpriːsɛpt) n **1** a rule or principle for action. **2** a guide or rule for morals; maxim. **3** a direction, esp. for a technical operation. **4** Law. **4a** a writ or warrant. **4b** (in England) an order to collect money under a rate. [C14: from L praeceptum injunction, from praecipere to admonish, from prae before + capere to take]
▶ **preˈceptive** adj

preceptor (prɪˈsɛptə) n Rare. a tutor or instructor.
▶ **preceptorial** (ˌpriːsɛpˈtɔːrɪəl) or **preˈceptoral** adj ▶ **preˈceptress** fem n

precession (prɪˈsɛʃən) n **1** the act of preceding. **2** See **precession of the equinoxes. 3** the motion of a spinning body, such as a top, gyroscope, or planet, in which it wobbles so that the axis of rotation sweeps out a cone. [C16: from LL praecessiō, from L praecēdere to precede]
▶ **preˈcessional** adj ▶ **preˈcessionally** adv

precession of the equinoxes n the slightly earlier occurrence of the equinoxes each year due to the slow continuous westward shift of the equinoctial points along the ecliptic.

precinct (ˈpriːsɪŋkt) n **1a** an enclosed area or building marked by a fixed boundary such as a wall. **1b** such a boundary. **2** an area in a town, often closed to traffic, that is designed or reserved for a particular activity: a shopping precinct. **3** US. **3a** a district of a city for administrative or police purposes. **3b** a polling district. [C15: from Med. L praecinctum (something) surrounded, from L praecingere to gird around]

precincts (ˈpriːsɪŋkts) pl n the surrounding region or area.

preciosity (ˌprɛʃɪˈɒsɪtɪ) n, pl **preciosities**. fastidiousness or affectation.

precious (ˈprɛʃəs) adj **1** beloved; dear; cherished. **2** very costly or valuable. **3** very fastidious or affected, as in speech, manners, etc. **4** Inf. worthless: you and your precious ideas! ◆ adv **5** Inf. (intensifier): there's precious little left. [C13: from OF precios, from L pretiōsus valuable, from pretium price]
▶ **ˈpreciously** adv ▶ **ˈpreciousness** n

precious metal n gold, silver, or platinum.

precious stone n any of certain rare minerals, such as diamond, ruby, or opal, that are highly valued as gemstones.

precipice (ˈprɛsɪpɪs) n **1** the steep sheer face of a cliff or crag. **2** the cliff or crag itself. [C16: from L praecipitium steep place, from praeceps headlong]
▶ **ˈprecipiced** adj

precipitant (prɪˈsɪpɪtənt) adj **1** hasty or impulsive; rash. **2** rushing or falling rapidly or without heed. **3** abrupt or sudden. ◆ n **4** Chem. a substance that causes a precipitate to form.
▶ **preˈcipitance** or **preˈcipitancy** n

precipitate vb (prɪˈsɪpɪˌteɪt), **precipitates, precipitating, precipitated. 1** (tr) to cause to happen too soon; bring on. **2** to throw or fall from or as from a height. **3** to cause (moisture) to condense and fall as snow, rain, etc., or (of moisture, rain, etc.) to condense and fall thus. **4** Chem. to undergo or cause to undergo a process in which a dissolved substance separates from solution as a fine suspension of solid particles. ◆ adj (prɪˈsɪpɪtɪt). **5** rushing ahead. **6** done rashly or with undue haste. **7** sudden and brief. ◆ n (prɪˈsɪpɪtɪt). **8** Chem. a precipitated solid. [C16: from L praecipitāre to throw down headlong, from praeceps steep, from prae before + caput head]
▶ **preˈcipitable** adj ▶ **preˌcipitaˈbility** n ▶ **preˈcipitately** adv ▶ **preˈcipiˌtator** n

precipitation (prɪˌsɪpɪˈteɪʃən) n Meteorol. **1a** rain, snow, sleet, dew, etc., formed by condensation of water vapour in the atmosphere. **1b** the deposition of these on the earth's surface. **2** the formation of a chemical precipitate. **3** the act of precipitating or the state of being precipitated. **4** rash or undue haste.

precipitous (prɪˈsɪpɪtəs) adj **1** resembling a precipice. **2** very steep. **3** hasty or precipitate.
▶ **preˈcipitously** adv ▶ **preˈcipitousness** n

USAGE NOTE The use of precipitous to mean hasty is thought by some people to be incorrect.

precis or **précis** (ˈpreɪsiː) n, pl **precis** or **précis** (ˈpreɪsiːz). **1** a summary of a text; abstract. ◆ vb **2** (tr) to make a precis of. [C18: from F: PRECISE]

precise (prɪˈsaɪs) adj **1** strictly correct in amount or value: a precise sum. **2** particular: this precise location. **3** using or operating with total accuracy: precise instruments. **4** strict in observance of rules, standards, etc.: a precise mind. [C16: from F précis, from L praecīdere to curtail, from prae before + caedere to cut]
▶ **preˈcisely** adv ▶ **preˈciseness** n

precision (prɪˈsɪʒən) n **1** the quality of being precise; accuracy. **2** (modifier) characterized by a high degree of exactness: precision grinding. [C17: from L praecīsiō a cutting off; see PRECISE]
▶ **preˈcisionism** n ▶ **preˈcisionist** n

preclassical (priːˈklæsɪkᵊl) adj (of music, literature, etc.) before a period regarded as classical.

preclude (prɪˈkluːd) vb **precludes, precluding, precluded.** (tr) **1** to exclude or debar. **2** to make impossible, esp. beforehand. [C17: from L praeclūdere to shut up, from prae before + claudere to close]
▶ **preclusion** (prɪˈkluːʒən) n ▶ **preclusive** (prɪˈkluːsɪv) adj

precocial (prɪˈkəʊʃəl) adj **1** denoting birds whose young, after hatching, are covered with down and capable of leaving the nest within a few days. ◆ n **2** a precocial bird. ◆ Cf. **altricial**.

precocious (prɪˈkəʊʃəs) adj **1** ahead in development, such as the mental development of a child. **2** Bot. flowering or ripening early. [C17: from L praecox, from prae early + coquere to ripen]
▶ **preˈcociously** adv ▶ **preˈcociousness** or **precocity** (prɪˈkɒsɪtɪ) n

★ people and places

precognition (ˌpriːkɒgˈnɪʃən) n Psychol. the alleged ability to foresee future events. [C17: from LL praecognitiō foreknowledge, from praecognoscere to foresee]
▸ **precognitive** (priːˈkɒgnɪtɪv) adj

preconceive (ˌpriːkənˈsiːv) vb preconceives, preconceiving, preconceived. (tr) to form an idea of beforehand.
▸ **preconception** (ˌpriːkənˈsepʃən) n

precondition (ˌpriːkənˈdɪʃən) n 1 a necessary or required condition; prerequisite. ◆ vb 2 (tr) Psychol. to present successively two stimuli to (an organism) without reinforcement so that they become associated; if a response is then conditioned to the second stimulus on its own, the same response will be evoked by the first stimulus.

preconize or **preconise** (ˈpriːkəˌnaɪz) vb preconizes, preconizing, preconized or preconises, preconising, preconised. (tr) 1 to announce or commend publicly. 2 to summon publicly. 3 (of the pope) to approve the appointment of (a nominee) to one of the higher dignities in the Roman Catholic Church. [C15: from Med. L praecōnīzāre to make an announcement, from L praecō herald]
▸ **ˌpreconiˈzation** or **ˌpreconiˈsation** n

precursor (prɪˈkɜːsə) n 1 a person or thing that precedes and announces someone or something to come. 2 a predecessor. 3 a chemical substance that gives rise to another more important substance. [C16: from L praecursor one who runs in front, from praecurrere, from prae in front + currere to run]

precursory (prɪˈkɜːsərɪ) or **precursive** adj 1 serving as a precursor. 2 preliminary.

pred. abbrev. for predicate.

predacious or **predaceous** (prɪˈdeɪʃəs) adj (of animals) habitually hunting and killing other animals for food. [C18: from L praeda plunder]
▸ **preˈdaciousness**, **preˈdaceousness**, or **predacity** (prɪˈdæsɪtɪ) n

predate (priːˈdeɪt) vb predates, predating, predated. (tr) 1 to affix a date to (a document, paper, etc.) that is earlier than the actual date. 2 to assign a date to (an event, period, etc.) that is earlier than the actual or previously assigned date of occurrence. 3 to be or occur at an earlier date than; precede in time.

predation (prɪˈdeɪʃən) n a relationship between two species of animal in a community, in which one hunts, kills, and eats the other.

predator (ˈpredətə) n 1 any carnivorous animal. 2 a predatory person or thing.

predatory (ˈpredətərɪ) adj 1 Zool. another word for **predacious**. 2 of or characterized by plundering, robbing, etc. [C16: from L praedātōrius rapacious, from praedārī to pillage, from praeda booty]
▸ **ˈpredatorily** adv ▸ **ˈpredatoriness** n

predecease (ˌpriːdɪˈsiːs) vb predeceases, predeceasing, predeceased. to die before (some other person).

predecessor (ˈpriːdɪˌsesə) n 1 a person who precedes another, as in an office. 2 something that precedes something else. 3 an ancestor. [C14: via OF from LL praedēcessor, from prae before + dēcēdere to go away]

predella (prɪˈdelə) n, pl predelle (-lɪ). 1 a painting or a series of small paintings in a long strip forming the lower edge of an altarpiece or the face of an altar step. 2 a platform in a church upon which the altar stands. [C19: from It.: step, prob. from OHG bret board]

predestinarian (ˌpriːˌdestɪˈnɛərɪən) n 1 a person who believes in divine predestination. ◆ adj 2 of or relating to predestination or those who believe in it.

predestinate vb (priːˈdestɪˌneɪt), predestinates, predestinating, predestinated. 1 another word for **predestine**. ◆ adj (priːˈdestɪnɪt, -ˌneɪt). 2 predestined.

predestination (priːˌdestɪˈneɪʃən) n 1 Christian theol. 1a the act of God foreordaining every event from eternity. 1b the doctrine or belief, esp. associated with Calvin, that the final salvation of some of mankind is foreordained from eternity by God. 2 the act of predestining or the state of being predestined.

predestine (priːˈdestɪn) or **predestinate** vb predestines, predestining, predestined or predestinates, predestinat-

ing, predestinated. (tr) 1 to determine beforehand. 2 Christian theol. (of God) to decree from eternity (any event, esp. the final salvation of individuals). [C14: from L praedestināre to resolve beforehand]

predetermine (ˌpriːdɪˈtɜːmɪn) vb predetermines, predetermining, predetermined. (tr) 1 to determine beforehand. 2 to influence or bias.
▸ **ˌpredeˈterminable** adj ▸ **ˌpredeˈterminate** adj ▸ **ˌpredeˌtermiˈnation** n

predicable (ˈpredɪkəbᵊl) adj 1 capable of being predicated or asserted. ◆ n 2 a quality that can be predicated. 3 Logic, obs. any of the five Aristotelian classes of predicates, namely genus, species, difference, property, and relation. [C16: from L praedicābilis, from praedicāre to assert publicly; see PREDICATE]
▸ **ˌpredicaˈbility** n

predicament n 1 (prɪˈdɪkəmənt) a perplexing, embarrassing, or difficult situation. 2 (ˈpredɪkəmənt) Logic. a logical category. [C14: from LL praedicāmentum what is predicated, from praedicāre to announce; see PREDICATE]

predicant (ˈpredɪkənt) adj 1 of or relating to preaching. ◆ n 2 a member of a religious order founded for preaching, esp. a Dominican. [C17: from L praedicāns preaching, from praedicāre to say publicly; see PREDICATE]

predicate vb (ˈpredɪˌkeɪt), predicates, predicating, predicated. (mainly tr) 1 (also intr; when tr, may take a clause as object) to declare or affirm. 2 to imply or connote. 3 (foll. by on or upon) Chiefly US. to base (a proposition, argument, etc.). 4 Logic. to assert (a property or condition) of the subject of a proposition. ◆ n (ˈpredɪkɪt). 5 Grammar. the part of a sentence in which something is asserted or denied of the subject of a sentence. 6 Logic. a term, property, or condition that is affirmed or denied concerning the subject of a proposition. ◆ adj (ˈpredɪkɪt). 7 of or relating to something that has been predicated. [C16: from L praedicāre to assert publicly, from prae in front + dīcere to say]
▸ **ˌprediˈcation** n

predicate calculus n the system of symbolic logic concerned not only with relations between propositions as wholes but also with the representation by symbols of individuals and predicates in propositions. See also **propositional calculus**.

predicative (prɪˈdɪkətɪv) adj Grammar. relating to or occurring within the predicate of a sentence: a predicative adjective. Cf. **attributive**.
▸ **preˈdicatively** adv

predict (prɪˈdɪkt) vb (tr; may take a clause as object) to state or make a declaration about in advance; foretell. [C17: from L praedīcere to mention beforehand]
▸ **preˈdictable** adj ▸ **preˌdictaˈbility** n ▸ **preˈdictably** adv ▸ **preˈdictive** adj ▸ **preˈdictor** n

prediction (prɪˈdɪkʃən) n 1 the act of predicting. 2 something predicted; a forecast.

predigest (ˌpriːdaɪˈdʒest, -dɪ-) vb (tr) to treat (food) artificially to aid subsequent digestion in the body.
▸ **ˌprediˈgestion** n

predikant (ˌpredɪˈkænt) n a minister in the Dutch Reformed Church, esp. in South Africa. [from Du., from OF predicant, from LL, from praedicāre to PREACH]

predilection (ˌpriːdɪˈlekʃən) n a predisposition, preference, or bias. [C18: from F prédilection, from Med. L praedīligere to prefer, from L prae before + dīligere to love]

predispose (ˌpriːdɪˈspəʊz) vb predisposes, predisposing, predisposed. (tr) (often foll. by to or towards) to incline or make (someone) susceptible to something beforehand.
▸ **ˌpredisˈposal** n ▸ **ˌpredispoˈsition** n

prednisolone (predˈnɪsəˌləʊn) n a steroid drug derived from prednisone and having the same uses as cortisone. [C20: altered from PREDNISONE]

prednisone (ˈprednɪˌsəʊn) n a steroid drug derived from cortisone and having the same uses. [C20: perhaps from PRE(GNANT) + -D(IE)N(E) + (CORT)ISONE]

predominant (prɪˈdɒmɪnənt) adj 1 superior in power, influence, etc., over others. 2 prevailing.
▸ **preˈdominance** n ▸ **preˈdominantly** adv

predominate vb (prɪˈdɒmɪˌneɪt), predominates, predomi-

nating, predominated. (*intr*) **1** (often foll. by *over*) to have power, influence, or control. **2** to prevail or preponderate. ◆ *adj* (prɪˈdɒmɪnɪt). **3** another word for **predominant**. [C16: from Med. L *praedominārī*, from L *prae* before + *domināri* to bear rule]
▸ pre'dominately *adv* ▸ pre,domi'nation *n*

pre-eclampsia (ˌpriːɪˈklæmpsɪə) *n* a serious condition that can occur late in pregnancy. If not treated it can lead to eclampsia.

pre-embryo (priːˈɛmbrɪˌəʊ) *n, pl* **pre-embryos**. the structure formed after fertilization of an ovum but before differentiation of embryonic tissue.

pre-eminent (prɪˈɛmɪnənt) *adj* extremely eminent or distinguished; outstanding.
▸ pre'eminence *n* ▸ pre'eminently *adv*

pre-empt (prɪˈɛmpt) *vb* **1** (*tr*) to acquire in advance of or to the exclusion of others; appropriate. **2** (*tr*) *Chiefly US.* to occupy (public land) in order to acquire a prior right to purchase. **3** (*intr*) *Bridge.* to make a high opening bid, often on a weak hand, to shut out opposition bidding.
▸ pre-'emptor *n*

pre-emption (prɪˈɛmpʃən) *n* **1** *Law.* the purchase of or right to purchase property in preference to others. **2** *International law.* the right of a government to intercept and seize property of the subjects of another state while in transit, esp. in time of war. [C16: from Med. L *praeemptiō*, from *praeemere* to buy beforehand]

pre-emptive (prɪˈɛmptɪv) *adj* **1** of, involving, or capable of pre-emption. **2** *Bridge.* (of a high bid) made to shut out opposition bidding. **3** *Mil.* designed to reduce or destroy an enemy's attacking strength before it can use it: *a pre-emptive strike.*

preen (priːn) *vb* **1** (of birds) to maintain (feathers) in a healthy condition by arrangement, cleaning, and other contact with the bill. **2** to dress or array (oneself) carefully; primp. **3** (usually foll. by *on*) to pride or congratulate (oneself). [C14 *preinen*, prob. from *prunen*, infl. by *prenen* to prick; suggestive of the pricking movement of the bird's beak]
▸ 'preener *n*

pre-exist (prɪɪɡˈzɪst) *vb* (*intr*) to exist at an earlier time.
▸ pre-ex'istent *adj* ▸ pre-ex'istence *n*

pref. *abbrev. for:* **1** preface. **2** prefatory. **3** preference. **4** preferred. **5** prefix.

prefab (ˈpriːˌfæb) *n* a building that is prefabricated, esp. a small house.

prefabricate (priːˈfæbrɪˌkeɪt) *vb* **prefabricates, prefabricating, prefabricated.** (*tr*) to manufacture sections of (a building) so that they can be easily transported to and rapidly assembled on a building site.
▸ pre,fabri'cation *n*

preface (ˈprɛfɪs) *n* **1** a statement written as an introduction to a literary or other work, typically explaining its scope, intention, method, etc.; foreword. **2** anything introductory. ◆ *vb* **prefaces, prefacing, prefaced.** (*tr*) **3** to furnish with a preface. **4** to serve as a preface to. [C14: from Med. L *praefātia*, from L *praefātiō* a saying beforehand, from *praefārī* to utter in advance]
▸ 'prefacer *n*

prefatory (ˈprɛfətərɪ, -trɪ) *or* **prefatorial** (ˌprɛfəˈtɔːrɪəl) *adj* of or serving as a preface; introductory. [C17: from L *praefārī* to say in advance]

prefect (ˈpriːfɛkt) *n* **1** (in France, Italy, etc.) the chief administrative officer in a department. **2** (in France, etc.) the head of a police force. **3** *Brit., Austral., & NZ.* a schoolchild appointed to a position of limited power over his fellows. **4** (in ancient Rome) any of several magistrates or military commanders. **5** *RC Church.* one of two senior masters in a Jesuit school or college. [C14: from L *praefectus* one put in charge, from *praeficere* to place in authority over, from *prae* before + *facere* to do]
▸ prefectorial (ˌpriːfɛkˈtɔːrɪəl) *adj*

prefecture (ˈpriːfɛkˌtjʊə) *n* **1** the office, position, or area of authority of a prefect. **2** the official residence of a prefect in France, etc.

prefer (prɪˈfɜː) *vb* **prefers, preferring, preferred. 1** (when *tr*, may take a clause as object or an infinitive) to like better or value more highly: *I prefer to stand.* **2** *Law.* (esp. of the po-

lice) to put (charges) before a court, magistrate, etc., for consideration and judgment. **3** (*tr; often passive*) to advance in rank over another or others; promote. [C14: from L *praeferre* to carry in front, prefer]

preferable (ˈprɛfərəbᵊl) *adj* preferred or more desirable.
▸ 'preferably *adv*

preference (ˈprɛfərəns, ˈprɛfrəns) *n* **1** the act of preferring. **2** something or someone preferred. **3** *International trade.* the granting of favour or precedence to particular foreign countries, as by levying differential tariffs.

preference shares *pl n Brit. & Austral.* fixed-interest shares issued by a company and giving their holders a prior right over ordinary shareholders to payment of dividend and to repayment of capital if the company is liquidated. US and Canad. name: **preferred stock.** Cf. **ordinary shares, preferred ordinary shares.**

preferential (ˌprɛfəˈrɛnʃəl) *adj* **1** showing or resulting from preference. **2** giving, receiving, or originating from preference in international trade.
▸ ,prefer'entially *adv*

preferment (prɪˈfɜːmənt) *n* **1** the act of promoting to a higher position, office, etc. **2** the state of being preferred for promotion or social advancement. **3** the act of preferring.

preferred ordinary shares *pl n Brit.* shares issued by a company that rank between preference shares and ordinary shares in the payment of dividends. Cf. **preference shares, ordinary shares.**

prefigure (priːˈfɪɡə) *vb* **prefigures, prefiguring, prefigured.** (*tr*) **1** to represent or suggest in advance. **2** to imagine beforehand.
▸ ,prefigu'ration *n* ▸ pre'figurement *n*

prefix *n* (ˈpriːfɪks). **1** *Grammar.* an affix that precedes the stem to which it is attached, as for example *un-* in *unhappy.* Cf. **suffix** (sense 1). **2** something coming or placed before. ◆ *vb* (priːˈfɪks, ˈpriːfɪks). (*tr*) **3** to put or place before. **4** *Grammar.* to add (a morpheme) as a prefix to the beginning of a word.
▸ prefixion (priːˈfɪkʃən) *n*

prefrontal (priːˈfrʌntᵊl) *adj* in or relating to the foremost part of the frontal lobe of the brain.

preglacial (priːˈɡleɪsɪəl, -ʃəl) *adj* formed or occurring before a glacial period, esp. before the Pleistocene epoch.

pregnable (ˈprɛɡnəbᵊl) *adj* capable of being assailed or captured. [C15 *prenable*, from OF *prendre* to take, from L *prehendere* to catch]

pregnant (ˈprɛɡnənt) *adj* **1** carrying a fetus or fetuses within the womb. **2** full of meaning or significance. **3** inventive or imaginative. **4** prolific or fruitful. [C16: from L *praegnāns* with child, from *prae* before + (*g*)*nascī* to be born]
▸ 'pregnancy *n* ▸ 'pregnantly *adv*

prehensile (prɪˈhɛnsaɪl) *adj* adapted for grasping, esp. by wrapping around a support: *a prehensile tail.* [C18: from F *préhensile*, from L *prehendere* to grasp]
▸ prehensility (ˌpriːhɛnˈsɪlɪtɪ) *n*

prehension (prɪˈhɛnʃən) *n* **1** the act of grasping. **2** apprehension by the mind.

prehistoric (ˌpriːhɪˈstɒrɪk) *or* **prehistorical** *adj* of or relating to man's development before the appearance of the written word.
▸ ,prehis'torically *adv* ▸ pre'history *n*

★ people and places

pre-ignition (ˌpriːɡˈnɪʃən) n ignition of all or part of the explosive charge in an internal-combustion engine before the exact instant necessary for correct operation.

prejudge (priːˈdʒʌdʒ) vb **prejudges, prejudging, prejudged.** (tr) to judge beforehand, esp. without sufficient evidence.

prejudice (ˈprɛdʒʊdɪs) n 1 an opinion formed beforehand, esp. an unfavourable one based on inadequate facts. 2 the act or condition of holding such opinions. 3 intolerance of or dislike for people of a specific race, religion, etc. 4 disadvantage or injury resulting from prejudice. 5 **in** (or **to**) **the prejudice of.** to the detriment of. 6 **without prejudice.** Law. without dismissing or detracting from an existing right or claim. ◆ vb **prejudices, prejudicing, prejudiced.** (tr) 7 to cause to be prejudiced. 8 to disadvantage or injure by prejudice. [C13: from OF préjudice, from L praejūdicium, from prae before + jūdicium sentence, from jūdex a judge]

prejudicial (ˌprɛdʒʊˈdɪʃəl) adj causing prejudice; damaging.
▸ ˌpreju'dicially adv

prelacy (ˈprɛləsɪ) n, pl **prelacies. 1** Also called: **prelature. 1a** the office or status of a prelate. **1b** prelates collectively. **2** Often derog. government of the Church by prelates.

prelapsarian (ˌpriːlæpˈsɛərɪən) adj of or relating to the human state before the Fall: prelapsarian innocence.

prelate (ˈprɛlɪt) n a Church dignitary of high rank, such as a cardinal, bishop, or abbot. [C13: from OF prélat, from Church L praelātus, from L praeferre to hold in special esteem]
▸ **prelatic** (prɪˈlætɪk) or **pre'latical** adj

preliminaries (prɪˈlɪmɪnərɪz) pl n the full word for **prelims.**

preliminary (prɪˈlɪmɪnərɪ) adj 1 (usually prenominal) occurring before or in preparation; introductory. ◆ n, pl **preliminaries. 2** a preliminary event or occurrence. **3** an eliminating contest held before the main competition. [C17: from NL praelīmināris, from L prae before + līmen threshold]
▸ pre'liminarily adv

prelims (ˈpriːlɪmz, prəˈlɪmz) pl n 1 Also called: **front matter.** the pages of a book, such as the title page and contents, before the main text. 2 the first public examinations taken for the bachelor's degree in some universities. 3 (in Scotland) the school examinations taken before public examinations. [C19: a contraction of PRELIMINARIES]

prelude (ˈprɛljuːd) n 1a a piece of music that precedes a fugue, or forms the first movement of a suite, or an introduction to an act in an opera, etc. 1b (esp. for piano) a self-contained piece of music. 2 an introduction or preceding event, occurrence, etc. ◆ vb **preludes, preluding, preluded. 3** to serve as a prelude to (something). **4** (tr) to introduce by a prelude. [C16: from Med. L praelūdium, from prae before + L lūdere to play]
▸ **preludial** (prɪˈljuːdɪəl) adj

premarital (priːˈmærɪtəl) adj (esp. of sexual relations) occurring before marriage.

premature (ˌprɛməˈtjʊə, ˈprɛməˌtjʊə) adj 1 occurring or existing before the normal or expected time. 2 impulsive or hasty: a premature judgment. 3 (of an infant) born before the end of the full period of gestation. [C16: from L praemātūrus very early from prae in advance + mātūrus ripe]
▸ ˌprema'turely adv

premedical (priːˈmɛdɪkəl) adj 1 of or relating to a course of study prerequisite for entering medical school. 2 of or relating to a person engaged in such a course of study.

premedication (ˌpriːmɛdɪˈkeɪʃən) n Surgery. any drugs administered to sedate and otherwise prepare a patient for general anaesthesia.

premeditate (prɪˈmɛdɪˌteɪt) vb **premeditates, premeditating, premeditated.** to plan or consider (something, such as a violent crime) beforehand.
▸ pre'medi,tator n

premeditation (prɪˌmɛdɪˈteɪʃən) n 1 Law. prior resolve

to do some act or to commit a crime. 2 the act of premeditating.

premenstrual syndrome or **tension** n symptoms, esp. nervous tension, that may be experienced because of hormonal changes in the days before a menstrual period starts. Abbrevs.: **PMS, PMT.**

premier (ˈprɛmjə) n 1 another name for **prime minister. 2** any of the heads of government of the Canadian provinces and the Australian states. ◆ adj (prenominal) 4 first in importance, rank, etc. 5 first in occurrence; earliest. [C15: from OF: first, from L prīmārius principal, from prīmus first]

premiere (ˈprɛmɪˌɛə, ˈprɛmɪə) n 1 the first public performance of a film, play, opera, etc. 2 the leading lady in a theatre company. ◆ vb **premieres, premiering, premiered. 3** (tr) to give a premiere of: the show will be premiered on Broadway. [C19: from F, fem of premier first]

premiership (ˈprɛmjəʃɪp) n 1 the office of premier. 2a championship competition held among a number of sporting clubs. 2b a victory in such a championship.

premillennialism (ˌpriːmɪˈlɛnɪəˌlɪzəm) n the doctrine or belief that the millennium will be preceded by the Second Coming of Christ.
▸ ˌpremil'lennialist n ▸ ˌpremille'narian n, adj

Preminger ★ (ˈprɛmɪndʒə) n Otto (**Ludwig**). 1906–86, US film director, born in Austria. His films include Carmen Jones (1954) and Anatomy of a Murder (1959).

premise n (ˈprɛmɪs), also **premiss. 1** Logic. a statement that is assumed to be true for the purpose of an argument from which a conclusion is drawn. ◆ vb (prɪˈmaɪz, ˈprɛmɪs), **premises, premising, premised. 2** (when tr, may take a clause as object) to state or assume (a proposition) as a premise in an argument, etc. [C14: from OF prémisse, from Med. L praemissa sent on before, from L praemittere to dispatch in advance]

premises (ˈprɛmɪsɪz) pl n 1 a piece of land together with its buildings, esp. considered as a place of business. 2 Law. (in a deed, etc.) the matters referred to previously; the aforesaid.

premium (ˈpriːmɪəm) n 1 an amount paid in addition to a standard rate, price, wage, etc.; bonus. 2 the amount paid or payable, usually in regular instalments, for an insurance policy. 3 the amount above nominal or par value at which something sells. 4 an offer of something free or at a reduced price as an inducement to buy a commodity or service. 5 a prize given to the winner of a competition. 6 US. an amount sometimes charged for a loan of money in addition to the interest. 7 great value or regard: to put a premium on someone's services. 8 **at a premium. 8a** in great demand, usually because of scarcity. **8b** above par. [C17: from L praemium prize]

Premium Savings Bonds pl n (in Britain) bonds issued by the Treasury since 1956 for purchase by the public. No interest is paid but there is a monthly draw for cash prizes of various sums. Also called: **premium bonds.**

premolar (priːˈməʊlə) adj 1 situated before a molar tooth. ◆ n 2 any one of eight bicuspid teeth in the human adult, two on each side of both jaws between the first molar and the canine.

premonition (ˌprɛməˈnɪʃən) n 1 an intuition of a future, usually unwelcome, occurrence; foreboding. 2 an early warning of a future event. [C16: from LL praemonitiō, from L praemonēre to admonish beforehand, from prae before + monēre to warn]
▸ **premonitory** (prɪˈmɒnɪtərɪ, -trɪ) adj

Premonstratensian (ˌpriːmɒnstrəˈtɛnsɪən) adj 1 of or denoting an order of regular canons founded in 1119 at Prémontré, in France. ◆ n 2 a member of this order.

prenatal (priːˈneɪtəl) adj 1 occurring or present before birth; during pregnancy. ◆ n 2 Inf. a prenatal examination. ◆ Also: **antenatal.**

prenominal (priːˈnɒmɪnəl) adj placed before a noun, esp. (of an adjective or sense of an adjective) used only before a noun.

prentice (ˈprɛntɪs) n an archaic word for **apprentice.**

prenuptial agreement n a contract made between a

man and woman before they marry, agreeing on the distribution of their assets in the event of divorce.

preoccupation (priːˌɒkjuˈpeɪʃən) *n* **1** the state of being preoccupied, esp. mentally. **2** something that preoccupies the mind.

preoccupied (priːˈɒkjuˌpaɪd) *adj* **1** engrossed or absorbed in something, esp. one's own thoughts. **2** already occupied or used.

preoccupy (priːˈɒkjuˌpaɪ) *vb* **preoccupies, preoccupying, preoccupied.** (*tr*) **1** to engross the thoughts or mind of. **2** to occupy before or in advance of another. [C16: from L *praeoccupāre* to capture in advance]

preordain (ˌpriːɔːˈdeɪn) *vb* (*tr*) to ordain, decree, or appoint beforehand.

prep (prep) *n Inf.* **1** short for **preparation** (sense 5) or (chiefly US) **preparatory school.** ◆ *vb* **preps, prepping, prepped.** **2** (*tr*) to prepare (a patient) for a medical operation or procedure.

prep. *abbrev. for:* **1** preparation. **2** preparatory. **3** preposition.

preparation (ˌprepəˈreɪʃən) *n* **1** the act or process of preparing. **2** the state of being prepared; readiness. **3** (*often pl*) a measure done in order to prepare for something; provision: *to make preparations for something.* **4** something that is prepared, esp. a medicine. **5** (esp. in a boarding school) **5a** homework. **5b** the period reserved for this. Usually shortened to **prep.** **6** *Music.* **6a** the anticipation of a dissonance so that the note producing it in one chord is first heard in the preceding chord as a consonance. **6b** a note so employed.

preparative (prɪˈpærətɪv) *adj* **1** preparatory. ◆ *n* **2** something that prepares.
▸ **preˈparatively** *adv*

preparatory (prɪˈpærətərɪ, -trɪ) *adj* **1** serving to prepare. **2** introductory. **3** occupied in preparation. **4 preparatory to.** before: *a drink preparatory to eating.*
▸ **preˈparatorily** *adv*

preparatory school *n* **1** (in Britain) a private school, usually single-sex and for children between the ages of 6 and 13, generally preparing pupils for public school. **2** (in the US) a private secondary school preparing pupils for college. ◆ Often shortened to **prep school.**

prepare (prɪˈpeə) *vb* **prepares, preparing, prepared. 1** to make ready or suitable in advance for some use, event, etc.: *to prepare a meal; to prepare to go.* **2** to put together using parts or ingredients; construct. **3** (*tr*) to equip or outfit, as for an expedition. **4** (*tr*) *Music.* to soften the impact of (a dissonant note) by the use of preparation. **5 be prepared.** (foll. by an *infinitive*) to be willing and able: *I'm not prepared to reveal these figures.* [C15: from L *praeparāre*, from *prae* before + *parāre* to make ready]
▸ **preˈparer** *n*

preparedness (prɪˈpeərɪdnɪs) *n* the state of being prepared, esp. militarily ready for war.

prepay (priːˈpeɪ) *vb* **prepays, prepaying, prepaid.** (*tr*) to pay for in advance.
▸ **preˈpayable** *adj*

prepense (prɪˈpens) *adj* (*postpositive*) (usually in legal contexts) premeditated (esp. in **malice prepense**). [C18: from Anglo-Norman *purpensé*, from OF *purpenser* to consider in advance, from L *pēnsāre* to consider]

preponderant (prɪˈpɒndərənt) *adj* greater in weight, force, influence, etc.
▸ **preˈponderance** *n* ▸ **preˈponderantly** *adv*

preponderate (prɪˈpɒndəˌreɪt) *vb* **preponderates, preponderating, preponderated.** (*intr*) **1** (often foll. by *over*) to be more powerful, important, numerous, etc. (than). **2** to be of greater weight than something else. [C17: from LL *praeponderāre* to be of greater weight, from *pondus* weight]
▸ **preˌponderˈation** *n*

preposition (ˌprepəˈzɪʃən) *n* a word or group of words used before a noun or pronoun to relate it grammatically or semantically to some other constituent of a sentence. [C14: from L *praepositiō* a putting before, from *pōnere* to place]
▸ **ˌprepoˈsitional** *adj* ▸ **ˌprepoˈsitionally** *adv*

prepossess (ˌpriːpəˈzes) *vb* (*tr*) **1** to preoccupy or engross mentally. **2** to influence in advance, esp. to make a favourable impression on beforehand.
▸ **ˌprepos'session** *n*

prepossessing (ˌpriːpəˈzesɪŋ) *adj* creating a favourable impression; attractive.

preposterous (prɪˈpɒstərəs) *adj* contrary to nature, reason, or sense; absurd; ridiculous. [C16: from L *praeposterus* reversed, from *prae* in front + *posterus* following]
▸ **preˈposterously** *adv* ▸ **preˈposterousness** *n*

prepotency (prɪˈpəʊtᵊnsɪ) *n* **1** the quality of possessing greater power or influence. **2** *Genetics.* the ability of one parent to transmit more characteristics to its offspring than the other parent. **3** *Bot.* the ability of pollen from one source to bring about fertilization more readily than that from other sources.
▸ **preˈpotent** *adj*

preppy (ˈprepɪ) *Inf.* ◆ *adj* **1** of or denoting a style of neat, understated, and often expensive clothes; young but classic. ◆ *n, pl* **preppies. 2** a person exhibiting such style. [C20: orig. US, from *preppy* a person who attends a PREPARATORY SCHOOL]

prep school *n Inf.* See **preparatory school.**

prepuce (ˈpriːpjuːs) *n* **1** the retractable fold of skin covering the tip of the penis. Nontechnical name: **foreskin. 2** a similar fold of skin covering the tip of the clitoris. [C14: from L *praepūtium*]

prequel (ˈpriːkwəl) *n* a film that is made about an earlier stage of a story or character's life because the later part of it has already made a successful film. [C20: from PRE- + (se)*quel*]

Pre-Raphaelite (ˌpriːˈræfəlaɪt) *n* **1** a member of the **Pre-Raphaelite Brotherhood,** an association of painters and writers founded in 1848 to revive the fidelity to nature and the vivid realistic colour considered typical of Italian painting before Raphael. ◆ *adj* **2** of, in the manner of, or relating to Pre-Raphaelite painting and painters.
▸ **ˌPre-ˈRaphaelitˌism** *n*

prerequisite (priːˈrekwɪzɪt) *adj* **1** required as a prior condition. ◆ *n* **2** something required as a prior condition.

prerogative (prɪˈrɒgətɪv) *n* **1** an exclusive privilege or right exercised by a person or group of people holding a particular office or hereditary rank. **2** any privilege or right. **3** a power, privilege, or immunity restricted to a sovereign or sovereign government. ◆ *adj* **4** having or able to exercise a prerogative. [C14: from L *praerogātīva* privilege, earlier: group with the right to vote first, from *prae* before + *rogāre* to ask]

pres. *abbrev. for:* **1** present (time). **2** presidential.

Pres. *abbrev. for* President.

presage *n* (ˈpresɪdʒ). **1** an intimation or warning of something about to happen; portent; omen. **2** a sense of what is about to happen; foreboding. ◆ *vb* (ˈpresɪdʒ, prɪˈseɪdʒ). **presages, presaging, presaged.** (*tr*) **3** to have a presentiment of. **4** to give a forewarning of; portend. [C14: from L *praesāgium*, from *praesāgīre* to perceive beforehand]
▸ **preˈsageful** *adj* ▸ **preˈsager** *n*

presale (ˈpriːˌseɪl) *n* the practice of arranging the sale of a product before it is available.
▸ **preˈsell** *vb* (*tr*)

presbyopia (ˌprezbɪˈəʊpɪə) *n* a progressively diminishing ability of the eye to focus, noticeable from middle to old age, caused by loss of elasticity of the crystalline lens. [C18: NL, from Gk *presbus* old man + *ōps* eye]
▸ **presbyopic** (ˌprezbɪˈɒpɪk) *adj*

presbyter (ˈprezbɪtə) *n* **1a** an elder of a congregation in the early Christian Church. **1b** (in some Churches having episcopal politics) an official who is subordinate to a

★ people and places

bishop and has administrative and sacerdotal functions. **2** (in some hierarchical Churches) another name for **priest. 3** (in the Presbyterian Church) an elder. [C16: from LL, from Gk *presbuteros* an older man, from *presbus* old man]
► ˌpresby'terial *adj*

presbyterian (ˌprezbɪ'tɪərɪən) *adj* **1** of or designating Church government by presbyters or lay elders. ♦ *n* **2** an upholder of this type of Church government.
► ˌpresby'terianism *n*

Presbyterian (ˌprezbɪ'tɪərɪən) *adj* **1** of or relating to any of various Protestant Churches governed by presbyters or lay elders and adhering to various modified forms of Calvinism. ♦ *n* **2** a member of a Presbyterian Church.
► ˌPresby'terianism *n*

presbytery ('prezbɪtərɪ) *n, pl* **presbyteries. 1** *Presbyterian Church.* **1a** a local Church court. **1b** the congregations within the jurisdiction of any such court. **2** the part of a church east of the choir, in which the main altar is situated; a sanctuary. **3** presbyters or elders collectively. **4** *RC Church.* the residence of a parish priest. [C15: from OF *presbiterie*, from Church L, from Gk *presbyterion; see* PRES-BYTER]

prescience ('presɪəns) *n* knowledge of events before they take place; foreknowledge. [C14: from L *praescīre* to foreknow]
► 'prescient *adj*

Prescott ★ ('preskət) *n* **1 John Leslie.** born 1938, British politician; deputy prime minister from 1997. **2 William Hickling** ('hɪklɪŋ). 1796–1859, US historian.

prescribe (prɪ'skraɪb) *vb* **prescribes, prescribing, prescribed. 1** (*tr*) to lay down as a rule or directive. **2** *Med.* to recommend or order the use of (a drug or other remedy). [C16: from L *praescrībere* to write previously]
► pre'scriber *n*

prescript ('priːskrɪpt) *n* something laid down or prescribed. [C16: from L *praescriptum* something written down beforehand, from *praescrībere* to PRESCRIBE]

prescription (prɪ'skrɪpʃən) *n* **1a** written instructions from a physician to a pharmacist stating the form, dosage, strength, etc., of a drug to be issued to a specific patient. **1b** the drug or remedy prescribed. **2a** written instructions for an optician specifying the lenses needed to correct defects of vision. **2b** (*as modifier*): *prescription glasses.* **3** the act of prescribing. **4** something that is prescribed. **5** a long-established custom or a claim based on one. **6** *Law.* **6a** the uninterrupted possession of property over a stated time, after which a right or title is acquired (**positive prescription**). **6b** the barring of adverse claims to property, etc., after a specified time has elapsed, allowing the possessor to acquire title (**negative prescription**). [C14: from legal L *praescriptiō* an order; see PRESCRIBE]

prescriptive (prɪ'skrɪptɪv) *adj* **1** making or giving directions, rules, or injunctions. **2** sanctioned by longstanding custom. **3** based upon legal prescription: *a prescriptive title.*
► pre'scriptively *adv* ► pre'scriptiveness *n*

presence ('prezəns) *n* **1** the state or fact of being present. **2** immediate proximity. **3** personal appearance or bearing, esp. of a dignified nature. **4** an imposing or dignified personality. **5** an invisible spirit felt to be nearby. **6** *Electronics.* a recording control that boosts mid-range frequencies. **7** *Obs.* assembly or company. [C14: via OF from L *praesentia* a being before, from *praeesse* to be before]

presence chamber *n* the room in which a great person, such as a monarch, receives guests, assemblies, etc.

presence of mind *n* the ability to remain calm and act constructively during times of crisis.

presenile dementia (priː'siːnaɪl) *n* a form of dementia, of unknown cause, starting before a person is old.

present[1] ('prez°nt) *adj* **1** (*prenominal*) in existence at the time at which something is spoken or written. **2** (*postpositive*) being in a specified place, thing, etc.: *the murderer is present in this room.* **3** (*prenominal*) now being dealt with or under discussion: *the present author.* **4** *Grammar.* denoting a tense of verbs used when the action or event described is occurring at the time of utterance or when the speaker does not wish to make any explicit temporal reference. **5** *Arch.* instant: *present help is at hand.* ♦ *n* **6** *Grammar.* **6a** the present tense. **6b** a verb in this tense. **7 at present.** now. **8 for the present.** for the time being; temporarily. **9 the present.** the time being; now. ♦ *See also* **presents.** [C13: from L *praesens,* from *praeesse* to be in front of]

present[2] *vb* (prɪ'zent). (*mainly tr*) **1** to introduce (a person) to another, esp. to someone of higher rank. **2** to introduce to the public: *to present a play.* **3** to introduce and compere (a radio or television show). **4** to show; exhibit: *he presented a brave face to the world.* **5** to bring or suggest to the mind: *to present a problem.* **6** to put forward; submit: *she presented a proposal for a new book.* **7** to award: *to present a prize; to present a university with a foundation scholarship.* **8** to offer formally: *to present one's compliments.* **9** to hand over for action or settlement: *to present a bill.* **10** to depict in a particular manner: *the actor presented Hamlet as a very young man.* **11** to salute someone with (one's weapon) (usually in **present arms**). **12** to aim (a weapon). **13** to nominate (a clergyman) to a bishop for institution to a benefice in his diocese. **14** to lay (a charge, etc.) before a court, magistrate, etc., for consideration or trial. **15** to bring a formal charge or accusation against (a person); indict. **16** (*intr*) *Med.* to seek treatment for a particular problem: *she presented with postnatal depression.* **17** (*intr*) *Inf.* to produce a specified impression: *she presents well in public.* **18 present oneself.** to appear, esp. at a specific time and place. ♦ *n* ('prez°nt). **19** a gift. [C13: from OF *presenter,* from L *praesentāre* to exhibit, from *praesens* PRESENT[1]]

presentable (prɪ'zentəb°l) *adj* **1** fit to be presented or introduced to other people. **2** fit to be displayed or offered.
► pre'sentableness *or* pre,senta'bility *n* ► pre'sentably *adv*

presentation (ˌprezən'teɪʃən) *n* **1** the act of presenting or state of being presented. **2** the manner of presenting; delivery or overall impression. **3** a verbal report, often with illustrative material: *a presentation on the company results.* **4a** an offering, as of a gift. **4b** (*as modifier*): *a presentation copy of a book.* **5** a performance or representation, as of a play. **6** the formal introduction of a person, as at court; debut. **7** the act or right of nominating a clergyman to a benefice.
► ˌpresen'tational *adj*

presentationism (ˌprezən'teɪʃə,nɪzəm) *n Philosophy.* the theory that objects are identical with our perceptions of them. Cf. **representationalism.**
► ˌpresen'tationist, *adj*

presentative (prɪ'zentətɪv) *adj* **1** *Philosophy.* able to be known or perceived immediately. **2** conferring the right of ecclesiastical presentation.

present-day *n* (*modifier*) of the modern day; current: *I don't like present-day fashions.*

presenter (prɪ'zentə) *n* **1** a person who presents something or someone. **2** *Radio, television.* a person who introduces a show, links items, etc.

presentient (prɪ'senʃənt) *adj* characterized by or experiencing a presentiment. [C19: from L *praesentiens,* from *praesentire,* from *prae-* PRE- + *sentire* to feel]

presentiment (prɪ'zentɪmənt) *n* a sense of something about to happen; premonition. [C18: from obs. F, from *pressentir* to sense beforehand]

presently ('prez°ntlɪ) *adv* **1** in a short while; soon. **2** at the moment. **3** an archaic word for **immediately.**

presentment (prɪ'zentmənt) *n* **1** the act of presenting or state of being presented; presentation. **2** something presented, such as a picture, play, etc. **3** *Law.* a statement on oath by a jury of circumstances within their own knowledge or observation. **4** *Commerce.* the presenting of a bill of exchange, promissory note, etc.

present participle ('prez°nt) *n* a participial form of verbs used adjectivally when the action it describes is contemporaneous with that of the main verb of a sentence and also used in the formation of certain compound tenses. In English this form ends in -*ing.*

present perfect ('prez°nt) *adj, n Grammar.* another term for **perfect** (senses 8, 10).

presents ('prɛzənts) *pl n Law.* used in a deed or document to refer to itself: *know all men by these presents.*

preservative (prɪ'zɜːvətɪv) *n* **1** something that preserves, esp. a chemical added to foods. ◆ *adj* **2** tending or intended to preserve.

preserve (prɪ'zɜːv) *vb* **preserves, preserving, preserved.** (*mainly tr*) **1** to keep safe from danger or harm; protect. **2** to protect from decay or dissolution; maintain: *to preserve old buildings.* **3** to maintain possession of; keep up: *to preserve a façade of indifference.* **4** to prevent from decomposition or chemical change. **5** to prepare (food), as by salting, so that it will resist decomposition. **6** to make preserves (of fruit, etc.). **7** to rear and protect (game) in restricted places for hunting or fishing. **8** (*intr*) to maintain protection for game in preserves. ◆ *n* **9** something that preserves or is preserved. **10** a special domain: *archaeology is the preserve of specialists.* **11** (*usually pl*) fruit, etc., prepared by cooking with sugar. **12** areas where game is reared for private hunting or fishing. [C14: via OF, from LL *praeservāre,* lit.: to keep safe in advance, from L *prae* before + *servāre* to keep safe]
▶ **pre'servable** *adj* ▶ **preservation** (ˌprɛzə'veɪʃən) *n* ▶ **pre'server** *n*

preset *vb* (priː'sɛt), **presets, presetting, preset.** (*tr*) **1** to set (a timing device) so that something begins to operate at the time specified. ◆ *n* ('priːsɛt). **2** *Electronics.* a control, such as a variable resistor, that is not as accessible as the main controls and is used to set initial conditions.

preshrunk (priː'ʃrʌŋk) *adj* (of fabrics) having undergone shrinking during manufacture so that further shrinkage will not occur.

preside (prɪ'zaɪd) *vb* **presides, presiding, presided.** (*intr*) **1** to sit in or hold a position of authority, as over a meeting. **2** to exercise authority; control. [C17: via F from L *praesidēre* to superintend, from *prae* before + *sedēre* to sit]

presidency ('prɛzɪdənsɪ) *n, pl* **presidencies.** **1** the office, dignity, or term of a president. **2** (*often cap.*) the office of president of a republic, esp. of the President of the US.

president ('prɛzɪdənt) *n* **1** (*often cap.*) the head of state of a republic, esp. of the US **2** (in the US) the chief executive officer of a company, corporation, etc. **3** a person who presides over an assembly, meeting, etc. **4** the chief executive officer of certain establishments of higher education. [C14: via OF from LL *praesidens* ruler; see PRESIDE]
▶ **presidential** (ˌprɛzɪ'dɛnʃəl) *adj* ▶ **presi'dentially** *adv* ▶ **'presidentship** *n*

presidium *or* **praesidium** (prɪ'sɪdɪəm) *n* **1** (*often cap.*) (in Communist countries) a permanent committee of a larger body, such as a legislature, that acts for it when it is in recess. **2** a collective presidency. [C20: from Russian *prezidium,* from L *praesidium,* from *praesidēre* to superintend; see PRESIDE]

Presley ★ ('prɛzlɪ) *n* **Elvis (Aaron** *or* **Aron).** 1935–77, US rock and roll singer. His recordings include "That's all Right (Mama)" (1954), "Heartbreak Hotel" (1956), "Hound Dog" (1956), numbers from the films *Loving You* and *Jailhouse Rock* (both 1957), and *Elvis is Back* (1960).

press[1] (prɛs) *vb* **1** to apply or exert weight, force, or steady pressure (on): *he pressed the button on the camera.* **2** (*tr*) to squeeze or compress so as to alter in shape. **3** to apply heat or pressure to (clothing) so as to smooth out creases. **4** to make (objects) from soft material by pressing with a mould, etc., esp. to make gramophone records from plastic. **5** (*tr*) to clasp; embrace. **6** (*tr*) to extract or force out (juice) by pressure (from). **7** (*tr*) to force or compel. **8** to importune (a person) insistently: *they pressed for an answer.* **9** to harass or cause harassment. **10** (*tr*) to plead or put forward strongly: *to press a claim.* **11** (*intr*) to be urgent. **12** (*tr; usually passive*) to have little of: *we're hard pressed for time.* **13** (when *intr,* often foll. by *on* or *forward*) to hasten or advance or cause to hasten or advance in a forceful manner. **14** (*intr*) to crowd; push. **15** (*tr*) *Arch.* to trouble or oppress. ◆ *n* **16** any machine that exerts pressure to form, shape, or cut materials or to extract liquids, compress solids, or hold components together while an adhesive joint is formed. **17** See **printing press. 18** the art or process of printing. **19 to (the) press.** to be printed: *when is this book going to press?* **20 the press. 20a** news media collectively, esp. newspapers. **20b** (*as modifier*): *press relations.* **21** the opinions and reviews in the newspapers, etc.: *the play received a poor press.* **22** the act of pressing or state of being pressed. **23** the act of crowding or pushing together. **24** a closely packed throng; crowd. **25** a cupboard, esp. a large one used for storing clothes or linen. **26** a wood or metal clamp to prevent tennis rackets, etc., from warping when not in use. [C14 *pressen,* from OF *presser,* from L, from *premere* to press]

press[2] (prɛs) *vb* (*tr*) **1** to recruit (men) by forcible measures for military service. **2** to use for a purpose other than intended (esp. in **press into service**). ◆ *n* **3** recruitment into military service by forcible measures, as by a press gang. [C16: back formation from *prest* to recruit soldiers; also infl. by PRESS[1]]

press agent *n* a person employed to obtain favourable publicity, such as notices in newspapers, for an organization, actor, etc.

press box *n* an area reserved for reporters, as in a sports stadium.

Pressburg ★ ('prɛsburk) *n* the German name for Bratislava.

Pressburger ★ ('prɛsˌbɜːgə) *n* **Emeric** ('ɛmərɪk). 1902–88, Hungarian film writer and producer, living in Britain: best known for his collaboration (1942–57) with Michael Powell. Films include *The Life and Death of Colonel Blimp* (1943), *I Know Where I'm Going* (1944), and *A Matter of Life and Death* (1945).

press conference *n* an interview for press reporters given by a politician, film star, etc.

press fit *n Engineering.* a type of fit for mating parts, usually tighter than a sliding fit, used when the parts do not have to move relative to each other.

press gallery *n* an area for newspaper reporters, esp. in a legislative assembly.

press gang *n* **1** (formerly) a detachment of men used to press civilians for service in the navy or army. ◆ *vb* **press-gang.** (*tr*) **2** to force (a person) to join the navy or army by a press gang. **3** to induce (a person) to perform a duty by forceful persuasion.

pressing ('prɛsɪŋ) *adj* **1** demanding immediate attention. **2** persistent or importunate. ◆ *n* **3** a large specified number of gramophone records produced at one time from a master record. **4** *Football.* the tactic of trying to stay very close to the opposition when they are in possession of the ball.
▶ **'pressingly** *adv*

pressman ('prɛsmən, -ˌmæn) *n, pl* **pressmen. 1** a journalist. **2** a person who operates a printing press.

press of sail *n Naut.* the most sail a vessel can carry under given conditions. Also called: **press of canvas.**

press release *n* an official announcement or account of a news item circulated to the press.

pressroom ('prɛsˌruːm, -ˌrʊm) *n* the room in a printing establishment that houses the printing presses.

press stud *n* a fastening device consisting of one part with a projecting knob that snaps into a hole on another like part, used esp. on clothing. Canad. equivalent: **dome fastener.**

press-up *n* an exercise in which the body is alternately raised from and lowered to the floor by the arms only, the trunk being kept straight. Also called (US and Canad.): **push-up.**

pressure ('prɛʃə) *n* **1** the state of pressing or being pressed. **2** the exertion of force by one body on the surface of another. **3** a moral force that compels: *to bring pressure to bear.* **4** urgent claims or demands: *to work under pressure.* **5** a burdensome condition that is hard to bear: *the pressure of grief.* **6** the force applied to a unit area of a surface, usually measured in pascals, millibars, torrs, or atmospheres. **7** short for **atmospheric pressure** or **blood pressure.** ◆ *vb* **pressures, pressuring, pressured.** (*tr*) **8** to constrain or compel, as by moral force. **9** another word for **pressurize.** [C14: from LL *pressūra* a pressing, from L *premere* to press]

pressure cooker *n* a strong hermetically sealed pot in

which food may be cooked quickly under pressure at a temperature above the normal boiling point of water.
▶ **'pressure-ˌcook** vb

pressure group n a group of people who seek to exert pressure on legislators, public opinion, etc., in order to promote their own ideas or welfare.

pressure point n any of several points on the body above an artery that, when firmly pressed, will control bleeding from the artery at a point farther away from the heart.

pressure suit n an inflatable suit worn by a person flying at high altitudes or in space, to provide protection from low pressure.

pressurize or **pressurise** ('preʃəˌraɪz) vb **pressurizes, pressurizing, pressurized** or **pressurises, pressurising, pressurised.** (tr) 1 to increase the pressure in (an enclosure, such as an aircraft cabin) in order to maintain approximately atmospheric pressure when the external pressure is low. 2 to increase pressure on (a fluid). 3 to make insistent demands of (someone); coerce.
▶ ˌpressuri'zation or ˌpressuri'sation n

pressurized-water reactor n a type of nuclear reactor that uses water under pressure as both coolant and moderator.

presswork ('preswɜːk) n the operation of, or matter printed by, a printing press.

Prestel ('prestel) n Trademark. (in Britain) the viewdata service operated by British Telecom.

Prester John ★ ('prestə) n a legendary Christian priest and king, believed in the Middle Ages to have ruled in the Far East, but identified in the 14th century with the king of Ethiopia. [C14 Prestre Johan, from Med. L presbyter Iohannes Priest John]

prestidigitation (ˌprestɪˌdɪdʒɪ'teɪʃən) n another name for **sleight of hand.** [C19: from F: quick-fingeredness, from L praestigiae tricks, prob. infl. by F preste nimble, & L digitus finger]
▶ ˌpresti'digiˌtator n

prestige (pre'stiːʒ) n 1 high status or reputation achieved through success, influence, wealth, etc.; renown. 2a the power to impress; glamour. 2b (modifier): a prestige car. [C17: via F from L praestigiae tricks]
▶ **prestigious** (pre'stɪdʒəs) adj

prestissimo (pre'stɪsɪˌməʊ) Music. ◆ adj, adv 1 to be played as fast as possible. ◆ n, pl **prestissimos.** 2 a piece to be played in this way. [C18: from It.: very quickly, from presto fast]

presto ('prestəʊ) adj, adv 1 Music. to be played very fast. ◆ adv 2 immediately (esp. in **hey presto**). ◆ n, pl **prestos.** 3 Music. a passage directed to be played very quickly. [C16: from It.: fast, from LL praestus (adj) ready to hand, L praestō (adv) present]

Preston ★ ('prestən) n a town in NW England, administrative centre of Lancashire, on the River Ribble: developed as a weaving centre (17th–18th centuries). Pop.: 177 660 (1991).

Prestonpans ★ (ˌprestən'pænz) n a small town and resort in SE Scotland, in East Lothian on the Firth of Forth: scene of the battle (1745) in which the Jacobite army of Prince Charles Edward defeated government forces under Sir John Cope. Pop.: 7014 (1991).

prestressed concrete (ˌpriː'strest) n concrete that contains steel wires that are stretched to counteract the stresses that will occur under load.

Prestwich ★ ('prestwɪtʃ) n a town in Bury, in NW England, in Greater Manchester. Pop.: 31 801 (1991).

Prestwick ★ ('prestwɪk) n a town in SW Scotland, in South Ayrshire on the Firth of Clyde; international airport, golf course: tourism. Pop.: 13 705 (1991).

presumably (prɪ'zjuːməblɪ) adv (sentence modifier) one supposes that: presumably he won't see you, if you're leaving tomorrow.

presume (prɪ'zjuːm) vb **presumes, presuming, presumed.** 1 (when tr, often takes a clause as object) to take (something) for granted; assume. 2 (when tr, often foll. by an infinitive) to dare (to do something): do you presume to copy my work? 3 (intr; foll. by on or upon) to rely or depend: don't presume

on his agreement. 4 (intr; foll. by on or upon) to take advantage (of): don't presume upon his good nature too far. 5 (tr) Law. to take as proved until contrary evidence is produced. [C14: via OF from L praesūmere to take in advance, from prae before + sūmere to ASSUME]
▶ **presumedly** (prɪ'zjuːmɪdlɪ) adv ▶ **pre'suming** adj

presumption (prɪ'zʌmpʃən) n 1 the act of presuming. 2 bold or insolent behaviour. 3 a belief or assumption based on reasonable evidence. 4 a basis on which to presume. 5 Law. an inference of the truth of a fact from other facts proved. [C13: via OF from L praesumptiō anticipation, from praesūmere to take beforehand; see PRESUME]

presumptive (prɪ'zʌmptɪv) adj 1 based on presumption or probability. 2 affording reasonable ground for belief.
▶ **pre'sumptively** adv

presumptuous (prɪ'zʌmptjʊəs) adj characterized by presumption or tending to presume; bold; forward.
▶ **pre'sumptuously** adv ▶ **pre'sumptuousness** n

presuppose (ˌpriːsə'pəʊz) vb **presupposes, presupposing, presupposed.** (tr) 1 to take for granted. 2 to require as a necessary prior condition.
▶ **presupposition** (ˌpriːsʌpə'zɪʃən) n

preteen (priː'tiːn) n a boy or girl approaching his or her teens.

pretence or US **pretense** (prɪ'tens) n 1 the act of pretending. 2 a false display; affectation. 3 a claim, esp. a false one, to a right, title, or distinction. 4 make-believe. 5 a pretext.

pretend (prɪ'tend) vb 1 (when tr, usually takes a clause as object or an infinitive) to claim or allege (something untrue). 2 (tr; may take a clause as object or an infinitive) to make believe, as in a play: you pretend to be Ophelia. 3 (intr; foll. by to) to present a claim, esp. a dubious one: to pretend to the throne. 4 (intr; foll. by to) Obs. to aspire as a candidate or suitor (for). ◆ adj 5 make-believe; imaginary. [C14: from L praetendere to stretch forth, feign]

pretender (prɪ'tendə) n 1 a person who pretends or makes false allegations. 2 a person who mounts a claim, as to a throne or title.

pretension (prɪ'tenʃən) n 1 (often pl) a false claim, esp. to merit, worth, or importance. 2 a specious or unfounded allegation; pretext. 3 the quality of being pretentious.

pretentious (prɪ'tenʃəs) adj 1 making claim to distinction or importance, esp. undeservedly. 2 ostentatious.
▶ **pre'tentiously** adv ▶ **pre'tentiousness** n

preterite or esp. US **preterit** ('pretərɪt) Grammar. ◆ n 1 a tense of verbs used to relate past action, formed in English by inflection of the verb, as jumped, swam. 2 a verb in this tense. ◆ adj 3 denoting this tense. [C14: from LL praeteritum (tempus) past (time), from L praeterīre to go by, from preter- beyond + īre to go]

preterm (priː'tɜːm) adj 1 (of a baby) born prematurely. ◆ adv 2 prematurely.

pretermit (ˌpriːtə'mɪt) vb **pretermits, pretermitting, pretermitted.** (tr) Rare. 1 to disregard. 2 to fail to do; neglect; omit. [C16: from L praetermittere to let pass, from preter- beyond + mittere to send]

preternatural (ˌpriːtə'nætʃrəl) adj 1 beyond what is ordinarily found in nature; abnormal. 2 another word for **supernatural.** [C16: from Med. L praeternātūrālis, from L praeter natūram beyond the scope of nature]
▶ ˌpreter'naturally adv

pretext ('priːtekst) n 1 a fictitious reason given in order to conceal the real one. 2 a pretence. [C16: from L praetextum disguise, from praetexere to weave in front, disguise]

pretor ('priːtə, -tɔː) n a variant (esp. US) spelling of **praetor.**

Pretoria ★ (prɪ'tɔːrɪə) n a city in N South Africa, the administrative capital of South Africa: two universities (1873, 1930); large steelworks. Pop.: 525 583 (1991).

Pretorius ★ (prɪ'tɔːrɪəs) n 1 **Andries Wilhelmus Jacobus** ('ɑndriːs wɪl'helmys jaː'koːbys). 1799–1853, a Boer leader in the Great Trek (1838) to escape British sovereignty; he also led an expedition to the Transvaal (1848). The town Pretoria was named after him. 2 his son, **Marthinus Wessels** (mar'tiːnys 'wesəls). 1819–1901, first president of the South African Republic (1857–71) and of the Orange Free State (1859–63).

prettify ('prɪtɪˌfaɪ) *vb* **prettifies, prettifying, prettified.** (*tr*) to make pretty, esp. in a trivial fashion; embellish.
▸ ˌpretti'fi'cation *n* ▸ 'pretti,fier *n*

pretty ('prɪtɪ) *adj* **prettier, prettiest. 1** pleasing or appealing in a delicate or graceful way. **2** dainty, neat, or charming. **3** *Inf., often ironical.* excellent, grand, or fine: *here's a pretty mess!* **4** commendable; good of its kind: *he replied with a pretty wit.* **5** *Inf.* effeminate; foppish. **6** *Arch. or Scot.* vigorous or brave. **7 sitting pretty.** *Inf.* well placed or established financially, socially, etc. ◆ *n, pl* **pretties. 8** a pretty person or thing. ◆ *adv Inf.* **9** fairly; somewhat. **10** very. ◆ *vb* **pretties, prettying, prettied. 11** (*tr*; often foll. by *up*) to make pretty; adorn. [OE *prættig* clever]
▸ 'prettily *adv* ▸ 'prettiness *n*

pretty-pretty *adj Inf.* excessively or ostentatiously pretty.

pretzel ('prɛtsəl) *n* a brittle savoury biscuit, in the form of a knot or stick, eaten esp. in Germany and the US. [C19: from G, from OHG *brezitella*]

Preussen ★ ('prɔysən) *n* the German name for **Prussia**.

prevail (prɪ'veɪl) *vb* (*intr*) **1** (often foll. by *over* or *against*) to prove superior; gain mastery: *skill will prevail.* **2** to be the most important feature; be prevalent. **3** to exist widely; be in force. **4** (often foll. by *on* or *upon*) to succeed in persuading or inducing. [C14: from L *praevalēre* to be superior in strength]
▸ pre'vailer *n*

prevailing (prɪ'veɪlɪŋ) *adj* **1** generally accepted; widespread: *the prevailing opinion.* **2** most frequent; predominant: *the prevailing wind is from the north.*
▸ pre'vailingly *adv*

prevalent ('prɛvələnt) *adj* **1** widespread or current. **2** superior in force or power; predominant.
▸ 'prevalence *n* ▸ 'prevalently *adv*

prevaricate (prɪ'værɪˌkeɪt) *vb* **prevaricates, prevaricating, prevaricated.** (*intr*) to speak or act falsely or evasively with intent to deceive. [C16: from L *praevāricārī* to walk crookedly, from *prae* beyond + *vāricare* to straddle the legs]
▸ preˌvari'cation *n* ▸ pre'vari,cator *n*

prevent (prɪ'vɛnt) *vb* **1** (*tr*) to keep from happening, esp. by taking precautionary action. **2** (*tr*; often foll. by *from*) to keep (someone from doing something). **3** (*intr*) to interpose or act as a hindrance. **4** (*tr*) *Arch.* to anticipate or precede. [C15: from L *praevenīre*, from *prae* before + *venīre* to come]
▸ pre'ventable *or* pre'ventible *adj* ▸ pre'ventably *or* pre'ventibly *adv*

prevention (prɪ'vɛnʃən) *n* **1** the act of preventing. **2** a hindrance or impediment.

preventive (prɪ'vɛntɪv) *adj* **1** tending or intended to prevent or hinder. **2** *Med.* tending to prevent disease; prophylactic. **3** (in Britain) of, relating to, or belonging to the customs and excise service or the coastguard. ◆ *n* **4** something that serves to prevent or hinder. **5** *Med.* any drug or agent that tends to prevent disease. Also (for senses 1, 2, 4, 5): **preventative.**
▸ pre'ventively *or* pre'ventatively *adv*

Prévert ★ (*French* prevεr) *n* **Jacques** (ʒak). 1900–77, Parisian poet, satirist, and writer of film scripts, noted esp. for his song poems. He was a member of the surrealist group from 1925 to 1929.

preview ('priːvjuː) *n* **1** an advance view or sight. **2** an advance showing before public presentation of a film, art exhibition, etc., usually before an invited audience. ◆ *vb* **3** (*tr*) to view in advance.

Previn ★ ('prɛvɪn) *n* **André** ('ɒndreɪ). born 1929, US orchestral conductor, born in Germany; living in Britain.

previous ('priːvɪəs) *adj* **1** (*prenominal*) existing or coming before something else. **2** (*postpositive*) *Inf.* taking place or done too soon; premature. **3 previous to.** before. [C17: from L *praevius* leading the way, from *prae* before + *via* way]
▸ 'previously *adv* ▸ 'previousness *n*

previous question *n* **1** (in the House of Commons) a

motion to drop the present topic under debate, put in order to prevent a vote. **2** (in the House of Lords and US legislative bodies) a motion to vote on a bill without delay.

previse (prɪ'vaɪz) *vb* **previses, prevising, prevised.** (*tr*) *Rare.* **1** to predict or foresee. **2** to notify in advance. [C16: from L *praevidēre* to foresee]
▸ **prevision** (prɪ'vɪʒən) *n*

Prévost d'Exiles ★ (*French* prevo dεgzil) *n* **Antoine François** (ɑ̃twan frɑ̃swa), known as *Abbé Prévost.* 1697–1763, French novelist, noted for his romance *Manon Lescaut* (1731), which served as the basis for operas by Puccini and Massenet.

prey (preɪ) *n* **1** an animal hunted or captured by another for food. **2** a person or thing that becomes the victim of a hostile person, influence, etc. **3 bird** *or* **beast of prey.** a bird or animal that preys on others for food. **4** an archaic word for **booty.** ◆ *vb* (*intr*; often foll. by *on* or *upon*) **5** to hunt food by killing other animals. **6** to make a victim (of others), as by profiting at their expense. **7** to exert a depressing or obsessive effect (on the mind, spirits, etc.). [C13: from OF *preie*, from L *praeda* booty]
▸ 'preyer *n*

Priam ★ ('praɪəm) *n Greek myth.* the last king of Troy, killed at its fall. He was father by Hecuba of Hector, Paris, and Cassandra.

priapic (praɪ'æpɪk, -'eɪ-) *or* **priapean** (ˌpraɪə'piːən) *adj* **1** (*sometimes cap.*) of or relating to Priapus. **2** a less common word for **phallic.**

priapism ('praɪəˌpɪzəm) *n Pathol.* prolonged painful erection of the penis, caused by neurological disorders, etc. [C17: from LL *priāpismus*, ult. from Gk PRIAPUS]

Priapus ★ (praɪ'eɪpəs) *n* **1** (in classical antiquity) the god of the male procreative power and of gardens and vineyards. **2** (*often not cap.*) a representation of the penis.

Pribilof Islands ★ ('prɪbɪləf) *pl n* a group of islands in the Bering Sea, off SW Alaska, belonging to the US: the breeding ground of the northern fur seal. Area: about 168 sq. km (65 sq. miles). Also called: **Fur Seal Islands.**

price (praɪs) *n* **1** the sum in money or goods for which anything is or may be bought or sold. **2** the cost at which anything is obtained. **3** the cost of bribing a person. **4** a sum of money offered as a reward for a capture or killing. **5** value or worth, esp. high worth. **6** *Gambling.* another word for **odds. 7 at any price.** whatever the price or cost. **8 at a price.** at a high price. **9 what price (something)?** what are the chances of (something) happening now? ◆ *vb* **prices, pricing, priced.** (*tr*) **10** to fix the price of. **11** to discover the price of. **12 price out of the market.** to charge so highly for as to prevent the sale, hire, etc., of. [C13 *pris*, from OF, from L *pretium*]
▸ 'pricer *n*

price control *n* the establishment and maintenance of maximum price levels for basic goods and services by a government.

price-dividend ratio *n* the ratio of the price of a share on a stock exchange to the dividends per share paid in the previous year, used as a measure of a company's potential as an investment. Abbrevs.: **P-D ratio, PDR.**

price-earnings ratio *n* the ratio of the price of a share on the stock exchange to the earnings per share, used as a measure of a company's future profitability. Abbrev.: **P-E ratio.**

price-fixing *n* **1** the setting of prices by agreement among producers and distributors. **2** another name for **price control** or **resale price maintenance.**

price leadership *n Marketing.* the setting of the price of a product or service by a dominant firm at a level that competitors can match, in order to avoid a price war.

priceless ('praɪslɪs) *adj* **1** of inestimable worth; invaluable. **2** *Inf.* extremely amusing or ridiculous.
▸ 'pricelessly *adv* ▸ 'pricelessness *n*

price ring *n* a group of traders formed to maintain the prices of their goods.

price-sensitive *adj* likely to affect the price of property, esp. shares and securities: *price-sensitive information.*

★ people and places

pricey or **pricy** ('praɪsɪ) adj **pricier**, **priciest**. an informal word for **expensive**.

prick (prɪk) vb (mainly tr) **1a** to make (a small hole) in (something) by piercing lightly with a sharp point. **1b** to wound in this manner. **2** (intr) to cause or have a piercing or stinging sensation. **3** to cause to feel a sharp emotional pain: *knowledge of such poverty pricked his conscience*. **4** to puncture. **5** to outline by or with points. **6** (also intr; usually foll. by up) to rise or raise erect: *the dog pricked his ears up*. **7** (usually foll. by out or off) to transplant (seedlings) into a larger container. **8** Arch. to urge on, esp. to spur a horse on. **9 prick up one's ears.** to start to listen attentively; become interested. ◆ n **10** the act of pricking or the sensation of being pricked. **11** a mark made by a sharp point; puncture. **12** a sharp emotional pain: *a prick of conscience*. **13** a taboo slang word for **penis**. **14** Sl., derog. an obnoxious or despicable person. **15** an instrument or weapon with a sharp point. **16** the track of an animal, esp. a hare. **17 kick against the pricks.** to hurt oneself by struggling against something in vain. [OE *prica* point, puncture]
▶ '**pricker** n

pricket ('prɪkɪt) n **1** a male deer in the second year of life having unbranched antlers. **2** a sharp metal spike on which to stick a candle. [C14 *priket*, from *prik* PRICK]

prickle ('prɪkᵊl) n **1** Bot. a pointed process arising from the outer layer of a stem, leaf, etc., and containing no woody tissue. Cf. **thorn**. **2** a pricking or stinging sensation. ◆ vb **prickles**, **prickling**, **prickled**. **3** to feel or cause to feel a stinging sensation. **4** (tr) to prick, as with a thorn. [OE *pricel*]

prickly ('prɪklɪ) adj **pricklier**, **prickliest**. **1** having or covered with prickles. **2** stinging. **3** irritable. **4** full of difficulties: *a prickly problem*.
▶ '**prickliness** n

prickly heat n a nontechnical name for **miliaria**.

prickly pear n **1** any of various tropical cactuses having flattened or cylindrical spiny joints and oval fruit that is edible in some species. **2** the fruit of any of these plants.

pride (praɪd) n **1** a feeling of honour and self-respect; a sense of personal worth. **2** excessive self-esteem; conceit. **3** a source of pride. **4** satisfaction or pleasure in one's own or another's success, achievements, etc. (esp. in **take (a) pride in**). **5** the better or superior part of something. **6** the most flourishing time. **7** a group (of lions). **8** courage; spirit. **9** Arch. pomp or splendour. **10 pride of place.** the most important position. ◆ vb **prides**, **priding**, **prided**. **11** (tr; foll. by on or upon) to take pride in (oneself) for. [OE *prȳda*]
▶ '**prideful** adj ▶ '**pridefully** adv

Pride ★ (praɪd) n **Thomas.** died 1658, soldier on the Parliamentary side during the Civil War. He expelled members of the Long Parliament hostile to the army (**Pride's Purge**, 1648) and signed Charles I's death warrant.

prie-dieu (priːˈdjɜː) n a piece of furniture consisting of a low surface for kneeling upon and a narrow front surmounted by a rest, for use when praying. [C18: from F, from *prier* to pray + *Dieu* God]

prier or **pryer** ('praɪə) n a person who pries.

priest (priːst) n **1** a person ordained to act as a mediator between God and man in administering the sacraments, preaching, etc. **2** (in episcopal Churches) a minister in the second grade of the hierarchy of holy orders, ranking below a bishop but above a deacon. **3** a minister of any religion. **4** an official who offers sacrifice on behalf of the people and performs other religious ceremonies. ◆ vb **5** (tr) to make a priest; ordain. [OE *prēost*, apparently from PRESBYTER]
▶ '**priestess** fem n ▶ '**priest,hood** n ▶ '**priest,like** adj
▶ '**priestly** adj

priestcraft ('priːst,krɑːft) n **1** the art and skills involved in the work of a priest. **2** Derog. the influence of priests upon politics.

priest-hole or **priest's hole** n a secret chamber in certain houses in England, built as a hiding place for Roman Catholic priests when they were proscribed in the 16th and 17th centuries.

Priestley ★ ('priːstlɪ) n **1 J(ohn) B(oynton)**. 1894–1984,

British author. His works include the novels *The Good Companions* (1929) and *Angel Pavement* (1930) and the comedy *Laburnum Grove* (1933). **2 Joseph**. 1733–1804, British chemist, political theorist, and clergyman, in the US from 1794. He discovered oxygen (1774) independently of Scheele and isolated and described many other gases.

prig[1] (prɪg) n a person who is smugly self-righteous and narrow-minded. [C18: from ?]
▶ '**priggery** or '**priggishness** n ▶ '**priggish** adj ▶ '**priggishly** adv

prig[2] (prɪg) Brit. arch. sl. ◆ vb **prigs**, **prigging**, **prigged**. **1** another word for **steal**. ◆ n **2** another word for **thief**. [C16: from ?]

Prigogine ★ (French prigɔʒin) n **Ilya** (ilja), Viscount. born 1917, Belgian chemist, born in Russia: Nobel prize for chemistry 1977 for his work on nonequilibrium thermodynamics.

prim (prɪm) adj **primmer**, **primmest**. **1** affectedly proper, precise, or formal. ◆ vb **prims**, **primming**, **primmed**. **2** (tr) to make prim. **3** to purse (the mouth) primly or (of the mouth) to be so pursed. [C18: from ?]
▶ '**primly** adv ▶ '**primness** n

prima ballerina ('priːmə) n a leading female ballet dancer. [from It., lit.: first ballerina]

primacy ('praɪməsɪ) n, pl **primacies**. **1** the state of being first in rank, grade, etc. **2** Christianity. the office, rank, or jurisdiction of a primate, senior bishop, or pope.

prima donna ('priːmə 'dɒnə) n, pl **prima donnas**. **1** a leading female operatic star. **2** Inf. a temperamental person. [C19: from It.: first lady]

prima facie ('praɪmə 'feɪʃɪ) adv at first sight; as it seems at first. [C15: from L, from *prīmus* first + *faciēs* FACE]

prima-facie evidence n Law. evidence that is sufficient to establish a fact or to raise a presumption of the truth unless controverted.

primal ('praɪməl) adj **1** first or original. **2** chief or most important. [C17: from Med. L *prīmālis*, from L *prīmus* first]

primaquine ('praɪmə,kwiːn) n a synthetic drug used in the treatment of malaria. [C20: from *prima-*, from L *prīmus* first + QUIN(OLIN)E]

primarily ('praɪmərɪlɪ, praɪˈmærɪlɪ, -ˈmɛərɪlɪ) adv **1** principally; chiefly; mainly. **2** at first; originally.

primary ('praɪmərɪ) adj **1** first in importance, degree, rank, etc. **2** first in position or time, as in a series. **3** fundamental; basic. **4** being the first stage; elementary. **5** (prenominal) of or relating to the education of children up to the age of 11. **6** (of the flight feathers of a bird's wing) growing from the manus. **7a** being the part of an electric circuit, such as a transformer, in which a changing current induces a current in a neighbouring circuit: *a primary coil*. **7b** (of a current) flowing in such a circuit. **8a** (of a product) consisting of a natural raw material; unmanufactured. **8b** (of production or industry) involving the extraction or winning of such products. **9** (of Latin, Greek, or Sanskrit tenses) referring to present or future time. **10** Geol., obs. relating to the Palaeozoic or earlier eras. ◆ n, pl **primaries**. **11** a person or thing that is first in rank, occurrence, etc. **12** (in the US) a preliminary election in which the voters of a state or region choose a party's convention delegates, nominees for office, etc. Full name: **primary election**. **13** short for **primary colour** or **primary school**. **14** any of the flight feathers growing from the manus of a bird's wing. **15** a primary coil, winding, inductance, or current in an electric circuit. **16** Astron. a celestial body around which one or more specified secondary bodies orbit: *the sun is the primary of the earth*. [C15: from L *prīmārius* principal, from *prīmus* first]

primary accent or **stress** n Linguistics. the strongest accent in a word or breath group, as that on the first syllable of *agriculture*.

primary cell n an electric cell that generates an electromotive force by the direct and usually irreversible conversion of chemical energy into electrical energy. Also called: **voltaic cell**.

primary colour n **1** any of three colours (usually red, green, and blue) that can be mixed to match any other colour, including white light but excluding black. **2** any one of the colours cyan, magenta, or yellow. An equal mixture of the three produces a black pigment. **3** any one of the colours red, yellow, green, or blue. All other colours look like a mixture of two or more of these colours.

primary school *n* **1** (in England and Wales) a school for children below the age of 11. It is usually divided into an infant and a junior section. **2** (in Scotland) a school for children below the age of 12. **3** (in the US and Canad.) a school equivalent to the first three or four grades of elementary school.

primate[1] ('praimeit) *n* **1** any placental mammal of the order *Primates*, typically having flexible hands, good eyesight, and, in the higher apes, a highly developed brain: includes lemurs, apes, and man. ◆ *adj* **2** of, relating to, or belonging to the order *Primates*. [C18: from NL *primates*, pl. of *prīmās* principal, from *prīmus* first]
▶ **primatial** (prai'meiʃəl) *adj*

primate[2] ('praimeit) *n* **1** another name for an **archbishop**. **2 Primate of all England.** the Archbishop of Canterbury. **3 Primate of England.** the Archbishop of York. [C13: from OF, from L *prīmās* principal, from *prīmus* first]

prime (praim) *adj* **1** (*prenominal*) first in quality or value; first-rate. **2** (*prenominal*) fundamental; original. **3** (*prenominal*) first in importance; chief. **4** *Maths.* **4a** having no factors except itself or one: $x^2 + x + 3$ *is a prime polynomial.* **4b** (foll. by *to*) having no common factors (with): *20 is prime to 21.* **5** *Finance.* having the best credit rating: *prime investments.* ◆ *n* **6** the time when a thing is at its best. **7** a period of power, vigour, etc. (esp. in **the prime of life**). **8** *Maths.* short for **prime number**. **9** *Chiefly RC Church.* the second of the seven canonical hours of the divine office, originally fixed for the first hour of the day, at sunrise. **10** the first of eight basic positions from which a parry or attack can be made in fencing. ◆ *vb* **primes, priming, primed. 11** to prepare (something). **12** (*tr*) to apply a primer, such as paint or size, to (a surface). **13** (*tr*) to fill (a pump) with its working fluid before starting, in order to expel air from it before starting. **14 prime the pump. 14a** See **pump priming. 14b** to make an initial input in order to set a process going. **15** (*tr*) to increase the quantity of fuel in the float chamber of (a carburettor) in order to facilitate the starting of an engine. **16** (*tr*) to insert a primer into (a gun, mine, etc.) preparatory to detonation or firing. **17** (*tr*) to provide with facts beforehand; brief. [(adj) C14: from L *prīmus* first; (n) C13: from L *prīma* (*hora*) the first (hour); (vb) C16: from ?]
▶ **'primeness** *n*

prime cost *n* the portion of the cost of a commodity that varies directly with the amount of it produced, principally comprising materials and labour. Also called: **variable cost.**

prime meridian *n* the 0° meridian from which the other meridians are calculated, usually taken to pass through Greenwich.

prime minister *n* **1** the head of a parliamentary government. **2** the chief minister of a sovereign or a state.

prime mover *n* **1** the original force behind an idea, enterprise, etc. **2a** the source of power, such as fuel, wind, electricity, etc., for a machine. **2b** the means of extracting power from such a source, such as a steam engine.

prime number *n* an integer that cannot be factorized into other integers but is only divisible by itself or 1, such as 2, 3, 7, and 11.

primer[1] ('praimə) *n* an introductory text, such as a school textbook. [C14: via Anglo-Norman, from Med. L *primārius* (*liber*) a first (book), from L *prīmārius* PRIMARY]

primer[2] ('praimə) *n* **1** a person or thing that primes. **2** a device, such as a tube containing explosive, for detonating the main charge in a gun, mine, etc. **3** a substance, such as paint, applied to a surface as a base, sealer, etc. [C15: see PRIME (vb)]

prime rate *n* the lowest commercial interest rate charged by a bank at a particular time.

primers ('praiməz) *n* (*functioning as sing*) *NZ inf.* the youngest classes in a primary school: *in the primers.*

prime time *n* the peak viewing time on television, for which advertising rates are the highest.

primeval *or* **primaeval** (prai'miːv'l) *adj* of or belonging to the first ages of the world. [C17: from L *prīmaevus* youthful, from *prīmus* first + *aevum* age]
▶ **pri'mevally** *or* **pri'maevally** *adv*

priming ('praimɪŋ) *n* **1** something used to prime. **2** a substance used to ignite an explosive charge.

primitive ('primitiv) *adj* **1** of or belonging to the beginning; original. **2** characteristic of an early state, esp. in being crude or uncivilized: *a primitive dwelling.* **3** *Anthropol.* denoting a preliterate and nonindustrial social system. **4** *Biol.* of, relating to, or resembling an early stage in development: *primitive amphibians.* **5** showing the characteristics of primitive painters; untrained, childlike, or naive. **6** *Geol.* of or denoting rocks formed in or before the Palaeozoic era. **7** denoting a word from which another word is derived, as for example *hope*, from which *hopeless* is derived. **8** *Protestant theol.* of or associated with a group that breaks away from a sect, denomination, or Church in order to return to what is regarded as the original simplicity of the Gospels. ◆ *n* **9** a primitive person or thing. **10a** an artist whose work does not conform to traditional standards of Western painting, such as a painter from an African civilization. **10b** a painter of the pre-Renaissance era in European painting. **10c** a painter of any era whose work appears childlike or untrained. ◆ Also called (for a, c): **naive. 11** a work by such an artist. **12** a word from which another word is derived. **13** *Maths.* a curve or other form from which another is derived. [C14: from L *prīmitīvus* earliest of its kind from *prīmus* first]
▶ **'primitively** *adv* ▶ **'primitiveness** *n*

primitivism ('primiti,vizəm) *n* **1** the condition of being primitive. **2** the belief that the value of primitive cultures is superior to that of the modern world.
▶ **'primitivist** *n, adj*

primo ('priːməʊ) *n, pl* **primos** *or* **primi** (-miː). *Music.* **1** the upper or right-hand part of a piano duet. **2 tempo primo.** at the same speed as at the beginning of the piece. [It.: first, from L *prīmus*]

Primo de Rivera ★ (*Spanish* 'primo de ri'βera) *n* **1 José Antonio** (xo'se an'tonjo). 1903–36, Spanish politician; founded Falangism in 1933. **2** his father, **Miguel** (mi'ɣel). 1870–1930, Spanish general; dictator of Spain (1923–30).

primogenitor (,praiməʊ'dʒenitə) *n* **1** a forefather; ancestor. **2** an earliest parent or ancestor, as of a race. [C17: alteration of PROGENITOR after PRIMOGENITURE]

primogeniture (,praiməʊ'dʒenitʃə) *n* **1** the state of being a first-born. **2** *Law.* the right of an eldest son to succeed to the estate of his ancestor to the exclusion of all others. [C17: from Med. L *prīmōgenitūra* birth of a first child, from L *prīmō* at first + LL *genitūra* a birth]
▶ **primogenitary** (,praiməʊ'dʒenitəri, -tri) *adj*

primordial (prai'mɔːdiəl) *adj* **1** existing at or from the beginning; primeval. **2** constituting an origin; fundamental. **3** *Biol.* relating to an early stage of development. [C14: from LL *prīmōrdiālis* original, from L *prīmus* first + *ōrdīrī* to begin]
▶ **pri,mordi'ality** *n* ▶ **pri'mordially** *adv*

primp (primp) *vb* to dress (oneself), esp. in fine clothes; prink. [C19: prob. from PRIM]

primrose ('prim,rəʊz) *n* **1** any of various temperate plants of the genus *Primula*, esp. a European variety which has pale yellow flowers. **2** short for **evening primrose. 3** Also called: **primrose yellow.** a light yellow, sometimes with a greenish tinge. ◆ *adj* **4** of or abounding in primroses. **5** of the colour primrose. [C15: from OF *primerose*, from Med. L *prīma rosa* first rose]

primrose path *n* (often preceded by *the*) a pleasurable way of life.

primula ('primjʊlə) *n* any plant of the N temperate genus *Primula*, having white, yellow, pink, or purple funnel-shaped flowers with five spreading petals: includes the primrose, oxlip, cowslip, and polyanthus. [C18: NL, from Med. L *prīmula* (*vēris*) little first one (of the spring)]

primum mobile *Latin.* ('praimʊm 'məʊbili) *n* **1** a prime mover. **2** *Astron.* the outermost empty sphere in the Ptolemaic system that was thought to revolve around the earth from east to west in 24 hours carrying with it the inner spheres of the planets, sun, moon, and fixed stars. [C15: from Med. L: first moving (thing)]

Primus ('praɪməs) *n Trademark.* a portable paraffin cooking stove, used esp. by campers. Also called: **Primus stove.**

prince (prɪns) *n* **1** (in Britain) a son of the sovereign or of one of the sovereign's sons. **2** a nonreigning male member of a sovereign family. **3** the monarch of a small territory that was at some time subordinate to an emperor or king. **4** any monarch. **5** a nobleman in various countries, such as Italy and Germany. **6** an outstanding member of a specified group: *a merchant prince.* [C13: via OF from L *princeps* first man, ruler]
  ▶ '**princedom** *n* ▶ '**prince,like** *adj*

Prince ★ (prɪns) *n* full name *Prince Rogers Nelson.* born 1958, US rock musician. His albums include *Dirty Mind* (1981), *Purple Rain* (1984), and *Emancipation* (1996). He changed his stage name to a symbol and is often referred to as 'The Artist (formerly known as Prince)'.

prince consort *n* the husband of a female sovereign, who is himself a prince.

Prince Edward Island ★ *n* an island in the Gulf of St Lawrence that constitutes the smallest Canadian province. Capital: Charlottetown. Pop.: 126 646 (1986). Area: 5656 sq. km (2184 sq. miles). Abbrev.: **PE.**
  ▶ **Prince Edward Islander** *n*

princeling ('prɪnslɪŋ) *n* **1** a young prince. **2** Also called: **princelet.** the ruler of an insignificant territory.

princely ('prɪnslɪ) *adj* **princelier, princeliest. 1** generous or lavish. **2** of or characteristic of a prince. ◆ *adv* **3** in a princely manner.
  ▶ '**princeliness** *n*

Prince of Darkness *n* another name for **Satan.**

Prince of Peace *n Bible.* the future Messiah (Isaiah 9:6): held by Christians to be Christ.

Prince of Wales[1] *n* the eldest son and heir apparent of the British sovereign.

Prince of Wales[2] ★ *n Cape.* a cape in W Alaska, on the Bering Strait opposite the coast of extreme NE Russia: the westernmost point of North America.

Prince of Wales Island ★ *n* **1** an island in N Canada, in the Northwest Territories. Area: about 36 000 sq. km (14 000 sq. miles). **2** an island in SE Alaska, the largest island in the Alexander Archipelago. Area: about 4000 sq. km (1500 sq. miles). **3** an island in NE Australia, in N Queensland in the Torres Strait. **4** The former name (until about 1867) of the island of **Penang.**

prince regent *n* a prince who acts as regent during the minority, disability, or absence of the legal sovereign.

Prince Regent ★ *n* George IV as regent of Great Britain and Ireland during the insanity of his father (1811–20).

Prince Rupert ★ *n* a port in W Canada, on the coast of British Columbia: one of the W termini of the Canadian National transcontinental railway. Pop.: 16 620 (1991).

prince's-feather *n* **1** a garden plant with spikes of bristly brownish-red flowers. **2** a tall tropical plant with hanging spikes of pink flowers.

princess (prɪn'sɛs) *n* **1** (in Britain) a daughter of the sovereign or of one of the sovereign's sons. **2** a nonreigning female member of a sovereign family. **3** the wife and consort of a prince. **4** *Arch.* a female sovereign. **5** Also: **princess dress.** a style of dress having a fitted bodice and A-line skirt without a seam at the waistline.

princess royal *n* **1** the eldest daughter of a British or (formerly) a Prussian sovereign. **2** (*caps.*) the title of Princess Anne.

Princeton ★ ('prɪnstən) *n* a town in central New Jersey: settled by Quakers in 1696; an important educational centre, seat of Princeton University (founded at Elizabeth in 1747 and moved here in 1756); scene of the battle (1777) during the War of American Independence in which Washington's troops defeated the British on the university campus. Pop.: 12 016 (1990).

principal ('prɪnsɪpᵊl) *adj* (*prenominal*) **1** first in importance, rank, value, etc. **2** denoting capital or property as

opposed to interest, etc. ◆ *n* **3** a person who is first in importance or directs some event, organization, etc. **4** *Law.* **4a** a person who engages another to act as his agent. **4b** an active participant in a crime. **4c** the person primarily liable to fulfil an obligation. **5** the head of a school or other educational institution. **6** (in Britain) a civil servant of an executive grade who is in charge of a section. **7** the leading performer in a play. **8** *Finance.* **8a** capital or property, as contrasted with income. **8b** the original amount of a debt on which interest is calculated. **9** a main roof truss or rafter. **10** *Music.* either of two types of open diapason organ stops. [C13: via OF from L *principālis* chief, from *princeps* chief man]
  ▶ '**principally** *adv* ▶ '**principalship** *n*

principal boy *n* the leading male role in a pantomime, traditionally played by a woman.

principality (,prɪnsɪ'pælɪtɪ) *n, pl* **principalities. 1** a territory ruled by a prince or from which a prince draws his title. **2** the authority of a prince.

principal nursing officer *n* a grade of nurse concerned with administration in the British National Health Service.

principal parts *pl n Grammar.* the main inflected forms of a verb, from which all other inflections may be deduced.

principate ('prɪnsɪ,peɪt) *n* **1** a state ruled by a prince. **2** a form of rule in the early Roman Empire in which some republican forms survived.

Principe ★ ('prɪnsɪpi:; *Portuguese* 'prĩsipə) *n* an island in the Gulf of Guinea, off the W coast of Africa: part of São Tomé e Principe. Area: 150 sq. km (58 sq. miles).

principle ('prɪnsɪpᵊl) *n* **1** a standard or rule of personal conduct: *he would stoop to anything - he has no principles.* **2** a set of such moral rules: *he was a man of principle.* **3** a fundamental or general truth. **4** the essence of something. **5** a source; origin. **6** a law concerning a natural phenomenon or the behaviour of a system: *the principle of the conservation of mass.* **7** *Chem.* a constituent of a substance that gives the substance its characteristics. **8** **in principle.** in theory. **9** **on principle.** because of or in demonstration of a principle. [C14: from L *principium* beginning, basic tenet]

principled ('prɪnsɪpᵊld) *adj* **a** having high moral principles. **b** (*in combination*): *high-principled.*

prink (prɪŋk) *vb* **1** to dress (oneself, etc.) finely; deck out. **2** (*intr*) to preen oneself. [C16: prob. changed from PRANK[2] (to adorn)]

print (prɪnt) *vb* **1** to reproduce (text, pictures, etc.), esp. in large numbers, by applying ink to paper or other material. **2** to produce or reproduce (a manuscript, data, etc.) in print, as for publication. **3** to write (letters, etc.) in the style of printed matter. **4** to mark or indent (a surface) by pressing (something) onto it. **5** to produce a photographic print from (a negative). **6** (*tr*) to fix in the mind or memory. **7** (*tr*) to make (a mark) by applying pressure. ◆ *n* **8** printed matter such as newsprint. **9** a printed publication such as a book. **10 in print.** **10a** in print or published form. **10b** (of a book, etc.) offered for sale by the publisher. **11 out of print.** no longer available from a publisher. **12** a design or picture printed from an engraved plate, wood block, or other medium. **13** printed text, esp. with regard to the typeface: *small print.* **14** a positive photographic image produced from a negative image on film. **15a** a fabric with a printed design. **15b** (*as modifier*): *a print dress.* **16a** a mark made by pressing something onto a surface. **16b** a stamp, die, etc., that makes such an impression. **17** See **fingerprint.** ◆ See also **print out.** [C13

priente, from OF: something printed, from *preindre* to make an impression, from L *premere* to press]
▶ '**printable** *adj*

printed circuit *n* an electronic circuit in which certain components and the connections between them are formed by etching a metallic coating or by electrodeposition on one or both sides of a thin insulating board.

printer ('printə) *n* **1** a person or business engaged in printing. **2** a machine or device that prints. **3** *Computing.* an output device for printing results on paper.

printer's devil *n* an apprentice or errand boy in a printing establishment.

printing ('printiŋ) *n* **1** the business or art of producing printed matter. **2** printed text. **3** Also called: **impression.** all the copies of a book, etc., printed at one time. **4** a form of writing in which letters resemble printed letters.

printing press *n* any of various machines used for printing.

printmaker ('print,meikə) *n* a person who makes print or prints, esp. a craftsman or artist.

print out *vb* (*tr, adv*) **1** (of a computer output device) to produce (printed information). ◆ *n* **print-out, printout. 2** such printed information.

print shop *n* a place in which printing is carried out.

prion ('pri:ɒn) *n* a protein in the brain, an abnormal transmissible form of which is thought to be the agent responsible for certain spongiform encephalopathies, such as BSE, scrapie, Creutzfeldt-Jakob disease, and kuru. [C20: from *pro*(*teinaceous*) *in*(*fectious particle*)]

prior[1] ('praiə) *adj* **1** (*prenominal*) previous. **2 prior to.** before; until. [C18: from L: previous]

prior[2] ('praiə) *n* **1** the superior of a community in certain religious orders. **2** the deputy head of a monastery or abbey, immediately below the abbot. [C11: from LL: head, from L (adj): previous, from OL *pri* before]
▶ '**priorate** *n* ▶ '**prioress** *fem n*

Prior ★ ('praiə) *n* **Matthew.** 1664–1721, English poet and diplomat, noted for his occasional verse.

priority (prai'ɒriti) *n, pl* **priorities. 1** the condition of being prior; antecedence; precedence. **2** the right of precedence over others. **3** something given specified attention: *my first priority.*

priory ('praiəri) *n, pl* **priories.** a religious house governed by a prior, sometimes being subordinate to an abbey. [C13: from Med. L *priōria*]

Pripet ★ ('pri:pɛt) *n* a river in E Europe, rising in the NW Ukraine and flowing northeast into Belarus across the **Pripet Marshes** (the largest swamp in Europe), then east into the Dnieper River. Length: about 800 km (500 miles). Russian name: **Pripyat** ('pripjət).

Priscian ★ ('prifiən) *n* Latin name *Priscianus Caesariensis.* 6th century A.D., Latin grammarian.

prise *or* **prize** (praiz) *vb* **prises, prising, prised** *or* **prizes, prizing, prized.** (*tr*) **1** to force open by levering. **2** to extract or obtain with difficulty: *they had to prise the news out of him.* [C17: from OF *prise* a taking, from *prendre* to take, from L *prehendere*; see PRIZE[1]]

prism ('prizəm) *n* **1** a transparent polygonal solid, often having triangular ends and rectangular sides, for dispersing light into a spectrum or for reflecting light: used in binoculars, periscopes, etc. **2** *Maths.* a polyhedron having parallel bases and sides that are parallelograms. [C16: from Med. L *prisma,* from Gk: something shaped by sawing, from *prizein* to saw]

prismatic (priz'mætik) *adj* **1** of or produced by a prism. **2** exhibiting bright spectral colours: *prismatic light.* **3** *Crystallog.* another word for **orthorhombic.**
▶ **pris'matically** *adv*

prison ('priz°n) *n* **1** a public building used to house convicted criminals and accused persons awaiting trial. **2** any place of confinement. [C12: from OF *prisun,* from L *prēnsiō* a capturing, from *prehendere* to lay hold of]

prisoner ('prizənə) *n* **1** a person kept in custody as a punishment for a crime, while awaiting trial, or for some other reason. **2** a person confined by any of various re-

straints: *we are all prisoners of time.* **3 take** (**someone**) **prisoner.** to capture and hold (someone) as a prisoner.

prisoner of war *n* a person, esp. a serviceman, captured by an enemy in time of war. Abbrev.: **POW.**

prisoner's base *n* a children's game involving two teams, members of which chase and capture each other.

prissy ('prisi) *adj* **prissier, prissiest.** fussy and prim, esp. in a prudish way. [C20: prob. from PRIM + SISSY]
▶ '**prissily** *adv* ▶ '**prissiness** *n*

Priština ★ (*Serbo-Croat* 'priftina) *n* a city in S Yugoslavia, in Serbia, capital of the Kosovo-Metohija autonomous region: under Turkish control until 1912; nearby is the 14th-century Gračanica monastery. Pop.: 155 499 (1991).

pristine ('pristain, -ti:n) *adj* **1** of or involving the earliest period, state, etc.; original. **2** pure; uncorrupted. **3** fresh, clean, and unspoiled: *his pristine new car.* [C15: from L *pristinus* primitive]

> **USAGE NOTE** The use of *pristine* to mean *fresh, clean, and unspoiled* is considered by some people to be incorrect.

Pritchett ★ ('pritfit) *n* Sir **V**(ictor) **S**(awdon). 1900–97, British short-story writer, novelist, essayist, and autobiographer.

prithee ('priði) *interj Arch.* pray thee; please. [C16: shortened from *I pray thee*]

privacy ('praivəsi, 'privəsi) *n* **1** the condition of being private. **2** secrecy.

private ('praivit) *adj* **1** not widely or publicly known: *they had private reasons for the decision.* **2** confidential; secret: *a private conversation.* **3** not for general or public use: *a private bathroom.* **4** of or provided by a private individual or organization rather than by the state. **5** (*prenominal*) individual; special: *my own private recipe.* **6** (*prenominal*) having no public office, rank, etc.: *a private man.* **7** (*prenominal*) denoting a soldier of the lowest military rank. **8** (of a place) retired; not overlooked. ◆ *n* **9** a soldier of the lowest rank in many armies and marine corps. **10 in private.** in secret. [C14: from L *prīvātus* belonging to one individual, withdrawn from public life, from *prīvāre* to deprive]
▶ '**privately** *adv*

private bill *n* a bill presented to Parliament or Congress on behalf of a private individual, corporation, etc.

private company *n* a limited company that does not issue shares for public subscription and whose owners do not enjoy an unrestricted right to transfer their shareholdings. Cf. **public company.**

private detective *n* an individual privately employed to investigate a crime or make other inquiries. Also called: **private investigator.**

private enterprise *n* economic activity undertaken by private individuals or organizations under private ownership.

privateer (,praivə'tiə) *n* **1** an armed privately owned vessel commissioned for war service by a government. **2** Also called: **privateersman.** a member of the crew of a privateer. ◆ *vb* **3** (*intr*) to serve as a privateer.

private eye *n Inf.* a private detective.

Private Finance Initiative *n* (in Britain) a government scheme to encourage private investment in public projects. Abbrev.: **PFI.**

private health insurance *n* insurance against the need for medical treatment as a private patient.

private hotel *n* **1** a hotel in which the proprietor has the right to refuse to accept a person as a guest. **2** *Austral. & NZ.* a hotel not having a licence to sell alcoholic liquor.

private income *n* an income from sources other than employment, such as investment. Also called: **private means.**

private life *n* the social life or personal relationships of an individual, esp. of a celebrity.

> ★ people and places

private member *n* a member of a legislative assembly not having an appointment in the government.

private member's bill *n* a parliamentary bill sponsored by a Member of Parliament who is not a government minister.

private parts *or* **privates** *pl n* euphemistic terms for **genitals**.

private patient *n* Brit. a patient receiving medical treatment not paid for by the National Health Service.

private pay bed *n* (in Britain) a hospital bed reserved for private patients who are charged by the health service for use of hospital facilities.

private practice *n* Brit. medical practice that is not part of the National Health Service.

private school *n* a school under the financial and managerial control of a private body, accepting mostly fee-paying pupils.

private secretary *n* **1** a secretary entrusted with the personal and confidential matters of a business executive. **2** a civil servant who acts as aide to a minister or senior government official.

private sector *n* the part of a country's economy that consists of privately owned enterprises.

privation (prɑɪ'veɪʃən) *n* **1** loss or lack of the necessities of life, such as food and shelter. **2** hardship resulting from this. **3** the state of being deprived. [C14: from L *prīvātiō* deprivation]

privative ('prɪvətɪv) *adj* **1** causing privation. **2** expressing lack or negation, as for example the English suffix *-less* and prefix *un-*. [C16: from L *prīvātīvus* indicating loss]
▶ **'privatively** *adv*

privatize *or* **privatise** ('praɪvɪ,taɪz) *vb* **privatizes, privatizing, privatized** *or* **privatises, privatising, privatised**. (tr) to take into, or return to, private ownership, a company or concern that has previously been owned by the state.
▶ ,**privati'zation** *or* ,**privati'sation** *n*

privet ('prɪvɪt) *n* **a** any of a genus of shrubs, esp. one having oval dark green leaves, white flowers, and purplish-black berries. **b** (as modifier): *a privet hedge.* [C16: from ?]

privilege ('prɪvɪlɪdʒ) *n* **1** a benefit, immunity, etc., granted under certain conditions. **2** the advantages and immunities enjoyed by a small usually powerful group or class, esp. to the disadvantage of others: *one of the obstacles to social harmony is privilege.* **3** US Stock Exchange. a speculative contract permitting its purchaser to make optional purchases or sales of securities at a specified time over a limited period. ◆ *vb* **privileges, privileging, privileged.** (tr) **4** to bestow a privilege or privileges upon. **5** (foll. by *from*) to free or exempt. [C12: from OF *privilège*, from L *prīvilēgium* law relevant to rights of an individual, from *prīvus* an individual + *lēx* law]

privileged ('prɪvɪlɪdʒd) *adj* **1** enjoying or granted as a privilege or privileges. **2** Law. **2a** not actionable as a libel or slander. **2b** (of a communication, document, etc.) that a witness cannot be compelled to divulge.

privity ('prɪvɪtɪ) *n, pl* **privities. 1** a legally recognized relationship existing between two parties, such as that between the parties to a contract: *privity of contract.* **2** secret knowledge that is shared. [C13: from OF *priveté*]

privy ('prɪvɪ) *adj* **privier, priviest. 1** (postpositive; foll. by *to*) participating in the knowledge of something secret. **2** Arch. secret, hidden, etc. ◆ *n, pl* **privies. 3** a lavatory, esp. an outside one. **4** Law. a person in privity with another. See **privity**. [C13: from OF *privé* something private, from L *prīvātus* PRIVATE]
▶ **'privily** *adv*

privy council *n* **1** the council of state of a monarch, esp. formerly. **2** Arch. a secret council.

Privy Council *n* **1** the private council of the British sovereign, consisting of all current and former ministers of the Crown and other distinguished subjects, all of whom are appointed for life. **2** (in Canada) a ceremonial body of advisers of the governor general, the chief of them being the Federal cabinet ministers.
▶ **Privy Counsellor** *n*

privy purse *n* (often cap.) **1** an allowance voted by Parliament for the private expenses of the monarch. **2** an offi-

cial of the royal household responsible for dealing with the monarch's private expenses. Full name: **Keeper of the Privy Purse.**

privy seal *n* (often cap.) (in Britain) a seal affixed to certain documents issued by royal authority: of less importance than the great seal.

Prix Goncourt (French pri) *n* an annual prize for a work of French fiction. [C20: after the Académie GONCOURT]

prize[1] (praɪz) *n* **1a** a reward or honour for having won a contest, competition, etc. **1b** (as modifier): *prize jockey; prize essay.* **2** something given to the winner of any game of chance, lottery, etc. **3** something striven for. **4** any valuable property captured in time of war, esp. a vessel. [C14: from OF *prise* a capture, from L *prehendere* to seize; infl. by ME *prise* reward]

prize[2] (praɪz) *vb* **prizes, prizing, prized.** (tr) to esteem greatly; value highly. [C15 *prise*, from OF *preisier* to PRAISE]

prize court *n* Law. a court having jurisdiction to determine how property captured at sea in wartime is to be distributed.

prizefight ('praɪz,faɪt) *n* a boxing match for a prize or purse.
▶ **'prize,fighter** *n* ▶ **'prize,fighting** *n*

prize ring *n* **1** the enclosed area or ring used by prizefighters. **2 the prize ring.** the sport of prizefighting.

pro[1] (prəʊ) *adv* **1** in favour of a motion, issue, course of action, etc. ◆ *prep* **2** in favour of. ◆ *n, pl* **pros. 3** (usually pl) an argument or vote in favour of a proposal or motion. See also **pros and cons.** [from L *prō* (prep) in favour of]

pro[2] (prəʊ) *n, pl* **pros,** *adj* Inf. **1** short for **professional. 2** a prostitute. [C19]

PRO *abbrev. for:* **1** Public Records Office. **2** public relations officer.

pro-[1] *prefix* **1** in favour of; supporting: *pro-Chinese.* **2** acting as a substitute for: *proconsul; pronoun.* [from L *prō* (adv & prep). In compound words borrowed from L, *prō-* indicates: forward, out (*project*); away from (*prodigal*); onward (*proceed*); in front of (*provide, protect*); on behalf of (*procure*); substitute for (*pronominal*); and sometimes intensive force (*promiscuous*)]

pro-[2] *prefix* before in time or position; anterior; forward: *prognathous.* [from Gk *pro* (prep) before (in time, position, etc.)]

proa ('prəʊə) *or* **prau** *n* any of several kinds of canoe-like boats used in the South Pacific, esp. one equipped with an outrigger and sails. [C16: from Malay *parāhu* a boat]

proactive (prəʊ'æktɪv) *adj* **1** tending to initiate change rather than reacting to events. **2** Psychol. of or denoting a mental process that affects a subsequent process. [C20: from PRO-[2] + (RE)ACTIVE]

pro-am ('prəʊ'æm) *adj* (of a golf tournament, etc.) involving both professional and amateur players.

probability (,prɒbə'bɪlɪtɪ) *n, pl* **probabilities. 1** the condition of being probable. **2** an event or other thing that is probable. **3** Statistics. a measure of the degree of confidence one may have in the occurrence of an event, measured on a scale from zero (impossibility) to one (certainty).

probable ('prɒbəb°l) *adj* **1** likely to be or to happen but not necessarily so. **2** most likely: *the probable cause of the accident.* ◆ *n* **3** a person who is probably to be chosen for a team, event, etc. [C14: via OF from L *probābilis* that may be proved, from *probāre* to prove]

probably ('prɒbəblɪ) *adv* **1** (sentence modifier) in all likelihood or probability: *I'll probably see you tomorrow.* ◆ *sentence substitute.* **2** I believe such a thing may be the case.

proband ('prəʊbænd) *n* another name (esp. US) for **propositus.** [C20: from L *probandus, probāre* to test]

probang ('prəʊbæŋ) *n* Surgery. a long flexible rod, often with a small sponge at one end, for inserting into the oesophagus, as to apply medication. [C17: var., apparently by association with PROBE, of *provang*, coined by W. Rumsey (1584–1660), Welsh judge, its inventor; from ?]

probate ('prəʊbɪt, -beɪt) *n* **1** the process of officially proving the validity of a will. **2** the official certificate stating a will to be genuine and conferring on the executors power to administer the estate. **3** (modifier) relating to

probate: *a probate court.* ◆ *vb* **probates, probating, probated.**
4 (*tr*) *Chiefly US.* to establish officially the validity of (a
will). [C15: from L *probāre* to inspect]

probation (prəˈbeɪʃən) *n* **1** a system of dealing with offenders by placing them under the supervision of a probation officer. **2 on probation. 2a** under the supervision of
a probation officer. **2b** undergoing a test period. **3** a trial
period, as for a teacher.
▸ pro'bational *or* pro'bationary *adj*

probationer (prəˈbeɪʃənə) *n* a person on probation.

probation officer *n* an officer of a court who supervises offenders placed on probation and assists and be-
friends them.

probe (prəʊb) *vb* **probes, probing, probed. 1** (*tr*) to search
into closely. **2** to examine (something) with or as if with
a probe. ◆ *n* **3** something that probes or tests. **4** *Surgery.* a
slender instrument for exploring a wound, sinus, etc. **5** a
thorough inquiry, such as one by a newspaper into corrupt practices. **6** *Electronics.* a lead connecting to or containing a monitoring circuit used for testing. **7** anything
which provides or acts as a coupling, esp. a flexible tube
extended from an aircraft to link it with another so that
it can refuel. **8** See **space probe.** [C16: from Med. L *proba*
investigation, from L *probāre* to test]
▸ 'probeable *adj* ▸ 'prober *n*

probity (ˈprəʊbɪtɪ) *n* confirmed integrity. [C16: from L
probitās honesty, from *probus* virtuous]

problem (ˈprɒbləm) *n* **1a** any thing, matter, person, etc.,
that is difficult to deal with. **1b** (*as modifier*): *a problem
child.* **2** a puzzle, question, etc., set for solution. **3** *Maths.*
a statement requiring a solution usually by means of
several operations or constructions. **4** (*modifier*) designating a literary work that deals with difficult moral
questions: *a problem play.* [C14: from LL *problēma,* from
Gk: something put forward]

problematic (ˌprɒbləˈmætɪk) *or* **problematical** *adj* **1**
having the nature of a problem; uncertain; questionable. **2** *Logic, obs.* (of a proposition) asserting that a property may or may not hold.
▸ ˌproblem'atically *adv*

pro bono publico *Latin.* (ˈprəʊ ˈbəʊnəʊ ˈpʊblɪkəʊ) for
the public good.

proboscidean *or* **proboscidian** (ˌprəʊbɒˈsɪdɪən) *adj*
1 of or belonging to an order of massive herbivorous placental mammals having tusks and a long trunk: contains the elephants. ◆ *n* **2** any proboscidean animal.

proboscis (prəʊˈbɒsɪs) *n, pl* **proboscises** *or* **proboscides**
(-sɪˌdiːz). **1** a long flexible prehensile trunk or snout, as of
an elephant. **2** the elongated mouthpart of certain insects. **3** any similar organ. **4** *Inf., facetious.* a person's
nose. [C17: via L from Gk *proboskis* trunk of an elephant, from *boskein* to feed]

procaine (ˈprəʊkeɪn, prəʊˈkeɪn) *n* a colourless or white
crystalline water-soluble substance used, as **procaine hydrochloride,** as a local anaesthetic. [C20: from PRO-[1] +
(CO)CAINE]

procathedral (ˌprəʊkəˈθiːdrəl) *n* a church serving as a
cathedral.

procedure (prəˈsiːdʒə) *n* **1** a way of acting or progressing, esp. an established method. **2** the established form
of conducting the business of a legislature, the enforcement of a legal right, etc. **3** *Computing.* another name for
subroutine.
▸ pro'cedural *adj* ▸ pro'cedurally *adv*

proceed (prəˈsiːd) *vb* (*intr*) **1** (often foll. by *to*) to advance
or carry on, esp. after stopping. **2** (often foll. by *with*) to
continue: *he proceeded with his reading.* **3** (often foll. by
against) to institute or carry on a legal action. **4** to originate; arise: *evil proceeds from the heart.* [C14: from L
prōcēdere to advance]
▸ pro'ceeder *n*

proceeding (prəˈsiːdɪŋ) *n* **1** an act or course of action. **2a**
a legal action. **2b** any step taken in a legal action. **3** (*pl*)
the minutes of the meetings of a society, etc. **4** (*pl*) legal
action; litigation. **5** (*pl*) the events of an occasion.

proceeds (ˈprəʊsiːdz) *pl n* **1** the profit or return derived
from a commercial transaction, investment, etc. **2** the

result, esp. the total sum, accruing from some undertaking.

process[1] (ˈprəʊsɛs) *n* **1** a series of actions which produce
a change or development: *the process of digestion.* **2** a
method of doing or producing something. **3** progress or
course of time. **4 in the process of.** during or in the course
of. **5a** a summons commanding a person to appear in
court. **5b** the whole proceedings in an action at law. **6** a
natural outgrowth or projection of a part or organism. **7**
(*modifier*) relating to the general preparation of a printing forme or plate by the use, at some stage, of photography. ◆ *vb* (*tr*) **8** to subject to a routine procedure;
handle. **9** to treat or prepare by a special method, esp. to
treat (food) in order to preserve it: *to process cheese.* **10a** to
institute legal proceedings against. **10b** to serve a process
on. **11** *Photog.* **11a** to develop, rinse, fix, wash, and dry
(exposed film, etc.). **11b** to produce final prints or slides
from (undeveloped film). **12** *Computing.* to perform operations on (data) according to programmed instructions
in order to obtain the required information. [C14: from
OF *procès,* from L *prōcessus* an advancing, from *prōcēdere*
to proceed]

process[2] (prəˈsɛs) *vb* (*intr*) to proceed in a procession.
[C19: back formation from PROCESSION]

process industry *n* a manufacturing industry, such as
oil refining, which converts bulk raw materials into a
workable form.

procession (prəˈsɛʃən) *n* **1** the act of proceeding in a regular formation. **2** a group of people or things moving
forwards in an orderly, regular, or ceremonial manner. **3**
Christianity. the emanation of the Holy Spirit. ◆ *vb* **4**
(*intr*) *Rare.* to go in procession. [C12: via OF from L
prōcessiō a marching forwards]

processional (prəˈsɛʃənəl) *adj* **1** of or suitable for a procession. ◆ *n* **2** *Christianity.* **2a** a book containing the
prayers, hymns, etc., prescribed for processions. **2b** a
hymn, etc., used in a procession.

processor (ˈprəʊsɛsə) *n* **1** *Computing.* another name for
central processing unit. **2** a person or thing that carries out
a process.

process-server *n* a sheriff's officer who serves legal
documents such as writs for appearance in court.

procès-verbal *French.* (prɔsɛverbal) *n, pl* **-baux** (-bo). a
written record of an official proceeding; minutes. [C17:
from F: see PROCESS, VERBAL]

pro-choice *adj* (of an organization, pressure group, etc.)
supporting the right of a woman to have an abortion.
Cf. **pro-life.**

prochronism (ˈprəʊkrəˌnɪzəm) *n* an error in dating that
places an event earlier than it actually occurred. [C17:
from PRO-[2] + Gk *khronos* time + -ISM, by analogy with
ANACHRONISM]

proclaim (prəˈkleɪm) *vb* (*tr*) **1** (*may take a clause as object*)
to announce publicly. **2** (*may take a clause as object*) to indicate plainly. **3** to praise or extol. [C14: from L
prōclāmāre to shout aloud]
▸ proclamation (ˌprɒkləˈmeɪʃən) *n* ▸ pro'claimer *n*
▸ proclamatory (prəˈklæmətərɪ, -trɪ) *adj*

proclitic (prəʊˈklɪtɪk) *adj* **1a** denoting a monosyllabic
word or form having no stress and pronounced as a prefix of the following word, as in English *'t* for *it* in *'twas.*
1b (in classical Greek) denoting a word that throws its
accent onto the following word. ◆ *n* **2** a proclitic word
or form. [C19: from NL *proclīticus,* from Gk *proklinein* to
lean forwards; on the model of ENCLITIC]

proclivity (prəˈklɪvɪtɪ) *n, pl* **proclivities.** a tendency or inclination. [C16: from L *prōclīvitās,* from *prōclīvis* steep,
from *clīvus* a slope]

Proclus ★ (ˈprəʊkləs, ˈprɒk-) *n* ?410–485 A.D., Greek Neo-
Platonist philosopher.

Procne ★ (ˈprɒknɪ) *n Greek myth.* a princess of Athens,
who punished her husband for raping her sister
Philomela by feeding him the flesh of their son. She was
changed at her death into a swallow. See **Philomela.**

proconsul (prəʊˈkɒnsəl) *n* **1** a governor of a colony or
other dependency. **2** (in ancient Rome) the governor of
a senatorial province.
▸ **proconsular** (prəʊˈkɒnsjʊlə) *adj*

Procopius ★ (prəʊ'kəʊpɪəs) n ?490–?562 A.D., Byzantine historian, noted for his account of the wars of Justinian I against the Persians, Vandals, and Ostrogoths.

procrastinate (prəʊ'kræstɪˌneɪt, prə-) vb **procrastinates, procrastinating, procrastinated.** (usually intr) to put off (an action) until later; delay. [C16: from L prōcrāstināre to postpone until tomorrow, from PRO-¹ + crās tomorrow]
▶ pro,crasti'nation n ▶ pro'crasti,nator n

procreate ('prəʊkrɪˌeɪt) vb **procreates, procreating, procreated. 1** to beget or engender (offspring). **2** (tr) to bring into being. [C16: from L prōcreāre, from PRO-¹ + creāre to create]
▶ 'procreant or 'procre,ative adj ▶ ,procre'ation n
▶ 'procre,ator n

Procrustean (prəʊ'krʌstɪən) adj tending or designed to produce conformity by violent or ruthless methods.

Procrustes ★ (prəʊ'krʌstiːz) n Greek myth. a robber, who put travellers in his bed, stretching or lopping off their limbs so that they fitted it. [C16: from Gk Prokroustēs the stretcher, from prokrouein to extend by hammering out]

proctology (prɒk'tɒlədʒɪ) n the branch of medical science concerned with the rectum. [from Gk prōktos rectum + -OLOGY]

proctor ('prɒktə) n **1** a member of the staff of certain universities having duties including the enforcement of discipline. **2** (formerly) an agent, esp. one engaged to conduct another's case in a court. **3** Church of England. one of the elected representatives of the clergy in Convocation. [C14: syncopated var. of PROCURATOR]
▶ proctorial (prɒk'tɔːrɪəl) adj

procumbent (prəʊ'kʌmbənt) adj **1** (of stems) trailing loosely along the ground. **2** leaning forwards or lying on the face. [C17: from L prōcumbere to fall forwards]

procurator ('prɒkjʊˌreɪtə) n **1** (in ancient Rome) a civil official of the emperor's administration, often employed as the governor of a minor province. **2** Rare. a person engaged by another to manage his affairs. [C13: from L: a manager, from prōcūrāre to attend to]
▶ **procuracy** ('prɒkjʊrəsɪ) or 'procu,ratorship n
▶ procuratorial (,prɒkjʊrə'tɔːrɪəl) adj

procurator fiscal n (in Scotland) a legal officer who performs the functions of public prosecutor and coroner.

procure (prə'kjʊə) vb **procures, procuring, procured. 1** (tr) to obtain or acquire; secure. **2** to obtain (women or girls) to act as prostitutes. [C13: from L prōcūrāre to look after]
▶ pro'curable adj ▶ pro'curement, pro'cural, or procuration (,prɒkju'reɪʃən) n

procurer (prə'kjʊərə) n a person who procures, esp. one who procures women as prostitutes.

prod (prɒd) vb **prods, prodding, prodded. 1** to poke or jab with or as if with a pointed object. **2** (tr) to rouse to action. ◆ n **3** the act or an instance of prodding. **4** a sharp object. **5** a stimulus or reminder. [C16: from ?]
▶ 'prodder n

prod. abbrev. for: **1** produce. **2** produced. **3** product.

prodigal ('prɒdɪgˀl) adj **1** recklessly wasteful or extravagant, as in disposing of goods or money. **2** lavish: prodigal of compliments. ◆ n **3** a person who spends lavishly or squanders money. [C16: from Med. L prōdigālis wasteful, from L, from prōdigere to squander, from agere to drive]
▶ ,prodi'gality n ▶ 'prodigally adv

prodigious (prə'dɪdʒəs) adj **1** vast in size, extent, power, etc. **2** wonderful or amazing. [C16: from L prōdigiōsus marvellous, from prodigium; see PRODIGY]
▶ pro'digiously adv ▶ pro'digiousness n

prodigy ('prɒdɪdʒɪ) n, pl **prodigies. 1** a person, esp. a child, of unusual or marvellous talents. **2** anything that is a cause of wonder. **3** something monstrous or abnormal. [C16: from L prōdigium an unnatural happening]

produce vb (prə'djuːs), **produces, producing, produced. 1** to bring (something) into existence; yield. **2** (tr) to make: she produced a delicious dinner. **3** (tr) to give birth to. **4** (tr) to present to view: to produce evidence. **5** (tr) to bring before the public: he produced a film last year. **6** (tr) to act as

producer of. **7** (tr) Geom. to extend (a line). ◆ n ('prɒdjuːs). **8** anything produced; a product. **9** agricultural products collectively: farm produce. [C15: from L prōdūcere to bring forward]
▶ pro'ducible adj ▶ pro,duci'bility n

producer (prə'djuːsə) n **1** a person or thing that produces. **2** Brit. a person responsible for the artistic direction of a play. **3** US & Canad. a person who organizes the stage production of a play, including the finance, management, etc. **4** the person who takes overall administrative responsibility for a film or television programme. Cf. **director** (sense 4). **5** the person who supervises the arrangement, recording, and mixing of a record. **6** Econ. a person or business enterprise that generates goods or services for sale. Cf. **consumer** (sense 1). **7** Chem. an apparatus or plant for making producer gas.

producer gas n a mixture of carbon monoxide and nitrogen produced by passing air over hot coke, used mainly as a fuel.

product ('prɒdʌkt) n **1** something produced by effort, or some mechanical or industrial process. **2** the result of some natural process. **3** a result or consequence. **4** Maths. the result of the multiplication of two or more numbers, quantities, etc. [C15: from L prōductum (something) produced, from prōdūcere to bring forth]

product differentiation n Commerce. the real or illusory distinction between competing products in a market.

production (prə'dʌkʃən) n **1** the act of producing. **2** anything that is produced; a product. **3** the amount produced or the rate at which it is produced. **4** Econ. the creation or manufacture of goods and services with exchange value. **5** any work created as a result of literary or artistic effort. **6** the presentation of a play, opera, etc. **7** Brit. the artistic direction of a play. **8** (modifier) manufactured by mass production: a production model of a car.
▶ pro'ductional adj

production line n a factory system in which parts or components of the end product are transported by a conveyor through a number of different sites at each of which a manual or machine operation is performed on them.

productive (prə'dʌktɪv) adj **1** producing or having the power to produce; fertile. **2** yielding favourable results. **3** Econ. **3a** producing goods and services that have exchange value: productive assets. **3b** relating to such production: the productive processes of an industry. **4** (postpositive; foll. by of) resulting in: productive of good results.
▶ pro'ductively adv ▶ pro'ductiveness n

productivity (,prɒdʌk'tɪvɪtɪ) n **1** the output of an industrial concern in relation to the materials, labour, etc., it employs. **2** the state of being productive.

product liability n the liability to the public of a manufacturer or trader for selling a faulty product.

product life cycle n Marketing. the four stages (introduction, growth, maturity, and decline) into one of which the sales of a product fall during its market life.

product line n Marketing. a group of related products marketed by the same company.

product placement n the practice of a company paying for its product to be placed in a prominent position in a film or television programme as a form of advertising.

proem ('prəʊɛm) n an introduction or preface, such as to a work of literature. [C14: from L prooemium introduction, from Gk prooimion, from PRO-² + hoimē song]
▶ proemial (prəʊ'iːmɪəl) adj

proenzyme (prəʊ'ɛnzaɪm) n the inactive form of an enzyme; zymogen.

Prof. abbrev. for Professor.

profane (prə'feɪn) adj **1** having or indicating contempt, irreverence, or disrespect for a divinity or something sacred. **2** not designed for religious purposes; secular. **3** not initiated into the inner mysteries or sacred rites. **4** coarse or blasphemous: profane language. ◆ vb **profanes, profaning, profaned.** (tr) **5** to treat (something sacred) with irrev-

erence. **6** to put to an unworthy use. [C15: from L *profānus* outside the temple]
▸ **profanation** (ˌprɒfəˈneɪʃən) *n* ▸ **proˈfanely** *adv* ▸ **proˈfaneness** *n* ▸ **proˈfaner** *n*

profanity (prəˈfænɪtɪ) *n, pl* **profanities. 1** the state or quality of being profane. **2** vulgar or irreverent action, speech, etc.

profess (prəˈfɛs) *vb* **1** (*tr*) to affirm or acknowledge: *to profess ignorance; to profess a belief in God.* **2** (*tr*) to claim (something), often insincerely or falsely: *to profess to be a skilled driver.* **3** to receive or be received into a religious order, as by taking vows. [C14: from L *prōfitērī* to confess openly]

professed (prəˈfɛst) *adj* (*prenominal*) **1** avowed or acknowledged. **2** alleged or pretended. **3** professing to be qualified as: *a professed philosopher.* **4** having taken vows of a religious order.
▸ **professedly** (prəˈfɛsɪdlɪ) *adv*

profession (prəˈfɛʃən) *n* **1** an occupation requiring special training in the liberal arts or sciences, esp. one of the three learned professions, law, theology, or medicine. **2** the body of people in such an occupation. **3** an avowal; declaration. **4** Also called: **profession of faith.** a declaration of faith in a religion, esp. as made on entering the Church or an order belonging to it. [C13: from Med. L *professiō* the taking of vows upon entering a religious order, from L: public acknowledgment; see PROFESS]

professional (prəˈfɛʃənəl) *adj* **1** of, suitable for, or engaged in as a profession. **2** engaging in an activity as a means of livelihood. **3a** extremely competent in a job, etc. **3b** (of a piece of work or anything performed) produced with competence or skill. **4** undertaken or performed by people who are paid. ◆ *n* **5** a person who belongs to one of the professions. **6** a person who engages for his livelihood in some activity also pursued by amateurs. **7** a person who engages in an activity with great competence. **8** an expert player of a game who gives instruction, esp. to members of a club by whom he is hired.
▸ **proˈfessionaˌlism** *n* ▸ **proˈfessionally** *adv*

professional foul *n Football.* a deliberate foul committed as a last-ditch tactic to prevent an opponent from scoring.

professor (prəˈfɛsə) *n* **1** the principal teacher in a field of learning at a university or college; a holder of a university chair. **2** *Chiefly US & Canad.* any teacher in a university or college. **3** a person who professes his opinions, beliefs, etc. [C14: from Med. L: one who has made his profession in a religious order, from L: a public teacher; see PROFESS]
▸ **professorial** (ˌprɒfɪˈsɔːrɪəl) *adj* ▸ **profesˈsorially** *adv* ▸ **proˈfesˈsoriate** *or* **proˈfessorship** *n*

proffer (ˈprɒfə) *vb* **1** (*tr*) to offer for acceptance. ◆ *n* **2** the act of proffering. [C13: from OF *proffrir*, from PRO-[1] + *offrir* to offer]

proficient (prəˈfɪʃənt) *adj* **1** having great facility (in an art, occupation, etc.); skilled. ◆ *n* **2** an expert. [C16: from L *prōficere* to make progress]
▸ **proˈficiency** *n* ▸ **proˈficiently** *adv*

profile (ˈprəʊfaɪl) *n* **1** a side view or outline of an object, esp. of a human head. **2** a short biographical sketch. **3** a graph, table, etc., representing the extent to which a person, field, or object exhibits various tested characteristics: *a population profile.* **4** a vertical section of soil or rock showing the different layers. **5** the outline of the shape of a river valley either from source to mouth (**long profile**) or at right angles to the flow of the river (**cross profile**). ◆ *vb* **profiles, profiling, profiled. 6** (*tr*) to draw, write, or make a profile of. [C17: from It. *profilo*, from *profilare* to sketch lightly, from L *filum* thread]
▸ **ˈprofiler** *or* **profilist** (ˈprəʊfɪlɪst) *n*

profile component *n Brit. education.* attainment targets in different subjects brought together for the general assessment of a pupil.

profit (ˈprɒfɪt) *n* **1** (*often pl*) excess of revenues over outlays and expenses in a business enterprise. **2** the monetary gain derived from a transaction. **3** income derived from property or an investment, as contrasted with capital gains. **4a** *Econ.* the income accruing to a success-

ful entrepreneur and held to be the motivating factor of a capitalist economy. **4b** (*as modifier*): *the profit motive.* **5** a gain, benefit, or advantage. ◆ *vb* **6** to gain or cause to gain profit. [C14: from L *prōfectus* advance, from *prōficere* to make progress]
▸ **ˈprofitless** *adj*

profitable (ˈprɒfɪtəbˀl) *adj* affording gain or profit.
▸ **ˌprofitaˈbility** *n* ▸ **ˈprofitably** *adv*

profit and loss *n Book-keeping.* an account compiled at the end of a financial year showing that year's revenue and expense items and indicating gross and net profit or loss.

profit centre *n* a section of a commercial organization which is allocated financial targets in its own right.

profiteer (ˌprɒfɪˈtɪə) *n* **1** a person who makes excessive profits, esp. by charging exorbitant prices for goods in short supply. ◆ *vb* **2** (*intr*) to make excessive profits.

profiterole (ˈprɒfɪtəˌrəʊl, prəˈfɪtəˌrəʊl) *n* a small case of choux pastry with a sweet or savoury filling. [C16: from F, lit.: a small profit]

profit-sharing *n* a system in which a portion of the net profit of a business is distributed to its employees, usually in proportion to their wages or their length of service.

profit taking *n* selling commodities, securities, etc., at a profit after a rise in market values or before an expected fall in values.

profligate (ˈprɒflɪgɪt) *adj* **1** shamelessly immoral or debauched. **2** wildly extravagant or wasteful. ◆ *n* **3** a profligate person. [C16: from L *prōflīgātus* corrupt, from *prōflīgāre* to overthrow, from PRO-[1] + *flīgere* to beat]
▸ **profligacy** (ˈprɒflɪgəsɪ) *n* ▸ **ˈprofligately** *adv*

pro forma (ˈprəʊ ˈfɔːmə) *adj* **1** prescribing a set form or procedure. ◆ *adv* **2** performed in a set manner. [L: for form's sake]

profound (prəˈfaʊnd) *adj* **1** penetrating deeply into subjects or ideas: *a profound mind.* **2** showing or requiring great knowledge or understanding: *a profound treatise.* **3** situated at or extending to a great depth. **4** stemming from the depths of one's nature: *profound regret.* **5** intense or absolute: *profound silence.* **6** thoroughgoing; extensive: *profound changes.* ◆ *n* **7** *Arch. or literary.* a great depth; abyss. [C14: from OF *profund*, from L *profundus* deep, from *fundus* bottom]
▸ **proˈfoundly** *adv* ▸ **profundity** (prəˈfʌndɪtɪ) *n*

Profumo ★ (prəˈfjuːməʊ) *n* **John** (**Dennis**). born 1915, British Conservative politician; secretary of state for war (1960–63). He resigned after a scandal that threatened Macmillan's government.

profuse (prəˈfjuːs) *adj* **1** plentiful or abundant: *profuse compliments.* **2** (often foll. by *in*) free or generous in the giving (of): *profuse in thanks.* [C15: from L *profundere* to pour lavishly]
▸ **proˈfusely** *adv* ▸ **proˈfuseness** *or* **proˈfusion** *n*

progenitive (prəʊˈdʒɛnɪtɪv) *adj* capable of bearing offspring.
▸ **proˈgenitiveness** *n*

progenitor (prəʊˈdʒɛnɪtə) *n* **1** a direct ancestor. **2** an originator or founder. [C14: from L: ancestor, from *gignere* to beget]

progeny (ˈprɒdʒɪnɪ) *n, pl* **progenies. 1** the immediate descendant or descendants of a person, animal, etc. **2** a result or outcome. [C13: from L *prōgeniēs* lineage; see PROGENITOR]

progesterone (prəʊˈdʒɛstəˌrəʊn) *n* a steroid hormone, secreted mainly by the corpus luteum in the ovary, that prepares and maintains the uterus for pregnancy. [C20: from PRO-[1] + GE(STATION) + STER(OL) + -ONE]

progestogen (prəʊˈdʒɛstədʒən) *or* **progestin** (prəˈdʒɛstɪn) *n* any of a group of steroid hormones with progesterone-like activity, used in oral contraceptives and in treating gynaecological disorders.

prognathous (prɒgˈneɪθəs) *or* **prognathic** (prɒgˈnæθɪk) *adj* having a projecting lower jaw. [C19: from PRO-[2] + Gk *gnathos* jaw]

prognosis (prɒgˈnəʊsɪs) *n, pl* **prognoses** (-ˈnəʊsiːz). **1** *Med.* a prediction of the course or outcome of a disease. **2** any prediction. [C17: via L from Gk: knowledge before-hand]

prognostic (prɒg'nɒstɪk) *adj* **1** of or serving as a prognosis. **2** predicting. ♦ *n* **3** *Med.* any symptom or sign used in making a prognosis. **4** a sign of some future occurrence. [C15: from OF *pronostique*, from L *prognōsticum*, from Gk, from *prognōskein* to know in advance]

prognosticate (prɒg'nɒstɪ,keɪt) *vb* **prognosticates, prognosticating, prognosticated. 1** to foretell (future events); prophesy. **2** (*tr*) to foreshadow or portend. [C16: from Med. L *prognōsticāre* to predict]
▸ **prog,nosti'cation** *n* ▸ **prog'nosticative** *adj* ▸ **prog'nosti,cator** *n*

program or (*sometimes*) **programme** ('prəʊgræm) *n* **1** a sequence of coded instructions fed into a computer, enabling it to perform specified logical and arithmetical operations on data. ♦ *vb* **programs** or **programmes, programming, programmed. 2** (*tr*) to feed a program into (a computer). **3** (*tr*) to arrange (data) in a suitable form so that it can be processed by a computer. **4** (*intr*) to write a program.
▸ **'programmer** *n*

programmable or **programable** (prəʊ'græməbəl) *adj* capable of being programmed for automatic operation or computer processing.

programme or *US* **program** ('prəʊgræm) *n* **1** a written or printed list of the events, performers, etc., in a public performance. **2** a performance presented at a scheduled time, esp. on radio or television. **3** a specially arranged selection of things to be done: *what's the programme for this afternoon?* **4** a plan, schedule, or procedure. **5** a syllabus or curriculum. ♦ *vb* **programmes, programming, programmed** or *US* **programs, programing, programed. 6** to design or schedule (something) as a programme. ♦ *n, vb* **7** *Computing.* a variant spelling of **program.** [C17: from LL *programma*, from Gk: written public notice, from PRO-² + *graphein* to write]
▸ **,program'matic** *adj*

programmed learning *n* a teaching method in which the material to be learned is broken down into easily understandable parts on which the pupil is able to test himself.

programme music *n* music that is intended to depict or evoke a scene or idea.

programme of study *n Brit. education.* the prescribed syllabus that pupils must be taught at each key stage in the National Curriculum.

programming language *n* a simple language system designed to facilitate the writing of computer programs.

program statement *n* a single instruction in a computer program.

program trading *n* trading on international stock exchanges using a computer program to exploit differences between stock index futures and actual share prices on world equity markets.

progress *n* ('prəʊgres). **1** movement forwards, esp. towards a place or objective. **2** satisfactory development or advance. **3** advance towards completion or perfection. **4** (*modifier*) of or relating to progress: *a progress report.* **5** (formerly) a stately royal journey. **6 in progress.** taking place. ♦ *vb* (prə'gres). **7** (*intr*) to move forwards or onwards. **8** (*intr*) to move towards completion or perfection. **9** (*tr*) to be responsible for the satisfactory progress of (a project, etc.) to completion. [C15: from L *prōgressus*, from *prōgredī* to advance, from *gradī* to step]

progression (prə'greʃən) *n* **1** the act of progressing; advancement. **2** the act or an instance of moving from one thing in a sequence to the next. **3** *Maths.* a sequence of numbers in which each term differs from the succeeding term by a constant relation. See also **arithmetic progression, geometric progression, harmonic progression. 4** *Music.* movement from one note or chord to the next.
▸ **pro'gressional** *adj*

progressive (prə'gresɪv) *adj* **1** of or relating to progress. **2** progressing by steps or degrees. **3** (*often cap.*) favouring or promoting political or social reform: *a progressive policy.* **4** denoting an educational system that allows flexibility in learning procedures, based on activities determined by the needs and capacities of the individual child. **5** (esp. of a disease) advancing in severity, complexity, or extent. **6** (of a dance, card game, etc.) involving a regular change of partners. **7** denoting an aspect of verbs in some languages, including English, used to express continuous activity: *a progressive aspect of the verb "to walk" is "is walking".* ♦ *n* **8** a person who advocates progress, as in education, politics, etc. **9a** the progressive aspect of a verb. **9b** a verb in this aspect.
▸ **pro'gressively** *adv* ▸ **pro'gressiveness** *n* ▸ **pro'gressivism** *n* ▸ **pro'gressivist** *n*

progress payment *n* an instalment of a larger payment made to a contractor for work carried out up to a specified stage of the job.

prohibit (prə'hɪbɪt) *vb* (*tr*) **1** to forbid by law or other authority. **2** to hinder or prevent. [C15: from L *prohibēre* to prevent, from PRO-¹ + *habēre* to hold]
▸ **pro'hibiter** or **pro'hibitor** *n*

prohibition (,prəʊɪ'bɪʃən) *n* **1** the act of prohibiting or state of being prohibited. **2** an order or decree that prohibits. **3** (*sometimes cap.*) (esp. in the US) a policy of legally forbidding the manufacture, sale, or consumption of alcoholic beverages. **4** *Law.* an order of a superior court forbidding an inferior court to determine a matter outside its jurisdiction.
▸ **,prohi'bitionary** *adj* ▸ **,prohi'bitionist** *n*

Prohibition (,prəʊɪ'bɪʃən) *n* the period (1920–33) when the manufacture, sale, and transportation of intoxicating liquors was banned in the US.
▸ **,Prohi'bitionist** *n*

prohibitive (prə'hɪbɪtɪv) or (*less commonly*) **prohibitory** (prə'hɪbɪtərɪ, -trɪ) *adj* **1** prohibiting or tending to prohibit. **2** (esp. of prices) tending or designed to discourage sale or purchase.
▸ **pro'hibitively** *adv* ▸ **pro'hibitiveness** *n*

project *n* ('prɒdʒekt). **1** a proposal, scheme, or design. **2a** a task requiring considerable or concerted effort, such as one by students. **2b** the subject of such a task. ♦ *vb* (prə'dʒekt). **3** (*tr*) to propose or plan. **4** (*tr*) to throw forwards. **5** to jut or cause to jut out. **6** (*tr*) to make a prediction based on known data and observations. **7** (*tr*) to transport in the imagination: *to project oneself into the future.* **8** (*tr*) to cause (an image) to appear on a surface. **9** to cause (one's voice) to be heard clearly at a distance. **10** *Psychol.* **10a** (*intr*) (esp. of a child) to believe that others share one's subjective mental life. **10b** to impute to others (one's hidden desires). **11** (*tr*) *Geom.* to draw a projection of. **12** (*intr*) to communicate effectively, esp. to a large gathering. [C14: from L *prōicere* to throw down]

projectile (prə'dʒektaɪl) *n* **1** an object thrown forwards. **2** any self-propelling missile, esp. a rocket. **3** any object that can be fired from a gun, such as a shell. ♦ *adj* **4** designed to be hurled forwards. **5** projecting forwards. **6** *Zool.* another word for **protrusile.** [C17: from NL *prōjectilis* jutting forwards]

projection (prə'dʒekʃən) *n* **1** the act of projecting or the state of being projected. **2** a part that juts out. **3** See **map projection. 4** the representation of a line, figure, or solid on a given plane as it would be seen from a particular direction or in accordance with an accepted set of rules. **5** a scheme or plan. **6** a prediction based on known evidence and observations. **7a** the process of showing film on a screen. **7b** the images shown. **8** *Psychol.* **8a** the belief that others share one's subjective mental life. **8b** the process of projecting one's own hidden desires and impulses.
▸ **pro'jectional** *adj* ▸ **pro'jective** *adj*

projectionist (prə'dʒekʃənɪst) *n* a person responsible for the operation of film projection machines.

projective geometry *n* the branch of geometry concerned with the properties of solids that are invariant under projection and section.

projector (prə'dʒektə) *n* **1** an optical instrument that projects an enlarged image of individual slides. Full name: **slide projector. 2** an optical instrument in which a film is wound past a lens so that the frames can be viewed as a continuously moving sequence. Full name: **film** or **cine projector. 3** a device for projecting a light beam. **4** a person who devises projects.

prokaryote or **procaryote** (prəʊˈkærɪɒt) n any organism of the kingdom Prokaryotae having cells in which the genetic material is in a single filament of DNA, not enclosed in a nucleus. Cf. **eukaryote**. [from PRO-² + KARYO- + -ote as in zygote]
▸ **prokaryotic** or **procaryotic** (prəʊˌkærɪˈɒtɪk) adj

Prokofiev ★ (prəˈkɒfɪˌef; Russian praˈkɔfjɪf) n **Sergei Sergeyevich** (sɪrˈgjej sɪrˈgjejɪvɪtʃ). 1891–1953, Soviet composer. His compositions include the orchestral fairy tale Peter and the Wolf (1936), the opera The Love for Three Oranges (1921), and seven symphonies.

Prokopyevsk ★ (Russian praˈkɔpjɪfsk) n a city in S Russia: the chief coal-mining centre of the Kuznetsk Basin. Pop.: 253 000 (1995 est.).

prolactin (prəʊˈlæktɪn) n a gonadotrophic hormone secreted by the anterior lobe of the pituitary gland. In mammals it stimulates the secretion of progesterone by the corpus luteum and initiates and maintains lactation.

prolapse (ˈprəʊlæps, prəʊˈlæps) Pathol. ◆ n **1** Also: **prolapsus** (prəʊˈlæpsəs). the sinking or falling down of an organ or part, esp. the womb. ◆ vb **prolapses, prolapsing, prolapsed.** (intr) **2** (of an organ, etc.) to sink from its normal position. [C17: from L prōlābī to slide along]

prolate (ˈprəʊleɪt) adj having a polar diameter of greater length than the equatorial diameter. Cf. **oblate**¹. [C17: from L prōferre to enlarge]
▸ **ˈprolately** adv

prole (prəʊl) n, adj Derog. sl., chiefly Brit. short for **proletarian**.

prolegomenon (ˌprəʊlɪˈɡɒmɪnən) n, pl **prolegomena** (-nə). (often pl) a preliminary discussion, esp. a formal critical introduction to a lengthy text. [C17: from Gk, from prolegein, from PRO-² + legein to say]
▸ **ˌproleˈgomenal** adj

prolepsis (prəʊˈlepsɪs) n, pl **prolepses** (-siːz). **1** a rhetorical device by which objections are anticipated and answered in advance. **2** use of a word after a verb in anticipation of its becoming applicable through the action of the verb, as flat in hammer it flat. [C16: via LL from Gk; anticipation, from prolambanein to anticipate, from PRO-² + lambanein to take]
▸ **proˈleptic** adj

proletarian (ˌprəʊlɪˈtɛərɪən) adj **1** of or belonging to the proletariat. ◆ n **2** a member of the proletariat. [C17: from L prōlētārius one whose only contribution to the state was his offspring, from prōlēs offspring]
▸ **ˌproleˈtarianism** n

proletariat (ˌprəʊlɪˈtɛərɪət) n **1** all wage-earners collectively. **2** the lower or working class. **3** (in Marxist theory) the class of wage-earners, esp. industrial workers, in a capitalist society, whose only possession of significant material value is their labour. **4** (in ancient Rome) the lowest class of citizens, who had no property. [C19: via F from L prōlētārius PROLETARIAN]

pro-life adj (of an organization, pressure group, etc.) supporting the right to life of the unborn; against abortion, experiments on embryos, etc.
▸ **ˌpro-ˈlifer** n

proliferate (prəˈlɪfəˌreɪt) vb **proliferates, proliferating, proliferated. 1** to grow or reproduce (new parts, cells, etc.) rapidly. **2** to grow or increase rapidly. [C19: from Med. L prōlifer having offspring, from L prōlēs offspring + ferre to bear]
▸ **proˌliferˈation** n ▸ **proˈliferative** adj

prolific (prəˈlɪfɪk) adj **1** producing fruit, offspring, etc., in abundance. **2** producing constant or successful results. **3** (often foll. by in or of) rich or fruitful. [C17: from Med. L prōlificus, from L prōlēs offspring]
▸ **proˈlifically** adv ▸ **proˈlificness** or **proˈlificacy** n

prolix (ˈprəʊlɪks, prəʊˈlɪks) adj **1** (of a speech, book, etc.) so long as to be boring. **2** long-winded. [C15: from L prōlixus stretched out widely, from līquī to flow]
▸ **proˈlixity** n ▸ **proˈlixly** adv

prolocutor (prəʊˈlɒkjʊtə) n a chairman, esp. of the lower house of clergy in a convocation of the Anglican Church. [C15: from L: advocate, from loqui to speak]
▸ **proˈlocutorship** n

PROLOG or **Prolog** (ˈprəʊlɒɡ) n a computer programming language based on mathematical logic. [C20: from pro(gramming in) log(ic)]

prologue or US (often) **prolog** (ˈprəʊlɒɡ) n **1** the prefatory lines introducing a play or speech. **2** a preliminary act or event. **3** (in early opera) **3a** an introductory scene in which a narrator summarizes the main action of the work. **3b** a brief independent play preceding the opera, esp. one in honour of a patron. ◆ vb **prologues, prologuing, prologued** or US **prologs, prologing, prologed. 4** (tr) to introduce with a prologue. [C13: from L prologus, from Gk, from PRO-² + logos discourse]

prolong (prəˈlɒŋ) vb (tr) to lengthen; extend. [C15: from LL prōlongāre to extend, from L PRO-¹ + longus long]
▸ **prolongation** (ˌprəʊlɒŋˈɡeɪʃən) n

prolusion (prəˈluːʒən) n **1** a preliminary written exercise. **2** an introductory essay. [C17: from L prōlūsiō, from prōlūdere to practise beforehand, from PRO-¹ + lūdere to play]
▸ **proˈlusory** (prəˈluːzərɪ) adj

prom (prɒm) n **1** Brit. short for **promenade** (sense 1) or **promenade concert. 2** US & Canad. inf. a formal dance held at a high school or college.

PROM (prɒm) n Computing. acronym for programmable read only memory.

promenade (ˌprɒməˈnɑːd) n **1** Chiefly Brit. a public walk, esp. at a seaside resort. **2** a leisurely walk, esp. one in a public place for pleasure or display. **3** a marchlike step in dancing. **4** a marching sequence in a square or country dance. ◆ vb **promenades, promenading, promenaded. 5** to take a promenade in or through (a place). **6** (intr) Dancing. to perform a promenade. **7** (tr) to display or exhibit (someone or oneself) on or as if on a promenade. [C16: from F, from promener to lead out for a walk, from LL prōmināre to drive (cattle) along, from mināre to drive, prob. from minārī to threaten]
▸ **ˌpromeˈnader** n

promenade concert n a concert at which some of the audience stand rather than sit.

promenade deck n an upper covered deck of a passenger ship for the use of the passengers.

promethazine (prəʊˈmeθəˌziːn) n an antihistamine drug used to treat allergies and to prevent vomiting. [C20: from PRO(PYL) + (di)meth(ylamine) + (phenothi)azine]

Promethean (prəˈmiːθɪən) adj **1** of or relating to Prometheus. **2** creative, original, or life-enhancing.

Prometheus ★ (prəˈmiːθɪəs) n Greek myth. a Titan, who stole fire from Olympus to give to mankind and in punishment was chained to a rock, where an eagle tore at his liver until Hercules freed him.

promethium (prəˈmiːθɪəm) n a radioactive element of the lanthanide series artificially produced by the fission of uranium. Symbol: Pm; atomic no.: 61; half-life of most stable isotope, ¹⁴⁵Pm: 17.7 years. [C20: NL from PROMETHEUS]

prominence (ˈprɒmɪnəns) n **1** the state of being prominent. **2** something that is prominent, such as a protuberance. **3** relative importance. **4** Astron. an eruption of incandescent gas from the sun's surface, visible during a total eclipse.

prominent (ˈprɒmɪnənt) adj **1** jutting or projecting outwards. **2** standing out from its surroundings; noticeable. **3** widely known; eminent. [C16: from L prōminēre to jut out, from PRO-¹ + ēminēre to project]
▸ **ˈprominently** adv

promiscuous (prəˈmɪskjʊəs) adj **1** indulging in casual and indiscriminate sexual relationships. **2** consisting of a number of dissimilar parts or elements mingled indiscriminately. **3** indiscriminate in selection. **4** casual or heedless. [C17: from L prōmiscuus indiscriminate, from PRO-¹ + miscēre to mix]
▸ **proˈmiscuously** adv ▸ **promiscuity** (ˌprɒmɪˈskjuːɪtɪ) or **proˈmiscuousness** n

promise (ˈprɒmɪs) vb **promises, promising, promised. 1** (often foll. by to; when tr, may take a clause as object or an infinitive) to give an assurance of (something to someone): I promise that I will come. **2** (tr) to undertake to give (something to someone): he promised me a car for my birthday. **3** (when tr, takes an infinitive) to cause people to ex-

---

★ people and places

pect that one is likely (to be or do something): *she promises to be a fine soprano.* **4** (*tr; usually passive*) *Obs.* to betroth: *I'm promised to Bill.* **5** (*tr*) to assure (someone) of the authenticity or inevitability of something: *there'll be trouble, I promise you.* ◆ *n* **6** an assurance given by one person to another agreeing or guaranteeing to do or not to do something. **7** indication of forthcoming excellence: *a writer showing considerable promise.* **8** the thing of which an assurance is given. [C14: from L *prōmissum* a promise, from *prōmittere* to send forth]
▶ ˌpromiˈsee *n* ▶ ˈpromiser *or* (*Law*) ˈpromisor *n*

romised Land ★ *n* **1** *Old Testament.* the land of Canaan, promised by God to Abraham and his descendants as their heritage (Genesis 12:7). **2** *Christianity.* heaven. **3** any longed-for place where one expects to find greater happiness.

romising (ˈprɒmɪsɪŋ) *adj* showing promise of future success.
▶ ˈpromisingly *adv*

romissory (ˈprɒmɪsərɪ) *adj* **1** containing, relating to, or having the nature of a promise. **2** *Insurance.* stipulating how the provisions of an insurance contract will be fulfilled.

romissory note *n Commerce, chiefly US.* a document containing a signed promise to pay a stated sum of money to a specified person at a designated date or on demand. Also called: **note, note of hand.**

romo (ˈprəʊməʊ) *n, pl* **promos.** *Inf.* something used to promote a product, esp. a videotape film used to promote a pop record. [C20: shortened from *promotion*]

romontory (ˈprɒməntərɪ, -trɪ) *n, pl* **promontories.** **1** a high point of land, esp. of rocky coast, that juts out into the sea. **2** *Anat.* any of various projecting structures. [C16: from L *prōmunturium* headland]

romote (prəˈməʊt) *vb* **promotes, promoting, promoted.** (*tr*) **1** to encourage the progress or existence of. **2** to raise to a higher rank, status, etc. **3** to advance (a pupil or student) to a higher course, class, etc. **4** to work for: *to promote reform.* **5** to encourage the sale of (a product) by advertising or securing financial support. [C14: from L *prōmovēre* to push onwards]
▶ proˈmotion *n* ▶ proˈmotional *adj*

romoter (prəˈməʊtə) *n* **1** a person or thing that promotes. **2** a person who helps to organize, develop, or finance an undertaking. **3** a person who organizes and finances a sporting event, esp. a boxing match.

rompt (prɒmpt) *adj* **1** performed or executed without delay. **2** quick or ready to act or respond. ◆ *adv* **3** *Inf.* punctually. ◆ *vb* **4** (*tr*) to urge (someone to do something). **5** to remind (an actor, singer, etc.) of lines forgotten during a performance. **6** (*tr*) to refresh the memory of. **7** (*tr*) to give rise to by suggestion: *his affairs will prompt discussion.* ◆ *n* **8** *Commerce.* **8a** the time limit allowed for payment of the debt incurred by purchasing on credit. **8b** Also called: **prompt note.** a memorandum sent to a purchaser to remind him of the time limit and the sum due. **9** anything that serves to remind. [C15: from L *promptus* evident, from *prōmere* to produce, from *emere* to buy]
▶ ˈpromptly *adv* ▶ ˈpromptness *n*

rompter (ˈprɒmptə) *n* **1** a person offstage who reminds the actors of forgotten lines or cues. **2** a person, thing, etc., that prompts.

romptitude (ˈprɒmptɪˌtjuːd) *n* the quality of being prompt; punctuality.

rompt side *n Theatre.* the side of the stage where the prompter is, usually to the actor's left in Britain and to his right in the United States.

romulgate (ˈprɒməlˌgeɪt) *vb* **promulgates, promulgating, promulgated.** (*tr*) **1** to put into effect (a law, decree, etc.), esp. by formal proclamation. **2** to announce officially. **3** to make widespread. [C16: from L *prōmulgāre* to bring to public knowledge]
▶ ˌpromulˈgation *n* ▶ ˈpromulˌgator *n*

ron. *abbrev. for:* **1** pronominal. **2** pronoun. **3** pronounced. **4** pronunciation.

ronate (prəʊˈneɪt) *vb* **pronates, pronating, pronated.** (*tr*) to

turn (the forearm or hand) so that the palmar surface is directed downwards. [C19: from LL *prōnāre* to bow]
▶ proˈnation *n* ▶ proˈnator *n*

prone (prəʊn) *adj* **1** lying flat or face downwards; prostrate. **2** sloping or tending downwards. **3** having an inclination to do something. [C14: from L *prōnus* bent forward, from PRO-¹]
▶ ˈpronely *adv* ▶ ˈproneness *n*

-prone *adj combining form.* liable or disposed to suffer: *accident-prone.*

prong (prɒŋ) *n* **1** a sharply pointed end of an instrument, such as on a fork. **2** any pointed projecting part. ◆ *vb* **3** (*tr*) to prick or spear with or as if with a prong. [C15]
▶ pronged *adj*

pronghorn (ˈprɒŋˌhɔːn) *n* a ruminant mammal inhabiting rocky deserts of North America and having small branched horns. Also called: **American antelope.**

pronominal (prəʊˈnɒmɪnˀl) *adj* relating to or playing the part of a pronoun. [C17: from LL *prōnōminālis*, from *prōnōmen* a PRONOUN]
▶ proˈnominally *adv*

pronoun (ˈprəʊˌnaʊn) *n* one of a class of words that serves to replace a noun or noun phrase that has already been or is about to be mentioned in the sentence or context. Abbrev.: **pron.** [C16: from L *prōnōmen*, from PRO-¹ + *nōmen* noun]

pronounce (prəˈnaʊns) *vb* **pronounces, pronouncing, pronounced.** **1** to utter or articulate (a sound or sounds). **2** (*tr*) to utter (words) in the correct way. **3** (*tr; may take a clause as object*) to proclaim officially: *I now pronounce you man and wife.* **4** (when *tr, may take a clause as object*) to declare as one's judgment: *to pronounce the death sentence upon someone.* [C14: from L *prōnuntiāre* to announce]
▶ proˈnounceable *adj* ▶ proˈnouncer *n*

pronounced (prəˈnaʊnst) *adj* **1** strongly marked or indicated. **2** (of a sound) articulated with vibration of the vocal cords; voiced.
▶ pronouncedly (prəˈnaʊnsɪdlɪ) *adv*

pronouncement (prəˈnaʊnsmənt) *n* **1** an official or authoritative announcement. **2** the act of declaring or uttering formally.

pronto (ˈprɒntəʊ) *adv Inf.* at once. [C20: from Sp.: quick, from L *promptus* PROMPT]

pronunciation (prəˌnʌnsɪˈeɪʃən) *n* **1** the act, instance, or manner of pronouncing sounds. **2** the supposedly correct manner of pronouncing sounds in a given language. **3** a phonetic transcription of a word.

proof (pruːf) *n* **1** any evidence that establishes or helps to establish the truth, validity, quality, etc., of something. **2** *Law.* the whole body of evidence upon which the verdict of a court is based. **3** *Maths, logic.* a sequence of steps or statements that establishes the truth of a proposition. **4** the act of testing the truth of something (esp. in **put to the proof**). **5** *Scots Law.* trial before a judge without a jury. **6** *Printing.* a trial impression made from composed type for the correction of errors. **7** (in engraving, etc.) a print made by an artist or under his supervision for his own satisfaction before he hands the plate over to a professional printer. **8** *Photog.* a trial print from a negative. **9a** the alcoholic strength of proof spirit. **9b** the strength of a liquor as measured on a scale in which the strength of proof spirit is 100 degrees. ◆ *adj* **10** (*usually postpositive; foll. by against*) impervious (to): *the roof is proof against rain.* **11** having the alcoholic strength of proof spirit. **12** of proved impenetrability: *proof armour.* ◆ *vb* **13** (*tr*) to take a proof from (type matter, a plate, etc.). **14** to proofread (text) or inspect (a print, etc.), as for approval. **15** to render (something) proof, esp. to waterproof. [C13: from OF *preuve* a test, from LL *proba*, from L *probāre* to test]

-proof *adj, vb combining form.* (to make) impervious to; secure against (damage by): *waterproof.* [from PROOF (*adj*)]

proofread (ˈpruːfˌriːd) *vb* **proofreads, proofreading, proofread** (-ˌred). to read (copy or printer's proofs) and mark errors to be corrected.
▶ ˈproofˌreader *n*

proof spirit *n* (in Britain) a mixture of alcohol and water or an alcoholic beverage that contains 49.28 per cent of alcohol by weight, 57.1 per cent by volume at 51°F: used until 1980 as a standard of alcoholic liquids.

prop[1] (prɒp) *vb* **props, propping, propped.** (*tr;* often foll. by *up*) **1** to support with a rigid object, such as a stick. **2** (usually also foll. by *against*) to place or lean. **3** to sustain or support. ◆ *n* **4** something that gives rigid support, such as a stick. **5** short for **clothes prop. 6** a person or thing giving support, as of a moral nature. **7** *Rugby.* either of the forwards at either end of the front row of a scrum. [C15: rel. to M Du. *proppe* vine prop]

prop[2] (prɒp) *n* short for **property** (sense 8).

prop[3] (prɒp) *n* an informal word for **propeller.**

prop. *abbrev. for:* **1** proper(ly). **2** property. **3** proposition. **4** proprietor.

propaedeutic (ˌprəʊpɪˈdjuːtɪk) *n* **1** (*often pl*) preparatory instruction basic to further study of an art or science. ◆ *adj also* **propaedeutical. 2** of, relating to, or providing such instruction. [C19: from Gk *propaideuein* to teach in advance, from PRO-[2] + *paideuein* to rear]

propaganda (ˌprɒpəˈɡændə) *n* **1** the organized dissemination of information, allegations, etc., to assist or damage the cause of a government, movement, etc. **2** such information, allegations, etc. [C18: from It., use of *propāgandā* in the NL title *Sacra Congregatio de Propaganda Fide* Sacred Congregation for Propagating the Faith]
▸ ˌpropaˈgandism *n* ▸ ˌpropaˈgandist *n, adj*

Propaganda (ˌprɒpəˈɡændə) *n RC Church.* a congregation responsible for directing the work of the foreign missions.

propagandize *or* **propagandise** (ˌprɒpəˈɡænˌdaɪz) *vb* **propagandizes, propagandizing, propagandized** *or* **propagandises, propagandising, propagandised. 1** (*tr*) to spread by, or subject to, propaganda. **2** (*intr*) to spread or organize propaganda.

propagate (ˈprɒpəˌɡeɪt) *vb* **propagates, propagating, propagated. 1** *Biol.* to reproduce or cause to reproduce; breed. **2** (*tr*) *Horticulture.* to produce (plants) by layering, grafting, cuttings, etc. **3** (*tr*) to promulgate. **4** *Physics.* to transmit, esp. in the form of a wave: *to propagate sound.* **5** (*tr*) to transmit (characteristics) from one generation to the next. [C16: from L *propāgāre* to increase (plants) by cuttings, from *propāgēs* a cutting, from *pangere* to fasten]
▸ ˌpropaˈgation *n* ▸ ˌpropaˈgational *adj* ▸ ˈpropagative *adj*
▸ ˈpropaˌgator *n*

propane (ˈprəʊpeɪn) *n* a flammable gaseous alkane found in petroleum and used as a fuel. Formula: $CH_3CH_2CH_3$. [C19: from PROPIONIC (ACID) + -ANE]

propanoic acid (ˌprəʊpəˈnəʊɪk) *n* a colourless liquid carboxylic acid used in inhibiting the growth of moulds in bread. Formula: CH_3CH_2COOH. Former name: **propionic acid.** [C20: from PROPANE + -OIC]

pro patria *Latin.* (ˈprəʊ ˈpætrɪˌɑː) for one's country.

propel (prəˈpɛl) *vb* **propels, propelling, propelled.** (*tr*) to impel, drive, or cause to move forwards. [C15: from L *prōpellere*]
▸ proˈpellant *or* proˈpellent *n*

propeller (prəˈpɛlə) *n* **1** a device having blades radiating from a central hub that is rotated to produce thrust to propel a ship, aircraft, etc. **2** a person or thing that propels.

propelling pencil *n* a pencil consisting of a metal or plastic case containing a replaceable lead. As the point is worn away the lead can be extended, usually by turning part of the case.

propene (ˈprəʊpiːn) *n* a colourless gaseous alkene obtained by cracking petroleum. Formula: $CH_3CH:CH_2$. Also called: **propylene.**

propensity (prəˈpɛnsɪtɪ) *n, pl* **propensities. 1** a natural tendency. **2** *Obs.* partiality. [C16: from L *prōpensus* inclined to, from *prōpendēre* to hang forwards]

proper (ˈprɒpə) *adj* **1** (*usually prenominal*) appropriate or usual: *in its proper place.* **2** suited to a particular purpose: *use the proper knife to cut the bread.* **3** correct in behaviour. **4** vigorously or excessively moral. **5** up to a required or regular standard. **6** (*immediately postpositive*) (of an object, quality, etc.) referred to so as to exclude anything not directly connected with it: *his claim is connected with*

the deed proper. **7** (*postpositive;* foll. by *to*) belonging to o characteristic of a person or thing. **8** (*prenominal*) *Brit.* in (intensifier): *I felt a proper fool.* **9** (*usually postpositive*) (c heraldic colours) considered correct for the natural col our of the object depicted: *three martlets proper.* **10** *Arch* pleasant or good. **11 good and proper.** *Inf.* thoroughly. ◆ ◆ **12** the parts of the Mass that vary according to the par ticular day or feast on which the Mass is celebrated [C13: via OF from L *prōprius* special]
▸ ˈproperly *adv* ▸ ˈproperness *n*

proper fraction *n* a fraction in which the numerato has a lower absolute value than the denominator, as ½ or $x/(3 + x^2)$.

proper motion *n* the very small continuous change i the direction of motion of a star relative to the sun.

proper noun *or* **name** *n* the name of a person, place, o object, as for example *Iceland, Patrick,* or *Uranus.* Cf. **com mon noun.**

propertied (ˈprɒpətɪd) *adj* owning land or property.

Propertius ★ (prəˈpɜːʃɪəs, -ʃəs) *n* **Sextus** (ˈsɛkstəs). ?50– ?15 B.C., Roman elegiac poet.

property (ˈprɒpətɪ) *n, pl* **properties. 1** something of value either tangible, such as land, or intangible, such as copy rights. **2** *Law.* the right to possess, use, and dispose c anything. **3** possessions collectively. **4a** land or real es tate. **4b** (*as modifier*): *property rights.* **5** *Chiefly Austral.* ranch or station. **6** a quality or characteristic attribute such as the density or strength of a material. **7** *Logic, obs* Also called: **proprium** (ˈprəʊprɪəm). an attribute that is no essential to a species but is common and peculiar to it. **8** any movable object used on the set of a stage play o film. Usually shortened to **prop.** [C13: from OF *propriété* from L *proprietās* something personal, from *proprius* one' own]

property bond *n* a bond issued by a life-assurance com pany, the premiums for which are invested in . property-owning fund.

property centre *n* a service for buying and sellin property, including conveyancing, provided by a grou of local solicitors. In full: **solicitors' property centre.**

property man *n* a member of the stage crew in charg of the stage properties. Usually shortened to **propman.**

prophecy (ˈprɒfɪsɪ) *n, pl* **prophecies. 1a** a message of di vine truth revealing God's will. **1b** the act of utterin such a message. **2** a prediction or guess. **3** the charis matic endowment of a prophet. [C13: ult. from G *prophētēs* PROPHET]

prophesy (ˈprɒfɪˌsaɪ) *vb* **prophesies, prophesying, prophe sied. 1** to foretell (something) by or as if by divine inspi ration. **2** (*intr*) *Arch.* to give instructions in religiou subjects. [C14 *prophecien,* from PROPHECY]
▸ ˈpropheˌsiable *adj* ▸ ˈpropheˌsier *n*

prophet (ˈprɒfɪt) *n* **1** a person who supposedly speaks b divine inspiration, esp. one through whom a divinit expresses his will. **2** a person who predicts the future: prophet of doom.* **3** a spokesman for a movement, doc trine, etc. [C13: from OF *prophète,* from L, from G *prophētēs* one who declares the divine will, from PRO-[2] *phanai* to speak]
▸ ˈprophetess *fem n*

Prophet (ˈprɒfɪt) *n* **the. 1** the principal designation o Mohammed as the founder of Islam. **2** a name for Josepl Smith as the founder of the Mormon Church.

prophetic (prəˈfɛtɪk) *adj* **1** of or relating to a prophet o prophecy. **2** of the nature of a prophecy; predictive.
▸ proˈphetically *adv*

prophylactic (ˌprɒfɪˈlæktɪk) *adj* **1** protecting from o preventing disease. **2** protective or preventive. ◆ *n* **3** a prophylactic drug or device. **4** *Chiefly US.* another nam for **condom.** [C16: via F from Gk *prophulaktikos,* fron *prophulassein* to guard by taking advance measures, from PRO-[2] + *phulax* a guard]

prophylaxis (ˌprɒfɪˈlæksɪs) *n* the prevention of diseas or control of its possible spread.

propinquity (prəˈpɪŋkwɪtɪ) *n* **1** nearness in place o time. **2** nearness in relationship. [C14: from l *propinquitās,* from *propinquus* near, from *prope* nearby]

★ people and places

propionic acid (ˌprəʊpɪˈɒnɪk) *n* the former name for **propanoic acid.** [C19: from Gk *pro-* first + *pionic,* from *piōn* fat, because it is first in order of the fatty acids]

propitiate (prəˈpɪʃɪˌeɪt) *vb* **propitiates, propitiating, propitiated.** (*tr*) to appease or make well disposed; conciliate. [C17: from L *propitiāre,* from *propitius* gracious] ▸ proˈpitiable *adj* ▸ proˌpitiˈation *n* ▸ proˈpitiative *adj* ▸ proˈpitiˌator *n* ▸ proˈpitiatory *adj*

propitious (prəˈpɪʃəs) *adj* **1** favourable; auguring well. **2** gracious or favourably inclined. [C15: from L *propitius* well disposed, from *prope* close to] ▸ proˈpitiously *adv* ▸ proˈpitiousness *n*

propjet (ˈprɒpˌdʒet) *n* another name for **turboprop.**

propolis (ˈprɒpəlɪs) *n* a greenish-brown resinous aromatic substance collected by bees from the buds of trees for use in the construction of hives. Also called: **bee glue, hive dross.** [C17: via L from Gk: suburb, bee glue, from *pro-* before + *polis* city]

proponent (prəˈpəʊnənt) *n* a person who argues in favour of something or puts forward a proposal, etc. [C16: from L *prōpōnere* to PROPOSE]

Propontis ★ (prəˈpɒntɪs) *n* the ancient name for (the Sea of) **Marmara.**

proportion (prəˈpɔːʃən) *n* **1** relative magnitude or extent; ratio. **2** correct or desirable relationship between parts; symmetry. **3** a part considered with respect to the whole. **4** (*pl*) dimensions or size: *a building of vast proportions.* **5** a share or quota. **6** a relationship that maintains a constant ratio between two variable quantities: *prices increase in proportion to manufacturing costs.* **7** *Maths.* a relationship between four numbers or quantities in which the ratio of the first pair equals the ratio of the second pair. ◆ *vb* (*tr*) **8** to adjust in relative amount, size, etc. **9** to cause to be harmonious in relationship of parts. [C14: from L *prōportiō,* from *prō portiōne,* lit.: for (its, one's) PORTION] ▸ proˈportionable *adj* ▸ proˈportionably *adv* ▸ proˈportionment *n*

proportional (prəˈpɔːʃənˀl) *adj* **1** of, involving, or being in proportion. ◆ *n* **2** *Maths.* an unknown term in a proportion: *in a/b = c/x, x is the fourth proportional.* ▸ proˌportionˈality *n* ▸ proˈportionally *adv*

proportional representation *n* representation of parties in an elective body in proportion to the votes they win. Abbrev.: **PR.** Cf. **first-past-the-post.** See also **Additional Member System, Alternative Vote, party list, Single Transferable Vote.**

proportionate *adj* (prəˈpɔːʃənɪt). **1** being in proper proportion. ◆ *vb* (prəˈpɔːʃəˌneɪt), **proportionates, proportionating, proportionated. 2** (*tr*) to make proportionate. ▸ proˈportionately *adv*

proposal (prəˈpəʊzˀl) *n* **1** the act of proposing. **2** something proposed, as a plan. **3** an offer, esp. of marriage.

propose (prəˈpəʊz) *vb* **proposes, proposing, proposed. 1** (when *tr,* may take a clause as object) to put forward (a plan, etc.) for consideration. **2** (*tr*) to nominate, as for a position. **3** (*tr*) to intend (to do something): *I propose to leave town now.* **4** (*tr*) to announce the drinking of (a toast). **5** (*intr;* often foll. by *to*) to make an offer of marriage. [C14: from OF *proposer,* from L *prōpōnere* to display, from PRO-[1] + *pōnere* to place] ▸ proˈposable *adj* ▸ proˈposer *n*

proposition (ˌprɒpəˈzɪʃən) *n* **1** a proposal for consideration. **2** *Philosophy.* the content of a sentence that affirms or denies something and is capable of being true or false. **3** *Maths.* a statement or theorem, usually containing its proof. **4** *Inf.* a person or matter to be dealt with: *he's a difficult proposition.* **5** *Inf.* an invitation to engage in sexual intercourse. ◆ *vb* **6** (*tr*) to propose a plan, deal, etc., to, esp. to engage in sexual intercourse. [C14 *proposicioun,* from L *prōpositiō* a setting forth; see PROPOSE] ▸ ˌpropoˈsitional *adj*

propositional calculus *n* the system of symbolic logic concerned only with the relations between propositions as wholes, taking no account of their internal structure. Cf. **predicate calculus.**

propositus (prəˈpɒzɪtəs) *or* (*fem*) **proposita** (prəˈpɒzɪtə) *n, pl* **propositi** (-ˌtaɪ) *or* (*fem*) **propositae** (-tiː).

Med. the first patient to be investigated in a family study, to whom all relationships are referred. Also called (esp. US): **proband.**

propound (prəˈpaʊnd) *vb* (*tr*) **1** to put forward for consideration. **2** *English law.* to produce (a will or similar instrument) to the proper court or authority for its validity to be established. [C16 *propone,* from L *prōpōnere* to set forth, from PRO-[1] + *pōnere* to place] ▸ proˈpounder *n*

propranolol (prəʊˈprænəˌlɒl) *n* a drug used in the treatment of heart disease.

proprietary (prəˈpraɪtərɪ, -trɪ) *adj* **1** of or belonging to property or proprietors. **2** privately owned and controlled. **3** *Med.* denoting a drug manufactured and distributed under a trade name. ◆ *n, pl* **proprietaries. 4** *Med.* a proprietary drug. **5** a proprietor or proprietors collectively. **6a** right to property. **6b** property owned. **7** (in Colonial America) an owner of a **proprietary colony,** a colony which was granted by the Crown to a particular person or group. [C15: from LL *proprietārius* an owner, from *proprius* one's own] ▸ proˈprietarily *adv*

proprietary name *n* a name which is restricted in use by virtue of being a trade name.

proprietor (prəˈpraɪətə) *n* **1** an owner of a business. **2** a person enjoying exclusive right of ownership to some property. ▸ proˌprieˈtorial (prəˌpraɪəˈtɔːrɪəl) *adj* ▸ proˈprietress *or* proˈprietrix *fem n*

propriety (prəˈpraɪətɪ) *n, pl* **proprieties. 1** the quality or state of being appropriate or fitting. **2** conformity to the prevailing standard of behaviour, speech, etc. **3 the proprieties.** the standards of behaviour considered correct by polite society. [C15: from OF *propriété,* from L *proprietās* a peculiarity, from *proprius* one's own]

proprioceptor (ˌprəʊprɪəˈseptə) *n Physiol.* any receptor, as in the gut, blood vessels, muscles, etc., that supplies information about the state of the body. [C20: from *proprio-,* from L *proprius* one's own + RECEPTOR] ▸ ˌproprioˈceptive *adj*

proptosis (prɒpˈtəʊsɪs) *n, pl* **proptoses** (-siːz). *Pathol.* the forward displacement of an organ or part, such as the eyeball. [C17: via LL from Gk, from *propiptein* to fall forwards]

propulsion (prəˈpʌlʃən) *n* **1** the act of propelling or the state of being propelled. **2** a propelling force. [C15: from L *prōpellere* to propel] ▸ proˈpulsive (prəˈpʌlsɪv) *or* proˈpulsory *adj*

propyl (ˈprəʊpɪl) *n* (*modifier*) of or containing the monovalent group of atoms C_3H_7 -. [C19: from PROP(IONIC ACID) + -YL]

propylaeum (ˌprɒpɪˈliːəm) *or* **propylon** (ˈprɒpɪˌlɒn) *n, pl* **propylaea** (-ˈliːə) *or* **propylons, propyla** (-lə). a portico, esp. one that forms the entrance to a temple. [C18: via L from Gk *propulaion* before the gate, from PRO-[2] + *pulē* gate]

propylene (ˈprəʊpɪˌliːn) *n* another name for **propene.** [C19]

propylene glycol *n* a colourless viscous compound used as an antifreeze and brake fluid. Formula: $CH_3CH(OH)CH_2OH$. Systematic name: **1,2-dihydroxy-propane.**

pro rata (ˈprəʊ ˈrɑːtə) in proportion. [Med. L]

prorate (prəʊˈreɪt, ˈprəʊreɪt) *vb* **prorates, prorating, prorated.** *Chiefly US & Canad.* to divide, assess, or distribute proportionately. [C19: from PRO RATA] ▸ proˈratable *adj* ▸ proˈration *n*

prorogue (prəˈrəʊg) *vb* **prorogues, proroguing, prorogued.** to discontinue the meetings of (a legislative body) without dissolving it. [C15: from L *prorogāre,* lit.: to ask publicly] ▸ prorogation (ˌprəʊrəˈgeɪʃən) *n*

prosaic (prəˈzeɪɪk) *adj* **1** lacking imagination. **2** having the characteristics of prose. [C16: from LL *prōsaicus,* from L *prōsa* PROSE] ▸ proˈsaically *adv*

pros and cons *pl n* the various arguments in favour of

and against a motion, course of action, etc. [C16: from L *prō* for + *con*, from *contrā* against]

proscenium (prə'si:nɪəm) *n, pl* **proscenia** (-nɪə) *or* **prosceniums. 1** the arch or opening separating the stage from the auditorium together with the area immediately in front of the arch. **2** (in ancient theatres) the stage itself. [C17: via L from Gk *proskēnion*, from *pro-* before + *skēnē* scene]

prosciutto (prəʊ'ʃuːtəʊ; *Italian* proˈʃutto) *n* cured ham from Italy: usually served as an hors d'oeuvre. [It., lit.: dried beforehand]

proscribe (prəʊ'skraɪb) *vb* **proscribes, proscribing, proscribed.** (*tr*) **1** to condemn or prohibit. **2** to outlaw; banish; exile. [C16: from L *prōscrībere* to put up a public notice, from *prō-* in public + *scrībere* to write]
▶ **proˈscriber** *n* ▶ **proscription** (prəʊ'skrɪpʃən) *n*

prose (prəʊz) *n* **1** spoken or written language distinguished from poetry by its lack of a marked metrical structure. **2** a passage set for translation into a foreign language. **3** commonplace or dull discourse, expression, etc. **4** (*modifier*) written in prose. **5** (*modifier*) matter-of-fact. ◆ *vb* **proses, prosing, prosed. 6** to write (something) in prose. **7** (*intr*) to speak or write in a tedious style. [C14: via OF from L *prōsa ōrātiō* straightforward speech, from *prorsus* prosaic, from *prōvertere* to turn forwards]
▶ **ˈproseˌlike** *adj*

prosecute ('prɒsɪˌkjuːt) *vb* **prosecutes, prosecuting, prosecuted. 1** (*tr*) to bring a criminal action against (a person). **2** (*intr*) **2a** to seek redress by legal proceedings. **2b** to institute or conduct a prosecution. **3** (*tr*) to practise (a profession or trade). **4** (*tr*) to continue to do (a task, etc.). [C15: from L *prōsequī* to follow]
▶ **ˈproseˌcutable** *adj* ▶ **ˈproseˌcutor** *n*

prosecution (ˌprɒsɪ'kjuːʃən) *n* **1** the act of prosecuting or the state of being prosecuted. **2a** the institution and conduct of legal proceedings against a person. **2b** the proceedings brought in the name of the Crown to put an accused on trial. **3** the lawyers acting for the Crown to put the case against a person. **4** the following up or carrying on of something begun.

proselyte ('prɒsɪˌlaɪt) *n* **1** a person newly converted to a religious faith, esp. a Gentile converted to Judaism. ◆ *vb* **proselytes, proselyting, proselyted. 2** a less common word for **proselytize.** [C14: from Church L *prosēlytus*, from Gk *prosēlutos* recent arrival, convert, from *proserchesthai* to draw near]
▶ **proselytism** ('prɒsɪlɪˌtɪzəm) *n* ▶ **proselytic** (ˌprɒsɪ'lɪtɪk) *adj*

proselytize *or* **proselytise** ('prɒsɪlɪˌtaɪz) *vb* **proselytizes, proselytizing, proselytized** *or* **proselytises, proselytising, proselytised.** to convert (someone) from one religious faith to another.
▶ **ˈproselytˌizer** *or* **ˈproselytˌiser** *n*

prosencephalon (ˌprɒsen'sefəlɒn) *n, pl* **prosencephala** (-lə). the part of the brain that develops from the anterior portion of the neural tube. Nontechnical name: **forebrain.** [C19: from NL, from Gk *prosō* forward + *enkephalos* brain]

prosenchyma (prɒs'eŋkɪmə) *n* a plant tissue consisting of long narrow cells with pointed ends: occurs in conducting tissue. [C19: from NL, from Gk *pros-* towards + *enkhuma* infusion]

Proserpina ★ (prəʊ'sɜːpɪnə) *n* the Roman goddess of the underworld. Greek counterpart: **Persephone.**

prosimian (prəʊ'sɪmɪən) *n* **1** any of a primitive suborder of primates, including lemurs, lorises, and tarsiers. ◆ *adj* **2** of or belonging to this suborder. [C19: via NL from L *sīmia* ape]

prosit *German.* ('proːzɪt) *sentence substitute.* good health! cheers! [G, from L, lit.: may it prove beneficial]

prosody ('prɒsədɪ) *n* **1** the study of poetic metre and of the art of versification. **2** a system of versification. **3** the patterns of stress and intonation in a language. [C15: from L *prosōdia* accent of a syllable, from Gk *prosōidia* song set to music, from *pros* towards + *ōidē*, from *aoidē* song; see ODE]
▶ **prosodic** (prə'sɒdɪk) *adj* ▶ **ˈprosodist** *n*

prosopopoeia *or* **prosopopeia** (ˌprɒsəpə'piːə) *n* **1**

Rhetoric. another word for **personification. 2** a figure of speech that represents an imaginary, absent, or dead person speaking or acting. [C16: via L from Gk *prosōpopoiia* dramatization, from *prosōpon* face + *poiein* to make]

prospect *n* ('prɒspekt). **1** (*sometimes pl*) a probability of future success. **2** a view or scene. **3** a mental outlook. **4** expectation, or what one expects. **5** a prospective buyer, project, etc. **6** a survey or observation. **7** *Mining.* **7a** a known or likely deposit of ore. **7b** the location of a deposit of ore. **7c** the yield of mineral obtained from a sample of ore. ◆ *vb* (prə'spekt). **8** (when *intr*, often foll. by *for*) to explore (a region) for gold or other valuable minerals. **9** (*tr*) to work (a mine) to discover its profitability. **10** (*intr*; often foll. by *for*) to search (for). [C15: from L *prōspectus* distant view, from *prōspicere* to look into the distance]

prospective (prə'spektɪv) *adj* **1** looking towards the future. **2** (*prenominal*) expected or likely.
▶ **pro'spectively** *adv*

prospector (prə'spektə) *n* a person who searches for gold, petroleum, etc.

prospectus (prə'spektəs) *n, pl* **prospectuses. 1** a formal statement giving details of a forthcoming event, such as the issue of shares. **2** a brochure giving details of courses, as at a school.

prosper ('prɒspə) *vb* (*usually intr*) to thrive, succeed, etc., or cause to thrive, etc., in a healthy way. [C15: from L *prosperāre* to succeed, from *prosperus* fortunate, from PRO-[1] + *spēs* hope]

prosperity (prɒ'sperɪtɪ) *n* the condition of prospering; success or wealth.

prosperous ('prɒspərəs) *adj* **1** flourishing; prospering. **2** wealthy.
▶ **ˈprosperously** *adv*

Prost ★ (*French* prɒst) *n* **Alain** (alɛ̃). born 1955, French motor-racing driver: world champion 1985, 1986, 1989, and 1993.

prostaglandin (ˌprɒstə'glændɪn) *n* any of a group of hormone-like compounds found in all mammalian tissues, which stimulate the muscles of the uterus and affect the blood vessels; used to induce abortion or birth. [C20: from *prosta(te)* gland + -IN; orig. believed to be secreted by the prostate gland]

prostate ('prɒsteɪt) *n* **1** Also called: **prostate gland.** a gland in male mammals that surrounds the neck of the bladder and secretes a liquid constituent of the semen. ◆ *adj* **2** Also: **prostatic** (prɒ'stætɪk). of the prostate gland. ◆ See also **PSA.** [C17: via Med. L from Gk *prostatēs* something standing in front (of the bladder), from *pro-* in front + *histanai* to cause to stand]

prosthesis ('prɒsθɪsɪs) *n, pl* **prostheses** (-ˌsiːz). **1** *Surgery.* **1a** the replacement of a missing bodily part with an artificial substitute. **1b** an artificial part such as a limb, eye, or tooth. **2** *Linguistics.* another word for **prothesis.** [C16: via LL from Gk: an addition, from *prostithenai* to add, from *pros-* towards + *tithenai* to place]
▶ **prosthetic** (prɒs'θetɪk) *adj* ▶ **pros'thetically** *adv*

prosthetics (prɒs'θetɪks) *n* (*functioning as sing*) the branch of surgery concerned with prosthesis.

prostitute ('prɒstɪˌtjuːt) *n* **1** a woman who engages in sexual intercourse for money. **2** a man who engages in such activity, esp. in homosexual practices. **3** a person who offers his talent for unworthy purposes. ◆ *vb* **prostitutes, prostituting, prostituted.** (*tr*) **4** to offer (oneself or another) in sexual intercourse for money. **5** to offer for unworthy purposes. [C16: from L *prōstituere* to expose to prostitution, from *prō-* in public + *statuere* to cause to stand]
▶ **ˌprostiˈtution** *n* ▶ **ˈprostiˌtutor** *n*

prostrate *adj* ('prɒstreɪt). **1** lying face downwards, as in submission. **2** exhausted physically or emotionally. **3** helpless or defenceless. **4** (of a plant) growing closely along the ground. ◆ *vb* (prɒ'streɪt), **prostrates, prostrating, prostrated.** (*tr*) **5** to cast (oneself) down, as in submission. **6** to lay or throw down flat. **7** to make helpless. **8** to make exhausted. [C14: from L *prōsternere* to throw to the ground, from *prō-* before + *sternere* to lay low]
▶ **pros'tration** *n*

prostyle ('prəʊstaɪl) *adj* **1** (of a building) having a row of columns in front, esp. as in the portico of a Greek temple. ◆ *n* **2** a prostyle building, portico, etc. [C17: from L *prostȳlos*, from Gk: with pillars in front, from PRO-² + *stulos* pillar]

prosy ('prəʊzɪ) *adj* **prosier, prosiest. 1** of the nature of or similar to prose. **2** dull, tedious, or long-winded. ▸ **'prosily** *adv* ▸ **'prosiness** *n*

Prot. *abbrev. for:* **1** Protectorate. **2** Protestant.

protactinium (ˌprəʊtækˈtɪnɪəm) *n* a toxic radioactive element that occurs in uranium ores and is produced by neutron irradiation of thorium. Symbol: Pa; atomic no.: 91; half-life of most stable isotope, ²³¹Pa: 32 500 years.

protagonist (prəʊˈtægənɪst) *n* **1** the principal character in a play, story, etc. **2** a supporter, esp. when important or respected, of a cause, party, etc. [C17: from Gk *prōtagōnistēs*, from *prōtos* first + *agōnistēs* actor] ▸ **pro'tagonism** *n*

Protagoras ★ (prəʊˈtægəˌræs) *n* ?485–?411 B.C., Greek philosopher and sophist, famous for his dictum "Man is the measure of all things."

protasis ('prɒtəsɪs) *n, pl* **protases** (-siːz). **1** *Logic, grammar.* the antecedent of a conditional statement, such as *it rains* in *if it rains the game will be cancelled.* **2** (in classical drama) the introductory part of a play. [C17: via L from Gk: a proposal, from *pro-* before + *teinein* to extend]

protea ('prəʊtɪə) *n* a shrub of tropical and southern Africa, having flowers with coloured bracts arranged in showy heads. [C20: from NL, from PROTEUS]

protean (prəʊˈtiːən, 'prəʊtɪən) *adj* readily taking on various shapes or forms; variable. [C16: from PROTEUS]

protease ('prəʊtɪˌeɪs) *n* any enzyme involved in proteolysis. [C20: from PROTEIN + -ASE]

protease inhibitor *n* any one of a class of antiviral drugs that impair the growth and replication of HIV by inhibiting the action of protease produced by the virus: used in the treatment of AIDS.

protect (prəˈtɛkt) *vb (tr)* **1** to defend from trouble, harm, etc. **2** *Econ.* to assist (domestic industries) by the imposition of protective tariffs on imports. **3** *Commerce.* to provide funds in advance to guarantee payment of (a note, etc.). [C16: from L *prōtegere* to cover before]

protectant (prəˈtɛktənt) *n* a chemical substance that affords protection, as against frost, rust, insects, etc.

protection (prəˈtɛkʃən) *n* **1** the act of protecting or the condition of being protected. **2** something that protects. **3a** the imposition of duties on imports, for the protection of domestic industries against overseas competition, etc. **3b** Also called: **protectionism.** the system or theory of such restrictions. **4** *Inf.* **4a** Also called: **protection money.** money demanded by gangsters for freedom from molestation. **4b** freedom from molestation purchased in this way. ▸ **pro'tection,ism** *n* ▸ **pro'tectionist** *n, adj*

protective (prəˈtɛktɪv) *adj* **1** giving or capable of giving protection. **2** *Econ.* of or intended for protection of domestic industries. ◆ *n* **3** something that protects. **4** a condom. ▸ **pro'tectively** *adv* ▸ **pro'tectiveness** *n*

protective coloration *n* the coloration of an animal that enables it to blend with its surroundings and therefore escape the attention of predators.

protector (prəˈtɛktə) *n* **1** a person or thing that protects. **2** *History.* a person who exercised royal authority during the minority, absence, or incapacity of the monarch. ▸ **pro'tectress** *fem n*

Protector (prəˈtɛktə) *n* short for **Lord Protector,** the title borne by Oliver Cromwell (1653–58) and by Richard Cromwell (1658–59) as heads of state during the period known as the Protectorate.

protectorate (prəˈtɛktərɪt) *n* **1a** a territory largely controlled by but not annexed to a stronger state. **1b** the relation of a protecting state to its protected territory. **2** the office or period of office of a protector.

protégé *or (fem)* **protégée** ('prəʊtɪˌʒeɪ) *n* a person who is protected and aided by the patronage of another. [C18: from F *protéger* to PROTECT]

protein ('prəʊtiːn) *n* any of a large group of nitrogenous compounds of high molecular weight that are essential constituents of all living organisms. [C19: via G from Gk *prōteios* primary, from *protos* first + -IN] ▸ ˌ**protein'aceous, pro'teinic,** *or* **pro'teinous** *adj*

pro tempore *Latin.* ('prəʊ 'tɛmpərɪ) *adv, adj* for the time being. Often shortened to **pro tem** ('prəʊ 'tɛm).

proteolysis (ˌprəʊtɪˈɒlɪsɪs) *n* the hydrolysis of proteins into simpler compounds by the action of enzymes. [C19: from NL, from proteo- (from PROTEIN) + -LYSIS] ▸ **proteolytic** (ˌprəʊtɪəˈlɪtɪk) *adj*

protest *n* ('prəʊtɛst). **1a** public, often organized, manifestation of dissent. **1b** *(as modifier): a protest march.* **2** a formal or solemn objection. **3** a formal notarial statement drawn up on behalf of a creditor and declaring that the debtor has dishonoured a bill of exchange, etc. **4** the act of protesting. ◆ *vb* (prəˈtɛst). **5** (when *intr,* foll. by *against, at, about,* etc.; when *tr, may take a clause as object*) to make a strong objection (to something, esp. a supposed injustice or offence). **6** (when *tr, may take a clause as object*) to disagree; object: *"I'm O.K." she protested.* **7** (when *tr, may take a clause as object*) to assert in a formal or solemn manner. **8** (*tr*) *Chiefly US.* to object forcefully to: *leaflets protesting Dr King's murder.* **9** (*tr*) to declare formally that (a bill of exchange or promissory note) has been dishonoured. [C14: from L *prōtestārī* to make a formal declaration, from *prō-* before + *testārī* to assert] ▸ **pro'testant** *adj, n* ▸ **pro'tester** *or* **pro'testor** *n* ▸ **pro'testingly** *adv*

Protestant ('prɒtɪstənt) *n* **a** an adherent of Protestantism. **b** *(as modifier): the Protestant Church.*

Protestantism ('prɒtɪstənˌtɪzəm) *n* the religion of any of the Churches of Western Christendom that are separated from the Roman Catholic Church and adhere substantially to principles established during the Reformation.

protestation (ˌprəʊtɛsˈteɪʃən) *n* **1** the act of protesting. **2** a strong declaration.

Proteus ★ ('prəʊtɪəs) *n Greek myth.* a prophetic sea god capable of changing his shape at will.

prothalamion (ˌprəʊθəˈleɪmɪən) *or* **prothalamium** *n, pl* **prothalamia** (-mɪə). a song or poem in celebration of a marriage. [C16: from Gk *pro-* before + *thalamos* marriage]

prothallus (prəʊˈθæləs) *or* **prothallium** (prəʊˈθælɪəm) *n, pl* **prothalli** (-laɪ) *or* **prothallia** (-lɪə). *Bot.* the small flat green disc of tissue that bears the reproductive organs of ferns, horsetails, and club mosses. [C19: from NL, from *pro-* before + Gk *thallus* a young shoot]

prothesis ('prɒθɪsɪs) *n, pl* **protheses** (-siːz). **1** a development of a language by which a syllable is prefixed to a word to facilitate pronunciation: *Latin "scala" gives Spanish "escala" by prothesis.* **2** *Eastern Orthodox Church.* the solemn preparation of the Eucharistic elements before consecration. [C16: via LL from Gk: a setting out in public, from *pro-* forth + *thesis* a placing] ▸ **prothetic** (prəˈθɛtɪk) *adj* ▸ **pro'thetically** *adv*

prothrombin (prəʊˈθrɒmbɪn) *n Biochemistry.* a zymogen found in blood that gives rise to thrombin on activation.

protist ('prəʊtɪst) *n* (in some classification systems) any organism belonging to a large group, including bacteria, protozoans, and fungi, regarded as distinct from plants and animals. The group is usually now restricted to protozoans, unicellular algae, and simple fungi. Cf. **protoctist.** [C19: from NL *Protista* most primitive organisms, from Gk *prōtistos* the very first, from *prōtos* first]

protium ('prəʊtɪəm) *n* the most common isotope of hydrogen, having a mass number of 1. [C20: NL, from PROTO- + -IUM]

proto- *or sometimes before a vowel* **prot-** *combining form.* **1** first: *protomartyr.* **2** primitive or original: *prototype.* **3** first in a series of chemical compounds: *protoxide.* [from Gk *prōtos* first, from *pro* before]

protocol ('prəʊtəˌkɒl) *n* **1** the formal etiquette and procedure for state and diplomatic ceremonies. **2** a record of an agreement, esp. in international negotiations, etc. **3a** an amendment to a treaty or convention. **3b** an annexe appended to a treaty to deal with subsidiary matters. **4** *Chiefly US.* a record of data or observations on a particular experiment or proceeding. **5** *Computing.* the set form in which data must be presented for handling by a particular computer configuration, esp. in the transmission of information between different computer systems. [C16: from Med. L *prōtocollum*, from LGk *prōtokollon* sheet glued to the front of a manuscript, from PROTO- + *kolla* glue]

protoctist (prəʊ'tɒktɪst) *n* (in modern biological classifications) any unicellular or simple multicellular organism belonging to the kingdom that includes protozoans, algae, and slime moulds. [C19: from NL *protoctista*, ?from Gk *prototokos* first born]

protohuman (ˌprəʊtəʊ'hjuːmən) *n* **1** any of various prehistoric primates that resembled modern man. ◆ *adj* **2** of these primates.

Proto-Indo-European *n* the prehistoric unrecorded language that was the ancestor of all Indo-European languages.

protomartyr (ˌprəʊtəʊ'mɑːtə) *n* **1** St Stephen as the first Christian martyr. **2** the first martyr to lay down his life in any cause.

proton ('prəʊtɒn) *n* a stable, positively charged elementary particle, found in atomic nuclei in numbers equal to the atomic number of the element. [C20: from Gk *prōtos* first]

protoplasm ('prəʊtəˌplæzəm) *n Biol.* the living contents of a cell: a complex translucent colourless colloidal substance. [C19: from NL, from PROTO- + Gk *plasma* form] ► ˌproto'plasmic, ˌproto'plasmal, *or* ˌprotoplas'matic *adj*

prototype ('prəʊtəˌtaɪp) *n* **1** one of the first units manufactured of a product, which is tested so that the design can be changed if necessary before the product is manufactured commercially. **2** a person or thing that serves as an example of a type. **3** *Biol.* the ancestral or primitive form of a species. ► ˌproto'typal, prototypic (ˌprəʊtə'tɪpɪk), *or* ˌproto'typical *adj*

protozoan (ˌprəʊtə'zəʊən) *n, pl* **protozoa** (-'zəʊə). **1** Also **protozoon.** any of various minute unicellular organisms formerly regarded as invertebrates of the phylum *Protozoa,* but now usually classified in certain phyla of protoctists. Protozoans include amoebas and foraminifers. ◆ *adj also* **protozoic. 2** of or belonging to protozoans. [C19: via NL from Gk PROTO- + *zoion* animal]

protract (prə'trækt) *vb* (*tr*) **1** to lengthen or extend (a speech, etc.). **2** (of a muscle) to draw, thrust, or extend (a part, etc.) forwards. **3** to plot using a protractor and scale. [C16: from L *prōtrahere* to prolong, from PRO-[1] + *trahere* to drag] ► pro'tracted *adj* ► protractedly *adv* ► pro'traction *n*

protractile (prə'træktaɪl) *adj* able to be extended: *protractile muscle.*

protractor (prə'træktə) *n* **1** an instrument for measuring or drawing angles, usually a flat semicircular transparent plastic sheet graduated in degrees. **2** *Anat.* a former term for **extensor.**

protrude (prə'truːd) *vb* **protrudes, protruding, protruded. 1** to thrust forwards or outwards. **2** to project or cause to project. [C17: from L, from PRO-[2] + *trudere* to thrust] ► pro'trusion *n* ► pro'trusive *adj*

protrusile (prə'truːsaɪl) *adj Zool.* capable of being thrust forwards: *protrusile jaws.*

protuberant (prə'tjuːbərənt) *adj* swelling out; bulging. [C17: from LL *prōtūberāre* to swell, from PRO-[1] + *tūber* swelling] ► pro'tuberance *or* pro'tuberancy *n* ► pro'tuberantly *adv*

proud (praʊd) *adj* **1** (foll. by *of,* an infinitive, or a clause) pleased or satisfied, as with oneself, one's possessions, achievements, etc. **2** feeling honoured or gratified by some distinction. **3** having an inordinately high opinion of oneself; haughty. **4** characterized by or proceeding from a sense of pride: *a proud moment.* **5** having a proper sense of self-respect. **6** stately or distinguished. **7** bold or fearless. **8** (of a surface, edge, etc.) projecting or protruding. **9** (of animals) restive or excited, often sexually. ◆ *adv* **10 do** (**someone**) **proud. 10a** to entertain (some-

one) on a grand scale: *they did us proud at the hotel.* **10b** to honour (someone): *his honesty did him proud.* [LOE *prūd,* from OF *prud, prod* brave, from LL *prōde* useful, from L *prōdesse* to be of value] ► 'proudly *adv* ► 'proudness *n*

proud flesh *n* a mass of tissue formed around a healing wound.

Proudhon ★ (French prudɔ̃) *n* **Pierre Joseph** (pjɛr ʒozɛf). 1809–65, French socialist, whose pamphlet *What is Property?* (1840) declared that property is theft.

Proust ★ (French prust) *n* **1 Joseph Louis** (ʒozɛf lwi). 1754–1826, French chemist, who formulated the law of constant proportions. **2 Marcel** (marsɛl). 1871–1922, French novelist whose long novel *À la recherche du temps perdu* (1913–27) deals with themes such as art, time, memory, and society.

Prov. *abbrev. for:* **1** Provençal. **2** *Bible.* Proverbs. **3** Province. **4** Provost.

prove (pruːv) *vb* **proves, proving, proved; proved** *or* **proven.** (*mainly tr*) **1** (*may take a clause as object or an infinitive*) to demonstrate the truth or validity of, esp. by using an established sequence of procedures. **2** to establish the quality of, esp. by experiment. **3** *Law.* to establish the genuineness of (a will). **4** to show (oneself) able or courageous. **5** (*copula*) to be found (to be): *this has proved useless.* **6** (*intr*) (of dough) to rise in a warm place before baking. [C12: from OF *prover,* from L *probāre* to test, from *probus* honest] ► 'provable *adj* ► 'provably *adv* ► ˌprova'bility *n*

proven ('pruːv°n, 'prəʊ-) *vb* **1** a past participle of **prove. 2** See **not proven.** ◆ *adj* **3** tried; tested: *a proven method.*

provenance ('prɒvɪnəns) *n* a place of origin, as of a work of art. [C19: from F, from *provenir,* from L *prōvenīre* to originate, from *venīre* to come]

Provençal (ˌprɒvɒn'sɑːl; French prɔvɑ̃sal) *adj* **1** denoting or characteristic of Provence, its inhabitants, their dialect of French, or their Romance language. ◆ *n* **2** a language of Provence, closely related to French and Italian, belonging to the Romance group of the Indo-European family. **3** a native or inhabitant of Provence.

Provence ★ (French prɔvɑ̃s) *n* a former province of SE France, on the Mediterranean, and the River Rhône: forms part of the administrative region of Provence-Alpes-Côte d'Azur.

provender ('prɒvɪndə) *n* **1** fodder for livestock. **2** food in general. [C14: from OF *provendre,* from LL *praebenda* grant, from L *praebēre* to supply]

proverb ('prɒvɜːb) *n* **1** a short memorable saying embodying some commonplace fact. **2** a person or thing exemplary of a characteristic: *Antarctica is a proverb for extreme cold.* **3** *Bible.* a wise saying providing guidance. [C14: via OF from L *prōverbium,* from *verbum* word]

proverbial (prə'vɜːbɪəl) *adj* **1** (*prenominal*) commonly or traditionally referred to as an example of some peculiarity, characteristic, etc. **2** of, embodied in, or resembling a proverb. ► pro'verbially *adv*

provide (prə'vaɪd) *vb* **provides, providing, provided.** (*mainly tr*) **1** to furnish or supply. **2** to afford; yield: *this meeting provides an opportunity to talk.* **3** (*intr*; often foll. by *for* or *against*) to take careful precautions: *he provided against financial ruin by wise investment.* **4** (*intr*; foll. by *for*) to supply means of support (to): *he provides for his family.* **5** (of a person, law, etc.) to state as a condition; stipulate. **6** to confer and induct into ecclesiastical offices. [C15: from L *prōvidēre* to provide for, from *prō-* beforehand + *vidēre* see] ► pro'vider *n*

providence ('prɒvɪdəns) *n* **1a** *Christianity.* God's foreseeing protection and care of his creatures. **1b** such protection and care as manifest by some other force. **2** a supposed manifestation of such care and guidance. **3** the foresight or care exercised by a person in the management of his affairs.

Providence[1] ('prɒvɪdəns) *n Christianity.* God, esp. as showing foreseeing care of his creatures.

Providence[2] ★ ('prɒvɪdəns) *n* a port in NE Rhode Island, capital of the state, at the head of Narragansett Bay:

founded by Roger Williams in 1636. Pop.: 150 639 (1994 est.).

provident ('prɒvɪdənt) adj **1** providing for future needs. **2** exercising foresight in the management of one's affairs. **3** characterized by foresight. [C15: from L prōvidens foreseeing, from prōvidēre to PROVIDE]
▸ 'providently adv

providential (,prɒvɪ'dɛnʃəl) adj characteristic of or presumed to proceed from or as if from divine providence.
▸ ,provi'dentially adv

provident society n a mutual insurance society catering esp. for those on a low income, providing sickness, death, and pension benefits.

providing (prə'vaɪdɪŋ) or **provided** conj (subordinating; sometimes foll. by that) on the condition or understanding (that): I'll play, providing you pay me.

province ('prɒvɪns) n **1** a territory governed as a unit of a country or empire. **2** (pl; usually preceded by the) those parts of a country lying outside the capital and other large cities and regarded as outside the mainstream of sophisticated culture. **3** an area of learning, activity, etc. **4** the extent of a person's activities or office. **5** an ecclesiastical territory, having an archbishop or metropolitan at its head. **6** an administrative and territorial subdivision of a religious order. **7** History. a region of the Roman Empire outside Italy ruled by a governor from Rome. [C14: from OF, from L prōvincia conquered territory]

Provincetown ★ ('prɒvɪns,taun) n a village in SE Massachusetts, at the tip of Cape Cod: scene of the first landing place of the Pilgrims (1620) and of the signing of the Mayflower Compact (1620). Pop.: 3374 (1990).

provincewide ('prɒvɪns,waɪd) Canad. ♦ adj **1** covering or available to the whole of a province: a provincewide referendum. ♦ adv **2** throughout a province: an advertising campaign to go provincewide.

provincial (prə'vɪnʃəl) adj **1** of or connected with a province. **2** characteristic of or connected with the provinces. **3** having attitudes and opinions supposedly common to people living in the provinces; unsophisticated; limited. **4** NZ. denoting a football team representing a province, one of the historical administrative areas of New Zealand. ♦ n **5** a person lacking the sophistications of city life; rustic or narrow-minded individual. **6** a person coming from or resident in a province or the provinces. **7** the head of an ecclesiastical province. **8** the head of a territorial subdivision of a religious order.
▸ provinciality (prə,vɪnʃɪ'ælɪtɪ) n ▸ pro'vincially adv

provincialism (prə'vɪnʃə,lɪzəm) n **1** narrowness of mind; lack of sophistication. **2** a word or attitude characteristic of a provincial. **3** attention to the affairs of one's local area rather than the whole nation. **4** the state or quality of being provincial.

provirus ('prəu,vaɪrəs) n the inactive form of a virus in a host cell.

provision (prə'vɪʒən) n **1** the act of supplying food, etc. **2** something that is supplied. **3** preparations (esp. in **make provision for**). **4** (pl) food and other necessities, as for an expedition. **5** a condition or stipulation incorporated in a document; proviso. **6** the conferring of and induction into ecclesiastical offices. ♦ vb **7** (tr) to supply with provisions. [C14: from L prōvīsiō a providing; see PROVIDE]
▸ pro'visioner n

provisional (prə'vɪʒənʃl) adj subject to later alteration; temporary or conditional: a provisional decision.
▸ pro'visionally adv

Provisional (prə'vɪʒənʃl) adj **1** designating one of the two factions of the IRA and Sinn Féin that have existed since a split in late 1969. The Provisional movement advocates terrorism to achieve Irish unity. ♦ n **2** Also called: **Provo.** a member of the Provisional IRA or Sinn Féin.

proviso (prə'vaɪzəu) n, pl **provisos** or **provisoes. 1** a clause in a document or contract that embodies a condition or stipulation. **2** a condition or stipulation. [C15: from Med. L prōvīsō quod it being provided that, from L prōvīsus provided]

provisory (prə'vaɪzərɪ) adj **1** containing a proviso; conditional. **2** provisional. **3** making provision.
▸ pro'visorily adv

Provo ('prəuvəu) n, pl **Provos**. another name for a **Provisional** (sense 2).

provocation (,prɒvə'keɪʃən) n **1** the act of provoking or inciting. **2** something that causes indignation, anger, etc.

provocative (prə'vɒkətɪv) adj serving or intended to provoke or incite, esp. to anger or sexual desire: a provocative look; a provocative remark.
▸ pro'vocatively adv

provoke (prə'vəuk) vb **provokes, provoking, provoked.** (tr) **1** to anger or infuriate. **2** to incite or stimulate. **3** to promote (anger, etc.) in a person. **4** to cause; bring about: the accident provoked an inquiry. [C15: from L prōvocāre to call forth]
▸ pro'voking adj ▸ pro'vokingly adv

provost ('prɒvəst) n **1** the head of certain university colleges or schools. **2** (in Scotland) the chairman and civic head of certain district councils or (formerly) of a burgh council. Cf. **convener** (sense 2). **3** Church of England. the senior dignitary of one of the more recent cathedral foundations. **4** RC Church. **4a** the head of a cathedral chapter. **4b** (formerly) the member of a monastic community second in authority under the abbot. **5** (in medieval times) an overseer, steward, or bailiff. [OE profost, from Med. L prōpositus placed at the head (of), from L praepōnere to place first]

provost marshal (prə'vəu) n the officer in charge of military police in a camp or city.

prow (prau) n the bow of a vessel. [C16: from OF proue, from L prora, from Gk prōra]

prowess ('prauɪs) n **1** outstanding or superior skill or ability. **2** bravery or fearlessness, esp. in battle. [C13: from OF proesce, from prou good]

prowl (praul) vb **1** (when intr, often foll. by around or about) to move stealthily around (a place) as if in search of prey or plunder. ♦ n **2** the act of prowling. **3** on the **prowl. 3a** moving around stealthily. **3b** pursuing members of the opposite sex. [C14 prollen, from ?]
▸ 'prowler n

prox. abbrev. for proximo (next month).

proximal ('prɒksɪməl) adj Anat. situated close to the centre, median line, or point of attachment or origin.
▸ 'proximally adv

proximate ('prɒksɪmɪt) adj **1** next or nearest in space or time. **2** very near; close. **3** immediately preceding or following in a series. **4** a less common word for **approximate**. [C16: from LL proximāre to draw near, from L proximus next, from prope near]
▸ 'proximately adv

proximity (prɒk'sɪmɪtɪ) n **1** nearness in space or time. **2** nearness or closeness in a series. [C15: from L proximitās closeness; see PROXIMATE]

proximo ('prɒksɪməu) adv Now rare except when abbreviated in formal correspondence. in or during the next or coming month: a letter of the seventh proximo. Abbrev.: **prox.** Cf. **instant, ultimo.** [C19: from L: in or on the next]

proxy ('prɒksɪ) n, pl **proxies. 1** a person authorized to act on behalf of someone else; agent: vote by proxy. **2** authority, esp. in the form of a document, given to a person to act on behalf of someone else. [C15 prokesye, from procuracy, from L prōcūrātiō procuration; see PROCURE]

Prozac ('prəuzæk) n Trademark. a drug that prolongs the action of serotonin in the brain; used as an antidepressant.

PRP abbrev. for: **1** performance-related pay. **2** profit-related pay.

PRT abbrev. for petroleum revenue tax.

prude (pru:d) n a person who affects or shows an excessively modest, prim, or proper attitude, esp. regarding sex. [C18: from F, from prudefemme, from OF prode femme respectable woman; see PROUD]
▸ 'prudery n ▸ 'prudish adj ▸ 'prudishly adv

prudence ('pru:dəns) n **1** caution in practical affairs; discretion. **2** care taken in the management of one's resources. **3** consideration for one's own interests. **4** the quality of being prudent.

prudent ('pruːdᵊnt) *adj* **1** discreet or cautious in managing one's activities; circumspect. **2** practical and careful in providing for the future. **3** exercising good judgment. [C14: from L *prūdēns* far-sighted, from *prōvidens* acting with foresight; see PROVIDENT]
▸ **'prudently** *adv*

prudential (pruː'dɛnʃəl) *adj* **1** characterized by or resulting from prudence. **2** exercising sound judgment.
▸ **pru'dentially** *adv*

Prudentius ★ (pruː'dɛnʃəs) *n* **Aurelius Clemens** (ɔː'riːlɪəs 'klemenz). 348–410 A.D., Latin Christian poet, born in Spain. His works include the allegory *Psychomachia*.

Prud'hon ★ (*French* prydɔ̃) *n* **Pierre Paul** (pjɛr pɔl). 1758–1823, French painter, noted for the romantic and mysterious aura of his portraits.

pruinose ('pruːɪˌnəʊs, -ˌnəʊz) *adj Bot.* coated with a powdery or waxy bloom. [C19: from L *pruīnōsus* frost-covered, from *pruīna* hoarfrost]

prune¹ (pruːn) *n* **1** a purplish-black partially dried fruit of any of several varieties of plum tree. **2** *Sl., chiefly Brit.* a dull or foolish person. **3 prunes and prisms.** denoting an affected and mincing way of speaking. [C14: from OF *prune*, from L *prūnum* plum, from Gk *prounon*]

prune² (pruːn) *vb* **prunes, pruning, pruned. 1** to remove (dead or superfluous twigs, branches, etc.) from (a tree, shrub, etc.), esp. by cutting off. **2** to remove (anything undesirable or superfluous) from (a book, etc.). [C15: from OF *proignier* to clip, prob. from *provigner* to prune vines, ult. from L *propāgo* a cutting]
▸ **'prunable** *adj* ▸ **'pruner** *n*

prunella (pruː'nɛlə) *n* a strong fabric, esp. a twill-weave worsted, formerly used for academic gowns and the uppers of some shoes. [C17: ?from *prunelle*, a green French liqueur, with reference to the colour of the cloth]

pruning hook *n* a tool with a curved steel blade terminating in a hook, used for pruning.

prurient ('prʊərɪənt) *adj* **1** unusually or morbidly interested in sexual thoughts or practices. **2** exciting lustfulness. [C17: from L *prūrīre* to lust after, itch]
▸ **'prurience** *n* ▸ **'pruriently** *adv*

prurigo (prʊə'raɪgəʊ) *n* a chronic inflammatory disease of the skin characterized by intense itching. [C19: from L: an itch]
▸ **pruriginous** (prʊə'rɪdʒɪnəs) *adj*

pruritus (prʊə'raɪtəs) *n Pathol.* any intense sensation of itching. [C17: from L: an itching; see PRURIENT]
▸ **pruritic** (prʊə'rɪtɪk) *adj*

Prus. *abbrev. for* Prussia(n).

Prussia ★ ('prʌʃə) *n* a former German state in N and central Germany, extending from France and the Low Countries to the Baltic Sea and Poland: developed as the chief military power of the Continent, leading the North German Confederation from 1867–71, when the German Empire was established; dissolved in 1947 and divided between East and West Germany, Poland, and the former Soviet Union. Area: (in 1939) 294 081 sq. km (113 545 sq. miles). German name: **Preussen.**

Prussian ('prʌʃən) *adj* **1** of Prussia, or its people, esp. of the Junkers and their military tradition. ◆ *n* **2** a native or inhabitant of Prussia. **3 Old Prussian.** the extinct Baltic language of the non-German inhabitants of Prussia.

Prussian blue *n* **1** any of a number of blue pigments containing ferrocyanide or ferricyanide ions. **2a** the blue or deep greenish-blue colour of this. **2b** (*as adj*): *a Prussian-blue carpet.*

prussic acid ('prʌsɪk) *n* the extremely poisonous aqueous solution of hydrogen cyanide. [C18: from F *acide prussique* Prussian acid, because obtained from Prussian blue]

Prut ★ (*Russian* prut) *n* a river in E Europe, rising in the SW Ukraine and flowing generally southeast, forming part of the border between Romania and Moldova, to join the River Danube. Length: 853 km (530 miles).

pry¹ (praɪ) *vb* **pries, prying, pried. 1** (*intr*; often foll. by *into*) to make an impertinent or uninvited inquiry (about a private matter, topic, etc.). ◆ *n, pl* **pries. 2** the act of prying. **3** a person who pries. [C14: from ?]

pry² (praɪ) *vb* **pries, prying, pried.** the US and Canad. word for **prise.** [C14: from ?]

pryer ('praɪə) *n* a variant spelling of **prier.**

Prynne ★ (prɪn) *n* **William.** 1600–69, English Puritan leader and pamphleteer, whose ears were cut off in punishment for his attacks on Laud.

Przemyśl ★ (*Polish* 'pʃɛmɪʃl) *n* a city in SE Poland, near the border with the Ukraine on the San River: a fortress in the early Middle Ages; belonged to Austria (1722–1918). Pop.: 67 000 (1989 est.).

Przewalski's horse (ˌpʃəˈʒəˈvælskɪz) *n* a wild horse of W Mongolia, having an erect mane and no forelock: extinct in the wild, a few survive in captivity. [C19: after the Russian explorer Nikolai *Przewalski* (1839–88), who discovered it]

PS *abbrev. for:* **1** Passenger Steamer. **2** Police Sergeant. **3** Also: **ps.** postscript. **4** private secretary. **5** prompt side.

Ps. *or* **Psa.** *Bible. abbrev. for* Psalm(s).

PSA *abbrev. for* prostatic specific antigen: an enzyme secreted by the prostate gland, increased levels of which are found in the blood of patients with cancer of the prostate.

psalm (sɑːm) *n* **1** (*often cap.*) any of the sacred songs that constitute a book (Psalms) of the Old Testament. **2** a musical setting of one of these. **3** any sacred song. [OE, from LL *psalmus*, from Gk *psalmos* song accompanied on the harp, from *psallein* to play (the harp)]
▸ **psalmic** ('sɑːmɪk, 'sæl-) *adj*

psalmist ('sɑːmɪst) *n* the composer of a psalm or psalms, esp. (*when cap.* and preceded by *the*) David, traditionally regarded as the author of The Book of Psalms.

psalmody ('sɑːmədɪ, 'sæl-) *n, pl* **psalmodies. 1** the act of singing psalms or hymns. **2** the art of setting psalms to music. [C14: via LL from Gk *psalmōdia* singing accompanied by a harp, from *psalmos* (see PSALM) + *ōidē* ODE]
▸ **'psalmodist** *n* ▸ **psalmodic** (sæl'mɒdɪk) *adj*

Psalter ('sɔːltə) *n* **1** another name for the Book of Psalms, esp. in the version in the Book of Common Prayer. **2** a translation, musical, or metrical version of the Psalms. **3** a book containing a version of Psalms. [OE *psealtere*, from LL *psaltērium*, from Gk *psaltērion* stringed instrument, from *psallein* to play a stringed instrument]

psalterium (sɔːl'tɪərɪəm) *n, pl* **psalteria** (-'tɪərɪə). the third compartment of the stomach of ruminants. Also called: **omasum.** [C19: from L *psaltērium* PSALTER; from the similarity of its folds to the pages of a book]

psaltery ('sɔːltərɪ) *n, pl* **psalteries.** *Music.* an ancient stringed instrument similar to the lyre, but having a trapezoidal sounding board over which the strings are stretched.

p's and q's *pl n* behaviour; manners (esp. in **mind one's p's and q's**). [altered from *p(lea)se* and *(than)k yous*]

PSBR (in Britain) *abbrev. for* public sector borrowing requirement; the money required by the public sector of the economy for expenditure on items that are not financed from income.

psephology (se'fɒlədʒɪ) *n* the statistical and sociological study of elections. [C20: from Gk *psephos* pebble, vote + -LOGY, from the ancient Greeks' custom of voting with pebbles]
▸ **psephological** (ˌsefə'lɒdʒɪk'l) *adj* ▸ **ˌpsepho'logically** *adv* ▸ **pse'phologist** *n*

pseud (sjuːd) *n* **1** *Inf.* a false or pretentious person. ◆ *adj* **2** another word for **pseudo.**

Pseudepigrapha (ˌsjuːdɪ'pɪgrəfə) *pl n* various Jewish writings from the first century B.C. to the first century A.D. that claim to have been divinely revealed but which have been excluded from the Greek canon of the Old Testament. [C17: from Gk *pseudepigraphos* falsely entitled, from PSEUDO- + *epigraphein* to inscribe]
▸ **Pseudepigraphic** (ˌsjuːdɛpɪ'græfɪk) *or* **ˌPseudepi'graphical** *adj*

pseudo ('sjuːdəʊ) *adj Inf.* not genuine.

pseudo- *or sometimes before a vowel* **pseud-** *combining form.* **1** false, pretending, or unauthentic: *pseudo-*

intellectual. **2** having a close resemblance to: *pseudopodium.* [from Gk *pseudēs* false, from *pseudein* to lie]

pseudocarp ('sju:dəʊ,kɑ:p) *n* a fruit, such as the apple, that includes parts other than the ripened ovary.
▸ ˌpseudo'carpous *adj*

pseudomorph ('sju:dəʊ,mɔ:f) *n* a mineral that has an uncharacteristic crystalline form as a result of assuming the shape of another mineral that it has replaced.
▸ ˌpseudo'morphic *or* ˌpseudo'morphous *adj* ▸ ˌpseudo-'morphism *n*

pseudonym ('sju:də,nɪm) *n* a fictitious name adopted esp. by an author. [C19: via F from Gk *pseudōnumon*]
▸ ˌpseudo'nymity *n* ▸ pseudonymous (sju:'dɒnɪməs) *adj*

pseudopodium (ˌsju:dəʊ'pəʊdɪəm) *n, pl* pseudopodia (-dɪə). a temporary projection from the cell of a protozoan, etc., used for feeding and locomotion.

pseudovector (ˌsju:dəʊ'vɛktə) *n Maths.* a variable quantity, such as angular momentum, that has magnitude and orientation with respect to an axis.

psf *abbrev. for* pounds per square foot.

pshaw (pʃɔ:) *interj Becoming rare.* an exclamation of disgust, impatience, disbelief, etc.

psi[1] (psaɪ) *n* **1** the 23rd letter of the Greek alphabet (Ψ, ψ), a composite consonant, transliterated as *ps*. **2** paranormal or psychic phenomena collectively.

psi[2] *abbrev. for* pounds per square inch.

psilocybin (ˌsɪlə'saɪbɪn, ˌsaɪlə-) *n* a crystalline phosphate ester that is the active principle of the hallucinogenic fungus *Psilocybe mexicana.* Formula: $C_{12}H_{17}N_2O_4P$. [C20: from NL *Psilocybe* (from Gk *psilos* bare + *kubē* head) + -IN]

psi particle *n* See **J/psi particle.**

psittacine ('sɪtə,saɪn, -sɪn) *adj* of, relating to, or resembling a parrot. [C19: from LL *psittacīnus*, from L *psittacus* a parrot]

psittacosis (ˌsɪtə'kəʊsɪs) *n* a disease of parrots that can be transmitted to man, in whom it produces pneumonia. Also called: **parrot fever.** [C19: from NL, from L *psittacus* a parrot, from Gk *psittakos*; see -OSIS]

Pskov ★ *(Russian* pskɔf) *n* **1** a city in NW Russia, on the Velikaya River: one of the oldest Russian cities, at its height in the 13th and 14th centuries. Pop.: 207 000 (1995 est.). **2** Lake. the S part of Lake Peipus in NW Russia, linked to the main part by a channel 24 km (15 miles) long. Area: about 1000 sq. km (400 sq. miles).

psoas ('səʊəs) *n* either of two muscles of the loins that aid in flexing and rotating the thigh. [C17: from NL, from Gk *psoai* (pl)]

psoriasis (sə'raɪəsɪs) *n* a skin disease characterized by the formation of reddish spots and patches covered with silvery scales. [C17: via NL from Gk: itching disease, from *psōra* itch]
▸ **psoriatic** (ˌsɔ:rɪ'ætɪk) *adj*

psst (pst) *interj* an exclamation made to attract someone's attention, esp. one made surreptitiously.

PST (in the US and Canada) *abbrev. for* Pacific Standard Time.

PSV (in Britain) *abbrev. for* public service vehicle (now called passenger carrying vehicle).

psych *or* **psyche** (saɪk) *vb* **psychs** *or* **psyches, psyching, psyched.** (*tr*) *Inf.* to psychoanalyse. See also **psych out, psych up.** [C20: shortened from PSYCHOANALYSE]

psyche ('saɪkɪ) *n* the human mind or soul. [C17: from L, from Gk *psukhē* breath, soul]

Psyche ★ ('saɪkɪ) *n Greek myth.* a beautiful girl loved by Eros (Cupid), who became the personification of the soul.

psychedelic (ˌsaɪkɪ'dɛlɪk) *adj* **1** relating to or denoting new or altered perceptions or sensory experiences, as through the use of hallucinogenic drugs. **2** denoting any of the drugs, esp. LSD, that produce these effects. **3** *Inf.* (of painting, etc.) having the vivid colours and complex patterns popularly associated with the visual effects of psychedelic states. [C20: from PSYCHE + Gk *delos* visible]
▸ ˌpsyche'delically *adv*

psychiatry (saɪ'kaɪətrɪ) *n* the branch of medicine con-

cerned with the diagnosis and treatment of mental disorders.
▸ **psychiatric** (ˌsaɪkɪ'ætrɪk) *or* ˌpsychi'atrical *adj*
▸ ˌpsychi'atrically *adv* ▸ psy'chiatrist *n*

psychic ('saɪkɪk) *adj* **1a** outside the possibilities defined by natural laws, as mental telepathy. **1b** (of a person) sensitive to forces not recognized by natural laws. **2** mental as opposed to physical. ♦ *n* **3** a person who is sensitive to parapsychological forces or influences.
▸ 'psychical *adj* ▸ 'psychically *adv*

psycho ('saɪkəʊ) *n, pl* psychos, *adj* an informal word for psychopath *or* psychopathic.

psycho- *or sometimes before a vowel* **psych-** *combining form.* indicating the mind or psychological or mental processes: *psychology.* [from Gk *psukhē* spirit, breath]

psychoactive (ˌsaɪkəʊ'æktɪv) *adj* (of drugs such as LSD and barbiturates) capable of affecting mental activity. Also: **psychotropic.**

psychoanalyse *or esp. US* **psychoanalyze** (ˌsaɪkəʊ-'ænə,laɪz) *vb* **psychoanalyses, psychoanalysing, psychoanalysed** *or US* **psychoanalyzes, psychoanalyzing, psychoanalyzed.** (*tr*) to examine or treat (a person) by psychoanalysis.

psychoanalysis (ˌsaɪkəʊə'nælɪsɪs) *n* a method of studying the mind and treating mental and emotional disorders based on revealing and investigating the role of the unconscious mind.
▸ **psychoanalyst** (ˌsaɪkəʊ'ænəlɪst) *n* ▸ **psychoanalytic** (ˌsaɪkəʊ,ænə'lɪtɪk) *or* ˌpsycho,ana'lytical *adj* ▸ ˌpsycho-ˌana'lytically *adv*

psychobiology (ˌsaɪkəʊbaɪ'ɒlədʒɪ) *n Psychol.* the attempt to understand the psychology of organisms in terms of their biological functions and structures.
▸ **psychobiological** (ˌsaɪkəʊ,baɪə'lɒdʒɪk°l) *adj* ▸ ˌpsycho-bi'ologist *n*

psychochemical (ˌsaɪkəʊ'kɛmɪk°l) *n* **1** any of various chemicals whose primary effect is the alteration of the normal state of consciousness. ♦ *adj* **2** of such compounds.

psychodrama ('saɪkəʊ,drɑːmə) *n* **1** *Psychiatry.* a form of group therapy in which individuals act out situations from their past. **2** a film, television drama, etc., in which the psychological development of the characters is emphasized.

psychodynamics (ˌsaɪkəʊdaɪ'næmɪks) *n* (*functioning as sing*) *Psychol.* the study of interacting motives and emotions.
▸ ˌpsychody'namic *adj*

psychogenic (ˌsaɪkəʊ'dʒɛnɪk) *adj Psychol.* (esp. of disorders or symptoms) of mental, rather than organic, origin.
▸ ˌpsycho'genically *adv*

psychokinesis (ˌsaɪkəʊkɪ'niːsɪs, -kaɪ-) *n* (in parapsychology) alteration of the state of an object supposedly by mental influence alone. [C20: from PSYCHO- + Gk *kinēsis* motion]

psycholinguistics (ˌsaɪkəʊlɪŋ'gwɪstɪks) *n* (*functioning as sing*) the psychology of language, including language acquisition by children, language disorders, etc.
▸ ˌpsycho'linguist *n*

psychological (ˌsaɪkə'lɒdʒɪk°l) *adj* **1** of or relating to psychology. **2** of or relating to the mind or mental activity. **3** having no real or objective basis; arising in the mind: *his backaches are all psychological.* **4** affecting the mind.
▸ ˌpsycho'logically *adv*

psychological moment *n* the most appropriate time for producing a desired effect.

psychological warfare *n* the application of psychology, esp. to attempts to influence morale in time of war.

psychologize *or US* **psychologise** (saɪ'kɒlə,dʒaɪz) *vb* **psychologizes, psychologizing, psychologized** *or US* **psychologises, psychologising, psychologised.** (*intr*) **1** to make interpretations of mental processes. **2** to carry out investigation in psychology.

psychology (saɪ'kɒlədʒɪ) *n, pl* psychologies. **1** the scientific study of all forms of human and animal behaviour.

2 *Inf.* the mental make-up of an individual that causes him to think or act in the way he does.
▸ **psy'chologist** *n*

psychometrics (ˌsaɪkəʊ'mɛtrɪks) *n* (*functioning as sing*) **1** the branch of psychology concerned with the design and use of psychological tests. **2** the application of statistical techniques to psychological testing.

psychometry (saɪ'kɒmɪtrɪ) *n Psychol.* **1** measurement and testing of mental states and processes. **2** (in parapsychology) the supposed ability to deduce facts about events by touching objects related to them.
▸ **psychometric** (ˌsaɪkəʊ'mɛtrɪk) *or* ˌpsycho'metrical *adj*
▸ ˌpsycho'metrically *adv*

psychomotor (ˌsaɪkəʊ'məʊtə) *adj* of, relating to, or characterizing movements of the body associated with mental activity.

psychoneuroimmunology (ˌsaɪkəʊˌnjʊərəʊˌɪmju-'nɒlədʒɪ) *n* the study of the psychological factors that affect the immune system. Abbrev.: **PNI**.

psychoneurosis (ˌsaɪkəʊnjʊə'rəʊsɪs) *n, pl* **psychoneuroses** (-'rəʊsiːz). another word for **neurosis**.

psychopath ('saɪkəʊˌpæθ) *n* a person with a personality disorder characterized by a tendency to commit antisocial and sometimes violent acts without feeling guilt.
▸ ˌpsycho'pathic *adj* ▸ ˌpsycho'pathically *adv*

psychopathology (ˌsaɪkəʊpə'θɒlədʒɪ) *n* the scientific study of mental disorders.
▸ **psychopathological** (ˌsaɪkəʊˌpæθə'lɒdʒɪkᵊl) *adj*

psychopathy (saɪ'kɒpəθɪ) *n* any mental disorder or disease.

psychopharmacology (ˌsaɪkəʊˌfɑːmə'kɒlədʒɪ) *n* the study of drugs that affect the mind.

psychophysics (ˌsaɪkəʊ'fɪzɪks) *n* (*functioning as sing*) the branch of psychology concerned with the relationship between physical stimuli and their effects in the mind.
▸ ˌpsycho'physical *adj*

psychophysiology (ˌsaɪkəʊˌfɪzɪ'ɒlədʒɪ) *n* the branch of psychology concerned with the physiological basis of mental processes.
▸ **psychophysiological** (ˌsaɪkəʊˌfɪzɪə'lɒdʒɪkᵊl) *adj*

psychosexual (ˌsaɪkəʊ'sɛksjʊəl) *adj* of or relating to the mental aspects of sex, such as sexual fantasies.
▸ ˌpsycho'sexually *adv*

psychosis (saɪ'kəʊsɪs) *n, pl* **psychoses** (-'kəʊsiːz). any form of severe mental disorder in which the individual's contact with reality becomes highly distorted. [C19: NL, from PSYCHO- + -OSIS]

psychosocial (ˌsaɪkəʊ'səʊʃəl) *adj* of or relating to processes or factors that are both social and psychological in origin.

psychosomatic (ˌsaɪkəʊsə'mætɪk) *adj* of disorders, such as stomach ulcers, thought to be caused or aggravated by psychological factors such as stress.

psychosurgery (ˌsaɪkəʊ'sɜːdʒərɪ) *n* any surgical procedure on the brain, such as a frontal lobotomy, to relieve serious mental disorders.
▸ **psychosurgical** (ˌsaɪkəʊ'sɜːdʒɪkᵊl) *adj*

psychotherapy (ˌsaɪkəʊ'θɛrəpɪ) *n* the treatment of nervous disorders by psychological methods.
▸ ˌpsychoˌthera'peutic *adj* ▸ ˌpsychoˌthera'peutically *adv*
▸ ˌpsycho'therapist *n*

psychotic (saɪ'kɒtɪk) *Psychiatry.* ◆ *adj* **1** of or characterized by psychosis. ◆ *n* **2** a person suffering from psychosis.
▸ **psy'chotically** *adv*

psychotomimetic (saɪˌkɒtəʊmɪ'mɛtɪk) *adj* (of drugs such as LSD and mescaline) capable of inducing psychotic symptoms.

psych out *vb* (*mainly tr, adv*) *Inf.* **1** to guess correctly the intentions of (another). **2** to analyse (a problem, etc.) psychologically. **3** to intimidate or frighten.

psychrometer (saɪ'krɒmɪtə) *n* a type of hygrometer consisting of two thermometers, one of which has a dry bulb and the other a bulb that is kept moist and ventilated.

psych up *vb* (*tr, adv*) *Inf.* to get (oneself or another) into a

state of psychological readiness for an action, performance, etc.

pt *abbrev. for:* **1** part. **2** patient. **3** payment. **4** point. **5** port. **6** pro tempore.

Pt *abbrev. for* (in place names): **1** Point. **2** Port. ◆ **3** *the chemical symbol for* platinum.

PT *abbrev. for:* **1** physical therapy. **2** physical training. **3** postal telegraph.

pt. *abbrev. for:* **1** pint. **2** preterite.

PTA *abbrev. for:* **1** Parent-Teacher Association. **2** (in Britain) Passenger Transport Authority.

Ptah ★ (ptɑː, tɑː) *n* (in ancient Egypt) a major god worshipped as the creative power, esp. at Memphis.

ptarmigan ('tɑːmɪgən) *n, pl* **ptarmigans** *or* **ptarmigan**. any of several arctic and subarctic grouse, esp. one which has a white winter plumage. [C16: changed (? infl. by Gk *pteron* wing) from Scot. Gaelic *tarmachan*, from ?]

Pte *Mil. abbrev. for* private.

pteridology (ˌtɛrɪ'dɒlədʒɪ) *n* the branch of botany concerned with the study of ferns. [C19: from *pterido-*, from Gk *pteris* fern + -LOGY]
▸ **pteridological** (ˌtɛrɪdəʊ'lɒdʒɪkᵊl) *adj*

pteridophyte ('tɛrɪdəʊˌfaɪt) *n* (in traditional classification) a plant, such as a fern, horsetail, or club moss, reproducing by spores and having vascular tissue, roots, stems, and leaves. In modern classifications these plants are placed in separate phyla. [C19: from *pterido-*, from Gk *pteris* fern + -PHYTE]

ptero- *combining form.* a wing, or a part resembling a wing: *pterodactyl*. [from Gk *pteron*]

pterodactyl (ˌtɛrə'dæktɪl) *n* an extinct flying reptile having membranous wings supported on an elongated fourth digit.

pteropod ('tɛrəˌpɒd) *n* a small marine gastropod mollusc in which the foot is expanded into two winglike lobes for swimming. Also called: **sea butterfly**.

pterosaur ('tɛrəˌsɔː) *n* any of an order of extinct flying reptiles of Jurassic and Cretaceous times: included the pterodactyls.

-pterous *or* **-pteran** *adj combining form.* indicating a specified number or type of wings: *dipterous*. [from Gk *-pteros*, from *pteron* wing]

pterygoid process ('tɛrɪˌgɔɪd) *n Anat.* either of two long bony plates extending downwards from each side of the sphenoid bone within the skull. [C18 *pterygoid*, from Gk *pterugoeidēs*, from *pterux* wing; see -OID]

PTN *abbrev. for* public telephone network: the telephone network provided in Britain by British Telecom.

PTO *or* **pto** *abbrev. for* please turn over.

Ptolemaic (ˌtɒlɪ'meɪɪk) *adj* **1** of or relating to the ancient astronomer Ptolemy or to his conception of the universe. **2** of or relating to the Macedonian dynasty that ruled Egypt from the death of Alexander the Great (323 B.C.) to the death of Cleopatra (30 B.C.).

Ptolemaic system *n* the theory of planetary motion developed by Ptolemy from the hypotheses of earlier philosophers, stating that the earth lay at the centre of the universe with the sun, the moon, and the known planets revolving around it in complicated orbits. Beyond the largest of these orbits lay a sphere of fixed stars.

Ptolemy ★ ('tɒlɪmɪ) *n* Latin name *Claudius Ptolemaeus*. 2nd-century A.D. Greek astronomer, mathematician, and geographer. His *Geography* was the standard geographical textbook until the discoveries of the 15th century. His system of astronomy (see **Ptolemaic system**) remained undisputed until Copernicus.

Ptolemy I ★ *n* called *Ptolemy Soter*. ?367–283 B.C., king of Egypt (323–285 B.C.), a general of Alexander the Great, who obtained Egypt on Alexander's death and founded the Ptolemaic dynasty.

Ptolemy II ★ *n* called *Philadelphus*. 309–246 B.C., the son of Ptolemy I; king of Egypt (285–246). Under his rule the power, prosperity, and culture of Egypt was at its height.

ptomaine *or* **ptomain** ('təʊmeɪn) *n* any of a group of amines formed by decaying organic matter. [C19: from It. *ptomaina*, from Gk *ptoma* corpse, from *piptein* to fall]

★ people and places

ptomaine poisoning *n* a popular term for **food poisoning**. Ptomaines were once erroneously thought to be a cause of food poisoning.

ptosis ('təʊsɪs) *n, pl* **ptoses** ('təʊsiːz). prolapse or drooping of a part, esp. the eyelid. [C18: from Gk: a falling]
▶ **ptotic** ('tɒtɪk) *adj*

PTSD *abbrev. for* post-traumatic stress disorder.

pty *Austral., NZ, & S. African. abbrev. for* proprietary.

ptyalin ('taɪəlɪn) *n Biochemistry.* an amylase secreted in the saliva of man and other animals. [C19: from Gk *ptualon* saliva, from *ptuein* to spit]

p-type *adj* **1** (of a semiconductor) having a density of mobile holes in excess of that of conduction electrons. **2** associated with or resulting from the movement of holes in a semiconductor: *p-type conductivity*.

Pu *the chemical symbol for* plutonium.

pub (pʌb) *n* **1** *Chiefly Brit.* a building with a bar and one or more public rooms licensed for the sale and consumption of alcoholic drink, often also providing light meals. Formal name: **public house. 2** *Austral. & NZ.* a hotel. ◆ *vb* **pubs, pubbing, pubbed. 3** (*intr*) *Inf.* to visit a pub or pubs (esp. in **go pubbing**).

pub. *abbrev. for:* **1** public. **2** publication. **3** published. **4** publisher. **5** publishing.

pub-crawl *Inf., chiefly Brit.* ◆ *n* **1** a drinking tour of a number of pubs or bars. ◆ *vb* **2** (*intr*) to make such a tour.

puberty ('pjuːbətɪ) *n* the period at the beginning of adolescence when the sex glands become functional. Also called: **pubescence.** [C14: from L *pūbertās* maturity, from *pūber* adult]
▶ **'pubertal** *adj*

pubes ('pjuːbiːz) *n, pl* **pubes. 1** the region above the external genital organs, covered with hair from the time of puberty. **2** pubic hair. **3** the pubic bones. **4** the plural of **pubis.** [from L]

pubescent (pjuː'bɛsᵊnt) *adj* **1** arriving or arrived at puberty. **2** (of certain plants and animals or their parts) covered with a layer of fine short hairs or down. [C17: from L *pūbēscere* to reach manhood, from *pūber* adult]
▶ **pu'bescence** *n*

pubic ('pjuːbɪk) *adj* of or relating to the pubes or pubis: *pubic hair.*

pubis ('pjuːbɪs) *n, pl* **pubes.** one of the three sections of the hipbone that forms part of the pelvis. [C16: shortened from NL *os pūbis* bone of the PUBES]

public ('pʌblɪk) *adj* **1** of or concerning the people as a whole. **2** open to all: *public gardens.* **3** performed or made openly: *public proclamation.* **4** (*prenominal*) well-known: *a public figure.* **5** (*usually prenominal*) maintained at the expense of, serving, or for the use of a community: *a public library.* **6** open, acknowledged, or notorious: *a public scandal.* **7 go public.** (of a private company) to issue shares for subscription by the public. ◆ *n* **8** the community or people in general. **9** a section of the community grouped because of a common interest, activity, etc.: *the racing public.* [C15: from L *pūblicus*, changed from *pōplicus* of the people, from *populus* people]
▶ **'publicly** *adv*

public-address system *n* a system of microphones, amplifiers, and loudspeakers for increasing the sound level, used in auditoriums, public gatherings, etc. Sometimes shortened to **PA system.**

publican ('pʌblɪkən) *n* **1** (in Britain) a person who keeps a public house. **2** (in ancient Rome) a public contractor, esp. one who farmed the taxes of a province. [C12: from OF *publicain*, from L *pūblicānus* tax gatherer, from *pūblicum* state revenues]

publication (ˌpʌblɪ'keɪʃən) *n* **1** the act or process of publishing a printed work. **2** any printed work offered for sale or distribution. **3** the act or an instance of making information public. [C14: via OF from L *pūblicātiō* confiscation of property, from *pūblicāre* to seize for public use]

public bar *n Brit.* a bar in a public house usually serving drinks at a cheaper price than in the lounge bar.

public company *n* a limited company whose shares

may be purchased by the public and traded freely on the open market and whose share capital is not less than a statutory minimum; public limited company. Cf. **private company.**

public convenience *n* a public lavatory.

public corporation *n* (in Britain) an organization established to run a nationalized industry or state-owned enterprise. The chairman and board members are appointed by a government minister, and the government has overall control.

public domain *n* **1** the status of a published work upon which the copyright has expired or which has not been subject to copyright. **2 in the public domain.** generally known or accessible.

public enemy *n* a notorious person, such as a criminal, who is regarded as a menace to the public.

public house *n* **1** *Brit.* the formal name for a **pub. 2** *US & Canad.* an inn, tavern, or small hotel.

publicist ('pʌblɪsɪst) *n* **1** a person who publicizes something, esp. a press or publicity agent. **2** a journalist. **3** *Rare.* a person learned in public or international law.

publicity (pʌ'blɪsɪtɪ) *n* **1a** the technique or process of attracting public attention to people, products, etc., as by the use of the mass media. **1b** (*as modifier*): *a publicity agent.* **2** public interest aroused by such a technique or process. **3** information used to draw public attention to people, products, etc. **4** the state of being public. [C18: via F from Med. L *pūblicitās;* see PUBLIC]

publicize *or* **publicise** ('pʌblɪˌsaɪz) *vb* **publicizes, publicizing, publicized** *or* **publicises, publicising, publicised.** (*tr*) to bring to public notice; advertise.

Public Lending Right *n* the right of authors to receive payment when their books are borrowed from public libraries.

public-liability insurance *n* (in Britain) a form of insurance, compulsory for any business in contact with the public, which pays compensation to a member of the public suffering injury or damage as a result of the policyholder or his employees failing to take reasonable care.

public limited company *n* another name for **public company.** Abbrev.: **plc** *or* **PLC.**

public nuisance *n* **1** *Law.* an illegal act causing harm to members of a community rather than to any individual. **2** *Inf.* a person generally considered objectionable.

public opinion *n* the attitude of the public, esp. as a factor in determining action, policy, etc.

public prosecutor *n Law.* an official in charge of prosecuting important cases.

Public Record Office *n* an institution in which official records are stored and kept available for inspection by the public.

public relations *n* (*functioning as sing or pl*) **1a** the practice of creating, promoting, or maintaining goodwill and a favourable image among the public towards an institution, public body, etc. **1b** the professional staff employed for this purpose. Abbrev.: **PR. 1c** the techniques employed. **1d** (*as modifier*): *the public-relations industry.* **2** the relationship between an organization and the public.

public school *n* **1** (in England and Wales) a private independent fee-paying secondary school. **2** in certain Canadian provinces, a public elementary school as distinguished from a separate school. **3** (in the US) any school that is part of a free local educational system.

public sector *n* the part of an economy which consists of state-owned institutions, including nationalized industries and services provided by local authorities.

public servant *n* **1** an elected or appointed holder of a public office. **2** the Austral. and NZ equivalent of **civil servant.**

public service *n* the Austral. and NZ equivalent of the civil service.

public-spirited *adj* having or showing active interest in the good of the community.

public utility *n* an enterprise concerned with the provision to the public of essentials, such as electricity or water. Also called (in the US): **public-service corporation.**

public works *pl n* engineering projects and other constructions, financed and undertaken by a government for the community.

publish ('pʌblɪʃ) *vb* **1** to produce and issue (printed matter) for distribution and sale. **2** (*intr*) to have one's written work issued for publication. **3** (*tr*) to announce formally or in public. **4** (*tr*) to communicate (defamatory matter) to someone other than the person defamed: *to publish a libel.* [C14: from OF *puplier,* from L *pūblicāre* to make PUBLIC]
▸ **'publishable** *adj*

publisher ('pʌblɪʃə) *n* **1** a company or person engaged in publishing periodicals, books, music, etc. **2** *US & Canad.* the proprietor of a newspaper.

Puccini ★ (pu'tʃi:nɪ) *n* **Giacomo** ('dʒa:komo). 1858–1924, Italian operatic composer, noted for the dramatic realism of his operas, which include *Manon Lescaut* (1893), *La Bohème* (1896), *Tosca* (1900), and *Madame Butterfly* (1904).

puce (pju:s) *n, adj* (of) a colour varying from deep red to dark purplish brown. [C18: shortened from F *couleur puce* flea colour, from L *pūlex* flea]

puck[1] (pʌk) *n* **1** a small disc of hard rubber used in ice hockey. **2** a stroke at the ball in hurling. **3** *Irish sl.* a sharp blow. ◆ *vb* (*tr*) **4** to strike (the ball) in hurling. **5** *Irish sl.* to strike hard; punch. [C19: from ?]

puck[2] (pʌk) *n* a mischievous or evil spirit. [OE *pūca,* from ?]
▸ **'puckish** *adj*

pucka ('pʌkə) *adj* a less common spelling of **pukka.**

pucker ('pʌkə) *vb* **1** to gather (a soft surface such as the skin) into wrinkles, or (of such a surface) to be so gathered. ◆ *n* **2** a wrinkle, crease, or irregular fold. [C16: ? rel. to POKE[2], from the baglike wrinkles]

pudding ('pʊdɪŋ) *n* **1** a sweetened usually cooked dessert made in many forms and of various ingredients. **2** a savoury dish, usually consisting partially of pastry or batter: *steak-and-kidney pudding.* **3** the dessert course in a meal. **4** a sausage-like mass of meat, oatmeal, etc., stuffed into a prepared skin or bag and boiled. [C13 *poding*]
▸ **'puddingy** *adj*

pudding stone *n* a conglomerate rock in which there is a difference in colour and composition between the pebbles and the matrix.

puddle ('pʌdᵊl) *n* **1** a small pool of water, esp. of rain. **2** a small pool of any liquid. **3** a worked mixture of wet clay and sand that is impervious to water and is used to line a pond or canal. ◆ *vb* **puddles, puddling, puddled.** (*tr*) **4** to make (clay, etc.) into puddle. **5** to subject (iron) to puddling. [C14 *podel,* dim. of OE *pudd* ditch, from ?]
▸ **'puddler** *n* ▸ **'puddly** *adj*

puddling ('pʌdlɪŋ) *n* a process for converting pig iron into wrought iron by heating it with ferric oxide in a furnace and stirring it to oxidize the carbon.

pudency ('pju:dᵊnsɪ) *n* modesty or prudishness. [C17: from LL *pudentia,* from L *pudēre* to feel shame]

pudendum (pju:'dɛndəm) *n, pl* **pudenda** (-də). (*often pl*) the human external genital organs collectively, esp. of a female. [C17: from LL, from L *pudenda* the shameful (parts), from *pudēre* to be ashamed]
▸ **pu'dendal** *or* **pudic** ('pju:dɪk) *adj*

pudgy ('pʌdʒɪ) *adj* **pudgier, pudgiest.** a variant spelling (esp. US) of **podgy.** [C19: from ?]
▸ **'pudgily** *adv* ▸ **'pudginess** *n*

Pudsey ★ ('pʌdzɪ) *n* a town in N England, in Leeds unitary authority, in West Yorkshire. Pop.: 31 636 (1991).

Puebla ★ (*Spanish* 'pweβla) *n* **1** an inland state of S central Mexico, situated on the Anáhuac Plateau. Capital: Puebla. Pop.: 4 624 239 (1995 est.). Area: 33 919 sq. km (13 096 sq. miles). **2** a city in S Mexico, capital of Puebla state: founded in 1532; university (1537). Pop.: 1 007 170 (1990). Full name: **Puebla de Zaragoza** (de θara'ɣoθa).

pueblo ('pwɛbləʊ; *Spanish* 'pweβlo) *n, pl* **pueblos** (-ləʊz; *Spanish* -los). **1** a communal village, built by certain Indians of the southwestern US and parts of Latin America, consisting of one or more flat-roofed houses. **2** (in Spanish America) a village or town. [C19: from Sp.: people, from L *populus*]

Pueblo[1] ('pwɛbləʊ) *n, pl* **Pueblo** *or* **Pueblos.** a member of any of the North American Indian peoples who live in pueblos.

Pueblo[2] ★ ('pwɛbləʊ) *n* a city in the US, in Colorado: a centre of the steel industry. Pop.: 100 471 (1994 est.).

puerile ('pjʊəraɪl) *adj* **1** exhibiting silliness; immature; trivial. **2** of or characteristic of a child. [C17: from L *puerīlis* childish, from *puer* a boy]
▸ **'puerilely** *adv* ▸ **puerility** (pjʊə'rɪlɪtɪ) *n*

puerperal (pju:'ɜ:pərəl) *adj* of or occurring during the period following childbirth. [C18: from NL *puerperālis,* from L *puerperium* childbirth, ult. from *puer* boy + *parere* to bear]

puerperal fever *n* a serious, formerly widespread, form of blood poisoning caused by infection contracted during childbirth.

puerperal psychosis *n* a mental disorder sometimes occurring in women after childbirth, characterized by deep depression.

Puerto Rico ★ ('pwɜ:təʊ 'ri:kəʊ, 'pwɛə-) *n* an autonomous commonwealth (in association with the US) occupying the smallest and easternmost of the Greater Antilles in the Caribbean: one of the most densely populated areas in the world; ceded by Spain to the US in 1899. Currency: US dollar. Capital: San Juan. Pop.: 3 809 000 (1997). Area: 9104 sq. km (3515 sq. miles). Former name (until 1932): **Porto Rico.** Abbrev.: **PR.**
▸ **Puerto Rican** *adj, n*

puff (pʌf) *n* **1** a short quick gust or emission, as of wind, smoke, etc. **2** the amount of wind, smoke, etc., released in a puff. **3** the sound made by a puff. **4** an instance of inhaling and expelling the breath as in smoking. **5** a light aerated pastry usually filled with cream, jam, etc. **6** a powder puff. **7** exaggerated praise, as of a book, product, etc., esp. through an advertisement. **8** a piece of clothing fabric gathered up so as to bulge in the centre while being held together at the edges. **9** a cylindrical roll of hair pinned in place in a coiffure. **10** *US.* a quilted bed cover. **11** one's breath (esp. in **out of puff**). **12** *Derog. sl.* a male homosexual. ◆ *vb* **13** to blow or breathe or cause to blow or breathe in short quick draughts. **14** (*tr; often foll. by out; usually passive*) to cause to be out of breath. **15** to take draws at (a cigarette, etc.). **16** (*intr*) to move with or by the emission of puffs: *the steam train puffed up the incline.* **17** (often foll. by *up, out,* etc.) to swell, as with air, pride, etc. **18** (*tr*) to praise with exaggerated empty words, often in advertising. **19** (*tr*) to apply (powder, dust, etc.) to (something). [OE *pyffan*]
▸ **'puffy** *adj*

puff adder *n* **1** a large venomous African viper that inflates its body when alarmed. **2** another name for **hognose snake.**

puffball ('pʌf,bɔ:l) *n* **1** any of various fungi having a round fruiting body that discharges a cloud of brown spores when mature. **2** short for **puffball skirt.**

puffball skirt *n* a skirt or a dress with a skirt that puffs out wide and is nipped into a narrow hem.

puffer ('pʌfə) *n* **1** a person or thing that puffs. **2** Also called: **blowfish, globefish.** a marine fish with an elongated spiny body that can be inflated to form a globe.

puffin ('pʌfɪn) *n* any of various northern diving birds, having a black-and-white plumage and a brightly coloured vertically flattened bill. [C14: ? of Cornish origin]

puff pastry *or US* **puff paste** *n* a dough used for making a rich flaky pastry.

puff-puff *n Brit.* a children's name for a steam locomotive or railway train.

pug[1] (pʌg) *n* a small compact breed of dog with a smooth coat, lightly curled tail, and a short wrinkled nose. [C16: from ?]
▸ **'puggish** *adj*

pug[2] (pʌg) *vb* **pugs, pugging, pugged.** (*tr*) **1** to mix (clay) with water to form a malleable mass or paste, often in a **pug mill**. **2** to fill or stop with clay or a similar substance. [C19: from ?]

ɔug[3] (pʌg) *n* a slang name for **boxer** (sense 1). [C20: shortened from PUGILIST]

Puget Sound ★ ('pjuːdʒɪt) *n* an inlet of the Pacific in NW Washington. Length: about 130 km (80 miles).

ɔugging ('pʌgɪŋ) *n* material such as clay, sawdust, etc., inserted between wooden flooring and ceiling to deaden sound. Also called: **pug**.

ɔuggree, pugree ('pʌgrɪ) *or* **puggaree, pugaree** ('pʌgərɪ) *n* **1** the usual Indian word for **turban**. **2** a scarf, usually pleated, around the crown of some hats, esp. sun helmets. [C17: from Hindi *pagrī*, from Sansk. *parikara*]

ɔugilism ('pjuːdʒɪˌlɪzəm) *n* the art, practice, or profession of fighting with the fists; boxing. [C18: from L *pugil* a boxer]
▶ **'pugilist** *n* ▶ **ˌpugi'listic** *adj* ▶ **ˌpugi'listically** *adv*

Pugin ★ ('pjuːdʒɪn) *n* **Augustus (Welby Northmore).** 1812–52, British architect; a leader of the Gothic Revival. He collaborated with Sir Charles Barry on the Palace of Westminster (begun 1836).

Puglia ★ ('puʎʎa) *n* the Italian name for **Apulia**.

pugnacious (pʌg'neɪʃəs) *adj* readily disposed to fight; belligerent. [C17: from L *pugnāx*]
▶ **pug'naciously** *adv* ▶ **pugnacity** (pʌg'næsɪtɪ) *n*

pug nose *n* a short stubby upturned nose. [C18: from PUG[1]]
▶ **'pug-ˌnosed** *adj*

puisne ('pjuːnɪ) *adj* (esp. of a subordinate judge) of lower rank. [C16: from Anglo-F, from OF *puisné* born later, from L *posteā* afterwards + *nascī* to be born]

puissance ('pjuːɪsˀns, 'pwiːsɑːns) *n* **1** a competition in showjumping that tests a horse's ability to jump large obstacles. **2** *Arch. or poetic.* power. [C15: from OF; see PUISSANT]

puissant ('pjuːɪsˀnt) *adj Arch. or poetic.* powerful. [C15: from OF, ult. from L *potēns* mighty, from *posse* to have power]
▶ **'puissantly** *adv*

puke (pjuːk) *Sl.* ◆ *vb* **pukes, puking, puked.** **1** to vomit. ◆ *n* **2** the act of vomiting. **3** the matter vomited. [C16: prob. imit.]

pukeko ('pukəkəʊ) *n, pl* **pukekos.** a New Zealand wading bird with bright plumage. [from Maori]

pukka *or* **pucka** ('pʌkə) *adj Anglo-Indian.* properly or perfectly done, constructed, etc.; good; genuine. [C17: from Hindi *pakkā* firm, from Sansk. *pakva*]

Pula ★ (*Serbo-Croat* 'puːla) *n* a port in NW Croatia, at the S tip of the Istrian Peninsula: made a Roman military base in 178 B.C.; became the main Austro-Hungarian naval station and passed to Italy in 1919, then to Yugoslavia (1947–91). Pop.: 62 300 (1991). Latin name: **Pietas Julia** (paɪˈeɪtæs ˈjuːlɪə). Italian name: **Pola**.

Pulau Pinang ★ ('pulaʊ pɪ'næŋ) *n* another name for **Penang**.

pulchritude ('pʌlkrɪˌtjuːd) *n Formal or literary.* physical beauty. [C15: from L *pulchritūdō*, from *pulcher* beautiful]
▶ **ˌpulchri'tudinous** *adj*

pule (pjuːl) *vb* **pules, puling, puled.** (*intr.*) to cry plaintively; whimper. [C16: ? imit.]
▶ **'puler** *n*

Pulitzer ★ ('pʊlɪtsə) *n* **Joseph.** 1847–1911, US newspaper publisher, born in Hungary. He established the Pulitzer prizes.

Pulitzer prize *n* one of a group of prizes established by Joseph Pulitzer and awarded yearly since 1917 for excellence in American journalism, literature, and music.

pull (pʊl) *vb* (*mainly tr*) **1** (*also intr*) to exert force on (an object) so as to draw it towards the source of the force. **2** to remove; extract: *to pull a tooth.* **3** to strip of feathers, hair, etc.; pluck. **4** to draw the entrails from (a fowl). **5** to rend or tear. **6** to strain (a muscle or tendon). **7** (usually foll. by *off*) *Inf.* to bring about: *to pull off a million-pound deal.* **8** (often foll. by *on*) *Inf.* to draw out (a weapon) for use: *he pulled a knife on his attacker.* **9** *Inf.* to attract: *the pop group*

pulled a crowd. **10** (*also intr*) *Sl.* to attract (a sexual partner). **11** (*intr;* usually foll. by *on* or *at*) to drink or inhale deeply: *to pull at one's pipe.* **12** to make (a grimace): *to pull a face.* **13** (*also intr;* foll. by *away, out, over,* etc.) to move (a vehicle) or (of a vehicle) to be moved in a specified manner. **14** (*intr*) to possess or exercise the power to move: *this car doesn't pull well on hills.* **15** to withdraw or remove: *the board decided to pull their support.* **16** *Printing.* to take (a proof) from type. **17** *Golf, baseball, etc.* to hit (a ball) so that it veers away from the direction in which the player intended to hit it. **18** *Cricket.* to hit (a ball) pitched straight or on the off side) to the leg side. **19** *Hurling.* to strike (a fast-moving ball) in the same direction as it is already moving. **20** (*also intr*) to row (a boat) or take a stroke of (an oar) in rowing. **21** (of a rider) to restrain (a horse), esp. to prevent it from winning a race. **22 pull a fast one.** *Sl.* to play a sly trick. **23 pull apart** or **to pieces.** to criticize harshly. **24 pull (one's) punches.** **24a** *Inf.* to restrain the force of one's criticisms or actions. **24b** *Boxing.* to restrain the force of one's blows. ◆ *n* **25** an act or an instance of pulling or being pulled. **26** the force or effort used in pulling: *the pull of the moon affects the tides.* **27** the act or an instance of taking in drink or smoke. **28** *Printing.* a proof taken from type: *the first pull was smudged.* **29** something used for pulling, such as a handle. **30** *Inf.* special advantage or influence: *his uncle is chairman of the company, so he has quite a lot of pull.* **31** *Inf.* the power to attract attention or support. **32** a period of rowing. **33** a single stroke of an oar in rowing. **34** the act of pulling the ball in golf, cricket, etc. **35** the act of reining in a horse. ◆ See also **pull down, pull in,** etc. [OE *pullian*]
▶ **'puller** *n*

pull down *vb* (*tr, adv*) to destroy or demolish: *the old houses were pulled down.*

pullet ('pʊlɪt) *n* a young hen of the domestic fowl, less than one year old. [C14: from OF *poulet* chicken, from L *pullus* a young animal or bird]

pulley ('pʊlɪ) *n* **1** a wheel with a grooved rim in which a rope can run in order to change the direction of a force applied to the rope, etc. **2** a number of such wheels pivoted in parallel in a block, used to raise heavy loads. **3** a wheel with a flat, convex, or grooved rim mounted on a shaft and driven by or driving a belt passing around it. [C14 *poley*, from OF *polie*, from Vulgar L *polidium* (unattested), apparently from LGk *polidion* (unattested) a little pole, from Gk *polos* axis]

pull in *vb* (*adv*) **1** (*intr;* often foll. by *to*) to reach a destination: *the train pulled in at the station.* **2** (*intr*) Also: **pull over.** (of a motor vehicle) **2a** to draw in to the side of the road. **2b** to stop (at a café, lay-by, etc.). **3** (*tr*) to attract: *his appearance will pull in the crowds.* **4** (*tr*) *Sl.* to arrest. **5** (*tr*) to earn or gain (money). ◆ *n* **pull-in. 6** *Brit.* a roadside café, esp. for lorry drivers.

Pullman ('pʊlmən) *n, pl* **Pullmans.** a luxurious railway coach. Also called: **Pullman car.** [C19: after G. M. *Pullman* (1831–97), its US inventor]

pull off *vb* (*tr*) **1** to remove (clothing) forcefully. **2** (*adv*) to succeed in performing (a difficult feat).

pull out *vb* (*adv*) **1** (*tr*) to extract. **2** (*intr*) to depart: *the train pulled out of the station.* **3** *Mil.* to withdraw or be withdrawn: *the troops were pulled out of the ruined city.* **4** (*intr*) (of a motor vehicle) **4a** to draw away from the side of the road. **4b** to draw out from behind another vehicle to overtake. **5** (*intr*) to abandon a position or situation. **6** (foll. by *of*) to level out (from a dive). ◆ *n* **pull-out. 7** an extra leaf of a book that folds out. **8** a removable section of a magazine, etc.

pullover ('pʊlˌəʊvə) *n* a garment, esp. a sweater, that is pulled on over the head.

pull through *vb* to survive or recover or cause to survive or recover, esp. after a serious illness or crisis. Also: **pull round.**

pull together *vb* **1** (*intr, adv*) to cooperate, or work harmoniously. **2 pull oneself together.** *Inf.* to regain one's self-control or composure.

pullulate ('pʌljʊˌleɪt) *vb* **pullulates, pullulating, pullulated.** (*intr*) **1** (of animals, etc.) to breed abundantly. **2** (of plants) to sprout, bud, or germinate. [C17: from L

pullulāre to sprout, from *pullulus* a baby animal, from *pullus* young animal]
▶ ‚pullu'lation *n*

pull up *vb* (*adv*) **1** (*tr*) to remove by the roots. **2** (often foll. by *with* or *on*) to move level (with) or ahead (of), esp. in a race. **3** to stop: *the car pulled up suddenly*. **4** (*tr*) to rebuke. ◆ *n* **pull-up. 5** *Brit.* a roadside café; pull-in.

pulmonary ('pʌlmənərɪ, 'pʊl-) *adj* **1** of or affecting the lungs. **2** having lungs or lunglike organs. [C18: from L *pulmōnārius*, from *pulmō* a lung]

pulmonary artery *n* either of the two arteries that convey oxygen-depleted blood from the heart to the lungs.

pulmonary vein *n* any one of the four veins that convey oxygen-rich blood from the lungs to the heart.

pulp (pʌlp) *n* **1** soft or fleshy plant tissue, such as the succulent part of a fleshy fruit. **2** a moist mixture of cellulose fibres, as obtained from wood, from which paper is made. **3a** a magazine or book containing trite or sensational material, and usually printed on cheap rough paper. **3b** (*as modifier*): *a pulp novel*. **4** *Dentistry*. the soft innermost part of a tooth, containing nerves and blood vessels. **5** any soft soggy mass. **6** *Mining*. pulverized ore. ◆ *vb* **7** to reduce (a material) to pulp or (of a material) to be reduced to pulp. **8** (*tr*) to remove the pulp from (fruit, etc.). [C16: from L *pulpa*]
▶ 'pulpy *adj*

pulpit ('pʊlpɪt) *n* **1** a raised platform, usually surrounded by a barrier, set up in churches as the appointed place for preaching, etc. **2** a medium for expressing an opinion, such as a newspaper column. **3** (usually preceded by *the*) **3a** the preaching of the Christian message. **3b** the clergy or their influence. [C14: from L *pulpitum* a platform]

pulpwood ('pʌlp‚wʊd) *n* pine, spruce, or any other soft wood used to make paper.

pulque ('pʊlkɪ) *n* a light alcoholic drink from Mexico made from the juice of various agave plants. [C17: from Mexican Sp., apparently from Nahuatl, from *puliuhqui* decomposed, since it will only keep for a day]

pulsar ('pʌl‚sɑː) *n* any of a number of very small stars first discovered in 1967, which rotate fast, emitting regular pulses of polarized radiation. [C20: from PULS(ATING ST)AR, on the model of QUASAR]

pulsate (pʌl'seɪt) *vb* **pulsates, pulsating, pulsated.** (*intr*) **1** to expand and contract with a rhythmic beat; throb. **2** *Physics.* to vary in intensity, magnitude, etc. **3** to quiver or vibrate. [C18: from L *pulsāre* to push]
▶ 'pulsative ('pʌlsətɪv) *adj* ▶ pul'sation *n* ▶ pul'sator *n*
▶ 'pulsatory ('pʌlsətərɪ, -trɪ) *adj*

pulsatilla (‚pʌlsə'tɪlə) *n* any of a genus of plants related to the anemone, with feathery or hairy foliage. [C16: from Med. L, from *pulsāta* beaten (by the wind)]

pulsating star *n* a type of variable star, the variation in brightness resulting from expansion and subsequent contraction of the star.

pulse[1] (pʌls) *n* **1** *Physiol.* **1a** the rhythmic contraction and expansion of an artery at each beat of the heart. **1b** a single such pulsation. **2** *Physics, electronics.* **2a** a transient sharp change in some quantity normally constant in a system. **2b** one of a series of such transient disturbances, usually recurring at regular intervals. **3a** a recurrent rhythmic series of beats, vibrations, etc. **3b** any single beat, wave, etc., in such a series. **4** an inaudible electronic "ping" to operate a slide projector. **5** bustle, vitality, or excitement: *the pulse of a city*. **6 keep one's finger on the pulse.** to be well informed about current events, opinions, etc. ◆ *vb* **pulses, pulsing, pulsed. 7** (*intr*) to beat, throb, or vibrate. **8** (*tr*) to provide an electronic pulse to operate (a slide projector). [C14 *pous*, from L *pulsus* a beating, from *pellere* to beat]
▶ 'pulseless *adj*

pulse[2] (pʌls) *n* **1** the edible seeds of any of several leguminous plants, such as peas, beans, and lentils. **2** the plant producing any of these. [C13 *pols*, from OF, from L *puls* pottage of pulse]

pulsejet ('pʌls‚dʒɛt) *n* a type of ramjet engine in which air is admitted through movable vanes that are closed by the pressure resulting from each intermittent explosion

of the fuel in the combustion chamber, thus causing pulsating thrust. Also called: **pulsejet engine, pulsojet.**

pulse modulation *n Electronics.* a type of modulation in which a train of pulses is used as the carrier wave, one or more of its parameters, such as amplitude, being modulated or modified in order to carry information.

pulsimeter (pʌl'sɪmɪtə) *n Med.* an instrument for measuring the rate of the pulse.

pulverize or **pulverise** ('pʌlvə‚raɪz) *vb* **pulverizes, pulverizing, pulverized** or **pulverises, pulverising, pulverised. 1** to reduce (a substance) to fine particles, as by grinding, or (of a substance) to be so reduced. **2** (*tr*) to destroy completely. [C16: from LL *pulverizare*, from L *pulvis* dust]
▶ 'pulver‚izable or 'pulver‚isable *adj* ▶ ‚pulveri'zation or ‚pulveri'sation *n* ▶ 'pulver‚izer or 'pulver‚iser *n*

pulverulent (pʌl'vɛrʊlənt) *adj* consisting of, covered with, or crumbling to dust or fine particles. [C17: from L *pulverulentus*, from *pulvis* dust]

puma ('pjuːmə) *n* a large American feline mammal that resembles a lion, having a plain greyish-brown coat and long tail. Also called: **cougar, mountain lion.** [C18: via Sp. from Quechua]

pumice ('pʌmɪs) *n* **1** Also called: **pumice stone.** a light porous volcanic rock used for scouring and, in powdered form, as an abrasive and for polishing. ◆ *vb* **pumices, pumicing, pumiced. 2** (*tr*) to rub or polish with pumice. [C15 *pomys*, from OF *pomis*, from L *pūmex*]
▶ pumiceous (pjuː'mɪʃəs) *adj*

pummel ('pʌməl) *vb* **pummels, pummelling, pummelled** or *U.S.* **pummels, pummeling, pummeled.** (*tr*) to strike repeatedly with or as if with the fists. Also (less commonly): **pommel** [C16: see POMMEL]

pump[1] (pʌmp) *n* **1** any device for compressing, driving, raising, or reducing the pressure of a fluid, esp. by means of a piston or set of rotating impellers. **2** *Biol.* a mechanism for the active transport of ions, such as protons calcium ions, and sodium ions, across cell membranes: *sodium pump.* ◆ *vb* **3** (when *tr*, usually foll. by *from*, *out*, etc.) to raise or drive (air, liquid, etc., esp. into or from something) with a pump. **4** (*tr*; usually foll. by *in* or *into*) to supply in large amounts: *to pump capital into a project.* **5** (*tr*) to deliver (bullets, etc.) repeatedly. **6** to operate (something, esp. a handle) in the manner of a pump or (of something) to work in this way: *to pump the pedals of a bicycle.* **7** (*tr*) to obtain (information) from (a person) by persistent questioning. **8** (*intr*; usually foll. by *from* or *out of*) (of liquids) to flow freely in large spurts: *oil pumped from the fissure.* **9 pump iron.** *Sl.* to exercise with weights; do body-building exercises. [C15: from MDu. *pumpe* pipe prob. from Sp. *bomba*, imit.]

pump[2] (pʌmp) *n* **1** a low-cut low-heeled shoe without fastenings, worn esp. for dancing. **2** a type of shoe with a rubber sole, used in games such as tennis; plimsoll [C16: from ?]

pumpernickel ('pʌmpə‚nɪk°l) *n* a slightly sour black bread, originating in Germany, made of coarse rye flour [C18: from G, from ?]

pumpkin ('pʌmpkɪn) *n* **1** any of several creeping plants of the genus *Cucurbita.* **2** the large round fruit of any of these plants, which has a thick orange rind, pulpy flesh and numerous seeds. [C17: from earlier *pumpion*, from OF, from L *pepo*, from Gk. from *peptein* to ripen]

pump priming *n* **1** the process of introducing fluid into a pump to improve starting and to expel air from it. **2** government expenditure designed to stimulate economic activity in stagnant or depressed areas. **3** another term for **deficit financing.**

pun[1] (pʌn) *n* **1** the use of words to exploit ambiguities and innuendoes for humorous effect; a play on words. An example is: *"Ben Battle was a soldier bold, And used to war's alarms: But a cannonball took off his legs, So he laid down his arms."* (Thomas Hood). ◆ *vb* **puns, punning, punned. 2** (*intr*) to make puns. [C17: ?from It. *puntiglio* wordplay; see PUNCTILIO]

pun[2] (pʌn) *vb* **puns, punning, punned.** (*tr*) *Brit.* to pack (earth, rubble, etc.) by pounding. [C16: var. of POUND[1]]

puna *Spanish.* ('puna) *n* **1** a high cold dry plateau. **2** an other name for **mountain sickness**. [C17: from American Sp., of Amerind origin]

Punakha or **Punaka** ★ ('puːnəkə) n a town in W central Bhutan: a former capital of the country.

punch[1] (pʌntʃ) vb **1** to strike at, esp. with a clenched fist. **2** (tr) Western US. to herd or drive (cattle), esp. for a living. **3** (tr) to poke with a stick, etc. ◆ n **4** a blow with the fist. **5** Inf. point or vigour: his arguments lacked punch. [C15: ? var. of pounce, from OF poinçonner to stamp]
▸ **'puncher** n

punch[2] (pʌntʃ) n **1** a tool or machine for piercing holes in a material. **2** a tool or machine used for stamping a design on something or shaping it by impact. **3** the solid die of a punching machine. **4** Computing. a device for making holes in a card or paper tape. ◆ vb **5** (tr) to pierce, cut, stamp, shape, or drive with a punch. [C14: shortened from puncheon, from OF ponçon; see PUNCHEON[2]]

punch[3] (pʌntʃ) n any mixed drink containing fruit juice and, usually, alcoholic liquor, generally hot and spiced. [C17: ?from Hindi pānch, from Sansk. pañca five; it orig. had five ingredients]

Punch (pʌntʃ) n the main character in the traditional children's puppet show **Punch and Judy**.

punchbag ('pʌntʃ,bæg) n a suspended stuffed bag that is punched for exercise, esp. boxing training. Also called (US and Canad.): **punching bag**.

punchball ('pʌntʃ,bɔːl) n **1** a stuffed or inflated ball, supported by a flexible rod, that is punched for exercise, esp. boxing training. **2** US. a game resembling baseball.

punchbowl ('pʌntʃ,bəʊl) n **1** a large bowl for serving punch, often having small drinking glasses hooked around the rim. **2** Brit. a bowl-shaped depression in the land.

punch-drunk adj **1** demonstrating or characteristic of the behaviour of a person who has suffered repeated blows to the head, esp. a professional boxer. **2** dazed; stupefied.

punched card or esp. US **punch card** n a card on which data can be coded in the form of punched holes, formerly used in computing.

punched tape or US (sometimes) **perforated tape** n other terms for **paper tape**.

puncheon[1] ('pʌntʃən) n a large cask of variable capacity, usually between 70 and 120 gallons. [C15 poncion, from OF ponchon, from ?]

puncheon[2] ('pʌntʃən) n **1** a short wooden post used as a vertical strut. **2** a less common word for **punch**[2] (sense 1). [C14 ponson, from OF ponçon, from L punctiō a puncture, from pungere to prick]

Punchinello (,pʌntʃɪ'nɛləʊ) n, pl **Punchinellos** or **Punchinelloes**. **1** a clown from Italian puppet shows, the prototype of Punch. **2** (sometimes not cap.) any grotesque or absurd character. [C17: from earlier Polichinello, from It. Polecenella, from pulcino chicken, ult. from L pullus young animal]

punch line n the culminating part of a joke, funny story, etc., that gives it its point.

punch-up n Brit. inf. a fight or brawl.

punchy ('pʌntʃɪ) adj **punchier**, **punchiest**. **1** an informal word for **punch-drunk**. **2** Inf. incisive or forceful.
▸ **'punchily** adv ▸ **'punchiness** n

punctate ('pʌŋkteɪt) adj having or marked with minute spots or depressions. [C18: from NL punctātus, from L punctum a point]
▸ **punc'tation** n

punctilio (pʌŋk'tɪlɪ,əʊ) n, pl **punctilios**. **1** strict attention to minute points of etiquette. **2** a petty formality or fine point of etiquette. [C16: from It. puntiglio small point, from L punctum point]

punctilious (pʌŋk'tɪlɪəs) adj **1** paying scrupulous attention to correctness in etiquette. **2** attentive to detail.
▸ **punc'tiliously** adv ▸ **punc'tiliousness** n

punctual ('pʌŋktjʊəl) adj **1** arriving or taking place at an arranged time. **2** (of a person) having the characteristic of always keeping to arranged times. **3** Obs. precise; exact. **4** Maths. consisting of or confined to a point.

[C14: from Med. L punctuālis concerning detail, from L punctum point]
▸ **,punctu'ality** n ▸ **'punctually** adv

punctuate ('pʌŋktjʊ,eɪt) vb **punctuates**, **punctuating**, **punctuated**. (mainly tr) **1** (also intr) to insert punctuation marks into (a written text). **2** to interrupt or insert at frequent intervals: a meeting punctuated by heckling. **3** to give emphasis to. [C17: from Med. L punctuāre to prick, from L, from pungere to puncture]

punctuation (,pʌŋktjʊ'eɪʃən) n **1** the use of symbols not belonging to the alphabet of a writing system to indicate aspects of the intonation and meaning not otherwise conveyed in the written language. **2** the symbols used for this purpose.

punctuation mark n any of the signs used in punctuation, such as a comma.

puncture ('pʌŋktʃə) n **1** a small hole made by a sharp object. **2** a perforation and loss of pressure in a pneumatic tyre. **3** the act of puncturing or perforating. ◆ vb **punctures**, **puncturing**, **punctured**. **4** (tr) to pierce a hole in (something) with a sharp object. **5** to cause (something pressurized, esp. a tyre) to lose pressure by piercing, or (of a tyre, etc.) to collapse in this way. **6** (tr) to depreciate (a person's self-esteem, pomposity, etc.). [C14: from L punctūra, from pungere to prick]

pundit ('pʌndɪt) n **1** an expert. **2** (formerly) a learned person. **3** Also: **pandit**. a Brahman learned in Sanskrit, Hindu religion, philosophy or law. [C17: from Hindi pandit, from Sansk. pandita learned man]

Pune ★ ('puːnə) n another name for **Poona**.

punga ('pʌŋə) n a variant spelling of **ponga**.

pungent ('pʌndʒənt) adj **1** having an acrid smell or sharp bitter flavour. **2** (of wit, satire, etc.) biting; caustic. **3** Biol. ending in a sharp point. [C16: from L pungens piercing, from pungere to prick]
▸ **'pungency** n ▸ **'pungently** adv

Punic ('pjuːnɪk) adj **1** of or relating to ancient Carthage or the Carthaginians. **2** treacherous; faithless. ◆ n **3** the language of the Carthaginians; a late form of Phoenician. [C15: from L Pūnicus, var. of Poenicus Carthaginian, from Gk Phoinix]

punish ('pʌnɪʃ) vb **1** to force (someone) to undergo a penalty for some crime or misdemeanour. **2** (tr) to inflict punishment for (some crime, etc.). **3** (tr) to treat harshly, esp. as by overexertion: to punish a horse. **4** (tr) Inf. to consume in large quantities: to punish the bottle. [C14 punisse, from OF punir, from L pūnīre to punish, from poena penalty]
▸ **'punishable** adj ▸ **'punisher** n ▸ **'punishing** adj

punishment ('pʌnɪʃmənt) n **1** a penalty for a crime or offence. **2** the act of punishing or state of being punished. **3** Inf. rough treatment.

punitive ('pjuːnɪtɪv) adj relating to, involving, or with the intention of inflicting punishment: a punitive expedition. [C17: from Med. L pūnītīvus concerning punishment, from L pūnīre to punish]
▸ **'punitively** adv

Punjab ★ (pʌn'dʒɑːb, 'pʌndʒɑːb) n **1** (formerly) a province in NW British India: divided between India and Pakistan in 1947. **2** a state of NW India: reorganized in 1966 as a Punjabi-speaking state, a large part forming the new state of Haryana; mainly agricultural. Capital: Chandigarh. Pop.: 21 695 000 (1994 est.). Area: 50 255 sq. km (19 403 sq. miles). **3** a province of W Pakistan: created in 1947. Capital: Lahore. Pop.: 54 000 000 (latest est.). Area: 205 344 sq. km (127 595 sq. miles).

Punjabi (pʌn'dʒɑːbɪ) n (pl **Punjabis**) **1** a member of the chief people of the Punjab. **2** the language of the Punjab, belonging to the Indic branch of the Indo-European family. ◆ adj **3** of the Punjab, its people, or their language.

Punjab States ★ pl n (formerly) a group of states in NW India, amalgamated in 1956 with Punjab state.

punk[1] (pʌŋk) n **1** a youth movement of the late 1970s, characterized by anti-Establishment slogans and outrageous clothes and hairstyles. **2** an inferior, rotten, or worthless person or thing. **3** worthless articles collectively. **4** short for **punk rock**. **5** Obs. a young male homosexual; catamite. **6** *Obs.* a prostitute. ◆ *adj* **7** rotten or worthless. [C16: from ?]

punk[2] (pʌŋk) *n* dried decayed wood or other substance that smoulders when ignited: used as tinder. [C18: from ?]

punka *or* **punkah** (ˈpʌŋkə) *n* **1** a fan made of a palm leaf or leaves. **2** a large fan made of palm leaves, etc., worked mechanically to cool a room. [C17: from Hindi *pankhā*, from Sansk. *paksaka* fan, from *paksa* wing]

punk rock *n* a fast abrasive style of rock music of the late 1970s, characterized by aggressive lyrics and performance, usually expressing rage and frustration.
▶ **punk rocker** *n*

punnet (ˈpʌnɪt) *n Chiefly Brit.* a small basket for fruit. [C19: ? dim. of dialect *pun* POUND[2]]

punster (ˈpʌnstə) *n* a person who is fond of making puns, esp. one who makes a tedious habit of this.

punt[1] (pʌnt) *n* **1** an open flat-bottomed boat with square ends, propelled by a pole. ◆ *vb* **2** to propel (a boat, esp. a punt) by pushing with a pole on the bottom of a river, etc. [OE *punt* shallow boat, from L *pontō* punt]

punt[2] (pʌnt) *n* **1** a kick in certain sports, such as rugby, in which the ball is released and kicked before it hits the ground. **2** any long high kick. ◆ *vb* **3** to kick (a ball, etc.) using a punt. [C19: ? var. of dialect *bunt* to push]

punt[3] (pʌnt) *Chiefly Brit.* ◆ *vb* **1** (*intr*) to gamble; bet. ◆ *n* **2** a gamble or bet, esp. against the bank, as in roulette, or on horses. **3** Also called: **punter**. a person who bets. **4 take a punt at.** *Austral. & NZ inf.* to make an attempt at. [C18: from F *ponter* to punt, from *ponte* bet laid against the banker, from Sp. *punto* point, from L *punctum*]

punt[4] (punt) *n* the Irish pound. [Irish Gaelic: pound]

Punta Arenas ★ (*Spanish* ˈpunta aˈrenas) *n* a port in S Chile, on the Strait of Magellan: the southernmost city in the world. Pop.: 117 206 (1995 est.). Former name: **Magallanes.**

punter[1] (ˈpʌntə) *n* a person who punts a boat.

punter[2] (ˈpʌntə) *n* a person who kicks a ball.

punter[3] (ˈpʌntə) *n* **1** a person who gambles or bets. **2** *Sl.* any client or customer, esp. a prostitute's client. **3** *Sl.* a victim of a con man.

puny (ˈpjuːnɪ) *adj* **punier, puniest. 1** small and weakly. **2** paltry; insignificant. [C16: from OF *puisne* PUISNE]
▶ **ˈpuniness** *n*

pup (pʌp) *n* **1a** a young dog; puppy. **1b** the young of various other animals, such as the seal. **2 in pup.** (of a bitch) pregnant. **3** *Inf., chiefly Brit.* a conceited young man (esp. in **young pup**). **4 sell (someone) a pup.** to swindle (someone) by selling him something worthless. ◆ *vb* **pups, pupping, pupped. 5** (of dogs, seals, etc.) to give birth to (young). [C18: back formation from PUPPY]

pupa (ˈpjuːpə) *n, pl* **pupae** (-piː) *or* **pupas.** an insect at the immobile nonfeeding stage of development between larva and adult, when many internal changes occur. [C19: via NL, from L: a doll]
▶ **ˈpupal** *adj*

pupate (pjuːˈpeɪt) *vb* **pupates, pupating, pupated.** (*intr*) (of an insect larva) to develop into a pupa.
▶ **puˈpation** *n*

pupil[1] (ˈpjuːpəl) *n* **1** a student who is taught by a teacher. **2** *Civil & Scots Law.* a boy under 14 or a girl under 12 who is in the care of a guardian. [C14: from L *pupillus* an orphan, from *pūpus* a child]
▶ **ˈpupillage** *or US* **ˈpupilage** *n* ▶ **ˈpupillary** *or* **ˈpupilary** *adj*

pupil[2] (ˈpjuːpəl) *n* the dark circular aperture at the centre of the iris of the eye, through which light enters. [C16: from L *pūpilla*, dim. of *pūpa* doll; from the tiny reflections in the eye]
▶ **ˈpupillary** *or* **ˈpupilary** *adj*

pupiparous (pjuːˈpɪpərəs) *adj* (of certain dipterous flies) producing young that have already reached the pupa stage at the time of hatching. [C19: from NL *pupiparus*, from PUPA + *parere* to bring forth]

puppet (ˈpʌpɪt) *n* **1a** a small doll or figure moved by strings attached to its limbs or by the hand inserted in its cloth body. **1b** (*as modifier*): *a puppet theatre.* **2a** a person, state, etc., that appears independent but is controlled by another. **2b** (*as modifier*): *a puppet government.* [C16 *popet,* ?from OF *poupette* little doll, ult. from L *pūpa* doll]

puppeteer (ˌpʌpɪˈtɪə) *n* a person who manipulates puppets.

puppetry (ˈpʌpɪtrɪ) *n* **1** the art of making and manipulating puppets and presenting puppet shows. **2** unconvincing or specious presentation.

puppy (ˈpʌpɪ) *n, pl* **puppies. 1** a young dog; pup. **2** *Inf., contemptuous.* a brash or conceited young man; pup. [C15 *popi,* from OF *popée* doll]
▶ **ˈpuppyhood** *n* ▶ **ˈpuppyish** *adj*

puppy fat *n* fatty tissue that develops in childhood or adolescence and usually disappears with maturity.

puppy love *n* another term for **calf love.**

Purana (puˈrɑːnə) *n* any of a class of Sanskrit writings not included in the Vedas, characteristically recounting the birth and deeds of Hindu gods and the creation of the universe. [C17: from Sansk.: ancient, from *purā* formerly]

Purbeck marble *or* **stone** (ˈpɜːbɛk) *n* a fossil-rich limestone that takes a high polish. [C15: after *Purbeck,* Dorset, where quarried]

purblind (ˈpɜːˌblaɪnd) *adj* **1** partly or nearly blind. **2** lacking in insight or understanding; obtuse. [C13: see PURE, BLIND]

Purcell ★ (ˈpɜːsˀl) *n* **1 Edward Mills.** 1912–97, US physicist, noted for his work on the magnetic moments of atomic nuclei: shared the Nobel prize for physics 1952. **2 Henry.** ?1659–95, English composer. His works include the opera *Dido and Aeneas* (1689), music for the theatrical pieces *King Arthur* (1691) and *The Fairy Queen* (1692) and several choral odes.

purchase (ˈpɜːtʃɪs) *vb* **purchases, purchasing, purchased.** (*tr*) **1** to obtain (goods, etc.) by payment. **2** to obtain by effort, sacrifice, etc.: *to purchase one's freedom.* **3** to draw or lift (a load) with mechanical apparatus. ◆ *n* **4** something that is purchased. **5** the act of buying. **6** acquisition of an estate by any lawful means other than inheritance. **7** the mechanical advantage achieved by a lever. **8** a firm foothold, grasp, etc., as for climbing something. [C13: from OF *porchacier* to strive to obtain; see CHASE[1]]
▶ **ˈpurchasable** *adj* ▶ **ˈpurchaser** *n*

purchase tax *n* (in Britain, formerly) a tax levied on nonessential consumer goods and added to selling prices by retailers.

purdah (ˈpɜːdə) *n* **1** the custom in some Muslim and Hindu communities of keeping women in seclusion, with clothing that conceals them completely when they go out. **2** a screen in a Hindu house used to keep the women out of view. [C19: from Hindi *parda* veil, from Persian *pardah*]

pure (pjuə) *adj* **1** not mixed with any extraneous or dissimilar materials, elements, etc. **2** free from tainting or polluting matter: *pure water.* **3** free from moral taint or defilement: *pure love.* **4** (*prenominal*) (intensifier): *a pure coincidence.* **5** (of a subject, etc.) studied in its theoretical aspects rather than for its practical applications: *pure mathematics.* **6** (of a vowel) pronounced with more or less unvarying quality without any glide. **7** (of a consonant) not accompanied by another consonant. **8** of unmixed descent. **9** *Genetics, biol.* breeding true; homozygous. [C13: from OF *pur,* from L *pūrus* unstained]
▶ **ˈpurely** *adv* ▶ **ˈpureness** *n*

purebred *adj* (ˈpjuəˈbrɛd). **1** denoting a pure strain obtained through many generations of controlled breeding. ◆ *n* (ˈpjuəˌbrɛd). **2** a purebred animal.

purée (ˈpjuəreɪ) *n* **1** a smooth thick pulp of sieved fruit, vegetables, meat, or fish. ◆ *vb* **purées, puréeing, puréed. 2** (*tr*) to make (cooked foods) into a purée. [C19: from F *purer* to PURIFY]

purfle (ˈpɜːfˀl) *vb* *also* **purfling. 1** a ruffled or curved ornamental band, as on clothing, furniture, etc. ◆ *vb* **purfles, purfling, purfled. 2** (*tr*) to decorate with such a band. [C14: from OF *purfiler* to decorate with a border, from *fil* thread, from L *filum*]

purgation (pɜːˈɡeɪʃən) n the act of purging or state of being purged; purification.

purgative (ˈpɜːɡətɪv) Med. ✦ n 1 a drug or agent for purging the bowels. ✦ adj 2 causing evacuation of the bowels.
► ˈpurgatively adv

purgatory (ˈpɜːɡətərɪ, -trɪ) n 1 Chiefly RC Church. a state or place in which the souls of those who have died in a state of grace are believed to undergo a limited amount of suffering to expiate their venial sins. 2 a place or condition of suffering or torment, esp. one that is temporary. [C13: from OF purgatoire, from Med. L pūrgātōrium, lit.: place of cleansing, from L pūrgāre to purge]
► ˌpurgaˈtorial adj

purge (pɜːdʒ) vb purges, purging, purged. 1 (tr) to rid (something) of (impure elements). 2 (tr) to rid (a state, political party, etc.) of (dissident people). 3 (tr) 3a to empty (the bowels) by evacuation of faeces. 3b to cause (a person) to evacuate his bowels. 4a to clear (a person) of a charge. 4b to free (oneself) of guilt, as by atonement. 5 (intr) to be purified. ✦ n 6 the act or process of purging. 7 the elimination of opponents or dissidents from a state, political party, etc. 8 a purgative drug or agent. [C14: from OF purger, from L pūrgāre to purify]

Puri ★ (ˈpʊəri, pʊəˈriː) n a port in E India, in Orissa on the Bay of Bengal: 12th-century temple of Jagannath. Pop.: 125 199 (1991).

purificator (ˈpjʊərɪfɪˌkeɪtə) n Christianity. a small white linen cloth used to wipe the chalice and paten at the Eucharist.

purify (ˈpjʊərɪˌfaɪ) vb purifies, purifying, purified. 1 to free (something) of contaminating or debasing matter. 2 (tr) to free (a person, etc.) from sin or guilt. 3 (tr) to make clean, as in a ritual. [C14: from OF purifier, from LL pūrificāre to cleanse, from pūrus pure + facere to make]
► ˌpurifiˈcation n ► purificatory (ˈpjʊərɪfɪˌkeɪtərɪ, -trɪ) adj
► ˈpuriˌfier n

Purim (ˈpʊərɪm; Hebrew puːˈriːm) n a Jewish holiday in February or March to commemorate the deliverance of the Jews from the massacre planned by Haman (Esther 9). [Heb. pūrīm, pl. of pūr lot; from the casting of lots by Haman]

purine (ˈpjʊəriːn) or **purin** (ˈpjʊərɪn) n 1 a colourless crystalline solid that can be prepared from uric acid. Formula: $C_5H_5N_4$. 2 Also called: purine base. any of a number of nitrogenous bases that are derivatives of purine. [C19: from G Purin]

puriri (puːˈriːriː) n a New Zealand tree with hard timber and red berries. [from Maori]

purism (ˈpjʊəˌrɪzəm) n insistence on traditional canons of correctness of form or purity of style or content.
► ˈpurist adj, n ► puˈristic adj

puritan (ˈpjʊərɪtən) n 1 a person who adheres to strict moral or religious principles, esp. one opposed to luxury and sensual enjoyment. ✦ adj 2 characteristic of a puritan. [C16: from LL pūritās purity]
► ˈpuritanˌism n

Puritan (ˈpjʊərɪtən) (in the late 16th and 17th centuries) ✦ n 1 any of the extreme English Protestants who wished to purify the Church of England of most of its ceremony and other aspects that they deemed to be Catholic. ✦ adj 2 of or relating to the Puritans.
► ˈPuritanˌism n

puritanical (ˌpjʊərɪˈtænɪkəl) adj 1 Usually disparaging. strict in moral or religious outlook, esp. in shunning sensual pleasures. 2 (sometimes cap.) of or relating to a puritan or the Puritans.
► ˌpuriˈtanically adv

purity (ˈpjʊərɪtɪ) n the state or quality of being pure.

purl[1] (pɜːl) n 1 a knitting stitch made by doing a plain stitch backwards. 2 a decorative border, as of lace. 3 gold or silver wire thread. ✦ vb 4 to knit in purl stitch. 5 to edge (something) with a purl. ✦ Also (for senses 2, 3, 5): pearl. [C16: from dialect pirl to twist into a cord]

purl[2] (pɜːl) vb 1 (intr) (of a stream, etc.) to flow with a gentle swirling or rippling movement and a murmuring sound. ✦ n 2 a swirling movement of water; eddy. 3 a

murmuring sound, as of a shallow stream. [C16: rel. to Norwegian purla to bubble]

purler[1] (ˈpɜːlə) n Inf. a headlong or spectacular fall (esp. in come a purler).

purler[2] (ˈpɜːlə) n Austral. sl. something outstanding in its class. [from ?]

purlieu (ˈpɜːljuː) n 1 English history. land on the edge of a forest once included within the bounds of the royal forest but later separated although still subject to some of the forest laws. 2 (usually pl) a neighbouring area; outskirts. 3 (often pl) a place one frequents; haunt. [C15 purlewe, from Anglo-F puralé a going through (infl. also by OF lieu place), from OF puraler, from pur through + aler to go]

purlin or **purline** (ˈpɜːlɪn) n a horizontal beam that supports the common rafters of a roof and is carried by the principal rafters or trusses. [C15: from ?]

purloin (pɜːˈlɔɪn) vb to steal. [C15: from OF porloigner to put at a distance, from por- for + loin distant, from L longus long]
► purˈloiner n

purple (ˈpɜːpəl) n 1 a colour between red and blue. 2 a dye or pigment producing such a colour. 3 cloth of this colour, often used to symbolize royalty or nobility. 4 (usually preceded by the) high rank; nobility. 5a the official robe of a cardinal. 5b the rank of a cardinal as signified by this. ✦ adj 6 of the colour purple. 7 (of writing) excessively elaborate or full of imagery: purple prose. [OE, from L purpura purple dye, from Gk porphura the purple fish (murex)]
► ˈpurpleness n ► ˈpurplish or ˈpurply adj

purple heart n 1 any of several tropical American trees. 2 Inf., chiefly Brit. a heart-shaped purple tablet consisting mainly of amphetamine.

Purple Heart n a decoration awarded to members of the US Armed Forces for a wound received in action.

purple patch n 1 Also called: purple passage. a section in a piece of writing characterized by fanciful or ornate language. 2 Sl. a period of good fortune.

purport vb (pɜːˈpɔːt). (tr) 1 to claim to be (true, official, etc.) by manner or appearance, esp. falsely. 2 (of speech or writing) to signify or imply. ✦ n (ˈpɜːpɔːt). 3 meaning; significance. 4 object; intention. [C15: from Anglo-F: contents, from OF porporter to convey, from L portāre]

purpose (ˈpɜːpəs) n 1 the reason for which anything is done, created, or exists. 2 a fixed design or idea that is the object of an action or other effort. 3 determination: a man of purpose. 4 practical advantage or use: to work to good purpose. 5 that which is relevant (esp. in to or from the purpose). 6 Arch. purport. 7 on purpose. intentionally. ✦ vb purposes, purposing, purposed. 8 (tr) to intend or determine to do (something). [C13: from OF porpos, from porposer to plan, from L prōpōnere to PROPOSE]
► ˈpurposeless adj

purpose-built adj made to serve a specific purpose.

purposeful (ˈpɜːpəsful) adj 1 having a definite purpose in view. 2 determined.
► ˈpurposefully adv ► ˈpurposefulness n

USAGE NOTE Purposefully is sometimes wrongly used where purposely is meant: he had purposely (not purposefully) left the door unlocked.

purposely (ˈpɜːpəslɪ) adv on purpose.

USAGE NOTE See at purposeful.

purposive (ˈpɜːpəsɪv) adj 1 having or indicating conscious intention. 2 serving a purpose; useful.
► ˈpurposively adv ► ˈpurposiveness n

purpura (ˈpɜːpjʊrə) n Pathol. any of several blood diseases causing purplish spots on the skin due to subcutaneous bleeding. [C18: via L from Gk porphura a shellfish yielding purple dye]

purr (pɜː) vb **1** (intr) (esp. of cats) to make a low vibrant sound, usually considered as expressing pleasure, etc. **2** (tr) to express (pleasure, etc.) by this sound or by a sound suggestive of purring. ◆ n **3** a purring sound. [C17: imit.]

purse (pɜːs) n **1** a small bag or pouch for carrying money, esp. coins. **2** US & Canad. a woman's handbag. **3** anything resembling a small bag or pouch in form or function. **4** wealth; funds; resources. **5** a sum of money that is offered, esp. as a prize. ◆ vb **purses, pursing, pursed.** **6** (tr) to contract (the mouth, lips, etc.) into a small rounded shape. [OE purs, prob. from LL bursa bag, ult. from Gk: leather]

purser ('pɜːsə) n an officer aboard a ship or aircraft who keeps the accounts and attends to the welfare of the passengers.

purse seine n a large net that encloses fish and is then closed at the bottom by means of a line resembling the string formerly used to draw shut the neck of a money pouch.

purse strings pl n control of expenditure (esp. in **hold** or **control the purse strings**).

purslane ('pɜːslɪn) n a plant with fleshy leaves used (esp. formerly) in salads and as a potherb. [C14 purcelane, from OF porcelaine, from LL, from L porcillāca, var. of portulāca]

pursuance (pə'sjuːəns) n the carrying out or pursuing of an action, plan, etc.

pursuant (pə'sjuːənt) adj **1** (usually postpositive; often foll. by to) Chiefly law. in agreement or conformity. **2** Arch. pursuing. [C17: rel. to ME poursuivant following after, from OF; see PURSUE]
▶ pur'suantly adv

pursue (pə'sjuː) vb **pursues, pursuing, pursued.** (mainly tr) **1** (also intr) to follow (a fugitive, etc.) in order to capture or overtake. **2** to follow closely or accompany: ill health pursued her. **3** to seek or strive to attain (some desire, etc.). **4** to follow the precepts of (a plan, policy, etc.). **5** to apply oneself to (studies, interests, etc.). **6** to follow persistently or seek to become acquainted with. **7** to continue to discuss or argue (a point, subject, etc.). [C13: from Anglo-Norman pursiwer, from OF poursivre, from L prōsequī to follow after]
▶ pur'suer n

pursuit (pə'sjuːt) n **1a** the act of pursuing. **1b** (as modifier): a pursuit plane. **2** an occupation or pastime. **3** (in cycling) a race in which the riders set off at intervals along the track and attempt to overtake each other. [C14: from OF poursieute, from poursivre to PURSUE]

pursuivant ('pɜːsɪvənt) n **1** the lowest rank of heraldic officer. **2** History. a state or royal messenger. **3** History. a follower or attendant. [C14: from OF, from poursivre to PURSUE]

purulent ('pjuərʊlənt) adj of, relating to, or containing pus. [C16: from L pūrulentus, from pūs]
▶ 'purulence n ▶ 'purulently adv

Purús ★ (Spanish, Portuguese pu'rus) n a river in NW central South America, rising in SE Peru and flowing northeast to the Amazon. Length: about 3200 km (2000 miles).

purvey (pə'veɪ) vb (tr) **1** to sell or provide (commodities, esp. foodstuffs) on a large scale. **2** to publish (lies, scandal, etc.). [C13: from OF porveeir, from L prōvidēre to PROVIDE]
▶ pur'veyor n

purveyance (pə'veɪəns) n **1** History. the collection or requisition of provisions for a sovereign. **2** Rare. the act of purveying.

purview ('pɜːvjuː) n **1** scope of operation. **2** breadth or range of outlook. **3** Law. the body of a statute, containing the enacting clauses. [C15: from Anglo-Norman purveu, from porveeir to furnish; see PURVEY]

pus (pʌs) n the yellow or greenish fluid product of inflammation. [C16: from L pūs]

Pusan ★ ('puː'sæn) n a port in SE South Korea, on the Korea Strait: the second largest city and chief port of the country; industrial centre; two universities. Pop.: 3 813 814 (1995).

Pusey ★ ('pjuːzɪ) n Edward Bouverie ('buːvərɪ). 1800–82, British ecclesiastic; a leader with Keble and Newman of the Oxford Movement.

push (pʊʃ) vb **1** (when tr, often foll. by off, away, etc.) to apply steady force to in order to move. **2** to thrust (one's way) through something, such as a crowd. **3** (tr) to encourage or urge (a person) to some action, decision, etc. **4** (when intr, often foll. by for) to be an advocate or promoter (of): to push for acceptance of one's theories. **5** (tr) to use one's influence to help (a person): to push one's own candidate. **6** to bear upon (oneself or another person) in order to achieve better results, etc. **7** Cricket, etc. to hit (a ball) with a stiff pushing stroke. **8** (tr) Inf. to sell (narcotic drugs) illegally. **9** (intr; foll. by out, into, etc.) to extend: the cliffs pushed out to the sea. **10 push one's luck** or **push it.** **10a** to take undue risks, esp. through overconfidence. **10b** (intr) to act overconfidently. ◆ n **11** the act of pushing; thrust. **12** a part or device that is pressed to operate some mechanism. **13** Inf. drive, energy, etc. **14** Inf. a special effort or attempt to advance, as of an army: to make a push. **15** Austral. sl. a group, gang, or clique. **16** Cricket, etc. a stiff pushing stroke. **17 at a push.** Inf. with difficulty; only just. **18 the push.** Inf., chiefly Brit. dismissal, esp. from employment. ◆ See also **push off, push in,** etc. [C13: from OF pousser, from L pulsāre, from pellere to drive]

push-bike n Brit. an informal name for **bicycle.**

push button n **1** an electrical switch operated by pressing a button, which closes or opens a circuit. ◆ modifier. **push-button.** **2a** operated by a push button: a push-button radio. **2b** initiated as simply as by pressing a button: push-button warfare.

pushcart ('pʊʃˌkɑːt) n another name (esp. US and Canad.) for **barrow**[1] (sense 3).

pushchair ('pʊʃˌtʃɛə) n a usually collapsible chair-shaped carriage for a small child. Also called: **baby buggy, buggy.** US and Canad. word: **stroller.** Austral. words: **pusher, stroller.**

pushed (pʊʃt) adj (often foll. by for) Inf. short (of) or in need of (time, money, etc.).

pusher ('pʊʃə) n **1** Inf. a person who sells illegal drugs, esp. narcotics such as heroin. **2** Inf. an aggressively ambitious person. **3** a person or thing that pushes. **4** Austral. the usual name for **pushchair.**

push in vb (intr, adv) to force one's way into a group of people, queue, etc.

pushing ('pʊʃɪŋ) adj **1** enterprising or aggressively ambitious. **2** impertinently self-assertive. ◆ adv **3** almost or nearly (a certain age, speed, etc.): pushing fifty.
▶ 'pushingly adv

Pushkin[1] ★ ('pʊʃkɪn) n a town in NW Russia: site of the imperial summer residence and Catherine the Great's palace. Pop.: 97 000 (1989). Former name: **Tsarskoye Selo** (1708–1937).

Pushkin[2] ★ ('pʊʃkɪn) n Aleksander Sergeyevich (alɪk'sandr sɪr'gjeɪvitʃ). 1799–1837, Russian poet, novelist, and dramatist. His works include the verse novel Eugene Onegin (1833), the tragedy Boris Godunov (1825), and the novel The Captain's Daughter (1836).

push money n a cash inducement provided by a manufacturer or distributor for a retailer or his staff, to reward successful selling.

push off vb (adv) **1** Also: **push out.** to move into open water, as by being cast off from a mooring. **2** (intr) Inf. to go away; leave.

pushover ('pʊʃˌəʊvə) n Inf. **1** something that is easily achieved. **2** a person, team, etc., that is easily taken advantage of or defeated.

push-pull n (modifier) using two similar electronic devices made to operate out of phase with each other to produce a signal that replicates the input waveform: a push-pull amplifier.

push-start vb (tr) **1** to start (a motor vehicle) by pushing it while it is in gear, thus turning the engine. ◆ n **2** this process.

★ people and places

push through *vb* (*tr*) to compel to accept: *the bill was pushed through Parliament.*

Pushto ('pʌʃtəʊ) *or* **Pushtu** ('pʌʃtuː) *n, adj* variant spellings of **Pashto**.

push-up *n* the US and Canad. term for **press-up**.

pushy ('pʊʃɪ) *adj* **pushier, pushiest.** *Inf.* **1** offensively assertive. **2** aggressively or ruthlessly ambitious.
  ► **'pushily** *adv* ► **'pushiness** *n*

pusillanimous (ˌpjuːsɪˈlænɪməs) *adj* characterized by a lack of courage or determination. [C16: from LL *pusillanimis* from L *pusillus* weak + *animus* courage]
  ► **pusillanimity** (ˌpjuːsɪləˈnɪmɪtɪ) *n* ► **ˌpusilˈlanimously** *adv*

puss (pʊs) *n* **1** an informal name for a **cat. 2** *Sl.* a girl or woman. **3** an informal name for a **hare.** [C16: rel. to MLow G *pūs*]

pussy[1] ('pʊsɪ) *n, pl* **pussies. 1** Also called: **puss, pussycat.** an informal name for a **cat. 2** a furry catkin. **3** *Taboo sl.* the female pudenda. [C18: from PUSS]

pussy[2] ('pʌsɪ) *adj* **pussier, pussiest.** containing or full of pus.

pussycat ('pʊsɪˌkæt) *n* **1** an informal or child's name for **cat**[1]. **2** *Brit. inf.* an endearing or gentle person.

pussyfoot ('pʊsɪˌfʊt) *vb* (*intr*) *Inf.* **1** to move about stealthily or warily like a cat. **2** to avoid committing oneself.

pussy willow ('pʊsɪ) *n* a willow tree with silvery silky catkins.

pustulant ('pʌstjʊlənt) *adj* **1** causing the formation of pustules. ♦ *n* **2** an agent causing such formation.

pustulate *vb* ('pʌstjʊˌleɪt), **pustulates, pustulating, pustulated. 1** to form or cause to form into pustules. ♦ *adj* ('pʌstjʊlɪt). **2** covered with pustules.
  ► **ˌpustuˈlation** *n*

pustule ('pʌstjuːl) *n* **1** a small inflamed elevated area of skin containing pus. **2** any spot resembling a pimple. [C14: from L *pustula* a blister, var. of *pūsula*]
  ► **pustular** ('pʌstjʊlə) *adj*

put (pʊt) *vb* **puts, putting, put.** (*mainly tr*) **1** to cause to be (in a position or place): *to put a book on the table.* **2** to cause to be (in a state, relation, etc.): *to put one's things in order.* **3** (foll. by *to*) to cause (a person) to experience or suffer: *to put to death.* **4** to set or commit (to an action, task, or duty), esp. by force: *to put him to work.* **5** to render or translate: *to put into English.* **6** to set (words) in a musical form (esp. in **put to music**). **7** (foll. by *at*) to estimate: *he put the distance at fifty miles.* **8** (foll. by *to*) to utilize: *he put his knowledge to use.* **9** (foll. by *to*) to couple (a female animal) with a male for breeding: *the farmer put his heifer to the bull.* **10** to express: *to put it bluntly.* **11** to make (an end or limit): *he put an end to the proceedings.* **12** to present for consideration; propose: *he put the question to the committee.* **13** to invest (money) in or expend (time, energy, etc.) on: *he put five thousand pounds into the project.* **14** to impart: *to put zest into a party.* **15** to throw or cast. **16 not know where to put oneself.** to feel embarrassed. **17 stay put.** to remain in one place; keep one's position. ♦ *n* **18** a throw, esp. in putting the shot. **19** Also called: **put option.** *Stock Exchange.* an option to sell a stated number of securities at a specified price during a limited period. ♦ *See* also **put about, put across,** etc. [C12 *puten* to push]

put about *vb* (*adv*) **1** *Naut.* to change course. **2** (*tr*) to make widely known: *he put about the news of the air disaster.* **3** (*tr; usually passive*) to disconcert or disturb.

put across *vb* (*tr*) **1** (*adv*) to communicate in a comprehensible way: *he couldn't put things across very well.* **2 put one across.** *Inf.* to get (someone) to believe a claim, excuse, etc., by deception: *they put one across their teacher.*

put aside *vb* (*tr, adv*) **1** to move (an object, etc.) to one side, esp. in rejection. **2** to save: *to put money aside for a rainy day.* **3** to disregard: *let us put aside our differences.*

putative ('pjuːtətɪv) *adj* (*prenominal*) **1** commonly regarded as being: *the putative father.* **2** considered to exist or have existed; inferred. [C15: from LL *putātīvus* supposed, from L *putāre* to consider]
  ► **'putatively** *adv*

put away *vb* (*tr, adv*) **1** to return (something) to the proper place. **2** to save: *to put away money for the future.* **3**

to lock up in a prison, mental institution, etc.: *they put him away for twenty years.* **4** to eat or drink, esp. in large amounts.

put back *vb* (*tr, adv*) **1** to return to its former place. **2** to move to a later time: *the wedding was put back a fortnight.* **3** to impede the progress of: *the strike put back production.*

put by *vb* (*tr, adv*) to set aside for the future; save.

put down *vb* (*tr, adv*) **1** to make a written record of. **2** to repress: *to put down a rebellion.* **3** to consider: *they put him down for an ignoramus.* **4** to attribute: *I put the mistake down to inexperience.* **5** to put (an animal) to death, because of old age or illness. **6** to table on the agenda: *the MPs put down a motion on the increase in crime.* **7** *Sl.* to reject or humiliate. ♦ *n* **put-down. 8** a cruelly crushing remark.

put forth *vb* (*tr, adv*) *Formal.* **1** to propose. **2** (of a plant) to produce or bear (leaves, etc.).

put forward *vb* (*tr, adv*) **1** to propose; suggest. **2** to offer the name of; nominate.

put in *vb* (*adv*) **1** (*intr*) *Naut.* to bring a vessel into port. **2** (often foll. by *for*) to apply (for a job, etc.). **3** (*tr*) to submit: *he put in his claims form.* **4** to intervene with (a remark) during a conversation. **5** (*tr*) to devote (time, effort, etc.): *he put in three hours overtime last night.* **6** (*tr*) to establish or appoint: *he put in a manager.* **7** (*tr*) *Cricket.* to cause to bat: *England won the toss and put the visitors in to bat.*

Putnam ★ ('pʌtnəm) *n* **1** *Israel.* 1718–90, American general in the War of Independence. **2** his cousin **Rufus.** 1738–1824, American soldier in the War of Independence; surveyor general of the US (1796–1803).

put off *vb* (*tr*) **1** (*adv*) to postpone: *they have put off the dance until tomorrow.* **2** (*adv*) to evade (a person) by postponement or delay: *they tried to put him off, but he came anyway.* **3** (*adv*) to cause aversion: *he was put off by her appearance.* **4** (*prep*) to cause to lose interest in: *the accident put him off driving.*

put on *vb* (*tr, mainly adv*) **1** to clothe oneself in. **2** (*usually passive*) to adopt (an attitude or feeling) insincerely: *his misery was just put on.* **3** to present (a play, show, etc.). **4** to add: *she put on weight.* **5** to cause (an electrical device) to function. **6** (*also prep*) to wager (money) on a horse race, game, etc. **7** (*also prep*) to impose: *to put a tax on cars.* **8** *Cricket.* to cause (a bowler) to bowl.

put out *vb* (*tr, adv*) **1** (*often passive*) **1a** to annoy; anger. **1b** to disturb; confuse. **2** to extinguish (a fire, light, etc.). **3** to poke forward: *to put out one's tongue.* **4** to be a source of inconvenience to: *I hope I'm not putting you out.* **5** to publish; broadcast: *the authorities put out a leaflet.* **6** to render unconscious. **7** to dislocate: *he put out his shoulder in the accident.* **8** to give out (work to be done) at different premises. **9** to lend (money) at interest. **10** *Cricket, etc.* to dismiss (a player or team).

put over *vb* (*tr, adv*) **1** *Inf.* to communicate (facts, information, etc.). **2** *Chiefly US.* to postpone. **3 put (a fast) one over on.** *Inf.* to get (someone) to believe a claim, excuse, etc., by deception: *he put one over on his boss.*

put-put ('pʌtˌpʌt) *Inf.* ♦ *n* **1** a light chugging or popping sound, as made by a petrol engine. ♦ *vb* **put-puts, put-putting, put-putted. 2** (*intr*) to make such a sound.

putrefy ('pjuːtrɪˌfaɪ) *vb* **putrefies, putrefying, putrefied.** (of organic matter) to decompose or rot with an offensive smell. [C15: from OF *putrefier* + L *putrefacere*, from *puter* rotten + *facere* to make]
  ► **putrefaction** (ˌpjuːtrɪˈfækʃən) *n* ► **ˌputreˈfactive** *or* **putrefacient** (ˌpjuːtrɪˈfeɪʃənt) *adj*

putrescent (pjuːˈtrɛsᵊnt) *adj* **1** becoming putrid; rotting. **2** characterized by or undergoing putrefaction. [C18: from L *putrescere* to become rotten]
  ► **puˈtrescence** *n*

putrid ('pjuːtrɪd) *adj* **1** (of organic matter) in a state of decomposition: *putrid meat.* **2** morally corrupt. **3** sickening; foul: *a putrid smell.* **4** *Inf.* deficient in quality or value: *a putrid film.* [C16: from L *putridus*, from *putrēre* to be rotten]
  ► **puˈtridity** *or* **'putridness** *n* ► **'putridly** *adv*

putsch (pʊtʃ) *n* a violent and sudden uprising; political revolt. [C20: from G, from Swiss G: a push, imit.]

putt (pʌt) *Golf.* ♦ *n* **1** a stroke on the green with a putter to roll the ball into or near the hole. ♦ *vb* **2** to strike (the ball) in this way. [C16: of Scot. origin]

puttee or **putty** ('pʌtɪ) *n, pl* **puttees** or **putties.** (*usually pl*) a strip of cloth worn wound around the leg from the ankle to the knee, esp. as part of a military uniform in World War I. [C19: from Hindi *pattī,* from Sansk. *pattikā,* from *patta* cloth]

putter[1] ('pʌtə) *n Golf.* **1** a club for putting, usually having a solid metal head. **2** a golfer who putts: *he is a good putter.*

putter[2] ('pʌtə) *vb* the usual US and Canad. word for **potter**[2].
▶ **'putterer** *n*

putter[3] ('putə) *n* **1** a person who puts: *the putter of a question.* **2** a person who puts the shot.

put through *vb* (*tr, mainly adv*) **1** to carry out to a conclusion: *he put through his plan.* **2** (*also prep*) to organize the processing of: *she put through his application to join the organization.* **3** to connect by telephone. **4** to make (a telephone call).

putting green ('pʌtɪŋ) *n* **1** (on a golf course) the area of closely mown grass at the end of a fairway where the hole is. **2** an area of smooth grass with several holes for putting games.

Puttnam ★ ('pʌtnəm) *n* **David,** Baron. born 1941, British film producer. Films include *Chariots of Fire* (1981), *The Killing Fields* (1984), and *Memphis Belle* (1990).

putto ('putəʊ) *n, pl* **putti** (-tiː). a representation of a small boy, a cherub or cupid, esp. in baroque painting or sculpture. [from It., from L *putus* boy]

putty ('pʌtɪ) *n, pl* **putties.** **1** a stiff paste made of whiting and linseed oil that is used to fix glass into frames and to fill cracks in woodwork, etc. **2** any substance with a similar function or appearance. **3** a mixture of lime and water with sand or plaster of Paris used on plaster as a finishing coat. **4** (*as modifier*): *a putty knife.* **5** a person who is easily influenced: *he's putty in her hands.* **6a** a colour varying from greyish yellow to greyish brown. **6b** (*as adj*): *putty wool.* ♦ *vb* **putties, puttying, puttied.** **7** (*tr*) to fix, fill, or coat with putty. [C17: from F *potée* a potful]

Putumayo ★ (*Spanish* putuˈmajo) *n* a river in NW South America, rising in S Colombia and flowing southeast as most of the border between Colombia and Peru, entering the Amazon in Brazil: scene of the Putumayo rubber scandal (1910–11) during the rubber boom, in which many Indians were enslaved and killed by rubber exploiters. Length: 1578 km (980 miles). Brazilian name: **Içá.**

put up *vb* (*adv, mainly tr*) **1** to build; erect: *to put up a statue.* **2** to accommodate or be accommodated: *can you put me up for tonight?* **3** to increase (prices). **4** to submit (a plan, case, etc.). **5** to offer: *to put a house up for sale.* **6** to give: *to put up a good fight.* **7** to provide (money) for: *they put up five thousand for the new project.* **8** to preserve or can (jam, etc.). **9** to pile up (long hair) on the head in any of several styles. **10** (*also intr*) to nominate or be nominated as a candidate: *he put up for president.* **11** *Arch.* to return (a weapon) to its holder: *put up your sword!* **12 put up to. 12a** to inform or instruct (a person) about (tasks, duties, etc.). **12b** to incite to. **13 put up with.** *Inf.* to endure; tolerate. ♦ *adj* **put-up. 14** dishonestly or craftily prearranged (esp. in **put-up job**).

put upon *vb* (*intr, prep; usually passive*) **1** to presume on (a person's generosity, good nature, etc.): *he's always being put upon.* **2** to impose hardship on: *he was sorely put upon.*

putz (pʌts) *n US sl.* a despicable or stupid person. [from Yiddish *puts* ornament]

Puvis de Chavannes ★ (*French* pyvis də ʃavan) *n* **Pierre Cécile** (pjer sesil). 1824–98, French mural painter.

Puy de Dôme ★ (pwi də dom) *n* **1** a department of central France in Auvergne region. Capital: Clermont-Ferrand. Pop.: 598 210 (1990). Area: 8016 sq. km (3094 sq. miles). **2** a mountain in central France, in the Auvergne Mountains: a volcanic plug. Height: 1485 m (4872 ft).

Puy de Sancy ★ (*French* pwi də sɑ̃si) *n* a mountain in S central France: highest peak of the Monts Dore. Height: 1886 m (6188 ft).

Pu-yi ★ ('puːˈjiː) *n* **Henry.** 1906–67, last emperor of China as Xuan-Tong (1908–12); emperor of the Japanese puppet state of Manchukuo as Kang-de (1934–45).

puzzle ('pʌzəl) *vb* **puzzles, puzzling, puzzled.** **1** to perplex or be perplexed. **2** (*intr; foll. by over*) to ponder about the cause of: *he puzzled over her absence.* **3** (*tr; usually foll. by out*) to solve by mental effort: *he puzzled out the meaning.* ♦ *n* **4** a person or thing that puzzles. **5** a problem that cannot be easily solved. **6** the state of being puzzled. **7** a toy, game, or question presenting a problem that requires skill or ingenuity for its solution. [C16: from ?]
▶ **'puzzlement** *n* ▶ **'puzzler** *n* ▶ **'puzzling** *adj* ▶ **'puzzlingly** *adv*

PVC *abbrev. for* polyvinyl chloride; a synthetic thermoplastic material made by polymerizing vinyl chloride. The flexible forms are used in insulation, shoes, etc. Rigid PVC is used for moulded articles.

PVS *abbrev. for:* **1** persistent vegetative state. **2** postviral syndrome.

Pvt. *Mil. abbrev. for* private.

PW *abbrev. for* policewoman.

PWA *abbrev. for* person with AIDS.

PWR *abbrev. for* pressurized-water reactor.

pyaemia or **pyemia** (paɪˈiːmɪə) *n* blood poisoning characterized by pus-forming microorganisms in the blood. [C19: from NL, from Gk *puon* pus + *haima* blood]
▶ **py'aemic** or **py'emic** *adj*

Pydna ★ ('pɪdnə) *n* a town in ancient Macedonia: site of a major Roman victory over the Macedonians, resulting in the downfall of their kingdom (168 B.C.).

pye-dog, pie-dog, or **pi-dog** ('paɪˌdɒg) *n* an ownerless half-wild Asian dog. [C19: Anglo-Indian, from Hindi *pāhī* outsider]

pyelitis (ˌpaɪəˈlaɪtɪs) *n* inflammation of the pelvis of the kidney. [C19: NL, from Gk *puelos* trough]
▶ **pye'litic** (ˌpaɪəˈlɪtɪk) *adj*

Pygmalion ★ (pɪgˈmeɪlɪən) *n Greek myth.* a king of Cyprus, who fell in love with the statue of a woman he had sculpted and which his prayers brought to life as Galatea.

pygmy or **pigmy** ('pɪgmɪ) *n, pl* **pygmies** or **pigmies.** **1** an abnormally undersized person. **2** something that is a very small example of its type. **3** a person of little importance or significance. **4** (*modifier*) very small. [C14: *pigmies* the Pygmies, from L *Pygmaeus* a Pygmy, from Gk *pugmaios* undersized, from *pugmē* fist]
▶ **pygmaean** or **pygmean** (pɪgˈmiːən) *adj*

Pygmy or **Pigmy** ('pɪgmɪ) *n, pl* **Pygmies** or **Pigmies.** a member of one of the dwarf peoples of Equatorial Africa, noted for their hunting and forest culture.

pyinkado (pjɪŋˈkɑːdəʊ) *n, pl* **pyinkados.** **1** a leguminous tree, native to India and Myanmar. **2** the heavy durable timber of this tree, used for construction. [C19: from Burmese]

pyjamas or *US* **pajamas** (pəˈdʒɑːməz) *pl n* **1** loose-fitting nightclothes comprising a jacket or top and trousers. **2** full loose-fitting ankle-length trousers worn by either sex in various Eastern countries. [C19: from Hindi, from Persian *pai* leg + *jāma* garment]

pyknic ('pɪknɪk) *adj* characterized by a broad squat fleshy physique with a large chest and abdomen. [C20: from Gk *puknos* thick]

pylon ('paɪlən) *n* **1** a large vertical steel tower-like structure supporting high-tension electrical cables. **2** a post or tower for guiding pilots or marking a turning point in a race. **3** a streamlined aircraft structure for attaching an engine pod, etc., to the main body of the aircraft. **4** a monumental gateway, such as one at the entrance to an ancient Egyptian temple. [C19: from Gk *pulōn* a gateway]

pylorus (paɪˈlɔːrəs) *n, pl* **pylori** (-raɪ). the small circular opening at the base of the stomach through which partially digested food passes to the duodenum. [C17: via LL from Gk *pulōrus* gatekeeper, from *pulē* gate + *ouros* guardian]

Pylos ★ ('paɪlɒs) *n* a port in SW Greece, in the SW Peloponnese: scene of a defeat of the Spartans by the

★ people and places

Athenians (425 B.C.) during the Peloponnesian War and of the Battle of Navarino (see **Navarino**). Italian name: **Navarino**. Modern Greek name: **Pílos**.

Pym ★ (pɪm) *n* **John. ?**1584–1643, leading English parliamentarian during the events leading to the Civil War: prominent in the impeachment of Buckingham (1626) and of Strafford and Laud (1640).

Pynchon ★ ('pɪntʃən) *n* **Thomas.** born 1937, US novelist, author of *V* (1963), *The Crying of Lot 49* (1967), *Gravity's Rainbow* (1973), and *Mason and Dixon* (1997).

pyo- *or before a vowel* **py-** *combining form.* denoting pus: *pyosis.* [from Gk *puon*]

Pyongyang *or* **P'yŏng-yang** ★ ('pjɒŋ'jæŋ) *n* the capital of North Korea, in the southwest on the Taedong River: industrial centre; university (1946). Pop.: 2 355 000 (1987 est.).

pyorrhoea *or esp. US* **pyorrhea** (ˌpaɪə'rɪə) *n* inflammation of the gums characterized by the discharge of pus and loosening of the teeth; periodontal disease.
   ▸ ˌpyor'rhoeal, ˌpyor'rhoeic *or esp. US* ˌpyor'rheal, ˌpyor-'rheic *adj*

pyracantha (ˌpaɪrə'kænθə) *n* any of a genus of shrubs with yellow, orange, or scarlet berries, widely cultivated for ornament. [C17: from Gk *purakantha*, from PYRO- + *akantha* thorn]

pyramid ('pɪrəmɪd) *n* **1** a huge masonry construction that has a square base and, as in the case of the ancient Egyptian royal tombs, four sloping triangular sides. **2** an object or structure resembling such a construction. **3** *Maths.* a solid having a polygonal base and triangular sides that meet in a common vertex. **4** *Crystallography.* a crystal form in which three planes intersect all three axes of the crystal. **5** *Finance.* a group of enterprises containing a series of holding companies structured so that the top holding company controls the entire group with a relatively small proportion of the total capital invested. **6** (*pl*) a game similar to billiards. ♦ *vb* **pyramids, pyramiding, pyramided. 7** to build up or be arranged in the form of a pyramid. **8** *Finance.* to form (companies) into a pyramid. [C16 (earlier *pyramis*): from L *pyramis*, from Gk *puramis*, prob. from Egyptian]
   ▸ **pyramidal** (pɪ'ræmɪd'l), ˌpyra'midical, *or* ˌpyra'midic *adj*
   ▸ **py'ramidally** *or* ˌpyra'midically *adv*

pyramid selling *n* a practice adopted by some manufacturers of advertising for distributors and selling them batches of goods. The first distributors then advertise for more distributors who are sold subdivisions of the original batches at an increased price. This process continues until the final distributors are left with a stock that is unsaleable except at a loss.

Pyramus and Thisbe ★ ('pɪrəməs; 'θɪzbɪ) *n* (in Greek legend) two lovers of Babylon: Pyramus, wrongly supposing Thisbe to be dead, killed himself and she, encountering him in his death throes, did the same.

pyre ('paɪə) *n* a pile of wood or other combustible material, esp. one for cremating a corpse. [C17: from L *pyra*, from Gk *pura* hearth, from *pur* fire]

Pyrenees ★ (ˌpɪrə'niːz) *pl n* a mountain range between France and Spain, extending from the Bay of Biscay to the Mediterranean. Highest peak: Pico de Aneto, 3404 m (11 168 ft).
   ▸ ˌPyre'nean *adj*

Pyrénées *or* **Pyrénées-Atlantiques** ★ (*French* pirenez-atlãtik) *n* a department of SW France in Aquitaine region. Capital: Pau. Pop.: 590 992 (1994 est.). Area: 7712 sq. km (3008 sq. miles). Former name: **Basses-Pyrénées.**

Pyrénées-Orientales ★ (*French* pirenezɔrjãtal) *n* a department of S France, in Languedoc-Roussillon region. Capital: Perpignan. Pop.: 375 018 (1994 est.). Area: 4144 sq. km (1616 sq. miles).

pyrethrin (paɪ'riːθrɪn) *n* either of two oily compounds found in pyrethrum and used as insecticides. [C19: from PYRETHRUM + -IN]

pyrethrum (paɪ'riːθrəm) *n* **1** any of several cultivated Eurasian chrysanthemums with white, pink, red, or purple flowers. **2** any insecticide prepared from the dried

flowers of any of these plants. [C16: via L from Gk *purethron* feverfew, prob. from *puretos* fever; see PYRETIC]

pyretic (paɪ'retɪk) *adj Pathology.* of, relating to, or characterized by fever. [C18: from NL *pyreticus*, from Gk *puretos* fever, from *pur* fire]

Pyrex ('paɪreks) *n Trademark.* **a** any of a variety of glasses that have low coefficients of expansion, making them suitable for heat-resistant glassware used in cookery and chemical apparatus. **b** (*as modifier*): *a Pyrex dish.*

pyrexia (paɪ'reksɪə) *n* a technical name for **fever.** [C18: from NL, from Gk *purexis*, from *puressein* to be feverish, from *pur* fire]
   ▸ py'rexial *or* py'rexic *adj*

pyridine ('pɪrɪˌdiːn) *n* a colourless hygroscopic liquid heterocyclic compound with a characteristic odour: used as a solvent and in preparing other organic chemicals. Formula: C_5H_5N. [C19: from PYRO- + -ID^2 + -INE^2]

pyridoxine (ˌpɪrɪ'dɒksiːn) *n Biochemistry.* a derivative of pyridine that is a precursor of the compounds pyridoxal and pyridoxamine. Also called: **vitamin B$_6$.**

pyrimidine (paɪ'rɪmɪˌdiːn) *n* **1** a liquid or crystalline organic compound with a penetrating odour. Formula: $C_4H_4N_2$. Also called: **pyrimidine base.** any of a number of similar compounds having a basic structure that is derived from pyrimidine, and which are constituents of nucleic acids. [C20: var. of PYRIDINE]

pyrite ('paɪraɪt) *n* a yellow mineral consisting of iron sulphide in cubic crystalline form. It occurs in igneous and metamorphic rocks and in veins, associated with various metals, and is used mainly in the manufacture of sulphuric acid and paper. Formula: FeS_2. Also called: **iron pyrites, pyrites.** [C16: from L *pyrites* flint, from Gk *puritēs* (*lithos*) fire(stone), from *pur* fire]
   ▸ **pyritic** (paɪ'rɪtɪk) *or* **py'ritous** *adj*

pyrites (paɪ'raɪtiːz; *in combination* 'paɪraɪts) *n, pl* **pyrites. 1** another name for **pyrite. 2** any of a number of other disulphides of metals, esp. of copper and tin.

pyro- *or before a vowel* **pyr-** *combining form.* **1** denoting fire or heat: *pyromania; pyrometer.* **2** *Chem.* denoting a new substance obtained by heating another: *pyroboric acid is obtained by heating boric acid.* **3** *Mineralogy.* **3a** having a property that changes upon the application of heat. **3b** having a flame-coloured appearance: *pyroxylin.* [from Gk *pur* fire]

pyroelectricity (ˌpaɪrəʊɪlek'trɪsɪtɪ) *n* the development of opposite charges at the ends of the axis of certain crystals as a result of a change in temperature.

pyrogallol (ˌpaɪrəʊ'gælɒl) *n* a crystalline soluble phenol with weakly acidic properties: used as a photographic developer and for absorbing oxygen in gas analysis. Formula: $C_6H_3(OH)_3$. [C20: from PYRO- + GALL(IC ACID) + -OL^1]

pyrogenic (ˌpaɪrəʊ'dʒenɪk) *or* **pyrogenous** (paɪ-'rɒdʒɪnəs) *adj* **1** produced by or producing heat. **2** *Pathology.* causing or resulting from fever. **3** *Geol.* less common words for **igneous.**

pyrography (paɪ'rɒgrəfɪ) *n* another name for **pokerwork.**

pyroligneous (ˌpaɪrəʊ'lɪgnɪəs) *or* **pyrolignic** *adj* (of a substance) produced by the action of heat on wood, esp. by destructive distillation.

pyrolysis (paɪ'rɒlɪsɪs) *n* **1** the application of heat to chemical compounds in order to cause decomposition. **2** such chemical decomposition.
   ▸ **pyrolytic** (ˌpaɪrəʊ'lɪtɪk) *adj*

pyromania (ˌpaɪrəʊ'meɪnɪə) *n Psychiatry.* the uncontrollable impulse and practice of setting things on fire.
   ▸ ˌpyro'mani,ac *n*

pyrometer (paɪ'rɒmɪtə) *n* an instrument for measuring high temperatures, esp. by measuring the brightness or total quantity of the radiation produced.
   ▸ **pyrometric** (ˌpaɪrəʊ'metrɪk) *or* ˌpyro'metrical *adj*
   ▸ ˌpyro'metrically *adv* ▸ py'rometry *n*

pyrope ('paɪrəʊp) *n* a deep yellowish-red garnet that consists of magnesium aluminium silicate and is used as a gemstone. [C14 (used loosely of a red gem; modern sense C19): from OF *pirope*, from L *pyrōpus* bronze, from Gk *purōpus* fiery-eyed]

pyrophoric (ˌpaɪrəʊˈfɒrɪk) *adj* **1** (of a chemical) igniting spontaneously on contact with air. **2** (of an alloy) producing sparks when struck or scraped: *lighter flints are made of pyrophoric alloy.* [C19: from NL *pyrophorus*, from Gk *purophoros* fire-bearing, from *pur* fire + *pherein* to bear]

pyrosis (paɪˈrəʊsɪs) *n Pathology.* a technical name for **heartburn.** [C18: from NL, from Gk: a burning, from *puroun* to burn, from *pur* fire]

pyrostat (ˈpaɪrəʊˌstæt) *n* **1** a device that activates an alarm or extinguisher in the event of a fire. **2** a thermostat for use at high temperatures.
▸ ˌpyroˈstatic *adj*

pyrotechnics (ˌpaɪrəʊˈtɛknɪks) *n* **1** (*functioning as sing*) the art of making fireworks. **2** (*functioning as sing or pl*) a firework display. **3** (*functioning as sing or pl*) brilliance of display, as in the performance of music.
▸ ˌpyroˈtechnic *or* ˌpyroˈtechnical *adj*

pyroxene (paɪˈrɒksiːn) *n* any of a large group of minerals consisting of the silicates of magnesium, iron, and calcium. They occur in basic igneous rocks. [C19: PYRO- + -*xene* from Gk *xenos* foreign, because mistakenly thought to have originated elsewhere when found in igneous rocks]

pyroxylin (paɪˈrɒksɪlɪn) *n* a yellow substance obtained by nitrating cellulose with a mixture of nitric and sulphuric acids; guncotton: used to make collodion, plastics, lacquers, and adhesives.

pyrrhic (ˈpɪrɪk) *Prosody.* ◆ *n* **1** a metrical foot of two short or unstressed syllables. ◆ *adj* **2** of or composed in pyrrhics. [C16: via L, from Gk *purrhikhē*, said to be after its inventor *Purrhikhos*]

Pyrrhic victory *n* a victory in which the victor's losses are as great as those of the defeated. Also called: **Cadmean victory.** [after PYRRHUS, who defeated the Romans at Asculum in 279 B.C. but suffered heavy losses]

Pyrrho ★ (ˈpɪrəʊ) *n* ?365–?275 B.C., Greek philosopher; founder of scepticism. He maintained that true wisdom and happiness lie in suspension of judgment, since certain knowledge is impossible to attain.
▸ ˈPyrrhonism *n* ▸ ˈPyrrhonist *n, adj*

Pyrrhus ★ (ˈpɪrəs) *n* **1** 319–272 B.C., king of Epirus (306–272). He invaded Italy but was ultimately defeated by the Romans (275 B.C.). **2** another name for **Neoptolemus.**
▸ ˈPyrrhic *adj*

pyruvic acid (paɪˈruːvɪk) *n* a liquid formed during the metabolism of proteins and carbohydrates, helping to release energy to the body. [C19: from PYRO- + L *ūva* grape]

Pythagoras ★ (paɪˈθæɡərəs) *n* ?580–?500 B.C., Greek philosopher and mathematician. He founded a religious brotherhood, which followed a life of strict asceticism and greatly influenced the development of mathematics and its application to music and astronomy.

Pythagoras' theorem *n* the theorem that in a right-angled triangle the square of the length of the hypotenuse equals the sum of the squares of the other two sides.

Pythagorean (paɪˌθæɡəˈriːən) *adj* **1** of or relating to Pythagoras. ◆ *n* **2** a follower of Pythagoras.

Pytheas ★ (ˈpɪθɪəs) *n* 4th century B.C., Greek navigator. He was the first Greek to visit and describe the coasts of Spain, France, and the British Isles and may have reached Iceland.

Pythia ★ (ˈpɪθɪə) *n Greek myth.* the priestess of Apollo at Delphi, who transmitted the oracles.

Pythian (ˈpɪθɪən) *adj also* **Pythic. 1** of or relating to Delphi or its oracle. ◆ *n* **2** the priestess of Apollo at the oracle of Delphi. [C16: via L *Pȳthius* from Gk *Puthios* of Delphi]

python (ˈpaɪθən) *n* any of a family of large non-venomous snakes of Africa, S Asia, and Australia. They can reach a length of more than 20 feet and kill their prey by constriction. [C19: NL, after PYTHON]
▸ **pythonic** (paɪˈθɒnɪk) *adj*

Python ★ (ˈpaɪθən) *n Greek myth.* a dragon, killed by Apollo at Delphi.

pythoness (ˈpaɪθənɛs) *n* a woman, such as Apollo's priestess at Delphi, believed to be possessed by an oracular spirit. [C14 *phitonesse*, ult. from Gk *Puthōn* PYTHON]

pyuria (paɪˈjʊərɪə) *n Pathol.* any condition characterized by the presence of pus in the urine. [C19: from NL, from Gk *puon* pus + *ouron* urine]

pyx (pɪks) *n* **1** Also called: **pyx chest.** the chest in which coins from the British mint are placed to be tested for weight, etc. **2** *Christianity.* any receptacle in which the Eucharistic Host is kept. [C14: from L *pyxis* small box, from Gk, from *puxos* box tree]

pyxidium (pɪkˈsɪdɪəm) *or* **pyxis** (ˈpɪksɪs) *n, pl* **pyxidia** (-ɪə) *or* **pyxides** (ˈpɪksɪˌdiːz). the dry fruit of such plants as the plantain: a capsule whose upper part falls off when mature so that the seeds are released. [C19: via NL from Gk *puxidion* a little box, from *puxis* box]

pyxis (ˈpɪksɪs) *n, pl* **pyxides** (ˈpɪksɪˌdiːz). **1** a small box used by the ancient Greeks and Romans to hold medicines, etc. **2** another name for **pyxidium.** [C14: via L from Gk: box]

★ people and places

Qq

q *or* **Q** (kju:) *n, pl* **q's, Q's,** *or* **Qs. 1** the 17th letter of the English alphabet. **2** a speech sound represented by this letter.

q *symbol for* quintal.

Q *symbol for:* **1** *Physics.* heat. **2** *Chess.* queen. **3** question.

q. *abbrev. for:* **1** quart. **2** quarter. **3** quarterly. **4** query. **5** question. **6** quire.

Q. *abbrev. for:* **1** quartermaster. **2** (*pl* **Qq., qq.**) Also: **q.** quarto. **3** Quebec. **4** Queen. **5** question. **6** *Electronics.* Q factor.

Qabis ★ ('kɑ:bɪs) *n* the Arabic name for **Gabès.**

Qaboos bin Said ★ (kə'buːs bɪn 'saɪd) *n* born 1940, sultan of Oman from 1970.

Qaddafi ★ (gə'dɑːfɪ) *n* Moamar al ('məʊə,mɑː: ,æl). See (Moamar al) **Gaddafi.**

qadi ('kɑːdɪ, 'keɪdɪ) *n, pl* **qadis.** a variant spelling of **cadi.**

Qairwan ★ (kaɪə'wɑːn) *n* a variant of **Kairouan.**

QANTAS ('kwɒntəs) *n* the national airline of Australia. [C20: from *Q(ueensland) a(nd) N(orthern) T(erritory) A(erial) S(ervices) Ltd.)*]

Qaraghandy ★ (*Kazakh* karaɣan'dɪ) *n* a variant transliteration of the Kazakh name for **Karaganda.**

QARANC *abbrev. for* Queen Alexandra's Royal Army Nursing Corps.

Qatar *or* **Katar** ★ (kæ'tɑː) *n* a state in E Arabia, occupying a peninsula in the Persian Gulf: under Persian rule until the 19th century; became a British protectorate in 1916; declared independence in 1971; exports petroleum and natural gas. Official language: Arabic. Official religion: (Sunni) Muslim. Currency: riyal. Capital: Doha. Pop.: 561 000 (1997). Area: about 11 000 sq. km (4250 sq. miles).
▸ **Qa'tari** *or* **Ka'tari** *adj, n*

Qattara Depression ★ (kə'tɑːrə) *n* an arid basin in the Sahara, in NW Egypt, impassable to vehicles. Area: about 18 000 sq. km (7000 sq. miles). Lowest point: 133 m (435 ft) below sea level.

qawwali (kə'vɑːlɪ) *n* an Islamic religious song, esp. in Asia.

QB *abbrev. for* Queen's Bench.

QC *abbrev. for* Queen's Counsel.

QED *abbrev. for:* **1** quantum electrodynamics. **2** quod erat demonstrandum. [L: which was to be shown or proved]

Qeshm ('keʃəm) *or* **Qishm** ★ *n* **1** the largest island in the Persian Gulf: part of Iran. Area: 1336 sq. km (516 sq. miles). **2** the chief town of this island.

Q factor *n* **1** a measure of the relationship between stored energy and rate of energy dissipation in certain electrical components, devices, etc. **2** Also called: **Q value.** the heat released in a nuclear reaction. ◆ Symbol: Q [C20: short for *quality factor*]

Q fever *n* an acute disease characterized by fever and pneumonia, transmitted to man by a rickettsia. [C20: from *q(uery) fever* (the cause being orig. unknown)]

qi (tʃiː) *n* a variant spelling of **chi².**

Qingdao ('tʃɪŋ'daʊ), **Tsingtao,** *or* **Chingtao** ★ *n* a port in E China, in E Shandong province on Jiazhou Bay, developed as a naval base and fort in 1891. Shandong university (1926). Pop.: 2 060 000 (1991 est.).

Qinghai, Tsinghai, *or* **Chinghai** ★ ('tʃɪŋ'haɪ) *n* **1** a province of NW China: consists largely of mountains and high plateaus. Capital: Xining. Pop.: 4 740 000 (1995 est.). Area: 721 000 sq. km (278 400 sq. miles). **2** the Pinyin transliteration of the Chinese name for **Koko Nor.**

Qiqihar, Chichihaerh, Ch'i-ch'i-haerh, *or* **Tsitsihar** ★ ('tʃiː,tʃiː'hɑː) *n* a city in NE China, in

Heilongjiang province on the Nonni River. Pop.: 1 380 000 (1991 est.).

Qishm ★ ('kɪʃəm) *n* a variant of **Qeshm.**

Qld *or* **QLD** *abbrev. for* Queensland.

QM *abbrev. for* Quartermaster.

QMG *abbrev. for* Quartermaster General.

QMV *abbrev. for* Qualified Majority Voting.

Qom (kɒm), **Qum,** *or* **Kum** ★ *n* a city in NW central Iran: a place of pilgrimage for Shiite Muslims. Pop.: 681 253 (1991).

qr. *pl* **qrs.** *abbrev. for:* **1** quarter. **2** quarterly. **3** quire.

Q-ship *n* a merchant ship with concealed guns, used to decoy enemy ships. [C20: from Q short for QUERY]

QSM (in New Zealand) *abbrev. for* Queen's Service Medal.

QSO *abbrev. for:* **1** quasi-stellar object. **2** (in New Zealand) Queen's Service Order.

qt *pl* **qt** *or* **qts** *abbrev. for* quart.

q.t. *Inf.* **1** *abbrev. for* quiet. **2 on the q.t.** secretly.

qua (kweɪ, kwɑː) *prep* in the capacity of; by virtue of being. [C17: from L, ablative sing (fem) of *qui* who]

quack¹ (kwæk) *vb* (*intr*) **1** (of a duck) to utter a harsh guttural sound. **2** to make a noise like a duck. ◆ *n* **3** the sound made by a duck. [C17: imit.]

quack² (kwæk) *n* **1a** an unqualified person who claims medical knowledge or other skills. **1b** (*as modifier*): *a quack doctor.* **2** *Brit., Austral., & NZ inf.* a doctor; physician or surgeon. ◆ *vb* **3** (*intr*) to act in the manner of a quack. [C17: short for QUACKSALVER]
▸ **'quackish** *adj*

quackery ('kwækərɪ) *n, pl* **quackeries.** the activities or methods of a quack.

quack grass *n* another name for **couch grass.**

quacksalver ('kwæk,sælvə) *n* an archaic word for **quack².** [C16: from Du., from *quack,* apparently: to hawk + *salf* SALVE]

quad¹ (kwɒd) *n* short for **quadrangle.**

quad² (kwɒd) *n* *Printing.* a block of type metal used for spacing. [C19: shortened from QUADRAT]

quad³ (kwɒd) *n* short for **quadruplet.**

quad⁴ (kwɒd) *n, adj Inf.* short for **quadraphonics** *or* **quadraphonic.**

quad bike *or* **quad** *n* a vehicle like a motorcycle, with four large wheels, designed for agricultural, sporting, and other off-road uses.

Quadragesima (,kwɒdrə'dʒesɪmə) *n* the first Sunday in Lent. Also called: **Quadragesima Sunday.** [C16: from Med. L *quadrāgēsima dies* the fortieth day]

Quadragesimal (,kwɒdrə'dʒesɪməl) *adj* of, relating to, or characteristic of Lent.

quadrangle ('kwɒd,ræŋɡ°l) *n* **1** *Geom.* a plane figure consisting of four points connected by four lines. **2** a rectangular courtyard, esp. one having buildings on all four sides. **3** the building surrounding such a courtyard. [C15: from LL *quadrangulum* figure having four corners]
▸ **quadrangular** (kwɒ'dræŋɡjulə) *adj*

quadrant ('kwɒdrənt) *n* **1** *Geom.* **1a** a quarter of the circumference of a circle. **1b** the area enclosed by two perpendicular radii of a circle. **1c** any of the four sections into which a plane is divided by two coordinate axes. **2** a piece of a mechanism in the form of a quarter circle. **3** an instrument formerly used in astronomy and navigation for measuring the altitudes of stars. [C14: from L *quadrāns* a quarter]
▸ **quadrantal** (kwɒ'drænt°l) *adj*

quadraphonics *or* **quadrophonics** (,kwɒdrə'fɒnɪks) *n* (*functioning as sing*) a system of sound recording and re-

quadrat ('kwɒdrət) n **1** Ecology. an area of vegetation selected at random for study. **2** Printing. an archaic name for quad². [C14 (meaning "a square"): var. of QUADRATE]

quadrate n ('kwɒdrɪt, -ˌdreɪt). **1** a cube, square, or a square or cubelike object. **2** one of a pair of bones of the upper jaw of fishes, amphibians, reptiles, and birds. ♦ adj ('kwɒdrɪt, -ˌdreɪt). **3** of or relating to this bone. **4** square or rectangular. ♦ vb (kwɒ'dreɪt), **quadrates, quadrating, quadrated. 5** (tr) to make square or rectangular. **6** (often foll. by with) to conform or cause to conform. [C14: from L quadrāre to make square]

quadratic (kwɒ'drætɪk) Maths. ♦ n **1** Also called: **quadratic equation**. an equation containing one or more terms in which the variable is raised to the power of two, but to no higher power. ♦ adj **2** of or relating to the second power.

quadrature ('kwɒdrətʃə) n **1** Maths. the process of determining a square having an area equal to that of a given figure or surface. **2** the process of making square or dividing into squares. **3** Astron. a configuration in which two celestial bodies form an angle of 90° with a third body. **4** Electronics. the relationship between two waves that are 90° out of phase.

quadrella (kwɒ'drelə) n Austral. a form of betting in which the punter must select the winner of four specified races.

quadrennial (kwɒ'drenɪəl) adj **1** occurring every four years. **2** lasting four years. ♦ n **3** a period of four years. ▶ quad'rennially adv

quadrennium (kwɒ'drenɪəm) n, pl **quadrenniums** or **quadrennia** (-nɪə). a period of four years. [C17: from L quadriennium, from QUADRI- + annus year]

quadri- or before a vowel **quadr-** combining form. four: quadrilateral. [from L, from quattuor four]

quadric ('kwɒdrɪk) Maths. ♦ adj **1** having or characterized by an equation of the second degree. **2** of the second degree. ♦ n **3** a quadric curve, surface, or function.

quadriceps ('kwɒdrɪˌseps) n, pl **quadricepses** (-ˌsepsɪz) or **quadriceps**. Anat. a large four-part muscle of the front of the thigh, which extends the leg. [C19: NL, from QUADRI- + -ceps as in BICEPS]

quadrifid ('kwɒdrɪfɪd) adj Bot. divided into four lobes or other parts: quadrifid leaves.

quadrilateral (ˌkwɒdrɪ'lætərəl) adj **1** having or formed by four sides. ♦ n **2** Also called: **tetragon**. a polygon having four sides.

quadrille¹ (kwɒ'drɪl) n **1** a square dance for four couples. **2** a piece of music for such a dance. [C18: via F from Sp. cuadrilla, dim. of cuadro square, from L quadra]

quadrille² (kwɒ'drɪl, kwə-) n an old card game for four players. [C18: from F, from Sp. cuartillo, from cuarto fourth, from L quartus, infl. by QUADRILLE¹]

quadrillion (kwɒ'drɪljən) n, pl **quadrillions** or **quadrillion**. **1** (in Britain, France, and Germany) the number represented as one followed by 24 zeros (10²⁴). US and Canad. word: **septillion**. **2** (in the US and Canada) the number represented as one followed by 15 zeros (10¹⁵). ♦ determiner **3** amounting to this number: a quadrillion atoms. [C17: from F quadrillon, from QUADRI- + -illion, on the model of million] ▶ quad'rillionth adj

quadrinomial (ˌkwɒdrɪ'nəumɪəl) n an algebraic expression containing four terms.

quadriplegia (ˌkwɒdrɪ'pliːdʒɪə) n paralysis of all four limbs. Also called: **tetraplegia**. [C20: from QUADRI- + Gk plēssein to strike] ▶ quadriplegic (ˌkwɒdrɪ'pliːdʒɪk) adj

quadrivalent (ˌkwɒdrɪ'veɪlənt) adj Chem. another word for **tetravalent**. ▶ ˌquadri'valency or ˌquadri'valence n

quadrivium (kwɒ'drɪvɪəm) n, pl **quadrivia** (-ɪə). (in medieval learning) a course consisting of arithmetic, geometry, astronomy, and music. [from Med. L, from L: crossroads, from QUADRI- + via way]

quadroon (kwɒ'druːn) n a person who is one-quarter Black. [C18: from Sp. cuarterón, from cuarto quarter, from L quartus]

quadrumanous (kwɒ'druːmənəs) adj (of monkeys and apes) having all four feet specialized for use as hands. [C18: from NL quadrumanus, from QUADRI- + L manus hand]

quadruped ('kwɒdruˌped) n **1** an animal, esp. a mammal, that has all four limbs specialized for walking. ♦ adj **2** having four feet. [C17: from L quadrupēs, from quadru- (see QUADRI-) + pēs foot] ▶ quadrupedal (kwɒ'druːpɪd'l) adj

quadruple ('kwɒdrup'l, kwɒ'druːp'l) vb **quadruples, quadrupling, quadrupled. 1** to multiply by four or increase fourfold. ♦ adj **2** four times as much or as many; fourfold. **3** consisting of four parts. **4** Music. having four beats in each bar. ♦ n **5** a quantity or number four times as great as another. [C16: via OF from L quadruplus, from quadru- (see QUADRI-) + -plus -fold] ▶ 'quadruply adv

quadruplet ('kwɒdruplɪt, kwɒ'druːplɪt) n **1** one of four offspring born at one birth. **2** a group of four similar things. **3** Music. a group of four notes to be played in a time value of three.

quadruplicate adj (kwɒ'druːplɪkɪt). **1** fourfold or quadruple. ♦ vb (kwɒ'druːplɪˌkeɪt), **quadruplicates, quadruplicating, quadruplicated. 2** to multiply or be multiplied by four. ♦ n (kwɒ'druːplɪkɪt). **3** a group or set of four things. [C17: from L quadruplicāre to increase fourfold]

quaestor ('kwiːstə) or US (sometimes) **questor** ('kwestə) n any of several magistrates of ancient Rome, usually a financial administrator. [C14: from L, from quaerere to inquire] ▶ quaestorial (kwe'stɔːrɪəl) adj

quaff (kwɒf) vb to drink heartily or in one draught. [C16: ? imit.; cf. MLow G quassen to eat or drink excessively] ▶ 'quaffer n

quag (kwæg) n a quagmire. [C16: ? rel. to QUAKE]

quagga ('kwægə) n, pl **quaggas** or **quagga**. a recently extinct member of the horse family of southern Africa: it had zebra-like stripes on the head and shoulders. [C18: from obs. Afrik., from Khoikhoi qǔagga]

quaggy ('kwægɪ) adj **quaggier, quaggiest. 1** resembling a quagmire; boggy. **2** soft or flabby.

quagmire ('kwæɡˌmaɪə) n **1** a soft wet area of land that gives way under the feet; bog. **2** an awkward, complex, or embarrassing situation. [C16: from QUAG + MIRE]

quahog ('kwɑːˌhɒg) n an edible clam native to the Atlantic coast of North America, having a large heavy rounded shell. [C18: from Amerind, short for poquauhock, from pohkeni dark + hogki shell]

quaich or **quaigh** (kweɪx) n Scot. a small shallow drinking cup, usually with two handles. [from Gaelic cuach cup]

Quai d'Orsay ★ (French ke dɔrsɛ) n the quay along the S bank of the Seine, Paris, where the French foreign office is situated.

quail¹ (kweɪl) n, pl **quails** or **quail**. any of various small Old World game birds having rounded bodies and small tails. [C14: from OF quaille, from Med. L quaccula, prob. imit.]

quail² (kweɪl) vb (intr) to shrink back with fear; cower. [C15: ?from OF quailler, from L coāgulāre to curdle]

quaint (kweɪnt) adj **1** attractively unusual, esp. in an old-fashioned style. **2** odd or inappropriate. [C13 (in the sense: clever): from OF cointe, from L cognitus known, from cognoscere to ascertain] ▶ 'quaintly adv ▶ 'quaintness n

quair (kweə) n Scot. a book. [var. of QUIRE¹]

quake (kweɪk) vb **quakes, quaking, quaked. (intr) 1** to shake or tremble with or as with fear. **2** to convulse or quiver, as from instability. ♦ n **3** a quaking. **4** Inf. an earthquake. [OE cwacian]

Quaker ('kweɪkə) n **1** a member of the Religious Society of Friends, a Christian sect founded by George Fox about 1650. Quakers reject sacraments, ritual, and formal min-

istry, and have promoted many causes for social reform.
◆ *adj* **2** of the Religious Society of Friends or its beliefs or practices. [C17: orig. a derog. nickname]
▶ **'Quakeress** *fem n* ▶ **'Quakerish** *adj* ▶ **'Quakerism** *n*

quaking ('kweɪkɪŋ) *adj* unstable or unsafe to walk on, as a bog or quicksand.

quaking grass *n* any of various grasses having delicate branches that shake in the wind.

quaky ('kweɪkɪ) *adj* **quakier, quakiest.** inclined to quake; shaky.
▶ **'quakiness** *n*

qualification (ˌkwɒlɪfɪˈkeɪʃən) *n* **1** an official record of achievement awarded on the successful completion of a course of training or passing of an examination. **2** an ability, quality, or attribute, esp. one that fits a person to perform a particular job or task. **3** a condition that modifies or limits; restriction. **4** a qualifying or being qualified.

qualified ('kwɒlɪˌfaɪd) *adj* **1** having the abilities, qualities, attributes, etc., necessary to perform a particular job or task. **2** limited, modified, or restricted; not absolute.

Qualified Majority Voting *n* a voting system, used by the EU Council of Ministers, by which resolutions concerning certain areas of policy may be passed without unanimity. Abbrev.: **QMV.**

qualify ('kwɒlɪˌfaɪ) *vb* **qualifies, qualifying, qualified. 1** to provide or be provided with the abilities or attributes necessary for a task, office, duty, etc.: *his degree qualifies him for the job.* **2** (*tr*) to make less strong, harsh, or violent; moderate or restrict. **3** (*tr*) to modify or change the strength or flavour of. **4** (*tr*) *Grammar.* another word for **modify. 5** (*tr*) to attribute a quality to; characterize. **6** (*intr*) to progress to the final stages of a competition, as by winning preliminary contests. [C16: from OF *qualifier*, from Med. L *quālificāre* to characterize, from L *quālis* of what kind + *facere* to make]
▶ **'quali,fiable** *adj* ▶ **'quali,fier** *n*

qualitative ('kwɒlɪtətɪv) *adj* involving or relating to distinctions based on quality or qualities.
▶ **'qualitatively** *adv*

qualitative analysis *n* See **analysis** (sense 4).

quality ('kwɒlɪtɪ) *n, pl* **qualities. 1** a distinguishing characteristic or attribute. **2** the basic character or nature of something. **3** a feature of personality. **4** degree or standard of excellence, esp. a high standard. **5** (formerly) high social status or the distinction associated with it. **6** musical tone colour; timbre. **7** *Logic.* the characteristic of a proposition that makes it affirmative or negative. **8** *Phonetics.* the distinctive character of a vowel, determined by the configuration of the mouth, tongue, etc. **9** (*modifier*) having or showing excellence or superiority: *a quality product.* [C13: from OF *qualité*, from L *quālitās* state, from *quālis* of what sort]

quality control *n* control of the quality of a manufactured product, usually by statistical sampling techniques.

quality time *n* a short period during the day in which a person gives the whole of his or her attention to some matter other than work, esp. family relationships.

qualm (kwɑːm) *n* **1** a sudden feeling of sickness or nausea. **2** a pang of doubt, esp. concerning moral conduct; scruple. **3** a sudden sensation of misgiving. [OE *cwealm* death or plague]
▶ **'qualmish** *adj*

quandary ('kwɒndrɪ) *n, pl* **quandaries.** a difficult situation; predicament. [C16: from ?; ? rel. to L *quandō* when]

quandong, quandang ('kwɒnˌdɒŋ), *or* **quantong** ('kwɒnˌtɒŋ) *n* **1** Also called: **native peach. 1a** a small Australian tree. **1b** the edible fruit or nut of this tree. **2** *Austral. sl.* a sponger or parasite. **3 silver quandong. 3a** an Australian tree. **3b** its timber. [from Abor.]

quango ('kwæŋɡəʊ) *n, pl* **quangos.** a semipublic government-financed administrative body whose members are appointed by the government. [C20: *qu(asi)-a(utonomous) n(on) g(overnmental) o(rganization)*]

quangocracy (kwæŋˈɡɒkrəsɪ) *n, pl* **quangocracies. 1** the

control or influence ascribed to quangos. **2** quangos collectively.

quant[1] (kwɒnt) *n* **1** a long pole for propelling a boat, esp. a punt. ◆ *vb* **2** to propel (a boat) with a quant. [C15: prob. from L *contus* pole, from Gk *kontos*]

quant[2] (kwɒnt) *n Inf.* a highly paid analyst with a degree in a quantitative science, employed by a financial house to predict price movements of securities, commodities, etc. [C20: from QUANTITATIVE]

Quant ★ (kwɒnt) *n* **Mary.** born 1934, British fashion designer.

quanta ('kwɒntə) *n* the plural of **quantum.**

quantic ('kwɒntɪk) *n* a homogeneous function of two or more variables in a rational and integral form. [C19: from L *quantus* how great]

quantifier ('kwɒntɪˌfaɪə) *n* **1** *Logic.* a symbol indicating the quantity of a term: *the existential quantifier corresponds to the words "there is something, such that".* **2** *Grammar.* a word or phrase, such as *some, all,* or *no,* expressing quantity.

quantify ('kwɒntɪˌfaɪ) *vb* **quantifies, quantifying, quantified.** (*tr*) **1** to discover or express the quantity of. **2** *Logic.* to specify the quantity of (a term) by using a quantifier, such as *all, some,* or *no.* [C19: from Med. L *quantificāre,* from L *quantus* how much + *facere* to make]
▶ **'quantifiable** *adj* ▶ ˌquantifiˈcation *n*

quantitative ('kwɒntɪtətɪv) *or* **quantitive** *adj* **1** involving or relating to considerations of amount or size. **2** capable of being measured. **3** *Prosody.* of a metrical system that is based on the length of syllables.
▶ **'quantitatively** *or* **'quantitively** *adv*

quantitative analysis *n* See **analysis** (sense 4).

quantity ('kwɒntɪtɪ) *n, pl* **quantities. 1a** a specified or definite amount, number, etc. **1b** (*as modifier*): *a quantity estimate.* **2** the aspect of anything that can be measured, weighed, counted, etc. **3 unknown quantity.** a person or thing whose action, effort, etc., is unknown or unpredictable. **4** a large amount. **5** *Maths.* an entity having a magnitude that may be denoted by a numerical expression. **6** *Physics.* a specified magnitude or amount. **7** *Logic.* the characteristic of a proposition that makes it universal or particular. **8** *Prosody.* the relative duration of a syllable or the vowel in it. [C14: from OF *quantité,* from L *quantitās* amount, from *quantus* how much]

USAGE NOTE The use of a plural noun after *quantity of* as in *a large quantity of bananas* was formerly considered incorrect, but is now acceptable.

quantity surveyor *n* a person who estimates the cost of the materials and labour necessary for a construction job.

quantize *or* **quantise** ('kwɒntaɪz) *vb* **quantizes, quantizing, quantized** *or* **quantises, quantising, quantised.** (*tr*) **1** *Physics.* to restrict (a physical quantity) to one of a set of fixed values. **2** *Maths.* to limit to values that are multiples of a basic unit.
▶ ˌquantiˈzation *or* ˌquantiˈsation *n*

quantum ('kwɒntəm) *n, pl* **quanta. 1** *Physics.* **1a** the smallest quantity of some physical property that a system can possess according to the quantum theory. **1b** a particle with such a unit of energy. **2** amount or quantity, esp. a specific amount. ◆ *adj* **3** of or designating a major breakthrough or sudden advance: *a quantum leap forward.* [C17: from L *quantus* (adj) how much]

quantum electrodynamics *n Physics.* the study of electromagnetic radiation and its interaction with charged particles in terms of quantum theory. Abbrev.: **QED.**

quantum mechanics *n* (*functioning as sing*) the branch of mechanics, based on the quantum theory, used for interpreting the behaviour of elementary particles and atoms, which do not obey Newtonian mechanics.

quantum meruit *Latin.* ('meruːɪt) as much as he has earned.

quantum number *n Physics.* one of a set of integers or half-integers characterizing the energy states of a particle or system of particles.

quantum theory *n* a theory concerning the behaviour of physical systems based on the idea that they can only possess certain properties, such as energy and angular momentum, in discrete amounts (quanta).

quaquaversal (ˌkwɑːkwəˈvɜːsəl) *adj Geol.* directed outwards in all directions from a common centre. [C18: from L *quāquā* in every direction + *versus* towards]

quarantine (ˈkwɒrənˌtiːn) *n* **1** a period of isolation or detention, esp. of persons or animals arriving from abroad, to prevent the spread of disease. **2** the place where such detention is enforced. **3** any period or state of enforced isolation. ◆ *vb* **quarantines, quarantining, quarantined. 4** (*tr*) to isolate in or as if in quarantine. [C17: from It. *quarantina* period of forty days, from *quaranta* forty, from L *quadrāgintā*]

quarantine flag *n Naut.* the yellow signal flag for the letter Q, flown alone from a vessel to indicate that there is no disease aboard or, with a second signal flag, to indicate that there is disease aboard. Also called: **yellow jack.**

quark[1] (kwɑːk) *n Physics.* any of a set of six elementary particles that, together with their antiparticles, are thought to be fundamental units of all baryons and mesons but unable to exist in isolation. [C20: coined by James JOYCE in the novel *Finnegans Wake*, and given special application in physics]

quark[2] (kwɑːk) *n* a type of low-fat soft cheese. [from G]

Quarles ★ (kwɔːlz, kwɑːlz) *n* Francis. 1592–1644, English poet.

quarrel[1] (ˈkwɒrəl) *n* **1** an angry disagreement; argument. **2** a cause of dispute; grievance. ◆ *vb* **quarrels, quarrelling, quarrelled** *or US* **quarrels, quarreling, quarreled.** (*intr*; often foll. by *with*) **3** to engage in a disagreement or dispute; argue. **4** to find fault; complain. [C14: from OF *querele*, from L *querēlla* complaint, from *querī* to complain] ▸ ˈ**quarreller** *or US* ˈ**quarreler** *n*

quarrel[2] (ˈkwɒrəl) *n* **1** an arrow having a four-edged head, fired from a crossbow. **2** a small square or diamond-shaped pane of glass. [C13: from OF *quarrel* pane, from Med. L *quadrellus*, dim. of L *quadrus* square]

quarrelsome (ˈkwɒrəlsəm) *adj* inclined to quarrel or disagree; belligerent.

quarrian *or* **quarrion** (ˈkwɒrɪən) *n* a cockatiel of inland Australia that feeds on seeds and grasses. [C20: prob. from Abor.]

quarry[1] (ˈkwɒrɪ) *n, pl* **quarries. 1** an open surface excavation for the extraction of building stone, slate, marble, etc. **2** a copious source, esp. of information. ◆ *vb* **quarries, quarrying, quarried. 3** to extract (stone, slate, etc.) from or as if from a quarry. **4** (*tr*) to excavate a quarry in. **5** to obtain (something) diligently and laboriously. [C15: from OF *quarriere*, from *quarre* (unattested) square-shaped stone, from L *quadrāre* to make square]

quarry[2] (ˈkwɒrɪ) *n, pl* **quarries. 1** an animal, etc., that is hunted, esp. by other animals; prey. **2** anything pursued. [C14: from *quire* entrails offered to the hounds, from OF *cuirée* what is placed on the hide, from *cuir* hide, from L *corium* leather; prob. also infl. by OF *coree* entrails, from L *cor* heart]

quarryman (ˈkwɒrɪmən) *n, pl* **quarrymen.** a man who works in or manages a quarry.

quarry tile *n* an unglazed floor tile.

quart (kwɔːt) *n* **1** a unit of liquid measure equal to a quarter of a gallon or two pints. 1 US quart (0.946 litre) is equal to 0.8326 UK quart. 1 UK quart (1.136 litres) is equal to 1.2009 US quarts. **2** a unit of dry measure equal to 2 pints or one eighth of a peck. [C14: from OF *quarte*, from L *quartus* fourth]

quartan (ˈkwɔːtᵊn) *adj* (of a fever) occurring every third day. [C13: from L *febris quartāna* fever occurring every fourth day, reckoned inclusively]

quarte (kɑːt) *n* the fourth of eight basic positions from which a parry or attack can be made in fencing. [C18: F from OF *quarte*, from L *quartus* fourth]

quarter (ˈkwɔːtə) *n* **1** one of four equal parts of an object,

quantity, etc. **2** the fraction equal to one divided by four (¼). **3** *US, Canad., etc.* a 25-cent piece. **4** a unit of weight equal to a quarter of a hundredweight. 1 US quarter is equal to 25 pounds; 1 Brit. quarter is equal to 28 pounds. **5** short for **quarter-hour. 6** a fourth part of a year; three months. **7** *Astron.* **7a** one fourth of the moon's period of revolution around the earth. **7b** either of two phases of the moon when half of the lighted surface is visible. **8** *Inf.* a unit of weight equal to a quarter of a pound or 4 ounces. **9** *Brit.* a unit of capacity for grain, etc., usually equal to 8 UK bushels. **10** *Sport.* one of the four periods into which certain games are divided. **11** *Naut.* the part of a vessel's side towards the stern. **12** a region or district of a town or city: *the Spanish quarter.* **13** a region, direction, or point of the compass. **14** (*sometimes pl*) an unspecified person or group of people: *to get word from the highest quarter.* **15** mercy or pity, as shown to a defeated opponent (esp. in **ask for** *or* **give quarter**). **16** any of the four limbs, including the adjacent parts, of a quadruped or bird. **17** *Heraldry.* one of four quadrants into which a shield may be divided. ◆ *vb* **18** (*tr*) to divide into four equal parts. **19** (*tr*) to divide into any number of parts. **20** (*tr*) (esp. formerly) to dismember (a human body). **21** to billet or be billeted in lodgings, esp. (of military personnel) in civilian lodgings. **22** (*intr*) (of hounds) to range over an area of ground in search of game or the scent of quarry. **23** (*intr*) *Naut.* (of the wind) to blow onto a vessel's quarter. **24** (*tr*) *Heraldry.* **24a** to divide (a shield) into four separate bearings. **24b** to place (one set of arms) in diagonally opposite quarters to another. ◆ *adj* **25** being or consisting of one of four equal parts. ◆ See also **quarters.** [C13: from OF *quartier*, from L *quartārius* a fourth part, from *quartus* fourth]

quarterback (ˈkwɔːtəˌbæk) *n* a player in American football who directs attacking play.

quarter-bound *adj* (of a book) having a binding consisting of two types of material, the better type being used on the spine.

quarter day *n* any of four days in the year when certain payments become due. In England, Wales, and Northern Ireland these are Lady Day, Midsummer's Day, Michaelmas, and Christmas. In Scotland they are Candlemas, Whit Sunday, Lammas, and Martinmas.

quarterdeck (ˈkwɔːtəˌdɛk) *n Naut.* the after part of the upper deck of a ship, traditionally the deck for official or ceremonial use.

quartered (ˈkwɔːtəd) *adj* **1** *Heraldry.* (of a shield) divided into four sections, each having contrasting arms or having two sets of arms, each repeated in diagonally opposite corners. **2** (of a log) sawn into four equal parts along two diameters at right angles to each other.

quarterfinal (ˌkwɔːtəˈfaɪnᵊl) *n* the round before the semifinal in a competition.

quarter-hour *n* **1** a period of 15 minutes. **2** either of the points on a timepiece that mark 15 minutes before or after the hour.

quartering (ˈkwɔːtərɪŋ) *n* **1** *Mil.* the allocation of accommodation to service personnel. **2** *Heraldry.* **2a** the marshalling of several coats of arms on one shield, usually representing intermarriages. **2b** any coat of arms marshalled in this way.

quarterlight (ˈkwɔːtəˌlaɪt) *n Brit.* a small pivoted window in the door of a car for ventilation.

quarterly (ˈkwɔːtəlɪ) *adj* **1** occurring, done, paid, etc., at intervals of three months. **2** of, relating to, or consisting of a quarter. ◆ *n, pl* **quarterlies. 3** a periodical issued every three months. ◆ *adv* **4** once every three months.

quartermaster (ˈkwɔːtəˌmɑːstə) *n* **1** an officer responsible for accommodation, food, and equipment in a military unit. **2** a rating in the navy, usually a petty officer, with particular responsibility for navigational duties.

quarter-miler *n* an athlete who specializes in running the quarter mile.

quartern (ˈkwɔːtən) *n* **1** a fourth part of certain weights or measures. **2** Also called: **quartern loaf.** *Brit.* **2a** a type of loaf 4 inches square. **2b** any loaf weighing 1600 g. [C13: from OF *quarteron*, from *quart* a quarter]

★ people and places

quarter note *n* the usual US and Canad. name for **crotchet** (sense 1).

quarter plate *n* a photographic plate measuring 3¼ × 4¼ inches (8.3 × 10.8 cm).

quarters ('kwɔːtəz) *pl n* **1** accommodation, esp. as provided for military personnel. **2** the stations assigned to crew members of a warship: *general quarters.*

quarter sessions *n* (*functioning as sing or pl*) (formerly) any of various courts held four times a year before justices of the peace or a recorder.

quarterstaff ('kwɔːtə,stɑːf) *n, pl* **quarterstaves** (-,steɪvz). a stout iron-tipped wooden staff about 6ft long, formerly used as a weapon. [C16: from ?]

quarter tone *n Music*. a quarter of a whole tone.

quartet *or* **quartette** (kwɔː'tɛt) *n* **1** a group of four singers or instrumentalists or a piece of music composed for such a group. **2** any group of four. [C18: from It. *quartetto*, dim. of *quarto* fourth]

quartic ('kwɔːtɪk) *adj, n* another word for **biquadratic**. [C19: from L *quartus* fourth]

quartile ('kwɔːtaɪl) *n* **1** *Statistics*. one of three values of a variable dividing its distribution into four groups with equal frequencies. ◆ *adj* **2** *Statistics*. of a quartile. **3** *Astrol*. denoting an aspect of two heavenly bodies when their longitudes differ by 90°. [C16: from Med. L *quartīlis*, from L *quartus* fourth]

quarto ('kwɔːtəʊ) *n, pl* **quartos**. a book size resulting from folding a sheet of paper into four leaves or eight pages. [C16: from NL *in quartō* in quarter]

quartz (kwɔːts) *n* a hard glossy mineral consisting of silicon dioxide in crystalline form. It occurs as colourless rock crystal and as several impure coloured varieties including agate, chalcedony, flint, and amethyst. Formula: SiO_2. [C18: from G *Quarz*, of Slavic origin]

quartz clock *or* **watch** *n* a clock or watch that is operated by a vibrating quartz crystal.

quartz crystal *n* a thin plate or rod cut from a piece of piezoelectric quartz and ground so that it vibrates at a particular frequency.

quartz glass *n* a colourless glass composed of almost pure silica, resistant to very high temperatures.

quartz-iodine lamp *or* **quartz lamp** *n* a type of tungsten-halogen lamp containing small amounts of iodine and having a quartz envelope, operating at high temperature and producing an intense light for use in car headlamps, etc.

quartzite ('kwɔːtsaɪt) *n* **1** a sandstone composed of quartz. **2** a very hard rock consisting of intergrown quartz crystals.

quasar ('kweɪzɑː, -sɑː) *n* any of a class of quasi-stellar objects that emit an immense amount of energy in the form of light, infrared radiation, etc., from a compact source. They are extremely distant and hence the youngest objects observed in the universe, and their energy generation is thought to involve a black hole located in a galaxy. [C20: *quasi(i-stell)ar (object)*]

quash (kwɒʃ) *vb* (*tr*) **1** to subdue forcefully and completely. **2** to annul or make void (a law, etc.). **3** to reject (an indictment, etc.) as invalid. [C14: from OF *quasser*, from L *quassāre* to shake]

quasi- *combining form*. **1** almost but not really; seemingly: *a quasi-religious cult*. **2** resembling but not actually being; so-called: *a quasi-scholar*. [from L, lit.: as if]

Quasimodo ★ (*Italian* kwa'zi:modo) *n* **Salvatore** (salva-'toːre). 1901–68, Italian poet: Nobel prize for literature 1959.

quasi-stellar object ('kwaːzɪ, 'kweɪsaɪ) *n* a member of any of several classes of astronomical bodies, including quasars and quasi-stellar galaxies, both of which have exceptionally large red shifts. Abbrev.: **QSO**.

quassia ('kwɒʃə) *n* **1** any of a genus of tropical American trees having bitter bark and wood. **2** the wood of this tree or a bitter compound extracted from it, formerly used as a tonic and vermifuge, now used in insecticides. [C18: from NL, after Graman *Quassi*, a slave who discovered (1730) the medicinal value of the root]

quatercentenary (,kwætəsɛn'tiːnərɪ) *n, pl* **quatercentenaries**. a 400th anniversary. [C19: from L *quater* four times + CENTENARY]
▸ **quatercentennial** (,kwætəsɛn'tɛnɪəl) *adj, n*

quaternary (kwə'tɜːnərɪ) *adj* **1** consisting of fours or by fours. **2** fourth in a series. **3** *Chem*. containing or being an atom bound to four other atoms or groups. ◆ *n, pl* **quaternaries**. **4** the number four or a set of four. [C15: from L *quaternārius* each containing four, from *quaternī* by fours, from *quattuor* four]

Quaternary (kwə'tɜːnərɪ) *adj* **1** of or denoting the most recent period of geological time, which succeeded the Tertiary period one million years ago. ◆ *n* **2** **the**. the Quaternary period or rock system.

quaternion (kwə'tɜːnɪən) *n* **1** *Maths*. a generalized complex number consisting of four components, $x = x_0 + x_1\mathbf{i} + x_2\mathbf{j} + x_3\mathbf{k}$, where x, $x_0...x_3$ are real numbers and $\mathbf{i}^2 = \mathbf{j}^2 = \mathbf{k}^2 = -1$, $\mathbf{ij} = -\mathbf{ji} = \mathbf{k}$, etc. **2** a set of four. [C14: from LL, from L *quaternī* four at a time]

Quathlamba ★ (kwaːt'laːmbaː) *n* the Sotho name for the **Drakensberg**.

quatrain ('kwɒtreɪn) *n* a stanza or poem of four lines. [C16: from F, from *quatre* four, from L *quattuor* four]

Quatre Bras ★ (*French* katrə bra) *n* a village in Belgium near Brussels; site of a battle in June 1815 where Wellington defeated the French under Marshal Ney, immediately preceding the battle of Waterloo.

quatrefoil ('kætrə,fɔɪl) *n* **1** a leaf composed of four leaflets. **2** *Archit*. a carved ornament having four foils arranged about a common centre. [C15: from OF, from *quatre* four + *-foil* leaflet]

quattrocento (,kwætrəʊ'tʃɛntəʊ) *n* the 15th century, esp. in reference to Renaissance Italian art and literature. [It., lit.: four hundred (short for fourteen hundred)]

quaver ('kweɪvə) *vb* **1** to say or sing (something) with a trembling voice. **2** (*intr*) (esp. of the voice) to quiver or tremble. **3** (*intr*) *Rare*. to sing or play trills. ◆ *n* **4** *Music*. a note having the time value of an eighth of a semibreve. Usual US and Canad. name: **eighth note**. **5** a tremulous sound or note. [C15 (in the sense: to vibrate): from *quaven* to tremble, of Gmc origin]
▸ **'quavering** *adj* ▸ **'quaveringly** *adv*

quay (kiː) *n* a wharf, typically one built parallel to the shoreline. [C14 *keye*, from OF *kai*, of Celtic origin]

quayage ('kiːɪdʒ) *n* **1** a system of quays. **2** a charge for the use of a quay.

Quayle ★ (kweɪl) *n* Sir (**John**) **Anthony**. 1913–89, British actor and producer: director (1948–56) of the Shakespeare Memorial Theatre.

quayside ('kiː,saɪd) *n* the edge of a quay along the water.

Que. *abbrev. for* Quebec.

quean (kwiːn) *n* **1** *Arch*. **1a** a boisterous impudent woman. **1b** a prostitute. **2** *Scot*. an unmarried girl. [OE *cwene*]

queasy ('kwiːzɪ) *adj* **queasier, queasiest**. **1** having the feeling that one is about to vomit; nauseous. **2** feeling or causing uneasiness. [C15: from ?]
▸ **'queasily** *adv* ▸ **'queasiness** *n*

Quebec ★ (kwɪ'bɛk, kə-, kɛ-) *n* **1** a province of E Canada: the largest Canadian province; a French colony from 1608 to 1763, when it passed to Britain; a large proportion of the population is French-speaking and there is a strong secessionist movement; lying mostly on the Canadian Shield, it has vast areas of forest and extensive tundra and is populated mostly in the plain around the St Lawrence River. Capital: Quebec. Pop.: 7 334 200 (1995 est.). Area: 1 540 680 sq. km (594 860 sq. miles). Abbrev.: **PQ**. **2** a port in E Canada, capital of the province of Quebec, situated on the St Lawrence River: founded in 1608 by Champlain; scene of the battle of the Plains of Abraham (1759), by which the British won Canada from the French. Pop.: 167 517 (1991).
▸ **Que'becker** *or* **Que'becer** *n*

Québecois (*French* kebɛkwa) *n, pl* **Québecois** (-kwa). a native or inhabitant of the province of Quebec, esp. a French-speaking one.

quebracho (keɪ'braːtʃəʊ) *n, pl* **quebrachos** (-tʃəʊz). **1** either of two South American trees having a tannin-rich hard wood used in tanning and dyeing. **2** a South American tree, whose bark yields alkaloids used in medicine and tanning. **3** the wood or bark of any of these trees. [C19: from American Sp., from *quiebracha*, from *quebrar* to break (from L *crepāre* to rattle) + *hacha* axe (from F)]

Quechua ('ketʃwə) *n* **1** (*pl* **Quechuas** *or* **Quechua**) a member of any of a group of South American Indian peoples of the Andes, including the Incas. **2** the language or family of languages spoken by these peoples.
▸ '**Quechuan** *adj, n*

queen (kwi:n) *n* **1** a female sovereign who is the official ruler or head of state. **2** the wife of a king. **3** a woman or a thing personified as a woman considered the best or most important of her kind: *the queen of ocean liners*. **4** *Sl.* an effeminate male homosexual. **5** the only fertile female in a colony of bees, ants, etc. **6** an adult female cat. **7** a playing card bearing the picture of a queen. **8** the most powerful chess piece, able to move in a straight line in any direction or diagonally. ◆ *vb* **9** *Chess.* to promote (a pawn) to a queen when it reaches the eighth rank. **10** (*tr*) to crown as queen. **11** (*intr*) to reign as queen. **12 queen it.** (often foll. by *over*) *Inf.* to behave in an overbearing manner. [OE *cwēn*]

Queen-Anne *n* **1** a style of furniture popular in England about 1700–20 and in America about 1720–70, characterized by walnut veneer and cabriole legs. ◆ *adj* **2** in or of this style. **3** of a style of architecture popular in early 18th-century England, characterized by red-brick construction with classical ornamentation.

Queen Anne's lace *n* another name for the **wild carrot**.

queen bee *n* **1** the fertile female bee in a hive. **2** *Inf.* a woman in a position of dominance over her associates.

Queenborough in Sheppey ★ ('kwi:nbərə; 'ʃɛpɪ) *n* a town in SE England, in Kent: formed in 1968 by the amalgamation of Queenborough, Sheerness, and Sheppey. Pop.: 30 790 (1991).

Queen Charlotte Islands ★ *pl n* a group of about 150 islands off the W coast of Canada: part of British Columbia. Pop.: 5316 (1991). Area: 9596 sq. km (3705 sq. miles).

queen consort *n* the wife of a reigning king.

queen dowager *n* the widow of a king.

Queen Elizabeth Islands ★ *pl n* a group of islands off the N coast of Canada: the northernmost islands of the Canadian Arctic archipelago, lying N of latitude 74°N; part of the Northwest Territories. Area: about 390 000 sq. km (150 000 sq. miles).

queenly ('kwi:nlɪ) *adj* **queenlier, queenliest. 1** resembling or appropriate to a queen. ◆ *adv* **2** in a manner appropriate to a queen.

Queen Mab ★ (mæb) *n* (in British folklore) a bewitching fairy who rules over men's dreams.

Queen Maud Land ★ (mɔːd) *n* the large section of Antarctica between Coats Land and Enderby Land: claimed by Norway in 1939.

Queen Maud Range ★ *n* a mountain range in Antarctica, in S Ross Dependency, extending for about 800 km (500 miles).

queen mother *n* the widow of a former king who is also the mother of the reigning sovereign.

queen olive *n* a variety of olive having large fleshy fruit suitable for pickling.

queen post *n* one of a pair of vertical posts that connect the tie beam of a truss to the principal rafters. Cf. **king post.**

Queens ★ (kwi:nz) *n* a borough of E New York City, on Long Island. Pop.: 1 951 598 (1990).

Queen's Award *n* either of two awards instituted by royal warrant (1976) for increased export earnings by a British firm (**Queen's Award for Export Achievement**) or for an advance in technology (**Queen's Award for Technological Achievement**).

Queen's Bench *n* (in England when the sovereign is female) one of the divisions of the High Court of Justice.

Queensberry rules ('kwi:nzbərɪ) *pl n* **1** the code of rules followed in modern boxing. **2** *Inf.* gentlemanly

conduct, esp. in a dispute. [C19: after the ninth Marquess of *Queensberry*, who originated the rules in 1869]

Queen's Counsel *n* (when the sovereign is female) **1** a barrister (in England and Wales) or an advocate (in Scotland) appointed Counsel to the Crown by the sovereign on the recommendation of the Lord Chancellor (in England and Wales) or the Lord President (in Scotland). **2** (in Australia) a similar appointment, usually made on the recommendation of the Chief Justice of each state, through the state governor. **3** (in Canada) an honorary title which may be bestowed by the government on lawyers with long experience.

Queen's County ★ *n* the former name of **Laois.**

Queen's English *n* (when the British sovereign is female) standard Southern British English.

queen's evidence *n* *English law.* (when the sovereign is female) evidence given for the Crown against his former associates in crime by an accomplice (esp. in **turn queen's evidence**). US equivalent: **state's evidence.**

Queen's Guide *n* (in Britain and the Commonwealth when the sovereign is female) a Guide who has passed the highest tests of proficiency.

queen's highway *n* **1** (in Britain when the sovereign is female) any public road or right of way. **2** (in Canada) a main road maintained by the provincial government.

queen-size *or* **queen-sized** *adj* (of a bed, etc.) larger or longer than normal size but smaller or shorter than king-size.

Queensland ★ ('kwi:nz,lænd, -lənd) *n* a state of NE Australia: fringed on the Pacific side by the Great Barrier Reef; the Great Dividing Range lies in the east, separating the coastal lowlands from the dry Great Artesian Basin in the south. Capital: Brisbane. Pop.: 3 339 000 (1996 est.). Area: 1 727 500 sq. km (667 000 sq. miles).
▸ '**Queens,lander** *n*

Queensland nut *n* another name for **macadamia.**

Queen's Scout *n* (in Britain and the Commonwealth when the sovereign is female) a Scout who has passed the highest tests of proficiency. US equivalent: **Eagle Scout.**

queer (kwɪə) *adj* **1** differing from the normal or usual; odd or strange. **2** dubious; shady. **3** faint, giddy, or queasy. **4** *Inf., derog.* homosexual. **5** *Inf.* eccentric or slightly mad. **6** *Sl.* worthless or counterfeit. ◆ *n* **7** *Inf., derog.* a homosexual. ◆ *vb* (*tr*) *Inf.* **8** to spoil or thwart (esp. in **queer someone's pitch**). **9** to put in a difficult position. [C16: ? from G *quer* oblique, ult. from OHG *twērh*]
▸ '**queerly** *adv* ▸ '**queerness** *n*

USAGE NOTE Although the term *queer* meaning homosexual is still considered derogatory when used by nonhomosexuals, it is now used by homosexuals of themselves as a positive term, as in *queer politics, queer cinema.*

---

queer fish *n* *Brit. inf.* an odd person.

queer street *n* (*sometimes cap.*) *Inf.* a difficult situation, such as debt or bankruptcy (in **in queer street**).

quell (kwɛl) *vb* (*tr*) **1** to suppress (rebellion, etc.); subdue. **2** to overcome or allay. [OE *cwellan* to kill]
▸ '**queller** *n*

Quelpart ★ ('kwɛl,pɑːt) *n* another name for **Cheju.**

Quemoy ★ (kɛ'mɔɪ) *n* an island in Formosa Strait, off the SE coast of China: administratively part of Taiwan. Pop.: 53 237 (1996 est.). Area: 130 sq. km (50 sq. miles).

quench (kwɛntʃ) *vb* (*tr*) **1** to satisfy (one's thirst, desires, etc.); slake. **2** to put out (a fire, etc.); extinguish. **3** to put down; suppress; subdue. **4** to cool (hot metal) by plunging it into cold water. [OE *ācwencan* to extinguish]
▸ '**quenchable** *adj* ▸ '**quencher** *n*

Queneau ★ (French kəno) *n* **Raymond** (rɛmɔ̃). 1903–76, French writer, whose novels include *Zazie dans le métro* (1959).

quenelle (kə'nɛl) *n* a ball of sieved meat or fish. [C19: from F, from G *Knödel* dumpling, from OHG *knodo* knot]

★ people and places

Querétaro ★ (*Spanish* keˈretaro) *n* **1** an inland state of central Mexico: economy based on agriculture and mining. Capital: Querétaro. Pop.: 1 248 844 (1995 est.). Area: 11 769 sq. km (4544 sq. miles). **2** a city in central Mexico, capital of Querétaro state: scene of the signing (1848) of the treaty ending the US-Mexican War and of the execution of Emperor Maximilian (1867). Pop.: 385 503 (1990).

querist (ˈkwɪərɪst) *n* a person who makes inquiries or queries; questioner.

quern (kwɜːn) *n* a stone hand mill for grinding corn. [OE *cweorn*]

quernstone (ˈkwɜːnˌstəʊn) *n* **1** another name for **millstone** (sense 1). **2** one of the two stones used in a quern.

querulous (ˈkwɛrʊləs, ˈkwɛrjʊ-) *adj* **1** inclined to make whining or peevish complaints. **2** characterized by or proceeding from a complaining fretful attitude or disposition.   [C15: from L *querulus,* from *querī* to complain]
▸ **ˈquerulously** *adv* ▸ **ˈquerulousness** *n*

query (ˈkwɪərɪ) *n, pl* **queries. 1** a question, esp. one expressing doubt. **2** a question mark. ◆ *vb* **queries, querying, queried.** (*tr*) **3** to express uncertainty, doubt, or an objection concerning (something). **4** to express as a query. **5** *US.* to put a question to (a person); ask.   [C17: from earlier *quere,* from L *quaerē* ask!, from *quaerere* to seek]

query language *n Computing.* the instructions and procedures used to retrieve information from a database.

Quesnay ★ (*French* kɛnɛ) *n* **François** (frāˈswa). 1694–1774, French political economist, encyclopedist, and physician, noted for his *Tableau économique* (1758).

quest (kwɛst) *n* **1** a looking for or seeking; search. **2** (in medieval romance) an expedition by a knight or knights to accomplish a task, such as finding the Holy Grail. **3** the object of a search; a goal or target. ◆ *vb* (*mainly intr*) **4** (foll. by *for* or *after*) to go in search (of). **5** (of dogs, etc.) to search for game. **6** (*also tr*) *Arch.* to seek.   [C14: from OF *queste,* from L *quaesita* sought, from *quaerere* to seek]
▸ **ˈquester** *n* ▸ **ˈquesting** *adj* ▸ **ˈquestingly** *adv*

question (ˈkwɛstʃən) *n* **1** a form of words addressed to a person in order to elicit information or evoke a response; interrogative sentence. **2** a point at issue: *it's only a question of time until she dies.* **3** a difficulty or uncertainty. **4** an act of asking. **4b** an investigation into some problem. **5** a motion presented for debate. **6 put the question.** to require members of a deliberative assembly to vote on a motion presented. **7** *Law.* a matter submitted to a court or other tribunal. **8 beyond (all) question.** beyond (any) dispute or doubt. **9 call in** or **into question. 9a** to make (something) the subject of disagreement. **9b** to cast doubt upon the truth, etc., of (something). **10 in question.** under discussion: *this is the man in question.* **11 out of the question.** beyond consideration; unthinkable or impossible. **12 put to the question.** (formerly) to interrogate by torture. ◆ *vb* (*mainly tr*) **13** to put a question or questions to (a person); interrogate. **14** to make (something) the subject of dispute. **15** to express uncertainty about the truth of (something); doubt.   [C13: via OF from L *quaestiō,* from *quaerere* to seek]
▸ **ˈquestioner** *n*

questionable (ˈkwɛstʃənəbᵊl) *adj* **1** (esp. of a person's morality or honesty) admitting of some doubt; dubious. **2** of disputable value or authority.
▸ **ˈquestionableness** *n* ▸ **ˈquestionably** *adv*

questioning (ˈkwɛstʃənɪŋ) *adj* **1** proceeding from or characterized by a feeling of doubt or uncertainty. **2** intellectually inquisitive: *a questioning mind.*
▸ **ˈquestioningly** *adv*

questionless (ˈkwɛstʃənlɪs) *adj* **1** blindly adhering; unquestioning. **2** a less common word for **unquestionable.**
▸ **ˈquestionlessly** *adv*

question mark *n* **1** the punctuation mark **?**, used at the end of questions and in other contexts where doubt or ignorance is implied. **2** this mark used for any other purpose, as to draw attention to a possible mistake.

question master *n Brit.* the chairman of a quiz or panel game.

questionnaire (ˌkwɛstʃəˈnɛə, ˌkɛs-) *n* a set of questions on a form, submitted to a number of people in order to collect statistical information.

question time *n* (in parliamentary bodies of the British type) the time set aside each day for questions to government ministers.

Quetta ★ (ˈkwɛtə) *n* a city in W central Pakistan, at an altitude of 1650 m (5500 ft): a summer resort, military station, and trading centre. Pop.: 300 000 (latest est.).

quetzal (ˈkɛtsəl) *n, pl* **quetzals** or **quetzales** (-ˈsɑːles). **1** a crested bird of Central and N South America, which has a brilliant green, red, and white plumage and, in the male, long tail feathers. **2** the standard monetary unit of Guatemala.   [via American Sp. from Nahuatl *quetzalli* brightly coloured tail feather]

Quetzalcoatl ★ (ˌkɛtsəlkəʊˈætᵊl) *n* a god of the Aztecs and Toltecs, represented as a feathered serpent.

queue (kjuː) *Chiefly Brit.* ◆ *n* **1** a line of people, vehicles, etc., waiting for something. **2** *Computing.* a list in which entries are deleted from one end and inserted at the other. **3** a pigtail. ◆ *vb* **queues, queuing** or **queueing, queued. 4** (*intr,* often foll. by *up*) to form or remain in a line while waiting. **5** *Computing.* to arrange (a number of programs) in a predetermined order for accessing by a computer. ◆ Usual US word (senses 1, 4): **line.** [C16 (in the sense: tail); C18 (in the sense: pigtail): via F from L *cauda* tail]

queue-jump *vb* (*intr*) **1** to take a place in a queue ahead of those already queuing; push in. **2** to obtain some advantage out of turn or unfairly.
▸ **ˈqueue-ˌjumper** *n*

Quezon City ★ (ˈkeɪzɒn) *n* a city in the Philippines, on central Luzon adjoining Manila: capital of the Philippines from 1948 to 1976; seat of the University of the Philippines (1908). Pop.: 1 676 644 (1994 est.).

Quezon y Molina ★ (ˈkeɪzɒn iː mɒˈliːnə; *Spanish* keˈθɒn i moˈlina) *n* **Manuel Luis** (maˈnwɛl lwis). 1878–1944, Philippine statesman: first president of the Philippines (from 1935) and head of the government in exile after the Japanese conquest in World War II.

quibble (ˈkwɪbᵊl) *vb* **quibbles, quibbling, quibbled.** (*intr*) **1** to make trivial objections. **2** *Arch.* to play on words; pun. ◆ *n* **3** a trivial objection or equivocation, esp. one used to avoid an issue. **4** *Arch.* a pun.   [C17: prob. from obs. *quib,* ?from L *quibus* (from *quī* who, which), as used in legal documents, with reference to their obscure phraseology]
▸ **ˈquibbler** *n* ▸ **ˈquibbling** *adj*

Quiberon ★ (*French* kibrɔ̃) *n* a peninsula of NW France, on the S coast of Brittany: a naval battle was fought off its coast in 1759 during the Seven Years' War, in which the British defeated the French.

quiche (kiːʃ) *n* an open savoury tart with an egg custard filling to which bacon, onion, cheese, etc., are added. [F, from G *Kuchen* cake]

quick (kwɪk) *adj* **1** performed or occurring during a comparatively short time: *a quick move.* **2** lasting a short time; brief. **3** accomplishing something in a time that is shorter than normal: *a quick worker.* **4** characterized by rapidity of movement; fast. **5** immediate or prompt. **6** (*postpositive*) eager or ready to perform (an action): *quick to criticize.* **7** responsive to stimulation; alert; lively. **8** eager or quick for learning. **9** easily excited or aroused. **10** nimble in one's movements or actions; deft: *quick fingers.* **11** *Arch.* **11a** alive; living. **11b** (*as n*) living people (esp. in **the quick and the dead**). **12 quick with child.** *Arch.* pregnant. ◆ *n* **13** any area of sensitive flesh, esp. that under a toenail or fingernail. **14** the most important part (of a thing). **15 cut (someone) to the quick.** to hurt (someone's) feelings deeply. ◆ *adv Inf.* **16** in a rapid manner; swiftly. **17** soon: *I hope he comes quick.* ◆ *sentence substitute.* **18** a command to perform an action immediately.   [OE *cwicu* living]
▸ **ˈquickly** *adv* ▸ **ˈquickness** *n*

quick-change artist *n* an actor or entertainer who undertakes several rapid changes of costume during his performance.

quicken ('kwɪkən) *vb* **1** to make or become faster; accelerate. **2** to impart to or receive vigour, enthusiasm, etc.: *science quickens man's imagination*. **3** to make or become alive; revive. **4a** (of an unborn fetus) to begin to show signs of life. **4b** (of a pregnant woman) to reach the stage of pregnancy at which movements of the fetus can be felt.

quick-freeze *vb* **quick-freezes, quick-freezing, quick-froze, quick-frozen.** (*tr*) to preserve (food) by subjecting it to rapid refrigeration at temperatures of 0°C or lower.

quickie ('kwɪkɪ) *n Inf.* **1** Also called (esp. Brit.): **quick one.** a speedily consumed alcoholic drink. **2a** anything made or done rapidly. **2b** (*as modifier*): *a quickie divorce*.

quicklime ('kwɪk,laɪm) *n* another name for **calcium oxide.**

quick march *n* **1** a march at quick time or the order to proceed at such a pace. ♦ *interj* **2** a command to commence such a march.

quicksand ('kwɪk,sænd) *n* a deep mass of loose wet sand that sucks anything on top of it inextricably into it.

quickset ('kwɪk,sɛt) *Chiefly Brit.* ♦ *n* **1a** a plant or cutting, esp. of hawthorn, set so as to form a hedge. **1b** such plants or cuttings collectively. **2** a hedge composed of such plants. ♦ *adj* **3** composed of such plants.

quicksilver ('kwɪk,sɪlvə) *n* **1** another name for **mercury** (sense 1). ♦ *adj* **2** rapid or unpredictable in movement or change.

quickstep ('kwɪk,stɛp) *n* **1** a modern ballroom dance in rapid quadruple time. **2** a piece of music composed for or in the rhythm of this dance. ♦ *vb* **quicksteps, quickstepping, quickstepped.** **3** (*intr*) to perform this dance.

quick-tempered *adj* readily roused to anger; irascible.

quickthorn ('kwɪk,θɔːn) *n* hawthorn, esp. when planted as a hedge. [C17: prob. from *quick* in the sense "fast-growing": cf. QUICKSET]

quick time *n Mil.* the normal marching rate of 120 paces to the minute.

quick-witted *adj* having a keenly alert mind, esp. as used to avert danger, make effective reply, etc.
▶ ,quick-'wittedly *adv* ▶ ,quick-'wittedness *n*

quid[1] (kwɪd) *n* a piece of tobacco, suitable for chewing. [OE *cwidu* chewing resin]

quid[2] (kwɪd) *n, pl* **quid.** *Brit. sl.* **1** a pound (sterling). **2** (**be**) **quids in.** (to be) in a very favourable or advantageous position. [C17: from ?]

quiddity ('kwɪdɪtɪ) *n, pl* **quiddities. 1** the essential nature of something. **2** a petty or trifling distinction; quibble. [C16: from Med. L *quidditās*, from L *quid* what]

quidnunc ('kwɪd,nʌŋk) *n* a person eager to learn news and scandal; gossipmonger. [C18: from L, lit.: what now]

quid pro quo ('kwɪd prəʊ 'kwəʊ) *n, pl* **quid pro quos. 1** a reciprocal exchange. **2** something given in compensation, esp. an advantage or object given in exchange for another. [C16: from L: something for something]

quiescent (kwɪ'esⁿnt) *adj* quiet, inactive, or dormant. [C17: from L *quiescere* to rest]
▶ qui'escence *or* qui'escency *n* ▶ qui'escently *adv*

quiet ('kwaɪət) *adj* **1** characterized by an absence of noise. **2** calm or tranquil: *the sea is quiet tonight*. **3** free from activities, distractions, etc.; untroubled: *a quiet life*. **4** short of work, orders, etc.; not busy: *business is quiet today*. **5** private; not public; secret: *a quiet word with someone*. **6** free from anger, impatience, or other extreme emotion. **7** free from pretentiousness; modest or reserved: *quiet humour*. **8** *Astron.* (of the sun) exhibiting a very low number of sunspots, solar flares, etc.; inactive. ♦ *n* **9** the state of being silent, peaceful, or untroubled. **10 on the quiet.** without other people knowing. ♦ *vb* **11** a less common word for **quieten.** [C14: from L *quiētus*, p.p. of *quiēscere* to rest, from *quiēs* repose]
▶ 'quietness *n*

quieten ('kwaɪətⁿn) *vb Chiefly Brit.* **1** (often foll. by *down*)

to make or become calm, silent, etc. **2** (*tr*) to allay (fear, doubts, etc.).

quietism ('kwaɪə,tɪzəm) *n* **1** a form of religious mysticism originating in Spain in the late 17th century, requiring complete passivity to God's will. **2** passivity and calmness of mind towards external events.
▶ 'quietist *n, adj*

quietly ('kwaɪətlɪ) *adv* **1** in a quiet manner. **2** just quietly. *Austral.* confidentially.

quietude ('kwaɪə,tjuːd) *n* the state or condition of being quiet, peaceful, calm, or tranquil.

quietus (kwaɪ'iːtəs, -'eɪtəs) *n, pl* **quietuses. 1** anything that serves to quash, eliminate, or kill. **2** a release from life; death. **3** the discharge or settlement of debts, duties, etc. [C16: from L *quiētus est*, lit.: he is at rest]

quiff (kwɪf) *n Brit.* a tuft of hair brushed up above the forehead. [C19: from ?]

quill (kwɪl) *n* **1a** any of the large stiff feathers of the wing or tail of a bird. **1b** the long hollow part of a feather; calamus. **2** Also called: **quill pen.** a feather made into a pen for writing. **3** any of the stiff hollow spines of a porcupine or hedgehog. **4** a device, formerly made from a crow quill, for plucking a harpsichord string. **5** a small roll of bark, esp. one of dried cinnamon. **6** a bobbin or spindle. **7** a fluted fold, as in a ruff. ♦ *vb* (*tr*) **8** to wind (thread, etc.) onto a spool or bobbin. **9** to make or press fluted folds in (a ruff, etc.). [C15 in the sense: hollow reed or pipe: from ?; cf. MLow G *quiele* quill]

Quilmes ★ (*Spanish* 'kilmes) *n* a city in E Argentina: a resort and suburb of Buenos Aires. Pop.: 509 445 (1991).

quilt (kwɪlt) *n* **1** a cover for a bed, consisting of a soft filling sewn between two layers of material, usually with crisscross seams. **2** short for **continental quilt. 3** a bedspread. **4** anything resembling a quilt. ♦ *vb* (*tr*) **5** to stitch together (two pieces of fabric) with (a thick padding or lining) between them. **6** to create (a garment, etc.) in this way. **7** to pad with material. [C13: from OF *coilte* mattress, from L *culcita* stuffed item of bedding]
▶ 'quilted *adj* ▶ 'quilter *n*

quilting ('kwɪltɪŋ) *n* **1** material for quilts. **2** the act of making a quilt. **3** quilted work.

Quimper ★ (*French* kɛ̃pɛr) *n* a city in NW France: capital of Finistère department. Pop.: 62 540 (1990).

quin (kwɪn) *n Brit.* short for **quintuplet** (sense 1). US and Canad. word: **quint.**

quinary ('kwaɪnərɪ) *adj* **1** of or by fives. **2** fifth in a series. **3** (of a number system) having a base of five. [C17: from L *quīnārius* containing five, from *quīnī* five each]

quince (kwɪns) *n* **1** a small widely cultivated Asian tree with edible pear-shaped fruits. **2** the fruit of this tree, much used in preserves. [C14 *qwince* pl. of *quyn*, from OF *coin*, from L *cotōneum*, from Gk *kudōnion* quince]

quincentenary (,kwɪnsɛn'tiːnərɪ) *n, pl* **quincentenaries.** a 500th anniversary. [C19: irregularly from L *quinque* five + CENTENARY]
▶ **quincentennial** (,kwɪnsɛn'tɛnɪəl) *adj, n*

quincunx ('kwɪnkʌŋks) *n* a group of five objects arranged in the shape of a rectangle with one at each of the four corners and the fifth in the centre. [C17: from L: five twelfths, from *quinque* five + *uncia* twelfth; in ancient Rome, this was a coin worth five twelfths of an AS[2] and marked with five spots]
▶ **quincuncial** (kwɪn'kʌnʃəl) *adj*

Quine ★ (kwaɪn) *n* **Willard van Orman.** born 1908, US philosopher. His works include *Word and Object* (1960), *Philosophy of Logic* (1970), *The Roots of Reference* (1973), and *The Logic of Sequences* (1990).

quinella (kwɪ'nɛlə) *n Austral.* a form of betting in which the punter must select the first and second place winners, in any order. [from American Sp. *quiniela*]

Qui Nhong ★ ('kwiː 'njɒŋ) *n* a port in SE Vietnam, on the South China Sea. Pop.: 163 385 (1992 est.).

quinidine ('kwɪnɪ,diːn) *n* a crystalline alkaloid drug used to treat heart arrhythmias.

quinine (kwɪ'niːn; *US* 'kwaɪnaɪn) *n* a bitter crystalline alkaloid extracted from cinchona bark, the salts of which are used as a tonic, analgesic, etc., and in malaria therapy. [C19: from Sp. *quina* cinchona bark, from Quechua *kina* bark]

Quinn ★ (kwɪn) *n* Anthony. born 1915, US film actor, born in Mexico: his films include *La Strada* (1954) and *Zorba the Greek* (1964).

quinol ('kwɪnɒl) *n* another name for hydroquinone.

quinoline ('kwɪnə,liːn, -lɪn) *n* an oily colourless insoluble compound synthesized by heating aniline, nitrobenzene, glycerol, and sulphuric acid: used as a food preservative and in the manufacture of dyes and antiseptics. Formula: C_9H_7N.

quinquagenarian (,kwɪŋkwədʒɪ'nɛərɪən) *n* **1** a person between 50 and 59 years old. ◆ *adj* **2** being between 50 and 59 years old. **3** of a quinquagenarian. [C16: from L *quinquāgēnārius* containing fifty, from *quinquāgēnī* fifty each]

Quinquagesima (,kwɪŋkwə'dʒɛsɪmə) *n* the Sunday preceding Lent. Also called: **Quinquagesima Sunday**. [C14: via Med. L from L *quinquāgēsima diēs* fiftieth day]

quinquecentenary (,kwɪŋkwɪsɛn'tiːnərɪ) *n, pl* **quinquecentenaries**. another name for quincentenary.

quinquennial (kwɪn'kwɛnɪəl) *adj* **1** occurring once every five years or over a period of five years. ◆ *n* **2** a fifth anniversary.
  ▸ **quin'quennially** *adv*

quinquennium (kwɪn'kwɛnɪəm) *n, pl* **quinquennia** (-nɪə). a period or cycle of five years. [C17: from L *quinque* five + *annus* year]

quinquereme (,kwɪŋkwɪ'riːm) *n* an ancient Roman galley with five banks of oars. [C16: from L *quinquerēmis*, from *quinque-* five + *rēmus* oar]

quinquevalent (,kwɪŋkwɪ'veɪlənt) *adj* Chem. another word for pentavalent.
  ▸ ,quinque'valency *or* ,quinque'valence *n*

quinsy ('kwɪnzɪ) *n* inflammation of the tonsils and surrounding tissues with the formation of abscesses. [C14: via OF & Med. L from Gk *kunankhē*, from *kuōn* dog + *ankhein* to strangle]

quint[1] *n* **1** (kwɪnt). an organ stop sounding a note a fifth higher. **2** (kɪnt). *Piquet*. a sequence of five cards in the same suit. [C17: from F *quinte*, from L *quintus* fifth]

quint[2] (kwɪnt) *n* the US and Canad. word for quin.

quintain ('kwɪntɪn) *n* (esp. in medieval Europe) a post or target set up for tilting exercises for mounted knights or foot soldiers. [C14: from OF *quintaine*, from L: street in a Roman camp between the fifth & sixth maniples (the maniple was a unit of 120–200 soldiers in ancient Rome), from *quintus* fifth]

quintal ('kwɪntᵊl) *n* **1** a unit of weight equal to (esp. in Britain) 112 pounds or (esp. in US) 100 pounds. **2** a unit of weight equal to 100 kilograms. [C15: via OF from Ar. *qintār*, possibly from L *centēnārius* consisting of a hundred]

quintan ('kwɪntən) *adj* (of a fever) occurring every fourth day. [C17: from L *febris quintāna* fever occurring every fifth day, reckoned inclusively]

Quintana Roo ★ (*Spanish* kin'tana 'rɔɔ) *n* a state of SE Mexico, on the E Yucatán Peninsula: hot, humid, forested, and inhabited chiefly by Maya Indians. Capital: Chetumal. Pop.: 703 442 (1995 est.). Area: 50 350 sq. km (19 463 sq. miles).

quinte (kænt) *n* the fifth of eight basic positions from which a parry or attack can be made in fencing. [C18: F from L *quintus* fifth]

quintessence (kwɪn'tɛsəns) *n* **1** the most typical representation of a quality, state, etc. **2** an extract of a substance containing its principle in its most concentrated form. **3** (in ancient philosophy) ether, the fifth essence or element, which was thought to be the constituent matter of the heavenly bodies and latent in all things. [C15: via F from Med. L *quinta essentia* the fifth essence, translation of Gk]
  ▸ **quintessential** (,kwɪntɪ'sɛnʃəl) *adj* ▸ ,quintes'sentially *adv*

quintet *or* **quintette** (kwɪn'tɛt) *n* **1** a group of five singers or instrumentalists or a piece of music composed for such a group. **2** any group of five. [C19: from It. *quintetto*, from *quinto* fifth]

quintillion (kwɪn'tɪljən) *n, pl* **quintillions** *or* **quintillion**. **1** (in Britain, France, and Germany) the number represented as one followed by 30 zeros (10^{30}). US and Canad. word: nonillion. **2** (in the US and Canada) the number represented as one followed by 18 zeros (10^{18}). Brit. word: trillion. [C17: from L *quintus* fifth + *-illion*, as in MILLION]
  ▸ **quin'tillionth** *adj*

quintuple ('kwɪntjʊpᵊl, kwɪn'tjuːpᵊl) *vb* **quintuples, quintupling, quintupled. 1** to multiply by five. ◆ *adj* **2** five times as much or as many; fivefold. **3** consisting of five parts. ◆ *n* **4** a quantity or number five times as great as another. [C16: from F, from L *quintus*, on the model of QUADRUPLE]

quintuplet ('kwɪntjʊplɪt, kwɪn'tjuːplɪt) *n* **1** one of five offspring born at one birth. **2** a group of five similar things. **3** *Music.* a group of five notes to be played in a time value of three or four.

quintuplicate *adj* (kwɪn'tjuːplɪkɪt). **1** fivefold or quintuple. ◆ *vb* (kwɪn'tjuːplɪ,keɪt), **quintuplicates, quintuplicating, quintuplicated. 2** to multiply or be multiplied by five. ◆ *n* (kwɪn'tjuːplɪkɪt). **3** a group or set of five things.

quip (kwɪp) *n* **1** a sarcastic remark. **2** a witty saying. **3** *Arch.* another word for quibble. ◆ *vb* **quips, quipping, quipped. 4** (*intr*) to make a quip. [C16: from earlier *quippy*, prob. from L *quippe* indeed, to be sure]
  ▸ 'quipster *n*

quire[1] ('kwaɪə) *n* **1** a set of 24 or 25 sheets of paper. **2** four sheets of paper folded to form 16 pages. **3** a set of all the sheets in a book. [C15 *quayer*, from OF *quaier*, from L *quaternī* four at a time, from *quater* four times]

quire[2] ('kwaɪə) *n* an obsolete spelling of choir.

Quirinal ★ ('kwɪrɪnᵊl) *n* one of the seven hills on which ancient Rome was built.

Quirinus ★ (kwɪ'raɪnəs) *n Roman myth.* a god of war, who came to be identified with the deified Romulus.

quirk (kwɜːk) *n* **1** a peculiarity of character; mannerism or foible. **2** an unexpected twist or turn: *a quirk of fate.* **3** a continuous groove in an architectural moulding. **4** a flourish, as in handwriting. [C16: from ?]
  ▸ 'quirky *adj* ▸ 'quirkiness *n*

quirt (kwɜːt) *US & S. African.* ◆ *n* **1** a whip with a leather thong at one end. ◆ *vb* (*tr*) **2** to strike with a quirt. [C19: from Sp. *cuerda* CORD]

quisling ('kwɪzlɪŋ) *n* a traitor who aids an occupying enemy force; collaborator. [C20: after Major Vidkun Quisling (1887–1945), Norwegian collaborator with the Nazis]

quit (kwɪt) *vb* **quits, quitting, quitted** *or* **quit. 1** (*tr*) to depart from; leave. **2** to resign; give up (a job). **3** (*intr*) (of a tenant) to give up occupancy of premises and leave them. **4** to desist or cease from (something or doing something). **5** (*tr*) to pay off (a debt). **6** (*tr*) *Arch.* to conduct or acquit (oneself); comport (oneself). ◆ *adj* **7** (*usually predicative*; foll. by *of*) free (from); released (from). [C13: from OF *quitter*, from L *quiētus* QUIET]

quitch grass (kwɪtʃ) *n* another name for couch grass. Sometimes shortened to **quitch**. [OE *cwice*; ? rel. to *cwicu* living, QUICK (with the implication that the grass cannot be killed)]

quitclaim ('kwɪt,kleɪm) *Law.* ◆ *n* **1** a renunciation of a claim or right. ◆ *vb* **2** (*tr*) to renounce (a claim). [C14: from Anglo-F *quiteclame*, from *quite* QUIT + *clamer* to declare (from L *clamāre* to shout)]

quite (kwaɪt) *adv* **1** completely or absolutely: *you're quite right.* **2** (*not used with a negative*) somewhat: *she's quite pretty.* **3** in actuality; truly. **4 quite a** *or* **an.** (*not used with a negative*) of an exceptional, considerable, or noticeable kind: *quite a girl.* **5 quite something.** a remarkable or noteworthy thing or person. ◆ *sentence substitute* **6** Also: **quite so.** an expression used to indicate agreement. [C14: adverbial use of *quite* (adj) QUIT]

USAGE NOTE See at **very.**

Quito ★ ('ki:təʊ; *Spanish* 'kito) *n* the capital of Ecuador, in the north at an altitude of 2850 m (9350 ft), just south of the equator: the oldest capital in South America, existing many centuries before the Incan conquest in 1487; a cultural centre since the beginning of Spanish rule (1534); two universities. Pop.: 1 487 513 (1997 est.).

quitrent ('kwɪt,rɛnt) *n* (formerly) a rent payable by a freeholder or copyholder to his lord in lieu of services.

quits (kwɪts) *adj* (*postpositive*) *Inf.* **1** on an equal footing; even. **2 call it quits.** to agree to end a dispute, contest, etc., agreeing that honours are even.

quittance ('kwɪt⁹ns) *n* **1** release from debt or other obligation. **2** a receipt or other document certifying this. [C13: from OF, from *quitter* to release from obligation; see QUIT]

quitter ('kwɪtə) *n* a person who gives up easily.

quiver[1] ('kwɪvə) *vb* **1** (*intr*) to shake with a tremulous movement; tremble. ◆ *n* **2** the state, process, or noise of shaking or trembling. [C15: from obs. *cwiver* quick, nimble]
▸ **'quivering** *adj* ▸ **'quivery** *adj*

quiver[2] ('kwɪvə) *n* a case for arrows. [C13: from OF *cuivre*]

qui vive (,ki: 'vi:v) *n* **on the qui vive.** on the alert; attentive. [C18: from F, lit.: long live who?, sentry's challenge (equivalent to "Whose side are you on?")]

Quixote ('kwɪksət; *Spanish* ki'xote) *n* See **Don Quixote.**

quixotic (kwɪk'sɒtɪk) *adj* preoccupied with an unrealistically optimistic or chivalrous approach to life; impractically idealistic. [C18: after DON QUIXOTE]
▸ **quix'otically** *adv*

quiz (kwɪz) *n*, *pl* **quizzes. 1a** an entertainment in which the knowledge of the players is tested by a series of questions. **1b** (*as modifier*): *a quiz programme.* **2** any set of quick questions designed to test knowledge. **3** an investigation by close questioning. **4** *Obs.* a practical joke. **5** *Obs.* a puzzling individual. **6** *Obs.* a person who habitually looks quizzically at others. ◆ *vb* **quizzes, quizzing, quizzed.** (*tr*) **7** to investigate by close questioning; interrogate. **8** *US & Canad. inf.* to test the knowledge of (a student or class). **9** (*tr*) *Obs.* to look quizzically at, esp. through a small monocle. [C18: from ?]
▸ **'quizzer** *n*

quizzical ('kwɪzɪk⁹l) *adj* questioning and mocking or supercilious.
▸ **'quizzically** *adv*

Qum ★ (kʊm) *n* a variant of **Qom.**

Qumran ★ ('kʊmrɑ:n) *n* See **Khirbet Qumran.**

Qungur ★ ('kʊŋgʊə) *n* a variant transliteration of the Chinese name for **Kongur Shan.**

quod (kwɒd) *n* *Chiefly Brit.* a slang word for **jail.** [C18: from ?]

quod erat demonstrandum *Latin.* ('kwɒd 'ɛræt ,dɛmən'strændʊm) (at the conclusion of a proof, esp. of a theorem in Euclidean geometry) which was to be proved. Abbrev.: **QED.**

quodlibet ('kwɒdlɪ,bɛt) *n* **1** a light piece of music. **2** a subtle argument, esp. one prepared as an exercise on a theological topic. [C14: from L, from *quod* what + *libet* pleases, that is, whatever you like]

quoin (kwɔɪn, kɔɪn) *n* **1** an external corner of a wall. **2** a stone forming the external corner of a wall. **3** another name for **keystone** (sense 1). **4** *Printing.* a wedge or an expanding device used to lock type up in a chase. **5** a wedge used for any of various other purposes. [C16: var. of *coin* (in former sense of corner)]

quoit (kɔɪt) *n* a ring of iron, plastic, etc., used in the game of quoits. [C15: from ?]

quoits (kɔɪts) *pl n* (*usually functioning as sing*) a game in which quoits are tossed at a stake in the ground in attempts to encircle it.

quokka ('kwɒkə) *n* a small wallaby of Western Australia, now rare. [of Abor. origin]

quondam ('kwɒndæm) *adj* (*prenominal*) of an earlier time; former. [C16: from L]

quorate ('kwɔ:,reɪt) *adj* *Brit.* consisting of or being a quorum: *the meeting was quorate.*

Quorn (kwɔ:n) *n* *Trademark.* a vegetable protein developed from a type of fungus and used as a meat substitute.

quorum ('kwɔ:rəm) *n* a minimum number of members in an assembly, etc., required to be present before any business can be transacted. [C15: from L, lit.: of whom, occurring in L commissions in the formula *quorum vos...duos* (etc.) *volumus* of whom we wish that you be...two (etc.)]

quota ('kwəʊtə) *n* **1** the proportional share or part that is due from, due to, or allocated to a person or group. **2** a prescribed number or quantity, as of items to be imported or students admitted to a college, etc. [C17: from L *quota pars* how big a share?, from *quotus* of what number]

quotable ('kwəʊtəb⁹l) *adj* apt or suitable for quotation.
▸ ,quota'bility *n*

quotation (kwəʊ'teɪʃən) *n* **1** a phrase or passage from a book, speech, etc., remembered and repeated, usually with an acknowledgment of its source. **2** the act or habit of quoting. **3a** a cost estimate for goods or services given to a prospective client. **3b** the current market price of a commodity, security, etc. **4** *Printing.* a quad used to fill up spaces.

quotation mark *n* either of the punctuation marks used to begin or end a quotation, respectively " and " or ' and '. Also called: **inverted comma.**

quote (kwəʊt) *vb* **quotes, quoting, quoted. 1** to recite a quotation. **2** (*tr*) to put quotation marks round (a phrase, etc.). **3a** to give (a cost estimate for specified goods or services) to a prospective client. **3b** to state (the current market price) of (a security or commodity). ◆ *n* **4** an informal word for **quotation. 5** (*often pl*) an informal word for **quotation mark.** ◆ *interj* **6** an expression used to indicate that the words that follow it form a quotation. [C14: from Med. L *quotāre* to assign reference numbers to passages, from L *quot* how many]

quoted company *n* a company whose shares are quoted on a stock exchange.

quote-driven *adj* denoting an electronic market system, esp. for stock exchanges, in which prices are determined by quotations made by market makers or dealers. Cf. **order-driven.**

quote-unquote *interj* an expression used before or part before and part after a quotation to identify it as such, and sometimes to dissociate the writer or speaker from it.

quoth (kwəʊθ) *vb* *Arch.* (used with all pronouns except *thou* and *you*, and with nouns) said. [OE *cwæth,* third person sing of *cwethan* to say]

quotha ('kwəʊθə) *interj* *Arch.* an expression of mild sarcasm, used in picking up a word or phrase used by someone else. [C16: from *quoth a* quoth he]

quotidian (kwəʊ'tɪdɪən) *adj* **1** (esp. of fever) recurring daily. **2** commonplace. ◆ *n* **3** a fever characterized by attacks that recur daily. [C14: from L *quotīdiānus,* var. of *cottīdiānus* daily]

quotient ('kwəʊʃənt) *n* **1a** the result of the division of one number or quantity by another. **1b** the integral part of the result of division. **2** a ratio of two numbers or quantities to be divided. [C15: from L *quotiens* how often]

quo vadis ('kwəʊ 'vɑːdɪs) whither goest thou? [L from the Vulgate version of John 16:5]

quo warranto ('kwəʊ wɒ'ræntəʊ) *n* *Law.* a proceeding initiated to determine or (formerly) a writ demanding by what authority a person claims an office, franchise, or privilege. [from Med. L: by what warrant]

Qur'an (kʊ'rɑːn, -'ræn) *n* a variant spelling of **Koran.**

q.v. (denoting a cross-reference) *abbrev. for* quod vide. [NL: which (word, item, etc.) see]

qwerty or **QWERTY keyboard** ('kwɜ:tɪ) *n* the standard English language typewriter keyboard layout with the characters q, w, e, r, t, and y at the top left of the keyboard.

★ people and places

Rr

r or **R** (ɑː) n, pl **r's, R's,** or **Rs. 1** the 18th letter of the English alphabet. **2** a speech sound represented by this letter. **3** See **three Rs.**

R symbol for: **1** Chem. gas constant. **2** Chem. radical. **3** Currency. **3a** rand. **3b** rupee. **4** Réaumur (scale). **5** Physics, electronics. resistance. **6** roentgen or röntgen. **7** Chess. rook. **8** Royal. **9** (in the US and Australia) **9a** restricted exhibition (used to describe a category of film certified as unsuitable for viewing by anyone under the age of 18). **9b** (as modifier): an R film.

r. abbrev. for: **1** rare. **2** recto. **3** Also: **r** rod (unit of length). **4** ruled. **5** Cricket. run(s).

R. abbrev. for: **1** rabbi. **2** rector. **3** Regiment. **4** Regina. [L: Queen] **5** Republican. **6** Rex. [L: King] **7** River. **8** Royal.

R. or **r.** abbrev. for: **1** radius. **2** railway. **3** registered (trademark). **4** right. **5** river. **6** road. **7** rouble.

Ra[1] the chemical symbol for radium.

Ra[2] (rɑː) or **Re** ★ n the ancient Egyptian sun god, depicted as a man with a hawk's head surmounted by a solar disc and serpent.

RA abbrev. for: **1** rear admiral. **2** Astron. right ascension. **3** (in Britain) Royal Academician or Academy. **4** (in Britain) Royal Artillery.

RAAF abbrev. for Royal Australian Air Force.

Rabat ★ (rəˈbɑːt) n the capital of Morocco, on the Atlantic coast, served by the port of Salé: became a fortified military centre in the 12th century and a Corsair republic in the 17th century. Pop. (with Salé): 1 386 000 (1994 est.).

Rabaul ★ (rɑːˈbaul) n a port in Papua New Guinea, on NE New Britain Island, in the Bismarck Archipelago: capital of the Territory of New Guinea until 1941; almost surrounded by volcanoes. Pop.: 17 022 (1990).

Rabbath Ammon ★ (ˈræbəθ ˈæmən) n Old Testament. the ancient royal city of the Ammonites, on the site of modern Amman.

rabbet (ˈræbɪt) or **rebate** n **1** a recess, groove, or step, usually of rectangular section, cut into a piece of timber to receive a mating piece. ♦ vb **rabbets, rabbeting, rabbeted** or **rebates, rebating, rebated.** (tr) **2** to cut a rabbet in (timber). **3** to join (pieces of timber) using a rabbet. [C15: from OF rabattre to beat down]

rabbi (ˈræbaɪ) n, pl **rabbis. 1** the spiritual leader of a Jewish congregation; the chief religious minister of a synagogue. **2** a scholar learned in Jewish Law, esp. one authorized to teach it. [Heb., from rabh master + -ī my]

rabbinate (ˈræbɪnɪt) n **1** the position, function, or tenure of office of a rabbi. **2** rabbis collectively.

rabbinic (rəˈbɪnɪk) or **rabbinical** (rəˈbɪnɪkᵊl) adj of or relating to the rabbis, their teachings, writings, views, language, etc.
▸ **rab'binically** adv

Rabbinic (rəˈbɪnɪk) n the form of the Hebrew language used by the rabbis of the Middle Ages.

rabbit (ˈræbɪt) n, pl **rabbits** or **rabbit. 1** any of various common gregarious burrowing mammals of Europe and North Africa. They are closely related to and similar to hares but are smaller and have shorter ears. **2** the fur of such an animal. **3** Brit. inf. a poor performer at a game or sport. ♦ vb **4** (intr) to hunt or shoot rabbits. **5** (intr) (often foll. by on or away) Brit. inf. to talk inconsequentially; chatter. [C14: ?from Walloon robett, dim. of Flemish robbe rabbit, from ?]

rabbit fever n Pathol. another name for **tularaemia.**

rabbit punch n a short sharp blow to the back of the neck that can cause loss of consciousness or even death. Austral. name: **rabbit killer.**

rabble (ˈræbᵊl) n **1** a disorderly crowd; mob. **2 the rabble.** Contemptuous. the common people. [C14 (in the sense: a pack of animals): from ?]

rabble-rouser n a person who manipulates the passions of the mob; demagogue.
▸ **'rabble-,rousing** adj, n

Rabelais ★ (ˈræbə,leɪ; French rablɛ) n François (frɑ̃swa). ?1494–1553, French writer, noted for his Gargantua and Pantagruel (1534).

Rabelaisian (,ræbəˈleɪzɪən, -ʒən) adj **1** of, relating to, or resembling the work of Rabelais, esp. by broad, often bawdy, humour and sharp satire. ♦ n **2** a student or admirer of Rabelais.
▸ ,Rabe'laisianism n

Rabi ★ (ˈrɑːbɪ) n Isidor Isaac. 1898–1988, US physicist, born in Austria, who devised the atomic and molecular beam resonance method of observing atomic spectra. Nobel prize for physics 1944.

rabid (ˈræbɪd, ˈreɪ-) adj **1** relating to or having rabies. **2** zealous; fanatical; violent; raging. [C17: from L rabidus frenzied, from rabere to be mad]
▸ **rabidity** (rəˈbɪdɪtɪ) or **'rabidness** n ▸ **'rabidly** adv

rabies (ˈreɪbiːz) n Pathol. an acute infectious viral disease of the nervous system transmitted by the saliva of infected animals, esp. dogs. [C17: from L: madness, from rabere to rave]
▸ **rabic** (ˈræbɪk) or **rabietic** (,reɪbɪˈɛtɪk) adj

Rabin ★ (ræˈbiːn) n Yitzhak (ˈjɪtzæk). 1922–95, Israeli statesman; prime minister (1974–77; 1992–95); shared Nobel peace prize 1994.

RAC abbrev. for: **1** Royal Armoured Corps. **2** Royal Automobile Club.

raccoon or **racoon** (rəˈkuːn) n, pl **raccoons, raccoon** or **racoons, racoon. 1** an omnivorous mammal, esp. the **North American raccoon,** inhabiting forests of North and Central America. Raccoons have a pointed muzzle, long tail, and greyish-black fur with black bands around the tail and across the face. **2** the fur of the raccoon. [C17: from Algonquian ärähkun, from ärähkuněm he scratches with his hands]

race[1] (reɪs) n **1** a contest of speed, as in running, etc. **2** any competition or rivalry. **3** rapid or constant onward movement: the race of time. **4** a rapid current of water, esp. one through a narrow channel that has a tidal range greater at one end than the other. **5** a channel of a stream, esp. one for conducting water to or from a water wheel for energy: a mill race. **6a** a channel or groove that contains ball bearings or roller bearings. **6b** the inner or outer cylindrical ring in a ball bearing or roller bearing. **7** Austral. & NZ. a narrow passage or enclosure in a sheep yard through which sheep pass individually, as to a sheep dip. **8** Austral. a wire tunnel through which footballers pass from the changing room onto a football field. **9** Arch. the span or course of life. ♦ vb **races, racing, raced. 10** to engage in a contest of speed with (another). **11** to cause (animals, etc.) to engage in a race: to race pigeons. **12** to move or go as fast as possible. **13** to run (an engine, propeller, etc.) or (of an engine, propeller, etc.) to run at high speed, esp. after reduction of the load. ♦ See also **races.** [C13: from ON rás running]

race[2] (reɪs) n **1** a group of people of common ancestry, distinguished from others by physical characteristics, such as hair type, colour of skin, stature, etc. **2 the human race.** human beings collectively. **3** a group of animals or plants having common characteristics that distinguish them from other members of the same species, usually forming a geographically isolated group; subspecies. **4** a group of people sharing the same interests, characteristics, etc.: race of authors. [C16: from F, from It. razza, from ?]

Race ★ (reɪs) n Cape. a cape at the SE extremity of Newfoundland, Canada.

racecard ('reɪsˌkɑːd) n a card at a race meeting with the races and runners, etc., printed on it.

racecourse ('reɪsˌkɔːs) n a long broad track, over which horses are raced. Also called (esp. US and Canad.): **racetrack**.

racehorse ('reɪsˌhɔːs) n a horse specially bred for racing.

raceme (rə'siːm) n an inflorescence in which the flowers are borne along the main stem. [C18: from L racēmus bunch of grapes]
▶ **racemose** ('ræsɪˌməʊs, -məʊz) adj

race meeting n a prearranged fixture for racing horses (or greyhounds) over a set course.

racemic (rə'siːmɪk, -'sɛm-) adj Chem. of, or being a mixture of dextrorotatory and laevorotatory isomers in such proportions that the mixture has no optical activity. [C19: from RACEME + -IC]
▶ **racemism** ('ræsɪˌmɪzəm) n

racer ('reɪsə) n 1 a person, animal, or machine that races. 2 a turntable used to traverse a heavy gun. 3 any of several slender nonvenomous North American snakes, such as the **striped racer**.

race relations n 1 (functioning as pl) the relations between members of two or more human races, esp. within a single community. 2 (functioning as sing) the branch of sociology concerned with such relations.

race riot n a riot among members of different races in the same community.

races ('reɪsɪz) pl n the races. a series of contests of speed between horses (or greyhounds) over a set course.

racetrack ('reɪsˌtræk) n 1 a circuit or course, esp. an oval one, used for motor racing, etc. 2 the usual US and Canad. word for **racecourse**.

raceway ('reɪsˌweɪ) n 1 another word for **race**¹ (senses 5, 6). 2 Chiefly US. a racetrack.

Rachel ★ ('reɪtʃəl) n Old Testament. the second wife of Jacob; mother of Joseph and Benjamin (Genesis 29–35).

rachis or **rhachis** ('reɪkɪs) n, pl **rachises, rhachises** or **rachides, rhachides** ('rækɪˌdiːz, 'reɪ-). 1 Bot. the main axis or stem of an inflorescence or compound leaf. 2 Ornithol. the shaft of a feather, esp. the part that carries the barbs. 3 another name for **spinal column**. [C17: via NL from Gk rhakhis ridge]
▶ **rachial, rhachial** ('reɪkɪəl) or **rachidial, rhachidial** (rə'kɪdɪəl) adj

rachitis (rə'kaɪtɪs) n Pathol. another name for **rickets**.
▶ **rachitic** (rə'kɪtɪk) adj

Rachmaninoff or **Rachmaninov** ★ (ræk'mænɪˌnɒf; Russian rax'maninəf) n Sergei Vassilievich (sɪr'gjej va-'siljɪvɪtʃ). 1873–1943, Russian pianist and composer, in the US from 1917. Works include three symphonies, four piano concertos, operas, and piano music.

Rachmanism ('rækməˌnɪzəm) n extortion or exploitation by a landlord of tenants of slum property. [C20: after Perec Rachman (1920–62), Brit. property-owner]

racial ('reɪʃəl) adj 1 denoting or relating to the division of the human species into races on grounds of physical characteristics. 2 characteristic of any such group.
▶ **racially** adv

Racine ★ (French rasin) n Jean Baptiste (ʒã batist). 1639–99, French poet and dramatist. His plays include Andromaque (1667) and Phèdre (1677).

racism ('reɪsɪzəm) or **racialism** ('reɪʃəˌlɪzəm) n 1 the belief that races have distinctive cultural characteristics determined by hereditary factors and that this endows some races with an intrinsic superiority. 2 abusive or aggressive behaviour towards members of another race on the basis of such a belief.
▶ **racist** or **racialist** n, adj

rack¹ (ræk) n 1 a framework for holding, carrying, or displaying a specific load or object. 2 a toothed bar designed to engage a pinion to form a mechanism that will adjust the position of something. 3 (preceded by the) an instrument of torture that stretched the body of the victim. 4 a cause or state of mental or bodily stress, suffering, etc. (esp. in **on the rack**). 5 US & Canad. (in pool, snooker, etc.) 5a the triangular frame used to arrange the balls for the opening shot. 5b the balls so grouped. Brit.

equivalent: **frame**. ◆ vb (tr) 6 to torture on the rack. 7 to cause great suffering to: guilt racked his conscience. 8 to strain or shake (something) violently: the storm racked the town. 9 to place or arrange in or on a rack. 10 to move (parts of machinery or a mechanism) using a toothed rack. 11 to raise (rents) exorbitantly. 12 **rack one's brains**. to strain in mental effort. [C14 rekke, prob. from MDu. rec framework]
▶ **racker** n

USAGE NOTE See at **wrack**¹.

rack² (ræk) n destruction; wreck (obs. except in **go to rack and ruin**). [C16: var. of WRACK¹]

rack³ (ræk) n another word for **single-foot**. [C16: ? based on ROCK²]

rack⁴ (ræk) n 1 a group of broken clouds moving in the wind. ◆ vb 2 (intr) (of clouds) to be blown along by the wind. [OE wræc what is driven]

rack⁵ (ræk) vb (tr) to clear (wine, beer, etc.) as by siphoning it off from the dregs. [C15: from OProvençal arraca, from raca dregs of grapes after pressing]

rack-and-pinion n 1 a device for converting rotary into linear motion and vice versa, in which a gearwheel (the pinion) engages with a flat toothed bar (the rack). ◆ adj 2 (of a type of steering gear in motor vehicles) having a track rod with a rack along part of its length that engages with a pinion attached to the steering column.

racket¹ ('rækɪt) n 1 a noisy disturbance or loud commotion; clamour; din. 2 an illegal enterprise carried on for profit, such as extortion, fraud, etc. 3 Sl. a business or occupation: what's your racket? 4 Music. a medieval woodwind instrument of deep bass pitch. ◆ vb 5 (intr; often foll. by about) Now rare. to go about gaily or noisily, in search of pleasure, etc. [C16: prob. imit.]
▶ **rackety** adj

racket² or **racquet** ('rækɪt) n 1 a bat consisting of an open network of strings stretched in an oval frame with a handle, used to strike a tennis ball, etc. 2 a snowshoe shaped like a tennis racket. ◆ vb 3 (tr) to strike (a ball, etc.) with a racket. ◆ See also **rackets**. [C16: from F raquette, from Ar. rāhat palm of the hand]

racketeer (ˌrækɪ'tɪə) n 1 a person engaged in illegal enterprises for profit. ◆ vb 2 (intr) to operate an illegal enterprise.
▶ **racketeering** n

racket press n a device consisting of a frame closed by a spring mechanism, for keeping taut the strings of a tennis racket, squash racket, etc.

rackets ('rækɪts) n (functioning as sing) a a game similar to squash played in a four-walled court by two or four players using rackets and a small hard ball. b (as modifier): a rackets court.

Rackham ★ ('rækəm) n Arthur. 1867–1939, British book illustrator, esp. of fairy tales.

rack railway n a steep mountain railway having a middle rail fitted with a rack that engages a pinion on the locomotive to provide traction. Also called: **cog railway**.

rack-rent n 1 a high rent that annually equals the value of the property upon which it is charged. 2 any extortionate rent. ◆ vb 3 to charge an extortionate rent for.
▶ **rack-renter** n

rack saw n Building trades. a wide-toothed saw.

racon ('reɪkɒn) n another name for **radar beacon**. [C20: from RA(DAR) + (BEA)CON]

raconteur (ˌrækɒn'tɜː) n a person skilled in telling stories. [C19: F, from raconter to tell]

racoon (rə'kuːn) n, pl **racoons** or **racoon**. a variant spelling of **raccoon**.

racquet ('rækɪt) n a variant spelling of **racket**².

racy ('reɪsɪ) adj **racier, raciest**. 1 (of a person's manner, literary style, etc.) having a distinctively lively and spirited quality. 2 having a characteristic or distinctive flavour: a racy wine. 3 suggestive; slightly indecent; risqué.
▶ **racily** adv ▶ **raciness** n

★ people and places

rad[1] (ræd) *n* a former unit of absorbed ionizing radiation dose equivalent to an energy absorption per unit mass of 0.01 joule per kilogram of irradiated material. [C20: from RADIATION]

rad[2] *symbol for* radian.

rad. *abbrev. for:* **1** radical. **2** radius.

RADA ('rɑːdə) *n* (in Britain) *acronym for* Royal Academy of Dramatic Art.

radar ('reɪdɑː) *n* **1** a method for detecting the position and velocity of a distant object. A narrow beam of extremely high-frequency radio pulses is transmitted and reflected by the object back to the transmitter. The direction of the reflected beam and the time between transmission and reception of a pulse determine the position of the object. **2** the equipment used in such detection. [C20: ra(dio) d(etecting) a(nd) r(anging)]

radar astronomy *n* the use of radar to map the surfaces of the planets, their satellites, and other bodies.

radar beacon *n* a device for transmitting a coded radar signal in response to a signal from an aircraft or ship. The coded signal is then used by the navigator to determine his position. Also called: **racon.**

radarscope ('reɪdɑːˌskəʊp) *n* a cathode-ray oscilloscope on which radar signals can be viewed.

radar trap *n* a device using radar to detect motorists who exceed the speed limit.

Radcliffe ★ ('rædklɪf) *n* **Ann.** 1764–1823, British novelist, noted for her Gothic romance *The Mysteries of Udolpho* (1794).

raddle ('rædªl) *vb* **raddles, raddling, raddled. 1** (*tr*) *Chiefly Brit.* to paint (the face) with rouge. ◆ *n, vb* **2** another word for **ruddle.** [C16: var. of RUDDLE]

raddled ('rædªld) *adj* (esp. of a person) unkempt or run-down in appearance.

Radetzky ★ (*German* raˈdɛtski) *n* Count **Joseph** ('joːzɛf). 1766–1858, Austrian field marshal: served in the war against Sardinia (1848–49): governor of Lombardy-Venetia in N Italy (1849-57).

radial ('reɪdɪəl) *adj* **1** (of lines, etc.) emanating from a common central point; arranged like the radii of a circle. **2** of, like, or relating to a radius or ray. **3** short for **radial-ply. 4** *Anat.* of or relating to the radius or forearm. **5** *Astron.* (of velocity) in a direction along the line of sight of a celestial object and measured by means of the red shift (or blue shift) of the spectral lines of the object. ◆ *n* **6** a radial part or section. [C16: from Med. L *radiālis,* from RADIUS]
▶ **'radially** *adv*

radial engine *n* an internal-combustion engine having a number of cylinders arranged about a central crankcase.

radial-ply *adj* (of a motor tyre) having the fabric cords in the outer casing running radially to enable the sidewalls to be flexible.

radial symmetry *n* a type of structure of an organism in which a vertical cut through the axis in any of two or more planes produces two halves that are mirror images of each other. Cf. **bilateral symmetry.**

radian ('reɪdɪən) *n* an SI unit of plane angle; the angle between two radii of a circle that cut off on the circumference an arc equal in length to the radius. 1 radian is equivalent to 57.296 degrees. Symbol: rad. [C19: from RADIUS]

radiance ('reɪdɪəns) *or* **radiancy** *n, pl* **radiances** *or* **radiancies. 1** the quality or state of being radiant. **2** a measure of the amount of electromagnetic radiation leaving or arriving at a point on a surface.

radiant ('reɪdɪənt) *adj* **1** sending out rays of light; bright; shining. **2** characterized by health, happiness, etc.: *a radiant smile.* **3** emitted or propagated by or as radiation; radiated: *radiant heat.* **4** sending out heat by radiation: *a radiant heater.* **5** *Physics.* (of a physical quantity in photometry) evaluated by absolute energy measurements: *radiant flux.* ◆ *n* **6** a point or object that emits radiation, esp. the part of a heater that gives out heat. **7** *Astron.* the point in the sky from which a meteor shower appears to emanate. [C15: from L *radiāre* to shine, from *radius* ray of light]
▶ **'radiancy** *n* ▶ **'radiantly** *adv*

radiant energy *n* energy that is emitted or propagated in the form of particles or electromagnetic radiation.

radiant heat *n* heat transferred in the form of electromagnetic radiation rather than by conduction or convection; infrared radiation.

radiata pine (ˌreɪdɪˈɑːtə) *n* a pine tree grown in Australia and New Zealand to produce building timber. Often shortened to **radiata.** [from NL]

radiate *vb* ('reɪdɪˌeɪt), **radiates, radiating, radiated. 1** Also: **eradiate.** to emit (heat, light, or other forms of radiation) or (of heat, light, etc.) to be emitted as radiation. **2** (*intr*) (of lines, beams, etc.) to spread out from a centre or be arranged in a radial pattern. **3** (*tr*) (of a person) to show (happiness, etc.) to a great degree. ◆ *adj* ('reɪdɪɪt, -ˌeɪt). **4** having rays; radiating. **5** (of a capitulum) consisting of ray flowers. **6** (of animals) showing radial symmetry. [C17: from L *radiāre* to emit rays]
▶ **'radiative** *adj*

radiation (ˌreɪdɪˈeɪʃən) *n* **1** *Physics.* **1a** the emission or transfer of radiant energy as particles, electromagnetic waves, sound, etc. **1b** the particles, etc., emitted, esp. the particles and gamma rays emitted in nuclear decay. **2** Also called: **radiation therapy.** *Med.* treatment using a radioactive substance. **3** the act, state, or process of radiating or being radiated.
▶ ˌradi'ational *adj*

radiation sickness *n* *Pathol.* illness caused by overexposure of the body to ionizing radiations from radioactive material or X-rays.

radiator ('reɪdɪˌeɪtə) *n* **1** a device for heating a room, building, etc., consisting of a series of pipes through which hot water or steam passes. **2** a device for cooling an internal-combustion engine, consisting of thin-walled tubes through which water passes. **3** *Electronics.* the part of an aerial or transmission line that radiates electromagnetic waves.

radical ('rædɪkªl) *adj* **1** of, relating to, or characteristic of the basic or inherent constitution of a person or thing; fundamental: *a radical fault.* **2** concerned with or tending to concentrate on fundamental aspects of a matter; searching or thoroughgoing: *radical thought.* **3** favouring or tending to produce extreme or fundamental changes in political, economic, or social conditions, institutions, etc.: *a radical party.* **4** *Med.* (of treatment) aimed at removing the source of a disease: *radical surgery.* **5** *Sl., chiefly US.* very good; excellent. **6** of or arising from the root or the base of the stem of a plant: *radical leaves.* **7** *Maths.* of, relating to, or containing roots of numbers or quantities. **8** *Linguistics.* of or relating to the root of a word. ◆ *n* **9** a person who favours extreme or fundamental change in existing institutions or in political, social, or economic conditions. **10** *Maths.* a root of a number or quantity, such as √5, √x. **11** *Chem.* **11a** short for **free radical. 11b** another name for **group** (sense 9). **12** *Linguistics.* another word for **root**[1] (sense 8). [C14: from LL *rādīcālis* having roots, from L *rādix* a root]
▶ **'radicalness** *n*

radicalism ('rædɪkəˌlɪzəm) *n* **1** the principles, desires, or practices of political radicals. **2** a radical movement, esp. in politics.
▶ ˌradical'istic *adj* ▶ ˌradical'istically *adv*

radically ('rædɪkəlɪ) *adv* thoroughly; completely; fundamentally: *to alter radically.*

radical sign *n* the symbol √ placed before a number or quantity to indicate the extraction of a root, esp. a square root. The value of a higher root is indicated by a raised digit in front of the symbol, as in ∛.

radicand ('rædɪˌkænd, ˌrædɪˈkænd) *n* a number or quantity from which a root is to be extracted, usually preceded by a radical sign: 3 *is the radicand of* √3. [C20: from L *rādīcandum,* lit.: that which is to be rooted, from *rādīcāre,* from *rādix* root]

radicchio (ræˈdiːkɪəʊ) *n, pl* **radicchios.** an Italian variety of chicory, having purple leaves streaked with white that are eaten raw in salads.

radices ('reɪdɪˌsiːz) *n* a plural of **radix**.

radicle ('rædɪkᵊl) *n* **1** *Bot.* **1a** the part of the embryo of seed-bearing plants that develops into the main root. **1b** a very small root or rootlike part. **2** *Anat.* any bodily structure resembling a rootlet, esp. one of the smallest branches of a vein or nerve. **3** *Chem.* a variant spelling of **radical** (sense 11). [C18: from L *rādīcula*, from *rādix* root]

Radiguet ★ (*French* radigε) *n* **Raymond** (rɛmɔ̃). 1903–23, French novelist; the author of *The Devil in the Flesh* (1923).

radii ('reɪdɪˌaɪ) *n* a plural of **radius**.

radio ('reɪdɪəu) *n, pl* **radios**. **1** the use of electromagnetic waves, lying in the radio-frequency range, for broadcasting, two-way communications, etc. **2** an electronic device designed to receive, demodulate, and amplify radio signals from sound broadcasting stations, etc. **3** the broadcasting, content, etc., of radio programmes: *he thinks radio is poor these days.* **4** the occupation or profession concerned with any aspect of the broadcasting of radio programmes. **5** short for **radiotelegraph, radiotelegraphy,** or **radiotelephone. 6** (*modifier*) **6a** of, relating to, or sent by radio signals: *a radio station.* **6b** of, concerned with, using, or operated by radio frequencies: *radio spectrum.* **6c** relating to or produced for radio: *radio drama.* ◆ *vb* **radios, radioing, radioed. 7** to transmit (a message, etc.) to (a person, etc.) by means of radio waves. ◆ Also called (esp. Brit.): **wireless.** [C20: short for *radiotelegraphy*]

radio- *combining form.* **1** denoting radio, broadcasting, or radio frequency: *radiogram.* **2** indicating radioactivity or radiation: *radiocarbon; radiochemistry.* [from F, from L *radius* ray]

radioactive (ˌreɪdɪəu'æktɪv) *adj* exhibiting, using, or concerned with radioactivity.
▸ ˌradio'actively *adv*

radioactive dating *n* another term for **radiometric dating.**

radioactive decay *n* disintegration of a nucleus that occurs spontaneously or as a result of electron capture. Also called: **disintegration.**

radioactive series *n Physics.* a series of nuclides each of which undergoes radioactive decay into the next member of the series, ending with a stable element, usually lead.

radioactive tracer *n Med.* See **tracer** (sense 3).

radioactive waste *n* any waste material containing radionuclides. Also called: **nuclear waste.**

radioactivity (ˌreɪdɪəuæk'tɪvɪtɪ) *n* the spontaneous emission of radiation from atomic nuclei. The radiation can consist of alpha, beta, or gamma radiation.

radio astronomy *n* a branch of astronomy in which a radio telescope is used to detect and analyse radio signals received on earth from radio sources in space.

radio beacon *n* a fixed radio transmitting station that broadcasts a characteristic signal by means of which a vessel or aircraft can determine its bearing or position.

radiobiology (ˌreɪdɪəubaɪ'ɒlədʒɪ) *n* the branch of biology concerned with the effects of radiation on living organisms and the study of biological processes using radioactive substances as tracers.
▸ **radiobiological** (ˌreɪdɪəuˌbaɪə'lɒdʒɪkᵊl) *adj* ▸ ˌradioˌbio'logically *adv* ▸ ˌradiobi'ologist *n*

radiocarbon (ˌreɪdɪəu'kɑːbᵊn) *n* a radioactive isotope of carbon, esp. carbon-14. See **carbon** (sense 1).

radiocarbon dating *n* See **carbon dating.**

radiochemistry (ˌreɪdɪəu'kɛmɪstrɪ) *n* the chemistry of radioactive elements and their compounds.
▸ ˌradio'chemical *adj* ▸ ˌradio'chemist *n*

radio compass *n* any navigational device that gives a bearing by determining the direction of incoming radio waves transmitted from a particular radio station or beacon. See also **goniometer** (sense 2).

radio control *n* remote control by means of radio signals from a transmitter.
▸ 'radio-con'trolled *adj*

radioelement (ˌreɪdɪəu'ɛlɪmənt) *n* an element that is naturally radioactive.

radio frequency *n* **1a** any frequency that lies in the range 10 kilohertz to 300 000 megahertz and can be used for broadcasting. Abbrevs.: **rf, RF. 1b** (*as modifier*): *a radio-frequency amplifier.* **2** the frequency transmitted by a particular radio station.

radio galaxy *n* a galaxy that is a strong emitter of radio waves.

radiogram ('reɪdɪəuˌgræm) *n* **1** *Brit.* a unit comprising a radio and record player. **2** a message transmitted by radiotelegraphy. **3** another name for **radiograph.**

radiograph ('reɪdɪəuˌgrɑːf) *n* an image produced on a specially sensitized photographic film or plate by radiation, usually by X-rays or gamma rays.

radiography (ˌreɪdɪ'ɒgrəfɪ) *n* the production of radiographs of opaque objects for use in medicine, surgery, industry, etc.
▸ ˌradi'ographer *n* ▸ **radiographic** (ˌreɪdɪəu'græfɪk) *adj* ▸ ˌradio'graphically *adv*

radio-immuno-assay ('reɪdɪəuˌɪmjunəu'æseɪ) *n* a sensitive immunological assay, making use of radioactive labelling, of such things as hormone levels in the blood.

radioisotope (ˌreɪdɪəu'aɪsətəup) *n* a radioactive isotope.
▸ **radioisotopic** (ˌreɪdɪəuˌaɪsə'tɒpɪk) *adj*

radiolarian (ˌreɪdɪəu'lɛərɪən) *n* any of various marine protozoans typically having a siliceous shell and stiff radiating cytoplasmic projections. [C19: from NL *Radiolaria,* from LL *radiolus* little sunbeam, from L *radius* ray]

radiology (ˌreɪdɪ'ɒlədʒɪ) *n* the use of X-rays and radioactive substances in the diagnosis and treatment of disease.
▸ ˌradi'ologist *n*

radiometer (ˌreɪdɪ'ɒmɪtə) *n* any instrument for the detection or measurement of radiant energy.
▸ **radiometric** (ˌreɪdɪəu'mɛtrɪk) *adj* ▸ ˌradi'ometry *n*

radiometric dating *n* any method of dating material based on the decay of its constituent radioactive atoms, such as potassium-argon dating or rubidium-strontium dating. Also called: **radioactive dating.**

radiopager ('reɪdɪəuˌpeɪdʒə) *n* a small radio receiver fitted with a buzzer to alert a person to telephone their home, office, etc., to receive a message.
▸ 'radioˌpaging *n*

radiopaque (ˌreɪdɪəu'peɪk) or **radio-opaque** *adj* not permitting X-rays or other radiation to pass through.
▸ **radiopacity** (ˌreɪdɪəu'pæsɪtɪ) or **radio-o'pacity** *n*

radio receiver *n* an apparatus that receives incoming modulated radio waves and converts them into sound.

radioscopy (ˌreɪdɪ'ɒskəpɪ) *n* another word for **fluoroscopy.**
▸ **radioscopic** (ˌreɪdɪəu'skɒpɪk) *adj* ▸ ˌradio'scopically *adv*

radiosonde ('reɪdɪəuˌsɒnd) *n* an airborne instrument to send meteorological information back to earth by radio. [C20: RADIO- + F *sonde* sounding line]

radio source *n* a celestial object, such as a supernova remnant or quasar, that is a source of radio waves.

radio spectrum *n* the range of electromagnetic frequencies used in radio transmission, between 10 kilohertz and 300 000 megahertz.

radio star *n* a former name for **radio source.**

radiotelegraphy (ˌreɪdɪəutɪ'lɛgrəfɪ) *n* a type of telegraphy in which messages (formerly in Morse code) are transmitted by radio waves.
▸ ˌradio'teleˌgraph *vb,* ▸ **radiotelegraphic** (ˌreɪdɪəuˌtɛlɪ'græfɪk) *adj*

radiotelephone (ˌreɪdɪəu'tɛlɪˌfəun) *n* **1** a device for communications by means of radio waves rather than by transmitting along wires or cables. ◆ *vb* **radiotelephones, radiotelephoning, radiotelephoned. 2** to telephone (a person) by radiotelephone.
▸ **radiotelephonic** (ˌreɪdɪəuˌtɛlɪ'fɒnɪk) *adj* ▸ **radiotelephony** (ˌreɪdɪəutɪ'lɛfənɪ) *n*

radio telescope *n* an instrument consisting of an antenna or system of antennas connected to one or more

★ people and places

radio receivers, used in radio astonomy to detect and analyse radio waves from space.

radioteletype (ˌreɪdɪəʊ'telɪˌtaɪp) *n* **1** a teleprinter that transmits or receives information by means of radio waves. **2** a network of such devices widely used for communicating news, messages, etc. Abbrevs.: **RTT, RTTY.**

radiotherapy (ˌreɪdɪəʊ'θerəpɪ) *n* the treatment of disease by means of alpha or beta particles emitted from an implanted or ingested radioisotope, or by means of a beam of high-energy radiation. Cf. **chemotherapy.**
▶ **radiotherapeutic** (ˌreɪdɪəʊˌθerə'pjuːtɪk) *adj* ▶ ˌradio-'therapist *n*

radio wave *n* an electromagnetic wave of radio frequency.

radish ('rædɪʃ) *n* **1** any of a genus of plants of Europe and Asia, with petals arranged like a cross, cultivated for their edible roots. **2** the root of this plant, which has a pungent taste and is eaten raw in salads. [OE *rædīc*, from L *rādīx* root]

radium ('reɪdɪəm) *n* **a** a highly radioactive luminescent white element of the alkaline earth group of metals. It occurs in pitchblende and other uranium ores. Symbol: Ra; atomic no.: 88; half-life of most stable isotope, ^{226}Ra: 1620 years. **b** (*as modifier*): *radium needle*. [C20: from L *radius* ray]

radium therapy *n* treatment of disease, esp. cancer, by exposing affected tissues to radiation from radium.

radius ('reɪdɪəs) *n, pl* **radii** *or* **radiuses. 1** a straight line joining the centre of a circle or sphere to any point on the circumference or surface. **2** the length of this line, usually denoted by the symbol *r*. **3** *Anat*. the outer, slightly shorter of the two bones of the human forearm, extending from the elbow to the wrist. **4** a corresponding bone in other vertebrates. **5** any of the veins of an insect's wing. **6** a group of ray flowers, occurring in such plants as the daisy. **7a** any radial or radiating part, such as a spoke. **7b** (*as modifier*): *a radius arm*. **8** a circular area of a size indicated by the length of its radius: *the police stopped every lorry within a radius of four miles*. **9** the operational limit of a ship, aircraft, etc. [C16: from L: rod, ray, spoke]

radix ('reɪdɪks) *n, pl* **radices** *or* **radixes. 1** *Maths*. any number that is the base of a number system or of a system of logarithms: *10 is the radix of the decimal system*. **2** *Biol*. the root or point of origin of a part or organ. **3** *Linguistics*. a less common word for **root**[1] (sense 8). [C16: from L *rādīx* root]

radix point *n* a point, such as the decimal point in the decimal system, separating the integral part of a number from the fractional part.

Radnorshire ('rædnəˌʃɪə, -ʃə) *or* **Radnor** ★ *n* (until 1974) a county of E Wales, now part of Powys.

Radom ★ (*Polish* 'radɔm) *n* a city in E Poland: under Austria from 1795 to 1815 and Russia from 1815 to 1918. Pop.: 232 300 (1995 est.).

radome ('reɪdəʊm) *n* a protective housing for a radar antenna made from a material that is transparent to radio waves. [C20: from RA(DAR) + DOME]

radon ('reɪdɒn) *n* a colourless radioactive element of the rare gas group, the most stable isotope of which, radon-222, is a decay product of radium. Symbol: Rn; atomic no.: 86; half-life of ^{222}Rn: 3.82 days. [C20: from RADIUM + -ON]

radula ('rædjʊlə) *n, pl* **radulae** (-ˌliː). a horny tooth-bearing strip on the tongue of molluscs that is used for rasping food. [C19: from LL: a scraping iron, from L *rādere* to scrape]
▶ 'radular *adj*

Raeburn ★ ('reɪˌbɜːn) *n* Sir **Henry**. 1756–1823, Scottish portrait painter.

RAF (*Not standard* ræf) *abbrev*. for Royal Air Force.

Rafferty ('ræfətɪ) *or* **Rafferty's rules** *pl n Austral. & NZ sl*. no rules at all. [C20: from ?]

raffia *or* **raphia** ('ræfɪə) *n* **1** a palm tree, native to Madagascar, that has large plumelike leaves, the stalks of which yield a useful fibre. **2** the fibre obtained from this plant, used for weaving, etc. **3** any of several related

palms or the fibre obtained from them. [C19: from Malagasy]

raffish ('ræfɪʃ) *adj* **1** careless or unconventional in dress, manners, etc.; rakish. **2** tawdry; flashy; vulgar. [C19: from *raff* rubbish, rabble]
▶ 'raffishly *adv* ▶ 'raffishness *n*

raffle ('ræf³l) *n* **1a** a lottery in which the prizes are goods rather than money. **1b** (*as modifier*): *a raffle ticket*. ◆ *vb* **raffles, raffling, raffled. 2** (*tr*; often foll. by *off*) to dispose of (goods) in a raffle. [C14 (a dice game): from OF, from ?]
▶ 'raffler *n*

Raffles ★ ('ræf³lz) *n* Sir **Thomas Stamford**. 1781–1826, British colonial administrator: founded Singapore (1819) as a station for the British East India Company.

rafflesia (ræ'fliːzɪə) *n* any of various tropical Asian parasitic leafless plants, the flowers of which grow up to 45 cm (18 inches) across, smell of putrid meat, and are pollinated by carrion flies. [C19: NL, after Sir Stamford RAFFLES, who discovered it]

Rafsanjani ★ (ˌræfsæn'dʒɑːnɪ) *n* **Ali Akbar Hashemi**. born 1934, Iranian politician: president of Iran (1989–97).

raft[1] (rɑːft) *n* **1** a buoyant platform of logs, planks, etc., used as a raft or moored platform. **2** a thick slab of reinforced concrete laid over soft ground to provide a foundation for a building. ◆ *vb* **3** to convey on or travel by raft, or make a raft from. [C15: from ON *raptr* RAFTER]

raft[2] (rɑːft) *n Inf*. a large collection or amount: *a raft of old notebooks discovered in a cupboard*.

rafter ('rɑːftə) *n* any one of a set of parallel sloping beams that form the framework of a roof. [OE *ræfter*]

RAFVR *abbrev*. for Royal Air Force Volunteer Reserve.

rag[1] (ræg) *n* **1a** a small piece of cloth, such as one torn from a discarded garment, or such pieces of cloth collectively. **1b** (*as modifier*): *a rag doll*. **2** a fragmentary piece of any material; scrap; shred. **3** *Inf*. a newspaper, esp. one considered as worthless, sensational, etc. **4** *Inf*. an item of clothing. **5** *Inf*. a handkerchief. **6** *Brit. sl., esp. naval*. a flag or ensign. **7 from rags to riches.** *Inf*. **7a** from poverty to great wealth. **7b** (*as modifier*): *a rags-to-riches tale*. [C14: prob. back formation from RAGGED from OE *raggig*]

rag[2] (ræg) *vb* **rags, ragging, ragged.** (*tr*) **1** to draw attention facetiously and persistently to the shortcomings of (a person). **2** *Brit*. to play rough practical jokes on. ◆ *n* **3** *Brit*. a boisterous practical joke. **4** (in British universities, etc.) **4a** a period in which various events are organized to raise money for charity. **4b** (*as modifier*): *rag day*. [C18: from ?]

rag[3] (ræg) *Jazz*. ◆ *n* **1** a piece of ragtime music. ◆ *vb* **rags, ragging, ragged. 2** (*tr*) to compose or perform in ragtime. [C20: from RAGTIME]

raga ('rɑːgə) *n* (in Indian music) **1** any of several conventional patterns of melody and rhythm that form the basis for freely interpreted compositions. **2** a composition based on one of these patterns. [C18: from Sansk. *rāga* tone, colour]

ragamuffin ('rægəˌmʌfɪn) *n* **1** a ragged unkempt person, esp. a child. **2** another name for **ragga**. [C14 *Ragamoffyn*, a demon in the poem *Piers Plowman* (1393); prob. based on RAG[1]]

rag-and-bone man *n Brit*. a man who buys and sells discarded clothing, etc. US equivalent: **junkman.**

ragbag ('rægˌbæg) *n* **1** a bag for storing odd rags. **2** a confused assortment; jumble.

ragbolt ('rægˌbəʊlt) *n* a bolt that has angled projections on it to prevent it working loose.

rage (reɪdʒ) *n* **1** intense anger; fury. **2** violent movement or action, esp. of the sea, wind, etc. **3** great intensity of hunger or other feelings. **4** a fashion or craze (esp. in **all the rage**). **5** *Austral. & NZ inf*. a dance or party. ◆ *vb* **rages, raging, raged.** (*intr*) **6** to feel or exhibit intense anger. **7** (esp. of storms, fires, etc.) to move or surge with great violence. **8** (esp. of a disease) to spread rapidly and uncontrollably. **9** *Austral. & NZ inf*. to have a good time. [C13: via OF from L *rabiēs* madness]

ragga ('rægə) *n* a dance-oriented style of reggae. Also called: **ragamuffin**. [C20: shortened from RAGAMUFFIN]

ragged ('rægɪd) *adj* **1** (of clothes) worn to rags; tattered. **2**

(of a person) dressed in tattered clothes. **3** having a neglected or unkempt appearance: *ragged weeds.* **4** having a rough or uneven surface or edge; jagged. **5** uneven or irregular: *a ragged beat; a ragged shout.* [C13: prob. from *ragge* RAG[1]]
▶ **'raggedly** *adv* ▶ **'raggedness** *n*

ragged robin *n* a plant related to the carnation family and native to Europe and Asia, that has pink or white flowers with ragged petals. See also **catchfly**.

raggedy ('rægɪdɪ) *adj Inf., chiefly US & Canad.* somewhat ragged; tattered: *a raggedy doll.*

ragi, raggee, *or* **raggy** ('rægɪ) *n* a cereal grass, cultivated in Africa and Asia for its edible grain. [C18: from Hindi]

raglan ('ræglən) *n* **1** a coat, jumper, etc., with sleeves that continue to the collar instead of having armhole seams. ◆ *adj* **2** cut in this design: *a raglan sleeve.* [C19: after Lord RAGLAN]

Raglan ★ ('ræglən) *n* Fitzroy James Henry Somerset, 1st Baron Raglan. 1788–1855, British field marshal: commanded British troops (1854–55) in the Crimean War.

ragout (ræ'gu:) *n* **1** a richly seasoned stew of meat and vegetables. ◆ *vb* **ragouts** (-'gu:z), **ragouting** (-'gu:ɪŋ), **ragouted** (-'gu:d). **2** (*tr*) to make into a ragout. [C17: from F, from *ragoûter* to stimulate the appetite again, from *ra-* RE- + *goûter* from L *gustāre* to taste]

rag-rolling *n* a decorating technique in which paint is applied with a roughly folded cloth in order to create a marbled effect.

ragtag ('ræg,tæg) *n Derog.* the common people; rabble (esp. in **ragtag and bobtail**). [C19: from RAG[1] + TAG[1]]

ragtime ('ræg,taɪm) *n* a style of jazz piano music, developed by Scott Joplin around 1900, having a two-four rhythm base and a syncopated melody. [C20: prob. from RAGGED + TIME]

rag trade *n Inf.* the clothing business.

Ragusa ★ (*Italian* ra'gu:za) *n* **1** an industrial town in SE Sicily. Pop.: 68 850 (1990). **2** the Italian name (until 1918) for **Dubrovnik**.

ragweed ('ræg,wi:d) *n* a North American plant of the composite family such as the **common ragweed**. Its green tassel-like flowers produce large amounts of pollen, which causes hay fever. Also called: **ambrosia**.

ragworm ('ræg,wɜːm) *n* any polychaete worm living chiefly in burrows in sand and having a flattened body with a row of fleshy lateral appendages along each side. US name: **clamworm**.

ragwort ('ræg,wɜːt) *n* any of several European plants of the composite family that have yellow daisy-like flowers. See also **groundsel**.

rah (rɑː) *interj Inf., chiefly US.* short for **hurrah**.

rai (raɪ) *n* a type of Algerian popular music based on traditional Algerian music influenced by modern Western pop. [C20: Ar., lit.: opinion]

raid (reɪd) *n* **1** a sudden surprise attack. **2** a surprise visit by police searching for criminals or illicit goods: *a fraud-squad raid.* See also **bear raid, dawn raid, ram raid**. ◆ *vb* **3** to make a raid against (a person, thing, etc.). **4** to sneak into (a place) in order to take something, steal, etc.: *raiding the larder.* [C15: Scot. dialect, from OE *rād* military expedition]
▶ **'raider** *n*

rail[1] (reɪl) *n* **1** a horizontal bar of wood, etc., supported by vertical posts, functioning as a fence, barrier, etc. **2** a horizontal bar fixed to a wall on which to hang things: *a picture rail.* **3** a horizontal framing member in a door. Cf. **stile**[2]. **4** short for **railing. 5** one of a pair of parallel bars laid on a track, roadway, etc., that serve as a guide and running surface for the wheels of a train, tramcar, etc. **6a** short for **railway. 6b** (*as modifier*): *rail transport.* **7** *Naut.* a trim for finishing the top of a bulwark. **8 off the rails. 8a** into or in a state of disorder. **8b** eccentric or mad. ◆ *vb* (*tr*) **9** to provide with a rail or railings. **10** (usually foll. by *in* or *off*) to fence (an area) with rails. [C13: from OF *raille* rod, from L *rēgula* ruler]

rail[2] (reɪl) *vb* (*intr*; foll. by *at* or *against*) to complain bit

terly or vehemently. [C15: from OF *railler* to mock, from OProvençal *ralhar* to chatter, from LL *ragere* to yell]
▶ **'railer** *n*

rail[3] (reɪl) *n* any of various small cranelike wading marsh birds with short wings and neck, long legs, and dark plumage. [C15: from OF *raale*, ?from L *rādere* to scrape]

railcar ('reɪl,kɑː) *n* a passenger-carrying railway vehicle consisting of a single coach with its own power unit.

railcard ('reɪl,kɑːd) *n Brit.* a card issued to students or senior citizens to entitle them to cheap rail fares.

railhead ('reɪl,hed) *n* **1** a terminal of a railway. **2** the farthest point reached by completed track on an unfinished railway.

railing ('reɪlɪŋ) *n* **1** (*often pl*) a fence, balustrade, or barrier that consists of rails supported by posts. **2** rails collectively or material for making rails.

raillery ('reɪlərɪ) *n, pl* **railleries. 1** light-hearted satire or ridicule; banter. **2** a bantering remark. [C17: from F, from *railler* to tease; see RAIL[2]]

railroad ('reɪl,rəʊd) *n* **1** the usual US word for **railway**. ◆ *vb* **2** (*tr*) *Inf.* to force (a person) into (an action) with haste or by unfair means.

railway ('reɪl,weɪ) *or US* **railroad** *n* **1** a permanent track composed of a line of parallel metal rails fixed to sleepers, for transport of passengers and goods in trains. **2** any track for the wheels of a vehicle to run on: *a cable railway.* **3** the entire equipment, rolling stock, buildings, property, and system of tracks used in such a transport system. **4** the organization responsible for operating a railway network. **5** (*modifier*) of, relating to, or used on a railway: *a railway engine.*

raiment ('reɪmənt) *n Arch. or poetic.* attire; clothing. [C15: from *arrayment*, from OF *areement*; see ARRAY]

rain (reɪn) *n* **1a** precipitation from clouds in the form of drops of water, formed by the condensation of water vapour in the atmosphere. **1b** a fall of rain; shower. **1c** (*in combination*): *a raindrop.* **2** a large quantity of anything falling rapidly or in quick succession: *a rain of abuse.* **3** (**come**) **rain or** (**come**) **shine.** regardless of the weather or circumstances. **4 right as rain.** *Brit. inf.* perfectly all right. ◆ *vb* **5** (*intr*; with *it* as subject) to be the case that rain is falling. **6** (*often with it* as subject) to fall or cause to fall like rain. **7** (*tr*) to bestow in large measure: *to rain abuse on someone.* **8 rained off.** cancelled or postponed on account of rain. US and Canad. term: **rained out.** ◆ See also **rains**. [OE *regn*]
▶ **'rainless** *adj*

rainbow ('reɪn,bəʊ) *n* **1a** a bow-shaped display in the sky of the colours of the spectrum, caused by the refraction and reflection of the sun's rays through rain. **1b** (*as modifier*): *a rainbow pattern.* **2** an illusory hope: *to chase rainbows.* **3** (*modifier*) of or relating to a political grouping together by several minorities, esp. of different races: *the rainbow coalition.*

Rainbow Bridge ★ *n* a natural stone bridge over a creek in SE Utah. Height: 94 m (309 ft). Span: 85 m (278 ft).

rainbow nation *n S. African.* an epithet, alluding to its multiracial population, of **South Africa**. [C20: coined by Nelson MANDELA following the end of apartheid]

rainbow trout *n* a freshwater trout of North American origin, marked with many black spots and two longitudinal red stripes.

rain check *n US & Canad.* **1** a ticket stub for a baseball game that allows readmission on a future date if the event is cancelled because of rain. **2** the deferral of acceptance of an offer. **3 take a rain check.** *Inf.* to accept or request the postponement of an offer.

raincoat ('reɪn,kəʊt) *n* a coat made of a waterproof material.

rainfall ('reɪn,fɔːl) *n* **1** precipitation in the form of raindrops. **2** *Meteorol.* the amount of precipitation in a specified place and time.

rainforest ('reɪn,fɒrɪst) *n* dense forest found in tropical areas of heavy rainfall.

rain gauge *n* an instrument for measuring rainfall over

★ people and places

snowfall, consisting of a cylinder covered by a funnel-like lid.

Rainier ★ ('reɪnɪə; reɪ'nɪə, rə-) *n* **Mount.** a mountain in W Washington State: the highest mountain in the state and in the Cascade Range. Height: 4392 m (14 410 ft).

Rainier III ★ ('reɪnɪˌeɪ; *French* rɛnje) *n* full name *Rainier Louis Henri Maxence Bertrand de Grimaldi.* born 1923, ruling prince of Monaco from 1949.

rainproof ('reɪnˌpruːf) *adj* **1** Also: **'rain,tight.** (of garments, materials, etc.) impermeable to rainwater. ◆ *vb* **2** (*tr*) to make rainproof.

rains (reɪnz) *pl n* **the rains.** the season of heavy rainfall, esp. in the tropics.

rain shadow *n* the relatively dry area on the leeward side of high ground in the path of rain-bearing winds.

rainstorm ('reɪnˌstɔːm) *n* a storm with heavy rain.

rainwater ('reɪnˌwɔːtə) *n* pure water from rain (as distinguished from spring water, tap water, etc., which may contain minerals and impurities).

rainy ('reɪnɪ) *adj* **rainier, rainiest. 1** characterized by a large rainfall: *a rainy climate.* **2** wet or showery; bearing rain. ▸ **'rainily** *adv* ▸ **'raininess** *n*

rainy day *n* a future time of need, esp. financial.

Rais *or* **Retz** ★ (*French* rɛ) *n* **Gilles de** (ʒil də). 1404–40, French nobleman who fought with Joan of Arc: marshal of France (1429–40). He was executed for the torture and murder of more than 140 children.

raise (reɪz) *vb* **raises, raising, raised.** (*mainly tr*) **1** to move or elevate to a higher position or level; lift. **2** to set or place in an upright position. **3** to construct, build, or erect: *to raise a barn.* **4** to increase in amount, size, value, etc.: *to raise prices.* **5** to increase in degree, strength, intensity, etc.: *to raise one's voice.* **6** to advance in rank or status; promote. **7** to arouse or awaken from sleep or death. **8** to stir up or incite; activate: *to raise a mutiny.* **9 raise Cain** (*or* **the devil, hell, the roof,** etc.). **9a** to create a disturbance, esp. by making a great noise. **9b** to protest vehemently. **10** to give rise to; cause or provoke: *to raise a smile.* **11** to put forward for consideration: *to raise a question.* **12** to cause to assemble or gather together: *to raise an army.* **13** to grow or cause to grow: *to raise a crop.* **14** to bring up; rear: *to raise a family.* **15** to cause to be heard or known; utter or express: *to raise a shout.* **16** to bring to an end; remove: *to raise a siege.* **17** to cause (bread, etc.) to rise, as by the addition of yeast. **18** *Poker.* to bet more than (the previous player). **19** *Bridge.* to bid (one's partner's suit) at a higher level. **20** *Naut.* to cause (something) to seem to rise above the horizon by approaching: *we raised land after 20 days.* **21** to establish radio communications with: *we raised Moscow last night.* **22** to obtain (money, funds, etc.). **23** to bring (a surface, a design, etc.) into relief; cause to project. **24** to cause (a blister, etc.) to form on the skin. **25** *Maths.* to multiply (a number) by itself a specified number of times: *8 is 2 raised to the power 3.* **26 raise one's glass (to).** to drink a toast (to). **27 raise one's hat.** *Old-fashioned.* to take one's hat briefly off one's head as a greeting or mark of respect. ◆ *n* **28** the act or an instance of raising. **29** *Chiefly US & Canad.* an increase, esp. in salary, wages, etc.; rise. [C12: from ON *reisa*] ▸ **'raisable** *or* **'raiseable** *adj*

raised beach *n* a wave-cut platform raised above the shoreline by a relative fall in the water level.

raisin ('reɪzᵊn) *n* a dried grape. [C13: from OF: grape, ult. from L *racēmus* cluster of grapes] ▸ **'raisiny** *adj*

raison d'être *French.* (rɛzɔ̃ dɛtrə) *n, pl* **raisons d'être** (rɛzɔ̃ dɛtrə). reason or justification for existence.

raita ('raɪtə) *n* an Indian dish of finely chopped cucumber, peppers, mint, etc., in yogurt, served with curries. [C20: from Hindi]

raj (rɑːdʒ) *n* **1** (in India) government; rule. **2** (cap. and preceded by *the*) the British government in India before 1947. [C19: from Hindi, from Sansk., from *rājati* he rules]

rajah *or* **raja** ('rɑːdʒə) *n* **1** (in India, formerly) a ruler: sometimes used as a title preceding a name. **2** a Malayan

or Javanese prince or chieftain. [C16: from Hindi, from Sansk. *rājan* king]

Rajasthan ★ (ˌrɑːdʒə'stɑːn) *n* a state of NW India, bordering on Pakistan: formed in 1958; contains the Thar Desert in the west. Capital: Jaipur. Pop.: 48 040 000 (1994 est.). Area: 342 239 sq. km (132 111 sq. miles).

Rajkot ★ ('rɑːdʒkəʊt) *n* a city in W India, in S Gujarat. Pop.: 559 407 (1991).

Rajput *or* **Rajpoot** ('rɑːdʒpʊt) *n Hinduism.* one of a Hindu military caste claiming descent from the Kshatriya, the original warrior caste. [C16: from Hindi, from Sansk. *rājan* king]

Rajputana ★ (ˌrɑːdʒpʊ'tɑːnə) *n* a former group of princely states in NW India: now mostly part of Rajasthan.

Rakata ★ (rə'kɑːtə) *n* another name for **Krakatoa.**

rake[1] (reɪk) *n* **1** a hand implement consisting of a row of teeth set in a headpiece attached to a long shaft and used for gathering hay, straw, etc., or for smoothing loose earth. **2** any of several mechanical farm implements equipped with rows of teeth or rotating wheels mounted with tines and used to gather hay, straw, etc. **3** any of various implements similar in shape or function. **4** the act of raking. ◆ *vb* **raises, raking, raked. 5** to scrape, gather, or remove (leaves, refuse, etc.) with a rake. **6** to level or prepare (a surface) with a rake. **7** (*tr*; sometimes foll. by *out*) to clear (ashes, etc.) from (a fire). **8** (*tr*; foll. by *up* or *together*) to gather (items or people) with difficulty, as from a scattered area or limited supply. **9** (*tr*; often foll. by *through, over,* etc.) to search or examine carefully. **10** (when *intr*, foll. by *against, along,* etc.) to scrape or graze: *the ship raked the side of the quay.* **11** (*tr*) to direct (gunfire) along the length of (a target): *machine-guns raked the column.* **12** (*tr*) to sweep (one's eyes) along the length of (something); scan. ◆ See also **rake in, rake-off,** etc. [OE *raca*] ▸ **'raker** *n*

rake[2] (reɪk) *n* a dissolute man, esp. one in fashionable society; roué. [C17: short for *rakehell* a dissolute man]

rake[3] (reɪk) *vb* **rakes, raking, raked.** (*mainly intr*) **1** to incline from the vertical by a perceptible degree, esp. (of a ship's mast) towards the stern. **2** (*tr*) to construct with a backward slope. ◆ *n* **3** the degree to which an object, such as a ship's mast, inclines from the perpendicular, esp. towards the stern. **4** *Theatre.* the slope of a stage from the back towards the footlights. **5** the angle between the working face of a cutting tool and a plane perpendicular to the surface of the workpiece. [C17: from ?; ? rel. to G *ragen* to project, Swedish *raka*]

rake in *vb* (*tr, adv*) *Inf.* to acquire (money) in large amounts.

rake-off *Sl.* ◆ *n* **1** a share of profits, esp. one that is illegal or given as a bribe. ◆ *vb* **rake off. 2** (*tr, adv*) to take or receive (such a share of profits).

rake up *vb* (*tr, adv*) to revive, discover, or bring to light (something forgotten): *to rake up an old quarrel.*

raki *or* **rakee** (rɑː'kiː, 'rækɪ) *n* a strong spirit distilled in Turkey from grain, usually flavoured with aniseed or other aromatics. [C17: from Turkish *rāqī*]

rakish[1] ('reɪkɪʃ) *adj* dissolute; profligate. [C18: from RAKE[2]] ▸ **'rakishly** *adv* ▸ **'rakishness** *n*

rakish[2] ('reɪkɪʃ) *adj* **1** dashing; jaunty: *a hat set at a rakish angle.* **2** *Naut.* (of a ship or boat) having lines suggestive of speed. [C19: prob. from RAKE[3]]

rale *or* **râle** (rɑːl) *n Med.* an abnormal crackling sound heard on auscultation of the chest, usually caused by the accumulation of fluid in the lungs. [C19: from F, from *râler* to breathe with a rattling sound]

Raleigh[1] ★ ('rɔːlɪ, 'rɑː-) *n* a city in E central North Carolina, capital of the state. Pop.: 236 707 (1994 est.).

Raleigh[2] *or* **Ralegh** ★ ('rɔːlɪ, 'rɑː-) *n* Sir **Walter.** ?1552–1618, English explorer and writer; favourite of Elizabeth I: introduced tobacco and potatoes into England. He was imprisoned (1603–16) for conspiracy against James I and subsequently beheaded.

rallentando (ˌrælɛn'tændəʊ) *adj, adv Music.* becoming

slower. Also: **ritardando**. [C19: It., from *rallentare* to slow down]

rally[1] ('rælɪ) *vb* **rallies, rallying, rallied. 1** to bring (a group, unit, etc.) into order, as after dispersal, or (of such a group) to reform and come to order. **2** (when *intr*, foll. by *to*) to organize (supporters, etc.) for a common cause or (of such people) to come together for a purpose. **3** to summon up (one's strength, spirits, etc.) or (of a person's health, strength, or spirits) to revive or recover. **4** (*intr*) *Stock Exchange*. to increase sharply after a decline. **5** (*intr*) *Tennis, squash, etc*. to engage in a rally. ♦ *n, pl* **rallies. 6** a large gathering of people for a common purpose. **7** a marked recovery of strength or spirits, as during illness. **8** a return to order after dispersal or rout, as of troops, etc. **9** *Stock Exchange*. a sharp increase in price or trading activity after a decline. **10** *Tennis, squash, etc*. an exchange of several shots before one player wins the point. **11** a type of motoring competition over public roads. [C16: from OF *rallier*, from RE- + *alier* to unite]
▸ 'rallier *n*

rally[2] ('rælɪ) *vb* **rallies, rallying, rallied.** to mock or ridicule (someone) in a good-natured way; chaff; tease. [C17: from OF *railler* to tease; see RAIL[2]]

rallycross ('rælɪ,krɒs) *n* a form of motor sport in which cars race over a one-mile circuit of rough grass with some hard-surfaced sections.

rally round *vb* (*intr*) to come to the aid of (someone); offer moral or practical support.

ram (ræm) *n* **1** an uncastrated adult male sheep. **2** a piston or moving plate, esp. one driven hydraulically or pneumatically. **3** the falling weight of a pile driver. **4** short for **battering ram. 5** a pointed projection in the stem of an ancient warship for puncturing the hull of enemy ships. **6** a warship equipped with a ram. ♦ *vb* **rams, ramming, rammed. 7** (*tr*; usually foll. by *into*) to force or drive, as by heavy blows: *to ram a post into the ground.* **8** (of a moving object) to crash with force (against another object) or (of two moving objects) to collide in this way. **9** (*tr*; often foll. by *in* or *down*) to stuff or cram (something into a hole, etc.). **10** (*tr*; foll. by *onto, against*, etc.) to thrust violently: *he rammed the books onto the desk.* **11** (*tr*) to present (an idea, argument, etc.) forcefully or aggressively (esp. in **ram** (something) **down someone's throat**). **12** (*tr*) to drive (a charge) into a firearm. [OE *ramm*]
▸ 'rammer *n*

Ram (ræm) *n* **the.** the constellation Aries, the first sign of the zodiac.

RAM[1] (ræm) *n Computing. acronym for* random access memory: semiconductor memory in which all storage locations can be rapidly accessed in the same amount of time. It forms the main memory of a computer, used by applications to perform tasks while the device is operating.

RAM[2] *abbrev. for* Royal Academy of Music.

Ramadan *or* **Rhamadhan** (,ræmə'dɑːn) *n* **1** the ninth month of the Muslim year, lasting 30 days, during which strict fasting is observed from sunrise to sunset. **2** the fast itself. [C16: from Ar., lit.: the hot month, from *ramad* dryness]

Ramakrishna ★ (,rɑːmə'krɪʃnə) *n* **Sri** (sriː). 1834–86, Hindu yogi and religious reformer.

Raman effect ('rɑːmən) *n* the change in wavelength of light that is scattered by electrons within a material: used in **Raman spectroscopy** for studying molecules. [C20: after Sir Chandasekhara *Raman* (1888–1970), Indian physicist]

Ramat Gan ★ (rɑː'mɑːt 'gɑːn) *n* a city in Israel, E of Tel Aviv. Pop.: 121 700 (1996 est.).

Rambert ★ ('rɒmbɛə) *n* Dame **Marie.** 1888–1982, British ballet dancer and teacher, born in Poland: founded the **Ballet Rambert** (1926).

ramble ('ræmb[ə]l) *vb* **rambles, rambling, rambled.** (*intr*) **1** to stroll about freely, as for relaxation, with no particular direction. **2** (of paths, streams, etc.) to follow a winding course; meander. **3** to grow or develop in a random fashion. **4** (of speech, writing, etc.) to lack organization. ♦ *n* **5** a leisurely stroll, esp. in the countryside. [C17: prob. rel. to MDu. *rammelen* to ROAM (of animals)]

rambler ('ræmblə) *n* **1** a weak-stemmed plant that straggles over other vegetation. **2** a person who rambles, esp. one who takes country walks. **3** a person who lacks organization in his speech or writing.

rambling ('ræmblɪŋ) *adj* **1** straggling or sprawling haphazardly: *a rambling old house.* **2** (of speech or writing) diffuse and disconnected. **3** (of a plant, esp. a rose) climbing and straggling. **4** nomadic; wandering.

Ramboesque (,ræmbəʊ'esk) *adj* looking or behaving like or characteristic of Rambo, a mindlessly brutal fictional film character.
▸ 'Rambo,ism *n*

Rambouillet ★ (*French* rãbujɛ) *n* a town in N France, in the Yvelines department: site of the summer residence of French presidents. Pop.: 25 300 (1990).

rambunctious (ræm'bʌŋk[ʃ]əs) *adj Inf.* boisterous; unruly. [C19: prob. from Icelandic *ram* (intensifying prefix) + -*bunctious*, from BUMPTIOUS]
▸ ram'bunctiousness *n*

rambutan (ræm'buːt[ə]n) *n* **1** a tree related to the soapberry, native to SE Asia, that has bright red edible fruit covered with hairs. **2** the fruit of this tree. [C18: from Malay, from *rambut* hair]

RAMC *abbrev. for* Royal Army Medical Corps.

Rameau ★ (*French* ramo) *n* **Jean Philippe** (ʒɑ̃ filip). 1683–1764, French composer. His works include the opera *Castor et Pollux* (1737) and his *Traité de l'harmonie* (1722) was important in the development of harmony.

ramekin *or* **ramequin** ('ræmɪkɪn) *n* **1** a savoury dish made from a cheese mixture baked in a fireproof container. **2** the container itself. [C18: F *ramequin*, of Gmc origin]

Rameses ★ ('ræmɪ,siːz) *n* a variant of **Ramses.**

ramification (,ræmɪfɪ'keɪʃən) *n* **1** the act or process of ramifying or branching out. **2** an offshoot or subdivision. **3** a structure of branching parts.

ramify ('ræmɪ,faɪ) *vb* **ramifies, ramifying, ramified. 1** to divide into branches or branchlike parts. **2** (*intr*) to develop complicating consequences. [C16: from F *ramifier*, from L *rāmus* branch + *facere* to make]

Ramillies ★ ('ræmɪliːz; *French* ramiji) *n* a village in central Belgium where the Duke of Marlborough defeated the French in 1706.

ramjet *or* **ramjet engine** ('ræm,dʒet) *n* **a** a type of jet engine in which fuel is burned in a duct using air compressed by the forward speed of the aircraft. **b** an aircraft powered by such an engine.

ramose ('reɪməʊs, ræ'məʊs) *or* **ramous** ('reɪməs) *adj* having branches. [C17: from L *rāmōsus*, from *rāmus* branch]
▸ 'ramosely *or* 'ramously *adv* ▸ ramosity (ræ'mɒsɪtɪ) *n*

ramp (ræmp) *n* **1** a sloping floor, path, etc., that joins two surfaces at different levels. **2** a place where the level of a road surface changes because of roadworks. **3** a movable stairway by which passengers enter and leave an aircraft. **4** the act of ramping. **5** *Brit. sl.* a swindle, esp. one involving exorbitant prices. ♦ *vb* **6** (*intr*) (often foll. by *about* or *around*) (esp. of animals) to rush around in a wild excited manner. **7** (*intr*) to act in a violent or threatening manner (esp. in **ramp and rage**). **8** (*tr*) *Finance*. to buy (a security) in the market with the object of raising its price and enhancing the image of the company behind it for financial gain. [C18 (n): from C13 *rampe*, from OF *ramper* to crawl or rear, prob. of Gmc origin]

rampage *vb* (ræm'peɪdʒ) **rampages, rampaging, rampaged. 1** (*intr*) to rush about in a violent or agitated fashion. ♦ *n* ('ræmpeɪdʒ, ræm'peɪdʒ). **2** angry or destructive behaviour. **3 on the rampage.** behaving violently or destructively. [C18: from Scot., from ?; ? based on RAMP]
▸ ram'pageous *adj* ▸ ram'pageously *adv* ▸ 'rampager *n*

rampant ('ræmpənt) *adj* **1** unrestrained or violent in behaviour, etc. **2** growing or developing unchecked. **3** (*postpositive*) *Heraldry*. (of a beast) standing on the hind legs, the right foreleg raised above the left. **4** (of an arch) having one abutment higher than the other. [C14: from OF *ramper* to crawl, rear; see RAMP]
▸ 'rampancy *n* ▸ 'rampantly *adv*

★ people and places

rampart ('ræmpɑːt) *n* **1** the surrounding embankment of a fort, often including any walls, parapets, etc., that are built on the bank. **2** any defence or bulwark. ◆ *vb* **3** (*tr*) to provide with a rampart; fortify. [C16: from OF, from RE- + *emparer* to take possession of, from OProvençal *antparar*, from L *ante* before + *parāre* to prepare]

rampike ('ræm,paɪk) *n* Canad. a tall tree that has been burned or is bare of branches.

rampion ('ræmpɪən) *n* a plant, native to Europe and Asia, that has clusters of bell-shaped bluish flowers and an edible white tuberous root used in salads. [C16: prob. from OF *raiponce*, from OIt. *raponzo*, from *rapa* turnip, from L *rāpum*]

Rampur ★ ('ræmpʊə) *n* a city in N India, in N Uttar Pradesh. Pop.: 243 742 (1991).

ram raid *n Inf.* a raid in which a stolen car is driven through a shop window in order to steal goods from the shop.
▶ **ram raiding** *n* ▶ **ram raider** *n*

ramrod ('ræm,rɒd) *n* **1** a rod for cleaning the barrel of a rifle, etc. **2** a rod for ramming in the charge of a muzzle-loading firearm.

Ramsay ★ ('ræmzɪ) *n* **1 Allan.** ?1686–1758, Scottish writer and bookseller, noted esp. for his comedy *The Gentle Shepherd* (1725). He introduced the circulating library to Scotland. **2** his son, **Allan.** 1713–84, Scottish portrait painter. **3 James Andrew Broun.** See (1st Marquis and 10th Earl of) **Dalhousie. 4** Sir **William.** 1852–1916, Scottish chemist. He discovered several rare gases: Nobel prize for chemistry 1904.

Ramses ('ræmsiːz) *or* **Rameses** ★ *n* any of 12 kings of ancient Egypt, who ruled from ?1315 to ?1090 B.C.

Ramses II *or* **Rameses II** ★ *n* died ?1225 B.C., king of ancient Egypt (?1292–?25). His reign was marked by the construction of such monuments as the temple at Abu Simbel.

Ramses III *or* **Rameses III** ★ *n* died ?1167 B.C., king of ancient Egypt (?1198–?67).

Ramsey ★ ('ræmzɪ) *n* Sir **Alf(red Ernest).** 1922–99, English footballer and football manager, who played for England 32 times and managed England when they won the World Cup (1966).

Ramsgate ★ ('ræmz,geɪt) *n* a port and resort in SE England, in E Kent on the North Sea coast. Pop.: 37 895 (1991).

ramshackle ('ræm,ʃækʰl) *adj* (esp. of buildings) rickety, shaky, or derelict. [C17 *ramshackled*, from obs. *ransackle* to RANSACK]

ramsons ('ræmzənz, -sənz) *pl n* (*usually functioning as sing*) **1** a broad-leaved garlic native to Europe and Asia. **2** the bulbous root of this plant, eaten as a relish. [OE *hramesa*]

ran (ræn) *vb* the past tense of **run.**

RAN *abbrev. for* Royal Australian Navy.

Rancagua ★ (*Spanish* raŋˈkagwa) *n* a city in central Chile. Pop.: 193 755 (1995 est.).

ranch (rɑːntʃ) *n* **1** a large tract of land, esp. one in North America, together with the necessary personnel, buildings, and equipment, for rearing livestock, esp. cattle. **2a** any large farm for the rearing of a particular kind of livestock or crop: *a mink ranch.* **2b** the buildings, land, etc., connected with it. ◆ *vb* **3** (*intr*) to run a ranch. **4** (*tr*) to raise (animals) on or as if on a ranch. [C19: from Mexican Sp. *rancho* small farm]
▶ **'rancher** *n*

rancherie ('rɑːntʃərɪ) *n* (in British Columbia, Canada) a settlement of North American Indians, esp. on a reserve. [from Sp. *ranchería*]

Ranchi ★ ('ræntʃɪ) *n* an industrial city in E India, in S Bihar between the coal and iron belts of the Chota Nagpur Plateau. Pop.: 599 306 (1991).

rancid ('rænsɪd) *adj* **1** (of food) having an unpleasant stale taste or smell as the result of decomposition. **2** (of a taste or smell) rank or sour; stale. [C17: from L *rancidus*, from *rancēre* to stink]
▶ **rancidity** (ræn'sɪdɪtɪ) *or* **'rancidness** *n*

rancour *or US* **rancor** ('ræŋkə) *n* malicious resentfulness or hostility; spite. [C14: from OF, from LL *rancor* rankness]
▶ **'rancorous** *adj* ▶ **'rancorously** *adv*

rand[1] (rænd, rɒnt) *n* the standard monetary unit of South Africa, divided into 100 cents. [C20: from Afrik., from WITWATERSRAND, referring to the gold-mining there; rel. to RAND[2]]

rand[2] (rænd) *n* **1** *Shoemaking.* a leather strip put in the heel of a shoe before the lifts are put on. **2** *Dialect.* **2a** a strip or margin; border. **2b** a strip of cloth; selvage. [OE; rel. to OHG *rant* border, rim of a shield, ON *rǫnd* shield, rim]

Rand ★ (rænd) *n* the. short for **Witwatersrand.**

R & B *abbrev. for* rhythm and blues.

R & D *abbrev. for* research and development.

Randers ★ (*Danish* 'randərs) *n* a port and industrial centre in Denmark, in E Jutland on **Randers Fjord** (an inlet of the Kattegat). Pop.: 61 435 (1995).

Randolph ★ ('rændɒlf, -dəlf) *n* **1 Edmund Jennings,** 1753–1813, US politician. He helped to frame the US constitution (1787), attorney general (1789–94), and secretary of state (1794–95). **2 John,** called *Randolph of Roanoke.* 1773–1833, US politician: opposed the Missouri Compromise (1820) that outlawed slavery. **3** Sir **Thomas,** 1st Earl of Moray. died 1332, Scottish soldier: regent after the death of Robert the Bruce (1329).

random ('rændəm) *adj* **1** lacking any definite plan or prearranged order; haphazard: *a random selection.* **2** *Statistics.* **2a** having a value which cannot be determined but only described in terms of probability: *a random variable.* **2b** chosen without regard to any characteristics of the individual members of the population so that each has an equal chance of being selected: *random sampling.* ◆ *n* **3 at random.** not following any prearranged order. [C14: from OF *randon*, from *randir* to gallop, of Gmc origin]
▶ **'randomly** *adv* ▶ **'randomness** *n*

random access *n* another name for **direct access.**

randomize *or* **randomise** ('rændə,maɪz) *vb* **randomizes, randomizing, randomized** *or* **randomises, randomising, randomised.** (*tr*) to set up (a selection process, sample, etc.) in a deliberately random way in order to enhance the statistical validity of any results obtained.
▶ **,randomi'zation** *or* **,randomi'sation** *n* ▶ **'random,izer** *or* **'random,iser** *n*

random walk theory *n Stock Exchange.* the theory that the future movement of share prices does not reflect past movements and therefore will not follow a discernible pattern.

R and R *US mil. abbrev. for* rest and recreation.

randy ('rændɪ) *adj* **randier, randiest. 1** *Inf., chiefly Brit.* sexually eager or lustful. **2** *Chiefly Scot.* lacking any sense of propriety; reckless. ◆ *n, pl* **randies. 3** *Chiefly Scot.* a rude or reckless person. [C17: prob. from obs. *rand* to RANT]
▶ **'randily** *adv* ▶ **'randiness** *n*

ranee ('rɑːnɪ) *n* a variant spelling of **rani.**

rang (ræŋ) *vb* the past tense of **ring**[2].

USAGE NOTE   See at **ring**[2].

rangatira (,rʌŋgə'tɪərə) *n NZ.* a Maori chief of either sex. [from Maori]

range (reɪndʒ) *n* **1** the limits within which a person or thing can function effectively: *the violin has a range of five octaves.* **2** the limits within which any fluctuation takes place: *a range of values.* **3** the total products of a manufacturer, designer, or stockist: *the new spring range.* **4a** the maximum effective distance of a projectile fired from a weapon. **4b** the distance between a target and a weapon. **5** an area set aside for shooting practice or rocket testing. **6** the total distance which a ship, aircraft, or land vehicle is capable of covering without taking on fresh fuel: *the range of this car is about 160 miles.* **7** *Maths.* (of a function or variable) the set of values that a function or variable can take. **8** *US & Canad.* **8a** an extensive tract of open land on which livestock can graze. **8b** (*as modifier*): *range cattle.* **9** the geographical region in which a species of plant or animal normally grows or lives. **10** a rank, row, or series of items. **11** a series or chain of mountains. **12** a large stove with burners and one or more ovens, usually heated by solid fuel. **13** the act or process of ranging. ◆ *vb* **ranges, ranging, ranged. 14** to establish or be situated in a line, row, or series. **15** (*tr; often reflexive*, foll. by *with*) to put into a specific category; classify: *she ranges herself with the angels.* **16** (foll. by *on*) to aim or point (a telescope, gun, etc.) or (of a gun, telescope, etc.) to be pointed or aimed. **17** to establish the distance of (a target) from (a weapon). **18** (*intr*) (of a gun or missile) to have a specified range. **19** (when *intr*, foll. by *over*) to wander about (in) an area; roam (over). **20** (*intr*; foll. by *over*) (of an animal or plant) to live or grow in its normal habitat. **21** (*tr*) to put (cattle) to graze on a range. **22** (*intr*) to fluctuate within specific limits. **23** (*intr*) to extend or run in a specific direction. **24** (*intr*) *Naut.* (of a vessel) to swing back and forth while at anchor. **25** (*tr*) to make (lines of printers' type) level or even at the margin. [C13: from OF: row, from *ranger* to position, from *renc* line]

rangefinder ('reɪndʒ,faɪndə) *n* an instrument for determining the distance of an object from the observer, esp. in order to sight a gun or focus a camera.

ranger ('reɪndʒə) *n* **1** (*sometimes cap.*) an official in charge of a forest, park, nature reserve, etc. **2** *Orig. US.* a person employed to patrol a State or national park. Brit. equivalent: **warden. 3** *US.* one of a body of armed troops employed to police a State or district: *a Texas ranger.* **4** (in the US) a commando specially trained in making raids. **5** a person who wanders about; a rover.

Ranger *or* **Ranger Guide** ('reɪndʒə) *n Brit.* a member of the senior branch of the Guides.

rangiora (,ræŋɡɪ'ɔːrə) *n* a broad-leaved shrub of New Zealand. [from Maori]

Rangoon ★ (ræŋ'ɡuːn) *n* the former name (until 1989) of **Yangon.**

rangy ('reɪndʒɪ) *adj* **rangier, rangiest. 1** having long slender limbs. **2** adapted to wandering or roaming. **3** allowing considerable freedom of movement; spacious.
▶ **'rangily** *adv* ▶ **'ranginess** *n*

rani *or* **ranee** ('rɑːnɪ) *n* an Indian queen or princess; the wife of a rajah. [C17: from Hindi: queen, from Sansk. *rājñī*]

Ranjit Singh ★ ('rʌndʒɪt 'sɪŋ) *n* called *the Lion of the Punjab.* 1780–1839; founder of the Sikh kingdom in the Punjab.

rank[1] (ræŋk) *n* **1** a position, esp. an official one, within a social organization: *the rank of captain.* **2** high social or other standing; status. **3** a line or row of people or things. **4** the position of an item in any ordering or sequence. **5** *Brit.* a place where taxis wait to be hired. **6** a line of soldiers drawn up abreast of each other. **7** any of the eight horizontal rows of squares on a chessboard. **8 close ranks.** to maintain discipline or solidarity. **9 pull rank.** to get one's own way by virtue of one's superior position or rank. **10 rank and file. 10a** the ordinary soldiers, excluding the officers. **10b** the great mass or majority of any group, as opposed to the leadership. **10c** (*modifier*): *rank-and-file support.* ◆ *vb* **11** (*tr*) to arrange (people or things) in rows or lines; range. **12** to accord or be accorded a specific position in an organization or group. **13** (*tr*) to array a set of objects as a sequence: *to rank students by their test scores.* **14** (*intr*) to be important; rate: *money ranks low in her order of priorities.* **15** *Chiefly US.* to take precedence or surpass in rank. [C16: from OF *ranc* row, rank, of Gmc origin]

rank[2] (ræŋk) *adj* **1** showing vigorous and profuse growth: *rank weeds.* **2** highly offensive or disagreeable, esp. in smell or taste. **3** (*prenominal*) complete or absolute; utter: *a rank outsider.* **4** coarse or vulgar; gross: *his language was rank.* [OE *ranc* straight, noble]
▶ **'rankly** *adv* ▶ **'rankness** *n*

Rank ★ *n* **1** (ræŋk). J(oseph) Arthur, 1st Baron. 1888–1972, British industrialist and film executive. **2** (German raŋk). Otto ('ɔto). 1884–1939, Austrian psychoanalyst.

ranker ('ræŋkə) *n* **1** a soldier in the ranks. **2** a commissioned officer who entered service as a noncommissioned recruit.

ranking ('ræŋkɪŋ) *adj* **1** *Chiefly US & Canad.* prominent; high ranking. **2** *Caribbean sl.* possessed of style; exciting. ◆ *n* **3** a position on a scale; rating: *a ranking in a tennis tournament.*

rankle ('ræŋk°l) *vb* **rankles, rankling, rankled.** (*intr*) to cause severe and continuous irritation, anger, or bitterness; fester. [C14 *ranclen*, from OF *draoncle* ulcer, from L *dracunculus* dim. of *dracō* serpent]

ransack ('rænsæk) *vb* (*tr*) **1** to search through every part of (a house, box, etc.); examine thoroughly. **2** to plunder; pillage. [C13: from ON *rann* house + *saka* to search]
▶ **'ransacker** *n*

ransom ('rænsəm) *n* **1** the release of captured prisoners, property, etc., on payment of a stipulated price. **2** the price demanded or stipulated for such a release. **3 hold to ransom. 3a** to keep (prisoners, etc.) in confinement until payment for their release is received. **3b** to attempt to force (a person) to comply with one's demands. **4 a king's ransom.** a very large amount of money or valuables. ◆ *vb* (*tr*) **5** to pay a stipulated price and so obtain the release of (prisoners, property, etc.). **6** to set free (prisoners, property, etc.) upon receiving the payment demanded. **7** to redeem; rescue: *Christ ransomed men from sin.* [C14: from OF *ransoun,* from L *redemptiō* a buying back]
▶ **'ransomer** *n*

Ransom ★ ('rænsəm) *n* **John Crowe.** 1888–1974, US poet and critic.

Ransome ★ ('rænsəm) *n* **Arthur.** 1884–1967, British writer, best known for his childrens' books, including *Swallows and Amazons* (1930).

rant (rænt) *vb* **1** to utter (something) in loud, violent, or bombastic tones. ◆ *n* **2** loud, declamatory, or extravagant speech; bombast. [C16: from Du. *ranten* to rave]
▶ **'ranter** *n* ▶ **'ranting** *adj, n* ▶ **'rantingly** *adv*

ranunculaceous (rə,nʌŋkjʊ'leɪʃəs) *adj* of, relating to, or belonging to a N temperate family of flowering plants typically having flowers with five petals and numerous anthers and styles. The family includes the buttercup, clematis, and columbine.

ranunculus (rə'nʌŋkjʊləs) *n, pl* **ranunculuses** *or* **ranunculi** (-,laɪ). any of a genus of ranunculaceous plants having finely divided leaves and typically yellow five-petalled flowers. The genus includes buttercup, crowfoot, and spearwort. [C16: from L: tadpole, from *rāna* frog]

RAOC *abbrev. for* Royal Army Ordnance Corps.

rap[1] (ræp) *vb* **raps, rapping, rapped. 1** to strike (a fist, stick, etc.) against (something) with a sharp quick blow; knock. **2** (*intr*) to make a sharp loud sound, esp. by knocking. **3** (*tr*) to rebuke or criticize sharply. **4** (*tr*; foll. by *out*) to put (forth) in sharp rapid speech; utter in an abrupt fashion: *to rap out orders.* **5** (*intr*) *Sl.* to talk, esp. volubly. **6** (*intr*) to perform a rhythmic monologue with musical backing. **7 rap over the knuckles.** to reprimand. ◆ *n* **8** a sharp quick blow or the sound produced by such a blow. **9** a sharp rebuke or criticism. **10** *Sl.* voluble talk; chatter. **11a** a fast, rhythmic monologue over a musical backing. **11b** (*as modifier*): *rap music.* **12 beat the rap.** *US & Canad. sl.* to escape punishment or be acquitted of a crime. **13 take the rap.** *Sl.* to suffer the punishment for a crime, whether guilty or not. [C14: prob. from ON; cf. Swedish *rappa* to beat]

rap[2] (ræp) *n* (*used with a negative*) the least amount (esp. in **not care a rap**). [C18: prob. from *ropaire* counterfeit coin formerly current in Ireland]

rap[3] (ræp) *vb* **raps, rapping, rapped.** *n Austral. inf.* a variant spelling of **wrap** (senses 8, 14).

rapacious (rə'peɪʃəs) *adj* **1** practising pillage or rapine. **2** greedy or grasping. **3** (of animals, esp. birds) subsisting by catching living prey. [C17: from L *rapāx*, from *rapere* to seize]
▶ **ra'paciously** *adv* ▶ **rapacity** (rə'pæsɪtɪ) *or* **ra'paciousness** *n*

Rapacki ★ (*Polish* ra'patski) *n* **Adam** ('adam). 1909–70, Polish politician: foreign minister (1956–68); his proposal to denuclearize eastern Europe (the **Rapacki Plan**) was rejected by the West because of Soviet predominance in conventional weapons.

Rapallo ★ (*Italian* ra'pallo) *n* a port and resort in NW

Italy, in Liguria on the **Gulf of Rapallo** (an inlet of the Ligurian Sea): scene of the signing of two treaties after World War I. Pop.: 30 000 (1990 est.).

Rapa Nui ★ ('rɑːpɑ: 'nuːɪ) *n* another name for **Easter Island**.

rape[1] (reɪp) *n* **1** the offence of forcing a person, esp. a woman, to submit to sexual intercourse against that person's will. **2** the act of despoiling a country in warfare. **3** any violation or abuse: *the rape of justice*. **4** *Arch.* abduction: *the rape of the Sabine women*. ◆ *vb* **rapes, raping, raped**. (*mainly tr*) **5** to commit rape upon (a person). **6** *Arch.* to carry off by force; abduct.   [C14: from L *rapere* to seize]
▶ **'rapist** *n*

rape[2] (reɪp) *n* a Eurasian plant that is cultivated for its seeds, **rapeseed**, which yield a useful oil, **rape oil**, and as a fodder plant. Also called: **colza, cole**.   [C14: from L *rāpum* turnip]

rape[3] (reɪp) *n* (*often pl*) the skins and stalks of grapes left after wine-making: used in making vinegar.   [C17: from F *râpe*, of Gmc origin]

Raphael ★ ('ræfeɪəl) *n* **1** *Bible*. one of the archangels; the angel of healing and the guardian of Tobias (Tobit 3:17; 5-12). Feast day: Sept. 29. **2** original name *Raffaello Santi* or *Sanzio*. 1483–1520, Italian painter and architect; his paintings include the *Sistine Madonna* (?1513).
▶ **,Raphael'esque** *adj*

raphia ('ræfɪə) *n* a variant spelling of **raffia**.

raphide ('reɪfaɪd) *or* **raphis** ('reɪfɪs) *n, pl* **raphides** ('ræfɪˌdiːz). needle-shaped crystals, usually of calcium oxalate, that occur in many plant cells.   [C18: from F, from Gk *rhaphis* needle]

rapid ('ræpɪd) *adj* **1** (of an action) performed or occurring during a short interval of time; quick. **2** acting or moving quickly; fast: *a rapid worker*. ◆ See also **rapids**.   [C17: from L *rapidus* tearing away, from *rapere* to seize]
▶ **'rapidly** *adv* ▶ **rapidity** (rə'pɪdɪtɪ) *or* **'rapidness** *n*

rapid eye movement *n* movement of the eyeballs during paradoxical sleep, while the sleeper is dreaming. Abbrev.: **REM**.

rapid fire *n* **1** a fast rate of gunfire. ◆ *adj* **rapid-fire. 2** firing shots rapidly. **3** done, delivered, or occurring in rapid succession.

rapids ('ræpɪdz) *pl n* part of a river where the water is very fast and turbulent.

rapier ('reɪpɪə) *n* **1** a long narrow two-edged sword with a guarded hilt, used as a thrusting weapon, popular in the 16th and 17th centuries. **2** a smaller single-edged 18th-century sword, used principally in France.   [C16: from OF *espee rapiere*, lit.: rasping sword]

rapine ('ræpaɪn) *n* the seizure of property by force; pillage.   [C15: from L *rapīna* plundering, from *rapere* to snatch]

rappee (ræ'piː) *n* a moist English snuff.   [C18: from F *tabac râpé*, lit.: scraped tobacco]

rappel (ræ'pɛl) *vb* **rappels, rappelling, rappelled**, *n* **1** another word for **abseil**. ◆ *n* **2** (formerly) a drumbeat to call soldiers to arms.   [C19: from F, from *rappeler* to call back, from L *appellāre* to summon]

rapport (ræ'pɔː) *n* (*often foll. by with*) a sympathetic relationship or understanding. See also **en rapport**.   [C15: from F, from *rapporter* to bring back, from RE- + *aporter*, from L *apportāre*, from *ad* to + *portāre* to carry]

rapprochement *French*. (raprɔʃmã) *n* a resumption of friendly relations, esp. between two countries.   [C19: lit.: bringing closer]

rapscallion (ræp'skæljən) *n* a disreputable person; rascal or rogue.   [C17: from earlier *rascallion*; see RASCAL]

rapt[1] (ræpt) *adj* **1** totally absorbed; engrossed; spellbound, carried away. **2** gone through or as if through emotion: *rapt with wonder*. **2** characterized by or proceeding from rapture: *a rapt smile*.   [C14: from L *raptus* carried away, from *rapere* to seize]
▶ **'raptly** *adv*

rapt[2] (ræpt) *adj Austral. inf.* Also: **wrapped**. very pleased; delighted.

raptor ('ræptə) *n* another name for **bird of prey**.   [C17: from L: plunderer, from *rapere* to take by force]

raptorial (ræp'tɔːrɪəl) *adj Zool.* **1** (of the feet of birds) adapted for seizing prey. **2** of or relating to birds of prey.   [C19: from L *raptor* robber, from *rapere* to snatch]

rapture ('ræptʃə) *n* **1** the state of mind resulting from feelings of high emotion; joyous ecstasy. **2** (*often pl*) an expression of ecstatic joy. **3** the act of transporting a person from one sphere of existence to another. ◆ *vb* **raptures, rapturing, raptured. 4** (*tr*) *Arch. or literary*. to enrapture.   [C17: from Med. L *raptūra*, from L *raptus* RAPT[1]]
▶ **'rapturous** *adj*

RAR *abbrev.* for Royal Australian Regiment.

rara avis ('reərə 'eɪvɪs) *n, pl* **rarae aves** ('reəri: 'eɪviːz). an unusual, uncommon, or exceptional person or thing.   [L: rare bird]

rare[1] (reə) *adj* **1** not widely known; not frequently used or experienced; uncommon or unusual: *a rare word*. **2** not widely distributed; not generally occurring: *a rare herb*. **3** (of a gas, esp. the atmosphere at high altitudes) having a low density; thin; rarefied. **4** uncommonly great; extreme: *kind to a rare degree*. **5** exhibiting uncommon excellence: *rare skill*.   [C14: from L *rārus* sparse]
▶ **'rareness** *n*

rare[2] (reə) *adj* (of meat, esp. beef) very lightly cooked.   [OE *hrēr*; rel. to *hreaw* RAW]

rarebit ('reəbɪt) *n* another term for **Welsh rabbit**.   [C18: by folk etymology from (WELSH) RABBIT; see RARE[2], BIT[1]]

rare earth *n* **1** any oxide of a lanthanide. **2** Also called: **rare-earth element**. any element of the lanthanide series.

raree show ('reəri:) *n* **1** a street show or carnival. **2** another name for **peepshow**.   [C17: *raree* from RARE[1]]

rarefaction (ˌreərɪ'fækʃən) *or* **rarefication** (ˌreərɪfɪ'keɪʃən) *n* the act or process of making less dense or the state of being less dense.
▶ **,rare'factive** *adj*

rarefied ('reərɪˌfaɪd) *adj* **1** exalted in nature or character; lofty: *a rarefied spiritual existence*. **2** current within only a small group. **3** thin: *air rarefied at altitude*.

rarefy ('reərɪˌfaɪ) *vb* **rarefies, rarefying, rarefied**. to make or become rarer or less dense; thin out.   [C14: from OF *raréfier*, from L *rārēfacere*, from *rārus* RARE[1] + *facere* to make]
▶ **'rare,fiable** *adj* ▶ **'rare,fier** *n*

rare gas *n* another name for **inert gas**.

rarely ('reəlɪ) *adv* **1** hardly ever; seldom. **2** to an unusual degree; exceptionally. **3** *Dialect*. uncommonly well; excellently: *he did rarely at market yesterday*.

> **USAGE NOTE**   Since *rarely* means *hardly ever*, one should not say something *rarely ever* happens.

raring ('reərɪŋ) *adj* ready; willing; enthusiastic (esp. in **raring to go**).   [C20: from *rare*, var. of REAR[2]]

rarity ('reərɪtɪ) *n, pl* **rarities. 1** a rare person or thing, esp. something valued because it is uncommon. **2** the state of being rare.

Rarotonga ★ (ˌreərə'tɒŋgə) *n* an island in the S Pacific, in the SW Cook Islands: the chief island of the group. Chief settlement: Avarua. Pop.: 9281 (1986). Area: 67 sq. km (26 sq. miles).

rasbora (ræz'bɔːrə) *n* any of the small cyprinid fishes of tropical Asia and East Africa. Many species are brightly coloured and are popular aquarium fishes.   [from NL, from an East Indian language]

rascal ('rɑːsk²l) *n* **1** a disreputable person; villain. **2** a mischievous or impish rogue. **3** an affectionate or mildly reproving term, esp. for a child: *you little rascal*. **4** *Obs.* a person of lowly birth. ◆ *adj* **5** (*prenominal*) *Obs.* **5a** belonging to the rabble. **5b** dishonest; knavish.   [C14: from OF *rascaille* rabble, ?from OF *rasque* mud]

rascality (rɑːs'kælɪtɪ) *n, pl* **rascalities**. mischievous or disreputable character or action.

rascally ('rɑːskəlɪ) *adj* **1** dishonest or mean; base. ◆ *adv* **2** in a dishonest or mean fashion.

rase (reɪz) *vb* **rases, rasing, rased**. a variant spelling of **raze**.

rash[1] (ræʃ) *adj* **1** acting without due thought; impetuous.

2 resulting from excessive haste or impetuosity: *a rash word.* [C14: from OHG *rasc* hurried, clever]
▸ 'rashly *adv* ▸ 'rashness *n*

rash[2] (ræʃ) *n* **1** *Pathol.* any skin eruption. **2** a series of unpleasant and unexpected occurrences: *a rash of forest fires.* [C18: from OF *rasche*, from *raschier* to scratch, from L *rādere* to scrape]

rasher ('ræʃə) *n* a thin slice of bacon or ham. [C16: from ?]

Rashid[1] ★ (ræ'ʃiːd) *n* the Egyptian name for **Rosetta**.

Rashid[2] ★ (ræ'ʃiːd) *n* Harun al-. See **Harun al-Rashid**.

Rasht (ræʃt) *or* **Resht** ★ *n* a city in NW Iran, near the Caspian Sea: agricultural and commercial centre in a rice-growing area. Pop.: 340 637 (1991).

Rask ★ (*Danish* rasg) *n* **Rasmus Christian** ('rasmus 'kresdjan). 1787–1832, Danish philologist. He pioneered comparative philology with his work on Old Norse (1818).

Rasmussen ★ (*Danish* 'rasmusən) *n* **Knud Johan Victor** (knuð jo'han 'viktər). 1879–1933, Danish arctic explorer and ethnologist. He led several expeditions through the Arctic in support of his theory that the North American Indians were originally migrants from Asia.

rasp (rɑːsp) *n* **1** a harsh grating noise. **2** a coarse file with rows of raised teeth. ◆ *vb* **3** (*tr*) to scrape or rub (something) roughly, esp. with a rasp; abrade. **4** to utter with or make a harsh grating noise. **5** to irritate (one's nerves); grate (upon). [C16: from OF *raspe*, of Gmc origin; cf. OHG *raspōn* to scrape]
▸ 'rasper *n* ▸ 'rasping *adj* ▸ 'raspish *adj*

raspberry ('rɑːzbərı, -brı) *n, pl* **raspberries**. **1** a prickly rosaceous shrub of North America and Europe that has pinkish-white flowers and typically red berry-like fruits (drupelets). See also **bramble**. **2a** the fruit of any such plant. **2b** (*as modifier*): *raspberry jelly.* **3a** a dark purplish-red colour. **3b** (*as adj*): *a raspberry dress.* **4** a spluttering noise made with the tongue and lips to express contempt (esp. in **blow a raspberry**). [C17: from earlier *raspis* raspberry, from ? + BERRY]

Rasputin ★ (ræ'spjuːtɪn; *Russian* ras'putin) *n* **Grigori Efimovich** (gri'gorij jɪ'fimavitʃ). ?1871–1916, Siberian monk, notorious for his debauchery and his influence over Tsarina Alexandra: assassinated by a group of Russian noblemen.

Ras Tafari ★ (ræs tə'fɑːrɪ) *n* See **Haile Selassie**.

Rastafarian (ˌræstə'feərɪən) *n* **1** a member of an originally Jamaican religion that regards Ras Tafari, the former emperor of Ethiopia, Haile Selassie, as God. ◆ *adj* **2** of, characteristic of, or relating to the Rastafarians. ◆ Often shortened to **Rasta**.

raster ('ræstə) *n* a pattern of horizontal scanning lines, esp. those traced by an electron beam on a television screen or those in a digitized bitmap image. [C20: via G from L: rake, from *rādere* to scrape]

rat (ræt) *n* **1** any of numerous long-tailed Old World rodents, that are similar to but larger than mice and are now distributed all over the world. **2** *Inf.* a person who deserts his friends or associates, esp. in time of trouble. **3** *Inf.* a worker who works during a strike; blackleg; scab. **4** *Inf.* a despicable person. **5 have** *or* **be rats**. Austral. sl. to be mad or eccentric. **6 smell a rat**. to detect something suspicious. ◆ *vb* **rats, ratting, ratted**. **7** (*intr*; usually foll. by *on*) **7a** to divulge secret information (about); betray the trust (of). **7b** to default (on); abandon. **8** to hunt and kill rats. [OE *ræt*]

rata ('rɑːtə) *n* a New Zealand tree with red flowers. [from Maori]

ratable *or* **rateable** ('reɪtəbᵊl) *adj* **1** able to be rated or evaluated. **2** *Brit.* (of property) liable to payment of rates.
▸ ˌrata'bility *or* ˌratea'bility *n* ▸ 'ratably *or* 'rateably *adv*

ratable value *n Brit.* (formerly) a fixed value assigned to a property by a local authority, on the basis of which variable annual rates are charged.

ratafia (ˌrætə'fɪə) *or* **ratafee** (ˌrætə'fiː) *n* **1** any liqueur made from fruit or from brandy with added fruit. **2** a flavouring essence made from almonds. **3** *Chiefly Brit.* Also

called: **ratafia biscuit**. a small macaroon flavoured with almonds. [C17: from West Indian Creole F]

ratan (ræ'tæn) *n* a variant spelling of **rattan**.

rat-arsed *adj Brit. sl.* drunk.

rat-a-tat-tat ('rætəˌtæt'tæt) *or* **rat-a-tat** ('rætə'tæt) *n* the sound of knocking on a door.

ratatouille (ˌrætə'twiː) *n* a vegetable casserole made of tomatoes, aubergines, peppers, etc., fried in oil and stewed slowly. [C19: from F, from *touiller* to stir, from L, from *tudes* hammer]

ratbag ('rætˌbæg) *n Sl.* an eccentric, stupid, or unreliable person.

rat-catcher *n* a person whose job is to destroy or drive away vermin, esp. rats.

ratchet ('rætʃɪt) *n* **1** a device in which a toothed rack or wheel is engaged by a pawl to permit motion in one direction only. **2** the toothed rack or wheel forming part of such a device. [C17: from F *rochet*, from OF *rocquet* blunt head of a lance, of Gmc origin]

ratchet effect *n Econ.* an effect that occurs when a price or wage increases as a result of temporary pressure but fails to fall back when the pressure is removed.

rate[1] (reɪt) *n* **1** a quantity or amount considered in relation to or measured against another quantity or amount: *a rate of 70 miles an hour.* **2a** a price or charge with reference to a standard or scale: *rate of interest.* **2b** (*as modifier*): *a rate card.* **3** a charge made per unit for a commodity, service, etc. **4** See **rates**. **5** the relative speed of progress or change of something variable; pace: *the rate of production has doubled.* **6a** relative quality; class or grade. **6b** (*in combination*): *first-rate ideas.* **7 at any rate**. in any case; at all events; anyway. ◆ *vb* **rates, rating, rated**. (*mainly tr*) **8** (*also intr*) to assign or receive a position on a scale of relative values; rank: *he is rated fifth in the world.* **9** to estimate the value of; evaluate: *we rate your services highly.* **10** to be worthy of; deserve: *this hotel does not rate four stars.* **11** to consider; regard: *I rate him among my friends.* **12** *Brit.* to assess the value of (property) for the purpose of local taxation. [C15: from OF, from Med. L *rata*, from L *prō ratā parte* according to a fixed proportion, from *ratus* fixed, from *rērī* to think, decide]

rate[2] (reɪt) *vb* **rates, rating, rated**. (*tr*) to scold or criticize severely; rebuke harshly. [C14: ? rel. to Swedish *rata* to chide]

rateable ('reɪtəbᵊl) *adj* a variant spelling of **ratable**.

rate-cap ('reɪtˌkæp) *vb* **rate-caps, rate-capping, rate-capped**. (*tr*) (formerly in Britain) to impose on (a local authority) an upper limit on the rate it may levy.
▸ 'rate-ˌcapping *n*

ratel ('reɪtᵊl) *n* **1** a carnivorous mammal related to the badger family, inhabiting wooded regions of Africa and S Asia. It has a massive body, strong claws, and a thick coat that is paler on the back. It feeds on honey and small animals. **2** *S. African.* a six-wheeled armoured vehicle. [C18: from Afrik.]

rate of exchange *n* See **exchange rate**.

rate of return *n Finance.* the ratio of the annual income from an investment to the original investment, often expressed as a percentage.

ratepayer ('reɪtˌpeɪə) *n Brit.* (formerly) a person who paid local rates, esp. a householder.

rates (reɪts) *pl n Brit.* a tax formerly levied on property by a local authority.

Rathenau ★ (*German* 'raːtənau) *n* **Walther** ('valtər). 1867–1922, German industrialist, who organized the war industries during World War I; minister of reconstruction (1921) and of foreign affairs (1922): largely responsible for the treaty of Rapallo with Russia: assassinated.

rather ('rɑːðə) *adv* (*in senses 1-4, not used with a negative*) **1** relatively or fairly; somewhat: *it's rather dull.* **2** to a significant or noticeable extent; quite: *she's rather pretty.* **3** to a limited extent or degree: *I rather thought that was the case.* **4** with better or more just cause: *this text is rather to be deleted than rewritten.* **5** more readily or willingly; sooner: *I would rather not see you tomorrow.* ◆ *sentence connector.* **6** on the contrary: *it's not cold. Rather, it's very hot.* ◆ *sentence substitute.* ('rɑː'ðɜː). **7** an expression of strong affir-

---

★ people and places

mation: *Is it worth seeing? Rather!* [OE *hrathor* comp. of *hræth* READY, quick]

> **USAGE NOTE** Both *would* and *had* are used with *rather* in sentences such as *I would rather* (or *had rather*) *go to the film than to the play*. *Had rather* is less common and now widely regarded as slightly old-fashioned.

ratify ('rætɪˌfaɪ) *vb* **ratifies, ratifying, ratified.** (*tr*) to give formal approval or consent to. [C14: via OF from L *ratus* fixed (see RATE[1]) + *facere* to make]
> ˈratiˌfiable *adj* ▸ ˌratifiˈcation *n* ▸ ˈratiˌfier *n*

rating[1] ('reɪtɪŋ) *n* **1** a classification according to order or grade; ranking. **2** an ordinary seaman. **3** *Sailing*. a handicap assigned to a racing boat based on its dimensions, draught, etc. **4** the estimated financial or credit standing of a business enterprise or individual. **5** *Radio, television, etc*. a figure based on statistical sampling indicating what proportion of the total audience tune in to a specific programme.

rating[2] ('reɪtɪŋ) *n* a sharp scolding or rebuke.

ratio ('reɪʃɪəʊ) *n, pl* **ratios. 1** a measure of the relative size of two classes expressible as a proportion: *the ratio of boys to girls is 2 to 1*. **2** *Maths*. a quotient of two numbers or quantities. See also **proportion** (sense 6). [C17: from L: a reckoning, from *rērī* to think]

ratiocinate (ˌrætɪˈɒsɪˌneɪt) *vb* **ratiocinates, ratiocinating, ratiocinated.** (*intr*) to think or argue logically and methodically; reason. [C17: from L *ratiōcinārī* to calculate, from *ratiō* REASON]
> ˌratiˌociˈnation *n* ▸ ˌratiˈociˌnative *adj* ▸ ˌratiˈociˌnator *n*

ration ('ræʃən) *n* **1a** a fixed allowance of food, provisions, etc., esp. a statutory one for civilians in time of scarcity or soldiers in time of war. **1b** (*as modifier*): *a ration book*. **2** a sufficient or adequate amount: *you've had your ration of television for today*. ◆ *vb* (*tr*) **3** (often foll. by *out*) to distribute (provisions), esp. to an army. **4** to restrict the distribution or consumption of (a commodity) (by people): *the government has rationed sugar.* ◆ See also **rations.** [C18: via F from L *ratiō* REASON]

rational ('ræʃənᵊl) *adj* **1** using reason or logic in thinking out a problem. **2** in accordance with the principles of logic or reason; reasonable. **3** of sound mind; sane: *the patient seemed rational.* **4** endowed with the capacity to reason: *rational beings.* **5** *Maths.* **5a** expressible as a ratio of two integers. **5b** (of an expression, equation, etc.) containing no variable either in irreducible radical form or raised to a fractional power. ◆ *n* **6** a rational number. [C14: from L *ratiōnālis*, from *ratiō* REASON]
> ˈratioˈnality *n* ▸ ˈrationally *adv* ▸ ˈrationalness *n*

rationale (ˌræʃəˈnɑːl) *n* a reasoned exposition, esp. one defining the fundamental reasons for an action, etc. [C17: from NL, from L *ratiōnālis*]

rationalism ('ræʃənəˌlɪzəm) *n* **1** reliance on reason rather than intuition to justify one's beliefs or actions. **2** *Philosophy*. the doctrine that knowledge is acquired by reason without regard to experience. **3** the belief that knowledge and truth are ascertained by rational thought and not by divine or supernatural revelation.
> ˈrationalist *n* ▸ ˌrationalˈistic *adj* ▸ ˌrationalˈistically *adv*

rationalize *or* **rationalise** ('ræʃənəˌlaɪz) *vb* **rationalizes, rationalizing, rationalized** *or* **rationalises, rationalising, rationalised. 1** to justify (one's actions) with plausible reasons, esp. after the event. **2** to apply logic or reason to (something). **3** (*tr*) to eliminate unnecessary equipment, etc., from (a group of businesses, factory, etc.), in order to make it more efficient. **4** (*tr*) *Maths.* to eliminate radicals without changing the value of (an expression) or the roots of (an equation).
> ˌrationaliˈzation *or* ˌrationaliˈsation *n* ▸ ˈrationalˌizer *or* ˈrationalˌiser *n*

rational number *n* any real number of the form a/b, where a and b are integers and b is not zero, as 7 or 7/3.

rations ('ræʃənz) *pl n* (*sometimes sing*) a fixed daily allowance of food, esp. to military personnel or when supplies are limited.

Ratisbon ★ ('rætɪzˌbɒn) *n* the former English name for **Regensburg.**

ratite ('rætaɪt) *adj* **1** (of flightless birds) having a breastbone that lacks a keel for the attachment of flight muscles. **2** of or denoting the flightless birds, that have a flat breastbone, feathers lacking vanes, and reduced wings. ◆ *n* **3** a bird, such as an ostrich that belongs to this group; a flightless bird. [C19: from L *ratis* raft]

rat kangaroo *n* any of several ratlike kangaroos that occur in Australia and Tasmania.

ratline *or* **ratlin** ('rætlɪn) *n Naut.* any of a series of light lines tied across the shrouds of a sailing vessel for climbing aloft. [C15: from ?]

ratoon *or* **rattoon** (ræ'tuːn) *n* **1** a new shoot that grows from near the root of crop plants, esp. the sugar cane, after the old growth has been cut back. ◆ *vb* **2** to propagate by such a growth. [C18: from Sp. *retoño*, from RE- + *otoñar* to sprout in autumn, from *otoño* AUTUMN]

ratpack ('rætˌpæk) *n Derog. sl.* those members of the press who pursue celebrities and give wide, often intrusive, coverage of their private lives: *the royal ratpack.*

rat race *n* a continual routine of hectic competitive activity: *working in the City is a real rat race.*

rat-running *n* the practice of driving through residential side streets to avoid congested main roads.
> **rat-run** *n* ▸ **rat-runner** *n*

ratsbane ('rætsˌbeɪn) *n* rat poison, esp. arsenic oxide.

rat-tail *n* **1a** a horse's tail that has no hairs. **1b** a horse having such a tail. **2** a style of spoon in which the line of the handle is prolonged in a tapering moulding along the back of the bowl.

rattan *or* **ratan** (ræ'tæn) *n* **1** a climbing palm having tough stems used for wickerwork and canes. **2** the stems of such a plant collectively. **3** a stick made from one of these stems. [C17: from Malay *rōtan*]

ratter ('rætə) *n* **1** a dog or cat that catches and kills rats. **2** another word for **rat** (sense 3).

Rattigan ★ ('rætɪgən) *n* Sir **Terence Mervyn.** 1911–77, British playwright. His plays include *The Winslow Boy* (1946) and *Ross* (1960).

rattle ('rætᵊl) *vb* **rattles, rattling, rattled. 1** to make a rapid succession of short sharp sounds, as of loose pellets colliding when shaken in a container. **2** to shake with such a sound. **3** to send, move, drive, etc., with such a sound: *the car rattled along the country road.* **4** (*intr*; foll. by *on*) to chatter idly: *he rattled on about his work.* **5** (*tr*; foll. by *off, out*, etc.) to recite perfunctorily or rapidly. **6** (*tr*) *Inf.* to disconcert; make frightened or anxious. ◆ *n* **7** a rapid succession of short sharp sounds. **8** a baby's toy filled with small pellets that rattle when shaken. **9** a series of loosely connected horny segments on the tail of a rattlesnake, vibrated to produce a rattling sound. **10** any of various European scrophulariaceous plants having a capsule in which the seeds rattle, such as the **red rattle** and the **yellow rattle. 11** idle chatter. **12** *Med.* another name for **rale.** [C14: from MDu. *ratelen*, imit.]
> ˈrattly *adj*

Rattle ★ ('rætᵊl) *n* Sir **Simon.** born 1955, British conductor.

rattler ('rætlə) *n* **1** a person or thing that rattles. **2** *Inf.* a rattlesnake.

rattlesnake ('rætᵊlˌsneɪk) *n* any of the venomous New World snakes such as the **black** or **timber rattlesnake** belonging to the family of pit vipers. They have a series of loose horny segments on the tail that are vibrated to produce a buzzing or whirring sound.

rattletrap ('rætᵊlˌtræp) *n Inf.* a broken-down old vehicle, esp. an old car.

rattling ('rætlɪŋ) *adv Inf.* (intensifier qualifying something good, fine, etc.): *a rattling good lunch.*

ratty ('rætɪ) *adj* **rattier, rattiest. 1** *Brit. & NZ inf.* irritable; annoyed. **2** *Inf.* (of the hair) straggly, unkempt, or greasy. **3** *US & Canad. sl.* shabby; dilapidated. **4** *Austral. sl.* mad, eccentric, or odd. **5** of, like, or full of rats.
> ˈrattily *adv* ▸ ˈrattiness *n*

Ratushinskaya ★ (ˌrætuˈʃɪnskaɪə) *n* **Irina** (ɪˈriːnə). born 1954, Russian poet and writer, living in Britain: imprisoned (1983–86) in a Soviet labour camp on charges of subversion. Her publications include *No, I'm Not Afraid* (1986), *Grey is the Colour of Hope* (1988), and *The Odessans* (1992).

raucous ('rɔːkəs) *adj* (of voices, cries, etc.) harshly or hoarsely loud. [C18: from L *raucus* hoarse]
▶ 'raucously *adv* ▶ 'raucousness *n*

raunchy ('rɔːntʃɪ) *adj* raunchier, raunchiest. *Sl.* 1 openly sexual; lusty; earthy. 2 *Chiefly US.* slovenly; dirty. [C20: from ?]
▶ 'raunchily *adv* ▶ 'raunchiness *n*

raupo ('raupəʊ) *n, pl* raupos. a marsh reed common in New Zealand. [from Maori]

Rauschenberg ★ ('raʊʃənbɜːɡ) *n* Robert. born 1925, US exponent of pop art.

rauwolfia (rɔːˈwʊlfɪə, raʊ-) *n* 1 a tropical flowering tree or shrub of SE Asia with latex in its stem. 2 the powdered root of this plant: a source of various drugs, esp. reserpine. [C19: NL, after Leonhard *Rauwolf* (died 1596), G botanist]

ravage ('rævɪdʒ) *vb* ravages, ravaging, ravaged. 1 to cause extensive damage to. ◆ *n* 2 (*often pl*) destructive action: *the ravages of time.* [C17: from F, from OF *ravir* to snatch away, RAVISH]
▶ 'ravager *n*

rave (reɪv) *vb* raves, raving, raved. 1 to utter (something) in a wild or incoherent manner, as when delirious. 2 (*intr*) to speak in an angry uncontrolled manner. 3 (*intr*) (of the sea, wind, etc.) to rage or roar. 4 (*intr*; foll. by *over* or *about*) *Inf.* to write or speak (about) with great enthusiasm. 5 (*intr*) *Brit. sl.* to enjoy oneself wildly or uninhibitedly. ◆ *n* 6 *Inf.* 6a enthusiastic or extravagant praise. 6b (*as modifier*): *a rave review.* 7 *Brit. sl.* 7a Also called: **rave-up**. a party. 7b a professionally organized party for young people, with electronic dance music, sometimes held in a field or disused building. 8 a name given to various types of dance music, such as techno, that feature fast electronic rhythm. [C14 *raven*, apparently from OF *resver* to wander]

ravel ('rævəl) *vb* ravels, ravelling, ravelled *or US* ravels, raveling, raveled. 1 to tangle (threads, fibres, etc.) or (of threads, etc.) to become entangled. 2 (*often foll. by out*) to tease or draw out (the fibres of a fabric) or (of a fabric) to fray out in loose ends; unravel. 3 (*tr;* usually foll. by *out*) to disentangle or resolve: *to ravel out a complicated story.* ◆ *n* 4 a tangle or complication. [C16: from MDu. *ravelen*]
▶ 'raveller *n* ▶ 'ravelly *adj*

Ravel ★ (*French* ravɛl) *n* Maurice (**Joseph**) (mɔris). 1875–1937, French composer, whose works include *Le Tombeau de Couperin* (1917) for piano, *Boléro* (1928) for orchestra, and the ballet *Daphnis et Chloé* (1912).

raven[1] ('reɪvʰn) *n* 1 a large passerine bird of the crow family, having a large straight bill, long wedge-shaped tail, and black plumage. 2a a shiny black colour. 2b (*as adj*): *raven hair.* [OE hræfn]

raven[2] ('rævʰn) *vb* 1 to seize or seek (plunder, prey, etc.). 2 to eat (something) voraciously or greedily. [C15: from OF *raviner* to attack impetuously; see RAVENOUS]

ravening ('rævənɪŋ) *adj* (of animals) voracious; predatory.
▶ 'raveningly *adv*

Ravenna ★ (rəˈvɛnə; *Italian* raˈvenna) *n* a city and port in NE Italy, in Emilia-Romagna: capital of the Western Roman Empire from 402 to 476, of the Goths from 493 to 526, and of the Byzantine province from 584 to 751; famous for its ancient mosaics. Pop.: 133 604 (1994 est.).

ravenous ('rævənəs) *adj* 1 famished; starving. 2 rapacious; voracious. [C16: from OF *ravineux*, from L *rapīna* plunder, from *rapere* to seize]
▶ 'ravenously *adv* ▶ 'ravenousness *n*

raver ('reɪvə) *n* 1 *Brit. sl.* a person who leads a wild or uninhibited social life. 2 *Sl.* a person who enjoys rave music, esp. one who frequents raves.

ravine (rəˈviːn) *n* a deep narrow steep-sided valley. [C15: from OF: torrent, from L *rapīna* robbery, infl. by L *rapidus* RAPID, both from *rapere* to snatch]

raving ('reɪvɪŋ) *adj* 1a delirious; frenzied. 1b (*as adv*): *raving mad.* 2 *Inf.* (intensifier): *a raving beauty.* ◆ *n* 3 (*usually pl*) frenzied or wildly extravagant talk or utterances.
▶ 'ravingly *adv*

ravioli (ˌrævɪˈəʊlɪ) *n* small squares of pasta containing a savoury mixture of meat, cheese, etc. [C19: It. dialect, lit.: little turnips, from It. *rava* turnip, from L *rāpa*]

ravish ('rævɪʃ) *vb* (*tr*) 1 (*often passive*) to enrapture. 2 to rape. 3 *Arch.* to carry off by force. [C13: from OF *ravir*, from L *rapere* to seize]
▶ 'ravisher *n* ▶ 'ravishment *n*

ravishing ('rævɪʃɪŋ) *adj* delightful; lovely; entrancing.
▶ 'ravishingly *adv*

raw (rɔː) *adj* 1 (of food) not cooked. 2 (*prenominal*) in an unfinished, natural, or unrefined state; not treated by manufacturing or other processes: *raw materials.* 3 (of the skin, a wound, etc.) having the surface exposed or abraded, esp. painfully. 4 (of an edge of material) unhemmed; liable to fray. 5 ignorant, inexperienced, or immature: *a raw recruit.* 6 (*prenominal*) not selected or modified: *raw statistics.* 7 frank or realistic: *a raw picture of a marriage.* 8 (of spirits) undiluted. 9 *Chiefly US.* coarse, vulgar, or obscene. 10 (of the weather) harshly cold and damp. 11 *Inf.* unfair; unjust (esp. in **a raw deal**). ◆ *n* 12 **in the raw.** 12a *Inf.* without clothes; naked. 12b in a natural or unmodified state. 13 **the raw.** *Brit. inf.* a sensitive point: *his criticism touched me on the raw.* [OE hrēaw]
▶ 'rawish *adj* ▶ 'rawly *adv* ▶ 'rawness *n*

Rawalpindi ★ (rɔːlˈpɪndɪ) *n* an ancient city in N Pakistan: interim capital of Pakistan (1959–67) during the building of Islamabad. Pop.: 1 290 000 (1995 est.).

rawboned ('rɔːˈbəʊnd) *adj* having a lean bony physique.

rawhide ('rɔːˌhaɪd) *n* 1 untanned hide. 2 a whip or rope made of strips cut from such a hide.

rawhide hammer *n* a hammer, used to avoid damaging a surface, having a head consisting of a metal tube from each end of which a tight roll of hide protrudes.

rawinsonde ('reɪwɪnˌsɒnd) *n* a hydrogen balloon carrying meteorological instruments and a radar target, enabling the velocity of winds in the atmosphere to be measured. [C20: blend of *radar* + *wind* + *radiosonde*]

Rawlplug ('rɔːlˌplʌɡ) *n* Trademark. a short fibre or plastic tube used to provide a fixing in a wall for a screw.

raw material *n* 1 material on which a particular manufacturing process is carried out. 2 a person or thing regarded as suitable for some particular purpose: *raw material for the army.*

raw silk *n* 1 untreated silk fibres reeled from the cocoon. 2 fabric woven from such fibres.

Rawsthorne ★ ('rɔːsˌθɔːn) *n* Alan. 1905–71, British composer, whose works include three symphonies, several concertos, and a set of *Symphonic Studies* (1939).

ray[1] (reɪ) *n* 1 a narrow beam of light; gleam. 2 a slight indication: *a ray of solace.* 3 *Maths.* a straight line extending from a point. 4 a thin beam of electromagnetic radiation or particles. 5 any of the bony or cartilaginous spines of the fin of a fish that form the support for the soft part of the fin. 6 any of the arms or branches of a starfish. 7 *Bot.* any strand of tissue that runs radially through the vascular tissue of some higher plants. ◆ *vb* 8 (of an object) to emit (light) in rays or (of light) to issue in the form of rays. 9 (*intr*) (of lines, etc.) to extend in rays or on radiating paths. 10 (*tr*) to adorn (an ornament, etc.) with rays or radiating lines. [C14: from OF *rai*, from L *radius* spoke]

ray[2] (reɪ) *n* any of various marine selachian fishes typically having a flattened body, greatly enlarged winglike pectoral fins, gills on the undersurface of the fins, and a long whiplike tail. [C14: from OF *raie*, from L *raia*]

ray[3] (reɪ) *n* Music. (in tonic sol-fa) the second degree of any major scale; supertonic. [C18: later variant of *re*; see GAMUT]

Ray[1] ★ (reɪ) *n* Cape. a promontory in SW Newfoundland, Canada.

Ray[2] ★ (reɪ) *n* 1 John. 1627–1705, English naturalist, noted for his botanical classification. 2 Man, real name

★ people and places

Emmanuel Rudnitsky. 1890–1976, US surrealist photographer. **3 Satyajit** ('sætjədʒɪt). 1921–92, Indian film director. His films include *Pather Panchali* (1955), *The World of Apu* (1959), and *The Stranger* (1992).

Raybans ('reɪˌbænz) *pl n Trademark.* a brand of sunglasses.

ray flower *or* **floret** *n* any of the small strap-shaped flowers in the flower head of certain composite plants, such as the daisy.

ray gun *n* (in science fiction) a gun that emits rays to paralyse, stun, or destroy.

Rayleigh ★ ('reɪlɪ) *n* **Lord,** title of *John William Strutt.* 1842–1919, British physicist: Nobel prize for physics (1904) for his work on sound and the scattering of radiation.

rayless ('reɪlɪs) *adj* **1** dark; gloomy. **2** lacking rays: *a rayless flower.*

raylet ('reɪlɪt) *n* a small ray.

rayon ('reɪɒn) *n* **1** any of a number of textile fibres made from wood pulp or other forms of cellulose. **2** any fabric made from such a fibre. **3** (*as modifier*): *a rayon shirt.* [C20: from F, from OF *rai* RAY¹]

raze *or* **rase** (reɪz) *vb* **razes, razing, razed** *or* **rases, rasing, rased.** (*tr*) **1** to demolish (buildings, etc.) completely (esp. in **raze to the ground**). **2** to delete; erase. **3** *Arch.* to graze. [C16: from OF *raser,* from L *rādere* to scrape]
▶ **'razer** *or* **'raser** *n*

razoo (rɑ:'zu:) *n, pl* **razoos.** *Austral. & NZ inf.* an imaginary coin: *not a brass razoo; they took every last razoo.* [C20: from ?]

razor ('reɪzə) *n* **1** a sharp implement used esp. for shaving the face. **2 on a razor's edge** *or* **razor-edge.** in an acute dilemma. ◆ *vb* **3** (*tr*) to cut or shave with a razor. [C13: from OF *raseor,* from *raser* to shave; see RAZE]

razorback ('reɪzəˌbæk) *n* **1** Also called: **finback.** another name for the **common rorqual** (see **rorqual**). **2** a wild pig of the US, having a narrow body, long legs, and a ridged back.

razorbill ('reɪzəˌbɪl) *or* **razor-billed auk** *n* a common auk of the North Atlantic, having a thick laterally compressed bill with white markings.

razor blade *n* a small rectangular piece of metal sharpened on one or both long edges for use in a razor for shaving.

razor-shell *n* any of various sand-burrowing bivalve molluscs which have a long tubular shell. US name: **razor clam.**

razor wire *n* strong wire with pieces of sharp metal set across it at close intervals.

razz (ræz) *US & Canad. sl.* ◆ *vb* **1** (*tr*) to make fun of; deride. ◆ *n* **2** short for **raspberry** (sense 4).

razzle-dazzle ('ræzˈlˈdæzˈl) *or* **razzmatazz** ('ræzmə-ˈtæz) *n Sl.* **1** noisy or showy fuss or activity. **2** a spree or frolic. [C19: rhyming compound from DAZZLE]

Rb *the chemical symbol for* rubidium.

RBT *abbrev. for* random breath testing.

RC *abbrev. for:* **1** Red Cross. **2** Roman Catholic.

RCA *abbrev. for:* **1** (formerly) Radio Corporation of America. **2** Royal College of Art.

RCAF *abbrev. for* Royal Canadian Air Force.

RC CH *abbrev. for* Roman Catholic Church.

RCM *abbrev. for* Royal College of Music.

RCMP *abbrev. for* Royal Canadian Mounted Police.

RCN *abbrev. for:* **1** Royal Canadian Navy. **2** Royal College of Nursing.

RCP *abbrev. for* Royal College of Physicians.

RCS *abbrev. for:* **1** Royal College of Science. **2** Royal College of Surgeons. **3** Royal Corps of Signals.

rd *abbrev. for:* **1** road. **2** rod (unit of length). **3** round. **4** *Physics.* rutherford.

Rd *abbrev. for* Road.

RDC (in Britain, formerly) *abbrev. for* Rural District Council.

re¹ (reɪ, ri:) *n Music.* the syllable used in the fixed system of solmization for the note D. [C14: see GAMUT]

re² (ri:) *prep* with reference to. [C18: from L *rē,* ablative case of *rēs* thing]

Re¹ ★ (reɪ) *n* another name for **Ra**².

Re² *the chemical symbol for* rhenium.

RE *abbrev. for:* **1** Religious Education. **2** Royal Engineers.

re- *prefix* **1** indicating return to a previous condition, withdrawal, etc.: *rebuild; renew.* **2** indicating repetition of an action: *remarry.* [L]

reach (ri:tʃ) *vb* **1** (*tr*) to arrive at or get to (a place, person, etc.) in the course of movement or action: *to reach the office.* **2** to extend as far as (a point or place): *to reach the ceiling; can you reach?* **3** (*tr*) to come to (a certain condition or situation): *to reach the point of starvation.* **4** (*intr*) to extend in influence or operation: *the Roman conquest reached throughout England.* **5** (*tr*) *Inf.* to pass or give (something to a person) with the outstretched hand. **6** (*intr*; foll. by *out, for,* or *after*) to make a movement (towards), as if to grasp or touch. **7** (*tr*) to make contact or communication with (someone): *we tried to reach him all day.* **8** (*tr*) to strike, esp. in fencing or boxing. **9** (*tr*) to amount to (a certain sum): *to reach five million.* **10** (*intr*) *Naut.* to sail on a tack with the wind on or near abeam. ◆ *n* **11** the act of reaching. **12** the extent or distance of reaching: *within reach.* **13** the range of influence, power, etc. **14** an open stretch of water, esp. on a river. **15** *Naut.* the direction or distance sailed by a vessel on one tack. **16** *Advertising.* the proportion of a market that an advertiser hopes to reach at least once in a campaign. [OE *ræcan*]
▶ **'reachable** *adj* ▶ **'reacher** *n*

reach-me-down *n* **1a** (*often pl*) a cheaply ready-made or second-hand garment. **1b** (*as modifier*): *reach-me-down finery.* **2** (*modifier*) unoriginal; derivative: *reach-me-down ideas.*

react (rɪ'ækt) *vb* **1** (*intr*; foll. by *to, upon,* etc.) (of a person or thing) to act in response to another person, a stimulus, etc. **2** (*intr*; foll. by *against*) to act in an opposing or contrary manner. **3** (*intr*) *Physics.* to exert an equal force in the opposite direction to an acting force. **4** *Chem.* to undergo or cause to undergo a chemical reaction. [C17: from LL *reagere,* from RE- + L *agere* to do]

re-act (ri:'ækt) *vb* (*tr*) to act or perform again.

reactance (rɪ'æktəns) *n* the opposition to the flow of alternating current by the capacitance or inductance of an electrical circuit.

reactant (rɪ'æktənt) *n* a substance that participates in a chemical reaction.

reaction (rɪ'ækʃən) *n* **1** a response to some foregoing action or stimulus. **2** the reciprocal action of two things acting together. **3** opposition to change, esp. political change, or a desire to return to a former system. **4** a response indicating a person's feelings or emotional attitude. **5** *Med.* **5a** any effect produced by the action of a drug. **5b** any effect produced by a substance (allergen) to which a person is allergic. **6** *Chem.* a process that involves changes in the structure and energy content of atoms, molecules, or ions. **7** the

equal and opposite force that acts on a body whenever it exerts a force on another body.
▸ re**'**actional *adj*

USAGE NOTE *Reaction* is used to refer both to an instant response (*her reaction was one of amazement*) and to a considered response in the form of a statement (*the Minister gave his reaction to the court's decision*). Some people think this second use is incorrect.

reactionary (rɪˈækʃənərɪ, -ʃənrɪ) *or* **reactionist** *adj* 1 of, relating to, or characterized by reaction, esp. against radical political or social change. ♦ *n, pl* **reactionaries** *or* **reactionists.** 2 a person opposed to radical change.
▸ re**'**actionism *n*

reaction engine *or* **motor** *n* an engine, such as a jet engine, that ejects gas at high velocity and develops its thrust from the ensuing reaction.

reaction turbine *n* a turbine in which the working fluid is accelerated by expansion in both the static nozzles and the rotor blades.

reactivate (rɪˈæktɪˌveɪt) *vb* **reactivates, reactivating, reactivated.** (*tr*) to make (something) active again.
▸ re**‚**acti**'**vation *n*

reactive (rɪˈæktɪv) *adj* 1 readily partaking in chemical reactions: *sodium is a reactive metal.* 2 of, concerned with, or having a reactance. 3 responsive to stimulus. 4 (of mental illnesses) precipitated by an external cause.
▸ **reactivity** (ˌriːækˈtɪvɪtɪ) *or* re**'**activeness *n*

reactor (rɪˈæktə) *n* 1 short for **nuclear reactor.** 2 a vessel in which a chemical reaction occurs. 3 a coil of low resistance and high inductance that introduces reactance into a circuit. 4 *Med.* a person sensitive to a particular drug or agent. 5 *Chem.* a substance that takes part in a reaction.

read[1] (riːd) *vb* **reads, reading, read** (rɛd). 1 to comprehend the meaning of (something written or printed) by looking at and interpreting the written or printed characters. 2 (when *tr*, often foll. by *out*) to look at, interpret, and speak aloud (something written or printed). 3 (*tr*) to interpret the significance or meaning of through scrutiny and recognition: *to read a map.* 4 (*tr*) to interpret or understand the meaning of (signs, characters, etc.) other than by visual means: *to read Braille.* 5 (*tr*) to have sufficient knowledge of (a language) to understand the written or printed word. 6 (*tr*) to discover or make out the true nature or mood of: *to read someone's mind.* 7 to interpret or understand (something read) in a specified way: *I read this speech as satire.* 8 (*tr*) to adopt as a reading in a particular passage: *for "boon" read "bone".* 9 (*intr*) to have or contain a certain form or wording: *the sentence reads as follows.* 10 to undertake a course of study in (a subject): *to read history.* 11 to gain knowledge by reading: *he read about the war.* 12 (*tr*) to register, indicate, or show: *the meter reads 100.* 13 (*tr*) to put into a specified condition by reading: *to read a child to sleep.* 14 (*tr*) to hear and understand, esp. when using a two-way radio: *we are reading you loud and clear.* 15 *Computing.* to obtain (data) from a storage device, such as magnetic tape. 16 **read a lesson** (*or* **lecture**). *Inf.* to censure or reprimand. ♦ *n* 17 matter suitable for reading: *this book is a very good read.* 18 the act or a spell of reading. ♦ See also **read into, read out,** etc. [OE *rǣdan* to advise, explain]

read[2] (rɛd) *vb* 1 the past tense and past participle of **read**[1]. ♦ *adj* 2 having knowledge gained from books (esp. in **widely read** and **well-read**). 3 **take (something) as read.** to take (something) for granted as a fact; understand or presume.

readable (ˈriːdəb'l) *adj* 1 (of handwriting, etc.) able to be read or deciphered; legible. 2 (of style of writing) interesting, easy, or pleasant to read.
▸ ‚read a**'**bility *or* **'**readableness *n* ▸ **'**readably *adv*

Reade ★ (riːd) *n* Charles. 1814–84, British novelist: author of *The Cloister and the Hearth* (1861).

reader (ˈriːdə) *n* 1 a person who reads. 2 *Chiefly Brit.* a member of staff below a professor but above a senior lecturer at a university. 3a a book that is part of a planned series for those learning to read. 3b a standard textbook, esp. for foreign-language learning. 4 a person who reads aloud in public. 5 a person who reads and assesses the merit of manuscripts submitted to a publisher. 6 a proofreader. 7 short for **lay reader.**

readership (ˈriːdəʃɪp) *n* all the readers collectively of a publication or author: *a readership of five million.*

reading (ˈriːdɪŋ) *n* 1a the act of a person who reads. 1b (*as modifier*): *a reading room.* 2a ability to read. 2b (*as modifier*): *a child of reading age.* 3 any matter that can be read; written or printed text. 4 a public recital or rendering of a literary work. 5 the form of a particular word or passage in a given text, esp. where more than one version exists. 6 an interpretation, as of a piece of music, a situation, or something said or written. 7 knowledge gained from books: *a person of little reading.* 8 a measurement indicated by a gauge, dial, scientific instrument, etc. 9 *Parliamentary procedure.* 9a the formal recital of the body or title of a bill in a legislative assembly in order to begin one of the stages of its passage. 9b one of the three stages in the passage of a bill through a legislative assembly. See **first reading, second reading, third reading.** 10 the formal recital of something written, esp. a will.

Reading ★ (ˈrɛdɪŋ) *n* a town and unitary authority in S England, on the River Thames: university (1892). Pop.: 213 474 (1991).

read into (riːd) *vb* (*tr, prep*) to discern in or infer from a statement (meanings not intended by the speaker or writer).

read out (riːd) *vb* (*adv*) 1 (*tr*) to read (something) aloud. 2 to retrieve (information) from a computer memory or storage device. 3 (*tr*) *US & Canad.* to expel (someone) from a political party or other society. ♦ *n* **read-out. 4a** the act of retrieving information from a computer memory or storage device. **4b** the information retrieved.

read up (riːd) *vb* (*adv*; when *intr*, often foll. by *on*) to acquire information about (a subject) by reading intensively.

read-write head (ˈriːdˈraɪt) *n Computing.* an electromagnet that can both read and write information on a magnetic tape or disk.

ready (ˈrɛdɪ) *adj* **readier, readiest.** 1 in a state of completion or preparedness, as for use or action. 2 willing or eager: *ready helpers.* 3 prompt or rapid: *a ready response.* 4 (*prenominal*) quick in perceiving; intelligent: *a ready mind.* 5 (*postpositive*) (foll. by *to*) on the point (of) or liable (to): *ready to collapse.* 6 (*postpositive*) conveniently near (esp. in **ready to hand**). 7 **make** *or* **get ready.** to prepare (oneself or something) for use or action. ♦ *n* 8 *Inf.* (often preceded by *the*) short for **ready money.** 9 **at** *or* **to the ready.** 9a (of a rifle) in the position adopted prior to aiming and firing. 9b poised for use or action: *with pen at the ready.* ♦ *vb* **readies, readying, readied.** 10 (*tr*) to put in a state of readiness; prepare. [OE (*ge*)*rǣde*]
▸ **'**readily *adv* ▸ **'**readiness *n*

ready-made *adj* 1 made for purchase and immediate use by any customer. 2 extremely convenient or ideally suited: *a ready-made solution.* 3 unoriginal or conventional: *ready-made phrases.* ♦ *n* 4 a ready-made article, esp. a garment.

ready-mix *n* 1 (*modifier*) consisting of ingredients blended in advance, esp. of food that is ready to cook or eat after addition of milk or water: *a ready-mix cake.* 2 concrete that is mixed before or during delivery to a building site.

ready money *or* **cash** *n* funds for immediate use; cash. Also: **the ready, the readies.**

ready reckoner *n* a table of numbers for facilitating simple calculations, esp. for working out interest, etc.

ready-to-wear *adj* (**ready to wear** when postpositive). 1 (of clothes) not tailored for the wearer; of a standard size. ♦ *n* 2 an article or suit of such clothes.

reafforest (ˌriːəˈfɒrɪst) *or* **reforest** *vb* (*tr*) to replant (an area that was formerly forested).
▸ ‚reaf‚forest**'**ation *or* ‚reforest**'**ation *n*

Reagan ★ (ˈreɪgən) *n* Ronald. born 1911, US film actor and Republican statesman: Governor of California (1966–74): 40th president of the US (1981–89).

★ people and places

reagent (ri:'eɪdʒənt) *n* a substance for use in a chemical reaction, esp. for use in chemical synthesis and analysis.

real[1] (rɪəl) *adj* **1** existing or occurring in the physical world; not imaginary, fictitious, or theoretical; actual. **2** (*prenominal*) true; actual; not false: *the real reason.* **3** (*prenominal*) deserving the name; rightly so called: *a real friend.* **4** not artificial or simulated; genuine: *real fur.* **5** (of food, etc.) traditionally made and having a distinct flavour: *real ale; real cheese.* **6** *Philosophy.* existent or relating to actual existence (as opposed to nonexistent, potential, contingent, or apparent). **7** (*prenominal*) *Econ.* (of prices, incomes, etc.) considered in terms of purchasing power rather than nominal currency value. **8** (*prenominal*) denoting or relating to immovable property such as land and tenements: *real estate.* **9** *Maths.* involving or containing real numbers alone; having no imaginary part. **10** *Inf.* (intensifier): *a real genius.* **11 the real thing.** the genuine article, not a substitute. ♦ *n* **12 for real.** *Sl.* not as a test or trial; in earnest. **13 the real.** that which exists in fact; reality. [C15: from OF *réel*, from LL *reālis*, from L *rēs* thing]
▶ **'realness** *n*

real[2] (reɪ'ɑ:l) *n, pl* **reals** or **reales** (*Spanish* re'ales). a former small Spanish or Spanish-American silver coin. [C17: from Sp., lit.: royal, from L *rēgālis*; see REGAL]

real ale *n* any beer which is allowed to ferment in the barrel and which is pumped up from the keg without using carbon dioxide.

real estate *n* another term, chiefly US and Canad., for **real property.**

realgar (rɪ'ælgə) *n* a rare orange-red soft mineral consisting of arsenic sulphide in monoclinic crystalline form. [C14: via Med. L from Ar. *rahj al-ghar* powder of the mine]

realism ('rɪə,lɪzəm) *n* **1** awareness or acceptance of the physical universe, events, etc., as they are, as opposed to the abstract or ideal. **2** a style of painting and sculpture that seeks to represent the familiar or typical in real life. **3** any similar style in other arts, esp. literature. **4** *Philosophy.* the thesis that general terms refer to entities that have a real existence separate from the individuals which fall under them. **5** *Philosophy.* the theory that physical objects continue to exist whether they are perceived or not.
▶ **'realist** *n*

realistic (,rɪə'lɪstɪk) *adj* **1** showing awareness and acceptance of reality. **2** practical or pragmatic rather than ideal or moral. **3** (of a book, etc.) depicting what is real and actual. **4** of or relating to philosophical realism.
▶ ,**real'istically** *adv*

reality (rɪ'ælɪtɪ) *n, pl* **realities. 1** the state of things as they are or appear to be, rather than as one might wish them to be. **2** something that is real. **3** the state of being real. **4** *Philosophy.* **4a** that which exists, independent of human awareness. **4b** the totality of facts. **5 in reality.** actually; in fact.

reality principle *n Psychoanal.* control of behaviour by the ego to meet the conditions imposed by the external world.

realize or **realise** ('rɪə,laɪz) *vb* **realizes, realizing, realized** or **realises, realising, realised. 1** (when *tr, may take a clause as object*) to become conscious or aware of (something). **2** (*tr, often passive*) to bring (a plan, ambition, etc.) to fruition. **3** (*tr*) to give (a drama or film) the appearance of reality. **4** (*tr*) (of goods, property, etc.) to sell for or make (a certain sum): *this table realized £800.* **5** (*tr*) to convert (property or goods) into cash. **6** (*tr*) (of a musicologist or performer) to reconstruct (a composition) from an incomplete set of parts.
▶ **'real,izable** or **'real,isable** *adj* ▶ **'real,izably** or **'real-,isably** *adv* ▶ ,**reali'zation** or ,**reali'sation** *n* ▶ **'real,izer** or **'real,iser** *n*

real life *n* actual human life, as lived by real people, esp. contrasted with the lives of fictional characters: *miracles don't happen in real life.*

really ('rɪəlɪ) *adv* **1** in reality; in actuality; assuredly: *it's really quite harmless.* **2** truly; genuinely: *really beautiful.* ♦ *interj* **3** an exclamation of dismay, disapproval, doubt,

surprise, etc. **4 not really?** an exclamation of surprise or polite doubt.

USAGE NOTE See at **very.**

---

realm (rɛlm) *n* **1** a royal domain; kingdom: *peer of the realm.* **2** a field of interest, study, etc.: *the realm of the occult.* [C13: from OF *reialme*, from L *regimen* rule, infl. by OF *reial*, from L *rēgālis* REGAL]

real number *n* any rational or irrational number. See **number.**

real presence *n* the doctrine that the body of Christ is actually present in the Eucharist.

real property *n Property law.* immovable property, esp. freehold land. Cf. **personal property.**

real tennis *n* an ancient form of tennis played in a four-walled indoor court.

real-time *adj* denoting or relating to a data-processing system in which a computer is on-line to a source of data and processes the data as it is generated.

realtor ('rɪəltə, -,tɔ:) *n* a US word for an **estate agent,** esp. an accredited one. [C20: from REALTY + -OR[1]]

realty ('rɪəltɪ) *n* another term for **real property.**

ream[1] (ri:m) *n* **1** a number of sheets of paper, formerly 480 sheets (**short ream**), now 500 sheets (**long ream**) or 516 sheets (**printer's ream** or **perfect ream**). One ream is equal to 20 quires. **2** (*often pl*) *Inf.* a large quantity, esp. of written matter: *he wrote reams.* [C14: from OF, from Sp., from Ar. *rizmah* bale]

ream[2] (ri:m) *vb* (*tr*) **1** to enlarge (a hole) by use of a reamer. **2** *US.* to extract (juice) from (a citrus fruit) using a reamer. [C19: ?from C14 *remen* to open up, from OE *rȳman* to widen]

reamer ('ri:mə) *n* **1** a steel tool with a cylindrical or tapered shank around which longitudinal teeth are ground, used for smoothing the bores of holes accurately to size. **2** *US.* a utensil with a conical projection used for extracting juice from citrus fruits.

reap (ri:p) *vb* **1** to cut or harvest (a crop) from (a field). **2** (*tr*) to gain or get (something) as a reward for or result of some action or enterprise. [OE *riopan*]
▶ **'reapable** *adj*

reaper ('ri:pə) *n* **1** a person who reaps or a machine for reaping. **2 the grim reaper.** death.

rear[1] (rɪə) *n* **1** the back or hind part. **2** the area or position that lies at the back: *a garden at the rear of the house.* **3** the section of a military force farthest from the front. **4** an informal word for **buttocks** (see **buttock**). **5 bring up the rear.** to be at the back in a procession, race, etc. **6 in the rear.** at the back. **7** (*modifier*) of or in the rear: *the rear side.* [C17: prob. from REARWARD or REARGUARD]

rear[2] (rɪə) *vb* **1** (*tr*) to care for and educate (children) until maturity; raise. **2** (*tr*) to breed (animals) or grow (plants). **3** (*tr*) to place or lift (a ladder, etc.) upright. **4** (*tr*) to erect (a monument, building, etc.). **5** (*intr; often foll. by up*) (esp. of horses) to lift the front legs in the air and stand nearly upright. **6** (*intr; often foll. by up* or *over*) (esp. of tall buildings) to rise high; tower. **7** (*intr*) to start with anger, resentment, etc. [OE *rǣran*]
▶ **'rearer** *n*

rear admiral *n* an officer holding flag rank in any of certain navies, junior to a vice admiral.

Reardon ★ ('rɪədən) *n* Ray. born 1932, Welsh snooker player: world champion 1970, 1973–76, 1978.

rearguard ('rɪə,gɑ:d) *n* **1** a detachment detailed to protect the rear of a military formation, esp. in retreat. **2** an entrenched or conservative element, as in a political party. **3** (*modifier*) of, relating to, or characteristic of a rearguard: *a rearguard action.* [C15: from OF *rereguarde*, from *rer*, from L *retro* back + *guarde* GUARD]

rear light or **lamp** *n* a red light, usually one of a pair, attached to the rear of a motor vehicle. Also called: **tail-light, tail lamp.**

---

rearm (riːˈɑːm) *vb* **1** to arm again. **2** (*tr*) to equip (an army, etc.) with better weapons.
▸ re'armament *n*

rearmost ('rɪəˌməʊst) *adj* nearest the rear; coming last.

rear-view mirror *n* a mirror on a motor vehicle enabling the driver to see traffic behind him.

rearward ('rɪəwəd) *adj, adv* **1** Also (for adv only): **rearwards.** towards or in the rear. ◆ *n* **2** a position in the rear, esp. the rear division of a military formation. [C14 (*as n:* the part of an army behind the main body of troops): from Anglo-F *rerewarde*, var. of *reregarde*; see REARGUARD]

Rea Silvia ★ ('rɪə 'sɪlvɪə) *n* a variant spelling of **Rhea Silvia.**

reason ('riːzᵊn) *n* **1** the faculty of rational argument, deduction, judgment, etc. **2** sound mind; sanity. **3** a cause or motive, as for a belief, action, etc. **4** an argument in favour or a justification for something. **5** *Philosophy.* the intellect regarded as a source of knowledge, as contrasted with experience. **6** *Logic.* a premise of an argument in favour of the given conclusion. **7 by reason of.** because of. **8** *in or within reason.* within moderate or justifiable bounds. **9 it stands to reason.** it is logical or obvious. **10 listen to reason.** to be persuaded peaceably. **11 reasons of State.** political justifications for an immoral act. ◆ *vb* **12** (when *tr, takes a clause as object*) to think logically or draw (logical conclusions) from facts or premises. **13** (*intr; usually foll. by with*) to seek to persuade by reasoning. **14** (*tr; often foll. by out*) to work out or resolve (a problem) by reasoning. [C13: from OF *reisun*, from L *ratiō* reckoning, from *rērī* to think]
▸ 'reasoner *n*

> **USAGE NOTE** The expression *the reason is because...* should be avoided. Instead one should say either *this is because...* or *the reason is that...*

reasonable ('riːzənəbᵊl) *adj* **1** showing reason or sound judgment. **2** having the ability to reason. **3** having modest or moderate expectations. **4** moderate in price. **5** fair; average: *reasonable weather.*
▸ 'reasonably *adv* ▸ 'reasonableness *n*

reasoned ('riːzᵊnd) *adj* well thought-out or well presented: *a reasoned explanation.*

reasoning ('riːzənɪŋ) *n* **1** the act or process of drawing conclusions from facts, evidence, etc. **2** the arguments, proofs, etc., so adduced.

reassure (ˌriːəˈʃʊə) *vb* reassures, reassuring, reassured. (*tr*) **1** to relieve (someone) of anxieties; restore confidence to. **2** to insure again.
▸ ˌreas'surance *n* ▸ ˌreas'surer *n* ▸ ˌreas'suringly *adv*

Réaumur ('reɪəˌmjʊə) *adj* indicating measurement on the Réaumur scale.

Réaumur scale *n* a scale of temperature in which the freezing point of water is taken as 0° and the boiling point as 80°. [C18: after René de *Réaumur* (1683–1757), F physicist, who introduced it]

reave (riːv) *vb* reaves, reaving, reaved *or* reft. *Arch.* **1** to carry off (property, prisoners, etc.) by force. **2** (*tr;* foll. by *of*) to deprive; strip. See **reive.** [OE *rēafian*]

rebarbative (rɪˈbɑːbətɪv) *adj* fearsome; forbidding. [C19: from F *rébarbatif*, from OF *rebarber* to repel (an enemy)]

rebate¹ *n* ('riːbeɪt). **1** a refund of a fraction of the amount payable; discount. ◆ *vb* (rɪˈbeɪt), **rebates, rebating, rebated.** (*tr*) **2** to deduct (a part) of a payment from (the total). **3** *Arch.* to reduce. [C15: from OF *rabattre* to beat down, hence reduce, from RE- + *abatre* to put down]
▸ re'batable *or* re'bateable *adj* ▸ 'rebater *n*

rebate² ('riːbeɪt, 'ræbɪt) *n, vb* rebates, rebating, rebated. another word for **rabbet.**

rebec *or* **rebeck** ('riːbɛk) *n* a medieval stringed instrument resembling the violin but having a lute-shaped body. [C16: from OF *rebebe*, from Ar. *rebāb*; ? infl. by OF *bec* beak]

Rebecca ★ (rɪˈbɛkə) *n Old Testament.* the sister of Laban, who became the wife of Isaac and the mother of Esau and Jacob (Genesis 24–27). Douay spelling: **Rebekah.**

rebel *vb* (rɪˈbɛl), **rebels, rebelling, rebelled.** (*intr;* often foll. by *against*) **1** to resist or rise up against a government or authority, esp. by force of arms. **2** to dissent from an accepted moral code or convention of behaviour, etc. **3** to show repugnance (towards). ◆ *n* ('rɛbᵊl). **4a** a person who rebels. **4b** (*as modifier*): *a rebel soldier.* **5** a person who dissents from some accepted moral code or convention of behaviour, etc. [C13: from OF *rebelle*, from L *rebellis* insurgent, from RE- + *bellum* war]

rebellion (rɪˈbɛljən) *n* **1** organized opposition to a government or other authority. **2** dissent from an accepted moral code or convention of behaviour, etc. [C14: via OF from L *rebelliō* revolt (of those conquered); see REBEL]

rebellious (rɪˈbɛljəs) *adj* **1** showing a tendency towards rebellion. **2** (of a problem, etc.) difficult to overcome; refractory.
▸ re'belliously *adv* ▸ re'belliousness *n*

rebirth (riːˈbɜːθ) *n* **1** a revival or renaissance: *the rebirth of learning.* **2** a second or new birth.

reboot (riːˈbuːt) *vb* to shut down and then restart (a computer system) or (of a computer system) to shut down and restart.

rebore *n* ('riːˌbɔː). **1** the process of boring out the cylinders of a worn reciprocating engine and fitting oversize pistons. ◆ *vb* (riːˈbɔː), **rebores, reboring, rebored. 2** (*tr*) to carry out this process.

rebound *vb* (rɪˈbaʊnd). (*intr*) **1** to spring back, as from a sudden impact. **2** to misfire, esp. so as to hurt the perpetrator. ◆ *n* ('riːbaʊnd). **3** the act or an instance of rebounding. **4 on the rebound. 4a** in the act of springing back. **4b** *Inf.* in a state of recovering from rejection, etc.: *he married her on the rebound from an unhappy love affair.* [C14: from OF *rebondir*, from RE- + *bondir* to BOUND²]

rebounder (rɪˈbaʊndə) *n* a type of small trampoline used for aerobic exercising.

rebozo (rɪˈbəʊzəʊ) *n, pl* rebozos. a long wool or linen scarf covering the shoulders and head, worn by Latin American women. [C19: from Sp., from *rebozar* to muffle]

rebrand (ˌriːˈbrænd) *vb* (*tr*) to change or update the image of (an organization or product).

rebuff (rɪˈbʌf) *vb* (*tr*) **1** to snub, reject, or refuse (help, sympathy, etc.). **2** to beat back (an attack); repel. ◆ *n* **3** a blunt refusal or rejection; snub. [C16: from OF *rebuffer*, from It., from *ribuffo* a reprimand, from *ri-* RE- + *buffo* puff, gust, apparently imit.]

rebuke (rɪˈbjuːk) *vb* rebukes, rebuking, rebuked. **1** (*tr*) to scold or reprimand (someone). ◆ *n* **2** a reprimand or scolding. [C14: from OF *rebuker*, from RE- + *buchier* to hack down, from *busche* log, of Gmc origin]
▸ re'bukable *adj* ▸ re'buker *n* ▸ re'bukingly *adv*

rebus ('riːbəs) *n, pl* rebuses. **1** a puzzle consisting of pictures, symbols, etc., representing syllables and words; the word *hear* might be represented by H and a picture of an ear. **2** a heraldic device that is a pictorial representation of the name of the bearer. [C17: from F *rébus*, from L *rēbus* by things, from RES]

rebut (rɪˈbʌt) *vb* **rebuts, rebutting, rebutted.** (*tr*) to refute or disprove, esp. by offering a contrary contention or argument. [C13: from OF *reboter*, from RE- + *boter* to thrust, BUTT³]
▸ re'buttable *adj* ▸ re'buttal *n*

rebutter (rɪˈbʌtə) *n* **1** *Law.* a defendant's pleading in reply to a plaintiff's surrejoinder. **2** a person who rebuts.

rec. *abbrev. for:* **1** receipt. **2** recipe. **3** record.

recalcitrant (rɪˈkælsɪtrənt) *adj* **1** not susceptible to control; refractory. ◆ *n* **2** a recalcitrant person. [C19: via F from L, from RE- + *calcitrāre* to kick, from *calx* heel]
▸ re'calcitrance *n*

recalescence (ˌriːkəˈlɛsəns) *n* a sudden increase in the temperature of cooling iron. [C19: from L *recalēscere* to grow warm again, from RE- + *calēscere*, from *calēre* to be hot]
▸ ˌreca'lesce *vb (intr)* ▸ ˌreca'lescent *adj*

recall (rɪˈkɔːl) *vb* (*tr*) **1** (*may take a clause as object*) to bring back to mind; recollect; remember. **2** to order to return.

> ★ people and places

3 to revoke or take back. **4** to cause (one's thoughts, attention, etc.) to return from a reverie or digression. ◆ *n* **5** the act of recalling or state of being recalled. **6** revocation or cancellation. **7** the ability to remember things; recollection. **8** *Mil.* (formerly) a signal to call back troops, etc. **9** *US.* the process by which elected officials may be deprived of office by popular vote.
▶ **re'callable** *adj*

recant (rɪ'kænt) *vb* to repudiate or withdraw (a former belief or statement), esp. formally in public. [C16: from L *recantāre*, from RE- + *cantāre* to sing]
▶ **recantation** (ˌriːkæn'teɪʃən) *n* ▶ **re'canter** *n*

recap *vb* ('riːˌkæp, riː'kæp), **recaps, recapping, recapped,** *n* ('riːˌkæp). *Inf.* short for **recapitulate** *or* **recapitulation**.
▶ **re'cappable** *adj*

recapitulate (ˌriːkə'pɪtjʊˌleɪt) *vb* **recapitulates, recapitulating, recapitulated. 1** to restate the main points of (an argument, speech, etc.). **2** (*tr*) (of an animal) to repeat (stages of its evolutionary development) during the embryonic stages of its life. [C16: from LL *recapitulāre*, lit.: to put back under headings; see CAPITULATE]
▶ **reca'pitulative** *or* **reca'pitulatory** *adj*

recapitulation (ˌriːkəˌpɪtjʊ'leɪʃən) *n* **1** the act of recapitulating, esp. summing up, as at the end of a speech. **2** Also called: **palingenesis.** *Biol.* the apparent repetition in the embryonic development of an animal of the changes that occurred during its evolutionary history. **3** *Music.* the repeating of earlier themes, esp. in the final section of a movement in sonata form.

recapture (riː'kæptʃə) *vb* **recaptures, recapturing, recaptured.** (*tr*) **1** to capture or take again. **2** to recover, renew, or repeat (a lost or former ability, sensation, etc.). ◆ *n* **3** the act of recapturing or fact of being recaptured.

recce ('rɛkɪ) *n, vb* **recces, recceing, recced** *or* **recceed.** a slang word for **reconnaissance** *or* **reconnoitre.**

recd *or* **rec'd** *abbrev. for* received.

recede (rɪ'siːd) *vb* **recedes, receding, receded.** (*intr*) **1** to withdraw from a point or limit; go back: *the tide receded*. **2** to become more distant: *hopes of rescue receded.* **3** to slope backwards: *apes have receding foreheads*. **4a** (of a man's hair) to cease to grow at the temples and above the forehead. **4b** (of a man) to start to go bald in this way. **5** to decline in value. **6** (usually foll. by *from*) to draw back or retreat, as from a promise. [C15: from L *recēdere* to go back, from RE- + *cēdere* to yield]

re-cede (riː'siːd) *vb* **re-cedes, re-ceding, re-ceded.** (*tr*) to restore to a former owner.

receipt (rɪ'siːt) *n* **1** a written acknowledgment by a receiver of money, goods, etc., that payment or delivery has been made. **2** the act of receiving or fact of being received. **3** (*usually pl*) an amount or article received. **4** *Obs.* another word for **recipe.** ◆ *vb* **5** (*tr*) to acknowledge payment of (a bill), as by marking it. [C14: from OF *receite*, from Med. L *recepta*, from L *recipere* to RECEIVE]

receivable (rɪ'siːvəbªl) *adj* **1** suitable for or capable of being received, esp. as payment or legal tender. **2** (of a bill, etc.) awaiting payment: *accounts receivable.* ◆ *n* **3** (*usually pl*) the part of the assets of a business represented by accounts due for payment.

receive (rɪ'siːv) *vb* **receives, receiving, received.** (*mainly tr*) **1** to take (something offered) into one's hand or possession. **2** to have (an honour, blessing, etc.) bestowed. **3** to accept delivery or transmission of (a letter, etc.). **4** to be informed of (news). **5** to hear and consent to or acknowledge (a confession, etc.). **6** (of a container) to take or hold (a substance, commodity, or certain amount). **7** to support or sustain (the weight of something); bear. **8** to apprehend or perceive (ideas, etc.). **9** to experience, undergo, or meet with: *to receive a crack on the skull.* **10** (*also intr*) to be at home to (visitors). **11** to greet or welcome (guests), esp. in formal style. **12** to admit (a person) to a place, society, condition, etc.: *he was received into the priesthood.* **13** to accept or acknowledge (a precept or principle) as true or valid. **14** to convert (incoming radio signals) into sounds, pictures, etc., by means of a receiver. **15** (*also intr*) *Tennis, etc.* to play at the other end from the server. **16** (*also intr*) to partake of (the Christian Eucharist). **17** (*intr*) *Chiefly Brit.* to buy and sell stolen

goods. [C13: from OF *receivre*, from L *recipere*, from RE- + *capere* to take]

received (rɪ'siːvd) *adj* generally accepted or believed: *received wisdom.*

Received Pronunciation *n* the accent of standard Southern British English. Abbrev.: **RP.**

receiver (rɪ'siːvə) *n* **1** a person who receives something; recipient. **2** a person appointed by a court to manage property pending the outcome of litigation, during the infancy of the owner, or after the owner has been declared bankrupt or insane. **3** *Chiefly Brit.* a person who receives stolen goods knowing that they have been stolen. **4** the equipment in a telephone, radio, or television that receives incoming electrical signals or modulated radio waves and converts them into the original audio or video signals. **5** the detachable part of a telephone that is held to the ear. **6** *Chem.* a vessel in which the distillate is collected during distillation. **7** *US sport.* a player whose function is to receive the ball.

receivership (rɪ'siːvəʃɪp) *n Law.* **1** the office or function of a receiver. **2** the condition of being administered by a receiver.

receiving order *n Brit.* a court order appointing a receiver to manage the property of a debtor or bankrupt.

recension (rɪ'sɛnʃən) *n* **1** a critical revision of a literary work. **2** a text revised in this way. [C17: from L *recēnsiō*, from *recēnsēre*, from RE- + *cēnsēre* to assess]

recent ('riːsªnt) *adj* having appeared, happened, or been made not long ago; modern, fresh, or new. [C16: from L *recens* fresh; rel. to Gk *kainos* new]
▶ **'recently** *adv* ▶ **'recentness** *or* **'recency** *n*

Recent ('riːsªnt) *adj, n Geol.* another word for **Holocene.**

receptacle (rɪ'sɛptəkªl) *n* **1** an object that holds something; container. **2** *Bot.* **2a** the enlarged or modified tip of the flower stalk that bears the parts of the flower. **2b** the part of lower plants that bears the reproductive organs or spores. [C15: from L *receptāculum* store-place, from *receptāre*, from *recipere* to RECEIVE]

reception (rɪ'sɛpʃən) *n* **1** the act of receiving or state of being received. **2** the manner in which something, such as a guest or a new idea, is received: *a cold reception.* **3** a formal party for guests, such as after a wedding. **4** an area in an office, hotel, etc., where visitors or guests are received and appointments or reservations dealt with. **5** short for **reception room. 6** the quality or fidelity of a received radio or television broadcast: *the reception was poor.* [C14: from L *receptiō*, from *recipere* to RECEIVE]

reception centre *n* a place to which distressed people, such as vagrants, addicts, victims of a disaster, refugees, etc., go pending more permanent arrangements.

receptionist (rɪ'sɛpʃənɪst) *n* a person employed in an office, surgery, etc., to receive clients or guests, arrange appointments, etc.

reception room *n* **1** a room in a private house suitable for entertaining guests. **2** a room in a hotel suitable for receptions, etc.

receptive (rɪ'sɛptɪv) *adj* **1** able to apprehend quickly. **2** tending to receive new ideas or suggestions favourably. **3** able to hold or receive.
▶ **re'ceptively** *adv* ▶ **receptivity** (ˌriːsɛp'tɪvɪtɪ) *or* **re'ceptiveness** *n*

receptor (rɪ'sɛptə) *n* **1** *Physiol.* a sensory nerve ending that changes specific stimuli into nerve impulses. **2** any of various devices that receive information, signals, etc.

recess *n* (rɪ'sɛs, 'riːsɛs). **1** a space, such as a niche or alcove, set back or indented. **2** (*often pl*) a secluded or secret place: *recesses of the mind.* **3** a cessation of business, such as the closure of Parliament during a vacation. **4** *Anat.* a small cavity or depression in a bodily organ. **5** *US & Canad.* a break between classes at a school. ◆ *vb* (rɪ'sɛs). **6** (*tr*) to place or set (something) in a recess. **7** (*tr*) to build a recess in (a wall, etc.). [C16: from L *recessus* a retreat, from *recēdere* to RECEDE]

recession¹ (rɪ'sɛʃən) *n* **1** a temporary depression in economic activity or prosperity. **2** the withdrawal of the clergy and choir in procession after a church service. **3**

the act of receding. **4** a part of a building, wall, etc., that recedes. [C17: from L *recessio*; see RECESS]

recession² (rɪˈsɛʃən) *n* the act of restoring possession to a former owner. [C19: from RE- + CESSION]

recessional (rɪˈsɛʃənᵊl) *adj* **1** of or relating to recession. ◆ *n* **2** a hymn sung as the clergy and choir withdraw after a church service.

recessive (rɪˈsɛsɪv) *adj* **1** tending to recede or go back. **2** *Genetics.* **2a** (of a gene) capable of producing its characteristic phenotype in the organism only when its allele is identical. **2b** (of a character) controlled by such a gene. Cf. **dominant** (sense 4). **3** *Linguistics.* (of stress) tending to be placed on or near the initial syllable of a polysyllabic word. ◆ *n* **4** *Genetics.* a recessive gene or character. ▸ re'cessively *adv* ▸ re'cessiveness *n*

recharge (ˌriːˈtʃɑːdʒ) *vb* **recharges, recharging, recharged.** (*tr*) **1** to cause (an accumulator, capacitor, etc.) to take up and store electricity again. **2** to revive or renew (one's energies) (esp. in **recharge one's batteries**). ▸ re'chargeable *adj*

recherché (rəˈʃɛəʃeɪ) *adj* **1** known only to connoisseurs; choice or rare. **2** studiedly refined or elegant. [C18: from F: p.p. of *rechercher* to make a thorough search for]

recidivism (rɪˈsɪdɪˌvɪzəm) *n* habitual relapse into crime. [C19: from L *recidīvus* falling back, from RE- + *cadere* to fall] ▸ re'cidivist *n, adj* ▸ re,cidi'vistic *or* re'cidivous *adj*

Recife ★ (rɛˈsiːfə) *n* a port at the easternmost point of Brazil on the Atlantic: capital of Pernambuco state; built partly on an island, with many waterways and bridges. Pop. (urban area): 3 168 000 (1995). Former name: **Pernambuco.**

recipe (ˈrɛsɪpɪ) *n* **1** a list of ingredients and directions for making something, esp. when preparing food. **2** *Med.* (formerly) a medical prescription. **3** a method for achieving some desired objective: *a recipe for success.* [C14: from L, lit.: take (it)! from *recipere* to take]

recipient (rɪˈsɪpɪənt) *n* **1** a person who or thing that receives. ◆ *adj* **2** receptive. [C16: via F from L, from *recipere* to RECEIVE] ▸ re'cipience *or* re'cipiency *n*

reciprocal (rɪˈsɪprəkᵊl) *adj* **1** of, relating to, or designating something given by each of two people, countries, etc., to the other; mutual: *reciprocal trade.* **2** given or done in return: *a reciprocal favour.* **3** (of a pronoun) indicating that action is given and received by each subject; for example, *each other* in *they started to shout at each other.* **4** *Maths.* of or relating to a number or quantity divided into one. ◆ *n* **5** something that is reciprocal. **6** Also called: **inverse.** *Maths.* a number or quantity that when multiplied by a given number or quantity gives a product of one: *the reciprocal of 2 is 0.5.* [C16: from L *reciprocus* alternating] ▸ re,cipro'cality *n* ▸ re'ciprocally *adv*

reciprocate (rɪˈsɪprəˌkeɪt) *vb* **reciprocates, reciprocating, reciprocated.** **1** to give or feel in return. **2** to move or cause to move backwards and forwards. **3** (*intr*) to be correspondent or equivalent. [C17: from L *reciprocāre*, from *reciprocus* RECIPROCAL] ▸ re,cipro'cation *n* ▸ re'cipro,cative *or* re'cipro,catory *adj* ▸ re'cipro,cator *n*

reciprocating engine *n* an engine in which one or more pistons move backwards and forwards inside a cylinder or cylinders.

reciprocity (ˌrɛsɪˈprɒsɪtɪ) *n* **1** reciprocal action or relation. **2** a mutual exchange of commercial or other privileges. [C18: via F from L *reciprocus* RECIPROCAL]

recision (rɪˈsɪʒən) *n* the act of cancelling or rescinding; annulment: *the recision of a treaty.* [C17: from L *recīsiō*, from *recīdere* to cut back]

recital (rɪˈsaɪtᵊl) *n* **1** a musical performance by a soloist or soloists. **2** the act of reciting or repeating something learned or prepared. **3** an account, narration, or description. **4** (*often pl*) *Law.* the preliminary statement in a deed showing the reason for its existence and explaining the operative part. ▸ re'citalist *n*

recitation (ˌrɛsɪˈteɪʃən) *n* **1a** the act of reciting from

memory. **1b** a formal reading of verse before an audience. **2** something recited.

recitative¹ (ˌrɛsɪtəˈtiːv) *n* a passage in a musical composition, esp. the narrative parts in an oratorio, reflecting the natural rhythms of speech. [C17: from It. *recitativo*; see RECITE]

recitative² (rɪˈsaɪtətɪv) *adj* of or relating to recital.

recite (rɪˈsaɪt) *vb* **recites, reciting, recited.** **1** to repeat (a poem, etc.) aloud from memory before an audience. **2** (*tr*) to give a detailed account of. **3** (*tr*) to enumerate (examples, etc.). [C15: from L *recitāre* to cite again, from RE- + *citāre* to summon] ▸ re'citable *adj* ▸ re'citer *n*

reck (rɛk) *vb Arch.* (*used mainly with a negative*) **1** to mind or care about (something): *to reck nought.* **2** (*usually impersonal*) to concern or interest (someone). [OE *reccan*]

reckless (ˈrɛklɪs) *adj* having or showing no regard for danger or consequences; heedless; rash: *a reckless driver.* [OE *recceleās*; see RECK, -LESS] ▸ 'recklessly *adv* ▸ 'recklessness *n*

Recklinghausen ★ (German rɛklɪŋˈhauzən) *n* an industrial city in NW Germany, in North Rhine-Westphalia on the N edge of the Ruhr. Pop.: 127 139 (1995 est.).

reckon (ˈrɛkən) *vb* **1** to calculate or ascertain by calculating; compute. **2** (*tr*) to include; count as part of a set or class. **3** (*usually passive*) to consider or regard: *he is reckoned clever.* **4** (when *tr*, takes a clause as object*) to think or suppose; be of the opinion: *I reckon you don't know.* **5** (*intr*; foll. by *with*) to settle accounts (with). **6** (*intr*; foll. by *with* or *without*) to take into account or fail to take into account: *they reckoned without John.* **7** (*intr*; foll. by *on* or *upon*) to rely or depend: *I reckon on your support.* **8** (*tr*) *Inf.* to have a high opinion of. **9 to be reckoned with.** of considerable importance or influence. [OE *(ge)recenian* recount]

reckoner (ˈrɛkənə) *n* any of various devices or tables used to facilitate reckoning, esp. a ready reckoner.

reckoning (ˈrɛkənɪŋ) *n* **1** the act of counting or calculating. **2** settlement of an account or bill. **3** a bill or account. **4** retribution for one's actions (esp. in **day of reckoning**). **5** *Navigation.* short for **dead reckoning.**

reclaim (rɪˈkleɪm) *vb* (*tr*) **1** to claim back: *reclaim baggage.* **2** to convert (desert, marsh, etc.) into land suitable for growing crops. **3** to recover (useful substances) from waste products. **4** to convert (someone) from sin, folly, vice, etc. ◆ *n* **5** the act of reclaiming or state of being reclaimed. [C13: from OF *réclamer*, from L *reclāmāre* to cry out, from RE- + *clāmāre* to shout] ▸ re'claimable *adj* ▸ re'claimant *or* re'claimer *n*

reclamation (ˌrɛkləˈmeɪʃən) *n* **1** the conversion of desert, marsh, etc., into land suitable for cultivation. **2** the recovery of useful substances from waste products. **3** the act of reclaiming or state of being reclaimed.

réclame *French.* (reklam) *n* **1** public acclaim or attention; publicity. **2** the capacity for attracting publicity.

reclinate (ˈrɛklɪˌneɪt) *adj Bot.* naturally curved or bent backwards so that the upper part rests on the ground. [C18: from L *reclīnātus* bent back]

recline (rɪˈklaɪn) *vb* **reclines, reclining, reclined.** to rest in a leaning position. [C15: from OF *recliner*, from L *reclīnāre*, from RE- + *clīnāre* to LEAN¹] ▸ re'clinable *adj* ▸ reclination (ˌrɛklɪˈneɪʃən) *n*

recliner (rɪˈklaɪnə) *n* a person or thing that reclines, esp. a type of armchair having a back that can be adjusted to slope at various angles.

recluse (rɪˈkluːs) *n* **1** a person who lives in seclusion, esp. to devote himself to prayer and religious meditation; a hermit. ◆ *adj* **2** solitary; retiring. [C13: from OF *reclus*, from LL *reclūdere* to shut away, from L RE- + *claudere* to close] ▸ re'clusion (rɪˈkluːʒən) *n* ▸ re'clusive *adj*

recognition (ˌrɛkəgˈnɪʃən) *n* **1** the act of recognizing or fact of being recognized. **2** acceptance or acknowledgment of a claim, duty, etc. **3** a token of thanks. **4** formal acknowledgment of a government or of the independence of a country. [C15: from L *recognitiō*, from *recognoscere*, from RE- + *cognoscere* to know] ▸ recognitive (rɪˈkɒgnɪtɪv) *or* re'cognitory *adj*

recognizance *or* **recognisance** (rɪˈkɒgnɪzəns) *n Law.* **a** a bond entered into before a court or magistrate by which a person binds himself to do a specified act, as to appear in court on a stated day, to keep the peace, or pay a debt. **b** a monetary sum pledged to the performance of such an act. [C14: from OF *reconoissance*, from *reconoistre* to RECOGNIZE]
▶ re**ˈcognizant** *or* re**ˈcognisant** *adj*

recognize *or* **recognise** (ˈrɛkəɡˌnaɪz) *vb* **recognizes, recognizing, recognized** *or* **recognises, recognising, recognised.** *(tr)* **1** to perceive (a person or thing) to be the same as or belong to the same class as something previously seen or known; know again. **2** to accept or be aware of (a fact, problem, etc.): *to recognize necessity.* **3** to give formal acknowledgment of the status or legality of (a government, a representative, etc.). **4** *Chiefly US & Canad.* to grant (a person) the right to speak in a deliberative body. **5** to give a token of thanks for (a service rendered, etc.). **6** to make formal acknowledgment of (a claim, etc.). **7** to show approval or appreciation of (something good). **8** to acknowledge or greet (a person). [C15: from L *recognoscere*, from RE- + *cognoscere* to know]
▶ **ˈrecog,nizable** *or* **ˈrecog,nisable** *adj* ▶ ˌrecog**ˈniza'bility** *or* ˌrecog**ˈnisaˈbility** *n* ▶ **ˈrecog,nizably** *or* **ˈrecog,nisably** *adv* ▶ **ˈrecog,nizer** *or* **ˈrecog,niser** *n*

recoil *vb* (rɪˈkɔɪl). *(intr)* **1** to jerk back, as from an impact or violent thrust. **2** (often foll. by *from*) to draw back in fear, horror, or disgust. **3** (foll. by *on* or *upon*) to go wrong, esp. so as to hurt the perpetrator. **4** (of an atom, etc.) to change momentum as a result of the emission of a particle. ♦ *n* (rɪˈkɔɪl, ˈriːkɔɪl). **5a** the backward movement of a gun when fired. **5b** the distance moved. **6** the motion acquired by an atom, etc., as a result of its emission of a particle. **7** the act of recoiling. [C13: from OF *reculer*, from RE- + *cul* rump, from L *cūlus*]
▶ re**ˈcoiler** *n*

recollect (ˌrɛkəˈlɛkt) *vb* (when *tr*, often takes a clause as object) to recall from memory; remember. [C16: from L *recolligere*, from RE- + *colligere* to COLLECT]
▶ ˌrecol**ˈlection** *n* ▶ ˌrecol**ˈlective** *adj* ▶ ˌrecol**ˈlectively** *adv*

recombinant (riːˈkɒmbɪnənt) *Genetics.* ♦ *adj* **1** produced by the combining of genetic material from more than one origin. ♦ *n* **2** a chromosome, cell, organism, etc., the genetic makeup of which results from recombination.

recombinant DNA *n* DNA molecules that are extracted from different sources and chemically joined together.

recombination (ˌriːkɒmbɪˈneɪʃən) *n Genetics.* any of several processes by which genetic material of different origins becomes combined.

recommend (ˌrɛkəˈmɛnd) *vb (tr)* **1** (may take a clause as object *or* an infinitive) to advise as the best course or choice; counsel. **2** to praise or commend: *to recommend a new book.* **3** to make attractive or advisable: *the trip has little to recommend it.* **4** *Arch.* to entrust (a person or thing) to someone else's care; commend. [C14: via Med. L from L RE- + *commendāre* to COMMEND]
▶ ˌrecom**ˈmendable** *adj* ▶ ˌrecom**ˈmendatory** *adj* ▶ ˌrecom**ˈmender** *n*

recommendation (ˌrɛkəmɛnˈdeɪʃən) *n* **1** the act of recommending. **2** something that recommends, esp. a letter. **3** something that is recommended, such as a course of action.

recommit (ˌriːkəˈmɪt) *vb* **recommits, recommitting, recommitted.** *(tr)* **1** to send (a bill) back to a committee for further consideration. **2** to commit again.
▶ ˌrecom**ˈmitment** *or* ˌrecom**ˈmittal** *n*

recompense (ˈrɛkəmˌpɛns) *vb* **recompenses, recompensing, recompensed.** *(tr)* **1** to pay or reward for service, work, etc. **2** to compensate for loss, injury, etc. ♦ *n* **3** compensation for loss, injury, etc. **4** reward, remuneration, or repayment. [C15: from OF *recompenser*, from L RE- + *compensāre* to balance in weighing]
▶ **ˈrecom,pensable** *adj* ▶ **ˈrecom,penser** *n*

reconcile (ˈrɛkənˌsaɪl) *vb* **reconciles, reconciling, reconciled.** *(tr)* **1** (*often passive;* usually foll. by *to*) to make (oneself or another) no longer opposed; cause to acquiesce in

something unpleasant: *she reconciled herself to poverty.* **2** to become friendly with (someone) after estrangement or to re-establish friendly relations between (two or more people). **3** to settle (a quarrel). **4** to make (two apparently conflicting things) compatible or consistent with each other. **5** to reconsecrate (a desecrated church, etc.). [C14: from L *reconciliāre*, from RE- + *conciliāre* to make friendly, CONCILIATE]
▶ **ˈrecon,cilement** *n* ▶ **ˈrecon,ciler** *n* ▶ **reconciliation** (ˌrɛkənˌsɪlɪˈeɪʃən) *n* ▶ **reconciliatory** (ˌrɛkənˈsɪlɪətərɪ, -trɪ) *adj*

recondite (rɪˈkɒndaɪt, ˈrɛkənˌdaɪt) *adj* **1** requiring special knowledge; abstruse. **2** dealing with abstruse or profound subjects. [C17: from L *reconditus* hidden away, from RE- + *condere* to conceal]
▶ re**ˈconditely** *adv* ▶ re**ˈconditeness** *n*

recondition (ˌriːkənˈdɪʃən) *vb (tr)* to restore to good condition or working order: *to recondition an engine.*
▶ ˌrecon**ˈditioned** *adj*

reconnaissance (rɪˈkɒnɪsəns) *n* **1** the act of reconnoitring. **2** the process of obtaining information about the position, etc., of an enemy. **3** a preliminary inspection of an area of land. [C18: from F, from OF *reconoistre* to explore, RECOGNIZE]

reconnoitre *or US* **reconnoiter** (ˌrɛkəˈnɔɪtə) *vb* **reconnoitres, reconnoitring, reconnoitred** *or US* **reconnoiters, reconnoitering, reconnoitered.** **1** to survey or inspect (an enemy's position, region of land, etc.). ♦ *n* **2** the act or process of reconnoitring; a reconnaissance. [C18: from obs. F *reconnoître* to inspect, explore; see RECOGNIZE]
▶ ˌrecon**ˈnoitrer** *or US* ˌrecon**ˈnoiterer** *n*

reconsider (ˌriːkənˈsɪdə) *vb* to consider (something) again, with a view to changing one's policy or course of action.
▶ ˌrecon,sider**ˈation** *n*

reconstitute (riːˈkɒnstɪˌtjuːt) *vb* **reconstitutes, reconstituting, reconstituted.** *(tr)* **1** to restore (food, etc.) to its former or natural state, as by the addition of water to a concentrate. **2** to reconstruct; form again.
▶ **reconstituent** (ˌriːkənˈstɪtjʊənt) *adj, n* ▶ ˌreconsti**ˈtution** *n*

reconstruct (ˌriːkənˈstrʌkt) *vb (tr)* **1** to construct or form again; rebuild. **2** to form a picture of (a crime, past event, etc.) by piecing together evidence.
▶ ˌrecon**ˈstructible** *adj* ▶ ˌrecon**ˈstruction** *n* ▶ ˌrecon**ˈstructive** *or* ˌrecon**ˈstructional** *adj* ▶ ˌrecon**ˈstructor** *n*

reconvert (ˌriːkənˈvɜːt) *vb (tr)* **1** to change (something) back to a previous state or form. **2** to bring (someone) back to his former religion.
▶ **reconversion** (ˌriːkənˈvɜːʃən) *n*

record *n* (ˈrɛkɔːd). **1** an account in permanent form, esp. in writing, preserving knowledge or information. **2** a written account of some transaction that serves as legal evidence of the transaction. **3** a written official report of the proceedings of a court of justice or legislative body. **4** anything serving as evidence or as a memorial: *the First World War is a record of human folly.* **5** (*often pl*) information or data on a specific subject collected methodically over a long period: *weather records.* **6a** the best or most outstanding amount, rate, height, etc., ever attained, as in some field of sport: *a world record.* **6b** (*as modifier*): *a record time.* **7** the sum of one's recognized achievements, career, or performance. **8** a list of crimes of which an accused person has previously been convicted. **9 have a record.** to be a known criminal. **10** Also called: **gramophone record, disc.** a thin disc of a plastic material upon which sound has been recorded. Each side has a spiral groove, which undulates in accordance with the frequency and amplitude of the sound. **11** the markings made by a recording instrument such as a seismograph. **12** *Computing.* a group of data or piece of information preserved as a unit in machine-readable form. **13 for the record.** for the sake of strict factual accuracy. **14 go on record.** to state one's views publicly. **15 off the record.** confidential or confidentially. **16 on record. 16a** stated in a public document. **16b** publicly known. **17 set** *or* **put the record straight.** to correct an error. ♦ *vb* (rɪˈkɔːd). (*mainly tr*) **18** to set down in some permanent form so as to preserve the true facts of: *to record the minutes of a meeting.* **19** to contain or serve to

relate (facts, information, etc.). **20** to indicate, show, or register: *his face recorded his disappointment.* **21** to remain as or afford evidence of: *these ruins record the life of the Romans in Britain.* **22** (*also intr*) to make a recording of (music, speech, etc.) for reproduction, esp. on a record player or tape recorder, or for later broadcasting. **23** (*also intr*) (of an instrument) to register or indicate (information) on a scale: *the barometer recorded a low pressure.* [C13: from OF *recorder*, from L *recordārī* to remember, from RE- + *cor* heart]
▶ re'cordable *adj*

recorded delivery *n* a Post Office service by which an official record of posting and delivery is obtained for a letter or package.

recorder (rɪ'kɔːdə) *n* **1** a person who records, such as an official or historian. **2** something that records, esp. an apparatus that provides a permanent record of experiments, etc. **3** short for **tape recorder. 4** *Music.* a wind instrument of the flute family, blown through a fipple in the mouth end, having a reedlike quality of tone. **5** (in England) a barrister or solicitor of at least ten years' standing appointed to sit as a part-time judge in the crown court.
▶ re'cordership *n*

recording (rɪ'kɔːdɪŋ) *n* **1a** the act or process of making a record, esp. of sound on a gramophone record or magnetic tape. **1b** (*as modifier*): *recording studio.* **2** the record or tape so produced. **3** something that has been recorded, esp. a radio or television programme.

Recording Angel *n* an angel who supposedly keeps a record of every person's good and bad acts.

record of achievement *n Brit.* a statement of the personal and educational development of each pupil.

record player *n* a device for reproducing the sounds stored on a record. A stylus vibrates in accordance with the undulations of the walls of the groove in the record as it rotates.

recount (rɪ'kaʊnt) *vb* (*tr*) to tell the story or details of; narrate. [C15: from OF *reconter*, from RE- + *conter* to tell; see COUNT¹]
▶ re'countal *n*

re-count *vb* (riː'kaʊnt). **1** to count (votes, etc.) again. ◆ *n* ('riː,kaʊnt). **2** a second or further count, esp. of votes in an election.

recoup (rɪ'kuːp) *vb* **1** to regain or make good (a financial or other loss). **2** (*tr*) to reimburse or compensate (someone), as for a loss. **3** *Law.* to keep back (something due), having rightful claim to do so. ◆ *n* **4** *Rare.* the act of recouping; recoupment. [C15: from OF *recouper* to cut back, from RE- + *couper*, from *coper* to behead]
▶ re'coupable *adj* ▶ re'coupment *n*

recourse (rɪ'kɔːs) *n* **1** the act of resorting to a person, course of action, etc., in difficulty (esp. in **have recourse to**). **2** a person, organization, or course of action that is turned to for help, etc. **3** the right to demand payment, esp. from the drawer or endorser of a bill of exchange or other negotiable instrument when the person accepting it fails to pay. **4 without recourse.** a qualified endorsement on such a negotiable instrument, by which the endorser protects himself from liability to subsequent holders. [C14: from OF *recours*, from LL *recursus* a running back, from RE- + L *currere* to run]

recover (rɪ'kʌvə) *vb* **1** (*tr*) to find again or obtain the return of (something lost). **2** to regain (loss of money, time, etc.). **3** (of a person) to regain (health, spirits, composure, etc.). **4** to regain (a former and better condition): *industry recovered after the war.* **5** *Law.* **5a** (*tr*) to gain (something) by the judgment of a court of law: *to recover damages.* **5b** (*intr*) to succeed in a lawsuit. **6** (*tr*) to obtain (useful substances) from waste. **7** (*intr*) (in fencing, rowing, etc.) to make a recovery. [C14: from OF *recoverer*, from L *recuperāre* RECUPERATE]
▶ re'coverable *adj* ▶ re,covera'bility *n* ▶ re'coverer *n*

re-cover (riː'kʌvə) *vb* (*tr*) **1** to cover again. **2** to provide (furniture, etc.) with a new cover.

recovery (rɪ'kʌvərɪ) *n*, *pl* **recoveries. 1** the act or process of recovering, esp. from sickness, a shock, or a setback. **2** restoration to a former or better condition. **3** the regain-

ing of something lost. **4** the extraction of useful substances from waste. **5** the retrieval of a space capsule after a spaceflight. **6** *Law.* the obtaining of a right, etc., by the judgment of a court. **7** *Fencing.* a return to the position of guard after making an attack. **8** *Swimming, rowing, etc.* the action of bringing the arm, an oar, etc., forward for another stroke. **9** *Golf.* a stroke played from the rough or a bunker to the fairway or green.

recovery stock *n Stock Exchange.* a security that has fallen in price but is believed to have the ability to recover.

recreant ('rɛkrɪənt) *Arch.* ◆ *adj* **1** cowardly; fainthearted. **2** disloyal. ◆ *n* **3** a disloyal or cowardly person. [C14: from OF, from *recroire* to surrender, from RE- + L *crēdere* to believe]
▶ 'recreance *or* 'recreancy *n* ▶ 'recreantly *adv*

recreate ('rɛkrɪ,eɪt) *vb* **recreates, recreating, recreated.** *Rare.* to amuse (oneself or someone else). [C15: from L *recreāre* to invigorate, renew, from RE- + *creāre* to CREATE]
▶ 'recreative *adj* ▶ 'recreatively *adv* ▶ 'recre,ator *n*

re-create (,riː'kreɪt) *vb* **re-creates, re-creating, re-created.** to create anew; reproduce.
▶ ,re-cre'ation *n* ▶ ,re-cre'ator *n*

recreation (,rɛkrɪ'eɪʃən) *n* **1** refreshment of health or spirits by relaxation and enjoyment. **2** an activity that promotes this. **3a** an interval of free time between school lessons. **3b** (*as modifier*): *recreation period.*

recreational (,rɛkrɪ'eɪʃənəl) *adj* **1** of, relating to, or used for recreation: *recreational facilities.* **2** (of a drug) taken for pleasure rather than for medical reasons or because of an addiction.

recreational vehicle *n Chiefly US.* a large vanlike vehicle equipped to be lived in. Abbrev.: **RV.**

recriminate (rɪ'krɪmɪ,neɪt) *vb* **recriminates, recriminating, recriminated.** (*intr*) to return an accusation against someone or engage in mutual accusations. [C17: via Med. L, from L *crīminārī* to accuse, from *crīmen* accusation]
▶ re,crimi'nation *n* ▶ re'criminative *or* re'criminatory *adj* ▶ re'crimi,nator *n*

recrudesce (,riːkruː'dɛs) *vb* **recrudesces, recrudescing, recrudesced.** (*intr*) (of a disease, trouble, etc.) to break out or appear again after a period of dormancy. [C19: from L *recrūdēscere*, from RE- + *crūdēscere* to grow worse, from *crūdus* bloody, raw]
▶ ,recru'descence *n*

recruit (rɪ'kruːt) *vb* **1a** to enlist (men) for military service. **1b** to raise or strengthen (an army, etc.) by enlistment. **2** (*tr*) to enrol or obtain (members, support, etc.). **3** to furnish or be furnished with a fresh supply; renew. **4** *Arch.* to recover (health, spirits, etc.). ◆ *n* **5** a newly joined member of a military service. **6** any new member or supporter. [C17: from F *recrute* lit.: new growth, from *recroître*, from L, from RE- + *crēscere* to grow]
▶ re'cruitable *adj* ▶ re'cruiter *n* ▶ re'cruitment *n*

recta ('rɛktə) *n* a plural of **rectum.**

rectal ('rɛktəl) *adj* of or relating to the rectum.
▶ 'rectally *adv*

rectangle ('rɛk,tæŋgᵊl) *n* a parallelogram having four right angles. [C16: from Med. L *rectangulum*, from *rectus* straight + *angulus* angle]

rectangular (rɛk'tæŋgjʊlə) *adj* **1** shaped like a rectangle. **2** having or relating to right angles. **3** mutually perpendicular: *rectangular coordinates.* **4** having a base or section shaped like a rectangle.
▶ rec,tangu'larity *n* ▶ rec'tangularly *adv*

rectangular coordinates *pl n* the Cartesian coordinates in a system of mutually perpendicular axes.

rectangular hyperbola *n* a hyperbola with perpendicular asymptotes.

recti ('rɛktaɪ) *n* the plural of **rectus.**

recti- *or before a vowel* **rect-** *combining form.* straight or right: *rectangle.* [from L *rectus*]

rectifier ('rɛktɪ,faɪə) *n* **1** an electronic device that converts an alternating current to a direct current. **2** *Chem.* an apparatus for condensing a hot vapour to a liquid in distillation; condenser. **3** a thing or person that rectifies.

rectify ('rɛktɪ,faɪ) *vb* **rectifies, rectifying, rectified.** (*tr*) **1** to

★ **people and places**

put right; correct; remedy. **2** to separate (a substance) from a mixture or refine (a substance) by fractional distillation. **3** to convert (alternating current) into direct current. **4** *Maths.* to determine the length of (a curve). [C14: via OF from Med. L *rectificāre*, from L *rectus* straight + *facere* to make]
▸ **'recti,fiable** ▸ **,rectifi'cation** *n*

rectilinear (,rɛktɪ'lɪnɪə) *or* **rectilineal** *adj* **1** in, moving in, or characterized by a straight line. **2** consisting of, bounded by, or formed by a straight line.
▸ **,recti'linearly** *or* **,recti'lineally** *adv*

rectitude ('rɛktɪ,tjuːd) *n* **1** moral or religious correctness. **2** correctness of judgment. [C15: from LL *rectitūdō*, from L *rectus* right, from *regere* to rule]

recto ('rɛktəʊ) *n*, *pl* **rectos**. **1** the front of a sheet of printed paper. **2** the right-hand pages of a book. Cf. **verso** (sense 1b). [C19: from L *rectō foliō* on the right-hand page]

rectocele ('rɛktə,siːl) *n* *Pathol.* a protrusion or herniation of the rectum into the vagina.

rector ('rɛktə) *n* **1** *Church of England.* a clergyman in charge of a parish in which, as its incumbent, he would formerly have been entitled to the whole of the tithes. **2** *RC Church.* a cleric in charge of a college, religious house, or congregation. **3** *Protestant Episcopal Church.* a clergyman in charge of a parish. **4** *Chiefly Brit.* the head of certain schools, colleges, or universities. **5** (in Scotland) a high-ranking official in a university. **6** (in South Africa) a principal of an Afrikaans university. [C14: from L: director, ruler, from *regere* to rule]
▸ **'rectorate** *n* ▸ **rectorial** (rɛk'tɔːrɪəl) *adj* ▸ **'rectorship** *n*

rectory ('rɛktərɪ) *n*, *pl* **rectories**. **1** the official house of a rector. **2** *Church of England.* the office and benefice of a rector.

rectrix ('rɛktrɪks) *n*, *pl* **rectrices** ('rɛktrɪ,siːz, rɛk'traɪsiːz). any of the large stiff feathers of a bird's tail, used in controlling the direction of flight. [C17: from LL, fem of L *rector* RECTOR]
▸ **rectricial** (rɛk'trɪʃəl) *adj*

rectum ('rɛktəm) *n*, *pl* **rectums** *or* **recta**. the lower part of the alimentary canal, between the sigmoid flexure of the colon and the anus. [C16: from NL *rectum intestinum* the straight intestine]

rectus ('rɛktəs) *n*, *pl* **recti**. *Anat.* a straight muscle. [C18: from NL *rectus musculus*]

recumbent (rɪ'kʌmbənt) *adj* **1** lying down; reclining. **2** (of an organ) leaning or resting against another organ. [C17: from L *recumbere* to lie back, from RE- + *cumbere* to lie]
▸ **re'cumbence** *or* **re'cumbency** *n* ▸ **re'cumbently** *adv*

recuperate (rɪ'kuːpə,reɪt, -'kjuː-) *vb* **recuperates, recuperating, recuperated**. **1** (*intr*) to recover from illness or exhaustion. **2** to recover (financial losses, etc.). [C16: from L *recuperāre* to recover, from RE- + *capere* to gain]
▸ **re,cuper'ation** *n* ▸ **re'cuperative** *adj*

recur (rɪ'kɜː) *vb* **recurs, recurring, recurred**. (*intr*) **1** to happen again. **2** (of a thought, etc.) to come back to the mind. **3** (of a problem, etc.) to come up again. **4** *Maths.* (of a digit or group of digits) to be repeated an infinite number of times at the end of a decimal fraction. [C15: from L *recurrere*, from RE- + *currere* to run]
▸ **re'curring** *adj*

recurrent (rɪ'kʌrənt) *adj* **1** tending to happen again or repeatedly. **2** *Anat.* (of certain nerves, etc.) turning back, so as to run in the opposite direction.
▸ **re'currence** *n* ▸ **re'currently** *adv*

recurrent fever *n* another name for **relapsing fever**.

recurring decimal *n* a rational number that contains a pattern of digits repeated indefinitely after the decimal point.

recursion (rɪ'kɜːʃən) *n* **1** the act or process of returning or running back. **2** *Maths, logic.* the application of a function to its own values to generate an infinite sequence of values. [C17: from L *recursio*, from *recurrere* RECUR]
▸ **re'cursive** *adj*

recurve (rɪ'kɜːv) *vb* **recurves, recurving, recurved**. to curve or bend (something) back or down or (of something) to be

so curved or bent. [C16: from L *recurvāre*, from RE- + *curvāre* to CURVE]

recusant ('rɛkjʊzənt) *n* **1** (in 16th to 18th century England) a Roman Catholic who did not attend the services of the Church of England. **2** any person who refuses to submit to authority. ◆ *adj* **3** (formerly, of Catholics) refusing to attend services of the Church of England. **4** refusing to submit to authority. [C16: from L *recūsāns* refusing, from *recūsāre*, from RE- + *causārī* to dispute, from *causa* a CAUSE]
▸ **'recusance** *or* **'recusancy** *n*

recycle (riː'saɪkªl) *vb* **recycles, recycling, recycled**. (*tr*) **1** to pass (a substance) through a system again for further treatment or use. **2** to reclaim (packaging or products with a limited useful life) for further use: *to recycle water.* ◆ *n* **3** the repetition of a fixed sequence of events.
▸ **re'cyclable** *or* **re'cycleable** *adj*

red[1] (rɛd) *n* **1** any of a group of colours, such as that of a ripe tomato or fresh blood. **2** a pigment or dye of or producing these colours. **3** red cloth or clothing: *dressed in red.* **4** a red ball in snooker, etc. **5** (in roulette) one of two colours on which players may place even bets. **6** *Inf.* red wine: *a bottle of red.* **7** **in the red.** *Inf.* in debt. **8** **see red.** *Inf.* to become very angry. ◆ *adj* **redder, reddest. 9** of the colour red. **10** reddish in colour or having parts or marks that are reddish: *red deer.* **11** having the face temporarily suffused with blood, being a sign of anger, shame, etc. **12** (of the complexion) rosy; florid. **13** (of the eyes) bloodshot. **14** (of the hands) stained with blood. **15** bloody or violent: *red revolution.* **16** denoting the highest degree of urgency in an emergency; used by the police and the army and informally (esp. in the phrase **red alert**). **17** (of wine) made from black grapes and coloured by their skins. ◆ *vb* **reds, redding, redded. 18** another word for **redden**. [OE *rēad*]
▸ **'reddish** *adj* ▸ **'redness** *n*

red[2] (rɛd) *vb* **reds, redding, red** *or* **redded**. (*tr*) a variant spelling of **redd**.

Red (rɛd) *Inf.* ◆ *adj* **1** Communist, Socialist, or Soviet. **2** radical, leftist, or revolutionary. ◆ *n* **3** a member or supporter of a Communist or Socialist Party or a national of the Soviet Union. **4** a radical, leftist, or revolutionary. [C19: from the colour chosen to symbolize revolutionary socialism]

redact (rɪ'dækt) *vb* (*tr*) **1** to compose or draft (an edict, proclamation, etc.). **2** to put (a literary work, etc.) into appropriate form for publication; edit. [C15: from L *redigere* to bring back, from RE- + *agere* to drive]
▸ **re'daction** *n* ▸ **re'dactional** *adj* ▸ **re'dactor** *n*

red admiral *n* a butterfly of temperate Europe and Asia, having black wings with red and white markings. See also **white admiral**.

red algae *pl n* the numerous algae which contain a red pigment in addition to chlorophyll. The group includes carrageen and dulse.

Red Army Faction *n* another name for **Baader-Meinhof Gang**.

redback ('rɛd,bæk) *n* *Austral.* a small, venomous spider, the female of which has a red stripe on its back. Also called: **redback spider**.

red bark *n* a kind of cinchona containing a high proportion of alkaloids.

red biddy *n* *Inf.* cheap red wine fortified with methylated spirits.

red blood cell *n* another name for **erythrocyte**.

red-blooded *adj Inf.* vigorous; virile.
▸ **,red-'bloodedness** *n*

red book *n* *Brit.* (sometimes caps.) a government publication bound in red, esp. the Treasury's annual forecast of revenue, expenditure, growth, and inflation.

redbreast ('rɛd,brɛst) *n* any of various birds having a red breast, esp. the Old World robin.

redbrick ('rɛd,brɪk) *n* (*modifier*) denoting, relating to, or characteristic of a provincial British university of relatively recent foundation.

Redbridge ★ ('rɛd,brɪdʒ) *n* a borough of NE Greater

London: includes part of Epping Forest. Pop.: 225 100 (1994 est.). Area: 56 sq. km (22 sq. miles).

redcap ('red,kæp) *n* **1** *Brit. inf.* a military policeman. **2** *US & Canad.* a porter at an airport or station.

Redcar and Cleveland ★ ('rɛdkɑː) *n* a unitary authority in NE England, in North Yorkshire. Pop.: 144 000 (1996 est.). Area: 240 sq. km (93 sq. miles).

red card *Soccer, etc.* ◆ *n* **1** a card of a red colour displayed by a referee to indicate that a player has been sent off. ◆ *vb* **red-card. 2** (*tr*) to send off (a player).

red carpet *n* **1** a strip of red carpeting laid for important dignitaries to walk on. **2a** deferential treatment accorded to a person of importance. **2b** (*as modifier*): *a red-carpet reception.*

red cedar *n* **1** any of several North American coniferous trees, esp. a juniper that has fragrant reddish wood. **2** the wood of any of these trees. **3** any of several Australian timber trees.

red cent *n* (*used with a negative*) *Inf., chiefly US.* a cent considered as a trivial amount of money (esp. in **not have a red cent**, etc.).

Red China ★ *n* an unofficial name for (the People's Republic of) **China.**

redcoat ('rɛd,kəʊt) *n* **1** (formerly) a British soldier. **2** *Canad. inf.* another name for **Mountie.**

red coral *n* any of several corals, the skeletons of which are pinkish red in colour and used to make ornaments, etc.

red corpuscle *n* another name for **erythrocyte.**

Red Crescent *n* the emblem of the Red Cross Society in a Muslim country.

Red Cross *n* **1** an international humanitarian organization (**Red Cross Society**) formally established by the Geneva Convention of 1864. **2** the emblem of this organization, consisting of a red cross on a white background.

redcurrant (,rɛd'kʌrənt) *n* **1** a N temperate shrub having greenish flowers and small edible rounded red berries. **2a** the fruit of this shrub. **2b** (*as modifier*): *redcurrant jelly.*

redd *or* **red** (rɛd) *Scot. & N English dialect.* ◆ *vb* **redds, redding, redd** *or* **redded. 1** (*tr*; often foll. by *up*) to bring order to; tidy (up). ◆ *n* **2** the act or an instance of redding. [C15: *redden* to clear, ? a variant of RID]
▸ **'redder** *n*

red deer *n* a large deer formerly widely distributed in the woodlands of Europe and Asia. The coat is reddish brown in summer and the short tail is surrounded by a patch of light-coloured hair.

Red Deer ★ *n* **1** a town in S Alberta on the Red Deer River: trade centre for mixed farming, dairying region, and natural gas processing. Pop: 58 134 (1991). **2** a river in W Canada, in SW Alberta, flowing southeast into the South Saskatchewan River. Length: about 620 km (385 miles). **3** a river in W Canada, flowing east through **Red Deer Lake** into Lake Winnipegosis. Length: about 225 km (140 miles).

redden ('rɛdˀn) *vb* **1** to make or become red. **2** (*intr*) to flush with embarrassment, anger, etc.

Redding ★ ('rɛdɪŋ) *n* **Otis.** 1941–67, US singer and songwriter. His recordings include "Respect" (1965).

Redditch ★ ('rɛdɪtʃ) *n* a town in W central England, in Hereford and Worcester: designated a new town in the mid-1960s; metal-working industries. Pop.: 73 372 (1991).

reddle ('rɛdˀl) *n, vb* **reddles, reddling, reddled.** a variant spelling of **ruddle.**

red duster *n Brit.* an informal name for the **Red Ensign.**

red dwarf *n* one of a class of stars of relatively small mass and low luminosity.

rede (riːd) *Arch.* ◆ *n* **1** advice or counsel. **2** an explanation. ◆ *vb* **redes, reding, reded.** (*tr*) **3** to advise; counsel. **4** to explain. [OE *rædan* to rule]

red earth *n* a clayey zonal soil of tropical savanna lands, formed by extensive chemical weathering and coloured by iron compounds.

redeem (rɪ'diːm) *vb* (*tr*) **1** to recover possession or owner-

ship of by payment of a price or service; regain. **2** to convert (bonds, shares, etc.) into cash. **3** to pay off (a loan, etc.). **4** to recover (something pledged, mortgaged, or pawned). **5** to convert (paper money) into bullion or specie. **6** to fulfil (a promise, pledge, etc.). **7** to exchange (coupons, etc.) for goods. **8** to reinstate in someone's estimation or good opinion: *he redeemed himself by his altruistic action.* **9** to make amends for. **10** to recover from captivity, esp. by a money payment. **11** *Christianity.* (of Christ as Saviour) to free (humanity) from sin by death on the Cross. [C15: from OF *redimer*, from L *redimere*, from *red-* RE- + *emere* to buy]
▸ **re'deemable** *or* **re'demptible** *adj* ▸ **re'deemer** *n*

Redeemer (rɪ'diːmə) *n* **the.** Jesus Christ as having brought redemption to mankind.

redeeming (rɪ'diːmɪŋ) *adj* serving to compensate for faults or deficiencies.

redemption (rɪ'dɛmpʃən) *n* **1** the act or process of redeeming. **2** the state of being redeemed. **3** *Christianity.* **3a** deliverance from sin through the incarnation, sufferings, and death of Christ. **3b** atonement for guilt. [C14: via OF from L *redemptiō* a buying back; see REDEEM]
▸ **re'demptional, re'demptive,** *or* **re'demptory** *adj* ▸ **re-'demptively** *adv*

redemption yield *n Stock Exchange.* the yield produced by a redeemable gilt-edged security taking into account the annual interest it pays and an annualized amount to account for any profit or loss when it is redeemed.

Red Ensign *n* the ensign of the British Merchant Navy, having the Union Jack on a red background at the upper corner of the vertical edge alongside the hoist. It was also the national flag of Canada until 1965.

redeploy (,riːdɪ'plɔɪ) *vb* to assign into new positions or tasks to (labour, troops, etc.).
▸ **,rede'ployment** *n*

redevelopment area (,riːdɪ'vɛləpmənt) *n* an urban area in which all or most of the buildings are demolished and rebuilt.

redeye ('rɛd,aɪ) *n* **1** *US sl.* inferior whisky. **2** *Sl., chiefly US.* a flight that departs late at night and arrives early next morning. **3** another name for **rudd.**

red-faced *adj* **1** flushed with embarrassment or anger. **2** having a florid complexion.
▸ **red-facedly** (,rɛd'feɪsɪdlɪ, -'feɪstlɪ) *adv*

redfin ('rɛd,fɪn) *n* any of various small cyprinid fishes with reddish fins.

redfish ('rɛd,fɪʃ) *n, pl* **redfish** *or* **redfishes. 1** a male salmon that has recently spawned. Cf. **blackfish** (sense 2). **2** *Canad.* another name for **kokanee.**

red flag *n* **1** a symbol of socialism, communism, or revolution. **2** a warning of danger or a signal to stop.

Redford ★ ('rɛdfəd) *n* **Robert.** born 1937, US film actor and director. His films as an actor include *Butch Cassidy and the Sundance Kid* (1969), *The Sting* (1973), and *Up Close and Personal* (1996) and as director *Ordinary People* (1980) and *The Horse Whisperer* (1998).

red fox *n* the common European fox which has a reddish-brown coat.

red giant *n* a giant star that emits red light.

Redgrave ★ ('rɛd,ɡreɪv) *n* **1 Lynn.** born 1944, British stage and film actress. Her films include *Georgy Girl* (1966) and *Getting It Right* (1989). **2** her father, Sir **Michael.** 1908–85, British actor. Among his films are *The Dam Busters* (1955) and *The Go-Between* (1971). **3** his elder daughter, **Vanessa.** born 1937, British actress, whose films include *Isadora* (1968), *Howard's End* (1992), and *Déjà Vu* (1998): noted also for her left-wing politics.

red grouse *n* a reddish-brown grouse of upland moors of Great Britain.

Red Guard *n* a member of a Communist Chinese youth movement that attempted to effect the Cultural Revolution (1966–69).

red-handed *adj* (*postpositive*) in the act of committing a crime or doing something wrong or shameful (esp. in **catch red-handed**). [C19 (earlier, C15 *red hand*)]
▸ **,red-'handedly** *adv* ▸ **,red-'handedness** *n*

★ people and places

red hat *n* the broad-brimmed crimson hat given to cardinals as the symbol of their rank.

redhead ('rɛd,hɛd) *n* a person with red hair.
▶ 'red,headed *adj*

red heat *n* 1 the temperature at which a substance is red-hot. 2 the state or condition of being red-hot.

red herring *n* 1 anything that diverts attention from a topic or line of inquiry. 2 a herring cured by salting and smoking.

red-hot *adj* 1 (esp. of metal) heated to the temperature at which it glows red. 2 extremely hot. 3 keen, excited, or eager. 4 furious; violent: *red-hot anger*. 5 very recent or topical: *red-hot information*. 6 *Austral. sl.* extreme, unreasonable, or unfair.

red-hot poker *n* a liliaceous plant: widely cultivated for its showy spikes of red or yellow flowers.

Red Indian *n, adj* another name, now considered offensive, for **American Indian**. [see REDSKIN]

redingote ('rɛdɪŋ,gəʊt) *n* 1 a man's full-skirted outer coat of the 18th and 19th centuries. 2 a woman's coat of the 18th century, with an open-fronted skirt, revealing a decorative underskirt. 3 a woman's coat with a close-fitting top and a full skirt. [C19: from F, from E *riding coat*]

redintegrate (rɛ'dɪntɪ,greɪt) *vb* **redintegrates, redintegrating, redintegrated**. (*tr*) to make whole or complete again; restore to a perfect state; renew. [C15: from L *redintegrāre* to renew, from *red-* RE- + *integer* complete]
▶ re,dinte'gration *n* ▶ red'integrative *adj*

redistribution (,riːdɪstrɪ'bjuːʃən) *n* 1 the act or an instance of distributing again. 2 a revision of the number of seats in the Canadian House of Commons allocated to each province, made every ten years on the basis of a new census.

redivivus (,rɛdɪ'vaɪvəs) *adj Rare.* returned to life; revived. [C17: from LL, from L *red-* RE- + *vīvus* alive]

red lead (lɛd) *n* a bright-red poisonous insoluble oxide of lead.

red-letter day *n* a memorably important or happy occasion. [C18: from the red letters used in ecclesiastical calendars to indicate saints' days and feasts]

red light *n* 1 a signal to stop, esp. a red traffic signal. 2 a danger signal. 3a a red lamp indicating that a house is a brothel. 3b (*as modifier*): *a red-light district*.

redline ('rɛd,laɪn) *vb* **redlines, redlining, redlined**. (*tr*) (esp. of a bank or group of banks) to refuse to consider giving a loan to (a person or country) because of the presumed risks involved.

red meat *n* any meat that is dark in colour, esp. beef and lamb. Cf. **white meat**.

Redmond ★ ('rɛdmənd) *n* **John Edward**. 1856–1918, Irish politician.

red mullet *n* a food fish of European waters with a pair of long barbels beneath the chin and a reddish coloration. US name: **goatfish**.

redneck ('rɛd,nɛk) *n Disparaging.* 1 (in the southwestern US) a poor uneducated White farm worker. 2 a person or institution that is extremely reactionary. ◆ *adj* 3 reactionary and bigoted: *redneck laws*.

redo (riː'duː) *vb* **redoes, redoing, redid, redone**. (*tr*) 1 to do over again. 2 *Inf.* to redecorate, esp. thoroughly: *we redid the house last summer*.

red ochre *n* any of various natural red earths containing ferric oxide: used as pigments.

redolent ('rɛdəʊlənt) *adj* 1 having a pleasant smell; fragrant. 2 (*postpositive*; foll. by *of* or *with*) having the odour or smell (of): *a room redolent of flowers*. 3 (*postpositive*; foll. by *of* or *with*) reminiscent or suggestive (of): *a picture redolent of the 18th century*. [C14: from L *redolens* smelling (of), from *redolēre* to give off an odour, from *red-* RE- + *olēre* to smell]
▶ 'redolence *or* 'redolency *n* ▶ 'redolently *adv*

Redon ★ (*French* rədɔ̃) *n* **Odilon** (ɔdilɔ̃). 1840–1916, French painter.

redouble (rɪ'dʌbʰl) *vb* **redoubles, redoubling, redoubled**. 1 to make or become much greater in intensity, number,

etc.: *to redouble one's efforts*. 2 to send back (sounds) or (of sounds) to be sent back. 3 *Bridge.* to double (an opponent's double). ◆ *n* 4 the act of redoubling.

redoubt (rɪ'daʊt) *n* 1 an outwork or fieldwork defending a hilltop, pass, etc. 2 a temporary defence work built inside a fortification as a last defensive position. [C17: via F from obs. It. *ridotta*, from Med. L *reductus* shelter, from L *redūcere* to lead]

redoubtable (rɪ'daʊtəbʰl) *adj* 1 to be feared; formidable. 2 worthy of respect. [C14: from OF, from *redouter* to dread, from RE- + *douter* to be afraid, DOUBT]
▶ re'doubtableness *n* ▶ re'doubtably *adv*

redound (rɪ'daʊnd) *vb* 1 (*intr*; foll. by *to*) to have an advantageous or disadvantageous effect (on): *brave deeds redound to your credit*. 2 (*intr*; foll. by *on* or *upon*) to recoil or rebound. 3 (*tr*) *Arch.* to reflect; bring: *his actions redound dishonour upon him*. [C14: from OF *redonder*, from L *redundāre* to stream over, from *red-* RE- + *undāre* to rise in waves]

redox ('riːdɒks) *n* (*modifier*) another term for **oxidation-reduction**. [C20: from RED(UCTION) + OX(IDATION)]

red pepper *n* 1 any of several varieties of the pepper plant cultivated for their hot pungent red podlike fruits. 2 the fruit of any of these plants. 3 the ripe red fruit of the sweet pepper. 4 another name for **cayenne pepper**.

Red Planet *n* the. an informal name for **Mars**[2].

redpoll ('rɛd,pɒl) *n* either of two widely distributed types of finches, having a greyish-brown plumage with a red crown and pink breast.

red rag *n* a provocation; something that infuriates. [so called because red objects supposedly infuriate bulls]

redress (rɪ'drɛs) *vb* (*tr*) 1 to put right (a wrong), esp. by compensation; make reparation for. 2 to correct or adjust (esp. in **redress the balance**). 3 to make compensation to (a person) for a wrong. ◆ *n* 4 the act or an instance of setting right a wrong; remedy or cure. 5 compensation, amends, or reparation for a wrong, injury, etc. [C14: from OF *redrecier* to set up again, from RE- + *drecier* to straighten; see DRESS]
▶ re'dressable *or* re'dressible *adj* ▶ re'dresser *or* re'dressor *n*

re-dress (riː'drɛs) *vb* (*tr*) to dress (something) again.

Red River ★ *n* 1 Also called: **Red River of the South**. a river in the S central US, flowing east from N Texas through Arkansas into the Mississippi in Louisiana. Length: 1639 km (1018 miles). 2 a river in the northern US, flowing north as the border between North Dakota and Minnesota and into Lake Winnipeg, Canada. Length: 515 km (320 miles). 3 a river in SE Asia, rising in SW China in Yünnan province and flowing southeast across N Vietnam to the Gulf of Tongkin: the chief river of N Vietnam, with an extensive delta. Length: 500 km (310 miles). Vietnamese name: **Song Koi**.

Red River cart *n Canad. history.* a strongly-built, two-wheeled, ox- or horse-drawn cart used in W Canada.

red rose *n English history.* the emblem of the House of Lancaster.

red salmon *n* any salmon having reddish flesh, esp. the sockeye salmon.

Red Sea ★ *n* a long narrow sea between Arabia and NE Africa, linked with the Mediterranean in the north by the Suez Canal and with the Indian Ocean in the south: occasionally reddish in appearance through algae. Area: 438 000 sq. km (169 000 sq. miles).

redshank ('rɛd,ʃæŋk) *n* any of various large common European sandpipers, esp. the **spotted redshank**, having red legs.

red shift *n* a shift in the lines of the spectrum of an astronomical object towards a longer wavelength (the red end of an optical spectrum), relative to the wavelength of these lines in the terrestrial spectrum, usually as a result of the Doppler effect caused by the recession of the object.

redskin ('rɛd,skɪn) *n* an informal name, now considered offensive, for an **American Indian**. [so called because one now extinct tribe painted themselves with red ochre]

red snapper *n* any of various marine percoid food fishes of the snapper family, having a reddish coloration, common in American coastal regions of the Atlantic.

red spider *n* short for **red spider mite** (see **spider mite**).

Red Spot *n* See **Great Red Spot**.

red squirrel *n* a reddish-brown squirrel, inhabiting woodlands of Europe and parts of Asia.

redstart ('red,stɑːt) *n* **1** a European songbird of the thrush family: the male has a black throat, orange-brown tail and breast, and grey back. **2** a North American warbler. [OE *rēad* red + *steort* tail]

red tape *n* obstructive official routine or procedure; time-consuming bureaucracy. [C18: from the red tape used to bind official government documents]

reduce (rɪ'djuːs) *vb* **reduces, reducing, reduced.** (*mainly tr*) **1** (*also intr*) to make or become smaller in size, number, etc. **2** to bring into a certain state, condition, etc.: *to reduce a forest to ashes; he was reduced to tears.* **3** (*also intr*) to make or become slimmer; lose or cause to lose excess weight. **4** to impoverish (esp. in **in reduced circumstances**). **5** to bring into a state of submission to one's authority; subjugate: *the whole country was reduced after three months.* **6** to bring down the price of (a commodity). **7** to lower the rank or status of; demote: *reduced to the ranks.* **8** to set out systematically as an aid to understanding; simplify: *his theories have been reduced in a treatise.* **9** *Maths.* to modify or simplify the form of (an expression or equation), esp. by substitution of one term by another. **10** *Cookery.* to make (a sauce, stock, etc.) more concentrated by boiling away some of the water in it. **11** to thin out (paint) by adding oil, turpentine, etc. **12** (*also intr*) *Chem.* **12a** to undergo or cause to undergo a chemical reaction with hydrogen. **12b** to lose or cause to lose oxygen atoms. **12c** to undergo or cause to undergo an increase in the number of electrons. **13** *Photog.* to lessen the density of (a negative or print). **14** *Surgery.* to manipulate or reposition (a broken or displaced bone, organ, or part) back to its normal site. [C14: from L *redūcere* to bring back, from RE- + *dūcere* to lead]
▸ re'ducible *adj* ▸ re,duci'bility *n* ▸ re'ducibly *adv*

reducer (rɪ'djuːsə) *n* **1** *Photog.* a chemical solution used to lessen the density of a negative or print by oxidizing some of the blackened silver to soluble silver compounds. **2** a pipe fitting connecting two pipes of different diameters. **3** a person or thing that reduces.

reducing agent *n Chem.* a substance that reduces another substance in a chemical reaction, being itself oxidized in the process.

reducing glass *n* a lens or curved mirror that produces an image smaller than the object observed.

reductase (rɪ'dʌkteɪz) *n* any enzyme that catalyses a biochemical reduction reaction. [C20: from REDUCTION + -ASE]

reductio ad absurdum (rɪ'dʌktɪəʊ æd æb'sɜːdəm) *n* **1** a method of disproving a proposition by showing that its inevitable consequences would be absurd. **2** a method of indirectly proving a proposition by assuming its negation to be true and showing that this leads to an absurdity. **3** application of a principle or proposed principle to an instance in which it is absurd. [L, lit.: reduction to the absurd]

reduction (rɪ'dʌkʃən) *n* **1** the act or process or an instance of reducing. **2** the state or condition of being reduced. **3** the amount by which something is reduced. **4** a form of an original resulting from a reducing process, such as a copy on a smaller scale. **5** *Maths.* **5a** the process of converting a fraction into its decimal form. **5b** the process of dividing out the common factors in the numerator and denominator of a fraction.
▸ re'ductive *adj*

reduction formula *n Maths.* a formula expressing the values of a trigonometric function of any angle greater than 90° in terms of a function of an acute angle.

reductionism (rɪ'dʌkʃə,nɪzəm) *n* **1** the analysis of complex things, data, etc., into less complex constituents. **2** *Often disparaging.* any theory or method that holds that a complex idea, system, etc., can be completely understood in terms of its simpler parts or components.
▸ re'ductionist *n, adj* ▸ re,duction'istic *adj*

redundancy (rɪ'dʌndənsɪ) *n, pl* **redundancies. 1a** the state or condition of being redundant or superfluous, esp. superfluous in one's job. **1b** (*as modifier*): *a redundancy payment.* **2** excessive proliferation or profusion, esp. of superfluity.

redundant (rɪ'dʌndənt) *adj* **1** surplus to requirements; unnecessary or superfluous. **2** verbose or tautological. **3** deprived of one's job because it is no longer necessary. [C17: from L *redundans* overflowing, from *redundāre* to stream over; see REDOUND]
▸ re'dundantly *adv*

red underwing *n* a large noctuid moth having hind wings coloured red and black.

reduplicate *vb* (rɪ'djuːplɪ,keɪt), **reduplicates, reduplicating, reduplicated. 1** to make or become double; repeat. **2** to repeat (a sound or syllable) in a word or (of a sound or syllable) to be repeated. ◆ *adj* (rɪ'djuːplɪkɪt). **3** doubled or repeated. **4** (of petals or sepals) having the margins curving outwards.
▸ re,dupli'cation *n* ▸ re'duplicative *adj*

red-water *n* a disease of cattle which destroys the red blood cells, characterized by the passage of red or blackish urine.

redwing ('red,wɪŋ) *n* a small European thrush having a speckled breast, reddish flanks, and brown back.

redwood ('red,wʊd) *n* a giant coniferous tree of coastal regions of California, having reddish fibrous bark and durable timber.

reebok ('riːbɒk, -bʊk) *n, pl* **reeboks** or **reebok.** a variant spelling of **rhebuck** or **rhebok.**

re-echo (riː'ɛkəʊ) *vb* **re-echoes, re-echoing, re-echoed. 1** to echo (a sound that is already an echo); resound. **2** (*tr*) to repeat like an echo.

reed (riːd) *n* **1** any of various widely distributed tall grasses that grow in swamps and shallow water and have jointed hollow stalks. **2** the stalk, or stalks collectively, of any of these plants, esp. as used for thatching. **3** *Music.* **3a** a thin piece of cane or metal inserted into the tubes of certain wind instruments, which sets in vibration the air column inside the tube. **3b** a wind instrument or organ pipe that sounds by means of a reed. **4** one of the several vertical parallel wires on a loom that may be moved upwards to separate the warp threads. **5** a small semicircular architectural moulding. **6** an archaic word for **arrow. 7 broken reed.** a weak, unreliable, or ineffectual person. ◆ *vb* (*tr*) **8** to fashion into or supply with reeds or reeding. **9** to thatch using reeds. [OE *hrēod*]

Reed ★ (riːd) *n* **1** Sir **Carol.** 1906–76, British film director. His films include *The Third Man* (1949) and *Oliver!* (1968). **2** Lou. born 1942, US rock singer, songwriter, and guitarist: member of the Velvet Underground (1965–70). His albums include *Transformer* (1972) and *Magic and Loss* (1992). **3** Walter. 1851–1902, US physician, who proved that yellow fever is transmitted by mosquitoes (1900).

reedbuck ('riːd,bʌk) *n, pl* **reedbucks** or **reedbuck.** an antelope of Africa south of the Sahara, having a buff-coloured coat and inward-curving horns.

reed bunting *n* a common European bunting that has a brown streaked plumage with, in the male, a black head.

reed grass *n* a tall perennial grass of rivers and ponds of Europe, Asia, and Canada.

reeding ('riːdɪŋ) *n* **1** a set of small semicircular architectural mouldings. **2** the milling on the edges of a coin.

reedling ('riːdlɪŋ) *n* a titlike Eurasian songbird, common in reed beds, which belongs to the family of Old World flycatchers and has a tawny back and tail and, in the male, a grey-and-black head. Also called: **bearded tit.**

reed mace *n* a tall reedlike marsh plant, with straplike leaves and flowers in long brown spikes. Also called: (popularly) **bulrush, cat's-tail.**

reed organ *n* **1** a wind instrument, such as the harmonium, accordion, or harmonica, in which the sound is produced by reeds, each reed producing one note only. **2** a type of pipe organ in which all the pipes are fitted with reeds.

reed pipe *n* an organ pipe sounded by a vibrating reed.

eed stop *n* an organ stop controlling a rank of reed pipes.

eed warbler *n* any of various common Old World warblers that inhabit marshy regions and have a brown plumage.

eedy ('riːdɪ) *adj* **reedier, reediest. 1** (of a place) abounding in reeds. **2** of or like a reed. **3** having a tone like a reed instrument; shrill or piping.
► **'reedily** *adv* ► **'reediness** *n*

eef[1] (riːf) *n* **1** a ridge of rock, sand, coral, etc., the top of which lies close to the surface of the sea. **2** a vein of ore, esp. one of gold-bearing quartz. **3** (*cap.*) **the. 3a** the Great Barrier Reef in Australia. **3b** the Witwatersrand in South Africa, a gold-bearing ridge. [C16: from MDu. *ref*, from ON *rif* RIB[1], REEF[2]]

eef[2] (riːf) *Naut.* ◆ *n* **1** the part gathered in when sail area is reduced, as in a high wind. ◆ *vb* **2** to reduce the area of (sail) by taking in a reef. **3** (*tr*) to shorten or bring inboard (a spar). [C14: from MDu. *rif*; rel. to ON *rif* reef, RIB[1]]

Reef ★ (riːf) *n* **the. 1** another name for **Great Barrier Reef. 2** another name for **Witwatersrand.**

eefer ('riːfə) *n* **1** *Naut.* a person who reefs, such as a midshipman. **2** another name for **reefing jacket. 3** *Sl.* a hand-rolled cigarette containing cannabis. [C19: from REEF[2]; applied to the cigarette from its resemblance to the rolled reef of a sail]

eefing jacket *n* a man's short double-breasted jacket of sturdy wool.

eef knot *n* a knot consisting of two overhand knots turned opposite ways. Also called: **square knot.**

eef point *n* *Naut.* one of several short lengths of line stitched through a sail for tying a reef.

eek (riːk) *vb* **1** (*intr*) to give off or emit a strong unpleasant odour; smell or stink. **2** (*intr*; often foll. by *of*) to be permeated (by): *the letter reeks of subservience.* **3** (*tr*) to treat with smoke; fumigate. **4** (*tr*) *Chiefly dialect.* to give off or emit (smoke, fumes, etc.). ◆ *n* **5** a strong offensive smell; stink. **6** *Chiefly dialect.* smoke or steam; vapour. [OE *rēocan*]
► **'reeky** *adj*

reel[1] (riːl, rɪəl) *n* **1** any of various cylindrical objects or frames that turn on an axis and onto which film, tape, wire, etc., may be wound. US equivalent: **spool. 2** *Angling.* a device for winding, casting, etc., consisting of a revolving spool with a handle, attached to a fishing rod. ◆ *vb* (*tr*) **3** to wind (cotton, thread, etc.) onto a reel. **4** (foll. by *in, out,* etc.) to wind or draw with a reel: *to reel in a fish.* [OE *hrēol*]
► **'reelable** *adj* ► **'reeler** *n*

reel[2] (riːl, rɪəl) *vb* (*mainly intr*) **1** to sway, esp. under the shock of a blow or through dizziness or drunkenness. **2** to whirl about or have the feeling of whirling about: *his brain reeled.* ◆ *n* **3** a staggering or swaying motion or sensation. [C14 *relen*, prob. from REEL[1]]

reel[3] (riːl, rɪəl) *n* **1** any of various lively Scottish dances for a fixed number of couples who combine in square and circular formations. **2** a piece of music composed for or in the rhythm of this dance. [C18: from REEL[2]]

reel-fed *adj* *Printing.* involving or printing on a web of paper: *a reel-fed press.*

reelman ('riːlmən, 'rɪəl-) *n, pl* **reelmen.** *Austral. & NZ.* (formerly) the member of a beach life-saving team who controlled the reel on which the line was wound.

reel off *vb* (*tr, adv*) to recite or write fluently and without apparent effort.

reel-to-reel *adj* **1** (of magnetic tape) wound from one reel to another in use. **2** (of a tape recorder) using magnetic tape wound from one reel to another, as opposed to cassettes.

re-entrant (riː'entrənt) *adj* **1** (of an angle) pointing inwards. ◆ *n* **2** an angle or part that points inwards.

re-entry (riː'entrɪ) *n, pl* **re-entries. 1** the act of retaking possession of land, etc. **2** the return of a spacecraft into the earth's atmosphere.

re-entry vehicle *n* the portion of a ballistic missile that

carries a nuclear warhead and re-enters the earth's atmosphere.

reeve[1] (riːv) *n* **1** *English history.* the local representative of the king in a shire until the early 11th century. **2** (in medieval England) a manorial steward who supervised the daily affairs of the manor. **3** *Canad. government.* (in some provinces) a president of a local council, esp. in a rural area. **4** (formerly) a minor local official in England and the US. [OE *gerēva*]

reeve[2] (riːv) *vb* **reeves, reeving, reeved** or **rove.** (*tr*) *Naut.* **1** to pass (a rope or cable) through an eye or other narrow opening. **2** to fasten by passing through or around something. [C17: ?from Du. *rēven* REEF[2]]

reeve[3] (riːv) *n* the female of the ruff (the bird). [C17: from ?]

re-export *vb* (ˌriːˈɪkˈspɔːt, ˌriːˈɛkspɔːt). **1** to export (imported goods, esp. after processing). ◆ *n* (riːˈɛkspɔːt). **2** the act of re-exporting. **3** a re-exported commodity.
► **ˌre-expor'tation** *n* ► **ˌre-ex'porter** *n*

ref (ref) *n* *Inf.* short for **referee.**

ref. *abbrev. for:* **1** referee. **2** reference. **3** reformed.

refection (rɪˈfɛkʃən) *n* refreshment with food and drink. [C14: from L *refectiō* a restoring, from *reficere*, from RE- + *facere* to make]

refectory (rɪˈfɛktərɪ, -trɪ) *n, pl* **refectories.** a dining hall in a religious or academic institution. [C15: from LL *refectōrium,* from L *refectus* refreshed]

refectory table *n* a long narrow dining table.

refer (rɪˈfɜː) *vb* **refers, referring, referred.** (often foll. by *to*). **1** (*intr*) to make mention (of). **2** (*tr*) to direct the attention of (someone) for information, facts, etc.: *the reader is referred to Chomsky, 1965.* **3** (*intr*) to seek information (from): *he referred to his notes.* **4** (*intr*) to be relevant (to); pertain or relate (to). **5** (*tr*) to assign or attribute: *Cromwell referred his victories to God.* **6** (*tr*) to hand over for consideration, reconsideration, or decision: *to refer a complaint to another department.* **7** (*tr*) to hand back to the originator as unacceptable or unusable. **8** (*tr*) *Brit.* to fail (a student) in an examination. **9 refer to drawer.** a request by a bank that the payee consult the drawer concerning a cheque payable by that bank. **10** (*tr*) to direct (a patient, client, etc.) to another doctor, agency, etc. [C14: from L *referre,* from RE- + *ferre* to BEAR[1]]
► **referable** ('refərəb'l) *or* **referrable** (rɪˈfɜːrəb'l) *adj* ► **re'ferral** *n* ► **re'ferrer** *n*

USAGE NOTE The common practice of adding *back* to *refer* is tautologous, since this meaning is already contained in the *re-* of *refer*: *this refers to* (not *back to*) *what has already been said.* However, when *refer* is used in the sense of passing a document or question for further consideration to the person from whom it was received, it may be appropriate to say *he referred the matter back.*

---

referee (ˌrefəˈriː) *n* **1** a person to whom reference is made, esp. for an opinion, information, or a decision. **2** the umpire or judge in any of various sports, esp. football and boxing. **3** a person who is willing to testify to the character or capabilities of someone. **4** *Law.* a person appointed by a court to report on a matter. ◆ *vb* **referees, refereeing, refereed. 5** to act as a referee (in); preside (over).

reference ('refərəns, 'refrəns) *n* **1** the act or an instance of referring. **2** something referred, esp. proceedings submitted to a referee in law. **3** a direction of the attention to a passage elsewhere or to another book, etc. **4** a book or passage referred to. **5** a mention or allusion: *this book contains several references to the Civil War.* **6** the relation between a word or phrase and the object or idea to which it refers. **7a** a source of information or facts. **7b** (*as modifier*): *a reference book; a reference library.* **8** a written testimonial regarding one's character or capabilities. **9** a person referred to for such a testimonial. **10a** (foll. by *to*) relation or delimitation, esp. to or by membership of a specific group: *without reference to sex or age.* **10b** (*as modifier*): *a reference group.* **11 terms of reference.** the specific limits of responsibility that determine the activities of an

investigating body, etc. ◆ *vb* **references, referencing, referenced.** (*tr*) **12** to furnish or compile a list of references for (a publication, etc.). **13** to make a reference to; refer to. ◆ *prep* **14** *Business jargon.* with reference to: *reference your letter of the 9th inst.* Abbrev.: **re.**
▸ **referential** (ˌrefəˈrenʃəl) *adj*

referendum (ˌrefəˈrendəm) *n, pl* **referendums** *or* **referenda** (-də). **1** submission of an issue of public importance to the direct vote of the electorate. **2** a vote on such a measure. ◆ See also **plebiscite.** [C19: from L: something to be carried back, from *referre* to REFER]

referent (ˈrefərənt) *n* the object or idea to which a word or phrase refers. [C19: from L *referens* from *referre* to REFER]

referred pain *n* *Psychol.* pain felt at some place other than its actual place of origin.

refill *vb* (riːˈfɪl). **1** to fill (something) again. ◆ *n* (ˈriːfɪl). **2** a replacement for a consumable substance in a permanent container. **3** a second or subsequent filling.
▸ **reˈfillable** *adj*

refine (rɪˈfaɪn) *vb* **refines, refining, refined. 1** to make or become free from impurities or foreign matter; purify. **2** (*tr*) to separate (a mixture) into pure constituents, as in an oil refinery. **3** to make or become elegant or polished. **4** (*intr*; often foll. by *on* or *upon*) to enlarge or improve (upon) by making subtle or fine distinctions. **5** (*tr*) to make (language) more subtle or polished. [C16: from RE- + FINE[1]]
▸ **reˈfinable** *adj* ▸ **reˈfiner** *n*

refined (rɪˈfaɪnd) *adj* **1** not coarse or vulgar; genteel, elegant, or polite. **2** subtle; discriminating. **3** freed from impurities; purified.

refinement (rɪˈfaɪnmənt) *n* **1** the act of refining or the state of being refined. **2** a fine or delicate point or distinction; a subtlety. **3** fineness or precision of thought, expression, manners, etc. **4** an improvement to a piece of equipment, etc.

refinery (rɪˈfaɪnərɪ) *n, pl* **refineries.** a factory for the purification of some crude material, such as sugar, oil, etc.

refit *vb* (riːˈfɪt), **refits, refitting, refitted. 1** to make or be made ready for use again by repairing, re-equipping, or re-supplying. ◆ *n* (ˈriːˌfɪt). **2** a repair or re-equipping, as of a ship, for further use.
▸ **reˈfitment** *n*

refl. *abbrev. for:* **1** reflection. **2** reflective. **3** reflex(ive).

reflate (riːˈfleɪt) *vb* **reflates, reflating, reflated.** to inflate or be inflated again. [C20: back formation from REFLATION]

reflation (riːˈfleɪʃən) *n* **1** an increase in economic activity. **2** an increase in the supply of money and credit designed to cause such economic activity. ◆ Cf. **inflation** (sense 2). [C20: from RE- + *-flation*, as in INFLATION]

reflect (rɪˈflekt) *vb* **1** to undergo or cause to undergo a process in which light, other electromagnetic radiation, sound, particles, etc., are thrown back after impinging on a surface. **2** (of a mirror, etc.) to form an image of (something) by reflection. **3** (*tr*) to show or express: *his tactics reflect his desire for power.* **4** (*tr*) to bring as a consequence: *their success reflected great credit on them.* **5** (*intr*; foll. by *on* or *upon*) to cause to be regarded in a specified way: *her behaviour reflects well on her.* **6** (*intr*; often foll. by *on* or *upon*) to cast dishonour or honour, credit or discredit, etc. (on). **7** (*intr*; usually foll. by *on*) to think, meditate, or ponder. [C15: from L *reflectere*, from RE- + *flectere* to bend]
▸ **reˈflectingly** *adv*

reflectance (rɪˈflektəns) *or* **reflection factor** *n* a measure of the ability of a surface to reflect light or other electromagnetic radiation, equal to the ratio of the reflected flux to the incident flux.

reflecting telescope *n* a type of telescope in which the initial image is formed by a concave mirror. Also called: **reflector.** Cf. **refracting telescope.**

reflection *or* **reflexion** (rɪˈflekʃən) *n* **1** the act of reflecting or the state of being reflected. **2** something reflected or the image so produced, as by a mirror. **3** careful or long consideration or thought. **4** attribution of discredit or blame. **5** *Maths.* a transformation in which the direction of one axis is reversed or changes the polar-

ity of one of the variables. **6** *Anat.* the bending back of a structure or part upon itself.
▸ **reˈflectional** *or* **reˈflexional** *adj*

reflection density *n* *Physics.* a measure of the extent to which a surface reflects light or other electromagnetic radiation. Symbol: *D*

reflective (rɪˈflektɪv) *adj* **1** characterized by quiet thought or contemplation. **2** capable of reflecting: *a reflective surface.* **3** produced by reflection.
▸ **reˈflectively** *adv*

reflectivity (ˌriːflekˈtɪvɪtɪ) *n* **1** *Physics.* a measure of the ability of a surface to reflect radiation, equal to the reflectance of a layer of material sufficiently thick for the reflectance not to depend on the thickness. **2** Also: **reflectiveness.** the quality or capability of being reflective.

reflector (rɪˈflektə) *n* **1** a person or thing that reflects. **2** a surface or object that reflects light, sound, heat, etc. **3** another name for **reflecting telescope.**

reflet (rəˈfleɪ) *n* an iridescent glow or lustre, as on ceramic ware. [C19: from F: a reflection, from It. *riflesso*, from L *reflexus*, from *reflectere* to reflect]

reflex *n* (ˈriːfleks). **1a** an immediate involuntary response, such as coughing, evoked by a given stimulus. **1b** (*as modifier*): *a reflex action.* See also **reflex arc. 2a** a mechanical response to a particular situation, involving no conscious decision. **2b** (*as modifier*): *a reflex response.* **3** a reflection; an image produced by or as if by reflection. ◆ *adj* (ˈriːfleks). **4** *Maths.* (of an angle) between 180° and 360°. **5** (*prenominal*) turned, reflected, or bent backwards. ◆ *vb* (rɪˈfleks). **6** (*tr*) to bend, turn, or reflect backwards. [C16: from L *reflexus* bent back, from *reflectere* to reflect]
▸ **reˈflexible** *adj* ▸ **reˌflexiˈbility** *n*

reflex arc *n* *Physiol.* the neural pathway over which impulses travel to produce a reflex action.

reflex camera *n* a camera in which the image is composed and focused on a ground-glass viewfinder screen.

reflexion (rɪˈflekʃən) *n Brit.* a less common spelling of **reflection.**
▸ **reˈflexional** *adj*

reflexive (rɪˈfleksɪv) *adj* **1** denoting a class of pronouns that refer back to the subject of a sentence or clause. Thus, in *that man thinks a great deal of himself,* the pronoun *himself* is reflexive. **2** denoting a verb used transitively with the reflexive pronoun as its direct object, as in *to dress oneself.* **3** *Physiol.* of or relating to a reflex. ◆ *n* **4** a reflexive pronoun or verb.
▸ **reˈflexively** *adv* ▸ **reˈflexiveness** *or* **reflexivity** (ˌriːflekˈsɪvɪtɪ) *n*

reflexology (ˌriːflekˈsɒlədʒɪ) *n* a form of therapy in alternative medicine in which the soles of the feet are massaged: designed to stimulate the blood supply and nerves and thus relieve tension.
▸ ˌ**reflexˈologist** *n*

reflux (ˈriːflʌks) *vb* **1** *Chem.* to boil or be boiled in a vessel attached to a condenser, so that the vapour condenses and flows back into the vessel. ◆ *n* **2** *Chem.* **2a** an act of refluxing. **2b** (*as modifier*): *a reflux condenser.* **3** the act or an instance of flowing back; ebb. [C15: from Med. L *refluxus,* from L *refluere* to flow back]

reflux oesophagitis (iːˌsɒfəˈdʒaɪtɪs) *n* inflammation of the gullet caused by regurgitation of stomach acids, producing heartburn: may be associated with a hiatus hernia.

reform (rɪˈfɔːm) *vb* **1** (*tr*) to improve (an existing institution, law, etc.) by alteration or correction of abuses. **2** to give up or cause to give up a reprehensible habit or immoral way of life. ◆ *n* **3** an improvement or change for the better, esp. as a result of correction of legal or political abuses or malpractices. **4** a principle, campaign, or measure aimed at achieving such change. **5** improvement of morals or behaviour. [C14: via OF from L *reformāre* to form again]
▸ **reˈformable** *adj* ▸ **reˈformative** *adj* ▸ **reˈformer** *n*

re-form (riːˈfɔːm) *vb* to form anew.
▸ ˌ**re-forˈmation** *n*

reformation (ˌrefəˈmeɪʃən) *n* **1** the act or an instance of reforming or the state of being reformed. **2** (*usually cap.*) a religious and political movement of 16th-century

★ **people and places**

Europe that began as an attempt to reform the Roman Catholic Church and resulted in the establishment of the Protestant Churches.
▸ ˌrefor'mational adj

eformatory (rɪ'fɔːmətərɪ, -trɪ) n, pl **reformatories. 1** Also called: **reform school.** (formerly) a place of instruction where young offenders were sent for corrective training. ◆ adj **2** having the purpose or function of reforming.

eformed (rɪ'fɔːmd) adj **1** of or designating a Protestant Church, esp. the Calvinist. **2** of or designating Reform Judaism.

eformism (rɪ'fɔːmɪzəm) n a doctrine advocating reform, esp. political or religious reform rather than abolition.
▸ re'formist n, adj

eform Judaism n a movement in Judaism that does not require strict observance of the law, but adapts to the contemporary world.

efract (rɪ'frækt) vb **1** to cause to undergo refraction. **2** (tr) to measure the amount of refraction of (the eye, a lens, etc.). [C17: from L refractus broken up, from refringere, from RE- + frangere to break]
▸ re'fractable adj ▸ re'fractive adj

efracting telescope n a type of telescope in which the image is formed by a set of lenses. Also called: **refractor.** Cf. **reflecting telescope.**

efraction (rɪ'frækʃən) n **1** Physics. the change in direction of a propagating wave, such as light or sound, in passing from one medium to another in which it has a different velocity. **2** the amount by which a wave is refracted. **3** the ability of the eye to refract light.
▸ re'fractional adj

efractive index n Physics. a measure of the extent to which a medium refracts light; the ratio of the speed of light in free space to that in the medium.

efractometer (ˌriːfræk'tɒmɪtə) n any instrument for measuring the refractive index.
▸ refractometric (rɪˌfræktə'metrɪk) adj ▸ ˌrefrac'tometry n

efractor (rɪ'fræktə) n **1** an object or material that refracts. **2** another name for **refracting telescope.**

efractory (rɪ'fræktərɪ) adj **1** unmanageable or obstinate. **2** Med. not responding to treatment. **3** Physiol. (of a nerve or muscle) incapable of responding to stimulation. **4** (of a material) able to withstand high temperatures without fusion or decomposition. ◆ n, pl **refractories. 5** a material, such as fire clay, that is able to withstand high temperatures.
▸ re'fractorily adv ▸ re'fractoriness n

efrain[1] (rɪ'freɪn) vb (intr; usually foll. by from) to abstain (from action); forbear. [C14: from L refrēnāre to check with a bridle, from RE- + frēnum a bridle]
▸ re'frainer n ▸ re'frainment n

efrain[2] (rɪ'freɪn) n **1** a regularly recurring melody, such as the chorus of a song. **2** a much repeated saying or idea. [C14: via OF, ult. from L refringere to break into pieces]

efrangible (rɪ'frændʒɪbʰl) adj capable of being refracted. [C17: from L refringere to break up, from RE- + frangere to break]
▸ reˌfrangi'bility or re'frangibleness n

efresh (rɪ'freʃ) vb **1** (usually tr or reflexive) to make or become fresh or vigorous, as through rest, drink, or food; revive or reinvigorate. **2** (tr) to enliven (something worn or faded), as by adding new decorations. **3** to pour cold water over previously blanched and drained food. **4** (tr) to stimulate (the memory, etc.). **5** (tr) to replenish, as with new equipment or stores. [C14: from OF refreschir; see RE-, FRESH]
▸ re'fresher n ▸ re'freshing adj

efresher course n a short educational course for people to review their subject and developments in it.

efreshment (rɪ'freʃmənt) n **1** the act of refreshing or the state of being refreshed. **2** (pl) snacks and drinks served as a light meal.

efrigerant (rɪ'frɪdʒərənt) n **1** a fluid capable of changes of phase at low temperatures: used as the working fluid of a refrigerator. **2** a cooling substance, such as ice or

solid carbon dioxide. **3** Med. an agent that provides a sensation of coolness or reduces fever. ◆ adj **4** causing cooling or freezing.

refrigerate (rɪ'frɪdʒə,reɪt) vb **refrigerates, refrigerating, refrigerated.** to make or become frozen or cold, esp. for preservative purposes; chill or freeze. [C16: from L refrīgerāre to make cold, from RE- + frīgus cold]
▸ reˌfriger'ation n ▸ re'frigerative adj ▸ re'frigeratory adj, n

refrigerator (rɪ'frɪdʒə,reɪtə) n a chamber in which food, drink, etc., are kept cool. Informal name: **fridge.**

refringent (rɪ'frɪndʒənt) adj Physics. of, concerned with, or causing refraction; refractive. [C18: from L refringere; see REFRACT]
▸ re'fringency or re'fringence n

reft (reft) vb a past tense and past participle of **reave.**

refuel (riː'fjuːəl) vb **refuels, refuelling, refuelled** or US **refuels, refueling, refueled.** to supply or be supplied with fresh fuel.

refuge ('refjuːdʒ) n **1** shelter or protection, as from the weather or danger. **2** any place, person, action, or thing that offers protection, help, or relief. [C14: via OF from L refugium, from refugere, from RE- + fugere to escape]

refugee (ˌrefjuː'dʒiː) n **a** a person who has fled from some danger or problem, esp. political persecution. **b** (as modifier): a refugee camp.
▸ ˌrefu'geeism n

refugee capital n Finance. money from abroad invested, esp. for a short term, in the country offering the highest interest rate.

refugium (rɪ'fjuːdʒɪəm) n, pl **refugia** (-dʒɪə). a geographical region that has remained unaltered by a climatic change affecting surrounding regions and that therefore forms a haven for relict fauna and flora. [C20: L: REFUGE]

refulgent (rɪ'fʌldʒənt) adj Literary. shining, brilliant, or radiant. [C16: from L refulgēre, from RE- + fulgēre to shine]
▸ re'fulgence or re'fulgency n ▸ re'fulgently adv

refund vb (rɪ'fʌnd). (tr) **1** to give back (money, etc.), as when an article purchased is unsatisfactory. **2** to reimburse (a person). ◆ n ('riː,fʌnd). **3** return of money to a purchaser or the amount so returned. [C14: from L refundere, from RE- + fundere to pour]
▸ re'fundable adj ▸ re'funder n

re-fund (riː'fʌnd) vb (tr) Finance. to discharge (an old or matured debt) by new borrowing, as by a new bond issue. [C20: from RE- + FUND]

refurbish (riː'fɜːbɪʃ) vb (tr) to renovate, re-equip, or restore.
▸ re'furbishment n

refusal (rɪ'fjuːzʰl) n **1** the act or an instance of refusing. **2** the opportunity to reject or accept; option.

refuse[1] (rɪ'fjuːz) vb **refuses, refusing, refused. 1** (tr) to decline to accept (something offered): to refuse promotion. **2** to decline to give or grant (something) to (a person, etc.). **3** (when tr, takes an infinitive) to express determination not (to do something); decline: he refuses to talk about it. **4** (of a horse) to be unwilling to take (a jump). [C14: from OF refuser, from L refundere to pour back]
▸ re'fusable adj ▸ re'fuser n

refuse[2] ('refjuːs) n a anything thrown away; waste; rubbish. **b** (as modifier): a refuse collection. [C15: from OF refuser to REFUSE[1]]

refusenik or **refusnik** (rɪ'fjuːznɪk) n **1** (formerly) a Jew in the Soviet Union who had been refused permission to emigrate. **2** a person who refuses to cooperate with a system or comply with a law because of a moral conviction. [C20: from REFUSE[1] + -NIK]

refute (rɪ'fjuːt) vb **refutes, refuting, refuted.** (tr) to prove (a statement, theory, charge, etc.) of (a person) to be false or incorrect; disprove. [C16: from L refūtāre to rebut]
▸ **refutable** ('refjutəbʰl, rɪ'fjuː-) adj ▸ 'refutably adv
▸ ˌrefu'tation n ▸ re'futer n

USAGE NOTE The use of refute to mean deny is thought by many people to be incorrect.

reg. *abbrev. for:* **1** regiment. **2** register(ed). **3** registrar. **4** regular(ly). **5** regulation.

regain (rɪˈɡeɪn) *vb* (*tr*) **1** to take or get back; recover. **2** to reach again.
▸ reˈgainer *n*

regal (ˈriːɡ°l) *adj* of, relating to, or befitting a king or queen; royal. [C14: from L *rēgālis*, from *rēx* king]
▸ reˈgality *n* ▸ ˈregally *adv*

regale (rɪˈɡeɪl) *vb* **regales, regaling, regaled.** (*tr; usually foll. by with*) **1** to give delight or amusement to: *he regaled them with stories.* **2** to provide with choice or abundant food or drink. ◆ *n* **3** *Arch.* **3a** a feast. **3b** a delicacy of food or drink. [C17: from F *régaler*, from *gale* pleasure]
▸ reˈgalement *n*

regalia (rɪˈɡeɪlɪə) *n* (*pl, sometimes functioning as sing*) **1** the ceremonial emblems or robes of royalty, high office, an order, etc. **2** any splendid or special clothes; finery. [C16: from Med. L: royal privileges, from L *rēgālis* REGAL]

regard (rɪˈɡɑːd) *vb* **1** to look closely or attentively at (something or someone); observe steadily. **2** (*tr*) to hold (a person or thing) in respect, admiration, or affection: *we regard your work very highly.* **3** (*tr*) to look upon or consider in a specified way: *she regarded her brother as her responsibility.* **4** (*tr*) to relate to; concern; have a bearing on. **5** to take notice of or pay attention to (something); heed: *he has never regarded the conventions.* **6 as regards.** (*prep*) in respect of; concerning. ◆ *n* **7** a gaze; look. **8** attention; heed: *he spends without regard to his bank balance.* **9** esteem, affection, or respect. **10** reference, relation, or connection (esp. in **with regard to** *or* **in regard to**). **11** (*pl*) good wishes or greetings (esp. in **with kind regards**, used at the close of a letter). **12 in this regard.** on this point. [C14: from OF *regarder* to look at, care about, from RE- + *garder* to GUARD]

regardant (rɪˈɡɑːd°nt) *adj* (*usually postpositive*) *Heraldry.* (of a beast) shown looking backwards over its shoulder. [C15: from OF; see REGARD]

regardful (rɪˈɡɑːdful) *adj* (*often foll. by of*) showing regard (for); heedful (of). **2** showing regard, respect, or consideration.
▸ reˈgardfully *adv*

regarding (rɪˈɡɑːdɪŋ) *prep* in respect of; on the subject of.

regardless (rɪˈɡɑːdlɪs) *adj* **1** (*usually foll. by of*) taking no regard or heed; heedless. ◆ *adv* **2** in spite of everything; disregarding drawbacks.
▸ reˈgardlessly *adv* ▸ reˈgardlessness *n*

regatta (rɪˈɡætə) *n* an organized series of races of yachts, rowing boats, etc. [C17: from obs. It. *rigatta* contest, from ?]

regd *abbrev. for* registered.

regelation (ˌriːdʒɪˈleɪʃən) *n* the rejoining together of two pieces of ice as a result of melting under pressure at the interface between them and subsequent refreezing.
▸ ˈregeˌlate *vb*

regency (ˈriːdʒənsɪ) *n, pl* **regencies.** **1** government by a regent. **2** the office of a regent. **3** a territory under the jurisdiction of a regent. [C15: from Med. L *regentia*, from L *regere* to rule]

Regency (ˈriːdʒənsɪ) *n* (*preceded by the*) **1** (in Britain) the period (1811–20) of the regency of the Prince of Wales (later George IV). **2** (in France) the period (1715-23) of the regency of Philip, Duke of Orleans. ◆ *adj* **3** characteristic of or relating to the Regency periods or to the styles of architecture, art, etc., produced in them.

regenerate *vb* (rɪˈdʒɛnəˌreɪt), **regenerates, regenerating, regenerated.** **1** to undergo or cause to undergo moral, spiritual, or physical renewal or invigoration. **2** to form or be formed again; come or bring into existence once again. **3** to replace (lost or damaged tissues or organs) by new growth, or to cause (such tissues) to be replaced. **4** (*tr*) *Electronics.* to use positive feedback to improve the demodulation and amplification of a signal. ◆ *adj* (rɪˈdʒɛnərɪt). **5** morally, spiritually, or physically renewed or reborn.
▸ reˈgeneracy *n* ▸ reˌgenerˈation *n* ▸ reˈgenerative *adj* ▸ reˈgeneratively *adv* ▸ reˈgenerˌator *n*

Regensburg ★ (*German* ˈreːɡənsbʊrk) *n* a city in SE Germany, in Bavaria on the River Danube: a free Impe-rial city from 1245 and the leading commercial city of S Germany in the 12th and 13th centuries; the Imperial Diet was held in the town hall from 1663 to 1806. Pop.: 125 608 (1995 est.). Former English name: **Ratisbon.**

regent (ˈriːdʒənt) *n* **1** the ruler or administrator of a country during the minority, absence, or incapacity of its monarch. **2** *US & Canad.* a member of the governing board of certain schools and colleges. ◆ *adj* **3** (*usually postpositive*) acting or functioning as a regent: *a queen regent.* [C14: from L *regēns*, from *regere* to rule]
▸ ˈregental *adj* ▸ ˈregentship *n*

regent-bird *n Austral.* a bowerbird, the male of which has showy yellow and velvety-black plumage. [after the PRINCE REGENT]

Regents Park ★ *n* a park in central London, laid out as Marylebone Park by John Nash; now known for the London Zoo, its open-air theatre, and Nash's curved terraces.

Reger ★ (*German* ˈreːɡər) *n* **Max** (maks). 1873–1916, German composer, esp. of organ works.

reggae (ˈrɛɡeɪ) *n* a type of West Indian popular music having four beats to the bar, the upbeat being strongly accented. [C20: of West Indian origin]

Reggio di Calabria ★ (*Italian* ˈreddʒo di kaˈlaːbrja) *n* a port in S Italy, in Calabria on the Strait of Messina: founded about 720 B.C. by Greek colonists. Pop.: 178 736 (1994 est.).

Reggio nell'Emilia ★ (*Italian* ˈreddʒo nɛlleˈmiːlja) *n* a city in N central Italy, in Emilia-Romagna: founded in the 2nd century B.C. by Marcus Aemilius Lepidus; ruled by the Este family in the 15th–18th centuries. Pop.: 134 169 (1994 est.).

regicide (ˈrɛdʒɪˌsaɪd) *n* **1** the killing of a king. **2** a person who kills a king. [C16: from L *rēx* king + -CIDE]
▸ ˌregiˈcidal *adj*

regime *or* **régime** (reɪˈʒiːm) *n* **1** a system of government or a particular administration: *a fascist regime.* **2** a social system or order. **3** another word for **regimen** (sense 1). [C18: from F, from L *regimen* guidance, from *regere* to rule]

regimen (ˈrɛdʒɪˌmɛn) *n* **1** Also called: **regime.** a systematic course of therapy, often including a recommended diet. **2** administration or rule. [C14: from L: guidance]

regiment *n* (ˈrɛdʒɪmənt). **1** a military formation varying in size from a battalion to a number of battalions. **2** a large number in regular or organized groups. ◆ *vb* (ˈrɛdʒɪˌmɛnt). (*tr*) **3** to force discipline or order on, esp. in a domineering manner. **4** to organize into a regiment. **5** to form into organized groups. [C14: via OF from LL *regimentum* government, from L *regere* to rule]
▸ ˌregiˈmental *adj* ▸ ˌregiˈmentally *adv* ▸ ˌregimenˈtation *n*

regimentals (ˌrɛdʒɪˈmɛnt°lz) *pl n* **1** the uniform and insignia of a regiment. **2** military dress.

Regin ★ (ˈreɪɡɪn) *n Norse myth.* a dwarf smith, tutor of Sigurd, whom he encouraged to kill Fafnir for the gold he guarded.

Regina[1] (rɪˈdʒaɪnə) *n* queen: now used chiefly in documents, inscriptions, etc. Cf. **Rex.** [L]

Regina[2] ★ (rɪˈdʒaɪnə) *n* a city in W Canada, capital and largest city of Saskatchewan: founded in 1882 as Pile O'Bones. Pop.: 179 178 (1991).

Regiomontanus ★ (ˌriːdʒɪəʊmɒnˈteɪnəs, -ˈtɑː-, -ˈtæn-) *n* original name *Johann Müller.* 1436–76, German mathematician and astronomer.

region (ˈriːdʒən) *n* **1** any large, indefinite, and continuous part of a surface or space. **2** an area considered as a unit for geographical, functional, social, or cultural reasons. **3** an administrative division of a country, or a Canadian province. **4** a realm or sphere of activity or interest. **5** range, area, or scope: *in what region is the price likely to be?* **6** a division or part of the body: *the lumbar region.* [C14: from L *regiō*, from *regere* to govern]

regional (ˈriːdʒən°l) *adj* of, characteristic of, or limited to a region.
▸ ˈregionally *adv*

egionalism ('riːdʒənəˌlɪzəm) n **1** division of a country into administrative regions having partial autonomy. **2** loyalty to one's home region; regional patriotism.
▸ **'regionalist** n, adj

égisseur French. (reʒiscœr) n an official in a dance company with varying duties, usually including directing productions. [F, from régir to manage]

egister ('rɛdʒɪstə) n **1** an official or formal list recording names, events, or transactions. **2** the book in which such a list is written. **3** an entry in such a list. **4** a recording device that accumulates data, totals sums of money, etc.: a cash register. **5** a movable plate that controls the flow of air into a furnace, chimney, room, etc. **6** Music. **6a** the timbre characteristic of a certain manner of voice production. **6b** any of the stops on an organ as classified in respect of its tonal quality: the flute register. **7** Printing. the exact correspondence of lines of type, etc., on the two sides of a printed sheet of paper. **8** a form of a language associated with a particular social situation or subject matter. **9** the act or an instance of registering. ◆ vb **10** (tr) to enter or cause someone to enter (an event, person's name, ownership, etc.) on a register. **11** to show or be shown on a scale or other measuring instrument: the current didn't register on the meter. **12** to show or be shown in a person's face, bearing, etc.: his face registered surprise. **13** (intr) Inf. to have an effect; make an impression: the news of her uncle's death just did not register. **14** to send (a letter, package, etc.) by registered post. **15** (tr) Printing. to adjust (a printing press, forme, etc.) to ensure that the printed matter is in register. [C14: from Med. L registrum, from L regerere to transcribe, from RE- + gerere to bear]
▸ **'registrable** adj

Registered General Nurse n (in Britain) a nurse who has completed a three-year training course and has been registered with the United Kingdom Central Council for Nursing, Midwifery, and Health Visiting. Abbrev.: **RGN**.

egistered post n **1** a Post Office service by which compensation is paid for loss or damage to mail for which a registration fee has been paid. **2** mail sent by this service.

Registered Trademark n See **trademark** (sense 1).

egister office n Brit. a government office where civil marriages are performed and births, marriages, and deaths are recorded. Often called: **registry office**.

egister ton n the full name for **ton**[1] (sense 6).

egistrar (ˌrɛdʒɪ'strɑː, 'rɛdʒɪˌstrɑː) n **1** a person who keeps official records. **2** an administrative official responsible for student records, enrolment procedure, etc., in a school, college, or university. **3** Brit. & NZ. a hospital doctor senior to a houseman but junior to a consultant. **4** Austral. the chief medical administrator of a large hospital. **5** Chiefly US. a person employed by a company to maintain a register of its security issues.
▸ **'regis,trarship** n

egistration (ˌrɛdʒɪ'streɪʃən) n **1a** the act of registering or state of being registered. **1b** (as modifier): a registration number. **2** an entry in a register. **3** a group of people, such as students, who register at a particular time. **4** Austral. **4a** a tax payable by the owner of a motor vehicle. **4b** the period paid for.

egistration document n Brit. a document giving identification details of a motor vehicle, including its manufacturer, date of registration, and owner's name.

egistration number n a sequence of letters and numbers assigned to a motor vehicle when it is registered, usually indicating the year and place of registration, displayed on numberplates at the front and rear of the vehicle.

egistration plate n Austral. & NZ. the numberplate of a vehicle.

egistry ('rɛdʒɪstrɪ) n, pl registries. **1** a place where registers are kept. **2** the registration of a ship's country of origin: a ship of Liberian registry. **3** another word for **registration**.

egistry office n Brit. another term for **register office**.

Regius professor ('riːdʒɪəs) n Brit. a person appointed by the Crown to a university chair founded by a royal patron. [C17: regius, from L: royal, from rex king]

reglet ('rɛglɪt) n **1** a flat narrow architectural moulding. **2** Printing. a strip of oiled wood used for spacing between lines. [C16: from OF, lit.: a little rule, from régle rule, from L rēgula]

regmaker ('rɛxˌmɑːkə) n S. African. a drink to relieve the symptoms of a hangover. [from Afrik., right maker]

regnal ('rɛgnəl) adj **1** of a sovereign or reign. **2** designating a year of a sovereign's reign calculated from the date of accession. [C17: from Med. L rēgnālis, from L rēgnum sovereignty; see REIGN]

regnant ('rɛgnənt) adj **1** (postpositive) reigning. **2** prevalent; current. [C17: from L regnāre to REIGN]
▸ **'regnancy** n

regorge (rɪ'gɔːdʒ) vb regorges, regorging, regorged. **1** (tr) to vomit up; disgorge. **2** (intr) (esp. of water) to flow or run back. [C17: from F regorger; see GORGE]

regress vb (rɪ'grɛs). **1** (intr) to return or revert, as to a former place, condition, or mode of behaviour. **2** (tr) Statistics. to measure the extent to which (a dependent variable) is associated with one or more independent variables. ◆ n ('riːgrɛs). **3** movement in a backward direction; retrogression. [C14: from L regressus, from regredī to go back, from RE- + gradī to go]
▸ **re'gressive** adj ▸ **re'gressor** n

regression (rɪ'grɛʃən) n **1** Psychol. the adoption by an adult of behaviour more appropriate to a child. **2** Statistics. **2a** the measure of the association between one variable (the dependent variable) and other variables (the independent variables). **2b** (as modifier): regression curve. **3** Geol. the retreat of the sea from the land. **4** the act of regressing.

regret (rɪ'grɛt) vb regrets, regretting, regretted. (tr) **1** (may take a clause as object or an infinitive) to feel sorry, repentant, or upset about. **2** to bemoan or grieve the death or loss of. ◆ n **3** a sense of repentance, guilt, or sorrow. **4** a sense of loss or grief. **5** (pl) a polite expression of sadness, esp. in a formal refusal of an invitation. [C14: from OF regreter, from ON]
▸ **re'gretful** adj ▸ **re'gretfully** adv ▸ **re'gretfulness** n ▸ **re'grettable** adj ▸ **re'grettably** adv

USAGE NOTE Regretful and regretfully are sometimes wrongly used where regrettable and regrettably are meant: he gave a regretful smile; he smiled regretfully; this is a regrettable (not a regretful) mistake; regrettably (not regretfully), I shall be unable to attend.

regroup (riː'gruːp) vb **1** to reorganize (military forces), esp. after an attack or a defeat. **2** (tr) to rearrange into a new grouping.

Regt abbrev. for: **1** Regent. **2** Regiment.

regulable ('rɛgjʊləbəl) adj able to be regulated.

regular ('rɛgjʊlə) adj **1** normal, customary, or usual. **2** according to a uniform principle, arrangement, or order. **3** occurring at fixed or regular intervals: a regular call on a customer. **4** following a set rule or normal practice; methodical or orderly. **5** symmetrical in appearance or form; even: regular features. **6** (prenominal) organized, elected, conducted, etc., in a proper or officially prescribed manner. **7** (prenominal) officially qualified or recognized: he's not a regular doctor. **8** (prenominal) (intensifier): a regular fool. **9** US & Canad. inf. likable, dependable, or nice: a regular guy. **10** denoting or relating to the personnel or units of the permanent military services: a regular soldier. **11** (of flowers) having any of their parts, esp. petals, alike in size, etc.; symmetrical. **12** Grammar. following the usual pattern of formation in a language. **13** Maths. **13a** (of a polygon) equilateral and equiangular. **13b** (of a polyhedron) having identical regular polygons as faces. **13c** (of a prism) having regular polygons as bases. **13d** (of a pyramid) having a regular polygon as a base and the altitude passing through the centre of the base. **14** Bot. (of a flower) having radial symmetry. **15** (postpositive) subject to the rule of an established religious order or community: canons regular. ◆ n **16** a professional long-term serviceman in a military

unit. **17** *Inf.* a person who does something regularly, such as attending a theatre. **18** a member of a religious order or congregation, as contrasted with a secular. [C14: from OF *reguler*, from L *rēgulāris* of a bar of wood or metal, from *rēgula* ruler, model]
▶ ˌregu'larity *n* ▶ 'regularˌize *or* 'regularˌise *vb* ▶ 'regularly *adv*

regulate ('regjuˌleɪt) *vb* **regulates, regulating, regulated.** (*tr*) **1** to adjust (the amount of heat, sound, etc.) as required; control. **2** to adjust (an instrument or appliance) so that it operates correctly. **3** to bring into conformity with a rule, principle, or usage. [C17: from LL *rēgulāre* to control, from L *rēgula* ruler]
▶ 'regulative *or* 'regulatory *adj* ▶ 'regulatively *adv*

regulation (ˌregju'leɪʃən) *n* **1** the act or process of regulating. **2** a rule, principle, or condition that governs procedure or behaviour. **3** (*modifier*) as required by official rules: *regulation uniform.* **4** (*modifier*) normal; usual; conforming to accepted standards: *a regulation haircut.*

regulator ('regjuˌleɪtə) *n* **1** a person or thing that regulates. **2** the mechanism by which the speed of a timepiece is regulated. **3** any of various mechanisms or devices, such as a governor valve, for controlling fluid flow, pressure, temperature, etc.

regulo ('regjuləʊ) *n* any of a number of temperatures to which a gas oven may be set: *cook at regulo 4.* [C20: from *Regulo*, trademark for a type of thermostatic control on gas ovens]

regulus ('regjuləs) *n, pl* **reguluses** *or* **reguli** (-ˌlaɪ). impure metal forming beneath the slag during the smelting of ores. [C16: from L: a petty king, from *rēx* king; formerly used for *antimony*, because it combines readily with gold, the king of metals]
▶ 'reguline *adj*

Regulus ★ ('regjuləs) *n* **Marcus Atilius** ('mɑːkəs ə'tɪliəs). died ?250 B.C., Roman general; consul (267; 256). Captured by the Carthaginians in the First Punic War, he was sent to Rome with the enemy's peace terms, which he advised the Senate to reject, and was tortured to death on his return to Carthage.

regurgitate (rɪ'gɜːdʒɪˌteɪt) *vb* **regurgitates, regurgitating, regurgitated. 1** to vomit forth (partially digested food). **2** (of some birds and animals) to bring back to the mouth (undigested or partly digested food to feed the young). **3** (*intr*) to be cast up or out, esp. from the mouth. **4** (*intr*) *Med.* (of blood) to flow in a direction opposite to the normal one, esp. through a defective heart valve. [C17: from Med. L *regurgitāre*, from RE- + *gurgitāre* to flood, from L *gurges* whirlpool]
▶ re'gurgitant *n, adj* ▶ reˌgurgi'tation *n*

rehabilitate (ˌriːə'bɪlɪˌteɪt) *vb* **rehabilitates, rehabilitating, rehabilitated.** (*tr*) **1** to help (a physically or mentally disabled person or an ex-prisoner) to readapt to society or a new job, as by vocational guidance, retraining, or therapy. **2** to restore to a former position or rank. **3** to restore the good reputation of. [C16: from Med. L *rehabilitāre* to restore, from RE- + L *habilitās* skill]
▶ ˌrehaˌbili'tation *n* ▶ ˌreha'bilitative *adj*

Rehabilitation Department *n NZ.* a government department set up after World War II to assist exservicemen. Often shortened to **rehab.**

rehash *vb* (riː'hæʃ). **1** (*tr*) to rework, reuse, or make over (old or already used material). ◆ *n* ('riːˌhæʃ). **2** something consisting of old, reworked, or reused material. [C19: from RE- + HASH¹ (to chop into pieces)]

rehearsal (rɪ'hɜːsᵊl) *n* **1** a session of practising a play, concert, etc., in preparation for public performance. **2 in rehearsal.** being prepared for public performance.

rehearse (rɪ'hɜːs) *vb* **rehearses, rehearsing, rehearsed. 1** to practise (a play, concert, etc.), in preparation for public performance. **2** (*tr*) to run through; recount; recite: *he rehearsed the grievances of the committee.* **3** (*tr*) to train or drill (a person) for public performance. [C16: from Anglo-Norman *rehearser*, from OF *rehercier* to harrow a second time, from RE- + *herce* harrow]
▶ re'hearser *n*

reheat *vb* (riː'hiːt). **1** to heat or be heated again: *to reheat yesterday's soup.* **2** (*tr*) to add fuel to (the exhaust gases of

an aircraft jet engine) to produce additional heat and thrust. ◆ *n* ('riːˌhiːt), *also* **reheating. 3** a process in which additional fuel is ignited in the exhaust gases of a jet engine to produce additional thrust.
▶ re'heater *n*

rehoboam (ˌriːə'bəʊəm) *n* a wine bottle holding the equivalent of six normal bottles. [after *Rehoboam*, a son of King Solomon, from Heb., lit.: the nation is enlarged]

Reich (raɪk) *n* **1** the Holy Roman Empire (962–1806) (**First Reich**). **2** the Hohenzollern empire in Germany from 1871 to 1918 (**Second Reich**). **3** the Nazi dictatorship (1933–45) in Germany (**Third Reich**). [G: kingdom]

Reichenberg ★ ('raiçənˌbɜːk) *n* the German name for **Liberec.**

Reichsmark ('raɪksˌmɑːk) *n, pl* **Reichsmarks** *or* **Reichsmark.** the standard monetary unit of Germany between 1924 and 1948.

Reichstag ('raiks,tɑːg) *n* **1** the legislative assembly of Germany (1867–1933). **2** the building in Berlin in which this assembly met.

Reid ★ (riːd) *n* **1** Sir **George Houston.** 1845–1918, Australian statesman, born in Scotland: premier of New South Wales (1894–99); prime minister of Australia (1904–05). **2 Thomas.** 1710–96, Scottish philosopher: his books include *Enquiry into the Human Mind on the Principles of Common Sense* (1764).

reify ('riːɪˌfaɪ) *vb* **reifies, reifying, reified.** (*tr*) to consider or make (an abstract idea or concept) real or concrete. [C19: from L *rēs* thing]
▶ ˌreifi'cation *n* ▶ ˌreifi'catory *adj* ▶ 'reiˌfier *n*

Reigate ★ ('raɪgɪt, -geɪt) *n* a town in S England, in Surrey at the foot of the North Downs. Pop.: 47 602 (1991).

reign (reɪn) *n* **1** the period during which a monarch is the official ruler of a country. **2** a period during which a person or thing is dominant or powerful: *the reign of violence.* ◆ *vb* (*intr*) **3** to exercise the power and authority of a sovereign. **4** to be accorded the rank and title of a sovereign without having ruling authority. **5** to predominate; prevail: *darkness reigns.* **6** (*usually present participle*) to be the most recent winner of a contest, etc.: *the reigning champion.* [C13: from OF *reigne*, from L *rēgnum* kingdom, from *rēx* king]

> **USAGE NOTE** *Reign* is sometimes wrongly written for *rein* in certain phrases: *he gave full rein* (not *reign*) *to his feelings; it will be necessary to rein in* (not *reign in*) *public spending.*

reiki ('reɪkɪ) *n* a form of therapy in which the practitioner is believed to channel energy into the patient in order to encourage healing or restore well-being. [Japanese, from *rei* universal + *ki* life force]

reimburse (ˌriːɪm'bɜːs) *vb* **reimburses, reimbursing, reimbursed.** (*tr*) to repay or compensate (someone) for (money already spent, losses, damages, etc.). [C17: from RE- + *imburse*, from Med. L *imbursāre* to put in a moneybag, from *bursa* PURSE]
▶ ˌreim'bursable *adj* ▶ ˌreim'bursement *n* ▶ ˌreim'burser *n*

reimport *vb* (ˌriːɪm'pɔːt, riː'ɪmpɔːt). **1** (*tr*) to import (goods manufactured from exported raw materials). ◆ *n* (riː'ɪmpɔːt). **2** the act of reimporting. **3** a reimported commodity.
▶ ˌreimpor'tation *n*

Reims *or* **Rheims** ★ (riːmz; *French* rɛ̃s) *n* a city in NE France: scene of the coronation of most French monarchs. Pop.: 185 164 (1990).

rein (reɪn) *n* **1** (*often pl*) one of a pair of long straps, usually connected together and made of leather, used to control a horse. **2** a similar device used to control a very young child. **3** any form or means of control: *to take up the reins of government.* **4** the direction in which a rider turns (in **on a left rein**). **5** something that restrains, controls, or guides. **6 give (a) free rein.** to allow considerable freedom; remove restraints. **7 keep a tight rein on.** to control carefully; limit: *we have to keep a tight rein on expenditure.* ◆ *vb* **8** (*tr*) to check, restrain, hold back, or halt with or as if with reins. **9** to control or guide (a horse) with a rein or reins: *they* *reined left.* ◆ See also **rein in.** [C13: from OF *resne*, from L *retinēre* to hold back, from RE- + *tenēre* to hold]

reincarnate *vb* (ˌriːɪnˈkɑːˌneɪt), **reincarnates, reincarnating, reincarnated.** (*tr; often passive*) **1** to cause to undergo reincarnation; be born again. ◆ *adj* (ˌriːɪnˈkɑːnɪt). **2** born again in a new body.

reincarnation (ˌriːɪnkɑːˈneɪʃən) *n* **1** the belief that on the death of the body the soul transmigrates to or is born again in another body. **2** the incarnation or embodiment of a soul in a new body after it has left the old one at physical death. **3** embodiment again in a new form, as of a principle or idea.
▸ ˌreincarˈnationist *n, adj*

reindeer (ˈreɪnˌdɪə) *n, pl* **reindeer** *or* **reindeers.** a large deer, having large branched antlers in the male and female and inhabiting the arctic regions. It also occurs in North America, where it is known as a caribou. [C14: from ON *hreindȳri*, from *hreinn* reindeer + *dȳr* animal]

Reindeer Lake ★ *n* a lake in W Canada, in Saskatchewan and Manitoba: drains into the Churchill River via the **Reindeer River.** Area: 6390 sq. km (2467 sq. miles).

reindeer moss *n* any of various lichens which occur in arctic and subarctic regions, providing food for reindeer.

reinforce (ˌriːɪnˈfɔːs) *vb* **reinforces, reinforcing, reinforced.** (*tr*) **1** to give added strength or support to. **2** to give added emphasis to; stress or increase: *his rudeness reinforced my determination.* **3** to give added support to (a military force) by providing more men, supplies, etc. [C17: from F *renforcer*]
▸ ˌreinˈforcement *n*

reinforced concrete *n* concrete with steel bars, mesh, etc., embedded in it to enable it to withstand tensile and shear stresses.

reinforced plastic *n* plastic with fibrous matter, such as carbon fibre, embedded in it to strengthen it.

Reinhardt ★ (ˈraɪnˌhɑːt) *n* **1** Django (ˈdʒæŋɡəʊ), real name *Jean Baptiste Reinhardt.* 1910–53, Belgian jazz guitarist, whose work was greatly influenced by Gypsy music. With Stéphane Grappelli, he led the quintet of the Hot Club of France between 1934 and 1939. **2** Max, original name *Max Goldmann.* 1873–1943, Austrian theatre producer and director, in the US after 1933.

rein in *vb* (*adv*) to stop (a horse) by pulling on the reins.

reins (reɪnz) *pl n* Arch. the kidneys or loins. [C14: from OF, from L *rēnēs* the kidneys]

reinstate (ˌriːɪnˈsteɪt) *vb* **reinstates, reinstating, reinstated.** (*tr*) to restore to a former rank or condition.
▸ ˌreinˈstatement *n* ▸ ˌreinˈstator *n*

reinsurer (ˌriːɪnˈʃʊərə) *n* an insurance company which will accept business from other insurance companies, thus enabling the risks to be spread.
▸ ˌreinˈsurance *n*

reinvent (ˌriːɪnˈvɛnt) *vb* (*tr*) **1** to replace (a product, etc.) with an entirely new version. **2** to duplicate (something that already exists) in what is therefore a wasted effort (esp. in **reinvent the wheel**).

reissue (ˌriːˈɪjuː) *n* **1** a book, record, etc., that is published or released again after being unavailable for a time. ◆ *vb* **2** (*tr*) to publish or release (a book, record, etc.) again after a period of unavailability.

reiterate (riːˈɪtəˌreɪt) *vb* **reiterates, reiterating, reiterated.** (*tr; may take a clause as object*) to say or do again or repeatedly. [C16: from L *reiterāre*, from RE- + *iterāre* to do again, from *iterum* again]
▸ reˌiterˈation *n* ▸ reˈiterative *adj* ▸ reˈiteratively *adv*

Reith ★ (riːθ) *n* John (Charles Walsham), 1st Baron. 1889–1971, British public servant: first general manager (1922–27) and first director general (1927–38) of the BBC.
▸ ˈReithian *or* ˈReithean *adj*

reive (riːv) *vb* **reives, reiving, reived.** (*intr*) Scot. & N English dialect. to go on a plundering raid. [var. of REAVE]
▸ ˈreiver *n*

reject *vb* (rɪˈdʒɛkt). (*tr*) **1** to refuse to accept, use, believe,

etc. **2** to throw out as useless or worthless; discard. **3** to rebuff (a person). **4** (of an organism) to fail to accept (a foreign tissue graft or organ transplant). ◆ *n* (ˈriːdʒɛkt). **5** something rejected as imperfect, unsatisfactory, or useless. [C15: from L *rēicere* to throw back, from RE- + *jacere* to hurl]
▸ reˈjecter *or* reˈjector *n* ▸ reˈjection *n* ▸ reˈjective *adj*

rejig (riːˈdʒɪg) *vb* **rejigs, rejigging, rejigged.** (*tr*) **1** to re-equip (a factory or plant). **2** Inf. to rearrange, manipulate, etc., sometimes in an unscrupulous way. ◆ *n* **3** the act or process of rejigging.
▸ reˈjigger *n*

rejoice (rɪˈdʒɔɪs) *vb* **rejoices, rejoicing, rejoiced.** (when *tr, takes a clause as object or an infinitive;* when *intr,* often foll. by *in*) to feel or express great joy or happiness. [C14: from OF *resjoir,* from RE- + *joir* to be glad, from L *gaudēre* to rejoice]
▸ reˈjoicer *n*

rejoin[1] (riːˈdʒɔɪn) *vb* **1** to come again into company with (someone or something). **2** (*tr*) to put or join together again; reunite.

rejoin[2] (rɪˈdʒɔɪn) *vb* (*tr*) **1** to answer or reply. **2** Law. to answer (a plaintiff's reply). [C15: from OF *rejoign-,* stem of *rejoindre;* see RE-, JOIN]

rejoinder (rɪˈdʒɔɪndə) *n* **1** a reply or response to a question or remark. **2** Law. (in pleading) the answer made by a defendant to the plaintiff's reply. [C15: from OF *rejoindre* to REJOIN[2]]

rejuvenate (rɪˈdʒuːvɪˌneɪt) *vb* **rejuvenates, rejuvenating, rejuvenated.** (*tr*) **1** to give new youth, restored vitality, or youthful appearance to. **2** (*usually passive*) Geog. to cause (a river) to begin eroding more vigorously to a new lower base level. [C19: from RE- + L *juvenis* young]
▸ reˌjuveˈnation *n* ▸ reˈjuveˌnator *n*

rejuvenesce (rɪˌdʒuːvəˈnɛs) *vb* **rejuvenesces, rejuvenescing, rejuvenesced.** **1** to make or become youthful or restored to vitality. **2** Biol. to convert (cells) or (of cells) to be converted into a more active form.
▸ reˌjuveˈnescence *n* ▸ reˌjuveˈnescent *adj*

rel. *abbrev. for:* **1** relating. **2** relative(ly). **3** released. **4** religion. **5** religious.

relapse (rɪˈlæps) *vb* **relapses, relapsing, relapsed.** (*intr*) **1** to lapse back into a former state or condition, esp. one involving bad habits. **2** to become ill again after apparent recovery. ◆ *n* **3** the act or an instance of relapsing. **4** the return of ill health after an apparent or partial recovery. [C16: from L *relabī,* from RE- + *labī* to slip, slide]
▸ reˈlapser *n*

relapsing fever *n* any of various infectious diseases characterized by recurring fever, caused by the bite of body lice or ticks. Also called: **recurrent fever.**

relata (rɪˈleɪtə) *n* the plural of **relatum.**

relate (rɪˈleɪt) *vb* **relates, relating, related.** **1** (*tr*) to tell or narrate (a story, etc.) **2** (*often foll. by to*) to establish association (between two or more things) or (of something) to have relation or reference (to something else). **3** (*intr;* often foll. by *to*) to form a sympathetic or significant relationship (with other people, things, etc.). [C16: from L *relātus* brought back, from *referre,* from RE- + *ferre* to bear]
▸ reˈlatable *adj* ▸ reˈlater *n*

related (rɪˈleɪtɪd) *adj* **1** connected; associated. **2** connected by kinship or marriage. **3** (in diatonic music) denoting or relating to a key that has notes in common with another key or keys.
▸ reˈlatedness *n*

relation (rɪˈleɪʃən) *n* **1** the state or condition of being related or the manner in which things are related. **2** connection by blood or marriage; kinship. **3** a person who is connected by blood or marriage; relative. **4** reference or regard (esp. in **in** or **with relation to**). **5** the position, association, connection, or status of one person or thing with regard to another. **6** the act of relating or narrating. **7** an account or narrative. **8** Law. the statement of grounds of complaint made by a relator. **9** Logic, maths. **9a** an association between ordered pairs of objects, numbers, etc., such as ... is greater than .... **9b** the set of ordered pairs whose members have such an association. ◆ See also

relations. [C14: from L *relātiō* a narration, a relation (between philosophical concepts)]

relational (rɪ'leɪʃənºl) *adj* **1** *Grammar.* indicating or expressing syntactic relation, as for example the case endings in Latin. **2** having relation or being related. **3** *Computing.* based on data that is interconnected, often in tabular form.

relations (rɪ'leɪʃənz) *pl n* **1** social, political, or personal connections or dealings between or among individuals, groups, nations, etc. **2** family or relatives. **3** *Euphemistic.* sexual intercourse.

relationship (rɪ'leɪʃənʃɪp) *n* **1** the state of being connected or related. **2** association by blood or marriage; kinship. **3** the mutual dealings, connections, or feelings that exist between two countries, people, etc. **4** an emotional or sexual affair or liaison.

relative ('relətɪv) *adj* **1** having meaning or significance only in relation to something else; not absolute. **2** (*prenominal*) (of a scientific quantity) being measured or stated relative to some other substance or measurement: *relative density.* **3** (*prenominal*) comparative or respective: *the relative qualities of speed and accuracy.* **4** (*postpositive; foll. by to*) in proportion (to); corresponding (to): *earnings relative to production.* **5** having reference (to); pertinent (to). **6** *Grammar.* denoting or belonging to a class of words that function as subordinating conjunctions in introducing relative clauses such as *who, which,* and *that.* Cf. **demonstrative. 7** *Grammar.* denoting or relating to a clause (**relative clause**) that modifies a noun or pronoun occurring earlier in the sentence. **8** (of a musical key or scale) having the same key signature as another key or scale. ♦ *n* **9** a person who is related by blood or marriage; relation. **10** a relative pronoun, clause, or grammatical construction. [C16: from LL *relātīvus* referring] ► **'relatively** *adv* ► **'relativeness** *n*

relative aperture *n Photog.* the ratio of the equivalent focal length of a lens to the effective aperture of the lens.

relative atomic mass *n* the ratio of the average mass per atom of the naturally occurring form of an element to one-twelfth of the mass of an atom of carbon-12. Symbol: A_r Abbrev.: **r.a.m.** Former name: **atomic weight.**

relative density *n* the ratio of the density of a substance to the density of a standard substance under specified conditions. For liquids and solids the standard is usually water at 4°C. For gases the standard is air or hydrogen at the same temperature and pressure as the substance. See also **specific gravity, vapour density.**

relative frequency *n Statistics.* the ratio of the actual number of favourable events to the total possible number of events.

relative humidity *n* the mass of water vapour present in the air expressed as a percentage of the mass present in an equal volume of saturated air at the same temperature.

relative majority *n Brit.* the excess of votes or seats won by the winner of an election over the runner-up when no candidate or party has more than 50 per cent. Cf. **absolute majority.**

relative molecular mass *n* the sum of all the relative atomic masses of the atoms in a molecule; the ratio of the average mass per molecule of a specified isotopic composition of a substance to one-twelfth the mass of an atom of carbon-12. Symbol: M_r Abbrev.: **r.m.m.** Former name: **molecular weight.**

relative permeability *n* the ratio of the permeability of a medium to that of free space.

relative permittivity *n* the ratio of the permittivity of a substance to that of free space.

relativism ('relətɪˌvɪzəm) *n* any theory holding that truth or moral or aesthetic value, etc., is not universal or absolute but may differ between individuals or cultures. ► **'relativist** *n, adj* ► **ˌrelativ'istic** *adj*

relativity (ˌrelə'tɪvɪtɪ) *n* **1** either of two theories developed by Albert Einstein, the **special theory of relativity,** which requires that the laws of physics shall be the same as seen by any two different observers in uniform relative motion, and the **general theory of relativity,** which considers observers with relative acceleration and leads

to a theory of gravitation. **2** the state or quality of being relative.

relator (rɪ'leɪtə) *n* **1** a person who relates a story; narrator. **2** *English law.* a person who gives information upon which the attorney general brings an action.

relatum (rɪ'leɪtəm) *n, pl* **relata** (-tə). *Logic.* one of the objects between which a relation is said to hold.

relax (rɪ'læks) *vb* **1** to make (muscles, a grip, etc.) less tense or rigid or (of muscles, a grip, etc.) to become looser or less rigid. **2** (*intr*) to take rest, as from work or effort. **3** to lessen the force of (effort, concentration) or (of effort) to become diminished. **4** to make (rules or discipline) less rigid or strict or (of rules, etc.) to diminish in severity. **5** (*intr*) (of a person) to become less formal; unbend. [C15: from L *relaxāre* to loosen, from RE- + *laxāre,* from *laxus* loose] ► **re'laxed** *adj* ► **relaxedly** (rɪ'læksɪdlɪ) *adv* ► **re'laxer** *n*

relaxant (rɪ'læksºnt) *n* **1** *Med.* a drug or agent that relaxes, esp. one that relaxes tense muscles. ♦ *adj* **2** of or tending to produce relaxation.

relaxation (ˌriːlæk'seɪʃən) *n* **1** rest or refreshment, as after work or effort; recreation. **2** a form of rest or recreation: *his relaxation is cricket.* **3** a partial lessening of a punishment, duty, etc. **4** the act of relaxing or state of being relaxed. **5** *Physics.* the return of a system to equilibrium after a displacement from this state.

relaxin (rɪ'læksɪn) *n* **1** a mammalian polypeptide hormone secreted during pregnancy, which relaxes the pelvic ligaments. **2** a preparation of this hormone, used to facilitate childbirth. [C20: from RELAX + -IN]

relay *n* ('riːleɪ). **1** a person or team of people relieving others, as on a shift. **2** a fresh team of horses, etc., posted along a route to relieve others. **3** the act of relaying or process of being relayed. **4** short for **relay race. 5** an automatic device that controls a valve, switch, etc., by means of an electric motor, solenoid, or pneumatic mechanism. **6** *Electronics.* an electrical device in which a small change in current or voltage controls the switching on or off of circuits. **7** *Radio.* **7a** a combination of a receiver and transmitter designed to receive radio signals and retransmit them. **7b** (*as modifier*): *a relay station.* ♦ *vb* (rɪ'leɪ). (*tr*) **8** to carry or spread (news or information) by relays. **9** to supply or replace with relays. **10** to retransmit (a signal) by means of a relay. **11** *Brit.* to broadcast (a performance) by sending out signals through a transmitting station. [C15 *relaien,* from OF *relaier* to leave behind, from RE- + *laier* to leave, ult. from L *laxāre* to loosen]

relay race *n* a race between two or more teams of contestants in which each contestant covers a specified portion of the distance.

release (rɪ'liːs) *vb* **releases, releasing, released.** (*tr*) **1** to free (a person or animal) from captivity or imprisonment. **2** to free (someone) from obligation or duty. **3** to free (something) from one's grip); let fall. **4** to issue (a record, film, or book) for sale or circulation. **5** to make (news or information) known or allow (news, etc.) to be made known. **6** *Law.* to relinquish (a right, claim, or title) in favour of someone else. ♦ *n* **7** the act of freeing or state of being freed. **8** the act of issuing for sale or publication. **9** something issued for sale or public showing, esp. a film or a record: *a new release from Bob Dylan.* **10** a news item, etc., made available for publication, broadcasting, etc. **11** *Law.* the surrender of a claim, right, title, etc., in favour of someone else. **12** a control mechanism for starting or stopping an engine. **13** the control mechanism for the shutter in a camera. [C13: from OF *relesser,* from L *relaxāre* to slacken] ► **re'leaser** *n*

relegate ('relɪˌɡeɪt) *vb* **relegates, relegating, relegated.** (*tr*) **1** to move to a position of less authority, importance, etc.; demote. **2** (*usually passive*) *Chiefly Brit.* to demote (a football team, etc.) to a lower division. **3** to assign or refer (a matter) to another. **4** (foll. by *to*) to banish or exile. **5** to assign (something) to a particular group or category. [C16: from L *relēgāre,* from RE- + *lēgāre* to send] ► **'rele,gatable** *adj* ► **ˌrele'gation** *n*

relent (rɪ'lent) *vb* (*intr*) **1** to change one's mind about some decision, esp. a harsh one; become more mild or amenable. **2** (of the pace or intensity of something) to slacken. **3** (of the weather) to become more mild. [C14: from RE- + L *lentāre* to bend, from *lentus* flexible]

relentless (rɪˈlɛntlɪs) *adj* **1** (of an enemy, etc.) implacable; inflexible; inexorable. **2** (of pace or intensity) sustained; unremitting.
▸ re'lentlessly *adv* ▸ re'lentlessness *n*

relevant (ˈrɛlɪvənt) *adj* having direct bearing on the matter in hand; pertinent. [C16: from Med. L *relevans*, from L *relevāre*, from RE- + *levāre* to raise, RELIEVE]
▸ 'relevance *or* 'relevancy *n* ▸ 'relevantly *adv*

reliable (rɪˈlaɪəbᵊl) *adj* able to be trusted; dependable.
▸ re,lia'bility *or* re'liableness *n* ▸ re'liably *adv*

reliance (rɪˈlaɪəns) *n* **1** dependence, confidence, or trust. **2** something or someone upon which one relies.
▸ re'liant *adj* ▸ re'liantly *adv*

relic (ˈrɛlɪk) *n* **1** something that has survived from the past, such as an object or custom. **2** something treasured for its past associations; keepsake. **3** (*usually pl*) a remaining part or fragment. **4** *RC Church, Eastern Church.* part of the body of a saint or his belongings, venerated as holy. **5** *Inf.* an old or old-fashioned person or thing. **6** (*pl*) *Arch.* the remains of a dead person; corpse. [C13: from OF *relique*, from L *reliquiae* remains, from *relinquere* to leave behind]

relict (ˈrɛlɪkt) *n* **1** *Ecology.* **1a** a group of animals or plants that exists as a remnant of a formerly widely distributed group. **1b** (*as modifier*): *a relict fauna.* **2** *Geol.* a mountain, lake, glacier, etc., that is a remnant of a pre-existing formation after a destructive process has occurred. **3** an archaic word for **widow.** **4** an archaic word for **relic.** [C16: from L *relictus* left behind, from *relinquere* to RELINQUISH]

relief (rɪˈliːf) *n* **1** a feeling of cheerfulness or optimism that follows the removal of anxiety, pain, or distress. **2** deliverance from or alleviation of anxiety, pain, etc. **3a** help or assistance, as to the poor or needy. **3b** (*as modifier*): *relief work.* **4** a diversion from monotony. **5** a person who replaces another at some task or duty. **6** a bus, plane, etc., that carries additional passengers when a scheduled service is full. **7** a road (**relief road**) carrying traffic round an urban area; bypass. **8a** the act of freeing a beleaguered town, fortress, etc.: *the relief of Mafeking.* **8b** (*as modifier*): *a relief column.* **9** Also called: **relievo, rilievo.** *Sculpture, archit.* **9a** the projection of forms or figures from a flat ground, so that they are partly or wholly free of it. **9b** a piece of work of this kind. **10** a printing process that employs raised surfaces from which ink is transferred to the paper. **11** any vivid effect resulting from contrast: *comic relief.* **12** variation in altitude in an area; difference between highest and lowest level. **13** *Law.* redress of a grievance or hardship: *to seek relief through the courts.* **14 on relief.** *US & Canad.* (of people) in receipt of government aid because of personal need. [C14: from OF, from *relever*; see RELIEVE]

relief map *n* a map that shows the configuration and height of the land surface, usually by means of contours.

relieve (rɪˈliːv) *vb* **relieves, relieving, relieved.** (*tr*) **1** to bring alleviation of (pain, distress, etc.) to (someone). **2** to bring aid or assistance to (someone in need, etc.). **3** to take over the duties or watch of (someone). **4** to bring aid or a relieving force to (a besieged town, etc.). **5** to free (someone) from an obligation. **6** to make (something) less unpleasant, arduous, or monotonous. **7** to bring into relief or prominence, as by contrast. **8** (foll. by *of*) *Inf.* to take from: *the thief relieved him of his watch.* **9 relieve oneself.** to urinate or defecate. [C14: from OF *relever*, from L *relevāre* to lift up, relieve, from RE- + *levāre* to lighten]
▸ re'lievable *adj* ▸ re'liever *n*

relieved (rɪˈliːvd) *adj* (*postpositive; often foll. by at, about*, etc.) experiencing relief, esp. from worry or anxiety.

religieuse *French.* (rəliʒjøz) *n* a nun. [C18: fem of RELIGIEUX]

religieux *French.* (rəliʒjø) *n, pl religieux* (-ʒjø). a member of a monastic order or clerical body. [C17: from L *religiōsus* religious]

religion (rɪˈlɪdʒən) *n* **1** belief in, worship of, or obedience to a supernatural power or powers considered to be di-

vine or to have control of human destiny. **2** any formal or institutionalized expression of such belief: *the Christian religion.* **3** the attitude and feeling of one who believes in a transcendent controlling power or powers. **4** *Chiefly RC Church.* the way of life entered upon by monks and nuns: *to enter religion.* **5** something of overwhelming importance to a person: *football is his religion.* [C12: via OF from L *religiō* fear of the supernatural, piety, prob. from *religāre*, from RE- + *ligāre* to bind]

religionism (rɪˈlɪdʒəˌnɪzəm) *n* extreme religious fervour.
▸ re'ligionist *n, adj*

religiose (rɪˈlɪdʒɪˌəʊs) *adj* affectedly or extremely pious; sanctimoniously religious.
▸ re'ligi,osely *adv* ▸ religiosity (rɪˌlɪdʒɪˈɒsɪtɪ) *n*

religious (rɪˈlɪdʒəs) *adj* **1** of, relating to, or concerned with religion. **2a** pious; devout; godly. **2b** (*as collective n*; preceded by *the*): *the religious.* **3** appropriate to or in accordance with the principles of a religion. **4** scrupulous, exact, or conscientious. **5** *Christianity.* of or relating to a way of life dedicated to religion and defined by a monastic rule. ♦ *n* **6** *Christianity.* a monk or nun.
▸ re'ligiously *adv* ▸ re'ligiousness *n*

Religious Society of Friends *n* the official name for the **Quakers.**

relinquish (rɪˈlɪŋkwɪʃ) *vb* (*tr*) **1** to give up (a task, struggle, etc.); abandon. **2** to surrender or renounce (a claim, right, etc.). **3** to release; let go. [C15: from F *relinquir*, from L *relinquere*, from RE- + *linquere* to leave]
▸ re'linquisher *n* ▸ re'linquishment *n*

reliquary (ˈrɛlɪkwərɪ) *n, pl reliquaries.* a receptacle or repository for relics, esp. relics of saints. [C17: from OF *reliquaire*, from *relique* RELIC]

relique (rəˈliːk, ˈrɛlɪk) *n* an archaic spelling of **relic.**

reliquiae (rɪˈlɪkwɪˌiː) *pl n* fossil remains of animals or plants. [C19: from L: remains]

relish (ˈrɛlɪʃ) *vb* (*tr*) **1** to savour or enjoy (an experience) to the full. **2** to anticipate eagerly; look forward to. **3** to enjoy the taste or flavour of (food, etc.); savour. ♦ *n* **4** liking or enjoyment, as of something eaten or experienced (esp. in **with relish**). **5** pleasurable anticipation: *he didn't have much relish for the idea.* **6** an appetizing or spicy food added to a main dish to enhance its flavour. **7** an appetizing taste or flavour. **8** a zestful trace or touch: *there was a certain relish in all his writing.* [C16: from earlier *reles* aftertaste, from OF, from *relaisser* to leave behind; see RELEASE]
▸ 'relishable *adj*

relive (riːˈlɪv) *vb* **relives, reliving, relived.** (*tr*) to experience (a sensation, event, etc.) again, esp. in the imagination.
▸ re'livable *adj*

relocate (ˌriːləʊˈkeɪt) *vb* **relocates, relocating, relocated.** to move or be moved to a new place, esp. (of an employee, a business, etc.) to a new area or place of employment.
▸ ,relo'cation *n*

reluctance (rɪˈlʌktəns) *or* **reluctancy** *n* **1** lack of eagerness or willingness; disinclination. **2** *Physics.* a measure of the resistance of a closed magnetic circuit to a magnetic flux. [C16: from L *reluctārī* to resist, from RE- + *luctārī* to struggle]

reluctant (rɪˈlʌktənt) *adj* not eager; unwilling; disinclined. [C17: from L *reluctārī* to resist]
▸ re'luctantly *adv*

reluctivity (ˌrɛlʌkˈtɪvɪtɪ) *n, pl reluctivities.* *Physics.* a specific or relative reluctance of a magnetic material. [C19: from obs. *reluct* to struggle + *-ivity*]

rely (rɪˈlaɪ) *vb* **relies, relying, relied.** (*intr*; foll. by *on* or *upon*) **1** to be dependent (on): *he relies on his charm.* **2** to have trust or confidence (in): *you can rely on us.* [C14: from OF *relier* to fasten together, from L *religāre*, from RE- + *ligāre* to tie]

REM *abbrev.* for rapid eye movement.

remain (rɪˈmeɪn) *vb* (*mainly intr*) **1** to stay behind or in the same place: *to remain at home.* **2** (*copula*) to continue to be: *to remain cheerful.* **3** to be left, as after use, the passage of time, etc. **4** to be left to be done, said, etc.: *it re-*

mains to be pointed out. [C14: from OF *remanoir*, from L *remanēre*, from RE- + *manēre* to stay]

remainder (rɪˈmeɪndə) *n* **1** a part or portion that is left, as after use, subtraction, expenditure, the passage of time, etc.: *the remainder of the milk.* **2** *Maths.* **2a** the amount left over when one quantity cannot be exactly divided by another: *for 10 ÷ 3, the remainder is 1.* **2b** another name for **difference** (sense 7). **3** *Property law.* a future interest in property; an interest in a particular estate that will pass to one at some future date, as on the death of the current possessor. **4** a number of copies of a book left unsold when demand ceases, which are sold at a reduced price. ◆ *vb* **5** (*tr*) to sell (copies of a book) as a remainder.

remains (rɪˈmeɪnz) *pl n* **1** any pieces, fragments, etc., that are left unused or still extant, as after use, consumption, the passage of time: *archaeological remains.* **2** the body of a dead person; corpse. **3** Also called: **literary remains.** the unpublished writings of an author at the time of his death.

remake *n* (ˈriːˌmeɪk). **1** something that is made again, esp. a new version of an old film. **2** the act of making again. ◆ *vb* (riːˈmeɪk), **remakes, remaking, remade. 3** (*tr*) to make again or anew.

remand (rɪˈmɑːnd) *vb* (*tr*) **1** *Law.* (of a court or magistrate) to send (a prisoner or accused person) back into custody. **2** to send back. ◆ *n* **3** the sending of a prisoner or accused person back into custody to await trial. **4** the act of remanding or state of being remanded. **5 on remand.** in custody or on bail awaiting trial. [C15: from Med. L *remandāre* to send back word, from L RE- + *mandāre* to command]

remand centre *n* (in Britain) an institution to which accused persons are sent for detention while awaiting appearance before a court.

remanence (ˈrɛmənəns) *n Physics.* the ability of a material to retain magnetization after the removal of the magnetizing field. [C17: from L *remanēre* to stay behind]

remark (rɪˈmɑːk) *vb* **1** (when *intr*, often foll. by *on* or *upon*; when *tr*, *may take a clause as object*) to pass a casual comment (about); reflect in informal speech or writing. **2** (*tr*; *may take a clause as object*) to perceive; observe; notice. ◆ *n* **3** a brief casually expressed thought or opinion. **4** notice, comment, or observation: *the event passed without remark.* **5** a variant of **remarque.** [C17: from OF *remarquer* to observe, from RE- + *marquer* to note, MARK[1]]
▶ **reˈmarker** *n*

remarkable (rɪˈmɑːkəbˀl) *adj* **1** worthy of note or attention: *a remarkable achievement.* **2** unusual, striking, or extraordinary: *a remarkable sight.*
▶ **reˈmarkableness** *n* ▶ **reˈmarkably** *adv*

remarque (rɪˈmɑːk) *n* a mark in the margin of an engraved plate to indicate the stage of production. [C19: from F; see REMARK]

Remarque ★ (rɪˈmɑːk) *n* Erich Maria (ˈeːrɪç maˈriːa). 1898–1970, US novelist, born in Germany, noted for his novel *All Quiet on the Western Front* (1929).

remaster (riːˈmɑːstə) *vb* (*tr*) to make a new master audio recording, now usually digital, from (an earlier original recording), in order to produce compact discs or stereo records with improved sound reproduction.

Rembrandt ★ (ˈrɛmbrænt) *n* full name *Rembrandt Harmensz (or Harmenszoon) van Rijn (or van Ryn).* 1606–69, Dutch painter, noted for his portraits, esp. *The Nightwatch* (1642).
▶ ˌRembrandtˈesque *adj*

REME (ˈriːmɪ) *n acronym for* Royal Electrical and Mechanical Engineers.

remedial (rɪˈmiːdɪəl) *adj* **1** affording a remedy; curative. **2** denoting or relating to special teaching for backward and slow learners: *remedial education.*
▶ **reˈmedially** *adv*

remedy (ˈrɛmɪdɪ) *n, pl* **remedies. 1** (usually foll. by *for* or *against*) any drug or agent that cures a disease or controls its symptoms. **2** (usually foll. by *for* or *against*) anything that serves to cure defects, improve conditions, etc.: *a remedy for industrial disputes.* **3** the legally permitted varia-

tion from the standard weight or quality of coins. ◆ (*tr*) **4** to relieve or cure (a disease, etc.) by a remedy. **5** to put to rights (a fault, error, etc.); correct. [C13: from Anglo-Norman *remedie*, from L *remedium* a cure, from *remedērī*, from RE- + *medērī* to heal]
▶ **remediable** (rɪˈmiːdɪəbˀl) *adj* ▶ **reˈmediably** *adv* ▶ **remediless** *adj*

remember (rɪˈmɛmbə) *vb* **1** to become aware of (something forgotten) again; bring back to one's consciousness. **2** to retain (an idea, intention, etc.) in one's conscious mind: *remember to do one's shopping.* **3** (*tr*) to give money, etc., to (someone), as in a will or in tipping. **4** (*tr*; foll. by *to*) to mention (a person's name) to another person, as by way of greeting: *remember me to your mother.* **5** (*tr*) to mention (a person) favourably, as in prayer. **6** (*tr*) to commemorate (a person, event, etc.): *to remember the dead of the wars.* **7 remember oneself.** to recover one's good manners after a lapse. [C14: from OF *remembrer*, from LL *rememorārī* to recall to mind, from L RE- + *memor* mindful]
▶ **reˈmemberer** *n*

remembrance (rɪˈmɛmbrəns) *n* **1** the act of remembering or state of being remembered. **2** something that is remembered; reminiscence. **3** a memento or keepsake. **4** the extent in time of one's power of recollection. **5** the act of honouring some past event, person, etc.

Remembrance Day *n* **1** (in Britain) another name for **Remembrance Sunday. 2** (in Canada) a statutory holiday observed on November 11 in memory of the dead of both World Wars.

remembrancer (rɪˈmɛmbrənsə) *n* **1** *Arch.* a reminder, memento, or keepsake. **2** (*usually cap.*) (in Britain) any of several officials of the Exchequer, esp. one (**Queen's** or **King's Remembrancer**) whose duties include collecting debts due to the Crown. **3** (*usually cap.*) an official (**City Remembrancer**) appointed by the Corporation of the City of London to represent its interests to Parliament.

Remembrance Sunday *n* (in Britain) the Sunday closest to November 11, on which the dead of both World Wars are commemorated. Also called: **Remembrance Day.**

remex (ˈriːmɛks) *n, pl* **remiges** (ˈrɛmɪˌdʒiːz). any of the large flight feathers of a bird's wing. [C18: from L: rower, from *rēmus* oar]
▶ **remigial** (rɪˈmɪdʒɪəl) *adj*

remind (rɪˈmaɪnd) *vb* (*tr*; usually foll. by *of*; may take a clause as object or an infinitive) to cause (a person) to remember (something or to do something); put (a person) in mind (of something): *remind me to phone home; flowers remind me of holidays.*
▶ **reˈminder** *n*

remindful (rɪˈmaɪndfʊl) *adj* **1** serving to remind. **2** (*postpositive*) mindful.

reminisce (ˌrɛmɪˈnɪs) *vb* **reminisces, reminiscing, reminisced.** (*intr*) to talk or write about old times, past experiences, etc.

reminiscence (ˌrɛmɪˈnɪsəns) *n* **1** the act of recalling or narrating past experiences. **2** (*often pl*) some past experience, event, etc., that is recalled. **3** an event, phenomenon, or experience that reminds one of something else. **4** *Philosophy.* the doctrine that the mind has seen the universal forms of all things in a previous disembodied existence.

reminiscent (ˌrɛmɪˈnɪsˀnt) *adj* **1** (*postpositive*; foll. by *of*) stimulating memories (of) or comparisons (with). **2** characterized by reminiscence. **3** (of a person) given to reminiscing. [C18: from L *reminiscī* to call to mind, from RE- + *mēns* mind]
▶ ˌremiˈniscently *adv*

remise (rɪˈmaɪz) *vb* **remises, remising, remised. 1** (*tr*) *Law.* to give up or relinquish (a right, claim, etc.). **2** (*intr*) *Fencing.* to make a remise. ◆ *n* **3** *Fencing.* a second thrust made on the same lunge after the first has missed. **4** *Obs.* a coach house. [C17: from F *remettre* to put back, from L *remittere*, from RE- + *mittere* to send]

remiss (rɪˈmɪs) *adj* (*postpositive*) **1** lacking in care or attention to duty; negligent. **2** lacking in energy. [C15: from L *remissus*, from *remittere*, from RE- + *mittere* to send]
▶ **reˈmissly** *adv* ▶ **reˈmissness** *n*

★ people and places

remissible (rɪ'mɪsɪb°l) *adj* able to be remitted. [C16: from L *remissibilis;* see REMIT]
▶ re,missi'bility *n*

remission (rɪ'mɪʃən) *or (less commonly)* **remittal** (rɪ'mɪt°l) *n* 1 the act of remitting or state of being remitted. 2 a reduction of the term of a sentence of imprisonment, as for good conduct. 3 forgiveness for sin. 4 discharge or release from penalty, obligation, etc. 5 lessening of intensity; abatement, as in the symptoms of a disease. 6 *Rare.* the act of sending a remittance.
▶ re'missive *adj* ▶ re'missively *adv*

remit *vb* (rɪ'mɪt), **remits, remitting, remitted.** *(mainly tr)* 1 *(also intr)* to send (payment, etc.), as for goods or service, esp. by post. 2 *Law.* (esp. of an appeal court) to send back (a case) to an inferior court for further consideration. 3 to cancel or refrain from exacting (a penalty or punishment). 4 *(also intr)* to relax (pace, intensity, etc.) or (of pace) to slacken or abate. 5 to postpone; defer. 6 *Arch.* to pardon or forgive (crime, sins, etc.). ◆ *n* ('riːmɪt, rɪ'mɪt). 7 area of authority (of a committee, etc.). 8 *Law.* the transfer of a case from one court or jurisdiction to another. 9 the act of remitting. [C14: from L *remittere,* from RE- + *mittere* to send]
▶ re'mittable *adj* ▶ re'mitter *n*

remittance (rɪ'mɪtəns) *n* 1 payment for goods or services received or as an allowance, esp. when sent by post. 2 the act of remitting.

remittance man *n* a man living abroad on money sent from home, esp. in the days of the British Empire.

remittent (rɪ'mɪt°nt) *adj* (of the symptoms of a disease) characterized by periods of diminished severity.
▶ re'mittence *n* ▶ re'mittently *adv*

remix *vb* (riː'mɪks). 1 to change the balance and separation of (a recording). ◆ *n* ('riː,mɪks). 2 a remixed version of a recording.

remnant ('rɛmnənt) *n* 1 *(often pl)* a part left over after use, processing, etc. 2 a surviving trace or vestige: *a remnant of imperialism.* 3 a piece of material from the end of a roll. ◆ *adj* 4 remaining; left over. [C14: from OF *remenant* remaining, from *remanoir* to REMAIN]

remonetize *or* **remonetise** (riː'mʌnɪ,taɪz) *vb* **remonetizes, remonetizing, remonetized** *or* **remonetises, remonetising, remonetised.** *(tr)* to reinstate as legal tender: *to remonetize silver.*
▶ re,moneti'zation *or* re,moneti'sation *n*

remonstrance (rɪ'mɒnstrəns) *n* 1 the act of remonstrating. 2 a protest or reproof, esp. a petition protesting against something.

remonstrant (rɪ'mɒnstrənt) *n* 1 a person who remonstrates, esp. one who signs a remonstrance. ◆ *adj* 2 *Rare.* remonstrating.

remonstrate ('rɛmən,streɪt) *vb* **remonstrates, remonstrating, remonstrated.** *(intr)* (usually foll. by *with, against,* etc.) to argue in protest or objection: *to remonstrate with the government.* [C16: from Med. L *remonstrāre* to point out (errors, etc.), from L RE- + *monstrāre* to show]
▶ ,remon'stration *n* ▶ remonstrative (rɪ'mɒnstrətɪv) *adj* ▶ 'remon,strator *n*

remontant (rɪ'mɒntənt) *adj* 1 (esp. of roses) flowering more than once in a single season. ◆ *n* 2 a rose having such a growth. [C19: from F: coming up again, from *remonter*]

remora ('rɛmərə) *n* a marine spiny-finned fish which has a flattened elongated body and attaches itself to larger fish, rocks, etc., by a sucking disc on the top of the head. [C16: from L, from RE- + *mora* delay; from its alleged habit of delaying ships]

remorse (rɪ'mɔːs) *n* 1 a sense of deep regret and guilt for some misdeed. 2 compunction; pity; compassion. [C14: from Med. L *remorsus* a gnawing, from L *remordēre,* from RE- + *mordēre* to bite]
▶ re'morseful *adj* ▶ re'morsefully *adv* ▶ re'morsefulness *n* ▶ re'morseless *adj*

remote (rɪ'məʊt) *adj* 1 located far away; distant. 2 far from society or civilization; out-of-the-way. 3 distant in time. 4 distantly related or connected: *a remote cousin.* 5 slight or faint (esp. in **not the remotest idea**). 6 (of a person's manner) aloof or abstracted. 7 operated from a dis-

tance; remote-controlled: *a remote monitor.* [C15: from L *remōtus* far removed, from *removēre,* from RE- + *movēre* to move]
▶ re'motely *adv* ▶ re'moteness *n*

remote access *n Computing.* access to a computer from a physically separate terminal.

remote control *n* control of a system or activity from a distance, usually by radio, ultrasonic, or electrical signals.
▶ re,mote-con'trolled *adj*

remote sensor *n* any instrument, such as a radar device or camera, that scans the earth or another planet from space in order to collect data about some aspect of it.
▶ remote sensing *adj, n*

rémoulade (,rɛmə'leɪd) *n* a mayonnaise sauce flavoured with herbs, mustard, and capers, served with salads, cold meat, etc. [C19: from F, from dialect *ramolas* horseradish, from L *armoracea*]

remould *vb* (,riː'məʊld). *(tr)* 1 to mould again. 2 to bond a new tread onto the casing of (a worn pneumatic tyre). ◆ *n* ('riː,məʊld). 3 a tyre made by this process.

remount *vb* (riː'maʊnt). 1 to get on (a horse, bicycle, etc.) again. 2 *(tr)* to mount (a picture, jewel, exhibit, etc.) again. ◆ *n* ('riː,maʊnt). 3 a fresh horse.

removal (rɪ'muːv°l) *n* 1 the act of removing or state of being removed. 2a a change of residence. 2b *(as modifier): a removal company.* 3 dismissal from office.

removalist (rɪ'muːvəlɪst) *n Austral.* a person or company that transports household effects to a new home.

remove (rɪ'muːv) *vb* **removes, removing, removed.** *(mainly tr)* 1 to take away and place elsewhere. 2 to dismiss (someone) from office. 3 to do away with; abolish; get rid of. 4 *Euphemistic.* to assassinate; kill. 5 *(intr) Formal.* to change the location of one's home or place of business. ◆ *n* 6 the act of removing, esp. (formal) a removal of one's residence or place of work. 7 the degree of difference: *only one remove from madness.* 8 *Brit.* (in certain schools) a class or form. [C14: from OF *removoir,* from L *removēre;* see MOVE]
▶ re'movable *adj* ▶ re,mova'bility *n* ▶ re'mover *n*

removed (rɪ'muːvd) *adj* 1 separated by distance or abstract distinction. 2 *(postpositive)* separated by a degree of descent or kinship: *the child of a person's first cousin is his first cousin once removed.*

Remscheid ★ *(German* 'rɛmʃaɪt) *n* an industrial city in W Germany, in North Rhine-Westphalia. Pop.: 123 069 (1995 est.).

remunerate (rɪ'mjuːnə,reɪt) *vb* **remunerates, remunerating, remunerated.** *(tr)* to reward or pay for work, service, etc. [C16: from L *remūnerārī* to reward, from RE- + *mūnerāre* to give, from *mūnus* a gift]
▶ re,muner'ation *n* ▶ re'munerable *adj* ▶ re'munerative *adj* ▶ re'muneratively *adv* ▶ re'muner,ator *n*

Remus ★ ('riːməs) *n Roman myth.* the brother of Romulus.

renaissance (rə'neɪsəns, 'rɛnə,sɑːns) *or* **renascence** *n* a revival or rebirth, esp. of culture and learning. [C19: from F, from L RE- + *nascī* to be born]

Renaissance (rə'neɪsəns, 'rɛnə,sɑːns) *n* 1 *the.* the great revival of art, literature, and learning in Europe in the 14th, 15th, and 16th centuries. 2 the spirit, culture, art, science, and thought of this period. ◆ *adj* 3 of, characteristic of, or relating to the Renaissance, its culture, etc.

renal ('riːn°l) *adj* of, relating to, resembling, or situated near the kidney. [C17: from F, from LL *rēnālis,* from L *rēnēs* kidneys, from ?]

renal pelvis *n* a small funnel-shaped cavity of the kidney into which urine is discharged before passing into the ureter.

Renan ★ *(French* rənā) *n* **(Joseph) Ernest** (ɛrnɛst). 1823–92, French philosopher, theologian, and historian; best known for his *Life of Jesus* (1863).

renascent (rɪ'næs°nt, -'neɪ-) *adj* becoming active or vigorous again; reviving: *renascent nationalism.* [C18: from L *renascī* to be born again]

rencounter (rɛn'kaʊntə) *Arch.* ◆ *n* also **rencontre** (rɛn'kɒntə). 1 an unexpected meeting. 2 a hostile clash, as of two armies, adversaries, etc.; skirmish. ◆ *vb* **3** to meet (someone) unexpectedly. [C16: from F *rencontre*, from *rencontrer*; as ENCOUNTER]

rend (rɛnd) *vb* **rends, rending, rent**. **1** to tear with violent force or to be torn in this way; rip. **2** (*tr*) to tear or pull (one's clothes, etc.), esp. as a manifestation of rage or grief. **3** (*tr*) (of a noise or cry) to disturb (the silence) with a shrill or piercing tone. [OE *rendan*]
▶ **'rendible** *adj*

Rendell ★ ('rɛndᵊl, rɛn'dɛl) *n* **Ruth (Barbara)**, Baroness. born 1930, British author of detective novels, such as *Wolf to the Slaughter* (1967), and psychological thrillers, such as *The Lake of Darkness* (1980) and (under the name Barbara Vine) *A Fatal Inversion* (1987) and *No Night is Too Long* (1994).

render ('rɛndə) *vb* (*tr*) **1** to present or submit (accounts, etc.) for payment, etc. **2** to give or provide (aid, charity, a service, etc.). **3** to show (obedience), as expected. **4** to give or exchange, as by way of return or requital: *to render blow for blow*. **5** to cause to become: *grief had rendered him simple-minded*. **6** to deliver (a verdict or opinion) formally. **7** to portray or depict (something), as in painting, music, or acting. **8** to translate (something). **9** (sometimes foll. by *up*) to yield or give: *the tomb rendered up its secret*. **10** (often foll. by *back*) to return (something); give back. **11** to cover the surface of (brickwork, etc.) with a coat of plaster. **12** (often foll. by *down*) to extract (fat) from (meat) by melting. ◆ *n* **13** a first thin coat of plaster applied to a surface. **14** one who or that which rends. [C14: from OF *rendre*, from L *reddere* to give back (infl. by L *prendere* to grasp), from RE- + *dare* to give]
▶ **'renderable** *adj* ▶ **'renderer** *n* ▶ **'rendering** *n*

rendezvous ('rɒndɪˌvuː) *n, pl* **rendezvous** (-ˌvuːz). **1** a meeting or appointment to meet at a specified time and place. **2** a place where people meet. ◆ *vb* (*intr*) **3** to meet at a specified time or place. [C16: from F, from *rendezvous!* present yourselves! from *se rendre* to present oneself; see RENDER]

rendition (rɛn'dɪʃən) *n* **1** a performance of a musical composition, dramatic role, etc. **2** a translation. **3** the act of rendering. [C17: from obs. F, from LL *redditiō*; see RENDER]

renegade ('rɛnɪˌgeɪd) *n* **1a** a person who deserts his cause or faith for another; traitor. **1b** (*as modifier*): *a renegade priest*. **2** any outlaw or rebel. [C16: from Sp. *renegado*, ult. from L RE- + *negāre* to deny]

renege *or* **renegue** (rɪ'niːg, -'neɪg) *vb* **reneges, reneging, reneged** *or* **renegues, reneguing, renegued**. **1** (*intr*; often foll. by *on*) to go back (on one's promise, etc.). ◆ *vb, n* **2** *Cards.* other words for **revoke**. [C16 (in the sense: to deny, renounce): from Med. L *renegāre* to renounce]
▶ **re'neger** *or* **re'neguer** *n*

renew (rɪ'njuː) *vb* (*mainly tr*) **1** to take up again. **2** (*also intr*) to begin (an activity) again; recommence. **3** to restate or reaffirm (a promise, etc.). **4** (*also intr*) to make (a lease, etc.) valid for a further period. **5** to regain or recover (vigour, strength, activity, etc.). **6** to restore to a new or fresh condition. **7** to replace (an old or worn-out part or piece). **8** to replenish (a supply, etc.).
▶ **re'newable** *adj* ▶ **re'newal** *n* ▶ **re'newer** *n*

renewable energy *n* another name for **alternative energy**.

renewables *pl n* sources of alternative energy, such as wind and wave power.

Renfrew ★ ('rɛnfruː) *n* an industrial town in W central Scotland, in Renfrewshire. Pop.: 20 764 (1991).

Renfrewshire ★ ('rɛnfruːˌʃɪə, -ʃə) *n* **1** a council area of W central Scotland, on the River Clyde W of Glasgow: corresponds to part of the historic county of Renfrewshire. Administrative centre: Paisley. Pop.: 178 550 (1996 est.). Area: 261 sq. km (101 sq. miles). **2** a historic county of W central Scotland, on the Firth of Clyde: now covered by the council areas of Renfrewshire, East Renfrewshire, and Inverclyde.

Reni ★ (*Italian* 'reːni) *n* **Guido** ('gwiːdo). 1575–1642, Italian baroque painter.

reni- *combining form.* kidney or kidneys: *reniform*. [from L *rēnēs*]

reniform ('rɛnɪˌfɔːm) *adj* having the shape or profile of a kidney: *a reniform leaf*.

renin ('riːnɪn) *n* a proteolytic enzyme secreted by the kidneys, which plays an important part in the maintenance of blood pressure. [C20: from RENI- + -IN]

Rennes ★ (*French* rɛn) *n* a city in NW France: the ancient capital of Brittany. Pop.: 203 533 (1990).

rennet ('rɛnɪt) *n* **1** the membrane lining the fourth stomach of a young calf. **2** a substance prepared esp. from the stomachs of calves and used for curdling milk in making cheese. [C15: rel. to OE *gerinnan* to curdle, RUN]

rennin ('rɛnɪn) *n* an enzyme that occurs in gastric juice and is an active constituent of rennet. It coagulates milk. [C20: from RENNET + -IN]

Reno ★ ('riːnəʊ) *n* a city in W Nevada, at the foot of the Sierra Nevada: noted as a divorce, wedding, and gambling centre by reason of its liberal laws. Pop.: 150 620 (1995 est.).

Renoir ★ ('rɛnwɑː; *French* rənwar) *n* **1 Jean** (ʒɑ̃). 1894–1979, French film director: his films include *La grande illusion* (1937) and *Diary of a Chambermaid* (1945). **2** his father, **Pierre Auguste** (pjɛr ogyst). 1841–1919, French impressionist painter, noted for such works as *Les Parapluies* and his later nudes.

renounce (rɪ'naʊns) *vb* **renounces, renouncing, renounced**. **1** (*tr*) to give up formally (a claim or right): *to renounce a title*. **2** (*tr*) to repudiate: *to renounce Christianity*. **3** (*tr*) to give up (some habit, etc.) voluntarily: *to renounce one's old ways*. **4** (*intr*) *Cards*. to fail to follow suit because one has no more cards of the suit led. ◆ *n* **5** *Cards*. a failure to follow suit. [C14: from OF *renoncer*, from L *renuntiāre*, from RE- + *nuntiāre* to announce, from *nuntius* messenger]
▶ **re'nouncement** *n* ▶ **re'nouncer** *n*

renovate ('rɛnəˌveɪt) *vb* **renovates, renovating, renovated**. (*tr*) **1** to restore (something) to good condition. **2** to revive or refresh (one's spirits, health, etc.). [C16: from L *renovāre*, from RE- + *novāre* to make new]
▶ **ˌreno'vation** *n* ▶ **'reno,vative** *adj* ▶ **'reno,vator** *n*

renown (rɪ'naʊn) *n* widespread reputation, esp. of a good kind; fame. [C14: from Anglo-Norman *renoun*, from OF *renom*, from *renomer* to celebrate, from RE- + *nomer* to name, from L *nōmināre*]
▶ **re'nowned** *adj*

rent[1] (rɛnt) *n* **1** a payment made periodically by a tenant to a landlord or owner for the occupation or use of land, buildings, etc. **2** *Econ.* the return derived from the cultivation of land in excess of production costs. **3 for rent**. *Chiefly US & Canad.* available for use and occupation subject to the payment of rent. ◆ *vb* **4** (*tr*) to grant (a person) the right to use one's property in return for periodic payments. **5** (*tr*) to occupy or use (property) in return for periodic payments. **6** (*intr*; often foll. by *at*) to be let or rented (for a specified rental). [C12: from OF *rente* revenue, from Vulgar L *rendere* (unattested) to yield; see RENDER]
▶ **'rentable** *adj* ▶ **'renter** *n*

rent[2] (rɛnt) *n* **1** a slit or opening made by tearing or rending. **2** a breach or division. ◆ *vb* **3** the past tense and past participle of **rend**.

rent-a- *prefix* **1** denoting a rental service. **2** *Derog. or facetious.* denoting a person or group that performs a function as if hired from a rental service: *rent-a-mob*.

rental ('rɛntᵊl) *n* **1a** the amount paid by a tenant as rent. **1b** an income derived from rents received. **2** property available for renting. ◆ *adj* **3** of or relating to rent.

rent boy *n* a young male prostitute.

rent control *n* regulation by law of the rent a landlord can charge for domestic accommodation and of his right to evict tenants.

rent-free *adj, adv* without payment of rent.

rentier *French.* (rɑ̃tje) *n* a person whose income consists primarily of fixed unearned amounts, such as rent or interest. [from *rente*; see RENT[1]]

rent-roll *n* **1** a register of lands and buildings owned by a person, company, etc., showing the rent due from each tenant. **2** the total income arising from rented property.

★ people and places

renunciation (rɪˌnʌnsɪˈeɪʃən) n 1 the act or an instance of renouncing. 2 a formal declaration renouncing something. 3 Stock Exchange. the surrender to another of the rights to buy new shares in a rights issue. [C14: from L renunciātiō a declaration, from renuntiāre to report]
▸ reˈnunciative or reˈnunciatory adj

rep[1] or **repp** (rɛp) n a silk, wool, rayon, or cotton fabric with a transversely corded surface. [C19: from F reps, ?from E ribs]
▸ **repped** adj

rep[2] (rɛp) n Theatre. short for **repertory company.**

rep[3] (rɛp) n 1 short for **representative** (sense 2). 2 NZ inf. a rugby player selected to represent his district.

rep[4] (rɛp) n US inf. short for **reputation.**

rep. abbrev. for: 1 report. 2 reporter. 3 reprint.

Rep. abbrev. for: 1 US. Representative. 2 Republic. 3 US. Republican.

repair[1] (rɪˈpɛə) vb (tr) 1 to restore (something damaged or broken) to good condition or working order. 2 to heal (a breach or division) in (something): to repair a broken marriage. 3 to make amends for (a mistake, injury, etc.). ◆ n 4 the act, task, or process of repairing. 5 a part that has been repaired. 6 state or condition: in good repair. [C14: from OF reparer, from L reparāre, from RE- + parāre to make ready]
▸ reˈpairable adj ▸ reˈpairer n

repair[2] (rɪˈpɛə) vb (intr) 1 (usually foll. by to) to go (to a place). 2 (usually foll. by to) to have recourse (to) for help, etc.: to repair to one's lawyer. ◆ n 3 a haunt or resort. [C14: from OF repairier, from LL repatriāre to return to one's native land, from L RE- + patria fatherland]

repairman (rɪˈpɛəˌmæn) n, pl **repairmen.** a man whose job it is to repair machines, etc.

repand (rɪˈpænd) adj Bot. having a wavy margin: a repand leaf. [C18: from L repandus bent backwards, from RE- + pandus curved]
▸ reˈpandly adv

reparable (ˈrɛpərəbəl, ˈrɛprə-) adj able to be repaired, recovered, or remedied. [C16: from L reparābilis, from reparāre to REPAIR[1]]
▸ ˈreparably adv

reparation (ˌrɛpəˈreɪʃən) n 1 the act or process of making amends. 2 (usually pl) compensation exacted as an indemnity from a defeated nation by the victors. 3 the act or process of repairing or state of having been repaired. [C14 reparacioun, ult. from L reparāre to REPAIR[1]]
▸ **reparative** (rɪˈpærətɪv) or reˈparatory adj

repartee (ˌrɛpɑːˈtiː) n 1 a sharp, witty, or aphoristic remark made as a reply. 2 skill in making sharp witty replies. [C17: from F repartie, from repartir to retort, from RE- + partir to go away]

repast (rɪˈpɑːst) n a meal or the food provided at a meal: a light repast. [C14: from OF, from repaistre to feed, from LL repāscere, from L RE- + pāscere to feed, pasture (of animals)]

repatriate vb (riːˈpætrɪˌeɪt), **repatriates, repatriating, repatriated.** (tr) 1 to send back (a refugee, prisoner of war, etc.) to the country of his birth or citizenship. 2 to send back (a sum of money previously invested abroad) to its country of origin. ◆ n (riːˈpætrɪɪt). 3 a person who has been repatriated. [C17: from LL repatriāre, from L RE- + patria fatherland]
▸ reˌpatriˈation n

repay (rɪˈpeɪ) vb **repays, repaying, repaid.** 1 to pay back (money, etc.) to (a person); refund or reimburse. 2 to make a return for (something): to repay kindness.
▸ reˈpayable adj ▸ reˈpayment n

repeal (rɪˈpiːl) vb (tr) 1 to annul or rescind officially; revoke: these laws were repealed. ◆ n 2 an instance or the process of repealing; annulment. [C14: from OF repeler, from RE- + apeler to call, APPEAL]
▸ reˈpealable adj ▸ reˈpealer n

repeat (rɪˈpiːt) vb 1 (when tr, may take a clause as object) to do or experience (something) again once or several times, esp. to say or write (something) again. 2 (intr) to occur more than once: the last figure repeats. 3 (tr; may take a clause as object) to reproduce (the words, sounds, etc.)

uttered by someone else; echo. 4 (tr) to utter (a poem, etc.) from memory; recite. 5 (intr) (of food) to be tasted again after ingestion as the result of belching. 6 (tr; may take a clause as object) to tell to another person (the secrets imparted to one by someone else). 7 (intr) (of a clock) to strike the hour or quarter-hour just past. 8 (intr) US. to vote (illegally) more than once in a single election. 9 **repeat oneself.** to say or do the same thing more than once, esp. so as to be tedious. ◆ n 10a the act or an instance of repeating. 10b (as modifier): a repeat performance. 11 a word, action, etc., that is repeated. 12 an order made out for goods, etc., that duplicates a previous order. 13 Radio, television. a broadcast of a programme which has been broadcast before. 14 Music. a passage that is an exact restatement of the passage preceding it. [C14: from OF repeter, from L repetere, from RE- + petere to seek]
▸ reˈpeatable adj

USAGE NOTE Since again is part of the meaning of repeat, one should not say something is repeated again.

repeated (rɪˈpiːtɪd) adj done, made, or said again and again; continual.
▸ reˈpeatedly adv

repeater (rɪˈpiːtə) n 1 a person or thing that repeats. 2 Also called: **repeating firearm.** a firearm capable of discharging several shots without reloading. 3 a timepiece that strikes the hour or quarter-hour just past, when a spring is pressed. 4 a device that amplifies incoming electrical signals and retransmits them.

repeating decimal n another name for **recurring decimal.**

repechage (ˌrɛpɪˈʃɑːʒ) n a heat of a competition, esp. in rowing or fencing, in which eliminated contestants have another chance to qualify for the next round or the final. [C19: from F repêchage, lit.: fishing out again, from RE- + pêcher to fish + -AGE]

repel (rɪˈpɛl) vb **repels, repelling, repelled.** (mainly tr) 1 to force or drive back (something or somebody). 2 (also intr) to produce a feeling of aversion or distaste in (someone or something); be disgusting (to). 3 to be effective in keeping away, controlling, or resisting: a spray that repels flies. 4 to have no affinity for; fail to mix with or absorb: water and oil repel each other. 5 to disdain to accept (something); turn away from or spurn: she repelled his advances. [C15: from L repellere, from RE- + pellere to push]
▸ reˈpeller n ▸ reˈpellingly adv

USAGE NOTE See at **repulse.**

repellent (rɪˈpɛlənt) adj 1 distasteful or repulsive. 2 driving or forcing away or back; repelling. ◆ n also **repellant.** 3 something, esp. a chemical substance, that repels: insect repellent. 4 a substance with which fabrics are treated to increase their resistance to water.
▸ reˈpellence or reˈpellency n ▸ reˈpellently adv

repent[1] (rɪˈpɛnt) vb to feel remorse (for); be contrite (about); show penitence (for). [C13: from OF repentir, from RE- + pentir, from L paenitēre to repent]
▸ reˈpenter n

repent[2] (ˈriːpənt) adj Bot. lying or creeping along the ground: repent stems. [C17: from L rēpere to creep]

repentance (rɪˈpɛntəns) n 1 remorse or contrition for one's past actions. 2 an act or the process of being repentant; penitence.
▸ reˈpentant adj

repercussion (ˌriːpəˈkʌʃən) n 1 (often pl) a result or consequence of an action or event: the repercussions of the war are still felt. 2 a recoil after impact; a rebound. 3 a reflection, esp. of sound; echo or reverberation. [C16: from L repercussiō, from repercutere to strike back]
▸ ˌreperˈcussive adj

repertoire (ˈrɛpəˌtwɑː) n 1 all the works collectively that a company, actor, etc., is competent to perform. 2 the entire stock of things available in a field or of a kind. **3 in repertoire.** denoting the performance of two or more plays, etc., by the same company in the same venue on different evenings over a period of time: *"Tosca" returns to Leeds next month in repertoire with "Wozzeck".* [C19: from F, from LL *repertōrium* inventory; see REPERTORY]

repertory ('rɛpətərɪ, -trɪ) *n, pl* **repertories. 1** the entire stock of things available in a field or of a kind; repertoire. **2** a place where a stock of things is kept; repository. **3** short for **repertory company.** [C16: from LL *repertōrium* storehouse, from L *reperīre* to obtain, from RE- + *parere* to bring forth]
▸ **repertorial** (,rɛpə'tɔːrɪəl) *adj*

repertory company *n* a theatrical company that performs plays from a repertoire. US name: **stock company.**

repetend ('rɛpɪ,tɛnd) *n* **1** *Maths.* the digit in a recurring decimal that repeats itself. **2** anything repeated. [C18: from L *repetendum* what is to be repeated, from *repetere* to REPEAT]

répétiteur French. (repetitœr) *n* a member of an opera company who coaches the singers.

repetition (,rɛpɪ'tɪʃən) *n* **1** the act or an instance of repeating; reiteration. **2** a thing, word, action, etc., that is repeated. **3** a replica or copy.
▸ **repetitive** (rɪ'pɛtɪtɪv) *adj*

repetitious (,rɛpɪ'tɪʃəs) *adj* characterized by unnecessary repetition.
▸ **repe'titiously** *adv* ▸ **repe'titiousness** *n*

repetitive strain *or* **stress injury** *n* a condition, characterized by arm or wrist pains, that can affect musicians, computer operators, etc., who habitually perform awkward hand movements. Abbrev.: **RSI.**

repine (rɪ'paɪn) *vb* **repines, repining, repined.** *(intr)* to be fretful or low-spirited through discontent. [C16: from RE- + PINE²]

replace (rɪ'pleɪs) *vb* **replaces, replacing, replaced.** *(tr)* **1** to take the place of; supersede. **2** to substitute a person or thing for (another); put in place of: *to replace an old pair of shoes.* **3** to restore to its rightful place.
▸ **re'placeable** *adj* ▸ **re'placer** *n*

replacement (rɪ'pleɪsmənt) *n* **1** the act or process of replacing. **2** a person or thing that replaces another.

replay *n* ('riː,pleɪ). **1** Also called: **action replay.** a showing again of a sequence of action in slow motion immediately after it happens. **2** a second match between a pair or group of contestants. ◆ *vb* (riː'pleɪ) **3** to play again (a record, sporting contest, etc.).

replenish (rɪ'plɛnɪʃ) *vb* *(tr)* **1** to make full or complete again by supplying what has been used up. **2** to put fresh fuel on (a fire). [C14: from OF *replenir*, from RE- + *plenir*, from L *plēnus* full]
▸ **re'plenisher** *n* ▸ **re'plenishment** *n*

replete (rɪ'pliːt) *adj* *(usually postpositive)* **1** (often foll. by *with*) copiously supplied (with); abounding (in). **2** having one's appetite completely or excessively satisfied; gorged; satiated. [C14: from L *replētus*, from *replēre*, from RE- + *plēre* to fill]
▸ **re'pletely** *adv* ▸ **re'pleteness** *n* ▸ **re'pletion** *n*

replevin (rɪ'plɛvɪn) *Law.* ◆ *n* **1** the recovery of goods unlawfully taken, made subject to establishing the validity of the recovery in a legal action and returning the goods if the decision is adverse. **2** (formerly) a writ of replevin. ◆ *vb* **3** another word for **replevy.** [C15: from Anglo-F, from OF *replevir* to give security for, from RE- + *plevir* to PLEDGE]

replevy (rɪ'plɛvɪ) *Law.* ◆ *vb* **replevies, replevying, replevied.** *(tr)* **1** to recover possession of (goods) by replevin. ◆ *n, pl* **replevies. 2** another word for **replevin.** [C15: from OF *replevir; see* REPLEVIN]
▸ **re'pleviable** *or* **re'plevisable** *adj*

replica ('rɛplɪkə) *n* an exact copy or reproduction, esp. on a smaller scale. [C19: from It., lit.: a reply, from *replicare*, from L: to bend back, repeat]

replicate *vb* ('rɛplɪ,keɪt), **replicates, replicating, replicated.** *(mainly tr)* **1** *(also intr)* to make or be a copy (of); reproduce. **2** to fold (something) over on itself; bend back.

◆ *adj* ('rɛplɪkɪt). **3** folded back on itself: *a replicate leaf.* [C19: from L *replicātus* bent back; see REPLICA]
▸ **repli'cation** *n* ▸ **'replicative** *adj*

reply (rɪ'plaɪ) *vb* **replies, replying, replied.** *(mainly intr)* **1** to make answer (to) in words or writing or by an action; respond. **2** *(tr; takes a clause as object)* to say (something) in answer: *he replied that he didn't want to come.* **3** *Law.* to answer a defendant's plea. **4** to return (a sound); echo. ◆ *n, pl* **replies. 5** an answer; response. **6** the answer made by a plaintiff or petitioner to a defendant's case. [C14: from OF *replier* to fold again, reply, from L *replicāre*, from RE- + *plicāre* to fold]
▸ **re'plier** *n*

repo ('riːpəʊ) *n Inf.* short for: **1** repurchase agreement. **2a** repossession of property. **2b** *(as modifier): a repo car.*

repoint (,riː'pɔɪnt) *vb* *(tr)* to repair the joints of (brickwork, masonry, etc.) with mortar or cement.

report (rɪ'pɔːt) *n* **1** an account prepared after investigation and published or broadcast. **2** a statement made widely known; rumour: *according to report, he is not dead.* **3** an account of the deliberations of a committee, body, etc.: *a report of parliamentary proceedings.* **4** *Brit.* a statement on the progress of each schoolchild. **5** a written account of a case decided at law. **6** comment on a person's character or actions; reputation: *he is of good report here.* **7** a sharp loud noise, esp. one made by a gun. ◆ *vb* (when *tr, may take a clause as object;* when *intr,* often foll. by *on*) **8** to give an account (of); describe. **9** to give an account of the results of an investigation (into): *to report on housing conditions.* **10** (of a committee, legislative body, etc.) to make a formal report on (a bill). **11** *(tr)* to complain about (a person), esp. to a superior. **12** to present (oneself) or be present at an appointed place or for a specific purpose: *report to the manager's office.* **13** *(intr)* to say or show that one is (in a certain state): *to report fit.* **14** *(intr;* foll. by *to)* to be responsible (to) and under the authority (of). **15** *(intr)* to act as a reporter. **16** *Law.* to take down in writing details of (the proceedings of a court of law, etc.) as a record or for publication. [C14: from OF, from L *reportāre*, from RE- + *portāre* to carry]
▸ **re'portable** *adj* ▸ **re'portedly** *adv*

reportage (rɪ'pɔːtɪdʒ, ,rɛpɔː'tɑːʒ) *n* **1** the act or process of reporting news or other events of general interest. **2** a journalist's style of reporting.

reported speech *n* another term for **indirect speech.**

reporter (rɪ'pɔːtə) *n* **1** a person who reports, esp. one employed to gather news for a newspaper or broadcasting organization. **2** a person authorized to report the proceedings of a legislature.

report stage *n* the stage preceding the third reading in the passage of a bill through Parliament.

repose¹ (rɪ'pəʊz) *n* **1** a state of quiet restfulness; peace or tranquillity. **2** dignified calmness of manner; composure. ◆ *vb* **reposes, reposing, reposed. 3** to lie or lay down at rest. **4** *(intr)* to lie when dead, as in the grave. **5** *(intr;* foll. by *on, in,* etc.) *Formal.* to be based (on): *your plan reposes on a fallacy.* [C15: from OF *reposer,* from LL *repausāre,* from RE- + *pausāre* to stop]
▸ **re'posal** *n* ▸ **re'poser** *n* ▸ **re'poseful** *adj* ▸ **re'posefully** *adv*

repose² (rɪ'pəʊz) *vb* **reposes, reposing, reposed.** *(tr)* **1** to put (trust) in a person or thing. **2** to place or put (an object) somewhere. [C15: from L *repōnere* to store up, from RE- + *pōnere* to put]
▸ **re'posal** *n*

reposition (,riːpə'zɪʃən) *n* **1** the act or process of depositing or storing. ◆ *vb* *(tr)* **2** to place in a new position. **3** to target (a product or brand) at a new market by changing its image.

repository (rɪ'pɒzɪtərɪ, -trɪ) *n, pl* **repositories. 1** a place or container in which things can be stored for safety. **2** a place where things are kept for exhibition; museum. **3** a place of burial; sepulchre. **4** a person to whom a secret is entrusted; confidant. [C15: from L *repositōrium,* from *repōnere* to place]

repossess (,riːpə'zɛs) *vb* *(tr)* to take back possession of (property), esp. for nonpayment of money due under a hire-purchase agreement.
▸ **repossession** (,riːpə'zɛʃən) *n* ▸ **,repos'sessor** *n*

★ **people and places**

epoussé (rə'puːseɪ) *adj* **1** raised in relief, as a design on a thin piece of metal hammered through from the underside. ♦ *n* **2** a design or surface made in this way. [C19: from F, from *repousser*, from RE- + *pousser* to PUSH]

epp (rep) *n* a variant spelling of **rep**[1].

eprehend (,reprɪ'hend) *vb* (*tr*) to find fault with; criticize. [C14: from L *reprehendere* to hold fast, rebuke, from RE- + *prendere* to grasp] ► ,repre'hender *n* ► ,repre'hension *n*

eprehensible (,reprɪ'hensɪb°l) *adj* open to criticism or rebuke; blameworthy. [C14: from LL *reprehensibilis*, from L *reprehendere*; see REPREHEND] ► ,repre,hensi'bility *n* ► ,repre'hensibly *adv*

epresent (,reprɪ'zent) *vb* (*tr*) **1** to stand as an equivalent of; correspond to. **2** to act as a substitute or proxy (for). **3** to act as or be the authorized delegate or agent for (a person, country, etc.): *an MP represents his constituency.* **4** to serve or use as a means of expressing: *letters represent the sounds of speech.* **5** to exhibit the characteristics of; exemplify; typify: *romanticism in music is represented by Beethoven.* **6** to present an image of through the medium of a picture or sculpture; portray. **7** to bring clearly before the mind. **8** to set forth in words; state or explain. **9** to describe as having a specified character or quality: *he represented her as a saint.* **10** to act out the part of on stage; portray. [C14: from L *repraesentāre* to exhibit, from RE- + *praesentāre* to PRESENT[2]] ► ,repre'sentable *adj* ► ,repre,senta'bility *n*

e-present (,riː'prɪ'zent) *vb* (*tr*) to present again. ► re-presentation (,riː,prezən'teɪʃən) *n*

epresentation (,reprɪzen'teɪʃən) *n* **1** the act or an instance of representing or the state of being represented. **2** anything that represents, such as a verbal or pictorial portrait. **3** anything that is represented, such as an image brought clearly to mind. **4** the principle by which delegates act for a constituency. **5** a body of representatives. **6** an instance of acting for another in a particular capacity, such as executor. **7** a dramatic production or performance. **8** (*often pl*) a statement of facts, true or alleged, esp. one set forth by way of remonstrance or expostulation.

epresentational (,reprɪzen'teɪʃən°l) *adj* **1** *Art.* depicting objects, scenes, etc., directly as seen; naturalistic. **2** of or relating to representation.

epresentationalism (,reprɪzen'teɪʃənə,lɪzəm) *or* **representationism** *n* *Philosophy.* the doctrine that in perceptions of objects what is before the mind is not the object but a representation of it. Cf. **presentationism. 2** *Art.* the practice of depicting objects, scenes, etc., directly as seen. ► ,represen,tational'istic *adj* ► ,represen'tationist *n, adj*

epresentative (,reprɪ'zentətɪv) *n* **1** a person or thing that represents another. **2** a person who represents and tries to sell the products or services of a firm. **3** a typical example. **4** a person representing a constituency in a deliberative, legislative, or executive body, esp. (*cap.*) a member of the **House of Representatives** (the lower house of Congress). ♦ *adj* **5** serving to represent; symbolic. **6a** exemplifying a class or kind; typical. **6b** containing or including examples of all the interests, types, etc., in a group. **7** acting as deputy or proxy for another. **8** representing a constituency or the whole people in the process of government: *a representative council.* **9** of or relating to the political representation of the people: *representative government.* **10** of or relating to a mental picture or representation. ► ,repre'sentatively *adv* ► ,repre'sentativeness *n*

epress (rɪ'pres) *vb* (*tr*) **1** to keep (feelings, etc.) under control; suppress or restrain. **2** to put into a state of subjugation: *to repress a people.* **3** *Psychol.* to banish (unpleasant thoughts) from one's conscious mind. [C14: from L *reprimere* to press back, from RE- + *premere* to PRESS[1]] ► re'pressed *adj* ► re'presser *or* re'pressor *n* ► re'pressible *adj* ► re'pression *n* ► re'pressive *adj*

eprieve (rɪ'priːv) *vb* reprieves, reprieving, reprieved. (*tr*) **1** to postpone or remit the punishment of (a person, esp. one condemned to death). **2** to give temporary relief to (a person or thing), esp. from otherwise irrevocable harm. ♦ *n* **3** a postponement or remission of punishment. **4** a

warrant granting a postponement. **5** a temporary relief from pain or harm; respite. [C16: from OF *repris* (something) taken back, from *reprendre*, from L *reprehendere*; ? also infl. by obs. E *repreve* to reprove] ► re'prievable *adj* ► re'priever *n*

reprimand ('reprɪ,mɑːnd) *n* **1** a reproof or formal admonition; rebuke. ♦ *vb* **2** (*tr*) to admonish or rebuke, esp. formally. [C17: from F *réprimande*, from L *reprimenda* (things) to be repressed; see REPRESS] ► ,repri'manding *adj*

reprint *n* ('riː,prɪnt). **1** a reproduction in print of any matter already published. **2** a reissue of a printed work using the same type, plates, etc., as the original. ♦ *vb* (riː'prɪnt). **3** (*tr*) to print again. ► re'printer *n*

reprisal (rɪ'praɪz°l) *n* **1** the act or an instance of retaliation in any form. **2** (*often pl*) retaliatory action against an enemy in wartime. **3** (formerly) the forcible seizure of the property or subjects of one nation by another. [C15: from OF *reprisaille*, from OIt., from *riprendere* to recapture, from L *reprehendere*; see REPREHEND]

reprise (rɪ'priːz) *Music.* ♦ *n* **1** the repeating of an earlier theme. ♦ *vb* reprises, reprising, reprised. **2** to repeat (an earlier theme). [C14: from OF, from *reprendre* to take back, from L *reprehendere*; see REPREHEND]

repro ('riːprəʊ) *n, pl* repros. **1** short for **reproduction** (sense 2): *repro furniture.* **2** short for **reproduction proof.**

reproach (rɪ'prəʊtʃ) *vb* (*tr*) **1** to impute blame to (a person) for an action or fault; rebuke. ♦ *n* **2** the act of reproaching. **3** rebuke or censure; reproof. **4** disgrace or shame: *to bring reproach upon one's family.* **5** *above* or *beyond* **reproach.** perfect; beyond criticism. [C15: from OF *reprochier*, from L RE- + *prope* near] ► re'proachable *adj* ► re'proacher *n* ► re'proachingly *adv*

reproachful (rɪ'prəʊtʃfʊl) *adj* full of or expressing reproach. ► re'proachfully *adv* ► re'proachfulness *n*

reprobate ('reprəʊ,beɪt) *adj* **1** morally unprincipled; depraved. **2** *Christianity.* condemned to eternal punishment in hell. ♦ *n* **3** an unprincipled, depraved, or damned person. **4** a disreputable or roguish person. ♦ *vb* reprobates, reprobating, reprobated. (*tr*) **5** to disapprove of; condemn. **6** (of God) to condemn to eternal punishment in hell. [C16: from LL *reprobātus* held in disfavour, from L RE- + *probāre* to test, APPROVE] ► reprobacy ('reprəbəsɪ) *n* ► 'repro,bater *n* ► ,repro'bation *n*

reprocess (riː'prəʊses) *vb* (*tr*) to treat again (something already made and used) in order to make it reusable in some form. ► re'processing *n, adj*

reproduce (,riːprə'djuːs) *vb* reproduces, reproducing, reproduced. (*mainly tr*) **1** to make a copy, representation, or imitation of; duplicate. **2** (*also intr*) *Biol.* to undergo or cause to undergo a process of reproduction. **3** to produce again; bring back into existence again; re-create. **4** (*intr*) to come out (well, badly, etc.) when copied. ► ,repro'ducer *n* ► ,repro'ducible *adj* ► ,repro'ducibly *adv* ► ,repro,duci'bility *n*

reproduction (,riːprə'dʌkʃən) *n* **1** *Biol.* any of various processes, either sexual or asexual, by which an animal or plant produces one or more individuals similar to itself. **2a** an imitation or facsimile of a work of art. **2b** (*as modifier*): *a reproduction portrait.* **3** the quality of sound from an audio system. **4** the act or process of reproducing.

reproduction proof *n* *Printing.* a proof of very good quality used for photographic reproduction to make a printing plate.

reproductive (,riːprə'dʌktɪv) *adj* of, relating to, characteristic of, or taking part in reproduction. ► ,repro'ductively *adv* ► ,repro'ductiveness *n*

reprography (rɪ'prɒgrəfɪ) *n* the art or process of copying, reprinting, or reproducing printed material. ► reprographic (,reprə'græfɪk) *adj* ► ,repro'graphically *adv*

reproof (rɪ'pruːf) *n* an act or expression of rebuke or censure. Also: **reproval** (rɪ'pruːvᵊl). [C14 *reproffe*, from OF *re-prove*, from LL *reprobāre* to disapprove of; see REPROBATE]

re-proof (riː'pruːf) *vb* (*tr*) **1** to treat (a coat, jacket, etc.) so as to renew its texture, waterproof qualities, etc. **2** to provide a new proof of (a book, galley, etc.).

reprove (rɪ'pruːv) *vb* **reproves, reproving, reproved**. (*tr*) to rebuke or scold. [C14: from OF *reprover*, from LL *reprobāre*, from L RE- + *probāre* to examine]
▸ **re'provable** *adj* ▸ **re'prover** *n* ▸ **re'provingly** *adv*

reptant ('reptənt) *adj Biol*. creeping, crawling, or lying along the ground. [C17: from L *reptāre* to creep]

reptile ('reptaɪl) *n* **1** any of the cold-blooded vertebrates characterized by lungs, an outer covering of horny scales or plates, and young produced in eggs, such as the tortoises, turtles, snakes, lizards, and crocodiles. **2** a grovelling insignificant person: *you miserable little reptile!*
◆ *adj* **3** creeping, crawling, or squirming. [C14: from LL *reptilis* creeping, from L *rēpere* to crawl]
▸ **reptilian** (rep'tɪlɪən) *n, adj*

Repton ★ ('reptᵊn) *n* **Humphry**. 1752–1818, British landscape gardener.

republic (rɪ'pʌblɪk) *n* **1** a form of government in which the people or their elected representatives possess the supreme power. **2** a political or national unit possessing such a form of government. **3** a constitutional form in which the head of state is an elected or nominated president. [C17: from F *république*, from L *rēspublica*, lit.: the public thing, from *rēs* thing + *publica* PUBLIC]

republican (rɪ'pʌblɪkən) *adj* **1** of, resembling, or relating to a republic. **2** supporting or advocating a republic. ◆ *n* **3** a supporter or advocate of a republic.

Republican (rɪ'pʌblɪkən) *adj* **1** of, belonging to, or relating to a Republican Party. **2** of, belonging to, or relating to the Irish Republican Army. ◆ *n* **3** a member or supporter of a Republican Party. **4** a member or supporter of the Irish Republican Army.

republicanism (rɪ'pʌblɪkə,nɪzəm) *n* **1** the principles or theory of republican government. **2** support for a republic. **3** (*often cap*.) support for a Republican Party.

Republican Party *n* **1** one of the two major political parties in the US: established around 1854. **2** any of a number of political parties in other countries, usually so named to indicate their opposition to monarchy.

Republic of Ireland ★ *n* See **Ireland**[1] (sense 2).

repudiate (rɪ'pjuːdɪ,eɪt) *vb* **repudiates, repudiating, repudiated**. (*tr*) **1** to reject the authority or validity of; refuse to accept or ratify. **2** to refuse to acknowledge or pay (a debt). **3** to cast off or disown (a son, lover, etc.). [C16: from L *repudiāre* to put away, from *repudium* separation, divorce, from RE- + *pudēre* to be ashamed]
▸ **re'pudiable** *adj* ▸ **re,pudi'ation** *n* ▸ **re'pudiative** *adj*
▸ **re'pudi,ator** *n*

repugnant (rɪ'pʌgnənt) *adj* **1** repellent to the senses; causing aversion. **2** distasteful; offensive; disgusting. **3** contradictory; inconsistent or incompatible. [C14: from L *repugnāns* resisting, from *repugnāre*, from RE- + *pugnāre* to fight]
▸ **re'pugnance** *n* ▸ **re'pugnantly** *adv*

repulse (rɪ'pʌls) *vb* **repulses, repulsing, repulsed**. (*tr*) **1** to drive back or ward off (an attacking force); repel; rebuff. **2** to reject with coldness and discourtesy: *she repulsed his advances*. ◆ *n* **3** the act or an instance of driving back or warding off; rebuff. **4** a cold discourteous rejection or refusal. [C16: from L *repellere* to drive back]
▸ **re'pulser** *n*

USAGE NOTE Some people think that the use of *repulse* in sentences such as *he was repulsed by what he saw* is incorrect and that the correct word is *repel*.

repulsion (rɪ'pʌlʃən) *n* **1** a feeling of disgust or aversion. **2** *Physics*. a force separating two objects, such as the force between two like electric charges.

repulsive (rɪ'pʌlsɪv) *adj* **1** causing or occasioning repugnance; loathsome; disgusting or distasteful. **2** tending to

repel, esp. by coldness and discourtesy. **3** *Physics*. concerned with, producing, or being a repulsion.
▸ **re'pulsively** *adv* ▸ **re'pulsiveness** *n*

repurchase (riː'pɜːtʃɪs) *vb* **1** (*tr*) to buy back or buy again (goods, securities, assets, etc.). ◆ *n* **2** an act or instance of repurchasing.

reputable ('repjutəb'l) *adj* **1** having a good reputation; honoured, trustworthy, or respectable. **2** (of words) acceptable as good usage; standard.
▸ **'reputably** *adv*

reputation (,repju'teɪʃən) *n* **1** the estimation in which a person or thing is generally held; opinion. **2** a high opinion generally held about a person or thing; esteem. **3** notoriety or fame, esp. for some specified characteristic. [C14: from L *reputātiō*, from *reputāre* to calculate; see RE-PUTE]

repute (rɪ'pjuːt) *vb* **reputes, reputing, reputed**. **1** (*tr; usually passive*) to consider (a person or thing) to be as specified: *he is reputed to be rich*. ◆ *n* **2** public estimation; reputation: *a writer of little repute*. [C15: from OF *reputer*, from L *reputāre*, from RE- + *putāre* to think]

reputed (rɪ'pjuːtɪd) *adj* (*prenominal*) generally reckoned or considered; supposed: *the reputed writer of two epic poems*.
▸ **re'putedly** *adv*

request (rɪ'kwɛst) *vb* (*tr*) **1** to express a desire for, esp. politely; ask for or demand: *to request a bottle of wine*. ◆ *n* **2** the act or an instance of requesting, esp. in the form of a written statement, etc.; petition or solicitation. **3 by request**. in accordance with someone's desire. **4 in request**. in demand; popular: *he is in request all over the world*. **5 on request**. on the occasion of a demand or request: *application forms are available on request*. [C14: from OF *requeste*, from Vulgar L *requaerere*; see REQUIRE, QUEST]
▸ **re'quester** *n*

request stop *n* a point on a route at which a bus, etc. will stop only if signalled to do so. US equivalent: **flag stop**.

Requiem ('rekwɪəm) *n* **1** *RC Church*. a Mass celebrated for the dead. **2** a musical setting of this Mass. **3** any piece of music composed or performed as a memorial to a dead person. [C14: from L *requiēs* rest, from the introit, *Requiem aeternam dona eis* Rest eternal grant unto them]

requiem shark *n* any of a family of sharks occurring mostly in tropical seas and characterized by a nictitating membrane.

requiescat (,rekwɪ'eskæt) *n* a prayer for the repose of the souls of the dead. [L, from *requiescat in pace* may he rest in peace]

require (rɪ'kwaɪə) *vb* **requires, requiring, required**. (*mainly tr, may take a clause as object or an infinitive*) **1** to have need of; depend upon; want. **2** to impose as a necessity; make necessary: *this work requires precision*. **3** (*also intr*) to make formal request (for); insist upon. **4** to call upon or oblige (a person) authoritatively; order or command: *to require someone to account for his actions*. [C14: from OF *requerre* via Vulgar L from L *requīrere* to seek to know; also infl. by *quaerere* to seek]
▸ **re'quirer** *n*

USAGE NOTE The use of *require to* as in *I require to see the manager* or *you require to complete a special form* is thought by many people to be incorrect: *I need to see the manager; you are required to complete a special form*.

requirement (rɪ'kwaɪəmənt) *n* **1** something demanded or imposed as an obligation. **2** a thing desired or needed. **3** the act or an instance of requiring.

requisite ('rekwɪzɪt) *adj* **1** absolutely essential; indispensable. ◆ *n* **2** something indispensable; necessity. [C15: from L *requisītus* sought after, from *requīrere* to seek for]
▸ **'requisitely** *adv*

requisition (,rekwɪ'zɪʃən) *n* **1** a request or demand, esp. an authoritative or formal one. **2** an official form on which such a demand is made. **3** the act of taking some

thing over, esp. temporarily for military or public use. ◆ *vb* (*tr*) **4** to demand and take for use, esp. by military or public authority. **5** (*may take an infinitive*) to require (someone) formally to do (something): *to requisition a soldier to drive an officer's car.*
▶ ˌrequiˈsitionary *adj* ▶ ˌrequiˈsitionist *n*

requite (rɪˈkwaɪt) *vb* **requites, requiting, requited.** (*tr*) to make return to (a person for a kindness or injury); repay with a similar action. [C16: RE- + obs. *quite* to discharge, repay; see QUIT]
▶ reˈquitable *adj* ▶ reˈquital *n* ▶ reˈquitement *n* ▶ reˈquiter *n*

reredos (ˈrɪədɒs) *n* **1** a screen or wall decoration at the back of an altar. **2** another word for **fireback**. [C14: from OF *areredos*, from *arere* behind + *dos* back, from L *dorsum*]

rerun *vb* (riːˈrʌn) **reruns, rerunning, reran, rerun.** (*tr*) **1** to broadcast or put on (a film, etc.) again. **2** to run (a race, etc.) again. ◆ *n* (ˈriːˌrʌn). **3** a film, etc., that is broadcast again; repeat. **4** a race that is run again. **5** *Computing.* the repeat of a part of a computer program.

res (reɪs) *n, pl* **res.** *Latin.* a thing, matter, or object.

res. *abbrev. for:* **1** research. **2** reserve. **3** residence. **4** resides. **5** resigned. **6** resolution.

resale price maintenance (ˈriːseɪl) *n* the practice by which a manufacturer establishes a fixed or minimum price for the resale of a brand product by retailers or other distributors. US equivalent: **fair trade.** Abbrev.: **rpm.**

reschedule (riːˈʃɛdjuːl; *also, esp. US* -ˈskɛdʒʊəl) *vb* (*tr*) **1** to change the time, date, or schedule of. **2** to arrange a revised schedule for repayment of (a debt).

rescind (rɪˈsɪnd) *vb* (*tr*) to annul or repeal. [C17: from L *rēscindere* to cut off, from *re-* (intensive) + *scindere* to cut]
▶ reˈscindable *adj* ▶ reˈscinder *n* ▶ reˈscindment *n*

rescission (rɪˈsɪʒən) *n* **1** the act of rescinding. **2** *Law.* the right to have a contract set aside if it has been entered into mistakenly, as a result of misrepresentation, undue influence, etc.

rescript (ˈriːˌskrɪpt) *n* **1** (in ancient Rome) a reply by the emperor to a question on a point of law. **2** any official announcement or edict; a decree. **3** something rewritten. [C16: from L *rēscriptum* reply, from *rēscribere* to write back]

rescue (ˈrɛskjuː) *vb* **rescues, rescuing, rescued.** (*tr*) **1** to bring (someone or something) out of danger, etc.; deliver or save. **2** to free (a person) from legal custody by force. **3** *Law.* to seize (goods) by force. ◆ *n* **4a** the act or an instance of rescuing. **4b** (*as modifier*): *a rescue party.* **5** the forcible removal of a person from legal custody. **6** *Law.* the forcible seizure of goods or property. [C14: from *rescowen*, from OF *rescourre*, from RE- + *escourre* to pull away, from L *excutere* to shake off, from *quatere* to shake]
▶ ˈrescuer *n*

research (rɪˈsɜːtʃ) *n* **1** systematic investigation to establish facts or collect information on a subject. ◆ *vb* **2** to carry out investigations into (a subject, etc.). [C16: from OF *recercher* to seek, search again, from RE- + *cercher* to SEARCH]
▶ reˈsearchable *adj* ▶ reˈsearcher *n*

research and development *n* a commercial company's application of scientific research to develop new products. Abbrev.: **R & D.**

reseat (riːˈsiːt) *vb* (*tr*) **1** to show (a person) to a new seat. **2** to put a new seat on (a chair, etc.). **3** to provide new seats for (a theatre, etc.). **4** to re-form the seating of (a valve).

resect (rɪˈsɛkt) *vb* (*tr*) *Surgery.* to cut out part of (a bone, organ, or other structure or part). [C17: from L *resecāre*, from RE- + *secāre* to cut]

resection (rɪˈsɛkʃən) *n* **1** *Surgery.* excision of part of a bone, organ, or other part. **2** *Surveying.* a method of fixing the position of a point by making angular observations to three fixed points.
▶ reˈsectional *adj*

resemblance (rɪˈzɛmbləns) *n* **1** the state or quality of resembling; likeness or similarity. **2** the degree or extent to which a likeness exists. **3** semblance; likeness.
▶ reˈsemblant *adj*

resemble (rɪˈzɛmbᵊl) *vb* **resembles, resembling, resembled.**

(*tr*) to possess some similarity to; be like. [C14: from OF *resembler*, from RE- + *sembler* to look like, from L *similis* like]
▶ reˈsembler *n*

resent (rɪˈzɛnt) *vb* (*tr*) to feel bitter, indignant, or aggrieved at. [C17: from F *ressentir*, from RE- + *sentir* to feel, from L *sentīre* to perceive; see SENSE]
▶ reˈsentful *adj* ▶ reˈsentment *n*

reserpine (ˈrɛsəpɪn) *n* an insoluble alkaloid, extracted from the roots of a rauwolfia, used medicinally to lower blood pressure and as a sedative and tranquillizer. [C20: from G *Reserpin*, prob. from the NL name of the plant]

reservation (ˌrɛzəˈveɪʃən) *n* **1** the act or an instance of reserving. **2** something reserved, esp. accommodation or a seat. **3** (*often pl*) a stated or unstated qualification of opinion that prevents one's wholehearted acceptance of a proposal, etc. **4** an area of land set aside, esp. (in the US) for American Indian peoples. **5** *Brit.* the strip of land between the two carriageways of a dual carriageway. **6** the act or process of keeping back, esp. for oneself; withholding. **7** *Law.* a right or interest retained by the grantor in property dealings.

reserve (rɪˈzɜːv) *vb* **reserves, reserving, reserved.** (*tr*) **1** to keep back or set aside, esp. for future use or contingency; withhold. **2** to keep for oneself; retain: *I reserve the right to question these men later.* **3** to obtain or secure by advance arrangement: *I have reserved two tickets for tonight's show.* **4** to delay delivery of (a judgment). ◆ *n* **5a** something kept back or set aside, esp. for future use or contingency. **5b** (*as modifier*): *a reserve stock.* **6** the state or condition of being reserved: *I have plenty in reserve.* **7** a tract of land set aside for a special purpose: *a nature reserve.* **8** *Austral. & NZ.* a public park. **9** the usual Canadian name for **reservation** (sense 4). **10** *Sport.* a substitute. **11** (*often pl*) **11a** a part of an army not committed to immediate action in a military engagement. **11b** that part of a nation's armed services not in active service. **12** coolness or formality of manner; restraint, silence, or reticence. **13** (*often pl*) *Finance.* liquid assets or a portion of capital not invested or a portion of profits not distributed by a bank or business enterprise and held to meet future liabilities or contingencies. **14 without reserve.** without reservations; fully. [C14: from OF *reserver*, from L *reservāre*, from RE- + *servāre* to keep]
▶ reˈservable *adj* ▶ reˈserver *n*

re-serve (riːˈsɜːv) *vb* **re-serves, re-serving, re-served.** (*tr*) to serve again.

reserve bank *n* one of the twelve banks forming part of the US Federal Reserve System.

reserve currency *n* foreign currency that is acceptable as a medium of international payments and is held in reserve by many countries.

reserved (rɪˈzɜːvd) *adj* **1** set aside for use by a particular person. **2** cool or formal in manner; restrained or reticent. **3** destined; fated: *a man reserved for greatness.*
▶ reˈservedly (rɪˈzɜːvɪdlɪ) *adv* ▶ reˈservedness *n*

reserved list *n Brit.* a list of retired naval, army, or airforce officers available for recall to active service in an emergency.

reserved occupation *n Brit.* an occupation from which one will not be called up for military service in time of war.

reserve-grade *adj Austral.* denoting a sporting team of the second rank in a club.

reserve price *n Brit.* the minimum price acceptable to the owner of property being auctioned or sold. Also called (*esp. Scot. and US*): **upset price.**

reserve tranche *n* the quota of 25 per cent to which a member of the IMF has unconditional access. Prior to 1978 it was paid in gold and known as the **gold tranche.**

reservist (rɪˈzɜːvɪst) *n* one who serves in the reserve formations of a nation's armed forces.

reservoir (ˈrɛzəˌvwɑː) *n* **1** a natural or artificial lake or large tank used for collecting and storing water for community use. **2** *Biol.* a cavity in an organism containing fluid. **3** a place where a great stock of anything is accumulated. **4** a large supply of something: *a reservoir of talent.* [C17: from F *réservoir*, from *réserver* to RESERVE]

reservoir rock *n* porous and permeable rock containing producible oil or gas in its pore spaces.

reset[1] *vb* (riː'sɛt), **resets, resetting, reset.** (*tr*) **1** to set again (a broken bone, matter in type, a gemstone, etc.). **2** to restore (a gauge, etc.) to zero. ♦ *n* ('riː,sɛt). **3** the act or an instance of setting again. **4** a thing that is set again.
▸ re'setter *n*

reset[2] *Scot.* ♦ *vb* (riː'sɛt), **resets, resetting, reset. 1** to receive or handle goods knowing they have been stolen. ♦ *n* ('riː,sɛt). **2** the receiving of stolen goods. [C14: from OF *receter*, from L *receptāre*, from *recipere* to receive]
▸ re'setter *n*

res gestae ('dʒɛstiː) *pl n* **1** things done or accomplished; achievements. **2** *Law.* incidental facts and circumstances that are admissible in evidence because they explain the matter at issue. [L]

Resht ★ (rɛʃt) *n* a variant of **Rasht**.

reside (rɪ'zaɪd) *vb* **resides, residing, resided.** (*intr*) *Formal.* **1** to live permanently (in a place); have one's home (in): *he resides in London.* **2** (of things, qualities, etc.) to be inherently present (in); be vested (in): *political power resides in military strength.* [C15: from L *residēre* to sit back, from RE- + *sedēre* to sit]
▸ re'sider *n*

residence ('rɛzɪdəns) *n* **1** the place in which one resides; abode or home. **2** a large imposing house; mansion. **3** the fact of residing in a place or a period of residing. **4 in residence. 4a** actually resident: *the Queen is in residence.* **4b** designating a creative artist resident and active for a set period at a college, gallery, etc.: *writer in residence.*

residency ('rɛzɪdənsɪ) *n, pl* **residencies. 1** a variant of **residence. 2** a regular series of concerts by a band or singer at one venue. **3** *US & Canad.* the period, following internship, during which a physician undergoes specialized training. **4** (in India, formerly) the official house of the governor general at the court of a native prince.

resident ('rɛzɪdənt) *n* **1** a person who resides in a place. **2** (esp. formerly) a representative of the British government in a British protectorate. **3** (in India, formerly) a representative of the British governor general at the court of a native prince. **4** a bird or animal that does not migrate. **5** *Brit. & NZ.* a junior doctor who lives in the hospital where he works. **6** *US & Canad.* a physician who lives in the hospital while undergoing specialist training after completing his internship. ♦ *adj* **7** living in a place; residing. **8** living or staying at a place in order to discharge a duty, etc. **9** (of qualities, etc.) existing or inherent (in). **10** (of birds and animals) not in the habit of migrating.
▸ 'residentship *n*

residential (,rɛzɪ'dɛnʃəl) *adj* **1** suitable for or allocated for residence: *a residential area.* **2** relating to residence.
▸ ,resi'dentially *adv*

residentiary (,rɛzɪ'dɛnʃərɪ) *adj* **1** residing in a place, esp. officially. **2** obliged to reside in an official residence: *a residentiary benefice.* ♦ *n, pl* **residentiaries. 3** a clergyman obliged to reside in the place of his official appointment.

residual (rɪ'zɪdjʊəl) *adj* **1** of, relating to, or designating a residue or remainder; remaining; leftover. **2** *US.* of or relating to the payment of residuals. ♦ *n* **3** something left over as a residue; remainder. **4** *Statistics.* **4a** the difference between the mean of a set of observations and one particular observation. **4b** the difference between the numerical value of one particular observation and the theoretical result. **5** (*often pl*) payment made to an actor, musician, etc., for subsequent use of film in which the person appears.
▸ re'sidually *adv*

residual unemployment *n* the unemployment that remains in periods of full employment, as a result of those mentally, physically, or emotionally unfit to work.

residuary (rɪ'zɪdjʊərɪ) *adj* **1** of, relating to, or constituting a residue; residual. **2** *Law.* entitled to the residue of an estate after payment of debts and distribution of specific gifts.

residue ('rɛzɪ,djuː) *n* **1** matter remaining after something has been removed. **2** *Law.* what is left of an estate after the discharge of debts and distribution of specific gifts. [C14: from OF *residu*, from L *residuus* remaining over, from *residēre* to stay behind]

residuum (rɪ'zɪdjʊəm) *n, pl* **residua** (-jʊə). a more formal word for **residue.**

resign (rɪ'zaɪn) *vb* **1** (when *intr*, often foll. by *from*) to give up tenure of (a job, office, etc.). **2** (*tr*) to reconcile (oneself) to; yield: *to resign oneself to death.* **3** (*tr*) to give up (a right, claim, etc.); relinquish. [C14: from OF *resigner*, from L *resignāre* to unseal, destroy, from RE- + *signāre* to seal]
▸ re'signer *n*

re-sign (riː'saɪn) *vb* to sign again.

resignation (,rɛzɪg'neɪʃən) *n* **1** the act of resigning. **2** a formal document stating one's intention to resign. **3** a submissive unresisting attitude; passive acquiescence.

resigned (rɪ'zaɪnd) *adj* characteristic of or proceeding from an attitude of resignation; acquiescent or submissive.
▸ re'signedly (rɪ'zaɪnɪdlɪ) *adv* ▸ re'signedness *n*

resile (rɪ'zaɪl) *vb* **resiles, resiling, resiled.** (*intr*) to spring or shrink back; recoil or resume original shape. [C16: from OF *resilir*, from L *resilīre* to jump back, from RE- + *salīre* to jump]
▸ re'silement *n*

resilient (rɪ'zɪlɪənt) *adj* **1** (of an object) capable of regaining its original shape or position after bending, stretching, or other deformation; elastic. **2** (of a person) recovering easily and quickly from illness, hardship, etc.
▸ re'silience *or* re'siliency *n* ▸ re'siliently *adv*

resin ('rɛzɪn) *n* **1** any of a group of solid or semisolid amorphous compounds that are obtained directly from certain plants as exudations. **2** any of a large number of synthetic, usually organic, materials that have a polymeric structure, esp. such a substance in a raw state before it is moulded or treated with plasticizer, etc. ♦ *vb* **3** (*tr*) to treat or coat with resin. [C14: from OF *resine*, from L *rēsīna*, from Gk *rhētinē* resin from a pine]
▸ 'resinous *adj* ▸ 'resinously *adv* ▸ 'resinousness *n*

resinate ('rɛzɪ,neɪt) *vb* **resinates, resinating, resinated.** (*tr*) to impregnate with resin.

resipiscence (,rɛsɪ'pɪsəns) *n* *Literary.* acknowledgment that one has been mistaken. [C16: from LL *resipiscentia*, from *resipiscere* to recover one's senses, from L *sapere* to know]
▸ ,resi'piscent *adj*

resist (rɪ'zɪst) *vb* **1** to stand firm (against); not yield (to); fight (against). **2** (*tr*) to withstand the deleterious action of; be proof against: *to resist corrosion.* **3** (*tr*) to oppose; refuse to accept or comply with: *to resist arrest.* **4** (*tr*) to refrain from, esp. in spite of temptation (esp. in **cannot resist (something)**). ♦ *n* **5** a substance used to protect something, esp. a coating that prevents corrosion. [C14: from L *resistere*, from RE- + *sistere* to stand firm]
▸ re'sister *n* ▸ re'sistible *adj* ▸ re,sisti'bility *n* ▸ re'sistibly *adv* ▸ re'sistless *adj*

resistance (rɪ'zɪstəns) *n* **1** the act or an instance of resisting. **2** the capacity to withstand something, esp. the body's natural capacity to withstand disease. **3a** the opposition to a flow of electric current through a circuit component, medium, or substance. It is measured in ohms. Symbol: R **3b** (*as modifier*): *a resistance thermometer.* **4** any force that tends to retard or oppose motion: *air resistance; wind resistance.* **5** line of least resistance. the easiest, but not necessarily the best or most honourable, course of action. **6** See **passive resistance.**
▸ re'sistant *adj, n*

Resistance (rɪ'zɪstəns) *n* **the.** an illegal organization fighting for national liberty in a country under enemy occupation.

resistance thermometer *n* an accurate type of thermometer in which temperature is calculated from the resistance of a coil of wire or of a semiconductor placed at the point at which the temperature is to be measured.

Resistencia ★ (*Spanish* resis'tenθja) *n* a city in NE Argentina, on the Paraná River. Pop.: 292 350 (1991).

resistivity (,riːzɪs'tɪvɪtɪ) *n* **1** the electrical property of a material that determines the resistance of a piece of given dimensions. It is measured in ohms. Former name: **specific resistance. 2** the power or capacity to resist; resistance.

resistor (rɪˈzɪstə) n an electrical component designed to introduce a known value of resistance into a circuit.

resit vb (riːˈsɪt), **resits, resitting, resat.** (tr) **1** to sit (an examination) again. ◆ n (ˈriːsɪt). **2** an examination which one must sit again.

res judicata (ˌdʒuːdɪˈkɑːtə) or **res adjudicata** n Law. a matter already adjudicated upon that cannot be raised again. [L]

Resnais ★ (French rɛnɛ) n **Alain** (alɛ̃). born 1922, French film director, whose films include *Hiroshima mon amour* (1959) and *Un Connait la chanson* (1998).

resoluble (rɪˈzɒljuˑbəl, ˈrɛzəl-) adj another word for **resolvable.**

re-soluble (riːˈsɒljubᵊl) adj capable of being dissolved again.
▸ **re-ˈsolubleness** or **re-ˌsoluˈbility** n ▸ **re-ˈsolubly** adv

resolute (ˈrɛzəˌluːt) adj **1** firm in purpose or belief; steadfast. **2** characterized by resolution; determined: *a resolute answer.* [C16: from L *resolutus*, from *resolvere* to RESOLVE]
▸ **ˈresoˌlutely** adv ▸ **ˈresoˌluteness** n

resolution (ˌrɛzəˈluːʃən) n **1** the act or an instance of resolving. **2** firmness or determination. **3** something resolved or determined; decision. **4** a formal expression of opinion by a meeting. **5** a judicial decision on some matter; verdict; judgment. **6** the act of separating something into its constituent parts or elements. **7** Med. subsidence of the symptoms of a disease, esp. the disappearance of inflammation without pus. **8** Music. the process in harmony whereby a dissonant note or chord is followed by a consonant one. **9** the ability of a television or film image to reproduce fine detail. **10** Physics. another word for **resolving power.**
▸ ˌreso'lutioner or ˌreso'lutionist n

resolvable (rɪˈzɒlvəbᵊl) or **resoluble** adj able to be resolved or analysed.
▸ **reˌsolvaˈbility, reˌsoluˈbility** or **reˈsolvableness, reˈsolubleness** n

resolve (rɪˈzɒlv) vb **resolves, resolving, resolved.** (mainly tr) **1** (takes a clause as object or an infinitive) to decide or determine firmly. **2** to express (an opinion) formally, esp. by a vote. **3** (also intr; usually foll. by into) to separate or cause to separate (into) (constituent parts). **4** (usually reflexive) to change; alter: *the ghost resolved itself into a tree.* **5** to make up the mind of; cause to decide: *the tempest resolved him to stay at home.* **6** to find the answer or solution to. **7** to explain away or dispel: *to resolve a doubt.* **8** to bring to an end; conclude: *to resolve an argument.* **9** Med. to cause (an inflammation) to subside, esp. without the formation of pus. **10** Music. (also intr) to follow (a dissonant note or chord) by one producing a consonance. **11** Physics. to distinguish between (separate parts) of (an image) as in a microscope, telescope, or other optical instrument. ◆ n **12** something determined or decided; resolution: *he had made a resolve to work all day.* **13** firmness of purpose; determination: *nothing can break his resolve.* [C14: from L *resolvere* to unfasten, reveal, from RE- + *solvere* to loosen]
▸ **reˈsolvable** adj ▸ **reˌsolvaˈbility** n ▸ **reˈsolver** n

resolved (rɪˈzɒlvd) adj fixed in purpose or intention; determined.
▸ **resolvedly** (rɪˈzɒlvɪdlɪ) adv ▸ **reˈsolvedness** n

resolvent (rɪˈzɒlvənt) adj **1** serving to dissolve or separate something into its elements; resolving. ◆ n **2** a drug or agent able to reduce swelling or inflammation.

resolving power n **1** Also called: **resolution.** Physics. the ability of a microscope or telescope to produce separate images of closely placed objects. **2** Photog. the ability of an emulsion to show up fine detail in an image.

resonance (ˈrɛzənəns) n **1** the condition or quality of being resonant. **2** sound produced by a body vibrating in sympathy with a neighbouring source of sound. **3** the condition of a body or system when it is subjected to a periodic disturbance of the same frequency as the natural frequency of the body or system. **4** amplification of speech sounds by sympathetic vibration in the bone

structure of the head and chest, resounding in the cavities of the nose, mouth, and pharynx. **5** Electronics. the condition of an electrical circuit when the frequency is such that the capacitive and inductive reactances are equal in magnitude. **6** Med. the sound heard when tapping a hollow bodily structure, esp. the chest or abdomen. **7** Chem. the phenomenon in which the electronic structure of a molecule can be represented by two or more hypothetical structures involving single, double, and triple chemical bonds. **8** Physics. the condition of a system in which there is a sharp maximum probability for the absorption of electromagnetic radiation or capture of particles. [C16: from L *resonāre* to RESOUND]

resonant (ˈrɛzənənt) adj **1** resounding or re-echoing. **2** producing resonance: *resonant walls.* **3** full of, or intensified by, resonance: *a resonant voice.*
▸ **ˈresonantly** adv

resonate (ˈrɛzəˌneɪt) vb **resonates, resonating, resonated. 1** to resound or cause to resound; reverberate. **2** Chem., electronics. to exhibit or cause to exhibit resonance. [C19: from L *resonāre*]
▸ ˌreso'nation n

resonator (ˈrɛzəˌneɪtə) n any body or system that displays resonance, esp. a tuned electrical circuit or a conducting cavity in which microwaves are generated by a resonant current.

resorb (rɪˈsɔːb) vb (tr) to absorb again. [C17: from L *resorbēre*, from RE- + *sorbēre* to suck in]
▸ **reˈsorbent** adj ▸ **reˈsorptive** adj

resorcinol (rɪˈzɔːsɪˌnɒl) n a colourless crystalline phenol, used in making dyes, drugs, resins, and adhesives. Formula: $C_6H_4(OH)_2$. [C19: NL, from RESIN + *orcinol*, a crystalline solid]
▸ **reˈsorcinal** adj

resorption (rɪˈsɔːpʃən) n **1** the process of resorbing or the state of being resorbed. **2** Geol. the remelting of a mineral by magma, resulting in a new crystal form being produced.

resort (rɪˈzɔːt) vb (intr) **1** (usually foll. by to) to have recourse (to) for help, use, etc.: *to resort to violence.* **2** to go, esp. often or habitually: *to resort to the beach.* ◆ n **3** a place to which many people go for recreation, etc.: *a holiday resort.* **4** the use of something as a means, help, or recourse. **5** last resort. the last possible course of action open to one. [C14: from OF *resortir*, from RE- + *sortir* to emerge]
▸ **reˈsorter** n

re-sort (riːˈsɔːt) vb (tr) to sort again.

resound (rɪˈzaʊnd) vb (intr) **1** to ring or echo with sound; reverberate. **2** to make a prolonged echoing noise: *the trumpet resounded.* **3** (of sounds) to echo or ring. **4** to be widely famous: *his fame resounded throughout India.* [C14: from OF *resoner*, from L *resonāre* to sound again]

re-sound (riːˈsaʊnd) vb to sound or cause to sound again.

resounding (rɪˈzaʊndɪŋ) adj **1** clear and emphatic: *a resounding vote of confidence.* **2** resonant; reverberating: *a resounding slap.*
▸ **reˈsoundingly** adv

resource (rɪˈzɔːs, -ˈsɔːs) n **1** capability, ingenuity, and initiative; quick-wittedness: *a man of resource.* **2** (often pl) a source of economic wealth, esp. of a country or business enterprise. **3** a supply or source of aid or support; something resorted to in time of need. **4** a means of doing something; expedient. [C17: from OF *ressource* relief, from *resourdre*, from L *resurgere*, from RE- + *surgere* to rise]
▸ **reˈsourceless** adj

resourceful (rɪˈzɔːsful, -ˈsɔːs-) adj ingenious, capable, and full of initiative.
▸ **reˈsourcefully** adv ▸ **reˈsourcefulness** n

respect (rɪˈspɛkt) n **1** an attitude of deference, admiration, or esteem; regard. **2** the state of being honoured or esteemed. **3** a detail, point, or characteristic: *they differ in some respects.* **4** reference or relation (esp. in **in respect of, with respect to**). **5** polite or kind regard; consideration: *respect for people's feelings.* **6** (often pl) an expression of esteem or regard (esp. in **pay one's respects**). ◆ vb (tr) **7** to have an attitude of esteem towards: *to respect one's elders.* **8** to pay proper attention to; not violate: *to respect Swiss*

neutrality. **9** *Arch.* to concern or refer to. [C14: from L *rēspicere* to look back, pay attention to, from RE- + *specere* to look]
▸ re'specter *n*

respectable (rɪ'spɛktəbəl) *adj* **1** having or deserving the respect of other people; estimable; worthy. **2** having good social standing or reputation. **3** having socially or conventionally acceptable morals, etc.: *a respectable woman.* **4** relatively or fairly good; considerable: *a respectable salary.* **5** fit to be seen by other people; presentable.
▸ re,specta'bility *n* ▸ re'spectably *adv*

respectful (rɪ'spɛktfʊl) *adj* full of, showing, or giving respect.
▸ re'spectfully *adv* ▸ re'spectfulness *n*

respecting (rɪ'spɛktɪŋ) *prep* concerning; regarding.

respective (rɪ'spɛktɪv) *adj* belonging or relating separately to each of several people or things; several: *we took our respective ways home.*
▸ re'spectiveness *n*

respectively (rɪ'spɛktɪvlɪ) *adv* (in listing a number of items or attributes that refer to another list) separately in the order given: *he gave Janet and John a cake and a chocolate respectively.*

Respighi ★ (*Italian* res'pi:gi) *n* **Ottorino** (otto'ri:no). 1879–1936, Italian composer, noted esp. for his operas and ballet music.

respirable ('rɛspɪrəbəl) *adj* **1** able to be breathed. **2** suitable or fit for breathing.
▸ ,respira'bility *n*

respiration (,rɛspɪ'reɪʃən) *n* **1** the process in living organisms of taking in oxygen from the surroundings and giving out carbon dioxide. **2** the chemical breakdown of complex organic substances that takes place in the cells and tissues of animals and plants, during which energy is released and carbon dioxide produced.
▸ respiratory ('rɛspɪrətərɪ, -trɪ) *or* ,respi'rational *adj*

respirator ('rɛspɪ,reɪtə) *n* **1** an apparatus for providing long-term artificial respiration. **2** a device worn over the mouth and nose to prevent inhalation of noxious fumes or to warm cold air before it is breathed.

respiratory failure *n* a condition in which the respiratory system is unable to provide an adequate supply of oxygen or to remove carbon dioxide efficiently.

respiratory quotient *n Biol.* the ratio of the volume of carbon dioxide expired to the volume of oxygen consumed by an organism, tissue, or cell in a given time.

respiratory system *n* the specialized organs, collectively, concerned with external respiration: in humans and other mammals it includes the trachea, bronchi, bronchioles, lungs, and diaphragm.

respire (rɪ'spaɪə) *vb* **respires, respiring, respired.** **1** to inhale and exhale (air); breathe. **2** (*intr*) to undergo the process of respiration. [C14: from L *rēspīrāre* to exhale, from RE- + *spīrāre* to breathe]

respite ('rɛspɪt, -paɪt) *n* **1** a pause from exertion; interval of rest. **2** a temporary delay. **3** a temporary stay of execution; reprieve. ◆ *vb* **respites, respiting, respited.** **4** (*tr*) to grant a respite to; reprieve. [C13: from OF *respit*, from L *respectus* a looking back; see RESPECT]

resplendent (rɪ'splɛndənt) *adj* having a brilliant or splendid appearance. [C15: from L *rēsplendēre*, from RE- + *splendēre* to shine]
▸ re'splendence *or* re'splendency *n* ▸ re'splendently *adv*

respond (rɪ'spɒnd) *vb* **1** to state or utter (something) in reply. **2** (*intr*) to act in reply; react: *to respond by issuing an invitation.* **3** (*intr*; foll. by *to*) to react favourably: *this patient will respond to treatment.* **4** an archaic word for **correspond.** ◆ *n* **5** *Archit.* a pilaster or an engaged column that supports an arch or a lintel. **6** *Christianity.* a choral anthem chanted in response to a lesson read. [C14: from OF *respondre*, from L *rēspondēre* to return like for like, from RE- + *spondēre* to pledge]
▸ re'spondence *or* re'spondency *n* ▸ re'sponder *n*

respondent (rɪ'spɒndənt) *n* **1** *Law.* a person against whom a petition is brought. ◆ *adj* **2** a less common word for **responsive.**

response (rɪ'spɒns) *n* **1** the act of responding; reply or

reaction. **2** *Bridge.* a bid replying to a partner's bid or double. **3** (*usually pl*) *Christianity.* a short sentence or phrase recited or sung in reply to the officiant at a church service. **4** *Electronics.* the ratio of the output to the input level of an electrical device. **5** a glandular, muscular, or electrical reaction that arises from stimulation of the nervous system. [C14: from L *rēsponsum* answer, from *rēspondēre* to RESPOND]
▸ re'sponseless *adj*

responser *or* **responsor** (rɪ'spɒnsə) *n* a radio or radar receiver used to receive and display signals from a transponder.

responsibility (rɪ,spɒnsɪ'bɪlɪtɪ) *n, pl* **responsibilities.** **1** the state or position of being responsible. **2** a person or thing for which one is responsible.

responsible (rɪ'spɒnsɪbəl) *adj* **1** (*postpositive; usually foll. by for*) having control or authority (over). **2** (*postpositive; foll. by to*) being accountable for one's actions and decisions (to): *responsible to one's commanding officer.* **3** (of a position, duty, etc.) involving decision and accountability. **4** (often foll. by *for*) being the agent or cause (of some action): *responsible for a mistake.* **5** able to take rational decisions without supervision; accountable for one's own actions. **6** able to meet financial obligations; of sound credit. [C16: from L *rēsponsus*, from *rēspondēre* to RESPOND]
▸ re'sponsibleness *n* ▸ re'sponsibly *adv*

responsive (rɪ'spɒnsɪv) *adj* **1** reacting or replying quickly or favourably, to a suggestion, initiative, etc. **2** (of an organism) reacting to a stimulus.
▸ re'sponsively *adv* ▸ re'sponsiveness *n*

responsory (rɪ'spɒnsərɪ) *n, pl* **responsories.** an anthem or chant recited or sung after a lesson in a church service. [C15: from LL *rēspōnsōrium*, from L *rēspondēre* to answer]

rest¹ (rest) *n* **1a** relaxation from exertion or labour. **1b** (*as modifier*): *a rest period.* **2** repose; sleep. **3** any relief or refreshment, as from worry. **4** calm; tranquillity. **5** death regarded as repose: *eternal rest.* **6** cessation from motion. **7 at rest. 7a** not moving. **7b** calm. **7c** dead. **7d** asleep. **8** a pause or interval. **9** a mark in a musical score indicating a pause of specific duration. **10** *Prosody.* a pause at the end of a line; caesura. **11** a shelter or lodging: *a seaman's rest.* **12** a thing or place on which to put something for support or to steady it. **13** *Billiards, snooker.* any of various special poles sometimes used as supports for the cue. **14 come to rest.** to slow down and stop. **15 lay to rest.** to bury (a dead person). **16 set (someone's mind) at rest.** to reassure (someone) or settle (someone's mind). ◆ *vb* **17** to take or give rest, as by sleeping, lying down, etc. **18** to place or position (oneself, etc.) for rest or relaxation. **19** (*tr*) to place or position for support or steadying: *to rest one's elbows on the table.* **20** (*intr*) to be at ease; be calm. **21** to cease or cause to cease from motion or exertion. **22** (*intr*) to remain without further attention or action: *let the matter rest.* **23** to direct (one's eyes) or (of one's eyes) to be directed: *her eyes rested on the child.* **24** to depend or cause to depend; base; rely: *the whole argument rests on one crucial fact.* **25** (*intr*; foll. by *with, on, upon*, etc.) to be a responsibility (of): *it rests with us to apportion blame.* **26** *Law.* to finish the introduction of evidence in (a case). **27** to put pastry in a cool place to allow the gluten to contract. **28 rest on one's oars.** to stop doing anything for a time. [OE *ræst, reste*, of Gmc origin]
▸ 'rester *n*

rest² (rest) *n* (usually preceded by *the*) **1** something left or remaining; remainder. **2** the others: *the rest of the world.* ◆ *vb* **3** (*copula*) to continue to be (as specified); remain: *rest assured.* [C15: from OF *rester* to remain, from L *rēstāre*, from RE- + *stāre* to stand]

rest area *n Austral. & NZ.* a motorists' stopping place, usually off a highway, equipped with tables, seats, etc.

restaurant ('rɛstə,rɒŋ, 'rɛstrɒŋ) *n* a commercial establishment where meals are prepared and served to customers. [C19: from F, from *restaurer* to RESTORE]

restaurant car *n Brit.* a railway coach in which meals are served. Also called: **dining car.**

restaurateur (,rɛstərə'tɜː) *n* a person who owns or runs a restaurant. [C18: via F from LL *restaurātor*, from L *restaurāre* to RESTORE]

★ people and places

rest-cure n 1 a rest taken as part of a course of medical treatment, so as to relieve stress, anxiety, etc. 2 an easy time or assignment: usually used with a negative: *it's no rest-cure, I assure you.*

restful ('restful) adj 1 giving or conducive to rest. 2 being at rest; tranquil; calm.
➤ **'restfully** adv ➤ **'restfulness** n

restharrow ('rest,hærəʊ) n any of a genus of Eurasian papilionaceous plants with tough woody stems and roots. [C16: from *rest*, var. of ARREST (to hinder, stop) + HARROW]

resting ('restɪŋ) adj 1 not moving or working; at rest. 2 *Euphemistic.* (of an actor) out of work. 3 (esp. of plant spores) undergoing a period of dormancy before germination.

restitution (,restɪ'tjuːʃən) n 1 the act of giving back something that has been lost or stolen. 2 *Law.* compensating for loss or injury by reverting as far as possible to the original position. 3 the return of an object or system to its original state, esp. after elastic deformation. [C13: from L *restitūtiō*, from *restituere* to rebuild, from RE- + *statuere* to set up]
➤ **,resti'tutive** or ,**resti'tutory** adj

restive ('restɪv) adj 1 restless, nervous, or uneasy. 2 impatient of control or authority. [C16: from OF *restif* balky, from *rester* to remain]
➤ **'restively** adv ➤ **'restiveness** n

restless ('restlɪs) adj 1 unable to stay still or quiet. 2 ceaselessly active or moving: *the restless wind.* 3 worried; anxious; uneasy. 4 not restful; without repose: *a restless night.*
➤ **'restlessly** adv ➤ **'restlessness** n

rest mass n the mass of an object that is at rest relative to an observer. It is the mass used in Newtonian mechanics.

restoration (,restə'reɪʃən) n 1 the act of restoring to a former or original condition, place, etc. 2 the giving back of something lost, stolen, etc. 3 something restored, replaced, or reconstructed. 4 a model or representation of an extinct animal, etc. 5 (*usually cap.*) *Brit. history.* the re-establishment of the monarchy in 1660 or the reign of Charles II (1660–85).

restorative (rɪ'stɒrətɪv) adj 1 tending to revive or renew health, spirits, etc. ♦ n 2 anything that restores or revives, esp. a drug.

restore (rɪ'stɔː) vb **restores, restoring, restored.** (tr) 1 to return (something) to its original or former condition. 2 to bring back to health, good spirits, etc. 3 to return (something lost, stolen, etc.) to its owner. 4 to reintroduce or re-enforce: *to restore discipline.* 5 to reconstruct (an extinct animal, etc.). [C13: from OF, from L *restaurāre* to rebuild, from RE- + *-staurāre*, as in *instaurāre* to renew]
➤ **re'storable** adj ➤ **re'storer** n

restrain (rɪ'streɪn) vb (tr) 1 to hold (someone) back from some action, esp. by force. 2 to deprive (someone) of liberty, as by imprisonment. 3 to limit or restrict. [C14 *restreyne*, from OF *restreindre*, from L *restringere*, from RE- + *stringere* to draw, bind]
➤ **re'strainable** adj ➤ **restrainedly** (rɪ'streɪnɪdlɪ) adv ➤ **re'strainer** n

restraint (rɪ'streɪnt) n 1 the ability to control or moderate one's impulses, passions, etc. 2 the act of restraining or the state of being restrained. 3 something that restrains; restriction. [C15: from OF *restreinte*, from *restreindre* to RESTRAIN]

restraint of trade n action interfering with the freedom to compete in business.

restrict (rɪ'strɪkt) vb (often foll. by *to*) to confine or keep within certain, often specified, limits or selected bounds. [C16: from L *restrictus* bound up, from *restringere*; see RESTRAIN]

restricted (rɪ'strɪktɪd) adj 1 limited or confined. 2 not accessible to the general public or (*esp. US*) out of bounds to military personnel. 3 *Brit.* denoting a zone in which a speed limit or waiting restrictions for vehicles apply.
➤ **re'strictedly** adv ➤ **re'strictedness** n

restriction (rɪ'strɪkʃən) n 1 something that restricts; a re-

strictive measure, law, etc. 2 the act of restricting or the state of being restricted.
➤ **re'strictionist** n, adj

restrictive (rɪ'strɪktɪv) adj 1 restricting or tending to restrict. 2 *Grammar.* denoting a relative clause or phrase that restricts the number of possible referents of its antecedent. The relative clause in *Americans who live in New York* is restrictive; the relative clause in *Americans, who are generally extrovert,* is nonrestrictive.
➤ **re'strictively** adv ➤ **re'strictiveness** n

restrictive practice n *Brit.* 1 a trading agreement against the public interest. 2 a practice of a union or other group tending to limit the freedom of other workers or employers.

rest room n a room in a public building with toilets, washbasins, and, sometimes, couches.

restructure (riː'strʌktʃə) vb (tr) to organize (a system, business, society, etc.) in a different way: *radical attempts to restructure the economy.*
➤ **re'structuring** n

result (rɪ'zʌlt) n 1 something that ensues from an action, policy, etc.; outcome; consequence. 2 a number, quantity, or value obtained by solving a mathematical problem. 3 *US.* a decision of a legislative body. 4 (*often pl*) the final score or outcome of a sporting contest. 5 a favourable result, esp. a victory or success. ♦ vb (intr) 6 (often foll. by *from*) to be the outcome or consequence (of). 7 (foll. by *in*) to issue or terminate (in a specified way, etc.); end: *to result in tragedy.* [C15: from L *resultāre* to rebound, spring from, from RE- + *saltāre* to leap]

resultant (rɪ'zʌltənt) adj 1 that results; resulting. ♦ n 2 *Maths, physics.* a single vector that is the vector sum of two or more other vectors.

resume (rɪ'zjuːm) vb **resumes, resuming, resumed.** 1 to begin again or go on with (something interrupted). 2 (tr) to occupy again, take back, or recover: *to resume one's seat; resume the presidency.* 3 *Arch.* to summarize; make a résumé of. [C15: from L *resūmere*, from RE- + *sūmere* to take up]
➤ **re'sumable** adj ➤ **re'sumer** n

résumé ('rezjʊ,meɪ) n 1 a short descriptive summary, as of events, etc. 2 *US & Canad.* another name for **curriculum vitae.** [C19: from F, from *résumer* to RESUME]

resumption (rɪ'zʌmpʃən) n the act of resuming or beginning again. [C15: via OF from LL *resumptiō*, from L *resūmere* to RESUME]
➤ **re'sumptive** adj ➤ **re'sumptively** adv

resupinate (rɪ'sjuːpɪnɪt) adj *Bot.* (of plant parts) reversed or inverted in position, so as to appear to be upside down. [C18: from L *resupinātus* bent back, from *resupīnāre*, from RE- + *supīnāre* to place on the back]
➤ **re,supi'nation** n

resurge (rɪ'sɜːdʒ) vb **resurges, resurging, resurged.** (intr) *Rare.* to rise again as if from the dead. [C16: from L *resurgere* to rise again, reappear, from RE- + *surgere* to lift, arise]

resurgent (rɪ'sɜːdʒənt) adj rising again, as to new life, vigour, etc.: *resurgent nationalism.*
➤ **re'surgence** n

resurrect (,rezə'rekt) vb 1 to rise or raise from the dead; bring or be brought back to life. 2 (tr) to bring back into use or activity; revive. 3 (tr) *Facetious.* (formerly) to exhume and steal (a body) from its grave.

resurrection (,rezə'rekʃən) n 1 a supposed act or instance of a dead person coming back to life. 2 belief in the possibility of this as part of a religious or mystical system. 3 the condition of those who have risen from the dead: *we shall all live in the resurrection.* 4 (*usually cap.*) *Christian theol.* the rising again of Christ from the tomb three days after his death. 5 (*usually cap.*) the rising again from the dead of all men at the Last Judgment. [C13: via OF from LL *resurrectiō*, from L *resurgere* to rise again]
➤ **,resur'rectional** or ,**resur'rectionary** adj

resurrectionism (,rezə'rekʃə,nɪzəm) n belief that men will rise again from the dead, esp. according to Christian doctrine.

resurrectionist (,rezə'rekʃənɪst) n 1 *Facetious.* (formerly) a body snatcher. 2 a person who believes in the Resurrection.

★ people and places

resurrection plant *n* any of several unrelated desert plants that form a tight ball when dry and unfold and bloom when moistened.

resuscitate (rɪ'sʌsɪˌteɪt) *vb* **resuscitates, resuscitating, resuscitated.** (*tr*) to restore to consciousness; revive. [C16: from L *resuscitāre*, from RE- + *suscitāre* to raise, from *sub*- up from below + *citāre* to rouse, from *citus* quick]
▸ re,susci'tation *n* ▸ re'suscitative *adj* ▸ re'susci,tator *n*

ret (rɛt) *vb* **rets, retting, retted.** (*tr*) to moisten or soak (flax, hemp, etc.) in order to separate the fibres from the woody tissue by beating. [C15: of Gmc origin]

ret. *abbrev. for:* **1** retain. **2** retired. **3** return(ed).

retable (rɪ'teɪbʰl) *n* an ornamental screenlike structure above and behind an altar. [C19: from F, from Sp. *retablo*, from L *retrō* behind + *tabula* board]

retail ('riːteɪl) *n* **1** the sale of goods individually or in small quantities to consumers. Cf. **wholesale.** ◆ *adj* **2** of, relating to, or engaged in such selling: *retail prices.* ◆ *adv* **3** in small amounts or at a retail price. ◆ *vb* **4** to sell or be sold in small quantities to consumers. **5** (rɪ'teɪl). (*tr*) to relate (gossip, scandal, etc.) in detail. [C14: from OF *retaillier*, from RE- + *taillier* to cut; see TAILOR]
▸ 'retailer *n*

retail price index *n* a measure of the changes in the average level of retail prices of selected goods, usually on a monthly basis. Abbrev.: **RPI.**

retain (rɪ'teɪn) *vb* (*tr*) **1** to keep in one's possession. **2** to be able to hold or contain: *soil that retains water.* **3** (of a person) to be able to remember (information, etc.) without difficulty. **4** to hold in position. **5** to keep for one's future use, as by paying a retainer or nominal charge. **6** *Law.* to engage the services of (a barrister) by payment of a preliminary fee. [C14: from OF *retenir*, from L *retinēre* to hold back, from RE- + *tenēre* to hold]
▸ re'tainable *adj* ▸ re'tainment *n*

retained object *n Grammar.* a direct or indirect object of a passive verb. The phrase *the drawings* in *she was given the drawings* is a retained object.

retainer (rɪ'teɪnə) *n* **1** *History.* a supporter or dependant of a person of rank. **2** a servant, esp. one who has been with a family for a long time. **3** a clip, frame, or similar device that prevents a part of a machine, etc., from moving. **4** a fee paid in advance to secure first option on the services of a barrister, jockey, etc. **5** a reduced rent paid for a flat, etc., to reserve it for future use.

retaining wall *n* a wall constructed to hold back earth, loose rock, etc. Also called: **revetment.**

retake *vb* (riː'teɪk), **retakes, retaking, retook, retaken.** (*tr*) **1** to take back or capture again: *to retake a fortress.* **2** *Films.* to shoot (a scene) again. **3** to tape (a recording) again. ◆ *n* ('riːˌteɪk). **4** *Films.* a rephotographed scene. **5** a retaped recording.
▸ re'taker *n*

retaliate (rɪ'tælɪˌeɪt) *vb* **retaliates, retaliating, retaliated.** (*intr*) **1** to take retributory action, esp. by returning some injury or wrong in kind. **2** to cast (accusations) back upon a person. [C17: from LL *retāliāre*, from L RE- + *tālis* of such kind]
▸ re,tali'ation *n* ▸ re'taliative *or* re'taliatory *adj*

retard (rɪ'tɑːd) *vb* (*tr*) to delay or slow down (the progress or speed) of (something). [C15: from OF *retarder*, from L *retardāre*, from RE- + *tardāre* to make slow, from *tardus* sluggish]

retardant (rɪ'tɑːdʰnt) *n* **1** a substance that reduces the rate of a chemical reaction. ◆ *adj* **2** having a slowing effect.

retardation (ˌriːtɑːˈdeɪʃən) *or* **retardment** (rɪ'tɑːdmənt) *n* **1** the act of retarding or the state of being retarded. **2** something that retards.
▸ re'tardative *or* re'tardatory *adj*

retarded (rɪ'tɑːdɪd) *adj* underdeveloped, usually mentally and esp. having an IQ of 70 to 85.

retarder (rɪ'tɑːdə) *n* **1** a person or thing that retards. **2** a substance added to slow down the rate of a chemical change, such as one added to cement to delay its setting.

retch (rɛtʃ, riːtʃ) *vb* **1** (*intr*) to undergo an involuntary spasm of ineffectual vomiting. ◆ *n* **2** an involuntary spasm of ineffectual vomiting. [OE *hræcan*; rel. to ON *hrækja* to spit]

retd *abbrev. for:* **1** retired. **2** retained. **3** returned.

rete ('riːtɪ) *n, pl* **retia** ('riːʃɪə, -tɪə). *Anat.* any network of nerves or blood vessels; plexus. [C14 (referring to a metal network used with an astrolabe): from L *rēte* net]
▸ retial ('riːʃɪəl) *adj*

retention (rɪ'tɛnʃən) *n* **1** the act of retaining or state of being retained. **2** the capacity to hold or retain liquid, etc. **3** the capacity to remember. **4** *Pathol.* the abnormal holding within the body of urine, faeces, etc. **5** *Commerce.* a sum of money owed to a contractor but not paid for an agreed period as a safeguard against the appearance of any faults. **6** (*pl*) *Account.* profits earned by a company but not distributed as dividends; retained earnings. [C14: from L *retentiō*, from *retinēre* to RETAIN]

retentive (rɪ'tɛntɪv) *adj* having the capacity to retain or remember.
▸ re'tentively *adv* ▸ re'tentiveness *n*

Réti ★ ('reɪtɪ) *n* Richard. 1889–1929, Hungarian chess player.

retiarius (ˌriːtɪ'ɛərɪəs, ˌriːʃɪ-) *n, pl* **retiarii** (-'ɛərɪˌaɪ). (in ancient Rome) a gladiator armed with a net and trident. [L, from *rēte* net]

reticent ('rɛtɪsənt) *adj* not communicative; not saying all that one knows; taciturn; reserved. [C19: from L *reticēre* to keep silent, from RE- + *tacēre* to be silent]
▸ 'reticence *n* ▸ 'reticently *adv*

reticle ('rɛtɪkʰl) *or* (*less commonly*) **reticule** *n* a network of fine lines, wires, etc., placed in the focal plane of an optical instrument. [C17: from L *rēticulum* a little net, from *rēte* net]

reticulate *adj* (rɪ'tɪkjʊlɪt) *also* **reticular.** **1** in the form of a network or having a network of parts: *a reticulate leaf.* ◆ *vb* (rɪ'tɪkjʊˌleɪt), **reticulates, reticulating, reticulated.** **2** to form or be formed into a net. [C17: from LL *rēticulātus* made like a net]
▸ re'ticulately *adv* ▸ re,ticu'lation *n*

reticule ('rɛtɪˌkjuːl) *n* **1** (formerly) a woman's small bag or purse, usually with a drawstring and made of net, beading, brocade, etc. **2** a less common variant of **reticle.** [C18: from F *réticule*, from L *rēticulum* RETICLE]

reticulum (rɪ'tɪkjʊləm) *n, pl* **reticula** (-lə). **1** any fine network, esp. one in the body composed of cells, fibres, etc. **2** the second compartment of the stomach of ruminants. [C17: from L: little net, from *rēte* net]

retiform ('riːtɪˌfɔːm, 'rɛt-) *adj Rare.* netlike; reticulate. [C17: from L *rēte* net + *forma* shape]

retina ('rɛtɪnə) *n, pl* **retinas** *or* **retinae** (-ˌniː). the light-sensitive membrane forming the inner lining of the posterior wall of the eyeball. [C14: from Med. L, ?from L *rēte* net]
▸ 'retinal *adj*

retinene ('rɛtɪˌniːn) *n* a yellow pigment, the aldehyde of vitamin A, that is involved in the formation of rhodopsin. [C20: from RETINA + -ENE]

retinitis (ˌrɛtɪ'naɪtɪs) *n* inflammation of the retina. [C20: from NL, from RETINA + -ITIS]

retinoscopy (ˌrɛtɪ'nɒskəpɪ) *n Ophthalmol.* a procedure for detecting errors of refraction in the eye by means of an instrument (**retinoscope**) that reflects a beam of light from a mirror into the eye.
▸ retinoscopic (ˌrɛtɪnə'skɒpɪk) *adj* ▸ ˌretino'scopically *adv* ▸ ˌreti'noscopist *n*

retinue ('rɛtɪˌnjuː) *n* a body of aides and retainers attending an important person. [C14: from OF *retenue*, from *retenir* to RETAIN]

retiral (rɪ'taɪərʰl) *n esp. Scot.* the act of retiring; retirement.

retire (rɪ'taɪə) *vb* **retires, retiring, retired.** (*mainly intr*) **1** (*also tr*) to give up or to cause (a person) to give up his work, esp. on reaching pensionable age. **2** to go away, as into seclusion, for recuperation, etc. **3** (*also tr*) to go to bed. **4** to recede or disappear: *the sun retired behind the clouds.* **5** to withdraw from a sporting contest, esp. because of injury. **6** (*also tr*) to pull back (troops, etc.) from battle or (of troops, etc.) to fall back. **7** (*tr*) to remove (money,

★ **people and places**

bonds, shares, etc.) from circulation. [C16: from F *retirer*, from OF RE- + *tirer* to pull, draw]
▶ **re'tired** *adj* ▶ **re'tirement** *n* ▶ **re'tirer** *n*

retirement pension *n Brit.* a weekly payment made by the government to a retired man over 65 or a woman over 60.

retirement relief *n* (in Britain) relief from capital-gains tax given to persons over 60 when disposing of business assets.

retiring (rɪˈtaɪərɪŋ) *adj* shunning contact with others; shy; reserved.
▶ **re'tiringly** *adv*

retool (riːˈtuːl) *vb* 1 to replace, re-equip, or rearrange the tools in (a factory, etc.). 2 (*tr*) *Chiefly US & Canad.* to revise or reorganize.

retort[1] (rɪˈtɔːt) *vb* 1 (when *tr*, takes a clause as object) to utter (something) quickly, wittily, or angrily, in response. 2 to use (an argument) against its originator. ◆ *n* 3 a sharp, angry, or witty reply. 4 an argument used against its originator. [C16: from L *retorquēre*, from RE- + *torquēre* to twist, wrench]
▶ **re'torter** *n*

retort[2] (rɪˈtɔːt) *n* 1 a glass vessel with a long tapering neck that is bent down, used for distillation. 2 a vessel used for heating ores in the production of metals or heating coal to produce gas. ◆ *vb* 3 (*tr*) to heat in a retort. [C17: from F *retorte*, from Med. L *retorta*, from L *retorquēre* to twist back; see RETORT[1]]

retouch (riːˈtʌtʃ) *vb* (*tr*) 1 to restore, correct, or improve (a painting, make-up, etc.) with new touches. 2 *Photog.* to alter (a negative or print) by painting over blemishes or adding details. ◆ *n* 3 the art or practice of retouching. 4 a detail that is the result of retouching. 5 a photograph, painting, etc., that has been retouched.
▶ **re'toucher** *n*

retrace (rɪˈtreɪs) *vb* **retraces, retracing, retraced.** (*tr*) 1 to go back over (one's steps, a route, etc.) again. 2 to go over (a past event) in the mind; recall. 3 to go over (a story, account, etc.) from the beginning.

re-trace (riːˈtreɪs) *vb* **re-traces, re-tracing, re-traced.** (*tr*) to trace (a map, etc.) again.

retract (rɪˈtrækt) *vb* 1 (*tr*) to draw in (a part or appendage): *a snail can retract its horns; to retract the landing gear of an aircraft.* 2 to withdraw (a statement, opinion, charge, etc.) as invalid or unjustified. 3 to go back on (a promise or agreement). [C16: from L *retractāre* to withdraw, from *tractāre*, from *trahere* to drag]
▶ **re'tractable** *or* **re'tractible** *adj* ▶ **re'traction** *n* ▶ **re-'tractive** *adj*

retractile (rɪˈtræktaɪl) *adj* capable of being drawn in: *the retractile claws of a cat.*
▶ **retractility** (ˌriːtrækˈtɪlɪtɪ) *n*

retractor (rɪˈtræktə) *n* 1 *Anat.* any of various muscles that retract an organ or part. 2 *Surgery.* an instrument for holding back an organ or part. 3 a person or thing that retracts.

retral (ˈriːtrəl, ˈretrəl) *adj Rare.* at, near, or towards the back. [C19: from L *retrō* backwards]
▶ **'retrally** *adv*

retread *vb* (riːˈtred) **retreads, retreading, retreaded.** 1 (*tr*) another word for **remould** (sense 2). ◆ *n* (ˈriːˌtred). 2 another word for **remould** (sense 3). 3 *NZ sl.* a pensioner who has resumed employment, esp. in the same profession as formerly.

re-tread (riːˈtred) *vb* **re-treads, re-treading, re-trod, re-trodden** *or* **re-trod.** (*tr*) to tread (one's steps, etc.) again.

retreat (rɪˈtriːt) *vb* (mainly intr) 1 *Mil.* to withdraw or retire in the face of or from action with an enemy. 2 to retire or withdraw, as to seclusion or shelter. 3 (of a person's features) to slope back; recede. 4 (*tr*) *Chess.* to move (a piece) back. ◆ *n* 5 the act of retreating or withdrawing. 6 *Mil.* 6a a withdrawal or retirement in the face of the enemy. 6b a bugle call signifying retirement or withdrawal. 7 retirement or seclusion. 8 a place to which one may retire for religious contemplation. 9 a period of seclusion, esp. for religious contemplation. 10 an institution for the care and treatment of the mentally ill, infirm, elderly,

etc. [C14: from OF *retret*, from *retraire* to withdraw, from L *retrahere* to pull back]

retrench (rɪˈtrentʃ) *vb* 1 to reduce (costs); economize. 2 (*tr*) to shorten, delete, or abridge. [C17: from OF *retrenchier*, from RE- + *trenchier* to cut, from L *truncāre* to lop]
▶ **re'trenchment** *n*

retribution (ˌretrɪˈbjuːʃən) *n* 1 the act of punishing or taking vengeance for wrongdoing, sin, or injury. 2 punishment or vengeance. [C14: via OF from Church L *retribūtiō*, from L *retribuere*, from RE- + *tribuere* to pay]
▶ **retributive** (rɪˈtrɪbjutɪv) *adj* ▶ **re'tributively** *adv*

retrieval (rɪˈtriːvəl) *n* 1 the act or process of retrieving. 2 the possibility of recovery, restoration, or rectification. 3 a computer operation that recalls data from a file.

retrieve (rɪˈtriːv) *vb* **retrieves, retrieving, retrieved.** (mainly tr) 1 to get or fetch back again; recover. 2 to bring back to a more satisfactory state; revive. 3 to rescue or save. 4 to recover or make newly available (stored information) from a computer system. 5 (*also intr*) (of dogs) to find and fetch (shot game, etc.). 6 *Tennis, etc.* to return successfully (a shot difficult to reach). 7 to recall; remember. ◆ *n* 8 the act of retrieving. 9 the chance of being retrieved. [C14: from OF *retrover*, from RE- + *trouver* to find, ?from Vulgar L *tropāre* (unattested) to compose]
▶ **re'trievable** *adj*

retriever (rɪˈtriːvə) *n* 1 one of a breed of large dogs that can be trained to retrieve game. 2 any dog used to retrieve shot game. 3 a person or thing that retrieves.

retro (ˈretrəʊ) *n, pl* **retros.** 1 short for **retrorocket.** ◆ *adj* 2 denoting something associated with or revived from the past: *retro fashion.*

retro- *prefix* 1 back or backwards: *retroactive.* 2 located behind: *retrochoir.* [from L *retrō* behind, backwards]

retroact (ˌretrəʊˈækt) *vb* (*intr*) 1 to act in opposition. 2 to influence or have reference to past events.
▶ **retro'action** *n*

retroactive (ˌretrəʊˈæktɪv) *adj* 1 applying or referring to the past: *retroactive legislation.* 2 effective from a date or for a period in the past.
▶ **retro'actively** *adv* ▶ **retroac'tivity** *n*

retrocede (ˌretrəʊˈsiːd) *vb* **retrocedes, retroceding, retroceded.** 1 (*tr*) to give back; return. 2 (*intr*) to go back; recede.
▶ **retrocession** (ˌretrəʊˈseʃən) *or* **retro'cedence** *n* ▶ **retro'cessive** *or* **retro'cedent** *adj*

retrochoir (ˈretrəʊˌkwaɪə) *n* the space in a large church or cathedral behind the high altar.

retrofire (ˈretrəʊˌfaɪə) *n* 1 the act of firing a retrorocket. 2 the moment at which it is fired.

retrofit (ˈretrəʊˌfɪt) *vb* **retrofits, retrofitting, retrofitted.** (*tr*) to equip (a vehicle, piece of equipment, etc.) with new parts, safety devices, etc., after manufacture.

retroflex (ˈretrəʊˌfleks) *or* **retroflexed** *adj* 1 bent or curved backwards. 2 *Phonetics.* of or involving retroflexion. [C18: from L *retrōflexus*, from *retrōflectere*, from RETRO- + *flectere* to bend]

retroflexion *or* **retroflection** (ˌretrəʊˈflekʃən) *n* 1 the act or condition of bending or being bent backwards. 2 the act of turning the tip of the tongue upwards and backwards in the articulation of a vowel or a consonant.

retrograde (ˈretrəʊˌgreɪd) *adj* 1 moving or bending backwards. 2 (esp. of order) reverse or inverse. 3 tending towards an earlier worse condition; declining or deteriorating. 4 *Astron.* 4a occurring or orbiting in a direction opposite to that of the earth's motion around the sun. Cf. **direct** (sense 18). 4b occurring or orbiting in a direction around a planet opposite to the planet's rotational direction. 4c appearing to move in a clockwise direction due to the rotational period exceeding the period of revolution around the sun: *Venus has retrograde rotation.* ◆ *vb* **retrogrades, retrograding, retrograded.** (*intr*) 5 to move in a retrograde direction; retrogress. [C14: from L *retrōgradī*, from *gradi* to walk, go]
▶ **retrogra'dation** *n* ▶ **retro'gradely** *adv*

retrogress (ˌretrəʊˈgres) *vb* (*intr*) 1 to go back to an earlier, esp. worse, condition; degenerate or deteriorate. 2

to move backwards; recede. [C19: from L *retrōgressus* having moved backwards; see RETROGRADE]
► ‚retro'gression *n* ► ‚retro'gressive *adj* ► ‚retro-'gressively *adv*

retrorocket ('rɛtrəʊ‚rɒkɪt) *n* a small auxiliary rocket engine on a larger rocket, missile, or spacecraft, that produces thrust in the opposite direction to the direction of flight in order to decelerate. Often shortened to **retro**.

retrorse (rɪ'trɔːs) *adj* (esp. of plant parts) pointing backwards. [C19: from L *retrōrsus*, from *retrōversus* turned back, from RETRO- + *vertere* to turn]
► re'trorsely *adv*

retrospect ('rɛtrəʊ‚spɛkt) *n* the act of surveying things past (often in **in retrospect**). [C17: from L *retrōspicere* to look back, from RETRO- + *specere* to look]
► ‚retro'spection *n*

retrospective (‚rɛtrəʊ'spɛktɪv) *adj* **1** looking or directed backwards, esp. in time; characterized by retrospection. **2** applying to the past; retroactive. ♦ *n* **3** an exhibition of an artist's life's work.
► ‚retro'spectively *adv*

retroussé (rə'truːseɪ) *adj* (of a nose) turned up. [C19: from F *retrousser* to tuck up]

retroversion (‚rɛtrəʊ'vɜːʃən) *n* **1** the act of turning or condition of being turned backwards. **2** the condition of a part or organ, esp. the uterus, that is turned backwards.
► 'retro‚verted *adj*

Retrovir ('rɛtrəʊ‚vɪə) *n Trademark.* the brand name for AZT.

retrovirus ('rɛtrəʊ‚vaɪrəs) *n* any of several viruses that are able to reverse the normal flow of genetic information from DNA to RNA by transcribing RNA into DNA: many retroviruses are known to cause cancer in animals.
► 'retro‚viral *adj*

retsina (rɛt'siːnə) *n* a Greek wine flavoured with resin. [Mod. Gk, from It. *resina* RESIN]

retune (riː'tjuːn) *vb* **retunes, retuning, retuned.** (*tr*) **1** to tune (a musical instrument) differently or again. **2** to tune (a radio, television, etc.) to another frequency.

return (rɪ'tɜːn) *vb* **1** (*intr*) to come back to a former place or state. **2** (*tr*) to give, take, or carry back; replace or restore. **3** (*tr*) to repay or recompense, esp. with something of equivalent value: *return the compliment.* **4** (*tr*) to earn or yield (profit or interest) as an income from an investment or venture. **5** (*intr*) to come back or revert in thought or speech: *I'll return to that later.* **6** (*intr*) to recur or reappear: *the symptoms have returned.* **7** to answer or reply. **8** (*tr*) to vote into office; elect. **9** (*tr*) *Law.* (of a jury) to deliver or render (a verdict). **10** (*tr*) to submit (a report, etc.) about (someone or something) to someone in authority. **11** (*tr*) *Cards.* to lead back (the suit led by one's partner). **12** (*tr*) *Ball games.* to hit, throw, or play (a ball) back. **13 return thanks.** (of Christians) to say grace before a meal. ♦ *n* **14** the act or an instance of coming back. **15** something that is given or sent back, esp. unsatisfactory merchandise or a theatre ticket for resale. **16** the act or an instance of putting, sending, or carrying back; replacement or restoration. **17** (*often pl*) the yield or profit from an investment or venture. **18** the act or an instance of reciprocation or repayment (esp. in **in return for**). **19** a recurrence or reappearance. **20** an official report, esp. of the financial condition of a company. **21a** a form (a **tax return**) on which a statement of one's taxable income is made. **21b** the statement itself. **22** (*often pl*) a statement of the votes counted at an election. **23** an answer or reply. **24** *Brit.* short for **return ticket**. **25** *Archit.* a part of a building that forms an angle with the façade. **26** *Law.* a report by a bailiff or other officer on the outcome of a formal document such as a writ, summons, etc. **27** *Cards.* a lead of a card in the suit that one's partner has previously led. **28** *Ball games.* the act of playing or throwing a ball, etc., back. **29 by return (of post).** *Brit.* by the next post back to the sender. **30 many happy returns (of the day).** a conventional birthday greeting. ♦ *adj* **31** of, relating to, or characterized by a return: *a return visit.* **32** denoting a second, reciprocal occasion: *a return match.* [C14: from OF *retorner*; see RE-, TURN]
► re'turnable *adj*

return crease *n Cricket.* one of two lines marked at

right-angles to each bowling crease, from inside which a bowler must deliver the ball.

returned soldier *n Austral. & NZ.* a soldier who has served abroad. Also (Austral. and Canad.): **returned man.**

returner (rɪ'tɜːnə) *n* **1** a person or thing that returns. **2** a person who goes back to work after a break, esp. a woman who has had children.

returning officer *n* (in Britain, Canada, Australia, etc.) an official in charge of conducting an election in a constituency, etc.

return ticket *n Brit., Austral., & NZ.* a ticket entitling a passenger to travel to his destination and back.

retuse (rɪ'tjuːs) *adj Bot.* having a rounded apex and a central depression. [C18: from L *retundere* to make blunt, from RE- + *tundere* to pound]

Retz ★ (*French* rɛ) *n* **Gilles de.** See (Gilles de) **Rais.**

Reuben ★ ('ruːbɪn) *n Old Testament.* **1** the eldest son of Jacob and Leah: one of the 12 patriarchs of Israel (Genesis 29:30). **2** the Israelite tribe descended from him. **3** the territory of this tribe, lying to the northeast of the Dead Sea. Douay spelling: **Ruben.**

reunify (riː'juːnɪ‚faɪ) *vb* **reunifies, reunifying, reunified.** (*tr*) to bring together again (something, esp. a country previously divided).
► ‚reunifi'cation *n*

reunion (riː'juːnjən) *n* **1** the act of coming together again. **2** the state or condition of having been brought together again. **3** a gathering of relatives, friends, or former associates.

Réunion ★ (riː'juːnjən; *French* reynjɔ̃) *n* an island in the Indian Ocean, in the Mascarene Islands: an overseas region of France, having been in French possession since 1642. Capital: Saint-Denis. Pop.: 681 000 (1997). Area: 2510 sq. km (970 sq. miles).

reunite (riː‚juː'naɪt) *vb* **reunites, reuniting, reunited.** to bring or come together again.
► ‚reu'nitable *adj*

Reus ★ (*Spanish* rɛus) *n* a city in NE Spain, northwest of Tarragona: became commercially important after the establishment of an English colony (about 1750). Pop.: 86 864 (1991).

Reuter ★ ('rɔɪtə) *n* Baron **Paul Julius von** (paul 'juːliʊs fɔn). original name *Israel Beer Josaphat.* 1816–99, German telegrapher, who founded a news agency in London (1851).

Reutlingen ★ (*German* 'rɔʏtlɪŋən) *n* a city in SW Germany, in Baden-Württemberg: founded in the 11th century; an Imperial free city from 1240 until 1802; textile industry. Pop.: 106 000 (1991).

rev (rɛv) *Inf.* ♦ *n* **1** revolution per minute. ♦ *vb* **revs, revving, revved. 2** (often foll. by *up*) to increase the speed of revolution of (an engine).

rev. *abbrev. for:* **1** revenue. **2** reverse(d). **3** review. **4** revise(d). **5** revision. **6** revolution. **7** revolving.

Rev. *abbrev. for:* **1** *Bible.* Revelation (of Saint John the Divine). **2** Reverend.

Reval ★ ('reːval) *n* the German name for **Tallinn.**

revalue (riː'væljuː) *or US* **revaluate** *vb* **revalues, revaluing, revalued** *or US* **revaluates, revaluating, revaluated. 1** to adjust the exchange value of (a currency), esp. upwards. Cf. **devalue. 2** (*tr*) to make a fresh valuation of.
► re‚valu'ation *n*

revamp (riː'væmp) *vb* (*tr*) **1** to patch up or renovate; repair or restore. ♦ *n* **2** something that has been renovated or revamped. **3** the act or process of revamping. [C19: from RE- + VAMP²]

revanchism (rɪ'væntʃɪzəm) *n* **1** a foreign policy aimed at revenge or the regaining of lost territories. **2** support for such a policy. [C20: from F *revanche* REVENGE]
► re'vanchist *n, adj*

rev counter *n Brit.* an informal name for **tachometer.**

Revd *abbrev. for* Reverend.

reveal (rɪ'viːl) *vb* (*tr*) **1** (*may take a clause as object or an infinitive*) to disclose (a secret); divulge. **2** to expose to view or show (something concealed). **3** (of God) to disclose (divine truths). ♦ *n* **4** *Archit.* the vertical side of an open-

ing in a wall, esp. the side of a window or door between the frame and the front of the wall. [C14: from OF *reveler*, from L *revēlāre* to unveil, from RE- + *vēlum* a VEIL]
▶ re'vealable *adj* ▶ re'vealer *n* ▶ re'vealment *n*

revealed religion *n* **1** religion based on the revelation by God to man of ideas that he would not have arrived at by reason alone. **2** religion in which the existence of God depends on revelation.

revealing (rɪ'viːlɪŋ) *adj* **1** of significance or import: *a very revealing experience.* **2** showing more of the body than is usual: *a revealing costume.*
▶ re'vealingly *adv*

reveille (rɪ'vælɪ) *n* **1** a signal, given by a bugle, drum, etc., to awaken soldiers or sailors in the morning. **2** the hour at which this takes place. [C17: from F *réveillez!* awake! from RE- + OF *esveillier* to be wakeful, ult. from L *vigilāre* to keep watch]

revel ('rɛv°l) *vb* **revels, revelling, revelled** or *US* **revels, reveling, reveled.** (intr) **1** (foll. by *in*) to take pleasure or wallow: *to revel in success.* **2** to take part in noisy festivities; make merry. ◆ *n* **3** (*often pl*) an occasion of noisy merrymaking. [C14: from OF *reveler* to be merry, noisy, from L *rebellāre* to revolt]
▶ 'reveller *n*

revelation (,rɛvə'leɪʃən) *n* **1** the act or process of disclosing something previously secret or obscure, esp. something true. **2** a fact disclosed or revealed, esp. in a dramatic or surprising way. **3** *Christianity.* God's disclosure of his own nature and his purpose for mankind. [C14: from Church L *revēlātiō*, from L *revēlāre* to REVEAL]
▶ ,reve'lational or ,reve'latory *adj*

Revelation (,rɛvə'leɪʃən) *n* (*popularly, often pl*) the last book of the New Testament, containing visionary descriptions of heaven, and of the end of the world. Also called: the **Apocalypse**, the **Revelation of Saint John the Divine.**

revelationist (,rɛvə'leɪʃənɪst) *n* a person who believes that God has revealed certain truths to man.

revelry ('rɛv°lrɪ) *n, pl* **revelries.** noisy or unrestrained merrymaking.

revenant ('rɛvɪnənt) *n* something, esp. a ghost, that returns. [C19: from F: ghost, from *revenir*, from L *revenīre*, from RE- + *venīre* to come]

revenge (rɪ'vɛndʒ) *n* **1** the act of retaliating for wrongs or injury received; vengeance. **2** something done as a means of vengeance. **3** the desire to take vengeance. **4** a return match, regarded as a loser's opportunity to even the score. ◆ *vb* **revenges, revenging, revenged.** (*tr*) **5** to inflict equivalent injury or damage for (injury received). **6** to take vengeance for (oneself or another); avenge. [C14: from OF *revenger*, from LL *revindicāre*, from RE- + *vindicāre* to VINDICATE]
▶ re'venger *n* ▶ re'venging *adj* ▶ re'vengingly *adv*

revengeful (rɪ'vɛndʒful) *adj* full of or characterized by desire for vengeance; vindictive.
▶ re'vengefully *adv* ▶ re'vengefulness *n*

revenue ('rɛvɪ,njuː) *n* **1** the income accruing from taxation to a government. **2a** a government department responsible for the collection of government revenue. **2b** (*as modifier*): *revenue men.* **3** the gross income from a business enterprise, investment, etc. **4** a particular item of income. **5** a source of income. [C16: from OF, from *revenir* to return, from L *revenīre*; see REVENANT]

revenue cutter *n* a small lightly armed boat used to enforce customs regulations and catch smugglers.

reverb (rɪ'vɜːb) *n* an electronic device that creates artificial acoustics.

reverberate (rɪ'vɜːbə,reɪt) *vb* **reverberates, reverberating, reverberated.** **1** (*intr*) to resound or re-echo. **2** to reflect or be reflected many times. **3** (*intr*) to rebound or recoil. **4** (*intr*) (of the flame or heat in a reverberatory furnace) to be deflected onto the metal or ore on the hearth. **5** (*tr*) to heat, melt, or refine (a metal or ore) in a reverberatory furnace. [C16: from L *reverberāre*, from RE- + *verberāre* to beat, from *verber* a lash]
▶ re'verberantly *adv* ▶ re,verber'ation *n* ▶ re'verberative *adj* ▶ re'verbe,rator *n* ▶ re'verberatory *adj*

reverberation time *n* a measure of the acoustic prop-

erties of a room, equal to the time taken for a sound to fall in intensity by 60 decibels. It is usually measured in seconds.

reverberatory furnace *n* a metallurgical furnace having a curved roof that deflects heat onto the charge so that the fuel is not in direct contact with the ore.

revere (rɪ'vɪə) *vb* **reveres, revering, revered.** (*tr*) to be in awe of and respect deeply; venerate. [C17: from L *reverērī*, from RE- + *verērī* to fear, be in awe of]

Revere ★ (rɪ'vɪə) *n* Paul. 1735–1818, American patriot and silversmith, known for his night ride on April 18, 1775, to warn the Massachusetts colonists that British troops were coming.

reverence ('rɛvərəns) *n* **1** a feeling or attitude of profound respect, usually reserved for the sacred or divine. **2** an outward manifestation of this feeling, esp. a bow or act of obeisance. **3** the state of being revered or commanding profound respect. ◆ *vb* **reverences, reverencing, reverenced.** **4** (*tr*) to revere or venerate.

Reverence ('rɛvərəns) *n* (preceded by *Your* or *His*) a title sometimes used to address or refer to a Roman Catholic priest.

reverend ('rɛvərənd) *adj* **1** worthy of reverence. **2** relating to or designating a clergyman. ◆ *n* **3** *Inf.* a clergyman. [C15: from L *reverendus* fit to be revered]

Reverend ('rɛvərənd) *adj* a title of respect for a clergyman. Abbrev.: **Rev., Revd.**

USAGE NOTE *Reverend* with a surname alone (*Reverend Smith*), as a term of address (*"Yes, Reverend"*), or in the salutation of a letter (*Dear Rev. Mr Smith*) are all generally considered to be wrong usage. Preferred are (*the*) *Reverend John Smith* or *Reverend Mr Smith* and *Dear Mr Smith*.

---

reverent ('rɛvərənt, 'rɛvrənt) *adj* feeling, expressing, or characterized by reverence. [C14: from L *reverēns* respectful]
▶ 'reverently *adv*

reverential (,rɛvə'rɛnʃəl) *adj* resulting from or showing reverence.
▶ ,rever'entially *adv*

reverie ('rɛvərɪ) *n* **1** an act or state of absent-minded daydreaming: *to fall into a reverie.* **2** a piece of instrumental music suggestive of a daydream. **3** *Arch.* a fanciful or visionary notion; daydream. [C14: from OF *resverie* wildness, from *resver* to behave wildly, from ?]

revers (rɪ'vɪə) *n, pl* **revers** (-'vɪəz). (*usually pl*) the turnedback lining of part of a garment, esp. of a lapel or cuff. [C19: from F, lit.: REVERSE]

reversal (rɪ'vɜːs°l) *n* **1** the act or an instance of reversing. **2** a change for the worse; reverse. **3** the state of being reversed. **4** the annulment of a judicial decision, esp. by an appeal court.

reverse (rɪ'vɜːs) *vb* **reverses, reversing, reversed.** (*mainly tr*) **1** to turn or set in an opposite direction, order, or position. **2** to change into something different or contrary; alter completely: *reverse one's policy.* **3** (*also intr*) to move or cause to move backwards or in an opposite direction: *to reverse a car.* **4** to run (machinery, etc.) in the opposite direction to normal. **5** to turn inside out. **6** *Law.* to revoke or set aside (a judgment, decree, etc.); annul. **7 reverse the charge(s).** to make a telephone call at the recipient's expense. ◆ *n* **8** the opposite or contrary of something. **9** the back or rear side of something. **10** a change to an opposite position, state, or direction. **11** a change for the worse; setback or defeat. **12a** the mechanism or gears by which machinery, a vehicle, etc., can be made to reverse its direction. **12b** (*as modifier*): *reverse gear.* **13** the side of a coin bearing a secondary design. **14a** printed matter in which normally black or coloured areas, esp. lettering, appear white, and vice versa. **14b** (*as modifier*): *reverse plates.* **15 in reverse.** in an opposite or backward direction. **16 the reverse of.** emphatically not; not at all: *he was the reverse of polite when I called.* ◆ *adj* **17** opposite or contrary in direction, position, order, nature, etc.; turned backwards. **18** back to front; inverted. **19** operating or mov-

ing in a manner contrary to that which is usual. **20** denoting or relating to a mirror image. [C14: from OF, from L *reversus*, from *revertere* to turn back]
▸ re'versely *adv* ▸ re'verser *n*

reverse-charge *adj* (*prenominal*) (of a telephone call) made at the recipient's expense.

reverse takeover *n Finance*. the purchase of a larger company by a smaller company, esp. of a public company by a private company.

reverse transcriptase (træn'skrɪpteɪz) *n* an enzyme present in retroviruses that copies RNA into DNA, thus reversing the usual flow of genetic information in which DNA is copied into RNA.

reverse video *n Computing*. highlighting by reversing the colours of normal characters and background on a visual display unit.

reversible (rɪ'vɜːsɪbᵊl) *adj* **1** capable of being reversed: *a reversible decision*. **2** capable of returning to an original condition. **3** *Chem., physics*. capable of assuming or producing either of two possible states and changing from one to the other: *a reversible reaction*. **4** (of a fabric or garment) woven, printed, or finished so that either side may be used as the outer side. ◆ *n* **5** a reversible garment, esp. a coat.
▸ re,versi'bility *n* ▸ re'versibly *adv*

reversing lights *pl n* lights on the rear of a motor vehicle that go on when the vehicle is being reversed.

reversion (rɪ'vɜːʃən) *n* **1** a return to an earlier condition, practice, or belief; act of reverting. **2** *Biol*. the return of individuals, organs, etc., to a more primitive condition or type. **3** *Property law*. **3a** an interest in an estate that reverts to the grantor or his heirs at the end of a period, esp. at the end of the life of a grantee. **3b** an estate so reverting. **3c** the right to succeed to such an estate. **4** the benefit payable on the death of a life-insurance policyholder.
▸ re'versionary *or* re'versional *adj*

reversionary bonus *n Insurance*. a bonus added to the sum payable on death or at the maturity of a with-profits assurance policy.

revert (rɪ'vɜːt) *vb* (*intr*; foll. by *to*). **1** to go back to a former practice, condition, belief, etc.: *he reverted to his old wicked ways*. **2** to take up again or come back to a former topic. **3** *Biol*. (of individuals, organs, etc.) to return to a more primitive, earlier, or simpler condition or type. **4** *Property law*. (of an estate or interest in land) to return to its former owner or his heirs. **5 revert to type**. to resume characteristics that were thought to have disappeared. [C13: from L *revertere*, from RE- + *vertere* to turn]
▸ re'verter *n* ▸ re'vertible *adj*

> **USAGE NOTE** Since *back* is part of the meaning of *revert*, one should not say that someone *reverts back* to a certain type of behaviour.

revet (rɪ'vet) *vb* **revets, revetting, revetted**. to face (a wall or embankment) with stones. [C19: from F *revêt*, from OF *revestir* to reclothe; see REVETMENT]

revetment (rɪ'vetmənt) *n* **1** a facing of stones, sandbags, etc., to protect a wall, embankment, or earthworks. **2** another name for **retaining wall**. [C18: from F *revêtement*, lit.: a reclothing, from *revêtir*; ult. from L RE- + *vestīre* to clothe]

review (rɪ'vjuː) *vb* (*mainly tr*) **1** to look at or examine again: *to review a situation*. **2** to look back upon (a period of time, sequence of events, etc.); remember: *he reviewed his achievements with pride*. **3** to inspect, esp. formally or officially: *the general reviewed his troops*. **4** *Law*. to re-examine (a decision) judicially. **5** to write a critical assessment of (a book, film, play, concert, etc.), esp. as a profession. ◆ *n* **6** Also called: **reviewal**. the act or an instance of reviewing. **7** a general survey or report: *a review of the political situation*. **8** a critical assessment of a book, film, play, concert, etc., esp. one printed in a newspaper or periodical. **9** a publication containing such articles. **10** a second consideration; re-examination. **11** a retrospective survey. **12** a formal or official inspection. **13** a

US and Canad. word for **revision** (sense 2). **14** *Law*. judicial re-examination of a case, esp. by a superior court. **15** a less common spelling of **revue**. [C16: from F, from *revoir* to see again, from L RE- + *vidēre* to see]
▸ re'viewer *n*

revile (rɪ'vaɪl) *vb* **reviles, reviling, reviled**. to use abusive or scornful language against (someone or something). [C14: from OF *reviler*, from RE- + *vil* VILE]
▸ re'vilement *n* ▸ re'viler *n*

revise (rɪ'vaɪz) *vb* **revises, revising, revised**. **1** (*tr*) to change or amend: *to revise one's opinion*. **2** *Brit*. to reread (a subject or notes on it) so as to memorize it, esp. for an examination. **3** (*tr*) to prepare a new version or edition of (a previously printed work). ◆ *n* **4** the act, process, or result of revising; revision. [C16: from L *revīsere*, from RE- + *vīsere* to inspect, from *vidēre* to see]
▸ re'visal *n* ▸ re'viser *n*

Revised Standard Version *n* a revision by American scholars of the American Standard Version of the Bible. The New Testament was published in 1946 and the entire Bible in 1953.

Revised Version *n* a revision of the Authorized Version of the Bible by two committees of British scholars, the New Testament being published in 1881 and the Old in 1885.

revision (rɪ'vɪʒən) *n* **1** the act or process of revising. **2** *Brit*. the process of rereading a subject or notes on it, esp. for an examination. **3** a corrected or new version of a book, article, etc.
▸ re'visionary *adj*

revisionism (rɪ'vɪʒə,nɪzəm) *n* **1** (*sometimes cap.*) **1a** a moderate, nonrevolutionary version of Marxism developed in Germany around 1900. **1b** (in Marxist-Leninist ideology) any dangerous departure from the true interpretation of Marx's teachings. **2** the advocacy of revision of some political theory, etc.
▸ re'visionist *n, adj*

revisory (rɪ'vaɪzərɪ) *adj* of, relating to, or having the power of revision.

revitalize *or* **revitalise** (riː'vaɪtᵊ,laɪz) *vb* **revitalizes, revitalizing, revitalized** *or* **revitalises, revitalising, revitalised**. (*tr*) to restore vitality or animation to.

revival (rɪ'vaɪvᵊl) *n* **1** the act or an instance of reviving or the state of being revived. **2** an instance of returning to life or consciousness; restoration of vigour or vitality. **3** a renewed use, acceptance of, or interest in (past customs, styles, etc.): *the Gothic revival*. **4** a new production of a play that has not been recently performed. **5** a reawakening of faith. **6** an evangelistic meeting or meetings intended to effect such a reawakening in those present.

revivalism (rɪ'vaɪvə,lɪzəm) *n* **1** a movement that seeks to reawaken faith. **2** the tendency or desire to revive former customs, styles, etc.
▸ re'vivalist *n* ▸ re,vival'istic *adj*

revive (rɪ'vaɪv) *vb* **revives, reviving, revived**. **1** to bring or be brought back to life, consciousness, or strength: *revived by a drop of whisky*. **2** to give or assume new vitality; flourish again or cause to flourish again. **3** to make or become operative or active again: *the youth movement was revived*. **4** to bring or come back to mind. **5** (*tr*) *Theatre*. to mount a new production of (an old play). [C15: from OF *revivre* to live again, from L *revīvere*, from RE- + *vīvere* to live]
▸ re'vivable *adj* ▸ re,viva'bility *n* ▸ re'viver *n* ▸ re'viving *adj*

revivify (rɪ'vɪvɪ,faɪ) *vb* **revivifies, revivifying, revivified**. (*tr*) to give new life or spirit to.
▸ re,vivifi'cation *n*

revocable ('revəkəbᵊl) *or* **revokable** (rɪ'vəʊkəbᵊl) *adj* capable of being revoked.
▸ ,revoca'bility *or* re,voka'bility *n* ▸ 'revocably *or* re'vokably *adv*

revocation (,revə'keɪʃən) *n* **1** the act of revoking or state of being revoked. **2a** the cancellation or annulment of a legal instrument. **2b** the withdrawal of an offer, power of attorney, etc.
▸ **revocatory** ('revəkətərɪ, -trɪ) *adj*

revoice (riː'vɔɪs) *vb* **revoices, revoicing, revoiced**. (*tr*) **1** to utter again; echo. **2** to adjust the design of (an organ

★ people and places

pipe or wind instrument) as after disuse or to conform with modern pitch.

evoke (ɪ'vəʊk) vb **revokes, revoking, revoked. 1** (tr) to take back or withdraw; cancel; rescind. **2** (intr) Cards. to break a rule by failing to follow suit when able to do so. ♦ n **3** Cards. the act of revoking. [C14: from L revocāre to call back, withdraw, from RE- + vocāre to call]
▶ re'voker n

evolt (ɪ'vəʊlt) n **1** a rebellion or uprising against authority. **2 in revolt.** in the process or state of rebelling. ♦ vb **3** (intr) to rise up in rebellion against authority. **4** (usually passive) to feel or cause to feel revulsion, disgust, or abhorrence. [C16: from F révolter, from OIt. rivoltare to overturn, ult. from L revolvere to roll back]

evolting (ɪ'vəʊltɪŋ) adj **1** causing revulsion; nauseating, disgusting, or repulsive. **2** Inf. unpleasant or nasty.
▶ re'voltingly adv

evolute ('revə,luːt) adj (esp. of the margins of a leaf) rolled backwards and downwards. [C18: from L revolūtus rolled back; see REVOLVE]

evolution (,revə'luːʃən) n **1** the overthrow or repudiation of a regime or political system by the governed. **2** (in Marxist theory) the inevitable, violent transition from one system of production in a society to the next. **3** a far-reaching and drastic change, esp. in ideas, methods, etc. **4a** movement in or as if in a circle. **4b** one complete turn in such a circle: 33 revolutions per minute. **5a** the orbital motion of one body, such as a planet, around another. **5b** one complete turn in such motion. **6** a cycle of successive events or changes. [C14: via OF from LL revolūtiō, from L revolvere to REVOLVE]

evolutionary (,revə'luːʃənərɪ) n, pl **revolutionaries. 1** a person who advocates or engages in revolution. ♦ adj **2** relating to or characteristic of a revolution. **3** advocating or engaged in revolution. **4** radically new or different: a revolutionary method of making plastics.

Revolutionary (,revə'luːʃənərɪ) adj **1** Chiefly US. of or relating to the War of American Independence (1775–83). **2** of or relating to any of various other Revolutions, esp. the **Russian Revolution** (1917) or the **French Revolution** (1789).

evolutionist (,revə'luːʃənɪst) n **1** a less common word for a **revolutionary.** ♦ adj **2** of or relating to revolution or revolutionaries.

evolutionize or **revolutionise** (,revə'luːʃə,naɪz) vb **revolutionizes, revolutionizing, revolutionized** or **revolutionises, revolutionising, revolutionised.** (tr) **1** to bring about a radical change in: science has revolutionized civilization. **2** to inspire or infect with revolutionary ideas: they revolutionized the common soldiers. **3** to cause a revolution in (a country, etc.).
▶ ,revo'lution,izer or ,revo'lution,iser n

evolve (ɪ'vɒlv) vb **revolves, revolving, revolved. 1** to move or cause to move around a centre or axis; rotate. **2** (intr) to occur periodically or in cycles. **3** to consider or be considered. **4** (intr; foll. by around or about) to be centred or focused (upon): Juliet's thoughts revolved around Romeo. ♦ n **5** Theatre. a circular section of a stage that can be rotated by electric power to provide a scene change. [C14: from L revolvere, from RE- + volvere to roll, wind]
▶ re'volvable adj

evolver (ɪ'vɒlvə) n a pistol having a revolving multichambered cylinder that allows several shots to be discharged without reloading.

evolving (ɪ'vɒlvɪŋ) adj **1** moving round a central axis: revolving door. **2** (of a fund) constantly added to from income from its investments to offset outgoing payments. **3** (of a letter of credit, loan, etc.) available to be repeatedly drawn on by the beneficiary provided that a specified amount is never exceeded.

evue (ɪ'vjuː) n a light entertainment consisting of topical sketches, songs, dancing, etc. [C20: from F; see REVIEW]

evulsion (ɪ'vʌlʃən) n **1** a sudden violent reaction in feeling, esp. one of extreme loathing. **2** the act or an instance of drawing back or recoiling from something. **3** the diversion of disease from one part of the body to another by cupping, counterirritants, etc. [C16: from L

revulsiō a pulling away, from revellere, from RE- + vellere to pull, tear]

revulsive (ɪ'vʌlsɪv) adj **1** of or causing revulsion. ♦ n **2** Med. a counterirritant.
▶ re'vulsively adv

reward (ɪ'wɔːd) n **1** something given in return for a deed or service rendered. **2** a sum of money offered, esp. for help in finding a criminal or for the return of lost or stolen property. **3** profit or return. **4** something received in return for good or evil; deserts. ♦ vb **5** (tr) to give something to (someone), esp. in gratitude for (a service rendered); recompense. [C14: from OF rewarder, from RE- + warder to care for, guard, of Gmc origin]
▶ re'wardless adj

reward claim n Austral. history. a claim granted to a miner who discovered gold in a new area.

rewarding (ɪ'wɔːdɪŋ) adj giving personal satisfaction; gratifying.

rewa-rewa ('reɪwə'reɪwə) n a tall tree of New Zealand, yielding reddish timber. [C19: from Maori]

rewind vb (riː'waɪnd) **rewinds, rewinding, rewound. 1** (tr) to wind back, esp. a film or tape onto the original reel. ♦ n ('riː,waɪnd, riː'waɪnd). **2** something rewound. **3** the act of rewinding.
▶ re'winder n

rewire (riː'waɪə) vb **rewires, rewiring, rewired.** (tr) to provide (a house, engine, etc.) with new wiring.
▶ re'wirable adj

reword (riː'wɜːd) vb (tr) to alter the wording of; express differently.

rework (riː'wɜːk) vb (tr) **1** to use again in altered form. **2** to rewrite or revise. **3** to reprocess for use again.

rewrite vb (riː'raɪt) **rewrites, rewriting, rewrote, rewritten.** (tr) **1** to write (material) again, esp. changing the words or form. ♦ n ('riː,raɪt). **2** Computing. to return (data) to a store when it has been erased during reading. **3** something rewritten.

Rex (reks) n king: part of the official title of a king, now used chiefly in documents, legal proceedings, on coins, etc. Cf. **Regina**[1]. [L]

Rexine ('reksiːn) n Trademark. a form of artificial leather.

Reye's syndrome (raɪz, reɪz) n a rare metabolic disease in children that can be fatal, involving damage to the brain, liver, and kidneys. [C20: after R.D.K. Reye (1912–78), Austral. paediatrician]

Reykjavik ★ ('reɪkjə,viːk) n the capital and chief port of Iceland, situated in the southwest: its buildings are heated by natural hot water. Pop.: 104 276 (1995 est.).

Reynard or **Renard** ('renəd, 'renɑːd) n a name for a fox, used in fables, etc.

Reynaud ★ (French reno) n Paul (pɔl). 1878–1966, French statesman: premier during the defeat of France by Germany (1940); later imprisoned by the Germans.

Reynolds ★ ('renəldz) n **1** Albert. born 1935, Irish politician: prime minister of the Republic of Ireland (1994–96). **2** Sir Joshua. 1723–92, British portrait painter; first president of the Royal Academy (1768).

Reynosa ★ (Spanish re'nosa) n a city in E Mexico, in Tamaulipas state on the Rio Grande. Pop.: 265 663 (1990).

RF abbrev. for radio frequency.

RFC abbrev. for: **1** Royal Flying Corps. **2** Rugby Football Club.

RGN (in Britain) abbrev. for Registered General Nurse.

RGS abbrev. for Royal Geographical Society.

rh or **RH** abbrev. for right hand.

Rh 1 the chemical symbol for rhodium. ♦ **2** abbrev. for rhesus (esp. in **Rh factor**).

RHA abbrev. for: **1** Regional Health Authority. **2** Royal Horse Artillery.

rhabdomancy ('ræbdə,mænsɪ) n divination for water or mineral ore by means of a rod or wand. [C17: via LL from LGk rhabdomanteia, from Gk rhabdos rod + manteia divination]
▶ 'rhabdo,mantist or 'rhabdo,mancer n

rhachis (ˈreɪkɪs) *n, pl* **rhachises** *or* **rhachides** (ˈrækɪˌdiːz, ˈreɪ-). a variant spelling of **rachis.**

Rhadamanthus *or* **Rhadamanthys** ★ (ˌrædəˈmænθəs) *n Greek myth.* one of the judges of the dead in the underworld.
▸ **ˌRhadaˈmanthine** *adj*

Rhaetia ★ (ˈriːʃɪə) *n* an Alpine province of ancient Rome including parts of present-day Tyrol and E Switzerland.
▸ **ˈRhaetian** *adj, n*

Rhaetian Alps ★ *pl n* a section of the central Alps along E Switzerland's borders with Austria and Italy. Highest peak: Piz Bernina, 4049 m (13 284 ft).

rhapsodic (ræpˈsɒdɪk) *adj* **1** of or like a rhapsody. **2** lyrical or romantic.

rhapsodize *or* **rhapsodise** (ˈræpsəˌdaɪz) *vb* **rhapsodizes, rhapsodizing, rhapsodized** *or* **rhapsodises, rhapsodising, rhapsodised. 1** to speak or write (something) with extravagant enthusiasm. **2** (*intr*) to recite or write rhapsodies.
▸ **ˈrhapsodist** *n*

rhapsody (ˈræpsədɪ) *n, pl* **rhapsodies. 1** *Music.* a composition free in structure and highly emotional in character. **2** an expression of ecstatic enthusiasm. **3** (in ancient Greece) an epic poem or part of an epic recited by a rhapsodist. **4** a literary work composed in an intense or exalted style. **5** rapturous delight or ecstasy. [C16: via L from Gk *rhapsōidia,* from *rhaptein* to sew together + *ōidē* song]

rhatany (ˈrætənɪ) *n, pl* **rhatanies. 1** either of two South American leguminous shrubs that have thick fleshy roots. **2** the dried roots used as an astringent. ◆ Also called: **krameria.** [C19: from NL *rhatānia,* ult. from Quechua *ratánya*]

rhea (rɪə) *n* either of two large fast-running flightless birds inhabiting the open plains of S South America. They are similar to but smaller than the ostrich. [C19: NL; arbitrarily after RHEA]

Rhea ★ (ˈrɪə) *n Greek myth.* a Titaness, wife of Cronus and mother of several of the gods, including Zeus: a fertility goddess. Roman counterpart: **Ops.**

Rhea Silvia *or* **Rea Silvia** ★ (ˈsɪlvɪə) *n Roman myth.* the mother of Romulus and Remus by Mars. See also **Ilia.**

rhebuck *or* **rhebok** (ˈriːbʌk) *n, pl* **rhebucks, rhebuck** *or* **rheboks, rhebok.** an antelope of southern Africa, having woolly brownish-grey hair. [C18: Afrik., from Du. *reebok* ROEBUCK]

Rhee ★ (riː) *n* **Syngman** (ˈsɪŋmən). 1875–1965, Korean statesman, leader of the campaign for independence from Japan; first president of South Korea (1948–60).

Rheims ★ (riːmz; *French* rɛ̃s) *n* a variant spelling of **Reims.**

Rhein ★ (raɪn) *n* the German name for the **Rhine.**

Rheinland ★ (ˈraɪnlant) *n* the German name for the **Rhineland.**

Rheinland-Pfalz ★ (ˈraɪnlantˈpfalts) *n* the German name for **Rhineland-Palatinate.**

Rhenish (ˈrɛnɪʃ, ˈriː-) *adj* **1** of or relating to the River Rhine or the lands adjacent to it. ◆ *n* **2** another word for **hock**^{2}.

rhenium (ˈriːnɪəm) *n* a dense silvery-white metallic element that has a high melting point. Symbol: Re; atomic no.: 75; atomic wt.: 186.2. [C19: NL, from *Rhēnus* the Rhine]

rheo- *combining form.* indicating stream, flow, or current: *rheostat.* [from Gk *rheos* stream, anything flowing, from *rhein* to flow]

rheology (rɪˈɒlədʒɪ) *n* the branch of physics concerned with the flow and change of shape of matter, esp. the viscosity of liquids.
▸ **rheological** (ˌriːəˈlɒdʒɪk^{ə}l) *adj* ▸ **rheˈologist** *n*

rheostat (ˈrɪəˌstæt) *n* a variable resistance, usually a coil of wire with a terminal at one end and a sliding contact that moves along the coil to tap off the current.
▸ **ˌrheoˈstatic** *adj*

Rhesus ★ (ˈriːsəs) *n Greek myth.* a king of Thrace, who arrived in the tenth year of the Trojan War to aid Troy. Odysseus and Diomedes stole his horses because an oracle had said that if they drank from the River Xanthus Troy would not fall.

rhesus baby (ˈriːsəs) *n* a baby suffering from haemolytic disease at birth as its red blood cells (which are Rh positive) have been attacked in the womb by antibodies from its Rh negative mother. [C20: see RH FACTOR]

rhesus factor *n* See **Rh factor.**

rhesus monkey *n* a macaque monkey of S Asia. [C19: NL, arbitrarily from Gk *Rhesos,* mythical Thracian king]

rhetoric (ˈrɛtərɪk) *n* **1** the study of the technique of using language effectively. **2** the art of using speech to persuade, influence, or please; oratory. **3** excessive ornamentation and contrivance in spoken or written discourse; bombast. **4** speech or discourse that pretends to significance but lacks true meaning: *mere rhetoric.* [C14: via L from Gk *rhētorikē* (*tekhnē*) (the art of) rhetoric, from *rhētōr* teacher of rhetoric, orator]

rhetorical (rɪˈtɒrɪk^{ə}l) *adj* **1** concerned with effect or style rather than content or meaning; bombastic. **2** of or relating to rhetoric or oratory.
▸ **rheˈtorically** *adv*

rhetorical question *n* a question to which no answer is required: used esp. for dramatic effect. An example is *Who knows?* (with the implication *Nobody knows*).

rhetorician (ˌrɛtəˈrɪʃən) *n* **1** a teacher of rhetoric. **2** a stylish or eloquent writer or speaker. **3** a pompous or extravagant speaker.

rheum (ruːm) *n* a watery discharge from the eyes or nose. [C14: from OF *reume,* ult. from Gk *rheuma* bodily humour, stream, from *rhein* to flow]
▸ **ˈrheumy** *adj*

rheumatic (ruːˈmætɪk) *adj* **1** of, relating to, or afflicted with rheumatism. ◆ *n* **2** a person afflicted with rheumatism. [C14: ult. from Gk *rheumatikos,* from *rheuma* a flow; see RHEUM]
▸ **rheuˈmatically** *adv*

rheumatic fever *n* a disease characterized by inflammation and pain in the joints.

rheumatics (ruːˈmætɪks) *n* (*functioning as sing*) *Inf.* rheumatism.

rheumatism (ˈruːməˌtɪzəm) *n* any painful disorder of joints, muscles, or connective tissue. [C17: from L *rheumatismus* catarrh, from Gk *rheumatismos;* see RHEUM]

rheumatoid (ˈruːməˌtɔɪd) *adj* (of symptoms) resembling rheumatism.

rheumatoid arthritis *n* a chronic disease characterized by inflammation and swelling of joints (esp. in the hands, wrists, knees, and feet), muscle weakness, and fatigue.

rheumatology (ˌruːməˈtɒlədʒɪ) *n* the study of rheumatic diseases.
▸ **rheumatological** (ˌruːmətəˈlɒdʒɪk^{ə}l) *adj*

Rh factor *n* an antigen commonly found in human blood: the terms **Rh positive** and **Rh negative** are used to indicate its presence or absence. It may cause a haemolytic reaction, esp. during pregnancy or following transfusion of blood that does not contain this antigen. Full name: **rhesus factor.** [after the rhesus monkey, in which it was first discovered]

rhinal (ˈraɪn^{ə}l) *adj* of or relating to the nose.

Rhine ★ (raɪn) *n* a river in central and W Europe, rising in SE Switzerland: flows through Lake Constance north through W Germany and west through the Netherlands to the North Sea. Length: about 1320 km (820 miles). Dutch name: **Rijn.** French name: **Rhin** (rɛ̃). German name **Rhein.**

Rhineland ★ (ˈraɪnˌlænd, -lənd) *n* the region of W Germany surrounding the Rhine. German name: **Rheinland.**

Rhineland-Palatinate ★ *n* a state of W Germany formed in 1946 from the S part of the Prussian Rhine province, the Palatinate, and parts of Rhine-Hesse and Hesse-Nassau; part of West Germany until 1990: agriculture and tourism are important. Capital: Mainz. Pop. 3 951 600 (1995 est.). Area: 19 832 sq. km (7657 sq miles). German name: **Rheinland-Pfalz.**

Rhine Palatinate ★ *n* See **Palatinate.**

rhinestone ('raɪn,stəʊn) *n* an imitation gem made of paste. [C19: translation of F *caillou du Rhin*, referring to Strasbourg, where such gems were made]

Rhine wine (raɪn) *n* any wine produced along the Rhine, characteristically a white table wine.

rhinitis (raɪ'naɪtɪs) *n* inflammation of the mucous membrane that lines the nose.
▸ **rhinitic** (raɪ'nɪtɪk) *adj*

rhino[1] ('raɪnəʊ) *n, pl* **rhinos** *or* **rhino**. short for **rhinoceros**.

rhino[2] ('raɪnəʊ) *n Brit.* a slang word for **money**. [C17: from ?]

rhino- *or before a vowel* **rhin-** *combining form.* the nose: *rhinology.* [from Gk *rhis, rhin*]

rhinoceros (raɪ'nɒsərəs, -'nɒsrəs) *n, pl* **rhinoceroses** *or* **rhinoceros**. any of several mammals constituting a family of SE Asia and Africa and having either one horn on the nose, like the **Indian rhinoceros**, or two horns, like the African **white rhinoceros**. They have a very thick skin and a massive body. [C13: via L from Gk *rhinokerōs*, from *rhis* nose + *keras* horn]
▸ **rhinocerotic** (,raɪnəʊsɪ'rɒtɪk) *adj*

rhinology (raɪ'nɒlədʒɪ) *n* the branch of medical science concerned with the nose.
▸ **rhinological** (,raɪn°'lɒdʒɪk°l) *adj* ▸ **rhi'nologist** *n*

rhinoplasty ('raɪnəʊ,plæstɪ) *n* plastic surgery of the nose.
▸ ,**rhino'plastic** *adj*

rhinoscopy (raɪ'nɒskəpɪ) *n Med.* examination of the nasal passages, esp. with a special instrument called a **rhinoscope** ('raɪnəʊ,skəʊp).

rhizo- *or before a vowel* **rhiz-** *combining form.* root: *rhizocarpous.* [from Gk *rhiza*]

rhizocarpous (,raɪzəʊ'kɑːpəs) *adj* **1** (of plants) producing subterranean flowers and fruit. **2** (of plants) having perennial roots but stems and leaves that wither.

rhizoid ('raɪzɔɪd) *n* any of various hairlike structures that function as roots in mosses, ferns, and fungi.
▸ **rhi'zoidal** *adj*

rhizome ('raɪzəʊm) *n* a thick horizontal underground stem whose buds develop into new plants. Also called: **rootstock, rootstalk.** [C19: from NL *rhizoma*, from Gk, from *rhiza* a root]
▸ **rhizomatous** (raɪ'zɒmətəs, -'zəʊ-) *adj*

rhizopod ('raɪzəʊ,pɒd) *n* **1** any of various protozoans characterized by naked protoplasmic processes (pseudopodia). ◆ *adj* **2** of, relating to, or belonging to rhizopods.

rho (rəʊ) *n, pl* **rhos**. the 17th letter in the Greek alphabet (P, ρ).

rhodamine ('rəʊdə,miːn, -mɪn) *n* any one of a group of synthetic red or pink basic dyestuffs used for wool and silk. [C20: from RHODO- + AMINE]

Rhode Island ★ (rəʊd) *n* a state of the northeastern US, bordering on the Atlantic: the smallest state in the US; mainly low-lying and undulating, with an indented coastline in the east and uplands in the northwest. Capital: Providence. Pop.: 990 225 (1994 est.). Area: 2717 sq. km (1049 sq. miles). Abbrevs.: **R.I.** or (with zip code) **RI**

Rhode Island Red *n* a breed of domestic fowl, originating in America, characterized by a dark reddish-brown plumage and the production of brown eggs.

Rhodes[1] ★ (rəʊdz) *n* **1** a Greek island in the SE Aegean Sea, about 16 km (10 miles) off the Turkish coast: the largest of the Dodecanese and the most easterly island in the Aegean. Capital: Rhodes. Pop.: 41 000 (latest est). Area: 1400 sq. km (540 sq. miles). **2** a port on this island, in the NE: founded in 408 B.C.; of great commercial and political importance in the 3rd century B.C.; suffered several earthquakes, notably in 225, when the Colossus was destroyed. Pop.: 40 656 (1981). ◆ Ancient Greek name: **Rhodos**. Modern Greek name: **Ródhos**.

Rhodes[2] ★ (rəʊdz) *n* **Cecil John**. 1853–1902, British colonial financier and statesman in South Africa; as prime minister of the Cape Colony (1890–96), he helped to extend British territory. He established the annual Rhodes scholarships.

Rhodesia ★ (rəʊ'diːʃə, -zɪə) *n* a former name (1964–79) for **Zimbabwe**.
▸ **Rho'desian** *adj, n*

Rhodesia and Nyasaland ★ *n* **Federation of.** a federation consisting of Northern Rhodesia, Southern Rhodesia, and Nyasaland, which existed from 1953 to 1963.

Rhodesian man *n* a type of early man, occurring in Africa in late Pleistocene times and resembling Neanderthal man.

Rhodes scholarship (rəʊdz) *n* one of 72 scholarships founded by Cecil Rhodes, awarded annually to Commonwealth and US students to study at Oxford University.
▸ **Rhodes scholar** *n*

Rhodian ('rəʊdɪən) *adj* **1** of or relating to the island of Rhodes. ◆ *n* **2** a native or inhabitant of Rhodes.

rhodium ('rəʊdɪəm) *n* a hard silvery-white element of the platinum metal group. Used as an alloying agent to harden platinum and palladium. Symbol: Rh; atomic no.: 45; atomic wt.: 102.90. [C19: NL, from Gk *rhodon* rose, from the pink colour of its compounds]

rhodo- *or before a vowel* **rhod-** *combining form.* rose or rose-coloured: *rhododendron; rhodolite.* [from Gk *rhodon* rose]

rhodochrosite (,rəʊdəʊ'krəʊsaɪt) *n* a pink, grey, or brown mineral that consists of manganese carbonate in hexagonal crystalline form. Formula: $MnCO_3$. [C19: from Gk *rhodokhrōs*, from *rhodon* rose + *khrōs* colour]

rhododendron (,rəʊdə'dendrən) *n* any of various shrubs native to S Asia but widely cultivated in N temperate regions. They are mostly evergreen and have clusters of showy red, purple, pink, or white flowers. [C17: from L: oleander, from Gk, from *rhodon* rose + *dendron* tree]

rhodolite ('rəʊdə,laɪt) *n* a pale violet or red variety of garnet, used as a gemstone.

rhodonite ('rəʊdə,naɪt) *n* a brownish translucent mineral consisting of manganese silicate in crystalline form with calcium, iron, or magnesium sometimes replacing the manganese. It is used as an ornamental stone, glaze, and pigment. [C19: from G *Rhodonit*, from Gk *rhodon* rose + -ITE[1]]

Rhodope Mountains ★ ('rɒdəpɪ, rɒ'dəʊ-) *pl n* a mountain range in SE Europe, in the Balkan Peninsula extending along the border between Bulgaria and Greece. Highest peak: Golyam Perelik (Bulgaria), 2191 m (7188 ft).

rhodopsin (rəʊ'dɒpsɪn) *n* a red pigment in the rods of the retina in vertebrates. Also called: **visual purple**. See also **iodopsin**. [C20: from RHODO- + Gk *opsis* sight + -IN]

Rhodos ★ ('rɒðɒs) *n* the Ancient Greek name for **Rhodes**[1].

rhomb (rɒm) *n* another name for **rhombus**.

rhombencephalon (,rɒmben'sefə,lɒn) *n* the part of the brain that develops from the posterior portion of the embryonic neural tube. Nontechnical name: **hindbrain**. [C20: from RHOMBUS + ENCEPHALON]

rhombic aerial *n* a directional travelling-wave aerial, usually horizontal, consisting of two conductors forming a rhombus.

rhombohedral (,rɒmbəʊ'hiːdrəl) *adj* **1** of or relating to a rhombohedron. **2** *Crystallog.* another term for **trigonal** (sense 2).

rhombohedron (,rɒmbəʊ'hiːdrən) *n, pl* **rhombohedrons** *or* **rhombohedra** (-drə) a six-sided prism whose sides are parallelograms. [C19: from RHOMBUS + -HEDRON]

rhomboid ('rɒmbɔɪd) *n* **1** a parallelogram having adjacent sides of unequal length. ◆ *adj also* **rhom'boidal. 2** having such a shape. [C16: from LL, from Gk *rhomboeidēs* shaped like a RHOMBUS]

rhombus ('rɒmbəs) *n, pl* **rhombuses** *or* **rhombi** (-baɪ). an oblique-angled parallelogram having four equal sides. Also called: **rhomb**. [C16: from Gk *rhombos* something that spins; rel. to *rhembein* to whirl]
▸ '**rhombic** *adj*

rhonchus ('rɒŋkəs) *n, pl* **rhonchi** (-kaɪ). a rattling or whistling respiratory sound resembling snoring, caused by secretions in the trachea or bronchi. [C19: from L, from Gk *rhenkhos* snoring]

Rhondda ★ ('rɒndə) *n* a town in S Wales, on two branches of the **Rhondda Valley**: developed into a major coal-mining centre after 1807 and grew to a population of 167 900 in 1924: the last mine closed in 1990. Pop.: 59 947 (1991).

Rhondda Cynon Taff ★ ('kʌnən tæf) *n* a county borough in S Wales, created in 1996. Pop.: 232 581 (1996 est.). Area: 558 sq. km (215 sq. miles).

Rhône ★ (rəʊn) *n* **1** a river in W Europe, rising in S Switzerland in the **Rhône glacier** and flowing to Lake Geneva, then into France through gorges between the Alps and Jura and south to its delta on the Gulf of Lions: important esp. for hydroelectricity and for wine production along its valley. Length: 812 km (505 miles). **2** a department of E central France, in the Rhône-Alpes region. Capital: Lyons. Pop.: 1 558 869 (1994 est.). Area: 3233 sq. km (1261 sq. miles).

Rhône-Alpes ★ (*French* rɔnalp) *n* a region of E France: mainly mountainous, rising to the edge of the Massif Central in the west and the French Alps in the east; drained by the Rivers Rhône, Saône, and Isère.

RHS *abbrev. for:* **1** Royal Historical Society. **2** Royal Horticultural Society. **3** Royal Humane Society.

rhubarb ('ruːbɑːb) *n* **1** any of several temperate and subtropical plants, esp. **common garden rhubarb,** which has long green and red acid-tasting edible leafstalks, usually eaten sweetened and cooked. **2** the leafstalks of this plant. **3** a related plant of central Asia, having a bittertasting underground stem that can be dried and used as a laxative or astringent. **4** *US & Canad. sl.* a heated discussion or quarrel. ♦ *interj, n, vb* **5** the noise made by actors to simulate conversation, esp. by repeating the word *rhubarb.* [C14: from OF *reubarbe,* from Med. L *reubarbarum,* prob. var. of *rha barbarum,* from *rha* rhubarb (from Gk, ?from *Rha,* ancient name of the Volga) + L *barbarus* barbarian]

rhumb (rʌm) *n* short for **rhumb line.**

rhumba ('rʌmbə, 'rʊm-) *n, pl* **rhumbas.** a variant spelling of **rumba.**

rhumb line *n* **1** an imaginary line on the surface of a sphere that intersects all meridians at the same angle. **2** the course navigated by a vessel or aircraft that maintains a uniform compass heading. [C16: from OSp. *rumbo,* apparently from MDu. *ruum* space, ship's hold, infl. by RHOMBUS]

rhyme *or (arch.)* **rime** (raɪm) *n* **1** identity of the terminal sounds in lines of verse or in words. **2** a word that is identical to another in its terminal sound: *"while" is a rhyme for "mile".* **3** a piece of poetry, esp. having corresponding sounds at the ends of the lines. **4 rhyme or reason.** sense, logic, or meaning. ♦ *vb* **rhymes, rhyming, rhymed** *or* **rimes, riming, rimed. 5** to use (a word) or (of a word) to be used so as to form a rhyme. **6** to render (a subject) into rhyme. **7** to compose (verse) in a metrical structure. ♦ See also **eye rhyme.** [C12: from OF *rime,* ult. from OHG *rīm* a number; spelling infl. by RHYTHM]

rhymester, rimester ('raɪmstə), **rhymer,** *or* **rimer** *n* a poet, esp. one considered to be mediocre; poetaster or versifier.

rhyming slang *n* slang in which a word is replaced by another word or phrase that rhymes with it; e.g. *apples and pears* meaning *stairs.*

rhyolite ('raɪəˌlaɪt) *n* a fine-grained igneous rock consisting of quartz, feldspars, and mica or amphibole. [C19: from Gk *rhuax* a stream of lava + -LITE]
▶ **rhyolitic** (ˌraɪə'lɪtɪk) *adj*

Rhys ★ (riːs) *n* **Jean (Ella Gwendolen Rees Williams).** ?1890–1979, British writer, born in Dominica. Her novels include *Wide Sargasso Sea* (1966).

rhythm ('rɪðəm) *n* **1a** the arrangement of the durations of and accents on the notes of a melody, usually laid out into regular groups (**bars**) of beats. **1b** any specific arrangement of such groupings; time: *quadruple rhythm.* **2** (in poetry) **2a** the arrangement of words into a sequence of stressed and unstressed or long and short syllables. **2b** any specific such arrangement; metre. **3** (in painting,

sculpture, etc.) a harmonious sequence or pattern of masses alternating with voids, of light alternating with shade, of alternating colours, etc. **4** any sequence of regularly recurring functions or events, such as certain physiological functions of the body. [C16: from L *rhythmus,* from Gk *rhuthmos;* rel. to *rhein* to flow]

rhythm and blues *n* (*functioning as sing*) any of various kinds of popular music derived from or influenced by the blues. Abbrev.: **R & B.**

rhythmic ('rɪðmɪk) *or* **rhythmical** ('rɪðmɪkᵊl) *adj* of, relating to, or characterized by rhythm, as in movement or sound; metrical, periodic, or regularly recurring.
▶ **'rhythmically** *adv* ▶ **rhythmicity** (rɪð'mɪsɪtɪ) *n*

rhythm method *n* a method of contraception by restricting sexual intercourse to those days in a woman's menstrual cycle on which conception is considered least likely to occur.

rhythm section *n* those instruments in a band or group (usually piano, double bass, and drums) whose prime function is to supply the rhythm.

RI *abbrev. for:* **1** Regina et Imperatrix. [L: Queen and Empress] **2** Rex et Imperator. [L: King and Emperor] **3** Royal Institution. **4** religious instruction.

ria (rɪə) *n* a long narrow inlet of the seacoast, being a former valley that was submerged by the sea. [C19: from Sp., from *rio* river]

Rialto ★ (rɪ'æltəʊ) *n* an island in Venice, Italy, linked with San Marco Island by the **Rialto Bridge** (1590) over the Grand Canal: the business centre of medieval and renaissance Venice.

riata *or* **reata** (rɪ'ɑːtə) *n South & West US.* a lariat or lasso. [C19: from American Sp., from Sp. *reatar* to tie together again, from RE- + *atar* to tie, from L *aptāre* to fit]

rib[1] (rɪb) *n* **1** any of the 24 elastic arches of bone that together form the chest wall in man. All are attached behind to the thoracic part of the spinal column. **2** the corresponding bone in other vertebrates. **3** a cut of meat including one or more ribs. **4** a part or element similar in function or appearance to a rib, esp. a structural member or a ridge. **5** a structural member in a wing that extends from the leading edge to the trailing edge. **6** a projecting moulding or band on the underside of a vault or ceiling. **7** one of a series of raised rows in knitted fabric. **8** a raised ornamental line on the spine of a book where the stitching runs across it. **9** any of the transverse stiffening timbers or joists forming the frame of a ship's hull. **10** any of the larger veins of a leaf. **11** a vein of ore in rock. **12** a projecting ridge of a mountain; spur. ♦ *vb* **ribs, ribbing, ribbed.** (*tr*) **13** to furnish or support with a rib or ribs. **14** to mark with or form into ribs or ridges. **15** to knit plain and purl stitches alternately in order to make raised rows in (knitting). [OE *ribb;* rel. to OHG *rippi,* ON *rif* REEF[1]]
▶ **'ribless** *adj*

rib[2] (rɪb) *vb* **ribs, ribbing, ribbed.** (*tr*) *Inf.* to tease or ridicule. [C20: short for *rib-tickle* (vb)]

RIBA *abbrev. for* Royal Institute of British Architects.

ribald ('rɪbᵊld) *adj* **1** coarse, obscene, or licentious, usually in a humorous or mocking way. ♦ *n* **2** a ribald person. [C13: from OF *ribauld,* from *riber* to live licentiously, of Gmc origin]

ribaldry ('rɪbᵊldrɪ) *n* ribald language or behaviour.

riband *or* **ribband** ('rɪbənd) *n* a ribbon, esp. one awarded for some achievement. [C14: var. of RIBBON]

Ribbentrop ★ (*German* 'rɪbəntrɒp) *n* **Joachim von** ('joːaxɪm fɒn). 1893–1946, German Nazi politician: foreign minister (1938–45), hanged as a war criminal at Nuremberg.

ribbing ('rɪbɪŋ) *n* **1** a framework or structure of ribs. **2** a pattern of ribs in woven or knitted material. **3** *Inf.* teasing.

Ribble ★ ('rɪbᵊl) *n* a river in NW England, flowing south and west through Lancashire to the Irish Sea. Length: 121 km (75 miles).

ribbon ('rɪbᵊn) *n* **1** a narrow strip of fine material, esp. silk, used for trimming, tying, etc. **2** something resembling a ribbon; a long strip. **3** a long thin flexible band of metal used as a graduated measure, spring, etc. **4** a long narrow strip of ink-impregnated cloth for making the impression of type characters on paper in a typewriter, etc. **5** (*pl*) ragged strips or shreds (esp. in **torn to ribbons**). **6** a small strip of coloured cloth signifying membership of an order or award of military decoration, prize, etc. **7** a small, usually looped, strip of coloured cloth worn to signify support for a charity or cause: *a red AIDS ribbon.* ◆ *vb* (*tr*) **8** to adorn with a ribbon or ribbons. **9** to mark with narrow ribbon-like marks. [C14 *ryban*, from OF *riban*, apparently of Gmc origin]

ribbon development *n Brit.* the building of houses in a continuous row along a main road.

ribbonfish ('rɪb⁹n,fɪʃ) *n, pl* **ribbonfish** *or* **ribbonfishes**. any of various soft-finned deep-sea fishes that have an elongated compressed body.

ribbonwood ('rɪb⁹n,wʊd) *n* a small evergreen malvaceous tree of New Zealand. Its wood is used in furniture making. Also: **lacebark**.

ribcage ('rɪb,keɪdʒ) *n* the bony structure of the ribs and their connective tissue that encloses the lungs, heart, etc.

Ribeirão Prêto ★ (*Portuguese* riβəi'rãu 'pretu) *n* a city in SE Brazil, in São Paulo state. Pop.: 416 186 (1991).

Ribera ★ (*Spanish* ri'βera) *n* **José de** (xo'se de) also called *Jusepe de Ribera*, Italian nickname *Lo Spagnoletto* (The Little Spaniard). 1591–1652, Spanish artist, living in Italy.

riboflavin *or* **riboflavine** (,raɪbəʊ'fleɪvɪn) *n* a vitamin of the B complex that occurs in green vegetables, milk, fish, egg yolk, liver, and kidney: used as a yellow or orange food colouring (**E 101**). Also called: **vitamin B₂**. [C20: from RIBOSE + FLAVIN]

ribonuclease (,raɪbəʊ'njuːklɪ,eɪz) *n* any of a group of enzymes that catalyse the hydrolysis of RNA. [C20: from RIBONUCLE(IC ACID) + -ASE]

ribonucleic acid (,raɪbəʊnjuː'kliːɪk, -'kleɪ-) *n* the full name of **RNA**. [C20: from RIBO(SE) + NUCLEIC ACID]

ribose ('raɪbəʊz, -bəʊs) *n* a sugar that occurs in RNA and riboflavin. [C20: changed from *arabinose*, from (GUM) ARAB(IC) + -IN+ -OSE²]

ribosomal RNA (,raɪbə'səʊməl) *n* a type of RNA thought to form the component of ribosomes on which the translation of messenger RNA into protein chains is accomplished.

ribosome ('raɪbə,səʊm) *n* any of numerous minute particles in the cytoplasm of cells that contain RNA and protein and are the site of protein synthesis. [C20: from RIBO(NUCLEIC ACID) + -SOME³]
▸ ,ribo'somal *adj*

rib-tickler *n* a very amusing joke or story.
▸ 'rib-,tickling *adj*

ribwort ('rɪb,wɜːt) *n* a Eurasian plant that has lancelike ribbed leaves. Also called: **ribgrass**. See also **plantain**¹.

Ricardo ★ (rɪ'kɑːdəʊ) *n* **David**. 1772–1823, British economist. His main work is *Principles of Political Economy and Taxation* (1817).
▸ Ri'cardian *adj, n*

Riccio ★ ('rɪtsɪəʊ) *n* a variant of **Rizzio**.

rice (raɪs) *n* **1** an erect grass that grows in warm climates on wet ground and has yellow oblong edible grains that become white when polished. **2** the grain of this plant. ◆ *vb* **rices, ricing, riced. 3** (*tr*) *US & Canad.* to sieve (potatoes or other vegetables) to a coarse mashed consistency. [C13 *rys*, via F, It., & L from Gk *orūza*, of Oriental origin]

Rice ★ (raɪs) *n* **Elmer**, original name *Elmer Reizenstein.* 1892–1967, US dramatist. His plays include *Street Scene* (1929).

rice bowl *n* **1** a small bowl used for eating rice. **2** a fertile rice-producing region.

rice paper *n* **1** a thin edible paper made from the straw of rice, on which macaroons and similar cakes are baked. **2** a thin delicate Chinese paper made from the **rice-paper plant**, the pith of which is pared and flattened into sheets.

ricercare (,riːtʃə'kɑːreɪ) *or* **ricercar** ('riːtʃə,kɑː) *n, pl* **ricercari** (-'kɑːriː) *or* **ricercars**. (in music of the 16th and 17th centuries) **1** an elaborate polyphonic composition making extensive use of contrapuntal imitation and usually very

slow in tempo. **2** an instructive composition to illustrate instrumental technique; étude. [It., lit.: to seek again]

rich (rɪtʃ) *adj* **1a** well supplied with wealth, property, etc.; owning much. **1b** (*as collective n; preceded by the*): *the rich.* **2** (when *postpositive*, usually foll. by *in*) having an abundance of natural resources, minerals, etc.: *a land rich in metals.* **3** producing abundantly; fertile: *rich soil.* **4** (when *postpositive*, foll. by *in* or *with*) well supplied (with desirable qualities); abundant (in): *a country rich with cultural interest.* **5** of great worth or quality: *a rich collection of antiques.* **6** luxuriant or prolific: *a rich growth of weeds.* **7** expensively elegant, elaborate, or fine; costly: *a rich display.* **8** (of food) having a large proportion of flavoursome or fatty ingredients. **9** having a full-bodied flavour: *a rich ruby port.* **10** (of a smell) pungent or fragrant. **11** (of colour) intense or vivid; deep: *a rich red.* **12** (of sound or a voice) full, mellow, or resonant. **13** (of a fuel-air mixture) containing a relatively high proportion of fuel. **14** very amusing or ridiculous: *a rich joke.* ◆ *n* **15** See **riches**. [OE *rīce* (orig. of persons: great, mighty), of Gmc origin, ult. from Celtic]

Rich ★ (rɪtʃ) *n* **Buddy**, real name *Bernard Rich.* 1917–87, US jazz drummer and band leader.

Richard ★ ('rɪtʃəd) *n* **Sir Cliff**, real name *Harry Rodger Webb.* born 1940, British pop singer. Film musicals include *Summer Holiday* (1962).

Richard I ★ *n* nicknamed *Cœur de Lion* or *the Lion-Heart.* 1157–99, king of England (1189–99); a leader of the third crusade (joining it in 1191). On his way home, he was captured in Austria (1192) and held to ransom. After a brief return to England (1194), he spent the rest of his life in France.

Richard II ★ *n* 1367–1400, king of England (1377–99); forced to abdicate in favour of Henry Bolingbroke, who became Henry IV.

Richard III ★ *n* 1452–85, king of England (1483–85), notorious as the suspected murderer of his two young nephews in the Tower of London; killed at the battle of Bosworth.

Richards ★ ('rɪtʃədz) *n* **1 I(vor) A(rmstrong).** 1893–1979, British critic and linguist, who, with C. K. Ogden, wrote *The Meaning of Meaning* (1923) and devised Basic English. **2** Sir **Gordon**. 1904–86, British jockey. **3 Viv**, full name *Isaac Vivian Alexander Richards.* born 1952, West Indian cricketer; captain of the West Indies (1985–91).

Richardson ★ ('rɪtʃədsən) *n* **1 Henry Handel**. pen name of *Ethel Florence Lindesay Richardson*, 1870–1946, Australian novelist; author of the trilogy *The Fortunes of Richard Mahony* (1917–29). **2** Sir **Owen Willans**. 1879–1959, British physicist; a pioneer in atomic physics: Nobel prize for physics 1928. **3** Sir **Ralph** (**David**). 1902–83, British actor. **4 Samuel**. 1689–1761, British novelist. His novels include *Pamela* (1740) and *Clarissa* (1747).

Richelieu ★ ('rɪʃə,ljɜː; *French* riʃəljø) *n* **Armand Jean du Plessis** (armã ʒã dy plesi). 1585–1642, French statesman and cardinal, principal minister to Louis XIII and virtual ruler of France (1624–42).

Richelieu River ★ *n* a river in E Canada, in S Quebec, rising in Lake Champlain and flowing north to the St Lawrence River. Length: 338 km (210 miles).

riches ('rɪtʃɪz) *pl n* wealth; an abundance of money, valuable possessions, or property.

Richler ★ ('rɪtʃlə) *n* **Mordecai**. born 1931, Canadian novelist. His novels include *Joshua Now and Then* (1981) and *Barney's Version* (1997).

richly ('rɪtʃlɪ) *adv* **1** in a rich or elaborate manner: *a richly decorated carving.* **2** fully and appropriately: *he was richly rewarded.*

Richmond ★ ('rɪtʃmənd) *n* **1** a borough of Greater London, on the River Thames: formed in 1965 by the amalgamation of Barnes, Richmond, and Twickenham; site of Hampton Court Palace and the Royal Botanic Gardens at Kew. Pop.: 172 000 (1994 est.). Area: 55 sq. km (21 sq. miles). Official name: **Richmond-upon-Thames**. **2** a town in N England, in North Yorkshire: Norman castle. Pop.: 7862 (1991). **3** a port in E Virginia, the state capital, at the falls of the James River: developed after the establishment of a trading post (1637); scene of the

---

Virginia Conventions of 1774 and 1775; Confederate capital in the American Civil War. Pop.: 201 108 (1994 est.). **4** a county of SW New York City: coextensive with Staten Island borough; consists of Staten Island and several smaller islands.

richness ('rɪtʃnɪs) *n* **1** the state or quality of being rich. **2** *Ecology*. the number of individuals of a species in a given area.

Richter ★ *n* **1** ('rɪktə). **Burton**. born 1931, US physicist; shared Nobel prize for physics (1976), for discovery of the J/psi particle. **2** (*German* 'rɪçtər). **Johann Friedrich** (joˈhan 'friːdrɪç), wrote under the name *Jean Paul*. 1763–1825, German novelist. His works include *Titan* (1800–03). **3** (*Russian* 'rixtɪr). **Sviatoslav** (svɪ̯ta'slaf). 1915–97, Ukrainian pianist.

Richter scale ('rɪktə) *n* a scale for expressing the magnitude of an earthquake, ranging from 0 to over 8. [C20: after Charles *Richter* (1900–85), US seismologist]

Richthofen ★ (*German* 'rɪçtho:fən) *n* Baron **Manfred von** ('manfreːt fɔn), nickname *the Red Baron*. 1892–1918, German aviator; commander during World War I of the 11th Chasing Squadron (**Richthofen's Flying Circus**); shot down after 80 victories.

rick[1] (rɪk) *n* **1** a large stack of hay, corn, etc., built in a regular-shaped pile, esp. with a thatched top. ♦ *vb* **2** (*tr*) to stack into ricks. [OE *hrēac*]

rick[2] (rɪk) *n* **1** a wrench or sprain, as of the back. ♦ *vb* **2** (*tr*) to wrench or sprain (a joint, a limb, the back, etc.). [C18: var. of *wrick*]

rickets ('rɪkɪts) *n* (*functioning as sing or pl*) a disease mainly of children, characterized by softening of developing bone, and hence bow legs, caused by a deficiency of vitamin D. [C17: from ?]

rickettsia (rɪ'kɛtsɪə) *n*, *pl* **rickettsiae** (-sɪˌiː) *or* **rickettsias**. any of a group of parasitic microorganisms, that live in the tissues of ticks, mites, etc., and cause disease when transmitted to man. [C20: after Howard T. *Ricketts* (1871–1910), US pathologist]
▸ **rick'ettsial** *adj*

rickettsial disease *n* any of several acute infectious diseases, such as typhus, caused by ticks, mites, or body lice infected with rickettsiae.

rickety ('rɪkɪtɪ) *adj* **1** (of a structure, piece of furniture, etc.) likely to collapse or break. **2** feeble. **3** resembling or afflicted with rickets. [C17: from RICKETS]
▸ **'ricketiness** *n*

rickrack *or* **ricrac** ('rɪkˌræk) *n* a zigzag braid used for trimming. [C20: reduplication of RACK[1]]

rickshaw ('rɪkʃɔː) *or* **ricksha** ('rɪkʃə) *n* **1** Also called: **jinrikisha**. a small two-wheeled passenger vehicle drawn by one or two men, used in parts of Asia. **2** Also called: **trishaw**. a similar vehicle with three wheels, propelled by a man pedalling as on a tricycle. [C19: shortened from JINRIKISHA]

ricochet ('rɪkəˌʃeɪ, 'rɪkəˌʃet) *vb* **ricochets** (-ˌʃeɪz), **ricocheting** (-ˌʃeɪɪŋ), **ricocheted** (-ˌʃeɪd) *or* **ricochets** (-ˌʃets), **ricochetting** (-ˌʃetɪŋ), **ricochetted** (-ˌʃetɪd). **1** (*intr*) (esp. of a bullet) to rebound from a surface, usually with a whining or zipping sound. ♦ *n* **2** the motion or sound of a rebounding object, esp. a bullet. **3** an object that ricochets. [C18: from F]

ricotta (rɪ'kɒtə) *n* a soft white unsalted cheese made from sheep's milk. [It., from L *recocta* recooked, from *recoquere*, from RE- + *coquere* to COOK]

RICS *abbrev. for* Royal Institution of Chartered Surveyors.

rictus ('rɪktəs) *n*, *pl* **rictus** *or* **rictuses**. **1** the gap or cleft of an open mouth or beak. **2** a fixed or unnatural grin or grimace as in horror or death. [C18: from L, from *ringī* to gape]
▸ **'rictal** *adj*

rid (rɪd) *vb* **rids**, **ridding**, **rid** *or* **ridded**. (*tr*) **1** (foll. by *of*) to relieve from something disagreeable or undesirable; make free (of). **2 get rid of**. to relieve or free oneself of (something unpleasant or undesirable). [C13 (meaning: to clear land): from ON *rythja*]

riddance ('rɪdⁿns) *n* the act of getting rid of something; removal (esp. in **good riddance**).

ridden ('rɪdⁿn) *vb* **1** the past participle of **ride**. ♦ *adj* **2** (*in combination*) afflicted or dominated by something specified: *disease-ridden*.

riddle[1] ('rɪdⁿl) *n* **1** a question, puzzle, or verse so phrased that ingenuity is required for elucidation of the answer or meaning. **2** a person or thing that puzzles, perplexes, or confuses. ♦ *vb* **riddles**, **riddling**, **riddled**. **3** to solve, explain, or interpret (a riddle). **4** (*intr*) to speak in riddles. [OE *rǣdelle*, *rǣdelse*, from *rǣd* counsel]
▸ **'riddler** *n*

riddle[2] ('rɪdⁿl) *vb* **riddles**, **riddling**, **riddled**. (*tr*) **1** (usually foll. by *with*) to pierce or perforate with numerous holes: *riddled with bullets*. **2** to put through a sieve; sift. ♦ *n* **3** a sieve, esp. a coarse one used for sand, grain, etc. [OE *hriddel* a sieve]
▸ **'riddler** *n*

ride (raɪd) *vb* **rides**, **riding**, **rode**, **ridden**. **1** to sit on and control the movements of (a horse or other animal). **2** (*tr*) to sit on and propel (a bicycle or similar vehicle). **3** (*intr*; often foll. by *on* or *in*) to be carried along or travel on or in a vehicle: *she rides to work on the bus*. **4** (*tr*) to travel over or traverse: *they rode the countryside in search of shelter*. **5** (*tr*) to take part in by riding: *to ride a race*. **6** to travel through or be carried across (sea, sky, etc.): *the small boat rode the waves; the moon was riding high*. **7** (*tr*) US & Canad. to cause to be carried: *to ride someone out of town*. **8** (*intr*) to be supported as if floating: *the candidate rode to victory on his new policies*. **9** (*intr*) (of a vessel) to lie at anchor. **10** (*tr*) (of a vessel) to be attached to (an anchor). **11** (*tr*) **11a** *Sl.* to have sexual intercourse with (someone). **11b** (of a male animal) to copulate with; mount. **12** (*tr; usually passive*) to tyrannize over or dominate: *ridden by fear*. **13** (*tr*) *Inf.* to persecute, esp. by constant or petty criticism: *don't ride me so hard*. **14** (*intr*) *Inf.* to continue undisturbed: *let it ride*. **15** (*tr*) to endure successfully; ride out. **16** (*tr*) to yield slightly to (a punch, etc.) to lessen its impact. **17** (*intr*; often foll. by *on*) (of a bet) to remain placed: *let your winnings ride on the same number*. **18 ride again**. *Inf.* to return to a former activity or scene. **19 ride for a fall**. to act in such a way as to invite disaster. **20 riding high**. confident, popular, and successful. ♦ *n* **21** a journey or outing on horseback or in a vehicle. **22** a path specially made for riding on horseback. **23** transport in a vehicle; lift: *can you give me a ride to the station?* **24** a device or structure, such as a roller coaster at a fairground, in which people ride for pleasure or entertainment. **25** *Sl.* an act of sexual intercourse. **26** *Sl.* a partner in sexual intercourse. **27 take for a ride**. *Inf.* **27a** to cheat, swindle, or deceive. **27b** to take (someone) away in a car and murder him. [OE *rīdan*]
▸ **'ridable** *or* **'rideable** *adj*

ride out *vb* (*tr, adv*) to endure successfully; survive (esp. in **ride out the storm**).

rider ('raɪdə) *n* **1** a person or thing that rides. **2** an additional clause, amendment, or stipulation added to a document, esp. (in Britain) a legislative bill at its third reading. **3** *Brit.* a statement made by a jury in addition to its verdict, such as a recommendation for mercy. **4** any of various objects or devices resting on or strengthening something else.
▸ **'riderless** *adj*

ride up *vb* (*intr, adv*) to work away from the proper position: *her new skirt rode up*.

ridge (rɪdʒ) *n* **1** a long narrow raised land formation with sloping sides. **2** any long narrow raised strip or elevation, as on a fabric or in ploughed land. **3** *Anat.* any elongated raised margin or border on a bone, tissue, etc. **4a** the top of a roof at the junction of two sloping sides. **4b** (*as modifier*): *a ridge tile*. **5** *Meteorol.* an elongated area of high pressure, esp. an extension of an anticyclone. Cf. **trough** (sense 4). ♦ *vb* **ridges**, **ridging**, **ridged**. **6** to form into a ridge or ridges. [OE *hrycg*]
▸ **'ridge,like** *adj* ▸ **'ridgy** *adj*

ridgepole ('rɪdʒˌpəʊl) *n* **1** a timber along the ridge of a roof, to which the rafters are attached. **2** the horizontal pole at the apex of a tent.

ridgeway ('rɪdʒˌweɪ) *n Brit.* a road or track along a ridge, esp. one of great antiquity.

ridicule ('rɪdɪˌkjuːl) *n* **1** language or behaviour intended to humiliate or mock. ♦ *vb* **ridicules**, **ridiculing**, **ridiculed**. **2**

★ people and places

(*tr*) to make fun of or mock. [C17: from F, from L *rīdiculus*, from *rīdēre* to laugh]

ridiculous (rɪ'dɪkjʊləs) *adj* worthy of or exciting ridicule; absurd, preposterous, laughable, or contemptible. [C16: from L *rīdiculōsus*, from *rīdēre* to laugh]
► ri'diculousness *n*

riding[1] ('raɪdɪŋ) *n* **1a** the art or practice of horsemanship. **1b** (*as modifier*): *a riding school.* **2** a track for riding.

riding[2] ('raɪdɪŋ) *n* (*cap. when part of a name*) any of the three former administrative divisions of Yorkshire: **North Riding**, **East Riding**, and **West Riding**. [from OE *thriding*, from ON *thrithjungr* a third]

riding crop *n* a short whip with a handle at one end for opening gates.

riding lamp *or* **light** *n* a light on a boat or ship showing that it is at anchor.

Ridley ★ ('rɪdlɪ). ♦ *n* **Nicholas.** ?1500–55, English bishop; burnt at the stake for refusing to disavow his Protestant beliefs when Mary I became queen.

Riefenstahl ★ (*German* 'riːfənʃtaːl) *n* **Leni** ('leːni). born 1902, German photographer and film director, known for her Nazi propaganda films.

Riemann ★ (*German* 'riːman) *n* **Georg Friedrich Bernhard** ('geːɔrk 'friːdrɪç 'bɛrnhart). 1826–66, German mathematician whose non-Euclidean geometry was used by Einstein.
► Rie'mannian *adj*

riempie ('rɪmpɪ) *n S. African*. a leather thong or lace used mainly to make chair seats. [C19: Afrik., dim. of *riem*, from Du.: RIM]

riesling ('riːzlɪŋ, 'raɪz-) *n* **1** a white wine from the Rhine valley in Germany and from certain districts in other countries. **2** the grape used to make this wine. [C19: from G, from earlier *Rüssling*, from ?]

rife (raɪf) *adj* (*postpositive*) **1** of widespread occurrence; current. **2** very plentiful; abundant. **3** (foll. by *with*) abounding (in): *a garden rife with weeds.* [OE *rīfe*]
► 'rifely *adv* ► 'rifeness *n*

riff (rɪf) *Jazz, rock*. ♦ *n* **1** an ostinato played over changing harmonies. ♦ *vb* **2** (*intr*) to play riffs. [C20: prob. altered from REFRAIN[2]]

riffle ('rɪfəl) *vb* **riffles, riffling, riffled**. **1** (when *intr*, often foll. by *through*) to flick rapidly through (pages of a book, etc.). **2** to shuffle (cards) by halving the pack and flicking the corners together. **3** to cause or form a ripple on water. ♦ *n* **4** *US & Canad*. a rapid in a stream. **4a** a rocky shoal causing a rapid. **4c** a ripple on water. **5** *Mining*. a contrivance on the bottom of a sluice, containing grooves for trapping particles of gold. **6** the act or an instance of riffling. [C18: prob. from RUFFLE[1], infl. by RIPPLE[1]]

riffraff ('rɪfˌræf) *n* (*sometimes functioning as pl*) worthless people, esp. collectively; rabble. [C15 *rif and raf*, from OF *rif et raf*; rel. to *rifler* to plunder, and *rafle* a sweeping up]

rifle[1] ('raɪfəl) *n* **1a** a firearm having a long barrel with a spirally grooved interior, which imparts to the bullet spinning motion and thus greater accuracy over a longer range. **1b** (*as modifier*): *rifle fire.* **2** (formerly) a large cannon with a rifled bore. **3** one of the grooves in a rifled bore. **4** (*pl*) **4a** a unit of soldiers equipped with rifles. **4b** (*cap. when part of a name*): *the King's Own Rifles.* ♦ *vb* **rifles, rifling, rifled**. (*tr*) **5** to make spiral grooves inside the barrel of (a gun). [C18: from OF *rifler* to scratch; rel. to Low G *rifeln* from *riefe* groove]

rifle[2] ('raɪfəl) *vb* **rifles, rifling, rifled**. (*tr*) **1** to search (a house, safe, etc.) and steal from it; ransack. **2** to steal and carry off: *to rifle goods.* [C14: from OF *rifler* to plunder, scratch, of Gmc origin]
► 'rifler *n*

riflebird ('raɪfəlˌbɜːd) *n* any of various Australian birds of paradise whose plumage has a metallic sheen.

rifleman ('raɪfəlmən) *n, pl* **riflemen**. **1.** a person skilled in the use of a rifle, esp. a soldier. **2** a wren of New Zealand.

rifle range *n* an area used for target practice with rifles.

rifling ('raɪflɪŋ) *n* **1** the cutting of spiral grooves on the inside of a firearm's barrel. **2** the series of grooves so cut.

rift (rɪft) *n* **1** a gap or space made by cleaving or splitting. **2** *Geol*. a fault produced by tension on either side of the fault plane. **3** a gap between two cloud masses; break or chink. **4** a break in friendly relations between people, nations, etc. ♦ *vb* **5** to burst or cause to burst open; split. [C13: from ON]

rift valley *n* a long narrow valley resulting from the subsidence of land between two faults.

rig (rɪg) *vb* **rigs, rigging, rigged**. (*tr*) **1** *Naut*. to equip (a vessel, mast, etc.) with (sails, rigging, etc.). **2** *Naut*. to set up or prepare ready for use. **3** to put the components of (an aircraft, etc.) into their correct positions. **4** to manipulate in a fraudulent manner, esp. for profit: *to rig prices.* ♦ *n* **5** *Naut*. the distinctive arrangement of the sails, masts, etc., of a vessel. **6** the installation used in drilling for and exploiting natural gas and oil deposits: *an oil rig.* **7** apparatus or equipment. **8** *US & Canad*. an articulated lorry. ♦ See also **rig out, rig up**. [C15: of Scand. origin; rel. to Norwegian *rigga* to wrap]

Riga ★ ('riːgə) *n* the capital of Latvia, on the **Gulf of Riga** at the mouth of the Western Dvina: a major trading centre of the Baltic since Viking times. Pop.: 839 670 (1995 est.).

rigadoon (ˌrɪgə'duːn) *n* **1** an old Provençal couple dance, light and graceful, in lively duple time. **2** a piece of music composed for or in the rhythm of this dance. [C17: from F, allegedly after *Rigaud*, a dancing master at Marseilles]

rigamarole ('rɪgəməˌrəʊl) *n* a variant of **rigmarole**.

-rigged *adj* (*in combination*) (of a sailing vessel) having a rig of a certain kind: *ketch-rigged; schooner-rigged.*

rigger ('rɪgə) *n* **1** a workman who rigs vessels, etc. **2** *Rowing*. a bracket on a boat to support a projecting rowlock. **3** a person skilled in the use of pulleys, cranes, etc.

rigging ('rɪgɪŋ) *n* **1** the shrouds, stays, etc., of a vessel. **2** the bracing wires, struts, and lines of a biplane, etc. **3** any form of lifting gear.

right (raɪt) *adj* **1** in accordance with accepted standards of moral or legal behaviour, justice, etc.: *right conduct.* **2** correct or true: *the right answer.* **3** appropriate, suitable, or proper: *the right man for the job.* **4** most favourable or convenient: *the right time to act.* **5** in a satisfactory condition: *things are right again now.* **6** indicating or designating the correct time: *the clock is right.* **7** correct in opinion or judgment. **8** sound in mind or body. **9** (*usually prenominal*) of, designating, or located near the side of something or someone that faces east when the front is turned towards the north. **10** (*usually prenominal*) worn on a right hand, foot, etc. **11** (*sometimes cap.*) of, designating, belonging to, or relating to the political or intellectual right (see sense 36). **12** (*sometimes cap.*) conservative: *the right wing of the party.* **13** *Geom.* **13a** formed by or containing a line or plane perpendicular to another line or plane. **13b** having the axis perpendicular to the base: *a right circular cone.* **13c** straight: *a right line.* **14** relating to or designating the side of cloth worn or facing outwards. **15** in one's right mind. **16** she'll be right. *Austral. & NZ inf.* that's all right; not to worry. **17 the right side of**. **17a** in favour with: *you'd better stay on the right side of him.* **17b** younger than: *she's still on the right side of fifty.* **18 too right**. *Austral. & NZ inf.* an exclamation of agreement. ♦ *adv* **19** in accordance with correctness or truth: *to guess right.* **20** in the appropriate manner: *do it right next time!* **21** in a straight line: *right to the top.* **22** in the direction of the east from the point of view of a person or thing facing north. **23** absolutely or completely: *he went right through the floor.* **24** all the way: *the bus goes right into town.* **25** without delay: *I'll be right over.* **26** exactly or precisely: *right here.* **27** in a manner consistent with a legal or moral code: *do right by me.* **28** in accordance with propriety; fittingly: *it serves you right.* **29** to good or favourable advantage: *it all came out right in the end.* **30** (esp. in religious titles) most or very: *right reverend.* **31 right, left, and centre**. on all sides. ♦ *n* **32** any claim, title, etc., that is morally just or legally granted as allowable or due to a person: *I know my rights.* **33** anything that accords with the principles of legal or moral justice. **34** the fact or state of being in accordance with reason, truth, or accepted standards (esp. in **in the right**). **35** the right side, di-

rection, position, area, or part: *the right of the army*. **36** (*often cap.* and preceded by *the*) the supporters or advocates of social, political, or economic conservatism or reaction. **37** *Boxing*. **37a** a punch with the right hand. **37b** the right hand. **38** (*often pl*) *Finance*. the privilege of a company's shareholders to subscribe for new issues of the company's shares on advantageous terms. **39 by right** (or **rights**). properly: *by rights you should be in bed*. **40 in one's own right**. having a claim or title oneself rather than through marriage or other connection. **41 to rights**. consistent with justice or orderly arrangement: *he put the matter to rights*. ◆ *vb* (*mainly tr*) **42** (*also intr*) to restore to or attain a normal, esp. an upright, position: *the raft righted in a few seconds*. **43** to make (something) accord with truth or facts. **44** to restore to an orderly state or condition. **45** to compensate for or redress (esp. in **right a wrong**). ◆ *interj* **46** an expression of agreement or compliance. [OE *riht, reoht*]
▶ **'rightable** *adj* ▶ **'righter** *n* ▶ **'rightness** *n*

right about *n* **1** a turn executed through 180°. ◆ *adj, adv* **2** in the opposite direction.

right angle *n* **1** the angle between radii of a circle that cut off on the circumference an arc equal in length to one quarter of the circumference; an angle of 90° or $\pi/2$ radians. **2 at right angles**. perpendicular or perpendicularly.
▶ **'right-,angled** *adj*

right-angled triangle *n* a triangle one angle of which is a right angle. US and Canad. name: **right triangle**.

right ascension *n Astron*. the angular distance measured eastwards along the celestial equator from the vernal equinox to the point at which the celestial equator intersects a great circle passing through the celestial pole and the heavenly object in question.

right away *adv* without delay.

righteous ('raɪtʃəs) *adj* **1a** characterized by, proceeding from, or in accordance with accepted standards of morality or uprightness: *a righteous man*. **1b** (*as collective n*; preceded by *the*): *the righteous*. **2** morally justifiable or right: *righteous indignation*. [OE *rīhtwīs*, from RIGHT + WISE²]
▶ **'righteously** *adv* ▶ **'righteousness** *n*

rightful ('raɪtfʊl) *adj* **1** in accordance with what is right. **2** (*prenominal*) having a legally or morally just claim: *the rightful owner*. **3** (*prenominal*) held by virtue of a legal or just claim: *my rightful property*.
▶ **'rightfully** *adv*

right-hand *adj* (*prenominal*) **1** of, located on, or moving towards the right: *a right-hand bend*. **2** for use by the right hand. **3 right-hand man**. one's most valuable assistant.

right-handed *adj* **1** using the right hand with greater skill or ease than the left. **2** performed with the right hand. **3** made for use by the right hand. **4** turning from left to right.
▶ **,right-'handedness** *n*

rightist ('raɪtɪst) *adj* **1** of, tending towards, or relating to the political right or its principles. ◆ *n* **2** a person who supports or belongs to the political right.
▶ **'rightism** *n*

rightly ('raɪtlɪ) *adv* **1** in accordance with the true facts. **2** in accordance with principles of justice or morality. **3** with good reason: *he was rightly annoyed with her*. **4** properly or suitably. **5** (*used with a negative*) *Inf*. with certainty (usually in **I don't rightly know**).

right-minded *adj* holding opinions or principles that accord with what is right or with the opinions of the speaker.

righto or **right oh** ('raɪt'əʊ) *sentence substitute*. *Brit. inf*. an expression of agreement or compliance.

right off *adv* immediately; right away.

right of way *n, pl* **rights of way**. **1** the right of one vehicle or vessel to take precedence over another, as laid down by law or custom. **2a** the legal right of someone to pass over another's land, acquired by grant or by long usage. **2b** the path used by this right. **3** *US*. the strip of land over which a power line, road, etc., extends.

right-on *adj Inf*. modern, trendy, and socially aware or relevant: *right-on green politics*.

Right Reverend *adj* (in Britain) a title of respect for an Anglican or Roman Catholic bishop.

rights issue *n Stock Exchange*. an issue of new shares offered by a company to its existing shareholders on favourable terms.

rightsize ('raɪt,saɪz) *vb* to restructure (an organization) to cut costs and improve effectiveness without ruthlessly downsizing.

right-thinking ('raɪt'θɪŋkɪŋ) *adj* possessing reasonable and generally acceptable opinions.

rightward ('raɪtwəd) *adj* **1** situated on or directed towards the right. ◆ *adv* **2** a variant of **rightwards**.

rightwards ('raɪtwədz) or **rightward** *adv* towards or on the right.

right whale *n* a large whalebone whale which is grey or black, has a large head and no dorsal fin, and is hunted as a source of whalebone and oil. See also **bowhead**. [C19: ? because it was *right* for hunting]

right wing *n* **1** (*often cap.*) the conservative faction of an assembly, party, etc. **2** the part of an army or field of battle on the right from the point of view of one facing the enemy. **3a** the right-hand side of the field of play from the point of view of a team facing its opponent's goal. **3b** a player positioned in this area in any of various games. ◆ *adj* **right-wing**. **4** of, belonging to, or relating to the right wing.
▶ **'right-'winger** *n*

Rigi ★ ('riːgɪ) *n* a mountain in the Alps of N central Switzerland, between Lakes Lucerne, Zug, and Lauerz.

rigid ('rɪdʒɪd) *adj* **1** physically inflexible or stiff: *a rigid piece of plastic*. **2** rigorously strict: *rigid rules*. [C16: from L *rigidus*, from *rigēre* to be stiff]
▶ **ri'gidity** *n* ▶ **'rigidly** *adv*

rigidify (rɪ'dʒɪdɪ,faɪ) *vb* **rigidifies, rigidifying, rigidified**. to make or become rigid.

rigmarole ('rɪgmə,rəʊl) or **rigamarole** *n* **1** any long complicated procedure. **2** a set of incoherent or pointless statements. [C18: from earlier *ragman roll* a list, prob. a roll used in a medieval game, wherein characters were described in verse, beginning with *Ragemon le bon* Ragman the good]

rigor ('raɪgɔː, 'rɪgə) *n* **1** *Med*. a sudden feeling of chilliness, often accompanied by shivering: it sometimes precedes a fever. **2** ('rɪgə). *Pathol*. rigidity of a muscle. **3** a state of rigidity assumed in reaction to shock. [see RIGOUR]

rigor mortis ('rɪgə 'mɔːtɪs) *n Pathol*. the stiffness of joints and muscular rigidity of a dead body. [C19: L, lit.: rigidity of death]

rigorous ('rɪgərəs) *adj* **1** harsh, strict, or severe: *rigorous discipline*. **2** severely accurate: *rigorous book-keeping*. **3** (esp. of weather) extreme or harsh. **4** *Maths, logic*. (of a proof) making the validity of each step explicit.
▶ **'rigorously** *adv*

rigour or US **rigor** ('rɪgə) *n* **1** harsh but just treatment or action. **2** a severe or cruel circumstance: *the rigours of famine*. **3** strictness, harshness, or severity of character. **4** strictness in judgment or conduct. [C14: from L *rigor*]

rig out *vb* **1** (*tr, adv*; often foll. by *with*) to equip or fit out (with): *his car is rigged out with gadgets*. **2** to dress or be dressed: *rigged out smartly*. ◆ *n* **rigout**. **3** *Inf*. a person's clothing or costume, esp. a bizarre outfit.

rig up *vb* (*tr, adv*) to erect or construct, esp. as a temporary measure: *cameras were rigged up*.

Rig-Veda (rɪg'veɪdə) *n* a compilation of Hindu poems dating from 2000 B.C. or earlier. [C18: from Sansk. *rigveda*, from *ric* song of praise + VEDA]

Rijeka ★ (rɪ'ɛkə; *Serbo-Croat* ri'jeka) *n* a port in NW Croatia: an ancient town, changing hands many times before passing to Yugoslavia in 1947 and to Croatia in 1991. Pop.: 167 964 (1991). Italian name: **Fiume**.

Rijksmuseum ★ ('raɪxsmju:,zɪəm) *n* a museum in Amsterdam housing the national art collection of the Netherlands.

Rijn ★ (rεjn) *n* the Dutch name for the **Rhine**.

Rijswijk ★ ('raɪsvaɪk; *Dutch* 'rεjswεjk) *n* a town in the SW Netherlands, in South Holland province on the SE outskirts of The Hague: scene of the signing (1697) of the **Treaty of Rijswijk,** ending the War of the Grand Alliance. Pop.: 48 000 (1991). English name: **Ryswick.**

rile (raɪl) *vb* **riles, riling, riled.** (*tr*) **1** to annoy or anger. **2** *US & Canad.* to agitate (water, etc.). [C19: var. of ROIL]

Riley ★ ('raɪlɪ) *n* **Bridget** (**Louise**). born 1931, British painter, best known for her black-and-white op art paintings of the 1960s.

Rilke ★ (*German* 'rɪlkə) *n* **Rainer Maria** ('raɪnər ma'riːa). 1875–1926, Austro-German poet, born in Prague. Author of the *Duino Elegies* (1922) and *Sonnets to Orpheus* (1923).

rill (rɪl) *n* **1** a brook or stream. **2** a channel or gulley, such as one formed during soil erosion. **3** Also: **rille.** one of many winding cracks on the moon. [C15: from Low G *rille*]

rim (rɪm) *n* **1** the raised edge of an object, esp. of something more or less circular such as a cup or crater. **2** the peripheral part of a wheel, to which the tyre is attached. **3** *Basketball.* the hoop from which the net is suspended. ◆ *vb* **rims, rimming, rimmed.** (*tr*) **4** to put a rim on (a pot, cup, wheel, etc.). **5** *Sl.* to lick, kiss, or suck the anus of (one's sexual partner). [OE *rima*]

Rimbaud ★ (*French* rɛ̃bo) *n* **Arthur** (artyr). 1854–91, French poet, whose work includes *A Season in Hell* (1873) and *Illuminations* (published 1884).

rime[1] (raɪm) *n* **1** frost formed by the freezing of water droplets in fog onto solid objects. ◆ *vb* **rimes, riming, rimed. 2** (*tr*) to cover with rime or something resembling rime. [OE *hrīm*]

rime[2] (raɪm) *n, vb* **rimes, riming, rimed.** an archaic spelling of **rhyme.**

rim-fire *adj* **1** (of a cartridge) having the primer in the rim of the base. **2** (of a firearm) adapted for such cartridges.

Rimini ★ ('rɪmɪnɪ) *n* a port and resort in NE Italy, in Emilia-Romagna on the N Adriatic coast. Pop.: 130 006 (1994 est.). Ancient name: **Ariminum.**

rimose (raɪ'məʊs, -'məʊz) *adj* (esp. of plant parts) having the surface marked by a network of cracks. [C18: from L *rīmōsus,* from *rīma* a split]

Rimsky-Korsakov ★ ('rɪmskɪ'kɔːsəkɒf; *Russian* 'rimskij-'kɔrsəkəf) *n* **Nikolai Andreyevich** (nika'laj an'drjejɪvitʃ). 1844–1908, Russian composer; noted for such works as the suite *Scheherazade* (1888).

rimu ('riːmuː) *n* a New Zealand tree. Also called: **red pine.** [from Maori]

rimy ('raɪmɪ) *adj* **rimier, rimiest.** coated with rime.

rind (raɪnd) *n* **1** a hard outer layer or skin on bacon, cheese, etc. **2** the outer layer of a fruit or of the spore-producing body of certain fungi. **3** the outer layer of the bark of a tree. [OE *rinde*]

rinderpest ('rɪndə,pɛst) *n* an acute contagious viral disease of cattle, characterized by severe inflammation of the intestinal tract and diarrhoea. [C19: from G *Rinderpest* cattle pest]

ring[1] (rɪŋ) *n* **1** a circular band of a precious metal often set with gems and worn upon the finger as an adornment or as a token of engagement or marriage. **2** any object or mark that is circular in shape. **3** a circular path or course: *to run around in a ring.* **4** a group of people or things standing or arranged so as to form a circle: *a ring of spectators.* **5** an enclosed space, usually circular in shape, where circus acts are performed. **6** a square raised platform, marked off by ropes, in which contestants box or wrestle. **7** **the ring.** the sport of boxing. **8** **throw one's hat in the ring.** to announce one's intention to be a candidate or contestant. **9** a group of people usually operating illegally and covertly: *a drug ring; a paedophile ring.* **10** (esp. at country fairs) an enclosure where horses, cattle, and other livestock are paraded and auctioned. **11** an area reserved for betting at a racecourse. **12** a circular strip of bark cut from a tree or branch. **13** a single turn in a spiral. **14** *Geom.* the area of space lying between two concentric circles. **15** *Maths.* a set that is subject to two binary operations, addition and multiplication, such that the set is a commutative group under addition and is closed under multiplication, this latter operation

being associative. **16** *Bot.* short for **annual ring. 17** *Chem.* a closed loop of atoms in a molecule. **18** *Astron.* any of the thin circular bands of small bodies orbiting a giant planet, esp. Saturn. **19** **run rings round.** *Inf.* to outclass completely. ◆ *vb* **rings, ringing, ringed.** (*tr*) **20** to surround with, or as if with, or form a ring. **21** to mark a bird with a ring or clip for subsequent identification. **22** to fit a ring in the nose of (a bull, etc.) so that it can be led easily. **23** to ringbark. [OE *hring*]
▸ **ringed** *adj*

ring[2] (rɪŋ) *vb* **rings, ringing, rang, rung. 1** to emit or cause to emit a resonant sound, characteristic of certain metals when struck. **2** to cause (a bell, etc.) to emit a ringing sound by striking it once or repeatedly or (of a bell) to emit such a sound. **3a** (*tr*) to cause (a large bell) to emit a ringing sound by pulling on a rope attached to a wheel on which the bell swings back and forth, being sounded by a clapper inside it. **3b** (*intr*) (of a bell) to sound by being swung in this way. **4** (*intr*) (of a building, place, etc.) to be filled with sound: *the church rang with singing.* **5** (*intr*; foll. by *for*) to call by means of a bell, etc.: *to ring for the butler.* **6** Also: **ring up.** *Chiefly Brit.* to call (a person) by telephone. **7** (*tr*) to strike or tap (a coin) in order to assess its genuineness by the sound produced. **8** *Sl.* to change the identity of (a stolen vehicle) by using the licence plate, serial number, etc., of another, usually disused, vehicle. **9** (*intr*) (of the ears) to have or give the sensation of humming or ringing. **10** **ring a bell.** to bring something to the mind or memory: *that rings a bell.* **11** **ring down the curtain. 11a** to lower the curtain at the end of a theatrical performance. **11b** (foll. by *on*) to put an end (to). **12** **ring false.** to give the impression of being false. **13** **ring true.** to give the impression of being true. ◆ *n* **14** the act of or a sound made by ringing. **15** a sound produced by or suggestive of a bell. **16** any resonant or metallic sound: *the ring of trumpets.* **17** *Inf., chiefly Brit.* a telephone call. **18** the complete set of bells in a tower or belfry: *a ring of eight bells.* **19** an inherent quality or characteristic: *his words had the ring of sincerity.* ◆ See also **ring in, ring off,** etc. [OE *hringan*]

> **USAGE NOTE** *Rang* and *sang* are the correct forms of the past tenses of *ring* and *sing,* although *rung* and *sung* are still heard informally and dialectally: *he rung (rang) the bell.*

ringbark ('rɪŋ,bɑːk) *vb* (*tr*) to kill (a tree) by cutting away a strip of bark from around the trunk.

ring binder *n* a loose-leaf binder with metal rings that can be opened to insert perforated paper.

ringbolt ('rɪŋ,bəʊlt) *n* a bolt with a ring fitted through an eye attached to the bolt head.

ringdove ('rɪŋ,dʌv) *n* **1** another name for **wood pigeon. 2** an Old World turtledove, having a black neck band.

ringed plover *n* a European shorebird with a greyish-brown back, white underparts, a black throat band, and orange legs.

ringer ('rɪŋə) *n* **1** a person or thing that rings a bell, etc. **2** Also called: **dead ringer.** *Sl.* a person or thing that is almost identical to another. **3** *Sl.* a stolen vehicle the identity of which has been changed by the use of the licence plate, serial number, etc., of another, usually disused, vehicle. **4** *Chiefly US.* a contestant, esp. a horse, entered in a competition under false representations of identity, record, or ability. **5** *Austral.* a stockman; station hand. **6** *Austral.* the fastest shearer in a shed. **7** *Austral. inf.* the fastest or best at anything. **8** a quoit thrown so as to encircle a peg. **9** such a throw.

ring-fence *vb* **1** to assign (money, a grant, fund, etc.) to one particular purpose, so as to restrict its use: *to ring-fence a financial allowance.* **2** to oblige (a person or organization) to use money for a particular purpose: *to ring-fence a local authority.* ◆ *n* **ring fence. 3** an agreement, contract, etc., in which the use of money is restricted to a particular purpose.

ring finger *n* the third finger, esp. of the left hand, on which a wedding ring is worn.

ring in *vb* (*adv*) **1** (*intr*) *Chiefly Brit.* to report to someone by telephone. **2** (*tr*) to accompany the arrival of with bells (esp. in **ring in the new year**). ◆ *n* **ring-in. 3** *Austral. & NZ inf.* a person or thing that is not normally a member of a particular group; outsider.

ringing tone *n Brit.* a sequence of pairs of tones heard by the dialler on a telephone when the number dialled is ringing. Cf. **engaged tone, dialling tone.**

ringleader ('rɪŋ,liːdə) *n* a person who leads others in unlawful or mischievous activity.

ringlet ('rɪŋlɪt) *n* **1** a lock of hair hanging down in a spiral curl. **2** a butterfly that occurs in S Europe and has dark brown wings marked with small black-and-white eyespots.
  ▸ 'ringleted *adj*

ring main *n* a domestic electrical supply in which outlet sockets are connected to the mains supply through a continuous closed circuit (**ring circuit**).

ringmaster ('rɪŋ,mɑːstə) *n* the master of ceremonies in a circus.

ring-necked *adj* (of animals, esp. birds and snakes) having a band of distinctive colour around the neck.

ring-necked pheasant *n* a common pheasant originating in Asia. The male has a bright plumage with a band of white around the neck and the female is mottled brown.

ring off *vb* (*intr, adv*) *Chiefly Brit.* to terminate a telephone conversation by replacing the receiver; hang up.

ring out *vb* (*adv*) **1** (*tr*) to accompany the departure of with bells (esp. in **ring out the old year**). **2** (*intr*) to send forth a loud resounding noise.

ring ouzel *n* a European thrush common in rocky areas. The male has a blackish plumage and the female is brown.

ring road *n* a main road that bypasses a town or town centre. US names: **belt, beltway.**

ringside ('rɪŋ,saɪd) *n* **1** the row of seats nearest a boxing or wrestling ring. **2a** any place affording a close uninterrupted view. **2b** (*as modifier*): *a ringside seat.*

ringtail ('rɪŋ,teɪl) *n Austral.* any of several tree-living phalangers having curling prehensile tails used to grasp branches while climbing.

ring up *vb* (*adv*) **1** *Chiefly Brit.* to make a telephone call (to). **2** (*tr*) to record on a cash register. **3 ring up the curtain. 3a** to begin a theatrical performance. **3b** (often foll. by *on*) to make a start (on).

ringworm ('rɪŋ,wɜːm) *n* any of various fungal infections of the skin or nails, often appearing as itching circular patches. Also called: **tinea.**

rink (rɪŋk) *n* **1** an expanse of ice for skating on, esp. one that is artificially prepared and under cover. **2** an area for roller-skating on. **3** a building or enclosure for ice-skating or roller-skating. **4** *Bowls.* a strip of the green on which a game is played. **5** *Curling.* the strip of ice on which the game is played. **6** (in bowls and curling) the players on one side in a game. [C14 (Scots): from OF *renc* row]

rinkhals ('rɪŋk,hæls) *or* **ringhals** ('rɪŋg,hæls) *n, pl* **rinkhals, rinkhalses, ringhals** *or* **ringhalses.** a venomous snake of southern Africa, which can spit venom over 2 m (7 ft). [Afrik., lit.: ring neck]

rink rat *n Canad. sl.* a youth who helps with odd chores around an ice-hockey rink in return for free admission to games, etc.

rinse (rɪns) *vb* **rinses, rinsing, rinsed.** (*tr*) **1** to remove soap from (clothes, etc.) by applying clean water in the final stage in washing. **2** to wash lightly, esp. without using soap. **3** to give a light tint to (hair). ◆ *n* **4** the act or an instance of rinsing. **5** *Hairdressing.* a liquid preparation put on the hair when wet to give a tint to it: *a blue rinse.* [C14: from OF *rincer*, from L *recens* fresh]
  ▸ 'rinser *n*

Rio Branco ★ (*Portuguese* 'riu 'brəŋku) *n* **1** a city in W Brazil, capital of Acre state. Pop.: 167 457 (1991). **2** a river in Brazil, flowing south to the Rio Negro. Length: 644 km (400 miles).

Río Bravo ★ ('rio 'braβo) *n* the Mexican name for the **Rio Grande.**

Rio de Janeiro ('riːəu də dʒə'nɪərəu) *or* **Rio** ★ *n* **1** a port in SE Brazil, on Guanabara Bay: the country's chief port and its capital from 1763 to 1960; backed by mountains, notably Sugar Loaf Mountain; founded by the French in 1555 and taken by the Portuguese in 1567. Pop. (urban area): 9 888 000 (1995). **2** a state of E Brazil. Capital: Rio de Janeiro. Pop.: 13 296 400 (1995 est.). Area: 42 911 sq. km (16 568 sq. miles).

Río de la Plata ★ ('riːəu də lɑː 'plɑːtə) *n* See **Plata.**

Río de Oro ★ (*Spanish* 'rio ðe 'oro) *n* a former region of W Africa: comprised the S part of the Spanish Sahara (now Western Sahara).

Rio Grande ★ *n* **1** ('riːəu 'grænd, 'grændɪ). a river in North America, rising in SW Colorado and flowing southeast to the Gulf of Mexico, forming the border between the US and Mexico. Length: about 3030 km (1885 miles). Mexican name: **Río Bravo. 2** (*Portuguese* 'riu 'grəndi). a port in SE Brazil, in SE Rio Grande do Sul state: serves as the port for Pôrto Alegre. Pop.: 157 608 (1991).

Rio Grande do Norte ★ (*Portuguese* 'riu 'grəndi do 'nɔrti) *n* a state of NE Brazil, on the Atlantic: much of it is semiarid plateau. Capital: Natal. Pop.: 2 582 300 (1995 est.). Area: 53 014 sq. km (20 469 sq. miles).

Rio Grande do Sul ★ (*Portuguese* 'riu 'grəndi du 'sul) *n* a state of S Brazil, on the Atlantic. Capital: Pôrto Alegre. Pop.: 9 578 600 (1995 est.). Area: 282 183 sq. km (108 951 sq. miles).

rioja (rɪ'əuxə) *n* a red or white wine, with a distinctive vanilla bouquet and flavour, produced around the Ebro river in central N Spain. [C20: from *La Rioja*, the area where it is produced]

Río Negro ★ ('riːəu 'neɪgrəu, 'nɛg-; *Spanish* 'rio 'neɣro) *n* See **Negro²**.

riot ('raɪət) *n* **1a** a disturbance made by an unruly mob or (in law) three or more persons. **1b** (*as modifier*): *a riot shield.* **2** unrestrained revelry. **3** an occasion of boisterous merriment. **4** *Sl.* a person who occasions boisterous merriment. **5** a dazzling display: *a riot of colour.* **6** *Hunting.* the indiscriminate following of any scent by hounds. **7** *Arch.* wanton lasciviousness. **8 run riot. 8a** to behave without restraint. **8b** (of plants) to grow profusely. ◆ *vb* **9** (*intr*) to take part in a riot. **10** (*intr*) to indulge in unrestrained revelry. **11** (*tr*; foll. by *away*) to spend (time or money) in wanton or loose living. [C13: from OF *riote* dispute, from *ruihoter* to quarrel, prob. from *ruir* to make a commotion, from L *rugīre* to roar]
  ▸ 'rioter *n*

Riot Act *n* **1** *Criminal law.* (formerly, in England) a statute of 1715 by which persons committing a riot had to disperse within an hour of the reading of the act by a magistrate. **2 read the riot act to.** to warn or reprimand severely.

riotous ('raɪətəs) *adj* **1** proceeding from or of the nature of riots or rioting. **2** characterized by wanton revelry: *riotous living.* **3** characterized by unrestrained merriment: *riotous laughter.*
  ▸ 'riotously *adv* ▸ 'riotousness *n*

riot shield *n* (in Britain) a shield used by police controlling crowds.

rip¹ (rɪp) *vb* **rips, ripping, ripped. 1** to tear or be torn violently or roughly. **2** (*tr*; foll. by *off* or *out*) to remove hastily or roughly. **3** (*intr*) *Inf.* to move violently or precipitously. **4** (*intr*; foll. by *into*) *Inf.* to pour violent abuse (on). **5** (*tr*) to saw or split (wood) in the direction of the grain. **6 let rip.** to act or speak without restraint. ◆ *n* **7** a tear or split. **8** short for **ripsaw.** ◆ See also **rip off.** [C15: ?from Flemish *rippen*]

rip² (rɪp) *n* short for **riptide.** [C18: ?from RIP¹]

rip³ (rɪp) *n Inf., arch.* **1** a debauched person. **2** an old worn-out horse. [C18: ?from *rep*, shortened from REPROBATE]

RIP *abbrev. for* requiescat *or* requiescant in pace. [L: may he, she, *or* they rest in peace]

riparian (raɪ'pɛərɪən) *adj* **1** of, inhabiting, or situated on the bank of a river. **2** denoting or relating to the legal rights of the owner of land on a river bank, such as fish-

---

★ people and places

ing. ◆ *n* **3** *Property law.* a person who owns land on a river bank. [C19: from L, from *rīpa* river bank]

ripcord ('rɪp,kɔːd) *n* **1** a cord that when pulled opens a parachute from its pack. **2** a cord on the gas bag of a balloon that when pulled enables gas to escape and the balloon to descend.

ripe (raɪp) *adj* **1** (of fruit, grain, etc.) mature and ready to be eaten or used. **2** mature enough to be eaten or used: *ripe cheese*. **3** fully developed in mind or body. **4** resembling ripe fruit, esp. in redness or fullness: *a ripe complexion*. **5** (*postpositive;* foll. by *for*) ready or eager (to undertake or undergo an action). **6** (*postpositive;* foll. by *for*) suitable: *the time is not yet ripe*. **7** mature in judgment or knowledge. **8** advanced but healthy (esp. in **a ripe old age**). **9** *Sl.* **9a** complete; thorough. **9b** excessive; exorbitant. **10** *Sl.* slightly indecent; risqué. [OE *rīpe*]
▸ '**ripely** *adv* ▸ '**ripeness** *n*

ripen ('raɪpʰn) *vb* to make or become ripe.

ripieno (,rɪpɪ'eɪnəʊ) *n*, *pl* **ripieni** (-niː) or **ripienos**. *Music.* a supplementary instrument or player. [It.]

rip off *vb* (*tr*) **1** to tear roughly (from). **2** (*adv*) *Sl.* to steal from or cheat (someone). ◆ *n* **rip-off. 3** *Sl.* a grossly overpriced article. **4** *Sl.* the act of stealing or cheating.

Ripon ★ ('rɪpʰn) *n* a city in N England, in North Yorkshire: cathedral (12th–16th centuries). Pop.: 13 806 (1991 est.).

riposte (rɪ'pɒst, rɪ'pəʊst) *n* **1** a swift sharp reply in speech or action. **2** *Fencing.* a counterattack made immediately after a successful parry. ◆ *vb* **ripostes, riposting, riposted. 3** (*intr*) to make a riposte. [C18: from F, from It., from *rispondere* to reply]

ripper ('rɪpə) *n* **1** a person or thing that rips. **2** a murderer who dissects or mutilates his victim's body. **3** *Inf., chiefly Austral. & NZ.* a fine or excellent person or thing.

ripping ('rɪpɪŋ) *adj Arch. Brit. sl.* excellent; splendid.
▸ '**rippingly** *adv*

ripple[1] ('rɪpʰl) *n* **1** a slight wave or undulation on the surface of water. **2** a small wave or undulation in fabric, hair, etc. **3** a sound reminiscent of water flowing quietly in ripples: *a ripple of laughter*. **4** *Electronics.* an oscillation of small amplitude superimposed on a steady value. **5** *US & Canad.* another word for **riffle** (sense 4). ◆ *vb* **ripples, rippling, rippled. 6** (*intr*) to form ripples or flow with an undulating motion. **7** (*tr*) to stir up (water) so as to form ripples. **8** (*tr*) to make ripple marks. **9** (*intr*) (of sounds) to rise and fall gently. [C17: ?from RIP[1]]
▸ '**rippler** *n* ▸ '**rippling** or '**ripply** *adj*

ripple[2] ('rɪpʰl) *n* **1** a special kind of comb designed to separate the seed from the stalks in flax or hemp. ◆ *vb* **ripples, rippling, rippled. 2** (*tr*) to comb with this tool. [C14: of Gmc origin]
▸ '**rippler** *n*

ripple effect *n* the repercussions of an event or situation experienced far beyond its immediate location.

ripple mark *n* one of a series of small wavy ridges of sand formed by waves on a beach, by a current in a sandy riverbed, or by wind on land: sometimes found fossilized on bedding planes of sedimentary rock.

rip-roaring *adj Inf.* characterized by excitement, intensity, or boisterous behaviour.

ripsaw ('rɪp,sɔː) *n* a handsaw for cutting along the grain of timber.

ripsnorter ('rɪp,snɔːtə) *n Sl.* a person or thing noted for intensity or excellence.
▸ '**rip,snorting** *adj*

riptide ('rɪp,taɪd) *n* **1** Also called: **rip**. a stretch of turbulent water in the sea, caused by the meeting of currents. **2** Also called: **rip current**. a strong current, esp. one flowing outwards from the shore.

rise (raɪz) *vb* **rises, rising, rose, risen** ('rɪzʰn). (*mainly intr*) **1** to get up from a lying, sitting, kneeling, or prone position. **2** to get out of bed, esp. to begin one's day: *he always rises early*. **3** to move from a lower to a higher place or position. **4** to ascend or appear above the horizon: *the sun is rising*. **5** to increase in height or level: *the water rose above the normal level*. **6** to attain higher rank, status, or reputation: *he will rise in the world*. **7** to be built or erected: *those*

blocks of flats are rising fast. **8** to appear: *new troubles rose to afflict her*. **9** to increase in strength, degree, etc.: *the wind is rising*. **10** to increase in amount or value: *house prices are always rising*. **11** to swell up: *dough rises*. **12** to become erect, stiff, or rigid: *the hairs on his neck rose in fear*. **13** (of one's stomach or gorge) to manifest nausea. **14** to revolt: *the people rose against their oppressors*. **15** to slope upwards: *the ground rises beyond the lake*. **16** to be resurrected. **17** to originate: *that river rises in the mountains*. **18** (of a session of a court, legislative assembly, etc.) to come to an end. **19** *Angling.* (of fish) to come to the surface of the water. **20** (often foll. by *to*) *Inf.* to respond (to teasing, etc.). ◆ *n* **21** the act or an instance of rising. **22** an increase in height. **23** an increase in rank, status, or position. **24** an increase in amount, cost, or value. **25** an increase in degree or intensity. **26** *Brit.* an increase in salary or wages. US and Canad. word: **raise. 27** the vertical height of a step or of a flight of stairs. **28** the vertical height of a roof above the walls or columns. **29** *Angling.* the act or instance of fish coming to the surface of the water to take flies, etc. **30** the beginning, origin, or source. **31** a piece of rising ground; incline. **32 get** *or* **take a rise out of.** *Sl.* to provoke an angry or petulant reaction from. **33 give rise to.** to cause the development of. [OE *rīsan*]

riser ('raɪzə) *n* **1** a person who rises, esp. from bed: *an early riser*. **2** the vertical part of a stair. **3** a vertical pipe, esp. one within a building.

rise to *vb* (*intr, prep*) to respond adequately to (the demands of something, esp. a testing challenge).

risibility (,rɪzɪ'bɪlɪtɪ) *n*, *pl* **risibilities. 1** a tendency to laugh. **2** hilarity; laughter.

risible ('rɪzɪbʰl) *adj* **1** having a tendency to laugh. **2** causing laughter; ridiculous. [C16: from LL *rīsibilis*, from L *rīdēre* to laugh]
▸ '**risibly** *adv*

rising ('raɪzɪŋ) *n* **1** a rebellion; revolt. **2** the leaven used to make dough rise in baking. ◆ *adj* (*prenominal*) **3** increasing in rank, status, or reputation: *a rising young politician*. **4** growing up to adulthood: *the rising generation*. ◆ *adv* **5** *Inf.* approaching: *he's rising 50*.

rising damp *n* capillary movement of moisture from the ground into the walls of buildings, resulting in damage up to a level of 3 feet.

rising trot *n* a horse's trot in which the rider rises from the saddle every second beat.

risk (rɪsk) *n* **1** the possibility of incurring misfortune or loss. **2** *Insurance.* **2a** chance of a loss or other event on which a claim may be filed. **2b** the type of such an event, such as fire or theft. **2c** the amount of the claim should such an event occur. **2d** a person or thing considered with respect to the characteristics that may cause an insured event to occur. **3 at risk.** vulnerable. **4 take** *or* **run a risk.** to proceed in an action without regard to the possibility of danger involved. ◆ *vb* (*tr*) **5** to expose to danger or loss. **6** to act in spite of the possibility of (injury or loss): *to risk a fall in climbing*. [C17: from F, from It., from *rischiare* to be in peril, from Gk *rhiza* cliff (from the hazards of sailing along rocky coasts)]

risk capital *n Chiefly Brit.* capital invested in an issue of ordinary shares, esp. of a speculative enterprise. Also called: **venture capital.**

risk factor *n Med.* a factor, such as a habit or an environmental condition, that predisposes an individual to develop a particular disease.

risky ('rɪskɪ) *adj* **riskier, riskiest.** involving danger.
▸ '**riskily** *adv* ▸ '**riskiness** *n*

risotto (rɪ'zɒtəʊ) *n*, *pl* **risottos.** a dish of rice cooked in stock and served variously with tomatoes, cheese, chicken, etc. [C19: from It., from *riso* RICE]

risqué ('rɪskeɪ) *adj* bordering on impropriety or indecency: *a risqué joke*. [C19: from F *risquer* to hazard, RISK]

rissole ('rɪsəʊl) *n* a mixture of minced cooked meat coated in egg and breadcrumbs and fried. [C18: from F, prob. ult. from L *russus* red]

risus sardonicus ('riːsəs sɑː'dɒnɪkəs) *n Pathol.* fixed contraction of the facial muscles resulting in a peculiar distorted grin, caused esp. by tetanus. Also called: **trismus cynicus** ('trɪzməs 'sɪnɪkəs). [C17: NL, lit.: sardonic laugh]

rit. *Music. abbrev. for:* **1** ritardando. **2** ritenuto.

ritardando (ˌrɪtɑːˈdændəʊ) *adj, adv* another term for **rallentando**. Abbrev.: **rit.** [C19: from It., from *ritardare* to slow down]

rite (raɪt) *n* **1** a formal act prescribed or customary in religious ceremonies: *the rite of baptism.* **2** a particular body of such acts, esp. of a particular Christian Church: *the Latin rite.* **3** a Christian Church: *the Greek rite.* [C14: from L *rītus* religious ceremony]

ritenuto (ˌrɪtəˈnuːtəʊ) *adj, adv Music.* **1** held back momentarily. **2** Abbrev.: **rit.** another term for **rallentando**. [C19: from It., from L *ritenēre* to hold back]

rite of passage *n* a ceremony performed in some cultures at times when an individual changes his status, as at puberty and marriage.

ritornello (ˌrɪtəˈnɛləʊ) *n, pl* **ritornellos** or **ritornelli** (-liː). *Music.* a short piece of instrumental music interpolated in a song. [It., lit.: a little return]

ritual (ˈrɪtjʊəl) *n* **1** the prescribed or established form of a religious or other ceremony. **2** such prescribed forms in general or collectively. **3** stereotyped activity or behaviour. **4** any formal act, institution, or procedure that is followed consistently: *the ritual of the law.* ♦ *adj* **5** of or characteristic of religious, social, or other rituals. [C16: from L *rītuālis*, from *rītus* RITE]
▸ **'ritually** *adv*

ritualism (ˈrɪtjʊəˌlɪzəm) *n* **1** exaggerated emphasis on the importance of rites and ceremonies. **2** the study of rites and ceremonies, esp. magical or religious ones.
▸ **'ritualist** *n* ▸ **ˌritual'istic** *adj* ▸ **ˌritual'istically** *adv*

ritualize or **ritualise** (ˈrɪtjʊəˌlaɪz) *vb* **ritualizes, ritualizing, ritualized** or **ritualises, ritualising, ritualised.** **1** (*intr*) to engage in ritualism or devise rituals. **2** (*tr*) to make (something) into a ritual.

ritzy (ˈrɪtsɪ) *adj* **ritzier, ritziest.** *Sl.* luxurious or elegant. [C20: after the hotels established by César *Ritz* (1850–1918), Swiss hotelier]
▸ **'ritzily** *adv* ▸ **'ritziness** *n*

rival (ˈraɪvəl) *n* **1a** a person, organization, team, etc., that competes with another for the same object or in the same field. **1b** (*as modifier*): *rival suitors.* **2** a person or thing that is considered the equal of another: *she is without rival in the field of physics.* ♦ *vb* **rivals, rivalling, rivalled** or *US* **rivals, rivaling, rivaled.** (*tr*) **3** to be the equal or near equal of: *an empire that rivalled Rome.* **4** to try to equal or surpass. [C16: from L *rīvalis*, lit.: one who shares the same brook, from *rīvus* a brook]

rivalry (ˈraɪvəlrɪ) *n, pl* **rivalries.** **1** the act of rivalling. **2** the state of being a rival or rivals.

rive (raɪv) *vb* **rives, riving, rived; rived** or **riven** (ˈrɪvən). (*usually passive*) **1** to split asunder: *a tree riven by lightning.* **2** to tear apart: *riven to shreds.* [C13: from ON *rīfa*]

river (ˈrɪvə) *n* **1a** a large natural stream of fresh water flowing along a definite course, usually into the sea, being fed by tributary streams. **1b** (*as modifier*): *river traffic.* **1c** (*in combination*): *riverside; riverbed.* Related adjs.: **fluvial, potamic.** **2** any abundant stream or flow: *a river of blood.* [C13: from OF, from L *rīpārius* of a river bank, from *rīpa* bank]
▸ **'riverless** *adj*

Rivera ★ (*Spanish* riˈβera) *n* **Diego** (ˈdjeɣo). 1886–1957, Mexican painter, noted for his monumental murals.

riverine (ˈrɪvəˌraɪn) *adj* **1** of, like, relating to, or produced by a river. **2** located or dwelling near a river; riparian.

Rivers ★ (ˈrɪvəz) *n* a state of S Nigeria, in the Niger River Delta on the Gulf of Guinea. Capital: Port Harcourt. Pop.: 4 103 372 (1995 est.). Area: 21 850 sq. km (8436 sq. miles).

Riverside ★ (ˈrɪvəˌsaɪd) *n* a city in SW California. Pop.: 211 000 (1989).

rivet (ˈrɪvɪt) *n* **1** a short metal pin for fastening two or more pieces together, having a head at one end, the other end being hammered flat after being passed through holes in the pieces. ♦ *vb* **rivets, riveting, riveted.** (*tr*) **2** to join by riveting. **3** to hammer in order to form into a head. **4** (*often passive*) to cause to be fixed, as in fas-cinated attention, horror, etc.: *to be riveted to the spot.* [C14: from OF, from *river* to fasten, from ?]
▸ **'riveter** *n* ▸ **'riveting** *adj*

riviera (ˌrɪvɪˈɛərə) *n* a coastal region reminiscent of the Riviera.

Riviera ★ (ˌrɪvɪˈɛərə) *n* the Mediterranean coastal region between Cannes, France, and La Spezia, Italy: contains some of Europe's most popular resorts. [C18: from It. lit.: shore, ult. from L *rīpa* bank, shore]

rivière (ˌrɪvɪˈɛə) *n* a necklace the diamonds or other precious stones of which gradually increase in size up to a large centre stone. [C19: from F: brook, RIVER]

rivulet (ˈrɪvjʊlɪt) *n* a small stream. [C16: from It. *rivoletto*, from L *rīvulus*, from *rīvus* stream]

Riyadh ★ (rɪˈjɑːd) *n* the joint capital (with Mecca) of Saudi Arabia, situated in a central oasis: the largest city in the country. Pop.: 1 800 000 (1991 est.).

riyal (rɪˈjɑːl) *n* the standard monetary and currency unit of Saudi Arabia or Yemen. [from Ar. *riyāl*, from Sp. *real*]

Rizal[1] ★ (*Spanish* riˈθal) *n* another name for **Pasay.**

Rizal[2] ★ (*Spanish* riˈθal) *n* **Jose** (xoˈse). 1861–96, Philippine nationalist, executed by the Spanish during the Philippine revolution.

Rizzio (ˈrɪtsɪəʊ) or **Riccio** ★ *n* **David.** ?1533–66, Italian musician who became the secretary of Mary, Queen of Scots; murdered at the instigation of a group of nobles.

RL *abbrev. for* Rugby League.

rly *abbrev. for* railway.

rm *abbrev. for:* **1** ream. **2** room.

RM *abbrev. for:* **1** Royal Mail. **2** Royal Marines. **3** (in Canada) Rural Municipality.

RMA *abbrev. for* Royal Military Academy (Sandhurst).

rms *abbrev. for* root mean square.

Rn *the chemical symbol for* radon.

RN *abbrev. for:* **1** (in Canada) Registered Nurse. **2** Royal Navy.

RNA *n Biochem.* ribonucleic acid; any of a group of nucleic acids, present in all living cells, that play an essential role in the synthesis of proteins.

RNAS *abbrev. for:* **1** Royal Naval Air Service(s). **2** Royal Naval Air Station.

RNIB (in Britain) *abbrev. for* Royal National Institute for the Blind.

RNID (in Britain) *abbrev. for* Royal National Institute for Deaf People.

RNLI *abbrev. for* Royal National Lifeboat Institution.

RNZAF *abbrev. for* Royal New Zealand Air Force.

RNZN *abbrev. for* Royal New Zealand Navy.

roach[1] (rəʊtʃ) *n, pl* **roaches** or **roach.** a European freshwater food fish having a deep compressed body and reddish ventral and tail fins. [C14: from OF *roche*, from ?]

roach[2] (rəʊtʃ) *n* **1** short for **cockroach.** **2** *Sl.* the butt of a cannabis cigarette.

roach[3] (rəʊtʃ) *n Naut.* the curve at the foot of a square sail. [C18: from ?]

roach clip *n Sl.* a small clip resembling tweezers, used to hold the butt of a cannabis cigarette, in order to avoid burning one's fingers.

road (rəʊd) *n* **1a** an open way, usually surfaced with tarmac or concrete, providing passage from one place to another. **1b** (*as modifier*): *road traffic; a road sign.* **1c** (*in combination*): *the roadside.* **2a** a street. **2b** (*cap. when part of a name*): *London Road.* **3** *Brit.* one of the tracks of a railway. **4** a way, path, or course: *the road to fame.* **5** (*often pl*) *Naut.* Also called: **roadstead.** a partly sheltered anchorage. **6** a drift or tunnel in a mine, esp. a level one. **7 hit the road.** *Sl.* to start or resume travelling. **8 one for the road.** *Inf.* a last alcoholic drink before leaving. **9 on the road. 9a** travelling about; on tour. **9b** leading a wandering life. **10 take** (**to**) **the road.** to begin a journey or tour. [OE *rād*; rel. to *rīdan* to RIDE]
▸ **'roadless** *adj*

road allowance *n Canad.* land reserved by the government to be used for public roads.

roadblock ('rəud,blɒk) *n* a barrier set up across a road by the police or military, in order to stop a fugitive, inspect traffic, etc.

road-fund licence *n Brit.* a paper disc showing that the tax in respect of a motor vehicle has been paid. [C20: from the former *road fund* for the maintenance of public highways]

road hog *n Inf.* a selfish or aggressive driver.

roadholding ('rəud,həuldɪŋ) *n* the extent to which a motor vehicle is stable and does not skid, esp. on sharp bends or wet roads.

roadhouse ('rəud,haus) *n* a pub, restaurant, etc., that is situated at the side of a road.

road hump *n* the official name for **sleeping policeman**.

roadie ('rəudɪ) *n Inf.* a person who transports and sets up equipment for a band or group. [C20: shortened from *road manager*]

road metal *n* crushed rock, broken stone, etc., used to construct a road.

road movie *n* a genre of film in which the chief character takes to the road, esp. to escape the law, his own past, etc.

road pricing *n* the practice of charging motorists for using certain stretches of road, in order to reduce congestion.

road rage *n* aggressive behaviour by a motorist in response to the actions of another road user.

roadroller ('rəud,rəulə) *n* a motor vehicle with heavy rollers for compressing road surfaces during roadmaking.

road show *n* **1** *Radio.* **1a** a live programme, usually with some audience participation, transmitted from a radio van taking a particular show on the road. **1b** the personnel and equipment needed for such a show. **2** a group of entertainers on tour. **3** any occasion when an organization attracts publicity while touring or visiting: *the royal road show.*

roadstead ('rəud,sted) *n Naut.* another word for **road** (sense 5).

roadster ('rəudstə) *n* **1** an open car, esp. one seating only two. **2** a kind of bicycle.

road tax *n* a tax paid, usually annually, on motor vehicles in use on the roads.

road test *n* **1** a test to ensure that a vehicle is roadworthy, esp. after repair or servicing, by driving it on roads. **2** a test of something in actual use. ◆ *vb* **road-test.** (*tr*) **3** to test (a vehicle, etc.) in this way.

road train *n Austral.* a truck pulling one or more large trailers, esp. on western roads.

roadway ('rəud,weɪ) *n* **1** the surface of a road. **2** the part of a road that is used by vehicles.

roadwork ('rəud,wɜːk) *n* sports training by running along roads.

roadworks ('rəud,wɜːks) *pl n* repairs to a road or cable under a road, esp. when forming a hazard or obstruction to traffic.

roadworthy ('rəud,wɜːðɪ) *adj* (of a motor vehicle) mechanically sound; fit for use on the roads.
▷ '**road,worthiness** *n*

roam (rəum) *vb* **1** to travel or walk about with no fixed purpose or direction. ◆ *n* **2** the act of roaming. [C13: from ?]
▷ '**roamer** *n*

roan (rəun) *adj* **1** (of a horse) having a bay (**red roan**), chestnut (**strawberry roan**), or black (**blue roan**) coat sprinkled with white hairs. ◆ *n* **2** a horse having such a coat. **3** a soft sheepskin leather used in bookbinding, etc. [C16: from OF, from Sp. *roano*, prob. from Gothic *rauths* red]

Roanoke Island ★ ('rəuə,nəuk) *n* an island off the coast of North Carolina: site of the first attempted English settlement in America. Length: 19 km (12 miles). Average width: 5 km (3 miles).

roar (rɔː) *vb* (*mainly intr*) **1** (of lions and other animals) to utter characteristic loud growling cries. **2** (*also tr*) (of people) to utter (something) with a loud deep cry, as in anger or triumph. **3** to laugh in a loud hearty unrestrained manner. **4** (of horses) to breathe with laboured rasping sounds. **5** (of the wind, waves, etc.) to blow or break loudly and violently, as during a storm. **6** (of a fire) to burn fiercely with a roaring sound. **7** (*tr*) to bring (oneself) into a certain condition by roaring: *to roar oneself hoarse.* ◆ *n* **8** a loud deep cry, uttered by a person or crowd, esp. in anger or triumph. **9** a prolonged loud cry of certain animals, esp. lions. **10** any similar noise made by a fire, the wind, waves, an engine, etc. [OE *rārian*]
▷ '**roarer** *n*

roaring ('rɔːrɪŋ) *adj* **1** *Inf.* very brisk and profitable (esp. in **a roaring trade**). ◆ *adv* **2** noisily or boisterously (esp. in **roaring drunk**). ◆ *n* **3** a loud prolonged cry.
▷ '**roaringly** *adv*

roast (rəust) *vb* (*mainly tr*) **1** to cook (meat or other food) by dry heat, usually with added fat and esp. in an oven. **2** to brown or dry (coffee, etc.) by exposure to heat. **3** *Metallurgy.* to heat (an ore) in order to produce a concentrate that is easier to smelt. **4** to heat (oneself or something) to an extreme degree, as when sunbathing, etc. **5** (*intr*) to be excessively and uncomfortably hot. **6** (*tr*) *Inf.* to criticize severely. ◆ *n* **7** something that has been roasted, esp. meat. [C13: from OF *rostir*, of Gmc origin]
▷ '**roaster** *n*

roasting ('rəustɪŋ) *Inf.* ◆ *adj* **1** extremely hot. ◆ *n* **2** severe criticism.

rob (rɒb) *vb* **robs, robbing, robbed. 1** to take something from (someone) illegally, as by force. **2** (*tr*) to plunder (a house, etc.). **3** (*tr*) to deprive unjustly: *to be robbed of an opportunity.* [C13: from OF *rober*, of Gmc origin]
▷ '**robber** *n*

Robbe-Grillet ★ (*French* rɔbgrijɛ) *n* **Alain** (alɛ̃). born 1922, French novelist; his novels include *Jealousy* (1957).

Robben Island ★ ('rɒbᵊn) *n* a small island in South Africa, 11 km (7 miles) off the Cape Peninsula: formerly used by the South African government to house political prisoners.

robbery ('rɒbərɪ) *n, pl* **robberies. 1** *Criminal law.* the stealing of property from a person by using or threatening to use force. **2** the act or an instance of robbing.

Robbia ★ ('rəubɪə; *Italian* 'rɔbbja) *n* **1 Andrea della** (an'drɛːa 'della). 1435–1525, Florentine sculptor. **2** his uncle, **Luca della** ('luːka 'della). ?1400–82, Florentine sculptor.

Robbins ★ ('rɒbɪnz) *n* **Jerome.** 1918–98, US ballet dancer and choreographer; noted for his choreography of *West Side Story* (1957).

robe (rəub) *n* **1** any loose flowing garment, esp. the official vestment of a peer, judge, or academic. **2** a dressing gown or bathrobe. ◆ *vb* **robes, robing, robed. 3** to put a robe, etc., on (oneself or someone else). [C13: from OF; of Gmc origin]

Robert I ★ ('rɒbət) *n* known as *Robert the Bruce.* 1274–1329, king of Scotland (1306–29): he defeated the English army of Edward II at Bannockburn (1314) and gained recognition of Scotland's independence (1328).

Robert II ★ *n* 1316–90, king of Scotland (1371–90).

Robert III ★ *n* ?1337–1406, king of Scotland (1390–1406), son of Robert II.

Roberts ★ ('rɒbəts) *n* **Frederick Sleigh,** 1st Earl. 1832–1914, British field marshal. He was awarded the Victoria Cross (1858) for his service during the Indian Mutiny and was commander in chief (1899–1900) in the second Boer War.

Robeson ★ ('rəubsən) *n* **Paul.** 1898–1976, US bass singer and actor.

Robespierre ★ ('rəubzpjɛə; *French* rɔbzpjɛr) *n* **Maximilien François Marie Isidore de** (maksimiljɛ̃ frɑ̃swa mari izidɔr də). 1758–94, French revolutionary and Jacobin leader: established the Reign of Terror: executed in the coup d'état of Thermidor (1794).

Robey ★ ('rəubɪ) *n* Sir **George,** original name *George Edward Wade,* known as *the prime minister of mirth.* 1869–1954, British music-hall comedian, who also appeared in films.

robin ('rɒbɪn) *n* **1** Also called: **robin redbreast.** a small Old

World songbird related to the thrushes. The adult has a brown back, orange-red breast and face, and grey underparts. **2** a North American thrush similar to but larger than the Old World robin. [C16: arbitrary use of name *Robin*]

Robin Goodfellow ★ (ˈrɒbɪn ˈgʊdˌfɛləʊ) *n* another name for **puck**[2].

Robin Hood ★ *n* a legendary English outlaw, who lived in Sherwood Forest (in the reign of Richard I) and robbed the rich to give to the poor.

robinia (rəˈbɪnɪə) *n* any tree of the leguminous genus *Robinia,* esp. the locust tree.

Robinson ★ (ˈrɒbɪnsən) *n* **1 Edward G.,** real name *Emanuel Goldenberg.* 1893–1973, US film actor, born in Romania. His films include *Little Caesar* (1930) and *All My Sons* (1948). **2 Edwin Arlington.** 1869–1935, US poet. **3 (William) Heath.** 1872–1944, British illustrator, noted for his drawings of fantastic machines. **4 John (Arthur Thomas).** 1919–83, British theologian; Bishop of Woolwich (1959–69); author of *Honest to God* (1963). **5 Mary.** born 1944, Irish stateswoman; president of the Republic of Ireland (1990–97). **6 Smokey,** real name *William Robinson.* born 1940, US Motown singer and songwriter. **7 "Sugar" Ray,** real name *Walker Smith.* 1921–89, US boxer, five-times world middleweight champion.

Robinson Crusoe ★ *n* the hero of Daniel Defoe's novel *Robinson Crusoe* (1719), who survived being shipwrecked on a desert island. See also **Selkirk.**

roborant (ˈrəʊbərənt, ˈrɒb-) *adj* **1** tending to fortify or increase strength. ♦ *n* **2** a drug or agent that increases strength. [C17: from L *roborāre* to strengthen, from *rōbur* an oak]

robot (ˈrəʊbɒt) *n* **1** any automated machine programmed to perform specific mechanical functions in the manner of a human. **2** (*modifier*) automatic: *a robot pilot.* **3** a person who works or behaves like a machine. **4** *S. African.* a set of traffic lights. [C20: used in *R.U.R.,* a play by Karel Čapek) from Czech *robota* work]
▸ roˈbotic *adj* ▸ ˈrobot-ˌlike *adj*

robot bomb *n* another name for the **V-1.**

robot dancing *or* **robotic dancing** (rəʊˈbɒtɪk) *n* a dance of the 1980s, characterized by jerky, mechanical movements. Also called: **robotics.**

robotics (rəʊˈbɒtɪks) *n* (*functioning as sing*) **1** the science or technology of designing, building, and using robots. **2** another name for **robot dancing.**

Rob Roy ★ (ˈrɒb ˈrɔɪ) *n* real name *Robert Macgregor.* 1671–1734, Scottish outlaw.

Robson[1] ★ (ˈrɒbsən) *n* **Mount.** a mountain in SW Canada, in E British Columbia: the highest peak in the Canadian Rockies. Height: 3954 m (12 972 ft).

Robson[2] ★ (ˈrɒbsən) *n* **1 Bobby,** full name *Robert William.* born 1933, English footballer and manager (1982–90). **2 Bryan.** born 1957, English footballer and manager: captain of England (1982–90). **3** Dame **Flora.** 1902–84, British actress.

robust (rəʊˈbʌst, ˈrəʊbʌst) *adj* **1** strong in constitution. **2** sturdily built: *a robust shelter.* **3** requiring or suited to physical strength: *a robust sport.* **4** (esp. of wines) having a full-bodied flavour. **5** rough or boisterous. **6** (of thought, intellect, etc.) straightforward. [C16: from L *rōbustus,* from *rōbur* an oak, strength]
▸ roˈbustly *adv*

robusta (rəʊˈbʌstə) *n* **1** a species of coffee tree, *Coffea canephora.* **2** coffee or coffee beans obtained from this plant. [from L *rōbustus* robust]

robustious (rəʊˈbʌstɪəs) *adj Arch.* **1** rough; boisterous. **2** strong, robust, or stout.
▸ roˈbustiously *adv* ▸ roˈbustiousness *n*

robustness (rəʊˈbʌstnɪs) *n* **1** the quality of being robust. **2** *Computing.* the ability of a computer system to cope with errors during execution.

roc (rɒk) *n* (in Arabian legend) a bird of enormous size and power. [C16: from Ar., from Persian *rukh*]

ROC *abbrev. for* Royal Observer Corps.

Roca ★ (ˈrəʊkə) *n* **Cape.** a cape in SW central Portugal,

near Lisbon: the westernmost point of continental Europe.

rocaille (rɒˈkaɪ) *n* decorative rock or shell work, esp. as ornamentation in a rococo fountain, grotto, or interior. [from F, from *roc* ROCK[1]]

rocambole (ˈrɒkəmˌbəʊl) *n* a variety of alliaceous plant whose garlic-like bulb is used for seasoning. [C17: from F, from G *Rockenbolle,* lit.: distaff bulb (with reference to its shape)]

Rocard ★ (*French* rɔkaːr) *n* **Michel.** born 1930, French politician: prime minister (1988–91).

Rochdale ★ (ˈrɒtʃˌdeɪl) *n* **1** a town in NW England, in Greater Manchester: former centre of textile industry. Pop.: 94 313 (1991). **2** a unitary authority in NW England, in Greater Manchester. Pop.: 207 100 (1996 est.). Area: 159 sq. km (61 sq. miles).

Rochelle salt (rɒˈʃɛl) *n* a white crystalline double salt used in Seidlitz powder. Formula: $KNaC_4H_4O_6.4H_2O$. [C18: after LA ROCHELLE]

roche moutonnée (rəʊʃ ˌmuːtəˈneɪ) *n, pl* **roches moutonnées** (rəʊʃ ˌmuːtəˈneɪz). a rounded mass of rock smoothed and striated by ice that has flowed over it. [C19: F, lit.: fleecy rock, from *mouton* sheep]

Rochester[1] ★ (ˈrɒtʃɪstə) *n* **1** a city in SE England, in Kent on the River Medway: with Chatham and Gillingham forms the conurbation of the Medway towns. Pop.: 23 971 (1991). **2** a city in the US, in NW New York State, on Lake Ontario. Pop.: 231 170 (1994 est.).

Rochester[2] ★ (ˈrɒtʃɪstə) *n* **2nd Earl of,** title of *John Wilmot.* 1647–80, English poet, wit, and libertine. His poems include satires, love lyrics, and bawdy verse.

rochet (ˈrɒtʃɪt) *n* a white surplice with tight sleeves, worn by bishops, abbots, and certain other Church dignitaries. [C14: from OF, from *roc* coat, of Gmc origin]

rock[1] (rɒk) *n* **1** *Geol.* any aggregate of minerals that makes up part of the earth's crust. It may be unconsolidated, such as a sand, clay, or mud, or consolidated, such as granite, limestone, or coal. **2** any hard mass of consolidated mineral matter, such as a boulder. **3** *US, Canad., & Austral.* a stone. **4** a person or thing suggesting a rock, esp. in being dependable, unchanging, or providing firm foundation. **5** *Brit.* a hard sweet, typically a long brightly coloured peppermint-flavoured stick, sold esp. in holiday resorts. **6** *Sl.* a jewel, esp. a diamond. **7** *Sl.* another name for **crack** (sense 28). **8 on the rocks. 8a** in a state of ruin or destitution. **8b** (of drinks, esp. whisky) served with ice. [C14: from OF *roche,* from ?]

rock[2] (rɒk) *vb* **1** to move or cause to move from side to side or backwards and forwards. **2** to reel or sway or cause (someone) to reel or sway, as with a violent shock or emotion. **3** (*tr*) to shake or move (something) violently. **4** (*intr*) to dance in the rock-and-roll style. ♦ *n* **5** a rocking motion. **6** short for **rock and roll. 7** Also called: **rock music.** any of various styles of pop music having a heavy beat, derived from rock and roll. [OE *roccian*]

Rock ★ (rɒk) *n* **the.** an informal name for **Gibraltar.**

rockabilly (ˈrɒkəˌbɪlɪ) *n* a fast, spare style of White rock music which originated in the mid-1950s in the US South. [C20: from ROCK (AND ROLL) + (HILL)BILLY]

Rockall ★ (ˈrɒkɔːl) *n* an uninhabited British island in the N Atlantic, 354 km (220 miles) W of the Outer Hebrides. Area: 0.07 ha (0.18 acres).

rock and roll *or* **rock'n'roll** *n* **1a** a type of pop music originating in the 1950s as a blend of rhythm and blues and country and western. **1b** (*as modifier*): *the rock-and-roll era.* **2** dancing performed to such music, with exaggerated body movements stressing the beat. ♦ *vb* **3** (*intr*) to perform this dance.
▸ **rock and roller** *or* **rock'n'roller** *n*

rock bass (bæs) *n* an eastern North American freshwater food fish, related to the sunfish family.

rock bottom *n* **a** the lowest possible level. **b** (*as modifier*): *rock-bottom prices.*

rock-bound *adj* hemmed in or encircled by rocks. Also (poetic): **rock-girt.**

rock cake *n* a small cake containing dried fruit and spice, with a rough surface supposed to resemble a rock.

rock crystal *n* a pure transparent colourless quartz, used in electronic and optical equipment.

rock dove *or* **pigeon** *n* a common dove from which domestic and feral pigeons are descended.

Rockefeller ★ (ˈrɒkəˌfɛlə) *n* **1 John D(avison)**. 1839–1937, US industrialist and philanthropist. **2** his son, **John D(avison)**. 1874–1960, US philanthropist. **3** his son, **Nelson (Aldrich)**. 1908–79, US politician; governor of New York State (1958–74); vice president (1974–76).

rocker (ˈrɒkə) *n* **1** any of various devices that transmit or operate with a rocking motion. See also **rocker arm. 2** another word for **rocking chair. 3** either of two curved supports on the legs of a chair on which it may rock. **4a** an ice skate with a curved blade. **4b** the curve itself. **5** a rock-music performer, fan, or song. **6** *Brit.* an adherent of a youth movement rooted in the 1950s, characterized by motorcycle trappings. **7 off one's rocker.** *Sl.* crazy.

rocker arm *n* a lever that rocks about a pivot, esp. a lever in an internal-combustion engine that transmits the motion of a pushrod or cam to a valve.

rockery (ˈrɒkərɪ) *n, pl* **rockeries.** a garden constructed with rocks, esp. one where alpine plants are grown.

rocket[1] (ˈrɒkɪt) *n* **1** a self-propelling device, esp. a cylinder containing a mixture of solid explosives, used as a firework, distress signal, etc. **2a** any vehicle that carries its own fuel and oxidant to burn in a rocket engine, esp. one used to carry a spacecraft, etc. **2b** (*as modifier*): *rocket launcher*. **3** *Brit. & NZ inf.* a severe reprimand (esp. in **get a rocket**). ◆ *vb* **rockets, rocketing, rocketed. 4** (*tr*) to propel (a missile, spacecraft, etc.) by means of a rocket. **5** (*intr*; foll. by *off, away,* etc.) to move off at high speed. **6** (*intr*) to rise rapidly: *he rocketed to the top.* [C17: from OF, from It. *rochetto*, dim. of *rocca* distaff, of Gmc origin]

rocket[2] (ˈrɒkɪt) *n* any of several plants of the mustard family, typically having yellowish flowers, such as **London rocket** and **yellow rocket.** See also **arugula, wall rocket.** [C16: from F *roquette*, from It. *rochetta*, from L *ērūca* hairy plant]

rocket engine *n* a reaction engine in which a fuel and oxidizer are burnt in a combustion chamber, the products of combustion expanding through a nozzle and producing thrust.

rocketry (ˈrɒkɪtrɪ) *n* the science and technology of the design, operation, maintenance, and launching of rockets.

rockfish (ˈrɒkˌfɪʃ) *n, pl* **rockfish** *or* **rockfishes. 1** any of various fishes that live among rocks, such as the goby, bass, etc. **2** *Brit.* any of several coarse fishes when used as food, esp. the dogfish or wolffish.

Rockford ★ (ˈrɒkfəd) *n* a city in N Illinois, on the Rock River. Pop.: 143 263 (1994 est.).

rock garden *n* a garden featuring rocks or rockeries.

Rockhampton ★ (rɒkˈhæmptən, -ˈhæmtən) *n* a port in Australia, in E Queensland on the Fitzroy River. Pop.: 65 868 (1993).

Rockies ★ (ˈrɒkɪz) *pl n* another name for the **Rocky Mountains.**

rocking chair *n* a chair set on curving supports so that the sitter may rock backwards and forwards.

Rockingham ★ (ˈrɒkɪŋəm) *n* **Marquess of,** title of *Charles Watson-Wentworth*. 1730–82, British statesman and opposition leader, whose supporters were known as the **Rockingham Whigs;** prime minister (1765–66; 1782).

rocking horse *n* a toy horse mounted on a pair of rockers on which a child can rock to and fro in a seesaw movement.

rocking stone *n* a boulder so delicately poised that it can be rocked.

rockling (ˈrɒklɪŋ) *n, pl* **rocklings** *or* **rockling.** a small gadoid fish which has an elongated body with barbels around the mouth and occurs mainly in the North Atlantic Ocean. [C17: from ROCK[1] + -LING[1]]

rock lobster *n* another name for the **spiny lobster.**

rock melon *n US, Austral., & NZ.* another name for **cantaloupe.**

rock pigeon *n* another name for **rock dove.**

rock plant *n* any plant that grows on rocks or in rocky ground.

rock rabbit *n S. African.* another name for **dassie.** See **hyrax.**

rockrose (ˈrɒkˌrəʊz) *n* any of various shrubs or herbaceous plants cultivated for their yellow-white or reddish roselike flowers.

rock salmon *n Brit.* a former term for **rockfish** (sense 2).

rock salt *n* another name for **halite.**

rock snake *or* **python** *n* any large Australasian python of the genus *Liasis.*

rock tripe *n Canad.* any of various edible lichens that grow on rocks and are used in the North as a survival food.

Rockwell ★ (ˈrɒkˌwɛl, -wəl) *n* **Norman.** 1894–1978, US illustrator.

rock wool *n* another name for **mineral wool.**

rocky[1] (ˈrɒkɪ) *adj* **rockier, rockiest. 1** consisting of or abounding in rocks: *a rocky shore.* **2** unyielding: *rocky determination.* **3** hard like rock: *rocky muscles.*
‣ **ˈrockiness** *n*

rocky[2] (ˈrɒkɪ) *adj* **rockier, rockiest. 1** weak or unstable. **2** *Inf.* (of a person) dizzy; nauseated.
‣ **ˈrockily** *adv* ‣ **ˈrockiness** *n*

Rocky Mountains *or* **Rockies** ★ *pl n* the chief mountain system of W North America, extending from British Columbia to New Mexico: forms the Continental Divide. Highest peak: Mount Elbert, 4399 m (14 431 ft). Mount McKinley (6194 m (20 320 ft)), in the Alaska Range, is not strictly part of the Rocky Mountains.

Rocky Mountain spotted fever *n* an acute rickettsial disease characterized by high fever, chills, pain in muscles and joints, etc. It is caused by the bite of an infected tick.

rococo (rəˈkəʊkəʊ) *n* (*often cap.*) **1** a style of architecture and decoration that originated in France in the early 18th century, characterized by elaborate but graceful ornamentation. **2** an 18th-century style of music characterized by prettiness and extreme use of ornamentation. **3** any florid or excessively ornamental style. ◆ *adj* **4** denoting, being in, or relating to the rococo. **5** florid or excessively elaborate. [C19: from F, from ROCAILLE, from *roc* ROCK[1]]

rod (rɒd) *n* **1** a slim cylinder of metal, wood, etc. **2** a switch or bundle of switches used to administer corporal punishment. **3** any of various staffs of insignia or office. **4** power, esp. of a tyrannical kind: *a dictator's iron rod.* **5** a straight slender shoot, stem, or cane of a woody plant. **6** See **fishing rod. 7** Also called: **pole, perch. 7a** a unit of length equal to 5½ yards. **7b** a unit of square measure equal to 30¼ square yards. **8** *Surveying.* another name (esp. US) for **staff**[1] (sense 8). **9** Also called: **retinal rod.** any of the elongated cylindrical cells in the retina of the eye, which are sensitive to dim light but not to colour. **10** any rod-shaped bacterium. **11** *US.* a slang name for **pistol. 12** short for **hot rod.** [OE *rodd*]
‣ **ˈrod-ˌlike** *adj*

Rodchenko ★ (rɒdˈtʃɛŋkəʊ) *n* **Alexander (Mikhailovich).** 1891–1956, Soviet painter, sculptor, designer, and photographer, noted for his abstract geometrical style: a member of the constructivist movement.

rode (rəʊd) *vb* the past tense of **ride.**

rodent (ˈrəʊdənt) *n* **a** any of the relatively small placental mammals having constantly growing incisor teeth specialized for gnawing. The group includes rats, mice, squirrels, etc. **b** (*as modifier*): *rodent characteristics.* [C19: from L *rōdere* to gnaw]
‣ **ˈrodent-ˌlike** *adj*

rodent ulcer *n* a slow-growing malignant tumour on the face, usually occurring at the edge of the eyelids, lips, or nostrils.

rodeo (ˈrəʊdɪˌəʊ) *n, pl* **rodeos.** *Chiefly US & Canad.* **1** a display of the skills of cowboys, including bareback riding. **2** the rounding up of cattle for branding, etc. **3** an enclosure for cattle that have been rounded up. [C19: from Sp., from *rodear* to go around, from *rueda* a wheel, from L *rota*]

Roderic ★ ('rɒdərɪk) *n* See **Rory O'Connor**.

Rodgers ★ ('rɒdʒəz) *n* **Richard**. 1902–79, US composer of musical comedies, including *Pal Joey* (1940; with Lorenz Hart) and *Oklahoma!* (1943; with Oscar Hammerstein II).

Ródhos ★ ('rɒðɔs) *n* transliteration of the Modern Greek name for **Rhodes**.

Rodin ★ (*French* rɔdɛ̃) *n* **Auguste** (ogyst). 1840–1917, French sculptor. His works include *The Kiss* (1886) and *The Thinker* (1905).

Rodney ★ ('rɒdnɪ) *n* **George Brydges**, 1st Baron Rodney. 1719–92, British admiral: captured Martinique (1762): defeated the Spanish at Cape St Vincent (1780) and the French off Dominica (1782), restoring British superiority in the Caribbean.

rodomontade (,rɒdəmɒn'teɪd, -'tɑːd) *Literary*. ◆ *n* **1a** boastful words or behaviour. **1b** (*as modifier*): *rodomontade behaviour*. ◆ *vb* **rodomontades, rodomontading, rodomontaded**. **2** (*intr*) to boast or rant. [C17: from F, from It. *rodomonte* a boaster, from *Rodomonte*, the name of a braggart king of Algiers in epic poems]

Rodrigo ★ (*Spanish* rɔ'ðriɣo) *n* **Joaquín** (xwa'kin). born 1902, Spanish composer. His works include *Concierto de Aranjuez* (1940) for guitar and orchestra.

roe[1] (rəʊ) *n* **1** Also called: **hard roe**. the ovary of a female fish filled with mature eggs. **2** Also called: **soft roe**. the testis of a male fish filled with mature sperm. [C15: from MDu. *roge*, from OHG *roga*]

roe[2] (rəʊ) *n, pl* **roes** *or* **roe**. short for **roe deer**. [OE *rā(ha)*]

Roe (rəʊ) *n* **Richard**. (formerly) the defendant in a fictitious action, Doe versus Roe, to test a point of law. See also **Doe**.

roebuck ('rəʊ,bʌk) *n, pl* **roebucks** *or* **roebuck**. the male of the roe deer.

roe deer *n* a small graceful deer of woodlands of Europe and Asia. The antlers are small and the summer coat is reddish-brown.

Roeg ★ (rəʊg) *n* **Nic(olas)**. born 1928, British film director and cinematographer. Films include *Walkabout* (1970), *Don't Look Now* (1972), and *Heart of Darkness* (1994).

roentgen *or* **röntgen** ('rɒntgən, -tjən, 'rɛnt-) *n* a unit of dose of electromagnetic radiation equal to the dose that will produce in air a charge of 0.258×10^{-3} coulomb on all ions of one sign. [C19: after W. K. ROENTGEN]

Roentgen *or* **Röntgen** ★ ('rɒntgən, -tjən, 'rɛnt-; *German* 'rœntgən) *n* **Wilhelm Konrad** ('vɪlhɛlm 'kɔnraːt). 1845–1923, German physicist, who discovered X-rays: Nobel prize for physics 1901.

roentgen ray *n* a former name for **X-ray**.

Roeselare ★ ('ruːsələrə) *n* the Flemish name for **Roulers**.

Roethke ★ ('rɛtkə) *n* **Theodore**. 1908–63, US poet, whose books include *The Far Field* (1964).

rogation (rəʊ'geɪʃən) *n* (*usually pl*) *Christianity*. a solemn supplication, esp. in a form of ceremony prescribed by the Church. [C14: from L *rogātiō*, from *rogāre* to ask, make supplication]

Rogation Days *pl n* April 25 (the **Major Rogation**) and the Monday, Tuesday, and Wednesday before Ascension Day, observed by Christians as days of solemn supplication and marked by processions and special prayers.

roger ('rɒdʒə) *interj* **1** (used in signalling, telecommunications, etc.) message received and understood. **2** an expression of agreement. ◆ *vb* **3** *Taboo sl*. (of a man) to copulate (with). [C20: from the name *Roger*, representing *R* for *received*]

Rogers ★ ('rɒdʒəz) *n* **1** **Ginger**, real name *Virginia McMath*. 1911–95, US dancer and film actress, who partnered Fred Astaire. **2** **Richard**, Baron Rogers of Riverside. born 1933, British architect. His works include the Pompidou Centre in Paris (1971–77; with Renzo Piano), the Lloyd's building in London (1986), and the Millennium Dome in Greenwich, London. **3** **William Penn Adair**, known as *Will*. 1879–1935, US actor and humorist.

Roget ★ ('rɒʒeɪ) *n* **Peter Mark**. 1779–1869, British physician, who on retirement devised a *Thesaurus of English Words and Phrases* (1852).

rogue (rəʊg) *n* **1** a dishonest or unprincipled person, esp.

a man. **2** *Often jocular*. a mischievous or wayward person, often a child. **3** a crop plant which is inferior, diseased, or of a different, unwanted variety. **4a** any inferior or defective specimen. **4b** (*as modifier*): *rogue heroin*. **5** *Arch*. a vagrant. **6a** an animal of vicious character that leads a solitary life. **6b** (*as modifier*): *a rogue elephant*. ◆ *vb* **rogues, roguing, rogued**. **7** (*tr*) to rid (a field or crop) of plants that are inferior, diseased, etc. [C16: from ?]

roguery ('rəʊgərɪ) *n, pl* **rogueries**. **1** behaviour characteristic of a rogue. **2** a roguish or mischievous act.

rogues' gallery *n* **1** a collection of photographs of known criminals kept by the police for identification purposes. **2** a group of undesirable people.

roguish ('rəʊgɪʃ) *adj* **1** dishonest or unprincipled. **2** mischievous.
► **'roguishly** *adv*

roil (rɔɪl) *vb* **1** (*tr*) to make (a liquid) cloudy or turbid by stirring up dregs or sediment. **2** (*intr*) (esp. of a liquid) to be agitated. **3** (*intr*) *Dialect*. to be noisy. **4** (*tr*) *Now rare*. another word for **rile** (sense 1). [C16: from ?]

roister ('rɔɪstə) *vb* (*intr*) **1** to engage in noisy or unrestrained merrymaking. **2** to brag, bluster, or swagger. [C16: from OF *rustre* lout, from *ruste* uncouth, from L *rusticus* rural]
► **'roisterer** *n* ► **'roisterous** *adj* ► **'roisterously** *adv*

Roland ★ ('rəʊlənd) *n* **1** the greatest of the legendary 12 peers or paladins (of whom Oliver was another) in attendance on Charlemagne. **2 a Roland for an Oliver**. an effective retort or retaliation.

role *or* **rôle** (rəʊl) *n* **1** a part or character in a play, film, etc., to be played by an actor or actress. **2** *Psychol*. the part played by a person in a particular social setting, influenced by his expectation of what is appropriate. **3** usual function: *what is his role in the organization?* [C17: from F *rôle* ROLL, an actor's script]

role model *n* a person regarded by others, esp. younger people, as a good example to follow.

role-playing *n* *Psychol*. activity in which a person imitates, consciously or unconsciously, a role uncharacteristic of himself. See also **psychodrama**.

Rolf (rɒlf) *or* **Rolf the Ganger** ★ *n* other names for **Rollo**.

Rolfe ★ (rɒlf) *n* **Frederick William**, also known as *Baron Corvo*. 1860–1913, British novelist. His best-known work is *Hadrian the Seventh* (1904).

roll (rəʊl) *vb* **1** to move or cause to move along by turning over and over. **2** to move or cause to move along on wheels or rollers. **3** to flow or cause to flow onwards in an undulating movement. **4** (*intr*) (of animals, etc.) to turn onto the back and kick. **5** (*intr*) to extend in undulations: *the hills roll down to the sea*. **6** (*intr*; usually foll. by *around*) to move or occur in cycles. **7** (*intr*) (of a planet, the moon, etc.) to revolve in an orbit. **8** (*intr*; foll. by *on*, *by*, etc.) to pass or elapse: *the years roll by*. **9** to rotate or cause to rotate wholly or partially: *to roll one's eyes*. **10** to curl, cause to curl, or admit of being curled, so as to form a ball, tube, or cylinder. **11** to make or form by shaping into a ball, tube, or cylinder: *to roll a cigarette*. **12** (often foll. by *out*) to spread or cause to spread out flat or smooth under or as if under a roller: *to roll pastry*. **13** to emit or utter with a deep prolonged reverberating sound: *the thunder rolled continuously*. **14** to trill or cause to be trilled: *to roll one's r's*. **15** (*intr*) (of a vessel, aircraft, rocket, etc.) to turn from side to side around the longitudinal axis. **16** to cause (an aircraft) to execute a roll or (of an aircraft) to execute a roll (sense 34). **17** (*intr*) to walk with a swaying gait, as when drunk. **18** *Chiefly US*. to throw (dice). **19** (*intr*) to operate or begin to operate: *the presses rolled*. **20** (*intr*) *Inf*. to make progress: *let the good times roll*. **21** (*tr*) *Inf*., *chiefly US & NZ*. to rob (a helpless person). ◆ *n* **22** the act or an instance of rolling. **23** anything rolled up in a cylindrical form: *a roll of newspaper*. **24** an official list or register, esp. of names: *an electoral roll*. **25** a rounded mass: *rolls of flesh*. **26** a cylinder used to flatten something; roller. **27** a small cake of bread for one person. **28** a flat pastry or cake rolled up with a meat (**sausage roll**), jam (**jam roll**), or other filling. **29** a swell or undulation on a surface: *the roll of the hills*. **30** a swaying, rolling, or unsteady movement or gait. **31** a deep prolonged reverberating sound: *the roll of thunder.* **32** a trilling sound; trill. **33** a very rapid beating of the sticks on a drum. **34** a flight manoeuvre in which an aircraft makes one complete rotation about its longitudinal axis without loss of height or change in direction. **35** *Sl.* an act of sexual intercourse or petting (esp. **in a roll in the hay**). **36** *US sl.* an amount of money, esp. a wad of paper money. **37 on a roll.** *Sl.* experiencing continued good luck or success. **38 strike off the roll(s).** expel from membership. **38a** to expel from membership. **38b** to debar (a solicitor) from practising, usually because of dishonesty. ◆ See also **roll in, roll on,** etc. [C14 *rollen,* from OF *roler,* from L *rotulus,* dim. of *rota* a wheel]

Rolland ★ (*French* rɔlɑ̃) *n* **Romain** (rɔmɛ̃). 1866–1944, French writer, noted for his novels about a musical genius, *Jean-Christophe* (1904–12): Nobel prize for literature 1915.

rollbar ('rəʊl,bɑː) *n* a bar that reinforces the frame of a car used for racing, rallying, etc., to protect the driver if the car should turn over.

roll call *n* the reading aloud of an official list of names, those present responding when their names are read out.

rolled gold *n* a metal, such as brass, coated with a thin layer of gold. Also (US): **filled gold.**

rolled-steel joist *n* a steel beam, esp. one with a cross section in the form of a letter *H* or *I.* Abbrev.: **RSJ.**

roller ('rəʊlə) *n* **1** a cylinder having an absorbent surface and a handle, used for spreading paint. **2** Also called: **garden roller.** a heavy cast-iron cylinder on an axle to which a handle is attached; used for flattening lawns. **3** a long heavy wave of the sea, advancing towards the shore. **4** a hardened cylinder of precision-ground steel that forms one of the rolling components of a roller bearing or of a linked driving chain. **5** a cylinder fitted on pivots, used to enable heavy objects to be easily moved. **6** *Printing.* a cylinder, usually of hard rubber, used to ink a plate before impression. **7** any of various other cylindrical devices that rotate about a cylinder, used for any of various purposes. **8** a small cylinder onto which a woman's hair may be rolled to make it curl. **9** *Med.* a bandage consisting of a long strip of muslin rolled tightly into a cylindrical form before application. **10** any of various Old World birds, such as the **European roller,** that have a blue, green, and brown plumage, a slightly hooked bill, and an erratic flight. **11** (*often cap.*) a variety of tumbler pigeon. **12** a person or thing that rolls. **13** short for **steamroller.**

rollerball ('rəʊlə,bɔːl) *n* a pen having a small moving nylon, plastic, or metal ball as a writing point.

roller bearing *n* a bearing in which a shaft runs on a number of hardened-steel rollers held within a cage.

Rollerblade ('rəʊlə,bleɪd) *n Trademark.* a type of roller skate in which the wheels are set in a single straight line under the boot.

roller chain *n Engineering.* a chain for transmitting power in which each link consists of two free-moving rollers held in position by pins connected to sideplates.

roller coaster *n* another term for **big dipper.**

roller derby *n* a race on roller skates, esp. one involving aggressive tactics.

roller skate *n* **1** a device having straps for fastening to a shoe and four small wheels that enable the wearer to glide swiftly over a floor. ◆ *vb* **roller-skate, roller-skates, roller-skating, roller-skated.** **2** (*intr*) to move on roller skates.
► **roller skater** *n*

roller towel *n* **1** a towel with the two ends sewn together, hung on a roller. **2** a towel wound inside a roller enabling a clean section to be pulled out when needed.

rollick ('rɒlɪk) *vb* **1** (*intr*) to behave in a carefree or boisterous manner. ◆ *n* **2** a boisterous or carefree escapade. [C19: Scot. dialect, prob. from ROMP + FROLIC]

rollicking[1] ('rɒlɪkɪŋ) *adj* boisterously carefree. [C19: from ROLLICK]

rollicking[2] ('rɒlɪkɪŋ) *n Brit. inf.* a very severe telling-off. [C20: from ROLLICK (vb) (in former sense: to be angry, make a fuss); ? infl. by BOLLOCKING]

roll in *vb* (*mainly intr*) **1** (*adv*) to arrive in abundance or in large numbers. **2** (*adv*) *Inf.* to arrive at one's destination. **3 be rolling in.** (*prep*) *Sl.* to abound or luxuriate in (wealth, money, etc.).

rolling ('rəʊlɪŋ) *adj* **1** having gentle rising and falling slopes: *rolling country.* **2** progressing by stages or by occurrences in different places in succession: *a rolling strike.* **3** subject to regular review and updating: *a rolling plan for overseas development.* **4** reverberating: *rolling thunder.* **5** *Sl.* extremely rich. **6** that may be turned up or down: *a rolling hat brim.* ◆ *adv* **7** *Sl.* swaying or staggering (in **rolling drunk**).

rolling launch *n Marketing.* the process of introducing a product onto a market gradually. Cf. **roll out** (sense 3).

rolling mill *n* **1** a mill or factory where ingots of heated metal are passed between rollers to produce sheets or bars of a required cross section and form. **2** a machine having rollers that may be used for this purpose.

rolling pin *n* a cylinder with handles at both ends used for rolling dough, pastry, etc., out flat.

rolling stock *n* the wheeled vehicles collectively used on a railway, including the locomotives, coaches, etc.

rolling stone *n* a restless or wandering person.

Rolling Stones ★ *pl n* **the.** British rock band (formed 1962): comprising Mick Jagger, Keith Richards (born 1943; guitar, vocals), Brian Jones (1942–69; guitar), Charlie Watts (born 1941; drums), Bill Wyman (born 1936; bass guitar), and subsequently Mick Taylor (born 1948; guitar; with the band 1969–74) and Ron Wood (born 1947; guitar; with the band from 1975). See also (Michael Philip) **Jagger.**

Rollins ★ ('rɒlɪnz) *n* **Sonny,** original name *Theodore Walter Rollins.* born 1930, US jazz tenor saxophonist.

rollmop ('rəʊl,mɒp) *n* a herring fillet rolled, usually around onion slices, and pickled in spiced vinegar. [C20: from G *Rollmops,* from *rollen* to ROLL + *Mops* pug dog]

rollneck ('rəʊl,nɛk) *adj* **1** (of a garment) having a high neck that may be rolled over. ◆ *n* **2** a rollneck sweater or other garment.

Rollo ★ ('rɒləʊ) *n* ?860–?930 A.D., Norse war leader who received from Charles the Simple a fief that formed the basis of the duchy of Normandy. Also called: **Rolf, Rolf the Ganger.**

roll of honour *n* a list of those who have died in war for their country.

roll on *vb* **1** *Brit.* used to express the wish that an eagerly anticipated event or date will come quickly: *roll on Saturday.* ◆ *adj* **roll-on. 2** (of a deodorant, etc.) dispensed by means of a revolving ball fitted into the neck of the container. ◆ *n* **roll-on. 3** a woman's foundation garment, made of elasticized material and having no fastenings.

roll-on/roll-off *adj* denoting a cargo ship or ferry designed so that vehicles can be driven on and off.

roll out *vb* (*tr, adv*) **1** to cause (pastry) to become flatter and thinner by pressure with a rolling pin. **2** to show (a new type of aircraft) to the public for the first time. **3** to launch (a new film, product, etc.) in a series of successive waves, as over the whole country. ◆ *n* **roll-out. 4** a presentation to the public of a new aircraft, product, etc.; a launch.

roll over *vb* (*adv*) **1** (*intr*) to overturn. **2** (*intr*) (of an animal, esp. a dog) to lie on its back while kicking its legs in the air. **3** (*tr*) to capitulate. **4** (*tr*) to allow (a loan, prize, etc.) to continue in force for a further period. ◆ *n* **rollover. 5** an instance of such continuance of a loan, prize, etc.

roll-top desk *n* a desk having a slatted wooden panel that can be pulled down over the writing surface when not in use.

roll up *vb* (*adv*) **1** to form or cause to form a cylindrical shape. **2** (*tr*) to wrap (an object) round on itself or on an axis: *to roll up a map.* **3** *Inf.* to arrive, esp. in a vehicle. **4** (*intr*) *Austral.* to assemble; congregate. ◆ *n* **roll-up. 5** *Brit. inf.* a cigarette made by hand from loose tobacco and cigarette papers. **6** *Austral.* the number attending a meeting, etc.

Rolodex ('rəʊləˌdɛks) *n Trademark, chiefly US.* a small file for holding names, addresses, and telephone numbers, consisting of cards attached horizontally to a rotatable central cylinder.

roly-poly ('rəʊlɪ'pəʊlɪ) *adj* 1 plump, buxom, or rotund. ♦ *n, pl* **roly-polies. 2** *Brit.* a strip of suet pastry spread with jam, fruit, or a savoury mixture, rolled up, and baked or steamed. [C17: apparently by reduplication from *roly,* from ROLL]

ROM (rɒm) *n Computing. acronym for* read only memory: a storage device that holds data permanently and cannot be altered by the programmer.

rom. *Printing. abbrev. for* roman (type).

Rom. *abbrev. for:* 1 Roman. 2 Romance (languages). 3 Romania(n). 4 *Bible.* Romans.

Roma ★ ('rɔːma) *n* the Italian name for **Rome.**

Romagna ★ (*Italian* rɔ'maɲɲa) *n* an area of N Italy: part of the Papal States up to 1860.

Romaic (rəʊ'meɪk) *Obs.* ♦ *n* 1 the modern Greek vernacular. ♦ *adj* 2 of or relating to Greek. [C19: from Gk *Rhōmaikos* Roman, with reference to the Eastern Roman Empire]

Romains ★ (*French* rɔmɛ̃) *n* **Jules** (ʒyl). pseudonym of *Louis Farigoule.* 1885–1972, French writer. His works include the novel *Men of Good Will* (1932–46).

roman ('rəʊmən) *adj* 1 of, relating to, or denoting a vertical style of printing type: the usual form of type for most printed matter. Cf. **italic.** ♦ *n* 2 roman type. [C16: so called because the style of letters is that used in ancient Roman inscriptions]

Roman ('rəʊmən) *adj* 1 of or relating to Rome or its inhabitants in ancient or modern times. 2 of or relating to Roman Catholicism or the Roman Catholic Church. ♦ *n* 3 a citizen or inhabitant of ancient or modern Rome.

***roman à clef** French.* (rɔmɑ̃ a kle) *n, pl* **romans à clef** (rɔmɑ̃ a kle). a novel in which real people are depicted under fictitious names. [lit.: novel with a key]

Roman alphabet *n* the alphabet evolved by the ancient Romans for the writing of Latin, derived ultimately from the Phoenicians. The alphabet serves for writing most of the languages of W Europe.

Roman blind *n* a window blind consisting of a length of material which, when drawn up, gathers into horizontal folds from the bottom.

Roman candle *n* a firework that produces a continuous shower of sparks punctuated by coloured balls of fire. [C19: it originated in Italy]

Roman Catholic *adj* 1 of or relating to the Roman Catholic Church. ♦ *n* 2 a member of this Church. ♦ Often shortened to **Catholic.**
▸ **Roman Catholicism** *n*

Roman Catholic Church *n* the Christian Church over which the pope presides, with administrative headquarters in the Vatican. Also called: **Catholic Church, Church of Rome.**

romance *n* (rə'mæns, 'rəʊmæns). 1 a love affair. 2 love, esp. romantic love idealized for its purity or beauty. 3 a spirit of or inclination for adventure or mystery. 4 a mysterious, exciting, sentimental, or nostalgic quality, esp. one associated with a place. 5 a narrative in verse or prose, written in a vernacular language in the Middle Ages, dealing with adventures of chivalrous heroes. 6 any similar narrative work dealing with events and characters remote from ordinary life. 7 a story, novel, film, etc., dealing with love, usually in an idealized or sentimental way. 8 an extravagant, absurd, or fantastic account. 9 a lyrical song or short instrumental composition having a simple melody. ♦ *vb* (rə'mæns). **romances, romancing, romanced. 10** (*intr*) to tell, invent, or write extravagant or romantic fictions. **11** (*intr*) to tell extravagant or improbable lies. **12** (*intr*) to have romantic thoughts. **13** (*intr*) (of a couple) to indulge in romantic behaviour. **14** (*tr*) to be romantically involved with. [C13: *romauns,* from OF *romans,* ult. from L *Rōmānicus* Roman]
▸ **ro'mancer** *n*

Romance (rə'mæns, 'rəʊmæns) *adj* 1 denoting, relating

to, or belonging to the languages derived from Latin, including Italian, Spanish, Portuguese, French, and Romanian. 2 denoting a word borrowed from a Romance language. ♦ *n* 3 this group of languages.

Roman Empire *n* 1 the territories ruled by ancient Rome. At its height the Roman Empire included W and S Europe, N Africa, and SW Asia. In 395 A.D. it was divided into the **Eastern Roman Empire,** whose capital was Byzantium, and the **Western Roman Empire,** whose capital was Rome. 2 the government of Rome and its dominions by the emperors from 27 B.C. 3 the Byzantine Empire. 4 the Holy Roman Empire.

Romanesque (ˌrəʊmə'nɛsk) *adj* 1 denoting or having the style of architecture used in W and S Europe from the 9th to the 12th century, characterized by the rounded arch and massive-masonry wall construction. 2 denoting a corresponding style in painting, sculpture, etc. [C18: see ROMAN, -ESQUE]

Roman holiday *n* entertainment or pleasure that depends on the suffering of others. [C19: from Byron's poem *Childe Harold* (IV, 141)]

Romania (rəʊ'meɪnɪə), **Rumania,** *or* **Roumania** ★ *n* a republic in SE Europe, bordering on the Black Sea: united in 1861; became independent in 1878; Communist government set up in 1945; became a socialist republic in 1965; a more democratic regime was installed after a revolution in 1989. It consists chiefly of a great central arc of the Carpathian Mountains and Transylvanian Alps, with the plains of Walachia, Moldavia, and Dobriya on the south and east and the Pannonian Plain in the west. Official language: Romanian. Religion: Christian (Romanian Orthodox) majority. Currency: leu. Capital: Bucharest. Pop.: 22 572 000 (1997). Area: 237 500 sq. km (91 699 sq. miles).

Romanian (rəʊ'meɪnɪən), **Rumanian,** *or* **Roumanian** *n* 1 the official language of Romania. 2 a native, citizen, or inhabitant of Romania. ♦ *adj* 3 relating to, denoting, or characteristic of Romania, its people, or their language.

Romanic (rəʊ'mænɪk) *adj* another word for **Roman** or **Romance.**

Romanism ('rəʊməˌnɪzəm) *n* Roman Catholicism, esp. when regarded as excessively or superstitiously ritualistic.
▸ **'Romanist** *n*

Romanize *or* **Romanise** ('rəʊməˌnaɪz) *vb* **Romanizes, Romanizing, Romanized** *or* **Romanises, Romanising, Romanised. 1** (*tr*) to impart a Roman Catholic character to (a ceremony, etc.). **2** (*intr*) to be converted to Roman Catholicism. **3** (*tr*) to transcribe (a language) into the Roman alphabet.
▸ **ˌRomani'zation** *or* **ˌRomani'sation** *n*

Roman law *n* the system of jurisprudence of ancient Rome, codified under Justinian and forming the basis of many modern legal systems.

Roman nose *n* a nose having a high prominent bridge.

Roman numerals *pl n* the letters used by the Romans for the representation of cardinal numbers, still used occasionally today. The integers are represented by the following letters: I (= 1), V (= 5), X (= 10), L (= 50), C (= 100), D (= 500), and M (= 1000). VI = 6 (V + I) but IV = 4 (V − I).

Romano ★ (*Italian* ro'maːno) *n* See **Giulio Romano.**

Romanov ★ ('rəʊmənɒf; *Russian* ra'manəf) *n* any of the Russian imperial dynasty that ruled from the crowning (1613) of Mikhail Fyodorovich to the abdication (1917) of Nicholas II during the February Revolution.

Romansch *or* **Romansh** (rəʊ'mænʃ) *n* a group of Romance dialects spoken in the Swiss canton of Grisons; an official language of Switzerland since 1938. [C17: from Romansch, lit.: Romance language]

romantic (rəʊ'mæntɪk) *adj* 1 of, relating to, imbued with, or characterized by romance. 2 evoking or given to thoughts and feelings of love, esp. idealized or sentimental love: *a romantic setting.* 3 impractical, visionary, or idealistic: *a romantic scheme.* 4 *Often euphemistic.* imaginary or fictitious: *a romantic account of one's war service.* 5 (*often cap.*) of or relating to a movement in European art,

music, and literature in the late 18th and early 19th centuries, characterized by an emphasis on feeling and content rather than order and form. ◆ *n* **6** a person who is romantic, as in being idealistic, amorous, or soulful. **7** a person whose tastes in art, literature, etc., lie mainly in romanticism. **8** (*often cap.*) a poet, composer, etc., of the romantic period or whose main inspiration is romanticism. [C17: from F, from obs. *romant* story, romance, from OF *romans* ROMANCE]
▸ ro'mantically *adv*

romanticism (rəʊ'mæntɪ,sɪzəm) *n* **1** (*often cap.*) the theory, practice, and style of the romantic art, music, and literature of the late 18th and early 19th centuries, usually opposed to classicism. **2** romantic attitudes, ideals, or qualities.
▸ ro'manticist *n*

romanticize *or* **romanticise** (rəʊ'mæntɪ,saɪz) *vb* **romanticizes, romanticizing, romanticized** *or* **romanticises, romanticising, romanticised.** **1** (*intr*) to think or act in a romantic way. **2** (*tr*) to interpret according to romantic precepts. **3** to make or become romantic, as in style.
▸ ro,mantici'zation *or* ro,mantici'sation *n*

Romany *or* **Romani** ('rɒmənɪ, 'rəʊ-) *n* **1a** (*pl* **Romanies** *or* **Romanis**) another name for a **Gypsy. 1b** (*as modifier*): *Romany customs.* **2** the language of the Gypsies, belonging to the Indic branch of the Indo-European family. [C19: from Romany *romani* (adj) Gypsy, ult. from Sansk. *domba* man of a low caste of musicians, of Dravidian origin]

romanza (rəʊ'mænzə) *n* a short instrumental piece or songlike character. [It.]

romaunt (rə'mɔːnt) *n Arch.* a verse romance. [C16: from OF; see ROMANTIC]

Romberg ★ ('rɒmbɜːɡ) *n* **Sigmund.** 1887–1951, Hungarian-born US composer of such operettas as *The Student Prince* (1924) and *The Desert Song* (1926).

Rome ★ (rəʊm) *n* **1** the capital of Italy, on the River Tiber: includes the independent state of the Vatican City; traditionally founded by Romulus on the Palatine Hill in 753 B.C., later spreading to six other hills east of the Tiber; capital of the Roman Empire; a great cultural and artistic centre, esp. during the Renaissance. Pop.: 2 687 881 (1994 est.). Italian name: **Roma. 2** the Roman Empire. **3** the Roman Catholic Church or Roman Catholicism.

Romeo ('rəʊmɪəʊ) *n, pl* **Romeos.** an ardent male lover. [after the hero of Shakespeare's *Romeo and Juliet* (1594)]

Romish ('rəʊmɪʃ) *adj Usually derog.* of or resembling Roman Catholic beliefs or practices.

Rommel ★ (*German* 'rɒməl) *n* **Erwin** ('ɛrviːn), nicknamed *the Desert Fox.* 1891–1944, German field marshal, noted for his leadership of the Afrika Corps (1941–42); committed suicide after the failure of the officers' plot against Hitler.

Romney ★ ('rɒmnɪ, 'rʌm-) *n* **George.** 1734–1802, British portrait painter.

Romney Marsh ★ ('rɒmnɪ, 'rʌm-) *n* a marshy area of SE England, on the Kent coast between New Romney and Rye: includes Dungeness.

romp (rɒmp) *vb* (*intr*) **1** to play or run about wildly, boisterously, or joyfully. **2 romp home** (*or* **in**). to win a race, etc., easily. ◆ *n* **3** a noisy or boisterous game or prank. **4** an instance of sexual activity between two or more people that is entered into light-heartedly and without emotional commitment: *naked sex romps.* **5** *Arch.* a playful or boisterous child, esp. a girl. **6** an easy victory. [C18: prob. var. of RAMP, from OF *ramper* to crawl, climb]

rompers ('rɒmpəz) *pl n* **1** a one-piece baby garment consisting of trousers and a bib with straps. **2** *NZ.* a type of costume worn by schoolgirls for games and gymnastics.

Romulus ★ ('rɒmjʊləs) *n Roman myth.* the founder of Rome, suckled with his twin brother Remus by a she-wolf after they were abandoned in infancy. Their parents were Rhea Silvia and Mars. Romulus later killed Remus in an argument over the new city.

Roncesvalles ★ ('rɒnsə,vælz; *Spanish* rɒnθez'βaʎes) *n* a village in N Spain, in the Pyrenees: a nearby pass was the

scene of the defeat of Charlemagne and death of Roland in 778. French name: **Roncevaux** (rɔ̃svo).

rondavel (,rɒn'dɑːvəl) *n S. African.* a circular, often thatched, building with a conical roof. [from ?]

rondeau ('rɒndəʊ) *n, pl* **rondeaux** (-dəʊ, -dəʊz). a poem consisting of 13 or 10 lines with two rhymes and having the opening words of the first line used as an unrhymed refrain. [C16: from OF, from *rondel* a little round, from *rond* ROUND]

rondel ('rɒndəl) *n* a rondeau consisting of three stanzas of 13 or 14 lines with a two-line refrain appearing twice or three times. [C14: from OF, lit.: a little circle, from *rond* ROUND]

rondo ('rɒndəʊ) *n, pl* **rondos.** a piece of music in which a refrain is repeated between episodes: often constitutes the form of the last movement of a sonata or concerto. [C18: from It., from F RONDEAU]

Rondônia ★ (*Portuguese* rõ'dɔnja) *n* a state of W Brazil: consists chiefly of tropical rainforest; a centre of the Amazon rubber boom until about 1912. Capital: Pôrto Velho. Pop.: 1 339 500 (1995 est.). Area: 243 043 sq. km (93 839 sq. miles). Former name (until 1956): **Guaporé.**

rone (rəʊn) *or* **ronepipe** *n Scot.* a drainpipe for carrying rainwater from a roof.

Ronsard ★ (*French* rɔ̃sar) *n* **Pierre de** (pjɛr də). 1524–85, French poet, foremost of the *Pléiade.*

röntgen ('rɒntɡən, -tjən, 'rɛnt-) *n* a variant spelling of **roentgen.**

Röntgen ★ ('rɒntɡən, -tjən, 'rɛnt-; *German* 'rœntɡən) *n* a variant spelling of (Wilhelm Konrad) **Roentgen.**

roo (ruː) *n Austral. inf.* a kangaroo.

rood (ruːd) *n* **1a** a crucifix, esp. one set on a beam or screen at the entrance to the chancel of a church. **1b** (*as modifier*): *rood screen.* **2** the Cross on which Christ was crucified. **3** a unit of area equal to one quarter of an acre or 0.10117 hectare. **4** a unit of area equal to 40 square rods. [OE *rōd*]

Roodepoort-Maraisburg ★ ('ruːdə,pʊət mə'reɪsbɜːɡ) *n* an industrial city in NE South Africa on the Witwatersrand. Pop.: 162 632 (1991).

roof (ruːf) *n, pl* **roofs** (ruːfs, ruːvz). **1a** a structure that covers or forms the top of a building. **1b** (*in combination*): *the rooftop.* **1c** (*as modifier*): *a roof garden.* **2** the top covering of a vehicle, oven, or other structure: *the roof of a car.* **3** *Anat.* any structure that covers an organ or part: *the roof of the mouth.* **4** a highest or topmost point or part: *Mount Everest is the roof of the world.* **5** a house or other shelter: *a poor man's roof.* **6 hit** (*or* **raise** *or* **go through**) **the roof.** *Inf.* to get extremely angry. ◆ *vb* **7** (*tr*) to provide or cover with a roof or rooflike part. [OE *hrōf*]
▸ 'roofer *n* ▸ 'roofless *adj*

roof garden *n* a garden on a flat roof of a building.

roofing ('ruːfɪŋ) *n* **1** material used to construct a roof. **2** the act of constructing a roof.

roof rack *n* a rack attached to the roof of a motor vehicle for carrying luggage, skis, etc.

rooftree ('ruːf,triː) *n* another name for **ridgepole.**

rooibos ('rɔɪ,bɒs, 'rʊɪ,bɒs) *n* any of various South African trees with red leaves. [from Afrik. *rooi* red + *bos* bush]

rooibos tea *n S. African.* a tealike drink made from the leaves of the rooibos.

rooikat ('rɔɪ,kæt, 'rʊɪ,kæt) *n* a South African lynx. [from Afrik. *rooi* red + *kat* cat]

rooinek ('rɔɪ,nɛk, 'rʊɪ,nɛk) *n S. African.* a contemptuous name for an **Englishman.** [C19: Afrik., lit.: red neck]

rook[1] (rʊk) *n* **1** a large Eurasian passerine bird, with a black plumage and a whitish base to its bill. **2** *Sl.* a swindler or cheat, esp. one who cheats at cards. ◆ *vb* **3** (*tr*) *Sl.* to overcharge, swindle, or cheat. [OE *hrōc*]

rook[2] (rʊk) *n* a chesspiece that may move any number of unoccupied squares in a straight line, horizontally or vertically. Also called: **castle.** [C14: from OF *rok*, ult. from Ar. *rukhkh*]

rookery ('rʊkərɪ) *n, pl* **rookeries.** **1** a group of nesting rooks. **2** a clump of trees containing rooks' nests. **3a** a breeding ground or communal living area of certain other birds or mammals, esp. penguins or seals. **3b** a colony of any such creatures. **4** *Arch.* an overcrowded slum.

rookie ('rʊkɪ) *n Inf.* a newcomer, esp. a raw recruit in the army. [C20: changed from RECRUIT]

room (ruːm, rʊm) *n* **1** space or extent, esp. unoccupied or unobstructed space for a particular purpose: *is there room to pass?* **2** an area within a building enclosed by a floor, a ceiling, and walls or partitions. **3** (*functioning as sing or pl*) the people present in a room: *the whole room was laughing.* **4** (foll. by *for*) opportunity or scope: *room for manoeuvre.* **5** (*pl*) a part of a house, hotel, etc., that is rented out as separate accommodation: *living in dingy rooms in Dalry.* ◆ *vb* **6** (*intr*) to occupy or share a room or lodging: *where does he room?* [OE *rūm*]
▸ '**roomer** *n*

roomful ('ruːm,fʊl, 'rʊm-) *n*, *pl* **roomfuls.** a number or quantity sufficient to fill a room: *a roomful of furniture.*

rooming house *n US & Canad.* a house having self-contained furnished rooms or flats for renting.

roommate ('ruːm,meɪt, 'rʊm-) *n* a person with whom one shares a room or lodging.

room service *n* service in a hotel providing meals, drinks, etc., in guests' rooms.

roomy ('ruːmɪ, 'rʊmɪ) *adj* **roomier, roomiest.** spacious.
▸ '**roomily** *adv* ▸ '**roominess** *n*

Roosevelt ★ ('rəʊzə,velt) *n* **1** (**Anna**) **Eleanor.** 1884–1962, US writer and diplomat: delegate to the United Nations (1945–52). **2** her husband, **Franklin Delano** ('delənəʊ), known as **FDR.** 1882–1945, 32nd president of the US (1933–45); elected four times. He instituted major reforms (the **New Deal**) and was a forceful leader during World War II. **3 Theodore.** 1858–1919, 26th president of the US (1901–09). He negotiated the right to build the Panama Canal (1903); Nobel peace prize (1906), for mediating in the Russo-Japanese war.

roost (ruːst) *n* **1** a place, perch, branch, etc., where birds, esp. domestic fowl, rest or sleep. **2** a temporary place to rest or stay. ◆ *vb* **3** (*intr*) to rest or sleep on a roost. **4** (*intr*) to settle down or stay. **5 come home to roost.** to have unfavourable repercussions. [OE *hrōst*]

Roost (ruːst) *n* **the.** a powerful current caused by conflicting tides around the Shetland and Orkney Islands. [C16: from ON *röst*]

rooster ('ruːstə) *n Chiefly US & Canad.* the male of the domestic fowl; a cock.

root[1] (ruːt) *n* **1a** the organ of a higher plant that anchors the rest of the plant in the ground and absorbs water and mineral salts from the soil. **1b** (loosely) any of the branches of such an organ. **2** any plant part, such as a tuber, that is similar to a root in function or appearance. **3a** the essential part or nature of something: *your analysis strikes at the root of the problem.* **3b** (*as modifier*): *the root cause of the problem.* **4** *Anat.* the embedded portion of a tooth, nail, hair, etc. **5** origin or derivation. **6** (*pl*) a person's sense of belonging in a community, place, etc., esp. the one in which he was born or brought up. **7** *Bible.* a descendant. **8** *Linguistics.* the form of a word that remains after removal of all affixes. **9** *Maths.* a quantity that when multiplied by itself a certain number of times equals a given quantity: *3 is a cube root of 27.* **10** Also called: **solution.** *Maths.* a number that when substituted for the variable satisfies a given equation. **11** *Music.* (in harmony) the note forming the foundation of a chord. **12** *Austral. & NZ sl.* sexual intercourse. **13 root and branch.** (*adv*) entirely; utterly. ◆ *Related adj:* **radical.** ◆ *vb* **14** (*intr*) Also: **take root.** to establish a root and begin to grow. **15** (*intr*) Also: **take root.** to become established, embedded, or effective. **16** (*tr*) to embed with or as if with a root or roots. **17** *Austral. & NZ sl.* to have sexual intercourse (with). ◆ *See also* **root out, roots.** [OE *rōt*, from ON]
▸ '**rooter** *n* ▸ '**root,like** *adj* ▸ '**rooty** *adj* ▸ '**rootiness** *n*

root[2] (ruːt) *vb* (*intr*) **1** (of a pig) to burrow in or dig up the earth in search of food, using the snout. **2** (foll. by *about, around, in,* etc.) *Inf.* to search vigorously but unsystematically. [C16: changed (through infl. of ROOT[1]) from earlier *wroot,* from OE *wrōtan;* rel. to OE *wrōt* snout]
▸ '**rooter** *n*

root[3] (ruːt) *vb* (*intr;* usually foll. by *for*) *Inf.* to give support

to (a contestant, team, etc.), as by cheering. [C19: ? var. of Scot. *rout* to make a loud noise, from ON *rauta* to roar]

root beer *n US & Canad.* an effervescent drink made from extracts of various roots and herbs.

root canal *n* the passage in the root of a tooth through which its nerves and blood vessels enter the pulp cavity.

root-canal therapy *n* another name for **root treatment.**

root climber *n* any of various climbing plants, such as the ivy, that adhere to a supporting structure by means of small roots growing from the side of the stem.

root crop *n* a crop, as of turnips or beets, cultivated for the food value of its roots.

rooted ('ruːtɪd) *adj* **1** having roots. **2** deeply felt: *rooted objections.*

root ginger *n* the raw underground stem of the ginger plant used finely chopped or grated, esp. in Chinese dishes.

root hair *n* any of the hollow hairlike outgrowths of the outer cells of a root, just behind the tip, that absorb water and salts from the soil.

rooting compound *n Horticulture.* a substance, usually a powder, containing auxins in which plant cuttings are dipped in order to promote root growth.

rootle ('ruːt°l) *vb* **rootles, rootling, rootled.** (*intr*) *Brit.* another word for **root**[2].

rootless ('ruːtlɪs) *adj* having no roots, esp. (of a person) having no ties with a particular place.

rootlet ('ruːtlɪt) *n* a small root.

root mean square *n* the square root of the average of the squares of a set of numbers or quantities: *the root mean square of* 1, 2, *and* 4 *is* $\sqrt{[(1^2 + 2^2 + 4^2)/3]} = \sqrt{7}$. Abbrev.: **rms.**

root nodule *n* a swelling on the root of a leguminous plant, such as clover, that contains bacteria capable of nitrogen fixation.

root out *vb* (*tr, adv*) to remove or eliminate completely: *we must root out inefficiency.*

roots (ruːts) *adj* (of popular music) going back to the origins of a style, esp. in being genuine and unpretentious: *roots rock.*

roots music *n* **1** another name for **world music.** **2** reggae, esp. when regarded as authentic and uncommercialized.

rootstock ('ruːt,stɒk) *n* **1** another name for **rhizome. 2** another name for **stock** (sense 7). **3** *Biol.* a basic structure from which offshoots have developed.

root treatment *n Dentistry.* a procedure, used for treating an abscess at the tip of the root of a tooth, in which the pulp is removed and a filling (**root filling**) inserted in the root canal. Also called: **root-canal therapy.**

ropable *or* **ropeable** ('rəʊpəb°l) *adj* **1** capable of being roped. **2** *Austral. & NZ inf.* **2a** angry. **2b** wild or intractable: *a ropable beast.*

rope (rəʊp) *n* **1a** a fairly thick cord made of intertwined hemp or other fibres or of wire or other strong material. **1b** (*as modifier*): *a rope ladder.* **2** a row of objects fastened to form a line: *a rope of pearls.* **3** a quantity of material wound in the form of a cord. **4** a filament or strand, esp. of something viscous or glutinous: *a rope of slime.* **5 give (someone) enough (*or* plenty of) rope to hang himself.** to allow (someone) to accomplish his own downfall by his own foolish acts. **6 know the ropes.** to have a thorough understanding of a particular sphere of activity. **7 on the ropes. 7a** *Boxing.* driven against the ropes enclosing the ring by an opponent's attack. **7b** in a hopeless position. **8 the rope. 8a** a rope halter used for hanging. **8b** death by hanging. ◆ *vb* **ropes, roping, roped. 9** (*tr*) to bind or fasten with or as if with a rope. **10** (*tr;* usually foll. by *off*) to enclose or divide by means of a rope. **11** (when *intr,* foll. by *up*) *Mountaineering.* to tie (climbers) together with a rope. [OE *rāp*]

rope in *vb* (*tr, adv*) **1** *Brit.* to persuade to take part in some activity. **2** *US & Canad.* to trick or entice into some activity.

rope's end *n* a short piece of rope, esp. as formerly used for flogging sailors.

★ people and places

ropewalk ('rəʊp,wɔːk) *n* a long narrow usually covered path or shed where ropes are made.

ropey *or* **ropy** ('rəʊpɪ) *adj* **ropier, ropiest. 1** *Brit. inf.* **1a** inferior. **1b** slightly unwell. **2** (of a viscous or sticky substance) forming strands. **3** resembling a rope.
▸ **'ropily** *adv* ▸ **'ropiness** *n*

Roquefort ('rɒkfɔː) *n* a blue-veined cheese with a strong flavour, made from ewe's and goat's milk. [C19: after *Roquefort*, village in S France]

roquet ('rəʊkɪ) *Croquet.* ◆ *vb* **roquets** (-kɪz), **roqueting** (-kɪŋ), **roqueted** (-kɪd). **1** to drive one's ball against (another person's ball) in order to be allowed to croquet. ◆ *n* **2** the act of roqueting. [C19: var. of CROQUET]

Roraima ★ (*Portuguese* rɔ'raima) *n* a state of N Brazil: chiefly rainforest. Capital: Boa Vista. Pop.: 262 200 (1995 est.). Area: 230 104 sq. km (89 740 sq. miles).

ro-ro ('rəʊrəʊ) *adj acronym for* roll-on/roll-off.

rorqual ('rɔːkwəl) *n* any of several whalebone whales that have a dorsal fin and a series of grooves along the throat and chest. Also called: **finback**. [C19: from F, from Norwegian *rörhval*, from ON *reytharhvalr*, from *reythr* (from *rauthr* red) + *hvalr* whale]

Rorschach test ('rɔːʃɑːk) *n Psychol.* a personality test consisting of a number of unstructured inkblots presented for interpretation. [C20: after Hermann Rorschach (1884–1922), Swiss psychiatrist]

rort (rɔːt) *Austral. inf.* ◆ *n* **1** a rowdy party or celebration. **2** a fraud; deception. ◆ *vb* (*tr*) **3** to take unfair advantage of (something): *our voting system can be rorted.* [C20: back formation from E dialect *rorty* (in the sense: good, splendid)]
▸ **'rorty** *adj*

Rory O'Connor ★ (,rɔːrɪ əʊ'kɒnə) *n* Also called *Roderic*. ?1116–98, king of Connaught and last High King of Ireland.

Rosa[1] ★ ('rəʊzə; *Italian* 'rɔːza) *n* **Monte** ('mɒntɪ; *Italian* 'monte). a mountain between Italy and Switzerland: the highest in the Pennine Alps. Height: 4634 m (15 204 ft).

Rosa[2] ★ (*Italian* 'rɔːza) *n* **Salvator** ('salvatɔr). 1615–73, Italian artist, noted esp. for his romantic landscapes.

rosace ('rəʊzeɪs) *n* **1** another name for **rose window. 2** another name for **rosette.** [C19: from F, from L *rosāceus* ROSACEOUS]

rosaceous (rəʊ'zeɪʃəs) *adj* **1** of or belonging to the Rosaceae, a family of plants typically having white, yellow, pink, or red five-petalled flowers. The family includes the rose, strawberry, blackberry, and many fruit trees. **2** like a rose, esp., rose-coloured. [C18: from L *rosāceus* composed of roses, from *rosa* ROSE[1]]

rosarian (rəʊ'zɛərɪən) *n* a person who cultivates roses, esp. professionally.

Rosario (rəʊ'sɑːrɪəʊ; *Spanish* rɔ'sarjo) *n* an inland port in E Argentina, on the Paraná River: the second largest city in the country; industrial centre. Pop.: 1 157 372 (1992 est.).

rosarium (rəʊ'zɛərɪəm) *n, pl* **rosariums** *or* **rosaria** (-'zɛərɪə). a rose garden. [C19: NL]

rosary ('rəʊzərɪ) *n, pl* **rosaries. 1** *RC Church.* **1a** a series of prayers counted on a string of beads, usually five or 15 decades of Aves, each decade beginning with a Paternoster and ending with a Gloria. **1b** a string of 55 or 165 beads used to count these prayers as they are recited. **2** (in other religions) a similar string of beads used in praying. **3** an archaic word for (a **garland** (of flowers, etc.). [C14: from L *rosārium* rose garden, from *rosārius* of roses, from *rosa* ROSE[1]]

Roscius ★ ('rɒskɪəs, -sɪəs) *n* **1** full name *Quintus Roscius Gallus.* died 62 B.C., Roman actor. **2** any actor.
▸ **'Roscian** *adj*

Roscommon ★ (rɒs'kɒmən) *n* an inland county of N central Republic of Ireland, in Connacht: economy based on cattle and sheep farming. County town: Roscommon. Pop.: 51 897 (1991). Area: 2463 sq. km (951 sq. miles).

rose[1] (rəʊz) *n* **1a** a shrub or climbing plant having prickly stems, compound leaves, and fragrant flowers. **1b** (*in combination*): *rosebush.* **2** the flower of any of these

plants. **3** any of various similar plants, such as the Christmas rose. **4a** a purplish-pink colour. **4b** (*as adj*): *rose paint.* **5** a rose, or a representation of one, as the national emblem of England. **6a** a cut for a gemstone, having a hemispherical faceted crown and a flat base. **6b** a gem so cut. **7** a perforated cap fitted to a watering can or hose, causing the water to issue in a spray. **8** a design or decoration shaped like a rose; rosette. **9** Also called: **ceiling rose.** *Electrical engineering.* a circular boss attached to a ceiling through which the flexible lead of an electric-light fitting passes. **10** *History.* See **red rose, white rose. 11 bed of roses.** a situation of comfort or ease. **12 under the rose.** in secret; privately; sub rosa. ◆ *vb* **roses, rosing, rosed. 13** (*tr*) to make rose-coloured; cause to blush or redden. [OE, from L *rosa*, prob. from Gk *rhodon* rose]
▸ **'rose,like** *adj*

rose[2] (rəʊz) *vb* the past tense of **rise.**

rosé ('rəʊzeɪ) *n* any pink wine, made either by removing the skins of red grapes after only a little colour has been extracted or by mixing red and white wines. [C19: from F, lit.: pink, from L *rosa* ROSE[1]]

roseate ('rəʊzɪ,eɪt) *adj* **1** of the colour rose or pink. **2** excessively or idealistically optimistic.

rosebay ('rəʊz,beɪ) *n* **1** any of several rhododendrons. **2 rosebay willowherb.** a perennial plant that has spikes of deep pink flowers and is widespread in N temperate regions. **3** another name for **oleander.**

Rosebery ★ ('rəʊzbərɪ, -brɪ) *n* **Earl of,** title of *Archibald Philip Primrose.* 1847–1929, British statesman; Liberal prime minister (1894–95).

rosebud ('rəʊz,bʌd) *n* **1** the bud of a rose. **2** *Literary.* a pretty young woman.

rose campion *n* a European plant widely cultivated for its pink flowers. Its stems and leaves are covered with white woolly down. Also called: **dusty miller.**

rose chafer *or* **beetle** *n* a British beetle that has a greenish-golden body with a metallic lustre and feeds on plants.

rose-coloured *adj* **1** of the colour rose; rosy. **2** Also: **rose-tinted.** excessively optimistic. **3 see through rose-coloured** *or* **rose-tinted glasses** (*or* **spectacles**). to view in an excessively optimistic light.

rose-cut *adj* (of a gemstone) cut with a hemispherical faceted crown and a flat base.

rosehip ('rəʊz,hɪp) *n* the berry-like fruit of a rose plant.

rosella (rəʊ'zɛlə) *n* any of various Australian parrots. [C19: prob. alteration of *Rose-hiller*, after *Rose Hill*, Parramatta, near Sydney]

rosemary ('rəʊzmərɪ) *n, pl* **rosemaries.** an aromatic European shrub widely cultivated for its grey-green evergreen leaves, which are used in cookery and in the manufacture of perfumes. It is the traditional flower of remembrance. [C15: earlier *rosmarine*, from L *rōs* dew + *marīnus* marine; modern form infl. by folk etymology, as if ROSE[1] + *Mary*]

Rosenberg ★ ('rəʊzən,bɜːg) *n* **1 Alfred.** 1893–1946, German Nazi politician and writer, who devised much of the racial ideology of Nazism: hanged for war crimes. **2 Isaac.** 1890–1918, British poet and painter, best known for his poems of World War I: died in action. **3 Julius.** 1918–53, US spy, who, with his wife **Ethel** (1914–53), was executed for passing information about nuclear weapons to the Russians.

rose of Sharon ('ʃærən) *n* a creeping shrub native to SE Europe but widely cultivated, having large yellow flowers. Also called: **Aaron's beard.**

roseola (rəʊ'ziːələ) *n Pathol.* **1** any red skin rash. **2** another name for **rubeola.** [C19: from NL, dim. of L *roseus* rosy]
▸ **ro'seolar** *adj*

rosery ('rəʊzərɪ) *n, pl* **roseries.** a bed or garden of roses.

Rosetta ★ (rəʊ'zɛtə) *n* a town in N Egypt, in the Nile delta. Pop.: 52 014 (1986). Egyptian name: **Rashid.**

Rosetta stone *n* a basalt slab discovered in 1799 at Rosetta, dating to the reign of Ptolemy V (196 B.C.) and carved with parallel inscriptions in hieroglyphics, Egyptian demotic, and Greek, which provided the key to the decipherment of ancient Egyptian texts.

rosette (rəʊ'zɛt) *n* **1** a decoration resembling a rose, esp. an arrangement of ribbons in a rose-shaped design worn as a badge or presented as a prize. **2** another name for **rose window**. **3** *Bot.* a circular cluster of leaves growing from the base of a stem. [C18: from OF: a little ROSE¹]

rose-water *n* **1** scented water made by the distillation of rose petals or by impregnation with oil of roses. **2** (*modifier*) elegant or delicate, esp. excessively so.

rose window *n* a circular window, esp. one that has ornamental tracery radiating from the centre to form a symmetrical roselike pattern. Also called: **wheel window, rosette.**

rosewood ('rəʊz,wʊd) *n* the hard dark wood of any of various tropical trees. It has a roselike scent and is used in cabinetwork.

Rosh Hashanah or **Rosh Hashana** ('rɒʃ həˈʃɑːnə; *Hebrew* 'rɒʃ haʃaˈna) *n* the Jewish New Year festival, celebrated on the first and second of Tishri. [from Heb., lit.: beginning of the year, from *rōsh* head + *hash-shānāh* year]

Rosicrucian (,rəʊzɪˈkruːʃən) *n* **1** a member of a society professing esoteric religious doctrines, venerating the rose and Cross as symbols of Christ's Resurrection and Redemption, and claiming various occult powers. ♦ *adj* **2** of or designating the Rosicrucians or Rosicrucianism. [C17: from L *Rosae Crucis* Rose of the Cross, translation of the G name Christian *Rosenkreuz*, supposed founder of the society]

rosin ('rɒzɪn) *n* **1** Also called: **colophony.** a translucent brittle amber substance produced in the distillation of crude turpentine oleoresin and used esp. in making varnishes, printing inks, and sealing waxes and for treating the bows of stringed instruments. **2** (not in technical usage) another name for **resin** (sense 1). ♦ *vb* **3** (*tr*) to treat or coat with rosin. [C14: var. of RESIN]
▸ **'rosiny** *adj*

Roskilde ★ (*Danish* 'rɔskilə) *n* a city in Denmark, on NE Sjælland west of Copenhagen: capital of Denmark from the 10th century to 1443; scene of the signing (1658) of the **Peace of Roskilde** between Denmark and Sweden. Pop.: 49 080 (1990).

ROSPA ('rɒspə) *n* (in Britain) *acronym for* Royal Society for the Prevention of Accidents.

Ross ★ (rɒs) *n* **1** Diana. born 1944, US Motown singer. **2** Sir **James Clark.** 1800–62, British naval officer and explorer, who located the north magnetic pole (1831) and discovered the Ross Sea (1839–43). **3** his uncle, Sir **John.** 1777–1856, Scottish naval officer and Arctic explorer. **4** Sir **Ronald.** 1857–1932, British bacteriologist, who discovered the transmission of malaria by mosquitoes: Nobel prize for physiology or medicine 1902.

Ross and Cromarty ★ ('krɒmətɪ) *n* a historic county of N Scotland, including the island of Lewis and many islets: now part of Highland and Western Isles council areas.

Ross Dependency ★ *n* a section of Antarctica administered by New Zealand: includes the coastal regions of Victoria Land and King Edward VII Land, the Ross Sea and islands, and the Ross Ice Shelf. Area: about 414 400 sq. km (160 000 sq. miles).

Rossellini ★ (,rɒsəˈliːnɪ) *n* Roberto. 1906–77, Italian film director. His films include *Rome, Open City* (1945) and *L'Amore* (1948).

Rossetti ★ (rɒˈzɛtɪ) *n* **1** Christina Georgina. 1830–94, British poet. **2** her brother, **Dante Gabriel.** 1828–82, British poet and painter: a leader of the Pre-Raphaelites.

Rossini ★ (rɒˈsiːnɪ) *n* Gioacchino Antonio (*Italian* dʒoakˈkiːno anˈtɔːnjo). 1792–1868, Italian composer, esp. of operas, such as *The Barber of Seville* (1816) and *William Tell* (1829).

Ross Island ★ *n* an island in the W Ross Sea: contains the active volcano Mount Erebus.

Rossiya ★ (raˈsiːjə) *n* transliteration of the Russian name for **Russia.**

Ross Sea ★ *n* a large arm of the S Pacific in Antarctica,

incorporating the Ross Ice Shelf and lying between Victoria Land and the Edward VII Peninsula.

Rostand ★ (*French* rɔstɑ̃) *n* Edmond (ɛdmɔ̃). 1868–1918, French playwright and poet; noted for his drama *Cyrano de Bergerac* (1897).

roster ('rɒstə) *n* **1** a list or register, esp. one showing the order of people enrolled for duty. ♦ *vb* **2** (*tr*) to place on a roster. [C18: from Du. *rooster* grating or list (the lined paper looking like a grid)]

Rostock ★ ('rɒstɒk) *n* a port in NE Germany, on the Warnow estuary 13 km (8 miles) from the Baltic and its outport, Warnemünde: formerly the chief port of East Germany; university (1419). Pop.: 232 634 (1995 est.).

Rostov or **Rostov-on-Don** ★ ('rɒstɒv) *n* a port in S Russia, on the River Don 48 km (30 miles) from the Sea of Azov: industrial centre. Pop.: 1 026 000 (1995 est.).

Rostropovich ★ (,rɒstrəˈpəʊvɪtʃ; *Russian* rəstraˈpovitʃ) *n* Mstislav Leopoldovich ('mɪstɪslɑːv; *Russian* mstiˈslaf leaˈpɔldavitʃ). born 1927, Soviet cellist and conductor; became a US citizen in 1978.

rostrum ('rɒstrəm) *n, pl* **rostrums** or **rostra** (-trə). **1** any platform on which public speakers stand to address an audience. **2** a platform in front of an orchestra on which the conductor stands. **3** another word for **ram** (sense 5). **4** the prow of an ancient Roman ship. **5** *Biol., zool.* a beak or beaklike part. [C16: from L *rōstrum* beak, ship's prow, from *rōdere* to nibble, gnaw; in pl, *rōstra* orator's platform, because this platform in the Roman forum was adorned with the prows of captured ships]
▸ **'rostral** *adj*

rosy ('rəʊzɪ) *adj* **rosier, rosiest. 1** of the colour rose or pink. **2** having a healthy pink complexion: *rosy cheeks.* **3** optimistic, esp. excessively so: *a rosy view of social improvements.* **4** resembling or abounding in roses.
▸ **'rosily** *adv* ▸ **'rosiness** *n*

rot (rɒt) *vb* **rots, rotting, rotted. 1** to decay or cause to decay as a result of bacterial or fungal action. **2** (*intr*; usually foll. by *off* or *away*) to crumble (off) or break (away), as from decay or long use. **3** (*intr*) to become weak or depressed through inertia, confinement, etc.; languish: *rotting in prison.* **4** to become or cause to become morally degenerate. ♦ *n* **5** the process of rotting or the state of being rotten. **6** something decomposed. Related adj: **putrid. 7** short for **dry rot. 8** *Pathol.* any putrefactive decomposition of tissues. **9** a condition in plants characterized by decay of tissues, caused by bacteria, fungi, etc. **10** *Vet. science.* a contagious fungal disease of sheep. **11** (*also interj*) nonsense; rubbish. [OE *rotian* (vb); rel. to ON, *rotna*; C13 (n), from ON]

rota ('rəʊtə) *n Chiefly Brit.* a register of names showing the order in which people take their turn to perform certain duties. [C17: from L: a wheel]

Rota ('rəʊtə) *n RC Church.* the supreme ecclesiastical tribunal.

rotachute ('rəʊtə,ʃuːt) *n* a device serving the same purpose as a parachute, in which the canopy is replaced by freely revolving rotor blades, used for the delivery of stores or recovery of missiles.

rotaplane ('rəʊtə,pleɪn) *n* an aircraft that derives its lift from freely revolving rotor blades.

rotary ('rəʊtərɪ) *adj* **1** operating by rotation. **2** turning; revolving. ♦ *n, pl* **rotaries. 3** a part of a machine that rotates about an axis. **4** *US & Canad.* another term for **roundabout** (sense 2). [C18: from Med. L *rotārius*, from L *rota* wheel]

Rotary Club *n* any of the local clubs that form **Rotary International,** an international association of professional and businessmen founded in the US in 1905 to promote community service.
▸ **Rotarian** (rəʊˈtɛərɪən) *n, adj*

rotary engine *n* **1** an internal-combustion engine having radial cylinders that rotate about a fixed crankshaft. **2** an engine, such as a turbine or wankel engine, in which power is transmitted directly to rotating components.

rotary plough or **tiller** *n* an implement with a series of blades mounted on a power-driven shaft which rotates so as to break up soil.

★ people and places

rotary press *n* a machine for printing from a revolving cylindrical forme, usually onto a continuous strip of paper.

rotary table *n* a chain or gear-driven unit, mounted in the derrick floor which rotates the drill pipe and bit.

rotate *vb* (rəʊˈteɪt), **rotates, rotating, rotated. 1** to turn or cause to turn around an axis; revolve or spin. **2** to follow or cause to follow a set sequence. **3** to replace (one set of personnel) with another. ◆ *adj* (ˈrəʊteɪt). **4** *Bot.* designating a corolla the petals of which radiate like the spokes of a wheel.
▸ **ˈroˈtatable** *adj*

rotation (rəʊˈteɪʃən) *n* **1** the act of rotating; rotary motion. **2** a regular cycle of events in a set order or sequence. **3** a planned sequence of cropping according to which the crops grown in successive seasons on the same land are varied so as to make a balanced demand on its fertility. **4** the spinning motion of a body, such as a planet, about an internal axis. **5** *Maths.* **5a** a circular motion of a configuration about a given point, without a change in shape. **5b** a transformation in which the coordinate axes are rotated by a fixed angle about the origin.
▸ **roˈtational** *adj*

rotator (rəʊˈteɪtə) *n* **1** a person, device, or part that rotates or causes rotation. **2** *Anat.* any of various muscles that revolve a part on its axis.

rotatory (ˈrəʊtətərɪ, -trɪ) *or (less commonly)* **rotative** *adj* of, possessing, or causing rotation.
▸ **ˈrotatorily** *adv*

Rotavator ★ (ˈrəʊtəˌveɪtə) *n Trademark.* a mechanical cultivator with rotary blades. [C20: from ROTA(RY) + (CULTI)VATOR]
▸ **ˈRotaˌvate** *vb* (*tr*)

rote (rəʊt) *n* **1** a habitual or mechanical routine or procedure. **2** by rote. by repetition; by heart (often in **learn by rote**). [C14: from ?]

rotenone (ˈrəʊtɪˌnəʊn) *n* a white odourless crystalline substance extracted from the roots of derris: a powerful insecticide. [C20: from Japanese *rōten* derris + -ONE]

rotgut (ˈrɒtˌɡʌt) *n Facetious sl.* alcoholic drink, esp. spirits, of inferior quality.

Roth ★ (rɒθ) *n* **Philip.** born 1933, US novelist. His works include *Portnoy's Complaint* (1969) and *I Married a Communist* (1998).

Rotherham ★ (ˈrɒðərəm) *n* **1** an industrial town in N England, in South Yorkshire. Pop.: 121 380 (1991). **2** a unitary authority in N England, in South Yorkshire. Pop.: 256 300 (1996 est.). Area: 283 sq. km (109 sq. miles).

Rothermere ★ (ˈrɒðəˌmɪə) *n* **Viscount.** title of *Harold Sidney Harmsworth.* 1868–1940, British newspaper magnate.

Rothesay ★ (ˈrɒθsɪ) *n* a town in SW Scotland, on the E coast of Bute Island. Pop.: 5264 (1991).

Rothko ★ (ˈrɒθkəʊ) *n* **Mark.** 1903–70, US expressionist painter, born in Russia.

Rothschild ★ (ˈrɒtʃaɪld, ˈrɒθs-) *n* a powerful family of European Jewish bankers, prominent members of which were: **1 Lionel Nathan,** Baron de Rothschild. 1809–79, British banker and first Jewish member of Parliament. **2** his grandfather **Meyer Amschel** (ˈmaɪər ˈamʃəl). 1743–1812, German financier and founder of the Rothschild bank. **3** his son, **Nathan Meyer,** Baron de Rothschild. 1777–1836, British banker, born in Germany.

rotifer (ˈrəʊtɪfə) *n* a minute aquatic multicellular invertebrate having a ciliated wheel-like organ used in feeding and locomotion: common constituents of freshwater plankton. Also called: **wheel animalcule.** [C18: from NL *Rotifera,* from L *rota* wheel + *ferre* to bear]
▸ **rotiferal** (rəʊˈtɪfərəl) *or* **roˈtiferous** *adj*

rotisserie (rəʊˈtɪsərɪ) *n* **1** a rotating spit on which meat, poultry, etc., can be cooked. **2** a shop or restaurant where meat is roasted to order. [C19: from F, from OF *rostir* to ROAST]

rotogravure (ˌrəʊtəʊɡrəˈvjʊə) *n* **1** a printing process using cylinders with many small holes, from which ink

is transferred to a moving web of paper, etc., in a rotary press. **2** printed material produced in this way, esp. magazines. [C20: from L *rota* wheel + GRAVURE]

rotor (ˈrəʊtə) *n* **1** the rotating member of a machine or device, such as the revolving arm of the distributor of an internal-combustion engine. **2** a rotating device having radiating blades projecting from a hub which produces thrust to lift and propel a helicopter. [C20: shortened form of ROTATOR]

Rotorua ★ (ˌrəʊtəˈruːə) *n* a city in New Zealand, on North Island at the SW end of Lake Rotorua: centre of forestry; noted for hydrothermal activity. Pop.: 54 700 (1994).

rotten (ˈrɒtⁿn) *adj* **1** decomposing, decaying, or putrid. **2** breaking up, esp. through age or hard use: *rotten ironwork.* **3** morally corrupt. **4** disloyal or treacherous. **5** *Inf.* unpleasant: *rotten weather.* **6** *Inf.* unsatisfactory or poor: *rotten workmanship.* **7** *Inf.* miserably unwell. **8** *Inf.* distressed and embarrassed: *I felt rotten breaking the bad news to him.* ◆ *adv Inf.* **9** extremely; very much: *men fancy her rotten.* [C13: from ON *rottin;* rel. to OE *rotian* to ROT]
▸ **ˈrottenly** *adv* ▸ **ˈrottenness** *n*

rotten borough *n* (before the Reform Act of 1832) any of certain English parliamentary constituencies with few or no electors.

rottenstone (ˈrɒtⁿnˌstəʊn) *n* a much-weathered limestone, rich in silica: used in powdered form for polishing metal.

rotter (ˈrɒtə) *n Sl., chiefly Brit.* a worthless, unpleasant, or despicable person.

Rotterdam ★ (ˈrɒtəˌdæm) *n* a port in the SW Netherlands, in South Holland province: the second largest city of the Netherlands and one of the world's largest ports; oil refineries, shipbuilding yards, etc. Pop.: 599 414 (1995).

Rottweiler (ˈrɒtˌwaɪlə, -ˌvaɪlə) *n* **1** a breed of large dog with a smooth black and tan coat, noted for strength and aggression. **2** (*often not cap.*) **2a** an aggressive and unscrupulous person. **2b** (*as modifier*): *rottweiler politics.* [G, from *Rottweil,* town in Swabia where the breed originated]

rotund (rəʊˈtʌnd) *adj* **1** rounded or spherical in shape. **2** plump. **3** sonorous or grandiloquent. [C18: from L *rotundus* round, from *rota* wheel]
▸ **roˈtundity** *n* ▸ **roˈtundly** *adv*

rotunda (rəʊˈtʌndə) *n* a circular building or room, esp. one that has a dome. [C17: from It. *rotonda,* from L *rotundus* round, from *rota* a wheel]

Rouault ★ (ruːˈəʊ; *French* rwo) *n* **Georges** (ʒɔrʒ). 1871–1958, French expressionist artist.

Roubaix ★ (*French* rubε) *n* a city in N France near the Belgian border: forms, with Tourcoing, a large industrial conurbation. Pop.: 97 746 (1990).

Roubiliac *or* **Roubillac** ★ (rubijak) *n* **Louis-François** (lwifrɑ̃swa). ?1695–1762, French sculptor: lived chiefly in England.

rouble *or* **ruble** (ˈruːbⁿl) *n* the unit monetary unit of Belarus, Russia, and Tajikistan. [C16: from Russian *rubl* silver bar, from ORussian *rublĭ* bar, block of wood, from *rubiti* to cut up]

roué (ˈruːeɪ) *n* a debauched or lecherous man; rake. [C19: from F, lit.: one broken on the wheel; with reference to the fate deserved by a debauchee]

Rouen ★ (*French* rwɑ̃) *n* a city in N France, on the River Seine: the chief river port of France; became capital of the duchy of Normandy in 912; scene of the burning of Joan of Arc (1431); university (1964). Pop.: 105 470 (1990).

rouge (ruːʒ) *n* **1** a red powder or cream, used as a cosmetic for adding redness to the cheeks. **2** short for **jeweller's rouge.** ◆ *vb* **rouges, rouging, rouged. 3** (*tr*) to apply rouge to. [C18: F: red, from L *rubeus*]

rouge et noir (ˈruːʒ eɪ ˈnwɑː) *n* a card game in which the players put their stakes on any of two red and two black diamond-shaped spots marked on the table. [F, lit.: red and black]

Rouget de Lisle ★ (*French* ruʒε də lil) *n* **Claude Joseph**

(klod ʒozɛf). 1760–1836, French army officer: composer of the *Marseillaise* (1792).

rough (rʌf) *adj* **1** (of a surface) not smooth; uneven or irregular. **2** (of ground) covered with scrub, boulders, etc. **3** denoting or taking place on uncultivated ground: *rough grazing*. **4** shaggy or hairy. **5** turbulent: *a rough sea*. **6** (of performance or motion) uneven; irregular: *a rough engine*. **7** (of behaviour or character) rude, coarse, or violent. **8** harsh or sharp: *rough words*. **9** *Inf.* severe or unpleasant: *a rough lesson*. **10** (of work, etc.) requiring physical rather than mental effort. **11** *Inf.* ill: *he felt rough after an evening of heavy drinking*. **12** unfair: *rough luck*. **13** harsh or grating to the ear. **14** without refinement, luxury, etc. **15** not perfected in any detail; rudimentary: *rough workmanship*; *rough justice*. **16** not prepared or dressed: *rough gemstones*. **17** (of a guess, etc.) approximate. **18** having the sound of *h*; aspirated. **19 rough on.** *Inf.*, *chiefly Brit.* **19a** severe towards. **19b** unfortunate for (a person). **20 the rough side of one's tongue.** harsh words; a rebuke. ◆ *n* **21** rough ground. **22** a sketch or preliminary piece of artwork. **23** unfinished or crude state (esp. in **in the rough**). **24 the rough.** *Golf.* the part of the course bordering the fairways where the grass is untrimmed. **25** *Inf.* a violent person; thug. **26** the unpleasant side of something (esp. in **take the rough with the smooth**). ◆ *adv* **27** roughly. **28 sleep rough.** to spend the night in the open; be without shelter. ◆ *vb* (*tr*) **29** to make rough; roughen. **30** (foll. by *out*, *in*, etc.) to prepare (a sketch, report, etc.) in preliminary form. **31 rough it.** *Inf.* to live without the usual comforts of life. ◆ See also **rough up.** [OE *rūh*]
▶ **'roughly** *adv* ▶ **'roughness** *n*

roughage ('rʌfɪdʒ) *n* **1** the coarse indigestible constituents of food, which provide bulk to the diet and aid digestion. **2** any rough material.

rough-and-ready *adj* **1** crude, unpolished, or hastily prepared, but sufficient for the purpose. **2** (of a person) without formality or refinement.

rough-and-tumble *n* **1** a fight or scuffle without rules. ◆ *adj* **2** characterized by disorderliness and disregard for rules.

rough breathing *n* (in Greek) the sign (͑) placed over an initial letter, indicating that (in ancient Greek) it was pronounced with an *h*.

roughcast ('rʌf,kɑːst) *n* **1** a mixture of plaster and small stones used to cover the surface of an external wall. **2** any rough or preliminary form, model, etc. ◆ *adj* **3** covered with roughcast. ◆ *vb* **roughcasts, roughcasting, roughcast. 4** to apply roughcast to (a wall, etc.). **5** to prepare in rough.
▶ **'rough,caster** *n*

rough-cut *n* a first basic edited version of a film with the scenes in sequence and the soundtrack synchronized.

rough diamond *n* **1** an unpolished diamond. **2** an intrinsically trustworthy or good person with uncouth manners or dress.

rough-dry *adj* **1** (of clothes or linen) dried ready for pressing. ◆ *vb* **rough-dries, rough-drying, rough-dried. 2** (*tr*) to dry (clothes, etc.) without ironing them.

roughen ('rʌfən) *vb* to make or become rough.

rough-hew *vb* **rough-hews, rough-hewing, rough-hewed; rough-hewed** or **rough-hewn.** (*tr*) to cut or shape roughly without finishing the surface.

roughhouse ('rʌf,haus) *n Sl.* rough, disorderly, or noisy behaviour.

roughish ('rʌfɪʃ) *adj* somewhat rough.

rough music *n* (formerly) a loud cacophony created with tin pans, drums, etc., esp. as a protest or demonstration of indignation outside someone's house.

roughneck ('rʌf,nɛk) *n Sl.* **1** a rough or violent person; thug. **2** a worker in an oil-drilling operation.

rough puff pastry *n* a rich flaky pastry.

roughrider ('rʌf,raɪdə) *n* a rider of wild or unbroken horses.

roughshod ('rʌf,ʃɒd) *adj* **1** (of a horse) shod with rough-bottomed shoes to prevent sliding. ◆ *adv* **2 ride roughshod over.** to domineer over or act with complete disregard for.

rough stuff *n Inf.* violence.

rough trade *n Sl.* (in homosexual use) a tough or violent sexual partner, esp. one casually picked up.

rough up *vb* (*tr*, *adv*) **1** *Inf.* to treat violently; beat up. **2** to cause (feathers, hair, etc.) to stand up by rubbing against the grain.

roulade (ruːˈlɑːd) *n* **1** something cooked in the shape of a roll, esp. a slice of meat. **2** an elaborate run in vocal music. [C18: from F, lit.: a rolling, from *rouler* to ROLL]

Roulers ★ (ruːˈlɛəz; *French* rulɛrs) *n* a city in NW Belgium, in West Flanders province. Pop.: 53 617 (1995 est.). Flemish name: **Roeselare.**

roulette (ruːˈlɛt) *n* **1** a gambling game in which a ball is dropped onto a spinning horizontal wheel divided into numbered slots, with players betting on the slot into which the ball will fall. **2** a toothed wheel for making a line of perforations. **3** a curve generated by a point on one curve rolling on another. ◆ *vb* **roulettes, rouletting, rouletted.** (*tr*) **4** to use a roulette on (something), as in engraving, making stationery, etc. [C18: from F, from *rouelle*, dim. of *roue* a wheel, from L *rota*]

Roumania ★ (ruːˈmeɪnɪə) *n* a variant of **Romania.**
▶ **Rou'manian** *adj, n*

round (raund) *adj* **1** having a flat circular shape, as a hoop. **2** having the shape of a ball. **3** curved; not angular. **4** involving or using circular motion. **5** (*prenominal*) complete: *a round dozen*. **6** *Maths.* **6a** forming or expressed by a whole number, with no fraction. **6b** expressed to the nearest ten, hundred, or thousand: *in round figures*. **7** (of a sum of money) considerable. **8** fully depicted or developed, as a character in a book. **9** full and plump: *round cheeks*. **10** (of sound) full and sonorous. **11** (of pace) brisk; lively. **12** (*prenominal*) (of speech) candid; unmodified: *a round assertion*. **13** (of a vowel) pronounced with rounded lips. ◆ *n* **14** a round shape or object. **15 in the round. 15a** in full detail. **15b** *Theatre.* with the audience all round the stage. **16** a session, as of a negotiation: *a round of talks*. **17** a series: *a giddy round of parties*. **18 the daily round.** the usual activities of one's day. **19** a stage of a competition: *he was eliminated in the first round*. **20** (*often pl*) a series of calls: *a milkman's round*. **21** a playing of all the holes on a golf course. **22** a single turn of play by each player, as in a card game. **23** one of a number of periods in a boxing, wrestling, or other match. **24** a single discharge by a gun. **25** a bullet or other charge of ammunition. **26** a number of drinks bought at one time for a group of people. **27a** a single slice of bread. **27b** a sandwich made from two slices of bread. **28** a general outburst of applause, etc. **29** movement in a circle. **30** *Music.* a part song in which the voices follow each other at equal intervals at the same pitch. **31** a sequence of bells rung in order of treble to tenor. **32** a cut of beef from the thigh. **33 go** or **make the rounds. 33a** to go from place to place, as in making social calls. **33b** (of information, rumour, etc.) to be passed around, so as to be generally known. ◆ *prep* **34** surrounding, encircling, or enclosing: *a band round her head*. **35** on all or most sides of: *to look round one*. **36** on or outside the circumference or perimeter of. **37** from place to place in: *driving round Ireland*. **38** reached by making a partial circuit about: *the shop round the corner*. **39** revolving round (a centre or axis): *the earth's motion round its axis*. ◆ *adv* **40** on all or most sides. **41** on or outside the circumference or perimeter: *the racing track is two miles round*. **42** to all members of a group: *pass the food round*. **43** in rotation or revolution: *the wheels turn round*. **44** by a circuitous route: *the road to the farm goes round by the pond*. **45** to a specific place: *she came round to see me*. **46 all year round.** throughout the year. ◆ *vb* **47** to make or become round. **48** (*tr*) to encircle; surround. **49** to move or cause to move with turning motion: *to round a bend*. **50** (*tr*) **50a** to pronounce (a speech sound) with rounded lips. **50b** to purse (the lips). ◆ See also **round down, round off,** etc. [C13: from OF *ront*, from L *rotundus* round, from *rota* a wheel]
▶ **'roundish** *adj* ▶ **'roundness** *n*

USAGE NOTE See at **around.**

★ people and places

roundabout ('raʊndə,baʊt) n 1 Brit. a revolving circular platform provided with wooden animals, seats, etc., on which people ride for amusement; merry-go-round. 2 a road junction in which traffic streams circulate around a central island. US and Canad. name: **traffic circle.** ◆ adj 3 indirect; devious. ◆ adv, prep **round about.** 4 on all sides: spectators standing round about. 5 approximately: at round about 5 o'clock.

round dance n 1 a dance in which the dancers form a circle. 2 a ballroom dance, such as the waltz, in which couples revolve.

round down vb (tr, adv) to lower (a number) to the nearest whole number or ten, hundred, or thousand below it.

rounded ('raʊndɪd) adj 1 round or curved. 2 mature or complete. 3 (of the lips) pursed. 4 (of a speech sound) articulated with rounded lips.

roundel ('raʊndəl) n 1 a form of rondeau consisting of three stanzas each of three lines with a refrain after the first and the third. 2 a circular identifying mark in national colours on military aircraft. 3 a small circular window, medallion, etc. 4 a round plate of armour used to protect the armpit. 5 another word for **roundelay.** [C13: from OF rondel; see RONDEL]

roundelay ('raʊndɪ,leɪ) n 1 Also called: **roundel.** a slow medieval dance performed in a circle. 2 a song in which a line or phrase is repeated as a refrain. [C16: from OF rondelet a little rondel, from rondel; also infl. by LAY[4]]

rounders ('raʊndəz) n (functioning as sing) Brit. a ball game in which players run between posts after hitting the ball, scoring a **rounder** if they run round all four before the ball is retrieved.

Roundhead ('raʊnd,hed) n English history. a supporter of Parliament against Charles I during the Civil War. [referring to their short-cut hair]

roundhouse ('raʊnd,haʊs) n 1 US & Canad. a building in which railway locomotives are serviced, radial tracks being fed by a central turntable. 2 US boxing sl. a swinging punch or style of punching. 3 an obsolete word for **jail.** 4 Obs. a cabin on the quarterdeck of a sailing ship.

rounding ('raʊndɪŋ) n Computing. a process in which a number is approximated as the closest number that can be expressed using the number of bits or digits available.

roundly ('raʊndlɪ) adv 1 frankly, bluntly, or thoroughly: to be roundly criticized. 2 in a round manner or so as to be round.

round off vb (tr, adv) 1 (often foll. by with) to complete, esp. agreeably: we rounded off the evening with a brandy. 2 to make less jagged.

round on vb (intr, prep) to attack or reply to (someone) with sudden irritation or anger.

round robin n 1 a petition or protest having the signatures in a circle to disguise the order of signing. 2 a tournament in which each player plays against every other player.

round-shouldered adj denoting a faulty posture characterized by drooping shoulders and a slight forward bending of the back.

roundsman ('raʊndzmən) n, pl **roundsmen.** 1 Brit. a person who makes rounds, as for inspection or to deliver goods. 2 Austral. & NZ. a reporter covering a particular district or topic.

round table n a a meeting of parties or people on equal terms for discussion. b (as modifier): a round-table conference.

Round Table n the. 1 (in Arthurian legend) the circular table of King Arthur, enabling his knights to sit around it without any having precedence. 2 Arthur and his knights collectively. 3 one of an organization of clubs of young business and professional men who meet in order to further charitable work.

round-the-clock adj (or as adv **round the clock**) throughout the day and night.

round tower n a freestanding circular stone belfry built in Ireland from the 10th century beside a monastery and used as a place of refuge.

round trip n a trip to a place and back again, esp. returning by a different route.

roundtripping ('raʊnd,trɪpɪŋ) n Finance. a form of trading in which a company borrows a sum of money from one source and takes advantage of a short-term rise in interest rates to make a profit by lending it to another.

round up vb (tr, adv) 1 to gather together: to round ponies up. 2 to raise (a number) to the nearest whole number or ten, hundred, or thousand above it. ◆ n **roundup.** 3 the act of gathering together livestock, esp. cattle, so that they may be branded, counted, or sold. 4 any similar act of bringing together: a roundup of today's news.

roundworm ('raʊnd,wɜːm) n a nematode worm that is a common intestinal parasite of man and pigs.

roup (raʊp) Scot. & N English dialect. ◆ vb (tr) 1 to sell by auction. ◆ n 2 an auction. [C16 (orig.: to shout): of Scand. origin]

rouse (raʊz) vb **rouses, rousing, roused.** 1 to bring (oneself or another person) out of sleep, etc., or (of a person) to come to consciousness in this way. 2 to provoke: to rouse someone's anger. 3 **rouse oneself.** to become energetic. 4 to start or cause to start from cover: to rouse game birds. 5 (intr; foll. by on) Austral. to scold or rebuke. [C15 (in sense of hawks ruffling their feathers): from ?]
▶ **'rouser** n

rouseabout ('raʊzə,baʊt) n 1 Austral. & NZ. an unskilled labourer in a shearing shed. 2 a variant of **roustabout** (sense 1).

rousing ('raʊzɪŋ) adj tending to excite; lively or vigorous: a rousing chorus.
▶ **'rousingly** adv

Rousseau ★ (French ruso) n 1 **Henri** (ɑ̃ri), known as le Douanier. 1844–1910, French painter, noted for such works as Sleeping Gypsy (1897) and Jungle with a Lion (1904–06). 2 **Jean Jacques** (ʒɑ̃ ʒak). 1712–78, French philosopher and writer, born in Switzerland. His works include Émile (1762) and Confessions (1782). 3 **Théodore** (teɔdɔr). 1812–67, French landscape painter.

Roussillon ★ (French rusijɔ̃) n a former province of S France: united with Aragon in 1172; passed to the French crown in 1659; now forms part of the region of Languedoc-Roussillon.

roust (raʊst) vb (tr; often foll. by out) to rout or stir, as out of bed. [C17: from ROUSE]

roustabout ('raʊstə,baʊt) n 1 an unskilled labourer, esp. on an oil rig. 2 Austral. & NZ. a variant of **rouseabout** (sense 1).

rout[1] (raʊt) n 1 an overwhelming defeat. 2 a disorderly retreat. 3 a noisy rabble. 4 Law. a group of three or more people proceeding to commit an illegal act. 5 Arch. a large party or social gathering. ◆ vb 6 (tr) to defeat and cause to flee in confusion. [C13: from Anglo-Norman rute, from OF: disorderly band, from L ruptus, from rumpere to burst]

rout[2] (raʊt) vb 1 to dig over or turn up (something), esp. (of an animal) with the snout; root. 2 (tr; usually foll. by out or up) to find by searching. 3 (tr; usually foll. by out) to drive out: they routed him out of bed at midnight. 4 (tr; often foll. by out) to hollow or gouge out. 5 (intr) to search, poke, or rummage. [C16: var. of ROOT[2]]

route (ruːt) n 1 the choice of roads taken to get to a place. 2 a regular journey travelled. 3 (cap.) US. a main road between cities: Route 66. ◆ vb **routes, routeing, routed.** (tr) 4 to plan the route of; send by a particular route. [C13: from OF rute, from Vulgar L rupta via (unattested), lit.: a broken (established) way, from L ruptus, from rumpere to break]

> **USAGE NOTE** When forming the present participle or verbal noun from the verb to route it is preferable to retain the e in order to distinguish the word from routing, the present participle or verbal noun from rout[1], to defeat or rout[2], to dig, rummage: the routeing of buses from the city centre to the suburbs. The spelling routing in this sense is, however, sometimes encountered, esp. in American English.

★ people and places

routemarch ('ru:t,mɑ:tʃ) n 1 Mil. a long training march. 2 Inf. any long exhausting walk.

router ('rautə) n any of various tools or machines for hollowing out, cutting grooves, etc.

routine (ru:'ti:n) n 1 a usual or regular method of procedure, esp. one that is unvarying. 2 Computing. a program or part of a program performing a specific function: an input routine. 3 a set sequence of dance steps. 4 Inf. a hackneyed or insincere speech. ◆ adj 5 relating to or characteristic of routine. [C17: from OF, from route a customary way, ROUTE]
▶ rou'tinely adv

roux (ru:) n a mixture of equal amounts of fat and flour, heated, blended, and used as a basis for sauces. [F: brownish, from L russus RUSSET]

rove¹ (rəuv) vb roves, roving, roved. 1 to wander about (a place) with no fixed direction; roam. 2 (intr) (of the eyes) to look around; wander. ◆ n 3 the act of roving. [C15 roven (in archery) to shoot at a target chosen at random (C16: to wander, stray), from ON]

rove² (rəuv) vb roves, roving, roved. 1 (tr) to pull out and twist (fibres of wool, cotton, etc.) lightly, as before spinning. ◆ n 2 wool, cotton, etc., thus prepared. [C18: from ?]

rove³ (rəuv) vb a past tense and past participle of reeve².

rover¹ ('rəuvə) n 1 a person who roves. 2 Archery. a mark selected at random for use as a target. 3 Australian Rules football. a player without a fixed position who, with the ruckmen, forms the ruck. [C15: from ROVE¹]

rover² ('rəuvə) n a pirate or pirate ship. [C14: prob. from MDu. or MLow G, from roven to rob]

Rover or **Rover Scout** ('rəuvə) n Brit. the former name for **Venture Scout**.

roving commission n authority or power given in a general area, without precisely defined terms of reference.

row¹ (rəu) n 1 an arrangement of persons or things in a line: a row of chairs. 2 Chiefly Brit. a street, esp. a narrow one lined with identical houses. 3 a line of seats, as in a cinema, theatre, etc. 4 Maths. a horizontal linear arrangement of numbers, quantities, or terms. 5 a horizontal rank of squares on a chessboard or draughtboard. 6 a hard row to hoe. a difficult task or assignment. 7 in a row. in succession; one after the other: he won two gold medals in a row. [OE rāw, ræw]

row² (rəu) vb 1 to propel (a boat) by using oars. 2 (tr) to carry (people, goods, etc.) in a rowing boat. 3 to be propelled by means of (oars or oarsmen). 4 (intr) to take part in the racing of rowing boats as a sport. 5 (tr) to race against in a boat propelled by oars: Oxford row Cambridge every year. ◆ n 6 an act, instance, period, or distance of rowing. 7 an excursion in a rowing boat. [OE rōwan]
▶ 'rower n

row³ (rau) n 1 a noisy quarrel. 2 a noisy disturbance: we couldn't hear the music for the row next door. 3 a reprimand. ◆ vb 4 (intr; often foll. by with) to quarrel noisily. 5 (tr) Arch. to reprimand. [C18: from ?]

rowan ('rəuən, 'rau-) n another name for the (European) **mountain ash**. [C16: of Scand. origin]

rowdy ('raudɪ) adj rowdier, rowdiest. 1 tending to create noisy disturbances; rough, loud, or disorderly: a rowdy gang of football supporters. ◆ n, pl rowdies. 2 a person who behaves in such a fashion. [C19: orig. US sl., ? rel. to ROW³]
▶ 'rowdily adv ▶ 'rowdiness or 'rowdyism n

Rowe ★ (rəu) n Nicholas. 1674–1718, English dramatist; poet laureate (1715–18). His plays include Tamerlane (1702) and The Fair Penitent (1703).

rowel ('rauəl) n 1 a small spiked wheel attached to a spur. 2 Vet. science. a piece of leather inserted under the skin of a horse to cause a discharge. ◆ vb rowels, rowelling, rowelled or US rowels, roweling, roweled. (tr) 3 to goad (a horse) using a rowel. 4 Vet. science. to insert a rowel in (the skin of a horse) to cause a discharge. [C14: from OF roel a little wheel, from roe a wheel, from L rota]

rowing boat ('rəuɪŋ) n Chiefly Brit. a small pleasure boat

propelled by one or more pairs of oars. Usual US and Canad. word: **rowboat**.

rowing machine ('rəuɪŋ) n a device with oars and a sliding seat, resembling a sculling boat, used to provide exercise.

Rowlandson ★ ('rəuləndsᵊn) n Thomas. 1756–1827, British caricaturist.

Rowley ★ ('rəulɪ, 'rau-) n Thomas. ?1586–?1642, English dramatist, who collaborated with John Ford and Thomas Dekker on The Witch of Edmonton (1621) and with Thomas Middleton on The Changeling (1622).

rowlock ('rɒlək) n a swivelling device attached to the gunwale of a boat that holds an oar in place. Usual US and Canad. word: **oarlock**.

Roxas y Acuña ★ (Spanish 'rɔxas i a'kuɲa) n Manuel (ma'nwel). 1892–1948, Philippine statesman; first president of the Republic of the Philippines (1946–48).

Roxburghshire ★ ('rɒksbərəʃɪə, -ʃə) n a historic county of SE Scotland, now part of Scottish Borders.

royal ('rɔɪəl) adj 1 of, relating to, or befitting a king, queen, or other monarch; regal. 2 (prenominal; often cap.) established by, chartered by, under the patronage of, or in the service of royalty: the Royal Society of St George. 3 being a member of a royal family. 4 above the usual or normal in standing, size, quality, etc. 5 Inf. unusually good or impressive; first-rate. 6 Naut. just above the topgallant (in **royal mast**). ◆ n 7 (sometimes cap.) a member of a royal family. 8 Also: **royal stag**. a stag with antlers having 12 or more branches. 9 Naut. a sail set next above the topgallant, on a royal mast. 10 a size of printing paper, 20 by 25 inches. [C14: from OF roial, from L rēgālis fit for a king, from rēx king; cf. REGAL]
▶ 'royally adv

Royal Academy n a society founded by George III in 1768 to foster a national school of painting, sculpture, and design in England. Full name: **Royal Academy of Arts**.

Royal Air Force n the air force of Great Britain. Abbrev.: **RAF**.

Royal and Ancient Club n the. a golf club, headquarters of the sport's ruling body, based in St Andrews, Scotland. Abbrev.: **R&A**.

royal assent n Brit. the formal signing of an act of Parliament by the sovereign, by which it becomes law.

royal blue n a a deep blue colour. b (as adj): a royal-blue carpet.

Royal Commission n (in Britain) a body set up by the monarch on the recommendation of the prime minister to gather information about the operation of existing laws or to investigate any social, educational, or other matter.

royal fern n a fern of damp regions, having large fronds up to 2 metres (7 feet) in height.

royal flush n Poker. a hand made up of the five top honours of a suit.

royalist ('rɔɪəlɪst) n 1 a supporter of a monarch or monarchy, esp. during the English Civil War. 2 Inf. an extreme reactionary: an economic royalist. ◆ adj 3 of or relating to royalists.
▶ 'royalism n

royal jelly n a substance secreted by the pharyngeal glands of worker bees and fed to all larvae when very young and to larvae destined to become queens throughout their development.

Royal Leamington Spa ★ n the official name of **Leamington Spa**.

Royal Marines pl n Brit. a corps of soldiers specially trained in amphibious warfare. Abbrev.: **RM**.

Royal Mint n a British organization having the sole right to manufacture coins since the 16th century. In 1968 it moved from London to Llantrisant in Wales.

Royal National Theatre ★ n a theatre complex in London, on the S bank of the Thames (opened 1976). The prefix Royal was added in 1988. It houses the Royal National Theatre Company.

Royal Navy n the navy of Great Britain. Abbrev.: **RN**.

royal palm n any of several palm trees of tropical Amer-

★ people and places

ica, having a tall trunk with a tuft of feathery pinnate leaves.

royal standard *n* a flag bearing the arms of the British sovereign, flown only when she or he is present.

royal tennis *n* another name for **real tennis**.

royalty ('rɔɪəltɪ) *n, pl* **royalties. 1** the rank, power, or position of a king or queen. **2a** royal persons collectively. **2b** a person who belongs to a royal family. **3** any quality characteristic of a monarch. **4** a percentage of the revenue from the sale of a book, performance of a theatrical work, use of a patented invention or of land, etc., paid to the author, inventor, or proprietor.

royal warrant *n* an authorization to a tradesman to supply goods to a royal household.

Royce ★ (rɔɪs) *n* Sir (**Frederick**) **Henry.** 1863–1933, British car designer, who with C. S. Rolls (1877–1910) founded Rolls-Royce Ltd.

rozzer ('rɒzə) *n Sl.* a policeman. [C19: from ?]

RPG *abbrev. for* report program generator: a business-oriented computer programming language.

RPI (in Britain) *abbrev. for* retail price index.

rpm *abbrev. for:* **1** resale price maintenance. **2** revolutions per minute.

RPV *abbrev. for* remotely piloted vehicle.

RR *abbrev. for:* **1** Right Reverend. **2** *Canad. & US.* rural route.

-rrhagia *n combining form.* (in pathology) an abnormal discharge: *menorrhagia.* [from Gk *-rrhagia* a bursting forth, from *rhēgnunai* to burst]

-rrhoea *or esp. US* **-rrhea** *n combining form.* (in pathology) a flow: *diarrhoea.* [from NL, from Gk *-rrhoia,* from *rhein* to flow]

r-RNA *abbrev. for* ribosomal RNA.

RRP *abbrev. for* recommended retail price.

Rs *symbol for* rupees.

RS (in Britain) *abbrev. for* Royal Society.

RSA *abbrev. for:* **1** Republic of South Africa. **2** (in New Zealand) Returned Services Association. **3** Royal Scottish Academician. **4** Royal Scottish Academy. **5** Royal Society of Arts.

RSFSR (formerly) *abbrev. for* Russian Soviet Federative Socialist Republic.

RSI *abbrev. for* repetitive strain injury.

RSL (in Australia) *abbrev. for* Returned Services League.

RSM *abbrev. for:* **1** regimental sergeant major. **2** Royal School of Music. **3** Royal Society of Medicine.

RSNZ *abbrev. for* Royal Society of New Zealand.

RSPB (in Britain) *abbrev. for* Royal Society for the Protection of Birds.

RSPCA (in Britain and Australia) *abbrev. for* Royal Society for the Prevention of Cruelty to Animals.

RSV *abbrev. for* Revised Standard Version (of the Bible).

RSVP *abbrev. for* répondez s'il vous plaît. [F: please reply]

rt *abbrev. for* right.

RTE *abbrev. for* Radio Telefis Éireann. [Irish Gaelic: Irish Radio and Television]

Rt Hon. *abbrev. for* Right Honourable.

Ru *the chemical symbol for* ruthenium.

RU *abbrev. for* Rugby Union.

RU486 *n Trademark.* a brand name for the **abortion pill.**

Ruanda-Urundi ★ (ru'ændəʊ'rʊndɪ) *n* a former territory of central Africa: part of German East Africa from 1890; a League of Nations mandate under Belgian administration from 1919; a United Nations trusteeship from 1946; divided into the independent states of Rwanda and Burundi in 1962.

rub (rʌb) *vb* **rubs, rubbing, rubbed. 1** to apply pressure and friction to (something) with a backward and forward motion. **2** to move (something) with pressure along, over, or against (a surface). **3** to chafe or fray. **4** (*tr*) to bring into a certain condition by rubbing: *rub it clean.* **5** (*tr*) to spread with pressure, esp. in order to cause to be

absorbed: *she rubbed ointment into his back.* **6** (*tr*) to mix (fat) into flour with the fingertips, as in making pastry. **7** (foll. by *off, out, away,* etc.) to remove or be removed by rubbing: *the mark would not rub off the chair.* **8** (*intr*) *Bowls.* (of a bowl) to be slowed or deflected by an uneven patch on the green. **9** (*tr;* often foll. by *together*) to move against each other with pressure and friction (esp. in **rub one's hands,** often a sign of glee, keen anticipation, or satisfaction, and **rub noses,** a greeting among Eskimos). **10 rub (up) the wrong way.** to arouse anger in; annoy. ♦ *n* **11** the act of rubbing. **12** (preceded by *the*) an obstacle or difficulty (esp. in **there's the rub**). **13** something that hurts the feelings or annoys; cut; rebuke. **14** *Bowls.* an uneven patch in the green. ♦ See also **rub along, rub down,** etc. [C15: ?from Low G *rubben,* from ?]

Rub' al Khali ★ ('rʊb æl 'kɑːlɪ) *n* a desert in S Arabia, mainly in Saudi Arabia, extending southeast from Nejd to Hadramaut and northeast from Yemen to the United Arab Emirates. Area: about 777 000 sq. km (300 000 sq. miles). English names: **Great Sandy Desert, Empty Quarter.** Also called: **Ar Rimal, Dahna.**

rub along *vb* (*intr, adv*) *Brit.* **1** to continue in spite of difficulties. **2** to maintain an amicable relationship; not quarrel.

rubato (ruː'bɑːtəʊ) *Music.* ♦ *n, pl* **rubatos. 1** flexibility of tempo in performance. ♦ *adj, adv* **2** to be played with a flexible tempo. [C19: from It. *tempo rubato,* lit.: stolen time, from *rubare* to ROB]

rubber[1] ('rʌbə) *n* **1** Also called: **India rubber, gum elastic, caoutchouc.** a cream to dark brown elastic material obtained by coagulating and drying the latex from certain plants, esp. the rubber tree. **2** any of a large variety of elastomers produced from natural rubber or by synthetic means. **3** *Chiefly Brit.* a piece of rubber used for erasing something written; eraser. **4** a cloth, pad, etc., used for polishing. **5** a person who rubs something in order to smooth, polish, or massage. **6** (*often pl*) *Chiefly US & Canad.* a rubberized waterproof overshoe. **7** *Sl.* a condom. **8** (*modifier*) made of or producing rubber: *a rubber ball; a rubber factory.* [C17: from RUB + -ER[1]; the tree was so named because its product was used for rubbing out writing]
► '**rubbery** *adj*

rubber[2] ('rʌbə) *n* **1** *Bridge, whist, etc.* **1a** a match of three games. **1b** the deal that wins such a match. **2** a series of matches or games in any of various sports. [C16: from ?]

rubber band *n* a continuous loop of thin rubber, used to hold papers, etc., together. Also called: **elastic band.**

rubber cement *n* any of a number of adhesives made by dissolving rubber in a solvent such as benzene.

rubberize *or* **rubberise** ('rʌbə,raɪz) *vb* **rubberizes, rubberizing, rubberized** *or* **rubberises, rubberising, rubberised.** (*tr*) to coat or impregnate with rubber.

rubberneck ('rʌbə,nek) *Sl.* ♦ *n* **1** a person who stares or gapes inquisitively. **2** a sightseer or tourist. ♦ *vb* **3** (*intr*) to stare in a naive or foolish manner.

rubber plant *n* **1** a plant with glossy leathery leaves that grows as a tall tree in India and Malaya but is cultivated as a house plant in Europe and North America. **2** any of several tropical trees, the sap of which yields crude rubber.

rubber stamp *n* **1** a device used for imprinting dates, etc., on forms, invoices, etc. **2** automatic authorization of a payment, proposal, etc. **3** a person who makes such automatic authorizations; a cipher or person of little account. ♦ *vb* **rubber-stamp.** (*tr*) **4** to imprint (forms, invoices, etc.) with a rubber stamp. **5** *Inf.* to approve automatically.

rubber tree *n* a tropical American tree cultivated throughout the tropics, esp. in Malaya, for the latex of its stem, which is the major source of commercial rubber.

rubbing ('rʌbɪŋ) *n* an impression taken of an incised or raised surface by laying paper over it and rubbing with wax, graphite, etc.

rubbish ('rʌbɪʃ) *n* **1** worthless, useless, or unwanted matter. **2** discarded or waste matter; refuse. **3** foolish words

or speech; nonsense. ◆ vb **4** (tr) Inf. to criticize; attack verbally. [C14 robys, from ?]
▸ 'rubbishy adj

rubble ('rʌbʰl) n **1** fragments of broken stones, bricks, etc. **2** debris from ruined buildings. **3** Also called: **rubblework**. masonry constructed of broken pieces of rock, stone, etc. [C14 robyl; ? rel. to RUBBISH, or to ME rubben to rub]
▸ 'rubbly adj

Rubbra ★ ('rʌbrə) n (Charles) **Edmund**. 1901–86, British composer; his works include 11 symphonies and a piano concerto.

rub down vb (adv) **1** to dry or clean (a horse, athlete, oneself, etc.) vigorously, esp. after exercise. **2** to make or become smooth by rubbing. **3** (tr) to prepare (a surface) for painting by rubbing it with sandpaper. ◆ n **rubdown**. **4** the act of rubbing down.

rube (ruːb) n US sl. an unsophisticated countryman. [C20: prob. from the name Reuben]

rubella (ruːˈbɛlə) n a mild contagious viral disease, somewhat similar to measles, characterized by cough, sore throat, and skin rash. Also called: **German measles**. [C19: from NL, from L rubellus reddish, from rubeus red]

rubellite ('ruːbɪˌlaɪt, ruːˈbɛl-) n a red transparent variety of tourmaline, used as a gemstone. [C18: from L rubellus reddish]

Rubens ★ ('ruːbɪnz) n Sir **Peter Paul**. 1577–1640, Flemish painter, appointed (1609) painter to Archduke Albert of Austria and knighted by Charles I of England in 1629. His works include Descent from the Cross (1611–14) and The Rape of the Sabines (1635).

rubeola (ruːˈbiːələ) n the technical name for **measles**. [C17: from NL, from L rubeus reddish]

Rubicon ★ ('ruːbɪkən) n **1** a stream in N Italy: in ancient times the boundary between Italy and Cisalpine Gaul. By leading his army across it and marching on Rome in 49 B.C., Julius Caesar committed himself to civil war with the senatorial party. **2** (sometimes not cap.) a point of no return. **3** a penalty in piquet by which the score of a player who fails to reach 100 points in six hands is added to his opponent's. **4 cross** (or **pass**) **the Rubicon**. to commit oneself irrevocably to some course of action.

rubicund ('ruːbɪkənd) adj of a reddish colour; ruddy; rosy. [C16: from L rubicundus, from rubēre to be ruddy, from ruber red]
▸ **rubicundity** (ˌruːbɪˈkʌndɪtɪ) n

rubidium (ruːˈbɪdɪəm) n a soft highly reactive radioactive element of the alkali metal group. It is used in electronic valves, photocells, and special glass. Symbol: Rb; atomic no.: 37; atomic wt.: 85.47; half-life of ^{87}Rb: 5×10^{11} years. [C19: from NL, from L rubidus dark red, with reference to the two red lines in its spectrum]
▸ **ru'bidic** adj

rubidium-strontium dating n a technique for determining the age of minerals based on the occurrence in natural rubidium of a fixed amount of the radioisotope ^{87}Rb which decays to the stable strontium isotope ^{87}Sr with a half-life of 5×10^{11} years.

rubiginous (ruːˈbɪdʒɪnəs) adj rust-coloured. [C17: from L rūbīginōsus, from rūbīgō rust, from ruber red]

rub in vb (tr, adv) **1** to spread with pressure, esp. in order to cause to be absorbed. **2 rub it in**. Inf. to harp on something distasteful to a person.

Rubinstein ('ruːbɪnˌstaɪn) n **1 Anton Grigorevich** (Russian anˈtɔn griˈgɔrjɪvitʃ). 1829–94, Russian composer and pianist. **2 Artur** (Polish 'artur). 1886–1982, US pianist, born in Poland.

ruble ('ruːbʰl) n a variant spelling of **rouble**.

rub off vb **1** to remove or be removed by rubbing. **2** (intr; often foll. by on or onto) to have an effect through close association or contact: her crude manners have rubbed off on you.

rub out vb (tr, adv) **1** to remove or be removed with a rubber. **2** US sl. to murder.

rubric ('ruːbrɪk) n **1** a title, heading, or initial letter in a book, manuscript, or section of a legal code, esp. one printed or painted in red ink or in some similarly distinguishing manner. **2** a set of rules of conduct or procedure. **3** a set of directions for the conduct of Christian church services, often printed in red in a prayer book or missal. [C15 rubrike red ochre, red lettering, from L rubrīca (terra) red (earth), ruddle, from ruber red]
▸ 'rubrical adj ▸ 'rubrically adv

ruby ('ruːbɪ) n, pl **rubies**. **1** a deep red transparent precious variety of corundum: used as a gemstone, in lasers, and for bearings and rollers in watchmaking. **2a** the deep-red colour of a ruby. **2b** (as adj): ruby lips. **3a** something resembling, made of, or containing a ruby. **3b** (as modifier): a ruby necklace. **4** (modifier) denoting a fortieth anniversary: our ruby wedding. [C14: from OF rubi, from L rubeus, from ruber red]

RUC abbrev. for Royal Ulster Constabulary.

ruche (ruːʃ) n a strip of pleated or frilled lawn, lace, etc., used to decorate blouses, dresses, etc. [C19: from F, lit.: beehive, from Med. L rūsca bark of a tree, of Celtic origin]

ruching ('ruːʃɪŋ) n **1** material used for a ruche. **2** a ruche or ruches collectively.

ruck[1] (rʌk) n **1** a large number or quantity; mass, esp. of undistinguished people or things. **2** (in a race) a group of competitors who are well behind the leaders. **3** Rugby. a loose scrum that forms around the ball when it is on the ground. **4** Australian Rules football. the three players who do not have fixed positions but follow the ball closely. ◆ vb **5** (intr) Rugby. to try to win the ball by mauling and scrummaging. [C13 (meaning "heap of firewood"): ?from ON]

ruck[2] (rʌk) n **1** a wrinkle, crease, or fold. ◆ vb **2** (usually foll. by up) to become or make wrinkled, creased, or puckered. [C18: of Scand. origin; rel. to ON hrukka]

ruckman ('rʌkmən) n, pl **ruckmen**. Australian Rules football. either of two players who, with the rover, form the ruck.

ruck-rover n Australian Rules football. a player playing a role midway between that of the rover and the ruckmen.

rucksack ('rʌkˌsæk) n a large bag, usually having two straps, carried on the back and often used by climbers, campers, etc. Also called: **backpack**. [C19: from G, lit.: back sack]

ruction ('rʌkʃən) n Inf. **1** an uproar; noisy or quarrelsome disturbance. **2** (pl) an unpleasant row; trouble. [C19: changed from INSURRECTION]

rudaceous (ruːˈdeɪʃəs) adj (of conglomerate, breccia, and similar rocks) composed of coarse-grained material. [C20: from L rudis coarse, rough + -ACEOUS]

Ruda Śląska ★ ('ruːdə ˈʃlɒnskə) n a town in SW Poland: coalmining. Pop.: 166 600 (1995 est.).

rudbeckia (rʌdˈbɛkɪə) n any of a genus of North American plants of the composite family, cultivated for their showy flowers, which have golden-yellow rays and green or black conical centres. See also **black-eyed Susan**. [C18: NL, after Olaus Rudbeck (1630–1702), Swedish botanist]

rudd (rʌd) n a European freshwater fish, having a compressed dark greenish body and reddish ventral and tail fins. [C17: prob. from dialect rud red colour, from OE rudu redness]

Rudd ★ (rʌd) n **Steele**, pen name of Arthur Hoey Davis, 1868–1935, Australian author. His works include On Our Selection (1899).

rudder ('rʌdə) n **1** Naut. a pivoted vertical vane that projects into the water at the stern and can be used to steer a vessel. **2** a vertical control surface attached to the rear of the fin used to steer an aircraft. **3** anything that guides or directs. [OE rōther]
▸ 'rudderless adj

rudderpost ('rʌdəˌpəʊst) n Naut. **1** a postlike member at the forward edge of a rudder. **2** the part of the stern frame of a vessel to which a rudder is fitted.

ruddle ('rʌdʰl), **raddle**, or **reddle** n **1** a red ochre, used esp. to mark sheep. ◆ vb **ruddles**, **ruddling**, **ruddled**. **2** (tr) to mark (sheep) with ruddle. [C16: dim. formed from OE rudu redness; see RUDD]

ruddy ('rʌdɪ) adj **ruddier**, **ruddiest**. **1** (of the complexion) having a healthy reddish colour. **2** coloured red or pink:

a ruddy sky. ◆ *adv, adj Inf., chiefly Brit.* **3** (intensifier) bloody; damned: *a ruddy fool.* [OE *rudig*, from *rudu* redness]
▶ **'ruddily** *adv* ▶ **'ruddiness** *n*

rude (ru:d) *adj* **1** insulting or uncivil; discourteous; impolite. **2** lacking refinement; coarse or uncouth. **3** vulgar or obscene: *a rude joke.* **4** unexpected and unpleasant: *a rude awakening.* **5** roughly or crudely made: *we made a rude shelter on the island.* **6** rough or harsh in sound, appearance, or behaviour. **7** humble or lowly. **8** (*prenominal*) robust or sturdy: *in rude health.* **9** (*prenominal*) approximate or imprecise: *a rude estimate.* [C14: via OF from L *rudis* coarse, unformed]
▶ **'rudely** *adv* ▶ **'rudeness** or (*inf.*) **'rudery** *n*

ruderal ('ru:dərəl) *n* **1** a plant that grows on waste ground. ◆ *adj* **2** growing in waste places. [C19: from NL *rūderālis*, from L *rūdus* rubble]

rudiment ('ru:dɪmənt) *n* **1** (*often pl*) the first principles or elementary stages of a subject. **2** (*often pl*) a partially developed version of something. **3** *Biol.* an organ or part in an embryonic or vestigial state. [C16: from L *rudīmentum* a beginning, from *rudis* unformed]

rudimentary (,ru:dɪ'mentərɪ, -trɪ) or **rudimental** *adj* **1** basic; fundamental. **2** incompletely developed; vestigial: *rudimentary leaves.*
▶ **,rudi'mentarily** or (*less commonly*) **,rudi'mentally** *adv*

rudish ('ru:dɪʃ) *adj* somewhat rude.

Rudolf ★ ('ru:dɒlf) *n* **Lake.** the former name (until 1979) of (Lake) **Turkana.**

Rudolf I or **Rudolph I** ★ ('ru:dɒlf) *n* 1218–91, king of Germany (1273–91): founder of the Hapsburg dynasty.

rue[1] (ru:) *vb* **rues, ruing, rued. 1** to feel sorrow, remorse, or regret for (one's own wrongdoing, past events, etc.). ◆ *n* **2** *Arch.* sorrow, pity, or regret. [OE *hrēowan*]
▶ **'ruer** *n*

rue[2] (ru:) *n* an aromatic Eurasian shrub with small yellow flowers and evergreen leaves which yield an acrid volatile oil, formerly used medicinally as a narcotic and stimulant. Archaic name: **herb of grace.** [C14: from OF, from L *rūta*, from Gk *rhutē*]

rueful ('ru:ful) *adj* **1** feeling or expressing sorrow or regret: *a rueful face.* **2** inspiring sorrow or pity.
▶ **'ruefully** *adv* ▶ **'ruefulness** *n*

ruff[1] (rʌf) *n* **1** a circular pleated or fluted collar of lawn, muslin, etc., worn by both men and women in the 16th and 17th centuries. **2** a natural growth of long or coloured hair or feathers around the necks of certain animals or birds. **3** an Old World shore bird of the sandpiper family, the male of which has a large erectile ruff of feathers in the breeding season. [C16: back formation from RUFFLE[1]]
▶ **'ruff,like** *adj*

ruff[2] (rʌf) *Cards.* ◆ *n, vb* **1** another word for **trump**[1] (senses 1, 4). ◆ *n* **2** an old card game similar to whist. [C16: from OF *roffle*; ? changed from It. *trionfa* TRUMP[1]]

ruffe or **ruff** (rʌf) *n* a European freshwater teleost fish of the perch family, having a single spiny dorsal fin. [C15: ? alteration of ROUGH (referring to its scales)]

ruffian ('rʌfɪən) *n* a violent or lawless person; hoodlum. [C16: from OF *rufien*, from It. *ruffiano* pander]
▶ **'ruffianism** *n* ▶ **'ruffianly** *adj*

ruffle[1] ('rʌf°l) *vb* **ruffles, ruffling, ruffled. 1** to make, be, or become irregular or rumpled: *a breeze ruffling the water.* **2** to annoy, irritate, or be annoyed or irritated. **3** (*tr*) to make into a ruffle; pleat. **4** (of a bird) to erect (its feathers) in anger, display, etc. **5** (*tr*) to flick (cards, pages, etc.) rapidly. ◆ *n* **6** an irregular or disturbed surface. **7** a strip of pleated material used as a trim. **8** *Zool.* another name for **ruff**[1] (sense 2). **9** annoyance or irritation. [C13: of Gmc origin; cf. MLow G *ruffelen* to crumple, ON *hrufla* to scratch]

ruffle[2] ('rʌf°l) *n* **1** a low continuous drumbeat. ◆ *vb* **ruffles, ruffling, ruffled. 2** (*tr*) to beat (a drum) with a low repetitive beat. [C18: from earlier *ruff*, imit.]

rufous ('ru:fəs) *adj* reddish-brown. [C18: from L *rūfus*]

rufty-tufty (,rʌftɪ 'tʌftɪ) *adj Sl.* rugged in appearance or manner.

rug (rʌg) *n* **1** a floor covering, smaller than a carpet and made of thick wool or of other material, such as an animal skin. **2** *Chiefly Brit.* a blanket, esp. one used for travellers. **3** *Sl.* a wig. **4 pull the rug out from under.** to betray, expose, or leave defenceless. [C16: of Scand. origin]

ruga ('ru:gə) *n, pl* **rugae** (-dʒi:). (*usually pl*) *Anat.* a fold, wrinkle, or crease. [C18: L]

rugby or **rugby football** ('rʌgbɪ) *n* **1** a form of football played with an oval ball in which the handling and carrying of the ball is permitted. Also called: **rugger. 2** *Canad.* another name for **Canadian football.** See also **rugby league, rugby union.** [after the public school at *Rugby*, where it was first played]

Rugby ★ ('rʌgbɪ) *n* a town in central England, in E Warwickshire: famous public school, founded in 1567. Pop.: 61 106 (1991).
▶ **'Rugbeian** *adj, n*

rugby league *n* a form of rugby football played between teams of 13 players.

rugby union *n* a form of rugby football played between teams of 15 players.

rugged ('rʌgɪd) *adj* **1** having an uneven or jagged surface. **2** rocky or steep: *rugged scenery.* **3** (of the face) strong-featured or furrowed. **4** rough, severe, or stern in character. **5** without refinement or culture; rude: *rugged manners.* **6** involving hardship; harsh: *he leads a rugged life in the mountains.* **7** difficult or hard: *a rugged test.* **8** (of equipment, machines, etc.) designed to withstand rough treatment or use in rough conditions. **9** *Chiefly US & Canad.* sturdy or strong; robust. [C14: from ON]
▶ **'ruggedly** *adv* ▶ **'ruggedness** *n*

rugger ('rʌgə) *n Chiefly Brit.* an informal name for **rugby.**

rugose ('ru:gəus, -gəuz) *adj* wrinkled: *rugose leaves.* [C18: from L *rūgōsus*, from *rūga* wrinkle]
▶ **'rugosely** *adv* ▶ **rugosity** (ru:'gɒsɪtɪ) *n*

rug rat *n US & Canad. inf.* a young child not yet walking.

Ruhr ★ (rʊə; *German* ru:r) *n* the chief coalmining and industrial region of Germany: in North Rhine-Westphalia around the valley of the **River Ruhr**, a tributary of the Rhine 235 km (146 miles) long. German name: **Ruhrgebiet** ('ru:rgə,bi:t).

ruin ('ru:ɪn) *n* **1** a destroyed or decayed building or town. **2** the state of being destroyed or decayed. **3** loss of wealth, position, etc., or something that causes such loss; downfall. **4** something that is severely damaged: *his life was a ruin.* **5** a person who has suffered a downfall, bankruptcy, etc. **6** *Arch.* loss of her virginity by a woman outside marriage. ◆ *vb* **7** (*tr*) to bring to ruin; destroy. **8** (*tr*) to injure or spoil: *the town has been ruined with tower blocks.* **9** (*intr*) *Arch. or poetic.* to fall into ruins; collapse. **10** (*tr*) *Arch.* to seduce and abandon (a woman). [C14: from OF *ruine*, from L *ruīna* a falling down, from *ruere* to fall violently]

ruination (,ru:ɪ'neɪʃən) *n* **1** the act of ruining or the state of being ruined. **2** something that causes ruin.

ruinous ('ru:ɪnəs) *adj* causing, tending to cause, or characterized by ruin or destruction.
▶ **'ruinously** *adv* ▶ **'ruinousness** *n*

Ruisdael or **Ruysdael** ★ ('ri:zdɑ:l, -deɪl, 'raɪz-; *Dutch* 'rœɪzdɑ:l) *n* **Jacob van** ('ja:kɔp van). ?1628–82, Dutch landscape painter.

rule (ru:l) *n* **1** an authoritative regulation or direction concerning method or procedure, as for a court of law, legislative body, game, or other activity: *judges' rules; play according to the rules.* **2** the exercise of governmental authority or control: *the rule of Caesar.* **3** the period of time in which a monarch or government has power: *his rule lasted 100 days.* **4** a customary form or procedure: *he made a morning swim his rule.* **5** (usually preceded by *the*) the common order of things: *violence was the rule rather than the exception.* **6** a prescribed method or procedure for solving a mathematical problem. **7** any of various devices with a straight edge for guiding or measuring; ruler: *a carpenter's rule.* **8** *Printing.* **8a** a printed or drawn character in the form of a long thin line. **8b** another name for **dash**[1] (sense 12): *en rule; em rule.* **8c** a strip of metal used to print such a line. **9** *Christianity.* a systematic body of prescriptions followed by members of a reli-

gious order. **10** *Law.* an order by a court or judge. **11 as a rule.** normally or ordinarily. ◆ *vb* **rules, ruling, ruled. 12** to exercise governing or controlling authority over (a people, political unit, individual, etc.). **13** (when *tr, often takes a clause as object*) to decide authoritatively; decree: *the chairman ruled against the proposal.* **14** (*tr*) to mark with straight parallel lines or one straight line. **15** (*tr*) to restrain or control. **16** (*intr*) to be customary or prevalent: *chaos rules in this school.* **17** (*intr*) to be pre-eminent or superior: *football rules in the field of sport.* **18 rule the roost** (*or* **roast**). to be pre-eminent; be in charge. [C13: from OF *riule*, from L *rēgula* a straight edge]
▶ **'rulable** *adj*

rule of three *n* a mathematical rule asserting that the value of one unknown quantity in a proportion is found by multiplying the denominator of each ratio by the numerator of the other.

rule of thumb *n* **a** a rough and practical approach, based on experience, rather than theory. **b** (*as modifier*): *a rule-of-thumb decision.*

rule out *vb* (*tr, adv*) **1** to dismiss from consideration. **2** to make impossible; preclude.

ruler ('ru:lə) *n* **1** a person who rules or commands. **2** Also called: **rule.** a strip of wood, metal, or other material, having straight edges, used for measuring and drawing straight lines.

Rules (ru:lz) *pl n* **1** short for **Australian Rules** (football). **2 the Rules.** *English history.* the neighbourhood around certain prisons in which trusted prisoners were allowed to live under specified restrictions.

ruling ('ru:lɪŋ) *n* **1** a decision of someone in authority, such as a judge. **2** one or more parallel ruled lines. ◆ *adj* **3** controlling or exercising authority. **4** predominant.

rum[1] (rʌm) *n* spirit made from sugar cane. [C17: ? shortened from C16 *rumbullion*, from ?]

rum[2] (rʌm) *adj* **rummer, rummest.** *Brit. sl.* strange; peculiar; odd. [C19: ?from Romany *rom* man]
▶ **'rumly** *adv* ▶ **'rumness** *n*

Rumania ★ (ru:'meɪnɪə) *n* a variant of **Romania.**
▶ **Ru'manian** *adj, n*

rumba *or* **rhumba** ('rʌmbə, 'rum-) *n* **1** a rhythmic and syncopated Cuban dance in duple time. **2** a ballroom dance derived from this. **3** a piece of music composed for or in the rhythm of this dance. [C20: from Sp.: lavish display, from ?]

rumble ('rʌmb°l) *vb* **rumbles, rumbling, rumbled. 1** to make or cause to make a deep resonant sound: *thunder rumbled in the sky.* **2** (*intr*) to move with such a sound: *the train rumbled along.* **3** (*tr*) to utter with a rumbling sound: *he rumbled an order.* **4** (*tr*) *Brit. sl.* to find out about (someone or something): *the police rumbled their plans.* **5** (*intr*) *US sl.* to be involved in a gang fight. ◆ *n* **6** a deep resonant sound. **7** a widespread murmur of discontent. **8** *US, Canad., & NZ sl.* a gang fight. [C14: ?from MDu. *rummelen*]
▶ **'rumbler** *n* ▶ **'rumbling** *adj*

rumble seat *n* a folding outside seat at the rear of some early cars; dicky.

rumbustious (rʌm'bʌstʃəs) *adj* boisterous or unruly. [C18: prob. var. of ROBUSTIOUS]
▶ **rum'bustiously** *adv* ▶ **rum'bustiousness** *n*

rumen ('ru:men) *n, pl* **rumens** *or* **rumina** (-mɪnə). the first compartment of the stomach of ruminants, in which food is partly digested before being regurgitated as cud. [C18: from L: gullet]

Rumford ★ ('rʌmfəd) *n* **Count.** See (Benjamin) **Thompson.**

ruminant ('ru:mɪnənt) *n* **1** any of a suborder of artiodactyl mammals which chew the cud and have a stomach of four compartments. The suborder includes deer, antelopes, cattle, sheep, and goats. **2** any other animal that chews the cud, such as a camel. ◆ *adj* **3** of, relating to, or belonging to this suborder. **4** (of members of this suborder and related animals, such as camels) chewing the cud; ruminating. **5** meditating or contemplating in a slow quiet way.

ruminate ('ru:mɪˌneɪt) *vb* **ruminates, ruminating, ruminated. 1** (of ruminants) to chew (the cud). **2** (when *intr, often*

foll. by *upon, on,* etc.) to meditate or ponder (upon). [C16: from L *rūmināre* to chew the cud, from RUMEN]
▶ **ˌrumiˈnation** *n* ▶ **'ruminative** *adj* ▶ **'ruminatively** *adv*
▶ **'rumiˌnator** *n*

rummage ('rʌmɪdʒ) *vb* **rummages, rummaging, rummaged. 1** (when *intr, often* foll. by *through*) to search (through) while looking for something, often causing disorder. ◆ *n* **2** an act of rummaging. **3** a jumble of articles. [C14 (in the sense: to pack a cargo): from OF *arrumage*, from *arrumer* to stow in a ship's hold, prob. of Gmc origin]
▶ **'rummager** *n*

rummage sale *n* **1** the US and Canad. term for **jumble sale.** **2** *US.* a sale of unclaimed property.

rummer ('rʌmə) *n* a drinking glass having an ovoid bowl on a short stem. [C17: from Du. *roemer* a glass for drinking toasts, from *roemen* to praise]

rummy ('rʌmɪ) *or* **rum** *n* a card game based on collecting sets and sequences. [C20: ?from RUM[2]]

rumour *or US* **rumor** ('ru:mə) *n* **1a** information, often a mixture of truth and untruth, passed around verbally. **1b** (*in combination*): *a rumourmonger.* **2** gossip or hearsay. ◆ *vb* **3** (*tr; usually passive*) to pass around or circulate in the form of a rumour: *it is rumoured that the Queen is coming.* [C14: via OF from L *rūmor* common talk]

rump (rʌmp) *n* **1** the hindquarters of a mammal, not including the legs. **2** the rear part of a bird's back, nearest to the tail. **3** a person's buttocks. **4** Also called: **rump steak.** a cut of beef from behind the loin. **5** an inferior remnant. [C15: from ON]
▶ **'rumpless** *adj*

Rumpelstiltskin ★ (ˌrʌmp°l'stɪltskɪn) *n* a dwarf in a German folktale who aids the king's bride on condition that she give him her first child or guess the dwarf's name. She guesses correctly and in his rage he destroys himself.

rumple ('rʌmp°l) *vb* **rumples, rumpling, rumpled. 1** to make or become crumpled or dishevelled. ◆ *n* **2** a wrinkle, fold, or crease. [C17: from MDu. *rompelen*; rel. to OE *gerumpen* wrinkled]
▶ **'rumply** *adj*

Rump Parliament *or* **the Rump** *n English history.* the remainder of the Long Parliament after Pride's Purge. It sat from 1648–53.

rumpus ('rʌmpəs) *n, pl* **rumpuses.** a noisy, confused, or disruptive commotion. [C18: from ?]

rumpus room *n* a room used for noisy activities, such as parties or children's games.

rumpy-pumpy ('rʌmpɪ'pʌmpɪ) *n Inf.* sexual intercourse.

run (rʌn) *vb* **runs, running, ran, run. 1** (*intr*) **1a** (of a two-legged creature) to move on foot at a rapid pace so that both feet are off the ground for part of each stride. **1b** (of a four-legged creature) to move at a rapid gait. **2** (*tr*) to pass over (a distance, route, etc.) in running: *to run a mile.* **3** (*intr*) to run in or finish a race as specified, esp. in a particular position: *John is running third.* **4** (*tr*) to perform as by running: *to run an errand.* **5** (*intr*) to flee; run away. **6** (*tr*) to bring into a specified state by running: *run oneself to a standstill.* **7** (*tr*) to track down or hunt (an animal): *to run a fox to earth.* **8** (*tr*) to set (animals) loose on (a field or tract of land) so as to graze freely: *he ran stock on that pasture last year.* **9** (*intr; often* foll. by *over, round,* or *up*) to make a short trip or brief visit: *I'll run over this afternoon.* **10** (*intr*) to move quickly and easily on wheels by rolling, or in any of certain other ways: *a sledge running over snow.* **11** to move or cause to move with a specified result: *to run a ship aground; run into a tree.* **12** (*often* foll. by *over*) to move or pass or cause to move or pass quickly: *to run one's eyes over a page.* **13** (*tr; foll. by into, out of, through,* etc.) to force, thrust, or drive: *she ran a needle into her finger.* **14** (*tr*) to drive or maintain and operate (a vehicle). **15** (*tr*) **3** to give a lift to (someone) in a vehicle: *he ran her to the station.* **16** to ply or cause to ply between places on a route: *the bus runs from Piccadilly to Golders Green.* **17** to function or cause to function: *the engine is running smoothly.* **18** (*tr*) to manage: *to run a company.* **19** to extend or continue or cause to extend or continue in a particular direction, for a particular dura-

★ people and places

tion or distance, etc.: *the road runs north; the play ran for two years.* **20** (*intr*) *Law.* to have legal force or effect: *the house lease runs for two more years.* **21** (*tr*) to be subjected to, be affected by, or incur: *to run a risk; run a temperature.* **22** (*intr*; often foll. by *to*) to be characterized (by); tend or incline: *to run to fat.* **23** (*intr*) to recur persistently or be inherent: *red hair runs in my family.* **24** to cause or allow (liquids) to flow or (of liquids) to flow: *the well has run dry.* **25** (*intr*) to melt and flow: *the wax grew hot and began to run.* **26** *Metallurgy.* **26a** to melt or fuse. **26b** (*tr*) to cast (molten metal): *to run lead into ingots.* **27** (*intr*) (of waves, tides, rivers, etc.) to rise high, surge, or be at a specified height: *a high sea was running that night.* **28** (*intr*) to be diffused: *the colours in my dress ran when I washed it.* **29** (*intr*) (of stitches) to unravel or come undone or (of a garment) to have stitches unravel or come undone. **30** (*intr*) (of growing creepers, etc.) to trail, spread, or climb: *ivy running over a cottage wall.* **31** (*intr*) to spread or circulate quickly: *a rumour ran through the town.* **32** (*intr*) to be stated or reported: *his story runs as follows.* **33** to publish or print or be published or printed in a newspaper, magazine, etc.: *they ran his story in the next issue.* **34** (often foll. by *for*) *Chiefly US & Canad.* to be a candidate or present as a candidate for political or other office: *Jones is running for president.* **35** (*tr*) to get past or through: *to run a blockade.* **36** (*tr*) to deal in (arms, etc.), esp. by importing illegally: *he runs guns for the rebels.* **37** *Naut.* to sail (a vessel, esp. a sailing vessel) or (of such a vessel) to be sailed with the wind coming from astern. **38** (*intr*) (of fish) to migrate upstream from the sea, esp. in order to spawn. **39** (*tr*) *Cricket.* to score (a run or number of runs) by hitting the ball and running between the wickets. **40** (*tr*) *Billiards, etc.* to make (a number of successful shots) in sequence. **41** (*tr*) *Golf.* to hit (the ball) so that it rolls along the ground. **42** (*tr*) *Bridge.* to cash (all one's winning cards in a long suit) successively. ◆ *n* **43** an act, instance, or period of running. **44** a gait, pace, or motion faster than a walk: *she went off at a run.* **45** a distance covered by running or a period of running: *a run of ten miles.* **46** an instance or period of travelling in a vehicle, esp. for pleasure: *to go for a run in the car.* **47** free and unrestricted access: *we had the run of the house.* **48a** a period of time during which a machine, computer, etc., operates. **48b** the amount of work performed in such a period. **49** a continuous or sustained period: *a run of good luck.* **50** a continuous sequence of performances: *the play had a good run.* **51** *Cards.* a sequence of winning cards in one suit: *a run of spades.* **52** tendency or trend: *the run of the market.* **53** type, class, or category: *the usual run of graduates.* **54** (usually foll. by *on*) a continuous and urgent demand: *a run on the dollar.* **55** a series of unravelled stitches, esp. in tights; ladder. **56** the characteristic pattern or direction of something: *the run of the grain on wood.* **57a** a period during which water or other liquid flows. **57b** the amount of such a flow. **58** a pipe, channel, etc., through which water or other liquid flows. **59** *US.* a small stream. **60** a steeply inclined course, esp. a snow-covered one used for skiing. **61** an enclosure for domestic fowls or other animals: *a chicken run.* **62** (esp. in Australia and New Zealand) a tract of land for grazing livestock. **63** the migration of fish upstream in order to spawn. **64** *Mil.* **64a** a mission in a warplane. **64b** Also called: **bombing run.** an approach by a bomber to a target. **65** the movement of an aircraft along the ground during takeoff or landing. **66** *Music.* a rapid scalelike passage of notes. **67** *Cricket.* a score of one, normally achieved by both batsmen running from one end of the wicket to the other after one of them has hit the ball. **68** *Baseball.* an instance of a batter touching all four bases safely, thereby scoring. **69** *Golf.* the distance that a ball rolls after hitting the ground. **70 a run for (one's) money.** *Inf.* **70a** a close competition. **70b** pleasure derived from an activity. **71 in the long run.** as the eventual outcome of a series of events, etc. **72 in the short run.** as the immediate outcome of a series of events, etc. **73 on the run. 73a** escaping from arrest; fugitive. **73b** in rapid flight; retreating: *the enemy is on the run.* **73c** hurrying from place to place. **74 the runs.** *Sl.* diarrhoea. ◆ See also **runabout, run across,** etc. [OE *runnen,* p.p. of (*ge*)*rinnan*]

runabout ('rʌnə,baʊt) *n* **1** a small light vehicle or aero-

plane. ◆ *vb* **run about. 2** (*intr, adv*) to move busily from place to place.

run across *vb* (*intr, prep*) to meet unexpectedly; encounter by chance.

run along *vb* (*intr, adv*) (often said patronizingly) to go away; leave.

run around *Inf.* ◆ *vb* (*intr, adv*) **1** (often foll. by *with*) to associate habitually (with). **2** to behave in a fickle or promiscuous manner. ◆ *n* **run-around. 3** deceitful or evasive treatment of a person (esp. in **give** *or* **get the run-around**).

run away *vb* (*intr, adv*) **1** to take flight; escape. **2** to go away; depart. **3** (of a horse) to gallop away uncontrollably. **4 run away with. 4a** to abscond or elope with: *he ran away with his boss's daughter.* **4b** to make off with; steal. **4c** to escape from the control of: *his enthusiasm ran away with him.* **4d** to win easily or be assured of victory in (a competition): *he ran away with the race.* ◆ *n* **runaway. 5a** a person or animal that runs away. **5b** (*as modifier*): *a runaway horse.* **6** the act or an instance of running away. **7** (*modifier*) rising rapidly, as prices: *runaway inflation.* **8** (*modifier*) (of a race, victory, etc.) easily won.

runcible spoon ('rʌnsɪb³l) *n* a forklike utensil with two broad prongs and one sharp curved prong. [*runcible* coined by Edward Lear, in a nonsense poem (1871)]

Runcorn ★ ('rʌŋ,kɔːn) *n* a town in NW England, in N Cheshire on the Manchester Ship Canal: port and industrial centre; designated a new town in 1964. Pop.: 64 154 (1991).

run down *vb* (*mainly adv*) **1** to allow (an engine, etc.) to lose power gradually and cease to function or (of an engine, etc.) to do this. **2** to decline or reduce in number or size: *the firm ran down its sales force.* **3** (*tr; usually passive*) to tire, sap the strength of, or exhaust: *he was thoroughly run down.* **4** (*tr*) to criticize adversely; decry. **5** (*tr*) to hit and knock to the ground with a moving vehicle. **6** (*tr*) *Naut.* to collide with and cause to sink. **7** (*tr*) to pursue and find or capture: *to run down a fugitive.* **8** (*tr*) to read swiftly or perfunctorily: *he ran down their list of complaints.* ◆ *adj* **run-down. 9** tired; exhausted. **10** worn-out, shabby, or dilapidated. ◆ *n* **rundown. 11** a brief review, résumé, or summary. **12** the process of a mechanism coming gradually to a standstill after the power is removed. **13** a reduction in number or size.

Rundstedt ★ ('rʊndʃtɛt; *German* 'rʊntʃtɛt) *n* **Karl Rudolf Gerd von** (karl 'ruːdɔlf gɛrt fɔn). 1875–1953, German field marshal; commanded the conquest of Poland and France and the Western Front (1942–44); led the Ardennes counteroffensive (Dec. 1944).

rune (ruːn) *n* **1** any of the characters of an ancient Germanic alphabet, in use, esp. in Scandinavia, from the 3rd century A.D. to the end of the Middle Ages. **2** any obscure piece of writing using mysterious symbols. **3** a kind of Finnish poem or a stanza in such a poem. [OE *rūn,* from ON *rūn* secret]
▸ '**runic** *adj*

rung[1] (rʌŋ) *n* **1** one of the bars or rods that form the steps of a ladder. **2** a crosspiece between the legs of a chair, etc. **3** *Naut.* a spoke on a ship's wheel or a handle projecting from the periphery. [OE *hrung*]
▸ '**rungless** *adj*

rung[2] (rʌŋ) *vb* the past participle of **ring**[2].

USAGE NOTE See at **ring**[2].

run in *vb* (*adv*) **1** to run (an engine) gently, usually when it is new. **2** (*tr*) to insert or include. **3** (*intr*) (of aircraft) to approach a point or target. **4** (*tr*) *Inf.* to take into custody; arrest. ◆ *n* **run-in. 5** *Inf.* an argument or quarrel. **6** an approach to the end of an event, etc.: *the run-in for the championship.* **7** *Printing.* matter inserted in an existing paragraph.

run into *vb* (*prep, mainly intr*) **1** (*also tr*) to collide with or cause to collide with: *her car ran into a tree.* **2** to encounter unexpectedly. **3** (*also tr*) to be beset by: *the project ran into financial difficulties.* **4** to extend to; be of the order of: *debts running into thousands.*

runnel ('rʌnəl) n Literary. a small stream. [C16: from OE rynele; rel. to RUN]

runner ('rʌnə) n 1 a person who runs, esp. an athlete. 2 a messenger for a bank, etc. 3 a person engaged in the solicitation of business. 4 a person on the run; fugitive. 5a a person or vessel engaged in smuggling. 5b (in combination): a gunrunner. 6 a person who operates, manages, or controls something. 7a either of the strips of metal or wood on which a sledge runs. 7b the blade of an ice skate. 8 a roller or guide for a sliding component. 9 Bot. 9a Also called: **stolon**. a slender horizontal stem, as of the strawberry, that grows along the surface of the soil and propagates by producing roots and shoots at the nodes or tip. 9b a plant that propagates in this way. 10 a strip of lace, linen, etc., placed across a table or dressing table for protection and decoration. 11 another word for **rocker** (on a rocking chair). 12 **do a runner**. Sl. to run away in order to escape trouble or to avoid paying for something.

runner bean n another name for **scarlet runner**.

runner-up n, pl **runners-up**. a contestant finishing a race or competition in second place.

running ('rʌnɪŋ) adj 1 maintained continuously; incessant: running commentary. 2 (postpositive) without interruption; consecutive: he lectured for two hours running. 3 denoting or relating to the scheduled operation of a public vehicle: the running time of a train. 4 accomplished at a run: a running jump. 5 moving or slipping easily, as a rope or a knot. 6 (of a wound, etc.) discharging pus. 7 prevalent; current: running prices. 8 repeated or continuous: a running design. 9 (of plants, plant stems, etc.) creeping along the ground. 10 flowing: running water. 11 (of handwriting) having the letters run together. ◆ n 12 management or organization: the running of a company. 13 operation or maintenance: the running of a machine. 14 competition or competitive situation (in **in the running, out of the running**). 15 **make the running**. to set the pace in a competition or race.

running board n a footboard along the side of a vehicle, esp. an early motorcar.

running head or **title** n Printing. a heading printed at the top of every page of a book.

running light n Naut. one of several lights displayed by vessels operating at night.

running mate n 1 US. a candidate for the subordinate of two linked positions, esp. a candidate for the vice-presidency. 2 a horse that pairs another in a team.

running repairs pl n repairs that do not, or do not greatly, interrupt operations.

runny ('rʌnɪ) adj runnier, runniest. 1 tending to flow; liquid. 2 (of the nose) exuding mucus.

Runnymede ★ ('rʌnɪ,miːd) n a meadow on the S bank of the Thames near Windsor, where King John met his rebellious barons in 1215 and acceded to Magna Carta.

run off vb (adv) 1 (intr) to depart in haste. 2 (tr) to produce quickly, as copies on a duplicating machine. 3 to drain (liquid) or (of liquid) to be drained. 4 (tr) to decide (a race) by a run-off. 5 **run off with**. 5a to steal; purloin. 5b to elope with. ◆ n run-off. 6 an extra race, contest, election, etc., to decide the winner after a tie. 7 NZ. grazing land for store cattle. 8 that portion of rainfall that runs into streams as surface water rather than being absorbed by the soil. 9 the overflow of a liquid from a container.

run-of-the-mill adj ordinary, average, or undistinguished in quality, character, or nature.

run on vb (adv) 1 (intr) to continue without interruption. 2 to write with linked-up characters. 3 Printing. to compose text matter without indentation or paragraphing. ◆ n run-on. 4 Printing. 4a text matter composed without indenting. 4b an additional quantity required in excess of the originally stated amount, whilst the job is being produced. 5a a word added at the end of a dictionary entry whose meaning can be easily inferred from the definition of the headword. 5b (as modifier): a run-on entry.

run out vb (adv) 1 (intr; often foll. by of) to exhaust (a supply of something) or (of a supply) to become exhausted. 2 **run out on**. Inf. to desert or abandon. 3 (tr) Cricket. to dis-

miss (a running batsman) by breaking the wicket with the ball, or with the ball in the hand, while he is out of his ground. ◆ n run-out. 4 Cricket. dismissal of a batsman by running him out.

run over vb 1 (tr, adv) to knock down (a person) with a moving vehicle. 2 (intr) to overflow the capacity of (a container). 3 (intr, prep) to examine hastily or make a rapid survey of. 4 (intr, prep) to exceed (a limit): we've run over our time.

runt (rʌnt) n 1 the smallest and weakest young animal in a litter, esp. the smallest piglet in a litter. 2 Derog. an undersized or inferior person. 3a a large pigeon, originally bred for eating. [C16: from ?] ▸ '**runtish** or '**runty** adj ▸ '**runtiness** n

run through vb 1 (tr, adv) to transfix with a sword or other weapon. 2 (intr, prep) to exhaust (money) by wasteful spending. 3 (intr, prep) to practise or rehearse: let's run through the plan. 4 (intr, prep) to examine hastily. ◆ n run-through. 5 a practice or rehearsal. 6 a brief survey.

run time n Computing. the time during which a computer program is executed.

run to vb (intr, prep) to be sufficient for: my income doesn't run to luxuries.

run up vb (tr, adv) 1 to amass; incur: to run up debts. 2 to make by sewing together quickly. 3 to hoist: to run up a flag. ◆ n run-up. 4 an approach run by an athlete for the long jump, pole vault, etc. 5 a preliminary or preparatory period: the run-up to the election.

runway ('rʌn,weɪ) n 1 a hard level roadway from which aircraft take off and on which they land. 2 Forestry, North American. a chute for sliding logs down. 3 Chiefly US. a narrow ramp extending from the stage into the audience in a theatre, etc. esp. as used by models in a fashion show.

Runyon ★ ('rʌnjən) n (**Alfred**) **Damon** ('deɪmən). 1884–1946, US writer, noted for his short stories, such as Guys and Dolls (1932), about Broadway characters.

rupee (ruː'piː) n the standard monetary unit of India, Mauritius, Nepal, Pakistan, the Seychelles, and Sri Lanka. [C17: from Hindi rupaīyā, from Sansk. rūpya coined silver, from rūpa shape, beauty]

Rupert ★ ('ruːpət) n **Prince**. 1619–82, German-born nephew of Charles I: Royalist general during the Civil War (until 1646) and commander of the Royalist fleet (1648–50).

Rupert's Land ★ n (formerly, in Canada) the territories granted by Charles II to the Hudson's Bay Company in 1670 and ceded to the Canadian Government in 1870, comprising all the land watered by rivers flowing into Hudson Bay.

rupiah (ruː'piːə) n, pl rupiah or rupiahs. the standard monetary unit of Indonesia. [from Hindi: RUPEE]

rupture ('rʌptʃə) n 1 the act of breaking or bursting or the state of being broken or burst. 2 a breach of peaceful or friendly relations. 3 Pathol. the breaking or tearing of a bodily structure or part. 3b another word for **hernia**. ◆ vb ruptures, rupturing, ruptured. 4 to break or burst. 5 to affect or be affected with a rupture or hernia. 6 to undergo or cause to undergo a breach in relations or friendship. [C15: from L ruptūra, from rumpere to burst forth] ▸ '**rupturable** adj

rural ('rʊərəl) adj 1 of, relating to, or characteristic of the country or country life. 2 living in the country. 3 of, relating to, or associated with farming. ◆ Cf. **urban**. [C15: via OF from L rūrālis, from rūs the country] ▸ '**ruralism** n ▸ '**ruralist** n ▸ ru'**rality** n ▸ '**rurally** adv

rural dean n Chiefly Brit. a clergyman having authority over a group of parishes.

rural district n (formerly) a rural division of a county.

ruralize or **ruralise** ('rʊərə,laɪz) vb ruralizes, ruralizing, ruralized or ruralises, ruralising, ruralised. 1 (tr) to make rural in character, appearance, etc. 2 (intr) to go into the country to live. ▸ ,rurali'**zation** or ,rurali'**sation** n

rural route n US & Canad. a mail service or route in a rural area, the mail being delivered by car or van.

Rurik or **Ryurik** ★ ('rʊərɪk) n died 879. Varangian (Scandinavian Viking) leader who founded the Russian monarchy. He gained control over Novgorod (?862) and his dynasty, the **Rurikids**, ruled until 1598.

Ruritania ★ (ˌrʊərɪˈteɪnɪə, -njə) n 1 an imaginary kingdom of central Europe: setting of several novels by Anthony Hope, esp. *The Prisoner of Zenda* (1894). 2 any setting of adventure, romance, and intrigue.
  ▸ ˌRuriˈtanian adj, n

Rus. *abbrev. for* Russia(n).

ruse (ruːz) n an action intended to mislead, deceive, or trick; stratagem. [C15: from OF: trick, esp. to evade capture, from *ruser* to retreat, from L *recūsāre* to refuse]

Ruse ★ (ˈruːseɪ) n a city in NE Bulgaria, on the River Danube: the chief river port and one of the largest industrial centres in Bulgaria. Pop.: 168 051 (1996 est.).

rush[1] (rʌʃ) vb 1 to hurry or cause to hurry; hasten. 2 (tr) to make a sudden attack upon (a fortress, position, person, etc.). 3 (when *intr*, often foll. by *at*, *in*, or *into*) to proceed or approach in a reckless manner. 4 **rush one's fences**. to proceed with precipitate haste. 5 (*intr*) to come, flow, swell, etc., quickly or suddenly: *tears rushed to her eyes*. 6 (*tr*) *Sl.* to cheat, esp. by grossly overcharging. 7 (*tr*) *US & Canad.* to make a concerted effort to secure the agreement, participation, etc., of (a person). 8 (*intr*) *American football*. to gain ground by running forwards with the ball. ◆ n 9 the act or condition of rushing. 10 a sudden surge towards someone or something: *a gold rush*. 11 a sudden surge of sensation, esp. from a drug. 12 a sudden demand. ◆ adj (*prenominal*) 13 requiring speed or urgency: *a rush job*. 14 characterized by much movement, business, etc.: *a rush period*. [C14 *ruschen*, from OF *ruser* to put to flight, from L *recūsāre* to refuse]
  ▸ ˈrusher n

rush[2] (rʌʃ) n 1 an annual or perennial plant growing in wet places and typically having grasslike cylindrical leaves and small green or brown flowers. 2 something valueless; a trifle; straw: *not worth a rush*. 3 short for **rush light**. [OE *risce*, *rysce*]
  ▸ ˈrush,like adj ▸ ˈrushy adj

Rushdie ★ (ˈrʊʃdɪ) n (**Ahmed**) **Salman** (ˈsælmən). born 1947, British writer, born in India. His novels include *The Satanic Verses* (1988), which some Muslims regard as blasphemous. He was forced into hiding (1989) after Ayatollah Khomeini called for his death in a fatwa; in 1998 the Iranian government withdrew its official support for the fatwa.

rushes (ˈrʌʃɪz) pl n (*sometimes sing*) (in film-making) the initial prints of a scene or scenes before editing, usually prepared daily.

rush hour n a period at the beginning and end of the working day when large numbers of people are travelling to or from work.

rush light or **candle** n a narrow candle, formerly in use, made of the pith of various types of rush dipped in tallow.

Rushmore ★ (ˈrʌʃmɔː) n **Mount**. a mountain in W South Dakota, in the Black Hills: a national memorial, with the faces of Washington, Lincoln, Jefferson, and Roosevelt carved into its side by Gutzon Borglum between 1927 and 1941. Height: 1841 m (6040 ft).

rusk (rʌsk) n a light bread dough, sweet or plain, baked twice until it is brown, hard, and crisp: often given to babies. [C16: from Sp. or Port. *rosca* screw, bread shaped in a twist, from ?]

Rusk ★ (rʌsk) n (**David**) **Dean**. 1909–94, US statesman: secretary of state (1961–69). He defended US military involvement in Vietnam.

Ruskin ★ (ˈrʌskɪn) n **John**. 1819–1900, British critic and social reformer. His works include *The Stones of Venice* (1851–53) and *Time and Tide* (1867).

Russ. *abbrev. for* Russia(n).

Russell ★ (ˈrʌsəl) n 1 **Bertrand** (**Arthur William**), 3rd Earl Russell. 1872–1970, British philosopher and mathematician. His books include *Principia Mathematica* (1910–13; with A. N. Whitehead), and *An Enquiry into Meaning and Truth* (1940): Nobel prize for literature 1950. 2 **George William**, pen name Æ. 1867–1935, Irish poet and journalist. 3 **John**, 1st Earl Russell. 1792–1878, British statesman;

prime minister (1846–52; 1865–66). 4 **Ken**. born 1927, film director. His films include *Women in Love* (1969) and *Valentino* (1977).

russet (ˈrʌsɪt) n 1 brown with a yellowish or reddish tinge. 2 a rough homespun fabric, reddish-brown in colour, formerly in use for clothing. 3 any of various apples with rough brownish-red skins. ◆ adj 4 *Arch.* simple; homely; rustic: *a russet life*. 5 of the colour russet: *russet hair*. [C13: from Anglo-Norman, from OF *rosset*, from L *russus*; rel. to L *ruber* red]
  ▸ ˈrussety adj

Russia ★ (ˈrʌʃə) n 1 the largest country in the world, covering N Eurasia and bordering on the Pacific and Arctic Oceans and the Baltic, Black, and Caspian Seas: ranges from arctic to subtropical in climate and includes tundra, forests, steppes, and arable land. Originating from the principality of Muscovy in the 17th century, it expanded to become the Russian Empire: became the Communist Russian Soviet Federative Socialist Republic after the overthrow of the tsar in 1917; merged with neighbouring Soviet Republics to form the Soviet Union in 1922; became an independent state following the disintegration of the Soviet Union in 1991. Official language: Russian. Religion: nonreligious and Christian (Russian Orthodox). Currency: rouble. Capital: Moscow. Pop.: 147 231 000 (1997). Area: 17 074 984 sq. km (6 592 658 sq. miles). Also called: **Russian Federation**. 2 another name for the **Russian Empire**. 3 (formerly) another name for the **Soviet Union**. 4 (formerly) another name for the **Russian Soviet Federative Socialist Republic**. ◆ Russian name: **Rossiya**.

Russia leather n a smooth dyed leather made from calfskin and scented with birch tar oil, originally produced in Russia.

Russian (ˈrʌʃən) n 1 the official language of Russia, and of the former Soviet Union: an Indo-European language belonging to the East Slavonic branch. 2 a native or inhabitant of Russia. ◆ adj 3 of, relating to, or characteristic of Russia, its people, or their language.

Russian doll n a hollow wooden figure, usually representing a Russian peasant woman, that comes apart to reveal a similar smaller figure, which itself contains another, and so on.

Russian Empire n the tsarist empire in Asia and E Europe, overthrown by the Russian Revolution of 1917.

Russian Federation ★ n See **Russia**.

Russianize or **Russianise** (ˈrʌʃəˌnaɪz) vb **Russianizes**, **Russianizing**, **Russianized** or **Russianises**, **Russianising**, **Russianised**. to make or become Russian in style, etc.
  ▸ ˌRussianiˈzation or ˌRussianiˈsation n

Russian roulette n 1 an act of bravado in which each person in turn spins the cylinder of a revolver loaded with only one cartridge and presses the trigger with the barrel against his own head. 2 any foolish or potentially suicidal undertaking.

Russian salad n a salad of cold diced cooked vegetables mixed with mayonnaise and pickles.

Russian Soviet Federative Socialist Republic ★ n (formerly) the largest administrative division of the Soviet Union. Abbrev.: **RSFSR**.

Russian Turkestan ★ n See **Turkestan**.

Russian Zone ★ n another name for the **Soviet Zone**.

Russo- (ˈrʌsəʊ) *combining form*. Russia or Russian: *Russo-Japanese*.

rust (rʌst) n 1 a reddish-brown oxide coating formed on iron or steel by the action of oxygen and moisture. 2 Also called: **rust fungus**. *Plant pathol.* **2a** any of a group of fungi which are parasitic on cereal plants, conifers, etc. **2b** any of various plant diseases characterized by reddish-brown discoloration of the leaves and stem, esp. that caused by the rust fungi. **3a** a strong brown colour, sometimes with a reddish or yellowish tinge. **3b** (*as adj*): *a rust carpet*. 4 any corrosive or debilitating influence, esp. lack of use. ◆ vb 5 to become or cause to become coated with a layer of rust. 6 to deteriorate or cause to deteriorate through some debilitating influence or lack of use: *he allowed his talent to rust over the years*. [OE *rūst*]
  ▸ ˈrustless adj

rust belt n an area where heavy industry is in decline, esp. in the Midwest of the US.

rustic ('rʌstɪk) adj **1** of, characteristic of, or living in the country; rural. **2** having qualities ascribed to country life or people; simple; unsophisticated: *rustic pleasures*. **3** crude, awkward, or uncouth. **4** made of untrimmed branches: *a rustic seat*. **5** (of masonry, etc.) having a rusticated finish. ◆ n **6** a person who comes from or lives in the country. **7** an unsophisticated, simple, or clownish person from the country. **8** Also called: **rusticwork**. brick or stone having a rough finish. [C16: from OF *rustique*, from L *rūsticus*, from *rūs* the country]
► 'rustically adv ► rusticity (rʌ'stɪsɪtɪ) n

rusticate ('rʌstɪ,keɪt) vb **rusticates, rusticating, rusticated**. **1** to banish or retire to the country. **2** to make or become rustic in style, etc. **3** (tr) Architect. to finish (an exterior wall) with large blocks of masonry separated by deep joints. **4** (tr) Brit. to send down from university for a specified time as a punishment. [C17: from L *rūsticārī*, from *rūs* the country]
► ,rusti'cation n ► 'rusti,cator n

rusticated ('rʌstɪ,keɪtɪd) or **rusticating** ('rʌstɪ,keɪtɪŋ) n (in New Zealand) a wide type of weatherboarding used in older houses.

rustle[1] ('rʌsᵊl) vb **rustles, rustling, rustled**. **1** to make or cause to make a low crisp whispering or rubbing sound, as of dry leaves or paper. **2** to move with such a sound. ◆ n **3** such a sound or sounds. [OE *hrūxlian*]

rustle[2] ('rʌsᵊl) vb **rustles, rustling, rustled**. **1** Chiefly US & Canad. to steal (cattle, horses, etc.). **2** Inf., US & Canad. to move swiftly and energetically. [C19: prob. special use of RUSTLE[1] (in the sense: to move with a quiet sound)]
► 'rustler n

rustle up vb (tr, adv) Inf. **1** to prepare (a meal, etc.) rapidly, esp. at short notice. **2** to forage for and obtain.

rustproof ('rʌst,pruːf) adj treated against rusting.

rusty ('rʌstɪ) adj **rustier, rustiest**. **1** covered with, affected by, or consisting of rust: *a rusty machine*. **2** of the colour rust. **3** discoloured by age: *a rusty coat*. **4** (of the voice) tending to croak. **5** old-fashioned in appearance: *a rusty old gentleman*. **6** impaired in skill or knowledge by inaction or neglect. **7** (of plants) affected by the rust fungus.
► 'rustily adv ► 'rustiness n

rut[1] (rʌt) n **1** a groove or furrow in a soft road, caused by wheels. **2** a narrow or predictable way of life; dreary or undeviating routine (esp. in **in a rut**). ◆ vb **ruts, rutting, rutted**. **3** (tr) to make a rut in. [C16: prob. from F *route* road]

rut[2] (rʌt) n **1** a recurrent period of sexual excitement and reproductive activity in certain male ruminants. ◆ vb **ruts, rutting, rutted**. **2** (intr) (of male ruminants) to be in a period of sexual excitement and activity. [C15: from OF *rut* noise, roar, from L *rugītus*, from *rugīre* to roar]

rutabaga (,ruːtə'beɪgə) n the US and Canad. name for **swede**. [C18: from Swedish dialect *rotabagge*, lit.: root bag]

rutaceous (ruː'teɪʃəs) adj of, relating to, or belonging to a family of tropical and temperate flowering plants many of which have aromatic leaves. The family includes rue, citrus trees, and dittany. [C19: from NL *Rutaceae*, from L *rūta* RUE[2]]

ruth (ruːθ) n Arch. **1** pity; compassion. **2** repentance; remorse. [C12: from *rewen* to RUE[1]]

Ruth ★ (ruːθ) n **1** Old Testament. **1a** a Moabite woman, who married a Hebrew and on his death remained with her mother-in-law Naomi, later becoming the wife of Boaz. **1b** the book in which these events are recounted. **2 George Herman**, nicknamed *Babe*. 1895–1948, US baseball player.

Ruthenia ★ (ruː'θiːnɪə) n a region of E Europe on the south side of the Carpathian Mountains: belonged to Hungary from the 14th century, to Czechoslovakia from 1918 to 1939, and to the Soviet Union from 1945 to 1991; now forms the Transcarpathian Region of the Ukraine. Also called: **Carpatho-Ukraine**.

ruthenium (ruː'θiːnɪəm) n a hard brittle white element of the platinum metal group. It is used to harden platinum and palladium. Symbol: Ru; atomic no.: 44; atomic

wt.: 101.07. [C19: from Med. L *Ruthenia* Russia, where it was discovered]

rutherford ('rʌðəfəd) n a former unit of activity equal to the quantity of a radioactive nuclide required to produce one million disintegrations per second. Abbrev.: **rd**. [C20: after E RUTHERFORD]

Rutherford ★ ('rʌðəfəd) n **Ernest**, 1st Baron Rutherford. 1871–1937, British physicist, born in New Zealand, who discovered the atomic nucleus (1909). Nobel prize for chemistry 1908.

rutherfordium (,rʌðə'fɔːdɪəm) n the US name for the element with the atomic no. 104. Soviet name **kurchatovium**. Symbol: Rf [C20: after E. RUTHERFORD]

ruthful ('ruːθfʊl) adj Arch. full of or causing sorrow or pity.
► 'ruthfully adv ► 'ruthfulness n

ruthless ('ruːθlɪs) adj feeling or showing no mercy; hardhearted.
► 'ruthlessly adv ► 'ruthlessness n

rutile ('ruːtaɪl) n a mineral consisting of titanium(IV) oxide (TiO_2) in tetragonal crystalline form. It is an important source of titanium. [C19: via F from G *Rutil*, from L *rutilus* red, glowing]

Rutland ★ ('rʌtlənd) n an inland county of central England. It became part of Leicestershire in 1974 but was reinstated as a unitary authority in 1997: mainly agricultural. Administrative centre: Oakham. Pop.: 33 600 (1994 est.). Area: 394 sq. km (152 sq. miles).

ruttish ('rʌtɪʃ) adj **1** (of an animal) in a condition of rut. **2** lascivious or salacious.
► 'ruttishly adv ► 'ruttishness n

rutty ('rʌtɪ) adj **ruttier, ruttiest**. full of ruts or holes: *a rutty track*.
► 'ruttily adv ► 'ruttiness n

Ruwenzori ★ (,ruːwɛn'zɔːrɪ) n a mountain range in central Africa, on the border between Uganda and the Democratic Republic of the Congo and between Lakes Edward and Albert: generally thought to be Ptolemy's "Mountains of the Moon". Highest peak: Mount Stanley, 5109 m (16 763 ft).

Ruysdael ★ ('riːzdɑːl, -deɪl, 'raɪz-; Dutch 'rœizdɑːl) n a variant spelling of **Ruisdael**.

Ruyter ★ ('raɪtə; Dutch 'rœitər) n **Michiel Adriaanszoon de** (miː'xiːl ,aːdri'aːnsun də). 1607–76, Dutch admiral, noted for his prevention of an Anglo-French invasion.

RV abbrev. for: **1** Chiefly US. recreational vehicle. **2** Revised Version (of the Bible).

Rwanda ★ (rʊ'ændə) n a republic in central Africa: part of German East Africa from 1899 until 1917, when Belgium took over the administration; became a republic in 1961 after the successful Hutu revolt against the Tutsi (1959); Tutsis from Uganda invaded in 1990; civil war broke out again in 1994. Official languages: Rwanda, French, and English. Religion: Roman Catholic, African Protestant, Muslim, and animist. Currency: Rwanda franc. Capital: Kigali. Pop.: 7 738 000 (1997). Area: 26 338 sq. km (10 169 sq. miles). Former name (until 1962): **Ruanda**.

-ry suffix forming nouns. a variant of **-ery**: *dentistry*.

Ryazan ★ (Russian rɪ'zanj) n a city in W central Russia: capital of a medieval principality; oil refineries and engineering industries. Pop.: 536 000 (1995 est.).

Rybinsk ★ (Russian 'ribinsk) n a city in W central Russia, on the River Volga: an important river port, terminal of the Mariinsk Waterway (between Saint Petersburg and the Volga) at the SE end of the **Rybinsk Reservoir** (area 4700 sq. km (1800 sq. miles)). Pop 248 000 (1995 est.). Former names: (from the Revolution until 1957) **Shcherbakov**, (1984–91) **Andropov**.

Rydal ★ ('raɪdᵊl) n a village in NW England, in Cumbria on **Rydal Water** (a small lake). **Rydal Mount**, home of Wordsworth from 1813 to 1850, is situated here.

Ryder ★ ('raɪdə) n **Susan**, Baroness Ryder of Warsaw. born 1923, British philanthropist; founder of the Sue Ryder Foundation for the Sick and Disabled; widow of Leonard Cheshire.

Ryder Cup n **the**. the trophy awarded in a professional golfing competition between teams representing Europe and the US. [**C20**: after Samuel *Ryder* (1859–1936), Brit. businessman and golf patron]

rye (raɪ) *n* **1** a tall hardy widely cultivated annual grass having bristly flower spikes and light brown grain. **2** the grain of this grass, used in making flour and whisky, and as a livestock food. **3** Also called: (esp. US): **rye whiskey.** whisky distilled from rye. **4** *US*. short for **rye bread.** [OE *ryge*]

Rye ★ (raɪ) *n* a resort in SE England, in East Sussex: one of the Cinque ports. Pop.: 3708 (1991).

rye bread *n* any of various breads made entirely or partly from rye flour, often with caraway seeds.

rye-grass *n* any of various grasses native to Europe, N Africa, and Asia, and widely cultivated as forage crops. They have flattened flower spikes and hairless leaves.

Ryle ★ (raɪl) *n* **1 Gilbert.** 1900–76, British philosopher; noted for his *Concept of Mind* (1949). **2** Sir **Martin.** 1918–84, British radio astronomer; Astronomer Royal (1972–82); shared Nobel prize for physics 1974.

Ryswick ★ ('rɪzwɪk) *n* the English name for **Rijswijk.**

Ryukyu Islands ★ (rɪ'uːkjuː) *pl n* a chain of 55 islands in the W Pacific, extending almost 650 km (400 miles) from S Japan to N Taiwan: an ancient kingdom, under Chinese rule from the late 14th century, Japanese supremacy from 1879 to 1945, and US control from 1945 to 1972; now part of Japan again. They are subject to frequent typhoons. Chief town: Naha City (on Okinawa). Pop.: 1 273 508 (1995). Area: 2196 sq. km (849 sq. miles).

Ryurik ★ ('rʊərɪk) *n* a variant spelling of **Rurik.**

Ss

s *or* **S** (εs) *n, pl* **s's, S's,** *or* **Ss. 1** the 19th letter of the English alphabet. **2** a speech sound represented by this letter, either voiceless, as in *sit*, or voiced, as in *dogs*. **3a** something shaped like an S. **3b** (*in combination*): *an S-bend in a road.*

s *symbol for* second (of time).

S *symbol for:* **1** small. **2** Society. **3** South. **4** *Chem.* sulphur. **5** *Physics.* **5a** entropy. **5b** siemens. **5c** strangeness. **6** *Currency.* Schilling.

s. *abbrev. for:* **1** shilling. **2** singular. **3** son. **4** succeeded.

s. *or* **S.** *Music. abbrev. for* soprano.

S. *abbrev. for:* **1** sabbath. **2** (*pl* **SS**) Saint. **3** Saturday. **4** Saxon. **5** school. **6** September. **7** Signor. **8** Sunday.

-s[1] *or* **-es** *suffix.* forming the plural of most nouns: *boys; boxes.* [from OE -*as*, pl. nominative and accusative ending of some masc nouns]

-s[2] *or* **-es** *suffix.* forming the third person singular present indicative tense of verbs: *he runs.* [from OE (northern dialect) -*es*, -*s*, orig. the ending of the second person singular]

-'s *suffix.* **1** forming the possessive singular of nouns and some pronouns: *man's; one's.* **2** forming the possessive plural of nouns whose plurals do not end in -*s*: *children's.* (The possessive plural of nouns ending in *s* and of some singular nouns is formed by the addition of an apostrophe after the final *s*: *girls'; for goodness' sake*.) **3** forming the plural of numbers, letters, or symbols: *20's.* **4** *Inf.* contraction of *is* or *has*: *it's gone.* **5** *Inf.* contraction of *us* with *let*: *let's.* **6** *Inf.* contraction of *does* in some questions: *what's he do?* [senses 1, 2: assimilated contraction from ME -*es*, from OE, masc and neuter genitive sing; sense 3, equivalent to -s[1]]

SA *abbrev. for:* **1** Salvation Army. **2** South Africa. **3** South America. **4** South Australia. **5** *Sturmabteilung*: the Nazi terrorist militia.

Saadi ★ (saːˈdiː) *n* a variant spelling of **Sadi.**

Saar ★ (saː; *German* zaːr) *n* **1** a river in W Europe, rising in the Vosges Mountains and flowing north to the Moselle River in Germany. Length: 246 km (153 miles). French name: **Sarre. 2** the **Saar.** another name for **Saarland.**

Saarbrücken ★ (*German* zaːrˈbrykən) *n* an industrial city in W Germany, capital of Saarland state, on the Saar River. Pop.: 189 012 (1995 est.).

Saarinen ★ (ˈsɑːrɪnən) *n* **Eero** (ˈeɪrəu). 1910–61, US architect, born in Finland.

Saarland ★ (*German* ˈzaːrlant) *n* a state of W Germany: formed in 1919; under League of Nations administration until 1935; occupied by France (1945–57); part of West Germany (1957–90): contains rich coal deposits and is a major industrial region. Capital: Saarbrücken. Pop.: 1 084 200 (1995 est.). Area: 2567 sq. km (991 sq. miles).

Saba ★ (ˈsɑːbə) *n* **1** an island in the NE Caribbean, in the Netherlands Antilles. Pop.: 1197 (1994 est.). Area: 13 sq. km (5 sq. miles). **2** another name for **Sheba**[1] (sense 1).

Sabadell ★ (*Spanish* saβaˈðel) *n* a town in NE Spain, near Barcelona: textile manufacturing. Pop.: 189 006 (1994 est.).

sabadilla (ˌsæbəˈdɪlə) *n* **1** a tropical American liliaceous plant. **2** the bitter brown seeds of this plant, which contain the alkaloid veratrine used in insecticides. [C19: from Sp. *cebadilla*, dim. of *cebada* barley, from L *cibāre* to feed, from *cibus* food]

Sabaean *or* **Sabean** (səˈbiːən) *n* **1** an inhabitant or native of ancient Saba. **2** the ancient Semitic language of Saba. ♦ *adj* **3** of or relating to ancient Saba, its inhabitants, or their language. [C16: from L *Sabaeus*, from Gk *Sabaios* belonging to Saba (Sheba)]

Sabah ★ (ˈsɑːbɑː) *n* a state of Malaysia, occupying N Borneo and offshore islands in the South China and Sulu Seas: became a British protectorate in 1888; gained independence and joined Malaysia in 1963. Capital: Kota Kinabalu. Pop.: 1 472 700 (1993 est.). Area: 76 522 sq. km (29 545 sq. miles). Former name (until 1963): **North Borneo.**

Sabatier ★ (*French* sabatje) *n* **Paul** (pɔl). 1854–1941, French chemist: shared the Nobel prize for chemistry (1912) for his organic hydrogenation process.

sabbat (ˈsæbæt, -ət) *n* another word for **Sabbath** (sense 4).

Sabbatarian (ˌsæbəˈtɛərɪən) *n* **1** a person advocating the strict religious observance of Sunday. **2** a person who observes Saturday as the Sabbath. ♦ *adj* **3** of the Sabbath or its observance. [C17: from LL *sabbatārius* a Sabbath-keeper]
▸ **ˌSabbaˈtarianism** *n*

Sabbath (ˈsæbəθ) *n* **1** the seventh day of the week, Saturday, devoted to worship and rest from work in Judaism and in certain Christian Churches. **2** Sunday, observed by Christians as the day of worship and rest. **3** (*not cap.*) a period of rest. **4** Also called: **sabbat, witches' Sabbath.** a midnight meeting for practitioners of witchcraft or devil worship. [OE *sabbat*, from L, from Gk *sabbaton*, from Heb., from *shābath* to rest]

sabbatical (səˈbætɪk[ə]l) *adj* **1** denoting a period of leave granted to university staff, teachers, etc., esp. originally every seventh year: *a sabbatical year.* ♦ *n* **2** any sabbatical period. [C16: from Gk *sabbatikos*; see SABBATH]

Sabbatical (səˈbætɪk[ə]l) *adj* of, relating to, or appropriate to the Sabbath as a day of rest and religious observance.

SABC *abbrev. for* South African Broadcasting Corporation.

saber (ˈseɪbə) *n, vb* the US spelling of **sabre.**

sabin (ˈsæbɪn, ˈseɪ-) *n Physics.* a unit of acoustic absorption. [C20: introduced by Wallace C. *Sabine* (1868–1919), US physicist]

Sabin ★ (ˈseɪbɪn) *n* **Albert Bruce.** 1906–93, US microbiologist, born in Poland. He developed the oral **Sabin vaccine** (1955) against poliomyelitis.

Sabine (ˈsæbaɪn) *n* **1** a member of an ancient people who lived in central Italy. ♦ *adj* **2** of or relating to this people or their language.

sabkha (ˈsæbxə, -kə) *n* a flat coastal plain with a salt crust, common in Arabia. [C19: from Ar.]

sable (ˈseɪb[ə]l) *n, pl* **sables** *or* **sable. 1** a marten of N Asian forests, with dark brown luxuriant fur. **2a** the highly valued fur of this animal. **2b** (*as modifier*): *a sable coat.* **3 American sable.** the brown, slightly less valuable fur of the American marten. **4** a dark brown to yellowish-brown colour. ♦ *adj* **5** of the colour of sable fur. **6** black; dark. **7** (*usually postpositive*) *Heraldry.* of the colour black. [C15: from OF, from OHG *zobel*, of Slavic origin]

Sable ★ (ˈseɪb[ə]l) *n* **Cape. 1** a cape at the S tip of Florida: the southernmost point of continental US. **2** the southernmost point of Nova Scotia, Canada.

sable antelope *n* a large black E African antelope with long backward-curving horns.

sabot (ˈsæbəu) *n* **1** a shoe made from a single block of wood. **2** a shoe with a wooden sole and a leather or cloth upper. **3** *Austral.* a small sailing boat with a shortened bow. [C17: from F, prob. from OF *savate* an old shoe, also infl. by *bot* BOOT[1]]

sabotage (ˈsæbəˌtɑːʒ) *n* **1** the deliberate destruction, disruption, or damage of equipment, a public service, etc., as by enemy agents, dissatisfied employees, etc. **2** any similar action. ♦ *vb* **sabotages, sabotaging, sabotaged. 3** (*tr*) to destroy or disrupt, esp. by secret means. [C20: from F, from *saboter* to spoil through clumsiness (lit.: to clatter in *sabots*)]

★ people and places

saboteur (ˌsæbəˈtɜː) *n* a person who commits sabotage. [C20: from F]

sabra (ˈsɑːbrə) *n* a native-born Israeli Jew. [from Heb. *Sabēr* prickly pear, common plant in the coastal areas of the country]

sabre *or US* **saber** (ˈseɪbə) *n* **1** a stout single-edged cavalry sword, having a curved blade. **2** a sword used in fencing, having a narrow V-shaped blade. ◆ *vb* **sabres, sabring, sabred** *or US* **sabers, sabering, sabered**. **3** (*tr*) to injure or kill with a sabre. [C17: via F from G (dialect) *Sabel*, from MHG *sebel*, ?from Magyar *száblya*]

sabre-rattling *n, adj Inf.* seeking to intimidate by an aggressive display of military power.

sabre-toothed tiger *or* **cat** *n* any of various extinct felines with long curved upper canine teeth.

sac (sæk) *n* a pouch, bag, or pouchlike part in an animal or plant. [C18: from F, from L *saccus*; see SACK¹] ► **saccate** (ˈsækɪt, -eɪt) *adj* ► **ˈsacˌlike** *adj*

saccharide (ˈsækəˌraɪd) *n* any sugar or other carbohydrate, esp. a simple sugar.

saccharimeter (ˌsækəˈrɪmɪtə) *n* any instrument for measuring the strength of sugar solutions. ► ˌsaccha'rimetry *n*

saccharin (ˈsækərɪn) *n* a very sweet white crystalline slightly soluble powder used as a nonfattening sweetener. [C19: from SACCHARO- + -IN]

saccharine (ˈsækəˌriːn) *adj* **1** excessively sweet; sugary: *a saccharine smile.* **2** of the nature of or containing sugar or saccharin.

saccharo- *or before a vowel* **racchar-** *combining form.* sugar. [via L from Gk *sakkharon*, ult. from Sansk. *śarkarā* sugar]

saccharose (ˈsækəˌrəʊz, -ˌrəʊs) *n* a technical name for **sugar** (sense 1).

saccule (ˈsækjuːl) *or* **sacculus** (ˈsækjʊləs) *n* **1** a small sac. **2** the smaller of the two parts of the membranous labyrinth of the internal ear. Cf. **utricle**. [C19: from L *sacculus* dim. of *saccus* SACK¹]

sacerdotal (ˌsæsəˈdəʊtˀl) *adj* of, relating to, or characteristic of priests. [C14: from L *sacerdōtālis*, from *sacerdōs* priest, from *sacer* sacred] ► ˌsacer'dotaˌlism *n* ► ˌsacer'dotally *adv*

sachem (ˈseɪtʃəm) *n* **1** *US.* a leader of a political party or organization. **2** another name for **sagamore**. [C17: from Amerind *săchim* chief]

sachet (ˈsæʃeɪ) *n* **1** a small sealed envelope, usually made of plastic, for containing shampoo, etc. **2a** a small soft bag containing perfumed powder, placed in drawers to scent clothing. **2b** the powder contained in such a bag. [C19: from OF: a little bag, from *sac* bag; see SACK¹]

Sachs ★ (*German* zaks) *n* **1** Hans (hans). 1494–1576, German master shoemaker and Meistersinger, portrayed by Wagner in *Die Meistersinger von Nürnberg.* **2** Nelly (Leonie). 1891–1970, German Jewish poet and dramatist, who escaped from Nazi Germany and settled in Sweden. Nobel prize for literature (1966) with Shmuel Yosef Agnon.

Sachsen ★ (ˈzaksən) *n* the German name for **Saxony**.

sack¹ (sæk) *n* **1** a large bag made of coarse cloth, thick paper, etc., used as a container. **2** Also called: **sackful**. the amount contained in a sack. **3a** a woman's loose tube-shaped dress. **3b** Also called: **sacque** (sæk). a woman's full loose hip-length jacket. **4 the sack.** *Inf.* dismissal from employment. **5** a slang word for **bed. 6 hit the sack.** *Sl.* to go to bed. ◆ *vb* (*tr*) **7** *Inf.* to dismiss from employment. **8** to put into a sack or sacks. [OE *sacc*, from L *saccus* bag, from Gk *sakkos*] ► ˈsackˌlike *adj*

sack² (sæk) *n* **1** the plundering of a place by an army or mob. **2** *American football.* a tackle on a quarterback that brings him down before he has passed the ball. ◆ *vb* (*tr*) **3** to plunder and partially destroy (a place). **4** *American football.* to tackle and bring down (a quarterback) before he has passed the ball. [C16: from F *mettre à sac*, lit.: to put (loot) in a sack, from L *saccus* SACK¹] ► ˈsacker *n*

sack³ (sæk) *n Arch. except in trademarks.* any dry white

wine from SW Europe. [C16 *wyne seck*, from F *vin sec* dry wine, from L *siccus* dry]

sackbut (ˈsækˌbʌt) *n* a medieval form of trombone. [C16: from F *saqueboute*, from OF *saquer* to pull + *bouter* to push]

sackcloth (ˈsækˌklɒθ) *n* **1** coarse cloth such as sacking. **2** garments made of such cloth, worn formerly to indicate mourning. **3 sackcloth and ashes.** a public display of extreme grief.

sacking (ˈsækɪŋ) *n* coarse cloth used for making sacks, woven from flax, hemp, jute, etc.

sack race *n* a race in which the competitors' legs and often bodies are enclosed in sacks.

Sackville ★ (ˈsækvɪl) *n* **Thomas**, 1st Earl of Dorset. 1536–1608, English poet, dramatist, and statesman.

Sackville-West ★ *n* **Victoria (Mary)**, known as *Vita.* 1892–1962, British writer, noted for the poem *The Land* (1931) and the novel *The Edwardians* (1930). Married to Harold Nicolson.

sacral¹ (ˈseɪkrəl) *adj* of or associated with sacred rites. [C19: from L *sacrum* sacred object]

sacral² (ˈseɪkrəl) *adj* of or relating to the sacrum. [C18: from NL *sacrālis* of the SACRUM]

sacrament (ˈsækrəmənt) *n* **1** an outward sign combined with a prescribed form of words and regarded as conferring grace upon those who receive it. The Protestant sacraments are baptism and the Lord's Supper. In the Roman Catholic and Eastern Churches they are baptism, penance, confirmation, the Eucharist, holy orders, matrimony, and the anointing of the sick (formerly extreme unction). **2** (*often cap.*) the Eucharist. **3** the consecrated elements of the Eucharist, esp. the bread. **4** something regarded as possessing a sacred significance. **5** a pledge. [C12: from Church L *sacrāmentum* vow, from L *sacrāre* to consecrate]

sacramental (ˌsækrəˈmɛntˀl) *adj* **1** of or having the nature of a sacrament. ◆ *n* **2** *RC Church.* a sacrament-like ritual action, such as the sign of the cross or the use of holy water. ► ˌsacraˈmentaˌlism *n* ► **sacramentality** (ˌsækrəmɛnˈtælɪtɪ) *n*

Sacramento ★ (ˌsækrəˈmɛntəʊ) *n* **1** an inland port in N central California, capital of the state at the confluence of the American and Sacramento Rivers: became a boom town in the gold rush of the 1850s. Pop.: 374 964 (1994 est.). **2** a river in N California, flowing generally south to San Francisco Bay. Length: 615 km (382 miles).

sacrarium (sæˈkrɛərɪəm) *n, pl* **sacraria** (-ˈkrɛərɪə). **1** the sanctuary of a church. **2** *RC Church.* a place near the altar of a church where materials used in the sacred rites are deposited or poured away. [C18: from L, from *sacer* sacred]

sacred (ˈseɪkrɪd) *adj* **1** exclusively devoted to a deity or to some religious ceremony or use. **2** worthy of or regarded with reverence and awe. **3** connected with or intended for religious use: *sacred music.* **4 sacred to.** dedicated to. [C14: from L *sacrāre* to set apart as holy, from *sacer* holy] ► ˈsacredly *adv* ► ˈsacredness *n*

sacred cow *n Inf.* a person, custom, etc., held to be beyond criticism. [alluding to the Hindu belief that cattle are sacred]

sacred mushroom *n* **1** any of various hallucinogenic mushrooms that have been eaten in rituals in various parts of the world. **2** a mescal button, used in a similar way.

sacrifice (ˈsækrɪˌfaɪs) *n* **1** a surrender of something of value as a means of gaining something more desirable or of preventing some evil. **2** a ritual killing of a person or animal with the intention of propitiating or pleasing a deity. **3** a symbolic offering of something to a deity. **4** the person, animal, or object killed or offered. **5** loss entailed by giving up or selling something at less than its value. **6** *Chess.* the act or an instance of sacrificing a piece. ◆ *vb* **sacrifices, sacrificing, sacrificed.** **7** to make a sacrifice (of). **8** *Chess.* to permit or force one's opponent to capture a piece freely, as in playing a gambit: *he sacrificed his queen and checkmated his opponent on the next move.*

[C13: via OF from L *sacrificium*, from *sacer* holy + *facere* to make]
▸ **'sacri,ficer** *n*

sacrifice paddock *n NZ.* a grassed field which is allowed to be grazed completely, so that it can be cultivated and resown later.

sacrificial (,sækrɪ'fɪʃəl) *adj* used in or connected with a sacrifice.
▸ **,sacri'ficially** *adv*

sacrilege ('sækrɪlɪdʒ) *n* **1** the misuse or desecration of anything regarded as sacred or as worthy of extreme respect. **2** the act or an instance of taking anything sacred for secular use. [C13: from OF, from L, from *sacrilegus* temple-robber, from *sacra* sacred things + *legere* to take]
▸ **sacrilegist** (,sækrɪ'liːdʒɪst) *n*

sacrilegious (,sækrɪ'lɪdʒəs) *adj* **1** of, relating to, or involving sacrilege. **2** guilty of sacrilege.
▸ **,sacri'legiously** *adv*

sacring bell ('seɪkrɪŋ) *n Chiefly RC Church.* a small bell rung at the elevation of the Host and chalice during Mass.

sacristan ('sækrɪstən) *or* **sacrist** ('sækrɪst, 'seɪ-) *n* **1** a person who has charge of the contents of a church. **2** a less common word for **sexton**. [C14: from Med. L *sacristānus*, ult. from L *sacer* holy]

sacristy ('sækrɪstɪ) *n, pl* **sacristies.** a room attached to a church or chapel where the sacred vessels, vestments, etc., are kept. [C17: from Med. L *sacristia*; see SACRISTAN]

sacroiliac (,seɪkrəʊ'ɪlɪ,æk) *Anat.* ◆ *adj* **1** of or relating to the sacrum and ilium or their articulation. ◆ *n* **2** the joint where these bones meet.

sacrosanct ('sækrəʊ,sæŋkt) *adj* very sacred or holy. [C17: from L *sacrōsanctus* made holy by sacred rite, from *sacer* holy + *sanctus*, from *sancīre* to hallow]
▸ **,sacro'sanctity** *n*

sacrum ('seɪkrəm) *n, pl* **sacra** (-krə). the large wedge-shaped bone, consisting of five fused vertebrae, in the lower part of the back. [C18: from L *os sacrum* holy bone, because it was used in sacrifices, from *sacer* holy]

sad (sæd) *adj* **sadder, saddest. 1** feeling sorrow; unhappy. **2** causing, suggestive, or expressive of such feelings: *a sad story.* **3** unfortunate; shabby: *her clothes were in a sad state.* **4** *Brit. inf.* ludicrously contemptible; pathetic: *a sad, boring little wimp.* [OE *sæd* weary]
▸ **'sadly** *adv* ▸ **'sadness** *n*

SAD *abbrev. for* seasonal affective disorder.

Sadat ★ (sə'dæt) *n* **(Mohammed) Anwar El** ('ænwɑː ɛl). 1918–81, Egyptian statesman: president of Egypt (1970–81): shared Nobel peace prize (1978) with Begin: assassinated.

sadden ('sæd°n) *vb* to make or become sad.

saddle ('sæd°l) *n* **1** a seat for a rider, usually made of leather, placed on a horse's back and secured with a girth under the belly. **2** a similar seat on a bicycle, tractor, etc. **3** a back pad forming part of the harness of a packhorse. **4** anything that resembles a saddle in shape, position, or function. **5** a cut of meat, esp. mutton, consisting of both loins. **6** the part of a horse or similar animal on which a saddle is placed. **7** the part of the back of a domestic chicken that is nearest to the tail. **8** another word for **col** (sense 1). **9 in the saddle.** in a position of control. ◆ *vb* **saddles, saddling, saddled. 10** (sometimes foll. by *up*) to put a saddle on (a horse). **11** (*intr*) to mount into the saddle. **12** (*tr*) to burden: *I didn't ask to be saddled with this job.* [OE *sadol, sædel*]
▸ **'saddle-,like** *adj*

saddleback ('sæd°l,bæk) *n* a marking resembling a saddle on the backs of various animals.
▸ **'saddle-,backed** *adj*

saddlebag ('sæd°l,bæg) *n* a pouch or small bag attached to the saddle of a horse, bicycle, etc.

saddlebill ('sæd°l,bɪl) *n* a large black-and-white stork of tropical Africa, having a heavy red bill with a black band around the middle. Also called: **jabiru**.

saddlebow ('sæd°l,bəʊ) *n* the pommel of a saddle.

saddlecloth ('sæd°l,klɒθ) *n* a light cloth put under a horse's saddle, so as to prevent rubbing.

saddle horse *n* a lightweight horse kept for riding only.

saddler ('sædlə) *n* a person who makes, deals in, or repairs saddles and other leather equipment for horses.

saddle roof *n* a roof that has a ridge and two gables.

saddlery ('sædlərɪ) *n, pl* **saddleries. 1** saddles, harness, and other leather equipment for horses collectively. **2** the business, work, or place of work of a saddler.

saddle soap *n* a soft soap containing neat's-foot oil used to preserve and clean leather.

saddletree ('sæd°l,triː) *n* the frame of a saddle.

Sadducee ('sædjʊ,siː) *n Judaism.* a member of an ancient Jewish sect that was opposed to the Pharisees, denying the resurrection of the dead and the validity of oral tradition. [OE *saddūcēas*, via L & Gk from LHeb. *sāddūqi*, prob. from *Sadoq* Zadok, high priest and supposed founder of the sect]
▸ **,Saddu'cean** *adj*

Sade ★ (sɑːd) *n* **Comte Donatien Alphonse François de** (*French* dɔnasjɛ̃ alfɔ̃s frɑ̃swa də), known as the *Marquis de Sade.* 1740–1814, French soldier and writer, whose exposition of sexual perversion gave rise to the term sadism.

sadhu *or* **saddhu** ('sɑːduː) *n* a Hindu wandering holy man. [Sansk., from *sādhu* good]

Sadi *or* **Saadi** ★ (sɑː'diː) *n* original name *Sheikh Muslih Addin.* ?1184–1292, Persian poet. His best-known works are *Gulistān* (Flower Garden) and *Būstān* (Tree Garden), long moralistic poems in prose and verse.

sadiron ('sæd,aɪən) *n* a heavy iron, pointed at both ends for pressing clothes. [C19: from SAD (in the obs. sense: heavy) + IRON]

sadism ('seɪdɪzəm) *n* the gaining of pleasure or sexual gratification from the infliction of pain and mental suffering on another person. Cf. **masochism**. [C19: from F, after the Marquis de SADE]
▸ **'sadist** *n* ▸ **sadistic** (sə'dɪstɪk) *adj* ▸ **sa'distically** *adv*

Sadler's Wells ★ ('sædləz welz) *n* (*functioning as sing*) a theatre in London. Renovated (1931) by Lilian Bayliss, it became the home of the Sadler's Wells Opera Company and the Sadler's Wells Ballet (now the Royal Ballet). [named after the medicinal *wells* on the site and its owner Thomas *Sadler*, who founded the original theatre on the site]

sadomasochism (,seɪdəʊ'mæsə,kɪzəm) *n* **1** the combination of sadistic and masochistic elements in one person. **2** sexual practice in which one partner adopts a sadistic role and the other a masochistic one.
▸ **,sadomaso'chistic** *adj*

Sadowa ★ ('sɑːdəʊvə) *n* a village in the W Czech Republic, in NE Bohemia: scene of the decisive battle of the Austro-Prussian war (1866) in which the Austrians were defeated by the Prussians. Czech name: **Sadová** ('sadɔva:).

s.a.e. *abbrev. for* stamped addressed envelope.

safari (sə'fɑːrɪ) *n, pl* **safaris. 1** an overland journey or hunting expedition, esp. in Africa. **2** the people, animals, etc., that go on the expedition. [C19: from Swahili: journey, from Ar., from *safara* to travel]

safari park *n* an enclosed park in which lions and other wild animals are kept uncaged in the open and can be viewed by the public from cars, etc.

safari suit *n* an outfit made of tough cotton, denim, etc., consisting of a bush jacket with matching trousers, shorts, or skirt.

safe (seɪf) *adj* **1** affording security or protection from harm: *a safe place.* **2** (*postpositive*) free from danger: *you'll be safe here.* **3** secure from risk: *a safe investment.* **4** worthy of trust: *a safe companion.* **5** tending to avoid controversy or risk: *a safe player.* **6** not dangerous: *water safe to drink.* **7 on the safe side.** as a precaution. ◆ *adv* **8** in a safe condition: *the children are safe in bed now.* **9 play safe.** to act in a way least likely to cause danger, controversy, or defeat. ◆ *n* **10** a strong container, usually of metal and provided with a secure lock, for storing money or valuables. **11** a small cupboard-like container for storing food. [C13: from OF *salf*, from L *salvus*]
▸ **'safely** *adv* ▸ **'safeness** *n*

safe-breaker *n* a person who breaks open and robs safes. Also called: **safe-cracker**.

★ people and places

safe-conduct n 1 a document giving official permission to travel through a region, esp. in time of war. 2 the protection afforded by such a document.

safe-deposit or **safety-deposit** n a a place with facilities for the safe storage of money. b (as modifier): a safe-deposit box.

safeguard ('seɪf,gɑːd) n 1 a person or thing that ensures protection against danger, injury, etc. 2 a safe-conduct. ◆ vb 3 (tr) to protect.

safe house n a place used secretly by undercover agents, terrorists, etc., as a refuge.

safekeeping ('seɪf'kiːpɪŋ) n the act of keeping or state of being kept in safety.

safe period n Inf. the period during the menstrual cycle when conception is considered least likely to occur.

safe seat n a Parliamentary seat that at an election is sure to be held by the same party as held it before.

safe sex n sexual intercourse using physical protection, such as a condom, or nonpenetrative methods to prevent the spread of such diseases as AIDS.

safety ('seɪftɪ) n, pl **safeties**. 1 the quality of being safe. 2 freedom from danger or risk of injury. 3 a contrivance designed to prevent injury. 4 American football. Also called: **safetyman**. either of two players who defend the area furthest back in the field.

safety belt n 1 another name for **seat belt** (sense 1). 2 a belt or strap worn by a person working at a great height to prevent him from falling.

safety curtain n a curtain made of fireproof material that can be lowered to separate the auditorium and stage in a theatre to prevent the spread of a fire.

safety factor n the ratio of the breaking stress of a material to the calculated maximum stress in use. Also called: **factor of safety**.

safety glass n glass that if broken will not shatter.

Safety Islands ★ pl n a group of three small French islands in the Atlantic, off the coast of French Guiana. French name: **Îles du Salut**.

safety lamp n an oil-burning miner's lamp in which the flame is surrounded by a metal gauze to prevent it from igniting combustible gas.

safety match n a match that will light only when struck against a specially prepared surface.

safety net n 1 a net used in a circus to catch high-wire and trapeze artistes if they fall. 2 any means of protection from hardship or loss.

safety pin n a spring wire clasp with a covering catch, made so as to shield the point when closed.

safety razor n a razor with a guard over the blade or blades to prevent deep cuts.

safety valve n 1 a valve in a pressure vessel that allows fluid to escape at excess pressure. 2 a harmless outlet for emotion, etc.

saffian ('sæfɪən) n leather tanned with sumach and usually dyed a bright colour. [C16: via Russian & Turkish from Persian *sakhtiyān* goatskin, from *sakht* hard]

safflower ('sæflaʊə) n 1 a thistle-like Eurasian annual plant having large heads of orange-yellow flowers and yielding a dye and an oil used in paints, medicines, etc. 2 a red dye used for cotton and for colouring foods and cosmetics. [C16: via Du. *saffloer* or G *safflor* from OF *saffleur*]

saffron ('sæfrən) n 1 an Old World crocus having purple or white flowers with orange stigmas. 2 the dried stigmas of this plant, used to flavour or colour food. 3 **meadow saffron**. another name for **autumn crocus**. 4a an orange to orange-yellow colour. 4b (as adj): a saffron dress. [C13: from OF *safran*, from Med. L *safranum*, from Ar. *za'farān*]

Safi ★ (French safi) n a port in W Morocco, 170 km (105 miles) northwest of Marrakech, to which it is the nearest port. Pop.: 278 000 (1993 est.).

Safid Rud ★ (sæ'fiːd 'ruːd) n a river in N Iran, flowing northeast to a delta on the Caspian Sea. Length: about 785 km (490 miles).

S.Afr. abbrev. for South Africa(n).

safranine or **safranin** ('sæfrənɪn) n any of a class of azine dyes used for textiles. [C19: from F *safran* SAFFRON + -INE²]

sag (sæg) vb **sags, sagging, sagged.** (mainly intr) 1 (also tr) to sink or cause to sink in parts, as under weight or pressure: the bed sags in the middle. 2 to fall in value: prices sagged to a new low. 3 to hang unevenly. 4 (of courage, etc.) to weaken. ◆ n 5 the act or an instance of sagging: a sag in profits. 6 Naut. the extent to which a vessel's keel sags at the centre. [C15: from ON] ▸ 'saggy adj

saga ('sɑːgə) n 1 any of several medieval prose narratives written in Iceland and recounting the exploits of a hero or a family. 2 any similar heroic narrative. 3 a series of novels about several generations or members of a family. 4 Inf. a series of events or a story stretching over a long period. [C18: from ON: a narrative]

sagacious (sə'geɪʃəs) adj having or showing sagacity; wise. [C17: from L *sagāx*, from *sāgīre* to be astute] ▸ sa'gaciously adv

sagacity (sə'gæsɪtɪ) n foresight, discernment, or keen perception; ability to make good judgments.

sagamore ('sægə,mɔː) n (among some North American Indians) a chief or eminent man. [C17: from Amerind *sāgimau*, lit.: he overcomes]

Sagan ★ (French sagã) n **Françoise** (frãswaz), original name **Françoise Quoirez**. born 1935, French writer, best-known for the novels *Bonjour Tristesse* (1954) and *Aimez-vous Brahms?* (1959).

sage¹ (seɪdʒ) n 1 a man revered for his profound wisdom. ◆ adj 2 profoundly wise or prudent. [C13: from OF, from L *sapere* to be sensible] ▸ 'sagely adv ▸ 'sageness n

sage² (seɪdʒ) n 1 a perennial Mediterranean plant having grey-green leaves and purple, blue, or white flowers. 2 the leaves of this plant, used in cooking for flavouring. 3 short for **sagebrush**. [C14: from OF *saulge*, from L *salvia*, from *salvus* in good health (from its curative properties)]

sagebrush ('seɪdʒ,brʌʃ) n any of a genus of aromatic plants of W North America, having silver-green leaves and large clusters of small white flowers.

saggar or **sagger** ('sægə) n a clay box in which ceramic wares are placed during firing. [C17: ? alteration of SAFEGUARD]

Saghalien ★ (sə'gɑːljən) n a variant of **Sakhalin**.

sagittal suture ('sædʒɪt³l) n a serrated line on the top of the skull that marks the junction of the two parietal bones.

Sagittarius (,sædʒɪ'tɛərɪəs) n, Latin genitive **Sagittarii** (,sædʒɪ'tɛərɪ,aɪ). 1 Astron. a S constellation. 2 Also called: the **Archer**. Astrol. the ninth sign of the zodiac. The sun is in this sign between Nov. 22 and Dec. 21. [C14: from L: an archer, from *sagitta* an arrow] ▸ **Sagittarian** (,sædʒɪ'tɛərɪən) adj

sagittate ('sædʒɪ,teɪt) adj (esp. of leaves) shaped like the head of an arrow. [C18: from NL *sagittātus*, from L *sagitta* arrow]

sago ('seɪgəʊ) n a starchy cereal obtained from the powdered pith of a palm (**sago palm**), used for puddings and as a thickening agent. [C16: from Malay *sāgū*]

saguaro (sə'gwɑːrəʊ) n, pl **saguaros**. a giant cactus of desert regions of Arizona, S California, and Mexico. [Mexican Sp., var. of *sahuaro*, an Indian name]

Saguenay ★ (,sægə'neɪ) n a river in SE Canada in S Quebec, rising as the Péribonca River on the central plateau and flowing south, then east to the St Lawrence. Length: 764 km (475 miles).

Sagunto ★ (Spanish sa'ɣunto) n an industrial town in E Spain, near Valencia: allied to Rome and made a heroic resistance to the Carthaginian attack led by Hannibal (219–218 B.C.). Pop.: 57 359 (1989). Ancient name: **Saguntum** (sə'gʌntəm).

Sahara ★ (sə'hɑːrə) n a desert in N Africa, extending from the Atlantic to the Red Sea and from the Mediterranean to central Mali, Niger, Chad, and the Sudan: the largest desert in the world, occupying over a quarter of Africa; rises to over 3300 m (11 000 ft) in the central mountain system of the Ahaggar and Tibesti massifs; large reserves of iron ore, oil, and natural gas. Area: 9 100 000 sq. km (3 500 000 sq. miles). Average annual rainfall: less than 254 mm (10 in.). Highest recorded temperature: 58°C (136.4°F).

▶ **Sa'haran** *n, adj*

sahib ('sɑːhɪb) *n* (in India) a form of address placed after a man's name, used as a mark of respect. [C17: from Urdu, from Ar. *çāhib*, lit.: friend]

said[1] (sɛd) *adj* **1** (*prenominal*) (in contracts, etc.) aforesaid.
♦ *vb* **2** the past tense and past participle of **say**.

said[2] ('sɑːɪd) *n* a variant of **sayyid**.

Saida ★ ('sɑːɪdə) *n* a port in SW Lebanon, on the Mediterranean: on the site of ancient Sidon; terminal of the Trans-Arabian pipeline from Saudi Arabia. Pop.: 100 000 (1991 est.).

saiga ('saɪgə) *n* either of two antelopes of the plains of central Asia, having a slightly elongated nose. [C19: from Russian]

Saigon ★ (saɪ'gɒn) *n* the former name (until 1976) of **Ho Chi Minh City**.

sail (seɪl) *n* **1** an area of fabric, usually Terylene or nylon (formerly canvas), with fittings for holding it in any suitable position to catch the wind, used for propelling certain kinds of vessels, esp. over water. **2** a voyage on such a vessel: *a sail down the river.* **3** a vessel with sails or such vessels collectively: *to travel by sail.* **4** a ship's sails collectively. **5** something resembling a sail in shape, position, or function, such as the part of a windmill that is turned by the wind. **6 in sail.** having the sail set. **7 make sail. 7a** to run up the sail or to run up more sail. **7b** to begin a voyage. **8 set sail. 8a** to embark on a voyage by ship. **8b** to hoist sail. **9 under sail. 9a** with sail hoisted. **9b** under way.
♦ *vb* (*mainly intr*) **10** to travel in a boat or ship: *we sailed to Le Havre.* **11** to begin a voyage: *we sail at 5 o'clock.* **12** (of a vessel) to move over the water. **13** (*tr*) to manoeuvre or navigate a vessel: *he sailed the schooner up the channel.* **14** (*tr*) to sail over: *she sailed the Atlantic single-handed.* **15** (often foll. by *over, through,* etc.) to move fast or effortlessly: *we sailed through customs.* **16** to move along smoothly; glide. **17** (often foll. by *in* or *into*) *Inf.* **17a** to begin (something) with vigour. **17b** to make an attack (on) violently. [OE *segl*]
▶ **'sailable** *adj* ▶ **'sailless** *adj*

sailboard ('seɪl,bɔːd) *n* the craft used for windsurfing, consisting of a moulded board to which a mast bearing a single sail is attached.

sailboarding ('seɪl,bɔːdɪŋ) *n* another name for **windsurfing**.

sailcloth ('seɪl,klɒθ) *n* **1** any of various fabrics from which sails are made. **2** a canvas-like cloth used for clothing, etc.

sailer ('seɪlə) *n* a vessel, with specified sailing characteristics: *a good sailer.*

sailfish ('seɪl,fɪʃ) *n, pl* **sailfish** or **sailfishes**. **1** any of several large game fishes of warm and tropical seas. They have an elongated upper jaw and a long sail-like dorsal fin. **2** another name for **basking shark**.

sailing ship *n* a large sailing vessel.

sailor ('seɪlə) *n* **1** any member of a ship's crew, esp. one below the rank of officer. **2** a person who sails, esp. with reference to the likelihood of his becoming seasick: *a good sailor.*

sailplane ('seɪl,pleɪn) *n* a high-performance glider.

sainfoin ('sænfɔɪn) *n* a Eurasian perennial plant, widely grown as a forage crop, having pale pink flowers and curved pods. [C17: from F, from Med. L *sānum faenum* wholesome hay, referring to its former use as a medicine]

saint (seɪnt; *unstressed* sənt) *n* **1** a person who after death is formally recognized by a Christian Church as having attained a specially exalted place'in heaven and the right to veneration. **2** a person of exceptional holiness. **3** (*pl*) *Bible.* the collective body of those who are righteous in God's sight. ♦ *vb* **4** (*tr*) to recognize formally as a saint. [C12: from OF, from L *sanctus* holy, from *sancīre* to hallow]
▶ **'sainthood** *n* ▶ **'saintlike** *adj*

Saint Agnes' Eve *n, usually abbreviated to* **St Agnes' Eve.** the night of Jan. 20, when according to tradition a woman can discover the identity of her future husband by performing certain rites.

Saint Albans ★ ('ɔːlbənz) *n, usually abbreviated to* **St Albans.** a city in SE England, in W Hertfordshire: founded in 948 A.D. around the Benedictine abbey first built in Saxon times on the site of the martyrdom (about 303 A.D.) of St Alban; present abbey built in 1077; Roman ruins. Pop.: 80 376 (1991). Latin name: **Verulamium**.

Saint Andrews ★ *n, usually abbreviated to* **St Andrews.** a city in E Scotland, in Fife on the North Sea: the oldest university in Scotland (1411); famous golf links. Pop.: 11 136 (1991).

Saint Andrew's Cross *n, usually abbreviated to* **St Andrew's Cross. 1** a diagonal cross with equal arms. **2** a white diagonal cross on a blue ground.

Saint Anthony's fire *n, usually abbreviated to* **St Anthony's fire.** *Pathol.* another name for **ergotism** or **erysipelas**.

Saint Augustine ★ ('ɔːgəs,tiːn) *n, usually abbreviated to* **St Augustine.** a resort in NE Florida, on the Intracoastal Waterway: the oldest town in North America (1565); the northernmost outpost of the Spanish colonial empire for over 200 years. Pop.: 11 692 (1990).

Saint Austell ★ ('ɔːstəl) *n, usually abbreviated to* **St Austell.** a town in SW England, in S Cornwall on **St Austell Bay** (an inlet of the English Channel): china clay industry; administratively part of St Austell with Fowey since 1968. Pop. (with Fowey): 21 622 (1991).

Saint Bernard *n, usually abbreviated to* **St Bernard.** a large breed of dog with a dense red-and-white coat, formerly used as a rescue dog in mountainous areas.

Saint Bernard Pass ★ *n, usually abbreviated to* **St Bernard Pass.** either of two passes over the Alps: the **Great St Bernard Pass**, 2472 m (8110 ft) high, east of Mont Blanc between Italy and Switzerland, or the **Little St Bernard Pass**, 2157 m (7077 ft) high, south of Mont Blanc between Italy and France.

Saint-Brieuc ★ (*French* sɛbriø) *n, usually abbreviated to* **St-Brieuc.** a market town in NW France, near the N coast of Brittany. Pop.: 47 370 (1990).

Saint Catharines ★ *n, usually abbreviated to* **St Catharines.** an industrial city in S central Canada, in S Ontario on the Welland Canal. Pop.: 129 300 (1991).

Saint Christopher ★ *n, usually abbreviated to* **St Christopher.** another name for **Saint Kitts.**

Saint Christopher-Nevis ★ *n, usually abbreviated to* **St Christopher-Nevis.** the official name of **Saint Kitts-Nevis.**

Saint Clair ★ (kleə) *n, usually abbreviated to* **St Clair. Lake.** a lake between SE Michigan and Ontario: linked with Lake Huron by the **St Clair River** and with Lake Erie by the Detroit River. Area: 1191 sq. km (460 sq. miles).

Saint-Cloud ★ (*French* sɛklu) *n, usually abbreviated to* **St-Cloud.** a residential suburb of Paris: former royal palace; Sèvres porcelain factory. Pop.: 28 670 (1990).

Saint Croix ★ (krɔɪ) *n, usually abbreviated to* **St Croix.** an island in the Caribbean, the largest of the Virgin Islands of the US: purchased by the US in 1917. Chief town: Christiansted. Pop.: 50 139 (1990). Area: 207 sq. km (80 sq. miles). Also called: **Santa Cruz** ('sæntə 'kruːz).

Saint Croix River ★ *n, usually abbreviated to* **St Croix River.** a river on the border between the northeast US and Canada, flowing from the Chiputneticook Lakes to Passamaquoddy Bay, forming the border between Maine, US, and New Brunswick, Canada. Length: 121 km (75 miles).

Saint David's ★ *n, usually abbreviated to* **St David's.** a town in SW Wales, in Pembrokeshire: its cathedral was a place of pilgrimage in medieval times. Pop.: 1627 (1991).

Saint-Denis ★ (*French* sɛdni) *n, usually abbreviated to* **St-Denis. 1** a town in N France, on the Seine: 12th-century Gothic abbey church, containing the tombs of many French monarchs; an industrial suburb of Paris. Pop.: 89 988 (1990). **2** the capital of the French overseas region of Réunion, a port on the N coast. Pop.: 207 158 (1995).

★ people and places

Sainte-Beuve ★ (*French* sɛ̃tbœv) *n* Charles Augustin (Jarl ogystɛ̃). 1804–69, French critic, best known for his collections of essays *Port Royal* (1840–59) and *Les Causeries du Lundi* (1851–62).

sainted ('seɪntɪd) *adj* **1** canonized. **2** like a saint in character or nature. **3** hallowed or holy.

Sainte Foy ★ (seɪnt 'fɔɪ, sənt) *n, usually abbreviated to* Ste Foy. a SW suburb of Quebec, on the St Lawrence River. Pop.: 71 133 (1991).

Saint Elias Mountains ★ *pl n, usually abbreviated to* St Elias Mountains. a mountain range between SE Alaska and the SW Yukon, Canada. Highest peak: Mount Logan, 6050 m (19 850 ft).

Saint Elmo's fire ('ɛlməʊz) *n, usually abbreviated to* St Elmo's fire. (not in technical usage) a luminous region that sometimes appears around church spires, the masts of ships, etc.

Saint-Étienne ★ (*French* sɛ̃tetjɛn) *n, usually abbreviated to* St-Étienne. a town in E central France: a major producer of textiles and armaments. Pop.: 201 569 (1990).

Saint-Exupéry ★ (*French* sɛ̃tɛgzyperi) *n* Antoine de (ɑ̃twan də). 1900–44, French novelist and aviator. His novels include *Vol de nuit* (1931): he also wrote the fairy tale *Le petit prince* (1943).

Saint Gall ★ (*French* sɛ̃ gal) *n, usually abbreviated to* St Gall. **1** a canton in NE Switzerland. Capital: St Gall. Pop.: 440 744 (1995 est.). Area: 2012 sq. km (777 sq. miles). **2** a town in NE Switzerland, capital of St Gall canton: an important educational centre in the Middle Ages. Pop.: 75 541 (1994). German name: **Sankt Gallen** (zaŋkt 'galən).

Saint George's ★ *n, usually abbreviated to* St George's. the capital of Grenada, a port in the southwest. Pop.: 4621 (1991).

Saint George's Channel ★ *n, usually abbreviated to* St George's Channel. a strait between Wales and Ireland, linking the Irish Sea with the Atlantic. Length: about 160 km (100 miles). Width: up to 145 km (90 miles).

Saint Gotthard ★ ('gɒtəd) *n, usually abbreviated to* St Gotthard. **1** a range of the Lepontine Alps in SE central Switzerland. **2** a pass over the St Gotthard mountains, in S Switzerland. Height: 2114 m (6935 ft).

Saint Helena ★ (ˌsɛntɪ'liːnə) *n, usually abbreviated to* St Helena. a volcanic island in the SE Atlantic, forming (with its dependencies Tristan da Cunha and Ascension) a United Kingdom overseas territory: discovered by the Portuguese in 1502 and annexed by England in 1651; scene of Napoleon's exile and death. Capital: Jamestown. Pop.: 5700 (1992). Area: 122 sq. km (47 sq. miles).

Saint Helens ★ *n, usually abbreviated to* St Helens. **1** a town in NW England, in Merseyside: glass industry. Pop.: 106 293 (1991). **2** a unitary authority in NW England, in Merseyside. Pop.: 181 000 (1994 est.). Area: 130 sq. km (50 sq. miles). **3 Mount.** a volcanic peak in S Washington state; it erupted in 1980 after lying dormant from 1857.

Saint Helier ★ ('hɛlɪə) *n, usually abbreviated to* St Helier. a market town and resort in the Channel Islands, on the S coast of Jersey. Pop.: 28 123 (1991).

Saint James's Palace ★ *n, usually abbreviated to* St James's Palace. a palace in Pall Mall, London: residence of British monarchs from 1697 to 1837.

Saint John ★ *n, usually abbreviated to* St John. **1** a port in E Canada, at the mouth of the St John River: the largest city in New Brunswick. Pop.: 90 457 (1991). **2** an island in the Caribbean, in the Virgin Islands of the US. Pop.: 3504 (1990). Area: 49 sq. km (19 sq. miles). **3 Lake.** a lake in Canada, in S Quebec: drained by the Saguenay River. Area: 971 sq. km (375 sq. miles). **4** a river in E North America, rising in Maine, US, and flowing northeast to New Brunswick, Canada, then generally southeast to the Bay of Fundy. Length: 673 km (418 miles).

Saint-John Perse ★ ('sɪndʒən 'pɜːs) *n* See (Saint-John) Perse.

Saint John's ★ *n, usually abbreviated to* St John's. **1** a port in Canada, capital of Newfoundland, on the E coast of the Avalon Peninsula. Pop.: 95 770 (1991). **2** the capital of Antigua and Barbuda: a port on the NW coast of the island of Antigua. Pop.: 21 514 (1991).

Saint John's wort *n, usually abbreviated to* St John's wort. any of a genus of shrubs or herbaceous plants, having yellow flowers.

Saint-Just ★ (*French* sɛ̃ʒyst) *n* Louis Antoine Léon de (lwi ɑ̃twan leɔ̃ də). 1767–94, French Revolutionary leader and orator. A member of the Committee of Public Safety (1793–94), he was guillotined with Robespierre.

Saint Kilda ★ ('kɪldə) *n, usually abbreviated to* St Kilda. **1** a group of volcanic islands in the Atlantic, in the Outer Hebrides: uninhabited since 1930; bird sanctuary. **2** the main island of this group. Also called: **Hirta**.

Saint Kitts ★ (kɪts) *n, usually abbreviated to* St Kitts. an island in the E Caribbean, in the Leeward Islands: part of the state of St Kitts-Nevis. Capital: Basseterre. Pop.: 40 618 (1991). Area: 168 sq. km (65 sq. miles). Also called: **Saint Christopher.**

Saint Kitts-Nevis ★ *n, usually abbreviated to* St Kitts-Nevis. an independent state in the E Caribbean, in the Caribbean; comprises the two islands of St Kitts and Nevis: with the island of Anguilla formed a colony (1882–1967) and a British associated state (1967–83); Anguilla formally separated from the group in 1983; gained full independence in 1983 as a member of the Commonwealth. Official language: English. Religion: Protestant majority. Currency: Eastern Caribbean dollar. Capital: Basseterre. Pop.: 39 406 (1996). Area: 262 sq. km (101 sq. miles).

Saint Laurent ★ (*French* sɛ̃ lɔrɑ̃) *n, usually abbreviated to* St Laurent. a W suburb of Montreal, Canada. Pop.: 72 402 (1991).

Saint-Laurent ★ (*French* sɛ̃lɔrɑ̃) *n* Yves (iv), full name Yves-Mathieu. born 1936, French couturier: popularized trousers for women for all occasions.

Saint Lawrence ★ *n, usually abbreviated to* St Lawrence. **1** a river in SE Canada, flowing northeast from Lake Ontario, forming part of the border between Canada and the US, to the Gulf of St Lawrence: commercially one of the most important rivers in the world as the easternmost link of the St Lawrence Seaway. Length: 1207 km (750 miles). Width at mouth: 145 km (90 miles). **2 Gulf of.** a deep arm of the Atlantic off the E coast of Canada between Newfoundland and the mainland coasts of Quebec, New Brunswick, and Nova Scotia.

Saint Lawrence Seaway ★ *n, usually abbreviated to* St Lawrence Seaway. an inland waterway of North America, passing through the Great Lakes, the St Lawrence River, and connecting canals and locks: one of the most important waterways in the world. Length: 3993 km (2480 miles).

Saint Leger ('lɛdʒə) *n, usually abbreviated to* St Leger. the. an annual horse race run at Doncaster, England, since 1776.

Saint Leonard ★ ('lɛnəd) *n, usually abbreviated to* St Leonard. a N suburb of Montreal, Canada. Pop.: 82 200 (latest est.).

Saint-Lô ★ (*French* sɛ̃lo) *n, usually abbreviated to* St-Lô. a market town in NW France: a Calvinist stronghold in the 16th century. Pop.: 22 819 (1990).

Saint Louis ★ ('lʊɪs) *n, usually abbreviated to* St Louis. a port in E Missouri, on the Mississippi River near its confluence with the Missouri: the largest city in the state; university; major industrial centre. Pop.: 368 215 (1994 est.).

Saint-Louis ★ (*French* sɛ̃lwi) *n, usually abbreviated to* St-Louis. a port in NW Senegal, on an island at the mouth of the Senegal River: the first French settlement in W Africa (1689); capital of Senegal until 1958. Pop.: 132 444 (1994 est.).

Saint Lucia ★ ('luːʃə) *n, usually abbreviated to* St Lucia. an island state in the Caribbean, in the Windward Islands group of the Lesser Antilles: a volcanic island; gained self-government in 1967 as a British Associated State; attained full independence within the Commonwealth in 1979. Official language: English. Religion: Roman Catholic majority. Currency: Eastern Caribbean dollar. Capital: Castries. Pop.: 144 000 (1996). Area: 616 sq. km (238 sq. miles).

saintly ('seɪntlɪ) *adj* like, relating to, or suitable for a saint.
▸ **'saintlily** *adv* ▸ **'saintliness** *n*

Saint Martin ★ *n, usually abbreviated to* **St Martin**. an island in the E Caribbean, in the Leeward Islands: administratively divided since 1648, the north belonging to France (as a dependency of Guadeloupe) and the south belonging to the Netherlands (as part of the Netherlands Antilles); salt industry. Pop.: (French) 28 518 (1990); (Dutch) 37 256 (1994 est.). Areas: (French) 52 sq. km (20 sq. miles); (Dutch) 33 sq. km (13 sq. miles). Dutch name: **Sint Maarten**.

Saint-Maur-des-Fossés ★ *(French* sɛmɔrdefose) *n, usually abbreviated to* **St-Maur-des-Fossés**. a town in N France, on the River Marne: a residential suburb of SE Paris. Pop.: 77 492 (1990).

Saint-Mihiel ★ *(French* sɛmjɛl) *n, usually abbreviated to* **St-Mihiel**. a village in NE France, on the River Meuse: site of a battle in World War I, in which the American army launched its first offensive in France.

Saint Moritz ★ (mə'rɪts) *n, usually abbreviated to* **St Moritz**. a village in E Switzerland, in Graubünden canton in the Upper Engadine, at an altitude of 1856 m (6089 ft): sports and tourist centre. Pop.: 5335 (1990 est.).

Saint-Nazaire ★ *(French* sɛnazɛr) *n, usually abbreviated to* **St-Nazaire**. a port in NW France, at the mouth of the River Loire: German submarine base in World War II; shipbuilding. Pop.: 64 812 (1990).

Saint-Ouen ★ *(French* sɛtwɛ̃) *n, usually abbreviated to* **St-Ouen**. a town in N France, on the Seine: an industrial suburb of Paris; famous flea market. Pop.: 42 611 (1990).

Saint Paul ★ *n, usually abbreviated to* **St Paul**. a port in SE Minnesota, capital of the state, at the head of navigation of the Mississippi: now contiguous with Minneapolis (the Twin Cities). Pop.: 262 071 (1994 est.).

saintpaulia (sənt'pɔːlɪə) *n* another name for **African violet**. [C20: NL, after Baron W. von *Saint Paul*, G soldier (died 1910), who discovered it]

Saint Paul's ★ *n, usually abbreviated to* **St Paul's**. a cathedral in central London, built between 1675 and 1710 to replace an earlier cathedral destroyed during the Great Fire (1666): regarded as Wren's masterpiece.

Saint Peter's ★ *n, usually abbreviated to* **St Peter's**. the basilica of the Vatican City, built between 1506 and 1615 to replace an earlier church: the largest church in the world, 188 m (615 ft) long, and chief pilgrimage centre of Europe; designed by many architects, notably Bramante, Raphael, Sangallo, Michelangelo, and Bernini.

Saint Petersburg ★ ('piːtəz,bɜːg) *n, usually abbreviated to* **St Petersburg**. **1** a city and port in NW Russia, on the Gulf of Finland at the mouth of the Neva River: founded by Peter the Great in 1703 and built on low-lying marshes subject to frequent flooding; capital of Russia from 1712 to 1918; a cultural and educational centre, with a university (1819); a major industrial centre, with engineering, shipbuilding, chemical, textile, and printing industries. Pop.: 4 838 500 (1995 est.). Former names: **Petrograd** (1914–24), **Leningrad** (1924–91). **2** a city and resort in W Florida, on Tampa Bay. Pop.: 238 585 (1994 est.).

Saint Pierre ★ *(French* sɛ pjɛr) *n, usually abbreviated to* **St Pierre**. a former town on the coast of the French island of Martinique, destroyed by the eruption of Mont Pelée in 1902.

Saint Pierre and Miquelon ★ (ˌmɪkə'lɒn; *French* miklɔ̃) *n, usually abbreviated to* **St Pierre and Miquelon**. an archipelago in the Atlantic, just off the S coast of Newfoundland: administratively an overseas department of France and the only remaining French possession in North America; consists of the islands of St Pierre, with most of the population, and Miquelon, about ten times as large; fishing industries. Capital: St Pierre. Pop.: 6392 (1990). Area: 242 sq. km (94 sq. miles).

Saint Pölten ★ ('pɜːltən) *n* See **Sankt Pölten**.

Saint-Quentin ★ *(French* sɛkɑ̃tɛ̃) *n, usually abbreviated to* **St-Quentin**. a town in N France, on the River Somme: textile industry. Pop.: 62 085 (1990).

Saint-Saëns ★ *(French* sɛsɑ̃s) *n* **(Charles) Camille** (kamij). 1835–1921, French composer. His works include the opera *Samson and Delilah* (1877), the suite *Carnival of Animals* (1886), five symphonies, and five piano concertos.

saint's day *n Christianity*. a day in the church calendar commemorating a saint.

Saint-Simon ★ *(French* sɛsimɔ̃) *n* **1 Comte de** (kɔ̃t də), title of *Claude Henri de Rouvroy*. 1760–1825, French social philosopher, generally regarded as the founder of French socialism. He thought society should be reorganized along industrial lines and that scientists should be the new spiritual leaders. His most important work is *Nouveau Christianisme* (1825). **2 Duc de** (dyk də), title of *Louis de Rouvroy*. 1675–1755, French soldier, statesman, and writer: his *Mémoires* are an outstanding account of the period 1694–1723, during the reigns of Louis XIV and Louis XV.

Saint Thomas ★ *n, usually abbreviated to* **St Thomas**. **1** an island in the E Caribbean, in the Virgin Islands of the US. Capital: Charlotte Amalie. Pop.: 48 166 (1990). Area: 83 sq. km (28 sq. miles). **2** the former name (1921–37) of **Charlotte Amalie**.

Saint Vincent ★ *n, usually abbreviated to* **St Vincent**. **1 Cape**. a headland at the SW extremity of Portugal: scene of several important naval battles, notably in 1797, when the British defeated the French and Spanish. **2 Gulf**. a shallow inlet of SE Australia, to the east of the Yorke Peninsula: salt industry.

Saint Vincent and the Grenadines ★ *n, usually abbreviated to* **St Vincent and the Grenadines**. an island state in the Caribbean, in the Windward Islands of the Lesser Antilles: comprises the island of St Vincent and the Northern Grenadines; formerly a British associated state (1969–79); gained full independence in 1979 as a member of the Commonwealth. Official language: English. Religion: Christian majority. Currency: East Caribbean dollar. Capital: Kingstown. Pop.: 113 000 (1996). Area: 389 sq. km (150 sq. miles).

Saint Vitus's dance ('vaɪtəsɪz) *n, usually abbreviated to* **St Vitus's dance**. *Pathol*. a nontechnical name for **Sydenham's chorea**.

Saipan ★ (saɪ'pæn) *n* an island in the W Pacific, in the S central Mariana Islands: administrative centre of the US Trust Territory of the Pacific Islands; captured by the Americans and used as a leading air base until the end of World War II; administered by the US since 1946. Pop.: 38 896 (1990). Area: 180 sq. km (70 sq. miles).

Saïs ★ ('seɪɪs) *n* (in ancient Egypt) a city in the W Nile delta; the royal capital of the 24th dynasty (about 730–715 B.C.) and the 26th dynasty (about 664–525 B.C.).
▸ **Saite** ('seɪaɪt) *n* ▸ **Saitic** (seɪ'ɪtɪk) *adj*

saith (seθ) *vb* (used with *he, she*, or *it*) *Arch*. a form of the present tense of **say**.

saithe (seɪθ) *n Brit*. another name for **coalfish**. [C19: from ON]

Sakai ★ (sɑː'kaɪ) *n* a port in S Japan, on S Honshu on Osaka Bay: a major port in the 16th century; an industrial satellite of Osaka. Pop.: 802 965 (1995).

sake[1] (seɪk) *n* **1** benefit or interest (esp. in **for (someone's or one's own) sake**). **2** the purpose of obtaining or achieving (esp. in **for the sake of (something)**). **3** used in various exclamations of impatience, urgency, etc. (esp. in *for heaven's sake*. [C13 (in the phrase *for the sake of*, prob. from legal usage): from OE *sacu* lawsuit (hence, a cause)]

sake[2], **saké**, *or* **saki** ('sækɪ) *n* a Japanese alcoholic drink made from fermented rice. [C17: from Japanese]

saker ('seɪkə) *n* a large falcon of E Europe and Asia. [C14 *sagre*, from OF *sacre*, from Ar. *saqr*]

Sakhalin (*Russian* səxa'lin) *or* **Saghalien** ★ *n* an island in the Sea of Okhotsk, off the SE coast of Russia north of Japan: fishing, forestry, and mineral resources (coal and petroleum). Capital: Yuzhno-Sakhalinsk. Pop.: 673 000 (1995 est.). Area: 76 000 sq. km (29 300 sq. miles). Japanese name (1905–24): **Karafuto**.

Sakha Republic ★ (*Russian* 'saxa) *n* an administrative division in E Russia, in NE Siberia on the Arctic Ocean. Capital: Yakutsk. Pop.: 1 060 700 (1994). Area:

3 103 200 sq. km (1 197 760 sq. miles). Former names: **Yakut Republic, Yakutia.**

Sakharov ★ (*Russian* zaˈxarəf) *n* **Andrei** (anˈdrjej). 1921–89, Soviet nuclear physicist and human-rights campaigner: Nobel peace prize 1975.

saki (ˈsɑːkɪ) *n* **1** any of several small mostly arboreal New World monkeys having a long bushy tail. **2** another name for **sake**[2]. [sense 1: C20: F, from Tupi *saqí*]

Saki ★ (ˈsɑːkɪ) *n* pen name of (Hector Hugh) **Munro.**

sal (sæl) *n* a pharmacological term for **salt** (sense 3). [L]

salaam (səˈlɑːm) *n* **1** a Muslim salutation consisting of a deep bow with the right palm on the forehead. **2** a salutation signifying peace. ◆ *vb* **3** to make a salaam (to). [C17: from Ar. *salām* peace, from *assalām ʿalaikum* peace be to you]

salable (ˈseɪləbʰl) *adj* the US spelling of **saleable.**

salacious (səˈleɪʃəs) *adj* **1** having an excessive interest in sex. **2** (of books, etc.) erotic, bawdy, or lewd. [C17: from L *salax* fond of leaping, from *salīre* to leap]
▸ **saˈlaciously** *adv* ▸ **saˈlaciousness** *or* **salacity** (səˈlæsɪtɪ) *n*

salad (ˈsæləd) *n* **1** a dish of raw vegetables, such as lettuce, tomatoes, etc., served as a separate course with cold meat, eggs, etc., or as part of a main course. **2** any dish of cold vegetables or fruit served with a dressing: *potato salad*. **3** any green vegetable or herb used in such a dish. [C15: from OF *salade*, from OProvençal *salada*, from *salar* to season with salt, from L *sal* salt]

salad days *pl n* a period of youth and inexperience.

salad dressing *n* a sauce for salad, such as oil and vinegar or mayonnaise.

salade niçoise (sælˈlɑːd niːˈswɑːz) *n* a cold dish consisting of a variety of ingredients, usually including hard-boiled eggs, anchovy fillets, olives, tomatoes, and sometimes tuna fish. [C20: from F, lit.: salad of or from NICE]

Saladin ★ (ˈsælədɪn) *n* Arabic name *Salah-ed-Din Yusuf ibn-Ayyub*. ?1137–93, sultan of Egypt and Syria. He defeated the Crusaders near Tiberias (1187) and captured Acre, Jerusalem, and Ashkelon. He fought against Richard I of England and Philip II of France during the Third Crusade (1189–92).

Salado ★ (*Spanish* saˈlaðo) *n* **1** a river in N Argentina, rising in the Andes as the Juramento and flowing southeast to the Paraná River. Length: 2012 km (1250 miles). **2** a river in W Argentina, rising near the Chilean border as the Desaguadero and flowing south to the Colorado River. Length: about 1365 km (850 miles).

Salamanca ★ (*Spanish* salaˈmaŋka) *n* a city in W Spain: a leading cultural centre of Europe till the end of the 16th century; market town. Pop.: 167 382 (1991).

salamander (ˈsæləˌmændə) *n* **1** any of various amphibians of central and S Europe. They have an elongated body, and only return to water to breed. **2** *Chiefly US & Canad.* any amphibian with a tail, as the newt. **3** a mythical reptilian creature supposed to live in fire. **4** an elemental fire-inhabiting being. [C14: from OF *salamandre*, from L *salamandra*, from Gk]

Salambria ★ (səˈlæmbrɪə, ˌsɑːlɑːmˈbrɪə) *n* a river in N Greece, in Thessaly, rising in the Pindus Mountains and flowing southeast and east to the Gulf of Salonika. Length: about 200 km (125 miles). Ancient name: **Peneus.** Modern Greek name: **Piniós.**

salami (səˈlɑːmɪ) *n* a highly seasoned type of sausage, usually flavoured with garlic. [C19: from It., pl of *salame*, from Vulgar L *salāre* (unattested) to salt, from L *sal* salt]

Salamis ★ (ˈsæləmɪs) *n* an island in the Saronic Gulf, Greece: scene of the naval battle in 480 B.C., in which the Greeks defeated the Persians. Pop.: 20 000 (latest est.). Area: 95 sq. km (37 sq. miles).

sal ammoniac *n* another name for **ammonium chloride.**

salaried (ˈsælərɪd) *adj* earning or yielding a salary: *a salaried worker; salaried employment*.

salary (ˈsælərɪ) *n, pl* **salaries**. **1** a fixed payment made by an employer, often monthly, for professional or office work. Cf. **wage.** ◆ *vb* **salaries, salarying, salaried**. **2** (*tr*) to pay a salary to. [C14: from Anglo-Norman *salarie*, from

L *salārium* the sum given to Roman soldiers to buy salt, from *sal* salt]

Salazar ★ (*Portuguese* sələˈzar) *n* **Antonio de Oliveira** (ənˈtonju ˈdɑː oliˈvəjrə). 1889–1970, Portuguese statesman; dictator (1932–68).

salchow (ˈsælkəʊ) *n Figure skating*. a jump from the inner backward edge of one foot with one, two, or three full turns in the air, returning to the outer backward edge of the opposite foot. [C20: after Ulrich *Salchow* (1877–1949), Swedish figure skater, who originated it]

Salduba ★ (sælˈduːbə, ˈsældəbə) *n* the pre-Roman (Celtiberian) name for **Zaragoza.**

sale (seɪl) *n* **1** the exchange of goods, property, or services for an agreed sum of money or credit. **2** the amount sold. **3** the opportunity to sell: *there was no sale for luxuries*. **4a** an event at which goods are sold at reduced prices, usually to clear old stocks. **4b** (*as modifier*): *sale bargains*. **5** an auction. [OE *sala*, from ON *sala*]

Sale ★ (seɪl) *n* **1** a town in NW England, in Greater Manchester: a residential suburb of Manchester. Pop.: 56 052 (1991). **2** a city in SE Australia, in SE Victoria: centre of an agricultural region. Pop.: 13 858 (1991).

Salé ★ (*French* sale) *n* a port in NW Morocco, on the Atlantic adjoining Rabat. Pop.: 521 000 (1993 est.).

saleable *or US* **salable** (ˈseɪləbʰl) *adj* fit for selling or capable of being sold.
▸ **ˌsaleaˈbility** *or US* **ˌsalaˈbility** *n*

Salem ★ (ˈseɪləm) *n* **1** a city in S India, in Tamil Nadu: textile industries. Pop.: 366 712 (1991). **2** a city in NE Massachusetts, on the Atlantic: scene of the execution of 19 witches after the witch hunts of 1692. Pop.: 38 091 (1990). **3** a city in the NW US, the state capital of Oregon. Pop.: 115 912 (1994 est.). **4** an Old Testament name for **Jerusalem.** (Genesis 14:18; Psalms 76:2).

sale of work *n* a sale of articles, often handmade, the proceeds of which benefit a charity or charities.

sale or return *n* an arrangement by which a retailer pays only for goods sold, returning those that are unsold.

Salerno ★ (*Italian* saˈlɛrno) *n* a port in SW Italy, in Campania on the **Gulf of Salerno**: first medical school of medieval Europe. Pop.: 146 546 (1994 est.).

saleroom (ˈseɪlˌruːm, -ˌrʊm) *n Chiefly Brit.* a room where objects are displayed for sale, esp. by auction.

salesclerk (ˈseɪlzˌklɜːk) *n US & Canad.* a shop assistant.

salesman (ˈseɪlzmən) *n, pl* **salesmen. 1** Also called: **saleswoman** (*fem*), **salesgirl** (*fem*), *or* **salesperson**. a person who sells merchandise or services in a shop. **2** short for **travelling salesman.**

salesmanship (ˈseɪlzmənʃɪp) *n* **1** the technique of, skill, or ability in selling. **2** the work of a salesman.

sales pitch *or* **talk** *n* an argument or other persuasion used in selling.

sales resistance *n* opposition of potential customers to selling, esp. aggressive selling.

sales tax *n* a tax levied on retail sales receipts and added to selling prices by retailers.

sales trader *n Stock Exchange*. a person employed by a market maker, or his firm, to find clients.

Salford ★ (ˈsɔːlfəd, ˈsɒl-) *n* **1** a city in NW England in Greater Manchester, on the Manchester Ship Canal: a major centre of the cotton industry in the 19th century; extensive docks. Pop.: 79 755 (1991). **2** a unitary authority in NW England, in Greater Manchester. Pop.: 230 700 (1996 est.). Area: 97 sq. km (37 sq. miles).

Salian (ˈseɪlɪən) *adj* **1** denoting or relating to a group of Franks (the **Salii**) who settled in the Netherlands in the 4th century A.D. ◆ *n* **2** a member of this group.

salicin (ˈsælɪsɪn) *n* a crystalline water-soluble glucoside obtained from the bark of poplar trees and used as a medical analgesic. [C19: from F, from L *salix* willow]

Salic law (ˈsælɪk) *n History*. **1** the code of laws of the Salian Franks and other Germanic tribes. **2** a law excluding women from succession to the throne in certain countries, such as France.

salicylate (səˈlɪsɪˌleɪt) *n* any salt or ester of salicylic acid.

---

salicylic acid (ˌsælɪˈsɪlɪk) *n* a white crystalline substance with a sweet taste and bitter aftertaste, used in the manufacture of aspirin, and as a fungicide. [C19: *salicyl* (from F, from L *salix* a willow + -YL) + -IC]

salient (ˈseɪlɪənt) *adj* 1 conspicuous or striking: *a salient feature*. 2 projecting outwards at an angle of less than 180°. 3 (esp. of animals) leaping. ◆ *n* 4 *Mil.* a projection of the forward line into enemy-held territory. 5 a salient angle. [C16: from L *salīre* to leap]
▶ ˈsalience *or* ˈsaliency *n* ▶ ˈsaliently *adv*

salientian (ˌseɪlɪˈɛnʃɪən) *n* 1 any of an order of vertebrates with no tail and long hind legs adapted for hopping, as the frog or the toad. ◆ *adj* 2 of or belonging to this order. [C19: from NL *Salientia*, lit.: leapers, from L *salīre* to leap]

Salieri ★ (*Italian* saˈljeːri) *n* **Antonio** (anˈtɔːnjo). 1750–1825, Italian composer and conductor, who worked in Vienna (from 1766). The suggestion that he poisoned Mozart has no foundation.

salina (səˈlaɪnə) *n* a salt marsh or lake. [C17: from Sp., from Med. L: salt pit, from LL *salīnus* SALINE]

saline (ˈseɪlaɪn) *adj* 1 of, consisting of, or containing common salt: *a saline taste*. 2 *Med.* of or relating to a saline. 3 of, consisting of, or containing any chemical salt, esp. sodium chloride. ◆ *n* 4 *Med.* a solution of sodium chloride and water. [C15: from LL *salīnus*, from L *sal* salt]
▶ **salinity** (səˈlɪnɪtɪ) *n*

Salinger ★ (ˈsælɪndʒə) *n* **J(erome) D(avid)**. born 1919, US writer, noted for his novel *The Catcher in the Rye* (1951). In 1997 he published *Hapworth 16, 1924*, his first novel for 34 years.

salinometer (ˌsælɪˈnɒmɪtə) *n* a hydrometer for determining the amount of salt in a solution.
▶ ˌsaliˈnometry *n*

Salisbury[1] ★ (ˈsɔːlzbərɪ, -brɪ) *n* 1 the former name (until 1982) of **Harare**. 2 a city in S Australia: an industrial suburb of N Adelaide. Pop.: 89 000 (latest est.). 3 a city in S England, in SE Wiltshire: nearby Old Sarum was the site of an Early Iron Age hill fort; its cathedral (1220–58) has the highest spire in England. Pop.: 39 268 (1991). Ancient name: **Sarum**. Official name: **New Sarum**.

Salisbury[2] ★ (ˈsɔːlzbərɪ, -brɪ) *n* **Robert Gascoyne Cecil** (ˈgæskɔɪn), 3rd Marquess of Salisbury. 1830–1903, British statesman; Conservative prime minister (1885–86; 1886–92; 1895–1902).

Salisbury Plain ★ *n* an open chalk plateau in S England, in Wiltshire: site of Stonehenge; military training area. Average height: 120 m (400 ft).

saliva (səˈlaɪvə) *n* the secretion of salivary glands, consisting of a clear usually slightly acid aqueous fluid of variable composition. [C17: from L, from ?]
▶ **salivary** (səˈlaɪvərɪ) *adj*

salivary gland *n* any of the glands in mammals that secrete saliva.

salivate (ˈsælɪˌveɪt) *vb* **salivates, salivating, salivated.** 1 (*intr*) to secrete saliva, esp. an excessive amount. 2 (*tr*) to cause (an animal, etc.) to produce saliva, as by the administration of mercury.
▶ ˌsaliˈvation *n*

Salk ★ (sɔːlk) *n* **Jonas Edward**. 1914–95, US virologist: developed the injectable **Salk vaccine** against poliomyelitis (1954).

sallee *or* **sally** (ˈsælɪ) *n Austral.* 1 a SE Australian eucalyptus tree with pale grey bark. 2 any of various acacia trees. [prob. from Abor.]

sallow[1] (ˈsæləʊ) *adj* 1 (esp. of human skin) of an unhealthy pale or yellowish colour. ◆ *vb* 2 (*tr*) to make sallow. [OE *salu*]
▶ ˈsallowish *adj* ▶ ˈsallowness *n*

sallow[2] (ˈsæləʊ) *n* 1 any of several small willow trees, esp. the common sallow, which has large catkins that appear before the leaves. 2 a twig or the wood of any of these trees. [OE *sealh*]
▶ ˈsallowy *adj*

Sallust ★ (ˈsæləst) *n* full name *Gaius Sallustius Crispus*. 86–?34 B.C., Roman historian and statesman.

sally (ˈsælɪ) *n, pl* **sallies.** 1 a sudden sortie, esp. by troops. 2 a sudden outburst or emergence into action or expression. 3 an excursion. 4 a jocular retort. ◆ *vb* **sallies, sallying, sallied.** (*intr*) 5 to make a sudden violent sortie. 6 (often foll. by *forth*) to go out on an expedition, etc. 7 to come or set out in an energetic manner. 8 to rush out suddenly. [C16: from OF *saillie*, from *saillir* to dash forwards, from L *salīre* to leap]

Sally Lunn (lʌn) *n* a flat round cake made from a sweet yeast dough. [C19: said to be after an 18th-century E baker who invented it]

salmagundi (ˌsælməˈgʌndɪ) *n* 1 a mixed salad dish of cooked meats, eggs, beetroot, etc., popular in 18th-century England. 2 a miscellany. [C17: from F *salmigondis*, ?from It. *salami conditi* pickled salami]

salmon (ˈsæmən) *n, pl* **salmons** *or* **salmon.** 1 a soft-finned fish of the Atlantic and the Pacific, which is an important food fish. Salmon occur in cold and temperate waters and many species migrate to fresh water to spawn. 2 *Austral.* any of several unrelated fish. [C13: from OF *saumon*, from L *salmō*]
▶ ˈsalmo,noid *adj*

salmonella (ˌsælməˈnɛlə) *n, pl* **salmonellae** (-ˌliː). any of a genus of rod-shaped aerobic bacteria including many species which cause food poisoning. [C19: NL, after Daniel E. *Salmon* (1850–1914), US veterinary surgeon]

salmon ladder *n* a series of steps designed to enable salmon to move upstream to their breeding grounds.

Salome ★ (səˈləʊmɪ) *n New Testament.* the daughter of Herodias, at whose instigation she beguiled Herod by her seductive dancing into giving her the head of John the Baptist.

salon (ˈsælɒn) *n* 1 a room in a large house in which guests are received. 2 an assembly of guests in a fashionable household, esp. a gathering of major literary, artistic, and political figures. 3 a commercial establishment in which hairdressers, etc., carry on their businesses. 4a a hall for exhibiting works of art. 4b such an exhibition, esp. one showing the work of living artists. [C18: from F, from It. *salone*, augmented form of *sala* hall, of Gmc origin]

Salonika *or* **Salonica** ★ (səˈlɒnɪkə) *n* the English name for **Thessaloníki**.

saloon (səˈluːn) *n* 1 Also called: **saloon bar**. *Brit.* another word for **lounge** (sense 5). 2 a large public room on a passenger ship. 3 any large public room used for a purpose: *a dancing saloon*. 4 *Chiefly US & Canad.* a place where alcoholic drink is sold and consumed. 5 a closed two-door or four-door car with four to six seats. US, Canad., and NZ name: **sedan**. [C18: from F SALON]

Salop ★ (ˈsæləp) *n* a former name (1974–80) of **Shropshire**.
▶ **Salopian** (səˈləʊpjən) *n, adj*

salopettes (ˌsæləˈpɛts) *pl n* a garment worn for skiing, consisting of quilted trousers held up by shoulder straps. [C20: from F]

salpiglossis (ˌsælpɪˈglɒsɪs) *n* any of a genus of plants, some species of which are cultivated for their bright funnel-shaped flowers. [C19: NL, from Gk *salpinx* trumpet + *glōssa* tongue]

salpinx (ˈsælpɪŋks) *n, pl* **salpinges** (sælˈpɪndʒiːz). *Anat.* another name for **Fallopian tube** *or* **Eustachian tube**. [C19: from Gk: trumpet]
▶ **salpingectomy** (ˌsælpɪnˈdʒɛktəmɪ) *n* ▶ **salpingitis** (ˌsælpɪnˈdʒaɪtɪs) *n*

salsa (ˈsælsə) *n* 1 a type of Latin American big-band dance music. 2 a dance performed to this. 3 *Cookery.* a spicy Mexican tomato-based sauce. [C20: from Sp.: sauce]

salsify (ˈsælsɪfɪ) *n, pl* **salsifies.** 1 Also called: **oyster plant, vegetable oyster**. a Mediterranean plant having grasslike leaves, purple flower heads, and a long white edible taproot. 2 the root of this plant, which tastes of oysters and is eaten as a vegetable. [C17: from F, from It. *sassefrica*, from LL, from L *saxum* rock + *fricāre* to rub]

sal soda *n* the crystalline decahydrate of sodium carbonate, $Na_2CO_3.10H_2O$.

★ people and places

alt (sɔːlt) n **1** a white powder or colourless crystalline solid, consisting mainly of sodium chloride and used for seasoning and preserving food. **2** (modifier) preserved in, flooded with, containing, or growing in salt or salty water: *salt pork*. **3** *Chem.* any of a class of crystalline solid compounds that are formed from, or can be regarded as formed from, an acid and a base. **4** liveliness or pungency: *his wit added salt to the discussion*. **5** dry or laconic wit. **6** an experienced sailor. **7** short for **saltcellar**. **8 rub salt into someone's wounds**. to make someone's pain, shame, etc., even worse. **9 salt of the earth**. a person or group of people regarded as the finest of their kind. **10 with a grain** (or **pinch**) **of salt**. with reservations. **11 worth one's salt**. worthy of one's pay. ◆ vb (tr) **12** to season or preserve with salt. **13** to scatter salt over (an iced road, etc.) to melt the ice. **14** to add zest to. **15** (often foll. by *down* or *away*) to preserve or cure with salt. **16** *Chem.* to treat with salt. **17** to give a false appearance of value to, esp. to introduce valuable ore fraudulently into (a mine, sample, etc.). ◆ adj **18** not sour, sweet, or bitter; salty. ◆ See also **salt away, salts**. [OE *sealt*]
► **'salt,like** adj ► **'saltness** n

SALT (sɔːlt) n acronym for Strategic Arms Limitation Talks or Treaty.

Salta ★ (Spanish 'salta) n a city in NW Argentina: thermal springs. Pop.: 370 904 (1991).

saltation (sæl'teɪʃən) n **1** *Biol.* an abrupt variation in the appearance of an organism, species, etc. **2** *Geol.* the leaping movement of sand or soil particles carried in water or by the wind. **3** a sudden abrupt movement. [C17: from L *saltātiō* a dance, from *saltāre* to leap about]
► **saltatorial** (,sæltə'tɔːrɪəl) or **'saltatory** adj

salt away or (less commonly) **down** vb (tr, adv) to hoard or save (money, valuables, etc.).

saltbush ('sɔːlt,bʊʃ) n any of certain shrubs that grow in alkaline desert regions.

salt cake n an impure form of sodium sulphate used in the manufacture of detergents, glass, and ceramic glazes.

saltcellar ('sɔːlt,selə) n **1** a small container for salt used at the table. **2** *Brit. inf.* either of the two hollows formed above the collarbones. [changed (through infl. of cellar) from C15 *salt saler; saler* from OF *saliere* container for salt, from L *salārius* belonging to salt, from *sal* salt]

salt dome or **plug** n a domelike structure of stratified rocks containing a central core of salt.

salted ('sɔːltɪd) adj seasoned, preserved, or treated with salt.

salt flat n a flat expanse of salt left by the total evaporation of a body of water.

saltigrade ('sæltɪ,greɪd) adj (of animals) adapted for moving in a series of jumps. [C19: from NL *Saltigradae*, name formerly applied to jumping spiders, from L *saltus* a leap + *gradī* to move]

Saltillo ★ (Spanish sal'tiʎo) n a city in N Mexico, capital of Coahuila state: resort and commercial centre of a mining region. Pop.: 420 947 (1990).

saltings ('sɔːltɪŋz) pl n meadow land or marsh that is periodically flooded by sea water.

saltire or **saltier** ('sɔːl,taɪə) n *Heraldry*. an ordinary consisting of a diagonal cross on a shield. [C14 *sawtoure*, from OF *sauteour* cross-shaped barricade, from *saulter* to jump, from L *saltāre*]

Salt Lake City ★ n a city in N central Utah, near the Great Salt Lake at an altitude of 1330 m (4300 ft): state capital; founded in 1847 by the Mormons as world capital of the Mormon Church; University of Utah (1850). Pop.: 171 849 (1994 est.).

salt lick n **1** a place where wild animals go to lick salt deposits. **2** a block of salt given to domestic animals to lick. **3** *Austral. & NZ.* a soluble cake of minerals used to supplement the diet of farm animals.

Salto ★ (Spanish 'salto) n a port in NW Uruguay, on the Uruguay River: Uruguay's second largest city. Pop.: 77 400 (1985).

saltpan ('sɔːlt,pæn) n a shallow basin, usually in a desert region, containing salt, gypsum, etc., that was deposited from an evaporated salt lake.

saltpetre or US **saltpeter** (,sɔːlt'piːtə) n **1** another name for **potassium nitrate. 2** short for **Chile saltpetre**. [C16: from OF *salpetre*, from L *sal petrae* salt of rock]

salt pork n pork, esp. taken from the back and belly, that has been cured with salt.

salts (sɔːlts) pl n **1** *Med.* any of various mineral salts, such as magnesium sulphate, for use as a cathartic. **2** short for **smelling salts. 3** like a dose of salts. *Inf.* very quickly.

saltus ('sæltəs) n, pl **saltuses**. a break in the continuity of a sequence. [L: a leap]

saltwater ('sɔːlt,wɔːtə) adj of or inhabiting salt water, esp. the sea: *saltwater fishes*.

saltworks ('sɔːlt,wɜːks) n (functioning as sing) a building or factory where salt is produced.

saltwort ('sɔːlt,wɜːt) n any of various plants, of beaches and salt marshes, having prickly leaves, striped stems, and small green flowers. Also called: **glasswort, kali**.

salty ('sɔːltɪ) adj **saltier, saltiest. 1** of, tasting of, or containing salt. **2** (esp. of humour) sharp. **3** relating to life at sea.
► **'saltiness** n

salubrious (sə'luːbrɪəs) adj conducive or favourable to health. [C16: from L, from *salūs* health]
► **sa'lubriously** adv ► **sa'lubrity** n

Saluki (sə'luːkɪ) n a tall breed of hound with a smooth coat and long fringes on the ears and tail. [C19: from Ar. *salūqīy* of Saluq, an ancient Arabian city]

salutary ('sæljʊtərɪ) adj **1** promoting or intended to promote an improvement: *a salutary warning*. **2** promoting or intended to promote health. [C15: from L *salūtāris* wholesome, from *salūs* safety]
► **'salutarily** adv

salutation (,sæljʊ'teɪʃən) n **1** an act, phrase, gesture, etc., that serves as a greeting. **2** a form of words used as an opening to a speech or letter, such as *Dear Sir*. [C14: from L *salūtātiō*, from *salūtāre* to greet; see SALUTE]

salutatory (sə'luːtətərɪ) adj of, relating to, or resembling a salutation.
► **sa'lutatorily** adv

salute (sə'luːt) vb **salutes, saluting, saluted. 1** (tr) to address or welcome with friendly words or gestures of respect, such as bowing. **2** (tr) to acknowledge with praise: *we salute your gallantry*. **3** *Mil.* to pay formal respect, as by raising the right arm. ◆ n **4** the act of saluting. **5** a formal military gesture of respect. [C14: from L *salūtāre* to greet, from *salūs* wellbeing]
► **sa'luter** n

salvable ('sælvəb'l) adj capable of or suitable for being saved or salvaged. [C17: from LL *salvāre* to save, from *salvus* safe]

Salvador ★ ('sælvə,dɔː; Portuguese salva'dor) n a port in E Brazil, capital of Bahia state: founded in 1549 as capital of the Portuguese colony, which it remained until 1763; a major centre of the African slave trade in colonial times. Pop.: 2 070 296 (1991). Former name: **Bahia**. Official name: **São Salvador da Bahia de Todos os Santos** (sãu salva'dor 'də: ba'ia 'də: 'tɔːduʃ uʃ 'sɐntuʃ).
► **,Salva'dorian** n, adj

salvage ('sælvɪdʒ) n **1** the act, process, or business of rescuing vessels or their cargoes from loss at sea. **2a** the act of saving any goods or property in danger of damage or destruction. **2b** (as modifier): *a salvage operation*. **3** the goods or property so saved. **4** compensation paid for the salvage of a vessel or its cargo. **5** the proceeds from the sale of salvaged goods. ◆ vb **salvages, salvaging, salvaged**. (tr) **6** to save or rescue (goods or property) from fire, shipwreck, etc. **7** to gain (something beneficial) from a failure. [C17: from OF, from Med. L *salvāgium*, from *salvāre* to SAVE[1]]
► **'salvageable** adj ► **'salvager** n

salvation (sæl'veɪʃən) n **1** the act of preserving or the state of being preserved from harm. **2** a person or thing that is the means of preserving from harm. **3** *Christianity*. deliverance by redemption from the power of sin. [C13: from OF, from LL *salvātiō*, from *salvātus* saved, from *salvāre* to SAVE[1]]

Salvation Army n a Christian body founded in 1865

by William Booth and organized on quasi-military lines for evangelism and social work among the poor.

salvationist (sæl'veɪʃənɪst) *n* **1** a member of an evangelical sect emphasizing the doctrine of salvation. **2** (*often cap.*) a member of the Salvation Army.

salve (sælv, sɑːv) *n* **1** an ointment for wounds, etc. **2** anything that heals or soothes. ◆ *vb* **salves, salving, salved.** (*tr*) **3** to apply salve to (a wound, etc.). **4** to soothe, comfort, or appease. [OE *sealf*]

salver ('sælvə) *n* a tray, esp. one of silver, on which food, letters, visiting cards, etc., are presented. [C17: from F *salve*, from Sp. *salva* tray from which the king's taster sampled food, from L *salvāre* to SAVE¹]

salvia ('sælvɪə) *n* any of a genus of herbaceous plants or small shrubs, such as the sage, grown for their medicinal or culinary properties or for ornament. [C19: from L: SAGE²]

salvo ('sælvəʊ) *n, pl* **salvos** or **salvoes.** **1** a discharge of fire from weapons in unison, esp. on a ceremonial occasion. **2** concentrated fire from many weapons, as in a naval battle. **3** an outburst, as of applause. [C17: from It. *salva*, from OF *salve*, from L *salvē!* greetings!, ult. from *salvus* safe]

Salvo ('sælvəʊ) *n, pl* **Salvos.** *Austral. sl.* a member of the Salvation Army.

sal volatile (vɒ'lætɪlɪ) *n* a solution of ammonium carbonate in alcohol and aqueous ammonia, used as smelling salts. Also called: **spirits of ammonia.** [C17: from NL: volatile salt]

Salween ★ ('sælwiːn) *n* a river in SW Asia, rising in the Tibetan Plateau and flowing south and east through SW China and Myanmar to the Gulf of Martaban. Length: 2400 km (1500 miles).

Salzburg ★ ('sæltsbɜːg; *German* 'zaltsburk) *n* **1** a city in W Austria, capital of Salzburg province: 7th-century Benedictine abbey; a centre of music since the Middle Ages and birthplace of Mozart; tourist centre. Pop.: 143 978 (1991). **2** a state of W Austria. Pop.: 504 258 (1994 est.). Area: 7154 sq. km (2762 sq. miles).

Salzgitter (*German* zalts'gɪtər) *n* an industrial city in central Germany, in SE Lower Saxony. Pop.: 117 842 (1995 est.).

SAM (sæm) *n acronym for* surface-to-air missile.

Sam. *Bible. abbrev. for* Samuel.

S.Am. *abbrev. for* South America(n).

Samar ★ ('sɑːmə) *n* an island in the E central Philippines, separated from S Luzon by the San Bernardino Strait: the third largest island in the republic. Capital: Catbalogan. Pop.: 1 300 000 (latest est.). Area: 13 080 sq. km (5050 sq. miles).

samara (sə'mɑːrə, 'sæmərə) *n* a dry winged one-seeded fruit: occurs in the ash, maple, etc. Also called: **key fruit.** [C16: from NL, from L: seed of an elm]

Samara ★ (*Russian* sa'marə) *n* a port in SW Russia, on the River Volga: centre of an important industrial complex; oil refining. Pop.: 1 184 000 (1995 est.). Former name (1935–91): **Kuibyshev** or **Kuybyshev.**

Samarang ★ (sə'mɑːrɑːŋ) *n* a variant spelling of **Semarang.**

Samaria ★ (sə'mɛərɪə) *n* **1** the region of ancient Palestine that extended from Judaea to Galilee and from the Mediterranean to the River Jordan; the N kingdom of Israel. **2** the capital of this kingdom; constructed northwest of Shechem in the 9th century B.C.

Samaritan (sə'mærɪt³n) *n* **1** a native or inhabitant of Samaria. **2** short for **Good Samaritan. 3** (in the UK) a member of a voluntary organization (**the Samaritans**) that offers counselling to people in despair, esp. by telephone.

samarium (sə'mɛərɪəm) *n* a silvery metallic element of the lanthanide series used in carbon-arc lighting, as a doping agent in laser crystals, and as a neutron-absorber. Symbol: Sm; atomic no.: 62; atomic wt.: 150.35. [C19: from NL, from mineral, *samarskite*, after Col. von *Samarski*, 19th-century Russian inspector of mines + -IUM]

Samarkand ★ ('sæmə,kænd; *Russian* səmar'kant) *n* a city in E Uzbekistan: under Tamerlane it became the

chief economic and cultural centre of central Asia, on trade routes from China and India (the "silk road"). Pop.: 368 000 (1996). Ancient name: **Maracanda.**

samba ('sæmbə) *n, pl* **sambas. 1** a modern ballroom dance from Brazil in bouncy duple time. **2** a piece of music composed for or in the rhythm of this dance. ◆ *vb* **sambas, sambaing, sambaed. 3** (*intr*) to perform such a dance. [Port., of African origin]

sambar or **sambur** ('sæmbə) *n, pl* **sambars, sambar** or **samburs, sambur.** a S Asian deer with three-tined antlers. [C17: from Hindi, from Sansk. *śambarra*, from ?]

Sambre ★ (*French* sɑ̃brə) *n* a river in W Europe, rising in N France and flowing east into Belgium to join the Meuse at Namur. Length: 190 km (118 miles).

Sam Browne belt (,sæm 'braʊn) *n* a military officer's wide belt supported by a strap passing from the left side of the belt over the right shoulder. [C20: after Sir *Samuel J. Browne* (1824–1901), British general, who devised it]

same (seɪm) *adj* (usually preceded by *the*) **1** being the very one: *she is wearing the same hat.* **2a** being the one previously referred to. **2b** (*as n*): *a note received about same.* **3a** identical in kind, quantity, etc.: *two girls of the same age.* **3b** (*as n*): *we'd like the same.* **4** unchanged in character or nature: *his attitude is the same as ever.* **5** all the same. **5a** Also: **just the same.** nevertheless; yet. **5b** immaterial: *it's all the same to me.* ◆ *adv* **6** in an identical manner. [C12: from ON *samr*]
▶ 'sameness *n*

samfoo ('sæmfuː) *n* a style of dress worn by Chinese women, consisting of a waisted blouse and trousers. [from Chinese *sam* dress + *foo* trousers]

Samian ('seɪmɪən) *adj* **1** of or relating to Samos, an island in the Aegean, or its inhabitants. ◆ *n* **2** a native or inhabitant of Samos.

Samian ware *n* a fine earthenware pottery, reddish-brown or black in colour, found in large quantities on Roman sites. [C19: after the island of SAMOS, source of a reddish earth similar to that from which the pottery was made]

samisen ('sæmɪ,sɛn) *n* a Japanese plucked stringed instrument with a long neck and a rectangular soundbox. [Japanese, from Chinese *san-hsien*, from *san* three + *hsien* string]

samite ('sæmaɪt) *n* a heavy fabric of silk, often woven with gold or silver threads, used in the Middle Ages. [C13: from OF *samit*, from Med. L *examitum*, from Gk, from *hexamitos* having six threads]

samizdat (*Russian* səmiz'dat) *n* (formerly, in the Soviet Union) **a** a system of clandestine printing and distribution of banned literature. **b** (*as modifier*): *a samizdat publication.* [from Russian]

Samnium ★ ('sæmnɪəm) *n* an ancient country of central Italy inhabited by Oscan-speaking Samnites: corresponds to the present-day regions of Abruzzi, Molise, and part of Campania.

Samoa ★ (sə'məʊə) *n* an independent state occupying four inhabited islands and five uninhabited islands in the S Pacific archipelago of the Samoa Islands: established as a League of Nations mandate under New Zealand administration in 1920 and a UN trusteeship in 1946; gained independence as Western Samoa in 1962: a member of the Commonwealth: changed its name to Samoa in 1997. Languages: Samoan and English. Religion: Christian. Currency: tala. Capital: Apia. Pop.: 167 400 (1996). Area: 2841 sq. km (1097 sq. miles). Former name (1962–97): **Western Samoa.**
▶ Sa'moan *adj, n*

Samoa Islands ★ *pl n* a group of islands in the S Pacific, northeast of Fiji: an independent kingdom until the mid 19th century, when it was divided administratively into **American Samoa** (in the east) and **German Samoa** (in the west); the latter was mandated to New Zealand in 1919 and gained full independence in 1962 as Western Samoa (now called **Samoa**). Area: 3038 sq. km (1173 sq. miles).

Samos ★ ('seimɒs) *n* an island in the E Aegean Sea, off the SW coast of Turkey: a leading commercial centre of ancient Greece. Pop.: 41 965 (1991). Area: 492 sq. km (190 sq. miles).

samosa (sə'məʊsə) *n, pl* **samosas** *or* **samosa**. (in Indian cookery) a small, fried, triangular spiced meat or vegetable pasty. [C20: from Hindi]

Samothrace ★ ('sæmə,θreɪs) *n* a Greek island in the NE Aegean Sea: mountainous. Pop.: 4000 (latest est.).

samovar ('sæmə,vɑː) *n* (esp. in Russia) a metal urn for making tea, in which the water is usually heated by an inner container. [C19: from Russian, from *samo-* self + *varit'* to boil]

Samoyed (,sæmə'jed) *n* 1 (*pl* **Samoyed** *or* **Samoyeds**) a member of a group of peoples who live chiefly in the area of the N Urals: related to the Finns. 2 the languages of these peoples. 3 (sə'mɔɪɛd) a white or cream breed of dog having a dense coat and a tightly curled tail. [C17: from Russian *Samoed*]

samp (sæmp) *n* S. *African*. crushed maize used for porridge. [from Amerind *nasaump* softened by water]

sampan ('sæmpæn) *n* a small skiff, widely used in the Orient, that is propelled by oars. [C17: from Chinese, from *san* three + *pan* board]

samphire ('sæm,faɪə) *n* 1 an umbelliferous plant of Eurasian coasts, having fleshy divided leaves and clusters of small white flowers. 2 **golden samphire**. a Eurasian coastal plant with fleshy leaves and yellow flower heads. 3 **marsh samphire**. another name for **glasswort** (sense 1). 4 any of several other plants of coastal areas. [C16 *sampiere*, from F *herbe de Saint Pierre* Saint Peter's herb]

sample ('sɑːmpªl) *n* 1a a small part of anything, intended as representative of the whole. 1b (*as modifier*): *a sample bottle*. 2 Also called: **sampling**. *Statistics*. a set of individuals or items selected from a population and analysed to test hypotheses about or yield estimates of the population. ◆ *vb* **samples, sampling, sampled**. 3 (*tr*) to take a sample or samples of. 4 *Music*. 4a to take a short extract from (one record) and mix it into a different backing track. 4b to record (a sound) and feed it into a computerized synthesizer so that it can be reproduced at any pitch. [C13: from OF *essample*, from L *exemplum* EXAMPLE]

sampler ('sɑːmplə) *n* 1 a person who takes samples. 2 a piece of embroidery done to show the embroiderer's skill in using many different stitches. 3 *Music*. a piece of electronic equipment used for sampling. 4 a recording comprising a collection of tracks from other albums, to stimulate interest in the featured products.

sampling ('sɑːmplɪŋ) *n* 1 the process of selecting a random sample. 2 a variant of **sample** (sense 2). 3 *Music*. the process of taking a short extract from a record and mixing it into a different backing track.

sampling distribution *n Statistics*. the distribution of a random, experimentally obtained sample.

Sampras ★ ('sæm,præs) *n* Pete. born 1971, US tennis player: US singles champion (1990; 1993; 1995; 1996); Wimbledon singles champion (1993; 1994; 1995; 1997; 1998).

Samson ★ ('sæmsən) *n* 1 a judge of Israel, who performed feats of strength until he was betrayed by his mistress Delilah (Judges 13–16). 2 any man of outstanding physical strength.

Samsun ★ (*Turkish* 'sɑmsun) *n* a port in N Turkey, on the Black Sea. Pop.: 326 900 (1994 est.). Ancient name: **Amisus** (ə'miːsəs).

Samuel ★ ('sæmjʊəl) *n Old Testament*. 1 a Hebrew prophet, seer, and judge, who anointed the first two kings of the Israelites (I Samuel 1–3; 8–15). 2 either of the two books named after him, **I** and **II Samuel**.

samurai ('sæmʊ,raɪ) *n, pl* **samurai**. 1 the Japanese warrior

caste from the 11th to the 19th centuries. 2 a member of this aristocratic caste. [C19: from Japanese]

samurai bond *n Finance*. a bond issued in Japan and denominated in yen, available for purchase by nonresidents of Japan. Cf. **shogun bond**.

San ★ (sɑːn) *n* a river in E central Europe, rising in the W Ukraine and flowing northwest across SE Poland to the Vistula River. Length: about 450 km (280 miles).

San'a *or* **Sanaa** ★ (sɑː'nɑː) *n* the administrative capital of Yemen, on the central plateau at an altitude of 2350 m (7700 ft). Pop.: 972 000 (1995 est.).

San Antonio ★ (sæn æn'təʊnɪ,əʊ) *n* a city in S Texas: site of the Alamo; the leading town in Texas until about 1930. Pop.: 998 905 (1994 est.).
▸ **San Antonian** *adj, n*

sanative ('sænətɪv) *adj, n* a less common word for **curative**. [C15: from Med. L *sānātīvus*, from L *sānāre* to heal, from *sānus* healthy]

sanatorium (,sænə'tɔːrɪəm) *or US* **sanitarium** *n, pl* **sanatoriums** *or* **sanatoria** (-rɪə). 1 an institution for the medical care and recuperation of persons who are chronically ill. 2 *Brit*. a room as in a boarding school where sick pupils may receive treatment. [C19: from NL, from L *sānāre* to heal]

San Bernardino ★ (sæn ,bɜːnə'diːnəʊ) *n* a city in SE California: founded in 1851 by Mormons from Salt Lake City. Pop.: 181 718 (1994 est.).

San Bernardino Pass ★ *n* a pass over the Lepontine Alps in SE Switzerland. Highest point: 2062 m (6766 ft).

San Blas ★ ('sɑːn 'blɑːs) *n* 1 **Isthmus of**. the narrowest part of the Isthmus of Panama. Width: about 50 km (30 miles). 2 **Gulf of**. an inlet of the Caribbean on the N coast of Panama.

San Cristóbal ★ (*Spanish* saŋ kri'stoβal) *n* 1 Also called: **Chatham Island**. an island in the Pacific, in the Galápagos Islands. Area: 505 sq. km (195 sq. miles). 2 a city in SW Venezuela: founded in 1561 by Spanish conquistadores. Pop.: 220 675 (1990).

sanctified ('sæŋktɪ,faɪd) *adj* 1 consecrated or made holy. 2 sanctimonious.

sanctify ('sæŋktɪ,faɪ) *vb* **sanctifies, sanctifying, sanctified**. (*tr*) 1 to make holy. 2 to free from sin. 3 to sanction (an action or practice) as religiously binding: *to sanctify a marriage*. 4 to declare or render (something) productive of or conductive to holiness or grace. [C14: from LL *sanctificāre*, from L *sanctus* holy + *facere* to make]
▸ ,sanctifi'cation *n* ▸ 'sancti,fier *n*

sanctimonious (,sæŋktɪ'məʊnɪəs) *adj* affecting piety or making a display of holiness. [C17: from L *sanctimonia* sanctity, from *sanctus* holy]
▸ ,sancti'moniously *adv* ▸ ,sancti'moniousness *or* 'sanctimony *n*

sanction ('sæŋkʃən) *n* 1 authorization. 2 aid or encouragement. 3 something, such as an ethical principle, that imparts binding force to a rule, oath, etc. 4 the penalty laid down in a law for contravention of its provisions. 5 (*often pl*) a coercive measure, esp. one taken by one or more states against another guilty of violating international law. ◆ *vb* (*tr*) 6 to give authority to. 7 to confirm. [C16: from L *sanctiō* the establishment of an inviolable decree, from *sancīre* to decree]

sanctitude ('sæŋktɪ,tjuːd) *n* saintliness; holiness.

sanctity ('sæŋktɪtɪ) *n, pl* **sanctities**. 1 the condition of being sanctified; holiness. 2 anything regarded as sanctified or holy. 3 the condition of being inviolable: *the sanctity of marriage*. [C14: from OF *saincteté*, from L *sanctitās*, from *sanctus* holy]

sanctuary ('sæŋktjʊərɪ) *n, pl* **sanctuaries**. 1 a holy place. 2 a consecrated building or shrine. 3 *Old Testament*. 3a the Israelite temple at Jerusalem. 3b the tabernacle in which the Ark was enshrined. 4 the chancel, or that part of a sacred building surrounding the main altar. 5a a sacred building where fugitives were formerly entitled to immunity from arrest or execution. 5b the immunity so afforded. 6 a place of refuge. 7 a place, protected by law, where animals can live and breed without interference.

[C14: from OF *sainctuarie*, from LL *sanctuārium* repository for holy things, from L *sanctus* holy]

sanctuary lamp *n Christianity.* a lamp, usually red, placed in a prominent position in the sanctuary of a church, which, when lit, indicates the presence of the Blessed Sacrament.

sanctum ('sæŋktəm) *n, pl* **sanctums** *or* **sancta** (-tə). **1** a sacred or holy place. **2** a room or place of total privacy. [C16: from L, from *sanctus* holy]

sanctum sanctorum (sæŋk'tɔːrəm) *n Bible.* another term for the **holy of holies**. **2** *Often facetious.* an especially private place. [C14: from L, lit.: holy of holies, rendering Heb. *qōdesh haqqodāshīm*]

Sanctus ('sæŋktəs) *n* **1** *Liturgy.* the hymn that occurs immediately after the preface in the celebration of the Eucharist. **2** a musical setting of this. [C14: from the hymn, *Sanctus sanctus sanctus* Holy, holy, holy, from L *sancīre* to consecrate]

Sanctus bell *n Chiefly RC Church.* a bell rung as the opening words of the Sanctus are pronounced.

sand (sænd) *n* **1** loose material consisting of rock or mineral grains, esp. rounded grains of quartz. **2** (*often pl*) a sandy area, esp. on the seashore or in a desert. **3a** a greyish-yellow colour. **3b** (*as adj*): *sand upholstery.* **4** the grains of sandlike material in an hourglass. **5** *US inf.* courage. **6 the sands are running out.** there is not much time left before the end. ♦ *vb* **7** (*tr*) to smooth or polish the surface of with sandpaper or sand. **8** (*tr*) to sprinkle or cover with or as if with sand. **9** to fill or cause to fill with sand: *the channel sanded up.* [OE]
▶ '**sand,like** *adj*

Sand ★ (*French* sɑ̃d) *n* **George** (ʒɔrʒ), pen name of *Amandine Aurore Lucie Dupin.* 1804–76, French novelist, author of such novels as *La Mare au diable* (1846): a champion of women's independence.

Sandage ★ ('sændɪdʒ) *n* **Allan Rex.** born 1926, US astronomer, who discovered the first quasar (1961).

Sandakan ★ (sɑːnˈdɑːkɑːn) *n* a port in Malaysia, on the NE coast of Sabah: capital (until 1947) of North Borneo. Pop.: 223 432 (1991).

sandal ('sænd*ə*l) *n* **1** a light shoe consisting of a sole held on the foot by thongs, straps, etc. **2** a strap passing over the instep or around the ankle to keep a low shoe on the foot. **3** another name for **sandalwood**. [C14: from L *sandalium*, from Gk, from *sandalon* sandal]
▶ '**sandalled** *adj*

sandalwood ('sænd*ə*l,wʊd) *or* **sandal** *n* **1** any of a genus of evergreen trees, esp. the **white sandalwood**, of S Asia and Australia, having hard light-coloured heartwood. **2** the wood of any of these trees, which is used for carving, is burned as incense, and yields an aromatic oil used in perfumery. **3** any of various similar trees or their wood, esp. a leguminous tree of SE Asia having dark red wood used as a dye. [C14 *sandal*, from Med. L, from LGk *sandanon*, from Sansk. *candana* sandalwood]

Sandalwood Island ★ *n* the former name for **Sumba**.

sandarac *or* **sandarach** ('sændə,ræk) *n* **1** a pinaceous tree of NW Africa, having hard fragrant dark wood. **2** a brittle pale yellow transparent resin obtained from the bark of this tree and used in making varnish and incense. [C16 *sandaracha*, from L *sandaraca* red pigment, from Gk *sandarakē*]

sandbag ('sænd,bæg) *n* **1** a sack filled with sand used for protection against gunfire, floodwater, etc., or as ballast in a balloon, etc. **2** a bag filled with sand and used as a weapon. ♦ *vb* **sandbags, sandbagging, sandbagged.** (*tr*) **3** to protect or strengthen with sandbags. **4** to hit with or as if with a sandbag. **5** *Finance.* to obstruct (an unwelcome takeover bid) by having prolonged talks in the hope that a more acceptable bidder will come forward.
▶ '**sand,bagger** *n*

sandbank ('sænd,bæŋk) *n* a bank of sand in a sea or river, that may be exposed at low tide.

sand bar *n* a ridge of sand in a river or sea, built up by the action of tides, currents, etc., and often exposed at low tide.

sandblast ('sænd,blɑːst) *n* **1** a jet of sand blown from a

nozzle under air or steam pressure. ♦ *vb* **2** (*tr*) to clean or decorate (a surface) with a sandblast.
▶ '**sand,blaster** *n*

sand-blind *adj* not completely blind. Cf. **stone-blind**. [C15: changed (through infl. of SAND) from OE *samblind* (unattested), from *sam-* half, + BLIND]
▶ '**sand-,blindness** *n*

sandbox ('sænd,bɒks) *n* **1** a container on a railway locomotive from which sand is released onto the rails to assist the traction. **2** a container of sand for small children to play in.

sandboy ('sænd,bɔɪ) *n* **happy** (*or* **jolly**) **as a sandboy.** very happy; high-spirited.

Sandburg ★ ('sændbɜːg, 'sænbɜːg) *n* **Carl.** 1878–1967, US writer, noted for his free verse.

sand castle *n* a mass of sand moulded into a castle-like shape, esp. by a child on the beach.

sand eel *or* **lance** *n* a silvery eel-like marine spiny-finned fish found burrowing in sand or shingle. Popular name: **launce**.

sander ('sændə) *n* **1** a power-driven tool for smoothing surfaces by rubbing with an abrasive disc. **2** a person who uses such a device.

sanderling ('sændəlɪŋ) *n* a small sandpiper that frequents sandy shores. [C17: ?from SAND + OE *erthling* *eorthling* inhabitant of earth]

Sanderson ★ ('sændəs*ə*n) *n* **Tessa.** born 1956, British javelin-thrower.

sand flea *n* another name for the **chigoe** or **sand hopper**.

sandfly ('sænd,flaɪ) *n, pl* **sandflies. 1** any of various small mothlike dipterous flies: the bloodsucking females transmit diseases including leishmaniasis. **2** any of various similar flies.

sandgrouse ('sænd,graʊs) *n* a bird of dry regions of the Old World, having very short feet, a short bill, and long pointed wings and tail.

sand hopper *n* any of various small hopping crustaceans, common in intertidal regions of seashores. Also called: **beach flea, sand flea.**

Sandhurst ★ ('sænd,hɜːst) *n* a village in S England, in Berkshire: seat of the Royal Military Academy for the training of officer cadets in the British Army. Pop.: 19 153 (1991).

San Diego ★ (,sæn dɪˈeɪgəʊ) *n* a port in S California, on the Pacific: naval base; two universities. Pop.: 1 151 977 (1994 est.).

sandman ('sænd,mæn) *n, pl* **sandmen.** (in folklore) a magical person supposed to put children to sleep by sprinkling sand in their eyes.

sand martin *n* a small brown European songbird with white underparts: it nests in tunnels bored in sand, river banks, etc.

sandpaper ('sænd,peɪpə) *n* **1** a strong paper coated with sand or other abrasive material for smoothing and polishing. ♦ *vb* **2** (*tr*) to polish or grind (a surface) with or as if with sandpaper.

sandpiper ('sænd,paɪpə) *n* **1** any of numerous N hemisphere shore birds having a long slender bill and legs and cryptic plumage. **2** any other bird of the family which includes snipes and woodcocks.

sandpit ('sænd,pɪt) *n* **1** a shallow pit or container holding sand for children to play in. **2** a pit from which sand is extracted.

Sandringham ★ ('sændrɪŋəm) *n* a village in E England, in Norfolk near the E shore of the Wash: site of **Sandringham House,** a residence of the royal family.

Sandrocottus ★ (,sændrəʊˈkɒtəs) *n* the Greek name of **Chandragupta.**

sandshoe ('sænd,ʃuː) *n* a light canvas shoe with a rubber sole.

sandstone ('sænd,stəʊn) *n* any of a group of common sedimentary rocks consisting of sand grains consolidated with such materials as quartz, haematite, and clay minerals.

sandstorm ('sænd,stɔːm) *n* a strong wind that whips up clouds of sand, esp. in a desert.

★ people and places

sand trap *n* another name (esp. US) for **bunker** (sense 2).

sand viper *n* a S European viper having a yellowish-brown coloration with a zigzag pattern along the back.

Sandwell ★ ('sændwɛl) *n* a unitary authority in central England, in the West Midlands. Pop.: 293 700 (1994 est.). Area: 86 sq. km (33 sq. miles).

sandwich ('sænwɪdʒ, -wɪtʃ) *n* **1** two or more slices of bread, usually buttered, with a filling of meat, cheese, etc. **2** anything that resembles a sandwich in arrangement. ◆ *vb* (*tr*) **3** to insert tightly between two other things. **4** to put into a sandwich. **5** to place between two dissimilar things. [C18: after 4th Earl of *Sandwich* (1718–92), who ate sandwiches rather than leave the gambling table for meals]

sandwich board *n* one of two connected boards that are hung over the shoulders in front of and behind a person to display advertisements.

sandwich course *n* any of several courses consisting of alternate periods of study and industrial work.

Sandwich Islands ★ *pl n* the former name of Hawaii.

sandwich man *n* a man who carries sandwich boards.

sandwort ('sænd,wɜːt) *n* **1** any of various plants which grow in dense tufts on sandy soil and have white or pink solitary flowers. **2** any of various related plants.

sandy ('sændɪ) *adj* **sandier, sandiest. 1** consisting of, containing, or covered with sand. **2** (esp. of hair) reddish-yellow. **3** resembling sand in texture.
▸ 'sandiness *n*

sand yacht *n* a wheeled boat with sails, built to be propelled over sand by the wind.

sandy blight *n Austral. inf.* any inflammation and irritation of the eye.

sane (seɪn) *adj* **1** free from mental disturbance. **2** having or showing reason or sound sense. [C17: from L *sānus* healthy]
▸ 'sanely *adv* ▸ 'saneness *n*

San Fernando ★ (*Spanish* san fɛr'nando) *n* **1** a port in Trinidad and Tobago, in SW Trinidad, on the Gulf of Paria: the second-largest town in the country. Pop.: 30 100 (1990). **2** an inland port in W Venezuela, on the Apure River. Pop.: 84 179 (1990 est.). Official name: **San Fernando de Apure. 3** a port in SW Spain, on the Isla de León SE of Cádiz; site of an arsenal (founded 1790) and of the most southerly observatory in Europe. Pop.: 85 191 (1991).

Sanforized *or* **Sanforised** ('sænfə,raɪzd) *adj Trademark.* (of a fabric) preshrunk using a patented process.

San Francisco ★ (,sæn fræn'sɪskəʊ) *n* a port in W California, situated around the Golden Gate: developed rapidly during the California gold rush; a major commercial centre and one of the world's finest harbours. Pop.: 734 676 (1994 est.).
▸ **San Franciscan** *n, adj*

San Francisco Bay ★ *n* an inlet of the Pacific in W California, linked with the open sea by the Golden Gate strait. Length: about 80 km (50 miles). Greatest width: 19 km (12 miles).

sang (sæŋ) *vb* the past tense of **sing.**

> **USAGE NOTE** See at **ring²**.

Sanger ★ ('sæŋə) *n* **1 Frederick.** born 1918, British biochemist, who determined the structure of insulin: awarded two Nobel prizes for chemistry (1958; 1980). **2 Margaret (Higgins).** 1883–1966, US leader of the birth-control movement.

sang-froid (*French* sɑ̃frwa) *n* composure; self-possession. [C18: from F, lit.: cold blood]

sangoma (sæŋ'gəʊmə) *n, pl* **sangomas.** *S. African.* a witch doctor. [from Bantu]

Sangraal (sæŋ'greɪl), **Sangrail,** *or* **Sangreal** ('sæŋgrɪəl) *n* another name for the **Holy Grail.**

Sangre de Cristo Mountains ★ ('sæŋgrɪ də 'krɪstəʊ) *pl n* a mountain range in S Colorado and N New Mexico:

part of the Rocky Mountains. Highest peak: Blanca Peak, 4364 m (14 317 ft).

sangria (sæŋ'griːə) *n* a Spanish drink of red wine, sugar, and orange or lemon juice, sometimes laced with brandy. [Sp.: a bleeding]

sanguinary ('sæŋgwɪnərɪ) *adj* **1** accompanied by much bloodshed. **2** bloodthirsty. **3** consisting of or stained with blood. [C17: from L *sanguinārius*]
▸ 'sanguinarily *adv* ▸ 'sanguinariness *n*

sanguine ('sæŋgwɪn) *adj* **1** cheerful and confident; optimistic. **2** (esp. of the complexion) ruddy in appearance. **3** blood-red. ◆ *n* **4** a red pencil containing ferric oxide, used in drawing. [C14: from L *sanguineus* bloody, from *sanguis* blood]
▸ 'sanguinely *adv* ▸ 'sanguineness *n*

sanguineous (sæŋ'gwɪnɪəs) *adj* **1** of, containing, or associated with blood. **2** a less common word for **sanguine.**
▸ san'guineousness *n*

Sanhedrin ('sænɪdrɪn) *n Judaism.* the supreme judicial, ecclesiastical, and administrative council of the Jews in New Testament times. [C16: from LHeb., from Gk *sunedrion* council, from *sun-* SYN- + *hedra* seat]

sanies ('seɪnɪ,iːz) *n Pathol.* a thin greenish foul-smelling discharge from a wound, ulcer, etc., containing pus and blood. [C16: from L, from ?]

San Ildefonso ★ (*Spanish* san ilde'fonso) *n* a town in central Spain, near Segovia: site of the 18th-century summer palace of the kings of Spain. Also called: **La Granja.**

sanitarium (,sænɪ'tɛərɪəm) *n, pl* **sanitariums** *or* **sanitaria** (-rɪə). the US word for **sanatorium.** [C19: from L *sānitās* health]

sanitary ('sænɪtərɪ) *adj* **1** of or relating to health and measures for the protection of health. **2** free from dirt, germs, etc.; hygienic. [C19: from F *sanitaire,* from L *sānitās* health]
▸ sanitarian (,sænɪ'tɛərɪən) *n* ▸ 'sanitariness *n*

sanitary engineering *n* the branch of civil engineering associated with the supply of water, disposal of sewage, and other public health services.
▸ sanitary engineer *n*

sanitary towel *or esp. US* **napkin** *n* an absorbent pad worn externally by women during menstruation to absorb the menstrual flow.

sanitation (,sænɪ'teɪʃən) *n* the study and use of practical measures for the preservation of public health.

sanitize *or* **sanitise** ('sænɪ,taɪz) *vb* **sanitizes, sanitizing, sanitized** *or* **sanitises, sanitising, sanitised.** (*tr*) **1** *Chiefly US & Canad.* to make hygienic, as by sterilizing. **2** to omit unpleasant details from (a news report, document, etc.) to make it more palatable to the recipients.
▸ ,saniti'zation *or* ,saniti'sation *n*

sanity ('sænɪtɪ) *n* **1** the state of being sane. **2** good sense or soundness of judgment. [C15: from L *sānitās* health, from *sānus* healthy]

San Jose ★ (,sæn həʊ'zeɪ) *n* a city in W central California: a leading world centre of the fruit drying and canning industry. Pop.: 816 884 (1994 est.).

San José ★ (*Spanish* saŋ xo'se) *n* the capital of Costa Rica, on the central plateau: a major centre of coffee production in the mid-19th century; University of Costa Rica (1843). Pop.: 321 193 (1995).

San Juan ★ (*Spanish* saŋ 'xwan) *n* **1** the capital and chief port of Puerto Rico, on the NE coast; University of Puerto Rico; manufacturing centre. Pop.: 437 745 (1990). **2** a city in W Argentina: almost completely destroyed by an earthquake in 1944. Pop.: 352 691 (1991).

San Juan Bautista ★ (*Spanish* saŋ 'xwan bau'tista) *n* the former name of **Villahermosa.**

San Juan Islands ★ (sæn 'wɑːn, 'hwɑːn) *pl n* a group of islands between NW Washington, US, and SE Vancouver Island, Canada: administratively part of Washington.

San Juan Mountains ★ *pl n* a mountain range in SW Colorado and N New Mexico: part of the Rocky Mountains. Highest peak: Uncompahgre Peak, 4363 m (14 314 ft).

★ people and places

sank (sæŋk) *vb* the past tense of **sink**.

Sankey ★ ('sæŋkɪ) *n* **Ira David**. 1840–1908, US evangelist and hymnodist.

Sankt Pölten ★ (*German* zaŋkt 'pœltən) *n, usually abbreviated to* **St Pölten**. a city in NE Austria, the capital of Lower Austria. Pop.: 50 026 (1991).

San Luis Potosí ★ (*Spanish* san 'lwis poto'si) *n* **1** a state of central Mexico: mainly high plateau; economy based on mining (esp. silver) and agriculture. Capital: San Luis Potosí. Pop.: 2 191 712 (1995 est.). Area: 62 849 sq. km (24 266 sq. miles). **2** an industrial city in central Mexico, capital of San Luis Potosí state, at an altitude of 1850 m (6000 ft). Pop.: 488 238 (1990).

San Marino ★ (ˌsæn məˈriːnəʊ) *n* a republic in S central Europe in the Apennines, forming an enclave in Italy: the smallest republic in Europe, according to tradition founded by St Marinus in the 4th century. Official language: Italian. Religion: Roman Catholic. Currency: lira. Capital: San Marino. Pop.: 25 300 (1996). Area: 62 sq. km (24 sq. miles).
▸ **San Marinese** (ˌsæn ˌmærɪˈniːz) *or* **Sammarinese** (sə-ˌmærɪˈniːz) *adj, n*

San Martín ★ (*Spanish* san marˈtin) *n* **José de** (xoˈse de). 1778–1850, South American patriot, who played an important part in gaining independence for Argentina, Chile, and Peru. He was protector of Peru (1821–22).

Sanmicheli ★ (*Italian* sanmiˈkɛːli) *n* **Michele** (miˈkɛːle). ?1484–1559, Italian mannerist architect.

San Pedro Sula ★ (*Spanish* san 'peðro 'sula) *n* a city in NW Honduras: the country's chief industrial centre. Pop.: 368 500 (1994).

San Remo ★ (*Italian* san 'rɛːmo) *n* a port and resort in NW Italy, in Liguria on the slopes of the Maritime Alps; flower market. Pop.: 60 800 (1987 est.).

sans (sænz) *prep* an archaic word for **without**. [C13: from OF *sanz*, from L *sine* without, but prob. also infl. by L *absentia* in the absence of]

Sans. *or* **Sansk.** *abbrev. for* Sanskrit.

San Salvador ★ (sæn 'sælvəˌdɔː; *Spanish* san salβaˈðor) *n* the capital of El Salvador, situated in the SW central part: became capital in 1841; ruined by earthquakes in 1854 and 1873; university (1841). Pop.: 422 570 (1992).

San Salvador Island ★ *n* an island in the central Bahamas: the first land in the New World seen by Christopher Columbus (1492). Area: 156 sq. km (60 sq. miles). Also called: **Watling Island**.

sans-culotte (ˌsænzkjʊˈlɒt) *n* **1** (during the French Revolution) **1a** (originally) a revolutionary of the poorer class. **1b** (later) any revolutionary. **2** any revolutionary extremist. [C18: from F, lit.: without knee breeches, because the revolutionaries wore pantaloons or trousers rather than knee breeches]

San Sebastián ★ (ˌsæn səˈbæstjən; *Spanish* san seβasˈtjan) *n* a port and resort in N Spain on the Bay of Biscay: former summer residence of the Spanish court. Pop.: 169 933 (1991).

sansevieria (ˌsænsɪˈvɪərɪə) *n* any of a genus of herbaceous perennial plants of Old World tropical regions: some are cultivated as house plants for their bayonet-like leaves; others yield a useful fibre. [NL, after Raimondo di Sangro (1710–71), It. scholar and prince of *San Severo*]

Sanskrit ('sænskrɪt) *n* an ancient language of India. It is the oldest recorded member of the Indic branch of the Indo-European family of languages. Although it is used only for religious purposes, it is one of the official languages of India. [C17: from Sansk. *samskrta* perfected, lit.: put together]
▸ **San'skritic** *adj*

sans serif *or* **sanserif** (sænˈsɛrɪf) *n* a style of printer's typeface in which the characters have no serifs.

San Stefano ★ (ˌsæn stɪˈfɑːnəʊ) *n* a village in NW Turkey, near Istanbul on the Sea of Marmara: scene of the signing (1878) of the treaty ending the Russo-Turkish War. Turkish name: **Yeşilköy**.

Santa ★ ('sæntə) *n Inf.* short for **Santa Claus**.

Santa Ana ★ *n* **1** (*Spanish* 'santa 'ana). a city in NW El

Salvador: the second largest city in the country; coffee-processing industry. Pop.: 202 337 (1992). **2** ('sæntə 'ænə). a city in SW California: commercial and processing centre of a rich agricultural region. Pop.: 290 827 (1994 est.).

Santa Anna *or* **Santa Ana** ★ (*Spanish* 'santa 'ana) *n* **Antonio López de** (aˈtonjo 'lopeθ de). ?1795–1876, Mexican general, revolutionary, and president (1833–36, 1841–?45, 1847–48, 1853–55).

Santa Catalina ★ ('sæntə ˌkætˀliːnə) *n* an island in the Pacific, off the coast of SW California: part of Los Angeles county: resort. Area: 181 sq. km (70 sq. miles). Also called: **Catalina Island**.

Santa Catarina ★ (*Portuguese* 'santə kətəˈrinə) *n* a state of S Brazil, on the Atlantic: consists chiefly of the Great Escarpment. Capital: Florianópolis. Pop.: 4 836 600 (1995 est.). Area: 95 985 sq. km (37 060 sq. miles).

Santa Clara ★ (*Spanish* 'santa 'klara) *n* a city in W central Cuba: sugar and tobacco industries. Pop.: 205 400 (1994 est.).

Santa Claus ★ ('sæntə ˌklɔːz) *n* the legendary patron saint of children, commonly identified with Saint Nicholas. Often shortened to **Santa**. Also called: **Father Christmas**.

Santa Cruz ★ ('sæntə 'kruːz; *Spanish* 'santa 'kruθ) *n* **1** a province of S Argentina, on the Atlantic: consists of a large part of Patagonia, with the forested foothills of the Andes in the west. Capital: Río Gallegos. Pop.: 180 115 (1995 est.). Area: 243 740 sq. km (94 186 sq. miles). **2** a city in E Bolivia: the second largest town in Bolivia. Pop.: 767 260 (1993 est.). **3** another name for **Saint Croix**.

Santa Cruz de Tenerife ★ ('sæntə 'kruːz də ˌtenəˈriːf; *Spanish* 'santa 'kruθ de teneˈrife) *n* a port and resort in the W Canary Islands, on NE Tenerife: oil refinery. Pop.: 211 389 (1986).

Santa Fe ★ *n* **1** ('sæntə 'feɪ). a city in N central New Mexico, capital of the state: one of the oldest European settlements in North America, founded in 1610 as the capital of the Kingdom of New Mexico; developed trade with the US by the Santa Fe Trail in the early 19th century. Pop.: 62 514 (1994 est.). **2** (*Spanish* 'santa 'fe). an inland port in E Argentina, on the Salado River: University of the Littoral (1920). Pop.: 406 388 (1991).
▸ **'Santa 'Fean** *adj, n*

Santa Gertrudis ('sæntə gəˈtruːdɪs) *n* one of a breed of red beef cattle developed in Texas.

Santa Isabel ★ (*Spanish* 'santa isaˈβel) *n* the former name (until 1973) of **Malabo**.

Santa Maria ★ *n* **1** (*Portuguese* 'səntə maˈria) a city in S Brazil, in Rio Grande do Sul state. Pop.: 193 294 (1991). **2** (*Spanish* 'santa ma'ria) an active volcano in SW Guatemala. Height: 3768 m (12 362 ft).

Santa Marta ★ (*Spanish* 'santa 'marta) *n* a port in NW Colombia, on the Caribbean: the oldest city in Colombia, founded in 1525; terminus of the Atlantic railway from Bogotá (opened 1961). Pop.: 309 372 (1995 est.).

Santa Maura ★ ('santa 'maura) *n* the Italian name for **Levkás**.

Santander ★ (*Spanish* santan'der) *n* a port and resort in N Spain, on an inlet of the Bay of Biscay: noted for its prehistoric collection from nearby caves; shipyards and an oil refinery. Pop.: 194 822 (1994 est.).

Santarém ★ (*Portuguese* sənta'rəj) *n* a port in N Brazil, in Pará state where the Tapajós River flows into the Amazon. Pop.: 168 153 (1991).

Santa Rosa de Copán ★ (*Spanish* 'santa 'rosa de co-'pan) *n* a village in W Honduras: noted for the ruined Mayan city of Copán, which lies to the west.

Santayana (ˌsæntɪ'ænə) *n* **George**. 1863–1952, US philosopher, poet, and critic, born in Spain. His works include *The Life of Reason* (1905–06) and *The Realms of Being* (1927–40).

Santee ★ (sæn'tiː) *n* a river in SE central South Carolina, formed by the union of the Congaree and Wateree Rivers: flows southeast to the Atlantic; part of the **Santee-Wateree-Catawba River System**, an inland waterway 866 km (538 miles) long. Length: 230 km (143 miles).

★ **people and places**

Santer ★ ('sæntə) n **Jacques.** born 1937, Luxembourg politician; prime minister of Luxembourg (1984–95); president of the European Commission (1994–99).

Santiago ★ (ˌsæntɪ'ɑːgəʊ; Spanish san'tjaɣo) n **1** the capital of Chile, at the foot of the Andes: commercial and industrial centre; two universities. Pop.: 5 076 808 (1995 est.). Official name: **Santiago de Chile** (de 'tʃile). **2** a city in the N Dominican Republic. Pop.: 375 000 (1991 est.). Official name: **Santiago de los Caballeros** (de los kaβa'ʎeros).

Santiago de Compostela ★ (Spanish de kɔmpɔs'tela) n a city in NW Spain: place of pilgrimage since the 9th century and the most visited (after Jerusalem and Rome) in the Middle Ages; cathedral built over the tomb of the apostle St James. Pop.: 87 472 (1991). Latin name: **Campus Stellae** ('kæmpəs 'steliː).

Santiago de Cuba ★ (Spanish de 'kuβa) n a port in SE Cuba, on **Santiago Bay** (a large inlet of the Caribbean): capital of Cuba until 1589; university (1947); industrial centre. Pop.: 440 084 (1994 est.).

Santiago del Estero ★ (Spanish del es'tero) n a city in N Argentina: the oldest continuous settlement in Argentina, founded in 1553 by Spaniards from Peru. Pop.: 263 471 (1991).

Santo Domingo ★ ('sæntəʊ də'mɪŋgəʊ; Spanish 'santo ðo'miŋgo) n **1** the capital and chief port of the Dominican Republic, on the S coast: the oldest continuous European settlement in the Americas, founded in 1496; university (1538). Pop. (capital district): 2 138 262 (1993). Former name (1936–61): **Ciudad Trujillo. 2** the former name (until 1844) of the **Dominican Republic. 3** another name (esp. in colonial times) for **Hispaniola.**

santonica (sæn'tɒnɪkə) n **1** an oriental wormwood plant. **2** the dried flower heads of this plant, formerly used as a vermifuge. ◆ Also called: **wormseed.** [C17: NL, from LL herba santonica herb of the Santones (prob. wormwood), from L Santonī a people of Aquitania]

santonin ('sæntənɪn) n a white crystalline soluble substance extracted from the dried flower heads of santonica and used in medicine as an anthelmintic. [C19: from SANTONICA + -IN]

Santos ★ (Portuguese 'sɐntuʃ) n a port in S Brazil, in São Paulo state: the world's leading coffee port. Pop.: 415 554 (1991).

São Francisco ★ (Portuguese sɐu frɐ'sisku) n a river in E Brazil, rising in SW Minas Gerais state and flowing northeast, then southeast to the Atlantic northeast of Aracajú. Length: 3200 km (1990 miles).

São Luís (Portuguese sɐu 'lwis) or **São Luíz** ★ ('lwiʃ) n a port in NE Brazil, capital of Maranhão state, on the W coast of São Luís Island: founded in 1612 by the French and taken by the Portuguese in 1615. Pop.: 164 334 (1991).

São Miguel ★ (Portuguese sɐu mi'ɣɛl) n an island in the E Azores: the largest of the group. Pop.: 126 388 (1991 est.). Area: 854 sq. km (333 sq. miles).

Saône ★ (French son) n a river in E France, rising in Lorraine and flowing generally south to join the Rhône at Lyon, as its chief tributary: canalized for 375 km (233 miles) above Lyon; linked by canals with the Rhine, Marne, Seine, and Loire Rivers. Length: 480 km (298 miles).

Saône-et-Loire ★ (French sonelwar) n a department of central France, in Burgundy region. Capital: Mâcon. Pop.: 555 348 (1994 est.). Area: 8627 sq. km (3365 sq. miles).

São Paulo ★ (Portuguese sɐum 'paulu) n **1** a state of SE Brazil: consists chiefly of tableland draining west into the Paraná River. Capital: São Paulo. Pop.: 33 699 600 (1995 est.). Area: 247 239 sq. km (95 459 sq. miles). **2** a city in S Brazil, capital of São Paulo state: the largest city and industrial centre in Brazil, with one of the busiest airports in the world; three universities; rapidly expanding population. Pop.: 25 000 (1874); 2 017 025 (1950); 9 393 753 (1991).

Saorstat Eireann ★ ('seəstɑːt 'eərən) n the Gaelic name for the **Irish Free State.**

São Salvador ★ (Portuguese sɐu salva'dor) n short for

São Salvador da Bahia de Todos os Santos, the official name for **Salvador.**

São Tomé e Principe ★ (Portuguese sɐun tu'mɛ 'ɛ: 'priːsipə) n a republic in the Gulf of Guinea, off the W coast of Africa, on the Equator: consists of the islands of Principe and São Tomé; colonized by the Portuguese in the late 15th century; became independent in 1975. Official language: Portuguese. Religion: Roman Catholic majority. Currency: dobra. Capital: São Tomé. Pop.: 134 000 (1996). Area: 1001 sq. km (386 sq. miles).

sap[1] (sæp) n **1** a solution of mineral salts, sugars, etc., that circulates in a plant. **2** any vital body fluid. **3** energy; vigour. **4** Sl. a gullible person. **5** another name for **sapwood.** ◆ vb **saps, sapping, sapped.** (tr) **6** to drain of sap. [OE sæp]

sap[2] (sæp) n **1** a deep and narrow trench used to approach or undermine an enemy position. ◆ vb **saps, sapping, sapped. 2** to undermine (a fortification, etc.) by digging saps. **3** (tr) to weaken. [C16 zappe, from It. zappa spade, from ?]

sapele (sə'piːlɪ) n **1** any of various W African trees yielding a hard timber resembling mahogany. **2** the timber of such a tree, used to make furniture. [C20: West African name]

sapid ('sæpɪd) adj **1** having a pleasant taste. **2** agreeable or engaging. [C17: from L sapidus, from sapere to taste]
► **sapidity** (sə'pɪdɪtɪ) n

sapient ('seɪpɪənt) adj Often used ironically. wise or sagacious. [C15: from L sapere to taste]
► **'sapience** n ► **'sapiently** adv

sapiential (ˌseɪpɪ'ɛnʃəl) adj showing, having, or providing wisdom.

sapling ('sæplɪŋ) n **1** a young tree. **2** Literary. a youth.

sapodilla (ˌsæpə'dɪlə) n **1** a large tropical American evergreen tree, the latex of which yields chicle. **2** Also called: **sapodilla plum.** the edible brown rough-skinned fruit of this tree. [C17: from Sp. zapotillo, dim. of zapote sapodilla fruit, from Nahuatl tsapotl]

saponaceous (ˌsæpəʊ'neɪʃəs) adj resembling soap. [C18: from NL, from L sāpō soap]

saponify (sə'pɒnɪˌfaɪ) vb **saponifies, saponifying, saponified.** Chem. **1** to undergo or cause to undergo a process in which a fat is converted into a soap by treatment with alkali. **2** to undergo or cause to undergo a reaction in which an ester is hydrolysed to an acid and an alcohol as a result of treatment with an alkali. [C19: from F saponifier, from L sāpō soap]
► **sa,poni fi'cation** n

saponin ('sæpənɪn) n any of a group of plant glycosides with a steroid structure that foam when shaken and are used in detergents. [C19: from F saponine, from L sāpō soap]

sappanwood or **sapanwood** ('sæpənˌwʊd) n **1** a small tree of S Asia producing wood that yields a red dye. **2** the wood of this tree. [C16: sapan, via Du. from Malay sapang]

sapper ('sæpə) n **1** a soldier who digs trenches, etc. **2** (in the British Army) a private of the Royal Engineers.

Sapper ★ ('sæpə) n real name Herman Cyril McNeile. 1888–1937, British novelist, author of the popular thriller Bulldog Drummond (1920) and its sequels.

Sapphic ('sæfɪk) adj **1** Prosody. denoting a metre associated with Sappho. **2** of or relating to Sappho or her poetry. **3** lesbian. ◆ n **4** Prosody. a verse, line, or stanza written in the Sapphic form of classical lyric poetry.

Sapphira ★ (sæ'faɪrə) n New Testament. the wife of Ananias, who together with her husband was struck dead for fraudulently concealing their wealth from the Church (Acts 5).

sapphire ('sæfaɪə) n **1a** any precious corundum gemstone that is not red, esp. the highly valued transparent blue variety. **1b** (as modifier): a sapphire ring. **2a** the blue colour of sapphire. **2b** (as adj): sapphire eyes. **3** (modifier) denoting a forty-fifth anniversary: our sapphire wedding. [C13 safir, from OF, from L sapphīrus, from Gk sappheiros, ?from Sansk. śanipriya, lit.: beloved of the planet Saturn]

Sappho ★ ('sæfəʊ) n 6th century B.C., Greek lyric poetess of Lesbos.

Sapporo ★ ('sɑːpəʊˌrəʊ) n a city in N Japan, on W Hokkaido: commercial centre; university (1918). Pop.: 1 756 968 (1995).

sappy ('sæpɪ) adj **sappier, sappiest. 1** (of plants) full of sap. **2** full of energy or vitality.

sapro- or before a vowel **sapr-** combining form. indicating dead or decaying matter: saprogenic. [from Gk sapros rotten]

saprogenic (ˌsæprəʊ'dʒenɪk) or **saprogenous** (sæ-'prɒdʒɪnəs) adj **1** producing or resulting from decay. **2** growing on decaying matter.

saprophyte ('sæprəʊˌfaɪt) n any plant that lives and feeds on dead organic matter.
  ▸ **saprophytic** (ˌsæprəʊ'fɪtɪk) adj

saprotroph ('sæprəʊˌtrəʊf) n any organism, esp. a fungus or bacterium, that lives and feeds on dead organic matter. Also called: **saprobe, saprobiont.**
  ▸ **saprotrophic** (ˌsæprəʊ'trəʊfɪk) adj ▸ ˌsapro'trophically adv

saprozoic (ˌsæprəʊ'zəʊɪk) adj (of animals or plants) feeding on dead organic matter.

sapsucker ('sæpˌsʌkə) n either of two North American woodpeckers that have white wing patches and feed on the sap from trees.

sapwood ('sæpˌwʊd) n the soft wood, just beneath the bark in tree trunks, that consists of living tissue.

Sar. abbrev. for Sardinia(n).

sarabande or **saraband** ('særəˌbænd) n **1** a decorous 17th-century courtly dance. **2** a piece of music composed for or in the rhythm of this dance, in slow triple time. [C17: from F sarabande, from Sp. zarabanda, from ?]

Saracen ('særəsən) n **1** History. a member of one of the nomadic Arabic tribes, esp. of the Syrian desert. **2a** a Muslim, esp. one who opposed the crusades. **2b** (in later use) any Arab. ♦ adj **3** of or relating to Arabs of either of these periods, regions, or types. [C13: from OF Sarrazin, from LL Saracēnus, from LGk Sarakēnos, ?from Ar. sharq sunrise]
  ▸ **Saracenic** (ˌsærə'senɪk) adj

Saragossa ★ (ˌsærə'gɒsə) n the English name for Zaragoza.

Sarah ★ ('seərə) n Old Testament. the wife of Abraham and mother of Isaac (Genesis 17:15–22).

Sarajevo (ˌsærə'jeɪvəʊ; Serbo-Croat 'sarajevɔ) or **Serajevo** ★ n the capital of Bosnia-Herzegovina: developed as a Turkish town in the 15th century; capital of the Turkish and Austro-Hungarian administrations in 1850 and 1878 respectively; scene of the assassination of Archduke Franz Ferdinand in 1914, precipitating World War I; besieged by Bosnian Serbs (1992–95). Pop.: 525 980 (1991).

Saransk ★ (Russian sa'ransk) n a city in W central Russia, capital of the Mordovian Republic: university (1957). Pop.: 320 000 (1995 est.).

Saratov ★ (Russian sa'rataf) n an industrial city in W Russia, on the River Volga: university (1919). Pop.: 895 000 (1995 est.).

Sarawak ★ (sə'rɑːwək) n a state of Malaysia, on the NW coast of Borneo on the South China Sea: granted to Sir James Brooke by the Sultan of Brunei in 1841 as a reward for helping quell a revolt; mainly agricultural. Capital: Kuching. Pop.: 1 648 217 (1991). Area: about 121 400 sq. km (48 250 sq. miles).

sarcasm ('sɑːkæzəm) n **1** mocking or ironic language intended to convey scorn or insult. **2** the use or tone of such language. [C16: from LL sarcasmus, from Gk, from sarkazein to rend the flesh, from sarx flesh]

sarcastic (sɑː'kæstɪk) adj **1** characterized by sarcasm. **2** given to the use of sarcasm.
  ▸ **sar'castically** adv

sarcenet or **sarsenet** ('sɑːsnɪt) n a fine soft silk fabric used for clothing, ribbons, etc. [C15: from OF sarzinet, from Sarrazin SARACEN]

sarco- or before a vowel **sarc-** combining form. indicating flesh: sarcoma. [from Gk sark-, sarx flesh]

sarcocarp ('sɑːkəʊˌkɑːp) n Bot. the fleshy mesocarp of such fruits as the peach or plum.

sarcoma (sɑː'kəʊmə) n, pl **sarcomata** (-mətə) or **sarcomas.** Pathol. a usually malignant tumour arising from connective tissue. [C17: via NL from Gk sarkōma fleshy growth]
  ▸ **sar'comatous** adj

sarcomatosis (sɑːˌkəʊmə'təʊsɪs) n Pathol. a condition characterized by the development of several sarcomas at various bodily sites. [C19: see SARCOMA, -OSIS]

sarcophagus (sɑː'kɒfəgəs) n, pl **sarcophagi** (-ˌgaɪ) or **sarcophaguses.** a stone or marble coffin or tomb, esp. one bearing sculpture or inscriptions. [C17: via L from Gk sarkophagos flesh-devouring; from the type of stone used, which was believed to destroy the flesh of corpses]

sarcoplasm ('sɑːkəʊˌplæzəm) n the cytoplasm of a muscle fibre.
  ▸ ˌsarco'plasmic adj

sarcous ('sɑːkəs) adj (of tissue) muscular or fleshy. [C19: from Gk sarx flesh]

sard (sɑːd) or **sardius** ('sɑːdɪəs) n an orange, red, or brown variety of chalcedony, used as a gemstone. Also called: **sardine.** [C14: from L sarda, from Gk sardios stone from Sardis]

sardar or **sirdar** (sə'dɑː) n (in India) **1** a title used before the name of Sikh men. **2** a leader. [Hindi, from Persian]

Sardegna ★ (sar'deɲɲa) n the Italian name for **Sardinia.**

sardine[1] (sɑː'diːn) n, pl **sardines** or **sardine. 1** any of various small fishes of the herring family, esp. a young pilchard. **2 like sardines.** very closely crowded together. [C15: via OF from L sardīna, dim. of sarda a fish suitable for pickling]

sardine[2] ('sɑːdiːn) n another name for **sard.** [C14: from LL sardinus, from Gk sardinos lithos Sardian stone, from Sardeis Sardis]

Sardinia ★ (sɑː'dɪnɪə) n the second largest island in the Mediterranean: forms, with offshore islands, an administrative region of Italy; ceded to Savoy by Austria in 1720 in exchange for Sicily and formed the Kingdom of Sardinia with Piedmont; became part of Italy in 1861. Capital: Cagliari. Pop.: 1 657 375 (1994 est.). Area: 24 089 sq. km (9301 sq. miles). Italian name: **Sardegna.**

Sardinian (sɑː'dɪnɪən) adj **1** of or relating to Sardinia, its inhabitants, or their language. ♦ n **2** a native or inhabitant of Sardinia. **3** the spoken language of Sardinia, sometimes regarded as a dialect of Italian but containing many loan words from Spanish.

Sardis ('sɑːdɪs) or **Sardes** ★ ('sɑːdiːz) n an ancient city of W Asia Minor: capital of Lydia.

sardonic (sɑː'dɒnɪk) adj characterized by irony, mockery, or derision. [C17: from F, from L, from Gk sardonios derisive, lit.: of Sardinia, alteration of Homeric sardanios scornful (laughter or smile)]
  ▸ **sar'donically** adv ▸ **sar'donicism** n

sardonyx ('sɑːdənɪks) n a variety of chalcedony with alternating reddish-brown and white parallel bands. [C14: via L from Gk sardonux, ?from sardion SARD + onux nail]

Sardou ★ (French sardu) n **Victorien** (viktɔrjɛ̃). 1831–1908, French dramatist. His plays include La Tosca (1887), the source of Puccini's opera.

Sargasso Sea ★ n a calm area of the N Atlantic, between the Caribbean and the Azores, where there is an abundance of sargassum.

sargassum (sɑː'gæsəm) n a floating brown seaweed having ribbon-like fronds containing air sacs, esp. abundant in the Sargasso Sea. [C16: from Port. sargaço from ?]

sarge (sɑːdʒ) n Inf. sergeant.

Sargent ★ ('sɑːdʒənt) n **1** Sir (**Harold**) **Malcolm** (**Watts**). 1895–1967, British conductor. **2 John Singer.** 1856–1925, US painter; in London from 1885.

Sargeson ★ ('sɑːdʒəsən) n **Frank.** 1903–82, New Zealand writer. His work includes the collection That Summer and Other Stories (1946).

Sargodha ★ (sɑː'gəʊdə) n a city in NE Pakistan: grain market. Pop.: 294 000 (latest est.).

★ people and places

Sargon II ★ ('sɑːgɒn) *n* died 705 B.C., king of Assyria (722–705).

sari *or* **saree** ('sɑːrɪ) *n, pl* **saris** *or* **sarees**. the traditional dress of women of India, Pakistan, etc., consisting of a very long piece of cloth swathed around the body. [C18: from Hindi *sārī*, from Sansk. *śātī*]

Sark ★ (sɑːk) *n* an island in the English Channel in the Channel Islands, consisting of **Great Sark** and **Little Sark**, connected by an isthmus: ruled by a hereditary seigneur or dame. Pop.: 550 (1986 est.). Area: 5 sq. km (2 sq. miles). French name: **Sercq**.

Sarka ★ ('zɑːkə) *n* a variant spelling of **Zarqa**.

sarking ('sɑːkɪŋ) *n Scot., northern English, & NZ*. flat planking supporting the roof cladding of a building. [C15 in England: from Scot. *sark* shirt]

sarky ('sɑːkɪ) *adj* **sarkier, sarkiest**. *Brit. inf.* sarcastic.

Sarmatia ★ (sɑː'meɪʃɪə) *n* the ancient name of a region of present-day Poland, Belarus, and SW Russia, between the Volga and Vistula Rivers.
▸ **Sar'matian** *n, adj* ▸ **Sarmatic** (sɑː'mætɪk) *adj*

sarmentose (sɑː'mɛntəʊs) *or* **sarmentous** (sɑː'mɛntəs) *adj* (of plants such as the strawberry) having stems in the form of runners. [C18: from L *sarmentōsus* full of twigs, from *sarmentum* brushwood, from *sarpere* to prune]

Sarnen ★ (*German* 'zarnən) *n* a town in central Switzerland, capital of Obwalden demicanton: resort. Pop.: 7200 (1980).

Sarnia ★ ('sɑːnɪə) *n* an inland port in S central Canada, in SW Ontario at the S end of Lake Huron: oil refineries. Pop.: 74 376 (1991).

sarnie ('sɑːnɪ) *n Brit. inf.* a sandwich. [C20: prob. from N or dialect pronunciation of first syllable of *sandwich*]

sarod (sæ'rəʊd) *n* an Indian stringed musical instrument that may be played with a bow or plucked. [C19: from Hindi]

sarong (sə'rɒŋ) *n* **1** a garment worn by men and women in the Malay Archipelago, Sri Lanka, etc., consisting of a long piece of cloth tucked around the waist or under the armpits. **2** a western adaptation of this garment, worn by women as beachwear. [C19: from Malay, lit.: sheath]

Saronic Gulf ★ (sə'rɒnɪk) *n* an inlet of the Aegean on the SE coast of Greece. Length: about 80 km (50 miles). Width: about 48 km (30 miles). Also called: (Gulf of) **Aegina**.

saros ('seɪrɒs) *n* a cycle of about 18 years 11 days (6585.32 days) in which eclipses of the sun and moon occur in the same sequence. [C19: from Gk, from Babylonian *šāru* 3600 (years); modern use apparently based on mistaken interpretation of *šāru* as a period of 18½ years]

Saros ★ ('sɑːrɒs) *n* **Gulf of**. an inlet of the Aegean in NW Turkey, north of the Gallipoli Peninsula. Length: 59 km (37 miles). Width: 35 km (22 miles).

Sarpedon ★ (sɑː'piːdɒn) *n Greek myth*. a son of Zeus and Laodameia, or perhaps Europa, and king of Lycia. He was slain by Patroclus while fighting on behalf of the Trojans.

Sarraute ★ (*French* sarot) *n* **Nathalie** (natali). born 1900, French novelist, noted for *Portrait of a Man Unknown* (1947): later works include *Les Fruits d'or* (1963). [C19: after *Sarrus*,

Sarre ★ (sar) *n* the French name for the **Saar**.

sarrusophone (sə'ruːzə,fəʊn) *n* a wind instrument resembling the oboe but made of brass. [C19: after *Sarrus*, F bandmaster, who invented it (1856)]

sarsaparilla (,sɑːsəpə'rɪlə) *n* **1** any of a genus of tropical American prickly climbing plants having large aromatic roots and heart-shaped leaves. **2** the dried roots of any of these plants, formerly used as a medicine. **3** a nonalcoholic drink prepared from these roots. [C16: from Sp. *sarzaparrilla*, from *zarza* a bramble + *-parrilla*, from *parra* a climbing plant]

sarsen ('sɑːs³n) *n* **1** *Geol.* a boulder of silicified sandstone, probably of Tertiary age. **2** such a stone used in a megalithic monument. ◆ Also called: **greywether**. [C17: prob. a var. of SARACEN]

sarsenet ('sɑːsnɪt) *n* a variant spelling of **sarcenet**.

Sarthe ★ (*French* sart) *n* a department of NW France, in Pays de la Loire region. Capital: Le Mans. Pop.: 520 615 (1994 est.). Area: 6245 sq. km (2436 sq. miles).

Sarto ★ (*Italian* 'sarto) *n* **Andrea del** (an'drɛːa del). 1486–1531, Florentine painter. His works include *The Nativity of the Virgin* (1514).

sartorial (sɑː'tɔːrɪəl) *adj* **1** of or relating to a tailor or to tailoring. **2** *Anat.* of the sartorius. [C19: from LL *sartōrius* from L *sartor* a patcher, from *sarcīre* to patch]
▸ **sar'torially** *adv*

sartorius (sɑː'tɔːrɪəs) *n, pl* **sartorii** (-'tɔːrɪ,aɪ). *Anat.* a long ribbon-shaped muscle that aids in flexing the knee. [C18: NL, from *sartorius musculus*, lit.: tailor's muscle, because it is used when one sits in the cross-legged position in which tailors traditionally sat while sewing]

Sartre ★ (*French* sartrə) *n* **Jean-Paul** (ʒãpɔl). 1905–80, French philosopher, novelist, and dramatist; exponent of existentialism. His works include the essay *Being and Nothingness* (1943), the novel *Nausea* (1938), and the play *Huis clos* (1944).

Sarum ★ ('sɛərəm) *n* the ancient name of **Salisbury**[1] (sense 3).

Sarum use *n* the distinctive local rite or system of rites used at Salisbury cathedral in late medieval times.

SAS *abbrev. for* Special Air Service.

Sasebo ★ ('sɑːsə,bəʊ) *n* a port in SW Japan, on NW Kyushu on Omura Bay: naval base. Pop.: 244 879 (1995).

sash[1] (sæʃ) *n* a long piece of ribbon, etc., worn around the waist or over one shoulder, as a symbol of rank. [C16: from Ar. *shāsh* muslin]

sash[2] (sæʃ) *n* **1** a frame that contains the panes of a window or door. **2** a complete frame together with panes of glass. ◆ *vb* **3** (*tr*) to furnish with a sash, sashes, or sash windows. [C17: orig. pl *sashes*, var. of *shashes*, from CHASSIS]

sashay (sæ'ʃeɪ) *vb* (*intr*) *Inf., chiefly US & Canad.* **1** to move, walk, or glide along casually. **2** to move or walk in a showy way; parade. [C19: from an alteration of *chassé*, a gliding dance step]

sash cord *n* a strong cord connecting a sash weight to a sliding sash.

sashimi ('sæʃɪmɪ) *n* a Japanese dish of thin fillets of raw fish. [C19: from Japanese *sashi* pierce + *mi* flesh]

sash saw *n* a small tenon saw used for cutting sashes.

sash weight *n* a weight used to counterbalance the weight of a sliding sash in a sash window and thus hold it in position at any height.

sash window *n* a window consisting of two sashes placed one above the other so that they can be slid past each other.

Saskatchewan ★ (sæs'kætʃɪwən) *n* **1** a province of W Canada: consists of Canadian Shield in the north and open prairie in the south; economy based chiefly on agriculture and mineral resources. Capital: Regina. Pop.: 1 015 600 (1995 est.). Area: 651 900 sq. km (251 700 sq. miles). Abbrev.: **Sask., SK**. **2** a river in W Canada, formed by the confluence of the North and South Saskatchewan Rivers: flows east to Lake Winnipeg. Length: 596 km (370 miles).
▸ **Saskatchewanian** (sæs,kætʃə'wɒnɪən) *n, adj*

Saskatoon ★ (,sæskə'tuːn) *n* a city in W Canada, in S Saskatchewan on the South Saskatchewan River: oil refining; university (1907). Pop.: 186 058 (1991).

sasquatch ('sæs,kwætʃ) *n* (in Canadian folklore) in British Columbia, a hairy beast or manlike monster said to leave huge footprints. [from Amerind]

sass (sæs) *US & Canad. inf.* ◆ *n* **1** impudent talk or behaviour. ◆ *vb* (*intr*) **2** to talk or answer back in such a way. [C20: back formation from SASSY]

sassaby ('sæsəbɪ) *n, pl* **sassabies**. an African antelope of grasslands and semideserts, having angular curved horns. [C19: from Bantu *tshêsêbê*]

sassafras ('sæsə,fræs) *n* **1** an aromatic deciduous tree of North America, having three-lobed leaves and dark blue fruits. **2** the aromatic dried root bark of this tree, used as a flavouring, and yielding **sassafras oil**. **3** *Austral.* any of several unrelated trees having a similar fragrant bark. [C16: from Sp. *sasafras*, from ?]

Sassari ★ (*Italian* 'sassari) *n* a city in NW Sardinia, Italy: the second-largest city on the island; university (1565). Pop.: 122 010 (1994 est.).

Sassenach ('sæsə,næx) *n Scot. & occasionally Irish.* an English person or Lowland Scot. [C18: from Gaelic *Sassunach*, from LL *saxonēs* Saxons]

Sassoon ★ (sæ'su:n) *n* Siegfried (**Lorraine**). 1886–1967, British poet and writer, best known for his poems of World War I. He also wrote a semiautobiographical trilogy *The Memoirs of George Sherston* (1928–36).

sassy ('sæsɪ) *adj* sassier, sassiest. *US & Canad. inf.* insolent; impertinent. [C19: var. of SAUCY]
▸ 'sassily *adv* ▸ 'sassiness *n*

sat (sæt) *vb* the past tense and past participle of **sit**.

Sat. *abbrev. for:* **1** Saturday. **2** Saturn.

Satan ('seɪt°n) *n* the devil, adversary of God, and tempter of mankind: sometimes identified with Lucifer (Luke 4:5–8). [OE, from LL, from Gk, from Heb.: plotter, from *sātan* to plot against]

satanic (sə'tænɪk) *adj* **1** of or relating to Satan. **2** supremely evil or wicked.
▸ sa'tanically *adv*

Satanism ('seɪt°,nɪzəm) *n* **1** the worship of Satan. **2** a form of such worship which includes blasphemous parodies of Christian prayers, etc. **3** a satanic disposition.
▸ 'Satanist *n, adj*

SATB *abbrev. for* soprano, alto, tenor, bass: a combination of voices in choral music.

satchel ('sætʃəl) *n* a rectangular bag, usually made of leather or cloth and provided with a shoulder strap, used for carrying school books. [C14: from OF *sachel*, from LL *saccellus*, from L *saccus* SACK¹]
▸ 'satchelled *adj*

sate¹ (seɪt) *vb* sates, sating, sated. (*tr*) **1** to satisfy (a desire or appetite) fully. **2** to supply beyond capacity or desire. [OE *sadian*]

sate² (sæt, seɪt) *vb Arch.* a past tense and past participle of **sit**.

sateen (sæ'ti:n) *n* a glossy linen or cotton fabric that resembles satin. [C19: changed from SATIN, on the model of VELVETEEN]

satellite ('sæt°,laɪt) *n* **1** a celestial body orbiting around a planet or star: *the earth is a satellite of the sun.* **2** a manmade device orbiting around the earth, moon, or another planet transmitting to earth scientific information or used for communication. **3** a country or political unit under the domination of a foreign power. **4** a subordinate area that is dependent upon a larger adjacent town. **5** (*modifier*) dependent upon another: *a satellite nation.* **6** (*modifier*) subordinate to or dependent upon another: *a satellite nation.* **7** (*modifier*) of, used in, or relating to the transmission of television signals from a satellite to the house: *a satellite dish aerial.* [C16: from L *satelles* an attendant, prob. of Etruscan origin]

satiable ('seɪʃɪəb°l) *adj* capable of being satiated.
▸ ,satia'bility *n* ▸ 'satiably *adv*

satiate ('seɪʃɪ,eɪt) *vb* satiates, satiating, satiated. (*tr*) **1** to fill or supply beyond capacity or desire. **2** to supply to capacity. [C16: from L *satiāre* to satisfy, from *satis* enough]
▸ ,sati'ation *n*

Satie ★ (*French* sati) *n* Erik (**Alfred Leslie**) (erik). 1866–1925, French composer. His music includes piano pieces and several ballets.

satiety (sə'taɪɪtɪ) *n* the state of being satiated. [C16: from L *satietās*, from *satis* enough]

satin ('sætɪn) *n* **1** a fabric of silk, rayon, etc., closely woven to show much of the warp, giving a smooth glossy appearance. **2** (*modifier*) like satin in texture: *a satin finish.* [C14: via OF from Ar. *zaitūnī*, Ar. rendering of Chinese *Tseutung* (now *Tsinkiang*), port from which the cloth was prob. first exported]
▸ 'satiny *adj*

satinet *or* **satinette** (,sætɪ'net) *n* a thin satin or satinlike fabric. [C18: from F: small satin]

satinflower ('sætɪn,flauə) *n* another name for **greater stitchwort** (see **stitchwort**).

satinwood ('sætɪn,wʊd) *n* **1** a tree that occurs in the East Indies and has hard wood with a satiny texture. **2** the wood of this tree, used in veneering, marquetry, etc.

satire ('sætaɪə) *n* **1** a novel, play, etc., in which topical issues, folly, or evil are held up to scorn by means of ridicule. **2** the genre constituted by such works. **3** the use of ridicule, irony, etc., to create such an effect. [C16: from L *satira* a mixture, from *satur* sated, from *satis* enough]

satirical (sə'tɪrɪk°l) *or* **satiric** *adj* **1** of, relating to, or containing satire. **2** given to the use of satire.
▸ sa'tirically *adv*

satirist ('sætərɪst) *n* **1** a person who writes satire. **2** a person given to the use of satire.

satirize *or* **satirise** ('sætə,raɪz) *vb* satirizes, satirizing, satirized *or* satirises, satirising, satirised. to deride (a person or thing) by means of satire.
▸ ,satiri'zation *or* ,satiri'sation *n*

satisfaction (,sætɪs'fækʃən) *n* **1** the act of satisfying or state of being satisfied. **2** the fulfilment of a desire. **3** the pleasure obtained from such fulfilment. **4** a source of fulfilment. **5** compensation for a wrong done or received. **6** *RC Church, Church of England.* the performance of a penance. **7** *Christianity.* the atonement for sin by the death of Christ.

satisfactory (,sætɪs'fæktərɪ) *adj* **1** adequate or suitable; acceptable. **2** giving satisfaction. **3** constituting or involving atonement or expiation for sin.
▸ ,satis'factorily *adv*

satisfice ('sætɪs,faɪs) *vb* satisfices, satisficing, satisficed. **1** (*intr*) to act in such a way as to satisfy the minimum requirements for achieving a particular result. **2** (*tr*) *Obs.* to satisfy. [C16: altered from SATISFY]
▸ 'satis,ficer *n*

satisficing behaviour *n Econ.* the form of behaviour demonstrated by firms who seek satisfactory profits and satisfactory growth rather than maximum profits.

satisfy ('sætɪs,faɪ) *vb* satisfies, satisfying, satisfied. (*mainly tr*) **1** (*also intr*) to fulfil the desires or needs of (a person). **2** to provide amply for (a need or desire). **3** to convince. **4** to dispel (a doubt). **5** to make reparation to or for. **6** to discharge or pay off (a debt) to (a creditor). **7** to fulfil the requirements of; comply with: *you must satisfy the terms of your lease.* **8** *Maths, logic.* to fulfil the conditions of (a theorem, assumption, etc.); to yield a truth by substitution of the given value. [C15: from OF *satisfier*, from L *satisfacere*, from *satis* enough + *facere* to make]
▸ 'satis,fiable *adj* ▸ 'satis,fying *adj* ▸ 'satis,fyingly *adv*

Sato Eisaku ★ ('sɑ:təʊ 'aɪsɑ:,ku:) *n* 1901–75, Japanese statesman: prime minister (1964–72): shared the Nobel peace prize (1974) for opposing the proliferation of nuclear weapons.

satori (sə'tɔ:rɪ) *n Zen Buddhism.* a state of sudden intuitive enlightenment. [from Japanese]

satrap ('sætrəp) *n* **1** (in ancient Persia) a provincial governor. **2** a subordinate ruler. [C14: from L *satrapa*, from Gk *satrapēs*, from OPersian *khshathrapāvan*, lit.: protector of the land]

satrapy ('sætrəpɪ) *n, pl* satrapies. the province, office, or period of rule of a satrap.

SATs (sæts) *pl n Brit. education.* acronym for standard assessment tasks: see **assessment tests**.

satsuma (sæt'su:mə) *n* **1** a small citrus tree cultivated, esp. in Japan, for its edible fruit. **2** the fruit of this tree, which has easily separable segments. [from SATSUMA]

Satsuma ('sætsu,mɑ:) *n* a former province of SW Japan, on S Kyushu: famous for its porcelain.

saturable ('sætʃərəb°l) *adj Chem.* capable of being saturated.
▸ ,satura'bility *n*

saturate *vb* ('sætʃə,reɪt), saturates, saturating, saturated. **1** to fill, soak, or imbue totally. **2** to make (a chemical compound, solution, etc.) saturated or (of a compound, etc.) to become saturated. **3** (*tr*) *Mil.* to bomb or shell heavily.

★ **people and places**

♦ *adj* ('sætʃərɪt, -,reɪt). **4** saturated. [C16: from L *saturāre*, from *satur* sated, from *satis* enough]

saturated ('sætʃə,reɪtɪd) *adj* **1** (of a solution or solvent) containing the maximum amount of solute that can normally be dissolved at a given temperature and pressure. **2** (of a chemical compound) containing no multiple bonds: *a saturated hydrocarbon.* **3** (of a fat) containing a high proportion of fatty acids having single bonds. **4** (of a vapour) containing the maximum amount of gaseous material at a given temperature and pressure.

saturation (,sætʃə'reɪʃən) *n* **1** the act of saturating or the state of being saturated. **2** *Chem.* the state of a chemical compound, solution, or vapour when it is saturated. **3** *Meteorol.* the state of the atmosphere in which it can hold no more water vapour at its particular temperature and pressure. **4** the attribute of a colour that enables an observer to judge its proportion of pure chromatic colour. **5** the level beyond which demand for a product or service is not expected to rise. ♦ *modifier.* **6** denoting the maximum possible intensity of coverage of an area: *saturation bombing.*

saturation point *n* the point at which no more can be absorbed, accommodated, used, etc.

Saturday ('sætədɪ) *n* the seventh and last day of the week: the Jewish Sabbath. [OE *sæternes dæg*, translation of L *Sāturnī diēs* day of Saturn]

Saturn[1] ★ ('sætɜːn) *n* the Roman god of agriculture and vegetation. Greek counterpart: **Cronus.**

Saturn[2] ('sætɜːn) *n* **1** the sixth planet from the sun, around which revolve planar concentric rings (**Saturn's rings**) consisting of small frozen particles. **2** the alchemical name for **lead**[2].
 ▸ **Saturnian** (sæ'tɜːnɪən) *adj*

Saturnalia (,sætə'neɪlɪə) *n, pl* **Saturnalia** or **Saturnalias. 1** an ancient Roman festival celebrated in December: renowned for its general merrymaking. **2** (*sometimes not cap.*) a period or occasion of wild revelry. [C16: from L *Sāturnālis* relating to SATURN[1]]
 ▸ **Satur'nalian** *adj*

saturnine ('sætə,naɪn) *adj* **1** having a gloomy temperament. **2** *Arch.* **2a** of or relating to lead. **2b** having lead poisoning. [C15: from F *saturnin*, from Med. L *sāturnīnus* (unattested), from L *Sāturnus* Saturn, from the gloomy influence attributed to the planet Saturn]
 ▸ **'satur,ninely** *adv*

satyagraha ('sɔːtjɑːgrɔːhɑː) *n* the policy of nonviolent resistance adopted by Mahatma Gandhi to oppose British rule in India. [via Hindi from Sansk., lit.: insistence on truth, from *satya* truth + *agraha* fervour]

satyr ('sætə) *n* **1** *Greek myth.* one of a class of sylvan deities, represented as goatlike men who drank and danced in the train of Dionysus and chased the nymphs. **2** a man who has strong sexual desires. **3** any of various butterflies, having dark wings often marked with eyespots. [C14: from L *satyrus*, from Gk *saturos*]
 ▸ **satyric** (sə'tɪrɪk) *adj*

satyriasis (,sætɪ'raɪəsɪs) *n* a neurotic compulsion in men to have sexual intercourse with many women without being able to have lasting relationships with them. [C17: via NL from Gk *saturiasis*]

sauce (sɔːs) *n* **1** any liquid or semiliquid preparation eaten with food to enhance its flavour. **2** anything that adds piquancy. **3** *US & Canad.* stewed fruit. **4** *Inf.* impudent language or behaviour. ♦ *vb* **sauces, saucing, sauced.** (*tr*) **5** to prepare (food) with sauce. **6** to add zest to. **7** *Inf.* to be saucy to. [C14: via OF from L *salsus* salted, from *sal* salt]

saucepan ('sɔːspən) *n* a metal or enamel pan with a long handle and often a lid, used for cooking food.

saucer ('sɔːsə) *n* **1** a small round dish on which a cup is set. **2** any similar dish. [C14: from OF *saussier* container for SAUCE]
 ▸ **'saucerful** *n*

saucy ('sɔːsɪ) *adj* **saucier, sauciest. 1** impertinent. **2** pert; jaunty: *a saucy hat.*
 ▸ **'saucily** *adv* ▸ **'sauciness** *n*

Saud ★ (saʊd) *n* full name *Saud ibn Abdul-Aziz.* 1902–69,

king of Saudi Arabia (1953–64); son of Ibn Saud. He was deposed by his brother Faisal.

Saudi Arabia ★ ('sɔːdɪ, 'saʊ-) *n* a kingdom in SW Asia, occupying most of the Arabian peninsula between the Persian Gulf and the Red Sea: founded in 1932 by Ibn Saud, who united Hejaz and Nejd; consists mostly of desert plateau; large reserves of petroleum and natural gas. Official language: Arabic. Official religion: (Sunni) Muslim. Currency: riyal. Capital: Riyadh (royal), Jidda (administrative). Pop.: 18 426 000 (1996). Area: 2 260 353 sq. km (872 722 sq. miles).
 ▸ **Saudi** or **Saudi Arabian** *adj, n*

sauerkraut ('saʊə,kraʊt) *n* finely shredded cabbage which has been fermented in brine. [G, from *sauer* sour + *Kraut* cabbage]

sauger ('sɔːgə) *n* a small North American pikeperch with a spotted dorsal fin: valued as a food and game fish. [C19: from ?]

Saul ★ (sɔːl) *n* **1** *Old Testament.* the first king of Israel (?1020–1000 B.C.). He led Israel successfully against the Philistines, but became afflicted with madness and died by his own hand; succeeded by David. **2** *New Testament.* the name borne by Paul prior to his conversion (Acts 9: 1–30).

sault (suː) *n Canad.* a waterfall or rapids. [C17: from Canad. F, from F *saut* a leap]

Sault Sainte Marie ★ ('suː seɪnt mə'riː) *n, usually abbreviated to* **Sault Ste Marie. 1** an inland port in central Canada, in Ontario on the St Mary's River, which links Lake Superior and Lake Huron, opposite Sault Ste Marie, Michigan: canal by-passing the rapids completed in 1895. Pop.: 81 476 (1991). **2** an inland port in NE Michigan, opposite Sault Ste Marie, Ontario: canal around the rapids completed in 1855, enlarged and divided in 1896 and 1919 (popularly called **Soo Canals**). Pop.: 14 689 (1990).

sauna ('sɔːnə) *n* **1** an invigorating bath originating in Finland in which the bather is subjected to hot steam, usually followed by a cold plunge. **2** the place in which such a bath is taken. [C20: from Finnish]

Saunders ★ ('sɔːndəz) *n* Dame **Cicely.** born 1918, British philanthropist: founder of the modern hospice movement. Her books include *Living with Dying* (1983).

saunter ('sɔːntə) *vb* **1** (*intr*) to walk in a casual manner; stroll. ♦ *n* a leisurely pace or stroll. [C17 (meaning: to wander aimlessly), C15 (to muse): from ?]
 ▸ **'saunterer** *n*

-saur or **-saurus** *n combining form.* lizard: *dinosaur.* [from NL *saurus*]

saurian ('sɔːrɪən) *adj* **1** of or resembling a lizard. ♦ *n* **2** a former name for **lizard.** [C15: from NL *Sauria*, from Gk *sauros*]

saury ('sɔːrɪ) *n, pl* **sauries.** a fish of tropical and temperate seas, having an elongated body and long toothed jaws. Also called: **skipper.** [C18: ?from LL *saurus*, from ?]

sausage ('sɒsɪdʒ) *n* **1** finely minced meat, esp. pork or beef, mixed with fat, cereal, and seasonings (**sausage meat**), and packed into a tube-shaped edible casing. **2** *Scot.* sausage meat. **3** an object shaped like a sausage. **4** **not a sausage.** nothing at all. [C15: from OF *saussiche*, from LL *salsīcia*, from L *salsus* salted; see SAUCE]

sausage dog *n* an informal name for **dachshund.**

sausage roll *n Brit.* a roll of sausage meat in pastry.

Saussure ★ (*French* sosyr) *n* **Ferdinand de** (ferdinɑ̃ də). 1857–1913, Swiss linguist, who pioneered structuralism in linguistics.
 ▸ **Saus'surean** *adj, n*

sauté ('səʊteɪ) *vb* **sautés, sautéing** or **sautéeing, sautéed. 1** to fry (food) quickly in a little fat. ♦ *n* **2** a dish of sautéed food, esp. meat that is browned and then cooked in a sauce. ♦ *adj* **3** sautéed until lightly brown: *sauté potatoes.* [C19: from F: tossed, from *sauter* to jump, from L, from *salīre* to spring]

Sava ('sɑːvə) or **Save** ★ (sɑːv) *n* a river in SE Europe, rising in NW Slovenia and flowing east and south to the Danube at Belgrade. Length: 940 km (584 miles).

savage ('sævɪdʒ) *adj* **1** wild; untamed: *savage beasts.* **2** fe-

rocious in temper: *a savage dog.* **3** uncivilized; crude: *savage behaviour.* **4** (of peoples) nonliterate or primitive: *a savage tribe.* **5** (of terrain) rugged and uncultivated. ◆ *n* **6** a member of a nonliterate society, esp. one regarded as primitive. **7** a fierce or vicious person or animal. ◆ *vb* **savages, savaging, savaged.** (*tr*) **8** to criticize violently. **9** to attack ferociously and wound. [C13: from OF *sauvage*, from L *silvāticus* belonging to a wood, from *silva* a wood]
▶ '**savagely** *adv* ▶ '**savageness** *n*

Savage ★ ('sævidʒ) *n* **Michael Joseph.** 1872–1940, New Zealand statesman; prime minister (1935-40).

Savage Island ★ *n* another name for **Niue.**

savagery ('sævidʒri) *n, pl* **savageries. 1** an uncivilized condition. **2** a savage act or nature. **3** savages collectively.

Savaii ★ (saː'vaiː) *n* the largest island in Samoa: mountainous and volcanic. Pop.: 44 930 (1986). Area: 1174 sq. km (662 sq. miles).

savanna *or* **savannah** (sə'vænə) *n* open grasslands, usually with scattered bushes or trees, characteristic of much of tropical Africa. [C16: from Sp. *zavana*, from Amerind *zabana*]

Savannah ★ (sə'vænə) *n* **1** a port in E Georgia, near the mouth of the Savannah River: port of departure of the *Savannah* for Liverpool (1819), the first steamship to cross the Atlantic. Pop.: 140 597 (1994 est.). **2** a river in the southeastern US, formed by the confluence of the Tugaloo and Seneca Rivers in NW South Carolina: flows southeast to the Atlantic. Length: 505 km (314 miles).

savant ('sævənt) *n* a man of great learning; sage. [C18: from F, from *savoir* to know, from L *sapere* to be wise]
▶ '**savante** *fem n*

savate (sə'væt) *n* a form of boxing in which blows may be delivered with the feet as well as the hands. [C19: from F, lit.: old worn-out shoe]

save[1] (seiv) *vb* **saves, saving, saved. 1** (*tr*) to rescue, preserve, or guard (a person or thing) from danger or harm. **2** to avoid the spending, waste, or loss of (money, possessions, etc.). **3** (*tr*) to deliver from sin; redeem. **4** (often foll. by *up*) to set aside or reserve (money, goods, etc.) for future use. **5** (*tr*) to treat with care so as to avoid or lessen wear or degeneration. **6** (*tr*) to prevent the necessity for; obviate the trouble of. **7** (*tr*) *Soccer, hockey, etc.* to prevent (a goal) by stopping (a struck ball or puck). ◆ *n* **8** *Soccer, hockey, etc.* the act of saving a goal. **9** *Computing.* an instruction to write information from the memory onto a tape or disk. [C13: from OF *salver*, via LL from L *salvus* safe]
▶ '**savable** *or* '**saveable** *adj* ▶ '**saver** *n*

save[2] (seiv) *Arch.* ◆ *prep* **1** (often foll. by *for*) Also: **saving.** with the exception of. ◆ *conj* **2** but. [C13 *sauf*, from OF, from L *salvō*, from *salvus* safe]

save as you earn *n* (in Britain) a savings scheme operated by the government, in which monthly contributions earn tax-free interest. Abbrev.: **SAYE.**

saveloy ('sævɪˌlɔɪ) *n* a smoked sausage made from salted pork, coloured red with saltpetre. [C19: prob. via F from It. *cervellato*, from *cervello* brain, from L, from *cerebrum* brain]

Savery ★ ('seɪvəri) *n* **Thomas.** ?1650–1715, English engineer, who built (1698) the first practical steam engine, used to pump water from mines.

savin *or* **savine** ('sævin) *n* **1** a small spreading juniper bush of Europe, N Asia, and North America. **2** the oil derived from the shoots and leaves of this plant, formerly used in medicine to treat rheumatism, etc. [C14: from OF *savine*, from L *herba Sabīna* the Sabine plant]

saving ('seɪvɪŋ) *adj* **1** tending to save or preserve. **2** redeeming or compensating (esp. in **saving grace**). **3** thrifty or economical. **4** *Law.* denoting or relating to an exception or reservation: *a saving clause in an agreement.* ◆ *n* **5** preservation or redemption. **6** economy or avoidance of waste. **7** reduction in cost or expenditure. **8** anything saved. **9** (*pl*) money saved for future use. ◆ *prep* **10** with the exception of. ◆ *conj* **11** except.
▶ '**savingly** *adv*

savings bank *n* a bank that accepts the savings of depositors and pays interest on them.

savings ratio *n Econ.* the ratio of personal savings to disposable income, esp. using the difference between national figures for disposable income and consumer spending as a measure of savings.

saviour *or US* **savior** ('seɪvjə) *n* a person who rescues another person or a thing from danger or harm. [C13 *saveour*, from OF, from Church L *Salvātor* the Saviour]

Saviour *or US* **Savior** ('seɪvjə) *n Christianity.* Jesus Christ regarded as the saviour of men from sin.

Savoie ★ (*French* savwa) *n* **1** a department of E France, in Rhône-Alpes region. Capital: Chambéry. Pop.: 365 392 (1994 est.). Area: 6188 sq. km (2413 sq. miles). **2** the French name for **Savoy**[1].

savoir-faire ('sævwɑː'fɛə) *n* the ability to do the right thing in any situation. [F, lit.: a knowing how to do]

Savona ★ (*Italian* sa'voːna) *n* a port in NW Italy, in Liguria on the Mediterranean: an important centre of the Italian iron and steel industry. Pop.: 69 806 (1990).

Savonarola ★ (*Italian* savona'rɔːla) *n* **Girolamo** (dʒi'rɔːlamo). 1452–98, Italian religious and political reformer. When the Medici were expelled from Florence (1494) he instituted a puritanical republic but lost the citizens' support after being excommunicated (1497); hanged as a heretic.

savory ('seɪvəri) *n, pl* **savories. 1** any of numerous aromatic plants, including the **winter savory** and **summer savory**, of the Mediterranean region, having narrow leaves and white, pink, or purple flowers. **2** the leaves of any of these plants, used as a potherb. [C14: prob. from OE *sætherie*, from L *satureia*, from ?]

savour *or US* **savor** ('seɪvə) *n* **1** the quality in a substance that is perceived by the sense of taste or smell. **2** a specific taste or smell: *the savour of lime.* **3** a slight but distinctive quality or trace. **4** the power to excite interest: *the savour of wit has been lost.* ◆ *vb* **5** (*intr*; often foll. by *of*) to possess the taste or smell (of). **6** (*intr*; often foll. by *of*) to have a suggestion (of). **7** (*tr*) to season. **8** (*tr*) to taste or smell, esp. appreciatively. **9** (*tr*) to relish or enjoy. [C13: from OF *savour*, from L *sapor* taste, from *sapere* to taste]
▶ '**savourless** *or US* '**savorless** *adj*

savoury *or US* **savory** ('seɪvəri) *adj* **1** attractive to the sense of taste or smell. **2** salty or spicy: *a savoury dish.* **3** pleasant. **4** respectable. ◆ *n, pl* **savouries** *or US* **savories.** Chiefly *Brit.* a savoury dish served as an hors d'oeuvre or dessert. [C13 *savure*, from OF, from *savourer* to SAVOUR]
▶ '**savouriness** *or US* '**savoriness** *n*

savoy (sə'vɔɪ) *n* a cultivated variety of cabbage having a compact head and wrinkled leaves. [C16: after the Savoy region]

Savoy[1] ★ (sə'vɔɪ) *n* an area of SE France, bordering on Italy, mainly in the Savoy Alps: a duchy in the late Middle Ages and part of the Kingdom of Sardinia from 1720 to 1860, when it became part of France. French name: **Savoie.**

Savoy[2] ★ (sə'vɔɪ) *n* a noble family of Italy that ruled over the duchy of Savoy and became the royal house of Italy (1861–1946): the oldest reigning dynasty in Europe before the dissolution of the Italian monarchy.

Savoy Alps ★ *pl n* a range of the Alps in SE France. Highest peak: Mont Blanc, 4807 m (15 772 ft).

Savoyard (sə'vɔɪɑːd; *French* savwajar) *n* **1** a native of Savoy. **2** the dialect of French spoken in Savoy. ◆ *adj* **3** of or relating to Savoy, its inhabitants, or their dialect.

savvy ('sævi) *Sl.* ◆ *vb* **savvies, savvying, savvied. 1** to understand or get the sense of (an idea, etc.). ◆ *n* **2** comprehension. ◆ *adj* **savvier, savviest. 3** Chiefly *US.* shrewd. [C18: corruption of Sp. *sabe* (*usted*) (you) know, from *saber* to know, from L *sapere* to be wise]

saw[1] (sɔː) *n* **1** any of various hand tools for cutting wood, metal, etc., having a blade with teeth along one edge. **2** any of various machines or devices for cutting by use of a toothed blade, such as a power-driven toothed band of metal. ◆ *vb* **saws, sawing, sawed; sawed** *or* **sawn. 3** to cut with a saw. **4** to form by sawing. **5** to cut as if wielding a saw: *to saw the air.* **6** to move (an object) from side to side as if moving a saw. [OE *sagu*: rel. to L *secare* to cut]
▶ '**sawer** *n* ▶ '**saw,like** *adj*

★ people and places

saw[2] (sɔː) *vb* the past tense of **see**[1].

saw[3] (sɔː) *n* a wise saying, maxim, or proverb. [OE *sagu* a saying]

sawbones ('sɔːˌbəʊnz) *n, pl* **sawbones** or **sawboneses**. *Sl.* a surgeon or doctor.

sawdust ('sɔːˌdʌst) *n* particles of wood formed by sawing.

sawfish ('sɔːˌfɪʃ) *n, pl* **sawfish** or **sawfishes**. a sharklike ray of subtropical coastal waters, having a serrated bladelike mouth.

sawfly ('sɔːˌflaɪ) *n, pl* **sawflies**. any of various hymenopterous insects, the females of which have a sawlike ovipositor.

sawhorse ('sɔːˌhɔːs) *n* a stand for timber during sawing.

sawmill ('sɔːˌmɪl) *n* an industrial establishment where timber is sawn into planks, etc.

sawn (sɔːn) *vb* a past participle of **saw**[1].

sawn-off or *esp. US* **sawed-off** *adj (prenominal)* (of a shotgun) having the barrel cut short, mainly to facilitate concealment of the weapon.

saw set *n* a tool used for setting the teeth of a saw, consisting of a clamp used to bend each tooth at a slight angle to the plane of the saw, alternate teeth being bent in the same direction.

sawyer ('sɔːjə) *n* a person who saws timber for a living. [C14 *sawier*, from SAW[1] + *-ier*, var. of -ER[1]]

sax (sæks) *n Inf.* short for **saxophone**.

Sax. *abbrev. for:* **1** Saxon. **2** Saxony.

Saxe[1] ★ (saks) *n* the French name for **Saxony**.

Saxe[2] ★ (*French* saks) *n* **Hermann Maurice** (ɛrman mɔris) comte de Saxe. 1696–1750, French marshal in the War of the Austrian Succession (1740–48).

saxe blue (sæks) *n* **a** a light greyish-blue colour. **b** (*as adj*): *a saxe-blue dress.* [C19: from F *Saxe* Saxony, source of a dye of this colour]

Saxe-Coburg-Gotha ★ (sæks'kəʊbɜːg'gəʊθə) *n* the ruling house of the former German duchy of Saxe-Coburg-Gotha (until 1918) and the name of the British royal family (1901–17) through Prince Albert.

saxhorn ('sæksˌhɔːn) *n* a valved brass instrument used chiefly in brass and military bands, having a tube of conical bore. It resembles the tuba. [C19: after Adolphe *Sax* (see SAXOPHONE), who invented it (1845)]

saxicolous (sæk'sɪkələs) *adj* living on or among rocks: *saxicolous plants.* Also: **saxicole** ('sæksɪˌkəʊl), **saxatile** ('sæksəˌtaɪl). [C19: from NL *saxicolus*, from L *saxum* rock + *colere* to dwell]

saxifrage ('sæksɪˌfreɪdʒ) *n* a plant having small white, yellow, purple, or pink flowers. [C15: from LL *saxifraga*, lit.: rock-breaker, from L *saxum* rock + *frangere* to break]

Saxo Grammaticus ★ ('sæksəʊ grə'mætɪkəs) *n* ?1150–?1220, Danish chronicler, noted for his *Gesta Danorum*, a partly legendary history of Denmark, which contains the Hamlet (Amleth) legend.

Saxon ('sæksən) *n* **1** a member of a West Germanic people who raided and settled parts of S Britain in the fifth and sixth centuries A.D. **2** a native or inhabitant of Saxony. **3a** the Low German dialect of Saxony. **3b** any of the West Germanic dialects spoken by the ancient Saxons. ◆ *adj* **4** of or characteristic of the ancient Saxons, the Anglo-Saxons, or their descendants. **5** of or characteristic of Saxony, its inhabitants, or their Low German dialect. [C13 (replacing OE *Seaxe*): via OF from LL *Saxon-*, *Saxo*, from Gk; of Gmc origin]

Saxony ★ ('sæksənɪ) *n* **1** a state in E Germany, formerly part of East Germany. Pop.: 4 584 300 (1995 est.). **2** a former duchy and electorate in SE and central Germany, whose territory changed greatly over the centuries. **3** (in the early Middle Ages) any territory inhabited or ruled by Saxons. ◆ Cf. **Saxony-Anhalt, Lower Saxony.** German name: **Sachsen.** French name: **Saxe.**

Saxony-Anhalt ★ ('sæksənɪ'ænhælt) *n* a state of E Germany: created in 1947 from the state of Anhalt and those parts of Prussia formerly ruled by the duchy of Saxony: part of East Germany until 1990. Pop.: 2 759 200 (1995 est.).

saxophone ('sæksəˌfəʊn) *n* a keyed single-reed wind instrument of mellow tone colour, used mainly in jazz and dance music. Often shortened to **sax.** [C19: after Adolphe *Sax* (1814–94), Belgian musical-instrument maker, who invented it (1846)]
▶ **saxophonic** (ˌsæksə'fɒnɪk) *adj* ▶ **saxophonist** (sæk-'sɒfənɪst) *n*

say (seɪ) *vb* **says, saying, said.** (*mainly tr*) **1** to speak, pronounce, or utter. **2** (*also intr*) to express (an idea, etc.) in words; tell. **3** (*also intr; may take a clause as object*) to state (an opinion, fact, etc.) positively. **4** to recite: *to say grace.* **5** (*may take a clause as object*) to report or allege: *they say we shall have rain today.* **6** (*may take a clause as object*) to suppose: *let us say that he is lying.* **7** (*may take a clause as object*) to convey by means of artistic expression. **8** to make a case for: *there is much to be said for it.* **9 go without saying.** to be so obvious as to need no explanation. **10 I say!** *Inf., chiefly Brit.* an exclamation of surprise. **11 not to say.** even. **12 that is to say.** in other words. **13 to say the least.** at the very least. ◆ *adv* **14** approximately: *there were, say, 20 people present.* **15** for example: *choose a number, say, four.* ◆ *n* **16** the right or chance to speak: *let him have his say.* **17** authority, esp. to influence a decision: *he has a lot of say.* **18** a statement of opinion: *you've had your say.* ◆ *interj* **19** *US & Canad. inf.* an exclamation to attract attention or express surprise. [OE *secgan*]
▶ **'sayer** *n*

Sayan Mountains ★ (sɑː'jæn) *pl n* a mountain range in S central Russia, in S Siberia. Highest peak: Munku-Sardyk, 3437 m (11 457 ft).

SAYE (in Britain) *abbrev. for* save as you earn.

Sayers ★ ('seɪəz) *n* **Dorothy L(eigh).** 1893–1957, British detective-story writer.

saying ('seɪɪŋ) *n* a maxim, adage, or proverb.

say-so *n Inf.* **1** an arbitrary assertion. **2** an authoritative decision. **3** the authority to make a final decision.

sayyid ('saɪɪd) or **said** *n* **1** a Muslim claiming descent from Mohammed's grandson Husain. **2** a Muslim honorary title. [C17: from Ar.: lord]

Sb *the chemical symbol for* antimony. [from NL *stibium*]

SBU *abbrev. for* strategic business unit: a division within an organization responsible for marketing its own range of products.

sc *Printing. abbrev. for* small capitals.

Sc *the chemical symbol for* scandium.

SC *abbrev. for:* **1** *NZ.* School Certificate. **2** Signal Corps. **3** *Canad.* Social Credit.

sc. *abbrev. for:* **1** scale. **2** scene. **3** science. **4** scilicet. **5** screw. **6** scruple (unit of weight).

scab (skæb) *n* **1** the dried crusty surface of a healing skin wound or sore. **2** a contagious disease of sheep resembling mange, caused by a mite. **3** a fungal disease of plants characterized by crusty spots on the fruits, leaves, etc. **4** *Derog.* **4a** Also called: **blackleg.** a person who refuses to support a trade union's actions, esp. strikes. **4b** (*as modifier*): *scab labour.* **5** a despicable person. ◆ *vb* **scabs, scabbing, scabbed.** (*intr*) **6** to become covered with a scab. **7** to replace a striking worker. [OE *sceabb*]

scabbard ('skæbəd) *n* a holder for a bladed weapon such as a sword or bayonet. [C13 *scauberc*, from Norman F *escaubers*, (pl) of Gmc origin]

scabby ('skæbɪ) *adj* **scabbier, scabbiest. 1** *Pathol.* having an area of the skin covered with scabs. **2** *Pathol.* having scabies. **3** *Inf.* despicable.
▶ **'scabbily** *adv* ▶ **'scabbiness** *n*

scabies ('skeɪbiːz) *n* a contagious skin infection caused by a mite, characterized by intense itching and inflammation. [C15: from L: scurf, from *scabere* to scratch]

scabious[1] ('skeɪbɪəs) *adj* **1** having or covered with scabs. **2** of, relating to, or resembling scabies. [C17: from L *scabiōsus*, from SCABIES]

scabious[2] ('skeɪbɪəs) *n* any of a genus of plants of the Mediterranean region, having blue, red, or whitish dome-shaped flower heads. [C14: from Med. L *scabiōsa herba* the scabies plant, referring to its use in treating scabies]

scabrous ('skeɪbrəs) *adj* **1** roughened because of small

projections. **2** indecent or salacious: *scabrous humour.* **3** difficult to deal with. [C17: from L *scaber* rough]
▶ '**scabrously** *adv*

scad (skæd) *n, pl* **scad** or **scads**. any of various marine fishes having a deeply forked tail, such as the large mackerel. [C17: from ?]

scads (skædz) *pl n Inf.* a large amount or number. [C19: from ?]

Scafell Pike ★ (skɔː'fel) *n* a mountain in NW England, in Cumbria in the Lake District: the highest peak in England. Height: 978 m (3209 ft).

scaffold ('skæfəld) *n* **1** a temporary framework that is used to support workmen and materials during the erection, repair, etc., of a building. **2** a raised wooden platform on which plays are performed, tobacco, etc., is dried, or (esp. formerly) criminals are executed. ◆ *vb (tr)* **3** to provide with a scaffold. **4** to support by means of a scaffold. [C14: from OF *eschaffaut*, from Vulgar L *catafalicum* (unattested)]
▶ '**scaffolder** *n*

scaffolding ('skæfəldɪŋ) *n* **1** a scaffold or system of scaffolds. **2** the building materials used to make scaffolds.

Scala ★ ('skaːla) *n* **La.** See **La Scala.**

scalable ('skeɪləbʰl) *adj* capable of being climbed.
▶ '**scalableness** *n* ▶ '**scalably** *adv*

scalar ('skeɪlə) *n* **1** a quantity, such as time or temperature, that has magnitude but not direction. **2** *Maths.* an element of a field associated with a vector space. ◆ *adj* **3** having magnitude but not direction. [C17 (meaning: resembling a ladder): from L *scālāris*, from *scāla* ladder]

scalar product *n* the product of two vectors to form a scalar, whose value is the product of the magnitudes of the vectors and the cosine of the angle between them. Also called: **dot product.**

scalawag ('skæləˌwæg) *n* a variant of **scallywag.**

scald[1] (skɔːld) *vb* **1** to burn or be burnt with or as if with hot liquid or steam. **2** (*tr*) to subject to the action of boiling water, so as to sterilize. **3** (*tr*) to heat (a liquid) almost to boiling point. **4** to plunge (tomatoes, etc.) into boiling water in order to skin them more easily. ◆ *n* **5** the act or result of scalding. **6** an abnormal condition in plants, caused by exposure to excessive sunlight, gases, etc. [C13: via OF from LL *excaldāre* to wash in warm water, from *calida* (*aqua*) warm (water), from *calēre* to be warm]
▶ '**scalder** *n*

scald[2] (skɔːld) *n* a variant spelling of **skald.**

scaldfish ('skɔːldˌfɪʃ, 'skaːld-) *n, pl* **scaldfish** or **scaldfishes.** a small European flatfish, covered with large fragile scales.

scale[1] (skeɪl) *n* **1** any of the numerous plates, made of various substances, covering the bodies of fishes. **2a** any of the horny or chitinous plates covering a part or the entire body of certain reptiles and mammals. **2b** any of the numerous minute structures covering the wings of lepidoptera. **3** a thin flat piece or flake. **4** a thin flake of dead epidermis shed from the skin. **5** a specialized leaf or bract, esp. the protective covering of a bud or the dry membranous bract of a catkin. **6** See **scale insect. 7** any oxide formed on a metal when heated. **8** tartar formed on the teeth. ◆ *vb* **scales, scaling, scaled. 9** (*tr*) to remove the scales or coating from. **10** to peel off or cause to peel off in flakes or scales. **11** (*intr*) to shed scales. **12** to cover or become covered with scales, incrustation, etc. [C14: from OF *escale*, of Gmc origin]

scale[2] (skeɪl) *n* **1** (*often pl*) a machine or device for weighing. **2** one of the pans of a balance. **3 tip the scales. 3a** to exercise a decisive influence. **3b** (foll. by *at*) to amount in weight (to). ◆ *vb* **scales, scaling, scaled.** (*tr*) **4** to weigh with or as if with scales. [C13: from ON *skál* bowl]

scale[3] (skeɪl) *n* **1** a sequence of marks either at regular intervals, or representing equal steps, used as a reference in making measurements. **2** a measuring instrument having such a scale. **3a** the ratio between the size of something real and that of a representation of it. **3b** (*as modifier*): *a scale model.* **4** a line, numerical ratio, etc., for showing this ratio. **5** a progressive or graduated table of things, wages, etc.: *a wage scale for carpenters.* **6** an estab-

lished standard. **7** a relative degree or extent: *he entertained on a grand scale.* **8** *Music.* a group of notes taken in ascending or descending order, esp. within the compass of one octave. **9** *Maths.* the notation of a given number system: *the decimal scale.* ◆ *vb* **scales, scaling, scaled. 10** to climb to the top of (a height) by or as if by a ladder. **11** (*tr*) to make or draw (a model, etc.) according to a particular ratio of proportionate reduction. **12** (*tr*; usually foll. by *up* or *down*) to increase or reduce proportionately in size, etc. **13** (*intr*) *Austral. inf.* to ride on public transport without paying a fare. [C15: via It. from L *scāla* ladder]

scaleboard ('skeɪlˌbɔːd) *n* a very thin piece of board, used for backing a picture, etc.

scale insect *n* a small insect which typically lives and feeds on plants and secretes a protective scale around itself. Many species are pests.

scalene ('skeɪliːn) *adj* **1** *Maths.* (of a triangle) having all sides of unequal length. **2** *Anat.* of or relating to any of the scalenus muscles. [C17: from LL *scalēnus* with unequal sides, from Gk *skalēnos*]

scalenus (skə'liːnəs) *n, pl* **scaleni** (-naɪ). *Anat.* any one of the three muscles situated on each side of the neck extending from the cervical vertebrae to the first or second pair of ribs. [C18: from NL; see SCALENE]

scaling ladder *n* a ladder used to climb high walls, esp. one used formerly to enter a besieged town, fortress, etc.

scallion ('skæljən) *n* any of various onions, such as the spring onion, that have a small bulb and long leaves and are eaten in salads. [C14: from Anglo-F *scalun*, from L *Ascalōnia* (*caepa*) Ascalonian (onion), from *Ascalo* Ascalon, a Palestinian port]

scallop ('skɒləp, 'skæl-) *n* **1** any of various marine bivalves having a fluted fan-shaped shell. **2** the edible adductor muscle of certain of these molluscs. **3** either of the shell valves of any of these molluscs. **4** a scallop shell in which fish, esp. shellfish, is cooked and served. **5** one of a series of curves along an edge. **6** the shape of a scallop shell used as the badge of a pilgrim, esp. in the Middle Ages. **7** *Chiefly Austral.* a potato cake fried in batter. ◆ *vb* **8** (*tr*) to decorate (an edge) with scallops. **9** to bake (food) in a scallop shell or similar dish. [C14: from OF *escalope* shell, of Gmc origin]
▶ '**scalloper** *n* ▶ '**scalloping** *n*

scally ('skælɪ) *n, pl* **scallies.** *Northwest English dialect.* a rascal; rogue. [C20: from SCALLYWAG]

scallywag ('skælɪˌwæg) *n Inf.* a scamp; rascal. ◆ Also: **scalawag, scallawag.** [C19: (orig. undersized animal): from ?]

scalp (skælp) *n* **1** *Anat.* the skin and subcutaneous tissue covering the top of the head. **2** (among North American Indians) a part of this removed as a trophy from a slain enemy. **3** a trophy or token signifying conquest. **4** *Scot. dialect.* a projection of bare rock from vegetation. ◆ *vb* (*tr*) **5** to cut the scalp from. **6** *Inf., chiefly US.* to purchase and resell (securities) quickly so as to make several small profits. **7** *Inf.* to buy (tickets) cheaply and resell at an inflated price. [C13: prob. from ON]
▶ '**scalper** *n*

scalpel ('skælpʰl) *n* a surgical knife with a short thin blade. [C18: from L *scalpellum*, from *scalper* a knife, from *scalpere* to scrape]

scaly ('skeɪlɪ) *adj* **scalier, scaliest. 1** resembling or covered in scales. **2** peeling off in scales.
▶ '**scaliness** *n*

scaly anteater *n* another name for **pangolin.**

Scamander ★ (skə'mændə) *n* the ancient name for the **Menderes** (sense 2).

scamp[1] (skæmp) *n* **1** an idle mischievous person. **2** a mischievous child. [C18: from *scamp* (vb) to be a highway robber, prob. from MDu. *schampen* to decamp, from OF *escamper*, from L *campus* field]
▶ '**scampish** *adj*

scamp[2] (skæmp) *vb* a less common word for **skimp.**
▶ '**scamper** *n*

scamper ('skæmpə) *vb* **1** (*intr*) to run about playfully. **2** (often foll. by *through*) to hurry through (a place, task, etc.) ◆ *n* **3** the act of scampering. [C17: prob. from *scamp* (vb); see SCAMP[1]]

scampi ('skæmpɪ) *n* (*usually functioning as sing*) large prawns, usually eaten fried in breadcrumbs. [It.: pl of *scampo* shrimp, from ?]

scan (skæn) *vb* **scans, scanning, scanned. 1** (*tr*) to scrutinize minutely. **2** (*tr*) to glance at quickly. **3** (*tr*) *Prosody*. to read or analyse (verse) according to the rules of metre and versification. **4** (*intr*) *Prosody*. to conform to the rules of metre and versification. **5** (*tr*) *Electronics*. to move a beam of light, electrons, etc., in a predetermined pattern over (a surface or region) to obtain information, esp. to reproduce a television image. **6** (*tr*) to examine data stored on (magnetic tape, etc.), usually in order to retrieve information. **7** to examine or search (a prescribed region) by systematically varying the direction of a radar or sonar beam. **8** *Med.* to obtain an image of (a part of the body) by means of a scanner. ◆ *n* **9** the act or an instance of scanning. **10** *Med.* **10a** the examination of a part of the body by means of a scanner: *a brain scan; an ultrasound scan*. **10b** the image produced by a scanner. [C14: from LL *scandere* to scan (verse), from L: to climb]
▸ 'scannable *adj*

Scand. or **Scan.** *abbrev.* for Scandinavia(n).

scandal ('skænd°l) *n* **1** a disgraceful action or event: *his negligence was a scandal*. **2** censure or outrage arising from an action or event. **3** a person whose conduct causes reproach or disgrace. **4** malicious talk, esp. gossip. **5** *Law*. a libellous action or statement. [C16: from LL *scandalum* stumbling block, from Gk *skandalon* a trap]
▸ 'scandalous *adj* ▸ 'scandalously *adv*

scandalize or **scandalise** ('skændə,laɪz) *vb* **scandalizes, scandalizing, scandalized** or **scandalises, scandalising, scandalised.** (*tr*) to shock, as by improper behaviour.
▸ ,scandali'zation or ,scandali'sation *n*

scandalmonger ('skænd°l,mʌŋgə) *n* a person who spreads or enjoys scandal, gossip, etc.

Scandinavia ★ (,skændɪ'neɪvɪə) *n* **1** Also called: **the Scandinavian Peninsula.** the peninsula of N Europe occupied by Norway and Sweden. **2** the countries of N Europe, esp. considered as a cultural unit and including Norway, Sweden, Denmark, and often Finland, Iceland, and the Faeroe Islands.
▸ ,Scandi'navian *adj, n*

scandium ('skændɪəm) *n* a rare silvery-white metallic element occurring in minute quantities in numerous minerals. Symbol: Sc; atomic no.: 21; atomic wt.: 44.96. [C19: from NL, from L *Scandia* Scandinavia, where discovered]

scanner ('skænə) *n* **1** a person or thing that scans. **2** a device, usually electronic, used to measure or sample the distribution of some quantity or condition in a particular system, region, or area. **3** an aerial or similar device designed to transmit or receive signals, esp. radar signals, inside a given solid angle of space. **4** any device used in medical diagnosis to obtain an image of an internal organ or part. **5** short for **optical scanner.**

scanning electron microscope *n* a type of electron microscope that produces a three-dimensional image.

scansion ('skænʃən) *n* the analysis of the metrical structure of verse. [C17: from L: climbing up, from *scandere* to climb]

scant (skænt) *adj* **1** scarcely sufficient: *he paid her scant attention*. **2** (*prenominal*) bare: *a scant ten inches*. **3** (*postpositive;* foll. by *of*) having a short supply (of). ◆ *vb* (*tr*) **4** to limit in size or quantity. **5** to provide with a limited supply of. **6** to treat in an inadequate manner. ◆ *adv* **7** scarcely; barely. [C14: from ON *skamt*, from *skammr* short]
▸ 'scantly *adv*

scantling ('skæntlɪŋ) *n* **1** a piece of sawn timber, such as a rafter, that has a small cross section. **2** the dimensions of a piece of building material or the structural parts of a ship or aircraft. **3** a building stone. **4** a small quantity or amount. [C16: changed (through infl. of SCANT & -LING[1]) from earlier *scantillon* a carpenter's gauge, from OF *escantillon*, ult. from L *scandere* to climb]

scanty ('skæntɪ) *adj* **scantier, scantiest. 1** limited; barely enough. **2** inadequate. **3** lacking fullness.
▸ 'scantily *adv* ▸ 'scantiness *n*

Scapa Flow ★ ('skɑːpə) *n* an extensive landlocked anchorage off the N coast of Scotland, in the Orkney Islands: major British naval base in both World Wars. Length: about 24 km (15 miles). Width: 13 km (8 miles).

scape or **'scape** (skeɪp) *vb* **scapes, scaping, scaped,** *n* an archaic word for **escape.**

-scape *suffix forming nouns.* indicating a scene or view of something: *seascape*. [from LANDSCAPE]

scapegoat ('skeɪp,gəʊt) *n* **1** a person made to bear the blame for others. **2** *Bible.* a goat symbolically laden with the sins of the Israelites and sent into the wilderness. ◆ *vb* **3** (*tr*) to make a scapegoat of. [C16: from ESCAPE + GOAT, coined by William Tyndale to translate Biblical Heb. *azāzēl* (prob.) goat for Azazel, mistakenly thought to mean "goat that escapes"]

scapegrace ('skeɪp,greɪs) *n* a mischievous person. [C19: from SCAPE + GRACE, alluding to a person who lacks God's grace]

scaphoid ('skæfɔɪd) *adj Anat.* an obsolete word for **navicular.** [C18: via NL from Gk *skaphoeidēs*, from *skaphē* boat]

scapula ('skæpjʊlə) *n, pl* **scapulae** (-liː) or **scapulas.** either of two large flat triangular bones, one on each side of the back part of the shoulder in man. Nontechnical name: **shoulder blade.** [C16: from LL: shoulder]

scapular ('skæpjʊlə) *adj* **1** *Anat.* of or relating to the scapula. ◆ *n* **2** part of the monastic habit worn by members of many Christian religious orders, consisting of a piece of woollen cloth worn over the shoulders, and hanging down to the ankles. **3** two small rectangular pieces of cloth joined by tapes passing over the shoulders and worn in token of affiliation to a religious order. **4** any of the small feathers of a bird that lie along the shoulder. ◆ Also called (for senses 2 and 3): **scapulary.**

scar[1] (skɑː) *n* **1** any mark left on the skin or other tissue following the healing of a wound, etc. **2** a permanent change in a person's character resulting from emotional distress. **3** the mark on a plant indicating the former point of attachment of a part. **4** a mark of damage. ◆ *vb* **scars, scarring, scarred. 5** to mark or become marked with a scar. **6** (*intr*) to heal leaving a scar. [C14: via LL from Gk *eskhara* scab]

scar[2] (skɑː) *n* a bare craggy rock formation. [C14: from ON *sker* low reef]

scarab ('skærəb) *n* **1** any scarabaeid beetle, esp. the **sacred scarab,** regarded by the ancient Egyptians as divine. **2** the scarab as represented on amulets, etc. [C16: from L *scarabaeus*]

scarabaeid (,skærə'biːɪd) *n* **1** any of a family of beetles including the sacred scarab and other dung beetles, the chafers, and rhinoceros beetles. ◆ *adj* **2** of or belonging to this family. [C19: from NL]

Scaramouch ('skærə,muːʃ) *n* a stock character who appears as a boastful coward in commedia dell'arte. [C17: via F from It. *Scaramuccia*, from *scaramuccia* a SKIRMISH]

Scarborough ★ ('skɑːbrə) *n* a fishing port and resort in NE England, in North Yorkshire on the North Sea: developed as a spa after 1660; ruined 12th-century castle. Pop.: 38 809 (1991).

scarce (skɛəs) *adj* **1** rarely encountered. **2** insufficient to meet the demand. **3 make oneself scarce.** *Inf.* to go away. ◆ *adv* **4** *Arch. or literary.* scarcely. [C13: from OF *scars*, from Vulgar L *excarpsus* (unattested) plucked out, from L *excerpere* to select]
▸ 'scarceness *n*

scarcely ('skɛəslɪ) *adv* **1** hardly at all. **2** *Often used ironically.* probably or definitely not: *that is scarcely justification for your actions.*

> **USAGE NOTE** See at **hardly.**

scarcity ('skɛəsɪtɪ) *n, pl* **scarcities. 1** inadequate supply. **2** rarity or infrequent occurrence.

scare (skɛə) *vb* **scares, scaring, scared. 1** to fill or be filled with fear or alarm. **2** (*tr;* often foll. by *away* or *off*) to drive (away) by frightening. ◆ *n* **3** a sudden attack of fear or alarm. **4** a period of general fear or alarm. ◆ *adj* **5** causing (needless) fear or alarm: *a scare story.* [C12: from ON *skirra*]
▶ 'scarer *n*

scarecrow ('skɛə,krəʊ) *n* **1** an object, usually in the shape of a man, made out of sticks and old clothes to scare birds away from crops. **2** a person or thing that appears frightening. **3** *Inf.* an untidy-looking person.

scaremonger ('skɛə,mʌŋgə) *n* a person who delights in spreading rumours of disaster.
▶ 'scare,mongering *n*

scarf[1] (skɑːf) *n, pl* **scarves** or **scarfs.** a rectangular, triangular, or long narrow piece of cloth worn around the head, neck, or shoulders for warmth or decoration. [C16: from ?]

scarf[2] (skɑːf) *n, pl* **scarfs. 1** Also called: **scarf joint, scarfed joint.** a lapped joint between two pieces of timber made by notching the ends and strapping or gluing the two pieces together. **2** the end of a piece of timber shaped to form such a joint. **3** *Whaling.* an incision made along a whale before stripping off the blubber. ◆ *vb* (*tr*) **4** to join (two pieces of timber) by means of a scarf. **5** to make a scarf on (a piece of timber). **6** to cut a scarf in (a whale). [C14: prob. from ON]

Scarfe ★ (skɑːf) *n* **Gerald.** born 1936, British cartoonist, famous for his scathing caricatures of politicians and celebrities.

scarfskin ('skɑːf,skɪn) *n* the outermost layer of the skin; epidermis or cuticle. [C17: from SCARF[1] (in the sense: an outer covering)]

Scargill ★ ('skɑːgɪl) *n* **Arthur.** born 1941, British trade-union leader; president of the National Union of Mineworkers (from 1982). He led the miners in a long and bitter strike (1984–85) against pit closures, but was unable to stop the closures.

scarify ('skɛərɪ,faɪ, 'skær-) *vb* **scarifies, scarifying, scarified.** (*tr*) **1** *Surgery.* to make tiny punctures or superficial incisions in (the skin or other tissue), as for inoculating. **2** *Agriculture.* to break up and loosen (soil) to a shallow depth. **3** to wound with harsh criticism. [C15: via OF from L *scarīfāre* to scratch open, from Gk *skariphasthai* to draw, from *skariphos* a pencil]
▶ ,scarifi'cation *n* ▶ 'scari,fier *n*

> **USAGE NOTE** *Scarify* is sometimes wrongly thought to mean the same as *scare*: *a frightening* (not *scarifying*) *film*.

scarlatina (,skɑːlə'tiːnə) *n* the technical name for **scarlet fever.** [C19: from NL, from It. *scarlattina,* dim. of *scarlatto* scarlet]

Scarlatti ★ (skɑː'lætɪ) *n* **1 Alessandro** (ales'sandro). ?1659–1725, Italian composer; regarded as the founder of modern opera. **2** his son, (**Giuseppe**) **Domenico** (do-'meːniko). 1685–1757, Italian composer, who wrote over 550 sonatas for harpsichord.

scarlet ('skɑːlɪt) *n* **1** a vivid orange-red colour. **2** cloth or clothing of this colour. ◆ *adj* **3** of the colour scarlet. **4** sinful or immoral. [C13: from OF *escarlate* fine cloth, from ?]

scarlet fever *n* an acute communicable disease characterized by fever, strawberry-coloured tongue, and a rash starting on the neck and chest and spreading to the abdomen and limbs. Technical name: **scarlatina.**

scarlet letter *n* (esp. among US Puritans) a scarlet letter *A* formerly worn by a person convicted of adultery.

scarlet pimpernel *n* a plant, related to the primrose, having small red, purple, or white star-shaped flowers that close in bad weather. Also called: **shepherd's** (or **poor man's**) **weatherglass.**

scarlet runner *n* a climbing perennial bean plant of South America, having scarlet flowers: widely cultivated for its long green edible pods containing edible seeds. Also: **runner bean.**

scarlet woman *n* **1** a sinful woman described in the Bible (Rev. 17), interpreted as a symbol of pagan Rome or of the Roman Catholic Church. **2** any sexually promiscuous woman.

scarp (skɑːp) *n* **1** a steep slope, esp. one formed by erosion or faulting. **2** *Fortifications.* the side of a ditch cut nearest to a rampart. ◆ *vb* **3** (*tr; often passive*) to wear or cut so as to form a steep slope. [C16: from It. *scarpa*]

scarper ('skɑːpə) *Brit. sl.* ◆ *vb* **1** (*intr*) to depart in haste. ◆ *n* **2** a hasty departure. [from ?]

Scarron ★ (*French* skarɔ̃) *n* **Paul** (pɔl). 1610–60, French dramatist and novelist, noted for his novel *Le Roman comique* (1651–57).

Scart or **SCART** (skɑːt) *n* *Electronics.* **a** a 21-pin plug-and-socket system which carries picture, sound, and other signals, used especially in home entertainment systems. **b** (*as modifier*): *a Scart cable.* [C20: after Syndicat des Constructeurs des Appareils Radiorécepteurs et Téléviseurs, the company that designed it]

scarves (skɑːvz) *n* a plural of **scarf**[1].

scary ('skɛərɪ) *adj* **scarier, scariest.** *Inf.* **1** causing fear or alarm. **2** timid.

scat[1] (skæt) *vb* **scats, scatting, scatted.** (*intr; usually imperative*) *Inf.* to go away in haste. [C19: ?from a hiss + *cat,* used to frighten away cats]

scat[2] (skæt) *n* **1** a type of jazz singing characterized by improvised vocal sounds instead of words. ◆ *vb* **scats, scatting, scatted. 2** (*intr*) to sing jazz in this way. [C20: ? imit.]

scathe (skeɪð) *vb* **scathes, scathing, scathed.** (*tr*) **1** *Rare.* to attack with severe criticism. **2** *Arch. or dialect.* to injure. ◆ *n* **3** *Arch. or dialect.* harm. [OE *sceatha*]

scathing ('skeɪðɪŋ) *adj* **1** harshly critical; scornful. **2** damaging.
▶ 'scathingly *adv*

scatology (skæ'tɒlədʒɪ) *n* **1** the scientific study of excrement, esp. in medicine and in palaeontology. **2** obscenity or preoccupation with obscenity, esp. in the form of references to excrement. [C19: from Gk *skat-* excrement + -LOGY]
▶ scatological (,skætə'lɒdʒɪkᵊl) *adj*

scatter ('skætə) *vb* **1** (*tr*) to throw about in various directions. **2** to separate and move or cause to separate and move in various directions. **3** to deviate or cause to deviate in many directions, as in the refraction of light. ◆ *n* **4** the act of scattering. **5** a substance or a number of objects scattered about. [C13: prob. a var. of SHATTER]
▶ 'scatterer *n*

scatterbrain ('skætə,breɪn) *n* a person who is incapable of serious thought or concentration.
▶ 'scatter,brained *adj*

scatter diagram *n* *Statistics.* a representation by a Cartesian graph of the correlation between two quantities, such as height and weight.

scattering ('skætərɪŋ) *n* **1** a small amount. **2** *Physics.* the process in which particles, atoms, etc., are deflected as a result of collision.

scatty ('skætɪ) *adj* **scattier, scattiest.** *Brit. inf.* **1** empty-headed or thoughtless. **2** distracted (esp. in **drive someone scatty**). [C20: from SCATTERBRAINED]
▶ 'scattily *adv* ▶ 'scattiness *n*

scaup or **scaup duck** (skɔːp) *n* either of two diving ducks, the **greater scaup** or the **lesser scaup,** of Europe and America, having a black-and-white plumage in the male. [C16: Scot. var. of SCALP]

scavenge ('skævɪndʒ) *vb* **scavenges, scavenging, scavenged. 1** to search for (anything usable) among discarded material. **2** (*tr*) to purify (a molten metal) by bubbling a suitable gas through it. **3** to clean up filth from (streets, etc.).

scavenger ('skævɪndʒə) *n* **1** a person who collects things discarded by others. **2** any animal that feeds on decaying organic matter. **3** a person employed to clean the streets. [C16: from Anglo-Norman *scawager,* from OF *escauwage* examination, from *escauwer* to scrutinize, of Gmc origin]
▶ 'scavengery *n*

ScD *abbrev. for* Doctor of Science.

> ★ people and places

SCE (in Scotland) *abbrev. for* Scottish Certificate of Education: either of two public examinations in specific subjects taken as school-leaving qualifications or as qualifying examinations for entry into a university, college, etc.

scena ('ʃeɪnə) *n, pl* **scene** (-ˌneɪ). a solo vocal piece of dramatic style and large scope, esp. in opera. [C19: It., from L *scēna* scene]

scenario (sɪ'nɑːrɪˌəʊ) *n, pl* **scenarios. 1** a summary of the plot of a play, etc., including information about its characters, scenes, etc. **2** a predicted sequence of events. [C19: via It. from L *scēnārium*, from *scēna*; see SCENE]

scene (siːn) *n* **1** the place where an action or event, real or imaginary, occurs. **2** the setting for the action of a play, novel, etc. **3** an incident or situation, real or imaginary, esp. as described or represented. **4a** a subdivision of an act of a play, in which the setting is fixed. **4b** a single event, esp. a significant one, in a play. **5** *Films.* a shot or series of shots that constitutes a unit of the action. **6** the backcloths, etc., for a play or film set. **7** the prospect of a place, landscape, etc. **8** a display of emotion. **9** *Inf.* the environment for a specific activity: *the fashion scene.* **10** *Inf.* interest or chosen occupation: *classical music is not my scene.* **11** *Rare.* the stage. **12 behind the scenes.** out of public view. [C16: from L *scēna* theatrical stage, from Gk *skēnē* tent, stage]

scene dock *or* **bay** *n* a place in a theatre where scenery is stored, usually near the stage.

scenery ('siːnərɪ) *n, pl* **sceneries. 1** the natural features of a landscape. **2** *Theatre.* the painted backcloths, etc., used to represent a location in a theatre or studio. [C18: from It. SCENARIO]

scenic ('siːnɪk) *adj* **1** of or relating to natural scenery. **2** having beautiful natural scenery: *a scenic drive.* **3** of or relating to the stage or stage scenery. **4** (in painting, etc.) representing a scene.
▶ '**scenically** *adv*

scenic railway *n* a miniature railway used for amusement in a park, zoo, etc.

scenic reserve *n* NZ. an area of natural beauty, set aside for public recreation.

scent (sɛnt) *n* **1** a distinctive smell, esp. a pleasant one. **2** a smell left in passing, by which a person or animal may be traced. **3** a trail, clue, or guide. **4** an instinctive ability for detecting. **5** another word (esp. Brit.) for **perfume.**
◆ *vb* **6** (*tr*) to recognize by or as if by the smell. **7** (*tr*) to have a suspicion of: *I scent foul play.* **8** (*tr*) to fill with odour or fragrance. **9** (*intr*) (of hounds, etc.) to hunt by the sense of smell. **10** to smell (at): *the dog scented the air.* [C14: from OF *sentir* to sense, from L *sentīre* to feel]
▶ '**scented** *adj*

sceptic *or arch. & US* **skeptic** ('skɛptɪk) *n* **1** a person who habitually doubts the authenticity of accepted beliefs. **2** a person who mistrusts people, ideas, etc., in general. **3** a person who doubts the truth of religion. [C16: from L *scepticus*, from Gk *skeptikos* one who reflects upon, from *skeptesthai* to consider]
▶ '**sceptical** *or arch. & US* '**skeptical** *adj* ▶ '**sceptically** *or arch. & US* '**skeptically** *adv* ▶ '**scepticism** *or arch. & US* '**skepticism** *n*

Sceptic *or arch. & US* **Skeptic** ('skɛptɪk) *n* **1** a member of one of the ancient Greek schools of philosophy, esp. that of Pyrrho, who believed that real knowledge of things is impossible. ◆ *adj* **2** of or relating to the Sceptics.
▶ '**Scepticism** *or arch. & US* '**Skepticism** *n*

sceptre *or US* **scepter** ('sɛptə) *n* **1** a ceremonial staff held by a monarch as the symbol of authority. **2** imperial authority; sovereignty. [C13: from OF *sceptre*, from L, from Gk *skeptron* staff]
▶ '**sceptred** *or US* '**sceptered** *adj*

Schaerbeek ★ (Flemish 'sxɑːrbeːk) *n* a city in central Belgium: an industrial suburb of Brussels. Pop.: 102 417 (1992 est.).

Schaffhausen ★ (German ʃaːfˈhauzən) *n* **1** a small canton of N Switzerland. Pop.: 73 894 (1995 est.). Area: 298 sq. km (115 sq. miles). **2** a town in N Switzerland, capital

of Schaffhausen canton, on the Rhine. Pop.: 70 000 (latest est.). French name: **Schaffhouse.**

Schaumburg-Lippe ★ (German 'ʃaumburkˈlɪpə) *n* a former state of NW Germany, between Westphalia and Hanover: part of Lower Saxony since 1946.

schedule ('ʃɛdjuːl; *also, esp. US* 'skɛdʒʊəl) *n* **1** a plan of procedure for a project. **2** a list of items: *a schedule of fixed prices.* **3** a list of times; timetable. **4** a list of tasks to be performed, esp. within a set period. **5** *Law.* a list or inventory. ◆ *vb* **schedules, scheduling, scheduled.** (*tr*) **6** to make a schedule of or place in a schedule. **7** to plan to occur at a certain time. [C14: earlier *cedule, sedule* via OF from LL *schedula* small piece of paper, from L *scheda* sheet of paper]

scheduled castes *pl n* certain classes in Indian society officially granted special concessions. See **Harijan.**

scheduled territories *pl n the.* another name for **sterling area.**

Scheele ★ (Swedish 'ʃeːlə) *n* **Karl Wilhelm** (kɑːrl 'vilhɛlm). 1742–86, Swedish chemist, who discovered oxygen.

scheelite ('ʃiːlaɪt) *n* a white, brownish, or greenish mineral, usually fluorescent, consisting of calcium tungstate with some tungsten often replaced by molybdenum. It is an important source of tungsten. [C19: from G *Scheelit*, after K. W. SCHEELE]

Scheldt ★ (ʃɛlt, skɛlt) *n* a river in W Europe, rising in NE France and flowing north and northeast through W Belgium to Antwerp, then northwest to the North Sea in the SW Netherlands. Length: 435 km (270 miles). Flemish and Dutch name: **Schelde** ('sxɛldə). French name: **Escaut.**

Schelling ★ (German 'ʃɛlɪŋ) *n* **Friedrich Wilhelm Joseph von** ('friːdrɪç 'vɪlhɛlm 'joːzɛf fɔn). 1775–1854, German philosopher. His works include *System of Transcendental Idealism* (1800).
▶ **Schellingian** (ʃɛ'lɪŋɪən) *adj*

schema ('skiːmə) *n, pl* **schemata** (-mətə). **1** a plan, diagram, or scheme. **2** (in the philosophy of Kant) a rule or principle that enables the understanding to unify experience. **3** *Logic.* **3a** a syllogistic figure. **3b** a representation of the form of an inference. [C19: from Gk: form]

schematic (skɪ'mætɪk) *adj* **1** of or relating to the nature of a diagram, plan, or schema. ◆ *n* **2** a schematic diagram, esp. of an electrical circuit, etc.
▶ **sche'matically** *adv*

schematize *or* **schematise** ('skiːməˌtaɪz) *vb* **schematizes, schematizing, schematized** *or* **schematises, schematising, schematised.** (*tr*) to form into or arrange in a scheme.
▶ '**schema,tism** *n* ▶ ,**schemati'zation** *or* ,**schemati'sation** *n*

scheme (skiːm) *n* **1** a systematic plan for a course of action. **2** a systematic arrangement of parts. **3** a secret plot. **4** a chart, diagram, or outline. **5** an astrological diagram giving the aspects of celestial bodies. **6** *Chiefly Brit.* a plan formally adopted by a commercial enterprise or governmental body, as for pensions, etc. **7** Short for **housing scheme.** ◆ *vb* **schemes, scheming, schemed. 8** (*tr*) to devise a system for. **9** to form intrigues (for) in an underhand manner. [C16: from L *schema*, from Gk *skhēma* form]
▶ '**schemer** *n*

scheming ('skiːmɪŋ) *adj* **1** given to making plots; cunning. ◆ *n* **2** intrigues.

Schengen Convention *or* **Agreement** ('ʃɛŋən) *n* an agreement, signed in 1985, but not implemented until 1995, to abolish border controls within Europe: thirteen countries had acceded by 1995; the UK is not a signatory.

scherzando (skeə'tsændəʊ) *Music.* ◆ *adj, adv* **1** to be performed in a light-hearted manner. ◆ *n, pl* **scherzandi** (-diː) *or* **scherzandos. 2** a movement, passage, etc., directed to be performed in this way. [It., lit.: joking; see SCHERZO]

scherzo ('skeətsəʊ) *n, pl* **scherzos** *or* **scherzi** (-tsiː). a brisk lively movement, developed from the minuet, with a contrasting middle section (a trio). [It.: joke, of Gmc origin]

Schiaparelli ★ (Italian skjapaˈrɛlli) *n* **1 Elsa** ('elsa). 1896–

1973, Italian couturière. **2 Giovanni Virginio** (dʒo'vanni vir'dʒiːnjo). 1835–1910, Italian astronomer, who discovered the asteroid Hesperia (1861).

Schick test (ʃɪk) *n Med.* a skin test to determine immunity to diphtheria. [C20: after Bela *Schick* (1877–1967), US paediatrician]

Schiedam ★ (*Dutch* sxiː'dɑm) *n* a port in the SW Netherlands, in South Holland province west of Rotterdam: gin distilleries. Pop.: 72 515 (1994).

Schiele ★ (*German* 'ʃiːlə) *n* **Egon** ('eːgɔn). 1890–1918, Austrian expressionist painter.

Schiller ★ (*German* 'ʃɪlər) *n* **Johann Christoph Friedrich von** (joˈhan 'krɪstɔf 'friːdrɪç fɔn). 1759–1805, German writer. His plays include the trilogy *Wallenstein* (1800) and *Maria Stuart* (1800).

schilling ('ʃɪlɪŋ) *n* the standard monetary unit of Austria. [C18: from G: SHILLING]

schism ('sɪzəm, 'skɪz-) *n* **1** the division of a group into opposing factions. **2** the factions so formed. **3** division within or separation from an established Church, not necessarily involving differences in doctrine. [C14: from Church L *schisma*, from Gk *skhisma* a cleft, from *skhizein* to split]

schismatic (sɪz'mætɪk, skɪz-) *or* **schismatical** *adj* **1** of or promoting schism. ♦ *n* **2** a person who causes schism or belongs to a schismatic faction.
▸ **schis'matically** *adv*

schist (ʃɪst) *n* any metamorphic rock that can be split into thin layers. [C18: from F *schiste*, from L *lapis schistos* stone that may be split, from Gk *skhizein* to split]
▸ **'schistose** *adj*

schistosome ('ʃɪstə,səum) *n* any of a genus of blood flukes which cause disease in man and domestic animals. Also called: **bilharzia**. [C19: from NL *Schistosoma*; see SCHIST, -SOME³]

schistosomiasis (,ʃɪstəsəu'maɪəsɪs) *n* a disease caused by infestation of the body with schistosomes. Also called: **bilharziasis**.

schizanthus (skɪz'ænθəs) *n* a flowering annual plant, native to Chile, that has finely divided leaves. [C19: NL from Gk *skhizein* to cut + *anthos* flower]

schizo ('skɪtsəu) *Offens.* ♦ *adj* **1** schizophrenic. ♦ *n, pl* **schizos**. **2** a schizophrenic person.

schizo- *or before a vowel* **schiz-** *combining form.* indicating a cleavage, split, or division: *schizophrenia*. [from Gk *skhizein* to split]

schizocarp ('skɪzə,kɑːp) *n Bot.* a dry fruit that splits into two or more one-seeded portions at maturity.
▸ **,schizo'carpous** *adj*

schizoid ('skɪtsɔɪd) *adj* **1** *Psychol.* denoting a personality disorder characterized by extreme shyness and oversensitivity. **2** *Inf.* characterized by conflicting or contradictory ideas, attitudes, etc. ♦ *n* **3** a person who has a schizoid personality.

schizomycete (,skɪtsəumaɪ'siːt) *n* any microscopic organism of the class *Schizomycetes*, which includes the bacteria.

schizophrenia (,skɪtsəu'friːnɪə) *n* **1** any of a group of psychotic disorders characterized by progressive deterioration of the personality, withdrawal from reality, hallucinations, emotional instability, etc. **2** *Inf.* behaviour that seems to be motivated by contradictory or conflicting principles. [C20: from SCHIZO- + Gk *phrēn* mind]
▸ **,schizo'phrenic** *adj, n*

schizothymia (,skɪtsəu'θaɪmɪə) *n Psychiatry.* the condition of being schizoid or introverted. It encompasses elements of schizophrenia. [C20: NL, from SCHIZO- + -*thymia*, from Gk *thumos* spirit]
▸ **,schizo'thymic** *adj*

Schlegel ★ (*German* 'ʃleːgəl) *n* **1 August Wilhelm von** ('august 'vɪlhɛlm fɔn). 1767–1845, German romantic critic and scholar, noted particularly for his translations of Shakespeare. **2** his brother, **Friedrich von** ('friːdrɪç fɔn). 1772–1829, German philosopher and critic; a founder of the romantic movement in Germany.

Schlesien ★ ('ʃleːziən) *n* the German name for **Silesia**.

Schlesinger ★ ('ʃlɛsɪndʒə) *n* **John (Richard)**. born 1926,

British film and theatre director. Films include *Billy Liar* (1963), *Midnight Cowboy* (1969), and *Eye for an Eye* (1995).

Schleswig ★ (*German* 'ʃleːsvɪç) *n* **1** a fishing port in N Germany, in Schleswig-Holstein state: on an inlet of the Baltic; formerly in West Germany. Pop.: 30 000 (1985 est.). **2** a former duchy, in the S Jutland Peninsula: annexed by Prussia in 1864; N part returned to Denmark after a plebiscite in 1920; S part forms part of the German state of Schleswig-Holstein. Danish name: **Slesvig**.

Schleswig-Holstein ★ (*German* 'ʃleːsvɪç'hɔlʃtaɪn) *n* a state of N Germany, formerly in West Germany: drained chiefly by the River Elbe; mainly agricultural. Capital: Kiel. Pop.: 2 708 400 (1995 est.). Area: 15 658 sq. km (6045 sq. miles).

Schlick ★ (*German* ʃlɪk) *n* **Moritz** ('moːrɪts). 1882–1936, German philosopher, working in Austria, who founded (1924) the Vienna Circle to develop the doctrine of logical positivism.

Schlieffen ★ (*German* 'ʃliːfən) *n* **Alfred** ('alfreːt), Count von Schlieffen. 1833–1913, German field marshal, who devised the **Schlieffen Plan** (1905) to ensure German victory over a Franco-Russian alliance by holding off Russia and swiftly defeating France by a flanking movement. A modified version was unsuccessfully used in World War I (1914).

Schliemann ★ (*German* 'ʃliːman) *n* **Heinrich** ('haɪnrɪç). 1822–90, German archaeologist, who discovered the nine superimposed cities of Troy (1871–90) and excavated Mycenae (1876).

schlieren ('ʃlɪərən) *n* **1** *Physics.* visible streaks produced in a transparent fluid as a result of variations in the fluid's density. **2** streaks or platelike masses of mineral in a rock mass. [G, pl of *Schliere* streak]

schmaltz *or* **schmalz** (ʃmælts, ʃmɔːlts) *n* excessive sentimentality. [C20: from G (*Schmalz*) & Yiddish: melted fat, from OHG *smalz*]
▸ **'schmaltzy** *or* **'schmalzy** *adj*

Schmidt ★ (ʃmɪt) *n* **Helmut (Heinrich Waldemar)** ('hɛlmuːt). born 1918, German Social Democrat statesman; chancellor of West Germany (1974–82).

Schmidt telescope *or* **camera** (ʃmɪt) *n* a catadioptric telescope designed to produce a very sharp image of a large area of sky in one photographic exposure. [C20: after B. V. *Schmidt* (1879–1935), Estonian-born G inventor]

Schnabel ★ ('ʃnɑːbᵊl) *n* **Artur** ('artur). 1882–1951, US pianist, born in Austria.

schnapper ('ʃnæpə) *n* a variant spelling of **snapper** (senses 1, 2).

schnapps *or* **schnaps** (ʃnæps) *n* **1** a Dutch spirit distilled from potatoes. **2** (in Germany) any strong spirit. [C19: from G *Schnaps*, from *schnappen* to SNAP]

schnauzer ('ʃnautsə) *n* a wire-haired breed of dog of the terrier type, originally from Germany, with a greyish coat. [C19: from G *Schnauze* snout]

Schnittke ★ ('ʃnɪtkə) *n* **Alfred**. 1934–98, Russian composer: his works include four symphonies, four violin concertos, choral, chamber, and film music.

schnitzel ('ʃnɪtsəl) *n* a thin slice of meat, esp. veal. [G: cutlet, from *schnitzen* to carve, *schnitzeln* to whittle]

schnorkel ('ʃnɔːkᵊl) *n, vb* **schnorkels, schnorkelling, schnorkelled.** a less common variant of **snorkel**.

schnozzle ('ʃnɒzᵊl) *n Chiefly US.* a slang word for **nose**. [alteration of Yiddish *shnoitsl*, from G *Schnauze* snout]

Schoenberg *or* **Schönberg** ★ ('ʃɜːnbɜːg; *German* 'ʃøːnbɛrk) *n* **Arnold** ('arnɔlt). 1874–1951, Austrian composer, in the US after 1933, who developed the twelve-tone technique. His works include the song cycle *Pierrot Lunaire* (1912) and the unfinished opera *Moses and Aaron*.

scholar ('skɒlə) *n* **1** a learned person, esp. in the humanities. **2** a person, esp. a child, who studies; pupil. **3** a student receiving a scholarship. **4** *S. African.* a school pupil. [C14: from OF *escoler*, via LL from L *schola* SCHOOL¹]
▸ **'scholarly** *adj* ▸ **'scholarliness** *n*

scholarship ('skɒlə,ʃɪp) *n* **1** academic achievement; learning. **2a** financial aid provided for a scholar because of academic merit. **2b** the position of a student who gains this financial aid. **2c** (*as modifier*): *a scholarship student*. **3** the qualities of a scholar.

scholastic (skə'læstɪk) *adj* **1** of or befitting schools, scholars, or education. **2** pedantic or precise. **3** (*often cap.*) characteristic of or relating to the medieval Schoolmen. ◆ *n* **4** a student or pupil. **5** a person who is given to logical subtleties. **6** (*often cap.*) a disciple or adherent of scholasticism; Schoolman. **7** a Jesuit student who is undergoing a period of probation prior to commencing his theological studies. [C16: via L from Gk *skholastikos* devoted to learning, ult. from *skholē* SCHOOL[1]]
▶ scho'lastically *adv*

scholasticism (skə'læstɪˌsɪzəm) *n* (*sometimes cap.*) the system of philosophy, theology, and teaching that dominated medieval western Europe and was based on the writings of the Church Fathers and Aristotle.

scholiast ('skəʊlɪˌæst) *n* a medieval annotator, esp. of classical texts. [C16: from LGk, ult. from Gk *skholē* school]
▶ ˌscholi'astic *adj*

Schönberg ★ ('ʃɜːnbɜːg; *German* 'ʃøːnberk) *n* See **Schoenberg**.

Schongauer ★ (*German* 'ʃoːngauər) *n* **Martin** ('martiːn). ?1445–91, German painter.

school[1] (skuːl) *n* **1a** an institution or building at which children and young people receive education. **1b** (*as modifier*): *school day*. **1c** (*in combination*): *schoolwork*. **2** any educational institution or building. **3** a faculty or department specializing in a particular subject: *a law school*. **4** the staff and pupils of a school. **5** the period of instruction in a school or one session of this: *he stayed after school to do extra work*. **6** a place or sphere of activity that instructs: *the school of hard knocks*. **7** a body of people or pupils adhering to a certain set of principles, doctrines, or methods. **8** a group of artists, writers, etc., linked by the same style, teachers, or aims. **9** a style of life: *a gentleman of the old school*. **10** *Inf.* a group assembled for a common purpose, esp. gambling or drinking. ◆ *vb* (*tr*) **11** to train or educate in or as in a school. **12** to discipline or control. [OE *scōl*, from L *schola* school, from Gk *skholē* leisure spent in the pursuit of knowledge]

school[2] (skuːl) *n* **1** a group of fish or other aquatic animals that swim together. ◆ *vb* **2** (*intr*) to form such a group. [OE *scolu* SHOAL[2]]

school board *n* **1** *English History*. an elected board of ratepayers who provided elementary schools (**board schools**). **2** (in the US and Canada) a local board of education.

schoolboy ('skuːlˌbɔɪ) *or* (*fem*) **schoolgirl** *n* a child attending school.

schoolhouse ('skuːlˌhaʊs) *n* **1** a building used as a school. **2** a house attached to a school.

schoolie ('skuːlɪ) *n Austral. sl.* **1** a schoolteacher. **2** a high school student.

schooling ('skuːlɪŋ) *n* **1** education, esp. when received at school. **2** the process of teaching or being taught in a school. **3** the training of an animal, esp. of a horse for dressage.

schoolman ('skuːlmən) *n, pl* **schoolmen**. (*sometimes cap.*) a scholar versed in the learning of the **Schoolmen**, the masters in the universities of the Middle Ages who were versed in scholasticism.

schoolmarm ('skuːlˌmɑːm) *n Inf.* **1** a woman schoolteacher. **2** any woman considered to be prim or old-fashioned.
▶ 'school,marmish *adj*

schoolmaster ('skuːlˌmɑːstə) *or* (*fem*) **schoolmistress** *n* **1** a person who teaches in or runs a school. **2** a person or thing that acts as an instructor.

schoolmate ('skuːlˌmeɪt) *or* **schoolfellow** *n* a companion at school; fellow pupil.

school of arts *n Austral.* a public building in a small town: orig. one used for adult education.

Schools (skuːlz) *pl n* **1 the Schools**. the medieval Schoolmen collectively. **2** (at Oxford University) **2a** the University building in which examinations are held. **2b** *Inf.* the

Second Public Examination for the degree of Bachelor of Arts.

schoolteacher ('skuːlˌtiːtʃə) *n* a person who teaches in a school.
▶ 'school,teaching *n*

school year *n* **1** a twelve-month period, usually of three terms, during which pupils remain in the same class. **2** the time during this period when the school is open.

schooner ('skuːnə) *n* **1** a sailing vessel with at least two masts, with all lower sails rigged fore-and-aft, and with the main mast stepped aft. **2** *Brit.* a large glass for sherry. **3** *US, Canad., Austral., & NZ.* a large glass for beer. [C18: from ?]

Schopenhauer ★ (*German* 'ʃoːpənhauər) *n* **Arthur** ('artur). 1788–1860, German philosopher, noted for his *The World as Will and Idea* (1819).
▶ **Schopenhauerian** (ˌʃəʊpənˈhaʊərɪən) *adj* ▶ 'Schopen,hauer,ism *n*

schottische (ʃɒˈtiːʃ) *n* **1** a 19th-century German dance resembling a slow polka. **2** a piece of music composed for or in the manner of this dance. [C19: from G *der schottische Tanz* the Scottish dance]

Schottky effect ('ʃɒtkɪ) *n Physics*. a reduction in the energy required to remove an electron from a solid surface in a vacuum when an electric field is applied to the surface. [C20: after W. *Schottky* (1886–1976), G physicist]

Schouten Islands ★ ('ʃaʊt°n) *pl n* a group of islands in the Pacific, off the N coast of Irian Jaya. Pop.: 25 487 (1966). Area: 3185 sq. km (1230 sq. miles).

Schreiner ★ ('ʃraɪnə) *n* **Olive** (**Emilie Albertina**). 1855–1920, South African novelist and feminist writer, whose works include the autobiographical *The Story of an African Farm* (1883).

Schrödinger ★ (*German* 'ʃrøːdɪŋər) *n* **Erwin** ('erviːn). 1887–1961, Austrian physicist, who discovered the **Schrödinger wave equation**: shared the Nobel prize for physics 1933.

Schubert ★ ('ʃuːbət) *n* **Franz** (**Peter**) (*German* frants). 1797–1828, Austrian composer; his many songs include the cycles *Die Winterreise* (1827); other works include symphonies and much piano and chamber music.

Schumacher ★ (*German* 'ʃuːmaxər) *n* **1 Ernst Friedrich** (ernst 'friːdrɪç). 1911–77, British economist, born in Germany, noted for his book *Small is Beautiful* (1973). **2 Michael**. born 1969, German motor-racing driver.

Schuman ★ *n* **1** (*French* ʃuman). **Robert** (rɔbɛr). 1886–1963, French statesman; prime minister (1947–48). **2** ('ʃuːmən). **William** (**Howard**). 1910–91, US composer.

Schumann ★ ('ʃuːmən) *n* **1 Elisabeth** (*German* eˈliːzabɛt). 1885–1952, German lieder singer. **2 Robert Alexander** (*German* 'roːbɛrt aleˈksandər). 1810–56, German composer, noted for his piano music, such as *Carneval* (1835), his songs, and four symphonies.

schuss (ʃʊs) *Skiing*. ◆ *n* **1** a straight high-speed downhill run. ◆ *vb* **2** (*intr*) to perform a schuss. [G: SHOT[1]]

Schütz ★ (*German* ʃyts) *n* **Heinrich** ('haɪnrɪç). 1585–1672, German composer, esp. of church music and madrigals.

schwa *or* **shwa** (ʃwɑː) *n* **1** a central vowel represented in the International Phonetic Alphabet by (ə). The sound occurs in unstressed syllables in English, as in *around* and *sofa*. **2** the symbol (ə) used to represent this sound. [C19: via G from Heb. *shewā*, a diacritic indicating lack of a vowel sound]

Schwaben ★ ('ʃvaːbən) *n* the German name for **Swabia**.

Schwarzkopf ★ *n* **1** (*German* ʃvarts'kɔpf). **Elisabeth** (eˈliːzabɛt). born 1915, Austro-British soprano, born in Germany. **2** ('ʃwɔːts,kɒpf). **Norman**, nicknamed *Stormin' Norman*. born 1934, US general: victorious commander-in-chief of the US-led forces in the Gulf War (1991).

Schwarzwald ★ ('ʃvartsvalt) *n* the German name for the **Black Forest**.

Schweinfurt ★ (*German* 'ʃvainfurt) *n* a city in central Germany, in N Bavaria on the River Main. Pop.: 54 520 (1991).

Schweitzer ★ ('ʃwaɪtsə, 'ʃvaɪt-) *n* **Albert**. 1875–1965, Franco-German physician, theologian, and organist, born in Alsace. He devoted most of his life after 1913 to a mission at Lambaréné, Gabon: Nobel peace prize 1952.

Schweiz ★ (ʃvaits) n the German name for **Switzerland.**

Schwerin ★ (German ʃveˈriːn) n a city in N Germany, in Mecklenburg-West Pomerania on **Lake Schwerin.** Pop.: 118 291 (1995 est.).

Schwitters ★ (German ˈʃvɪtərs) n **Kurt** (kʊrt). 1887–1948, German Dadaist painter and poet.

Schwyz ★ (German ʃviːts) n **1** a canton of central Switzerland: played an important part in the formation of the Swiss confederation, to which it gave its name. Capital: Schwyz. Pop.: 120 576 (1995 est.). Area: 908 sq. km (351 sq. miles). **2** a town in E central Switzerland, capital of Schwyz canton: tourism. Pop.: 12 740 (1990).

sci. abbrev. for: **1** science. **2** scientific.

sciatic (saɪˈætɪk) adj **1** Anat. of or relating to the hip or the hipbone. **2** of or afflicted with sciatica. [C16: from F, from LL, from L ischiadicus relating to pain in the hip, from Gk, from iskhia hip-joint]

sciatica (saɪˈætɪkə) n a form of neuralgia characterized by intense pain along the body's longest nerve (**sciatic nerve**), extending from the back of the thigh down to the calf of the leg. [C15: from LL sciatica; see SCIATIC]

science (ˈsaɪəns) n **1** the systematic study of the nature and behaviour of the material and physical universe, based on observation, experiment, and measurement. **2** the knowledge so obtained or the practice of obtaining it. **3** any particular branch of this knowledge: the applied sciences. **4** any body of knowledge organized in a systematic manner. **5** skill or technique. **6** Arch. knowledge. [C14: via OF from L scientia knowledge, from scīre to know]

science fiction n **a** a literary genre that makes imaginative use of scientific knowledge. **b** (as modifier): a science-fiction writer.

Science Museum n a museum in London, originating from 1852 and given its present name and site in 1899: contains collections relating to the history of science, technology, and industry.

science park n an area where scientific research and commercial development are carried on in cooperation.

scienter (saɪˈɛntə) adv Law. knowingly; wilfully. [from L]

sciential (saɪˈɛnʃəl) adj **1** of or relating to science. **2** skilful or knowledgeable.

scientific (ˌsaɪənˈtɪfɪk) adj **1** (prenominal) of, derived from, or used in science: scientific equipment. **2** (prenominal) occupied in science: scientific manpower. **3** conforming with the methods used in science.
▸ ˌscienˈtifically adv

scientism (ˈsaɪənˌtɪzəm) n **1** the application of the scientific method. **2** the uncritical application of scientific methods to inappropriate fields of study.
▸ ˌscienˈtistic adj

scientist (ˈsaɪəntɪst) n a person who studies or practises any of the sciences or who uses scientific methods.

Scientology (ˌsaɪənˈtɒlədʒɪ) n Trademark. the philosophy of the Church of Scientology, a nondenominational movement founded in the US in the 1950s, which emphasizes self-knowledge as a means of realizing full spiritual potential. [C20: from L scient(ia) SCIENCE + -LOGY]
▸ ˌScienˈtologist n

sci-fi (ˈsaɪˈfaɪ) n short for **science fiction.**

scilicet (ˈsɪlɪˌsɛt) adv namely: used esp. in explaining an obscure text or supplying a missing word. [L: from scīre licet it is permitted to know]

scilla (ˈsɪlə) n any of a genus of liliaceous plants having small bell-shaped flowers. See also **squill** (sense 3). [C19: via L from Gk skilla]

Scilly Isles, Scilly Islands (ˈsɪlɪ), or **Scillies** ★ (ˈsɪlɪz) pl n a group of about 140 small islands (only five inhabited) off the extreme SW coast of England; tourist centre. Capital: Hugh Town. Pop.: 2900 (1991). Area: 16 sq. km (6 sq. miles).
▸ **Scillonian** (sɪˈləʊnɪən) adj, n

scimitar (ˈsɪmɪtə) n an oriental sword with a curved

blade broadening towards the point. [C16: from OIt. prob. from Persian shimshīr, from ?]

scintigraphy (ˌsɪnˈtɪgrəfɪ) n Med. a diagnostic technique using a radioactive tracer and scintillation counter for producing pictures (**scintigrams**) of internal parts of the body. [C20: from SCINTI(LLATION) + -GRAPHY]

scintilla (sɪnˈtɪlə) n a minute amount; hint, trace, or particle. [C17: from L: a spark]

scintillate (ˈsɪntɪˌleɪt) vb **scintillates, scintillating, scintillated.** (mainly intr) **1** (also tr) to give off (sparks); sparkle. **2** to be animated or brilliant. **3** Physics. to give off flashes of light as a result of the impact of photons. [C17: from L scintillāre, from scintilla a spark]
▸ ˈscintillant adj ▸ ˈscintilˌlating adj

scintillation (ˌsɪntɪˈleɪʃən) n **1** the act of scintillating. **2** a spark or flash. **3** the twinkling of stars. **4** Physics. a flash of light produced when a material scintillates.

scintillation counter n an instrument for detecting and measuring the intensity of high-energy radiation. It consists of a phosphor with which particles collide producing flashes of light that are converted into pulses of electric current that are counted by electronic equipment.

sciolism (ˈsaɪəˌlɪzəm) n Rare. the practice of opinionating on subjects of which one has only superficial knowledge. [C19: from LL sciolus someone with a smattering of knowledge, from L scīre to know]
▸ ˈsciolist n ▸ ˌscioˈlistic adj

scion (ˈsaɪən) n **1** a descendant or young member of a family. **2** a shoot of a plant used to form a graft. [C14: from OF cion, of Gmc origin]

Scipio ★ (ˈskɪpɪˌəʊ, ˈsɪpɪˌəʊ) n **1** full name Publius Cornelius Scipio Africanus Major. 237–183 B.C., Roman general. He commanded the Roman invasion of Carthage in the Second Punic War, defeating Hannibal at Zama (202). **2** his grandson by adoption, full name Publius Cornelius Scipio Aemilianus Africanus Minor. ?185–129 B.C., Roman statesman and general; commanded an army in the last Punic War and destroyed Carthage (146).

scirrhus (ˈsɪrəs) n, pl **scirrhi** (-raɪ) or **scirrhuses.** Pathol. a firm cancerous growth composed of fibrous tissues. [C17: from NL, from L scirros, from Gk, from skiros hard]
▸ **scirrhoid** (ˈsɪrɔɪd) adj

scission (ˈsɪʒən) n the act or an instance of cutting, splitting, or dividing. [C15: from LL scissiō, from scindere to split]

scissor (ˈsɪzə) vb to cut (an object) with scissors.

scissors (ˈsɪzəz) pl n **1** Also called: **pair of scissors.** a cutting instrument used for cloth, hair, etc., having two crossed pivoted blades that cut by a shearing action. **2** a wrestling hold in which a wrestler wraps his legs round his opponent's body or head and squeezes. **3** any gymnastic feat in which the legs cross and uncross in a scissor-like movement. [C14 sisoures, from OF cisoires, from Vulgar L cīsōria (unattested), ult. from L caedere to cut]

scissors kick n a type of swimming kick in which one leg is moved forward and the other bent back and they are then brought together again in a scissor-like action.

sciurine (ˈsaɪjʊrɪn, -ˌraɪn) adj of or belonging to a family of rodents inhabiting most parts of the world except Australia and southern South America: includes squirrels, marmots, and chipmunks. [C19: from L sciūrus, from Gk skiouros squirrel, from skia a shadow + oura a tail]

sclera (ˈsklɪərə) n the firm white fibrous membrane that forms the outer covering of the eyeball. Also called: **sclerotic.** [C19: from NL, from Gk sklēros hard]
▸ **scleˈritis** n

sclerenchyma (sklɪəˈrɛŋkɪmə) n a supporting tissue in plants consisting of dead cells with very thick lignified walls. [C19: from SCLERO- + PARENCHYMA]

sclero- or before a vowel **scler-** combining form. **1** indicating hardness: sclerosis. **2** of the sclera: sclerotomy. [from Gk sklēros hard]

scleroderma (ˌsklɪərəʊˈdɜːmə) or **sclerodermia** (ˌsklɪərəʊˈdɜːmɪə) n a chronic disease common among women, characterized by thickening and hardening of the skin.

scleroma (sklɪə'rəumə) n, pl **scleromata** (-mətə). Pathol. any small area of abnormally hard tissue, esp. in a mucous membrane. [C17: from NL, from Gk, from sklēroun to harden, from sklēros hard]

scleroprotein (,sklɪərəu'prəuti:n) n any of a group of insoluble stable proteins such as keratin that occur in skeletal and connective tissues. Also called: **albuminoid**.

sclerosis (sklɪə'rəusɪs) n, pl **scleroses** (-si:z). **1** Pathol. a hardening or thickening of organs, tissues, or vessels from inflammation, degeneration, or (esp. on the inner walls of arteries) deposition of fatty plaques. **2** the hardening of a plant cell wall or tissue. [C14: via Med. L from Gk sklērōsis a hardening]

sclerotic (sklɪə'rɒtɪk) adj **1** of or relating to the sclera. **2** of, relating to, or having sclerosis. ◆ n **3** another name for **sclera**. [C16: from Med. L sclērōticus, from Gk; see SCLEROMA]

sclerous ('sklɪərəs) adj Anat., pathol. hard; bony; indurated. [C19: from Gk sklēros hard]

SCM (in Britain) abbrev. for: **1** State Certified Midwife. **2** Student Christian Movement.

scoff[1] (skɒf) vb **1** (intr; often foll. by at) to speak contemptuously (about); mock. **2** (tr) Obs. to regard with derision. ◆ n **3** an expression of derision. **4** an object of derision. [C14: prob. from ON] ▸ 'scoffer n ▸ 'scoffing adj, n

scoff[2] (skɒf) Inf., chiefly Brit. ◆ vb **1** to eat (food) fast and greedily. ◆ n **2** food or rations. [C19: var of scaff food]

Scofield ★ ('skəufi:ld) n (David) Paul. born 1922, English stage and film actor.

scold (skəuld) vb **1** to find fault with or reprimand (a person) harshly. **2** (intr) to use harsh or abusive language. ◆ n **3** a person, esp. a woman, who constantly finds fault. [C13: from ON skald] ▸ 'scolder n ▸ 'scolding n

scoliosis (,skɒlɪ'əusɪs) n Pathol. an abnormal lateral curvature of the spine. [C18: from NL, from Gk: a curving, from skolios bent] ▸ scoliotic (,skɒlɪ'ɒtɪk) adj

scollop ('skɒləp) n, vb a variant spelling of **scallop**.

scombroid ('skɒmbrɔɪd) adj **1** of, relating to, or belonging to the Scombroidea, a suborder of marine spiny-finned fishes having a forked powerful tail: includes the mackerels, tunnies, and sailfish. ◆ n **2** any fish belonging to the suborder Scombroidea. [C19: from Gk skombros a mackerel; see -OID]

sconce[1] (skɒns) n **1** a bracket fixed to a wall for holding candles or lights. **2** a flat candlestick with a handle. [C14: from OF esconse hiding place, lantern, or from LL sconsa, from absconsa dark lantern]

sconce[2] (skɒns) n a small protective fortification, such as an earthwork. [C16: from Du. schans, from MHG schanze bundle of brushwood]

scone (skɒn, skəun) n a light plain doughy cake made from flour with very little fat, cooked in an oven or (esp. originally) on a griddle. [C16: Scot., ?from MDu. schoonbrot fine bread]

Scone ★ (sku:n) n a parish in E Scotland near Perth, consisting of the two villages of New Scone and Old Scone, formerly the site of the Pictish capital and the stone upon which medieval Scottish kings were crowned. The stone was removed to Westminster Abbey by Edward I in 1296: it was returned to Scotland in 1996 and placed in Edinburgh Castle. Scone Palace was rebuilt in the neogothic style in the 19th century.

scoop (sku:p) n **1** a utensil used as a shovel or ladle, esp. a small shovel with deep sides and a short handle, used for taking up flour, etc. **2** a utensil with a long handle and round bowl used for dispensing liquids, etc. **3** anything that resembles a scoop in action, such as the bucket on a dredge. **4** a utensil used for serving mashed potatoes, ice cream, etc. **5** a spoonlike surgical instrument for extracting foreign matter, etc., from the body. **6** the quantity taken up by a scoop. **7** the act of scooping, dredging, etc. **8** a hollow cavity. **9** Sl. a large quick gain, as of money. **10**

a news story reported in one newspaper before all the others. ◆ vb (mainly tr) **11** (often foll. by up) to take up and remove (an object or substance) with or as if with a scoop. **12** (often foll. by out) to hollow out with or as if with a scoop. **13** to make (a large sudden profit). **14** to beat (rival newspapers) in uncovering a news item. [C14: via MDu. schōpe from Gmc] ▸ 'scooper n ▸ 'scoop,ful n

scoot (sku:t) vb **1** to go or cause to go quickly or hastily; dart or cause to dart off or away. ◆ n **2** the act of scooting. [C19 (US): from ?]

scooter ('sku:tə) n **1** a child's vehicle consisting of a low footboard on wheels, steered by handlebars. **2** See **motor scooter**.

Scopas ★ ('skəupəs) n 4th century B.C., Greek sculptor and architect.

scope (skəup) n **1** opportunity for exercising the faculties or abilities. **2** range of view or grasp. **3** the area covered by an activity, topic, etc.: the scope of his thesis was vast. **4** Naut. slack left in an anchor cable. **5** Logic. the part of a formula that follows a quantifier or an operator. **6** Inf. short for **telescope, microscope, oscilloscope**, etc. **7** Arch. purpose. [C16: from It. scopo goal, from L scopus, from Gk skopos target]

-scope n combining form. indicating an instrument for observing or detecting: microscope. [from NL -scopium, from Gk -skopion, from skopein to look at] ▸ -scopic adj combining form.

scopolamine (skə'pɒlə,mi:n) n a colourless viscous liquid alkaloid extracted from certain plants, such as henbane: used in preventing travel sickness and as a sedative and truth serum. Also called: **hyoscine**. [C20: scopol- from NL scopolia Japonica Japanese belladonna (from which the alkaloid is extracted), after G. A. Scopoli (1723–88), It. naturalist, + AMINE]

Scopus ★ ('skəupəs) n Mount. a mountain in central Israel, east of Jerusalem: a N extension of the Mount of Olives; site of the Hebrew University (1925). Height: 834 m (2736 ft).

-scopy n combining form. indicating a viewing or observation: microscopy. [from Gk -skopia, from skopein to look at]

scorbutic (skɔ:'bju:tɪk) adj of or having scurvy. [C17: from NL scorbūticus, from Med. L scorbūtus, prob. of Gmc origin] ▸ scor'butically adv

scorch (skɔ:tʃ) vb **1** to burn or become burnt, esp. so as to affect the colour, taste, etc. **2** to wither or parch or cause to wither from exposure to heat. **3** (intr) Inf. to be very hot: it is scorching outside. **4** (tr) Inf. to criticize harshly. ◆ n **5** a slight burn. **6** a mark caused by the application of too great heat. **7** Horticulture. a mark on fruit, etc., caused by pests or insecticides. [C15: prob. from ON skorpna to shrivel up] ▸ 'scorching adj

scorched earth policy n **1** the policy in warfare of removing or destroying everything that might be useful to an invading enemy. **2** Business. a manoeuvre by a company expecting an unwelcome takeover bid in which apparent profitability is greatly reduced by a reversible operation, such as borrowing at an exorbitant interest rate.

scorcher ('skɔ:tʃə) n **1** a person or thing that scorches. **2** something caustic. **3** Inf. a very hot day. **4** Brit. inf. something remarkable.

score (skɔ:) n **1** a numerical record of a competitive game or match. **2** the total number of points made by a side or individual in a game. **3** the act of scoring, esp. a point or points. **4 the score**. Inf. the actual situation. **5** a group or set of twenty: three score years and ten. **6** (usually pl; foll. by of) lots: I have scores of things to do. **7** Music. **7a** the printed form of a composition in which the instrumental and vocal parts appear on separate staves vertically arranged on large pages (**full score**) or in a condensed version, usually for piano (**short score**) or voices and piano (**vocal score**). **7b** the incidental music for a film or play. **7c** the songs, music, etc., for a stage or film musical. **8** a mark or notch, esp. one made in keeping a tally. **9** an account of

amounts due. **10** an amount recorded as due. **11** a reason: *the book was rejected on the score of length.* **12** a grievance. **13a** a line marking a division or boundary. **13b** (*as modifier*): *score line.* **14 over the score.** *Inf.* excessive; unfair. **15 settle** *or* **pay off a score.** **15a** to avenge a wrong. **15b** to repay a debt. ◆ *vb* **scores, scoring, scored.** **16** to gain (a point or points) in a game or contest. **17** (*tr*) to make a total score of. **18** to keep a record of the score (of). **19** (*tr*) to be worth (a certain amount) in a game. **20** (*tr*) to record by making notches in. **21** to make (cuts, lines, etc.) in or on. **22** (*intr*) *Sl.* to obtain something desired, esp. to purchase an illegal drug. **23** (*intr*) *Sl.* (of men) to be successful in seducing a person. **24** (*tr*) **24a** to arrange (a piece of music) for specific instruments or voices. **24b** to write the music for (a film, play, etc.). **25** to achieve (success or an advantage): *your idea scored with the boss.* [OE *scora*]
▶ **'scorer** *n*

scoreboard ('skɔːˌbɔːd) *n Sport, etc.* a board for displaying the score of a game or match.

scorecard ('skɔːˌkɑːd) *n* **1** a card on which scores are recorded, as in golf. **2** a card identifying the players in a sports match, esp. cricket.

score off *vb* (*intr, prep*) to gain an advantage at someone else's expense.

scoria ('skɔːrɪə) *n, pl* **scoriae** (-rɪˌiː). **1** a mass of solidified lava containing many cavities. **2** refuse obtained from smelted ore. [C17: from L: dross, from Gk *skōria*, from *skōr* excrement]

scorify ('skɔːrɪˌfaɪ) *vb* **scorifies, scorifying, scorified.** to remove (impurities) from metals by forming scoria.
▶ ˌscorifiˈcation *n* ▶ 'scoriˌfier *n*

scoring ('skɔːrɪŋ) *n* another name for **orchestration** (see **orchestrate**).

scorn (skɔːn) *n* **1** open contempt for a person or thing. **2** an object of contempt or derision. ◆ *vb* **3** to treat with contempt or derision. **4** (*tr*) to reject with contempt. [C12 *schornen*, from OF *escharnir*, of Gmc origin]
▶ 'scorner *n* ▶ 'scornful *adj* ▶ 'scornfully *adv*

Scorpio ('skɔːpɪˌəʊ) *n* **1** Also called: **Scorpius.** *Astron.* a large S constellation. **2** Also called: the **Scorpion.** *Astrol.* the eighth sign of the zodiac. The sun is in this sign between about Oct. 23 and Nov. 21. [L: SCORPION]

scorpion ('skɔːpɪən) *n* **1** an arachnid of warm dry regions, having a segmented body with a long tail terminating in a venomous sting. **2 false scorpion.** a small nonvenomous arachnid that superficially resembles the scorpion but lacks the long tail. **3** *Bible.* a barbed scourge (I Kings 12:11). [C13: via OF from L *scorpiō*, from Gk *skorpios*, from ?]

Scorpion ('skɔːpɪən) *n* **the.** the constellation Scorpio, the eighth sign of the zodiac.

scorpion fish *n* any of a genus of fish of temperate and tropical seas, having venomous spines on the dorsal and anal fins.

Scorsese ★ (skɔːˈseɪzɪ) *n* **Martin.** born 1942, US film director, whose films include *Taxi Driver* (1976), *Casino* (1995), *Kundun* (1998), and the controversial *The Last Temptation of Christ* (1988).

Scot (skɒt) *n* **1** a native or inhabitant of Scotland. **2** a member of a tribe of Celtic raiders from the north of Ireland who eventually settled in N Britain during the 5th and 6th centuries.

Scot. *abbrev. for:* **1** Scotch (whisky). **2** Scotland. **3** Scottish.

scot and lot *n Brit. history.* a municipal tax paid by burgesses that came to be regarded as a qualification for the borough franchise in parliamentary elections. [C13 *scot* tax, from Gmc]

scotch[1] (skɒtʃ) *vb* (*tr*) **1** to put an end to; crush: *bad weather scotched our plans.* **2** *Obs.* to cut or score. ◆ *n* **3** *Arch.* a gash. **4** a line marked down, as for hopscotch. [C15: from ?]

scotch[2] (skɒtʃ) *vb* **1** (*tr*) to block, prop, or prevent from moving with or as if with a wedge. ◆ *n* **2** a block or wedge to prevent motion. [C17: from ?]

Scotch[1] (skɒtʃ) *adj* **1** another word for **Scottish.** ◆ *n* **2** the Scots or their language.

USAGE NOTE In the north of England and in Scotland, *Scotch* is not used outside fixed expressions such as *Scotch whisky*. The use of *Scotch* for *Scots* or *Scottish* is otherwise felt to be incorrect, esp. when applied to people.

Scotch[2] (skɒtʃ) *n* whisky distilled from fermented malted barley and made in Scotland. Also called: **Scotch whisky.**

Scotch broth *n Brit.* a thick soup made from mutton or beef stock, vegetables, and pearl barley.

Scotch egg *n Brit.* a hard-boiled egg enclosed in a layer of sausage meat, covered in egg and crumbs, and fried.

Scotchman ('skɒtʃmən) *or* (*fem*) **Scotchwoman** *n, pl* **Scotchmen** *or* **Scotchwomen.** (*regarded as bad usage by the Scots*) another word for **Scotsman** *or* **Scotswoman.**

Scotch mist *n* **1** a heavy wet mist. **2** drizzle.

Scotch snap *n Music.* a rhythmic pattern consisting of a short note followed by a long one. Also called: **Scotch catch.**

Scotch terrier *n* another name for **Scottish terrier.**

scoter ('skəʊtə) *n, pl* **scoters** *or* **scoter.** a sea duck of northern regions. The male plumage is black with white patches around the head and eyes. [C17: from ?]

scot-free *adv, adj* (*predicative*) without harm, loss, or penalty. [C16: see SCOT AND LOT]

Scotland ★ ('skɒtlənd) *n* a country that is part of the United Kingdom, occupying the north of Great Britain: the English and Scottish thrones were united under one monarch in 1603 and the parliaments in 1707. The establishment of a separate Scottish parliament was approved in a referendum in 1997. It consists of the Highlands in the north, the central Lowlands, and hilly uplands in the south; has a deeply indented coastline, about 800 offshore islands (mostly in the west), and many lochs. Capital: Edinburgh. Pop.: 4 998 567 (1991). Area: 78 768 sq. km (30 412 sq. miles).

Scotland Yard *n* the headquarters of the police force of metropolitan London. Official name: **New Scotland Yard.**

scotoma (skəˈtəʊmə) *n, pl* **scotomas** *or* **scotomata** (-mətə). **1** *Pathol.* a blind spot. **2** *Psychol.* a mental blind spot. [C16: via Med. L from Gk *skotōma* giddiness, from *skotoun* to make dark, from *skotos* darkness]

Scots (skɒts) *adj* **1** of or characteristic of Scotland, its people, their English dialects, or their Gaelic language. ◆ *n* **2** any of the English dialects spoken or written in Scotland.

Scotsman ('skɒtsmən) *or* (*fem*) **Scotswoman** *n, pl* **Scotsmen** *or* **Scotswomen.** a native or inhabitant of Scotland.

Scots pine *or* **Scotch pine** *n* **1** a coniferous tree of Europe and W and N Asia, having blue-green needle-like leaves and brown cones with a small prickle on each scale. **2** the wood of this tree.

Scott ★ (skɒt) *n* **1** Sir **George Gilbert.** 1811–78, British Gothic-Revival architect, who designed the Albert Memorial (1863) and St Pancras Station (1865). **2** his grandson, Sir **Giles Gilbert.** 1880–1960, British architect, who designed the Anglican cathedral in Liverpool (1904–78). **3 Paul (Mark).** 1920–78, British novelist, noted for his "Raj Quartet": *The Jewel in the Crown* (1966), *The Day of the Scorpion* (1968), *The Towers of Silence* (1972), and *A Division of the Spoils* (1975). **4** Sir **Peter (Markham).** 1909–89, British wildlife artist and conservationist. He founded (1946) the Slimbridge waterfowl refuge in Gloucestershire. **5 Robert Falcon.** 1868–1912, British naval officer who commanded two Antarctic expeditions (1901–04; 1910–12), reaching the South Pole on Jan. 18, 1912, shortly after Amundsen; he and his party died on the return journey. **6** Sir **Walter.** 1771–1832, Scottish novelist, best known for his "Waverley" novels, including *Waverley* (1814), *The Heart of Midlothian* (1818), and *Redgauntlet* (1824).

Scotticism ('skɒtɪˌsɪzəm) *n* a Scottish idiom, word, etc.

★ people and places

Scottie or **Scotty** ('skɒtɪ) n, pl **Scotties**. **1** See **Scottish terrier**. **2** Inf. a Scotsman.

Scottish ('skɒtɪʃ) adj of, relating to, or characteristic of Scotland, its people, their Gaelic language, or their English dialects.

Scottish Borders ★ n a council area in SE Scotland, on the English border. Administrative centre: Newtown St Boswells. Pop.: 106 100 (1996 est.). Area: 4734 sq. km (1827 sq. miles).

Scottish Certificate of Education n See SCE.

Scottish Gaelic n the Goidelic language of the Celts of Scotland, used esp. in the Highlands and Western Isles.

Scottish National Party n a political party advocating the independence of Scotland. Abbrev.: SNP.

Scottish terrier n a small but sturdy long-haired breed of terrier, usually with a black coat.

Scotus ★ ('skəʊtəs) n See **Duns Scotus**.

scoundrel ('skaʊndrəl) n a worthless or villainous person. [C16: from ?]

scour[1] ('skaʊə) vb **1** to clean or polish (a surface) by washing and rubbing. **2** to remove dirt from or have the dirt removed from. **3** (tr) to clear (a channel) by the force of water. **4** (tr) to remove by or as if by rubbing. **5** (tr) to cause (livestock) to purge their bowels. ♦ n **6** the act of scouring. **7** the place scoured, esp. by running water. **8** something that scours, such as a cleansing agent. **9** (often pl) prolonged diarrhoea in livestock, esp. cattle. [C13: via MLow G schüren, from OF escurer, from LL excūrāre to cleanse, from cūrāre; see CURE]
▶ **'scourer** n

scour[2] ('skaʊə) vb **1** to range over (territory), as in making a search. **2** to move swiftly or energetically over (territory). [C14: from ON skūr]

scourge (skɜːdʒ) n **1** a person who harasses or causes destruction. **2** a means of inflicting punishment or suffering. **3** a whip used for inflicting punishment or torture. ♦ vb **scourges, scourging, scourged**. (tr) **4** to whip. **5** to punish severely. [C13: from Anglo-F, from OF escorgier (unattested) to lash, from es- EX-[1] + L corrigia whip]
▶ **'scourger** n

scourings ('skaʊərɪŋz) pl n **1** the residue left after cleaning grain. **2** residue that remains after scouring.

scouse (skaʊs) n Liverpool dialect. a stew made from leftover meat. [C19: shortened from LOBSCOUSE]

Scouse (skaʊs) Brit. inf. ♦ n **1** Also: **Scouser**. a person who comes from Liverpool. **2** the dialect spoken by such a person. ♦ adj **3** of or from Liverpool. [C20: from SCOUSE]

scout[1] (skaʊt) n **1** a person, ship, or aircraft sent out to gain information. **2** Mil. a person or unit despatched to reconnoitre the position of the enemy, etc. **3** the act or an instance of scouting. **4** (esp. at Oxford University) a college servant. **5** Inf. a fellow. ♦ vb **6** to examine or observe (anything) in order to obtain information. **7** (tr; sometimes foll. by out or up) to seek. **8** (intr; foll. by about or around) to go in search (for). [C14: from OF ascouter to listen to, from L auscultāre to AUSCULTATE]
▶ **'scouter** n

scout[2] (skaʊt) vb to reject (a person, etc.) with contempt. [C17: from ON skūta derision]

Scout (skaʊt) n (sometimes not cap.) a boy or (in some countries) a girl who is a member of a worldwide movement (the **Scout Association**) founded as the Boy Scouts in England in 1908 by Lord Baden-Powell.
▶ **'Scouting** n

Scouter ('skaʊtə) n the leader of a troop of Scouts. Also called (esp. formerly): **Scoutmaster**.

scow (skaʊ) n an unpowered barge used for freight, etc.; lighter. [C18: via Du. schouw from Low G schalde]

scowl (skaʊl) vb **1** (intr) to contract the brows in a threatening or angry manner. ♦ n **2** a gloomy or threatening expression. [C14: prob. from ON]
▶ **'scowler** n

SCPS (in Britain) abbrev. for Society of Civil and Public Servants.

scrabble ('skræbəl) vb **scrabbles, scrabbling, scrabbled**.

1 (intr; often foll. by about or at) to scrape (at) or grope (for), as with hands or claws. **2** to struggle (with). **3** (intr; often foll. by for) to struggle to gain possession. **4** to scribble. ♦ n **5** the act or an instance of scrabbling. **6** a scribble. **7** a disorderly struggle. [C16: from MDu. shrabbelen, frequentative of shrabben to scrape]
▶ **'scrabbler** n

Scrabble ('skræbəl) n Trademark. a game in which words are formed by placing lettered tiles in a pattern similar to a crossword puzzle.

scrag (skræg) n **1** a thin or scrawny person or animal. **2** the lean end of a neck of veal or mutton. **3** Inf. the neck of a human being. ♦ vb **scrags, scragging, scragged**. **4** (tr) Inf. to wring the neck of. [C16: ? var. of CRAG]

scraggly ('skræglɪ) adj **scragglier, scraggliest**. Chiefly US. untidy or irregular.

scraggy ('skrægɪ) adj **scraggier, scraggiest**. **1** lean or scrawny. **2** rough; unkempt.
▶ **'scraggily** adv ▶ **'scragginess** n

scram[1] (skræm) vb **scrams, scramming, scrammed**. (intr; often imperative) Inf. to go away hastily. [C20: from SCRAMBLE]

scram[2] (skræm) n **1** an emergency shutdown of a nuclear reactor. ♦ vb **scrams, scramming, scrammed**. **2** (of a nuclear reactor) to shut down or be shut down in an emergency. [C20: ?from SCRAM[1]]

scramble ('skræmbəl) vb **scrambles, scrambling, scrambled**. **1** (intr) to climb or crawl, esp. by using the hands to aid movement. **2** to proceed hurriedly or in a disorderly fashion. **3** (intr; often foll. by for) to compete with others, esp. in a disordered manner. **4** (intr; foll. by through) to deal with hurriedly. **5** (tr) to throw together in a haphazard manner. **6** (tr) to collect in a hurried or disorganized manner. **7** (tr) to cook (eggs that have been whisked up with milk) in a pan containing a little melted butter. **8** Mil. to order (a crew or aircraft) to take off immediately or (of a crew or aircraft) to take off immediately. **9** (tr) to render (speech) unintelligible during transmission by means of an electronic scrambler. ♦ n **10** the act of scrambling. **11** a climb or trek over difficult ground. **12** a disorderly struggle, esp. to gain possession. **13** Mil. an immediate preparation for action, as of crew, aircraft, etc. **14** Brit. a motorcycle rally in which competitors race across rough open ground. [C16: blend of SCRABBLE & RAMP]

scrambler ('skræmblə) n an electronic device that renders speech unintelligible during transmission, by altering frequencies.

Scranton ★ ('skræntən) n an industrial city in NE Pennsylvania: university (1988). Pop.: 77 964 (1994 est.).

scrap[1] (skræp) n **1** a small piece of something larger; fragment. **2** an extract from something written. **3a** waste material or used articles, esp. metal, often collected and reprocessed. **3b** (as modifier): scrap iron. **4** (pl) pieces of discarded food. ♦ vb **scraps, scrapping, scrapped**. (tr) **5** to discard as useless. [C14: from ON skrap]

scrap[2] (skræp) Inf. ♦ n **1** a fight or argument. ♦ vb **scraps, scrapping, scrapped**. **2** (intr) to quarrel or fight. [C17: ?from SCRAPE]

scrapbook ('skræp,bʊk) n a book or album of blank pages in which to mount newspaper cuttings, pictures, etc.

scrape (skreɪp) vb **scrapes, scraping, scraped**. **1** to move (a rough or sharp object) across (a surface), esp. to smooth or clean. **2** (tr; often foll. by away or off) to remove (a layer) by rubbing. **3** to produce a harsh or grating sound by rubbing against (a surface, etc.). **4** (tr) to injure or damage by rough contact: to scrape one's knee. **5** (intr) to be very economical (esp. in scrimp and scrape). **6** (intr) to draw the foot backwards in making a bow. **7 scrape acquaintance with**. to contrive an acquaintance with. ♦ n **8** the act of scraping. **9** a scraped place. **10** a harsh or grating sound. **11** Inf. an awkward or embarrassing predicament. **12** Inf. a conflict or struggle. [OE scrapian]
▶ **'scraper** n

scraperboard ('skreɪpə,bɔːd) n thin card covered with a layer of china clay and a top layer of Indian ink, which can be scraped away with a special tool to leave a white line.

scrape through vb (adv) **1** (intr) to manage or survive with difficulty. **2** to succeed in with difficulty or by a narrow margin.

scrape together or **up** vb (tr, adv) to collect with difficulty: to scrape together money for a new car.

scrapheap ('skræp,hi:p) n **1** a pile of discarded material. **2 on the scrapheap.** (of people or things) having outlived their usefulness.

scrappy ('skræpɪ) adj **scrappier, scrappiest.** fragmentary; disjointed.
▶ 'scrappily adv

scratch (skrætʃ) vb **1** to mark or cut (the surface of something) with a rough or sharp instrument. **2** (often foll. by at, out, off, etc.) to scrape (the surface of something), as with claws, nails, etc. **3** to scrape (the surface of the skin) with the nails, as to relieve itching. **4** to chafe or irritate (a surface, esp. the skin). **5** to make or cause to make a grating sound. **6** (tr; sometimes foll. by out) to erase by or as if by scraping. **7** (tr) to write or draw awkwardly. **8** (intr; sometimes foll. by along) to earn a living, manage, etc., with difficulty. **9** to withdraw (an entry) from a race, (US) election, etc. ◆ n **10** the act of scratching. **11** a slight injury. **12** a mark made by scratching. **13** a slight grating sound. **14** (in a handicap sport) a competitor or the status of a competitor who has no allowance. **15a** the line from which competitors start in a race. **15b** (formerly) a line drawn on the floor of a prize ring at which the contestants stood to begin fighting. **16** Billiards, etc. a lucky shot. **17 from scratch.** Inf. from the very beginning. **18 up to scratch.** (usually used with a negative) Inf. up to standard. ◆ adj **19** Sport. (of a team) assembled hastily. **20** (in a handicap sport) with no allowance or penalty. **21** Inf. rough or haphazard. [C15: via OF escrater from Gmc]
▶ 'scratcher n ▶ 'scratchy adj

scratchcard ('skrætʃ,kɑːd) n a ticket that reveals whether or not the holder is eligible for a prize when the surface is removed by scratching.

scratch file n Computing. a temporary store for use during the execution of a program.

scratching ('skrætʃɪŋ) n a percussive effect obtained by rotating a gramophone record manually: a disc-jockey and dub technique.

scratch pad n **1** Chiefly US & Canad. a notebook, esp. one with detachable leaves. **2** Computing. a small semiconductor memory for temporary storage.

scratch video n the recycling of images from films or television to make collages.

scrawl (skrɔːl) vb **1** to write or draw (words, etc.) carelessly or hastily. ◆ n **2** careless or scribbled writing or drawing. [C17: ? a blend of SPRAWL & CRAWL[1]]
▶ 'scrawly adj

scrawny ('skrɔːnɪ) adj **scrawnier, scrawniest. 1** very thin and bony. **2** meagre or stunted. [C19: var. of dialect scranny]
▶ 'scrawnily adv ▶ 'scrawniness n

scream (skriːm) vb **1** to utter or emit (a sharp piercing cry or similar sound), esp. as of fear, pain, etc. **2** (intr) to laugh wildly. **3** (intr) to speak, shout, or behave in a wild manner. **4** (tr) to bring (oneself) into a specified state by screaming: she screamed herself hoarse. **5** (intr) to be extremely conspicuous: these orange curtains scream; you need something more restful. ◆ n **6** a sharp piercing cry or sound, esp. one denoting fear or pain. **7** Inf. a person or thing that causes great amusement. [C13: from Gmc]

screamer ('skriːmə) n **1** a person or thing that screams. **2** a goose-like aquatic bird, such as the **crested screamer** of tropical and subtropical South America. **3** Inf. (in printing) an exclamation mark. **4** someone or something that raises screams of laughter or astonishment. **5** US & Canad. sl. a sensational headline. **6** Austral. sl. a person or thing that is excellent of its kind.

scree (skriː) n an accumulation of rock fragments at the foot of a cliff or hillside, often forming a sloping heap. [OE scrīthan to slip; rel. to ON skrītha to slide]

screech[1] (skriːtʃ) n **1** a shrill or high-pitched sound or cry. ◆ vb **2** to utter with or produce a screech. [C16: var. of earlier scritch, imit.]
▶ 'screecher n ▶ 'screechy adj

screech[2] (skriːtʃ) n Canad. sl. (esp. in Newfoundland) a dark rum. [?from SCREECH[1]]

screech owl n **1** Brit. another name for **barn owl**. **2** a small North American owl having a reddish-brown or grey plumage.

screed (skriːd) n **1** a long or prolonged speech or piece of writing. **2** a strip of wood, plaster, or metal placed on a surface to act as a guide to the thickness of the cement or plaster coat to be applied. **3** a mixture of cement, sand, and water applied to a concrete slab, etc., to give a smooth surface finish. [C14: prob. var. of OE scrēade shred]

screen (skriːn) n **1** a light movable frame, panel, or partition serving to shelter, divide, hide, etc. **2** anything that serves to shelter, protect, or conceal. **3** a frame containing a mesh that is placed over a window to keep out insects. **4** a decorated partition, esp. in a church around the choir. **5** a sieve. **6** the wide end of a cathode-ray tube, esp. in a television set, on which a visible image is formed. **7** a white or silvered surface, placed in front of a projector to receive the enlarged image of a film or of slides. **8 the screen.** the film industry or films collectively. **9** Photog. a plate of ground glass in some types of camera on which the image of a subject is focused. **10** men or ships deployed around and ahead of a larger military formation to warn of attack. **11** Electronics. See **screen grid.** ◆ vb (tr) **12** (sometimes foll. by off) to shelter, protect, or conceal. **13** to sieve or sort. **14** to test or check (an individual or group) so as to determine suitability for a task, etc. **15** to examine for the presence of a disease, weapons, etc. **16** to provide with a screen or screens. **17** to project (a film) onto a screen, esp. for public viewing. [C15: from OF escren (F écran)]
▶ 'screenable adj ▶ 'screener n ▶ 'screenful n

screen grid n Electronics. an electrode placed between the control grid and anode of a valve which acts as an electrostatic shield, thus increasing the stability of the device. Sometimes shortened to **screen.**

screenings ('skriːnɪŋz) pl n refuse separated by sifting.

screening test n a simple test performed on a large number of people to identify those who have or are likely to develop a specified disease.

screenplay ('skriːn,pleɪ) n the script for a film, including instructions for sets and camera work.

screen process n a method of printing using a fine mesh of silk, nylon, etc., treated with an impermeable coating except in the areas through which ink is subsequently forced onto the paper behind. Also called: **silk-screen printing.**

screensaver ('skriːn,seɪvə) n Computing. a computer program that reduces screen damage resulting from an unchanging display, when the computer is switched on but not in use, by blanking the screen or generating moving patterns, pictures, etc.

screenwriter ('skriːn,raɪtə) n a person who writes screenplays.

screw (skruː) n **1** a device used for fastening materials together, consisting of a threaded shank that has a slotted head by which it may be rotated so as to cut its own thread. **2** Also called: **screw-bolt.** a threaded cylindrical rod that engages with a similarly threaded cylindrical hole. **3** a thread in a cylindrical hole corresponding with that on the screw with which it is designed to engage. **4** anything resembling a screw in shape or spiral form. **5** a twisting movement of or resembling that of a screw. **6** Also called: **screw-back.** Billiards, etc. a stroke in which the cue ball moves backward after striking the object ball. **7** another name for **propeller** (sense 1). **8** Sl. a prison guard. **9** Brit. sl. salary, wages, or earnings. **10** Brit. a small amount of salt, tobacco, etc., in a twist of paper. **11** Sl. a person who is mean with money. **12** Sl. an old or worthless horse. **13** (often pl) Sl. force or compulsion (esp. in **put the screws on**). **14** Taboo sl. sexual intercourse. **15 have a screw loose.** Inf. to be insane. ◆ vb **16** (tr) to rotate (a screw or bolt) so as to drive it into or draw it out of a material. **17** (tr) to cut a screw thread in (a rod or hole) with a tap or die or on a lathe. **18** to turn or cause to turn in the manner of a screw. **19** (tr) to attach or fasten with a screw or screws. **20** (tr) Inf. to take advantage of; cheat. **21**

(*tr;* often foll. by *up*) *Inf.* to distort or contort: *he screwed his face into a scowl.* **22** (*tr;* often foll. by *from* or *out of*) *Inf.* to coerce or force out of; extort. **23** *Taboo sl.* to have sexual intercourse (with). **24** (*tr*) *Sl.* to burgle. **25 have one's head screwed on the right way.** *Inf.* to be sensible. ◆ See also **screw up.** [C15: from F *escroe*, from Med. L *scrōfa* screw, from L: sow, presumably because the thread of the screw is like the spiral of the sow's tail]
▶ **'screwer** *n*

screwball ('skruː,bɔːl) *Sl., chiefly US & Canad.* ◆ *n* **1** an odd or eccentric person. ◆ *adj* **2** odd; eccentric.

screwdriver ('skruː,draivə) *n* **1** a tool used for turning screws, usually having a steel shank with a flattened square-cut tip that fits into a slot in the head of the screw. **2** an alcoholic beverage consisting of orange juice and vodka.

screwed (skruːd) *adj* **1** fastened by a screw or screws. **2** having spiral grooves like a screw. **3** twisted or distorted. **4** *Brit. sl.* drunk.

screw eye *n* a wood screw with its shank bent into a ring.

screw pine *n* any of various tropical Old World plants having a spiral mass of pineapple-like leaves and conelike fruits.

screw propeller *n* an early form of ship's propeller in which an Archimedes' screw is used to produce thrust by accelerating a flow of water.

screw top *n* **1** a bottle top that screws onto the bottle, allowing the bottle to be resealed after use. **2** a bottle with such a top.
▶ **'screw-,top** *adj*

screw up *vb* (*tr, adv*) **1** to twist out of shape or distort. **2** to summon up: *to screw up one's courage.* **3** (*also intr*) *Inf.* to mishandle or bungle.

screwy ('skruːɪ) *adj* **screwier, screwiest.** *Inf.* odd, crazy, or eccentric.

Scriabin ★ ('skriæbɪn; *Russian* 'skrjabin) *n* **Aleksandr Nikolayevich** (alɪk'sandr nikaˈlajɪvitʃ). 1872–1915, Russian composer, who wrote many piano works; his orchestral compositions include *Prometheus* (1911).

scribble ('skrɪbᵊl) *vb* **scribbles, scribbling, scribbled. 1** to write or draw in a hasty or illegible manner. **2** to make meaningless or illegible marks (on). **3** *Derog. or facetious.* to write poetry, novels, etc. ◆ *n* **4** hasty careless writing or drawing. **5** meaningless or illegible marks. [C15: from Med. L *scrībillāre* to write hastily, from L *scrībere* to write]
▶ **'scribbler** *n* ▶ **'scribbly** *adj*

scribbly gum *n Austral.* a eucalypt with smooth white bark, marked with random patterns made by wood-boring insects.

scribe (skraib) *n* **1** a person who copies documents, esp. a person who made handwritten copies before the invention of printing. **2** a clerk or public copyist. **3** *Bible.* a recognized scholar and teacher of the Jewish Law. ◆ *vb* **scribes, scribing, scribed. 4** to score a line on (a surface) with a pointed instrument, as in metalworking. [(in the senses: writer, etc.) C14: from L *scrība* clerk, from *scrībere* to write; C17 (vb): ?from INSCRIBE]
▶ **'scribal** *adj*

Scribe ★ (*French* skrib) *n* **Augustin Eugène** (ogystɛ øʒɛn). 1791–1861, French writer of comedies and libretti for light opera.

scriber ('skraibə) *n* a pointed steel tool used to score materials as a guide to cutting, etc. Also called: **scribe.**

scrim (skrɪm) *n* a fine open-weave fabric, used in upholstery, lining, building, and in the theatre to create the illusion of a solid wall. [C18: from ?]

scrimmage ('skrɪmɪdʒ) *n* **1** a rough or disorderly struggle. **2** *American football.* the clash of opposing linemen at every down. ◆ *vb* **scrimmages, scrimmaging, scrimmaged. 3** (*intr*) to engage in a scrimmage. **4** (*tr*) to put (the ball) into a scrimmage. [C15: from earlier *scrimish*, var. of SKIRMISH]
▶ **'scrimmager** *n*

scrimp (skrɪmp) *vb* **1** (when *intr*, sometimes foll. by *on*) to be very sparing in the use (of) (esp. in **scrimp and save**). **2**

(*tr*) to treat meanly: *he is scrimping his children.* [C18: Scot., from ?]
▶ **'scrimpy** *adj* ▶ **'scrimpiness** *n*

scrimshank ('skrɪm,ʃæŋk) *vb* (*intr*) *Brit. mil. sl.* to shirk work. [C19: from ?]

scrimshaw ('skrɪm,ʃɔː) *n* **1** the art of decorating or carving shells, bone, ivory, etc., done by sailors as a leisure activity. **2** an article or articles made in this manner. [C19: from ?]

scrip¹ (skrɪp) *n* **1** a written certificate, list, etc. **2** a small scrap, esp. of paper with writing on it. **3** *Finance.* **3a** a certificate representing a claim to part of a share of stock. **3b** the shares issued by a company (**scrip** or **bonus issue**) without charge and distributed among existing shareholders. [C18: in some senses, prob. from SCRIPT; otherwise, short for *subscription receipt*]

scrip² (skrɪp) *or* **script** *n Inf.* a medical prescription. [C20: from PRESCRIPTION]

script (skrɪpt) *n* **1** handwriting as distinguished from print. **2** the letters, characters, or figures used in writing by hand. **3** any system or style of writing. **4** written copy for the use of performers in films and plays. **5** *Law.* an original or principal document. **6** an answer paper in an examination. **7** another word for **scrip²**. ◆ *vb* **8** (*tr*) to write a script for. [C14: from L *scriptum* something written, from *scrībere* to write]

Script. *abbrev. for* Scripture(s).

scriptorium (skrɪp'tɔːrɪəm) *n, pl* **scriptoriums** *or* **scriptoria** (-rɪə). a room, esp. in a monastery, set apart for the copying of manuscripts. [from Med. L]

scripture ('skrɪptʃə) *n* a sacred, solemn, or authoritative book or piece of writing. [C13: from L *scriptūra* written material, from *scrībere* to write]
▶ **'scriptural** *adj*

Scripture ('skrɪptʃə) *n* **1** Also called: **Holy Scripture, Holy Writ, the Scriptures.** *Christianity.* the Old and New Testaments. **2** any book or body of writings, esp. when regarded as sacred by a particular religious group.

scriptwriter ('skrɪpt,raitə) *n* a person who prepares scripts, esp. for a film.
▶ **'script,writing** *n*

scrivener ('skrɪvnə) *n Arch.* **1** a person who writes out deeds, etc. **2** a notary. [C14: from *scrivein* clerk, from OF *escrivain*, ult. from L *scrība* SCRIBE]

scrod (skrɒd) *n US.* a young cod or haddock. [C19: ? from obs. Du. *schrood,* from MDu. *schrode* SHRED (*n*); the name perhaps refers to the method of preparing the fish for cooking]

scrofula ('skrɒfjulə) *n Pathol.* (*no longer in technical use*) tuberculosis of the lymphatic glands. Also called (formerly): (the) **king's evil.** [C14: from Med. L, from LL *scrōfulae* swollen glands in the neck, lit.: little sows (sows were thought to be particularly prone to the disease), from L *scrōfa* sow]
▶ **'scrofulous** *adj*

scroll (skrəʊl) *n* **1** a roll of parchment, etc., usually inscribed with writing. **2** an ancient book in the form of a roll of parchment, papyrus, etc. **3** a decorative carving or moulding resembling a scroll. ◆ *vb* **4** (*tr*) to saw into scrolls. **5** to roll up like a scroll. **6** *Computing.* to move (text) on a screen in order to view a section that cannot be fitted into a single display. [C15 *scrowle,* from *scrowe,* from OF *escroe* scrap of parchment, but also infl. by ROLL]

scroll saw *n* a saw with a narrow blade for cutting intricate ornamental curves in wood.

scrollwork ('skrəʊl,wɜːk) *n* ornamental work in scroll-like patterns.

Scrooge (skruːdʒ) *n* a mean or miserly person. [C19: after a character in Dickens' story *A Christmas Carol* (1843)]

scrophulariaceous (,skrɒfjuˌlɛərɪ'eiʃəs) *adj* of or belonging to the *Scrophulariaceae,* a family of plants including figwort, snapdragon, foxglove, and mullein. [C19: from NL (*herba*) *scrophularia* scrofula (plant), from the use of such plants in treating scrofula]

scrotum ('skrəʊtəm) *n, pl* **scrota** (-tə) *or* **scrotums.** the

pouch of skin containing the testes in most mammals. [C16: from L]
▸ **'scrotal** *adj*

scrounge (skraʊndʒ) *vb* **scrounges, scrounging, scrounged.** *Inf.* **1** (when *intr*, sometimes foll. by *around*) to search in order to acquire (something) without cost. **2** to obtain or seek to obtain (something) by begging. [C20: var. of dialect *scrunge* to steal, from ?]
▸ **'scrounger** *n*

scrub[1] (skrʌb) *vb* **scrubs, scrubbing, scrubbed. 1** to rub (a surface, etc.) hard, with or as if with a brush, soap, and water, in order to clean it. **2** to remove (dirt) by rubbing, esp. with a brush and water. **3** (*intr;* foll. by *up*) (of a surgeon) to wash the hands and arms thoroughly before operating. **4** (*tr*) to purify (a gas) by removing impurities. **5** (*tr*) *Inf.* to delete or cancel. ◆ *n* **6** the act of or an instance of scrubbing. [C14: from MLow G *schrubben*, or MDu. *schrobben*]

scrub[2] (skrʌb) *n* **1a** vegetation consisting of stunted trees, bushes, and other plants growing in an arid area. **1b** (*as modifier*): *scrub vegetation.* **2** an area of arid land covered with such vegetation. **3a** an animal of inferior breeding or condition. **3b** (*as modifier*): *a scrub bull.* **4** a small person. **5** anything stunted or inferior. **6** *Sport, US & Canad.* a player not in the first team. **7 the scrub.** *Austral. inf.* a remote or uncivilized place. ◆ *adj* (*prenominal*) **8** small or inferior. **9** *Sport, US.* **9a** (of a player) not in the first team. **9b** (of a team) composed of such players. [C16: var. of SHRUB[1]]

scrubber ('skrʌbə) *n* **1** a person or thing that scrubs. **2** an apparatus for purifying a gas. **3** *Derog. sl.* a promiscuous woman.

scrubby ('skrʌbɪ) *adj* **scrubbier, scrubbiest. 1** covered with or consisting of scrub. **2** (of trees, etc.) stunted in growth. **3** *Brit. inf.* messy.

scrubland ('skrʌb,lænd) *n* an area of scrub vegetation.

scrub turkey *n* another term for **megapode.**

scrub typhus *n* a disease characterized by severe headache, skin rash, chills, and swelling of the lymph nodes, caused by the bite of mites infected with a microorganism: occurs mainly in Asia and Australia.

scruff[1] (skrʌf) *n* the nape of the neck (esp. in **by the scruff of the neck**). [C18: var. of *scuft,* ?from ON *skoft* hair]

scruff[2] (skrʌf) *n Inf.* **1** an untidy scruffy person. **2** a disreputable person; ruffian.

scruffy ('skrʌfɪ) *adj* **scruffier, scruffiest.** unkempt or shabby.

scrum (skrʌm) *n* **1** *Rugby.* the act or method of restarting play when the two opposing packs of forwards group together with heads down and arms interlocked and push to gain ground while the scrum half throws the ball in and the hookers attempt to scoop it out to their own team. **2** *Inf.* a disorderly struggle. ◆ *vb* **scrums, scrumming, scrummed. 3** (*intr;* usually foll. by *down*) *Rugby.* to form a scrum. [C19: from SCRUMMAGE]

scrum half *n Rugby.* **1** a player who puts in the ball at scrums and tries to get it away to his three-quarter backs. **2** this position in a team.

scrummage ('skrʌmɪdʒ) *n, vb* **scrummages, scrummaging, scrummaged. 1** *Rugby.* another word for **scrum. 2** a variant of **scrimmage.** [C19: var. of SCRIMMAGE]

scrump (skrʌmp) *vb Dialect.* to steal (apples) from an orchard or garden. [var. of SCRIMP]

scrumptious ('skrʌmpʃəs) *adj Inf.* very pleasing; delicious. [C19: prob. changed from SUMPTUOUS]
▸ **'scrumptiously** *adv*

scrumpy ('skrʌmpɪ) *n* a rough dry cider, brewed esp. in the West Country of England. [from *scrump,* var. of SCRIMP (in obs. sense: withered), referring to the apples used]

scrunch (skrʌntʃ) *vb* **1** to crumple or crunch or to be crumpled or crunched. ◆ *n* **2** the act or sound of scrunching. [C19: var. of CRUNCH]

scrunchie ('skrʌntʃɪ) *n* a loop of elastic covered loosely with fabric, used to hold the hair in a ponytail.

scruple ('skruːpᵊl) *n* **1** (*often pl*) a doubt or hesitation as to what is morally right in a certain situation. **2** *Arch.* a very

small amount. **3** a unit of weight equal to 20 grains (1.296 grams). ◆ *vb* **scruples, scrupling, scrupled. 4** (*obs when tr*) to have doubts (about), esp. from a moral compunction. [C16: from L *scrupulus* a small weight, from *scrupus* rough stone]

scrupulous ('skruːpjʊləs) *adj* **1** characterized by careful observation of what is morally right. **2** very careful or precise. [C15: from L *scrupulōsus* punctilious]
▸ **'scrupulously** *adv* ▸ **'scrupulousness** *n*

scrutineer (,skruːtɪ'nɪə) *n* a person who examines, esp. one who scrutinizes the conduct of an election poll.

scrutinize *or* **scrutinise** ('skruːtɪ,naɪz) *vb* **scrutinizes, scrutinizing, scrutinized** *or* **scrutinises, scrutinising, scrutinised.** (*tr*) to examine carefully or in minute detail.
▸ **'scruti,nizer** *or* **'scruti,niser** *n*

scrutiny ('skruːtɪnɪ) *n, pl* **scrutinies. 1** close or minute examination. **2** a searching look. **3** (in the early Christian Church) a formal testing that catechumens had to undergo before being baptized. [C15: from LL *scrūtinium* an investigation, from *scrūtārī* to search (orig. referring to rag-and-bone men), from *scrūta* rubbish]

scry (skraɪ) *vb* **scries, scrying, scried.** (*intr*) to divine, esp. by crystal gazing. [C16: from DESCRY]

scuba ('skjuːbə) *n* an apparatus used in skin diving, consisting of a cylinder or cylinders containing compressed air attached to a breathing apparatus. [C20: from the initials of *self-contained underwater breathing apparatus*]

scud (skʌd) *vb* **scuds, scudding, scudded.** (*intr*) **1** (esp. of clouds) to move along swiftly and smoothly. **2** *Naut.* to run before a gale. ◆ *n* **3** the act of scudding. **4a** a formation of low ragged clouds driven by a strong wind beneath rain-bearing clouds. **4b** a sudden shower or gust of wind. [C16: prob. of Scand. origin]

scuff (skʌf) *vb* **1** to drag (the feet) while walking. **2** to scratch (a surface) or (of a surface) to become scratched. **3** (*tr*) *US.* to poke at (something) with the foot. ◆ *n* **4** the act or sound of scuffing. **5** a rubbed place caused by scuffing. **6** a backless slipper. [C19: prob. imit.]

scuffle ('skʌfᵊl) *vb* **scuffles, scuffling, scuffled.** (*intr*) **1** to fight in a disorderly manner. **2** to move by shuffling. ◆ *n* **3** a disorderly struggle. **4** the sound made by scuffling. [C16: of Scand. origin; cf. Swedish *skuff, skuffa* to push]

scull (skʌl) *n* **1** a single oar moved from side to side over the stern of a boat to propel it. **2** one of a pair of short-handled oars, both of which are pulled by one oarsman. **3** a racing shell propelled by an oarsman or oarsmen pulling two oars. **4** an act, instance, period, or distance of sculling. ◆ *vb* **5** to propel (a boat) with a scull. [C14: from ?]
▸ **'sculler** *n*

scullery ('skʌlərɪ) *n, pl* **sculleries.** *Chiefly Brit.* a small room or part of a kitchen where washing-up, vegetable preparation, etc., is done. [C15: from Anglo-Norman *squillerie,* from OF, from *escuele* a bowl, from L *scutella,* from *scutra* a flat tray]

Scullin ★ ('skʌlɪn) *n* James Henry. 1876–1953, Australian statesman; prime minister of Australia (1929–31).

scullion ('skʌljən) *n* **1** a mean or despicable person. **2** *Arch.* a servant employed to work in a kitchen. [C15: from OF *escouillon* cleaning cloth, from *escouve* a broom, from L *scōpa* a broom, twig]

sculpt (skʌlpt) *vb* **1** a variant of **sculpture. 2** (*intr*) to practise sculpture. ◆ Also: **sculp.** [C19: from F *sculpter,* from L *sculpere* to carve]

sculptor ('skʌlptə) *or* (*fem*) **sculptress** *n* a person who practises sculpture.

sculpture ('skʌlptʃə) *n* **1** the art of making figures or designs in relief or the round by carving wood, moulding plaster, etc., or casting metals, etc. **2** works or a work made in this way. **3** ridges or indentations as on a shell, formed by natural processes. ◆ *vb* **sculptures, sculpturing, sculptured.** (*mainly tr*) **4** (*also intr*) to carve, cast, or fashion (stone, bronze, etc.) three-dimensionally. **5** to portray (a person, etc.) by means of sculpture. **6** to form in the manner of sculpture. **7** to decorate with sculpture. [C14: from L *sculptūra* a carving]
▸ **'sculptural** *adj*

★ people and places

sculpturesque (ˌskʌlptʃəˈrɛsk) *adj* resembling sculpture.
> ˌsculptur'esquely *adv*

scum (skʌm) *n* **1** a layer of impure matter that forms on the surface of a liquid, often as the result of boiling or fermentation. **2** the greenish film of algae and similar vegetation surface of a stagnant pond. **3** the skin of oxides or impurities on the surface of a molten metal. **4** waste matter. **5** a worthless person or group of people. ♦ *vb* **scums, scumming, scummed. 6** (*tr*) to remove scum from. **7** (*intr*) *Rare.* to form a layer of or become covered with scum. [C13: of Gmc origin]
> 'scummy *adj*

scumbag ('skʌmˌbæg) *n Sl* an offensive or despicable person. [C20: ?from earlier US sense: condom, from US slang *scum* semen + *bag*]

scumble ('skʌmbˀl) *vb* **scumbles, scumbling, scumbled. 1** (in painting and drawing) to soften or blend (an outline or colour) with an upper coat of opaque colour, applied very thinly. **2** to produce an effect of broken colour on doors, panelling, etc., by exposing coats of paint below the top coat. ♦ *n* **3** the upper layer of colour applied in this way. [C18: prob. from SCUM]

scuncheon ('skʌntʃən) *n* the inner part of a door jamb or window frame. [C15: from OF *escoinson*, from *coin* angle]

scungy ('skʌndʒɪ) *adj* **scungier, scungiest.** *Austral. & NZ sl.* miserable; sordid; dirty. [C20: from ?]

scunner ('skʌnə) *Dialect, chiefly Scot.* ♦ *vb* **1** (*intr*) to feel aversion. **2** (*tr*) to produce a feeling of aversion in. ♦ *n* **3** a strong aversion (often in **take a scunner**). **4** an object of dislike; nuisance. [C14: from Scot. *skunner*, from ?]

Scunthorpe ★ ('skʌn,θɔːp) *n* a town in E England, in North Lincolnshire: developed rapidly after the discovery of local iron ore (1871); iron and steel industries have declined. Pop.: 75 982 (1991).

scup (skʌp) *n* a common fish of American coastal regions of the Atlantic. [C19: from Amerind *mishcup*, from *mishe* big + *kuppe* close together; from the form of the scales]

scupper[1] ('skʌpə) *n Naut.* a drain or spout allowing water on the deck of a vessel to flow overboard. [C15 *skopper*, from ?]

scupper[2] ('skʌpə) *vb* (*tr*) *Brit. sl.* **1** to overwhelm, ruin, or disable. **2** to sink (one's ship) deliberately. [C19: from ?]

scurf (skɜːf) *n* **1** another name for **dandruff. 2** flaky or scaly matter adhering to or peeling off a surface. [OE *scurf*]
> 'scurfy *adj*

scurrilous ('skʌrɪləs) *adj* **1** grossly or obscenely abusive or defamatory. **2** characterized by gross or obscene humour. [C16: from L *scurrīlis* derisive, from *scurra* buffoon]
> scurrility (skəˈrɪlɪtɪ) *n* > 'scurrilously *adv*

scurry ('skʌrɪ) *vb* **scurries, scurrying, scurried. 1** to move about hurriedly. **2** (*intr*) to whirl about. ♦ *n, pl* **scurries. 3** the act or sound of scurrying. **4** a brisk light whirling movement, as of snow. [C19: prob. from *hurry-scurry*, from HURRY]

scurvy ('skɜːvɪ) *n* **1** a disease caused by a lack of vitamin C, characterized by anaemia, spongy gums, and bleeding beneath the skin. ♦ *adj* **scurvier, scurviest. 2** mean or despicable. [C16: see SCURF]
> 'scurvily *adv* > 'scurviness *n*

scurvy grass *n* any of various plants of Europe and North America, formerly used to treat scurvy.

scut (skʌt) *n* the short tail of animals such as the deer and rabbit. [C15: prob. from ON]

scutage ('skjuːtɪdʒ) *n* (in feudal society) a payment sometimes exacted by a lord from his vassal in lieu of military service. [C15: from Med. L *scūtāgium*, lit.: shield dues, from L *scūtum* a shield]

Scutari ★ *n* **1** ('skuːtərɪ, skuːˈtɑːrɪ). the former name of **Üsküdar. 2** ('skuːtarɪ). the Italian name for **Shkodër.**

scutate ('skjuːteɪt) *adj* **1** (of animals) covered with large bony or horny plates. **2** *Bot.* shaped like a round shield. [C19: from L *scūtātus* armed with a shield, from *scūtum* a shield]

scutcheon ('skʌtʃən) *n* **1** a variant of **escutcheon. 2** any rounded or shield-shaped structure.

scutch grass (skʌtʃ) *n* another name for **couch grass.** [var. of COUCH GRASS]

scute (skjuːt) *n Zool.* a horny plate that makes up part of the exoskeleton in armadillos, turtles, etc. [C14 (the name of a F coin; C19 in zoological sense): from L *scūtum* shield]

scutellum (skjuːˈtɛləm) *n, pl* **scutella** (-lə). *Biol.* **1** the last of three plates into which an insect's thorax is divided. **2** one of the scales on the tarsus of a bird's leg. **3** the cotyledon of a developing grass seed. [C18: from NL: a little shield, from L *scūtum* a shield]
> **scutellate** ('skjuːtɪ,leɪt, -lɪt) *adj*

scutter ('skʌtə) *vb, n Brit. inf.* scurry. [C18: prob. from SCUTTLE[2], with -ER[1] as in SCATTER]

scuttle[1] ('skʌtˀl) *n* **1** See **coal scuttle. 2** *Dialect, chiefly Brit.* a shallow basket, esp. for carrying vegetables. **3** the part of a motorcar body lying immediately behind the bonnet. [OE *scutel* trencher, from L *scutella* bowl, dim. of *scutra* platter]

scuttle[2] ('skʌtˀl) *vb* **scuttles, scuttling, scuttled. 1** (*intr*) to run or move about with short hasty steps. ♦ *n* **2** a hurried pace or run. [C15: ?from SCUD, infl. by SHUTTLE]

scuttle[3] ('skʌtˀl) *vb* **scuttles, scuttling, scuttled.** (*tr*) *Naut.* to cause (a vessel) to sink by opening the seacocks or making holes in the bottom. **2** to give up (hopes, plans, etc.). ♦ *n* **3** *Naut.* a small hatch or its cover. [C15 (n): via OF from Sp. *escotilla* a small opening, from *escote* opening in a piece of cloth, from *escotar* to cut out]

scuttlebutt ('skʌtˀl,bʌt) *n Naut.* **1** a drinking fountain. **2** (formerly) a cask of drinking water aboard a ship. **3** *Chiefly US sl.* gossip.

scutum ('skjuːtəm) *n, pl* **scuta** (-tə). **1** the middle of three plates into which an insect's thorax is divided. **2** another word for **scute.** [L: shield]

scuzzy ('skʌzɪ) *adj* **scuzzier, scuzziest.** *Sl., chiefly US.* unkempt, dirty, or squalid. [C20: ?from *disgusting* or ?from blend of *scum & fuzz*]

Scylla ★ ('sɪlə) *n* **1** *Greek myth.* a sea nymph transformed into a sea monster believed to drown sailors navigating the Strait of Messina. Cf. **Charybdis. 2 between Scylla and Charybdis.** in a predicament in which avoidance of either of two dangers means exposure to the other.

Scyros ★ ('skɪrəs) *n* a variant spelling of **Skyros.**

scythe (saɪð) *n* **1** a long-handled implement for cutting grass, etc., having a curved sharpened blade that moves in a plane parallel to the ground. ♦ *vb* **scythes, scything, scythed. 2** (*tr*) to cut (grass, etc.) with a scythe. [OE *sigthe*]

Scythia ★ ('sɪðɪə) *n* an ancient region of SE Europe and Asia, north of the Black Sea: now part of the Ukraine.
> 'Scythian *adj, n*

SD *abbrev. for:* **1** South Dakota. **2** Also: **sd.** *Statistics.* standard deviation.

S. Dak. *abbrev. for* South Dakota.

SDI *abbrev. for* Strategic Defense Initiative. See **Star Wars.**

SDLP *abbrev. for* Social Democratic and Labour Party (of Ulster).

SDP *abbrev. for* Social Democratic Party.

SDRs *Finance. abbrev. for* special drawing rights.

Se *the chemical symbol for* selenium.

SE *symbol for* southeast(ern).

sea (siː) *n* **1a** (usually preceded by *the*) the mass of salt water on the earth's surface as differentiated from the land. Related adjs.: **marine, maritime. 1b** (*as modifier*): *sea air.* **2** (*cap. when part of place name*) **2a** one of the smaller areas of ocean: *the Irish Sea.* **2b** a large inland area of water: *the Caspian Sea.* **3** turbulence or swell: *heavy seas.* **4** (*cap. when part of a name*) *Astron.* any of many huge dry plains on the surface of the moon: *Sea of Serenity.* See also **mare**[2]. **5** anything resembling the sea in size or apparent limitlessness. **6 at sea. 6a** on the ocean. **6b** in a state of confusion. **7 go to sea.** to become a sailor. **8 put (out) to sea.** to embark on a sea voyage. [OE *sǣ*]

sea anchor *n Naut.* any device, such as a bucket,

dragged in the water to keep a vessel heading into the wind or reduce drifting.

sea anemone *n* any of various coelenterates having a polypoid body with oral rings of tentacles.

sea bag *n* a canvas bag used by a seaman for his belongings.

sea bass (bæs) *n* any of various American coastal fishes having an elongated body with a long spiny dorsal fin almost divided into two.

sea bird *n* a bird such as a gull, that lives on the sea.

seaboard ('siː,bɔːd) *n* land bordering on the sea.

Seaborg ★ ('siː,bɔːg) *n* **Glenn Theodore**. 1912–99, US chemist. With E. M. McMillan, he discovered several transuranic elements: shared the Nobel prize for chemistry 1951.

seaborgium ('siːbɔːgɪəm) *n* a synthetic transuranic element, synthesized and identified in 1974. Symbol: Sg; atomic no.: 106. [C20: after Glenn SEABORG]

seaborne ('siː,bɔːn) *adj* **1** carried on or by the sea. **2** transported by ship.

sea bream *n* a fish of European seas, valued as a food fish.

sea breeze *n* a wind blowing from the sea to the land, esp. during the day when the land surface is warmer.

SEAC ('siːæk) *n* (in Britain) *acronym for* School Examination and Assessment Council.

sea change *n* a seemingly magical change. [from Ariel's song "Full Fathom Five" in *The Tempest* (1611)]

seacoast ('siː,kəʊst) *n* land bordering on the sea; a coast.

seacock ('siː,kɒk) *n Naut.* a valve in the hull of a vessel below the water line for admitting sea water or for pumping out bilge water.

sea cow *n* **1** a dugong or manatee. **2** an archaic name for the **walrus**.

sea cucumber *n* an echinoderm having an elongated body covered with a leathery skin and a cluster of tentacles at the oral end.

sea dog *n* an experienced or old sailor.

sea eagle *n* any of various fish-eating eagles of coastal areas, esp. the **European sea eagle**, having a brown plumage and white tail.

seafarer ('siː,fɛərə) *n* **1** a traveller who goes by sea. **2** a sailor.

seafaring ('siː,fɛərɪŋ) *adj* (*prenominal*) **1** travelling by sea. **2** working as a sailor. ◆ *n* **3** the act of travelling by sea. **4** the work of a sailor.

seafood ('siː,fuːd) *n* edible saltwater fish or shellfish.

seafront ('siː,frʌnt) *n* a built-up area facing the sea.

sea-girt *adj Literary*. surrounded by the sea.

seagoing ('siː,gəʊɪŋ) *adj* intended for or used at sea.

sea green *n* **a** a moderate green colour, sometimes with a bluish or yellowish tinge. **b** (*as adj*): *a sea-green carpet*.

sea gull *n* **1** a popular name for the **gull** (the bird). **2** *NZ inf.* a casual dock worker.

sea holly *n* a European plant of sandy shores, having bluish-green stems and blue flowers.

sea horse *n* **1** a marine teleost fish of temperate and tropical waters, having a bony-plated body, a prehensile tail, and a horselike head and swimming in an upright position. **2** an archaic name for the **walrus**. **3** a fabled sea creature with the tail of a fish and the front parts of a horse.

sea-island cotton *n* **1** a cotton plant of the Sea Islands, off the Florida coast, widely cultivated for its fine long fibres. **2** the fibre of this plant or the material woven from it.

Sea Islands ★ *pl n* a chain of islands in the Atlantic off the coasts of South Carolina, Georgia, and Florida.

sea kale *n* a European coastal plant with broad fleshy leaves and white flowers: cultivated for its edible asparagus-like shoots. Cf. **kale**.

seal[1] (siːl) *n* **1** a device impressed on a piece of wax, etc., fixed to a letter, etc., as a mark of authentication. **2** a stamp, ring, etc., engraved with a device to form such an

impression. **3** a substance, esp. wax, so placed over an envelope, etc., that it must be broken before the object can be opened or used. **4** any substance or device used to close or fasten tightly. **5** a small amount of water contained in the trap of a drain to prevent the passage of foul smells. **6** anything that gives a pledge or confirmation. **7** a token; sign: *seal of death*. **8** a decorative stamp sold in aid of charity. **9** *RC Church*. Also called: **seal of confession**. the obligation never to reveal anything said in confession. **10** set one's seal on (*or* to). **10a** to mark with one's sign or seal. **10b** to endorse. ◆ *vb* **11** to affix a seal to, as proof of authenticity, etc. **12** to stamp with or as if with a seal. **13** to approve or authorize. **14** (sometimes foll. by *up*) to close or secure with or as if with a seal: *to seal one's lips*. **15** (foll. by *off*) to enclose (a place) with a fence, etc. **16** to decide irrevocably. **17** to close tightly so as to render airtight or watertight. **18** to subject (the outside of meat, etc.) to fierce heat so as to retain the juices during cooking. **19** to paint (a porous material) with a nonporous coating. **20** *Austral*. to cover (a road) with bitumen, asphalt, tarmac, etc. [C13 *seel*, from OF, from L *sigillum* little figure, from *signum* a sign] ► 'sealable *adj*

seal[2] (siːl) *n* **1** a fish-eating mammal with four flippers which is aquatic but comes on shore to breed. **2** sealskin. ◆ *vb* **3** (*intr*) to hunt for seals. [OE *seolh*] ► 'sealer *n* ► 'seal-,like *adj*

sea lane *n* an established route for ships.

sealant ('siːlənt) *n* **1** any substance, such as wax, used for sealing documents, bottles, etc. **2** any of a number of substances used for stopping leaks, waterproofing wood, etc.

sea lavender *n* any of various plants found on temperate salt marshes, having spikes of white, pink, or mauve flowers.

sealed-beam *adj* (esp. of a car headlight) having a lens and prefocused reflector sealed in the lamp vacuum.

sealed road *n Austral. & NZ.* a road surfaced with bitumen or some other hard material.

sea legs *pl n Inf.* **1** the ability to maintain one's balance on board ship. **2** the ability to resist seasickness.

sea level *n* the level of the surface of the sea with respect to the land, taken to be the mean level between high and low tide.

sea lily *n* any of various echinoderms in which the body consists of a long stalk bearing a central disc with delicate radiating arms.

sealing wax *n* a hard material made of shellac, turpentine, and pigment that softens when heated.

sea lion *n* any of various large eared seals, such as the **Californian sea lion**, of the N Pacific, often used as a performing animal.

Sea Lord *n* (in Britain) either of the two serving naval officers (**First** and **Second Sea Lords**) who sit on the admiralty board of the Ministry of Defence.

seal ring *n* another term for **signet ring**.

sealskin ('siːl,skɪn) *n* **a** the skin or pelt of a fur seal, esp. when dressed with the outer hair removed and the underfur dyed dark brown. **b** (*as modifier*): *a sealskin coat*.

Sealyham terrier ('siːlɪəm) *n* a short-legged short-haired breed of terrier with a medium-length white coat. [C19: after *Sealyham*, village in S Wales]

seam (siːm) *n* **1** the line along which pieces of fabric, etc., are joined, esp. by stitching. **2** a ridge or line made by joining two edges. **3** a stratum of coal, ore, etc. **4** a linear indentation, such as a wrinkle or scar. **5** (*modifier*) *Cricket*. of or relating to a style of bowling in which the bowler utilizes the stitched seam round the ball in order to make it swing in flight and after touching the ground: *a seam bowler*. **6** bursting at the seams. full to overflowing. ◆ *vb* **7** (*tr*) to join or sew together by or as if by a seam. **8** to mark or become marked with or as if with a seam or wrinkle. [OE]

seaman ('siːmən) *n*, *pl* **seamen**. **1** a naval rating trained in seamanship. **2** a man who serves as a sailor. **3** a person skilled in seamanship. ► 'seamanly *adj, adv* ► 'seaman-,like *adj*

★ people and places

seamanship ('siːmənʃɪp) *n* skill in and knowledge of the work of navigating, maintaining, and operating a vessel.

Seami ★ (siˈɑːmɪ) *n* a variant spelling of **Zeami**.

sea mile *n* a unit of distance used in navigation, defined as the length of one minute of arc, measured along the meridian, in the latitude of the position. Its actual length varies slightly with latitude, but is about 1853 metres (6080 feet). See also **nautical mile**.

seamless ('siːmlɪs) *adj* **1** (of a garment) having no seams. **2** continuous or flowing: *seamless output; a seamless performance*.

sea mouse *n* any of various large worms having a broad flattened body covered dorsally with a dense mat of iridescent hairlike setae.

seamstress ('semstrɪs) *or (rarely)* **sempstress** ('sempstrɪs) *n* a woman who sews and makes clothes, esp. professionally.

seamy ('siːmɪ) *adj* **seamier, seamiest.** showing the least pleasant aspect; sordid.
▸ **'seaminess** *n*

Seanad Éireann ('ʃænəð 'eːrən) *n* (in the Republic of Ireland) the upper chamber of parliament. [from Irish, lit.: senate of Ireland]

seance *or* **séance** ('seɪɑːns) *n* a meeting at which spiritualists attempt to receive messages from the spirits of the dead. [C19: from F, lit.: a sitting, from OF *seoir* to sit, from L *sedēre*]

sea otter *n* a large marine otter of N Pacific coasts, formerly hunted for its thick brown fur.

sea pink *n* another name for **thrift** (the plant).

seaplane ('siːˌpleɪn) *n* any aircraft that lands on and takes off from water.

seaport ('siːˌpɔːt) *n* **1** a port or harbour accessible to seagoing vessels. **2** a town or city located at such a place.

SEAQ ('siːˌæk) *n* acronym for Stock Exchange Automated Quotations: an electronic system that collects and displays information needed to trade in equities.

sear (sɪə) *vb* (*tr*) **1** to scorch or burn the surface of. **2** to brand with a hot iron. **3** to cause to wither. **4** *Rare.* to make unfeeling. ◆ *adj* **5** *Poetic.* dried up. [OE *sēarian* to become withered, from *sēar* withered]

search (sɜːtʃ) *vb* **1** to look through (a place, etc.) thoroughly in order to find someone or something. **2** (*tr*) to examine (a person) for concealed objects. **3** to look at or examine (something) closely: *to search one's conscience*. **4** (*tr*; foll. by *out*) to discover by investigation. **5** *Surgery.* to probe (a wound, etc.). **6** *Computing.* to review (a file) to locate specific information. **7** *Arch.* to penetrate. **8 search me.** *Inf.* I don't know. ◆ *n* **9** the act or an instance of searching. **10** the examination of a vessel by the right of search. **11 right of search.** *International law.* the right possessed by the warships of a belligerent state to search merchant vessels to ascertain whether ship or cargo is liable to seizure. [C14: from OF *cerchier*, from LL *circāre* to go around, from L *circus* circle]
▸ **'searchable** *adj* ▸ **'searcher** *n*

search engine *n Computing.* a service provided on the Internet that carries out searches and locates information on the Internet.

searching ('sɜːtʃɪŋ) *adj* keenly penetrating: *a searching look*.
▸ **'searchingly** *adv*

searchlight ('sɜːtʃˌlaɪt) *n* **1** a device that projects a powerful beam of light in a particular direction. **2** the beam of light produced by such a device.

search party *n* a group of people taking part in an organized search, as for a lost, missing, or wanted person.

search warrant *n* a written order issued by a justice of the peace authorizing a constable to enter and search premises for stolen goods, etc.

Searle ★ (sɜːl) *n* Ronald (William Fordham). born 1920, British cartoonist, best known as the creator of the schoolgirls of St Trinian's.

seascape ('siːˌskeɪp) *n* a sketch, etc., of the sea.

sea scorpion *n* any of various northern marine fishes

having a tapering body and a large head covered with bony plates and spines.

Sea Scout *n* a Scout belonging to any of a number of Scout troops whose main activities are canoeing, sailing, etc.

sea serpent *n* a huge legendary creature of the sea resembling a snake or dragon.

sea shanty *n* another name for **shanty**[2].

seashell ('siːˌʃel) *n* the empty shell of a marine mollusc.

seashore ('siːˌʃɔː) *n* **1** land bordering on the sea. **2** *Law.* the land between the marks of high and low water.

seasick ('siːˌsɪk) *adj* suffering from nausea and dizziness caused by the motion of a ship at sea.
▸ **'sea,sickness** *n*

seaside ('siːˌsaɪd) *n* **a** any area bordering on the sea, esp. one regarded as a resort. **b** (*as modifier*): *a seaside hotel*.

sea snail *n* a small spiny-finned fish of cold seas, having a soft scaleless tadpole-shaped body with the pelvic fins fused into a sucker.

sea snake *n* a venomous snake of tropical seas that swims by means of a laterally compressed oarlike tail.

season ('siːzⁿn) *n* **1** one of the four equal periods into which the year is divided by the equinoxes and solstices. These periods (spring, summer, autumn, and winter) have characteristic weather conditions, and occur at opposite times of the year in the N and S hemispheres. **2** a period of the year characterized by particular conditions or activities: *the rainy season*. **3** the period during which any particular species of animal, bird, or fish is legally permitted to be caught or killed: *open season on red deer*. **4** a period during which a particular entertainment, sport, etc., takes place: *the football season*. **5** any definite or indefinite period. **6** any of the major periods into which the ecclesiastical calendar is divided, such as Lent or Easter. **7** fitting or proper time. **8 in good season.** early enough. **9 in season. 9a** (of game) permitted to be killed. **9b** (of fresh food) readily available. **9c** Also: **in** *or* **on heat.** (of some female mammals) sexually receptive. **9d** appropriate. ◆ *vb* **10** (*tr*) to add herbs, salt, pepper, or spice to (food). **11** (*tr*) to add zest to. **12** (in the preparation of timber) to undergo or cause to undergo drying. **13** (*tr; usually passive*) to make or become experienced: *seasoned troops*. **14** (*tr*) to mitigate or temper. [C13: from OF *seson*, from L *satiō* a sowing, from *serere* to sow]
▸ **'seasoned** *adj* ▸ **'seasoner** *n*

seasonable ('siːzənəbⁿl) *adj* **1** suitable for the season: *a seasonable Christmas snow scene*. **2** taking place at the appropriate time.
▸ **'seasonableness** *n* ▸ **'seasonably** *adv*

seasonal ('siːzənⁿl) *adj* of, relating to, or occurring at a certain season or seasons of the year: *seasonal labour*.
▸ **'seasonally** *adv*

seasonal affective disorder *n* a state of depression sometimes experienced by people in winter, thought to be related to lack of sunlight. Abbrev.: **SAD.**

seasoning ('siːzənɪŋ) *n* **1** something that enhances the flavour of food, such as salt or herbs. **2** another term (not now in technical usage) for **drying**.

season ticket *n* a ticket for a series of events, number of journeys, etc., within a limited time, usually obtained at a reduced rate.

sea squirt *n* a minute primitive marine animal, most of which are sedentary, having a saclike body with openings through which water enters and leaves.

sea swallow *n* a popular name for **tern.**

seat (siːt) *n* **1** a piece of furniture designed for sitting on, such as a chair or sofa. **2** the part of a chair, bench, etc., on which one sits. **3** a place to sit, esp. one that requires a ticket: *I have two seats for the film tonight*. **4** the buttocks. **5** the part of a garment covering the buttocks. **6** the part or area serving as the base of an object. **7** the part or surface on which the base of an object rests. **8** the place or centre in which something is located: *a seat of government*. **9** a place of abode, esp. a country mansion. **10** a membership or the right to membership in a legislative or similar body. **11** *Chiefly Brit.* a parliamentary constituency. **12** the manner in which a rider sits on a horse. ◆ *vb* **13** (*tr*) to bring to or place on a seat. **14** (*tr*) to provide with seats. **15** (*tr; often passive*) to place or centre: *the ministry is seated in the capital.* **16** (*tr*) to set firmly in place. **17** (*tr*) to fix or install in a position of power. **18** (*intr*) (of garments) to sag in the area covering the buttocks: *your skirt has seated badly.* [OE *gesete*]

seat belt *n* **1** Also called: **safety belt.** a belt or strap worn in a vehicle to restrain forward motion in the event of a collision. **2** a similar belt or strap worn in an aircraft at takeoff and landing.

seating ('si:tɪŋ) *n* **1** the act of providing with a seat or seats. **2a** the provision of seats, as in a theatre, etc. **2b** (*as modifier*): *seating arrangements.* **3** material used for covering seats. **4** a surface on which a part, such as a valve, is supported.

Seaton Valley ★ ('si:t°n) *n* a region in NE England, in SE Northumberland: consists of a group of former coalmining villages. Pop.: 45 000 (latest est.).

sea trout *n* a silvery marine variety of the brown trout that migrates to fresh water to spawn.

Seattle ★ (sɪ'æt°l) *n* a port in W Washington, on the isthmus between Lake Washington and Puget Sound: the largest city in the state and chief commercial centre of the Northwest; two universities. Pop.: 520 947 (1994 est.).

sea urchin *n* any echinoderm such as the **edible sea urchin,** having a globular body enclosed in a rigid spiny test and occurring in shallow marine waters.

sea vegetables *pl n* edible seaweed.

sea wall *n* a wall or embankment built to prevent encroachment or erosion by the sea.

seaward ('si:wəd) *adv* **1** Also called: **seawards.** towards the sea. ◆ *adj* **2** directed or moving towards the sea. **3** (esp. of a wind) coming from the sea.

seaway ('si:,weɪ) *n* **1** a waterway giving access to an inland port. **2** a vessel's progress. **3** a route across the sea.

seaweed ('si:,wi:d) *n* any of numerous multicellular marine algae that grow on the seashore, in salt marshes, in brackish water, or submerged in the ocean.

seaworthy ('si:,wɜ:ðɪ) *adj* in a fit condition or ready for a sea voyage.
▸ '**sea,worthiness** *n*

sebaceous (sɪ'beɪʃəs) *adj* **1** of or resembling sebum, fat, or tallow. **2** secreting fat. [C18: from LL *sēbāceus,* from SEBUM]

sebaceous glands *pl n* the small glands in the skin that secrete sebum into hair follicles and onto most of the body surface except the soles of the feet and the palms of the hands.

Sebastian ★ (sɪ'bæstjən) *n* **Saint.** died ?288 A.D., Christian martyr. According to tradition, he was first shot with arrows and then beaten to death. Feast day: Jan. 20.

Sebastopol ★ (sɪ'bæstəpəl) *n* the English name for Sevastopol.

seborrhoea *or esp. US* **seborrhea** (,sɛbə'rɪə) *n* a disease of the sebaceous glands characterized by excessive secretion of sebum.

sebum ('si:bəm) *n* the oily secretion of the sebaceous glands that acts as a lubricant for the hair and skin and provides some protection against bacteria. [C19: from NL, from L: tallow]

sec[1] (sɛk) *adj* **1** (of wines) dry. **2** (of champagne) of medium sweetness. [C19: from F, from L *siccus*]

sec[2] (sɛk) *n Inf.* short for **second**[2]: *wait a sec.*

sec[3] (sɛk) *abbrev. for* secant.

SEC *abbrev. for* Securities and Exchange Commission.

sec. *abbrev. for:* **1** second (of time). **2** secondary. **3** secretary. **4** section. **5** sector.

secant ('si:kənt) *n* **1** (of an angle) a trigonometric function that in a right-angled triangle is the ratio of the length of the hypotenuse to that of the adjacent side; the reciprocal of cosine. Abbrev.: **sec. 2** a line that intersects a curve. [C16: from L *secāre* to cut]

secateurs ('sɛkətəz) *pl n Chiefly Brit.* a small pair of shears for pruning, having a pair of pivoted handles and

usually a single cutting blade that closes against a flat surface. [C19: pl of F *sécateur,* from L *secāre* to cut]

secede (sɪ'si:d) *vb* **secedes, seceding, seceded.** (*intr; often foll. by from*) (of a person, section, etc.) to make a formal withdrawal of membership, as from a political alliance, etc. [C18: from L *sēcēdere* to withdraw, from *sē-* apart + *cēdere* to go]
▸ se'**ceder** *n*

secession (sɪ'sɛʃən) *n* **1** the act of seceding. **2** (*often cap.*) *Chiefly US.* the withdrawal in 1860–61 of 11 Southern states from the Union to form the Confederacy, precipitating the American Civil War. [C17: from L *sēcessiō* a withdrawing, from *sēcēdere* to SECEDE]
▸ se'**cession,ism** *n* ▸ se'**cessionist** *n, adj*

sech (ʃɛk, sɛtʃ, 'sɛk'eɪtʃ) *n* hyperbolic secant.

seclude (sɪ'klu:d) *vb* **secludes, secluding, secluded.** (*tr*) **1** to remove from contact with others. **2** to shut off or screen from view. [C15: from L *sēclūdere* to shut off, from *sē-* + *claudere* to imprison]

secluded (sɪ'klu:dɪd) *adj* **1** kept apart from the company of others: *a secluded life.* **2** private.
▸ se'**cludedly** *adv* ▸ se'**cludedness** *n*

seclusion (sɪ'klu:ʒən) *n* **1** the act of secluding or the state of being secluded. **2** a secluded place. [C17: from Med. L *sēclūsiō;* see SECLUDE]

second[1] ('sɛkənd) *adj* (*usually prenominal*) **1a** coming directly after the first in numbering or counting order, position, time, etc.; being the ordinal number of *two:* often written 2nd. **1b** (*as n*): *the second in line.* **2** graded or ranked between the first and third levels. **3** alternate: *every second Thursday.* **4** extra: *a second opportunity.* **5** resembling a person or event from an earlier period of history: *a second Wagner.* **6** of lower quality; inferior. **7** denoting the lowest but one forward ratio of a gearbox in a motor vehicle. **8** *Music.* denoting a musical part, voice, or instrument subordinate to or lower in pitch than another (the first): *the second tenors.* **9 at second hand.** by hearsay. ◆ *n* **10** *Brit. education.* an honours degree of the second class, usually further divided into an upper and lower designation. Full term: **second-class honours degree. 11** the lowest but one forward ratio of a gearbox in a motor vehicle. **12** (in boxing, duelling, etc.) an attendant who looks after a competitor. **13** a speech seconding a motion or the person making it. **14** *Music.* the interval between one note and another lying next above or below it in the diatonic scale. **15** (*pl*) goods of inferior quality. **16** (*pl*) *Inf.* a second helping of food. **17** (*pl*) the second course of a meal. ◆ *vb* (*tr*) **18** to give aid or backing to. **19** (in boxing, etc.) to act as second to (a competitor). **20** to express formal support for (a motion already proposed). ◆ *adv* **21** Also: **secondly.** in the second place. ◆ *sentence connector.* **22** Also: **secondly.** as the second point. [C13: via OF from L *secundus* coming next in order, from *sequī* to follow]
▸ '**seconder** *n*

second[2] ('sɛkənd) *n* **1a** 1/60 of a minute of time. **1b** the basic SI unit of time: the duration of 9 192 631 770 periods of radiation corresponding to the transition between two hyperfine levels of the ground state of caesium-133. Symbol: s **2** 1/60 of a minute of angle. Symbol: ″ **3** a very short period of time. [C14: from OF, from Med. L *pars minūta secunda* the second small part (a minute being the first small part of an hour); see SECOND[1]]

second[3] (sɪ'kɒnd) *vb* (*tr*) *Brit.* **1** to transfer (an employee) temporarily to another branch, etc. **2** *Mil.* to transfer (an officer) to another post. [C19: from F *en second* in second rank (or position)]
▸ se'**condment** *n*

secondary ('sɛkəndərɪ) *adj* **1** one grade or step after the first. **2** derived from or depending on what is primary or first: *a secondary source.* **3** below the first in rank, importance, etc. **4** (*prenominal*) of or relating to the education of young people between the ages of 11 and 18: *secondary education.* **5** (of the flight feathers of a bird's wing) growing from the ulna. **6a** being the part of an electric circuit, such as a transformer or induction coil, in which a current is induced by a changing current in a neighbouring coil: *a secondary coil.* **6b** (of a current) flowing in such a circuit. **7** *Chem.* **7a** (of an amine) containing the group

NH. **7b** (of a salt) derived from a tribasic acid by replacement of two acidic hydrogen atoms with metal atoms. ◆ *n, pl* **secondaries. 8** a person or thing that is secondary. **9** a subordinate, deputy, or inferior. **10** a secondary coil, winding, inductance, or current in an electric circuit. **11** *Ornithol.* any of the flight feathers that grow from the ulna of a bird's wing. **12** *Astron.* a celestial body that orbits around a specified primary body: *the moon is the secondary of the earth.* **13** *American football.* **13a** (usually preceded by *the*) cornerbacks and safeties collectively. **13b** their area in the field. **14** short for **secondary colour.** ▸ 'secondarily *adv* ▸ 'secondariness *n*

secondary cell *n* an electric cell that can be recharged and can therefore be used to store electrical energy in the form of chemical energy.

secondary colour *n* a colour formed by mixing two primary colours.

secondary emission *n Physics.* the emission of electrons (**secondary electrons**) from a solid as a result of bombardment with a beam of electrons, ions, or metastable atoms.

secondary picketing *n* the picketing by striking workers of a factory, distribution outlet, etc., that supplies goods to or distributes goods from their employer.

secondary sexual characteristic *n* any of various features distinguishing individuals of different sex but not directly concerned in reproduction. Examples are the antlers of a stag and the beard of a man.

second ballot *n* an electoral procedure in which, after a first ballot, candidates at the bottom of the poll are eliminated and another ballot is held among the remaining candidates.

second-best *adj* **1** next to the best. **2 come off second best.** *Inf.* to be worsted by someone. ◆ *n* **3 second best.** an inferior alternative.

second chamber *n* the upper house of a bicameral legislative assembly.

second childhood *n* dotage; senility (esp. in **in his, her,** etc., **second childhood**).

second class *n* **1** the class or grade next in value, quality, etc., to the first. ◆ *adj* (**second-class** *when prenominal*). **2** of the class or grade next to the best in quality, etc. **3** shoddy or inferior. **4** of or denoting the class of accommodation in a hotel or on a train, etc., lower in quality and price than first class. **5** (in Britain) of mail that is processed more slowly than first-class mail. **6** *Education.* See **second**¹ (sense 10). ◆ *adv* **7** by second-class mail, transport, etc.

second-class citizen *n* a person whose rights and opportunities are treated as less important than those of other people in the same society.

Second Coming *n* the prophesied return of Christ to earth at the Last Judgment.

second cousin *n* the child of a first cousin of either of one's parents.

second-degree burn *n Pathol.* a burn in which blisters appear on the skin.

seconde (sɪ'kɒnd) *n* the second of eight positions from which a parry or attack can be made in fencing. [C18: from F *seconde parade* the second parry]

Second Empire *n* the style of furniture and decoration of the Second Empire in France (1852–70), reviving the Empire style, but with fussier ornamentation.

second fiddle *n Inf.* **1a** the second violin in a string quartet or an orchestra. **1b** the musical part assigned to such an instrument. **2** a person who has a secondary status.

second floor *n Brit.* the storey of a building immediately above the first and two floors up from the ground. US and Canad. term: **third floor.**

second generation *n* **1** offspring of parents born in a given country. **2** (*modifier*) of a refined stage of development in manufacture: *a second-generation robot.*

second growth *n* natural regrowth of a forest after fire, cutting, etc.

second hand *n* a pointer on the face of a timepiece that indicates the seconds.

second-hand *adj* **1** previously owned or used. **2** not from an original source or experience. **3** dealing in or selling goods that are not new: *a second-hand car dealer.* ◆ *adv* **4** from a source of previously owned or used goods: *he prefers to buy second-hand.* **5** not directly: *he got the news second-hand.*

second language *n* **1** a language other than the mother tongue used for business transactions, teaching, debate, etc. **2** a language that is officially recognized in a country, other than the main national language.

second lieutenant *n* an officer holding the lowest commissioned rank in the armed forces of certain nations.

secondly ('sɛkəndlɪ) *adv* another word for **second**¹, usually used to precede the second item in a list of topics.

second nature *n* a habit, characteristic, etc., long practised or acquired so as to seem innate.

second person *n* a grammatical category of pronouns and verbs used when referring to or describing the individual or individuals being addressed.

second-rate *adj* **1** not of the highest quality; mediocre. **2** second in importance, etc.

second reading *n* the second presentation of a bill in a legislative assembly, as to approve its general principles (in Britain), or to discuss a committee's report on it (in the US).

second sight *n* the alleged ability to foresee the future, see actions taking place elsewhere, etc. ▸ 'second-'sighted *adj*

second string *n* **1** *Chiefly Brit.* an alternative course of action, etc., intended to come into use should the first fail (esp. in **a second string to one's bow**). **2** *Chiefly US & Canad.* a substitute or reserve player or team.

second thought *n* (*usually pl*) a revised opinion or idea on a matter already considered.

second wind (wɪnd) *n* **1** the return of the ability to breathe at a comfortable rate, esp. following a period of exertion. **2** renewed ability to continue in an effort.

secrecy ('si:krɪsɪ) *n, pl* **secrecies. 1** the state or quality of being secret. **2** the state of keeping something secret. **3** the ability or tendency to keep things secret.

secret ('si:krɪt) *adj* **1** kept hidden or separate from the knowledge of others. Related adj: **cryptic. 2** known only to initiates: *a secret password.* **3** hidden from general view or use: *a secret garden.* **4** able or tending to keep things private or to oneself. **5** operating without the knowledge of outsiders: *a secret society.* ◆ *n* **6** something kept or to be kept hidden. **7** something unrevealed; a mystery. **8** an underlying explanation, reason, etc.: *the secret of success.* **9** a method, plan, etc., known only to initiates. **10** *Liturgy.* a prayer said by the celebrant of the Mass after the offertory and before the preface. [C14: via OF from L *sēcrētus* concealed, from *sēcernere* to sift] ▸ 'secretly *adv*

secret agent *n* a person employed in espionage.

secretaire (ˌsɛkrɪ'tɛə) *n* an enclosed writing desk, usually having an upper cabinet section. [C19: from F; see SECRETARY]

secretariat (ˌsɛkrɪ'tɛərɪət) *n* **1a** an office responsible for the secretarial, clerical, and administrative affairs of a legislative body or international organization. **1b** the staff of such an office. **2** a body of secretaries. **3** a secretary's place of work; office. **4** the position of a secretary. [C19: via F from Med. L *sēcrētāriātus*, from *sēcrētārius* SECRETARY]

secretary ('sɛkrətrɪ) *n, pl* **secretaries. 1** a person who handles correspondence, keeps records, and does general clerical work for an individual, organization, etc. **2** the official manager of the day-to-day business of a society or board. **3** (in Britain) a senior civil servant who assists a government minister. **4** (in the US) the head of a government administrative department. **5** (in Britain) See **secretary of state. 6** Another name for **secretaire.** [C14: from Med. L *sēcrētārius*, from L *sēcrētum* something hidden; see SECRET] ▸ secretarial (ˌsɛkrɪ'tɛərɪəl) *adj* ▸ 'secretaryship *n*

secretary bird *n* a large African long-legged bird of

prey having a crest and tail of long feathers and feeding chiefly on snakes.

secretary-general *n, pl* **secretaries-general**. a chief administrative official, as of the United Nations.

secretary of state *n* **1** (in Britain) the head of any of several government departments. **2** (in the US) the head of the government department in charge of foreign affairs (**State Department**).

secrete[1] (sɪ'kriːt) *vb* **secretes, secreting, secreted**. (of a cell, organ, etc.) to synthesize and release (a secretion). [C18: back formation from SECRETION]
▸ **se'cretor** *n* ▸ **se'cretory** *adj*

secrete[2] (sɪ'kriːt) *vb* **secretes, secreting, secreted**. (*tr*) to put in a hiding place. [C18: var. of obs. *secret* to hide away]

secretion (sɪ'kriːʃən) *n* **1** a substance that is released from a cell, esp. a glandular cell. **2** the process involved in producing and releasing such a substance from the cell. [C17: from Med. L *sēcrētiō*, from L: a separation]

secretive ('siːkrɪtɪv) *adj* inclined to secrecy.
▸ **'secretively** *adv* ▸ **'secretiveness** *n*

secretory (sɪ'kriːtərɪ) *adj* of, relating to, or producing a secretion: *secretory function*.

secret police *n* a police force that operates relatively secretly to check subversion or political dissent.

secret service *n* a government agency or department that conducts intelligence or counterintelligence operations.

sect (sɛkt) *n* **1** a subdivision of a larger religious group (esp. the Christian Church as a whole) the members of which have to some extent diverged from the rest by developing deviating beliefs, practices, etc. **2** *Often disparaging.* **2a** a schismatic religious body. **2b** a religious group regarded as extreme or heretical. **3** a group of people with a common interest, doctrine, etc. [C14: from L *secta* faction, from *sequī* to follow]

-sect *vb combining form*. to cut or divide, esp. into a specified number of parts: *trisect*. [from L *sectus* cut, from *secāre* to cut]

sectarian (sɛk'tɛərɪən) *adj* **1** of, relating to, or characteristic of sects or sectaries. **2** adhering to a particular sect, faction, or doctrine. **3** narrow-minded, esp. as a result of adherence to a particular sect. ♦ *n* **4** a member of a sect or faction, esp. one who is intolerant towards other sects, etc.
▸ **sec'tarian,ism** *n*

sectary ('sɛktərɪ) *n, pl* **sectaries**. **1** a member of a sect, esp. a religous sect. **2** a member of a Nonconformist denomination, esp. one that is small. [C16: from Med. L *sectārius*, from L *secta* SECT]

section ('sɛkʃən) *n* **1** a part cut off or separated from the main body of something. **2** a part or subdivision of a piece of writing, book, etc.: *the sports section of the newspaper*. **3** one of several component parts. **4** a distinct part of a country, community, etc. **5** *US & Canad.* an area one mile square. **6** *NZ.* a plot of land for building, esp. in a suburban area. **7** the section of a railway track that is controlled by a particular signal box. **8** the act or process of cutting or separating by cutting. **9** a representation of an object cut by an imaginary vertical plane so as to show its construction and interior. **10** *Geom.* a plane surface formed by cutting through a solid. **11** a thin slice of biological tissue, etc., prepared for examination by microscope. **12** a segment of an orange or other citrus fruit. **13** a small military formation. **14** *Austral. & NZ.* a fare stage on a bus, tram, etc. **15** *Music.* **15a** an extended division of a composition or movement: *the development section*. **15b** a division in an orchestra, band, etc., containing instruments belonging to the same class: *the brass section*. **16** Also called: **signature, gathering.** a folded printing sheet or sheets ready for gathering and binding. ♦ *vb* (*tr*) **17** to cut or divide into sections. **18** to cut through so as to reveal a section. **19** (in drawing, esp. mechanical drawing) to shade so as to indicate sections. [C16: from L *sectiō*, from *secāre* to cut]

sectional ('sɛkʃən°l) *adj* **1** composed of several sections. **2** of or relating to a section. **3** of or concerned with a particular group within a community, esp. to the exclusion of others.
▸ **'sectiona,lize** *or* **'sectiona,lise** *vb* (*tr*) ▸ **'sectionally** *adv*

sectionalism ('sɛkʃənə,lɪzəm) *n* excessive or narrow minded concern for local or regional interests.
▸ **'sectionalist** *n, adj*

sector ('sɛktə) *n* **1** a part or subdivision, esp. of a society or an economy: *the private sector*. **2** *Geom.* either portion of a circle included between two radii and an arc. **3** a measuring instrument consisting of two graduated arms hinged at one end. **4** a part or subdivision of an area of military operations. **5** *Computing.* the smallest addressable portion of the track on a magnetic tape, disk, or drum store. [C16: from LL: sector, from L: a cutter, from *secāre* to cut]
▸ **'sectoral** *adj*

sectorial (sɛk'tɔːrɪəl) *adj* **1** of or relating to a sector. **2** *Zool.* adapted for cutting: *the sectorial teeth of carnivores*.

secular ('sɛkjʊlə) *adj* **1** of or relating to worldly as opposed to sacred things. **2** not concerned with or related to religion. **3** not within the control of the Church. **4** (of an education, etc.) having no particular religious affinities. **5** (of clerics) not bound by religious vows to a monastic or other order. **6** occurring or appearing once in an age or century. **7** lasting for a long time. **8** *Astron.* occurring slowly over a long period of time. ♦ *n* **9** a member of the secular clergy. [C13: from OF *seculer*, from L *saeculāris* temporal, from L: concerning an age, from *saeculum* an age]
▸ **secularity** (,sɛkjʊ'lærɪtɪ) *n* ▸ **'secularly** *adv*

secularism ('sɛkjʊlə,rɪzəm) *n* **1** *Philosophy.* a doctrine that rejects religion, esp. in ethics. **2** the attitude that religion should have no place in civil affairs.
▸ **'secularist** *n, adj*

secularize *or* **secularise** ('sɛkjʊlə,raɪz) *vb* **secularizes, secularizing, secularized** *or* **secularises, secularising, secularised**. (*tr*) **1** to change from religious or sacred to secular functions, etc. **2** to dispense from allegiance to a religious order. **3** *Law.* to transfer (property) from ecclesiastical to civil possession or use.
▸ **,seculari'zation** *or* **,seculari'sation** *n*

secund (sɪ'kʌnd) *adj Bot.* having parts arranged on one turned to one side of the axis. [C18: from L *secundus* following, from *sequī* to follow]

Secunderabad ★ (sə'kʌndərə,bæd, -,bɑːd) *n* a former town in S central India, in N Andra Pradesh: one of the largest British military stations in India: now part of Hyderabad city.

secure (sɪ'kjʊə) *adj* **1** free from danger, damage, etc. **2** free from fear, care, etc. **3** in safe custody. **4** not likely to fail, become loose, etc. **5** able to be relied on: *a secure investment*. **6** *Arch.* overconfident. ♦ *vb* **secures, securing, secured**. **7** (*tr*) to obtain: *I will secure some good seats*. **8** (when *intr*, often foll. by *against*) to make or become free from danger, fear, etc. **9** (*tr*) to make fast or firm. **10** (when *intr* often foll. by *against*) to make or become certain: *this plan will secure your happiness*. **11** (*tr*) to assure (a creditor) of payment, as by giving security. **12** (*tr*) to make (a military position) safe from attack. **13** *Naut.* to make (a vessel or its contents) safe or ready by battening down hatches, etc. [C16: from L *sēcūrus* free from care]
▸ **se'curable** *adj* ▸ **se'curely** *adv* ▸ **se'curement** *n* ▸ **se'curer** *n*

Securities and Investment Board *n* a British regulatory body set up in 1986 to oversee London's financial markets, each of which has its own self-regulatory organization. Abbrev.: **SIB**.

securitization *or* **securitisation** (sɪ,kjʊərɪtaɪ'zeɪʃən) *n Finance.* the use of such securities as eurobonds to enable investors to lend directly to borrowers with a minimum of risk but without using banks as intermediaries.

security (sɪ'kjʊərɪtɪ) *n, pl* **securities**. **1** the state of being secure. **2** assured freedom from poverty or want: *he needs the security of a permanent job*. **3** a person or thing that secures, guarantees, etc. **4** precautions taken to ensure against theft, espionage, etc. **5** (*often pl*) **5a** a certificate of creditorship or property carrying the right to receive interest or dividend, such as shares or bonds. **5b** the finan cial asset represented by such a certificate. **6** the specific asset that a creditor can claim in the event of default on an obligation. **7** something given or pledged to secure the fulfilment of a promise or obligation. **8** the protection of data to ensure that only authorised personnel have access to computer files.

security blanket *n* **1** a policy of temporary secrecy by police or those in charge of security, in order to protect a person, place, etc., threatened with danger, from further risk. **2** a baby's blanket, soft toy, etc., to which a baby or young child becomes very attached, using it as a comforter. **3** *Inf.* anything used or thought of as providing reassurance.

Security Council *n* an organ of the United Nations established to maintain world peace.

security guard *n* someone employed to protect buildings, people, etc., and to collect and deliver large sums of money.

security risk *n* a person deemed to be a threat to state security in that he could be open to pressure, have subversive political beliefs, etc.

secy. *or* **sec'y.** *abbrev. for* secretary.

sedan (sɪ'dæn) *n* **1** *US, Canad., & NZ.* a saloon car. **2** short for **sedan chair.** [C17: from ?]

Sedan ★ (*French* sədā; *English* sɪ'dæn) *n* a town in NE France, on the River Meuse: passed to France in 1642; a Protestant stronghold (16th–17th centuries); scene of a French defeat (1870) during the Franco-Prussian War and of a battle (1940) in World War II, which began the German invasion of France. Pop.: 22 400 (1990).

sedan chair *n* a closed chair for one passenger, carried on poles by two bearers, commonly used in the 17th and 18th centuries.

sedate[1] (sɪ'deɪt) *adj* **1** habitually calm and composed in manner. **2** sober or decorous. [C17: from L *sēdāre* to soothe]
▸ **se'dately** *adv* ▸ **se'dateness** *n*

sedate[2] (sɪ'deɪt) *vb* **sedates, sedating, sedated.** (*tr*) to administer a sedative to. [C20: back formation from SEDATIVE]

sedation (sɪ'deɪʃən) *n* **1** a state of calm or reduced nervous activity. **2** the administration of a sedative.

sedative ('sɛdətɪv) *adj* **1** having a soothing or calming effect. **2** of or relating to sedation. ◆ *n* **3** *Med.* a sedative drug or agent. [C15: from Med. L *sēdātīvus*, from L *sēdātus* assuaged; see SEDATE[1]]

Seddon ★ ('sɛd°n) *n* **Richard John,** known as **King Dick.** 1845–1906, New Zealand statesman, born in England; prime minister (1893–1906).

sedentary ('sɛd°ntərɪ) *adj* **1** characterized by or requiring a sitting position: *sedentary work.* **2** tending to sit about without taking much exercise. **3** (of animals) moving about very little. **4** (of birds) not migratory. [C16: from L *sedentārius,* from *sedēre* to sit]
▸ **'sedentarily** *adv* ▸ **'sedentariness** *n*

Seder ('seɪdə) *n Judaism.* a ceremonial meal on the first night or first two nights of Passover. [from Heb. *sēdher* order]

sedge (sɛdʒ) *n* a grasslike plant growing on wet ground and having rhizomes, triangular stems, and minute flowers in spikelets. [OE *secg*]
▸ **'sedgy** *adj*

Sedgemoor ★ ('sɛdʒ,mʊə) *n* a plain in SW England, in central Somerset: scene of the defeat (1685) of the Duke of Monmouth.

sedge warbler *n* a European songbird of reed beds and swampy areas, having a streaked brownish plumage with white eye stripes.

Sedgwick ★ ('sɛdʒwɪk) *n* **Adam.** 1785–1873, British geologist, who helped to establish the geological time scale.

sedilia (sɛ'daɪlɪə) *n* (*functioning as sing*) the group of three seats, each called a **sedile** (sɛ'daɪlɪ) on the south side of a sanctuary where the celebrant and ministers sit during High Mass. [C18: from L, from *sedīle* a chair, from *sedēre* to sit]

sediment ('sɛdɪmənt) *n* **1** matter that settles to the bottom of a liquid. **2** material that has been deposited from

water, ice, or wind. [C16: from L *sedimentum* a settling, from *sedēre* to sit]
▸ **,sedimen'tation** *n*

sedimentary (,sɛdɪ'mɛntərɪ) *adj* **1** characteristic of, resembling, or containing sediment. **2** (of rocks) formed by the accumulation of mineral and organic fragments that have been deposited by water, ice, or wind.
▸ **,sedi'mentarily** *adv*

sedimentation tank *n* a tank into which sewage is passed to allow suspended solid matter to separate out.

sedition (sɪ'dɪʃən) *n* **1** speech or behaviour directed against the peace of a state. **2** an offence that tends to undermine the authority of a state. **3** an incitement to public disorder. [C14: from L *sēditiō* discord, from *sēd-* apart + *itiō* a going, from *īre* to go]
▸ **se'ditionary** *n, adj*

seditious (sɪ'dɪʃəs) *adj* **1** of, like, or causing sedition. **2** inclined to or taking part in sedition.

seduce (sɪ'djuːs) *vb* **seduces, seducing, seduced.** (*tr*) **1** to persuade to engage in sexual intercourse. **2** to lead astray, as from the right action. **3** to win over, attract, or lure. [C15: from L *sēdūcere* to lead apart]
▸ **se'ducible** *adj*

seducer (sɪ'djuːsə) *or* (*fem*) **seductress** (sɪ'dʌktrɪs) *n* a person who entices, allures, or seduces, esp. one who entices another to engage in sexual intercourse.

seduction (sɪ'dʌkʃən) *n* **1** the act of seducing or the state of being seduced. **2** a means of seduction.

seductive (sɪ'dʌktɪv) *adj* tending to seduce or capable of seducing; enticing; alluring.
▸ **se'ductively** *adv* ▸ **se'ductiveness** *n*

sedulous ('sɛdjʊləs) *adj* assiduous; diligent. [C16: from L *sēdulus,* from ?]
▸ **sedulity** (sɪ'djuːlɪtɪ) *or* **'sedulousness** *n* ▸ **'sedulously** *adv*

sedum ('siːdəm) *n* a rock plant having thick fleshy leaves and clusters of white, yellow, or pink flowers. [C15: from L: houseleek]

see[1] (siː) *vb* **sees, seeing, saw, seen.** **1** to perceive with the eyes. **2** (when *tr, may take a clause as object*) to understand: *I explained the problem but he could not see it.* **3** (*tr*) to perceive with any or all of the senses: *I hate to see you so unhappy.* **4** (*tr; may take a clause as object*) to foresee: *I can see what will happen if you don't help.* **5** (when *tr, may take a clause as object*) to ascertain or find out (a fact): *see who is at the door.* **6** (when *tr, takes a clause as object; when intr, foll. by to*) to make sure (of something) or take care (of something): *see that he gets to bed early.* **7** (when *tr, may take a clause as object*) to consider, deliberate, or decide: *see if you can come next week.* **8** (*tr*) to have experience of: *he had seen much unhappiness in his life.* **9** (*tr*) to allow to be in a specified condition: *I cannot stand by and see a child in pain.* **10** (*tr*) to be characterized by: *this period of history has seen much unrest.* **11** (*tr*) to meet or pay a visit to: *to see one's solicitor.* **12** (*tr*) to receive: *the Prime Minister will see the deputation now.* **13** (*tr*) to frequent the company of: *she is seeing a married man.* **14** (*tr*) to accompany: *I saw her to the door.* **15** (*tr*) to refer to or look up: *for further information see the appendix.* **16** (in gambling, esp. in poker) to match (another player's bet) or match the bet of (another player) by staking an equal sum. **17 as far as I can see.** to the best of my judgment. **18 see fit.** (*takes an infinitive*) to consider proper, etc.: *I don't see fit to allow her to come here.* **19 see (someone) hanged** *or* **damned first.** *Inf.* to refuse absolutely to do what one has been asked. **20 see you, see you later,** *or* **be seeing you.** an expression of farewell. ◆ See also **see about, see into,** etc. [OE *sēon*]

see[2] (siː) *n* the diocese of a bishop, or the place within it where his cathedral is situated. [C13: from OF *sed,* from L *sēdēs* a seat]

see about *vb* (*intr, prep*) **1** to take care of: *he couldn't see about the matter because he was ill.* **2** to investigate: *to see about a new car.*

Seebeck effect ('siːbɛk) *n* the phenomenon in which a current is produced in a circuit containing two or more different metals when the junctions between the metals are maintained at different temperatures. Also called: **thermoelectric effect.** [C19: after Thomas *Seebeck* (1770–1831), G physicist]

★ people and places

seed (siːd) n **1** Bot. a mature fertilized plant ovule, consisting of an embryo and its food store surrounded by a protective seed coat (testa). Related adj: **seminal. 2** the small hard seedlike fruit of plants such as wheat. **3** any propagative part of a plant, such as a tuber, spore, or bulb. **4** the source, beginning, or germ of anything: *the seeds of revolt.* **5** *Chiefly Bible.* descendants: *the seed of Abraham.* **6** an archaic term for **sperm** or **semen. 7** *Sport.* a seeded player. **8** *Chem.* a small crystal added to a supersaturated solution to induce crystallization. **9 go** *or* **run to seed. 9a** (of plants) to produce and shed seeds. **9b** to lose vigour, usefulness, etc. ♦ vb **10** to plant (seeds, grain, etc.) in (soil): *we seeded this field with oats.* **11** (intr) (of plants) to form or shed seeds. **12** (tr) to remove the seeds from (fruit, etc.). **13** (tr) *Chem.* to add a small crystal to (a supersaturated solution) in order to cause crystallization. **14** (tr) to scatter certain substances, such as silver iodide, in (clouds) in order to cause rain. **15** (tr) to arrange (the draw of a tournament) so that outstanding teams or players will not meet in the early rounds. [OE *sǣd*]
▷ **'seeder** n ▷ **'seedless** adj

seedbed ('siːd,bɛd) n **1** a plot of land in which seedlings are grown before being transplanted. **2** the place where something develops.

seedcake ('siːd,keɪk) n a sweet cake flavoured with caraway seeds and lemon rind or essence.

seed capital n *Finance.* a small amount of capital required to finance the research necessary to produce a business plan for a new company.

seed coral n small pieces of coral used in jewellery, etc.

seed corn n **1** the good quality ears or kernels of corn that are used as seed. **2** assets that are expected to provide future benefits.

seed leaf n the nontechnical name for **cotyledon.**

seedling ('siːdlɪŋ) n a plant produced from a seed, esp. a very young plant.

seed money n money used for the establishment of an enterprise.

seed oyster n a young oyster, esp. a cultivated oyster, ready for transplantation.

seed pearl n a tiny pearl weighing less than a quarter of a grain.

seed pod n a carpel or pistil enclosing the seeds of a plant, esp. a flowering plant.

seed potato n a potato tuber used for planting.

seed vessel n *Bot.* a dry fruit, such as a capsule.

seedy ('siːdɪ) adj **seedier, seediest. 1** shabby in appearance: *seedy clothes.* **2** (of a plant) at the stage of producing seeds. **3** *Inf.* not physically fit.
▷ **'seedily** adv ▷ **'seediness** n

Seeger ★ ('siːgə) n Pete. born 1919, US folk singer and songwriter, noted for his protest songs, which include "Where Have all the Flowers Gone?" (1961) and "If I Had a Hammer" (1962).

seeing ('siːɪŋ) n **1** the sense or faculty of sight. **2** *Astron.* the condition of the atmosphere with respect to observation of stars, planets, etc. ♦ conj **3** (subordinating; often foll. by *that*) in light of the fact (that).

USAGE NOTE   The use of *seeing as how* as in *seeing as (how) the bus is always late, I don't need to hurry* is generally thought to be incorrect or nonstandard.

see into vb (intr, prep) to discover the true nature of: *I can't see into your thoughts.*

seek (siːk) vb **seeks, seeking, sought.** (mainly tr) **1** (when intr, often foll. by *for* or *after*) to try to find by searching: *to seek a solution.* **2** (also intr) to try to obtain or acquire: *to seek happiness.* **3** to attempt (to do something): *I'm only seeking to help.* **4** (also intr) to inquire about or request (something). **5** to resort to: *to seek the garden for peace.* [OE *sēcan*]
▷ **'seeker** n

seek out vb (tr, adv) to search hard for and find a specific person or thing: *she sought out her friend from amongst the crowd.*

Seeland ★ ('zeːlant) n the German name for **Sjælland.**

seem (siːm) vb (may take an infinitive) **1** (copula) to appear to the mind or eye; look: *the car seems to be running well.* **2** to appear to be: *there seems no need for all this nonsense.* **3** used to diminish the force of a following infinitive to be polite, more noncommittal, etc.: *I can't seem to get through to you.* [C12: ?from ON *soma* to beseem, from *sœmr* befitting]

USAGE NOTE   See at **like.**

seeming ('siːmɪŋ) adj **1** (prenominal) apparent but not actual or genuine. ♦ n **2** outward or false appearance.
▷ **'seemingly** adv

seemly ('siːmlɪ) adj **seemlier, seemliest. 1** proper or fitting. **2** *Obs.* pleasing in appearance. ♦ adv **3** *Arch.* decorously. [C13: from ON *sœmiligr*, from *sœmr* befitting]

seen (siːn) vb the past participle of **see**[1].

see off vb (tr, adv) **1** to be present at the departure of (a person making a journey). **2** *Inf.* to cause to leave or depart, esp. by force.

seep (siːp) vb **1** (intr) to pass gradually or leak as if through small openings. ♦ n **2** a small spring or place where water, oil, etc., has oozed through the ground. [OE *sīpian*]
▷ **'seepage** n

seer[1] (sɪə) n **1** a person who can supposedly see into the future. **2** a person who professes supernatural powers. **3** a person who sees.

seer[2] (sɪə) n a varying unit of weight used in India, usually about two pounds or one kilogram. [from Hindi]

seersucker ('sɪə,sʌkə) n a light cotton, linen, or other fabric with a crinkled surface and often striped. [C18: from Hindi *śīrśakar*, from Persian *shīr o shakkar*, lit.: milk and sugar]

seesaw ('siː,sɔː) n **1** a plank balanced in the middle so that two people seated on the ends can ride up and down by pushing on the ground with their feet. **2** the pastime of riding up and down on a seesaw. **3** an up-and-down or back-and-forth movement. ♦ vb **4** (intr) to move up and down or back and forth in such a manner. [C17: reduplication of SAW[1], alluding to the movement from side to side, as in sawing]

seethe (siːð) vb **seethes, seething, seethed. 1** (intr) to boil or to foam as if boiling. **2** (intr) to be in a state of extreme agitation, esp. through anger. **3** (tr) to soak in liquid. **4** (tr) *Arch.* to cook by boiling. [OE *sēothan*]
▷ **'seething** adj ▷ **'seethingly** adv

see through vb **1** (tr) to help out in time of need or trouble. **2** (tr, adv) to remain with until the end or completion: *let's see the job through.* **3** (intr, prep) to perceive the true nature of: *I can see through your evasion.* ♦ adj **seethrough. 4** partly or wholly transparent or translucent, esp. (of clothes) in a titillating way.

Seferis ★ (sə'fɛərɪs) n George. pen name of *Georgios Seferiades.* 1900–71, Greek poet and diplomat: Nobel prize for literature 1963.

Sefton ★ ('sɛft°n) n a unitary authority in NW England, in Merseyside. Pop.: 292 400 (1994 est.). Area: 150 sq. km (58 sq. miles).

segment n ('sɛgmənt). **1** *Maths.* **1a** a part of a line or curve between two points. **1b** a part of a plane or solid figure cut off by an intersecting line, plane, or planes. **2** one of several parts or sections into which an object is divided. **3** *Zool.* any of the parts into which the body or appendages of an annelid or arthropod are divided. **4** *Linguistics.* a speech sound considered in isolation. ♦ vb (sɛg'mɛnt). **5** to cut or divide (a whole object) into segments. [C16: from L *segmentum*, from *secāre* to cut]
▷ **seg'mental** adj ▷ **'segmentary** adj

segmentation (,sɛgmɛn'teɪʃən) n **1** the act or an instance of dividing into segments. **2** *Embryol.* another name for **cleavage** (sense 4).

★ people and places

Segovia[1] ★ (sɪ'gəʊvɪə; *Spanish* se'ɣoβja) *n* a town in central Spain: site of a Roman aqueduct, still in use, and the fortified palace of the kings of Castile (the Alcázar). Pop.: 58 060 (1991).

Segovia[2] ★ (sɪ'gəʊvɪə; *Spanish* se'ɣoβja) *n* **Andrés** (an'dres), Marquis of Salobreña. 1893–1987, Spanish classical guitarist.

Segrè ★ (sə'greɪ) *n* **Emilio** (ɪ'miːlɪəʊ). 1905–89, US physicist, born in Italy, who was the first to produce an artificial element. He shared the Nobel prize for physics (1959) with Owen Chamberlain for their discovery (1955) of the antiproton.

segregate ('segrɪ,geɪt) *vb* **segregates, segregating, segregated.** **1** to set or be set apart from others or from the main group. **2** (*tr*) to impose segregation on (a racial or minority group). **3** *Genetics.* to undergo or cause to undergo segregation. [C16: from L *sēgregāre,* from *sē-* apart + *grex* a flock]
▶ **'segre,gative** *adj* ▶ **'segre,gator** *n*

segregation (,segrɪ'geɪʃən) *n* **1** the act of segregating or state of being segregated. **2** *Sociol.* the practice or policy of creating separate facilities within the same society for the use of a particular group. **3** *Genetics.* the separation at meiosis of the two members of any pair of alleles into separate gametes.
▶ ,segre'gational *adj* ▶ ,segre'gationist *n*

segue ('seɪgwɪ) *vb* **segues, segueing, segued.** (*intr*) **1** (often foll. by *into*) to proceed from one piece of music to another without a break. ♦ *n* **2** the practice or an instance of segueing. [from It: follows, from *seguire* to follow, from L *sequī*]

seguidilla (,segɪ'diːljə) *n* **1** a Spanish dance in a fast triple rhythm. **2** a piece of music composed for or in the rhythm of this dance. [Sp.: a little dance, from *seguida* a dance, from *seguir* to follow, from L *sequī*]

seiche (seɪʃ) *n* a tide-like movement of a body of water caused by barometric pressure, earth tremors, etc. [C19: from Swiss F, from ?]

Seidlitz powder *or* **powders** ('sedlɪts) *n* a laxative consisting of two powders, tartaric acid and a mixture of sodium bicarbonate and Rochelle salt. [C19: after *Seidlitz,* a village in Bohemia with mineral springs having similar laxative effects]

seif dune (seɪf) *n* (in deserts, esp. the Sahara) a long ridge of blown sand, often several miles long. [*seif,* from Ar.: sword, from the shape of the dune]

seigneur (sɛ'njɜː; *French* sɛɲœr) *n* a feudal lord, esp. in France. [C16: from OF, from Vulgar L *senior,* from L: an elderly man; see SENIOR]
▶ **sei'gneurial** *adj*

seigneury ('seɪnjərɪ) *n, pl* **seigneuries.** the estate of a seigneur.

seignior ('seɪnjə) *n* **1** a less common name for a **seigneur.** **2** (in England) the lord of a seigniory. [C14: from Anglo-F *segnour*]
▶ **seigniorial** (seɪ'njɔːrɪəl) *adj*

seigniory ('seɪnjərɪ) *or* **signory** ('siːnjərɪ) *n, pl* **seigniories** *or* **seignories.** **1** less common names for a **seigneury. 2** (in England) the fee or manor of a seignior; a feudal domain. **3** the authority of a seignior.

seine (seɪn) *n* **1** a large fishing net that hangs vertically in the water by means of floats at the top and weights at the bottom. ♦ *vb* **seines, seining, seined. 2** to catch (fish) using this net. [OE *segne,* from L *sagēna,* from Gk *sagēnē*]

Seine ★ (seɪn; *French* sɛn) *n* a river in N France, rising on the Plateau de Langres and flowing northwest through Paris to the English Channel: the second longest river in France, linked by canal with the Rivers Somme, Scheldt, Meuse, Rhine, Saône, and Loire. Length: 776 km (482 miles).

Seine-et-Marne ★ (*French* sɛnemarn) *n* a department of N central France, in Île-de-France region. Capital: Melun. Pop.: 1 171 313 (1994 est.). Area: 5931 sq. km (2313 sq. miles).

Seine-Maritime ★ (*French* sɛnmaritim) *n* a department of N France, in Haute-Normandie region. Capital:

Rouen. Pop.: 1 239 973 (1994 est.). Area: 6342 sq. km (2473 sq. miles).

Seine-Saint-Denis ★ (*French* sɛnsɛdni) *n* a department of N central France, in Île-de-France region. Capital: Bobigny. Pop.: 1 404 430 (1994 est.). Area: 236 sq. km (92 sq. miles).

seise *or US* **seize** (siːz) *vb* **seises, seising, seised** *or US* **seizes, seizing, seized.** to put into legal possession of (property, etc.).
▶ **'seiser** *n*

seisin *or US* **seizin** ('siːzɪn) *n Property law.* feudal possession of an estate in land. [C13: from OF *seisine,* from *seisir* to SEIZE]

seismic ('saɪzmɪk) *adj* relating to or caused by earthquakes or artificially produced earth tremors.

seismo- *or before a vowel* **seism-** *combining form.* earthquake: *seismology.* [from Gk *seismos*]

seismograph ('saɪzmə,grɑːf) *n* an instrument that registers and records earthquakes. A **seismogram** is the record from such an instrument.
▶ seismographic (,saɪzmə'græfɪk) *adj* ▶ seismographer (saɪz'mɒgrəfə) *n* ▶ seis'mography *n*

seismology (saɪz'mɒlədʒɪ) *n* the branch of geology concerned with the study of earthquakes.
▶ seismologic (,saɪzmə'lɒdʒɪk) *or* ,seismo'logical *adj* ▶ ,seismo'logically *adv* ▶ seis'mologist *n*

seize[1] (siːz) *vb* **seizes, seizing, seized.** (*mainly tr*) **1** (also *intr,* foll. by *on*) to hold of quickly; grab. **2** (sometimes foll. by *on* or *upon*) to grasp mentally, esp. rapidly: *she immediately seized his idea.* **3** to take mental possession of: *alarm seized the crowd.* **4** to take possession of rapidly and forcibly: *the thief seized the woman's purse.* **5** to take legal possession of. **6** to take by force or capture: *the army seized the undefended town.* **7** to take immediate advantage of: *to seize an opportunity.* **8** *Naut.* to bind (two ropes together). **9** (*intr;* often foll. by *up*) (of mechanical parts) to become jammed, esp. because of excessive heat. [C13 *saisen,* from OF *saisir,* from Med. L *sacīre* to position, of Gmc origin]
▶ **'seizable** *adj*

seize[2] (siːz) *vb* **seizes, seizing, seized.** the US spelling of **seise.**

seizure ('siːʒə) *n* **1** the act or an instance of seizing or the state of being seized. **2** *Pathol.* a sudden manifestation or recurrence of a disease, such as an epileptic convulsion.

Sekondi ★ (,sekən'diː) *n* a port in SW Ghana, 8 km (5 miles) northeast of Takoradi: linked administratively with Takoradi in 1946. Pop. (with Takoradi): 103 600 (1988 est.).

selachian (sɪ'leɪkɪən) *adj* of or belonging to a large subclass of cartilaginous fishes including the sharks, rays, dogfish, and skates. [C19: from NL *Selachii,* from Gk *selakhē* a shark]

Selangor ★ (sə'læŋə) *n* a state of Peninsular Malaysia, on the Strait of Malacca: established as a British protectorate in 1874, became a Federated Malay State in 1896 and part of Malaysia in 1946; tin producer. Capital: Shah Alam. Pop.: 1 981 090 (1993 est.). Area: 8203 sq. km (3167 sq. miles).

Selby ★ ('selbɪ) *n* an inland port in N England, in N Yorkshire, on the River Ouse: centre for a major coalfield since 1983: agricultural products. Pop.: 15 292 (1991).

seldom ('seldəm) *adv* rarely. [OE *seldon*]

select (sɪ'lekt) *vb* **1** to choose (someone or something) in preference to another or others. ♦ *adj also* **selected. 2** chosen in preference to others. **3** of particular quality. **4** limited as to membership or entry: *a select gathering.* ♦ *n Austral. history.* **5** a piece of land acquired by a freeselector. **6** the process of free-selection. [C16: from L *sēligere* to sort, from *sē-* apart + *legere* to choose]
▶ se'lectness *n* ▶ se'lector *n*

select committee *n* (in Britain) a small committee of members of parliament, set up to investigate and report on a specified matter.

selection (sɪ'lekʃən) *n* **1** the act or an instance of selecting or the state of being selected. **2** a thing or number of things that have been selected. **3** a range from which something may be selected: *a good selection of clothes*. **4** *Biol.* the process by which certain organisms or characters are reproduced and perpetuated in the species in preference to others.

selective (sɪˈlɛktɪv) *adj* **1** of or characterized by selection. **2** tending to choose carefully or characterized by careful choice. **3** *Electronics.* occurring at or operating at a particular frequency or band of frequencies.
▶ se'**lectively** *adv*

selectivity (sɪˌlɛkˈtɪvɪtɪ) *n* **1** the state or quality of being selective. **2** the degree to which a radio receiver, etc., can respond to the frequency of a desired signal.

Selene ★ (sɪˈliːnɪ) *n* the Greek goddess of the moon. Roman counterpart: **Luna.**

selenite (ˈsɛlɪˌnaɪt) *n* a colourless glassy variety of gypsum.

selenium (sɪˈliːnɪəm) *n* a nonmetallic element that exists in several allotropic forms. The common form is a grey crystalline solid that is photoconductive, photovoltaic, and semiconducting: used in photocells, solar cells, and in xerography. Symbol: Se; atomic no.: 34; atomic wt.: 78.96. [C19: from NL, from Gk *selēnē* moon; by analogy to TELLURIUM (from L *tellus* earth)]

seleno- *or before a vowel* **selen-** *combining form.* denoting the moon: *selenography.* [from Gk *selēnē* moon]

selenography (ˌsiːlɪˈnɒɡrəfɪ) *n* the branch of astronomy concerned with the description and mapping of the surface features of the moon.
▶ ˌsele'**nographer** *n* ▶ **selenographic** (sɪˌliːnəʊˈɡræfɪk) *adj*

Seles ★ (ˈsɛlɛʃ, -lɛz) *n* **Monica.** born 1973, US tennis player, born in Yugoslavia.

Seleucia ★ (sɪˈluːʃɪə) *n* **1** an ancient city in Mesopotamia, on the River Tigris: founded by Seleucus Nicator in 312 B.C.; became the chief city of the Seleucid empire; sacked by the Romans around 162 A.D. **2** an ancient city in SE Asia Minor, on the River Calycadnus (modern Goksu Nehri): captured by the Turks in the 13th century; site of present-day Silifke (Turkey). Official name: **Seleucia Tracheotis** (ˌtrækɪˈəʊtɪs) or **Trachea** (trəˈkɪə). **3** an ancient port in Syria, on the River Orontes: the port of Antioch, of military importance during the wars between the Ptolemies and Seleucids; largely destroyed by earthquake in 526; site of present-day Samandağ (Turkey). Official name: **Seleucia Pieria** (paɪˈiːrɪə).

Seleucus I ★ (sɪˈluːkəs) *n* surname *Nicator.* ?358–280 B.C., Macedonian general under Alexander the Great, who founded the Seleucid kingdom.

self (sɛlf) *n, pl* **selves. 1** the distinct individuality or identity of a person or thing. **2** a person's typical bodily make-up or personal characteristics: *she's looking her old self again.* **3** one's own welfare or interests: *he only thinks of self.* **4** an individual's consciousness of his own identity or being. **5** a bird, animal, etc., that is a single colour throughout. ♦ *pron* **6** *Not standard.* myself, yourself, etc.: *seats for self and wife.* ♦ *adj* **7** of the same colour or material. **8** *Obs.* the same. [OE *seolf*]

self- *combining form.* **1** of oneself or itself: *self-defence.* **2** by, to, in, due to, for, or from the self: *self-employed; self-respect.* **3** automatic or automatically: *self-propelled.*

self-abnegation *n* the denial of one's own interests in favour of the interests of others.

self-absorption *n* **1** preoccupation with oneself to the exclusion of others. **2** *Physics.* the process in which some of the radiation emitted by a material is absorbed by the material itself.

self-abuse *n* **1** disparagement or misuse of one's own abilities, etc. **2** a censorious term for **masturbation.**

self-acting *adj* not requiring an external influence or control to function; automatic.

self-addressed *adj* **1** addressed for return to the sender. **2** directed to oneself: *a self-addressed remark.*

self-aggrandizement *n* the act of increasing one's own power, importance, etc.
▶ ˌself-ag'gran,dizing *adj*

self-appointed *adj* having assumed authority without the agreement of others: *a self-appointed critic.*

self-assertion *n* the act or an instance of putting forward one's own opinions, etc., esp. in an aggressive or conceited manner.
▶ ˌself-as'serting *adj* ▶ ˌself-as'sertive *adj*

self-assurance *n* confidence in the validity, value, etc., of one's own ideas, opinions, etc.
▶ ˌself-as'sured *adj* ▶ ˌself-as'suredly *adv*

self-centred *adj* totally preoccupied with one's own concerns.
▶ ˌself-'centredness *n*

self-certification *n* (in Britain) a formal assertion by a worker to his employer that absence from work for up to seven days was due to sickness.

self-coloured *adj* **1** having only a single and uniform colour: *a self-coloured dress.* **2** (of cloth, etc.) having the natural or original colour.

self-command *n* another term for **self-control.**

self-confessed *adj* according to one's own testimony or admission: *a self-confessed liar.*

self-confidence *n* confidence in one's own powers, judgment, etc.
▶ ˌself-'confident *adj* ▶ ˌself-'confidently *adv*

self-conscious *adj* **1** unduly aware of oneself as the object of the attention of others. **2** conscious of one's existence.
▶ ˌself-'consciously *adv* ▶ ˌself-'consciousness *n*

self-contained *adj* **1** containing within itself all parts necessary for completeness. **2** (of a flat) having its own kitchen, bathroom, and lavatory not shared by others. **3** able or tending to keep one's feelings, thoughts, etc., to oneself.
▶ ˌself-con'tainedness *n*

self-contradictory *adj Logic.* (of a proposition) both asserting and denying a given proposition.

self-control *n* the ability to exercise restraint or control over one's feelings, emotions, reactions, etc.
▶ ˌself-con'trolled *adj*

self-deception *or* **self-deceit** *n* the act or an instance of deceiving oneself.
▶ ˌself-de'ceptive *adj*

self-defence *n* **1** the act of defending oneself, one's actions, ideas, etc. **2** boxing as a means of defending the person (esp. in **noble art of self-defence**). **3** *Law.* the right to defend one's person, family, or property against attack or threat of attack.
▶ ˌself-'fensive *adj*

self-denial *n* the denial or sacrifice of one's own desires.
▶ ˌself-de'nying *adj*

self-deprecating *or* **self-depreciating** *adj* having a tendency to disparage oneself.

self-determination *n* **1** the ability to make a decision for oneself without influence from outside. **2** the right of a nation or people to determine its own form of government.
▶ ˌself-de'termined *adj* ▶ ˌself-de'termining *adj*

self-discipline *n* the act of disciplining or power to discipline one's own feelings, desires, etc.
▶ ˌself-'disciplined *adj*

self-drive *adj* denoting or relating to a hired car that is driven by the hirer.

self-educated *adj* **1** educated through one's own efforts without formal instruction. **2** educated at one's own expense.

self-effacement *n* the act of making oneself, one's actions, etc., inconspicuous, esp. because of timidity.
▶ ˌself-ef'facing *adj*

self-employed *adj* earning one's living in one's own business or through freelance work, rather than as the employee of another.
▶ ˌself-em'ployment *n*

self-esteem *n* **1** respect for or a favourable opinion of oneself. **2** an unduly high opinion of oneself.

self-evident *adj* containing its own evidence or proof without need of further demonstration.
▶ ˌself-'evidence *n* ▶ ˌself-'evidently *adv*

self-existent *adj Philosophy.* existing independently of any other being or cause.

★ people and places

self-explanatory *adj* understandable without explanation; self-evident.

self-expression *n* the expression of one's own personality, feelings, etc., as in painting or poetry.
▶ ˌself-exˈpressive *adj*

self-government *n* **1** the government of a country, nation, etc., by its own people. **2** the state of being self-controlled.
▶ ˌself-ˈgoverned *adj* ▶ ˌself-ˈgoverning *adj*

selfheal (ˈsɛlfˌhiːl) *n* **1** a low-growing European herbaceous plant with tightly clustered violet-blue flowers and reputedly having healing powers. **2** any of several other plants thought to have healing powers.

self-help *n* **1** the act or state of providing the means to help oneself without relying on the assistance of others. **2a** the practice of solving one's problems by joining or forming a group designed to help those suffering from a particular problem. **2b** (*as modifier*): *a self-help group*.

self-image *n* one's own idea of oneself or sense of one's worth.

self-important *adj* having or showing an unduly high opinion of one's own abilities, importance, etc.
▶ ˌself-imˈportantly *adv* ▶ ˌself-imˈportance *n*

self-improvement *n* the improvement of one's status, position, education, etc., by one's own efforts.

self-induced *adj* **1** induced or brought on by oneself or itself. **2** *Electronics*. produced by self-induction.

self-induction *n* the production of an electromotive force in a circuit when the magnetic flux linked with the circuit changes as a result of a change in current in the same circuit.

self-indulgent *adj* tending to indulge one's own desires, etc.
▶ ˌself-inˈdulgence *n*

self-interest *n* **1** one's personal interest or advantage. **2** the act or an instance of pursuing one's own interest.
▶ ˌself-ˈinterested *adj*

selfish (ˈsɛlfɪʃ) *adj* **1** chiefly concerned with one's own interest, advantage, etc., esp. to the exclusion of the interests of others. **2** relating to or characterized by self-interest.
▶ ˈselfishly *adv* ▶ ˈselfishness *n*

self-justification *n* the act or an instance of justifying or providing excuses for one's own behaviour, etc.

selfless (ˈsɛlflɪs) *adj* having little concern for one's own interests.
▶ ˈselflessly *adv* ▶ ˈselflessness *n*

self-loading *adj* (of a firearm) utilizing some of the force of the explosion to eject the empty shell and replace it with a new one.
▶ ˌself-ˈloader *n*

self-love *n* the instinct to seek one's own well-being or to further one's own interest.

self-made *adj* **1** having achieved wealth, status, etc., by one's own efforts. **2** made by oneself.

self-opinionated *adj* **1** having an unduly high regard for oneself or one's own opinions. **2** clinging stubbornly to one's own opinions.

self-pity *n* the act or state of pitying oneself, esp. in an exaggerated or self-indulgent manner.
▶ ˌself-ˈpitying *adj* ▶ ˌself-ˈpityingly *adv*

self-pollination *n* the transfer of pollen from the anthers to the stigma of the same flower.
▶ ˌself-ˈpolliˌnated *adj*

self-possessed *adj* having control of one's emotions, etc.
▶ ˌself-posˈsession *n*

self-preservation *n* the preservation of oneself from danger or injury.

self-pronouncing *adj* (in a phonetic transcription) of or denoting a word that, except for marks of stress, keeps the letters of its ordinary orthography to represent its pronunciation.

self-propelled *adj* (of a vehicle) provided with its own source of tractive power rather than requiring an external means of propulsion.
▶ ˌself-proˈpelling *adj*

self-raising *adj* (of flour) having a raising agent, such as baking powder, already added.

self-realization *n* the realization or fulfilment of one's own potential or abilities.

self-regard *n* **1** concern for one's own interest. **2** proper esteem for oneself.

self-regulating organization *n* one of several British organizations set up in 1986 under the auspices of the Securities and Investment Board to regulate the activities of London investment markets. Abbrev.: **SRO**.

self-reliance *n* reliance on one's own abilities, decisions, etc.
▶ ˌself-reˈliant *adj*

self-reproach *n* the act of finding fault with or blaming oneself.
▶ ˌself-reˈproachful *adj*

self-respect *n* a proper sense of one's own dignity and integrity.
▶ ˌself-reˈspecting *adj*

self-restraint *n* restraint imposed by oneself on one's own feelings, desires, etc.

self-righteous *adj* having an exaggerated awareness of one's own virtuousness.
▶ ˌself-ˈrighteously *adv* ▶ ˌself-ˈrighteousness *n*

self-rule *n* another term for **self-government** (sense 1).

self-sacrifice *n* the sacrifice of one's own desires, etc., for the sake of duty or for the well-being of others.
▶ ˌself-ˈsacriˌficing *adj*

selfsame (ˈsɛlfˌseɪm) *adj* (*prenominal*) the very same.

self-satisfied *adj* having or showing a complacent satisfaction with oneself, one's own actions, behaviour, etc.
▶ ˌself-ˌsatisˈfaction *n*

self-sealing *adj* (esp. of an envelope) designed to become sealed with the application of pressure only.

self-seeking *n* **1** the act or an instance of seeking one's own profit or interest. ◆ *adj* **2** having or showing an exclusive preoccupation with one's own profit or interest: *a self-seeking attitude*.
▶ ˌself-ˈseeker *n*

self-service *adj* **1** of or denoting a shop, restaurant, petrol station, etc., where the customer serves himself. ◆ *n* **2** the practice of serving oneself, as in a shop, etc.

self-serving *adj* habitually seeking one's own advantage, esp. at the expense of others.

self-sown *adj* (of plants) growing from seed dispersed by any means other than by the agency of man or animals. Also: **self-seeded**.

self-starter *n* **1** an electric motor used to start an internal-combustion engine. **2** the switch that operates this motor. **3** a person who is strongly motivated and shows initiative, esp. at work.

self-styled *adj* (*prenominal*) claiming to be of a specified nature, quality, profession, etc.: *a self-styled expert*.

self-sufficient *or* **self-sufficing** *adj* **1** able to provide for or support oneself without the help of others. **2** *Rare*. having undue confidence in oneself.
▶ ˌself-sufˈficiency *n* ▶ ˌself-sufˈficiently *adv*

self-supporting *adj* **1** able to support or maintain oneself without the help of others. **2** able to stand up or hold firm without support, props, attachments, etc.

self-tender *n* an offer by a company to buy back some or all of its shares from its shareholders, esp. as a protection against an unwelcome takeover bid.

self-will *n* stubborn adherence to one's own will, desires, etc., esp. at the expense of others.
▶ ˌself-ˈwilled *adj*

self-winding *adj* (of a wrist watch) having a mechanism in which a rotating or oscillating weight rewinds the mainspring.

Seljuk (sɛlˈdʒuːk) *n* **1** a member of any of the pre-Ottoman Turkish dynasties ruling over large parts of Asia in the 11th, 12th, and 13th centuries A.D. ◆ *adj* **2** of or relating to these dynasties. [C19: from Turkish]

Selkirk ★ (ˈsɛlˌkɜːk) *n* Alexander. original name *Alexander*

Selcraig. 1676–1721, Scottish sailor, who was marooned on one of the islets of Juan Fernández and is regarded as the prototype of Defoe's Robinson Crusoe.

Selkirk Mountains ★ *pl n* a mountain range in SW Canada, in SE British Columbia. Highest peak: Mount Sir Sandford, 3533 m (11 590 ft).

Selkirkshire ★ ('sɛlkɜːkˌʃɪə, -ʃə) *n* a historic county of SE Scotland, now part of Scottish Borders.

sell (sɛl) *vb* **sells, selling, sold. 1** to dispose of or transfer or be disposed of or transferred to a purchaser in exchange for money or other consideration. **2** to deal in (objects, property, etc.): *he sells used cars.* **3** (*tr*) to give up or surrender for a price or reward: *to sell one's honour.* **4** to promote or facilitate the sale of (objects, property, etc.): *publicity sells many products.* **5** to gain acceptance of: *to sell an idea.* **6** (*intr*) to be in demand on the market: *these dresses sell well.* **7** (*tr*) *Inf.* to deceive. **8 sell down the river.** *Inf.* to betray. **9 sell oneself. 9a** to convince someone else of one's potential or worth. **9b** to give up one's moral standards, etc. **10 sell short. 10a** *Inf.* to belittle. **10b** *Finance.* to sell securities or goods without owning them in anticipation of buying them before delivery at a lower price. ◆ *n* **11** the act or an instance of selling: *a soft sell.* **12** *Inf.* a hoax or deception. ◆ See also **sell off, sell out,** etc. [OE *sellan* to lend, deliver]
▸ **'sellable** *adj* ▸ **'seller** *n*

Sellafield ★ ('sɛləˌfiːld) *n* the site of an atomic power station and nuclear reprocessing plant in NW England, in W Cumbria. Former name: **Windscale.**

sell-by date *n* **1** a date printed on the packaging of perishable goods, indicating the date after which the goods should not be offered for sale. **2 past one's sell-by date.** *Inf.* beyond one's prime.

Sellers ★ ('sɛləz) *n* **Peter.** 1925–80, British actor, noted for his part in *The Goon Show* (BBC Radio, 1952–60). His films include *I'm All Right, Jack* (1959), *The Pink Panther* (1963), and *Being There* (1979).

selling race *or* **plate** *n* a horse race in which the winner must be offered for sale at auction.

sell off *vb* (*tr, adv*) to sell (remaining or unprofitable items), esp. at low prices.

Sellotape ('sɛləˌteɪp) *n* **1** *Trademark.* a type of transparent adhesive tape. ◆ *vb* **Sellotapes, Sellotaping, Sellotaped.** (*tr*) **2** to seal or stick using adhesive tape.

sell out *vb* (*adv*) **1** Also (*chiefly Brit.*): **sell up.** to dispose of (something) completely by selling. **2** (*tr*) *Inf.* to betray. **3** (*intr*) *Inf.* to abandon one's principles, standards, etc. ◆ *n* **sellout. 4** *Inf.* a performance for which all tickets are sold. **5** a commercial success. **6** *Inf.* a betrayal.

sell-through *adj* **1** (of prerecorded video cassettes) sold without first being available for hire only. ◆ *n* **2** the sale of prerecorded video cassettes in this way.

sell up *vb* (*adv*) *Chiefly Brit.* **1** (*tr*) to sell all (the possessions) of (a bankrupt debtor) in order to discharge his debts. **2** (*intr*) to sell a business.

selsyn ('sɛlsɪn) *n* another name for **synchro.** [from SEL(F-) + SYN(CHRONOUS)]

Seltzer ('sɛltsə) *n* **1** a natural effervescent water with a high content of minerals. **2** a similar synthetic water, used as a beverage. [C18: changed from G *Selterser Wasser* water from (*Nieder*) *Selters,* district where mineral springs are located, near Wiesbaden, Germany]

selva ('sɛlvə) *n* **1** dense equatorial forest, esp. in the Amazon basin, characterized by tall broad-leaved evergreen trees. **2** a tract of such forest. [C19: from Sp. & Port., from L *silva* forest]

selvage *or* **selvedge** ('sɛlvɪdʒ) *n* **1** the finished nonfraying edge of a length of woven fabric. **2** a similar strip of material allowed in fabricating a metal or plastic article. [C15: from SELF + EDGE]
▸ **'selvaged** *adj*

selves (sɛlvz) *n* **a** the plural of **self. b** (*in combination*): *ourselves, yourselves, themselves.*

Sem. *abbrev. for:* **1** Seminary. **2** Semitic.

semantic (sɪ'mæntɪk) *adj* **1** of or relating to the meanings of different words or symbols. **2** of or relating to se-

mantics. [C19: from Gk *sēmantikos* having significance, from *sēmainein* to signify, from *sēma* a sign]
▸ **se'mantically** *adv*

semantics (sɪ'mæntɪks) *n* (*functioning as sing*) **1** the branch of linguistics that deals with the study of meaning. **2** the study of the relationships between signs and symbols and what they represent. **3** *Logic.* the principles that determine the truth-values of the formulas in a logical system.
▸ **se'manticist** *n*

semaphore ('sɛməˌfɔː) *n* **1** an apparatus for conveying information by means of visual signals, as with flags, etc. **2** a system of signalling by holding a flag in each hand and moving the arms to designated positions for each letter of the alphabet. ◆ *vb* **semaphores, semaphoring, semaphored. 3** to signal (information) by means of semaphore. [C19: via F, from Gk *sēma* a signal + -PHORE]
▸ **semaphoric** (ˌsɛmə'fɒrɪk) *adj*

Semarang *or* **Samarang** ★ (sə'mɑːrɑːŋ) *n* a port in S Indonesia, in N Java on the Java Sea. Pop.: 1 005 316 (1990).

semasiology (sɪˌmeɪsɪ'ɒlədʒɪ) *n* another name for **semantics.** [C19: from Gk *sēmasia* meaning, from *sēmainein* to signify + -LOGY]

sematic (sɪ'mætɪk) *adj* (of the conspicuous coloration of certain animals) acting as a warning. [C19: from Gk *sēma* a sign]

semblance ('sɛmbləns) *n* **1** outward appearance, esp. without any inner substance. **2** a resemblance. [C13: from OF, from *sembler* to seem, from L *simulāre* to imitate, from *similis* like]

Semele ★ ('sɛmɪlɪ) *n* Greek myth. mother of Dionysus by Zeus.

sememe ('siːmiːm) *n* Linguistics. the meaning of a morpheme. [C20 (coined in 1933 by L. Bloomfield, US linguist): from Gk *sēma* a sign + -EME]

semen ('siːmɛn) *n* **1** the thick whitish fluid containing spermatozoa that is ejaculated from the male genital tract. **2** another name for **sperm**[1]. [C14: from L: seed]

Semeru *or* **Semeroe** ★ (sə'mɛruː) *n* a volcano in Indonesia: the highest peak in Java. Height: 3676 m (12 060 ft).

semester (sɪ'mɛstə) *n* **1** Chiefly US & Canad. either of two divisions of the academic year. **2** (in German universities) a session of six months. [C19: via G from L *sēmestris* half-yearly, from *sex* six + *mensis* a month]

semi ('sɛmɪ) *n, pl* **semis.** *Inf.* **1** Brit. short for **semidetached (house). 2** short for **semifinal.**

semi- *prefix* **1** half: *semicircle.* **2** partially, partly, or almost: *semiprofessional.* **3** occurring twice in a specified period of time: *semiweekly.* [from L]

semiannual (ˌsɛmɪ'ænjʊəl) *adj* **1** occurring every half-year. **2** lasting for half a year.
▸ **ˌsemi'annually** *adv*

semiarid (ˌsɛmɪ'ærɪd) *adj* characterized by scanty rainfall and scrubby vegetation, often occurring in continental interiors.

semiautomatic (ˌsɛmɪˌɔːtə'mætɪk) *adj* **1** partly automatic. **2** (of a firearm) self-loading but firing only one shot at each pull of the trigger. ◆ *n* **3** a semiautomatic firearm.
▸ **ˌsemiˌauto'matically** *adv*

semibreve ('sɛmɪˌbriːv) *n* Music. a note, now the longest in common use, having a time value that may be divided by any power of 2 to give all other notes. Usual US and Canad. name: **whole note.**

semicircle ('sɛmɪˌsɜːk^əl) *n* **1a** one half of a circle. **1b** half the circumference of a circle. **2** anything having the shape or form of half a circle.
▸ **semicircular** (ˌsɛmɪ'sɜːkjʊlə) *adj*

semicircular canal *n* Anat. any of the three looped fluid-filled membranous tubes, at right angles to one another, that comprise the labyrinth of the ear.

semicolon (ˌsɛmɪ'kəʊlən) *n* the punctuation mark ; used to indicate a pause intermediate in value or length between that of a comma and that of a full stop.

semiconductor (ˌsɛmɪkən'dʌktə) *n* **1** a substance, such as germanium or silicon, that has an electrical conductivity that increases with temperature. **2a** a device, such as a transistor or integrated circuit, that depends on the properties of such a substance. **2b** (as modifier): a semiconductor diode.

semiconscious (ˌsɛmɪˈkɒnʃəs) adj not fully conscious. ▸ ˌsemiˈconsciously adv ▸ ˌsemiˈconsciousness n

semidetached (ˌsɛmɪdɪˈtætʃt) adj **a** (of a building) joined to another building on one side by a common wall. **b** (as n): they live in a semidetached.

semifinal (ˌsɛmɪˈfaɪnᵊl) n **a** the round before the final in a competition. **b** (as modifier): the semifinal draw. ▸ ˌsemiˈfinalist n

semifluid (ˌsɛmɪˈfluːɪd) adj **1** having properties between those of a liquid and those of a solid. ◆ n **2** a substance that has such properties because of high viscosity: tar is a semifluid. ◆ Also: **semiliquid**.

semiliterate (ˌsɛmɪˈlɪtərɪt) adj **1** hardly able to read or write. **2** able to read but not to write.

semilunar (ˌsɛmɪˈluːnə) adj shaped like a crescent or half-moon.

semilunar valve n Anat. either of two crescent-shaped valves, one in the aorta and one in the pulmonary artery, that prevent regurgitation of blood into the heart.

seminal (ˈsɛmɪnəl) adj **1** potentially capable of development. **2** highly original and important. **3** rudimentary or unformed. **4** of or relating to semen: seminal fluid. **5** Biol. of or relating to seed. [C14: from LL sēminālis belonging to seed, from L sēmen seed] ▸ ˈseminally adv

seminar (ˈsɛmɪˌnɑː) n **1** a small group of students meeting regularly under the guidance of a tutor, professor, etc. **2** one such meeting or the place in which it is held. **3** a higher course for postgraduates. **4** any group or meeting for holding discussions or exchanging information. [C19: via G from L sēminārium SEMINARY]

seminary (ˈsɛmɪnərɪ) n, pl **seminaries**. **1** an academy for the training of priests, etc. **2** Arch. a private secondary school, esp. for girls. [C15: from L sēminārium a nursery garden, from sēmen seed] ▸ ˌsemiˈnarial adj ▸ seminarian (ˌsɛmɪˈnɛərɪən) n

seminiferous (ˌsɛmɪˈnɪfərəs) adj **1** containing, conveying, or producing semen. **2** (of plants) bearing or producing seeds.

semiotics (ˌsɛmɪˈɒtɪks) n (functioning as sing) **1** the study of signs and symbols, esp. the relations between written or spoken signs and their referents in the physical world or the world of ideas. **2** the scientific study of the symptoms of disease. ◆ Also called: **semiology**. [from Gk sēmeiōtikos, from sēmeion a sign] ▸ ˌsemiˈotic adj

Semipalatinsk ★ (Russian sɪmipaˈlatinsk) n a city in NE Kazakhstan, on the Irtysh River. Pop.: 320 200 (1995 est.).

semipermeable (ˌsɛmɪˈpɜːmɪəbᵊl) adj (esp. of a cell membrane) selectively permeable. ▸ ˌsemiˌpermeaˈbility n

semiprecious (ˌsɛmɪˈprɛʃəs) adj (of certain stones) having less value than a precious stone.

semiprofessional (ˌsɛmɪprəˈfɛʃənᵊl) adj **1** (of a person) engaged in an activity or sport part-time but for pay. **2** (of an activity or sport) engaged in by semiprofessional people. **3** of or relating to a person whose activities are professional in some respects. ◆ n **4** a semiprofessional person. ▸ ˌsemiproˈfessionally adv

semiquaver (ˈsɛmɪˌkweɪvə) n Music. a note having the time value of one-sixteenth of a semibreve. Usual US and Canad. name: **sixteenth note.**

Semiramis ★ (sɛˈmɪrəmɪs) n the legendary founder of Babylon and wife of Ninus, king of Assyria, which she ruled with great skill after his death.

semirigid (ˌsɛmɪˈrɪdʒɪd) adj **1** partly but not wholly rigid. **2** (of an airship) maintaining shape by means of a main supporting keel and internal gas pressure.

semiskilled (ˌsɛmɪˈskɪld) adj partly skilled or trained but not sufficiently so to perform specialized work.

semisolid (ˌsɛmɪˈsɒlɪd) adj having a viscosity and rigidity intermediate between that of a solid and a liquid.

semisolus (ˌsɛmɪˈsəʊləs) n an advertisement that appears on the same page as another advertisement but not adjacent to it.

semisweet (ˈsɛmɪˌswiːt) adj (of biscuits, etc.) slightly sweetened.

Semite (ˈsiːmaɪt) n a member of the group of peoples who speak a Semitic language, including the Jews and Arabs as well as the ancient Babylonians, Assyrians, and Phoenicians. [C19: from NL sēmīta descendant of Shem, via Gk Sēm, from Heb. SHEM]

Semitic (sɪˈmɪtɪk) n **1** a branch or subfamily of the Afro-Asiatic family of languages that includes Arabic, Hebrew, Aramaic, and such ancient languages as Phoenician. ◆ adj **2** denoting or belonging to this group of languages. **3** denoting or characteristic of any of the peoples speaking a Semitic language, esp. the Jews or the Arabs. **4** another word for **Jewish.**

semitone (ˈsɛmɪˌtəʊn) n an interval denoting the pitch difference between certain adjacent degrees of the diatonic scale (**diatonic semitone**) or between one note and its sharpened or flattened equivalent (**chromatic semitone**); minor second. Also called (US and Canad.): **half step.** Cf. **whole tone.** ▸ ˌsemiˈtonic (ˌsɛmɪˈtɒnɪk) adj

semitrailer (ˈsɛmɪˌtreɪlə) n a type of trailer or articulated lorry that has wheels only at the rear, the front end being supported by the towing vehicle.

semitropical (ˌsɛmɪˈtrɒpɪkᵊl) adj partly tropical. ▸ ˌsemiˈtropics pl n

semivowel (ˈsɛmɪˌvaʊəl) n Phonetics. a vowel-like sound that acts like a consonant. In English and many other languages the chief semivowels are (w) in well and (j), represented as y, in yell. Also called: **glide.**

semiyearly (ˌsɛmɪˈjɪəlɪ) adj another word for **semiannual.**

Semmelweis ★ (ˈzɛmᵊlˌvaɪs) n Ignaz Philipp (ˈɪɡnɑːts ˈfiːlɪp). 1818–65, Hungarian obstetrician, who discovered the cause of puerperal infection and pioneered the use of antiseptics.

semolina (ˌsɛməˈliːnə) n the large hard grains of wheat left after flour has been bolted, used for puddings, soups, etc. [C18: from It. semolino, dim. of semola bran, from L simila very fine wheat flour]

Sempach ★ (German ˈzɛmpax) n a village in central Switzerland, in Lucerne canton on **Lake Sempach**: scene of the victory (1386) of the Swiss over the Hapsburgs.

sempervivum (ˌsɛmpəˈvaɪvəm) n any of a genus of hardy perennials including the houseleek. [C16 (used of the houseleek, adopted C18 by Linnaeus (1707-78), Swedish botanist, for the genus): L, from sempervivus ever-living]

sempiternal (ˌsɛmpɪˈtɜːnᵊl) adj Literary. everlasting; eternal. [C15: from OF, from LL sempiternālis, from L, from semper always + aeternus ETERNAL] ▸ ˌsempiˈternally adv

semplice (ˈsɛmplɪtʃɪ) adj, adv Music. to be performed in a simple manner. [It.: simple, from L simplex]

sempre (ˈsɛmprɪ) adv Music. (preceding a tempo or dynamic marking) always; consistently. It is used to indicate that a specified volume, tempo, etc., is to be sustained throughout a piece or passage. [It.: always, from L semper]

sempstress (ˈsɛmpstrɪs) n a rare word for **seamstress.**

Semtex (ˈsɛmtɛks) n a pliable plastic explosive. [orig. a trade name]

SEN (in Britain) abbrev. for: **1** (formerly) State Enrolled Nurse. **2** special educational needs: needs arising from any of a wide range of problems that affect a pupil's normal educational development and for which special provisions are made.

Sen. or **sen.** abbrev. for: **1** senate. **2** senator. **3** senior.

senate (ˈsɛnɪt) n **1** any legislative body considered to resemble a Senate. **2** the main governing body at some universities. [C13: from L senātus council of the elders, from senex an old man]

Senate ('sɛnɪt) *n* (*sometimes not cap.*) **1** the upper chamber of the legislatures of the US, Canada, Australia, and many other countries. **2** the legislative council of ancient Rome.

senator ('sɛnətə) *n* **1** (*often cap.*) a member of a Senate or senate. **2** any legislator.
▸ **senatorial** (ˌsɛnə'tɔːrɪəl) *adj*

send (sɛnd) *vb* **sends, sending, sent. 1** (*tr*) to cause or order (a person or thing) to be taken, directed, or transmitted to another place: *to send a letter.* **2** (when *intr*, foll. by *for*; when *tr*, takes an *infinitive*) to dispatch a request or command (for something or to do something): *he sent for a bottle of wine.* **3** (*tr*) to direct or cause to go to a place or point: *his blow sent the champion to the floor.* **4** (*tr*) to bring to a state or condition: *this noise will send me mad.* **5** (*tr*; often foll. by *forth, out,* etc.) to cause to issue: *his cooking sent forth a lovely smell.* **6** (*tr*) to cause to happen or come: *misery sent by fate.* **7** to transmit (a message) by radio. **8** (*tr*) *Sl.* to move to excitement or rapture: *this music really sends me.* ◆ *n* **9** another word for **swash** (sense 4). [OE *sendan*]
▸ **'sendable** *adj* ▸ **'sender** *n*

Sendai ★ (sɛn'daɪ) *n* a city in central Japan, on NE Honshu: university (1907). Pop.: 971 263 (1995).

send down *vb* (*tr, adv*) **1** *Brit.* to expel from a university. **2** *Inf.* to send to prison.

sendoff ('sɛnd‚ɒf) *n Inf.* **1** a demonstration of good wishes to a person about to set off on a journey, etc. ◆ *vb* **send off.** (*tr, adv*) **2** to cause to depart. **3** *Soccer, rugby,* etc. (of the referee) to dismiss (a player) from the field of play for some offence. **4** *Inf.* to give a sendoff to.

send up *vb* (*tr, adv*) **1** *Sl.* to send to prison. **2** *Brit. inf.* to make fun of, esp. by doing an imitation or parody of. ◆ *n* **send-up. 3** *Brit. inf.* a parody or imitation.

Seneca ★ ('sɛnɪkə) *n* **1 Lucius Annaeus** ('luːsɪəs ə'niːəs), called *the Younger.* ?4 B.C.–65 A.D., Roman philosopher, statesman, and dramatist; tutor and adviser to Nero, in whose murder he was implicated; committed suicide. **2** his father, **Marcus** ('maːkəs) *or* **Lucius Annaeus**, called *the Elder* or *the Rhetorician.* ?55 B.C.–?39 A.D., Roman writer.

Senegal ★ (ˌsɛnɪ'gɔːl) *n* a republic in West Africa, on the Atlantic: made part of French West Africa in 1895; became fully independent in 1960; mostly low-lying, with semidesert in the north and tropical forest in the southwest. Official language: French. Religion: Muslim majority. Currency: franc. Capital: Dakar. Pop.: 8 532 000 (1996). Area: 197 160 sq. km (76 124 sq. miles).
▸ **Senegalese** (ˌsɛnɪgə'liːz) *adj, n*

Senegambia ★ (ˌsɛnə'gæmbɪə) *n* a region of W Africa, between the Senegal and Gambia Rivers: now mostly in Senegal.

Senegambia Confederation *n* an economic and political union (1982–89) between Senegal and The Gambia.

senescent (sɪ'nɛsᵊnt) *adj* **1** growing old. **2** characteristic of old age. [C17: from L *senēscere* to grow old, from *senex* old]
▸ **se'nescence** *n*

seneschal ('sɛnɪʃəl) *n* **1** a steward of the household of a medieval prince or nobleman. **2** *Brit.* a cathedral official. [C14: from OF, from Med. L *siniscalcus,* of Gmc origin]

Senghor ★ (*French* sɑ̃gɔr) *n* **Léopold Sédar** (leɔpɔl sedar). born 1906, Senegalese statesman and writer; president of Senegal (1960–80).

senile ('siːnaɪl) *adj* **1** of or characteristic of old age. **2** mentally or physically weak or infirm on account of old age. [C17: from L *senīlis,* from *senex* an old man]
▸ **senility** (sɪ'nɪlɪtɪ) *n*

senile dementia *n* dementia starting in old age with no clear physical cause.

senior ('siːnjə) *adj* **1** higher in rank or length of service. **2** older in years: *senior citizens.* **3** of or relating to maturity or old age: *senior privileges.* **4** *Education.* **4a** of or designating more advanced or older pupils. **4b** of or relating to a secondary school. **4c** *US.* denoting a student in the last year of school or university. ◆ *n* **5** a senior person. **6** a senior pupil, student, etc. [C14: from L: older, from *senex* old]

Senior ('siːnjə) *adj Chiefly US.* being the older: used to distinguish the father from the son: *Charles Parker, Senior.* Abbrevs.: **Sr., Sen.**

senior aircraftman *n* a rank in the Royal Air Force comparable to that of a private in the army, though not the lowest rank in the Royal Air Force.

senior citizen *n* an old age pensioner.

senior common room *n* (in British universities, colleges, etc.) a common room for the use of academic staff.

seniority (ˌsiːnɪ'ɒrɪtɪ) *n, pl* **seniorities. 1** the state of being senior. **2** precedence in rank, etc., due to senior status.

senior service *n Brit.* the Royal Navy.

Senlac ★ ('sɛnlæk) *n* a hill in Sussex: site of the Battle of Hastings in 1066.

senna ('sɛnə) *n* **1** any of a genus of tropical plants having typically yellow flowers and long pods. **2 senna leaf.** the dried leaflets of any of these plants, used as a cathartic and laxative. **3 senna pods.** the dried fruits of any of these plants, used as a cathartic and laxative. [C16: via NL from Ar. *sanā*]

Senna ★ ('sɛnə) *n* **Ayrton** ('eətən). 1960–94, Brazilian racing driver: world champion (1988, 1990, 1991).

Sennacherib ★ (se'nækərɪb) *n* died 681 B.C., king of Assyria (705–681); son of Sargon II. He defeated Babylon and rebuilt Nineveh.

Sennar ★ ('sɛnɑː, se'nɑː) *n* **1** a region of the E Sudan, between the White Nile and the Blue Nile: a kingdom from the 16th to 19th centuries. **2** a town in this region, on the Blue Nile: the nearby **Sennar Dam** (1925) supplies irrigation water to Gezira. Pop.: 8000 (latest est.).

sennight *or* **se'nnight** ('sɛnaɪt) *n* an archaic word for **week.** [OE *seofan nihte;* see SEVEN, NIGHT]

señor (se'njɔː; *Spanish* se'ɲor) *n, pl* **señors** *or* **señores** (*Spanish* -'ɲores). a Spaniard: a title of address equivalent to *Mr* when placed before a name or *sir* when used alone. [Sp., from L *senior* an older man, SENIOR]

señora (se'njɔːrə; *Spanish* 'ɲora) *n, pl* **señoras** (-rəz; *Spanish* -ras). a married Spanish woman: a title of address equivalent to *Mrs* when placed before a name or *madam* when used alone.

señorita (ˌsenjɔː'riːtə; *Spanish* ˌseɲo'rita) *n, pl* **señoritas** (-təz; *Spanish* -tas). an unmarried Spanish woman: title of address equivalent to *Miss* when placed before a name or *madam* or *miss* when used alone.

sensation (sɛn'seɪʃən) *n* **1** the power of perceiving through the senses. **2** a physical experience resulting from the stimulation of one of the sense organs. **3** a general feeling or awareness: *a sensation of fear.* **4** a state of widespread public excitement: *his announcement caused a sensation.* **5** anything that causes such a state: *your speech was a sensation.* [C17: from Med. L, from LL *sensātus* endowed with SENSE]

sensational (sɛn'seɪʃənᵊl) *adj* **1** causing or intended to cause intense feelings, esp. of curiosity, horror, etc.: *sensational disclosures in the press.* **2** *Inf.* extremely good: *a sensational skater.* **3** of or relating to the faculty of sensation.
▸ **sen'sationally** *adv*

sensationalism (sɛn'seɪʃənᵊˌlɪzəm) *n* **1** the use of sensational language, etc., to arouse an intense emotional response. **2** such sensational matter itself. **3** *Philosophy.* the doctrine that knowledge cannot go beyond the analysis of experience.
▸ **sen'sationalist** *n* ▸ **sen‚sational'istic** *adj*

sensationalize *or* **sensationalise** (sɛn'seɪʃənᵊˌlaɪz) *vb* **sensationalizes, sensationalizing, sensationalized** *or* **sensationalises, sensationalising, sensationalised.** (*tr*) to cause (events, esp. in newspaper reports) to seem more vivid, shocking, etc., than they really are.

sense (sɛns) *n* **1** any of the faculties by which the mind receives information about the external world or the state of the body. The five traditional senses are sight, hearing, touch, taste, and smell. **2** the ability to perceive. **3** a feeling perceived through one of the senses: *a sense of warmth.* **4** a mental perception or awareness: *a sense of happiness.* **5** moral discernment: *a sense of right and wrong.* **6** (*sometimes pl*) sound practical judgment or intelligence. **7** reason or purpose: *what is the sense of going out?* **8**

★ **people and places**

meaning: *what is the sense of this proverb?* **9** specific meaning; definition: *in what sense are you using the word?* **10** an opinion or consensus. **11** *Maths.* one of two opposite directions in which a vector can operate. **12 make sense.** to be understandable. **13 take leave of one's senses.** *Inf.* to go mad. ◆ *vb* **senses, sensing, sensed.** (*tr*) **14** to perceive through one or more of the senses. **15** to apprehend or detect without or in advance of the evidence of the senses. **16** to understand. **17** *Computing.* **17a** to test or locate the position of (a part of computer hardware). **17b** to read (data). [C14: from L *sēnsus*, from *sentīre* to feel]

sense datum *n* a unit of sensation, such as a sharp pain, detached both from any information it may convey and from its putative source in the external world.

senseless ('sɛnslɪs) *adj* **1** foolish: *a senseless plan.* **2** lacking in feeling; unconscious. **3** lacking in perception. ▸ **'senselessly** *adv* ▸ **'senselessness** *n*

sense organ *n* a structure in animals that is specialized for receiving external or internal stimuli and transmitting them in the form of nervous impulses to the brain.

sensibility (ˌsɛnsɪ'bɪlɪtɪ) *n, pl* **sensibilities. 1** the ability to perceive or feel. **2** (*often pl*) the capacity for responding to emotion, etc. **3** (*often pl*) the capacity for responding to aesthetic stimuli. **4** discernment; awareness. **5** (*usually pl*) emotional or moral feelings: *cruelty offends most people's sensibilities.*

sensible ('sɛnsɪbəl) *adj* **1** having or showing good sense or judgment. **2** (of clothing) serviceable; practical. **3** having the capacity for sensation; sensitive. **4** capable of being apprehended by the senses. **5** perceptible to the mind. **6** (sometimes foll. by *of*) having perception; aware: *sensible of your kindness.* **7** readily perceived: *a sensible difference.* [C14: from OF, from LL *sēnsibilis*, from L *sentīre* to sense] ▸ **'sensibleness** *n* ▸ **'sensibly** *adv*

sensitive ('sɛnsɪtɪv) *adj* **1** having the power of sensation. **2** responsive to or aware of feelings, moods, etc. **3** easily irritated; delicate. **4** affected by external conditions or stimuli. **5** easily offended. **6** of or relating to the senses or the power of sensation. **7** capable of registering small differences or changes in amounts, etc.: *a sensitive instrument.* **8** *Photog.* responding readily to light: *a sensitive emulsion.* **9** *Chiefly US.* connected with matters affecting national security. **10** (of a stock market or prices) quickly responsive to external influences. [C14: from Med. L *sēnsitīvus*, from L *sentīre* to feel] ▸ **'sensitively** *adv* ▸ **ˌsensi'tivity** *n*

sensitive plant *n* a tropical American mimosa plant, the leaflets and stems of which fold if touched.

sensitize *or* **sensitise** ('sɛnsɪˌtaɪz) *vb* **sensitizes, sensitizing, sensitized** *or* **sensitises, sensitising, sensitised. 1** to make or become sensitive. **2** (*tr*) to render (an individual) sensitive to a drug, etc. **3** (*tr*) *Photog.* to make (a material) sensitive to light by coating it with a photographic emulsion often containing special chemicals, such as dyes. ▸ ˌsensiti'zation *or* ˌsensiti'sation *n* ▸ 'sensiˌtizer *or* 'sensiˌtiser *n*

sensitometer (ˌsɛnsɪ'tɒmɪtə) *n* an instrument for measuring the sensitivity to light of a photographic material over a range of exposures.

sensor ('sɛnsə) *n* anything, such as a photoelectric cell, that receives a signal or stimulus and responds to it. [C19: from L *sēnsus* perceived, from *sentīre* to observe]

sensorimotor (ˌsɛnsərɪ'məʊtə) *or* **sensomotor** (ˌsɛnsə'məʊtə) *adj* of or relating to both the sensory and motor functions of an organism or to the nerves controlling them.

sensorium (sɛn'sɔ:rɪəm) *n, pl* **sensoriums** *or* **sensoria** (-rɪə). **1** the area of the brain considered responsible for receiving and integrating sensations from the outside world. **2** *Physiol.* the entire sensory and intellectual apparatus of the body. [C17: from LL, from L *sēnsus* felt, from *sentīre* to perceive]

sensory ('sɛnsərɪ) *adj* of or relating to the senses or the power of sensation. [C18: from L *sensōrius*, from *sentīre* to feel]

sensual ('sɛnsjʊəl) *adj* **1** of or relating to any of the senses or sense organs; bodily. **2** strongly or unduly inclined to gratification of the senses. **3** tending to arouse the bodily appetites, esp. the sexual appetite. [C15: from LL *sensuālis*, from L *sēnsus* SENSE] ▸ **'sensually** *adv*

sensualism ('sɛnsjʊəˌlɪzəm) *n* **1** the quality or state of being sensual. **2** the doctrine that the ability to gratify the senses is the only criterion of goodness.

sensuality (ˌsɛnsjʊ'ælɪtɪ) *n, pl* **sensualities. 1** the quality or state of being sensual. **2** excessive indulgence in sensual pleasures. ▸ **sensualist** ('sɛnsjʊəlɪst) *n*

sensuous ('sɛnsjʊəs) *adj* **1** aesthetically pleasing to the senses. **2** appreciative of qualities perceived by the senses. **3** of or derived from the senses. [C17, but not common until C19: apparently coined by Milton to avoid the sexual overtones of SENSUAL] ▸ **'sensuously** *adv* ▸ **'sensuousness** *n*

sent (sɛnt) *vb* the past tense and past participle of **send.**

sentence ('sɛntəns) *n* **1** a sequence of words capable of standing alone to make an assertion, ask a question, or give a command, usually consisting of a subject and a predicate. **2** the judgment formally pronounced upon a person convicted in criminal proceedings, esp. the decision as to what punishment is to be imposed. **3** *Music.* a passage or division of a piece of music, usually consisting of two or more contrasting musical phrases and ending in a cadence. **4** *Arch.* a proverb, maxim, or aphorism. ◆ *vb* **sentences, sentencing, sentenced. 5** (*tr*) to pronounce sentence on (a convicted person) in a court of law. [C13: via OF from L *sententia* a way of thinking, from *sentīre* to feel] ▸ **sentential** (sɛn'tɛnʃəl) *adj*

sentence connector *n* a word or phrase that introduces a clause or sentence and serves as a transition between it and a previous clause or sentence, as for example *also* in *I'm buying eggs and also I'm looking for a dessert for tonight.*

sentence substitute *n* a word or phrase, esp. one traditionally classified as an adverb, that is used in place of a finite sentence, such as *yes, no, certainly,* and *never.*

sententious (sɛn'tɛnʃəs) *adj* **1** characterized by or full of aphorisms or axioms. **2** constantly using aphorisms, etc. **3** tending to indulge in pompous moralizing. [C15: from L *sententiōsus* full of meaning, from *sententia*; see SENTENCE] ▸ **sen'tentiously** *adv* ▸ **sen'tentiousness** *n*

sentient ('sɛnʃənt, 'sɛntɪənt) *adj* **1** having the power of sense perception or sensation; conscious. ◆ *n* **2** *Rare.* a sentient person or thing. [C17: from L *sentiēns* feeling, from *sentīre* to perceive] ▸ **sentience** ('sɛnʃəns) *n*

sentiment ('sɛntɪmənt) *n* **1** susceptibility to tender or romantic emotion: *she has too much sentiment to be successful.* **2** (*often pl*) a thought, opinion, or attitude. **3** exaggerated or mawkish feeling or emotion. **4** an expression of response to deep feeling, esp. in art. **5** a feeling or awareness: *a sentiment of pity.* **6** a mental attitude determined by feeling: *there is a strong revolutionary sentiment in his country.* **7** a feeling conveyed, or intended to be conveyed, in words. [C17: from Med. L *sentīmentum*, from L *sentīre* to feel]

sentimental (ˌsɛntɪ'mɛntəl) *adj* **1** tending to indulge the emotions excessively. **2** making a direct appeal to the emotions, esp. to romantic feelings. **3** relating to or characterized by sentiment. ▸ ˌsenti'menta,lism *n* ▸ ˌsenti'mentalist *n* ▸ ˌsenti'mentally *adv*

sentimentality (ˌsɛntɪmɛn'tælɪtɪ) *n, pl* **sentimentalities. 1** the state, quality, or an instance of being sentimental. **2** an act, statement, etc., that is sentimental.

sentimentalize *or* **sentimentalise** (ˌsɛntɪ'mɛntəˌlaɪz) *vb* **sentimentalizes, sentimentalizing, sentimentalized** *or* **sentimentalises, sentimentalising, sentimentalised.** to make sentimental or behave sentimentally. ▸ ˌsentiˌmentali'zation *or* ˌsentiˌmentali'sation *n*

sentimental value *n* the value of an article in terms of its sentimental associations for a particular person.

sentinel ('sɛntɪn°l) n **1** a person, such as a sentry, assigned to keep guard. ♦ vb **sentinels, sentinelling, sentinelled** or US **sentinels, sentineling, sentineled.** (tr) **2** to guard as a sentinel. **3** to post as a sentinel. [C16: from OF sentinelle, from OIt., from sentina watchfulness, from sentire to notice, from L]

sentry ('sɛntrɪ) n, pl **sentries.** a soldier who guards or prevents unauthorized access to a place, etc. [C17: ? shortened from obs. centrinel, C16 var. of SENTINEL]

sentry box n a small shelter with an open front in which a sentry may stand to be sheltered from the weather.

senza ('sɛntsɑ:) prep Music. omitting. [It.]

Seoul ★ (səul) n the capital of South Korea, in the west on the Han River: capital of Korea from 1392 to 1910, then seat of the Japanese administration until 1945; became capital of South Korea in 1948; cultural and educational centre. Pop.: 10 229 262 (1995). Also called: **Kyongsong.** Japanese name: **Keijo.**

Sep. abbrev. for: **1** September. **2** Septuagint.

sepal ('sɛp°l) n any of the separate parts of the calyx of a flower. [C19: from NL sepalum: sep- from Gk skepē a covering + -alum, from NL petalum PETAL]

-sepalous adj combining form. having sepals of a specified type or number: polysepalous.
▸ **-sepaly** n combining form.

separable ('sɛpərəb°l) adj able to be separated, divided, or parted.
▸ ,separa'bility or 'separableness n ▸ 'separably adv

separate vb ('sɛpə,reɪt), **separates, separating, separated. 1** (tr) to act as a barrier between: a range of mountains separates the two countries. **2** to part or be parted from a mass or group. **3** (tr) to discriminate between: to separate the men from the boys. **4** to divide or be divided into component parts. **5** to sever or be severed. **6** (intr) (of a married couple) to cease living together. ♦ adj ('sɛprɪt, 'sɛpərɪt). **7** existing or considered independently: a separate problem. **8** disunited or apart. **9** set apart from the main body or mass. **10** distinct, individual, or particular. **11** solitary or withdrawn. [C15: from L sēparāre, from sē- apart + parāre to obtain]
▸ 'separately adv ▸ 'separateness n ▸ 'separative adj
▸ 'sepa,rator n

separates ('sɛprɪts, 'sɛpərɪts) pl n women's outer garments that only cover part of the body; skirts, blouses, jackets, trousers, etc.

separate school n **1** (in certain Canadian provinces) a school for a large religious minority financed by provincial grants in addition to the education tax. **2** a Roman Catholic school.

separation (,sɛpə'reɪʃən) n **1** the act of separating or state of being separated. **2** the place or line where a separation is made. **3** a gap that separates. **4** Family law. the cessation of cohabitation between a man and wife, either by mutual agreement or under a decree of a court.

separatist ('sɛpərətɪst) n **a** a person who advocates secession from an organization, federation, union, etc. **b** (as modifier): a separatist movement.
▸ 'separa,tism n

Sephardi (sɪ'fɑ:dɪ) n, pl **Sephardim** (-dɪm). Judaism. **1** a Jew of Spanish, Portuguese, or North African descent. **2** the pronunciation of Hebrew used by these Jews, and in Modern Hebrew as spoken in Israel. ♦ Cf. **Ashkenazi.** [C19: from LHeb., from Heb. sepharad a region mentioned in Obadiah 20, thought to have been Spain]
▸ Se'phardic adj

sepia ('si:pɪə) n **1** a dark reddish-brown pigment obtained from the inky secretion of the cuttlefish. **2** a brownish tone imparted to a photograph, esp. an early one. **3** a brownish-grey to dark yellowish-brown colour. **4** a drawing or photograph in sepia. ♦ adj **5** of the colour sepia or done in sepia: a sepia print. [C16: from L: a cuttlefish, from Gk]

sepoy ('si:pɔɪ) n (formerly) an Indian soldier in the service of the British. [C18: from Port. sipaio, from Urdu sipāhī, from Persian: horseman, from sipāh army]

seppuku (se'pu:ku:) n another word for **hara-kiri.** [from Japanese, from Chinese ch'ieh to cut + fu bowels]

sepsis ('sɛpsɪs) n the presence of pus-forming bacteria in the body. [C19: via NL from Gk sēpsis a rotting]

sept (sɛpt) n **1** Anthropol. a clan that believes itself to be descended from a common ancestor. **2** a branch of a tribe, esp. in Ireland or Scotland. [C16: ? a var. of SECT]

Sept. abbrev. for: **1** September. **2** Septuagint.

septa ('sɛptə) n the plural of **septum.**

septal ('sɛptəl) adj of or relating to a septum.

September (sɛp'tɛmbə) n the ninth month of the year, consisting of 30 days. [OE, from L: the seventh (month) according to the original calendar of ancient Rome, from septem seven]

septenary ('sɛptɪnərɪ) adj **1** of or relating to the number seven. **2** forming a group of seven. ♦ n, pl **septenaries. 3** the number seven. **4** a group of seven things. **5** a period of seven years. [C16: from L septēnārius, from septēnī seven each, from septem seven]

septennial (sɛp'tɛnɪəl) adj **1** occurring every seven years. **2** relating to or lasting seven years. [C17: from L, from septem seven + annus a year]

septet (sɛp'tɛt) n **1** Music. a group of seven singers or instrumentalists or a piece of music composed for such a group. **2** a group of seven people or things. [C19: from G, from L septem seven]

septic ('sɛptɪk) adj **1** of or caused by sepsis. **2** of or caused by putrefaction. ♦ n **3** Austral. & NZ inf. short for **septic tank.** [C17: from L sēpticus, from Gk, from sēptos decayed, from sēpein to make rotten]
▸ 'septically adv ▸ **septicity** (sɛp'tɪsɪtɪ) n

septicaemia or US **septicemia** (,sɛptɪ'si:mɪə) n any of various diseases caused by microorganisms in the blood. Nontechnical name: **blood poisoning.** [C19: from NL, from Gk sēptik(os) SEPTIC + -AEMIA]
▸ ,septi'caemic or US ,septi'cemic adj

septic tank n a tank, usually below ground, for containing sewage to be decomposed by anaerobic bacteria. Also called (Austral.): **septic system.**

septillion (sɛp'tɪljən) n, pl **septillions** or **septillion. 1** (in Britain, France, and Germany) the number represented as one followed by 42 zeros (10^{42}). **2** (in the US and Canada) the number represented as one followed by 24 zeros (10^{24}). Brit. word: **quadrillion.** [C17: from F, from sept seven + -illion, on the model of million]
▸ sep'tillionth adj, n

septime ('sɛpti:m) n the seventh of eight basic positions from which a parry or attack can be made in fencing. [C19: from L septimus seventh, from septem seven]

septuagenarian (,sɛptjʊədʒɪ'nɛərɪən) n **1** a person who is from 70 to 79 years old. ♦ adj **2** being between 70 and 79 years old. **3** of or relating to a septuagenarian. [C18: from L, from septuāgintā seventy]

Septuagesima (,sɛptjʊə'dʒɛsɪmə) n the third Sunday before Lent. [C14: from Church L septuāgēsima (diēs) the seventieth (day)]

Septuagint ('sɛptjʊə,dʒɪnt) n the principal Greek version of the Old Testament, including the Apocrypha, believed to have been translated by 70 or 72 scholars. [C16: from L septuāgintā seventy]

septum ('sɛptəm) n, pl **septa.** Biol., anat. a dividing partition between two tissues or cavities. [C18: from L saeptum wall, from saepīre to enclose]

septuple ('sɛptjʊp°l) adj **1** seven times as much or as many. **2** consisting of seven parts or members. ♦ vb **septuples, septupling, septupled. 3** (tr) to multiply by seven. [C17: from LL septuplus, from septem seven]
▸ **septuplicate** (sɛp'tju:plɪkɪt) n, adj

sepulchral (sɪ'pʌlkrəl) adj **1** suggestive of a tomb; gloomy. **2** of or relating to a sepulchre.
▸ se'pulchrally adv

sepulchre or US **sepulcher** ('sɛpəlkə) n **1** a burial vault, tomb, or grave. **2** Also called: **Easter sepulchre.** an alcove in some churches in which the Eucharistic elements were kept from Good Friday until Easter. ♦ vb **sepulchres, sepulchring, sepulchred** or US **sepulchers, sepul-**

chering, sepulchered. 3 (*tr*) to bury in a sepulchre.   [C12: from OF *sépulcre*, from L *sepulcrum*, from *sepelīre* to bury]

sepulture ('sɛpəltʃə) *n* the act of placing in a sepulchre.   [C13: via OF from L *sepultūra*, from *sepultus* buried, from *sepelīre* to bury]

seq. *abbrev. for:* **1** sequel. **2** sequens.   [L: the following (one)]

sequel ('si:kwəl) *n* **1** anything that follows from something else. **2** a consequence. **3** a novel, play, etc., that continues a previously related story.   [C15: from LL *sequēla*, from L *sequī* to follow]

sequela (sɪ'kwi:lə) *n, pl* **sequelae** (-li:). (*often pl*) *Med.* **1** any abnormal bodily condition or disease arising from a preexisting disease. **2** any complication of a disease.   [C18: from L: SEQUEL]

sequence ('si:kwəns) *n* **1** an arrangement of two or more things in a successive order. **2** the successive order of two or more things: *chronological sequence*. **3** an action or event that follows another or others. **4a** *Cards.* a set of three or more consecutive cards, usually of the same suit. **4b** *Bridge.* a set of two or more consecutive cards. **5** *Music.* an arrangement of notes or chords repeated several times at different pitches. **6** *Maths.* an ordered set of numbers or other mathematical entities in one-to-one correspondence with the integers 1 to *n* **7** a section of a film constituting a single continuous uninterrupted episode. **8** *Biochem.* the unique order of amino acids in a protein or of nucleotides in DNA or RNA. ♦ *vb* (*tr*) **9** to arrange in a sequence.   [C14: from Med. L *sequentia* that which follows, from L *sequī* to follow]

sequence of tenses *n Grammar.* the sequence according to which the tense of a subordinate verb in a sentence is determined by the tense of the principal verb, as in *I believe he is lying, I believed he was lying*, etc.

sequencing ('si:kwənsɪŋ) *n Biochem.* the procedure of determining the order of amino acids in the polypeptide chain of a protein (**protein sequencing**) or of nucleotides in a DNA section comprising a gene (**gene sequencing**).

sequent ('si:kwənt) *adj* **1** following in order or succession. **2** following as a result. ♦ *n* **3** something that follows.   [C16: from L *sequēns*, from *sequī* to follow]
▸ '**sequently** *adv*

sequential (sɪ'kwɛnʃəl) *adj* **1** characterized by or having a regular sequence. **2** another word for **sequent**.
▸ **sequentiality** (sɪ,kwɛnʃɪ'ælɪtɪ) *n* ▸ **se'quentially** *adv*

sequential access *n* a method of reading data from a computer file by reading through the file from the beginning.

sequester (sɪ'kwɛstə) *vb* (*tr*) **1** to remove or separate. **2** (*usually passive*) to retire into seclusion. **3** *Law.* to take (property) temporarily out of the possession of its owner, esp. until creditors are satisfied or a court order is complied with. **4** *International law.* to appropriate (enemy property).   [C14: from LL *sequestrāre* to surrender for safekeeping, from L *sequester* a trustee]

sequestrate (sɪ'kwɛstreɪt) *vb* **sequestrates, sequestrating, sequestrated.** (*tr*) *Law.* a variant of **sequester** (sense 3).   [C16: from LL *sequestrāre* to SEQUESTER]
▸ **sequestrator** ('si:kwɛs,treɪtə) *n*

sequestration (,si:kwɛ'streɪʃən) *n* **1** the act of sequestering or state of being sequestered. **2** *Law.* the sequestering of property. **3** *Chem.* the effective removal of ions from a solution by coordination with another type of ion or molecule to form complexes.

sequestrum (sɪ'kwɛstrəm) *n, pl* **sequestra** (-trə). *Pathol.* a detached piece of dead bone that often migrates to a wound, etc.   [C19: from NL, from L: something deposited]
▸ **se'questral** *adj*

sequin ('si:kwɪn) *n* **1** a small piece of shiny often coloured metal foil, usually round, used to decorate garments, etc. **2** a gold coin formerly minted in Italy.   [C17: via F from It. *zecchino*, from *zecca* mint, from Ar. *sikkah* die for striking coins]
▸ '**sequined** *adj*

sequoia (sɪ'kwɔɪə) *n* either of two giant Californian coniferous trees, the **redwood**, or the **big tree** or **giant sequoia**.   [C19: NL, after *Sequoya*, known also as George Guess, (?1770–1843), American Indian scholar and leader]

Sequoia National Park ★ *n* a national park in central California, in the Sierra Nevada Mountains: established in 1890 to protect groves of giant sequoias, some of which are about 4000 years old. Area: 1556 sq. km (601 sq. miles).

sérac ('sɛræk) *n* a pinnacle of ice among crevasses on a glacier, usually on a steep slope.   [C19: from Swiss F: a variety of white cheese (hence the ice that resembles it), from Med. L *serācium*, from L *serum* whey]

seraglio (sɛ'rɑ:lɪ,əʊ) or **serail** (sə'raɪ) *n, pl* **seraglios** or **serails. 1** the harem of a Muslim house or palace. **2** a sultan's palace, esp. in the former Turkish empire.   [C16: from It. *serraglio* animal cage, from Med. L *serrāculum* bolt, from L *sera* a door bar; associated also with Turkish *seray* palace]

Serajevo ★ (*Serbo-Croat* 'sɛrajɛvɔ) *n* a variant of **Sarajevo**.

Seram or **Ceram** ★ (sɪ'ræm) *n* an island in Indonesia, in the Moluccas, separated from New Guinea by the **Ceram Sea**: mountainous and densely forested. Area: 17 150 sq. km (6622 sq. miles). Also called: **Serang** (sə'ræŋ).

serape (sə'rɑ:pɪ) *n* **1** a blanket-like shawl, often of brightly coloured wool, worn by men in Latin America. **2** a large shawl worn around the shoulders by women as a fashion garment.   [C19: Mexican Sp.]

seraph ('sɛrəf) *n, pl* **seraphs** or **seraphim** (-əfɪm). *Theol.* a member of the highest order of angels in the celestial hierarchies, often depicted as the winged head of a child.   [C17: back formation from pl *seraphim*, via LL from Heb.]
▸ **seraphic** (sɪ'ræfɪk) *adj*

Serapis ★ ('sɛrəpɪs) *n* a Graeco-Egyptian god combining attributes of Apis and Osiris.

Serb (sɜ:b) *n, adj* another word for **Serbian**.   [C19: from Serbian *Srb*]

Serb. *abbrev. for* Serbia(n).

Serbia ★ ('sɜ:bɪə) *n* a constituent republic of Yugoslavia: declared a kingdom in 1882; precipitated World War I by the conflict with Austria; became part of the Kingdom of the Serbs, Croats, and Slovenes (later called Yugoslavia) in 1918; remained united with Montenegro to form the Federal Republic of Yugoslavia when the other constituent republics became independent in 1991–92. Capital: Belgrade. Pop.: 5 806 000 (1995 est.). Area: 88 361 sq. km (34 109 sq. miles). Former name: **Servia**. Serbian name: **Srbija**.

Serbian ('sɜ:bɪən) *adj* **1** of, relating to, or characteristic of Serbia, its people, or their dialect of Serbo-Croat. ♦ *n* **2** the dialect of Serbo-Croat spoken in Serbia. **3** a native or inhabitant of Serbia.

Serbo-Croat or **Serbo-Croatian** ('sɜ:bəʊ-) *n* **1** the language of the Serbs and the Croats. The Serbian dialect is usually written in the Cyrillic alphabet, the Croatian in Roman. ♦ *adj* **2** of or relating to this language.

SERC (in Britain) *abbrev. for* Science and Engineering Research Council.

Sercq ★ (sɛrk) *n* the French name for **Sark**.

sere[1] (sɪə) *adj* **1** *Arch.* dried up. ♦ *vb* **seres, sering, sered**, *n* **2** a rare spelling of **sear**.   [OE *sēar*]

sere[2] (sɪə) *n* the series of changes occurring in the ecological succession of a community.   [C20: from SERIES]

Seremban ★ (sə'rɛmbən) *n* a town in Peninsular Malaysia, capital of Negri Sembilan state. Pop.: 182 584 (1991).

serenade (,sɛrɪ'neɪd) *n* **1** a piece of music characteristically played outside the house of a woman. **2** a piece of music suggestive of this. **3** an extended composition in several movements similar to the modern suite. ♦ *vb* **serenades, serenading, serenaded. 4** (*tr*) to play a serenade for (someone). **5** (*intr*) to play a serenade.   [C17: from F *sérénade*, from It. *serenata*, from *sereno* peaceful, from L *serēnus*; also infl. in meaning by It. *sera* evening, from L *sērus* late]
▸ ,**sere'nader** *n*

serendipity (,sɛrən'dɪpɪtɪ) *n* the faculty of making fortunate discoveries by accident.   [C18: coined by Horace Walpole, from the Persian fairytale *The Three Princes of Serendip*, in which the heroes possess this gift]
▸ ,**seren'dipitous** *adj*

serene (sɪ'ri:n) *adj* **1** peaceful or tranquil; calm. **2** clear or

bright: *a serene sky.* **3** (*often cap.*) honoured: *His Serene Highness.* [C16: from L *serēnus*]
▸ se'renely *adv* ▸ serenity (sɪ'rɛnɪtɪ) *n*

serf (sɜːf) *n* (esp. in medieval Europe) an unfree person, esp. one bound to the land. [C15: from OF, from L *servus* a slave]
▸ 'serfdom *or* 'serfhood *n*

serge (sɜːdʒ) *n* **1** a twill-weave woollen or worsted fabric used for clothing. **2** a similar twilled cotton, silk, or rayon fabric. [C14: from OF *sarge*, from Vulgar L *sārica* (unattested), from L *sēricum*, from Gk *sērikon* silk, ult. from *sēr* silkworm]

sergeant ('sɑːdʒənt) *n* **1** a noncommissioned officer in certain armies, air forces, and marine corps, usually ranking immediately above a corporal. **2a** (in Britain) a police officer ranking between constable and inspector. **2b** (in the US) a police officer ranking below a captain. **3** a court or municipal officer who has ceremonial duties. ◆ Also: **serjeant.** [C12: from OF *sergent*, from L *serviēns*, lit.: serving, from *servīre* to SERVE]

sergeant at arms *n* an officer of a legislative or fraternal body responsible for maintaining internal order. Also: **sergeant, serjeant at arms.**

Sergeant Baker ('beɪkə) *n* a large brightly coloured Australian sea fish.

sergeant major *n* the chief administrative noncommissioned officer of a military headquarters. See also **warrant officer.**

Sergipe ★ (*Portuguese* ser'ʒipi) *n* a state of NE Brazil: the smallest Brazilian state; a centre of resistance to Dutch conquest (17th century). Capital: Aracajú. Pop.: 1 605 300 (1995 est.). Area: 13 672 sq. km (8492 sq. miles).

Sergt *abbrev. for* Sergeant.

serial ('sɪərɪəl) *n* **1** a novel, film, etc., presented in instalments at regular intervals. **2** a publication, regularly issued and consecutively numbered. ◆ *adj* **3** of or resembling a series. **4** published or presented as a serial. **5** of or relating to such publication or presentation. **6** *Computing.* of or operating on items of information, etc., in the order in which they occur. **7** of or using the techniques of serialism. [C19: from NL *seriālis*, from L *seriēs* SERIES]
▸ 'serially *adv*

serialism ('sɪərɪəˌlɪzəm) *n* (in 20th-century music) the use of a sequence of notes in a definite order as a thematic basis for a composition. See also **twelve-tone.**

serialize *or* **serialise** ('sɪərɪəˌlaɪz) *vb* **serializes, serializing, serialized** *or* **serialises, serialising, serialised.** (*tr*) to publish or present in the form of a serial.
▸ ˌseriali'zation *or* ˌseriali'sation *n*

serial killer *n* a person who carries out a series of murders, selecting victims at random or according to a perverse pattern.

serial monogamy *n* the practice of having a number of long-term monogamous romantic or sexual relationships or marriages in succession.

serial number *n* any of the consecutive numbers assigned to machines, tools, books, etc.

seriate ('sɪərɪt) *adj* forming a series.

seriatim (ˌsɪərɪ'ætɪm) *adv* one after another in order. [C17: from Med. L, from L *seriēs* SERIES]

sericeous (sɪ'rɪʃəs) *adj Bot.* **1** covered with a layer of small silky hairs: *a sericeous leaf.* **2** silky. [C18: from LL *sēriceus* silken, from L *sēricus*; see SERGE]

sericulture ('sɛrɪˌkʌltʃə) *n* the rearing of silkworms for the production of raw silk. [C19: via F; *seri-* from L *sēricum* silk, ult. from Gk *sēr* a silkworm]
▸ ˌseri'cultural *adj* ▸ ˌseri'culturist *n*

series ('sɪəriːz) *n, pl* **series. 1** a group or succession of related things, usually arranged in order. **2** a set of radio or television programmes having the same characters but different stories. **3** a set of books having the same format, related content, etc., published by one firm. **4** a set of stamps, coins, etc., issued at a particular time. **5** *Maths.* the sum of a finite or infinite sequence of numbers or quantities. **6** *Electronics.* an arrangement of two or more

components connected in a circuit so that the same current flows in turn through each of them (esp. in **in series**). Cf. **parallel** (sense 10). **7** *Geol.* a stratigraphical unit that represents the rocks formed during an epoch. [C17: from L: a row, from *serere* to link]

series-wound ('sɪərɪˌzˌwaʊnd) *adj* (of a motor or generator) having the field and armature circuits connected in series.

serif ('sɛrɪf) *n Printing.* a small line at the extremities of a main stroke in a type character. [C19: ?from Du. *schreef* dash, prob. of Gmc origin]

serigraph ('sɛrɪˌɡrɑːf) *n* a colour print made by an adaptation of the silk-screen process. [C19: from *seri-*, from L *sēricum* silk + -GRAPH]
▸ serigraphy (sə'rɪɡrəfɪ) *n*

serin ('sɛrɪn) *n* any of various small yellow-and-brown finches of parts of Europe. [C16: from F, ?from OProvençal *sirena* a bee-eater, from L *sīrēn*, a kind of bird, from SIREN]

seringa (sə'rɪŋɡə) *n* **1** any of a Brazilian genus of trees that yield rubber. **2** a deciduous tree of southern Africa with a graceful shape. [C18: from Port., var. of SYRINGA]

Seringapatam ★ (sə,rɪŋɡəpə'tæm) *n* a small town in S India, in Karnataka on **Seringapatam Island** in the Cauvery River: capital of Mysore from 1610 to 1799, when it was besieged and captured by the British. Pop.: 21 902 (1991 est.).

seriocomic (ˌsɪərɪəʊ'kɒmɪk) *adj* mixing serious and comic elements.
▸ ˌserio'comically *adv*

serious ('sɪərɪəs) *adj* **1** grave in nature or disposition: *a serious person.* **2** marked by deep feeling; sincere: *is he serious or joking?* **3** concerned with important matters: *a serious conversation.* **4** requiring effort or concentration: *a serious book.* **5** giving rise to fear or anxiety: *a serious illness.* **6** *Inf.* worthy of regard because of substantial quantity or quality: *serious money; serious wine.* **7** *Inf.* extreme or remarkable: *a serious haircut.* [C15: from LL *sēriōsus*, from L *sērius*]
▸ 'seriousness *n*

seriously ('sɪərɪəslɪ) *adv* **1** in a serious manner or to a serious degree. **2** *Inf.* extremely or remarkably: *seriously tall.*

serjeant ('sɑːdʒənt) *n* a variant spelling of **sergeant.**

serjeant at law *n* (formerly, in England) a barrister of a special rank. Also: **serjeant, sergeant at law, sergeant.**

sermon ('sɜːmən) *n* **1a** an address of religious instruction or exhortation, often based on a passage from the Bible, esp. one delivered during a church service. **1b** a written version of such an address. **2** a serious speech, esp. one administering reproof. [C12: via OF from L *sermō* discourse, prob. from *serere* to join together]

sermonize *or* **sermonise** ('sɜːməˌnaɪz) *vb* **sermonizes, sermonizing, sermonized** *or* **sermonises, sermonising, sermonised.** to address (a person or audience) as if delivering a sermon.
▸ 'sermonˌizer *or* 'sermonˌiser *n*

Sermon on the Mount *n Bible.* a major discourse delivered by Christ, including the Beatitudes and the Lord's Prayer (Matthew 5–7).

sero- *combining form.* indicating a serum: *serology.*

seroconvert (ˌsɪərəʊkən'vɜːt) *vb* (*intr*) (of an individual) to produce antibodies specific to, and in response to the presence in the blood of, a particular antigen, such as a virus or vaccine.
▸ ˌserocon'version *n*

serology (sɪ'rɒlədʒɪ) *n* the branch of science concerned with serums.
▸ serologic (ˌsɪərə'lɒdʒɪk) *or* ˌsero'logical *adj*

seropositive (ˌsɪərəʊ'pɒzɪtɪv) *adj* (of a person whose blood has been tested for a specific disease, such as AIDS) showing a serological reaction indicating the presence of the disease.

serotine ('sɛrəˌtaɪn) *adj* **1** *Biol.* produced, flowering, or developing late in the season. ◆ *n* **2** a reddish-coloured European insectivorous bat. [C16: from L *sērōtinus* late, from *sērus* late; applied to the bat because it flies late in the evening]

★ people and places

serotonin (ˌsɛrəˈtəʊnɪn) *n* a compound that occurs in the brain, intestines, and blood platelets and induces vasoconstriction.

serous (ˈsɪərəs) *adj* of, producing, or containing serum. [C16: from L *serōsus*]
▸ **serosity** (sɪˈrɒsɪtɪ) *n*

serous fluid *n* a thin watery fluid found in many body cavities.

serous membrane *n* any of the smooth moist delicate membranes, such as the pleura, that line the closed cavities of the body.

serow (ˈsɛrəʊ) *n* either of two antelopes of mountainous regions of S and SE Asia, having a dark coat and conical backward-pointing horns. [C19: from native name *să-ro* Tibetan goat]

serpent (ˈsɜːpənt) *n* 1 a literary word for **snake. 2** *Bible.* a manifestation of Satan as a guileful tempter (Genesis 3:1–5). 3 a sly or unscrupulous person. 4 an obsolete wind instrument resembling a snake in shape. [C14: via OF from L *serpēns* a creeping thing, from *serpere* to creep]

serpentine¹ (ˈsɜːpənˌtaɪn) *adj* 1 of, relating to, or resembling a serpent. 2 twisting; winding. [C14: from LL *serpentīmus*, from *serpēns* SERPENT]

serpentine² (ˈsɜːpənˌtaɪn) *n* any of several secondary minerals, consisting of hydrated magnesium silicate, that are green to brown in colour and greasy to the touch. [C15 *serpentyn*, from Med. L *serpentīnum* SERPENTINE¹; referring to the snakelike patterns of these minerals]

serpigo (sɜːˈpaɪɡəʊ) *n Pathol.* any progressive skin eruption, such as ringworm or herpes. [C14: from Med. L, from L *serpere* to creep]

SERPS or **Serps** (sɜːps) *n* (in Britain) *acronym for* state earnings-related pension scheme.

serrate *adj* (ˈsɛrɪt, -eɪt). 1 (of leaves) having a margin of forward pointing teeth. 2 having a notched or sawlike edge. ◆ *vb* (sɛˈreɪt), **serrates, serrating, serrated. 3** (*tr*) to make serrate. [C17: from L *serrātus* saw-shaped, from *serra* a saw]
▸ **ser'rated** *adj*

serration (sɛˈreɪʃən) *n* 1 the state or condition of being serrated. 2 a row of toothlike projections on an edge. 3 a single notch.

serried (ˈsɛrɪd) *adj* in close or compact formation: *serried ranks of troops.* [C17: from OF *serré* close-packed, from *serrer* to shut up]

serriform (ˈsɛrɪˌfɔːm) *adj Biol.* resembling a notched or sawlike edge. [*serri-*, from L *serra* saw]

serrulate (ˈsɛruˌleɪt, -lɪt) *adj* (esp. of leaves) minutely serrate. [C18: from NL *serrulātus*, from L *serrula* dim. of *serra* a saw]
▸ ˌ**serru'lation** *n*

Sertorius ★ (sɜːˈtɔːrɪəs) *n* **Quintus** (ˈkwɪntəs). ?123–72 B.C., Roman soldier who led an insurrection in Spain against Sulla; assassinated.

serum (ˈsɪərəm) *n*, *pl* **serums** or **sera** (-rə). 1 Also called: **blood serum.** blood plasma from which the clotting factors have been removed. 2 antitoxin obtained from the blood serum of immunized animals. 3 *Physiol., zool.* clear watery fluid, esp. that exuded by serous membranes. 4 a less common word for **whey.** [C17: from L: whey]

serum albumin *n* a form of albumin that is the most abundant protein constituent of blood plasma.

serum hepatitis *n* a former name for **hepatitis B.**

serum sickness *n* an allergic reaction, such as vomiting, skin rash, etc., that sometimes follows injection of a foreign serum.

serval (ˈsɜːvᵊl) *n*, *pl* **servals** or **serval.** a slender feline mammal of the African bush, having an orange-brown coat with black spots. [C18: via F from LL *cervālis* staglike, from L *cervus* a stag]

servant (ˈsɜːvᵊnt) *n* 1 a person employed to work for another, esp. one who performs household duties. 2 See **public servant.** [C13: via OF from *servant* serving, from *servir* to SERVE]

serve (sɜːv) *vb* **serves, serving, served. 1** to be in the service

of (a person). 2 to render or be of service to (a person, cause, etc.); help. 3 to attend to (customers) in a shop, etc. 4 (*tr*) to provide (guests, etc.) with food, drink, etc.: *she served her guests with cocktails.* 5 to distribute or provide (food, etc.) for guests, etc.: *do you serve coffee?* 6 (*tr*; sometimes foll. by *up*) to present (food, etc.) in a specified manner: *peaches served with cream.* 7 (*tr*) to provide with a regular supply of. 8 (*tr*) to work actively for: to *serve the government.* 9 (*tr*) to pay homage to: *to serve God.* 10 to suit: *this will serve my purpose.* 11 (*intr; may take an infinitive*) to function: *this wood will serve to build a fire.* 12 to go through (a period of service, enlistment, etc.). 13 (*intr*) (of weather, conditions, etc.) to be suitable. 14 (*tr*) Also: **service.** (of a male animal) to copulate with (a female animal). 15 *Tennis, squash, etc.* to put (the ball) into play. 16 (*tr*) to deliver (a legal document) to (a person). 17 (*tr*) *Naut.* to bind (a rope, etc.) with fine cord to protect it from chafing, etc. 18 **serve (a person) right.** *Inf.* to pay (a person) back, esp. for wrongful or foolish treatment or behaviour. ◆ *n* 19 *Tennis, squash, etc.* short for **service. 20** *Austral. inf.* hostile or critical remarks. [C13: from OF *servir*, from L *servīre*, from *servus* a slave]
▸ '**servable** or '**serveable** *adj*

server (ˈsɜːvə) *n* 1 a person who serves. 2 *RC Church.* a person who assists the priest at Mass. 3 something that is used in serving food and drink. 4 the player who serves in racket games. 5 *Computing.* a computer or program that supplies data or resources to other machines on a network.

Servetus ★ (sɜːˈviːtəs) *n* **Michael,** Spanish name *Miguel Serveto.* 1511–53, Spanish theologian and physician. He was burnt at the stake by order of Calvin for denying the doctrine of the Trinity and the divinity of Christ.

Servia ★ (ˈsɜːvɪə) *n* the former name of **Serbia.**
▸ '**Servian** *adj, n*

service (ˈsɜːvɪs) *n* 1 an act of help or assistance. 2 an organized system of labour and material aids used to supply the needs of the public: *telephone service.* 3 the supply, installation, or maintenance of goods carried out by a dealer. 4 the state of availability for use by the public (esp. in **into** or **out of service**). 5 a periodic overhaul made on a car, etc. 6 the act or manner of serving guests, customers, etc., in a shop, hotel, etc. 7 a department of public employment and its employees: *civil service.* 8 employment in or performance of work for another: *in the service of his firm.* 9a one of the branches of the armed forces. 9b (*as modifier*): *service life.* 10 the state or duties of a domestic servant (esp. in **in service**). 11 the act or manner of serving food. 12 a set of dishes, cups, etc., for use at table. 13 public worship carried out according to certain prescribed forms: *divine service.* 14 the prescribed form according to which a specific kind of religious ceremony is to be carried out: *the burial service.* 15 *Tennis, squash, etc.* 15a the act, manner, or right of serving a ball. 15b the game in which a particular player serves: *he has lost his service.* 16 the serving of a writ, summons, etc., upon a person. 17 (of male animals) the act of mating. 18 (*modifier*) of or for the use of servants or employees. 19 (*modifier*) serving the public rather than producing goods: *service industry.* ◆ *vb* **services, servicing, serviced.** (*tr*) 20 to provide service or services to. 21 to make fit for use. 22 to supply with assistance. 23 to overhaul (a car, machine, etc.). 24 (of a male animal) to mate with (a female). 25 *Brit.* to meet interest on (debt). ◆ See also **services.** [C12 *servise,* from OF, from L *servitium* condition of a slave, from *servus* a slave]

serviceable (ˈsɜːvɪsəbᵊl) *adj* 1 capable of or ready for service. 2 capable of giving good service.
▸ ˌ**servicea'bility** *n* ▸ '**serviceably** *adv*

service area *n* a place on a motorway providing garage services, restaurants, toilet facilities, etc.

service car *n NZ.* a bus operating on a long-distance route.

service charge *n* a percentage of a bill, as at a hotel, added to the total to pay for service.

service contract *n* a contract between an employer and a senior employee, esp. a director, executive, etc.

service flat *n Brit.* a flat in which domestic services are provided by the management. Also called (esp. Austral.): **serviced flat.**

serviceman ('sɜːvɪsmən) *n, pl* **servicemen. 1** a person who serves in the armed services of a country. **2** a man employed to service and maintain equipment.
▶ **'service,woman** *fem n*

service road *n Brit.* a narrow road running parallel to a main road and providing access to houses, shops, etc., situated along its length.

services ('sɜːvɪsɪz) *pl n* **1** work performed for remuneration. **2** (usually preceded by *the*) the armed forces. **3** (*sometimes sing*) *Econ.* commodities, such as banking, that are mainly intangible and usually consumed concurrently with their production. **4** a system of providing the public with gas, water, etc.

service station *n* a place that supplies fuel, oil, etc., for motor vehicles and often carries out repairs, servicing, etc.

service tree *n* **1** Also called: **sorb.** a Eurasian rosaceous tree, cultivated for its white flowers and brown edible apple-like fruits. **2 wild service tree.** a similar and related Eurasian tree. [*service* from OE *syrfe*, from Vulgar L *sorbea* (unattested), from L *sorbus* sorb]

serviette (,sɜːvɪ'ɛt) *n Chiefly Brit.* a small square of cloth or paper used while eating to protect the clothes, etc. [C15: from OF, from *servir* to SERVE; on the model of OUBLI-ETTE]

servile ('sɜːvaɪl) *adj* **1** obsequious or fawning in attitude or behaviour. **2** of or suitable for a slave. **3** existing in or relating to a state of slavery. **4** (when *postpositive*, foll. by *to*) submitting or obedient. [C14: from L *servīlis*, from *servus* slave]
▶ **servility** (sɜː'vɪlɪtɪ) *n*

serving ('sɜːvɪŋ) *n* a portion or helping of food or drink.

servitor ('sɜːvɪtə) *n Arch.* a person who serves another. [C14: from OF, from LL, from L *servīre* to SERVE]

servitude ('sɜːvɪ,tjuːd) *n* **1** the state or condition of a slave. **2** the state or condition of being subjected to or dominated by a person or thing. **3** *Law.* a burden attaching to an estate for the benefit of an adjoining estate or of some definite person. See also **easement.** [C15: via OF from L *servitūdō*, from *servus* slave]

servo ('sɜːvəʊ) *adj* (*prenominal*) of or activated by a servomechanism: *servo brakes.* ◆ *n, pl* **servos. 2** *Inf.* short for **servomechanism.** [from *servomotor* from F, from L *servus* slave + F *moteur* motor]

servomechanism ('sɜːvəʊ,mɛkə,nɪzəm) *n* a mechanical or electromechanical system for control of the position or speed of an output transducer.

servomotor ('sɜːvəʊ,məʊtə) *n* any motor that supplies power to a servomechanism.

servqual ('sɜːv,kwɒl) *n Marketing.* the provision of high-quality products by an organization backed by a high level of service for consumers. [C20: from SERV(ICE) + QUAL(ITY)]

sesame ('sɛsəmɪ) *n* **1** a tropical herbaceous plant of the East Indies, cultivated, esp. in India, for its small oval seeds. **2** the seeds of this plant, used in flavouring bread and yielding an edible oil (**benne oil** or **gingili**). [C15: from L *sēsamum*, from Gk *sēsamon, sēsamē,* of Semitic origin]

sesamoid ('sɛsə,mɔɪd) *adj Anat.* **1** of or relating to various small bones formed in tendons, such as the patella. **2** of or relating to any of various small cartilages, esp. those of the nose. [C17: from L *sēsamoīdēs* like sesame (seed), from Gk]

Sesostris I ★ (sɛ'sɒstrɪs) *n* 20th century B.C., king of Egypt of the 12th dynasty. He conquered Nubia and brought ancient Egypt to the height of its prosperity.

sesqui- *prefix* **1** indicating one and a half: *sesquicentennial.* **2** (in a chemical compound) indicating a ratio of two to three. [from L, contraction of SEMI- + *as* AS[2] + *-que* and]

sesquicentennial (,sɛskwɪsɛn'tɛnɪəl) *adj* **1** of a period of 150 years. ◆ *n* **2** a period of 150 years. **3** a 150th anniversary or its celebration.
▶ **,sesquicen'tennially** *adv*

sessile ('sɛsaɪl) *adj* **1** (of flowers or leaves) having no stalk. **2** (of animals such as the barnacle) permanently attached. [C18: from L *sessilis* concerning sitting, from *sedēre* to sit]
▶ **sessility** (sɛ'sɪlɪtɪ) *n*

sessile oak *n* another name for the **durmast.**

session ('sɛʃən) *n* **1** the meeting of a court, legislature, judicial body, etc., for the execution of its function or the transaction of business. **2** a single continuous meeting of such a body. **3** a series or period of such meetings. **4** *Education.* **4a** the time during which classes are held. **4b** a school or university year. **5** *Presbyterian Church.* the body presiding over a local congregation and consisting of the minister and elders. **6** a meeting of a group of musicians to record in a studio. **7** any period devoted to an activity. [C14: from L *sessiō* a sitting, from *sedēre* to sit]
▶ **'sessional** *adj*

Sessions ★ ('sɛʃənz) *n* Roger (**Huntington**). 1896–1985, US composer.

sesterce ('sɛstəs) *or* **sestertius** (sɛ'stɜːtɪəs) *n* a silver or, later, bronze coin of ancient Rome worth a quarter of a denarius. [C16: from L *sestertius* a coin worth two and a half asses, from *sēmis* half + *tertius* a third]

sestet (sɛ'stɛt) *n* **1** *Prosody.* the last six lines of a sonnet. **2** another word for **sextet** (sense 1). [C19: from It., from *sesto* sixth, from L, from *sex* six]

sestina (sɛ'stiːnə) *n* an elaborate verse form of Italian origin in which the six final words of the lines in the first stanza are repeated in a different order in each of the remaining five stanzas. [C19: from It., from *sesto* sixth, from L *sextus*]

Sestos ★ ('sɛstɒs) *n* a ruined town in NW Turkey, at the narrowest point of the Dardanelles: N terminus of the bridge of boats built by Xerxes in 481 B.C. for the crossing of his armies of invasion.

set[1] (sɛt) *vb* **sets, setting, set.** (*mainly tr*) **1** to put or place in position or into a specified state or condition: *to set someone free.* **2** (*also intr*; foll. by *to* or *on*) to put or be put (to); apply or be applied: *he set fire to the house.* **3** to put into order or readiness for use: *to set the table for dinner.* **4** (*also intr*) to put, form, or be formed into a jelled, firm, or rigid state: *the jelly set in three hours.* **5** (*also intr*) to put or be put into a position that will restore a normal state: *to set a broken bone.* **6** to adjust (a clock or other instrument) to a position. **7** to establish: *we have set the date for our wedding.* **8** to prescribe (an undertaking, course of study, etc.): *the examiners have set "Paradise Lost".* **9** to arrange in a particular fashion, esp. an attractive one: *she set her hair.* **10** Also: **set to music.** to provide music for (a poem or other text to be sung). **11** Also: **set up.** *Printing.* to arrange or produce (type, film, etc.) from (text or copy). **12** to arrange (a stage, television studio, etc.) with scenery and props. **13** to describe (a scene or the background to a literary work, etc.) in words: *his novel is set in Russia.* **14** to present as a model of good or bad behaviour (esp. in **set an example**). **15** (foll. by *on* or *by*) to value (something) at a specified price or estimation of worth: *he set a high price on his services.* **16** (*also intr*) to give or be given a particular direction: *his course was set to the East.* **17** (*also intr*) to rig (a sail) or (of a sail) to be rigged so as to catch the wind. **18** (*intr*) (of the sun, moon, etc.) to disappear beneath the horizon. **19** to leave (dough, etc.) in one place so that it may prove. **20** to sink (the head of a nail) below the surface surrounding it by using a nail set. **21** *Computing.* to give (a binary circuit) the value 1. **22** (of plants) to produce (fruits, seeds, etc.) after pollination or (of fruits or seeds) to develop after pollination. **23** to plant (seeds, seedlings, etc.). **24** to place (a hen) on (eggs) for the purpose of incubation. **25** (*intr*) (of a gun dog) to turn in the direction of game. **26** *Bridge.* to defeat (one's opponents) in their attempt to make a contract. **27** a dialect word for **sit.** ◆ *n* **28** the act of setting or the state of being set. **29** a condition of firmness or hardness. **30** bearing, carriage, or posture: *the set of a gun dog when pointing.* **31** the scenery and other props used in a dramatic production, film, etc. **32** Also called: **set width.** *Printing.* **32a** the width of the body of a piece of type. **32b** the width of the lines of type in a page or column. **33** *Psychol.* a temporary bias disposing an organism to react to a stimulus in one way rather than in others. **34** a seedling, cutting, or similar part that

★ people and places

is ready for planting: *onion sets.* **35** a variant spelling of **sett.** ◆ *adj* **36** fixed or established by authority or agreement: *set hours of work.* **37** (*usually postpositive*) rigid or inflexible: *she is set in her ways.* **38** unmoving; fixed: *a set expression on his face.* **39** conventional, artificial, or stereotyped: *she made her apology in set phrases.* **40** (*postpositive;* foll. by *on* or *upon*) resolute in intention: *he is set upon marrying.* **41** (of a book, etc.) prescribed for students' preparation for an examination. ◆ See also **set about, set against,** etc. [OE *settan,* causative of *sittan* to SIT]

set² (set) *n* **1** a number of objects or people grouped or belonging together, often having certain features or characteristics in common: *a set of coins.* **2** a group of people who associate together, etc.: *he's part of the jet set.* **3** *Maths.* a collection of numbers, objects, etc., that are treated as an entity: {3, the moon} is the set the two members of which are the number 3 and the moon. **4** any apparatus that receives or transmits television or radio signals. **5** *Tennis, squash, etc.* one of the units of a match, in tennis, one in which a player or pair of players must win at least six games: *Hingis lost the first set.* **6a** the number of couples required for a formation dance. **6b** a series of figures that make up a formation dance. **7a** a band's or performer's concert repertoire on a given occasion: *the set included no new songs.* **7b** a continuous performance: *the Who played two sets.* **8 make a dead set at. 8a** to attack by arguing or ridiculing. **8b** (of a woman) to try to gain the affections of (a man). ◆ *vb* **sets, setting, set. 9** (*intr*) (in square and country dancing) to perform a sequence of steps while facing towards another dancer. **10** (*usually tr*) to divide into sets: *in this school we set our older pupils for English.* [C14 (in the obs. sense: a religious sect): from OF *sette,* from L *secta* SECT; later sense infl. by the verb SET¹]

seta ('si:tə) *n, pl* **setae** (-ti:). (in invertebrates and plants) any bristle or bristle-like appendage. [C18: from L]
► **setaceous** (sɪ'teɪʃəs) *adj*

set about *vb* (*intr, prep*) **1** to start or begin. **2** to attack physically or verbally.

set against *vb* (*tr, prep*) **1** to balance or compare. **2** to cause to be unfriendly to.

set aside *vb* (*tr, adv*) **1** to reserve for a special purpose. **2** to discard or quash. ◆ *n* **set-aside. 3a** (in the European Union) a scheme in which a proportion of farmland is taken out of production in order to reduce surpluses or maintain or increase prices of a specific crop. **3b** (*as modifier*): *set-aside land.*

set back *vb* (*tr, adv*) **1** to hinder; impede. **2** *Inf.* to cost (a person) a specified amount. ◆ *n* **setback. 3** anything that serves to hinder or impede. **4** a recession in the upper part of a high building. **5** a steplike shelf where a wall is reduced in thickness.

set down *vb* (*tr, adv*) **1** to record. **2** to judge or regard: *he set him down as an idiot.* **3** (foll. by *to*) to attribute: *his attitude was set down to his illness.* **4** to rebuke. **5** to snub. **6** *Brit.* to allow (passengers) to alight from a bus, etc.

set forth *vb* (*adv*) *Formal or arch.* **1** (*tr*) to state, express, or utter. **2** (*intr*) to start out on a journey.

Seth ★ (sεθ) *n Old Testament.* Adam's third son, given by God in place of the murdered Abel (Genesis 4:25).

SETI ('sεtɪ) *n* acronym for Search for Extraterrestrial Intelligence; a scientific programme attempting, by radio transmissions, to make contact with beings from other planets.

setiferous (sɪ'tɪfərəs) *or* **setigerous** (sɪ'tɪdʒərəs) *adj Biol.* bearing bristles. [C19: see SETA, -FEROUS, -GEROUS]

set in *vb* (*intr, adv*) **1** to become established: *the winter has set in.* **2** (of wind) to blow or (of current) to move towards shore. ◆ *adj* **set-in. 3** (of a part) made separately and then added to a larger whole: *a set-in sleeve.*

setline ('sεt,laɪn) *n* any of various types of fishing line that consist of a long suspended line having shorter hooked and baited lines attached.

set off *vb* (*adv*) **1** (*intr*) to embark on a journey. **2** (*tr*) to cause (a person) to act or do something, such as laugh. **3** (*tr*) to cause to explode. **4** (*tr*) to act as a foil or contrast to: *that brooch sets your dress off well.* **5** (*tr*) *Accounting.* to cancel a credit on (one account) against a debit on another.

◆ *n* **setoff. 6** anything that serves as a counterbalance. **7** anything that serves to contrast with or enhance something else; foil. **8** a cross claim brought by a debtor that partly offsets the creditor's claim.

set-off *n Printing.* a fault in which ink is transferred from a heavily inked or undried printed sheet to the sheet next to it in a pile.

set on *vb* **1** (*prep*) Also: **set upon.** to attack or cause to attack: *they set the dogs on him.* **2** (*tr, adv*) to instigate or incite; urge.

Seton ★ ('si:t°n) *n* Ernest Thompson. 1860–1946, US author and illustrator of animal books, born in England.

Seto Naikai ★ ('setəʊ 'naɪkaɪ) *n* transliteration of the Japanese name for the **Inland Sea.**

setose ('si:təʊs) *adj Biol.* covered with setae; bristly. [C17: from L *saetōsus,* from *saeta* a bristle]

set out *vb* (*adv, mainly tr*) **1** to present, arrange, or display. **2** to give a full account of: *he set out the matter in full.* **3** to plan or lay out (a garden, etc.). **4** (*intr*) to begin or embark on an undertaking, esp. a journey.

set piece *n* **1** a work of literature, music, etc., often having a conventional or prescribed theme, intended to create an impressive effect. **2** a display of fireworks. **3** *Sport.* a rehearsed team manoeuvre usually attempted at a restart of play.

setscrew ('sεt,skru:) *n* a screw that fits into the boss or hub of a wheel, coupling, cam, etc., and prevents motion of the part relative to the shaft on which it is mounted.

set square *n* a thin flat piece of plastic, metal, etc., in the shape of a right-angled triangle, used in technical drawing.

sett *or* **set** (set) *n* **1** a small rectangular paving block made of stone. **2** the burrow of a badger. **3a** a square in a pattern of tartan. **3b** the pattern itself. [C19: var. of SET¹ (n)]

settee (sε'ti:) *n* a seat, for two or more people, with a back and usually with arms. [C18: changed from SETTLE²]

setter ('sεtə) *n* any of various breeds of large long-haired gun dog trained to point out game by standing rigid.

set theory *n Maths.* the branch of mathematics concerned with the properties and interrelationships of sets.

setting ('sεtɪŋ) *n* **1** the surroundings in which something is set. **2** the scenery, properties, or background used to create the location for a stage play, film, etc. **3** *Music.* a composition consisting of a certain text and music arranged for it. **4** the metal mounting and surround of a gem. **5** the tableware, cutlery, etc., for a single place at table. **6** any of a set of points on a scale or dial that can be selected to control the speed, temperature, etc., at which a machine operates.

settle¹ ('sεt°l) *vb* **settles, settling, settled. 1** (*tr*) to put in order: *he settled his affairs before he died.* **2** to arrange or be arranged in a fixed or comfortable position: *he settled himself by the fire.* **3** (*intr*) to come to rest or a halt: *a bird settled on the hedge.* **4** to take up or cause to take up residence: *the family settled in the country.* **5** to establish or become established in a way of life, job, etc. **6** (*tr*) to migrate to and form a community; colonize. **7** to make or become quiet, calm, or stable. **8** to cause (sediment) to sink to the bottom, as in a liquid, or (of sediment) to sink thus. **9** to subside or cause to subside: *the dust settled.* **10** (sometimes foll. by *up*) to pay off or account for (a bill, debt, etc.). **11** (*tr*) to decide or dispose of: *to settle an argument.* **12** (*intr;* often foll. by *on* or *upon*) to agree or fix: *to settle upon a plan.* **13** (*tr;* usually foll. by *on* or *upon*) to secure (title, property, etc.) to a person: *he settled his property on his wife.* **14** to determine (a legal dispute, etc.) by agreement of the parties without resort to court action (esp. in **settle out of court**). [OE *setlan*]
► **'settleable** *adj*

settle² ('sεt°l) *n* a seat, for two or more people, usually made of wood with a high back and arms, and sometimes having a storage space in the boxlike seat. [OE *setl*]

settle down *vb* (*adv, mainly intr*) **1** (*also tr*) to make or become quiet and orderly. **2** (often foll. by *to*) to apply oneself diligently: *please settle down to work.* **3** to adopt an orderly and routine way of life, esp. after marriage.

settle for *vb (intr, prep)* to accept or agree to in spite of dispute or dissatisfaction.

settlement ('sɛt^əlmənt) *n* **1** the act or state of settling or being settled. **2** the establishment of a new region; colonization. **3** a place newly settled; colony. **4** a community formed by members of a group, esp. of a religious sect. **5** a public building used to provide educational and general welfare facilities for persons living in deprived areas. **6** a subsidence of all or part of a structure. **7a** the payment of an outstanding account, invoice, charge, etc. **7b** *(as modifier): settlement day.* **8** an agreement reached in matters of finance, business, etc. **9** *Law.* **9a** a conveyance, usually to trustees, of property to be enjoyed by several persons in succession. **9b** the deed conveying such property.

settler ('sɛtlə) *n* a person who settles in a new country or a colony.

settlings ('sɛtlɪŋz) *pl n* any matter that has settled at the bottom of a liquid.

set to *vb (intr, adv)* **1** to begin working. **2** to start fighting.
♦ *n* **set-to. 3** *Inf.* a brief disagreement or fight.

set-top box *n* a device which converts the signals from a digital television broadcast into a form which can be viewed on a standard analogue television set.

Setúbal ★ *(Portuguese* sə'tuβal) *n* a port in SW Portugal, on **Setúbal Bay** south of Lisbon: an earthquake in 1755 destroyed most of the old town. Pop.: 83 550 (1991).

set up *vb (adv, mainly tr)* **1** *(also intr)* to put into a position of power, etc. **2** *(also intr)* to begin or enable (someone) to begin a new venture), as by acquiring or providing means, etc. **3** to build or construct: *to set up a shed.* **4** to raise or produce: *to set up a wail.* **5** to advance or propose: *to set up a theory.* **6** to restore the health of: *the sea air will set you up again.* **7** to establish (a record). **8** *Inf.* to cause (a person) to be blamed, accused, etc. ♦ *n* **setup. 9** *Inf.* the way in which anything is organized or arranged. **10** *Sl.* an event the result of which is prearranged: *it's a setup.* **11** a prepared arrangement of materials, machines, etc., for a job or undertaking. ♦ *adj* **set-up. 12** physically well-built.

Seurat ★ *(French* sœra) *n* Georges (ʒɔrʒ). 1859–91, French painter. He developed the pointillist technique, as in *Dimanche à la Grande-Jatte* (1886).

Sevan ★ (sɛ'vɑːn) *n* Lake. a lake in Armenia, at an altitude of 1914 m (6279 ft). Area: 1417 sq. km (547 sq. miles).

Sevastopol ★ *(Russian* sɪvas'tɔpəlj) *n* a port, naval base, and resort in the S Ukraine, on the Black Sea: captured and destroyed by British, French, and Turkish forces after a siege of 11 months (1854–55) during the Crimean War; taken by the Germans after a siege of 8 months (1942) during World War II. Pop.: 365 000 (1996 est.). English name: **Sebastopol.**

seven ('sɛv^ən) *n* **1** the cardinal number that is the sum of six and one and is a prime number. **2** a numeral, 7, VII, etc., representing this number. **3** the amount or quantity that is one greater than six. **4** anything representing, represented by, or consisting of seven units, such as a playing card with seven symbols on it. **5** Also called: **seven o'clock.** seven hours after noon or midnight. ♦ *determiner* **6a** amounting to seven: *seven swans a-swimming.* **6b** *(as pron): you've eaten seven already.* ♦ See also **sevens.** [OE *seofon*]

Seven against Thebes ★ *pl n Greek myth.* the seven members of an expedition undertaken to regain for Polynices, a son of Oedipus, his share in the throne of Thebes from his usurping brother Eteocles. The seven are usually listed as Polynices, Adrastus, Amphiaraus, Capaneus, Hippomedon, Tydeus, and Parthenopaeus. The campaign failed and the warring brothers killed each other in single combat before the Theban walls. See also **Adrastus.**

seven deadly sins *pl n* a fuller name for the **deadly sins.**

sevenfold ('sɛv^ən,fəʊld) *adj* **1** equal to or having seven times as many or as much. **2** composed of seven parts.
♦ *adv* **3** by or up to seven times as many or as much.

Seven Hills of Rome ★ *pl n* the hills on which the an-

cient city of Rome was built: the Palatine, Capitoline, Quirinal, Caelian, Aventine, Esquiline, and Viminal.

sevens ('sɛv^ənz) *n (functioning as sing)* a rugby union match or competition played with seven players on each side.

seven seas *pl n* the oceans of the world considered as the N and S Pacific, the N and S Atlantic, and the Arctic, Antarctic, and Indian Oceans.

seven-segment display *n* an arrangement of seven bars forming a square figure of eight, used in electronic displays of alphanumeric characters: any letter or figure can be represented by illuminating selected bars.

Seven Sleepers ★ *pl n* seven Christian youths from Ephesus who were walled up in a cave by the Emperor Decius in 250 A.D. and, according to legend, slept for 187 years.

seventeen ('sɛv^ən'tiːn) *n* **1** the cardinal number that is the sum of ten and seven and is a prime number. **2** a numeral, 17, XVII, etc., representing this number. **3** the amount or quantity that is seven more than ten. **4** something represented by, representing, or consisting of 17 units. ♦ *determiner* **5a** amounting to seventeen: *seventeen attempts.* **5b** *(as pron): seventeen were sold.* [OE *seofontíene*]
▶ 'seven'teenth *adj, n*

seventh ('sɛv^ənθ) *adj* **1** *(usually prenominal)* **1a** coming after the sixth and before the eighth in numbering, position, etc.; being the ordinal number of *seven:* often written 7th. **1b** *(as n): she left on the seventh.* ♦ *n* **2a** one of seven equal parts of an object, quantity, measurement, etc. **2b** *(as modifier): a seventh part.* **3** the fraction equal to one divided by seven (1/7). **4** *Music.* **4a** the interval between one note and another seven notes away from it in a diatonic scale. **4b** one of two notes constituting such an interval in relation to the other. ♦ *adv* **5** Also: **seventhly.** after the sixth person, event, etc.

Seventh-Day Adventist *n* a member of that branch of the Adventists which constituted itself as a separate body after the expected Second Coming of Christ failed to be realized in 1844. They believe that Christ's coming is imminent and observe Saturday instead of Sunday as their Sabbath.

seventh heaven *n* **1** the final state of eternal bliss. **2** a state of supreme happiness.

seventy ('sɛv^əntɪ) *n, pl* **seventies. 1** the cardinal number that is the product of ten and seven. **2** a numeral, 70, LXX, etc., representing this number. **3** *(pl)* the numbers 70–79, esp. the 70th to the 79th year of a person's life or of a particular century. **4** the amount or quantity that is seven times as big as ten. **5** something represented by, representing, or consisting of 70 units. ♦ *determiner* **6a** amounting to seventy: *the seventy varieties of fabric.* **6b** *(as pron): to invite seventy to the wedding.* [OE *seofontig*]
▶ 'seventieth *adj, n*

Seven Wonders of the World *pl n* the seven structures considered by ancient and medieval scholars to be the most wondrous of the ancient world. The list varies, but generally consists of the Pyramids of Egypt, the Hanging Gardens of Babylon, Phidias' statue of Zeus at Olympia, the temple of Artemis at Ephesus, the mausoleum of Halicarnassus, the Colossus of Rhodes, and the Pharos (or lighthouse) of Alexandria.

Seven Years' War *n* the war (1756–63) of Britain and Prussia, who emerged in the ascendant, against France and Austria, resulting from commercial and colonial rivalry between Britain and France and from the conflict in Germany between Prussia and Austria.

sever ('sɛvə) *vb* **1** to put or be put apart. **2** to divide or be divided into parts. **3** *(tr)* to break off or dissolve (a tie, relationship, etc.). [C14 *severen,* from OF, from L *sēparāre* to SEPARATE]
▶ 'severable *adj*

several ('sɛvrəl) *determiner* **1a** more than a few: *several people objected.* **1b** *(as pronoun; functioning as pl): several of them know.* ♦ *adj* **2** *(prenominal)* various; separate: *the members with their several occupations.* **3** *(prenominal)* distinct; different: *three several times.* **4** *Law.* capable of being dealt with separately. [C15: via Anglo-F from Med. L *sēparālis,* from L *sēpar,* from *sēparāre* to SEPARATE]

★ people and places

severally ('sɛvrəlı) *adv* **1** separately or distinctly. **2** each in turn.

severalty ('sɛvrəltı) *n, pl* **severalties. 1** the state of being several or separate. **2** (usually preceded by *in*) *Property law.* the tenure of property, esp. land, in a person's own right.

severance ('sɛvərəns) *n* **1** the act of severing or state of being severed. **2** a separation. **3** *Law.* the division into separate parts of a joint estate, contract, etc.

severance pay *n* compensation paid by a firm to employees for loss of employment.

severe (sɪ'vɪə) *adj* **1** rigorous or harsh in the treatment of others: *a severe parent.* **2** serious in appearance or manner. **3** critical or dangerous: *a severe illness.* **4** causing discomfort by its harshness: *severe weather.* **5** strictly restrained in appearance: *a severe way of dressing.* **6** hard to perform or accomplish: *a severe test.* [C16: from L *sevērus*]
► **se'verely** *adv* ► **severity** (sɪ'vɛrɪtɪ) *n*

Severn ★ ('sɛvᵊn) *n* **1** a river in E Wales and W England, rising in Powys and flowing northeast and east into England, then south to the Bristol Channel. Length: about 290 km (180 miles). **2** a river in SE central Canada, in Ontario, flowing northeast to Hudson Bay. Length: about 676 km (420 miles).

Severnaya Zemlya ★ (*Russian* 'sjevɪrnəjə zɪm'lja) *n* an archipelago in the Arctic Ocean off the coast of N central Russia.

Severus ★ (sɪ'vɪərəs) *n* **Lucius Septimius** (sɛp'tɪmɪəs). 146–211 A.D., Roman soldier and emperor (193–211). He waged war successfully against the Parthians (197–202) and spent his last years in Britain (208–11).

Seveso ★ (sə'veɪzəυ) *n* a town in N Italy, near Milan: evacuated in 1976 after contamination by a poisonous cloud of dioxin gas released from a factory.

Sévigné ★ (*French* seviɲe) *n* **Marquise de,** title of *Marie de Rabutin-Chantal.* 1626–96, French writer, whose correspondence with her daughter provides an account of society during the reign of Louis XIV.

Seville ★ (sə'vɪl) *n* a port in SW Spain, on the Guadalquivir River: chief town of S Spain under the Vandals and Visigoths (5th–8th centuries); centre of Spanish colonial trade (16th–17th centuries); tourist centre. Pop.: 714 148 (1991). Ancient name: **Hispalis.** Spanish name: **Sevilla** (se'βiʎa).

Seville orange *n* **1** an orange tree of tropical and semitropical regions: grown for its bitter fruit, which is used to make marmalade. **2** the fruit of this tree.

Sèvres (*French* sɛvrə) *n* porcelain ware manufactured at Sèvres, near Paris, from 1756, characterized by the use of clear colours and elaborate decorative detail.

sew (səʊ) *vb* **sews, sewing, sewed; sewn** *or* **sewed. 1** to join or decorate (pieces of fabric, etc.) by means of a thread repeatedly passed through with a needle. **2** (*tr;* often foll. by *on* or *up*) to attach, fasten, or close by sewing. **3** (*tr*) to make (a garment, etc.) by sewing. ◆ See also **sew up.** [OE *sēowan*]

sewage ('suːɪdʒ) *n* waste matter from domestic or industrial establishments that is carried away in sewers or drains. [C19: back formation from SEWER¹]

sewage farm *n* a place where sewage is treated, esp. for use as manure.

Seward ★ ('sjuːəd) *n* **William Henry.** 1801–72, US statesman; secretary of state (1861–69); an opponent of slavery, he was also responsible for the purchase of Alaska (1867).

Seward Peninsula ★ *n* a peninsula of W Alaska, on the Bering Strait. Length: about 290 km (180 miles).

Sewell ★ ('suːəl) *n* **Henry.** 1807–79, New Zealand statesman, born in England: first prime minister of New Zealand (1856).

sewer¹ (sʊə) *n* **1** a drain or pipe, esp. one that is underground, used to carry away surface water or sewage. ◆ *vb* **2** (*tr*) to provide with sewers. [C15: from OF, from *essever* to drain, from Vulgar L *exaquāre* (unattested), from L EX-¹ + *aqua* water]

sewer² ('səʊə) *n* a person or thing that sews.

sewerage ('sʊərɪdʒ) *n* **1** an arrangement of sewers. **2** the removal of surface water or sewage by means of sewers. **3** another word for **sewage.**

sewing ('səʊɪŋ) *n* **a** a piece of cloth, etc., that is sewn or to be sewn. **b** (*as modifier*): *sewing basket.*

sewing machine *n* any machine designed to sew material. It is now usually driven by electric motor but is sometimes operated by a foot treadle or by hand.

sewn (səʊn) *vb* a past participle of **sew.**

sew up *vb* (*tr, adv*) **1** to fasten or mend completely by sewing. **2** *US.* to acquire sole use or control of. **3** *Inf.* to complete or negotiate successfully: *to sew up a deal.*

sex (sɛks) *n* **1** the sum of the characteristics that distinguish organisms on the basis of their reproductive function. **2** either of the two categories, male or female, into which organisms are placed on this basis. **3** short for **sexual intercourse. 4** feelings or behaviour resulting from the urge to gratify the sexual instinct. **5** sexual matters in general. ◆ *modifier.* **6** of or concerning sexual matters: *sex education.* **7** based on or arising from the difference between the sexes: *sex discrimination.* ◆ *vb* **8** (*tr*) to ascertain the sex of. [C14: from L *sexus*]

sex- *combining form.* six: *sexcentenary.* [from L]

sexagenarian (,sɛksədʒɪ'nɛərɪən) *n* **1** a person from 60 to 69 years old. ◆ *adj* **2** being from 60 to 69 years old. **3** of or relating to a sexagenarian. [C18: from L, from *sexāgēnī* sixty each, from *sexāgintā* sixty]

Sexagesima (,sɛksə'dʒɛsɪmə) *n* the second Sunday before Lent. [C16: from L: sixtieth, from *sexāgintā* sixty]

sexagesimal (,sɛksə'dʒɛsɪməl) *adj* **1** relating to or based on the number 60: *sexagesimal measurement of angles.* ◆ *n* **2** a fraction in which the denominator is some power of 60.

sex-and-shopping *adj* (*prenominal*) (of a novel) belonging to a genre of novel in which the central character, a woman, has a number of sexual encounters, and the author mentions the name of many upmarket products.

sex appeal *n* the quality or power of attracting the opposite sex.

sexcentenary (,sɛksɛn'tiːnərɪ) *adj* **1** of or relating to 600 or a period of 600 years. **2** of or celebrating a 600th anniversary. ◆ *n, pl* **sexcentenaries. 3** a 600th anniversary or its celebration. [C18: from L *sexcentēnī* six hundred each]

sex chromosome *n* either of the chromosomes determining the sex of animals.

sexed (sɛkst) *adj* **1** (*in combination*) having a specified degree of sexuality: *undersexed.* **2** of, relating to, or having sexual differentiation.

sex hormone *n* an animal hormone affecting development and growth of reproductive organs and related parts.

sexism ('sɛksɪzəm) *n* discrimination on the basis of sex, esp. the oppression of women by men.
► **'sexist** *n, adj*

sexless ('sɛkslɪs) *adj* **1** having or showing no sexual differentiation. **2** having no sexual desires. **3** sexually unattractive.

sex linkage *n Genetics.* the condition in which a gene is located on a sex chromosome so that the character controlled by the gene is associated with either of the sexes.
► **'sex-,linked** *adj*

sex object *n* someone, esp. a woman, regarded only from the point of view of someone else's sexual desires.

sexology (sɛk'sɒlədʒɪ) *n* the study of sexual behaviour in human beings.
► **sex'ologist** *n* ► **sexological** (,sɛksə'lɒdʒɪkᵊl) *adj*

sexpartite (sɛks'pɑːtaɪt) *adj* **1** (esp. of vaults, arches, etc.) divided into or composed of six parts. **2** involving six participants.

sex shop *n* a shop selling aids to sexual activity, pornographic material, etc.

sext (sɛkst) *n Chiefly RC Church.* the fourth of the seven canonical hours of the divine office or the prayers prescribed for it. [C15: from Church L *sexta hōra* the sixth hour]

sextan ('sɛkstən) *adj* (of a fever) marked by paroxysms that recur every fifth day. [C17: from Med. L *sextana* (*febris*) (fever) of the sixth (day)]

sextant ('sɛkstənt) *n* **1** an instrument used in navigation and consisting of a telescope through which a sighting of a heavenly body is taken, with protractors for determining its angular distance above the horizon. **2** a sixth part of a circle. [C17: from L *sextāns* one sixth of a unit]

sextet *or* **sextette** (sɛks'tɛt) *n* **1** *Music.* a group of six singers or instrumentalists or a piece of music composed for such a group. **2** a group of six people or things. [C19: var. of SESTET]

sextillion (sɛks'tɪljən) *n, pl* **sextillions** *or* **sextillion. 1** (in Britain, France, and Germany) the number represented as one followed by 36 zeros (10^{36}). **2** (in the US and Canada) the number represented as one followed by 21 zeros (10^{21}). [C17: from F, from SEX- + -*illion*, on the model of SEPTILLION]

sexto ('sɛkstəʊ) *n, pl* **sextos** another word for **sixmo.**

sexton ('sɛkstən) *n* a person employed to act as caretaker of a church and often also as a bell-ringer, grave-digger, etc. [C14: from OF, from Med. L *sacristānus* SACRISTAN]

sextuple ('sɛkstjʊpʰl) *n* **1** a quantity or number six times as great as another. ◆ *adj* **2** six times as much or as many. **3** consisting of six parts or members. [C17: L *sextus* sixth + -*uple*, as in QUADRUPLE]

sextuplet ('sɛkstjʊplɪt) *n* **1** one of six offspring at one birth. **2** a group of six. **3** *Music.* a group of six notes played in a time value of four.

sexual ('sɛksjʊəl) *adj* **1** of or characterized by sex. **2** (of reproduction) characterized by the union of male and female gametes. Cf. **asexual** (sense 2). [C17: from LL *sexuālis*]
▸ **sexuality** (ˌsɛksjʊ'ælɪtɪ) *n* ▸ '**sexually** *adv*

sexual harassment *n* the persistent unwelcome directing of sexual remarks and looks, and unnecessary physical contact, at a person, usually a woman, esp. in the work place.

sexual intercourse *n* the sexual act in which the male's erect penis is inserted into the female's vagina; copulation; coitus.

sexually transmitted disease *n* any of various diseases, such as syphilis or gonorrhoea, transmitted by sexual intercourse. Also called: **venereal disease.**

sexual selection *n* an evolutionary process in animals, in which selection by females of males with certain characters results in the preservation of these characters in the species.

sexy ('sɛksɪ) *adj* **sexier, sexiest.** *Inf.* **1** provoking or intended to provoke sexual interest: *a sexy dress.* **2** feeling sexual interest; aroused. **3** interesting, exciting, or trendy: *a sexy project; a sexy new car.*
▸ '**sexily** *adv* ▸ '**sexiness** *n*

Seychelles ★ (seɪ'ʃɛl, -'ʃɛlz) *pl n* a group of volcanic islands in the W Indian Ocean: taken by the British from the French in 1744: became an independent republic within the Commonwealth in 1976, incorporating the British Indian Ocean Territory islands of Aldabra, Farquhar and Desroches. Languages: Creole, English, and French. Religion: Roman Catholic majority. Currency: rupee. Capital: Victoria. Pop.: 76 100 (1996). Area: 455 sq. km (176 sq. miles).

Seyhan ★ (seɪ'hɑːn) *n* another name for **Adana.**

Seymour ★ ('siːmɔː) *n* **Jane.** ?1509–37, third wife of Henry VIII of England; mother of Edward VI.

sf *or* **sfz** *Music. abbrev. for* sforzando.

SF *or* **sf** *abbrev. for* science fiction.

SFA *abbrev. for:* **1** Scottish Football Association. **2** sweet Fanny Adams. See **fanny adams.**

Sfax ★ (sfæks) *n* a port in E Tunisia, on the Gulf of Gabès: the second largest town in Tunisia; commercial centre of a phosphate region. Pop.: 230 900 (1994).

SFO *abbrev. for* Serious Fraud Office: the department of the British government which investigates cases of serious financial fraud.

Sforza ★ (*Italian* 'sfɔrtsa) *n* **1** Count **Carlo** ('karlo). 1873–

1952, Italian statesman; leader of the anti-Fascist opposition. **2 Francesco** (fran'tʃesko). 1401–66, duke of Milan (1450–66). **3** his father **Giacomuzzo** (dʒako'muttso) *or* **Muzio** ('muttsjo), original name *Attendolo.* 1369–1424, Italian condottiere and founder of the dynasty that ruled Milan (1450–1535). **4 Lodovico** (lodo'viːko), called *the Moor.* 1451–1508, duke of Milan (1494–1500), but effective ruler from 1480; patron of Leonardo da Vinci.

sforzando (sfɔː'tsɑːndəʊ) *or* **sforzato** (sfɔː'tsɑːtəʊ) *Music.* ◆ *adj, adv* **1** to be played with strong initial attack. Abbrevs.: **sf, sfz.** ◆ *n* **2** a symbol, mark, etc., indicating this. [C19: from It., from *sforzare* to force, from Vulgar L *fortiāre* (unattested) to FORCE]

SG *abbrev. for* solicitor general.

sgd *abbrev. for* signed.

S. Glam *abbrev. for* South Glamorgan.

SGML *abbrev. for* standard generalized mark-up language: an international standard used in publishing for defining the structure and formatting of documents.

sgraffito ★ (sgræ'fiːtəʊ) *n, pl* **sgraffiti** (-tɪ). **1** a technique in mural or ceramic decoration in which the top layer of glaze, plaster, etc., is incised with a design to reveal parts of the ground. **2** such a decoration. [C18: from It., from *sgraffire* to scratch]

's Gravenhage ★ (sxraːvən'haːxə) *n* the Dutch name for (The) **Hague.**

Sgt *abbrev. for* Sergeant.

sh (*spelling pron* ʃʃʃ) *interj* an exclamation to request silence or quiet.

sh. *abbrev. for:* **1** *Stock Exchange.* share. **2** sheep. **3** *Bookbinding.* sheet.

Shaanxi ('ʃæn'ʃiː) *or* **Shensi** ★ *n* a province of NW China: one of the earliest centres of Chinese civilization; largely mountainous. Capital: Xi An. Pop.: 34 810 000 (1995 est.). Area: 195 800 sq. km (75 598 sq. miles).

Shaba ★ ('ʃaːbə) *n* a region of the SE Democratic Republic of the Congo: site of secessionist movement during the 1960s and declared itself independent again in 1993: important for hydroelectric power and rich mineral resources (copper and tin ore). Area: 496 964 sq. km (191 878 sq. miles). Former name (until 1972): **Katanga.**

shabby ('ʃæbɪ) *adj* **shabbier, shabbiest. 1** threadbare or dilapidated in appearance. **2** wearing worn and dirty clothes. **3** mean or unworthy: *shabby treatment.* **4** dirty or squalid. [C17: from OE *sceabb* scab]
▸ '**shabbily** *adv* ▸ '**shabbiness** *n*

Shache ('ʃæ'tʃeɪ), **Soche,** *or* **So-ch'e** ★ *n* a town in W China, in the W Xinjiang Uygur AR: a centre of the caravan trade between China, India, and Transcaspian areas. Also called: **Yarkand.**

shack (ʃæk) *n* **1** a roughly built hut. ◆ *vb* **2** See **shack up.** [C19: ?from dialect *shackly* ramshackle, from dialect *shack* to shake]

shackle ('ʃækʰl) *n* **1** (*often pl*) a metal ring or fastening, usually part of a pair used to secure a person's wrists or ankles. **2** (*often pl*) anything that confines or restricts freedom. **3** a U-shaped bracket, the open end of which is closed by a bolt (**shackle pin**), used for securing ropes, chains, etc. ◆ *vb* **shackles, shackling, shackled.** (*tr*) **4** to confine with or as if with shackles. **5** to fasten or connect with a shackle. [OE *sceacel*]
▸ '**shackler** *n*

Shackleton ★ ('ʃækəltən) *n* Sir **Ernest Henry.** 1874–1922, British explorer. He commanded three expeditions to the Antarctic (1907–09; 1914–17; 1921–22), during which the south magnetic pole was located (1909).

shack up *vb* (*intr, adv;* usually foll. by *with*) *Sl.* to live, esp. with a lover.

shad (ʃæd) *n, pl* **shad** *or* **shads.** any of various herring-like food fishes that migrate from the sea to fresh water to spawn. [OE *sceadd*]

Shadbolt ★ ('ʃæd,bəʊlt) *n* **Maurice.** born 1932, New Zealand novelist.

shaddock ('ʃædək) *n* another name for **pomelo** (sense 1). [C17: after Captain *Shaddock*, who brought its seed from the East Indies to Jamaica in 1696]

★ people and places

shade (ʃeɪd) n 1 relative darkness produced by the blocking out of light. 2 a place made relatively darker or cooler than other areas by the blocking of light, esp. sunlight. 3 a position of relative obscurity. 4 something used to provide a shield or protection from a direct source of light, such as a lampshade. 5 a darker area indicated in a painting, drawing, etc., by shading. 6 a colour that varies slightly from a standard colour: *a darker shade of green.* 7 a slight amount: *a shade of difference.* 8 *Literary.* a ghost. ♦ vb **shades, shading, shaded.** (*mainly tr*) 9 to screen or protect from heat, light, view, etc. 10 to make darker or dimmer. 11 to represent (a darker area) in (a painting, etc.), by means of hatching, etc. 12 (*also intr*) to change or cause to change slightly. 13 to lower (a price) slightly. [OE *sceadu*]
▸ 'shadeless *adj*

shades (ʃeɪdz) *pl n* 1 gathering darkness at nightfall. 2 *Sl.* sunglasses. 3 (*often cap.*; preceded by *the*) a literary term for **Hades.** 4 (foll. by *of*) undertones: *shades of my father!*

shading ('ʃeɪdɪŋ) n the graded areas of tone, lines, dots, etc., indicating light and dark in a painting or drawing.

shadoof (ʃə'duːf) n a mechanism for raising water, consisting of a pivoted pole with a bucket at one end and a counterweight at the other, esp. as used in Egypt. [C19: from Egyptian Ar.]

shadow ('ʃædəʊ) n 1 a dark image or shape cast on a surface by the interception of light rays by an opaque body. 2 an area of relative darkness. 3 the dark portions of a picture. 4 a hint or faint semblance: *beyond a shadow of a doubt.* 5 a remnant or vestige: *a shadow of one's past self.* 6 a reflection. 7 a threatening influence: *a shadow over one's happiness.* 8 a spectre. 9 an inseparable companion. 10 a person who trails another in secret, such as a detective. 11 *Med.* a dark area on an X-ray film representing an opaque structure or part. 12 (in Jungian psychology) the archetype that represents man's animal ancestors. 13 *Arch.* shelter. 14 (*modifier*) *Brit.* designating a member or members of the main opposition party in Parliament who would hold ministerial office if their party were in power: *shadow cabinet.* ♦ vb (*tr*) 15 to cast a shadow over. 16 to make dark or gloomy. 17 to shade from light. 18 to follow or trail secretly. 19 (often foll. by *forth*) to represent vaguely. [OE *sceadwe*, oblique case of *sceadu* shade]
▸ 'shadower n

shadow-box vb (*intr*) *Boxing.* to practise blows and footwork against an imaginary opponent.
▸ 'shadow-ˌboxing n

shadowgraph ('ʃædəʊˌɡrɑːf) n 1 a silhouette made by casting a shadow on a lighted surface. 2 another name for **radiograph.**

shadow play n a theatrical entertainment using shadows thrown by puppets or actors onto a lighted screen.

shadow price n *Econ.* the calculated price of a good or service for which no market price exists.

shadowy ('ʃædəʊɪ) *adj* 1 dark; shady. 2 resembling a shadow in faintness. 3 illusory or imaginary. 4 mysterious or secretive: *a shadowy underworld figure.*
▸ 'shadowiness n

Shadrach ★ ('ʃædræk, 'ʃeɪ-) n *Old Testament.* one of Daniel's three companions, who, together with Meshach and Abednego, was miraculously saved from destruction in Nebuchadnezzar's fiery furnace (Daniel 3:12–30).

shady ('ʃeɪdɪ) *adj* **shadier, shadiest.** 1 shaded. 2 affording or casting a shade. 3 quiet or concealed. 4 *Inf.* questionable as to honesty or legality.
▸ 'shadily *adv* ▸ 'shadiness n

SHAEF (ʃeɪf) (in WWII) n acronym for Supreme Headquarters Allied Expeditionary Forces.

Shaffer ★ ('ʃæfə) n Peter. born 1926, British dramatist. His plays include *The Royal Hunt of the Sun* (1964), *Equus* (1973), and *Amadeus* (1979).

shaft (ʃɑːft) n 1 the long narrow pole that forms the body of a spear, arrow, etc. 2 something directed at a person in the manner of a missile. 3 a ray or streak, esp. of light. 4 a rod or pole forming the handle of a hammer, golf club, etc. 5 a revolving rod that transmits motion or power. 6 one of the two wooden poles by which an animal is harnessed to a vehicle. 7 *Anat.* the middle part of a long

bone. 8 the middle part of a column or pier, between the base and the capital. 9 *Archit.* a column that supports a vaulting rib, sometimes one of a set. 10 a vertical passageway through a building, as for a lift. 11 a vertical passageway into a mine. 12 *Ornithol.* the central rib of a feather. 13 an archaic or literary word for **arrow.** ♦ vb 14 *US & Canad. sl.* to trick or cheat. [OE *sceaft*]

Shaftesbury ★ ('ʃɑːftsbərɪ, -brɪ) n 1 **1st Earl of,** title of Anthony Ashley Cooper. 1621–83, English statesman, a major figure in the Whig opposition to Charles II. 2 **7th Earl of,** title of Anthony Ashley Cooper. 1801–85, British evangelical churchman and social reformer.

shag[1] (ʃæɡ) n 1 a matted tangle, esp. of hair, etc. 2 a napped fabric, usually a rough wool. 3 shredded coarse tobacco. [OE *sceacga*]

shag[2] (ʃæɡ) n another name for **green cormorant** (*Phalacrocorax aristotelis*). [C16: special use of SHAG[1], with reference to its crest]

shag[3] (ʃæɡ) *Brit. sl.* ♦ vb **shags, shagging, shagged.** 1 *Taboo.* to have sexual intercourse with (a person). 2 (*tr;* often foll. by *out; usually passive*) to exhaust. ♦ n 3 *Taboo.* an act of sexual intercourse. [C20: from ?]

shaggy ('ʃæɡɪ) *adj* **shaggier, shaggiest.** 1 having or covered with rough unkempt fur, hair, wool, etc.: *a shaggy dog.* 2 rough or unkempt.
▸ 'shaggily *adv* ▸ 'shagginess n

shaggy dog story n *Inf.* a long rambling joke ending in a deliberate anticlimax, such as a pointless punch line.

shagreen (ʃæ'ɡriːn) n 1 the rough skin of certain sharks and rays, used as an abrasive. 2 a rough grainy leather made from certain animal hides. [C17: from F *chagrin*, from Turkish *çagri rump*]

shah (ʃɑː) n a ruler of certain Middle Eastern countries, esp. (formerly) Iran. [C16: from Persian: king]
▸ 'shahdom n

Shah Jahan ★ (dʒə'hɑːn) n 1592–1666, Mogul emperor (1628–58), who created the Taj Mahal and the Pearl Mosque at Agra.

Shahjahanpur ★ (ˌʃɑːdʒəˌhɑːn'pʊə) n a city in N India, in central Uttar Pradesh: founded in 1647 in the reign of Shah Jahan. Pop.: 237 713 (1991).

Shah of Iran ★ (ʃɑː) n See (Mohammed Reza) **Pahlavi**[1].

Shaka or **Chaka** ★ ('ʃaka) n died 1828, Zulu military leader, who founded the Zulu Empire in southern Africa.

shake (ʃeɪk) vb **shakes, shaking, shook, shaken.** 1 to move or cause to move up and down or back and forth with short quick movements. 2 to sway or totter or cause to sway or totter. 3 to clasp or grasp (the hand) of (a person) in greeting, agreement, etc.: *he shook John's hand.* 4 **shake hands.** to clasp hands in greeting, agreement, etc. 5 **shake on it.** *Inf.* to shake hands in agreement, reconciliation, etc. 6 to bring or come to a specified condition by or as if by shaking: *he shook free and ran.* 7 (*tr*) to wave or brandish: *he shook his sword.* 8 (*tr;* often foll. by *up*) to rouse or agitate. 9 (*tr*) to shock, disturb, or upset: *he was shaken by the news.* 10 (*tr*) to undermine or weaken: *the crisis shook his faith.* 11 to mix (dice) by rattling in a cup or the hand before throwing. 12 *Austral. old-fashioned sl.* to steal. 13 (*tr*) *US & Canad. inf.* to get rid of. 14 *Music.* to perform a trill on (a note). 15 **shake in one's shoes.** to tremble with fear or apprehension. 16 **shake one's head.** to indicate disagreement or disapproval by moving the head from side to side. ♦ n 17 the act or an instance of shaking. 18 a tremor or vibration. 19 **the shakes.** *Inf.* a state of uncontrollable trembling or a condition that causes it, such as a fever. 20 *Inf.* a very short period of time: *in half a shake.* 21 a fissure or crack in timber or rock. 22 an instance of shaking dice before casting. 23 *Music.* another word for **trill** (sense 1). 24 an informal name for **earthquake.** 25 short for **milk shake. 26 no great shakes.** *Inf.* of no great merit or value. ♦ See also **shake down, shake off, shake up.** [OE *sceacan*]
▸ 'shakable or 'shakeable *adj*

shake down vb (*adv*) 1 to fall or settle or cause to fall or settle by shaking. 2 (*tr*) *US sl.* to extort money from, esp. by blackmail. 3 (*tr*) *Inf., chiefly US.* to submit (a vessel, etc.) to a shakedown test. 4 (*intr*) to go to bed, esp. to a makeshift bed. ◆ *n* **shakedown. 5** *US sl.* a swindle or act of extortion. **6** a makeshift bed, esp. of straw, blankets, etc. **7** *Inf., chiefly US.* **7a** a voyage to test the performance of a ship or aircraft or to familiarize the crew with their duties. **7b** (*as modifier*): *a shakedown run.*

shake off *vb* (*adv*) **1** to remove or be removed with or as if with a quick movement: *she shook off her depression.* **2** (*tr*) to escape from; elude: *they shook off the police.*

shaker ('ʃeɪkə) *n* **1** a person or thing that shakes. **2** a container from which a condiment is shaken. **3** a container in which the ingredients of alcoholic drinks are shaken together.

Shakers ('ʃeɪkəz) *pl n* **the.** an American millenarian sect, founded in 1747 as an offshoot of the Quakers, given to ecstatic shaking and practising common ownership of property.

Shakespeare ★ ('ʃeɪkspɪə) *n* **William.** 1564–1616, English dramatist and poet. He was born and died at Stratford-upon-Avon but spent most of his life as an actor and playwright in London. His plays with approximate dates of composition are: *Henry VI, Parts I–III* (1590); *Richard III* (1592); *The Comedy of Errors* (1592); *Titus Andronicus* (1593); *The Taming of the Shrew* (1593); *The Two Gentlemen of Verona* (1594); *Love's Labour's Lost* (1594); *Romeo and Juliet* (1594); *Richard II* (1595); *A Midsummer Night's Dream* (1595); *King John* (1596); *The Merchant of Venice* (1596); *Henry IV, Parts I–II* (1597); *Much Ado about Nothing* (1598); *Henry V* (1598); *Julius Caesar* (1599); *As You Like It* (1599); *Twelfth Night* (1599); *Hamlet* (1600); *The Merry Wives of Windsor* (1600); *Troilus and Cressida* (1601); *All's Well that ends Well* (1602); *Measure for Measure* (1604); *Othello* (1604); *King Lear* (1605); *Macbeth* (1605); *Antony and Cleopatra* (1606); *Coriolanus* (1607); *Timon of Athens* (1607); *Pericles* (1608); *Cymbeline* (1609); *The Winter's Tale* (1610); *The Tempest* (1611); and, possibly in collaboration with John Fletcher, *Two Noble Kinsmen* (1612) and *Henry VIII* (1612). His *Sonnets*, variously addressed to a fair young man and a dark lady, were published in 1609.

Shakespearean *or* **Shakespearian** (ʃeɪk'spɪərɪən) *adj* **1** of, relating to, or characteristic of Shakespeare or his works. ◆ *n* **2** a student of or specialist in Shakespeare's works.

Shakespearean sonnet *n* a sonnet form developed in 16th-century England and employed by Shakespeare, having the rhyme scheme a b a b c d c d e f e f g g.

shake up *vb* (*tr, adv*) **1** to shake in order to mix. **2** to reorganize drastically. **3** to stir. **4** to restore the shape of (a pillow, etc.). **5** *Inf.* to shock mentally or physically. ◆ *n* **shake-up. 6** *Inf.* a radical reorganization.

Shakhty ★ (*Russian* 'ʃaxtɪ) *n* an industrial city in W Russia: the chief town of the E Donets Basin. Pop.: 230 000 (1995 est.).

shako ('ʃækəʊ) *n, pl* **shakos** *or* **shakoes.** a tall usually cylindrical military headdress, having a plume and often a peak. [C19: via F from Hungarian *csákó*, from MHG *zacke* a sharp point]

shaky ('ʃeɪkɪ) *adj* **shakier, shakiest. 1** tending to shake or tremble. **2** liable to prove defective. **3** uncertain or questionable: *your arguments are very shaky.*
▶ **'shakily** *adv* ▶ **'shakiness** *n*

shale (ʃeɪl) *n* a dark fine-grained sedimentary rock formed by compression of successive layers of clay. [OE *scealu* shell]
▶ **'shaly** *adj*

shale oil *n* an oil distilled from shales and used as fuel.

shall (ʃæl; *unstressed* ʃəl) *vb past* **should.** (takes an infinitive without *to* or an implied infinitive) used as an auxiliary: **1** (esp. with *I* or *we* as subject) to make the future tense: *we shall see you tomorrow.* Cf. **will**[1] (sense 1). **2** (with *you, he, she, it, they,* or a noun as subject) **2a** to indicate determination on the part of the speaker, as in issuing a threat: *you shall pay for this!* **2b** to indicate compulsion, now esp. in official documents. **2c** to indicate certainty or inevitability: *our day shall come.* **3** (with *any noun or pronoun as subject, esp. in conditional clauses or clauses expressing doubt*) to indicate nonspecific futurity: *I don't think I shall ever see her again.* [OE *sceal*]

shallop ('ʃæləp) *n* a light boat used for rowing in shallow water. [C16: from F *chaloupe*, from Du. *sloep* sloop]

shallot (ʃə'lɒt) *n* **1** an alliaceous plant cultivated for its edible bulb. **2** the bulb of this plant, which divides into small sections and is used in cooking for flavouring. [C17: from OF, from *eschaloigne*, from L *Ascalōnia caepa* Ascalonian onion, from *Ascalon,* a Palestinian town]

shallow ('ʃæləʊ) *adj* **1** having little depth. **2** lacking intellectual or mental depth or subtlety. ◆ *n* **3** (*often pl*) a shallow place in a body of water. ◆ *vb* **4** to make or become shallow. [C15: rel. to OE *sceald* shallow]
▶ **'shallowly** *adv* ▶ **'shallowness** *n*

shalom aleichem Hebrew. (ʃa'lɒm a'lexɛm) *sentence substitute.* peace be to you: used by Jews as a greeting or farewell. Often shortened to **shalom.**

shalt (ʃælt) *vb Arch. or dialect.* (used with the pronoun *thou*) a singular form of the present tense (indicative mood) of **shall.**

sham (ʃæm) *n* **1** anything that is not what it appears to be. **2** something false or fictitious that purports to be genuine. **3** a person who pretends to be something other than he is. ◆ *adj* **4** counterfeit or false. ◆ *vb* **shams, shamming, shammed. 5** to assume the appearance of (something); counterfeit: *to sham illness.* [C17: ? a N English dialect var. of SHAME]

shaman ('ʃæmən) *n* **1** a priest of shamanism. **2** a medicine man of a similar religion, esp. among certain tribes of North American Indians. [C17: from Russian *shaman,* ult. from Sansk. *śrama* religious exercise]

shamanism ('ʃæmə,nɪzəm) *n* **1** the religion of certain peoples of northern Asia, based on the belief that the world is pervaded by good and evil spirits who can be influenced or controlled only by the shamans. **2** any similar religion involving forms of spiritualism.
▶ **'shamanist** *n, adj*

Shamash ★ ('ʃɑːmæʃ) *n* the sun god of Assyria and Babylonia. [from Akkadian: sun]

shamateur ('ʃæmətə) *n* a sportsperson who is officially an amateur but accepts payment. [C20: from SHAM + AMATEUR]

shamble ('ʃæmb°l) *vb* **shambles, shambling, shambled. 1** (*intr*) to walk or move along in an awkward or unsteady way. ◆ *n* **2** an awkward or unsteady walk. [C17: from *shamble* (adj) ungainly, ?from *shamble legs* legs resembling those of a meat vendor's table; see SHAMBLES]
▶ **'shambling** *adj, n*

shambles ('ʃæmb°lz) *n* (*functioning as sing or pl*) **1** a place of great disorder: *the room was a shambles after the party.* **2** a place where animals are brought to be slaughtered. **3** any place of slaughter or carnage. [C14 *shamble* table used by meat vendors, from OE *sceamel* stool, from LL *scamellum* a small bench, from L *scamnum* stool]

shambolic (ʃæm'bɒlɪk) *adj Inf.* completely disorganized; chaotic. [C20: from SHAMBLES]

shame (ʃeɪm) *n* **1** a painful emotion resulting from an awareness of having done something dishonourable, unworthy, etc. **2** capacity to feel such an emotion. **3** ignominy or disgrace. **4** a person or thing that causes this. **5** an occasion for regret, disappointment, etc.: *it's a shame you can't come with us.* **6 put to shame. 6a** to disgrace. **6b** to surpass totally. ◆ *vb* **shames, shaming, shamed.** (*tr*) **7** to cause to feel shame. **8** to bring shame on. **9** (often foll. by *into*) to compel through a sense of shame. ◆ *interj* **10**

★ people and places

S. African inf. **10a** an expression of sympathy. **10b** an expression of pleasure or endearment. [OE *scamu*]
▶ '**shamable** or '**shameable** adj

shamefaced ('ʃeɪmˌfeɪst) adj **1** bashful or modest. **2** showing a sense of shame. [C16: alteration of earlier *shamefast*, from OE *sceamfæst*]
▶ **shamefacedly** (ˌʃeɪm'feɪsɪdlɪ) adv

shameful ('ʃeɪmful) adj causing or deserving shame.
▶ '**shamefully** adv ▶ '**shamefulness** n

shameless ('ʃeɪmlɪs) adj **1** having no sense of shame. **2** without decency or modesty.
▶ '**shamelessly** adv ▶ '**shamelessness** n

Shamir ★ (ʃæ'mɪə) n **Yitzhak** ('jɪtzæk). born 1915, Israeli statesman, born in Poland: prime minister (1983–84; 1986–92).

shammy ('ʃæmɪ) n, pl **shammies**. *Inf.* another word for chamois (sense 3). Also called: **shammy leather**. [C18: variant of CHAMOIS]

Shamo ★ ('ʃɑː'məʊ) n transliteration of the Chinese name for the **Gobi**.

shampoo (ʃæm'puː) n **1** a preparation of soap or detergent to wash the hair. **2** a similar preparation for washing carpets, etc. **3** the process of shampooing. ◆ vb **shampoos, shampooing, shampooed**. (tr) **4** to wash (the hair, etc.) with such a preparation. [C18: from Hindi, from *chāmpnā* to knead]

shamrock ('ʃæmˌrɒk) n a plant having leaves divided into three leaflets: the national emblem of Ireland. [C16: from Irish Gaelic *seamróg*, dim. of *seamar* clover]

shamus ('ʃɑːməs, 'ʃeɪ-) n, pl **shamuses**. *US sl.* a police or private detective. [prob. from *shammes* caretaker of a synagogue, infl. by Irish *Séamas* James]

Shandong ('ʃæn'dʌŋ) or **Shantung** ★ n a province of NE China, on the Yellow Sea and the Gulf of Chihli: part of the earliest organized state of China (1520–1030 B.C.); consists chiefly of the fertile plain of the lower Yellow River, with mountains over 1500 m (5000 ft) high in the centre. Capital: Jinan. Pop.: 86 710 000 (1995 est.). Area: 153 300 sq. km (59 189 sq. miles).

shandy ('ʃændɪ) n, pl **shandies**. an alcoholic drink made of beer and ginger beer or lemonade. [C19: from ?]

Shang ★ (ʃæŋ) n **1** the dynasty ruling in China from about the 18th to the 12th centuries B.C. ◆ adj **2** of or relating to the pottery produced during the Shang dynasty.

shanghai ('ʃæŋhaɪ, ˌʃæŋ'haɪ) *Sl.* ◆ vb **shanghais, shanghaiing, shanghaied.** (tr) **1** to kidnap (a man or seaman) for enforced service at sea. **2** to force or trick (someone) into doing something, etc. **3** *Austral. & NZ.* to shoot with a catapult. ◆ n **4** *Austral. & NZ.* a catapult. [C19: from the city of SHANGHAI; from the forceful methods formerly used to collect crews for voyages to the Orient]

Shanghai ★ ('ʃæŋ'haɪ) n a port in E China, in SE Jiangsu near the estuary of the Yangtze: the largest city in China and one of the largest ports in the world; a major cultural and industrial centre, with two universities. Pop.: 7 830 000 (1991 est.).

Shangri-la (ˌʃæŋgrɪ'lɑː) n a remote or imaginary utopia. [C20: from the name of an imaginary valley in the Himalayas, from *Lost Horizon* (1933), a novel by James Hilton]

shank (ʃæŋk) n **1** *Anat.* the shin. **2** the corresponding part of the leg in vertebrates other than man. **3** a cut of meat from the top part of an animal's shank. **4** the main part of a tool, between the working part and the handle. **5** the part of a bolt between the thread and the head. **6** the ring or stem on the back of some buttons. **7** the stem or long narrow part of a key, hook, spoon handle, nail, etc. **8** the band of a ring as distinguished from the setting. **9** the part of a shoe connecting the wide part of the sole with the heel. **10** *Printing.* the body of a piece of type. ◆ vb **11** (intr) (of fruits, roots, etc.) to show disease symptoms, esp. discoloration. **12** (tr) *Golf.* to mishit (the ball) with the foot of the shaft. [OE *scanca*]

Shankar ★ ('ʃæŋkɑː) n **Ravi** ('rɑːviː). born 1920, Indian sitarist.

Shankaracharya (ˌʃʌŋkərɑː'tʃɑːrjə) or **Shankara** ★

(ˈʃʌŋkərə) n 9th century A.D., Hindu philosopher and teacher; chief exponent of Vedanta philosophy.

Shankly ★ ('ʃæŋklɪ) n **Bill.** 1913–81, Scottish footballer and manager of Liverpool FC (1959–74).

shanks's pony or *US* **shanks's mare** ('ʃæŋksɪz) n *Inf.* one's own legs as a means of transportation.

Shannon[1] ★ ('ʃænən) n a river in the Republic of Ireland, rising in NW Co. Cavan and flowing south to the Atlantic by an estuary 113 km (70 miles) long: the longest river in the Republic of Ireland. Length: 260 km (161 miles).

Shannon[2] ★ ('ʃænən) n **Claude (Elwood)**. born 1916, US mathematician, who was responsible for the development of information theory.

shanny ('ʃænɪ) n, pl **shannies**. a European blenny of rocky coastal waters. [C19: from ?]

Shansi ★ ('ʃæn'siː) n a variant transliteration of the Chinese name for **Shanxi**.

Shan State ★ (ʃɑːn, ʃæn) n an administrative division of E Myanmar: formed in 1947 from the joining of the Federation of Shan States with the Wa States; consists of the **Shan plateau**, crossed by forested mountain ranges reaching over 2100 m (7000 ft). Pop.: 4 416 000 (1994 est.). Area: 149 743 sq. km (57 816 sq. miles).

shan't (ʃɑːnt) contraction of shall not.

Shantou or **Shantow** ★ ('ʃæn'taʊ) n a port in SE China, in E Guangdong near the mouth of the Han River: became a treaty port in 1869. Pop.: 578 630 (1990 est.). Also called: **Swatow**.

shantung (ˌʃæn'tʌŋ) n **1** a heavy silk fabric with a knobbly surface. **2** a cotton or rayon imitation of this. [C19: after SHANTUNG]

Shantung ★ ('ʃæn'tʌŋ) n a variant transliteration of the Chinese name for **Shandong**.

shanty[1] ('ʃæntɪ) n, pl **shanties**. **1** a ramshackle hut; crude dwelling. **2** *Austral. & NZ.* a public house, esp. an unlicensed one. [C19: from Canad. F *chantier* cabin built in a lumber camp, from OF *gantier* GANTRY]

shanty[2] ('ʃæntɪ) or **chanty** n, pl **shanties** or **chanties**. a song originally sung by sailors, esp. a rhythmic one forming an accompaniment to work. [C19: from F *chanter* to sing; see CHANT]

shantytown ('ʃæntɪˌtaʊn) n a town or section of a town or city inhabited by very poor people living in shanties.

Shanxi or **Shansi** ★ ('ʃæn'ʃiː) n a province of N China: China's richest coal reserves and much heavy industry. Capital: Taiyuan. Pop.: 30 450 000 (1995 est.). Area: 157 099 sq. km (60 656 sq. miles).

shape (ʃeɪp) n **1** the outward form of an object defined by outline. **2** the figure or outline of the body of a person. **3** a phantom. **4** organized or definite form: *my plans are taking shape*. **5** the form that anything assumes. **6** pattern; mould. **7** condition or state of efficiency: *to be in good shape*. **8** out of shape. **8a** in bad physical condition. **8b** bent, twisted, or deformed. **9 take shape**. to assume a definite form. ◆ vb **shapes, shaping, shaped**. **10** (when intr, often foll. by *into* or *up*) to receive or cause to receive shape or form. **11** (tr) to mould into a particular pattern or form. **12** (tr) to plan, devise, or prepare: *to shape a plan of action*. ◆ See also **shape up**. [OE *gesceap*, lit.: that which is created, from *sceppan* to create]
▶ '**shapable** or '**shapeable** adj ▶ '**shaper** n

SHAPE (ʃeɪp) n acronym for Supreme Headquarters Allied Powers Europe.

-shaped (ʃeɪpt) adj combining form. having the shape of: *an L-shaped room; a pear-shaped figure*.

shapeless ('ʃeɪplɪs) adj **1** having no definite shape or form: *a shapeless mass*. **2** lacking a symmetrical or aesthetically pleasing shape: *a shapeless figure*.
▶ '**shapelessness** n

shapely ('ʃeɪplɪ) adj **shapelier, shapeliest**. (esp. of a woman's body or legs) pleasing or attractive in shape.
▶ '**shapeliness** n

shape up vb (intr, adv) *Inf.* **1** to proceed or develop satisfactorily. **2** to develop a definite or proper form.

shard (ʃɑːd) or **sherd** n **1** a broken piece or fragment of a brittle substance, esp. of pottery. **2** *Zool.* a tough sheath, scale, or shell, esp. the elytra of a beetle. [OE *sceard*]

share[1] (ʃɛə) *n* **1** a part or portion of something owned or contributed by a person or group. **2** (*often pl*) any of the equal parts, usually of low par value, into which the capital stock of a company is divided. **3 go shares.** *Inf.* to share (something) with another or others. ◆ *vb* **shares, sharing, shared. 4** (*tr;* often foll. by *out*) to divide or apportion, esp. equally. **5** (when *intr*, often foll. by *in*) to receive or contribute a portion of: *we can share the cost of the petrol.* **6** to join with another or others in the use of (something): *can I share your umbrella? [OE *sceanu*]
▶ '**sharable** *or* '**shareable** *adj* ▶ '**sharer** *n*

share[2] (ʃɛə) *n* short for **ploughshare**. [OE *scear*]

sharecrop ('ʃɛə,krɒp) *vb* **sharecrops, sharecropping, share-cropped.** *Chiefly US.* to cultivate (farmland) as a sharecrop-per.

sharecropper ('ʃɛə,krɒpə) *n Chiefly US.* a farmer, esp. a tenant farmer, who pays over a proportion of a crop or crops as rent.

shared ownership *n* (in Britain) a form of house purchase whereby the purchaser buys a proportion of the dwelling, usually from a local authority or housing association, and rents the rest.

share-farmer *n Chiefly Austral.* a farmer who pays a fee to another in return for use of land to raise crops, etc.

shareholder ('ʃɛə,həʊldə) *n* the owner of one or more shares in a company.

share index *n* an index showing the movement of share prices. See **FT Index.**

share-milker *n* (in New Zealand) a person who lives on a dairy farm and milks the farmer's herd in return for an agreed share of the profits.

share option *n* a scheme giving employees an option to buy shares in the company for which they work at a favourable price or discount.

share premium *n Brit.* the excess of the amount actually subscribed for an issue of corporate capital over its par value.

share shop *n* a stockbroker, bank, or other financial intermediary that handles the buying and selling of shares for members of the public, esp. during a privatization issue.

shareware ('ʃɛə,wɛə) *n Computing.* software available to all users without the need for a licence and for which a token fee is requested.

Shari ★ ('ʃɑːrɪ) *n* a variant spelling of **Chari** (the river).

sharia *or* **sheria** (ʃə'riːə) *n* the body of doctrines that regulate the lives of those who profess Islam. [Ar.]

sharif (ʃæ'riːf) *n* a variant transliteration of **sherif**.

shark[1] (ʃɑːk) *n* any of various usually ferocious fishes, with a long body, two dorsal fins, and rows of sharp teeth. [C16: from ?]
▶ '**shark,like** *adj*

shark[2] (ʃɑːk) *n* a person who preys on or victimizes others, esp. by swindling or extortion. [C18: prob. from G *Schurke* rogue]

shark repellent *n* **1** any of various substances used by divers to deter shark attack. **2** (*pl*) *Finance.* another name for **porcupine provisions.**

sharkskin ('ʃɑːk,skɪn) *n* a smooth glossy fabric of acetate rayon, used for sportswear, etc.

shark watcher *n Inf.* a business consultant who assists companies in identifying and preventing unwelcome takeover bids.

Sharon ★ ('ʃærən) *n* **Plain of.** a plain in W Israel, between the Mediterranean and the hills of Samaria, extending from Haifa to Tel Aviv.

sharon fruit ('ʃærən) *n* another name for **persimmon** (sense 2).

sharp (ʃɑːp) *adj* **1** having a keen edge suitable for cutting. **2** having an edge or point. **3** involving a sudden change, esp. in direction: *a sharp bend.* **4** moving, acting, or reacting quickly, etc.: *sharp reflexes.* **5** clearly defined. **6** mentally acute; keen-witted; attentive. **7** sly or artful: *sharp practice.* **8** bitter or harsh: *sharp words.* **9** shrill or penetrat-

ing: *a sharp cry.* **10** having an acrid taste. **11** keen; biting: *a sharp wind.* **12** *Music.* **12a** (*immediately postpositive*) denoting a note that has been raised in pitch by one chromatic semitone: *F sharp.* **12b** (of an instrument, voice, etc.) out of tune by being too high in pitch. Cf. **flat**[1] (sense 20). **13** *Inf.* **13a** stylish. **13b** too smart. **14 at the sharp end.** involved in the most competitive or difficult aspect of any activity. ◆ *adv* **15** in a sharp manner. **16** exactly: *six o'clock sharp.* **17** *Music.* **17a** higher than a standard pitch. **17b** out of tune by being too high in pitch: *she sings sharp.* Cf. **flat**[1] (sense 25). ◆ *n* **18** *Music.* **18a** an accidental that raises the pitch of a note by one chromatic semitone. Usual symbol: ♯ **18b** a note affected by this accidental. Cf. **flat**[1] (sense 31). **19** a thin needle with a sharp point. **20** *Inf.* a sharper. ◆ *vb* **21** *Music.* the usual US and Canad. word for **sharpen.** [OE *scearp*]
▶ '**sharply** *adv* ▶ '**sharpness** *n*

Sharp ★ (ʃɑːp) *n* Cecil (**James**). 1859–1924, British musician, best known for collecting, editing, and publishing English folk songs.

sharpbender ('ʃɑːp,bɛndə) *n Inf.* an organization that has been underperforming its competitors but suddenly becomes more successful, often as a result of new management or changes in its business strategy. [C20: from the sharp upward bend in its sales or profits]

sharpen ('ʃɑːpⁿn) *vb* **1** to make or become sharp or sharper. **2** *Music.* to raise the pitch of (a note), esp. by one semitone.
▶ '**sharpener** *n*

sharper ('ʃɑːpə) *n* a person who cheats or swindles; fraud.

Sharpeville ★ ('ʃɑːpvɪl) *n* a town in E South Africa: scene of riots in 1960, when 69 demonstrators died, in 1984, and in 1985, when 19 died.

sharpish ('ʃɑːpɪʃ) *adj* **1** rather sharp. ◆ *adv* **2** *Inf.* quickly; fairly sharply: *quick sharpish.*

sharp-set *adj* **1** set to give an acute cutting angle. **2** keenly hungry. **3** keen or eager.

sharpshooter ('ʃɑːp,ʃuːtə) *n* an expert marksman.
▶ '**sharp,shooting** *n*

sharp-tongued *adj* bitter or critical in speech; sarcastic.

sharp-witted *adj* having or showing a keen intelligence; perceptive.
▶ ,**sharp-'wittedly** *adv* ▶ ,**sharp-'wittedness** *n*

Shasta daisy ('ʃæstə) *n* a plant widely cultivated for its large white daisy-like flowers.

shastra ('ʃɑːstrə), **shaster** ('ʃɑːstə), *or* **sastra** ('ʃɑːstrə) *n* any of the sacred writings of Hinduism. [C17: from Sansk. *śāstra*, from *śās* to teach]

shat (ʃæt) *vb Taboo.* a past tense and past participle of **shit.**

Shatt-al-Arab ★ ('ʃætæl'ærəb) *n* a river in SE Iraq, formed by the confluence of the Tigris and Euphrates Rivers: flows southeast as part of the border between Iraq and Iran to the Persian Gulf. Length: 193 km (120 miles).

shatter ('ʃætə) *vb* **1** to break or be broken into many small pieces. **2** (*tr*) to impair or destroy: *his nerves were shattered by the torture.* **3** (*tr*) to dumbfound or thoroughly upset: *she was shattered by the news.* **4** (*tr*) *Inf.* to cause to be tired out or exhausted. [C12: ? obscurely rel. to SCATTER]
▶ '**shattered** *adj* ▶ '**shattering** *adj* ▶ '**shatteringly** *adv*

shatterproof ('ʃætə,pruːf) *adj* designed to resist shattering.

shave (ʃeɪv) *vb* **shaves, shaving, shaved; shaved** *or* **shaven.** (*mainly tr*) **1** (*also intr*) to remove (the beard, hair, etc.) from (the face, head, or body) by scraping the skin with a razor. **2** to cut or trim very closely. **3** to reduce to shavings. **4** to remove thin slices from (wood, etc.) with a sharp cutting tool. **5** to touch or graze in passing. **6** *Inf.* to reduce (a price) by a slight amount. ◆ *n* **7** the act or an instance of shaving. **8** any tool for scraping. **9** a thin slice or shaving. [OE *sceafan*]
▶ '**shavable** *or* '**shaveable** *adj*

shaveling ('ʃeɪvlɪŋ) *n Arch.* **1** *Derog.* a priest or clergyman with a shaven head. **2** a young fellow; youth.

shaven ('ʃeɪvⁿn) *adj* **a** closely shaved or tonsured. **b** (*in combination*): *clean-shaven.*

shaver ('ʃeɪvə) *n* **1** a person or thing that shaves. **2** Also

★ people and places

called: **electric razor**, **electric shaver**. an electrically powered implement for shaving, having rotating blades behind a fine metal comb. **3** *Inf.* a youngster, esp. a young boy.

Shavian ('ʃeɪvɪən) *adj* **1** of or like George Bernard Shaw (1856–1950), Irish dramatist, his works, ideas, etc. ◆ *n* **2** an admirer of Shaw or his works.

shaving ('ʃeɪvɪŋ) *n* **1** a thin paring or slice, esp. of wood, that has been shaved from something. ◆ *modifier.* **2** used when shaving the face, etc.: *shaving cream*.

Shavuot *or* **Shabuoth** (ʃəˈvuːəs, -əus; *Hebrew* ʃavuːˈɔt) *n* the Hebrew name for **Pentecost** (sense 2). [from Heb. *shābhū'ōth*, pl of *shābhūā'* week]

Shaw ★ (ʃɔː) *n* **1** George Bernard, often known as *GBS*. 1856–1950, Irish dramatist and critic, in England from 1876. His plays include *Arms and the Man* (1894), *Man and Superman* (1903), *Pygmalion* (1913), *Back to Methuselah* (1921), and *St Joan* (1923): Nobel prize for literature 1925. **2** **Richard Norman**. 1831–1912, British architect. **3** **Thomas Edward**. the name assumed by (T. E.) **Lawrence** after 1927.

shawl (ʃɔːl) *n* a piece of fabric or knitted or crocheted material worn around the shoulders by women or wrapped around a baby. [C17: from Persian *shāl*]

shawm (ʃɔːm) *n Music.* a medieval form of the oboe with a conical bore and flaring bell. [C14 *shalmye*, from OF *chalemie*, ult. from L *calamus* a reed, from Gk *kalamos*]

shay (ʃeɪ) *n* a dialect word for **chaise**. [C18: back formation from CHAISE, mistaken for pl]

Shcheglovsk ★ (*Russian* ʃtʃɪgˈlɔfsk) *n* the former name (until 1932) of **Kemerovo**.

Shcherbakov ★ (*Russian* ʃtʃɪrbaˈkɔf) *n* the former name (from the Revolution until 1957) of **Rybinsk**.

she (ʃiː) *pron (subjective)* **1** refers to a female person or animal: *she is a doctor*. **2** refers to things personified as feminine, such as cars, ships, and nations. **3** *Austral. & NZ.* a pronoun often used instead of *it*, as in **she'll be right** (it will be all right). ◆ *n* **4a** a female person or animal. **4b** *(in combination)*: *she-cat*. [OE *sīe*, accusative of *sēo*, fem. demonstrative pron]

shea (ʃɪə) *n* **1** a tropical African tree with oily seeds. **2 shea butter.** the white butter-like fat obtained from the seeds of this plant and used as food, etc. [C18: from W African *si*]

sheading ('ʃiːdɪŋ) *n* any of the six subdivisions of the Isle of Man. [var. of *shedding*]

sheaf (ʃiːf) *n, pl* **sheaves. 1** a bundle of reaped but unthreshed corn tied with one or two bonds. **2** a bundle of objects tied together. **3** the arrows contained in a quiver. ◆ *vb* **4** (*tr*) to bind or tie into a sheaf. [OE *sceaf*]

shear (ʃɪə) *vb* **shears, shearing, sheared** *or (arch., Austral., & NZ)* sometimes **shore; sheared** *or* **shorn. 1** (*tr*) to remove (the fleece or hair) of (sheep, etc.) by cutting or clipping. **2** to cut or cut through (something) with shears or a sharp instrument. **3** *Engineering.* to cause (a part, member, etc.) to deform or fracture or (of a part, etc.) to deform or fracture as a result of excess torsion. **4** (*tr*; often foll. by *of*) to strip or divest: *to shear someone of his power*. **5** (when *intr*, foll. by *through*) to move through (something) by or as if by cutting. ◆ *n* **6** the act, process, or an instance of shearing. **7** a shearing of a sheep or flock of sheep: *a sheep of two shears*. **8** a form of deformation or fracture in which parallel planes in a body slide over one another. **9** *Physics.* the deformation of a body, part, etc., expressed as the lateral displacement between two points in parallel planes divided by the distance between the planes. **10** either one of the blades of a pair of shears, scissors, etc. ◆ See also **shears**. [OE *sceran*]
▸ **'shearer** *n*

shearling ('ʃɪəlɪŋ) *n* **1** a young sheep after its first shearing. **2** the skin of such an animal.

shear pin *n* an easily replaceable pin in a machine designed to break and stop the machine if the stress becomes too great.

shears (ʃɪəz) *pl n* **1a** large scissors, as for cutting cloth, jointing poultry, etc. **1b** a large scissor-like and usually hand-held cutting tool with flat blades, as for cutting hedges. **2** any of various analogous cutting implements.

shearwater ('ʃɪə,wɔːtə) *n* any of several oceanic birds specialized for an aerial or aquatic existence.

sheatfish ('ʃiːt,fɪʃ) *n, pl* **sheatfish** *or* **sheatfishes.** another name for **European catfish** (see **silurid** (sense 1)). [C16: var. of *sheathfish*; ? infl. by G *Schaid* sheatfish]

sheath (ʃiːθ) *n, pl* **sheaths** (ʃiːðz). **1** a case or covering for the blade of a knife, sword, etc. **2** any similar close-fitting case. **3** *Biol.* an enclosing or protective structure. **4** the protective covering on an electric cable. **5** a figure-hugging dress with a narrow tapering skirt. **6** another name for **condom**. [OE *scēath*]

sheathe (ʃiːð) *vb* **sheathes, sheathing, sheathed.** (*tr*) **1** to insert (a knife, sword, etc.) into a sheath. **2** (esp. of cats) to retract (the claws). **3** to surface with or encase in a sheath or sheathing.

sheathing ('ʃiːðɪŋ) *n* **1** any material used as an outer layer, as on a ship's hull. **2** boarding, etc., used to cover a timber frame.

sheath knife *n* a knife carried in or protected by a sheath.

sheave[1] (ʃiːv) *vb* **sheaves, sheaving, sheaved.** (*tr*) to gather or bind into sheaves.

sheave[2] (ʃiːv) *n* a wheel with a grooved rim, esp. one used as a pulley. [C14: of Gmc origin]

sheaves (ʃiːvz) *n* the plural of **sheaf**.

Sheba[1] ★ ('ʃiːbə) *n* **1** Also called: **Saba**. the ancient kingdom of the Sabeans: a rich trading nation dealing in gold, spices, and precious stones (I Kings 10). **2** the region inhabited by this nation, located in the SW corner of the Arabian peninsula: modern Yemen.

Sheba[2] ★ ('ʃiːbə) *n* **Queen of.** *Old Testament.* a queen of the Sabeans, who visited Solomon (I Kings 10:1–13).

shebang (ʃɪˈbæŋ) *n Sl., chiefly US & Canad.* a situation or affair (esp. in **the whole shebang**). [C19: from ?]

shebeen *or* **shebean** (ʃəˈbiːn) *n* **1** *Irish, Scot., & S. African.* a place where alcoholic drink is sold illegally. **2** (in Ireland) alcohol, esp. home-distilled whiskey, sold without a licence. **3** (in South Africa) a place where Black African men engage in social drinking. [C18: from Irish Gaelic *síbín* beer of poor quality]

shebeen king *or (fem)* **shebeen queen** *n* (in South Africa) the proprietor of a shebeen.

Shechem ★ ('ʃɛkəm, -ɛm) *n* the ancient name of **Nablus**.

shed[1] (ʃɛd) *n* **1** a small building or lean-to of light construction, used for storage, shelter, etc. **2** a large roofed structure, esp. one with open sides, used for storage, repairing locomotives, etc. **3** *Austral. & NZ.* the building in which sheep are shorn. [OE *sced*; prob. var. of *scead* shelter]

shed[2] (ʃɛd) *vb* **sheds, shedding, shed.** (*mainly tr*) **1** to pour forth or cause to pour forth: *to shed tears*. **2 shed light on** *or* **upon.** to clarify (a problem, etc.). **3** to cast off or lose: *the snake sheds its skin*. **4** (of a lorry) to drop (its load) on the road by accident. **5** to repel: *this coat sheds water*. **6** to separate or divide a group of sheep: *a good dog can shed his sheep in minutes*. **7** *Dialect.* to make a parting in (the hair). ◆ *n* **8** short for **watershed**. **9** the action of separating or dividing a group of sheep: *the old dog was better at the shed than the young one*. [OE *sceadan*]
▸ **'shedable** *or* **'sheddable** *adj*

she'd (ʃiːd) *contraction of* she had *or* she would.

shedder[1] ('ʃɛdə) *n* **1** a person or thing that sheds. **2** an animal, such as a llama, snake, or lobster, that moults.

shedder[2] ('ʃɛdə) *n NZ.* a person who milks cows in a cow shed.

shed hand *n Chiefly Austral.* an unskilled worker in a sheepshearing shed.

shed out *vb* (*tr, adv*) *NZ.* to separate off (sheep that have lambed) and move them to better pasture.

sheen (ʃiːn) *n* **1** a gleaming or glistening brightness; lustre. **2** *Poetic.* splendid clothing. ◆ *adj* **3** *Rare.* beautiful. [OE *sciene*]
▸ **'sheeny** *adj*

sheep (ʃiːp) *n, pl* **sheep. 1** any of a genus of ruminant mammals having transversely ribbed horns and a narrow face. **2 Barbary sheep.** another name for **aoudad. 3** a

meek or timid person. **4 separate the sheep from the goats.** to pick out the members of a group who are superior in some respects. [OE *sceap*]
▶ 'sheep,like *adj*

sheepcote ('ʃiːp,kəʊt) *n Chiefly Brit.* another word for **sheepfold.**

sheep-dip *n* **1** any of several liquid disinfectants and insecticides in which sheep are immersed. **2** a deep trough containing such a liquid.

sheepdog ('ʃiːp,dɒg) *n* **1** a dog used for herding sheep. **2** any of various breeds of dog reared originally for herding sheep. See **Old English sheepdog, Shetland sheepdog.**

sheepdog trial *n* (*often pl*) a competition in which sheepdogs are tested in their tasks.

sheepfold ('ʃiːp,fəʊld) *n* a pen or enclosure for sheep.

sheepish ('ʃiːpɪʃ) *adj* **1** abashed or embarrassed, esp. through looking foolish. **2** resembling a sheep in timidity.
▶ 'sheepishly *adv* ▶ 'sheepishness *n*

sheepo ('ʃiːpəʊ) *n, pl* **sheepos.** *NZ.* a person employed to bring sheep to the catching pen in a shearing shed.

sheep's eyes *pl n Old-fashioned.* amorous or inviting glances.

sheepshank ('ʃiːp,ʃæŋk) *n* a knot made in a rope to shorten it temporarily.

sheepskin ('ʃiːp,skɪn) *n* **a** the skin of a sheep, esp. when used for clothing, etc. **b** (*as modifier*): *a sheepskin coat.*

sheepwalk ('ʃiːp,wɔːk) *n Chiefly Brit.* a tract of land for grazing sheep.

sheer[1] (ʃɪə) *adj* **1** perpendicular; very steep: *a sheer cliff.* **2** (of textiles) so fine as to be transparent. **3** (*prenominal*) absolute: *sheer folly.* **4** *Obs.* bright. ◆ *adv* **5** steeply. **6** completely or absolutely. [OE *scīr*]
▶ 'sheerly *adv* ▶ 'sheerness *n*

sheer[2] (ʃɪə) *vb* (foll. by *off* or *away* (*from*)). **1** to deviate or cause to deviate from a course. **2** (*intr*) to avoid an unpleasant person, thing, topic, etc. ◆ *n* **3** *Naut.* the position of a vessel relative to its mooring. [C17: ? var. of SHEAR]

sheerlegs *or* **shearlegs** ('ʃɪə,legz) *n* (*functioning as sing*) a device for lifting weights consisting of two spars lashed together at the upper ends from which a lifting tackle is suspended. Also called: **shears.** [C19: var. of *shear legs*]

Sheerness ★ (,ʃɪə'nes) *n* a port and resort in SE England, in N Kent at the junction of the Medway estuary and the Thames: administratively part of Queenborough in Sheppey since 1968.

sheet[1] (ʃiːt) *n* **1** a large rectangular piece of cloth, generally one of a pair used as inner bedclothes. **2a** a thin piece of a substance such as paper or glass, usually rectangular in form. **2b** (*as modifier*): *sheet iron.* **3** a broad continuous surface: *a sheet of water.* **4** a newspaper, esp. a tabloid. **5** a piece of printed paper to be folded into a section for a book. ◆ *vb* **6** (*tr*) to provide with, cover, or wrap in a sheet. [OE *sciete*]

sheet[2] (ʃiːt) *n Naut.* a line or rope for controlling the position of a sail relative to the wind. [OE *scēata* corner of a sail]

sheet anchor *n* **1** *Naut.* a large strong anchor for use in emergency. **2** a person or thing to be relied on in an emergency. [C17: from earlier *shute anker*, from *shoot* (obs.) the sheet of a sail]

sheet bend *n* a knot used esp. for joining ropes of different sizes.

sheeting ('ʃiːtɪŋ) *n* fabric from which sheets are made.

sheet lightning *n* lightning that appears as a broad sheet, caused by the reflection of more distant lightning.

sheet metal *n* metal in the form of a sheet, the thickness being intermediate between that of plate and that of foil.

sheet music *n* **1** the printed or written copy of a short composition or piece. **2** music in its written or printed form.

Sheffield ★ ('ʃefiːld) *n* **1** a city in N England, in South Yorkshire on the River Don: important centre of steel manufacture and of the cutlery industry; university

(1905). Pop.: 431 607 (1991). **2** a unitary authority in N England, in South Yorkshire. Pop.: 530 100 (1994 est.). Area: 368 sq. km (142 sq. miles).

sheikh *or* **sheik** (ʃeɪk) *n* (in Muslim countries) **a** the head of an Arab tribe, village, etc. **b** a religious leader. [C16: from Ar. *shaykh* old man]
▶ 'sheikhdom *or* 'sheikdom *n*

sheila ('ʃiːlə) *n Austral. & NZ old-fashioned.* an informal word for **girl** or **woman.** [C19: from the girl's name *Sheila*]

shekel ('ʃekəl) *n* **1** the standard monetary unit of modern Israel, divided into 100 agorot. **2** any of several former coins and units of weight of the Near East. **3** (*often pl*) *Inf.* any coin or money. [C16: from Heb. *sheqel*]

Shelburne ★ ('ʃelbɜːn) *n* **2nd Earl of,** title of *William Petty Fitzmaurice,* also called (from 1784) *1st Marquess of Lansdowne.* 1737–1805, British statesman; prime minister (1782–83).

shelduck ('ʃel,dʌk) *or* (*masc*) **sheldrake** ('ʃel,dreɪk) *n, pl* **shelducks, shelduck** *or* **sheldrakes, sheldrake.** any of various large usually brightly coloured gooselike ducks of the Old World. [C14: *shel,* prob. from dialect *sheld* pied]

shelf (ʃelf) *n, pl* **shelves. 1** a thin flat plank of wood, metal, etc., fixed horizontally against a wall, etc., for the purpose of supporting objects. **2** something resembling this in shape or function. **3** the objects placed on a shelf: *a shelf of books.* **4** a projecting layer of ice, rock, etc., on land or in the sea. **5** See **off the shelf. 6** **on the shelf.** put aside or abandoned; used esp. of unmarried women considered to be past the age of marriage. [OE *scylfe* ship's deck]
▶ 'shelf,like *adj*

shelf life *n* the length of time a packaged food, etc., will last without deteriorating.

shell (ʃel) *n* **1** the protective outer layer of an egg, esp. a bird's egg. **2** the hard outer covering of many molluscs. **3** any other hard outer layer, such as the exoskeleton of many arthropods. **4** the hard outer layer of some fruits, esp. of nuts. **5** any hard outer case. **6** a hollow artillery projectile filled with explosive primed to explode either during flight or on impact. **7** a small-arms cartridge. **8** a pyrotechnic cartridge designed to explode in the air. **9** *Rowing.* a very light narrow racing boat. **10** the external structure of a building, esp. one that is unfinished. **11** *Physics.* **11a** a class of electron orbits in an atom in which the electrons have the same principal quantum number and little difference in their energy levels. **11b** an analogous energy state of nucleons in certain theories (**shell models**) of the structure of the atomic nucleus. **12 come** (*or* **bring**) **out of one's shell.** to become (or help to become) less shy and reserved. ◆ *vb* **13** to divest or be divested of a shell, husk, etc. **14** to separate or be separated from an ear, husk, etc. **15** (*tr*) to bombard with artillery shells. ◆ See also **shell out.** [OE *sciell*]
▶ 'shell-less *adj* ▶ 'shell-,like *adj* ▶ 'shelly *adj*

she'll (ʃiːl; *unstressed* ʃɪl) *contraction of* she will *or* she shall.

shellac (ʃə'læk, 'ʃelæk) *n* **1** a yellowish resin secreted by the lac insect, esp. a commercial preparation of this used in varnishes, polishes, etc. **2** Also called: **shellac varnish.** a varnish made by dissolving shellac in ethanol or a similar solvent. ◆ *vb* **shellacs, shellacking, shellacked.** (*tr*) **3** to coat (an article) with a shellac varnish. [C18: SHELL + LAC[1], translation of F *laque en écailles,* lit.: lac in scales, that is, in thin plates]

shellback ('ʃel,bæk) *n* an experienced or old sailor.

shell company *n Business.* **1** a near-defunct company, esp. one with a stock-exchange listing, used as a vehicle for a thriving company. **2** a company that has ceased to trade but retains its registration and is sold for a small sum to enable its new owners to avoid the cost and trouble of registering a new company.

Shelley ★ ('ʃeli) *n* **1** *Mary Wollstonecraft* **(Godwin)** ('wʊl-stən,krɑːft). 1797–1851, British writer; author of *Frankenstein* (1818); the daughter of William Godwin and Mary Wollstonecraft, she eloped with Percy Bysshe Shelley. **2** *Percy Bysshe* (bɪʃ). 1792–1822, British Romantic poet. His works include *Queen Mab* (1813) and the verse drama *Prometheus Unbound* (1820): shorter lyrics include the

★ people and places

odes *To the West Wind* and *To a Skylark* (both 1820). He was drowned off Leghorn.

shellfire ('ʃɛl,faɪə) *n* the firing of artillery shells.

shellfish ('ʃɛl,fɪʃ) *n, pl* **shellfish** or **shellfishes**. any aquatic invertebrate having a shell or shell-like carapace, esp. such an animal used as human food. Examples are crustaceans such as crabs and lobsters and molluscs such as oysters.

shell out *vb* (*adv*) *Inf.* to pay out or hand over (money).

shell program *n Computing.* a basic low-cost computer program that provides a framework within which the user can develop the program to suit his personal requirements.

shellproof ('ʃɛl,pruːf) *adj* designed, intended, or able to resist shellfire.

shell shock *n* loss of sight, etc., resulting from psychological strain during prolonged engagement in warfare. ▶ 'shell-,shocked *adj*

shell suit *n* a lightweight tracksuit consisting of an inner cotton layer covered by a waterproof nylon layer.

Shelta ('ʃɛltə) *n* a secret language used by some itinerant tinkers in Ireland and parts of Britain, based on Gaelic. [C19: from earlier *sheldrū*, ? an arbitrary alteration of OIrish *bēlre* speech]

shelter ('ʃɛltə) *n* 1 something that provides cover or protection, as from weather or danger. 2 the protection afforded by such a cover. 3 the state of being sheltered. ◆ *vb* 4 (*tr*) to provide with or protect by a shelter. 5 (*intr*) to take cover, as from rain. 6 (*tr*) to act as a shelter for. [C16: from ?] ▶ 'shelterer *n*

sheltered ('ʃɛltəd) *adj* 1 protected from wind or weather. 2 protected from outside influences: *a sheltered upbringing.* 3 specially designed to provide a safe environment for the elderly, handicapped, or disabled: *sheltered housing.*

sheltie or **shelty** ('ʃɛltɪ) *n, pl* **shelties**. another name for **Shetland pony** or **Shetland sheepdog**. [C17: prob. from Orkney dialect *sjalti*, from ON *Hjalti* Shetlander, from *Hjaltland* Shetland]

shelve[1] (ʃɛlv) *vb* **shelves, shelving, shelved**. (*tr*) 1 to place on a shelf. 2 to provide with shelves. 3 to put aside or postpone from consideration. 4 to dismiss or cause to retire. [C16: from *shelves*, pl of SHELF] ▶ 'shelver *n*

shelve[2] (ʃɛlv) *vb* **shelves, shelving, shelved**. (*intr*) to slope away gradually. [C16: from ?]

shelves (ʃɛlvz) *n* the plural of **shelf**.

shelving ('ʃɛlvɪŋ) *n* 1 material for making shelves. 2 a set of shelves; shelves collectively.

Shem ★ (ʃɛm) *n Old Testament.* the eldest of Noah's three sons (Genesis 10:21). Douay spelling: **Sem** (sɛm).

shemozzle (ʃɪ'mɒz²l) *n Inf.* a noisy confusion or dispute; uproar. [C19: ?from Yiddish *shlimazl* misfortune]

shenanigan (ʃɪ'nænɪgən) *n Inf.* 1 (*usually pl*) roguishness; mischief. 2 an act of treachery; deception. [C19: from ?]

Shensi ★ (ʃɛn'siː) *n* a variant transliteration of the Chinese name for **Shaanxi**.

Shenyang ★ ('ʃɛn'jæŋ) *n* a walled city in NE China in S Manchuria, capital of Liaoning province: capital of the Manchu dynasty from 1644–1912; seized by the Japanese in 1931. Pop.: 4 540 000 (1991 est.). Former name: **Mukden**.

she-oak *n* any of various Australian trees of the genus *Casuarina*. See **casuarina**. [C18: *she* (in the sense: inferior) + OAK]

Sheol ('ʃiːəʊl, -ɒl) *n Bible.* 1 the abode of the dead. 2 (*often not cap.*) hell. [C16: from Heb. *shĕ'ōl*]

Shepard ★ ('ʃɛpəd) *n* 1 **Alan Bartlett, Jr.** 1923–98, US naval officer; first US astronaut in space (1961). 2 **Sam**, original name *Samuel Shepard Rogers*. born 1943, US dramatist, film actor, and director.

shepherd ('ʃɛpəd) *n* 1 a person employed to tend sheep. Fem. equivalent: **shepherdess**. 2 a person, such as a clergyman, who watches over a group of people. ◆ *vb* (*tr*) 3 to

guide or watch over in the manner of a shepherd. 4 *Australian Rules, rugby, etc.* to prevent opponents from tackling (a member of one's own team) by blocking their path: illegal in rugby.

shepherd dog *n* another term for **sheepdog** (sense 1).

shepherd's pie *n Chiefly Brit.* a baked dish of minced meat covered with mashed potato.

shepherd's-purse *n* a plant having small white flowers and flattened triangular seed pods.

shepherd's weatherglass *n Brit.* another name for the **scarlet pimpernel**.

Sheppey ★ ('ʃɛpɪ) *n* **Isle of.** an island in SE England, off the N coast of Kent in the Thames estuary: separated from the mainland by **The Swale**, a narrow channel. Chief towns: Sheerness, Minster. Pop.: 32 000 (latest est.). Area: 80 sq. km (30 sq. miles).

Sheraton[1] ★ ('ʃɛrətən) *n* **Thomas**. 1751–1806, British furniture maker, author of the influential *Cabinet-Maker and Upholsterer's Drawing Book* (1791).

Sheraton[2] ('ʃɛrətən) *adj* denoting furniture made by or in the style of Thomas Sheraton, characterized by lightness, elegance, and the extensive use of inlay.

sherbet ('ʃɜːbət) *n* 1 a fruit-flavoured slightly effervescent powder, eaten as a sweet or used to make a drink. 2 another word (esp. US and Canad.) for **sorbet** (sense 1). 3 *Austral. sl.* beer. 4 a cooling Oriental drink of sweetened fruit juice. [C17: from Turkish, from Persian, from Ar. *sharbah* drink, from *shariba* to drink]

Sherborne ★ ('ʃɜːbɔːn) *n* a town in S England in Dorset: noted for its medieval abbey, ruined medieval castle, and **Sherborne Castle**, a mansion built by Sir Walter Raleigh in 1594. Pop.: 7606 (1991).

Sherbrooke ★ ('ʃɜː,brʊk) *n* a city in E Canada, in S Quebec: industrial and commercial centre. Pop.: 76 429 (1991).

sherd (ʃɜːd) *n* a variant of **shard**.

Sheridan ★ ('ʃɛrɪdən) *n* 1 **Philip Henry**. 1831–88, American Union cavalry commander in the Civil War. He forced Lee's surrender to Grant (1865). 2 **Richard Brinsley** ('brɪnzlɪ). 1751–1816, Irish dramatist and politician, noted for his comedies *The Rivals* (1775), *School for Scandal* (1777), and *The Critic* (1779).

sherif or **shereef** (ʃɛ'riːf) or **sharif** *n Islam.* 1 a descendant of Mohammed through his daughter Fatima. 2 an honorific title accorded to any Muslim ruler. [C16: from Ar. *sharīf* noble]

sheriff ('ʃɛrɪf) *n* 1 (in the US) the chief elected law-enforcement officer in a county. 2 (in Canada) a municipal official who enforces court orders, escorts convicted criminals to prison, etc. 3 (in England and Wales) the chief executive officer of the Crown in a county, having chiefly ceremonial duties. 4 (in Scotland) a judge in any of the sheriff courts. 5 (in New Zealand) an officer of the High Court. [OE *scīrgerēfa*, from *scīr* SHIRE + *gerēfa* REEVE[1]] ▶ 'sheriffdom *n*

sheriff court *n* (in Scotland) a court having jurisdiction to try all but the most serious crimes and to deal with most civil actions.

Sherman ★ ('ʃɜːmən) *n* **William Tecumseh** (tɪ'kʌmsə). 1820–91, American Union commander during the Civil War. He led the victorious march through Georgia (1864).

Sherpa ('ʃɜːpə) *n, pl* **Sherpas** or **Sherpa**. a member of a people of Mongolian origin living on the southern slopes of the Himalayas in Nepal, noted as mountaineers.

Sherrington ★ ('ʃɛrɪŋtən) *n* **Sir Charles Scott**. 1857–1952, British physiologist, noted for his work on reflex action: shared the Nobel prize for physiology or medicine 1932.

sherry ('ʃɛrɪ) *n, pl* **sherries**. a fortified wine, originally only from the Jerez region of southern Spain. [C16: from earlier *sherris* (assumed to be pl), from Sp. *Xeres*, now *Jerez*]

's Hertogenbosch ★ (*Dutch* shɛrtoːxən'bɒs) *n* a city in the S Netherlands, capital of North Brabant province: birthplace of Hieronymus Bosch. Pop.: 95 448 (1994). Also called: **Den Bosch**. French name: **Bois-le-Duc**.

sherwani (ʃɛə'wɑːnɪ) *n* a long coat closed up to the neck, worn by men in India. [Hindi]

Sherwood ★ ('ʃɜːˌwʊd) n Robert Emmet. 1896–1955, US dramatist. His plays include *The Petrified Forest* (1935) and *There Shall be no Night* (1940).

Sherwood Forest ★ n an ancient forest in central England, in Nottinghamshire: formerly a royal hunting ground and much more extensive; famous as the home of Robin Hood.

she's (ʃiːz) *contraction of* she is *or* she has.

Shetland *or* **Shetland Islands** ★ ('ʃetlənd) pl n a group of about 100 islands (fewer than 20 inhabited), off the N coast of Scotland, which constitute an island authority of Scotland: a Norse dependency from the 8th century until 1472; noted for the breeding of Shetland ponies, knitwear manufacturing, and fishing; oil-related industries. Administrative centre: Lerwick. Pop.: 23 020 (1996 est.). Area: 1426 sq. km (550 sq. miles). Official name (until 1974): **Zetland**.

Shetland pony n a very small sturdy breed of pony with a long shaggy mane and tail. Also called: **sheltie**.

Shetland sheepdog n a small dog similar in appearance to a collie. Also called: **sheltie**.

Shevardnadze ★ (ˌʃevəd'nɑːdze) n **Eduard (Amvrosiyevich)**. born 1928, Georgian statesman; Soviet minister of foreign affairs (1985–91 and from 1991), who played an important part in arms negotiations with the US; president of Georgia from 1992.

shew (ʃəʊ) vb shews, shewing, shewed; shewn *or* shewed. an archaic spelling of **show**.

shewbread *or* **showbread** ('ʃəʊˌbred) n Bible. the loaves of bread placed every Sabbath on the table beside the altar of incense in the tabernacle or temple of ancient Israel.

SHF *or* **shf** Radio. abbrev. for superhigh frequency.

Shiah *or* **Shia** ('ʃiːə) n 1 one of the two main branches of Islam (the other being the Sunni), now mainly in Iran, which regards Mohammed's cousin Ali and his successors as the true imams. ◆ adj 2 designating or characteristic of this sect or its beliefs and practices. [C17: from Ar. *shī'ah* sect, from *shā'a* to follow]

shiatsu (ʃiː'ætsuː) n a type of massage in which pressure is applied to the same points of the body as in acupuncture. Also called: **acupressure**. [Japanese from Chinese *chǐ* finger + *yā* pressure]

shibboleth ('ʃɪbəˌleθ) n 1 a slogan or catch phrase, usually considered outworn, characteristic of a particular party or sect. 2 a custom, phrase, or use of language that acts as a test of belonging to, or as a stumbling block to joining a particular social class, profession, etc. [C14: from Heb., lit.: ear of grain; the word is used in the Old Testament by the Gileadites as a test word for the Ephraimites, who could not pronounce the sound *sh*]

shickered ('ʃɪkəd) adj Austral. & NZ sl. drunk; intoxicated. [via Yiddish from Heb.]

shied (ʃaɪd) vb the past tense and past participle of **shy**¹ and **shy**².

shield (ʃiːld) n 1 any protection used to intercept blows, missiles, etc., such as a tough piece of armour carried on the arm. 2 any similar protective device. 3 Heraldry. a pointed stylized shield used for displaying armorial bearings. 4 anything that resembles a shield in shape, such as a prize in a sports competition. 5 Physics. a structure of concrete, lead, etc., placed around a nuclear reactor. 6 a broad stable plateau of ancient Precambrian rocks forming the rigid nucleus of a particular continent. 7 the shield. NZ. the Bledisloe Shield, a trophy competed for by provincial rugby teams. ◆ vb 8 (tr) to protect, hide, or conceal (something) from danger or harm. [OE *scield*]
▸ 'shield,like adj

Shield (ʃiːld) n the. Canad. another term for the **Canadian Shield**.

shield match n 1 Austral. a cricket match for the Sheffield Shield. 2 NZ. a rugby match for the Ranfurly Shield.

shield volcano n a broad volcano built up from the repeated nonexplosive eruption of basalt to form a low dome or shield, usually having a large caldera at the summit.

shieling ('ʃiːlɪŋ) *or* **shiel** (ʃiːl) n Chiefly Scot. 1 a temporary shelter used by people tending cattle on high or remote ground. 2 pasture land for the grazing of cattle in summer. [C16: from earlier *shiel*, from ME *shale* hut, from ?]

shier ('ʃaɪə) adj a comparative of **shy**¹.

shiest ('ʃaɪɪst) adj a superlative of **shy**¹.

shift (ʃɪft) vb 1 to move or cause to move from one place or position to another. 2 (tr) to change for another or others. 3 to change (gear) in a motor vehicle. 4 (intr) (of a sound or set of sounds) to alter in a systematic way. 5 (intr) to provide for one's needs (esp. in **shift for oneself**). 6 to remove or be removed, esp. with difficulty: *no detergent can shift these stains*. 7 (intr) Sl. to move quickly. 8 (tr) Computing. to move (bits held in a store location) to the left or right. ◆ n 9 the act or an instance of shifting. 10 a group of workers who work for a specific period. 11 the period of time worked by such a group. 12 an expedient, contrivance, or artifice. 13 an underskirt or dress with little shaping. [OE *sciftan*]
▸ 'shifter n

shiftless ('ʃɪftlɪs) adj lacking in ambition or initiative.
▸ 'shiftlessness n

shifty ('ʃɪftɪ) adj shiftier, shiftiest. 1 given to evasions. 2 furtive in character or appearance.
▸ 'shiftily adv ▸ 'shiftiness n

shigella (ʃɪ'gelə) n any of a genus of rod-shaped bacteria, some species of which cause dysentery. [C20: after K. *Shiga* (1870–1957), Japanese bacteriologist, who discovered them]

Shiite ('ʃiːaɪt) *or* **Shiah** Islam. ◆ n 1 an adherent of Shiah. ◆ adj 2 of or relating to Shiah.
▸ **Shiism** ('ʃiːɪzəm) n ▸ **Shiitic** (ʃiː'ɪtɪk) adj

Shijiazhuang ('ʃiːdʒɑː'dʒwæŋ), **Shihchiachuang**, *or* **Shihkiachwang** ★ (ˌʃiːtʃjɑː'tʃwæŋ) n a city in NE China, capital of Hebei province: textile manufacturing. Pop.: 1 320 000 (1991 est.).

Shikoku ★ ('ʃiːkəʊˌkuː) n the smallest of the four main islands of Japan, separated from Honshu by the Inland Sea: mostly forested and mountainous. Pop.: 4 183 000 (1995). Area: 17 759 sq. km (6857 sq. miles).

shillelagh *or* **shillala** (ʃə'leɪlə, -lɪ) n (in Ireland) a stout club or cudgel. [C18: from Irish Gaelic *sail* cudgel + *éille* leash, thong]

shilling ('ʃɪlɪŋ) n 1 a former British or Australian silver or cupronickel coin worth one twentieth of a pound, not minted in Britain since 1970. Abbrevs.: **s., sh.** 2 the standard monetary unit of Kenya, Somalia, Tanzania, and Uganda. [OE *scilling*]

Shillong ★ (ʃɪ'lɒŋ) n a city in NE India, capital of Meghalaya: situated on the **Shillong Plateau** at an altitude of 1520 m (4987 ft); destroyed by earthquake in 1897 and rebuilt. Pop.: 131 719 (1991).

shillyshally ('ʃɪlɪˌʃælɪ) Inf. ◆ vb shillyshallies, shillyshallying, shillyshallied. 1 (intr) to be indecisive, esp. over unimportant matters. ◆ adv 2 in an indecisive manner. ◆ adj 3 indecisive or hesitant. ◆ n, pl shillyshallies. 4 vacillation. [C18: from *shill I shall I*, by reduplication of *shall I*]
▸ 'shilly,shallier n

Shiloh ★ ('ʃaɪləʊ) n a town in central ancient Palestine, in Canaan on the E slope of Mount Ephraim: keeping place of the tabernacle and the ark; destroyed by the Philistines.

shily ('ʃaɪlɪ) adv a less common spelling of **shyly**. See **shy**¹.

shim (ʃɪm) n 1 a thin washer or strip often used with a number of similar washers or strips to adjust a clearance for gears, etc. ◆ vb shims, shimming, shimmed. 2 (tr) to modify clearance on (a gear, etc.) by use of shims. [C18: from ?]

shimmer ('ʃɪmə) vb 1 (intr) to shine with a glistening or tremulous light. ◆ n 2 a faint, glistening, or tremulous light. [OE *scimerian*]
▸ 'shimmering *or* 'shimmery adj

shimmy ('ʃɪmɪ) n, pl shimmies. 1 an American ragtime dance with much shaking of the hips and shoulders. 2 abnormal wobbling motion in a motor vehicle, esp. in the front wheels or steering. ◆ vb shimmies, shimmying

shimmied. (*intr*) **3** to dance the shimmy. **4** to vibrate or wobble. [C19: changed from CHEMISE, mistaken for pl]

Shimonoseki ★ (ˌʃɪmənəʊˈsɛkɪ) *n* a port in SW Japan, on SW Honshu: scene of the peace treaty (1895) ending the Sino-Japanese War; a heavy industrial centre. Pop.: 259 791 (1995).

shin (ʃɪn) *n* **1** the front part of the lower leg. **2** the front edge of the tibia. **3** *Chiefly Brit.* a cut of beef, the lower foreleg. ♦ *vb* **shins, shinning, shinned. 4** (when *intr*, often foll. by *up*) to climb (a pole, tree, etc.) by gripping with the hands or arms and the legs and hauling oneself up. **5** (*tr*) to kick (a person) in the shins. [OE *scinu*]

Shinar ★ (ˈʃaɪnə) *n Old Testament.* the southern part of the valley of the Tigris and Euphrates, often identified with Sumer; Babylonia.

shinbone (ˈʃɪnˌbəʊn) *n* the nontechnical name for **tibia** (sense 1).

shindig (ˈʃɪnˌdɪg) or **shindy** (ˈʃɪndɪ) *n, pl* **shindigs** or **shindies.** *Sl.* **1** a noisy party, dance, etc. **2** a quarrel or commotion. [C19: var. of SHINTY]

shine (ʃaɪn) *vb* **shines, shining, shone. 1** (*intr*) to emit light. **2** (*intr*) to glow or be bright with reflected light. **3** (*tr*) to direct the light of (a lamp, etc.): *he shone the torch in my eyes.* **4** (*tr*; *p.t. & p.p.* **shined**) to cause to gleam by polishing: *to shine shoes.* **5** (*intr*) to excel: *she shines at tennis.* **6** (*intr*) to appear clearly. ♦ *n* **7** the state or quality of shining; sheen; lustre. **8** *Inf.* a liking or fancy (esp. in **take a shine to**). [OE *scīnan*]

shiner (ˈʃaɪnə) *n* **1** something that shines, such as a polishing device. **2** any of numerous small North American freshwater cyprinid fishes. **3** *Inf.* a black eye. **4** *NZ.* old-fashioned *inf.* a tramp.

shingle[1] (ˈʃɪŋgəl) *n* **1** a thin rectangular tile, esp. one made of wood, that is laid with others in overlapping rows to cover a roof or a wall. **2** a woman's short-cropped hairstyle. **3** *US & Canad.* a small signboard placed outside the office of a doctor, lawyer, etc. ♦ *vb* **shingles, shingling, shingled.** (*tr*) **4** to cover (a roof or a wall) with shingles. **5** to cut (the hair) in a short-cropped style. [C12 *scingle*, from LL *scindula* a split piece of wood, from L *scindere* to split]
▸ **'shingler** *n*

shingle[2] (ˈʃɪŋgəl) *n* **1** coarse gravel, esp. the pebbles found on beaches. **2** a place or area strewn with shingle. [C16: of Scand. origin]
▸ **'shingly** *adj*

shingles (ˈʃɪŋgəlz) *n* (*functioning as sing*) an acute viral disease characterized by inflammation, pain, and skin eruptions along the course of affected nerves. Technical names: **herpes zoster, zoster.** [C14: from Med. L *cingulum* girdle, rendering Gk *zōnē* zone]

Shinto (ˈʃɪntəʊ) *n* the indigenous religion of Japan, incorporating the worship of a number of ethnic divinities. [C18: from Japanese: the way of the gods, from Chinese *shên* gods + *tao* way]
▸ **'Shintoism** *n* ▸ **'Shintoist** *n, adj*

shinty (ˈʃɪntɪ) *n* **1** a game resembling hockey played with a ball and sticks curved at the lower end. **2** (*pl* **shinties**) the stick used in this game. [C17: ? from Scot. Gaelic *sinteag* a pace, bound]

shiny (ˈʃaɪnɪ) *adj* **shinier, shiniest. 1** glossy or polished; bright. **2** (of clothes or material) worn to a smooth and glossy state, as by continual rubbing.
▸ **'shininess** *n*

ship (ʃɪp) *n* **1** a vessel propelled by engines or sails for navigating on the water, esp. a large vessel. **2** *Naut.* a large sailing vessel with three or more square-rigged masts. **3** the crew of a ship. **4** short for **airship** or **spaceship. 5 when one's ship comes in** (*or* **home**). when one has become successful. ♦ *vb* **ships, shipping, shipped. 6** to place, transport, or travel on any conveyance, esp. aboard a ship. **7** (*tr*) *Naut.* to take (water) over the side. **8** to bring or go aboard a vessel: *to ship oars.* **9** (*tr*; often foll. by *off*) *Inf.* to send away: *they shipped the children off to boarding school.* **10** (*intr*) to engage to serve aboard a ship: *I shipped aboard a Liverpool liner.* [OE *scip*]
▸ **'shippable** *adj*

-ship *suffix forming nouns.* **1** indicating state or condition:

fellowship. **2** indicating rank, office, or position: *lordship.* **3** indicating craft or skill: *scholarship.* [OE -*scipe*]

shipboard (ˈʃɪpˌbɔːd) *n* (*modifier*) taking place, used, or intended for use aboard a ship: *a shipboard encounter.*

shipbuilder (ˈʃɪpˌbɪldə) *n* a person or business engaged in building ships.
▸ **'ship,building** *n*

ship chandler *n* a person or business dealing in supplies for ships.
▸ **ship chandlery** *n*

Shipka Pass ★ (ˈʃɪpkə) *n* a pass over the Balkan Mountains in central Bulgaria: scene of a bloody Turkish defeat in the Russo-Turkish War (1877–78). Height: 1334 m (4376 ft).

shipload (ˈʃɪpˌləʊd) *n* the quantity carried by a ship.

shipmaster (ˈʃɪpˌmɑːstə) *n* the master or captain of a ship.

shipmate (ˈʃɪpˌmeɪt) *n* a sailor who serves on the same ship as another.

shipment (ˈʃɪpmənt) *n* **1a** goods shipped together as part of the same lot: *a shipment of grain.* **1b** (*as modifier*): *a shipment schedule.* **2** the act of shipping cargo.

ship money *n English history.* a tax levied to finance the fitting out of warships: abolished 1640.

ship of the line *n Naut.* (formerly) a warship large enough to fight in the first line of battle.

shipowner (ˈʃɪpˌəʊnə) *n* a person who owns or has shares in a ship or ships.

shipper (ˈʃɪpə) *n* a person or company in the business of shipping freight.

shipping (ˈʃɪpɪŋ) *n* **1a** the business of transporting freight, esp. by ship. **1b** (*as modifier*): *a shipping magnate; shipping line.* **2** ships collectively: *there is a lot of shipping in the Channel.*

ship's biscuit *n* another name for **hardtack.**

shipshape (ˈʃɪpˌʃeɪp) *adj* **1** neat; orderly. ♦ *adv* **2** in a neat and orderly manner.

shipworm (ˈʃɪpˌwɜːm) *n* any of a genus of wormlike marine bivalve molluscs that bore into wooden piers, ships, etc., by means of drill-like shell valves.

shipwreck (ˈʃɪpˌrɛk) *n* **1** the partial or total destruction of a ship at sea. **2** a wrecked ship or part of such a ship. **3** ruin or destruction: *the shipwreck of all my hopes.* ♦ *vb* (*tr*) **4** to wreck or destroy (a ship). **5** to bring to ruin or destruction. [OE *scipwræc*, from SHIP + *wræc* something driven by the sea]

shipwright (ˈʃɪpˌraɪt) *n* an artisan skilled in one or more of the tasks required to build vessels.

shipyard (ˈʃɪpˌjɑːd) *n* a place or facility for the building, maintenance, and repair of ships.

shiralee (ˌʃɪrəˈliː) *n Austral. sl.* a swagman's bundle. [from ?]

Shiraz ★ (ʃɪəˈrɑːz) *n* a city in SW Iran, at an altitude of 1585 m (5200 ft): an important Muslim cultural centre in the 14th century; university (1948); noted for fine carpets. Pop.: 965 117 (1991).

shire (ˈʃaɪə) *n* **1a** one of the British counties. **1b** (*in combination*): *Yorkshire.* **2** (in Australia) a rural district having its own local council. **3** See **shire horse. 4 the Shires.** the Midland counties of England, famous for hunting, etc. [OE *scīr* office]

Shiré ★ (ˈʃɪəreɪ) *n* a river in E central Africa, flowing from Lake Malawi through Malawi and Mozambique to the Zambezi. Length: 596 km (370 miles).

Shiré Highlands ★ *pl n* an upland area of S Malawi. Average height: 900 m (3000 ft).

shire horse *n* a large heavy breed of carthorse with long hair on the fetlocks.

shirk (ʃɜːk) *vb* **1** to avoid discharging (work, a duty, etc.); evade. ♦ *n also* **shirker. 2** a person who shirks. [C17: prob. from G *Schurke* rogue]

shirr (ʃɜː) *vb* **1** to gather (fabric) into two or more parallel rows to decorate a dress, blouse, etc., often using elastic thread. **2** (*tr*) to bake (eggs) out of their shells. ♦ *n also*

shirring. 3 a series of gathered rows decorating a dress, blouse, etc. [C19: from ?]

shirt (ʃɜːt) *n* **1** a garment worn on the upper part of the body, esp. by men, usually having a collar and sleeves and buttoning up the front. **2** short for **nightshirt. 3 keep your shirt on.** *Inf.* refrain from losing your temper. **4 put** *or* **lose one's shirt on.** *Inf.* to bet or lose all one has on (a horse, etc.). [OE *scyrte*]

shirting (ˈʃɜːtɪŋ) *n* fabric used in making men's shirts.

shirt-lifter *n Derog. sl.* a male homosexual.

shirtsleeve (ˈʃɜːtˌsliːv) *n* **1** the sleeve of a shirt. **2 in one's shirtsleeves.** not wearing a jacket.

shirt-tail *n* the part of a shirt that extends below the waist.

shirtwaister (ˈʃɜːtˌweɪstə) *or US* **shirtwaist** *n* a woman's dress with a tailored bodice resembling a shirt.

shirty (ˈʃɜːtɪ) *adj* **shirtier, shirtiest.** *Sl., chiefly Brit.* bad-tempered or annoyed. [C19: ? based on such phrases as *to get someone's shirt out* to annoy someone]
▸ **ˈshirtily** *adv*

shish kebab (ˈʃiːʃ kəˈbæb) *n* a dish consisting of small pieces of meat and vegetables threaded onto skewers and grilled. [from Turkish *şiş kebab*, from *şiş* skewer; see KEBAB]

shit (ʃɪt) *Taboo.* ◆ *vb* **shits, shitting; shitted, shit,** *or* **shat. 1** to defecate. **2** (usually foll. by *on*) *Sl.* to give the worst possible treatment (to). ◆ *n* **3** faeces; excrement. **4** an act of defecation. **5** *Sl.* rubbish; nonsense. **6** *Sl.* an obnoxious or worthless person. ◆ *interj* **7** *Sl.* an exclamation expressing anger, disgust, etc. [OE *scite* (unattested) dung, *scītan* to defecate, of Gmc origin]
▸ **ˈshitty** *adj*

Shittim ★ (ˈʃɪtɪm) *n Old Testament.* the site to the east of the Jordan and northeast of the Dead Sea where the Israelites encamped before crossing the Jordan (Numbers 25:1–9).

shiv (ʃɪv) *n* a variant of **chiv.**

Shiva ★ (ˈʃiːvə, ˈʃɪvə) *n* a variant spelling of **Siva.**

shivaree (ˌʃɪvəˈriː) *n* a variant spelling (esp. US and Canad.) of **charivari.**

shiver[1] (ˈʃɪvə) *vb* (*intr*) **1** to shake or tremble, as from cold or fear. ◆ *n* **2** the act of shivering; a tremulous motion. **3 the shivers.** an attack of shivering, esp. through fear or illness. [C13 *chiveren*, ? var. of *chevelen* to chatter (used of teeth), from OE *ceafl* jowl]
▸ **ˈshiverer** *n* ▸ **ˈshivering** *n, adj* ▸ **ˈshivery** *adj*

shiver[2] (ˈʃɪvə) *vb* **1** to break or cause to break into fragments. ◆ *n* **2** a splintered piece. [C13: of Gmc origin]

Shizuoka ★ (ˌʃɪzuːˈəʊkə) *n* a city in central Japan, on S Honshu: a centre for green tea; university (1949). Pop.: 474 089 (1995).

Shkodër ★ (*Albanian* ˈʃkodər) *n* a market town in NW Albania, on **Lake Shkodër:** an Illyrian capital in the first millennium B.C. Pop.: 83 700 (1991 est.). Italian name: **Scutari.**

shoal[1] (ʃəʊl) *n* **1** a stretch of shallow water. **2** a sandbank or rocky area, esp. one that is visible at low water. ◆ *vb* **3** to make or become shallow. **4** (*intr*) *Naut.* to sail into shallower water. ◆ *adj also* **shoaly. 5** a less common word for **shallow.** [OE *sceald* shallow]

shoal[2] (ʃəʊl) *n* **1** a large group of fish. **2** a large group of people or things. ◆ *vb* **3** (*intr*) to collect together in such a group. [OE *scolu*]

shock[1] (ʃɒk) *vb* **1** to experience or cause to experience extreme horror, disgust, surprise, etc.: *the atrocities shocked us.* **2** to cause a state of shock in (a person). **3** to come or cause to come into violent contact. ◆ *n* **4** a sudden and violent jarring blow or impact. **5** something that causes a sudden and violent disturbance in the emotions. **6** *Pathol.* a state of bodily collapse, as from severe bleeding, burns, fright, etc. **7** Also: **electric shock.** pain and muscular spasm as the physical reaction to an electric current passing through the body. [C16: from OF *choc*, from *choquier* to make violent contact with, of Gmc origin]
▸ **ˈshockable** *adj* ▸ ˌshockaˈbility *n*

shock[2] (ʃɒk) *n* **1** a number of sheaves set on end in a field

to dry. **2** a pile or stack of unthreshed corn. ◆ *vb* **3** (*tr*) to set up (sheaves) in shocks. [C14: prob. of Gmc origin]

shock[3] (ʃɒk) *n* a thick bushy mass, esp. of hair. [C19: ?from SHOCK[2]]

shock absorber *n* any device designed to absorb mechanical shock, esp. one fitted to a motor vehicle to damp the recoil of the road springs.

shocker (ˈʃɒkə) *n Inf.* **1** a person or thing that shocks. **2** a sensational novel, film, or play.

shockheaded (ˈʃɒkˌhɛdɪd) *adj* having a head of bushy or tousled hair.

shock-horror *adj Facetious.* (esp. of newspaper headlines) sensationalistic: *shock-horror stories about the British diet.*

shocking (ˈʃɒkɪŋ) *adj* **1** causing shock, horror, or disgust. **2 shocking pink. 2a** of a garish shade of pink. **2b** (*as n*): *dressed in shocking pink.* **3** *Inf.* very bad or terrible: *shocking weather.*
▸ **ˈshockingly** *adv*

Shockley ★ (ˈʃɒklɪ) *n* **William Bradfield.** 1910–89, US physicist, born in Britain, who shared the Nobel prize for physics (1956) with John Bardeen and Walter Brattain for developing the transistor. He also held controversial views on the connection between race and intelligence.

shockproof (ˈʃɒkˌpruːf) *adj* capable of absorbing shock without damage.

shock therapy *or* **treatment** *n* the treatment of certain psychotic conditions by injecting drugs or by passing an electric current through the brain (**electroconvulsive therapy**) to produce convulsions or coma.

shock troops *pl n* soldiers specially trained and equipped to carry out an assault.

shock wave *n* a region across which there is a rapid pressure, temperature, and density rise caused by a body moving supersonically in a gas or by a detonation. See also **sonic boom.**

shod (ʃɒd) *vb* the past participle of **shoe.**

shoddy (ˈʃɒdɪ) *adj* **shoddier, shoddiest. 1** imitating something of better quality. **2** of poor quality. ◆ *n, pl* **shoddies. 3** a yarn or fabric made from wool waste or clippings. **4** anything of inferior quality that is designed to simulate superior quality. [C19: from ?]
▸ **ˈshoddily** *adv* ▸ **ˈshoddiness** *n*

shoe (ʃuː) *n* **1a** one of a matching pair of coverings shaped to fit the foot, esp. one ending below the ankle, having an upper of leather, plastic, etc., on a sole and heel of heavier material. **1b** (*as modifier*): *shoe cleaner.* **2** anything resembling a shoe in shape, function, position, etc., such as a horseshoe. **3** a band of metal or wood on the bottom of the runner of a sledge. **4** *Engineering.* a lining to protect from wear: see **brake shoe. 5 be in** (*a person's*) **shoes.** *Inf.* to be in (another person's) situation. ◆ *vb* **shoes, shoeing, shod.** (*tr*) **6** to furnish with shoes. **7** to fit (a horse) with horseshoes. **8** to furnish with a hard cover, such as a metal plate, for protection against friction or bruising. [OE *scōh*]

shoeblack (ˈʃuːˌblæk) *n* (esp. formerly) a person who shines boots and shoes.

shoehorn (ˈʃuːˌhɔːn) *n* **1** a smooth curved implement of horn, metal, plastic, etc., inserted at the heel of a shoe to ease the foot into it. ◆ *vb* (*tr*) **2** to cram (people or things) into a small space.

shoelace (ˈʃuːˌleɪs) *n* a cord for fastening shoes.

shoe leather *n* **1** leather used to make shoes. **2 save shoe leather.** to avoid wearing out shoes, as by taking a bus rather than walking.

shoemaker (ˈʃuːˌmeɪkə) *n* a person who makes or repairs shoes or boots.
▸ **ˈshoeˌmaking** *n*

shoer (ˈʃuːə) *n Rare.* a person who shoes horses; farrier.

shoeshine (ˈʃuːˌʃaɪn) *n* the act or an instance of polishing a pair of shoes.

shoestring (ˈʃuːˌstrɪŋ) *n* **1** another word for **shoelace. 2** *Inf.* a very small or petty amount of money (esp. in **on a shoestring**).

★ people and places

shoetree ('ʃuː,triː) *n* a wooden or metal form inserted into a shoe or boot to stretch it or preserve its shape.

shofar *or* **shophar** (*Hebrew* ʃo'far) *n, pl* **shofars, shophars** *or* **shofroth, shophroth** (*Hebrew* -'frɔt). *Judaism*. a ram's horn sounded on certain religious occasions. [from Heb. *shōphār* ram's horn]

shogun ('ʃəʊ,guːn) *n Japanese history*. (from about 1192 to 1867) any of a line of hereditary military dictators who relegated the emperors to a position of purely theoretical supremacy. [C17: from Japanese, from Chinese *chiang chün* general, from *chiang* to lead + *chün* army]
▸ **'shogunate** *n*

shogun bond *n* a bond sold on the Japanese market by a foreign institution and denominated in a foreign currency. Cf. **samurai bond**.

Sholapur ★ ('ʃəʊlə,pʊə) *n* a city in SW India, in S Maharashtra: major textile centre. Pop.: 604 215 (1991).

Sholem Aleichem ★ ('ʃɒlɛm ɑː'leɪçɛm) *n* See (Sholem) Aleichem.

Sholokhov ★ (*Russian* 'ʃɒləxəf) *n* **Mikhail Aleksandrovich** (mixa'il alık'sandrəvitʃ). 1905–84, Soviet author, noted for *And Quiet Flows the Don* (1934) and *The Don Flows Home to the Sea* (1940): Nobel prize for literature 1965.

shone (ʃɒn; *US* ʃəʊn) *vb* a past tense and past participle of **shine**.

shoo (ʃuː) *sentence substitute*. **1** go away!: used to drive away unwanted or annoying people, animals, etc. ◆ *vb* **shoos, shooing, shooed**. **2** (*tr*) to drive away by or as if by crying "shoo". **3** (*intr*) to cry "shoo". [C15: imit.]

shoo-in *n US & Canad*. **1** a person or thing that is certain to win or succeed. **2** a match or contest that is easy to win.

shook[1] (ʃʊk) *n* **1** a set of parts ready for assembly, esp. of a barrel. **2** a group of sheaves piled together on end; shock. [C18: from ?]

shook[2] (ʃʊk) *vb* the past tense of **shake**.

shoon (ʃuːn) *n Dialect, chiefly Scot*. a plural of **shoe**.

shoot (ʃuːt) *vb* **shoots, shooting, shot**. **1** (*tr*) to hit, wound, damage, or kill with a missile discharged from a weapon. **2** to discharge (a missile or missiles) from a weapon. **3** to fire (a weapon) or (of a weapon) to be fired. **4** to send out or be sent out as if from a weapon: *he shot questions at her*. **5** (*intr*) to move very rapidly. **6** (*tr*) to slide or push into or out of a fastening: *to shoot a bolt*. **7** to emit (a ray of light) or (of a ray of light) to be emitted. **8** (*tr*) to go or pass quickly over or through: *to shoot rapids*. **9** (*intr*) to hunt game with a gun for sport. **10** (*tr*) to pass over (an area) in hunting game. **11** (*intr*) (of a plant) to produce (buds, branches, etc.). **12** to photograph or record (a sequence, etc.). **13** (*tr; usually passive*) to variegate or streak, as with colour. **14** *Soccer, hockey, etc*. to hit or propel (the ball, etc.) towards the goal. **15** (*tr*) *Sport, chiefly US & Canad*. to score (strokes, etc.): *he shot 72 on the first round*. **16** (*tr*) to measure the altitude of (a celestial body). **17** (often foll. by *up*) *Sl*. to inject (someone, esp. oneself) with (a drug, esp. heroin). **18 shoot a line**. *Sl*. to boast. **18a** to tell a lie. **19 shoot oneself in the foot**. *Inf*. to damage one's own cause inadvertently. ◆ *n* **20** the act of shooting. **21** the action or motion of something that is shot. **22** the first aerial part of a plant to develop from a germinating seed. **23** any new growth of a plant, such as a bud, etc. **24** *Chiefly Brit*. a meeting or party organized for hunting game with guns. **25** an area where game can be hunted with guns. **26** a steep descent in a stream; rapid. **27** *Inf*. a photographic assignment **28 the whole shoot**. *Sl*. everything. ◆ *interj* **29** *US & Canad*. an exclamation expressing disbelief, scepticism, disappointment, etc. ◆ See also **shoot down, shoot through**. [OE *scēotan*]

shoot down *vb* (*tr, adv*) **1** to shoot callously. **2** to defeat or disprove: *he shot down her argument*.

shoot-'em-up *or* **shoot-em-up** *n Inf*. **1** a type of computer game, the object of which is to shoot as many enemies, targets, etc. as possible. **2** a fast-moving film involving many gunfights, battles, etc.

shooter ('ʃuːtə) *n* **1** a person or thing that shoots. **2** *Sl*. a gun.

shooting box *n* a small country house providing ac-

commodation for a shooting party. Also called: **shooting lodge**.

shooting brake *n Brit*. another name for **estate car**.

shooting star *n Inf*. a meteor.

shooting stick *n* a device that resembles a walking stick, having a spike at one end and a folding seat at the other.

shoot through *vb* (*intr, adv*) *Austral. inf*. to leave; go away.

shop (ʃɒp) *n* **1** a place, esp. a small building, for the retail sale of goods and services. **2** an act or instance of shopping. **3** a place for the performance of a specified type of work; workshop. **4 all over the shop**. *Inf*. **4a** in disarray: *his papers were all over the shop*. **4b** in every direction: *they searched for it all over the shop*. **5 shut up shop**. to close business at the end of the day or permanently. **6 talk shop**. *Inf*. to discuss one's business, profession, etc., esp. on a social occasion. ◆ *vb* **shops, shopping, shopped**. **7** (*intr; often foll. by* for) to visit a shop or shops in search of (goods) with the intention of buying them. **8** (*tr*) *Sl., chiefly Brit*. to inform on (someone), esp. to the police. [OE *sceoppa* stall]
▸ **'shopping** *n*

shop around *vb* (*intr, adv*) *Inf*. **1** to visit a number of shops or stores to compare goods and prices. **2** to consider a number of possibilities before making a choice.

shop assistant *n* a person who serves in a shop.

shop floor *n* **1** the part of a factory housing the machines and men directly involved in production. **2** workers, esp. factory workers organized in a union.

shopkeeper ('ʃɒp,kiːpə) *n* a person who owns or manages a shop or small store.
▸ **'shop,keeping** *n*

shoplifter ('ʃɒp,lɪftə) *n* a customer who steals goods from a shop.
▸ **'shop,lifting** *n*

shopper ('ʃɒpə) *n* **1** a person who buys goods in a shop. **2** a bag for shopping.

shopping centre *n* **1** a purpose-built complex of stores, restaurants, etc. **2** the area of a town where most of the shops are situated.

shopping mall *n* a large enclosed shopping centre.

shopping plaza *n Chiefly US & Canad*. a shopping centre, esp. a small group of stores built as a strip.

shopsoiled ('ʃɒp,sɔɪld) *adj* worn, faded, etc., from being displayed in a shop or store.

shop steward *n* an elected representative of the union workers in a shop, factory, etc.

shoptalk ('ʃɒp,tɔːk) *n* conversation concerning one's work, esp. when carried on outside business hours.

shopwalker ('ʃɒp,wɔːkə) *n Brit*. a person employed by a departmental store to supervise sales personnel, assist customers, etc.

shoran ('ʃɔːræn) *n* a short-range radar system by which an aircraft, ship, etc., can accurately determine its position. [C20: *sho(rt-)ra(nge) n(avigation)*]

shore[1] (ʃɔː) *n* **1** the land along the edge of a sea, lake, or wide river. Related adj: **littoral**. **2a** land, as opposed to water. **2b** (*as modifier*): *shore duty*. **3** *Law*. the tract of coastland lying between the ordinary marks of high and low water. **4** (*often pl*) a country: *his native shores*. [C14: prob. from MLow G, MDu. *schōre*]

shore[2] (ʃɔː) *n* **1** a prop or beam used to support a wall, building, etc. ◆ *vb* **shores, shoring, shored**. **2** (*tr; often foll. by* up) to make safe with or as if with a shore. [C15: from MDu. *schōre*]
▸ **'shoring** *n*

shore[3] (ʃɔː) *vb Arch., Austral., & NZ*. a past tense of **shear**.

shore bird *n* any of various birds that live close to water, esp. plovers, sandpipers, etc. Also called (Brit.): **wader**.

shore leave *n Naval*. **1** permission to go ashore. **2** time spent ashore during leave.

shoreless ('ʃɔːlɪs) *adj* **1** without a shore suitable for landing. **2** *Poetic*. boundless; vast.

shoreline ('ʃɔː,laɪn) *n* the edge of a body of water.

shoreward ('ʃɔːwəd) *adj* **1** near or facing the shore. ◆ *adv also* **shorewards. 2** towards the shore.

shorn (ʃɔːn) *vb* a past participle of **shear.**

short (ʃɔːt) *adj* **1** of little length; not long. **2** of little height; not tall. **3** of limited duration. **4** deficient: *the number of places laid at the table was short by four.* **5** (*postpositive; often foll. by of or on*) lacking (in) or needful (of): *I'm always short of money.* **6** concise; succinct. **7** (of drinks) consisting chiefly of a spirit, such as whisky. **8** *Cricket.* (of a fielding position) near the batsman: *short leg.* **9** lacking in the power of retentiveness: *a short memory.* **10** abrupt to the point of rudeness: *the salesgirl was very short with him.* **11** (of betting odds) almost even. **12** *Finance.* **12a** not possessing the securities or commodities that have been sold under contract and therefore obliged to make a purchase before the delivery date. **12b** of or relating to such sales, which depend on falling prices for profit. **13** *Phonetics.* **13a** denoting a vowel of relatively brief temporal duration. **13b** (in popular usage) denoting the qualities of the five English vowels represented orthographically in the words *pat, pet, pit, pot, put,* and *putt.* **14** *Prosody.* **14a** denoting a vowel that is phonetically short or a syllable containing such a vowel. **14b** (of a vowel or syllable in verse) not carrying emphasis or accent. **15** (of pastry) crumbly in texture. **16 in short supply.** scarce. **17 short and sweet.** unexpectedly brief. **18 short for.** an abbreviation for. ◆ *adv* **19** abruptly: *to stop short.* **20** briefly or concisely. **21** rudely or curtly. **22** *Finance.* without possessing the securities or commodities at the time of their contractual sale: *to sell short.* **23 caught** or **taken short.** having a sudden need to urinate or defecate. **24 go short.** not to have a sufficient amount, etc. **25 short of.** except: *nothing short of a miracle can save him now.* ◆ *n* **26** anything that is short. **27** a drink of spirits. **28** *Phonetics, prosody.* a short vowel or syllable. **29** *Finance.* **29a** a short contract or sale. **29b** a short seller. **30** a short film, usually of a factual nature. **31** See **short circuit. 32 for short.** *Inf.* as a shortened form: *he is called J.R. for short.* **33 in short. 33a** as a summary. **33b** in a few words. ◆ *vb* **34** See **short circuit** (sense 2). ◆ See also **shorts.** [OE *scort*] ▸ '**shortness** *n*

short-acting *adj* (of a drug) quickly effective, but requiring regularly repeated doses for long-term treatment. Cf. **intermediate-acting, long-acting.**

shortage ('ʃɔːtɪdʒ) *n* a deficiency or lack in the amount needed, expected, or due; deficit.

shortbread ('ʃɔːt,brɛd) *n* a rich crumbly biscuit made with a large proportion of butter.

shortcake ('ʃɔːt,keɪk) *n* **1** shortbread. **2** a dessert made of layers of biscuit or cake filled with fruit and cream.

short-change *vb* **short-changes, short-changing, short-changed.** (*tr*) **1** to give less than correct change to. **2** *Sl.* to treat unfairly or dishonestly, esp. by giving less than is expected or deserved.

short circuit *n* **1** a faulty or accidental connection between two points of different potential in an electric circuit, establishing a path of low resistance through which an excessive current can flow. ◆ *vb* **short-circuit. 2** to develop or cause to develop a short circuit. **3** (*tr*) to bypass (a procedure, etc.). **4** (*tr*) to hinder or frustrate (plans, etc.). ◆ Sometimes (for senses 1, 2) shortened to **short.**

shortcoming ('ʃɔːt,kʌmɪŋ) *n* a failing, defect, or deficiency.

short corner *n Hockey.* another name for **penalty corner.**

short covering *n* the purchase of securities or commodities by a short seller to meet delivery requirements.

shortcrust pastry ('ʃɔːt,krʌst) *n* a basic type of pastry that has a crisp but crumbly texture. Also: **short pastry.**

short cut *n* **1** a route that is shorter than the usual one. **2** a means of saving time or effort. ◆ *vb* **short-cut, short-cuts, short-cutting, short-cut. 3** (*intr*) to use a short cut.

short-dated *adj* (of a gilt-edged security) having less than five years to run before redemption. Cf. **medium-dated, long-dated.**

short-day *adj* (of plants) able to flower only if exposed to short periods of daylight, each followed by a long dark period. Cf. **long-day.**

shorten ('ʃɔːt³n) *vb* **1** to make or become short or shorter.

2 (*tr*) *Naut.* to reduce the area of (sail). **3** (*tr*) to make (pastry, etc.) short, by adding fat. **4** *Gambling.* to cause (the odds) to lessen or (of odds) to become less.

shortening ('ʃɔːt³nɪŋ) *n* butter or other fat, used in a dough, etc., to make the mixture short.

Shorter Catechism *n Chiefly Presbyterian Church.* the more widely used of two catechisms of religious instruction drawn up in 1647.

shortfall ('ʃɔːt,fɔːl) *n* **1** failure to meet a goal or a requirement. **2** the amount of such a failure.

shorthand ('ʃɔːt,hænd) *n* **a** a system of rapid handwriting employing simple strokes and other symbols to represent words or phrases. **b** (*as modifier*): *a shorthand typist.*

short-handed *adj* **1** lacking the usual or necessary number of assistants, workers, etc. **2** *Sport, US & Canad.* with less than the full complement of players.

shorthand typist *n Brit.* a person skilled in the use of shorthand and in typing. US and Canad. name: **stenographer.**

short head *n Horse racing.* a distance shorter than the length of a horse's head.

shorthorn ('ʃɔːt,hɔːn) *n* a short-horned breed of cattle with several regional varieties.

shortie *or* **shorty** ('ʃɔːtɪ) *n, pl* **shorties.** *Inf.* **a** a person or thing that is extremely short. **b** (*as modifier*): *a shortie nightdress.*

short list *Chiefly Brit.* ◆ *n* **1** Also called (Scot.): **short leet.** a list of suitable applicants for a job, post, etc., from which the successful candidate will be selected. ◆ *vb* **short-list.** (*tr*) **2** to put (someone) on a short list.

short-lived *adj* living or lasting only for a short time.

shortly ('ʃɔːtlɪ) *adv* **1** in a short time; soon. **2** briefly. **3** in a curt or rude manner.

short-order *adj Chiefly US.* of or connected with food that is easily and quickly prepared.

short-range *adj* of small or limited extent in time or distance: *a short-range forecast.*

shorts (ʃɔːts) *pl n* **1** trousers reaching the top of the thigh or partway to the knee, worn by both sexes for sport, etc. **2** *Chiefly US & Canad.* men's underpants that usually reach mid-thigh. **3** short-dated gilt-edged securities. **4** short-term bonds. **5** securities or commodities that have been sold short. **6** a livestock feed containing a large proportion of bran and wheat germ.

short shrift *n* **1** brief and unsympathetic treatment. **2** (formerly) a brief period allowed to a condemned prisoner to make confession. **3 make short shrift of.** to dispose of quickly.

short-sighted *adj* **1** relating to or suffering from myopia. **2** lacking foresight: *a short-sighted plan.* ▸ ,short-'sightedly *adv* ▸ ,short-'sightedness *n*

short-spoken *adj* tending to be abrupt in speech.

short story *n* a prose narrative of shorter length than the novel.

short-tempered *adj* easily moved to anger.

short-term *adj* **1** of, for, or extending over a limited period. **2** *Finance.* extending over, maturing within, or required within a short period of time, usually twelve months: *short-term credit; short-term capital.*

short-termism (-'tɜːmɪzəm) *n* the tendency to focus attention on short-term gains, often at the expense of long-term success or stability.

short time *n* the state or condition of working less than the normal working week, esp. because of a business recession.

short ton *n* the full name for **ton**[1] (sense 2).

short-waisted *adj* unusually short from the shoulders to the waist.

short wave *n* **a** a radio wave with a wavelength in the range 10–100 metres. **b** (*as modifier*): *a short-wave broadcast.*

short-winded *adj* **1** tending to run out of breath, esp. after exertion. **2** (of speech or writing) terse or abrupt.

Shostakovich ★ (,ʃɒstə'kəʊvɪtʃ; *Russian* ʃɒsta'kɔvitʃ) *n* **Dmitri Dmitriyevich** ('dmitrij 'dmitrijɪvitʃ). 1906–75, Soviet composer, noted esp. for his 15 symphonies and his chamber music.

shot[1] (ʃɒt) *n* **1** the act or an instance of discharging a projectile. **2** (*pl* **shot**) a solid missile, such as an iron ball or a lead pellet, discharged from a firearm. **3a** small round pellets of lead collectively, as used in cartridges. **3b** metal in the form of coarse powder or small pellets. **4** the distance that a discharged projectile travels or is capable of travelling. **5** a person who shoots, esp. with regard to his ability: *he is a good shot.* **6** *Inf.* an attempt. **7** *Inf.* a guess. **8** any act of throwing or hitting something, as in certain sports. **9** the launching of a rocket, etc., esp. to a specified destination: *a moon shot.* **10a** a single photograph. **10b** a length of film taken by a single camera without breaks. **11** *Inf.* an injection, as of a vaccine or narcotic drug. **12** *Inf.* a glass of alcoholic drink, esp. spirits. **13** *Sport.* a heavy metal ball used in the shot put. **14 call the shots.** *Sl.* to have control over an organization, etc. **15 have a shot at.** *Inf.* to attempt. **16 like a shot.** very quickly, esp. willingly. **17 shot in the arm.** *Inf.* anything that regenerates, increases confidence or efficiency, etc. **18 shot in the dark.** a wild guess. [OE *scot*]

shot[2] (ʃɒt) *vb* **1** the past tense and past participle of **shoot.** ◆ *adj* **2** (of textiles) woven to give a changing colour effect: *shot silk.* **3** streaked with colour.

shotgun (ˈʃɒtˌɡʌn) *n* **1** a shoulder firearm with unrifled bore used mainly for hunting small game. **2** *American football.* an offensive formation in which the quarterback lines up for a snap unusually far behind the line of scrimmage. ◆ *adj* **3** *Chiefly US.* involving coercion or duress: *a shotgun merger.*

shotgun wedding *n Inf.* a wedding into which one or both partners are coerced, usually because the woman is pregnant.

shot put *n* an athletic event in which contestants hurl or put a heavy metal ball or shot as far as possible.
▶ **'shot-,putter** *n*

shotten (ˈʃɒtᵊn) *adj* **1** (of fish, esp. herring) having recently spawned. **2** *Arch.* worthless. [C15: from obs. p.p. of SHOOT]

shot tower *n* a building formerly used in the production of shot, in which molten lead was graded and dropped from a great height into water, thus cooling it and forming the shot.

should (ʃʊd) *vb* the past tense of **shall:** used as an auxiliary verb to indicate that an action is considered by the speaker to be obligatory (*you should go*) or to form the subjunctive mood with *I* or *we* (*I should like to see you*). [OE *sceold*]

> **USAGE NOTE** *Should* has, as its most common meaning in modern English, the sense *ought* as in *I should go to the graduation, but I don't see how I can.* However, the older sense of the subjunctive of *shall* is often used with *I* or *we* to indicate a more polite form than *would*: *I should like to go, but I can't.* In much speech and writing, *should* has been replaced by *would* in contexts of this kind, but it remains in formal English when a conditional subjunctive is used: *should he choose to remain, he would be granted asylum.*

shoulder (ˈʃəʊldə) *n* **1** the part of the vertebrate body where the arm or a corresponding forelimb joins the trunk. **2** the joint at the junction of the forelimb with the pectoral girdle. **3** a cut of meat including the upper part of the foreleg. **4** *Printing.* the flat surface of a piece of type from which the face rises. **5** the part of a garment that covers the shoulder. **6** anything that resembles a shoulder in shape or position. **7** the strip of unpaved land that borders a road. **8 a shoulder to cry on.** a person one turns to for sympathy with one's troubles. **9 give (someone) the cold shoulder.** *Inf.* to treat in a cold manner; snub. **9a** to ignore or shun. **10 put one's shoulder to the wheel.** *Inf.* to work very hard. **11 rub shoulders with.** *Inf.* to mix with socially or associate with. **12 shoulder to shoulder. 12a** side by side. **12b** in a corporate effort. ◆ *vb* **13** (*tr*) to bear or carry (a burden, etc.) as if on one's shoul-

ders. **14** to push (something) with or as if with the shoulder. **15** (*tr*) to lift or carry on the shoulders. **16 shoulder arms.** *Mil.* to bring the rifle vertically close to the right side with the muzzle uppermost. [OE *sculdor*]

shoulder blade *n* the nontechnical name for **scapula.**

shoulder strap *n* a strap over the shoulders, as to hold up a garment or to support a bag, etc.

shouldn't (ˈʃʊdᵊnt) *contraction of* should not.

shouldst (ʃʊdst) *or* **shouldest** (ˈʃʊdɪst) *vb Arch. or dialect.* (used with the pronoun *thou*) a form of the past tense of **shall.**

shout (ʃaʊt) *n* **1** a loud cry, esp. to convey emotion or a command. **2** *Inf.* **2a** a round, esp. of drinks. **2b** one's turn to buy a round of drinks. ◆ *vb* **3** to utter (something) in a loud cry. **4** (*intr*) to make a loud noise. **5** (*tr*) *Austral. & NZ inf.* to treat (someone) to (something, esp. a round of drinks). [C14: prob. from ON *skūta* taunt]
▶ **'shouter** *n*

shout down *vb* (*tr, adv*) to drown, overwhelm, or silence by talking loudly.

shove (ʃʌv) *vb* **shoves, shoving, shoved. 1** to give a thrust or push to (a person or thing). **2** (*tr*) to give a violent push to. **3** (*intr*) to push one's way roughly. **4** (*tr*) *Inf.* to put (something) somewhere: *shove it in the bin.* ◆ *n* **5** the act or an instance of shoving. ◆ See also **shove off.** [OE *scūfan*]
▶ **'shover** *n*

shove-halfpenny *n Brit.* a game in which players try to propel coins, originally old halfpennies, with the hand into lined sections of a wooden board.

shovel (ˈʃʌvᵊl) *n* **1** an instrument for lifting or scooping loose material, such as earth, coal, etc., consisting of a curved blade or a scoop attached to a handle. **2** any machine or part resembling a shovel in action. **3** Also called: **shovelful.** the amount that can be contained in a shovel. ◆ *vb* **shovels, shovelling, shovelled** *or US* **shovels, shoveling, shoveled. 4** to lift (earth, etc.) with a shovel. **5** (*tr*) to clear or dig (a path) with or as if with a shovel. **6** (*tr*) to gather, load, or unload in a hurried or careless way. [OE *scofl*]
▶ **'shoveller** *or US* **'shoveler** *n*

shoveler (ˈʃʌvələ) *n* a duck of ponds and marshes, having a spoon-shaped bill, a blue patch on each wing, and in the male a green head, white breast, and reddish-brown body.

shovelhead (ˈʃʌvᵊlˌhɛd) *n* a common shark of the Atlantic and Pacific Oceans, having a shovel-shaped head.

shove off *vb* (*intr, adv; often imperative*) **1** to move from the shore in a boat. **2** *Inf.* to go away; depart.

show (ʃəʊ) *vb* **shows, showing, showed; shown** *or* **showed. 1** to make, be, or become visible or noticeable: *to show one's dislike.* **2** (*tr*) to exhibit: *he showed me a picture.* **3** (*tr*) to indicate or explain; prove: *to show that the earth moves round the sun.* **4** (*tr*) to present (oneself or itself) in a specific character: *to show oneself to be trustworthy.* **5** (*tr*; foll. by *how* and an infinitive) to instruct by demonstration: *show me how to swim.* **6** (*tr*) to indicate: *a barometer shows changes in the weather.* **7** (*tr*) to grant or bestow: *to show favour to someone.* **8** (*intr*) to appear: *to show to advantage.* **9** to exhibit, display, or offer (goods, etc.) for sale: *three artists were showing at the gallery.* **10** (*tr*) to allege, as in a legal document: *to show cause.* **11** to present (a film, etc.) or (of a play, etc.) to be presented, as at a theatre or cinema. **12** (*tr*) to guide or escort: *please show me to my room.* **13 show in** *or* **out.** to conduct a person into or out of a room or building by opening the door for him. **14** (*intr*) *Inf.* to arrive. ◆ *n* **15** a display or exhibition. **16** a public spectacle. **17** an ostentatious display. **18** a theatrical or other entertainment. **19** a trace or indication. **20** *Obstetrics.* a discharge of blood at the onset of labour. **21** *US, Austral., & NZ inf.* a chance (esp. in **give someone a show**). **22** *Sl., chiefly Brit.* a thing or affair (esp. in **good show, bad show,** etc.). **23 for show.** in order to attract attention. **24 run the show.** *Inf.* to take charge of or manage an affair, business, etc. **25 steal the show.** *Inf.* to be looked upon as the most interesting, popular, etc., esp. unexpectedly. ◆ See also **show off, show up.** [OE *scēawian*]

showboat (ˈʃəʊˌbəʊt) *n* **1** a paddle-wheel river steamer with a theatre and a repertory company. ◆ *vb* **2** (*intr*) to perform or behave in a showy flamboyant way.

showbread ('ʃəʊˌbrɛd) *n* a variant spelling of **shewbread**.

show business *n* the entertainment industry, including theatre, films, television, and radio. Informal term: **show biz.**

show card *n Commerce.* a card containing a tradesman's advertisement; poster.

showcase ('ʃəʊˌkeɪs) *n* **1** a glass case used to display objects in a museum or shop. **2** a setting in which anything may be displayed to best advantage. ◆ *vb* **showcases, showcasing, showcased. 3** (*tr*) to display or exhibit.

show day *n* (in Australia) a public holiday in a state on the date of its annual agricultural and industrial show.

showdown ('ʃəʊˌdaʊn) *n* **1** *Inf.* an action that brings matters to a head or acts as a conclusion. **2** *Poker.* the exposing of the cards in the players' hands at the end of the game.

shower[1] ('ʃaʊə) *n* **1** a brief period of rain, hail, sleet, or snow. **2** a sudden abundant fall or downpour, as of tears, sparks, or light. **3** a rush: *a shower of praise.* **4a** a kind of bath in which a person stands upright and is sprayed with water from a nozzle. **4b** the room, booth, etc., containing such a bath. Full name: **shower bath. 5** *Brit. sl.* a derogatory term applied to a person or group. **6** *US, Canad., Austral., & NZ.* a party held to honour and present gifts to a person, as to a prospective bride. **7** a large number of particles formed by the collision of a cosmic-ray particle with a particle in the atmosphere. **8** *NZ.* a light fabric put over a tea table to protect the food from flies, etc. ◆ *vb* **9** (*tr*) to sprinkle or spray with or as if with a shower. **10** (often with *it* as subject) to fall or cause to fall in the form of a shower. **11** (*tr*) to give (gifts, etc.) in abundance or present (a person) with (gifts, etc.): *they showered gifts on him.* **12** (*intr*) to take a shower. [OE *scūr*]
▶ 'showery *adj*

shower[2] ('ʃəʊə) *n* a person or thing that shows.

showgirl ('ʃəʊˌgɜːl) *n* a girl who appears in variety shows, nightclub acts, etc.

show house *n* a house on a newly built estate that is decorated and furnished for prospective buyers to view.

showing ('ʃəʊɪŋ) *n* **1** a presentation, exhibition, or display. **2** manner of presentation.

showjumping ('ʃəʊˌdʒʌmpɪŋ) *n* the riding of horses in competitions to demonstrate skill in jumping over or between various obstacles.
▶ 'show-ˌjumper *n*

showman ('ʃəʊmən) *n, pl* **showmen. 1** a person who presents or produces a theatrical show, etc. **2** a person skilled at presenting anything in an effective manner.
▶ 'showmanship *n*

shown (ʃəʊn) *vb* a past participle of **show.**

show off *vb* (*adv*) **1** (*tr*) to exhibit or display so as to invite admiration. **2** (*intr*) *Inf.* to behave in such a manner as to make an impression. ◆ *n* **show-off. 3** *Inf.* a person who makes a vain display of himself.

showpiece ('ʃəʊˌpiːs) *n* **1** anything displayed or exhibited. **2** anything prized as a very fine example of its type.

showplace ('ʃəʊˌpleɪs) *n* a place exhibited or visited for its beauty, historic interest, etc.

showroom ('ʃəʊˌruːm, -ˌrʊm) *n* a room in which goods for sale, such as cars, are on display.

show up *vb* (*adv*) **1** to reveal or be revealed clearly. **2** (*tr*) to expose or reveal the faults or defects of by comparison. **3** (*tr*) *Inf.* to put to shame; embarrass. **4** (*intr*) *Inf.* to appear or arrive.

showy ('ʃəʊɪ) *adj* **showier, showiest. 1** gaudy or ostentatious. **2** making an imposing display.
▶ 'showily *adv* ▶ 'showiness *n*

shrank (ʃræŋk) *vb* a past tense of **shrink.**

shrapnel ('ʃræpn°l) *n* **1** a projectile containing a number of small pellets or bullets exploded before impact. **2** fragments from this type of shell. [C19: after H. *Shrapnel* (1761–1842), E army officer, who invented it]

shred (ʃrɛd) *n* **1** a long narrow strip or fragment torn or cut off. **2** a very small piece or amount. ◆ *vb* **shreds,**

shredding, shredded or **shred. 3** (*tr*) to tear or cut into shreds. [OE *scread*]
▶ 'shredder *n*

Shreveport ★ ('ʃriːvˌpɔːt) *n* a city in NW Louisiana, on the Red River: centre of an oil and natural-gas region. Pop.: 196 982 (1994 est.).

shrew (ʃruː) *n* **1** Also called: **shrewmouse.** a small mouselike long-snouted insectivorous mammal. **2** a bad-tempered or mean-spirited woman. [OE *scrēawa*]

shrewd (ʃruːd) *adj* **1** astute and penetrating, often with regard to business. **2** artful: *a shrewd politician.* **3** *Obs.* piercing: *a shrewd wind.* [C14: from *shrew* (obs. vb) to curse, from SHREW]
▶ 'shrewdly *adv* ▶ 'shrewdness *n*

shrewish ('ʃruːɪʃ) *adj* (esp. of a woman) bad-tempered and nagging.

Shrewsbury ★ ('ʃrəʊzbərɪ, -brɪ, 'ʃruːz-) *n* a town in W central England, administrative centre of Shropshire, on the River Severn: strategically situated near the Welsh border; market town. Pop.: 90 900 (1991).

shriek (ʃriːk) *n* **1** a shrill and piercing cry. ◆ *vb* **2** to produce or utter (words, sounds, etc.) in a shrill piercing tone. [C16: prob. from ON *skrækja* to screech]
▶ 'shrieker *n*

shrieval ('ʃriːv°l) *adj* of or relating to a sheriff.

shrievalty ('ʃriːvəltɪ) *n, pl* **shrievalties. 1** the office or term of office of a sheriff. **2** the jurisdiction of a sheriff. [C16: from arch. *shrieve* sheriff, on the model of *mayoralty*]

shrift (ʃrɪft) *n Arch.* the act or an instance of shriving or being shriven. See also **short shrift.** [OE *scrift*, from L *scriptum* SCRIPT]

shrike (ʃraɪk) *n* an Old World songbird having a heavy hooked bill and feeding on smaller animals which it sometimes impales on thorns, etc. Also called: **butcherbird.** [OE *scrīc* thrush]

shrill (ʃrɪl) *adj* **1** sharp and high-pitched in quality. **2** emitting a sharp high-pitched sound. ◆ *vb* **3** to utter (words, sounds, etc.) in a shrill tone. [C14: prob. from OE *scrallettan*]
▶ 'shrillness *n* ▶ 'shrilly *adv*

shrimp (ʃrɪmp) *n* **1** any of a genus of chiefly marine decapod crustaceans having a slender flattened body with a long tail and a single pair of pincers. **2** *Inf.* a diminutive person, esp. a child. ◆ *vb* **3** (*intr*) to fish for shrimps. [C14: prob. of Gmc origin]
▶ 'shrimper *n*

shrine (ʃraɪn) *n* **1** a place of worship hallowed by association with a sacred person or object. **2** a container for sacred relics. **3** the tomb of a saint or other holy person. **4** a place or site venerated for its association with a famous person or event. **5** *RC Church.* a building, alcove, or shelf arranged as a setting for a statue, picture, etc., of Christ, the Virgin Mary, or a saint. ◆ *vb* **shrines, shrining, shrined. 6** short for **enshrine.** [OE *scrīn*, from L *scrīnium* bookcase]
▶ 'shrine-ˌlike *adj*

shrink (ʃrɪŋk) *vb* **shrinks, shrinking; shrank** or **shrunk; shrunk** or **shrunken. 1** to contract or cause to contract as from wetness, heat, cold, etc. **2** to become or cause to become smaller in size. **3** (*intr*; often foll. by *from*) **3a** to recoil or withdraw: *to shrink from the sight of blood.* **3b** to feel great reluctance (at). ◆ *n* **4** the act or an instance of shrinking. **5** a slang word for **psychiatrist.** [OE *scrincan*]
▶ 'shrinkable *adj* ▶ 'shrinker *n* ▶ 'shrinking *adj*

shrinkage ('ʃrɪŋkɪdʒ) *n* **1** the act or fact of shrinking. **2** the amount by which anything decreases in size, value, weight, etc. **3** *Commerce.* the loss of merchandise through shoplifting or damage.

shrinking violet *n Inf.* a shy person.

shrink-wrap *vb* **shrink-wraps, shrink-wrapping, shrink-wrapped.** (*tr*) to package a product in a flexible plastic wrapping designed to shrink about its contours to protect and seal it.

shrive (ʃraɪv) *vb* **shrives, shriving; shrove** or **shrived; shriven** ('ʃrɪv°n) or **shrived.** *Chiefly RC Church.* **1** to hear the confession of (a penitent). **2** (*tr*) to impose a penance upon (a penitent) and grant him absolution. **3** (*intr*) to confess

one's sins to a priest in order to obtain forgiveness. [OE *scrifan*, from L *scrībere* to write]
> 'shriver *n*

shrivel ('ʃrɪvªl) *vb* **shrivels, shrivelling, shrivelled** *or US* **shrivels, shriveling, shriveled. 1** to make or become shrunken and withered. **2** to lose or cause to lose vitality. [C16: prob. of Scand. origin]

Shropshire ★ ('ʃrɒp͵ʃɪə, -ʃə) *n* a county of W central England: mainly agricultural. Administrative centre: Shrewsbury. Pop.: 416 500 (1994 est.). Area: 3490 sq. km (1347 sq. miles).

shroud (ʃraʊd) *n* **1** a garment or piece of cloth used to wrap a dead body. **2** anything that envelops like a garment: *a shroud of mist.* **3** a protective covering for a piece of equipment. **4** *Astronautics.* a streamlined protective covering used to protect the payload during a rocket-powered launch. **5** *Naut.* one of a pattern of ropes or cables used to stay a mast. ♦ *vb* (*tr*) **6** to wrap in a shroud. **7** to cover, envelop, or hide. [OE *scrūd* garment]
> 'shroudless *adj*

shrove (ʃrəʊv) *vb* a past tense of **shrive.**

Shrovetide ('ʃrəʊv͵taɪd) *n* the Sunday, Monday, and Tuesday before Ash Wednesday, formerly a time when confessions were made for Lent.

shrub[1] (ʃrʌb) *n* a woody perennial plant, smaller than a tree, with several major branches arising from near the base of the main stem. [OE *scrybb*]
> 'shrub͵like *adj*

shrub[2] (ʃrʌb) *n* a mixed drink of rum, fruit juice, sugar, and spice. [C18: from Ar. *sharāb,* var. of *shurb* drink; see SHERBET]

shrubbery ('ʃrʌbərɪ) *n, pl* **shrubberies. 1** a place where a number of shrubs are planted. **2** shrubs collectively.

shrubby ('ʃrʌbɪ) *adj* **shrubbier, shrubbiest. 1** consisting of, planted with, or abounding in (shrubs). **2** resembling a shrub.
> 'shrubbiness *n*

shrug (ʃrʌg) *vb* **shrugs, shrugging, shrugged. 1** to draw up and drop (the shoulders) abruptly in a gesture expressing indifference, ignorance, etc. ♦ *n* **2** the gesture so made. [C14: from ?]

shrug off *vb* (*tr, adv*) **1** to minimize the importance of; dismiss. **2** to get rid of.

shrunk (ʃrʌŋk) *vb* a past participle and past tense of **shrink.**

shrunken ('ʃrʌŋkªn) *vb* **1** a past participle and past tense of **shrink.** ♦ *adj* **2** (*usually prenominal*) reduced in size.

shtoom (ʃtʊm) *adj Sl.* silent, dumb (esp. in **keep shtoom**). [from Yiddish, from G *stumm* silent]

shuck (ʃʌk) *n* **1** the outer covering of something, such as the husk of a grain of maize, a pea pod, or an oyster shell. ♦ *vb* (*tr*) **2** to remove the shucks from. [C17: US dialect, from ?]
> 'shucker *n*

shucks (ʃʌks) *interj US & Canad. inf.* an exclamation of disappointment, annoyance, etc.

shudder ('ʃʌdə) *vb* **1** (*intr*) to shake or tremble suddenly and violently, as from horror, fear, aversion, etc. ♦ *n* **2** a convulsive shiver. [C18: from MLow G *schöderen*]
> 'shuddering *adj* > 'shudderingly *adv* > 'shuddery *adj*

shuffle ('ʃʌfªl) *vb* **shuffles, shuffling, shuffled. 1** to walk or move (the feet) with a slow dragging motion. **2** to change the position of (something), esp. in order to deceive others. **3** (*tr*) to mix together in a careless manner: *he shuffled the papers nervously.* **4** to mix up (cards in a pack) to change their order. **5** (*intr*) to behave in an evasive or underhand manner. **6** (when *intr*, foll. by *into* or *out of*) to move or cause to move clumsily: *he shuffled out of the door.* ♦ *n* **7** the act or an instance of shuffling. **8** a rearrangement: *a Cabinet shuffle.* **9** a dance or dance step with short dragging movements of the feet. [C16: prob. from Low G *schüffeln*]
> 'shuffler *n*

shuffleboard ('ʃʌfªl͵bɔːd) *n* a game in which players push wooden or plastic discs with a long cue towards numbered scoring sections marked on a floor, esp. a ship's deck.

shuffle off *vb* (*tr, adv*) to thrust off or put aside: *shuffle off responsibility.*

shuffle play *n* a facility on a compact disc player that selects tracks at random from a number of compact discs.

shufty *or* **shufti** ('ʃʊftɪ, 'ʃʌftɪ) *n, pl* **shufties.** *Brit. sl.* a look; peep. [C20: from Ar.]

Shufu *or* **Sufu** ★ ('ʃuː'fuː) *n* transliteration of the Chinese name for **Kashi.**

shun (ʃʌn) *vb* **shuns, shunning, shunned.** (*tr*) to avoid deliberately. [OE *scunian,* from ?]

shunt (ʃʌnt) *vb* **1** to turn or cause to turn to one side. **2** *Railways.* to transfer (rolling stock) from track to track. **3** *Electronics.* to divert or be diverted through a shunt. **4** (*tr*) to evade by putting off onto someone else. ♦ *n* **5** the act or an instance of shunting. **6** a railway point. **7** *Electronics.* a low-resistance conductor connected in parallel across a part of a circuit to provide an alternative path for a known fraction of the current. **8** *Med.* a channel that bypasses the normal circulation of the blood. **9** *Brit. inf.* a collision that occurs when a vehicle runs into the back of the vehicle in front. [C13: ?from *shunen* to SHUN]

shunt-wound ('ʃʌnt͵waʊnd) *adj Electrical engineering.* (of a motor or generator) having the field and armature circuits connected in parallel.

shush (ʃuʃ) *interj* **1** be quiet! hush! ♦ *vb* **2** to silence or calm (someone) by or as if by saying "shush". [C20: reduplication of SH, infl. by HUSH]

Shushan ★ ('ʃuː͵ʃæn) *n* the Biblical name for **Susa.**

shut (ʃʌt) *vb* **shuts, shutting, shut. 1** to move (something) so as to cover an aperture: *to shut a door.* **2** to close (something) by bringing together the parts: *to shut a book.* **3** (*tr*; often foll. by *up*) to close or lock the doors of: *to shut up a house.* **4** (*tr*; foll. by *in, out,* etc.) to confine, enclose, or exclude. **5** (*tr*) to prevent (a business, etc.) from operating. **6 shut the door on. 6a** to refuse to think about. **6b** to render impossible. ♦ *adj* **7** closed or fastened. ♦ *n* **8** the act or time of shutting. ♦ See also **shutdown, shut-off,** etc. [OE *scyttan*]

shutdown ('ʃʌt͵daʊn) *n* **1a** the closing of a factory, shop, etc. **1b** (*as modifier*): *shutdown costs.* ♦ *vb* **shut down.** (*adv*) **2** to cease or cause to cease operation. **3** (*tr*) to close by lowering.

Shute ★ (ʃuːt) *n* Nevil, real name *Nevil Shute Norway.* 1899–1960, British novelist, in Australia after World War II: noted for his novels *A Town like Alice* (1950) and *On the Beach* (1957).

shuteye ('ʃʌt͵aɪ) *n* a slang term for **sleep.**

shut-in *n Chiefly US.* **a** a person confined indoors by illness. **b** (*as modifier*): *a shut-in patient.*

shut-off *n* **1** a device that shuts something off, esp. a machine control. **2** a stoppage or cessation. ♦ *vb* **shut off.** (*tr, adv*) **3** to stem the flow of. **4** to block off the passage through. **5** to isolate or separate.

shutout ('ʃʌt͵aʊt) *n* **1** a less common word for **lockout. 2** *Sport.* a match in which the opposition does not score. ♦ *vb* **shut out.** (*tr, adv*) **3** to keep out or exclude. **4** to conceal from sight: *we planted trees to shut out the view of the road.*

shutter ('ʃʌtə) *n* **1** a hinged doorlike cover, often louvred and usually one of a pair, for closing off a window. **2 put up the shutters.** to close business at the end of the day or permanently. **3** *Photog.* an opaque shield in a camera that, when tripped, admits light to expose the film or plate for a predetermined period, usually a fraction of a second. **4** *Music.* one of the louvred covers over the mouths of organ pipes, operated by the swell pedal. **5** a person or thing that shuts. ♦ *vb* (*tr*) **6** to close with a shutter or shutters. **7** to equip with a shutter or shutters.

shuttering ('ʃʌtərɪŋ) *n* another word (esp. *Brit.*) for **formwork.**

shuttle ('ʃʌtªl) *n* **1** a bobbin-like device used in weaving for passing the weft thread between the warp threads. **2** a small bobbin-like device used to hold the thread in a sewing machine, etc. **3a** a bus, train, aircraft, etc., that plies between two points. **3b** short for **space shuttle. 4a** the movement between various countries of a diplomat in order to negotiate with rulers who refuse to meet each other. **4b** (*as modifier*): *shuttle diplomacy*. **5** *Badminton*, *etc*. short for **shuttlecock**. ◆ *vb* **shuttles, shuttling, shuttled. 6** to move or cause to move by or as if by a shuttle. [OE *scytel* bolt]

shuttlecock ('ʃʌt²l,kɒk) *n* **1** a light cone consisting of a cork stub with feathered flights, struck to and fro in badminton and battledore. **2** anything moved to and fro, as in an argument.

shut up *vb* (*adv*) **1** (*tr*) to prevent all access to. **2** (*tr*) to confine or imprison. **3** *Inf.* to cease to talk or make a noise or cause to cease to talk or make a noise: often used in commands.

shwa (ʃwɑ:) *n* a variant spelling of **schwa**.

shy¹ (ʃaɪ) *adj* **shyer, shyest** *or* **shier, shiest. 1** not at ease in the company of others. **2** easily frightened; timid. **3** (often foll. by *of*) watchful or wary. **4** (foll. by *of*) *Inf.*, chiefly *US & Canad.* short (of). **5** (*in combination*) showing reluctance or disinclination: *workshy*. ◆ *vb* **shies, shying, shied.** (*intr*) **6** to move suddenly, as from fear: *the horse shied at the snake in the road*. **7** (usually foll. by *off* or *away*) to draw back. ◆ *n*, *pl* **shies. 8** a sudden movement, as from fear. [OE *sceoh*]
▸ **'shyer** *n* ▸ **'shyly** *adv* ▸ **'shyness** *n*

shy² (ʃaɪ) *vb* **shies, shying, shied. 1** to throw (something) with a sideways motion. ◆ *n*, *pl* **shies. 2** a quick throw. **3** *Inf.* a gibe. **4** *Inf.* an attempt. [C18: of Gmc origin]
▸ **'shyer** *n*

Shylock ('ʃaɪ,lɒk) *n* a heartless or demanding creditor. [C19: after *Shylock*, the heartless usurer in Shakespeare's *The Merchant of Venice* (1596)]

shyster ('ʃaɪstə) *n Sl.*, chiefly *US.* a person, esp. a lawyer or politician, who uses discreditable methods. [C19: prob. based on *Scheuster*, a disreputable 19th-cent. New York lawyer]

si (si:) *n Music.* the syllable used in the fixed system of solmization for the note B. [C14: see GAMUT]

Si¹ (ʃi:) *or* **Si Kiang** ★ *n* a variant transliteration of the Chinese name for the **Xi**.

Si² the chemical symbol for silicon.

SI **1** symbol for Système International (d'Unités). See **SI unit. 2** *NZ abbrev.* for South Island.

sial ('saɪəl) *n* the silicon-rich and aluminium-rich rocks of the earth's continental upper crust. [C20: *si(licon)* + *al(uminium)*]
▸ **sialic** (saɪ'ælɪk) *adj*

Sialkot ★ (sɪ'ælkɒt) *n* a city in NE Pakistan: shrine of Guru Nanak. Pop.: 296 000 (1981).

Siam ★ (saɪ'æm, 'saɪæm) *n* **1** the former name (until 1939 and 1945–49) of **Thailand. 2 Gulf of.** an arm of the South China Sea between the Malay Peninsula and Indochina.

siamang ('saɪə,mæŋ) *n* a large black gibbon of Sumatra and the Malay Peninsula, having the second and third toes united. [C19: from Malay]

Siamese (,saɪə'mi:z) *n*, *pl* **Siamese. 1** See **Siamese cat.** ◆ *adj* **2** characteristic of, relating to, or being a Siamese twin. ◆ *adj*, *n*, *pl* **Siamese. 3** another word for **Thai.**

Siamese cat *n* a short-haired breed of cat with a tapering tail, blue eyes, and dark ears, mask, tail, and paws.

Siamese fighting fish *n* a brightly coloured labyrinth fish of Thailand and Malaysia: the males are very pugnacious.

Siamese twins *pl n* twin babies born joined together at some point, such as at the hips.

Sian ★ (ʃjɑ:n) *n* a variant transliteration of the Chinese name for **Xi An.**

Siang ★ (ʃjɑ:ŋ) *n* a variant transliteration of the Chinese name for the **Xiang.**

Siangtan ★ ('ʃjɑ:ŋ'tɑ:n) *n* a variant transliteration of the Chinese name for **Xiangtan.**

sib (sɪb) *n* **1** a blood relative. **2** kinsmen collectively; kindred. [OE *sibb*]

SIB (in Britain) *abbrev.* for Securities and Investments Board: a body that regulates financial dealings in the City of London.

Sib. *abbrev.* for Siberia(n).

Sibelius ★ (sɪ'beɪlɪəs) *n* Jean (ʒɑn). 1865–1957, Finnish composer, noted for his seven symphonies, his symphonic poems, such as *Finlandia* (1900), and his violin concerto (1905).

Siberia ★ (saɪ'bɪərɪə) *n* a vast region of Russia and N Kazakhstan: extends from the Ural Mountains to the Pacific and from the Arctic Ocean to the borders with China and Mongolia; colonized rapidly after the building of the Trans-Siberian Railway. Area: 13 807 037 sq. km (5 330 896 sq. miles).
▸ **Si'berian** *n*, *adj*

sibilant ('sɪbɪlənt) *adj* **1** *Phonetics.* relating to or denoting the consonants (s, z, ʃ, ʒ), all pronounced with a characteristic hissing sound. **2** having a hissing sound. ◆ *n* **3** a sibilant consonant. [C17: from L *sibilāre* to hiss, imit.]
▸ **'sibilance** *or* **'sibilancy** *n* ▸ **'sibilantly** *adv*

sibilate ('sɪbɪ,leɪt) *vb* **sibilates, sibilating, sibilated.** to pronounce or utter (words or speech) with a hissing sound.
▸ **,sibi'lation** *n*

Sibiu ★ (*Romanian* si'biu) *n* an industrial town in W central Romania: originally a Roman city, refounded by German colonists in the 12th century. Pop.: 168 619 (1993 est.). German name: **Hermannstadt.** Hungarian name: **Nagyszeben.**

sibling ('sɪblɪŋ) *n* **a** a person's brother or sister. **b** (*as modifier*): *sibling rivalry*. [C19: specialized modern use of OE *sibling* relative, from SIB]

sibyl ('sɪbɪl) *n* **1** (in ancient Greece and Rome) any of a number of women believed to be oracles or prophetesses. **2** a witch, fortune-teller, or sorceress. [C13: ult. from Gk *Sibulla*, from ?]
▸ **sibylline** ('sɪbɪ,laɪn) *adj*

sic¹ (sɪk) *adv* so or thus: inserted in brackets in a text to indicate that an odd or questionable reading is what was actually written or printed. [L]

sic² (sɪk) *vb* **sics, sicking, sicked.** (*tr*) **1** to attack: used only in commands, as to a dog. **2** to urge (a dog) to attack. [C19: dialect var. of SEEK]

Sic. *abbrev. for:* **1** Sicilian. **2** Sicily.

Sica ★ (*Italian* 'si:ka) *n* **Vittorio de.** See (Vittorio) **de Sica.**

siccative ('sɪkətɪv) *n* a substance added to a liquid to promote drying: used in paints and some medicines. [C16: from LL *siccātīvus*, from L *siccāre* to dry up, from *siccus* dry]

Sichuan ('sɪ'tʃwɑ:n) *or* **Szechwan** ★ *n* a province of SW China: the most populous administrative division in the country, esp. in the central Red Basin, where it is crossed by three main tributaries of the Yangtze. Capital: Chengdu. Pop.: 112 140 000 (1995 est.). Area: about 569 800 sq. km (220 000 sq. miles).

Sicilia ★ (si'tʃi:lja) *n* the Latin and Italian name for **Sicily.**

siciliano (,si:tʃi:'ljɑ:nəu) *n*, *pl* **sicilianos. 1** an old dance in six-beat or twelve-beat time. **2** a piece of music composed for or in the rhythm of this dance. [It.]

Sicily ★ (sɪsɪlɪ) *n* the largest island in the Mediterranean, separated from the tip of SW Italy by the Strait of Messina: administratively an autonomous region of Italy; settled by Phoenicians, Greeks, and Carthaginians before the Roman conquest of 241 B.C.; under Normans (12th–13th centuries); formed the **Kingdom of the Two Sicilies** with Naples in 1815; mountainous and volcanic. Capital: Palermo. Pop.: 5 025 280 (1994 est.). Area: 25 460 sq. km (9830 sq. miles). Latin names: **Sicilia, Trinacria.** Italian name: **Sicilia.**
▸ **Sicilian** (sɪ'sɪlɪən) *adj*, *n*

sick¹ (sɪk) *adj* **1** inclined or likely to vomit. **2a** suffering from ill health. **2b** (*as collective n*; preceded by *the*): *the sick*. **3a** of or used by people who are unwell: *sick benefits*. **3b** (*in combination*): *a sickroom*. **4** deeply affected with a mental or spiritual feeling akin to physical sickness: *sick at heart*. **5** mentally or spiritually disturbed. **6** *Inf.* delighting in or catering for the macabre: *sick humour*. **7** Also: **sick and tired.** (often foll. by *of*) *Inf.* disgusted or weary: *I am sick of his everlasting laughter*. **8** (often foll. by *for*) weary with longing: *I am sick for my own country*. **9** pallid or sickly. **10** not in working order. ◆ *n*, *vb* **11** an informal word for **vomit.** [OE *sēoc*]
▸ **'sickish** *adj*

sick[2] (sɪk) *vb* a variant spelling of **sic**[2].

sickbay ('sɪk,beɪ) *n* a room for the treatment of the sick or injured, as on board a ship or at a boarding school.

sick building syndrome *n* a group of symptoms, such as headaches, eye irritation, and lethargy, that may be experienced by workers in offices that are totally air-conditioned.

sicken ('sɪkən) *vb* **1** to make or become nauseated or disgusted. **2** (*intr*; often foll. by *for*) to show symptoms (of an illness).
▸ '**sickener** *n*

sickening ('sɪkənɪŋ) *adj* **1** causing sickness or revulsion. **2** *Inf.* extremely annoying.
▸ '**sickeningly** *adv*

Sickert ★ ('sɪkət) *n* **Walter Richard**. 1860–1942, British impressionist painter.

sick headache *n* **1** a headache accompanied by nausea. **2** a nontechnical name for **migraine**.

sickie ('sɪkɪ) *n Inf.* a day of sick leave from work. [C20: from SICK[1] + -IE]

sickle ('sɪk°l) *n* an implement for cutting grass, corn, etc., having a curved blade and a short handle. [OE *sicol*, from L *secula*]

sick leave *n* leave of absence from work through illness.

sicklebill ('sɪk°l,bɪl) *n* any of various birds having a markedly curved bill, such as certain hummingbirds and birds of paradise.

sickle-cell anaemia *n* a hereditary form of anaemia occurring mainly in Black populations, in which a large number of red blood cells become sickle-shaped.

sick list *n* **1** a list of the sick, esp. in the army or navy. **2** **on the sick list**. ill.

sickly ('sɪklɪ) *adj* **sicklier, sickliest. 1** disposed to frequent ailments; not healthy; weak. **2** of or caused by sickness. **3** (of a smell, taste, etc.) causing revulsion or nausea. **4** (of light or colour) faint or feeble. **5** mawkish; insipid.
♦ *adv* **6** in a sick or sickly manner.
▸ '**sickliness** *n*

sick-making *adj Inf.* galling; sickening.

sickness ('sɪknɪs) *n* **1** an illness or disease. **2** nausea or queasiness. **3** the state or an instance of being sick.

sick pay *n* wages paid to an employee while he is on sick leave.

sic transit gloria mundi *Latin.* ('sɪk 'trænsɪt 'glɔːrɪ,ɑː 'mʊndiː) thus passes the glory of the world.

Sicyon ★ ('sɪsɪ,ɒn, 'sɪʃɪən) *n* an ancient city in S Greece, in the NE Peloponnese near Corinth: declined after 146 B.C.

sidalcea (sɪ'dælsɪə) *n* any of a genus of hardy perennial plants with pink flowers. Also called **Greek mallow**. [from NL]

Siddhartha ★ (sɪ'dɑːtə) *n* the personal name of the **Buddha**.

Siddons ★ ('sɪd°nz) *n* **Sarah**. 1755–1831, British tragedienne.

side (saɪd) *n* **1** a line or surface that borders anything. **2** *Geom.* **2a** any line segment forming part of the perimeter of a plane geometric figure. **2b** another name for **face** (sense 13). **3** either of two parts into which an object, surface, area, etc., can be divided: *the right side and the left side*. **4** either of the two surfaces of a flat object: *the right and wrong side of the cloth*. **5** a surface or part of an object that extends vertically: *the side of a cliff*. **6** either half of a human or animal body, esp. the area around the waist: *I have a pain in my side*. **7** the area immediately next to a person or thing: *he stood at her side*. **8** a district, point, or direction within an area identified by reference to a central point: *the south side of the city*. **9** the area at the edge of a room, road, etc. **10** aspect or part: *look on the bright side*. **11** one of two or more contesting factions, teams, etc. **12** a page in an essay, etc. **13** a position, opinion, etc., held in opposition to another in a dispute. **14** line of descent: *he gets his brains from his mother's side*. **15** *Inf.* a television channel. **16** *Billiards, etc.* spin imparted to a ball by striking it off-centre with the cue. **17** *Brit. sl.* insolence or pretentiousness: *to put on side*. **18** **on one side**. set apart from

the rest, as provision for emergencies, etc. **19** **on the side.** **19a** apart from or in addition to the main object. **19b** as a sideline. **19c** *US.* as a side dish. **20** **take sides**. to support one person, opinion, etc., as against another. ♦ *adj* **21** being on one side; lateral. **22** from or viewed as if from one side. **23** directed towards one side. **24** subordinate or incidental: *side road*. ♦ *vb* **sides, siding, sided**. **25** (*intr*; usually foll. by *with*) to support or associate oneself (with a faction, interest, etc.). [OE *sīde*]

side arms *pl n* weapons carried on the person, by belt or holster, such as a sword, pistol, etc.

sideband ('saɪd,bænd) *n* the frequency band either above (**upper sideband**) or below (**lower sideband**) the carrier frequency, within which fall the components produced by modulation of a carrier wave.

sideboard ('saɪd,bɔːd) *n* a piece of furniture intended to stand at the side of a dining room, with drawers, cupboards, and shelves to hold silver, china, linen, etc.

sideboards ('saɪd,bɔːdz) *pl n* another term for **sideburns**.

sideburns ('saɪd,bɜːnz) *pl n* a man's whiskers grown down either side of the face in front of the ears. Also called: **sideboards, side whiskers**, (*Austral.*) **sidelevers**.

sidecar ('saɪd,kɑː) *n* a small car attached on one side to a motorcycle, the other side being supported by a single wheel.

side chain *n Chem.* a group of atoms bound to an atom, usually a carbon atom, that forms part of a larger chain or ring in a molecule.

-sided *adj* (*in combination*) having a side or sides as specified: *three-sided; many-sided*.

side deal *n* a transaction between two people for their private benefit, which is subsidiary to a contract negotiated by them on behalf of the organizations they represent.

side dish *n* a portion of food served in addition to the main dish.

side drum *n* a small double-headed drum carried at the side with snares that produce a rattling effect.

side effect *n* **1** any unwanted nontherapeutic effect caused by a drug. **2** any secondary effect, esp. an undesirable one.

side-foot *Soccer.* ♦ *n* **1** a shot or pass played with the side of the foot. ♦ *vb* **2** (*tr*) to strike (a ball) with the side of the foot.

sidekick ('saɪd,kɪk) *n Inf.* a close friend or follower who accompanies another on adventures, etc.

sidelight ('saɪd,laɪt) *n* **1** light coming from the side. **2** a side window. **3** either of the two navigational running lights used by vessels at night, a red light on the port and a green on the starboard. **4** *Brit.* either of two small lights on the front of a motor vehicle. **5** additional or incidental information.

sideline ('saɪd,laɪn) *n* **1** *Sport.* a line that marks the side boundary of a playing area. **2** a subsidiary interest or source of income. **3** an auxiliary business activity or line of merchandise. ♦ *vb* **sidelines, sidelining, sidelined. 4** (*tr*) *Chiefly US & Canad.* to prevent (a player) from taking part in a game.

sidelines ('saɪd,laɪnz) *pl n* **1** *Sport.* the area immediately outside the playing area, where substitute players sit. **2** the peripheral areas of any region, organization, etc.

sidelong ('saɪd,lɒŋ) *adj* (*prenominal*) **1** directed or inclining to one side. **2** indirect or oblique. ♦ *adv* **3** from the side; obliquely.

sidereal (saɪ'dɪərɪəl) *adj* **1** of or involving the stars. **2** determined with reference to one or more stars: *the sidereal day*. [C17: from L *sīdereus*, from *sīdus* a star]
▸ si'**dereally** *adv*

sidereal day *n* See **day** (sense 5).

sidereal period *n Astron.* the period of revolution of a body about another with respect to one or more stars.

sidereal time *n* time based upon the rotation of the earth with respect to a particular star, the **sidereal day** being the unit of measurement.

sidereal year *n* See **year** (sense 5).

siderite ('saɪdə,raɪt) *n* **1** a pale yellow to brownish-black mineral consisting chiefly of iron(II) carbonate. It occurs mainly in ore veins and sedimentary rocks and is an important source of iron. Formula: $FeCO_3$. **2** a meteorite consisting principally of metallic iron.

sidero- *or before a vowel* **sider-** *combining form.* indicating iron: *siderolite.* [from Gk *sidēros*]

siderolite ('saɪdərə‚laɪt) *n* a meteorite consisting of a mixture of iron, nickel, and such ferromagnesian minerals as olivine.

siderosis (‚saɪdə'rəʊsɪs) *n* a lung disease caused by breathing in fine particles of iron or other metallic dust.

siderostat ('saɪdərəʊ‚stæt) *n* an astronomical instrument consisting of a plane mirror rotated by a clock mechanism about two axes so that light from a celestial body, esp. the sun, is reflected along a constant direction for a long period of time. [C19: from *sidero-*, from L *sidus* a star + -STAT]

side-saddle *n* **1** a riding saddle originally designed for women riders in skirts who sit with both legs on the near side of the horse. ◆ *adv* **2** on or as if on a side-saddle.

sideshow ('saɪd‚ʃəʊ) *n* **1** a small show or entertainment offered in conjunction with a larger attraction, as at a circus or fair. **2** a subordinate event or incident.

sideslip ('saɪd‚slɪp) *n* **1** a sideways skid, as of a motor vehicle. ◆ *vb* **sideslips, sideslipping, sideslipped. 2** another name for **slip**[1] (sense 11).

sidesman ('saɪdzmən) *n, pl* **sidesmen.** *Church of England.* a man elected to help the parish church-warden.

side-splitting *adj* **1** producing great mirth. **2** (of laughter) uproarious or very hearty.

sidestep ('saɪd‚step) *vb* **sidesteps, sidestepping, sidestepped. 1** to step aside from or out of the way of (something). **2** (*tr*) to dodge or circumvent. ◆ *n* **side step. 3** a movement to one side, as in dancing, boxing, etc.
▸ 'side‚stepper *n*

sidestroke ('saɪd‚strəʊk) *n* a type of swimming stroke in which the swimmer lies sideways in the water making a scissors kick with his legs.

sideswipe ('saɪd‚swaɪp) *n* **1** a glancing blow or hit along or from the side. **2** an unexpected criticism of someone or something while discussing another subject. ◆ *vb* **sideswipes, sideswiping, sideswiped. 3** to strike (someone) with a glancing blow from the side.
▸ 'side‚swiper *n*

sidetrack ('saɪd‚træk) *vb* **1** to distract or be distracted from a main subject or topic. ◆ *n* **2** *US & Canad.* a railway siding. **3** a digression.

side-valve engine *n* a type of internal-combustion engine in which the inlet and exhaust valves are in the cylinder block at the side of the pistons.

sidewalk ('saɪd‚wɔːk) *n* the US and Canad. word for **pavement.**

sidewall ('saɪd‚wɔːl) *n* either of the sides of a pneumatic tyre between the tread and the rim.

sideward ('saɪdwəd) *adj* **1** directed or moving towards one side. ◆ *adv also* **sidewards. 2** towards one side.

sideways ('saɪd‚weɪz) *adv* **1** moving, facing, or inclining towards one side. **2** from one side; obliquely. **3** with one side forward. ◆ *adj* (*prenominal*) **4** moving or directed to or from one side. **5** towards or from one side.

side whiskers *pl n* another name for **sideburns.**

sidewinder ('saɪd‚waɪndə) *n* **1** a North American rattlesnake that moves forwards by a sideways looping motion. **2** *Boxing, US.* a heavy swinging blow from the side.

Sidi-bel-Abbès ★ (*French* sidibɛlabɛs) *n* a city in NW Algeria: headquarters of the Foreign Legion until Algerian independence (1962). Pop.: 152 778 (1987).

siding ('saɪdɪŋ) *n* **1** a short stretch of railway track connected to a main line, used for storing rolling stock. **2** a short railway line giving access to the main line for freight from a factory, etc. **3** *US & Canad.* material attached to the outside of a building to make it weatherproof.

sidle ('saɪdᵊl) *vb* **sidles, sidling, sidled.** (*intr*) **1** to move in a furtive or stealthy manner. **2** to move along sideways. [C17: back formation from obs. *sideling* sideways]

Sidmouth ★ ('sɪdməθ) *n* **1st Viscount.** See (Henry) Addington.

Sidney *or* **Sydney** ★ ('sɪdnɪ) *n* Sir **Philip.** 1554–86, English poet, courtier, and soldier. His works include the romance *Arcadia* (1590) and the sonnet sequence *Astrophel and Stella* (1591).

Sidon ★ ('saɪdᵊn) *n* the chief city of ancient Phoenicia: founded in the third millennium B.C.; wealthy through trade and the making of glass and purple dyes; now the Lebanese city of Saïda.
▸ **Sidonian** (saɪ'dəʊnɪən) *adj, n*

Sidra ★ ('sɪdrə) *n* **Gulf of.** a wide inlet of the Mediterranean on the N coast of Libya.

SIDS *abbrev. for* sudden infant death syndrome. See **cot death.**

Siegbahn ★ ('siːɡbɑːn) *n* **1 Kai** (kaɪ). born 1918, Swedish physicist who worked on electron spectroscopy: Nobel prize for physics 1981. **2** his father, **Karl Manne Georg** (kɑːrl 'manə 'jeːɔrj). 1886–1978, Swedish physicist: Nobel prize for physics (1924) for his work on X-ray spectroscopy.

siege (siːdʒ) *n* **1a** the offensive operations carried out to capture a fortified place by surrounding it and deploying weapons against it. **1b** (*as modifier*): *siege warfare.* **2** a persistent attempt to gain something. **3** *Obs.* a seat or throne. **4 lay siege to. 4a** to besiege. **4b** to importune. [C13: from OF *sege* a seat, from Vulgar L *sēdicāre* (unattested) to sit down, from L *sedēre*]

siege mentality *n* a state of mind in which a person believes that he or she is being constantly oppressed or attacked.

Siegen ★ ('ziːɡən) *n* a city in NW Germany, in North Rhine-Westphalia: manufacturing centre: birthplace of Rubens. Pop.: 111 541 (1995 est.).

Siegfried ★ ('siːɡfriːd; *German* 'ziːkfriːt) *n German myth.* a German prince, the son of Sigmund and husband of Kriemhild, who, in the *Nibelungenlied*, assumes possession of the treasure of the Nibelungs by slaying the dragon that guards it, wins Brunhild for King Gunther, and is eventually killed by Hagen. Norse equivalent: **Sigurd.**

siemens ('siːmənz) *n, pl* **siemens.** the derived SI unit of electrical conductance equal to 1 reciprocal ohm. Symbol: S Formerly called: **mho.**

Siemens ★ ('siːmənz) *n* **1 Ernst Werner von** (ɛrnst 'vɛrnər fɔn). 1816–92, German engineer. His inventions include the self-excited dynamo and electrolytic refining. **2** his brother, Sir **William**, original name *Karl Wilhelm Siemens.* 1823–83, British engineer, born in Germany, who invented the open-hearth steel furnace.

Siena ★ (sɪ'ɛnə; *Italian* 'sjɛːna) *n* a walled city in central Italy, in Tuscany: founded by the Etruscans; important artistic centre (13th–14th centuries); university (13th century). Pop.: 58 278 (1990).

Sienkiewicz ★ (*Polish* ʃɛn'kjɛvitʃ) *n* **Henryk** ('xɛnrik). 1846–1916, Polish novelist. His works include *Quo Vadis?* (1896) and the war trilogy *With Fire and Sword* (1884): Nobel prize for literature 1905.

sienna (sɪ'ɛnə) *n* **1** a natural earth containing ferric oxide used as a yellowish-brown pigment when untreated (**raw sienna**) or a reddish-brown pigment when roasted (**burnt sienna**). **2** the colour of this pigment. [C18: from It. *terra di Siena* earth of SIENA]

sierra (sɪ'ɛərə) *n* a range of mountains with jagged peaks, esp. in Spain or America. [C17: from Sp., lit.: saw, from L *serra*]
▸ **si'erran** *adj*

Sierra Leone ★ (sɪ'ɛərə lɪ'əʊnɪ, lɪ'əʊn) *n* a republic in W Africa, on the Atlantic: became a British colony in 1808 and gained independence (within the Commonwealth) in 1961; declared a republic in 1971; became a one-party state in 1978; multiparty democracy restored in 1991 but civil unrest followed: consists of coastal swamps rising to a plateau in the east. Official language: English. Religion: Muslim majority and animist. Currency: leone. Capital: Freetown. Pop.: 4 617 000 (1996). Area: 71 740 sq. km (27 699 sq. miles).
▸ **Sierra Leonean** *adj, n*

★ people and places

Sierra Madre ★ (*Spanish* 'sjerra 'maðre) *n* (*functioning as sing*) the main mountain system of Mexico, extending for 2500 km (1500 miles) southeast from the N border: consists of the **Sierra Madre Oriental** in the east, the **Sierra Madre Occidental** in the west, and the **Sierra Madre del Sur** in the south. Highest peak: Citlaltépetl, 5699 m (18 698 ft).

Sierra Morena ★ (*Spanish* 'sjerra mo'rena) *n* (*functioning as sing*) a mountain range in SW Spain, between the Guadiana and Guadalquivir Rivers. Highest peak: Estrella, 1299 m (4262 ft).

Sierra Nevada ★ *n* (*functioning as sing*) **1** (sɪ'ɛərə nɪ'vɑːdə). a mountain range in E California, parallel to the Coast Ranges. Highest peak: Mount Whitney, 4418 m (14 495 ft). **2** (*Spanish* 'sjerra ne'βaða). a mountain range in SE Spain, mostly in Granada and Almería provinces. Highest peak: Cerro de Mulhacén, 3478 m (11 411 ft).

siesta (sɪ'ɛstə) *n* a rest or nap, usually taken in the early afternoon, as in hot countries. [C17: from Sp., from L *sexta hōra* the sixth hour, i.e. noon]

sieve (sɪv) *n* **1** a device for separating lumps from powdered material, straining liquids, etc., consisting of a container with a mesh or perforated bottom through which the material is shaken or poured. ◆ *vb* **sieves, sieving, sieved. 2** to pass or cause to pass through a sieve. **3** (*tr*; often foll. by *out*) to separate or remove (lumps, materials, etc.) by use of a sieve. [OE *sife*]
▸ **'sieve,like** *adj*

Sieyès ★ (*French* sjejes) *n* **Emmanuel Joseph** (ɛmanɥel ʒozef), called *Abbé Sieyès*. 1748–1836, French statesman and churchman, prominent during the Revolution. He was instrumental in bringing Napoleon I to power (1799).

sift (sɪft) *vb* **1** (*tr*) to sieve (sand, flour, etc.) in order to remove the coarser particles. **2** to scatter (something) over a surface through a sieve. **3** (*tr*) to separate with or as if with a sieve. **4** (*tr*) to examine minutely: *to sift evidence*. **5** (*intr*) to move as if through a sieve. [OE *siftan*]
▸ **'sifter** *n*

siftings ('sɪftɪŋz) *pl n* material or particles separated out by or as if by a sieve.

sigh (saɪ) *vb* **1** (*intr*) to draw in and exhale audibly a deep breath as an expression of weariness, relief, etc. **2** (*intr*) to make a sound resembling this. **3** (*intr*; often foll. by *for*) to yearn, long, or pine. **4** (*tr*) to utter or express with sighing. ◆ *n* **5** the act or sound of sighing. [OE *sīcan*, from ?]
▸ **'sigher** *n*

sight (saɪt) *n* **1** the power or faculty of seeing; vision. Related adj: **visual. 2** the act or an instance of seeing. **3** the range of vision: *within sight of land*. **4** point of view; judgment: *in his sight she could do no wrong*. **5** a glimpse or view (esp. in **catch** *or* **lose sight of**). **6** anything that is seen. **7** (*often pl*) anything worth seeing: *the sights of London*. **8** *Inf.* anything unpleasant or undesirable to see: *his room was a sight!* **9** any of various devices or instruments used to assist the eye in making alignments or directional observations, esp. such a device used in aiming a gun. **10** an observation or alignment made with such a device. **11** a **sight.** *Inf.* a great deal: *she's a sight too good for him.* **12** a **sight for sore eyes.** a person or thing that one is pleased or relieved to see. **13** **at** *or* **on sight.** as soon as seen. **13b** on presentation: *a bill payable at sight.* **14** **know by sight.** to be familiar with the appearance of without having personal acquaintance. **15** **not by a long sight.** *Inf.* on no account. **16** **set one's sights on.** to have (a specified goal) in mind. **17** **sight unseen.** without having seen the object at issue: *to buy a car sight unseen.* ◆ *vb* **18** (*tr*) to see, view, or glimpse. **19** (*tr*) **19a** to furnish with a sight or sights. **19b** to adjust the sight of. **20** to aim (a firearm) using the sight. [OE *sihth*]
▸ **'sightable** *adj*

sighted ('saɪtɪd) *adj* **1** not blind. **2** (*in combination*) having sight of a specified kind: *short-sighted*.

sighting ('saɪtɪŋ) *n* **1** an occasion on which something is seen, esp. something rare or unusual. **2** another name for **sight** (sense 10).

sighting shot *n* an experimental shot made to assist gunmen in setting their sights.

sightless ('saɪtlɪs) *adj* **1** blind. **2** invisible.
▸ **'sightlessly** *adv* ▸ **'sightlessness** *n*

sightly ('saɪtlɪ) *adj* **sightlier, sightliest.** pleasing or attractive to see.
▸ **'sightliness** *n*

sight-read ('saɪt,riːd) *vb* **sight-reads, sight-reading, sight-read** (-,red). to sing or play (music in a printed or written form) without previous preparation.
▸ **'sight-,reader** *n* ▸ **'sight-,reading** *n*

sightscreen ('saɪt,skriːn) *n Cricket.* a large white screen placed near the boundary behind the bowler to help the batsman see the ball.

sightsee ('saɪt,siː) *vb* **sightsees, sightseeing, sightsaw, sightseen.** to visit the famous or interesting sights of (a place).
▸ **'sight,seeing** *n* ▸ **'sight,seer** *n*

Sigismund ★ ('sɪgɪsmənd) *n* 1368–1437, king of Hungary (1387–1437) and of Bohemia (1419–37); Holy Roman Emperor (1411–37).

sigla ('sɪglə) *n* the list of symbols used in a book, usually collected together as part of the preliminaries. [L: pl of *siglum*, dim. of *signum* sign]

sigma ('sɪgmə) *n* **1** the 18th letter in the Greek alphabet (Σ, σ, or, when final, ς), a consonant, transliterated as *S*. **2** *Maths.* the symbol Σ, indicating summation of the numbers of quantities indicated. [C17: from Gk]

sigma notation *n* an algebraic notation in which a capital Greek sigma (Σ) is used to indicate that all values of the expression following the sigma are to be added together (usually for values of a variable between specified limits).

sigmoid ('sɪgmɔɪd) *or* **sigmoidal** *adj* **1** shaped like the letter S. **2** of or relating to the sigmoid flexure of the large intestine. [C17: from Gk *sigmoeidēs* sigma-shaped]

sigmoid flexure *n* the S-shaped bend in the final portion of the large intestine.

Sigmund ★ ('sɪgmʊnd, 'siːgmʊnd; *German* 'ziːkmʊnt) *n* **1** *Norse myth.* the father of the hero Sigurd. **2** Also called: **Siegmund** (*German* 'ziːkmʊnt). *German myth.* king of the Netherlands, father of Siegfried.

sign (saɪn) *n* **1** something that indicates a fact, condition, etc., that is not immediately or outwardly observable. **2** an action or gesture intended to convey information, a command, etc. **3a** a board, placard, etc., displayed in public and intended to inform, warn, etc. **3b** (*as modifier*): *a sign painter*. **4** an arbitrary mark or device that stands for a word, phrase, etc. **5** *Maths, logic.* **5a** any symbol used to indicate an operation: *a plus sign*. **5b** the positivity or negativity of a number, expression, etc. **6** an indication or vestige: *the house showed no signs of being occupied*. **7** a portentous or significant event. **8** the scent or spoor of an animal. **9** *Med.* any objective evidence of the presence of a disease or disorder. **10** *Astrol.* See **sign of the zodiac.** ◆ *vb* **11** to write (one's name) as a signature to (a document, etc.) in attestation, confirmation, etc. **12** (*intr*; often foll. by *to*) to make a sign. **13** to engage or be engaged by written agreement, as a player for a team, etc. **14** (*tr*) to outline in gestures a sign over, esp. the sign of the cross. **15** (*tr*) to indicate by or as if by a sign; betoken. ◆ See also **sign away, sign in,** etc. [C13: from OF, from L *signum* a sign]
▸ **'signable** *adj* ▸ **'signer** *n*

Signac ★ (*French* siɲak) *n* **Paul** (pɔl). 1863–1935, French painter.

signal ('sɪgnəl) *n* **1** any sign, gesture, etc., that serves to communicate information. **2** anything that acts as an incitement to action: *the rise in prices was a signal for rebellion*. **3a** a variable parameter, such as a current or electromagnetic wave, by which information is conveyed through an electronic circuit, etc. **3b** the information so conveyed. **3c** (*as modifier*): *a signal generator*. ◆ *adj* **4** distinguished or conspicuous. **5** used to give or act as a signal. ◆ *vb* **signals, signalling, signalled** *or US* **signals, signaling, signaled. 6** to communicate (a message, etc.) to (a person). [C16: from OF *seignal*, from Med. L *signāle*, from L *signum* sign]
▸ **'signaller** *or US* **'signaler** *n*

signal box *n* **1** a building containing signal levers for all the railway lines in its section. **2** a control point for a large area of a railway system.

signalize *or* **signalise** ('sɪgnə,laɪz) *vb* **signalizes, signalizing, signalized** *or* **signalises, signalising, signalised**. (*tr*) **1** to make noteworthy. **2** to point out carefully.

signally ('sɪgnəlɪ) *adv* conspicuously or especially.

signalman ('sɪgⁿlmən) *n, pl* **signalmen**. a railway employee in charge of the signals and points within a section.

signal-to-noise ratio *n* the ratio of one parameter, such as power of a wanted signal, to the same parameter of the noise at a specified point in an electronic circuit, etc.

signatory ('sɪgnətərɪ, -trɪ) *n, pl* **signatories**. **1** a person who has signed a document such as a treaty or an organization, state, etc., on whose behalf such a document has been signed. ◆ *adj* **2** having signed a document, treaty, etc. [C17: from L *signātōrius* concerning sealing, from *signāre* to seal, from *signum* a mark]

signature ('sɪgnɪtʃə) *n* **1** the name of a person or a mark or sign representing his name. **2** the act of signing one's name. **3** a distinctive mark, characteristic, etc., that identifies a person or thing. **4** *Music.* See **key signature, time signature. 5** *Printing.* **5a** a sheet of paper printed with several pages that upon folding will become a section or sections of a book. **5b** such a sheet so folded. **5c** a mark, esp. a letter, printed on the first page of a signature. [C16: from OF, from Med. L *signātūra*, from L *signāre* to sign]

signature tune *n Brit.* a melody used to introduce or identify a television or radio programme, a performer, etc.

sign away *vb* (*tr, adv*) to dispose of by or as if by signing a document.

signboard ('saɪn,bɔːd) *n* a board carrying a sign or notice, esp. one used to advertise a product, event, etc.

signet ('sɪgnɪt) *n* **1** a small seal, esp. one as part of a finger ring. **2** a seal used to stamp or authenticate documents. **3** the impression made by such a seal. [C14: from Med. L *signētum* a little seal, from L *signum* a sign]

signet ring *n* a finger ring bearing a signet.

significance (sɪg'nɪfɪkəns) *n* **1** consequence or importance. **2** something expressed or intended. **3** the state or quality of being significant. **4** *Statistics.* a measure of the confidence that can be placed in a result as not being merely a matter of chance.

significant (sɪg'nɪfɪkənt) *adj* **1** having or expressing a meaning. **2** having a covert or implied meaning. **3** important or momentous. **4** *Statistics.* of or relating to a difference between a result derived from a hypothesis and its observed value that is too large to be attributed to chance. [C16: from L *significāre* to SIGNIFY]
▶ **sig'nificantly** *adv*

significant figures *pl n* **1** the figures of a number that express a magnitude to a specified degree of accuracy: *3.141 59 to four significant figures is 3.142.* **2** the number of such figures: *3.142 has four significant figures.*

significant other *n US inf.* a spouse or lover.

signification (,sɪgnɪfɪ'keɪʃən) *n* **1** meaning or sense. **2** the act of signifying.

signify ('sɪgnɪ,faɪ) *vb* **signifies, signifying, signified**. (when *tr, may take a clause as object*) **1** (*tr*) to indicate or suggest. **2** (*tr*) to imply or portend: *the clouds signified the coming storm.* **3** (*tr*) to stand as a symbol, sign, etc. (*for*). **4** (*intr*) to be important. [C13: from OF, from L *significāre*, from *signum* a mark + *facere* to make]
▶ **sig'nificative** *adj* ▶ **'signi,fier** *n*

sign in *vb* (*adv*) **1** to sign or cause to sign a register, as at a hotel, club, etc. **2** to make or become a member, as of a club.

signing ('saɪnɪŋ) *n* a specific set of manual signs used to communicate with deaf people.

sign language *n* any system of communication by manual signs or gestures, such as one used by deaf people.

sign off *vb* (*adv*) **1** (*intr*) to announce the end of a radio or television programme, esp. at the end of a day. **2** (*tr*) (of a

doctor) to declare (someone) unfit for work, because of illness. **3** (*intr*) *Brit.* to terminate one's claim to social security benefits.

sign of the zodiac *n* any of the 12 equal areas into which the zodiac can be divided, named after the 12 zodiacal constellations. In astrology, it is thought that a person's attitudes to life can be correlated with the sign in which the sun lay at the moment of their birth. Also called: **sign, star sign, sun sign.**

sign on *vb* (*adv*) **1** (*tr*) to hire or employ. **2** (*intr*) to commit oneself to a job, activity, etc. **3** (*intr*) *Brit.* to claim social security benefits.

signor *or* **signior** ('siːnjɔː; *Italian* siɲ'ɲor) *n, pl* **signors** *or* **signori** (*Italian* -'ɲori). an Italian man: usually used before a name as a title equivalent to *Mr*.

signora (siː'njɔːrə; *Italian* siɲ'ɲora) *n, pl* **signoras** *or* **signore** (*Italian* -re). a married Italian woman: a title of address equivalent to *Mrs* when placed before a name or *madam* when used alone. [It., fem of SIGNORE]

signore (siː'njɔːreɪ; *Italian* siɲ'ɲore) *n, pl* **signori** (-rɪ; *Italian* -ri). an Italian man: a title of respect equivalent to *sir* when used alone. [It., ult. from L *senior* an elder, from *senex* an old man]

Signorelli ★ (*Italian* siɲɲo'rɛlli) *n* **Luca** ('luːka). ?1441–1523, Italian painter.

Signoret ★ (*French* siɲɔrɛ) *n* **Simone** (simɔn), original name *Simone Kaminker*. 1921–85, French actress, whose films include *La Ronde* (1950) and *Ship of Fools* (1965): married to the actor and singer Yves Montand (1921–91).

signorina (,siːnjɔːˈriːnə; *Italian* siɲɲoˈrina) *n, pl* **signorinas** *or* **signorine** (*Italian* -ne). an unmarried Italian woman: a title of address equivalent to *Miss* when placed before a name or *madam* or *miss* when used alone. [It., dim. of SIGNORA]

signory ('siːnjərɪ) *n, pl* **signories**. a variant spelling of **seigniory.**

sign out *vb* (*adv*) to sign (one's name) to indicate that one is leaving a place: *he signed out for the evening.*

signpost ('saɪn,pəust) *n* **1** a post bearing a sign that shows the way, as at a roadside. **2** something that serves as a clue or indication. ◆ *vb* (*tr; usually passive*) **3** to mark with signposts. **4** to indicate direction towards.

sign up *vb* (*adv*) to enlist or cause to enlist, as for military service.

Sigurd ★ ('sɪguəd; *German* 'ziːgurt) *n Norse myth.* a hero who killed the dragon Fafnir to gain the treasure of Andvari, won Brynhild for Gunnar by deception, and then was killed by her when she discovered the fraud. His wife was Gudrun. German counterpart: **Siegfried.**

Sihanouk ★ ('siːanuk) *n* King **Norodom** (,nɔrə'dɔm). born 1922, Cambodian statesman; king of Cambodia (1941–55 and from 1993); prime minister (1955–60); head of state (1960–70, 1975–76); head of the transitional government (1991–93).

sika ('siːkə) *n* a Japanese forest-dwelling deer, now introduced into Britain, having a brown coat and a large white patch on the rump. [from Japanese *shika*]

Sikang ★ ('ʃiːˈkæŋ) *n* a former province of W China: established in 1928 from part of W Sichuan and E Tibet; dissolved in 1955.

Sikh (siːk) *n* **1** a member of an Indian religion that separated from Hinduism and was founded in the 16th century, that teaches monotheism and rejects the authority of the Vedas. ◆ *adj* **2** of or relating to the Sikhs or their religious beliefs. [C18: from Hindi, lit.: disciple, from Sansk. *śiksati* he studies]
▶ **'Sikh,ism** *n*

Si Kiang ★ ('ʃiː 'kjæŋ, kaɪ'æŋ) *n* See **Xi.**

Siking ★ ('siːˈkɪŋ) *n* a former name for **Xi An.**

Sikkim ★ ('sɪkɪm) *n* a state of NE India: under British control (1861–1947); became an Indian protectorate in 1950 and an Indian state in 1975; lies in the Himalayas, rising to 8600 m (28 216 ft) at Kanchenjunga in the north. Capital: Gangtok. Pop.: 444 000 (1994 est.). Area: 7096 sq. km (2740 sq. miles).
▶ **,Sikki'mese** *adj, n*

★ people and places

Sikorski ★ (sɪˈkɔːskɪ) *n* **Władysław** (ˈvlædɪˌslæf). 1881–1943, Polish general and statesman: prime minister (1922–23) and prime minister of the Polish government in exile during World War II: died in an air crash.

Sikorsky ★ (sɪˈkɔːskɪ) *n* **Igor**. 1889–1972, US aeronautical engineer, born in Russia. He designed the first successful helicopter (1939).

silage (ˈsaɪlɪdʒ) *n* any crop harvested while green for fodder and kept succulent by partial fermentation in a silo. Also called: **ensilage**. [C19: alteration (infl. by SILO) of ENSILAGE]

sild (sɪld) *n* any of various small young herrings, esp. when prepared and canned in Norway. [Norwegian]

silence (ˈsaɪləns) *n* **1** the state or quality of being silent. **2** the absence of sound or noise. **3** refusal or failure to speak, etc., when expected: *his silence on their promotion was alarming.* **4** a period of time without noise. **5** oblivion or obscurity. ◆ *vb* **silences, silencing, silenced.** (*tr*) **6** to bring to silence. **7** to put a stop to: *to silence all complaint.*

silencer (ˈsaɪlənsə) *n* **1** any device designed to reduce noise, esp. the device in the exhaust system of a motor vehicle. US and Canad. name: **muffler. 2** a device fitted to the muzzle of a firearm to deaden the report. **3** a person or thing that silences.

silene (saɪˈliːnɪ) *n* any of a genus of plants with pink or white flowers and slender leaves. [C18: NL, from L]

silent (ˈsaɪlənt) *adj* **1** characterized by an absence or near absence of noise or sound: *a silent house.* **2** tending to speak very little or not at all. **3** unable to speak. **4** failing to speak, communicate, etc., when expected: *the witness chose to remain silent.* **5** not spoken or expressed. **6** (of a letter) used in the orthography of a word but no longer pronounced in that word: *the "k" in "know" is silent.* **7** denoting a film that has no accompanying soundtrack. [C16: from L *silēns*, from *silēre* to be quiet] ▸ **ˈsilently** *adv* ▸ **ˈsilentness** *n*

silent cop *n Austral. sl.* a small raised hemispherical marker in the middle of a crossroads.

silent majority *n* a presumed moderate majority of the citizens who are too passive to make their views known.

Silenus ★ (saɪˈliːnəs; ˈsɪleɪnəs) *n Greek myth.* **1** chief of the satyrs and foster father to Dionysus. **2** (*pl* **Sileni** (saɪˈliːnaɪ; ˈsɪleɪniː)). (*often not cap.*) one of a class of woodland deities, closely similar to the satyrs.

Silesia ★ (saɪˈliːʃɪə) *n* a region of central Europe around the upper and middle Oder valley: mostly annexed by Prussia in 1742 but became almost wholly Polish in 1945; rich coal and iron-ore deposits. Polish name: **Śląsk.** Czech name: **Slezsko.** German name: **Schlesien.** ▸ **Siˈlesian** *adj, n*

silex (ˈsaɪlɛks) *n* a type of heat-resistant glass made from fused quartz. [C16: from L: hard stone]

silhouette (ˌsɪluˈɛt) *n* **1** the outline of a solid figure as cast by its shadow. **2** an outline drawing filled in with black, often a profile portrait cut out of black paper and mounted on a light ground. ◆ *vb* **silhouettes, silhouetting, silhouetted. 3** (*tr*) to cause to appear in silhouette. [C18: after Étienne de *Silhouette* (1709–67), F politician]

silica (ˈsɪlɪkə) *n* the dioxide of silicon (SiO$_2$), occurring naturally as quartz. It is a refractory insoluble material used in the manufacture of glass, ceramics, and abrasives. [C19: NL, from L *silex* hard stone]

silica gel *n* an amorphous form of silica capable of absorbing large quantities of water: used esp. in drying gases and oils.

silicate (ˈsɪlɪkɪt, -ˌkeɪt) *n* a salt or ester that can be regarded as derived from silicic acid. Silicates constitute a large proportion of the earth's minerals and are present in cement and glass.

siliceous or **silicious** (sɪˈlɪʃəs) *adj* **1** of, relating to, or containing silica: *a siliceous clay.* **2** (of plants) growing in soil rich in silica.

silicic (sɪˈlɪsɪk) *adj* of or containing silicon or an acid obtained from silicon.

silicic acid *n* a white gelatinous substance obtained by adding an acid to a solution of sodium silicate. It is best regarded as hydrated silica.

silicify (sɪˈlɪsɪˌfaɪ) *vb* **silicifies, silicifying, silicified.** to convert or be converted into silica: *silicified wood.* ▸ **siˌlicifiˈcation** *n*

silicon (ˈsɪlɪkən) *n* **a** a brittle metalloid element that exists in two allotropic forms; occurs principally in sand, quartz, granite, feldspar, and clay. It is usually a grey crystalline solid but is also found as a brown amorphous powder. It is used in transistors, solar cells, and alloys. Its compounds are widely used in glass manufacture and the building industry. Symbol: Si; atomic no.: 14; atomic wt.: 28.09. **b** (*modifier; sometimes cap.*) denoting an area of a country that contains much high-technology industry. [C19: from SILICA, on the model of *boron, carbon*]

silicon carbide *n* an extremely hard bluish-black insoluble crystalline substance produced by heating carbon with sand at a high temperature and used as an abrasive and refractory material. Very pure crystals are used as semiconductors. Formula: SiC.

silicon chip *n* another term for **chip** (sense 7).

silicon-controlled rectifier *n* a semiconductor rectifier whose forward current between two electrodes, the anode and cathode, is initiated by means of a signal applied to a third electrode, the gate. The current subsequently becomes independent of the signal. Also called: **thyristor.**

silicone (ˈsɪlɪˌkəʊn) *n Chem.* **a** any of a large class of polymeric synthetic materials that usually have resistance to temperature, water, and chemicals, and good insulating and lubricating properties, making them suitable for wide use as oils, water repellents, resins, etc. **b** (*as modifier*): *silicone rubber.*

Silicon Valley ★ *n* **1** an industrial strip in W California, extending S of San Francisco, in which the US information technology industry is concentrated. **2** any area in which industries associated with information technology are concentrated.

silicosis (ˌsɪlɪˈkəʊsɪs) *n Pathol.* a form of pneumoconiosis caused by breathing in tiny particles of silica, quartz, or slate, and characterized by shortness of breath.

siliqua (sɪˈliːkwə, ˈsɪlɪkwə) or **silique** (sɪˈliːk, ˈsɪlɪk) *n, pl* **siliquae** (-ˈliːkwiː), **siliquas,** or **siliques.** the long dry dehiscent fruit of cruciferous plants, such as the wallflower. [C18: via F from L *siliqua* a pod] ▸ **siliquose** (ˈsɪlɪˌkwəʊs) or **siliquous** (ˈsɪlɪkwəs) *adj*

silk (sɪlk) *n* **1** the very fine soft lustrous fibre produced by a silkworm to make its cocoon. **2a** thread or fabric made from this fibre. **2b** (*as modifier*): *a silk dress.* **3** a garment made of this. **4** a very fine fibre produced by a spider to build its web, nest, or cocoon. **5** the tuft of long fine styles on an ear of maize. **6** *Brit.* **6a** the gown worn by a Queen's (or King's) Counsel. **6b** *Inf.* a Queen's (or King's) Counsel. **6c take silk.** to become a Queen's (or King's) Counsel. [OE *sioluc;* ult. from Chinese *ssŭ* silk] ▸ **ˈsilkˌlike** *adj*

silk cotton *n* another name for **kapok.**

silk-cotton tree *n* any of a genus of tropical trees having seeds covered with silky hairs from which kapok is obtained. Also called: **kapok tree.**

silken (ˈsɪlkən) *adj* **1** made of silk. **2** resembling silk in smoothness or gloss. **3** dressed in silk. **4** soft and delicate.

silk hat *n* a man's top hat covered with silk.

silkworm (ˈsɪlkˌwɜːm) *n* **1** the larva of the Chinese moth that feeds on the leaves of the mulberry tree: widely cultivated as a source of silk. **2** any of various similar or related larvae.

silky (ˈsɪlkɪ) *adj* **silkier, silkiest. 1** resembling silk in texture; glossy. **2** made of silk. **3** (of a voice, manner, etc.) suave; smooth. **4** *Bot.* covered with long fine soft hairs: *silky leaves.* ▸ **ˈsilkily** *adv* ▸ **ˈsilkiness** *n*

silky oak *n* any of an Australian genus of trees having divided leaves and showy clusters of orange, red, or white flowers: cultivated in the tropics as shade trees.

sill (sɪl) *n* **1** a shelf at the bottom of a window inside a room. **2** a horizontal piece along the outside lower member of a window, that throws water clear of the wall below. **3** the lower horizontal member of a window or door frame. **4** a horizontal member placed on top of a foundation wall in order to carry a timber framework. **5** a mass of igneous rock, situated between two layers of older sedimentary rock. [OE *syll*]

sillabub ('sɪlə,bʌb) *n* a variant spelling of **syllabub**.

Sillanpää ★ (*Finnish* 'sɪllɑmpæ:) *n* **Frans Eemil** (frans 'eːmil). 1888–1964, Finnish writer, noted for his novels *Meek Heritage* (1919) and *The Maid Silja* (1931): Nobel prize for literature 1939.

Sillitoe ★ ('sɪlɪtəʊ) *n* **Alan**. born 1928, British novelist. His works include *The Loneliness of the Long Distance Runner* (1959).

silly ('sɪlɪ) *adj* **sillier, silliest. 1** lacking in good sense; absurd. **2** frivolous, trivial, or superficial. **3** feeble-minded. **4** dazed, as from a blow. ◆ *n* **5** (*modifier*) Cricket. (of a fielding position) near the batsman's wicket: *silly mid-on.* **6** (*pl* **sillies**) Also called: **silly-billy.** *Inf.* a foolish person. [C15 (in the sense: pitiable, hence the later senses: foolish): from OE *sælig* (unattested) happy, from *sæl* happiness]
▶ 'silliness *n*

silly season *n Brit.* a period, usually during the summer months, when journalists fill space reporting on frivolous events and activities.

silo ('saɪləʊ) *n, pl* **silos. 1** a pit, trench, or tower, often cylindrical in shape, in which silage is made and stored. **2** an underground position in which missile systems are sited for protection. [C19: from Sp., ? of Celtic origin]

Siloam ★ (saɪ'ləʊəm, sɪ-) *n Bible.* a pool in Jerusalem where Jesus cured a man of his blindness (John 9).

Silone ★ (*Italian* si'loːne) *n* **Ignazio** (iɲ'ɲattsjo). 1900–78, Italian writer, noted for his novels *Fontamara* (1933) and *Bread and Wine* (1937).

silt (sɪlt) *n* **1** a fine deposit of mud, clay, etc., esp. one in a river or lake. ◆ *vb* **2** (usually foll. by *up*) to fill or become filled with silt; choke. [C15: from ON]
▶ 'silt'ation *n* ▶ 'silty *adj*

Silurian (saɪ'lʊərɪən) *adj* **1** of or formed in the third period of the Palaeozoic era, during which fishes first appeared. ◆ *n* **2** the. the Silurian period or rock system. [C19: from *Silures,* a Welsh tribe who opposed the Romans]

silurid (saɪ'lʊərɪd) *n* **1** any freshwater teleost fish of the family Siluridae, such as the **European catfish,** which has an elongated body, naked skin, and a long anal fin. ◆ *adj* **2** of, relating to, or belonging to the family Siluridae. [C19: from L *silūrus,* from Gk *silouros* a river fish]

silva ('sɪlvə) *n* a variant spelling of **sylva**.

silvan ('sɪlvən) *adj, n* a variant spelling of **sylvan**.

Silvanus *or* **Sylvanus** ★ (sɪl'veɪnəs) *n Roman myth.* the Roman god of woodlands, fields, and flocks. Greek counterpart: **Pan**. [L: from *silva* woodland]

silver ('sɪlvə) *n* **1a** a ductile malleable brilliant greyish-white element having the highest electrical and thermal conductivity of any metal. It occurs free and in argentite and other ores: used in jewellery, tableware, coinage, electrical contacts, and electroplating. Symbol: Ag; atomic no.: 47; atomic wt.: 107.870. **1b** (*as modifier*): *a silver coin.* Related adj: **argent. 2** coin made of, or having the appearance of, this metal. **3** cutlery, whether made of silver or not. **4** any household articles made of silver. **5** short for **silver medal. 6a** a brilliant or light greyish-white colour. **6b** (*as adj*): *silver hair.* ◆ *adj* **7** well-articulated: *silver speech.* **8** (*prenominal*) denoting the 25th in a series: *a silver wedding anniversary.* ◆ *vb* **9** (*tr*) to coat with silver or a silvery substance: *to silver a spoon.* **10** to become or cause to become silvery in colour. [OE *siolfor*]
▶ 'silvering *n*

silver age *n* **1** (in Greek and Roman mythology) the second of the world's major epochs, inferior to the preceding golden age. **2** the postclassical period of Latin literature, occupying the early part of the Roman imperial era.

silver beet *n* an Australian and New Zealand variety of beet, cultivated for its edible leaves with white stems.

silver bell *n* any of various deciduous trees of North

America and China, having white bell-shaped flowers. Also called: **snowdrop tree.**

silver birch *n* a tree of N temperate regions of the Old World, having silvery-white peeling bark.

silver bromide *n* a yellowish powder that darkens when exposed to light: used in making photographic emulsions. Formula: AgBr.

silver chloride *n* a white powder that darkens on exposure to light: used in making photographic emulsions and papers. Formula: AgCl.

silver disc *n* (in Britain) an album certified to have sold 60 000 copies or a single certified to have sold 200 000 copies.

silver-eye *n Austral. & NZ.* another name for **waxeye** or **white-eye.**

silver fern *n NZ.* **1** another name for **ponga. 2** a formalized spray of fern leaf, silver on a black background: the symbol of New Zealand sporting teams.

silver fir *n* any of various fir trees the leaves of which have a silvery undersurface.

silverfish ('sɪlvə,fɪʃ) *n, pl* **silverfish** *or* **silverfishes. 1** a silver variety of the goldfish. **2** any of various other silvery fishes, such as the moonfish. **3** any of various small primitive wingless insects that have long antennae and tail appendages and occur in buildings, feeding on food scraps, book-bindings, etc.

silver fox *n* **1** an American red fox in a colour phase in which the fur is black with long silver-tipped hairs. **2** the valuable fur or pelt of this animal.

silver-gilt *n* silver covered with a thin film of gold.

silver iodide *n* a yellow powder that darkens on exposure to light: used in photography and artificial rainmaking. Formula: AgI.

silver lining *n* a hopeful aspect of an otherwise desperate or unhappy situation (esp. in the phrase **every cloud has a silver lining**).

silver medal *n* a medal of silver awarded to a competitor who comes second in a contest or race.

silver nitrate *n* a white crystalline soluble poisonous substance used in making photographic emulsions and as a medical antiseptic and astringent. Formula: AgNO₃.

silver plate *n* **1** a thin layer of silver deposited on a base metal. **2** articles, esp. tableware, made of silver plate. ◆ *vb* **silver-plate, silver-plates, silver-plating, silver-plated. 3** (*tr*) to coat (a metal, object, etc.) with silver, as by electroplating.

silver screen *n* the. *Inf.* **1** films collectively or the film industry. **2** the screen onto which films are projected.

silver service *n* (in restaurants) a style of serving food using a spoon and fork in one hand like a pair of tongs.

silverside ('sɪlvə,saɪd) *n* **1** *Brit. & NZ.* a cut of beef below the aitchbone and above the leg. **2** a small marine or freshwater teleost fish related to the grey mullets.

silversmith ('sɪlvə,smɪθ) *n* a craftsman who makes or repairs articles of silver.
▶ 'silver,smithing *n*

silverware ('sɪlvə,wɛə) *n* articles, esp. tableware, made of or plated with silver.

silverweed ('sɪlvə,wiːd) *n* **1** a rosaceous perennial creeping plant with silvery pinnate leaves and yellow flowers. **2** any of various twining shrubs of SE Asia and Australia, having silvery leaves and showy purple flowers.

silvery ('sɪlvərɪ) *adj* **1** of or having the appearance of silver: *the silvery moon.* **2** containing or covered with silver. **3** having a clear ringing sound.
▶ 'silveriness *n*

silviculture ('sɪlvɪ,kʌltʃə) *n* the branch of forestry that is concerned with the cultivation of trees. [C20: *silvi-,* from L *silva* woodland + CULTURE]
▶ ,silvi'cultural *adj* ▶ ,silvi'culturist *n*

sima ('saɪmə) *n* **1** the silicon-rich and magnesium-rich rocks of the earth's oceanic crust. **2** the earth's continental lower crust. [C20: from SI(LICA) + MA(GNESIA)]

Simbirsk ★ (*Russian* sim'birsk) *n* a city in W central Russia, on the River Volga: birthplace of Lenin (V. I.

★ people and places

Ulyanov). Pop.: 678 000 (1995 est.). Former name (1924–91): **Ulyanovsk.**

Simenon ★ ('sɪmənɒn; *French* simnɔ̃) *n* **Georges** (ʒɔrʒ). 1903–89, Belgian writer, who wrote over two hundred novels, including a detective series featuring Maigret.

Simeon ★ ('sɪmɪən) *n* **1a** *Old Testament*. the second son of Jacob and Leah. **1b** the tribe descended from him. **1c** the territory once occupied by this tribe in the extreme south of the land of Canaan. **2** *New Testament*. a devout Jew, who recognized the infant Jesus as the Messiah and uttered the canticle *Nunc Dimittis* over him in the Temple (Luke 2:25–35).

Simeon Stylites ★ (staɪ'laɪtiːz) *n* **Saint**. ?390–459 A.D., Syrian monk, first of the ascetics who lived on pillars. Feast day: Jan. 5 or Sept. 1.

Simferopol ★ (*Russian* sɪmfɪ'rɔpəlj) *n* a city in the S Ukraine, on the S Crimean Peninsula: a Scythian town in the 1st century B.C.; seized by the Russians in 1736. Pop.: 348 000 (1996 est.).

simian ('sɪmɪən) *adj* **1** of or resembling a monkey or ape. ◆ *n* **2** a monkey or ape. [C17: from L *sīmia* an ape, prob. from Gk *sīmos* flat-nosed]

similar ('sɪmɪlə) *adj* **1** showing resemblance in qualities, characteristics, or appearance. **2** *Geom.* (of two or more figures) having corresponding angles equal and all corresponding sides in the same ratio. [C17: from OF, from L *similis*]
▶ **similarity** (ˌsɪmɪ'lærɪtɪ) *n* ▶ **'similarly** *adv*

> **USAGE NOTE** *As* should not be used after *similar: Wilson held a similar position to Jones* (not *a similar position as Jones*); *the system is similar to the one in France* (not *similar as in France*).

simile ('sɪmɪlɪ) *n* a figure of speech that expresses the resemblance of one thing to another of a different category, usually introduced by *as* or *like*. Cf. **metaphor**. [C14: from L *simile* something similar, from *similis* like]

similitude (sɪ'mɪlɪˌtjuːd) *n* **1** likeness. **2** a thing or sometimes a person that is like or the counterpart of another. **3** *Arch.* a simile or parable. [C14: from L *similitūdō*, from *similis* like]

Simla ('sɪmlə) *n* a city in N India, capital of Himachal Pradesh state: summer capital of India (1865–1939); hill resort and health centre. Pop.: 109 860 (1991).

simmer ('sɪmə) *vb* **1** to cook (food) gently at or just below the boiling point. **2** (*intr*) to be about to break out in rage or excitement. ◆ *n* **3** the act, sound, or state of simmering. [C17: ? imit.]

simmer down *vb* (*adv*) **1** (*intr*) *Inf.* to grow calmer, as after intense rage. **2** (*tr*) to reduce the volume of (a liquid) by boiling slowly.

simnel cake ('sɪmn°l) *n Brit.* a fruit cake covered with a layer of marzipan, traditionally eaten during Lent or at Easter. [C13 *simenel*, from OF, from L *simila* fine flour, prob. of Semitic origin]

Simon ★ ('saɪmən) *n* **1** the original name of (Saint) **Peter.** **2** *New Testament*. **2a** See **Simon Zelotes. 2b** a relative of Jesus, who may have been identical with Simon Zelotes (Matthew 13:55). **2c** Also called: **Simon the Tanner.** a Christian of Joppa with whom Peter stayed (Acts of the Apostles 9:43). **3 John (Allsebrook)**, 1st Viscount Simon. 1873–1954, British statesman and lawyer. He was Liberal home secretary (1915–16) and, as a leader of the National Liberals, foreign secretary (1931–35), home secretary (1935–37), Chancellor of the Exchequer (1937–40), Lord Chancellor (1940–45). **4 (Marvin) Neil.** born 1927, US dramatist and librettist: his plays include *Barefoot in the Park* (1963) and *London Suite* (1995). **5 Paul.** born 1942, US pop singer and songwriter. His albums include: with Art Garfunkel (born 1941), *Bridge over Troubled Water* (1970); and, solo, *Graceland* (1986).

Simonides ★ (saɪ'mɒnɪˌdiːz) *n* ?556–?468 B.C., Greek lyric poet and epigrammatist, noted for his odes to victory.

Simon Magus ★ *n New Testament*. a Samaritan sorcerer,

probably from Gitta, of the 1st century A.D. After being converted to Christianity, he tried to buy miraculous powers from the apostles (Acts of the Apostles 8:9–24). He is also identified as the founder of a Gnostic sect.

Simon Peter ★ *n New Testament*. the full name of the apostle Peter, a combination of his original name and the name given him by Christ (Matthew 16:17–18).

simon-pure ('saɪmən-) *adj Rare*. authentic; genuine. [C19: from *the real Simon Pure*, a character in the play *A Bold Stroke for a Wife* (1717) by Susannah Centlivre (1669–1723), who is impersonated by another character in some scenes]

simony ('saɪmənɪ) *n Christianity*. the practice, now usually regarded as a sin, of buying or selling spiritual or Church benefits such as pardons, relics, etc. [C13: from OF *simonie*, from LL *sīmōnia*, from SIMON MAGUS]

Simon Zelotes ★ (zɪ'ləʊtiːz) *n Saint*. one of the 12 apostles, who had probably belonged to the Zealot party before becoming a Christian (Luke 6:15). Owing to a misinterpretation of two similar Aramaic words he is also, but mistakenly, called *the Canaanite* (Matthew 10:4). Feast day: Oct. 28 or May 10.

simoom (sɪ'muːm) *or* **simoon** (sɪ'muːn) *n* a strong suffocating sand-laden wind of the deserts of Arabia and North Africa. [from Ar. *samūm* poisonous, from Aramaic *sammā* poison]

simpatico (sɪm'pɑːtɪˌkəʊ) *adj Inf.* **1** pleasant or congenial. **2** of similar mind or temperament. [It.: from *simpatia* SYMPATHY]

simper ('sɪmpə) *vb* **1** (*intr*) to smile coyly, affectedly, or in a silly self-conscious way. **2** (*tr*) to utter (something) in such a manner. ◆ *n* **3** a simpering smile; smirk. [C16: prob. from Du. *simper* affected]
▶ **'simpering** *adj* ▶ **'simperingly** *adv*

simple ('sɪmp°l) *adj* **1** easy to understand or do: *a simple problem*. **2** plain; unadorned: *a simple dress*. **3** not combined or complex: *a simple mechanism*. **4** unaffected or unpretentious: *despite his fame, he remained a simple man*. **5** sincere; frank: *her simple explanation was readily accepted*. **6** of humble condition or rank: *the peasant was of simple birth*. **7** feeble-minded. **8** (*prenominal*) without additions or modifications: *the witness told the simple truth*. **9** (*prenominal*) straightforward: *a simple case of mumps*. **10** *Chem.* (of a substance) consisting of only one chemical compound. **11** *Maths.* (of an equation) containing variables to the first power only. **12** *Biol.* **12a** not divided into parts: *a simple leaf*. **12b** formed from only one ovary: *simple fruit*. **13** *Music*. relating to or denoting a time where the number of beats per bar may be two, three, or four. ◆ *n Arch.* **14** a simpleton. **15** a plant having medicinal properties. [C13: via OF from L *simplex* plain]
▶ **simplicity** (sɪm'plɪsɪtɪ) *n*

simple fraction *n* a fraction in which the numerator and denominator are both integers. Also called: **common fraction, vulgar fraction.**

simple fracture *n* a fracture in which the broken bone does not pierce the skin.

simple harmonic motion *n* a form of periodic motion of a particle, etc., in which the acceleration is always directed towards some equilibrium point and is proportional to the displacement from this point. Abbrev.: **SHM.**

simple-hearted *adj* free from deceit; frank.

simple interest *n* interest paid on the principal alone. Cf. **compound interest.**

simple machine *n* a simple device for altering the magnitude or direction of a force. The six basic types are the lever, wheel and axle, pulley, screw, wedge, and inclined plane.

simple-minded *adj* **1** stupid; foolish; feeble-minded. **2** unsophisticated; artless.
▶ ˌsimple-'mindedly *adv* ▶ ˌsimple-'mindedness *n*

simple sentence *n* a sentence consisting of a single main clause.

simpleton ('sɪmp°ltən) *n* a foolish or ignorant person.

simplify ('sɪmplɪˌfaɪ) *vb* **simplifies, simplifying, simplified.** (*tr*) **1** to make less complicated or easier. **2** *Maths.* to re-

duce (an equation, fraction, etc.) to its simplest form. [C17: via F from Med. L *simplificāre*, from L *simplus* simple + *facere* to make]
▶ ,**simplifi'cation** *n*

simplistic (sɪm'plɪstɪk) *adj* 1 characterized by extreme simplicity. 2 making unrealistically simple judgments or analyses.
▶ '**simplism** *n* ▶ sim'**plistically** *adv*

> USAGE NOTE Since *simplistic* already has *too* as part of its meaning, it is tautologous to talk about something being *too simplistic* or *oversimplistic*.

Simplon Pass ★ ('sɪmplɒn) *n* a pass over the Lepontine Alps in S Switzerland, between Brig (Switzerland) and Iselle (Italy). Height: 2009 m (6590 ft).

simply ('sɪmplɪ) *adv* 1 in a simple manner. 2 merely. 3 absolutely; altogether: *a simply wonderful holiday.* 4 (*sentence modifier*) frankly.

Simpson ★ ('sɪmpsᵊn, 'sɪmsᵊn) *n* 1 Sir **James Young.** 1811–70, Scottish obstetrician, who pioneered the use of chloroform as an anaesthetic. 2 **Wallis (Warfield).** See **Edward VIII.**

Simpson Desert ★ *n* an uninhabited arid region in central Australia, mainly in the Northern Territory. Area: about 145 000 sq. km (56 000 sq. miles).

simulacrum (,sɪmju'leɪkrəm) *n*, *pl* **simulacra** (-krə). *Arch.* 1 any image or representation of something. 2 a superficial likeness. [C16: from L: likeness, from *simulāre* to imitate, from *similis* like]

simulate ('sɪmju,leɪt) *vb* **simulates, simulating, simulated.** (*tr*) 1 to make a pretence of: *to simulate anxiety.* 2 to reproduce the conditions of (a situation, etc.), as in carrying out an experiment: *to simulate weightlessness.* 3 to have the appearance of. ◆ *adj* ('sɪmjulɪt, -,leɪt). 4 *Arch.* assumed. [C17: from L *simulāre* to copy, from *similis* like]
▶ ,**simu'lation** *n* ▶ '**simulative** *adj*

simulated ('sɪmju,leɪtɪd) *adj* 1 (of fur, leather, pearls, etc.) being an imitation of the genuine article, usually made from cheaper material. 2 (of actions, emotions, etc.) imitated; feigned.

simulator ('sɪmju,leɪtə) *n* 1 any device that simulates specific conditions for the purposes of research or operator training: *space simulator.* 2 a person who simulates.

simulcast ('sɪməl,kɑːst) *vb* 1 (*tr*) to broadcast (a programme, etc.) simultaneously on radio and television. ◆ *n* 2 a programme, etc., so broadcast. [C20: from SIMUL(TANEOUS) + (BROAD)CAST]

simultaneous (,sɪməl'teɪnɪəs) *adj* occurring, existing, or operating at the same time. [C17: on the model of INSTANTANEOUS from L *simul* at the same time]
▶ ,**simul'taneously** *adv* ▶ ,**simul'taneousness** *or* **simultaneity** (,sɪməltə'niːɪtɪ) *n*

> USAGE NOTE See at **unique.**

simultaneous equations *pl n* a set of equations that are all satisfied by the same values of the variables, the number of variables being equal to the number of equations.

sin[1] (sɪn) *n* **1a** transgression of God's known will or any principle or law regarded as embodying this. **1b** the condition of estrangement from God arising from such transgression. 2 any serious offence, as against a religious or moral principle. 3 any offence against a principle or standard. 4 **live in sin.** *Inf.* (of an unmarried couple) to live together. ◆ *vb* **sins, sinning, sinned.** (*intr*) 5 to commit a sin. 6 (usually foll. by *against*) to commit an offence (against a person, etc.). [OE *synn*]
▶ '**sinner** *n*

sin[2] (saɪn) *Maths. abbrev. for* sine.

SIN (in Canada) *abbrev. for* Social Insurance Number.

Sinai ★ ('saɪnaɪ) *n* 1 a mountainous peninsula of NE Egypt at the N end of the Red Sea, between the Gulf of Suez and the Gulf of Aqaba: occupied by Israel in 1967; fully restored by 1982. 2 **Mount.** the mountain where Moses received the Law from God (Exodus 19–20): often identified as Jebel Musa, sometimes as Jebel Serbal, both on the S Sinai Peninsula.
▶ **Sinaitic** (,saɪnɪ'ɪtɪk) *or* **Sinaic** (sɪ'neɪɪk) *adj*

Sinaloa ★ (,siːnɑ'ləuə, ,sɪn-; *Spanish* sina'loa) *n* a state of W Mexico. Capital: Culiacán. Pop.: 2 424 745 (1995 est.). Area: 58 092 sq. km (22 425 sq. miles).

sinanthropus (sɪn'ænθrəpəs) *n* a primitive apelike man of the genus *Sinanthropus,* now considered a subspecies of *Homo erectus.* [C20: from NL, from LL *Sīnae* the Chinese + *-anthropus,* from Gk *anthrōpos* man]

Sinatra ★ (sɪ'nɑːtrə) *n* Frank, full name *Francis Albert Sinatra.* 1915–98, US popular singer and film actor. His recordings include "My Way" (1969).

sin bin *n* 1 *Sl.* (in ice hockey, etc.) an area off the field of play where a player who has committed a foul can be sent to sit for a specified period. 2 *Inf.* a separate unit for disruptive schoolchildren.

since (sɪns) *prep* 1 during or throughout the period of time after: *since May it has only rained once.* ◆ *conj* (*subordinating*) 2 (sometimes preceded by *ever*) continuously from or starting from the time when. 3 seeing that; because. ◆ *adv* 4 since that time: *I haven't seen him since.* [OE *sīththan,* lit.: after that]

> USAGE NOTE See at **ago.**

sincere (sɪn'sɪə) *adj* 1 not hypocritical or deceitful; genuine: *sincere regret.* 2 *Arch.* pure; unmixed. [C16: from L *sincērus*]
▶ sin'**cerely** *adv* ▶ **sincerity** (sɪn'serɪtɪ) *or* sin'**cereness** *n*

sinciput ('sɪnsɪ,pʌt) *n*, *pl* **sinciputs** *or* **sincipita** (sɪn'sɪpɪtə). *Anat.* the forward upper part of the skull. [C16: from L: half a head, from SEMI- + *caput* head]
▶ sin'**cipital** *adj*

Sinclair ★ (sɪn'kleə, 'sɪŋkleə) *n* Upton (Beall). 1878–1968, US novelist, noted for *The Jungle* (1906) and his series *World's End* (1940–53).

Sind ★ (sɪnd) *n* a province of SE Pakistan, mainly in the lower Indus valley: formerly a province of British India; became a province of Pakistan in 1947; divided in 1955 between Hyderabad and Khairpur; reunited as a province in 1970. Capital: Karachi. Pop.: 21 682 000 (1985 est.). Area: 140 914 sq. km (54 407 sq. miles).

sine[1] (saɪn) *n* (of an angle) a trigonometric function that in a right-angled triangle is the ratio of the length of the opposite side to that of the hypotenuse. [C16: from L *sinus* a bend; in NL, *sinus* was mistaken as a translation of Ar. *jiba* sine (from Sansk. *jīva,* lit.: bowstring) because of confusion with Ar. *jaib* curve]

sine[2] ('saɪnɪ) *prep* (esp. in Latin phrases or legal terms) lacking; without.

sinecure ('saɪnɪ,kjuə) *n* 1 a paid office or post involving minimal duties. 2 a Church benefice to which no spiritual charge is attached. [C17: from Med. L (*beneficium*) *sine cūrā* (benefice) without cure (of souls), from L *sine* without + *cūra* cure]
▶ '**sine,curism** *n* ▶ '**sine,curist** *n*

sine curve (saɪn) *n* a curve of the equation $y = \sin x$. Also called: **sinusoid.**

sine die *Latin.* ('saɪnɪ 'daɪɪ) *adv, adj* without a day fixed. [lit.: without a day]

sine qua non *Latin.* ('saɪnɪ kweɪ 'nɒn) *n* an essential requirement. [lit.: without which not]

sinew ('sɪnju:) *n* 1 *Anat.* another name for **tendon. 2** (*often pl*) **2a** a source of strength or power. **2b** a literary word for **muscle.** [OE *sionu*]
▶ '**sinewless** *adj*

sine wave (saɪn) *n* any oscillation, such as an alternating current, whose waveform is that of a sine curve.

sinewy ('sɪnjuɪ) *adj* 1 consisting of or resembling a tendon or tendons. 2 muscular. 3 (esp. of language, style, etc.) forceful. 4 (of meat, etc.) tough.
▶ '**sinewiness** *n*

★ people and places

sinfonia (ˌsɪnfəˈnɪə) n, pl **sinfonie** (-ˈniːeɪ) or **sinfonias**. 1 another word for **symphony** (senses 2, 3). 2 (cap. when part of a name) a symphony orchestra. [It.]

sinfonietta (ˌsɪnfənˈjetə) n 1 a short or light symphony. 2 (cap. when part of a name) a small symphony orchestra. [It.: a little symphony]

sinful (ˈsɪnful) adj 1 having committed or tending to commit sin: a sinful person. 2 characterized by or being a sin: a sinful act. ▶ 'sinfully adv ▶ 'sinfulness n

sing (sɪŋ) vb **sings, singing, sang, sung.** 1 to produce or articulate (sounds, words, a song, etc.) with musical intonation. 2 (when intr, often foll. by to) to perform (a song) to the accompaniment (of): to sing to a guitar. 3 (intr; foll. by of) to tell a story in song (about): I sing of a maiden. 4 (intr) to perform songs for a living. 5 (intr) (esp. of certain birds and insects) to utter calls or sounds reminiscent of music. 6 (when intr, usually foll. by of) to tell (something), esp. in verse: the poet who sings of the war. 7 (intr) to make a whining, ringing, or whistling sound: the arrow sang past his ear. 8 (intr) (of the ears) to experience a continuous ringing. 9 (tr) to bring to a given state by singing: to sing a child to sleep. 10 (intr) Sl., chiefly US. to confess or act as an informer. ◆ n 11 Inf. an act or performance of singing. ◆ See also **sing out.** [OE singan] ▶ 'singable adj ▶ 'singer n ▶ 'singing adj, n

> **USAGE NOTE** See at **ring²**.

sing. abbrev. for singular.

Singapore ★ (ˌsɪŋəˈpɔː, ˌsɪŋgə-) n 1 a republic in SE Asia, occupying one main island and about 58 small islands at the S end of the Malay Peninsula: established as a British trading post in 1819 and became part of the Straits Settlements in 1826; occupied by the Japanese (1942–45); a British colony from 1946, becoming self-governing in 1959; part of the Federation of Malaysia from 1963 to 1965, when it became an independent republic (within the Commonwealth). Official languages: Chinese, Malay, English, and Tamil. Religion: Buddhist, Taoist, traditional beliefs, and Muslim. Currency: Singapore dollar. Capital: Singapore. Pop.: 3 045 000 (1996). Area: 648 sq. km (250 sq. miles). 2 the capital of the republic of Singapore: a major international port. Pop.: 2 413 945 (1980). ▶ ˌSingaˈporean adj, n

singe (sɪndʒ) vb **singes, singeing, singed.** 1 to burn or be burnt superficially; scorch: to singe one's clothes. 2 (tr) to burn the ends of (hair, etc.). 3 (tr) to expose (a carcass) to flame to remove bristles or hair. ◆ n 4 a superficial burn. [OE sengan]

Singer ★ (ˈsɪŋə) n 1 Isaac Bashevis. 1904–91, US writer of Yiddish novels, born in Poland. His works include The Family Moskrat (1950) and The King of the Fields (1989): Nobel prize for literature 1978. 2 Isaac Merritt. 1811–75, US inventor, who originated a chain-stitch sewing machine (1852).

Singh (sɪŋ) n a title assumed by a Sikh when he becomes a full member of the community. [from Hindi, from Sansk. sinhá a lion]

Singhalese (ˌsɪŋəˈliːz) n, pl **Singhaleses** or **Singhalese,** adj a variant spelling of **Sinhalese.**

singing telegram n a a service by which a person is employed to present greetings or congratulations by singing. b the greetings or congratulations presented thus.

single (ˈsɪŋgəl) adj (usually prenominal) 1 existing alone; solitary: upon the hill stood a single tower. 2 distinct from other things. 3 composed of one part. 4 designed or sufficient for one user: a single bed. 5 (also postpositive) unmarried. 6 connected with the condition of being unmarried: he led a single life. 7 (esp. of combat) involving two individuals. 8 even one: there wasn't a single person on the beach. 9 (of a flower) having only one set or whorl of petals. 10 single-minded: a single devotion to duty. 11 Rare. honest or sincere. ◆ n 12 something forming one individual unit. 13 (often pl) 13a an unmarried person. 13b (as modifier): singles bar. 14 a gramophone record, CD, or cassette with a short recording, usually of pop music, on it. 15 Cricket. a hit from which one run is scored. 16a Brit. a pound note. 16b US & Canad. a dollar note. 17 See single ticket. ◆ vb singles, singling, singled. 18 (tr; usually foll. by out) to select from a group of people or things: he singled him out for special mention. ◆ See also singles. [C14: from OF sengle, from L singulus individual] ▶ 'singleness n

single-acting adj (of a reciprocating engine or pump) having a piston or pistons pressurized on one side only.

single-breasted adj (of a garment) having the fronts overlapping only slightly and with one row of fastenings.

single cream n cream having a low fat content that does not thicken with beating.

single-decker n Brit. inf. a bus with only one passenger deck.

single-end n Scot. a dwelling consisting of a single room.

single entry n a a book-keeping system in which transactions are entered in one account only. b (as modifier): a single-entry account.

single file n a line of persons, animals, or things ranged one behind the other.

single-foot n 1 a rapid showy gait of a horse in which each foot strikes the ground separately. ◆ vb 2 to move or cause to move at this gait.

single-handed adj, adv 1 unaided or working alone: a single-handed crossing of the Atlantic. 2 having or operated by one hand or one person only. ▶ ˌsingle-'handedly adv ▶ ˌsingle-'handedness n

single-lens reflex n See reflex camera.

single-minded adj having but one aim or purpose; dedicated. ▶ ˌsingle-'mindedly adv ▶ ˌsingle-'mindedness n

single-parent family n a household consisting of at least one dependent child and the mother or father, the other parent being dead or permanently absent. Also called: **one-parent family.**

singles (ˈsɪŋgəlz) pl n Tennis, etc. a match played with one person on each side.

singles bar n a bar or club that is a social meeting place for single people.

single-sex adj (of schools, etc.) admitting members of one sex only.

single sideband transmission n a method of transmitting radio waves in which either the upper or the lower sideband is transmitted, the carrier being either wholly or partially suppressed.

singlestick (ˈsɪŋgəlˌstɪk) n 1 a wooden stick used instead of a sword for fencing. 2 fencing with such a stick. 3 any short heavy stick.

singlet (ˈsɪŋglɪt) n 1 a sleeveless undergarment covering the body from the shoulders to the hips. 2 a garment worn with shorts by athletes, boxers, etc. [C18: from SINGLE, on the model of doublet]

single ticket n Brit. a ticket entitling a passenger to travel only to his destination, without returning.

singleton (ˈsɪŋgəltən) n 1 Bridge, etc. an original holding of one card only in a suit. 2 a single object, etc., distinguished from a pair or group. 3 Maths. a set containing only one member. [C19: from SINGLE, on the model of SIMPLETON]

single-track adj 1 (of a railway) having only a single pair of lines, so that trains can travel in only one direction at a time. 2 (of a road) only wide enough for one vehicle.

Single Transferable Vote n (modifier) of or relating to a system of voting in which voters list the candidates in order of preference. Abbrev.: STV. See proportional representation.

singletree (ˈsɪŋgəlˌtriː) n US & Austral. another word for **swingletree.**

singly (ˈsɪŋglɪ) adv 1 one at a time; one by one. 2 apart from others; separately; alone.

sing out *vb* (*tr, adv*) to call out in a loud voice; shout.

singsong ('sɪŋ,sɒŋ) *n* **1** an accent or intonation that is characterized by an alternately rising and falling rhythm, such as in a person's voice. **2** *Brit.* an informal session of singing, esp. of popular songs. ◆ *adj* **3** having a monotonous rhythm: *a singsong accent*.

singular ('sɪŋgjʊlə) *adj* **1** remarkable; extraordinary: *a singular feat*. **2** unusual; odd: *a singular character*. **3** unique. **4** denoting a word or an inflected form of a word indicating that one referent is being referred to or described. **5** *Logic.* (of a proposition) referring to a specific thing or person. ◆ *n* **6** *Grammar.* **6a** the singular number. **6b** a singular form of a word. [C14: from L *singulāris* single]
▸ **'singularly** *adv*

singularity (,sɪŋgjʊ'lærɪtɪ) *n, pl* **singularities. 1** the state or quality of being singular. **2** something distinguishing a person or thing from others. **3** something unusual. **4** *Maths.* a point at which a function is not differentiable although it is differentiable in a neighbourhood of that point. **5** *Astron.* a hypothetical point in space-time at which matter is infinitely compressed to infinitesimal volume.

singularize *or* **singularise** ('sɪŋgjʊlə,raɪz) *vb* **singularizes, singularizing, singularized** *or* **singularises, singularising, singularised.** (*tr*) **1** to make (a word, etc.) singular. **2** to make conspicuous.
▸ ,singulari'zation *or* ,singulari'sation *n*

singultus (sɪŋ'gʌltəs) *n, pl* **singultuses.** a technical name for **hiccup.** [C18: from L, lit.: a sob]

sinh (ʃaɪn, sɪnʃ) *n* hyperbolic sine. [C20: from SIN(E)[1] + H(YPERBOLIC)]

Sinhailien ★ ('ʃɪn'haɪ'ljen) *n* a variant transliteration of the Chinese name for **Lianyungang.**

Sinhalese (,sɪnhə'liːz) *or* **Singhalese** *n* **1** (*pl* **Sinhaleses** *or* **Sinhalese**) a member of a people living chiefly in Sri Lanka, where they constitute the majority of the population. **2** the language of this people: the official language of Sri Lanka. ◆ *adj* **3** of or relating to this people or their language.

Sining ★ ('ʃiː'nɪŋ) *n* variant transliteration of the Chinese name for **Xining.**

sinister ('sɪnɪstə) *adj* **1** threatening or suggesting evil or harm: *a sinister glance*. **2** evil or treacherous. **3** (*usually postpositive*) *Heraldry.* of, on, or starting from the left side from the bearer's point of view. **4** *Arch.* located on the left side. [C15: from L *sinister* on the left-hand side, considered by Roman augurs to be the unlucky one]
▸ **'sinisterly** *adv* ▸ **'sinisterness** *n*

sinistral ('sɪnɪstrəl) *adj* **1** of or located on the left side, esp. the left side of the body. **2** a technical term for **left-handed. 3** (of the shells of certain molluscs) coiling in a clockwise direction from the apex.
▸ **'sinistrally** *adv*

sinistrorse ('sɪnɪ,strɔːs, ,sɪnɪ'strɔːs) *adj* (of some climbing plants) growing upwards in a spiral from right to left. [C19: from L *sinistrōrsus* turned towards the left, from *sinister* on the left + *vertere* to turn]
▸ **,sinis'trorsal** *adj*

Sinitic (sɪ'nɪtɪk) *n* **1** a branch of the Sino-Tibetan family of languages, consisting of the various dialects of Chinese. ◆ *adj* **2** belonging to this group of languages.

sink (sɪŋk) *vb* **sinks, sinking, sank; sunk** *or* **sunken. 1** to descend or cause to descend, esp. beneath the surface of a liquid. **2** (*intr*) to appear to move down towards or descend below the horizon. **3** (*intr*) to slope downwards. **4** (*intr; often foll. by* in *or* into) to pass into a specified lower state or condition: *to sink into apathy*. **5** to make or become lower in volume, pitch, etc. **6** to make or become lower in value, price, etc. **7** (*intr*) to become weaker in health, strength, etc. **8** (*intr*) to seep or penetrate. **9** (*tr*) to dig, cut, drill, bore, or excavate (a hole, shaft, etc.). **10** (*tr*) to drive into the ground: *to sink a stake*. **11** (*tr; usually foll. by* in *or* into) **11a** to invest (money). **11b** to lose (money) in an unwise investment. **12** (*tr*) to pay (a debt). **13** (*intr*) to become hollow: *his cheeks had sunk during his illness*. **14** (*tr*) to hit or propel (a ball) into a hole, pocket, etc.: *he sank a 15-foot putt*. **15** (*tr*) *Brit. inf.* to drink, esp. quickly: *he sank three pints in half an hour*. **16 sink or swim.**

to take risks where the alternatives are loss or success. ◆ *n* **17** a fixed basin, esp. in a kitchen, made of stone, metal, etc., used for washing. **18** a place of vice or corruption. **19** an area of ground below that of the surrounding land, where water collects. **20** *Physics.* a device by which energy is removed from a system: *a heat sink*. ◆ *adj* **21** *Inf.* (of a housing estate or school) deprived or having low standards of achievement. [OE *sincan*]
▸ **'sinkable** *adj*

sinker ('sɪŋkə) *n* **1** a weight attached to a fishing line, net, etc., to cause it to sink in water. **2** a person who sinks shafts, etc.

sinkhole ('sɪŋk,həʊl) *n* **1** Also called (esp. in Britain): **swallow hole.** a depression in the ground surface, esp. in limestone, where a surface stream disappears underground. **2** a place into which foul matter runs.

Sinkiang-Uighur Autonomous Region ★ ('sɪn'kjæŋ'wiː,gʊə) *n* a variant transliteration of the Chinese name for the **Xinjiang Uygur Autonomous Region.**

sink in *vb* (*intr, adv*) to enter or penetrate the mind: *eventually the news sank in*.

sinking ('sɪŋkɪŋ) *n* **a** a feeling in the stomach caused by hunger or uneasiness. **b** (*as modifier*): *a sinking feeling*.

sinking fund *n* a fund accumulated out of a business enterprise's earnings or a government's revenue and invested to repay a long-term debt.

sinless ('sɪnlɪs) *adj* free from sin or guilt; pure.
▸ **'sinlessly** *adv* ▸ **'sinlessness** *n*

Sinn Féin (ʃɪn 'feːn) *n* an Irish republican political movement founded about 1905 and linked to the revolutionary Irish Republican Army. [C20: from Irish Gaelic: we ourselves]
▸ **'Sinn 'Féiner** *n* ▸ **'Sinn 'Féinism** *n*

Sino- *combining form.* Chinese: *Sino-Tibetan; Sinology*. [from F, from LL *Sīnae* the Chinese, from LGk, from Ar. *Sīn* China, prob. from Chinese *Ch'in*]

Sinology (saɪ'nɒlədʒɪ) *n* the study of Chinese history, language, culture, etc.
▸ **Sinological** (,saɪnə'lɒdʒɪk°l) *adj* ▸ **Si'nologist** *n* ▸ **Sinologue** ('saɪnə,lɒg) *n*

Sino-Tibetan ('saɪnəʊ-) *n* **1** a family of languages that includes most of the languages of China, as well as Tibetan, Burmese, and possibly Thai. ◆ *adj* **2** belonging to or relating to this family of languages.

sinsemilla (,sɪnsə'miːljə) *n* **1** a type of marijuana with a very high narcotic content. **2** the plant from which it is obtained, a strain of *Cannabis sativa*. [C20: from American Sp., lit.: without seed]

sinter ('sɪntə) *n* **1** a whitish porous incrustation, usually consisting of silica, that is deposited from hot springs. **2** the product of a sintering process. ◆ *vb* **3** (*tr*) to form large particles, lumps, or masses from (metal powders) by heating or pressure or both. [C18: from G *Sinter* CINDER]

Sint Maarten ★ (sɪnt 'maːrtə) *n* the Dutch name for **Saint Martin.**

Sintra ★ ('sɪntrə) *n* a town in central Portugal, near Lisbon, in the Sintra mountains: noted for its castles and palaces and the beauty of its setting: tourism. Former name: **Cintra.**

sinuate ('sɪnjʊɪt, -,eɪt) *adj* **1** Also: **sinuous.** (of leaves) having a strongly waved margin. **2** another word for **sinuous.** [C17: from L *sinuātus* curved]
▸ **'sinuately** *adv*

Sinŭiju (,sɪ,nuːɪ'dʒuː) *n* a port in North Korea, on the Yalu River opposite Andong, China: developed by the Japanese during their occupation (1910–45); industrial centre. Pop.: 289 000 (1987 est.).

sinuous ('sɪnjʊəs) *adj* **1** full of turns or curves. **2** devious; not straightforward. **3** supple. [C16: from L *sinuōsus* winding, from *sinus* a curve]
▸ **'sinuously** *adv* ▸ **sinuosity** (,sɪnjʊ'ɒsɪtɪ) *n*

sinus ('saɪnəs) *n, pl* **sinuses. 1** *Anat.* **1a** any bodily cavity or hollow space. **1b** a large channel for venous blood, esp. between the brain and the skull. **1c** any of the air cavities in the cranial bones. **2** *Pathol.* a passage leading to a cavity containing pus. [C16: from L: a curve]

sinusitis (ˌsaɪnəˈsaɪtɪs) n inflammation of the membrane lining a sinus, esp. a nasal sinus.

sinusoid (ˈsaɪnəˌsɔɪd) n 1 any of the irregular terminal blood vessels that replace capillaries in certain organs, such as the liver, heart, spleen, and pancreas. 2 another name for **sine curve**. ◆ adj 3 resembling a sinus. [C19: from F sinusoïde. See SINUS, -OID]

sinusoidal projection n an equal-area map projection on which all parallels are straight lines and all except the prime meridian are sine curves, often used to show tropical latitudes.

Sion ★ n 1 (French sjɔ̃). a town in SW Switzerland, capital of Valais canton, on the River Rhône. Pop.: 24 538 (1990). Latin name: **Sedunum. 2** (ˈsaɪən). a variant of **Zion**.

Siouan (ˈsuːən) n a family of North American Indian languages, including Sioux.

Sioux (suː) n 1 (pl **Sioux** (suː, suːz)). a member of a group of North American Indian peoples. 2 any of the languages of the Sioux. [from F, shortened from Nadowessioux]

sip (sɪp) vb **sips, sipping, sipped. 1** to drink (a liquid) by taking small mouthfuls. ◆ n 2 a small quantity of a liquid taken into the mouth and swallowed. 3 an act of sipping. [C14: prob. from Low G sippen]
▶ 'sipper n

siphon or **syphon** (ˈsaɪfⁿn) n 1 a tube placed with one end at a certain level in a vessel of liquid and the other end outside the vessel below this level, so that atmospheric pressure forces the liquid through the tube and out of the vessel. 2 See **soda siphon. 3** Zool. any of various tubular organs in different aquatic animals, such as molluscs, through which water passes. ◆ vb 4 (often foll. by off) to draw off through or as if through a siphon. [C17: from L sīphō, from Gk siphōn]
▶ 'siphonal or siphonic (saɪˈfɒnɪk) adj

siphon bottle n another name (esp. US) for **soda siphon**.

siphonophore (ˈsaɪfənəˌfɔː) n any of an order of marine colonial hydrozoans, including the Portuguese man-of-war. [C19: from NL, from Gk siphōnophoros tube-bearing]

Siple ★ (ˈsaɪpⁿl) n Mount. a mountain in Antarctica, on the coast of Byrd Land. Height: 3100 m (10 171 ft).

sippet (ˈsɪpɪt) n a small piece of something, esp. a piece of toast or fried bread served with soup or gravy. [C16: used as dim. of SOP]

sir (sɜː) n 1 a formal or polite term of address for a man. 2 Arch. a gentleman of high social status. [C13: var. of SIRE]

Sir (sɜː) n 1 a title of honour placed before the name of a knight or baronet: Sir Walter Raleigh. 2 Arch. a title placed before the name of a figure from ancient history.

Siracusa ★ (siraˈkuːza) n the Italian name for **Syracuse**.

Siraj-ud-daula ★ (sɪˈrɑːdʒʊdˈdaʊlə) n ?1728–57, Indian leader who became the Great Mogul's deputy in Bengal (1756); opponent of English colonization. He captured Calcutta (1756) from the English and many of his prisoners suffocated in a crowded room that became known as the Black Hole of Calcutta. He was defeated (1757) by a group of Indian nobles in alliance with Robert Clive.

sirdar (ˈsɜːdɑː) n 1 a general or military leader in Pakistan and India. 2 (formerly) the title of the British commander in chief of the Egyptian Army. 3 a variant of **sardar**. [from Hindi sardār, from Persian, from sar head + dār possession]

sire (saɪə) n 1 a male parent, esp. of a horse or other domestic animal. 2 a respectful term of address, now used only in addressing a male monarch. ◆ vb **sires, siring, sired. 3** (tr) (esp. of a domestic animal) to father. [C13: from OF, from L senior an elder, from senex an old man]

siren (ˈsaɪərən) n 1 a device for emitting a loud wailing sound, esp. as a warning or signal, consisting of a rotating perforated metal drum through which air or steam is passed under pressure. 2 (sometimes cap.) Greek myth. one of several sea nymphs whose singing was believed to lure sailors to destruction on the rocks the nymphs inhabited. 3 a woman considered to be dangerously alluring or seductive. 4 an aquatic eel-like salamander of North America, having external gills, no hind limbs, and

reduced forelimbs. [C14: from OF sereine, from L sīrēn, from Gk seirēn]

sirenian (saɪˈriːnɪən) adj 1 of or belonging to the Sirenia, an order of aquatic herbivorous placental mammals having forelimbs modified as paddles and a horizontally flattened tail: contains only the dugong and manatees. ◆ n 2 an animal belonging to this order; sea cow.

Siret ★ (sɪˈret) n a river in SE Europe, rising in the Ukraine and flowing southeast through E Romania to the Danube. Length: about 450 km (280 miles).

Sirius (ˈsɪrɪəs) n the brightest star in the sky, lying in the constellation Canis Major. Also called: the **Dog Star**. [C14: via L from Gk Seirios, from ?]

sirloin (ˈsɜːˌlɔɪn) n a prime cut of beef from the loin, esp. the upper part. [C16 surloyn, from OF surlonge, from sur above + longe, from loigne LOIN]

sirocco (sɪˈrɒkəʊ) n, pl **siroccos**. a hot oppressive and often dusty wind usually occurring in spring, beginning in N Africa and reaching S Europe. [C17: from It., from Ar. sharq east wind]

sironize or **sironise** (ˈsaɪrəˌnaɪz) vb **sironizes, sironizing, sironized** or **sironises, sironising, sironised. (tr)** Austral. to treat (a woollen fabric) chemically to prevent it wrinkling after being washed. [C20: from (C)SIRO + -n- + -IZE]

siroset (ˈsaɪrəʊˌset) adj Austral. of or relating to the chemical treatment of woollen fabrics to give a permanent-press effect, or a garment so treated.

sirrah (ˈsɪrə) n Arch. a contemptuous term used in addressing a man or boy. [C16: prob. var. of SIRE]

sirree (səˈriː) interj (sometimes cap.) US inf. an exclamation used with yes or no.

sirup (ˈsɪrəp) n US. a less common spelling of **syrup**.

sis (sɪs) n Inf. short for **sister**.

SIS (in Britain) abbrev. for Secret Intelligence Service. Also called: **MI6**.

sisal (ˈsaɪsⁿl) n 1 a Mexican agave plant cultivated for its large fleshy leaves, which yield a stiff fibre used for making rope. 2 the fibre of this plant. ◆ Also called: **sisal hemp**. [C19: from Mexican Sp., after Sisal, a port in Yucatán, Mexico]

Sisera ★ (ˈsɪsərə) n a defeated leader of the Canaanites, who was assassinated by Jael (Judges 4:17–21).

siskin (ˈsɪskɪn) n 1 a yellow-and-black Eurasian finch. 2 **pine siskin**. a North American finch, having a streaked yellowish-brown plumage. [C16: from MDu. sīseken, from MLow G sīsek]

Sisley ★ (ˈsɪslɪ; French sisle) n **Alfred** (alfrɛd). 1839–99, French painter, esp. of landscapes; one of the originators of impressionism.

sissy or **cissy** (ˈsɪsɪ) n, pl **sissies. 1** an effeminate, weak, or cowardly boy or man. ◆ adj 2 effeminate, weak, or cowardly.

sister (ˈsɪstə) n 1 a female person having the same parents as another person. 2 a female person who belongs to the same group, trade union, etc., as another or others. 3 a senior nurse. 4 Chiefly RC Church. a nun or a title given to a nun. 5 a woman fellow member of a religious body. 6 (modifier) belonging to the same class, fleet, etc., as another or others: a sister ship. 7 (modifier) Biol. denoting any of the cells or cell components formed by division of a parent cell or cell component: sister nuclei. [OE sweostor]

sisterhood (ˈsɪstəˌhʊd) n 1 the state of being related as a sister or sisters. 2 a religious body or society of sisters.

sister-in-law n, pl **sisters-in-law. 1** the sister of one's husband or wife. 2 the wife of one's brother.

sisterly (ˈsɪstəlɪ) adj of or suitable to a sister, esp. in showing kindness.
▶ 'sisterliness n

Sistine Chapel ★ (ˈsɪstaɪn, -tiːn) n the chapel of the pope in the Vatican at Rome, built for Sixtus IV and decorated with frescoes by Michelangelo and others. [Sistine, from It. Sistino relating to Sisto Sixtus (Pope Sixtus IV)]

sistrum (ˈsɪstrəm) n, pl **sistra** (-trə). a musical instrument of ancient Egypt consisting of a metal rattle. [C14: via L from Gk *seistron,* from *seiein* to shake]

Sisyphean (ˌsɪsɪˈfiːən) *adj* **1** relating to Sisyphus. **2** actually or seemingly endless and futile.

Sisyphus ★ (ˈsɪsɪfəs) *n Greek myth.* a king of Corinth, punished in Hades for his misdeeds by eternally having to roll a heavy stone up a hill: every time he approached the top, the stone escaped his grasp and rolled to the bottom.

sit (sɪt) *vb* **sits, sitting, sat.** *(mainly intr)* **1** *(also tr; when intr, often foll. by down, in,* or *on)* to adopt a posture in which the body is supported on the buttocks and the torso is more or less upright: *to sit on a chair.* **2** *(tr)* to cause to adopt such a posture. **3** (of an animal) to adopt or rest in a posture with the hindquarters lowered to the ground. **4** (of a bird) to perch or roost. **5** (of a hen or other bird) to cover eggs to hatch them. **6** to be situated or located. **7** (of the wind) to blow from the direction specified. **8** to adopt and maintain a posture for one's portrait to be painted, etc. **9** to occupy or be entitled to a seat in some official capacity, as a judge, etc. **10** (of a deliberative body) to be in session. **11** to remain inactive or unused: *his car sat in the garage.* **12** (of a garment) to fit or hang as specified: *that dress sits well on you.* **13** to weigh, rest, or lie as specified: *greatness sits easily on him.* **14** *(tr)* Chiefly *Brit.* to take (an examination): *he's sitting his bar finals.* **15** (usually foll. by *for*) Chiefly *Brit.* to be a candidate (for a qualification): *he's sitting for a BA.* **16** *(intr; in combination)* to look after a specified person or thing for someone else: *granny-sit.* **17** *(tr)* to have seating capacity for. **18 sit tight.** *Inf.* **18a** to wait patiently. **18b** to maintain one's stand, opinion, etc., firmly. ◆ See also **sit back, sit down,** etc. [OE *sittan*]

sitar (sɪˈtɑː) *n* a stringed musical instrument, esp. of India, having a long neck, a rounded body, and movable frets. [from Hindi *sitār,* lit.: three-stringed]
▸ **siˈtarist** *n*

sit back *vb* *(intr, adv)* to relax, as when action should be taken: *many people just sit back and ignore the problems of today.*

sitcom (ˈsɪtˌkɒm) *n* an informal term for **situation comedy.**

sit down *vb* *(adv)* **1** to adopt or cause (oneself or another) to adopt a sitting posture. **2** *(intr;* foll. by *under)* to suffer (insults, etc.) without protests or resistance. ◆ *n* **sit-down. 3** a form of civil disobedience in which demonstrators sit down in a public place. **4** See **sit-down strike.** ◆ *adj* **sit-down. 5** (of a meal, etc.) eaten while sitting down at a table.

sit-down strike *n* a strike in which workers refuse to leave their place of employment until a settlement is reached.

site (saɪt) *n* **1a** the piece of land where something was, is, or is intended to be located: *a building site.* **1b** *(as modifier):* site office. **2** *Computing.* an Internet location where information relating to a specific subject or group of subjects can be accessed. ◆ *vb* **sites, siting, sited. 3** *(tr)* to locate or install (something) in a specific place. [C14: from L *situs* situation, from *sinere* to be placed]

sith (sɪθ) *adv, conj, prep* an archaic word for **since.** [OE *siththa*]

sit-in *n* **1** a form of civil disobedience in which demonstrators occupy seats in a public place and refuse to move. **2** another term for **sit-down strike.** ◆ *vb* **sit in.** *(intr, adv)* **3** (often foll. by *for*) to deputize (for). **4** (foll. by *on*) to take part (in) as a visitor or guest. **5** to organize or take part in a sit-in.

Sitka ★ (ˈsɪtkə) *n* a town in SE Alaska, in the Alexander Archipelago on W Baranof Island: capital of Russian America (1804–67) and of Alaska (1867–1906). Pop.: 8588 (1990).

sitkamer (ˈsɪtˌkɑːmə) *n S. African.* a sitting room. [from Afrik.]

sitka spruce (ˈsɪtkə) *n* a tall North American spruce tree having yellowish-green needle-like leaves. [from SITKA]

sit on *vb* *(intr, prep)* **1** to be a member of (a committee, etc.). **2** *Inf.* to suppress. **3** *Inf.* to check or rebuke.

sit out *vb* *(tr, adv)* **1** to endure to the end: *I sat out the play*

although it was terrible. **2** to remain seated throughout (a dance, etc.).

Sitsang ★ (ˈsiːˈtsæŋ) *n* a Chinese name for **Tibet.**

sitter (ˈsɪtə) *n* **1** a person or animal that sits. **2** a person who is posing for his or her portrait to be painted, etc. **3** a broody hen that is sitting on its eggs to hatch them. **4** *(in combination)* a person who looks after a specified person or thing for someone else: *flat-sitter.* **5** *US.* short for **baby-sitter. 6** anyone, other than the medium, taking part in a seance. **7** anything that is extremely easy, such as an easy catch in cricket.

Sitter ★ (ˈsɪtə) *n* Willem de (ˈwɪləm də). 1872–1934, Dutch astronomer, who calculated the size of the universe and conceived of it as expanding.

sitting (ˈsɪtɪŋ) *n* **1** a continuous period of being seated: *I read his novel at one sitting.* **2** such a period in a restaurant, canteen, etc.: *dinner will be served in two sittings.* **3** the act or period of posing for one's portrait to be painted, etc. **4** a meeting, esp. of an official body, to conduct business. **5** the incubation period of a bird's eggs during which the mother sits on them. ◆ *adj* **6** in office: *a sitting councillor.* **7** seated: *in a sitting position.*

Sitting Bull ★ *n* Indian name *Tatanka Yotanka* ?1831–90, American Indian chief of the Teton Dakota Sioux. Resisting White encroachment on his people's hunting grounds, he led the Sioux tribes against the US Army in the Sioux War (1876–77). The hunger of the Sioux, whose food came from the diminishing buffalo, forced his surrender (1881).

sitting duck *n Inf.* a person or thing in a defenceless or vulnerable position. Also called: **sitting target.**

sitting room *n* a room in a private house or flat used for relaxation and entertainment of guests.

sitting tenant *n* a tenant occupying a house, flat, etc.

situate (ˈsɪtjʊˌeɪt) *vb* **situates, situating, situated. 1** *(tr; often passive)* to place. ◆ *adj* **2** (now used esp. in legal contexts) situated. [C16: from LL *situāre* to position, from L *situs* a SITE]

situation (ˌsɪtjʊˈeɪʃən) *n* **1** physical placement, esp. with regard to the surroundings. **2a** state of affairs. **2b** a complex or critical state of affairs in a novel, play, etc. **3** social or financial status, position, or circumstances. **4** a position of employment.
▸ **ˌsituˈational** *adj*

situation comedy *n* (on television or radio) a comedy series involving the same characters in various day-to-day situations which are developed as separate stories for each episode. Also called: **sitcom.**

sit up *vb* *(adv)* **1** to raise (oneself or another) from a recumbent to an upright posture. **2** *(intr)* to remain out of bed and awake, esp. until a late hour. **3** *(intr) Inf.* to become suddenly interested: *devaluation of the dollar made the money market sit up.* ◆ *n* **sit-up. 4** a physical exercise in which the body is brought into a sitting position from one of lying on the back. Also called: **trunk curl.**

Sitwell ★ (ˈsɪtwəl) *n* **1** Dame **Edith.** 1887–1964, British poet, noted for her collection *Façade* (1922). **2** her brother, Sir **Osbert.** 1892–1969, British writer, best known for his autobiographical books. **3** his brother, Sir **Sacheverell** (səˈʃɛvərəl). 1897–1988, British writer on art, architecture, and travel.

sitz bath (sɪts, zɪts) *n* a bath in which the buttocks and hips are immersed in hot water. [half translation of G *Sitzbad,* from *Sitz* seat + *Bad* bath]

SI unit *n* any of the units adopted for international use under the Système International d'Unités, now employed for all scientific and most technical purposes. There are seven fundamental units: the metre, kilogram, second, ampere, kelvin, candela, and mole; and two supplementary units: the radian and the steradian. All other units are derived by multiplication or division of these units.

Siva ('siːvə) *n Hinduism.* the destroyer, one of the three chief divinities of the later Hindu pantheon. [from Sansk. *Śiva*, lit.: the auspicious (one)]
▶ **'Siva,ism** *n*

Sivas ★ (*Turkish* 'sivɑs) *n* a city in central Turkey, at an altitude of 1347 m (4420 ft): one of the chief cities in Asia Minor in ancient times; scene of the national congress (1919) leading to the revolution that established modern Turkey. Pop.: 240 100 (1994 est.).

six (sɪks) *n* **1** the cardinal number that is the sum of five and one. **2** a numeral, 6, VI, etc., representing this number. **3** something representing, represented by, or consisting of six units, such as a playing card with six symbols on it. **4** *Also:* **six o'clock.** six hours after noon or midnight. **5** *Cricket.* **5a** a stroke from which the ball crosses the boundary without bouncing. **5b** the six runs scored for such a stroke. **6** a division of a Brownie Guide or Cub Scout pack. **7 at sixes and sevens. 7a** in disagreement. **7b** in a state of confusion. **8 knock (someone) for six.** *Inf.* to upset or overwhelm (someone) completely. **9 six of one and half a dozen of the other.** a situation in which the alternatives are considered equivalent. ◆ *determiner* **10a** amounting to six: *six nations.* **10b** (*as pron*): *set the table for six.* [OE *siex*]

Six (*French* sis) *n* **Les** (le). a group of six young composers in France, who from about 1916 formed a temporary association. Its members were Darius Milhaud, Arthur Honegger, Francis Poulenc, Georges Auric, Louis Durey, and Germaine Tailleferre.

Six Counties ★ *pl n* the counties of Northern Ireland.

sixer ('sɪksə) *n* the leader of a group of six Cub Scouts or Brownie Guides.

sixfold ('sɪks,fəʊld) *adj* **1** equal to or having six times as many or as much. **2** composed of six parts. ◆ *adv* **3** by or up to six times as many or as much.

sixmo ('sɪksməʊ) *n, pl* **sixmos.** a book size resulting from folding a sheet of paper into six leaves or twelve pages, each one sixth the size of the sheet. Often written: **6mo, 6°.** Also called: **sexto.**

Six Nations ★ *pl n* (in North America) the Indian confederacy of the Cayugas, Mohawks, Oneidas, Onondagas, Senecas, and Tuscaroras. Also called: **Iroquois.**

sixpence ('sɪkspəns) *n* (formerly) a small British cupronickel coin with a face value of six old pennies, worth 2½ pence.

six-shooter *n US inf.* a revolver with six chambers. Also called: **six-gun.**

sixte (sɪkst) *n* the sixth of eight basic positions from which a parry or attack can be made in fencing. [from F: (the) sixth (parrying position), from L *sextus* sixth]

sixteen ('sɪks'tiːn) *n* **1** the cardinal number that is the sum of ten and six. **2** a numeral, 16, XVI, etc., representing this number. **3** something represented by, representing, or consisting of 16 units. ◆ *determiner* **4a** amounting to sixteen: *sixteen tons.* **4b** (*as pron*): *sixteen are known to the police.* [OE *sextyne*]
▶ **'six'teenth** *adj, n*

sixteenmo ('sɪks'tiːnməʊ) *n, pl* **sixteenmos.** a book size resulting from folding a sheet of paper into 16 leaves or 32 pages. Often written: **16mo, 16°.** Also called: **sextodecimo.**

sixteenth note *n* the usual US and Canad. name for **semiquaver.**

sixth (sɪksθ) *adj* **1** (*usually prenominal*) **1a** coming after the fifth and before the seventh in numbering, position, time, etc.; being the ordinal number of *six*: often written 6th. **1b** (*as n*): *the sixth to go.* ◆ *n* **2a** one of six parts of an object, quantity, measurement, etc. **2b** (*as modifier*): *a sixth part.* **3** the fraction equal to one divided by six (1/6). **4** *Music.* **4a** the interval between one note and another six notes away from it in the diatonic scale. **4b** one of two notes constituting such an interval in relation to the other. ◆ *adv* **5** *Also:* **sixthly.** after the fifth person, posi-

tion, etc. ◆ *sentence connector.* **6** *Also:* **sixthly.** as the sixth point.

sixth form *n* (in England and Wales) **a** the most senior level in a secondary school to which pupils, usually above the legal leaving age, may proceed to take A levels, retake GCSEs, etc. **b** (*as modifier*): *a sixth-form college.*
▶ **'sixth-,former** *n*

sixth sense *n* any supposed means of perception, such as intuition, other than the five senses of sight, hearing, touch, taste, and smell.

Sixtus V ★ ('sɪkstəs) *n* original name *Felice Peretti.* 1520–90, Italian ecclesiastic; pope (1585–90).

sixty ('sɪkstɪ) *n, pl* **sixties. 1** the cardinal number that is the product of ten and six. **2** a numeral, 60, LX, etc., representing sixty. **3** something represented by, representing, or consisting of 60 units. ◆ *determiner* **4a** amounting to sixty: *sixty soldiers.* **4b** (*as pron*): *sixty are dead.* [OE *sixtig*]
▶ **'sixtieth** *adj, n*

sixty-fourmo (,sɪkstɪ'fɔːməʊ) *n, pl* **sixty-fourmos.** a book size resulting from folding a sheet of paper into 64 leaves or 128 pages, each one sixty-fourth the size of the sheet. Often written **64mo, 64°.**

sixty-fourth note *n* the usual US and Canad. name for **hemidemisemiquaver.**

sixty-nine *n* another term for **soixante-neuf.**

sizable *or* **sizeable** ('saɪzəb°l) *adj* quite large.
▶ **'sizably** *or* **'sizeably** *adv*

size[1] (saɪz) *n* **1** the dimensions, amount, or extent of something. **2** large dimensions, etc. **3** one of a series of graduated measurements, as of clothing: *she takes size 4 shoes.* **4** *Inf.* state of affairs as summarized: *he's bankrupt, that's the size of it.* ◆ *vb* **sizes, sizing, sized. 5** to sort according to size. **6** (*tr*) to cut to a particular size or sizes. [C13: from OF *sise,* shortened from *assise* ASSIZE]
▶ **'sizer** *n*

> **USAGE NOTE** The use of *-size* and *-sized* after *large* or *small* is redundant, except when describing something which is made in specific sizes: *a large* (not *large-size*) *organization.* Similarly, *in size* is redundant in the expressions *large in size* and *small in size.*

size[2] (saɪz) *n* **1** *Also called:* **sizing.** a thin gelatinous mixture, made from glue, clay, or wax, that is used as a sealer on paper or plaster surfaces. ◆ *vb* **sizes, sizing, sized. 2** (*tr*) to treat or coat (a surface) with size. [C15: ?from OF *sise*; see SIZE[1]]

sized (saɪzd) *adj* of a specified size: *medium-sized.*

> **USAGE NOTE** See at **size**[1].

size up *vb* (*adv*) **1** (*tr*) *Inf.* to make an assessment of (a person, problem, etc.). **2** to conform to or make so as to conform to certain specifications of dimension.

sizzle ('sɪz°l) *vb* **sizzles, sizzling, sizzled.** (*intr*) **1** to make the hissing sound characteristic of frying fat. **2** *Inf.* to be very hot. **3** *Inf.* to be very angry. ◆ *n* **4** a hissing sound. [C17: imit.]
▶ **'sizzler** *n* ▶ **'sizzling** *adj*

SJ *abbrev.* for Society of Jesus.

SJA *abbrev.* for Saint John's Ambulance (Brigade *or* Association).

Sjælland ★ (*Danish* 'sjɛlan) *n* the Danish name for **Zealand.**

sjambok ('ʃæmbʌk) *n* (in South Africa) a heavy whip of rhinoceros or hippopotamus hide. [C19: from Afrik., ult. from Urdu *chābuk* horsewhip]

SK *abbrev.* for Saskatchewan.

ska (skɑː) *n* a type of West Indian pop music: a precursor of reggae. [C20: from ?]

skaapsteker ('skɑːp,stɪəkə) *n* any of several back-fanged venomous South African snakes. [from Afrik. *skaap* sheep + *steek* to pierce]

Skagen ★ ('skɑːgən) *n* **Cape.** another name for the **Skaw.**

Skagerrak ★ ('skægə,ræk) *n* an arm of the North Sea between Denmark and Norway, merging with the Kattegat in the southeast.

skald *or* **scald** (skɔːld) *n* (in ancient Scandinavia) a bard or minstrel. [from ON, from ?]
▶ 'skaldic *or* 'scaldic *adj*

Skara Brae ★ ('skærə) *n* a neolithic village in NE Scotland, in the Orkney Islands: one of Europe's most perfectly preserved Stone Age villages, buried by a sand dune until uncovered by a storm in 1850.

skat (skæt) *n* a three-handed card game using 32 cards, popular in German-speaking communities. [C19: from G, from It. *scarto* played cards, from *scartare* to discard, from L *charta* CARD[1]]

skate[1] (skeɪt) *n* **1** See **roller skate, ice skate. 2** the steel blade or runner of an ice skate. **3** such a blade fitted with straps for fastening to a shoe. **4 get one's skates on.** to hurry. ◆ *vb* **skates, skating, skated.** (*intr*) **5** to glide swiftly on skates. **6** to slide smoothly over a surface. **7 skate on thin ice.** to place oneself in a dangerous situation. [C17: via Du. from OF *éschasse* stilt, prob. of Gmc origin]
▶ 'skater *n*

skate[2] (skeɪt) *n, pl* **skate** *or* **skates.** any of a family of large rays of temperate and tropical seas, having two dorsal fins, a short spineless tail, and a long snout. [C14: from ON *skata*]

skateboard ('skeɪt,bɔːd) *n* **1** a board mounted on roller-skate wheels, usually ridden while standing up. ◆ *vb* **2** (*intr*) to ride on a skateboard.
▶ 'skate,boarder *n* ▶ 'skate,boarding *n*

skate over *vb* (*intr, prep*) **1** to cross on or as if on skates. **2** to avoid dealing with (a matter) fully.

Skaw ★ (skɔː) *n* **the.** a cape at the N tip of Denmark. Also called: (Cape) **Skagen.**

skean-dhu (ˌskiːən'duː) *n* a dirk worn in the stocking as part of Highland dress. [C19: from Gaelic *sgian dubh* black knife]

skedaddle (skɪ'dæd⁰l) *Inf.* ◆ *vb* **skedaddles, skedaddling, skedaddled. 1** (*intr*) to run off hastily. ◆ *n* **2** a hasty retreat. [C19: from ?]

skeet (skiːt) *n* a form of clay-pigeon shooting in which targets are hurled from two traps at varying speeds and angles. [C20: changed from ON *skeyti* a thrown object, from *skjōta* to shoot]

skein (skeɪn) *n* **1** a length of yarn, etc., wound in a long coil. **2** something resembling this, such as a lock of hair. **3** a flock of geese flying. [C15: from OF *escaigne*, from ?]

skeleton ('skɛlɪtən) *n* **1** a hard framework consisting of inorganic material that supports and protects the soft parts of an animal's body: may be internal, as in vertebrates, or external, as in arthropods. **2** *Inf.* a very thin emaciated person or animal. **3** the essential framework of any structure, such as a building or leaf. **4** an outline consisting of bare essentials: *the skeleton of a novel.* **5** (*modifier*) reduced to a minimum: *a skeleton staff.* **6 skeleton in the cupboard** *or* US & Canad. **closet.** a scandalous fact or event in the past that is kept secret. [C16: via NL from Gk: something desiccated, from *skellein* to dry up]
▶ 'skeletal *or* 'skeleton-,like *adj*

skeletonize *or* **skeletonise** ('skɛlɪtə,naɪz) *vb* **skeletonizes, skeletonizing, skeletonized** *or* **skeletonises, skeletonising, skeletonised.** (*tr*) **1** to reduce to a minimum framework or outline. **2** to create the essential framework of.

skeleton key *n* a key with the serrated edge filed down so that it can open numerous locks. Also called: **passkey.**

Skelmersdale ★ ('skɛlməz,deɪl) *n* a town in NW England, in Lancashire: designated a new town in 1962. Pop.: 42 104 (1991).

Skelton ★ ('skɛltən) *n* **John.** ?1460–1529, English poet, noted for his colloquial speech rhythms.
▶ **Skel'tonic** (skɛl'tɒnɪk) *adj*

skep (skɛp) *n* **1** a beehive, esp. one constructed of straw. **2**

Now chiefly *dialect.* a large basket of wickerwork or straw. [OE *sceppe*]

skeptic ('skɛptɪk) *n, adj* an archaic and the usual US spelling of **sceptic.**

skerrick ('skɛrɪk) *n* US, Austral., & NZ. a small fragment or amount (esp. in **not a skerrick**). [C20: N English dialect, prob. of Scand. origin]

skerry ('skɛrɪ) *n, pl* **skerries.** Chiefly Scot. **1** a small rocky island. **2** a reef. [C17: Orkney dialect, from ON *sker* scar (rock formation)]

sketch (skɛtʃ) *n* **1** a rapid drawing or painting. **2** a brief usually descriptive essay or other literary composition. **3** a short play, often comic, forming part of a revue. **4** a short evocative piece of instrumental music. **5** any brief outline. ◆ *vb* **6** to make a rough drawing (of). **7** (*tr*; often foll. by *out*) to make a brief description of. [C17: from Du. *schets*, via It. from L *schedius* hastily made, from Gk *skhedios* unprepared]
▶ 'sketcher *n*

sketchbook ('skɛtʃ,bʊk) *n* **1** a book of plain paper containing sketches or for making sketches in. **2** a book of literary sketches.

sketchy ('skɛtʃɪ) *adj* **sketchier, sketchiest. 1** existing only in outline. **2** superficial or slight.
▶ 'sketchily *adv* ▶ 'sketchiness *n*

skew (skjuː) *adj* **1** placed in or turning into an oblique position or course. **2** *Machinery.* having a component that is at an angle to the main axis of an assembly: *a skew bevel gear.* **3** *Maths.* composed of or being elements that are neither parallel nor intersecting. **4** (of a statistical distribution) not having equal probabilities above and below the mean. **5** distorted or biased. ◆ *n* **6** an oblique, slanting, or indirect course or position. ◆ *vb* **7** to take or cause to take an oblique course or direction. **8** (*intr*) to look sideways. **9** (*tr*) to distort. [C14: from OF *escuer* to shun, of Gmc origin]
▶ 'skewness *n*

skewback ('skjuː,bæk) *n* Archit. the sloping surface on both sides of a segmental arch that takes the thrust.

skewbald ('skjuː,bɔːld) *adj* **1** marked or spotted in white and any colour except black. ◆ *n* **2** a horse with this marking. [C17: see SKEW, PIEBALD]

skewer (skjʊə) *n* **1** a long pin for holding meat in position while being cooked, etc. **2** a similar pin having some other function. ◆ *vb* **3** to drive a skewer through or fasten with a skewer. [C17: prob. from dialect *skiver*]

skewwhiff ('skjuː'wɪf) *adj* (*postpositive*) Brit. inf. not straight. [C18: prob. infl. by ASKEW]

ski (skiː) *n, pl* **skis** *or* **ski. 1a** one of a pair of wood, metal, or plastic runners that are used for gliding over snow. **1b** (*as modifier*): *a ski boot.* **2** a water-ski. ◆ *vb* **skis, skiing; skied** *or* **ski'd. 3** (*intr*) to travel on skis. [C19: from Norwegian, from ON *skith* snowshoes]
▶ 'skier *n* ▶ 'skiing *n*

skibob ('skiː,bɒb) *n* a vehicle made of two short skis, the forward one having a steering handle and the rear one supporting a low seat, for gliding down snow slopes.
▶ 'skibobber *n*

skid (skɪd) *vb* **skids, skidding, skidded. 1** to cause (a vehicle) to slide sideways or (of a vehicle) to slide sideways while in motion, esp. out of control. **2** (*intr*) to slide without revolving, as the wheel of a moving vehicle after sudden braking. ◆ *n* **3** an instance of sliding, esp. sideways. **4** a support on which heavy objects may be stored and moved short distances by sliding. **5** a shoe or drag used to apply pressure to the metal rim of a wheel to act as a brake. [C17: ? of Scand. origin]

Skidoo ('skɪduː) *n* Canad., trademark. another name for **snowmobile.**

skid row (rəʊ) *or* **skid road** *n* Sl., chiefly US & Canad. a dilapidated section of a city inhabited by vagrants, etc.

skied[1] (skaɪd) *vb* the past tense and past participle of **sky.**

skied[2] (skiːd) *vb* a past tense and past participle of **ski.**

Skien ★ (Norwegian 'ʃeːən) *n* a port in S Norway, on the **Skien River:** one of the oldest towns in Norway; timber industry. Pop.: 47 870 (1990).

skiff (skɪf) n a small narrow boat. [C18: from F esquif, from OIt. schifo a boat, of Gmc origin]

skiffle ('skɪfᵊl) n a style of popular music of the 1950s, played chiefly on guitars and improvised percussion instruments. [C20: from ?]

skijoring (skiː'dʒɔːrɪŋ, -'jɔːrɪŋ) n a sport in which a skier is pulled over snow or ice, usually by a horse. [Norwegian skikjöring, lit.: ski-driving]
▸ ski'jorer n

ski jump n 1 a high ramp overhanging a slope from which skiers compete to make the longest jump. ◆ vb ski-jump. 2 (intr) to perform a ski jump.
▸ ski jumper n

Skikda ★ ('skɪkdɑː) n a port in NE Algeria, on an inlet of the Mediterranean: founded by the French in 1838 on the site of a Roman city. Pop.: 128 747 (1987). Former name: **Philippeville**.

skilful or US **skillful** ('skɪlful) adj 1 possessing or displaying accomplishment or skill. 2 involving or requiring accomplishment or skill.
▸ 'skilfully or US 'skillfully adv

ski lift n any device for carrying skiers up a slope, such as a chairlift.

skill (skɪl) n 1 special ability in a sport, etc., esp. ability acquired by training. 2 something, esp. a trade or technique, requiring special training or manual proficiency. [C12: from ON skil distinction]
▸ 'skill-less or 'skilless adj

skilled (skɪld) adj 1 demonstrating accomplishment or special training. 2 (prenominal) involving skill or special training: a skilled job.

skillet ('skɪlɪt) n 1 a small frying pan. 2 Chiefly Brit. a saucepan. [C15: prob. from skele bucket, from ON]

skilly ('skɪlɪ) n Chiefly Brit. a thin soup or gruel. [C19: from skilligallee, from ?]

skim (skɪm) vb skims, skimming, skimmed. 1 (tr) to remove floating material from the surface of (a liquid), as with a spoon: to skim milk. 2 to glide smoothly or lightly over (a surface). 3 (tr) to throw (something) in a path over a surface, so as to bounce or ricochet: to skim stones over water. 4 (when intr, usually foll. by through) to read (a book) in a superficial manner. ◆ n 5 the act or process of skimming. 6 material skimmed off a liquid, esp. off milk. 7 any thin layer covering a surface. [C15 skimmen, prob. from scumen to skim]

skimmed milk n milk from which the cream has been removed. Also called: **skim milk**.

skimmer ('skɪmə) n 1 a person or thing that skims. 2 any of several mainly tropical coastal aquatic birds having a bill with an elongated lower mandible for skimming food from the surface of the water. 3 a flat perforated spoon used for skimming fat from liquids.

skimmia ('skɪmɪə) n any of a genus of rutaceous shrubs grown for their ornamental red berries and evergreen foliage. [C18: NL from Japanese (mijama-) shikimi, a native name of the plant]

skimp (skɪmp) vb 1 to be extremely sparing or supply (someone) sparingly. 2 to perform (work, etc.) carelessly or with inadequate materials. [C17: ? a combination of SCANT & SCRIMP]

skimpy ('skɪmpɪ) adj skimpier, skimpiest. 1 made of too little material. 2 excessively thrifty; mean.
▸ 'skimpily adv ▸ 'skimpiness n

skin (skɪn) n 1 the tissue forming the outer covering of the vertebrate body: it consists of two layers, the outermost of which may be covered with hair, scales, feathers, etc. 2 a person's complexion: a fair skin. 3 any similar covering in a plant or lower animal. 4 any coating or film, such as one that forms on the surface of a liquid. 5 the outer covering of a fur-bearing animal, dressed and finished with the hair on. 6 a container made from animal skin. 7 the outer covering surface of a vessel, rocket, etc. 8 a person's skin regarded as his life: to save one's skin. 9 (often pl) Inf. (in jazz or pop use) a drum. 10 Inf. short for skinhead. 11 by the skin of one's teeth. only just. 12 get under one's skin. Inf. to irritate. 13 no skin off one's nose. Inf. not a matter that affects one adversely. 14 skin and bone. ex-

tremely thin. 15 thick (or thin) skin. an insensitive (or sensitive) nature. ◆ vb skins, skinning, skinned. 16 (tr) to remove the outer covering from (fruit, etc.). 17 (tr) to scrape a small piece of skin from (a part of oneself) in falling, etc.: he skinned his knee. 18 (often foll. by over) to cover (something) with skin or a skinlike substance or (of something) to become covered in this way. 19 (tr) Sl. to swindle. ◆ adj 20 of or for the skin: skin cream. [OE scinn]
▸ 'skinless adj ▸ 'skin,like adj

skin-deep adj 1 superficial; shallow. ◆ adv 2 superficially.

skin diving n the sport or activity of diving and underwater swimming without wearing a diver's costume.
▸ 'skin-,diver n

skin flick n Sl. a film containing much nudity and explicit sex for sensational purposes.

skinflint ('skɪn,flɪnt) n an ungenerous or niggardly person. [C18: referring to a person so avaricious that he would skin (swindle) a flint]

skinful ('skɪn,ful) n, pl skinfuls. Sl. sufficient alcoholic drink to make one drunk.

skin graft n a piece of skin removed from one part of the body and surgically grafted at the site of a severe burn or similar injury.

skinhead ('skɪn,hed) n 1 a member of a group of White youths, noted for their closely cropped hair, aggressive behaviour, and overt racism. 2 a closely cropped hairstyle.

skink (skɪŋk) n any of a family of lizards commonest in tropical Africa and Asia, having an elongated body covered with smooth scales. [C16: from L scincus a lizard, from Gk skinkos]

skinned (skɪnd) adj 1 stripped of the skin. 2a having a skin as specified. 2b (in combination): thick-skinned.

Skinner ★ ('skɪnə) n B(urrhus) F(rederic). 1904–90, US behavioural psychologist.

skinny ('skɪnɪ) adj skinnier, skinniest. 1 lacking in flesh; thin. 2 consisting of or resembling skin.

skint (skɪnt) adj (usually postpositive) Brit. sl. without money. [var. of skinned, p.p. of SKIN]

skin test n Med. any test to determine immunity to a disease or hypersensitivity by introducing a small amount of the test substance beneath the skin.

skintight ('skɪn'taɪt) adj (of garments) fitting tightly over the body; clinging.

skip¹ (skɪp) vb skips, skipping, skipped. 1 (when intr, often foll. by over, into, etc.) to spring or move lightly, esp. to move by hopping from one foot to the other. 2 (intr) to jump over a skipping-rope. 3 to cause (a stone, etc.) to skim over a surface or (of a stone) to move in this way. 4 to omit (intervening matter): he skipped a chapter of the book. 5 (intr; foll. by through) Inf. to read or deal with quickly or superficially. 6 skip it! Inf. it doesn't matter! 7 (tr) Inf. to miss deliberately: to skip school. 8 (tr) Inf., chiefly US & Canad. to leave (a place) in haste: to skip town. ◆ n 9 a skipping movement or gait. 10 the act of passing over or omitting. [C13: prob. from ON]

skip² (skɪp) n, vb skips, skipping, skipped. Inf. short for skipper¹.

skip³ (skɪp) n 1 a large open container for transporting building materials, etc. 2 a cage used as a lift in mines, etc. [C19: var. of SKEP]

ski pants pl n stretch trousers, worn for skiing or as a fashion garment, kept taut by a strap under the foot.

skip distance n the shortest distance between a transmitter and a receiver that will permit reception of radio waves of a specified frequency by one reflection from the ionosphere.

skipjack ('skɪp,dʒæk) n, pl skipjack or skipjacks. 1 Also called: skipjack tuna. an important food fish that has a striped abdomen and occurs in all tropical seas. 2 black skipjack. a small spotted tuna of Indo-Pacific seas.

skiplane ('skiː,pleɪn) n an aircraft fitted with skis to enable it to land on and take off from snow.

skipper¹ ('skɪpə) n 1 the captain of any vessel. 2 the captain of an aircraft. **3** a leader, as of a sporting team. ◆ *vb* **4** to act as skipper (of). [C14: from MLow G, MDu. *schipper* shipper]

skipper[2] ('skɪpə) *n* **1** a person or thing that skips. **2** a small butterfly having a hairy mothlike body and erratic darting flight.

skipping ('skɪpɪŋ) *n* the act of jumping over a rope that is held either by the person jumping or by two other people, as a game or for exercise.

skipping-rope *n Brit.* a cord, usually having handles at each end, that is held in the hands and swung round and down so that the holder or others can jump over it.

Skipton ★ ('skɪptən) *n* a market town in N England, in North Yorkshire: 11th-century castle. Pop.: 13 583 (1991).

skip-tooth saw *n* a saw with alternate teeth absent.

skip zone *n* a region surrounding a broadcasting station that cannot receive transmissions either directly or by reflection off the ionosphere.

skirl (skɜːl) *Scot. & N English dialect.* ◆ *vb* **1** (*intr*) (esp. of bagpipes) to emit a shrill sound. ◆ *n* **2** the sound of bagpipes. [C14: prob. from ON]

skirmish ('skɜːmɪʃ) *n* **1** a minor short-lived military engagement. **2** any brisk clash or encounter. ◆ *vb* **3** (*intr*; often foll. by *with*) to engage in a skirmish. [C14: from OF *eskirmir*, of Gmc origin]
▸ 'skirmisher *n*

Skíros ★ ('skɪrɒs) *n* transliteration of the Modern Greek name for **Skyros**.

skirt (skɜːt) *n* **1** a garment hanging from the waist, worn chiefly by women and girls. **2** the part of a dress below the waist. **3** Also called: **apron.** a circular flap, as round the base of a hovercraft. **4** the flaps on a saddle. **5** *Brit.* a cut of beef from the flank. **6** (*often pl*) an outlying area. **7 bit of skirt.** *Sl.* a girl or woman. ◆ *vb* **8** (*tr*) to form the edge of. **9** (*tr*) to provide with a border. **10** (when *intr*, foll. by *around, along,* etc.) to pass (by) or be situated (near) the outer edge of (an area, etc.). **11** (*tr*) to avoid (a difficulty, etc.): *he skirted the issue.* **12** *Chiefly Austral. & NZ.* to trim the ragged edges from (a fleece). [C13: from ON *skyrta* shirt]
▸ 'skirted *adj*

skirting ('skɜːtɪŋ) *n* **1** a border, esp. of wood or tiles, fixed round the base of an interior wall to protect it. **2** material used for skirts.

skirting board *n* a skirting made of wood.

skirtings ('skɜːtɪŋz) *pl n* ragged edges trimmed from the fleece of a sheep.

ski stick *or* **pole** *n* a stick, usually with a metal point, used by skiers to gain momentum and maintain balance.

skit (skɪt) *n* **1** a brief satirical theatrical sketch. **2** a short satirical piece of writing. [C18: rel. to earlier verb *skit* to move rapidly, hence to score a satirical hit, prob. of Scand. origin]

skite[1] (skaɪt) *Scot. dialect.* ◆ *vb* **skites, skiting, skited. 1** (*intr*) to slide or slip, as on ice. **2** (*tr*) to strike with a sharp blow. ◆ *n* **3** an instance of slipping or sliding. **4** a sharp blow. [C18: from ?]

skite[2] (skaɪt) *Austral. & NZ inf.* ◆ *vb* **skites, skiting, skited.** (*intr*) **1** to boast. ◆ *n* **2** boastful talk. **3** a person who boasts. [C19: from Scot. & N English dialect]

ski tow *n* a device for pulling skiers uphill, usually a motor-driven rope grasped by the skier while riding on his skis.

skitter ('skɪtə) *vb* **1** (*intr*; often foll. by *off*) to move or run rapidly or lightly. **2** to skim or cause to skim lightly and rapidly. **3** (*intr*) *Angling.* to draw a bait lightly over the surface of water. [C19: prob. from dialect *skite* to dash about]

skittish ('skɪtɪʃ) *adj* **1** playful, lively, or frivolous. **2** difficult to handle or predict. [C15: prob. from ON]
▸ 'skittishly *adv* ▸ 'skittishness *n*

skittle ('skɪt°l) *n* **1** a wooden or plastic pin, typically widest just above the base. **2** (*pl; functioning as sing*) Also called (esp. US): **ninepins.** a bowling game in which play-

ers knock over as many skittles as possible by rolling a wooden ball at them. [C17: from ?]

skive[1] (skaɪv) *vb* **skives, skiving, skived.** (*tr*) to shave or remove the surface of (leather). [C19: of Scand. origin, from *skifa*]
▸ 'skiver *n*

skive[2] (skaɪv) *vb* **skives, skiving, skived.** (when *intr*, often foll. by *off*) *Brit. inf.* to evade (work or responsibility). [C20: from ?]
▸ 'skiver *n*

skivvy[1] ('skɪvɪ) *n, pl* **skivvies. 1** *Chiefly Brit., often contemptuous.* a servant, esp. a female; drudge. ◆ *vb* **skivvies, skivvying, skivvied. 2** (*intr*) *Brit.* to work as a skivvy. [C20: from ?]

skivvy[2] ('skɪvɪ) *n, pl* **skivvies.** *Austral. & NZ.* a lightweight sweater-like garment with long sleeves and a polo neck. [from ?]

skol (skɒl) *or* **skoal** (skəʊl) *sentence substitute* good health! (a drinking toast). [C16: from Danish *skaal* bowl, of Scand. origin, from *skal*]

skookum ('skuːkəm) *adj W Canad.* large or big. [from Chinook Jargon]

Skopje ★ ('skɔːpjɛ) *n* the capital of (the Former Yugoslav Republic of) Macedonia, on the Vardar River: became capital of Serbia in 1346 and of Macedonia in 1945; suffered a severe earthquake in 1963. Pop.: 41 280 (1994). Serbo-Croat name: **Skoplje** ('skɔpljɛ). Turkish name (1392–1913): **Üsküb.**

Skryabin ★ ('skrɪəbɪn; *Russian* 'skrjabɪn) *n* a variant spelling of **Scriabin.**

Skt, Skt., Skr, *or* **Skr.** *abbrev. for* Sanskrit.

skua ('skjuːə) *n* any of various predatory aquatic gull-like birds having a dark plumage and long tail. [C17: from NL, from Faeroese *skúgvur*, of Scand. origin, from *skúfi*]

skulduggery *or US* **skullduggery** (skʌl'dʌgərɪ) *n Inf.* underhand dealing; trickery. [C18: from earlier Scot. *skulduddery*, of ?]

skulk (skʌlk) *vb* (*intr*) **1** to move stealthily so as to avoid notice. **2** to lie in hiding; lurk. **3** to shirk duty or evade responsibilities. ◆ *n* **4** a person who skulks. **5** *Obs.* a pack of foxes. [C13: from ON]
▸ 'skulker *n*

skull (skʌl) *n* **1** the bony skeleton of the head of vertebrates. **2** *Often derog.* the head regarded as the mind or intelligence: *to have a dense skull.* **3** a picture of a skull used to represent death or danger. [C13: from ON]

skull and crossbones *n* a picture of the human skull above two crossed thighbones, formerly on the pirate flag, now used as a warning of danger or death.

skullcap ('skʌl,kæp) *n* **1** a rounded brimless hat fitting the crown of the head. **2** the top part of the skull. **3** any of a genus of perennial plants, that have helmet-shaped flowers.

skunk (skʌŋk) *n, pl* **skunks** *or* **skunk. 1** any of various American mammals having a black-and-white coat and bushy tail: they eject an unpleasant-smelling fluid from the anal gland when attacked. **2** *Inf.* a despicable person. [C17: of Amerind origin]

skunk cabbage *n* a low-growing fetid aroid swamp plant of E North America, having broad leaves and minute flowers enclosed in a greenish spathe.

sky (skaɪ) *n, pl* **skies. 1** (*sometimes pl*) the apparently dome-shaped expanse extending upwards from the horizon that is blue or grey during the day and black at night. **2** outer space, as seen from the earth. **3** (*often pl*) weather, as described by the appearance of the upper air: *sunny skies.* **4** heaven. **5** *Inf.* the highest level of attainment: *the sky's the limit.* **6 to the skies.** extravagantly. ◆ *vb* **skies, skying, skied. 7** *Rowing.* to lift (the blade of an oar) too high before a stroke. **8** (*tr*) *Inf.* to hit (a ball) high in the air. [C13: from ON *skȳ*]

sky blue *n, adj* (of) a light or pale blue colour.

skydiving ('skaɪ,daɪvɪŋ) *n* the sport of parachute jumping, in which participants perform manoeuvres before opening the parachute.
▸ 'sky,dive *vb* 'sky,dives, 'sky,diving, 'sky,dived *or US* 'sky,dove; 'sky,dived ▸ 'sky,diver *n*

★ people and places

Skye ★ (skaɪ) *n* a mountainous island off the NW coast of Scotland, the largest island of the Inner Hebrides: tourist centre. Chief town: Portree. Pop.: 7500 (latest est.). Area: 1735 sq. km (670 sq. miles).

Skye terrier *n* a short-legged long-bodied breed of terrier with long wiry hair and erect ears.

sky-high *adj, adv* **1** at or to an unprecedented level: *prices rocketed sky-high.* ♦ *adv* **2** high into the air. **3 blow sky-high.** to destroy.

skyjack ('skaɪ,dʒæk) *vb* (tr) to hijack (an aircraft). [C20: from SKY + HIJACK]

skylark ('skaɪ,lɑːk) *n* **1** an Old World lark, noted for singing while hovering at a great height. ♦ *vb* **2** (intr) Inf. to romp or play jokes.

skylight ('skaɪ,laɪt) *n* a window placed in a roof or ceiling to admit daylight. Also called: **fanlight.**

skyline ('skaɪ,laɪn) *n* **1** the line at which the earth and sky appear to meet. **2** the outline of buildings, trees, etc., seen against the sky.

sky pilot *n Sl.* a clergyman, esp. a chaplain.

skyrocket ('skaɪ,rɒkɪt) *n* **1** another word for **rocket**[1] (sense 1). ♦ *vb* **2** (intr) Inf. to rise rapidly, as in price.

Skyros or **Scyros** ★ ('skiːrɒs) *n* a Greek island in the Aegean, the largest island in the N Sporades. Pop.: 3000 (latest est.). Area: 199 sq. km (77 sq. miles). Modern Greek name: **Skíros.**

skysail ('skaɪ,seɪl) *n Naut.* a square sail set above the royal on a square-rigger.

skyscraper ('skaɪ,skreɪpə) *n* a tall multistorey building.

skyward ('skaɪwəd) *adj* **1** directed or moving towards the sky. ♦ *adv* **2** Also: **skywards.** towards the sky.

skywriting ('skaɪ,raɪtɪŋ) *n* **1** the forming of words in the sky by the release of smoke or vapour from an aircraft. **2** the words so formed.
  ▶ '**sky,writer** *n*

slab (slæb) *n* **1** a broad flat thick piece of wood, stone, or other material. **2** a thick slice of cake, etc. **3** any of the outside parts of a log that are sawn off while the log is being made into planks. **4** Austral. & NZ. **4a** a rough-hewn wooden plank. **4b** (as modifier): *a slab hut.* **5** *Inf., chiefly Brit.* an operating or mortuary table. ♦ *vb* **slabs, slabbing, slabbed.** (tr) **6** to cut or make into a slab or slabs. **7** to saw slabs from (a log). [C13: from ?]

slack[1] (slæk) *adj* **1** not tight, tense, or taut. **2** negligent or careless. **3** (esp. of water, etc.) moving slowly. **4** (of trade, etc.) not busy. **5** *Phonetics.* another term for **lax** (sense 4). ♦ *adv* **6** in a slack manner. ♦ *n* **7** a part of a rope, etc., that is slack: *take in the slack.* **8** a period of decreased activity. ♦ *vb* **9** to neglect (one's duty, etc.). **10** (often foll. by *off*) to loosen. ♦ See also **slacks.** [OE *slæc, sleac*]
  ▶ '**slackly** *adv* ▶ '**slackness** *n*

slack[2] (slæk) *n* small pieces of coal with a high ash content. [C15: prob. from MLow G *slecke*]

slacken ('slækən) *vb* (often foll. by *off*) **1** to make or become looser. **2** to make or become slower, less intense, etc.

slacker ('slækə) *n* a person who evades work or duty; shirker.

slacks (slæks) *pl n* informal trousers worn by both sexes.

slack water *n* the period of still water around the turn of the tide, esp. at low tide.

slag (slæg) *n* **1** Also called: **cinder.** the fused material formed during the smelting or refining of metals. It usually consists of a mixture of silicates with calcium, phosphorus, sulphur, etc. **2** the mass of rough fragments of rock derived from volcanic lava. **3** a mixture of shale, clay, coal dust, etc., produced during coal mining. **4** *Brit. sl.* a coarse or dissipated woman or girl. ♦ *vb* **slags, slagging, slagged. 5** to convert into or become slag. **6** (tr; sometimes foll. by *off*) *Sl.* to make disparaging comments about; slander. [C16: from MLow G *slagge*, ?from *slagen* to slay]
  ▶ '**slagging** *n* ▶ '**slaggy** *adj*

slag heap *n* a hillock of waste matter from coal mining, etc.

slain (sleɪn) *vb* the past participle of **slay.**

slake (sleɪk) *vb* **slakes, slaking, slaked. 1** (tr) Literary. to satisfy (thirst, desire, etc.). **2** (tr) Poetic. to cool or refresh. **3** to undergo or cause to undergo the process in which lime reacts with water to produce calcium hydroxide. [OE *slacian*, from *slæc* SLACK[1]]
  ▶ '**slakable** or '**slakeable** *adj*

slaked lime *n* another name for **calcium hydroxide.**

slalom ('slɑːləm) *n Skiing, canoeing, etc.* a race over a winding course marked by artificial obstacles. [Norwegian, from *slad* sloping + *lom* path]

slam[1] (slæm) *vb* **slams, slamming, slammed. 1** to cause (a door or window) to close noisily or (of a door, etc.) to close in this way. **2** (tr) to throw (something) down violently. **3** (tr) Sl. to criticize harshly. **4** (intr; usually foll. by *into* or *out of*) Inf. to go (into or out of a room, etc.) in violent haste or anger. **5** (tr) to strike with violent force. **6** (tr) Inf. to defeat easily. ♦ *n* **7** the act or noise of slamming. [C17: of Scand. origin]

slam[2] (slæm) *n* a the winning of all (**grand slam**) or all but one (**little** or **small slam**) of the 13 tricks at bridge or whist. **b** the bid to do so in bridge. [C17: from ?]

slam-dance *vb* **slam-dances, slam-dancing, slam-danced.** (intr) to hurl oneself repeatedly into or through a crowd at a rock-music concert.

slammer ('slæmə) *n* **the.** *Sl.* prison.

slander ('slɑːndə) *n* **1** *Law.* **1a** defamation in some transient form, as by spoken words, gestures, etc. **1b** a slanderous statement, etc. **2** any defamatory words spoken about a person. ♦ *vb* **3** to utter or circulate slander (about). [C13: via Anglo-F from OF *escandle*, from LL *scandalum* a cause of offence; see SCANDAL]
  ▶ '**slanderer** *n* ▶ '**slanderous** *adj*

slang (slæŋ) *n* **1a** vocabulary, idiom, etc., that is not appropriate to the standard form of a language or to formal contexts and may be restricted as to social status or distribution. **1b** (as modifier): *a slang word.* ♦ *vb* **2** to abuse (someone) with vituperative language. [C18: from ?]
  ▶ '**slangy** *adj* ▶ '**slanginess** *n*

slant (slɑːnt) *vb* **1** to incline or be inclined at an oblique or sloping angle. **2** (tr) to write or present (news, etc.) with a bias. **3** (intr; foll. by *towards*) (of a person's opinions) to be biased. ♦ *n* **4** an inclined or oblique line or direction. **5** a way of looking at something. **6** a bias or opinion, as in an article. **7 on a** (or **the**) **slant.** sloping. ♦ *adj* **8** oblique; sloping. [C17: short for ASLANT, prob. of Scand. origin]
  ▶ '**slanting** *adj*

slantwise ('slɑːnt,waɪz) or **slantways** *adv, adj* (prenominal) in a slanting or oblique direction.

slap (slæp) *n* **1** a sharp blow or smack, as with the open hand, something flat, etc. **2** the sound made by or as if by such a blow. **3** (a bit of) **slap and tickle.** *Brit. inf.* sexual play. **4 a slap in the face.** an insult or rebuff. **5 a slap on the back.** congratulation. ♦ *vb* **slaps, slapping, slapped. 6** (tr) to strike (a person or thing) sharply, as with the open hand or something flat. **7** (tr) to bring down (the hand, etc.) sharply. **8** (when intr, usually foll. by *against*) to strike (something) with or as if with a slap. **9** (tr) Inf., chiefly Brit. to apply in large quantities, haphazardly, etc.: *she slapped butter on the bread.* **10 slap on the back.** to congratulate. ♦ *adv Inf.* **11** exactly: *slap on time.* **12** forcibly or abruptly: *to fall slap on the floor.* [C17: from Low G *slapp*, G *Schlappe*, imit.]

slapdash ('slæp,dæʃ) *adv* **1** in a careless, hasty, or haphazard manner. ♦ *adj* **2** careless, hasty, or haphazard. ♦ *n* **3** slapdash activity or work.

slaphappy ('slæp,hæpɪ) *adj* **slaphappier, slaphappiest.** *Inf.* **1** cheerfully irresponsible or careless. **2** dazed or giddy from or as if from repeated blows.

slaphead ('slæp,hed) *n Derog. sl.* a bald person. [C20: from ?]

slapstick ('slæp,stɪk) *n* **1a** comedy characterized by horseplay and physical action. **1b** (as modifier): *slapstick humour.* **2** a pair of paddles formerly used in pantomime to strike a blow with a loud sound but without injury.

slap-up *adj* (prenominal) *Brit. inf.* (esp. of meals) lavish; excellent; first-class.

slash (slæʃ) vb (tr) **1** to cut or lay about (a person or thing) with sharp sweeping strokes, as with a sword, etc. **2** to lash with a whip. **3** to make large gashes in: *to slash tyres.* **4** to reduce (prices, etc.) drastically. **5** to criticize harshly. **6** to slit (the outer fabric of a garment) so that the lining material is revealed. **7** to clear (scrub or undergrowth) by cutting. ◆ *n* **8** a sharp sweeping stroke, as with a sword or whip. **9** a cut or rent made by such a stroke. **10** a decorative slit in a garment revealing the lining material. **11** *US & Canad.* littered wood chips that remain after trees have been cut down. **12** another name for **solidus**. **13** *Brit. sl.* the act of urinating. [C14 *slaschen*, ?from OF *esclachier* to break]

slasher ('slæʃə) *n* **1** a person or thing that slashes. **2** *Austral. & NZ.* a tool or machine used for cutting scrub or undergrowth in the bush.

slasher movie *n Sl.* a film in which victims, usually women, are slashed with knives, razors, etc. Also called: **stalk-and-slash movie.**

slashing ('slæʃɪŋ) *adj* aggressively or harshly critical (esp. in **slashing attack**).

Śląsk ★ (ʃlõsk) *n* the Polish name for **Silesia.**

slat (slæt) *n* **1** a narrow thin strip of wood or metal, as used in a Venetian blind, etc. **2** a movable or fixed aerofoil attached to the leading edge of an aircraft wing to increase lift. [C14: from OF *esclat* splinter, from *esclater* to shatter]

slate¹ (sleɪt) *n* **1a** a compact fine-grained metamorphic rock that can be split into thin layers and is used as a roofing and paving material. **1b** (*as modifier*): *a slate tile.* **2** a roofing tile of slate. **3** (formerly) a writing tablet of slate. **4** a dark grey colour. **5** *Chiefly US & Canad.* a list of candidates in an election. **6 clean slate.** a record without dishonour. **7 have a slate loose.** *Brit. & Irish inf.* to be eccentric or crazy. **8 on the slate.** *Brit. inf.* on credit. ◆ *vb* **slates, slating, slated.** (*tr*) **9** to cover (a roof) with slates. **10** *Chiefly US.* to enter (a person's name) on a list, esp. on a political slate. ◆ *adj* **11** of the colour slate. [C14: from OF *esclate*, from *esclat* a fragment]
▶ 'slaty *adj*

slate² (sleɪt) *vb* **slates, slating, slated.** (*tr*) *Inf., chiefly Brit.* to criticize harshly. [C19: prob. from SLATE¹]
▶ 'slating *n*

slater ('sleɪtə) *n* **1** a person trained in laying roof slates. **2** another name for **woodlouse.**

slather ('slaːðə) *n* **1** (*usually pl*) *Inf., chiefly US & Canad.* a large quantity. **2 open slather.** *Austral. & NZ sl.* a free-for-all. [C19: from ?]

slattern ('slætən) *n* a slovenly woman or girl. [C17: prob. from *slattering*, from dialect *slatter* to slop]
▶ 'slatternly *adj* ▶ 'slatternliness *n*

slaughter ('slɔːtə) *n* **1** the killing of animals, esp. for food. **2** the savage killing of a person. **3** the indiscriminate or brutal killing of large numbers of people, as in war. ◆ *vb* (*tr*) **4** to kill (animals), esp. for food. **5** to kill in a brutal manner. **6** to kill indiscriminately or in large numbers. [OE *sleaht*]
▶ 'slaughterer *n* ▶ 'slaughterous *adj*

slaughterhouse ('slɔːtəˌhaus) *n* a place where animals are butchered for food; abattoir.

Slav (slɑːv) *n* a member of any of the peoples of E Europe or NW Asia who speak a Slavonic language. [C14: from Med. L *Sclāvus* a captive Slav; see SLAVE]

slave (sleɪv) *n* **1** a person legally owned by another and having no freedom of action or right to property. **2** a person who is forced to work for another against his will. **3** a person under the domination of another person or some habit or influence. **4** a drudge. **5** a device that is controlled by or that duplicates the action of another similar device. ◆ *vb* **slaves, slaving, slaved. 6** (*intr; often foll. by away*) to work like a slave. [C13: via OF from Med. L *Sclāvus* a Slav, one held in bondage (the Slavonic races were frequently conquered in the Middle Ages), from LGk *Sklabos* a Slav]

Slave Coast ★ *n* the coast of W Africa between the Volta River and Mount Cameroon, chiefly along the Bight of Benin: the main source of African slaves (16th–19th centuries).

slave cylinder *n* a small cylinder containing a piston that operates the brake shoes or pads in hydraulic brakes or the working part in any other hydraulically operated system.

slave-driver *n* **1** (esp. formerly) a person forcing slaves to work. **2** an employer who demands excessively hard work from his employees.

slaveholder ('sleɪvˌhəuldə) *n* a person who owns slaves.
▶ 'slave,holding *n*

slaver¹ ('sleɪvə) *n* **1** an owner of or dealer in slaves. **2** another name for **slave ship.**

slaver² ('slævə) *vb* (*intr*) **1** to dribble saliva. **2** (often foll. by *over*) **2a** to fawn or drool (over someone). **2b** to show great desire (for). ◆ *n* **3** saliva dribbling from the mouth. **4** *Inf.* drivel. [C14: prob. from Low Du.]
▶ 'slaverer *n*

Slave River ★ *n* a river in W Canada, in the Northwest Territories and NE Alberta, flowing from Lake Athabaska northwest to Great Slave Lake. Length: about 420 km (260 miles). Also called: **Great Slave River.**

slavery ('sleɪvərɪ) *n* **1** the state or condition of being a slave. **2** the subjection of a person to another person, esp. in being forced into work. **3** the condition of being subject to some influence or habit. **4** work done in harsh conditions for low pay.

slave ship *n* a ship used to transport slaves, esp. formerly from Africa to the New World.

Slave State *n US history.* any of the 15 Southern states in which slavery was legal until the Civil War.

slave trade *n* the business of trading in slaves, esp. the transportation of Black Africans to America from the 16th to 19th centuries.
▶ 'slave-,trader *n* ▶ 'slave-,trading *n*

slavey ('sleɪvɪ) *n Brit. inf.* a female general servant.

Slavic ('slɑːvɪk) *n, adj* another word (esp. US) another word (esp. US) for **Slavonic.**

slavish ('sleɪvɪʃ) *adj* **1** of or befitting a slave. **2** being or resembling a slave. **3** unoriginal; imitative.
▶ 'slavishly *adv*

Slavkov ★ ('slafkɔf) *n* the Czech name for **Austerlitz.**

Slavonia ★ (slə'vəunɪə) *n* a region of Croatia, mainly between the Drava and Sava Rivers.
▶ Sla'vonian *adj, n*

Slavonic (slə'vɒnɪk) *or esp. US* **Slavic** *n* **1** a branch of the Indo-European family of languages, usually divided into three subbranches: **South Slavonic** (including Bulgarian), **East Slavonic** (including Russian), and **West Slavonic** (including Polish and Czech). ◆ *adj* **2** of or relating to this group of languages. **3** of or relating to the people who speak these languages.

slaw (slɔː) *n Chiefly US & Canad.* short for **coleslaw.** [C19: from Danish *sla*, short for *salade* SALAD]

slay (sleɪ) *vb* **slays, slaying, slew, slain.** (*tr*) **1** *Arch. or literary.* to kill, esp. violently. **2** *Sl.* to impress (someone of the opposite sex). [OE *slēan*]
▶ 'slayer *n*

SLCM *abbrev. for* sea-launched cruise missile: a type of cruise missile that can be launched from either a submarine or a surface ship.

SLD *abbrev. for* Social and Liberal Democrats.

sleaze (sliːz) *n Inf.* **1** sleaziness. **2** dishonest, disreputable, or immoral behaviour, esp. of public officials or employees: *political sleaze.*

sleazy ('sliːzɪ) *adj* **sleazier, sleaziest. 1** disreputable: *a sleazy nightclub.* **2** flimsy, as cloth. [C17: from ?]
▶ 'sleazily *adv* ▶ 'sleaziness *n*

sledge¹ (slɛdʒ) *or esp. US & Canad.* **sled** (slɛd) *n* **1** Also called: **sleigh.** a vehicle mounted on runners, drawn by horses or dogs, for transporting people or goods, esp. over snow. **2** a light wooden frame used, esp. by children, for sliding over snow. ◆ *vb* **sledges, sledging, sledged. 3** to convey, travel, or go by sledge. [C17: from MDu. *sleedse*; C14 *sled*, from MLow G, from ON *slethi*]
▶ 'sledger *n*

sledge² (slɛdʒ) *n* short for **sledgehammer.**

sledge³ (slɛdʒ) *vb* **sledges, sledging, sledged.** (*tr*) *Austral.*

★ people and places

bait (an opponent, esp. a batsman in cricket) in order to upset his concentration. [from ?]

sledgehammer ('slɛdʒ,hæmə) n 1 a large heavy hammer with a long handle used with both hands for heavy work such as breaking rocks, etc. 2 (modifier) resembling the action of a sledgehammer in power, etc.: a sledgehammer blow. [C15: sledge, from OE slecg a large hammer]

sleek (sliːk) adj 1 smooth and shiny. 2 polished in speech or behaviour. 3 (of an animal or bird) having a shiny healthy coat or feathers. 4 (of a person) having a prosperous appearance. ◆ vb (tr) 5 to make smooth and glossy, as by grooming, etc. 6 (usually foll. by over) to gloss (over). [C16: var. of SLICK]
▶ 'sleekly adv ▶ 'sleekness n ▶ 'sleeky adj

sleep (sliːp) n 1 a periodic state of physiological rest during which consciousness is suspended. 2 Bot. the nontechnical name for **nyctitropism**. 3 a period spent sleeping. 4 a state of quiescence or dormancy. 5 a poetic word for **death**. ◆ vb sleeps, sleeping, slept. 6 (intr) to be in or as in the state of sleep. 7 (intr) (of plants) to show nyctitropism. 8 (intr) to be inactive or quiescent. 9 (tr) to have sleeping accommodation for (a certain number): the boat could sleep six. 10 (tr; foll. by away) to pass (time) sleeping. 11 (intr) Poetic. to be dead. 12 **sleep on it.** to give (something) extended consideration, esp. overnight. ◆ See also **sleep around, sleep in,** etc. [OE slǣpan]

sleep around vb (intr, adv) Inf. to be sexually promiscuous.

sleeper ('sliːpə) n 1 a person, animal, or thing that sleeps. 2 a railway sleeping car or compartment. 3 Brit. one of the blocks supporting the rails on a railway track. 4 a heavy timber beam, esp. one that is laid horizontally on the ground. 5 Chiefly Brit. a small plain gold circle worn in a pierced ear lobe to prevent the hole from closing up. 6 Inf. a person or thing that achieves unexpected success after an initial period of obscurity. 7 a spy planted in advance for future use.

sleep in vb (intr, adv) 1 Brit. to sleep longer than usual. 2 to sleep at the place of one's employment.

sleeping bag n a large well-padded bag designed for sleeping in, esp. outdoors.

sleeping car n a railway carriage fitted with compartments containing bunks for people to sleep in.

sleeping partner n a partner in a business who does not play an active role. Also called: **silent partner.**

sleeping pill n a pill or tablet containing a sedative drug, such as a barbiturate, used to induce sleep.

sleeping policeman n a bump built across a road to deter motorists from speeding. Official name: **road hump.**

sleeping sickness n 1 Also called: **African sleeping sickness.** an African disease transmitted by the bite of the tsetse fly, characterized by fever and sluggishness. 2 Also called: **sleepy sickness.** an epidemic viral form of encephalitis characterized by extreme drowsiness. Technical name: **encephalitis lethargica.**

sleepless ('sliːplɪs) adj 1 without sleep or rest: a sleepless journey. 2 unable to sleep. 3 always alert. 4 Chiefly poetic. always active or moving.
▶ 'sleeplessly adv ▶ 'sleeplessness n

sleep off vb (tr, adv) Inf. to lose by sleeping: to sleep off a hangover.

sleep out vb (intr, adv) 1 (esp. of a tramp) to sleep in the open air. 2 to sleep away from the place of one's employment. ◆ n sleep-out. 3 Austral. & NZ. an area of a veranda partitioned off so that it may be used as a bedroom.

sleepwalk ('sliːp,wɔːk) vb (intr) to walk while asleep.
▶ 'sleep,walker n ▶ 'sleep,walking n, adj

sleep with vb (intr, prep) to have sexual intercourse with (usually) spend the night with. Also: **sleep together.**

sleepy ('sliːpɪ) adj sleepier, sleepiest. 1 inclined to or needing sleep. 2 characterized by or exhibiting drowsiness, etc. 3 conducive to sleep. 4 without activity or bustle: a sleepy town.
▶ 'sleepily adv ▶ 'sleepiness n

sleet (sliːt) n 1 partly melted falling snow or hail or (esp. US) partly frozen rain. 2 Chiefly US. the thin coat of ice

that forms when sleet or rain freezes on cold surfaces. ◆ vb 3 (intr) to fall as sleet. [C13: of Gmc origin]
▶ 'sleety adj

sleeve (sliːv) n 1 the part of a garment covering the arm. 2 a tubular piece that is shrunk into a cylindrical bore to reduce its bore or to line it with a different material. 3 a tube fitted externally over two cylindrical parts in order to join them. 4 a flat cardboard container to protect a gramophone record. US name: **jacket.** 5 **(have a few tricks) up one's sleeve.** (to have options, etc.) secretly ready. 6 **roll up one's sleeves.** to prepare oneself for work, a fight, etc. ◆ vb sleeves, sleeving, sleeved. 7 (tr) to provide with a sleeve or sleeves. [OE slīf, slēf]
▶ 'sleeveless adj ▶ 'sleeve,like adj

sleeve board n a small ironing board for pressing sleeves, fitted onto an ironing board or table.

sleeving ('sliːvɪŋ) n Electronics, chiefly Brit. tubular flexible insulation into which bare wire can be inserted.

sleigh (sleɪ) n 1 another name for **sledge**[1] (sense 1). ◆ vb 2 (intr) to travel by sleigh. [C18: from Du. slee, var. of slede SLEDGE[1]]

sleight (slaɪt) n Arch. 1 skill; dexterity. 2 a trick or stratagem. 3 cunning. [C14: from ON slægth, from slægr SLY]

sleight of hand n 1 manual dexterity used in performing conjuring tricks. 2 the performance of such tricks.

slender ('slɛndə) adj 1 of small width relative to length or height. 2 (esp. of a person's figure) slim and wellformed. 3 small or inadequate in amount, size, etc.: slender resources. 4 (of hopes, etc.) feeble. 5 very small: a slender margin. [C14 slendre, from ?]
▶ 'slenderly adv ▶ 'slenderness n

slenderize or **slenderise** ('slɛndə,raɪz) vb slenderizes, slenderizing, slenderized or slenderises, slenderising, slenderised. Chiefly US & Canad. to make or become slender.

slept (slɛpt) vb the past tense and past participle of **sleep.**

Slesvig ★ ('sleːsvi) n the Danish name for **Schleswig.**

sleuth (sluːθ) n 1 an informal word for **detective.** 2 short for **sleuthhound** (sense 1). ◆ vb 3 (tr) to track or follow. [C19: short for sleuthhound, from C12 sleuth trail, from ON sloth]

sleuthhound ('sluːθ,haʊnd) n 1 a dog trained to track people, esp. a bloodhound. 2 an informal word for **detective.**

S level n Brit. the Special level of a subject taken for the General Certificate of Education: usually taken at the same time as A levels as an additional qualification.

slew[1] (sluː) vb the past tense of **slay.**

slew[2] or esp. US **slue** (sluː) vb 1 to twist or be twisted sideways, esp. awkwardly. 2 Naut. to cause (a mast) to rotate in its step or (of a mast) to rotate in its step. ◆ n 3 the act of slewing. [C18: from ?]

slew[3] (sluː) n a variant spelling (esp. US) of **slough**[1] (sense 2).

slew[4] or **slue** (sluː) n Inf., chiefly US & Canad. a great number. [C20: from Irish Gaelic sluagh]

Slezsko ★ ('slɛskɔ) n the Czech name for **Silesia.**

slice (slaɪs) n 1 a thin flat piece cut from something having bulk: a slice of pork. 2 a share or portion: a slice of the company's revenue. 3 any of various utensils having a broad flat blade and resembling a spatula. 4 (in golf, tennis, etc.) 4a the flight of a ball that travels obliquely. 4b the action of hitting such a shot. 4c the shot so hit. ◆ vb slices, slicing, sliced. 5 to divide or cut (something) into parts or slices. 6 (when intr, usually foll. by through) to cut in a clean and effortless manner. 7 (when intr, foll. by into or through) to move or go (through something) like a knife. 8 (usually foll. by off, from, away, etc.) to cut or be cut (from) a larger piece. 9 (tr) to remove by use of a slicing implement. 10 to hit (a ball) with a slice. [C14: from OF esclice a piece split off, from esclicier to splinter]
▶ 'sliceable adj ▶ 'slicer n

slick (slɪk) adj 1 flattering and glib: a slick salesman. 2 adroitly devised or executed: a slick show. 3 Inf., chiefly US & Canad. shrewd; sly. 4 Inf. superficially attractive: a slick publication. 5 Chiefly US & Canad. slippery. ◆ n 6 a slippery area, esp. a patch of oil floating on water. ◆ vb (tr) 7

Chiefly US & Canad. to make smooth or sleek. [C14: prob. from ON]
▷ **'slickly** *adv* ▷ **'slickness** *n*

slicker ('slɪkə) *n* **1** *Inf.* a sly or untrustworthy person (esp. in **city slicker**). **2** *US & Canad.* a shiny raincoat, esp. an oilskin.

slide (slaɪd) *vb* **slides, sliding, slid** (slɪd); **slid** *or* **slidden** ('slɪdᵊn). **1** to move or cause to move smoothly along a surface in continual contact with it: *doors that slide open.* **2** (*intr*) to lose grip or balance: *he slid on his back.* **3** (*intr;* usually foll. by *into, out of, away from,* etc.) to pass or move unobtrusively: *she slid into the room.* **4** (*intr;* usually foll. by *into*) to go (into a specified condition) by degrees, etc.: *he slid into loose living.* **5** (foll. by *in, into,* etc.) to move (an object) unobtrusively or (of an object) to move in this way: *he slid the gun into his pocket.* **6 let slide.** to allow to deteriorate: *to let things slide.* ◆ *n* **7** the act or an instance of sliding. **8** a smooth surface, as of ice or mud, for sliding on. **9** a construction incorporating an inclined smooth slope for sliding down in playgrounds, etc. **10** a small glass plate on which specimens are mounted for microscopical study. **11** Also called: **diapositive, transparency.** a positive photograph on a transparent base, mounted in a frame, that can be viewed by means of a slide projector. **12** Also called: **hair slide.** *Chiefly Brit.* an ornamental clip to hold hair in place. **13** *Machinery.* a sliding part or member. **14** *Music.* a portamento. **15** *Music.* the sliding curved tube of a trombone that is moved in or out. **16** *Music* **16a** a tube placed over a finger held against the frets of a guitar to produce a portamento. **16b** the style of guitar playing using a slide. **17** *Geol.* **17a** the downward movement of a large mass of earth, rocks, etc. **17b** the mass of material involved in this descent. See also **landslide.** [OE *slīdan*]
▷ **'slidable** *adj* ▷ **'slider** *n*

slide over *vb* (*intr, prep*) **1** to cross as if by sliding. **2** to avoid dealing with (a matter) fully.

slide rule *n* a mechanical calculating device consisting of two strips, one sliding along a central groove in the other, each strip graduated in two or more logarithmic scales of numbers, trigonometric functions, etc.

sliding scale *n* a variable scale according to which specified wages, prices, etc., fluctuate in response to changes in some other factor.

slier ('slaɪə) *adj* a comparative of **sly.**

sliest ('slaɪɪst) *adj* a superlative of **sly.**

slight (slaɪt) *adj* **1** small in quantity or extent. **2** of small importance. **3** slim and delicate. **4** lacking in strength or substance. ◆ *vb* (*tr*) **5** to show disregard for (someone); snub. **6** to treat as unimportant or trifling. **7** *US.* to devote inadequate attention to (work, duties, etc.). ◆ *n* **8** an act or omission indicating supercilious neglect. [C13: from ON *slēttr* smooth]
▷ **'slightingly** *adv* ▷ **'slightly** *adv* ▷ **'slightness** *n*

Sligo ★ ('slaɪgəu) *n* **1** a county of NW Republic of Ireland, on the Atlantic: has a deeply indented low-lying coast; livestock and dairy farming. County town: Sligo. Pop.: 54 756 (1991). Area: 1795 sq. km (693 sq. miles). **2** a port in NW Republic of Ireland, county town of Co. Sligo on **Sligo Bay.** Pop.: 17 300 (1991).

slily ('slaɪlɪ) *adv* a variant spelling of **slyly.**

slim (slɪm) *adj* **slimmer, slimmest. 1** small in width relative to height or length. **2** poor; meagre: *slim chances of success.* ◆ *vb* **3** to make or become slim, esp. by diets and exercise. **4** (*tr*) to reduce in size: *the workforce was slimmed.* [C17: from Du.: crafty, from MDu. *slimp* slanting]
▷ **'slimmer** *n* ▷ **'slimming** *n* ▷ **'slimness** *n*

Slim[1] (slɪm) *n* the E African name for **AIDS.** [from its wasting effects]

Slim[2] ★ (slɪm) *n* **William Joseph,** 1st Viscount. 1891–1970, British field marshal, who commanded (1943–45) the 14th Army in recapturing Burma from the Japanese; governor general of Australia (1953–60).

slim down *vb* (*adv*) **1** to make or become slim, esp. intentionally. **2** to make (an organization) more efficient or (of an organization) to become more efficient, esp. by cutting staff. ◆ *n* **slimdown. 3** an instance of an organization slimming down.

slime (slaɪm) *n* **1** soft thin runny mud or filth. **2** any moist viscous fluid, esp. when noxious or unpleasant. **3** a mucous substance produced by various organisms, such as fish, slugs, and fungi. ◆ *vb* **slimes, sliming, slimed.** (*tr*) **4** to cover with slime. [OE *slīm*]

slimline ('slɪm,laɪn) *adj* slim or conducive to slimness.

slimy ('slaɪmɪ) *adj* **slimier, slimiest. 1** characterized by, covered with, secreting, or resembling slime. **2** offensive or repulsive. **3** *Chiefly Brit.* characterized by servility.

sling[1] (slɪŋ) *n* **1** a simple weapon consisting of a loop of leather, etc., in which a stone is whirled and then let fly. **2** a rope or strap by which something may be secured or lifted. **3** *Med.* a wide piece of cloth suspended from the neck for supporting an injured hand or arm. **4** a loop or band attached to an object for carrying. **5** the act of slinging. ◆ *vb* **slings, slinging, slung. 6** (*tr*) to hurl with or as if with a sling. **7** to attach a sling or slings to (a load, etc.). **8** (*tr*) to carry or hang loosely from or as if from a sling: *to sling washing from the line.* **9** (*tr*) *Inf.* to throw. [C13: ?from ON]
▷ **'slinger** *n*

sling[2] (slɪŋ) *n* a mixed drink with a spirit base, usually sweetened. [C19: from ?]

slingback ('slɪŋ,bæk) *n* a shoe with a strap instead of a full covering for the heel.

sling off *vb* (*intr, adv;* often foll. by *at*) *Austral. & NZ inf.* to mock; deride; jeer (at).

slingshot ('slɪŋ,ʃɒt) *n* **1** the US and Canad. name for **catapult** (sense 1). **2** another name for **sling**[1] (sense 1).

slink (slɪŋk) *vb* **slinks, slinking, slunk. 1** (*intr*) to move or act in a furtive manner from or as if from fear, guilt, etc. **2** (*intr*) to move in a sinuous alluring manner. **3** (*tr*) (of animals, esp. cows) to give birth to prematurely. ◆ *n* **4** an animal, esp. a calf, born prematurely. [OE *slincan*]

slinky ('slɪŋkɪ) *adj* **slinkier, slinkiest.** *Inf.* **1** moving in a sinuously graceful or provocative way. **2** (of clothes) figure-hugging.
▷ **'slinkily** *adv* ▷ **'slinkiness** *n*

slip[1] (slɪp) *vb* **slips, slipping, slipped. 1** to move or cause to move smoothly and easily. **2** (*tr*) to place, insert, or convey quickly or stealthily. **3** (*tr*) to put on or take off easily or quickly: *to slip on a sweater.* **4** (*intr*) to lose balance and slide unexpectedly: *he slipped on the ice.* **5** to let loose or be let loose. **6** to be released from (something). **7** (*tr*) to let go (mooring or anchor lines) over the side. **8** (when *intr,* often foll. by *from* or *out of*) to pass out of (the mind or memory). **9** (*intr*) to move or pass swiftly or unperceived: *to slip quietly out of the room.* **10** (*intr;* sometimes foll. by *up*) to make a mistake. **11** Also: **sideslip.** to cause (an aircraft) to slide sideways or (of an aircraft) to slide sideways. **12** (*intr*) to decline in health, mental ability, etc. **13** (*intr*) (of an intervertebral disc) to become displaced from the normal position. **14** (*tr*) to dislocate (a bone). **15** (of animals) to give birth to (offspring) prematurely. **16** (*tr*) to pass (a stitch) from one needle to another without knitting it. **17a** (*tr*) to operate (the clutch of a motor vehicle) so that it partially disengages. **17b** (*intr*) (of the clutch of a motor vehicle) to fail to engage, esp. as a result of wear. **18 let slip. 18a** to allow to escape. **18b** to say unintentionally. ◆ *n* **19** the act or an instance of slipping. **20** a mistake or oversight: *a slip of the pen.* **21** a moral lapse or failing. **22** a woman's sleeveless undergarment, worn as a lining for a dress. **23** a pillowcase. **24** See **slipway. 25** *Cricket.* **25a** the position of the fielder who stands a little way behind and to the offside of the wicketkeeper. **25b** the fielder himself. **26** the relative movement of rocks along a fault plane. **27** *Metallurgy, crystallog.* the deformation of a metallic crystal caused when one part glides over another part along a plane. **28** a landslide. **29** the deviation of a propeller from its helical path through a fluid. **30** another name for **sideslip** (sense 1). **31 give someone the slip.** to elude or escape from someone. ◆ See also **slip up.** [C13: from MLow G or Du. *slippen*]
▷ **'slipless** *adj*

slip[2] (slɪp) *n* **1** a narrow piece; strip. **2** a small piece of paper: *a receipt slip.* **3** a part of a plant that, when detached from the parent, will grow into a new plant; cutting. **4** a young slender person: *a slip of a child.* **5** *Printing.*

★ people and places

5a a long galley. **5b** a galley proof. ◆ *vb* **slips, slipping, slipped. 6** (*tr*) to detach (portions of stem, etc.) from (a plant) for propagation. [C15: prob. from MLow G, MDu. *slippe* to cut, strip]

slip[3] (slɪp) *n* clay mixed with water to a creamy consistency, used for decorating or patching a ceramic piece. [OE *slyppe* slime]

slipcase ('slɪpˌkeɪs) *n* a protective case for a book or set of books that is open at one end so that only the spines of the books are visible.

slipcover ('slɪpˌkʌvə) *n US & Canad.* **1** a loose cover. **2** a book jacket; dust cover.

slipe (slaɪp) *n NZ.* **a** wool removed from the pelt of a slaughtered sheep by immersion in a chemical bath. **b** (*as modifier*): *slipe wool.* [C14 in England: from *slype* to strip, skin]

slipknot ('slɪpˌnɒt) *n* **1** Also called: **running knot.** a nooselike knot tied so that it will slip along the rope round which it is made. **2** a knot that can be easily untied by pulling one free end.

slip-on *adj* **1** (of a garment or shoe) made so as to be easily and quickly put on or taken off. ◆ *n* **2** a slip-on garment or shoe.

slipover ('slɪpˌəʊvə) *adj* **1** of or denoting a garment that can be put on easily over the head. ◆ *n* **2** such a garment, esp. a sleeveless pullover.

slippage ('slɪpɪdʒ) *n* **1** the act or an instance of slipping. **2** the amount of slipping or the extent to which slipping occurs. **3a** an instance of not reaching a target, etc. **3b** the extent of this.

slipped disc *n Pathol.* a herniated intervertebral disc, often resulting in pain because of pressure on the spinal nerves.

slipper ('slɪpə) *n* **1** a light shoe of some soft material, for wearing around the house. **2** a woman's evening shoe. ◆ *vb* **3** (*tr*) *Inf.* to hit or beat with a slipper.
▸ 'slippered *adj*

slipper bath *n* a bath in the shape of a slipper, with a covered end.

slipperwort ('slɪpəˌwɜːt) *n* another name for **calceolaria.**

slippery ('slɪpərɪ, -prɪ) *adj* **1** causing or tending to cause objects to slip: *a slippery road.* **2** liable to slip from the grasp, etc. **3** not to be relied upon: *a slippery character.* **4** (esp. of a situation) unstable. [C16: prob. coined by Coverdale to translate G *schlipfferig* in Luther's Bible (Psalm 35:6)]
▸ 'slipperiness *n*

slippery elm *n* **1** a North American tree, having notched winged fruits and a mucilaginous inner bark. **2** the bark of this tree, used medicinally as a demulcent. ◆ Also called: **red elm.**

slippy ('slɪpɪ) *adj* **slippier, slippiest. 1** *Inf. or dialect.* another word for **slippery** (senses 1, 2). **2** *Brit. inf.* alert; quick.
▸ 'slippiness *n*

slip rail *n Austral. & NZ.* a rail in a fence that can be slipped out of place to make an opening.

slip road *n Brit.* a short road connecting a motorway to another road.

slipshod ('slɪpˌʃɒd) *adj* **1** (of an action) negligent; careless. **2** (of a person's appearance) slovenly; down-at-heel. [C16: from SLIP[1] + SHOD]

slip-slop *n S. African.* the usual name for **flip-flop** (sense 5).

slipstream ('slɪpˌstriːm) *n* Also called: **airstream. a** the stream of air forced backwards by an aircraft propeller. **b** a stream of air behind any moving object.

slip up *Inf.* ◆ *vb* (*intr, adv*) **1** to make a blunder or mistake. ◆ *n* **slip-up. 2** a mistake or mishap.

slipware ('slɪpˌwɛə) *n* pottery that has been decorated with slip and glazed.

slipway ('slɪpˌweɪ) *n* **1** the sloping area in a shipyard, containing the ways. **2** the ways on which a vessel is launched.

slit (slɪt) *vb* **slits, slitting, slit.** (*tr*) **1** to make a straight long incision in. **2** to cut into strips lengthwise. ◆ *n* **3** a long narrow cut. **4** a long narrow opening. [OE *slītan* to slice]
▸ 'slitter *n*

slither ('slɪðə) *vb* **1** to move or slide or cause to move or slide unsteadily, as on a slippery surface. **2** (*intr*) to travel with a sliding motion. ◆ *n* **3** a slithering motion. [OE *slidrian*, from *slīdan* to slide]
▸ 'slithery *adj*

slit trench *n Mil.* a narrow trench dug for the protection of a small number of people.

sliver ('slɪvə) *n* **1** a thin piece that is cut or broken off lengthwise. **2** a loose fibre obtained by carding. ◆ *vb* **3** to divide or be divided into splinters. **4** (*tr*) to form (wool, etc.) into slivers. [C14: from *sliven* to split]

Sloan ★ (sləʊn) *n John.* 1871–1951, US painter, a leading member of the Ash Can School.

Sloane Ranger (sləʊn) *n* (in Britain) *Inf.* a young upper-class person having a home in London and in the country, characterized as wearing expensive informal clothes. Also called: **Sloane.** [C20: pun on *Sloane* Square, London, and *Lone Ranger*, television cowboy character]

slob (slɒb) *n* **1** *Inf.* a slovenly, unattractive, and lazy person. **2** *Irish.* mire. [C19: from Irish Gaelic *slab* mud]
▸ 'slobbish *adj*

slobber ('slɒbə) *or* **slabber** *vb* **1** to dribble (saliva, food, etc.) from the mouth. **2** (*intr*) to speak or write mawkishly. **3** (*tr*) to smear with matter dribbling from the mouth. ◆ *n* **4** liquid or saliva spilt from the mouth. **5** maudlin language or behaviour. [C15: from MLow G, MDu. *slubberen*]
▸ 'slobberer *or* 'slabberer *n* ▸ 'slobbery *or* 'slabbery *adj*

sloe (sləʊ) *n* **1** the small sour blue-black fruit of the blackthorn. **2** another name for **blackthorn.** [OE *slāh*]

sloe-eyed *adj* having dark slanted or almond-shaped eyes.

sloe gin *n* gin flavoured with sloe juice.

slog (slɒg) *vb* **slogs, slogging, slogged. 1** to hit with heavy blows, as in boxing. **2** (*intr*) to work hard; toil. **3** (*intr*; foll. by *down, up,* etc.) to move with difficulty. **4** *Cricket.* to take large swipes at the ball. ◆ *n* **5** a tiring walk. **6** long exhausting work. **7** a heavy blow or swipe. [C19: from ?]
▸ 'slogger *n*

slogan ('sləʊgən) *n* **1** a distinctive or topical phrase used in politics, advertising, etc. **2** *Scot. history.* a Highland battle cry. [C16: from Gaelic *sluagh-ghairm* war cry]

sloop (sluːp) *n* a single-masted sailing vessel, rigged fore-and-aft. [C17: from Du. *sloep*]

sloot (sluːt) *n S. African.* a ditch for irrigation or drainage. [from Afrik., from Du. *sluit, sluis* SLUICE]

slop[1] (slɒp) *vb* **slops, slopping, slopped. 1** (when *intr*, often foll. by *about*) to cause (liquid) to splash or spill or (of liquid) to splash or spill. **2** (*intr;* foll. by *along, through,* etc.) to tramp (through) mud or slush. **3** (*tr*) to feed slop or swill to: *to slop the pigs.* **4** (*tr*) to ladle or serve, esp. clumsily. **5** (*intr;* foll. by *over*) *Inf., chiefly US & Canad.* to be unpleasantly effusive. ◆ *n* **6** a puddle of spilt liquid. **7** (*pl*) wet feed, esp. for pigs, made from kitchen waste, etc. **8** (*pl*) waste food or liquid refuse. **9** (*often pl*) *Inf.* liquid or semiliquid food of low quality. **10** soft mud, snow, etc. [C14: from OE *-sloppe* COWSLIP]

slop[2] (slɒp) *n* **1** (*pl*) sailors' clothing and bedding issued from a ship's stores. **2** any loose article of clothing, esp. a smock. **3** (*pl*) shoddy manufactured clothing. [OE *oferslop* surplice]

slop basin *n* a bowl or basin into which the dregs from teacups are emptied at the table.

slope (sləʊp) *vb* **slopes, sloping, sloped. 1** to lie or cause to lie at a slanting or oblique angle. **2** (*intr*) (esp. of natural features) to follow an inclined course: *many paths sloped down the hillside.* **3** (*intr;* foll. by *off, away,* etc.) to go furtively. **4** (*tr*) *Mil.* to hold (a rifle) in the slope position. ◆ *n* **5** an inclined portion of ground. **6** (*pl*) hills or foothills. **7** any inclined surface or line. **8** the degree or amount of such inclination. **9** *Maths.* (of a line) the tangent of the angle between the line and another line parallel to the x-axis. **10** (formerly) the position adopted for military drill when the rifle is rested on the shoulder. [C15: short for *aslope,* ?from the p.p. of OE *āslūpan* to slip away]
▸ 'sloper *n* ▸ 'sloping *adj*

slop out *vb* (*intr, adv*) (of prisoners) to empty chamber pots and collect water for washing.

sloppy ('slɒpɪ) *adj* **sloppier, sloppiest. 1** (esp. of the ground, etc.) wet; slushy. **2** *Inf.* careless; untidy. **3** *Inf.* mawkishly sentimental. **4** (of food or drink) watery and unappetizing. **5** splashed with slops. **6** (of clothes) loose; baggy.
▶ '**sloppily** *adv* ▶ '**sloppiness** *n*

slosh (slɒʃ) *n* **1** watery mud, snow, etc. **2** *Brit. sl.* a heavy blow. **3** the sound of splashing liquid. ◆ *vb* **4** (*tr;* foll. by *around, on, in,* etc.) *Inf.* to throw or pour (liquid). **5** (when *intr,* often foll. by *about* or *around*) *Inf.* **5a** to shake or stir (something) in a liquid. **5b** (of a person) to splash (around) in water, etc. **6** (*tr*) *Brit. sl.* to deal a heavy blow to. **7** (usually foll. by *about* or *around*) *Inf.* to shake (a container of liquid) or (of liquid within a container) to be shaken. [C19: var. of SLUSH, infl. by SLOP¹]
▶ '**sloshy** *adj*

sloshed (slɒʃt) *adj Chiefly Brit. sl.* drunk.

slot¹ (slɒt) *n* **1** an elongated aperture or groove, such as one in a vending machine for inserting a coin. **2** *Inf.* a place in a series or scheme. ◆ *vb* **slots, slotting, slotted. 3** (*tr*) to furnish with a slot or slots. **4** (usually foll. by *in* or *into*) to fit or adjust in a slot. **5** *Inf.* to situate or be situated in a series. [C13: from OF *esclot* the depression of the breastbone, from ?]
▶ '**slotter** *n*

slot² (slɒt) *n* the trail of an animal, esp. a deer. [C16: from OF *esclot* horse's hoofprint, prob. of Scand. origin]

sloth (sləʊθ) *n* **1** any of a family of shaggy-coated arboreal edentate mammals, such as the three-toed sloth or ai or the two-toed sloth or unau, of Central and South America. They are slow-moving, hanging upside down by their long arms and feeding on vegetation. **2** reluctance to exert oneself. [OE *slǣwth,* from *slǣw,* var. of *slāw* slow]

sloth bear *n* a bear of forests of S India and Sri Lanka, having an elongated snout specialized for feeding on termites.

slothful ('sləʊθfʊl) *adj* lazy; indolent.
▶ '**slothfully** *adv* ▶ '**slothfulness** *n*

slot machine *n* a machine, esp. one for gambling, activated by placing a coin in a slot.

slouch (slaʊtʃ) *vb* **1** (*intr*) to sit or stand with a drooping bearing. **2** (*intr*) to walk or move with an awkward slovenly gait. **3** (*tr*) to cause (the shoulders) to droop. ◆ *n* **4** a drooping carriage. **5** (*usually used in negative constructions*) *Inf.* an incompetent or slovenly person: *he's no slouch at football.* [C16: from ?]
▶ '**slouching** *adj*

slouch hat *n* any soft hat with a brim that can be pulled down over the ears, esp. an Australian army hat with the left side of the brim turned up.

slough¹ (slaʊ) *n* **1** a hollow filled with mud; bog. **2** (sluː) Also: **slew** (esp. US), **slue.** *North American.* a large hole where water collects or a marshy inlet. **3** despair or degradation. [OE *slōh*]
▶ '**sloughy** *adj*

slough² (slʌf) *n* **1** any outer covering that is shed, such as the dead outer layer of the skin of a snake, the cellular debris in a wound, etc. ◆ *vb* **2** (often foll. by *off*) to shed (a skin, etc.) or (of a skin, etc.) to be shed. [C13: of Gmc origin]
▶ '**sloughy** *adj*

Slough ★ (slaʊ) *n* an industrial town and unitary authority in SE central England, in NE Berkshire. Pop.: 110 708 (1991).

slough off (slʌf) *vb* (*tr, adv*) to cast off (cares, etc.).

Slovak ('sləʊvæk) *adj* **1** of or characteristic of Slovakia, its people, or their language. ◆ *n* **2** the official language of Slovakia. Slovak is closely related to Czech; they are mutually intelligible. **3** a native or inhabitant of Slovakia.

Slovakia ★ (sləʊ'vækɪə) *n* a country in central Europe: part of Hungary from the 11th century until 1918, when it united with Bohemia and Moravia to form Czechoslovakia; it became independent in 1993. Official language: Slovak. Religion: Roman Catholic majority. Currency:

koruna. Capital: Bratislava. Pop.: 5 372 000 (1996). Area: 49 036 sq. km (18 940 sq. miles).
▶ Slo'vakian *adj, n*

sloven ('slʌvᵊn) *n* a person who is habitually negligent in appearance, hygiene, or work. [C15: prob. rel. to Flemish *sloef* dirty, Du. *slof* negligent]

Slovene (sləʊ'viːn) *adj* **1** Also **Slovenian.** of or characteristic of Slovenia, its people, or their language. ◆ *n* **2** Also **Slovenian.** the official language of Slovenia. **3** a native or inhabitant of Slovenia.

Slovenia ★ (sləʊ'viːnɪə) *n* a republic in S central Europe: settled by the Slovenes in the 6th century; joined Yugoslavia in 1918 and became an autonomous republic in 1946; declared independence in 1991 (internationally recognized in 1992): rises over 2800 m (9000 ft) in the Julian Alps. Official language: Slovene. Religion: Roman Catholic majority. Currency: tolar. Capital: Ljubljana. Pop.: 1 958 746 (1996). Area: 20 251 sq. km (7819 sq. miles).

slovenly ('slʌvənlɪ) *adj* **1** frequently or habitually unclean or untidy. **2** negligent and careless: *slovenly manners.* ◆ *adv* **3** in a negligent or slovenly manner.
▶ '**slovenliness** *n*

slow (sləʊ) *adj* **1** performed or occurring during a comparatively long interval of time. **2** lasting a comparatively long time: *a slow journey.* **3** characterized by lack of speed: *a slow walker.* **4** (*prenominal*) adapted to or productive of slow movement: *the slow lane of a motorway.* **5** (of a clock, etc.) indicating a time earlier than the correct time. **6** not readily responsive to stimulation: *a slow mind.* **7** dull or uninteresting: *the play was very slow.* **8** not easily aroused: *a slow temperament.* **9** lacking promptness or immediacy: *a slow answer.* **10** unwilling to perform an action or enter into a state: *slow to anger.* **11** behind the times. **12** (of trade, etc.) unproductive; slack. **13** (of a fire) burning weakly. **14** (of an oven) cool. **15** *Photog.* requiring a relatively long time of exposure to produce a given density: *a slow lens.* **16** *Sport.* (of a court, track, etc.) tending to reduce the speed of the ball or the competitors. **17** *Cricket.* (of a bowler, etc.) delivering the ball slowly, usually with spin. ◆ *adv* **18** in a manner characterized by lack of speed; slowly. ◆ *vb* **19** (often foll. by *up, down,* etc.) to decrease or cause to decrease in speed, efficiency, etc. [OE *slāw* sluggish]
▶ '**slowly** *adv* ▶ '**slowness** *n*

slowcoach ('sləʊ,kəʊtʃ) *n Brit. inf.* a person who moves or works slowly. US and Canad. equivalent: **slowpoke.**

slow handclap *n Brit.* slow rhythmic clapping, esp. used by an audience to indicate dissatisfaction or impatience.

slow march *n Mil.* a march in **slow time,** usually 65 or 75 paces to the minute.

slow match *or* **fuse** *n* a match or fuse that burns slowly without flame.

slow-mo *or* **slo-mo** ('sləʊ,məʊ) *n, adj Inf.* short for **slow motion** *or* **slow-motion.**

slow motion *n* **1** *Films, television, etc.* action that is made to appear slower than normal by passing the film through the camera at a faster rate or by replaying a video recording more slowly. ◆ *adj* **slow-motion. 2** of or relating to such action. **3** moving or functioning at considerably less than usual speed.

slow virus *n* a type of virus that is present in the body for a long time before it becomes active or infectious.

slowworm ('sləʊ,wɜːm) *n* a Eurasian legless lizard with a brownish-grey snakelike body. Also called: **blindworm.**

SLR *abbrev. for* single-lens reflex: see **reflex camera.**

SLSC *Austral. abbrev. for* Surf Life Saving Club.

slub (slʌb) *n* **1** a lump in yarn or fabric, often intentionally to give a knobbly effect. **2** a loosely twisted roll of fibre prepared for spinning. ◆ *vb* **slubs, slubbing, slubbed. 3** (*tr*) to draw out and twist (a sliver of fibre). ◆ *adj* **4** (of material) having an irregular appearance. [C18: from ?]

sludge (slʌdʒ) *n* **1** soft mud, snow, etc. **2** any deposit or sediment. **3** a surface layer of ice that is not frozen solid but has a slushy appearance. **4** (in sewage disposal) the

solid constituents of sewage that are removed for purification. [C17: prob. rel. to SLUSH]
▶ 'sludgy *adj*

lue[1] (sluː) *n*, *vb* slues, sluing, slued. a variant spelling (esp. US) of slew[2].

lue[2] (sluː) *n* a variant spelling of slough[1] (sense 2).

slug[1] (slʌg) *n* 1 any of various terrestrial gastropod molluscs in which the body is elongated and the shell is absent or very much reduced. 2 any of various other invertebrates having a soft slimy body, esp. the larvae of certain sawflies. [C15 (in the sense: a slow person or animal): prob. from ON]

slug[2] (slʌg) *n* 1 an fps unit of mass; the mass that will acquire an acceleration of 1 foot per second per second when acted upon by a force of 1 pound. 2 *Metallurgy.* a metal blank from which small forgings are worked. 3 a bullet. 4 *Chiefly US & Canad.* a metal token for use in slot machines, etc. 5 *Printing.* 5a a thick strip of type metal that is used for spacing. 5b a metal strip containing a line of characters as produced by a Linotype machine. 6 a draught of a drink, esp. an alcoholic one. [C17 (bullet), C19 (printing): ?from SLUG[1], with allusion to the shape of the animal]

slug[3] (slʌg) *vb* slugs, slugging, slugged. 1 *Chiefly US & Canad.* to hit very hard and solidly. 2 (*tr*) *Austral. & NZ inf.* to charge (someone) an exorbitant price. ◆ *n* 3 *US & Canad.* a heavy blow. 4 *Austral. & NZ inf.* an exorbitant price. [C19: ?from SLUG[2] (bullet)]

luggard ('slʌgəd) *n* 1 a person who is habitually indolent. ◆ *adj* 2 lazy. [C14 *slogarde*]
▶ 'sluggardly *adj*

luggish ('slʌgɪʃ) *adj* 1 lacking energy; inactive. 2 functioning at below normal rate or level. 3 exhibiting poor response to stimulation.
▶ 'sluggishly *adv* ▶ 'sluggishness *n*

luice (sluːs) *n* 1 Also called: sluiceway. a channel that carries a rapid current of water, esp. one that has a sluicegate to control the flow. 2 the body of water controlled by a sluicegate. 3 See sluicegate. 4 *Mining.* an inclined trough for washing ores. 5 an artificial channel through which logs can be floated. ◆ *vb* sluices, sluicing, sluiced. 6 (*tr*) to draw out or drain (water, etc.) from (a pond, etc.) by means of a sluice. 7 (*tr*) to wash or irrigate with a stream of water. 8 (*tr*) *Mining.* to wash in a sluice. 9 (*tr*) to send (logs, etc.) down a sluice. 10 (*intr*; often foll. by *away* or *out*) (of water, etc.) to run or flow from or as if from a sluice. 11 (*tr*) to provide with a sluice. [C14: from OF *escluse*, from LL *exclūsa aqua* water shut out, from L *exclūdere* to shut out]
▶ 'sluice,like *adj*

luicegate ('sluːs,geɪt) *n* a valve or gate fitted to a sluice to control the rate of flow of water. See also floodgate (sense 1).

lum (slʌm) *n* 1 a squalid overcrowded house, etc. 2 (*often pl*) a squalid section of a city, characterized by inferior living conditions. 3 (*modifier*) of or characteristic of slums: *slum conditions.* ◆ *vb* slums, slumming, slummed. (*intr*) 4 to visit slums, esp. for curiosity. 5 Also: slum it. to suffer conditions below those to which one is accustomed. [C19: orig. sl., from ?]
▶ 'slummy *adj*

lumber ('slʌmbə) *vb* 1 (*intr*) to sleep, esp. peacefully. 2 (*intr*) to be quiescent or dormant. 3 (*tr*; foll. by *away*) to spend (time) sleeping. ◆ *n* 4 (*sometimes pl*) sleep. 5 a dormant or quiescent state. [OE *slūma* sleep (n)]
▶ 'slumberer *n* ▶ 'slumbering *adj*

lumberous ('slʌmbərəs) or **slumbrous** *adj Chiefly poetic.* 1 sleepy; drowsy. 2 inducing sleep.
▶ 'slumberously *adv* ▶ 'slumberousness *n*

lump (slʌmp) *vb* (*intr*) 1 to sink or fall heavily and suddenly. 2 to relax ungracefully. 3 (of business activity, etc.) to decline suddenly. 4 (of health, interest, etc.) to deteriorate or decline suddenly. ◆ *n* 5 a sudden or marked decline or failure, as in progress or achievement. 6 a decline in commercial activity, prices, etc.; depression. 7 the act of slumping. [C17: prob. of Scand. origin]

lung (slʌŋ) *vb* the past tense and past participle of sling[1].

lunk (slʌŋk) *vb* the past tense and past participle of slink.

slur (slɜː) *vb* slurs, slurring, slurred. (*mainly tr*) 1 (often foll. by *over*) to treat superficially, hastily, or without due deliberation. 2 (*also intr*) to pronounce or utter (words, etc.) indistinctly. 3 to speak disparagingly of. 4 *Music.* to execute (a melodic interval of two or more notes) smoothly, as in legato performance. ◆ *n* 5 an indistinct sound or utterance. 6 a slighting remark. 7 a stain or disgrace, as upon one's reputation. 8a *Music.* a performance or execution of a melodic interval of two or more notes in a part. 8b the curved line (⌒ or ⌣) indicating this. [C15: prob. from MLow G]

slurp (slɜːp) *Inf.* ◆ *vb* 1 to eat or drink (something) noisily. ◆ *n* 2 a sound produced in this way. [C17: from MDu. *slorpen* to sip]

slurry ('slʌrɪ) *n*, *pl* slurries. a suspension of solid particles in a liquid, as in a mixture of cement, coal dust, manure, meat, etc. with water. [C15 *slory*]

slush (slʌʃ) *n* 1 any watery muddy substance, esp. melting snow. 2 *Inf.* sloppily sentimental language. ◆ *vb* 3 (*intr*; often foll. by *along*) to make one's way through or as if through slush. [C17: rel. to Danish *slus* sleet, Norwegian *slusk* slops]
▶ 'slushy *adj* ▶ 'slushiness *n*

slush fund *n* a fund for financing political or commercial corruption.

slushy ('slʌʃɪ) *adj* slushier, slushiest. of, resembling, or consisting of slush.
▶ 'slushiness *n*

slut (slʌt) *n* 1 a dirty slatternly woman. 2 an immoral woman. [C14: from ?]
▶ 'sluttish *adj* ▶ 'sluttishness *n*

Sluter ★ (*Dutch* 'slyːtər) *n* Claus (klaus). ?1345–1406, Dutch sculptor, working in Burgundy. He is best known for the portal sculptures and the *Well of Moses* in the Carthusian monastery at Champnol.

sly (slaɪ) *adj* slyer, slyest *or* slier, sliest. 1 crafty; artful: *a sly dodge.* 2 insidious; furtive: *a sly manner.* 3 roguish: *sly humour.* ◆ *n* 4 on the sly. in a secretive manner. [C12: from ON *slægr* clever, lit.: able to strike, from *slā* to slay]
▶ 'slyly *or* 'slily *adv* ▶ 'slyness *n*

slype (slaɪp) *n* a covered passage in a church that connects the transept to the chapterhouse. [C19: prob. from MFlemish *slijpen* to slip]

Sm the chemical symbol for samarium.

SM *abbrev. for* 1 sergeant major. 2 sadomasochism.

smack[1] (smæk) *n* 1 a smell or flavour that is distinctive though faint. 2 a distinctive trace: *the smack of corruption.* 3 a small quantity, esp. a taste. 4 a slang word for heroin. ◆ *vb* (*intr*; foll. by *of*) 5 to have the characteristic smell or flavour (of something): *to smack of the sea.* 6 to have an element suggestive (of something): *his speeches smacked of bigotry.* [OE *smæc*]

smack[2] (smæk) *vb* 1 (*tr*) to strike or slap smartly, with or as if with the open hand. 2 to strike or send forcibly or loudly or to be struck or sent forcibly or loudly. 3 to open and close (the lips) loudly, esp. to show pleasure. ◆ *n* 4 a sharp resounding slap or blow with something flat, or the sound of such a blow. 5 a loud kiss. 6 a sharp sound made by the lips, as in enjoyment. 7 have a smack at. *Inf., chiefly Brit.* to attempt. 8 smack in the eye. *Inf., chiefly Brit.* a snub or setback. ◆ *adv Inf.* 9 directly; squarely. 10 sharply and unexpectedly. [C16: from MLow G or MDu. *smacken*, prob. imit.]

smack[3] (smæk) *n* a sailing vessel, usually sloop-rigged, used in coasting and fishing along the British coast. [C17: from Low G *smack* or Du. *smak*, from ?]

smacker ('smækə) *n Sl.* 1 a loud kiss; smack. 2 a pound note or dollar bill.

small (smɔːl) *adj* 1 limited in size, number, importance, etc. 2 of little importance or on a minor scale: *a small business.* 3 lacking in moral or mental breadth or depth: *a small mind.* 4 modest or humble: *small beginnings.* 5 of low or inferior status, esp. socially. 6 feel small. to be humiliated. 7 (of a child or animal) young; not mature. 8 unimportant; trivial: *a small matter.* 9 of or designating the ordinary modern minuscule letter used in printing and cursive writing. 10 lacking great strength or force: *a small effort.* 11 in fine particles: *small gravel.* ◆ *adv* 12 into

small pieces: *cut it small.* **13** in a small or soft manner. ◆ *n* **14** (often preceded by *the*) an object, person, or group considered to be small: *the small or the large?* **15** a small slender part, esp. of the back. **16** (*pl*) *Inf., chiefly Brit.* items of personal laundry, such as underwear. [OE *smæl*]
▸ 'smallish *adj* ▸ 'smallness *n*

small arms *pl n* portable firearms of relatively small calibre.

small beer *n Inf., chiefly Brit.* people or things of no importance.

small change *n* **1** coins, esp. those of low value. **2** a person or thing that is not outstanding or important.

small circle *n* a circular section of a sphere that does not contain the centre of the sphere.

small claims court *n Brit. & Canad.* a local court with jurisdiction to try civil actions involving small claims.

small fry *pl n* **1** people or things regarded as unimportant. **2** young children. **3** young or small fishes.

small goods *pl n Austral. & NZ.* meats bought from a delicatessen, such as sausages.

smallholding ('smɔːlˌhəʊldɪŋ) *n* a holding of agricultural land smaller than a small farm.
▸ 'smallˌholder *n*

small hours *pl n* **the.** the early hours of the morning, after midnight and before dawn.

small intestine *n* the longest part of the alimentary canal, in which digestion is completed. Cf. **large intestine.**

small-minded *adj* narrow-minded; intolerant.
▸ ˌsmall-'mindedly *adv* ▸ ˌsmall-'mindedness *n*

smallpox ('smɔːlˌpɒks) *n* a highly contagious viral disease characterized by high fever and a rash changing to pustules, which dry up and form scabs that are cast off, leaving pitted depressions. Technical name: **variola.**

small print *n* matter in a contract, etc., printed in small type, esp. when considered to be a trap for the unwary.

small-scale *adj* **1** of limited size or scope. **2** (of a map, model, etc.) giving a relatively small representation of something.

small screen *n* an informal name for **television.**

small slam *n Bridge.* another name for **little slam.**

small talk *n* light conversation for social occasions.

small-time *adj Inf.* insignificant; minor: *a small-time criminal.*
▸ 'small-'timer *n*

smalt (smɔːlt) *n* **1** a type of silica glass coloured deep blue with cobalt oxide. **2** a pigment made by crushing this glass, used in colouring enamels. [C16: via F from It. *smalto* coloured glass, of Gmc origin]

smarm (smɑːm) *vb Brit. inf.* **1** (*tr*; often foll. by *down*) to flatten (the hair, etc.) with grease. **2** (when *intr*, foll. by *up* to) to ingratiate oneself (with). [C19: from ?]

smarmy ('smɑːmɪ) *adj* **smarmier, smarmiest.** *Brit. inf.* obsequiously flattering or unpleasantly suave.
▸ 'smarmily *adv* ▸ 'smarminess *n*

smart (smɑːt) *adj* **1** astute, as in business. **2** quick, witty, and often impertinent in speech: *a smart talker.* **3** fashionable; chic: *a smart hotel.* **4** well-kept; neat. **5** causing a sharp stinging pain. **6** vigorous or brisk. **7** (of systems) operating as if by human intelligence by using automatic computer control. **8** (of a weapon, etc.) containing a device which enables it to be guided to its target: *smart bombs.* ◆ *vb* (*mainly intr*) **9** to feel, cause, or be the source of a sharp stinging physical pain or keen mental distress: *he smarted under their abuse.* **10** (often foll. by *for*) to suffer a harsh penalty. ◆ *n* **11** a stinging pain or feeling. ◆ *adv* **12** in a smart manner. ◆ See also **smarts.** [OE *smeortan*]
▸ 'smartly *adv* ▸ 'smartness *n*

Smart ★ (smɑːt) *n* **Christopher.** 1722–71, British poet, author of *A Song to David* (1763) and *Jubilate Agno* (written 1758–63, published 1939). He was confined (1756–63) for religious mania and died in a debtors' prison.

smart aleck ('ælɪk) *n Inf.* **a** an irritatingly oversmart person. **b** (*as modifier*): *a smart-aleck remark.* [C19: from *Aleck, Alec,* short for *Alexander*]
▸ 'smart-ˌalecky *adj*

smart card *n* a plastic card with integrated circuits used for storing and processing computer data. Also called: **laser card, intelligent card.**

smart drug *n* any of various drugs that are claimed to improve the intelligence or memory of the person taking them.

smarten ('smɑːt⁽ᵊ⁾n) *vb* (usually foll. by *up*) **1** (*intr*) to make oneself neater. **2** (*tr*) to make quicker or livelier.

smart money *n* **1** money bet or invested by experienced gamblers or investors. **2** money paid in order to extricate oneself from an unpleasant situation or agreement, esp. from military service. **3** *Law.* damages awarded to a plaintiff where the wrong was aggravated by fraud, malice, etc.

smarts (smɑːts) *pl n Sl., chiefly US.* know-how, intelligence, or wits: *street smarts.*

smart set *n* (*functioning as sing or pl*) fashionable people considered as a group.

smash (smæʃ) *vb* **1** to break into pieces violently and usually noisily. **2** (when *intr*, foll. by *against, through, into,* etc.) to throw or crash (against) vigorously, causing shattering: *he smashed the equipment.* **3** (*tr*) to hit forcefully and suddenly. **4** (*tr*) *Tennis, etc.* to hit (the ball) fast and powerfully, esp. with an overhead stroke. **5** (*tr*) to defeat (persons, theories, etc.). **6** to make or become bankrupt. **7** (*intr*) to collide violently; crash. ◆ *n* **8** an act, instance, or sound of smashing or the state of being smashed. **9** a violent collision, esp. of vehicles. **10** a total failure or collapse, as of a business. **11** *Tennis, etc.* a fast and powerful overhead stroke. **12** *Inf.* **12a** something having popular success. **12b** (*in combination*): *smash-hit.* ◆ *adv* **13** with a smash. ◆ See also **smash-up.** [C18: prob. from SM(ACK² + M)ASH]
▸ 'smashable *adj*

smash-and-grab *adj Inf.* of or relating to a robbery in which a shop window is broken and the contents removed.

smashed (smæʃt) *adj Sl.* drunk or under the influence of a drug.

smasher ('smæʃə) *n Inf., chiefly Brit.* a person or thing that is very attractive or outstanding.

smashing ('smæʃɪŋ) *adj Inf., chiefly Brit.* excellent or first-rate: *we had a smashing time.*

smash-up *Inf.* ◆ *n* **1** a bad collision, esp of cars. ◆ *vb* **smash up. 2** (*tr, adv*) to damage to the point of complete destruction: *they smashed the place up.*

smatter ('smætə) *n* **1** a smattering. ◆ *vb* **2** (*tr*) *Arch.* to dabble in. [C14 (in the sense: to prattle): from ?]
▸ 'smatterer *n*

smattering ('smætərɪŋ) *n* **1** a slight or superficial knowledge. **2** a small amount.

smear (smɪə) *vb* (*mainly tr*) **1** to bedaub or cover with oil, grease, etc. **2** to rub over or apply thickly. **3** to rub so as to produce a smudge. **4** to slander. **5** (*intr*) to be or become smeared or dirtied. ◆ *n* **6** a dirty mark or smudge. **7a** a slanderous attack. **7b** (*as modifier*): *smear tactics.* **8** a preparation of blood, secretions, etc., smeared onto a glass slide for examination under a microscope. [OE *smeoru(n)*]
▸ 'smeary *adj* ▸ 'smearily *adv* ▸ 'smeariness *n*

smear test *n Med.* another name for **Pap test.**

smectic ('smɛktɪk) *adj Chem.* (of a substance) existing in or having a mesomorphic state in which the molecules are oriented in layers. [C17: via L from Gk *smēktikos,* from *smēkhein* to wash; from the soaplike consistency of a smectic substance]

smegma ('smɛgmə) *n Physiol.* a whitish sebaceous secretion that accumulates beneath the prepuce. [C19: via L from Gk *smēgma* detergent, from *smekhein* to wash]

smell (smɛl) *vb* **smells, smelling, smelt** *or* **smelled. 1** (*tr*) to perceive the scent of (a substance) by means of the olfactory nerves. **2** (*copula*) to have a specified smell: *the curry smells very spicy.* **3** (*intr*; often foll. by *of*) to emit an odour (of): *the park smells of flowers.* **4** (*intr*) to emit an unpleasant odour. **5** (*tr*; often foll. by *out*) to detect through shrewdness or instinct. **6** (*intr*) to have or use the sense of smell; sniff. **7** (*intr*; foll. by *of*) to give indications (of): *he*

★ people and places

smells of money. **8** (*intr; foll.* by *around, about,* etc.) to search, investigate, or pry. **9** (*copula*) to be or seem to be untrustworthy. ◆ *n* **10** that sense (olfaction) by which scents or odours are perceived. Related adj: **olfactory. 11** anything detected by the sense of smell. **12** a trace or indication. **13** the act or an instance of smelling. [C12: from ?]
▶ 'smeller *n*

smelling salts *pl n* a pungent preparation containing crystals of ammonium carbonate that has a stimulant action when sniffed in cases of faintness, headache, etc.

smelly ('smɛlɪ) *adj* **smellier, smelliest.** having a strong or nasty smell.
▶ 'smelliness *n*

smelt[1] (smɛlt) *vb* (*tr*) to extract (a metal) from (an ore) by heating. [C15: from MLow G, MDu. *smelten*]

smelt[2] (smɛlt) *n, pl* **smelt** or **smelts.** a marine or freshwater salmonoid food fish having a long silvery body and occurring in temperate and cold northern waters. [OE *smylt*]

smelt[3] (smɛlt) *vb* a past tense and past participle of **smell.**

smelter ('smɛltə) *n* **1** a person engaged in smelting. **2** Also called: **smeltery.** an industrial plant in which smelting is carried out.

smetana ★ (*Czech* 'smɛtana) *n* **Bedřich** ('bɛdr̝ɪx). 1824–84, Czech composer, founder of his country's national school of music. His works include *My Fatherland* (1874–79), a cycle of six symphonic poems, and the opera *The Bartered Bride* (1866).

smew (smju:) *n* a merganser of N Europe and Asia, having a male plumage of white with black markings. [C17: from ?]

smidgen or **smidgin** ('smɪdʒən) *n Inf., chiefly US.* a very small amount. [C20: from ?]

smilax ('smaɪlæks) *n* **1** any of a genus of climbing shrubs having slightly lobed leaves, small greenish or yellow flowers, and berry-like fruits: includes the sarsaparilla plant and greenbrier. **2** a fragile, much branched vine of southern Africa: cultivated for its glossy green foliage. [C17: via L from Gk: bindweed]

smile (smaɪl) *n* **1** a facial expression characterized by an upturning of the corners of the mouth, usually showing amusement, friendliness, etc. **2** favour or blessing: *the smile of fortune.* ◆ *vb* **smiles, smiling, smiled. 3** (*intr*) to wear or assume a smile. **4** (*intr; foll.* by *at*) **4a** to look (at) with a kindly expression. **4b** to look derisively (at). **4c** to bear (troubles, etc.) patiently. **5** (*intr;* foll. by *on* or *upon*) to show approval. **6** (*tr*) to express by means of a smile: *she smiled a welcome.* **7** (*tr;* often foll. by *away*) to drive away or change by smiling. **8 come up smiling.** to recover cheerfully from misfortune. [C13: prob. from ON]
▶ 'smiler *n* ▶ 'smiling *adj* ▶ 'smilingly *adv*

Smiles ★ (smaɪlz) *n* **Samuel.** 1812–1904, British writer: author of the didactic work *Self-Help* (1859).

smiley ('smaɪlɪ) *adj* **1** given to smiling; cheerful. **2** depicting a smile: *a smiley badge.* ◆ *n* **3** any of a group of symbols depicting a smile, or other facial expression, used in electronic mail.

smirch (smɜːtʃ) *vb* (*tr*) **1** to dirty; soil. ◆ *n* **2** the act of smirching or state of being smirched. **3** a smear or stain. [C15 *smorchen,* from ?]

smirk (smɜːk) *n* **1** a smile expressing scorn, smugness, etc., rather than pleasure. ◆ *vb* **2** (*intr*) to give such a smile. **3** (*tr*) to express with such a smile. [OE *smearcian*]
▶ 'smirker *n* ▶ 'smirking *adj* ▶ 'smirkingly *adv*

smite (smaɪt) *vb* **smites, smiting, smote;** **smitten** or **smit** (smɪt). (*mainly tr*) *Now arch.* in most senses. **1** to strike with a heavy blow. **2** to damage with or as if with blows. **3** to affect severely: *smitten with flu.* **4** to afflict in order to punish. **5** (*intr;* foll. by *on*) to strike forcibly or abruptly: *the sun smote down on him.* [OE *smītan*]
▶ 'smiter *n*

smith (smɪθ) *n* **1a** a person who works in metal. **1b** (*in combination*): *a silversmith.* **2** See **blacksmith.** [OE]

Smith ★ (smɪθ) *n* **1 Adam.** 1723–90, Scottish economist and philosopher, whose *The Wealth of Nations* (1776) advocated free trade. **2 Bessie,** known as *Empress of the Blues.*

1894–1937, US blues singer. **3 F. E.** See (1st Earl of) **Birkenhead. 4 Ian** (**Douglas**). born 1919, Zimbabwean statesman; prime minister of Rhodesia (1964–79). He declared independence from Britain unilaterally (1965). **5 John.** ?1580–1631, English explorer, who helped found the North American colony of Jamestown, Virginia. **6 John.** 1938–94, British Labour politician; leader of the Labour Party (1992–94). **7 Joseph.** 1805–44, US religious leader; founder of the Mormon Church. **8 Dame Maggie.** born 1934, British actress. Her films include *The Prime of Miss Jean Brodie* (1969), *The Lonely Passion of Judith Hearne* (1988), and *The Secret Garden* (1993). **9 Stevie,** real name *Florence Margaret Smith.* 1902–71, British poet. Her poems include 'A Good Time was had by All' (1937) and 'Not Waving but Drowning' (1957). **10 Sydney.** 1771–1845, British clergyman and writer, noted for *The Letters of Peter Plymley* (1807–08), advocating Catholic emancipation. **11 William.** 1769–1839, British geologist, who founded the science of stratigraphy.

smithereens (ˌsmɪðə'riːnz) *pl n* little shattered pieces or fragments. [C19: from Irish Gaelic *smidirín,* from *smiodar*]

smithery ('smɪθərɪ) *n, pl* **smitheries. 1** the trade or craft of a blacksmith. **2** a rare word for **smithy.**

Smithson ★ ('smɪθsən) *n* **James.** original name *James Lewes Macie.* 1765–1829, British chemist, who left a bequest to found the Smithsonian Institution, Washington DC.

smithy ('smɪðɪ) *n, pl* **smithies.** a place in which metal, usually iron or steel, is worked by heating and hammering; forge. [OE *smiththe*]

smitten ('smɪtˀn) *vb* **1** a past participle of **smite.** ◆ *adj* **2** (*postpositive*) affected by love (for).

smock (smɒk) *n* **1** any loose protective garment, worn by artists, laboratory technicians, etc. **2** a woman's loose blouselike garment, reaching to below the waist, worn over slacks, etc. **3** Also called: **smock frock.** a loose protective overgarment decorated with smocking, worn formerly esp. by farm workers. **4** *Arch.* a woman's loose undergarment. ◆ *vb* **5** to ornament (a garment) with smocking. [OE *smocc*]
▶ 'smock,like *adj*

smocking ('smɒkɪŋ) *n* ornamental needlework used to gather and stitch material in a honeycomb pattern so that the part below the gathers hangs in even folds.

smog (smɒg) *n* a mixture of smoke, fog, and chemical fumes. [C20: from SM(OKE + F)OG[1]]
▶ 'smoggy *adj*

smoke (sməʊk) *n* **1** the product of combustion, consisting of fine particles of carbon carried by hot gases and air. **2** any cloud of fine particles suspended in a gas. **3a** the act of smoking tobacco, esp. as a cigarette. **3b** the duration of smoking such substances. **4** *Inf.* a cigarette or cigar. **5** something with no concrete or lasting substance: *everything turned to smoke.* **6** a thing or condition that obscures. **7 go** *or* **end up in smoke.** 7a to come to nothing. **7b** to burn up vigorously. **7c** to flare up in anger. ◆ *vb* **smokes, smoking, smoked. 8** (*intr*) to emit smoke or the like, sometimes excessively or in the wrong place. **9** to draw in on (a burning cigarette, etc.) and exhale the smoke. **10** (*tr*) to bring (oneself) into a specified state by smoking. **11** (*tr*) to subject or expose to smoke. **12** (*tr*) to cure (meat, fish, etc.) by treating with smoke. **13** (*tr*) to fumigate or purify the air of (rooms, etc.). **14** (*tr*) to darken (glass, etc.) by exposure to smoke. ◆ See also **smoke out.** [OE *smoca* (n)]
▶ 'smokable *or* 'smokeable *adj*

Smoke (sməʊk) *n* **the.** short for the **Big Smoke.**

smoke-dried *adj* (of fish, etc.) cured in smoke.

smoked rubber *n* a type of crude natural rubber in the form of brown sheets obtained by coagulating latex with an acid, rolling it into sheets, and drying over open wood fires. It is the main raw material for natural rubber products.

smokeho ('sməʊkəʊ) *n* a variant spelling of **smoko.**

smokehouse ('sməʊk,haʊs) *n* a building or special construction for curing meat, fish, etc., by smoking.

★ people and places

smokeless ('sməʊklɪs) *adj* having or producing little or no smoke: *smokeless fuel.*

smokeless zone *n* an area where only smokeless fuels are permitted to be used.

smoke out *vb* (*tr, adv*) **1** to subject to smoke in order to drive out of hiding. **2** to bring into the open: *they smoked out the plot.*

smoker ('sməʊkə) *n* **1** a person who habitually smokes tobacco. **2** *Also called:* **smoking compartment.** a compartment of a train where smoking is permitted. **3** an informal social gathering, as at a club.

smoke screen *n* **1** *Mil.* a cloud of smoke produced to obscure movements. **2** something said or done in order to hide the truth.

smokestack ('sməʊk,stæk) *n* a tall chimney that conveys smoke into the air.

smokestack industry *n Inf.* any of the traditional British industries, esp. heavy engineering or manufacturing, as opposed to such modern industries as electronics.

smoking jacket *n* (formerly) a man's comfortable jacket of velvet, etc., closed by a tie belt or fastenings, worn at home.

smoko *or* **smokeho** ('sməʊkəʊ) *n, pl* **smokos** *or* **smokehos**. *Austral. & NZ inf.* **1** a short break from work for tea, a cigarette, etc. **2** refreshment taken during this break.

smoky ('sməʊkɪ) *adj* **smokier, smokiest. 1** emitting or resembling smoke. **2** emitting smoke excessively or in the wrong place: *a smoky fireplace.* **3** having the flavour of having been cured by smoking. **4** made dirty or hazy by smoke: *a smoky atmosphere.*
▶ '**smokily** *adv* ▶ '**smokiness** *n*

Smoky Mountains ★ *pl n* See **Great Smoky Mountains.**

smolder ('sməʊldə) *vb, n* the US spelling of **smoulder.**

Smolensk ★ (*Russian* sma'ljɛnsk; *English* 'smɒlɛnsk) *n* a city in W Russia, on the Dnieper River: a major commercial centre in medieval times; scene of severe fighting (1941 and 1943) in World War II. Pop.: 353 000 (1995 est.).

Smollett ★ ('smɒlɪt) *n* **Tobias George.** 1721–71, Scottish novelist, whose satires include *Roderick Random* (1748) and *Humphry Clinker* (1771).

smolt (sməʊlt) *n* a young salmon at the stage when it migrates from fresh water to the sea. [C14: Scot., from ?]

smooch (smuːtʃ) *Sl.* ◆ *vb* (*intr*) **1** *Also* (*Austral. and NZ*): **smoodge, smooge.** (of two people) to kiss and cuddle. **2** *Brit.* to dance very slowly and amorously with one's arms around another person or (of two people) to dance together in such a way. ◆ *n* **3** the act of smooching. [C20: var. of dialect *smouch*, imit.]

smoodge *or* **smooge** (smuːdʒ) *vb* **smoodges, smoodging, smoodged** *or* **smooges, smooging, smooged.** (*intr*) *Austral. & NZ.* **1** another word for **smooch** (sense 1). **2** to seek to ingratiate oneself.

smooth (smuːð) *adj* **1** without bends or irregularities. **2** silky to the touch: *smooth velvet.* **3** lacking roughness of surface; flat. **4** tranquil or unruffled: *smooth temper.* **5** lacking obstructions or difficulties. **6a** suave or persuasive, esp. as suggestive of insincerity. **6b** (*in combination*): *smooth-tongued.* **7** (of the skin) free from hair. **8** of uniform consistency: *smooth batter.* **9** free from jolts: *smooth driving.* **10** not harsh or astringent: *a smooth wine.* **11** having all projections worn away: *smooth tyres.* **12** *Phonetics.* without preliminary aspiration. **13** *Physics.* (of a plane, etc.) regarded as being frictionless. ◆ *adv* **14** in a calm or even manner. ◆ *vb* (*mainly tr*) **15** (*also intr;* often foll. by *down*) to make or become flattened or without roughness. **16** (often foll. by *out* or *away*) to take or rub (away) in order to make smooth: *she smoothed out the creases in her dress.* **17** to make calm; soothe. **18** to make easier: *smooth his path.* ◆ *n* **19** the smooth part of something. **20** the act of smoothing. **21** *Tennis, etc.* the side of a racket on which the binding strings form a continuous line.
◆ See also **smooth over.** [OE *smōth*]
▶ '**smoother** *n* ▶ '**smoothly** *adv* ▶ '**smoothness** *n*

smoothbore ('smuːð,bɔː) *n* (*modifier*) (of a firearm) having an unrifled bore: *a smoothbore shotgun.*
▶ '**smooth,bored** *adj*

smooth breathing *n* (in Greek) the sign (ʼ) placed over an initial vowel, indicating that (in ancient Greek) it was not pronounced with an *h.*

smoothen ('smuːðən) *vb* to make or become smooth.

smooth hound *n* any of several small sharks of North Atlantic coastal regions.

smoothie *or* **smoothy** ('smuːðɪ) *n, pl* **smoothies.** *Sl., usually derog.* a person, esp. a man, who is suave or slick, esp. in speech, dress, or manner.

smoothing iron *n* a former name for **iron** (sense 3).

smooth muscle *n* muscle that is capable of slow rhythmic involuntary contractions: occurs in the walls of the blood vessels, etc.

smooth over *vb* (*tr*) to ease or gloss over: *to smooth over a difficulty.*

smooth snake *n* any of several slender nonvenomous European snakes having very smooth scales and a reddish-brown coloration.

smooth-spoken *adj* speaking or spoken in a gently persuasive or competent manner.

smooth-tongued *adj* suave or persuasive in speech.

smorgasbord ('smɔːgəsˌbɔːd) *n* a variety of cold or hot savoury dishes served in Scandinavia as hors d'oeuvres or as a buffet meal. [Swedish, from *smörgås* sandwich + *bord* table]

smote (sməʊt) *vb* the past tense of **smite.**

smother ('smʌðə) *vb* **1** to suffocate or stifle by cutting off or being cut off from the air. **2** (*tr*) to surround (with) or envelop (in): *he smothered her with love.* **3** (*tr*) to extinguish (a fire) by covering so as to cut it off from the air. **4** to be or cause to be suppressed or stifled: *smother a giggle.* **5** (*tr*) to cook or serve (food) thickly covered with sauce, etc. ◆ *n* **6** anything, such as a cloud of smoke, that stifles. **7** a profusion or turmoil. [OE *smorian* to suffocate]
▶ '**smothery** *adj*

smothered mate *n Chess.* checkmate given by a knight when the king is prevented from moving by surrounding men.

smoulder *or US* **smolder** ('sməʊldə) *vb* (*intr*) **1** to burn slowly without flame, usually emitting smoke. **2** (esp. of anger, etc.) to exist in a suppressed state. **3** to have strong repressed feelings, esp. anger. ◆ *n* **4** a smouldering fire. [C14: from *smolder* (n), from ?]

SMP *abbrev. for* statutory maternity pay.

smudge (smʌdʒ) *vb* **smudges, smudging, smudged. 1** to smear or soil or cause to do so. **2** (*tr*) *Chiefly US & Canad.* to fill (an area) with smoke in order to drive insects away. ◆ *n* **3** a smear or dirty mark. **4** a blurred form or area: *that smudge in the distance is a quarry.* **5** *Chiefly US & Canad.* a smoky fire for driving insects away or protecting plants from frost. [C15: from ?]
▶ '**smudgy** *adj* ▶ '**smudgily** *adv* ▶ '**smudginess** *n*

smug (smʌg) *adj* **smugger, smuggest.** excessively self-satisfied or complacent. [C16: of Gmc origin]
▶ '**smugly** *adv* ▶ '**smugness** *n*

smuggle ('smʌgəl) *vb* **smuggles, smuggling, smuggled. 1** to import or export (prohibited or dutiable goods) secretly. **2** (*tr;* often foll. by *into* or *out of*) to bring or take secretly, as against the law or rules. [C17: from Low G *smukkelen* & Du. *smokkelen,* ?from OE *smūgen* to creep]
▶ '**smuggler** *n* ▶ '**smuggling** *n*

smut (smʌt) *n* **1** a small dark smudge or stain, esp. one caused by soot. **2** a speck of soot or dirt. **3** something obscene or indecent. **4a** any of various fungal diseases of flowering plants, esp. cereals, in which black sooty masses of spores cover the affected parts. **4b** any parasitic fungus that causes such a disease. ◆ *vb* **smuts, smutting, smutted. 5** to mark or become marked or smudged, as with soot. **6** to affect (grain, etc.) or (of grain) to be affected with smut. [OE *smitte;* associated with SMUDGE SMUTCH]
▶ '**smutty** *adj* ▶ '**smuttily** *adv* ▶ '**smuttiness** *n*

smutch (smʌtʃ) *vb* **1** (*tr*) to smudge; mark. ◆ *n* **2** a mark; smudge. **3** soot; dirt. [C16: prob. from MHG *smutzen* to soil]
▶ '**smutchy** *adj*

Smuts ★ (smʌts) *n* **Jan Christiaan** (jan 'kristiˌan). 1870–

1950, South African statesman; prime minister (1919–24; 1939–48). After fighting for the Boers in the Boer War, he advocated Anglo-Boer reconciliation and served the Allies in World Wars I and II.

Smyrna ★ ('smɜːnə) *n* an ancient city on the W coast of Asia Minor: a major trading centre in the ancient world; a centre of early Christianity. Modern name: **Izmir**.

Sn *the chemical symbol for* tin. [from NL *stannum*]

snack (snæk) *n* **1** a light quick meal eaten between or in place of main meals. **2** a sip or bite. ◆ *vb* **3** (*intr*) to eat a snack. [C15: prob. from MDu. *snacken*, var. of *snappen* to snap]

snack bar *n* a place where light meals or snacks can be obtained, often with a self-service system.

snaffle ('snæf'l) *n* **1** Also called: **snaffle bit**. a simple jointed bit for a horse. ◆ *vb* **snaffles, snaffling, snaffled**. (*tr*) **2** *Brit. inf.* to steal or take for oneself. **3** to equip or control with a snaffle. [C16: from ?]

snafu (snæ'fuː) *Sl., chiefly mil.* ◆ *n* **1** confusion or chaos regarded as the normal state. ◆ *adj* **2** (*postpositive*) confused or muddled up, as usual. ◆ *vb* **snafus, snafuing, snafued**. **3** (*tr*) *US & Canad.* to throw into chaos. [C20: from *s(ituation) n(ormal): a(ll) f(ucked) u(p)*]

snag[1] (snæg) *n* **1** a difficulty or disadvantage: *the snag is that I have nothing suitable to wear.* **2** a sharp protuberance, such as a tree stump. **3** a small loop or hole in a fabric caused by a sharp object. **4** *Chiefly US & Canad.* a tree stump in a riverbed that is dangerous to navigation. **5** *US & Canad.* a standing dead tree, esp. one used as a perch by an eagle. ◆ *vb* **snags, snagging, snagged**. **6** (*tr*) to hinder or impede. **7** (*tr*) to tear or catch (fabric). **8** (*intr*) to develop a snag. **9** (*intr*) *Chiefly US & Canad.* (of a boat) to strike a snag. **10** (*tr*) *Chiefly US & Canad.* to clear (a stretch of water) of snags. **11** (*tr*) *US.* to seize (an opportunity, etc.). [C16: of Scand. origin]
▸ **'snaggy** *adj*

snag[2] (snæg) *n* (*usually pl*) *Austral. sl.* a sausage. [from ?]

snaggletooth ('snæg'l,tuːθ) *n, pl* **snaggleteeth**. a tooth that is broken or projecting.

snail (sneɪl) *n* **1** any of numerous terrestrial or freshwater gastropod molluscs with a spirally coiled shell, esp. the **garden snail**. **2** any other gastropod with a spirally coiled shell, such as a whelk. **3** a slow-moving person or animal. [OE *snægl*]
▸ **'snail-,like** *adj*

snail mail *Inf. n* **1** the conventional postal system, as opposed to electronic mail. ◆ *vb* **snail-mail**. **2** (*tr*) to send by the conventional postal system, rather than by electronic mail. [C20: so named because of the relative slowness of the conventional postal system]

snail's pace *n* a very slow speed or rate.

snake (sneɪk) *n* **1** a reptile having a scaly cylindrical limbless body, fused eyelids, and a jaw modified for swallowing large prey: includes venomous forms such as cobras and rattlesnakes, large nonvenomous constrictors (boas and pythons), and small harmless types such as the grass snake. **2** Also: **snake in the grass**. a deceitful or treacherous person. **3** anything resembling a snake in appearance or action. **4** (in the European Union) a group of currencies, any one of which can only fluctuate within narrow limits, but each can fluctuate more against other currencies. **5** a tool in the form of a long flexible wire for unblocking drains. ◆ *vb* **snakes, snaking, snaked**. **6** (*intr*) to glide or move like a snake. **7** (*tr*) to move in or follow (a sinuous course). [OE *snaca*]
▸ **'snake,like** *adj*

snakebird ('sneɪk,bɜːd) *n* another name for **darter** (the bird).

snakebite ('sneɪk,baɪt) *n* **1** a bite inflicted by a snake, esp. a venomous one. **2** a drink of cider and lager.

snake charmer *n* an entertainer, esp. in Asia, who charms or appears to charm snakes by playing music.

Snake River ★ *n* a river in the northwestern US, rising in NW Wyoming and flowing west through Idaho, turning north as part of the border between Idaho and Oregon, and flowing west to the Columbia River near Pasco, Washington. Length: 1670 km (1038 miles).

snakeroot ('sneɪk,ruːt) *n* **1** any of various North American plants the roots or rhizomes of which have been used as a remedy for snakebite. **2** the rhizome or root of any such plant.

snakes and ladders *n* (*functioning as sing*) a board game in which players move counters along a series of squares according to throws of a dice. A ladder provides a short cut to a square nearer the finish and a snake obliges a player to return to a square nearer the start.

snake's head *n* a European fritillary plant of damp meadows, having purple-and-white flowers.

snakeskin ('sneɪk,skɪn) *n* the skin of a snake, esp. when made into a leather valued for handbags, shoes, etc.

snaky ('sneɪkɪ) *adj* **snakier, snakiest. 1** of or like a snake. **2** treacherous or insidious. **3** infested with snakes. **4** *Austral. & NZ sl.* angry or bad-tempered.
▸ **'snakily** *adv* ▸ **'snakiness** *n*

snap (snæp) *vb* **snaps, snapping, snapped. 1** to break or cause to break suddenly, esp. with a sharp sound. **2** to make or cause to make a sudden sharp cracking sound. **3** (*intr*) to give way or collapse suddenly, esp. from strain. **4** to move, close, etc., or cause to move, close, etc., with a sudden sharp sound. **5** to move or cause to move in a sudden or abrupt way. **6** (*intr*; often foll. by *at* or *up*) to seize something suddenly or quickly. **7** (when *intr*, often foll. by *at*) to bite at (something) bringing the jaws rapidly together. **8** to speak (words) sharply or abruptly. **9** to take a snapshot of (something). **10** (*tr*) *American football*. to put (the ball) into play by sending it back from the line of scrimmage. **11** snap one's fingers at. *Inf*. **11a** to dismiss with contempt. **11b** to defy. **12** snap out of it. *Inf*. to recover quickly, esp. from depression or anger. ◆ *n* **13** the act of breaking suddenly or the sound produced by a sudden breakage. **14** a sudden sharp sound, esp. of bursting, popping, or cracking. **15** a catch, clasp, or fastener that operates with a snapping sound. **16** a sudden grab or bite. **17** a thin crisp biscuit: *ginger snaps*. **18** *Inf*. See **snapshot**. **19** *Inf*. vigour, liveliness, or energy. **20** *Inf*. a task or job that is easy or profitable to do. **21** a short spell or period, esp. of cold weather. **22** *Brit*. a card game in which the word *snap* is called when two cards of equal value are turned up on the separate piles dealt by each player. **23** *American football*. the start of each play when the centre passes the ball back from the line of scrimmage to a teammate. **24** (*modifier*) done on the spur of the moment: *a snap decision*. **25** (*modifier*) closed or fastened with a snap. ◆ *adv* **26** with a snap. ◆ *interj* **27a** *Cards*. the word called while playing snap. **27b** an exclamation used to draw attention to the similarity of two things. ◆ See also **snap up**. [C15: from MLow G or MDu. *snappen* to seize]
▸ **'snapless** *adj* ▸ **'snappingly** *adv*

snapdragon ('snæp,drægən) *n* any of several plants of the genus *Antirrhinum* having spikes of showy white, yellow, pink, red, or purplish flowers. Also called: **antirrhinum**.

snap fastener *n* another name for **press stud**.

snapper ('snæpə) *n, pl* **snapper** or **snappers. 1** any large sharp-toothed percoid food fish of warm and tropical coastal regions. See also **red snapper. 2** a food fish of Australia and New Zealand that has a pinkish body covered with blue spots. **3** another name for the **snapping turtle. 4** a person or thing that snaps. ◆ Also (for sense 1, 2): **schnapper**.

snapping turtle *n* any large aggressive North American river turtle having powerful hooked jaws and a rough shell. Also called: **snapper**.

snappy ('snæpɪ) *adj* **snappier, snappiest. 1** Also: **snappish**. apt to speak sharply or irritably. **2** Also: **snappish**. apt to snap or bite. **3** crackling in sound: *a snappy fire*. **4** brisk, sharp, or chilly: *a snappy pace*. **5** smart and fashionable: *a snappy dresser*. **6 make it snappy**. *Sl*. hurry up!
▸ **'snappily** *adv* ▸ **'snappiness** *n*

snap ring *n* *Mountaineering*. another name for **karabiner**.

snapshot ('snæp,ʃɒt) *n* an informal photograph taken with a simple camera. Often shortened to **snap**.

snap shot *n* *Sport*. a sudden, fast shot at goal.

snap up *vb* (*tr, adv*) **1** to avail oneself of eagerly and quickly: *she snapped up the bargains.* **2** to interrupt abruptly.

snare[1] (snɛə) *n* **1** a device for trapping birds or small animals, esp. a flexible loop that is drawn tight around the prey. **2** a surgical instrument for removing certain tumours, consisting of a wire loop that may be drawn tight around their base to sever them. **3** anything that traps or entangles someone or something unawares. ◆ *vb* **snares, snaring, snared.** (*tr*) **4** to catch (birds or small animals) with a snare. **5** to catch or trap in or as if in a snare. [OE *sneare*]
▶ **'snarer** *n*

snare[2] (snɛə) *n Music.* a set of gut strings wound with wire fitted against the lower drumhead of a snare drum. They produce a rattling sound when the drum is beaten. [C17: from MDu. *snaer* or MLow G *snare* string]

snare drum *n Music.* a cylindrical drum with two drumheads, the upper of which is struck and the lower fitted with a snare. See **snare**[2].

snarl[1] (snɑːl) *vb* **1** (*intr*) (of an animal) to growl viciously, baring the teeth. **2** to speak or express (something) viciously. ◆ *n* **3** a vicious growl or facial expression. **4** the act of snarling. [C16: from Gmc origin]
▶ **'snarler** *n* ▶ **'snarling** *adj* ▶ **'snarly** *adj*

snarl[2] (snɑːl) *n* **1** a tangled mass of thread, hair, etc. **2** a complicated or confused state or situation. **3** a knot in wood. ◆ *vb* **4** (often foll. by *up*) to be, become, or make tangled or complicated. **5** (*tr*; often foll. by *up*) to confuse mentally. **6** (*tr*) to emboss (metal) by hammering on a tool held against the under surface. [C14: from ON]
▶ **'snarler** *n* ▶ **'snarly** *adj*

snarl-up *n Inf., chiefly Brit.* a confusion, obstruction, or tangle, esp. a traffic jam.

snatch (snætʃ) *vb* **1** (*tr*) to seize or grasp (something) suddenly or peremptorily: *he snatched the chocolate.* **2** (*intr*; usually foll. by *at*) to seize or attempt to seize suddenly. **3** (*tr*) to take hurriedly: *to snatch some sleep.* **4** (*tr*) to remove suddenly: *she snatched her hand away.* **5** (*tr*) to gain, win, or rescue, esp. narrowly: *they snatched victory in the closing seconds.* ◆ *n* **6** an act of snatching. **7** a fragment or incomplete part: *snatches of conversation.* **8** a brief spell: *snatches of time off.* **9** *Weightlifting.* a lift in which the weight is raised in one quick motion from the floor to an overhead position. **10** *Sl., chiefly US.* an act of kidnapping. **11** *Brit. sl.* a robbery: *a diamond snatch.* [C13 *snacchen*]
▶ **'snatcher** *n*

snatchy ('snætʃɪ) *adj* **snatchier, snatchiest.** disconnected or spasmodic.
▶ **'snatchily** *adv*

snazzy ('snæzɪ) *adj* **snazzier, snazziest.** *Inf.* (esp. of clothes) stylishly and often flashily attractive. [C20: ?from SN(APPY + J)AZZY]
▶ **'snazzily** *adv* ▶ **'snazziness** *n*

sneak (sniːk) *vb* **1** (*intr*; often foll. by *along, off, in,* etc.) to move furtively. **2** (*intr*) to behave in a cowardly or underhand manner. **3** (*tr*) to bring, take, or put stealthily. **4** (*intr*) *Inf., chiefly Brit.* to tell tales (esp. in schools). **5** (*tr*) *Inf.* to steal. **6** (*intr*; foll. by *off, out, away,* etc.) *Inf.* to leave unobtrusively. ◆ *n* **7** a person who acts in an underhand or cowardly manner, esp. an informer. **8a** a stealthy act. **8b** (*as modifier*): *a sneak attack.* [OE *snīcan* to creep]
▶ **'sneaky** *adj* ▶ **'sneakily** *adv* ▶ **'sneakiness** *n*

sneakers ('sniːkəz) *pl n Chiefly US & Canad.* canvas shoes with rubber soles worn informally.

sneaking ('sniːkɪŋ) *adj* **1** acting in a furtive or cowardly way. **2** secret: *a sneaking desire to marry a millionaire.* **3** slight but nagging (esp. in **a sneaking suspicion**).
▶ **'sneakingly** *adv*

sneak thief *n* a person who steals paltry articles from premises, which he enters through open doors, windows, etc.

sneer (snɪə) *n* **1** a facial expression of scorn or contempt, typically with the upper lip curled. **2** a scornful or contemptuous remark or utterance. ◆ *vb* **3** (*intr*) to assume a facial expression of scorn or contempt. **4** to say or utter (something) in a scornful manner. [C16: ?from Low Du.]
▶ **'sneerer** *n* ▶ **'sneering** *adj, n*

sneeze (sniːz) *vb* **sneezes, sneezing, sneezed.** **1** (*intr*) to expel air from the nose involuntarily, esp. as the result of irritation of the nasal mucous membrane. ◆ *n* **2** the act or sound of sneezing. [OE *fnēosan* (unattested)]
▶ **'sneezer** *n* ▶ **'sneezy** *adj*

sneeze at *vb* (*intr, prep*; usually with a negative) *Inf.* to dismiss lightly: *his offer is not to be sneezed at.*

sneezewood ('sniːz,wʊd) *n* **1** a South African tree. **2** its exceptionally hard wood, used for furniture, gateposts and railway sleepers.

sneezewort ('sniːz,wɜːt) *n* a Eurasian plant having daisy-like flowers and long grey-green leaves, which cause sneezing when powdered.

snick (snɪk) *n* **1** a small cut; notch. **2** *Cricket.* **2a** a glancing blow off the edge of the bat. **2b** the ball so hit. ◆ *vb* (*tr*) **3** to cut a small corner or notch in (material, etc.). **4** *Cricket.* to hit (the ball) with a snick. [C18: prob. of Scand. origin]

snicker ('snɪkə) *n, vb* **1** another word (esp. US and Canad.) for **snigger.** ◆ *vb* **2** (*intr*) (of a horse) to whinny. [C17: prob. imit.]

snide (snaɪd) *adj* **1** Also: **snidey** ('snaɪdɪ). (of a remark, etc.) maliciously derogatory. **2** counterfeit. ◆ *n* **3** *Sl.* sham jewellery. [C19: from ?]
▶ **'snidely** *adv* ▶ **'snideness** *n*

sniff (snɪf) *vb* **1** to inhale through the nose, usually in short rapid audible inspirations, as for clearing a congested nasal passage or for taking a drug. **2** (when *intr*, often foll. by *at*) to perceive or attempt to perceive (a smell) by inhaling through the nose. ◆ *n* **3** the act or sound of sniffing. **4** a smell perceived by sniffing, esp. a faint scent. ◆ See also **sniff at, sniff out.** [C14: prob. rel. to *snivelen* to snivel]
▶ **'sniffer** *n* ▶ **'sniffing** *n, adj*

sniff at *vb* (*intr, prep*) to express contempt or dislike for.

sniffer dog *n* a police dog trained to detect drugs or explosives by smell.

sniffle ('snɪf°l) *vb* **sniffles, sniffling, sniffled.** **1** (*intr*) to breathe audibly through the nose, as when the nasal passages are congested. ◆ *n* **2** the act, sound, or an instance of sniffling.
▶ **'sniffler** *n* ▶ **'sniffly** *adj*

sniffles ('snɪf°lz) or **snuffles** *pl n Inf.* **the.** a cold in the head.

sniff out *vb* (*tr, adv*) to detect through shrewdness or instinct.

sniffy ('snɪfɪ) *adj* **sniffier, sniffiest.** *Inf.* contemptuous or disdainful.
▶ **'sniffily** *adv* ▶ **'sniffiness** *n*

snifter ('snɪftə) *n* **1** a pear-shaped glass with a bowl that narrows towards the top so that the aroma of brandy or a liqueur is retained. **2** *Inf.* a small quantity of alcoholic drink. [C19: ?from dialect *snifter* to sniff, ? of Scand. origin]

snig (snɪg) *vb* **snigs, snigging, snigged.** (*tr*) *NZ.* to drag (a felled log) by a chain or cable. [from E dialect]

snigger ('snɪgə) *n* **1** a sly or disrespectful laugh, esp. one partly stifled. ◆ *vb* (*intr*) **2** to utter such a laugh. [C18: var. of SNICKER]
▶ **'sniggering** *n, adj*

snigging chain *n Austral. & NZ.* a chain attached to a log when being hauled out of the bush.

snip (snɪp) *vb* **snips, snipping, snipped.** **1** to cut or clip with a small quick stroke or a succession of small quick strokes, esp. with scissors or shears. ◆ *n* **2** the act of snipping. **3** the sound of scissors or shears closing. **4** Also called: **snipping.** a small piece of anything. **5** a small cut made by snipping. **6** *Chiefly Brit.* an informal word for **bargain.** **7** *Inf.* something easily done; cinch. ◆ See also **snips.** [C16: from Low G, Du. *snippen*]

snipe (snaɪp) *n, pl* **snipe** or **snipes.** **1** any of a genus of birds, such as the common snipe, of marshes and river banks, having a long straight bill. **2** a shot, esp. a gunshot, fired from a place of concealment. ◆ *vb* **snipes, sniping, sniped.** **3** (when *intr*, often foll. by *at*) to attack (a person or persons) with a rifle from a place of concealment. **4** (*intr*; often foll. by *at*) to criticize a person or persons from a

position of security. **5** (*intr*) to hunt or shoot snipe. [C14: from ON *snīpa*]
▶ **'sniper** *n*

snipefish ('snaɪp,fɪʃ) *n, pl* **snipefish** *or* **snipefishes**. a teleost fish of tropical and temperate seas, having a deep body, long snout, and a single long dorsal fin. Also called: **bellows fish**.

snippet ('snɪpɪt) *n* a small scrap or fragment of fabric, news, etc.
▶ **'snippetiness** *n* ▶ **'snippety** *adj*

snips (snɪps) *pl n* a small pair of shears used for cutting sheet metal.

snitch (snɪtʃ) *Sl.* ◆ *vb* **1** (*tr*) to steal; take, esp. in an underhand way. **2** (*intr*) to act as an informer. ◆ *n* **3** an informer. **4** the nose. [C17: from ?]

snitchy ('snɪtʃɪ) *adj* **snitchier, snitchiest.** *NZ inf.* bad-tempered or irritable.

snivel ('snɪvˀl) *vb* **snivels, snivelling, snivelled** *or US* **snivels, sniveling, sniveled. 1** (*intr*) to sniffle as a sign of distress. **2** to utter (something) tearfully; whine. **3** (*intr*) to have a runny nose. ◆ *n* **4** an instance of snivelling. [C14 *snivelen*]
▶ **'sniveller** *n* ▶ **'snivelling** *adj, n*

snob (snɒb) *n* **1a** a person who strives to associate with those of higher social status and who behaves condescendingly to others. **1b** (*as modifier*): *snob appeal.* **2** a person having similar pretensions with regard to his tastes, etc.: *an intellectual snob.* [C18 (in the sense: shoemaker; hence, C19: a person who flatters those of higher station, etc.): from ?]
▶ **'snobbery** *n* ▶ **'snobbish** *adj* ▶ **'snobbishly** *adv*

SNOBOL ('snəʊbɒl) *n* String Oriented Symbolic Language: a computer-programming language for handling strings of symbols.

Sno-Cat ('snəʊ,kæt) *n Trademark.* a type of snowmobile.

snoek (snʊk) *n* a South African edible marine fish. [Afrik., from Du. *snoek* pike]

snog (snɒg) *Brit. sl.* ◆ *vb* **snogs, snogging, snogged. 1** to kiss and cuddle (someone). ◆ *n* **2** the act of kissing and cuddling. [from ?]

snood (snuːd) *n* **1** a pouchlike hat, often of net, loosely holding a woman's hair at the back. **2** a headband, esp. one formerly worn by young unmarried women in Scotland. [OE *snōd*; from ?]

snook¹ (snuːk) *n, pl* **snook** *or* **snooks. 1** any of a genus of large game fishes of tropical American marine and fresh waters. **2** *Austral.* the sea pike. [C17: from Du. *snoek* pike]

snook² (snuːk) *n Brit.* a rude gesture, made by putting one thumb to the nose with the fingers of the hand outstretched (esp. in **cock a snook**). [C19: from ?]

snooker ('snuːkə) *n* **1** a game played on a billiard table with 15 red balls, six balls of other colours, and a white cue ball. The object is to pot the balls in a certain order. **2** a shot in which the cue ball is left in a position such that another ball blocks the target ball. ◆ *vb* (*tr*) **3** to leave (an opponent) in an unfavourable position by playing a snooker. **4** to place (someone) in a difficult situation. **5** (*often passive*) to thwart; defeat. [C19: from ?]

snoop (snuːp) *Inf.* ◆ *vb* **1** (*intr*; often foll. by *about* or *around*) to pry into the private business of others. ◆ *n* **2** a person who pries into the business of others. **3** an act or instance of snooping. [C19: from Du. *snoepen* to eat furtively]
▶ **'snooper** *n* ▶ **'snoopy** *adj*

snooperscope ('snuːpə,skəʊp) *n Mil., US.* an instrument that enables the user to see objects in the dark by illuminating the object with infrared radiation.

snoot (snuːt) *n Sl.* the nose. [C20: var. of SNOUT]

snooty ('snuːtɪ) *adj* **snootier, snootiest.** *Inf.* **1** aloof or supercilious. **2** snobbish: *a snooty restaurant.*
▶ **'snootily** *adv* ▶ **'snootiness** *n*

snooze (snuːz) *Inf.* ◆ *vb* **snoozes, snoozing, snoozed. 1** (*intr*) to take a brief light sleep. ◆ *n* **2** a nap. [C18: from ?]
▶ **'snoozer** *n* ▶ **'snoozy** *adj*

snore (snɔː) *vb* **snores, snoring, snored. 1** (*intr*) to breathe through the mouth and nose while asleep with snorting

sounds caused by the soft palate vibrating. ◆ *n* **2** the act or sound of snoring. [C14: imit.]
▶ **'snorer** *n*

snorkel ('snɔːkˀl) *n* **1** a device allowing a swimmer to breathe while face down on the surface of the water, consisting of a bent tube fitting into the mouth and projecting above the surface. **2** (on a submarine) a retractable vertical device containing air-intake and exhaust pipes for the engines and general ventilation. ◆ *vb* **snorkels, snorkelling, snorkelled** *or US* **snorkels, snorkeling, snorkeled. 3** (*intr*) to swim with a snorkel. [C20: from G *Schnorchel*]

Snorri Sturluson ★ ('snɔːrɪ 'stɜːləsˀn) *n* 1179–1241, Icelandic historian and poet; author of *Younger* or *Prose Edda* (?1222) and the *Heimskringla* sagas of the Norwegian kings.

snort (snɔːt) *vb* **1** (*intr*) to exhale forcibly through the nostrils, making a characteristic noise. **2** (*intr*) (of a person) to express contempt or annoyance by such an exhalation. **3** (*tr*) to utter in a contemptuous or annoyed manner. **4** *Sl.* to inhale (a powdered drug) through the nostrils. ◆ *n* **5** a forcible exhalation of air through the nostrils, esp. (of persons) as a noise of contempt. **6** *Sl.* an instance of snorting a drug. [C14 *snorten*]
▶ **'snorting** *n, adj* ▶ **'snortingly** *adv*

snorter ('snɔːtə) *n* **1** a person or animal that snorts. **2** *Brit. sl.* something outstandingly impressive or difficult.

snot (snɒt) *n* (*usually considered vulgar*) **1** nasal mucus or discharge. **2** *Sl.* a contemptible person. [OE *gesnot*]

snotty ('snɒtɪ) *adj* **snottier, snottiest.** (*considered vulgar*) **1** dirty with nasal discharge. **2** *Sl.* contemptible; nasty. **3** snobbish; conceited.
▶ **'snottily** *adv* ▶ **'snottiness** *n*

snout (snaʊt) *n* **1** the part of the head of a vertebrate, esp. a mammal, consisting of the nose, jaws, and surrounding region. **2** the corresponding part of the head of such insects as weevils. **3** anything projecting like a snout, such as a nozzle. **4** *Sl.* a person's nose. **5** *Brit. sl.* a cigarette or tobacco. **6** *Sl.* an informer. [C13: of Gmc origin]
▶ **'snouted** *adj* ▶ **'snoutless** *adj* ▶ **'snout,like** *adj*

snout beetle *n* another name for **weevil**.

snow (snəʊ) *n* **1** precipitation from clouds in the form of flakes of ice crystals formed in the upper atmosphere. **2** a layer of snowflakes on the ground. **3** a fall of such precipitation. **4** anything resembling snow in whiteness, softness, etc. **5** the random pattern of white spots on a television or radar screen, occurring when the signal is weak. **6** *Sl.* cocaine. ◆ *vb* **7** (*intr*, with *it* as subject) to be the case that snow is falling. **8** (*tr*; usually passive, foll. by *over, under, in,* or *up*) to cover or confine with a heavy fall of snow. **9** (*often with it* as subject) to fall or cause to fall as or like snow. **10** (*tr*) *US & Canad. sl.* to overwhelm with elaborate often insincere talk. **11 be snowed under.** to be overwhelmed, esp. with paperwork. [OE *snāw*]
▶ **'snowless** *adj* ▶ **'snow,like** *adj*

Snow ★ (snəʊ) *n* C(harles) P(ercy), Baron. 1905–80, British novelist and physicist. His novels include the series *Strangers and Brothers* (1949–70).

snowball ('snəʊ,bɔːl) *n* **1** snow pressed into a ball for throwing, as in play. **2** a drink made of advocaat and lemonade. ◆ *vb* **3** to increase rapidly in size, importance, etc. **4** (*tr*) to throw snowballs at.

snowball tree *n* any of several shrubs of the genus *Viburnum*, with spherical clusters of white or pinkish flowers.

snowberry ('snəʊbərɪ) *n, pl* **snowberries. 1** a shrub cultivated for its small pink flowers and white berries. **2** Also called: **waxberry**. any of the berries of such a plant.

snow-blind *adj* having temporarily impaired vision because of the intense reflection of sunlight from snow.
▶ **snow blindness** *n*

snowblower ('snəʊ,bləʊə) *n* a snow-clearing machine that draws the snow in and blows it away.

snowboard ('snəʊ,bɔːd) *n* a shaped board, resembling a skateboard without wheels, on which a person can stand to slide across snow. [C20: on the model of SURFBOARD]
▶ **'snow,boarding** *n*

snowbound ('snəʊ,baʊnd) *adj* confined to one place by heavy falls or drifts of snow; snowed in.

snow bunting *n* a bunting of northern and arctic regions, having a white plumage with dark markings on the wings, back, and tail.

snowcap ('snəʊ,kæp) *n* a cap of snow, as on top of a mountain.
▸ 'snow,capped *adj*

Snowdon ★ ('snəʊdˀn) *n* a mountain in NW Wales, in Gwynedd: the highest peak in Wales. Height: 1085 m (3560 ft).

Snowdonia ★ (snəʊ'dəʊnɪə) *n* 1 a massif in NW Wales, in Gwynedd, the highest peak being Snowdon. 2 a national park in NW Wales, in Gwynedd and Conwy: includes the Snowdonia massif in the north. Area: 2189 sq. km (845 sq. miles).

snowdrift ('snəʊ,drɪft) *n* a bank of deep snow driven together by the wind.

snowdrop ('snəʊ,drɒp) *n* a Eurasian plant having drooping white bell-shaped flowers that bloom in early spring.

snowfall ('snəʊ,fɔːl) *n* 1 a fall of snow. 2 *Meteorol.* the amount of snow received in a specified place and time.

snow fence *n* a lath-and-wire fence put up in winter beside windy roads to prevent snowdrifts.

snowfield ('snəʊ,fiːld) *n* a large area of permanent snow.

snowflake ('snəʊ,fleɪk) *n* 1 one of the mass of small thin delicate arrangements of ice crystals that fall as snow. 2 any of various European plants that have white nodding bell-shaped flowers.

snow goose *n* a North American goose having a white plumage with black wing tips.

snow gum *n* any of several eucalypts of mountainous regions of SE Australia.

snow-in-summer *n* a plant of SE Europe and Asia having white flowers and downy stems and leaves: cultivated as a rock plant.

snow leopard *n* a large feline mammal of mountainous regions of central Asia, closely related to the leopard but having a long pale brown coat marked with black rosettes.

snow lily *n Canad.* another name for **dogtooth violet**.

snow line *n* the altitudinal or latitudinal limit of permanent snow.

snowman ('snəʊ,mæn) *n, pl* **snowmen**. a figure resembling a man, made of packed snow.

snowmobile ('snəʊmə,biːl) *n* a motor vehicle for travelling on snow, esp. one with caterpillar tracks and front skis.

snowplough *or esp. US* **snowplow** ('snəʊ,plaʊ) *n* an implement or vehicle for clearing away snow.

snowshoe ('snəʊ,ʃuː) *n* 1 a device to facilitate walking on snow, esp. a racket-shaped frame with a network of thongs stretched across it. ◆ *vb* **snowshoes, snowshoeing, snowshoed**. 2 (*intr*) to walk or go using snowshoes.
▸ 'snow,shoer *n*

snowstorm ('snəʊ,stɔːm) *n* a storm with heavy snow.

snow tyre *n* a motor-vehicle tyre with deep treads to give improved grip on snow and ice.

snow-white *adj* 1 white as snow. 2 pure as white snow.

snowy ('snəʊɪ) *adj* **snowier, snowiest**. 1 covered with or abounding in snow: *snowy hills*. 2 characterized by snow: *snowy weather*. 3 resembling snow in whiteness, purity, etc.
▸ 'snowily *adv* ▸ 'snowiness *n*

Snowy Mountains ★ *pl n* a mountain range in SE Australia, part of the Australian Alps: famous hydroelectric scheme. Also called (Austral. informal): **the Snowy, the Snowies**.
▸ **Snowy Mountain** *adj*

snowy owl *n* a large owl of tundra regions, having a white plumage flecked with brown.

Snowy River ★ *n* a river in SE Australia, rising in SE New South Wales: waters diverted through a system of dams and tunnels across the watershed into the Murray and Murrumbidgee Rivers for hydroelectric power and to provide water for irrigation. Length: 426 km (265 miles).

SNP *abbrev. for* Scottish National Party.

Snr *or* **snr** *abbrev. for* senior.

snub (snʌb) *vb* **snubs, snubbing, snubbed.** (*tr*) 1 to insult (someone) deliberately. 2 to stop or check the motion of (a boat, horse, etc.) by taking turns of a rope around a post. ◆ *n* 3 a deliberately insulting act or remark. 4 *Naut.* an elastic shock absorber attached to a mooring line. ◆ *adj* 5 short and blunt. See also **snub-nosed**. [C14: from ON *snubba* to scold]
▸ 'snubber *n* ▸ 'snubby *adj*

snub-nosed *adj* 1 having a short turned-up nose. 2 (of a pistol) having an extremely short barrel.

snuff[1] (snʌf) *vb* 1 (*tr*) to inhale through the nose. 2 (when *intr*, often foll. by *at*) (esp. of an animal) to examine by sniffing. ◆ *n* 3 an act or the sound of snuffing. [C16: prob. from MDu. *snuffen* to snuffle, ult. imit.]
▸ 'snuffer *n*

snuff[2] (snʌf) *n* 1 finely powdered tobacco, esp. for sniffing up the nostrils. 2 a small amount of this. 3 **up to snuff.** *Inf.* 3a in good health or in good condition. 3b *Chiefly Brit.* not easily deceived. ◆ *vb* 4 (*intr*) to use or inhale snuff. [C17: from Du. *snuf*, shortened from *snuftabale*, lit.: tobacco for snuffing]

snuff[3] (snʌf) *vb* (*tr*) 1 (often foll. by *out*) to extinguish (a light from a candle). 2 to cut off the charred part of (the wick of a candle, etc.). 3 (usually foll. by *out*) *Inf.* to put an end to. 4 **snuff it.** *Brit. inf.* to die. ◆ *n* 5 the burned portion of the wick of a candle. [C14 *snoffe*, from ?]

snuffbox ('snʌf,bɒks) *n* a container, often of elaborate ornamental design, for holding small quantities of snuff.

snuff-dipping *n* the practice of absorbing nicotine by holding in one's mouth, between the cheek and the gum, a small amount of tobacco.

snuffer ('snʌfə) *n* 1 a cone-shaped implement for extinguishing candles. 2 (*pl*) an instrument resembling a pair of scissors for trimming the wick or extinguishing the flame of a candle.

snuffle ('snʌfˀl) *vb* **snuffles, snuffling, snuffled.** 1 (*intr*) to breathe noisily or with difficulty. 2 to say or speak in a nasal tone. 3 (*intr*) to snivel. ◆ *n* 4 an act or the sound of snuffling. 5 a nasal voice. 6 **the snuffles.** a condition characterized by snuffling. [C16: from Low G or Du. *snuffelen*]
▸ 'snuffly *adj*

snuff movie *or* **film** *n Sl.* a pornographic film in which an unsuspecting actress or actor is murdered as the climax of the film.

snuffy ('snʌfɪ) *adj* **snuffier, snuffiest**. 1 of or resembling snuff. 2 covered with or smelling of snuff. 3 disagreeable.
▸ 'snuffiness *n*

snug (snʌg) *adj* **snugger, snuggest**. 1 comfortably warm and well protected; cosy: *the children were snug in bed*. 2 small but comfortable: *a snug cottage*. 3 well ordered; compact: *a snug boat*. 4 sheltered and secure: *a snug anchorage*. 5 fitting closely and comfortably. 6 offering safe concealment. ◆ *n* 7 (in Britain and Ireland) one of the bars in certain pubs, offering intimate seating for only a few persons. ◆ *vb* **snugs, snugging, snugged**. 8 to make or become comfortable and warm. [C16 (in the sense: prepared for storms (used of a ship)) from O Icelandic *snöggr* short-haired, from Swedish *snygg* tidy]
▸ 'snugly *adv* ▸ 'snugness *n*

snuggery ('snʌgərɪ) *n, pl* **snuggeries**. 1 a cosy and comfortable place or room. 2 another name for **snug** (sense 7).

snuggle ('snʌgˀl) *vb* **snuggles, snuggling, snuggled**. 1 (usually *intr*; usually foll. by *down, up,* or *together*) to nestle into or draw close to (somebody or something) for warmth or from affection. ◆ *n* 2 the act of snuggling. [C17: frequentative of SNUG (vb)]

so[1] (səʊ) *adv* 1 (foll. by an adjective or adverb and a correlative clause often introduced by *that*) to such an extent: *the river is so dirty that it smells*. 2 (*used with a negative; it replaces the first as in an equative comparison*) to the

★ people and places

same extent as: *she is not so old as you.* **3** (intensifier): *it's so lovely.* **4** in the state or manner expressed or implied: *they're happy and will remain so.* **5** (*not used with a negative;* foll. by an auxiliary verb or *do, have,* or *be* used as main verbs) also: *I can speak Spanish and so can you.* **6** *Dialect.* indeed: used to contradict a negative statement: *"you didn't phone her." "I did so!"* **7** *Arch.* provided that. **8 and so on** or **forth.** and continuing similarly. **9 or so.** approximately: *fifty or so people came to see me.* **10 so be it.** used to express agreement or resignation. **11 so much. 11a** a certain degree or amount (of). **11b** a lot (of): *it's just so much non- sense.* **12 so much for. 12a** no more can or need be said about. **12b** used to express contempt for something that has failed. ◆ *conj* (*subordinating; often foll. by that*) **13** in order (that): *to die so that you might live.* **14** with the conse- quence (that): *he was late home, so there was trouble.* **15 so as.** (*takes an infinitive*) in order (to): *to diet so as to lose weight.* ◆ *sentence connector.* **16** in consequence: *she wasn't needed, so she left.* **17** thereupon: *and so we ended up in France.* **18 so what!** *Inf.* what importance does that have? ◆ *pron* **19** used to substitute for a clause or sen- tence, which may be understood: *you'll stop because I said so.* ◆ *adj* **20** (used with *is, was,* etc.) factual: *it can't be so.* ◆ *interj* **21** an exclamation of surprise, etc. [OE *swā*]

> **USAGE NOTE** In formal English, *so* is not used as a conjunction, to indicate either purpose (*he left by a back door so he could avoid photographers*) or re- sult (*the project was abandoned so his services were no longer needed*). In the former case *to* or *in order to* should be used instead, and in the latter case *and so* or *and therefore.*

so[2] (səʊ) *n Music.* a variant spelling of **soh**.

So. *abbrev. for* south(ern).

soak (səʊk) *vb* **1** to make, become, or be thoroughly wet or saturated, esp. by immersion in a liquid. **2** (when *intr,* usually foll. by *in* or *into*) (of a liquid) to penetrate or per- meate. **3** (*tr;* usually foll. by *in* or *up*) (of a permeable solid) to take in (a liquid) by absorption: *the earth soaks up rainwater.* **4** (*tr;* foll. by *out* or *out of*) to remove by immer- sion in a liquid: *she soaked the stains out of the dress.* **5** *Inf.* to drink excessively or make or become drunk. **6** (*tr*) *Sl.* to overcharge. ◆ *n* **7** the act of immersing in a liquid or the period of immersion. **8** the liquid in which some- thing may be soaked. **9** *Austral.* a natural depression holding rainwater, esp. just beneath the surface of the ground. **10** *Sl.* a person who drinks to excess. [OE *sōcian* to cook]
> ▸ '**soaker** *n* ▸ '**soaking** *n, adj* ▸ '**soakingly** *adv*

soakaway ('səʊkə,weɪ) *n* a pit filled with rubble, etc., into which waste water drains.

so-and-so *n, pl* **so-and-sos.** *Inf.* **1** a person whose name is forgotten or ignored. **2** *Euphemistic.* a person or thing re- garded as unpleasant: *which so-and-so broke my razor?*

Soane ★ (səʊn) *n* Sir **John.** 1753–1837, British architect. His work includes Dulwich College Art Gallery (1811– 14) and his own house in Lincoln's Inn Fields, London (1812–13), which is now the Sir John Soane Museum.

soap (səʊp) *n* **1** a cleaning agent made by reacting animal or vegetable fats or oils with potassium or sodium hy- droxide. Soaps act by emulsifying grease and lowering the surface tension of water, so that it more readily pene- trates open materials such as textiles. **2** any metallic salt of a fatty acid, such as palmitic or stearic acid. **3** *Sl.* flat- tery or persuasive talk (esp. in **soft soap**). **4** *Inf.* short for **soap opera. 5 no soap.** *Sl.* not possible. ◆ *vb* (*tr*) **6** to apply soap to. **7** (often foll. by *up*) *Sl.* to flatter. [OE *sāpe*]
> ▸ '**soapless** *adj* ▸ '**soap,like** *adj*

soapberry ('səʊp,berɪ) *n, pl* **soapberries. 1** any of various chiefly tropical American trees having pulpy fruit con- taining saponin. **2** the fruit of any of these trees.

soapbox ('səʊp,bɒks) *n* **1** a box or crate for packing soap. **2** a crate used as a platform for speech-making. **3** a child's home-made racing cart.

soap opera *n* a serialized drama, usually dealing with domestic themes, broadcast on radio or television.

Often shortened to **soap.** [C20: so called because manu- facturers of soap were typical sponsors]

soapstone ('səʊp,stəʊn) *n* a massive compact soft vari- ety of talc, used for making table tops, hearths, orna- ments, etc. Also called: **steatite**.

soapsuds ('səʊp,sʌdz) *pl n* foam or lather made from soap.
> ▸ '**soap,sudsy** *adj*

soapwort ('səʊp,wɜːt) *n* a Eurasian plant having rounded clusters of fragrant pink or white flowers and leaves that were formerly used as a soap substitute. Also called: **bouncing Bet**.

soapy ('səʊpɪ) *adj* **soapier, soapiest. 1** containing or cov- ered with soap: *soapy water.* **2** resembling or characteris- tic of soap. **3** *Sl.* flattering.
> ▸ '**soapily** *adv* ▸ '**soapiness** *n*

soar (sɔː) *vb* (*intr*) **1** to rise or fly upwards into the air. **2** (of a bird, aircraft, etc.) to glide while maintaining altitude by the use of ascending air currents. **3** to rise or increase in volume, size, etc.: *soaring prices.* [C14: from OF *essorer,* from Vulgar L *exaurāre* (unattested) to expose to the breezes, from L EX-[1] + *aura* breeze]
> ▸ '**soarer** *n* ▸ '**soaring** *n, adj* ▸ '**soaringly** *adv*

Soares ★ (*Portuguese* 'swarɪʃ) *n* **Mário** ('marju). born 1924, Portuguese statesman; prime minister (1976–77; 1978– 80; 1983–86); president (1986–96).

sob (sɒb) *vb* **sobs, sobbing, sobbed. 1** (*intr*) to weep with con- vulsive gasps. **2** (*tr*) to utter with sobs. **3** to cause (oneself) to be in a specified state by sobbing: *to sob oneself to sleep.* ◆ *n* **4** a convulsive gasp made in weeping. [C12: prob. from Low G]
> ▸ '**sobbing** *n, adj*

sober ('səʊbə) *adj* **1** not drunk. **2** not given to excessive indulgence in drink or any other activity. **3** sedate and rational: *a sober attitude to a problem.* **4** (of colours) plain and dull or subdued. **5** free from exaggeration or specu- lation: *he told us the sober truth.* ◆ *vb* **6** (usually foll. by *up*) to make or become less intoxicated. [C14 *sobre,* from OF, from L *sōbrius*]
> ▸ '**sobering** *n, adj* ▸ '**soberly** *adv*

Sobers ★ ('səʊbəz) *n* Sir **Garfield St Auburn,** known as *Gary.* born 1936, West Indian cricketer.

sobriety (səʊ'braɪətɪ) *n* **1** the state or quality of being sober. **2** the quality of refraining from excess. **3** the qual- ity of being serious or sedate.

sobriquet or **soubriquet** ('səʊbrɪ,keɪ) *n* a humorous epithet, assumed name, or nickname. [C17: from F *sou- briquet,* from ?]

sob story *n* a tale of personal distress intended to arouse sympathy.

Soc. or **soc.** *abbrev. for:* **1** socialist. **2** society.

soca ('səʊkə) *n* a mixture of soul and calypso music typi- cal of the E Caribbean. [C20: a blend of *soul* + *calypso*]

socage ('sɒkɪdʒ) *n English legal history.* the tenure of land by certain services, esp. of an agricultural nature. [C14: from Anglo-F, from *soc* SOKE]

so-called *adj* **a** (*prenominal*) designated or styled by the name or word mentioned, esp. (in the speaker's opin- ion) incorrectly: *a so-called genius.* **b** (also used parenthe- tically after a noun): *these experts, so-called, are no help.*

soccer ('sɒkə) *n* **a** a game in which two teams of eleven players try to kick or head a ball into their opponents' goal, only the goalkeeper on either side being allowed to touch the ball with his hands and arms, except in the case of throw-ins. **b** (*as modifier*): *a soccer player.* ◆ Also called: **Association Football.** [C19: from *Assoc*(*iation Foot- ball*) + -ER[1]]

socceroo (,sɒkə'ruː) *n, pl* **socceroos.** *Austral. sl.* a member of the Australian national soccer team. [C20: from SOC- CER + (KANGAR)OO]

Soche or **So-ch'e** ★ (səʊ'tʃe) *n* a variant transliteration of the Chinese name for **Shache.**

Sochi ★ (*Russian* 'sɒtʃi) *n* a city and resort in SW Russia, in the Krasnodar Territory on the Black Sea: hot mineral springs. Pop.: 355 000 (1995 est.).

sociable ('səʊʃəbᵊl) *adj* **1** friendly or companionable. **2** (of an occasion) providing the opportunity for friendli-

ness and conviviality. ◆ *n* **3** *Chiefly US.* a social. **4** a type of open carriage with two seats facing each other. [C16: via F from L, from *sociāre* to unite, from *socius* an associate]
▶ ˌsocia'bility *n* ▶ 'sociably *adv*

social ('səʊʃəl) *adj* **1** living or preferring to live in a community rather than alone. **2** denoting or relating to human society or any of its subdivisions. **3** of or characteristic of the behaviour and interaction of persons forming groups. **4** relating to or having the purpose of promoting companionship, communal activities, etc.: *a social club.* **5** relating to or engaged in social services: *a social worker.* **6** relating to or considered appropriate to a certain class of society. **7** (esp. of certain species of insects) living together in organized colonies: *social bees.* **8** (of plant species) growing in clumps. ◆ *n* **9** an informal gathering, esp. of an organized group. [C16: from L *sociālis* companionable, from *socius* a comrade]
▶ 'socially *adv*

Social and Liberal Democrats *pl n* (in Britain) a political party formed in 1988 by the merging of the Liberal Party and part of the Social Democratic Party; in 1989 it changed its name to the Liberal Democrats.

social anthropology *n* the branch of anthropology that deals with cultural and social phenomena such as kinship systems or beliefs.

Social Chapter *n* the section of the **Maastricht Treaty** concerning working conditions, consultation of workers, employment rights, and social security.

Social Charter *n* a declaration of the rights, minimum wages, maximum hours, etc., of workers in the European Union, codified in the Maastricht Treaty (1992).

social climber *n* a person who seeks advancement to a higher social class, esp. by obsequious behaviour.
▶ social climbing *n*

social contract *or* **compact** *n* (in the theories of Locke, Hobbes, Rousseau, and others) an agreement, entered into by individuals, that results in the formation of the state, the prime motive being the desire for protection, which entails the surrender of some personal liberties.

Social Credit *n* **1** (esp. in Canada) a right-wing Populist political party, movement, or doctrine. **2 Social Credit League.** (in New Zealand) a middle-of-the-road political party, in favour of free enterprise. **3 Social Credit Rally.** (in Canada) a political party formed in 1963 from a splinter group of the Social Credit Party.

social democrat *n* **1** any socialist who believes in the gradual transformation of capitalism into democratic socialism. **2** (*usually cap.*) a member of a Social Democratic Party.
▶ social democracy *n*

Social Democratic and Labour Party *n* a Northern Irish political party, which advocates peaceful union with the Republic of Ireland. Abbrev.: **SDLP.**

Social Democratic Party *n* **1** (in Britain, 1981–90) a political party founded by ex-members of the Labour Party. It formed an alliance with the Liberal Party and continued in a reduced form after many members left to join the Social and Liberal Democrats in 1988. **2** one of the two major political parties in Germany, favouring gradual reform. **3** any of the parties in many other countries similar to that of Germany.

social engineering *n* the manipulation of the social position and function of individuals in order to manage change in a society.

social fund *n* (in Britain) a social security fund from which loans or payments may be made to people in cases of extreme need.

social insurance *n* government insurance providing coverage for the unemployed, the injured, the old, etc.: usually financed by contributions from employers and employees.

Social Insurance Number *n Canad.* an identification number issued to individuals by the government in connection with income tax and social insurance.

socialism ('səʊʃəˌlɪzəm) *n* **1** an economic theory or system in which the means of production, distribution,

and exchange are owned by the community collectively, usually through the state. Cf. **capitalism. 2** any of various social or political theories or movements in which the common welfare is to be achieved through the establishment of a socialist economic system. **3** (in Leninist theory) a transitional stage in the development of a society from capitalism to communism: characterized by the distribution of income according to work rather than need.

socialist ('səʊʃəlɪst) *n* **1** a supporter or advocate of socialism or any party promoting socialism (**socialist party**). ◆ *adj* **2** of, implementing, or relating to socialism. **3** (*sometimes cap.*) of or relating to socialists or a socialist party.
▶ ˌsocia'listic *adj*

Socialist International *n* an international association of largely anti-Communist Social Democratic Parties founded in Frankfurt in 1951.

socialist realism *n* (in Communist countries, esp. formerly) the doctrine that art, literature, etc., should present an idealized portrayal of reality, which glorifies the achievements of the Communist Party.

socialite ('səʊʃəˌlaɪt) *n* a person who is or seeks to be prominent in fashionable society.

sociality (ˌsəʊʃɪ'ælɪtɪ) *n, pl* **socialities. 1** the tendency of groups and persons to develop social links and live in communities. **2** the quality or state of being social.

socialize *or* **socialise** ('səʊʃəˌlaɪz) *vb* **socializes, socializing, socialized** *or* **socialises, socialising, socialised. 1** (*intr*) to behave in a friendly or sociable manner. **2** (*tr*) to prepare for life in society. **3** (*tr*) *Chiefly US.* to alter or create so as to be in accordance with socialist principles.

social market *n* an economic system in which industry and commerce are run by private enterprise within limits set by the government to ensure equality of opportunity and social and environmental responsibility. **b** (*as modifier*): *a social-market economy.*

social realism *n* **1** the use of realist art, literature, etc., as a medium for social or political comment. **2** another name for **socialist realism.**

social science *n* **1** the study of society and of the relationship of individual members within society, including economics, history, political science, psychology, anthropology, and sociology. **2** any of these subjects studied individually.
▶ social scientist *n*

social secretary *n* **1** a member of an organization who arranges its social events. **2** a personal secretary who deals with private correspondence, etc.

social security *n* **1** public provision for the economic welfare of the aged, unemployed, etc., esp. through pensions and other monetary assistance. **2** (*often cap.*) a government programme designed to provide such assistance.

social services *pl n* welfare activities organized by the state or a local authority and carried out by trained personnel.

social studies *n* (*functioning as sing*) the study of how people live and organize themselves in society, embracing geography, history, economics, and other subjects.

social welfare *n* **1** social services provided by a state for the benefit of its citizens. **2** (*caps.*) (in New Zealand) a government department concerned with pensions and benefits for the elderly, the sick, etc.

social work *n* any of various social services designed to alleviate the conditions of the poor and aged and to increase the welfare of children.
▶ social worker *n*

societal (sə'saɪətəl) *adj* of or relating to society, esp. human society.
▶ so'cietally *adv*

societal marketing *n* **1** marketing that takes into account society's long-term welfare. **2** the marketing of a social or charitable cause, such as an anti-apartheid campaign.

society (sə'saɪətɪ) *n, pl* **societies. 1** the totality of social relationships among organized groups of human beings or animals. **2** a system of human organizations generating distinctive cultural patterns and institutions. **3** such a system with reference to its mode of social and economic organization or its dominant class: *middle-class society*. **4** those with whom one has companionship. **5** an organized group of people associated for some specific purpose or on account of some common interest: *a learned society*. **6a** the privileged class of people in a community, esp. as considered superior or fashionable. **6b** (*as modifier*): *a society woman*. **7** the social life and intercourse of such people: *to enter society*. **8** companionship: *I enjoy her society*. **9** *Ecology*. a small community of plants within a larger association. [C16: via OF *societé* from L *societās*, from *socius* a comrade]

Society Islands ★ *pl n* a group of islands in the S Pacific: administratively part of French Polynesia; consists of the Windward Islands and the Leeward Islands; became a French protectorate in 1843 and a colony in 1880. Pop.: 162 573 (1988). Area: 1595 sq. km (616 sq. miles).

Society of Jesus *n* the religious order of the Jesuits, founded by Ignatius Loyola.

socio- *combining form*. denoting social or society: *socioeconomic; sociopolitical; sociology*.

sociobiology (ˌsəʊsɪəʊbaɪˈɒlədʒɪ) *n* the study of social behaviour in animals and humans.
▶ ˌsociobiˈologist *n*

socioeconomic (ˌsəʊsɪəʊˌiːkəˈnɒmɪk, -ˌɛkə-) *adj* of, relating to, or involving both economic and social factors.
▶ ˌsocioˌecoˈnomically *adv*

sociolinguistics (ˌsəʊsɪəʊlɪŋˈgwɪstɪks) *n* (*functioning as sing*) the study of language in relation to its social context.
▶ ˌsocioˈlinguist *n*

sociology (ˌsəʊsɪˈɒlədʒɪ) *n* the study of the development, organization, functioning, and classification of human societies.
▶ sociological (ˌsəʊsɪəˈlɒdʒɪkˀl) *adj* ▶ ˌsociˈologist *n*

sociometry (ˌsəʊsɪˈɒmɪtrɪ) *n* the study of sociological relationships within groups.
▶ sociometric (ˌsəʊsɪəˈmɛtrɪk) *adj* ▶ ˌsociˈometrist *n*

sociopath (ˈsəʊsɪəˌpæθ) *n* *Psychiatry*. another term for **psychopath.**
▶ ˌsocioˈpathic *adj* ▶ **sociopathy** (ˌsəʊsɪˈɒpəθɪ) *n*

sociopolitical (ˌsəʊsɪəʊpəˈlɪtɪkˀl) *adj* of or involving both political and social factors.

sock¹ (sɒk) *n* **1** a cloth covering for the foot, reaching to between the ankle and knee and worn inside a shoe. **2** an insole put in a shoe, so as to make it fit better. **3** a light shoe worn by actors in ancient Greek and Roman comedy. **4 pull one's socks up.** *Brit. inf.* to make a determined effort, esp. to improve one's behaviour or performance. **5 put a sock in it.** *Brit. sl.* be quiet! [OE *socc* a light shoe, from L *soccus*, from Gk *sukkhos*]

sock² (sɒk) *Sl.* ◆ *vb* **1** (*usually tr*) to hit with force. **2 sock it to.** *Sl.* to make a forceful impression on. ◆ *n* **3** a forceful blow. [C17: from ?]

socket (ˈsɒkɪt) *n* **1** a device into which an electric plug can be inserted in order to make a connection in a circuit. **2** *Chiefly Brit.* such a device mounted on a wall and connected to the electricity supply; power point. **3** a part with an opening or hollow into which some other part can be fitted. **4** *Anat.* **4a** a bony hollow into which a part or structure fits: *an eye socket*. **4b** the receptacle of a ball-and-socket joint. ◆ *vb* **5** (*tr*) to furnish with or place into a socket. [C13: from Anglo-Norman *soket* a little ploughshare, from *soc*, of Celtic origin]

socket set *n* a set of tools consisting of a handle into which various interchangeable heads can be fitted.

sockeye (ˈsɒkˌaɪ) *n* a Pacific salmon having red flesh and valued as a food fish. Also called: **red salmon.** [by folk etymology from *sukkegh*, of Amerind origin]

socle (ˈsəʊkˀl) *n* another name for **plinth** (sense 1). [C18: via F *zoccolo*, from L *socculus* a little shoe, from *soccus* a SOCK¹]

Socotra, Sokotra, *or* **Suqutra** ★ (səˈkəʊtrə) *n* an island in the Indian Ocean, about 240 km (150 miles) off

Cape Guardafui, Somalia: administratively part of Yemen. Area: 3100 sq. km (1200 sq. miles).

Socrates ★ (ˈsɒkrəˌtiːz) *n* ?470–399 B.C., Athenian philosopher; his beliefs that virtue is based on knowledge, attained by a dialectical process, are known through the writings of his pupils Plato and Xenophon. He was condemned to death for impiety and corruption of youth (399) and died by drinking hemlock.

Socratic (sɒˈkrætɪk) *adj* **1** of or relating to Socrates, his methods, etc. ◆ *n* **2** a person who follows the teachings of Socrates.
▶ **Soˈcratically** *adv* ▶ **Soˈcratiˌcism** *n* ▶ **Socratist** (ˈsɒkrətɪst) *n*

Socratic irony *n* *Philosophy*. a means by which the feigned ignorance of a questioner leads the person answering to expose his own ignorance.

Socratic method *n* *Philosophy*. the method of instruction by question and answer used by Socrates in order to elicit from his pupils truths he considered to be implicitly known by all rational beings.

sod¹ (sɒd) *n* **1** a piece of grass-covered surface soil held together by the roots of the grass; turf. **2** *Poetic*. the ground. ◆ *vb* **sods, sodding, sodded. 3** (*tr*) to cover with sods. [C15: from Low G]

sod² (sɒd) *Sl., chiefly Brit.* ◆ *n* **1** a person considered to be obnoxious. **2** a jocular word for a **person. 3 sod all.** *Sl.* nothing. ◆ *interj* **4 sod it.** a strong exclamation of annoyance. See also **sod off.** [C19: shortened from SODOMITE]
▶ ˈsodding *adj*

soda (ˈsəʊdə) *n* **1** any of a number of simple inorganic compounds of sodium, such as sodium carbonate (**washing soda**), sodium bicarbonate (**baking soda**), and sodium hydroxide (**caustic soda**). **2** See **soda water. 3** *US & Canad.* a fizzy drink. [C16: from Med. L, from *sodanum* barilla, a plant that was burned to obtain a type of sodium carbonate, ?from Ar.]

soda ash *n* the anhydrous commercial form of sodium carbonate.

soda bread *n* a type of bread leavened with sodium bicarbonate combined with milk and cream of tartar.

soda fountain *n* *US & Canad.* **1** a counter that serves drinks, snacks, etc. **2** an apparatus dispensing soda water.

sodality (səʊˈdælɪtɪ) *n, pl* **sodalities. 1** *RC Church.* a religious society. **2** fellowship. [C16: from L *sodālitās* fellowship, from *sodālis* a comrade]

sodamide (ˈsəʊdəˌmaɪd) *n* a white crystalline compound used as a dehydrating agent and in making sodium cyanide. Formula: $NaNH_2$.

soda siphon *n* a sealed bottle containing and dispensing soda water. The water is forced up a tube reaching to the bottom of the bottle by the pressure of gas above the water.

soda water *n* an effervescent beverage made by charging water with carbon dioxide under pressure. Sometimes shortened to **soda.**

sodden (ˈsɒdˀn) *adj* **1** completely saturated. **2a** dulled, esp. by excessive drinking. **2b** (*in combination*): *a drink-sodden mind*. **3** doughy, as bread is when improperly cooked. ◆ *vb* **4** to make or become sodden. [C13 *soden*, p.p. of SEETHE]
▶ ˈsoddenness *n*

Soddy ★ (ˈsɒdɪ) *n* **Frederick.** 1877–1956, British chemist, who discovered isotopes: Nobel prize for chemistry 1921.

sodium (ˈsəʊdɪəm) *n* **a** a very reactive soft silvery-white element of the alkali metal group occurring principally in common salt, Chile saltpetre, and cryolite. It is used in the production of chemicals, in metallurgy, and, alloyed with potassium, as a cooling medium in nuclear reactors. Symbol: Na; atomic no.: 11; atomic wt.: 22.99. **b** (*as modifier*): *sodium light*. [C19: NL, from SODA + -IUM]

sodium amytal *n* another name for **Amytal.**

sodium benzoate *n* a white crystalline soluble compound used in preserving food (**E 211**), as an antiseptic, and in making dyes.

sodium bicarbonate *n* a white crystalline soluble

compound used in effervescent drinks, baking powders, fire-extinguishers, and in medicine as an antacid; sodium hydrogen carbonate. Formula: $NaHCO_3$. Systematic name: **sodium hydrogencarbonate**. Also called: **bicarbonate of soda, baking soda**.

sodium carbonate *n* a colourless or white odourless soluble crystalline compound used in the manufacture of glass, ceramics, soap, and paper, and as a cleansing agent. Formula: Na_2CO_3.

sodium chlorate *n* a colourless crystalline soluble compound used as a bleaching agent, antiseptic, and weedkiller. Formula: $NaClO_3$.

sodium chloride *n* common table salt; a soluble colourless crystalline compound widely used as a seasoning and preservative for food and in the manufacture of chemicals, glass, and soap. Formula: NaCl. Also called: **salt**.

sodium cyanide *n* a white odourless crystalline soluble poisonous compound used for extracting gold and silver from their ores and for case-hardening steel. Formula: NaCN.

sodium glutamate ('glu:tə,meɪt) *n* another name for **monosodium glutamate**.

sodium hydrogencarbonate *n* the systematic name for **sodium bicarbonate**.

sodium hydroxide *n* a white strongly alkaline solid used in the manufacture of rayon, paper, aluminium, soap, and sodium compounds. Formula: NaOH. Also called: **caustic soda**.

sodium hyposulphite *n* another name (not in technical usage) for **sodium thiosulphate**.

sodium lamp *n* another name for **sodium-vapour lamp**.

sodium nitrate *n* a white crystalline soluble solid compound used in matches, explosives, and rocket propellants, as a fertilizer, and as a curing salt for preserving food (**E 251**). Formula: $NaNO_3$.

Sodium Pentothal *n Trademark*. another name for **thiopentone sodium**.

sodium silicate *n* **1** Also called: **soluble glass**. See **water glass**. **2** any sodium salt of a silicic acid.

sodium sulphate *n* a solid white substance used in making glass, detergents, and pulp. Formula: Na_2SO_4. See **salt cake** and **Glauber's salt**.

sodium thiosulphate *n* a white soluble substance used in photography as a fixer to dissolve unchanged silver halides and also to remove excess chlorine from chlorinated water. Formula: $Na_2S_2O_3$. Also called (not in technical usage): **sodium hyposulphite, hypo**.

sodium-vapour lamp *n* a type of electric lamp consisting of a glass tube containing neon and sodium vapour at low pressure through which an electric current is passed to give an orange light: used in street lighting.

sod off *Brit. taboo sl.* ♦ *interj* **1** a forceful expression of dismissal. ♦ *vb* **sods, sodding, sodded. 2** (*intr, adv*) to go away.

Sodom ★ ('sɒdəm) *n* **1** *Old Testament.* a city destroyed by God for its wickedness that, with Gomorrah, traditionally typifies depravity (Genesis 19:24). **2** this city as representing homosexuality. **3** any place notorious for depravity.

sodomite ('sɒdə,maɪt) *n* a person who practises sodomy.

sodomize *or* **sodomise** ('sɒdə,maɪz) *vb* **sodomizes, sodomizing, sodomized** *or* **sodomises, sodomising, sodomised.** (*tr*) to have anal intercourse with (a person).

sodomy ('sɒdəmɪ) *n* anal intercourse committed by a man with another man or a woman. [C13: via OF *sodomie* from L (Vulgate) *Sodoma* Sodom]

Sod's law (sɒdz) *n Inf.* a facetious precept stating that if something can go wrong or turn out inconveniently it will.

Soekarno ★ (su:'kɑːnəu) *n* a variant spelling of (Achmed) **Sukarno**.

Soemba ★ ('su:mbə) *n* a variant spelling of **Sumba**.

Soembawa ★ (su:m'bɑːwə) *n* a variant spelling of **Sumbawa**.

Soenda Islands ★ ('su:ndə) *pl n* a variant spelling of **Sunda Islands**.

Soenda Strait ★ *n* a variant spelling of **Sunda Strait**.

Soerabaja ★ (,suərə'baɪə) *n* a variant spelling of **Surabaya**.

soever (səu'evə) *adv* in any way at all: used to emphasize or make less precise a word or phrase, usually in combination with *what, where, when, how*, etc., or else separated by intervening words. Cf. **whatsoever**.

sofa ('səufə) *n* an upholstered seat with back and arms for two or more people. [C17 (in the sense: dais upholstered as a seat): from Ar. *suffah*]

soffit ('sɒfɪt) *n* the underside of a part of a building or a structural component, such as an arch, beam, stair, etc. [C17: via F from It. *soffitto*, from L *suffixus* something fixed underneath, from *suffigere*, from *sub-* under + *figere* to fasten]

Sofia ★ ('səufɪə) *n* the capital of Bulgaria, in the west: colonized by the Romans in 29 A.D.; became capital of Bulgaria in 1879; university (1880). Pop.: 1 116 823 (1996 est.). Ancient name: **Serdica**. Bulgarian name: **Sofiya** ('sɒfi,ja).

S. of Sol. *Bible. abbrev. for* Song of Solomon.

soft (sɒft) *adj* **1** easy to dent, work, or cut without shattering; malleable. **2** not hard; giving little or no resistance to pressure or weight. **3** fine, light, smooth, or fluffy to the touch. **4** gentle; tranquil. **5** (of music, sounds, etc.) low and pleasing. **6** (of light, colour, etc.) not excessively bright or harsh. **7** (of a breeze, climate, etc.) temperate, mild, or pleasant. **8** slightly blurred; not sharply outlined: *soft focus*. **9** (of a diet) consisting of easily digestible foods. **10** kind or lenient, often excessively so. **11** easy to influence or impose upon. **12** prepared to compromise; not doctrinaire: *the soft left*. **13** *Inf.* feeble or silly; simple (often in **soft in the head**). **14** unable to endure hardship, esp. through pampering. **15** physically out of condition; flabby: *soft muscles*. **16** loving; tender: *soft words*. **17** *Inf.* requiring little exertion; easy: *a soft job*. **18** *Chem.* (of water) relatively free of mineral salts and therefore easily able to make soap lather. **19** (of a drug such as cannabis) nonaddictive. **20** *Phonetics.* (not in technical usage) denoting the consonants *c* and *g* in English when they are pronounced as palatal or alveolar fricatives or affricates (s, dʒ, ʃ, ð, tʃ) before *e* and *i*, rather than as velar stops (k, g). **21** *Finance, chiefly US.* (of prices, a market, etc.) unstable and tending to decline. **22** (of currency) in relatively little demand, esp. because of a weak balance of payments situation. **23** (of radiation, such as X-rays and ultraviolet radiation) having low energy and not capable of deep penetration of materials. **24 soft on** *or* **about. 24a** gentle, sympathetic, or lenient towards. **24b** feeling affection or infatuation for. ♦ *adv* **25** in a soft manner: *to speak soft.* ♦ *n* **26** a soft object, part, or piece. **27** *Inf.* **softie.** ♦ *sentence substitute. Arch.* **28** quiet! **29** wait! [OE *sōfte*]
► 'softly *adv* ► 'softness *n*

softa ('sɒftə) *n* a Muslim student of divinity and jurisprudence, esp. in Turkey. [C17: from Turkish, from Persian *sōkhtah* aflame (with love of learning)]

softball ('sɒft,bɔ:l) *n* a variation of baseball using a larger softer ball, pitched underhand.

soft ball *n Cookery*. a term used for sugar syrup boiled to a consistency at which it may be rubbed into balls after dipping in cold water.

soft-boiled *adj* (of an egg) boiled for a short time so that the yolk is still soft.

soft coal *n* another name for **bituminous coal**.

soft commodities *pl n* nonmetal commodities, such as cocoa, sugar, and grains, bought and sold on a futures market. Also called: **softs**.

soft-core *adj* (of pornography) suggestive and titillating through not being totally explicit.

soft-cover *adj* a less common word for **paperback**.

soft drink *n* a nonalcoholic drink.

soften ('sɒf°n) *vb* **1** to make or become soft or softer. **2** to make or become more gentle.
► 'softener *n*

softening of the brain n an abnormal softening of the tissues of the cerebrum characterized by mental impairment.

soft-focus lens n Photog. a lens designed to produce an image that is slightly out of focus: typically used for portrait work.

soft furnishings pl n Brit. curtains, hangings, rugs, etc.

soft goods pl n textile fabrics and related merchandise. Also called (US and Canad.): **dry goods**.

soft-headed adj **1** Inf. feeble-minded; stupid; simple. **2** (of a stick or hammer for playing a percussion instrument) having a soft head.
  ▶ ‚soft-'headedness n

softhearted (‚sɒft'hɑ:tɪd) adj easily moved to pity.
  ▶ ‚soft'heartedly adv ▶ ‚soft'heartedness n

softie or **softy** ('sɒftɪ) n, pl **softies**. Inf. a person who is sentimental, weakly foolish, or lacking in physical endurance.

soft landing n **1** a landing by a spacecraft on the moon or a planet at a sufficiently low velocity for the equipment or occupants to remain unharmed. **2** a painless resolution of a problem, esp. an economic problem. Cf. **hard landing**.

soft option n in a number of choices, the one involving the least difficulty or exertion.

soft palate n the posterior fleshy portion of the roof of the mouth.

soft paste n a artificial porcelain made from clay, bone ash, etc. **b** (as modifier): softpaste porcelain.

soft-pedal vb **soft-pedals, soft-pedalling, soft-pedalled** or US **soft-pedals, soft-pedaling, soft-pedaled**. (tr) **1** to mute the tone of (a piano) by depressing the soft pedal. **2** Inf. to make (something, esp. something unpleasant) less obvious by deliberately failing to emphasize or allude to it. ◆ n **soft pedal**. **3** a foot-operated lever on a piano, the left one of two, that either moves the whole action closer to the strings so that the hammers strike with less force or causes fewer of the strings to sound.

soft porn n Inf. soft-core pornography.

softs (sɒfts) pl n another name for **soft commodities**.

soft sell n a method of selling based on indirect suggestion or inducement.

soft shoulder or **verge** n a soft edge along the side of a road that is unsuitable for vehicles to drive on.

soft soap n **1** Med. Also called: **green soap**. a soft or liquid alkaline soap used in treating certain skin disorders. **2** Inf. flattering, persuasive, or cajoling talk. ◆ vb **soft-soap**. **3** Inf. to use such talk on (a person).

soft-spoken adj **1** speaking or said with a soft gentle voice. **2** able to persuade or impress by glibness of tongue.

soft spot n a sentimental fondness (esp. in **have a soft spot for**).

soft touch n Inf. a person easily persuaded or imposed on, esp. to lend money.

software ('sɒft‚weə) n Computing. the programs that can be used with a particular computer system. Cf. **hardware** (sense 2).

softwood ('sɒft‚wʊd) n **1** the open-grained wood of any of numerous coniferous trees, such as pine and cedar. **2** any tree yielding this wood.

SOGAT ('səʊgæt) n (formerly, in Britain) acronym for Society of Graphical and Allied Trades.

Sogdiana ★ (‚sɒgdɪ'ɑ:nə) n a region of ancient central Asia. Its chief city was Samarkand.
  ▶ 'Sogdian adj, n

soggy ('sɒgɪ) adj **soggier, soggiest**. **1** soaked with liquid. **2** (of bread, pastry, etc.) moist and heavy. **3** Inf. lacking in spirit or positiveness. [C18: prob. from dialect sog marsh, from ?]
  ▶ 'soggily adv ▶ 'sogginess n

soh or **so** (səʊ) n Music. (in tonic sol-fa) the name used for the fifth note or dominant of any scale. [C14: later variant of sol; see GAMUT]

Soho ★ ('səʊhəʊ) n a district of central London, in the City of Westminster: a foreign quarter since the late 17th century, now chiefly known for restaurants, nightclubs, striptease clubs, etc.

soi-disant French. (swadizɑ̃) adj so-called; self-styled. [lit.: calling oneself]

soigné or (fem) **soignée** (swɑːnjeɪ) adj well-groomed; elegant. [F, from soigner to take good care of, of Gmc origin]

soil[1] (sɔɪl) n **1** the top layer of the land surface of the earth that is composed of disintegrated rock particles, humus, water, and air. **2** a type of this material having specific characteristics: loamy soil. **3** land, country, or region: one's native soil. **4 the soil**. life and work on a farm; land: he belonged to the soil. **5** any place or thing encouraging growth or development. [C14: from Anglo-Norman, from L solium a seat, but confused with L solum the ground]

soil[2] (sɔɪl) vb **1** to make or become dirty or stained. **2** (tr) to pollute with sin or disgrace; sully; defile. ◆ n **3** the state or result of soiling. **4** refuse, manure, or excrement. [C13: from OF soillier to defile, from soil pigsty, prob. from L sūs a swine]

soil[3] (sɔɪl) vb (tr) to feed (livestock) green fodder to fatten or purge them. [C17: ?from obs. vb (C16) soil to manure, from SOIL[2] (n)]

soil pipe n a pipe that conveys sewage or waste water from a toilet, etc., to a soil drain or sewer.

soiree ('swɑːreɪ) n an evening party or gathering, usually at a private house, esp. where guests listen to, play, or dance to music. [C19: from F, from OF soir evening, from L sērum a late time, from sērus late]

Soissons ★ (French swasɔ̃) n a city in N France, on the Aisne River: has Roman remains and an 11th-century abbey. Pop.: 32 144 (1990).

soixante-neuf French. (swasɑ̃tnœf) n a sexual activity in which two people simultaneously stimulate each other's genitalia with their mouths. Also called: **sixty-nine**. [lit.: sixty-nine, from the position adopted by the participants]

sojourn ('sɒdʒɜːn, 'sʌdʒ-) n **1** a temporary stay. ◆ vb **2** (intr) to stay or reside temporarily. [C13: from OF sojorner, from Vulgar L subdiurnāre (unattested) to spend a day, from L sub- during + LL diurnum day]
  ▶ 'sojourner n

soke (səʊk) n English legal history. **1** the right to hold a local court. **2** the territory under the jurisdiction of a particular court. [C14: from Med. L sōca, from OE sōcn a seeking]

Sokoto ★ ('səʊkə‚təʊ) n **1** a state of NW Nigeria. Capital: Sokoto. Pop.: 4 524 162 (1992 est.). Area: 65 735 sq. km (25 380 sq. miles). **2** a town in NW Nigeria, capital of Sokoto state: capital of the Fulah Empire in the 19th century; Muslim place of pilgrimage. Pop.: 185 500 (1992 est.).

Sokotra ★ (sə'kəʊtrə) n a variant spelling of **Socotra**.

sol[1] (sɒl) n Music. the syllable used in the fixed system of solmization for the note G. [C14: see GAMUT]

sol[2] (sɒl) n a colloid that has a continuous liquid phase, esp. one in which a solid is suspended in a liquid. [C20: shortened from SOLUTION]

Sol ★ (sɒl) n **1** the Roman god personifying the sun. **2** a poetic word for the **sun**.

sol. abbrev. for: **1** soluble. **2** solution.

Sol. abbrev. for: **1** Also: **Solr.** solicitor. **2** Bible. Solomon.

sola Latin. ('səʊlə) adj the feminine form of **solus**.

solace ('sɒlɪs) n **1** comfort in misery, disappointment, etc. **2** something that gives comfort or consolation. ◆ vb **solaces, solacing, solaced**. **3** to give comfort or cheer to (a person) in time of sorrow, distress, etc. **4** to alleviate (sorrow, misery, etc.). [C13: from OF solas, from L sōlātium comfort, from sōlārī to console]
  ▶ 'solacer n

solan or **solan goose** ('səʊlən) n an archaic name for the **gannet**. [C15 soland, from ON]

solanaceous (‚sɒlə'neɪʃəs) adj of or relating to the Solanaceae, a family of plants having typically tubular flowers, protruding anthers, and often poisonous or narcotic properties: includes the potato, tobacco, and several nightshades. [C19: from NL *Sōlānāceae*, from L *sōlānum* nightshade]

solanum (səʊ'leɪnəm) *n* any tree, shrub, or herbaceous plant of the mainly tropical solanaceous genus *Solanum*: includes the potato and certain nightshades. [C16: from L: nightshade]

solar ('səʊlə) *adj* **1** of or relating to the sun. **2** operating by or utilizing the energy of the sun: *solar cell*. **3** *Astron*. determined from the motion of the earth relative to the sun: *solar year*. **4** *Astrol*. subject to the influence of the sun. [C15: from L *sōlāris*, from *sōl* the sun]

solar cell *n* a cell that produces electricity from the sun's rays, used esp. in spacecraft.

solar constant *n* the rate at which the sun's energy is received per unit area at the top of the earth's atmosphere when the sun is at its mean distance from the earth and atmospheric absorption has been corrected for.

solar day *n* See under **day** (sense 6).

solar energy *n* energy obtained from solar power.

solar flare *n* a brief powerful eruption of intense high-energy radiation from the sun's surface, associated with sunspots and causing radio and magnetic disturbances on earth.

solarium (səʊ'lɛərɪəm) *n, pl* **solariums** *or* **solaria** (-'lɛərɪə) **1** a room built largely of glass to afford exposure to the sun. **2** a bed equipped with ultraviolet lights used for acquiring an artificial suntan. **3** an establishment offering such facilities. [C19: from L: a terrace, from *sōl* sun]

solar month *n* See under **month** (sense 4).

solar plexus *n* **1** *Anat*. the network of nerves situated behind the stomach that supply the abdominal organs. **2** (not in technical usage) the part of the stomach beneath the diaphragm; pit of the stomach. [C18: referring to resemblance between the radial network of nerves & ganglia & the rays of the sun]

solar power *n* radiation from the sun used to heat a fluid or to generate electricity using solar cells.

solar system *n* the system containing the sun and the bodies held in its gravitational field, including the planets (Mercury, Venus, earth, Mars, Jupiter, Saturn, Uranus, Neptune, Pluto), the asteroids, and comets.

solar wind (wɪnd) *n* the stream of charged particles, such as protons, emitted by the sun at high velocities, its intensity increasing during periods of solar activity.

solar year *n* See under **year** (sense 4).

solatium (səʊ'leɪʃəm) *n, pl* **solatia** (-ʃɪə). *Law, chiefly US & Scot.* compensation awarded for injury to the feelings as distinct from physical suffering and pecuniary loss. [C19: from L: see SOLACE]

sold (səʊld) *vb* **1** the past tense and past participle of **sell**. ◆ *adj* **2 sold on.** *Sl.* uncritically attached to or enthusiastic about.

solder ('sɒldə; *US* 'sɒdər) *n* **1** an alloy used for joining two metal surfaces by melting the alloy so that it forms a thin layer between the surfaces. **2** something that joins things together firmly; a bond. ◆ *vb* **3** to join or mend or be joined or mended with or as if with solder. [C14: via OF from L *solidāre* to strengthen, from *solidus* solid]
▸ **'solderable** *adj* ▸ **'solderer** *n*

soldering iron *n* a hand tool consisting of a handle fixed to a copper tip that is heated and used to melt and apply solder.

soldier ('səʊldʒə) *n* **1a** a person who serves or has served in an army. **1b** Also called: **common soldier.** a noncommissioned member of an army as opposed to a commissioned officer. **2** a person who works diligently for a cause. **3** *Zool.* an individual in a colony of social insects, esp. ants, that has powerful jaws adapted for defending the colony, crushing food, etc. ◆ *vb* **4** (*intr*) to serve as a soldier. [C13: from OF *soudier*, from *soude* (army) pay, from LL *solidus* a gold coin, from L: firm]
▸ **'soldierly** *adj*

soldier of fortune *n* a man who seeks money or adventure as a soldier; mercenary.

soldier on *vb* (*intr, adv*) to persist in one's efforts in spite of difficulties, pressure, etc.

soldiery ('səʊldʒərɪ) *n, pl* **soldieries. 1** soldiers collectively. **2** a group of soldiers. **3** the profession of being a soldier.

sole[1] (səʊl) *adj* **1** (*prenominal*) being the only one; only. **2** (*prenominal*) of or relating to one individual or group and no other: *sole rights*. **3** *Law.* having no wife or husband. **4** an archaic word for **solitary**. [C14: from OF *soule*, from L *sōlus* alone]
▸ **'soleness** *n*

sole[2] (səʊl) *n* **1** the underside of the foot. **2** the underside of a shoe. **3a** the bottom of a furrow. **3b** the bottom of a plough. **4** the underside of a golf-club head. ◆ *vb* **soles, soling, soled.** (*tr*) **5** to provide (a shoe) with a sole. [C14: via OF from L *solea* sandal]

sole[3] (səʊl) *n, pl* **sole** *or* **soles.** any of various tongue-shaped flatfishes, esp. the **European sole**: most common in warm seas and highly valued as food fishes. [C14: via OF from Vulgar L *sola* (unattested), from L *solea* a sandal (from the fish's shape)]

solecism ('sɒlɪˌsɪzəm) *n* **1a** the nonstandard use of a grammatical construction. **1b** any mistake, incongruity, or absurdity. **2** a violation of good manners. [C16: from L *soloecismus*, from Gk, from *soloikos* speaking incorrectly, from *Soloi* an Athenian colony of Cilicia where the inhabitants spoke a corrupt form of Greek]
▸ **'solecist** *n* ▸ ˌsole'cistic *adj* ▸ ˌsole'cistically *adv*

solely ('səʊllɪ) *adv* **1** only; completely. **2** without others; singly. **3** for one thing only.

solemn ('sɒləm) *adj* **1** characterized or marked by seriousness or sincerity: *a solemn vow*. **2** characterized by pomp, ceremony, or formality. **3** serious, glum, or pompous. **4** inspiring awe: *a solemn occasion*. **5** performed with religious ceremony. **6** gloomy or sombre: *solemn colours*. [C14: from OF *solempne*, from L *sōllemnis* appointed, ?from *sollus* whole]
▸ **'solemnly** *adv* ▸ **'solemnness** *or* **'solemness** *n*

solemnify (sə'lɛmnɪˌfaɪ) *vb* **solemnifies, solemnifying, solemnified.** (*tr*) to make serious or grave.
▸ soˌlemnifi'cation *n*

solemnity (sə'lɛmnɪtɪ) *n, pl* **solemnities. 1** the state or quality of being solemn. **2** (*often pl*) solemn ceremony, observance, etc. **3** *Law.* a formality necessary to validate a deed, contract, etc.

solemnize *or* **solemnise** ('sɒləmˌnaɪz) *vb* **solemnizes, solemnizing, solemnized** *or* **solemnises, solemnising, solemnised.** (*tr*) **1** to celebrate or observe with rites or formal ceremonies, as a religious occasion. **2** to celebrate or perform the ceremony of (marriage). **3** to make solemn or serious. **4** to perform or hold (ceremonies, etc.) in due manner.
▸ ˌsolemni'zation *or* ˌsolemni'sation *n* ▸ 'solemˌnizer *or* 'solemˌniser *n*

solenodon (sə'lɛnədən) *n* either of two rare shrewlike nocturnal mammals of the Caribbean having a long hairless tail and an elongated snout. [C19: from NL, from L *sōlēn* sea mussel (from Gk: pipe) + Gk *odōn* tooth]

solenoid ('səʊlɪˌnɔɪd) *n* **1** a coil of wire, usually cylindrical, in which a magnetic field is set up by passing a current through it. **2** a coil of wire, partially surrounding an iron core, that is made to move inside the coil by the magnetic field set up by a current: used to convert electrical to mechanical energy, as in the operation of a switch. [C19: from F *solénoïde*, from Gk *sōlēn* a tube]
▸ ˌsole'noidal *adj*

Solent ★ ('səʊlənt) *n* **the.** a strait of the English Channel between the coast of Hampshire (on the English mainland) and the Isle of Wight. Width: up to 6 km (4 miles).

Soleure ★ (sɔlœr) *n* the French name for **Solothurn**.

sol-fa ('sɒl'fɑː) *n* **1** short for **tonic sol-fa.** ◆ *vb* **sol-fas, sol-faing, sol-faed. 2** *US.* to use tonic sol-fa syllables in singing (a tune). [C16: see GAMUT]

solfatara (ˌsɒlfə'tɑːrə) *n* a volcanic vent emitting only sulphurous gases and water vapour or sometimes hot mud. [C18: from It.: a sulphurous volcano near Naples, from *solfo* sulphur]

solfeggio (sɒl'fɛdʒɪəʊ) *or* **solfège** (sɒl'fɛʒ) *n, pl* **solfeggi**

(-'fɛdʒiː), **solfeggios,** or **solfèges.** *Music.* **1** a voice exercise in which runs, scales, etc., are sung to the same syllable or syllables. **2** solmization, esp. the French or Italian system, in which the names correspond to the notes of the scale of C major. [C18: from It. *solfeggiare* to use the syllables sol-fa; see GAMUT]

soli ('səʊlɪ) *adj, adv Music.* (of a piece or passage) (to be performed) by or with soloists.

solicit (sə'lɪsɪt) *vb* **solicits, soliciting, solicited. 1** (when *intr,* foll. by *for*) to make a request, application, etc., to (a person for business, support, etc.). **2** to accost (a person) with an offer of sexual relations in return for money. **3** to provoke or incite (a person) to do something wrong or illegal. [C15: from OF *solliciter* to disturb, from L *sollicitāre* to harass, from *sollus* whole + *ciēre* to excite]
► so,lici'tation *n*

solicitor (sə'lɪsɪtə) *n* **1** (in Britain) a lawyer who advises clients on matters of law, draws up legal documents, prepares cases for barristers, etc. **2** (in the US) an officer responsible for the legal affairs of a town, city, etc. **3** a person who solicits.
► so'licitor,ship *n*

Solicitor General *n, pl* **Solicitors General. 1** (in Britain) the law officer of the Crown ranking next to the Attorney General (in Scotland to the Lord Advocate) and acting as his assistant. **2** (in New Zealand) the government's chief lawyer.

solicitous (sə'lɪsɪtəs) *adj* **1** showing consideration, concern, attention, etc. **2** keenly anxious or willing; eager. [C16: from L *sollicitus* anxious; see SOLICIT]
► so'licitousness *n*

solicitude (sə'lɪsɪ,tjuːd) *n* **1** the state or quality of being solicitous. **2** (*often pl*) something that causes anxiety or concern. **3** anxiety or concern.

solid ('sɒlɪd) *adj* **1** of, concerned with, or being a substance in a physical state in which it resists changes in size and shape. Cf. **gas** (sense 1), **liquid** (sense 1). **2** consisting of matter all through. **3** of the same substance all through: *solid rock.* **4** sound; proved or provable: *solid facts.* **5** reliable or sensible; upstanding: *a solid citizen.* **6** firm, strong, compact, or substantial: *a solid table; solid ground.* **7** (of a meal or food) substantial. **8** (*often postpositive*) without interruption or respite: *solid bombardment.* **9** financially sound or solvent: *a solid institution.* **10** strongly linked or consolidated: *a solid relationship.* **11 solid for.** unanimously in favour of. **12** *Geom.* having or relating to three dimensions. **13** (of a word composed of two or more elements) written or printed as a single word without a hyphen. **14** *Printing.* with no space or leads between lines of type. **15** (of a writer, work, etc.) adequate; sensible. **16** of or having a single uniform colour or tone. **17** *Austral. & NZ inf.* excessively severe or unreasonable. ◆ *n* **18** *Geom.* **18a** a closed surface in three-dimensional space. **18b** such a surface together with the volume enclosed by it. **19** a solid substance, such as wood, iron, or diamond. [C14: from OF *solide,* from L *solidus* firm]
► **solidity** (sə'lɪdɪtɪ) *n* ► **solidly** *adv* ► **solidness** *n*

solidago (,sɒlɪ'deɪɡəʊ) *n, pl* **solidagos.** any plant of a chiefly American genus, which includes the goldenrods. [C18: via NL from Med. L *solidago* a plant reputed to have healing properties, from *soldāre* to strengthen, from L *solidāre,* from *solidus* solid]

solid angle *n* an area subtended in three dimensions by lines intersecting at a point on a sphere whose radius is the distance to the point. See also **steradian.**

solidarity (,sɒlɪ'dærɪtɪ) *n, pl* **solidarities.** unity of interests, sympathies, etc., as among members of the same class.

solid fuel *n* **1** a fuel, such as coal or coke, that is a solid rather than an oil or gas. **2** Also called: **solid propellant.** a rocket fuel that is a solid rather than a liquid or a gas.

solid geometry *n* the branch of geometry concerned with three-dimensional geometric figures.

solidify (sə'lɪdɪ,faɪ) *vb* **solidifies, solidifying, solidified. 1** to make or become solid or hard. **2** to make or become strong, united, determined, etc.
► so,lidifi'cation *n* ► so'lidi,fier *n*

solid-state *n* (*modifier*) **1** (of an electronic device) activated by a semiconductor component in which current flow is through solid material rather than in a vacuum. **2** of, concerned with, characteristic of, or consisting of solid matter.

solid-state physics *n* (*functioning as sing*) the branch of physics concerned with the properties of solids, such as superconductivity, photoconductivity, and ferromagnetism.

solidus ('sɒlɪdəs) *n, pl* **solidi** (-,daɪ). **1** Also called: **diagonal, oblique, separatrix, shilling mark, slash, stroke, virgule.** a short oblique stroke used in text to separate items of information, such as days, months, and years in dates (*18/7/80*), alternative words (*and/or*), numerator from denominator in fractions (*55/103*), etc. **2** a gold coin of the Byzantine empire. [C14: from LL *solidus* (*nummus*) a gold coin (from *solidus* solid); in Med. L, *solidus* referred to a shilling and was indicated by a long *s,* which ult. became the virgule]

solifluction or **solifluxion** ('sɒlɪ,flʌkʃən, 'səʊlɪ-) *n* slow downhill movement of soil, saturated with meltwater, over a permanently frozen subsoil in tundra regions. [C20: from L *solum* soil + *fluctio* act of flowing]

Solihull ★ (,səʊlɪ'hʌl) *n* **1** a town in central England, in the S West Midlands near Birmingham: mainly residential. Pop.: 94 531 (1991). **2** a unitary authority in central England, in the West Midlands. Pop.: 202 000 (1994 est.). Area 180 sq. km (70 sq. miles).

soliloquize or **soliloquise** (sə'lɪlə,kwaɪz) *vb* **soliloquizes, soliloquizing, soliloquized** or **soliloquises, soliloquising, soliloquised.** (*intr*) to utter a soliloquy.
► so'liloquist *n* ► so'lilo,quizer or so'lilo,quiser *n*

soliloquy (sə'lɪləkwɪ) *n, pl* **soliloquies. 1** the act of speaking alone or to oneself, esp. as a theatrical device. **2** a speech in a play that is spoken in soliloquy. [C17: via LL *sōliloquium,* from L *sōlus* sole + *loquī* to speak]

> **USAGE NOTE** *Soliloquy* is sometimes wrongly used where *monologue* is meant. Both words refer to a long speech by one person, but a *monologue* can be addressed to other people, whereas in a *soliloquy* the speaker is always talking to himself or herself.

Soliman ★ ('sɒlɪmən) *n* a variant spelling of **Suleiman I.**

Solimões ★ (suli'mõəʃ) *n* **the.** the Brazilian name for the Amazon from the Peruvian border to the Rio Negro.

Solingen ★ (*German* 'zoːlɪŋən) *n* a city in W Germany, in North Rhine-Westphalia: a major European centre of the cutlery industry. Pop.: 165 973 (1995 est.).

solipsism ('sɒlɪp,sɪzəm) *n Philosophy.* the extreme form of scepticism which denies the possibility of any knowledge other than of one's own existence. [C19: from L *sōlus* alone + *ipse* self]
► 'solipsist *n, adj* ► ,solip'sistic *adj*

solitaire ('sɒlɪ,teə, ,sɒlɪ'teə) *n* **1** Also called: **pegboard.** a game played by one person, esp. one involving moving and taking pegs in a pegboard with the object of being left with only one. **2** the US name for **patience** (the card game). **3** a gem, esp. a diamond, set alone in a ring. **4** any of several extinct birds related to the dodo. **5** any of several dull grey North American songbirds. [C18: from OF: SOLITARY]

solitary ('sɒlɪtərɪ, -trɪ) *adj* **1** following or enjoying a life of solitude: *a solitary disposition.* **2** experienced or performed alone: *a solitary walk.* **3** (of a place) unfrequented. **4** (*prenominal*) single; sole: *a solitary cloud.* **5** having few companions; lonely. **6** (of animals) not living in organized colonies or large groups: *solitary bees.* **7** (of flowers) growing singly. ◆ *n, pl* **solitaries. 8** a person who lives in seclusion; hermit. **9** *Inf.* short for **solitary confinement.** [C14: from L *sōlitārius,* from *sōlus* SOLE[1]]
► 'solitarily *adv* ► 'solitariness *n*

solitary confinement *n* isolation imposed on a prisoner, as by confinement in a special cell.

solitude ('sɒlɪ,tjuːd) *n* **1** the state of being solitary or se-

cluded. **2** *Poetic.* a solitary place. [C14: from L *sōlitūdō*, from *sōlus* alone, SOLE[1]]
▶ ‚soli'tudinous *adj*

solmization *or* **solmisation** (‚sɒlmɪ'zeɪʃən) *n Music.* a system of naming the notes of a scale by syllables instead of letters, which assigns the names *ut* (or *do*), *re*, *mi*, *fa*, *sol*, *la*, *si* (or *ti*) to the degrees of the major scale of C (**fixed system**) or (excluding the syllables *ut* and *si*) to the major scale in any key (**movable system**). See also **tonic solfa**. [C18: from F *solmisation*, from *solmiser* to use the sol-fa syllables, from SOL[1] + MI]

solo ('səʊləʊ) *n, pl* **solos. 1** (*pl* **solos** or **soli** (-liː)). a musical composition for one performer with or without accompaniment. **2** any of various card games in which each person plays on his own, such as solo whist. **3** a flight in which an aircraft pilot is unaccompanied. **4a** any performance carried out by an individual without assistance. **4b** (*as modifier*): *a solo attempt.* ◆ *adj* **5** *Music.* unaccompanied: *a sonata for cello solo.* ◆ *adv* **6** by oneself; alone: *to fly solo.* ◆ *vb* **7** (*intr*) to operate an aircraft alone. [C17: via It. from L *sōlus* alone]
▶ **soloist** ('səʊləʊɪst) *n*

Solomon ★ ('sɒləmən) *n* 10th century B.C., king of Israel, son of David and Bathsheba, credited with great wisdom.
▶ **Solomonic** (‚sɒlə'mɒnɪk) *or* **Solomonian** (‚sɒlə'məʊnɪən) *adj*

Solomon Islands ★ *pl n* an independent state in the SW Pacific comprising an archipelago extending for almost 1450 km (900 miles) in a northwest–southeast direction: the northernmost islands of the archipelago (Buka and Bougainville) form part of Papua New Guinea; the main islands are Guadalcanal, Malaita, San Cristobal, New Georgia, Santa Isabel, and Choiseul: a member of the Commonwealth. Official language: English. Religion: Christian majority. Currency: Solomon Islands dollar. Capital: Honiara. Pop.: 411 000 (1997). Area: 29 785 sq. km (11 500 sq. miles).

Solomon's seal *n* **1** another name for **Star of David. 2** any of several plants of N temperate regions, having greenish or yellow paired flowers, long narrow waxy leaves, and prominent leaf scars. [C16: translation of Med. L *sigillum Solomonis*, ?from resemblance of the leaf scars to seals]

Solon ★ ('səʊlən) *n* ?638–?559 B.C., Athenian statesman, who introduced economic, political, and legal reforms.
▶ **Solonian** (səʊ'ləʊnɪən) *or* **Solonic** (səʊ'lɒnɪk) *adj*

so long *sentence substitute.* **1** *Inf.* farewell; goodbye. ◆ *adv* **2** *S. African sl.* for the time being; meanwhile.

Solothurn ★ (*German* 'zoːloturn) *n* **1** a canton of NW Switzerland. Capital: Solothurn. Pop.: 237 338 (1995 est.). Area: 793 sq. km (306 sq. miles). **2** a town in NW Switzerland, capital of Solothurn canton, on the Aare River. Pop.: 15 480 (1990 est.). ◆ French name: **Soleure.**

solo whist *n* a version of whist for four players acting independently, each of whom may bid to win or lose a fixed number of tricks.

solstice ('sɒlstɪs) *n* **1** either the shortest day of the year (**winter solstice**) or the longest day of the year (**summer solstice**). **2** either of the two points on the ecliptic at which the sun is overhead at the tropic of Cancer or Capricorn at the summer and winter solstices. [C13: via OF from L *sōlstitium*, lit.: the (apparent) standing still of the sun, from *sōl* sun + *sistere* to stand still]
▶ **solstitial** (sɒl'stɪʃəl) *adj*

Solti ★ ('ʃɒltɪ) *n* Sir **Georg** ('geːɔrk). 1912–97, British conductor, born in Hungary.

soluble ('sɒljʊb'l) *adj* **1** (of a substance) capable of being dissolved, esp. easily dissolved. **2** capable of being solved or answered. [C14: from LL *solūbilis*, from L *solvere* to dissolve]
▶ ‚solu'bility *n* ▶ 'solubly *adv*

solus ('səʊləs) *adj* **1** alone; separate. **2** of or denoting the position of an advertising poster or press advertisement that is separated from competing advertisements: *a solus position.* **3** of or denoting a retail outlet, such as a petrol station, that sells the products of one company exclu-

sively: *a solus site.* **4** (*fem* **sola**) alone; by oneself (formerly used in stage directions). [C17: from L *sōlus* alone]

solute ('sɒljuːt) *n* **1** the substance in a solution that is dissolved. ◆ *adj* **2** *Bot.* loose or unattached; free. [C16: from L *solūtus* free, from *solvere* to release]

solution (sə'luːʃən) *n* **1** a homogeneous mixture of two or more substances in which the molecules or atoms of the substances are completely dispersed. **2** the act or process of forming a solution. **3** the state of being dissolved (esp. in **in solution**). **4** a mixture of substances in which one or more components are present as small particles with colloidal dimension: *a colloidal solution.* **5** a specific answer to or way of answering a problem. **6** the act or process of solving a problem. **7** *Maths.* **7a** the unique set of values that yield a true statement when substituted for the variables in an equation. **7b** a member of a set of assignments of values to variables under which a given statement is satisfied; a member of a solution set. [C14: from L *solūtiō* an unloosing, from *solūtus*; see SOLUTE]

solution set *n* another name for **truth set.**

Solutrean (sə'luːtrɪən) *adj* of or relating to an Upper Palaeolithic culture of Europe. [C19: after *Solutré*, village in central France where traces of this culture were orig found]

solvation (sɒl'veɪʃən) *n* the process in which there is some chemical association between the molecules of a solute and those of the solvent.

Solvay process ('sɒlveɪ) *n* an industrial process for manufacturing sodium carbonate. Carbon dioxide is passed into a solution of sodium chloride saturated with ammonia. Sodium bicarbonate is precipitated and heated to form the carbonate. [C19: after Ernest *Solvay* (1838–1922), Belgian chemist who invented it]

solve (sɒlv) *vb* **solves, solving, solved.** (*tr*) **1** to find the explanation for or solution to (a mystery, problem, etc.). **2** *Maths.* **2a** to work out the answer to (a problem). **2b** to obtain the roots of (an equation). [C15: from L *solvere* to loosen]
▶ 'solvable *adj*

solvent ('sɒlvənt) *adj* **1** capable of meeting financial obligations. **2** (of a substance, esp. a liquid) capable of dissolving another substance. ◆ *n* **3** a liquid capable of dissolving another substance. **4** something that solves. [C17: from L *solvēns* releasing, from *solvere* to free]
▶ 'solvency *n*

solvent abuse *n* the deliberate inhaling of intoxicating fumes given off by certain solvents.

Solway Firth ★ ('sɒlweɪ) *n* an inlet of the Irish Sea between SW Scotland and NW England. Length: about 56 km (35 miles).

Solyman ★ ('sɒlɪmən) *n* a variant spelling of **Suleiman I.**

Solzhenitsyn ★ (*Russian* səlʒə'nitsin; ‚sɒlʒə'nɪtsɪn) *n* **Alexander Isayevich** (alɪk'sandr i'sajɪvitʃ). born 1918, Russian novelist. His books include *One Day in the Life of Ivan Denisovich* (1962), *Cancer Ward* (1968), and *The Gulag Archipelago* (1974). Critical of the Soviet regime, he was imprisoned (1945–53), exiled to Siberia (1953–56), and deported to the West (1974). He returned to Russia in 1994. Nobel prize for literature 1970.

Som. *abbrev. for* Somerset.

soma[1] **★** ('səʊmə) *n, pl* **somata** (-mətə) *or* **somas.** the body of an organism, as distinct from the germ cells. [C19: via NL from Gk *sōma* body]

soma[2] ('səʊmə) *n* an intoxicating plant juice drink used in Vedic rituals. [from Sansk.]

Somali (səʊ'mɑːlɪ) *n* **1** (*pl* **Somalis** or **Somali**) a member of a tall dark-skinned people inhabiting Somalia. **2** the Cushitic language of this people. ◆ *adj* **3** of, relating to, or characteristic of Somalia, the Somalis, or their language.

Somalia ★ (səʊ'mɑːlɪə) *n* a republic in NE Africa, on the Indian Ocean and the Gulf of Aden: the north became a British protectorate in 1884; the east and south were established as an Italian protectorate in 1889; gained independence and united as the Somali Republic in 1960. In 1991 the former British Somaliland region in the north unilaterally declared itself independent but this was not

officially recognized. Factional fighting has continued. Official languages: Arabic and Somali. Official religion: (Sunni) Muslim. Currency: Somali shilling. Capital: Mogadishu. Pop.: 6 870 000 (1997). Area: 637 541 sq. km (246 154 sq. miles).
▸ **So'malian** adj, n

Somaliland ★ (sǝu'mɑːlɪˌlænd) n a former region of E Africa, between the equator and the Gulf of Aden: includes Somalia, Djibouti, and SE Ethiopia.

somatic (sǝu'mætɪk) adj **1** of or relating to the soma: somatic cells. **2** of or relating to an animal body or body wall as distinct from the viscera, limbs, and head. **3** of or relating to the human body as distinct from the mind: a somatic disease. [C18: from Gk sōmatikos concerning the body, from sōma the body]
▸ **so'matically** adv

somato- or before a vowel **somat-** combining form. body: somatotype. [from Gk sōma, sōmat- body]

somatogenic (sǝˌmætǝu'dʒenɪk) adj Med. originating in the cells of the body: of organic, rather than mental, origin: a somatogenic disorder.

somatotype ('sǝumǝtǝˌtaɪp) n a type or classification of physique or body build. See **endomorph, mesomorph, ectomorph.**

sombre or US **somber** ('sɒmbǝ) adj **1** dismal; melancholy: a sombre mood. **2** dim, gloomy, or shadowy. **3** (of colour, clothes, etc.) sober, dull, or dark. [C18: from F, from Vulgar L subumbrāre (unattested) to shade, from L sub beneath + umbra shade]
▸ **'sombrely** or US **'somberly** adv ▸ **'sombreness** or US **'somberness** n ▸ **sombrous** ('sɒmbrǝs) adj

sombrero (sɒm'breǝrǝu) n, pl **sombreros.** a hat with a wide brim, as worn in Mexico. [C16: from Sp., from sombrero de sol shade from the sun]

some (sʌm; unstressed sǝm) determiner **1a** (a) certain unknown or unspecified: some people can learn. **1b** (as pron; functioning as sing or pl): some can teach and others can't. **2a** an unknown or unspecified quantity or amount of: there's some rice on the table; he owns some horses. **2b** (as pron; functioning as sing or pl): we'll buy some. **3a** a considerable number or amount of: he lived some years afterwards. **3b** a little: show him some respect. **4** (usually stressed) Inf. an impressive or remarkable: that was some game! ◆ adv **5** about; approximately: some thirty pounds. **6** a certain amount (more) (in **some more** and (inf.) **and then some**). **7** US, not standard. to a certain degree or extent: I like him some. [OE sum]

-some¹ suffix forming adjectives. characterized by; tending to: awesome; tiresome. [OE -sum]

-some² suffix forming nouns. indicating a group of a specified number of members: threesome. [OE sum, special use of SOME (determiner)]

-some³ (-sǝum) n combining form. a body: chromosome. [from Gk sōma body]

somebody ('sʌmbǝdɪ) pron **1** some person; someone. ◆ n, pl **somebodies. 2** a person of great importance: he is somebody in this town.

USAGE NOTE See at **everyone.**

someday ('sʌmˌdeɪ) adv at some unspecified time in the (distant) future.

somehow ('sʌmˌhau) adv **1** in some unspecified way. **2** Also: **somehow or other.** by any means that are necessary.

someone ('sʌmˌwʌn, -wǝn) pron some person; somebody.

USAGE NOTE See at **everyone.**

someplace ('sʌmˌpleɪs) adv US & Canad. inf. in, at, or to some unspecified place or region.

somersault or **summersault** ('sʌmǝˌsɔːlt) n **1a** a forward roll in which the head is placed on the ground and the trunk and legs are turned over it. **1b** a similar roll in a backward direction. **2** an acrobatic feat in which either

of these rolls is performed in midair, as in diving or gymnastics. **3** a complete reversal of opinion, policy, etc. ◆ vb **4** (intr) to perform a somersault. [C16: from OF soubresault, prob. from OProvençal sobresaut, from sobre over (from L super) + saut a jump, leap (from L saltus)]

Somerset¹ ★ ('sʌmǝsɪt, -ˌset) n a county of SW England, on the Bristol Channel; includes the unitary authorities of North Somerset and Bath and North East Somerset. The Mendip Hills lie in the north and Exmoor in the west; mainly agricultural (esp. dairying and fruit). Administrative centre: Taunton. Pop.: 680 925 (1996 est.). Area: 4196 sq. km (1620 sq. miles).

Somerset² ★ ('sʌmǝset) n **1st Duke of,** title of Edward Seymour. ?1500–52, English statesman, protector of England (1547–49) during Edward VI's minority. He defeated the Scots (1547) and furthered the Protestant Reformation: executed.

something ('sʌmθɪŋ) pron **1** an unspecified or unknown thing; some thing: take something warm with you. **2** something or other. one unspecified thing or an alternative thing. **3** an unspecified or unknown amount: something less than a hundred. **4** an impressive or important person, thing, or event: isn't that something? ◆ adv **5** to some degree; a little; somewhat: to look something like me. **6** (foll. by an adj) Inf. (intensifier): it hurts something awful. **7** **something else.** Sl., chiefly US. a remarkable person or thing.

-something n combining form. **a** a person whose age can be approximately expressed by a specified decade. **b** (as modifier): the thirtysomething market. [C20: from the US television series thirtysomething]

sometime ('sʌmˌtaɪm) adv **1** at some unspecified point of time. ◆ adj **2** (prenominal) having been at one time; former: the sometime President.

USAGE NOTE The form sometime should not be used to refer to a fairly long period of time: he has been away for some time (not for sometime).

sometimes ('sʌmˌtaɪmz) adv **1** now and then; from time to time. **2** Obs. formerly; sometime.

someway ('sʌmˌweɪ) adv in some unspecified manner.

somewhat ('sʌmˌwɒt) adv (not used with a negative) rather; a bit: she found it somewhat odd.

somewhere ('sʌmˌweǝ) adv **1** in, to, or at some unknown or unspecified place or point: somewhere in England; somewhere between 3 and 4 o'clock. **2 get somewhere.** Inf. to make progress.

Somme ★ (French sɔm) n **1** a department of N France, in Picardy region. Capital: Amiens. Pop.: 552 398 (1994 est.). Area: 6277 sq. km (2448 sq. miles). **2** a river in N France, rising in Aisne department and flowing west to Amiens, then northwest to the English Channel: scene of heavy fighting in World War I. Length: 245 km (152 miles).

sommelier ('sɒmǝlˌjeɪ) n a wine waiter. [F: butler, via OF from OProvençal saumalier pack-animal driver, from LL sagma a packsaddle, from Gk]

somnambulate (sɒm'næmbjuˌleɪt) vb **somnambulates, somnambulating, somnambulated.** (intr) to walk while asleep. [C19: from L somnus sleep + ambulāre to walk]
▸ **som'nambulance** n ▸ **som'nambulant** adj, n ▸ **somˌnambu'lation** n ▸ **som'nambuˌlator** n

somnambulism (sɒm'næmbjuˌlɪzǝm) n a condition characterized by walking while asleep or in a hypnotic trance. Also called: **noctambulism.**
▸ **som'nambulist** n

somniferous (sɒm'nɪfǝrǝs) or **somnific** adj Rare. tending to induce sleep.

somnolent ('sɒmnǝlǝnt) adj **1** drowsy; sleepy. **2** causing drowsiness. [C15: from L somnus sleep]
▸ **'somnolence** or **'somnolency** n ▸ **'somnolently** adv

Somnus ★ ('sɒmnǝs) n the Roman god of sleep. Greek counterpart: **Hypnos.**

son (sʌn) n **1** a male offspring; a boy or man in relation to his parents. **2** a male descendant. **3** (often cap.) a familiar

term of address for a boy or man. **4** a male from a certain country, environment, etc.: *a son of the circus.* ◆ Related adj: **filial.** [OE *sunu*]
▸ **'sonless** *adj*

Son (sʌn) *n Christianity.* the second person of the Trinity, Jesus Christ.

sonant ('səunənt) *adj* **1** *Phonetics.* denoting a voiced sound capable of forming a syllable or syllable nucleus. **2** inherently possessing, exhibiting, or producing a sound. **3** *Rare.* resonant; sounding. ◆ *n* **4** *Phonetics.* a voiced sound belonging to the class of frictionless continuants or nasals (l, r, m, n, ŋ) considered from the point of view of being a vowel and, in this capacity, able to form a syllable or syllable nucleus. [C19: from L *sonāns* sounding, from *sonāre* to make a noise, resound]
▸ **'sonance** *n*

sonar ('səʊnɑː) *n* a communication and position-finding device used in underwater navigation and target detection using echolocation. [C20: from *so(und) na(vigation and) r(anging)*]

sonata (sə'nɑːtə) *n* **1** an instrumental composition, usually in three or more movements, for piano alone (**piano sonata**) or for any other instrument with or without piano accompaniment (**violin sonata, cello sonata,** etc.). See also **sonata form. 2** a one-movement keyboard composition of the baroque period. [C17: from It., from *sonare* to sound, from L]

sonata form *n* a musical structure consisting of an expanded ternary form whose three sections (exposition, development, and recapitulation), followed by a coda, are characteristic of the first movement in a sonata, symphony, string quartet, concerto, etc.

sondage (sɒn'dɑːʒ) *n, pl* **sondages** (-'dɑːʒɪz, -'dɑːʒ). *Archaeol.* a deep trial trench for inspecting stratigraphy. [C20: from F: a sounding, from *sonder* to sound]

sonde (sɒnd) *n* a rocket, balloon, or probe used for observing in the upper atmosphere. [C20: from F: plummet, plumb line; see SOUND³]

Sondheim ★ ('sɒndhaɪm) *n* **Stephen (Joshua).** born 1930, US songwriter. He wrote the lyrics for *West Side Story* (1957), the score for *Company* (1971), and both for *Into the Woods* (1987).

sone (səʊn) *n* a unit of loudness equal to 40 phons. [C20: from L *sonus* a sound]

son et lumière (sɒn eɪ 'luːmɪˌɛə) *n* an entertainment staged at night at a famous building, historical site, etc., whereby the history of the location is presented by means of lighting effects, sound effects, and narration. [F, lit.: sound and light]

song (sɒŋ) *n* **1a** a piece of music, usually employing a verbal text, composed for the voice, esp. one intended for performance by a soloist. **1b** the whole repertory of such pieces. **1c** (*as modifier*): *a song book.* **2** poetical composition; poetry. **3** the characteristic tuneful call or sound made by certain birds or insects. **4** the act or process of singing: *they raised their voices in song.* **5 for a song.** at a bargain price. **6 on song.** *Brit. inf.* performing at peak efficiency or ability. [OE *sang*]

Song ★ (sʊŋ) *n* the Pinyin transliteration of the Chinese name for **Sung.**

song and dance *n Inf.* **1** *Brit.* a fuss, esp. one that is unnecessary. **2** *US & Canad.* a long or elaborate story or explanation.

songbird ('sɒŋˌbɜːd) *n* **1** any of a suborder of passerine birds having highly developed vocal organs and, in most, a musical call. **2** any bird having a musical call.

song cycle *n* any of several groups of songs written during and after the Romantic period, each series relating a story or grouped around a central motif.

Songhua ★ ('sʌŋ'wɑː) *n* a river in NE China, rising in SE Jilin province and flowing north and northeast to the Amur River near Tongjiang: the chief river of Manchuria and largest tributary of the Amur; frozen from November to April. Length: over 1300 km (800 miles). Also called: **Sungari.**

Song Koi *or* **Song Coi ★** ('sɒŋ 'kɔɪ) *n* transliteration of the Vietnamese name for the **Red River** (sense 3).

songololo (ˌsɒŋgʊ'lɒlʊ) *n, pl* **songololos.** *S. African.* a millipede. [from Nguni, from *ukusonga* to roll up]

songster ('sɒŋstə) *n* **1** a singer or poet. **2** a singing bird; songbird.
▸ **'songstress** *fem n*

song thrush *n* a common Old World thrush with a spotted breast, noted for its song.

songwriter ('sɒŋˌraɪtə) *n* a person who composes songs in a popular idiom.

sonic ('sɒnɪk) *adj* **1** of, involving, or producing sound. **2** having a speed about equal to that of sound in air. [C20: from L *sonus* sound]

sonic barrier *n* another name for **sound barrier.**

sonic boom *n* a loud explosive sound caused by the shock wave of an aircraft, etc., travelling at supersonic speed.

sonic depth finder *n* an instrument for detecting the depth of water or of a submerged object by means of sound waves; Fathometer.

sonics ('sɒnɪks) *n* (*functioning as sing*) *Physics.* the study of mechanical vibrations in matter.

son-in-law *n, pl* **sons-in-law.** the husband of one's daughter.

sonnet ('sɒnɪt) *Prosody.* ◆ *n* **1** a verse form consisting of 14 lines in iambic pentameter with a fixed rhyme scheme, usually divided into octave and sestet or, in the English form, into three quatrains and a couplet. ◆ *vb* **2** (*intr*) to compose sonnets. **3** (*tr*) to celebrate in a sonnet. [C16: via It. from OProvençal *sonet* a little poem, from *son* song, from L *sonus* a sound]

sonneteer (ˌsɒnɪ'tɪə) *n* a writer of sonnets.

sonny ('sʌnɪ) *n, pl* **sonnies.** *Often patronizing.* a familiar term of address to a boy or man.

sonobuoy ('səʊnəˌbɔɪ) *n* a buoy equipped to detect underwater noises and transmit them by radio. [SONIC + BUOY]

Son of Man ★ *n Bible.* a title of Jesus Christ.

Sonora ★ (*Spanish* so'nora) *n* a state of NW Mexico, on the Gulf of California: consists of a narrow coastal plain rising inland to the Sierra Madre Occidental; an important mining area in colonial times. Capital: Hermosillo. Pop.: 2 083 630 (1995 est.). Area: 184 934 sq. km (71 403 sq. miles).

sonorant ('sɒnərənt) *n Phonetics.* **1** one of the frictionless continuants or nasals (l, r, m, n, ŋ) having consonantal or vocalic functions depending on its situation within the syllable. **2** either of the two consonants represented in English orthography by *w* or *y* and regarded as either consonantal or vocalic articulations of the vowels (iː) and (uː).

sonorous (sə'nɔːrəs, 'sɒnərəs) *adj* **1** producing or capable of producing sound. **2** (of language, sound, etc.) deep or resonant. **3** (esp. of speech) high-flown; grandiloquent. [C17: from L *sonōrus* loud, from *sonor* a noise]
▸ **sonority** (sə'nɒrɪtɪ) *n* ▸ **so'norously** *adv* ▸ **so'norousness** *n*

sonsy *or* **sonsie** ('sɒnsɪ) *adj* **sonsier, sonsiest.** *Scot., Irish, & English dialect.* **1** plump; buxom. **2** cheerful; good-natured. **3** lucky. [C16: from Gaelic *sonas* good fortune]

Sontag ★ ('sɒntæg) *n* **Susan.** born 1933, US intellectual and essayist, noted esp. for her writings on modern culture. Her works include "Notes on Camp" (1964), *On Photography* (1977), *Illness as Metaphor* (1979), and *The Volcano Lover* (1992).

Soo Canals ★ (suː) *pl n* **the.** the two ship canals linking Lakes Superior and Huron. There is a canal on the Canadian and on the US side of the rapids of the St Mary's River. See also **Sault Sainte Marie.**

Soochow ★ ('suː'tʃaʊ) *n* a variant transliteration of the Chinese name for **Suzhou.**

sook (sʊk) *n* **1** *SW English dialect.* a baby. **2** *Derog.* a coward. [?from OE *sūcan* to suck, infl. by Welsh *swci swead* tame]

sool (suːl) *vb* (*tr*) *Austral. & NZ sl.* **1** to incite (esp. a dog) to attack. **2** to attack.
▸ **'sooler** *n*

soon (suːn) *adv* **1** in or after a short time; in a little while; before long. **2 as soon as.** at the very moment that: *as soon as she saw him.* **3 as soon … as.** used to indicate that the second alternative is not preferable to the first: *I'd just as soon go by train as drive.* [OE *sōna*]

sooner ('suːnə) *adv* **1** the comparative of **soon:** *he came sooner than I thought.* **2** rather; in preference: *I'd sooner die than give up.* **3 no sooner … than.** immediately after or when: *no sooner had he got home than the rain stopped.* **4 sooner or later.** eventually; inevitably.

> **USAGE NOTE** *When* is sometimes used instead of *than* after *no sooner*, but this use is generally regarded as incorrect: *no sooner had he arrived than* (not *when*) *the telephone rang.*

Soong *or* **Song** ★ (suŋ) *n* an influential Chinese family, notably **Soong Ch'ing-ling** (1890–1981), who married **Sun Yat-sen** and became a vice-chairman of the People's Republic of China (1959); and **Soong Mei-ling** (born 1898), who married **Chiang Kai-shek.**

soot (sut) *n* **1** finely divided carbon deposited from flames during the incomplete combustion of organic substances such as coal. ◆ *vb* **2** (*tr*) to cover with soot. [OE *sōt*]

sooth (suːθ) *Arch. or poetic.* ◆ *n* **1** truth or reality (esp. in **in sooth**). ◆ *adj* **2** true or real. [OE *sōth*]

soothe (suːð) *vb* **soothes, soothing, soothed. 1** (*tr*) to make calm or tranquil. **2** (*tr*) to relieve or assuage (pain, longing, etc.). **3** (*intr*) to bring tranquillity or relief. [C16 (in the sense: to mollify): from OE *sōthian* to prove]
> ► '**soother** *n*   ► '**soothing** *adj*   ► '**soothingly** *adv*   ► '**soothingness** *n*

soothsayer ('suːθ,seɪə) *n* a seer or prophet.

sooty ('sutɪ) *adj* **sootier, sootiest. 1** covered with soot. **2** resembling or consisting of soot.
> ► '**sootily** *adv*   ► '**sootiness** *n*

sop (sɒp) *n* **1** (*often pl*) food soaked in a liquid before being eaten. **2** a concession, bribe, etc., given to placate or mollify: *a sop to one's feelings.* **3** *Inf.* a stupid or weak person. ◆ *vb* **sops, sopping, sopped. 4** (*tr*) to dip or soak (food) in liquid. **5** (when *intr*, often foll. by *in*) to soak or be soaked. **6** (*tr*; often foll. by *up*) to mop or absorb (liquid) as with a sponge. [OE *sopp*]

SOP *abbrev. for* standard operating procedure.

sop. *abbrev. for* soprano.

Soper ★ ('səupə) *n* **Donald (Oliver)**, Baron. 1903–98, British Methodist minister and publicist, noted esp. for his pacifist convictions.

Sophia ★ (səu'faɪə) *n* 1630–1714, electress of Hanover (1658–1714), in whom the Act of Settlement (1701) vested the English Crown. She was a granddaughter of James I of England and her son became George I of Great Britain and Ireland.

sophism ('sɒfɪzəm) *n* an instance of sophistry. Cf. **paralogism.** [C14: from L *sophisma*, from Gk: ingenious trick, from *sophizesthai* to use clever deceit, from *sophos* wise]

sophist ('sɒfɪst) *n* **1** a person who uses clever or quibbling but unsound arguments. **2** one of the pre-Socratic philosophers who were prepared to enter into debate on any subject however specious. [C16: from L *sophista*, from Gk *sophistēs* a wise man, from *sophizesthai* to act craftily]

sophistic (sə'fɪstɪk) *or* **sophistical** *adj* **1** of or relating to sophists or sophistry. **2** consisting of sophisms or sophistry; specious.
> ► so'**phistically** *adv*

sophisticate *vb* (sə'fɪstɪ,keɪt), **sophisticates, sophisticating, sophisticated. 1** (*tr*) to make (someone) less natural or innocent, as by education. **2** to pervert or corrupt (an argument, etc.) by sophistry. **3** (*tr*) to make more complex or refined. **4** *Rare.* to falsify (a text, etc.) by alterations. ◆ *n* (sə'fɪstɪ,keɪt, -kɪt). **5** a sophisticated person. [C14: from Med. L *sophisticāre*, from L *sophisticus* sophistic]
> ► so,**phisti'cation** *n*   ► so'**phisti,cator** *n*

sophisticated (sə'fɪstɪ,keɪtɪd) *adj* **1** having refined or cultured tastes and habits. **2** appealing to sophisticates: *a sophisticated restaurant.* **3** unduly refined or cultured. **4** pretentiously or superficially wise. **5** (of machines, methods, etc.) complex and refined.

sophistry ('sɒfɪstrɪ) *n, pl* **sophistries. 1a** a method of argument that is seemingly plausible though actually invalid and misleading. **1b** the art of using such arguments. **2** subtle but unsound or fallacious reasoning. **3** an instance of this.

Sophocles ★ ('sɒfə,kliːz) *n* ?496–406 B.C., Greek dramatist; author of seven extant tragedies, including *Oedipus Rex, Electra,* and *Oedipus at Colonus.*
> ► **Sophoclean** (,sɒfə'kliːən) *adj*

sophomore ('sɒfə,mɔː) *n Chiefly US & Canad.* a second-year student at a secondary (high) school or college. [C17: ?from earlier *sophumer*, from *sophum*, var. of SOPHISM, + -ER[1]]

Sophy *or* **Sophi** ('səufɪ) *n, pl* **Sophies.** (formerly) a title of the Persian monarchs. [C16: from L *sophī* wise men, from Gk *sophos* wise]

-sophy *n combining form.* indicating knowledge or an intellectual system: *philosophy.* [from Gk, from *sophia* wisdom, from *sophos* wise]
> ► -**sophic** *or* -**sophical** *adj combining form.*

soporific (,sɒpə'rɪfɪk) *adj also* (*arch.*) ,**sopor'iferous. 1** inducing sleep. **2** drowsy; sleepy. ◆ *n* **3** a drug or other agent that induces sleep. [C17: from F, from L *sopor* sleep + -FIC]

sopping ('sɒpɪŋ) *adj* completely soaked; wet through. Also: **sopping wet.**

soppy ('sɒpɪ) *adj* **soppier, soppiest. 1** wet or soggy. **2** *Brit. inf.* silly or sentimental. **3 soppy on.** *Brit. inf.* foolishly charmed or affected by.
> ► '**soppily** *adv*   ► '**soppiness** *n*

sopranino (,sɒprə'niːnəu) *n, pl* **sopraninos. a** the instrument with the highest possible pitch in a family of instruments. **b** (*as modifier*): *a sopranino recorder.* [It., dim. of SOPRANO]

soprano (sə'prɑːnəu) *n, pl* **sopranos** *or* **soprani** (-'prɑːniː). **1** the highest adult female voice. **2** the voice of a young boy before puberty. **3** a singer with such a voice. **4** the highest part of a piece of harmony. **5a** the highest or second highest instrument in a family of instruments. **5b** (*as modifier*): *a soprano saxophone.* ◆ See also **treble.** [C18: from It., from *sopra* above, from L *suprā*]

soprano clef *n* the clef that establishes middle C as being on the bottom line of the staff.

Sopwith ★ ('sɒpwɪθ) *n* Sir **Thomas Octave Murdoch.** 1888–1989, British aircraft designer, who built the Sopwith Camel biplane used during World War I. He was chairman (1935–63) of the Hawker Siddeley Group, which developed the Hurricane fighter and Lancaster bomber.

Sorata ★ (*Spanish* so'rata) *n* **Mount.** a mountain in W Bolivia, in the Andes: the highest mountain in the Cordillera Real, with two peaks, Ancohuma, 6550 m (21 490 ft), and Illampu, 6485 m (21 276 ft).

sorb (sɔːb) *n* **1** another name for **service tree. 2** any of various related trees, esp. the mountain ash. **3** Also called: **sorb apple.** the fruit of any of these trees. [C16: from L *sorbus*]

sorbefacient (,sɔːbɪ'feɪʃənt) *adj* **1** inducing absorption. ◆ *n* **2** a sorbefacient drug. [C19: from L *sorbē(re)* to absorb + -FACIENT]

sorbet ('sɔːbeɪ, -bɪt) *n* **1** a water ice made from fruit juice, egg whites, etc. **2** a US word for **sherbet** (sense 1). [C16: from F, from OIt. *sorbetto*, from Turkish *şerbet*, from Ar. *sharbah* a drink]

sorbic acid ('sɔːbɪk) *n* a white crystalline carboxylic acid found in berries of the mountain ash and used to inhibit the growth of moulds and as an additive (**E 200**) for certain synthetic coatings. [C19: from SORB (the tree), from its discovery in berries of the mountain ash]

sorbitol ('sɔːbɪ,tɒl) *n* a white crystalline alcohol, found in certain fruits and berries and manufactured by the catalytic hydrogenation of sucrose: used as a sweetener

(E 420) and in the manufacture of ascorbic acid and synthetic resins. [C19: from SORB + -ITOL]

Sorbonne ★ (French sɔrbɔn) n **the.** a part of the University of Paris containing the faculties of science and literature: founded in 1253 by Robert de Sorbon as a theological college; given to the university in 1808.

sorbo rubber ('sɔːbəʊ) n Brit. a spongy form of rubber. [C20: from ABSORB]

sorcerer ('sɔːsərə) or (fem) **sorceress** ('sɔːsərɪs) n a person who seeks to control and use magic powers; a wizard or magician. [C16: from OF sorcier, from Vulgar L sortiārius (unattested) caster of lots, from L sors lot]

sorcery ('sɔːsərɪ) n, pl **sorceries.** the art, practices, or spells of magic, esp. black magic. [C13: from OF sorcerie, from sorcier SORCERER]

sordid ('sɔːdɪd) adj **1** dirty, foul, or squalid. **2** degraded; vile; base. **3** selfish and grasping: sordid avarice. [C16: from L sordidus, from sordēre to be dirty]
► **'sordidly** adv ► **'sordidness** n

sordino (sɔːˈdiːnəʊ) n, pl **sordini** (-niː). **1** a mute for a stringed or brass musical instrument. **2** any of the dampers in a piano. **3 con sordino** or **sordini.** a musical direction to play with a mute. **4 senza sordino** or **sordini.** a musical direction to remove or play without the mute or (on the piano) with the sustaining pedal pressed down. [It.: from sordo deaf, from L surdus]

sore (sɔː) adj **1** (esp. of a wound, injury, etc.) painfully sensitive; tender. **2** causing annoyance: a sore point. **3** resentful; irked. **4** urgent; pressing: in sore need. **5** (postpositive) grieved; distressed. **6** causing grief or sorrow. ◆ n **7** a painful or sensitive wound, injury, etc. **8** any cause of distress or vexation. ◆ adv **9** Arch. direly; sorely (now only in such phrases as **sore afraid**). [OE sār]
► **'soreness** n

sorehead ('sɔːˌhɛd) n Inf., chiefly US & Canad. a peevish or disgruntled person.

sorely ('sɔːlɪ) adv **1** painfully or grievously: sorely wounded. **2** pressingly or greatly: to be sorely taxed.

sorghum ('sɔːgəm) n any grass of the Old World genus Sorghum, having glossy seeds: cultivated for grain, hay, and as a source of syrup. [C16: from NL, from It. sorgo, prob. from Vulgar L Syricum grānum (unattested) Syrian grain]

Sorocaba ★ (Portuguese soroˈkaba) n a city in S Brazil, in São Paulo state: industrial centre. Pop.: 348 952 (1991).

soroptimist (səˈrɒptɪmɪst) n a member of Soroptimist International, an organization of clubs for professional and executive businesswomen.

sorority (səˈrɒrɪtɪ) n, pl **sororities.** Chiefly US. a social club or society for university women. [C16: from Med. L sorōritās, from L soror sister]

sorption ('sɔːpʃən) n the process in which one substance takes up or holds another; adsorption or absorption. [C20: back formation from ABSORPTION, ADSORPTION]

sorrel[1] ('sɒrəl) n **1a** a light brown to brownish-orange colour. **1b** (as adj): a sorrel carpet. **2** a horse of this colour. [C15: from OF sorel, from sor a reddish brown, of Gmc origin]

sorrel[2] ('sɒrəl) n **1** any of several plants of Eurasia and North America, having acid-tasting leaves used in salads and sauces. **2** short for **wood sorrel.** [C14: from OF surele, from sur sour, of Gmc origin]

Sorrento ★ (səˈrɛntəʊ; Italian sorˈrɛnto) n a port in SW Italy, in Campania on a mountainous peninsula between the Bay of Naples and the Gulf of Salerno: a resort since Roman times. Pop.: 17 500 (1990).

sorrow ('sɒrəʊ) n **1** the feeling of sadness, grief, or regret associated with loss, bereavement, sympathy for another's suffering, etc. **2** a particular cause or source of this. **3** Also called: **sorrowing.** the outward expression of grief or sadness. ◆ vb **4** (intr) to mourn or grieve. [OE sorg]
► **'sorrowful** adj ► **'sorrowfully** adv ► **'sorrowfulness** n

sorry ('sɒrɪ) adj **sorrier, sorriest. 1** (usually postpositive; often foll. by for) feeling or expressing pity, sympathy, grief, or regret: I feel sorry for him. **2** pitiful, wretched, or deplorable: a sorry sight. **3** poor; paltry: a sorry excuse. **4** affected

by sorrow; sad. **5** causing sorrow or sadness. ◆ interj **6** an exclamation expressing apology. [OE sārig]
► **'sorrily** adv ► **'sorriness** n

sort (sɔːt) n **1** a class, group, kind, etc., as distinguished by some common quality or characteristic. **2** Inf. a type or character, nature, etc.: he's a good sort. **3** Austral. sl. a person, esp. a girl. **4** a more or less definable or adequate example: it's a sort of review. **5** (often pl) Printing. any of the individual characters making up a fount of type. **6** Arch. manner; way: in this sort we struggled home. **7 after a sort.** to some extent. **8 of sorts** or **of a sort. 8a** of an inferior kind. **8b** of an indefinite kind. **9 out of sorts.** not in normal good health, temper, etc. **10 sort of.** in some way or other; as it were; rather. ◆ vb **11** (tr) to arrange according to class, type, etc. **12** (tr) to put (something) into working order. **13** to arrange (computer information) by machine in an order convenient to the user. **14** (intr) Arch. to agree; accord. [C14: from OF, from Med. L sors kind, from L: fate]
► **'sortable** adj ► **'sorter** n

USAGE NOTE See at **kind**[2].

sortie ('sɔːtɪ) n **1a** (of troops, etc.) the act of attacking from a contained or besieged position. **1b** the troops doing this. **2** an operational flight made by one aircraft. **3** a short or relatively short return trip. ◆ vb **sorties, sortieing, sortied. 4** (intr) to make a sortie. [C17: from F: a going out, from sortir to go out]

sortilege ('sɔːtɪlɪdʒ) n the act or practice of divination by drawing lots. [C14: via OF from Med. L sortilegium, from L sortilegus a soothsayer, from sors fate + legere to select]

sort out vb (tr, adv) **1** to find a solution to (a problem, etc.), esp. to make clear or tidy: to sort out the mess. **2** to take or separate, as from a larger group: to sort out the likely ones. **3** to organize into an orderly and disciplined group. **4** Inf. to beat or punish.

SOS n **1** an internationally recognized distress signal in which the letters SOS are repeatedly spelt out, as by radiotelegraphy: used esp. by ships and aircraft. **2** a message broadcast in an emergency for people otherwise unobtainable. **3** Inf. a call for help.

sosatie (səˈsɑːtɪ) n S. African. curried meat on skewers. [from Afrik., from Du.]

Sosnowiec ★ (Polish sɔsˈnɔvjɛts) n an industrial town in S Poland. Pop.: 248 900 (1995 est.).

so-so Inf. ◆ adj **1** (postpositive) neither good nor bad. ◆ adv **2** in an average or indifferent manner.

sostenuto (ˌsɒstəˈnuːtəʊ) adj, adv Music. to be performed in a smooth sustained manner. [C18: from It., from sostenere to sustain, from L sustinēre]

sot (sɒt) n **1** a habitual or chronic drunkard. **2** a person stupefied by or as if by drink. [OE, from Med. L sottus]
► **'sottish** adj

soteriology (sɒˌtɪərɪˈɒlədʒɪ) n Christian theol. the doctrine of salvation. [C19: from Gk sōtēria deliverance (from sōtēr a saviour) + -LOGY]

Soto ★ ('səʊtəʊ; Spanish 'soto) n See (Hernando) **De Soto.**

sotto voce ('sɒtəʊ 'vəʊtʃɪ) adv in an undertone. [C18: from It.: under (one's) voice]

sou (suː) n **1** a former French coin of low denomination. **2** a very small amount of money: I haven't a sou. [C19: from F, from OF sol, from L: SOLIDUS]

soubrette (suːˈbrɛt) n **1** a minor female role in comedy, often that of a pert lady's maid. **2** any pert or flirtatious girl. [C18: from F: maidservant, from Provençal, from soubret conceited, from soubra to exceed, from L superāre to surmount]

soubriquet ('səʊbrɪˌkeɪ) n a variant spelling of **sobriquet.**

Soudan ★ (sudɑ̃) n the French name for the **Sudan.**

soufflé ('suːfleɪ) n **1** a light fluffy dish made with beaten egg whites combined with cheese, fish, etc. **2** a similar sweet or savoury cold dish, set with gelatine. ◆ adj also **souffléed. 3** made light and puffy, as by beating and cooking. [C19: from F, from souffler to blow, from L sufflāre]

Soufrière ★ (French sufrjɛr) n **1** a volcano in the Caribbean, on N St Vincent: erupted in 1902, killing about

2000 people. Height: 1234 m (4048 ft). **2** a volcano in the Caribbean, on S Montserrat: the highest point on the island: erupted in 1997 killing 19 people and destroying the island's capital. Height: 915 m (3002 ft). **3** a volcano in the Caribbean, on Guadeloupe. Height: 1484 m (4869 ft).

sough (sau) *vb* **1** (*intr*) (esp. of the wind) to make a sighing sound. ◆ *n* **2** a soft continuous murmuring sound. [OE *swōgan* to resound]

sought (sɔːt) *vb* the past tense and past participle of **seek**.

souk (suːk) *n* an open-air marketplace in Muslim countries, esp. North Africa and the Middle East. [from Ar.]

soukous ('suːkʊs) *n* a style of African popular music that originated in Zaïre (now the Democratic Republic of the Congo), characterized by syncopated rhythms and intricate contrasting guitar melodies. [C20: ? from F *secouer* to shake]

soul (səul) *n* **1** the spirit or immaterial part of man, the seat of human personality, intellect, will, and emotions: regarded as an entity that survives the body after death. **2** *Christianity*. the spiritual part of a person, capable of redemption from sin through divine grace. **3** the essential part or fundamental nature of anything. **4** a person's feelings or moral nature. **5a** Also called: **soul music**. a type of Black music resulting from the addition of jazz, gospel, and pop elements to the urban blues style. **5b** (as *modifier*): *a soul singer.* **6** (*modifier*) of or relating to Black Americans and their culture: *soul food.* **7** nobility of spirit or temperament: *a man of great soul.* **8** an inspiring or leading figure, as of a movement. **9** a person regarded as typifying some characteristic or quality: *the soul of discretion.* **10** a person; individual: *an honest soul.* **11 upon my soul!** an exclamation of surprise. [OE *sāwol*]

soul-destroying *adj* (of an occupation, situation, etc.) unremittingly monotonous.

soul food *n Inf.* food, such as chitterlings, yams, etc., traditionally eaten by African-Americans.

soulful ('səulful) *adj* expressing profound thoughts or feelings.
▶ 'soulfully *adv* ▶ 'soulfulness *n*

soulless ('səullıs) *adj* lacking humanizing qualities or influences; mechanical: *soulless work.* **2** (of a person) lacking in sensitivity or nobility.
▶ 'soullessness *n*

soul mate *n* a person for whom one has a deep affinity, esp. a lover, wife, husband, etc.

soul-searching *n* **1** deep or critical examination of one's motives, actions, beliefs, etc. ◆ *adj* **2** displaying the characteristics of this.

sound[1] (saund) *n* **1a** a periodic disturbance in the pressure or density of a fluid or in the elastic strain of a solid, produced by a vibrating object. It travels as longitudinal waves. **1b** (as *modifier*): *a sound wave.* **2** the sensation produced by such a periodic disturbance in the organs of hearing. **3** anything that can be heard. **4** (*modifier*) of or relating to radio as distinguished from television: *sound broadcasting.* **5** a particular instance or type of sound: *the sound of running water.* **6** volume or quality of sound: *a radio with poor sound.* **7** the area or distance over which something can be heard: *within the sound of Big Ben.* **8** impression or implication: *I don't like the sound of that.* **9** (*often pl*) *Sl.* music, esp. rock, jazz, or pop. ◆ *vb* **10** to cause (an instrument, etc.) to make a sound or (of an instrument, etc.) to emit a sound. **11** to announce or be announced by a sound: *to sound the alarm.* **12** (*intr*) (of a sound) to be heard. **13** (*intr*) to resonate with a certain quality or intensity: *to sound loud.* **14** (*copula*) to give the impression of being as specified: *to sound reasonable.* **15** (*tr*) to pronounce distinctly or audibly: *to sound one's consonants.* [C13: from OF *soner* to make a sound, from L *sonāre*, from *sonus* a sound]
▶ 'soundable *adj*

sound[2] (saund) *adj* **1** free from damage, injury, decay, etc. **2** firm; substantial: *a sound basis.* **3** financially safe or stable: *a sound investment.* **4** showing good judgment or reasoning; wise: *sound advice.* **5** valid, logical, or justifiable: *a sound argument.* **6** holding approved beliefs; ethically correct; honest. **7** (of sleep) deep; peaceful; unbroken. **8**

thorough: *a sound examination.* ◆ *adv* **9** soundly; deeply: now archaic except when applied to sleep. [OE *sund*]
▶ 'soundly *adv* ▶ 'soundness *n*

sound[3] (saund) *vb* **1** to measure the depth of (a well, the sea, etc.) by plumb line, sonar, etc. **2** to seek to discover (someone's views, etc.), as by questioning. **3** (*intr*) (of a whale, etc.) to dive downwards swiftly and deeply. **4** *Med.* **4a** to probe or explore (a bodily cavity or passage) by means of a sound. **4b** to examine (a patient) by means of percussion and auscultation. ◆ *n* **5** *Med.* an instrument for insertion into a bodily cavity or passage to dilate strictures, dislodge foreign material, etc. ◆ See also **sound out**. [C14: from OF *sonder*, from *sonde* sounding line, prob. of Gmc origin]
▶ 'sounder *n*

sound[4] (saund) *n* **1** a relatively narrow channel between two larger areas of sea or between an island and the mainland. **2** an inlet or deep bay of the sea. **3** the air bladder of a fish. [OE *sund* swimming, narrow sea]

Sound ★ (saund) *n* **the**. a strait between SW Sweden and Sjælland (Denmark), linking the Kattegat with the Baltic: busy shipping lane. Length: 113 km (70 miles). Narrowest point: 5 km (3 miles). Swedish and Danish name: **Øresund**.

soundalike ('saundə,laık) *n* **a** a person or thing that sounds like another, often well-known, person or thing. **b** (as *modifier*): *a soundalike band.*

sound barrier *n* (not in technical usage) a hypothetical barrier to flight at or above the speed of sound, when a sudden large increase in drag occurs. Also called: **sonic barrier**.

sound bite *n* a short pithy sentence or phrase extracted from a longer speech for use on radio or television.

soundbox ('saund,bɒks) *n* the resonating chamber of the hollow body of a violin, guitar, etc.

sound effect *n* any sound artificially produced, reproduced from a recording, etc., to create a theatrical effect, as in plays, films, etc.

sounding[1] ('saundıŋ) *adj* **1** resounding; resonant. **2** having an imposing sound and little content; pompous: *sounding phrases.*

sounding[2] ('saundıŋ) *n* **1** (*sometimes pl*) the act or process of measuring depth of water or examining the bottom of a river, lake, etc., as with a sounding line. **2** an observation or measurement of atmospheric conditions, as made using a sonde. **3** (*often pl*) measurements taken by sounding. **4** (*pl*) a place where a sounding line will reach the bottom, esp. less than 100 fathoms in depth.

sounding board *n* **1** Also called: **soundboard**. a thin wooden board in a violin, piano, etc., serving to amplify the vibrations produced by the strings passing across it. **2** Also called: **soundboard**. a thin screen suspended over a pulpit, stage, etc., to reflect sound towards an audience. **3** a person, group, experiment, etc., used to test a new idea, policy, etc.

sounding line *n* a line marked off to indicate its length and having a **sounding lead** at one end. It is dropped over the side of a vessel to determine the depth of the water.

soundless ('saundlıs) *adj* extremely still or silent.
▶ 'soundlessness *n*

sound out *vb* (*tr, adv*) to question (someone) in order to discover (opinions, facts, etc.).

soundpost ('saund,pəust) *n Music.* a small wooden post in guitars, violins, etc., that joins the front to the back and helps support the bridge.

soundproof ('saund,pruːf) *adj* **1** not penetrable by sound. ◆ *vb* **2** (*tr*) to render soundproof.

sound spectrograph *n* an electronic instrument that produces a record (**sound spectrogram**) of the frequencies and intensities of the components of a sound.

sound system *n* **1** any system of sounds, as in the speech of a language. **2** integrated equipment for producing amplified sound, as in a hi-fi or mobile disco, or as a public-address system on stage.

soundtrack ('saund,træk) *n* **1** the recorded sound accompaniment to a film. **2** a narrow strip along the side of a spool of film, which carries the sound accompaniment.

sound wave *n* a wave that propagates sound.

Souness ★ ('suːnɪs) *n* **Graeme.** born 1953, Scottish football player and manager.

soup (suːp) *n* **1** a liquid food made by boiling or simmering meat, fish, vegetables, etc. **2** *Inf.* a photographic developer. **3** *Inf.* anything resembling soup, esp. thick fog. **4** a slang name for **nitroglycerine. 5 in the soup.** *Sl.* in trouble or difficulties. [C17: from OF *soupe*, from LL *suppa*, of Gmc origin]
  ▶ **'soupy** *adj*

soupçon *French.* (supsɔ̃) *n* a slight amount; dash. [C18: from F, ult. from L *suspicio* SUSPICION]

Souphanouvong ★ (ˌsuːfænuːˈvɒŋ) *n* **Prince.** 1902–95, Laotian statesman; president of Laos (1975–86).

soup kitchen *n* **1** a place or mobile stall where food and drink, esp. soup, is served to destitute people. **2** *Mil.* a mobile kitchen.

soup plate *n* a deep plate with a wide rim, used esp. for drinking soup.

soup up *vb* (*tr, adv*) *Sl.* to modify the engine of (a car or motorcycle) in order to increase its power. Also: **hot up,** (esp. US and Canad.) **hop up.**

sour ('saʊə) *adj* **1** having or denoting a sharp biting taste like that of lemon juice or vinegar. **2** made acid or bad, as in the case of milk, by the action of microorganisms. **3** having a rancid or unwholesome smell. **4** (of a person's temperament) sullen, morose, or disagreeable. **5** (esp. of the weather) harsh and unpleasant. **6** disagreeable; distasteful: *a sour experience.* **7** (of land, etc.) lacking in fertility, esp. due to excessive acidity. **8** (of petrol, gas, etc.) containing a relatively large amount of sulphur compounds. **9 go** *or* **turn sour.** to become unfavourable or inharmonious: *his marriage went sour.* ◆ *n* **10** something sour. **11** *Chiefly US.* an iced drink usually made with spirits, lemon juice, and ice: *a whiskey sour.* **12** an acid used in bleaching clothes or in curing skins. ◆ *vb* **13** to make or become sour. [OE *sūr*]
  ▶ **'sourish** *adj* ▶ **'sourly** *adv* ▶ **'sourness** *n*

Sour ★ (sʊə) *n* a variant spelling of **Sur.**

source (sɔːs) *n* **1** the point or place from which something originates. **2a** a spring that forms the starting point of a stream. **2b** the area where the headwaters of a river rise. **3** a person, group, etc., that creates, issues, or originates something: *the source of a complaint.* **4a** any person, book, organization, etc., from which information, evidence, etc., is obtained. **4b** (*as modifier*): *source material.* **5** anything, such as a story or work of art, that provides a model or inspiration for a later work. **6 at source.** at the point of origin. ◆ *vb* **sources, sourcing, sourced.** (*tr*) **7** to establish an originator or source of (a product, etc.). **8** (foll. by *from*) to originate from. [C14: from OF *sors*, from *sourdre* to spring forth, from L *surgere* to rise]

source program *n* an original computer program written by a programmer that is converted into the equivalent object program, written in machine language.

sour cherry *n* **1** a Eurasian tree with white flowers: cultivated for its tart red fruits. **2** the fruit.

sour cream *n* cream soured by lactic acid bacteria, used in making salads, dips, etc.

sourdough ('saʊəˌdəʊ) *Dialect.* ◆ *adj* **1** (of bread) made with fermented dough used as leaven. ◆ *n* **2** (in the Western US, Canada, and Alaska) an old-time prospector or pioneer.

sour gourd *n* **1** a large tree of N Australia, having gourdlike fruit. **2** the acid-tasting fruit. **3** the fruit of the baobab tree.

sour grapes *n* (*functioning as sing*) the attitude of affecting to despise something because one cannot have it oneself.

sourpuss ('saʊəˌpʊs) *n Inf.* a person who is habitually gloomy or sullen.

sourveld ('saʊəˌfelt) *n* (in South Africa) a type of grazing characterized by long coarse grass. [from Afrik. *suur* sour + *veld* grassland]

Sousa ★ ('suːzə) *n* **John Philip.** 1854–1932, US composer of military marches, such as *The Stars and Stripes Forever* (1897).

sousaphone ('suːzəˌfəʊn) *n* a large tuba that encircles the player's body and has a bell facing forwards. [C20: after J. P. SOUSA]
  ▶ **'sousa,phonist** *n*

souse (saʊs) *vb* **souses, sousing, soused. 1** to plunge (something) into water or other liquid. **2** to drench or be drenched. **3** (*tr*) to pour or dash (liquid) over (a person or thing). **4** to steep or cook (food) in a marinade. **5** (*tr*) *Sl.* to make drunk. ◆ *n* **6** the liquid used in pickling. **7** the act or process of sousing. **8** *Sl.* a drunkard. [C14: from OF *sous*, of Gmc origin]

Sousse (suːs), **Susa,** *or* **Susah** ★ *n* a port in E Tunisia, on the Mediterranean: founded by the Phoenicians in the 9th century B.C. Pop.: 125 000 (1994). Ancient name: **Hadrumetum** (ˌhædrəˈmiːtəm).

soutane (suːˈtæn) *n RC Church.* a priest's cassock. [C19: from F, from OIt. *sottana*, from Med. L *subtanus* (adj) (worn) beneath, from L *subtus* below]

souterrain ('suːtəˌreɪn) *n Archaeol.* an underground chamber or passage. [C18: from F]

south (saʊθ) *n* **1** one of the four cardinal points of the compass, at 180° from north and 90° clockwise from east and anticlockwise from west. **2** the direction along a meridian towards the South Pole. **3 the south.** (*often cap.*) any area lying in or towards the south. **4** (*usually cap.*) *Cards.* the player or position corresponding to south on the compass. ◆ *adj* **5** in, towards, or facing the south. **6** (esp. of the wind) from the south. ◆ *adv* **7** in, to, or towards the south. [OE *sūth*]

South (saʊθ) *n* **the. 1** the southern part of England, generally regarded as lying to the south of an imaginary line between the Wash and the Severn. **2** (in the US) **2a** the states south of the Mason-Dixon Line that formed the Confederacy during the Civil War. **2b** the Confederacy itself. **3** the countries of the world that are not economically and technically advanced. ◆ *adj* **4** of or denoting the southern part of a specified country, area, etc.

South Africa ★ *n* **Republic of.** a republic occupying the southernmost part of the African continent: the Dutch Cape Colony (1652) was acquired by Britain in 1806 and British victory in the Boer War resulted in the formation of the Union of South Africa in 1910, which became a republic in 1961; implementation of the apartheid system began in 1948 and was abolished, following an intense civil rights campaign, in 1993 with multiracial elections held in 1994; a member of the Commonwealth, it withdrew in 1961 because of opposition to apartheid but was re-admitted in 1994: mainly plateau with mountains in the south and east. Mineral production includes gold, diamonds, coal, and copper. Official languages: Afrikaans; English; Ndebele, Pedi; South Sotho; Swazi; Tsonga; Tswana; Venda; Xhosa; Zulu. Religion: chiefly Christian. Currency: rand. Capitals: Cape Town (legislative), Pretoria (administrative), Bloemfontein (judicial). Pop.: 42 446 000 (1997). Area: 1 221 044 sq. km (471 445 sq. miles). Former name (1910–61): **Union of South Africa.**
  ▶ **South African** *adj, n*

South America ★ *n* the fourth largest of the continents, bordering on the Caribbean in the north, the Pacific in the west, and the Atlantic in the east and joined to Central America by the Isthmus of Panama. It is dominated by the Andes Mountains, which extend over 7250 km (4500 miles) and include many volcanoes; ranges from dense tropical jungle, desert, and temperate plains to the cold wet windswept region of Tierra del Fuego. It comprises chiefly developing countries undergoing great changes. Pop.: 317 846 000 (1996). Area: 17 816 600 sq. km (6 879 000 sq. miles).
  ▶ **South American** *adj, n*

Southampton ★ (saʊθˈæmptən, -ˈhæmp-) *n* **1** a port in S England, in Hampshire on **Southampton Water** (an inlet of the English Channel): chief English passenger port; university (1952); shipyards and oil refinery. Pop.: 210 138 (1991). **2** a unitary authority in S England, in

---

★ people and places

Hampshire. Pop.: 211 700 (1994 est.). Area: 49 sq. km (19 sq. miles).

Southampton Island ★ *n* an island in N Canada, in the Northwest Territories at the entrance to Hudson Bay: inhabited chiefly by Inuit. Area: 49 470 sq. km (19 100 sq. miles).

South Arabia ★ *n* **Federation of.** the former name (1959–67) of **South Yemen** (excluding Aden).
▶ **South Arabian** *adj, n*

South Australia ★ *n* a state of S central Australia, on the Great Australian Bight: generally arid, with the Great Victoria Desert in the west central part, the Lake Eyre basin in the northeast, and the Flinders Ranges, Murray River basin, and salt lakes in the southeast. Capital: Adelaide. Pop.: 1 477 700 (1996 est.). Area: 984 395 sq. km (380 070 sq. miles).
▶ **South Australian** *adj, n*

South Bend ★ *n* a city in the US, N Indiana: university (1842). Pop.: 105 092 (1994 est.).

southbound ('sauθ,baund) *adj* going or leading towards the south.

south by east *n* **1** one point on the compass east of south. ◆ *adj, adv* **2** in, from, or towards this direction.

south by west *n* **1** one point on the compass west of south. ◆ *adj, adv* **2** in, from, or towards this direction.

South Carolina ★ *n* a state of the southeastern US, on the Atlantic: the first state to secede from the Union in 1860; consists largely of low-lying coastal plains, rising in the northwest to the Blue Ridge Mountains; the largest US textile producer. Capital: Columbia. Pop.: 3 698 746 (1996 est.). Area: 78 282 sq. km (30 225 sq. miles). Abbrev. (and zip code): **SC**
▶ **South Carolinian** *adj, n*

South China Sea ★ *n* part of the Pacific surrounded by SE China, Vietnam, the Malay Peninsula, Borneo, and the Philippines.

Southcott ★ ('sauθkɒt) *n* **Joanna.** 1750–1814, British religious fanatic, who claimed that she would give birth to the second Messiah.

South Dakota ★ *n* a state of the western US: lies mostly in the Great Plains; the chief US producer of gold and beryl. Capital: Pierre. Pop.: 732 405 (1996 est.). Area: 196 723 sq. km (75 955 sq. miles). Abbrevs.: **S. Dak.** or (with zip code) **SD**
▶ **South Dakotan** *adj, n*

Southdown ('sauθ,daun) *n* an English breed of sheep with short wool and a greyish-brown face and legs. [C18: so called because it was originally bred on the SOUTH DOWNS]

South Downs ★ *pl n* a range of low hills in S England, extending from E Hampshire to East Sussex.

southeast (,sauθ'i:st; *Naut.* ,sau'i:st) *n* **1** the point of the compass or the direction midway between south and east. **2** (*often cap.*; usually preceded by *the*) any area lying in or towards this direction. ◆ *adj also* **southeastern. 3** (*sometimes cap.*) of or denoting the southeastern part of a specified country, area, etc. **4** in, towards, or facing the southeast. **5** (esp. of the wind) from the southeast. ◆ *adv* **6** in, to, or towards the southeast.
▶ ,south'easternmost *adj*

Southeast ★ (,sauθ'i:st) *n* (usually preceded by *the*) the southeastern part of Britain, esp. the London area.

Southeast Asia ★ *n* a region including Brunei, Cambodia, Indonesia, Laos, Malaysia, Myanmar, the Philippines, Thailand, and Vietnam.
▶ **Southeast Asian** *adj, n*

southeast by east *n* **1** one point on the compass north of southeast. ◆ *adj, adv* **2** in, from, or towards this direction.

southeast by south *n* **1** one point on the compass south of southeast. ◆ *adj, adv* **2** in, from, or towards this direction.

southeaster (,sauθ'i:stə; *Naut.* ,sau'i:stə) *n* a strong wind or storm from the southeast.

southeasterly (,sauθ'i:stəlɪ; *Naut.* ,sau'i:stəlɪ) *adj, adv* **1** in, towards, or (esp. of the wind) from the southeast.

◆ *n, pl* **southeasterlies. 2** a strong wind or storm from the southeast.

southeastward (,sauθ'i:stwəd; *Naut.* ,sau'i:stwəd) *adj* **1** towards or (esp. of a wind) from the southeast. ◆ *n* **2** a direction towards or area in the southeast. ◆ *adv* **3** Also: **southeastwards.** towards the southeast.

Southend-on-Sea ★ (,sauθ'end-) *n* a town and unitary authority in SE England, in SE Essex on the Thames estuary: one of England's largest resorts, extending for about 11 km (7 miles) along the coast. Pop.: 158 517 (1991).

souther ('sauðə) *n* a strong wind or storm from the south.

southerly ('sʌðəlɪ) *adj* **1** of or situated in the south. ◆ *adv, adj* **2** towards the south. **3** from the south. ◆ *n, pl* **southerlies. 4** a wind from the south.
▶ 'southerliness *n*

southern ('sʌðən) *adj* **1** in or towards the south. **2** (of a wind, etc.) coming from the south. **3** native to or inhabiting the south.
▶ 'southern,most *adj*

Southern ('sʌðən) *adj* of, relating to, or characteristic of the south of a particular region or country.

Southern Alps ★ *pl n* a mountain range in New Zealand, on South Island: the highest range in Australasia. Highest peak: Mount Cook, 3764 m (12 349 ft).

Southern Cross *n* a small constellation in the S hemisphere whose four brightest stars form a cross. It is represented on the national flags of Australia and New Zealand.

Southerner ('sʌðənə) *n* (*sometimes not cap.*) a native or inhabitant of the south of any specified region, esp. the South of England or the Southern states of the US.

southern hemisphere *n* (*often caps.*) that half of the earth lying south of the equator.

Southern Ireland ★ *n* See **Ireland**[1] (sense 2).

southern lights *pl n* another name for **aurora australis.**

Southern Ocean ★ *n* another name for the **Antarctic Ocean.**

Southern Rhodesia ★ *n* the former name (until 1964) of **Zimbabwe.**
▶ **Southern Rhodesian** *adj, n*

Southern Uplands ★ *pl n* a hilly region extending across S Scotland: includes the Lowther, Moorfoot, and Lammermuir hills.

Southey ★ ('sauðɪ, 'sʌðɪ) *n* **Robert.** 1774–1843, British poet; poet laureate (1813–43).

South Georgia ★ *n* an island in the S Atlantic, about 1300 km (800 miles) southeast of the Falkland Islands; a United Kingdom overseas territory. Area: 3755 sq. km (1450 sq. miles).
▶ **South Georgian** *adj*

South Glamorgan ★ *n* a former county of S Wales, created in 1974 and replaced by two county boroughs in 1996.

South Gloucestershire ★ *n* a unitary authority of SW England, in Gloucestershire. Pop.: 220 000 (1996 est.). Area: 510 sq. km (197 sq. miles).

South Holland ★ *n* a province of the SW Netherlands, on the North Sea: lying mostly below sea level, it has a coastal strip of dunes and is drained chiefly by distributaries of the Rhine, with large areas of reclaimed land; the most densely populated province in the country, intensively cultivated and industrialized. Capital: The Hague. Pop.: 3 325 064 (1995 est.). Area: 3196 sq. km (1234 sq. miles). Dutch name: **Zuidholland.**

southing ('sauðɪŋ) *n* **1** *Navigation.* movement, deviation, or distance covered in a southerly direction. **2** *Astron.* a south or negative declination.

South Island ★ *n* **the.** the largest island of New Zealand, separated from the North Island by Cook Strait. Pop.: 926 350 (1996). Area: 153 947 sq. km (59 439 sq. miles).

South Korea ★ *n* a republic in NE Asia: established as a republic in 1948; invaded by North Korea and Chinese Communists in 1950 but division remained unchanged at the end of the war (1953); includes over 3000 islands; rapid industrialization. Language: Korean. Religions:

Buddhist, Christian, Confucianist, Shamanist, and Chondokyo. Currency: won. Capital: Seoul. Pop.: 45 232 000 (1996). Area: 98 477 sq. km (38 022 sq. miles). Korean name: **Hanguk**.
▶ **South Korean** *adj, n*

South Lanarkshire ★ *n* a council area of S Scotland. Administrative centre: Hamilton. Pop.: 307 450 (1996 est.). Area: 1771 sq. km (684 sq. miles).

South Orkney Islands ★ *pl n* a group of islands in the S Atlantic, southeast of Cape Horn: formerly a dependency of the Falkland Islands; part of British Antarctic Territory since 1962. Area: 621 sq. km (240 sq. miles).

South Ossetia ★ (ə'siːʃən) *n* an administrative division of Georgia, on the S slopes of the Caucasus Mountains. Capital: Tskhinvali. Pop.: 99 800 (1990). Area: 3900 sq. km (1500 sq. miles). Official name: **Tskhinvali**.

southpaw ('sauθ,pɔː) *Inf.* ◆ *n* **1** a left-handed boxer. **2** any left-handed person. ◆ *adj* **3** of or relating to a southpaw.

South Pole ★ *n* **1** the southernmost point on the earth's axis, at the latitude of 90°S. **2** *Astron.* the point of intersection of the earth's extended axis and the southern half of the celestial sphere. **3** (*usually not caps.*) the south-seeking pole of a freely suspended magnet.

Southport ★ ('sauθ,pɔːt) *n* a town and resort in NW England, in Merseyside on the Irish Sea. Pop.: 90 959 (1991).

South Saskatchewan ★ *n* a river in S central Canada, rising in S Alberta and flowing east and northeast to join the North Saskatchewan River, forming the Saskatchewan River. Length: 1392 km (865 miles).

South Sea Bubble *n Brit. history.* the financial crash that occurred in 1720 after the **South Sea Company** had taken over the national debt in return for a monopoly of trade with the South Seas, causing feverish speculation in their stocks.

South Sea Islands ★ *pl n* the islands in the S Pacific.

South Seas ★ *pl n* the seas south of the equator.

South Shetland Islands ★ *pl n* a group of islands in the S Atlantic, north of the Antarctic Peninsula: formerly a dependency of the Falkland Islands; part of British Antarctic Territory since 1962. Area: 4662 sq. km (1800 sq. miles).

South Shields ★ *n* a port in NE England, in Tyne and Wear on the Tyne estuary opposite North Shields. Pop.: 83 704 (1991).

south-southeast *n* **1** the point on the compass or the direction midway between southeast and south. ◆ *adj, adv* **2** in, from, or towards this direction.

south-southwest *n* **1** the point on the compass or the direction midway between south and southwest. ◆ *adj, adv* **2** in, from, or towards this direction.

South Tyneside ★ *n* a unitary authority of NE England, in Tyne and Wear. Pop.: 156 700 (1994 est.). Area: 64 sq. km (25 sq. miles).

South Tyrol *or* **Tirol** ★ *n* a former part of the Austrian state of Tyrol: ceded to Italy in 1919, becoming the Bolzano and Trento provinces of the Trentino-Alto Adige Autonomous Region. Area: 14 037 sq. km (5420 sq. miles).

South Vietnam ★ *n* a former republic (1955–76) occupying the S of present-day Vietnam, on the South China Sea and the Gulf of Siam.
▶ **South Vietnamese** *adj, n*

southward ('sauθwəd; *Naut.* 'sʌðəd) *adj* **1** situated, directed, or moving towards the south. ◆ *n* **2** the southward part, direction, etc. ◆ *adv* **3** Also: **southwards**. towards the south.

Southwark ★ ('sʌðək) *n* a borough of S central Greater London, on the River Thames: site of the Globe Theatre; docks and warehouses. Pop.: 228 800 (1994 est.). Area: 29 sq. km (11 sq. miles).

Southwell ★ ('sauθwel) *n* **Saint Robert.** ?1561–95, English poet and Roman Catholic martyr, who was imprisoned, tortured, and executed for his Jesuit activities. His best known poem is "The Burning Babe".

southwest (,sauθ'west; *Naut.* ,sau'west) *n* **1** the point of the compass or the direction midway between west and

south. **2** (*often cap.*; usually preceded by *the*) any area lying in or towards this direction. ◆ *adj also* **southwestern. 3** (*sometimes cap.*) of or denoting the southwestern part of a specified country, area, etc.: *southwest Italy.* **4** in or towards the southwest. **5** (esp. of the wind) from the southwest. ◆ *adv* **6** in, to, or towards the southwest.
▶ ,**south'westernmost** *adj*

Southwest ★ (,sauθ'west) *n* (usually preceded by *the*) the southwestern part of Britain, esp. Cornwall, Devon, and Somerset.

South West Africa ★ *n* another name for **Namibia.**

southwest by south *n* **1** one point on the compass south of southwest. ◆ *adj, adv* **2** in, from, or towards this direction.

southwest by west *n* **1** one point on the compass north of southwest. ◆ *adj, adv* **2** in, from, or towards this direction.

southwester (,sauθ'westə; *Naut.* ,sau'westə) *n* a strong wind or storm from the southwest.

southwesterly (,sauθ'westəlɪ; *Naut.* ,sau'westəlɪ) *adj, adv* **1** in, towards, or (esp. of a wind) from the southwest. ◆ *n, pl* **southwesterlies. 2** a wind or storm from the southwest.

southwestward (,sauθ'westwəd; *Naut.* ,sau'westwəd) *adj* **1** from or towards the southwest. ◆ *adv* **2** Also: **southwestwards.** towards the southwest. ◆ *n* **3** a direction towards or area in the southwest.

South Yemen ★ *n* a former republic (1967–90) in SW Arabia, on the Gulf of Aden: now part of Yemen. Official name: **People's Democratic Republic of Yemen.** Name from 1963 to 1967 (excluding Aden): Federation of **South Arabia.** See also **Yemen, North Yemen.**

South Yorkshire ★ *n* a metropolitan county of N England, administered since 1986 by the unitary authorities of Barnsley, Doncaster, Sheffield, and Rotherham. Area: 1560 sq. km (602 sq. miles).

Soutine ★ (*French* sutin) *n* **Chaim** ('xaɪɪm). 1893–1943, French expressionist painter, born in Russia.

souvenir (,suːvəˈnɪə, 'suːvə,nɪə) *n* **1** an object that recalls a certain place, occasion, or person; memento. **2** *Rare.* a thing recalled. ◆ *vb* **3** (*tr*) *Austral. & NZ. sl.* to steal or keep for one's own use; purloin. [C18: from F, from (*se*) *souvenir* to remember, from L *subvenīre* to come to mind]

sou'wester (sau'westə) *n* a waterproof hat having a very broad rim behind, worn esp. by seamen. [C19: a contraction of SOUTHWESTER]

sovereign ('sɒvrɪn) *n* **1** a person exercising supreme authority, esp. a monarch. **2** a former British gold coin worth one pound sterling. ◆ *adj* **3** supreme in rank or authority: *a sovereign lord.* **4** excellent or outstanding: *a sovereign remedy.* **5** of or relating to a sovereign. **6** independent of outside authority: *a sovereign state.* [C13: from OF *soverain*, from Vulgar L *superānus* (unattested), from L *super* above; also infl. by REIGN]
▶ **'sovereignly** *adv*

sovereignty ('sɒvrəntɪ) *n, pl* **sovereignties. 1** supreme and unrestricted power, as of a state. **2** the position, dominion, or authority of a sovereign. **3** an independent state.

Sovetsk ★ (*Russian* sa'vjetsk) *n* a town in W Russia, in the Kaliningrad Region on the Neman River: scene of the signing of the treaty (1807) between Napoleon I and Tsar Alexander I; passed from East Prussia to the Soviet Union in 1945 and to Russia in 1991. Former name (until 1945): **Tilsit.**

soviet ('səuvɪət, 'sɒv-) *n* **1** (in the former Soviet Union) an elected government council at the local, regional, and national levels, culminating in the Supreme Soviet. ◆ *adj* **2** of or relating to a soviet. [C20: from Russian *sovyet* council, from ORussian *sŭvĕtŭ*]
▶ **'sovie,tism** *n*

Soviet ('səuvɪət, 'sɒv-) *adj* of or relating to the former Soviet Union, its people, or its government.

Soviet Central Asia ★ *n* (formerly) the region of the Soviet Union now occupied by Kazakhstan, Kyrgyzstan, Tajikistan, Turkmenistan, and Uzbekistan. Also called: **Russian Turkestan, West Turkestan.**

★ people and places

sovietize or **sovietise** ('səʊvɪɪˌtaɪz, 'sɒv-) vb **sovietizes, sovietizing, sovietized** or **sovietises, sovietising, sovietised.** (tr) (often cap.) **1** to bring (a country, person, etc.) under Soviet control or influence. **2** to cause (a country) to conform to the Soviet model in its social, political, and economic structure.
  ▸ ˌsovieti'zation or ˌsovieti'sation n

Soviet Russia ★ n (formerly) another name for the **Russian Soviet Federative Socialist Republic** or the **Soviet Union.**

Soviets ('səʊvɪəts, 'sɒv-) pl n the people or government of the former Soviet Union.

Soviet Union ★ n a former federal republic in E Europe and central and N Asia: established in 1922 as a Communist state, following the revolution of 1917; dissolved at the end of 1991, following the collapse of Communist Party rule earlier in that year and the declarations of independence by many of the constituent republics. Area: 22 402 202 sq. km (8 649 489 sq. miles). Official name: **Union of Soviet Socialist Republics.** Also called: **Russia, Soviet Russia.** Abbrev.: **USSR.**

Soviet Zone ★ n that part of Germany occupied by the Soviet forces in 1945–49: transformed into the German Democratic Republic in 1949–50. Also called: **Russian Zone.**

sow[1] (səʊ) vb **sows, sowing, sowed; sown** or **sowed. 1** to scatter or place (seed, a crop, etc.) in or on (a piece of ground, field, etc.) so that it may grow: to sow wheat; to sow a strip of land. **2** (tr) to implant or introduce: to sow a doubt in someone's mind. [OE sāwan]
  ▸ 'sower n

sow[2] (saʊ) n **1** a female adult pig. **2** the female of certain other animals, such as the mink. **3** Metallurgy. **3a** the channels for leading molten metal to the moulds in casting pig iron. **3b** iron that has solidified in these channels. [OE sugu]

Soweto ★ (sə'wɛtəʊ, -'weɪtəʊ) n a contiguous group of Black African townships southwest of Johannesburg, South Africa: the largest purely Black African urban settlement in southern Africa: scene of riots (1976) following protests against the use of Afrikaans in schools for Black African children. Area: 62 sq. km (24 sq. miles). Pop.: 596 632 (1991). [C20: from so(uth) we(st) to(wnship)]

sown (səʊn) vb a past participle of **sow**[1].

sow thistle (saʊ) n any of various plants of an Old World genus, having milky juice, prickly leaves, and heads of yellow flowers.

soya bean ('sɔɪə) or US & Canad. **soybean** ('sɔɪˌbiːn) n **1** an Asian bean plant cultivated for its nutritious seeds, for forage, and to improve the soil. **2** the seed, used as food, forage, and as the source of an oil. [C17 soya, via Du. from Japanese shōyu, from Chinese chiang yu, from chiang paste + yu sauce]

Soyinka ★ (sɔ'jɪŋkə) n **Wole** ('wɔːle). born 1934, Nigerian writer. His works include the play Kongi's Harvest (1966), the novel The Interpreters (1965), and the essays collected in The Burden of Memory, the Muse of Forgiveness (1999). Nobel prize for literature 1986.

soy sauce (sɔɪ) n a salty dark brown sauce made from fermented soya beans, used esp. in Chinese cookery. Also called: **soya sauce.**

sozzled ('sɒzəld) adj an informal word for **drunk.** [C19: ?from obs. sozzle stupor]

SP abbrev. for starting price.

sp. abbrev. for: **1** special. **2** (pl **spp.**) species. **3** specific. **4** specimen. **5** spelling.

Sp. abbrev. for: **1** Spain. **2** Spaniard. **3** Spanish.

spa (spɑː) n a mineral spring or a place or resort where such a spring is found. [C17: after SPA]

Spa ★ (spɑː) n a town in E Belgium, in Liège province: a resort with medicinal mineral springs (discovered in the 14th century). Pop.: 10 140 (1991).

Spaak ★ (spɑːk) n **Paul Henri** (pɔl ɑ̃ri). 1899–1972, Belgian statesman, socialist prime minister (1937–38); president of the consultative assembly of the Council of Europe (1949–51) and secretary-general of NATO (1957–61).

space (speɪs) n **1** the unlimited three-dimensional ex-

panse in which all material objects are located. Related adj: **spatial. 2** an interval of distance or time between two points, objects, or events. **3** a blank portion or area. **4a** unoccupied area or room: there is no space for a table. **4b** (in combination): space-saving. Related adj: **spacious. 5a** the region beyond the earth's atmosphere containing other planets, stars, galaxies, etc.; universe. **5b** (as modifier): a space probe. **6** a seat or place, as on a train, aircraft, etc. **7** Printing. a piece of metal, less than type-high, used to separate letters or words. **8** Music. any of the gaps between the lines that make up the staff. **9** Also called: **spacing.** Telegraphy. the period of time that separates characters in Morse code. ◆ vb **spaces, spacing, spaced.** (tr) **10** to place or arrange at intervals or with spaces between. **11** to divide into or by spaces: to space one's time evenly. **12** Printing. to separate (letters, words, or lines) by the insertion of spaces. [C13: from OF espace, from L spatium]
  ▸ 'spacer n

space age n **1** the period in which the exploration of space has become possible. ◆ adj **space-age. 2** (usually prenominal) futuristic or ultramodern.

space-bar n a horizontal bar on a typewriter that is depressed in order to leave a space between words, letters, etc.

space capsule n a vehicle, sometimes carrying people or animals, designed to obtain scientific information from space, planets, etc., and be recovered on returning to earth.

spacecraft ('speɪsˌkrɑːft) n a manned or unmanned vehicle designed to orbit the earth or travel to celestial objects.

spaced out adj Sl. intoxicated through or as if through taking a drug. Often shortened to **spaced.**

space heater n a heater used to warm the air in an enclosed area, such as a room.

Space Invaders n Trademark. a video or computer game, the object of which is to destroy attacking alien spacecraft.

spaceman ('speɪsˌmæn) or (fem) **spacewoman** n, pl **spacemen** or (fem) **spacewomen.** a person who travels in outer space.

space platform n another name for **space station.**

spaceport ('speɪsˌpɔːt) n a base equipped to launch, maintain, and test spacecraft.

space probe n a vehicle, such as a satellite, equipped to obtain scientific information, normally transmitted back to earth by radio, about a planet, conditions in space, etc.

spaceship ('speɪsˌʃɪp) n a manned spacecraft.

space shuttle n any of a series of reusable US space vehicles (Columbia, Challenger (exploded 1986), Discovery, Atlantis, Endeavor) that can be launched into earth orbit transporting astronauts and equipment for a period of observation, research, etc., before re-entry and an unpowered landing on a runway; the first operational flight was in 1982.

space station n any large manned artificial satellite designed to orbit the earth during a long period of time thus providing a base for scientific research in space and a construction site, launch pad, and docking arrangements for spacecraft.

spacesuit ('speɪsˌsuːt, -ˌsjuːt) n a sealed and pressurized suit worn by astronauts providing an artificial atmosphere, acceptable temperature, radiocommunication link, and protection from radiation.

space-time or **space-time continuum** n Physics. the four-dimensional continuum having three spatial coordinates and one time coordinate that together completely specify the location of a particle or an event.

spacewalk ('speɪsˌwɔːk) n **1** the act or an instance of floating and manoeuvring in space, outside but attached by a lifeline to a spacecraft. Technical name: **extravehicular activity.** ◆ vb **2** (intr) to engage in this activity.

spacey ('speɪsɪ) adj **spacier, spaciest.** Sl. vague and dreamy, as if under the influence of drugs. [C20: SPACE + -EY]

spacial ('speɪʃəl) *adj* a variant spelling of **spatial**.

spacing ('speɪsɪŋ) *n* **1** the arrangement of letters, words, spaces, etc., on a page. **2** the arrangement of objects in a space.

spacious ('speɪʃəs) *adj* having a large capacity or area.
▶ **'spaciously** *adv* ▶ **'spaciousness** *n*

spade[1] (speɪd) *n* **1** a tool for digging, typically consisting of a flat rectangular steel blade attached to a long wooden handle. **2** something resembling a spade. **3** a cutting tool for stripping the blubber from a whale or skin from a carcass. **4 call a spade a spade.** to speak plainly and frankly. ◆ *vb* **spades, spading, spaded. 5** (*tr*) to use a spade on. [OE *spadu*]
▶ **'spader** *n*

spade[2] (speɪd) *n* **1a** the black symbol on a playing card resembling a heart-shaped leaf with a stem. **1b** a card with one or more of these symbols or (*when pl*) the suit of cards so marked, usually the highest ranking of the four. **2** a derogatory word for a **Black**[1]. **3 in spades.** *Inf.* in an extreme or emphatic way. [C16: from It. *spada* sword, used as an emblem on playing cards, from L *spatha*, from Gk *spathē* blade]

spadework ('speɪd,wɜːk) *n* dull or routine preparatory work.

spadix ('speɪdɪks) *n, pl* **spadices** (speɪ'daɪsiːz). a spike of small flowers on a fleshy stem, the whole being enclosed in a spathe. [C18: from L: pulled-off branch of a palm, with its fruit, from Gk: torn-off frond]

spaghetti (spə'gɛtɪ) *n* pasta in the form of long strings. [C19: from It.: little cords, from *spago* a cord]

spaghetti junction *n* a junction, usually between motorways, in which there are a large number of intersecting roads used by a large volume of high-speed traffic. [C20: from the nickname given to the Gravelly Hill Interchange, Birmingham, where the M6, A38M, A38, and A5127 intersect]

spaghetti western *n* a cowboy film made in Europe, esp. by an Italian director.

spahi *or* **spahee** ('spɑːhiː, 'spɑːiː) *n, pl* **spahis** *or* **spahees. 1** (formerly) an irregular cavalryman in the Turkish army. **2** (formerly) a member of a body of native Algerian cavalry in the French army. [C16: from OF, from Turkish *sipahi*, from Persian *sipāhī* soldier]

Spain ★ (speɪn) *n* a kingdom of SW Europe, occupying the Iberian peninsula between the Mediterranean and the Atlantic: a leading European power in the 16th century, with many overseas possessions, esp. in the New World; became a republic in 1931; under the fascist dictatorship of Franco following the Civil War (1936–39) until his death in 1975; a member of the European Union. It consists chiefly of a central plateau (the Meseta), with the Pyrenees and the Cantabrian Mountains in the north and the Sierra Nevada in the south. Official languages: Castilian Spanish, with Catalan, Galician, and Basque official regional languages. Religion: Roman Catholic. Currency: peseta and euro. Capital: Madrid. Pop.: 39 323 000 (1997). Area: 504 748 sq. km (194 883 sq. miles). Spanish name: **España**.

spake (speɪk) *vb Arch.* a past tense of **speak**.

Spalato ★ ('spɑːlato) *n* the Italian name for **Split**.

Spalding ★ ('spɔːldɪŋ) *n* a town in E England, in S Lincolnshire: noted for its bulbfields. Pop.: 18 731 (1991).

spam (spæm) *vb* **spams, spamming, spammed.** *Computing sl.* to send unsolicited electronic mail simultaneously to a number of newsgroups on the Internet. [C20: from the repeated use of the word *Spam* in a popular sketch from the Brit. television show *Monty Python's Flying Circus*, first broadcast in 1969]

Spam (spæm) *n Trademark.* a kind of tinned luncheon meat, made largely from pork.

span[1] (spæn) *n* **1** the interval, space, or distance between two points, such as the ends of a bridge or arch. **2** the complete duration or extent: *the span of his life.* **3** *Psychol.* the amount of material that can be processed in a single

mental act: *span of attention.* **4** short for **wingspan. 5** a unit of length based on the width of an expanded hand, usually taken as nine inches. ◆ *vb* **spans, spanning, spanned.** (*tr*) **6** to stretch or extend across, over, or around. **7** to provide with something that spans: *to span a river with a bridge.* **8** to measure or cover, esp. with the extended hand. [OE *spann*]

span[2] (spæn) *n* a team of horses or oxen, esp. two matched animals. [C16 (in the sense: yoke): from MDu.: something stretched, from *spannen* to stretch]

span[3] (spæn) *vb Arch. or dialect.* a past tense of **spin**.

Span. *abbrev. for* Spanish.

spandrel *or* **spandril** ('spændrəl) *n Archit.* **1** an approximately triangular surface bounded by the outer curve of an arch and the adjacent wall. **2** the surface area between two adjacent arches and the horizontal cornice above them. [C15 *spaundrell*, from Anglo-F *spaundre*, from OF *spandre* to spread]

spangle ('spæŋgʲl) *n* **1** a small thin piece of metal or other shiny material used as a decoration, esp. on clothes; sequin. **2** any glittering or shiny spot or object. ◆ *vb* **spangles, spangling, spangled. 3** (*intr*) to glitter or shine with or like spangles. **4** (*tr*) to cover with spangles. [C15: dim. of *spange*, ?from MDu.: clasp]
▶ **'spangly** *adj*

Spaniard ('spænjəd) *n* a native or inhabitant of Spain.

spaniel ('spænjəl) *n* **1** any of several breeds of gundog with long drooping ears and a silky coat. **2** an obsequiously devoted person. [C14: from OF *espaigneul* Spanish (dog), from OProvençal *espanhol*, ult. from L *Hispāniolus* Spanish]

Spanish ('spænɪʃ) *n* **1** the official language of Spain, Mexico, and most countries of South and Central America except Brazil. Spanish is an Indo-European language belonging to the Romance group. **2 the Spanish.** (*functioning as pl*) the natives, citizens, or inhabitants of Spain. ◆ *adj* **3** of or relating to the Spanish language or its speakers. **4** of or relating to Spain or Spaniards.

Spanish America ★ *n* the parts of America colonized by Spaniards and now chiefly Spanish-speaking: includes most of South and Central America, Mexico, and much of the Caribbean.

Spanish-American *adj* **1** of or relating to any of the Spanish-speaking countries or peoples of the Americas. ◆ *n* **2** a native or inhabitant of Spanish America. **3** a Spanish-speaking person in the US.

Spanish customs *or* **practices** *pl n Inf.* irregular practices among a group of workers to gain increased financial allowances, reduced working hours, etc.

Spanish fly *n* **1** a European blister beetle, the dried body of which yields cantharides. **2** another name for **cantharides.**

Spanish Guinea ★ *n* the former name (until 1964) of **Equatorial Guinea.**

Spanish guitar *n* the classic form of the guitar; a six-stringed instrument with a waisted body and a central sound hole.

Spanish Main ★ *n* **1** the mainland of Spanish America, esp. the N coast of South America. **2** the Caribbean Sea, the S part of which in colonial times was the haunt of pirates.

Spanish Morocco ★ *n* a former Spanish colony on the N coast of Morocco: part of the kingdom of Morocco since 1956.
▶ **Spanish Moroccan** *adj*

Spanish moss *n* **1** an epiphytic plant growing in tropical and subtropical regions as long bluish-grey strands suspended from the branches of trees. **2** a tropical lichen growing as long trailing green threads from the branches of trees.

Spanish omelette *n* an omelette containing green peppers, onions, tomato, etc.

Spanish rice *n* rice cooked with tomatoes, onions, green peppers, etc.

Spanish Sahara ★ *n* the former name (until 1975) of **Western Sahara.**

Spanish West Africa ★ *n* a former overseas territory

★ people and places

of Spain in NW Africa: divided in 1958 into the overseas provinces of Ifni and Spanish Sahara.
▶ **Spanish West African** *adj, n*

spank[1] (spæŋk) *vb* **1** (*tr*) to slap with the open hand, esp. on the buttocks. ◆ *n* **2** one or a series of these slaps. [C18: prob. imit.]

spank[2] (spæŋk) *vb* (*intr*) to go at a quick and lively pace. [C19: back formation from SPANKING[2]]

spanker ('spæŋkə) *n* **1** a person or thing that spanks. **2** *Naut.* a fore-and-aft sail or a mast that is aftermost in a sailing vessel. **3** *Inf.* something outstandingly fine or large.

spanking[1] ('spæŋkɪŋ) *n* a series of spanks, usually as a punishment for children.

spanking[2] ('spæŋkɪŋ) *adj* (*prenominal*) **1** *Inf.* outstandingly fine, smart, large, etc. **2** quick and energetic. **3** (esp. of a breeze) fresh and brisk.

spanner ('spænə) *n* **1** a steel hand tool with jaws or a hole, designed to grip a nut or bolt head. **2 spanner in the works.** *Brit. inf.* an impediment or annoyance. [C17: from G, from *spannen* to stretch]

span roof *n* a roof consisting of two equal sloping sides.

spanspek ('spæn,spek) *n* *S. African.* the sweet melon. [C19: possibly from Afrik.: literally, Spanish bacon]

spar[1] (spɑː) *n* **1** any piece of nautical gear resembling a pole and used as a mast, boom, gaff, etc. **2** a principal supporting structural member of an aerofoil that runs from tip to tip or root to tip. [C13: from ON *sperra* beam]

spar[2] (spɑː) *vb* **spars, sparring, sparred.** (*intr*) **1** *Boxing & martial arts.* to box using light blows, as in training. **2** to dispute or argue. **3** (of gamecocks, etc.) to fight with the feet or spurs. ◆ *n* **4** an unaggressive fight. **5** an argument or wrangle. [OE, ? from SPUR]

spar[3] (spɑː) *n* any of various minerals, such as feldspar, that are light-coloured, crystalline, and easily cleavable. [C16: from MLow G *spar*]

sparaxis (spər'æksɪs) *n* a South African plant of the iris family, having lacerated spathes and showy flowers. [C19: NL, from Gk, from *sparassō* to tear]

spare (speə) *vb* **spares, sparing, spared.** **1** (*tr*) to refrain from killing, punishing, or injuring. **2** (*tr*) to release or relieve, as from pain, suffering, etc. **3** (*tr*) to refrain from using: *spare the rod, spoil the child.* **4** (*tr*) to be able to afford or give: *I can't spare the time.* **5** (*usually passive*) (esp. of Providence) to allow to survive: *I'll see you next year if we are spared.* **6** (*intr*) Now rare. to act or live frugally. **7 not spare oneself.** to exert oneself to the full. **8 to spare.** more than is required: *two minutes to spare.* ◆ *adj* **9** (*often immediately postpositive*) in excess of what is needed; additional. **10** able to be used when needed: *a spare part.* **11** (of a person) thin and lean. **12** scanty or meagre. **13** (*postpositive*) *Brit. sl.* upset, angry, or distracted (esp. in **go spare**). ◆ *n* **14** a duplicate kept as a replacement in case of damage or loss. **15** a spare tyre. **16** *Tenpin bowling.* **16a** the act of knocking down all the pins with the two bowls of a single frame. **16b** the score thus made. [OE *sparian* to refrain from injuring]
▶ 'sparely *adv* ▶ 'spareness *n* ▶ 'sparer *n*

spare-part surgery *n* surgical replacement of defective or damaged organs by transplant or insertion of artificial devices.

sparerib (,speə'rɪb) *n* a cut of pork ribs with most of the meat trimmed off.

spare tyre *n* **1** an additional tyre carried by a motor vehicle in case of puncture. **2** *Brit. sl.* a deposit of fat just above the waist.

sparing ('speərɪŋ) *adj* **1** (sometimes foll. by *of*) economical or frugal (with). **2** scanty; meagre. **3** merciful or lenient.
▶ 'sparingly *adv* ▶ 'sparingness *n*

spark[1] (spɑːk) *n* **1** a fiery particle thrown out or left by burning material or caused by the friction of two hard surfaces. **2a** a momentary flash of light accompanied by a sharp crackling noise, produced by a sudden electrical discharge through the air or some other insulating medium between two points. **2b** the electrical discharge itself. **2c** (*as modifier*): *a spark gap.* **3** anything that serves to animate or kindle. **4** a trace or hint: *a spark of interest.* **5** vivacity, enthusiasm, or humour. **6** a small piece of diamond, as used in cutting glass. ◆ *vb* **7** (*intr*) to give off sparks. **8** (*intr*) (of the sparking plug or ignition system of an internal-combustion engine) to produce a spark. **9** (*tr*; often foll. by *off*) to kindle or animate. ◆ See also **sparks**. [OE *spearca*]

spark[2] (spɑːk) *n* **1** *Rare.* a fashionable or gallant young man. **2 bright spark.** *Brit., usually ironic.* a person who appears clever or witty. [C16 (in the sense: beautiful or witty woman): ? of Scand. origin]
▶ 'sparkish *adj*

Spark ★ (spɑːk) *n* Dame **Muriel.** born 1918, British novelist; her works include *Memento Mori* (1959), *The Prime of Miss Jean Brodie* (1961), and *Reality and Dreams* (1996).

spark gap *n* the space between two electrodes across which a spark can jump.

sparking plug *n* a device screwed into the cylinder head of an internal-combustion engine to ignite the explosive mixture by means of an electric spark. Also called: **spark plug.**

sparkle ('spɑːk°l) *vb* **sparkles, sparkling, sparkled.** **1** to issue or reflect or cause to issue or reflect bright points of light. **2** (*intr*) (of wine, mineral water, etc.) to effervesce. **3** (*intr*) to be vivacious or witty. ◆ *n* **4** a point of light, spark, or gleam. **5** vivacity or wit. [C12 *sparklen*, frequentative of *sparken* to SPARK[1]]

sparkler ('spɑːklə) *n* **1** a type of firework that throws out sparks. **2** *Inf.* a sparkling gem.

sparkling wine *n* a wine made effervescent by carbon dioxide gas added artificially or produced naturally by secondary fermentation.

spark plug *n* another name for **sparking plug.**

sparks (spɑːks) *n* (*functioning as sing*) *Inf.* **1** an electrician. **2** a radio officer, esp. on a ship.

sparky ('spɑːkɪ) *adj* **sparkier, sparkiest.** lively, vivacious, spirited.

sparring partner ('spɑːrɪŋ) *n* **1** a person who practises with a boxer during training. **2** a person with whom one has friendly arguments.

sparrow ('spærəʊ) *n* **1** any of various weaverbirds, esp. the house sparrow, having a brown or grey plumage and feeding on seeds or insects. **2** *US & Canad.* any of various North American finches, such as the chipping sparrow, that have a dullish streaked plumage. ◆ See also **hedge sparrow, tree sparrow.** [OE *spearwa*]

sparrowgrass ('spærəʊ,grɑːs) *n* a dialect or popular name for **asparagus.**

sparrowhawk ('spærəʊ,hɔːk) *n* any of several small hawks of Eurasia and N Africa that prey on smaller birds.

sparrow hawk *n* a very small North American falcon, closely related to the kestrels.

sparse (spɑːs) *adj* scattered or scanty; not dense. [C18: from L *sparsus*, from *spargere* to scatter]
▶ 'sparsely *adv* ▶ 'sparseness *or* 'sparsity *n*

Sparta ★ ('spɑːtə) *n* an ancient Greek city in the S Peloponnese, famous for the discipline and military prowess of its citizens and for their austere way of life.

Spartacus ★ ('spɑːtəkəs) *n* died 71 B.C., Thracian slave, who led an unsuccessful revolt of gladiators against Rome (73–71 B.C.).

Spartan ('spɑːt°n) *adj* **1** of or relating to Sparta or its citizens. **2** (*sometimes not cap.*) very strict or austere: *a Spartan upbringing.* **3** (*sometimes not cap.*) possessing courage and resolve. ◆ *n* **4** a citizen of Sparta. **5** (*sometimes not cap.*) a disciplined or brave person.

spasm ('spæzəm) *n* **1** an involuntary muscular contraction, esp. one resulting in cramp or convulsion. **2** a sudden burst of activity, emotion, etc. [C14: from L *spasmus*, from Gk *spasmos* a cramp, from *span* to tear]

spasmodic (spæz'mɒdɪk) *or* (*rarely*) **spasmodical** *adj* **1** taking place in sudden brief spells. **2** of or characterized by spasms. [C17: NL, from Gk *spasmos* SPASM]
▶ spas'modically *adv*

Spassky ★ ('spæskɪ; *Russian* 'spaskij) *n* **Boris** (ba'ris).

born 1937, Russian chess player; world champion (1969–72).

spastic ('spæstɪk) *n* **1** a person who is affected by spasms or convulsions, esp. one who has cerebral palsy. **2** *Offens. sl.* a clumsy, incapable, or incompetent person. ◆ *adj* **3** affected by or resembling spasms. **4** *Offens. sl.* clumsy, incapable, or incompetent. [C18: from L *spasticus*, from Gk, from *spasmos* SPASM]
▶ '**spastically** *adv* ▶ **spas'ticity** (spæs'tɪsɪtɪ) *n*

spat[1] (spæt) *n* **1** *Now rare.* a slap or smack. **2** a slight quarrel. ◆ *vb* **spats, spatting, spatted.** **3** *Rare.* to slap (someone). **4** (*intr*) *US, Canad., & NZ.* to have a slight quarrel. [C19: prob. imit.]

spat[2] (spæt) *vb* a past tense and past participle of **spit**[1].

spat[3] (spæt) *n* another name for **gaiter** (sense 2). [C19: short for SPATTERDASH]

spat[4] (spæt) *n* **1** a larval oyster or similar bivalve mollusc. **2** such oysters or other molluscs collectively. [C17: from Anglo-Norman *spat*]

spatchcock ('spætʃˌkɒk) *n* **1** a chicken or game bird split down the back and grilled. ◆ *vb* (*tr*) **2** to interpolate (words, a story, etc.) into a sentence, narrative, etc., esp. inappropriately. [C18: ? var. of *spitchcock* eel when prepared & cooked]

spate (speɪt) *n* **1** a fast flow, rush, or outpouring: *a spate of words.* **2** *Chiefly Brit.* a sudden flood: *the rivers were in spate.* **3** *Chiefly Brit.* a sudden heavy downpour. [C15 (Scot. & N Engl): from ?]

spathe (speɪð) *n* a large bract that encloses the inflorescence of several members of the lily family. [C18: from L *spatha*, from Gk *spathē* a blade]
▶ **spathaceous** (spə'θeɪʃəs) *adj*

spathic ('spæθɪk) *or* **spathose** ('spæθəus) *adj* (of minerals) resembling spar, esp. in having good cleavage. [C18: from G *Spat* SPAR[3]]

spatial *or* **spacial** ('speɪʃəl) *adj* **1** of or relating to space. **2** existing or happening in space.
▶ **spatiality** (ˌspeɪʃɪ'ælɪtɪ) *n* ▶ '**spatially** *adv*

spatiotemporal (ˌspeɪʃɪəu'tempərəl) *adj* **1** of or existing in both space and time. **2** of or concerned with space-time.
▶ ˌspatio'temporally *adv*

spatter ('spætə) *vb* **1** to scatter or splash (a substance, esp. a liquid) or (of a substance) to splash (something) in scattered drops: *to spatter mud on the car; mud spattered in her face.* **2** (*tr*) to sprinkle, cover, or spot (with a liquid). **3** (*tr*) to slander or defame. **4** (*intr*) to shower or rain down: *bullets spattered around them.* ◆ *n* **5** the sound of spattering. **6** something spattered, such as a spot or splash. **7** the act or an instance of spattering. [C16: imit.]

spatterdash ('spætəˌdæʃ) *n* **1** *US.* another name for **roughcast.** **2** (*pl*) long leather leggings worn in the 18th century, as to protect from mud when riding. [C17: see SPATTER, DASH[1]]

spatula ('spætjulə) *n* a utensil with a broad flat blade, used for lifting, spreading, or stirring foods, etc. [C16: from L: a broad piece, from *spatha* a flat wooden implement; see SPATHE]
▶ '**spatular** *adj*

spatulate ('spætjulɪt) *adj* **1** shaped like a spatula; having thickened rounded ends: *spatulate fingers.* **2** Also: **spathulate.** *Bot.* having a narrow base and a broad rounded apex.

spavin ('spævɪn) *n* enlargement of the hock of a horse by a bony growth (**bony spavin**) or distension of the ligament (**bog spavin**), often resulting in lameness. [C15: from OF *espavin*, from ?]
▶ '**spavined** *adj*

spawn (spɔːn) *n* **1** the mass of eggs deposited by fish, amphibians, or molluscs. **2** *Often derog.* offspring, product, or yield. **3** *Bot.* the nontechnical name for **mycelium.** ◆ *vb* **4** (of fish, amphibians, etc.) to produce or deposit (eggs). **5** *Often derog.* (of people) to produce (offspring). **6** (*tr*) to produce or engender. [C14: from Anglo-Norman *espaundre*, from OF *spandre* to spread out]
▶ '**spawner** *n*

spay (speɪ) *vb* (*tr*) to remove the ovaries from (a female

animal). [C15: from OF *espeer* to cut with the sword, from *espee* sword, from L *spatha*]

SPCK (in Britain) *abbrev. for* Society for Promoting Christian Knowledge.

speak (spiːk) *vb* **speaks, speaking, spoke, spoken. 1** to make (verbal utterances); utter (words). **2** to communicate or express (something) in or as if in words. **3** (*intr*) to deliver a speech, discourse, etc. **4** (*tr*) to know how to talk in (a language or dialect): *he does not speak German.* **5** (*intr*) to make a characteristic sound: *the clock spoke.* **6** (*intr*) (of hounds used in hunting) to give tongue; bark. **7** (*tr*) *Naut.* to hail and communicate with (another vessel) at sea. **8** (*intr*) (of a musical instrument) to produce a sound. **9 on speaking terms.** on good terms; friendly. **10 so to speak.** in a manner of speaking; as it were. **11 speak one's mind.** to express one's opinions frankly and plainly. **12 to speak of.** of a significant or worthwhile nature: *no support to speak of.* ◆ See also **speak for, speak out, speak to.** [OE *specan*]
▶ '**speakable** *adj*

speakeasy ('spiːkˌiːzɪ) *n, pl* **speakeasies.** *US.* a place where alcoholic drink was sold illicitly during Prohibition.

speaker ('spiːkə) *n* **1** a person who speaks, esp. at a formal occasion. **2** See **loudspeaker.**
▶ '**speakership** *n*

Speaker ('spiːkə) *n* the presiding officer in any of numerous legislative bodies.

speak for *vb* (*intr, prep*) **1** to speak as a representative of (other people). **2 speak for itself.** to be so evident that no further comment is necessary. **3 speak for yourself.** *Inf.* (used as an imperative) do not presume that other people agree with you.

speaking ('spiːkɪŋ) *adj* **1** (*prenominal*) eloquent, impressive, or striking. **2a** able to speak. **2b** (*in combination*) able to speak a particular language: *French-speaking.*

speaking clock *n Brit.* a telephone service that gives a verbal statement of the time.

speaking in tongues *n* another term for **gift of tongues.**

speaking tube *n* a tube for conveying a person's voice from one room or building to another.

speak out *or* **up** *vb* (*intr, adv*) **1** to state one's beliefs, objections, etc., bravely and firmly. **2** to speak more loudly and clearly.

speak to *vb* (*intr, prep*) **1** to address (a person). **2** to reprimand. **3** *Formal.* to give evidence of or comments on (a subject).

spear[1] (spɪə) *n* **1** a weapon consisting of a long shaft with a sharp pointed end of metal, stone, or wood that may be thrown or thrust. **2** a similar implement used to catch fish. **3** another name for **spearman.** ◆ *vb* **4** to pierce (something) with or as if with a spear. [OE *spere*]

spear[2] (spɪə) *n* a shoot, stalk, or blade, as of grass. [C16: prob. var. of SPIRE[1], infl. by SPEAR[1]]

spear grass *n* **1** Also called: **wild Spaniard.** a New Zealand grass with sharp leaves that grows on mountains. **2** any of various other grasses with sharp stiff blades or seeds.

spear gun *n* a device for shooting spears underwater.

spearhead ('spɪəˌhɛd) *n* **1** the pointed head of a spear. **2** the leading force in a military attack. **3** any person or thing that leads or initiates an attack, campaign, etc. ◆ *vb* **4** (*tr*) to lead or initiate (an attack, campaign, etc.).

spearman ('spɪəmən) *n, pl* **spearmen.** a soldier armed with a spear.

spearmint ('spɪəmɪnt) *n* a purple-flowered mint plant of Europe, having leaves that yield an oil used for flavouring.

spec (spɛk) *n* **1 on spec.** *Inf.* as a speculation or gamble: *all the tickets were sold so I went to the theatre on spec.* ◆ *adj* **2** (*prenominal*) *Austral. & NZ inf.* speculative: *a spec developer.*

spec. *abbrev. for:* **1** special. **2** specification. **3** speculation.

special ('spɛʃəl) *adj* **1** distinguished from, set apart from, or excelling others of its kind. **2** (*prenominal*) designed or reserved for a particular purpose. **3** not usual or commonplace. **4** (*prenominal*) particular or primary: *his special interest was music.* **5** of or relating to the education of handicapped children: *a special school.* ◆ *n* **6** a special person or thing, such as an extra edition of a newspaper

or a train reserved for a particular purpose. **7** a dish or meal given prominence, esp. at a low price, in a café, etc. **8** short for **special constable. 9** *US, Canad., Austral., & NZ inf.* an item in a store advertised at a reduce price. ◆ *vb* **specials, specialling, specialled.** (*tr*) **10** (of a nurse) to give a (gravely ill patient) constant individual care. **11** *NZ inf.* to advertise and sell (an item) at a reduced price. [C13: from OF *especial*, from L *speciālis* individual, special, from *speciēs* appearance]
► **'specially** *adv* ► **'specialness** *n*

USAGE NOTE   See at especial.

Special Branch *n* (in Britain) the department of the police force that is concerned with political security.

special clearing *n Banking.* (in Britain) the clearing of a cheque through a bank in less than the usual three days, for an additional charge.

special constable *n* a person recruited for temporary or occasional police duties, esp. in time of emergency.

special delivery *n* the delivery of a piece of mail outside the time of a scheduled delivery.

special drawing rights *pl n* (*sometimes caps.*) the reserve assets of the International Monetary Fund on which member nations may draw.

special effects *pl n Films.* techniques used in the production of scenes that cannot be achieved by normal techniques.

specialist ('speʃəlɪst) *n* a person who specializes in a particular activity, field of research, etc.
► **'special,ism** *n* ► **,special'istic** *adj*

speciality (,speʃɪ'ælɪtɪ) *or esp. US & Canad.* **specialty** *n, pl* **specialities** *or esp. US & Canad.* **specialties. 1** a special interest or skill. **2a** a service or product specialized in, as at a restaurant. **2b** (*as modifier*): *a speciality dish.* **3** a special feature or characteristic.

specialize *or* **specialise** ('speʃə,laɪz) *vb* **specializes, specializing, specialized** *or* **specialises, specialising, specialised. 1** (*intr*) to train in or devote oneself to a particular area of study, occupation, or activity. **2** (*usually passive*) to cause (organisms or parts) to develop in a way most suited to a particular environment or way of life or (of organisms, etc.) to develop in this way. **3** (*tr*) to modify for a special use or purpose.
► **,speciali'zation** *or* **,speciali'sation** *n*

special licence *n Brit.* a licence permitting a marriage to take place by dispensing with the usual legal conditions.

special pleading *n Law.* **1** a pleading that alleges new facts that offset those put forward by the other side rather than directly admitting or denying those facts. **2** a pleading that emphasizes the favourable aspects of a case while omitting the unfavourable.

special school *n Brit.* a school for children who are unable to benefit from ordinary schooling because they have learning difficulties, physical or mental handicaps, etc.

special team *n American football.* any of several predetermined permutations of the players within a team that play in situations, such as kickoffs and attempts at field goals, where the standard offensive and defensive formations are not appropriate.

specialty ('speʃəltɪ) *n, pl* **specialties. 1** *Law.* a formal contract or obligation expressed in a deed. **2** a variant (esp. US and Canad.) of **speciality.**

speciation (,spiːʃɪ'eɪʃən) *n* the evolutionary development of a biological species.

specie ('spiːʃiː) *n* **1** coin money, as distinguished from bullion or paper money. **2a** **in specie.** **2a** (of money) in coin. **2b** in kind. [C16: from L *in speciē* in kind]

species ('spiːʃiːz; *Latin* 'spiːʃɪ,iːz) *n, pl* **species. 1** *Biol.* **1a** any of the taxonomic groups into which a genus is divided, the members of which are capable of interbreeding. Abbrev.: **sp. 1b** the animals of such a group. **1c** any group of related animals or plants not necessarily of this taxonomic rank. **2** (*modifier*) denoting a plant that is a

natural member of a species rather than a hybrid or cultivar: *a species clematis.* **3** *Logic.* a group of objects or individuals, all sharing common attributes, that forms a subdivision of a genus. **4** a kind, sort, or variety: *a species of treachery.* **5** *Chiefly RC Church.* the outward form of the bread and wine in the Eucharist. **6** *Obs.* an outward appearance or form. [C16: from L: appearance, from *specere* to look]

specif. *abbrev. for* specifically.

specific (spɪ'sɪfɪk) *adj* **1** explicit, particular, or definite. **2** relating to a specified or particular thing: *a specific treatment for arthritis.* **3** of or relating to a biological species. **4** (of a disease) caused by a particular pathogenic agent. **5** *Physics.* **5a** characteristic of a property of a substance, esp. in relation to the same property of a standard reference substance: *specific gravity.* **5b** characteristic of a property of a substance per unit mass, length, area, etc.: *specific heat.* **5c** (of an extensive physical quantity) divided by mass: *specific volume.* **6** denoting a tariff levied at a fixed sum per unit of weight, quantity, volume, etc., irrespective of value. ◆ *n* **7** (*sometimes pl*) a designated quality, thing, etc. **8** *Med.* any drug used to treat a particular disease. [C17: from Med. L *specificus*, from L SPECIES]
► **spe'cifically** *adv* ► **specificity** (,spesɪ'fɪsɪtɪ) *n*

specification (,spesɪfɪ'keɪʃən) *n* **1** the act or an instance of specifying. **2** (in patent law) a written statement accompanying an application for a patent that describes the nature of an invention. **3** a detailed description of the criteria for the constituents, construction, appearance, performance, etc., of a material, apparatus, etc., or of the standard of workmanship required in its manufacture. **4** an item, detail, etc., specified.

specific charge *n Physics.* the charge-to-mass ratio of an elementary particle.

specific gravity *n* the ratio of the density of a substance to that of water.

specific heat capacity *n* the heat required to raise unit mass of a substance by unit temperature interval under specified conditions, such as constant pressure. Also called: **specific heat.**

specific humidity *n* the mass of water vapour in a sample of moist air divided by the mass of the sample.

specific volume *n Physics.* the volume of matter per unit mass.

specify ('spesɪ,faɪ) *vb* **specifies, specifying, specified.** (*tr; may take a clause as object*) **1** to refer to or state specifically. **2** to state as a condition. **3** to state or include in the specification of. [C13: from Med. L *specificāre* to describe]
► **'speci,fiable** *adj* ► **specificative** ('spesɪfɪ,keɪtɪv) *adj*

specimen ('spesɪmɪn) *n* **1a** an individual, object, or part regarded as typical of its group or class. **1b** (*as modifier*): *a specimen page.* **2** *Med.* a sample of tissue, blood, urine, etc., taken for diagnostic examination or evaluation. **3** the whole or a part of an organism, plant, rock, etc., collected and preserved as an example of its class, species, etc. **4** *Inf., often derog.* a person. [C17: from L: mark, proof, from *specere* to look at]

specious ('spiːʃəs) *adj* **1** apparently correct or true, but actually wrong or false. **2** deceptively attractive in appearance. [C14: (orig.: fair): from L *speciōsus* plausible, from *speciēs* outward appearance, from *specere* to look at]
► **'speciously** *adv* ► **speciosity** (,spiːʃɪ'ɒsɪtɪ) *or* **'speciousness** *n*

speck (spek) *n* **1** a very small mark or spot. **2** a small or tiny piece of something. ◆ *vb* **3** (*tr*) to mark with specks or spots. [OE *specca*]

speckle ('spek³l) *n* **1** a small mark usually of a contrasting colour, as on the skin, eggs, etc. ◆ *vb* **speckles, speckling, speckled. 2** (*tr*) to mark with or as if with speckles. [C15: from MDu. *spekkel*]
► **'speckled** *adj*

specs (speks) *pl n Inf.* short for **spectacles.**

spectacle ('spektək³l) *n* **1** a public display or performance, esp. a showy or ceremonial one. **2** a thing or person seen, esp. an unusual one: *he makes a spectacle of himself.* **3** a strange or interesting object or phenomenon. [C14: via OF from L *spectaculum* a show, from *spectāre* to watch, from *specere* to look at]

spectacles ('spektək⁹lz) *pl n* a pair of glasses for correcting defective vision. Often (informal) shortened to **specs.**
▸ **'spectacled** *adj*

spectacular (spek'tækjʊlə) *adj* **1** of or resembling a spectacle; impressive, grand, or dramatic. **2** unusually marked or great: *a spectacular increase.* ◆ *n* **3** a lavishly produced performance.
▸ **spec'tacularly** *adv*

spectate (spek'teɪt) *vb* **spectates, spectating, spectated.** (*intr*) to be a spectator; watch. [C20: back formation from SPECTATOR]

spectator (spek'teɪtə) *n* a person viewing anything; onlooker; observer. [C16: from L, from *spectāre* to watch; see SPECTACLE]

spectator sport *n* a sport that attracts more people as spectators than as participants.

Spector ★ ('spektə) *n Phil.* born 1940, US record producer and songwriter, noted for the densely orchestrated "Wall of Sound" in his work with groups such as the Ronettes and the Crystals.

spectra ('spektrə) *n* the plural of **spectrum.**

spectral ('spektrəl) *adj* **1** of or like a spectre. **2** of or relating to a spectrum.
▸ **spectrality** (spek'trælɪtɪ) *n* ▸ **'spectrally** *adv*

spectral type *or* **class** *n* any of various groups into which stars are classified according to characteristic spectral lines and bands.

spectre *or US* **specter** ('spektə) *n* **1** a ghost; phantom; apparition. **2** an unpleasant or menacing mental image: *the spectre of redundancy.* [C17: from L *spectrum,* from *specere* to look at]

spectro- *combining form.* indicating a spectrum: *spectrogram.*

spectrograph ('spektrəʊ‚grɑːf) *n* a spectroscope or spectrometer that produces a photographic record (**spectrogram**) of a spectrum. See also **sound spectrograph.**
▸ **‚spectro'graphic** *adj* ▸ **‚spectro'graphically** *adv* ▸ **spectrography** (spek'trɒgrəfɪ) *n*

spectroheliograph (‚spektrəʊ'hiːlɪə‚grɑːf) *n* an instrument used to take a photograph (**spectroheliogram**) of the sun in light of a particular wavelength, usually that of calcium or hydrogen, to show the distribution of the element over the surface and in the atmosphere.
▸ **‚spectro‚helio'graphic** *adj*

spectrometer (spek'trɒmɪtə) *n* any instrument for producing a spectrum, esp. one in which wavelength, energy, intensity, etc., can be measured. See also **mass spectrometer.**
▸ **spectrometric** (‚spektrəʊ'metrɪk) *adj* ▸ **spec'trometry** *n*

spectrophotometer (‚spektrəʊfəʊ'tɒmɪtə) *n* an instrument for producing or recording a spectrum and measuring the photometric intensity of each wavelength present.
▸ **spectrophotometric** (‚spektrəʊ‚fəʊtə'metrɪk) *adj* ▸ **‚spectropho'tometry** *n*

spectroscope ('spektrə‚skəʊp) *n* any of a number of instruments for dispersing electromagnetic radiation and thus forming or recording a spectrum.
▸ **spectroscopic** (‚spektrə'skɒpɪk) *or* **‚spectro'scopical** *adj*

spectroscopy (spek'trɒskəpɪ) *n* the science and practice of using spectrometers and spectroscopes and of analysing spectra.
▸ **spec'troscopist** *n*

spectrum ('spektrəm) *n, pl* **spectra. 1** the distribution of colours produced when white light is dispersed by a prism or diffraction grating. There is a continuous change in wavelength from red, the longest wavelength, to violet, the shortest. Seven colours are usually distinguished: violet, indigo, blue, green, yellow, orange, and red. **2** the whole range of electromagnetic radiation with respect to its wavelength or frequency. **3** any particular distribution of electromagnetic radiation often showing lines or bands characteristic of the substance emitting the radiation or absorbing it. **4** any similar distribution or record of the energies, velocities, masses, etc., of atoms, ions, electrons, etc.: *a mass spectrum.* **5** any range or scale, as of capabilities, emotions, or moods. **6** another name for an **afterimage.** [C17: from L: image, from *spectāre* to observe, from *specere* to look at]

spectrum analysis *n* the analysis of a spectrum to determine the properties of its source.

specular ('spekjʊlə) *adj* **1** of, relating to, or having the properties of a mirror. **2** of or relating to a speculum. [C16: from L *speculāris,* from *speculum* a mirror, from *specere* to look at]

speculate ('spekjʊ‚leɪt) *vb* **speculates, speculating, speculated. 1** (when *tr, takes a clause as object*) to conjecture without knowing the complete facts. **2** (*intr*) to buy or sell securities, property, etc., in the hope of deriving capital gains. **3** (*intr*) to risk loss for the possibility of considerable gain. **4** (*intr*) NZ. in rugby football, to make an emergency undirected forward kick at the ball. [C16: from L *speculārī* to spy out, from *specula* a watchtower, from *specere* to look at]

speculation (‚spekjʊ'leɪʃən) *n* **1** the act or an instance of speculating. **2** a supposition, theory, or opinion arrived at through speculating. **3** investment involving high risk but also possible high profits.
▸ **'speculative** *adj*

speculator ('spekjʊ‚leɪtə) *n* **1** a person who speculates. **2** NZ rugby. an undirected kick of the ball.

speculum ('spekjʊləm) *n, pl* **specula** (-lə) *or* **speculums. 1** a mirror, esp. one made of polished metal for use in a telescope, etc. **2** Med. an instrument for dilating a bodily cavity or passage to permit examination of its interior. **3** a patch of distinctive colour on the wing of a bird. [C16: from L: mirror, from *specere* to look at]

sped (sped) *vb* a past tense and past participle of **speed.**

speech (spiːtʃ) *n* **1a** the act or faculty of speaking. **1b** (*as modifier*): *speech therapy.* **2** that which is spoken; utterance. **3** a talk or address delivered to an audience. **4** a person's characteristic manner of speaking. **5** a national or regional language or dialect. **6** Linguistics. another word for **parole.** [OE *spēc*]

speech day *n* Brit. (in schools) an annual day on which prizes are presented, speeches are made by guest speakers, etc.

speechify ('spiːtʃɪ‚faɪ) *vb* **speechifies, speechifying, speechified.** (*intr*) **1** to make a speech or speeches. **2** to talk pompously and boringly.
▸ **'speechi‚fier** *n*

speechless ('spiːtʃlɪs) *adj* **1** not able to speak. **2** temporarily deprived of speech. **3** not expressed or able to be expressed in words: *speechless fear.*
▸ **'speechlessly** *adv* ▸ **'speechlessness** *n*

speed (spiːd) *n* **1** the act or quality of acting or moving fast; rapidity. **2** the rate at which something moves, is done, or acts. **3** Physics. **3a** a scalar measure of the rate of movement of a body expressed either as the distance travelled divided by the time taken (**average speed**) or the rate of change of position with respect to time at a particular point (**instantaneous speed**). **3b** another word for **velocity** (sense 2). **4** a rate of rotation, usually expressed in revolutions per unit time. **5a** a gear ratio in a motor vehicle, bicycle, etc. **5b** (*in combination*): *a three-speed gear.* **6** Photog. a numerical expression of the sensitivity to light of a particular type of film, paper, or plate. See also **ISO rating. 7** Photog. a measure of the ability of a lens to pass light from an object to the image position. **8** a slang word for **amphetamine. 9** Arch. prosperity or success. **10** at speed. quickly. ◆ *vb* **speeds, speeding; sped** *or* **speeded. 11** to move or go or cause to move or go quickly. **12** (*tr*) to drive (a motor vehicle) at a high speed, esp. above legal limits. **13** (*tr*) to help further the success or completion of. **14** (*intr*) Sl. to take or be under the influence of amphetamines. **15** (*intr*) to operate or run at a high speed. **16** Arch. **16a** (*intr*) to prosper or succeed. **16b** (*tr*) to wish success to. ◆ See also **speed up.** [OE *spēd* (orig. in the sense: success)]
▸ **'speeder** *n*

speedball ('spiːd‚bɔːl) *n Sl.* a mixture of heroin with amphetamine or cocaine.

speedboat ('spiːdˌbəʊt) n a high-speed motorboat.

speed chess n a form of chess in which each player's game is limited to a total stipulated time, usually half an hour; the first player to exceed the time limit loses.

speed limit n the maximum permitted speed at which a vehicle may travel on certain roads.

speedo ('spiːdəʊ) n, pl **speedos.** an informal name for **speedometer.**

speed of light n the speed at which electromagnetic radiation travels in a vacuum; 2.997 924 58 × 10[8] metres per second exactly. Symbol: c Also called (not in technical usage): **velocity of light.**

speedometer (spɪˈdɒmɪtə) n a device fitted to a vehicle to measure and display the speed of travel. See also **mileometer.**

speed up vb (adv) **1** to increase or cause to increase in speed or rate; accelerate. ◆ n **speed-up. 2** an instance of this; acceleration.

> **USAGE NOTE** The past tense and past participle of *speed up* is *speeded up*, not *sped up.*

speedway ('spiːdˌweɪ) n **1** the sport of racing on light powerful motorcycles round cinder tracks. **2** the track or stadium where such races are held. **3** US & Canad. **3a** a racetrack for cars. **3b** a road on which fast driving is allowed.

speedwell ('spiːdˌwel) n any of various temperate plants, such as the **common speedwell** and the **germander speedwell,** having small blue or pinkish-white flowers.

speedy ('spiːdɪ) adj **speedier, speediest. 1** characterized by speed. **2** done or decided without delay.
> **'speedily** adv ▸ **'speediness** n

spek (spɛk) n S. African. bacon. [from Afrik., from Du.]

speleology or **spelaeology** (ˌspiːlɪˈɒlədʒɪ) n **1** the scientific study of caves. **2** the sport or pastime of exploring caves. [C19: from L spēlaeum cave]
> **speleological** or **spelaeological** (ˌspiːlɪəˈlɒdʒɪk'l) adj
> **ˌspeleˈologist** or **ˌspelaeˈologist** n

spell[1] (spɛl) vb **spells, spelling; spelt** or **spelled. 1** to write or name in correct order the letters that comprise the conventionally accepted form of (a word). **2** (tr) (of letters) to go to make up the conventionally established form of (a word) when arranged correctly: d-o-g spells dog. **3** (tr) to indicate or signify: such actions spell disaster. ◆ See also **spell out.** [C13: from OF espeller, of Gmc origin]
> **'spellable** adj

spell[2] (spɛl) n **1** a verbal formula considered as having magical force. **2** any influence that can control the mind or character; fascination. **3** a state induced as by the pronouncing of a spell; trance: to break the spell. **4** under a spell. held in or as if in a spell. [OE spell speech]

spell[3] (spɛl) n **1** an indeterminate, usually short, period of time: a spell of cold weather. **2** a period or tour of duty after which one person or group relieves another. **3** Scot., Austral., & NZ. a period or interval of rest. ◆ vb **4** (tr) to take over from (a person) for an interval of time; relieve temporarily. [OE spelian to take the place of, from ?]

spellbind ('spɛlˌbaɪnd) vb **spellbinds, spellbinding, spellbound.** (tr) to cause to be spellbound; entrance or enthral.
> **'spellˌbinder** n

spellbound ('spɛlˌbaʊnd) adj having one's attention held as though one is bound by a spell.

spellchecker ('spɛlˌtʃɛkə) n Computing. a program that highlights any word in a word-processed document that is not recognized as being correctly spelt.

speller ('spɛlə) n **1** a person who spells words in the manner specified: a bad speller. **2** a book designed to teach or improve spelling.

spelling ('spɛlɪŋ) n **1** the act or process of writing words by using the letters conventionally accepted for their formation; orthography. **2** the art or study of orthography. **3** the way in which a word is spelt. **4** the ability of a person to spell.

spelling bee n a contest in which players are required to spell words.

spell out vb (tr, adv) **1** to make clear, distinct, or explicit; clarify in detail: let me spell out the implications. **2** to read laboriously or with difficulty, working out each word letter by letter. **3** to discern by study; puzzle out.

spelt[1] (spɛlt) vb a past tense and past participle of **spell**[1].

spelt[2] (spɛlt) n a species of wheat that was formerly much cultivated and was used to develop present-day cultivated wheats. [OE]

spelter ('spɛltə) n impure zinc. [C17: prob. from MDu. speauter, from ?]

spelunker (spɪˈlʌŋkə) n a person whose hobby is the exploration of caves. [C20: from L spēlunca, from Gk spēlunx a cave]
> **speˈlunking** n

Spence ★ (spɛns) n Sir Basil (Unwin). 1907–76, British architect, born in India; designed Coventry Cathedral (1951).

spencer[1] ('spɛnsə) n **1** a short fitted coat or jacket. **2** a woman's knitted vest. [C18: after Earl Spencer (1758–1834)]

spencer[2] ('spɛnsə) n Naut. a large loose-footed gaffsail on a square-rigger or barque. [C19: ?from a proper name]

Spencer ★ ('spɛnsə) n **1** Herbert. 1820–1903, British philosopher, who applied evolutionary theory to the study of society. **2** Sir Stanley. 1891–1959, British painter, noted for his paintings of Christ in a contemporary British setting.

Spencer Gulf ★ n an inlet of the Indian Ocean in S Australia, between the Eyre and Yorke Peninsulas. Length: about 320 km (200 miles). Greatest width: about 145 km (90 miles).

spend (spɛnd) vb **spends, spending, spent. 1** to pay out (money, wealth, etc.). **2** (tr) to concentrate (time, effort, etc.) upon an object, activity, etc. **3** (tr) to pass (time) in a specific way, place, etc. **4** (tr) to use up completely: the hurricane spent its force. **5** (tr) to give up (one's blood, life, etc.) in a cause. [OE spendan, from L expendere; infl. also by OF despendre to spend; see EXPEND, DISPENSE]
> **'spendable** adj ▸ **'spender** n

Spender ★ ('spɛndə) n Sir Stephen. 1909–95, British poet; coeditor of Horizon (1939–41) and of Encounter (1953–67).

spendthrift ('spɛndˌθrɪft) n **1** a person who spends money in an extravagant manner. ◆ adj **2** (usually prenominal) of or like a spendthrift.

Spengler ★ ('spɛŋlə; German 'ʃpɛŋlər) n Oswald ('ɔsvalt). 1880–1936, German philosopher, noted for The Decline of the West (1918–22).

Spenser ★ ('spɛnsə) n Edmund. ?1552–99, English poet celebrated for the allegorical The Faerie Queene (1590; 1596). His other verse includes the collection of eclogues The Shephearde's Calendar (1579).

Spenserian (spɛnˈsɪərɪən) adj **1** relating to or characteristic of Edmund Spenser or his poetry. ◆ n **2** a student or imitator of Edmund Spenser.

Spenserian stanza n Prosody. the stanza form used by the poet Spenser in his poem The Faerie Queene, consisting of eight lines in iambic pentameter and a concluding Alexandrine, rhyming a b a b b c b c c.

spent (spɛnt) vb **1** the past tense and past participle of **spend.** ◆ adj **2** used up or exhausted; consumed. **3** (of a fish) exhausted by spawning.

sperm[1] (spɜːm) n, pl **sperms** or **sperm. 1** another name for **semen. 2** a male reproductive cell; male gamete. [C14: from LL sperma, from Gk]

sperm[2] (spɜːm) n short for **sperm whale, spermaceti,** or **sperm oil.**

-sperm n combining form. (in botany) a seed: gymnosperm.
> **-spermous** or **-spermal** adj combining form.

spermaceti (ˌspɜːməˈsɛtɪ, -ˈsiːtɪ) n a white waxy substance obtained from oil from the head of the sperm whale. [C15: from Med. L sperma cētī whale's sperm, from sperma SPERM[1] + L cētus whale, from Gk kētos]

spermatic (spɜːˈmætɪk), **spermic** ('spɜːmɪk), or

spermous ('spɜːməs) *adj* **1** of or relating to spermatozoa: *spermatic fluid*. **2** of or relating to the testis: *the spermatic artery*. [C16: from LL *spermaticus*, from Gk *spermatikos* concerning seed, from *sperma* seed]
▸ sper'matically *adv*

spermatid ('spɜːmətɪd) *n Zool.* any of four immature male gametes that are formed from a spermatocyte, each of which develops into a spermatozoon.

spermato-, spermo- *or before a vowel* **spermat-, sperm-** *combining form.* **1** indicating sperm: *spermatozoon*. **2** indicating seed: *spermatophyte*. [from Gk *sperma, spermat-* seed]

spermatocyte ('spɜːmətəʊˌsaɪt) *n* an immature male germ cell.

spermatogenesis (ˌspɜːmətəʊˈdʒɛnɪsɪs) *n* the formation and maturation of spermatozoa in the testis.
▸ spermatogenetic (ˌspɜːmətəʊdʒɪˈnɛtɪk) *adj*

spermatogonium (ˌspɜːmətəʊˈgəʊnɪəm) *n, pl* spermatogonia (-nɪə). *Zool.* an immature male germ cell that divides to form many spermatocytes.

spermatophyte ('spɜːmətəʊˌfaɪt) *or* **spermophyte** *n* (in traditional classifications) any seed-bearing plant. Former name: **phanerogam**.
▸ spermatophytic (ˌspɜːmətəʊˈfɪtɪk) *adj*

spermatozoon (ˌspɜːmətəʊˈzəʊɒn) *n, pl* spermatozoa (-zəʊə). any of the male reproductive cells released in the semen during ejaculation. Also called: **sperm, zoosperm**.
▸ ˌspermatoˈzoal, ˌspermatoˈzoan, *or* ˌspermatoˈzoic *adj*

spermicide ('spɜːmɪˌsaɪd) *n* any agent that kills spermatozoa.
▸ ˌspermiˈcidal *adj*

sperm oil *n* an oil obtained from the head of the sperm whale, used as a lubricant.

spermous ('spɜːməs) *adj* **1** of or relating to the sperm whale or its products. **2** another word for **spermatic**.

sperm whale *n* a large toothed whale, having a square-shaped head and hunted for sperm oil, spermaceti, and ambergris. Also called: **cachalot**. [C19: short for SPERMA-CETI *whale*]

spew (spjuː) *vb* **1** to eject (the contents of the stomach) involuntarily through the mouth; vomit. **2** to spit (spittle, phlegm, etc.) out of the mouth. **3** (usually foll. by *out*) to send or be sent out in a stream: *flames spewed out*. ◆ *n* **4** something ejected from the mouth. ◆ Also (archaic): **spue**. [OE *spīwan*]
▸ 'spewer *n*

Spey ★ (speɪ) *n* a river in E Scotland, flowing generally northeast through the Grampian Mountains to the Moray Firth: salmon fishing. Length: 172 km (107 miles).

Speyer ★ (*German* ˈʃpaɪər) *n* a port in SW Germany, in Rhineland-Palatinate on the Rhine: the scene of 50 imperial diets. Pop.: 47 450 (1991). English name: **Spires**.

sp. gr. *abbrev. for* specific gravity.

sphagnum ('sfægnəm) *n* any moss of the genus *Sphagnum*, of temperate bogs: layers of these mosses decay to form peat. Also called: **peat moss, bog moss**. [C18: from NL, from Gk *sphagnos* a variety of moss]
▸ 'sphagnous *adj*

sphairee (sfaɪriː) *n Austral.* a game resembling tennis played with wooden bats and a perforated plastic ball. [from Gk *sphaira* a ball]

sphalerite ('sfæləˌraɪt, 'sfeɪlə-) *n* a yellow to brownish-black mineral consisting mainly of zinc sulphide in cubic crystalline form: the chief source of zinc. Formula: ZnS. Also called: **zinc blende**. [C19: from Gk *sphaleros* deceitful, from *sphallein* to cause to stumble]

sphene (sfiːn) *n* a brown, yellow, green, or grey lustrous mineral consisting of calcium titanium silicate in monoclinic crystalline form. Also called: **titanite**. [C19: from F *sphène*, from Gk *sphēn* a wedge, alluding to its crystals]

sphenoid ('sfiːnɔɪd) *adj also* **sphenoidal**. **1** wedge-shaped. **2** of or relating to the sphenoid bone. ◆ *n* **3** See **sphenoid bone**.

sphenoid bone *n* the large butterfly-shaped compound bone at the base of the skull.

sphere (sfɪə) *n* **1** *Maths.* **1a** a three-dimensional closed surface such that every point on the surface is equidistant from a given point, the centre. **1b** the solid figure bounded by this surface or the space enclosed by it. **2** any object having approximately this shape; a globe. **3** the night sky considered as a vaulted roof; firmament. **4** any heavenly object such as a planet, natural satellite, or star. **5** (in the Ptolemaic or Copernican systems of astronomy) one of a series of revolving hollow globes, arranged concentrically, on whose transparent surfaces the sun, the moon, the planets, and fixed stars were thought to be set. **6** a particular field of activity; environment. **7** a social class or stratum of society. ◆ *vb* **spheres, sphering, sphered**. (*tr*) *Chiefly poetic.* **8** to surround or encircle. **9** to place aloft or in the heavens. [C14: from LL *sphēra*, from L *sphaera* globe, from Gk *sphaira*]
▸ 'spherical *adj*

-sphere *n combining form.* **1** having the shape or form of a sphere: *bathysphere*. **2** indicating a spherelike enveloping mass: *atmosphere*.
▸ -spheric *adj combining form.*

spherical ('sfɛrɪkʰl) *or* **spheric** *adj* **1** shaped like a sphere. **2** of or relating to a sphere: *spherical geometry*. **3** *Geom.* formed on the surface of or inside a sphere: *a spherical triangle*. **4a** of or relating to heavenly bodies. **4b** of or relating to the spheres of the Ptolemaic or the Copernican system.
▸ 'spherically *adv* ▸ 'sphericalness *n*

spherical aberration *n Physics.* a defect of optical systems that arises when light striking a mirror or lens near its edge is focused at different points on the axis to the light striking near the centre. The effect occurs when the mirror or lens has spherical surfaces.

spherical angle *n* an angle formed at the intersection of two great circles of a sphere.

spherical coordinates *pl n* three coordinates that define the location of a point in space in terms of its radius vector, *r*, the angle, θ, which this vector makes with one axis, and the angle, φ, which the plane of this vector makes with a mutually perpendicular axis.

spherical trigonometry *n* the branch of trigonometry concerned with the measurement of the angles and sides of spherical triangles.

spheroid ('sfɪərɔɪd) *n* **1** another name for **ellipsoid of revolution**. ◆ *adj* **2** shaped like but not exactly a sphere.
▸ spher'oidal *adj* ▸ ˌspheroid'icity *n*

spherometer (sfɪəˈrɒmɪtə) *n* an instrument for measuring the curvature of a surface.

spherule ('sfɛruːl) *n* a very small sphere. [C17: from LL *sphaerula*]
▸ 'spherular *adj*

spherulite ('sfɛruˌlaɪt) *n* any of several spherical masses of radiating needle-like crystals of one or more minerals occurring in rocks such as obsidian.
▸ spherulitic (ˌsfɛruˈlɪtɪk) *adj*

sphincter ('sfɪŋktə) *n Anat.* a ring of muscle surrounding the opening of a hollow organ or body and contracting to close it. [C16: from LL, from Gk *sphinkter*, from *sphingein* to grip tightly]
▸ 'sphincteral *adj*

sphinx (sfɪŋks) *n, pl* sphinxes *or* sphinges ('sfɪndʒiːz). **1** any of a number of huge stone statues built by the ancient Egyptians, having the body of a lion and the head of a man. **2** an inscrutable person.

Sphinx ★ (sfɪŋks) *n the.* **1** *Greek myth.* a monster with a woman's head and a lion's body. She lay outside Thebes, asking travellers a riddle and killing them when they failed to answer it. Oedipus answered the riddle and the Sphinx then killed herself. **2** the huge statue of a sphinx near the pyramids at El Gîza in Egypt. [C16: via L from Gk, apparently from *sphingein* to hold fast]

sphragistics (sfrəˈdʒɪstɪks) *n* (*functioning as sing*) the study of seals and signet rings. [C19: from Gk *sphragistikos*, from *sphragizein* to seal, from *sphragis* a seal]
▸ sphra'gistic *adj*

sphygmo- *or before a vowel* **sphygm-** *combining form* indicating the pulse: *sphygmograph*. [from Gk *sphugmo-* pulsation, from *sphuzein* to throb]

★ people and places

sphygmograph ('sfɪgməʊˌgrɑːf) *n Med.* an instrument for making a recording (**sphygmogram**) of variations in blood pressure and pulse.
▶ **sphygmographic** (ˌsfɪgməʊ'græfɪk) *adj* ▶ **sphygmography** (sfɪg'mɒgrəfɪ) *n*

sphygmomanometer (ˌsfɪgməʊmə'nɒmɪtə) *n Med.* an instrument for measuring arterial blood pressure.

spicate ('spaɪkeɪt) *adj Bot.* having, arranged in, or relating to spikes: *a spicate inflorescence.* [C17: from L *spīcātus* having spikes, from *spīca* a point]

spiccato (spɪ'kɑːtəʊ) *Music.* ♦ *n* **1** a style of playing a bowed stringed instrument in which the bow bounces lightly off the strings. ♦ *adj, adv* **2** (to be played) in this manner. [It.: detached]

spice (spaɪs) *n* **1a** any of a variety of aromatic vegetable substances, such as ginger, cinnamon, or nutmeg, used as flavourings. **1b** these substances collectively. **2** something that represents or introduces zest, charm, or gusto. **3** *Rare.* a small amount. ♦ *vb* **spices, spicing, spiced.** (*tr*) **4** to prepare or flavour (food) with spices. **5** to introduce charm or zest into. [C13: from OF *espice*, from LL *speciēs* (pl) spices, from L *speciēs* (sing) kind; also associated with LL *spīcea* (unattested) fragrant herb, from L *spīceus* having spikes of foliage]

spicebush ('spaɪsˌbʊʃ) *n* a North American shrub having aromatic leaves and bark.

Spice Islands ★ *pl n* the former name of the **Moluccas**.

spick-and-span *or* **spic-and-span** ('spɪkən'spæn) *adj* **1** extremely neat and clean. **2** new and fresh. [C17: shortened from *spick-and-span-new*, from obs. *spick* spike + *span-new*, from ON *spānnȳr* absolutely new]

spicule ('spɪkjuːl) *n* **1** Also called: **spiculum.** a small slender pointed structure or crystal, esp. any of the calcareous or siliceous elements of the skeleton of sponges, corals, etc. **2** *Astron.* a spiked ejection of hot gas above the sun's surface. [C18: from L *spiculum* small, sharp point]
▶ **spiculate** ('spɪkjuˌleɪt, -lɪt) *adj*

spicy ('spaɪsɪ) *adj* **spicier, spiciest.** **1** seasoned with or containing spice. **2** highly flavoured; pungent. **3** *Inf.* suggestive of scandal or sensation.
▶ **'spicily** *adv* ▶ **'spiciness** *n*

spider ('spaɪdə) *n* **1** any of various predatory silk-producing arachnids, having four pairs of legs and a rounded unsegmented body. **2** any of various similar or related arachnids. **3** any implement or tool having the shape of a spider. **4** any part of a machine having a number of radiating spokes, tines, or arms. **5** Also called: **octopus.** *Brit.* a cluster of elastic straps fastened at a central point and used to hold a load on a car rack, motorcycle, etc. **6** *Snooker, etc.* a rest having long legs, used to raise the cue above the level of the height of the ball. [OE *spīthra*]
▶ **'spidery** *adj*

spider crab *n* any of various crabs having a small triangular body and very long legs.

spiderman ('spaɪdəˌmæn) *n, pl* **spidermen.** *Inf., chiefly Brit.* a person who erects the steel structure of a building.

spider mite *n* any of various plant-feeding mites, esp. the **red spider mite**, which is a serious orchard pest.

spider monkey *n* **1** any of several arboreal New World monkeys of Central and South America, having very long legs, a long prehensile tail, and a small head. **2 woolly spider monkey.** a rare related monkey of SE Brazil.

spider plant *n* a house plant having long narrow leaves with a light central stripe.

spiderwort ('spaɪdəˌwɜːt) *n* **1** any of various American plants having blue, purplish, or pink flowers and widely grown as house plants. See also **tradescantia. 2** any of various similar or related plants.

spiel (ʃpiːl) *n* **1** glib plausible talk, associated esp. with salesmen. ♦ *vb* **2** (*intr*) to deliver a prepared spiel. **3** (*tr;* usually foll. by *off*) to recite (a prepared oration). [C19: from G *Spiel* play]
▶ **'spieler** *n*

Spielberg ★ ('spiːlbɜːg) *n* **Steven.** born 1947, US film director, noted for such films as *Jaws* (1975), *Close Encoun-*

ters of the Third Kind (1977), E.T. (1982), Schindler's List (1993), and Saving Private Ryan (1998).

spier ('spaɪə) *n Arch.* a person who spies or scouts.

spiffing ('spɪfɪŋ) *adj Brit. sl., old-fashioned.* excellent; splendid. [C19: prob. from dialect *spiff* spruce, smart]

spiffy ('spɪfɪ) *adj* **spiffier, spiffiest.** *US & Canad. sl.* smart; stylish. [C19: from dialect *spiff* smartly dressed]
▶ **'spiffily** *adv*

spigot ('spɪgət) *n* **1** a stopper for the vent hole of a cask. **2** a tap, usually of wood, fitted to a cask. **3** a US name for **tap**[2] (sense 1). **4** a short projection on one component designed to fit into a hole on another, esp. the male part of a joint between two pipes. [C14: prob. from OProvençal *espiga* a head of grain, from L *spīca* a point]

spike[1] (spaɪk) *n* **1** a sharp point. **2** any sharp-pointed object, esp. one made of metal. **3** a long metal nail. **4** (*pl*) shoes with metal projections on the sole and heel for greater traction, as used by athletes. **5** *Brit. sl.* another word for **dosshouse.** ♦ *vb* **spikes, spiking, spiked.** (*tr*) **6** to secure or supply with or as with spikes. **7** to render ineffective or block the intentions of; thwart. **8** to impale on a spike. **9** to add alcohol to (a drink). **10** *Volleyball.* to hit (a ball) sharply downwards with an overarm motion from the front of one's own court into the opposing court. **11** (formerly) to render (a cannon) ineffective by blocking its vent with a spike. **12 spike (someone's) guns.** to thwart (someone's) purpose. [C13 *spyk*]
▶ **'spiky** *adj*

spike[2] (spaɪk) *n Bot.* **1** an inflorescence consisting of a raceme of sessile flowers. **2** an ear of wheat, etc. [C14: from L *spīca* ear of corn]

spikelet ('spaɪklɪt) *n Bot.* a small spike, esp. the inflorescence of most grasses and sedges.

spikenard ('spaɪknɑːd, 'spaɪkəˌnɑːd) *n* **1** an aromatic Indian plant, having rose-purple flowers. **2** an aromatic ointment obtained from this plant. **3** any of various similar or related plants. **4** a North American plant having small green flowers and an aromatic root. ♦ Also called (for senses 1, 2): **nard.** [C14: from Med. L *spīca nardī*; see SPIKE[2], NARD]

spile (spaɪl) *n* **1** a heavy timber stake or pile. **2** *US.* a spout for tapping sap from the sugar maple tree. **3** a plug or spigot. ♦ *vb* **spiles, spiling, spiled.** (*tr*) **4** to provide or support with a spile. **5** *US.* to tap (a tree) with a spile. [C16: prob. from MDu. *spile* peg]

spill[1] (spɪl) *vb* **spills, spilling; spilt** *or* **spilled.** (*mainly tr*) **1** (when *intr,* usually foll. by *from, out of,* etc.) to fall or cause to fall from or as from a container, esp. unintentionally. **2** to disgorge (contents, occupants, etc.) or (of contents, occupants, etc.) to be disgorged. **3** to shed (blood). **4** Also: **spill the beans.** *Inf.* to divulge something confidential. **5** *Naut.* to let (wind) escape from a sail or (of the wind) to escape from a sail. ♦ *n* **6** *Inf.* a fall or tumble. **7** short for **spillway. 8** a spilling of liquid, etc., or the amount spilt. **9** *Austral.* the declaring of several political jobs vacant when one higher up becomes so. [OE *spillan* to destroy]
▶ **'spillage** *n* ▶ **'spiller** *n*

spill[2] (spɪl) *n* a splinter of wood or strip of twisted paper with which pipes, fires, etc., are lit. [C13: of Gmc origin]

Spillane ★ (spɪ'leɪn) *n* **Mickey,** original name *Frank Morrison Spillane.* born 1918, US detective-story writer, best known for his books featuring the detective Mike Hammer, for example *I, the Jury* (1947).

spillikin, spilikin, *or* **spellican** ('spɪlɪkɪn), ('spɛlɪkən) *n* a thin strip of wood, cardboard, or plastic, esp. one used in spillikins.

spillikins ('spɪlɪkɪnz) *n* (*functioning as sing*) *Brit.* a game in which players try to pick each spillikin from a heap without moving any of the others. Also called: **jackstraws.**

spill over *vb* **1** (*intr, adv*) to overflow or be forced out of an area, container, etc. ♦ *n* **spillover.** *Chiefly US & Canad.* **2** the act of spilling over. **3** the excess part of something.

spillway ('spɪlˌweɪ) *n* a channel that carries away surplus water, as from a dam.

spilt (spɪlt) *vb* a past tense and past participle of **spill**[1].

spin (spɪn) *vb* **spins, spinning, spun. 1** to rotate or cause to rotate rapidly, as on an axis. **2a** to draw out and twist (natural fibres, as of silk or cotton) into a long continuous thread. **2b** to make such a thread or filament from (synthetic resins, etc.), usually by forcing through a nozzle. **3** (of spiders, silkworms, etc.) to form (webs, cocoons, etc.) from a silky fibre exuded from the body. **4** (*tr*) to shape (metal) into a rounded form on a lathe. **5** (*tr*) *Inf.* to tell (a tale, story, etc.) by drawing it out at great length (esp. in **spin a yarn**). **6** to bowl, pitch, hit, or kick (a ball) so that it rotates in the air and changes direction or speed on bouncing, or (of a ball) to be projected in this way. **7** (*intr*) (of wheels) to revolve rapidly without causing propulsion. **8** to cause (an aircraft) to dive in a spiral descent or (of an aircraft) to dive in a spiral descent. **9** (*intr*; foll. by *along*) to drive or travel swiftly. **10** (*tr*) Also: **spin-dry.** to rotate (clothes) in a washing machine in order to extract surplus water. **11** (*intr*) to reel or grow dizzy, as from turning around: *my head is spinning.* **12** (*intr*) to fish by drawing a revolving lure through the water. **13** (*intr*) *Inf.* to present news or information in a way that creates a favourable impression. ◆ *n* **14** a swift rotating motion; instance of spinning. **15** *Physics.* **15a** the intrinsic angular momentum of an elementary particle or atomic nucleus. **15b** a quantum number determining values of this angular momentum. **16** a condition of loss of control of an aircraft or an intentional flight manoeuvre in which the aircraft performs a continuous spiral descent. **17** a spinning motion imparted to a ball, etc. **18** *Inf.* a short or fast drive, ride, etc., esp. in a car, for pleasure. **19 flat spin.** *Inf., chiefly Brit.* a state of agitation or confusion. **20** *Austral. & NZ inf.* a period of a specified kind of fortune: *a bad spin.* **21** *Inf.* the practice of presenting news or information in a way that creates a favourable impression. ◆ See also **spin out.** [OE *spinnan*]

spina bifida ('spaɪnə 'bɪfɪdə) *n* a congenital condition in which the meninges of the spinal cord protrude through a gap in the backbone, sometimes causing enlargement of the skull and paralysis. [NL; see SPINE, BIFID]

spinach ('spɪnɪdʒ, -ɪtʃ) *n* **1** an annual plant cultivated for its dark green edible leaves. **2** The leaves, eaten as a vegetable. [C16: from OF *espinache,* from OSp., from Ar. *isfānākh,* from Persian]

spinal ('spaɪn°l) *adj* **1** of or relating to the spine or the spinal cord. ◆ *n* **2** short for **spinal anaesthesia.**
  ▸ **'spinally** *adv*

spinal anaesthesia *n* **1** anaesthesia of the lower half of the body produced by injecting an anaesthetic beneath the arachnoid membrane. Cf. **epidural** (sense 2). **2** loss of sensation in part of the body as the result of injury of the spinal cord.

spinal canal *n* the passage through the spinal column that contains the spinal cord.

spinal column *n* a series of contiguous or interconnecting bony or cartilaginous segments that surround and protect the spinal cord. Also called: **spine, vertebral column.** Nontechnical name: **backbone.**

spinal cord *n* the thick cord of nerve tissue within the spinal canal, which together with the brain forms the central nervous system.

spin bowler *n* another name for **spinner** (sense 2b).

spindle ('spɪnd°l) *n* **1** a rod or stick that has a notch in the top, used to draw out natural fibres for spinning into thread, and a long narrow body around which the thread is wound when spun. **2** one of the thin rods or pins bearing bobbins upon which spun thread is wound in a spinning machine. **3** any of various parts in the form of a rod, esp. a rotating rod that acts as an axle, etc. **4** a piece of wood that has been turned, such as a table leg. **5** a small square metal shaft that passes through the lock of a door and to which the door knobs or handles are fixed. **6** *Biol.* a spindle-shaped structure formed in a cell during mitosis or meiosis which draws the duplicated chromosomes apart during cell division. **7** a device consisting of a sharp upright spike on a pedestal on which bills, order forms, etc., are impaled. ◆ *vb* **spindles, spindling, spindled. 8** (*tr*) to form into a spindle or equip with spindles. **9** (*intr*) *Rare.* (of a plant, stem, shoot, etc.) to grow rapidly and become elongated and thin. [OE *spinel*]

spindlelegs ('spɪnd°l,legz) *or* **spindleshanks** *n* **1** (*functioning as pl*) long thin legs. **2** (*functioning as sing*) a person who has such legs.

spindle tree *n* any of various shrubs or trees of Europe and W Asia, typically having red fruits and yielding a hard wood formerly used in making spindles.

spindly ('spɪndlɪ) *adj* **spindlier, spindliest.** tall, slender, and frail; attenuated.

spin doctor *n* *Inf.* a person who provides a favourable slant to an item of news, potentially unpopular policy, etc., esp. on behalf of a political personality or party. [C20: from the spin given to a ball in various sports to make it go in the desired direction]

spindrift ('spɪn,drɪft) *n* spray blown up from the sea. Also: **spoondrift.** [C16: Scot. var. of *spoondrift,* from *spoon* to scud + DRIFT]

spin-dry *vb* **spin-dries, spin-drying, spin-dried.** (*tr*) to extract water from (wet washing) by spinning in a washing machine or spin-dryer.

spin-dryer *n* a device that extracts water from clothes, etc., by spinning them in a perforated drum.

spine (spaɪn) *n* **1** the spinal column. **2** the sharply pointed tip or outgrowth of a leaf, stem, etc. **3** *Zool.* a hard pointed process or structure, such as the quill of a porcupine. **4** the back of a book, record sleeve, etc. **5** a ridge, esp. of a hill. **6** strength of endurance, will, etc. **7** anything resembling the spinal column in function or importance; main support or feature. [C14: from OF *espine* spine, from L *spīna* thorn, backbone]
  ▸ **spined** *adj*

spine-chiller *n* a book, film, etc., that arouses terror.
  ▸ **'spine-,chilling** *adj*

spinel (spɪ'nel) *n* any of a group of hard glassy minerals of variable colour consisting of oxides of aluminium, magnesium, iron, zinc, or manganese: used as gemstones. [C16: from F *spinelle,* from It. *spinella,* dim. of *spina* a thorn, from L; so called from the shape of the crystals]

spineless ('spaɪnlɪs) *adj* **1** lacking a backbone. **2** having no spiny processes: *spineless stems.* **3** lacking character, resolution, or courage.
  ▸ **'spinelessly** *adv* ▸ **'spinelessness** *n*

spinet (spɪ'net, 'spɪnɪt) *n* a small type of harpsichord having one manual. [C17: from It. *spinetta,* ? from Giovanni *Spinetti,* 16th-cent. It. maker of musical instruments & its supposed inventor]

spinifex ('spɪnɪ,feks) *n* **1** any of various Australian grasses having pointed leaves and spiny seed heads. **2** Also called: **porcupine grass.** *Austral.* any of various coarse spiny-leaved inland grasses. [C19: from NL, from L *spīna* a thorn + *-fex* maker, from *facere* to make]

spinnaker ('spɪnəkə; *Naut.* 'spæŋkə) *n* a large light triangular racing sail set from the foremast of a yacht. [C19: prob. from SPIN + (MO)NIKER, but traditionally from *Sphinx,* the yacht that first adopted this type of sail]

spinner ('spɪnə) *n* **1** a person or thing that spins. **2** *Cricket.* **2a** a ball that is bowled with a spinning motion. **2b** a bowler who specializes in bowling such balls. **3** a streamlined fairing that fits over the hub of an aircraft propeller. **4** a fishing lure with a fin or wing that revolves.

spinneret ('spɪnə,ret) *n* **1** any of several organs in spiders and certain insects through which silk threads are exuded. **2** a finely perforated dispenser through which a liquid is extruded in the production of synthetic fibres.

spinney ('spɪnɪ) *n* *Chiefly Brit.* a small wood or copse. [C16: from OF *espinei,* from *espine* thorn, from L *spīna*]

spinning ('spɪnɪŋ) *n* **1** the act or process of spinning. **2** the act or technique of casting and drawing a revolving lure through the water so as to imitate a live fish, etc.

spinning jenny *n* an early type of spinning frame with several spindles, invented in 1764.

spinning wheel *n* a wheel-like machine for spinning at home, having one hand- or foot-operated spindle.

spin-off *n* **1** any product or development derived incidentally from the application of existing knowledge or enterprise. **2** a book, film, or television series derived from a similar successful book, film, or television series.

spinose ('spaɪnəʊs, spaɪ'nəʊs) *adj* (esp. of plants) bearing many spines. [C17: from L *spīnōsus* prickly, from *spīna* a thorn]

spin out *vb* (*tr, adv*) **1** to extend or protract (a story, etc.) by including superfluous detail. **2** to spend or pass (time). **3** to contrive to cause (money, etc.) to last as long as possible.

Spinoza ★ (spɪ'nəʊzə) *n* Baruch (bə'ruːk). 1632–77, Dutch pantheistic rationalist philosopher. His chief work is *The Ethics* (1677).

spinster ('spɪnstə) *n* **1** an unmarried woman. **2** a woman regarded as being beyond the age of marriage. **3** (formerly) a woman who spins thread for her living. [C14 (in the sense: a person, esp. a woman, whose occupation is spinning; C17: a woman still unmarried): from SPIN + -STER]
► **'spinster,hood** *n* ► **'spinsterish** *adj*

spiny ('spaɪnɪ) *adj* **spinier, spiniest. 1** (of animals) having or covered with quills or spines. **2** (of plants) covered with spines; thorny. **3** troublesome; puzzling.
► **'spininess** *n*

spiny anteater *n* another name for **echidna**.

spiny-finned *adj* (of certain fishes) having fins that are supported by stiff bony spines.

spiny lobster *n* any of various large edible marine decapod crustaceans having a very tough spiny carapace. Also called: **rock lobster, crawfish, langouste**.

spiracle ('spaɪərək³l, 'spaɪrə-) *n* **1** any of several paired apertures in the cuticle of an insect, by which air enters and leaves the trachea. **2** a small paired rudimentary gill slit in skates, rays, and related fishes. **3** any similar respiratory aperture, such as the blowhole in whales. [C14 (orig.: breath): from L *spīrāculum* vent, from *spīrāre* to breathe]
► **spiracular** (spɪ'rækjʊlə) *adj* ► **spi'raculate** *adj*

spiraea *or esp. US* **spirea** (spaɪ'rɪə) *n* any of various rosaceous plants having sprays of small white or pink flowers. See also **meadowsweet** (sense 2). [C17: via L from Gk *speiraia*, from *speira* SPIRE²]

spiral ('spaɪərəl) *n* **1** *Geom.* one of several plane curves formed by a point winding about a fixed point at an ever-increasing distance from it. **2** a curve that lies on a cylinder or cone, at a constant angle to the line segments making up the surface; helix. **3** something that pursues a winding, usually upward, course or that displays a twisting form or shape. **4** a flight manoeuvre in which an aircraft descends describing a helix of comparatively large radius with the angle of attack within the normal flight range. **5** *Econ.* a continuous upward or downward movement in economic activity or prices, caused by interaction between prices, wages, demand, and production. ◆ *adj* **6** having the shape of a spiral. ◆ *vb* **spirals, spiralling, spiralled** *or US* **spirals, spiraling, spiraled. 7** to assume or cause to assume a spiral course or shape. **8** (*intr*) to increase or decrease with steady acceleration: *prices continue to spiral.* [C16: via F from Med. L *spīrālis*, from L *spīra* a coil; see SPIRE²]
► **'spirally** *adv*

spiral galaxy *n* a galaxy consisting of an ellipsoidal nucleus of old stars from opposite sides of which arms, containing younger stars, spiral outwards around the nucleus.

spirant ('spaɪrənt) *adj* **1** *Phonetics.* another word for **fricative.** ◆ *n* **2** a fricative consonant. [C19: from L *spīrāns* breathing, from *spīrāre* to breathe]

spire¹ ('spaɪə) *n* **1** Also called: **steeple.** a tall structure that tapers upwards to a point, esp. one on a tower or roof or one that forms the upper part of a steeple. **2** a slender tapering shoot or stem, such as a blade of grass. **3** the apical part of any tapering formation; summit. ◆ *vb* **spires, spiring, spired. 4** (*intr*) to assume the shape of a spire; point up. **5** (*tr*) to furnish with a spire or spires. [OE *spīr* blade]
► **'spiry** *adj*

spire² ('spaɪə) *n* **1** any of the coils or turns in a spiral struc-

ture. **2** the apical part of a spiral shell. [C16: from L *spīra* a coil, from Gk *speira*]

Spires ★ ('spaɪəz) *n* the English name for **Speyer.**

spirillum (spaɪ'rɪləm) *n, pl* **spirilla** (-lə). **1** any bacterium having a curved or spirally twisted rodlike body. **2** any bacterium of the genus *Spirillum*, such as *S. minus*, which causes ratbite fever. [C19: from NL, lit.: a little coil, from *spīra* a coil]

spirit¹ ('spɪrɪt) *n* **1** the force or principle of life that animates the body of living things. **2** temperament or disposition: *truculent in spirit.* **3** liveliness; mettle: *they set to it with spirit.* **4** the fundamental, emotional, and activating principle of a person; will: *the experience broke his spirit.* **5** a sense of loyalty or dedication: *team spirit.* **6** the prevailing element; feeling: *a spirit of joy pervaded the atmosphere.* **7** state of mind or mood; attitude: *he did it in the wrong spirit.* **8** (*pl*) an emotional state, esp. with regard to exaltation or dejection: *in high spirits.* **9** a person characterized by some activity, quality, or disposition: *a leading spirit of the movement.* **10** the deeper more significant meaning as opposed to a pedantic interpretation: *the spirit of the law.* **11** a person's intangible being as contrasted with his physical presence: *I shall be with you in spirit.* **12a** an incorporeal being, esp. the soul of a dead person. **12b** (*as modifier*): *spirit world.* ◆ *vb* (*tr*) (usually foll. by *away* or *off*) to carry off mysteriously or secretly. **14** (often foll. by *up*) to impart animation or determination to. [C13: from OF *esperit*, from L *spīritus* breath, spirit]
► **'spiritless** *adj*

spirit² ('spɪrɪt) *n* **1** (*often pl*) any distilled alcoholic liquor, such as whisky or gin. **2** *Chem.* **2a** an aqueous solution of ethanol, esp. one obtained by distillation. **2b** the active principle or essence of a substance, extracted as a liquid, esp. by distillation. **3** *Pharmacol.* a solution of a volatile substance, esp. a volatile oil, in alcohol. **4** *Alchemy.* any of the four substances sulphur, mercury, sal ammoniac, or arsenic. [C14: special use of SPIRIT¹, name applied to alchemical substances (as in sense 4), hence extended to distilled liquids]

Spirit ('spɪrɪt) *n* **the. a** another name for the **Holy Spirit. b** God, esp. when regarded as transcending material limitations.

spirited ('spɪrɪtɪd) *adj* **1** displaying animation, vigour, or liveliness. **2** (*in combination*) characterized by mood, temper, or disposition as specified: *high-spirited; public-spirited.*
► **'spiritedly** *adv* ► **'spiritedness** *n*

spirit gum *n* a glue made from gum dissolved in ether used to affix a false beard, etc.

spiritism ('spɪrɪ,tɪzəm) *n* a less common word for **spiritualism.**
► **'spiritist** *n* ► ,spirit'istic *adj*

spirit lamp *n* a lamp that burns methylated or other spirits instead of oil.

spirit level *n* a device for setting horizontal surfaces, consisting of a block of material in which a sealed tube partially filled with liquid is set so that the air bubble rests between two marks on the tube when the block is horizontal.

spiritous ('spɪrɪtəs) *adj* a variant of **spirituous.**

spirits of ammonia *n* (*functioning as sing or pl*) another name for **sal volatile.**

spirits of hartshorn *n* (*functioning as sing or pl*) a solution of ammonia gas in water. See **ammonium hydroxide.** Also called: **aqueous ammonia.**

spirits of salt *n* (*functioning as sing or pl*) a solution of hydrochloric acid in water.

spiritual ('spɪrɪtjʊəl) *adj* **1** relating to the spirit or soul and not to physical nature or matter; intangible. **2** of or relating to sacred things, the Church, religion, etc. **3** standing in a relationship based on communication between souls or minds: *a spiritual father.* **4** having a mind or emotions of a high and delicately refined quality. ◆ *n* **5** Also called: **Negro spiritual.** a type of religious song originating among Black slaves in the American South. **6** (*often pl*) the sphere of religious, spiritual, or ecclesiastical matters, or such matters in themselves.
► ,spiritu'ality *n* ► 'spiritually *adv*

spiritualism ('spɪrɪtjʊəˌlɪzəm) n 1 the belief that the disembodied spirits of the dead, surviving in another world, can communicate with the living in this world, esp. through mediums. 2 the doctrines and practices associated with this belief. 3 Philosophy. the belief that because reality is to some extent immaterial it is therefore spiritual. 4 any doctrine that prefers the spiritual to the material.
▸ 'spiritualist n

spiritualize or **spiritualise** ('spɪrɪtjʊəˌlaɪz) vb **spiritualizes, spiritualizing, spiritualized** or **spiritualises, spiritualising, spiritualised.** (tr) to make spiritual or infuse with spiritual content.
▸ ˌspirituali'zation or ˌspirituali'sation n ▸ 'spiritualˌizer or 'spiritualˌiser n

spirituel (ˌspɪrɪtjʊ'ɛl) adj having a refined and lively mind or wit. Also (fem): **spirituelle.** [C17: from F]

spirituous ('spɪrɪtjʊəs) adj 1 characterized by or containing alcohol. 2 (of a drink) being a spirit.
▸ spirituosity (ˌspɪrɪtjʊ'ɒsɪtɪ) or 'spirituousness n

spirochaete or US **spirochete** ('spaɪrəˌkiːt) n any of a group of spirally coiled rodlike bacteria that includes the causative agent of syphilis. [C19: from NL, from spiro-, from L spira, from Gk speira a coil + chaeta, from Gk khaitē long hair]

spirograph ('spaɪrəˌgrɑːf) n Med. an instrument for recording the movements of breathing. [C20: NL, from spiro-, from L spīrāre to breathe + -GRAPH]
▸ ˌspiro'graphic adj

spirogyra (ˌspaɪrə'dʒaɪrə) n any of various green freshwater multicellular algae containing spirally coiled chloroplasts. [C20: from NL, from spiro-, from L spīra, from Gk speira a coil + Gk guros a circle]

spirt (spɜːt) n a variant spelling of **spurt.**

spiry ('spaɪərɪ) adj Poetic. of spiral form; helical.

spit[1] (spɪt) vb **spits, spitting, spat** or **spit. 1** (intr) to expel saliva from the mouth; expectorate. **2** (intr) Inf. to show disdain or hatred by spitting. **3** (of a fire, hot fat, etc.) to eject (sparks, etc.) violently and with an explosive sound. **4** (intr) to rain very lightly. **5** (tr; often foll. by out) to eject or discharge (something) from the mouth: he spat the food out. **6** (tr; often foll. by out) to utter (short sharp words or syllables), esp. in a violent manner. **7 spit it out!** Brit. inf. a command given to someone that he should speak forthwith. ◆ n **8** another name for **spittle. 9** a light or brief fall of rain, snow, etc. **10** the act or an instance of spitting. **11** Inf., chiefly Brit. another word for **spitting image.** [OE spittan]
▸ 'spitter n

spit[2] (spɪt) n **1** a pointed rod on which meat is skewered and roasted before or over an open fire. **2** Also called: **rotisserie, rotating spit.** a similar device fitted onto a cooker. **3** an elongated often hooked strip of sand or shingle projecting from a shore. ◆ vb **spits, spitting, spitted. 4** (tr) to impale on or transfix with or as if with a spit. [OE spitu]

spit and polish n Inf. punctilious attention to neatness, discipline, etc., esp. in the armed forces.

spite (spaɪt) n **1** maliciousness; venomous ill will. **2** an instance of such malice; grudge. **3 in spite of.** (prep) in defiance of; regardless of; notwithstanding. ◆ vb **spites, spiting, spited.** (tr) **4** to annoy in order to vent spite. [C13: var. of DESPITE]
▸ 'spiteful adj

spitfire ('spɪtˌfaɪə) n a person given to outbursts of spiteful temper, esp. a woman or girl.

Spithead ★ (ˌspɪt'hɛd) n an extensive anchorage between the mainland of England and the Isle of Wight, off Portsmouth.

Spitsbergen ★ ('spɪtsˌbɜːgən) n another name for **Svalbard.**

spitting image n Inf. a person who bears a strong physical resemblance to another. Also called: **spit, spit and image.** [C19: modification of spit and image, from SPIT[1] (as in the very spit of) the exact likeness of)]

spitting snake n another name for the **rinkhals.**

spittle ('spɪtəl) n **1** the fluid secreted in the mouth; saliva. **2** Also called: **cuckoo spit, frog spit.** the frothy substance se-

creted on plants by the larvae of certain froghoppers. [OE spætl saliva]

spittoon (spɪ'tuːn) n a receptacle for spittle, usually in a public place.

spitz (spɪts) n any of various breeds of dog characterized by a stocky build, a pointed muzzle, erect ears, and a tightly-curled tail. [C19: from G Spitz, from spitz pointed]

Spitz ★ (spɪts) n **Mark.** born 1950, US swimmer, who won seven gold medals at the 1972 Olympic Games.

spiv (spɪv) n Brit. sl. a person who makes a living by underhand dealings or swindling; black marketeer. [C20: back formation from dialect spiving smart]
▸ 'spivvy adj

splake (spleɪk) n a type of hybrid trout bred by Canadian zoologists. [from sp(eckled) + lake (trout)]

splanchnic ('splæŋknɪk) adj of or relating to the viscera: a splanchnic nerve. [C17: from NL splanchnicus, from Gk, from splankhna the entrails]

splash (splæʃ) vb **1** to scatter (liquid) about in blobs; spatter. **2** to descend or cause to descend upon in scattered blobs: he splashed his jacket; rain splashed against the window. **3** to make (one's) way by or as if by splashing: he splashed through the puddle. **4** (tr) to print (a story or photograph) prominently in a newspaper. ◆ n **5** an instance or sound of splashing. **6** an amount splashed. **7** a mark or patch created by or as if by splashing. **8** Inf. an extravagant display, usually for effect (esp. in **make a splash). 9** a small amount of soda water, etc., added to an alcoholic drink. [C18: alteration of PLASH]
▸ 'splashy adj

splashdown ('splæʃˌdaʊn) n **1** the controlled landing of a spacecraft on water at the end of a space flight. **2** the time scheduled for this event. ◆ vb **splash down. 3** (intr, adv) (of a spacecraft) to make a splashdown.

splat[1] (splæt) n a wet slapping sound. [C19: imit.]

splat[2] (splæt) n a wide flat piece of wood, esp. one that is the upright central part of a chair back. [C19: ? rel. to OE splātan to split]

splatter ('splætə) vb **1** to splash with small blobs. ◆ n **2** a splash of liquid, mud, etc.

splatter movie n Sl. a film in which the main feature is the graphic and gory murder of numerous victims.

splay (spleɪ) adj **1** spread out; broad and flat. **2** turned outwards in an awkward manner. ◆ vb **3** to spread out; turn out or expand. ◆ n **4** a surface of a wall that forms an oblique angle to the main flat surfaces, esp. at a doorway or window opening. [C14: short for DISPLAY]

splayfoot ('spleɪˌfʊt) n, pl **splayfeet.** Pathol. another word for **flatfoot.**
▸ 'splayˌfooted adj

spleen (spliːn) n **1** a spongy highly vascular organ situated near the stomach in man. It forms lymphocytes, produces antibodies, and filters bacteria and foreign particles from the blood. **2** the corresponding organ in other animals. **3** spitefulness or ill humour: to vent one's spleen. **4** Arch. the organ in the human body considered to be the seat of the emotions. **5** Arch. another word for **melancholy.** [C13: from OF esplen, from L splēn, from Gk]
▸ 'spleenish or 'spleeny adj

spleenwort ('spliːnˌwɜːt) n any of various ferns that often grow on walls.

splendent ('splɛndənt) adj Arch. **1** shining brightly; lustrous: a splendent sun. **2** famous; illustrious. [C15: from L splendēns brilliant, from splendēre to shine]

splendid ('splɛndɪd) adj **1** brilliant or fine, esp. in appearance. **2** characterized by magnificence. **3** glorious or illustrious: a splendid reputation. **4** brightly gleaming; radiant: splendid colours. **5** very good or satisfactory: a splendid time. [C17: from L splendidus, from splendēre to shine]
▸ 'splendidly adv ▸ 'splendidness n

splendiferous (splɛn'dɪfərəs) adj Facetious. grand; splendid: a really splendiferous meal. [C15: from Med. L splendiferus, from L splendor radiance + ferre to bring]

splendour or US **splendor** ('splɛndə) n **1** the state or quality of being splendid. **2 sun in splendour.** Heraldry. a representation of the sun with rays and a human face.

★ people and places

splenetic (splɪ'nɛtɪk) *adj* **1** of or relating to the spleen. **2** spiteful or irritable; peevish. ♦ *n* **3** a spiteful or irritable person.
▸ sple'netically *adv*

splenic ('splɛnɪk, 'spliː-) *adj* **1** of, relating to, or in the spleen. **2** having a disease or disorder of the spleen.

splenius ('spliːnɪəs) *n, pl* **splenii** (-nɪˌaɪ). either of two muscles at the back of the neck that rotate, flex, and extend the head and neck. [C18: via NL from Gk *splēnion* a plaster]
▸ 'splenial *adj*

splenomegaly (ˌspliːnəʊ'mɛgəlɪ) *n* abnormal enlargement of the spleen. [C20: NL, from Gk *splēn* spleen + *megal-*, stem of *megas* big]

splice (splaɪs) *vb* **splices, splicing, spliced.** (*tr*) **1** to join (two ropes) by intertwining the strands. **2** to join up the trimmed ends of (two pieces of wire, film, etc.) with solder or an adhesive material. **3** to join (timbers) by overlapping and binding or bolting the ends together. **4** (*passive*) *Inf.* to enter into marriage: *the couple got spliced*. **5 splice the mainbrace.** *Naut. hist.* to issue and partake of an extra allocation of alcoholic spirits. ♦ *n* **6** a join made by splicing. **7** the place where such a join occurs. **8** the wedge-shaped end of a cricket-bat handle that fits into the blade. [C16: prob. from MDu. *splissen*]
▸ 'splicer *n*

spline (splaɪn) *n* **1** any one of a series of narrow keys formed longitudinally around a shaft that fit into corresponding grooves in a mating part: used to prevent movement between two parts, esp. in transmitting torque. **2** a long narrow strip of wood, metal, etc.; slat. **3** a thin narrow strip made of wood, metal, or plastic fitted into a groove in the edge of a board, tile, etc., to connect it to another. ♦ *vb* **splines, splining, splined. 4** (*tr*) to provide (a shaft, part, etc.) with splines. [C18: East Anglian dialect; ? rel. to OE *splin* spindle]

splint (splɪnt) *n* **1** a rigid support for restricting movement of an injured part, esp. a broken bone. **2** a thin sliver of wood, esp. one used to light cigars, a fire, etc. **3** a thin strip of wood woven with others to form a chair seat, basket, etc. **4** *Vet. science.* a bony enlargement of the cannon bone of a horse. ♦ *vb* **5** to apply a splint to (a broken arm, etc.). [C13: from MLow G *splinte*]

splinter ('splɪntə) *n* **1** a small thin sharp piece of wood, glass, etc., broken off from a whole. **2** a metal fragment from a shell, bomb, etc., thrown out during an explosion. ♦ *vb* **3** to reduce or be reduced to sharp fragments. **4** to break or be broken off in small sharp fragments. [C14: from MDu. *splinter;* see SPLINT]
▸ 'splintery *adj*

splinter group *n* a number of members of an organization, political party, etc., who split from the main body and form an independent association of their own.

split (splɪt) *vb* **splits, splitting, split. 1** to break or cause to break, esp. forcibly, by cleaving into separate pieces, often into two roughly equal pieces. **2** to separate or be separated from a whole: *he split a piece of wood from the block*. **3** to separate or be separated into factions, usually through discord. **4** (often foll. by *up*) to separate or cause to separate through a disagreement. **5** (when *tr*, often foll. by *up*) to divide or be divided among two or more persons: *split up the pie among us*. **6** *Sl.* to depart; leave: *let's split*. **7** (*tr*) to separate (something) into its components by interposing something else: *to split a word with hyphens*. **8** (*intr*; usually foll. by *on*) *Sl.* to betray; inform: *he split on me to the cops*. **9** (*tr*) *US politics.* to mark (a ballot, etc.) so as to vote for the candidates of more than one party: *he split the ticket*. **10 split one's sides.** to laugh very heartily. ♦ *n* **11** the act or process of splitting. **12** a gap or rift caused or a piece removed by the process of splitting. **13** a breach or schism in a group or the faction resulting from such a breach. **14** a dessert of sliced fruit and ice cream, covered with whipped cream, nuts, etc.: *banana split*. **15** See **Devonshire split. 16** *Tenpin bowling.* a formation of the pins after the first bowl in which there is a large gap between two pins or groups of pins. **17** *Inf.* an arrangement or process of dividing up loot or money. ♦ *adj* **18** having been split; divided: *split logs*. **19** having a

split or splits: *hair with split ends*. ♦ See also **splits, split up.** [C16: from MDu. *splitten* to cleave]
▸ 'splitter *n*

Split ★ (*Serbo-Croat* split) *n* a port and resort in W Croatia on the Adriatic: became part of Yugoslavia in 1918 after Austrian rule since 1797: remains of the palace of Diocletian (295–305). Pop.: 200 459 (1991). Italian name: **Spalato.**

split infinitive *n* (in English grammar) an infinitive used with another word between *to* and the verb itself, as in *to really finish it*.

> **USAGE NOTE** The traditional rule against placing an adverb between *to* and its verb is gradually disappearing. Although it is true that a split infinitive may result in a clumsy sentence (*he decided to firmly and definitively deal with the problem*), this is not enough to justify the absolute condemnation that this practice has attracted. Indeed, very often the most natural position of the adverb is between *to* and the verb (*he decided to really try next time*) and to change it would result in an artificial and awkward construction (*he decided really to try next time*). The current view is therefore that the split infinitive is not a grammatical error. Nevertheless, many writers prefer to avoid splitting infinitives in formal written English, since readers with a more traditional point of view are likely to interpret this type of construction as incorrect.

split-level *adj* (of a house, room, etc.) having the floor level of one part about half a storey above the floor level of an adjoining part.

split pea *n* a pea dried and split and used in soups, pease pudding, or as a vegetable.

split personality *n* **1** the tendency to change rapidly in mood or temperament. **2** a nontechnical term for **multiple personality.**

split pin *n* a metal pin made by bending double a wire, often of hemispherical section, so that it can be passed through a hole in a nut, shaft, etc., to secure another part by bending back the ends of the wire.

split ring *n* a steel ring having two helical turns, often used as a key ring.

splits (splɪts) *n* (*functioning as sing*) (in gymnastics, etc.) the act of sinking to the floor to achieve a sitting position in which both legs are straight, pointing in opposite directions, and at right angles to the body.

split-screen technique *n* a cinematic device by which two or more complete images are projected simultaneously onto separate parts of the screen. Also called: **split screen.**

split second *n* **1** an extremely small period of time; instant. ♦ *adj* **split-second.** (*prenominal*) **2** made or arrived at in an extremely short time: *a split-second decision*. **3** depending upon minute precision: *split-second timing*.

split shift *n* a work period divided into two parts that are separated by an interval longer than a normal rest period.

splitting ('splɪtɪŋ) *adj* **1** (of a headache) intolerably painful; acute. **2** (of the head) assailed by an overpowering unbearable pain.

split up *vb* (*adv*) **1** (*tr*) to separate out into parts; divide. **2** (*intr*) to become parted through disagreement: *they split up after years of marriage*. **3** to break down or be capable of being broken down into constituent parts. ♦ *n* **split-up. 4** the act or an instance of separating.

splodge (splɒdʒ) *n* **1** a large irregular spot or blot. ♦ *vb* **splodges, splodging, splodged. 2** (*tr*) to mark (something) with such a blot or blots. [C19: alteration of earlier SPLOTCH]
▸ 'splodgy *adj*

splotch (splɒtʃ) *n, vb* the usual US word for **splodge.** [C17: ? a blend of SPOT + BLOTCH]
▸ 'splotchy *adj*

splurge (spl3ːdʒ) n 1 an ostentatious display, esp. of wealth. 2 a bout of unrestrained extravagance. ♦ vb **splurges, splurging, splurged. 3** (often foll. by *out*) to spend (money) extravagantly. [C19: from ?]

splutter ('splʌtə) vb 1 to spit out (saliva, food particles, etc.) from the mouth in an explosive manner, as through choking or laughing. 2 to utter (words) with spitting sounds, as through rage or choking. 3 to eject or be ejected in an explosive manner: *sparks spluttered from the fire.* 4 (tr) to bespatter (a person) with tiny particles explosively ejected. ♦ n 5 the process or noise of spluttering. 6 spluttering incoherent speech. 7 anything ejected through spluttering. [C17: var. of SPUTTER, infl. by SPLASH]
▸ 'splutterer n

Spock ★ (spɒk) n Benjamin, known as Dr Spock. 1903–98, US paediatrician, who wrote the permissive *The Common Sense Book of Baby and Child Care* (1946).

spode (spəʊd) n (*sometimes cap.*) china or porcelain manufactured by Josiah Spode (1754–1827), English potter, or his company.

spoil (spɔɪl) vb **spoils, spoiling, spoilt** *or* **spoiled. 1** (tr) to cause damage to (something), in regard to its value, beauty, usefulness, etc. 2 (tr) to weaken the character of (a child) by complying unrestrainedly with its desires. 3 (intr) (of perishable substances) to become unfit for consumption or use. 4 (intr) Sport. to disrupt the play or style of an opponent, as to prevent him from settling into a rhythm. 5 Arch. to strip (a person or place) of (property) by force. 6 **be spoiling for.** to have an aggressive desire for (a fight, etc.). ♦ n 7 waste material thrown up by an excavation. 8 any treasure accumulated by a person. 9 Obs. the act of plundering. ♦ See also **spoils.** [C13: from OF *espoillier*, from L *spoliāre* to strip, from *spolium* booty]

spoilage ('spɔɪlɪdʒ) n 1 the act or an instance of spoiling or the state or condition of being spoilt. 2 an amount of material that has been wasted by being spoilt: *considerable spoilage.*

spoiler ('spɔɪlə) n 1 a plunderer or robber. 2 a person or thing that causes spoilage or corruption. 3 a device fitted to an aircraft wing to increase drag and reduce lift. 4 a similar device fitted to a car. 5 Sport. a competitor who adopts spoiling tactics. 6 a magazine, newspaper, etc., produced specifically to coincide with the production of a rival magazine, newspaper, etc., in order to divert public interest and reduce its sales.

spoils (spɔɪlz) pl n 1 (*sometimes sing*) valuables seized by violence, esp. in war. 2 Chiefly US. the rewards and benefits of public office regarded as plunder for the winning party or candidate. See also **spoils system.**

spoilsport ('spɔɪl,spɔːt) n Inf. a person who spoils the pleasure of other people.

spoils system n Chiefly US. the practice of filling appointive public offices with friends and supporters of the ruling political party.

spoilt (spɔɪlt) vb a past tense and past participle of **spoil.**

Spokane ★ (spəʊ'kæn) n a city in E Washington: commercial centre of an agricultural region. Pop.: 192 781 (1994 est.).

spoke[1] (spəʊk) vb 1 the past tense of **speak.** 2 Arch. or dialect. a past participle of **speak.**

spoke[2] (spəʊk) n 1 a radial member of a wheel, joining the hub to the rim. 2 a radial projection from the rim of a wheel, as in a ship's wheel. 3 a rung of a ladder. 4 **put a spoke in someone's wheel.** Brit. to thwart someone's plans. ♦ vb **spokes, spoking, spoked. 5** (tr) to equip with or as if with spokes. [OE *spaca*]

spoken ('spəʊkən) vb 1 the past participle of **speak.** ♦ adj 2 uttered in speech. 3 (*in combination*) having speech as specified: *soft-spoken.* 4 **spoken for.** engaged or reserved.

spokeshave ('spəʊk,ʃeɪv) n a small plane with two handles, one on each side of its blade, used for shaping or smoothing cylindrical wooden surfaces, such as spokes.

spokesman ('spəʊksmən), **spokesperson** ('spəʊks-,pɜːs°n), *or* **spokeswoman** ('spəʊks,wʊmən) n, pl **spokesmen, spokespersons** *or* **spokespeople,** *or* **spokeswomen.** a person authorized to speak on behalf of another person or group.

spoliation (,spəʊlɪ'eɪʃən) n 1 the act or an instance of despoiling or plundering. 2 the authorized plundering of neutral vessels on the seas by a belligerent state in time of war. 3 Law. the material alteration of a document so as to render it invalid. 4 English ecclesiastical law. the taking of the fruits of a benefice by a person not entitled to them. [C14: from L *spoliātiō,* from *spoliāre* to SPOIL]
▸ **spoliatory** ('spəʊlɪətərɪ, -trɪ) adj

spondee ('spɒndiː) n Prosody. a metrical foot consisting of two long syllables (--). [C14: from OF *spondée,* from L *spondēus,* from Gk, from *spondē* ritual libation; from use of spondee in the music for such ceremonies]
▸ **spondaic** (spɒn'deɪɪk) adj

spondylitis (,spɒndɪ'laɪtɪs) n inflammation of the vertebrae. [C19: from NL, from Gk *spondulos* vertebra; see -ITIS]

sponge (spʌndʒ) n 1 any of various multicellular typically marine animals, usually occurring in complex sessile colonies, in which the porous body is supported by a fibrous, calcareous, or siliceous skeletal framework. 2 a piece of the light porous highly absorbent elastic skeleton of certain sponges, used in bathing, cleaning, etc. 3 any of a number of light porous elastic materials resembling a sponge. 4 another word for **sponger** (sense 1). 5 Inf. a person who indulges in heavy drinking. 6 leavened dough, esp. before kneading. 7 See **sponge cake.** 8 Also called: **sponge pudding.** Brit. a light steamed or baked spongy pudding. 9 porous metal capable of absorbing large quantities of gas: *platinum sponge.* 10 a rub with a sponge. 11 **throw in the sponge** (*or* **towel**). See **throw in** (sense 3). ♦ vb **sponges, sponging, sponged. 12** (tr; often foll. by *off* or *down*) to clean (something) by wiping or rubbing with a damp or wet sponge. 13 (tr; usually foll. by *off, away, out,* etc.) to remove (marks, etc.) by rubbing with a damp or wet sponge or cloth. 14 (when tr, often foll. by *up*) to absorb (liquids, esp. when spilt) in the manner of a sponge. 15 (intr) to go collecting sponges. 16 (foll. by *off*) to get (something) from someone by presuming on his generosity: *to sponge a meal off someone.* 17 (foll. by *off* or *on*) to obtain one's subsistence, etc., unjustifiably (from): *he sponges off his friends.* [OE, from L *spongia,* from Gk]
▸ **'spongy** adj

sponge bag n a small waterproof bag made of plastic, etc., that holds toilet articles, used esp. when travelling.

sponge bath n a washing of the body with a wet sponge or cloth, without immersion in water.

sponge cake n a light porous cake, made of eggs, sugar, flour, and flavourings, without any fat.

sponger ('spʌndʒə) n 1 Inf. a person who lives off other people by continually taking advantage of their generosity; parasite or scrounger. 2 a person or ship employed in collecting sponges.

spongiform ('spʌndʒɪ,fɔːm) adj 1 resembling a sponge in appearance, esp. in having many holes. 2 denoting diseases characterized by this appearance of affected tissues.

sponsion ('spɒnʃən) n 1 the act or process of becoming surety; sponsorship. 2 (*often pl*) International law. an unauthorized agreement made by a public officer, requiring ratification by his government. 3 any act or promise, esp. one made on behalf of someone else. [C17: from L *sponsiō,* from *spondēre* to pledge]

sponson ('spɒnsən) n 1 Naval. an outboard support for a gun, etc. 2 a structural projection from the side of a paddle steamer for supporting a paddle wheel. 3 a float or flotation chamber along the gunwale of a boat or ship. 4 a structural unit attached to a helicopter fuselage by struts, housing the landing gear and flotation bags. [C19: ?from EXPANSION]

sponsor ('spɒnsə) n 1 a person or group that promotes either another person or group in an activity or the activity itself, either for profit or for charity. 2 Chiefly US & Canad. a person or business firm that pays the costs of a radio or television programme in return for advertising time. 3 a legislator who presents and supports a bill, motion, etc. 4 Also called: **godparent. 4a** an authorized witness who makes the required promises on behalf of a person to be baptized and thereafter assumes responsi-

bility for his Christian upbringing. **4b** a person who presents a candidate for confirmation. ♦ *vb* **5** (*tr*) to act as a sponsor for. [C17: from L, from *spondēre* to promise solemnly]
▶ **sponsorial** (spɒnˈsɔːrɪəl) *adj* ▶ **'sponsor,ship** *n*

sponsored ('spɒnsəd) *adj* denoting an activity organized to raise money for a charity in which sponsors agree to donate money on completion of the activity by participants.

spontaneity (,spɒntəˈniːɪtɪ, -ˈneɪ-) *n, pl* **spontaneities. 1** the state or quality of being spontaneous. **2** (*often pl*) the exhibiting of spontaneous actions, impulses, or behaviour.

spontaneous (spɒnˈteɪnɪəs) *adj* **1** occurring, produced, or performed through natural processes without external influence. **2** arising from an unforced personal impulse; voluntary; unpremeditated. **3** (of plants) growing naturally; indigenous. [C17: from LL *spontāneus*, from L *sponte* voluntarily]
▶ **spon'taneously** *adv* ▶ **spon'taneousness** *n*

spontaneous combustion *n* the ignition of a substance or body as a result of internal oxidation processes, without the application of an external source of heat.

spontaneous generation *n* another name for **abiogenesis.**

spoof (spuːf) *Inf.* ♦ *n* **1** a mildly satirical mockery or parody; lampoon. **2** a good-humoured deception or trick. ♦ *vb* **3** to indulge in a spoof of (a person or thing). [C19: coined by A. Roberts (1852–1933), E comedian]
▶ **'spoofer** *n*

spook (spuːk) *Inf.* ♦ *n* **1** a ghost. **2** *US & Canad.* a spy. **3** a strange or frightening person. ♦ *vb* (*tr*) *US & Canad.* **4** to frighten: *to spook horses; to spook a person.* **5** (of a ghost) to haunt. [C19: from Du. *spook,* from MLow G *spōk* ghost]
▶ **'spooky** *adj*

spool (spuːl) *n* **1** a device around which magnetic tape, film, cotton, etc., can be wound, with flanges at top and bottom to prevent it from slipping off. **2** anything round which other materials, esp. thread, are wound. ♦ *vb* **3** (sometimes foll. by *up*) to wind or be wound onto a spool. [C14: of Gmc origin]

spoon (spuːn) *n* **1** a utensil having a shallow concave part, usually elliptical in shape, attached to a handle, used in eating or serving food, stirring, etc. **2** Also called: **spoonbait.** an angling lure consisting of a bright piece of metal which swivels on a trace to which are attached a hook or hooks. **3** *Golf.* a former name for a No. 3 wood. **4 be born with a silver spoon in one's mouth.** to inherit wealth or social standing. **5** *Rowing.* a type of oar blade that is curved at the edge and tip. ♦ *vb* **6** (*tr*) to scoop up or transfer (food, liquid, etc.) from one container to another with or as if with a spoon. **7** (*intr*) *Old-fashioned sl.* to kiss and cuddle. **8** *Sport.* to hit (a ball) with a weak lifting motion, as in golf, cricket, etc. [OE *spōn* splinter]

spoonbill ('spuːn,bɪl) *n* any of several wading birds of warm regions, having a long horizontally flattened bill.

spoondrift ('spuːn,drɪft) *n* a less common spelling of **spindrift.**

spoonerism ('spuːnə,rɪzəm) *n* the transposition of the initial consonants or consonant clusters of a pair of words, often resulting in an amusing ambiguity, such as *hush my brat* for *brush my hat.* [C20: after W. A. Spooner (1844–1930), E clergyman renowned for this]

spoon-feed *vb* **spoon-feeds, spoon-feeding, spoon-fed.** (*tr*) **1** to feed with a spoon. **2** to overindulge or spoil. **3** to provide (a person) with ready-made opinions, judgments, etc.

spoonful ('spuːn,fʊl) *n, pl* **spoonfuls. 1** the amount that a spoon is able to hold. **2** a small quantity.

spoony *or* **spooney** ('spuːnɪ) *Inf., old-fashioned.* ♦ *adj* **spoonier, spooniest. 1** foolishly or stupidly amorous. ♦ *n, pl* **spoonies. 2** a fool or silly person, esp. one in love.

spoor (spʊə, spɔː) *n* **1** the trail of an animal or person, esp. as discernible to the eye. ♦ *vb* **2** to track (an animal) by following its trail. [C19: from Afrik., from MDu. *spor;* rel. to OE *spor* track]

Sporades ★ ('spɒrə,diːz) *pl n* two groups of Greek islands

in the Aegean: the **Northern Sporades,** lying northeast of Euboea, and the **Southern Sporades,** which include the Dodecanese and lie off the SW coast of Turkey.

sporadic (spəˈrædɪk) *adj* **1** occurring at irregular points in time; intermittent: *sporadic firing.* **2** scattered; isolated: *a sporadic disease.* [C17: from Med. L *sporadicus,* from Gk, from *sporas* scattered]
▶ **spo'radically** *adv*

sporangium (spəˈrændʒɪəm) *n, pl* **sporangia** (-dʒɪə). any organ, esp. in fungi, in which asexual spores are produced. [C19: from NL, from SPORO- + Gk *angeion* receptacle]
▶ **spo'rangial** *adj*

spore (spɔː) *n* **1** a reproductive body, produced by bacteria, fungi, some protozoans and many plants, that develops into a new individual. A **sexual spore** is formed after the fusion of gametes and an **asexual spore** is the result of asexual reproduction. **2** a germ cell, seed, dormant bacterium, or similar body. ♦ *vb* **spores, sporing, spored. 3** (*intr*) to produce, carry, or release spores. [C19: from NL *spora,* from Gk: a sowing; rel. to Gk *speirein* to sow]

spore case *n* the nontechnical name for **sporangium.**

sporo- *or before a vowel* **spor-** *combining form.* spore: *sporophyte.* [from NL *spora*]

sporogenesis (,spɔːrəʊˈdʒɛnɪsɪs, ,spɒ-) *n* the process of spore formation in plants and animals.
▶ **sporogenous** (spɔːˈrɒdʒɪnəs, ,spɒ-) *adj*

sporogonium (,spɔːrəʊˈgəʊnɪəm, ,spɒ-) *n, pl* **sporogonia** (-nɪə). a structure in mosses and liverworts consisting of a spore-bearing capsule on a short stalk that arises from the parent plant.

sporophyll *or* **sporophyl** ('spɔːrəʊfɪl, 'spɒ-) *n* a leaf in mosses, ferns, and related plants that bears the sporangia.

sporophyte ('spɔːrəʊ,faɪt, 'spɒ-) *n* the diploid form of plants that have alternation of generations. It produces asexual spores.
▶ **sporophytic** (,spɔːrəˈfɪtɪk, ,spɒ-) *adj*

-sporous *adj combining form.* (in botany) having a specified type or number of spores.

sporozoan (,spɔːrəˈzəʊən, ,spɒ-) *n* **1** any parasitic protozoan of a phylum that includes the malaria parasite. ♦ *adj* **2** of or relating to the sporozoans.

sporran ('spɒrən) *n* a large pouch, usually of fur, worn hanging from a belt in front of the kilt in Scottish Highland dress. [C19: from Scot. Gaelic *sporan* purse]

sport (spɔːt) *n* **1** an individual or group activity pursued for exercise or pleasure, often taking a competitive form. **2** such activities considered collectively. **3** any pastime indulged in for pleasure. **4** the pleasure derived from a pastime, esp. hunting, shooting, or fishing. **5** playful or good-humoured joking: *to say a thing in sport.* **6** derisive mockery or the object of such mockery: *to make sport of someone.* **7** someone or something that is controlled by external influences: *the sport of fate.* **8** *Inf.* (sometimes qualified by *good, bad,* etc.) a person who reacts cheerfully in the face of adversity, esp. a good loser. **9** *Inf.* a person noted for being scrupulously fair and abiding by the rules of a game. **10** *Inf.* a person who leads a merry existence, esp. a gambler: *he's a bit of a sport.* **11** *Austral. & NZ inf.* a form of address used esp. between males. **12** *Biol.* **12a** an animal or plant that differs conspicuously from other organisms of the same species, usually because of a mutation. **12b** an anomalous characteristic of such an organism. ♦ *vb* **13** (*tr*) *Inf.* to wear or display in an ostentatious or proud manner: *she was sporting a new hat.* **14** (*intr*) to skip about or frolic happily. **15** to amuse (oneself), esp. in outdoor physical recreation. **16** (*intr*; often foll. by *with*) *Arch.* to make fun (of). **17** (*intr*) *Biol.* to produce or undergo a mutation. ♦ See also **sports.** [C15 *sporten,* var. of *disporten* to DISPORT]
▶ **'sporter** *n* ▶ **'sportful** *adj* ▶ **'sportfully** *adv*
▶ **'sportfulness** *n*

sporting ('spɔːtɪŋ) *adj* **1** (*prenominal*) of, relating to, or used or engaged in a sport or sports. **2** relating or conforming to sportsmanship; fair. **3** of or relating to gambling. **4** willing to take a risk.
▶ **'sportingly** *adv*

sportive ('spɔːtɪv) adj 1 playful or joyous. 2 done in jest rather than seriously.
▸ 'sportively adv ▸ 'sportiveness n

sports (spɔːts) n 1 (modifier) relating to, concerned with, or used in sports: sports equipment. 2 Also called: **sports day**. Brit. a meeting held at a school or college for competitions in various athletic events.

sports car n a production car designed for speed and manoeuvrability, having a low body and usually seating only two persons.

sportscast ('spɔːts,kɑːst) n US. a broadcast consisting of sports news.
▸ 'sports,caster n

sports jacket n a man's informal jacket, made esp. of tweed. Also called (US, Austral., and NZ): **sports coat.**

sportsman ('spɔːtsmən) n, pl **sportsmen**. 1 a man who takes part in sports, esp. of the outdoor type. 2 a person who exhibits fairness, generosity, observance of the rules, and good humour when losing.
▸ 'sportsman-,like or 'sportsmanly adj ▸ 'sportsman,ship n

sports medicine n the branch of medicine concerned with injuries sustained through sport.

sportswear ('spɔːts,wɛə) n clothes worn for sport or outdoor leisure wear.

sportswoman ('spɔːts,wumən) n, pl **sportswomen**. a woman who takes part in sports, esp. of the outdoor type.

sporty ('spɔːtɪ) adj **sportier, sportiest**. 1 (of a person) fond of sport or outdoor activities. 2 (of clothes) having the appearance of sportswear. 3 (of a car) having the performance or appearance of a sports car.
▸ 'sportily adv ▸ 'sportiness n

sporule ('spɒruːl) n a very small spore. [C19: from NL sporula]

spot (spɒt) n 1 a small mark on a surface, such as a circular patch or stain, differing in colour or texture from its surroundings. 2 a location: this is the exact spot. 3 a blemish of the skin, esp. a pimple or one occurring through some disease. 4 a blemish on the character of a person; moral flaw. 5 Inf. a place of entertainment: a night spot. 6 Inf., chiefly Brit. a small quantity or amount: a spot of lunch. 7 Inf. an awkward situation: that puts me in a spot. 8 a short period between regular television or radio programmes that is used for advertising. 9 a position or length of time in a show assigned to a specific performer. 10 short for **spotlight**. 11 (in billiards) 11a Also called: **spot ball**. the white ball that is distinguished from the plain by a mark or spot. 11b the player using this ball. 12 Billiards, snooker, etc. one of the marked places where the ball is placed. 13 (modifier) 13a denoting or relating to goods, currencies, or securities available for immediate delivery and payment: spot goods. See also **spot price. 13b** involving immediate cash payment: spot sales. **14 change one's spots.** (used mainly in negative constructions) to reform one's character. **15 high spot.** an outstanding event: the high spot of the holiday. **16 knock spots off.** to outstrip or outdo with ease. **17 on the spot. 17a** immediately. **17b** at the place in question. **17c** in the best position to deal with a situation. **17d** in an awkward predicament. **17e** (as modifier): our on-the-spot reporter. **18 tight spot.** a serious, difficult, or dangerous situation. **19 weak spot. 19a** some aspect of a character or situation that is susceptible to criticism. **19b** a flaw in a person's knowledge. ◆ vb **spots, spotting, spotted. 20** (tr) to observe or perceive suddenly; discern. **21** to put stains or spots upon (something). **22** (intr) (of some fabrics) to be susceptible to spotting by or as if by water: silk spots easily. **23** Billiards. to place (a ball) on one of the spots. **24** to look out for and note (trains, talent, etc.). **25** (intr) to rain slightly; spit. [C12 (in the sense: moral blemish): from G]
▸ 'spotless adj ▸ 'spotlessly adv ▸ 'spotlessness n

spot check n 1 a quick random examination. 2 a check made without prior warning. ◆ vb **spot-check. 3** (tr) to perform a spot check on.

spot height n a mark on a map indicating the height of a hill, mountain, etc.

spotlight ('spɒt,laɪt) n 1 a powerful light focused so as to illuminate a small area. **2 the.** the focus of attention.
◆ vb **spotlights, spotlighting, spotlit or spotlighted.** (tr) **3** to direct a spotlight on. **4** to focus attention on.

spot-on adj Brit. inf. absolutely correct; very accurate.

spot price n the price of goods, currencies, or securities that are offered for immediate delivery and payment.

spotted ('spɒtɪd) adj 1 characterized by spots or marks, esp. in having a pattern of spots. 2 stained or blemished; soiled or bespattered.

spotted dick or **dog** n Brit. a steamed or boiled suet pudding containing dried fruit and shaped into a roll.

spotted fever n any of various severe febrile diseases characterized by small irregular spots on the skin.

spotted gum n 1 an Australian eucalyptus tree. 2 the wood of this tree, used for shipbuilding, sleepers, etc.

spotter ('spɒtə) n 1a a person or thing that watches or observes. 1b (as modifier): a spotter plane. 2 a person who makes a hobby of watching for and noting numbers or types of trains, buses, etc.: a train spotter. 3 Mil. a person who advises adjustment of fire on a target by observations. 4 a person, esp. one engaged in civil defence, who watches for enemy aircraft.

spottie ('spɒtɪ) n NZ. a young deer of up to three months of age.

spotty ('spɒtɪ) adj **spottier, spottiest. 1** abounding in or characterized by spots or marks, esp. on the skin. **2** not consistent or uniform; irregular or uneven.
▸ 'spottily adv ▸ 'spottiness n

spot-weld vb **1** (tr) to join (two pieces of metal) by small circular welds by means of heat, usually electrically generated, and pressure. ◆ n **2** a weld so formed.
▸ 'spot-,welder n

spousal ('spauzᵊl) n **1** (often pl) **1a** the marriage ceremony. **1b** a wedding. ◆ adj **2** of or relating to marriage.
▸ 'spousally adv

spouse n (spaus, spauz). **1** a person's partner in marriage. Related adj: **spousal.** ◆ vb (spauz, spaus), **spouses, spousing, spoused. 2** (tr) Obs. to marry. [C12: from OF spus (masc), spuse (fem), from L sponsus, sponsa betrothed man or woman, from spondēre to promise solemnly]

spout (spaut) vb **1** to discharge (a liquid) in a continuous jet or in spurts, esp. through a narrow gap or under pressure, or (of a liquid) to gush thus. **2** (of a whale, etc.) to discharge air through the blowhole in a spray at the surface of the water. **3** Inf. to utter (a stream of words) on a subject. ◆ n **4** a tube, pipe, chute, etc., allowing the passage or pouring of liquids, grain, etc. **5** a continuous stream or jet of liquid. **6** short for **waterspout. 7 up the spout.** Sl. **7a** ruined or lost: any hope of rescue is right up the spout. **7b** pregnant. [C14: ?from MDu. spouten, from ON spyta to spit]
▸ 'spouter n

spouting ('spautɪŋ) n NZ. **a** a rainwater downpipe on the exterior of a building. **b** such pipes collectively.

SPQR abbrev. for Senatus Populusque Romanus. [L: the Senate and People of Rome]

sprag (spræg) n **1** a chock or steel bar used to prevent a vehicle from running backwards on an incline. **2** a support or post used in mining. [C19: from ?]

sprain (spreɪn) vb **1** (tr) to injure (a joint) by a sudden twisting or wrenching of its ligaments. ◆ n **2** the injury characterized by swelling and temporary disability. [C17: from ?]

sprang (spræŋ) vb a past tense of **spring**.

sprat (spræt) n **1** Also called: **brisling**. a small marine food fish of the herring family. **2** any of various small or young herrings. [C16: var. of OE sprott]

sprawl (sprɔːl) vb **1** (intr) to sit or lie in an ungainly manner with one's limbs spread out. **2** to fall down or knock down with the limbs spread out in an ungainly way. **3** to spread out or cause to spread out in a straggling fashion: his handwriting sprawled all over the paper. ◆ n **4** the act or an instance of sprawling. **5** a sprawling posture or arrangement of items. **6a** the urban area formed by the expansion of a town or city into surrounding countryside: the urban sprawl. **6b** the process by which this has happened. [OE spreawlian]
▸ 'sprawling or 'sprawly adj

spray[1] (spreɪ) n **1** fine particles of a liquid. **2a** a liquid, such as perfume, paint, etc., designed to be discharged from an aerosol or atomizer: *hair spray*. **2b** the aerosol or atomizer itself. **3** a quantity of small objects flying through the air: *a spray of bullets.* ◆ vb **4** to scatter (liquid) in the form of fine particles. **5** to discharge (a liquid) from an aerosol or atomizer. **6** (tr) to treat or bombard with a spray: *to spray the lawn.* [C17: from MDu. *sprāien*]
▶ **'sprayer** n

spray[2] (spreɪ) n **1** a single slender shoot, twig, or branch that bears buds, leaves, flowers, or berries. **2** an ornament or floral design like this. [C13: of Gmc origin]

spray gun n a device that sprays a fluid in a finely divided form by atomizing it in an air jet.

spread (spred) vb **spreads, spreading, spread. 1** to extend or unfold or be extended or unfolded to the fullest width: *she spread the map.* **2** to extend or cause to extend over a larger expanse: *the milk spread all over the floor; the political unrest spread over several years.* **3** to apply or be applied in a coating: *butter does not spread very well when cold.* **4** to distribute or be distributed over an area or region. **5** to display or be displayed in its fullest extent: *the landscape spread before us.* **6** (tr) to prepare (a table) for a meal. **7** (tr) to lay out (a meal) on a table. **8** to send or be sent out in all directions; disseminate or be disseminated: *someone was spreading rumours; the disease spread quickly.* **9** (of rails, wires, etc.) to force or be forced apart. **10** to increase the breadth of (a part), esp. to flatten the head of a rivet by pressing, hammering, or forging. **11** (tr) *Agriculture.* **11a** to lay out (hay) in a relatively thin layer to dry. **11b** to scatter (seed, manure, etc.) over an area. **12** (tr; often foll. by *around*) *Inf.* to make (oneself) agreeable to a large number of people. ◆ n **13** the act or process of spreading; diffusion, dispersion, expansion, etc. **14** *Inf.* the wingspan of an aircraft. **15** an extent of space or time; stretch: *a spread of 50 years.* **16** *Inf., chiefly US & Canad.* a ranch or large tract of land. **17** the limit of something fully extended: *the spread of a bird's wings.* **18** a covering for a table or bed. **19** *Inf.* a large meal or feast, esp. when it is laid out on a table. **20** a food which can be spread on bread, etc.: *salmon spread.* **21** two facing pages in a book or other publication. **22** a widening of the hips and waist: *middle-age spread.* ◆ adj **23** extended or stretched out, esp. to the fullest extent. [OE *sprǣdan*]
▶ **'spreadable** adj ▶ **'spreader** n

spread betting n a form of gambling in which stakes are placed not on the results of contests but on the number of points scored, etc. Winnings and losses are calculated according to the accuracy or inaccuracy of the prediction.

spread eagle n **1** the representation of an eagle with outstretched wings, used as an emblem of the US. **2** an acrobatic skating figure.

spread-eagle adj also **spread-eagled. 1** lying or standing with arms and legs outstretched. ◆ vb **spread-eagles, spread-eagling, spread-eagled. 2** to assume or cause to assume the shape of a spread eagle. **3** (intr) *Skating.* to execute a spread eagle.

spreadsheet ('spred,ʃiːt) n a computer program that allows easy entry and manipulation of figures, equations, and text: used esp. for financial planning.

Sprechgesang (German 'ʃprɛçɡəzaŋ) n *Music.* a type of vocalization between singing and recitation. [C20: from G *Sprechgesang*, lit.: speaking-song]

spree (spriː) n **1** a session of considerable overindulgence, esp. in drinking, squandering money, etc. **2** a romp. [C19: ? changed from Scot. *spreath* plundered cattle, ult. from L *praeda* booty]

sprig (sprɪɡ) n **1** a shoot, twig, or sprout of a tree, shrub, etc.; spray. **2** an ornamental device resembling a spray of leaves or flowers. **3** Also called: **dowel pin.** a small wire nail without a head. **4** *Inf., rare.* a youth. **5** *Inf., rare.* a person considered as the descendant of an established family, social class, etc. **6** *NZ.* another word for **stud**[1] (sense 5). ◆ vb **sprigs, sprigging, sprigged.** (tr) **7** to fasten or secure with sprigs. **8** to ornament (fabric, etc.) with a design of sprigs. [C15: prob. of Gmc origin]
▶ **'sprigger** n ▶ **'spriggy** adj

sprightly ('spraɪtlɪ) adj **sprightlier, sprightliest. 1** full of vitality; lively and active. ◆ adv **2** *Obs.* in an active or lively manner. [C16: from *spright*, var. of SPRITE + -LY[1]]
▶ **'sprightliness** n

spring (sprɪŋ) vb **springs, springing, sprang** or **sprung; sprung. 1** to move or cause to move suddenly upwards or forwards in a single motion. **2** to release or be released from a forced position by elastic force: *the bolt sprang back.* **3** (tr) to leap or jump over. **4** (intr) to come or arise suddenly. **5** (intr) (of a part of a mechanism, etc.) to jump out of place. **6** to make (wood, etc.) warped or split or (of wood, etc.) to become warped or split. **7** to happen or cause to happen unexpectedly: *to spring a surprise.* **8** (intr; usually foll. by *from*) to originate; be descended: *the idea sprang from a chance meeting; he sprang from peasant stock.* **9** (intr; often foll. by *up*) to come into being or appear suddenly: *factories springing up.* **10** (tr) (of a gundog) to rouse (game) from cover. **11** (intr) (of game or quarry) to start or rise suddenly from cover. **12** to explode (a mine) or (of a mine) to explode. **13** (tr) to provide with a spring or springs. **14** (tr) *Inf.* to arrange the escape of (someone) from prison. **15** (intr) *Arch. or poetic.* (of daylight or dawn) to begin to appear. ◆ n **16** the act or an instance of springing. **17** a leap, jump, or bound. **18a** the quality of resilience; elasticity. **18b** (as modifier): *spring steel.* **19** the act or an instance of moving rapidly back from a position of tension. **20a** a natural outflow of ground water, as forming the source of a stream. **20b** (as modifier): *spring water.* **21a** a device, such as a coil or strip of steel, that stores potential energy when it is compressed, stretched, or bent and releases it when the restraining force is removed. **21b** (as modifier): *a spring mattress.* **22** a structural defect such as a warp or bend. **23a** (sometimes cap.) the season of the year between winter and summer, astronomically from the March equinox to the June solstice in the N hemisphere and from the September equinox to the December solstice in the S hemisphere. **23b** (as modifier): *spring showers.* Related adj: **vernal. 24** the earliest or freshest time of something. **25** a source or origin. **26** Also called: **spring line.** *Naut.* a mooring line, usually one of a pair that cross amidships. [OE *spring*]
▶ **'springless** adj ▶ **'spring,like** adj

spring balance or esp. US **spring scale** n a device in which an object to be weighed is attached to the end of a helical spring, the extension of which indicates the weight of the object on a calibrated scale.

springboard ('sprɪŋ,bɔːd) n **1** a flexible board, usually projecting low over the water, used for diving. **2** a similar board used for gaining height or momentum in gymnastics. **3** *Austral. & NZ.* a board inserted into the trunk of a tree at some height above the ground on which a lumberjack stands to chop down the tree. **4** anything that serves as a point of departure or initiation.

springbok ('sprɪŋ,bɒk) n, pl **springbok** or **springboks.** an antelope of semidesert regions of southern Africa, which moves in leaps. [C18: from Afrik., from Du. *springen* to spring + *bok* goat]

Springbok ('sprɪŋ,bɒk, -,bɒk) n a person who has represented South Africa in a national sports team.

spring chicken n **1** *Chiefly US.* a young chicken, tender for cooking, esp. one from two to ten months old. **2 he or she is no spring chicken.** *Inf.* he or she is no longer young.

spring-clean vb **1** to clean (a house) thoroughly: traditionally at the end of winter. ◆ n **2** an instance of this.
▶ ,**spring-'cleaning** n

springe (sprɪndʒ) n **1** a snare set to catch small wild animals or birds and consisting of a loop attached to a bent twig or branch under tension. ◆ vb **springes, springeing, springed. 2** (tr) to catch (animals or birds) with this. [C13: rel. to OE *springan* to spring]

springer ('sprɪŋə) n **1** a person or thing that springs. **2** short for **springer spaniel. 3** *Archit.* **3a** the first and lowest stone of an arch. **3b** the impost of an arch.

springer spaniel n either of two breeds of spaniel with a slightly domed head and ears of medium length.

Springfield ★ ('sprɪŋ,fiːld) n **1** a city in S Massachusetts, on the Connecticut River: the site of the US arsenal and armoury (1794–1968), which developed the Springfield and Garand rifles. Pop.: 149 164 (1994 est.). **2** a city in SW Missouri. Pop.: 149 727 (1994 est.). **3** a city in central

Illinois, capital of the state: the home and burial place of Abraham Lincoln. Pop.: 105 938 (1994 est.).

springhaas ('sprɪŋˌhɑːs) *n*, *pl* **springhaas** or **springhase** (-ˌhɑːzə). a small S and E African nocturnal kangaroo-like rodent. [from Afrik.: spring hare]

springing ('sprɪŋɪŋ) *n Archit.* the level where an arch or vault rises from a support.

spring lock *n* a type of lock having a spring-loaded bolt, a key being required only to unlock it.

spring onion *n* an immature form of the onion, widely cultivated for its tiny bulb and long green leaves which are eaten in salads, etc. Also called: **scallion**.

spring roll *n* a Chinese dish consisting of a savoury mixture rolled up in a thin pancake and fried.

Springs ★ (sprɪŋz) *n* a city in E South Africa: developed around a coal mine established in 1885 and later became a major world gold-mining centre, now with uranium extraction. Pop.: 68 235 (1985).

Springsteen ★ ('sprɪŋˌstiːn) *n Bruce.* born 1949, US rock singer, songwriter, and guitarist. His albums with the E Street Band include *Born to Run* (1975), *Darkness on the Edge of Town* (1978), and *Born in the USA* (1984).

springtail ('sprɪŋˌteɪl) *n* any of various primitive wingless insects having a forked springing organ.

spring tide *n* **1** either of the two tides that occur at or just after new moon and full moon: the greatest rise and fall in tidal level. Cf. **neap tide. 2** any great rush or flood.

springtime ('sprɪŋˌtaɪm) *n* **1** Also called: **springtide**. the season of spring. **2** the earliest, usually the most attractive, period of the existence of something.

springy ('sprɪŋɪ) *adj* **springier, springiest. 1** possessing or characterized by resilience or bounce. **2** (of a place) having many springs of water.
▶ **'springily** *adv* ▶ **'springiness** *n*

sprinkle ('sprɪŋk°l) *vb* **sprinkles, sprinkling, sprinkled. 1** to scatter (liquid, powder, etc.) in tiny particles or droplets over (something). **2** (*tr*) to distribute over (something): *the field was sprinkled with flowers*. **3** (*intr*) to drizzle slightly. ◆ *n* **4** the act or an instance of sprinkling or a quantity that is sprinkled. **5** a slight drizzle. [C14: prob. from MDu. *sprenkelen*]
▶ **'sprinkler** *n*

sprinkler system *n* a fire-extinguishing system that releases water from overhead nozzles opened automatically by a temperature rise.

sprinkling ('sprɪŋklɪŋ) *n* a small quantity or amount: *a sprinkling of common sense.*

sprint (sprɪnt) *n* **1** *Athletics.* a short race run at top speed. **2** a fast finishing speed at the end of a longer race, as in running or cycling, etc. **3** any quick run. ◆ *vb* **4** (*intr*) to go at top speed, as in running, cycling, etc. [C16: of Scand. origin]
▶ **'sprinter** *n*

sprit (sprɪt) *n Naut.* a light spar pivoted at the mast and crossing a fore-and-aft quadrilateral sail diagonally to the peak. [OE *spreot*]

sprite (spraɪt) *n* **1** (in folklore) a nimble elflike creature, esp. one associated with water. **2** a small dainty person. [C13: from OF *esprit*, from L *spīritus* SPIRIT[1]]

spritsail ('sprɪtˌseɪl; *Naut.* 'sprɪtsəl) *n Naut.* a sail mounted on a sprit or bowsprit.

spritzer ('sprɪtsə) *n* a drink, usually white wine, with soda water added. [from G *spritzen* to splash]

sprocket ('sprɒkɪt) *n* **1** Also called: **sprocket wheel.** a relatively thin wheel having teeth projecting radially from the rim, esp. one that drives or is driven by a chain. **2** an individual tooth on such a wheel. **3** a cylindrical wheel with teeth on one or both rims for pulling film through a camera or projector. [C16: from ?]

sprout (spraʊt) *vb* **1** (of a plant, seed, etc.) to produce (new leaves, shoots, etc.). **2** (*intr*; often foll. by *up*) to begin to grow or develop. ◆ *n* **3** a new shoot or bud. **4** something that grows like a sprout. **5** See **Brussels sprout**. [OE *sprūtan*]

spruce[1] (spruːs) *n* **1** any coniferous tree of a N temperate genus, cultivated for timber and for ornament. They grow in a pyramidal shape and have needle-like leaves and light-coloured wood. See also **Norway spruce. 2** the wood of any of these trees. [C17: short for *Spruce fir*, from C14 *Spruce* Prussia, changed from *Pruce*, via OF from L *Prussia*]

spruce[2] (spruːs) *adj* neat, smart, and trim. [C16: ?from *Spruce leather*, a fashionable leather imported from Prussia; see SPRUCE[1]]
▶ **'sprucely** *adv* ▶ **'spruceness** *n*

spruce beer *n* an alcoholic drink made of fermented molasses flavoured with spruce twigs and cones.

spruce up *vb* **spruces, sprucing, spruced.** (*adv*) to make (oneself, a person, or thing) smart and neat.

sprue[1] (spruː) *n* **1** a vertical channel in a mould through which plastic or molten metal is introduced or out of which it flows when the mould is filled. **2** plastic or metal that solidifies in a sprue. [C19: from ?]

sprue[2] (spruː) *n* a chronic disease, esp. of tropical climates, characterized by diarrhoea and emaciation. [C19: from Du. *spruw*]

spruik ('spruːɪk) *vb* (*intr*) *Austral. sl.* to describe or hold forth like a salesman; spiel or advertise loudly. [C20: from ?]
▶ **'spruiker** *n*

spruit (spreɪt) *n S. African.* a small tributary stream or watercourse. [Afrik. *sprint* offshoot, tributary]

sprung (sprʌŋ) *vb* a past tense and past participle of **spring**.

sprung rhythm *n Prosody.* a type of poetic rhythm characterized by metrical feet of irregular composition, each having one strongly stressed syllable, often the first, and an indefinite number of unstressed syllables.

spry (spraɪ) *adj* **spryer, spryest** or **sprier, spriest.** active and brisk; nimble. [C18: ? of Scand. origin]
▶ **'spryly** *adv* ▶ **'spryness** *n*

spud (spʌd) *n* **1** an informal word for **potato. 2** a narrow-bladed spade for cutting roots, digging up weeds, etc. ◆ *vb* **spuds, spudding, spudded. 3** (*tr*) to eradicate (weeds) with a spud. **4** (*intr*) to drill the first foot of an oil well. [C15 *spudde* short knife, from ?; applied later to a digging tool, & hence to a potato]

Spud Island ★ *n* a slang name for **Prince Edward Island**.

spue (spjuː) *vb* **spues, spuing, spued.** an archaic spelling of **spew**.
▶ **'spuer** *n*

spume (spjuːm) *n* **1** foam or surf, esp. on the sea; froth. ◆ *vb* **spumes, spuming, spumed. 2** (*intr*) to foam or froth. [C14: from OF *espume*, from L *spūma*]
▶ **'spumous** or **'spumy** *adj*

spun (spʌn) *vb* **1** the past tense and past participle of **spin**. ◆ *adj* **2** formed or manufactured by spinning: *spun gold; spun glass.*

spunk (spʌŋk) *n* **1** *Inf.* courage or spirit. **2** *Brit. taboo sl.* semen. **3** touchwood or tinder. [C16 (in the sense: a spark): from Scot. Gaelic *spong* tinder, sponge, from L *spongia* sponge]
▶ **'spunky** *adj* ▶ **'spunkily** *adv*

spun silk *n* shiny yarn or fabric made from silk waste.

spur (spɜː) *n* **1** a pointed device or sharp spiked wheel fixed to the heel of a rider's boot to enable him to urge his horse on. **2** anything serving to urge or encourage. **3** a sharp horny projection from the leg in male birds, such as the domestic cock. **4** a pointed process in any of various animals. **5** a tubular extension at the base of the corolla in flowers such as larkspur. **6** a short or stunted branch of a tree. **7** a ridge projecting laterally from a mountain or mountain range. **8** another name for **groyne. 9** Also called: **spur track.** a railway branch line or siding. **10** a short side road leading off a main road. **11** a sharp cutting instrument attached to the leg of a gamecock. **12 on the spur of the moment.** on impulse. **13 win one's spurs. 13a** to prove one's ability; gain distinction. **13b** *History.* to earn knighthood. ◆ *vb* **spurs, spurring, spurred. 14** (*tr*) to goad or urge with or as if with spurs. **15** (*intr*) to go or ride quickly; press on. **16** (*tr*) to provide with a spur or spurs. [OE *spura*]

spurge (spɜːdʒ) *n* any of various plants that have milky sap and small flowers typically surrounded by conspicuous bracts. [C14: from OF *espurge*, from *espurgier* to purge, from L *expurgāre* to cleanse]

pur gear *or* **wheel** *n* a gear having involuted teeth either straight or helically cut on a cylindrical surface.

purious ('spjʊərɪəs) *adj* **1** not genuine or real. **2** (of a plant part or organ) resembling another part in appearance only; false: *a spurious fruit*. **3** *Rare.* illegitimate. [C17: from L *spurius* of illegitimate birth]
▸ **'spuriously** *adv* ▸ **'spuriousness** *n*

purn (spɜːn) *vb* **1** to reject (a person or thing) with contempt. **2** (when *intr*, often foll. by *against*) *Arch.* to kick (at). ◆ *n* **3** an instance of spurning. **4** *Arch.* a kick or thrust. [OE *spurnan*]
▸ **'spurner** *n*

purt *or* **spirt** (spɜːt) *vb* **1** to gush or cause to gush forth in a sudden stream or jet. **2** (*intr*) to make a sudden effort. ◆ *n* **3** a sudden stream or jet. **4** a short burst of activity, speed, or energy. [C16: ? rel. to MHG *sprützen* to squirt]

putnik ('spʊtnɪk, 'spʌt-) *n* any of a series of Soviet artificial satellites, **Sputnik 1** (launched in 1957) being the first man-made satellite to orbit the earth. [C20: from Russian, lit.: fellow traveller, from *s-* with + *put* path + *-nik*, suffix indicating agent]

putter ('spʌtə) *vb* **1** another word for **splutter** (senses 1–3). **2** *Physics.* **2a** to undergo or cause to undergo a process in which atoms of a solid are removed from its surface by the impact of high-energy ions. **2b** to coat (a metal) onto (a solid surface) by this process. ◆ *n* **3** the process or noise of sputtering. **4** incoherent stammering speech. **5** something ejected while sputtering. [C16: from Du. *sputteren*, imit.]
▸ **'sputterer** *n*

putum ('spjuːtəm) *n, pl* **sputa** (-tə). saliva ejected from the mouth, esp. mixed with mucus. [C17: from L: spittle, from *spuere* to spit out]

py (spaɪ) *n, pl* **spies.** **1** a person employed by a state or institution to obtain secret information from rival countries, organizations, companies, etc. **2** a person who keeps secret watch on others. **3** *Obs.* a close view. ◆ *vb* **spies, spying, spied.** **4** (*intr*; usually foll. by *on*) to keep a secret or furtive watch (on). **5** (*intr*) to engage in espionage. **6** (*tr*) to catch sight of; descry. [C13 *spien*, from OF *espier*, of Gmc origin]

pyglass ('spaɪˌglɑːs) *n* a small telescope.

py out *vb* (*tr, adv*) **1** to discover by careful observation. **2** to make a close scrutiny of.

q. *abbrev. for:* **1** sequence. **2** square. **3** (*pl* **sqq.**) the following one. [from L *sequens*]

q. *abbrev. for:* **1** Squadron. **2** Square.

QL *abbrev. for* structured query language: a computer programming language used for database management.

squab (skwɒb) *n, pl* **squabs** *or* **squab.** **1** a young unfledged bird, esp. a pigeon. **2** a short fat person. **3a** a well-stuffed bolster or cushion. **3b** a sofa. ◆ *adj* **4** (of birds) unfledged. **5** short and fat. [C17: prob. of Gmc origin]
▸ **'squabby** *adj*

squabble ('skwɒbᵊl) *vb* **squabbles, squabbling, squabbled.** **1** (*intr*) to quarrel over a small matter. ◆ *n* **2** a petty quarrel. [C17: prob. of Scand. origin]
▸ **'squabbler** *n*

squad (skwɒd) *n* **1** the smallest military formation, typically a dozen soldiers, esp. a drill formation. **2** any small group of people engaged in a common pursuit. **3** *Sport.* a number of players from which a team is to be selected. [C17: from OF *esquade*, from OSp. *escuadra*, from *escuadrar* to SQUARE, from the square formations used]

squaddie *or* **squaddy** ('skwɒdɪ) *n, pl* **squaddies.** *Brit. sl.* a private soldier. [C20: from SQUAD]

squadron ('skwɒdrən) *n* **1** a subdivision of a naval fleet detached for a particular task. **2** a cavalry unit comprising two or more troops. **3** the basic tactical and administrative air force unit comprising two or more flights. [C16: from It. *squadrone* soldiers drawn up in square formation, from *squadro* square]

squadron leader *n* an officer holding commissioned rank, between flight lieutenant and wing commander in the air forces of Britain and certain other countries.

squalene ('skweɪˌliːn) *n Biochemistry.* a terpene first found in the liver of sharks but also present in the livers of most higher animals. [C20: from NL *squalus*, genus name of the shark]

squalid ('skwɒlɪd) *adj* **1** dirty and repulsive, esp. as a result of neglect or poverty. **2** sordid. [C16: from L *squālidus*, from *squālēre* to be stiff with dirt]
▸ **squa'lidity** *or* **'squalidness** *n* ▸ **'squalidly** *adv*

squall[1] (skwɔːl) *n* **1** a sudden strong wind or brief turbulent storm. **2** any sudden commotion. ◆ *vb* **3** (*intr*) to blow in a squall. [C18: ? a special use of SQUALL[2]]
▸ **'squally** *adj*

squall[2] (skwɔːl) *vb* **1** (*intr*) to cry noisily; yell. ◆ *n* **2** a shrill or noisy yell or howl. [C17: prob. of Scand. origin]
▸ **'squaller** *n*

squalor ('skwɒlə) *n* the condition or quality of being squalid; disgusting filth. [C17: from L]

squama ('skweɪmə) *n, pl* **squamae** (-miː). *Biol.* a scale or scalelike structure. [C18: from L]
▸ **squamate** ('skweɪmeɪt) *adj* ▸ **squa'mation** *n*
▸ **'squamose** *or* **'squamous** *adj*

squander ('skwɒndə) *vb* (*tr*) to spend wastefully or extravagantly; dissipate. [C16: from ?]
▸ **'squanderer** *n*

square (skwɛə) *n* **1** a plane geometric figure having four equal sides and four right angles. **2** any object, part, or arrangement having this or a similar shape. **3** an open area in a town, sometimes including the surrounding buildings, which may form a square. **4** *Maths.* the product of two equal factors; the second power: *9 is the square of 3*, written 3^2. **5** an instrument having two strips of wood, metal, etc., set in the shape of a T or L, used for constructing or testing right angles. **6** *Cricket.* the closely-cut area in the middle of a ground on which wickets are prepared. **7** *Inf.* a person who is old-fashioned in views, customs, appearance, etc. **8** *Obs.* a standard, pattern, or rule. **9 back to square one.** indicating a return to the starting point because of failure, lack of progress, etc. **10 on the square.** **10a** at right angles. **10b** *Inf.* honestly and openly. **11 out of square.** **11a** not at right angles or not having a right angle. **11b** not in order or agreement. ◆ *adj* **12** being a square in shape or section. **13** having or forming one or more right angles or being at right angles to something. **14a** (*prenominal*) denoting a measure of area of any shape: *a circle of four square feet*. **14b** (*immediately postpositive*) denoting a square having a specified length on each side: *a board four feet square*. **15** fair and honest (esp. in **a square deal**). **16** straight, even, or level: *a square surface.* **17** *Cricket.* at right angles to the wicket: *square leg.* **18** *Soccer, hockey, etc.* in a straight line across the pitch: *a square pass.* **19** *Naut.* (of the sails of a square-rigged ship) set at right angles to the keel. **20** *Inf.* old-fashioned. **21** stocky or sturdy: *square shoulders.* **22** (*postpositive*) having no remaining debts or accounts to be settled. **23** (*prenominal*) unequivocal or straightforward: *a square contradiction.* **24** (*postpositive*) neat and tidy. **25** *Maths.* (of a matrix) having the same number of rows and columns. **26 all square.** on equal terms; even in score. **27 square peg (in a round hole).** *Inf.* a person or thing that is a misfit. ◆ *vb* **squares, squaring, squared.** (*mainly tr*) **28** to make into a square or similar shape. **29** *Maths.* to raise (a number or quantity) to the second power. **30** to test or adjust for deviation with respect to a right angle, plane surface, etc. **31** (sometimes foll. by *off*) to divide into squares. **32** to position so as to be rectangular, straight, or level: *to square the shoulders.* **33** (sometimes foll. by *up*) to settle (debts, accounts, etc.). **34** to level (the score) in a game, etc. **35** (*also intr*; often foll. by *with*) to agree or cause to agree: *your ideas don't square with mine.* **36** to arrange (something) or come to an arrangement with (someone) as by bribery. **37 square the circle.** to attempt the impossible (in reference to the insoluble problem of constructing a square having exactly the same area as a given circle). ◆ *adv* **38** in order to be square. **39** at right angles. **40** *Soccer, hockey, etc.* in a straight line across the pitch: *to pass the ball square.* **41** *Inf.* squarely. ◆ See also **square away, square off, square up.** [C13: from OF *esquare*,

from Vulgar L *exquadra* (unattested), from L *quadrāre* to make square]
▸ 'squareness *n* ▸ 'squarer *n*

square away *vb* (*adv*) **1** to set the sails of (a square-rigged ship) at right angles to the keel. **2** (*tr*) *US & Canad.* to make neat and tidy.

square-bashing *n Brit. mil. sl.* drill on a barracks square.

square bracket *n* **1** either of a pair of characters [ ], used to enclose a section of writing or printing to separate it from the main text. **2** Also called: **bracket**. either of these characters used as a sign of aggregation in mathematical or logical expressions.

square dance *n* **1** any of various formation dances in which the couples form squares. ◆ *vb* **square-dance, square-dances, square-dancing, square-danced.** **2** (*intr*) to perform such a dance.
▸ 'square-,dancer *n*

square knot *n* another name for **reef knot**.

square leg *n Cricket.* **1** a fielding position on the on side approximately at right angles to the batsman. **2** a person who fields in this position.

squarely ('skwεəlɪ) *adv* **1** in a direct way; straight: *he hit me squarely on the nose.* **2** in an honest, frank, and just manner. **3** at right angles.

square meal *n* a substantial meal consisting of enough to satisfy.

square measure *n* a unit or system of units for measuring areas.

square number *n* an integer, such as 1, 4, 9, or 16, that is the square of an integer.

square off *vb* (*intr, adv*) to assume a posture of offence or defence, as in boxing.

square of opposition *n Logic.* the diagrammatic representation of the relationships between the four types of proposition found in the syllogism.

square-rigged *adj Naut.* rigged with square sails. See **square sail**.

square root *n* a number or quantity that when multiplied by itself gives a given number or quantity: *the square roots of 4 are 2 and –2.*

square sail *n Naut.* a rectangular or square sail set on a horizontal yard rigged more or less at right angles to the keel.

square shooter *n Inf., chiefly US.* an honest or frank person.
▸ **square shooting** *adj*

square up *vb* (*adv*) **1** to pay or settle (bills, debts, etc.). **2** *Inf.* to arrange or be arranged satisfactorily. **3** (*intr*; foll. by *to*) to prepare to be confronted (with), esp. courageously. **4** (*tr*; foll. by *to*) to adopt a position of readiness to fight (an opponent). **5** *Scot.* to tidy up.

squarrose ('skwærəʊz, 'skwɒ-) *adj* **1** *Biol.* having a rough surface, caused by projecting hairs, scales, etc. **2** *Bot.* having or relating to overlapping parts that are pointed or recurved. [C18: from L *squarrōsus* scabby]

squash[1] (skwɒʃ) *vb* **1** to press or squeeze or be pressed or squeezed in or down so as to crush, distort, or pulp. **2** (*tr*) to suppress or overcome. **3** (*tr*) to humiliate or crush (a person), esp. with a disconcerting retort. **4** (*intr*) to make a sucking, splashing, or squelching sound. **5** (often foll. by *in* or *into*) to enter or insert in a confined space. ◆ *n* **6** *Brit.* a still drink made from fruit juice or fruit syrup diluted with water. **7** a crush, esp. of people in a confined space. **8** something squashed. **9** the act or sound of squashing or the state of being squashed. **10** Also called: **squash rackets.** a game for two or four players played in an enclosed court with a small rubber ball and light long-handled rackets. **11** Also called: **squash tennis.** a similar game played with larger rackets and a larger pneumatic ball. [C16: from OF *esquasser*, from Vulgar L *exquassāre* (unattested), from L EX-[1] + *quassāre* to shatter]
▸ 'squasher *n*

squash[2] (skwɒʃ) *n, pl* **squashes** or **squash.** *US & Canad.* **1** any of various marrow-like plants, the fruits of which have a hard rind surrounding edible flesh. **2** the fruit, eaten as a

vegetable. [C17: of Amerind origin, from *askutasquash*, lit.: green vegetable eaten green]

squashy ('skwɒʃɪ) *adj* **squashier, squashiest.** **1** easily squashed; pulpy: *a squashy peach.* **2** soft and wet; marshy: *squashy ground.*
▸ 'squashily *adv* ▸ 'squashiness *n*

squat (skwɒt) *vb* **squats, squatting, squatted.** (*intr*) **1** to rest in a crouching position with the knees bent and the weight on the feet. **2** to crouch down, esp. in order to hide. **3** *Law.* to occupy land or property to which the occupant has no legal title. ◆ *adj* **4** Also: **squatty.** short and broad. ◆ *n* **5** a squatting position. **6** a house occupied by squatters. [C13: from OF *esquater*, from *es-* EX-[1] + *catir* to press together, from Vulgar L *coactīre* (unattested), from L *cōgere* to compress]
▸ 'squatly *adv* ▸ 'squatness *n*

squatter ('skwɒtə) *n* **1** a person who occupies property or land to which he has no legal title. **2** (in Australia) **2a** a grazier with extensive holdings. **2b** *History.* a person occupying land as tenant of the Crown. **3** (in New Zealand) a 19th-century settler who took up large acreage on a crown lease.

squat thrust *n* an exercise in which the hands are kept on the floor with the arms held straight while the legs are straightened out behind and quickly drawn in towards the body again.

squattocracy (skwɒ'tɒkrəsɪ) *n Austral.* squatters collectively, regarded as rich and influential. See **squatter** (sense 2a). [C19: from SQUATTER + -CRACY]

squaw (skwɔː) *n* **1** *Offens.* a North American Indian woman. **2** *Sl., usually facetious.* a woman or wife. [C17: of Amerind origin]

squawk (skwɔːk) *n* **1** a loud raucous cry; screech. **2** *Inf.* a loud complaint. ◆ *vb* **3** to utter (with) a squawk. **4** (*intr*) *Inf.* to complain loudly. [C19: imit.]
▸ 'squawker *n*

squaw man *n Derog.* a White man married to a North American Indian woman.

squeak (skwiːk) *n* **1** a short shrill cry or high-pitched sound. **2** *Inf.* an escape (esp. in **narrow squeak, near squeak**). **3** *Inf.* (*usually used with a negative*) a word; a slight sound. ◆ *vb* **4** to make or cause to make a squeak. **5** (*intr*; usually foll. by *through* or *by*) to pass with only a narrow margin: *to squeak through an examination.* **6** (*intr*) *Inf.* to confess information about oneself or another. **7** (*tr*) to utter with a squeak. [C17: prob. of Scand. origin]
▸ 'squeaky *adj* ▸ 'squeakily *adv* ▸ 'squeakiness *n*

squeaky-clean *adj* **1** (of hair) washed so clean that wet strands squeak when rubbed. **2** completely clean. **3** *Inf., derog.* (of a person) cultivating a virtuous and wholesome image.

squeal (skwiːl) *n* **1** a high shrill yelp, as of pain. **2** a screaming sound. ◆ *vb* **3** to utter (with) a squeal. **4** (*intr*) *Sl.* to confess information about another. **5** (*intr*) *Inf., chiefly Brit.* to complain loudly. [C13 *squelen*, imit.]
▸ 'squealer *n*

squeamish ('skwiːmɪʃ) *adj* **1** easily sickened or nauseated. **2** easily shocked; prudish. **3** easily frightened: *squeamish about spiders.* [C15: from Anglo-F *escoymous*, from ?]
▸ 'squeamishly *adv* ▸ 'squeamishness *n*

squeegee ('skwiːdʒiː) *n* **1** an implement with a rubber blade used for wiping away surplus water from a surface, such as a windowpane. **2** any of various similar devices used in photography for pressing water out of wet prints or negatives or for squeezing prints onto a glazing surface. ◆ *vb* **squeegees, squeegeeing, squeegeed.** **3** to remove (liquid) from (something) by use of a squeegee. [C19: prob. imit., infl. by SQUEEZE]

squeeze (skwiːz) *vb* **squeezes, squeezing, squeezed.** (*mainly tr*) **1** to grip or press firmly, esp. so as to crush or distort. **2** to crush or press (something) so as to extract (a liquid): *to squeeze juice from an orange; to squeeze an orange.* **3** to apply gentle pressure to, as in affection or reassurance: *he squeezed her hand.* **4** to push or force in a confined space: *to squeeze six lettuces into one box; to squeeze through a crowd.* **5** to hug closely. **6** to oppress with exacting demands, such as excessive taxes. **7** to exert pressure on (someone)

★ people and places

in order to extort (something): *to squeeze money out of a victim by blackmail.* **8** *Bridge, whist.* to lead a card that forces (opponents) to discard potentially winning cards. ◆ *n* **9** the act or an instance of squeezing or of being squeezed. **10** a hug or handclasp. **11** a crush of people in a confined space. **12** *Chiefly Brit.* a condition of restricted credit imposed by a government to counteract price inflation. **13** an amount extracted by squeezing: *a squeeze of lemon juice.* **14** *Inf.* pressure brought to bear in order to extort something (esp. in **put the squeeze on**). **15** *Commerce.* any action taken by a trader or traders on a market that forces buyers to make purchases and prices to rise. **16** Also called: **squeeze play.** *Bridge, whist.* a manoeuvre that forces opponents to discard potentially winning cards. [C16: from ME *queysen* to press, from OE *cwȳsan*]
▶ **'squeezable** *adj* ▶ **'squeezer** *n*

squelch (skweltʃ) *vb* **1** (*intr*) to walk laboriously through soft wet material or with wet shoes, making a sucking noise. **2** (*intr*) to make such a noise. **3** (*tr*) to crush completely; squash. **4** (*tr*) *Inf.* to silence, as by a crushing retort. ◆ *n* **5** a squelching sound. **6** something that has been squelched. **7** *Inf.* a crushing remark. [C17: imit.]
▶ **'squelcher** *n* ▶ **'squelchy** *adj*

squib (skwɪb) *n* **1** a firework that burns with a hissing noise and culminates in a small explosion. **2** a short witty attack; lampoon. **3 damp squib.** something intended but failing to impress. ◆ *vb* **squibs, squibbing, squibbed. 4** (*intr*) to sound, move, or explode like a squib. **5** (*intr*) to let off or shoot a squib. **6** to write a squib against (someone). [C16: prob. imit. of a light explosion]

squid (skwɪd) *n, pl* **squid** *or* **squids.** any of various ten-limbed pelagic cephalopod molluscs of most seas, having a torpedo-shaped body ranging from about 10 centimetres to 16.5 metres long. See also **cuttlefish.** [C17: from ?]

squiffy ('skwɪfɪ) *adj* **squiffier, squiffiest.** *Brit. inf.* slightly drunk. [C19: from ?]

squiggle ('skwɪgᵊl) *n* **1** a mark or movement in the form of a wavy line; curlicue. **2** an illegible scrawl. ◆ *vb* **squiggles, squiggling, squiggled. 3** (*intr*) to wriggle. **4** (*intr*) to form or draw squiggles. **5** (*tr*) to make into squiggles. [C19: ? a blend of SQUIRM + WIGGLE]
▶ **'squiggler** *n* ▶ **'squiggly** *adj*

squilgee ('skwɪldʒiː) *n* a variant spelling of **squeegee.** [C19: ?from SQUEEGEE, infl. by SQUELCH]

squill (skwɪl) *n* **1** Also called: **sea squill.** a Mediterranean plant of the lily family. **2** any of various related Old World plants. **3** Also called: **scilla.** the bulb of the sea squill, which is sliced, dried, and used medicinally, as an expectorant. [C14: from L *squilla* sea onion, from Gk *skilla,* from ?]

squinch (skwɪntʃ) *n* a small arch, corbelling, etc., across an internal corner of a tower, used to support a spire, etc. Also called: **squinch arch.** [C15: from obs. *scunch,* from ME *sconcheon,* from OF *escoinson,* from *es-* EX-¹ + *coin* corner]

squint (skwɪnt) *vb* **1** (*usually intr*) to cross or partly close (the eyes). **2** (*intr*) to have a squint. **3** (*intr*) to look or glance sideways or askance. ◆ *n* **4** the nontechnical name for **strabismus. 5** the act or an instance of squinting; glimpse. **6** a narrow oblique opening in a wall or pillar of a church to permit a view of the main altar from a side aisle or transept. **7** *Inf.* a quick look; glance. ◆ *adj* **8** having a squint. **9** *Inf.* askew; crooked. [C14: short for ASQUINT]
▶ **'squinter** *n* ▶ **'squinty** *adj*

squire ('skwaɪə) *n* **1** a country gentleman in England, esp. the main landowner in a rural community. **2** *Feudal history.* a young man of noble birth, who attended upon a knight. **3** *Rare.* a man who courts or escorts a woman. **4** *Inf., chiefly Brit.* a term of address used by one man to another. ◆ *vb* **squires, squiring, squired. 5** (*tr*) (of a man) to escort (a woman). [C13: from OF *esquier;* see ESQUIRE]

squirearchy *or* **squirarchy** ('skwaɪəˌrɑːkɪ) *n, pl* **squirearchies** *or* **squirarchies. 1** government by squires. **2** squires collectively, esp. as a political or social force.
▶ **squire'archal, squir'archal** *or* **squire'archical, squir'archical** *adj*

squireen (skwaɪ'riːn) *or* **squireling** ('skwaɪəlɪŋ) *n Rare.*

a petty squire. [C19: from SQUIRE + -*een,* Anglo-Irish dim. suffix]

squirm (skwɜːm) *vb* (*intr*) **1** to move with a wriggling motion; writhe. **2** to feel deep mental discomfort, guilt, embarrassment, etc. ◆ *n* **3** a squirming movement. [C17: imit. (? infl. by WORM)]
▶ **'squirmer** *n* ▶ **'squirmy** *adj*

squirrel ('skwɪrəl) *n, pl* **squirrels** *or* **squirrel. 1** any of various arboreal rodents having a bushy tail and feeding on nuts, seeds, etc. **2** any of various related rodents, such as a ground squirrel or a marmot. **3** the fur of such an animal. **4** *Inf.* a person who hoards things. ◆ *vb* **squirrels, squirrelling, squirrelled** *or US* **squirrels, squirreling, squirreled. 5** (*tr* ; usually foll. by *away*) *Inf.* to store for future use; hoard. [C14: from OF *esquireul,* from LL *sciūrus,* from Gk *skiouros,* from *skia* shadow + *oura* tail]

squirrel cage *n* **1** a cage consisting of a cylindrical framework that is made to rotate by a small animal running inside the framework. **2** a repetitive purposeless task, way of life, etc. **3** Also called: **squirrel-cage motor.** *Electrical engineering.* the rotor of an induction motor with a cylindrical winding having copper bars around the periphery parallel to the axis.

squirt (skwɜːt) *vb* **1** to force (a liquid) or (of a liquid) to be forced out of a narrow opening. **2** (*tr*) to cover or spatter with liquid so ejected. ◆ *n* **3** a jet or amount of liquid so ejected. **4** the act or an instance of squirting. **5** an instrument used for squirting. **6** *Inf.* **6a** a person regarded as insignificant or contemptible. **6b** a short person. [C15: imit.]
▶ **'squirter** *n*

squirting cucumber *n* a hairy plant of the Mediterranean region, having a fruit that discharges seeds explosively when ripe.

squish (skwɪʃ) *vb* **1** (*tr*) to crush, esp. so as to make a soft splashing noise. **2** (*intr*) (of mud, etc.) to make a splashing noise. ◆ *n* **3** a soft squashing sound. [C17: imit.]
▶ **'squishy** *adj*

squit (skwɪt) *n Brit. sl.* **1** an insignificant person. **2** nonsense. [C19: var. of SQUIRT]

squiz (skwɪz) *n, pl* **squizzes.** *Austral. & NZ sl.* a look or glance, esp. an inquisitive one. [C20: ? blend of SQUINT + QUIZ]

sr *Maths. abbrev. for* steradian.

Sr *abbrev. for:* **1** (after a name) senior. **2** Señor. **3** Sir. **4** Sister (religious). **5** *the chemical symbol for* strontium.

Sra *abbrev. for* Señora.

Srbija ★ ('sᵊrbija) *n* the Serbian name for **Serbia.**

SRC (in Britain) *abbrev. for* Science Research Council.

Sri Lanka ★ (ˌsriː ˈlæŋkə) *n* a republic in S Asia, occupying the island of Ceylon: settled by the Sinhalese from S India in about 550 B.C.; became a British colony 1802; gained independence in 1948, becoming a republic within the Commonwealth in 1972. Exports include tea, cocoa, cinnamon, and copra. Official languages: Sinhalese and Tamil; English is also widely spoken. Religion: Hinayana Buddhist majority. Currency: Sri Lanka rupee. Capital: Colombo (administrative), Sri Jayewardenepura Kotte (legislative). Pop.: 18 663 000 (1997). Area: 65 610 sq. km (25 332 sq. miles). Official name (since 1978): **Democratic Socialist Republic of Sri Lanka.** Former name (until 1972): **Ceylon.**
▶ **Sri Lankan** *adj, n*

Srinagar ★ (sriːˈnʌgə) *n* a city in N India, the summer capital of the state of Jammu and Kashmir, at an altitude of 1600 m (5250 ft) on the Jhelum River: seat of the University of Jammu and Kashmir (1948). Pop.: 586 038 (1991).

SRN (formerly, in Britain) *abbrev. for* State Registered Nurse.

SRO *abbrev. for:* **1** standing room only. **2** (in Britain) Statutory Rules and Orders. **3** self-regulatory organization.

Srta *abbrev. for* Señorita.

SS *abbrev. for:* **1** Saints. **2** a paramilitary organization within the Nazi party that provided Hitler's bodyguard, security forces, concentration-camp guards, etc. [G *Schutzstaffel* protection squad] **3** steamship.

★ people and places

SSE *symbol for* south-southeast.

ssp. (*pl* **sspp.**) *Biol. abbrev. for* subspecies.

SSR (formerly) *abbrev. for* Soviet Socialist Republic.

SSRC (formerly in Britain) *abbrev. for* Social Science Research Council.

SST *abbrev. for* supersonic transport.

SSW *symbol for* south-southwest.

St *abbrev. for:* **1** Saint (all entries that are usually preceded by *St* are in this dictionary listed alphabetically under **Saint**). **2** statute. **3** Strait. **4** Street.

st. *abbrev. for:* **1** stanza. **2** statute. **3** stone. **4** *Cricket.* stumped by.

s.t. *abbrev. for* short ton.

-st *suffix.* a variant of **-est**[2].

Sta (in the names of places or churches) *abbrev. for* Saint (female). [It. *Santa*]

stab (stæb) *vb* **stabs, stabbing, stabbed. 1** (*tr*) to pierce or injure with a sharp pointed instrument. **2** (*tr*) (of a sharp pointed instrument) to pierce or wound. **3** (when *intr*, often foll. by *at*) to make a thrust (at); jab. **4** (*tr*) to inflict with a sharp pain. **5 stab in the back. 5a** (*vb*) to damage the reputation of (a person, esp. a friend) in a surreptitious way. **5b** (*n*) a treacherous action or remark that causes the downfall of or injury to a person. ♦ *n* **6** the act or an instance of stabbing. **7** an injury or rift made by stabbing. **8** a sudden sensation, esp. an unpleasant one: *a stab of pity.* **9** *Inf.* an attempt (esp. in **make a stab at**). [C14: from *stabbe* stab wound]
  ▸ **'stabber** *n*

Stabat Mater (ˈstɑːbæt ˈmɑːtə) *n* **1** *RC Church.* a Latin hymn commemorating the sorrows of the Virgin Mary at the crucifixion. **2** a musical setting of this hymn. [from opening words, lit.: the mother was standing]

stabile (ˈsteɪbaɪl) *n* **1** *Arts.* a stationary abstract construction, usually of wire, metal, wood, etc. ♦ *adj* **2** fixed; stable. **3** resistant to chemical change. [C18: from L *stabilis*]

stability (stəˈbɪlɪtɪ) *n, pl* **stabilities. 1** the quality of being stable. **2** the ability of an aircraft to resume its original flight path after inadvertent displacement.

stabilize *or* **stabilise** (ˈsteɪbɪˌlaɪz) *vb* **stabilizes, stabilizing, stabilized** *or* **stabilises, stabilising, stabilised. 1** to make or become stable or more stable. **2** to keep or be kept stable. **3** (*tr*) to put or keep (an aircraft, vessel, etc.) in equilibrium by one or more special devices or (of an aircraft, etc.) to become stable.
  ▸ ˌstabiliˈzation *or* ˌstabiliˈsation *n*

stabilizer *or* **stabiliser** (ˈsteɪbɪˌlaɪzə) *n* **1** any device for stabilizing an aircraft. **2** a substance added to something to maintain it in a stable or unchanging state, such as an additive that preserves the texture of food. **3** *Naut.* **3a** a system of pairs of fins projecting from the hull of a ship and controllable to counteract roll. **3b** See **gyrostabilizer**. **4** either of a pair of small wheels fitted to the back wheel of a bicycle to help a beginner to maintain balance. **5** *Econ.* a measure, such as progressive taxation, interest-rate control, or unemployment benefit, used to restrict swings in prices, employment, production, etc., in a free economy. **6** a person or thing that stabilizes.

stable[1] (ˈsteɪbʰl) *n* **1** a building, usually consisting of stalls, for the lodging of horses or other livestock. **2** the animals lodged in such a building, collectively. **3a** the racehorses belonging to a particular establishment or owner. **3b** the establishment itself. **3c** (*as modifier*): *stable companion.* **4** *Inf.* a source of training, such as a school, theatre, etc.: *the two athletes were out of the same stable.* **5** a number of people considered as a source of a particular talent: *a stable of writers.* **6** (*modifier*) of, relating to, or suitable for a stable: *stable door.* ♦ *vb* **stables, stabling, stabled. 7** to put, keep, or be kept in a stable. [C13: from OF *estable* cowshed, from L *stabulum* shed, from *stāre* to stand]

stable[2] (ˈsteɪbʰl) *adj* **1** steady in position or balance; firm. **2** lasting: *a stable relationship.* **3** steadfast or firm of purpose. **4** (of an elementary particle, etc.) not undergoing decay; not radioactive. **5** (of a chemical compound) not

readily partaking in a chemical change. [C13: from OF *estable*, from L *stabilis* steady, from *stāre* to stand]
  ▸ **'stableness** *n* ▸ **'stably** *adv*

stableboy (ˈsteɪbʰlˌbɔɪ), **stablegirl** (ˈsteɪbʰlˌɡɜːl), *or* **stableman** (ˈsteɪbʰlˌmæn, -mən) *n, pl* **stableboys, stablegirls,** *or* **stablemen.** a boy, girl, or man who works in a stable.

stable door *n* a door with an upper and lower leaf that may be opened separately. US and Canad. equivalent: **Dutch door.**

Stableford (ˈsteɪbʰlfəd) *n* *Golf.* **a** a scoring system in which points are awarded according to the number of strokes taken at each hole, whereby a hole completed in one stroke over par counts as one point, a hole completed in level par counts as two points, etc. **b** (*as modifier*): *a Stableford competition.* ♦ Cf. **match play, stroke play.** [C20: after its inventor Dr Frank *Stableford* (1870–1959), E amateur golfer]

stable lad *n* a person who looks after the horses in a racing stable.

stabling (ˈsteɪblɪŋ) *n* stable buildings or accommodation.

stablish (ˈstæblɪʃ) *vb* an archaic variant of **establish**.

Stabroek ★ (Dutch ˈstɑːbruːk) *n* the former name (until 1812) of **Georgetown** (sense 1).

staccato (stəˈkɑːtəʊ) *adj* **1** *Music.* (of notes) short, clipped, and separate. **2** characterized by short abrupt sounds, as in speech: *a staccato command.* ♦ *adv* **3** (esp. used as a musical direction) in a staccato manner. [C18: from It., from *staccare* to detach, shortened from *distaccare*]

stachys (ˈstækɪs) *n* any plant of the herbaceous genus *Stachys.* See also **woundwort**. [C16: from L, from Gk: ear of corn]

stack (stæk) *n* **1** an ordered pile or heap. **2** a large orderly pile of hay, straw, etc., for storage in the open air. **3** (*often pl*) compactly spaced bookshelves, used to house collections of books in an area usually prohibited to library users. **4** a number of aircraft circling an airport at different altitudes, awaiting their signal to land. **5** a large amount. **6** *Mil.* a pile of rifles or muskets in the shape of a cone. **7** *Brit.* a measure of coal or wood equal to 108 cubic feet. **8** See **chimney stack, smokestack. 9** a vertical pipe, such as the funnel of a ship or the soil pipe attached to the side of a building. **10** a high column of rock, esp. one isolated from the mainland by the erosive action of the sea. **11** an area in a computer memory for temporary storage. ♦ *vb* (*tr*) **12** to place in a stack; pile. **13** to load or fill up with piles of something: *to stack a lorry with bricks.* **14** to control a number of aircraft waiting to land at an airport so that each flies at a different altitude. **15 stack the cards.** to prearrange the order of a pack of cards secretly so as to cheat. [C13: from ON *stakkr* haystack, of Gmc origin]
  ▸ **'stackable** *adj* ▸ **'stacker** *n*

stacked (stækt) *adj Sl.* a variant of **well-stacked**.

stadholder *or* **stadtholder** (ˈstædˌhəʊldə) *n* **1** the chief magistrate of the former Dutch republic or any of its provinces (from about 1580 to 1802). **2** a viceroy or governor of a province. [C16: from Du. *stad houder*, from *stad* city + *houder* holder]

stadia[1] (ˈsteɪdɪə) *n* **1** measurement of distance using a telescopic surveying instrument and a graduated staff calibrated to correspond with the distance from the observer. **2** the two parallel cross hairs or **stadia hairs** in the eyepiece of the instrument used. **3** the staff used. [C19: prob. from STADIA[2]]

stadia[2] (ˈsteɪdɪə) *n* a plural of **stadium**.

stadium (ˈsteɪdɪəm) *n, pl* **stadiums** *or* **stadia. 1** a sports arena with tiered seats for spectators. **2** (in ancient Greece) a course for races, usually located between two hills providing slopes for tiers of seats. **3** an ancient Greek measure of length equivalent to about 607 feet or 184 metres. [C16: via L from Gk *stadion*, changed from *spadion* racecourse, from *spān* to pull; infl. by Gk *stadios* steady]

Staël ★ (French stal) *n* **Madame de.** full name *Baronne Anne Louise Germaine (née Necker) de Staël-Holstein.* 1766–1817,

French writer, whose works, esp. *De l'Allemagne* (1810), anticipated French romanticism.

staff[1] (sta:f) *n, pl* **staffs** *for senses 1–4;* **staffs** *or* **staves** *for senses 5–9.* **1** a group of people employed by a company, individual, etc., for executive, clerical, sales work, etc. **2** (*modifier*) attached to or provided for the staff of an establishment: *a staff doctor.* **3** the body of teachers or lecturers of an educational institution. **4** *Mil.* the officers appointed to assist a commander, service, or central headquarters organization. **5** a stick with some special use, such as a walking stick or an emblem of authority. **6** something that sustains or supports: *bread is the staff of life.* **7** a pole on which a flag is hung. **8** *Chiefly Brit.* a graduated rod used in surveying, esp. for sighting to with a levelling instrument. **9** Also called: **stave.** *Music.* **9a** the system of horizontal lines grouped into sets of five (four in plainsong) upon which music is written. The spaces between them are employed in conjunction with a clef in order to give a graphic indication of pitch. **9b** any set of five lines in this system together with its clef: *the treble staff.* ◆ *vb* **10** (*tr*) to provide with a staff. [OE *stæf*]

staff[2] (sta:f) *n US.* a mixture of plaster and hair used to cover the external surface of temporary structures and for decoration. [C19: from ?]

Staffa ★ ('stæfə) *n* an island in W Scotland, in the Inner Hebrides west of Mull: site of Fingal's Cave.

staff corporal *n* a noncommissioned rank in the British Army above that of staff sergeant and below that of warrant officer.

staff nurse *n* a qualified nurse ranking immediately below a sister.

staff officer *n* a commissioned officer serving on the staff of a commander, service, or central headquarters.

Stafford[1] ★ ('stæfəd) *n* a market town in central England, administrative centre of Staffordshire. Pop.: 61 381 (1991).

Stafford[2] ★ ('stæfəd) *n* Sir **Edward William.** 1819–1901, New Zealand statesman, born in Scotland: prime minister (1856–61; 1865–69; 1872).

Staffordshire ★ ('stæfəd,ʃɪə, -ʃə) *n* a county of central England, includes the unitary authority of Stoke-on-Trent: coalfields lie in the east and south and the Pennine uplands in the north; important in the history of industry, coal and iron having been worked at least since the 13th century. Administrative centre: Stafford. Pop.: 1 054 400 (1994). Area: 2716 sq. km (1048 sq. miles).

Staffordshire bull terrier *n* a breed of smooth-coated terrier with a stocky frame and generally a pied or brindled coat.

Staffs. (stæfs) *abbrev. for* Staffordshire.

staff sergeant *n Mil.* **1** *Brit.* a noncommissioned officer holding a rank between sergeant and warrant officer and employed on administrative duties. **2** *US.* a noncommissioned officer who ranks: **2a** (in the Army) above sergeant and below sergeant first class. **2b** (in the Air Force) above airman first class and below technical sergeant. **2c** (in the Marine Corps) above sergeant and below gunnery sergeant.

stag (stæg) *n* **1** the adult male of a deer. **2** a man unaccompanied by a woman at a social gathering. **3** *Stock Exchange, Brit.* a speculator who applies for shares in a new issue in anticipation of a rise in its price and thus a quick profit on resale. **4** (*modifier*) (of a social gathering) attended by men only. ◆ *adv* **5** without a female escort. ◆ *vb* **stags, stagging, stagged.** (*tr*) **6** *Stock Exchange.* to apply for (shares in a new issue) with the intention of selling them for a quick profit when trading commences. [OE *stagga* (unattested); rel. to ON *steggr* male bird]

stag beetle *n* any of various beetles, the males of which have large branched mandibles.

stage (steɪdʒ) *n* **1** a distinct step or period of development, growth, or progress. **2** a raised area or platform. **3** the platform in a theatre where actors perform. **4 the. the** theatre as a profession. **5** any scene regarded as a setting for an event or action. **6** a portion of a journey or a stopping place after such a portion. **7** short for **stagecoach. 8** *Brit.* a division of a bus route for which there is a fixed

fare. **9** one of the separate propulsion units of a rocket that can be jettisoned when it has burnt out. **10** a small stratigraphical unit; a subdivision of a rock series or system. **11** the platform on a microscope on which the specimen is mounted for examination. **12** *Electronics.* a part of a complex circuit, esp. a transistor with the associated elements required to amplify a signal in an amplifier. **13 by** *or* **in easy stages.** not hurriedly: *he learned French by easy stages.* ◆ *vb* **stages, staging, staged.** (*tr*) **14** to perform (a play), esp. on a stage: *to stage "Hamlet".* **15** to set the action of (a play) in a particular time or place. **16** to plan, organize, and carry out (an event). [C13: from OF *estage* position, from Vulgar L *staticum* (unattested), from L *stāre* to stand]

stagecoach ('steɪdʒ,kəʊtʃ) *n* a large four-wheeled horse-drawn vehicle formerly used to carry passengers, mail, etc., on a regular route.

stagecraft ('steɪdʒ,krɑːft) *n* skill in or the art of writing or staging plays.

stage direction *n* an instruction to an actor or director, written into the script of a play.

stage door *n* a door at a theatre leading backstage.

stage fright *n* nervousness or panic that may beset a person about to appear in front of an audience.

stagehand ('steɪdʒ,hænd) *n* a person who sets the stage, moves props, etc., in a theatrical production.

stage left *n* the part of the stage to the left of a performer facing the audience.

stage-manage *vb* **stage-manages, stage-managing, stage-managed.** **1** to work as stage manager (for a play, etc.). **2** (*tr*) to arrange, present, or supervise from behind the scenes.

stage manager *n* a person who supervises the stage arrangements of a theatrical production.

stager ('steɪdʒə) *n* **1** a person of experience; veteran (esp. in **old stager**). **2** an archaic word for **actor.**

stage right *n* the part of the stage to the right of a performer facing the audience.

stage-struck *adj* infatuated with the glamour of theatrical life, esp. with the desire to act.

stage whisper *n* **1** a loud whisper from one actor to another onstage intended to be heard by the audience. **2** any loud whisper that is intended to be overheard.

stagflation (stæg'fleɪʃən) *n* a situation in which inflation is combined with stagnant or falling output and employment. [C20: blend of *stagnation* + *inflation*]

stagger ('stægə) *vb* **1** (*usually intr*) to walk or cause to walk unsteadily as if about to fall. **2** (*tr*) to astound or overwhelm, as with shock: *I am staggered by his ruthlessness.* **3** (*tr*) to place or arrange in alternating or overlapping positions or time periods to prevent confusion or congestion: *a staggered junction; to stagger holidays.* **4** (*intr*) to falter or hesitate: *his courage staggered in the face of the battle.* ◆ *n* **5** the act or an instance of staggering. [C13: from dialect *stacker,* from ON *staka* to push]
► '**staggerer** *n* ► '**staggering** *adj* ► '**staggeringly** *adv*

staggered directorships *pl n Business.* a defence against unwelcome takeover bids in which a company resolves that its directors should serve staggered terms of office and that no director can be removed from office without just cause, thus preventing a bidder from controlling the board for some years.

staggers ('stægəz) *n* (*functioning as sing or pl*) **1** a form of vertigo associated with decompression sickness. **2** Also called: **blind staggers.** a disease of horses and some other domestic animals characterized by a swaying unsteady gait, caused by infection or lesions of the central nervous system.

staging ('steɪdʒɪŋ) *n* any temporary structure used in the process of building, esp. the horizontal platforms supported by scaffolding.

staging area *n* a checkpoint or regrouping area for military formations in transit.

staging post *n* a place where a journey is usually broken, esp. a stopover on a flight.

Stagira ★ (stə'dʒaɪrə) *n* an ancient city on the coast of Chalcidice in Macedonia: the birthplace of Aristotle.

stagnant ('stægnənt) *adj* **1** (of water, etc.) standing still; without flow or current. **2** brackish and foul from standing still. **3** stale, sluggish, or dull from inaction. **4** not growing or developing; static. [C17: from L *stagnāns*, from *stagnāre* to be stagnant, from *stagnum* a pool]
▶ '**stagnancy** *n*

stagnate (stæg'neɪt) *vb* **stagnates, stagnating, stagnated.** (*intr*) to be or become stagnant.
▶ **stag'nation** *n*

stag night *or* **party** *n* a party for men only, esp. one held for a man just before he is married.

stagy *or US* **stagey** ('steɪdʒɪ) *adj* **stagier, stagiest.** excessively theatrical or dramatic.
▶ '**stagily** *adv* ▶ '**staginess** *n*

staid (steɪd) *adj* of a settled, sedate, and steady character. [C16: obs. p.p. of STAY¹]
▶ '**staidly** *adv* ▶ '**staidness** *n*

stain (steɪn) *vb* (*mainly tr*) **1** to mark or discolour with patches of something that dirties. **2** to dye with a penetrating dyestuff or pigment. **3** to bring disgrace or shame on: *to stain one's honour.* **4** to colour (specimens) for microscopic study by treatment with a dye or similar reagent. **5** (*intr*) to produce indelible marks or discoloration: *does ink stain?* ◆ *n* **6** a spot, mark, or discoloration. **7** a moral taint; blemish or slur. **8** a dye or similar reagent, used to colour specimens for microscopic study. **9** a solution or liquid used to penetrate the surface of a material, esp. wood, and impart a rich colour without covering up the surface or grain. **10** any dye used to colour textiles and hides. [C14 *steynen* (vb), shortened from *disteynen* to remove colour from, from OF *desteindre* to discolour, ult. from L *tingere* to tinge]
▶ '**stainable** *adj* ▶ '**staina'bility** *n* ▶ '**stainer** *n*

stained glass *n* a glass that has been coloured, as by fusing with a film of metallic oxide or burning pigment into the surface. **b** (*as modifier*): *a stained-glass window.*

Stainer ★ ('steɪnə) *n* Sir **John.** 1840–1901, British composer and organist, noted for his sacred music, esp. the oratorio *The Crucifixion* (1887).

Staines ★ (steɪnz) *n* a town in SE England, in N Surrey on the River Thames. Pop.: 51 167 (1991).

stainless ('steɪnlɪs) *adj* **1** resistant to discoloration, esp. that resulting from corrosion; rust-resistant: *stainless steel.* **2** having no blemish: *stainless reputation.*
▶ '**stainlessly** *adv*

stainless steel *n* **a** a type of steel resistant to corrosion as a result of the presence of large amounts of chromium. **b** (*as modifier*): *stainless-steel cutlery.*

stair (steə) *n* **1** one of a flight of stairs. **2** a series of steps: *a narrow stair.* ◆ See also **stairs.** [OE *stæger*]

staircase ('steə,keɪs) *n* a flight of stairs, its supporting framework, and, usually, a handrail or banisters.

stairs (steəz) *pl n* **1** a flight of steps leading from one storey or level to another, esp. indoors. **2 below stairs.** *Brit.* in the servants' quarters.

stairway ('steə,weɪ) *n* a means of access consisting of stairs; staircase or flight of steps.

stairwell ('steə,wel) *n* a vertical shaft or opening that contains a staircase.

stake¹ (steɪk) *n* **1** a stick or metal bar driven into the ground as a marker, part of a fence, support for a plant, etc. **2** one of a number of vertical posts that fit into sockets around a flat truck or railway wagon to hold the load in place. **3** a method or the practice of executing a person by binding him to a stake in the centre of a pile of wood that is then set on fire. **4 pull up stakes.** to leave one's home or resting place and move on. ◆ *vb* **stakes, staking, staked.** (*tr*) **5** to tie, fasten, or tether with or to a stake. **6** (often foll. by *out* or *off*) to fence or surround with stakes. **7** (often foll. by *out*) to lay (a claim) to land, rights, etc. **8** to support with a stake. [OE *staca* pin]

stake² (steɪk) *n* **1** the money or valuables that a player must hazard in order to buy into a gambling game or make a bet. **2** an interest, often financial, held in something: *a stake in the company's future.* **3** (*often pl*) the money that a player has available for gambling. **4** (*often pl*) a prize in a race, etc., esp. one made up of contribu-

tions from contestants or owners. **5** (*pl*) a horse race in which all owners of competing horses contribute to the prize. **6** *US & Canad. inf.* short for **grubstake. 7 at stake.** at risk: *lives are at stake.* **8 raise the stakes. 8a** to increase the amount of money or valuables hazarded in a gambling game. **8b** to increase the costs, risks, or considerations involved in taking an action or reaching a conclusion.
◆ *vb* **stakes, staking, staked.** (*tr*) **9** to hazard (money, etc.) on a result. **10** to invest in or support with money, etc.: *to stake a business.* [C16: from ?]

Staked Plain ★ *n* another name for the **Llano Estacado.**

stakeholder ('steɪk,həʊldə) *n* **1** a person or group owning a significant percentage of a company's shares. **2** a person or group not owning shares in an enterprise but affected by or having an interest in its operations, such as the employees, customers, local community, etc. ◆ *adj* **3** of or relating to policies intended to allow people to participate in and benefit from decisions made by enterprises in which they have a stake: *a stakeholder economy.*

stakeout ('steɪkaʊt) *Chiefly US & Canad. sl.* ◆ *n* **1** a police surveillance. **2** an area or house kept under such surveillance. ◆ *vb* **stake out. 3** (*tr, adv*) to keep under surveillance.

Stakhanovism (stæ'kænə,vɪzəm) *n* (in the former Soviet Union) a system designed to raise production by offering incentives to efficient workers. [C20: after A. G. *Stakhanov* (1906–77), Soviet miner, the worker first awarded benefits under the system in 1935]
▶ Sta'khanov,ite *n, adj*

stalactite ('stælək,taɪt) *n* a cylindrical mass of calcium carbonate hanging from the roof of a limestone cave: formed by precipitation from continually dripping water. Cf. **stalagmite.** [C17: from NL *stalactites*, from Gk *stalaktos* dripping, from *stalassein* to drip]
▶ **stalactiform** (stə'læktɪ,fɔ:m) *adj* ▶ **stalactitic** (,stælək'tɪtɪk) *or* ,stalac'titical *adj*

stalag ('stæleɪg) *n* a German prisoner-of-war camp in World War II, esp. for men from the ranks. [short for *Stammlager* base camp]

stalagmite ('stæleɪg,maɪt) *n* a cylindrical mass of calcium carbonate projecting upwards from the floor of a limestone cave: formed by precipitation from continually dripping water. Cf. **stalactite.** [C17: from NL *stalagmites*, from Gk *stalagmos* dripping; rel. to Gk *stalassein* to drip]
▶ **stalagmitic** (,stæleɪg'mɪtɪk) *or* ,stalag'mitical *adj*

stale¹ (steɪl) *adj* **1** (esp. of food) hard, musty, or dry from being kept too long. **2** (of beer, etc.) flat and tasteless from being kept too long. **3** (of air) stagnant; foul. **4** uninteresting from overuse: *stale clichés.* **5** no longer new: *stale news.* **6** lacking in energy or ideas through overwork or lack of variety. **7** *Banking.* (of a cheque) not negotiable by a bank as a result of not having been presented within six months of being written. **8** *Law.* (of a claim, etc.) having lost its effectiveness or force, as by failure to act or by the lapse of time. ◆ *vb* **stales, staling, staled. 9** to make or become stale. [C13 (orig. applied to liquor in the sense: well matured): prob. from OF *estale* (unattested) motionless, of Frankish origin]
▶ '**staleness** *n*

stale² (steɪl) *vb* **stales, staling, staled. 1** (*intr*) (of livestock) to urinate. ◆ *n* **2** the urine of horses or cattle. [C15: ?from OF *estaler* to stand in one position]

stale bull *n Business.* a dealer or speculator who holds unsold commodities after a rise in market prices but who cannot trade because there are no buyers at the new levels and because his financial commitments prevent him from making further purchases.

stalemate ('steɪl,meɪt) *n* **1** a chess position in which any of a player's possible moves would place his king in check: in this position the game ends in a draw. **2** a situation in which two opposing forces find that further action is impossible or futile; deadlock. ◆ *vb* **stalemates, stalemating, stalemated. 3** (*tr*) to subject to a stalemate. [C18: from obs. *stale*, from OF *estal* STALL¹ + (CHECK)MATE]

Stalin¹ ★ ('stɑ:lɪn) *n* **1** Also called: **Stalino.** a former name (from after the Revolution until 1961) of **Donetsk. 2** the former name (1950–61) of **Braşov**. **3** the former name (1949–56) of **Varna**.

Stalin[2] ★ ('stɑːlɪn) *n* **Joseph**. original name *Iosif Vissarionovich Dzhugashvili*. 1879–1953, Soviet leader; general secretary of the Communist Party of the Soviet Union (1922–53). He succeeded Lenin and created a totalitarian state, crushing all opposition, esp. in the purges of 1934–37. He instigated rapid industrialization and the collectivization of agriculture and established the Soviet Union as a world power.

Stalinabad ★ (*Russian* stəlina'bat) *n* the former name (1929–61) of **Dushanbe**.

Stalingrad ★ ('stɑːlɪnˌgræd; *Russian* stəlin'grat) *n* the former name (1925–61) of **Volgograd**.

Stalinism ('stɑːlɪˌnɪzəm) *n* the theory and form of government associated with Joseph Stalin: a variant of Marxism-Leninism characterized by totalitarianism, rigid bureaucracy, and loyalty to the state.
▸ '**Stalinist** *n, adj*

Stalinogrod ★ (*Polish* stali'nɔgrɔt) *n* the former name (1953–56) for **Katowice**.

Stalin Peak ★ *n* a former name for **Kommunizma Peak**.

Stalinsk ★ (*Russian* 'stalinsk) *n* the former name (1932–61) of **Novokuznetsk**.

stalk[1] (stɔːk) *n* **1** the main stem of a herbaceous plant. **2** any of various subsidiary plant stems, such as a leafstalk or flower stalk. **3** a slender supporting structure in animals such as crinoids and barnacles. **4** any long slender supporting shaft or column. [C14: prob. dim. from OE *stalu* upright piece of wood]
▸ **stalked** *adj* ▸ '**stalk**ˌl**ike** *adj*

stalk[2] (stɔːk) *vb* **1** to follow or approach (game, prey, etc.) stealthily and quietly. **2** to pursue persistently and, sometimes, attack (a person with whom one is obsessed, often a celebrity). **3** to spread over (a place) in a menacing or grim manner: *fever stalked the camp*. **4** (*intr*) to walk in a haughty, stiff, or threatening way. **5** to search (a piece of land) for prey. ♦ *n* **6** the act of stalking. **7** a stiff or threatening stride. [OE *bestealcian* to walk stealthily]
▸ '**stalker** *n*

stalk-and-slash movie *n* another name for **slasher movie**.

stalking-horse *n* **1** a horse or an imitation one used by a hunter to hide behind while stalking. **2** something serving as a means of concealing plans; pretext. **3** a candidate put forward to divide the opposition or mask the candidacy of another person for whom the stalking-horse would then withdraw.

stalky ('stɔːkɪ) *adj* **stalkier, stalkiest**. **1** like a stalk; slender and tall. **2** having or abounding in stalks.
▸ '**stalkily** *adv* ▸ '**stalkiness** *n*

stall[1] (stɔːl) *n* **1a** a compartment in a stable or shed for a single animal. **1b** another name for **stable**[1] (sense 1). **2** a small often temporary stand or booth for the sale of goods. **3a** (in a church) one of a row of seats usually divided by armrests or a small screen, for the choir or clergy. **3b** a pen. **4** an instance of an engine stalling. **5** a condition of an aircraft in flight in which a reduction in speed or an increase in the aircraft's angle of attack causes a sudden loss of lift resulting in a downward plunge. **6** any small room or compartment. **7a** a seat in a theatre or cinema, usually fixed to the floor. **7b** (*pl*) the area of seats on the ground floor of a theatre or cinema nearest to the stage or screen. **8** a tubelike covering for a finger. **9** (*pl*) short for **starting stalls**. ♦ *vb* **10** to cause (a motor vehicle or its engine) to stop, usually by incorrect use of the clutch or incorrect adjustment of the fuel mixture, or (of an engine or motor vehicle) to stop, usually for these reasons. **11** to cause (an aircraft) to go into a stall or (of an aircraft) to go into a stall. **12** to stick or cause to stick fast, as in mud or snow. **13** (*tr*) to confine (an animal) in a stall. [OE *steall* a place for standing]

stall[2] (stɔːl) *vb* **1** to employ delaying tactics towards (someone); be evasive. ♦ *n* **2** an evasive move; pretext. [C16: from Anglo-F *estale* bird used as a decoy, infl. by STALL[1]]

stall-feed *vb* **stall-feeds, stall-feeding, stall-fed**. (*tr*) to keep

and feed (an animal) in a stall, esp. as an intensive method of fattening it for slaughter.

stallholder ('stɔːl,həʊldə) *n* a person who sells goods at a market stall.

stallion ('stæljən) *n* an uncastrated male horse, esp. one used for breeding. [C14 *staloun*, from OF *estalon*, of Gmc origin]

stalwart ('stɔːlwət) *adj* **1** strong and sturdy; robust. **2** solid, dependable, and courageous. **3** resolute and firm. ♦ *n* **4** a stalwart person, esp. a supporter. [OE *stælwirthe* serviceable, from *stæl*, from *stathol* support + *wierthe* WORTH]
▸ '**stalwartly** *adv* ▸ '**stalwartness** *n*

Stambul *or* **Stamboul** ★ (stæm'buːl) *n* the old part of Istanbul, Turkey, south of the Golden Horn: the site of ancient Byzantium; sometimes used as a name for the whole city.

stamen ('steimɛn) *n, pl* **stamens** *or* **stamina**. the male reproductive organ of a flower, consisting of a stalk (filament) bearing an anther in which pollen is produced. [C17: from L: the warp in an upright loom, from *stāre* to stand]
▸ **staminiferous** (ˌstæmɪ'nɪfərəs) *adj*

Stamford ★ ('stæmfəd) *n* a city in SW Connecticut, on Long Island Sound: major chemical research laboratories. Pop.: 107 199 (1994 est.).

Stamford Bridge ★ *n* a village in N England, east of York: site of a battle (1066) in which King Harold of England defeated his brother Tostig and King Harald Hardrada of Norway, three weeks before the Battle of Hastings.

stamina[1] ('stæmɪnə) *n* enduring energy, strength, and resilience. [C19: identical with STAMINA[2], from L *stāmen* thread, hence the threads of life spun out by the Fates, hence energy, etc.]

stamina[2] ('stæmɪnə) *n* a plural of **stamen**.

staminate ('stæmɪnɪt, -ˌneit) *adj* (of plants) having stamens, esp. having stamens but no carpels; male.

stammer ('stæmə) *vb* **1** to speak or say (something) in a hesitant way, esp. as a result of a speech disorder or through fear, stress, etc. ♦ *n* **2** a speech disorder characterized by involuntary repetitions and hesitations. [OE *stamerian*]
▸ '**stammerer** *n* ▸ '**stammering** *n, adj*

stamp (stæmp) *vb* **1** (when *intr*, often foll. by *on*) to bring (the foot) down heavily (on the ground, etc.). **2** (*intr*) to walk with heavy or noisy footsteps. **3** (*intr*; foll. by *on*) to repress or extinguish: *he stamped on criticism*. **4** (*tr*) to impress or mark (a device or sign) on (something). **5** to mark (something) with an official seal or device: *to stamp a passport*. **6** (*tr*) to fix or impress permanently: *the date was stamped on her memory*. **7** (*tr*) to affix a postage stamp to. **8** (*tr*) to distinguish or reveal: *that behaviour stamps him as a cheat*. **9** to pound or crush (ores, etc.). ♦ *n* **10** the act or an instance of stamping. **11a** See **postage stamp**. **11b** a mark applied to postage stamps for cancellation. **12** a similar piece of gummed paper used for commercial or trading purposes. **13** a block, die, etc., used for imprinting a design or device. **14** a design, device, or mark that has been stamped. **15** a characteristic feature or trait; hallmark: *the stamp of authenticity*. **16** a piece of gummed paper or other mark applied to official documents to indicate payment, validity, ownership, etc. **17** *Brit. inf.* a national insurance contribution, formerly recorded by means of a stamp on an official card. **18** type or class: *men of his stamp*. **19** an instrument or machine for crushing or pounding ores, etc., or the pestle in such a device. ♦ See also **stamp out**. [OE *stampe*]
▸ '**stamper** *n*

stamp duty *or* **tax** *n* a tax on legal documents, publications, etc., the payment of which is certified by the attaching or impressing of official stamps.

stampede (stæm'piːd) *n* **1** an impulsive headlong rush of startled cattle or horses. **2** headlong rush of a crowd. **3** any sudden large-scale action, such as a rush of people to support a candidate. **4** *W US & Canad.* a rodeo event featuring fairground and social elements. ♦ *vb* **stampedes, stampeding, stampeded**. **5** to run away or cause to run away

in a stampede. [C19: from American Sp. *estampida*, from Sp.: a din, from *estampar* to stamp, of Gmc origin]
▸ **stam'peder** *n*

stamping ground *n* a habitual or favourite meeting or gathering place.

stamp mill *n* a machine for crushing ore.

stamp out *vb* (*tr, adv*) **1** to put out or extinguish by stamping: *to stamp out a fire.* **2** to suppress by force: *to stamp out a rebellion.*

stance (stæns, stɑːns) *n* **1** the manner and position in which a person or animal stands. **2** *Sport.* the posture assumed when about to play the ball, as in golf, cricket, etc. **3** emotional or intellectual attitude: *a leftist stance.* **4** *Chiefly Scot.* a place where a vehicle waits: *taxi stance.* [C16: via F from It. *stanza* place for standing, from L *stāns*, from *stāre* to stand]

stanch (stɑːntʃ) *vb* a variant of **staunch²**.

stanchion ('stɑːnʃən) *n* **1** any vertical pole, beam, rod, etc., used as a support. ◆ *vb* **2** (*tr*) to provide or support with a stanchion or stanchions. [C15: from OF *estanchon*, from *estance*, from Vulgar L *stantia* (unattested) a standing, from L *stāre* to stand]

stand (stænd) *vb* **stands, standing, stood.** (*mainly intr*) **1** (*also tr*) to be or cause to be in an erect or upright position. **2** to rise to, assume, or maintain an upright position. **3** (*copula*) to have a specified height when standing: *to stand six feet tall.* **4** to be situated or located: *the house stands in the square.* **5** to be in a specified state or condition: *to stand in awe of someone.* **6** to adopt or remain in a resolute position or attitude. **7** (*may take an infinitive*) to be in a specified position: *I stand to lose money in this venture.* **8** to remain in force or continue in effect: *my orders stand.* **9** to come to a stop or halt, esp. temporarily. **10** (of water, etc.) to collect and remain without flowing. **11** (often foll. by *at*) (of a score, account, etc.) to indicate the specified position: *the score stands at 20 to 1.* **12** (*also tr; when intr*, foll. by *for*) to tolerate or bear: *I won't stand for your nonsense; I can't stand spiders.* **13** (*tr*) to resist; survive: *to stand the test of time.* **14** (*tr*) to submit to: *to stand trial.* **15** (often foll. by *for*) *Chiefly Brit.* to be or become a candidate: *stand for Parliament.* **16** to navigate in a specified direction: *we were standing for Madeira.* **17** (of a gun dog) to point at game. **18** to halt, esp. to give action, repel attack, or disrupt an enemy advance when retreating. **19** (*tr*) *Inf.* to bear the cost of; pay for: *to stand someone a drink.* **20 stand a chance.** to have a hope or likelihood of winning, succeeding, etc. **21 stand fast.** to maintain one's position firmly. **22 stand one's ground.** to maintain a stance or position in the face of opposition. **23 stand still. 23a** to remain motionless. **23b** (foll. by *for*) *US.* to tolerate: *I won't stand still for your threats.* **24 stand to (someone).** *Irish inf.* to be useful to (someone): *your knowledge of English will stand to you.* ◆ *n* **25** the act or an instance of standing. **26** an opinion, esp. a resolutely held one: *he took a stand on capital punishment.* **27** a halt or standstill. **28** a place where a person or thing stands. **29** *Austral. & NZ.* **29a** a position on the floor of a shearing shed allocated to one shearer. **29b** the shearer's equipment. **30** a structure on which people can sit or stand. **31** a frame or rack on which such articles as coats and hats may be hung. **32** a small table or piece of furniture where articles may be placed or stored: *a music stand.* **33** a supporting framework, esp. for a tool or instrument. **34** a stall, booth, or counter from which goods may be sold. **35** a halt to give action, etc., esp. during a retreat and having some duration or success. **36** *Cricket.* an extended period at the wicket by two batsmen. **37** a growth of plants in a particular area, esp. trees in a forest or a crop in a field. **38** a stop made by a touring theatrical company, pop group, etc., to give a performance (esp. in **one-night stand**). **39** (of a gun dog) the act of pointing at game. ◆ See also **stand by, stand down,** etc. [OE *standan*]
▸ **'stander** *n*

standard ('stændəd) *n* **1** an accepted or approved example of something against which others are judged or measured. **2** (*often pl*) a principle of propriety, honesty, and integrity. **3** a level of excellence or quality. **4** any distinctive flag or device, etc., as of a nation, sovereign, or special cause, etc., or the colours of a cavalry regiment. **5** a flag or emblem formerly used to show the central or

rallying point of an army in battle. **6** the commodity or commodities in which is stated the value of a basic monetary unit: *the gold standard; the silver standard.* **7** an authorized model of a unit of measure or weight. **8** a unit of board measure equal to 1980 board feet. **9** (in coinage) the prescribed proportion by weight of precious metal and base metal that each coin must contain. **10** an upright pole or beam. **11a** a piece of furniture consisting of an upright pole or beam on a base or support. **11b** (*as modifier*): *a standard lamp.* **12a** a plant, esp. a fruit tree, that is trained so that it has an upright stem free of branches. **12b** (*as modifier*): *a standard cherry.* **13** a song or piece of music that has remained popular for many years. **14** a form or grade in an elementary school. ◆ *adj* **15** of the usual, regularized, medium, or accepted kind: *a standard size.* **16** of recognized authority, competence, or excellence: *the standard work on Greece.* **17** denoting or characterized by idiom, vocabulary, etc., that is regarded as correct and acceptable by educated native speakers. **18** *Brit.* (formerly) (of eggs) of a size that is smaller than *large* and larger than *medium*. [C12: from OF *estandart* gathering place, flag to mark such a place, prob. of Gmc origin]

standard assessment tasks *pl n Brit. education.* the formal name for assessment tests. Acronym: **SATs.**

standard-bearer *n* **1** a man who carries a standard. **2** a leader of a cause or party.

standard cell *n* a voltaic cell producing a constant and accurately known electromotive force that can be used to calibrate voltage-measuring instruments.

standard cost *n* the predetermined budgeted cost of a manufacturing process against which actual costs are compared.

standard deviation *n Statistics.* a measure of dispersion obtained by extracting the square root of the mean of the squared deviations of the observed values from their mean in a frequency distribution.

standard error of the mean *n Statistics.* the standard deviation of the distribution of means of samples chosen from a larger population; equal to the standard deviation of the whole population divided by the square root of the sample size.

standard function *n Computing.* a subprogram provided by a translator that carries out a task, for example the computation of a mathematical function, such as sine, square root, etc.

standard gauge *n* **1** a railway track with a distance of 4 ft. 8½ in. (1.435 m) between the lines; used on most railways. ◆ *adj* **standard-gauge** or **standard-gauged.** **2** of, relating to, or denoting a railway with a standard gauge.

Standard Grade *n* (in Scotland) an examination designed to test skills and the application of knowledge, which replaced O grade.

standardize or **standardise** ('stændə,daɪz) *vb* **standardizes, standardizing, standardized** or **standardises, standardising, standardised.** **1** to make or become standard. **2** (*tr*) to test by or compare with a standard.
▸ **,standardi'zation** or **,standardi'sation** *n* ▸ **'standard,izer** or **'standard,iser** *n*

standard model *n Physics.* a theory of fundamental interactions in which the electromagnetic, weak, and strong interactions are described in terms of the exchange of virtual particles.

standard of living *n* a level of subsistence or material welfare of a community, class, or person.

standard time *n* the official local time of a region or country determined by the distance from Greenwich of a line of longitude passing through the area.

stand by *vb* (*intr*) **1** (*adv*) to be available and ready to act if needed. **2** (*adv*) to be an onlooker without taking any action: *he stood by at the accident.* **3** (*prep*) to be faithful to: *to stand by one's principles.* ◆ *n* **stand-by. 4a** a person or thing that is ready for use or can be relied on in an emergency. **4b** (*as modifier*): *stand-by provisions.* **5** on **stand-by.** in a state of readiness for action or use. ◆ *adj* **stand-by. 6** not booked in advance but awaiting or subject to availability: *a stand-by ticket.*

stand down *vb* (*adv*) **1** (*intr*) to resign or withdraw, esp.

in favour of another. **2** (*intr*) to leave the witness box in a court of law after giving evidence. **3** *Chiefly Brit.* to go or be taken off duty.

stand for *vb* (*intr, prep*) **1** to represent or mean. **2** *Chiefly Brit.* to be or become a candidate for. **3** to support or recommend. **4** *Inf.* to tolerate or bear: *he won't stand for it.*

stand in *vb* **1** (*intr, adv;* usually foll. by *for*) to act as a substitute. **2 stand** (*someone*) **in good stead.** to be of benefit or advantage to (someone). ◆ *n* **stand-in. 3a** a person or thing that serves as a substitute. **3b** (*as modifier*): *a stand-in teacher.* **4** a person who substitutes for an actor during intervals of waiting or in dangerous stunts.

standing ('stændɪŋ) *n* **1** social or financial position, status, or reputation: *a man of some standing.* **2** length of existence, experience, etc. **3** (*modifier*) used to stand in or on: *standing room.* ◆ *adj* **4** *Athletics.* **4a** (of the start of a race) begun from a standing position. **4b** (of a jump, leap, etc.) performed from a stationary position without a run-up. **5** (*prenominal*) permanent, fixed, or lasting. **6** (*prenominal*) still or stagnant: *a standing pond.* **7** *Printing.* (of type) set and stored for future use.

standing army *n* a permanent army of paid soldiers maintained by a nation.

standing order *n* **1** Also called: **banker's order.** an instruction to a bank by a depositor to pay a stated sum at regular intervals. Cf. **direct debit. 2** a rule or order governing the procedure, conduct, etc., of an organization. **3** *Mil.* one of a number of orders which have long-term validity.

standing rigging *n* the stays, shrouds, and other more or less fixed, though adjustable, ropes that support the masts of a sailing vessel.

standing wave *n* *Physics.* a wave that has unchanging amplitude at each point along its axis. Also called: **stationary wave.**

Standish ★ ('stændɪʃ) *n* **Myles** (or **Miles**). ?1584–1656, English military leader of the Pilgrim Fathers at Plymouth, New England.

standoff ('stænd,ɒf) *n* **1** *US & Canad.* the act or an instance of standing off or apart. **2** a deadlock or stalemate. **3** *Rugby.* short for **stand-off half.** ◆ *vb* **stand off.** (*adv*) **4** (*intr*) to navigate a vessel so as to avoid the shore, an obstruction, etc. **5** (*tr*) to keep or cause to keep at a distance. **6** (*intr*) to reach a deadlock or stalemate. **7** (*tr*) to dismiss (workers), esp. temporarily.

stand-off half *n* *Rugby.* **1** a player who acts as a link between his scrum half and three-quarter backs. **2** this position. ◆ Also called: **fly half.**

standoffish (,stænd'ɒfɪʃ) *adj* reserved, haughty, or aloof.
▶ ,stand'offishness *n*

stand on *vb* (*intr*) **1** (*adv*) to continue to navigate a vessel on the same heading. **2** (*prep*) to insist on: *to stand on ceremony.*

stand out *vb* (*intr, adv*) **1** to be distinctive or conspicuous. **2** to refuse to agree or comply: *they stood out for a better price.* **3** to protrude or project. **4** to navigate a vessel away from a port, harbour, etc. ◆ *n* **standout. 5** *Inf.* **5a** a person or thing that is distinctive or outstanding. **5b** (*as modifier*): *the standout track from the album.*

stand over *vb* (*tr, prep*) **1** to supervise closely. **2** *Austral. & NZ inf.* to threaten or intimidate.

standover man ('stænd,əʊvə) *n* *Austral.* a person who extorts money by intimidation.

standpipe ('stænd,paɪp) *n* **1** a vertical pipe, open at the upper end, attached to a pipeline or tank serving to limit the pressure head to that of the height of the pipe. **2** a temporary freshwater outlet installed in a street when household water supplies are cut off.

standpoint ('stænd,pɔɪnt) *n* a physical or mental position from which things are viewed.

standstill ('stænd,stɪl) *n* a complete cessation of movement; halt: *come to a standstill.*

stand to *vb* **1** (*adv*) *Mil.* to assume positions or cause to assume positions to resist a possible attack. **2 stand to reason.** to conform with the dictates of reason: *it stands to reason.*

stand up *vb* (*adv*) **1** (*intr*) to rise to the feet. **2** (*intr*) to resist or withstand wear, criticism, etc. **3** (*tr*) *Inf.* to fail to keep an appointment with, esp. intentionally. **4 stand up for.** to support, side with, or defend. **5 stand up to. 5a** to confront or resist courageously. **5b** to withstand or endure (wear, criticism, etc.). ◆ *adj* **stand-up.** (*prenominal*) **6** having or being in an erect position: *a stand-up collar.* **7** done, taken, etc., while standing: *a stand-up meal.* **8** (of comedy or a comedian) performed or performing solo. ◆ *n* **stand-up. 9** a stand-up comedian. **10** stand-up comedy.

Stanford ★ ('stænfəd) *n* Sir **Charles** (**Villiers**). 1852–1924, Anglo-Irish composer and conductor: noted esp. for his church music, oratorios, and cantatas.

Stanford-Binet test (-bɪ'neɪ) *n* *Psychol.* a revision, esp. for US use, of the Binet-Simon scale designed to measure mental ability by comparing the performance of an individual with the average performance for his age group. See also **Binet-Simon scale, intelligence test.** [C20: after *Stanford University*, California, & Alfred *Binet* (1857–1911), F psychologist]

stanhope ('stænəp) *n* a light one-seater carriage with two or four wheels. [C18: after Fitzroy *Stanhope* (1787–1864), E clergyman for whom it was first built]

Stanislavsky *or* **Stanislavski** (,stænɪ'slævskɪ; *Russian* stani'slafskij) *n* **Konstantin** (kənstan'tin). 1863–1938, Russian actor, cofounder of the Moscow Art Theatre (1897) and creator of the Method theory of acting.

Stanisław (*Polish* sta'niswaf) *or* **Stanislaus** ★ ('stænɪslaus) *n* **Saint.** 1030–79, the patron saint of Poland. As Bishop of Cracow (1072–79) he excommunicated King Bolesław II, who arranged his murder. Feast day: May 11.

stank (stæŋk) *vb* a past tense of **stink.**

Stanley[1] ★ ('stænlɪ) *n* **1** the capital of the Falkland Islands, in NE East Falkland Island: scene of fighting in the Falklands War of 1982. Pop.: 1557 (1991). **2** a town in NE England, in N Durham. Pop.: 18 905 (1991). **3 Mount.** a mountain in central Africa, between Uganda and the Democratic Republic of the Congo: the highest peak of the Ruwenzori range. Height: 5109 m (16 763 ft). Congolese name: **Ngaliema Mountain.**

Stanley[2] ★ ('stænlɪ) *n* Sir **Henry Morton.** 1841–1904, British explorer, who led an expedition to Africa in search of Livingstone, whom he found on Nov. 10, 1871. He led three further expeditions in Africa (1874–77; 1879–84; 1887–89).

Stanley Falls ★ *pl n* the former name of **Boyoma Falls.**

Stanley knife *n* *Trademark.* a type of knife used for carpet fitting, etc., consisting of a thick hollow metal handle with a short, very sharp, replaceable blade inserted in one end. [C19: after F. T. *Stanley*, US businessman and founder of the Stanley Rule and Level Company]

Stanley Pool ★ *n* a lake between the Democratic Republic of the Congo and the Congo, formed by a widening of the River Congo. Area: 829 sq. km (320 sq. miles). Congolese name: **Pool Malebo.**

Stanleyville ★ ('stænlɪ,vɪl) *n* the former name (until 1966) of **Kisangani.**

stann- *combining form.* denoting tin: *stannite.* [from LL *stannum* tin]

Stannaries ★ ('stænərɪz) *n* (*sometimes functioning as sing*) **the.** a former tin-mining district of Devon and Cornwall, under the jurisdiction of special courts.

stannary ('stænərɪ) *n, pl* **stannaries.** a place or region where tin is mined or worked. [C15: from Med. L *stannāria*, from LL *stannum* tin]

stannic ('stænɪk) *adj* of or containing tin, esp. in the tetravalent state; designating a tin(IV) compound. [C18: from LL *stannum* tin]

stannite ('stænaɪt) *n* a grey metallic mineral that consists of a sulphide of tin, copper, and iron and is a source of tin. Formula: Cu_2FeSnS_4. [C19: from LL *stannum* tin + -ITE[1]]

stannous ('stænəs) *adj* of or containing tin, esp. in the divalent state; designating a tin(II) compound.

Stanovoi Range *or* **Stanovoy Range** ★ (*Russian*

stənə'vɔj) *n* a mountain range in SE Russia: forms part of the watershed between rivers flowing to the Arctic and the Pacific. Highest peak: Mount Skalisty, 2482 m (8143 ft).

Stans ★ (*German* ʃtans) *n* a town in central Switzerland, capital of Nidwalden demicanton, 11 km (7 miles) southeast of Lucerne: tourist centre. Pop.: 5700 (latest est.).

stanza ('stænzə) *n* **1** *Prosody.* a fixed number of verse lines arranged in a definite metrical pattern, forming a unit of a poem. **2** *US & Austral.* a half or a quarter in a football match. [C16: from It.: halting place, from Vulgar L *stantia* (unattested) station, from L *stāre* to stand]
▸ 'stanzaed *adj* ▸ stanzaic (stæn'zeɪɪk) *adj*

stapelia (stə'piːlɪə) *n* any of various fleshy cactus-like leafless African plants having large fetid flowers. [C18: from NL, after J. B. van *Stapel* (died 1636), Du. botanist]

stapes ('steɪpiːz) *n, pl* **stapes** *or* **stapedes** (stæ'piːdiːz). the stirrup-shaped bone that is the innermost of three small bones in the middle ear of mammals. Nontechnical name: **stirrup bone.** Cf. **incus, malleus.** [C17: via NL from Med. L, ? var. of *stapeda* stirrup, infl. by L *stāre* to stand + *pēs* a foot]

staphylo- *combining form.* **1** uvula: *staphyloplasty.* **2** resembling a bunch of grapes: *staphylococcus.* [from Gk *staphulē* bunch of grapes, uvula]

staphylococcus (,stæfɪləʊ'kɒkəs) *n, pl* **staphylococci** (-'kɒkaɪ; *US* -'kɒksaɪ). any spherical Gram-positive bacterium of the genus *Staphylococcus,* typically occurring in clusters and causing boils, infection in wounds, and septicaemia. Often shortened to **staph.**
▸ ,staphylo'coccal *adj*

staphyloplasty ('stæfɪləʊ,plæstɪ) *n* plastic surgery or surgical repair involving the soft palate or the uvula.
▸ ,staphylo'plastic *adj*

staple[1] ('steɪp^əl) *n* **1** a short length of thin wire bent into a square U-shape, used to fasten papers, cloth, etc. **2** a short length of stiff wire formed into a U-shape with pointed ends, used for holding a hasp to a post, securing electric cables, etc. ◆ *vb* **staples, stapling, stapled. 3** (*tr*) to secure (papers, wire, etc.) with staples. [OE *stapol* prop, of Gmc origin]
▸ 'stapler *n*

staple[2] ('steɪp^əl) *adj* **1** of prime importance; principal: *staple foods.* **2** (of a commodity) forming a predominant element in the product, consumption, or trade of a nation, region, etc. ◆ *n* **3** a staple commodity. **4** a main constituent; integral part. **5** *Chiefly US & Canad.* a principal raw material produced or grown in a region. **6** the fibre of wool, cotton, etc., graded as to length and degree of fineness. ◆ *vb* **staples, stapling, stapled. 7** (*tr*) to arrange or sort (wool, cotton, etc.) according to length and fineness. [C15: from MDu. *stapel* warehouse]

staple gun *n* a mechanism that fixes staples to a surface.

star (stɑː) *n* **1** any of a vast number of celestial objects visible in the clear night sky as points of light. **2a** a hot gaseous mass, such as the sun, that radiates energy, esp. as light and infrared radiation, and in some cases as ultraviolet, radio waves, and X-rays. **2b** (*as modifier*): *a star catalogue.* Related adjs.: **astral, sidereal, stellar. 3** *Astrol.* **3a** a celestial body, esp. a planet, supposed to influence events, personalities, etc. **3b** (*pl*) another name for **horoscope** (sense 1). **4** an emblem shaped like a conventionalized star, often used as a symbol of rank, an award, etc. **5** a small white blaze on the forehead of an animal, esp. a horse. **6a** a distinguished or glamorous celebrity, often from the entertainment world. **6b** (*as modifier*): *star quality.* **7** another word for **asterisk. 8** see **stars.** to see or seem to see bright moving pinpoints of light, as from a blow on the head, increased blood pressure, etc. ◆ *vb* **stars, starring, starred. 9** (*tr*) to mark or decorate with a star or stars. **10** to feature or be featured as a star: *"Greed" starred Erich von Stroheim; Olivier starred in "Hamlet".* [OE *steorra*]
▸ 'starless *adj* ▸ 'star,like *adj*

Stara Zagora ★ (*Bulgarian* 'stara za'gɔra) *n* a city in central Bulgaria: ceded to Bulgaria by Turkey in 1877. Pop.: 149 666 (1996 est.).

starboard ('stɑːbəd, -,bɔːd) *n* **1** the right side of an aero-

plane or vessel when facing the nose or bow. Cf. **port**[2] (sense 1). ◆ *adj* **2** relating to or on the starboard. ◆ *vb* **3** to turn or be turned towards the starboard. [OE *stēorbord,* lit.: steering side, from *stēor* steering paddle + *bord* side; from the fact that boats were formerly steered by a paddle held over the right-hand side]

starburst ('stɑː,bɜːst) *n* **1** a pattern of rays or lines radiating from a light source. **2** *Photog.* a lens attachment which produces a starburst effect.

starch (stɑːtʃ) *n* **1** a polysaccharide composed of glucose units that occurs widely in plant tissues in the form of storage granules. **2** a starch obtained from potatoes and some grain: it is fine white powder that, in solution with water, is used to stiffen fabric. **3** any food containing a large amount of starch, such as rice and potatoes. **4** stiff or pompous formality. ◆ *vb* **5** (*tr*) to stiffen with or soak in starch. [OE *stercan* (unattested except by the p.p. *sterced*) to stiffen]
▸ 'starcher *n*

Star Chamber *n* **1** *English history.* the Privy Council sitting as a court of equity; abolished 1641. **2** (*sometimes not caps.*) any arbitrary tribunal dispensing summary justice. **3** (*sometimes not caps.*) (in Britain, in a Conservative government) a group of senior ministers who make the final decision on the public spending of each government department.

starch-reduced *adj* (of food, esp. bread) having the starch content reduced, as in proprietary slimming products.

starchy ('stɑːtʃɪ) *adj* **starchier, starchiest. 1** of or containing starch. **2** extremely formal, stiff, or conventional: *a starchy manner.* **3** stiffened with starch.
▸ 'starchily *adv* ▸ 'starchiness *n*

star connection *n* a connection used in a polyphase electrical device or system of devices in which the windings each have one end connected to a common junction, the **star point,** and the other end to a separate terminal.

star-crossed *adj* dogged by ill luck; destined to misfortune.

stardom ('stɑːdəm) *n* **1** the fame and prestige of being a star in films, sport, etc. **2** the world of celebrities.

stardust ('stɑː,dʌst) *n* **1** a large number of distant stars appearing to the observer as a cloud of dust. **2** a dreamy romantic or sentimental quality or feeling.

stare (steə) *vb* **stares, staring, stared. 1** (*intr*) (often foll. by *at*) to look or gaze fixedly, often with hostility or rudeness. **2** (*intr*) to stand out as obvious; glare. **3 stare one in the face.** to be glaringly obvious or imminent. ◆ *n* **4** the act or an instance of staring. [OE *starian*]
▸ 'starer *n*

starfish ('stɑː,fɪʃ) *n, pl* **starfish** *or* **starfishes.** any of various echinoderms, typically having a flattened body covered with a flexible test and five arms radiating from a central disc.

star fruit *n* another name for **carambola.**

stargaze ('stɑː,geɪz) *vb* **stargazes, stargazing, stargazed.** (*intr*) **1** to observe the stars. **2** to daydream.
▸ 'star,gazer *n* ▸ 'star,gazing *n, adj*

stark (stɑːk) *adj* **1** (*usually prenominal*) devoid of any elaboration; bare: *the stark facts.* **2** grim; desolate: *a stark landscape.* **3** (*usually prenominal*) utter; absolute: *stark folly.* **4** *Arch.* severe; violent. **5** *Arch. or poetic.* rigid, as in death (esp. in **stiff and stark, stark dead**). **6** short for **stark-naked.** ◆ *adv* **7** completely: *stark mad.* **8** *Rare.* starkly. [OE *stearc* stiff]
▸ 'starkly *adv* ▸ 'starkness *n*

Stark ★ *n* **1** (stɑːk). Dame **Freya** (**Madeline**) ('freɪə). 1893–1993, British traveller and writer. **2** (*German* ʃtark). **Johannes** (jo'hanəs). 1874–1957, German physicist, who discovered the splitting of spectrum lines in a strong electrostatic field (**Stark effect,** 1913): Nobel prize for physics 1919.

stark-naked *adj* completely naked. Informal word (*postpositive*): **starkers.** [C13 *stert naket,* lit.: tail naked; *stert,* from OE *steort* tail]

★ people and places

starlet ('stɑːlɪt) *n* **1** a young actress who is projected as a potential star. **2** a small star.

starlight ('stɑː,laɪt) *n* **1** the light emanating from the stars. ◆ *adj also* **starlighted**. **2** of or like starlight. **3** Also: **starlit** ('stɑː,lɪt). illuminated by starlight.

starling ('stɑːlɪŋ) *n* any gregarious passerine songbird of an Old World family, esp. the **common starling**, which has a blackish iridescent plumage and a short tail. [OE *stærlinc*, from *stær* starling + *-line* -LING[1]]

star-of-Bethlehem *n* **1** Also: **starflower**. a Eurasian liliaceous plant having narrow leaves and starlike white flowers. **2** any of several similar and related plants.

Star of David *n* an emblem symbolizing Judaism and consisting of a six-pointed star formed by superimposing one inverted equilateral triangle upon another of equal size.

Starr ★ (stɑː) *n* **1** (**Myra**) **Belle**. 1848–89, US outlaw, a famous rustler of horses and cattle. **2 Ringo**, original name *Richard Starkey*. born 1940, British rock musician; drummer (1962–70) with the Beatles.

starry ('stɑːrɪ) *adj* **starrier, starriest**. **1** filled, covered with, or illuminated by stars. **2** of, like, or relating to a star or stars.
▸ 'starriness *n*

starry-eyed *adj* given to naive wishes, judgments, etc.; full of unsophisticated optimism.

Stars and Stripes *n* (*functioning as sing*) **the**. the national flag of the United States of America, consisting of 50 white stars representing the present states on a blue field and seven red and six white horizontal stripes representing the original states. Also called: the **Star-Spangled Banner**.

star sapphire *n* a sapphire showing a starlike figure in reflected light because of its crystalline structure.

star sign *n* another name for **sign of the zodiac**.

Star-Spangled Banner *n* **the**. **1** the national anthem of the United States of America. **2** another term for the **Stars and Stripes**.

star stream *n* one of two main streams of stars that, because of the rotation of the Milky Way, appear to move in opposite directions.

star-studded *adj* featuring a large proportion of well-known performers: *a star-studded cast*.

start (stɑːt) *vb* **1** to begin or cause to begin (something or to do something); come or cause to come into being, operation, etc.: *he started a quarrel; they started to work*. **2** (when *intr*, sometimes foll. by *on*) to make or cause to make a beginning of (a process, series of actions, etc.): *they started on the project*. **3** (sometimes foll. by *up*) to set or be set in motion: *he started up the machine*. **4** (*intr*) to make a sudden involuntary movement, as from fright; jump. **5** (*intr*; sometimes foll. by *up, away*, etc.) to spring or jump suddenly from a position or place. **6** to establish or be established; set up: *to start a business*. **7** (*tr*) to support (someone) in the first part of a venture, career, etc. **8** to work or cause to work loose. **9** to enter or be entered in a race. **10** (*intr*) to flow violently from a source: *wine started from a hole in the cask*. **11** (*tr*) to rouse (game) from a hiding place, lair, etc. **12** (*intr*) (esp. of eyes) to bulge; pop. **13** (*intr*) *Brit. inf.* to commence quarrelling or causing a disturbance. **14 to start with**. in the first place. ◆ *n* **15** the beginning or first part of a journey, series of actions or operations, etc. **16** the place or time of starting, as of a race or performance. **17** a signal to proceed, as in a race. **18** a lead or advantage, either in time or distance, in a competitive activity: *he had an hour's start on me*. **19** a slight involuntary movement, as through fright, surprise, etc.: *she gave a start as I entered*. **20** an opportunity to enter a career, undertake a project, etc. **21** *Inf.* a surprising incident. **22 for a start**. in the first place. ◆ *See also* **start in, start off**, etc. [OE *styrtan*]

starter ('stɑːtə) *n* **1** Also called: **self-starter**. a device for starting an internal-combustion engine, usually consisting of a powerful electric motor that engages with the flywheel. **2** a person who supervises and signals the start of a race. **3** a competitor who starts in a race or contest. **4** *Inf., chiefly Austral.* an acceptable or practicable proposition, plan, idea, etc. **5** *Chiefly Brit.* the first course of a

meal. **6** (*modifier*) designed to be used by a novice: *a starter kit*. **7 for starters**. *Sl.* in the first place. **8 under starter's orders**. **8a** (of horses in a race) awaiting the start signal. **8b** (of a person) eager or ready to begin.

starter home *n* a compact flat or house marketed by price and size specifications to suit the requirements of first-time home buyers.

start in *vb* (*adv*) to undertake (something or doing something); commence or begin.

starting block *n* one of a pair of adjustable devices with pads or blocks against which a sprinter braces his feet in crouch starts.

starting gate *n* **1** a movable barrier so placed on the starting line of a racecourse that the raising of it releases all the contestants simultaneously. **2** the US name for **starting stalls**.

starting grid *n Motor racing*. a marked section of the track at the start where the cars line up according to their times in practice, the fastest occupying the front position.

starting price *n* (esp. in horse racing) the latest odds offered by bookmakers at the start of a race.

starting stalls *pl n Brit.* a line of stalls in which horses are enclosed at the start of a race and from which they are released by the simultaneous springing open of retaining barriers at the front of each stall.

startle ('stɑːt°l) *vb* **startles, startling, startled**. to be or cause to be surprised or frightened, esp. so as to start involuntarily. [OE *steartlian* to stumble]
▸ 'startler *n* ▸ 'startling *adj*

start off *vb* (*adv*) **1** (*intr*) to set out on a journey. **2** to be or make the first step in (an activity); initiate: *he started the show off with a lively song*. **3** (*tr*) to cause (a person) to act or do something, such as to laugh, to tell stories, etc.

start on *vb* (*intr, prep*) *Brit. inf.* to pick a quarrel with; upbraid.

start out *vb* (*intr, adv*) **1** to set out on a journey. **2** to take the first steps, as in life, one's career, etc.: *he started out as a salesman*. **3** to take the first actions in an activity in a particular way or with a specified aim: *they started out wanting a house, but eventually bought a flat*.

start up *vb* (*adv*) **1** to come or cause to come into being for the first time; originate. **2** (*intr*) to spring or jump suddenly. **3** to set in or go into motion, activity, etc.: *he started up the engine*. ◆ *adj* **start-up**. **4** of or relating to input, usually financial, made to establish a new project or business: *a start-up mortgage*.

starve (stɑːv) *vb* **starves, starving, starved**. **1** to die or cause to die from lack of food. **2** to deprive (a person or animal) or (of a person, etc.) to be deprived of food. **3** (*intr*) *Inf.* to be very hungry. **4** (foll. by *of* or *for*) to deprive or be deprived (of something), esp. so as to cause suffering or malfunctioning: *the engine was starved of fuel*. **5** (*tr*; foll. by *into*) to bring (to) a specified condition by starving: *to starve someone into submission*. **6** *Arch. or dialect.* to be or cause to be extremely cold. [OE *steorfan* to die]
▸ 'star'vation *n*

starveling ('stɑːvlɪŋ) *Arch.* ◆ *n* **1a** a starving or poorly fed person, animal, etc. **1b** (*as modifier*): *a starveling child*. ◆ *adj* **2** insufficient; meagre; scant.

Star Wars *n* (*functioning as sing*) (in the US) a proposed system of artificial satellites armed with lasers to destroy enemy missiles in space. [C20: popularly named after the science-fiction film *Star Wars* (1977)]

starwort ('stɑː,wɜːt) *n* **1** any of several plants with star-shaped flowers, esp. the stitchwort. **2** any of several aquatic plants having a star-shaped rosette of floating leaves.

stash (stæʃ) *vb* **1** (*tr*; often foll. by *away*) *Inf.* to put or store (money, valuables, etc.) in a secret place, as for safekeeping. ◆ *n* **2** *Inf., chiefly US & Canad.* a secret store or the place where this is hidden. **3** *Sl.* drugs kept for personal consumption. [C20: from ?]

stasis ('steɪsɪs) *n* **1** *Pathol.* a stagnation in the normal flow of bodily fluids, such as the blood or urine. **2** a state or condition in which there is no action or progress.

[C18: via NL from Gk: a standing, from *histanai* to cause to stand]

-stat *n combining form.* indicating a device that causes something to remain stationary or constant: *thermostat.* [from Gk *-statēs,* from *histanai* to cause to stand]

state (steɪt) *n* **1** the condition of a person, thing, etc., with regard to main attributes. **2** the structure or form of something: *a solid state.* **3** any mode of existence. **4** position in life or society; estate. **5** ceremonious style, as befitting wealth or dignity: *to live in state.* **6** a sovereign political power or community. **7** the territory occupied by such a community. **8** the sphere of power in such a community: *affairs of state.* **9** (*often cap.*) one of a number of areas or communities having their own governments and forming a federation under a sovereign government, as in the US. **10** (*often cap.*) the body politic of a particular sovereign power, esp. as contrasted with a rival authority such as the Church. **11** *Obs.* a class or order; estate. **12** *Inf.* a nervous, upset, or excited condition (esp. in **in a state**). **13 lie in state.** (of a body) to be placed on public view before burial. **14 state of affairs.** a situation; circumstances or condition. ◆ *modifier.* **15** controlled or financed by a state: *state university.* **16** of, relating to, or concerning the State: *State trial.* **17** involving ceremony or concerned with a ceremonious occasion: *state visit.* ◆ *vb* **states, stating, stated.** (*tr; may take a clause as object*) **18** to articulate in words; utter. **19** to declare formally or publicly. [C13: from OF *estat,* from L *status* a standing, from *stāre* to stand]
  ▸ '**statable** *or* '**stateable** *adj*   ▸ '**statehood** *n*

state bank *n* (in the US) a commercial bank incorporated under a State charter and not required to be a member of the Federal Reserve System.

statecraft ('steɪtˌkrɑːft) *n* the art of conducting public affairs; statesmanship.

state duma *n* another name for **duma** (sense 3).

state house *n NZ.* a house built by the government and rented to a **state tenant.** Brit. equivalent: **council house.**

Statehouse ('steɪtˌhaʊs) *n* (in the US) the building which houses a state legislature.

stateless ('steɪtlɪs) *adj* **1** without nationality: *stateless persons.* **2** without a state or states.
  ▸ '**statelessness** *n*

stately ('steɪtlɪ) *adj* **statelier, stateliest. 1** characterized by a graceful, dignified, and imposing appearance or manner. ◆ *adv* **2** in a stately manner.
  ▸ '**stateliness** *n*

stately home *n Brit.* a large mansion, esp. one open to the public.

statement ('steɪtmənt) *n* **1** the act of stating. **2** something that is stated, esp. a formal prepared announcement or reply. **3** *Law.* a declaration of matters of fact. **4** an account containing a summary of bills or invoices and displaying the total amount due. **5** an account prepared by a bank for a client, usually at regular intervals, to show all credits and debits and the balance at the end of the period. **6** a computer instruction written in a source language, such as FORTRAN, which is converted into one or more machine-code instructions by a compiler. **7** *Logic.* the content of a sentence that affirms or denies something and may be true or false. **8** *Brit. education.* a legally binding account of the provisions that will be made to meet the needs of a pupil with special educational needs.

statement of attainment *n Brit. education.* a programme of specific objectives that pupils should achieve within their own levels of attainment in a particular subject.

statement of claim *n Law.* (in England) the first pleading made by the plaintiff in a High Court action.

Staten Island ★ ('stæt°n) *n* an island in SE New York State, in New York Harbor: a borough of New York city; heavy industry. Pop.: 378 977 (1990). Area: 155 sq. km (60 sq. miles).

state of the art *n* **1** the level of knowledge and development achieved in a technique, science, etc., esp. at present. ◆ *adj* **state-of-the-art.** (*prenominal*) **2** the most re-

cent and therefore considered the best; up-to-the-minute: *a state-of-the-art amplifier.*

State Registered Nurse *n* (formerly, in Britain) a nurse who had extensive training and was qualified to perform all nursing services. See **Registered General Nurse.**

stateroom ('steɪtˌruːm, -ˌrʊm) *n* **1** a private cabin or room on a ship, train, etc. **2** *Chiefly Brit.* a large room in a palace or other building for use on state occasions.

States ★ (steɪts) *n* (*functioning as sing or pl*) **the.** an informal name for the **United States of America.**

state school *n* any school maintained by the state, in which education is free.

stateside ('steɪtˌsaɪd) *adj, adv* (*sometimes cap.*) *US.* of, in, to, or towards the US.

statesman ('steɪtsmən) *n, pl* **statesmen. 1** a political leader whose wisdom, integrity, etc., win great respect. **2** a person active and influential in the formulation of high government policy.
  ▸ '**statesman-ˌlike** *or* '**statesmanly** *adj*   ▸ '**statesmanship** *n*
  ▸ '**states,woman** *fem n*

state socialism *n* a variant of socialism in which the power of the state is employed for the purpose of creating an egalitarian society by means of public control of major industries, banks, etc.
  ▸ **state socialist** *n*

state trooper *n US.* a state policeman.

static ('stætɪk) *adj also* **statical. 1** not active or moving; stationary. **2** (of a weight, force, or pressure) acting but causing no movement. **3** of or concerned with forces that do not produce movement. **4** relating to or causing stationary electric charges; electrostatic. **5** of or relating to interference in the reception of radio or television transmissions. **6** of or concerned with statics. **7** *Computing.* (of a memory) not needing its contents refreshed periodically. ◆ *n* **8** random hissing or crackling or a speckled picture caused by interference in the reception of radio or television transmissions. **9** electric sparks or crackling produced by friction. [C16: from NL *staticus,* from Gk *statikos* causing to stand, from *histanai* to stand]
  ▸ '**statically** *adv*

statice ('stætɪsɪ) *n* another name for **sea lavender.**

static electricity *n* electricity that is not dynamic or flowing as a current.

statics ('stætɪks) *n* (*functioning as sing*) the branch of mechanics concerned with the forces that produce a state of equilibrium in a system.

station ('steɪʃən) *n* **1** the place or position at which a thing or person stands. **2a** a place along a route or line at which a bus, train, etc., stops for fuel or to pick up or let off passengers or goods, esp. one with ancillary buildings and services. **2b** (*as modifier*): *a station buffet.* **3a** the headquarters or local offices of an organization such as the police or fire services. **3b** (*as modifier*): *a station sergeant.* See **police station, fire station. 4** a building, depot, etc., with special equipment for some particular purpose: *power station; petrol station.* **5** *Mil.* a place of duty: *an action station.* **6** *Navy.* **6a** a location to which a ship or fleet is assigned for duty. **6b** an assigned location for a member of a ship's crew. **7** a television or radio channel. **8** a position or standing, as in a particular society or organization. **9** the type of one's occupation; calling. **10** (in British India) a place where the British district officials or garrison officers resided. **11** *Biol.* the habitat occupied by a particular animal or plant. **12** *Austral. & NZ.* a large sheep or cattle farm. **13** (*sometimes cap.*) *RC Church.* **13a** one of the stations of the Cross. **13b** any of the churches (**station churches**) in Rome used as points of assembly for religious processions and ceremonies on particular days (**station days**). ◆ *vb* **14** (*tr*) to place in or assign to a station. [C14: via OF from L *statiō* a standing still, from *stāre* to stand]

stationary ('steɪʃənərɪ) *adj* **1** not moving; standing still. **2** not able to be moved. **3** showing no change: *the doctors said his condition was stationary.* **4** tending to remain in one place. [C15: from L *statiōnārius,* from *statiō* STATION]

USAGE NOTE   Avoid confusion with **stationery.**

★ people and places

stationary orbit *n Astronautics.* a synchronous orbit lying in or approximately in the plane of the equator.

stationary wave *n* another name for **standing wave.**

stationer ('steɪʃənə) *n* a person who sells stationery or a shop where stationery is sold. [C14: from Med. L *stationarius* a person having a regular station, hence a shopkeeper (esp. a bookseller) as distinguished from an itinerant tradesman; see STATION]

stationery ('steɪʃənərɪ) *n* any writing materials, such as paper, envelopes, pens, ink, rulers, etc.

USAGE NOTE Avoid confusion with **stationary.**

station house *n Chiefly US.* a house that is situated by or serves as a station, esp. as a police or fire station.

stationmaster ('steɪʃən,mɑːstə) *n* the senior official in charge of a railway station.

Stations of the Cross *pl n RC Church.* **1** a series of 14 crosses, often accompanied by 14 pictures or carvings, arranged around the walls of a church, to commemorate 14 stages in Christ's journey to Calvary. **2** a devotion of 14 prayers relating to each of these stages.

station wagon *n* another name (less common in Britain) for **estate car.**

statism ('steɪtɪzəm) *n* the theory or practice of concentrating economic and political power in the state.
▶ 'statist *n*

statistic (stə'tɪstɪk) *n* a datum capable of exact numerical representation, such as the correlation coefficient of two series or the standard deviation of a sample.
▶ sta'tistical *adj* ▶ sta'tistically *adv* ▶ statistician (,stætɪ'stɪʃən) *n*

statistical mechanics *n* (*functioning as sing*) the study of the properties of physical systems as predicted by the statistical behaviour of their constituent particles.

statistics (stə'tɪstɪks) *n* **1** (*functioning as sing*) a science concerned with the collection, classification, and interpretation of quantitative data and with the application of probability theory to the analysis and estimation of population parameters. **2** the quantitative data themselves. [C18 (orig. "science dealing with facts of a state"): via G *Statistik*, from NL *statisticus* concerning state affairs, from L *status* STATE]

Statius ★ ('steɪʃɪəs) *n* **Publius Papinius** ('pʌblɪəs pə'pɪnɪəs). ?45–96 A.D., Roman poet.

stator ('steɪtə) *n* the stationary part of a rotary machine or device, esp. of a motor or generator. [C20: from L: one who stands (by), from *stāre* to stand]

statoscope ('stætə,skəʊp) *n* a very sensitive form of aneroid barometer used to detect and measure small variations in atmospheric pressure, such as one used in an aircraft to indicate small changes in altitude.

statuary ('stætjʊərɪ) *n* **1** statues collectively. **2** the art of making statues. ◆ *adj* **3** of or for statues. [C16: from L *statuārius*]

statue ('stætjuː) *n* a wooden, stone, metal, plaster, or other sculpture of a human or animal figure, usually life-size or larger. [C14: via OF from L *statua*, from *statuere* to set up; cf. STATUTE]

statuesque (,stætjʊ'esk) *adj* like a statue, esp. in possessing great formal beauty or dignity.
▶ ,statu'esquely *adv* ▶ ,statu'esqueness *n*

statuette (,stætjʊ'et) *n* a small statue.

stature ('stætʃə) *n* **1** height, esp. of a person or animal when standing. **2** the degree of development of a person: *the stature of a champion.* **3** intellectual or moral greatness: *a man of stature.* [C13: via OF from L *statūra*, from *stāre* to stand]

status ('steɪtəs) *n, pl* **statuses. 1** a social or professional position, condition, or standing. **2** the relative position or standing of a person or thing. **3** a high position or standing: *he has acquired a new status in that job.* **4** the legal standing or condition of a person. **5** a state of affairs. [C17: from L: posture, from *stāre* to stand]

status quo (kwəʊ) *n* (usually preceded by *the*) the existing state of affairs. [lit.: the state in which]

status symbol *n* a possession which is regarded as proof of the owner's social position, wealth, prestige, etc.

statute ('stætjuːt) *n* **1a** an enactment of a legislative body expressed in a formal document. **1b** this document. **2** a permanent rule made by a body or institution. [C13: from OF *estatut*, from LL *statūtum*, from L *statuere* to set up, decree, ult. from *stāre* to stand]

statute book *n Chiefly Brit.* a register of enactments passed by the legislative body of a state: *not on the statute book.*

statute law *n* **1** a law enacted by a legislative body. **2** a particular example of this. ◆ Cf. **common law, equity.**

statute mile *n* a legal or formal name for **mile** (sense 1).

statute of limitations *n* a legislative enactment prescribing the period of time within which proceedings must be instituted to enforce a right or bring an action at law.

statutory ('stætjʊtərɪ, -trɪ) *adj* **1** of, relating to, or having the nature of a statute. **2** prescribed or authorized by statute. **3** (of an offence) **3a** recognized by statute. **3b** subject to a punishment or penalty prescribed by statute.
▶ 'statutorily *adv*

statutory order *n* a statute that applies further legislation to an existing act.

Stauffenberg ★ (German 'ʃtaʊfənberk) *n* **Claus** (klaʊs), **Graf von.** 1907–44, German army officer, who tried to assassinate Hitler (1944). He and his fellow conspirators were executed.

staunch[1] (stɔːntʃ) *adj* **1** loyal, firm, and dependable: *a staunch supporter.* **2** solid or substantial in construction. **3** *Rare.* (of a ship, etc.) watertight; seaworthy. [C15 (orig.: watertight): from OF *estanche*, from *estanchier* to STANCH]
▶ 'staunchly *adv* ▶ 'staunchness *n*

staunch[2] (stɔːntʃ) *or* **stanch** (stɑːntʃ) *vb* **1** to stem the flow of (a liquid, esp. blood) or (of a liquid) to stop flowing. **2** to prevent the flow of a liquid, esp. blood, from (a hole, wound, etc.). [C14: from OF *estanchier*, from Vulgar L *stanticāre* (unattested) to cause to stand, from L *stāre* to halt]
▶ 'staunchable *or* 'stanchable *adj* ▶ 'stauncher *or* 'stancher *n*

Stavanger ★ (Norwegian sta'vaŋər) *n* a port in SW Norway: canning and shipbuilding industries. Pop.: 104 322 (1996).

stave (steɪv) *n* **1** any one of a number of long strips of wood joined together to form a barrel, bucket, boat hull, etc. **2** any of various bars, slats, or rods, usually of wood, such as a rung of a ladder. **3** any stick, staff, etc. **4** a stanza or verse of a poem. **5** *Music.* **5a** *Brit.* an individual group of five lines and four spaces used in staff notation. **5b** another word for **staff**[1] (sense 9). ◆ *vb* **staves, staving, staved** *or* **stove. 6** (often foll. by *in*) to break or crush (the staves of a boat, barrel, etc.) or (of the staves of a boat) to be broken or crushed. **7** (*tr*; usually foll. by *in*) to burst or force (a hole in something). **8** (*tr*) to provide (a ladder, chair, etc.) with staves. [C14: back formation from *staves*, pl. of STAFF[1]]

stave off *vb* (*tr, adv*) to avert or hold off, esp. temporarily: *to stave off hunger.*

staves (steɪvz) *n* a plural of **staff**[1] or **stave.**

stavesacre ('steɪvz,eɪkə) *n* **1** a Eurasian ranunculaceous plant having poisonous seeds. **2** the seeds, which have strong emetic and cathartic properties. [C14 *staphisagre*, from L *staphis agria*, from Gk, from *staphis* raisin + *agria* wild]

Stavropol ★ (Russian 'stavrəpəlj) *n* **1** a city in SW Russia: founded as a fortress in 1777. Pop.: 342 000 (1995 est.). Former name (1940–43): **Voroshilovsk. 2** the former name (until 1964) of **Togliatti.**

stay[1] (steɪ) *vb* **1** (*intr*) to continue or remain in a certain place, position, etc.: *to stay outside.* **2** (*copula*) to continue to be; remain: *to stay awake.* **3** (*intr*; often foll. by *at*) to reside temporarily: *to stay at a hotel.* **4** (*tr*) to remain for a

specified period: *to stay the weekend.* **5** (*intr*) *Scot. & S. African.* to reside permanently or habitually; live. **6** *Arch.* to stop or cause to stop. **7** (*intr*) to wait, pause, or tarry. **8** (*tr*) to delay or hinder. **9** (*tr*) **9a** to discontinue or suspend (a judicial proceeding). **9b** to hold in abeyance or restrain from enforcing (an order, decree, etc.). **10** to endure (something testing or difficult, such as a race): *stay the course.* **11** (*tr*) to hold back or restrain: *to stay one's anger.* **12** (*tr*) to satisfy or appease (an appetite, etc.) temporarily. ◆ *n* **13** the act of staying or sojourning in a place or the period during which one stays. **14** the act of stopping or restraining or state of being stopped, etc. **15** the suspension of a judicial proceeding, etc.: *stay of execution.* [C15 *staien*, from Anglo-F *estaier* to stay, from OF *ester* to stay, from L *stāre* to stand]
▸ 'stayer *n*

stay[2] (steɪ) *n* **1** anything that supports or steadies, such as a prop or buttress. **2** a thin strip of metal, plastic, bone, etc., used to stiffen corsets, etc. See also **stays** (sense 1). ◆ *vb* (*tr*) **3** (often foll. by *up*) to prop or hold. **4** (often foll. by *up*) to comfort or sustain. **5** (foll. by *on* or *upon*) to cause to rely or depend. [C16: from OF *estaye*, of Gmc origin]

stay[3] (steɪ) *n* a rope, cable, or chain, usually one of a set, used for bracing uprights, such as masts, funnels, flagpoles, chimneys, etc.; guy. ◆ See also **stays** (senses 2, 3). [OE *stæg*]

stay-at-home *adj* **1** (of a person) enjoying a quiet, settled, and unadventurous use of leisure. ◆ *n* **2** a stay-at-home person.

staying power *n* endurance; stamina.

stays (steɪz) *pl n* **1** old-fashioned corsets with bones in them. **2** a position of a sailing vessel relative to the wind so that the sails are luffing or aback. **3 miss** *or* **refuse stays.** (of a sailing vessel) to fail to come about.

staysail ('steɪ,seɪl; *Naut.* 'steɪsəl) *n* an auxiliary sail, often triangular, set on a stay.

STD *abbrev. for:* **1** Doctor of Sacred Theology. **2** sexually transmitted disease. **3** subscriber trunk dialling.

STD code *n Brit.* a code of four or more digits, other than those comprising a subscriber's local telephone number, that determines the routing of a call. [C20: *s(ubscriber) t(runk) d(ialling)*]

Ste *abbrev. for* Saint (female). [F *Sainte*]

stead (stɛd) *n* **1** (preceded by *in*) *Rare.* the place, function, or position that should be taken by another: *to come in someone's stead.* **2 stand (someone) in good stead.** to be useful or of good service to (someone). ◆ *vb* **3** (*tr*) *Arch.* to help or benefit. [OE *stede*]

Stead ★ (stɛd) *n* **Christina (Ellen).** 1902–83, Australian novelist. Her works include *The Man who Loved Children* (1940).

steadfast *or* **stedfast** ('stɛdfəst, -,fɑːst) *adj* **1** (esp. of a person's gaze) fixed in intensity or direction; steady. **2** unwavering or determined in purpose, loyalty, etc.: *steadfast resolve.*
▸ 'steadfastly *or* 'stedfastly *adv* ▸ 'steadfastness *or* 'stedfastness *n*

steading ('stɛdɪŋ) *n* another name for **farmstead**.

steady ('stɛdɪ) *adj* **steadier, steadiest. 1** not able to be moved or disturbed easily; stable. **2** free from fluctuation. **3** not easily excited; imperturbable. **4** staid; sober. **5** regular; habitual: *a steady drinker.* **6** continuous: *a steady flow.* **7** *Naut.* (of a vessel) keeping upright, as in heavy seas. ◆ *vb* **steadies, steadying, steadied. 8** to make or become steady. ◆ *adv* **9** in a steady manner. **10 go steady.** *Inf.* to date one person regularly. ◆ *n, pl* **steadies. 11** *Inf.* one's regular boyfriend or girlfriend. ◆ *interj* **12** *Naut.* an order to the helmsman to stay on a steady course. **13** a warning to keep calm, be careful, etc. **14** *Brit.* a command to get set to start, as in a race: *ready, steady, go!* [C16: from STEAD + -Y[1]]
▸ 'steadily *adv* ▸ 'steadiness *n* ▸ 'steadying *adj*

steady state *n Physics.* the condition of a system when some or all of the quantities describing it are independent of time but not necessarily in thermodynamic or chemical equilibrium.

steady-state theory *n* a theory postulating that the universe exists throughout time in a steady state such that the average density of matter does not vary with distance or time. Matter is continuously created in the space left by the receding stars and galaxies of the expanding universe. Cf. **big-bang theory.**

steak (steɪk) *n* **1** See **beefsteak. 2** any of various cuts of beef, for braising, stewing, etc. **3** a thick slice of pork, veal, cod, salmon, etc. **4** minced meat prepared in the same way as steak: *hamburger steak.* [C15: from ON *steik* roast]

steakhouse ('steɪk,haʊs) *n* a restaurant that has steaks as its speciality.

steak tartare (tɑː'tɑː) *or* **tartar** *n* raw minced steak, mixed with onion, seasonings, and raw egg. Also called: **tartare steak, tartar steak.**

steal (stiːl) *vb* **steals, stealing, stole, stolen. 1** to take (something) from someone, etc., without permission or unlawfully, esp. in a secret manner. **2** (*tr*) to obtain surreptitiously. **3** (*tr*) to appropriate (ideas, etc.) without acknowledgment, as in plagiarism. **4** to move or convey stealthily: *they stole along the corridor.* **5** (*intr*) to pass unnoticed: *the hours stole by.* **6** (*tr*) to win or gain by strategy or luck, as in various sports: *to steal a few yards.* ◆ *n Inf.* **7** the act of stealing. **8** something stolen or acquired easily or at little cost. [OE *stelan*]
▸ 'stealer *n*

stealth (stɛlθ) *n* **1** the act or characteristic of moving with extreme care and quietness, esp. so as to avoid detection. **2** cunning or underhand procedure or dealing. [C13 *stelthe*; see STEAL, -TH[1]]
▸ 'stealthy *adj*

Stealth (stɛlθ) *n* (*modifier*) *Inf.* denoting or referring to technology that aims to reduce the radar, thermal, and acoustic recognizability of aircraft and missiles.

Stealth bomber *or* **plane** *n* a type of US military aircraft using advanced technology to render it virtually undetectable to sight, radar, or infrared sensors. Also called: **B-2.**

steam (stiːm) *n* **1** the gas or vapour into which water is changed when boiled. **2** the mist formed when such gas or vapour condenses in the atmosphere. **3** any vaporous exhalation. **4** *Inf.* power, energy, or speed. **5 get up steam. 5a** (of a ship, etc.) to work up a sufficient head of steam in a boiler to drive an engine. **5b** *Inf.* to go quickly. **6 let off steam.** *Inf.* to release pent-up energy, feelings, etc. **7 under one's own steam.** without the assistance of others. **8** (*modifier*) driven, operated, heated, powered, etc., by steam: *a steam radiator.* **9** (*modifier*) treated by steam: *steam-ironed.* **10** (*modifier*) *Humorous.* old-fashioned; outmoded: *steam radio.* ◆ *vb* **11** to emit or be emitted as steam. **12** (*intr*) to generate steam, as a boiler, etc. **13** (*intr*) *Inf.* to move or travel by steam power, as a ship, etc. **14** (*intr*) *Inf.* to proceed quickly and sometimes forcefully. **15** to cook or be cooked in steam. **16** (*tr*) to treat with steam or apply steam to, as in cleaning, pressing clothes, etc. ◆ See also **steam up.** [OE]

steam bath *n* **1** a room or enclosure that can be filled with steam in which people bathe to induce sweating and refresh or cleanse themselves. **2** an act of taking such a bath.

steamboat ('stiːm,bəʊt) *n* a boat powered by a steam engine.

steam boiler *n* a vessel in which water is boiled to generate steam.

steam engine *n* an engine that uses steam to produce mechanical work, esp. one in which steam from a boiler is expanded in a cylinder to drive a reciprocating piston.

steamer ('stiːmə) *n* **1** a boat or ship driven by steam engines. **2** a vessel used to cook food by steam. **3** *Austral. sl.* a rough clash between sports teams.

steaming ('stiːmɪŋ) *adj* **1** very hot. **2** *Inf.* angry. **3** *Sl.* drunk. ◆ *n* **4** *Inf.* robbery, esp. of passengers in a railway carriage or bus, by a large gang of armed youths.

steam iron *n* an electric iron that emits steam from channels in the iron face to facilitate pressing and ironing, the steam being produced from water contained within the iron.

steam jacket n Engineering. a jacket containing steam that surrounds and heats a cylinder.

steam organ n a type of organ powered by steam, once common at fairgrounds, played either by a keyboard or by a moving punched card. US name: **calliope**.

steam point n the temperature at which the maximum vapour pressure of water is equal to one atmosphere (1.01325×10^5 N/m^2). It has the value of 100° on the Celsius scale.

steam reforming n Chem. a process in which methane from natural gas is heated, with steam, usually with a catalyst, to produce a mixture of carbon monoxide and hydrogen used in organic synthesis and as a fuel.

steamroller ('sti:m,rəʊlə) n **1a** a steam-powered vehicle with heavy rollers used for compressing road surfaces during road-making. **1b** another word for **roadroller**. **2a** an overpowering force or person that overcomes all opposition. **2b** (as modifier): steamroller tactics. ◆ vb **3** (tr) to crush (opposition, etc.) by overpowering force.

steamship ('sti:m,ʃɪp) n a ship powered by one or more steam engines.

steam shovel n a steam-driven mechanical excavator.

steam turbine n a turbine driven by steam.

steam up vb (adv) **1** to cover (windows, etc.) or (of windows, etc.) to become covered with a film of condensed steam. **2** (tr; usually passive) Sl. to excite or make angry: he's all steamed up about the delay.

steamy ('sti:mɪ) adj **steamier**, **steamiest**. **1** of, resembling, full of, or covered with steam. **2** Inf. lustful or erotic: steamy nightlife.
▸ 'steaminess n

steapsin (stɪ'æpsɪn) n Biochem. a pancreatic lipase. [C19: from Gk stear fat + PEPSIN]

stearic (stɪ'ærɪk) adj **1** of or relating to suet or fat. **2** of, consisting of, containing, or derived from stearic acid.

stearic acid n a colourless odourless insoluble waxy carboxylic acid used for making candles and suppositories. Formula: $CH_3(CH_2)_{16}COOH$. Systematic name: **octadecanoic acid**.

stearin or **stearine** ('stɪərɪn) n **1** Also called: **tristearin**. a colourless crystalline ester of glycerol and stearic acid, present in fats and used in soap and candles. **2** another name for **stearic acid**. **3** fat in its solid form. [C19: from F stéarine, from Gk stear fat + -IN]

steatite ('stɪə,taɪt) n another name for **soapstone**. [C18: from L steatītēs, from Gk stear fat + -ITE¹]
▸ **steatitic** (,stɪə'tɪtɪk) adj

steato- combining form. denoting fat. [from Gk stear, steat- fat, tallow]

steatolysis (,stɪə'tɒlɪsɪs) n Physiol. **1** the digestive process whereby fats are emulsified and then hydrolysed to fatty acids and glycerine. **2** the breaking down of fat.

steatopygia (,stɪətəʊ'pɪdʒɪə, -'paɪ-) or **steatopyga** (,stɪətəʊ'paɪgə) n excessive fatness of the buttocks. [C19: from NL, from STEATO- + Gk pugē the buttocks]
▸ ,steato'pygic or steato'pygous (,stɪə'tɒpɪgəs) adj

Stębark ★ ('stɛmbark) n the Polish name for **Tannenberg**.

stedfast ('stɛdfəst, -,fɑ:st) adj a less common spelling of **steadfast**.

steed (sti:d) n Arch. or literary. a horse, esp. one that is spirited or swift. [OE stēda stallion]

steel (sti:l) n **1a** any of various alloys based on iron containing carbon and often small quantities of other elements such as sulphur, manganese, chromium, and nickel. Steels exhibit a variety of properties, such as strength, malleability, etc., depending on their composition and the way they have been treated. **1b** (as modifier): steel girders. See also **stainless steel**. **2** something that is made of steel. **3** a steel stiffener in a corset, etc. **4** a ridged steel rod used for sharpening knives. **5** the quality of hardness, esp. with regard to a person's character or attitudes. **6** Canad. a railway track or line. **7** **cold steel**. bladed weapons. ◆ vb (tr) **8** to fit, plate, edge, or point with steel. **9** to make hard and unfeeling: he steeled his heart against her sorrow; he steeled himself for the blow. [OE stēli]
▸ 'steely adj ▸ 'steeliness n

Steel ★ (sti:l) n **David** (**Martin Scott**), Baron. born 1938, British politician; leader of the Liberal Party (1976–88).

steel band n Music. a type of band, popular in the Caribbean Islands, consisting mainly of percussion instruments made from oil drums, hammered or embossed to obtain different notes.

steel blue n **a** a dark bluish-grey colour. **b** (as adj): steel-blue eyes.

Steele ★ (sti:l) n Sir **Richard**. 1672–1729, British essayist and dramatist, born in Ireland.

steel engraving n **a** a method or art of engraving (letters, etc.) on a steel plate. **b** a print made from such a plate.

steel grey n **a** a dark grey colour, usually slightly purple. **b** (as adj): a steel-grey suit.

steelhead ('sti:l,hɛd) n, pl **steelheads** or **steelhead**. a silvery North Pacific variety of the rainbow trout.

steel wool n a tangled or woven mass of fine steel fibres, used for cleaning or polishing.

steelworks ('sti:l,wɜ:ks) n (functioning as sing or pl) a plant in which steel is made from iron ore and rolled or forged into bars, sheets, etc.
▸ 'steel,worker n

steelyard ('sti:l,jɑ:d) n a portable balance consisting of a pivoted bar with two unequal arms. The load is suspended from the shorter one and the bar is returned to the horizontal by sliding a weight along the longer, graduated arm.

Steen ★ (steɪn) n **Jan** (jɑn). 1626–79, Dutch genre painter.

steenbok ('sti:n,bɒk) n, pl **steenboks** or **steenbok**. a small antelope of central and southern Africa, having a reddish-brown coat and straight horns. [C18: from Afrik., from Du. steen stone + bok BUCK¹]

steep¹ (sti:p) adj **1a** having or being a slope or gradient approaching the perpendicular. **1b** (as n): the steep. **2** Inf. (of a fee, price, demand, etc.) unduly high; unreasonable (esp. in **that's a bit steep**). **3** Inf. excessively demanding or ambitious: a steep task. **4** Brit. inf. (of a statement) extreme or far-fetched. [OE steap]
▸ 'steeply adv ▸ 'steepness n

steep² (sti:p) vb **1** to soak or be soaked in a liquid in order to soften, cleanse, extract an element, etc. **2** (tr; usually passive) to saturate; imbue: steeped in ideology. ◆ n **3** an instance or the process of steeping or the condition of being steeped. **4** a liquid or solution used for the purpose of steeping something. [OE stēpan]
▸ 'steeper n

steepen ('sti:pᵊn) vb to become or cause to become steep or steeper.

steeple ('sti:pᵊl) n **1** a tall ornamental tower that forms the superstructure of a church, temple, etc. **2** such a tower with the spire above it. **3** any spire or pointed structure. [OE stēpel]
▸ 'steepled adj

steeplechase ('sti:pᵊl,tʃeɪs) n **1** a horse race over a course equipped with obstacles to be jumped. **2** a track race in which the runners have to leap hurdles, a water jump, etc. **3** Arch. **3a** a horse race across a stretch of open countryside including obstacles to be jumped. **3b** a rare word for **point-to-point**. ◆ vb **steeplechases**, **steeplechasing**, **steeplechased**. **4** (intr) to take part in a steeplechase.
▸ 'steeple,chaser n ▸ 'steeple,chasing n

steeplejack ('sti:pᵊl,dʒæk) n a person trained and skilled in the construction and repair of steeples, chimneys, etc.

steer¹ (stɪə) vb **1** to direct the course of (a vehicle or vessel) with a steering wheel, rudder, etc. **2** (tr) to guide with tuition: his teachers steered him through his exams. **3** (tr) to direct the movements or course of (a person, conversation, etc.). **4** to pursue (a specified course). **5** (intr) (of a vessel, vehicle, etc.) to admit of being guided in a specified fashion: this boat does not steer properly. **6** **steer clear of**. to keep away from; shun. ◆ n **7** Chiefly US. guidance; information (esp. in a **bum steer**). [OE stieran]
▸ 'steerable adj ▸ 'steerer n

steer[2] (stɪə) *n* a castrated male ox or bull; bullock. [OE *stēor*]

steerage ('stɪərɪdʒ) *n* **1** the cheapest accommodation on a passenger ship, originally the compartments containing steering apparatus. **2** an instance or the practice of steering and its effect on a vessel or vehicle.

steerageway ('stɪərɪdʒ,weɪ) *n Naut.* enough forward movement to allow a vessel to be steered.

steering committee *n* a committee set up to prepare and arrange topics to be discussed, the order of business, etc., for a legislative assembly or other body.

steering wheel *n* a wheel turned by the driver of a motor vehicle, ship, etc., when he wishes to change direction.

steersman ('stɪəzmən) *n, pl* **steersmen.** the helmsman of a vessel.

Stefansson ★ ('stɛfənsən) *n* **Vilhjalmur** ('vɪl,hjaʊmɛr) 1879–1962, Canadian explorer, noted for his books on the Inuit.

Steffens ★ ('stɛfənz) *n* **(Joseph) Lincoln.** 1866–1936, US political analyst, known for his exposure of political corruption.

stegosaur ('stɛgə,sɔː) *or* **stegosaurus** (,stɛgə'sɔːrəs) *n* any of various quadrupedal herbivorous dinosaurs of Jurassic and early Cretaceous times, having an armour of bony plates. [C19: from Gk *stegos* roof + -SAUR]

Steier ★ (*German* 'ʃtaiər) *n* a variant spelling of **Steyr.**

Steiermark ★ ('ʃtaiər,mark) *n* the German name for **Styria.**

stein (staɪn) *n* an earthenware beer mug, esp. of a German design. [from G *Stein*, lit.: stone]

Stein ★ *n* **1** (staɪn). **Gertrude.** 1874–1946, US writer, resident in Paris (1903–1946). Her works include *The Autobiography of Alice B. Toklas* (1933). **2** (*German* ʃtain). **Heinrich Friedrich Carl** ('hainrɪç 'friːdrɪç karl), **Baron.** 1757–1831, Prussian statesman; a leader of the European coalition against Napoleon (1813–15).

Steinbeck ★ ('staɪnbɛk) *n* **John (Ernst).** 1902–68, US writer, noted for his novel *The Grapes of Wrath* (1939): Nobel prize for literature 1962.

steinbok ('staɪn,bɒk) *n, pl* **steinboks** *or* **steinbok.** a variant of **steenbok.**

Steiner ★ ('staɪnə; *German* 'ʃtainər) *n* **Rudolf** ('ruːdɔlf). 1861–1925, Austrian philosopher, founder of anthroposophy. He was particularly influential in education. See also **anthroposophy.**

Steinitz ★ ('staɪnɪts; *German* 'ʃtainɪts) *n* **Wilhelm** ('vɪlhɛlm). 1836–1900, US chess player, born in Prague; world champion (1866–94).

Steinway ★ ('staɪnweɪ) *n* **Henry (Engelhard)**, original name *Heinrich Engelhardt Steinweg.* 1797–1871, US piano maker, born in Germany.

stele ('stiːlɪ, stiːl) *n, pl* **stelae** ('stiːliː) *or* **steles.** **1** an upright stone slab or column decorated with figures or inscriptions, common in prehistoric times. **2** a prepared vertical surface that has a commemorative inscription or design, esp. one on the face of a building. **3** the conducting tissue of the stems and roots of plants, which is in the form of a cylinder. ◆ Also called (for senses 1, 2): **stela.** [C19: from Gk *stēlē*]
▸ '**stelar** *adj*

stellar ('stɛlə) *adj* **1** of, relating to, or resembling a star or stars. **2** of or relating to star entertainers. **3** *Inf.* outstanding or immense: *companies are registering stellar profits.* [C17: from LL *stellāris*, from L *stella* star]

stellar evolution *n Astron.* the sequence of changes that occurs in a star as it ages.

stellate ('stɛlɪt, -eɪt) *or* **stellated** *adj* resembling a star in shape; radiating from the centre: *a stellate arrangement of petals.* [C16: from L *stellātus* starry, from *stellāre* to stud with stars, from *stella* a star]
▸ '**stellately** *adv*

stellular ('stɛljʊlə) *adj* **1** displaying or abounding in small stars: *a stellular pattern.* **2** resembling a little star or little stars. [C18: from LL *stellula*, dim. of L *stella* star]
▸ '**stellularly** *adv*

stem[1] (stɛm) *n* **1** the main axis of a plant, which bears the leaves, axillary buds, and flowers and contains a hollow cylinder of vascular tissue. **2** any similar subsidiary structure in such plants that bears a flower, fruit, or leaf. **3** a corresponding structure in algae and fungi. **4** any long slender part, such as the hollow part of a tobacco pipe between the bit and the bowl. **5** the main line of descent or branch of a family. **6** any shank or cylindrical pin or rod, such as the pin that carries the winding knob on a watch. **7** *Linguistics.* the form of a word that remains after removal of all inflectional affixes. **8** the main, usually vertical, stroke of a letter or of a musical note such as a minim. **9a** the main upright timber or structure at the bow of a vessel. **9b** the very forward end of a vessel (esp. in **from stem to stern**). ◆ *vb* **stems, stemming, stemmed. 10** (*intr*; usually foll. by *from*) to be derived; originate. **11** (*tr*) to make headway against (a tide, wind, etc.). **12** (*tr*) to remove or disengage the stem or stems from. [OE *stemn*]
▸ '**stem,like** *adj*

stem[2] (stɛm) *vb* **stems, stemming, stemmed. 1** (*tr*) to restrain or stop (the flow of something) by or as if by damming up. **2** (*tr*) to pack tightly or stop up. **3** *Skiing.* to manoeuvre (a ski or skis), as in performing a stem. ◆ *n* **4** *Skiing.* a technique in which the heel of one ski or both skis is forced outwards from the direction of movement in order to slow down or turn. [C15 *stemmen*, from ON *stemma*]

stem cell *n Histology.* an undifferentiated cell that gives rise to specialized cells, such as blood cells.

stem ginger *n* choice pieces of the underground stem of the ginger plant which are crystallized or preserved in syrup and eaten as a sweetmeat.

stemma ('stɛmə) *n* a family tree; pedigree. [C19: via L from Gk *stema* garland, wreath, from *stephein* to crown, wreathe]

stemmed (stɛmd) *adj* **1a** having a stem. **1b** (*in combination*): *a long-stemmed glass.* **2** having had the stem or stems removed.

stem turn *n Skiing.* a turn in which the heel of one ski is stemmed and the other ski is brought parallel. Also called: **stem.**

stench (stɛntʃ) *n* a strong and extremely offensive odour; stink. [OE *stenc*]

stencil ('stɛnsᵊl) *n* **1** a device for applying a design, characters, etc., to a surface, consisting of a thin sheet of plastic, metal, etc., in which the design or characters have been cut so that ink or paint can be applied through the incisions onto the surface. **2** a design or characters produced in this way. ◆ *vb* **stencils, stencilling, stencilled** *or US* **stencils, stenciling, stenciled.** (*tr*) **3** to mark (a surface) with a stencil. **4** to produce (characters or a design) with a stencil. [C14 *stanselen* to decorate with bright colours, from OF *estenceler*, from *estencele* a spark, from L *scintilla*]

Stendhal ★ (*French* stɛ̃dal) *n* original name *Marie Henri Beyle.* 1783–1842, French writer. His two chief novels are *Le Rouge et le noir* (1830) and *La Chartreuse de Parme* (1839).

Sten gun (stɛn) *n* a light 9mm sub-machine-gun formerly used in the British Army. [C20: from *S & T* (initials of Shepherd & Turpin, the inventors) + *-en*, as in BREN GUN]

steno- *or before a vowel* **sten-** *combining form.* indicating narrowness or contraction: *stenography; stenosis.* [from Gk *stenos* narrow]

stenograph ('stɛnə,grɑːf) *n* **1** any of various keyboard machines for writing in shorthand. **2** any character used in shorthand. ◆ *vb* **3** (*tr*) to record (minutes, letters, etc.) in shorthand.

stenographer (stə'nɒgrəfə) *n* the US & Canad. name for **shorthand typist.**

stenography (stə'nɒgrəfɪ) *n* **1** the act or process of writing in shorthand by hand or machine. **2** matter written in shorthand.
▸ **stenographic** (,stɛnə'græfɪk) *adj*

stenosis (stɪ'nəʊsɪs) *n, pl* **stenoses** (-siːz). *Pathol.* an abnormal narrowing of a bodily canal or passage. [C19: via NL from Gk *stenōsis*, ult. from *stenos* narrow]
▸ **stenotic** (stɪ'nɒtɪk) *adj*

stenotype ('stɛnə,taɪp) n **1** Trademark. a machine with a keyboard for recording speeches, etc., in a phonetic shorthand. **2** any machine resembling this. **3** the phonetic symbol typed in one stroke of such a machine.

stenotypy ('stɛnə,taɪpɪ) n a form of shorthand in which alphabetic combinations are used to represent groups of sounds or short common words.
▸ 'steno,typist n

Stentor ★ ('stɛntɔ:) n **1** Greek myth. a Greek herald with a powerful voice who died after he lost a shouting contest with Hermes, herald of the gods. **2** (not cap.) any person with an unusually loud voice.

stentorian (stɛn'tɔ:rɪən) adj (of the voice, etc.) uncommonly loud: stentorian tones. [C17: after STENTOR]

step (stɛp) n **1** the act of raising the foot and setting it down again in coordination with the transference of the weight of the body. **2** the distance or space covered by such a motion. **3** the sound made by such a movement. **4** the impression made by such movement of the foot; footprint. **5** the manner of walking or moving the feet; gait: a proud step. **6** a sequence of foot movements that make up a particular dance or part of a dance: the steps of the waltz. **7** any of several paces or rhythmic movements in marching, dancing, etc.: the goose step. **8** (pl) a course followed by a person in walking or as walking: they followed in their leader's steps. **9** one of a sequence of separate consecutive stages in the progression towards some goal. **10** a rank or grade in a series or scale. **11** an object or device that offers support for the foot when ascending or descending. **12** (pl) a flight of stairs, esp. out of doors. **13** (pl) another name for **stepladder**. **14** a very short easily walked distance: it is only a step. **15** Music. a melodic interval of a second. **16** an offset or change in the level of a surface similar to the step of a stair. **17** a strong block or frame bolted onto the keel of a vessel and fitted to receive the base of a mast. **18** a ledge cut in mining or quarrying excavations. **19 break step. 20 in step. 20a** marching, dancing, etc., in conformity with a specified pace or moving in unison with others. **20b** Inf. in agreement or harmony. **21 keep step.** to remain walking, marching, dancing, etc., in unison or in a specified rhythm. **22 out of step. 22a** not moving in conformity with a specified pace or in accordance with others. **22b** Inf. not in agreement; out of harmony. **23 step by step.** with care and deliberation; gradually. **24 take steps.** to take measures (to do something). **25 watch one's step. 25a** Inf. to conduct oneself with caution and good behaviour. **25b** to walk or move carefully. ◆ vb **steps, stepping, stepped. 26** (intr) to move by raising the foot and then setting it down in a different position, transferring the weight of the body to this foot and repeating the process with the other foot. **27** (intr; often foll. by in, out, etc.) to move or go on foot, esp. for a short distance: step this way. **28** (intr) Inf., chiefly US. to move, often in an attractive graceful manner, as in dancing: he can really step around. **29** (intr; usually foll. by on or upon) to place or press the foot; tread: to step on the accelerator. **30** (intr; usually foll. by into) to enter (into a situation) apparently with ease: she stepped into a life of luxury. **31** (tr) to walk or take (a number of paces, etc.): to step ten paces. **32** (tr) to perform the steps of: they step the tango well. **33** (tr) to set or place (the foot). **34** (tr; usually foll. by off or out) to measure (some distance of ground) by stepping. **35** (tr) to arrange in or supply with a series of steps so as to avoid coincidence or symmetry. **36** (tr) to raise (a mast) and fit it into its step. ◆ See also **step down**, **step in**, etc. [OE stepe, stæpe]
▸ 'step,like adj

Step (stɛp) n **a** a set of aerobic exercises designed to improve the cardiovascular system, which consists of stepping on and off a special box of adjustable height. **b** (as modifier): Step aerobics.

step- combining form. indicating relationship through the previous marriage of a spouse or parent: stepson; stepfather. [OE stēop-]

stepbrother ('stɛp,brʌðə) n a son of one's stepmother or stepfather by a union with someone other than one's father or mother.

stepchild ('stɛp,tʃaɪld) n, pl **stepchildren**. a stepson or stepdaughter.

stepdaughter ('stɛp,dɔ:tə) n a daughter of one's husband or wife by a former union.

step down vb (adv) **1** (tr) to reduce gradually. **2** (intr) Inf. to resign or abdicate (from a position). **3** (intr) Inf. to assume an inferior or less senior position. ◆ adj **step-down.** (prenominal) **4** (of a transformer) reducing a high voltage to a lower voltage. Cf. **step-up** (sense 3). ◆ n **step-down. 5** Inf. a decrease in quantity or size.

stepfather ('stɛp,fɑːðə) n a man who has married one's mother after the death or divorce of one's father.

stephanotis (,stɛfə'nəʊtɪs) n any of various climbing shrubs of Madagascar and Malaya, cultivated for their fragrant white waxy flowers. [C19: via NL from Gk: fit for a crown, from stephanos a crown]

Stephen ★ ('stiːvⁿn) n **1** ?1097–1154, king of England (1135–54); grandson of William the Conqueror. He seized the throne on the death of Henry I, causing civil war with Henry's daughter Matilda. He eventually recognized her son (later Henry II) as his successor. **2 Saint.** died ?35 A.D., the first Christian martyr. Feast day: Dec. 26 or 27. **3 Saint,** Hungarian name István. ?975–1038 A.D., first king of Hungary as Stephen I (997–1038). Feast day: Aug. 16. **4** Sir **Leslie.** 1832–1904, British biographer and first editor of the Dictionary of National Biography; father of Virginia Woolf.

Stephenson ★ ('stiːvənsən) n **1 George.** 1781–1848, British inventor of the first successful steam locomotive (1814); constructed the first railway to carry passengers, the Stockton and Darlington Railway (opened 1825). **2** his son, **Robert.** 1803–59, British engineer, noted for his construction of locomotives, railway bridges, and viaducts.

step in vb **1** (intr, adv) Inf. to intervene or involve oneself. ◆ adj **step-in. 2** (prenominal) (of garments, etc.) put on by being stepped into; without fastenings. **3** (of a ski binding) engaging automatically when the boot is positioned on the ski. ◆ n **step-in. 4** (often pl) a step-in garment, esp. underwear.

stepladder ('stɛp,lædə) n a folding portable ladder that is made of broad flat steps fixed to a supporting frame hinged at the top to another supporting frame.

stepmother ('stɛp,mʌðə) n a woman who has married one's father after the death or divorce of one's mother.

step on vb (intr, prep) **1** to place or press the foot on. **2** Inf. to behave harshly or contemptuously towards. **3 step on it.** Inf. to go more quickly; hurry up.

step out vb (intr, adv) **1** to go outside or leave a room, etc., esp. briefly. **2** to begin to walk more quickly and take longer strides. **3** US & Canad. inf. to withdraw from involvement.

step-parent ('stɛp,pɛərənt) n a stepfather or stepmother.
▸ 'step-,parenting n

steppe (stɛp) n (often pl) an extensive grassy plain usually without trees. [C17: from ORussian step lowland]

stepper ('stɛpə) n a person who or animal that steps, esp. a horse or a dancer.

Steppes ★ (stɛps) pl n **the. 1** the huge grasslands of Eurasia, chiefly in the Ukraine and Russia. **2** another name for **Kyrgyz Steppe.**

stepping stone n **1** one of a series of stones acting as footrests for crossing streams, marshes, etc. **2** a circumstance that assists progress towards some goal.

stepsister ('stɛp,sɪstə) n a daughter of one's stepmother or stepfather by a union with someone other than one's father or mother.

stepson ('stɛp,sʌn) n a son of one's husband or wife by a former union.

step up vb (adv) Inf. **1** (tr) to increase or raise by stages; accelerate. **2** (intr) to make progress or effect an advancement; be promoted. ◆ adj **step-up.** (prenominal) **3** (of a transformer) increasing a low voltage to a higher voltage. Cf. **step-down** (sense 4). ◆ n **step-up. 4** Inf. an increment in quantity, size, etc.

-ster suffix forming nouns. **1** indicating a person who is engaged in a certain activity: prankster; songster. **2** indicating a person associated with or being something specified: mobster; youngster. [OE -estre]

steradian (stə'reɪdɪən) *n* an SI unit of solid angle; the angle that, having its vertex in the centre of a sphere, cuts off an area of the surface of the sphere equal to the square of the length of the radius. Symbol: sr [C19: from STEREO- + RADIAN]

stercoraceous (ˌstɜːkə'reɪʃəs) *adj* of, relating to, or consisting of dung or excrement. [C18: from L *stercus* dung + -ACEOUS]

stere (stɪə) *n* a unit used to measure volumes of stacked timber equal to one cubic metre (35.315 cubic feet). [C18: from F *stère*, from Gk *stereos* solid]

stereo ('stɛrɪəu, 'stɪər-) *adj* 1 short for **stereophonic** or **stereoscopic**. ◆ *n, pl* **stereos**. 2 stereophonic sound: *to broadcast in stereo*. 3 a stereophonic record player, tape recorder, etc. 4 *Photog*. 4a stereoscopic photography. 4b a stereoscopic photograph. 5 *Printing*. short for **stereotype**. [C20: shortened form]

stereo- *or sometimes before a vowel* **stere-** *combining form.* indicating three-dimensional quality or solidity: *stereoscope.* [from Gk *stereos* solid]

stereochemistry (ˌstɛrɪəu'kɛmɪstrɪ, ˌstɪər-) *n* the study of the spatial arrangement of atoms in molecules and its effect on chemical properties.

stereograph ('stɛrɪəˌgrɑːf, 'stɪər-) *n* two almost identical pictures, or one special picture, that when viewed through special glasses or a stereoscope form a single three-dimensional image. Also called: **stereogram.**

stereoisomer (ˌstɛrɪəu'aɪsəmə, ˌstɪər-) *n Chem.* an isomer that exhibits stereoisomerism.

stereoisomerism (ˌstɛrɪəuaɪ'sɒməˌrɪzəm, ˌstɪər-) *n Chem.* isomerism caused by differences in the spatial arrangement of atoms in molecules.

stereophonic (ˌstɛrɪə'fɒnɪk, ˌstɪər-) *adj* (of a system for recording, reproducing, or broadcasting sound) using two or more separate microphones to feed two or more loudspeakers through separate channels in order to give a spatial effect to the sound. Often shortened to **stereo.** ▸ ˌstereo'phonically *adv* ▸ **stereophony** (ˌstɛrɪ'ɒfənɪ, ˌstɪər-) *n*

stereoscope ('stɛrɪəˌskəup, 'stɪər-) *n* an optical instrument for viewing two-dimensional pictures, giving an illusion of depth and relief. It has a binocular eyepiece through which two slightly different pictures of an object are viewed, one with each eye. ▸ **stereoscopic** (ˌstɛrɪə'skɒpɪk, ˌstɪər-) *adj*

stereoscopy (ˌstɛrɪ'ɒskəpɪ, ˌstɪər-) *n* 1 the viewing or appearance of objects in or as if in three dimensions. 2 the study and use of the stereoscope. ▸ ˌstere'oscopist *n*

stereospecific (ˌstɛrɪəuspɪ'sɪfɪk, ˌstɪər-) *adj Chem.* relating to or having fixed position in space, as in the spatial arrangements of atoms in certain polymers.

stereotype ('stɛrɪəˌtaɪp, 'stɪər-) *n* 1a a method of producing cast-metal printing plates from a mould made from a forme of type. 1b the plate so made. 2 another word for **stereotypy**. 3 an idea, convention, etc., that has grown stale through fixed usage. 4 a standardized image or conception of a type of person, etc. ◆ *vb* **stereotypes, stereotyping, stereotyped.** (*tr*) 5a to make a stereotype of. 5b to print from a stereotype. 6 to impart a fixed usage or convention to. ▸ 'stereoˌtyper *or* 'stereoˌtypist *n*

stereotyped ('stɛrɪəˌtaɪpt, 'stɪər-) *adj* 1 lacking originality or individuality; conventional; trite. 2 reproduced from or on a stereotype printing plate.

stereotypy ('stɛrɪəˌtaɪpɪ, 'stɪər-) *n* 1 the act or process of making stereotype printing plates. 2 a tendency to think or act in rigid, repetitive, and often meaningless patterns.

stereovision (ˌstɛrɪəu'vɪʒən, ˌstɪər-) *n* the perception or exhibition of three-dimensional objects in three dimensions.

steric ('stɛrɪk, 'stɪər-) *or* **sterical** *adj Chem.* of or caused by the spatial arrangement of atoms in a molecule. [C19: from STEREO- + -IC]

sterile ('stɛraɪl) *adj* 1 unable to produce offspring; permanently infertile. 2 free from living, esp. pathogenic, mi-

croorganisms. 3 (of plants or their parts) not producing or bearing seeds, fruit, spores, stamens, or pistils. 4 lacking inspiration or vitality; fruitless. [C16: from L *sterilis*] ▸ 'sterilely *adv* ▸ **sterility** (stɛ'rɪlɪtɪ) *n*

sterilize *or* **sterilise** ('stɛrɪˌlaɪz) *vb* **sterilizes, sterilizing, sterilized** *or* **sterilises, sterilising, sterilised.** (*tr*) to render sterile; make infertile or barren. ▸ ˌsterili'zation *or* ˌsterili'sation *n* ▸ 'steriˌlizer *or* 'steriˌliser *n*

sterling ('stɜːlɪŋ) *n* 1a British money: *pound sterling.* 1b (*as modifier*): *sterling reserves.* 2 the official standard of purity of British coins. 3a short for **sterling silver**. 3b (*as modifier*): *a sterling bracelet.* 4 an article or articles manufactured from sterling silver. ◆ *adj* 5 (*prenominal*) genuine and reliable: first-class: *sterling quality.* [C13: prob. from OE *steorra* star + -LING[1]; referring to a small star on early Norman pennies]

sterling area *n* a group of countries that use sterling as a medium of international payments. Also called: **scheduled territories.**

sterling silver *n* 1 an alloy containing not less than 92.5 per cent of silver. 2 sterling-silver articles collectively.

Sterlitamak ★ (*Russian* stjɛrlitə'mak) *n* an industrial city in W Russia, in the Bashkir Republic. Pop.: 259 000 (1995 est.).

stern[1] (stɜːn) *adj* 1 showing uncompromising or inflexible resolve; firm or authoritarian. 2 lacking leniency or clemency. 3 relentless; unyielding: *the stern demands of parenthood.* 4 having an austere or forbidding appearance or nature. [OE *styrne*] ▸ 'sternly *adv* ▸ 'sternness *n*

stern[2] (stɜːn) *n* 1 the rear or after part of a vessel, opposite the bow or stem. 2 the rear part of any object. ◆ *adj* 3 relating to or located at the stern. [C13: from ON *stjōrn* steering]

Stern ★ (stɜːn) *n* **Isaac.** born 1920, US violinist, born in Russia.

Sternberg ★ ('stɜːn,bɜːg, 'ʃtɜːn-) *n* See (Joseph) **von Sternberg.**

Sterne ★ (stɜːn) *n* **Laurence.** 1713–68, British novelist, born in Ireland, author of *The Life and Opinions of Tristram Shandy, Gentleman* (1759–67).

sternforemost ('stɜːn'fɔːməust) *adv Naut.* backwards.

sternmost ('stɜːn,məust) *adj Naut.* 1 farthest to the stern; aftmost. 2 nearest the stern.

sternpost ('stɜːn,pəust) *n Naut.* the main upright timber or structure at the stern of a vessel.

stern sheets *pl n Naut.* the part of an open boat near the stern.

sternum ('stɜːnəm) *n, pl* **sterna** (-nə) *or* **sternums.** 1 (in man) a long flat vertical bone in front of the thorax, to which are attached the collarbone and the first seven pairs of ribs. Nontechnical name: **breastbone.** 2 the corresponding part in many other vertebrates. [C17: via NL from Gk *sternon* breastbone] ▸ 'sternal *adj*

sternutation (ˌstɜːnju'teɪʃən) *n* a sneeze or the act of sneezing. [C16: from LL *sternūtāre* to sneeze, from *sternuere* to sputter (of a light)]

sternutator ('stɜːnju,teɪtə) *n* a substance that causes sneezing, coughing, and tears; used in chemical warfare. ▸ **sternutatory** (stɜː'njuːtətərɪ, -trɪ) *adj, n*

sternwards ('stɜːnwədz) *or* **sternward** *adv Naut.* towards the stern; astern.

sternway ('stɜːn,weɪ) *n Naut.* movement of a vessel sternforemost.

stern-wheeler *n* a vessel, esp. a river boat, propelled by a large paddle wheel at the stern.

steroid ('stɪərɔɪd, 'stɛr-) *n Biochem.* any of a large group of organic compounds containing a characteristic chemical ring system, including sterols, bile acids, many hormones, and the D vitamins. [C20: from STEROL + -OID] ▸ ste'roidal *adj*

sterol ('stɛrɒl) *n Biochem.* any of a group of natural steroid alcohols, such as cholesterol and ergosterol, that are waxy insoluble substances. [C20: shortened from CHO-LESTEROL, ERGOSTEROL, etc.]

tertorous ('stɜːtərəs) adj **1** marked by heavy snoring. **2** breathing in this way. [C19: from L stertere to snore]
▸ **'stertorously** adv ▸ **'stertorousness** n

tet (stɛt) n **1** a word or mark indicating that certain deleted typeset or written matter is to be retained. ◆ vb **stets, stetting, stetted. 2** (tr) to mark (matter) thus. [L, lit.: let it stand]

stethoscope ('stɛθə,skəʊp) n Med. an instrument for listening to the sounds made within the body, typically consisting of a hollow disc that transmits the sound through hollow tubes to earpieces. [C19: from F, from Gk stēthos breast + -SCOPE]
▸ **stethoscopic** (,stɛθə'skɒpɪk) adj ▸ **stethoscopy** (stɛ'θɒskəpɪ) n

Stetson ('stɛts°n) n Trademark. a type of felt hat with a broad brim and high crown, worn mainly by cowboys. [C20: after John Stetson (1830–1906), US hat-maker]

Stettin ★ (ʃtɛ'tiːn) n the German name for **Szczecin**.

stevedore ('stiːvɪ,dɔː) n **1** a person employed to load or unload ships. ◆ vb **stevedores, stevedoring, stevedored. 2** to load or unload (a ship, ship's cargo, etc.). [C18: from Sp. estibador a packer, from estibar to load (a ship), from L stīpāre to pack full]

Stevenage ★ ('stiːvənɪdʒ) n a town in SE England, in N Hertfordshire on the Great North Road: developed chiefly as the first of the new towns (1946). Pop.: 76 064 (1991).

Stevenson ★ ('stiːvənsən) n **1 Adlai Ewing** ('ædleɪ 'juːɪŋ). 1900–68, US statesman: twice defeated as Democratic presidential candidate (1952; 1956); US delegate at the United Nations (1961–65). **2 Robert Louis (Balfour).** 1850–94, Scottish writer: his novels include Treasure Island (1883), Kidnapped (1886), and The Master of Ballantrae (1889).

stew[1] (stjuː) n **1a** a dish of meat, fish, or other food, cooked by stewing. **1b** (as modifier): stew pot. **2** Inf. a difficult or worrying situation or a troubled state (esp. in **in a stew). 3** a heterogeneous mixture: a stew of people of every race. **4** (usually pl) Arch. a brothel. ◆ vb **5** to cook or cause to cook by long slow simmering. **6** (intr) Inf. to be troubled or agitated. **7** (intr) Inf. to be oppressed with heat or crowding. **8** to cause (tea) to become bitter or (of tea) to become bitter through infusing for too long. **9 stew in one's own juice.** to suffer unaided the consequences of one's actions. [C14 stuen to take a very hot bath, from OF estuver, from Vulgar L extūfāre (unattested), from EX-[1] + (unattested) tūfus vapour, from Gk tuphos]

stew[2] (stjuː) n Brit. **1** a fishpond or fishtank. **2** an artificial oyster bed. [C14: from OF estui, from estoier to confine, ult. from L studium STUDY]

steward (stjʊəd) n **1** a person who administers the property, house, finances, etc., of another. **2** a person who manages the eating arrangements, staff, or service at a club, hotel, etc. **3** a waiter on a ship or aircraft. **4** a mess attendant in a naval mess. **5** a person who helps to supervise some event or proceedings in an official capacity. **6** short for **shop steward.** ◆ vb **7** to act or serve as a steward (of something). [OE stigweard, from stig hall + weard WARD]
▸ **'stewardship** n

stewardess ('stjʊədɪs, ,stjʊə'dɛs) n a woman steward on an aircraft or ship.

Stewart ★ ('stjʊət) n **1** the usual spelling for the royal house of **Stuart** before the reign of Mary Queen of Scots (Mary Stuart). **2 Jackie,** full name John Young Stewart. born 1939, Scottish motor-racing driver: world champion 1969, 1971, and 1973. **3 James (Maitland).** 1908–97, US film actor: films include The Philadelphia Story (1940) and Shenandoah (1965). **4 Rod.** born 1945, British rock singer: vocalist with the Faces (1969–75). His albums include Every Picture Tells a Story (1971).

Stewart Island ★ n the third largest island of New Zealand, in the SW Pacific off the S tip of South Island. Pop.: 450 (1989 est.). Area: 1735 sq. km (670 sq. miles).

stewed (stjuːd) adj **1** (of meat, fish, etc.) cooked by stewing. **2** Brit. (of tea) bitter through having been left to infuse for too long. **3** a slang word for **drunk** (sense 1).

Steyr or **Steier** ★ (German 'ʃtaɪər) n an industrial city in N central Austria, in Upper Austria. Pop.: 39 542 (1991).

stg abbrev. for sterling.

sthenic ('sθɛnɪk) adj abounding in energy or bodily strength; active or strong. [C18: from NL sthenicus, from Gk sthenos force, on the model of asthenic]

Stheno ★ ('sθiːnəʊ, 'sθɛnəʊ) n Greek myth. one of the three Gorgons.

stibine ('stɪbaɪn) n **1** a colourless poisonous gas with an offensive odour: made by the action of hydrochloric acid on an alloy of antimony and zinc. **2** any one of a class of stibine derivatives in which one or more hydrogen atoms have been replaced by organic groups. [C19: from L stibium antimony + -INE[2]]

stibnite ('stɪbnaɪt) n a soft greyish mineral consisting of antimony sulphide in crystalline form: the chief ore of antimony. [C19: from obs. stibine stibnite + -ITE[1]]

-stichous adj combining form. having a certain number of rows. [from LL -stichus, from Gk -stikhos, from stikhos row]

stick[1] (stɪk) n **1** a small thin branch of a tree. **2a** any long thin piece of wood. **2b** such a piece of wood having a characteristic shape for a special purpose: a walking stick; a hockey stick. **2c** a baton, wand, staff, or rod. **3** an object or piece shaped like a stick: a stick of celery. **4** In full: **control stick.** the lever by which a pilot controls the movements of an aircraft. **5** Inf. the lever used to change gear in a motor vehicle. **6** Naut. a mast or yard. **7a** a group of bombs arranged to fall at intervals across a target. **7b** a number of paratroops jumping in sequence. **8** Sl. **8a** verbal abuse, criticism: I got some stick for that blunder. **8b** physical power, force (esp. in **give it some stick). 9** (usually pl) a piece of furniture: these few sticks are all I have. **10** (pl) Inf. a rural area considered remote or backward (esp. in **in the sticks). 11** (pl) Hockey. a declaration made by the umpire if a player's stick is above the shoulders. **12** (pl) goalposts. **13** Inf. a dull boring person. **14** (usually preceded by old) Inf. a familiar name for a person: not a bad old stick. **15** punishment; beating. **16 in a cleft stick.** in a difficult position. **17 wrong end of the stick.** a complete misunderstanding of a situation, explanation, etc. ◆ vb **sticks, sticking, sticked. 18** to support (a plant) with sticks; stake. [OE sticca]

stick[2] (stɪk) vb **sticks, sticking, stuck. 1** (tr) to pierce or stab with or as if with something pointed. **2** to thrust or push (a sharp or pointed object) or (of a sharp or pointed object) to be pushed into or through another object. **3** (tr) to fasten in position by pushing or forcing a point into something: to stick a peg in a hole. **4** (tr) to fasten in position by or as if by pins, nails, etc.: to stick a picture on the wall. **5** (tr) to transfix or impale on a pointed object. **6** (tr) to cover with objects piercing or set in the surface. **7** (when intr, foll. by out, up, through, etc.) to put forward or be put forward; protrude or cause to protrude: to stick one's head out. **8** (tr) Inf. to place or put in a specified position: stick your coat on this chair. **9** to fasten or be fastened by or as if by an adhesive substance: stick the pages together; they won't stick. **10** (tr) Inf. to cause to become sticky. **11** (when tr, usually passive) to come or cause to come to a standstill: stuck in a traffic jam; the wheels stuck. **12** (intr) to remain for a long time: the memory sticks in my mind. **13** (tr) Sl., chiefly Brit. to tolerate; abide: I can't stick that man. **14** (intr) to be reluctant. **15** (tr; usually passive) Inf. to cause to be at a loss; baffle or puzzle: I was totally stuck for an answer. **16** (tr) Sl. to force or impose something unpleasant on: they stuck me with the bill. **17** (tr) to kill by piercing or stabbing. **18 stick to the ribs.** Inf. (of food) to be hearty and satisfying. ◆ n **19** the state or condition of adhering. **20** Inf. a substance causing adhesion. **21** Obs. something that causes delay or stoppage. ◆ See also **stick around, stick by,** etc. [OE stician]

stick around or **about** vb (intr, adv) Inf. to remain in a place, esp. awaiting something.

stick by vb (intr, prep) to remain faithful to; adhere to.

sticker ('stɪkə) n **1** an adhesive label, poster, or paper. **2** a person or thing that sticks. **3** a persevering or industrious person. **4** something prickly, such as a thorn, that clings to one's clothing, etc. **5** Inf. something that perplexes. **6** Inf. a knife used for stabbing or piercing.

stickhandle ('stɪk,hændªl) *vb* **stickhandles, stickhandling, stickhandled.** *Ice hockey.* to manoeuvre (the puck) deftly.

sticking plaster *n* a thin cloth with an adhesive substance on one side, used for covering slight or superficial wounds.

stick insect *n* any of various mostly tropical insects that have an elongated cylindrical body and long legs and resemble twigs.

stick-in-the-mud *n Inf.* a conservative person who lacks initiative or imagination.

stickle ('stɪkªl) *vb* **stickles, stickling, stickled.** (*intr*) **1** to dispute stubbornly, esp. about minor points. **2** to refuse to agree or concur, esp. by making petty stipulations. [C16 *stightle* (in the sense: to arbitrate): frequentative of OE *stihtan* to arrange]

stickleback ('stɪkªl,bæk) *n* any of various small fishes that have a series of spines along the back and occur in cold and temperate northern regions. [C15: from OE *stickel* prick, sting + BACK]

stickler ('stɪklə) *n* **1** (usually foll. by *for*) a person who makes insistent demands: *a stickler for accuracy.* **2** a problem or puzzle.

stick out *vb* (*adv*) **1** to project or cause to project. **2** (*tr*) *Inf.* to endure (something disagreeable) (esp. in **stick it out**). **3 stick out a mile** *or* **like a sore thumb.** *Inf.* to be extremely obvious. **4 stick out for.** to insist on (a demand), refusing to yield until it is met.

stick shift *n US & Canad.* **1a** a manually operated transmission system in a motor vehicle. **1b** a motor vehicle having manual transmission. **2** a gear lever.

stick to *vb* (*prep, mainly intr*) **1** (*also tr*) to adhere or cause to adhere to. **2** to continue constantly at. **3** to remain faithful to. **4** not to move or digress from: *the speaker stuck closely to his subject.* **5 stick to someone's fingers.** *Inf.* to be stolen by someone.

stick-up *n* **1** *Sl., chiefly US.* a robbery at gunpoint; holdup. ◆ *vb* **stick up.** (*adv*) **2** (*tr*) *Sl., chiefly US.* to rob, esp. at gunpoint. **3** (*intr*; foll. by *for*) *Inf.* to support or defend: *stick up for oneself.*

sticky ('stɪkɪ) *adj* **stickier, stickiest. 1** covered or daubed with an adhesive or viscous substance: *sticky fingers.* **2** having the property of sticking to a surface. **3** (of weather or atmosphere) warm and humid; muggy. **4** *Inf.* difficult, awkward, or painful: *a sticky business.* ◆ *vb* **stickies, stickying, stickied. 5** (*tr*) *Inf.* to make sticky.
▸ 'stickily *adv* ▸ 'stickiness *n*

stickybeak ('stɪkɪ,biːk) *Austral. & NZ inf.* ◆ *n* **1** an inquisitive person. ◆ *vb* **2** (*intr*) to pry.

sticky end *n Inf.* an unpleasant finish or death (esp. in **come to** *or* **meet a sticky end**).

sticky wicket *n* **1** a cricket pitch that is rapidly being dried by the sun after rain and is particularly conducive to spin. **2** *Inf.* a difficult or awkward situation.

Stieglitz ★ ('stiːɡlɪts) *n* **Alfred.** 1864–1946, US photographer, whose work helped to develop photography as an art: among his best photographs are those of his wife, Georgia O'Keeffe.

stiff (stɪf) *adj* **1** not easily bent; rigid; inflexible. **2** not working or moving easily or smoothly: *a stiff handle.* **3** difficult to accept in its severity or harshness: *a stiff punishment.* **4** moving with pain or difficulty; not supple: *a stiff neck.* **5** difficult; arduous: *a stiff climb.* **6** unrelaxed or awkward; formal. **7** firmer than liquid in consistency; thick or viscous. **8** powerful; strong: *a stiff breeze; a stiff drink.* **9** excessively high: *a stiff price.* **10** lacking grace or attractiveness. **11** stubborn or stubbornly maintained: *a stiff fight.* **12** *Obs.* tightly stretched; taut. **13** *Sl.* intoxicated. **14 stiff with.** *Inf.* amply provided with. ◆ *n* **15** *Sl.* a corpse. **16** *Sl.* anything thought to be a loser or a failure; flop. ◆ *adv* **17** completely or utterly: *bored stiff; frozen stiff.* ◆ *vb* **18** (*intr*) *Sl.* to fail: *the film stiffed.* **19** (*tr*) *Sl., chiefly US.* to cheat or swindle. [OE *stīf*]
▸ 'stiffish *adj* ▸ 'stiffly *adv* ▸ 'stiffness *n*

stiffen ('stɪfªn) *vb* **1** to make or become stiff or stiffer. **2** (*intr*) to become suddenly tense or unyielding.
▸ 'stiffener *n*

stiff-necked *adj* haughtily stubborn or obstinate.

stifle ('staɪfªl) *vb* **stifles, stifling, stifled. 1** (*tr*) to smother or suppress: *stifle a cough.* **2** to feel or cause to feel discomfort and difficulty in breathing. **3** to prevent or be prevented from breathing so as to cause death. **4** (*tr*) to crush or stamp out. [C14: var. of *stuflen*, prob. from OF *estouffer* to smother]

stigma ('stɪɡmə) *n, pl* **stigmas** *or* **stigmata** ('stɪɡmətə, stɪɡ'mɑːtə). **1** a distinguishing mark of social disgrace: *the stigma of having been in prison.* **2** a small scar or mark such as a birthmark. **3** *Pathol.* any mark on the skin, such as one characteristic of a specific disease. **4** *Bot.* the terminal part of the ovary, at the end of the style, where deposited pollen enters the gynoecium. **5** *Zool.* **5a** a pigmented eyespot in some invertebrates. **5b** the spiracle of an insect. **6** *Arch.* a mark branded on the skin. **7** (*pl*) *Christianity.* marks resembling the wounds of the crucified Christ, believed to appear on the bodies of certain individuals. [C16: via L from Gk: brand, from *stizein* to tattoo]

stigmatic (stɪɡ'mætɪk) *adj* **1** relating to or having a stigma or stigmata. **2** another word for **anastigmatic.** ◆ *n also* **stigmatist** ('stɪɡmətɪst). **3** *Chiefly RC Church.* a person marked with the stigmata.

stigmatism ('stɪɡmə,tɪzəm) *n* **1** *Physics.* the state or condition of being anastigmatic. **2** *Pathol.* the condition resulting from or characterized by stigmata.

stigmatize *or* **stigmatise** ('stɪɡmə,taɪz) *vb* **stigmatizes, stigmatizing, stigmatized** *or* **stigmatises, stigmatising, stigmatised. 1** (*tr*) to mark out or describe (as something bad). **2** to mark with a stigma or stigmata.
▸ ,stigmati'zation *or* ,stigmati'sation *n* ▸ 'stigma,tizer *or* 'stigma,tiser *n*

stilbene ('stɪlbiːn) *n* a colourless or slightly yellow crystalline unsaturated hydrocarbon used in the manufacture of dyes. [C19: from Gk *stilbos* glittering + -ENE]

stilboestrol *or US* **stilbestrol** (stɪl'biːstrəl) *n* a synthetic hormone having derivatives with oestrogenic properties. Also called: **diethylstilboestrol.** [C20: from STILBENE + OESTRUS + -OL¹]

stile¹ (staɪl) *n* **1** a set of steps or rungs in a wall or fence to allow people, but not animals, to pass over. **2** short for **turnstile.** [OE *stigel*]

stile² (staɪl) *n* a vertical framing member in a door, window frame, etc. [C17: prob. from Du. *stijl* pillar, ult. from L *stilus* writing instrument]

stiletto (stɪ'letəu) *n, pl* **stilettos. 1** a small dagger with a slender tapered blade. **2** a sharply pointed tool used to make holes in leather, cloth, etc. **3** Also called: **spike heel, stiletto heel.** a very high heel on a woman's shoe, tapering to a very narrow tip. ◆ *vb* **stilettoes, stilettoeing, stilettoed. 4** (*tr*) to stab with a stiletto. [C17: from It., from *stilo* a dagger, from L *stilus* a stake, pen]

Stilicho ★ ('stɪlɪkəu) *n* **Flavius** ('fleɪvɪəs). ?365–408 A.D., Roman general and statesman, born a Vandal: effective ruler of the Western Roman Empire (395–408).

still¹ (stɪl) *adj* **1** (*usually predicative*) motionless; stationary. **2** undisturbed or tranquil; silent and calm. **3** not sparkling or effervescent. **4** gentle or quiet; subdued. **5** *Obs.* (of a child) dead at birth. ◆ *adv* **6** continuing now or in the future as in the past: *do you still love me?* **7** up to this or that time; yet: *I still don't know your name.* **8** (often used with a comparative) even or yet: *still more insults.* **9** quietly or without movement: *sit still.* **10** *Poetic & dialect.* always. ◆ *n* **11** *Poetic.* silence or tranquillity: *the still of the night.* **12a** a still photograph, esp. of a scene from a film. **12b** (*as modifier*): *a still camera.* ◆ *vb* **13** to make or become still, quiet, or calm. **14** (*tr*) to allay or relieve: *her fears were stilled.* ◆ *sentence connector.* **15** even then; nevertheless: *the child has some new toys and still cries.* [OE *stille*]
▸ 'stillness *n*

still² (stɪl) *n* an apparatus for carrying out distillation, used esp. in the manufacture of spirits. [C16: from OF *stiller* to drip, from L *stillāre*, from *stilla* a drip]

stillage ('stɪlɪdʒ) *n* **1** a frame or stand for keeping things off the ground, such as casks in a brewery. **2** a container in which goods, machinery, etc., are transported. [C16:

prob. from Du. *stillagie* frame, scaffold, from *stellen* to stand; see -AGE]

stillborn ('stɪl,bɔːn) *adj* **1** (of a fetus) dead at birth. **2** (of an idea, plan, etc.) fruitless; abortive; unsuccessful.
▶ 'still,birth *n*

still life *n*, *pl* **still lifes**. **1a** a painting or drawing of inanimate objects, such as fruit, flowers, etc. **1b** (*as modifier*): *a still-life painting*. **2** the genre of such paintings.

still room *n Brit*. **1** a room in which distilling is carried out. **2** a pantry or storeroom, as in a large house.

Stillson wrench ('stɪls°n) *n Trademark*. a large wrench having adjustable jaws that tighten as the pressure on the handle is increased.

stilly *adv* ('stɪlɪ). **1** *Arch*. or *literary*. quietly or calmly. ◆ *adj* ('stɪlɪ). **2** *Poetic*. still, quiet, or calm.

stilt (stɪlt) *n* **1** either of a pair of two long poles with footrests on which a person stands and walks, as used by circus clowns. **2** a long post or column that is used with others to support a building above ground level. **3** any of several shore birds similar to the avocets but having a straight bill. ◆ *vb* **4** (*tr*) to raise or place on or as if on stilts. [C14 (in the sense: crutch, handle of a plough): rel. to Low G *stilte* pole]

stilted ('stɪltɪd) *adj* **1** (of speech, writing, etc.) formal, pompous, or bombastic. **2** not flowing continuously or naturally: *stilted conversation*. **3** *Archit*. (of an arch) having vertical piers between the impost and the springing.
▶ 'stiltedly *adv* ▶ 'stiltedness *n*

Stilton ('stɪltən) *n Trademark*. either of two rich cheeses, blue-veined (**blue Stilton**) or white (**white Stilton**), both very strong in flavour. [C18: named after *Stilton*, Cambridgeshire, where it was orig. sold]

Stilwell ★ ('stɪlwel) *n* **Joseph W(arren)**, known as *Vinegar Joe*. 1883–1946, US general, who was (1941–44) Chiang Kai-shek's chief of staff and commander of all US forces in China, Burma, and India.

stimulant ('stɪmjʊlənt) *n* **1** a drug or similar substance that increases physiological activity, esp. of a particular organ. **2** any stimulating agent or thing. ◆ *adj* **3** stimulating. [C18: from L *stimulāns* goading, from *stimulāre* to urge on]

stimulate ('stɪmjʊ,leɪt) *vb* **stimulates, stimulating, stimulated**. **1** (*tr*) to arouse or quicken the activity or senses of. **2** (*tr*) *Physiol*. to excite (a nerve, organ, etc.) with a stimulus. **3** (*intr*) to act as a stimulant or stimulus. [C16: from L *stimulāre*]
▶ 'stimu,lating *adj* ▶ ,stimu'lation *n* ▶ 'stimulative *adj, n*
▶ 'stimu,lator *n*

stimulus ('stɪmjʊləs) *n*, *pl* **stimuli** (-,laɪ, -,liː). **1** something that stimulates or acts as an incentive. **2** any drug, agent, electrical impulse, or other factor able to cause a response in an organism. [C17: from L: a cattle goad]

sting (stɪŋ) *vb* **stings, stinging, stung**. **1** (of certain animals and plants) to inflict a wound on (an organism) by the injection of poison. **2** to feel or cause to feel a sharp mental or physical pain. **3** (*tr*) to goad or incite (esp. in **sting into action**). **4** (*tr*) *Inf*. to cheat, esp. by overcharging. ◆ *n* **5** a skin wound caused by the poison injected by certain insects or plants. **6** pain caused by or as if by the sting of a plant or animal. **7** a mental pain or pang: *a sting of conscience*. **8** a sharp pointed organ, such as the ovipositor of a wasp, by which poison can be injected. **9** the ability to sting: *a sharp sting in his criticism*. **10** something as painful or swift of action as a sting: *the sting of death*. **11** a sharp stimulus or incitement. **12** *Sl*. a swindle or fraud. **13** *Sl*. a police trap, esp. one whereby a person is enticed into committing a crime for which he is then arrested. [OE *stingan*]
▶ 'stinger *n* ▶ 'stinging *adj*

stinging nettle *n* See **nettle** (sense 1).

stingray ('stɪŋ,reɪ) *n* any of various rays having a whiplike tail bearing a serrated venomous spine capable of inflicting painful weals.

stingy[1] ('stɪndʒɪ) *adj* **stingier, stingiest**. **1** unwilling to spend or give. **2** insufficient or scanty. [C17 (? in the sense: ill-tempered): ?from *stinge*, dialect var. of STING]
▶ 'stingily *adv* ▶ 'stinginess *n*

stingy[2] ('stɪŋɪ) *adj* **stingier, stingiest**. *Inf*. stinging or capable of stinging.

stink (stɪŋk) *n* **1** a strong foul smell; stench. **2** *Sl*. a great deal of trouble (esp. in **make** *or* **raise a stink**). **3** **like stink**. intensely; furiously. ◆ *vb* **stinks, stinking, stank** *or* **stunk; stunk**. (*mainly intr*) **4** to emit a foul smell. **5** *Sl*. to be thoroughly bad or abhorrent: *this town stinks*. **6** *Inf*. to have a very bad reputation: *his name stinks*. **7** to be of poor quality. **8** (foll. by *of or with*) *Sl*. to have or appear to have an excessive amount (of money). **9** (*tr*; usually foll. by *up*) *Inf*. to cause to stink. ◆ See also **stink out**. [OE *stincan*]
▶ 'stinky *adj*

stink bomb *n* a small glass globe used by practical jokers: it releases a liquid with an offensive smell when broken.

stinker ('stɪŋkə) *n* **1** a person or thing that stinks. **2** *Sl*. a difficult or very unpleasant person or thing. **3** *Sl*. something of very poor quality. **4** *Inf*. any of several fulmars or related birds that feed on carrion.

stinkhorn ('stɪŋk,hɔːn) *n* any of various fungi having an unpleasant odour.

stinking ('stɪŋkɪŋ) *adj* **1** having a foul smell. **2** *Inf*. unpleasant or disgusting. **3** (*postpositive*) *Sl*. very drunk. **4 cry stinking fish**. to decry something, esp. one's own products. ◆ *adv* **5** *Inf*. (intensifier, expressing contempt): *stinking rich*.
▶ 'stinkingly *adv* ▶ 'stinkingness *n*

stinko ('stɪŋkəʊ) *adj* (*postpositive*) *Sl*. drunk.

stink out *vb* (*tr, adv*) **1** to drive out or away by a foul smell. **2** *Brit*. to cause to stink: *the smell of orange peel stinks out the room*.

stinkweed ('stɪŋk,wiːd) *n* **1** Also called: **wall mustard**. a cruciferous plant, naturalized in Britain and S and central Europe, having pale yellow flowers and a disagreeable smell when bruised. **2** any of various other illsmelling plants.

stinkwood ('stɪŋk,wʊd) *n* **1** any of various trees having offensive-smelling wood, esp. a southern African lauraceous tree yielding a hard wood used for furniture. **2** the heavy durable wood of any of these trees.

stint[1] (stɪnt) *vb* **1** to be frugal or miserly towards (someone) with (something). **2** *Arch*. to stop or check (something). ◆ *n* **3** an allotted or fixed amount of work. **4** a limitation or check. [OE *styntan* to blunt]
▶ 'stinter *n*

stint[2] (stɪnt) *n* any of various small sandpipers of a chiefly northern genus. [OE]

stipe (staɪp) *n* **1** a stalk in plants that bears reproductive structures, esp. the stalk bearing the cap of a mushroom. **2** the stalk that bears the leaflets of a fern or the thallus of a seaweed. **3** *Zool*. any stalklike part; stipes. [C18: via F from L *stīpes* tree trunk]

stipel ('staɪp°l) *n* a small paired leaflike structure at the base of certain leaflets; secondary stipule. [C19: via NL from L *stipula*, dim. of *stīpes* a log]
▶ **stipellate** (staɪ'pelɪt, -eɪt) *adj*

stipend ('staɪpend) *n* a fixed or regular amount of money paid as a salary or allowance, as to a clergyman. [C15: from OF *stipende*, from L *stīpendium* tax, from *stips* a contribution + *pendere* to pay out]

stipendiary (staɪ'pendɪərɪ) *adj* **1** receiving or working for regular pay: *a stipendiary magistrate*. **2** paid for by a stipend. ◆ *n*, *pl* **stipendiaries**. **3** a person who receives regular payment. [C16: from L *stīpendiārius* concerning tribute, from *stīpendium* STIPEND]

stipes ('staɪpiːz) *n*, *pl* **stipites** ('stɪpɪ,tiːz). *Zool*. **1** the second maxillary segment in insects and crustaceans. **2** the eyestalk of a crab or similar crustacean. **3** any similar stemlike structure. [C18: from L]
▶ **stipiform** ('staɪpɪ,fɔːm) *or* **stipitiform** ('stɪpɪtɪ,fɔːm) *adj*

stipple ('stɪp°l) *vb* **stipples, stippling, stippled**. (*tr*) **1** to draw, engrave, or paint using dots or flecks. **2** to apply paint, powder, etc., to (something) with many light dabs. ◆ *n* **3** also **stippling**. **3** the technique of stippling or a picture produced by or using stippling. [C18: from Du. *stippelen*, from *stippen* to prick, from *stip* point]
▶ 'stippler *n*

stipulate ('stɪpjʊˌleɪt) *vb* **stipulates, stipulating, stipulated. 1** (*tr; may take a clause as object*) to specify, often as a condition of an agreement. **2** (*intr;* foll. by *for*) to insist (on) as a term of an agreement. **3** (*tr; may take a clause as object*) to guarantee or promise. [C17: from L *stipulārī*, prob. from OL *stipulus* firm]
▶ ˌstipu'lation *n* ▶ 'stipuˌlator *n*

stipule ('stɪpjuːl) *n* a small paired usually leaflike outgrowth occurring at the base of a leaf or its stalk. [C18: from L; see STIPE]
▶ **stipular** ('stɪpjʊlə) *adj*

stir[1] (stɜː) *vb* **stirs, stirring, stirred. 1** to move an implement such as a spoon around in (a liquid) so as to mix up the constituents. **2** to change or cause to change position; disturb or be disturbed. **3** (*intr;* often foll. by *from*) to venture or depart (from one's usual or preferred place). **4** (*intr*) to be active after a rest; be up and about. **5** (*tr*) to excite or stimulate, esp. emotionally. **6** to move (oneself) briskly or vigorously; exert (oneself). **7** (*tr*) to rouse or awaken: *to stir someone from sleep; to stir memories.* **8** (when *tr,* foll. by *up*) to cause or incite others to cause (trouble, arguments, etc.). **9 stir one's stumps.** to move or become active. ◆ *n* **10** the act or an instance of stirring or the state of being stirred. **11** a strong reaction, esp. of excitement: *his publication caused a stir.* **12** a slight movement. **13** *NZ inf.* a noisy party. ◆ See also **stir up.** [OE *styrian*]

stir[2] *vb* **1** a slang word for **prison:** *in stir.* **2 stir-crazy.** *Sl., chiefly US & Canad.* mentally disturbed as a result of being in prison. [C19: from ?]

Stir. *abbrev. for* Stirlingshire.

stir-fry *vb* **stir-fries, stir-frying, stir-fried. 1** to cook (chopped meat, vegetables, etc.) rapidly by stirring them in a wok or frying pan over a high heat. ◆ *n, pl* **stir-fries. 2** a dish cooked in this way.

stirk (stɜːk) *n* **1** a heifer of 6 to 12 months old. **2** a yearling heifer or bullock. [OE *stierc*]

Stirling ★ ('stɜːlɪŋ) *n* **1** a town in central Scotland, on the River Forth: its castle was a regular residence of many Scottish monarchs between the 12th century and 1603. Pop.: 30 515 (1991). **2** a council area of central Scotland. Administrative centre: Stirling. Pop.: 82 750 (1996 est.). Area: 2173 sq. km (839 sq. miles).

Stirlingshire ★ ('stɜːlɪŋˌʃɪə, -ʃə) *n* a historic county of central Scotland, now part of Stirling and Falkirk council areas.

stirps (stɜːps) *n, pl* **stirpes** ('stɜːpiːz). **1** *Genealogy.* a line of descendants from an ancestor. **2** *Bot.* a race or variety. [C17: from L: root, family origin]

stirrer ('stɜːrə) *n* **1** a person or thing that stirs. **2** *Inf.* a person who deliberately causes trouble. **3** *Austral. & NZ inf.* a political activist or agitator.

stirring ('stɜːrɪŋ) *adj* **1** exciting the emotions; stimulating. **2** active, lively, or busy.
▶ 'stirringly *adv*

stirrup ('stɪrəp) *n* **1** Also called: **stirrup iron.** either of two metal loops on a riding saddle, with a flat footpiece through which a rider puts his foot for support. They are attached to the saddle by **stirrup leathers. 2** a U-shaped support or clamp. **3** *Naut.* one of a set of ropes fastened to a yard at one end and having a thimble at the other through which a footrope is reeved for support. [OE *stigrāp,* from *stīg* step + *rāp* rope]

stirrup cup *n* a cup containing an alcoholic drink offered to a horseman ready to ride away.

stirrup pump *n* a hand-operated pump, the base of the cylinder of which is placed in a bucket of water: used in fighting fires.

stir up *vb* (*tr, adv*) to set in motion; instigate: *he stirred up trouble.*

stitch (stɪtʃ) *n* **1** a link made by drawing a thread through material by means of a needle. **2** a loop of yarn formed around an implement used in knitting, crocheting, etc. **3** a particular method of stitching or shape of stitch. **4** a sharp spasmodic pain in the side resulting from running or exercising. **5** (*usually used with a negative*) *Inf.* the least fragment of clothing: *he wasn't wearing a stitch.* **6** *Agriculture.* the ridge between two furrows. **7 drop a stitch.** to allow a loop of wool to fall off a knitting needle acciden-

tally while knitting. **8 in stitches.** *Inf.* laughing uncontrollably. ◆ *vb* **9** (*tr*) to sew, fasten, etc., with stitches. **10** (*intr*) to be engaged in sewing. **11** (*tr*) to bind together (the leaves of a book, pamphlet, etc.) with wire staples or thread. ◆ *n, vb* **12** an informal word for **suture** (senses 1b, 5). [OE *stice* sting]
▶ 'stitcher *n*

stitch up *vb* (*tr, adv*) **1** to join or mend by means of stitches or sutures. **2** *Sl.* **2a** to incriminate (someone) on a false charge by manufacturing evidence. **2b** to betray, cheat, or defraud. **3** *Sl.* to prearrange (something) in a clandestine manner. ◆ *n* **stitch-up. 4** *Sl.* a matter that has been prearranged clandestinely.

stitchwort ('stɪtʃˌwɜːt) *n* any of several low-growing N temperate herbaceous plants having small white star-shaped flowers.

stiver ('staɪvə) *n* **1** a former Dutch coin worth one twentieth of a guilder. **2** a small amount, esp. of money. [C16: from Du. *stuiver*]

St John ★ ('sɪndʒən) *n* Henry. See (1st Viscount) **Bolingbroke.**

stoa ('stəʊə) *n, pl* **stoae** ('stəʊiː) *or* **stoas.** a covered walk that has a colonnade on one or both sides, esp. as in ancient Greece. [C17: from Gk]

stoat (stəʊt) *n* a small Eurasian mammal, closely related to the weasels, having a brown coat and a black-tipped tail: in the northern parts of its range it has a white winter coat and is then known as an ermine. [C15: from ?]

stochastic (stɒ'kæstɪk) *adj* **1** *Statistics.* **1a** (of a random variable) having a probability distribution, usually with finite variance. **1b** (of a process) involving a random variable the successive values of which are not independent. **1c** (of a matrix) square with non-negative elements that add to unity in each row. **2** *Rare.* involving conjecture. [C17: from Gk *stokhastikos* capable of guessing, from *stokhazesthai* to aim at, conjecture, from *stokhos* a target]

stock (stɒk) *n* **1a** (*sometimes pl*) the total goods or raw material kept on the premises of a shop or business. **1b** (*as modifier*): *a stock book.* **2** a supply of something stored for future use. **3** *Finance.* **3a** the capital raised by a company through the issue and subscription of shares entitling their holders to dividends, partial ownership, and usually voting rights. **3b** the proportion of such capital held by an individual shareholder. **3c** the shares of a specified company or industry. **4** standing or status. **5a** farm animals, such as cattle and sheep, bred and kept for their meat, skins, etc. **5b** (*as modifier*): *stock farming.* **6** the trunk or main stem of a tree or other plant. **7** *Horticulture.* **7a** a rooted plant into which a scion is inserted during grafting. **7b** a plant or stem from which cuttings are taken. **8** the original type from which a particular race, family, group, etc., is derived. **9** a race, breed, or variety of animals or plants. **10** (*often pl*) a small pen in which a single animal can be confined. **11** a line of descent. **12** any of the major subdivisions of the human species; race or ethnic group. **13** the part of a rifle, etc., into which the barrel is set: held by the firer against the shoulder. **14** the handle of something, such as a whip or fishing rod. **15** the main body of a tool, such as the block of a plane. **16** short for **diestock, gunstock,** or **rolling stock. 17** (formerly) the part of a plough to which the irons and handles were attached. **18** the main upright part of a supporting structure. **19** a liquid or broth in which meat, fish, bones, or vegetables have been simmered for a long time. **20** film material before exposure and processing. **21** Also called: **gillyflower.** any of several cruciferous plants such as **evening** or **night-scented stock,** of the Mediterranean region: cultivated for their brightly coloured flowers. **22 Virginian stock.** a similar and related North American plant. **23** a long usually white neckcloth wrapped around the neck, worn in the 18th century and as part of modern riding dress. **24a** the repertoire of plays available to a repertory company. **24b** (*as modifier*): *a stock play.* **25** a log or block of wood. **26** See **laughing stock. 27 in stock. 27a** stored on the premises or available for sale or use. **27b** supplied with goods of a specified kind. **28 out of stock. 28a** not immediately available for sale or use. **28b** not having goods of a specified kind immediately available. **29 take stock. 29a** to make an inventory. **29b** to make a general ap-

praisal, esp. of prospects, resources, etc. **30 take stock in.** to attach importance to. ◆ *adj* **31** staple; standard: *stock sizes in clothes.* **32** (*prenominal*) being a cliché; hackneyed: *a stock phrase.* ◆ *vb* **33** (*tr*) to keep (goods) for sale. **34** (*intr; usually foll.* by *up* or *up on*) to obtain a store of (something) for future use or sale: *to stock up on beer.* **35** (*tr*) to supply with live animals, fish, etc.: *to stock a farm.* **36** (*intr*) (of a plant) to put forth new shoots. **37** (*tr*) *Obs.* to punish by putting in the stocks. ◆ See also **stocks.** [OE *stocc* trunk (of a tree), stem, stick (the various senses developed from these meanings, as trunk of a tree, hence line of descent; structures made of timber; a store of timber or other goods for future use, hence an aggregate of goods, animals, etc.)]
▶ '**stocker** *n*

stockade (stɒ'keɪd) *n* **1** an enclosure or barrier of stakes and timbers. ◆ *vb* **stockades, stockading, stockaded.** **2** (*tr*) to surround with a stockade. [C17: from Sp. *estacada*, from *estaca* a stake, of Gmc origin]

stockbreeder ('stɒk,briːdə) *n* a person who breeds or rears livestock as an occupation.
▶ '**stock,breeding** *n*

stockbroker ('stɒk,brəʊkə) *n* a person who buys and sells securities on a commission basis for customers.
▶ '**stock,brokerage** *or* '**stock,broking** *n*

stockbroker belt *n Brit. inf.* the area outside a city, esp. London, in which rich commuters live.

stock car *n* **1** a car, usually a production saloon, strengthened and modified for a form of racing in which the cars often collide. **2** *US & Canad.* a railway wagon for carrying livestock.

stock dove *n* a European dove, smaller than the wood pigeon and having a grey plumage.

stock exchange *n* **1a** a highly organized market facilitating the purchase and sale of securities and operated by professional stockbrokers and market makers according to fixed rules. **1b** a place where securities are regularly traded. **1c** (*as modifier*): *a stock-exchange operator; stock-exchange prices.* **2** the prices or trading activity of a stock exchange: *the stock exchange fell heavily today.* ◆ Also called: **stock market.**

stockfish ('stɒk,fɪʃ) *n, pl* **stockfish** *or* **stockfishes.** fish cured by splitting and drying in the air.

Stockhausen ★ (*German* 'ʃtɒkhauzən) *n* **Karlheinz** (karl-'haints). born 1928, German composer. His avant-garde works include *Gruppen* (1959) for three orchestras and *Stimmung* (1968) for six vocalists.

stockholder ('stɒk,həʊldə) *n* **1** an owner of corporate capital stock. **2** *Austral.* a person who keeps livestock.
▶ '**stock,holding** *n*

Stockholm ★ ('stɒkhəʊm; *Swedish* 'stɔkhɔlm) *n* the capital of Sweden, a port in the E central part at the outflow of Lake Mälar into the Baltic: situated partly on the mainland and partly on islands; traditionally founded about 1250; university (1877). Pop.: 711 119 (1996 est.).

stockhorse ('stɒk,hɔːs) *n Austral.* a stockman's horse.

stockinet (,stɒkɪ'net) *n* a machine-knitted elastic fabric used, esp. formerly, for stockings, underwear, etc. [C19: ?from earlier *stocking-net*]

stocking ('stɒkɪŋ) *n* **1** one of a pair of close-fitting garments made of knitted yarn to cover the foot and part or all of the leg. **2** something resembling this in position, function, etc. **3 in** (**one's**) **stocking** *or* **stockinged feet.** wearing stockings or socks but no shoes. [C16: from dialect *stock* stocking + -ING¹]
▶ '**stockinged** *adj*

stocking cap *n* a conical knitted cap, often with a tassel.

stocking filler *n Brit.* a present of a size suitable for inclusion in a Christmas stocking.

stock in trade *n* **1** goods in stock necessary for carrying on a business. **2** anything constantly used by someone as a part of his profession, occupation, or trade: *friendliness is the salesman's stock in trade.*

stockist ('stɒkɪst) *n Commerce, Brit.* a dealer who undertakes to maintain stocks of a specified product at or

above a certain minimum in return for favourable buying terms granted by the manufacturer of the product.

stockjobber ('stɒk,dʒɒbə) *n* **1** *Brit.* (formerly) a wholesale dealer on a stock exchange who sold securities to brokers without transacting directly with the public. See **market maker. 2** *US, disparaging.* a stockbroker, esp. one dealing in worthless securities.
▶ '**stock,jobbery** *or* '**stock,jobbing** *n*

stockman ('stɒkmən, -,mæn) *n, pl* **stockmen. 1a** a man engaged in the rearing or care of farm livestock, esp. cattle. **1b** an owner of cattle or other livestock. **2** *US & Canad.* a man employed in a warehouse or stockroom.

stock market *n* another name for **stock exchange.**

stockpile ('stɒk,paɪl) *vb* **stockpiles, stockpiling, stockpiled. 1** to acquire and store a large quantity of (something). ◆ *n* **2** a large store or supply accumulated for future use.
▶ '**stock,piler** *n*

Stockport ★ ('stɒk,pɔːt) *n* **1** a town in NW England, in Greater Manchester: an early textile centre and scene of several labour disturbances in the early 19th century. Pop.: 132 813 (1991). **2** a unitary authority in NW England, in Greater Manchester. Pop.: 291 400 (1994 est.). Area: 126 sq. km (49 sq. miles).

stockpot ('stɒk,pɒt) *n Chiefly Brit.* a pot in which stock for soup, etc., is made or kept.

stockroom ('stɒk,ruːm, -,rʊm) *n* a room in which a stock of goods is kept, as in a shop or factory.

stock route *n Austral. & NZ.* a route designated for droving sheep or cattle.

stocks (stɒks) *pl n* **1** *History.* an instrument of punishment consisting of a heavy wooden frame with holes in which the feet, hands, or head of an offender were locked. **2** a frame used to support a boat while under construction. **3** *Naut.* a vertical post or shaft at the forward edge of a rudder, extended upwards for attachment to the steering controls. **4 on the stocks.** in preparation or under construction.

stock-still *adv* absolutely still; motionless.

stocktaking ('stɒk,teɪkɪŋ) *n* **1** the examination, counting, and valuing of goods on hand in a shop or business. **2** a reassessment of one's current situation, progress, prospects, etc.

Stockton¹ ★ ('stɒktən) *n* an inland port in central California, on the San Joaquin River: seat of the University of the Pacific (1851). Pop.: 222 633 (1994 est.).

Stockton² ★ ('stɒktən) *n* **1st Earl of.** title of (Maurice Harold) **Macmillan.**

Stockton-on-Tees ★ *n* **1** a port in NE England, on the River Tees: industrial centre, famous for the **Stockton-Darlington Railway** (1825), the first passenger-carrying railway in the world. Pop.: 83 576 (1991). **2** a unitary authority in NE England, in Co. Durham. Pop.: 176 600 (1996 est.). Area: 195 sq. km (75 sq. miles).

stock watering *n Business.* the creation of more new shares in a company than is justified by its assets.

stock whip *n* a whip with a long lash and a short handle, used to herd cattle, etc.

stocky ('stɒkɪ) *adj* **stockier, stockiest.** (usually of a person) thickset; sturdy.
▶ '**stockily** *adv* ▶ '**stockiness** *n*

stockyard ('stɒk,jɑːd) *n* a large yard with pens or covered buildings where farm animals are assembled, sold, etc.

stodge (stɒdʒ) *Inf.* ◆ *n* **1** heavy filling starchy food. **2** a dull person or subject. ◆ *vb* **stodges, stodging, stodged. 3** to stuff (oneself or another) with food. [C17: ? blend of STUFF + *podge*, from *podgy* fat]

stodgy ('stɒdʒɪ) *adj* **stodgier, stodgiest. 1** (of food) heavy or uninteresting. **2** excessively formal and conventional. [C19: from STODGE]
▶ '**stodgily** *adv* ▶ '**stodginess** *n*

stoep (stuːp) *n S. African.* a veranda. [from Afrik., from Du.]

stoic ('stəʊɪk) *n* **1** a person who maintains stoical qualities. ◆ *adj* **2** a variant of **stoical.**

Stoic ('stəʊɪk) n **1** a member of the ancient Greek school of philosophy founded by Zeno, holding that virtue and happiness can be attained only by submission to destiny and the natural law. ◆ adj **2** of or relating to the doctrines of the Stoics. [C16: via L from Gk *stōikos*, from *stoa,* the porch in Athens where Zeno taught]

stoical ('stəʊɪk°l) adj characterized by impassivity or resignation.
▶ '**stoically** adv

stoichiometry or **stoicheiometry** (ˌstɔɪkɪ'ɒmɪtrɪ) n the branch of chemistry concerned with the proportions in which elements are combined in compounds and the quantitative relationships between reactants and products in chemical reactions. [C19: from Gk *stoikheion* element + -METRY]
▶ ˌ**stoichio'metric** or ˌ**stoicheio'metric** adj

stoicism ('stəʊɪˌsɪzəm) n **1** indifference to pleasure and pain. **2** (cap.) the philosophy of the Stoics.

stoke (stəʊk) vb **stokes, stoking, stoked. 1** to feed, stir, and tend (a fire, furnace, etc.). **2** (tr) to tend the furnace of; act as a stoker for. [C17: back formation from STOKER]

stokehold ('stəʊkˌhəʊld) n Naut. **1** a coal bunker for a ship's furnace. **2** the hold for a ship's boilers; fire room.

stokehole ('stəʊkˌhəʊl) n **1** another word for **stokehold. 2** a hole in a furnace through which it is stoked.

Stoke-on-Trent ★ (stəʊk-) n **1** a city in central England, in N Staffordshire on the River Trent: a major centre of the pottery industry. Pop.: 266 543 (1991). **2** a unitary authority in central England, in N Staffordshire. Pop.: 245 200 (1994 est.). Area: 93 sq. km (36 sq. miles).

stoker ('stəʊkə) n a person employed to tend a furnace, as on a steamship. [C17: from Du., from *stoken* to stoke]

Stoker ★ ('stəʊkə) n **Bram,** original name *Abraham Stoker.* 1847–1912, Irish novelist, author of *Dracula* (1897).

stoke up vb (adv) **1** to feed and tend (a fire, etc.) with fuel. **2** (intr) to fill oneself with food.

Stokowski ★ (stə'kɒfskɪ) n **Leopold.** 1887–1977, US conductor, born in Britain.

STOL (stɒl) n **1** a system in which an aircraft can take off and land in a short distance. **2** an aircraft using this system. Cf. **VTOL** [C20: s(hort) t(ake)o(ff and) l(anding)]

stole[1] (stəʊl) vb the past tense of **steal.**

stole[2] (stəʊl) n **1** a long scarf or shawl, worn by women. **2** a long narrow scarf worn by various officiating clergymen. [OE *stole,* from L *stola,* from Gk *stolē* clothing]

stolen ('stəʊlən) vb the past participle of **steal.**

stolid ('stɒlɪd) adj showing little or no emotion or interest. [C17: from L *stolidus* dull]
▶ **stolidity** (stɒ'lɪdɪtɪ) or '**stolidness** n ▶ '**stolidly** adv

stolon ('stəʊlən) n **1** another name for **runner** (sense 9). **2** a branching structure in lower animals, esp. the anchoring rootlike part of colonial organisms. [C17: from L *stolō* shoot]
▶ **stoloniferous** (ˌstəʊlə'nɪfərəs) adj

Stolypin ★ (Russian sta'ljipin) n **Petr Arkadievich** (pjɔtr ar-'kadijɪvitʃ). 1863–1911, Russian conservative statesman: prime minister (1906–11). He instituted agrarian reforms but was ruthless in suppressing rebellion: assassinated.

stoma ('stəʊmə) n, pl **stomata. 1** Bot. an epidermal pore in plant leaves, that controls the passage of gases into and out of a plant. **2** Zool., anat. a mouth or mouthlike part. **3** Surgery. an artificial opening made in a tubular organ, esp. the colon or ileum. See **colostomy, ileostomy.** [C17: via NL from Gk: mouth]

stomach ('stʌmək) n **1** (in vertebrates) the enlarged muscular saclike part of the alimentary canal in which food is stored until it has been partially digested. Related adj: **gastric. 2** the corresponding organ in invertebrates. **3** the abdominal region. **4** desire, appetite, or inclination: *I have no stomach for arguments.* ◆ vb (tr; used mainly in negative constructions) **5** to tolerate; bear: *I can't stomach his bragging.* **6** to eat or digest: *he cannot stomach oysters.* [C14: from OF *stomaque,* from L *stomachus,* from Gk *stomakhos,* from *stoma* mouth]

stomachache ('stʌməkˌeɪk) n pain in the stomach, as

from acute indigestion. Also called: **stomach upset, upset stomach.**

stomacher ('stʌməkə) n a decorative V-shaped panel of stiff material worn over the chest and stomach by men and women in the 16th century, later only by women.

stomachic (stə'mækɪk) adj also **stomachical. 1** stimulating gastric activity. **2** of or relating to the stomach. ◆ n **3** a stomachic medicine.

stomach pump n Med. a suction device for removing stomach contents by a tube inserted through the mouth.

stomata ('stəʊmətə, 'stɒm-, stəʊ'mɑːtə) n the plural of **stoma.**

stomatitis (ˌstəʊmə'taɪtɪs, ˌstɒm-) n inflammation of the mouth.
▶ **stomatitic** (ˌstəʊmə'tɪtɪk, ˌstɒm-) adj

stomato- or before a vowel **stomat-** combining form. indicating the mouth or a mouthlike part: *stomatology.* [from Gk *stoma, stomat-*]

stomatology (ˌstəʊmə'tɒlədʒɪ) n the branch of medicine concerned with the mouth.
▶ **stomatological** (ˌstəʊmətə'lɒdʒɪk°l) adj

-stome n combining form. indicating a mouth or opening resembling a mouth: *peristome.* [from Gk *stoma* mouth, & *stomion* little mouth]

-stomous adj combining form. having a specified type of mouth.

stomp (stɒmp) vb **1** (intr) to tread or stamp heavily. ◆ n **2** a rhythmic stamping jazz dance. [var. of STAMP]
▶ '**stomper** n

-stomy n combining form. indicating a surgical operation performed to make an artificial opening into or for a specified part: *cytostomy.* [from Gk -*stomia,* from *stoma* mouth]

stone (stəʊn) n **1** the hard compact nonmetallic material of which rocks are made. **2** a small lump of rock; pebble. **3** short for **gemstone. 4a** a piece of rock designed or shaped for some particular purpose. **4b** (in combination): *gravestone; millstone.* **5a** something that resembles a stone. **5b** (in combination): *hailstone.* **6** the woody central part of such fruits as the peach and plum, that contains the seed; endocarp. **7** any similar hard part of a fruit, such as the stony seed of a date. **8** (pl **stone**) Brit. a unit of weight, used esp. to express human body weight, equal to 14 pounds or 6.350 kilograms. **9** Also called: **granite.** the rounded heavy mass of granite or iron used in the game of curling. **10** Pathol. a nontechnical name for **calculus. 11** Printing. a table with a very flat iron or stone surface upon which pages are composed. **12** (modifier) relating to or made of stone: *a stone house.* **13** (modifier) made of stoneware: *a stone jar.* **14 cast a stone** (at). cast aspersions (upon). **15 heart of stone.** an obdurate or unemotional nature. **16 leave no stone unturned.** to do everything possible to achieve an end. ◆ vb **stones, stoning, stoned.** (tr) **17** to throw stones at, esp. to kill. **18** to remove the stones from. **19** to furnish or provide with stones. [OE *stān*]
▶ '**stoner** n

Stone ★ (stəʊn) n **1 Oliver.** born 1946, US film director: his films include *Platoon* (1986), *JFK* (1991), and *U-Turn* (1998). **2 Sharon.** born 1958, US film actress: her films include *Casino* (1995) and *Sphere* (1998).

stone- prefix very, completely: *stone-blind, stone-cold.* [from STONE in sense of "like a stone"]

Stone Age n **1** a period in human culture identified by the use of stone implements. ◆ modifier. **Stone-Age. 2** (sometimes not caps.) of or relating to this period.

stone-blind adj completely blind. Cf. **sand-blind.**

stonechat ('stəʊnˌtʃæt) n an Old World songbird having a black plumage with a reddish-brown breast. [C18: from its cry, which sounds like clattering pebbles]

stone-cold adj **1** completely cold. **2 stone-cold sober.** completely sober.

stonecrop ('stəʊnˌkrɒp) n any of various N temperate plants having fleshy leaves and typically red, yellow, or white flowers.

★ people and places

stone curlew *n* any of several brownish shore birds having a large head and eyes. Also called: **thick-knee**.

stonecutter ('stəʊnˌkʌtə) *n* **1** a person who is skilled in cutting and carving stone. **2** a machine used to dress stone.
▸ 'stone,cutting *n*

stoned (stəʊnd) *adj Sl.* under the influence of drugs or alcohol.

stone-deaf *adj* completely deaf.

stonefish ('stəʊnˌfɪʃ) *n, pl* **stonefish** *or* **stonefishes**. a venomous tropical marine fish that resembles a piece of rock on the seabed.

stonefly ('stəʊnˌflaɪ) *n, pl* **stoneflies**. any of various insects, in which the larvae are aquatic, living beneath stones.

stone fruit *n* the nontechnical name for **drupe**.

Stonehenge ★ (ˌstəʊn'hɛndʒ) *n* a prehistoric ruin in S England, in Wiltshire on Salisbury Plain: constructed over the period of roughly 2500–1500 B.C.; one of the most important megalithic monuments in Europe; believed to have had religious and astronomical purposes.

stonemason ('stəʊnˌmeɪsᵊn) *n* a person who is skilled in preparing stone for building.
▸ 'stone,masonry *n*

stone pine *n* a pine tree with a short bole and radiating branches forming an umbrella shape.

Stones ★ (stəʊnz) *pl n* **the.** See **Rolling Stones.**

stone's throw *n* a short distance.

stonewall (ˌstəʊn'wɔːl) *vb* **1** (*intr*) *Cricket.* (of a batsman) to play defensively. **2** to obstruct (an investigation, etc.), esp. by giving uncommunicative answers to questioning. **3** to obstruct or hinder (parliamentary business).
▸ ,stone'waller *n*

stoneware ('stəʊnˌwɛə) *n* **1** a hard opaque pottery, fired at a very high temperature. ◆ *adj* **2** made of stoneware.

stonewashed ('stəʊnˌwɒʃt) *adj* (of clothes or fabric) given a worn faded look by being subjected to the abrasive action of many small pieces of pumice.

stonework ('stəʊnˌwɜːk) *n* **1** any structure or part of a building made of stone. **2** the process of dressing or setting stones.
▸ 'stone,worker *n*

stonkered ('stɒŋkəd) *adj Sl.* completely exhausted or beaten. [C20: from *stonker* to beat, from ?]

stony *or* **stoney** ('stəʊnɪ) *adj* **stonier, stoniest. 1** of or resembling stone. **2** abounding in stone or stones. **3** unfeeling or obdurate. **4** short for **stony-broke.**
▸ 'stonily *adv* ▸ 'stoniness *n*

stony-broke *adj Brit. sl.* completely without money; penniless.

stony-hearted *adj* unfeeling; hardhearted.
▸ ,stony-'heartedness *n*

stood (stʊd) *vb* the past tense and past participle of **stand.**

stooge (stuːdʒ) *n* **1** an actor who feeds lines to a comedian or acts as his butt. **2** *Sl.* someone who is taken advantage of by another. ◆ *vb* **stooges, stooging, stooged. 3** (*intr*) *Sl.* to act as a stooge. [C20: from ?]

stook (stuːk) *n* **1** a number of sheaves set upright in a field to dry with their heads together. ◆ *vb* **2** (*tr*) to set up (sheaves) in stooks. [C15: var. of *stouk*, of Gmc origin]
▸ 'stooker *n*

stool (stuːl) *n* **1** a backless seat or footrest consisting of a small flat piece of wood, etc., resting on three or four legs, a pedestal, etc. **2** a rootstock or base of a plant from which shoots, etc., are produced. **3** a cluster of shoots growing from such a base. **4** *Chiefly US.* a decoy used in hunting. **5** waste matter evacuated from the bowels. **6** a lavatory seat. **7** (in W Africa, esp. Ghana) a chief's throne. **8 fall between two stools. 8a** to fail through vacillation between two alternatives. **8b** to be in an unsatisfactory situation through not belonging to either of two categories or groups. ◆ *vb* (*intr*) **9** (of a plant) to send up shoots from the base of the stem, rootstock, etc. **10** to lure wildfowl with a decoy. [OE *stōl*]

stool ball *n* a game resembling cricket, still played by girls and women in Sussex, England.

stool pigeon *n* **1** an informer for the police. **2** *Sl.* a person acting as a decoy. [C19: from use of pigeon fixed to a stool as a decoy]

stoop¹ (stuːp) *vb* (*mainly intr*) **1** (*also tr*) to bend (the body) forward and downward. **2** to carry oneself with head and shoulders habitually bent forward. **3** (often foll. by *to*) to abase or degrade oneself. **4** (often foll. by *to*) to condescend; deign. **5** (of a bird of prey) to swoop down. ◆ *n* **6** the act, position, or characteristic of stooping. **7** a lowering from a position of dignity or superiority. **8** a downward swoop, esp. of a bird of prey. [OE *stūpan*]
▸ 'stooping *adj*

stoop² (stuːp) *n US.* an open porch or small platform with steps leading up to it at the entrance to a building. [C18: from Du. *stoep*, of Gmc origin]

stop (stɒp) *vb* **stops, stopping, stopped. 1** to cease from doing or being (something); discontinue. **2** to cause (something moving) to halt or (of something moving) to come to a halt. **3** (*tr*) to prevent the continuance or completion of. **4** (*tr*; often foll. by *from*) to prevent or restrain: *to stop George from fighting.* **5** (*tr*) to keep back: *to stop supplies.* **6** (*tr*) to intercept or hinder in transit: *to stop a letter.* **7** (*tr*; often foll. by *up*) to block or plug, esp. so as to close: *to stop up a pipe.* **8** (*tr*; often foll. by *up*) to fill a hole or opening in: *to stop up a wall.* **9** (*tr*) to staunch or stem: *to stop a wound.* **10** (*tr*) to instruct a bank not to honour (a cheque). **11** (*tr*) to deduct (money) from pay. **12** (*tr*) *Brit.* to provide with punctuation. **13** (*tr*) *Boxing.* to beat (an opponent) by a knockout. **14** (*tr*) *Inf.* to receive (a blow, hit, etc.). **15** (*intr*) to stay or rest: *we stopped at the Robinsons'.* **16** (*tr*) *Rare.* to defeat, beat, or kill. **17** (*tr*) *Music.* **17a** to alter the vibrating length of (a string on a violin, guitar, etc.) by pressing down on it at some point with the finger. **17b** to alter the vibrating length of an air column in a wind instrument by closing (a finger hole, etc.). **17c** to produce (a note) in this manner. **18** *Bridge.* to have a protecting card or winner in (a suit in which one's opponents are strong). **19 stop at nothing.** to be prepared to do anything; be unscrupulous or ruthless. ◆ *n* **20** an arrest of movement or progress. **21** the act of stopping or the state of being stopped. **22** a place where something halts or pauses: *a bus stop.* **23** a stay in or as if in the course of a journey. **24** the act or an instance of blocking or obstructing. **25** a plug or stopper. **26** a block, screw, etc., that prevents, limits, or terminates the motion of a mechanism or moving part. **27** *Brit.* a punctuation mark, esp. a full stop. **28** *Music.* **28a** the act of stopping the string, finger hole, etc., of an instrument. **28b** a set of organ pipes or harpsichord strings that may be allowed to sound as a group by muffling or silencing all other such sets. **28c** a knob, lever, or handle on an organ, etc., that is operated to allow sets of pipes to sound. **28d** an analogous device on a harpsichord or other instrument with variable registers, such as an electronic instrument. **29 pull out all the stops. 29a** to play at full volume. **29b** to spare no effort. **30** Also called: **stop consonant.** *Phonetics.* any of a class of consonants articulated by first making a complete closure at some point of the vocal tract and then releasing it abruptly with audible plosion. **31** Also called: **f-stop.** *Photog.* **31a** a setting of the aperture of a camera lens, calibrated to the corresponding f-number. **31b** another name for **diaphragm** (sense 4). **32** Also called: **stopper.** *Bridge.* a protecting card or winner in a suit in which one's opponents are strong.
◆ See also **stop off, stop out, stopover.** [C14: from OE *stoppian* (unattested), as in *forstoppian* to plug the ear, ult. from LL *stuppāre* to stop with tow, from L *stuppa* tow, from Gk *stuppē*]
▸ 'stoppable *adj*

stopbank ('stɒpˌbæŋk) *n NZ.* an embankment to prevent flooding.

stop bath *n* a weakly acidic solution used to stop the action of a developer on a film, plate, or paper before the material is immersed in fixer.

stopcock ('stɒpˌkɒk) *n* a valve used to control or stop the flow of a fluid in a pipe.

stope (stəʊp) *n* **1** a steplike excavation made in a mine to extract ore. ◆ *vb* **stopes, stoping, stoped. 2** to mine (ore, etc.) in stopes. [C18: prob. from Low G *stope*]

Stopes ★ (stəʊps) *n* **Marie Carmichael.** 1880–1958, British pioneer of birth control, who established the first clinic in Britain (1921).

stopgap ('stɒp,gæp) *n* **a** a temporary substitute. **b** (*as modifier*): *a stopgap programme.*

stop-go *adj Brit.* (of economic policy) characterized by deliberate alternate expansion and contraction of aggregate demand in an effort to curb inflation and eliminate balance-of-payments deficits, and yet maintain full employment.

stoplight ('stɒp,laɪt) *n* **1** a red light on a traffic signal indicating that vehicles or pedestrians coming towards it should stop. **2** another word for **brake light.**

stop-loss *adj Business.* of or relating to an order to a broker in a commodity or security market to close an open position at a specified price in order to limit any loss.

stop off *vb also* **stop in,** (esp. US) **stop by. 1** (*intr, adv; often foll. by at*) to halt and call somewhere, as on a visit or errand, esp. en route to another place. ◆ *n* **stopoff. 2a** a break in a journey. **2b** (*as modifier*): *stopoff point.*

stop out *vb* (*adv*) **1** (*tr*) to cover (part of the area) of a piece of cloth, printing plate, etc., to prevent it from being dyed, etched, etc. **2** (*intr*) to remain out of a house, esp. overnight.

stopover ('stɒp,əʊvə) *n* **1** a stopping place on a journey. ◆ *vb* **stop over. 2** (*intr, adv*) to make a stopover.

stoppage ('stɒpɪdʒ) *n* **1** the act of stopping or the state of being stopped. **2** something that stops or blocks. **3** a deduction of money, as from pay. **4** an organized cessation of work, as during a strike.

stoppage time *n Soccer, rugby, etc.* another name for **injury time.**

Stoppard ★ ('stɒpɑːd) *n* **Sir Tom.** born 1937, British playwright, born in Czechoslovakia: his works include *Rosencrantz and Guildenstern are Dead* (1967), *Jumpers* (1972), and *Invention of Love* (1997).

stopped (stɒpt) *adj* (of a pipe, esp. an organ pipe) closed at one end and thus sounding an octave lower than an open pipe of the same length.

stopper ('stɒpə) *n* **1** Also called: **stopple.** a plug or bung for closing a bottle, pipe, duct, etc. **2** a person or thing that stops or puts an end to something. **3** *Bridge.* another name for **stop** (sense 32). ◆ *vb* **4** (*tr*) Also: **stopple.** to close or fit with a stopper.

stopping ('stɒpɪŋ) *n* **1** Brit. inf. a dental filling. ◆ *adj* **2** *Chiefly Brit.* making many stops in a journey: *a stopping train.*

stop press *n Brit.* **1** news items inserted into a newspaper after the printing has been started. **2** the space regularly left blank for this.

stopwatch ('stɒp,wɒtʃ) *n* a type of watch used for timing sporting events, etc., accurately, having a device for stopping the hands instantly.

storage ('stɔːrɪdʒ) *n* **1** the act of storing or the state of being stored. **2** space or an area reserved for storing. **3** a charge made for storing. **4** *Computing.* **4a** the act or process of storing information in a computer memory or on a disk, etc. **4b** (*as modifier*): *storage capacity.*

storage battery *n* another name (esp. US) for **accumulator** (sense 1).

storage capacity *n* the maximum number of bits, bytes, words, etc., that can be held in a memory system such as that of a computer or of the brain.

storage device *n* a piece of computer equipment, such as a magnetic tape, disk, drum, etc., in or on which information can be stored.

storage heater *n* an electric device capable of accumulating and radiating heat generated by off-peak electricity.

storax ('stɔːræks) *n* **1** any of numerous trees or shrubs of tropical and subtropical regions, having drooping showy white flowers. **2** a vanilla-scented solid resin obtained from one of these trees, formerly used as incense and in perfumery and medicine. **3** a liquid aromatic balsam obtained from liquidambar trees and used in perfumery and medicine. [C14: via LL from Gk *sturax*]

store (stɔː) *vb* **stores, storing, stored. 1** (*tr*) to keep, set aside, or accumulate for future use. **2** (*tr*) to place in a warehouse, depository, etc., for safekeeping. **3** (*tr*) to supply, provide, or stock. **4** (*intr*) to be put into storage. **5** *Computing.* to enter or retain (information) in a storage device. ◆ *n* **6a** an establishment for the retail sale of goods and services. **6b** (*in combination*): *storefront.* **7** a large supply or stock kept for future use. **8** short for **department store. 9a** a storage place such as a warehouse or depository. **9b** (*in combination*): *storeman.* **10** the state of being stored (esp. in **in store**). **11** a large amount or quantity. **12** *Computers, chiefly Brit.* another name for **memory** (sense 7). **13 in store.** forthcoming or imminent. **14 lay, put,** or **set store by.** to value or reckon as important. ◆ *adj* **15** (of cattle, sheep, etc.) bought lean to be fattened up for market. ◆ See also **stores.** [C13: from OF *estor*, from *estorer* to restore, from L *instaurāre* to refresh]
▸ **'storable** *adj*

Store Bælt ★ ('sdɔːrə 'bɛld) *n* the Danish name for the **Great Belt.**

store card *n* another name for **charge card.**

storehouse ('stɔː,haʊs) *n* a place where things are stored.

storekeeper ('stɔː,kiːpə) *n* a manager, owner, or keeper of a store.
▸ **'store,keeping** *n*

store of value *n Econ.* the function of money that enables goods and services to be paid for a considerable time after they have been acquired.

storeroom ('stɔː,ruːm, -,rʊm) *n* **1** a room in which things are stored. **2** room for storing.

stores (stɔːz) *pl n* supply or stock of something, esp. essentials, for a specific purpose.

storey *or esp. US* **story** ('stɔːrɪ) *n, pl* **storeys** *or* **stories. 1** a floor or level of a building. **2** a set of rooms on one level. [C14: from Anglo-L *historia*, picture, from L: narrative, prob. from the pictures on medieval windows]

Storey ★ ('stɔːrɪ) *n* **David** (**Malcolm**). born 1933, British novelist and dramatist. His works include the novel *This Sporting Life* (1960) and the plays *Home* (1970) and *Stages* (1992).

storeyed *or US* **storied** ('stɔːrɪd) *adj* **a** having a storey or storeys. **b** (*in combination*): *a two-storeyed house.*

storied ('stɔːrɪd) *adj* **1** recorded in history or in a story. **2** decorated with narrative scenes.

stork (stɔːk) *n* any of a family of large wading birds, chiefly of warm regions of the Old World, having very long legs and a long stout pointed bill, and typically having a white-and-black plumage. [OE *storc*]

storksbill ('stɔːks,bɪl) *n* a plant related to the geranium, having pink or reddish-purple flowers and fruits with a beaklike process.

storm (stɔːm) *n* **1a** a violent weather condition of strong winds, rain, hail, thunder, lightning, blowing sand, snow, etc. **1b** (*as modifier*): *storm cloud.* **1c** (*in combination*): *stormproof.* **2** *Meteorol.* a wind of force 10 on the Beaufort scale, reaching speeds of 55 to 63 mph. **3** a strong or violent reaction: *a storm of protest.* **4** a direct assault on a stronghold. **5** a heavy discharge or rain, as of bullets or missiles. **6** short for **storm window. 7** storm in a teacup. *Brit.* a violent fuss or disturbance over a trivial matter. **8 take by storm. 8a** to capture or overrun by a violent assault. **8b** to overwhelm and enthral. ◆ *vb* **9** to attack or capture (something) suddenly and violently. **10** (*intr*) to be vociferously angry. **11** (*intr*) to move or rush violently or angrily. **12** (*intr; with it* as subject) to rain, hail, or snow hard and be very windy, often with thunder and lightning. [OE]

stormbound ('stɔːm,baʊnd) *adj* detained or harassed by storms.

storm centre *n* **1** the centre of a cyclonic storm, etc., where pressure is lowest. **2** the centre of any disturbance or trouble.

storm cloud *n* **1** a heavy dark cloud presaging rain or a storm. **2** a herald of disturbance, anger, etc.: *the storm clouds of war.*

storm-cock *n* another name for **mistle thrush.**

storm cone *n Brit.* a canvas cone hoisted as a warning of high winds.

storm door *n* an additional door outside an ordinary door, providing extra insulation against wind, cold, rain, etc.

storming ('stɔːmɪŋ) *adj Inf.* characterized by or displaying dynamism, speed, and energy: *a storming performance.*

storm lantern *n* another name for **hurricane lamp.**

Stormont ★ ('stɔːmənt) *n* a suburb of Belfast: site of Parliament House (1928–30), formerly the seat of the parliament of Northern Ireland (1922–72) and (from 1998) seat of the Northern Ireland Assembly; Stormont House, formerly the residence of the prime minister of Northern Ireland; and Stormont Castle.

storm trooper *n* **1** a member of the Nazi SA. **2** a member of a force of shock troops.

storm window *n* **1** an additional window fitted outside an ordinary window to provide insulation against wind, cold, rain, etc. **2** a type of dormer window.

stormy ('stɔːmɪ) *adj* **stormier, stormiest. 1** characterized by storms. **2** involving or characterized by violent disturbance or emotional outburst.
▸ **'stormily** *adv* ▸ **'storminess** *n*

stormy petrel *n* **1** Also called: **storm petrel.** any of various small petrels typically having dark plumage and paler underparts. **2** a person who brings or portends trouble.

Stornoway ★ ('stɔːnə,weɪ) *n* a port in NW Scotland, on the E coast of Lewis in the Outer Hebrides, administrative centre of the Western Isles. Pop.: 5975 (1991).

Storting *or* **Storthing** ('stɔːtɪŋ) *n* the parliament of Norway. [C19: Norwegian, from *stor* great + *thing* assembly]

story[1] ('stɔːrɪ) *n, pl* **stories. 1** a narration of a chain of events told or written in prose or verse. **2** Also called: **short story.** a piece of fiction, briefer and usually less detailed than a novel. **3** Also called: **story line.** the plot of a book, film, etc. **4** an event that could be the subject of a narrative. **5** a report or statement on a matter or event. **6** the event or material for such a report. **7** *Inf.* a lie, fib, or untruth. **8 cut** (*or* **make**) **a long story short.** to leave out details in a narration. **9 the same old story.** *Inf.* the familiar or regular course of events. **10 the story goes.** it is commonly said or believed. ◆ *vb* **stories, storying, storied.** (*tr*) **11** to decorate (a pot, wall, etc.) with scenes from history or legends. [C13: from Anglo-F *estorie*, from L *historia*; see HISTORY]

story[2] ('stɔːrɪ) *n, pl* **stories.** another spelling (esp. US) of **storey.**

storyboard ('stɔːrɪ,bɔːd) *n* (in films, television, etc.) a series of sketches or photographs showing the sequence of shots or images planned for a film.

storybook ('stɔːrɪ,bʊk) *n* **1** a book containing stories, esp. for children. ◆ *adj* **2** unreal or fantastic: *a storybook world.*

storyteller ('stɔːrɪ,telə) *n* **1** a person who tells stories. **2** *Inf.* a liar.
▸ **'story,telling** *n*

Stoss ★ (*German* ʃtoːs) *n Viet* (faɪət). ?1445–1533, German Gothic sculptor and woodcarver. His masterpiece is the high altar in the Church of St Mary, Cracow (1477–89).

stoup *or* **stoop** (stuːp) *n* **1** a small basin for holy water. **2** *Dialect.* a bucket or cup. [C14 (in the sense: bucket): from ON]

Stour ★ ('staʊə) *n* any of several rivers in England, including the Great Stour in Kent.

Stourbridge ★ ('staʊə,brɪdʒ) *n* an industrial town in W central England, in the West Midlands. Pop.: 55 624 (1991).

stoush (staʊʃ) *Austral. & NZ sl.* ◆ *vb* **1** (*tr*) to hit or punch. ◆ *n* **2** fighting, violence, or a fight. [C19: from ?]

stout (staʊt) *adj* **1** solidly built or corpulent. **2** (*prenominal*) resolute or valiant: *stout fellow.* **3** strong, sub-

stantial, and robust. **4 a stout heart.** courage; resolution. ◆ *n* **5** strong porter highly flavoured with malt. [C14: from OF *estout* bold, of Gmc origin]
▸ **'stoutly** *adv* ▸ **'stoutness** *n*

Stout ★ (staʊt) *n* Sir **Robert.** 1844–1930, New Zealand statesman, born in Scotland: prime minister of New Zealand (1884–87).

stouthearted (,staʊt'hɑːtɪd) *adj* valiant; brave.
▸ **,stout'heartedly** *adv* ▸ **,stout'heartedness** *n*

stove[1] (staʊv) *n* **1** another word for **cooker** (sense 1). **2** any heating apparatus, such as a kiln. [OE *stofa* bathroom]

stove[2] (staʊv) *vb* a past tense and past participle of **stave.**

stove enamel *n* a type of enamel made heatproof by treatment in a stove.

stovepipe ('staʊv,paɪp) *n* **1** a pipe that serves as a flue to a stove. **2** Also called: **stovepipe hat.** a man's tall silk hat.

stow (staʊ) *vb* (*tr*) **1** (often foll. by *away*) to pack or store. **2** to fill by packing. **3** *Naut.* to pack or put away (cargo, sails, etc.). **4** to have enough room for. **5** (*usually imperative*) *Brit. sl.* to cease from: *stow your noise!* [OE *stōwian* to keep, from *stōw* a place]

Stow ★ (staʊ) *n* **John.** 1525–1605, English antiquary, noted for his *Survey of London and Westminster* (1598; 1603).

stowage ('staʊɪdʒ) *n* **1** space, room, or a charge for stowing goods. **2** the act or an instance of stowing or the state of being stowed. **3** something that is stowed.

stowaway ('staʊə,weɪ) *n* **1** a person who hides aboard a vehicle, ship, or aircraft in order to gain free passage. ◆ *vb* **stow away. 2** (*intr, adv*) to travel in such a way.

Stowe ★ (staʊ) *n* **Harriet Elizabeth Beecher.** 1811–96, US writer, whose bestselling novel *Uncle Tom's Cabin* (1852) contributed to the antislavery cause.

STP *abbrev. for:* **1** Professor of Sacred Theology. [from L: *Sanctae Theologiae Professor*] **2** *Trademark.* scientifically treated petroleum: an oil substitute promising renewed power for an internal-combustion engine. **3** standard temperature and pressure. ◆ *n* **4** a synthetic hallucinogenic drug related to mescaline. [from humorous reference to the extra power resulting from scientifically treated petroleum]

Strabane ★ (strə'bæn) *n* a district of W Northern Ireland, bordering the Irish Republic: agriculture, textiles. Administrative centre: Strabane. Pop.: 36 141 (1991). Area: 862 sq. km (333 sq. miles).

strabismus (strə'bɪzməs) *n* abnormal alignment of one or both eyes, characterized by a turning inwards or outwards from the nose: caused by paralysis of an eye muscle, etc. Also called: **squint.** [C17: via NL from Gk *strabismos*, from *strabizein* to squint, from *strabos* crosseyed]
▸ **stra'bismal, stra'bismic,** *or* **stra'bismical** *adj*

Strabo ★ ('streɪbəʊ) *n* ?63 B.C.–?23 A.D., Greek geographer and historian, noted for his *Geographica.*

Strachey ★ ('streɪtʃɪ) *n* (**Giles**) **Lytton.** 1880–1932, British biographer, best known for *Eminent Victorians* (1918) and *Queen Victoria* (1921).

straddle ('stræd'l) *vb* **straddles, straddling, straddled. 1** (*tr*) to have one leg, part, or support on each side of. **2** (*tr*) *US & Canad. inf.* to be in favour of both sides of (something). **3** (*intr*) to stand, walk, or sit with the legs apart. **4** (*tr*) to spread (the legs) apart. **5** *Gunnery.* to fire a number of shots slightly beyond and slightly short of (a target) to determine the correct range. **6** (*intr*) (in poker, of the second player after the dealer) to double the ante before looking at one's cards. ◆ *n* **7** the act or position of straddling. **8** a noncommittal attitude or stand. **9** *Business.* a contract or option permitting its purchaser either to sell or buy securities or commodities within a specified period of time at specified prices. **10** *Athletics.* a high-jumping technique in which the body is parallel with the bar and the legs straddle it at the highest point of the jump. **11** (in poker) the stake put up after the ante in poker by the second player after the dealer. [C16: from obs. *strad-* (OE *strode*), past stem of STRIDE]
▸ **'straddler** *n*

Stradivari ★ (ˌstrædɪˈvɑːrɪ) n **Antonio** (anˈtɔːnjo). ?1644–1737, Italian violin, viola, and cello maker.

Stradivarius (ˌstrædɪˈvɛərɪəs) n any of a number of violins manufactured by Antonio Stradivari or his family. Often shortened to (informal) **Strad**.

strafe (streɪf, strɑːf) vb **strafes, strafing, strafed**. (tr) **1** to machine-gun (troops, etc.) from the air. **2** Sl. to punish harshly. ♦ n **3** an act or instance of strafing. [C20: from G strafen to punish]
▶ ˈstrafer n

Strafford ★ (ˈstræfəd) n **Thomas Wentworth**, Earl of. 1593–1641, English statesman. Lord deputy of Ireland (1632–39) and a chief adviser to Charles I, he was impeached by Parliament and executed.

straggle (ˈstræg³l) vb **straggles, straggling, straggled**. (intr) **1** to go, come, or spread in a rambling or irregular way. **2** to linger behind or wander from a main line or part. [C14: from ?]
▶ ˈstraggler n ▶ ˈstraggly adj

straight (streɪt) adj **1** not curved or crooked; continuing in the same direction without deviating. **2** straightforward, outright, or candid: a straight rejection. **3** even, level, or upright. **4** in keeping with the facts; accurate. **5** honest, respectable, or reliable. **6** accurate or logical: straight reasoning. **7** continuous; uninterrupted. **8** (esp. of an alcoholic drink) undiluted; neat. **9** not crisp, kinked, or curly: straight hair. **10** correctly arranged; orderly. **11** (of a play, acting style, etc.) straightforward or serious. **12** Boxing. (of a blow) delivered with an unbent arm: a straight left. **13** (of the cylinders of an internal-combustion engine) in line, rather than in a V-formation or in some other arrangement: a straight eight. **14** a slang word for **heterosexual**. **15** Inf. no longer owing or being owed something: if you buy the next round we'll be straight. **16** Sl. conventional in views, customs, appearance, etc. **17** Sl. not using narcotics. ♦ adv **18** in a straight line or direct course. **19** immediately; at once: he came straight back. **20** in an even, level, or upright position. **21** without cheating, lying, or unreliability: tell it to me straight. **22** continuously; uninterruptedly. **23** (often foll. by out) frankly; candidly: he told me straight out. **24 go straight**. Inf. to reform after having been dishonest or a criminal. ♦ n **25** the state of being straight. **26** a straight line, form, part, or position. **27** Brit. a straight part of a racetrack. **28** Poker. **28a** five cards that are in sequence irrespective of suit. **28b** a hand containing such a sequence. **28c** (as modifier): a straight flush. **29** Sl. a conventional person. **30** a slang word for **heterosexual**. **31** Sl. a cigarette containing only tobacco, without marijuana, etc. [C14: from p.p. of OE streccan to stretch]
▶ ˈstraightly adv ▶ ˈstraightness n

straight and narrow n Inf. the proper, honest, and moral path of behaviour.

straight angle n an angle of 180°.

straightaway adv (ˌstreɪtəˈweɪ). also **straight away**. **1** at once. ♦ n (ˈstreɪtəˌweɪ). **2** the US word for **straight** (sense 27).

straight chair n a straight-backed side chair.

straightedge (ˈstreɪtˌɛdʒ) n a stiff strip of wood or metal with one edge straight, used for ruling and testing straight lines.

straighten (ˈstreɪt³n) vb (sometimes foll. by up or out) **1** to make or become straight. **2** (tr) to make neat or tidy.
▶ ˈstraightener n

straighten out vb (adv) **1** to make or become less complicated or confused. **2** US & Canad. to reform or become reformed.

straight face n a serious facial expression, esp. one that conceals the impulse to laugh.
▶ ˌstraight-ˈfaced adj

straight fight n a contest between two candidates only.

straight flush n (in poker) five consecutive cards of the same suit.

straightforward (ˌstreɪtˈfɔːwəd) adj **1** (of a person) honest, frank, or simple. **2** Chiefly Brit. (of a task, etc.) simple; easy. ♦ adv, adj **3** in a straight course.
▶ ˌstraightˈforwardly adv ▶ ˌstraightˈforwardness n

straightjacket (ˈstreɪtˌdʒækɪt) n a less common spelling of **straitjacket**.

straight-laced adj a variant spelling of **strait-laced**.

straight man n a subsidiary actor who acts as stooge to a comedian.

straight-out adj US inf. **1** complete; thoroughgoing. **2** frank or honest.

straight razor n another name for **cut-throat** (sense 2).

straightway (ˈstreɪtˌweɪ) adv Arch. at once.

strain[1] (streɪn) vb **1** to draw or be drawn taut; stretch tight. **2** to exert, tax, or use (resources) to the utmost extent. **3** to injure or damage or be injured or damaged by overexertion: he strained himself. **4** to deform or be deformed as a result of a stress. **5** (intr) to make intense or violent efforts; strive. **6** to subject or be subjected to mental tension or stress. **7** to pour or pass (a substance) or (of a substance) to be poured or passed through a sieve, filter, or strainer. **8** (tr) to draw off or remove (one part of a substance or mixture from another) by or as if by filtering. **9** (tr) to clasp tightly; hug. **10** (intr; foll. by at) to push, pull, or work with violent exertion (upon). ♦ n **11** the act or an instance of straining. **12** the damage resulting from excessive exertion. **13** an intense physical or mental effort. **14** (often pl) Music. a theme, melody, or tune. **15** a great demand on the emotions, resources, etc. **16** a way of speaking; tone of voice: don't go on in that strain. **17** tension or tiredness resulting from overwork, worry, etc.; stress. **18** Physics. the change in dimension of a body under load expressed as the ratio of the total deflection or change in dimension to the original unloaded dimension. [C13: from OF estreindre to press together, from L stringere to bind tightly]

strain[2] (streɪn) n **1** the main body of descendants from one ancestor. **2** a group of organisms within a species or variety, distinguished by one or more minor characteristics. **3** a variety of bacterium or fungus, esp. one used for a culture. **4** a streak; trace. **5** Arch. a kind, type, or sort. [OE strēon]

strained (streɪnd) adj **1** (of an action, expression, etc.) not natural or spontaneous. **2** (of an atmosphere, relationship, etc.) not relaxed; tense.

strainer (ˈstreɪnə) n **1** a sieve used for straining sauces, vegetables, tea, etc. **2** a gauze or simple filter used to strain liquids.

strait (streɪt) n **1** (often pl) a narrow channel of the sea linking two larger areas of sea. **2** (often pl) a position of acute difficulty (often in **in dire** or **desperate straits**). **3** Arch. a narrow place or passage. ♦ adj **4** Arch. (of spaces, etc.) affording little room. [C13: from OF estreit narrow, from L strictus constricted, from stringere to bind tightly]
▶ ˈstraitly adv ▶ ˈstraitness n

straiten (ˈstreɪt³n) vb **1** (tr; usually passive) to embarrass or distress, esp. financially. **2** (tr) to limit, confine, or restrict. **3** Arch. to make or become narrow.

straitjacket (ˈstreɪtˌdʒækɪt) n **1** Also: **straightjacket**. a jacket made of strong canvas material with long sleeves for binding the arms of violent prisoners or mental patients. **2** a restriction or limitation. ♦ vb **3** (tr) to confine in or as if in a straitjacket.

strait-laced or **straight-laced** adj prudish or puritanical.

Straits Settlements ★ (streɪts) n (functioning as sing) (formerly) a British crown colony of SE Asia that included Singapore, Penang, Malacca, Labuan, and some smaller islands.

strake (streɪk) n **1a** a curved metal plate forming part of the metal rim on a wooden wheel. **1b** any metal plate let into a rubber tyre. **2** Also called: **streak**. Naut. one of a continuous range of planks or plates forming the side of a vessel. [C14: rel. to OE streccan to stretch]

Stralsund ★ (German ˈtraːlzʊnt) n a port in NE Germany, on a strait of the Baltic: one of the leading towns of the Hanseatic League. Pop.: 71 620 (1991).

stramonium (strəˈməʊnɪəm) n **1** a preparation of the dried leaves and flowers of the thorn apple, containing hyoscyamine and used as a drug to treat nervous disor-

---

★ people and places

ders. **2** another name for **thorn apple** (sense 1). [C17: from NL, from ?]

strand[1] (strænd) *vb* **1** to leave or drive (ships, fish, etc.) aground or ashore or (of ships, etc.) to be left or driven ashore. **2** (*tr; usually passive*) to leave helpless, as without transport, money, etc. ◆ *n* **3** *Chiefly poetic.* a shore or beach. [OE]

strand[2] (strænd) *n* **1** a set of or one of the individual fibres or threads of string, wire, etc., that form a rope, cable, etc. **2** a single length of string, hair, wool, wire, etc. **3** a string of pearls or beads. **4** a constituent element of something. ◆ *vb* **5** (*tr*) to form (a rope, cable, etc.) by winding strands together. [C15: from ?]

Strand ★ (strænd) *n* **the.** a street in W central London, parallel to the Thames: famous for its hotels and theatres.

strange (streɪndʒ) *adj* **1** odd, unusual, or extraordinary; peculiar. **2** not known, seen, or experienced before; unfamiliar. **3** not easily explained. **4** (usually foll. by *to*) inexperienced (in) or unaccustomed (to): *strange to a task*. **5** not of one's own kind, locality, etc.; alien; foreign. **6** shy; distant; reserved. **7 strange to say.** it is unusual or surprising (that). **8** *Physics.* **8a** denoting a particular flavour of quark. **8b** denoting or relating to a hypothetical form of matter composed of such quarks: *strange matter; a strange star.* ◆ *adv* **9** *Not standard.* in a strange manner. [C13: from OF *estrange*, from L *extrāneus* foreign; see EXTRANEOUS]
▸ **'strangely** *adv*

strangeness ('streɪndʒnɪs) *n* **1** the state or quality of being strange. **2** *Physics.* a property of certain elementary particles characterized by a quantum number (**strangeness number**) conserved in strong but not in weak interactions.

stranger ('streɪndʒə) *n* **1** any person whom one does not know. **2** a person who is new to a particular locality, from another region, town, etc. **3** a guest or visitor. **4** (foll. by *to*) a person who is unfamiliar (with) or new (to) something: *he is no stranger to computing.*

strangle ('stræŋg°l) *vb* **strangles, strangling, strangled.** (*tr*) **1** to kill by or by compressing the windpipe; throttle. **2** to prevent or inhibit the growth or development of: *to strangle originality.* **3** to suppress (an utterance) by or as if by swallowing suddenly: *to strangle a cry.* ◆ See also **strangles.** [C13: via OF, ult. from Gk *strangalē* a halter]
▸ **'strangler** *n*

stranglehold ('stræŋg°l,həʊld) *n* **1** a wrestling hold in which a wrestler's arms are pressed against his opponent's windpipe. **2** complete power or control over a person or situation.

strangles ('stræŋg°lz) *n* (*functioning as sing*) an acute infectious bacterial disease of horses, characterized by inflammation of the respiratory tract. Also called: **equine distemper.**

strangulate ('stræŋgjʊ,leɪt) *vb* **strangulates, strangulating, strangulated.** (*tr*) **1** to constrict (a hollow organ, vessel, etc.) so as to stop the flow of air, blood, etc., through it. **2** another word for **strangle.**
▸ **,strangu'lation** *n*

strangury ('stræŋgjʊrɪ) *n Pathol.* painful excretion of urine, drop by drop. [C14: from L *strangūria*, from Gk, from *stranx* a drop squeezed out + *ouron* urine]

Stranraer ★ (stræn'rɑː) *n* a market town in SW Scotland, in W Dumfries and Galloway: fishing port with a ferry service to Northern Ireland. Pop.: 11 348 (1991).

strap (stræp) *n* **1** a long strip of leather or similar material, for binding trunks, baggage, etc. **2** a strip of leather or similar material used for carrying, lifting, or holding. **3** a loop of leather, rubber, etc., suspended from the roof in a bus or train for standing passengers to hold on to. **4** a razor strop. **5** short for **shoulder strap. 6** *Business.* a triple option on a security or commodity consisting of one put option and two call options at the same price and for the same period. Cf. **strip**[2] (sense 4). **7** *Irish, derog. sl.* a shameless or promiscuous woman. **8 the strap.** a beating with a strap as a punishment. ◆ *vb* **straps, strapping, strapped.** (*tr*) **9** to tie or bind with a strap. **10** to beat with a

strap. **11** to sharpen with a strap or strop. [C16: var. of STROP]

straphanger ('stræp,hæŋə) *n Inf.* a passenger in a bus, train, etc., who has to travel standing, esp. holding on to a strap.
▸ **'strap,hanging** *n*

strapping ('stræpɪŋ) *adj* (*prenominal*) tall and sturdy. [C17: from STRAP (in the arch. sense: to work vigorously)]

strapwork ('stræp,wɜːk) *n Archit.* decorative work resembling interlacing straps.

Strasbourg ★ (*French* strasbur; *English* 'stræzbɜːg) *n* a city in NE France, on the Rhine: the chief French inland port; under German rule (1870–1918); university (1567); seat of the Council of Europe and of the European Parliament. Pop.: 255 937 (1990). German name: **Strassburg** ('ʃtrɑːsbʊrk).

strata ('strɑːtə) *n* a plural of **stratum.**

> **USAGE NOTE** *Strata* is sometimes wrongly used as a singular noun: *this stratum* (not *strata*) *of society is often disregarded.*

stratagem ('strætɪdʒəm) *n* a plan or trick, esp. to deceive an enemy. [C15: ult. from Gk *stratēgos* a general, from *stratos* an army + *agein* to lead]

strategic (strə'tiːdʒɪk) *or* **strategical** *adj* **1** of or characteristic of strategy. **2** important to strategy. **3** (of weapons, esp. missiles) directed against an enemy's homeland rather than used on a battlefield. Cf. **tactical.**
▸ **stra'tegically** *adv*

strategics (strə'tiːdʒɪks) *n* (*functioning as sing*) strategy, esp. in a military sense.

strategist ('strætɪdʒɪst) *n* a specialist or expert in strategy.

strategy ('strætɪdʒɪ) *n, pl* **strategies. 1** the art or science of the planning and conduct of a war. **2** a particular long-term plan for success, esp. in politics, business, etc. **3** a plan or stratagem. [C17: from F *stratégie*, from Gk *stratēgia* function of a general; see STRATAGEM]

Stratford-on-Avon *or* **Stratford-upon-Avon** ★ ('strætfəd-) *n* a market town in central England, in SW Warwickshire on the River Avon: the birthplace and burial place of William Shakespeare and home of the Royal Shakespeare Company; tourist centre. Pop.: 22 231 (1991).

strath (stræθ) *n Scot.* a flat river valley. [C16: from Scot. & Irish Gaelic *srath*]

Strathclyde Region ★ (stræθ'klaɪd) *n* a former local government region in W Scotland, formed in 1975 and replaced in 1996 by twelve council areas: Glasgow, Renfrewshire, East Renfrewshire, Inverclyde, North Lanarkshire, South Lanarkshire, Argyll and Bute, East Dunbartonshire, West Dunbartonshire, North Ayrshire, South Ayrshire, and East Ayrshire.

strathspey (stræθ'speɪ) *n* **1** a Scottish dance with gliding steps, slower than a reel. **2** a piece of music composed for or in the rhythm of this dance. [after *Strathspey*, valley of the river Spey]

strati- *combining form.* indicating stratum or strata: *stratigraphy.*

straticulate (strə'tɪkjʊlɪt, -,leɪt) *adj* (of a rock formation) composed of very thin even strata. [C19: from NL *strāticulum* (unattested), dim. of L *strātum* something strewn; see STRATUS]
▸ **stra,ticu'lation** *n*

stratify ('strætɪ,faɪ) *vb* **stratifies, stratifying, stratified. 1** to form or be formed in layers or strata. **2** *Sociol.* to divide (a society) into status groups or (of a society) to develop such groups. [C17: from F *stratifier*, from NL *stratificāre*, from L STRATUM]
▸ **,stratifi'cation** *n* ▸ **'strati,fied** *adj*

stratigraphy (strə'tɪgrəfɪ) *n* **1** the study of the composition, relative positions, etc., of rock strata in order to determine their geological history. **2** *Archaeol.* a vertical section through the earth showing the relative positions

of the human artefacts and therefore the chronology of successive levels of occupation.
 ▸ **stratigraphic** (ˌstrætɪ'græfɪk) or ˌ**strati'graphical** adj

stratocumulus (ˌstrætəʊ'kju:mjʊləs) n, pl **stratocumuli** (-ˌlaɪ). Meteorol. a uniform stretch of cloud containing dark grey globular masses.

stratopause ('strætə,pɔ:z) n Meteorol. the transitional zone of maximum temperature between the stratosphere and the mesosphere.

stratosphere ('strætə,sfɪə) n the atmospheric layer lying between the troposphere and the mesosphere, in which temperature generally increases with height.
 ▸ **stratospheric** (ˌstrætə'sfɛrɪk) or ˌ**strato'spherical** adj

stratum ('strɑːtəm) n, pl **strata** or **stratums**. 1 (usually pl) any of the distinct layers into which sedimentary rocks are divided. 2 Biol. a single layer of tissue or cells. 3 a layer of any material, esp. one of several parallel layers. 4 a layer of ocean or atmosphere either naturally or arbitrarily demarcated. 5 a level of a social hierarchy. [C16: via NL from L: something strewn, from sternere to scatter]
 ▸ **'stratal** adj

stratus ('streɪtəs) n, pl **strati** (-taɪ). a grey layer cloud. [C19: via NL from L: strewn, from sternere to extend]

Straus ★ (straʊs) n Oscar (ɔskar). 1870–1954, French composer, born in Austria, noted for such operettas as Waltz Dream (1907) and The Chocolate Soldier (1908).

Strauss ★ (straʊs; German ʃtraʊs) n 1 **David Friedrich** ('daːfrɪt 'fri:drɪç). 1808–74, German Protestant theologian, noted for his Life of Jesus (1835–36). 2 **Johann** (jo'han). 1804–49, Austrian composer, noted for his waltzes. 3 his son, **Johann**, called the Waltz King. 1825–99, Austrian composer, whose works include The Blue Danube Waltz (1867) and the operetta Die Fledermaus (1874). 4 **Richard** ('rɪçart). 1864–1949, German composer, noted esp. for his symphonic poems, including Till Eulenspiegel (1895), his operas, such as Der Rosenkavalier (1911), and his Four Last Songs (1948).

Stravinsky ★ (Russian stra'vinskij) n Igor Fyodorovich ('igərj 'fjɔdərəvitʃ). 1882–1971, US composer, born in Russia. He created ballet scores, such as The Firebird (1910), Petrushka (1911), and The Rite of Spring (1913), for Diaghilev. Later works include Requiem Canticles (1966).

straw (strɔː) n **1a** stalks of threshed grain, esp. of wheat, rye, oats, or barley, used in plaiting hats, baskets, etc., or as fodder. **1b** (as modifier): a straw hat. **2** a single dry or ripened stalk, esp. of a grass. **3** a long thin hollow paper or plastic tube, used for sucking up liquids into the mouth. **4** (usually used with a negative) anything of little value or importance: I wouldn't give a straw for our chances. **5** a measure or remedy that one turns to in desperation (esp. in **clutch** or **grasp at a straw** or **straws**). **6a** a pale yellow colour. **6b** (as adj): straw hair. **7 draw the short straw**. to be the person to whom an unpleasant task falls. **8 straw in the wind**. a hint or indication. **9 the last straw**. a small incident, setback, etc., that coming after others proves insufferable. [OE strēaw]
 ▸ **'strawy** adj

Straw ★ (strɔː) n Jack, full name John Whitaker Straw. born 1946, British Labour politician; Home Secretary from 1997.

strawberry ('strɔːbərɪ, -brɪ) n, pl **strawberries**. 1 any of various low-growing rosaceous plants which have red edible fruits and spread by runners. **2a** the fruit of any of these plants, consisting of a sweet fleshy receptacle bearing small seedlike parts (the true fruits). **2b** (as modifier): strawberry ice cream. **3a** a purplish-red colour. **3b** (as adj): strawberry shoes. [OE strēawberige; ?from the strawlike appearance of the runners]

strawberry blonde adj 1 (of hair) reddish blonde. ◆ n 2 a woman with such hair.

strawberry mark n a soft vascular red birthmark. Also called: **strawberry**.

strawberry tomato n 1 a tropical annual plant having bell-shaped whitish-yellow flowers and small edible round yellow berries. **2** the fruit of this plant, eaten fresh or made into preserves or pickles. ◆ Also called: **Cape gooseberry**.

strawberry tree n a S European evergreen tree having white or pink flowers and red strawberry-like berries. See also **arbutus**.

strawboard ('strɔːˌbɔːd) n a board made of compressed straw and adhesive.

strawflower ('strɔːˌflaʊə) n an Australian plant in which the coloured bracts retain their colour when the plant is dried. See also **immortelle**.

straw man n Chiefly US. 1 a figure of a man made from straw. **2** a person of little substance. **3** a person used as a cover for some dubious plan or enterprise.

straw poll or esp. US, Canad., & NZ. **vote** n an unofficial poll or vote taken to determine the opinion of a group or the public on some issue.

Strawson ★ ('strɔːsən) n Sir **Peter** (**Frederick**). born 1919, British philosopher. His early work deals with the relationship between language and logic, his later work with metaphysics. His books include The Bounds of Sense (1966) and Freedom and Resentment (1974).

strawweight ('strɔːˌweɪt) n **a** a professional boxer weighing not more than 47.6 kg (105 pounds). **b** (as modifier): the strawweight title. ◆ Also called: **miniflyweight**.

stray (streɪ) vb (intr) **1** to wander away, as from the correct path or from a given area. **2** to wander haphazardly. **3** to digress from the point, lose concentration, etc. **4** to deviate from certain moral standards. ◆ n **5a** a domestic animal, fowl, etc., that has wandered away from its place of keeping and is lost. **5b** (as modifier): stray dogs. **6** a lost or homeless person, esp. a child: waifs and strays. **7** an occurrence, specimen, etc., that is out of place or outside the usual pattern. ◆ adj **8** scattered, random, or haphazard. [C14: from OF estraier, from Vulgar L estragāre (unattested), from L extrā- outside + vagāri to roam]
 ▸ **'strayer** n

Strayhorn ★ ('streɪˌhɔːn) n **Billy**, full name William Strayhorn. 1915–67, US jazz composer and pianist, noted esp. for his association (1939–67) with Duke Ellington.

strays (streɪz) pl n **1** Also called: **stray capacitance**. Electronics. undesired capacitance in equipment. **2** another word for **static** (sense 8).

streak (stri:k) n **1** a long thin mark, stripe, or trace of some contrasting colour. **2** (of lightning) a sudden flash. **3** an element or trace, as of some quality or characteristic. **4** a strip, vein, or layer. **5** a short stretch or run, esp. of good or bad luck. **6** Inf. an act or the practice of running naked through a public place. ◆ vb **7** (tr) to mark or daub with a streak or streaks. **8** (intr) to form streaks or become streaked. **9** (intr) to move rapidly in a straight line. **10** (intr) Inf. to run naked through a public place in order to shock or amuse. [OE strica]
 ▸ **streaked** adj ▸ **'streaker** n ▸ **'streak,like** adj

streaky ('stri:kɪ) adj **streakier**, **streakiest**. **1** marked with streaks. **2** occurring in streaks. **3** (of bacon) having alternate layers of meat and fat. **4** of varying or uneven quality.
 ▸ **'streakiness** n

stream (stri:m) n **1** a small river; brook. **2** any steady flow of water or other fluid. **3** something that resembles a stream in moving continuously in a line or particular direction. **4** a rapid or unbroken flow of speech, etc.: a stream of abuse. **5** Brit., Austral., & NZ. any of several parallel classes of schoolchildren, or divisions of children within a class, grouped together because of similar ability. **6 go** (or **drift**) **with the stream**. to conform to the accepted standards. **7 on** (or **off**) **stream**. (of an industrial plant, manufacturing process, etc.) in (or not in) operation or production. ◆ vb **8** to emit or be emitted in a continuous flow: his nose streamed blood. **9** (intr) to move in unbroken succession, as a crowd of people, vehicles, etc. **10** (intr) to float freely or with a waving motion: bunting streamed in the wind. **11** (tr) to unfurl (a flag, etc.). **12** Brit. education. to group or divide (children) in streams. [OE]
 ▸ **'streamlet** n

streamer ('stri:mə) n **1** a long narrow flag or part of a flag. **2** a long narrow coiled ribbon of coloured paper that becomes unrolled when tossed. **3** a stream of light, esp. one appearing in some forms of the aurora. **4** Jour-

---

★ people and places

nalism. a large heavy headline printed across the width of a page. **5** *Computing.* another word for **tape streamer.**

streamline ('stri:m,laɪn) *n* **1** a contour on a body that offers the minimum resistance to a gas or liquid flowing around it. ◆ *vb* **streamlines, streamlining, streamlined. 2** (*tr*) to make streamlined.

streamlined ('stri:m,laɪnd) *adj* **1** offering or designed to offer the minimum resistance to the flow of a gas or liquid. **2** made more efficient, esp. by simplifying.

stream of consciousness *n* **1** *Psychol.* the continuous flow of ideas, thoughts, and feelings forming the content of an individual's consciousness. **2** a literary technique that reveals the flow of thoughts and feelings of characters through long passages of soliloquy.

streamy ('stri:mɪ) *adj* **streamier, streamiest.** *Chiefly poetic.* **1** (of an area, land, etc.) having many streams. **2** flowing or streaming.

Streep ★ (stri:p) *n* **Meryl**, original name *Mary Louise Streep.* born 1949, US actress. Her films include *Kramer vs Kramer* (1979), *The French Lieutenant's Woman* (1981), *Sophie's Choice* (1982), *Out of Africa* (1986), and *Dancing at Lughnasa* (1998).

street (stri:t) *n* **1a** a public road that is usually lined with buildings, esp. in a town: *Oxford Street.* **1b** (*as modifier*): *a street directory.* **2** the buildings lining a street. **3** the part of the road between the pavements, used by vehicles. **4** the people living, working, etc., in a particular street. **5** (*modifier*) of or relating to the urban counterculture. **6 on the streets. 6a** earning a living as a prostitute. **6b** homeless. **7** (**right**) **up one's street.** *Inf.* (just) what one knows or likes best. **8 streets ahead of.** *Inf.* superior to, more advanced than, etc. **9 streets apart.** *Inf.* markedly different. [OE *stræt*, from L *via strāta* paved way (*strāta,* from *strātus,* p.p. of *sternere* to stretch out)]

street Arab *n* *Literary & old-fashioned.* a homeless child, esp. one who survives by begging and stealing; urchin.

streetcar ('stri:t,kɑ:) *n* the usual US and Canad. name for **tram** (sense 1).

street credibility *n* a command of the style, knowledge, etc., associated with urban counter-culture. Often shortened to **street cred.**
▸ ,street-'credible *adj*

street cry *n* (*often pl*) the cry of a street hawker.

street furniture *n* pieces of equipment, such as street lights and pillar boxes, placed in the street for the benefit of the public.

street value *n* the monetary worth of a commodity, usually an illicit one, considered as the price it would fetch when sold to the ultimate user.

streetwalker ('stri:t,wɔ:kə) *n* a prostitute who solicits on the streets.
▸ 'street,walking *n, adj*

streetwise ('stri:t,waɪz) *adj* adept at surviving in an urban, poor, and often criminal environment.

Streicher ★ (*German* 'ʃtraɪçər) *n* **Julius** ('ju:lɪus). 1885–1946, German Nazi journalist and politician, who spread anti-Semitic propaganda as editor of *Der Stürmer* (1923–45). He was hanged as a war criminal.

Streisand ★ ('straɪsænd) *n* **Barbra.** born 1942, US singer, film actress, and film director: her films as an actress include *Funny Girl* (1968), *A Star is Born* (1976), and as actress and director *Yentl* (1983) and *The Mirror has Two Faces* (1996).

strelitzia (strɛ'lɪtsɪə) *n* any of various southern African perennial herbaceous plants, cultivated for their showy flowers: includes the bird-of-paradise flower. [C18: after Charlotte of Mecklenburg-*Strelitz* (1744–1818), queen of Great Britain & Ireland]

strength (strɛŋθ) *n* **1** the state or quality of being physically or mentally strong. **2** the ability to withstand or exert great force, stress, or pressure. **3** something regarded as beneficial or a source of power: *their chief strength is technology.* **4** potency, as of a drink, drug, etc. **5** power to convince; cogency: *the strength of an argument.* **6** degree of intensity or concentration of colour, light, sound, flavour, etc. **7** the full or part of the full complement as specified: *at full strength; below strength.* **8 from**

strength to strength. with ever-increasing success. **9 in strength.** in large numbers. **10 on the strength of.** on the basis of or relying upon. **11 the strength of.** *Austral. & NZ inf.* the essential facts about. [OE *strengthu*]

strengthen ('strɛŋθən) *vb* to make or become stronger.
▸ 'strengthener *n*

strenuous ('strɛnjʊəs) *adj* **1** requiring or involving the use of great energy or effort. **2** characterized by great activity, effort, or endeavour. [C16: from L *strēnuus* brisk]
▸ 'strenuously *adv* ▸ 'strenuousness *n*

strep (strɛp) *n* *Inf.* short for **streptococcus.**

strepitoso (,strɛpɪ'təʊsəʊ) *adv* *Music.* boisterously. [It.]

strepto- *combining form.* **1** indicating a shape resembling a twisted chain: *streptococcus.* **2** indicating streptococcus. [from Gk *streptos* twisted, from *strephein* to twist]

streptocarpus (,strɛptəʊ'kɑ:pəs) *n* any of various mostly African plants having spirally-twisted capsules. [C19: from NL, from Gk *streptos* twisted + *karpos* fruit]

streptococcus (,strɛptəʊ'kɒkəs) *n, pl* **streptococci** (-'kɒkaɪ; *US* -'kɒksaɪ). any spherical bacterium of the genus *Streptococcus,* typically occurring in chains and including many pathogenic species. Often shortened to **strep.**
▸ streptococcal (,strɛptəʊ'kɒk'l) *or* streptococcic (,strɛptəʊ'kɒksɪk) *adj*

streptomycin (,strɛptəʊ'maɪsɪn) *n* an antibiotic obtained from the bacterium *Streptomyces griseus:* used in the treatment of tuberculosis and other bacterial infections.

streptothricin (,strɛptəʊ'θraɪsɪn) *n* an antibiotic produced by the bacterium *Streptomyces lavendulae.*

Stresemann ★ (*German* 'ʃtreːsəman) *n* **Gustav.** 1878–1929, German statesman; chancellor (1923) and foreign minister (1923–29) of the Weimar Republic. He gained (1926) Germany's admission to the League of Nations and shared the Nobel peace prize (1926) with Aristide Briand.

stress (strɛs) *n* **1** special emphasis or significance. **2** mental, emotional, or physical strain or tension. **3** emphasis placed upon a syllable by pronouncing it more loudly than those that surround it. **4** such emphasis as part of a rhythm in music or poetry. **5** a syllable so emphasized. **6** *Physics.* **6a** force or a system of forces producing deformation or strain. **6b** the force acting per unit area. ◆ *vb* (*tr*) **7** to give emphasis or prominence to. **8** to pronounce (a word or syllable) more loudly than those that surround it. **9** to subject to stress. [C14 *stresse,* shortened from DISTRESS]
▸ 'stressful *adj*

-stress *suffix forming nouns.* indicating a woman who performs or is engaged in a certain activity: *songstress; seamstress.* [from -ST(E)R + -ESS]

stretch (strɛtʃ) *vb* **1** to draw out or extend or be drawn out or extended in length, area, etc. **2** to extend or be extended to an undue degree, esp. so as to distort or lengthen permanently. **3** to extend (the limbs, body, etc.). **4** (*tr*) to reach or suspend (a rope, etc.) from one place to another. **5** (*tr*) to draw tight; tighten. **6** (often foll. by *out, forward,* etc.) to reach or hold (out); extend. **7** (*intr;* usually foll. by *over*) to reach or extend in time: *the course stretched over three months.* **8** (*intr;* foll. by *for, over,* etc.) (of a region, etc.) to extend in length or area. **9** (*intr*) (esp. of a garment) to be capable of expanding, as to a larger size: *socks that will stretch.* **10** (*tr*) to put a great strain upon or extend to the limit. **11** to injure (a muscle, tendon, etc.) by means of a strain or sprain. **12** (*tr;* often foll. by *out*) to make do with (limited resources): *to stretch one's budget.* **13** (*tr*) *Inf.* to expand or elaborate (a story, etc.) beyond what is credible or acceptable. **14** (*tr; often passive*) to extend, as to the limit of one's abilities or talents. **15** *Arch. or sl.* to hang or be hanged by the neck. **16 stretch a point. 16a** to make a concession or exception not usually made. **16b** to exaggerate. ◆ *n* **17** the act of stretching or state of being stretched. **18** a large or continuous expanse or distance: *a stretch of water.* **19** extent in time, length, area, etc. **20a** capacity for being stretched, as in some garments. **20b** (*as modifier*): *stretch pants.* **21** the section or sections of a racecourse that are straight, esp. the final section leading to the finishing line. **22** *Sl.* a term of

imprisonment. **23 at a stretch.** *Chiefly Brit.* **23a** with some difficulty; by making a special effort. **23b** if really necessary or in extreme circumstances. **23c** at one time: *he sometimes read for hours at a stretch.* [OE *streccan*]
▸ '**stretchable** *adj* ▸ ,**stretcha'bility** *n*

stretcher ('strɛtʃə) *n* **1** a device for transporting the ill, wounded, or dead, consisting of a frame covered by canvas or other material. **2** a strengthening often decorative member joining the legs of a chair, table, etc. **3** the wooden frame on which canvas is stretched and fixed for oil painting. **4** a tie beam or brace used in a structural framework. **5** a brick or stone laid horizontally with its length parallel to the length of a wall. **6** *Rowing*. a fixed board across a boat on which an oarsman braces his feet. **7** *Austral. & NZ*. a camp bed. ◆ *vb* (*tr*) **8** to transport (a sick or injured person) on a stretcher.

stretcher-bearer *n* a person who helps to carry a stretcher, esp. in wartime.

stretch limo *n Inf.* a limousine that has been lengthened to provide extra seating accommodation and more legroom. In full: **stretch limousine.**

stretchmarks ('strɛtʃ,mɑːks) *pl n* marks that remain visible on the abdomen after its distension in pregnancy.

stretchy ('strɛtʃɪ) *adj* **stretchier, stretchiest.** characterized by elasticity.
▸ '**stretchiness** *n*

Stretford ★ ('strɛtfəd) *n* an industrial town in NW England, in Trafford, in Greater Manchester. Pop.: 43 953 (1991).

stretto ('strɛtəʊ) *n, pl* **strettos** or **stretti** (-tiː). **1** (in a fugue) the close overlapping of two parts or voices, the second one entering before the first has completed its statement. **2** Also called: **stretta.** a concluding passage, played at a faster speed than earlier material. [C17: from It., from L *strictus* tightly bound; see STRICT]

strew (struː) *vb* **strews, strewing, strewed; strewn** or **strewed.** to spread or scatter or be spread or scattered, as over a surface or area. [OE *strēowian*]
▸ '**strewer** *n*

strewth (struːθ) *interj* an expression of surprise or dismay. [C19: alteration of *God's truth*]

stria ('straɪə) *n, pl* **striae** ('straɪiː). (*often pl*) **1** Also called: **striation.** *Geol.* any of the parallel scratches or grooves on the surface of a rock over which a glacier has flowed or on the surface of a crystal. **2** *Biol., anat.* a narrow band of colour or a ridge, groove, or similar linear mark. **3** *Archit.* a narrow channel, such as a flute on the shaft of a column. [C16: from L: a groove]

striate *adj* ('straɪɪt), *also* **striated.** **1** marked with striae; striped. ◆ *vb* ('straɪeɪt), **striates, striating, striated.** **2** (*tr*) to mark with striae. [C17: from L *strīāre* to make grooves]

striation (straɪ'eɪʃən) *n* **1** an arrangement or pattern of striae. **2** the condition of being striate. **3** another word for **stria** (sense 1).

stricken ('strɪkən) *adj* **1** laid low, as by disease or sickness. **2** deeply affected, as by grief, love, etc. **3** *Arch.* wounded or injured. **4 stricken in years.** made feeble by age. [C14: p.p. of STRIKE]
▸ '**strickenly** *adv*

strict (strɪkt) *adj* **1** adhering closely to specified rules, ordinances, etc. **2** complied with or enforced stringently; rigorous: *a strict code of conduct.* **3** severely correct in attention to conduct or morality: *a strict teacher.* **4** (of a punishment, etc.) harsh; severe. **5** (*prenominal*) complete; absolute: *strict secrecy.* [C16: from L *strictus*, from *stringere* to draw tight]
▸ '**strictly** *adv* ▸ '**strictness** *n*

strict implication *n Logic.* a form of implication in which the proposition "if A then B" is true only when B is deducible from A.

stricture ('strɪktʃə) *n* **1** a severe criticism; censure. **2** *Pathol.* an abnormal constriction of a tubular organ or part. [C14: from L *strictūra* contraction; see STRICT]
▸ '**strictured** *adj*

stride (straɪd) *n* **1** a long step or pace. **2** the space measured by such a step. **3** a striding gait. **4** an act of forward movement by an animal. **5** progress or development

(esp. in **make rapid strides**). **6** a regular pace or rate of progress: *to get into one's stride; to be put off one's stride.* **7** Also: **stride piano.** *Jazz.* a piano style characterized by single bass notes on the first and third beats and chords on the second and fourth. **8** (*pl*) *Inf., chiefly Austral. & NZ.* men's trousers. **9 take (something) in one's stride.** to do (something) without difficulty or effort. ◆ *vb* **strides, striding, strode, stridden** ('strɪdⁿn). **10** (*intr*) to walk with long regular or measured paces, as in haste, etc. **11** (*tr*) to cover or traverse by striding: *he strode thirty miles.* **12** (often foll. by *over, across*, etc.) to cross (over a space, obstacle, etc.) with a stride. **13** *Arch. or poetic.* to straddle or bestride. [OE *strīdan*]
▸ '**strider** *n*

strident ('straɪdⁿnt) *adj* **1** (of a shout, voice, etc.) loud or harsh. **2** urgent, clamorous, or vociferous: *strident demands.* [C17: from L *strīdēns*, from *strīdere* to make a grating sound]
▸ '**stridence** or '**stridency** *n* ▸ '**stridently** *adv*

stridor ('straɪdɔː) *n* **1** *Pathol.* a high-pitched whistling sound made during respiration, caused by obstruction of the air passages. **2** *Chiefly literary.* a harsh or shrill sound. [C17: from L; see STRIDENT]

stridulate ('strɪdjʊ,leɪt) *vb* **stridulates, stridulating, stridulated.** (*intr*) (of insects such as the cricket) to produce sounds by rubbing one part of the body against another. [C19: back formation from *stridulation*, from L *strīdulus* creaking, from *strīdere* to make a harsh noise]
▸ ,**stridu'lation** *n* ▸ '**stridu,lator** *n*

stridulous ('strɪdjʊləs) or **stridulant** *adj* **1** making a harsh, shrill, or grating noise. **2** *Pathol.* of, relating to, or characterized by stridor.
▸ '**stridulousness** or '**stridulance** *n*

strife (straɪf) *n* **1** angry or violent struggle; conflict. **2** rivalry or contention, esp. of a bitter kind. **3** *Austral. & NZ inf.* trouble or discord of any kind. **4** *Arch.* striving. [C13: from OF *estrif*, prob. from *estriver* to STRIVE]

strigil ('strɪdʒɪl) *n* a curved blade used by the ancient Romans and Greeks to scrape the body after bathing. [C16: from L *strigilis*, from *stringere* to graze]

strigose ('straɪgəʊs) *adj* **1** *Bot.* bearing stiff hairs or bristles. **2** *Zool.* marked with fine closely set grooves or ridges. [C18: via NL *strigōsus*, from *striga* a bristle, from L: grain cut down]

strike (straɪk) *vb* **strikes, striking, struck. 1** to deliver (a blow or stroke) to (a person). **2** to come or cause to come into sudden or violent contact (with). **3** (*tr*) to make an attack on. **4** to produce (fire, sparks, etc.) or (of fire, sparks, etc.) to be produced by ignition. **5** to cause (a match) to light by friction or (of a match) to be lighted. **6** to press (the key of a piano, organ, etc.) or to sound (a specific note) in this or a similar way. **7** to indicate (a specific time) by the sound of a hammer striking a bell or by any other percussive sound. **8** (of a venomous snake) to cause injury by biting. **9** (*tr*) to affect or cause to affect deeply, suddenly, or radically: *her appearance struck him as strange.* **10** (*past participle* **struck** or **stricken**) (*tr; passive*) usually foll. by *with*) to render incapable or nearly so: *stricken with grief.* **11** (*tr*) to enter the mind of: *it struck me that he had become very quiet.* **12** (*past participle* **struck** or **stricken**) to render: *struck dumb.* **13** (*tr*) to be perceived by; catch: *the glint of metal struck his eye.* **14** to arrive at or come upon (something), esp. suddenly or unexpectedly: *to strike the path for home; to strike upon a solution.* **15** (*intr*; sometimes foll. by *out*) to set (out) or proceed, esp. upon a new course: *to strike out for the coast.* **16** (*tr; usually passive*) to afflict with a disease, esp. unexpectedly: *he was struck with polio.* **17** (*tr*) to discover or come upon a source of (ore, petroleum, etc.). **18** (*tr*) (of a plant) to produce or send down (a root or roots). **19** (*tr*) to take apart or pack up; break (esp. in **strike camp**). **20** (*tr*) to take down or dismantle (a stage set, etc.). **21** (*tr*) *Naut.* **21a** to lower or remove (a specified piece of gear). **21b** to haul down or dip (a flag, sail, etc.) in salute or in surrender. **22** to attack (an objective). **23** to impale the hook in the mouth of (a fish) by suddenly tightening or jerking the line after the bait has been taken. **24** (*tr*) to form or impress (a coin, metal, etc.) by or as if by stamping. **25** to level (a surface) by use of a flat board. **26** (*tr*) to assume or take up (an attitude, posture, etc.). **27** (*intr*) (of workers in a factory, etc.) to cease work collectively as a protest against working conditions, low pay, etc. **28** (*tr*) to reach by agreement: *to strike a bargain*. **29** (*tr*) to form a (jury, esp. a special jury) by cancelling certain names among those nominated for jury service until only the requisite number remains. **30 strike home. 30a** to deliver an effective blow. **30b** to achieve the intended effect. **31 strike it rich.** *Inf.* **31a** to discover an extensive deposit of a mineral, petroleum, etc. **31b** to have an unexpected financial success. ♦ *n* **32** an act or instance of striking. **33** a cessation of work, as a protest against working conditions or low pay: *on strike*. **34** a military attack, esp. an air attack on a surface target: *air strike*. **35** *Baseball.* a pitched ball judged good but missed or not swung at, three of which cause a batter to be out. **36** Also called: **ten-strike.** *Tenpin bowling.* **36a** the act or an instance of knocking down all the pins with the first bowl of a single frame. **36b** the score thus made. **37** a sound made by striking. **38** the mechanism that makes a clock strike. **39** the discovery of a source of ore, petroleum, etc. **40** the horizontal direction of a fault, rock stratum, etc. **41** *Angling.* the act or an instance of striking. **42** *Inf.* an unexpected or complete success, esp. one that brings financial gain. **43 take strike.** *Cricket.* (of a batsman) to prepare to play a ball delivered by the bowler. ♦ See also **strike down, strike off**, etc. [OE *strīcan*]

strikebound ('straɪk,baʊnd) *adj* (of a factory, etc.) closed or made inoperative by a strike.

strikebreaker ('straɪk,breɪkə) *n* a person who tries to make a strike ineffectual by working or by taking the place of those on strike.
▸ 'strike,breaking *n*, *adj*

strike down *vb* (*tr*, *adv*) to cause to die, esp. suddenly: *he was struck down in his prime.*

strike off *vb* (*tr*) **1** to remove or erase from (a list, record, etc.) by or as if by a stroke of the pen. **2** (*adv*) to cut off or separate by or as if by a blow: *she was struck off from the inheritance.*

strike out *vb* (*adv*) **1** (*tr*) to remove or erase. **2** (*intr*) to start out or begin: *to strike out on one's own*. **3** *Baseball.* to put out or be put out on strikes. **4** (*intr*) *US inf.* to fail utterly.

strike pay *n* money paid to strikers from the funds of a trade union.

striker ('straɪkə) *n* **1** a person who is on strike. **2** the hammer in a timepiece that rings a bell or alarm. **3** any part in a mechanical device that strikes something, such as the firing pin of a gun. **4** *Soccer, inf.* an attacking player, esp. one who generally positions himself near his opponent's goal in the hope of scoring. **5** *Cricket.* the batsman who is about to play a ball.

strike up *vb* (*adv*) **1** (of a band, orchestra, etc.) to begin to play or sing **2** (*tr*) to bring about; cause to begin: *to strike up a friendship.*

striking ('straɪkɪŋ) *adj* **1** attracting attention; fine; impressive: *a striking beauty*. **2** conspicuous; noticeable: *a striking difference.*
▸ 'strikingly *adv* ▸ 'strikingness *n*

striking circle *n Hockey.* the semicircular area in front of each goal, which an attacking player must have entered before scoring a goal.

Strimmer ('strɪmə) *n Trademark.* an electrical tool for trimming the edges of lawns.

Strimon ★ ('strɪmɒn) *n* a transliteration of the Greek name for the **Struma.**

Strindberg ★ ('strɪndbɜːg; *Swedish* 'strɪndbærj) *n* **August** ('aʊɡəst). 1849–1912, Swedish dramatist and novelist, whose plays include *The Father* (1887), *Miss Julie* (1888), and *The Ghost Sonata* (1907).

Strine (straɪn) *n* a humorous transliteration of Australian pronunciation, as in *Gloria Soame* for *glorious home*. [C20: a jocular rendering of the Australian pronunciation of *Australian*]

string (strɪŋ) *n* **1** a thin length of cord, twine, fibre, or similar material used for tying, hanging, binding, etc. **2** a group of objects threaded on a single strand: *a string of beads*. **3** a series or succession of things, events, etc.: *a string of oaths*. **4** a number, chain, or group of similar

things, animals, etc., owned by or associated with one person or body: *a string of girlfriends*. **5** a tough fibre or cord in a plant. **6** *Music.* a tightly stretched wire, cord, etc., found on stringed instruments, such as the violin, guitar, and piano. **7** short for **bowstring. 8** *Archit.* short for **string course** or **stringer** (sense 1). **9** (*pl;* usually preceded by *the*) **9a** violins, violas, cellos, and double basses collectively. **9b** the section of a symphony orchestra constituted by such instruments. **10** a group of characters that can be treated as a unit by a computer program. **11** *Physics.* a one-dimensional entity postulated to be a fundamental component of matter in some theories of particle physics. See also **cosmic string. 12** (*pl*) complications or conditions (esp. in **no strings attached**). **13** (*modifier*) composed of stringlike strands woven in a large mesh: *a string bag; a string vest*. **14 first** (**second**, etc.) **string.** a person or thing regarded as a primary (secondary, etc.) source of strength. **15 keep on a string.** to have control or a hold over (a person), esp. emotionally. **16 pull strings.** *Inf.* to exert power or influence, esp. secretly or unofficially. **17 pull the strings.** to have real or ultimate control of something. ♦ *vb* **strings, stringing, strung. 18** (*tr*) to provide with a string or strings. **19** (*tr*) to suspend or stretch from one point to another. **20** (*tr*) to thread on a string. **21** (*tr*) to form or extend in a line or series. **22** (foll. by *out*) to space or spread out at intervals. **23** (*tr;* usually foll. by *up*) *Inf.* to kill (a person) by hanging. **24** (*tr*) to remove the stringy parts from (vegetables, esp. beans). **25** (*intr*) (esp. of viscous liquids) to become stringy or ropey. **26** (*tr;* often foll. by *up*) to cause to be tense or nervous. [OE *streng*]
▸ 'string,like *adj*

string along *vb* (*adv*) *Inf.* **1** (*intr;* often foll. by *with*) to agree or appear to be in agreement (with). **2** (*intr;* often foll. by *with*) to accompany. **3** to deceive or hoax, esp. in order to gain time.

stringboard ('strɪŋ,bɔːd) *n* a skirting that covers the ends of the steps in a staircase. Also called: **stringer.**

string course *n Archit.* an ornamental projecting band or continuous moulding along a wall. Also called: **cordon.**

stringed (strɪŋd) *adj* (of musical instruments) having or provided with strings.

stringendo (strɪn'dʒɛndəʊ) *adj, adv Music.* to be performed with increasing speed. [It., from *stringere* to compress, from L: to draw tight]

stringent ('strɪndʒənt) *adj* **1** requiring strict attention to rules, procedure, detail, etc. **2** *Finance.* characterized by or causing a shortage of credit, loan capital, etc. [C17: from L *stringere* to bind]
▸ 'stringency *n* ▸ 'stringently *adv*

stringer ('strɪŋə) *n* **1** *Archit.* **1a** a long horizontal beam that is used for structural purposes. **1b** another name for **stringboard. 2** *Naut.* a longitudinal structural brace for strengthening the hull of a vessel. **3** a journalist retained by a newspaper or news service on a part-time basis to cover a particular town or area.

stringhalt ('strɪŋ,hɔːlt) *n Vet. science.* a sudden spasmodic lifting of the hind leg of a horse. Also called: **springhalt.** [C16: prob. STRING + HALT²]

stringpiece ('strɪŋ,piːs) *n* a long horizontal timber beam used to strengthen or support a framework.

string quartet *n Music.* **1** an instrumental ensemble consisting of two violins, one viola, and one cello. **2** a piece of music for such a group.

string tie *n* a very narrow tie.

stringy ('strɪŋɪ) *adj* **stringier, stringiest. 1** made of strings or resembling strings. **2** (of meat, etc.) fibrous. **3** (of a person's build) wiry; sinewy. **4** (of liquids) forming in strings.
▸ 'stringily *adv* ▸ 'stringiness *n*

stringy-bark *n Austral.* any of several eucalyptus trees having fibrous bark.

strip¹ (strɪp) *vb* **strips, stripping, stripped. 1** to take or pull (the covering, clothes, etc.) off (oneself, another person, or thing). **2** (*intr*) **2a** to remove all one's clothes. **2b** to perform a striptease. **3** (*tr*) to denude or empty completely. **4** (*tr*) to deprive: *he was stripped of his pride*. **5** (*tr*) to rob or plunder. **6** (*tr*) to remove (paint, etc.) from (a surface, furniture, etc.): *stripped pine*. **7** (*tr*) to pull out the old coat of hair from (dogs of certain long- and wire-haired breeds). **8a** to remove the leaves from the stalks of (tobacco, etc.). **8b** to separate the leaves from the stems of (tobacco, etc.). **9** (*tr*) *Agriculture*. to draw the last milk from (a cow). **10** to dismantle (an engine, mechanism, etc.). **11** to tear off or break (the thread) from (a screw, bolt, etc.) or (the teeth) from (a gear). **12** (often foll. by *down*) to remove the accessories from (a motor vehicle): *his car was stripped down*. ◆ *n* **13** the act or an instance of undressing or of performing a striptease. [OE *bestrīepan* to plunder]

strip[2] (strɪp) *n* **1** a relatively long, flat, narrow piece of something. **2** short for **airstrip**. **3** the clothes worn by the members of a team, esp. a football team. **4** *Business*. a triple option on a security or commodity consisting of one call option and two put options at the same price and for the same period. Cf. **strap** (sense 6). **5 tear (someone) off a strip.** *Inf.* to rebuke (someone) angrily. ◆ *vb* **strips, stripping, stripped. 6** to cut or divide into strips. [C15: from MDu. *strīpe* STRIPE[1]]

strip cartoon *n* a sequence of drawings in a newspaper, magazine, etc., relating a humorous story or an adventure. Also called: **comic strip.**

strip club *n* a small club in which striptease performances take place.

stripe[1] (straɪp) *n* **1** a relatively long band of colour or texture that differs from the surrounding material or background. **2** a fabric having such bands. **3** a strip, band, or chevron worn on a uniform, etc., esp. to indicate rank. **4** *Chiefly US & Canad.* kind; type: *a man of a certain stripe*. ◆ *vb* **stripes, striping, striped. 5** (*tr*) to mark with stripes. [C17: prob. from MDu. *strīpe*]
▸ **striped** *adj*

stripe[2] (straɪp) *n* a stroke from a whip, rod, cane, etc. [C15: ?from MLow G *strippe*]

striped muscle *n* a type of contractile tissue that is marked by transverse striations. Also called: **striated muscle.**

strip lighting *n* electric lighting by means of long glass tubes that are fluorescent lamps or that contain long filaments.

stripling (ˈstrɪplɪŋ) *n* a lad. [C13: from STRIP[2] + -LING[1]]

strip mining *n* another term (esp. US) for **opencast mining.**

stripper (ˈstrɪpə) *n* **1** a striptease artiste. **2** a person or thing that strips. **3** a device or substance for removing paint, varnish, etc.

strip-search *vb* **1** (*tr*) (of police, customs officials, etc.) to strip (a prisoner or suspect) naked to search him or her for contraband, narcotics, etc. ◆ *n* **2** a search that involves stripping a person naked.
▸ **'strip-searching** *n*

striptease (ˈstrɪpˌtiːz) *n* **a** a form of erotic entertainment in which a person gradually undresses to music. **b** (*as modifier*): *a striptease club*.
▸ **'strip,teaser** *n*

stripy *or* **stripey** (ˈstraɪpɪ) *adj* **stripier, stripiest.** marked by or with stripes; striped.

strive (straɪv) *vb* **strives, striving, strove, striven** (ˈstrɪvən). **1** (*may take a clause as object or an infinitive*) to make a great and tenacious effort. **2** (*intr*) to fight; contend. [C13: from OF *estriver*, of Gmc origin]
▸ **'striver** *n*

strobe (strəʊb) *n* short for **strobe lighting** or **stroboscope.**

strobe lighting *n* **1** a high-intensity flashing beam of light produced by rapid electrical discharges in a tube or by a perforated disc rotating in front of an intense light source. **2** the use of or the apparatus for producing such light. Sometimes shortened to **strobe.**

strobilus (ˈstrəʊbɪləs) *or* **strobile** (ˈstrəʊbaɪl) *n, pl* **strobiluses, strobili** (-bɪlaɪ), *or* **strobiles.** *Bot.* the technical name for **cone** (sense 3). [C18: via LL from Gk *strobilos* a fir cone]

stroboscope (ˈstrəʊbəˌskəʊp) *n* **1** an instrument producing an intense flashing light, the frequency of which

can be synchronized with some multiple of the frequency of rotation, vibration, or operation of an object, etc., making it appear stationary. Sometimes shortened to **strobe. 2** a similar device synchronized with the shutter of a camera so that a series of still photographs can be taken of a moving object. [C19: from *strobo-*, from Gk *strobos* a whirling + -SCOPE]
▸ **stroboscopic** (ˌstrəʊbəˈskɒpɪk) *or* **strobo'scopical** *adj*
▸ **strobo'scopically** *adv*

strode (strəʊd) *vb* the past tense of **stride.**

stroganoff (ˈstrɒɡəˌnɒf) *n* a dish of sliced beef cooked with onions and mushrooms, served in a sour-cream sauce. Also called: **beef stroganoff.** [C19: after Count *Stroganoff*, 19th-century Russian diplomat]

stroke (strəʊk) *n* **1** the act or an instance of striking; a blow, knock, or hit. **2** a sudden action, movement, or occurrence: *a stroke of luck.* **3** a brilliant or inspired act or feat: *a stroke of genius.* **4** *Pathol.* apoplexy; rupture of a blood vessel in the brain resulting in loss of consciousness, often followed by paralysis, or embolism or thrombosis affecting a cerebral vessel. **5a** the striking of a clock. **5b** the hour registered by this: *on the stroke of three.* **6** a mark made by a writing implement. **7** another name for **solidus** (sense 1), used esp. when dictating or reading aloud. **8** a light touch or caress, as with the fingers. **9** a pulsation, esp. of the heart. **10** a single complete movement or one of a series of complete movements. **11** *Sport.* the act or manner of striking the ball with a club, bat, etc. **12** any one of the repeated movements used by a swimmer. **13** a manner of swimming, esp. one of several named styles such as the crawl. **14a** any one of a series of linear movements of a reciprocating part, such as a piston. **14b** the distance travelled by such a part from one end of its movement to the other. **15** a single pull on an oar or oars in rowing. **16** manner or style of rowing. **17** the oarsman who sits nearest the stern of a shell, facing the cox, and sets the rate of rowing. **18 a stroke (of work).** (*usually used with a negative*) a small amount of work. **19 at a stroke.** one action. **20 off one's stroke.** performing or working less well than usual. **21 on the stroke.** punctually. ◆ *vb* **strokes, stroking, stroked. 22** (*tr*) to touch, brush, etc. lightly or gently. **23** (*tr*) to mark a line or a stroke on or through. **24** to act as the stroke of (a racing shell). **25** (*tr*) *Sport.* to strike (a ball) with a smooth swinging blow. [OE *strācian*]

stroke play *n Golf.* **a** a scoring by counting the strokes taken. **b** (*as modifier*): *a strokeplay tournament.* ◆ Also called: **medal play.** Cf. **match play, Stableford.**

stroll (strəʊl) *vb* **1** to walk about in a leisurely manner. **2** (*intr*) to wander about. ◆ *n* **3** a leisurely walk. [C17: prob. from dialect G *strollen*, from ?]

stroller (ˈstrəʊlə) *n* the usual US, Canad., and Austral. word for **pushchair.**

stroma (ˈstrəʊmə) *n, pl* **stromata** (-mətə). *Biol.* **1** the dense colourless framework of a chloroplast and certain cells. **2** the fibrous connective tissue forming the matrix of the mammalian ovary and testis. **3** a dense mass of hyphae that is produced by certain fungi and gives rise to spore-producing bodies. [C19: via NL from LL: a mattress, from Gk]
▸ **stromatic** (strəʊˈmætɪk) *or* **stromatous** *adj*

Strombolian (strɒmˈbəʊlɪən) *adj* relating to or denoting a type of volcanic eruption characterized by repeated small explosions caused by gas escaping through lava.

strong (strɒŋ) *adj* **stronger** (ˈstrɒŋɡə), **strongest** (ˈstrɒŋɡɪst). **1** involving or possessing strength. **2** solid or robust; not easily broken or injured. **3** resolute or morally firm. **4** intense in quality; not faint or feeble: *a strong voice; a strong smell.* **5** easily defensible; incontestable or formidable. **6** concentrated; not weak or diluted. **7a** (*postpositive*) containing or having a specified number: *a navy 40 000*

strong. **7b** (*in combination*): *a 40 000-strong navy.* **8** having an unpleasantly powerful taste or smell. **9** having an extreme or drastic effect: *strong discipline.* **10** emphatic or immoderate: *strong language.* **11** convincing, effective, or cogent. **12** (of a colour) having a high degree of saturation or purity; produced by a concentrated quantity of colouring agent. **13** *Grammar.* **13a** of or denoting a class of verbs, in certain languages including the Germanic languages, whose conjugation shows vowel gradation, as *sing, sang, sung.* **13b** belonging to any part-of-speech class, in various languages, whose inflections follow the less regular of two possible patterns. Cf. **weak** (sense 10). **14** (of a wind, current, etc.) moving fast. **15** (of a syllable) accented or stressed. **16** (of an industry, etc.) firm in price or characterized by firm or increasing prices. **17** (of certain acids and bases) producing high concentrations of hydrogen or hydroxide ions in aqueous solution. **18 have a strong stomach.** not to be prone to nausea. ◆ *adv* **19** *Inf.* in a strong way; effectively: *going strong.* **20 come on strong.** to make a forceful or exaggerated impression. [OE *strang*]
▶ **'strongly** *adv* ▶ **'strongness** *n*

strong-arm *Inf.* ◆ *n* **1** (*modifier*) of or involving physical force or violence: *strong-arm tactics.* ◆ *vb* **2** (*tr*) to show violence towards.

strongbox ('strɒŋ,bɒks) *n* a box or safe in which valuables are locked for safety.

strong breeze *n Meteorol.* a wind of force 6 on the Beaufort scale, reaching speeds of 25 to 31 mph.

strong drink *n* alcoholic drink.

strong-eye dog *n NZ.* See **eye dog.**

strong gale *n Meteorol.* a wind of force 9 on the Beaufort scale, reaching speeds of 47 to 54 mph.

stronghold ('strɒŋ,həʊld) *n* **1** a defensible place; fortress. **2** a major centre or area of predominance.

strong interaction or **force** *n Physics.* an interaction between elementary particles responsible for the forces between nucleons in the nucleus. Also called: **strong nuclear interaction** or **force.** See **interaction** (sense 2). Cf. **weak interaction.**

strong-minded *adj* having strength of mind; firm, resolute, and determined.
▶ ,**strong-'mindedly** *adv* ▶ **strong-'mindedness** *n*

strong point *n* something at which one excels; forte.

strongroom ('strɒŋ,ruːm, -,rʊm) *n* a specially designed room in which valuables are locked for safety.

strong-willed *adj* having strength of will.

strontium ('strɒntɪəm) *n* a soft silvery-white element of the alkaline earth group of metals. The radioisotope **strontium-90,** with a half-life of 28.1 years, is used in nuclear power sources and is a hazardous nuclear fallout product. Symbol: Sr; atomic no.: 38; atomic wt.: 87.62. [C19: from NL, after *Strontian,* in the Highlands of Scotland, where discovered]

strontium unit *n* a unit expressing the concentration of strontium-90 in an organic medium, such as soil, bone, etc., relative to the concentration of calcium in the medium.

strop (strɒp) *n* **1** a leather strap or an abrasive strip for sharpening razors. **2** a rope or metal band around a block or deadeye for support. ◆ *vb* **strops, stropping, stropped. 3** (*tr*) to sharpen (a razor, etc.) on a strop. [C14 (in nautical use: a strip of rope): via MLow G or MDu. *strop,* ult. from L *stroppus,* from Gk *strophos* cord]

strophanthin (strəʊ'fænθɪn) *n* a toxic glycoside or mixture of glycosides obtained from the ripe seeds of certain species of strophanthus. [C19: NL, from STROPHANTH(US) + -IN]

strophanthus (strəʊ'fænθəs) *n* **1** any of various small trees or shrubs of tropical Africa and Asia, having strap-shaped twisted petals. **2** the seeds of any of these plants. [C19: NL, from Gk *strophos* twisted cord + *anthos* flower]

strophe ('strəʊfɪ) *n Prosody.* (in ancient Greek drama) **a** the first of two movements made by a chorus during the performance of a choral ode. **b** the first part of a choral ode sung during this movement. ◆ See **antistrophe,**

epode. [C17: from Gk: a verse, lit.: a turning, from *strephein* to twist]
▶ **strophic** ('strɒfɪk, 'strəʊ-) *adj*

stroppy ('strɒpɪ) *adj* **stroppier, stroppiest.** *Brit. inf.* angry or awkward. [C20: changed & shortened from OBSTREPEROUS]
▶ **'stroppily** *adv* ▶ **'stroppiness** *n*

strove (strəʊv) *vb* the past tense of **strive.**

strow (strəʊ) *vb* **strows, strowing, strowed; strown** or **strowed.** an archaic variant of **strew.**

struck (strʌk) *vb* **1** the past tense and past participle of **strike.** ◆ *adj* **2** *Chiefly US & Canad.* (of an industry, factory, etc.) shut down or otherwise affected by a labour strike.

structural ('strʌktʃərəl) *adj* **1** of, relating to, or having structure or a structure. **2** of, relating to, or forming part of the structure of a building. **3** of or relating to the structure of the earth's crust. **4** of or relating to the structure of organisms. **5** *Chem.* of or involving the arrangement of atoms in molecules.
▶ **'structurally** *adv*

structural formula *n* a chemical formula showing the composition and structure of a molecule.

structuralism ('strʌktʃərə,lɪzəm) *n* **1** an approach to social sciences and to literature in terms of oppositions, contrasts, and hierarchical structures, esp. as they might reflect universal mental characteristics or organizing principles. **2** an approach to linguistics that analyses and describes the structure of language, as distinguished from its comparative and historical aspects.
▶ **'structuralist** *n, adj*

structural linguistics *n* (*functioning as sing*) a descriptive approach to an analysis of language on the basis of its structure as reflected by irreducible units of phonological, morphological, and semantic features.

structural unemployment *n Econ.* unemployment resulting from changes in the structure of an industry as a result of changes in either technology or taste.

structure ('strʌktʃə) *n* **1** a complex construction or entity. **2** the arrangement and interrelationship of parts in a construction. **3** the manner of construction or organization. **4** *Chem.* the arrangement of atoms in a molecule of a chemical compound. **5** *Geol.* the way in which a mineral, rock, etc., is made up of its component parts. ◆ *vb* **structures, structuring, structured.** (*tr*) **6** to impart a structure to. [C15: from L *structūra,* from *struere* to build]

structured interview *n Marketing.* an interview in which the respondent answers only "yes", "no", or "don't know".

strudel ('struːdəl) *n* a thin sheet of filled dough rolled up and baked: *apple strudel.* [G, from MHG *strodel* whirlpool, from the way the pastry is rolled]

struggle ('strʌgˀl) *vb* **struggles, struggling, struggled.** (*intr*) **1** (usually foll. by *for* or *against; may take an infinitive*) to exert strength, energy, and force; work or strive. **2** to move about strenuously so as to escape from something confining. **3** to contend, battle, or fight. **4** to go or progress with difficulty. ◆ *n* **5** a laboured or strenuous exertion or effort. **6** a fight or battle. **7** the act of struggling. [C14: from ?]
▶ **'struggling** *adj*

strum (strʌm) *vb* **strums, strumming, strummed. 1** to sound (the strings of a guitar, etc.) with a downward or upward sweep of the thumb or of a plectrum. **2** to play (chords, a tune, etc.) in this way. [C18: prob. imit.]
▶ **'strummer** *n*

struma ('struːmə) *n, pl* **strumae** (-miː). **1** an abnormal enlargement of the thyroid gland; goitre. **2** *Bot.* a swelling, esp. at the base of a moss capsule. **3** another word for **scrofula.** [C16: from L: scrofulous tumour, from *struere* to heap up]
▶ **'strumous** ('struːməs) or **strumose** ('struːməʊs) *adj*

Struma ★ ('struːmə) *n* a river in S Europe, rising in SW Bulgaria near Sofia and flowing generally southeast through Greece to the Aegean. Length: 362 km (225 miles). Greek names: **Strimon, Strymon.**

strumpet ('strʌmpɪt) *n Arch.* a prostitute or promiscuous woman. [C14: from ?]

strung (strʌŋ) *vb* **1** a past tense and past participle of **string**. ◆ *adj* **2a** (of a piano, etc.) provided with strings. **2b** (*in combination*): *gut-strung*. **3 highly strung.** very nervous or volatile in character.

strung up *adj* (*postpositive*) *Inf.* tense or nervous.

strut (strʌt) *vb* **struts, strutting, strutted. 1** (*intr*) to walk in a pompous manner; swagger. **2** (*tr*) to support or provide with struts. ◆ *n* **3** a structural member, esp. as part of a framework. **4** an affected, proud, or stiff walk. [C14 *strouten* (in the sense: swell, stand out; C16: to walk stiffly), from OE *strūtian* to stand stiffly] ▸ **'strutter** *n* ▸ **'strutting** *adj* ▸ **'struttingly** *adv*

struthious ('struːθɪəs) *adj* **1** (of birds) related to or resembling the ostrich. **2** of, relating to, or designating all flightless birds. [C18: from LL *strūthiō*, from Gk *strouthiōn*, from *strouthos* ostrich]

Struve ★ ('struːvə) *n* **Otto.** 1897–1963, US astronomer, born in Russia, noted for his work in stellar spectroscopy and his discovery (1937) of interstellar hydrogen.

strychnine ('strɪkniːn) *n* a white crystalline very poisonous alkaloid, obtained from the plant nux vomica: formerly used in small quantities as a stimulant. [C19: via F from NL *Strychnos*, from Gk *strukhnos* nightshade]

Strymon ★ ('straɪmən) *n* transliteration of the Greek name for the **Struma.**

Stuart ★ ('stjʊət) *n* **1** the royal house that ruled in Scotland from 1371 to 1714 and in England from 1603 to 1714. See also **Stewart** (sense 1). **2 Charles Edward,** called *the Young Pretender* or *Bonnie Prince Charlie.* 1720–88, pretender to the British throne. He led the Jacobite Rebellion (1745–46) in an attempt to re-establish the Stuart succession. **3** his father, **James Francis Edward,** called *the Old Pretender.* 1688–1766, pretender to the British throne; son of James II (James VII of Scotland) and his second wife, Mary of Modena. He made two unsuccessful attempts to realize his claim to the throne (1708; 1715). **4** Mary. See **Mary, Queen of Scots.**

stub (stʌb) *n* **1** a short piece remaining after something has been cut, removed, etc.: *a cigar stub.* **2** the residual piece or section of a receipt, ticket, cheque, etc. **3** the usual US and Canad. word for **counterfoil. 4** any short projection or blunted end. **5** the stump of a tree or plant. ◆ *vb* **stubs, stubbing, stubbed.** (*tr*) **6** to strike (one's toe, foot, etc.) painfully against a hard surface. **7** (usually foll. by *out*) to put (out a cigarette or cigar) by pressing the end against a surface. **8** to clear (land) of stubs. **9** to dig up (the roots) of (a tree or bush). [OE *stubb*]

stub axle *n* a short axle that carries one of the front steered wheels of a motor vehicle.

stubble ('stʌbᵊl) *n* **1a** the stubs of stalks left in a field where a crop has been harvested. **1b** (*as modifier*): *a stubble field.* **2** any bristly growth. [C13: from OF *estuble*, from L *stupula*, var. of *stipula* stalk] ▸ **'stubbled** *or* **'stubbly** *adj*

stubble-jumper *n Canad. sl.* a prairie grain farmer.

stubborn ('stʌbᵊn) *adj* **1** refusing to comply, agree, or give in. **2** difficult to handle, treat, or overcome. **3** persistent and dogged. [C14 *stoborne*, from ?] ▸ **'stubbornly** *adv* ▸ **'stubbornness** *n*

Stubbs ★ (stʌbz) *n* **George.** 1724–1806, British painter, esp. of horses.

stubby ('stʌbɪ) *adj* **stubbier, stubbiest. 1** short and broad; stumpy or thickset. **2** bristling and stiff. ◆ *n* **3** *Austral. sl.* Also: **stubbie.** a small bottle of beer. ▸ **'stubbily** *adv* ▸ **'stubbiness** *n*

stucco ('stʌkəʊ) *n, pl* **stuccoes** *or* **stuccos. 1** a weather-resistant mixture of dehydrated lime, powdered marble, and glue, used in decorative mouldings on buildings. **2** any of various types of cement or plaster used for coating outside walls. **3** Also called: **stuccowork.** decorative work moulded in stucco. ◆ *vb* **stuccoes** *or* **stuccos, stuccoing, stuccoed. 4** (*tr*) to apply stucco to. [C16: from It., of Gmc origin]

stuck (stʌk) *vb* **1** the past tense and past participle of **stick²**. ◆ *adj* **2** *Inf.* baffled or nonplussed. **3** (foll. by *on*) *Sl.*

keen (on) or infatuated (with). **4 get stuck in** *or* **into.** *Inf.* **4a** to perform (a task) with determination. **4b** to attack (a person).

stuck-up *adj Inf.* conceited, arrogant, or snobbish. ▸ **'stuck-'upness** *n*

stud¹ (stʌd) *n* **1** a large-headed nail or other projection protruding from a surface, usually as decoration. **2** a type of fastener consisting of two discs at either end of a short shank, used to fasten shirtfronts, collars, etc. **3** a vertical member used with others to construct the framework of a wall. **4** the crossbar in the centre of a link of a heavy chain. **5** one of a number of rounded projections on the sole of a boot or shoe to give better grip, as on a football boot. ◆ *vb* **studs, studding, studded.** (*tr*) **6** to provide, ornament, or make with studs. **7** to dot or cover (with): *the park was studded with daisies.* **8** to provide or support (a wall, partition, etc.) with studs. [OE *studu*]

stud² (stʌd) *n* **1** a group of pedigree animals, esp. horses, kept for breeding purposes. **2** any male animal kept principally for breeding purposes, esp. a stallion. **3** a farm or stable where a stud is kept. **4** the state or condition of being kept for breeding purposes: *at stud; put to stud.* **5** (*modifier*) of or relating to such animals or the place where they are kept: *a stud farm; a stud horse.* **6** *Sl.* a virile or sexually active man. **7** short for **stud poker.** [OE *stōd*]

studbook ('stʌd,bʊk) *n* a written record of the pedigree of a purebred stock, esp. of racehorses.

studding ('stʌdɪŋ) *n* **1** studs collectively, esp. as used to form a wall or partition. **2** material used to form or serve as studs.

studdingsail ('stʌdɪŋ,seɪl; *Naut.* 'stʌns²l) *n Naut.* a light auxiliary sail set outboard on spars on either side of a square sail. Also called: **stunsail, stuns'l.** [C16: *studding*, ?from MLow G, MDu. *stōtinge*, from *stōten* to thrust]

student ('stjuːdᵊnt) *n* **1a** a person following a course of study, as in a school, college, university, etc. **1b** (*as modifier*): *student teacher.* **2** a person who makes a thorough study of a subject. [C15: from L *studēns* diligent, from *studēre* to be zealous]

Student's t *n* a statistic often used to test the hypothesis that a random sample of normally distributed observations has a given mean. [after *Student*, pen name of W. S. Gosset (1876–1937), Brit. mathematician]

studhorse ('stʌd,hɔːs) *n* another word for **stallion.**

studied ('stʌdɪd) *adj* carefully practised, designed, or premeditated: *a studied reply.* ▸ **'studiedly** *adv* ▸ **'studiedness** *n*

studio ('stjuːdɪəʊ) *n, pl* **studios. 1** a room in which an artist, photographer, or musician works. **2** a room used to record television or radio programmes, make films, etc. **3** (*pl*) the premises of a radio, television, or film company. [C19: from It., lit.: study, from L *studium* diligence]

studio couch *n* an upholstered couch, usually backless, convertible into a double bed.

studio flat *n* a flat with one main room.

studious ('stjuːdɪəs) *adj* **1** given to study. **2** of a serious, thoughtful, and hard-working character. **3** showing deliberation, care, or precision. [C14: from L *studiōsus* devoted to, from *studium* assiduity] ▸ **'studiously** *adv* ▸ **'studiousness** *n*

stud poker *n* a variety of poker in which the first card is dealt face down before each player and the next four are dealt face up (**five-card stud**) or in which the first two cards and the last card are dealt face down and the intervening four cards are dealt face up (**seven-card stud**).

study ('stʌdɪ) *vb* **studies, studying, studied. 1** to apply the mind to the learning or understanding of (a subject), esp. by reading. **2** (*tr*) to investigate or examine, as by observation, research, etc. **3** (*tr*) to look at minutely; scrutinize. **4** (*tr*) to give much careful or critical thought to. **5** to take a course in (a subject), as at a college. **6** (*tr*) to try to memorize: *to study a part for a play.* **7** (*intr*) to meditate or contemplate; reflect. ◆ *n, pl* **studies. 8a** the act or process of studying. **8b** (*as modifier*): *study group.* **9** a room used for studying, reading, writing, etc. **10** (*often pl*) work relating to a particular discipline: *environmental studies.* **11** an investigation and analysis of a subject, institution

---

★ people and places

etc. **12** a product of studying, such as a written paper or book. **13** a drawing, sculpture, etc., executed for practice or in preparation for another work. **14** a musical composition intended to develop one aspect of performing technique. **15** *Inf.* **in a brown study.** in a reverie or daydream. [C13: from OF *estudie,* from L *studium* zeal, from *studēre* to be diligent]

stuff (stʌf) *vb* (*mainly tr*) **1** to pack or fill completely; cram. **2** (*intr*) to eat large quantities. **3** to force, shove, or squeeze: *to stuff money into a pocket.* **4** to fill (food such as poultry or tomatoes) with a stuffing. **5** to fill (an animal's skin) with material so as to restore the shape of the live animal. **6** *Taboo sl.* to have sexual intercourse with (a woman). **7** *US & Canad.* to fill (a ballot box) with fraudulent votes. **8** *Sl.* to ruin, frustrate, or defeat. ◆ *n* **9** the raw material or fabric of something. **10** woollen cloth or fabric. **11** any general or unspecified substance or accumulation of objects. **12** stupid or worthless actions, speech, etc. **13** subject matter, skill, etc.: *he knows his stuff.* **14** a slang word for **money. 15** *Sl.* a drug, esp. cannabis. **16** *Inf.* **do one's stuff.** to do what is expected of one. **17 that's the stuff.** that is what is needed. **18** *Brit. sl.* a girl or woman considered sexually (esp. in **bit of stuff**). [C14: from OF *estoffe,* from *estoffer* to furnish, of Gmc origin]
▶ **'stuffer** *n*

stuffed (stʌft) *adj* **1** filled with something, esp. (of poultry and other food) filled with stuffing. **2** (foll. by *up*) having the nasal passages blocked with mucus. **3 get stuffed!** *Brit. taboo sl.* an exclamation of contemptuous anger or annoyance against another person.

stuffed shirt *n Inf.* a pompous person.

stuff gown *n Brit.* a woollen gown worn by a barrister who has not taken silk.

stuffing ('stʌfɪŋ) *n* **1** the material with which something is stuffed. **2** a mixture of ingredients with which poultry, meat, etc., is stuffed before cooking. **3 knock the stuffing out of (someone).** to defeat (someone) utterly.

stuffing box *n* a small chamber in which packing is compressed around a reciprocating or rotating rod or shaft to form a seal.

stuffy ('stʌfɪ) *adj* **stuffier, stuffiest. 1** lacking fresh air. **2** excessively dull, staid, or conventional. **3** (of the nasal passages) blocked with mucus.
▶ **'stuffily** *adv* ▶ **'stuffiness** *n*

stultify ('stʌltɪˌfaɪ) *vb* **stultifies, stultifying, stultified.** (*tr*) **1** to make useless, futile, or ineffectual, esp. by routine. **2** to cause to appear absurd or inconsistent. [C18: from L *stultus* stupid + *facere* to make]
▶ ˌstultifiˈcation *n* ▶ 'stultiˌfier *n*

stum (stʌm) (in wine-making) ◆ *n* **1** a less common word for **must**². **2** partly fermented wine added to fermented wine as a preservative. ◆ *vb* **stums, stumming, stummed. 3** to preserve (wine) by adding stum. [C17: from Du. *stom* dumb]

stumble ('stʌmbᵊl) *vb* **stumbles, stumbling, stumbled.** (*intr*) **1** to trip or fall while walking or running. **2** to walk in an awkward, unsteady, or unsure way. **3** to make mistakes or hesitate in speech or actions. **4** (foll. by *across* or *upon*) to come (across) by accident. ◆ *n* **5** a false step, trip, or blunder. **6** the act of stumbling. [C14: rel. to Norwegian *stumla,* Danish dialect *stumle*]
▶ **'stumbler** *n* ▶ **'stumbling** *adj* ▶ **'stumblingly** *adv*

stumbling block *n* any impediment or obstacle.

stumer ('stjuːmə) *n* **1** *Sl.* a forgery or cheat. **2** *Irish dialect.* a poor bargain. **3** *Scot.* a stupid person. **4 come a stumer.** *Austral. sl.* to crash financially. [from ?]

stump (stʌmp) *n* **1** the base of a tree trunk left standing after the tree has been felled or has fallen. **2** the part of something, such as a tooth, limb, or blade, that remains after a larger part has been removed. **3** (*often pl*) *Inf.*, *facetious.* a leg (esp. in **stir one's stumps**). **4** *Cricket.* any of three upright wooden sticks that, with two bails laid across them, form a wicket (the **stumps**). **5** Also called: **tortillon.** a short sharply-pointed stick of cork or rolled paper or leather, used in drawing and shading. **6** a heavy tread or the sound of heavy footsteps. **7** a platform used by an orator when addressing a meeting. ◆ *vb* **8** (*tr*) to stop, confuse, or puzzle. **9** (*intr*) to plod or trudge

heavily. **10** (*tr*) *Cricket.* to dismiss (a batsman) by breaking his wicket with the ball or with the ball in the hand while he is out of his crease. **11** *Chiefly US & Canad.* to campaign or canvass (an area), esp. by political speechmaking. [C14: from MLow G *stump*]
▶ **'stumper** *n*

stump up *vb* (*adv*) *Brit. inf.* to give (the money required).

stumpy ('stʌmpɪ) *adj* **stumpier, stumpiest. 1** short and thickset like a stump; stubby. **2** full of stumps.
▶ **'stumpiness** *n*

stun (stʌn) *vb* **stuns, stunning, stunned.** (*tr*) **1** to render unconscious, as by a heavy blow or fall. **2** to shock or overwhelm. **3** to surprise or astound. ◆ *n* **4** the state or effect of being stunned. [C13 *stunen,* from OF *estoner* to daze, ult. from L EX-¹ + *tonāre* to thunder]

stung (stʌŋ) *vb* the past tense and past participle of **sting**.

stunk (stʌŋk) *vb* a past tense and past participle of **stink**.

stunner ('stʌnə) *n Inf.* a person or thing of great beauty, quality, size, etc.

stunning ('stʌnɪŋ) *adj Inf.* very attractive, impressive, astonishing, etc.
▶ **'stunningly** *adv*

stunsail or **stuns'l** ('stʌnsᵊl) *n* another word for **studdingsail**.

stunt¹ (stʌnt) *vb* **1** (*tr*) to prevent or impede (the growth or development) of (a plant, animal, etc.). ◆ *n* **2** the act or an instance of stunting. **3** a person, animal, or plant that has been stunted. [C17 (as vb: to check the growth of): ?from C15 *stont* of short duration, from OE *stunt* foolish; sense prob. infl. by ON *stuttr* dwarfed]
▶ **'stunted** *adj* ▶ **'stuntedness** *n*

stunt² (stʌnt) *n* **1** a feat of daring or skill. **2a** an acrobatic or dangerous piece of action in a film, etc. **2b** (*as modifier*): *a stunt man.* **3** anything spectacular or unusual done for attention. ◆ *vb* **4** (*intr*) to perform a stunt or stunts. [C19: US student slang, from ?]

stupa ('stuːpə) *n* a domed edifice housing Buddhist or Jain relics. [C19: from Sansk.: dome]

stupe (stjuːp) *n Med.* a hot damp cloth, usually sprinkled with an irritant, applied to the body to relieve pain by counterirritation. [C14: from L *stuppa* flax, from Gk *stuppē*]

stupefacient (ˌstjuːpɪˈfeɪʃɪənt) *n* **1** a drug that causes stupor. ◆ *adj* **2** of, relating to, or designating this type of drug. [C17: from L *stupefaciēns,* from *stupēre* to be stunned + *facere* to make]

stupefaction (ˌstjuːpɪˈfækʃən) *n* **1** astonishment. **2** the act of stupefying or the state of being stupefied.

stupefy ('stjuːpɪˌfaɪ) *vb* **stupefies, stupefying, stupefied.** (*tr*) **1** to render insensitive or lethargic. **2** to confuse or astound. [C16: from OF *stupefier,* from L *stupefacere;* see STUPEFACIENT]
▶ **'stupeˌfying** *adj*

stupendous (stjuːˈpɛndəs) *adj* astounding, wonderful, huge, etc. [C17: from L *stupēre* to be amazed]
▶ **stu'pendously** *adv* ▶ **stu'pendousness** *n*

stupid ('stjuːpɪd) *adj* **1** lacking in common sense, perception, or intelligence. **2** (*usually postpositive*) dazed or stupefied: *stupid from lack of sleep.* **3** slow-witted. **4** trivial, silly, or frivolous. ◆ *n* **5** *Inf.* a stupid person. [C16: from F *stupide,* from L *stupidus* silly, from *stupēre* to be amazed]
▶ **stu'pidity** or **'stupidness** *n*

stupor ('stjuːpə) *n* **1** a state of unconsciousness. **2** mental dullness; torpor. [C17: from L, from *stupēre* to be aghast]
▶ **'stuporous** *adj*

sturdy ('stɜːdɪ) *adj* **sturdier, sturdiest. 1** healthy, strong, and vigorous. **2** strongly built; stalwart. [C13 (in the sense: rash, harsh): from OF *estordi* dazed, from *estordir* to stun]
▶ **'sturdily** *adv* ▶ **'sturdiness** *n*

sturgeon ('stɜːdʒən) *n* any of various primitive bony fishes of temperate waters of the N hemisphere, having an elongated snout and rows of spines along the body. [C13: from OF *estourgeon,* of Gmc origin]

Sturt ★ (stɜːt) *n* **Charles.** 1795–1869, British explorer, who led three expeditions (1828–29; 1829; 1844–45) into the Australian interior, discovering the Darling River (1828).

Sturt's desert pea (stɜːts) *n* another name for **desert pea**.

stutter ('stʌtə) *vb* **1** to speak (a word, phrase, etc.) with recurring repetition of consonants, esp. initial ones. **2** to make (an abrupt sound) repeatedly: *the gun stuttered.* ◆ *n* **3** the act or habit of stuttering. **4** a stuttering sound. [C16]
▸ **'stutterer** *n* ▸ **'stuttering** *n, adj* ▸ **'stutteringly** *adv*

Stuttgart ★ (*German* 'ʃtʊtgart) *n* an industrial city in W Germany, capital of Baden-Württemberg state, on the River Neckar: developed around a stud farm (*Stuotgarten*) of the Counts of Württemberg. Pop.: 588 482 (1995 est.).

Stuyvesant ★ ('staɪvɪsˀnt) *n* **Peter.** ?1610–72, Dutch colonial administrator of New Netherland (later New York) (1646–64).

sty (staɪ) *n, pl* **sties.** **1** a pen in which pigs are housed. **2** any filthy or corrupt place. ◆ *vb* **sties, stying, stied.** **3** to enclose or be enclosed in a sty. [OE *stig*]

stye *or* **sty** (staɪ) *n, pl* **styes** *or* **sties.** inflammation of a sebaceous gland of the eyelid. [C15 *styanye* (mistaken as *sty on eye*), from OE *stīgend* rising, hence swelling, + *ye* eye]

Stygian ('stɪdʒɪən) *adj* **1** of or relating to the Styx. **2** *Chiefly literary.* dark, gloomy, or hellish. [C16: from L *Stygius*, from Gk *Stugios*, from *Stux* STYX]

style (staɪl) *n* **1** a form of appearance, design, or production; type or make. **2** the way in which something is done: *good style.* **3** the manner in which something is expressed or performed, considered as separate from its intrinsic content, meaning, etc. **4** a distinctive, formal, or characteristic manner of expression in words, music, painting, etc. **5** elegance or refinement of manners, dress, etc. **6** prevailing fashion in dress, looks, etc. **7** a fashionable or ostentatious mode of existence: *to live in style.* **8** the particular mode of orthography, punctuation, design, etc., followed in a book, journal, etc., or in a printing or publishing house. **9** *Chiefly Brit.* the distinguishing title or form of address of a person or firm. **10** *Bot.* the long slender extension of the ovary, bearing the stigma. **11** a method of expressing or calculating dates. See **Old Style, New Style.** **12** another word for **stylus** (sense 1). **13** the arm of a sundial. ◆ *vb* **styles, styling, styled.** (*mainly tr*) **14** to design, shape, or tailor: *to style hair.* **15** to adapt or make suitable for. **16** to make consistent or correct according to a printing or publishing style. **17** to name or call; designate: *to style a man a fool.* [C13: from L *stylus, stilus* writing implement, hence characteristics of the writing, style]
▸ **'stylar** *adj* ▸ **'styler** *n*

stylebook ('staɪl,bʊk) *n* a book containing rules and examples of punctuation, typography, etc., for the use of writers, editors, and printers.

stylet ('staɪlɪt) *n Surgery.* **1** a wire for insertion into a catheter, etc., to maintain its rigidity during passage. **2** a slender probe. [C17: from F *stilet,* from Olt. STILETTO; infl. by L *stylus* style]

styling mousse *n* a light foamy substance applied to the hair before styling in order to retain the style.

stylish ('staɪlɪʃ) *adj* having style; smart; fashionable.
▸ **'stylishly** *adv* ▸ **'stylishness** *n*

stylist ('staɪlɪst) *n* **1** a person who performs, writes, or acts with attention to style. **2** a designer of clothes, décor, etc. **3** a hairdresser who styles hair.

stylistic (staɪ'lɪstɪk) *adj* of or relating to style, esp. artistic or literary style.
▸ **sty'listically** *adv*

stylite ('staɪlaɪt) *n Christianity.* one of a class of recluses who in ancient times lived on the top of high pillars. [C17: from LGk *stulitēs,* from Gk *stulos* a pillar]
▸ **stylitic** (staɪ'lɪtɪk) *adj*

stylize *or* **stylise** ('staɪlaɪz) *vb* **stylizes, stylizing, stylized** *or* **stylises, stylising, stylised.** (*tr*) to give a conventional or established stylistic form to.
▸ **,styli'zation** *or* **,styli'sation** *n*

stylo- *or before a vowel* **styl-** *combining form.* **1** (in biology) a style. **2** indicating a column or point: *stylobate; stylograph.* [from Gk *stulos* column]

stylobate ('staɪlə,beɪt) *n* a continuous horizontal course of masonry that supports a colonnade. [C17: from L *stylobatēs,* from Gk *stulos* pillar + *-batēs,* from *bainein* to walk]

stylograph ('staɪlə,grɑːf) *n* a fountain pen having a fine hollow tube as the writing point instead of a nib. [C19: from STYL(US) + -GRAPH]

styloid ('staɪlɔɪd) *adj* **1** resembling a stylus. **2** *Anat.* of or relating to a projecting process of the temporal bone. [C18: from NL *styloides,* from Gk *stuloeidēs* like a stylus; infl. by Gk *stulos* pillar]

stylops ('staɪlɒps) *n, pl* **stylopes** (-lə,piːz). any of various insects living as a parasite in other insects, esp. bees and wasps. [C19: NL, from Gk, from *stulos* a pillar + *ōps* an eye, from the fact that the male has stalked eyes]

stylus ('staɪləs) *n, pl* **styli** (-laɪ) *or* **styluses. 1** Also called: **style.** a pointed instrument for engraving, drawing, or writing. **2** a tool used in ancient times for writing on wax tablets, which was pointed at one end and blunt at the other for erasing. **3** Also called: **needle.** a device attached to the cartridge in the pick-up arm of a record player that rests in the groove in the record, transmitting the vibrations to the sensing device in the cartridge. [C18: from L, var. of *stilus* writing implement]

stymie *or* **stymy** ('staɪmɪ) *vb* **stymies, stymieing** *or* **stymying, stymied.** (*tr; often passive*) **1** to hinder or thwart. **2** *Golf.* (formerly) to impede with a stymie. ◆ *n, pl* **stymies. 3** *Golf.* (formerly) a situation in which an opponent's ball is blocking the line between the hole and the ball about to be played. **4** a situation of obstruction. [C19: from ?]

styptic ('stɪptɪk) *adj* **1** contracting the blood vessels or tissues. ◆ *n* **2** a styptic drug. [C14: via LL, from Gk *stuptikos* capable of contracting, from *stuphein* to contract]

styrene ('staɪriːn) *n* a colourless oily volatile flammable liquid made from ethylene and benzene. It readily polymerizes and is used in making synthetic plastics and rubbers. Formula: $C_6H_5CH:CH_2$. Systematic name: **phenylethene.** [C20: from Gk *sturax* tree of the genus *Styrax* + -ENE]

Styria ★ ('stɪərɪə) *n* a mountainous state of SE Austria: rich mineral resources. Capital: Graz. Pop.: 1 203 993 (1994 est.). Area: 16 384 sq. km (6326 sq. miles). German name: **Steiermark.**

Styx ★ (stɪks) *n Greek myth.* a river in Hades across which Charon ferried the souls of the dead. [from Gk *Stux;* related to *stugein* to hate]

suable ('sjuːəbˀl) *adj* liable to be sued in a court.
▸ **,sua'bility** *n*

Suakin ★ ('suːəkɪn) *n* a port in the NE Sudan, on the Red Sea: formerly the chief port of the African Red Sea; now obstructed by a coral reef. Pop.: 6000 (latest est.).

suasion ('sweɪʒən) *n* a rare word for **persuasion.** [C14: from L *suāsiō,* from *suādēre* to PERSUADE]
▸ **'suasive** *adj*

suave (swɑːv) *adj* (esp. of a man) displaying smoothness and sophistication in manner; urbane. [C16: from L *suāvis* sweet]
▸ **'suavely** *adv* ▸ **suavity** ('swɑːvɪtɪ) *or* **'suaveness** *n*

sub (sʌb) *n* **1** short for several words beginning with *sub-,* such as **subeditor, submarine, subordinate, subscription,** and **substitute. 2** *Brit. inf.* an advance payment of wages or salary. Formal term: **subsistence allowance.** ◆ *vb* **subs, subbing, subbed. 3** (*intr*) to serve or act as a substitute. **4** *Brit. inf.* to grant or receive (an advance payment of wages or salary). **5** (*tr*) *Inf.* short for **subedit.**

sub. *abbrev. for:* **1** subeditor. **2** *Music.* subito. **3** subscription. **4** substitute.

sub- *prefix* **1** situated under or beneath: *subterranean.* **2** secondary in rank; subordinate: *subeditor.* **3** falling short of; less than or imperfectly: *subarctic; subhuman.* **4** forming a subdivision or subordinate part: *subcommittee.* **5** (in chemistry) **5a** indicating that a compound contains a relatively small proportion of a specified element: *suboxide.* **5b** indicating that a salt is basic salt: *subacetate.* [from L *sub*]

subacid (sʌbˈæsɪd) adj (esp. of some fruits) moderately acid or sour.
▸ **subacidity** (ˌsʌbəˈsɪdɪtɪ) or **subˈacidness** n

subadar or **subahdar** (ˈsuːbəˌdɑː) n (formerly) the chief native officer of a company of Indian soldiers in the British service. [C17: via Urdu from Persian, from *sūba* province + *-dār* holding]

subalpine (sʌbˈælpaɪn) adj **1** situated in or relating to the regions at the foot of mountains. **2** (of plants) growing below the tree line in mountainous regions.

subaltern (ˈsʌbˀltən) n **1** a commissioned officer below the rank of captain in certain armies, esp. the British. ◆ adj **2** of inferior position or rank. **3** *Logic*. (of a proposition) particular, esp. in relation to a universal of the same quality. [C16: from LL *subalternus*, from L SUB- + *alternus* alternate, from *alter* the other]

subalternation (ˌsʌbɔːltəˈneɪʃən) n *Logic*. the relation between a universal and a particular proposition of the same quality where the universal proposition implies the particular proposition.

subantarctic (ˌsʌbæntˈɑːktɪk) adj of or relating to latitudes immediately north of the Antarctic Circle.

subaqua (sʌbˈækwə) adj of or relating to underwater sport: *subaqua swimming*.

subaqueous (sʌbˈeɪkwɪəs, -ˈækwɪ-) adj occurring, formed, or used under water.

subarctic (sʌbˈɑːktɪk) adj of or relating to latitudes immediately south of the Arctic Circle.

subatomic (ˌsʌbəˈtɒmɪk) adj **1** of, relating to, or being a particle making up an atom or a process occurring within atoms. **2** having dimensions smaller than atomic dimensions.

subbasement (ˈsʌbˌbeɪsmənt) n a storey of a building beneath the main basement.

subclass (ˈsʌbˌklɑːs) n **1** a principal subdivision of a class. **2** a taxonomic group that is a subdivision of a class. **3** *Maths*. another name for **subset.**

subclavian (sʌbˈkleɪvɪən) adj *Anat*. (of an artery, vein, etc.) below the clavicle. [C17: from NL *subclāvius*, from L SUB- + *clavis* key]

subclinical (sʌbˈklɪnɪkˀl) adj *Med*. of or relating to the stage in the course of a disease before the symptoms are first noted.
▸ **subˈclinically** adv

subconscious (sʌbˈkɒnʃəs) adj **1** acting or existing without one's awareness. ◆ n **2** *Psychol*. that part of the mind on the fringe of consciousness which contains material it is possible to become aware of by redirecting attention.
▸ **subˈconsciously** adv ▸ **subˈconsciousness** n

subcontinent (sʌbˈkɒntɪnənt) n a large land mass that is a distinct part of a continent, such as India is of Asia.
▸ **subcontinental** (ˌsʌbkɒntɪˈnentˀl) adj

subcontract n (sʌbˈkɒntrækt). **1** a subordinate contract under which the supply of materials, labour, etc., is let out to someone other than a party to the main contract. ◆ vb (ˌsʌbkənˈtrækt). **2** (intr; often foll. by *for*) to enter into or make a subcontract. **3** (tr) to let out (work) on a subcontract.
▸ **ˌsubconˈtractor** n

subcontrary (sʌbˈkɒntrərɪ) *Logic*. ◆ adj **1** (of a pair of propositions) related such that they cannot both be false at once, although they may be true together. ◆ n, pl **subcontraries**. **2** a statement which cannot be false when a given statement is false.

subcritical (sʌbˈkrɪtɪkˀl) adj *Physics*. (of a nuclear reaction, power station, etc.) having or involving a chain reaction that is not self-sustaining; not yet critical.

subculture (ˈsʌbˌkʌltʃə) n a subdivision of a national culture or an enclave within it with a distinct integrated network of behaviour, beliefs, and attitudes.
▸ **subˈcultural** adj

subcutaneous (ˌsʌbkjuːˈteɪnɪəs) adj *Med*. situated, used, or introduced beneath the skin.
▸ **ˌsubcuˈtaneously** adv

subdeacon (ˌsʌbˈdiːkən) n *Chiefly RC Church*. **1** a cleric who assists at High Mass. **2** (formerly) a person ordained to the lowest of the major orders.
▸ **subdeaconate** (sʌbˈdiːkənɪt) n

subdivide (ˌsʌbdɪˈvaɪd, ˈsʌbdɪˌvaɪd) vb **subdivides, subdividing, subdivided**. to divide (something) resulting from an earlier division.
▸ **ˈsubdiˌvision** n

subdominant (sʌbˈdɒmɪnənt) *Music*. ◆ n **1** the fourth degree of a major or minor scale. **2** a key or chord based on this. ◆ adj **3** of or relating to the subdominant.

subdue (səbˈdjuː) vb **subdues, subduing, subdued**. (tr) **1** to establish ascendancy over by force. **2** to overcome and bring under control, as by intimidation or persuasion. **3** to hold in check or repress (feelings, etc.). **4** to render less intense or less conspicuous. [C14 *sobdue*, from OF *soduire* to mislead, from L *subdūcere* to remove; infl. by L *subdere* to subject]
▸ **subˈduable** adj ▸ **subˈdual** n

subdued (səbˈdjuːd) adj **1** cowed, passive, or shy. **2** gentle or quiet: *a subdued whisper*. **3** (of colours, lighting, etc.) not harsh or bright.

subdural (sʌbˈdjuərəl) adj *Anat*. between the dura mater and the arachnoid: *subdural haematoma*.

subedit (sʌbˈɛdɪt) vb **subedits, subediting, subedited**. to edit and correct (written or printed material).

subeditor (sʌbˈɛdɪtə) n a person who checks and edits copy, esp. on a newspaper.

subequatorial (ˌsʌbˌɛkwəˈtɔːrɪəl) adj in or characteristic of regions immediately north or south of equatorial regions.

suberose (ˈsjuːbəˌrəus), **subereous** (sjuːˈbɛrɪəs), or **suberic** (sjuːˈbɛrɪk) adj *Bot*. relating to, resembling, or consisting of cork; corky. [C19: from L *sūber* cork + -OSE¹]

subfamily (ˈsʌbˌfæmɪlɪ) n, pl **subfamilies**. **1** *Biol*. a taxonomic group that is a subdivision of a family. **2** a subdivision of a family of languages.

subfusc (ˈsʌbfʌsk) adj **1** devoid of brightness or appeal; drab, dull, or dark. ◆ n **2** (at Oxford University) formal academic dress. [C18: from L *subfuscus* dusky, from *fuscus* dark]

subgenus (ˈsʌbˌdʒiːnəs, -ˌdʒɛn-) n, pl **subgenera** (-ˈdʒɛnərə) or **subgenuses**. *Biol*. a subdivision of a genus that is of higher rank than a species.
▸ **subgeneric** (ˌsʌbdʒəˈnɛrɪk) adj

subheading (ˈsʌbˌhɛdɪŋ) or **subhead** n **1** the heading or title of a subdivision or subsection of a printed work. **2** a division subordinate to a main heading or title.

subhuman (sʌbˈhjuːmən) adj **1** of or designating animals below man (*Homo sapiens*) in evolutionary development. **2** less than human.

subindex (sʌbˈɪndɛks) n, pl **subindices** (-dɪˌsiːz) or **subindexes**. another word for **subscript** (sense 2).

subitize or **subitise** (ˈsʌbɪˌtaɪz) vb **subitizes, subitizing, subitized** or **subitises, subitising, subitised**. *Psychol*. to perceive the number of (a group of items) at a glance and without counting: *the maximum number of items that can be subitized is about five*. [C20: from L *subitus* sudden + -IZE]

subito (ˈsuːbɪˌtəu) adv *Music*. suddenly; immediately. [C18: via It. from L: suddenly, from *subitus* sudden, from *subīre* to approach]

subj. *abbrev. for:* **1** subject. **2** subjective(ly). **3** subjunctive.

subjacent (sʌbˈdʒeɪsˀnt) adj **1** forming a foundation; underlying. **2** lower than. [C16: from L *subjacēre* to lie close, be under]
▸ **subˈjacency** n ▸ **subˈjacently** adv

subject n (ˈsʌbdʒɪkt). **1** the predominant theme or topic, as of a book, discussion, etc. **2** any branch of learning considered as a course of study. **3** *Grammar, logic*. a word, phrase, etc., about which something is predicated or stated in a sentence; for example, *the cat* in the sentence *The cat catches mice*. **4** a person or thing that undergoes experiment, treatment, etc. **5** a person under the rule of a monarch, government, etc. **6** an object, figure, scene, etc., as portrayed by an artist or photographer. **7** *Philosophy*. **7a** that which thinks or feels as opposed to the object of thinking and feeling; the self or the mind. **7b** a

substance as opposed to its attributes. **8** Also called: **theme.** *Music.* the principal motif of a fugue, the basis from which the musical material is derived in a sonata-form movement, or the recurrent figure in a rondo. **9** *Logic.* the term of a proposition about which something is asserted. **10** an originating motive. **11 change the subject.** to select a new topic of conversation. ◆ *adj* ('sʌbdʒɪkt). (*usually postpositive;* foll. by *to*) **12** being under the power or sovereignty of a ruler, government, etc.: *subject peoples.* **13** showing a tendency (towards): *a child subject to indiscipline.* **14** exposed or vulnerable: *subject to ribaldry.* **15** conditional upon: *the results are subject to correction.* ◆ *adv* ('sʌbdʒɪkt). **16 subject to.** (*prep*) under the condition that: *we accept, subject to her agreement.* ◆ *vb* (səb'dʒɛkt). (*tr*) **17** (foll. by *to*) to cause to undergo: *they subjected him to torture.* **18** (*often passive;* foll. by *to*) to expose or render vulnerable or liable (to some experience): *he was subjected to great danger.* **19** (foll. by *to*) to bring under the control or authority (of): *to subject a soldier to discipline.* **20** *Rare.* to present for consideration; submit. [C14: from L *subjectus* brought under, from *subicere* to place under, from SUB- + *jacere* to throw]
▸ sub'jectable *adj* ▸ sub'jection *n*

subjective (səb'dʒɛktɪv) *adj* **1** of, proceeding from, or relating to the mind of the thinking subject and not the nature of the object being considered. **2** of, relating to, or emanating from a person's emotions, prejudices, etc. **3** relating to the inherent nature of a person or thing; essential. **4** existing only as perceived and not as a thing in itself. **5** *Med.* (of a symptom, condition, etc.) experienced only by the patient and incapable of being recognized or studied by anyone else. **6** *Grammar.* denoting a case of nouns and pronouns, esp. in languages having only two cases, that identifies the subject of a finite verb and (in formal use in English) is selected for predicate complements, as in *It is I.* ◆ *n* **7** *Grammar.* **7a** the subjective case. **7b** a subjective word or speech element. Cf. **objective.**
▸ sub'jectively *adv* ▸ ,subjec'tivity *or* sub'jectiveness *n*

subjectivism (səb'dʒɛktɪ,vɪzəm) *n Philosophy.* the doctrine that there are no absolute moral values but that these are variable in the same way that taste is.
▸ sub'jectivist *n*

subjoin (sʌb'dʒɔɪn) *vb* (*tr*) to add or attach at the end of something spoken, written, etc. [C16: from F *subjoindre,* from L *subjungere* to add to, from *sub-* in addition + *jungere* to join]
▸ sub'joinder *n*

sub judice ('dʒuː'dɪsɪ) *adj* (*usually postpositive*) before a court of law or a judge; under judicial consideration. [L]

subjugate ('sʌbdʒʊ,geɪt) *vb* subjugates, subjugating, subjugated. (*tr*) **1** to bring into subjection. **2** to make subservient or submissive. [C15: from LL *subjugāre* to subdue, from L SUB- + *jugum* yoke]
▸ 'subjugable *adj* ▸ ,subju'gation *n* ▸ 'subju,gator *n*

subjunctive (səb'dʒʌŋktɪv) *Grammar.* ◆ *adj* **1** denoting a mood of verbs used when the content of the clause is being doubted, supposed, feared true, etc., rather than being asserted. In the following sentence, *were* is in the subjunctive: *I'd think seriously about it if I were you.* Cf. **indicative.** ◆ *n* **2a** the subjunctive mood. **2b** a verb in this mood. [C16: via LL *subjunctīvus,* from L *subjungere* to SUBJOIN]
▸ sub'junctively *adv*

sublease *n* ('sʌb,liːs). **1** a lease of property made by a lessee or tenant of that property. ◆ *vb* (sʌb'liːs), subleases, subleasing, subleased. **2** to grant a sublease of (property); sublet. **3** (*tr*) to obtain or hold by sublease.
▸ sublessee (,sʌble'siː) *n* ▸ sublessor (,sʌble'sɔː) *n*

sublet (sʌb'lɛt) *vb* sublets, subletting, sublet. **1** to grant a sublease of (property). **2** to let out (work, etc.) under a subcontract.

sublieutenant (,sʌblə'tɛnənt) *n* the most junior commissioned officer in the Royal Navy and certain other navies.
▸ ,sublieu'tenancy *n*

sublimate ('sʌblɪ,meɪt) *vb* sublimates, sublimating, sublimated. **1** *Psychol.* to direct the energy of (a primitive impulse) into activities that are socially more acceptable. **2**

(*tr*) to make purer; refine. ◆ *n* **3** *Chem.* the material obtained when a substance is sublimed. [C16: from L *sublīmāre* to elevate, from *sublīmis* lofty; see SUBLIME]
▸ ,subli'mation *n*

sublime (sə'blaɪm) *adj* **1** of high moral, intellectual, or spiritual value; noble; exalted. **2** inspiring deep veneration or awe. **3** unparalleled; supreme. **4** *Poetic.* of proud bearing or aspect. **5** *Arch.* raised up. ◆ *n* **the sublime. 6** something that is sublime. **7** the ultimate degree or perfect example: *the sublime of folly.* ◆ *vb* sublimes, subliming, sublimed. **8** (*tr*) to make higher or purer. **9** to change or cause to change directly from a solid to a vapour or gas without first melting. **10** to undergo or cause to undergo this process followed by a reverse change directly from a vapour to a solid: *to sublime iodine onto glass.* [C14: from L *sublīmis* lofty, ?from *sub-* up to + *līmen* lintel]
▸ sub'limely *adv* ▸ sublimity (sə'blɪmɪtɪ) *n*

subliminal (sʌb'lɪmɪn°l) *adj* **1** resulting from processes of which the individual is not aware. **2** (of stimuli) less than the minimum intensity or duration required to elicit a response. [C19: from L *sub-* below + *līmen* threshold]
▸ sub'liminally *adv*

subliminal advertising *n* advertising on film or television that employs subliminal images to influence the viewer unconsciously.

sublingual (sʌb'lɪŋgwəl) *adj Anat.* situated beneath the tongue.

sublunary (sʌb'luːnərɪ) *adj* **1** between the moon and the earth. **2** of or relating to the earth. [C16: via LL, from L SUB- + *lūna* moon]

sub-machine-gun *n* a portable automatic or semiautomatic light gun with a short barrel, designed to be fired from the hip or shoulder.

submarginal (sʌb'mɑːdʒɪn°l) *adj* **1** below the minimum requirements. **2** (of land) infertile and unprofitable.
▸ sub'marginally *adv*

submarine ('sʌbmə,riːn, ,sʌbmə'riːn) *n* **1** a vessel, esp. a warship, capable of operating below the surface of the sea. **2** (*modifier*) **2a** of or relating to a submarine: *a submarine captain.* **2b** below the surface of the sea: *a submarine cable.*
▸ submariner (sʌb'mærɪnə) *n*

submaxillary gland (,sʌbmæk'sɪlərɪ) *n* (in mammals) either of a pair of salivary glands situated on each side behind the lower jaw.

submediant (sʌb'miːdɪənt) *Music.* ◆ *n* **1** the sixth degree of a major or minor scale. **2** a key or chord based on this. ◆ *adj* **3** of or relating to the submediant.

submerge (səb'mɜːdʒ) *or* **submerse** (səb'mɜːs) *vb* submerges, submerging, submerged *or* submerses, submersing, submersed. **1** to plunge, sink, or dive or cause to plunge, sink, or dive below the surface of water, etc. **2** (*tr*) to cover with water or other liquid. **3** (*tr*) to hide; suppress. **4** (*tr*) to overwhelm, as with work, etc. [C17: from L *submergere*]
▸ sub'mergence *or* sub'mersion *n*

submersible (səb'mɜːsɪb°l) *or* **submergible** (səb'mɜːdʒɪb°l) *adj* **1** able to be submerged. **2** capable of operating under water, etc. ◆ *n* **3** a vessel designed to operate under water for short periods. **4** a submarine designed and equipped to carry out work below the level that divers can work.
▸ sub,mersi'bility *or* sub,mergi'bility *n*

subminiature (sʌb'mɪnɪətʃə) *adj* smaller than miniature.

subminiature camera *n* a pocket-sized camera, usually using 16 millimetre film.

submission (səb'mɪʃən) *n* **1** an act or instance of submitting. **2** something submitted; a proposal, etc. **3** the quality or condition of being submissive. **4** the act of referring a document, etc., for the consideration of someone else.

submissive (səb'mɪsɪv) *adj* of, tending towards, or indicating submission, humility, or servility.
▸ sub'missively *adv* ▸ sub'missiveness *n*

submit (səb'mɪt) *vb* submits, submitting, submitted. **1** (often

foll. by *to*) to yield (oneself), as to the will of another person, a superior force, etc. **2** (foll. by *to*) to subject or be voluntarily subjected (to analysis, treatment, etc.). **3** (*tr*; often foll. by *to*) to refer (something to someone) for judgment or consideration. **4** (*tr*; *may take a clause as object*) to state, contend, or propose deferentially. **5** (*intr*; often foll. by *to*) to defer or accede (to the decision, etc., of another). [C14: from L *submittere* to place under]
▶ **sub'mittable** *or* **sub'missible** *adj* ▶ **sub'mittal** *n* ▶ **sub'mitter** *n*

submultiple (sʌb'mʌltɪpªl) *n* **1** a number that can be divided into another number an integral number of times without a remainder: *three is a submultiple of nine.* ◆ *adj* **2** being a submultiple of a quantity or number.

subnormal (sʌb'nɔːməl) *adj* **1** less than the normal. **2** having a low intelligence. ◆ *n* **3** a subnormal person.
▶ **subnormality** (ˌsʌbnɔː'mælɪtɪ) *n*

subnuclear (sʌb'njuːklɪə) *adj* in or smaller than the nucleus of an atom.

suborbital (sʌb'ɔːbɪtªl) *adj* **1** (of a rocket, missile, etc.) having a flight path that is less than an orbit of the earth or other celestial body. **2** *Anat.* situated beneath the orbit of the eye.

suborder ('sʌb,ɔːdə) *n Biol.* a subdivision of an order.
▶ **sub'ordinal** *adj*

subordinate *adj* (sə'bɔːdɪnɪt). **1** of lesser order or importance. **2** under the authority or control of another: *a subordinate functionary.* ◆ *n* (sə'bɔːdɪnɪt). **3** a person or thing that is subordinate. ◆ *vb* (sə'bɔːdɪˌneɪt), **subordinates, subordinating, subordinated.** (*tr*; usually foll. by *to*) **4** to put in a lower rank or position (than). **5** to make subservient: *to subordinate mind to heart.* [C15: from Med. L *subordināre*, from L SUB- + *ordō* rank]
▶ **sub'ordinately** *adv* ▶ **sub,ordi'nation** *n* ▶ **sub'ordinative** *adj*

subordinate clause *n Grammar.* a clause with an adjectival, adverbial, or nominal function, rather than one that functions as a separate sentence in its own right.

subordinating conjunction *n* a conjunction that introduces subordinate clauses, such as *if, because, although,* and *until.*

suborn (sə'bɔːn) *vb* (*tr*) **1** to bribe, incite, or instigate (a person) to commit a wrongful act. **2** *Law.* to induce (a witness) to commit perjury. [C16: from L *subornāre*, from *sub-* secretly + *ornāre* to furnish]
▶ **subornation** (ˌsʌbɔː'neɪʃən) *n* ▶ **subornative** (sʌ'bɔːnətɪv) *adj* ▶ **sub'orner** *n*

Subotica ★ (*Serbo-Croat* 'subɔtitsa) *n* a town in NE Yugoslavia, in Serbia near the border with Hungary: agricultural and industrial centre. Pop.: 100 386 (1991). Hungarian name: **Szabadka.**

suboxide (sʌb'ɒksaɪd) *n* an oxide of an element containing less oxygen than the common oxide formed by the element: *carbon suboxide,* C_2O_3.

subplot ('sʌb,plɒt) *n* a subordinate or auxiliary plot in a novel, play, film, etc.

subpoena (səb'piːnə) *n* **1** a writ issued by a court of justice requiring a person to appear before the court at a specified time. ◆ *vb* **subpoenas, subpoenaing, subpoenaed. 2** (*tr*) to serve with a subpoena. [C15: from L: under penalty]

subrogate ('sʌbrə,geɪt) *vb* **subrogates, subrogating, subrogated.** (*tr*) *Law.* to put (one person or thing) in the place of another in respect of a right or claim. [C16: from L *subrogāre*, from *sub-* in place of + *rogāre* to ask]
▶ ,**subro'gation** *n*

sub rosa ('rəuzə) *adv* in secret. [L, lit.: under the rose; from use of the rose in ancient times as a token of secrecy]

subroutine ('sʌbruːˌtiːn) *n* a section of a computer program that is stored only once but can be used at several different points in the program. Also called: **procedure.**

sub-Saharan *adj* in, of, or relating to Africa south of the Sahara desert.

subscribe (səb'skraɪb) *vb* **subscribes, subscribing, subscribed. 1** (usually foll. by *to*) to pay or promise to pay (money) as a contribution (to a fund, for a magazine, etc.), esp. at regular intervals. **2** to sign (one's name, etc.) at the end of a document. **3** (*intr*; foll. by *to*) to give support or approval: *to subscribe to the theory of reincarnation.* [C15: from L *subscrībere* to write underneath]
▶ **sub'scriber** *n*

subscriber trunk dialling *n Brit.* a service by which telephone subscribers can obtain trunk calls by dialling direct without the aid of an operator. Abbrev.: **STD.**

subscript ('sʌbskrɪpt) *Printing.* ◆ *adj* **1** (of a character) written or printed below the base line. Cf. **superscript.**
◆ *n* **2** Also called: **subindex.** a subscript character.

subscription (səb'skrɪpʃən) *n* **1** a payment or promise of payment for consecutive issues of a magazine, newspaper, book, etc., over a specified period of time. **2a** the advance purchase of tickets for a series of concerts, etc. **2b** (*as modifier*): *a subscription concert.* **3** money paid or promised, as to a charity, or the fund raised in this way. **4** an offer to buy shares or bonds issued by a company. **5** the act of signing one's name to a document, etc. **6** a signature or other appendage attached to the bottom of a document, etc. **7** agreement or acceptance expressed by or as if by signing one's name. **8** a signed document, statement, etc. **9** *Chiefly Brit.* the membership dues or fees paid to a society or club. **10** an advance order for a new product. **11a** the sale of books, etc., prior to publishing. **11b** (*as modifier*): *a subscription edition.*
▶ **sub'scriptive** *adj* ▶ **sub'scriptively** *adv*

subsequence ('sʌbsɪkwəns) *n* **1** the fact or state of being subsequent. **2** a subsequent incident or occurrence.

subsequent ('sʌbsɪkwənt) *adj* occurring after; succeeding. [C15: from L *subsequēns* following on, from *subsequī*, from *sub-* near + *sequī* to follow]
▶ **'subsequently** *adv* ▶ **'subsequentness** *n*

subserve (səb'sɜːv) *vb* **subserves, subserving, subserved.** (*tr*) to be helpful or useful to. [C17: from L *subservīre* to be subject to, from SUB- + *servīre* to serve]

subservient (səb'sɜːvɪənt) *adj* **1** obsequious. **2** serving as a means to an end. **3** a less common word for **subordinate** (sense 2). [C17: from L *subserviēns* complying with, from *subservīre* to SUBSERVE]
▶ **sub'serviently** *adv* ▶ **sub'servience** *or* **sub'serviency** *n*

subset ('sʌb,sɛt) *n* a mathematical set contained within a larger set.

subshrub ('sʌb,ʃrʌb) *n* a small bushy plant that is woody except for the tips of the branches.

subside (səb'saɪd) *vb* **subsides, subsiding, subsided.** (*intr*) **1** to become less loud, excited, violent, etc.; abate. **2** to sink or fall to a lower level. **3** (of the surface of the earth, etc.) to cave in; collapse. **4** (of sediment, etc.) to sink or descend to the bottom; settle. [C17: from L *subsīdere* to settle down]
▶ **sub'sider** *n*

subsidence (səb'saɪdªns, 'sʌbsɪdªns) *n* **1** the act or process of subsiding or the condition of having subsided. **2** *Geol.* the gradual sinking of landforms to a lower level.

subsidiarity (səb,sɪdɪ'ærɪtɪ) *n* the principle of devolving political decisions to the lowest practical level.

subsidiary (səb'sɪdɪərɪ) *adj* **1** serving to aid or supplement; auxiliary. **2** of lesser importance; subordinate.
◆ *n, pl* **subsidiaries. 3** a subsidiary person or thing. **4** Also called: **subsidiary company.** a company with at least half of its capital stock owned by another company. [C16: from L *subsidiārius* supporting, from *subsidium* SUBSIDY]
▶ **sub'sidiarily** *adv* ▶ **sub'sidiariness** *n*

subsidize *or* **subsidise** ('sʌbsɪ,daɪz) *vb* **subsidizes, subsidizing, subsidized** *or* **subsidises, subsidising, subsidised.** (*tr*) **1** to aid or support with a subsidy. **2** to obtain the aid of by means of a subsidy.
▶ ,**subsidi'zation** *or* ,**subsidi'sation** *n* ▶ **'subsi,dizer** *or* **'subsi,diser** *n*

subsidy ('sʌbsɪdɪ) *n, pl* **subsidies. 1** a financial aid supplied by a government, as to industry, for public welfare, the balance of payments, etc. **2** *English history.* a financial grant made originally for special purposes by Parliament to the Crown. **3** any monetary aid, grant, or contribution. [C14: from Anglo-Norman *subsidie*, from L *subsidium* assistance, from *subsidēre* to remain, from *sub-* down + *sedēre* to sit]

subsist (səb'sɪst) *vb* (*mainly intr*) **1** (often foll. by *on*) to be sustained; manage to live: *to subsist on milk*. **2** to continue in existence. **3** (foll. by *in*) to lie or reside by virtue (of); consist. **4** (*tr*) *Obs.* to provide with support. [C16: from L *subsistere* to stand firm]
▸ sub'sistent *adj*

subsistence (səb'sɪstəns) *n* **1** the means by which one maintains life. **2** the act or condition of subsisting.

subsistence farming *n* a type of farming in which most of the produce (**subsistence crop**) is consumed by the farmer and his family.

subsistence level *n* a standard of living barely adequate to support life.

subsistence wage *n* the lowest wage upon which a worker and his family can survive.

subsoil ('sʌb,sɔɪl) *n* **1** Also called: **undersoil**. the layer of soil beneath the surface soil and overlying the bedrock. ♦ *vb* **2** (*tr*) to plough (land) to a depth so as to break up the subsoil.

subsonic (sʌb'sɒnɪk) *adj* being, having, or travelling at a velocity below that of sound.

subspecies ('sʌb,spiːʃiːz) *n*, *pl* **subspecies**. *Biol*. a subdivision of a species: usually occurs because of isolation within a species.

substance ('sʌbstəns) *n* **1** the tangible basic matter of which a thing consists. **2** a specific type of matter, esp. a homogeneous material with definite or fairly definite chemical composition. **3** the essence, meaning, etc., of a discourse, thought, or written article. **4** solid or meaningful quality: *an education of substance*. **5** material density or body: *free space has no substance*. **6** material possessions or wealth: *a man of substance*. **7** *Philosophy*. the supposed immaterial substratum of anything that can receive modifications and in which attributes and accidents inhere. **8 in substance**. with regard to the salient points. [C13: via OF from L *substantia*, from *substāre*, from SUB- + *stāre* to stand]

substandard (sʌb'stændəd) *adj* **1** below an established or required standard. **2** another word for **nonstandard**.

substantial (səb'stænʃəl) *adj* **1** of a considerable size or value: *substantial funds*. **2** worthwhile; important; telling: *a substantial reform*. **3** having wealth or importance: *a substantial member of the community*. **4** (of food or a meal) sufficient and nourishing. **5** solid or strong: *a substantial door*. **6** real; actual; true: *substantial evidence*. **7** of or relating to the basic or fundamental substance or aspects of a thing. ♦ *n* **8** (*often pl*) *Rare*. an essential or important element.
▸ **substantiality** (səb,stænʃɪ'ælɪtɪ) *or* **sub'stantialness** *n*
▸ sub'stantially *adv*

substantialism (səb'stænʃə,lɪzəm) *n* *Philosophy*. the doctrine that a substantial reality underlies phenomena.
▸ sub'stantialist *n*

substantiate (səb'stænʃɪ,eɪt) *vb* **substantiates, substantiating, substantiated**. (*tr*) **1** to establish as valid or genuine. **2** to give form or real existence to. [C17: from NL *substantiāre*, from L *substantia* SUBSTANCE]
▸ sub,stanti'ation *n*

substantive ('sʌbstəntɪv) *n* **1** *Grammar*. a noun or pronoun used in place of a noun. ♦ *adj* **2** of, relating to, containing, or being the essential element of a thing. **3** having independent function, resources, or existence. **4** of substantial quantity. **5** solid in foundation or basis. **6** *Grammar*. denoting, relating to, or standing in place of a noun. **7** (səb'stæntɪv). (of a dye or colour) staining the material directly without use of a mordant. [C15: from LL *substantīvus*, from L *substāre* to stand beneath]
▸ **substantival** (,sʌbstən'taɪvᵊl) *adj* ▸ ,substan'tivally *adv*
▸ 'substantively *adv*

substantive rank *n* a permanent rank in the armed services.

substation ('sʌb,steɪʃən) *n* **1** a subsidiary station. **2** an installation at which electrical energy is received from one or more power stations for conversion from alternating to direct current, stepping down the voltage, or switching before distribution by a low-tension network.

substituent (sʌb'stɪtjʊənt) *n* **1** *Chem*. an atom or group that replaces another atom or group in a molecule or can be regarded as replacing an atom in a parent compound. ♦ *adj* **2** substituted or substitutable. [C19: from L *substituere* to SUBSTITUTE]

substitute ('sʌbstɪ,tjuːt) *vb* **substitutes, substituting, substituted**. **1** (often foll. by *for*) to serve or cause to serve in place of another person or thing. **2** *Chem*. to replace (an atom or group in a molecule) with (another atom or group). ♦ *n* **3a** a person or thing that serves in place of another, such as a player in a game who takes the place of an injured colleague. **3b** (*as modifier*): *a substitute goalkeeper*. [C16: from L *substituere*, from *sub-* in place of + *statuere* to set up]
▸ ,substi'tutable *adj* ▸ 'substi,tutive *adj*

> **USAGE NOTE** *Substitute* is sometimes wrongly used where *replace* is meant: *he replaced* (not *substituted*) *the worn tyre with a new one*.

substitution (,sʌbstɪ'tjuːʃən) *n* **1** the act of substituting or state of being substituted. **2** something or someone substituted.

substrate ('sʌbstreɪt) *n* **1** *Biochem*. the substance upon which an enzyme acts. **2** another word for **substratum**.

substratum (sʌb'strɑːtəm, -'streɪ-) *n*, *pl* **substrata** (-'strɑːtə, -'streɪtə). **1** any layer or stratum lying underneath another. **2** a basis or foundation; groundwork. [C17: from NL, from L *substrātus* strewn beneath, from *substernere* to spread under]
▸ sub'strative *or* sub'stratal *adj*

substructure ('sʌb,strʌktʃə) *n* **1** a structure, pattern, etc., that forms the basis of anything. **2** a structure forming a foundation or framework for a building or other construction.
▸ sub'structural *adj*

subsume (səb'sjuːm) *vb* **subsumes, subsuming, subsumed**. (*tr*) **1** to incorporate (an idea, case, etc.) under a comprehensive or inclusive classification. **2** to consider (an instance of something) as part of a general rule. [C16: from NL *subsumere*, from L SUB- + *sumere* to take]
▸ sub'sumable *adj* ▸ **subsumption** (səb'sʌmpʃən) *n*

subtemperate (sʌb'tempərɪt) *adj* of or relating to the colder temperate regions.

subtenant (sʌb'tenənt) *n* a person who rents or leases property from a tenant.
▸ sub'tenancy *n*

subtend (səb'tend) *vb* (*tr*) **1** *Geom*. to be opposite to and delimit (an angle or side). **2** (of a bract, stem, etc.) to have (a bud or similar part) growing in its axil. [C16: from L *subtendere* to extend beneath]

subterfuge ('sʌbtə,fjuːdʒ) *n* a stratagem employed to conceal something, evade an argument, etc. [C16: from LL *subterfugium*, from L *subterfugere* to escape by stealth, from *subter* secretly + *fugere* to flee]

subterminal (sʌb'tɜːmɪnᵊl) *adj* almost at an end.

subterranean (,sʌbtə'reɪnɪən) *adj* **1** Also: **subterraneous**, **subterrestrial**. situated, living, or operating below the surface of the earth. **2** existing or operating in concealment. [C17: from L *subterrāneus*, from SUB- + *terra* earth]
▸ ,subter'raneanly *or* ,subter'raneously *adv*

subtext ('sʌb,tekst) *n* **1** an underlying theme in a piece of writing. **2** a message which is not stated directly but can be inferred.

subtile ('sʌtᵊl) *adj* a rare spelling of **subtle**.
▸ 'subtilely *adv* ▸ **subtility** (sʌb'tɪlɪtɪ) *or* 'subtileness *n*
▸ 'subtilty *n*

subtilize *or* **subtilise** ('sʌtɪ,laɪz) *vb* **subtilizes, subtilizing, subtilized** *or* **subtilises, subtilising, subtilised**. **1** (*tr*) to bring to a purer state; refine. **2** to debate subtly. **3** (*tr*) to make (the mind, etc.) keener.
▸ ,subtili'zation *or* ,subtili'sation *n*

subtitle ('sʌb,taɪtᵊl) *n* **1** an additional subordinate title given to a literary or other work. **2** (*often pl*) **2a** text superimposed on a film or television broadcast, either a translation of foreign dialogue or as an aid for the hard of hearing. **2b** Also called: **caption**. explanatory text on a silent film. ♦ *vb* **subtitles, subtitling, subtitled**. **3** (*tr; usually passive*) to provide a subtitle for.

subtle ('sʌtᵊl) *adj* **1** not immediately obvious or comprehensible. **2** difficult to detect or analyse, often through being delicate or highly refined: *a subtle scent*. **3** showing or making or capable of showing or making fine distinctions of meaning. **4** marked by or requiring mental acuteness or ingenuity; discriminating. **5** delicate or faint: *a subtle shade*. **6** cunning or wily: *a subtle rogue*. **7** operating or executed in secret: *a subtle intrigue*. [C14: from OF *soutil*, from L *subtīlis* finely woven]
▶ **'subtleness** *n* ▶ **'subtly** *adv*

subtlety ('sʌtᵊltɪ) *n, pl* **subtleties**. **1** the state or quality of being subtle; delicacy. **2** a fine distinction. **3** something subtle.

subtonic (sʌb'tɒnɪk) *n Music*. the seventh degree of a major or minor scale.

subtotal (sʌb'təutᵊl, 'sʌb,təutᵊl) *n* **1** the total made up by a column of figures, etc., forming part of the total made up by a larger column. ♦ *vb* **subtotals, subtotalling, subtotalled** *or US* **subtotals, subtotaling, subtotaled**. **2** to work out a subtotal for (a column, etc.).

subtract (səb'trækt) *vb* **1** to calculate the difference between (two numbers or quantities) by subtraction. **2** to remove (a part of a thing, quantity, etc.) from the whole. [C16: from L *subtractus* withdrawn, from *subtrahere* to draw away from beneath]
▶ **sub'tracter** *n* ▶ **sub'tractive** *adj*

subtraction (səb'trækʃən) *n* **1** the act or process of subtracting. **2** a mathematical operation in which the difference between two numbers or quantities is calculated.

subtrahend ('sʌbtrə,hɛnd) *n* the number to be subtracted from another number (the **minuend**). [C17: from L *subtrahendus*, from *subtrahere* to SUBTRACT]

subtropics (sʌb'trɒpɪks) *pl n* the region lying between the tropics and temperate lands.
▶ **sub'tropical** *adj*

subulate ('su:bjəlɪt, -,leɪt) *adj* (esp. of plant parts) tapering to a point; awl-shaped. [C18: from NL *subulatus* like an awl, from L *sūbula* awl]

suburb ('sʌbɜ:b) *n* a residential district situated on the outskirts of a city or town. [C14: from L *suburbium*, from *sub*- close to + *urbs* a city]

suburban (sə'bɜ:bᵊn) *adj* **1** of, in, or inhabiting a suburb or the suburbs. **2** characteristic of a suburb or the suburbs. **3** *Mildly derog*. narrow or unadventurous in outlook.
▶ **su'burban,ite** *n* ▶ **su'burban,ize** *or* **su'burban,ise** *vb* (*tr*)

suburbia (sə'bɜ:bɪə) *n* **1** suburbs or the people living in them considered as an identifiable community or class in society. **2** the life, customs, etc., of suburbanites.

subvention (səb'vɛnʃən) *n* **1** a grant, aid, or subsidy, as from a government. **2** *Sport*. a fee paid indirectly to a supposedly amateur athlete for appearing at a meeting. [C15: from LL *subventiō* assistance, from L *subvenīre*, from *sub*- under + *venīre* to come]

subversion (səb'vɜ:ʃən) *n* **1** the act or an instance of subverting a legally constituted government, institution, etc. **2** the state of being subverted; destruction or ruin. [C14: from LL *subversiō* destruction, from L *subvertere* to overturn]

subversive (səb'vɜ:sɪv) *adj* **1** liable to subvert or overthrow a government, legally constituted institution, etc. ♦ *n* **2** a person engaged in subversive activities, etc.
▶ **sub'versively** *adv* ▶ **sub'versiveness** *n*

subvert (səb'vɜ:t) *vb* (*tr*) **1** to bring about the complete downfall or ruin of (something existing by a system of law, etc.). **2** to undermine the moral principles of (a person, etc.). [C14: from L *subvertere* to overturn]
▶ **sub'verter** *n*

subway ('sʌb,weɪ) *n* **1** *Brit*. an underground tunnel enabling pedestrians to cross a road, railway, etc. **2** an underground tunnel for traffic, power supplies, etc. **3** an underground railway.

succedaneum (,sʌksɪ'deɪnɪəm) *n, pl* **succedanea** (-nɪə). something that is used as a substitute, esp. any medical drug or agent that may be taken or prescribed in place of another. [C17: from L *succēdāneus* following after; see SUCCEED]
▶ **,succe'daneous** *adj*

succeed (sək'si:d) *vb* **1** (*intr*) to accomplish an aim, esp. in the manner desired. **2** (*intr*) to happen in the manner desired: *the plan succeeded*. **3** (*intr*) to acquit oneself satisfactorily or do well, as in a specified field. **4** (when *intr*, often foll. by *to*) to come next in order (after someone or something). **5** (when *intr*, often foll. by *to*) to take over an office, post, etc. (from a person). **6** (*intr*; usually foll. by *to*) to come into possession (of property, etc.); inherit. **7** (*intr*) to have a result according to a specified manner: *the plan succeeded badly*. [C15: from L *succēdere* to follow after]
▶ **suc'ceeder** *n* ▶ **suc'ceedingly** *adv*

success (sək'sɛs) *n* **1** the favourable outcome of something attempted. **2** the attainment of wealth, fame, etc. **3** an action, performance, etc., that is characterized by success. **4** a person or thing that is successful. [C16: from L *successus* an outcome; see SUCCEED]

successful (sək'sɛsful) *adj* **1** having succeeded in one's endeavours. **2** marked by a favourable outcome. **3** having obtained fame, wealth, etc.
▶ **suc'cessfully** *adv* ▶ **suc'cessfulness** *n*

succession (sək'sɛʃən) *n* **1** the act or an instance of one person or thing following another. **2** a number of people or things following one another in order. **3** the act, process, or right by which one person succeeds to the office, etc., of another. **4** the order that determines how one person or thing follows another. **5** a line of descent to a title, etc. **6 in succession**. in a manner such that one thing is followed uninterruptedly by another. [C14: from L *successio*; see SUCCEED]
▶ **suc'cessional** *adj*

successive (sək'sɛsɪv) *adj* **1** following another without interruption. **2** of or involving succession: *a successive process*.
▶ **suc'cessively** *adv* ▶ **suc'cessiveness** *n*

successor (sək'sɛsə) *n* a person or thing that follows, esp. a person who succeeds another.

succinct (sək'sɪŋkt) *adj* marked by brevity and clarity; concise. [C15: from L *succinctus* girt about, from *succingere* to gird from below]
▶ **suc'cinctly** *adv* ▶ **suc'cinctness** *n*

succinic acid (sʌk'sɪnɪk) *n* a colourless odourless water-soluble acid found in plant and animal tissues, deriving from amber. Formula: $HOOC(CH_2)_2COOH$. Systematic name: **butanedioic acid**. [C19: from L *succinum* amber]

succotash ('sʌkə,tæʃ) *n US & Canad*. a mixture of cooked sweet corn kernels and lima beans, served as a vegetable. [C18: of Amerind origin, from *msiquatash*, lit.: broken pieces]

succour *or US* **succor** ('sʌkə) *n* **1** help or assistance, esp. in time of difficulty. **2** a person or thing that provides help. ♦ *vb* **3** (*tr*) to give aid to. [C13: from OF *sucurir*, from L *succurrere* to hurry to help]

succubus ('sʌkjubəs) *n, pl* **succubi** (-,baɪ). **1** Also called: **succuba**. a female demon fabled to have sexual intercourse with sleeping men. Cf. **incubus**. **2** any evil demon. [C16: from Med. L, from LL *succuba* harlot, from *succubāre* to lie beneath]

succulent ('sʌkjulənt) *adj* **1** juicy. **2** (of plants) having thick fleshy leaves or stems. ♦ *n* **3** a plant that can exist in arid conditions by using water stored in its fleshy tissues. [C17: from L *succulentus*, from *sūcus* juice]
▶ **'succulence** *or* **'succulency** *n* ▶ **'succulently** *adv*

succumb (sə'kʌm) *vb* (*intr*; often foll. by *to*) **1** to give way to the force (of) or desire (for). **2** to be fatally overwhelmed (by disease, etc.); die (of). [C15: from L *succumbere* to be overcome, from SUB- + -*cumbere*, from *cubāre* to lie down]

succursal (sʌ'kɜ:sᵊl) *adj* **1** (esp. of a religious establishment) subsidiary. ♦ *n* **2** a subsidiary establishment. [C19: from F, from Med. L *succursus*, from *succurrere* to SUCCOUR]

such (sʌtʃ) (often foll. by a corresponding subordinate clause introduced by *that* or *as*) ♦ *determiner* **1a** of the sort specified or understood: *such books.* **1b** (*as pronoun*): *such is life; robbers, rapists, and such.* **2** so great; so much: *such a help.* **3 as such. 3a** in the capacity previously specified or understood: *a judge as such hasn't so much power.* **3b** in itself or themselves: *intelligence as such can't guarantee success.* **4 such and such.** specific, but not known or named: *at such and such a time.* **5 such as. 5a** for example: *animals, such as tigers.* **5b** of a similar kind as; like: *people such as your friend.* **5c** of the (usually small) amount, etc.: *the food, such as there was, was excellent.* **6 such that.** so that: used to express purpose or result: *power such that it was effortless.* ◆ *adv* **7** (intensifier): *such a nice person.* [OE *swilc*]

suchlike ('sʌtʃ,laɪk) *adj* **1** (*prenominal*) of such a kind; similar: *John, Ken, and other suchlike idiots.* ◆ *n* **2** such or similar persons or things: *hyenas, jackals, and suchlike.*

Su-chou ★ ('su:'tʃaʊ) *n* a variant transliteration of the Chinese name for **Suzhou.**

Süchow ★ ('ʃu:'tʃaʊ) *n* a variant transliteration of the Chinese name for **Xuzhou.**

suck (sʌk) *vb* **1** to draw (a liquid or other substance) into the mouth by creating a partial vacuum in the mouth. **2** to draw in (fluid, etc.) by or as if by a similar action: *plants suck moisture from the soil.* **3** to drink milk from (a mother's breast); suckle. **4** (*tr*) to extract fluid content from (a solid food): *to suck a lemon.* **5** (*tr*) to take into the mouth and moisten, dissolve, or roll around with the tongue: *to suck one's thumb.* **6** (*tr; often foll. by* **down, in,** etc.) to draw by using irresistible force. **7** (*intr*) (of a pump) to draw in air because of a low supply level or leaking valves, etc. **8** (*tr*) to assimilate or acquire (knowledge, comfort, etc.). **9** (*intr*) *Sl.* to be contemptible or disgusting. ◆ *n* **10** the act or an instance of sucking. **11** something that is sucked, esp. milk from the mother's breast. **12 give suck to.** to give (a baby or young animal) milk from the breast or udder. **13** an attracting or sucking force. **14** a sound caused by sucking. ◆ See also **suck in, sucks, suck up to.** [OE *sūcan*]

sucker ('sʌkə) *n* **1** a person or thing that sucks. **2** *Sl.* a person who is easily deceived or swindled. **3** *Sl.* a person who cannot resist the attractions of a particular type of person or thing: *he's a sucker for blondes.* **4** a young animal that is not yet weaned. **5** *Zool.* an organ specialized for sucking or adhering. **6** a cup-shaped device, generally made of rubber, that may be attached to articles allowing them to adhere to a surface by suction. **7** *Bot.* **7a** a strong shoot that arises in a mature plant from a root, rhizome, or the base of the main stem. **7b** a short branch of a parasitic plant that absorbs nutrients from the host. **8** a pipe or tube through which a fluid is drawn by suction. **9** any of various small mainly North American cyprinoid fishes having a large sucking mouth. **10** any of certain fishes that have sucking discs, esp. the sea snail. **11** a piston in a suction pump or the valve in such a piston. ◆ *vb* **12** (*tr*) to strip the suckers from (a plant). **13** (*intr*) (of a plant) to produce suckers.

suck in *vb* (*adv*) **1** (*tr*) to attract by using an inexorable force, inducement, etc. **2** to draw in (one's breath) sharply.

suckle ('sʌkəl) *vb* **suckles, suckling, suckled. 1** to give (a baby or young animal) milk from the breast or (of a baby, etc.) to suck milk from the breast. **2** (*tr*) to bring up; nurture. [C15: prob. back formation from SUCKLING] ▸ **'suckler** *n*

suckling ('sʌklɪŋ) *n* **1** an infant or young animal that is still taking milk from the mother. **2** a very young child. [C15: see SUCK, -LING[1]]

Suckling ★ ('sʌklɪŋ) *n* Sir **John.** 1609–42, English Cavalier poet and dramatist.

sucks (sʌks) *interj Sl.* **1** an expression of disappointment. **2** an exclamation of defiance or derision (esp. in **yah boo sucks to you**).

suck up to *vb* (*intr, adv + prep*) *Inf.* to flatter for one's own profit; toady.

sucrase ('sju:kreɪz) *n* another name for **invertase.** [C19: from F *sucre* sugar + -ASE]

sucre (*Spanish* 'sukre) *n* the standard monetary unit of Ecuador. [C19: after Antonio José de SUCRE]

Sucre[1] ★ (*Spanish* 'sukre) *n* the legal capital of Bolivia, in the south central part of the country in the E Andes: university (1624). Pop.: 144 994 (1993 est.). Former name (until 1839): **Chuquisaca.**

Sucre[2] ★ (*Spanish* 'sukre) *n* **Antonio José de** (an'tonjo xo'se de). 1795–1830, South American liberator, born in Venezuela, who assisted Bolivar in the colonial revolt against Spain; first president of Bolivia (1826–28).

sucrose ('sju:krəʊz, -krəʊs) *n* the technical name for **sugar** (sense 1). [C19: F *sucre* sugar + -OSE[2]]

suction ('sʌkʃən) *n* **1** the act or process of sucking. **2** the force produced by a pressure difference, as the force holding a sucker onto a surface. **3** the act or process of producing such a force. [C17: from LL *suctiō* a sucking, from L *sūgere* to suck] ▸ **'suctional** *adj*

suction pump *n* a pump for raising water or a similar fluid by suction. It usually consists of a cylinder containing a piston fitted with a flap valve.

suctorial (sʌk'tɔːrɪəl) *adj* **1** specialized for sucking or adhering. **2** relating to or possessing suckers or suction. [C19: from NL *suctōrius*, from L *sūgere* to suck]

Sudan ★ (su:'dɑːn, -'dæn) *n* **the. 1** a republic in NE Africa, on the Red Sea: the largest country in Africa; conquered by Mehemet Ali of Egypt (1820–22) and made an Anglo-Egyptian condominium in 1899 after joint forces defeated the Mahdist revolt; became a republic in 1956; civil war has been waged between separatists, in the mainly Christian south, and the government since independence, apart from a period of peace (1972–83). It consists mainly of a plateau, with the Nubian Desert in the north. Official language: Arabic. Official religion: Muslim; there are large Christian and animist minorities. Currency: Sudanese dinar. Capital: Khartoum. Pop.: 32 594 000 (1997). Area: 2 505 805 sq. km (967 491 sq. miles). Former name (1899–1956): **Anglo-Egyptian Sudan.** French name: **Soudan. 2** a region stretching across Africa south of the Sahara and north of the tropical zone: inhabited chiefly by Negroid tribes rather than Arabs. ▸ **Sudanese** (,su:d°'ni:z) *adj, n*

sudarium (sju'dɛərɪəm) *n, pl* **sudaria** (-'dɛərɪə). another word for **sudatorium.** [C17: from L, from *sūdāre* to sweat]

sudatorium (,sju:də'tɔːrɪəm) *or* **sudatory** *n, pl* **sudatoria** (-'tɔːrɪə) *or* **sudatories.** a room, esp. in a Roman bathhouse, where sweating is induced by heat. [C18: from L, from *sūdāre* to sweat]

sudatory ('sju:dətərɪ, -trɪ) *adj* **1** relating to or producing sweating. ◆ *n, pl* **sudatories. 2** a sudatory agent. **3** another word for **sudatorium.**

Sudbury ★ ('sʌdbərɪ, -brɪ) *n* a city in central Canada, in Ontario: a major nickel-mining centre. Pop.: 92 884 (1991).

sudd (sʌd) *n* floating masses of reeds and weeds that occur on the White Nile and obstruct navigation. [C19: from Ar., lit.: obstruction]

sudden ('sʌd°n) *adj* **1** occurring or performed quickly and without warning. **2** marked by haste; abrupt. **3** *Rare.* rash; precipitate. ◆ *n* **4** *Arch.* an abrupt occurrence (in on **a sudden**). **5 all of a sudden.** without warning; unexpectedly. [C13: via F from LL *subitāneus*, from L *subitus* unexpected, from *subīre* to happen unexpectedly, from *sub-* secretly + *īre* to go] ▸ **'suddenly** *adv* ▸ **'suddenness** *n*

sudden death *n* **1** (in sports, etc.) an extra game or contest to decide the winner of a tied competition. **2** an unexpected or quick death.

sudden infant death syndrome *n* a technical name for **cot death.** Abbrev.: **SIDS.**

Sudetenland ★ (su:'deɪt°n,lænd) *n* a mountainous region of the N Czech Republic: part of Czechoslovakia (1919–38; 1945–93); occupied by Germany (1938–45). Also called: **the Sudeten.**

Sudetes (su:'di:ti:z) *or* **Sudeten Mountains** ★ *pl n* a mountain range in E central Europe, along the N border of the Czech Republic, extending into Germany and Poland: rich in minerals, esp. coal. Highest peak: Schneekoppe, 1603 m (5259 ft).

★ people and places

sudor ('sju:dɔ:) *n* a technical name for **sweat**. [L]
▶ **sudoral** ('sju:dərəl) *adj*

sudoriferous (ˌsju:də'rɪfərəs) *adj* producing or conveying sweat. Also: ˌsudo'riparous. [C16: via NL from SUDOR + L *ferre* to bear]
▶ ˌsudor'iferousness *n*

sudorific (ˌsju:də'rɪfɪk) *adj* 1 producing or causing sweating. ◆ *n* 2 a sudorific agent. [C17: from NL *sūdōrificus*, from SUDOR + L *facere* to make]

suds (sʌdz) *pl n* 1 the bubbles on the surface of water in which soap, detergents, etc., have been dissolved; lather. 2 soapy water. [C16: prob. from MDu. *sudse* marsh]
▶ **sudsy** *adj*

sue (sju:, su:) *vb* **sues, suing, sued**. 1 to institute legal proceedings (against). 2 to make suppliant requests of (someone for something). [C13: from OF *sivre*, from L *sequī* to follow]
▶ **suer** *n*

Sue ★ (French sy) *n* **Eugène** (øʒɛn). original name *Marie-Joseph Sue*. 1804–57, French novelist, whose works include *Les mystères de Paris* (1842–43) and *Le juif errant* (1844–45).

suede (sweɪd) *n* **a** a leather with a fine velvet-like nap on the flesh side, produced by abrasive action. **b** (*as modifier*): *a suede coat*. [C19: from F *gants de Suède*, lit.: gloves from Sweden]

suet ('su:ɪt, 'sju:ɪt) *n* a hard waxy fat around the kidneys and loins in sheep, cattle, etc., used in cooking and making tallow. [C14: from OF *seu*, from L *sēbum*]
▶ **suety** *adj*

Suetonius ★ (swiː'təʊnɪəs) *n* full name *Gaius Suetonius Tranquillus*. 75–150 A.D., Roman biographer and historian, whose chief works were *Concerning Illustrious Men* and *The Lives of the Caesars* (from Julius Caesar to Domitian).

suet pudding *n Brit.* any of a variety of puddings made with suet and steamed or boiled.

Suez ★ ('su:ɪz) *n* 1 a port in NE Egypt, at the head of the Gulf of Suez at the S end of the Suez Canal: an ancient trading site and a major naval station under the Ottoman Empire; port of departure for pilgrims to Mecca; oil-refining centre. It suffered severely in the Arab–Israeli conflicts of 1967 and 1973. Pop.: 388 000 (1992 est.). 2 **Isthmus of.** a strip of land in NE Egypt, between the Mediterranean and the Red Sea: links Africa and Asia and is crossed by the Suez Canal. 3 **Gulf of.** the NW arm of the Red Sea: linked with the Mediterranean by the Suez Canal.

Suez Canal ★ *n* a sea-level canal in NE Egypt, crossing the Isthmus of Suez and linking the Mediterranean with the Red Sea: built (1854–69) by de Lesseps with French and Egyptian labour; nationalized in 1956 by the Egyptians. Length: 163 km (101 miles).

Suff. *abbrev. for:* 1 Suffolk. 2 Suffragan.

suffer ('sʌfə) *vb* 1 to undergo or be subjected to (pain, punishment, etc.). 2 (*tr*) to undergo or experience (anything): *to suffer a change of management*. 3 (*intr*) to be set at a disadvantage: *this author suffers in translation*. 4 (*tr*) *Arch.* to tolerate; permit (someone to do something): *suffer the little children to come unto me*. 5 **suffer from**. 5a to be ill with, esp. recurrently. 5b to be given to: *he suffers from a tendency to exaggerate*. [C13: from OF *soffrir*, from L *sufferre*, from SUB- + *ferre* to bear]
▶ **sufferer** *n* ▶ **suffering** *n*

sufferable ('sʌfərəbᵊl, 'sʌfrə-) *adj* able to be tolerated or suffered; endurable.

sufferance ('sʌfərəns, 'sʌfrəns) *n* 1 tolerance arising from failure to prohibit; tacit permission. 2 capacity to endure pain, injury, etc. 3 the state or condition of suffering. 4 **on sufferance**. tolerated with reluctance. [C13: via OF from LL *sufferentia* endurance, from L *sufferre* to SUFFER]

suffice (sə'faɪs) *vb* **suffices, sufficing, sufficed**. 1 to be adequate or satisfactory for (something). 2 **suffice it to say that**. (*takes a clause as object*) let us say no more than that; I shall just say that. [C14: from OF *suffire*, from L *sufficere* from *sub-* below + *facere* to make]

sufficiency (sə'fɪʃənsɪ) *n, pl* **sufficiencies**. 1 the quality or condition of being sufficient. 2 an adequate amount. 3 *Arch.* efficiency.

sufficient (sə'fɪʃənt) *adj* 1 enough to meet a need or purpose; adequate. 2 *Logic*. (of a condition) assuring the truth of a statement; requiring but not necessarily caused by some other state of affairs. Cf. **necessary** (sense 3b). 3 *Arch.* competent; capable. ◆ *n* 4 a sufficient quantity. [C14: from L *sufficiens* supplying the needs of, from *sufficere* to SUFFICE]
▶ **suf'ficiently** *adv*

suffix *n* ('sʌfɪks). 1 *Grammar.* an affix that follows the stem to which it is attached, as for example *-s* and *-ness* in *dogs* and *softness*. Cf. **prefix** (sense 1). 2 anything added at the end of something else. ◆ *vb* ('sʌfɪks, sə'fɪks). 3 (*tr*) *Grammar*. to add (a morpheme) as a suffix to a word. [C18: from NL *suffixum*, from L *suffixus* fastened below, from *suffigere* to fasten below]

suffocate ('sʌfə,keɪt) *vb* **suffocates, suffocating, suffocated**. 1 to kill or be killed by the deprivation of oxygen, as by obstruction of the air passage. 2 to block the air passages or have the air passages blocked. 3 to feel or cause to feel discomfort from heat and lack of air. [C16: from L *suffōcāre*, from SUB- + *faucēs* throat]
▶ **'suffo,cating** *adj* ▶ ˌsuffo'cation *n*

Suffolk ★ ('sʌfək) *n* a county of SE England, on the North Sea: its coast is flat and marshy, indented by broad tidal estuaries. Administrative centre: Ipswich. Pop.: 649 500 (1994 est.). Area: 3800 sq. km (1467 sq. miles).

Suffolk punch *n* a breed of draught horse with a chestnut coat and short legs.

suffragan ('sʌfrəgən) *adj* 1a (of any bishop of a diocese) subordinate to and assisting his superior archbishop or metropolitan. 1b (of any assistant bishop) assisting the bishop of his diocese but having no ordinary jurisdiction in that diocese. ◆ *n* 2 a suffragan bishop. [C14: from Med. L *suffragāneus*, from *suffrāgium* assistance, from L: suffrage]
▶ **'suffraganship** *n*

suffrage ('sʌfrɪdʒ) *n* 1 the right to vote, esp. in public elections; franchise. 2 the exercise of such a right; casting a vote. 3 a short intercessory prayer. [C14: from L *suffrāgium*]

suffragette (ˌsʌfrə'dʒɛt) *n* a female advocate of the extension of the franchise to women, esp. a militant one, as in Britain at the beginning of the 20th century. [C20: from SUFFRAG(E) + -ETTE]

suffragist ('sʌfrədʒɪst) *n* an advocate of the extension of the franchise, esp. to women.
▶ **'suffragism** *n*

suffruticose (sə'fru:tɪˌkəʊz) *adj* (of a plant) having a permanent woody base and herbaceous branches. [C18: from NL *suffruticōsus*, from L SUB- + *frutex* shrub]

suffuse (sə'fju:z) *vb* **suffuses, suffusing, suffused**. (*tr; usually passive*) to spread or flood through or over (something). [C16: from L *suffūsus* overspread with, from *suffundere*, from SUB- + *fundere* to pour]
▶ **suffusion** (sə'fju:ʒən) *n* ▶ **suf'fusive** *adj*

Sufi ('su:fɪ) *n, pl* **Sufis**. an adherent of any of various Muslim mystical orders or teachings, which emphasize the direct personal experience of God. [C17: from Ar. *sūfiy*, lit.: (man) of wool; prob. from the ascetic's woollen garments]
▶ **'Sufic** *adj* ▶ **'Sufism** *n*

Sufu ★ ('fu:'fu:) *n* a variant spelling of **Shufu**.

sugar ('ʃʊgə) *n* 1 Also called: **sucrose, saccharose**. a white crystalline sweet carbohydrate, a disaccharide, found in many plants: used esp. as a sweetening agent in food and drinks. Related adj: **saccharine**. 2 any of a class of simple water-soluble carbohydrates, such as sucrose, lactose, and fructose. 3 *Inf., chiefly US & Canad*. a term of affection, esp. for one's sweetheart. ◆ *vb* 4 (*tr*) to add sugar to; make sweet. 5 (*tr*) to cover or sprinkle with sugar. 6 (*intr*) to produce sugar. 7 **sugar the pill** *or* **medicine**. to make something unpleasant more agreeable by adding something pleasant. [C13 *suker*, from OF *çucre*, from Med. L *zuccārum*, ult. from Sansk. *śarkarā*]
▶ **'sugared** *adj*

sugar beet *n* a variety of beet cultivated for its white roots from which sugar is obtained.

sugar candy *n* **1** Also called: **rock candy.** large crystals of sugar formed by suspending strings in a strong sugar solution that hardens on the strings, used chiefly for sweetening coffee. **2** *Chiefly US.* confectionery; sweets.

sugar cane *n* a coarse perennial grass of Old World tropical regions, having tall stout canes that yield sugar: cultivated chiefly in the Caribbean and the southern US.

sugar-coat *vb* (*tr*) **1** to coat or cover with sugar. **2** to cause to appear more attractive.

sugar diabetes *n* an informal name for **diabetes mellitus** (see **diabetes**).

sugar glider *n* a common Australian phalanger that glides from tree to tree feeding on insects and nectar.

sugaring off *n Canad.* the boiling down of maple sap to produce sugar, traditionally a social event in early spring.

sugar loaf *n* **1** a large conical mass of hard refined sugar. **2** something resembling this.

Sugar Loaf Mountain ★ *n* a mountain in SE Brazil, in Rio de Janeiro on Guanabara Bay. Height: 390 m (1280 ft). Portuguese name: **Pão de Açúcar.**

sugar maple *n* a North American maple tree, grown as a source of sugar, which is extracted from the sap, and for its hard wood.

sugar of lead (lɛd) *n* another name for **lead acetate**.

sugarplum (ˈʃugəˌplʌm) *n* a crystallized plum.

sugary (ˈʃugərɪ) *adj* **1** of, like, or containing sugar. **2** excessively sweet. **3** deceptively pleasant; insincere.
  ▸ **ˈsugariness** *n*

Suger ★ (suːˈʒɛr) *n* 1081–1151, French ecclesiastic and statesman, who acted as adviser to Louis VI and regent (1147–49) to Louis VII. As abbot of Saint-Denis (1122–51) he influenced the development of Gothic architecture.

suggest (səˈdʒɛst) *vb* (*tr; may take a clause as object*) **1** to put forward (a plan, idea, etc.) for consideration: *I suggest Smith for the post; a plan suggested itself.* **2** to evoke (a person, thing, etc.) in the mind by the association of ideas: *that painting suggests home to me.* **3** to give an indirect or vague hint of: *his face always suggests his peace of mind.* [C16: from L *suggerere* to bring up]
  ▸ **sugˈgester** *n*

suggestible (səˈdʒɛstɪbᵊl) *adj* **1** easily influenced by ideas provided by other persons. **2** characteristic of something that can be suggested.
  ▸ **sugˌgestiˈbility** *n*

suggestion (səˈdʒɛstʃən) *n* **1** something that is suggested. **2** a hint or indication: *a suggestion of the odour of violets.* **3** *Psychol.* the process whereby the mere presentation of an idea to a receptive individual leads to the acceptance of that idea. See also **autosuggestion**.

suggestive (səˈdʒɛstɪv) *adj* **1** (*postpositive; foll. by of*) conveying a hint (of something). **2** tending to suggest something improper or indecent.
  ▸ **sugˈgestively** *adv* ▸ **sugˈgestiveness** *n*

Suharto ★ (suˈhɑːtəu) *n* born 1921, Indonesian general and statesman; president (1968–98).

suicidal (ˌsuːɪˈsaɪdᵊl, ˌsjuː-) *adj* **1** involving, indicating, or tending towards suicide. **2** liable to result in suicide: *a suicidal attempt.* **3** liable to destroy one's own interests or prospects; dangerously rash.
  ▸ **ˌsuiˈcidally** *adv*

suicide (ˈsuːɪˌsaɪd, ˈsjuː-) *n* **1** the act or an instance of killing oneself intentionally. **2** the self-inflicted ruin of one's own prospects or interests: *a merger would be financial suicide.* **3** a person who kills himself intentionally. **4** (*modifier*) reckless; extremely dangerous: *a suicide mission.* **5** (*modifier*) (of an action) undertaken or (of a person) undertaking an action in the knowledge that it will result in the death of the person performing it in order that maximum damage may be inflicted: *suicide bomber.* [C17: from NL *suicīdium*, from L *suī* of oneself + *-cīdium*, from *caedere* to kill]

sui generis (ˌsuːaɪ ˈdʒɛnərɪs) *adj* unique. [L, lit.: of its own kind]

suint (ˈsuːɪnt, swɪnt) *n* a water-soluble substance found in the fleece of sheep, formed from dried perspiration. [C18: from F *suer* to sweat, from L *sūdāre*]

Suisse ★ (sɥis) *n* the French name for **Switzerland**.

suit (suːt, sjuːt) *n* **1** any set of clothes of the same or similar material designed to be worn together, now usually (for men) a jacket with matching trousers or (for women) a jacket with matching or contrasting skirt or trousers. **2** (*in combination*) any outfit worn for a specific purpose: *a spacesuit.* **3** any set of items, such as parts of personal armour. **4** any of the four sets of 13 cards in a pack of playing cards, being spades, hearts, diamonds, and clubs. **5** a civil proceeding; lawsuit. **6** the act or process of suing in a court of law. **7** a petition or appeal made to a person of superior rank or status or the act of making such a petition. **8** a man's courting of a woman. **9** *Sl.* an executive, manager, or bureaucrat, esp. one considered faceless or dull. **10 follow suit. 10a** to play a card of the same suit as the card played immediately before it. **10b** to act in the same way as someone else. **11 strong** *or* **strongest suit.** something that one excels in. ◆ *vb* **12** to make or be fit or appropriate for: *that dress suits your figure.* **13** to meet the requirements or standards (of). **14** to be agreeable or acceptable to (someone). **15 suit oneself.** to pursue one's own intentions without reference to others. [C13: from OF *sieute* set of things, from *sivre* to follow]

suitable (ˈsuːtəbᵊl, ˈsjuːt-) *adj* appropriate; proper; fit.
  ▸ **ˌsuitaˈbility** *or* **ˈsuitableness** *n* ▸ **ˈsuitably** *adv*

suitcase (ˈsuːtˌkeɪs, ˈsjuːt-) *n* a portable rectangular travelling case for clothing, etc.

suite (swiːt) *n* **1** a series of items intended to be used together; set. **2** a set of connected rooms in a hotel. **3** a matching set of furniture, esp. of two armchairs and a settee. **4** a number of attendants or followers. **5** *Music.* **5a** an instrumental composition consisting of several movements in the same key based on or derived from dance rhythms, esp. in the baroque period. **5b** an instrumental composition in several movements less closely connected than a sonata. [C17: from F, from OF *sieute*; see **suit**]

suiting (ˈsuːtɪŋ, ˈsjuːt-) *n* a fabric used for suits.

suitor (ˈsuːtə, ˈsjuːt-) *n* **1** a man who courts a woman; wooer. **2** *Law.* a person who brings a suit in a court of law; plaintiff. [C13: from Anglo-Norman *suter*, from L *secūtor* follower, from *sequī* to follow]

Suiyüan ★ (ˈswiːˈjɑːn) *n* a former province in N China: now part of the Inner Mongolian Autonomous Region.

Sukarnapura ★ (suˌkɑːnəˈpuərə) *n* a former name of **Jayapura**.

Sukarno *or* **Soekarno** ★ (suːˈkɑːnəu) *n* Achmed (ˈɑːkmɛd). 1901–70, Indonesian statesman; first president of the Republic of Indonesia (1945–67).

Sukarno Peak ★ *n* a former name of (Mount) **Jaya**.

Sukhumi ★ (*Russian* suˈxumi) *n* a port and resort in W Georgia, on the Black Sea: site of an ancient Greek colony. Pop.: 112 000 (1993).

sukiyaki (ˌsuːkɪˈjɑːkɪ) *n* a Japanese dish consisting of very thinly sliced beef or other meat, vegetables, and seasonings cooked together quickly, usually at the table. [from Japanese]

Sukkoth *or* **Succoth** (ˈsukəut, -kəuθ; *Hebrew* suːˈkɔt) *n* an eight-day Jewish harvest festival beginning on Tishri 15, which commemorates the period when the Israelites lived in the wilderness. Also called: **Feast of Tabernacles**. [from Heb., lit.: tabernacles]

Sulawesi ★ (ˌsuːləˈweɪsɪ) *n* an island in E Indonesia: mountainous and forested, with volcanoes and hot springs. Pop.: 12 520 711 (1990). Area (including adjacent islands): 229 108 sq. km (88 440 sq. miles). Also called: **Celebes**.

sulcate (ˈsʌlkeɪt) *adj Biol.* marked with longitudinal parallel grooves. [C18: via L *sulcātus* from *sulcāre* to plough, from *sulcus* a furrow]

sulcus (ˈsʌlkəs) *n, pl* **sulci** (-saɪ). **1** a linear groove, furrow, or slight depression. **2** any of the narrow grooves on the surface of the brain that mark the cerebral convolutions. [C17: from L]

Suleiman I (ˌsuːlɪˈmɑːn, -leɪ-), **Soliman,** or **Solyman** ★ n called *the Magnificent.* ?1495–1566, sultan of the Ottoman Empire (1520–66), noted for his military power and cultural achievements.

sulf- *combining form.* a US variant of **sulph-**.

sulfur (ˈsʌlfə) n the US spelling of **sulphur**.

sulk (sʌlk) vb **1** (*intr*) to be silent and resentful because of a wrong done to one; brood sullenly: *the child sulked after being slapped.* ♦ n **2** (*often pl*) a state or mood of feeling resentful or sullen: *he's in a sulk; he's got the sulks.* **3** Also: **sulker.** a person who sulks. [C18: ? back formation from SULKY¹]

sulky¹ (ˈsʌlkɪ) adj **sulkier, sulkiest. 1** sullen, withdrawn, or moody, through or as if through resentment. **2** dull or dismal: *sulky weather.* [C18: ?from obs. *sulke* sluggish]
▸ ˈsulkily *adv* ▸ ˈsulkiness *n*

sulky² (ˈsʌlkɪ) n, pl **sulkies.** a light two-wheeled vehicle for one person, usually drawn by one horse. [C18: from SULKY¹]

Sulla ★ (ˈsʌlə) n full name *Lucius Cornelius Sulla Felix.* 138–78 B.C., Roman general and dictator (82–79).

sullage (ˈsʌlɪdʒ) n **1** filth or waste, esp. sewage. **2** sediment deposited by running water. [C16: ?from F *souiller* to sully]

sullen (ˈsʌlən) adj **1** unwilling to talk or be sociable; sulky; morose. **2** sombre; gloomy: *a sullen day.* ♦ n **3** (*pl*) *Arch.* a sullen mood. [C16: ?from Anglo-F *solain* (unattested), ult. rel. to L *sōlus* alone]
▸ ˈsullenly *adv* ▸ ˈsullenness *n*

Sullivan ★ (ˈsʌlɪvⁿn) n **1** Sir **Arthur (Seymour).** 1842–1900, British composer of such operettas as *H.M.S. Pinafore* (1878) and *The Mikado* (1885), with W. S. Gilbert as librettist. **2 Louis (Henri).** 1856–1924, US pioneer of modern architecture.

Sullom Voe ★ (ˈsʌləm vəʊ) n a deep coastal inlet in the Shetland Islands, on the N coast of Mainland. It is used for the storage and transshipment of oil.

sully (ˈsʌlɪ) vb **sullies, sullying, sullied.** (*tr*) to stain or tarnish (a reputation, etc.) or (of a reputation) to become stained or tarnished. [C16: prob. from F *souiller* to soil]

Sully ★ (ˈsʌlɪ; *French* sylli) n **Maximilien de Béthune** (maksimiljɛ̃ də betyn), Duc de Sully. 1559–1641, French statesman; minister of Henry IV.

Sully-Prudhomme ★ (*French* sylli prydɔm) n **René François Armand** (rəne frɑ̃swa armɑ̃). 1839–1907, French poet: Nobel prize for literature 1901.

sulph- or US **sulf-** *combining form.* containing sulphur: *sulphate.*

sulpha or US **sulfa drug** (ˈsʌlfə) n any of a group of sulphonamides that inhibit the activity of bacteria and are used to treat bacterial infections.

sulphadiazine or US **sulfadiazine** (ˌsʌlfəˈdaɪəˌziːn) n an important sulpha drug used chiefly in combination with an antibiotic. [from SULPH- + DIAZ(O) + -INE²]

sulphanilamide or US **sulfanilamide** (ˌsʌlfəˈnɪləˌmaɪd) n a white crystalline compound formerly used in the treatment of bacterial infections. [from SULPH- + ANIL(INE) + AMIDE]

sulphate or US **sulfate** (ˈsʌlfeɪt) n **1** any salt or ester of sulphuric acid. ♦ vb **sulphates, sulphating, sulphated** or US **sulfates, sulfating, sulfated. 2** (*tr*) to treat with a sulphate or convert into a sulphate. **3** to undergo or cause to undergo the formation of a layer of lead sulphate on the plates of an accumulator. [C18: from NL *sulfātum*]
▸ sulˈphation or US sulˈfation n

sulphide or US **sulfide** (ˈsʌlfaɪd) n a compound of sulphur with a more electropositive element.

sulphite or US **sulfite** (ˈsʌlfaɪt) n any salt or ester of sulphurous acid.
▸ **sulphitic** or US **sulfitic** (sʌlˈfɪtɪk) adj

sulphonamide or US **sulfonamide** (sʌlˈfɒnəˌmaɪd) n any of a class of organic compounds that are amides of sulphonic acids containing the group -SO₂NH₂ or a

group derived from this. An important class of sulphonamides are the sulpha drugs.

sulphone or US **sulfone** (ˈsʌlfəʊn) n any of a class of organic compounds containing the divalent group SO_2 linked to two other organic groups.

sulphonic or US **sulfonic acid** (sʌlˈfɒnɪk) n any of a large group of strong organic acids that contain the group -SO_2OH and are used in the manufacture of dyes and drugs.

sulphonmethane or US **sulfonmethane** (ˌsʌlfɒnˈmiːθeɪn) n a colourless crystalline compound used medicinally as a hypnotic. Formula: $C_7H_{16}O_4S_2$.

sulphur or US **sulfur** (ˈsʌlfə) n **a** an allotropic nonmetallic element, occurring free in volcanic regions and in combined state in gypsum, pyrite, and galena. It is used in the production of sulphuric acid, in the vulcanization of rubber, and in fungicides. Symbol: S; atomic no.: 16; atomic wt.: 32.066. **b** (*as modifier*): *sulphur springs.* [C14 *soufre,* from OF, from L *sulfur*]
▸ **sulphuric** or US **sulfuric** (sʌlˈfjʊərɪk) adj

sulphurate or US **sulfurate** (ˈsʌlfjuˌreɪt) vb **sulphurates, sulphurating, sulphurated.** (*tr*) to combine or treat with sulphur or a sulphur compound.
▸ ˌsulphuˈration or US ˌsulfuˈration n

sulphur-bottom n another name for **blue whale**.

sulphur dioxide n a colourless soluble pungent gas. It is both an oxidizing and a reducing agent and is used in the manufacture of sulphuric acid, the preservation of foodstuffs (**E 220**), bleaching, and disinfecting. Formula: SO_2. Systematic name: **sulphur(IV) oxide.**

sulphureous or US **sulfureous** (sʌlˈfjʊərɪəs) adj **1** another word for **sulphurous** (sense 1). **2** of the yellow colour of sulphur.

sulphuretted or US **sulfureted hydrogen** (ˈsʌlfjuˌretɪd) n another name for **hydrogen sulphide**.

sulphuric acid n a colourless dense oily corrosive liquid used in accumulators and in the manufacture of fertilizers, dyes, and explosives. Formula: H_2SO_4. Systematic name: **tetraoxosulphuric(VI) acid.**

sulphurize, sulphurise, or US **sulfurize** (ˈsʌlfjuˌraɪz) vb **sulphurizes, sulphurizing, sulphurized, sulphurises, sulphurising, sulphurised** or US **sulfurizes, sulfurizing, sulfurized.** (*tr*) to combine or treat with sulphur or a sulphur compound.
▸ ˌsulphuriˈzation, ˌsulphuriˈsation, or US ˌsulfuriˈzation n

sulphurous or US **sulfurous** (ˈsʌlfərəs) adj **1** Also: **sulphureous.** of, relating to, or resembling sulphur: *a sulphurous colour.* **2** (sʌlˈfjʊərəs). of or containing sulphur with an oxidation state of 4: *sulphurous acid.* **3** of or relating to hellfire. **4** hot-tempered.
▸ ˈsulphurously or US ˈsulfurously adv ▸ ˈsulphurousness or US ˈsulfurousness n

sulphurous acid n an unstable acid produced when sulphur dioxide dissolves in water: used as a preservative for food and a bleaching agent. Formula: H_2SO_3. Systematic name: **sulphuric(IV) acid.**

sulphur trioxide n a colourless reactive fuming solid that forms sulphuric acid with water. Formula: SO_3. Systematic name: **sulphur(VI) oxide.**

sultan (ˈsʌltən) n **1** the sovereign of a Muslim country, esp. of the former Ottoman Empire. **2** a small domestic fowl with a white crest and heavily feathered legs and feet: originated in Turkey. [C16: from Med. L *sultānus,* from Ar. *sultān* rule, from Aramaic *salita* to rule]

sultana (sʌlˈtɑːnə) n **1a** the dried fruit of a small white seedless grape, originally produced in SW Asia; seedless raisin. **1b** the grape itself. **2** Also called: **sultaness.** a wife, concubine, or female relative of a sultan. **3** a mistress; concubine. [C16: from It., fem of *sultano* SULTAN]

sultanate (ˈsʌltəˌneɪt) n **1** the territory or a country ruled by a sultan. **2** the office, rank, or jurisdiction of a sultan.

sultry (ˈsʌltrɪ) adj **sultrier, sultriest. 1** (of weather or climate) oppressively hot and humid. **2** characterized by or emitting oppressive heat. **3** displaying or suggesting passion; sensual: *sultry eyes.* [C16: from obs. *sulter* to swelter + -Y¹]
▸ ˈsultrily *adv* ▸ ˈsultriness *n*

Sulu Archipelago ★ ('suːluː) *n* a chain of over 500 islands in the SW Philippines, separating the Sulu Sea from the Celebes Sea: formerly a sultanate, ceded to the Philippines in 1940. Capital: Jolo. Pop.: 555 239 (1980). Area: 2686 sq. km (1037 sq. miles).

Sulu Sea ★ *n* part of the W Pacific between Borneo and the central Philippines.

sum (sʌm) *n* **1** the result of the addition of numbers, quantities, objects, etc. **2** one or more columns or rows of numbers to be added, subtracted, multiplied, or divided. **3** *Maths.* the limit of the first *n* terms of a converging infinite series as *n* tends to infinity. **4** a quantity, esp. of money: *he borrows enormous sums.* **5** the essence or gist of a matter (esp. in **in sum, in sum and substance**). **6** a less common word for **summary. 7** (*modifier*) complete or final (esp. in **sum total**). ◆ *vb* **sums, summing, summed. 8** (often foll. by *up*) to add or form a total of (something). **9** (*tr*) to calculate the sum of (the terms in a sequence). ◆ See also **sum up.** [C13 *summe*, from OF, from L *summa* the top, sum, from *summus* highest, from *super* above]

sumach *or US* **sumac** ('suːmæk, 'ʃuː-) *n* **1** any of various temperate or subtropical shrubs or small trees, having compound leaves and red hairy fruits. See also **poison sumach. 2** a preparation of powdered leaves of certain species of sumach, used in dyeing and tanning. **3** the wood of any of these plants. [C14: via OF from Ar. *summāq*]

Sumatra ★ (su'mɑːtrə) *n* a mountainous island in W Indonesia, in the Greater Sunda Islands, separated from the Malay Peninsula by the Strait of Malacca: Dutch control began in the 16th century; joined Indonesia in 1945. Pop.: 22 706 200 (1995 est.). Area: 473 606 sq. km (182 821 sq. miles).
▸ **Su'matran** *adj, n*

Sumba *or* **Soemba** ★ ('suːmbə) *n* an island in Indonesia, in the Lesser Sunda Islands, separated from Flores by the **Sumba Strait**: formerly important for sandalwood exports. Pop.: 355 000 (1990 est.). Area: 11 153 sq. km (4306 sq. miles). Former name: **Sandalwood Island.**

Sumbawa *or* **Soembawa** ★ (suːm'bɑːwə) *n* a mountainous island in Indonesia, in the Lesser Sunda Islands, between Lombok and Flores Islands. Pop.: 373 000 (1990 est.). Area: 14 750 sq. km (5695 sq. miles).

Sumer ★ ('suːmə) *n* the S region of Babylonia; seat of a civilization of city-states that reached its height in the 3rd millennium B.C.

Sumerian (su'mɪərɪən, -'mɛər-) *n* **1** a member of a people who established a civilization in Sumer during the 4th millennium B.C. **2** the extinct language of this people. ◆ *adj* **3** of or relating to ancient Sumer, its inhabitants, or their language or civilization.

summa cum laude ('sumɑː kʊm 'laʊdeɪ) *adv, adj Chiefly US.* with the utmost praise: the highest designation for achievement in examinations. In Britain it is sometimes used to designate a first-class honours degree. [from L]

summarize *or* **summarise** ('sʌmə,raɪz) *vb* **summarizes, summarizing, summarized** *or* **summarises, summarising, summarised.** (*tr*) to make or be a summary of; express concisely.
▸ ,summari'zation *or* ,summari'sation *n* ▸ 'summa,rizer, 'summa,riser, *or* 'summarist *n*

summary ('sʌmərɪ) *n, pl* **summaries. 1** a brief account giving the main points of something. ◆ *adj* (*usually prenominal*). **2** performed arbitrarily and quickly, without formality: *a summary execution.* **3** (of legal proceedings) short and free from the complexities and delays of a full trial. **4 summary jurisdiction.** the right a court has to adjudicate immediately upon some matter. **5** giving the gist or essence. [C15: from L *summārium*, from *summa* SUM]
▸ 'summarily *adv* ▸ 'summariness *n*

summary offence *n* an offence that is triable in a magistrates' court.

summation (sʌ'meɪʃən) *n* **1** the act or process of determining a sum; addition. **2** the result of such an act or process. **3** a summary. **4** *US law.* the concluding statements made by opposing counsel in a case before a court. [C18: from Med. L *summātiō*, from *summāre* to total, from L *summa* SUM]
▸ sum'mational *adj* ▸ 'summative *adj*

summative assessment *n Brit. education.* general assessment of a pupil's achievements over a range of subjects by means of a combined appraisal of formative assessments.

summer ('sʌmə) *n* **1** (*sometimes cap.*) **1a** the warmest season of the year, between spring and autumn, astronomically from the June solstice to the September equinox in the N hemisphere and at the opposite time of year in the S hemisphere. **1b** (*as modifier*): *summer flowers.* Related adj: **aestival. 2** the period of hot weather associated with the summer. **3** a time of blossoming, greatest happiness, etc. **4** *Chiefly poetic.* a year represented by this season: *a child of nine summers.* ◆ *vb* **5** (*intr*) to spend the summer (at a place). **6** (*tr*) to keep or feed (farm animals) during the summer: *they summered their cattle on the mountain slopes.* [OE *sumor*]
▸ 'summerly *adj* ▸ 'summery *adj*

summerhouse ('sʌmə,haʊs) *n* a small building in a garden or park, used for shade or recreation in the summer.

summer pudding *n Brit.* a pudding made by filling a bread-lined basin with a purée of fruit.

summersault ('sʌmə,sɔːlt) *n, vb* a variant spelling of **somersault.**

summer school *n* a school, academic course, etc., held during the summer.

summer solstice *n* **1** the time at which the sun is at its northernmost point in the sky (southernmost point in the S hemisphere). It occurs about June 21 (December 22 in the S hemisphere). **2** *Astron.* the point on the celestial sphere, opposite the **winter solstice**, at which the ecliptic is furthest north from the celestial equator.

summertime ('sʌmə,taɪm) *n* the period or season of summer.

summer time *n Brit.* any daylight-saving time, esp. British Summer Time.

summerweight ('sʌmə,weɪt) *adj* (of clothes) suitable in weight for wear in the summer.

summing-up *n* **1** a review or summary of the main points of an argument, speech, etc. **2** concluding statements made by a judge to the jury before they retire to consider their verdict.

summit ('sʌmɪt) *n* **1** the highest point or part, esp. of a mountain; top. **2** the highest possible degree or state; peak or climax: *the summit of ambition.* **3** the highest level, importance, or rank: *a meeting at the summit.* **4a** a meeting of chiefs of governments or other high officials. **4b** (*as modifier*): *a summit conference.* [C15: from OF *somet*, dim. of *som*, from L *summum*; see SUM]

summon ('sʌmən) *vb* (*tr*) **1** to order to come; send for, esp. to attend court, by issuing a summons. **2** to order or instruct (to do something) or call (to something): *the bell summoned them to their work.* **3** to call upon to meet or convene. **4** (often foll. by *up*) to muster or gather (one's strength, courage, etc.). **5** *Arch.* to call upon to surrender. [C13: from L *summonēre* to give a discreet reminder, from *monēre* to advise]

summons ('sʌmənz) *n, pl* **summonses. 1** a call, signal, or order to do something, esp. to attend at a specified place or time. **2a** an official order requiring a person to attend court, either to answer a charge or to give evidence. **2b** the writ making such an order. **3** a call or command given to the members of an assembly to convene a meeting. ◆ *vb* **4** to take out a summons against (a person). [C13: from OF *somonse*, from *somondre* to SUMMON]

summum bonum *Latin.* ('sumʊm 'bɒnʊm) *n* the principle of goodness in which all moral values are included or from which they are derived; highest or supreme good.

sumo ('suːməʊ) *n* the national style of wrestling of Japan, in which two contestants of great height and weight attempt to force each other to touch the ground with any part of the body except the soles of the feet or to step out of the ring. [from Japanese *sumō*]

sump (sʌmp) *n* **1** a receptacle, as in the crankcase of an internal-combustion engine, into which liquids, esp. lubricants, can drain to form a reservoir. **2** another name for **cesspool** (sense 1). **3** *Mining.* a depression at the bottom of a shaft where water collects. [C17: from MDu. *somp* marsh]

★ people and places

sumpter ('sʌmptə) n Arch. a packhorse, mule, or other beast of burden. [C14: from OF sometier driver of a baggage horse, from Vulgar L sagmatārius (unattested), from LL sagma packsaddle]

sumptuary ('sʌmptjʊərɪ) adj relating to or controlling expenditure or extravagance. [C17: from L sumptuārius concerning expense, from sumptus expense, from sūmere to spend]

sumptuous ('sʌmptjʊəs) adj 1 expensive or extravagant: sumptuous costumes. 2 magnificent; splendid: a sumptuous scene. [C16: from OF somptueux, from L sumptuōsus costly, from sumptus; see SUMPTUARY]
▶ **'sumptuously** adv ▶ **'sumptuousness** n

Sumter ★ ('sʌmtə) n See **Fort Sumter.**

sum up vb (adv) 1 to summarize (the main points of an argument, etc.). 2 (tr) to form a quick opinion of: I summed him up in five minutes.

Sumy ★ (Russian 'sumi) n a city in the NE Ukraine, on the River Pysol: site of early Slav settlements. Pop.: 304 000 (1996 est.).

sun (sʌn) n 1 the star that is the source of heat and light for the planets in the solar system. Related adj: **solar.** 2 any star around which a planetary system revolves. 3 the sun as it appears at a particular time or place: the winter sun. 4 the radiant energy, esp. heat and light, received from the sun; sunshine. 5 a person or thing considered as a source of radiant warmth, glory, etc. 6 a pictorial representation of the sun, often depicted with a human face. 7 Poetic. a year or a day. 8 Poetic. a climate. 9 Arch. sunrise or sunset (esp. in **from sun to sun**). 10 **catch the sun.** to become slightly sunburnt. 11 **place in the sun.** a prominent or favourable position. 12 **take** or **shoot the sun.** Naut. to measure the altitude of the sun in order to determine latitude. 13 **touch of the sun.** slight sunstroke. 14 **under** or **beneath the sun.** on earth; at all: nobody under the sun eats more than you. ◆ vb **suns, sunning, sunned.** 15 to expose (oneself) to the sunshine. 16 (tr) to expose to the sunshine in order to warm, etc. [OE sunne]

Sun. abbrev. for Sunday.

sunbaked ('sʌn,beɪkt) adj 1 (esp. of roads, etc.) dried or cracked by the sun's heat. 2 baked hard by the heat of the sun: sunbaked bricks.

sun bath n the exposure of the body to the rays of the sun or a sun lamp, esp. in order to get a suntan.

sunbathe ('sʌn,beɪð) vb **sunbathes, sunbathing, sunbathed.** (intr) to bask in the sunshine, esp. in order to get a suntan.
▶ **'sun,bather** n

sunbeam ('sʌn,biːm) n a beam, ray, or stream of sunlight.
▶ **'sun,beamed** or **'sun,beamy** adj

Sunbelt ★ ('sʌn,belt) n the southern states of the USA.

sunbird ('sʌn,bɜːd) n any of various small songbirds of tropical regions of the Old World, esp. Africa, having a long slender curved bill and a bright plumage in the males.

sunbonnet ('sʌn,bɒnɪt) n a hat that shades the face and neck from the sun, esp. one of cotton with a projecting brim, now worn esp. by babies.

sunburn ('sʌn,bɜːn) n 1 inflammation of the skin caused by overexposure to the sun. 2 another word for **suntan.**
▶ **'sun,burnt** or **'sun,burned** adj

sunburst ('sʌn,bɜːst) n 1 a burst of sunshine, as through a break in the clouds. 2 a pattern or design resembling that of the sun. 3 a jewelled brooch with this pattern.

Sunbury-on-Thames ★ ('sʌnbərɪ, -brɪ) n a town in SE England, in N Surrey. Pop.: 27 392 (1991).

sun-cured adj cured or preserved by exposure to the sun.

sundae ('sʌndɪ, -deɪ) n ice cream topped with a sweet sauce, nuts, whipped cream, etc. [C20: from ?]

Sunda Islands ('sʌndə) or **Soenda Islands** ★ pl n a chain of islands in the Malay Archipelago, consisting of the **Greater Sunda Islands** (chiefly Sumatra, Java, Borneo, and Sulawesi) and **Nusa Tenggara** (formerly the Lesser Sunda Islands).

Sunda Strait or **Soenda Strait** ★ n a strait between Sumatra and Java, linking the Java Sea with the Indian Ocean. Narrowest point: about 26 km (16 miles).

Sunday ('sʌndɪ) n the first day of the week and the Christian day of worship. [OE sunnandæg, translation of L diēs sōlis day of the sun, translation of Gk hēmera hēliou]

Sunday best n one's best clothes, esp. regarded as those most suitable for churchgoing.

Sunday school n 1a a school for the religious instruction of children on Sundays, usually held in a church hall. 1b (as modifier): a Sunday-school outing. 2 the members of such a school.

sunder ('sʌndə) Arch. or literary. ◆ vb 1 to break or cause to break apart or in pieces. ◆ n 2 **in sunder.** into pieces; apart. [OE sundrian]

Sunderland ★ ('sʌndələnd) n 1 a port in NE England, in Tyne and Wear at the mouth of the River Wear: shipbuilding and marine engineering. Pop.: 183 310 (1991). 2 a unitary authority in NE England, in Tyne and Wear. Pop.: 297 200 (1994 est.). Area: 138 sq. km (53 sq. miles).

sundew ('sʌn,djuː) n any of several bog plants having leaves covered with sticky hairs that trap and digest insects. [C16: translation of L ros solis]

sundial ('sʌn,daɪəl) n a device indicating the time during the hours of sunlight by means of a stationary arm (the **gnomon**) that casts a shadow onto a plate or surface marked in hours.

sun disc n a disc symbolizing the sun, esp. one flanked by two serpents and the extended wings of a vulture: a religious figure in ancient Egypt.

sundog ('sʌn,dɒg) n another word for **parhelion.**

sundown ('sʌn,daʊn) n another name for **sunset.**

sundowner ('sʌn,daʊnə) n 1 Austral. sl. a tramp, esp. one who seeks food and lodging at sundown when it is too late to work. 2 Inf., chiefly Brit. an alcoholic drink taken at sunset.

sundress ('sʌn,drɛs) n a dress for hot weather that exposes the shoulders, arms, and back.

sun-dried adj dried or preserved by exposure to the sun.

sundry ('sʌndrɪ) determiner 1 several or various; miscellaneous. ◆ pron 2 **all and sundry.** everybody, individually and collectively. ◆ n, pl **sundries.** 3 (pl) miscellaneous unspecified items. 4 the Austral. term for **extra** (sense 6). [OE syndrig separate]

Sundsvall ★ (Swedish 'sundsval) n a port in E Sweden, on the Gulf of Bothnia: icebound in winter; cellulose industries. Pop.: 94 815 (1994).

sunfast ('sʌn,fɑːst) adj Chiefly US & Canad. not fading in sunlight.

sunfish ('sʌn,fɪʃ) n, pl **sunfish** or **sunfishes.** 1 any of various large fishes of temperate and tropical seas, esp. one which has a large rounded compressed body, long pointed dorsal and anal fins, and a fringelike tail fin. 2 any of various small predatory North American freshwater percoid fishes, typically having a compressed brightly coloured body.

sunflower ('sʌn,flaʊə) n 1 any of several American plants having very tall thick stems, large flower heads with yellow rays, and seeds used as food, esp. for poultry. See also **Jerusalem artichoke.** 2 **sunflower seed oil.** the oil extracted from sunflower seeds, used as a salad oil, in margarine, etc.

sung (sʌŋ) vb 1 the past participle of **sing.** ◆ adj 2 produced by singing: a sung syllable.

USAGE NOTE See at **ring².**

Sung or **Song** ★ (suŋ) n an imperial dynasty of China (960–1279 A.D.), notable for its art, literature, and philosophy.

Sungari ★ ('suŋgərɪ) n another name for the **Songhua.**

Sungkiang ★ ('suŋ'kjæŋ, -kaɪ'æŋ) n a former province of NE China: now part of the Inner Mongolian AR.

sunglass ('sʌn,glɑːs) n another name for **burning glass.**

★ people and places

sunglasses ('sʌn,glɑ:sɪz) *pl n* glasses with darkened or polarizing lenses that protect the eyes from the sun's glare.

sun-god *n* **1** the sun considered as a personal deity. **2** a deity associated with the sun or controlling its movements.

sunk (sʌŋk) *vb* **1** a past participle of **sink**. ◆ *adj* **2** *Inf.* with all hopes dashed; ruined.

sunken ('sʌŋkən) *vb* **1** a past participle of **sink**. ◆ *adj* **2** unhealthily hollow: *sunken cheeks*. **3** situated at a lower level than the surrounding or usual one: *a sunken bath*. **4** situated under water; submerged. **5** depressed; low: *sunken spirits*.

sunk fence *n* another name for **ha-ha**².

Sun King ★ *n* the. an epithet of **Louis XIV**.

sun lamp *n* **1** a lamp that generates ultraviolet rays, used for obtaining an artificial suntan, for muscular therapy, etc. **2** a lamp used in film studios, etc., to give an intense beam of light by means of parabolic mirrors.

sunless ('sʌnlɪs) *adj* **1** without sun or sunshine. **2** gloomy; depressing.
  ▸ **'sunlessly** *adv*

sunlight ('sʌnlaɪt) *n* **1** the light emanating from the sun. **2** an area or the time characterized by sunshine.
  ▸ **'sunlit** *adj*

sun lounge *or US* **sun parlor** *n* a room with large windows positioned to receive as much sunlight as possible.

Sunna ('sʌnə) *n* the body of traditional Islamic law accepted by most orthodox Muslims as based on the words and acts of Mohammed. [C18: from Ar. *sunnah* rule]

Sunni ('sʌnɪ) *n* **1** one of the two main branches of orthodox Islam (the other being the Shiah), consisting of those who acknowledge the authority of the Sunna. **2** (*pl* **Sunni**) a less common word for **Sunnite**.

Sunnite ('sʌnaɪt) *n* an adherent of the Sunni.

sunny ('sʌnɪ) *adj* **sunnier, sunniest**. **1** full of or exposed to sunlight. **2** radiating good humour. **3** of or resembling the sun.
  ▸ **'sunnily** *adv* ▸ **'sunniness** *n*

sunrise ('sʌn,raɪz) *n* **1** the daily appearance of the sun above the horizon. **2** the atmospheric phenomena accompanying this appearance. **3** Also called (esp. US): **sunup**. the time at which the sun rises at a particular locality.

sunrise industry *n* any of the high-technology industries, such as electronics, that hold promise of future development.

sunroof ('sʌn,ru:f) *or* **sunshine roof** *n* a panel, often translucent, that may be opened in the roof of a car.

sunset ('sʌn,sɛt) *n* **1** the daily disappearance of the sun below the horizon. **2** the atmospheric phenomena accompanying this disappearance. **3** Also called: **sundown**. the time at which the sun sets at a particular locality. **4** the final stage or closing period, as of a person's life.

sunshade ('sʌn,ʃeɪd) *n* a device, esp. a parasol or awning, serving to shade from the sun.

sunshine ('sʌn,ʃaɪn) *n* **1** the light received directly from the sun. **2** the warmth from the sun. **3** a sunny area. **4** a light-hearted or ironic term of address.
  ▸ **'sun,shiny** *adj*

sun sign *n* another name for **sign of the zodiac**.

sunspot ('sʌn,spɒt) *n* **1** any of the dark cool patches that appear on the surface of the sun and last about a week. **2** *Inf.* a sunny holiday resort. **3** *Austral.* a small cancerous spot produced by overexposure to the sun.

sunstroke ('sʌn,strəʊk) *n* heatstroke caused by prolonged exposure to intensely hot sunlight.

sunsuit ('sʌn,su:t, -,sju:t) *n* a child's outfit consisting of a brief top and shorts or skirt.

suntan ('sʌn,tæn) *n* **a** a brownish colouring of the skin caused by the formation of the pigment melanin within the skin on exposure to the ultraviolet rays of the sun or a sun lamp. Often shortened to **tan**. **b** (*as modifier*): *suntan oil*.
  ▸ **'sun,tanned** *adj*

suntrap ('sʌn,træp) *n* a very sunny sheltered place.

sunward ('sʌnwəd) *adj* **1** directed or moving towards the sun. ◆ *adv* **2** Also: **sunwards**. towards the sun.

Sun Yat-sen ★ ('sʊn 'jɑːt'sɛn) *n* 1866–1925, Chinese statesman, who was instrumental in the overthrow of the Manchu dynasty and was the first president of the Republic of China (1911). He reorganized the Kuomintang.

Suomi ★ ('suɒmi) *n* the Finnish name for **Finland**.

sup¹ (sʌp) *vb* **sups, supping, supped**. (*intr*) *Arch.* to have supper. [C13: from OF *soper*]

sup² (sʌp) *vb* **sups, supping, supped**. **1** to partake of (liquid) by swallowing a little at a time. **2** *Scot. & N English dialect*. to drink. ◆ *n* **3** a sip. [OE *sūpan*]

sup. *abbrev. for:* **1** above. [from L *supra*] **2** superior. **3** *Grammar*. superlative. **4** supplement. **5** supplementary. **6** supply.

super (su:pə) *adj* **1** *Inf.* outstanding; exceptional. ◆ *n* **2** petrol with a high octane rating. **3** *Inf.* a supervisor. **4** *Austral. & NZ inf.* superannuation benefits. **5** *Austral & NZ inf.* superphosphate. ◆ *interj* **6** *Brit. inf.* an enthusiastic expression of approval. [from L: above]

super. *abbrev. for:* **1** superfine. **2** superior.

super- *prefix* **1** placed above or over: *superscript*. **2** surpassing others; outstanding: *superstar*. **3** of greater size, extent, quality, etc.: *supermarket*. **4** beyond a standard or norm: *supersonic*. **5** indicating that a chemical compound contains a specified element in a higher proportion than usual: *superphosphate*. [from L *super* above]

superable ('su:pərəbʰl) *adj* able to be surmounted or overcome. [C17: from L *superābilis*, from *superāre* to overcome]
  ▸ **,supera'bility** *or* **'superableness** *n* ▸ **'superably** *adv*

superannuate (,su:pər'ænju,eɪt) *vb* **superannuates, superannuating, superannuated**. (*tr*) **1** to pension off. **2** to discard as obsolete or old-fashioned.

superannuated (,su:pər'ænju,eɪtɪd) *adj* **1** discharged, esp. with a pension, owing to age or illness. **2** too old to serve usefully. **3** obsolete. [C17: from Med. L *superannātus* aged more than one year, from L SUPER- + *annus* a year]

superannuation (,su:pər,ænju'eɪʃən) *n* **1a** the amount deducted regularly from employees' incomes in a contributory pension scheme. **1b** the pension finally paid. **2** the act or process of superannuating or the condition of being superannuated.

superb (sʊ'pɜːb, sju-) *adj* **1** surpassingly good; excellent. **2** majestic or imposing. **3** magnificently rich; luxurious. [C16: from OF *superbe*, from L *superbus* distinguished, from *super* above]
  ▸ **su'perbly** *adv* ▸ **su'perbness** *n*

Super Bowl *n American football*. the championship game held annually between the best team of the American Football Conference and that of the National Football Conference.

supercalender (,su:pə'kæləndə) *n* **1** a calender that gives a high gloss to paper. ◆ *vb* **2** (*tr*) to finish (paper) in this way.
  ▸ **,super'calendered** *adj*

supercargo (,su:pə'kɑ:gəʊ) *n, pl* **supercargoes**. an officer on a merchant ship who supervises commercial matters and is in charge of the cargo. [C17: changed from Sp. *sobrecargo*, from *sobre* over + *cargo* CARGO]

supercharge ('su:pə,tʃɑːdʒ) *vb* **supercharges, supercharging, supercharged**. (*tr*) **1** to increase the intake pressure of (an internal-combustion engine) with a supercharger; boost. **2** to charge (the atmosphere, a remark, etc.) with an excess amount of (tension, emotion, etc.). **3** to apply pressure to (a fluid); pressurize.

supercharger ('su:pə,tʃɑːdʒə) *n* a device that increases the mass of air drawn into an internal-combustion engine by raising the intake pressure. Also called: **blower, booster**.

superciliary (,su:pə'sɪlɪərɪ) *adj* over the eyebrow or a corresponding region in lower animals. [C18: from NL *superciliaris*, from L, from SUPER- + *cilium* eyelid]

supercilious (,su:pə'sɪlɪəs) *adj* displaying arrogant

pride, scorn, or indifference. [C16: from L, from *supercilium* eyebrow]
▶ ˌsuper'ciliously *adv* ▶ ˌsuper'ciliousness *n*

superclass ('su:pəˌklɑ:s) *n* a taxonomic group that is a subdivision of a subphylum.

supercolumnar (ˌsu:pəkə'lʌmnə) *adj Archit.* 1 having one colonnade above another. 2 placed above a colonnade or a column.
▶ ˌsupercol,umni'ation *n*

superconductivity (ˌsu:pəˌkɒndʌk'tɪvɪtɪ) *n Physics.* the property of certain substances that have no electrical resistance. In metals it occurs at very low temperatures; higher-temperature superconductivity occurs in some ceramic materials.
▶ **superconduction** (ˌsu:pəkən'dʌkʃən) *n* ▶ ˌsupercon-'ducting *or* ˌsupercon'ducting *adj* ▶ ˌsupercon'ductor *n*

supercontinent ('su:pəˌkɒntɪnənt) *n* a great landmass thought to have existed in the geological past and to have split into smaller landmasses, which drifted and formed the present continents.

supercool (ˌsu:pə'ku:l) *vb Chem.* to cool or be cooled without freezing or crystallization to a temperature below that at which freezing or crystallization should occur.

supercritical (ˌsu:pə'krɪtɪkªl) *adj* 1 *Physics.* (of a fluid) brought to a temperature and pressure higher than its critical temperature and pressure, so that its physical and chemical properties change. 2 *Nuclear physics.* of or containing more than the critical mass.

superdense theory (ˌsu:pə'dɛns) *n Astron.* another name for the **big-bang theory.**

super-duper (ˌsu:pə'du:pə) *adj Inf.* extremely pleasing, impressive, etc.: often used as an exclamation.

superego (ˌsu:pər'i:gəʊ, -'ɛgəʊ) *n, pl* **superegos.** *Psychoanal.* that part of the unconscious mind that acts as a conscience for the ego.

superelevation (ˌsu:pərˌɛlɪ'veɪʃən) *n* 1 another name for **bank**[2] (sense 8). 2 The difference between the heights of the sides of a road or railway track on a bend.

supereminent (ˌsu:pər'ɛmɪnənt) *adj* of distinction, dignity, or rank superior to that of others; pre-eminent.
▶ ˌsuper'eminence *n* ▶ ˌsuper'eminently *adv*

supererogation (ˌsu:pərˌɛrə'geɪʃən) *n* 1 the performance of work in excess of that required or expected. 2 *RC Church.* supererogatory prayers, devotions, etc.

supererogatory (ˌsu:pərɛ'rɒgətərɪ, -trɪ) *adj* 1 performed to an extent exceeding that required or expected. 2 exceeding what is needed; superfluous. 3 *RC Church.* of or relating to prayers, good works, etc., performed over and above those prescribed as obligatory. [C16: from Med. L *superērogātōrius,* from L *supererogāre* to spend over and above]

superfamily ('su:pəˌfæmɪlɪ) *n, pl* **superfamilies.** 1 *Biol.* a subdivision of a suborder. 2 any analogous group, such as a group of related languages.

superfecundation (ˌsu:pəˌfi:kən'deɪʃən) *n Physiol.* the fertilization of two or more ova, produced during the same menstrual cycle, by sperm ejaculated during two or more acts of sexual intercourse.

superfetation (ˌsu:pəfi:'teɪʃən) *n Physiol.* the presence in the uterus of two fetuses developing from ova fertilized at different times. [C17 *superfetate,* from L *superfētāre* to fertilize when already pregnant, from *fētus* offspring]

superficial (ˌsu:pə'fɪʃəl) *adj* 1 of, near, or forming the surface: *superficial bruising.* 2 displaying a lack of thoroughness or care: *a superficial inspection.* 3 only outwardly apparent rather than genuine or actual: *the similarity was merely superficial.* 4 of little substance or significance: *superficial differences.* 5 lacking profundity: *the film's plot was quite superficial.* 6 (of measurements) involving only the surface area. [C14: from LL *superficiālis* of the surface, from L SUPERFICIES]
▶ **superficiality** (ˌsu:pəˌfɪʃɪ'ælɪtɪ) *n* ▶ ˌsuper'ficially *adv*

superficies (ˌsu:pə'fɪʃi:z) *n, pl* **superficies.** 1 a surface or outer face. 2 the outward form of a thing. [C16: from L: upper side]

superfine (ˌsu:pə'faɪn) *adj* 1 of exceptional fineness or quality. 2 excessively refined.
▶ ˌsuper'fineness *n*

superfix (ˌsu:pəˌfɪks) *n Linguistics.* a type of feature distinguishing the meaning or grammatical function of one word or phrase from that of another, as stress does for example between the noun *conduct* and the verb *conduct.*

superfluid (ˌsu:pə'flu:ɪd) *n* 1 *Physics.* a fluid in a state characterized by a very low viscosity, high thermal conductivity, high capillarity, etc. The only known example is that of liquid helium at temperatures close to absolute zero. ◆ *adj* 2 being or relating to a superfluid.
▶ ˌsuperflu'idity *n*

superfluity (ˌsu:pə'flu:ɪtɪ) *n* 1 the condition of being superfluous. 2 a quantity or thing that is in excess of what is needed. 3 a thing that is not needed. [C14: from OF *superfluité,* via LL from L *superfluus* SUPERFLUOUS]

superfluous (su:'pɜ:fluəs) *adj* 1 exceeding what is sufficient or required. 2 not necessary or relevant; uncalled for. [C15: from L *superfluus* overflowing, from *fluere* to flow]
▶ su'perfluously *adv* ▶ su'perfluousness *n*

Super-G *n Skiing.* a type of slalom in which the course is shorter than in a standard slalom and the obstacles are farther apart than in a giant slalom. [C20: from SUPER- + G(IANT)]

supergiant ('su:pəˌdʒaɪənt) *n* any of a class of extremely bright stars which have expanded to a large diameter and are eventually likely to explode as supernovas.

superglue ('su:pəˌglu:) *n* any of various adhesives that quickly make an exceptionally strong bond.

supergrass ('su:pəˌgrɑ:s) *n* an informer whose information implicates a large number of people.

supergravity (ˌsu:pə'grævɪtɪ) *n Physics.* any of various theories in which supersymmetry is applied to the theory of gravitation.

superheat (ˌsu:pə'hi:t) *vb (tr)* 1 to heat (a vapour, esp. steam) to a temperature above its saturation point for a given pressure. 2 to heat (a liquid) to a temperature above its boiling point without boiling occurring. 3 to heat excessively; overheat.
▶ ˌsuper'heater *n*

superheavy (ˌsu:pə'hɛvɪ) *adj Physics.* denoting or relating to elements of high atomic number (above 109) postulated to exist with special stability as a consequence of the shell model of the nucleus.

superheterodyne receiver (ˌsu:pə'hɛtərəˌdaɪn) *n* a radio receiver that combines two radio-frequency signals by heterodyne action, to produce a signal above the audible frequency limit. Sometimes shortened to **superhet.** [C20: from SUPER(SONIC) + HETERODYNE]

superhigh frequency ('su:pəˌhaɪ) *n* a radio-frequency band or radio frequency lying between 30 000 and 3000 megahertz.

superhuman (ˌsu:pə'hju:mən) *adj* 1 having powers above and beyond those of mankind. 2 exceeding normal human ability or experience.
▶ ˌsuper'humanly *adv*

superimpose (ˌsu:pərɪm'pəʊz) *vb* **superimposes, superimposing, superimposed.** *(tr)* 1 to set or place on or over something else. 2 (usually foll. by *on* or *upon*) to add (to).
▶ ˌsuper,impo'sition *n*

superinduce (ˌsu:pərɪn'dju:s) *vb* **superinduces, superinducing, superinduced.** *(tr)* to introduce as an additional feature, factor, etc.
▶ **superinduction** (ˌsu:pərɪn'dʌkʃən) *n*

superintend (ˌsu:pərɪn'tɛnd) *vb* to undertake the direction or supervision (of); manage. [C17: from Church L *superintendere,* from L SUPER- + *intendere* to give attention to]
▶ ˌsuperin'tendence *n*

superintendent (ˌsu:pərɪn'tɛndənt) *n* 1 a person who directs and manages an organization, office, etc. 2 (in Britain) a senior police officer higher in rank than an inspector but lower than a chief superintendent. 3 (in the US) the head of a police department. 4 *Chiefly US &*

Canad. a caretaker, esp. of a block of apartments. ◆ *adj* **5** of or relating to supervision; superintending. [C16: from Church L *superintendens* overseeing]
▶ ,superin'tendency *n*

superior (su:'pɪərɪə) *adj* **1** greater in quality, quantity, etc. **2** of high or extraordinary worth, merit, etc. **3** higher in rank or status. **4** displaying a conscious sense of being above or better than others; supercilious. **5** (*often postpositive;* foll. by *to*) not susceptible (to) or influenced (by). **6** placed higher up; further from the base. **7** *Astron.* (of a planet) having an orbit further from the sun than the orbit of the earth. **8** (of a plant ovary) situated above the calyx and other floral parts. **9** *Printing.* (of a character) written or printed above the line; superscript. ◆ *n* **10** a person or thing of greater rank or quality. **11** *Printing.* a character set in a superior position. **12** (*often cap.*) the head of a community in a religious order. [C14: from L, from *superus* placed above, from *super* above]
▶ su'perioress *fem n* ▶ superiority (su:,pɪərɪ'ɒrɪtɪ) *n*

USAGE NOTE *Superior* should not be used with *than: he is a better* (not *a superior*) *poet than his brother; his poetry is superior to* (not *superior than*) *his brother's.*

Superior ★ (su:'pɪərɪə, sju:-) *n* **Lake.** a lake in the N central US and S Canada: one of the largest freshwater lakes in the world and westernmost of the Great Lakes. Area: 82 362 sq. km (31 800 sq. miles).

superior court *n* **1** (in England) a higher court not subject to control by any other court except by way of appeal. See also **Supreme Court of Judicature. 2** (in several states of the US) a court of general jurisdiction ranking above the inferior courts and below courts of last resort.

superiority complex *n Inf.* an inflated estimate of one's own merit, usually manifested in arrogance.

superior planet *n* any of the six planets (Mars, Jupiter, Saturn, Uranus, Neptune, and Pluto) whose orbit lies outside that of the earth.

superl. *abbrev. for* superlative.

superlative (su:'pɜːlətɪv) *adj* **1** of outstanding quality, degree, etc.; supreme. **2** *Grammar.* denoting the form of an adjective or adverb that expresses the highest or a very high degree of quality. In English this is usually marked by the suffix *-est* or the word *most,* as in *loudest* or *most loudly.* **3** (of language or style) excessive; exaggerated. ◆ *n* **4** a thing that excels all others or is of the highest quality. **5** *Grammar.* the superlative form of an adjective or adverb. **6** the highest degree; peak. [C14: from OF *superlatif,* via LL from L *superlātus* extravagant, from *superferre* to carry beyond]
▶ su'perlatively *adv* ▶ su'perlativeness *n*

superlunar (,su:pə'lu:nə) *adj* beyond the moon; celestial.
▶ ,super'lunary *adj*

superman ('su:pə,mæn) *n, pl* **supermen. 1** (in the philosophy of Nietzsche) an ideal man who would rise above good and evil and who represents the goal of human evolution. **2** any man of apparently superhuman powers.

supermarket ('su:pə,mɑːkɪt) *n* a large self-service store selling food and household supplies.

supermembrane (,su:pə'membreɪn) *n Physics.* a type of membrane postulated in certain theories of elementary particles that involve supersymmetry.

supermodel ('su:pə,mɒdˀl) *n* a very successful and well-known photographic or catwalk model.

supermundane (,su:pə'mʌndeɪn) *adj* elevated above earthly things.

supernal (su:'pɜːnˀl, sju:-) *adj Literary.* **1** divine; celestial. **2** of, from above, or from the sky. [C15: from Med. L *supernālis,* from L *supernus* that is on high, from *super* above]
▶ su'pernally *adv*

supernatant (,su:pə'neɪtˀnt) *adj* **1** floating on the surface or over something. **2** *Chem.* (of a liquid) lying above

a sediment or precipitate. [C17: from L *supernatāre* to float, from SUPER- + *natāre* to swim]
▶ ,superna'tation *n*

supernatural (,su:pə'nætʃərəl) *adj* **1** of or relating to things that cannot be explained according to natural laws. **2** of or caused as if by a god; miraculous. **3** of or involving occult beings. **4** exceeding the ordinary; abnormal. ◆ *n* **5** the supernatural. supernatural forces, occurrences, and beings collectively.
▶ ,super'naturally *adv* ▶ ,super'naturalness *n*

supernaturalism (,su:pə'nætʃərəlɪzəm) *n* **1** the quality or condition of being supernatural. **2** belief in supernatural forces or agencies as producing effects in this world.
▶ ,super'naturalist *n, adj* ▶ ,super,natural'istic *adj*

supernormal (,su:pə'nɔːməl) *adj* greatly exceeding the normal.
▶ supernormality (,su:pənɔː'mælɪtɪ) *n* ▶ ,super'normally *adv*

supernova (,su:pə'nəʊvə) *n, pl* **supernovae** (-vi:) *or* **supernovas.** a star that explodes owing to instabilities following the exhaustion of its nuclear fuel, becoming for a few days up to one hundred million times brighter than the sun. Cf. **nova.**

supernumerary (,su:pə'nju:mərərɪ) *adj* **1** exceeding a regular or proper number; extra. **2** functioning as a substitute or assistant with regard to a regular body or staff. ◆ *n, pl* **supernumeraries. 3** a person or thing that exceeds the required or regular number. **4** a substitute or assistant. **5** an actor who has no lines, esp. a nonprofessional one. [C17: from LL *supernumerārius,* from L SUPER- + *numerus* number]

superorder ('su:pər,ɔːdə) *n Biol.* a subdivision of a subclass.

superordinate (,su:pər'ɔːdɪnɪt) *adj* **1** of higher status or condition. ◆ *n* **2** a person or thing that is superordinate. **3** a word the meaning of which includes the meaning of another word or words: "red" is the superordinate of "scarlet" and "crimson".

superphosphate (,su:pə'fɒsfeɪt) *n* **1** a mixture of the diacid calcium salt of orthophosphoric acid with calcium sulphate and small quantities of other phosphates, used as a fertilizer. **2** a salt of phosphoric acid formed by incompletely replacing its acidic hydrogen atoms.

superpose (,su:pə'pəʊz) *vb* **superposes, superposing, superposed.** (*tr*) *Geom.* to transpose (the coordinates of one geometric figure) to coincide with those of another. [C19: from F *superposer,* from L *superpōnere,* from *pōnere* to place]

superposition (,su:pəpə'zɪʃən) *n* **1** the act of superposing or state of being superposed. **2** *Geol.* the principle that in any sequence of sedimentary rocks that has not been disturbed the lowest strata are the oldest.

superpower ('su:pə,paʊə) *n* **1** an extremely powerful state, such as the US. **2** extremely high power, esp. electrical or mechanical.
▶ 'super,powered *adj*

supersaturated (,su:pə'sætʃə,reɪtɪd) *adj* **1** (of a solution) containing more solute than a saturated solution. **2** (of a vapour) containing more material than a saturated vapour.
▶ ,super,satu'ration *n*

superscribe (,su:pə'skraɪb) *vb* **superscribes, superscribing, superscribed.** (*tr*) to write (an inscription, name, etc.) above, on top of, or outside. [C16: from L *superscrībere,* from *scrībere* to write]
▶ superscription (,su:pə'skrɪpʃən) *n*

superscript ('su:pə,skrɪpt) *Printing.* ◆ *adj* **1** (of a character) written or printed above the line; superior. Cf. **subscript.** ◆ *n* **2** a superscript or superior character. [C16: from L *superscriptus*]

supersede (,su:pə'si:d) *vb* **supersedes, superseding, superseded.** (*tr*) **1** to take the place of (something old fashioned or less appropriate); supplant. **2** to replace in function, office, etc.; succeed. **3** to discard or set aside or cause to be set aside as obsolete or inferior. [C15: via OF from L *supersedēre* to sit above]
▶ ,super'sedence *n* ▶ supersedure (,su:pə'si:dʒə) *n*
▶ supersession (,su:pə'seʃən) *n*

supersex ('su:pə,sɛks) n *Genetics*. a sterile organism in which the ratio between the sex chromosomes is disturbed.

supersonic (,su:pə'sɒnɪk) *adj* being, having, or capable of a velocity in excess of the velocity of sound.
▶ ,**super'sonically** *adv*

supersonics (,su:pə'sɒnɪks) n (*functioning as sing*) **1** the study of supersonic motion. **2** a less common name for **ultrasonics.**

superstar ('su:pə,stɑː) n an extremely popular film star, pop star, etc.
▶ '**super,stardom** n

superstition (,su:pə'stɪʃən) n **1** irrational belief usually founded on ignorance or fear and characterized by obsessive reverence for omens, charms, etc. **2** a notion, act, or ritual that derives from such belief. **3** any irrational belief, esp. with regard to the unknown. [C15: from L *superstitiō*, from *superstāre* to stand still by something (as in amazement)]

superstitious (,su:pə'stɪʃəs) *adj* **1** disposed to believe in superstition. **2** of or relating to superstition.
▶ ,**super'stitiously** *adv* ▶ ,**super'stitiousness** n

superstore ('su:pə,stɔː) n a large supermarket.

superstratum (,su:pə'strɑːtəm, -'streɪ-) n, *pl* **superstrata** (-tə) *or* **superstratums.** *Geol.* a layer or stratum overlying another layer or similar structure.

superstring ('su:pə,strɪŋ) n *Physics*. a type of string postulated in certain theories of elementary particles that involve supersymmetry.

superstructure ('su:pə,strʌktʃə) n **1** the part of a building above its foundation. **2** any structure or concept erected on something else. **3** *Naut.* any structure above the main deck of a ship with sides flush with the sides of the hull. **4** the part of a bridge supported by the piers and abutments.
▶ '**super,structural** *adj*

supersymmetry (,su:pə'sɪmɪtrɪ) n *Physics*. a symmetry of elementary particles having a higher order than that in the standard model, postulated to encompass the behaviour of both bosons and fermions.

supertanker ('su:pə,tæŋkə) n a large fast tanker of more than 275 000 tons capacity.

supertax ('su:pə,tæks) n a tax levied in addition to the basic tax, esp. on incomes above a certain level.

supertonic (,su:pə'tɒnɪk) n *Music*. **1** the second degree of a major or minor scale. **2** a key or chord based on this.

supervene (,su:pə'vi:n) *vb* **supervenes, supervening, supervened.** (*intr*) **1** to follow closely; ensue. **2** to occur as an unexpected or extraneous development. [C17: from L *supervenīre* to come upon]
▶ ,**super'venience** *or* **supervention** (,su:pə'vɛnʃən) n
▶ ,**super'venient** *adj*

supervise ('su:pə,vaɪz) *vb* **supervises, supervising, supervised.** (*tr*) **1** to direct or oversee the performance or operation of. **2** to watch over so as to maintain order, etc. [C16: from Med. L *supervidēre*, from L SUPER- + *vidēre* to see]
▶ **supervision** (,su:pə'vɪʒən) n

supervisor ('su:pə,vaɪzə) n **1** a person who manages or supervises. **2** a foreman or forewoman. **3** (in some British universities) a tutor supervising the work, esp. research work, of a student. **4** (in some US schools) an administrator running a department of teachers.
▶ '**super,visorship** n ▶ '**super,visory** *adj*

supinate ('su:pɪ,neɪt, 'sjuː-) *vb* **supinates, supinating, supinated.** to turn (the hand and forearm) so that the palm faces up or forwards. [C19: from L *supīnāre* to lay on the back, from *supīnus* supine]
▶ ,**supi'nation** n

supine *adj* (suː'paɪn, sjuː-; 'suːpaɪn, 'sjuː-). **1** lying or resting on the back with the face, palm, etc., upwards. **2** displaying no interest or animation; lethargic. ◆ n ('suːpaɪn, 'sjuː-). **3** *Grammar*. a noun form derived from a verb in Latin, often used to express purpose with verbs of motion. [C15: from L *supīnus* rel. to *sub* under, up; (in grammatical sense) from *verbum supīnum* supine word (from ?)]
▶ **su'pinely** *adv* ▶ **su'pineness** n

supp. *or* **suppl.** *abbrev. for* supplement(ary).

supper ('sʌpə) n **1** an evening meal, esp. a light one. **2** an evening social event featuring a supper. **3 sing for one's supper.** to obtain something by performing a service. [C13: from OF *soper*]
▶ '**supperless** *adj*

Suppiluliumas I ★ (,sʌpɪlʌlɪ'uːməs) n king of the Hittites (?1375–?1335 B.C.); founder of the Hittite empire.

supplant (sə'plɑːnt) *vb* (*tr*) to take the place of, often by trickery or force. [C13: via OF from L *supplantāre* to trip up, from *sub-* from below + *planta* sole of the foot]
▶ **sup'planter** n

supple ('sʌpᵊl) *adj* **1** bending easily without damage. **2** capable of or showing easy or graceful movement; lithe. **3** mentally flexible; responding readily. **4** disposed to agree, sometimes to the point of servility. ◆ *vb* **supples, suppling, suppled. 5** *Rare*. to make or become supple. [C13: from OF *souple*, from L *supplex* bowed]
▶ '**suppleness** n

supplejack ('sʌpᵊl,dʒæk) n **1** a North American twining woody vine that has greenish-white flowers and purple fruits. **2** a bush plant of New Zealand having tough climbing vines. **3** a tropical American woody vine having strong supple wood. **4** any of various other vines with strong supple stems. **5** *US.* a walking stick made from the wood of the tropical supplejack.

supplement n ('sʌplɪmənt). **1** an addition designed to complete, make up for a deficiency, etc. **2** a section appended to a publication to supply further information, correct errors, etc. **3** a magazine or section inserted into a newspaper or periodical, such as one issued every week. **4** *Geom.* **4a** either of a pair of angles whose sum is 180°. **4b** an arc of a circle that when added to another arc forms a semicircle. ◆ *vb* ('sʌplɪ,ment). **5** (*tr*) to provide a supplement to, esp. in order to remedy a deficiency. [C14: from L *supplēmentum*, from *supplēre* to SUPPLY]
▶ ,**supplemen'tation** n

supplementary (,sʌplɪ'mentərɪ) *adj* **1** Also (*less commonly*): **supplemental** (,sʌplə'mentᵊl). forming or acting as a supplement. ◆ n, *pl* **supplementaries. 2** a person or thing that is a supplement.
▶ ,**supple'mentarily** *or* (*less commonly*) ,**supple'mentally** *adv*

supplementary angle n either of two angles whose sum is 180°. Cf. **complementary angle.**

suppliant ('sʌplɪənt) *adj* **1** expressing entreaty or supplication. ◆ n, *adj* **2** another word for **supplicant.** [C15: from F *supplier* to beseech, from L *supplicāre* to kneel in entreaty]
▶ '**suppliantly** *adv*

supplicant ('sʌplɪkənt) *or* **suppliant** n **1** a person who supplicates. ◆ *adj* **2** entreating humbly; supplicating. [C16: from L *supplicāns* beseeching]

supplicate ('sʌplɪ,keɪt) *vb* **supplicates, supplicating, supplicated. 1** to make a humble request to (someone); plead. **2** (*tr*) to ask for or seek humbly. [C15: from L *supplicāre* to beg on one's knees]
▶ ,**suppli'cation** n ▶ '**suppli,catory** *adj*

supply[1] (sə'plaɪ) *vb* **supplies, supplying, supplied. 1** (*tr;* often foll. by *with*) to furnish with something required. **2** (*tr;* often foll. by *to* or *for*) to make available or provide (something desired or lacking): *to supply books to the library*. **3** (*tr*) to provide for adequately; satisfy: *who will supply their needs?* **4** to serve as a substitute, usually temporary, in (another's position, etc.): *there are no clergymen to supply the pulpit*. **5** (*tr*) *Brit*. to fill (a vacancy, position, etc.). ◆ n, *pl* **supplies. 6a** the act of providing or something provided. **6b** (*as modifier*): *a supply dump*. **7** (*often pl*) an amount available for use; stock. **8** (*pl*) food, equipment, etc., needed for a campaign or trip. **9** *Econ.* **9a** willingness and ability to offer goods and services for sale. **9b** the amount of a commodity that producers are willing and able to offer for sale at a specified price. Cf. **demand** (sense 9). **10** *Mil.* **10a** the management and disposal of food and equipment. **10b** (*as modifier*): *supply routes*. **11** (*often pl*) a grant of money voted by a legislature for government expenses. **12** (in Parliament and similar legislatures) the money voted annually for the expenses of the civil service and armed forces. **13a** a person who acts as a

temporary substitute. **13b** (*as modifier*): *a supply vicar*. **14** a source of electricity, gas, etc. [C14: from OF *souppleier*, from L *supplēre* to complete, from *sub-* up + *plēre* to fill]
▶ sup'pliable *adj* ▶ sup'plier *n*

supply[2] ('sʌplɪ) *or* **supplely** ('sʌpᵊlɪ) *adv* in a supple manner.

supply-side economics (sə'plaɪ-) *n* (*functioning as sing*) a school of economic thought that emphasizes the importance to a strong economy of policies that remove impediments to supply.

support (sə'pɔ:t) *vb* (*tr*) **1** to carry the weight of. **2** to bear (pressure, weight, etc.). **3** to provide the necessities of life for (a family, person, etc.). **4** to tend to establish (a theory, statement, etc.) by providing new facts. **5** to speak in favour of (a motion). **6** to give aid or courage to. **7** to give approval to (a cause, principle, etc.); subscribe to. **8** to endure with forbearance: *I will no longer support bad behaviour.* **9** to give strength to; maintain: *to support a business.* **10** (in a concert) to perform earlier than (the main attraction). **11** *Films, theatre.* **11a** to play a subordinate role to. **11b** to accompany (the feature) in a film programme. **12** to act or perform (a role or character). ◆ *n* **13** the act of supporting or the condition of being supported. **14** a thing that bears the weight or part of the weight of a construction. **15** a person who or thing that furnishes aid. **16** the means of maintenance of a family, person, etc. **17** a band or entertainer not topping the bill. **18** (often preceded by *the*) an actor or group of actors playing subordinate roles. **19** *Med.* an appliance worn to ease the strain on an injured bodily structure or part. **20** Also: **athletic support.** a more formal term for **jockstrap.** [C14: from OF *supporter*, from L *supportāre* to bring, from *sub-* up + *portāre* to carry]
▶ sup'portable *adj* ▶ sup'portive *adj*

supporter (sə'pɔ:tə) *n* **1** a person who or thing that acts as a support. **2** a person who backs a sports team, politician, etc. **3** a garment or device worn to ease the strain on or restrict the movement of a bodily structure or part. **4** *Heraldry.* a figure or beast in a coat of arms depicted as holding up the shield.

supporting (sə'pɔ:tɪŋ) *adj* **1** (of a role) being a fairly important but not leading part. **2** (of an actor or actress) playing a supporting role.

suppose (sə'pəʊz) *vb* **supposes, supposing, supposed.** (*tr; may take a clause as object*) **1** to presume (something) to be true without certain knowledge: *I suppose he meant to kill her.* **2** to consider as a possible suggestion for the sake of discussion, etc.: *suppose that he wins.* **3** (of theories, etc.) to imply the inference or assumption (of): *your policy supposes full employment.* [C14: from OF *supposer*, from Med. L *suppōnere*, from L: to substitute, from SUB- + *pōnere* to put]
▶ sup'posable *adj* ▶ sup'poser *n*

supposed (sə'pəʊzd, -'pəʊzɪd) *adj* **1** (*prenominal*) presumed to be true without certain knowledge. **2** (*prenominal*) believed to be true on slight grounds; highly doubtful. **3** (sə'pəʊzd). (*postpositive; foll. by to*) expected or obliged (to): *I'm supposed to be there.* **4** (sə'pəʊzd). (*postpositive; used in negative; foll. by to*) expected or obliged not (to): *you're not supposed to walk on the grass.*
▶ supposedly (sə'pəʊzɪdlɪ) *adv*

supposition (ˌsʌpə'zɪʃən) *n* **1** the act of supposing. **2** a fact, theory, etc., that is supposed.
▶ ˌsuppo'sitional *adj* ▶ ˌsuppo'sitionally *adv*

supposititious (ˌsʌpə'zɪʃəs) *adj* deduced from supposition; hypothetical.
▶ ˌsuppo'sitiously *adv* ▶ ˌsuppo'sitiousness *n*

supposititious (sə,pɒzɪ'tɪʃəs) *adj* substituted with intent to mislead or deceive.
▶ sup,posi'titiously *adv* ▶ sup,posi'titiousness *n*

suppositive (sə'pɒzɪtɪv) *adj* **1** of, involving, or arising out of supposition. **2** *Grammar.* denoting a conjunction introducing a clause expressing a supposition, as for example *if, supposing,* or *provided that.* ◆ *n* **3** *Grammar.* a suppositive conjunction.
▶ sup'positively *adv*

suppository (sə'pɒzɪtərɪ, -trɪ) *n, pl* **suppositories.** *Med.* a solid medication for insertion into the vagina, rectum, or urethra, where it melts and releases the active sub-

stance. [C14: from Med. L *suppositōrium,* from L *suppositus* placed beneath]

suppress (sə'prɛs) *vb* (*tr*) **1** to put an end to; prohibit. **2** to hold in check; restrain: *I was obliged to suppress a smile.* **3** to withhold from circulation or publication: *to suppress seditious pamphlets.* **4** to stop the activities of; crush: *to suppress a rebellion.* **5** *Electronics.* **5a** to reduce or eliminate (unwanted oscillations) in a circuit. **5b** to eliminate (a particular frequency or frequencies) in a signal. **6** *Psychiatry.* to resist consciously (an idea or a desire entering one's mind). [C14: from L *suppressus* held down, from *supprimere* to restrain, from *sub-* down + *premere* to press]
▶ sup'pressible *adj* ▶ sup'pressive *adj* ▶ sup'presser *n*

suppressant (sə'prɛsənt) *adj* **1** tending to suppress or restrain an action or condition. ◆ *n* **2** a suppressant drug or agent: *a cough suppressant.*

suppression (sə'prɛʃən) *n* **1** the act or process of suppressing or the condition of being suppressed. **2** *Psychiatry.* the conscious avoidance of unpleasant thoughts.

suppressor (sə'prɛsə) *n* **1** a person or thing that suppresses. **2** a device fitted to an electrical appliance to suppress unwanted electrical interference to audiovisual signals.

suppurate ('sʌpjʊˌreɪt) *vb* **suppurates, suppurating, suppurated.** (*intr*) *Pathol.* (of a wound, sore, etc.) to discharge pus; fester. [C16: from L *suppūrāre,* from SUB- + *pūs* pus]
▶ ˌsuppu'ration *n* ▶ 'suppurative *adj*

supra- *prefix* over, above, beyond, or greater than: *supranational.* [from L *suprā* above]

supraliminal (ˌsuːprə'lɪmɪnᵊl, ˌsjuː-) *adj* of or relating to any stimulus that is above the threshold of sensory awareness.
▶ ˌsupra'liminally *adv*

supramolecular (ˌsuːprəmə'lɛkjʊlə, ˌsjuː-) *adj* **1** more complex than a molecule. **2** consisting of more than one molecule.

supranational (ˌsuːprə'næʃᵊnᵊl, ˌsjuː-) *adj* beyond the authority or jurisdiction of one national government: *the supranational institutions of the EU.*
▶ ˌsupra'nationalism *n*

supraorbital (ˌsuːprə'ɔ:bɪtᵊl, ˌsjuː-) *adj Anat.* situated above the orbit.

suprarenal (ˌsuːprə'riːnᵊl, ˌsjuː-) *adj Anat.* situated above a kidney.

suprarenal gland *n* another name for **adrenal gland.**

supremacist (sʊ'prɛməsɪst, sjuː-) *n* **1** a person who promotes or advocates the supremacy of any particular group. ◆ *adj* **2** characterized by belief in the supremacy of any particular group.
▶ su'prematism *n*

supremacy (sʊ'prɛməsɪ, sjuː-) *n* **1** supreme power; authority. **2** the quality or condition of being supreme.

supreme (sʊ'priːm, sjuː-) *adj* **1** of highest status or power. **2** (*usually prenominal*) of highest quality, importance, etc. **3** greatest in degree; extreme: *supreme folly.* **4** (*prenominal*) final or last; ultimate: *the supreme judgment.* [C16: from L *suprēmus* highest, from *superus* that is above, from *super* above]
▶ su'premely *adv*

Supreme Being *n* God.

Supreme Court *n* (in the US) **1** the highest Federal court. **2** (in many states) the highest state court.

Supreme Court of Judicature *n* (in England) a court formed in 1873 by the amalgamation of several superior courts into two divisions, the High Court of Justice and the Court of Appeal.

supreme sacrifice *n the.* the sacrifice of one's life.

Supreme Soviet *n* (in the former Soviet Union) **1** the bicameral legislature, comprising the **Soviet of the Union** and the **Soviet of the Nationalities. 2** a similar legislature in each former Soviet republic.

supremo (sʊ'priːməʊ, sjuː-) *n, pl* **supremos.** *Brit. inf.* a person in overall authority. [C20: from SUPREME]

Supt *or* **supt** *abbrev. for* superintendent.

Suqutra ★ (sə'kəʊtrə) *n* a variant spelling of **Socotra.**

★ people and places

Sur or **Sour** ★ (sʊə) n transliteration of the Arabic name for **Tyre**.

sur-¹ prefix over; above; beyond: *surcharge; surrealism*. Cf. **super-**. [from OF, from L SUPER-]

sur-² prefix a variant of **sub-** before r: *surrogate*.

sura ('sʊərə) n any of the 114 chapters of the Koran. [C17: from Ar. *sūrah* section]

Surabaya, Surabaja, or **Soerabaja** ★ (ˌsʊərə'baɪə) n a port in Indonesia, on E Java on the **Surabaya Strait**: the country's second port and chief naval base; university (1954); fishing and ship-building industries; oil refinery. Pop.: 2 421 016 (1990).

surah ('sʊərə) n a twill-weave fabric of silk or rayon. [C19: from F pronunciation of *Surat*, a port in W India where orig. made]

Surakarta ★ (ˌsʊərə'kɑːtə) n a town in Indonesia, on central Java: textile manufacturing. Pop.: 504 176 (1990).

sural ('sjʊərəl) adj Anat. of or relating to the calf of the leg. [C17: via NL from L *sūra* calf]

Surat ★ (sʊ'ræt, 'sʊərət) n a port in W India, in W Gujarat: a major port in the 17th century; textile manufacturing. Pop.: 1 498 817 (1991).

surbase ('sɜːˌbeɪs) n the uppermost part, such as a moulding, of a pedestal, base, or skirting.

surcease (sɜː'siːs) Arch. ◆ n 1 cessation or intermission. ◆ vb **surceases, surceasing, surceased. 2** to desist from (some action). **3** to cease or cause to cease. [C16: from earlier *sursesen*, from OF *surseoir*, from L *supersedēre* to sit above]

surcharge n ('sɜːˌtʃɑːdʒ). **1** a charge in addition to the usual payment, tax, etc. **2** an excessive sum charged, esp. when unlawful. **3** an extra and usually excessive burden or supply. **4** an overprint that alters the face value of a postage stamp. ◆ vb (sɜː'tʃɑːdʒ, 'sɜːˌtʃɑːdʒ), **surcharges, surcharging, surcharged.** (tr) **5** to charge an additional sum, tax, etc. **6** to overcharge (a person) for something. **7** to put an extra physical burden upon; overload. **8** to fill to excess; overwhelm. **9** Law. to insert credits that have been omitted in (an account). **10** to overprint a surcharge on (a stamp).

surcingle ('sɜːˌsɪŋɡᵊl) n a girth for a horse which goes around the body, used esp. with a racing saddle. [C14: from OF *surcengle*, from sur- over + *cengle* a belt, from L *cingulum*]

surcoat ('sɜːˌkəʊt) n 1 a tunic, often embroidered with heraldic arms, worn by a knight over his armour during the Middle Ages. **2** (formerly) an outer coat or other garment.

surculose ('sɜːkjʊˌləʊs) adj (of a plant) bearing suckers. [C19: from L *surculōsus* woody, from *surculus* twig, from *sūrus* a branch]

surd (sɜːd) n 1 Maths. a number containing an irrational root, such as 2√3; irrational number. **2** Phonetics. a voiceless consonant, such as (t). ◆ adj **3** of or relating to a surd. [C16: from L *surdus* muffled]

sure (ʃʊə, ʃɔː) adj 1 (sometimes foll. by *of*) free from hesitancy or uncertainty (with regard to a belief, conviction, etc.): *we are sure of the accuracy of the statement; I am sure that he is lying*. **2** (foll. by *of*) having no doubt, as of the occurrence of a future state or event: *sure of success*. **3** always effective; unfailing: *a sure remedy*. **4** reliable in indication or accuracy: *a sure criterion*. **5** (of persons) worthy of trust or confidence: *a sure friend*. **6** not open to doubt: *sure proof*. **7** admitting of no vacillation or doubt: *he is sure in his beliefs*. **8** bound to be or occur; inevitable: *victory is sure*. **9** (postpositive) bound inevitably (to be or do something); certain: *she is sure to be there*. **10** physically secure or dependable: *a sure footing*. **11 be sure.** (usually imperative or dependent imperative; takes a clause as object or an infinitive, sometimes with *to* replaced by *and*) to be careful or certain: *be sure and shut the door; be sure to shut the door*. **12 for sure.** without a doubt; surely. **13 make sure. 13a** (takes a clause as object) to make certain; ensure. **13b** (foll. by *of*) to establish or confirm power or possession (over). **14 sure enough.** Inf. as might have been confidently expected; definitely: often used as a sentence substitute. **15 to be sure. 15a** without doubt; certainly. **15b** it has to be acknowledged; admittedly. ◆ adv **16** (sentence modifier) US & Canad. inf. without question; certainly. ◆ sentence substitute. **17** US & Canad. inf. willingly; yes. [C14: from OF *seur*, from L *sēcūrus* SECURE]
 ▸ '**sureness** n

sure-fire adj (usually prenominal) Inf. certain to succeed or meet expectations; assured.

sure-footed adj 1 unlikely to fall, slip, or stumble. **2** not likely to err or fall.
 ▸ ˌsure-'footedly adv ▸ ˌsure-'footedness n

surely ('ʃʊəlɪ, 'ʃɔː-) adv 1 without doubt; assuredly. **2** without fail; inexorably (esp. **in slowly but surely**). **3** (sentence modifier) am I not right in thinking that?; I am sure that: *surely you don't mean it?* **4** Rare. in a sure manner. **5** Arch. safely; securely. ◆ sentence substitute. **6** Chiefly US & Canad. willingly; yes.

sure thing Inf. ◆ sentence substitute. **1** Chiefly US. used to express enthusiastic assent. ◆ n **2** something guaranteed to be successful.

surety ('ʃʊətɪ, 'ʃʊərɪtɪ) n, pl **sureties. 1** a person who assumes legal responsibility for another's debt or obligation and himself becomes liable if the other defaults. **2** security given against loss or damage or as a guarantee that an obligation will be met. **3** Obs. the quality or condition of being sure. **4 stand surety.** to act as a surety. [C14: from OF *seurte*, from L *sēcūritās* security]
 ▸ '**suretyship** n

surf (sɜːf) n 1 waves breaking on the shore or on a reef. **2** foam caused by the breaking of waves. ◆ vb (intr) **3** to take part in surfing. **4** to move rapidly and easily through a particular medium: *surfing the Internet*. **5** Inf. to be carried on top of something: *that guy's surfing the audience*. [C17: prob. var. of SOUGH]

surface ('sɜːfɪs) n 1a the exterior face of an object or one such face. **1b** (as modifier): *surface gloss*. **2** the area or size of such a face. **3** material resembling such a face, with length and width but without depth. **4a** the superficial appearance as opposed to the real nature. **4b** (as modifier): *a surface resemblance*. **5** Geom. **5a** the complete boundary of a solid figure. **5b** a continuous two-dimensional configuration. **6a** the uppermost level of the land or sea. **6b** (as modifier): *surface transportation*. **7 come to the surface.** to emerge; become apparent. **8 on the surface.** to all appearances. ◆ vb **surfaces, surfacing, surfaced. 9** to rise or cause to rise to or as if to the surface (of water, etc.). **10** (tr) to treat the surface of, as by polishing, smoothing, etc. **11** (tr) to furnish with a surface. **12** (intr) to become apparent; emerge. **13** (intr) Inf. **13a** to wake up. **13b** to get up. [C17: from F, from *sur* on + *face* FACE]
 ▸ '**surfacer** n

surface-active adj (of a substance, esp. a detergent) capable of lowering the surface tension of a liquid. See also **surfactant.**

surface mail n mail transported by land or sea. Cf. **airmail.**

surface structure n Generative grammar. a representation of a string of words or morphemes as they occur in a sentence, together with labels and brackets that represent syntactic structure. Cf. **deep structure.**

surface tension n 1 a property of liquids caused by intermolecular forces near the surface leading to the apparent presence of a surface film and to capillarity, etc. **2** a measure of this.

surface-to-air adj of or relating to a missile launched from the surface of the earth against airborne targets.

surfactant (sɜː'fæktənt) n 1 Also called: **surface-active agent.** a substance, such as a detergent, that can reduce the surface tension of a liquid and thus allow it to foam or penetrate solids; a wetting agent. ◆ adj **2** having the properties of a surfactant. [C20: *surf*(ace)-*act*(ive) *a*(ge)*nt*]

surfboard ('sɜːfˌbɔːd) n a long narrow board used in surfing.

surfboat ('sɜːfˌbəʊt) n a boat with a high bow and stern and flotation chambers, equipped for use in rough surf.

surfcasting ('sɜːfˌkɑːstɪŋ) n fishing from the shore by casting into the surf.
 ▸ '**surfˌcaster** n

surfeit ('sɜːfɪt) *n* **1** (usually foll. by *of*) an excessive amount. **2** overindulgence, esp. in eating or drinking. **3** disgust, nausea, etc., caused by such overindulgence. ◆ *vb* **4** (*tr*) to supply or feed excessively; satiate. **5** (*intr*) *Arch.* to eat, drink, or be supplied to excess. [C13: from F *sourfait,* from *sourfaire* to overdo, from SUR-¹ + *faire,* from L *facere* to do]

surfie ('sɜːfɪ) *n Austral. & NZ sl.* a young person whose main interest in life is surfing.

surfing ('sɜːfɪŋ) *n* the sport of riding towards shore on the crest of a wave by standing or lying on a surfboard.
▸ **'surfer** or **'surf,rider** *n*

surf mat *n Austral. inf.* a small inflatable rubber mattress used to ride on waves.

surg. *abbrev. for:* **1** surgeon. **2** surgery. **3** surgical.

surge (sɜːdʒ) *n* **1** a strong rush or sweep; sudden increase: *a surge of anger.* **2** the rolling swell of the sea. **3** a heavy rolling motion or sound: *the surge of the trumpets.* **4** an undulating rolling surface, as of hills. **5** a billowing cloud or volume. **6** *Naut.* a temporary release or slackening of a rope or cable. **7** a large momentary increase in the voltage or current in an electric circuit. **8** an instability or unevenness in the power output of an engine. ◆ *vb* **surges, surging, surged. 9** (*intr*) (of waves, the sea, etc.) to rise or roll with a heavy swelling motion. **10** (*intr*) to move like a heavy sea. **11** *Naut.* to slacken or temporarily release (a rope or cable) from a capstan or (of a rope, etc.) to be slackened or released and slip back. **12** (*intr*) (of an electric current or voltage) to undergo a large momentary increase. **13** (*tr*) *Rare.* to cause to move in or as if in a wave or waves. [C15: from L *surgere* to rise, from *sub-* up + *regere* to lead]
▸ **'surger** *n*

surgeon ('sɜːdʒən) *n* **1** a medical practitioner who specializes in surgery. **2** a medical officer in the Royal Navy. [C14: from Anglo-Norman *surgien,* from OF *cirurgien;* see SURGERY]

surgeonfish ('sɜːdʒən,fɪʃ) *n, pl* **surgeonfish** or **surgeonfishes.** any of various tropical marine spiny-finned fishes, having a compressed brightly coloured body with knife-like spines at the base of the tail.

surgeon general *n, pl* **surgeons general. 1** (esp. in the British and US armies and navies) the senior officer of the medical service. **2** the head of the US public health service.

surgery ('sɜːdʒərɪ) *n, pl* **surgeries. 1** the branch of medicine concerned with manual or operative procedures, esp. incision into the body. **2** the performance of such procedures by a surgeon. **3** *Brit.* a place where, or time when, a doctor, dentist, etc., can be consulted. **4** *Brit.* an occasion when an MP, lawyer, etc., is available for consultation. **5** *US & Canad.* an operating theatre. [C14: via OF from L *chirurgia,* from Gk *kheirurgia,* from *kheir* hand + *ergon* work]

surgical ('sɜːdʒɪkˀl) *adj* of, relating to, involving, or used in surgery.
▸ **'surgically** *adv*

surgical boot *n* a specially designed boot or shoe that compensates for deformities of the foot or leg.

surgical spirit *n* methylated spirit used medically for sterilizing.

Suribachi ★ (ˌsʊərɪ'bɑːtʃɪ) *n Mount.* a volcanic hill in the Volcano Islands, on Iwo Jima: site of a US victory (1945) over the Japanese in World War II.

suricate ('sjʊərɪ,keɪt) *n* another name for **slender-tailed meerkat** (see **meerkat**). [C18: from F *surikate,* prob. from a native South African word]

Surinam ★ (ˌsʊərɪ'næm) *n* a republic in NE South America, on the Atlantic: became a self-governing part of the Netherlands in 1954 and fully independent in 1975. Official language: Dutch; English is also widely spoken. Religion: Hindu, Christian, and Muslim. Currency: guilder. Capital: Paramaribo. Pop.: 424 000 (1997). Area: 163 820 sq. km (63 251 sq. miles). Former names: **Dutch Guiana, Netherlands Guiana.**

surly ('sɜːlɪ) *adj* **surlier, surliest. 1** sullenly ill-tempered or rude. **2** (of an animal) ill-tempered or refractory. [C16: from obs. *sirly* haughty]
▸ **'surlily** *adv* ▸ **'surliness** *n*

surmise *vb* (sɜː'maɪz), **surmises, surmising, surmised. 1** (when *tr, may take a clause as object*) to infer (something) from incomplete or uncertain evidence. ◆ *n* (sɜː'maɪz, 'sɜːmaɪz). **2** an idea inferred from inconclusive evidence. [C15: from OF, from *surmettre* to accuse, from L *supermittere* to throw over]
▸ **surmisedly** (sɜː'maɪzɪdlɪ) *adv*

surmount (sɜː'maʊnt) *vb* (*tr*) **1** to prevail over; overcome. **2** to ascend and cross to the opposite side of. **3** to lie on top of or rise above. **4** to put something on top of or above. [C14: from OF *surmonter,* from SUR-¹ + *monter* to mount]
▸ **sur'mountable** *adj*

surname ('sɜː,neɪm) *n* **1** Also called: **last name, second name.** a family name as opposed to a first or Christian name. **2** (formerly) a descriptive epithet attached to a person's name to denote a personal characteristic, profession, etc.; nickname. ◆ *vb* **surnames, surnaming, surnamed. 3** (*tr*) to furnish with or call by a surname.
▸ **'sur,namer** *n*

surpass (sɜː'pɑːs) *vb* (*tr*) **1** to be greater than in degree, extent, etc. **2** to be superior to in achievement or excellence. **3** to overstep the limit or range of: *the theory surpasses my comprehension.* [C16: from F *surpasser,* from SUR-¹ + *passer* to PASS]
▸ **sur'passable** *adj*

surpassing (sɜː'pɑːsɪŋ) *adj* **1** exceptional; extraordinary. ◆ *adv* **2** *Obs.* or *poetic.* (intensifier): *surpassing fair.*
▸ **sur'passingly** *adv*

surplice ('sɜːplɪs) *n* a loose wide-sleeved liturgical vestment of linen, reaching to the knees, worn over the cassock by clergymen, choristers, and acolytes. [C13: from OF *sourpelis,* from Med. L *superpellīcium,* from SUPER- + *pellīcium* coat made of skins, from L *pellis* a skin]

surplus ('sɜːpləs) *n, pl* **surpluses. 1** a quantity or amount in excess of what is required. **2** *Accounting.* **2a** an excess of total assets over total liabilities. **2b** an excess of actual net assets over the nominal value of capital stock. **2c** an excess of revenues over expenditures. **3** *Econ.* **3a** an excess of government revenues over expenditures. **3b** an excess of receipts over payments on the balance of payments. ◆ *adj* **4** being in excess; extra. [C14: from OF, from Med. L *superplūs,* from L SUPER- + *plūs* more]

surprise (sə'praɪz) *vb* **surprises, surprising, surprised.** (*tr*) **1** to cause to feel amazement or wonder. **2** to encounter or discover unexpectedly or suddenly. **3** to capture or assault suddenly and without warning. **4** to present with something unexpected, such as a gift. **5** (foll. by *into*) to provoke (someone) to unintended action by a trick, etc. **6** (often foll. by *from*) to elicit by unexpected behaviour or by a trick: *to surprise information from a prisoner.* ◆ *n* **7** the act or an instance of surprising; the act of taking unawares. **8** a sudden or unexpected event, gift, etc. **9** the feeling or condition of being surprised; astonishment. **10** (*modifier*) causing, characterized by, or relying upon surprise: *a surprise move.* **11 take by surprise. 11a** to come upon suddenly and without warning. **11b** to capture unexpectedly or catch unprepared. **11c** to astonish; amaze. [C15: from OF, from *surprendre* to overtake, from SUR-¹ + *prehendere* to grasp]
▸ **sur'prisal** *n* ▸ **sur'prised** *adj* ▸ **surprisedly** (sə'praɪzɪdlɪ) *adv*

surprising (sə'praɪzɪŋ) *adj* causing surprise; unexpected or amazing.
▸ **sur'prisingly** *adv*

surra ('sʊərə) *n* a tropical febrile disease of cattle, horses, camels, and dogs. [from Marathi, a language of India]

surrealism (sə'rɪə,lɪzəm) *n* (*sometimes cap.*) a movement in art and literature in the 1920s, which developed esp. from Dada, characterized by the evocative juxtaposition of incongruous images in order to include unconscious and dream elements. [C20: from F *surréalisme,* from SUR-¹ + *réalisme* realism]
▸ **sur'real** *adj* ▸ **sur'realist** *n, adj* ▸ **sur,real'istic** *adj*

surrebutter (ˌsɜːrɪ'bʌtə) *n Law.* (in pleading) the plaintiff's reply to the defendant's rebutter.
▸ **,surre'buttal** *n*

surrejoinder (ˌsɜːrɪ'dʒɔɪndə) *n Law.* (in pleading) the plaintiff's reply to the defendant's rejoinder.

surrender (sə'rɛndə) *vb* **1** (*tr*) to relinquish to another under duress or on demand: *to surrender a city*. **2** (*tr*) to relinquish or forego (an office, position, etc.), esp. as a voluntary concession to another: *he surrendered his place to a lady*. **3** to give (oneself) up physically, as to an enemy. **4** to allow (oneself) to yield, as to a temptation, influence, etc. **5** (*tr*) to give up (hope, etc.). **6** (*tr*) *Law*. to give up or restore (an estate), esp. to give up a lease before expiration of the term. **7 surrender to bail**. to present oneself at court at the appointed time after having been on bail. ◆ *n* **8** the act or instance of surrendering. **9** *Insurance*. the voluntary discontinuation of a life policy by its holder in return for a consideration (the **surrender value**). **10** *Law*. **10a** the yielding up or restoring of an estate, esp. the giving up of a lease before its term has expired. **10b** the giving up to the appropriate authority of a fugitive from justice. **10c** the act of surrendering or being surrendered to bail. **10d** the deed by which a legal surrender is effected. [C15: from OF *surrendre* to yield]

surreptitious (ˌsʌrəp'tɪʃəs) *adj* **1** done, acquired, etc., in secret or by improper means. **2** operating by stealth. [C15: from L *surreptīcius* furtive, from *surripere* to steal, from *sub*- secretly + *rapere* to snatch]
▶ ˌsurrep'titiously *adv* ▶ ˌsurrep'titiousness *n*

surrey ('sʌrɪ) *n* a light four-wheeled horse-drawn carriage having two or four seats. [C19: from *Surrey cart*, after SURREY[1] where orig. made]

Surrey[1] ★ ('sʌrɪ) *n* a county of SE England, on the River Thames: urban in the northeast; crossed from east to west by the North Downs and drained by tributaries of the Thames. Administrative centre: Kingston upon Thames. Pop.: 1 041 200 (1994 est.). Area: 1679 sq. km (648 sq. miles).

Surrey[2] ★ ('sʌrɪ) *n* **Earl of**, title of *Henry Howard*. ?1517–47, English courtier and poet; one of the first in England to write sonnets. He was beheaded for high treason.

surrogate *n* ('sʌrəgɪt). **1** a person or thing acting as a substitute. **2** *Chiefly Brit*. a deputy, such as a clergyman appointed to deputize for a bishop in granting marriage licences. **3** (in some US states) a judge with jurisdiction over the probate of wills, etc. **4** (*modifier*) of, relating to, or acting as a surrogate: *a surrogate pleasure*. ◆ *vb* ('sʌrəˌgeɪt), **surrogates**, **surrogating**, **surrogated**. (*tr*) **5** to put in another's position as a deputy, substitute, etc. [C17: from L *surrogāre* to substitute]
▶ 'surrogateship *n* ▶ ˌsurro'gation *n*

surrogate motherhood *or* **surrogacy** ('sʌrəgəsɪ) *n* the role of a woman who bears a child on behalf of a childless couple, either by artificial insemination or implantation of an embryo.
▶ **surrogate mother** *n*

surround (sə'raʊnd) *vb* (*tr*) **1** to encircle or enclose or cause to be encircled or enclosed. **2** to deploy forces on all sides of (a place or military formation), so preventing access or retreat. **3** to exist around: *the people who surround her*. ◆ *n* **4** *Chiefly Brit*. a border, esp. the area of uncovered floor between the walls of a room and the carpet or around an opening or panel. **5** *Chiefly US*. **5a** a method of capturing wild beasts by encircling the area in which they are believed to be. **5b** the area so encircled. [C15 *surrounden* to overflow, from OF *suronder*, from LL, from L SUPER- + *undāre* to abound, from *unda* a wave]
▶ **sur'rounding** *adj*

surroundings (sə'raʊndɪŋz) *pl n* the conditions, scenery, etc., around a person, place, or thing; environment.

sursum corda ('sɜːsəm 'kɔːdə) *n* **1** *RC Church*. a Latin versicle meaning *Lift up your hearts*, said by the priest at Mass. **2** a cry of exhortation, hope, etc.

surtax ('sɜːˌtæks) *n* **1** a tax, usually highly progressive, levied on the amount by which a person's income exceeds a specific level. **2** an additional tax on something that has already been taxed. ◆ *vb* **3** (*tr*) to assess for liability to surtax; charge with an extra tax.

Surtees ★ ('sɜːtiːz) *n* **1 John**. born 1934, British racing motorcyclist and motor-racing driver; motorcycling world champion (1956, 1958–60) and world champion motor-racing driver (1964). **2 Robert Smith**. 1803–64, British journalist and novelist, who satirized the sporting

life of the English gentry in such works as *Jorrocks's Jaunts and Jollities* (1838).

surtitles ('sɜːˌtaɪtªlz) *pl n* brief translations of the text of an opera or play that is being sung or spoken in a foreign language, projected above the stage.

surtout ('sɜːtuː) *n* a man's overcoat resembling a frock coat, popular in the late 19th century. [C17: from F, from *sur* over + *tout* all]

surveillance (sɜː'veɪləns) *n* close observation or supervision of a person, group, etc., esp. one in custody or under suspicion. [C19: from F, from *surveiller* to watch over, from SUR-[1] + *veiller* to keep watch (from L *vigilāre*; see VIGIL)]
▶ **sur'veillant** *adj*, *n*

survey *vb* (sɜː'veɪ, 'sɜːveɪ). **1** (*tr*) to view or consider in a comprehensive or general way. **2** (*tr*) to examine carefully, in order to or as if to appraise condition and value. **3** to plot a detailed map of (an area of land) by measuring or calculating distances and height. **4** *Brit*. to inspect a building to determine its condition and value. **5** to examine a vessel thoroughly in order to determine its seaworthiness. **6** (*tr*) to run a statistical survey on (incomes, opinions, etc.). ◆ *n* ('sɜːveɪ). **7** a comprehensive or general view. **8** a critical, detailed, and formal inspection. **9** *Brit*. an inspection of a building to determine its condition and value. **10** a report incorporating the results of such an inspection. **11a** a body of surveyors. **11b** an area surveyed. [C15: from F *surveoir*, from SUR-[1] + *veoir* to see, from L *vidēre*]

surveying (sɜː'veɪɪŋ) *n* **1** the study or practice of making surveys of land. **2** the setting out on the ground of the positions of proposed construction or engineering works.

surveyor (sɜː'veɪə) *n* **1** a person whose occupation is to survey land or buildings. See also **quantity surveyor**. **2** *Chiefly Brit*. a person concerned with the official inspection of something for purposes of measurement and valuation. **3** a person who carries out surveys, esp. of ships (**marine surveyor**) to determine seaworthiness, etc. **4** a customs official. **5** *Arch*. a supervisor.
▶ **sur'veyorship** *n*

surveyor's measure *n* the system of measurement based on the **surveyor's chain** (66 feet) as a unit.

survival (sə'vaɪvªl) *n* **1** a person or thing that survives, such as a custom. **2a** the act or fact of surviving or condition of having survived. **2b** (*as modifier*): *survival kit*.

survival bag *n* a large plastic bag carried by climbers for use in an emergency as protection against exposure.

survivalist (sə'vaɪvəlɪst) *n* *Chiefly US*. **a** a person who believes in ensuring his personal survival of a catastrophic event by arming himself and often by living in the wild. **b** (*as modifier*): *survivalist weapons*.
▶ **sur'vival,ism** *n*

survival of the fittest *n* a popular term for **natural selection**.

survive (sə'vaɪv) *vb* **survives**, **surviving**, **survived**. **1** (*tr*) to live after the death of (another). **2** to continue in existence or use after (a passage of time, adversity, etc.). **3** *Inf*. to endure (something): *I don't know how I survive such an awful job*. [C15: from OF *sourvivre*, from L *supervīvere*, from SUPER- + *vīvere* to live]
▶ **sur'vivor** *n*

sus (sʌs) *Brit. sl.* ◆ *n* **1** short for **suspicion**, with reference to former police powers (**sus laws**) of detaining for questioning, searching, etc., any person suspected of criminal intent: *he was picked up on sus*. ◆ *vb* **susses**, **sussing**, **sussed**. **2** a variant spelling of **suss** (sense 2).

Susa ★ ('suːsə) *n* an ancient city north of the Persian Gulf: capital of Elam and of the Persian Empire; flourished as a Greek polis under the Seleucids and Parthians. Biblical name: **Shushan**.

Susah *or* **Susa** ★ ('suːzə) *n* other names for **Sousse**.

Susanna ★ (suː'zænə) *n Apocrypha*. **1** the wife of Joachim, who was condemned to death for adultery because of a false accusation, but saved by Daniel's sagacity. **2** the book of the Apocrypha containing this story.

susceptance (sə'sɛptəns) *n Physics*. the imaginary component of the admittance. [C19: from *suscept(ibility)* + -ANCE]

susceptibility (sə,septə'bɪlɪtɪ) *n, pl* **susceptibilities. 1** the quality or condition of being susceptible. **2** the ability or tendency to be impressed by emotional feelings. **3** (*pl*) emotional sensibilities; feelings. **4** *Physics.* **4a** Also called: **electric susceptibility.** (of a dielectric) the amount by which the relative permittivity differs from unity. **4b** Also called: **magnetic susceptibility.** (of a magnetic medium) the amount by which the relative permeability differs from unity.

susceptible (sə'septəb³l) *adj* **1** (*postpositive;* foll. by *of* or *to*) yielding readily (to); capable (of): *hypotheses susceptible of refutation; susceptible to control.* **2** (*postpositive;* foll. by *to*) liable to be afflicted (by): *susceptible to colds.* **3** easily impressed emotionally. [C17: from LL *susceptibilis,* from L *suscipere* to take up]
  ▸ **sus'ceptibly** *adv*

sushi ('su:ʃɪ) *n* a Japanese dish consisting of small cakes of cold rice with a topping, esp. of raw fish. [Japanese]

suslik ('sʌslɪk) *or* **souslik** *n* a central Eurasian ground squirrel having large eyes and small ears. [from Russian]

suspect *vb* (sə'spɛkt). **1** (*tr*) to believe guilty of a specified offence without proof. **2** (*tr*) to think false, questionable, etc.: *she suspected his sincerity.* **3** (*tr; may take a clause as object*) to surmise to be the case; think probable: *to suspect fraud.* **4** (*intr*) to have suspicion. ♦ *n* ('sʌspɛkt). **5** a person under suspicion. ♦ *adj* ('sʌspɛkt). **6** causing or open to suspicion. [C14: from L *suspicere* to mistrust, from SUB- + *specere* to look]

suspend (sə'spɛnd) *vb* **1** (*tr*) to hang from above. **2** (*tr; passive*) to cause to remain floating or hanging: *a cloud of smoke was suspended over the town.* **3** (*tr*) to render inoperative or cause to cease, esp. temporarily. **4** (*tr*) to hold in abeyance; postpone action on. **5** (*tr*) to debar temporarily from privilege, office, etc., as a punishment. **6** (*tr*) *Chem.* to cause (particles) to be held in suspension in a fluid. **7** (*tr*) *Music.* to continue (a note) until the next chord is sounded, with which it usually forms a dissonance. See **suspension** (sense 11). **8** (*intr*) to cease payment, as from incapacity to meet financial obligations. [C13: from L *suspendere* from SUB- + *pendere* to hang]
  ▸ **sus'pendible** *or* **sus'pensible** *adj* ▸ **sus,pendi'bility** *n*

suspended animation *n* a temporary cessation of the vital functions, as by freezing an organism.

suspended sentence *n* a sentence of imprisonment that is not served by an offender unless he commits a further offence during its currency.

suspender (sə'spɛndə) *n* **1** (*often pl*) *Brit.* **1a** an elastic strap attached to a belt or corset having a fastener at the end, for holding up women's stockings. **1b** a similar fastener attached to a garter worn by men in order to support socks. **2** (*pl*) the US and Canad. name for **braces. 3** a person or thing that suspends, such as one of the vertical cables in a suspension bridge.

suspender belt *n* a belt with suspenders hanging from it to hold up women's stockings.

suspense (sə'spɛns) *n* **1** the condition of being insecure or uncertain. **2** mental uncertainty; anxiety: *their father's illness kept them in a state of suspense.* **3** excitement felt at the approach of the climax: *a play of terrifying suspense.* **4** the condition of being suspended. [C15: from Med. L *suspensum* delay, from L *suspendere* to hang up]
  ▸ **sus'penseful** *adj*

suspense account *n Book-keeping.* an account in which entries are made until determination of their proper disposition.

suspension (sə'spɛnʃən) *n* **1** an interruption or temporary revocation: *the suspension of a law.* **2** a temporary debarment, as from position, privilege, etc. **3** a deferment, esp. of a decision, judgment, etc. **4** *Law.* a postponement of execution of a sentence or the deferring of a judgment, etc. **5** cessation of payment of business debts, esp. as a result of insolvency. **6** the act of suspending or the state of being suspended. **7** a system of springs, shock absorbers, etc., that supports the body of a wheeled or tracked vehicle and insulates it from shocks transmitted

by the wheels. **8** a device or structure, usually a wire or spring, that serves to suspend or support something, such as the pendulum of a clock. **9** *Chem.* a dispersion of fine solid or liquid particles in a fluid, the particles being supported by buoyancy. See also **colloid. 10** the process by which eroded particles of rock are transported in a river. **11** *Music.* one or more notes of a chord that are prolonged until a subsequent chord is sounded, usually to form a dissonance.

suspension bridge *n* a bridge suspended from cables or chains that hang between two towers and are anchored at both ends.

suspensive (sə'spɛnsɪv) *adj* **1** having the power of deferment; effecting suspension. **2** causing, characterized by, or relating to suspense.
  ▸ **sus'pensively** *adv* ▸ **sus'pensiveness** *n*

suspensory (sə'spɛnsərɪ) *n, pl* **suspensories. 1** Also called: **suspensor.** *Anat.* a ligament or muscle that holds a structure or part in position. **2** a bandage, sling, etc., for supporting a dependent part. ♦ *adj* **3** suspending or supporting. **4** *Anat.* (of a ligament or muscle) supporting or holding a structure or part in position.

suspicion (sə'spɪʃən) *n* **1** the act or an instance of suspecting; belief without sure proof, esp. that something is wrong. **2** the feeling of mistrust of a person who suspects. **3** the state of being suspected: *to be shielded from suspicion.* **4** a slight trace. **5 above suspicion.** in such a position that no guilt may be thought or implied, esp. through having an unblemished reputation. **6 on suspicion.** as a suspect. **7 under suspicion.** regarded with distrust. [C14: from OF *sospeçon,* from L *suspīciō* distrust, from *suspicere;* see SUSPECT]
  ▸ **sus'picional** *adj*

suspicious (sə'spɪʃəs) *adj* **1** exciting or liable to excite suspicion; questionable. **2** disposed to suspect something wrong. **3** indicative or expressive of suspicion.
  ▸ **sus'piciously** *adv* ▸ **sus'piciousness** *n*

Susquehanna ★ (,sʌskwɪ'hænə) *n* a river in the eastern US, rising in Otsego Lake and flowing generally south to Chesapeake Bay at Havre de Grace: the longest river in the eastern US. Length: 714 km (444 miles).

suss (sʌs) *Sl.* ♦ *vb* (*tr*) **1** (often foll. by *out*) to attempt to work out (a situation, person's character, etc.), esp. using one's intuition. **2** Also: **sus.** to become aware of; suspect (esp. in **suss it**). ♦ *n* **3** sharpness of mind; social astuteness. [C20: shortened from SUSPECT]

Sussex ★ ('sʌsɪks) *n* **1** (until 1974) a county of SE England, now divided into the separate counties of East Sussex and West Sussex. **2** (in Anglo-Saxon England) the kingdom of the South Saxons, which became a shire of the kingdom of Wessex in the early 9th century A.D. **3** a breed of red beef cattle originally from Sussex. **4** a heavy and long-established breed of domestic fowl used principally as a table bird.

sustain (sə'steɪn) *vb* (*tr*) **1** to hold up under; withstand: *to sustain great provocation.* **2** to undergo (an injury, loss, etc.); suffer: *to sustain a broken arm.* **3** to maintain or prolong: *to sustain a discussion.* **4** to support physically from below. **5** to provide for or give support to, esp. by supplying necessities: *to sustain one's family.* **6** to keep up the vitality or courage of. **7** to uphold or affirm the justice or validity of: *to sustain a decision.* **8** to establish the truth of; confirm. ♦ *n* **9** *Music.* the prolongation of a note, by playing technique or electronics. [C13: via OF from L *sustinēre* to hold up]
  ▸ **sus'tained** *adj* ▸ **sustainedly** (sə'steɪnɪdlɪ) *adv* ▸ **sus-'tainer** *n* ▸ **sus'taining** *adj* ▸ **sus'tainment** *n*

sustainable (sə'steɪnəb³l) *adj* **1** capable of being sustained. **2** (of economic development, energy sources, etc.) capable of being maintained at a steady level without exhausting natural resources or causing severe ecological damage: *sustainable development.*

sustaining pedal *n Music.* a foot-operated lever on a piano that keeps the dampers raised from the strings when keys are released, allowing them to continue to vibrate.

sustenance ('sʌstɪnəns) *n* **1** means of sustaining health or life; nourishment. **2** means of maintenance; livelihood. **3** Also: **sustention** (sə'stɛnʃən). the act or process of sustaining or the quality of being sustained. [C13: from OF *sostenance*, from *sustenir* to SUSTAIN]

sustentation (ˌsʌstɛnˈteɪʃən) *n* a less common word for **sustenance.** [C14: from L *sustentātio*, from *sustentāre*, frequentative of *sustinēre* to SUSTAIN]

susurrate (ˈsjuːsəˌreɪt) *vb* **susurrates, susurrating, susurrated.** (*intr*) *Literary.* to make a soft rustling sound; whisper; murmur. [C17: from L *susurrāre* to whisper]
▸ ˌsusurˈration *or* susurrus (sjuːˈsʌrəs) *n*

Sutcliffe ★ (ˈsʌtˌklɪf) *n* **Herbert.** 1894–1978, English cricketer, who played for Yorkshire.

Suth. *abbrev. for* Sutherland.

Sutherland[1] ★ (ˈsʌðələnd) *n* (until 1975) a county of N Scotland, now part of Highland.

Sutherland[2] ★ (ˈsʌðələnd) *n* **1 Graham.** 1903–80, British artist, noted for his tapestry *Christ in Majesty* (1962) in Coventry Cathedral. **2** Dame **Joan,** known as *La Stupenda.* born 1926, Australian soprano.

Sutherland Falls ★ *n* a waterfall in New Zealand, on SW South Island. Height: 580 m (1904 ft).

Sutlej ★ (ˈsʌtlɪdʒ) *n* a river in S Asia, rising in SW Tibet and flowing west through the Himalayas: crosses Himachal Pradesh and the Punjab (India), enters Pakistan, and joins the Chenab west of Bahawalpur: the longest of the five rivers of the Punjab. Length: 1368 km (850 miles).

sutler (ˈsʌtlə) *n* (formerly) a merchant who accompanied an army in order to sell provisions to the soldiers. [C16: from obs. Du. *soeteler*, ult. from MHG *sudelen* to do dirty work]

sutra (ˈsuːtrə) *n* **1** *Hinduism.* Sanskrit sayings or collections of sayings on Vedic doctrine dating from about 200 A.D. onwards. **2** (*modifier*) *Hinduism.* **2a** of or relating to the last of the Vedic literary periods, from about 500 to 100 B.C.: *the sutra period.* **2b** of or relating to the sutras or compilations of sutras of about 200 A.D. onwards. **3** *Buddhism.* collections of dialogues and discourses of classic Mahayana Buddhism dating from the 2nd to the 6th century A.D. [C19: from Sansk.: list of rules]

suttee (sʌˈtiː, ˈsʌtiː) *n* **1** the former Hindu custom whereby a widow burnt herself to death on her husband's funeral pyre. **2** a widow performing this. [C18: from Sansk. *satī* virtuous woman, from *sat* good]
▸ sutˈteeism *n*

Sutton ★ (ˈsʌt°n) *n* a borough of S Greater London. Pop.: 173 400 (1994 est.). Area: 43 sq. km (17 sq. miles).

Sutton Coldfield ★ (ˈkəʊldˌfiːld) *n* a town in central England, in Birmingham, in the N West Midlands. Pop.: 86 494 (1981).

Sutton-in-Ashfield ★ (-ˈæʃˌfiːld) *n* a market town in N central England, in W Nottinghamshire. Pop.: 37 890 (1991).

suture (ˈsuːtʃə) *n* **1** *Surgery.* **1a** catgut, silk thread, or wire used to stitch together two bodily surfaces. **1b** the surgical seam formed after stitching. **2** *Anat.* a type of immovable joint, esp. between the bones of the skull (**cranial suture**). **3** a seam or joining, as in sewing. **4** *Zool.* a line of junction in a molluscan shell. ◆ *vb* **sutures, suturing, sutured.** **5** (*tr*) *Surgery.* to join (the edges of a wound, etc.) by means of sutures. [C16: from L *sūtūra*, from *suere* to sew]
▸ ˈsutural *adj*

Suu Kyi ★ *n* Aung San. See Aung San Suu Kyi.

Suva ★ (ˈsuːvə) *n* the capital and chief port of Fiji, on the SE coast of Viti Levu. Pop.: 200 000 (1990 est.).

Suvorov ★ (*Russian* suˈvɔrəf) *n* **Aleksandr Vasilyevich** (alɪkˈsandr vaˈsiljɪvitʃ). 1729–1800, Russian field marshal, who fought successfully against the Turks (1787–91), the Poles (1794), and the French in Italy (1798–99).

Suwannee (suˈwɒnɪ) *or* **Swanee** ★ *n* a river in the southeastern US, rising in SE Georgia and flowing across Florida to the Gulf of Mexico at **Suwannee Sound.** Length: about 400 km (250 miles).

suzerain (ˈsuːzəˌreɪn) *n* **1a** a state or sovereign exercising some degree of dominion over a dependent state, usually controlling its foreign affairs. **1b** (*as modifier*): *a suzerain power.* **2a** a feudal overlord. **2b** (*as modifier*): *suzerain*

lord. [C19: from F, from *sus* above (from L *sursum* turned upwards) + *-erain,* as in *souverain* sovereign]

suzerainty (ˈsuːzərəntɪ) *n, pl* **suzerainties. 1** the position, power, or dignity of a suzerain. **2** the relationship between suzerain and subject.

Suzhou (ˈsuːˈdʒəʊ), **Su-chou,** *or* **Soochow** ★ *n* a city in E China, in S Jiangsu on the Grand Canal: noted for its gardens; produces chiefly silk. Pop.: 706 459 (1990 est.). Also called: **Wuhsien.**

sv *abbrev. for:* **1** sailing vessel. **2** side valve. **3** sub verbo *or* voce. [L: under the word *or* voice]

Svalbard ★ (*Norwegian* ˈsvɑːlbɑr) *n* a Norwegian archipelago in the Arctic Ocean, about 650 km (400 miles) north of Norway: consists of the main group (Spitsbergen, North East Land, Edge Island, Barents Island, and Prince Charles Foreland) and a number of outlying islands; sovereignty long disputed but granted to Norway in 1920; coal mining. Administrative centre: Longyearbyen. Area: 62 050 sq. km (23 958 sq. miles). Also called: **Spitsbergen.**

svelte (svɛlt, sfɛlt) *adj* attractively or gracefully slim; slender. [C19: from F, from It. *svelto,* from *svellere* to pull out, from L *ēvellere*]

Svengali (svɛnˈɡɑːlɪ) *n* a person who controls another's mind, usually with sinister intentions. [after a character in George Du Maurier's novel *Trilby* (1894)]

Sverdlovsk ★ (*Russian* svɪrˈdlɒfsk) *n* the former name (1924–91) for **Yekaterinburg.**

Sverige ★ (ˈsværjə) *n* the Swedish name for **Sweden.**

Svevo ★ (*Italian* ˈzveːvo) *n* **Italo** (ˈiːtalo), original name **Ettore Schmitz.** 1861–1928, Italian novelist and short-story writer, best known for the novel *Confessions of Zeno* (1923).

Svizzera ★ (ˈzvittsera) *n* the Italian name for **Switzerland.**

Svizzra ★ (ˈzvitsra) *n* the Romansch name for **Switzerland.**

SW 1 *symbol for* southwest(ern). **2** *abbrev. for* short wave.

Sw. *abbrev. for:* **1** Sweden. **2** Swedish.

swab (swɒb) *n* **1** *Med.* **1a** a small piece of cotton, gauze, etc., for use in applying medication, cleansing a wound, or obtaining a specimen of a secretion, etc. **1b** the specimen so obtained. **2** a mop for cleaning floors, decks, etc. **3** a brush used to clean a firearm's bore. **4** *Sl.* an uncouth or worthless fellow. ◆ *vb* **swabs, swabbing, swabbed. 5** (*tr*) to clean or medicate with or as if with a swab. **6** (*tr*; foll. by *up*) to take up with a swab. [C16: prob. from MDu. *swabbe* mop]
▸ ˈswabber *n*

Swabia ★ (ˈsweɪbɪə) *n* a region and former duchy (from the 10th century to 1313) of S Germany: now in Baden-Württemberg and Bavaria; part of West Germany until 1990. German name: **Schwaben** (ˈʃvaːbᵊn).
▸ ˈSwabian *adj, n*

swaddle (ˈswɒdᵊl) *vb* **swaddles, swaddling, swaddled.** (*tr*) **1** to wind a bandage round. **2** to wrap (a baby) with swaddling clothes. **3** to restrain as if by wrapping with bandages; smother. ◆ *n* **4** *Chiefly US.* swaddling clothes. [C15: from OE *swæthel* swaddling clothes]

swaddling clothes *pl n* **1** long strips of linen or other cloth formerly wrapped round a newly born baby. **2** restrictions or supervision imposed on the immature.

swaddy *or* **swaddie** (ˈswɒdɪ) *n Brit. sl., old-fashioned.* a soldier. [C19: from E dialect *swad* country bumpkin, soldier]

swag (swæg) *n* **1** *Sl.* property obtained by theft or other illicit means. **2** *Sl.* goods; valuables. **3** an ornamental festoon of fruit, flowers, or drapery or a representation of this. **4** a swaying movement; lurch. **5** *Austral. & NZ inf.* a swagman's pack containing personal belongings, etc. **6 swags of.** *Austral. & NZ inf.* lots of. ◆ *vb* **swags, swagging, swagged. 7** *Chiefly Brit.* to lurch or sag or cause to lurch or sag. **8** (*tr*) to adorn or arrange with swags. [C17: ? of Scand. origin]

swage (sweɪdʒ) *n* **1** a shaped tool or die used in forming cold metal by hammering, pressing, etc. ◆ *vb* **swages, swaging, swaged. 2** (*tr*) to form (metal) with a swage. [C19: from F *souage,* from ?]
▸ ˈswager *n*

swage block *n* an iron block with holes, grooves, etc., to assist in the cold-working of metal.

swagger ('swægə) *vb* **1** (*intr*) to walk or behave in an arrogant manner. **2** (*intr*; often foll. by *about*) to brag loudly. ◆ *n* **3** an arrogant gait or manner. ◆ *adj* **4** *Brit. inf., rare.* elegantly fashionable. [C16: prob. from SWAG]
▸ **'swaggerer** *n* ▸ **'swaggering** *adj* ▸ **'swaggeringly** *adv*

swagger stick *or esp. Brit.* **swagger cane** *n* a short cane or stick carried on occasion mainly by army officers.

swaggie ('swægɪ) *n Austral. sl.* short for **swagman**.

swagman ('swæg,mæn, -mən) *n, pl* **swagmen**. *Austral. & NZ inf.* a tramp or vagrant worker who carries his possessions on his back. Also called: **swaggie**.

Swahili (swɑː'hiːlɪ) *n* **1** a language of E Africa that is an official language of Kenya and Tanzania and is widely used as a lingua franca throughout E and central Africa. Also called: **Kiswahili**. **2** (*pl* **Swahilis** *or* **Swahili**) a member of a people speaking this language, living chiefly in Zanzibar. Also called: **Mswahili** (*pl* **Waswahili**). ◆ *adj* **3** of or relating to the Swahilis or their language. [C19: from Ar. *sawāhil* coasts]
▸ **Swa'hilian** *adj*

swain (sweɪn) *n Arch. or poetic.* **1** a male lover or admirer. **2** a country youth. [OE *swān* swineherd]

swallow[1] ('swɒləʊ) *vb* (*mainly tr*) **1** to pass (food, drink, etc.) through the mouth to the stomach by means of the muscular action of the oesophagus. **2** (often foll. by *up*) to engulf or destroy as if by ingestion. **3** *Inf.* to believe gullibly: *he will never swallow such an excuse.* **4** to refrain from uttering or manifesting: *to swallow one's disappointment.* **5** to endure without retaliation. **6** to enunciate (words, etc.) indistinctly; mutter. **7** (often foll. by *down*) to eat or drink reluctantly. **8** (*intr*) to perform or simulate the act of swallowing, as in gulping. ◆ *n* **9** the act of swallowing. **10** the amount swallowed at any single time; mouthful. **11** *Rare.* another word for **throat** or **gullet**. [OE *swelgan*]
▸ **'swallowable** *adj* ▸ **'swallower** *n*

swallow[2] ('swɒləʊ) *n* any of various passerine songbirds having long pointed wings, a forked tail, short legs, and a rapid flight. [OE *swealwe*]

swallow dive *n* a type of dive in which the diver arches back while in the air, keeping his legs straight and together and his arms outstretched, finally entering the water headfirst. US and Canad. equivalent: **swan dive**.

swallow hole *n Chiefly Brit.* another word for **sinkhole** (sense 1).

swallowtail ('swɒləʊ,teɪl) *n* **1** any of various butterflies of Europe, having a tail-like extension of each hind wing. **2** the forked tail of a swallow or similar bird. **3** short for **swallow-tailed coat**.
▸ **'swallow-,tailed** *adj*

swallow-tailed coat *n* another name for **tail coat**.

swam (swæm) *vb* the past tense of **swim**.

swami ('swɑːmɪ) *n, pl* **swamies** *or* **swamis**. (in India) a title of respect for a Hindu saint or religious teacher. [C18: from Hindi *svāmī*, from Sansk. *svāmin* master, from *sva* one's own]

swamp (swɒmp) *n* **1** permanently waterlogged ground that is usually overgrown and sometimes partly forested. Cf. **marsh**. ◆ *vb* **2** to drench or submerge or be drenched or submerged. **3** *Naut.* to cause (a boat) to sink or fill with water or (of a boat) to sink or fill with water. **4** to overburden or overwhelm or be overburdened or overwhelmed, as by excess work or great numbers. **5** (*tr*) to render helpless. [C17: prob. from MDu. *somp*]
▸ **'swampy** *adj*

swamp boat *n* a shallow-draught boat powered by an aeroplane engine mounted on a raised structure for use in swamps. Also called: **airboat**.

swamp cypress *n* a North American deciduous coniferous tree that grows in swamps. Also called: **bald cypress**.

swamp fever *n* **1** Also called: **equine infectious anaemia**. a viral disease of horses. **2** *US.* another name for **malaria**.

swampland ('swɒmp,lænd) *n* a permanently waterlogged area; marshland.

swan (swɒn) *n* **1** any of various large aquatic birds having a long neck and usually a white plumage. **2** *Rare, literary.* **2a** a poet. **2b** (*cap. when part of a title or epithet*): *the Swan of Avon* (Shakespeare). ◆ *vb* **swans, swanning, swanned. 3** (*intr*; usually foll. by *around* or *about*) *Inf.* to wander idly. [OE]
▸ **'swan,like** *adj*

Swan[1] ★ (swɒn) *n* a river in SW Western Australia, rising as the Avon northeast of Narrogin and flowing northwest and west to the Indian Ocean below Perth. Length: about 240 km (150 miles).

Swan[2] ★ (swɒn) *n* Sir **Joseph Wilson**. 1828–1914, British physicist and chemist, who developed the incandescent electric light (1880).

swan dive *n* the US and Canad. name for **swallow dive**.

Swanee ★ ('swɒnɪ) *n* a variant spelling of **Suwannee**.

swank (swæŋk) *Inf.* ◆ *vb* **1** (*intr*) to show off or swagger. ◆ *n* **2** Also called: **swankpot**. *Brit.* a swaggering or conceited person. **3** *Chiefly US.* showy elegance or style. **4** swagger; ostentation. ◆ *adj* **5** another word (esp. US) for **swanky**. [C19: ?from MHG *swanken* to sway]

swanky ('swæŋkɪ) *adj* **swankier, swankiest.** *Inf.* **1** expensive and showy; stylish: *a swanky hotel.* **2** boastful or conceited.
▸ **'swankily** *adv* ▸ **'swankiness** *n*

swan neck *n* a tube, rail, etc., curved like a swan's neck.

swannery ('swɒnərɪ) *n, pl* **swanneries.** a place where swans are kept and bred.

swan's-down *n* **1** the fine soft down feathers of a swan, used to trim powder puffs, clothes, etc. **2** a thick soft fabric of wool with silk, cotton, or rayon, used for infants' clothing, etc. **3** a cotton fabric with a heavy nap.

Swansea ('swɒnzɪ) *n* **1** a port in S Wales, on an inlet of the Bristol Channel (**Swansea Bay**); a metallurgical and oil-refining centre; university (1920). Pop.: 171 038 (1991). **2** a county of S Wales, on the Bristol Channel; created in 1996 from part of West Glamorgan. Administrative centre: Swansea. Pop.: 230 600 (1996 est.). Area: 378 sq. km (146 sq. miles).

swan song *n* **1** the last act, publication, etc., of a person before retirement or death. **2** the song that a dying swan is said to sing

swan-upping *n Brit.* **1** the practice or action of marking nicks in swans' beaks as a sign of ownership. **2** the annual swan-upping of royal cygnets on the River Thames.

swap *or* **swop** (swɒp) *vb* **swaps, swapping, swapped** *or* **swops, swopping, swopped. 1** to trade or exchange (something or someone) for another. ◆ *n* **2** an exchange. **3** something that is exchanged. **4** *Finance.* Also called: **swap option, swaption.** a contract in which the parties to it exchange liabilities on outstanding debts, often exchanging fixed-interest-rate for floating-rate debts (**debt swap**), either as a means of debt management or in trading (**swap trading**). [C14 (in the sense: to shake hands on a bargain, strike): prob. imit.]
▸ **'swapper** *or* **'swopper** *n*

SWAPO *or* **Swapo** ('swɑːpəʊ) *n acronym for* South-West Africa People's Organization.

swaption ('swɒpʃən) *n* another name for **swap** (sense 4).

swaraj (swə'rɑːdʒ) *n* (in British India) self-government; independence. [C20: from Sansk. *svarāj*, from *sva* self + *rājya* rule]
▸ **swa'rajism** *n* ▸ **swa'rajist** *n, adj*

sward (swɔːd) *n* **1** turf or grass or a stretch of turf or grass. ◆ *vb* **2** to cover or become covered with grass. [OE *sweard* skin]

swarf (swɔːf, swɑːf) *n* material removed by cutting or grinding tools in the machining of metals, stone, etc. [C16: of Scand. origin]

swarm[1] (swɔːm) *n* **1** a group of bees, led by a queen, that has left the parent hive to start a new colony. **2** a large mass of small animals, esp. insects. **3** a throng or mass, esp. when moving or in turmoil. ◆ *vb* **4** (*intr*) (of small animals, esp. bees) to move in or form a swarm. **5** (*intr*) to congregate, move about or proceed in large numbers. **6** (when *intr*, often foll. by *with*) to overrun or be overrun (with): *swarming with rats*. **7** (*tr*) to cause to swarm. [OE *swearm*]

swarm² (swɔːm) *vb* (when *intr*, usually foll. by *up*) to climb (a ladder, etc.) by gripping with the hands and feet: *the boys swarmed up the rigging*. [C16: from ?]

swart (swɔːt) *or* **swarth** (swɔːθ) *adj Arch. or dialect*. swarthy. [OE *sweart*]

swarthy ('swɔːðɪ) *adj* **swarthier, swarthiest**. dark-hued or dark-complexioned. [C16: from obs. *swarty*]
▸ 'swarthily *adv* ▸ 'swarthiness *n*

swash (swɒʃ) *vb* **1** (*intr*) (esp. of water or things in water) to wash or move with noisy splashing. **2** (*tr*) to dash (a liquid, esp. water) against or upon. **3** (*intr*) *Arch.* to swagger. ◆ *n* **4** Also called: **send**. the dashing movement or sound of water, as of waves on a beach. **5** Also called: **swash channel**. a channel of moving water cutting through or running behind a sandbank. **6** *Arch.* swagger or bluster. [C16: prob. imit.]

swashbuckler ('swɒʃ,bʌklə) *n* **1** a swaggering or flamboyant adventurer. **2** a film, book, play, etc., depicting excitement and adventure, esp. in a historical setting. [C16: from SWASH (in archaic sense: to make the noise of a sword striking a shield) + BUCKLER]
▸ 'swash,buckling *adj*

swash letter *n Printing*. a decorative letter, esp. an ornamental italic capital. [C17: from *aswash* aslant]

swastika ('swɒstɪkə) *n* **1** a primitive religious symbol or ornament in the shape of a Greek cross, usually having the ends of the arms bent at right angles. **2** this symbol with clockwise arms, the emblem of Nazi Germany. [C19: from Sansk. *svastika*, from *svasti* prosperity; from belief that it brings good luck]

swat (swɒt) *vb* **swats, swatting, swatted**. (*tr*) **1** to strike or hit sharply: *to swat a fly*. ◆ *n* **2** a sharp or violent blow. ◆ Also: **swot**. [C17: N English dialect & US var. of SQUAT]
▸ 'swatter *n*

Swat ★ (swɒt) *n* **1** a former princely state of NW India: passed to Pakistan in 1947. **2** a river in Pakistan, rising in the north and flowing south to the Kabul River north of Peshawar. Length: about 640 km (400 miles).

swatch (swɒtʃ) *n* **1** a sample of cloth or other material. **2** a number of such samples, usually fastened together in book form. [C16: Scot. & N English, from ?]

swath (swɔːθ) *or* **swathe** (sweɪð) *n*, *pl* **swaths** (swɔːðz) *or* **swathes**. **1** the width of one sweep of a scythe or of the blade of a mowing machine. **2** the strip cut by these in one course. **3** the quantity of cut grass, hay, etc., left in one such course. **4** a long narrow strip or belt. [OE *swæth*]

swathe (sweɪð) *vb* **swathes, swathing, swathed**. (*tr*) **1** to bandage (a wound, limb, etc.), esp. completely. **2** to wrap a band, garment, etc., around, esp. so as to cover completely; swaddle. **3** to envelop. ◆ *n* **4** a bandage or wrapping. **5** a variant spelling of **swath**. [OE *swathian*]

Swatow ★ ('swɒ'tau) *n* a variant transliteration of the Chinese name for **Shantou**.

sway (sweɪ) *vb* **1** (*usually intr*) to swing or cause to swing to and fro: *the door swayed in the wind*. **2** (*usually intr*) to lean or incline or cause to lean or incline to one side or in different directions in turn. **3** (*usually intr*) to vacillate or cause to vacillate between two or more opinions. **4** to be influenced or swerve or influence or cause to swerve to or from a purpose or opinion. **5** *Arch. or poetic*. to rule or wield power (over). ◆ *n* **6** control; power. **7** a swinging or leaning movement. **8** *Arch.* dominion; governing authority. **9 hold sway**. to be master; reign. [C16: prob. from ON *sveigja* to bend]

sway-back *n* an abnormal sagging or concavity of the spine in horses.
▸ 'sway-,backed *adj*

Swaziland ★ ('swɑːzɪ,lænd) *n* a kingdom in southern Africa: made a protectorate of the Transvaal by Britain in 1894; gained independence in 1968; a member of the Commonwealth. Official languages: Swazi and English. Religion: Christian majority, traditional beliefs. Currency: lilangeni (*pl* emalangeni). Capital: Mbabane (administrative); Lobamba (legislative). Pop.: 1 032 000 (1997). Area: 17 363 sq. km (6704 sq. miles).

Swazi Territory ★ *n* the former name of **KaNgwane**.

swear (sweə) *vb* **swears, swearing, swore, sworn. 1** to declare or affirm (a statement) as true, esp. by invoking a deity, etc., as witness. **2** (foll. by *by*) **2a** to invoke (a deity, etc.) by name as a witness or guarantee to an oath. **2b** to trust implicitly; have complete confidence (in). **3** (*intr*; often foll. by *at*) to curse, blaspheme, or use swearwords. **4** (when *tr*, *may take a clause as object or an infinitive*) to promise solemnly on oath; vow. **5** (*tr*) to assert or affirm with great emphasis or earnestness. **6** (*intr*) to give evidence or make any statement or solemn declaration on oath. **7** to take an oath in order to add force or solemnity to (a statement or declaration). ◆ *n* **8** a period of swearing. [OE *swerian*]
▸ 'swearer *n*

swear in *vb* (*tr*, *adv*) to administer an oath to (a person) on his assuming office, entering the witness box to give evidence, etc.

swear off *vb* (*intr*, *prep*) to promise to abstain from something: *to swear off drink*.

swearword ('sweə,wɜːd) *n* a socially taboo word of a profane, obscene, or insulting character.

sweat (swɛt) *n* **1** the secretion from the sweat glands, esp. when profuse and visible, as during strenuous activity, from excessive heat, etc.; perspiration. **2** the act or process of secreting this fluid. **3** the act of inducing the exudation of moisture. **4** drops of moisture given forth or gathered on the surface of something. **5** *Inf.* a state or condition of worry or eagerness (esp. in **in a sweat**). **6** *Sl.* drudgery or hard labour: *mowing lawns is a real sweat*! **7** *Sl.*, *chiefly Brit.* a soldier, esp. one who is old and experienced. **8 no sweat!** *Sl.* an expression conveying consent or assurance. ◆ *vb* **sweats, sweating, sweat** *or* **sweated. 9** to secrete (sweat) through the pores of the skin, esp. profusely; perspire. **10** (*tr*) to make wet or stain with perspiration. **11** to give forth or cause to give forth (moisture) in droplets: *the maple sweats sap*. **12** (*intr*) to collect and condense moisture on an outer surface: *a glass of beer sweating*. **13** (*intr*) (of a liquid) to pass through a porous surface in droplets. **14** (of tobacco leaves, hay, etc.) to exude moisture and, sometimes, begin to ferment or to cause (tobacco leaves, etc.) to exude moisture. **15** (*tr*) to heat (food, esp. vegetables) slowly in butter in a tightly closed saucepan. **16** (*tr*) to join (pieces of metal) by pressing together and heating. **17** (*tr*) to heat (solder) until it melts. **18** (*tr*) to heat (partially fused metal) to extract an easily fusible constituent. **19** *Inf.* to suffer anxiety, impatience, or distress. **20** *Inf.* to overwork or be overworked. **21** (*tr*) *Inf.* to employ at very low wages and under bad conditions. **22** (*tr*) *Inf.* to extort, esp. by torture: *to sweat information out of a captive*. **23** (*intr*) *Inf.* to suffer punishment: *you'll sweat for this!* **24 sweat blood**. *Inf.* **24a** to work very hard. **24b** to be filled with anxiety or impatience. ◆ See also **sweat off**, **sweat out**, **sweats**. [OE *swætan* to sweat, from *swāt* sweat]

sweatband ('swɛt,bænd) *n* **1** a band of material set in a hat or cap to protect it from sweat. **2** a piece of cloth tied around the forehead to keep sweat out of the eyes or around the wrist to keep the hands dry, as in sports.

sweated ('swɛtɪd) *adj* **1** made by exploited labour: *sweated goods*. **2** (of workers, etc.) forced to work in poor conditions for low pay.

sweater ('swɛtə) *n* **1** a garment made of knitted or crocheted material covering the upper part of the body, esp. a heavy one worn for warmth. **2** a person or thing that sweats. **3** an employer who overworks and underpays his employees.

sweat gland *n* any of the coiled tubular subcutaneous glands that secrete sweat.

sweating sickness *n* an acute infectious febrile disease that was widespread in Europe during the late 15th century, characterized by profuse sweating.

sweat off *or* **away** *vb* (*tr*, *adv*) *Inf.* to get rid of (weight) by strenuous exercise or sweating.

sweat out *vb* (*tr*, *adv*) **1** to cure or lessen the effects of (a cold, respiratory infection, etc.) by sweating. **2** *Inf.* to endure (hardships) for a time (often in **sweat it out**). **3 sweat one's guts out**. *Inf.* to work extremely hard.

sweats (swɛts) *pl n* sweatshirts and sweat-suit trousers: *jeans and sweats.*

sweatshirt ('swɛtˌʃɜːt) *n* a long-sleeved knitted cotton sweater worn by athletes, etc.

sweatshop ('swɛtˌʃɒp) *n* a workshop where employees work long hours under bad conditions for low wages.

sweat suit *n* a suit worn by athletes for training comprising knitted cotton trousers and a light cotton sweater.

sweaty ('swɛtɪ) *adj* **sweatier, sweatiest. 1** covered with perspiration; sweating. **2** smelling of or like sweat. **3** causing sweat.
▶ '**sweatily** *adv* ▶ '**sweatiness** *n*

swede (swiːd) *n* **1** a Eurasian plant cultivated for its bulbous edible root, which is used as a vegetable and as cattle fodder. **2** the root of this plant. ◆ Also called: **Swedish turnip.** [C19: so called after being introduced into Scotland from Sweden in the 18th century]

Swede (swiːd) *n* a native, citizen, or inhabitant of Sweden.

Sweden ★ ('swiːdᵊn) *n* a kingdom in NW Europe, occupying the E part of the Scandinavian Peninsula, on the Gulf of Bothnia and the Baltic: first united during the Viking period (8th–11th centuries); a member of the European Union. About 50 per cent of the total area is forest and 9 per cent lakes. Exports include timber, pulp, paper, iron ore, and steel. Official language: Swedish. Official religion: Church of Sweden (Lutheran Christian). Currency: krona. Capital: Stockholm. Pop.: 8 863 000 (1997). Area: 449 793 sq. km (173 665 sq. miles). Swedish name: **Sverige.**

Swedenborg ★ ('swiːdᵊnˌbɔːɡ; *Swedish* 'sveːdənbɔrj) *n* **Emanuel** (e'manuel). original surname **Svedberg.** 1688–1772, Swedish scientist and theologian.

Swedish ('swiːdɪʃ) *adj* **1** of, relating to, or characteristic of Sweden, its people, or their language. ◆ *n* **2** the official language of Sweden.

Sweelinck ★ (*Dutch* 'sweːlɪŋk) *n* **Jan Pieterszoon** (jɑn 'piːtərˌzoːn). 1562–1621, Dutch composer, noted for his organ works.

sweep (swiːp) *vb* **sweeps, sweeping, swept. 1** to clean or clear (a space, chimney, etc.) with a brush, broom, etc. **2** (often foll. by *up*) to remove or collect (dirt, rubbish, etc.) with a brush, broom, etc. **3** to move in a smooth or continuous manner, esp. quickly or forcibly: *cars swept along the road.* **4** to move in a proud or dignified fashion: *she swept past.* **5** to spread or pass rapidly across, through, or along (a region, area, etc.): *the news swept through the town.* **6** (*tr*) to direct (the gaze, line of fire, etc.) over; survey. **7** (*tr*; foll. by *away* or *off*) to overwhelm emotionally: *she was swept away by his charm.* **8** to brush or lightly touch (a surface, etc.): *the dress swept along the ground.* **9** (*tr*; often foll. by *away*) to convey, clear, or abolish, esp. with strong or continuous movements: *the sea swept the sandcastle away; secondary modern schools were swept away.* **10** (*intr*) to extend gracefully or majestically, esp. in a wide circle: *the plains sweep down to the sea.* **11** to search (a body of water) for mines, etc., by dragging. **12** (*tr*) to win overwhelmingly, esp. in an election: *Labour swept the country.* **13** (*tr*) to propel (a boat) with sweeps. **14 sweep the board. 14a** (in gambling) to win all the cards or money. **14b** to win every event or prize in a contest. **15 sweep (something) under the carpet.** to conceal (something, esp. a problem) in the hope that it will be overlooked by others. ◆ *n* **16** the act or an instance of sweeping; removal by or as if by a brush or broom. **17** a swift or steady movement, esp. in an arc. **18** the distance, arc, etc., through which something, such as a pendulum, moves. **19** a wide expanse or scope: *the sweep of the plains.* **20** any curving line or contour. **21** short for **sweepstake. 22a** a long oar used on an open boat. **22b** *Austral.* a person steering a surf boat with such an oar at the stern. **23** any of the sails of a windmill. **24** *Electronics.* a steady horizontal or circular movement of an electron beam across or around the fluorescent screen of a cathode-ray tube. **25** a curving driveway. **26** *Chiefly Brit.* See **chimney sweep. 27** another name for **swipe** (sense 6). **28 clean sweep. 28a** an overwhelming victory or success. **28b** a complete change; purge: *to make a clean sweep.* [C13 *swepen*]
▶ '**sweepy** *adj*

sweeper ('swiːpə) *n* **1** a person employed to sweep, such as a roadsweeper. **2** any device for sweeping: *a carpet sweeper.* **3** *Inf.*, soccer. a player who supports the main defenders, as by intercepting loose balls, etc.

sweep hand *n Horology.* a long hand that registers seconds or fractions of seconds on the perimeter of the dial.

sweeping ('swiːpɪŋ) *adj* **1** comprehensive and wide-ranging: *sweeping reforms.* **2** indiscriminate or without reservations: *sweeping statements.* **3** decisive or overwhelming: *a sweeping victory.* **4** taking in a wide area: *a sweeping glance.* **5** driving steadily onwards, esp. over a large area: *a sweeping attack.*
▶ '**sweepingly** *adv* ▶ '**sweepingness** *n*

sweep-saw *n* a saw with a thin blade that can be used for cutting curved shapes.

sweepstake ('swiːpˌsteɪk) *or esp. US* **sweepstakes** *n* **1a** a lottery in which the stakes of the participants constitute the prize. **1b** the prize itself. **2** any event involving such a lottery, esp. a horse race. ◆ Often shortened to **sweep.** [C15: orig. referring to someone who *sweeps* or takes all the stakes in a game]

sweet (swiːt) *adj* **1** having or denoting a pleasant taste like that of sugar. **2** agreeable to the senses or the mind: *sweet music.* **3** having pleasant manners; gentle: *a sweet child.* **4** (of wine, etc.) having a relatively high sugar content; not dry. **5** (of foods) not decaying or rancid: *sweet milk.* **6** not salty: *sweet water.* **7** free from unpleasant odours: *sweet air.* **8** containing no corrosive substances: *sweet soil.* **9** (of petrol) containing no sulphur compounds. **10** sentimental or unrealistic. **11** *Jazz.* performed with a regular beat, with the emphasis on clearly outlined melody and little improvisation. **12** *Arch.* respected; dear (used in polite forms of address): *sweet sir.* **13** smooth and precise; perfectly executed: *a sweet shot.* **14 at one's own sweet will.** as it suits oneself alone. **15 keep (someone) sweet.** to ingratiate oneself in order to ensure cooperation. **16 sweet on.** fond of or infatuated with. ◆ *adv* **17** *Inf.* in a sweet manner. ◆ *n* **18** a sweet taste or smell; sweetness in general. **19** (*often pl*) *Brit.* any of numerous kinds of confectionery consisting wholly or partly of sugar, esp. of sugar boiled and crystallized (**boiled sweets**). **20** *Brit.* any sweet dish served as a dessert. **21** dear; sweetheart (used as a form of address). **22** anything that is sweet. **23** (*often pl*) a pleasurable experience, state, etc.: *the sweets of success.* [OE *swēte*]
▶ '**sweetish** *adj* ▶ '**sweetly** *adv* ▶ '**sweetness** *n*

Sweet ★ (swiːt) *n* **Henry.** 1845–1912, British philologist; a pioneer of modern phonetics. His books include *A History of English Sounds* (1874).

sweet alyssum *n* a Mediterranean plant having clusters of small fragrant white or violet flowers. See also **alyssum.**

sweet-and-sour *adj* (of food) cooked in a sauce made from sugar and vinegar and other ingredients.

sweet bay *n* a small tree of SE North America, belonging to the magnolia family and having large fragrant white flowers. Sometimes shortened to **bay.**

sweetbread ('swiːtˌbrɛd) *n* the pancreas or the thymus gland of an animal, used for food. [C16: SWEET + BREAD, ? from OE *brǣd* meat]

sweetbrier ('swiːtˌbraɪə) *n* a Eurasian rose having a tall bristly stem, fragrant leaves, and single pink flowers. Also called: **eglantine.**

sweet cherry *n* either of two types of cherry tree that are cultivated for their edible sweet fruit.

sweet chestnut *n* See **chestnut** (sense 1).

sweet cicely ('sɪsəlɪ) *n* **1** Also called: **myrrh.** an aromatic European plant, having compound leaves and clusters of small white flowers. **2** the leaves, formerly used in cookery for their flavour of aniseed. **3** any of various related plants of Asia and America, having aromatic roots.

sweet corn *n* **1** a variety of maize whose kernels are rich in sugar and eaten as a vegetable when young. **2** the unripe ears of maize, esp. the sweet kernels removed from the cob, cooked as a vegetable.

sweeten ('swiːtᵊn) *vb* (*mainly tr*) **1** (*also intr*) to make or become sweet or sweeter. **2** to mollify or soften (a person). **3** to make more agreeable. **4** (*also intr*) *Chem.* to free or be freed from unpleasant odours, acidic or corrosive substances, or the like.

sweetener ('swi:t°nə) *n* **1** a sweetening agent, esp. one that does not contain sugar. **2** *Inf.* a bribe. **3** *Inf.* a financial inducement.

sweetening ('swi:t°nɪŋ) *n* something that sweetens.

sweet flag *n* an aroid marsh plant, having swordlike leaves, small greenish flowers, and aromatic roots. Also called: **calamus.**

sweet gale *n* a shrub of northern swamp regions, having yellow catkin-like flowers and aromatic leaves. Also called: **bog myrtle.** Often shortened to **gale.**

sweet gum *n* **1** a North American liquidambar tree, having prickly spherical fruit clusters and fragrant sap: the wood (called **satin walnut**) is used to make furniture. **2** the sap of this tree. ◆ Also called: **red gum.**

sweetheart ('swi:t,hɑ:t) *n* **1** a person loved by another. **2** *Inf.* a lovable, generous, or obliging person. **3** a term of endearment.

sweetheart agreement *n Austral. inf.* an industrial agreement on pay and conditions concluded without resort to arbitration.

sweetie ('swi:tɪ) *n Inf.* **1** sweetheart; darling: used as a term of endearment. **2** *Brit.* another word for **sweet** (sense 19). **3** *Chiefly Brit.* an endearing person. **4** a large seedless variety of grapefruit that has a green-to-yellow rind and juicy sweet pulp.

sweeting ('swi:tɪŋ) *n* **1** a variety of sweet apple. **2** an archaic word for **sweetheart.**

sweet marjoram *n* another name for **marjoram** (sense 1).

sweetmeat ('swi:t,mi:t) *n* a sweetened delicacy, such as a preserve, sweet, or, formerly, a cake or pastry.

sweet pea *n* a climbing plant of S Europe, widely cultivated for its butterfly-shaped fragrant flowers of delicate pastel colours.

sweet pepper *n* **1** a pepper plant with large bell-shaped fruits that are eaten unripe (**green pepper**) or ripe (**red pepper**). **2** the fruit of this plant.

sweet potato *n* **1** a twining plant of tropical America, cultivated in the tropics for its edible fleshy yellow root. **2** the root of this plant.

sweet shop *n Chiefly Brit.* a shop solely or largely selling sweets, esp. boiled sweets.

sweetsop ('swi:t,sɒp) *n* **1** a small West Indian tree, having yellowish-green fruit. **2** the fruit, which has a sweet edible pulp. ◆ Also called: **custard apple.**

sweet spot *n Sport.* the centre area of a racket, golf club, etc., from which the cleanest shots are made.

sweet-talk *Inf.* ◆ *vb* **1** to coax, flatter, or cajole (someone). ◆ *n* **sweet talk. 2** cajolery; coaxing.

sweet tooth *n* a strong liking for sweet foods.

sweetveld ('swi:t,felt) *n* (in South Africa) a type of grazing characterized by high-quality grass. [pron. from Afrik. *soetveld*]

sweet william ('wɪljəm) *n* a widely cultivated Eurasian plant with flat clusters of white, pink, red, or purple flowers.

swell (swel) *vb* **swells, swelling, swelled; swollen** *or* **swelled. 1** to grow or cause to grow in size, esp. as a result of internal pressure. **2** to expand or cause to expand at a particular point or above the surrounding level; protrude. **3** to grow or cause to grow in size, amount, intensity, or degree: *the party is swelling with new recruits.* **4** to puff or be puffed up with pride or another emotion. **5** (*intr*) (of seas or lakes) to rise in waves. **6** (*intr*) to well up or overflow. **7** (*tr*) to make (a musical phrase) increase gradually in volume and then diminish. ◆ *n* **8a** the undulating movement of the surface of the open sea. **8b** a succession of waves or a single large wave. **9** a swelling or being swollen; expansion. **10** an increase in quantity or degree; inflation. **11** a bulge; protuberance. **12** a gentle hill. **13** *Inf.* a person very fashionably dressed. **14** *Inf.* a man of high social or political standing. **15** *Music.* a crescendo followed by an immediate diminuendo. **16** Also called: **swell organ.** *Music.* **16a** a set of pipes on an organ housed

in a box (**swell box**) fitted with a shutter operated by a pedal, which can be opened or closed to control the volume. **16b** the manual on an organ controlling this. ◆ *adj* **17** *Inf.* stylish or grand. **18** *Sl.* excellent; first-class. [OE *swellan*]

swelled head *or* **swollen head** *Inf.* ◆ *n* **1** an inflated view of one's own worth, often caused by sudden success. ◆ *adj* **swelled-headed, swell-headed,** *or* **swollen-headed. 2** conceited.

swelling ('swelɪŋ) *n* **1** the act of expansion or inflation. **2** the state of being or becoming swollen. **3** a swollen or inflated part or area. **4** an abnormal enlargement of a bodily structure or part, esp. as the result of injury. ◆ Related adj: **tumescent.**

swelter ('sweltə) *vb* **1** (*intr*) to suffer under oppressive heat, esp. to perspire and feel faint. **2** (*tr*) *Rare.* to cause to suffer under oppressive heat. ◆ *n* **3** a sweltering condition (esp. in **in a swelter**). **4** oppressive humid heat. [C15 *swelten,* from OE *sweltan* to die]

sweltering ('sweltərɪŋ) *adj* oppressively hot and humid: *a sweltering day.* ▸ '**swelteringly** *adv*

swept (swept) *vb* the past tense and past participle of **sweep.**

sweptback ('swept,bæk) *adj* (of an aircraft wing) inclined backwards towards the rear of the fuselage.

sweptwing ('swept,wɪŋ) *adj* (of an aircraft, etc.) having wings swept (usually) backwards.

swerve (swɜ:v) *vb* **swerves, swerving, swerved. 1** to turn or cause to turn aside, usually sharply or suddenly, from a course. ◆ *n* **2** the act, instance, or degree of swerving. [OE *sweorfan* to scour] ▸ '**swervable** *adj* ▸ '**swerver** *n* ▸ '**swerving** *adj*

Sweyn ★ (sweɪn) *n* known as *Sweyn Forkbeard.* died 1014, king of Denmark (?986–1014). He conquered England, forcing Ethelred II to flee (1013); father of Canute.

SWG *abbrev. for* Standard Wire Gauge; a notation for the diameters of metal rods or thickness of metal sheet ranging from 16 mm to 0.02 mm or from 0.5 inch to 0.001 inch.

swift (swɪft) *adj* **1** moving or able to move quickly; fast. **2** occurring or performed quickly or suddenly; instant. **3** (*postpositive;* foll. by *to*) prompt to act or respond: *swift to take revenge.* ◆ *adv* **4a** swiftly or quickly. **4b** (*in combination*): *swift-moving.* ◆ *n* **5** any of various insectivorous birds of the Old World. They have long narrow wings and spend most of the time on the wing. **6** any of various North American lizards of the iguana family that can run very rapidly. **7** the main cylinder in a carding machine. **8** an expanding circular frame used to hold skeins of silk, wool, etc. [OE, from *swīfan* to turn] ▸ '**swiftly** *adv* ▸ '**swiftness** *n*

Swift ★ (swɪft) *n* **1** Graham Colin. born 1949, British novelist: his books include *Last Orders* (1996). **2 Jonathan.** 1667–1745, Anglo-Irish satirist and churchman, who became dean of St Patrick's, Dublin, in 1713. His works include *Gulliver's Travels* (1726).

swiftlet ('swɪftlɪt) *n* any of various small swifts of an Asian genus that often live in caves and use echolocation.

swig (swɪg) *Inf.* ◆ *n* **1** a large swallow or deep drink, esp. from a bottle. ◆ *vb* **swigs, swigging, swigged. 2** to drink (some liquid) deeply, esp. from a bottle. [C16: from ?] ▸ '**swigger** *n*

swill (swɪl) *vb* **1** to drink large quantities of (liquid, esp. alcoholic drink); guzzle. **2** (*tr;* often foll. by *out*) *Chiefly Brit.* to drench or rinse in large amounts of water. **3** (*tr*) to feed swill to (pigs, etc.). ◆ *n* **4** wet feed, esp. for pigs, consisting of kitchen waste, skimmed milk, etc. **5** refuse, esp. from a kitchen. **6** a deep drink, esp. beer. **7** any liquid mess. **8** the act of swilling. [OE *swilian* to wash out] ▸ '**swiller** *n*

swim (swɪm) *vb* **swims, swimming, swam, swum. 1** (*intr*) to move along in water by means of movements of the body, the arms and legs, or (in the case of fish) tail and fins. **2** (*tr*) to cover (a distance or stretch of water) in this way. **3** (*tr*) to compete in (a race) in this way. **4** (*intr*) to be supported by and on a liquid; float. **5** (*tr*) to use (a

particular stroke) in swimming. **6** (*intr*) to move smoothly, usually through air or over a surface. **7** (*intr*) to reel or seem to reel: *my head swam; the room swam around me.* **8** (*intr*; often foll. by *in* or *with*) to be covered or flooded with water or other liquid. **9** (*intr*; often foll. by *in*) to be liberally supplied (with): *he's swimming in money.* **10** (*tr*) to cause to float or swim. **11 swim with** (or **against**) **the stream** or **tide.** to conform to (or resist) prevailing opinion. ◆ *n* **12** the act, an instance, or period of swimming. **13** any graceful gliding motion. **14** a condition of dizziness; swoon. **15** a pool in a river good for fishing. **16 in the swim.** *Inf.* fashionable or active in social or political activities. [OE *swimman*]
▸ **'swimmable** *adj* ▸ **'swimmer** *n* ▸ **'swimming** *n, adj*

swim bladder *n Ichthyol.* another name for **air bladder** (sense 1).

swimmeret ('swɪmə,rɛt) *n* any of the small paired appendages on the abdomen of crustaceans, used chiefly in locomotion.

swimming bath *n* (*often pl*) an indoor swimming pool.

swimming costume or **bathing costume** *n Chiefly Brit.* any garment worn for swimming or sunbathing, such as a woman's one-piece garment covering most of the torso but not the limbs.

swimmingly ('swɪmɪŋlɪ) *adv* successfully, effortlessly, or well (esp. in **go swimmingly**).

swimming pool *n* an artificial pool for swimming.

swimsuit ('swɪm,suːt, -,sjuːt) *n* a woman's one-piece swimming garment that leaves the arms and legs bare.

Swinburne ★ ('swɪn,bɜːn) *n* **Algernon Charles.** 1837–1909, British poet and critic.

swindle ('swɪndᵊl) *vb* **swindles, swindling, swindled. 1** to cheat (someone) of money, etc.; defraud. **2** (*tr*) to obtain (money, etc.) by fraud. ◆ *n* **3** a fraudulent scheme or transaction. [C18: back formation from G *Schwindler*, from *schwindeln*, from OHG *swintilōn*, from *swintan* to disappear]
▸ **'swindler** *n*

swindle sheet *n* a slang term for **expense account.**

Swindon ★ ('swɪndən) *n* a town and unitary authority in S England, in NE Wiltshire: railway workshops. Pop.: 145 236 (1991).

swine (swaɪn) *n* **1** (*pl* **swine** or **swines**). a coarse or contemptible person. **2** (*pl* **swine**). another name for a **pig.** [OE *swīn*]
▸ **'swinish** *adj* ▸ **'swinishly** *adv* ▸ **'swinishness** *n*

swine fever *n* an infectious viral disease of pigs, characterized by fever and diarrhoea.

swineherd ('swaɪn,hɜːd) *n Arch.* a person who looks after pigs.

swing (swɪŋ) *vb* **swings, swinging, swung. 1** to move or cause to move rhythmically to and fro, as a free-hanging object; sway. **2** (*intr*) to move, walk, etc., with a relaxed and swaying motion. **3** to pivot or cause to pivot, as on a hinge. **4** to move or cause to move in a curve: *the car swung around the bend.* **5** to move or cause to move by suspending or being suspended. **6** to hang or be hung so as to be able to turn freely. **7** (*intr*) *Sl.* to be hanged: *he'll swing for it.* **8** to alter or cause to alter habits, a course, etc. **9** (*tr*) *Inf.* to influence or manipulate successfully: *I hope he can swing the deal.* **10** (*tr*; foll. by *up*) to raise or hoist, esp. in a sweeping motion. **11** (*intr*; often foll. by *at*) to hit out or strike (at), esp. with a sweeping motion. **12** (*tr*) to wave (a weapon, etc.) in a sweeping motion; flourish. **13** to arrange or play (music) with the rhythmically flexible and compulsive quality associated with jazz. **14** (*intr*) (of popular music, esp. jazz, or of the musicians who play it) to have this quality. **15** *Sl.* to be lively and modern. **16** (*intr*) *Cricket.* to bowl (a ball) with swing or (of a ball) to move with a swing. **17 swing the lead.** *Inf.* to malinger or make up excuses. ◆ *n* **18** the act or manner of swinging or the distance covered while swinging: *a wide swing.* **19** a sweeping stroke or blow. **20** *Boxing.* a wide punch from the side similar to but longer than a hook. **21** *Cricket.* the lateral movement of a bowled ball through the air. **22** any free-swaying motion. **23** any curving movement; sweep. **24** something that swings or is swung, esp. a suspended seat on which a person may

swing back and forth. **25** a kind of popular dance music influenced by jazz, usually played by big bands and originating in the 1930s. **26** *Prosody.* a steady distinct rhythm or cadence in prose or verse. **27** *Inf.* the normal round or pace: *the swing of things.* **28a** a fluctuation, as in some business activity, voting pattern, etc. **28b** (*modifier*) able to bring about a swing in a voting pattern. **29** *Canad.* (in the North) a train of freight sleighs or canoes. **30** *Chiefly US.* a circular tour. **31 go with a swing.** to go well; be successful. **32 in full swing.** at the height of activity. **33 swings and roundabouts.** equal advantages and disadvantages. [OE *swingan*]

swingboat ('swɪŋ,bəʊt) *n* a piece of fairground equipment consisting of a boat-shaped carriage for swinging in.

swing bridge *n* a low bridge that can be rotated about a vertical axis to permit the passage of ships, etc.

swinge (swɪndʒ) *vb* **swinges, swingeing** or **swinging, swinged.** (*tr*) *Arch.* to beat, flog, or punish. [OE *swengan*]

swingeing ('swɪndʒɪŋ) *adj Chiefly Brit.* punishing; severe.

swinger ('swɪŋə) *n Sl.* **1** a person regarded as being modern and lively. **2** a person who swaps sexual partners in a group, esp. habitually.
▸ **'swinging** *adj* ▸ **'swingingly** *adv*

swingle ('swɪŋᵊl) *n* **1** a flat-bladed wooden instrument used for beating and scraping flax or hemp to remove coarse matter from it. ◆ *vb* **swingles, swingling, swingled. 2** (*tr*) to use a swingle on. [OE *swingel* stroke]

swingletree ('swɪŋᵊl,triː) *n* a crossbar in a horse's harness to which the ends of the traces are attached. Also called: **whippletree.**

swing shift *n US & Canad. inf.* the usual US and Canad. term for **back shift.**

swing-wing *adj* **1** of or relating to a variable-geometry aircraft. ◆ *n* **2a** such an aircraft. **2b** either of the two wings of such an aircraft.

swipe (swaɪp) *vb* **swipes, swiping, swiped. 1** (when *intr,* usually foll. by *at*) *Inf.* to hit hard with a sweeping blow. **2** (*tr*) *Sl.* to steal. **3** (*tr*) to pass a machine-readable card, such as a credit card, debit card, etc., through a machine that electronically interprets the information encoded on it, usu. in a magnetic strip. ◆ *n* **4** *Inf.* a hard blow. **5** an unexpected criticism of someone or something while discussing another subject. **6** Also called: **sweep.** a type of lever for raising and lowering a weight, such as a bucket in a well. [C19: ? rel. to SWEEP]

swirl (swɜːl) *vb* **1** to turn or cause to turn in a twisting spinning fashion. **2** (*intr*) to be dizzy; swim: *my head was swirling.* ◆ *n* **3** a whirling or spinning motion, esp. in water. **4** a whorl; curl. **5** the act of swirling or stirring. **6** dizzy confusion or disorder. [C15: prob. from Du. *zwirrelen*]
▸ **'swirling** *adj* ▸ **'swirly** *adj*

swish (swɪʃ) *vb* **1** to move with or make or cause to move with or make a whistling or hissing sound. **2** (*intr*) (esp. of fabrics) to rustle. **3** (*tr*) *Sl., now rare.* to whip; flog. **4** (*tr,* foll. by *off*) to cut with a swishing blow. ◆ *n* **5** a hissing or rustling sound or movement. **6** a rod for flogging or a blow from this. ◆ *adj* **7** *Inf., chiefly Brit.* fashionable; smart. [C18: imit.]
▸ **'swishy** *adj*

Swiss (swɪs) *adj* **1** of, relating to, or characteristic of Switzerland, its inhabitants, or their dialects of German French, and Italian. ◆ *n, pl* **Swiss. 2** a native, inhabitant or citizen of Switzerland.

Swiss chard *n* another name for **chard.**

Swiss cheese plant *n* See **monstera.**

swiss roll *n* a sponge cake spread with jam, cream, o some other filling, and rolled up.

switch (swɪtʃ) *n* **1** a mechanical, electrical, or electronic device for opening or closing a circuit or for diverting a current from one part of a circuit to another. **2** a swift and usually sudden shift or change. **3** an exchange or swap. **4** a flexible rod or twig, used esp. for punishment **5** the sharp movement or blow of such an instrument. **6** a tress of false hair used to give added length or bulk to a

---

★ people and places

woman's own hair-style. **7** the tassel-like tip of the tail of cattle and certain other animals. **8** any of various card games in which the suit is changed during play. **9** *US & Canad.* a railway siding. **10** *US & Canad.* a railway point. **11** *Austral. inf.* short for **switchboard** (sense 1). ◆ *vb* **12** to shift, change, turn aside, or change the direction of (something). **13** to exchange (places); replace (something by something else). **14** *Chiefly US & Canad.* to transfer (rolling stock) from one railway track to another. **15** (*tr*) to cause (an electric current) to start or stop flowing or to change its path by operating a switch. **16** (*tr*) to lash or whip with or as if with a switch. ◆ See also **switch off, switch on.** [C16: ?from MDu. *swijch* twig]
▶ 'switcher *n*

switchback ('swɪtʃˌbæk) *n* **1** a mountain road, railway, or track which rises and falls sharply many times or a sharp rise and fall on such a road, railway, or track. **2** another word (esp. Brit.) for **big dipper.**

switchblade *or* **switchblade knife** ('swɪtʃˌbleɪd) *n* another name (esp. US and Canad.) for **flick knife.**

switchboard ('swɪtʃˌbɔːd) *n* **1** an installation in a telephone exchange, office, etc., at which the interconnection of telephone lines is manually controlled. **2** an assembly of switchgear for the control of power supplies in an installation or building.

switchgear ('swɪtʃˌɡɪə) *n Electrical engineering.* any of several devices used for opening and closing electric circuits, esp. those that pass high currents.

switchman ('swɪtʃmən) *n, pl* **switchmen.** the US and Canad. name for **pointsman.**

switch off *vb* (*adv*) **1** to cause (a device) to stop operating as by moving a switch, knob, etc. **2** *Inf.* to cease to interest or be interested; make or become bored, alienated, etc.

switch on *vb* (*adv*) **1** to cause (a device) to operate as by moving a switch, knob, or lever. **2** (*tr*) *Inf.* to produce (charm, tears, etc.) suddenly or automatically. **3** (*tr*) *Inf.* (now dated) to make up-to-date, esp. in outlook, dress, etc.

swither ('swɪðə) *Scot.* ◆ *vb* (*intr*) **1** to hesitate; vacillate; be perplexed. ◆ *n* **2** hesitation; perplexity; agitation. [C16: from ?]

Swithin *or* **Swithun** ★ ('swɪðɪn, 'swɪθ-) *n Saint.* died 862 A.D., English ecclesiastic: bishop of Winchester (?852–862). Feast day: July 15.

Switz. *or* **Swit.** *abbrev. for* Switzerland.

Switzer ★ ('swɪtsə) *n* a less common word for **Swiss.** [C16: from MHG, from *Swīz* Switzerland]

Switzerland ★ ('swɪtsələnd) *n* a federal republic in W central Europe: the cantons of Schwyz, Uri, and Unterwalden formed a defensive league against the Hapsburgs in 1291, later joined by other cantons; gained independence in 1499; adopted a policy of permanent neutrality from 1516; a leading centre of the Reformation in the 16th century. It lies in the Jura Mountains and the Alps, with a plateau between the two ranges. Official languages: German, French and Italian; Romansch is also spoken. Religion: mostly Protestant and Roman Catholic. Currency: Swiss franc. Capital: Bern. Pop.: 7 116 000 (1997). Area: 41 288 sq. km (15 941 sq. miles). German name: **Schweiz.** French name: **Suisse.** Italian name: **Svizzera.** Romansch name: **Svizra.** Latin name: **Helvetia** (hɛlˈviːʃə).

swivel ('swɪvəl) *n* **1** a coupling device which allows an attached object to turn freely. **2** such a device made of two parts which turn independently, such as a compound link of a chain. **3a** a pivot on which is mounted a gun that may be swung horizontally from side to side. **3b** Also called: **swivel gun.** the gun itself. ◆ *vb* **swivels, swivelling, swivelled** *or US* **swivels, swiveling, swiveled.** **4** to turn or swing on or as if on a pivot. **5** (*tr*) to provide with, secure by, or support with a swivel. [C14: from OE *swīfan* to turn]

swivel chair *n* a chair, the seat of which is joined to the legs by a swivel and which thus may be spun round.

swivel pin *n* another name for **kingpin** (sense 2).

swiz *or* **swizz** (swɪz) *n Brit. inf.* a swindle or disappointment; swizzle.

swizzle ('swɪzəl) *n* **1** an alcoholic drink containing gin or rum. **2** *Brit. inf.* a swiz. ◆ *vb* **swizzles, swizzling, swizzled.** **3** (*tr*) to stir a swizzle stick in (a drink). **4** *Brit. inf.* to swindle; cheat. [C19: from ?]

swizzle stick *n* a small rod used to agitate an effervescent drink to facilitate the escape of carbon dioxide.

swob (swɒb) *n, vb* **swobs, swobbing, swobbed.** a less common word for **swab.**

swollen ('swəʊlən) *vb* **1** a past participle of **swell.** ◆ *adj* **2** tumid or enlarged as by swelling. **3** turgid or bombastic.
▶ 'swollenness *n*

swoon (swuːn) *vb* (*intr*) **1** a literary word for **faint.** **2** to become ecstatic. ◆ *n* **3** an instance of fainting. ◆ Also (archaic or dialect): **swound** (swaʊnd). [OE *geswōgen* insensible, p.p. of *swōgan* (unattested except in compounds) suffocate]
▶ 'swooning *adj*

swoop (swuːp) *vb* **1** (*intr*; usually foll. by *down*, *on*, or *upon*) to sweep or pounce suddenly. **2** (*tr*; often foll. by *up*, *away*, or *off*) to seize or scoop suddenly. ◆ *n* **3** the act of swooping. **4** a swift descent. [OE *swāpan* to sweep]

swoosh (swuʃ) *vb* **1** to make or cause to make a rustling or swirling sound, esp. when moving or pouring out. ◆ *n* **2** a swirling or rustling sound or movement. [C20: imit.]

swop (swɒp) *vb* **swops, swopping, swopped,** *n* a variant spelling of **swap.**

sword (sɔːd) *n* **1** a thrusting, striking, or cutting weapon with a long blade having one or two cutting edges, a hilt, and usually a crosspiece or guard. **2** such a weapon worn on ceremonial occasions as a symbol of authority. **3** something resembling a sword, such as the snout of a swordfish. **4 the sword. 4a** violence or power, esp. military power. **4b** death; destruction: *to put to the sword.* [OE *sweord*]

swordbearer ('sɔːdˌbɛərə) *n* an official who carries a ceremonial sword.

sword dance *n* a dance in which the performers dance nimbly over swords on the ground or brandish them in the air.
▶ **sword dancer** *n* ▶ **sword dancing** *n*

swordfish ('sɔːdˌfɪʃ) *n, pl* **swordfish** *or* **swordfishes.** a large fish with a very long upper jaw: valued as a food and game fish.

sword grass *n* any of various grasses and other plants having sword-shaped sharp leaves.

sword knot *n* a loop on the hilt of a sword by which it was attached to the wrist, now purely decorative.

sword lily *n* another name for **gladiolus.**

Sword of Damocles *n* a closely impending disaster. [see DAMOCLES]

swordplay ('sɔːdˌpleɪ) *n* **1** the action or art of fighting with a sword. **2** verbal sparring.

swordsman ('sɔːdzmən) *n, pl* **swordsmen.** one who uses or is skilled in the use of a sword.
▶ 'swordsmanship *n*

swordstick ('sɔːdˌstɪk) *n* a hollow walking stick containing a short sword or dagger.

swordtail ('sɔːdˌteɪl) *n* any of several small freshwater fishes of Central America having a long swordlike tail.

swore (swɔː) *vb* the past tense of **swear.**

sworn (swɔːn) *vb* **1** the past participle of **swear.** ◆ *adj* **2** bound, pledged, or made inveterate, by or as if by an oath: *a sworn statement; he was sworn to God.*

swot[1] (swɒt) *Brit. inf.* ◆ *vb* **swots, swotting, swotted.** **1** (often foll. by *up*) to study (a subject) intensively, as for an examination; cram. ◆ *n* **2** Also called: **swotter.** a person who works or studies hard. **3** hard work or grind. ◆ Also: **swat.** [C19: var. of SWEAT (n)]

swot[2] (swɒt) *vb* **swots, swotting, swotted,** *n* a variant of **swat.**

SWOT (swɒt) *n acronym for* strengths, weaknesses, opportunities, and threats: an analysis of a product made before it is marketed.

swounds *or* **'swounds** (zwaʊndz, zaʊndz) *interj Arch.* less common spellings of **zounds.**

swum (swʌm) *vb* the past participle of **swim**.

swung (swʌŋ) *vb* the past tense and past participle of swing.

swy (swaɪ) *n Austral.* another name for **two-up**. [C20: from G *zwei* two]

Sybaris ★ ('sɪbərɪs) *n* a Greek colony in S Italy, on the Gulf of Taranto: notorious for its luxurious living, founded about 720 B.C. and sacked in 510.
▸ 'Sybarite *n* ▸ Sybaritic (ˌsɪbə'rɪtɪk) *adj*

sybarite ('sɪbəˌraɪt) *n* **1** (*sometimes cap.*) a devotee of luxury and the sensual vices. ◆ *adj* **2** luxurious; sensuous. [C16: from L *Sybarīta*, from Gk *Subarītēs* inhabitant of SYBARIS]
▸ sybaritic (ˌsɪbə'rɪtɪk) *adj* ▸ ˌsyba'ritically *adv* ▸ 'sybaritism *n*

sycamore ('sɪkəˌmɔː) *n* **1** a Eurasian maple tree, naturalized in Britain and North America, having five-lobed leaves and two-winged fruits. **2** *US & Canad.* an American plane tree. See **plane tree**. **3** a tree of N Africa and W Asia, having an edible figlike fruit. [C14: from OF *sicamor*, from L *sӯcomorus*, from Gk, from *sukon* fig + *moron* mulberry]

syconium (saɪ'kəʊnɪəm) *n, pl* **syconia** (-nɪə). *Bot.* the fleshy fruit of the fig, consisting of an enlarged receptacle. [C19: from NL, from Gk *sukon* fig]

sycophant ('sɪkəfənt) *n* a person who uses flattery to win favour from individuals wielding influence; toady. [C16: from L *sӯcophanta*, from Gk *sukophantēs*, lit.: person showing a fig, apparently referring to the fig sign used in accusation, from *sukon* fig + *phainein* to show; sense prob. developed from "accuser" to "informer, flatterer"]
▸ 'sycophancy *n* ▸ sycophantic (ˌsɪkə'fæntɪk) *adj* ▸ ˌsyco'phantically *adv*

sycosis (saɪ'kəʊsɪs) *n* chronic inflammation of the hair follicles, esp. those of the beard. [C16: via NL from Gk *sukōsis*, from *sukon* fig]

Sydenham's chorea ('sɪd³nəmz) *n* a form of chorea affecting children, often associated with rheumatic fever. Nontechnical name: **Saint Vitus's dance**. [after T. Sydenham (1624–89), E physician]

Sydney[1] ★ ('sɪdnɪ) *n* **1** a port in SE Australia, capital of New South Wales, on an inlet of the S Pacific: the largest city in Australia and the first British settlement, established as a penal colony in 1788; developed rapidly after 1820 with the discovery of gold in its hinterland; large wool market; three universities. Pop.: 3 772 700 (1995 est.). **2** a port in SE Canada, in Nova Scotia on NE Cape Breton Island: capital of Cape Breton Island until 1820, when the island united administratively with Nova Scotia. Pop.: 26 063 (1991).

Sydney[2] ★ ('sɪdnɪ) *n* a variant spelling of (Sir Philip) **Sidney**.

Syene ★ (saɪ'iːnɪ) *n* transliteration of the Ancient Greek name for **Aswan**.

syenite ('saɪəˌnaɪt) *n* a light-coloured coarse-grained igneous rock consisting of feldspars with hornblende. [C18: from F, from L *syēnītēs lapis* stone from *Syene* (Aswan), where orig. quarried]
▸ syenitic (ˌsaɪə'nɪtɪk) *adj*

Syktyvkar ★ (*Russian* siktif'kar) *n* a city in NW Russia, capital of the Komi Republic: timber industry. Pop.: 229 000 (1995 est.).

syllabary ('sɪləbərɪ) *n, pl* **syllabaries. 1** a table or list of syllables. **2** a set of symbols used in certain writing systems, such as one used for Japanese, in which each symbol represents a spoken syllable. [C16: from NL *syllabārium*, from L *syllaba* SYLLABLE]

syllabi ('sɪləˌbaɪ) *n* a plural of **syllabus**.

syllabic (sɪ'læbɪk) *adj* **1** of or relating to syllables or the division of a word into syllables. **2** denoting a kind of verse line based on a specific number of syllables rather than being regulated by stresses or quantities. **3** (of a consonant) constituting a syllable. ◆ *n* **4** a syllabic consonant.
▸ syl'labically *adv*

syllabify (sɪ'læbɪˌfaɪ) *or* **syllabicate** *vb* **syllabifies, syl-** labifying, syllabified *or* **syllabicates, syllabicating, syllabicated.** (*tr*) to divide (a word) into its constituent syllables.
▸ sylˌlabifi'cation *or* sylˌlabi'cation *n*

syllable ('sɪləb³l) *n* **1** a combination or set of one or more units of sound in a language that must consist of a sonorous element (a sonant or vowel) and may or may not contain less sonorous elements (consonants or semivowels) flanking it: for example "paper" has two syllables. **2** (in the writing systems of certain languages, esp. ancient ones) a symbol or set of symbols standing for a syllable. **3** the least mention: *don't breathe a syllable of it.* **4 in words of one syllable.** simply; bluntly. ◆ *vb* **syllables, syllabling, syllabled. 5** to pronounce syllables of (a text); articulate. **6** (*tr*) to write down in syllables. [C14: via OF from L *syllaba*, from Gk *sullabē*, from *sullambanein* to collect together]

syllabub *or* **sillabub** ('sɪləˌbʌb) *n* **1** a spiced drink made of milk with rum, port, brandy, or wine, often hot. **2** *Brit.* a cold dessert made from milk or cream beaten with sugar, wine, and lemon juice. [C16: from ?]

syllabus ('sɪləbəs) *n, pl* **syllabuses** *or* **syllabi** (-ˌbaɪ). **1** an outline of a course of studies, text, etc. **2** *Brit., Austral., & NZ.* **2a** the subjects studied for a particular course. **2b** a list of these subjects. [C17: from LL, erroneously from L *sittybus* parchment strip giving title and author, from Gk *sittuba*]

syllepsis (sɪ'lɛpsɪs) *n, pl* **syllepses** (-siːz). **1** (in grammar or rhetoric) the use of a single sentence construction in which a verb, adjective, etc., is made to cover two syntactical functions, as *have* in *she and they have promised to come.* **2** another word for **zeugma**. [C16: from LL, from Gk *sullēpsis*, from *sul-* SYN- + *lēpsis*, from *lambanein* to take]
▸ syl'leptic *adj* ▸ syl'leptically *adv*

syllogism ('sɪləˌdʒɪzəm) *n* **1** a deductive inference consisting of two premises and a conclusion, all of which are categorical propositions. The subject of the conclusion is the **minor term** and its predicate the **major term;** the **middle term** occurs in both premises but not the conclusion. There are 256 such arguments but only 24 are valid. *Some men are mortal; some men are angelic; so some mortals are angelic* is invalid, while *some temples are in ruins; all ruins are fascinating; so some temples are fascinating* is valid. Here *fascinating, in ruins,* and *temples* are respectively major, middle, and minor terms. **2** a piece of deductive reasoning from the general to the particular. [C14: via L from Gk *sullogismos*, from *sullogizesthai* to reckon together, from *logos* a discourse]
▸ ˌsyllo'gistic *adj* ▸ 'sylloˌgize *or* 'sylloˌgise *vb*

sylph (sɪlf) *n* **1** a slender graceful girl or young woman. **2** any of a class of imaginary beings assumed to inhabit the air. [C17: from NL *sylphus*, prob. coined from L *silva* wood + Gk *numphē* nymph]
▸ 'sylph,like *adj*

sylva *or* **silva** ('sɪlvə) *n, pl* **sylvas** *or* **sylvae** (-viː). the trees growing in a particular region. [C17: from L *silva* a wood]

sylvan *or* **silvan** ('sɪlvən) *Chiefly poetic.* ◆ *adj* **1** of or consisting of woods or forests. **2** in woods or forests. **3** idyllically rural or rustic. ◆ *n* **4** an inhabitant of the woods, esp. a spirit. [C16: from L *silvānus*, from *silva* forest]

sylvanite ('sɪlvəˌnaɪt) *n* a silver-white mineral consisting of a compound of tellurium with gold and silver in the form of elongated crystals. [C18: from (TRAN)SYLVAN(IA) + -ITE[1], with reference to the region where first found]

Sylvanus ★ (sɪl'veɪnəs) *n* a variant spelling of **Silvanus**.

Sylvester II ★ (sɪl'vɛstə) *n* original name *Gerbert of Aurillac. c.* 940–1003 A.D., French ecclesiastic and scholar; pope (909–1003): noted for his achievements in mathematics and astronomy.

sylviculture ('sɪlvɪˌkʌltʃə) *n* a variant spelling of **silviculture**.

sym- *prefix* a variant of **syn-** before *b, p,* and *m.*

symbiont ('sɪmbɪˌɒnt) *n* an organism living in a state of symbiosis. [C19: from Gk *sumbioun* to live together, from *bioun* to live]
▸ ˌsymbi'ontic *adj* ▸ ˌsymbi'ontically *adv*

symbiosis (ˌsɪmbɪ'əʊsɪs) *n* **1** a close association of two

★ people and places

interdependent animal or plant species. **2** a similar relationship between persons or groups. [C19: via NL from Gk: a living together]
▸ ˌsymbiˈotic *adj*

symbol ('sɪmbˀl) *n* **1** something that represents or stands for something else, usually by convention or association, esp. a material object used to represent something abstract. **2** an object, person, etc., used in a literary work, film, etc., to stand for or suggest something else with which it is associated. **3** a letter, figure, or sign used in mathematics, music, etc., to represent a quantity, phenomenon, operation, function, etc. ◆ *vb* **symbols, symbolling, symbolled** *or US* **symbols, symboling, symboled. 4** (*tr*) another word for **symbolize**. [C15: from Church L *symbolum*, from Gk *sumbolon* sign, from *sumballein* to throw together, from SYN- + *ballein* to throw]

symbolic (sɪm'bɒlɪk) *or* **symbolical** *adj* **1** of or relating to a symbol or symbols. **2** serving as a symbol. **3** characterized by the use of symbols or symbolism.
▸ **sym'bolically** *adv*

symbolic logic *n* another name for **formal logic.**

symbolism ('sɪmbə,lɪzəm) *n* **1** the representation of something in symbolic form or the attribution of symbolic character to something. **2** a system of symbols or symbolic representation. **3** a symbolic significance or quality. **4** (*often cap.*) a late 19th-century movement in art that sought to express mystical or abstract ideas through the symbolic use of images.

symbolist ('sɪmbəlɪst) *n* **1** a person who uses or can interpret symbols, esp. as a means to revealing aspects of truth and reality. **2** an artist or writer who practises symbolism in his work. **3** (*usually cap.*) a writer associated with the symbolist movement. **4** (*often cap.*) an artist associated with the symbolist movement. ◆ *adj* **5** of, relating to, or characterizing symbolism or symbolists.
▸ ˌsymbol'istic *adj* ▸ ˌsymbol'istically *adv*

symbolist movement *n* (*usually cap.*) a movement beginning in French and Belgian poetry towards the end of the 19th century with Mallarmé, Valéry, Verlaine, Rimbaud, and others, and seeking to express states of mind rather than objective reality by the power of words and images to suggest as well as denote.

symbolize *or* **symbolise** ('sɪmbə,laɪz) *vb* **symbolizes, symbolizing, symbolized** *or* **symbolises, symbolising, symbolised. 1** (*tr*) to serve as or be a symbol of. **2** (*tr*; *usually foll. by by*) to represent by a symbol or symbols. **3** (*intr*) to use symbols. **4** (*tr*) to treat or regard as symbolic.
▸ ˌsymboli'zation *or* ˌsymboli'sation *n*

symbol retailer *n* any member of a voluntary group of independent retailers, often using a common name or symbol, formed to obtain better prices from wholesalers or manufacturers in competition with supermarket chains. Also called: **voluntary retailer.**

symmetrical (sɪ'mɛtrɪkˀl) *adj* possessing or displaying symmetry.

symmetry ('sɪmɪtrɪ) *n, pl* **symmetries. 1** similarity, correspondence, or balance among systems or parts of a system. **2** *Maths.* an exact correspondence in position or form about a given point, line, or plane. **3** beauty or harmony of form based on a proportionate arrangement of parts. [C16: from L *symmetria*, from Gk *summetria* proportion, from SYN- + *metron* measure]

Symonds ★ ('sɪməndz) *n* **John Addington** ('ædɪŋtən). 1840–93, British writer, noted for his *Renaissance in Italy* (1875–86) and for studies of homosexuality.

Symons ★ ('saɪmənz) *n* **Arthur.** 1865–1945, British poet and critic, who helped to introduce the French symbolists to England.

sympathectomy (ˌsɪmpə'θɛktəmɪ) *n, pl* **sympathectomies.** the surgical excision or chemical destruction (**chemical sympathectomy**) of one or more parts of the sympathetic nervous system. [C20: from SYMPATHETIC + -ECTOMY]

sympathetic (ˌsɪmpə'θɛtɪk) *adj* **1** characterized by, feeling, or showing sympathy; understanding. **2** in accord with the subject's personality or mood; congenial: *a sympathetic atmosphere.* **3** (when *postpositive*, often foll. by *to* or *towards*) showing agreement (with) or favour (towards). **4** *Anat., physiol.* of or relating to the division of

the autonomic nervous system that acts in opposition to the parasympathetic system accelerating the heartbeat, dilating the bronchi, inhibiting the smooth muscles of the digestive tract, etc. Cf. **parasympathetic. 5** relating to vibrations occurring as a result of similar vibrations in a neighbouring body: *sympathetic strings on a sitar.*
▸ ˌsympa'thetically *adv*

sympathetic magic *n* a type of magic in which it is sought to produce a large-scale effect, often at a distance, by performing some small-scale ceremony resembling it, such as the pouring of water on an altar to induce rainfall.

sympathize *or* **sympathise** ('sɪmpə,θaɪz) *vb* **sympathizes, sympathizing, sympathized** *or* **sympathises, sympathising, sympathised.** (*intr*; often foll. *by with*) **1** to feel or express compassion or sympathy (for); commiserate: *he sympathized with my troubles.* **2** to share or understand the sentiments or ideas (of); be in sympathy (with).
▸ 'sympa,thizer *or* 'sympa,thiser *n*

sympatholytic (ˌsɪmpəθəʊ'lɪtɪk) *Med.* ◆ *adj* **1a** inhibiting or antagonistic to nerve impulses of the sympathetic nervous system. **1b** of or relating to such inhibition. ◆ *n* **2** a sympatholytic drug. Cf. **sympathomimetic.** [C20: from SYMPATH(ETIC) + -LYTIC]

sympathomimetic (ˌsɪmpəθəʊmɪ'mɛtɪk) *Med.* ◆ *adj* **1** causing a physiological effect similar to that produced by stimulation of the sympathetic nervous system. ◆ *n* **2** a sympathomimetic drug. Cf. **sympatholytic.** [C20: from SYMPATH(ETIC) + MIMETIC]

sympathy ('sɪmpəθɪ) *n, pl* **sympathies. 1** the sharing of another's emotions, esp. of sorrow or anguish; compassion. **2** affinity or harmony, usually of feelings or interests, between persons or things: *to be in sympathy with someone.* **3** mutual affection or understanding arising from such a relationship. **4** the condition of a physical system or body when its behaviour is similar or corresponds to that of a different system that influences it, such as the vibration of sympathetic strings. **5** (*sometimes pl*) a feeling of loyalty, support, or accord, as for an idea, cause, etc. **6** *Physiol.* the relationship between two organs or parts whereby a change in one affects the other. [C16: from L *sympathīa*, from Gk, from *sumpathēs*, from SYN- + *pathos* suffering]

sympathy strike *n* a strike organized in support of another strike or cause. Also called: **sympathetic strike.**

symphonic poem *n Music.* an extended orchestral composition, originated by Liszt, based on nonmusical material, such as a work of literature or folk tale. Also called: **tone poem.**

symphony ('sɪmfənɪ) *n, pl* **symphonies. 1** an extended large-scale orchestral composition, usually with several movements, at least one of which is in sonata form. **2** a piece of instrumental music in up to three very short movements, used as an overture to or interlude in a baroque opera. **3** any purely orchestral movement in a vocal work, such as a cantata or oratorio. **4** short for **symphony orchestra. 5** anything distinguished by a harmonious composition: *the picture was a symphony of green.* **6** *Arch.* harmony in general; concord. [C13: from OF *symphonie*, from L *symphōnia* concord, from Gk, from SYN- + *phōnē* sound]
▸ **symphonic** (sɪm'fɒnɪk) *adj* ▸ **sym'phonically** *adv*

symphony orchestra *n Music.* an orchestra capable of performing symphonies, esp. a large orchestra comprising strings, brass, woodwind, harp and percussion.

symphysis ('sɪmfɪsɪs) *n, pl* **symphyses** (-,siːz). **1** *Anat., bot.* a growing together of parts or structures, such as two bony surfaces joined by an intermediate layer of fibrous cartilage. **2** a line marking this growing together. **3** *Pathol.* an abnormal adhesion of two or more parts or structures. [C16: via NL from Gk *sumphusis*, from *sumphuein*, from SYN- + *phuein* to grow]
▸ **symphysial** *or* **symphyseal** (sɪm'fɪzɪəl) *adj*

sympodium (sɪm'pəʊdɪəm) *n, pl* **sympodia** (-dɪə). the main axis of growth in the grapevine and similar plants: a number of lateral branches that arise from just behind the apex of the main stem, which ceases to grow. [C19: from NL, from SYN- + Gk *podion* a little foot]
▸ **sym'podial** *adj* ▸ **sym'podially** *adv*

symposium (sɪm'pəʊzɪəm) *n, pl* **symposiums** *or* **symposia** (-zɪə). **1** a conference or meeting for the discussion of some subject, esp. an academic topic or social problem. **2** a collection of scholarly contributions on a given subject. **3** (in classical Greece) a drinking party with intellectual conversation, music, etc. [C16: via L from Gk *sumposion*, from *sumpinein* to drink together]

symptom ('sɪmptəm) *n* **1** *Med.* any sensation or change in bodily function experienced by a patient that is associated with a particular disease. **2** any phenomenon or circumstance accompanying something and regarded as evidence of its existence; indication. [C16: from LL *symptōma*, from Gk *sumptōma* chance, from *sumpiptein* to occur, from SYN- + *piptein* to fall]

symptomatic (,sɪmptə'mætɪk) *adj* **1** being a symptom; indicative: *symptomatic of insanity*. **2** of, relating to, or according to symptoms: *a symptomatic analysis.*
▸ ,**sympto'matically** *adv*

symptomatology (,sɪmptəmə'tɒlədʒɪ) *n* the branch of medicine concerned with the study and classification of the symptoms of disease.

syn. *abbrev. for* synonym(ous).

syn- *prefix* **1** with or together: *synecology*. **2** fusion: *syngamy*. [from Gk *sun* together]

synaeresis (sɪ'nɪərɪsɪs) *n* a variant spelling of **syneresis**.

synaesthesia *or US* **synesthesia** (,sɪniːs'θiːzɪə) *n* **1** *Physiol.* a sensation experienced in a part of the body other than the part stimulated. **2** *Psychol.* the subjective sensation of a sense other than the one being stimulated. [C19: from NL, from SYN- + *-esthesia*, from Gk *aisthēsis* sensation]
▸ **synaesthetic** *or US* **synesthetic** (,sɪniːs'θɛtɪk) *adj*

synagogue ('sɪnə,gɒg) *n* **1a** a building for Jewish religious services and religious instruction. **1b** (*as modifier*): *synagogue services.* **2** a congregation of Jews who assemble for worship or religious study. **3** the religion of Judaism as organized in such congregations. [C12: from OF, from LL *synagōga*, from Gk *sunagōgē* a gathering, from *sunagein* to bring together]
▸ **synagogical** (,sɪnə'gɒdʒɪk^əl) *or* **synagogal** ('sɪnə,gɒg^əl) *adj*

synapse ('saɪnæps) *n* the point at which a nerve impulse is relayed from the terminal portion of an axon to the dendrites of an adjacent neuron.

synapsis (sɪ'næpsɪs) *n, pl* **synapses** (-siːz). **1** *Cytology.* the association in pairs of homologous chromosomes at the start of meiosis. **2** another word for **synapse**. [C19: from NL, from Gk *sunapsis* junction, from *sunaptein* to join together]
▸ **synaptic** (sɪ'næptɪk) *adj* ▸ **syn'aptically** *adv*

synarthrosis (,sɪnɑː'θrəʊsɪs) *n, pl* **synarthroses** (-siːz). *Anat.* any of various joints which lack a synovial cavity and are virtually immovable; a fixed joint. [C16: via NL from Gk *sunarthrōsis*, from *sunarthrousthai* to be connected by joints, from *sun-* SYN- + *arthron* a joint]
▸ ,**synar'throdial** *adj*

sync *or* **synch** (sɪŋk) *Films, television, computing.* ♦ *vb* **1** an informal word for **synchronize**. ♦ *n* **2** an informal word for **synchronization** (esp. in **in** or **out of sync**).

syncarp ('sɪnkɑːp) *n Bot.* a fleshy multiple fruit, formed from two or more carpels of one flower or the aggregated fruits of several flowers. [C19: from NL *syncarpium*, from SYN- + Gk *karpos* fruit]

syncarpous (sɪn'kɑːpəs) *adj* **1** (of the ovaries of certain flowering plants) consisting of united carpels. **2** of or relating to a syncarp.

synchro ('sɪŋkrəʊ) *n, pl* **synchros**. **1** Also called: **selsyn**. any of a number of electrical devices in which the angular position of a rotating part is transformed into a voltage, or vice versa. **2** short for **synchronized swimming**.

synchro- *combining form.* indicating synchronization: *synchromesh*.

synchrocyclotron (,sɪŋkrəʊ'saɪklə,trɒn) *n* a cyclotron in which the frequency of the electric field is modulated to allow for relativistic effects at high velocities and thus produce higher energies.

synchromesh ('sɪŋkrəʊ,mɛʃ) *adj* **1** (of a gearbox, etc.) having a system of clutches that synchronizes the speeds of the driving and driven members before engagement to avoid shock in gear changing and to reduce noise and wear. ♦ *n* **2** a gear system having these features. [C20: shortened from *synchronized mesh*]

synchronic (sɪn'krɒnɪk) *adj* **1** concerned with the events or phenomena at a particular period without considering historical antecedents: *synchronic linguistics*. Cf. **diachronic**. **2** synchronous.
▸ **syn'chronically** *adv* ▸ **synchronicity** (,sɪnkrə'nɪsɪtɪ) *n*

synchronicity (,sɪnkrə'nɪsɪtɪ) *n* an apparently meaningful coincidence in time of two or more similar or identical events that are causally unrelated. [C20: coined by Carl Jung from SYNCHRONIC + -ITY]

synchronism ('sɪŋkrə,nɪzəm) *n* **1** the quality or condition of being synchronous. **2** a chronological list of historical persons and events, arranged to show parallel or synchronous occurrence. **3** the representation in a work of art of one or more incidents that occurred at separate times. [C16: from Gk *sunkhronismos*]
▸ ,**synchro'nistic** *or* ,**synchro'nistical** *adj* ▸ ,**synchro'nistically** *adv*

synchronize *or* **synchronise** ('sɪŋkrə,naɪz) *vb* **synchronizes, synchronizing, synchronized** *or* **synchronises, synchronising, synchronised**. **1** (when *intr*, usually foll. by *with*) to occur or recur or cause to occur or recur at the same time or in unison. **2** to indicate or cause to indicate the same time: *synchronize your watches.* **3** (*tr*) *Films.* to establish (the picture and soundtrack records) in their correct relative position. **4** (*tr*) to designate (events) as simultaneous.
▸ ,**synchroni'zation** *or* ,**synchroni'sation** *n* ▸ '**synchro,nizer** *or* '**synchro,niser** *n*

synchronized swimming *n* a sport in which swimmers move in patterns in time to music. Sometimes shortened to **synchro** *or* **synchro swimming**.

synchronous ('sɪŋkrənəs) *adj* **1** occurring at the same time. **2** *Physics.* (of periodic phenomena, such as voltages) having the same frequency and phase. **3** occurring or recurring exactly together and at the same rate. [C17: from LL *synchronus*, from Gk *sunkhronos*, from SYN- + *khronos* time]
▸ '**synchronously** *adv* ▸ '**synchronousness** *n*

synchronous machine *n* an electrical machine whose rotating speed is proportional to the frequency of the alternating-current supply and independent of the load.

synchronous motor *n* an alternating-current motor that runs at a speed that is equal to or is a multiple of the frequency of the supply.

synchrony ('sɪŋkrənɪ) *n* the state of being synchronous; simultaneity.

synchrotron ('sɪŋkrə,trɒn) *n* a particle accelerator having an electric field of fixed frequency and a changing magnetic field. [C20: from SYNCHRO- + (ELEC)TRON]

syncline ('sɪŋklaɪn) *n* a downward fold of stratified rock in which the strata slope towards a vertical axis. [C19: from SYN- + Gk *klīnein* to lean]
▸ **syn'clinal** *adj*

Syncom ('sɪn,kɒm) *n* a communications satellite in stationary orbit. [C20: from *syn(chronous) com(munication)*]

syncopate ('sɪŋkə,peɪt) *vb* **syncopates, syncopating, syncopated**. (*tr*) **1** *Music.* to modify or treat (a beat, rhythm, note, etc.) by syncopation. **2** to shorten (a word) by omitting sounds or letters from the middle. [C17: from Med. L *syncopāre* to omit a letter or syllable, from LL *syncopa* SYNCOPE]
▸ '**synco,pator** *n*

syncopation (,sɪŋkə'peɪʃən) *n* **1** *Music.* **1a** the displacement of the usual rhythmic accent away from a strong beat onto a weak beat. **1b** a note, beat, rhythm, etc., produced by syncopation. **2** another word for **syncope** (sense 2).

syncope ('sɪŋkəpɪ) *n* **1** a technical word for a **faint**. **2** the omission of sounds or letters from the middle of a word. [C16: from LL *syncopa*, from Gk *sunkopē* a cutting off, from SYN- + *koptein* to cut]
▸ **syncopic** (sɪn'kɒpɪk) *or* '**syncopal** *adj*

★ people and places

syncretism ('sɪŋkrɪˌtɪzəm) n **1** the tendency to syncretize. **2** the historical tendency of languages to reduce their use of inflection, as in the development of Old English into Modern English. [C17: from NL *syncrētismus*, from Gk *sunkrētismos* alliance of Cretans, from *sunkrētizein* to join forces (in the manner of the Cretan towns), from SYN- + *Krēs* a Cretan]
▶ **syncretic** (sɪŋ'krɛtɪk) or ˌsyncre'tistic adj ▶ 'syncretist n

syncretize or **syncretise** ('sɪŋkrɪˌtaɪz) vb **syncretizes, syncretizing, syncretized** or **syncretises, syncretising, syncretised.** to attempt to combine the characteristic teachings, beliefs, or practices of (differing systems of religion or philosophy).
▶ ˌsyncreti'zation or ˌsyncreti'sation n

syndactyl (sɪn'dæktɪl) adj **1** (of certain animals) having two or more digits growing fused together. ◆ n **2** an animal with this arrangement of digits.
▶ syn'dactylism n

syndesmosis (ˌsɪndɛs'məʊsɪs) n, pl **syndesmoses** (-siːz). *Anat.* a type of joint in which the articulating bones are held together by a ligament of connective tissue. [C18: NL, from Gk *sundein* to bind together]
▶ **syndesmotic** (ˌsɪndɛs'mɒtɪk) adj

syndetic (sɪn'dɛtɪk) adj denoting a grammatical construction in which two clauses are connected by a conjunction. [C17: from Gk *sundetikos*, from *sundetos* bound together]
▶ **syndesis** (sɪn'diːsɪs) n ▶ syn'detically adv

syndic ('sɪndɪk) n **1** *Brit.* a business agent of some universities or other bodies. **2** (in several countries) a government administrator or magistrate with varying powers. [C17: via OF from LL *syndicus*, from Gk *sundikos* defendant's advocate, from SYN- + *dikē* justice]
▶ 'syndical adj

syndicalism ('sɪndɪkəˌlɪzəm) n **1** a revolutionary movement and theory advocating seizure of the means of production and distribution by syndicates of workers, esp. by a general strike. **2** an economic system resulting from such action.
▶ 'syndical adj ▶ 'syndicalist adj, n ▶ ˌsyndical'istic adj

syndicate n ('sɪndɪkɪt). **1** an association of business enterprises or individuals organized to undertake a joint project. **2** a news agency that sells articles, photographs, etc., to a number of newspapers for simultaneous publication. **3** any association formed to carry out an enterprise of common interest to its members. **4** a board of syndics or the office of syndic. ◆ vb ('sɪndɪˌkeɪt) **syndicates, syndicating, syndicated. 5** (tr) to sell (articles, photographs, etc.) to several newspapers for simultaneous publication. **6** (tr) *US.* to sell (a programme or programmes) to several local commercial stations. **7** to form a syndicate of (people). [C17: from OF *syndicat* office of a SYNDIC]
▶ ˌsyndi'cation n

syndicated research n *Marketing.* a large-scale marketing research project undertaken without being commissioned and subsequently offered to interested parties.

syndrome ('sɪndrəʊm) n **1** *Med.* any combination of signs and symptoms that are indicative of a particular disease or disorder. **2** a symptom, characteristic, or set of symptoms or characteristics indicating the existence of a condition, problem, etc. [C16: via NL from Gk *sundrom*, lit.: a running together, from SYN- + *dramein* to run]
▶ **syndromic** (sɪn'drɒmɪk) adj

syne or **sync** (saɪn) adv, prep, conj a Scottish word for **since.** [C14: prob. rel. to OE *sīth* since]

synecdoche (sɪn'ɛkdəkɪ) n a figure of speech in which a part is substituted for a whole or a whole for a part, as in *50 head of cattle* for *50 cows,* or *the army* for *a soldier.* [C14: via L from Gk *sunekdokhē*, from SYN- + *ekdokhē* interpretation, from *dekhesthai* to accept]
▶ **synecdochic** (ˌsɪnɛk'dɒkɪk) or ˌsynec'dochical adj

synecious (sɪ'niːʃəs) adj a variant spelling of **synoecious.**

synecology (ˌsɪnɪ'kɒlədʒɪ) n the ecological study of communities of plants and animals.
▶ **synecologic** (sɪnˌɛkə'lɒdʒɪk) or synˌeco'logical adj ▶ synˌeco'logically adv

syneresis or **synaeresis** (sɪ'nɪərɪsɪs) n **1** *Chem.* the process in which a gel contracts on standing and exudes liquid, as in the separation of whey in cheese-making. **2** the contraction of two vowels into a diphthong. [C16: via LL from Gk *sunairesis* a shortening, from *sunairein* to draw together, from SYN- + *hairein* to take]

synergism ('sɪnəˌdʒɪzəm, sɪ'nɜː-) n **1** Also called: **synergy.** the working together of two or more drugs, muscles, etc., to produce an effect greater than the sum of their individual effects. **2** another name for **synergy** (sense 1). [C18: from NL *synergismus*, from Gk *sunergos*, from SYN- + *ergon* work]
▶ ˌsyner'getic adj ▶ 'synergist n, adj

synergy ('sɪnədʒɪ) n, pl **synergies. 1** Also called: **synergism.** the potential ability of individual organizations or groups to be more successful or productive as a result of a merger. **2** another name for **synergism** (sense 1). [C19: from NL *synergia*, from Gk *sunergos*; see SYNERGISM]
▶ sy'nergic adj

synesis ('sɪnɪsɪs) n a grammatical construction in which the inflection or form of a word is conditioned by the meaning rather than the syntax, as for example the plural form *have* with the singular noun *group* in the sentence *the group have already assembled.* [via NL from Gk *sunesis* union, from *sunienai* to bring together, from SYN- + *hienai* to send]

synesthesia (ˌsɪniːs'θiːzɪə) n the usual US spelling of **synaesthesia.**

syngamy ('sɪŋgəmɪ) or **syngenesis** (sɪn'dʒɛnɪsɪs) n reproduction involving the fusion of a male and female haploid gamete. Also called: **sexual reproduction.**
▶ **syngamic** (sɪŋ'gæmɪk) or **syngamous** ('sɪŋgəməs) adj

Synge ★ (sɪŋ) n **John Millington.** 1871–1909, Irish playwright. His plays, marked by vivid colloquial Irish speech, include *Riders to the Sea* (1904) and *The Playboy of the Western World,* produced amidst uproar at the Abbey Theatre, Dublin, in 1907.

synod ('sɪnəd, 'sɪnɒd) n **1** a special ecclesiastical council, esp. of a diocese, formally convened to discuss ecclesiastical affairs. **2** *Rare.* any council, esp. for discussion. [C14: from LL *synodus*, from Gk SYN- + *hodos* a way]
▶ 'synodal adj

synodic (sɪ'nɒdɪk) adj relating to or involving a conjunction or two successive conjunctions of the same star, planet, or satellite.

synodic month n See **month** (sense 6).

synoecious or **synecious** (sɪ'niːʃəs) adj (of plants) having male and female organs on the same flower or structure. [C19: SYN- + -*oecious,* from Gk *oikion* dim. of *oikos* house]

synonym ('sɪnənɪm) n **1** a word that means the same or nearly the same as another word, such as *bucket* and *pail.* **2** a word or phrase used as another name for something, such as *Hellene* for a Greek.
▶ ˌsyno'nymic or ˌsyno'nymical adj ▶ ˌsyno'nymity n

synonymous (sɪ'nɒnɪməs) adj **1** (often foll. by *with*) being a synonym (of). **2** (*postpositive;* foll. by *with*) closely associated (with) or suggestive (of): *his name was synonymous with greed.*
▶ syn'onymously adv ▶ syn'onymousness n

synonymy (sɪ'nɒnɪmɪ) n, pl **synonymies. 1** the study of synonyms. **2** the character of being synonymous; equivalence. **3** a list or collection of synonyms, esp. one in which their meanings are discriminated.

synopsis (sɪ'nɒpsɪs) n, pl **synopses** (-siːz). a brief review of a subject; summary. [C17: via LL from Gk *sunopsis*, from SYN- + *opsis* view]

synopsize or **synopsise** (sɪ'nɒpsaɪz) vb **synopsizes, synopsizing, synopsized** or **synopsises, synopsising, synopsised.** (tr) **1** *US.* variants of **epitomize. 2** *US & Canad.* to make a synopsis of.

synoptic (sɪ'nɒptɪk) adj **1** of or relating to a synopsis. **2** (*often cap.*) *Bible.* **2a** (of the Gospels of Matthew, Mark, and Luke) presenting the narrative of Christ's life, ministry, etc., from a point of view held in common by all three, and with close similarities in content, order, etc. **2b** of or relating to these three Gospels. **3** *Meteorol.* concerned with the distribution of meteorological condi-

tions over a wide area at a given time: *a synoptic chart.*
♦ *n* **4** (*often cap.*) *Bible.* **4a** any of the three synoptic Gospels. **4b** any of the authors of these. [C18: from Gk *sunoptikos*]
▸ syn'optically *adv* ▸ syn'optist *n*

synovia (saɪˈnəʊvɪə, sɪ-) *n* a transparent viscid lubricating fluid, secreted by the membrane lining joints, tendon sheaths, etc. [C17: from NL, prob. from SYN- + L *ōvum* egg]
▸ syn'ovial *adj*

synovitis (ˌsaɪnəʊˈvaɪtɪs, ˌsɪn-) *n* inflammation of the membrane surrounding a joint.
▸ synovitic (ˌsaɪnəʊˈvɪtɪk, ˌsɪn-) *adj*

synroc (ˈsɪnˌrɒk) *n* a titanium-ceramic substance that can incorporate nuclear waste in its crystals. [from *syn*(*thetic*) + *roc*(*k*)]

syntactics (sɪnˈtæktɪks) *n* (*functioning as sing*) the branch of semiotics that deals with the formal properties of symbol systems; proof theory.

syntagma (sɪnˈtægmə) *or* **syntagm** (ˈsɪnˌtæm) *n, pl* **syntagmata** (-ˈtægmətə) *or* **syntagms.** **1** a word or phrase forming a syntactic unit. **2** a systematic collection of statements or propositions. [C17: from LL, from Gk, from *suntassein* to put in order; see SYNTAX]
▸ ˌsyntag'matic *adj*

syntax (ˈsɪntæks) *n* **1** the branch of linguistics that deals with the grammatical arrangement of words and morphemes in sentences. **2** the totality of facts about the grammatical arrangement of words in a language. **3** a systematic statement of the rules governing the grammatical arrangement of words and morphemes in a language. **4** a systematic statement of the rules governing the properly formed formulas of a logical system. [C17: from LL *syntaxis*, from Gk *suntaxis*, from *suntassein* to put in order, from SYN- + *tassein* to arrange]
▸ syn'tactic *or* syn'tactical *adj* ▸ syn'tactically *adv*

synth (sɪnθ) *n* short for **synthesizer.**

synthesis (ˈsɪnθɪsɪs) *n, pl* **syntheses** (-ˌsiːz). **1** the process of combining objects or ideas into a complex whole. **2** the combination or whole produced by such a process. **3** the process of producing a compound by a chemical reaction or series of reactions, usually from simpler starting materials. **4** *Linguistics.* the use of inflections rather than word order and function words to express the syntactic relations in a language. [C17: via L from Gk *sunthesis*, from *suntithenai* to put together, from SYN- + *tithenai* to place]
▸ 'synthesist *n*

synthesis gas *n Chem.* **1** a mixture of carbon dioxide, carbon monoxide, and hydrogen formerly made by reacting water gas with steam to enrich the proportion of hydrogen in the synthesis of ammonia. **2** a similar mixture of gases made by steam reforming natural gas, used for synthesizing organic chemicals and as a fuel.

synthesize (ˈsɪnθɪˌsaɪz), **synthetize**, *or* **synthesise, synthetise** *vb* **synthesizes, synthesizing, synthesized; synthetizes, synthetizing, synthetized** *or* **synthesises, synthesising, synthesised; synthetises, synthetising, synthetised.** **1** to combine or cause to combine into a whole. **2** (*tr*) to produce by synthesis.
▸ ˌsynthesi'zation, ˌsynthetiˈzation *or* ˌsynthesi'sation, ˌsyntheti'sation *n*

synthesizer (ˈsɪnθɪˌsaɪzə) *n* **1** an electronic musical instrument, usually operated by means of a keyboard, in which sounds are produced by oscillators, filters, and amplifiers. **2** a person or thing that synthesizes.

synthetic (sɪnˈθetɪk) *adj also* **synthetical.** **1** (of a substance or material) made artificially by chemical reaction. **2** not genuine; insincere: *synthetic compassion.* **3** denoting languages, such as Latin, whose morphology is characterized by synthesis. **4** *Philosophy.* **4a** (of a proposition) having a truth-value that is not determined solely by virtue of the meanings of the words, as in *all men are arrogant.* **4b** contingent. ♦ *n* **5** a synthetic substance or material. [C17: from NL *syntheticus*, from Gk *sunthetikos* expert in putting together, from *suntithenai* to put together; see SYNTHESIS]
▸ syn'thetically *adv*

syphilis (ˈsɪfɪlɪs) *n* a sexually transmitted disease caused by infection with the microorganism *Treponema pallidum:* characterized by an ulcerating chancre, usually on the genitals and progressing through the lymphatic system to nearly all tissues of the body, producing serious clinical manifestations. [C18: from NL *Syphilis* (*sive Morbus Gallicus*) "Syphilis (or the French disease)", title of a poem (1530) by G. Fracastoro, It. physician and poet, in which a shepherd *Syphilus* is portrayed as the first victim of the disease]
▸ syphilitic (ˌsɪfɪˈlɪtɪk) *adj* ▸ 'syphiˌloid *adj*

syphon (ˈsaɪfˀn) *n, vb* a variant spelling of **siphon.**

Syr. *abbrev. for:* **1** Syria. **2** Syriac. **3** Syrian.

Syracuse ★ *n* **1** (ˈsaɪrəˌkjuːz). a port in SW Italy, in SE Sicily on the Ionian Sea: founded in 734 B.C. by Greeks from Corinth and taken by the Romans in 212 B.C., after a siege of three years. Pop.: 127 496 (1994 est.). Italian name: **Siracusa.** **2** (ˈsɪrəˌkjuːs). a city in central New York State, on Lake Onondaga: site of the capital of the Iroquois Indian federation. Pop.: 159 895 (1994 est.).

Syr Darya ★ (*Russian* si darjˈja) *n* a river in central Asia, formed from two headstreams rising in the Tian Shan: flows generally west to the Aral Sea: the longest river in central Asia. Length: (from the source of the Naryn) 2900 km (1800 miles). Ancient name: **Jaxartes.**

Syria ★ *n* **1** a republic in W Asia, on the Mediterranean: ruled by the Ottoman Turks (1516–1918); made a French mandate in 1920; became independent in 1944; joined Egypt in the United Arab Republic (1958–61). Official language: Arabic. Religion: Muslim majority. Currency: Syrian pound. Capital: Damascus. Pop.: 15 009 000 (1997). Area: 185 180 sq. km (71 498 sq. miles). **2** (formerly) the region between the Mediterranean, the Euphrates, the Taurus, and the Arabian Desert.

Syriac (ˈsɪrɪˌæk) *n* a dialect of Aramaic spoken in Syria until about the 13th century A.D.

Syrian (ˈsɪrɪən) *adj* **1** of or relating to Syria, its people, or their dialect of Arabic. ♦ *n* **2** a native or inhabitant of Syria.

syringa (sɪˈrɪŋgə) *n* another name for **mock orange** (sense 1) or **lilac** (sense 1). [C17: from NL, from Gk *surinx* tube, from use of its hollow stems for pipes]

syringe (ˈsɪrɪndʒ, sɪˈrɪndʒ) *n* **1** *Med.* a hypodermic syringe or a rubber ball with a slender nozzle, for use in withdrawing or injecting fluids, cleaning wounds, etc. **2** any similar device for injecting, spraying, or extracting liquids by means of pressure or suction. ♦ *vb* **syringes, syringing, syringed.** **3** (*tr*) to cleanse, inject, or spray with a syringe. [C15: from LL, from L: SYRINX]

syringomyelia (səˌrɪŋgəʊmaɪˈiːlɪə) *n* a chronic progressive disease of the spinal cord in which cavities form in the grey matter: characterized by loss of the sense of pain and temperature. [C19: *syringo*-, from Gk: SYRINX + *-myelia* from Gk *muelos* marrow]
▸ syringomyelic (səˌrɪŋgəʊmaɪˈelɪk) *adj*

syrinx (ˈsɪrɪŋks) *n, pl* **syringes** (sɪˈrɪndʒiːz) *or* **syrinxes. 1** the vocal organ of a bird, situated in the lower part of the trachea. **2** (in classical Greek music) a panpipe or set of panpipes. [C17: via L from Gk *surinx* pipe]
▸ syringeal (sɪˈrɪndʒɪəl) *adj*

Syrinx ★ (ˈsɪrɪŋks) *n Greek myth.* a nymph who was changed into a reed to save her from the amorous pursuit of Pan. From this reed Pan then fashioned his musical pipes.

syrup (ˈsɪrəp) *n* **1** a solution of sugar dissolved in water and often flavoured with fruit juice: used for sweetening fruit, etc. **2** any of various thick sweet liquids prepared for cooking or table use from molasses, sugars, etc. **3** *Inf.* cloying sentimentality. **4** a liquid medicine containing a sugar solution for flavouring or preservation. ♦ *Also:* **sirup.** [C15: from Med. L *syrupus*, from Ar. *sharāb* a drink, from *shariba* to drink]
▸ 'syrupy *adj*

syssarcosis (ˌsɪsɑːˈkəʊsɪs) *n, pl* **syssarcoses** (-siːz). *Anat.* the union or articulation of bones by muscle. [C17: from NL, from Gk *sussarkōsis*, from *sus-* SYN- + *sarkoun* to become fleshy, from *sarx* flesh]
▸ syssarcotic (ˌsɪsɑːˈkɒtɪk) *adj*

systaltic (sı'stæltık) *adj* (esp. of the action of the heart) of, relating to, or characterized by alternate contractions and dilations; pulsating. [C17: from LL *systalticus*, from Gk, from *sustellein* to contract, from SYN- + *stellein* to place]

system ('sıstəm) *n* **1** a group or combination of interrelated, interdependent, or interacting elements forming a collective entity; a methodical or coordinated assemblage of parts, facts, etc. **2** any scheme of classification or arrangement. **3** a network of communications, transportation, or distribution. **4** a method or complex of methods: *he has a perfect system at roulette*. **5** orderliness; an ordered manner. **6 the system.** (*often cap.*) society seen as an environment exploiting, restricting, and repressing individuals. **7** an organism considered as a functioning entity. **8** any of various bodily parts or structures that are anatomically or physiologically related: *the digestive system*. **9** one's physiological or psychological constitution: *get it out of your system*. **10** any assembly of electronic, mechanical, etc., components with interdependent functions, usually forming a self-contained unit: *a brake system*. **11** a group of celestial bodies that are associated as a result of natural laws, esp. gravitational attraction: *the solar system*. **12** a point of view or doctrine used to interpret a branch of knowledge. **13** *Mineralogy*. one of a group of divisions into which crystals may be placed on the basis of the lengths and inclinations of their axes. **14** *Geol*. a stratigraphical unit for the rock strata formed during a period of geological time. [C17: from F, from LL *systēma*, from Gk *sustēma*, from SYN- + *histanai* to cause to stand]

systematic (,sıstı'mætık) *adj* **1** characterized by the use of order and planning; methodical: *a systematic administrator*. **2** comprising or resembling a system: *systematic theology*. **3** Also: **systematical**. *Biol*. of or relating to taxonomic classification.
▸ ,system'atically *adv* ▸ 'systema,tism *n* ▸ 'systematist *n*

systematics (,sıstı'mætıks) *n* (*functioning as sing*) the study of systems and the principles of classification and nomenclature.

systematize ('sıstımə,taız), **systemize** *or* **systematise, systemise** *vb* systematizes, systematizing, systematized; systemizes, systemizing, systemized *or* systematises, systematising, systematised; systemises, systemising, systemised. (*tr*) to arrange in a system.
▸ ,systemati'zation, ,systemati'sation *or* ,systemi'zation, ,systemi'sation *n* ▸ 'systema,tizer, 'systema,tiser *or* 'syste,mizer, 'syste,miser *n*

system building *n* a method of building in which prefabricated components are used to speed the construction of buildings.
▸ ,system 'built *adj*

Système International d'Unités (*French* sistεm ε̃tεrnasjɔnal dynite) *n* the International System of units. See **SI unit.**

systemic (sı'stεmık, -'sti:-) *adj* **1** another word for **system-atic** (senses 1, 2). **2** *Physiol*. (of a poison, disease, etc.) affecting the entire body. **3** (of an insecticide, fungicide, etc.) designed to be absorbed by a plant into its tissues.
◆ *n* **4** a systemic insecticide, fungicide, etc.
▸ sys'temically *adv*

systems analysis *n* the analysis of the requirements of a task and the expression of these in a form that permits the assembly of computer hardware and software to perform the task.
▸ **systems analyst** *n*

systems engineering *n* the branch of engineering, based on systems analysis and information theory, concerned with the design of integrated systems.

systole ('sıstəlı) *n* contraction of the heart, during which blood is pumped into the aorta and the arteries. Cf. **diastole.** [C16: via LL from Gk *sustolē*, from *sustellein* to contract; see SYSTALTIC]
▸ **systolic** (sı'stɒlık) *adj*

Syzran ★ (*Russian* 'sizrənj) *n* a port in W central Russia, in Samara Region on the Volga River: oil refining. Pop.: 177 000 (1995 est.).

syzygy ('sızıdʒı) *n, pl* **syzygies. 1** either of the two positions (conjunction or opposition) of a celestial body when sun, earth, and the body lie in a straight line: *the moon is at syzygy when full*. **2** *Rare*. any pair, usually of opposites. [C17: from LL, from Gk *suzugia*, from *suzugos* yoked together, from SYN- + *zugon* a yoke]
▸ **syzygial** (sı'zıdʒıəl), **syzygetic** (,sızı'dʒεtık), *or* **syzygal** ('sızıg'l) *adj* ▸ ,syzy'getically *adv*

Szabadka ★ ('sɔbɔtkɔ) *n* the Hungarian name for **Subotica.**

Szczecin ★ (*Polish* 'ʃtʃεtʃin) *n* a port in NW Poland, on the River Oder: the busiest Polish port and leading coal exporter; shipbuilding. Pop.: 419 600 (1995 est.). German name: **Stettin.**

Szechwan ★ ('sεt'ʃwɑ:n) *n* a variant transliteration of the Chinese name for **Sichuan.**

Szeged ★ (*Hungarian* 'sεgεd) *n* an industrial city in S Hungary, on the Tisza River. Pop.: 167 000 (1996).

Szell ★ (sεl) *n* **George.** 1897–1970, US conductor, born in Hungary.

Szent-Györgyi ★ (*Hungarian* 'sεntdjørdji) *n* **Albert (von Nagyrapolt).** 1893–1986, US biochemist, born in Hungary, who isolated ascorbic acid and identified it as vitamin C. Nobel prize for physiology or medicine 1937.

Szilard ★ ('sıla:d) *n* **Leo.** 1898–1964, US physicist, born in Hungary, who worked on the atomic bomb during World War II.

Szombathely ★ (*Hungarian* 'sombɔthεj) *n* a city in W Hungary: site of the Roman capital of Pannonia. Pop.: 84 000 (1995 est.).

Szymanowski ★ (*Polish* ʃima'nɔfski) *n* **Karol** ('karɔl). 1882–1937, Polish composer, whose works include the opera *King Roger* (1926), two violin concertos, symphonies, piano music, and songs.

★ people and places

Tt

t *or* **T** (tiː) *n, pl* **t's, T's,** *or* **Ts. 1** the 20th letter of the English alphabet. **2** a speech sound represented by this letter. **3** something shaped like a T. **4 to a T.** in every detail; perfectly.

t *symbol for:* **1** *Statistics.* distribution. **2** tonne(s). **3** troy (weight).

T *symbol for:* **1** absolute temperature. **2** surface tension. **3** tera-. **4** tesla. **5** *Chem.* tritium. **6** *Biochem.* thymine.

t. *abbrev. for:* **1** *Commerce.* tare. **2** teaspoon(ful). **3** temperature. **4** *Music.* tempo. **5** *Music.* Also: **T.** tenor. **6** *Grammar.* tense. **7** ton(s). **8** transitive.

't *contraction of* it.

ta (taː) *interj Brit. inf.* thank you.   [C18: imit. of baby talk]

Ta the chemical symbol for tantalum.

TA (in Britain) *abbrev. for* Territorial Army (now superseded by **TAVR**).

taal (taːl) *n S. African* language: usually, by implication, Afrikaans. [Afrik. from Du.]

Taal ★ (taːˈɑːl) *n* an active volcano in the Philippines, on S Luzon on an island in the centre of **Lake Taal**. Height: 300 m (984 ft). Area of lake: 243 sq. km (94 sq. miles).

tab[1] (tæb) *n* **1** a small flap of material, esp. one on a garment for decoration or for fastening to a button. **2** any similar flap, such as a piece of paper attached to a file for identification. **3** *Brit. mil.* the insignia on the collar of a staff officer. **4** *Chiefly US & Canad.* a bill, esp. for a meal or drinks. **5 keep tabs on.** *Inf.* to keep a watchful eye on.   ◆ *vb* **tabs, tabbing, tabbed. 6** (*tr*) to supply with a tab or tabs. [C17: from ?]

tab[2] (tæb) *n* short for **tabulator** or **tablet**.

TAB *abbrev. for:* **1** *Austral. & NZ.* Totalizator Agency Board. **2** typhoid-paratyphoid A and B (vaccine).

tabard ('tæbəd) *n* a sleeveless or short-sleeved jacket, esp. one worn by a herald, bearing a coat of arms, or by a knight over his armour. [C13: from OF *tabart*, from ?]

tabaret ('tæbərɪt) *n* a hard-wearing fabric of silk or similar cloth with stripes of satin or moire, used esp. for upholstery. [C19: ? from TABBY[1]]

Tabasco[1] (təˈbæskəʊ) *n Trademark.* a very hot red sauce made from matured capsicums.

Tabasco[2] ★ (*Spanish* taˈβasko) *n* a state in SE Mexico, on the Gulf of Campeche: mostly flat and marshy with extensive jungles; hot and humid climate. Capital: Villahermosa. Pop.: 1 748 664 (1995 est.). Area: 24 661 sq. km (9520 sq. miles).

tabby[1] ('tæbɪ) *n* a fabric with a watered pattern, esp. silk or taffeta. [C17: from OF *tabis* silk cloth, from Ar. *al-'attabiya*, lit.: the quarter of (Prince) 'Attab, the part of Baghdad where the fabric was first made]

tabby[2] ('tæbɪ) *adj* **1** (esp. of cats) brindled with dark stripes or wavy markings on a lighter background. **2** having a wavy or striped pattern, particularly in colours of grey and brown.   ◆ *n, pl* **tabbies. 3** a tabby cat. **4** any female domestic cat. [C17: from *Tabby,* pet form of the girl's name *Tabitha,* prob. infl. by TABBY[1]]

tabernacle ('tæbə,nækəl) *n* **1** (*often cap.*) *Old Testament.* **1a** the portable sanctuary in which the ancient Israelites carried the Ark of the Covenant. **1b** the Jewish Temple. **2** any place of worship that is not called a church. **3** *RC Church.* a receptacle in which the Blessed Sacrament is kept. **4** *Chiefly RC Church.* a canopied niche. **5** *Naut.* a strong framework for holding the foot of a mast, allowing it to be swung down to pass under low bridges, etc. [C13: from L *tabernāculum* a tent, from *taberna* a hut]
▸ **taber'nacular** *adj*

tabes ('teɪbiːz) *n, pl* **tabes. 1** a wasting of a bodily organ or part. **2** short for **tabes dorsalis**. [C17: L: a wasting away]
▸ **tabetic** (təˈbɛtɪk) *adj*

tabescent (təˈbɛsənt) *adj* **1** progressively emaciating; wasting away. **2** of, relating to, or having tabes. [C19: from L *tābēscere,* from TABES]
▸ **ta'bescence** *n*

tabes dorsalis (dɔːˈsɑːlɪs) *n* a form of late syphilis that attacks the spinal cord causing degeneration of the nerve fibres, paralysis of the leg muscles, acute abdominal pain, etc. [NL, lit.: tabes of the back]

tabla ('tʌblə, 'tɑːblɑː) *n* a musical instrument of India consisting of a pair of drums whose pitches can be varied. [Hindu, from Ar. *tabla* drum]

tablature ('tæblətʃə) *n Music.* any of a number of forms of musical notation, esp. for playing the lute, consisting of letters and signs indicating rhythm and fingering. [C16: from F, ult. from L *tabulātum* wooden floor, from *tabula* a plank]

table ('teɪbəl) *n* **1** a flat horizontal slab or board, usually supported by one or more legs. **2a** such a slab or board on which food is served. **2b** (*as modifier*): table linen. **3** food as served in a particular household, etc.: *a good table.* **4** such a piece of furniture specially designed for any of various purposes: *a bird table.* **5a** a company of persons assembled for a meal, game, etc. **5b** (*as modifier*): table talk. **6** any flat or level area, such as a plateau. **7** a rectangular panel set below or above the face of a wall. **8** *Archit.* another name for **string course. 9** any of various flat surfaces, as an upper horizontal facet of a cut gem. **10** *Music.* the sounding board of a violin, guitar, etc. **11a** an arrangement of words, numbers, or signs, usually in parallel columns. **11b** See **multiplication table. 12** a tablet on which laws were inscribed by the ancient Romans, the Hebrews, etc. **13 turn the tables.** to cause a complete reversal of circumstances. **14 under the table. 14a** (**under-the-table** *when prenominal*) done illicitly and secretly. **14b** *Sl.* drunk.   ◆ *vb* **tables, tabling, tabled.** (*tr*) **15** to place on a table. **16** *Brit.* to submit (a bill, etc.) for consideration by a legislative body. **17** *US.* to suspend discussion of (a bill, etc.) indefinitely. **18** to enter in or form into a list. [C12: via OF from L *tabula* a writing tablet]

tableau ('tæbləʊ) *n, pl* **tableaux** (-ləʊ, -ləʊz) *or* **tableaus. 1** See **tableau vivant. 2** a pause on stage when all the performers briefly freeze in position. **3** any dramatic group or scene. [C17: from F, from OF *tablel* a picture, dim. of TABLE]

tableau vivant *French.* (tablo vivɑ̃) *n, pl* **tableaux vivants** (tablo vivɑ̃). a representation of a scene by a person or group posed silent and motionless. [C19, lit.: living picture]

Table Bay ★ *n* the large bay on which Cape Town is situated, on the SW coast of South Africa.

tablecloth ('teɪbəl,klɒθ) *n* a cloth for covering the top of a table, esp. during meals.

table d'hôte ('tɑːbəl 'dəʊt) *adj* **1** (of a meal) consisting of a set number of courses with limited choice of dishes offered at a fixed price. Cf. **à la carte.**   ◆ *n, pl* **tables d'hôte** ('tɑːbəlz 'dəʊt). **2** a table d'hôte meal or menu. [C17: from F, lit.: the host's table]

tableland ('teɪbəl,lænd) *n* flat elevated land.

table licence *n* a licence authorizing the sale of alcoholic drinks with meals only.

Table Mountain ★ *n* a mountain in SW South Africa, overlooking Cape Town and Table Bay: flat-topped and steep-sided. Height: 1087 m (3567 ft).

tablespoon ('teɪbəl,spuːn) *n* **1** a spoon, larger than a dessertspoon, used for serving food, etc. **2** Also called: **tablespoonful.** the amount contained in such a spoon. **3** a unit of capacity used in cooking, etc., equal to half a fluid ounce.

tablet ('tæblɪt) *n* **1** a pill made of a compressed medicinal substance. **2** a flattish cake of some substance, such as soap. **3** a slab of stone, wood, etc., esp. one used for inscriptions. **4a** a rigid sheet, as of bark, etc., used for similar purposes. **4b** (*often pl*) a set of these fastened together. **5** a pad of writing paper. **6** *Scot.* a sweet made from butter, sugar, and condensed milk, usually shaped into flat oblong cakes. [C14: from OF *tablete* a little table, from L *tabula* a board]

table tennis *n* a miniature form of tennis played on a table with bats and a hollow ball.

table-turning *n* the movement of a table attributed by spiritualists to the power of spirits.

tableware ('teɪbˌlˌwɛə) *n* articles such as dishes, plates, knives, forks, etc., used at meals.

tabloid ('tæblɔɪd) *n* **1** a newspaper with pages about 30 cm (12 inches) by 40 cm (16 inches), usually with many photographs and a concise and often sensational style. **2** (*modifier*) designed to appeal to a mass audience or readership; sensationalist: *the tabloid press; tabloid television.* [C20: from earlier *Tabloid*, a trademark for a medicine in tablet form]

taboo *or* **tabu** (tə'bu:) *adj* **1** forbidden or disapproved of: *taboo words.* **2** (in Polynesia) marked off as sacred and forbidden. ◆ *n, pl* **taboos** *or* **tabus**. **3** any prohibition resulting from social or other conventions. **4** ritual restriction or prohibition, esp. of something that is considered holy or unclean. ◆ *vb* **5** (*tr*) to place under a taboo. [C18: from Tongan *tapu*]

tabor *or* **tabour** ('teɪbə) *n* a small drum used esp. in the Middle Ages, struck with one hand while the other held a pipe. [C13: from OF *tabour*, ?from Persian *tabīr*]

Tabor ★ ('teɪbə) *n* **Mount.** a mountain in N Israel, near Nazareth: traditionally regarded as the mountain where the Transfiguration took place. Height: 588 m (1929 ft).

taboret *or* **tabouret** ('tæbərɪt) *n* **1** a low stool. **2** a frame for stretching out cloth while it is being embroidered. **3** a small tabor. [C17: from F *tabouret*, dim. of TABOR]

Tabriz ★ (tæ'bri:z) *n* a city in NW Iran: an ancient city, situated in a volcanic region of hot springs; university (1947); carpet manufacturing. Pop.: 1 088 985 (1991). Ancient name: **Tauris** ('tɔ:rɪs).

tabular ('tæbjʊlə) *adj* **1** arranged in systematic or table form. **2** calculated from or by means of a table. **3** like a table in form; flat. [C17: from L *tabulāris* concerning boards, from *tabula* a board]
▸ **'tabularly** *adv*

tabula rasa ('tæbjʊlə 'rɑːsə) *n, pl* **tabulae rasae** ('tæbjuːliː 'rɑːsiː). **1** the mind in its uninformed original state. **2** an opportunity for a fresh start; clean slate. [L: a scraped tablet]

tabulate *vb* ('tæbjuˌleɪt), **tabulates, tabulating, tabulated.** (*tr*) **1** to set out, arrange, or write in tabular form. **2** to form or cut with a flat surface. ◆ *adj* ('tæbjʊlɪt, -ˌleɪt) **3** having a flat surface. [C18: from L *tabula* a board]
▸ **'tabulable** *adj* ▸ **ˌtabu'lation** *n*

tabulator ('tæbjuˌleɪtə) *n* **1** a device for setting the stops that locate the column margins on a typewriter. **2** *Computing.* a machine that reads data from one medium, such as punched cards, producing lists, tabulations, or totals.

tacamahac ('tækəməˌhæk) *or* **tacmahack** *n* **1** any of several strong-smelling resinous gums used in ointments, incense, etc. **2** any tree yielding this resin. [C16: from Sp. *tacamahaca*, from Nahuatl *tecomahca* aromatic resin]

tacet ('teɪsɛt, 'tæs-) *vb* (*intr*) (on a musical score) a direction indicating that a particular instrument or singer does not take part. [C18: from L: it is silent, from *tacēre* to be quiet]

tacheometer (ˌtækɪ'ɒmɪtə) *or* **tachymeter** *n* *Surveying.* a type of theodolite designed for the rapid measurement of distances, elevations, and directions.
▸ **ˌtache'ometry** *n*

tachisme ('tɑːʃɪzəm) *n* a type of action painting in which haphazard dabs and blots of colour are treated as a means of unconscious expression. [C20: F, from *tache* stain]

tachistoscope (tæ'kɪstəˌskəʊp) *n* an instrument for displaying visual images for very brief intervals, usually a fraction of a second. [C20: from Gk *takhistos* swiftest + -SCOPE]
▸ **tachistoscopic** (tæˌkɪstə'skɒpɪk) *adj*

tacho- *combining form.* speed: *tachograph; tachometer.* [from Gk *takhos*]

tachograph ('tækəˌgrɑːf) *n* a tachometer that produces a record (**tachogram**) of its readings, esp. a device for recording the speed of and distance covered by a vehicle. Often shortened to **tacho.**

tachometer (tæ'kɒmɪtə) *n* any device for measuring speed, esp. the rate of revolution of a shaft. Tachometers are often fitted to cars to indicate the number of revolutions per minute of the engine.
▸ **ta'chometry** *n*

tachy- *or* **tacheo-** *combining form.* swift or accelerated: *tachyon.* [from Gk *takhus* swift]

tachycardia (ˌtækɪ'kɑːdɪə) *n* abnormally rapid beating of the heart.

tachygraphy (tæ'kɪgrəfɪ) *n* shorthand, esp. as used in ancient Rome or Greece.

tachymeter (tæ'kɪmɪtə) *n* another name for **tacheometer.**

tachyon ('tækɪˌɒn) *n* *Physics.* a hypothetical elementary particle capable of travelling faster than the velocity of light. [C20: from TACHY- + -ON]

tachyphylaxis (ˌtækɪfɪ'læksɪs) *n* very rapid development of tolerance or immunity to the effects of a drug. [NL, from TACHY- + *phylaxis* on the model of *prophylaxis*; see PROPHYLACTIC]

tacit ('tæsɪt) *adj* implied or inferred without direct expression; understood: *a tacit agreement.* [C17: from L *tacitus*, p.p. of *tacēre* to be silent]
▸ **'tacitly** *adv*

taciturn ('tæsɪˌtɜːn) *adj* habitually silent, reserved, or uncommunicative. [C18: from L *taciturnus*, from *tacēre* to be silent]
▸ **ˌtaci'turnity** *n* ▸ **'taciˌturnly** *adv*

Tacitus ★ ('tæsɪtəs) *n* **Publius Cornelius** ('pʌblɪəs kɔː'niːljəs). ?55–?120 A.D., Roman historian. His works include the *Histories* and the *Annals.*

tack[1] (tæk) *n* **1** a short sharp-pointed nail, with a large flat head. **2** *Brit.* a long loose temporary stitch used in dressmaking, etc. **3** See **tailor's-tack. 4** a temporary fastening. **5** stickiness. **6** *Naut.* the heading of a vessel sailing to windward, stated in terms of the side of the sail against which the wind is pressing. **7** *Naut.* **7a** a course sailed with the wind blowing from forward of the beam. **7b** one such course or a zigzag pattern of such courses. **8** *Naut.* **8a** a sheet for controlling the weather clew of a course. **8b** the weather clew itself. **9** *Naut.* the forward lower clew of a fore-and-aft sail. **10** a course of action or policy. **11 on the wrong tack.** under a false impression. ◆ *vb* **12** (*tr*) to secure by a tack or tacks. **13** *Brit.* to sew (something) with long loose temporary stitches. **14** (*tr*) to attach or append. **15** *Naut.* to change the heading of (a sailing vessel) to the opposite tack. **16** *Naut.* to steer (a sailing vessel) on alternate tacks. **17** (*intr*) *Naut.* (of a sailing vessel) to proceed on a different tack or to alternate tacks. **18** (*intr*) to follow a zigzag route; keep changing one's course of action. [C14 *tak* fastening, nail]
▸ **'tacker** *n*

tack[2] (tæk) *n* riding harness for horses, such as saddles, bridles, etc. [C20: shortened from TACKLE]

tack hammer *n* a light hammer for driving tacks.

tackies *or* **takkies** ('tækɪz) *pl n, sing* **tacky.** *S. African inf.* tennis shoes or plimsolls. [C20: prob. from TACKY[1], from their nonslip rubber soles]

tackle ('tæk[ə]l) *n* **1** an arrangement of ropes and pulleys designed to lift heavy weights. **2** the equipment required for a particular occupation, etc. **3** *Naut.* the halyards and other running rigging aboard a vessel. **4** *Sport.* a physical challenge to an opponent, as to prevent his progress with the ball. **5** *American football.* a defensive lineman. ◆ *vb* **tackles, tackling, tackled. 6** (*tr*) to undertake (a task, etc.). **7** (*tr*) to confront (esp. an opponent) with a difficult proposition. **8** *Sport.* to challenge (an opponent) with a tackle. [C13: rel. to MLow G *takel* ship's rigging]
▸ **'tackler** *n*

tack rag n *Building trades.* a cotton cloth impregnated with an oil, used to remove dust from a surface prior to painting.

tacky[1] ('tækɪ) *adj* **tackier, tackiest.** slightly sticky or adhesive. [C18: from TACK[1] (in the sense: stickiness)]
► **'tackily** *adv* ► **'tackiness** *n*

tacky[2] ('tækɪ) *adj* **tackier, tackiest.** *Inf.* **1** shabby or shoddy. **2** ostentatious and vulgar. **3** *US.* (of a person) dowdy; seedy. [C19: from dialect *tacky* an inferior horse, from ?]
► **'tackiness** *n*

Tacna-Arica ★ (*Spanish* 'takna'rika) *n* a coastal desert region of W South America, long disputed by Chile and Peru: divided in 1929 into the Peruvian department of Tacna and the Chilean department of Arica.

tacnode ('tæk,nəʊd) *n* another name for **osculation** (sense 1). [C19: from L *tactus* touch (from *tangere* to touch) + NODE]

Tacoma ★ (tə'kəʊmə) *n* a port in W Washington, on Puget Sound: industrial centre. Pop.: 183 060 (1994 est.).

tact (tækt) *n* **1** a sense of what is fitting and considerate in dealing with others, so as to avoid giving offence. **2** skill in handling difficult situations; diplomacy. [C17: from L *tactus* a touching, from *tangere* to touch]
► **'tactful** *adj* ► **'tactfulness** *n* ► **'tactless** *adj* ► **'tactlessness** *n*

tactic ('tæktɪk) *n* a piece of tactics; tactical move. See also **tactics.**

-tactic *adj combining form.* having a specified kind of pattern or arrangement or having an orientation determined by a specified force: *syndiotactic; phototactic.* [from Gk *taktikos* relating to order; see TACTICS]

tactical ('tæktɪkᵊl) *adj* **1** of, relating to, or employing tactics: *a tactical error.* **2** (of missiles, bombing, etc.) for use in or supporting limited military operations; short-range. **3** skilful, adroit, or diplomatic.
► **'tactically** *adv*

tactical voting *n* (in an election) the practice of casting one's vote not for the party of one's choice but for the second strongest contender in a constituency in order to defeat the likeliest winner.

tactics ('tæktɪks) *pl n* **1** (*functioning as sing*) *Mil.* the art and science of the detailed direction and control of movement of forces in battle to achieve an aim or task. **2** the manoeuvres used to achieve an aim or task. **3** plans followed to achieve a particular short-term aim. [C17: from NL *tactica*, from Gk, from *taktikos* concerning arrangement, from *taktos* arranged (for battle), from *tassein* to arrange]
► **tac'tician** *n*

tactile ('tæktaɪl) *adj* **1** of, relating to, affecting, or having a sense of touch. **2** *Now rare.* tangible. [C17: from L *tactilis*, from *tangere* to touch]
► **tactility** (tæk'tɪlɪtɪ) *n*

Tadmor ★ ('tædmɔː) *n* the biblical name for **Palmyra.**

tadpole ('tæd,pəʊl) *n* the aquatic larva of frogs, toads, etc., which develops from a limbless tailed form with external gills into a form with internal gills, limbs, and a reduced tail. [C15 *taddepol*, from *tadde* toad + *pol* head]

Tadzhik ★ *n* a variant spelling of **Tajik.**

Tadzhikistan ★ *n* a variant spelling of **Tajikistan.**

taedium vitae ('tiːdɪəm 'viːtaɪ, 'vaɪtiː) *n* the feeling that life is boring and dull. [L, lit.: weariness of life]

Taegu ★ (te'guː) *n* a city in SE South Korea: textile and agricultural trading centre. Pop.: 2 449 139 (1995).

Taejon ★ (te'dʒɒn) *n* a city in W South Korea: market centre of an agricultural region. Pop.: 1 272 143 (1995).

tae kwon do ('taɪ 'kwɒn 'dəʊ, 'teɪ) *n* a Korean martial art that resembles karate. [C20: Korean *tae* kick + *kwon* fist + *do* way, method]

tael (teɪl) *n* **1** a unit of weight, used in the Far East. **2** (formerly) a Chinese monetary unit. [C16: from Port., from Malay *tahil* weight, ?from Sansk.]

ta'en (teɪn) *vb* a Scot. or poetic contraction of **taken.**

taenia *or US* **tenia** ('tiːnɪə) *n, pl* **taeniae** *or US* **teniae** (-nɪˌiː). **1** (in ancient Greece) a headband. **2** *Archit.* the fillet between the architrave and frieze of a Doric entablature. **3** *Anat.* any bandlike structure or part. **4** any of a genus of tapeworms. [C16: via L from Gk *tainia* narrow strip]

taeniasis *or US* **teniasis** (tiː'naɪəsɪs) *n Pathol.* infestation with tapeworms of the genus *Taenia.*

taffeta ('tæfɪtə) *n* a thin crisp lustrous plain-weave fabric of silk, etc., used esp. for women's clothes. [C14: from Med. L *taffata*, from Persian *tāftah* spun, from *tāftan* to spin]

taffrail ('tæf,reɪl) *n Naut.* a rail at the stern of a vessel. [C19: changed from earlier *tafferel*, from Du. *taffereel* panel (hence applied to the part of a vessel decorated with carved panels), from *tafel* table]

Taffy ('tæfɪ) *n, pl* **Taffies.** a slang word or nickname for a **Welshman.** [C17: from the supposed Welsh pronunciation of *Davy* (from *David*, Welsh *Dafydd*), a common Welsh Christian name]

tafia *or* **taffia** ('tæfɪə) *n* a type of rum, esp. from Guyana or the Caribbean. [C18: from F, from West Indian Creole, prob. from RATAFIA]

Tafilelt (tæ'fiːlelt) *or* **Tafilalet** ★ (,tæfɪ'lɑːlet) *n* an oasis in SE Morocco, the largest in the Sahara. Area: about 1300 sq. km (500 sq. miles).

Taft ★ (tæft) *n* **William Howard.** 1857–1930, US statesman; 27th president of the US (1909–13).

tag[1] (tæg) *n* **1** a piece of paper, leather, etc., for attaching to something as a mark or label: *a price tag.* **2** Also called: **electronic tag.** an electronic device worn by an offender serving a noncustodial sentence, which monitors the offender's whereabouts by means of a link to a central computer through the telephone system. **3** a small piece of material hanging from a part or piece. **4** a point of metal, etc., at the end of a cord or lace. **5** an epithet or verbal appendage, the refrain of a song, the moral of a fable, etc. **6** a brief quotation. **7** an ornamental flourish. **8** the tip of an animal's tail. **9** a matted lock of wool or hair. **10** *Sl.* a graffito consisting of a nickname or personal symbol. ♦ *vb* **tags, tagging, tagged.** (*mainly tr*) **11** to mark with a tag. **12** to monitor the whereabouts of (an offender) by means of an electronic tag. **13** to add or append as a tag. **14** to supply (prose or blank verse) with rhymes. **15** (*intr*; usually foll. by *on* or *along*) to trail (behind). **16** to name or call (someone something). **17** to cut the tags of wool or hair from (an animal). [C15: from ?]

tag[2] (tæg) *n* **1** Also called: **tig.** a children's game in which one player chases the others in an attempt to catch one of them who will then become the chaser. **2** the act of tagging one's partner in tag wrestling. **3** (*modifier*) denoting a wrestling contest between two teams of two wrestlers, in which only one from each team may be in the ring at one time. The contestant outside the ring may change places with his team-mate inside the ring after touching his hand. ♦ *vb* **tags, tagging, tagged.** (*tr*) **4** to catch (another child) in the game of tag. **5** (in tag wrestling) to touch the hand of (one's partner). [C18: ?from TAG[1]]

Tagalog (tə'gɑːlɒg) *n* **1** (*pl* **Tagalogs** *or* **Tagalog**) a member of a people of the Philippines. **2** the language of this people. ♦ *adj* **3** of or relating to this people or their language.

Taganrog ★ (*Russian* təgan'rɔk) *n* a port in SW Russia, on the Gulf of Taganrog (an inlet of the Sea of Azov): founded in 1698 as a naval base and fortress by Peter the Great: industrial centre. Pop.: 292 000 (1995 est.).

tag end *n* **1** the last part of something. **2** a loose end of cloth, thread, etc.

tagetes (tæ'dʒiːtiːz) *n, pl* **tagetes.** any of a genus of plants with yellow or orange flowers, including the French and African marigolds. [from NL, from *Tages*, an Etruscan god]

tagliatelle (,tæljə'telɪ) *n* a form of pasta made in narrow strips. [It., from *tagliare* to cut]

tag line *n* **1** an amusing or memorable phrase designed to catch attention in an advert. **2** another name for **punch line.**

Tagore ★ (tə'gɔː) *n* **Rabindranath** (rə'biːndrəˌnɑːt). 1861–1941, Indian poet and philosopher. His works include *Gitanjali* (1910; 1912): Nobel prize for literature 1913.

Tagus ★ ('teɪgəs) *n* a river in SW Europe, rising in E central Spain and flowing west to the border with Portugal, then southwest to the Atlantic at Lisbon: the longest river of the Iberian Peninsula. Length: 1007 km (626 miles). Portuguese name: **Tejo**. Spanish name: **Tajo**.

Tahiti ★ (tə'hi:tɪ) *n* an island in the S Pacific, in the Windward group of the Society Islands: the largest and most important French possession in French Polynesia; became a French protectorate in 1842 and a colony in 1880. Capital: Papeete. Pop.: 115 820 (1988). Area: 1005 sq. km (388 sq. miles).
▶ **Tahitian** (tə'hi:tɪən, tə'hi:ʃən) *adj, n*

Tahoe ★ ('tɑ:həʊ, 'teɪ-) *n* **Lake.** a lake between E California and W Nevada, in the Sierra Nevada Mountains at an altitude of 1899 m (6229 ft). Area: about 520 sq. km (200 sq. miles).

tahr *or* **thar** (tɑ:) *n* any of several goatlike mammals of S and SW Asia, having a shaggy coat and curved horns. [from Nepali *thār*]

tahsil (tə'si:l) *n* an administrative division in certain states in India. [Urdu, from Ar.: collection]

Tai (taɪ) *adj, n* a variant spelling of **Thai**.

taiaha ('taɪə,hɑ:) *n* NZ. a carved weapon in the form of a staff, now used in Maori ceremonial oratory. [from Maori]

t'ai chi ch'uan ('taɪ dʒi: 'tʃwɑ:n) *n* a Chinese system of callisthenics characterized by coordinated and rhythmic movements. Often shortened to **t'ai chi** ('taɪ 'dʒi:). [Chinese, lit.: great art of boxing]

Taichung *or* **T'ai-chung** ★ ('taɪ'tʃʊŋ) *n* a city in W Taiwan (Republic of China): commercial centre of an agricultural region. Pop.: 857 590 (1996 est.).

taiga ('taɪgə) *n* the coniferous forests extending across much of subarctic North America and Eurasia. [from Russian, of Turkic origin]

taihoa ('taɪhəʊə) *sentence substitute*. NZ. hold on! no hurry! [Maori]

tail[1] (teɪl) *n* **1** the rear part of the vertebrate body that contains an elongation of the vertebral column, esp. forming a flexible appendage. **2** anything resembling such an appendage; the bottom, lowest, or rear part. **3** the last part or parts: *the tail of the storm*. **4** the rear part of an aircraft including the fin, tailplane, and control surfaces. **5** *Astron.* the luminous stream of gas and dust particles driven from the head of a comet when close to the sun. **6** the rear portion of a bomb, rocket, missile, etc., usually fitted with guiding or stabilizing vanes. **7** a line of people or things. **8** a long braid or tress of hair: *a pigtail.* **9** a final short line in a stanza. **10** *Inf.* a person employed to follow and spy upon another. **11** an informal word for **buttocks. 12** *Taboo sl.* **12a** the female genitals. **12b** a woman considered sexually (esp. in **piece of tail, bit of tail**). **13** the foot of a page. **14** the lower end of a pool or part of a stream. **15** *Inf.* the course or track of a fleeing person or animal. **16** (*modifier*) coming from or situated in the rear: *a tail wind.* **17 turn tail.** to run away; escape. **18 with one's tail between one's legs.** in a state of utter defeat or confusion. ♦ *vb* **19** to form or cause to form the tail. **20** to remove the tail of (an animal). **21** (*tr*) to remove the stalk of. **22** (*tr*) to connect (objects, ideas, etc.) together by or as if by the tail. **23** (*tr*) *Inf.* to follow stealthily. **24** (*intr*) (of a vessel) to assume a specified position, as when at a mooring. **25** to build the end of (a brick, joist, etc.) into a wall or (of a brick, etc.) to have one end built into a wall.
♦ See also **tail off, tail out, tails.** [OE *tægel*]
▶ **'tailless** *adj*

tail[2] (teɪl) *Law.* ♦ *n* **1** the limitation of an estate or interest to a person and the heirs of his body. ♦ *adj* **2** (*immediately postpositive*) limited in this way. [C15: from OF *taille* a division; see TAILOR]
▶ **'tailless** *adj*

tailback ('teɪl,bæk) *n* a queue of traffic stretching back from an obstruction.

tailboard ('teɪl,bɔ:d) *n* a board at the rear of a lorry, etc., that can be removed or let down.

tail coat *n* **1** a man's black coat having a horizontal cut over the hips and a tapering tail with a vertical slit up to the waist. **2** a cutaway frock coat, part of morning dress.

tail covert *n* any of the covert feathers of a bird covering the bases of the tail feathers.

tail end *n* the last, endmost, or final part.

tailgate ('teɪl,geɪt) *n* **1** another name for **tailboard. 2** a door at the rear of a hatchback vehicle. ♦ *vb* **tailgates, tailgating, tailgated. 3** to drive very close behind (a vehicle).
▶ **'tail,gater** *n*

tail gate *n* a gate that is used to control the flow of water at the lower end of a lock.

tailing ('teɪlɪŋ) *n* the part of a beam, rafter, projecting brick, etc., embedded in a wall.

tailings ('teɪlɪŋz) *pl n* waste left over after certain processes, such as from an ore-crushing plant or in milling grain.

tail-light ('teɪl,laɪt) *or* **tail lamp** *n* other names for **rear light.**

tail off *or* **away** *vb* (*adv; usually intr*) to decrease or cause to decrease in quantity, degree, etc., esp. gradually.

tailor ('teɪlə) *n* **1** a person who makes, repairs, or alters outer garments, esp. menswear. Related adj: **sartorial. 2** a voracious and active marine food fish of Australia. ♦ *vb* **3** to cut or style (material, etc.) to satisfy certain requirements. **4** (*tr*) to adapt so as to make suitable. **5** (*intr*) to work as a tailor. [C13: from Anglo-Norman *taillour*, from OF *taillier* to cut, from L *tālea* a cutting]
▶ **'tailored** *adj*

tailorbird ('teɪlə,bɜ:d) *n* any of several tropical Asian warblers that build nests by sewing together large leaves using plant fibres.

tailor-made *adj* **1** made by a tailor to fit exactly. **2** perfectly meeting a particular purpose. ♦ *n* **3** a tailor-made garment. **4** *Inf.* a factory-made cigarette.

tailor's chalk *n* pipeclay used by tailors and dressmakers to mark seams, darts, etc., on material.

tailor's-tack *n* one of a series of loose looped stitches used to transfer markings for seams, darts, etc., from a paper pattern to material.

tail out *vb* (*tr, adv*) NZ. to guide (timber) as it emerges from a circular saw.

tailpiece ('teɪl,pi:s) *n* **1** an extension or appendage that lengthens or completes something. **2** a decorative design at the foot of a page or end of a chapter. **3** *Music.* a piece of wood to which the strings of a violin, etc., are attached at their lower end. **4** a short beam or rafter that has one end embedded in a wall.

tailpipe ('teɪl,paɪp) *n* a pipe from which exhaust gases are discharged, esp. the terminal pipe of the exhaust system of a motor vehicle.

tailplane ('teɪl,pleɪn) *n* a small horizontal wing at the tail of an aircraft to provide longitudinal stability. Also called (esp. US): **horizontal stabilizer.**

tailrace ('teɪl,reɪs) *n* a channel that carries water away from a water wheel, turbine, etc.

tail rotor *n* a small propeller fitted to the rear of a helicopter to counteract the torque reaction of the main rotor and thus prevent the body of the helicopter from rotating in an opposite direction.

tails (teɪlz) *pl n* **1** an informal name for **tail coat.** ♦ *interj, adv* **2** with the reverse side of a coin uppermost.

tailskid ('teɪl,skɪd) *n* **1** a runner under the tail of an aircraft. **2** a rear-wheel skid of a motor vehicle.

tailspin ('teɪl,spɪn) *n* **1** *Aeronautics.* another name for **spin** (sense 16). **2** *Inf.* a state of confusion or panic.

tailstock ('teɪl,stɒk) *n* a casting that slides on the bed of a lathe and is locked in position to support the free end of a workpiece.

tailwind ('teɪl,wɪnd) *n* a wind blowing in the same direction as the course of an aircraft or ship.

Taimyr Peninsula ★ (Russian taj'mir) *n* a large peninsula of the N central Soviet Union, between the Kara Sea and the Laptev Sea. Also: **Taymyr Peninsula.**

Tainan *or* **T'ai-nan** ★ ('taɪ'næn) *n* a city in SW Taiwan (Republic of China): an early centre of Chinese emigration from the mainland; largest city and capital of the island (1638–1885); Chengkung University. Pop.: 707 658 (1996 est.).

Taínaron ★ ('tɛnarən) *n* transliteration of the Modern Greek name for (Cape) **Matapan.**

Taino ('taɪnəu) *n* **1** (*pl* **Tainos** or **Taino**) a member of an extinct American Indian people of the West Indies. **2** the language of this people.

taint (teɪnt) *vb* **1** to affect or be affected by pollution or contamination. **2** to tarnish (someone's reputation, etc.). ◆ *n* **3** a defect or flaw. **4** a trace of contamination or infection. [C14: (infl. by *attaint* infected, from ATTAIN) from OF *teindre* to dye, from L *tingere*]
▸ **'taintless** *adj*

taipan ('taɪˌpæn) *n* a large highly venomous Australian snake. [C20: from Abor.]

Taipei or **T'ai-pei** ★ ('taɪ'peɪ) *n* the capital of Taiwan (Republic of China), at the N tip of the island: became capital in 1885; industrial centre; two universities. Pop.: 2 626 138 (1996 est.).

Taisho (taɪ'ʃəu) *n* **1** the period of Japanese history and artistic style associated with the reign of Emperor Yoshihito (1912–26). **2** the throne name of Yoshihito (1879–1926), emperor of Japan (1912–26).

Taiwan ★ ('taɪ'wɑːn) *n* **1** an island in SE Asia between the East China Sea and the South China Sea, off the SE coast of the People's Republic of China: the principal territory of the Republic of China. Pop.: 21 616 000 (1997). Former name: **Formosa. 2** another name for the Republic of **China** (sense 2).
▸ ˌ**Taiwan'ese** *adj, n*

Taiwan Strait ★ *n* another name for **Formosa Strait.**

Taiyuan or **T'ai-yüan** ★ ('taɪjuːˈɑːn) *n* a city in N China, capital of Shanxi: founded before 450 A.D.; an industrial centre, surrounded by China's largest reserves of high-grade bituminous coal. Pop.: 1 500 000 (1991 est.).

Ta'izz ★ (tæˈɪz, teɪˈiːz) *n* a town in SW Yemen, formerly in North Yemen: agricultural trading centre. Pop.: 178 043 (1995 est.).

taj (tɑːdʒ) *n* a tall conical cap worn as a mark of distinction by Muslims. [via Ar. from Persian: crown]

Tajik or **Tadzhik** ★ ('tɑːdʒɪk, tɑːˈdʒiːk) *n* **1** a member of a Muslim people of Tajikistan. **2** the language of this people.

Tajikistan or **Tadzhikistan** ★ (tɑːˌdʒɪkɪˈstɑːn) *n* a republic in central Asia: under Uzbek rule from the 15th century until taken by Russia in the 1860s; a Soviet republic from 1929 until gaining independence in 1991; mountainous. Language: Tajik. Religion: nonreligious and Muslim. Currency: rouble. Capital: Dushanbe. Pop.: 6 054 000 (1997). Area: 143 100 sq. km (55 240 sq. miles).

Taj Mahal ★ ('tɑːdʒ məˈhɑːl) *n* a marble mausoleum in central India, in Agra: built (1632–43) by the emperor Shah Jahan in memory of his wife. [Urdu, lit.: crown of buildings]

Tajo ★ ('taxo) *n* the Spanish name for the **Tagus.**

takahe ('tɑːkəˌhiː) *n* a rare flightless New Zealand rail. Also called: **notornis.** [from Maori]

Takamatsu ★ (ˌtækəˈmætsuː) *n* a port in SW Japan, on NE Shikoku on the Inland Sea. Pop.: 330 997 (1995).

Takao ★ (tæˈkau) *n* the Japanese name for **Gaoxiong.**

take (teɪk) *vb* **takes, taking, took, taken.** (*mainly tr*) **1** (*also intr*) to gain possession of (something) by force or effort. **2** to appropriate or steal. **3** to receive or accept into a relationship with oneself: *to take a wife.* **4** to pay for or buy. **5** to rent or lease. **6** to obtain by regular payment. **7** to win. **8** to obtain or derive from a source. **9** to assume the obligations of: *to take office.* **10** to endure, esp. with fortitude: *to take punishment.* **11** to adopt as a symbol of duty, etc.: *to take the veil.* **12** to receive in a specified way: *she took the news very well.* **13** to adopt as one's own: *to take someone's part in a quarrel.* **14** to receive and make use of: *to take advice.* **15** to receive into the body, as by eating, inhaling, etc. **16** to eat, drink, etc., esp. habitually. **17** to have or be engaged in for one's benefit or use: *to take a rest.* **18** to work at or study: *to take economics at college.* **19** to make, do, or perform (an action). **20** to make use of: *to take an*

opportunity. **21** to put into effect: *to take measures.* **22** (*also intr*) to make a photograph of or admit of being photographed. **23** to act or perform. **24** to write down or copy: *to take notes.* **25** to experience or feel: *to take offence.* **26** to consider or regard: *I take him to be honest.* **27** to accept as valid: *I take your point.* **28** to hold or maintain in the mind: *his father took a dim view of his career.* **29** to deal or contend with. **30** to use as a particular case: *take hotels for example.* **31** (*intr;* often foll. by *from*) to diminish or detract: *the actor's bad performance took from the effect of the play.* **32** to confront successfully: *the horse took the jump at the third attempt.* **33** (*intr*) to have or produce the intended effect: *her vaccination took.* **34** (*intr*) (of plants, etc.) to start growing successfully. **35** to aim or direct: *he took a swipe at his opponent.* **36** to deal a blow to in a specified place. **37** *Arch.* to have sexual intercourse with (a woman). **38** to remove from a place. **39** to carry along or have in one's possession. **40** to convey or transport. **41** to use as a means of transport: *I shall take the bus.* **42** to conduct or lead. **43** to escort or accompany. **44** to bring or deliver to a state, position, etc.: *his ability took him to the forefront.* **45** to seek: *to take cover.* **46** to ascertain by measuring, etc.: *to take a pulse.* **47** (*intr*) (of a mechanism) to catch or engage (a part). **48** to put an end to: *she took her own life.* **49** to come upon unexpectedly. **50** to contract: *he took a chill.* **51** to attack or attack: *the fever took him one night.* **52** (*copula*) to become suddenly or be rendered (ill): *he was taken sick.* **53** (*also intr*) to absorb or become absorbed by something: *the material took a polish.* **54** (*usually passive*) to charm: *she was very taken with the puppy.* **55** (*intr*) to be or become popular; win favour. **56** to require: *that task will take all your time.* **57** to subtract or deduct. **58** to hold: *the suitcase won't take all your clothes.* **59** to quote or copy. **60** to proceed to occupy: *to take a seat.* **61** (often foll. by *to*) to use or employ: *to take steps to ascertain the answer.* **62** to win or capture (a trick, piece, etc.). **63** *Sl.* to cheat, deceive, or victimize. **64 take five** (or **ten**) *Inf., chiefly US & Canad.* to take a break of five (or ten) minutes. **65 take it. 65a** to assume; believe. **65b** *Inf.* to stand up to or endure criticism, harsh treatment, etc. **66 take one's time.** to use as much time as is needed. **67 take (someone's) name in vain. 67a** to use a name, esp. of God, disrespectfully or irreverently. **67b** *Jocular.* to say (someone's) name. **68 take upon oneself.** to assume the right to do or responsibility for something. ◆ *n* **69** the act of taking. **70** the number of quarry killed or captured. **71** *Inf., chiefly US.* the amount of anything taken, esp. money. **72** *Films, music.* **72a** one of a series of recordings from which the best will be selected. **72b** the process of taking one such recording. **72c** a scene photographed without interruption. **73** *Inf., chiefly US.* a version or interpretation: *Cronenberg's harsh take on the sci-fi story.* ◆ See also **take after, take against,** etc. [OE *tacan*]
▸ **'takable** or **'takeable** *adj* ▸ **'taker** *n*

take after *vb* (*intr, prep*) to resemble in appearance, character, behaviour, etc.

take against *vb* (*intr, prep*) to start to dislike, esp. without good reason.

take apart *vb* (*tr, adv*) **1** to separate (something) into component parts. **2** to criticize severely.

take away *vb* (*tr, adv*) **1** to subtract: *take away four from nine to leave five.* ◆ *prep* **2** minus: *nine take away four is five.* ◆ *adj* **takeaway.** *Brit., Austral., & NZ.* **3** sold for consumption away from the premises: *a takeaway meal.* **4** selling food for consumption away from the premises: *a takeaway Indian restaurant.* ◆ *n* **takeaway.** *Brit., Austral., & NZ.* **5** a shop or restaurant that sells such food. **6** a meal bought at such a shop or restaurant: *we'll have a Chinese takeaway tonight.* ◆ *Scot.* word for senses 3–6): **carry out.** US and Canad. word (for senses 3–6): **takeout.**

take back *vb* (*adv, mainly tr*) **1** to retract or withdraw (something said, promised, etc.). **2** to regain possession of. **3** to return for exchange. **4** to accept (someone) back (into one's home, affections, etc.). **5** to remind one of the past: *that tune really takes me back.* **6** (*also intr*) *Printing.* to move (copy) to the previous line.

take down *vb* (*tr, adv*) **1** to record in writing. **2** to dismantle or tear down. **3** to lower or reduce in power, arrogance, etc. (esp. in **take down a peg**). ◆ *adj* **take-down.** made or intended to be disassembled.

★ people and places

take for *vb* (*tr, prep*) *Inf.* to consider or suppose to be, esp. mistakenly: *the fake coins were taken for genuine; who do you take me for?*

take-home pay *n* the remainder of one's pay after all income tax and other compulsory deductions have been made.

take in *vb* (*tr, adv*) **1** to understand. **2** to include. **3** to receive into one's house in exchange for payment: *to take in lodgers.* **4** to make (clothing, etc.) smaller by altering seams. **5** *Inf.* to cheat or deceive. **6** *US.* to go to: *let's take in a movie tonight.*

taken ('teɪkən) *vb* **1** the past participle of **take.** ◆ *adj* **2** (*postpositive*; foll. by *with*) enthusiastically impressed (by); infatuated (with).

take off *vb* (*adv*) **1** (*tr*) to remove (a garment). **2** (*intr*) (of an aircraft) to become airborne. **3** *Inf.* to set out or cause to set out on a journey: *they took off for Spain.* **4** (*tr*) (of a disease) to kill. **5** (*tr*) *Inf.* to mimic. **6** (*intr*) *Inf.* to become successful or popular. ◆ *n* **takeoff. 7** the act or process of making an aircraft airborne. **8** the stage of a country's economic development when rapid and sustained economic growth is first achieved. **9** *Inf.* an act of mimicry.

take on *vb* (*adv, mainly tr*) **1** to employ or hire. **2** to assume or acquire: *his voice took on a plaintive note.* **3** to agree to do; undertake. **4** to compete against; fight. **5** (*intr*) *Inf.* to exhibit great emotion, esp. grief.

take out *vb* (*tr, adv*) **1** to extract or remove. **2** to obtain or secure (a licence, patent, etc.). **3** to go out with; escort. **4** *Bridge.* to bid a different suit from (one's partner) in order to rescue him from a difficult contract. **5** *Sl.* to kill or destroy. **6** *Austral. inf.* to win, esp. in sport. **7 take it** *or* **a lot out of.** *Inf.* to sap the energy or vitality of. **8 take out on.** *Inf.* to vent (anger, etc.) on. **9 take someone out of himself.** *Inf.* to make someone forget his anxieties, problems, etc. ◆ *adj* **takeout. 10** *Bridge.* of or designating a conventional informatory bid, asking one's partner to bid another suit. ◆ *adj, n* **takeout. 11** the US and Canad. word for **takeaway** (senses 3–6).

take over *vb* (*adv*) **1** to assume the control or management of. **2** *Printing.* to move (copy) to the next line. ◆ *n* **takeover.** the act of seizing or assuming power, control, etc.

take to *vb* (*intr, prep*) **1** to make for; flee to: *to take to the hills.* **2** to form a liking for. **3** to have recourse to: *to take to the bottle.*

take up *vb* (*adv, mainly tr*) **1** to adopt the study, practice, or activity of: *to take up gardening.* **2** to shorten (a garment). **3** to pay off (a note, mortgage, etc.). **4** to agree to or accept (an invitation, etc.). **5** to pursue further or resume (something): *he took up French where he left off.* **6** to absorb (a liquid). **7** to act as a patron to. **8** to occupy or fill (space or time). **9** to interrupt, esp. in order to contradict or criticize. **10** *Austral. & NZ.* to occupy and break in (uncultivated land): *he took up some hundreds of acres in the back country.* **11 take up on. 11a** to argue with (someone): *can I take you up on two points in your talk?* **11b** to accept what is offered by (someone): *let me take you up on your invitation.* **12 take up with. 12a** to discuss with (someone); refer to. **12b** (*intr*) to begin to keep company or associate with. ◆ *n* **take-up. 13a** the claiming of something, esp. a state benefit. **13b** (*as modifier*): *take-up rate.*

takin ('tɑːkiːn) *n* a massive bovid mammal of S Asia, having a shaggy coat, short legs, and horns. [C19: from Tibetan native name]

taking ('teɪkɪŋ) *adj* **1** charming, fascinating, or intriguing. **2** *Inf.* infectious; catching. ◆ *n* **3** something taken. **4** (*pl*) receipts; earnings. ▸ **'takingly** *adv* ▸ **'takingness** *n*

Takoradi ★ (ˌtɑːkəˈrɑːdɪ) *n* the chief port of Ghana, in the southwest on the Gulf of Guinea: modern harbour opened in 1928. Pop. (with Sekondi): 103 600 (1988 est.).

talapoin ('tælə,pɔɪn) *n* **1** a small W African monkey. **2** (in Myanmar and Thailand) a Buddhist monk. [C16: from F, lit.: Buddhist monk, from Port. *talapão*; orig. jocular, from the appearance of the monkey]

Ilaria (təˈlɛərɪə) *pl n Greek myth.* winged sandals. [C16:

from L, from *tālāris* belonging to the ankle, from *tālus* ankle]

Talavera de la Reina ★ (*Spanish* talaˈβera ðe la ˈreina) *n* a walled town in central Spain, on the Tagus River: scene of the defeat of the French by British and Spanish forces (1809) during the Peninsular War; agricultural processing centre. Pop.: 68 640 (1991).

Talbot ★ ('tɔːlbət) *n* (**William Henry**) Fox. 1800–77, British pioneer of photography.

talc (tælk) *n also* **talcum. 1** See **talcum powder. 2** a soft mineral, consisting of magnesium silicate, used in the manufacture of ceramics and paints and as a filler in talcum powder, etc. ◆ *vb* **talcs, talcking, talcked** *or* **talcs, talcing, talced. 3** (*tr*) to apply talc to. [C16: from Med. L *talcum*, from Ar. *talq* mica, from Persian *talk*] ▸ **'talcose** *or* **'talcous** *adj*

Talca ★ (*Spanish* 'talka) *n* a city in central Chile: scene of the declaration of Chilean independence (1818). Pop.: 169 448 (1995 est.).

Talcahuano ★ (*Spanish* talkaˈwano) *n* a port in S central Chile, near Concepción on an inlet of the Pacific: oil refinery. Pop.: 260 915 (1995 est.).

talcum powder ('tælkəm) *n* a powder made of purified talc, usually scented, used for perfuming the body and for absorbing excess moisture. Often shortened to **talcum** or **talc.**

tale (teɪl) *n* **1** a report, narrative, or story. **2** one of a group of short stories. **3a** a malicious or meddlesome rumour or piece of gossip. **3b** (*in combination*): *talebearer; taleteller.* **4** a fictitious or false statement. **5 tell tales. 5a** to tell fanciful lies. **5b** to report malicious stories, trivial complaints, etc., esp. to someone in authority. **6 tell a tale.** to reveal something important. **7 tell its own tale.** to be self-evident. **8** *Arch.* a number; amount. [OE *talu* list]

talent ('tælənt) *n* **1** innate ability, aptitude, or faculty; above average ability: *a talent for cooking; a child with talent.* **2** a person or persons possessing such ability. **3** any of various ancient units of weight and money. **4** *Inf.* members of the opposite sex collectively: *the local talent.* [OE *talente*, from L *talenta*, pl. of *talentum* sum of money, from Gk *talanton* unit of money; in Med. L the sense was extended to ability through the infl. of the parable of the talents (Matthew 25:14–30)] ▸ **'talented** *adj*

talent scout *n* a person whose occupation is the search for talented sportsmen, performers, etc., for engagements as professionals.

tales ('teɪliːz) *n Law.* **1** (*functioning as pl*) a group of persons summoned to fill vacancies on a jury panel. **2** (*functioning as sing*) the writ summoning such jurors. [C15: from Med. L *tālēs dē circumstantibus* such men from among the bystanders, from L *tālis* such] ▸ **'talesman** *n*

Taliban *or* **Taleban** ('tælɪˌbæn) *n* a militant Islamic organization in Afghanistan. [C20: from Ar. *tāliban* seekers]

Taliesin ★ (ˌtælɪˈɛsɪn) *n* 6th century A.D., Welsh bard; reputed author of the *Book of Taliesin.*

taligrade ('tælɪˌɡreɪd) *adj* (of mammals) walking on the outer side of the foot. [C20: from NL, from L *tālus* ankle, heel + -GRADE]

talion ('tælɪən) *n* the system or legal principle of making the punishment correspond to the crime; retaliation. [C15: via OF from L *tāliō*, from *tālis* such]

talipes ('tælɪˌpiːz) *n* **1** a congenital deformity of the foot by which it is twisted in any of various positions. **2** a technical name for **club foot.** [C19: NL, from L *tālus* ankle + *pēs* foot]

talipot *or* **talipot palm** ('tælɪˌpɒt) *n* a palm tree of the East Indies, having large leaves that are used for fans, thatching houses, etc. [C17: from Bengali: palm leaf, from Sansk. *tālī* fan palm + *pattra* leaf]

talisman ('tælɪzmən) *n, pl* **talismans. 1** a stone or other small object, usually inscribed or carved, believed to protect the wearer from evil influences. **2** anything thought to have magical or protective powers. [C17: via F or Sp. from Ar. *tilsam*, from Med. Gk *telesma* ritual,

from Gk: consecration, from *telein* to perform a rite, complete]
▸ **talismanic** (ˌtælɪzˈmænɪk) *adj*

talk (tɔːk) *vb* **1** (*intr*; often foll. by *to* or *with*) to express one's thoughts, feelings, or desires by means of words (to). **2** (*intr*) to communicate by other means: *lovers talk with their eyes.* **3** (*intr*; usually foll. by *about*) to exchange ideas or opinions (about). **4** (*intr*) to articulate words. **5** (*tr*) to give voice to; utter: *to talk rubbish.* **6** (*tr*) to discuss: *to talk business.* **7** (*intr*) to reveal information. **8** (*tr*) to know how to communicate in (a language or idiom): *he talks English.* **9** (*intr*) to spread rumours or gossip. **10** (*intr*) to make sounds suggestive of talking. **11** (*intr*) to be effective or persuasive: *money talks.* **12 now you're talking.** *Inf.* at last you're saying something agreeable. **13 talk big.** to boast. **14 you can talk.** *Inf.* **14a** you don't have to worry about doing a particular thing yourself. **14b** Also: **you can't talk.** you yourself are guilty of offending in the very matter you are upholding or decrying. ◆ *n* **15** a speech or lecture. **16** an exchange of ideas or thoughts. **17** idle chatter, gossip, or rumour. **18** a subject of conversation; theme. **19** (*often pl*) a conference, discussion, or negotiation. **20** a specific manner of speaking: *children's talk.* ◆ See also **talk about, talk back,** etc. [C13 *talkien*]
▸ **'talker** *n*

talk about *vb* (*intr*, *prep*) **1** to discuss. **2** used informally and often ironically to add emphasis to a statement: *all his plays have such ridiculous plots – talk about good drama!*

talkative ('tɔːkətɪv) *adj* given to talking a great deal.
▸ **'talkatively** *adv* ▸ **'talkativeness** *n*

talk back *vb* (*intr*, *adv*) **1** to answer boldly or impudently. **2** *NZ.* to conduct a telephone dialogue for immediate transmission over the air. ◆ *n* **talkback. 3** *Television, radio.* a system of telephone links enabling spoken directions to be given during the production of a programme. **4** *NZ.* a broadcast telephone dialogue.

talk down *vb* (*adv*) **1** (*intr*; often foll. by *to*) to behave (towards) in a superior manner. **2** (*tr*) to override (a person) by continuous or loud talking. **3** (*tr*) to give instructions to (an aircraft) by radio to enable it to land.

talkie ('tɔːkɪ) *n Inf.* an early film with a soundtrack. Full name: **talking picture.**

Talking Book *n Trademark.* a recording of a book, designed to be used by blind people.

talking head *n* (on television) a person, shown only from the shoulders up, who speaks without illustrative material.

talking-to *n Inf.* a session of criticism, as of a subordinate by a person in authority.

talk into *vb* (*tr*, *prep*) to persuade to by talking: *I talked him into buying the house.*

talk out *vb* (*tr*, *adv*) **1** to resolve or eliminate by talking. **2** *Brit.* to block (a bill, etc.) in a legislative body by lengthy discussion. **3 talk out of.** to dissuade from by talking.

talk round *vb* **1** (*tr*, *adv*) Also: **talk over.** to persuade to one's opinion. **2** (*intr*, *prep*) to discuss (a subject), esp. without coming to a conclusion.

talk shop *vb* to talk about one's profession, esp. at a social occasion.

talk show *n* another name for **chat show.**

tall (tɔːl) *adj* **1** of more than average height. **2** (*postpositive*) having a specified height: *five feet tall.* [C14 (in the sense: big, comely, valiant)]
▸ **'tallness** *n*

tallage ('tælɪdʒ) *n English history.* **a** a tax levied by kings on Crown lands and royal towns. **b** a toll levied by a lord upon his tenants or by a feudal lord upon his vassals. [C13: from OF *taillage*, from *taillier* to cut; see TAILOR]

Tallahassee (ˌtæləˈhæsɪ) *n* a city in N Florida, capital of the state: two universities. Pop.: 133 718 (1994 est.).

tallboy ('tɔːlˌbɔɪ) *n* **1** a high chest of drawers made in two sections placed one on top of the other. **2** a fitting on the top of a chimney to prevent downdraughts.

Talleyrand-Périgord ★ ('tælɪˌrændˈperɪɡɔː; *French* talɛrɑ̃-periɡɔr) *n* **Charles Maurice** (Jarl mɔrɪs). 1754–1838, French statesman; foreign minister (1797–1807; 1814–15).

Tallinn *or* **Tallin** ★ ('tælɪn) *n* the capital of Estonia, on the Gulf of Finland: founded by the Danes in 1219; naval base. Pop.: 434 763 (1995 est.). German name: **Reval.**

Tallis ★ ('tælɪs) *n* **Thomas.** ?1505–85, English composer; noted for his Anglican liturgical music.

tallith ('tælɪθ) *n* a shawl with fringed corners worn by Jewish males, esp. during religious services. [C17: from Heb. *tallīt*]

tall order *n Inf.* a difficult or unreasonable request.

tallow ('tæləʊ) *n* **1** a fatty substance extracted chiefly from the suet of sheep and cattle: used for making soap, candles, food, etc. ◆ *vb* **2** (*tr*) to cover or smear with tallow. [OE *tælg*, a dye]
▸ **'tallowy** *adj*

tallowwood ('tæləʊˌwʊd) *n Austral.* a tall eucalyptus tree having soft fibrous bark and a greasy timber.

tall poppy *n Austral. inf.* a prominent or highly paid person.

tall poppy syndrome *n Austral. inf.* a tendency to disparage any person who has achieved great prominence or wealth.

tall ship *n* any square-rigged sailing ship.

tall story *n Inf.* an exaggerated or incredible account.

tally ('tælɪ) *vb* **tallies, tallying, tallied. 1** (*intr*) to correspond one with the other: *the two stories don't tally.* **2** (*tr*) to supply with an identifying tag. **3** (*intr*) to keep score. **4** (*tr*) *Obs.* to record or mark. ◆ *n, pl* **tallies. 5** any record of debit, credit, the score in a game, etc. **6** *Austral. & NZ.* the number of sheep shorn in a specified period. **7** an identifying label or mark. **8** a counterpart or duplicate of something. **9** a stick used (esp. formerly) as a record of the amount of a debt according to the notches cut in it. **10** a notch or mark made on such a stick. **11** a mark used to represent a certain number in counting. [C15: from Med. L *tālea*, from L: cutting]

tally clerk *n Austral. & NZ.* a person, esp. on a wharf or in an airport, who checks the count of goods being loaded or unloaded.

tally-ho (ˌtælɪˈhəʊ) *interj* **1** the cry of a participant at a hunt when the quarry is sighted. ◆ *n, pl* **tally-hos. 2** an instance of crying tally-ho. **3** another name for a **four-in-hand** (sense 1). ◆ *vb* **tally-hos, tally-hoing, tally-hoed** *or* **tally-ho'd. 4** (*intr*) to make the cry of tally-ho. [C18: ?from F *taïaut* cry used in hunting]

tallyman ('tælɪmən) *n, pl* **tallymen. 1** a scorekeeper or recorder. **2** *Dialect.* a travelling salesman for a firm specializing in hire-purchase.
▸ **'tally,woman** *fem n*

Talmud ('tælmʊd) *n Judaism.* the primary source of Jewish religious law, consisting of the Mishnah and the Gemara. [C16: from Heb. *talmūdh*, lit.: instruction, from *lāmadh* to learn]
▸ **Tal'mudic** *or* **Tal'mudical** *adj* ▸ **'Talmudism** *n* ▸ **'Talmudist** *n*

talon ('tælən) *n* **1** a sharply hooked claw, esp. of a bird of prey. **2** anything resembling this. **3** the part of a lock that the key presses on when it is turned. **4** *Piquet, etc.* the pile of cards left after the deal. **5** *Archit.* another name for **ogee. 6** *Stock Exchange.* a printed slip attached to some bearer bonds to enable the holder to apply for a new sheet of coupons. [C14: from OF: heel, from L *tālus*]
▸ **'taloned** *adj*

Talos ★ ('teɪlɒs) *n Greek myth.* the nephew and apprentice of Daedalus, who surpassed his uncle as an inventor and was killed by him out of jealousy.

talus[1] ('teɪləs) *n, pl* **tali** (-laɪ). the bone of the ankle that articulates with the leg bones to form the ankle joint; anklebone. [C18: from L: ankle]

talus[2] ('teɪləs) *n, pl* **taluses. 1** *Geol.* another name for **scree. 2** *Fortifications.* the sloping side of a wall. [C17: from F, from L *talūtium* slope, ? of Iberian origin]

tam (tæm) *n* short for **tam-o'-shanter.**

tamale (təˈmɑːlɪ) *n* a Mexican dish made of minced meat mixed with crushed maize and seasonings, wrapped in maize husks and steamed. [C19: erroneously for *tamal*, from Mexican Sp., from Nahuatl *tamalli*]

★ **people and places**

tamandua (ˌtæmənˈdʊə) *n* a small arboreal mammal of Central and South America, having a tubular mouth specialized for feeding on termites. Also called: **lesser anteater**. [C17: via Port. from Tupi: ant trapper, from *taixi* ant + *mondê* to catch]

tamarack (ˈtæməˌræk) *n* **1** any of several North American larches. **2** the wood of any of these trees. [C19: of Amerind origin]

tamari (təˈmɑːrɪ) *n* a Japanese variety of soy sauce. [Japanese]

tamarillo (ˌtæməˈrɪləʊ) *n, pl* **tamarillos**. another name for **tree tomato**.

tamarin (ˈtæmərɪn) *n* any of numerous small monkeys of South and Central American forests; similar to the marmosets. [C18: via F, of Amerind origin]

tamarind (ˈtæmərɪnd) *n* **1** a tropical evergreen tree having yellow flowers and brown pods. **2** the fruit of this tree, used as a food and to make beverages and medicines. **3** the wood of this tree. [C16: from Med. L *tamarindus*, ult. from Ar. *tamr hindī* Indian date]

tamarisk (ˈtæmərɪsk) *n* any of a genus of trees and shrubs of the Mediterranean region and S and SE Asia, having scalelike leaves, slender branches, and feathery flower clusters. [C15: from LL *tamariscus*, from L *tamarix*]

Tamatave ★ (*French* tamatav) *n* the former name (until 1979) of **Toamasina**.

Tamaulipas ★ (*Spanish* tamauˈlipas) *n* a state of NE Mexico, on the Gulf of Mexico. Capital: Ciudad Victoria. Pop.: 2 526 387 (1995 est.). Area: 79 829 sq. km (30 822 sq. miles).

Tambo ★ (ˈtæmbəʊ) *n* **Oliver**. 1917–93, South African politician; president (1977–91) of the African National Congress.

Tambora ★ (ˈtæmbəˌrɑː) *n* a volcano in Indonesia, on N Sumbawa: violent eruption of 1815 reduced its height from about 4000 m (13 000 ft) to 2850 m (9400 ft).

tambour (ˈtæmbʊə) *n* **1** *Real Tennis*. the sloping buttress on one side of the receiver's end of the court. **2** a small embroidery frame, consisting of two hoops over which the fabric is stretched while being worked. **3** embroidered work done on such a frame. **4** a sliding door on desks, cabinets, etc., made of thin strips of wood glued onto a canvas backing. **5** *Archit.* a wall that is circular in plan, esp. one that supports a dome or one that is surrounded by a colonnade. **6** a drum. ◆ *vb* **7** to embroider on a tambour. [C15: from F, from *tabour* TABOR]

tamboura (tæmˈbʊərə) *n* a stringed instrument with a long neck used in Indian music to provide a drone. [from Persian *tanbūr*, from Ar. *tunbūr*]

tambourin (ˈtæmbʊrɪn) *n* **1** an 18th-century Provençal folk dance. **2** a piece of music composed for or in the rhythm of this dance. **3** a small drum. [C18: from F: a little drum]

tambourine (ˌtæmbəˈriːn) *n* *Music*. a percussion instrument consisting of a single drumhead of skin stretched over a circular wooden frame hung with pairs of metal discs that jingle when it is struck or shaken. [C16: from MFlemish *tamborijn* a little drum, from OF: TAMBOURIN]
▶ ˌtambouˈrinist *n*

Tambov ★ (*Russian* tamˈbɔf) *n* an industrial city in W Russia: founded in 1636 as a Muscovite fort. Pop.: 316 000 (1995 est.).

Tamburlaine ★ (ˈtæmbəˌleɪn) *n* a variant of **Tamerlane**.

tame (teɪm) *adj* **1** changed by man from a wild state into a domesticated or cultivated condition. **2** (of animals) not fearful of human contact. **3** meek or submissive. **4** flat, insipid, or uninspiring. ◆ *vb* **tames, taming, tamed**. (*tr*) **5** to make tame; domesticate. **6** to break the spirit of, subdue, or curb. **7** to tone down, soften, or mitigate. [OE *tam*]
▶ ˈtamable *or* ˈtameable *adj* ▶ ˈtamely *adv* ▶ ˈtameness *n*
▶ ˈtamer *n*

Tamerlane (ˈtæməˌleɪn) *or* **Tamburlaine** ★ *n* Turkic name *Timur* (tiːˈmʊə). ?1336–1405, Mongol conqueror; ruler of Samarkand (1369–1405): died while invading China.

Tameside ★ (ˈteɪmˌsaɪd) *n* a unitary authority of NW England, in Greater Manchester. Pop.: 221 800 (1994 est.). Area: 103 sq. km (40 sq. miles).

Tamil (ˈtæmɪl) *n* **1** (*pl* **Tamils** *or* **Tamil**) a member of a mixed Dravidian and Caucasoid people of S India and Sri Lanka. **2** the language of this people. ◆ *adj* **3** of or relating to this people or their language.

Tamil Nadu ★ (ˈtæmɪl nɑːˈduː) *n* a state of SE India, on the Coromandel Coast: reorganized in 1956 and 1960 and made smaller; consists of a coastal plain backed by hills, including the Nilgiri Hills in the west. Capital: Madras. Pop.: 58 840 000 (1994 est.). Area: 130 058 sq. km (50 216 sq. miles). Former name (until 1968): **Madras**.

Tammerfors ★ (tamərˈfɔrs) *n* the Swedish name for **Tampere**.

tammy[1] (ˈtæmɪ) *n, pl* **tammies**. another word for **tam-o'-shanter**.

tammy[2] (ˈtæmɪ) *n, pl* **tammies**. (esp. formerly) a woollen cloth used for straining sauces, soups, etc. [C18: changed from F *tamis*, ? of Celtic origin]

tam-o'-shanter (ˌtæməˈʃæntə) *n* a Scottish brimless wool or cloth cap with a bobble in the centre. [C19: after the hero of Burns's poem *Tam o' Shanter* (1790)]

tamoxifen (təˈmɒksɪˌfen) *n* a drug that antagonizes the action of oestrogen and is used to treat breast cancer and some types of infertility in women. [C20: from T(RANS-) + AM(INE) + OXY-[2] + PHEN(OL)]

tamp (tæmp) *vb* (*tr*) **1** to force or pack down firmly by repeated blows. **2** to pack sand, earth, etc., into (a drill hole) over an explosive. [C17: prob. back formation from *tampin* (obs. var. of TAMPION), taken as a present participle *tamping*]

Tampa ★ (ˈtæmpə) *n* a port and resort in W Florida, on **Tampa Bay** (an arm of the Gulf of Mexico): two universities. Pop.: 285 523 (1994 est.).

tamper[1] (ˈtæmpə) *vb* (*intr*) **1** (usually foll. by *with*) to interfere or meddle. **2** to use bribery or blackmail. **3** (usually foll. by *with*) to attempt to influence, esp. by bribery. [C16: alteration of TEMPER (vb)]
▶ ˈtamperer *n*

tamper[2] (ˈtæmpə) *n* **1** a person or thing that tamps, esp. an instrument for packing down tobacco in a pipe. **2** a casing around the core of a nuclear weapon to increase its efficiency by reflecting neutrons and delaying the expansion.

Tampere ★ (*Finnish* ˈtampɛre) *n* a city in SW Finland: the second largest town in Finland; textile manufacturing. Pop.: 182 742 (1996 est.). Swedish name: **Tammerfors**.

Tampico ★ (*Spanish* tamˈpiko) *n* a port and resort in E Mexico, in Tamaulipas on the Pánuco River: oil refining. Pop.: 272 690 (1990).

tampion (ˈtæmpɪən) *or* **tompion** *n* a plug placed in a gun's muzzle when the gun is not in use. [C15: from F: TAMPON]

tampon (ˈtæmpɒn) *n* **1** a plug of lint, cotton wool, etc., inserted into a wound or body cavity to stop the flow of blood, absorb secretions, etc. ◆ *vb* **2** (*tr*) to plug (a wound, etc.) with a tampon. [C19: via F from OF *tapon* a little plug, of Gmc origin]
▶ **tamponage** (ˈtæmpənɪdʒ) *n*

tam-tam *n* another name for **gong** (sense 1). [from Hindi; see TOM-TOM]

Tamworth ★ (ˈtæmwəθ) *n* **1** a market town in W central England, in SE Staffordshire. Pop.: 68 440 (1991). **2** a city in SE Australia, in E central New South Wales: industrial centre of an agricultural region. Pop.: 34 000 (latest est.).

tan[1] (tæn) *n* **1** the brown colour produced by the skin after exposure to ultraviolet rays, esp. those of the sun. **2** a yellowish-brown colour. **3** short for **tanbark**. ◆ *vb* **tans, tanning, tanned**. **4** to go brown or cause to go brown after exposure to ultraviolet rays. **5** to convert (a skin or hide) into leather by treating it with a tanning agent. **6** (*tr*) *Sl.* to beat or flog. ◆ *adj* **tanner, tannest**. **7** of the colour tan. [OE *tannian* (unattested as infinitive, attested as *getanned*, p.p.), from Med. L *tannāre*, from *tannum* tanbark, ? of Celtic origin]
▶ ˈtannable *adj* ▶ ˈtannish *adj*

tan[2] (tæn) *abbrev. for* tangent (sense 2).

Tana ★ ('tɑːnə) *n* **1 Lake.** Also called: (Lake) **Tsana.** a lake in NW Ethiopia, on a plateau 1800 m (6000 ft) high: the largest lake of Ethiopia; source of the Blue Nile. Area: 3673 sq. km (1418 sq. miles). **2** a river in E Kenya, rising in the Aberdare Range and flowing in a wide curve east to the Indian Ocean: the longest river in Kenya. Length: 708 km (440 miles). **3** a river in NE Norway, flowing generally northeast as part of the border between Norway and Finland into the Arctic Ocean by Tana Fjord. Length: about 320 km (200 miles). Finnish name: **Teno.**

tanager ('tænədʒə) *n* any of a family of American songbirds having a short thick bill and, in the male, a brilliantly coloured plumage. [C19: from NL *tanagra*, based on Amerind *tangara*]

Tanagra ★ ('tænəgrə) *n* a town in ancient Boeotia, famous for terracotta figurines of the same name, first discovered in its necropolis.

Tanana ★ ('tænənɑː) *n* a river in central Alaska, rising in the Wrangell Mountains and flowing northwest to the Yukon River. Length: about 765 km (475 miles).

Tananarive ★ (*French* tananariv) *n* the former name of **Antananarivo.**

tanbark ('tæn,bɑːk) *n* the bark of certain trees, esp. the oak, used as a source of tannin.

Tancred ★ ('tæŋkrɪd) *n* died 1112, Norman hero of the First Crusade, who played a prominent part in the capture of Jerusalem (1099).

tandem ('tændəm) *n* **1** a bicycle with two sets of pedals and two saddles, arranged one behind the other for two riders. **2** a two-wheeled carriage drawn by two horses harnessed one behind the other. **3** a team of two horses so harnessed. **4** any arrangement of two things in which one is placed behind the other. **5 in tandem.** together or in conjunction. ◆ *adj* **6** *Brit.* used as, used in, or routed through an intermediate automatic telephone exchange. ◆ *adv* **7** one behind the other. [C18: whimsical use of L *tandem* at length, to indicate a long vehicle]

Tandjungpriok *or* **Tanjungpriok** ★ (,tændʒuŋ'priːɒk) *n* a port in Indonesia, on the NW coast of Java adjoining the capital, Jakarta: a major shipping and distributing centre for the whole archipelago.

tandoori (tæn'dʊərɪ) *n* an Indian method of cooking meat or vegetables on a spit in a clay oven. [from Urdu, from *tandoor* an oven]

tang (tæŋ) *n* **1** a strong taste or flavour. **2** a pungent or characteristic smell. **3** a trace, touch, or hint of something. **4** the pointed end of a tool, such as a chisel, file, knife, etc., which is fitted into a handle, shaft, or stock. [C14: from ON *tangi* point]

Tang ★ (tæŋ) *n* the imperial dynasty of China from 618–907 A.D.

Tanga ★ ('tæŋgə) *n* a port in N Tanzania, on the Indian Ocean: Tanzania's second port. Pop.: 187 155 (1988).

Tanganyika (,tæŋgə'njiːkə) *n* **1** a former state in E Africa: became part of German East Africa in 1884; ceded to Britain as a League of Nations mandate in 1919 and as a UN trust territory in 1946; gained independence in 1961 and united with Zanzibar in 1964 as the United Republic of Tanzania. **2 Lake.** a lake in central Africa between Tanzania and the Democratic Republic of the Congo, bordering also on Burundi and Zambia, in the Great Rift Valley: the longest freshwater lake in the world. Area: 32 893 sq. km (12 700 sq. miles). Length: 676 km (420 miles).
▶ ,Tangan'yikan *adj, n*

Tange ★ ('tæŋgə) *n* Kenzo. born 1913, Japanese architect. His buildings include the Kurashiki city hall (1960) and St Mary's Cathedral in Tokyo (1962–64).

tangent ('tændʒənt) *n* **1** a geometric line, curve, plane, or curved surface that touches another curve or surface at one point but does not intersect it. **2** (of an angle) a trigonometric function that in a right-angled triangle is the ratio of the length of the opposite side to that of the adjacent side; the ratio of sine to cosine. Abbrev.: **tan.** **3** *Music.* a small piece of metal that strikes the string of a clavichord. **4 on** *or* **at a tangent.** on a completely different or divergent course, esp. of thought. ◆ *adj* **5a** of or in-

volving a tangent. **5b** touching at a single point. **6** touching. [C16: from L *līnea tangēns* the touching line, from *tangere* to touch]
▶ 'tangency *n*

tangent galvanometer *n* a galvanometer having a vertical coil of wire with a horizontal magnetic needle at its centre. The current to be measured is passed through the coil and produces a proportional magnetic field which deflects the needle.

tangential (tæn'dʒenʃəl) *adj* **1** of, being, or in the direction of a tangent. **2** *Astron.* (of velocity) in a direction perpendicular to the line of sight of a celestial object. **3** of superficial relevance only; digressive.
▶ tan,genti'ality *n* ▶ tan'gentially *adv*

tangerine (,tændʒə'riːn) *n* **1** an Asian citrus tree cultivated for its small orange-like fruits. **2** the fruit of this tree, having sweet spicy flesh. **3a** a reddish-orange colour. **3b** (*as adj*): *a tangerine door.* [C19: from TANGIER]

tangi ('tæŋiː) *n NZ.* **1** a Maori funeral ceremony. **2** *Inf.* a lamentation.

tangible ('tændʒɪbəl) *adj* **1** capable of being touched or felt. **2** capable of being clearly grasped by the mind. **3** having a physical existence: *tangible assets.* [C16: from LL *tangibilis*, from L *tangere* to touch]
▶ ,tangi'bility *or* 'tangibleness *n* ▶ 'tangibly *adv*

Tangier ★ (tæn'dʒɪə) *n* a port in N Morocco, on the Strait of Gibraltar: a Phoenician trading post in the 15th century B.C.; a neutral international zone (1923–56); made the summer capital of Morocco and a free port in 1962; commercial and financial centre. Pop.: 307 000 (1993 est.).
▶ ,Tange'rine *n, adj*

tangle ('tæŋgəl) *n* **1** a confused or complicated mass of hairs, lines, fibres, etc., knotted or coiled together. **2** a complicated problem, condition, or situation. ◆ *vb* **tangles, tangling, tangled. 3** to become or cause to become twisted together in a confused mass. **4** (*intr*; often foll. by *with*) to come into conflict; contend. **5** (*tr*) to involve in matters which hinder or confuse. **6** (*tr*) to ensnare or trap, as in a net. [C14 *tangilen*, var. of *tagilen*, prob. from ON]
▶ 'tangled *or* 'tangly *adj*

tango ('tæŋgəʊ) *n, pl* **tangos. 1** a Latin-American dance characterized by long gliding steps and sudden pauses. **2** a piece of music composed for or in the rhythm of this dance. ◆ *vb* **tangoes, tangoing, tangoed. 3** (*intr*) to perform this dance. [C20: from American Sp., prob. of Niger-Congo origin]

tangram ('tæŋgræm) *n* a Chinese puzzle in which a square, cut into a parallelogram, a square, and five triangles, is formed into figures. [C19: ?from Chinese *t'ang* Chinese + -GRAM]

Tangshan ★ ('tæŋ'ʃæn) *n* an industrial city in NE China, in Hebei province. Pop.: 1 500 000 (1991 est.).

Tanguy ★ (*French* tɑ̃gi) *n* Yves (iv). 1900–55, US surrealist painter, born in France.

tangy ('tæŋɪ) *adj* **tangier, tangiest.** having a pungent, fresh, or briny flavour or aroma.

tanh (θæn, tænʃ) *n* hyperbolic tangent; a hyperbolic function that is the ratio of sinh to cosh. [C20: from TAN(GENT) + H(YPERBOLIC)]

Tanis ★ ('teɪnɪs) *n* an ancient city located in the E part of the Nile delta: abandoned after the 6th century B.C.; at one time the capital of Egypt. Biblical name: **Zoan.**

Tanjore ★ (tæn'dʒɔː) *n* the former name of **Thanjavur.**

Tanjungpriok ★ (,tændʒuŋ'priːɒk) *n* a variant spelling of **Tandjungpriok.**

tank (tæŋk) *n* **1** a large container or reservoir for liquids or gases. **2** an armoured combat vehicle moving on tracks and armed with guns, etc. **3** *Brit. or US dialect.* a reservoir, lake, or pond. **4** *Sl., chiefly US.* a jail. **5** Also called: **tankful.** the quantity contained in a tank. **6** *Austral.* a reservoir formed by excavation and damming. ◆ *vb* **7** (*tr*) to put or keep in a tank. **8** *Sl.* to defeat heavily. ◆ See also **tank up.** [C17: from Gujarati (a language of W India) *tānkh* artificial lake, but infl. also by Port. *tanque*, from *estanque* pond, ult. from Vulgar L *stanticāre* (unattested) to block]

tanka ('tɑːŋkə) *n, pl* **tankas** *or* **tanka**. a Japanese verse form consisting of five lines, the first and third having five syllables, the others seven. [C19: from Japanese, from *tan* short + *ka* verse]

tankage ('tæŋkɪdʒ) *n* **1** the capacity or contents of a tank or tanks. **2** the act of storing in a tank or tanks, or a fee charged for this. **3** *Agriculture*. **3a** fertilizer consisting of the dried and ground residues of animal carcasses. **3b** a protein supplement feed for livestock.

tankard ('tæŋkəd) *n* a large one-handled drinking vessel sometimes fitted with a hinged lid. [C14]

tank engine *or* **locomotive** *n* a steam locomotive that carries its water supply in tanks mounted around its boiler.

tanker ('tæŋkə) *n* a ship, lorry, or aeroplane designed to carry liquid in bulk, such as oil.

tank farming *n* another name for **hydroponics**.
▸ **tank farmer** *n*

tank top *n* a sleeveless upper garment with wide shoulder straps and a low neck. [C20: after *tank suits*, one-piece bathing costumes of the 1920s worn in tanks or swimming pools]

tank up *vb* (*adv*) *Chiefly Brit*. **1** to fill the tank of (a vehicle) with petrol. **2** *Sl.* to imbibe or cause to imbibe a large quantity of alcoholic drink.

tank wagon *or esp. US & Canad.* **tank car** *n* a form of railway wagon carrying a tank for the transport of liquids.

Tannenberg ★ (German 'tanənbɛrk) *n* a village in N Poland, formerly in East Prussia: site of a decisive defeat of the Teutonic Knights by the Poles in 1410 and of a decisive German victory over the Russians in 1914. Polish name: **Stębark**.

tanner[1] ('tænə) *n* a person who tans skins and hides.

tanner[2] ('tænə) *n Brit*. an informal word for **sixpence**. [C19: from ?]

tannery ('tænərɪ) *n, pl* **tanneries**. a place or building where skins and hides are tanned.

Tannhäuser ★ ('tæn,hɔɪzə) *n* 13th-century German minnesinger, identified with a legendary knight. The legend forms the basis of an opera by Wagner.

tannic ('tænɪk) *adj* of, relating to, containing, or produced from tan, tannin, or tannic acid.

tannin ('tænɪn) *n* any of a class of yellowish compounds found in many plants and used as tanning agents, mordants, medical astringents, etc. Also called: **tannic acid**. [C19: from F *tanin*, from TAN[1]]

Tannoy ('tænɔɪ) *n Trademark*. a type of public-address system.

Tans (tænz) *pl n* **the**. *Irish inf.* short for the **Black and Tans**.

tansy ('tænzɪ) *n, pl* **tansies**. any of numerous plants having yellow flowers in flat-topped clusters and formerly used in medicine and for seasoning. [C15: from OF *tanesie*, from Med. L *athanasia* (from its alleged power to prolong life) from Gk: immortality]

Tanta ★ ('tæntə) *n* a city in N Egypt, on the Nile delta: noted for its Muslim festivals. Pop.: 380 000 (1992 est.).

tantalite ('tæntə,laɪt) *n* a heavy brownish mineral: it occurs in coarse granite and is an ore of tantalum. [C19: from TANTALUM + -ITE[1]]

tantalize *or* **tantalise** ('tæntə,laɪz) *vb* **tantalizes, tantalizing, tantalized** *or* **tantalises, tantalising, tantalised**. (*tr*) to tease or make frustrated, as by tormenting with the sight of something desired but inaccessible. [C16: from TANTALUS]
▸ **,tantali'zation** *or* **,tantali'sation** *n* ▸ **'tanta,lizing** *or* **'tanta,lising** *adj* ▸ **'tanta,lizingly** *or* **'tanta,lisingly** *adv*

tantalum ('tæntələm) *n* a hard greyish-white metallic element: used in electrolytic rectifiers and in alloys to increase hardness and chemical resistance, esp. in surgical instruments. Symbol: Ta; atomic no.: 73; atomic wt.: 180.95. [C19: after TANTALUS, from the metal's incapacity to absorb acids]

tantalus ('tæntələs) *n Brit*. a case in which bottles may be locked with their contents tantalizingly visible.

Tantalus ★ ('tæntələs) *n Greek myth*. a king, the father of Pelops, punished in Hades for his misdeeds by having to stand in water that recedes when he tries to drink it and under fruit that moves away as he reaches for it.

tantamount ('tæntə,maunt) *adj* (*postpositive; foll. by to*) as good (as); equivalent in effect (to). [C17: from Anglo-F *tant amunter* to amount to as much]

tantara ('tæntərə, tæn'tɑːrə) *n* a fanfare or blast, as on a trumpet or horn. [C16: from L *taratantara*, imit. of the sound of the tuba]

tantivy (tæn'tɪvɪ) *adv* **1** at full speed; rapidly. ◆ *n, pl* **tantivies**, *sentence substitute*. **2** a hunting cry, esp. at full gallop. [C17: ? imit. of galloping hooves]

tant mieux French. (tɑ̃ mjø) so much the better.

tanto ('tæntəu) *adv Music*. too much; excessively. [It.]

tant pis French. (tɑ̃ pi) so much the worse.

Tantrism ('tæntrɪzəm) *n* **1** a movement within Hinduism combining magical and mystical elements and with sacred writings of its own (**the Tantra**). **2** a similar movement within Buddhism. [C18: from Sansk. *tantra*, lit.: warp, hence doctrine]
▸ **'Tantric** *adj* ▸ **'Tantrist** *n*

tantrum ('tæntrəm) *n* (*often pl*) a childish fit of rage; outburst of bad temper. [C18: from ?]

Tan-tung ★ ('tæn'tuŋ) *n* a variant transliteration of the Chinese name for **Andong**.

Tanzania ★ (,tænzə'nɪə) *n* a republic in E Africa, on the Indian Ocean: formed by the union of the independent states of Tanganyika and Zanzibar in 1964; a member of the Commonwealth. Exports include coffee, tea, sisal, and cotton. Official languages: Swahili and English. Religions: Christian, Muslim, and animist. Currency: Tanzanian shilling. Capital: Dodoma. Pop.: 29 461 000 (1997). Area: 945 203 sq. km (364 943 sq. miles).
▸ **,Tanza'nian** *adj, n*

Tao (tau) *n* (in the philosophy of Taoism) **1** that in virtue of which all things happen or exist. **2** the rational basis of human conduct. **3** the course of life and its relation to eternal truth. [Chinese, lit.: path, way]

Taoiseach ('ti:ʃæx) *n* the prime mininster of the Irish Republic. [from Irish, lit.: leader]

Taoism ('tauɪzəm) *n* a system of religion and philosophy based on the teachings of Lao Zi and advocating a simple honest life and noninterference with the course of natural events.
▸ **'Taoist** *n, adj* ▸ **,Tao'istic** *adj*

taonga (tɑ'ɒŋgə) *n NZ*. anything highly prized. [Maori]

tap[1] (tæp) *vb* **taps, tapping, tapped**. **1** to strike (something) lightly and usually repeatedly. **2** (*tr*) to produce by striking in this way: *to tap a rhythm*. **3** (*tr*) to strike lightly with (something): *to tap one's finger on the desk*. **4** (*intr*) to walk with a tapping sound. **5** (*tr*) to attach reinforcing pieces to (the toe or heel of a shoe). ◆ *n* **6** a light blow or knock, or the sound made by it. **7** the metal piece attached to the toe or heel of a shoe used for tap-dancing. **8** short for **tap-dancing**. ◆ See also **taps**. [C13 *tappen*, prob. from OF *taper*, of Gmc origin]

tap[2] (tæp) *n* **1** a valve by which a fluid flow from a pipe can be controlled. US names: **faucet, spigot**. **2** a stopper to plug a cask or barrel. **3** a particular quality of alcoholic drink, esp. when contained in casks: *an excellent tap*. **4** *Brit*. short for **taproom**. **5** the withdrawal of fluid from a bodily cavity. **6** a tool for cutting female screw threads. **7** *Electronics, chiefly US & Canad.* a connection made at some point between the end terminals of an inductor, resistor, etc. Usual Brit. name: **tapping**. **8** *Stock Exchange*. **8a** an issue of a government security released slowly onto the market when its market price reaches a predetermined level. **8b** (*as modifier*): *tap stock; tap issue*. **9** a concealed listening or recording device connected to a telephone or telegraph wire. **10 on tap. 10a** *Inf.* ready for use. **10b** (of drinks) on draught. ◆ *vb* **taps, tapping, tapped**. (*tr*) **11** to furnish with a tap. **12** to draw off with or as if with a tap. **13** to cut into (a tree) and draw off sap from it. **14** *Brit. inf.* **14a** to ask (someone) for money: *he tapped me for a fiver*. **14b** to obtain (money) from someone. **15** to connect a tap to (a telephone or telegraph wire). **16** to make a connection to (a pipe, drain, etc.). **17** to cut a female screw thread in (an object or material) by use of a

tap. **18** *Inf.* (of a sports team or an employer) to make an illicit attempt to recruit (a player or employee bound by an existing contract). [OE *tæppa*]
▸ 'tapper *n*

tapa ('tɑːpə) *n* **1** the inner bark of the paper mulberry. **2** a cloth made from this in the Pacific islands. [C19: from native Polynesian name]

Tapajós ★ (*Portuguese* tapa'ʒɔs) *n* a river in N Brazil, rising in N central Mato Grosso and flowing northeast to the Amazon. Length: about 800 km (500 miles).

tapas ('tæpəs) *pl n* **a** light snacks or appetizers, usually eaten with drinks. **b** (*as modifier*): *a tapas bar*. [from Sp. *tapa* cover, lid]

tap dance *n* **1** a step dance in which the performer wears shoes equipped with taps that make a rhythmic sound on the stage as he dances. ◆ *vb* **tap-dance, tap-dances, tap-dancing, tap-danced.** (*intr*) **2** to perform a tap dance.
▸ 'tap-,dancer *n* ▸ 'tap-,dancing *n*

tape (teɪp) *n* **1** a long thin strip of cotton, linen, etc., used for binding, fastening, etc. **2** a long narrow strip of paper, metal, etc. **3** a string stretched across the track at the end of a race course. **4** See **magnetic tape, ticker tape, paper tape, tape recording.** ◆ *vb* **tapes, taping, taped.** (*mainly tr*) **5** (*also intr*) Also: **tape record.** to record (speech, music, etc.). **6** to furnish with tapes. **7** to bind, measure, secure, or wrap with tape. **8** (*usually passive*) *Brit. inf.* to take stock of (a person or situation). [OE *tæppe*]
▸ 'tape,like *adj* ▸ 'taper *n*

tape deck *n* **1** a tape recording unit in a hi-fi system. **2** the platform supporting the spools, cassettes, or cartridges of a tape recorder, incorporating the motor and the playback, recording, and erasing heads.

tape machine *n* **1** another word for **tape recorder. 2** a telegraphic device that records current stock quotations electronically or on ticker tape. US equivalent: **ticker.**

tape measure *n* a tape or length of metal marked off in inches, centimetres, etc., used for measuring. Also called (esp. US): **tapeline.**

tapenade ('tæpənɑːd) *n* a savoury paste made from capers, olives, and anchovies, with olive oil and lemon juice. [C20: F, from Provençal *tapéo* capers]

taper ('teɪpə) *vb* **1** to become or cause to become narrower towards one end. **2** (often foll. by *off*) to become or cause to become smaller or less significant. ◆ *n* **3** a thin candle. **4** a thin wooden or waxed strip for transferring a flame; spill. **5** a narrowing. **6** any feeble light. [OE *tapor*, prob. from L *papyrus* papyrus (from its use as a wick)]
▸ 'taperer *n* ▸ 'tapering *adj*

tape recorder *n* an electrical device used for recording sounds on magnetic tape and usually also for reproducing them.

tape recording *n* **1** the act of recording on magnetic tape. **2** the magnetized tape used for this. **3** the speech, music, etc., so recorded.

tape streamer *n Computing.* an electromechanical device that enables data to be copied byte by byte from a hard disk onto magnetic tape for security or storage.

tapestry ('tæpɪstrɪ) *n, pl* **tapestries. 1** a heavy woven fabric, often in the form of a picture, used for wall hangings, furnishings, etc. **2** another word for **needlepoint** (sense 1). **3** a colourful and complicated situation: *the rich tapestry of life.* [C15: from OF *tapisserie* carpeting, from OF *tapiz*; see TAPIS]
▸ 'tapestried *adj*

tapeworm ('teɪp,wɜːm) *n* any of a class of parasitic ribbon-like flatworms. The adults inhabit the intestines of vertebrates.

taphole ('tæp,həʊl) *n* a hole in a furnace for running off molten metal or slag.

taphouse ('tæp,haʊs) *n Now rare.* an inn.

tapioca (,tæpɪ'əʊkə) *n* a beadlike starch obtained from cassava root, used in cooking as a thickening agent, esp. in puddings. [C18: via Port. from Tupi *tipioca* pressed-out juice, from *tipi* residue + *ok* to squeeze out]

tapir ('teɪpə) *n, pl* **tapirs** *or* **tapir.** any of various mammals of South and Central America and SE Asia, having an elon-

gated snout, three-toed hind legs, and four-toed forelegs. [C18: from Tupi *tapiira*]

tapis ('tæpiː) *n, pl* **tapis. 1** tapestry or carpeting, esp. as formerly used to cover a table. **2 on the tapis.** currently under consideration. [C17: from F, from OF *tapiz*, from Gk *tapētion* rug, from *tapēs* carpet]

tappet ('tæpɪt) *n* a mechanical part that reciprocates to receive or transmit intermittent motion. [C18: from TAP¹ + -ET]

taproom ('tæp,ruːm, -,rʊm) *n* a bar, as in a hotel or pub.

taproot ('tæp,ruːt) *n* the main root of plants such as the dandelion, which grows vertically downwards and bears smaller lateral roots.

taps (tæps) *n* (*functioning as sing*) **1** *Chiefly US.* **1a** (in army camps, etc.) a signal given on a bugle, drum, etc., indicating that lights are to be put out. **1b** any similar signal, as at a military funeral. **2** (in the Guide movement) a closing song sung at an evening camp fire or at the end of a meeting.

tapster ('tæpstə) *n* **1** *Rare.* a barman. **2** (in W Africa) a man who taps palm trees. [OE *tæppestre*, fem. of *tæppere*, from *tappian* to TAP²]

tap water *n* water drawn off through taps from pipes in a house, as distinguished from distilled water, mineral water, etc.

tar¹ (tɑː) *n* **1** any of various dark viscid substances obtained by the destructive distillation of organic matter such as coal, wood, or peat. **2** another name for **coal tar.** ◆ *vb* **tars, tarring, tarred.** (*tr*) **3** to coat with tar. **4 tar and feather.** to punish by smearing tar and feathers over (someone). **5 tarred with the same brush.** regarded as having the same faults. [OE *teoru*]
▸ 'tarry *adj* ▸ 'tarriness *n*

tar² (tɑː) *n* an informal word for **seaman.** [C17: short for TARPAULIN]

Tara ★ ('tærə, 'tɑːrə) *n* a village in Co. Meath near Dublin, by the **Hill of Tara,** the historic seat of the ancient Irish kings.

Tarabulus el Gharb ★ (tə'rɑːbələs ɛl 'gɑːb) *n* transliteration of the Arabic name for **Tripoli** (Libya).

Tarabulus esh Sham ★ (tə'rɑːbələs ɛʃ 'ʃæm) *n* transliteration of the Arabic name for **Tripoli** (Lebanon).

taradiddle ('tærə,dɪdˌl) *n* a variant spelling of **tarradiddle.**

tarakihi *or* **terakihi** ('tærə,kiːhiː) *n, pl* **tarakihis.** a common edible sea fish of New Zealand waters. [from Maori]

taramasalata (,tærəməsə'lɑːtə) *n* a creamy pale pink paté, made from the roe of grey mullet or smoked cod and served as an hors d'oeuvre. [C20: from Mod. Gk, from *tarama* cod's roe]

tarantass (,tɑːrən'tæs) *n* a four-wheeled Russian carriage without springs. [C19: from Russian *tarantas*]

tarantella (,tærən'tɛlə) *n* **1** a peasant dance from S Italy. **2** a piece of music composed for or in the rhythm of this dance. [C18: from It., from TARANTO]

tarantism ('tærən,tɪzəm) *n* a nervous disorder marked by uncontrollable bodily movement, widespread in S Italy during the 15th to 17th centuries: popularly thought to be caused by the bite of a tarantula. [C17: from NL *tarantismus*, from TARANTO]

Taranto ★ (tə'ræntəʊ; *Italian* 'tɑːranto) *n* a port in SE Italy, in Apulia on the **Gulf of Taranto** (an inlet of the Ionian Sea): the chief city of Magna Graecia; taken by the Romans in 272 B.C. Pop.: 213 933 (1994 est.). Latin name: **Tarentum.**

tarantula (tə'ræntjʊlə) *n, pl* **tarantulas** *or* **tarantulae** (-,liː) **1** any of various large hairy spiders of tropical America. **2** a large hairy spider of S Europe. [C16: from Med. L, from Olt. *tarantola*, from TARANTO]

Tarawa ★ (tə'rɑːwə) *n* an atoll in Kiribati, occupying a chain of islets surrounding a lagoon in the W central Pacific: the capital of Kiribati, Bairiki, is on this atoll. Pop.: 29 028 (1990).

taraxacum (tə'ræksəkəm) *n* **1** any of a genus of perennial plants of the composite family, such as the dandelion. **2** the dried root of the dandelion, used as a laxative,

★ people and places

diuretic, and tonic. [C18: from Med. L, from Ar. *tarakhshaqūn* wild chicory, ? of Persian origin]

Tarbes ★ (*French* tarb) *n* a town in SW France: noted for the breeding of Anglo-Arab horses. Pop.: 50 228 (1990).

tarboosh (tɑːˈbuːʃ) *n* a felt or cloth brimless cap, usually red and often with a silk tassel, worn by Muslim men. [C18: from Ar. *tarbūsh*]

tarboy (ˈtɑːˌbɔɪ) *n Austral. & NZ inf.* a boy who applies tar to the skin of sheep cut during shearing.

Tardenoisian (ˌtɑːdəˈnɔɪzɪən) *adj* of or referring to a Mesolithic culture characterized by small flint instruments. [C20: after *Tardenois*, France, where implements were found]

tardigrade (ˈtɑːdɪˌɡreɪd) *n* any of various minute aquatic segmented eight-legged invertebrates occurring in soil, ditches, etc. Popular name: **water bear**. [C17: via L *tardigradus*, from *tardus* sluggish + *gradī* to walk]

tardy (ˈtɑːdɪ) *adj* **tardier, tardiest. 1** occurring later than expected. **2** slow in progress, growth, etc. [C15: from OF *tardif*, from L *tardus* slow]
▸ **ˈtardily** *adv* ▸ **ˈtardiness** *n*

tare[1] (teə) *n* **1** any of various vetch plants of Eurasia and N Africa. **2** the seed of any of these plants. **3** *Bible.* a weed, thought to be the darnel. [C14: from ?]

tare[2] (teə) *n* **1** the weight of the wrapping or container in which goods are packed. **2** a deduction from gross weight to compensate for this. **3** the weight of an unladen vehicle. ◆ *vb* **tares, taring, tared. 4** (*tr*) to weigh (a package, etc.) in order to calculate the amount of tare. [C15: from OF: waste, from Med. L *tara*, from Ar. *tarhah* something discarded, from *taraha* to reject]

Tarentum ★ (təˈrɛntəm) *n* the Latin name of **Taranto**.

targe (tɑːdʒ) *n* an archaic word for **shield**. [C13: from OF, of Gmc origin]

target (ˈtɑːɡɪt) *n* **1a** an object or area at which an archer or marksman aims, usually a round flat surface marked with concentric rings. **1b** (*as modifier*): *target practice.* **2a** any point or area aimed at. **2b** (*as modifier*): *target area; target company.* **3** a fixed goal or objective. **4** a person or thing at which an action or remark is directed or the object of a person's feelings. **5** a joint of lamb consisting of the breast and neck. **6** (*formerly*) a small round shield. **7** *Physics, electronics.* **7a** a substance subjected to bombardment by electrons or other particles, or to irradiation. **7b** an electrode in a television camera tube whose surface is scanned by the electron beam. **8** *Electronics.* an object detected by the reflection of a radar or sonar signal, etc. ◆ *vb* **targets, targeting, targeted.** (*tr*) **9** to make a target of. **10** to direct or aim: *to target benefits at those most in need.* [C14: from OF *targette* a little shield, from OF TARGE]

tariff (ˈtærɪf) *n* **1a** a tax levied by a government on imports or occasionally exports. **1b** a system or list of such taxes. **2** any schedule of prices, fees, fares, etc. **3** *Chiefly Brit.* **3a** a method of charging for the supply of services such as gas and electricity. **3b** a schedule of such charges. **4** *Chiefly Brit.* a bill of fare with prices listed; menu. ◆ *vb* (*tr*) **5** to set a tariff on. **6** to price according to a schedule of tariffs. [C16: from It. *tariffa*, from Ar. *ta'rīfa* to inform]

tariff office *n Insurance.* a company whose premiums are based on a tariff agreed with other insurance companies.

Tarim ★ (ˈtɑːˈriːm) *n* a river in NW China, in Xinjiang Uygur AR: flows east along the N edge of the Taklimakan Shama desert, dividing repeatedly and forming lakes among the dunes, finally disappearing in the Lop Nor depression; the chief river of Xinjiang Uygur AR: drains the great **Tarim Basin** between the Tian Shan and Kunlun mountain systems of central Asia, an area of about 906 500 sq. km (350 000 sq. miles). Length: 2190 km (1360 miles).

Tarkington ★ (ˈtɑːkɪŋtən) *n* (**Newton**) Booth. 1869–1946, US novelist. His works include *Monsieur Beaucaire* (1900) and *The Magnificent Ambersons* (1918).

Tarkovsky ★ (tɑːˈkɒfskɪ) *n* Andrei (*Russian* anˈdrjej). 1932–86, Soviet film director, whose films include *Andrei Rublev* (1966) and *The Sacrifice* (1986).

tarlatan (ˈtɑːlətən) *n* an open-weave cotton fabric, used

for stiffening garments. [C18: from F *tarlatane*, var. of *tarnatane* type of muslin, ? of Indian origin]

Tarmac (ˈtɑːmæk) *n* **1** *Trademark.* (*often not cap.*) a paving material that consists of crushed stone rolled and bound with a mixture of tar and bitumen, esp. as used for a road, airport runway, etc. Full name: **Tarmacadam** (ˌtɑːməˈkædəm). See also **macadam.** ◆ *vb* **Tarmacs, Tarmacking, Tarmacked.** (*tr*) **2** (*usually not cap.*) to apply Tarmac to.

tarn (tɑːn) *n* a small mountain lake or pool. [C14: from ON]

Tarn ★ (*French* tarn) *n* **1** a department of S France, in Midi-Pyrénées region. Capital: Albi. Pop.: 341 954 (1994 est.). Area: 5780 sq. km (2254 sq. miles). **2** a river in SW France, rising in the Massif Central and flowing generally west to the Garonne River. Length: 375 km (233 miles).

tarnation (tɑːˈneɪʃən) *n* a euphemism for **damnation.**

Tarn-et-Garonne ★ (*French* tarnegarɔn) *n* a department of SW France, in Midi-Pyrénées region. Capital: Montauban. Pop.: 204 732 (1994 est.). Area: 3731 sq. km (1455 sq. miles).

tarnish (ˈtɑːnɪʃ) *vb* **1** to lose or cause to lose the shine, esp. by exposure to air or moisture resulting in surface oxidation; discolour. **2** to stain or become stained; taint. ◆ *n* **3** a tarnished condition, surface, or film. [C16: from OF *ternir* to make dull, from *terne* lustreless of Gmc origin]
▸ **ˈtarnishable** *adj*

Tarnopol ★ (tarˈnɔpɔl) *n* the Polish name for **Ternopol.**

Tarnów ★ (*Polish* ˈtarnuf) *n* an industrial city in SE Poland. Pop.: 121 600 (1995 est.).

taro (ˈtɑːrəʊ) *n, pl* **taros. 1** a plant cultivated in the tropics for its large edible rootstock. **2** the rootstock of this plant. ◆ Also called: **eddo.** [C18: from Tahitian & Maori]

tarot (ˈtærəʊ) *n* **1** one of a special pack of cards, now used mainly for fortune-telling. **2** a card in a tarot pack with distinctive symbolic design. ◆ *adj* **3** relating to tarot cards. [C16: from F, from OIt. *tarocco*, from ?]

tarpan (ˈtɑːpæn) *n* a European wild horse, now extinct. [from Tatar]

tarpaulin (tɑːˈpɔːlɪn) *n* **1** a heavy waterproof fabric made of canvas or similar material coated with tar, wax, or paint. **2** a sheet of this fabric. **3** a hat made of or covered with this fabric, esp. a sailor's hat. **4** a rare word for **seaman.** [C17: prob. from TAR[1] + PALL[1] + -ING[1]]

Tarpeia ★ (tɑːˈpiːə) *n* (in Roman legend) a vestal virgin, who betrayed Rome to the Sabines and was killed by them when she requested a reward.

Tarpeian Rock ★ (tɑːˈpiːən) *n* (in ancient Rome) a cliff on the Capitoline hill from which traitors were hurled.

tarpon (ˈtɑːpən) *n, pl* **tarpons** or **tarpon.** a large silvery game fish of warm oceans. [C17: ?from Du. *tarpoen*, from ?]

Tarquin ★ (ˈtɑːkwɪn) *n* **1** Latin name *Lucius Tarquinius Priscus.* fifth legendary king of Rome (616–578 B.C.). **2** Latin name *Lucius Tarquinius Superbus.* seventh and last legendary king of Rome (534–510 B.C.).

tarradiddle (ˈtærəˌdɪdəl) *n* **1** a trifling lie. **2** nonsense; twaddle. [C18: from ?]

tarragon (ˈtærəɡən) *n* **1** an aromatic plant of the Old World, having leaves which are used as seasoning. **2** the leaves of this plant. [C16: from F *targon*, from Med. L *tarcon*, ? ult. from Gk *drakontion* adderwort]

Tarragona ★ (*Spanish* tarraˈɣona) *n* a port in NE Spain, on the Mediterranean: one of the richest seaports of the Roman Empire; destroyed by the Moors (714). Pop.: 110 003 (1994 est.). Latin name: **Tarraco** (təˈrɑːkəʊ).

Tarrasa ★ (*Spanish* taˈrrasa) *n* a city in NE Spain: textile centre. Pop.: 161 428 (1994 est.).

tarry (ˈtærɪ) *vb* **tarries, tarrying, tarried. 1** (*intr*) to delay; linger. **2** (*intr*) to remain temporarily or briefly. **3** (*intr*) to wait or stay. **4** (*tr*) *Arch. or poetic.* to await. [C14 *tarien*, from ?]
▸ **ˈtarrier** *n*

tarsal ('tɑːs°l) *adj* **1** of the tarsus or tarsi. ◆ *n* **2** a tarsal bone.

tarseal ('tɑːˌsiːl) *n NZ*. **1** the bitumen surface of a road. **2 the tarseal.** the main highway.

Tarshish ★ ('tɑːʃɪʃ) *n Old Testament*. an ancient port, mentioned in I Kings 10:22, situated in Spain or in one of the Phoenician colonies in Sardinia.

tarsia ('tɑːsɪə) *n* another term for **intarsia**. [C17: from It., from Ar. *tarsi'*]

tarsier ('tɑːsɪə) *n* any of several nocturnal arboreal primates of Indonesia and the Philippines, having huge eyes, long hind legs, and digits ending in pads to facilitate climbing. [C18: from F, from *tarse* the flat of the foot; see TARSUS]

tarsus ('tɑːsəs) *n, pl* **tarsi** (-saɪ). **1** the bones of the ankle and heel, collectively. **2** the corresponding part in other mammals and in amphibians and reptiles. **3** the connective tissue supporting the free edge of each eyelid. **4** the part of an insect's leg that lies distal to the tibia. [C17: from NL, from Gk *tarsos* flat surface, instep]

Tarsus ★ ('tɑːsəs) *n* **1** a city in SE Turkey, on the Tarsus River: site of ruins of ancient Tarsus, capital of Cilicia, and birthplace of St Paul. Pop.: 225 000 (1994 est.). **2** a river in SE Turkey, in Cilicia, rising in the Taurus Mountains and flowing south past Tarsus to the Mediterranean. Ancient name: **Cydnus**. Length: 153 km (95 miles).

tart[1] (tɑːt) *n* a pastry case often having no top crust, with a filling of fruit, custard, etc. [C14: from OF *tarte*, from ?]

tart[2] (tɑːt) *adj* **1** (of a flavour, etc.) sour; acid. **2** cutting; sharp: *a tart remark*. [OE *teart* rough]
▸ **'tartly** *adv* ▸ **'tartness** *n*

tart[3] (tɑːt) *n Inf*. a promiscuous woman, esp. a prostitute. See also **tart up**. [C19: shortened from SWEETHEART]
▸ **'tarty** *adj*

tartan ('tɑːt°n) *n* **1a** a design of straight lines, crossing at right angles to give a chequered appearance, esp. the distinctive design or designs associated with each Scottish clan. **1b** (*as modifier*): *a tartan kilt*. **2** a fabric or garment with this design. [C16: ?from OF *tertaine* linsey-woolsey, from OSp. *tiritaña* a fine silk fabric, from *tiritar* to rustle]
▸ **'tartaned** *adj*

tartar[1] ('tɑːtə) *n* **1** a hard deposit on the teeth, consisting of food, cellular debris, and mineral salts. **2** a brownish-red substance consisting mainly of potassium hydrogen tartrate, deposited during the fermentation of wine. [C14: from Med. L *tartarum*, from Med. Gk *tartaron*]

tartar[2] ('tɑːtə) *n* (*sometimes cap.*) a fearsome or formidable person. [C16: special use of TARTAR]

Tartar ('tɑːtə) *n, adj* a variant spelling of **Tatar**.

Tartarean (tɑːˈtɛərɪən) *adj Literary*. of or relating to Tartarus; infernal.

tartar emetic *n* antimony potassium tartrate, a poisonous, crystalline salt used as a mordant and in medicine.

tartaric (tɑːˈtærɪk) *adj* of, containing, or derived from tartar or tartaric acid.

tartaric acid *n* a colourless crystalline acid which is found in many fruits: used as a food additive (**E334**) in soft drinks, confectionery, and baking powders, and in tanning and photography. Formula: $(CHOH)_2(COOH)_2$. Systematic name: **2,3-dihydroxybutanedioic acid.**

tartar sauce *n* a mayonnaise sauce mixed with hard-boiled egg yolks, chopped herbs, capers, etc. [from F *sauce tartare*, from TARTAR]

Tartarus ★ ('tɑːtərəs) *n Greek myth*. **1** an abyss under Hades where the Titans were imprisoned. **2** a part of Hades reserved for evildoers. **3** the underworld; Hades. **4** a primordial god who became the father of the monster Typhon. [C16: from L, from Gk *Tartaros*, of obscure origin]

Tartary ★ ('tɑːtərɪ) *n* a variant spelling of **Tatary**.

tartlet ('tɑːtlɪt) *n Brit*. an individual pastry case with a sweet or savoury filling.

tartrate ('tɑːtreɪt) *n* any salt or ester of tartaric acid.

tartrated ('tɑːtreɪtɪd) *adj* being in the form of a tartrate.

tartrazine ('tɑːtrəˌziːn, -zɪn) *n* an azo dye that produces a yellow colour: used as a food additive (**E102**), in drugs, and to dye textiles.

Tartu ★ (*Russian* 'tartu) *n* a city in Estonia; university (1632). Pop.: 104 907 (1995). Former name (11th century until 1918): **Yurev.** German name: **Dorpat.**

tart up *vb* (*tr; adv*) *Brit. inf*. **1** to dress and make (oneself) up in a provocative or promiscuous way. **2** to decorate or improve the appearance of: *to tart up a bar*.

tarwhine ('tɑːˌwaɪn) *n* any of various Australian marine food fishes, esp. the sea bream. [?from Abor.]

Tarzan ('tɑːzən) *n* (*sometimes not cap.*) *Inf., often ironical*. a man with great physical strength, agility, and virility. [C20: after the hero of a series of stories by E. R. BURROUGHS]

Tas. *abbrev. for* Tasmania.

Tashkent ★ (*Russian* taʃˈkjent) *n* the capital of Uzbekistan: one of the oldest cities in central Asia; taken by the Russians in 1865; cotton textile manufacturing. Pop.: 2 106 000 (1994 est.).

tasimeter (təˈsɪmɪtə) *n* a device for measuring small temperature changes. It depends on the changes of pressure resulting from expanding or contracting solids. [C19 *tasi-*, from Gk *tasis* tension + -METER]
▸ **tasimetric** (ˌtæsɪˈmɛtrɪk) *adj* ▸ **taˈsimetry** *n*

task (tɑːsk) *n* **1** a specific piece of work required to be done. **2** an unpleasant or difficult job or duty. **3** any piece of work. **4 take to task.** to criticize or reprove. ◆ *vb* (*tr*) **5** to assign a task to. **6** to subject to severe strain; tax. [C13: from OF *tasche*, from Med. L *tasca*, from *taxa* tax, from L *taxāre* to TAX]

task force *n* **1** a temporary grouping of military units formed to undertake a specific mission. **2** any organization set up to carry out a continuing task.

taskmaster ('tɑːskˌmɑːstə) *n* a person, discipline, etc., that enforces work, esp. hard or continuous work.
▸ **'taskˌmistress** *fem n*

taskwork ('tɑːskˌwɜːk) *n* **1** hard or unpleasant work. **2** a rare word for **piecework**.

Tasman ★ ('tæzmən) *n* **Abel Janszoon** ('abəl 'jansuːn). 1603–59, Dutch navigator, who discovered Tasmania, New Zealand, and the Tonga and Fiji Islands (1642–43).

Tasmania ★ (tæzˈmeɪnɪə) *n* an island in the S Pacific, south of mainland Australia: forms, with offshore islands, the smallest state of Australia; discovered by the Dutch explorer Tasman in 1642; used as a penal colony by the British (1803–53); mostly forested and mountainous. Capital: Hobart. Pop.: 473 200 (1996 est.). Area: 68 332 sq. km (26 383 sq. miles). Former name (1642–1855): **Van Diemen's Land.**
▸ **Tasˈmanian** *adj, n*

Tasmanian devil *n* a small ferocious carnivorous marsupial of Tasmania.

Tasmanian wolf *or* **tiger** *n* other names for **thylacine**.

Tasman Sea ★ *n* the part of the Pacific between SE Australia and NW New Zealand.

tass (tæs) *or* **tassie** ('tæsɪ) *n Scot. & N English dialect*. **1** a cup or glass. **2** its contents. [C15: from OF *tasse* cup, from Ar. *tassah* basin, from Persian *tast*]

Tass (tæs) *n* (formerly) the principal news agency of the Soviet Union: replaced in 1992 by Itar Tass. [T(*elegrafnoye*) a(*gentstvo*) S(*ovetskogo*) S(*oyuza*) Telegraphic Agency of the Soviet Union]

tassel ('tæs°l) *n* **1** a tuft of loose threads secured by a knot or knob, used to decorate soft furnishings, clothes, etc. **2** anything resembling this, esp. the tuft of stamens at the tip of a maize inflorescence. ◆ *vb* **tassels, tasselling, tasselled** *or US* **tassels, tasseling, tasseled. 3** (*tr*) to adorn with tassels. **4** (*intr*) (of maize) to produce stamens in a tuft. [C13: from OF, from Vulgar L *tassellus* (unattested), changed from L *taxillus* a small die]

Tassie *or* **Tassy** ★ ('tæzɪ) *n, Austral. inf*. **1** Tasmania. **2** (*pl* **Tassies**) a native or inhabitant of Tasmania.

Tasso ★ (*Italian* 'tasso) *n* **Torquato** (torˈkwaːto). 1544–95, Italian poet.

taste (teɪst) *n* **1** the sense by which the qualities and flavour of a substance are distinguished by the taste buds **2**

★ people and places

the sensation experienced by means of the taste buds. **3** the act of tasting. **4** a small amount eaten, drunk, or tried on the tongue. **5** a brief experience of something: *a taste of the whip.* **6** a preference or liking for something. **7** the ability to make discerning judgments about aesthetic, artistic, and intellectual matters. **8** judgment of aesthetic or social matters according to a generally accepted standard: *bad taste.* **9** discretion; delicacy: *that remark lacks taste.* ◆ *vb* **tastes, tasting, tasted. 10** to distinguish the taste of (a substance) by means of the taste buds. **11** (*usually tr*) to take a small amount of (a food, liquid, etc.) into the mouth, esp. in order to test the quality. **12** (often foll. by *of*) to have a specific flavour or taste. **13** (when *intr*, usually foll. by *of*) to have an experience of (something): *to taste success.* **14** (*tr*) an archaic word for **enjoy.** [C13: from OF *taster,* ult. from L *taxāre* to appraise]
▸ **'tastable** *adj*

taste bud *n* any of the elevated sensory organs on the surface of the tongue, by means of which the sensation of taste is experienced.

tasteful ('teɪstful) *adj* indicating good taste: *a tasteful design.*
▸ **'tastefully** *adv* ▸ **'tastefulness** *n*

tasteless ('teɪstlɪs) *adj* **1** lacking in flavour; insipid. **2** lacking social or aesthetic taste.
▸ **'tastelessly** *adv* ▸ **'tastelessness** *n*

taster ('teɪstə) *n* **1** a person who samples food or drink for quality. **2** any device used in tasting or sampling. **3** a person employed, esp. formerly, to taste food and drink prepared for a king, etc., to test for poison. **4** a sample or preview of a product, experience, etc., intended to stimulate interest in the product, experience, etc., itself: *the single serves as a taster for the band's new album.*

tasty ('teɪstɪ) *adj* **tastier, tastiest.** having a pleasant flavour.
▸ **'tastily** *adv* ▸ **'tastiness** *n*

tat[1] (tæt) *vb* **tats, tatting, tatted.** to make (something) by tatting. [C19: from ?]

tat[2] (tæt) *n* **1** tatty articles or a tatty condition. **2** tasteless articles. **3** a tangled mass. [C20: back formation from TATTY]

tat[3] (tæt) *n* See **tit for tat.**

ta-ta (tæ'tɑ:) *sentence substitute. Brit. inf.* goodbye; farewell. [C19: from ?]

Tatar or **Tartar** ('tɑːtə) *n* **1a** a member of a Mongoloid people who established a powerful state in central Asia in the 13th century. **1b** a descendant of this people, now scattered throughout Russia and N central Asia. **2** any of the Turkic languages spoken by the present-day Tatars. ◆ *adj* **3** of or relating to the Tatars. [C14: from OF *Tartare,* from Med. L *Tartarus* (associated with L *Tartarus* the underworld), from Persian *Tātār*]
▸ **Tatarian** (tɑː'tɛərɪən), **Tar'tarian** or **Tataric** (tɑː'tærɪk), **Tar'taric** *adj*

Tatar Republic ★ *n* a constituent republic of W Russia, around the confluence of the Volga and Kama Rivers. Capital: Kazan. Pop.: 3 755 000 (1995 est.). Area: 68 000 sq. km (26 250 sq. miles).

Tatar Strait ★ *n* an arm of the Pacific between the mainland of SE Russia and Sakhalin Island, linking the Sea of Japan with the Sea of Okhotsk. Length: about 560 km (350 miles). Also called: **Gulf of Tatary.**

Tatary or **Tartary** ★ ('tɑːtərɪ) *n* **1** a historical region (with indefinite boundaries) in E Europe and Asia, inhabited by Bulgars until overrun by the Tatars in the mid-13th century: extended as far east as the Pacific under Genghis Khan. **2** Gulf of. another name for the **Tatar Strait.**

Tate ★ (teɪt) *n* **1** Sir Henry. 1819–99, British sugar refiner and philanthropist; founder of the Tate Gallery. **2** (**John Orley**) **Allen.** 1899–1979, US poet and critic.

Tate Gallery ★ *n* an art gallery in London, built in 1897.

tater ('teɪtə) *n* a dialect word for **potato.**

Tati ★ (*French* tati) *n* **Jacques** (ʒak), real name *Jacques Tatischeff.* 1908–82, French actor, creator of the character Monsieur Hulot.

tatouay ('tætu,eɪ) *n* a large armadillo of South America.

[C16: from Sp. *tatuay,* from Guarani, from *tatu* armadillo + *ai* worthless (because inedible)]

Tatra Mountains ★ ('tɑːtrə, 'tæt-) *pl n* a mountain range along the border between Slovakia and Poland, extending for about 64 km (40 miles): the highest range of the central Carpathians. Highest peak: Gerlachovka, 2663 m (8737 ft). Also called: **High Tatra.**

tatter ('tætə) *vb* **1** to make or become ragged or worn to shreds. ◆ *n* **2** a torn or ragged piece, esp. of material. [C14: from ON]

tatterdemalion (,tætədɪ'meɪljən) *n Rare.* a person dressed in ragged clothes. [C17: from TATTER + -*demalion,* from ?]

tattersall ('tætə,sɔːl) *n* a fabric having stripes or bars in a checked or squared pattern. [C19: after *Tattersall's,* a horse market in London founded by Richard *Tattersall* (died 1795), Brit. horseman; the horse blankets at the market orig. had this pattern]

Tattersall's ('tætə,sɔːlz) *n Austral.* **1** Also called (inf.): **Tatt's.** a lottery now based in Melbourne. **2** a name used for sportsmen's clubs. [after *Tattersall's* horse market; see TATTERSALL]

tatting ('tætɪŋ) *n* **1** an intricate type of lace made by looping a thread of cotton or linen by means of a hand shuttle. **2** the act or work of producing this. [C19: from ?]

tattle ('tæt³l) *vb* **tattles, tattling, tattled. 1** (*intr*) to gossip about another's personal matters. **2** (*tr*) to reveal by gossiping. **3** (*intr*) to talk idly; chat. ◆ *n* **4** the act or an instance of tattling. **5** a scandalmonger; gossip. [C15 (in the sense: to stammer, hesitate): from MDu. *tatelen* to prate, imit.]
▸ **'tattler** *n*

tattletale ('tæt³l,teɪl) *Chiefly US & Canad. n* **1** a scandalmonger or gossip. **2** another word for **telltale** (sense 1).

tattoo[1] (tæ'tuː) *n, pl* **tattoos. 1** (formerly) a signal by drum or bugle ordering the military to return to their quarters. **2** a military display or pageant. **3** any similar beating on a drum, etc. [C17: from Du. *taptoe,* from *tap toe!* turn off the taps! from *tap* tap of a barrel + *toe* to shut]

tattoo[2] (tæ'tuː) *vb* **tattoos, tattooing, tattooed. 1** to make (pictures or designs) on (the skin) by pricking and staining with indelible colours. ◆ *n, pl* **tattoos. 2** a design made by this process. **3** the practice of tattooing. [C18: from Tahitian *tatau*]
▸ **tat'tooer** or **tat'tooist** *n*

tatty ('tætɪ) *adj* **tattier, tattiest.** *Chiefly Brit.* worn out, shabby, or unkempt. [C16: of Scot. origin]
▸ **'tattily** *adv* ▸ **'tattiness** *n*

Tatum ★ ('teɪtəm) *n Art,* full name *Arthur Tatum.* 1910–56, US jazz pianist.

tau (tɔː, taʊ) *n* the 19th letter in the Greek alphabet (T or τ). [C13: from Gk]

tau cross *n* a cross shaped like the Greek letter tau. Also called: **Saint Anthony's cross.**

taught (tɔːt) *vb* the past tense and past participle of **teach.**

taunt (tɔːnt) *vb* (*tr*) **1** to provoke or deride with mockery, contempt, or criticism. **2** to tease; tantalize. ◆ *n* **3** a jeering remark. [C16: from F *tant pour tant* like for like]
▸ **'taunting** *adj*

Taunton ★ ('tɔːntən) *n* a market town in SW England, administrative centre of Somerset: scene of Judge Jeffreys' "Bloody Assize" (1685) after the Battle of Sedgemoor. Pop.: 55 855 (1991).

tau particle *n Physics.* a type of elementary particle classified as a lepton.

taupe (təʊp) *n* **a** a brownish-grey colour. **b** (*as adj*): *a taupe coat.* [C20: from F, lit.: mole, from L *talpa*]

Taupo ★ ('taʊpəʊ) *n Lake.* a lake in New Zealand, on central North Island: the largest lake of New Zealand. Area: 616 sq. km (238 sq. miles).

Tauranga ★ (taʊ'ræŋə) *n* a port in New Zealand, on NE North Island on the Bay of Plenty: exports dairy produce, meat, and timber. Pop.: 76 100 (1994).

taurine ('tɔːraɪn) *adj* of or resembling a bull. [C17: from L *taurīnus,* from *taurus* a bull]

tauromachy (tɔːˈrɒməkɪ) *n* the art or act of bullfighting. [C19: Gk *tauromakhia*, from *tauros* bull + *makhē* fight]

Taurus (ˈtɔːrəs) *n* **1** *Astron.* a constellation in the N hemisphere. **2** *Astrol.* Also called: the **Bull**. the second sign of the zodiac. The sun is in this sign between about April 20 and May 20. [C14: from L: bull]

Taurus Mountains ★ *pl n* a mountain range in S Turkey, parallel to the Mediterranean coast: crossed by the Cilician Gates; continued in the northeast by the Anti-Taurus range. Highest peak: Kaldi Dağ, 3734 m (12 251 ft).

taut (tɔːt) *adj* **1** tightly stretched; tense. **2** showing nervous strain; stressed. **3** *Chiefly naut.* in good order; neat. [C14 *tought*]
▸ **ˈtautly** *adv* ▸ **ˈtautness** *n*

tauten (ˈtɔːtᵊn) *vb* to make or become taut.

tauto- *or before a vowel* **taut-** *combining form.* identical or same: *tautology.* [from Gk *tauto,* from *to auto*]

tautog (tɔːˈtɒg) *n* a large dark-coloured food fish of the North American coast of the Atlantic Ocean. [C17: from Narraganset *tautauog,* pl. of *tautau* sheepshead]

tautology (tɔːˈtɒlədʒɪ) *n, pl* **tautologies. 1** the use of words that merely repeat elements of the meaning already conveyed, as in *Will these supplies be adequate enough?* in place of *Will these supplies be adequate?* **2** *Logic.* a statement that is always true, as in *either the sun is out or the sun is not out.* [C16: from LL *tautologia,* from Gk, from *tautologos*]
▸ **tautological** (ˌtɔːtᵊˈlɒdʒɪkᵊl) *or* **tauˈtologous** *adj*

tautomerism (tɔːˈtɒməˌrɪzəm) *n* the ability of certain chemical compounds to exist as a mixture of two interconvertible isomers in equilibrium. [C19: from TAUTO- + ISOMERISM]
▸ **tautomer** (ˈtɔːtəmə) *n* ▸ **tautomeric** (ˌtɔːtəˈmɛrɪk) *adj*

tautonym (ˈtɔːtənɪm) *n Biol.* a taxonomic name in which the generic and specific components are the same, as in *Rattus rattus* (black rat).
▸ **ˌtautoˈnymic** *or* **tautonymous** (tɔːˈtɒnəməs) *adj* ▸ **tauˈtonymy** *n*

Tavener ★ (ˈtævənə) *n* **John** (**Kenneth**). born 1944, British composer, whose works include the cantata *The Whale* (1966), the opera *Thérèse* (1979), and the choral work *The Last Discourse* (1998).

tavern (ˈtævən) *n* **1** a less common word for **pub. 2** *US, E Canad., & NZ.* a place licensed for the sale and consumption of alcoholic drink. [C13: from OF *taverne,* from L *taberna* hut]

taverna (təˈvɜːnə) *n* **1** (in Greece) a guesthouse that has its own bar. **2** a Greek restaurant. [C20: Mod. Gk, from L *taberna*]

Taverner ★ (ˈtævənə) *n* **John.** ?1495–1545, English composer, esp. of church music.

TAVR *abbrev. for* Territorial and Army Volunteer Reserve.

taw[1] (tɔː) *n* **1** a large marble used for shooting. **2** a game of marbles. **3** the line from which the players shoot in marbles. **4 back to taws.** *Austral. inf.* back to the beginning. [C18: from ?]

taw[2] (tɔː) *vb* (*tr*) to convert (skins) into leather by treatment with alum and salt rather than by normal tanning processes. [OE *tawian*]
▸ **ˈtawer** *n*

tawa (ˈtɑːwə) *n* a New Zealand timber tree with edible berries. [from Maori]

tawdry (ˈtɔːdrɪ) *adj* **tawdrier, tawdriest.** cheap, showy, and of poor quality: *tawdry jewellery.* [C16 *tawdry lace,* shortened & altered from *Seynt Audries lace,* finery sold at the fair of St *Audrey* (Etheldrida), 7th-century queen of Northumbria]
▸ **ˈtawdrily** *adv* ▸ **ˈtawdriness** *n*

tawny (ˈtɔːnɪ) *n* **a** a light brown to brownish-orange colour. **b** (*as adj*): *tawny port.* [C14: from OF *tané,* from *taner* to tan]
▸ **ˈtawniness** *n*

tawny owl *n* a European owl having a reddish-brown plumage and a round head.

tawse *or* **taws** (tɔːz) *n Chiefly Scot.* a leather strap having one end cut into thongs, formerly used as an instrument of punishment by a schoolteacher. [C16: prob. pl of obs. *taw* strip of leather; see TAW[2]]

tax (tæks) *n* **1** a compulsory financial contribution imposed by a government to raise revenue, levied on income or property, on the prices of goods and services, etc. **2** a heavy demand on something; strain. ◆ *vb* (*tr*) **3** to levy a tax on (persons, companies, etc.). **4** to make heavy demands on; strain. **5** to accuse or blame. **6** *Law.* to determine (the amount legally chargeable or allowable to a party to a legal action): *to tax costs.* **7** *Sl.* to demand money or goods from (someone) with menaces. [C13: from OF *taxer,* from L *taxāre* to appraise, from *tangere* to touch]
▸ **ˈtaxable** *adj* ▸ **ˈtaxer** *n*

taxation (tækˈseɪʃən) *n* **1** the act or principle of levying taxes or the condition of being taxed. **2a** an amount assessed as tax. **2b** a tax rate. **3** revenue from taxes.
▸ **taxˈational** *adj*

tax avoidance *n* reduction or minimization of tax liability by lawful methods.

tax-deductible *adj* legally deductible from income or wealth before tax assessment.

tax disc *n* a paper disc displayed on the windscreen of a motor vehicle showing that the tax due on it has been paid.

taxeme (ˈtæksiːm) *n Linguistics.* any element of speech that may differentiate one utterance from another with a different meaning, such as the occurrence of a particular phoneme, the presence of a certain intonation, or a distinctive word order. [C20: from Gk *taxis* order, arrangement + -EME]
▸ **ˈtaxˈemic** *adj*

tax evasion *n* reduction or minimization of tax liability by illegal methods.

tax exile *n* a person having a high income who chooses to live abroad so as to avoid paying high taxes.

tax haven *n* a country or state having a lower rate of taxation than elsewhere.

tax holiday *n* a period during which tax concessions are made for some reason; examples include an export incentive or an incentive to start a new business given by some governments, in which a company is excused all or part of its tax liability.

taxi (ˈtæksɪ) *n, pl* **taxis** *or* **taxies. 1** Also called: **cab, taxicab.** a car, usually fitted with a taximeter, that may be hired, along with its driver, to carry passengers to any specified destination. ◆ *vb* **taxis** *or* **taxies, taxiing** *or* **taxying, taxied. 2** to cause (an aircraft) to move along the ground, esp. before takeoff and after landing, or (of an aircraft) to move along the ground in this way. **3** (*intr*) to travel in a taxi. [C20: shortened from *taximeter cab*]

taxidermy (ˈtæksɪˌdɜːmɪ) *n* the art or process of preparing, stuffing, and mounting animal skins so that they have a lifelike appearance. [C19: from Gk *taxis* arrangement + -*dermy,* from Gk *derma* skin]
▸ **ˌtaxiˈdermal** *or* **ˌtaxiˈdermic** *adj* ▸ **ˈtaxiˌdermist** *n*

taximeter (ˈtæksɪˌmiːtə) *n* a meter fitted to a taxi to register the fare, based on the length of the journey. [C19: from F *taximètre*; see TAX, -METER]

taxing (ˈtæksɪŋ) *adj* demanding, onerous, and wearing.
▸ **ˈtaxingly** *adv*

taxi rank *n* a place where taxis wait to be hired.

taxis (ˈtæksɪs) *n* **1** the movement of an organism in response to an external stimulus. **2** *Surgery.* the repositioning of a displaced part by manual manipulation only. [C18: via NL from Gk: arrangement, from *tassein* to place in order]

-taxis *or* **-taxy** *n combining form.* **1** indicating movement towards or away from a specified stimulus: *thermotaxis.* **2** order or arrangement: *phyllotaxis.* [from NL, from Gk *taxis* order]
▸ **-tactic** *or* **-taxic** *adj combining form.*

taxiway (ˈtæksɪˌweɪ) *n* a marked path along which aircraft taxi to or from a runway, parking area, etc.

tax loss *n* a loss sustained by a company that can be set against future profits for tax purposes.

taxman (ˈtæksˌmæn) *n, pl* **-men. 1** a collector of taxes. **2**

★ people and places

Inf. a tax-collecting body personified: *he was convicted of conspiring to cheat the taxman of five million pounds.*

axon ('tækson) *n, pl* **taxa** ('tæksə). *Biol.* any taxonomic group or rank. [C20: back formation from TAXONOMY]

axonomy (tæk'sɒnəmɪ) *n* **1** the branch of biology concerned with the classification of organisms into groups based on similarities of structure, origin, etc. **2** the science or practice of classification. [C19: from F *taxonomie*, from Gk *taxis* order + -NOMY]
▸ **taxonomic** (,tæksə'nɒmɪk) *or* ,taxo'nomical *adj* ▸ ,taxo-'nomically *adv* ▸ tax'onomist *n*

taxpayer ('tæks,peɪə) *n* a person or organization that pays taxes.

ax relief *n* remission of income tax due on a proportion of income earned.

tax return *n* a declaration of personal income used as a basis for assessing an individual's liability for taxation.

tax shelter *n* a form into which business activities may be organized to minimize taxation.

taxy *n combining form.* a variant of **-taxis.**

Tay ★ (teɪ) *n* **1 Firth of.** the estuary of the River Tay on the North Sea coast of Scotland. Length: 40 km (25 miles). **2** a river in central Scotland, flowing northeast through Loch Tay, then southeast to the Firth of Tay: the longest river in Scotland; noted for salmon fishing. Length: 193 km (120 miles). **3 Loch.** a lake in central Scotland, in Stirling council area. Length: 23 km (14 miles).

Taylor ★ ('teɪlə) *n* **1 A(lan) J(ohn) P(ercivale).** 1906–90, British historian; his works include *The Origins of the Second World War* (1961). **2 Brook.** 1685–1731, English mathematician, who laid the foundations of differential calculus. **3 Elizabeth.** born 1932, US film actress, born in England: films include *Cat on a Hot Tin Roof* (1958) and *Who's Afraid of Virginia Woolf?* (1966). **4 Zachary.** 1784–1850, 12th president of the US (1849–50); hero of the Mexican War.

Taymyr Peninsula ★ (taɪ'mɪə) *n* a variant spelling of **Taimyr Peninsula.**

Tay-Sachs disease (,teɪ'sæks) *n* an inherited disorder, caused by a faulty recessive gene, in which lipids accumulate in the brain, leading to mental retardation and blindness. [C20: after W. *Tay* (1843–1927), Brit. physician, and B. *Sachs* (1858–1944), US neurologist]

Tayside Region ★ ('teɪ,saɪd) *n* (until 1996) a local government region in E Scotland: replaced by the council areas of Angus, City of Dundee, and Perth and Kinross.

tazza ('tætsə) *n* a wine cup with a shallow bowl and a circular foot. [C19: from It., prob. from Ar. *tassah* bowl]

Tb *the chemical symbol for* terbium.

TB *abbrev. for:* **1** torpedo boat. **2** *Also:* **tb.** tuberculosis.

T-bar *n* **1** a T-shaped wrench for use with a socket. **2** a T-shaped bar on a ski tow which skiers hold on to while being pulled up slopes.

Tbilisi ★ (dbɪ'liːsɪ) *n* the capital of Georgia, on the Kura River: founded in 458; taken by the Russians in 1801; university (1918); a major industrial centre. Pop.: 1 253 100 (1994). Russian name: **Tiflis.**

T-bone steak *n* a large choice steak cut from the sirloin of beef, containing a T-shaped bone.

tbs. *or* **tbsp.** *abbrev. for* tablespoon(ful).

TBT *abbrev. for* tri-*n*-butyl tin: a biocide used in marine paints to prevent fouling.

Tc *the chemical symbol for* technetium.

T-cell *n* a type of lymphocyte that matures in the thymus gland and is responsible for killing cells infected by a virus. Also called: **T-lymphocyte.**

Tchad ★ (tʃad) *n* the French name for **Chad.**

Tchaikovsky ★ (tʃaɪ'kɒfskɪ; *Russian* tʃɪj'kɒfskɪj) *n* **Pyotr Ilyich** (pjɔtr ilj'jitʃ). 1840–93, Russian composer. His works include six symphonies, three piano concertos, a violin concerto, ballets, and operas.

t.d.c. *abbrev. for* top dead-centre.

t distribution *n* See **Student's t.**

te *or* **ti** (tiː) *n Music.* (in tonic sol-fa) the syllable used for

the seventh note or subtonic of any scale. [later variant of *si*; see GAMUT]

Te *the chemical symbol for* tellurium.

tea (tiː) *n* **1** an evergreen shrub of tropical and subtropical Asia, having white fragrant flowers: family *Theaceae.* **2a** the dried leaves of this shrub, used to make a beverage by infusion in boiling water. **2b** such a beverage, served hot or iced. **3a** any of various similar plants or any plants that are used to make a tealike beverage. **3b** any such beverage. **4** *Chiefly Brit.* **4a** *Also called:* **afternoon tea.** a light meal eaten in mid-afternoon, usually consisting of tea and cakes, etc. **4b** *Also called:* **high tea.** afternoon tea that also includes a light cooked dish. **5** *Brit., Austral., & NZ.* the main evening meal. **6** *US & Canad. dated sl.* marijuana. **7 tea and sympathy.** *Inf.* a caring attitude, esp. to someone in trouble. [C17: from Chinese (Amoy) *t'e,* from Ancient Chinese *d'a*]

tea bag *n* a small bag containing tea leaves, infused in boiling water to make tea.

tea ball *n Chiefly US.* a perforated metal ball filled with tea leaves and used to make tea.

tea break *n* a short rest period during working hours during which tea, coffee, etc., is drunk.

teacake ('tiː,keɪk) *n Brit.* a flat bun, usually eaten toasted and buttered.

teach (tiːtʃ) *vb* **teaches, teaching, taught. 1** (*tr; may take a clause as object or an infinitive; often foll. by how*) to help to learn; tell or show (how). **2** to give instruction or lessons in (a subject) to (a person or animal). **3** (*tr; may take a clause as object or an infinitive*) to cause to learn or understand: *experience taught him that he could not be a journalist.* [OE *tæcan*]
▸ 'teachable *adj*

teacher ('tiːtʃə) *n* a person whose occupation is teaching others, esp. children.

teach-in *n* an informal conference, esp. on a topical subject, usually held at a university or college and involving a panel of visiting speakers, lecturers, students, etc.

teaching ('tiːtʃɪŋ) *n* **1** the art or profession of a teacher. **2** (*sometimes pl*) something taught; precept. **3** (*modifier*) denoting a person or institution that teaches: *a teaching hospital.* **4** (*modifier*) used in teaching: *teaching aids.*

teaching machine *n* a machine that presents information and questions to the user, registers the answers, and indicates whether these are correct or acceptable.

tea cloth *n* another name for **tea towel.**

tea cosy *n* a covering for a teapot to keep the contents hot.

teacup ('tiː,kʌp) *n* **1** a cup out of which tea may be drunk. **2** *Also called:* **teacupful.** the amount a teacup will hold, about four fluid ounces.

tea dance *n* a dance held in the afternoon at which tea is served.

teahouse ('tiː,haʊs) *n* a restaurant, esp. in Japan or China, where tea and light refreshments are served.

teak (tiːk) *n* **1** a large tree of the East Indies. **2** the hard resinous yellowish-brown wood of this tree, used for furniture making, etc. [C17: from Port. *teca,* from Malayalam *tēkka*]

teakettle ('tiː,ket°l) *n* a kettle for boiling water to make tea.

teal (tiːl) *n, pl* **teals** *or* **teal. 1** any of various small freshwater ducks that are related to the mallard. **2** a greenish-blue colour. [C14]

tea lady *n* a woman employed in a factory, office, etc., to make tea during a tea break.

tea leaf *n* **1** the dried leaf of the tea shrub, used to make tea. **2** (*usually pl*) shredded parts of these leaves, esp. after infusion.

team (tiːm) *n* (*sometimes functioning as pl*) **1** a group of people organized to work together. **2** a group of players forming one of the sides in a sporting contest. **3** two or more animals working together, as to pull a vehicle. **4** such animals and the vehicle. ◆ *vb* **5** (when *intr,* often foll. by *up*) to make or cause to make a team. **6** (*tr*) *US &*

Canad. to drag or transport in or by a team. **7** (*intr*) *US & Canad.* to drive a team. [OE *team* offspring]

tea-maker *n* a spoon with a perforated cover used to infuse tea in a cup of boiling water.

team-mate *n* a fellow member of a team.

team spirit *n* willingness to cooperate as part of a team.

teamster ('ti:mstə) *n* **1** a driver of a team of horses. **2** *US & Canad.* the driver of a lorry.

team teaching *n* a system whereby two or more teachers pool their skills, knowledge, etc., to teach combined classes.

teamwork ('ti:m,wɜːk) *n* **1** the cooperative work done by a team. **2** the ability to work efficiently as a team.

teapot ('ti:,pɒt) *n* a container with a lid, spout, and handle, in which tea is made and from which it is served.

teapoy ('ti:pɔɪ) *n* a small table with a tripod base. [C19: from Hindi *tipāī*, from Sansk. *tri* three + *pāda* foot]

tear[1] (tɪə) *n* **1** a drop of the secretion of the lacrimal glands. See **tears**. **2** something shaped like a hanging drop: *a tear of amber.* ◆ Also called: **teardrop**. [OE *tēar*]
▶ 'tearless *adj*

tear[2] (tɛə) *vb* **tears, tearing, tore, torn**. **1** to cause to come apart or to come apart; rip. **2** (*tr*) to make (a hole or split) in (something). **3** (*intr*; often foll. by *along*) to hurry or rush. **4** (*tr*; usually foll. by *away* or *from*) to remove or take by force. **5** (when *intr*, often foll. by *at*) to cause pain, distress, or anguish (to). **6 tear one's hair**. *Inf.* to be angry, frustrated, very worried, etc. ◆ *n* **7** a hole, cut, or split. **8** the act of tearing. ◆ See also **tear away, tear down**, etc. [OE *teran*]
▶ 'tearable *adj* ▶ 'tearer *n*

tear away (tɛə) *vb* **1** (*tr, adv*) to persuade (oneself or someone else) to leave. ◆ *n* **tearaway. 2** *Brit.* a reckless impetuous unruly person.

tear down (tɛə) *vb* (*tr, adv*) to destroy or demolish: *to tear down an argument.*

tear duct (tɪə) *n* a short tube in the inner corner of the eyelid through which tears drain into the nose. Technical name: **lacrimal duct.**

tearful ('tɪəful) *adj* **1** crying or about to cry. **2** tending to produce tears; sad.
▶ 'tearfully *adv* ▶ 'tearfulness *n*

tear gas (tɪə) *n* a gas that makes the eyes smart and water, causing temporary blindness; used in warfare and to control riots.

tearing ('tɛərɪŋ) *adj* violent or furious (esp. in **tearing hurry** or **rush**).

tear into (tɛə) *vb* (*intr, prep*) *Inf.* to attack vigorously and damagingly.

tear-jerker ('tɪə,dʒɜːkə) *n Inf.* an excessively sentimental film, play, book, etc.

tearoom ('ti:,ruːm, -,rʊm) *n Brit.* a restaurant where tea and light refreshments are served. Also called: **teashop.**

tea rose *n* any of several varieties of hybrid rose that have pink or yellow flowers with a scent resembling that of tea.

tears (tɪəz) *pl n* **1** the clear salty solution secreted by the lacrimal glands that lubricates and cleanses the surface of the eyeball. **2** a state of intense frustration (esp. in **bored to tears**). **3 in tears**. weeping.

tear sheet (tɛə) *n* a page in a newspaper or periodical that is cut or perforated so that it can be easily torn out.

tease (ti:z) *vb* **teases, teasing, teased. 1** to annoy (someone) by deliberately offering something with the intention of delaying or withdrawing the offer. **2** to vex (someone) maliciously or playfully. **3** (*tr*) to separate the fibres of; comb; card. **4** (*tr*) to raise the nap of (a fabric) with a teasel. **5** another word (esp. US and Canad.) for **backcomb. 6** (*tr*) to loosen or pull apart (biological tissues, etc.). ◆ *n* **7** a person or thing that teases. **8** the act of teasing. ◆ See also **tease out**. [OE *tǣsan*]
▶ 'teasing *adj* ▶ 'teasingly *adv*

teasel, teazel, or **teazle** ('ti:zˀl) *n* **1** any of various plants (esp. the **fuller's teasel**) of Eurasia and N Africa, having prickly leaves and prickly heads of yellow or purple flowers. **2a** the dried flower head of the fuller's teasel,

used for teasing. **2b** any implement used for the same purpose. ◆ *vb* **teasels, teaselling, teaselled** or *US* **teasels, teaseling, teaseled. 3** (*tr*) to tease (a fabric). [OE *tǣsel*]
▶ 'teaseller *n*

tease out *vb* (*tr, adv*) to extract (information) with difficulty.

teaser ('ti:zə) *n* **1** a person who teases. **2** a difficult question. **3** a preliminary advertisement in a campaign that attracts attention by making people curious to know what product is being advertised.

tea service or **set** *n* the china or pottery articles used in serving tea, including a teapot, cups, saucers, etc.

teashop ('ti:,ʃɒp) *n Brit.* another name for **tearoom.**

teaspoon ('ti:,spuːn) *n* **1** a small spoon used for stirring tea, etc. **2** Also called: **teaspoonful** the amount contained in such a spoon. **3** a unit of capacity used in cooking, medicine, etc., equal to about 5 ml.

teat (ti:t) *n* **1a** the nipple of a mammary gland. **1b** (in cows, etc.) any of the projections from the udder. **2** something resembling a teat such as the rubber mouthpiece of a feeding bottle. [C13: from OF *tete*, of Gmc origin]

tea towel or **cloth** *n* a towel for drying dishes, etc. US name: **dishtowel.**

tea tree *n* any of various trees of Australia and New Zealand that yield an oil used as an antiseptic.

tea trolley *n Brit.* a trolley from which tea is served.

TEC (tɛk) *n acronym for* Training and Enterprise Council. See **Training Agency.**

tech (tɛk) *n Inf.* a technical college.

tech. *abbrev. for:* **1** technical. **2** technology.

technetium (tɛk'ni:ʃɪəm) *n* a silvery-grey metallic element, artificially produced by bombardment of molybdenum by deuterons. The radioisotope **technetium-99m** is used in radiotherapy. Symbol: Tc; atomic no.: 43; half-life of most stable isotope, ^{97}Tc: 2.6×10^6 years. [C20: NL, from Gk *tekhnētos* manmade, from *tekhnasthai* to devise artificially, from *tekhnē* skill]

technic *n* **1** (tɛk'ni:k). another word for **technique. 2** ('tɛknɪk). another word for **technics**. [C17: from L *technicus*, from Gk *tekhnikos*, from *tekhnē* skill]

technical ('tɛknɪkˀl) *adj* **1** of or specializing in industrial, practical, or mechanical arts and applied sciences. **2** skilled in practical arts rather than abstract thinking. **3** relating to a particular field of activity: *the technical jargon of linguistics.* **4** existing by virtue of a strict application of the rules or a strict interpretation of the wording: *a technical loophole in the law.* **5** of or showing technique: *technical brilliance.*
▶ 'technically *adv* ▶ 'technicalness *n*

technical college *n Brit.* an institution for further education that provides courses in technology, art, secretarial skills, agriculture, etc.

technical drawing *n* the study and practice of the basic techniques of draughtsmanship, as employed in mechanical drawing, architecture, etc.

technicality (,tɛknɪ'kælɪtɪ) *n, pl* **technicalities. 1** a petty formal point arising from a strict interpretation of rules, etc. **2** the state or quality of being technical. **3** technical methods and vocabulary.

technical knockout *n Boxing.* a judgment of a knockout given when a boxer is in the referee's opinion too badly beaten to continue without risk of serious injury.

technician (tɛk'nɪʃən) *n* **1** a person skilled in mechanical or industrial techniques or in a particular technical field. **2** a person employed in a laboratory, etc., to do mechanical and practical work. **3** a person having specific artistic or mechanical skill, esp. if lacking flair.

Technicolor ('tɛknɪ,kʌlə) *n Trademark.* the process of producing colour film by means of superimposing synchronized films of the same scene, each of which has a different colour filter.

technics ('tɛknɪks) *n* (*functioning as sing*) the study or theory of industry and industrial arts; technology.

technique (tɛk'ni:k) *n* **1** a practical method, skill, or art applied to a particular task. **2** proficiency in a practical or

★ people and places

mechanical skill. **3** special facility; knack. [C19: from F, from *technique* (adj): see TECHNIC]

echno ('tɛknəʊ) *n* a type of fast disco music, using electronic sounds and having a strong technological influence.

echno- *combining form*. **1** craft or art: *technology; technography.* **2** technological or technical: *technocracy.* [from Gk *tekhnē* skill]

echnocracy (tɛk'nɒkrəsɪ) *n, pl* technocracies. government by scientists, engineers, and other such experts.
▶ **technocrat** ('tɛknə,kræt) *n* ▶ ,techno'cratic *adj*

echnology (tɛk'nɒlədʒɪ) *n, pl* technologies. **1** the application of practical or mechanical sciences to industry or commerce. **2** the methods, theory, and practices governing such application. **3** the total knowledge and skills available to any human society. [C17: from Gk *tekhnologia* systematic treatment, from *tekhnē* skill]
▶ **technological** (,tɛknə'lɒdʒɪk²l) *adj* ▶ **tech'nologist** *n*

echnophile ('tɛknəʊ,faɪl) *n* **1** a person who is enthusiastic about technology. ◆ *adj* **2** enthusiastic about technology.

echnophobe (,tɛknəʊ'fəʊb) *n* **1** someone who fears the effects of technological development on society or the environment. **2** someone who is afraid of using technological devices, such as computers.

echy ('tɛtʃɪ) *adj* techier, techiest. a variant spelling of tetchy.
▶ 'techily *adv* ▶ 'techiness *n*

ectonic (tɛk'tɒnɪk) *adj* **1** denoting or relating to building. **2** *Geol*. **2a** (of landforms, etc.) resulting from distortion of the earth's crust due to forces within it. **2b** (of processes, movements, etc.) occurring within the earth's crust and causing structural deformation. [C17: from LL *tectonicus*, from Gk *tektonikos* belonging to carpentry, from *tektōn* a builder]

ectonics (tɛk'tɒnɪks) *n* (*functioning as sing*) **1** the art and science of construction or building. **2** the study of the processes by which the earth's surface has attained its present structure.

ectrix ('tɛktrɪks) *n, pl* tectrices ('tɛktrɪ,siːz). (*usually pl*) *Ornithol*. another name for covert (sense 5). [C19: NL, from L *tector* plasterer, from *tegere* to cover]
▶ **tectricial** (tɛk'trɪʃəl) *adj*

Tecumseh ★ (tɪ'kʌmsə) *n* ?1768–1813, American Indian chief of the Shawnee tribe; killed fighting for the British in the War of 1812.

ted[1] (tɛd) *vb* teds, tedding, tedded. to shake out (hay), so as to dry it. [C15: from ON *tethja*]

ted[2] (tɛd) *n Inf*. short for teddy boy.

edder ('tɛdə) *n* **1** a machine equipped with a series of small rotating forks for tedding hay. **2** a person who teds.

Tedder ★ ('tɛdə) *n* Arthur William, 1st Baron Tedder of Glenguin. 1890–1967, British marshal of the Royal Air Force; deputy commander of the Allied Expeditionary Force (1944–45).

eddy ('tɛdɪ) *n, pl* teddies. a woman's one-piece undergarment, incorporating a chemise top and panties.

eddy bear *n* a stuffed toy bear. Often shortened to **teddy**. [C20: from *Teddy*, from *Theodore*, after Theodore ROOSEVELT, well known as a hunter of bears]

eddy boy *n* **1** (in Britain, esp. in the mid-1950s) one of a cult of youths who wore mock Edwardian fashions. **2** any tough or delinquent youth. [C20: from *Teddy*, from *Edward*, referring to the Edwardian dress]

Te Deum (,tiː 'diːəm) *n* **1** an ancient Latin hymn in rhythmic prose. **2** a musical setting of this hymn. **3** a service of thanksgiving in which the recital of this hymn forms a central part. [from the L canticle beginning *Tē Deum laudāmus*, lit.: Thee, God, we praise]

edious ('tiːdɪəs) *adj* causing fatigue or tedium; monotonous.
▶ 'tediousness *n*

edium ('tiːdɪəm) *n* the state of being bored or the quality of being boring; monotony. [C17: from L *taedium*, from *taedēre* to weary]

tee[1] (tiː) *n* **1** a pipe fitting in the form of a letter T, used to join three pipes. **2** a metal section with a cross section in the form of a letter T.

tee[2] (tiː) *Golf.* ◆ *n* **1** an area from which the first stroke of a hole is made. **2** a support for a golf ball, usually a small wooden or plastic peg, used when teeing off or in long grass, etc. ◆ *vb* tees, teeing, teed. **3** (when *intr*, often foll. by *up*) to position (the ball) ready for striking, on or as if on a tee. ◆ See also **tee off**. [C17 *teaz*, from ?]

tee[3] (tiː) *n* a mark used as a target in certain games such as curling and quoits. [C18: ?from T-shaped marks, which may have orig. been used in curling]

tee-hee or **te-hee** ('tiː'hiː) *interj* **1** an exclamation of laughter, esp. when mocking. ◆ *n* **2** a chuckle. ◆ *vb* tee-hees, tee-heeing, tee-heed or te-hees, te-heeing, te-heed. **3** (*intr*) to snigger or laugh, esp. derisively. [C14: imit.]

teem[1] (tiːm) *vb* (*intr*; usually foll. by *with*) to be prolific or abundant (in). [OE *tēman* to produce offspring; rel. to West Saxon *tīeman*; see TEAM]

teem[2] (tiːm) *vb* **1** (*intr*; often foll. by *down* or *with rain*) to pour in torrents. **2** (*tr*) to pour or empty out. [C15 *temen* to empty, from ON *tœma*]

teen (tiːn) *adj Inf*. another word for teenage.

teenage ('tiːn,eɪdʒ) *adj* (*prenominal*) of or relating to the time in a person's life between the ages of 13 and 19. Also: **teenaged**.

teenager ('tiːn,eɪdʒə) *n* a person between the ages of 13 and 19 inclusive.

teens (tiːnz) *pl n* **1** the years of a person's life between the ages of 13 and 19 inclusive. **2** all the numbers that end in -teen.

teeny ('tiːnɪ) *adj* teenier, teeniest. *Inf*. extremely small; tiny. Also: **teeny-weeny** ('tiːnɪ'wiːnɪ) or **teensy-weensy** ('tiːnzɪ'wiːnzɪ). [C19: var. of TINY]

teenybopper ('tiːnɪ,bɒpə) *n Sl*. a young teenager, usually a girl, who avidly follows fashions in clothes and pop music. [C20: *teeny*, from teenage + -*bopper*; see BOP]

tee off *vb* (*adv*) **1** *Golf*. to strike (the ball) from a tee. **2** *Inf*. to begin; start.

teepee ('tiːpiː) *n* a variant spelling of tepee.

Tees ★ (tiːz) *n* a river in N England, rising in the N Pennines and flowing southeast and east to the North Sea at Middlesbrough. Length: 113 km (70 miles).

tee shirt *n* a variant of T-shirt.

Teesside ★ ('tiːz,saɪd) *n* the industrial region around the lower Tees valley and estuary: a county borough, containing Middlesbrough, from 1968 to 1974.

teeter ('tiːtə) *vb* **1** to move or cause to move unsteadily; wobble. ◆ *n, vb* **2** another word for seesaw. [C19: from ME *titeren*]

teeth (tiːθ) *n* **1** the plural of tooth. **2** the most violent part: *the teeth of the gale*. **3** the power to produce a desired effect: *that law has no teeth*. **4 get one's teeth into.** to become engrossed in. **5 in the teeth of.** in direct opposition to; against. **6 to the teeth.** to the greatest possible degree: *armed to the teeth*. **7 show one's teeth.** to threaten.

teethe (tiːð) *vb* teethes, teething, teethed. (*intr*) to cut one's baby (deciduous) teeth.

teething ring *n* a hard ring on which babies may bite while teething.

teething troubles *pl n* the problems that arise during the initial stages of a project, etc.

teetotal (tiː'təʊt²l) *adj* **1** of or practising abstinence from alcoholic drink. **2** *Dialect*. complete. [C19: allegedly coined in 1833 by Richard Turner, E advocate of total abstinence from alcohol; prob. from TOTAL, with emphatic reduplication]
▶ **tee'totaller** *n* ▶ **tee'totalism** *n*

teetotum (tiː'təʊtəm) *n Arch*. a spinning top bearing letters of the alphabet on its four sides. [C18: from *T totum*, from *T* initial on one of the faces + *totum* the name of the toy, from L *tōtum* the whole]

teff (tɛf) *n* an annual grass of NE Africa, grown for its grain. [C18: from Amharic *ṭēf*]

TEFL ('tɛf²l) *acronym for* Teaching (of) English as a Foreign Language.

Teflon ('tɛflɒn) *n* a trademark for **polytetrafluoroethylene.**

teg (tɛg) *n* **1** a two-year-old sheep. **2** the fleece of a two-year-old sheep. [C16: from ?]

tegmen ('tɛgmən) *n, pl* **tegmina** (-mɪnə). **1** either of the leathery forewings of the cockroach and related insects. **2** the delicate inner covering of a seed. **3** any similar covering or layer. [C19: from L: a cover, from *tegere* to cover]
▸ **'tegminal** *adj*

Tegucigalpa ★ (*Spanish* teɣuθi'ɣalpa) *n* the capital of Honduras, in the south on the Choluteca River: founded about 1579; university (1847). Pop.: 775 300 (1994).

tegument ('tɛgjumənt) *n* a less common word for **integument.** [C15: from L *tegumentum* a covering, from *tegere* to cover]

te-hee (tiː'hiː) *interj, n, vb* a variant of **tee-hee.**

Tehran *or* **Teheran** ★ (tɛə'rɑːn, -'ræn) *n* the capital of Iran, at the foot of the Elburz Mountains: built on the site of the ancient capital Ray, destroyed by Mongols in 1220; became capital in the 1790s; three universities. Pop.: 11 000 000 (1994 est.).

Tehuantepec ★ (tə'wɑːntə,pek) *n* **Isthmus of.** the narrowest part of S Mexico, with the Bay of Campeche on the north coast and the **Gulf of Tehuantepec** (an inlet of the Pacific) on the south coast.

Teide *or* **Teyde** ★ (*Spanish* 'teiðe) *n* **Pico de** ('piko de). a volcanic mountain in the Canary Islands, on Tenerife. Height: 3718 m (12 198 ft).

te **igitur** *Latin.* (teɪ 'ɪgɪ,tʊə; *English* teɪ 'ɪdʒɪtʊə) *n* RC Church. the first prayer of the canon of the Mass, which begins *Te igitur clementissime Pater* (Thee, therefore, most merciful Father).

Teilhard de Chardin ★ (*French* tejar də ʃardɛ̃) *n* **Pierre** (pjɛr). 1881–1955, French Jesuit priest and palaeontologist, noted for his *The Phenomenon of Man* (1938–40).

Tejo ★ ('təʒu) *n* the Portuguese name for the **Tagus.**

Te Kanawa ★ (teɪ 'kɑːnəwə) *n* Dame **Kiri** ('kɪrɪ). born 1944, New Zealand soprano.

tektite ('tɛktaɪt) *n* a small dark glassy object found in several areas around the world, thought to be a product of meteorite impact. [C20: from Gk *tēktos* molten]

tel. *abbrev. for:* **1** telegram. **2** telegraph(ic). **3** telephone.

tel- *combining form.* a variant of **tele-** and **telo-** before a vowel.

telaesthesia *or US* **telesthesia** (,tɛlɪs'θiːzɪə) *n* the alleged perception of events that are beyond the normal range of perceptual processes.
▸ **telaesthetic** *or US* **telesthetic** (,tɛlɪs'θɛtɪk) *adj*

telamon ('tɛləmən) *n, pl* **telamones** (,tɛlə'məʊniːz) *or* **telamons.** a column in the form of a male figure, used to support an entablature. [C18: via L from Gk, from *tlēnai* to bear]

Telamon ★ ('tɛləmən, -,mɒn) *n Greek myth.* a king of Salamis; brother of Peleus and father of Teucer and Ajax.

Telanaipura ★ (,tɛlənaɪ'pʊərə) *n* another name for **Jambi.**

telangiectasis (tɪ,lændʒɪ'ɛktəsɪs) *or* **telangiectasia** (tɪ,lændʒɪɛk'teɪzɪə) *n, pl* **telangiectases** (-,siːz). *Pathol.* an abnormal dilation of the capillaries or terminal arteries producing blotched red spots, esp. on the face or thighs. [C19: NL, from Gk *telos* end + *angeion* vessel + *ektasis* dilation]
▸ **telangiectatic** (tɪ,lændʒɪɛk'tætɪk) *adj*

Tel Aviv ★ ('tɛl ə'viːv) *n* a city in W Israel, on the Mediterranean: the largest city and chief financial centre in Israel; incorporated the city of Jaffa in 1950; university (1953): the capital of Israel in international law. Pop.: 355 900 (1996 est.). Official name: **Tel Aviv-Jaffa** ('tɛl ə'viːv'dʒæfə).

tele- *combining form.* **1** at or over a distance; distant: *telescope; telekinesis.* **2** television: *telecast.* **3** by means of or via telephone or television: *telesales.* [from Gk *tele* far]

telecast ('tɛlə,kɑːst) *vb* **telecasts, telecasting, telecast** *or* **telecasted. 1** to broadcast by television. ◆ *n* **2** a television broadcast.
▸ **'tele,caster** *n*

telecom ('tɛlɪ,kɒm) *or* **telecoms** ('tɛlɪ,kɒmz) *n (functioning as sing)* short for **telecommunications.**

telecommunications (,tɛlɪkə,mjuːnɪ'keɪʃənz) *n (functioning as sing)* the science and technology of communications by telephony, radio, television, etc.

telecommuting (,tɛlɪkə'mjuːtɪŋ) *n* another name for **teleworking.**
▸ **,telecom'muter** *n*

teledu ('tɛlɪ,duː) *n* a badger of SE Asia and Indonesia, having dark brown hair with a white stripe along the back and producing a fetid secretion when attacked. [C19: from Malay]

telegenic (,tɛlɪ'dʒɛnɪk) *adj* having or showing a pleasant television image. [C20: from TELE(VISION) + (PHOTO)GENIC]
▸ **,tele'genically** *adv*

telegnosis (,tɛlə'nəʊsɪs, ,tɛləg-) *n* knowledge about distant events alleged to have been obtained without the use of any normal sensory mechanism. [C20: from TELE- + -*gnosis*, from Gk *gnōsis* knowledge]

Telegonus ★ (tɪ'lɛgənəs) *n Greek myth.* a son of Odysseus and Circe, who sought his father and mistakenly killed him, later marrying Odysseus' widow Penelope.

telegony (tɪ'lɛgənɪ) *n Genetics.* the supposed influence of a previous sire on offspring borne by a female to other sires.
▸ **telegonic** (,tɛlɪ'gɒnɪk) *or* **te'legonous** *adj*

telegram ('tɛlɪ,græm) *n* a communication transmitted by telegraph.

telegraph ('tɛlɪ,grɑːf) *n* **1a** a device, system, or process by which information can be transmitted over a distance, esp. using radio signals or coded electrical signals sent along a transmission line. **1b** (*as modifier*): *telegraph pole.* ◆ *vb* **2** to send a telegram to (a person or place); wire. **3** (*tr*) to transmit or send by telegraph. **4** (*tr*) to give advance notice of (anything), esp. unintentionally. **5** (*tr*) *Canad. inf.* to cast (votes) illegally by impersonating registered voters.
▸ **telegraphist** (tɪ'lɛgrə,fɪst) *or* **telegrapher** (tɪ'lɛgrəfə) *n* ▸ **tele'graphic** *adj*

telegraph plant *n* a small tropical Asian shrub having small leaflets that turn in various directions during the day and droop at night.

telegraphy (tɪ'lɛgrəfɪ) *n* **1** a system of telecommunications involving any process providing reproduction at a distance of written, printed, or pictorial matter. **2** the skill or process of operating a telegraph.

Telegu (,tɛlə,guː) *n, adj* a variant spelling of **Telugu.**

telekinesis (,tɛlɪkaɪ'niːsɪs) *n* **1** the movement of a body caused by thought or willpower without the application of a physical force. **2** the ability to cause such movement.
▸ **telekinetic** (,tɛlɪkɪ'nɛtɪk) *adj*

Telemachus ★ (tɪ'lɛməkəs) *n Greek myth.* the son of Odysseus and Penelope, who helped his father slay his mother's suitors.

Telemann ★ (*German* 'teːləman) *n* **Georg Philipp** ('geːɔrk 'fiːlɪp). 1681–1767, German composer.

telemark ('tɛlɪ,mɑːk) *n Skiing.* a turn in which one ski is placed far forward of the other and turned gradually inwards. [C20: after *Telemark,* county in Norway]

telemarketing ('tɛlɪ,mɑːkɪtɪŋ) *n* another name for **telesales.**
▸ **'tele,marketer** *n*

telemedicine ('tɛlɪ,mɛdɪsɪn, -,mɛdsɪn) *n* the treatment of disease or injury by consultation with a specialist in a distant place, esp. by means of a computer or satellite link.

Telemessage ('tɛlɪ,mɛsɪdʒ) *n Trademark.* a message sent by telephone or telex and delivered in printed form.

telemeter (tɪ'lɛmɪtə) *n* **1** any device for recording or measuring a distant event and transmitting the data to a receiver. **2** any device used to measure a distance without directly comparing it with a measuring rod, etc. ◆ *vb* **3** (*tr*) to obtain and transmit (data) from a distant source.
▸ **telemetric** (,tɛlɪ'mɛtrɪk) *adj*

★ people and places

elemetry (tɪˈlɛmɪtrɪ) *n* **1** the use of radio waves, telephone lines, etc., to transmit the readings of measuring instruments to a device on which the readings can be indicated or recorded. **2** the measurement of linear distance using a tellurometer.

elencephalon (ˌtɛlɛnˈsɛfəˌlɒn) *n* the cerebrum together with related parts of the hypothalamus and the third ventricle.
▶ **telencephalic** (ˈtɛlɛnsɪˈfælɪk) *adj*

eleology (ˌtɛlɪˈɒlədʒɪ, ˌtiːlɪ-) *n* **1** *Philosophy*. **1a** the doctrine that there is evidence of purpose or design in the universe, and esp. that this provides proof of the existence of a Designer. **1b** the belief that certain phenomena are best explained in terms of purpose rather than cause. **2** *Biol.* the belief that natural phenomena have a predetermined purpose and are not determined by mechanical laws. [C18: from NL *teleologia*, from Gk *telos* end + -LOGY]
▶ **teleological** (ˌtɛlɪəˈlɒdʒɪkəl, ˌtiːlɪ-) *adj* ▶ ˌtele·ˈologist *n*

eleost (ˈtɛlɪˌɒst, ˈtiːlɪ-) *n* any of a subclass of bony fishes having rayed fins and a swim bladder, as herrings, carps, eels, cod, perches, etc. [C19: from NL *teleosteī* (pl) creatures having complete skeletons, from Gk *teleos* complete + *osteon* bone]

elepathy (tɪˈlɛpəθɪ) *n* the communication between people of thoughts, feelings, etc., involving mechanisms that cannot be understood in terms of known scientific laws.
▶ **telepathic** (ˌtɛlɪˈpæθɪk) *adj* ▶ te'lepathist *n* ▶ te'lepa-ˌthize *or* ▶ te'lepaˌthise *vb* (*intr*)

elephone (ˈtɛlɪˌfəʊn) *n* **1** an electrical device for transmitting speech, consisting of a microphone and receiver mounted on a handset. **2a** a worldwide system of communications using telephones. The microphone in one telephone converts sound waves into electrical signals that are transmitted along a telephone wire or by radio to one or more distant sets. **2b** (*as modifier*): *a telephone exchange.* ◆ *vb* **3** to call or talk to (a person) by telephone. **4** to transmit (a message, etc.) by telephone.
▶ 'teleˌphoner *n* ▶ **telephonic** (ˌtɛlɪˈfɒnɪk) *adj*

telephone banking *n* a facility enabling customers to make use of banking services, such as oral payment instructions, account movements, raising loans, etc., over the telephone rather than by personal visit.

telephone box *n* an enclosure from which a paid telephone call can be made. Also called: **telephone kiosk, telephone booth.**

telephone directory *n* a book listing the names, addresses, and telephone numbers of subscribers in a particular area.

telephone number *n* **1** a set of figures identifying the telephone of a particular subscriber, and used in making connections to that telephone. **2** (*pl*) extremely large numbers, esp. in reference to salaries or prices.

telephone selling *n* another name for **telesales.**

telephonist (tɪˈlɛfənɪst) *n Brit.* a person who operates a telephone switchboard. Also called (esp. US): **telephone operator.**

telephony (tɪˈlɛfənɪ) *n* a system of telecommunications for the transmission of speech or other sounds.

telephotography (ˌtɛlɪfəˈtɒɡrəfɪ) *n* the process or technique of photographing distant objects using a telephoto lens.

telephoto lens (ˈtɛlɪˌfəʊtəʊ) *n* a compound camera lens in which the focal length is greater than that of a simple lens and thus produces a magnified image of a distant object.

teleprinter (ˈtɛlɪˌprɪntə) *n* **1** a telegraph apparatus consisting of a keyboard transmitter, which converts a typed message into coded pulses for transmission along a wire or cable, and a printing receiver, which converts incoming signals and prints out the message. US name: **teletypewriter. 2** a network of such devices: no longer widely used. **3** a similar device used for direct input/output of data into a computer at a distant location.

Teleprompter (ˈtɛlɪˌprɒmptə) *n Trademark*. a device for displaying a television script so that the speaker can read it while appearing to look at the camera.

Teleran (ˈtɛləˌræn) *n Trademark*. an electronic navigational aid in which the image of a ground-based radar system is televised to aircraft. [C20: from *Tele(vision) R(adar) A(ir) N(avigation)*]

telesales (ˈtɛlɪˌseɪlz) *n* (*functioning as sing*) the selling or attempted selling of a particular commodity or service by a salesman who makes his initial approach by telephone. Also called: **telemarketing, telephone selling.**

telescope (ˈtɛlɪˌskəʊp) *n* **1** an optical instrument for making distant objects appear closer by use of a combination of lenses (**refracting telescope**) or lenses and curved mirrors (**reflecting telescope**). **2** any instrument, such as a radio telescope, for collecting, focusing, and detecting electromagnetic radiation from space. ◆ *vb* **telescopes, telescoping, telescoped. 3** to crush together or be crushed together, as in a collision. **4** to fit together like a set of cylinders that slide into one another, thus allowing extension and shortening. **5** to make or become smaller or shorter. [C17: from It. *telescopio* or NL *telescopium*, lit.: far-seeing instrument]

telescopic (ˌtɛlɪˈskɒpɪk) *adj* **1** of or relating to a telescope. **2** seen through or obtained by means of a telescope. **3** visible only with a telescope. **4** able to see far. **5** having parts that telescope.
▶ ˌtele'scopically *adv*

telescopic sight *n* a telescope mounted on a rifle, etc., used for sighting.

telescopy (tɪˈlɛskəpɪ) *n* the branch of astronomy concerned with the use and design of telescopes.

telespectroscope (ˌtɛlɪˈspɛktrəˌskəʊp) *n* a combination of a telescope and a spectroscope, used for spectroscopic analysis of radiation from stars and other celestial bodies.

telestereoscope (ˌtɛlɪˈstɪərɪəˌskəʊp, -ˈstɛrɪə-) *n* an optical instrument for obtaining stereoscopic images of distant objects.

telestich (tɪˈlɛstɪk, ˈtɛlɪˌstɪk) *n* a short poem in which the last letters of each successive line form a word. [C17: from Gk *telos* end + *stikhos* row]

Teletext (ˈtɛlɪˌtɛkst) *n Trademark*. a form of Videotex in which information is broadcast by a television station and received on an adapted television set. **Ceefax** is provided by the BBC and **Oracle** by ITV.

telethon (ˈtɛlɪˌθɒn) *n* a lengthy television programme to raise charity funds, etc. [C20: from TELE- + MARATHON]

Teletype (ˈtɛlɪˌtaɪp) *n* **1** *Trademark*. a type of teleprinter. **2** (*sometimes not cap.*) a network of such devices. ◆ *vb* **Teletypes, Teletyping, Teletyped. 3** (*sometimes not cap.*) to transmit (a message) by Teletype.

teletypewriter (ˌtɛlɪˈtaɪpˌraɪtə, ˈtɛlɪˌtaɪp-) *n* a US name for **teleprinter.**

televangelist (ˌtɛlɪˈvændʒəlɪst) *n US*. an evangelical preacher who appears regularly on television, preaching the gospel and appealing for donations from viewers. [C20: from TELE(VISION + E)VANGELIST]

televise (ˈtɛlɪˌvaɪz) *vb* **televises, televising, televised. 1** to put on television. **2** (*tr*) to transmit by television.

television (ˈtɛlɪˌvɪʒən) *n* **1** the system or process of producing on a distant screen a series of transient visible images, usually with an accompanying sound signal. Electrical signals, converted from optical images by a camera tube, are transmitted by radio waves or by cable and reconverted into optical images by means of a television tube inside a television set. **2** Also called: **television set**. a device designed to receive and convert incoming electrical signals into a series of visible images on a screen together with accompanying sound. **3** the content, etc., of television programmes. **4** the occupation or profession concerned with any aspect of the broadcasting of television programmes. **5** (*modifier*) of, relating to, or used in the transmission or reception of video and audio UHF or VHF radio signals: *a television transmitter.*
◆ Abbrev.: **TV.**

television tube *n* a cathode-ray tube designed for the reproduction of television pictures. Sometimes shortened to **tube.**

televisual (ˌtɛlɪ'vɪʒʊəl, -zjʊ-) *adj* relating to or suitable for production on television.
▸ ˌtele'visually *adv*

teleworking (ˈtɛlɪˌwɜːkɪŋ) *n* the use of home computers, telephones, etc., to enable a person to work from home while maintaining contact with colleagues, customers, or a central office. Also called: **telecommuting.**
▸ 'tele,worker *n*

telex ('tɛlɛks) *n* **1** an international telegraph service in which teleprinters are rented out to subscribers. **2** a teleprinter used in such a service. **3** a message transmitted or received by telex. ◆ *vb* **4** to transmit (a message) to (a person, etc.) by telex. [C20: from *tel(eprinter) ex(change)*]

Telford[1] ★ ('tɛlfəd) *n* a town in W central England, in Shropshire: designated a new town in 1963: forms a unitary authority with the Wrekin. Pop.: 119 340 (1991).

Telford[2] ★ ('tɛlfəd) *n* **Thomas.** 1757–1834, Scottish civil engineer, noted for the Menai suspension bridge (1825).

Telidon ('tɛlɪˌdɒn) *n Trademark.* a Canadian interactive viewdata service.

tell[1] (tɛl) *vb* **tells, telling, told. 1** (when *tr*, *may take a clause as object*) to let know or notify. **2** (*tr*) to order or instruct. **3** (when *intr*, usually foll. by *of*) to give an account or narration (of). **4** (*tr*) to communicate by words: *tell lies.* **5** (*tr*) to make known: *to tell fortunes.* **6** (*intr*; often foll. by *of*) to serve as an indication: *her blush told of her embarrassment.* **7** (*tr*; used with *can*, etc.; *may take a clause as object*) to discover or discern: *I can tell what is wrong.* **8** (*tr*; used with *can*, etc.) to distinguish or discriminate: *he couldn't tell chalk from cheese.* **9** (*intr*) to have or produce an impact, effect, or strain: *every step told on his bruised feet.* **10** (*intr*; sometimes foll. by *on*) *Inf.* to reveal secrets or gossip (about). **11** (*tr*) to assure: *I tell you, I've had enough!* **12** (*tr*) to count (votes). **13 tell the time.** to read the time from a clock. **14 you're telling me.** *Sl.* I know that very well. ◆ See also **tell apart, tell off.** [OE *tellan*]
▸ 'tellable *adj*

tell[2] (tɛl) *n* a large mound resulting from the accumulation of rubbish on a long-settled site, esp. in the Middle East. [C19: from Ar. *tall*]

Tell ★ (tɛl) *n* **William,** German name *Wilhelm Tell.* legendary Swiss patriot, who shot an apple from his son's head on the order of an Austrian governor.

tell apart *vb* (*tr, adv*) to distinguish between.

Tell el Amarna ★ ('tɛl ɛl ə'mɑːnə) *n* a group of ruins and rock tombs in Upper Egypt, on the Nile below Asyut: site of the capital of Amenhotep IV, built about 1375 B.C.; excavated from 1891 onwards.

teller ('tɛlə) *n* **1** a bank cashier. **2** a person appointed to count votes. **3** a person who tells; narrator.

Teller ★ ('tɛlə) *n* **Edward.** born 1908, US nuclear physicist, born in Hungary: contributed to the development of the hydrogen bomb (1952).

telling ('tɛlɪŋ) *adj* **1** having a marked effect or impact. **2** revealing.
▸ 'tellingly *adv*

tell off *vb* (*tr, adv*) **1** *Inf.* to reprimand; scold. **2** to count and select for duty.

telltale ('tɛlˌteɪl) *n* **1** a person who tells tales about others. **2a** an outward indication of something concealed. **2b** (*as modifier*): *a telltale paw mark.* **3** a device used to monitor a process, machine, etc.

tellurian (tɛ'lʊərɪən) *adj* **1** of the earth. ◆ *n* **2** (esp. in science fiction) an inhabitant of the earth. [C19: from L *tellūs* the earth]

telluric[1] (tɛ'lʊərɪk) *adj* of or originating on or in the earth or soil; terrestrial. [C19: from L *tellūs* the earth]

telluric[2] (tɛ'lʊərɪk) *adj* of or containing tellurium, esp. in a high valence state. [C20: from TELLUR(IUM) + -IC]

tellurion *or* **tellurian** (tɛ'lʊərɪən) *n* an instrument that shows how day and night, etc., result from the earth's rotation on its axis, etc. [C19: from L *tellūs* the earth]

tellurium (tɛ'lʊərɪəm) *n* a brittle silvery-white nonmetallic element. Symbol: Te; atomic no.: 52; atomic wt.: 127.60. [C19: NL, from L *tellūs* the earth, by analogy with URANIUM]

tellurometer (ˌtɛljʊ'rɒmɪtə) *n Surveying.* an electronic instrument for measuring distances by the transmission of radio waves. [C20: from L *tellūs* the earth + -METER]

Tellus ★ ('tɛləs) *n* the Roman goddess of the earth; protectress of marriage, fertility, and the dead.

telly ('tɛlɪ) *n, pl* **tellies.** *Inf.*, *chiefly Brit.* short for **television.**

telo- *or before a vowel* **tel-** *combining form.* **1** complete; final; perfect. **2** end; at the end. [from Gk *telos* end]

telpherage ('tɛlfərɪdʒ) *n* an overhead transport system in which an electrically driven truck runs along a rail or cable, the load being suspended in a car beneath. Also called: **telpher.** [C19: changed from *telephore*, from TELE- + -PHORE + -AGE]

telson ('tɛlsən) *n* the last segment or an appendage on the last segment of the body of crustaceans and arachnids. [C19: from Gk: a boundary]

Telugu *or* **Telegu** ('tɛlɪˌguː) *n* **1** a language of SE India, belonging to the Dravidian family of languages. **2** (*pl* **Telugus** *or* **Telugu**) a member of the people who speak this language. ◆ *adj* **3** of or relating to this people or their language.

Telukbetung *or* **Teloekbetoeng** ★ (təˌlukbə'tuŋ) *n* a port in Indonesia, in S Sumatra on the Sunda Strait. Pop.: 285 000 (latest est.).

Tema ★ ('tiːmə) *n* a port in SE Ghana on the Atlantic: new harbour opened in 1962; oil-refining. Pop.: 110 000 (1988 est.).

temazepam (tə'mæzəˌpæm) *n* a sedative in the form of a gel-like capsule, which is taken orally or melted and injected by drug users.

Témbi ★ ('tembiː) *n* transliteration of the Modern Greek name for **Tempe.**

temblor ('tɛmblə, -blɔː) *n, pl* **temblors** *or* **temblores** (tɛm'blɔːreɪz). *Chiefly US.* an earthquake or earth tremor. [C19: American Sp., from Sp. *temblar* to shake, tremble]

temerity (tɪ'mɛrɪtɪ) *n* rashness or boldness. [C15: from L *temeritās* accident, from *temere* at random]
▸ **temerarious** (ˌtɛmə'rɛərɪəs) *adj*

Temesvár ★ ('tɛmɛʃˌvɑːr) *n* the Hungarian name for Timişoara.

temp (tɛmp) *Inf.* ◆ *n* **1** a person, esp. a typist or other office worker, employed on a temporary basis. ◆ *vb* (*intr*) **2** to work as a temp.

temp. *abbrev. for:* **1** temperature. **2** temporary. **3** tempore. [L: in the time of]

Tempe ★ ('tɛmpɪ) *n* **Vale of.** a wooded valley in E Greece, in Thessaly between the mountains Olympus and Ossa. Modern Greek name: **Témbi.**

temper ('tɛmpə) *n* **1** a frame of mind; mood or humour. **2** a sudden outburst of anger. **3** a tendency to exhibit anger; irritability. **4** a mental condition of moderation and calm (esp. in **keep one's temper** *or* **lose one's temper**). **5** the degree of hardness, elasticity, etc., of a metal. ◆ *vb* (*tr*) **6** to make more acceptable or suitable by adding something else; moderate: *he tempered his criticism with sympathy.* **7** to reduce the brittleness of (a hardened metal) by reheating it and allowing it to cool. **8** *Music.* **8a** to adjust the frequency differences between the notes of a scale on (a keyboard instrument). **8b** to make such an adjustment to the pitches of notes in (a scale). [OE *temprian* to mingle, from L *temperāre* to mix, prob. from *tempus* time]
▸ 'temperable *adj* ▸ 'temperer *n*

tempera ('tɛmpərə) *n* **1** a painting medium for powdered pigments, consisting usually of egg yolk and water. **2a** any emulsion used as a painting medium, with casein, glue, wax, etc., as a base. **2b** the paint made from this. **3** the technique of painting with tempera. [C19: from It. *pingere a tempera* painting in tempera, from *temperare* to mingle; see TEMPER]

temperament ('tɛmpərəmənt) *n* **1** a person's character, disposition, and tendencies. **2** excitability, moodiness, or anger. **3** the characteristic way an individual behaves, esp. towards other people. **4a** an adjustment made to the frequency differences between notes on a keyboard instrument to allow modulation to other keys. **4b** any of several systems of such adjustment, esp. **equal temperament,** a system giving a scale based on an octave divided

★ people and places

into twelve exactly equal semitones. **5** *Obs.* the characteristic way an individual behaves, viewed as the result of the influence of the four humours. [C15: from L *temperāmentum* a mixing in proportion, from *temperāre* to TEMPER]

emperamental (ˌtɛmpərəˈmɛntªl) *adj* **1** easily upset or irritated; excitable. **2** of or caused by temperament. **3** *Inf.* working erratically and inconsistently; unreliable.
▸ ˌtempera'mentally *adv*

emperance ('tɛmpərəns) *n* **1** restraint or moderation, esp. in yielding to one's appetites or desires. **2** abstinence from alcoholic drink. [C14: from L *temperantia*, from *temperāre* to regulate]

emperate ('tɛmpərɪt) *adj* **1** having a climate intermediate between tropical and polar; moderate or mild in temperature. **2** mild in quality or character; exhibiting temperance. [C14: from L *temperātus*]
▸ 'temperately *adv* ▸ 'temperateness *n*

emperate Zone *n* those parts of the earth's surface lying between the Arctic Circle and the tropic of Cancer and between the Antarctic Circle and the tropic of Capricorn.

emperature ('tɛmprɪtʃə) *n* **1** the degree of hotness of a body, substance, or medium, esp. as measured on a scale that has one or more fixed reference points. **2** *Inf.* a body temperature in excess of the normal. [C16 (orig.: a mingling): from L *temperātūra* proportion, from *temperāre* to TEMPER]

emperature gradient *n* the rate of change in temperature in a given direction.

emperature-humidity index *n* an index of the effect on human comfort of temperature and humidity levels, 65 being the highest comfortable level.

tempered ('tɛmpəd) *adj* **1** *Music.* adjusted in accordance with a system of temperament. **2** (*in combination*) having a temper or temperament as specified: *ill-tempered*.

tempest ('tɛmpɪst) *n* **1** *Chiefly literary.* a violent wind or storm. **2** a violent commotion, uproar, or disturbance. [C13: from OF *tempeste*, from L *tempestās* storm, from *tempus* time]

tempestuous (tɛmˈpɛstjʊəs) *adj* **1** of or relating to a tempest. **2** violent or stormy.
▸ tem'pestuously *adv* ▸ tem'pestuousness *n*

tempi ('tɛmpiː) *n* (in musical senses) the plural of **tempo**.

Templar ('tɛmplə) *n* **1** a member of a military order (**Knights of the Temple of Solomon**) founded by Crusaders in Jerusalem around 1118; suppressed in 1312. **2** (*sometimes not cap.*) *Brit.* a lawyer who has chambers in the Temple in London. [C13: from Med. L *templārius* of the TEMPLE; applied to the order because their house adjoined the site of the Temple of Solomon]

template or **templet** ('tɛmplɪt) *n* **1** a gauge or pattern, cut out in wood or metal, used in woodwork, etc., to help shape something accurately. **2** a pattern cut out in card or plastic, used to reproduce shapes. **3** a short beam that is used to spread a load, as over a doorway. **4** *Biochem.* the molecular structure of a compound that serves as a pattern for the production of another compound. [C17 *templet* (later spelling infl. by PLATE), prob. from F, dim. of TEMPLE³]

temple¹ ('tɛmpªl) *n* **1** a building or place dedicated to the worship of a deity or deities. **2** a Mormon church. **3** *US.* another name for a **synagogue**. **4** a Christian church. **5** any place or object regarded as a shrine where God makes himself present. **6** a building regarded as the focus of an activity, interest, or practice: *a temple of the arts*. [OE *tempel*, from L *templum*]

temple² ('tɛmpªl) *n* the region on each side of the head in front of the ear and above the cheek bone. [C14: from OF *temple*, from L *tempora* the temples, from *tempus* temple of the head]

temple³ ('tɛmpªl) *n* the part of a loom that keeps the cloth being woven stretched to the correct width. [C15: from F, from L *templum* a small timber]

Temple¹ ★ ('tɛmpªl) *n* **1** a building in London that belonged to the Templars: it now houses two law societies.

2 any of three buildings erected by the Jews in ancient Jerusalem for the worship of Jehovah.

Temple² ★ ('tɛmpªl) *n* **1** **Shirley**, married name *Shirley Temple Black*. born 1928, US child film star and (later) politician. She became US ambassador to Ghana (1974–76) and to Czechoslovakia (from 1989). **2** Sir **William**. 1628–99, English diplomat. He negotiated the Triple Alliance (1668) and the marriage of William of Orange to Mary II. **3** **William**. 1881–1944, British prelate and advocate of social reform; archbishop of Canterbury (1942–44).

Temple of Artemis ★ *n* the large temple at Ephesus, on the W coast of Asia Minor: one of the Seven Wonders of the World.

tempo ('tɛmpəʊ) *n, pl* **tempos** or **tempi** (-piː). **1** the speed at which a piece of music is meant to be played. **2** rate or pace. [C18: from It., from L *tempus* time]

temporal¹ ('tɛmpərəl) *adj* **1** of or relating to time. **2** of secular as opposed to spiritual or religious affairs. **3** lasting for a relatively short time. **4** *Grammar.* of or relating to tense or the linguistic expression of time. [C14: from L *temporālis*, from *tempus* time]
▸ 'temporally *adv*

temporal² ('tɛmpərəl) *adj Anat.* of or near the temple or temples. [C16: from LL *temporālis* belonging to the temples; see TEMPLE²]

temporal bone *n* either of two compound bones forming the sides of the skull.

temporality (ˌtɛmpəˈrælɪtɪ) *n, pl* **temporalities**. **1** the state or quality of being temporal. **2** something temporal. **3** (*often pl*) a secular possession or revenue belonging to a Church.

temporal lobe *n* the laterally protruding portion of each cerebral hemisphere, situated below the parietal lobe and associated with sound perception and interpretation.

temporary ('tɛmpərərɪ) *adj* **1** not permanent; provisional. **2** lasting only a short time. ◆ *n, pl* **temporaries**. **3** a person employed on a temporary basis. [C16: from L *temporārius*, from *tempus* time]
▸ 'temporarily *adv* ▸ 'temporariness *n*

temporize or **temporise** ('tɛmpəˌraɪz) *vb* **temporizes, temporizing, temporized** or **temporises, temporising, temporised.** (*intr*) **1** to delay, act evasively, or protract a negotiation, etc., esp. in order to gain time or effect a compromise. **2** to adapt oneself to the circumstances, as by temporary or apparent agreement. [C16: from F *temporiser*, from Med. L *temporizāre*, from *tempus* time]
▸ ˌtempori'zation or ˌtempori'sation *n* ▸ 'tempoˌrizer or 'tempoˌriser *n*

tempt (tɛmpt) *vb* (*tr*) **1** to entice to do something, esp. something morally wrong or unwise. **2** to allure or attract. **3** to give rise to a desire in (someone) to do something; dispose. **4** to risk provoking (esp. in **tempt fate**). [C13: from OF *tempter*, from L *temptāre* to test]
▸ 'temptable *adj* ▸ 'tempter *n* ▸ 'temptress *fem n*

temptation (tɛmpˈteɪʃən) *n* **1** the act of tempting or the state of being tempted. **2** a person or thing that tempts.

tempting ('tɛmptɪŋ) *adj* attractive or inviting: *a tempting meal.*
▸ 'temptingly *adv*

tempus fugit *Latin.* ('tɛmpəs 'fjuːdʒɪt) time flies.

Temuco ★ (*Spanish* teˈmuko) *n* a city in S Chile: agricultural trading centre. Pop.: 239 340 (1995 est.).

ten (tɛn) *n* **1** the cardinal number that is the sum of nine and one. It is the base of the decimal number system and the base of the common logarithm. **2** a numeral, 10, X, etc., representing this number. **3** something representing or consisting of ten units. **4** Also called: **ten o'clock**. ten hours after noon or midnight. ◆ *determiner* **5** amounting to ten. ◆ Related adj: **decimal**. [OE *tēn*]

ten. *Music. abbrev. for:* **1** tenor. **2** tenuto.

tenable ('tɛnəbªl) *adj* able to be upheld, believed, maintained, or defended. [C16: from OF, from *tenir* to hold, from L *tenēre*]
▸ ˌtena'bility or 'tenableness *n* ▸ 'tenably *adv*

tenace ('teneɪs) *n Bridge, whist.* a holding of two

nonconsecutive high cards of a suit, such as the ace and queen. [C17: from F, from Sp. *tenaza* forceps, ult. from L *tenāx* holding fast, from *tenēre* to hold]

tenacious (tɪ'neɪʃəs) *adj* **1** holding firmly: *a tenacious grip*. **2** retentive: *a tenacious memory*. **3** stubborn or persistent. **4** holding together firmly; cohesive. **5** tending to stick or adhere. [C16: from L *tenāx*, from *tenēre* to hold]
▶ te'naciously *adv* ▶ te'naciousness *or* tenacity (tɪ'næsɪtɪ) *n*

tenaculum (tɪ'nækjʊləm) *n*, *pl* tenacula (-lə). a hooked surgical instrument for grasping and holding parts. [C17: from LL, from L *tenēre* to hold]

tenancy ('tɛnənsɪ) *n*, *pl* tenancies. **1** the temporary possession or holding by a tenant of lands or property owned by another. **2** the period of holding or occupying such property. **3** the period of holding office, a position, etc.

tenant ('tɛnənt) *n* **1** a person who holds, occupies, or possesses land or property, esp. from a landlord. **2** a person who has the use of a house, etc., subject to the payment of rent. **3** any holder or occupant. ♦ *vb* **4** (*tr*) to hold as a tenant. [C14: from OF, lit.: (one who is) holding, from *tenir* to hold, from L *tenēre*]
▶ 'tenantable *adj* ▶ 'tenantless *adj*

tenant farmer *n* a person who farms land rented from another, the rent usually taking the form of crops or livestock.

tenantry ('tɛnəntrɪ) *n* **1** tenants collectively. **2** the status or condition of being a tenant.

tench (tɛntʃ) *n* a European freshwater game fish of the carp family. [C14: from OF *tenche*, from LL *tinca*]

Ten Commandments *pl n* the. *Old Testament*. the commandments summarizing the basic obligations of man towards God and his fellow men, delivered to Moses on Mount Sinai engraved on two tables of stone (Exodus 20:1–17).

tend[1] (tɛnd) *vb* (when *intr*, usually foll. by *to* or *towards*) **1** (when *tr*, takes an *infinitive*) to have a general disposition (to do something); be inclined: *children tend to prefer sweets to meat*. **2** (*intr*) to have or be an influence (towards a specific result). **3** (*intr*) to go or move (in a particular direction): *to tend to the south*. [C14: from OF *tendre*, from L *tendere* to stretch]

tend[2] (tɛnd) *vb* **1** (*tr*) to care for. **2** (when *intr*, often foll. by *on* or *to*) to attend (to). **3** (*tr*) to handle or control. **4** (*intr*; often foll. by *for*) *Inf.*, *chiefly US & Canad.* to pay attention. [C14: var. of ATTEND]

tendency ('tɛndənsɪ) *n*, *pl* tendencies. **1** (often foll. by *to*) an inclination, predisposition, propensity, or leaning. **2** the general course, purport, or drift of something, esp. a written work. [C17: from Med. L *tendentia*, from L *tendere* to TEND[1]]

tendentious *or* **tendencious** (tɛn'dɛnʃəs) *adj* having or showing an intentional tendency or bias, esp. a controversial one. [C20: from TENDENCY]
▶ ten'dentiously *or* ten'denciously *adv* ▶ ten'dentiousness *or* ten'denciousness *n*

tender[1] ('tɛndə) *adj* **1** easily broken, cut, or crushed; soft. **2** easily damaged; vulnerable or sensitive: *at a tender age*. **3** having or expressing warm feelings. **4** kind or sympathetic: *a tender heart*. **5** arousing warm feelings; touching. **6** gentle and delicate: *a tender breeze*. **7** requiring care in handling: *a tender question*. **8** painful or sore. **9** sensitive to moral or spiritual feelings. **10** (*postpositive*; foll. by *of*) protective: *tender of one's emotions*. [C13: from OF *tendre*, from L *tener* delicate]
▶ 'tenderly *adv* ▶ 'tenderness *n*

tender[2] ('tɛndə) *vb* **1** (*tr*) to give, present, or offer: *to tender a bid*. **2** (*intr*; foll. by *for*) to make a formal offer or estimate (for a job or contract). **3** (*tr*) *Law*. to offer (money or goods) in settlement of a debt or claim. ♦ *n* **4** the act or an instance of tendering; offer. **5** a formal offer to supply specified goods or services at a stated cost or rate. **6** something, esp. money, used as an official medium of payment: *legal tender*. [C16: from Anglo-F *tendre*, from L *tendere* to extend]
▶ 'tenderer *n*

tender[3] ('tɛndə) *n* **1** a small boat towed or carried by a

ship. **2** a vehicle drawn behind a steam locomotive to carry the fuel and water. **3** a person who tends. [C15: var. of *attender*]

tenderfoot ('tɛndə,fʊt) *n*, *pl* tenderfoots *or* tenderfeet. **1** a newcomer, esp. to the mines or ranches of the southwestern US. **2** (formerly) a beginner in the Scouts or Guides.

tenderhearted (,tɛndə'hɑːtɪd) *adj* having a compassionate, kindly, or sensitive disposition.

tenderize *or* **tenderise** ('tɛndə,raɪz) *vb* tenderizes, tenderizing, tenderized *or* tenderises, tenderising, tenderised. (*tr*) to make (meat) tender, as by pounding it or adding a substance to break down the fibres.
▶ ,tenderi'zation *or* ,tenderi'sation *n* ▶ 'tender,izer *or* 'tender,iser *n*

tenderloin ('tɛndə,lɔɪn) *n* a tender cut of pork or other meat from between the sirloin and ribs.

tendon ('tɛndən) *n* a cord or band of tough tissue that attaches a muscle to a bone or some other part; sinew. [C16: from Med. L *tendō*, from L *tendere* to stretch]

tendril ('tɛndrɪl) *n* a threadlike leaf or stem that attaches climbing plants to a support by twining or adhering. [C16: ?from OF *tendron* tendril (confused with OF *tendron* bud), from Med. L *tendō* TENDON]

tenebrism ('tɛnə,brɪzəm) *n* (*sometimes cap.*) a school, style, or method of painting, adopted chiefly by 17th-century Spanish and Neapolitan painters, characterized by large areas of dark colours, usually relieved with a shaft of light.
▶ 'tenebrist *n*, *adj*

tenebrous ('tɛnəbrəs) *or* **tenebrious** (tə'nɛbrɪəs) *adj* gloomy, shadowy, or dark. [C15: from L *tenebrōsus* from *tenebrae* darkness]

Tenedos ★ ('tɛnɪ,dɒs) *n* an island in the NE Aegean, near the entrance to the Dardanelles: in Greek legend the base of the Greek fleet during the siege of Troy. Modern Turkish name: **Bozcaada**.

tenement ('tɛnəmənt) *n* **1** Also called: **tenement building**. a large building divided into rooms or flats. **2** a dwelling place or residence. **3** *Chiefly Brit.* a room or flat for rent. **4** *Property law*. any form of permanent property, such as land, dwellings, offices, etc. [C14: from Med. L *tenementum*, from L *tenēre* to hold]
▶ tene'mental (,tɛnə'mɛntəl) *adj*

Tenerife ★ (,tɛnə'riːf; *Spanish* tene'rife) *n* a Spanish island in the Atlantic, off the NW coast of Africa: the largest of the Canary Islands; volcanic and mountainous; tourism and agriculture. Capital: Santa Cruz. Pop.: 560 000 (latest est.). Area: 2058 sq. km (795 sq. miles).

tenesmus (tɪ'nɛzməs) *n* an ineffective painful straining to empty the bowels or bladder. [C16: from Med. L, from L *tēnesmos*, from Gk, from *teinein* to strain]
▶ te'nesmic *adj*

tenet ('tɛnɪt, 'tiːnɪt) *n* a belief, opinion, or dogma. [C17: from L, lit.: he (it) holds, from *tenēre* to hold]

tenfold ('tɛn,fəʊld) *adj* **1** equal to or having 10 times as many or as much. **2** composed of 10 parts. ♦ *adv* **3** by or up to 10 times as many or as much.

ten-gallon hat *n* (in the US) a cowboy's broad-brimmed felt hat with a very high crown.

Teng Hsiao-ping ★ ('tɛŋ sjaʊ 'pɪŋ) *n* a variant transliteration of the Chinese name for **Deng Xiaoping**.

Tengri Khan ★ ('tɛŋgrɪ 'kɑːn) *n* a mountain in central Asia, on the border between Kyrgyzstan and the Xinjiang Uygur Autonomous Region of W China. Height: 6995 m (22 951 ft).

Tengri Nor ★ ('tɛŋgrɪ 'nɔː) *n* another name for **Nam Co**.

Ten Gurus ★ *pl n* the ten leaders of the Sikh religion, from its founder Guru Nanak (1469–1539) to Guru Govind Singh (1666–1708).

Teniers ★ ('tɛnɪəz) *n* David ('dɑːvɪt), called *the Elder*, 1582–1649, and his son **David**, called *the Younger*, 1610–90, Flemish painters.

tenner ('tɛnə) *n* *Inf.* **1** *Brit.* **1a** a ten-pound note. **1b** the sum of ten pounds. **2** *US.* a ten-dollar bill.

Tennessee ★ (,tɛnɪ'siː) *n* **1** a state of the E central US:

★ people and places

consists of a lowland plain in the west, rising to the Appalachians and the Cumberland Plateau in the east. Capital: Nashville. Pop.: 5 319 654 (1996 est.). Area: 109 412 sq. km (42 244 sq. miles). Abbrevs.: **Tenn.** or (with zip code) **TN 2** a river in the E central US, flowing southwest from E Tennessee into N Alabama, then west and north to the Ohio River at Paducah: the longest tributary of the Ohio; includes a series of dams and reservoirs under the Tennessee Valley Authority. Length: 1049 km (652 miles).
▸ ˌTennesˈsean *adj, n*

enniel ★ (ˈtɛnjəl) *n* Sir **John.** 1820–1914, British illustrator of Lewis Carroll's *Alice* books and political cartoonist in *Punch.*

ennis (ˈtɛnɪs) *n* **a** a racket game played between two players or pairs of players who hit a ball to and fro over a net on a rectangular court of grass, asphalt, clay, etc. See also **lawn tennis, real tennis, table tennis. b** (*as modifier*): *tennis court; tennis racket.* [C14: prob. from Anglo-F *tenetz* hold (imperative), from OF *tenir* to hold, from L *tenēre*]

ennis elbow *n* inflammation of the elbow caused by exertion in playing tennis, etc.

ennis shoe *n* a rubber-soled canvas shoe tied with laces.

ennyson ★ (ˈtɛnɪsˀn) *n* **Alfred,** Lord Tennyson. 1809–92, British poet; poet laureate (1850–92). His poems include *The Lady of Shalott* (1832) and *Idylls of the King* (1859).
▸ **Tennysonian** (ˌtɛnɪˈsəʊnɪən) *adj, n*

ˈeno ★ (ˈtɛnə) *n* the Finnish name for **Tana** (sense 3).

eno- *or before a vowel* **ten-** *combining form.* tendon: *tenosynovitis.* [from Gk *tenōn*]

enochtitlán ★ (tɛˌnɒːtʃtiːˈtlɑːn) *n* an ancient city and capital of the Aztec empire on the present site of Mexico City; razed by Cortés in 1521.

enon (ˈtɛnən) *n* **1** the projecting end of a piece of wood formed to fit into a corresponding mortise in another piece. ◆ *vb* (*tr*) **2** to form a tenon on (a piece of wood). **3** to join with a tenon and mortise. [C15: from OF, from *tenir* to hold, from L *tenēre*]
▸ ˈtenoner *n*

enon saw *n* a small fine-toothed saw with a strong back, used esp. for cutting tenons.

enor (ˈtɛnə) *n* **1** *Music.* **1a** the male voice intermediate between alto and baritone. **1b** a singer with such a voice. **1c** a saxophone, horn, etc., intermediate between the alto and baritone or bass. **2** general drift of thought; purpose. **3** a settled course of progress. **4** *Arch.* general tendency. **5** *Finance.* the time required for a bill of exchange or promissory note to become due for payment. **6** *Law.* **6a** the exact words of a deed, etc. **6b** an exact copy. [C13 (orig.: general sense): from OF *tenour*, from L *tenor* a holding to a course, from *tenēre* to hold; musical sense via It. *tenore*, referring to the voice part that was continuous, that is, to which the melody was assigned]

enor clef *n* the clef that establishes middle C as being on the fourth line of the staff.

enorrhaphy (tɪˈnɒrəfɪ) *n, pl* **tenorrhaphies.** *Surgery.* the union of torn or divided tendons by means of sutures. [C19: from TENO- + Gk *raphē* a sewing]

enosynovitis (ˈtɛnəʊˌsaɪnəʊˈvaɪtɪs) *n* painful swelling and inflammation of tendons, usually of the wrist, often the result of repetitive movements such as typing.

enotomy (təˈnɒtəmɪ) *n, pl* **tenotomies.** surgical division of a tendon.
▸ teˈnotomist *n*

enpin bowling (ˈtɛnˌpɪn) *n* a bowling game in which bowls are rolled down a lane to knock over the ten target pins. Also called (esp. US and Canad.): **tenpins.**

enrec (ˈtɛnrɛk) *n* any of a family of small mammals of Madagascar resembling hedgehogs or shrews. [C18: via F from Malagasy *tràndraka*]

ense[1] (tɛns) *adj* **1** stretched or stressed tightly; taut or rigid. **2** under mental or emotional strain. **3** producing mental or emotional strain: *a tense day.* **4** *Phonetics.* Also: **narrow.** pronounced with considerable muscular effort, as the vowel (iː) in "beam". ◆ *vb* **tenses, tensing, tensed.**

(often foll. by *up*) **5** to make or become tense. [C17: from L *tensus* taut, from *tendere* to stretch]
▸ ˈtensely *adv* ▸ ˈtenseness *n*

tense[2] (tɛns) *n Grammar.* a category of the verb or verbal inflections, such as present, past, and future, that expresses the temporal relations between what is reported in a sentence and the time of its utterance. [C14: from OF *tens* time, from L *tempus*]
▸ ˈtenseless *adj*

tense logic *n Logic.* the study of temporal relations between propositions, usually pursued by considering the logical properties of symbols representing the tenses of natural languages.

tensile (ˈtɛnsaɪl) *adj* **1** of or relating to tension. **2** sufficiently ductile to be stretched or drawn out. [C17: from NL *tensilis*, from L *tendere* to stretch]
▸ **tensility** (tɛnˈsɪlɪtɪ) *or* ˈtensileness *n*

tensile strength *n* a measure of the ability of a material to withstand a longitudinal stress, expressed as the greatest stress that the material can stand without breaking.

tensimeter (tɛnˈsɪmɪtə) *n* a device that measures differences in vapour pressures. [C20: from TENSI(ON) + -METER]

tensiometer (ˌtɛnsɪˈɒmɪtə) *n* **1** an instrument for measuring the tensile strength of a wire, beam, etc. **2** an instrument used to compare the vapour pressures of two liquids. **3** an instrument for measuring the surface tension of a liquid. **4** an instrument for measuring the moisture content of soil.

tension (ˈtɛnʃən) *n* **1** the act of stretching or the state or degree of being stretched. **2** mental or emotional strain; stress. **3** a situation or condition of hostility, suspense, or uneasiness. **4** *Physics.* a force that tends to produce an elongation of a body or structure. **5** *Physics.* voltage, electromotive force, or potential difference. **6** a device for regulating the tension in a part, string, thread, etc., as in a sewing machine. **7** the degree of tightness or looseness with which a person knits. [C16: from L *tensiō*, from *tendere* to strain]
▸ ˈtensional *adj* ▸ ˈtensionless *adj*

tensor (ˈtɛnsə, -sɔː) *n* **1** *Anat.* any muscle that can cause a part to become firm or tense. **2** *Maths.* a set of components, functions of the coordinates of any point in space, that transform linearly between coordinate systems. [C18: from NL, lit.: a stretcher]
▸ **tensorial** (tɛnˈsɔːrɪəl) *adj*

tent (tɛnt) *n* **1** a portable shelter of canvas, plastic, etc., supported on poles and fastened to the ground by pegs and ropes. **2** something resembling this in function or shape. ◆ *vb* **3** (*intr*) to camp in a tent. **4** (*tr*) to cover with or as if with a tent or tents. **5** (*tr*) to provide with a tent as shelter. [C13: from OF *tente*, from L *tentōrium* something stretched out, from *tendere* to stretch]
▸ ˈtentage *n* ▸ ˈtented *adj*

tentacle (ˈtɛntək°l) *n* **1** any of various elongated flexible organs that occur near the mouth in many invertebrates and are used for feeding, grasping, etc. **2** any of the hairs on the leaf of an insectivorous plant that are used to capture prey. **3** something resembling a tentacle, esp. in its ability to reach out or grasp. [C18: from NL *tentāculum*, from L *tentāre*, var. of *temptāre* to feel]
▸ ˈtentacled *adj* ▸ **tentacular** (tɛnˈtækjʊlə) *adj*

tentation (tɛnˈteɪʃən) *n* a method of achieving the correct adjustment of a mechanical device by a series of trials. [C14: from L *tentātiō*, variant of *temptātiō* TEMPTATION]

tentative (ˈtɛntətɪv) *adj* **1** provisional or experimental. **2** hesitant, uncertain, or cautious. [C16: from Med. L *tentātīvus*, from L *tentāre* to test]
▸ ˈtentatively *adv* ▸ ˈtentativeness *n*

tenter (ˈtɛntə) *n* **1** a frame on which cloth is stretched in order that it may retain its shape while drying. **2** a person who stretches cloth on a tenter. ◆ *vb* **3** (*tr*) to stretch (cloth) on a tenter. [C14: from Med. L *tentōrium*, from L *tentus* stretched, from *tendere* to stretch]

tenterhook (ˈtɛntəˌhʊk) *n* **1** one of a series of hooks used to hold cloth on a tenter. **2 on tenterhooks.** in a state of tension or suspense.

tenth (tɛnθ) *adj* **1** (*usually prenominal*) **1a** coming after the ninth in numbering, position, etc.; being the ordinal number of *ten:* often written 10th. **1b** (*as n*): *see you on the tenth.* ♦ *n* **2a** one of 10 equal parts of something. **2b** (*as modifier*): *a tenth part.* **3** the fraction equal to one divided by ten (1/10). ♦ *adv* **4** Also: **tenthly.** after the ninth person, position, event, etc. [C12 *tenthe*, from OE *tēotha*]

tent stitch *n* another term for **petit point.** [C17: from ?]

tenuis ('tɛnjʊɪs) *n, pl* **tenues** ('tɛnju,iːz). (in classical Greek) a voiceless stop (k, p, t). [C17: from L: thin]

tenuous ('tɛnjʊəs) *adj* **1** insignificant or flimsy: *a tenuous argument.* **2** slim, fine, or delicate: *a tenuous thread.* **3** diluted or rarefied in consistency or density: *a tenuous fluid.* [C16: from L *tenuis*]
▶ **tenuity** (tɛ'njuːɪtɪ) *or* **'tenuousness** *n* ▶ **'tenuously** *adv*

tenure ('tɛnjʊə, 'tɛnjə) *n* **1** the possession or holding of an office or position. **2** the length of time an office, position, etc., lasts. **3** *Chiefly US & Canad.* the improved security status of a person after having been in the employ of the same company or institution for a specified period. **4** the right to permanent employment until retirement, esp. for teachers, etc. **5a** the holding of property, esp. realty, in return for services rendered, etc. **5b** the duration of such holding. [C15: from OF, from Med. L *tenitūra*, ult. from L *tenēre* to hold]
▶ **ten'urial** *adj*

tenuto (tɪ'njuːtəʊ) *adj, adv Music.* (of a note) to be held for or beyond its full time value. [from It., lit.: held, from *tenere* to hold, from L *tenēre*]

Tenzing Norgay ★ ('tɛnsɪŋ 'nɔːgeɪ) *n* 1914–86, Nepalese mountaineer. With Sir Edmund Hillary, he was the first to reach the summit of Mount Everest (1953).

teocalli (,tiːəʊ'kælɪ) *n, pl* **teocallis.** any of various truncated pyramids built by the Aztecs as bases for their temples. [C17: from Nahuatl, from *teotl* god + *calli* house]

tepee *or* **teepee** ('tiːpiː) *n* a cone-shaped tent of animal skins used by American Indians. [C19: from Siouan *tipī*, from *ti* to dwell + *pi* used for]

tephra ('tɛfrə) *n Chiefly US.* solid matter ejected during a volcanic eruption. [C20: Gk, lit.: ashes]

Tepic ★ (*Spanish* te'pik) *n* a city in W central Mexico, capital of Nayarit state: agricultural, trading and processing centre. Pop.: 206 967 (1990).

tepid ('tɛpɪd) *adj* **1** slightly warm; lukewarm. **2** relatively unenthusiastic or apathetic. [C14: from L *tepidus*, from *tepēre* to be lukewarm]
▶ **tepidity** (tɛ'pɪdɪtɪ) *or* **'tepidness** *n* ▶ **'tepidly** *adv*

tequila (tɪ'kiːlə) *n* **1** a spirit that is distilled in Mexico from an agave plant and forms the basis of many mixed drinks. **2** the plant from which this drink is made. [C19: from Mexican Sp., from *Tequila*, region of Mexico]

ter. *abbrev. for:* **1** terrace. **2** territory.

ter- *combining form.* three, third, or three times. [from L *ter* thrice]

tera- *prefix* denoting 10^{12}: *terameter.* Symbol: T [from Gk *teras* monster]

Terai ★ (tə'raɪ) *n* **1** (in India) a belt of marshy land at the foot of mountains, esp. at the foot of the Himalayas in Uttar Pradesh. **2** a felt hat with a wide brim worn in subtropical regions.

terat- *or* **terato-** *combining form.* indicating a monster or something abnormal: *teratism.* [from Gk *terat-, teras* monster, prodigy]

teratism ('tɛrə,tɪzəm) *n* a malformed animal or human, esp. in the fetal stage; monster.

teratogen ('tɛrətədʒən, tɪ'rætə-) *n* any substance, organism, or process that causes malformations in a fetus. Teratogens include certain drugs (such as thalidomide), infections (such as German measles), and ionizing radiation.
▶ **,terato'genic** *adj*

teratoid ('tɛrə,tɔɪd) *adj Biol.* resembling a monster.

teratology (,tɛrə'tɒlədʒɪ) *n* **1** the branch of medical science concerned with the development of physical abnormalities during the fetal or early embryonic stage. **2** the branch of biology concerned with the structure, development, etc., of monsters. **3** a collection of tales about mythical or fantastic creatures, monsters, etc.
▶ **,tera'tologist** *n*

teratoma (,tɛrə'təʊmə) *n, pl* **teratomata** (-mətə) *or* **teratomas.** a tumour composed of tissue foreign to the site of growth.

terbium ('tɜːbɪəm) *n* a soft malleable silvery-grey element of the lanthanide series of metals. Symbol: Tb; atomic no.: 65; atomic wt.: 158.925. [C19: from NL, after *Ytterby*, Sweden, village where discovered]
▶ **'terbic** *adj*

terbium metal *n Chem.* any of a group of related lanthanides, including terbium, europium, and gadolinium.

Ter Borch *or* **Terborch** ★ (*Dutch* ter 'bɔrx) *n* Gerard ('xeːrɑrt). 1617–81, Dutch genre and portrait painter.

terce (tɜːs) *or* **tierce** *n Chiefly RC Church.* the third of the seven canonical hours, originally fixed at the third hour of the day, about 9 a.m. [C14: var. of TIERCE]

Terceira ★ (*Portuguese* tər'sɐɪrə) *n* an island in the N Atlantic, in the Azores: NATO military air base. Pop.: 60 000 (latest est.). Area: 397 sq. km (153 sq. miles).

tercel ('tɜːsəl) *or* **tiercel** *n* a male falcon or hawk, esp. as used in falconry. [C14: from OF, from Vulgar L *tertiolus* (unattested), from L *tertius* third, from the tradition that only one egg in three hatched a male chick]

tercentenary (,tɜːsɛn'tiːnərɪ) *or* **tercentennial** *adj* **1** of a period of 300 years. **2** of a 300th anniversary. ♦ *n, pl* **tercentenaries** *or* **tercentennials.** **3** an anniversary of 300 years.

tercet ('tɜːsɪt, tɜː'sɛt) *n* a group of three lines of verse that rhyme together or are connected by rhyme with adjacent groups of three lines. [C16: from F, from It. *terzetto,* dim. of *terzo* third, from L *tertius*]

terebene ('tɛrə,biːn) *n* a mixture of hydrocarbons prepared from oil of turpentine and sulphuric acid, used to make paints and varnishes and medicinally as an expectorant and antiseptic. [C19: from TEREB(INTH) + -ENE]

terebinth ('tɛrɪbɪnθ) *n* a small Mediterranean tree that yields a turpentine. [C14: from L *terebinthus,* from Gk *terebinthos* turpentine tree]

terebinthine (,tɛrɪ'bɪnθaɪn) *adj* **1** of or relating to terebinth or related plants. **2** of, consisting of, or resembling turpentine.

teredo (te'riːdəʊ) *n, pl* **teredos** *or* **teredines** (-dɪ,niːz). any of a genus of marine bivalve molluscs. See **shipworm.** [C17: via L from Gk *terēdōn* wood-boring worm]

Terence ★ ('tɛrəns) *n* Latin name *Publius Terentius Afer.* ?190–159 B.C., Roman dramatist.

Terengganu (tɛrɛŋ'gɑːnuː) *n* a variant spelling of **Trengganu.**

Teresa *or* **Theresa** ★ (tə'riːzə; *Spanish* te'resa) *n* **1 Saint,** known as *Teresa of Avila.* 1515–82, Spanish nun, who reformed the Carmelite order. Her writings include *The Way to Perfection.* Feast day: Oct. 15. **2 Mother,** original name *Agnes Gonxha Bojaxhiu.* 1910–97, Indian Roman Catholic missionary, born in Skopje, now in the Former Yugoslav Republic of Macedonia, of Albanian parents: noted for her relief work in Calcutta; Nobel peace prize 1979. ♦ See also **Thérèse de Lisieux.**

Tereshkova ★ (*Russian* tɪrɪʃ'kɔvə) *n* **Valentina Vladimirovna** (vəlɪn'tinə vlɑ'dimirəvnə). born 1937, Soviet cosmonaut; first woman in space (1963).

Teresina ★ (*Portuguese* tere'zinɐ) *n* an inland port in NE Brazil, capital of Piauí state, on the Parnaíba River: chief commercial centre of the Parnaíba valley. Pop.: 556 073 (1991). Former name: **Therezina.**

terete ('teriːt) *adj* (esp. of plant parts) cylindrical and tapering. [C17: from L *teres* smooth, from *terere* to rub]

tergiversate ('tɜːdʒɪvə,seɪt) *vb* **tergiversates, tergiversating, tergiversated.** (*intr*) **1** to change sides or loyalties. **2** to be evasive or ambiguous. [C17: from L *tergiversārī* to turn one's back, from *tergum* back + *vertere* to turn]
▶ **,tergiver'sation** *n* ▶ **'tergiver,sator** *n*

tergum ('tɜːgəm) *n, pl* **terga** (-gə). a cuticular plate cover-

★ people and places

ing the dorsal surface of a body segment of an arthropod. [C19: from L: the back]
▸ **'tergal** *adj*

term (tɜːm) *n* **1** a name, expression, or word used for some particular thing, esp. in a specialized field of knowledge: *a medical term*. **2** any word or expression. **3** a limited period of time: *a prison term*. **4** any of the divisions of the academic year during which a school, college, etc., is in session. **5** a point in time determined for an event or for the end of a period. **6** the period at which childbirth is imminent. **7** *Law*. **7a** an estate or interest in land limited to run for a specified period. **7b** the duration of an estate, etc. **7c** (formerly) a period of time during which sessions of courts of law are held. **7d** time allowed to a debtor to settle. **8** *Maths*. any distinct quantity making up a fraction or proportion, or contained in a polynomial, sequence, series, etc. **9** *Logic*. **9a** the word or phrase that forms either the subject or predicate of a proposition. **9b** a name or variable, as opposed to a predicate. **9c** any of the three subjects or predicates occurring in a syllogism. **10** *Archit*. a sculptured post, esp. one in the form of an armless bust or an animal on the top of a square pillar. ◆ *vb* **11** (*tr*) to designate; call: *he was termed a thief*. ◆ See also **terms**. [C13: from OF *terme*, from L *terminus* end]
▸ **'termly** *adj, adv*

termagant ('tɜːməgənt) *n* a shrewish woman; scold. [C13: from earlier *Tervagaunt*, from OF *Tervagan*, from It. *Trivigante*; after an arrogant character in medieval mystery plays who was supposed to be a Muslim deity]

-termer *n* (*in combination*) a person serving a specified length of time in prison: *a short-termer*.

terminable ('tɜːmɪnəbʰl) *adj* **1** able to be terminated. **2** terminating after a specific period or event.
▸ ˌtermina'bility *or* 'terminableness *n* ▸ 'terminably *adv*

terminal ('tɜːmɪnʰl) *adj* **1** of, being, or situated at an end, terminus, or boundary. **2** of or occurring after or in a term: *terminal examinations*. **3** (of a disease) terminating in death. **4** *Inf*. extreme: *terminal boredom*. **5** of or relating to the storage or delivery of freight at a warehouse. ◆ *n* **6** a terminating point, part, or place. **7a** a point at which current enters or leaves an electrical device, such as a battery or a circuit. **7b** a conductor by which current enters or leaves at such a point. **8** *Computing*. a device having input/output links with a computer. **9** *Archit*. **9a** an ornamental carving at the end of a structure. **9b** another name for **term** (sense 10). **10a** a point or station at the end of the line of a railway or at an airport, serving as an important access point for passengers or freight. **10b** a less common name for **terminus** (sense 2). **11** a reception and departure building at the terminus of a bus, sea, or air transport route. **12** a site where raw material is unloaded and processed, esp. an onshore installation designed to receive offshore oil or gas. [C15: from L *terminālis*, from *terminus* end]
▸ **'terminally** *adv*

terminal market *n* a commodity market in a trading centre rather than at a producing centre.

terminal velocity *n* **1** the constant maximum velocity reached by a body falling under gravity through a fluid, esp. the atmosphere. **2** the velocity of a missile or projectile when it reaches its target. **3** the maximum velocity attained by a rocket, missile, or shell flying in a parabolic flight path. **4** the maximum velocity that an aircraft can attain.

terminate ('tɜːmɪˌneɪt) *vb* **terminates, terminating, terminated**. (when *intr*, often foll. by *in* or *with*) to form, be, or put an end (to); conclude. [C16: from L *terminātus* limited, from *termināre* to set boundaries, from *terminus* end]
▸ **'terminative** *adj* ▸ **'termiˌnator** *n*

termination (ˌtɜːmɪ'neɪʃən) *n* **1** the act of terminating or the state of being terminated. **2** something that terminates. **3** a final result.

terminology (ˌtɜːmɪ'nɒlədʒɪ) *n, pl* **terminologies**. **1** the body of specialized words relating to a particular subject. **2** the study of terms. [C19: from Med. L *terminus* term from L: end]
▸ **terminological** (ˌtɜːmɪnə'lɒdʒɪkʰl) *adj* ▸ ˌtermi'nologist *n*

term insurance *n* life assurance, usually low in cost

and offering no cash value, that provides for the payment of a specified sum of money only if the insured dies within a stipulated time.

terminus ('tɜːmɪnəs) *n, pl* **termini** (-naɪ) *or* **terminuses**. **1** the last or final part or point. **2** either end of a railway, bus route, etc., or a station or town at such a point. **3** a goal aimed for. **4** a boundary or boundary marker. **5** *Archit*. another name for **term** (sense 10). [C16: from L: end]

Terminus ★ ('tɜːmɪnəs) *n* the Roman god of boundaries.

terminus ad quem *Latin*. ('tɜːmɪˌnʊs æd 'kwem) *n* the aim or terminal point. [lit.: the end to which]

terminus a quo *Latin*. ('tɜːmɪˌnʊs ɑː 'kwəʊ) *n* the starting point; beginning. [lit.: the end from which]

termitarium (ˌtɜːmɪ'tɛərɪəm) *n, pl* **termitaria** (-ɪə). the nest of a termite colony. [C20: from TERMITE + -ARIUM]

termite ('tɜːmaɪt) *n* any of an order of whitish antlike social insects of warm and tropical regions. Some species feed on wood, causing damage to buildings, trees, etc. [C18: from NL *termitēs* white ants, pl of *termes*, from L: a woodworm]
▸ **termitic** (tɜː'mɪtɪk) *adj*

termless ('tɜːmlɪs) *adj* **1** without limit or boundary. **2** unconditional. **3** an archaic word for **indescribable**.

termor *or* **termer** ('tɜːmə) *n Property law*. a person who holds an estate for a term of years or until he dies.

terms (tɜːmz) *pl n* **1** (usually specified prenominally) the actual language or mode of presentation used: *he described the project in loose terms*. **2** conditions of an agreement. **3** a sum of money paid for a service. **4** (usually preceded by *on*) mutual relationship or standing: *they are on affectionate terms*. **5** **bring to terms**. to cause to agree or submit. **6** **come to terms**. to reach acceptance or agreement. **7** **in terms of**. as expressed by; regarding: *in terms of money he was no better off*.

terms of trade *pl n Economics, Brit*. the ratio of export prices to import prices.

tern (tɜːn) *n* any of several aquatic birds related to the gulls, having a forked tail, long narrow wings, and a typically black-and-white plumage. [C18: from ON *therna*]

ternary ('tɜːnərɪ) *adj* **1** consisting of three or groups of three. **2** *Maths*. (of a number system) to the base three. [C14: from L *ternārius*, from *ternī* three each]

ternary form *n* a musical structure consisting of two contrasting sections followed by a repetition of the first; the form *aba*.

ternate ('tɜːnɪt, -neɪt) *adj* **1** (esp. of a leaf) consisting of three leaflets or other parts. **2** (esp. of plants) having groups of three members. [C18: from NL *ternātus*, from Med. L *ternāre* to increase threefold]
▸ **'ternately** *adv*

terne (tɜːn) *n* **1** an alloy of lead containing tin and antimony. **2** Also called: **terne plate**. steel plate coated with this alloy. [C16: ?from F *terne* dull, from OF *ternir* to TARNISH]

Terni ★ (*Italian* 'tɛrni) *n* an industrial city in central Italy, in Umbria: site of waterfalls created in Roman times. Pop.: 108 294 (1994 est.).

Ternopol ★ (*Russian* tɪr'nɔpəlj) *n* a town in the W Ukraine: formerly under Polish rule. Pop.: 235 000 (1996 est.). Polish name: **Tarnopol**.

terotechnology (ˌtɪərəʊtek'nɒlədʒɪ, ter-) *n* a branch of technology that utilizes management, financial, and engineering expertise in the installation, efficient operation, and maintenance of equipment and machinery. [C20: from Gk *tērein* to care for + TECHNOLOGY]

terpene ('tɜːpiːn) *n* any one of a class of unsaturated hydrocarbons, such as pinene and the carotenes, that are found in the essential oils of many plants, esp. conifers. [C19: terp- from obs. *terpentine* turpentine + -ENE]

terpineol (tɜː'pɪnɪˌɒl) *n* a terpene alcohol with an odour of lilac, existing in three isomeric forms that occur in several essential oils. [C20: from TERPENE + -INE² + -OL¹]

Terpsichore ★ (tɜːp'sɪkərɪ) *n* the Muse of the dance and of choral song. [C18: via L from Gk, from *terpsikhoros* delighting in the dance, from *terpein* to delight + *khoros* dance]

Terpsichorean (ˌtɜːpsɪkəˈrɪən, -ˈkɔːrɪən) *Often used facetiously.* ♦ *adj also* **Terpsichoreal.** **1** of or relating to dancing. ♦ *n* **2** a dancer.

terra (ˈtɛrə) *n* (in legal contexts) earth or land. [from L]

terra alba (ˈælbə) *n* **1** a white finely powdered form of gypsum, used to make paints, paper, etc. **2** any of various other white earthy substances, such as kaolin, pipeclay, and magnesia. [from L, lit.: white earth]

terrace (ˈtɛrəs) *n* **1** a horizontal flat area of ground, often one of a series in a slope. **2a** a row of houses, usually identical and having common dividing walls, or the street onto which they face. **2b** (*cap. when part of a street name*): *Grosvenor Terrace.* **3** a paved area alongside a building, serving partly as a garden. **4** a balcony or patio. **5** the flat roof of a house built in a Spanish or Oriental style. **6** a flat area bounded by a short steep slope formed by the down-cutting of a river or by erosion. **7** (*usually pl*) unroofed tiers around a football pitch on which the spectators stand. ♦ *vb* **terraces, terracing, terraced. 8** (*tr*) to make into or provide with a terrace or terraces. [C16: from OF *terrasse*, from OProvençal *terrassa* pile of earth, from *terra* earth, from L]

terraced house *n Brit.* a house that is part of a terrace. US and Canad. name: **row house.**

terracing (ˈtɛrəsɪŋ) *n* **1** a series of terraces, esp. one dividing a slope into a steplike system of flat narrow fields. **2** the act of making a terrace or terraces. **3** another name for **terrace** (sense 7).

terra cotta (ˈkɒtə) *n* **1** a hard unglazed brownish-red earthenware, or the clay from which it is made. **2** something made of terra cotta, such as a sculpture. **3** a strong reddish-brown to brownish-orange colour. [C18: from It., lit.: baked earth]
▸ ˈterra-ˈcotta *adj*

terra firma (ˈfɜːmə) *n* the solid earth; firm ground. [C17: from L]

terrain (təˈreɪn) *n* a piece of ground, esp. with reference to its physical character or military potential: *a rocky terrain.* [C18: from F, ult. from L *terrēnum* ground, from *terra* earth]

terra incognita *Latin.* (ˈtɛrə ɪnˈkɒɡnɪtə) *n* an unexplored or unknown land, region, or area.

Terramycin (ˌtɛrəˈmaɪsɪn) *n Trademark.* a broad-spectrum antibiotic used in treating various infections.

terrapin (ˈtɛrəpɪn) *n* any of various web-footed reptiles that live on land and in fresh water and feed on small aquatic animals. Also called: **water tortoise.** [C17: of Amerind origin]

terrarium (tɛˈrɛərɪəm) *n, pl* **terrariums** *or* **terraria** (-ˈrɛərɪə). **1** an enclosure for small land animals. **2** a glass container, often a globe, in which plants are grown. [C19: NL, from L *terra* earth]

terra sigillata (ˌsɪdʒɪˈlɑːtə) *n* **1** a reddish-brown clayey earth found on the Aegean island of Lemnos: formerly used as an astringent and in the making of earthenware pottery. **2** any similar earth resembling this. **3** earthenware pottery made from this or a similar earth, esp. Samian ware. [from L: sealed earth]

terrazzo (tɛˈrætsəʊ) *n, pl* **terrazzos.** a floor made by setting marble chips into a layer of mortar and polishing the surface. [C20: from It.: TERRACE]

terrene (tɛˈriːn) *adj* **1** of the earth; worldly; mundane. **2** *Rare.* of earth; earthy. ♦ *n* **3** a land. **4** a rare word for **earth.** [C14: from Anglo-Norman, from L *terrēnus*, from *terra* earth]

terreplein (ˈtɛəˌpleɪn) *n* the top of a rampart where guns are placed behind the parapet. [C16: from F, from Med. L *terrā plēnus* filled with earth]

terrestrial (təˈrɛstrɪəl) *adj* **1** of the earth. **2** of the land as opposed to the sea or air. **3** (of animals and plants) living or growing on the land. **4** earthly, worldly, or mundane. **5** *Television.* denoting or using signals sent over the earth's surface from a transmitter on land, rather than by satellite. ♦ *n* **6** an inhabitant of the earth. [C15: from L *terrestris*, from *terra* earth]
▸ terˈrestrially *adv* ▸ terˈrestrialness *n*

terrestrial telescope *n* a telescope for use on earth rather than for making astronomical observations. Such telescopes contain an additional lens or prism system to produce an erect image.

terret (ˈtɛrɪt) *n* **1** either of the two rings on a harness through which the reins are passed. **2** the ring on a dog's collar for attaching the lead. [C15: var. of *toret*, from OF, dim. of *tor* loop]

terre-verte (ˈtɛəˌvɜːt) *n* **1** a greyish-green pigment used in paints. It is made from a mineral found in greensand and similar rocks. ♦ *adj* **2** of a greyish-green colour. [C17: from F, lit.: green earth]

terrible (ˈtɛrəbᵊl) *adj* **1** very serious or extreme. **2** *Inf.* of poor quality; unpleasant or bad. **3** causing terror. **4** causing awe. [C15: from L *terribilis*, from *terrēre* to terrify]
▸ ˈterribleness *n* ▸ ˈterribly *adv*

terricolous (tɛˈrɪkələs) *adj* living on or in the soil. [C19: from L *terricola*, from *terra* earth + *colere* to inhabit]

terrier[1] (ˈtɛrɪə) *n* any of several usually small, active, and short-bodied breeds of dog, originally trained to hunt animals living underground. [C15: from OF *chien terrier* earth dog, from Med. L *terrārius* belonging to the earth, from L *terra* earth]

terrier[2] (ˈtɛrɪə) *n English legal history.* a register or survey of land. [C15: from OF, from Med. L *terrārius* of the land, from L *terra* land]

terrific (təˈrɪfɪk) *adj* **1** very great or intense. **2** *Inf.* very good; excellent. **3** very frightening. [C17: from L *terrificus*, from *terrēre* to frighten]
▸ terˈrifically *adv*

terrify (ˈtɛrɪˌfaɪ) *vb* **terrifies, terrifying, terrified.** (*tr*) to inspire fear or dread in; frighten greatly. [C16: from L *terrificāre*, from *terrēre* to alarm + *facere* to cause]
▸ ˈterriˌfying *adj* ▸ ˈterriˌfyingly *adv*

terrigenous (tɛˈrɪdʒɪnəs) *adj* **1** of or produced by the earth. **2** (of geological deposits) formed in the sea from material derived from the land by erosion. [C17: from L *terrigenus*, from *terra* earth + *gignere* to beget]

terrine (tɛˈriːn) *n* **1** an oval earthenware cooking dish with a tightly fitting lid used for pâtés, etc. **2** the food cooked or served in such a dish, esp. pâté. [C18: earlier form of TUREEN]

territorial (ˌtɛrɪˈtɔːrɪəl) *adj* **1** of or relating to a territory or territories. **2** restricted to or owned by a particular territory. **3** local or regional. **4** *Zool.* establishing and defending a territory. **5** pertaining to a territorial army, providing a reserve of trained men for use in emergency.
▸ ˌterriˌtoriˈality *n* ▸ ˌterriˈtorially *adv*

Territorial (ˌtɛrɪˈtɔːrɪəl) *n* a member of a Territorial Army.

Territorial Army *n* (in Britain) a standing reserve army originally organized between 1907 and 1908. Full name: **Territorial and Volunteer Reserve.**

Territorial Council *n* (in Canada) an elected body responsible for local government in the Northwest Territories or the Yukon.

territorial waters *pl n* the waters over which a nation exercises jurisdiction and control.

territory (ˈtɛrɪtərɪ) *n, pl* **territories. 1** any tract of land; district. **2** the geographical domain under the jurisdiction of a political unit, esp. of a sovereign state. **3** the district for which an agent, etc., is responsible. **4** an area inhabited and defended by an animal or a pair of animals. **5** an area of knowledge. **6** (in football, hockey, etc.) the area defended by a team. **7** (*often cap.*) a region of a country, esp. of a federal state, that enjoys less autonomy and a lower status than most constituent parts of the state. **8** (*often cap.*) a protectorate or other dependency of a country. [C15: from L *territōrium* land surrounding a town, from *terra* land]

terror (ˈtɛrə) *n* **1** great fear, panic, or dread. **2** a person or thing that inspires great dread. **3** *Inf.* a troublesome person or thing, esp. a child. **4** terrorism. [C14: from OF *terreur*, from L *terror*, from *terrēre* to frighten]
▸ ˈterrorful *adj* ▸ ˈterrorless *adj*

terrorism (ˈtɛrəˌrɪzəm) *n* **1** the systematic use of violence and intimidation to achieve some goal. **2** the act of terrorizing. **3** the state of being terrorized.
▸ ˈterrorist *n, adj*

★ people and places

errorize or **terrorise** ('tɛrə,raɪz) vb **terrorizes, terrorizing, terrorized** or **terrorises, terrorising, terrorised**. (tr) **1** to coerce or control by violence, fear, threats, etc. **2** to inspire with dread; terrify.
▶ ,terrori'zation or ,terrori'sation n ▶ 'terror,izer or 'terror,iser n

terror-stricken or **terror-struck** adj in a state of terror.

terry ('tɛrɪ) n, pl **terries**. **1** an uncut loop in the pile of towelling or a similar fabric. **2** a fabric with such a pile. [C18: ? var. of TERRET]

Terry ★ ('tɛrɪ) n Dame **Ellen**. 1847–1928, British actress.

terse (tɜːs) adj **1** neatly brief and concise. **2** curt; abrupt. [C17: from L tersus precise, from tergēre to polish]
▶ 'tersely adv ▶ 'terseness n

tertial ('tɜːʃəl) adj, n another word for **tertiary** (senses 5, 6). [C19: from L tertius third, from ter thrice, from trēs three]

tertian ('tɜːʃən) adj **1** (of a fever) occurring every other day. ◆ n **2** a tertian fever. [C14: from L febris tertiāna fever occurring every third day, from tertius third]

tertiary ('tɜːʃərɪ) adj **1** third in degree, order, etc. **2** (of an industry) involving services as opposed to extraction or manufacture, such as transport, finance, etc. **3** RC Church. of or relating to a Third Order. **4** Chem. **4a** (of an organic compound) having a functional group attached to a carbon atom that is attached to three other groups. **4b** (of an amine) having three organic groups attached to a nitrogen atom. **4c** (of a salt) derived from a tribasic acid by replacement of all its acidic hydrogen atoms with metal atoms or electropositive groups. **5** Ornithol., rare. of or designating any of the small flight feathers attached to the part of the humerus nearest to the body. ◆ n, pl **tertiaries**. **6** Ornithol., rare. any of the tertiary feathers. **7** RC Church. a member of a Third Order. [C16: from L tertiārius containing one third, from tertius third]

Tertiary ('tɜːʃərɪ) adj **1** of, denoting, or formed in the first period of the Cenozoic era. ◆ n **2** the. the Tertiary period or rock system.

tertiary college n Brit. a college system incorporating the secondary school sixth form and vocational courses.

tertiary colour n a colour formed by mixing two secondary colours.

tertium quid ('tɜːtɪəm) n an unknown or indefinite thing related in some way to two known or definite things, but distinct from both. [C18: from LL, rendering Gk triton ti some third thing]

Tertullian ★ (tɜː'tʌlɪən) n Latin name Quintus Septimius Florens Tertullianus. ?160–?220 A.D., Carthaginian Christian theologian.

Teruel ★ (Spanish te'rwel) n a city in E central Spain: 15th-century cathedral; scene of fierce fighting during the Spanish Civil War. Pop.: 31 000 (1991).

tervalent (tɜː'veɪlənt) adj Chem. another word for **trivalent**.
▶ ter'valency n

Terylene ('tɛrɪ,liːn) n Trademark. a synthetic polyester fibre or fabric. US name (trademark): **Dacron**.

terza rima ('tɛətsə 'riːmə) n, pl **terze rime** ('tɛətseɪ 'riːmeɪ). a verse form consisting of a series of tercets in which the middle line of one tercet rhymes with the first and third lines of the next. [C19: from It., lit.: third rhyme]

TESL ('tesˀl) acronym for Teaching (of) English as a Second Language.

tesla ('tɛslə) n the derived SI unit of magnetic flux density equal to a flux of 1 weber in an area of 1 square metre. Symbol: T [C20: after Nikola TESLA]

Tesla ★ ('tɛslə) n Nikola ('nɪkələ). 1857–1943, US electrical engineer, born in Smiljan, now in Croatia. His inventions include a transformer, generators, and dynamos.

tesla coil n a step-up transformer with an air core, used for producing high voltages at high frequencies.

Tessa ('tɛsə) n (in Britain) acronym for Tax Exempt Special Savings Account; a savings scheme introduced in 1991 enabling interest on up to £1800 p.a. to be paid tax free if the capital remains intact for five years.

tessellate ('tɛsɪ,leɪt) vb **tessellates, tessellating, tessellated**. **1** (tr) to construct, pave, or inlay with a mosaic of small tiles. **2** (intr) (of identical shapes) to fit together exactly. [C18: from L tessellātus checked, from tessella small stone cube, from TESSERA]

tessera ('tɛsərə) n, pl **tesserae** (-sə,riː). **1** a small square tile of stone, glass, etc., used in mosaics. **2** a die, tally, etc., used in classical times, made of bone or wood. [C17: from L, from Ionic Gk tesseres four]
▶ 'tesseral adj

Tessin ★ (tɛ'siːn) n the German name for **Ticino**.

tessitura (,tɛsɪ'tʊərə) n Music. the general pitch level of a piece of vocal music. [It.: texture, from L textura; see TEXTURE]

test¹ (tɛst) vb **1** to ascertain (the worth, capability, or endurance) of (a person or thing) by subjection to certain examinations, etc.; try. **2** (often foll. by for) to carry out an examination on (a substance, material, or system) to indicate the presence of a substance or the possession of a property: to test food for arsenic. **3** (tr) to put under severe strain: the long delay tested my patience. **4** (intr) to achieve a specified result in a test: he tested positive for the AIDS virus. ◆ n **5** a method, practice, or examination designed to test a person or thing. **6** a series of questions or problems designed to test a specific skill or knowledge. **7** a standard of judgment; criterion. **8a** a chemical reaction or physical procedure for testing a substance, material, etc. **8b** a chemical reagent used in such a procedure. **8c** the result of the procedure or the evidence gained from it. **9** Sport. See **test match**. **10** Arch. a declaration of truth, loyalty, etc. **11** (modifier) performed as a test: test drive. [C14 (in the sense: vessel used in treating metals): from L testum earthen vessel]
▶ 'testable adj ▶ 'testing adj

test² (tɛst) n the hard outer covering of certain invertebrates and tunicates. [C19: from L testa shell]

testa ('tɛstə) n, pl **testae** (-tiː). the hard outer layer of a seed. [C18: from L: shell]

testaceous (tɛ'steɪʃəs) adj Biol. **1** of or possessing a test or testa. **2** of the reddish-brown colour of terra cotta. [C17: from L testācens, from TESTA]

testament ('tɛstəmənt) n **1** Law. a will (esp. in **last will and testament**). **2** a proof, attestation, or tribute. **3a** a covenant instituted between God and man. **3b** a copy of either the Old or the New Testament, or of the complete Bible. [C14: from L testamentum a will, from testārī to bear witness, from testis a witness]
▶ ,testa'mental adj ▶ ,testa'mentary adj

Testament ('tɛstəmənt) n **1** either of the two main parts of the Bible; the Old Testament or the New Testament. **2** the New Testament as distinct from the Old.

testate ('tɛsteɪt, 'tɛstɪt) adj **1** having left a legally valid will at death. ◆ n **2** a person who dies testate. [C15: from L testārī to make a will; see TESTAMENT]
▶ 'testacy ('tɛstəsɪ) n

testator (tɛ'steɪtə) or (fem) **testatrix** (tɛ'steɪtrɪks) n a person who makes a will, esp. one who dies testate. [C15: from Anglo-F testatour, from LL testātor, from L testārī to make a will]

test ban n an agreement among nations to forgo tests of nuclear weapons.

test-bed n Engineering. an area used for testing machinery, etc., under working conditions.

test card or **pattern** n a complex pattern used to test the characteristics of a television transmission system.

test case n a legal action that serves as a precedent in deciding similar succeeding cases.

test-drive vb **test-drives, test-driving, test-drove, test-driven**. (tr) to drive (a car or other motor vehicle) for a limited period in order to assess it.

tester¹ ('tɛstə) n a person or thing that tests.

tester² ('tɛstə) n a canopy over a bed. [C14: from Med. L testerium, from LL testa a skull, from L: shell]

testes ('tɛstiːz) n the plural of **testis**.

testicle ('tɛstɪkˀl) n either of the two male reproductive glands, in most mammals enclosed within the scrotum, that produce spermatozoa. [C15: from L testiculus, dim. of testis]
▶ **testicular** (tɛ'stɪkjulə) adj

testiculate (tɛˈstɪkjʊlɪt) *adj Bot.* having an oval shape: *the testiculate tubers of certain orchids.* [C18: from LL *testiculātus;* see TESTICLE]

testify (ˈtɛstɪˌfaɪ) *vb* **testifies, testifying, testified. 1** (when *tr, may take a clause as object*) to state (something) formally as a declaration of fact. **2** *Law.* to declare or give (evidence) under oath, esp. in court. **3** (when *intr,* often foll. by *to*) to be evidence (of); serve as witness (to). **4** (*tr*) to declare or acknowledge openly. [C14: from L *testificārī,* from *testis* witness]
▸ **ˌtestifiˈcation** *n* ▸ **ˈtestiˌfier** *n*

testimonial (ˌtɛstɪˈməʊnɪəl) *n* **1a** a recommendation of the character, ability, etc., of a person or of the quality of a product or service. **1b** (*as modifier*): *testimonial advertising.* **2** a formal statement of truth or fact. **3** a tribute given for services or achievements. **4** a sports match to raise money for a particular player. ◆ *adj* **5** of or relating to a testimony or testimonial.

USAGE NOTE *Testimonial* is sometimes wrongly used where *testimony* is meant: *his re-election is a testimony* (not *a testimonial*) *to his popularity with his constituents.*

testimony (ˈtɛstɪmənɪ) *n, pl* **testimonies. 1** a declaration of truth or fact. **2** *Law.* evidence given by a witness, esp. in court under oath. **3** evidence testifying to something: *her success was a testimony to her good luck.* **4** *Old Testament.* the Ten Commandments. [C15: from L *testimōnium,* from *testis* witness]

testis (ˈtɛstɪs) *n, pl* **testes.** another word for **testicle.** [C17: from L, lit.: witness (to masculinity)]

test match *n* (in various sports, esp. cricket) an international match, esp. one of a series.

testosterone (tɛˈstɒstəˌrəʊn) *n* a potent steroid hormone secreted mainly by the testes. [C20: from TESTIS + STEROL + -ONE]

test paper *n* **1** *Chem.* paper impregnated with an indicator for use in chemical tests. **2a** the question sheet of a test. **2b** the paper completed by a test candidate.

test pilot *n* a pilot who flies aircraft of new design to test their performance in the air.

test tube *n* **1** a cylindrical round-bottomed glass tube open at one end: used in scientific experiments. **2** (*modifier*) made synthetically in, or as if in, a test tube: *a test-tube product.*

test-tube baby *n* **1** a fetus that has developed from an ovum fertilized in an artificial womb. **2** a baby conceived by artificial insemination.

testudinal (tɛˈstjuːdɪnᵊl) *adj* of or resembling a tortoise. [C19: from L TESTUDO]

testudo (tɛˈstjuːdəʊ) *n, pl* **testudines** (-dɪˌniːz). a form of shelter used by the ancient Roman Army as protection against attack from above, consisting of a mobile arched structure or of overlapping shields held by the soldiers over their heads. [C17: from L: a tortoise, from *testa* a shell]

testy (ˈtɛstɪ) *adj* **testier, testiest.** irritable or touchy. [C14: from Anglo-Norman *testif* headstrong, from OF *teste* head, from LL *testa* skull, from L: shell]
▸ **ˈtestily** *adv* ▸ **ˈtestiness** *n*

tetanus (ˈtɛtənəs) *n* **1** Also called: **lockjaw.** an acute infectious disease in which sustained muscular spasm, contraction, and convulsion are caused by the release of toxins from a bacterium. **2** *Physiol.* any tense contraction of a muscle. [C16: via L from Gk *tetanos,* ult. from *teinein* to stretch]
▸ **ˈtetanal** *adj* ▸ **ˈtetaˌnoid** *adj*

tetany (ˈtɛtənɪ) *n* an abnormal increase in the excitability of nerves and muscles caused by a deficiency of parathyroid secretion. [C19: from F; see TETANUS]

tetchy (ˈtɛtʃɪ) *adj* **tetchier, tetchiest.** being or inclined to be cross, irritable, or touchy. [C16: prob. from obs. *tetch* defect, from OF *tache* spot, of Gmc origin]
▸ **ˈtetchily** *adv* ▸ **ˈtetchiness** *n*

tête-à-tête (ˌteɪtəˈteɪt) *n, pl* **tête-à-têtes** *or* **tête-à-tête. 1a** a private conversation between two people. **1b** (*as modifier*): *a tête-à-tête conversation.* **2** a small sofa for two people, esp. one that is S-shaped in plan so that the sitters are almost face to face. ◆ *adv* **3** intimately; in private. [C17: from F, lit.: head to head]

tête-bêche (tɛtˈbɛʃ) *adj Philately.* (of an unseparated pair of stamps) printed so that one is inverted in relation to the other. [C19: from F, from *tête* head + *bêche,* from obs. *béchevet* double-headed (orig. of a bed)]

tether (ˈtɛðə) *n* **1** a rope, chain, etc., by which an animal is tied to a particular spot. **2** the range of one's endurance, etc. **3 at the end of one's tether.** distressed or exasperated to the limit of one's endurance. ◆ *vb* **4** (*tr*) to tie with or as if with a tether. [C14: from ON *tjothr*]

Tethys[1] ★ (ˈtiːθɪs, ˈtɛθ-) *n Greek myth.* a Titaness and sea goddess, wife of Oceanus.

Tethys[2] ★ (ˈtiːθɪs, ˈtɛθ-) *n* the sea that lay between the two ancient supercontinents, Laurasia and Gondwanaland, and which can be regarded as the predecessor of today's smaller Mediterranean.

Teton Range ★ (ˈtiːtᵊn) *n* a mountain range in the N central US, mainly in NW Wyoming. Highest peak: Grand Teton, 4196 m (13 766 ft).

tetra- *or before a vowel* **tetr-** *combining form.* four: *tetrameter.* [from Gk]

tetrabasic (ˌtɛtrəˈbeɪsɪk) *adj* (of an acid) containing four replaceable hydrogen atoms.
▸ **tetrabasicity** (ˌtɛtrəbeɪˈsɪsɪtɪ) *n*

tetrachloromethane (ˈtɛtrəklɔːrəʊˌmiːθeɪn) *n* the systematic name for **carbon tetrachloride.**

tetrachord (ˈtɛtrəˌkɔːd) *n Music.* any of several groups of four notes in descending order, in which the first and last notes form a perfect fourth. [C17: from Gk *tetrakhordos* four-stringed]
▸ **ˌtetraˈchordal** *adj*

tetracyclic (ˌtɛtrəˈsaɪklɪk) *adj Chem.* containing four rings in its molecular structure.

tetracycline (ˌtɛtrəˈsaɪklaɪn, -klɪn) *n* an antibiotic synthesized from chlortetracycline or derived from a bacterium. [C20: from TETRA- + CYCL(IC) + -INE[2]]

tetrad (ˈtɛtræd) *n* a group or series of four. [C17: from Gk *tetras,* from *tettares* four]

tetraethyl lead (ˌtɛtrəˈiːθaɪl lɛd) *n* a colourless oily insoluble liquid used in petrol to prevent knocking. Systematic name: **lead tetraethyl.**

tetrafluoroethene (ˈtɛtrəˌflʊərəʊˈɛθiːn) *n Chem.* a dense colourless gas that is polymerized to make polytetrafluorethene (PTFE). Formula: $F_2C{:}CF_2$. Also called: **tetrafluoroethylene.** [C20: from TETRA- + FLUORO- + ETHENE]

tetragon (ˈtɛtrəˌgɒn) *n* a less common name for **quadrilateral** (sense 2). [C17: from Gk *tetragōnon*]

tetragonal (tɛˈtrægənᵊl) *adj* **1** *Crystallog.* relating or belonging to the crystal system characterized by three mutually perpendicular axes of which only two are equal. **2** of or shaped like a quadrilateral.
▸ **teˈtragonally** *adv*

Tetragrammaton (ˌtɛtrəˈgræmətᵊn) *n Bible.* the Hebrew name for God consisting of the four consonants Y H V H (or Y H W H). It is usually transliterated as *Jehovah* or *Yahweh.* Sometimes shortened to **Tetragram.** [C14: from Gk, from *tetragrammatos* having four letters]

tetrahedron (ˌtɛtrəˈhiːdrən) *n, pl* **tetrahedrons** *or* **tetrahedra** (-drə). a solid figure having four triangular plane faces. A **regular tetrahedron** has faces that are equilateral triangles. [C16: from NL, from LGk *tetraedron*]
▸ **ˌtetraˈhedral** *adj*

tetralogy (tɛˈtrælədʒɪ) *n, pl* **tetralogies.** a series of four related works, as in drama or opera. [C17: from Gk *tetralogia*]

tetramerous (tɛˈtræmərəs) *adj Biol.* having or consisting of four parts. [C19: from NL *tetramerus,* from Gk *tetramerēs*]

tetrameter (tɛˈtræmɪtə) *n Prosody.* **1** a line of verse consisting of four metrical feet. **2** a verse composed of such lines.

etraplegia (ˌtetrəˈpliːdʒɪə) *n* another name for **quadriplegia**.
▶ ˌtetraˈplegic *adj*

etraploid ('tetrəˌplɔɪd) *Genetics*. ◆ *adj* **1** having four times the haploid number of chromosomes in the nucleus. ◆ *n* **2** a tetraploid organism, nucleus, or cell.

etrapod ('tetrəˌpɒd) *n* **1** any vertebrate that has four limbs. **2** a device consisting of four arms radiating from a central point: three arms form a supporting tripod and the fourth is vertical.

etrapterous (teˈtræptərəs) *adj* having four wings. [C19: from NL tetrapterus, from Gk tetrapteros, from TETRA- + pteron wing]

etrarch ('tetrɑːk) *n* **1** the ruler of one fourth of a country. **2** a subordinate ruler. **3** any of four joint rulers. [C14: from Gk tetrarkhēs; see TETRA-, -ARCH]
▶ **tetrarchate** (teˈtrɑːˌkeɪt, -kɪt) *n* ▶ **teˈtrarchic** *adj* ▶ 'tetrarchy *n*

etrastich ('tetrəˌstɪk) *n* a poem, stanza, or strophe that consists of four lines. [C16: via L from Gk tetrastikhon, from TETRA- + stikhos row]
▶ **tetrastichic** (ˌtetrəˈstɪkɪk) *or* **tetrastichal** (teˈtræstɪkˀl) *adj*

etravalent (ˌtetrəˈveɪlənt) *adj Chem.* **1** having a valency of four. **2** Also: **quadrivalent**. having four valencies.
▶ ˌtetraˈvalency *n*

etrazzini ★ (*Italian* tetratˈtsiːni) *n* **Luisa** (luˈiːza). 1871–1940, Italian soprano.

etrode ('tetrəʊd) *n* an electronic valve having four electrodes.

etroxide (teˈtrɒksaɪd) *n* any oxide that contains four oxygen atoms per molecule.

etryl ('tetrɪl) *n* a yellow crystalline explosive solid, trinitrophenylmethylnitramine, used in detonators.

Tetuán ★ (teˈtwɑːn) *n* a city in N Morocco: capital of Spanish Morocco (1912–56). Pop.: 272 000 (1993 est.).

Tetzel *or* **Tezel ★** ('tetsˀl) *n* **Johann** (joˈhan). ?1465–1519, German Dominican monk. His preaching on papal indulgences provoked Luther's 95 theses at Wittenberg (1517).

Teucer ★ ('tjuːsə) *n Greek myth.* **1** a Cretan leader, who founded Troy. **2** a son of Telamon and Hesione, who distinguished himself by his archery on the side of the Greeks in the Trojan War.

Teucrian ('tjuːkrɪən) *n, adj* another word for **Trojan**.

Teut. *abbrev. for* Teuton(ic).

Teutoburger Wald ★ (*German* 'tɔytoburgər valt) *n* a low wooded mountain range in N Germany.

Teuton ('tjuːtən) *n* **1** a member of an ancient Germanic people from Jutland who migrated to S Gaul in the 2nd century B.C. **2** a member of any people speaking a Germanic language, esp. a German. ◆ *adj* **3** Teutonic. [C18: from L Teutonī the Teutons, of Gmc origin]

Teutonic (tjuːˈtɒnɪk) *adj* **1** characteristic of or relating to the German people. **2** of the ancient Teutons. **3** (not used in linguistics) of or relating to the Germanic languages.

Tevere ★ ('teːvere) *n* the Italian name for the **Tiber**.

Tewkesbury ★ ('tjuːksbəri, -bri) *n* a town in W England, in N Gloucestershire at the confluence of the Rivers Severn and Avon: scene of a decisive battle (1471) in the Wars of the Roses in which the Yorkists defeated the Lancastrians; 12th-century abbey. Pop.: 9488 (1991).

Tex. *abbrev. for:* **1** Texan. **2** Texas.

Texas ★ ('teksəs) *n* a state of the southwestern US, on the Gulf of Mexico: the second largest state; part of Mexico from 1821 to 1836, when it was declared an independent republic; joined the US in 1845; consists chiefly of a plain, with a wide flat coastal belt rising up to the semiarid Sacramento and Davis Mountains of the southwest; a major producer of cotton, rice, and livestock; the chief US producer of oil and gas; a leading world supplier of sulphur. Capital: Austin. Pop.: 19 128 261 (1996 est.). Area: 678 927 sq. km (262 134 sq. miles). Abbrevs.: **Tex.** or (with zip code) **TX**
▶ 'Texan *n, adj*

Tex-Mex ('teksˌmeks) *adj* of, relating to, or denoting the Texan version of something Mexican, such as music, food, or language.

text (tekst) *n* **1** the main body of a printed or written work as distinct from commentary, notes, illustrations, etc. **2** the words of something printed, written, or displayed on a visual display unit. **3** the original exact wording of a work as distinct from a revision or translation. **4** a short passage of the Bible used as a starting point for a sermon. **5** the topic or subject of a discussion or work. **6** short for **textbook**. **7** any novel, play, etc., prescribed as part of a course of study. [C14: from Med. L textus version, from L textus texture, from texere to compose]

textbook ('tekstˌbʊk) *n* a book used as a standard source of information on a particular subject.
▶ 'text,bookish *adj*

textile ('tekstaɪl) *n* **1** any fabric or cloth, esp. woven. **2** raw material suitable to be made into cloth. ◆ *adj* **3** of or relating to fabrics. [C17: from L textilis woven, from texere to weave]

textual ('tekstjʊəl) *adj* **1** of or relating to a text or texts. **2** based on a text.
▶ 'textually *adv*

textual criticism *n* **1** the scholarly study of manuscripts, esp. of the Bible, in an effort to establish the original text. **2** literary criticism emphasizing a close analysis of the text.

textualism ('tekstjʊəˌlɪzəm) *n* **1** doctrinaire adherence to a text, esp. of the Bible. **2** textual criticism, esp. of the Bible.
▶ 'textualist *n, adj*

texture ('tekstʃə) *n* **1** the surface of a material, esp. as perceived by the sense of touch. **2** the structure, appearance, and feel of a woven fabric. **3** the general structure and disposition of the constituent parts of something: *the texture of a cake*. **4** the distinctive character or quality of something: *the texture of life in America*. ◆ *vb* **textures, texturing, textured**. **5** (*tr*) to give a distinctive texture to. [C15: from L textūra web, from texere to weave]
▶ 'textural *adj* ▶ 'texturally *adv*

Teyde ★ (*Spanish* 'teiðe) *n* a variant spelling of **Teide**.

Tezel ('tetsˀl) *n* a variant spelling of (Johann) **Tetzel**.

TGAT ('tiːgæt) *n* (in Britain) *acronym for* Task Group on Assessment and Testing: a group that advises on assessment and testing within the National Curriculum.

TGV (ˌtiːdʒiːˈviː, *French* teʒeve) (in France) *abbrev. for* train à grande vitesse: a high-speed passenger train.

TGWU (in Britain) *abbrev. for* Transport and General Workers' Union.

Th *the chemical symbol for* thorium.

Th. *abbrev. for* Thursday.

-th[1] *suffix forming nouns.* **1** (*from verbs*) indicating an action or its consequence: *growth*. **2** (*from adjectives*) indicating a quality: *width*. [from OE -thu, -tho]

-th[2] *or* **-eth** *suffix.* forming ordinal numbers: *fourth; thousandth*. [from OE -(o)tha, -(o)the]

Thabana-Ntlenyana ★ (tɑːˈbɑːnəˀnˈtlenjənə) *n* a mountain in Lesotho: the highest peak of the Drakensberg Mountains. Height: 3482 m (11 425 ft). Also called: **Thadentsonyane, Thabantshonyana**.

Thackeray ★ ('θækəri) *n* **William Makepeace**. 1811–63, British novelist, born in India. His novels include *Vanity Fair* (1848), *Pendennis* (1850), and *The Newcomes* (1855).

Thaddeus *or* **Thadeus ★** ('θædɪəs) *n New Testament*. one of the 12 apostles (Matthew 10:3; Mark 3:18), traditionally identified with Jude.

Thadentsonyane ★ (ˌtɑːdənˈtsɒnjənə) *n* another name for **Thabana-Ntlenyana**.

Thai (taɪ) *adj* **1** of Thailand, its people, or their language. ◆ *n* **2** (*pl* **Thais** *or* **Thai**) a native or inhabitant of Thailand. **3** the language of Thailand, sometimes classified as belonging to the Sino-Tibetan family.

Thailand ★ ('taɪˌlænd) *n* a kingdom in SE Asia, on the Andaman Sea and the Gulf of Siam: united as a kingdom in 1350 and became a major SE Asian power; consists chiefly of a central plain around the Chao Phraya river system, mountains rising over 2400 m (8000 ft) in the northwest, and rainforest the length of the S peninsula. Official language: Thai. Official religion: (Hinayana) Buddhist. Currency: baht. Capital: Bangkok. Pop.:

60 602 000 (1997). Area: 513 998 sq. km (198 455 sq. miles). Former name (until 1939 and 1945–49): **Siam.**

Thaïs ★ ('θeɪɪs) *n* 4th-century B.C. Athenian courtesan; mistress of Alexander the Great.

thalamus ('θæləməs) *n, pl* **thalami** (-ˌmaɪ). **1** either of the two contiguous egg-shaped masses of grey matter at the base of the brain. **2** both of these masses considered as a functional unit. **3** the receptacle or torus of a flower. [C18: from L, from Gk *thalamos* inner room]
▸ **thalamic** (θəˈlæmɪk) *adj*

thalassaemia *or US* **thalassemia** (ˌθælə'si:mɪə) *n* a hereditary disease resulting from defects in the synthesis of the red blood pigment haemoglobin. [NL, from Gk *thalassa* sea + -AEMIA, it being esp. prevalent round the eastern Mediterranean]

thalassic (θə'læsɪk) *adj* of or relating to the sea, esp. to small or inland seas. [C19: from F *thalassique*, from Gk *thalassa* sea]

thaler ('tɑːlə) *n, pl* **thaler** *or* **thalers.** a former German, Austrian, or Swiss silver coin. [from G; see DOLLAR]

Thales ★ ('θeɪliːz) *n* ?624–?546 B.C., Greek philosopher, mathematician, and astronomer, born in Miletus. He held that water was the origin of all things and he predicted the solar eclipse of May 28, 585 B.C.

Thalia ★ (θə'laɪə) *n Greek myth.* **1** the Muse of comedy and pastoral poetry. **2** one of the three Graces, the others are Aglaia and Euphrosyne. [C17: via L from Gk, from *thaleia* blooming]

thalidomide (θə'lɪdəˌmaɪd) *n* **a** a drug formerly used as a sedative and hypnotic but withdrawn from use when found to cause abnormalities in developing fetuses. **b** (*as modifier*): *a thalidomide baby*. [C20: from *thali(mi)do-(glutari)mide*]

thallium ('θælɪəm) *n* a soft malleable highly toxic white metallic element. Symbol: Tl; atomic no.: 81; atomic wt.: 204.37. [C19: from NL, from Gk *thallos* a green shoot; from the green line in its spectrum]

thallus ('θæləs) *n, pl* **thalli** ('θælaɪ) *or* **thalluses.** the undifferentiated vegetative body of algae, fungi, and lichens. [C19: from L, from Gk *thallos* green shoot, from *thallein* to bloom]
▸ **'thalloid** *adj*

thalweg *or* **talweg** ('tɑːlveg) *n Geog., rare.* **1** the longitudinal outline of a riverbed from source to mouth. **2** the line of steepest descent from any point on the land surface. [C19: from G *Thal* or *Tal* valley + *Weg* way]

Thames ★ *n* **1** (tɛmz). a river in S England, rising in the Cotswolds and flowing east through London to the North Sea by a large estuary. Length: 346 km (215 miles). Ancient name: **Tamesis** ('tæməsɪs). **2** (teɪmz, θeɪmz). a river in SE Canada, in Ontario, flowing south to London, then southwest to Lake St Clair. Length: 217 km (135 miles).

than (ðæn; *unstressed* ðən) *conj* (*coordinating*), *prep* **1** used to introduce the second element of a comparison, the first element of which expresses difference: *shorter than you*. **2** used after adverbs such as *rather* or *sooner* to introduce a rejected alternative in an expression of preference: *rather than be imprisoned, I shall die*. [OE *thanne*]

thanatology (ˌθænə'tɒlədʒɪ) *n* the scientific study of death and its related phenomena. [C19: from Gk *thanatos* death + -LOGY]

thanatopsis (ˌθænə'tɒpsɪs) *n* a meditation on death, as in a poem. [C19: from Gk *thanatos* death + *opsis* a view]

Thanatos ★ ('θænəˌtɒs) *n* the Greek personification o death: son of Nyx, goddess of night. Roman counter part: **Mors.** Cf. **Eros.**
▸ **Thanatotic** (ˌθænə'tɒtɪk) *adj*

thane *or* (*less commonly*) **thegn** (θeɪn) *n* **1** (in Anglo Saxon England) a member of an aristocratic class whe held land from the king or from another nobleman in return for certain services. **2** (in medieval Scotland) a person of rank holding land from the king. [OE *thegn*]
▸ **thanage** ('θeɪnɪdʒ) *n*

Thanet ★ ('θænɪt) *n* **Isle of.** an island in SE England, in NE Kent, separated from the mainland by two branches o the River Stour: scene of many Norse invasions. Area 109 sq. km (42 sq. miles).

Thanjavur ★ (ˌtʌndʒə'vʊə) *n* a city in SE India, in I Tamil Nadu: headquarters of the earliest Protestant missions in India. Pop.: 202 013 (1991). Former name **Tanjore.**

thank (θæŋk) *vb* (*tr*) **1** to convey feelings of gratitude to. **2** to hold responsible: *he has his creditors to thank for his bankruptcy*. [OE *thancian*]

thankful ('θæŋkful) *adj* grateful and appreciative.
▸ **'thankfully** *adv* ▸ **'thankfulness** *n*

thankless ('θæŋklɪs) *adj* **1** receiving no thanks or appreciation. **2** ungrateful.
▸ **'thanklessly** *adv* ▸ **'thanklessness** *n*

thanks (θæŋks) *pl n* **1** an expression of appreciation o gratitude. **2** **thanks to.** because of: *thanks to him we lost the match*. ♦ *interj* **3** *Inf.* an exclamation expressing gratitude.

thanksgiving ('θæŋksˌgɪvɪŋ; *US* θæŋks'gɪv-) *n* **1** the act of giving thanks. **2** a formal public expression of thanks to God.

Thanksgiving Day *n* an annual day of holiday celebrated in thanksgiving to God on the fourth Thursday of November in the United States, and on the second Monday of October in Canada. Often shortened to **Thanksgiving.**

Thapsus ★ ('θæpsəs) *n* an ancient town near Carthage in North Africa: site of Caesar's victory over Pompey in 46 B.C.

thar (tɑː) *n* a variant spelling of **tahr.**

Thar Desert ★ (tɑː) *n* a desert in NW India, mainly in NW Rajasthan state and extending into Pakistan. Area: over 260 000 sq. km (100 000 sq. miles). Also called: **Indian Desert, Great Indian Desert.**

Thásos ★ ('θæsɒs) *n* a Greek island in the N Aegean: colonized by Greeks from Paros in the 7th century B.C. as a gold-mining centre; under Turkish rule (1455–1912). Pop.: 13 110 (1981). Area: 379 sq. km (146 sq. miles).

that (ðæt; *unstressed* ðət) *determiner* (*used before a sing n*) **1a** used preceding a noun that has been mentioned or is understood: *that idea of yours*. **1b** (*as pronoun*): *don't eat that*. **2a** used preceding a noun that denotes something more remote or removed: *that building over there is for sale*. **2b** (*as pronoun*): *that is John and this is his wife*. **3** used to refer to something that is familiar: *that old chap from across the street*. **4 and (all) that.** *Inf.* everything connected with the subject mentioned: *he knows a lot about building and that*. **5 at that.** (*completive-intensive*) additionally, all things considered, or nevertheless: *I might decide to go at that*. **6 like that.** **6a** effortlessly: *he gave me the answer just like that*. **6b** of such a nature, character, etc.: *he paid for all our tickets — he's like that*. **7 that is.** **7a** to be precise. **7b** in other words. **7c** for example. **8 that's that.** there is no more to be done, discussed, etc. ♦ *conj* (*subordinating*) **9** used to introduce a noun clause: *I believe that you'll come*. **10** used to introduce: **10a** a clause of purpose: *they fought that others might have peace*. **10b** a clause of result: *he laughed so hard that he cried*. **10c** a clause after an understood sentence expressing desire, indignation, or amazement: *oh, that I had never lived!* ◆ *adv* **11** used to reinforce the specification of a precise degree already mentioned: *go just that fast and you should be safe.* **12** Also: **all that.** (*usually used with a negative*) *Inf.* (intensifier): *he wasn't that upset at the news.* **13** *Dialect.* (intensifier): *the cat was that weak after the fight.* ◆ *pron* **14** used to introduce a restrictive relative clause: *the book that we want.* **15** used to introduce a clause with the verb *to be* to emphasize the extent to which the preceding noun is applicable: *genius that she is, she outwitted the computer.* [OE *thæt*]

> **USAGE NOTE** Precise stylists maintain a distinction between *that* and *which: that* is used as a relative pronoun in restrictive clauses and *which* in nonrestrictive clauses. In *the book that is on the table is mine,* the clause *that is on the table* is used to distinguish one particular book (the one on the table) from another or others (which may be anywhere, but not on the table). In *the book, which is on the table, is mine,* the *which* clause is merely descriptive or incidental. The more formal the level of language, the more important it is to preserve the distinction between the two relative pronouns; but in informal or colloquial usage, the words are often used interchangeably.

hatch ('θætʃ) *n* **1a** Also called: **thatching.** a roofing material that consists of straw, reed, etc. **1b** a roof made of such material. **2** anything resembling this, such as the hair of the head. **3** Also called: **thatch palm.** any of various palms with leaves suitable for thatching. ◆ *vb* **4** to cover with thatch. [OE *theccan* to cover]
> ▸ 'thatcher *n*

Thatcher ★ ('θætʃə) *n* **Margaret** (**Hilda**), Baroness (née *Roberts*). born 1925, British stateswoman; leader of the Conservative Party (1975–90); prime minister (1979–90).

Thatcherism ('θætʃə,rɪzəm) *n* the policies of monetarism, privatization, and self-help promoted by Margaret Thatcher.
> ▸ '**Thatcher**,**ite** *n*, *adj*

thaumatology (,θɔ:mə'tɒlədʒɪ) *n* the study of or a treatise on miracles. [C19: from Gk *thaumato-* combining form of *thauma* a wonder, marvel + -LOGY]

thaumatrope ('θɔ:mə,trəup) *n* a toy in which partial pictures on the two sides of a card appear to merge when the card is twirled rapidly. [C19: from Gk *thaumato-* (see THAUMATOLOGY) + -TROPE]
> ▸ **thaumatropical** (,θɔ:mə'trɒpɪkᵃl) *adj*

thaumaturge ('θɔ:mə,tɜ:dʒ) *n Rare.* a performer of miracles; magician. [C18: from Med. L *thaumaturgus,* from Gk *thaumatourgos* miracle-working]
> ▸ ,**thauma**'**turgic** *adj* ▸ '**thauma**,**turgy** *n*

thaw (θɔ:) *vb* **1** to melt or cause to melt: *the snow thawed.* **2** to become or cause to become unfrozen; defrost. **3** (*intr*) to be the case that the ice or snow is melting: *it's thawing fast.* **4** (*intr*) to become more relaxed or friendly. ◆ *n* **5** the act or process of thawing. **6** a spell of relatively warm weather, causing snow or ice to melt. **7** an increase in relaxation or friendliness. [OE *thawian*]

ThD *abbrev.* for Doctor of Theology.

the¹ (*stressed or emphatic* ði:; *unstressed before a consonant* ðə; *unstressed before a vowel* ðɪ) *determiner* (*article*) **1** used preceding a noun that has been previously specified: *the pain should disappear soon.* Cf. a¹. **2** used to indicate a particular person, object, etc.: *ask the man standing outside.* Cf. a¹. **3** used preceding certain nouns associated with one's culture, society, or community: *to go to the doctor; to listen to the news.* **4** used preceding present participles and adjectives when they function as nouns: *the singing is awful.* **5** used preceding titles and certain names uniquely specific or proper nouns: *the United States; the Chairman.* **6** used preceding a qualifying adjective or noun in certain names or titles: *Edward the First.* **7** used preceding a noun to make it refer to its class generically: *the white seal is hunted for its fur.* **8** used instead of *my, your, her,* etc., with parts of the body: *take me by the hand.* **9** (usually stressed) the best, only, or most remarkable: *Harry's is the club in*

this town. **10** used with proper nouns when qualified: *written by the young Hardy.* **11** another word for **per:** *fifty pence the pound.* **12** *Often facetious or derog.* my; our: *the wife goes out on Thursdays.* **13** used preceding a unit of time in phrases or titles indicating an outstanding person, event, etc.: *housewife of the year.* [ME, from OE *thē,* a demonstrative adjective that later superseded *sē* (masculine singular) and *sēo, sio* (feminine singular)]

the² (ðə, ðɪ) *adv* **1** (often foll. by *for*) used before comparative adjectives or adverbs for emphasis: *she looks the happier for her trip.* **2** used correlatively before each of two comparative adjectives or adverbs to indicate equality: *the sooner you come, the better; the more I see you, the more I love you.* [OE *thī, thȳ*]

theanthropism (θi:'ænθrə,pɪzəm) *n* **1** the ascription of human traits or characteristics to a god or gods. **2** *Christian theol.* the doctrine of the union of the divine and human natures in the single person of Christ. [C19: from Ecclesiastical Gk *theanthrōpos* (from *theos* god + *anthrōpos* man) + -ISM]
> ▸ **theanthropic** (,θi:æn'θrɒpɪk) *adj*

thearchy ('θi:ɑ:kɪ) *n, pl* **thearchies.** rule or government by God or gods; theocracy. [C17: from Church Gk *thearkhia;* see THEO-, -ARCHY]

theatre *or US* **theater** ('θɪətə) *n* **1** a building designed for the performance of plays, operas, etc. **2** a large room or hall, usually with a raised platform and tiered seats for an audience. **3** a room in a hospital equipped for surgical operations. **4** plays regarded collectively as a form of art. **5 the theatre.** the world of actors, theatrical companies, etc. **6** a setting for dramatic or important events. **7** writing that is suitable for dramatic presentation: *a good piece of theatre.* **8** *US, Austral., & NZ.* the usual word for **cinema** (sense 1). **9** a major area of military activity. **10** a circular or semicircular open-air building with tiers of seats. [C14: from L *theātrum,* from Gk *theatron* place for viewing, from *theasthai* to look at]

theatre-in-the-round *n, pl* **theatres-in-the-round.** a theatre with seats arranged around a central acting area.

theatre of cruelty *n* a type of theatre that seeks to communicate a sense of pain, suffering, and evil, using gesture, movement, sound, and symbolism rather than language.

theatre of the absurd *n* drama in which normal conventions and dramatic structure are modified in order to present life as irrational.

theatrical (θɪ'ætrɪkᵊl) *adj* **1** of or relating to the theatre or dramatic performances. **2** exaggerated and affected in manner or behaviour; histrionic.
> ▸ **the**,**atri**'**cality** *or* **the**'**atricalness** *n* ▸ **the**'**atrically** *adv*

theatricals (θɪ'ætrɪkᵊlz) *pl n* dramatic performances, esp. as given by amateurs.

theatrics (θɪ'ætrɪks) *n* (*functioning as sing*) **1** the art of staging plays. **2** exaggerated mannerisms or displays of emotions.

Thebaid ★ ('θi:beɪd, -bɪ-) *n* the territory around ancient Thebes in Egypt, or sometimes around Thebes in Greece.

thebaine ('θi:bə,i:n) *n* a poisonous white crystalline alkaloid, extracted from opium. [C19: from NL *thebaia* opium of Thebes (with reference to Egypt as a chief source of opium) + -INE²]

Thebes ★ (θi:bz) *n* **1** (in ancient Greece) the chief city of Boeotia, destroyed by Alexander the Great (336 B.C.). **2** (in ancient Egypt) a city on the Nile: at various times capital of Upper Egypt or of the entire country.
> ▸ **Thebaic** (θɪ'beɪɪk) *adj* ▸ '**Theban** *adj, n*

theca ('θi:kə) *n, pl* **thecae** (-si:). **1** *Bot.* an enclosing organ, cell, or spore case. **2** *Zool.* a hard outer covering, such as the container of a coral polyp. [C17: from L *thēca,* from Gk *thēkē* case]
> ▸ '**thecate** *adj*

thecodont ('θi:kə,dɒnt) *adj* **1** (of mammals and certain reptiles) having teeth that grow in sockets. **2** of or relating to teeth of this type. ◆ *n* **3** any of various extinct reptiles of Triassic times, having teeth set in sockets: they gave rise to the dinosaurs, crocodiles, pterodactyls, and birds. [C20: NL *Thecodontia,* from Gk *thēkē* case + -ODONT]

> ★ people and places

thé dansant *French.* (te dāsā) *n, pl* **thés dansants** (te dāsā). a dance held while afternoon tea is served, popular in the 1920s and 1930s.   [lit.: dancing tea]

thee (ðiː) *pron* **1** the objective form of **thou**[1]. **2** (*subjective*) *Rare.* refers to the person addressed: used mainly by members of the Society of Friends.   [OE *thē*]

theft (θeft) *n* **1** the dishonest taking of property belonging to another person with the intention of depriving the owner permanently of its possession. **2** *Rare.* something stolen.   [OE *thēofth*]

thegn (θeɪn) *n* a less common variant of **thane**.

Theiler ★ ('taɪlə) *n* **Max.** 1899–1972, US virologist, born in South Africa: Nobel prize for physiology or medicine (1951) for developing a vaccine against yellow fever.

theine ('θiːiːn, -ɪn) *n* caffeine, esp. when present in tea.   [C19: from NL *thea* tea + -INE[2]]

their (ðɛə) *determiner* **1** of or associated in some way with them: *their own clothes; she tried to combat their mocking her.* **2** belonging to or associated with people in general: *in many countries they wash their clothes in the river.* **3** belonging to or associated with an indefinite antecedent such as *one, whoever,* or *anybody: everyone should bring their own lunch.*   [C12: from ON *theira*]

> **USAGE NOTE** See at **they.**

theirs (ðɛəz) *pron* **1** something or someone belonging to or associated with them: *theirs is difficult.* **2** something or someone belonging to or associated with an indefinite antecedent such as *one, whoever,* or *anybody: everyone thinks theirs is best.* **3 of theirs.** belonging to or associated with them.

theism ('θiːɪzəm) *n* **1** the belief in one God as the creator and ruler of the universe. **2** the belief in the existence of a God or gods.   [C17: from Gk *theos* god + -ISM]
> ► '**theist** *n, adj* ► **the'istic** *or* **the'istical** *adj*

them (ðɛm; *unstressed* ðəm) *pron* **1** (*objective*) refers to things or people other than the speaker or people addressed: *I'll kill them; what happened to them?* ◆ *determiner* **2** a nonstandard word for **those:** *three of them oranges.*   [OE *thǣm,* infl. by ON *theim*]

> **USAGE NOTE** See at **me**[1], **they.**

thematic apperception test *n Psychol.* a projective test in which drawings of interacting people are shown and the person being tested is asked to make up a story about them.

theme (θiːm) *n* **1** an idea or topic expanded in a discourse, discussion, etc. **2** (in literature, music, art, etc.) a unifying idea, image, or motif, repeated or developed throughout a work. **3** *Music.* a group of notes forming a recognizable melodic unit, often used as the basis of the musical material in a composition. **4** a short essay, esp. one set as an exercise for a student. **5** *Grammar.* another word for **root**[1] (sense 8) or **stem**[1] (sense 7). **6** (*modifier*) planned or designed round one unifying subject, image, etc.: *a theme holiday.* ◆ *vb* **themes, theming, themed.** (*tr*) **7** to design, decorate, etc., in accordance with a theme.   [C13: from L *thema,* from Gk: deposit, from *tithenai* to lay down]
> ► **thematic** (θɪ'mætɪk) *adj*

theme park *n* an area planned as a leisure attraction, in which all the displays, buildings, activities, etc., are based on one subject.

theme song *n* **1** a melody used, esp. in a film score, to set a mood, introduce a character, etc. **2** another term for **signature tune.**

Themis ★ ('θiːmɪs) *n Greek myth.* a goddess of order and justice.

Themistocles ★ (θə'mɪstə,kliːz) *n* ?527–?460 B.C., Athenian statesman, who led the Athenians in their victory against the Persians at Salamis (480): ostracized in 470.

themselves (ðəm'sɛlvz) *pron* **1a** the reflexive form of *they* or *them.* **1b** (intensifier): *the team themselves voted on*

it. **2** (*preceded by a copula*) their normal or usual selves: *they don't seem themselves any more.* **3** Also: **themself.** *Not standard.* a reflexive form of an indefinite antecedent such as *one, whoever,* or *anybody: everyone has to look after themselves.*

then (ðɛn) *adv* **1** at that time; over that period of time. **2** (*sentence modifier*) in that case; that being so: *then why don't you ask her? go on then, take it.* ◆ *sentence connector.* **3** after that; with that: *then John left the room.* ◆ *n* **4** that time: *from then on.* ◆ *adj* **5** (*prenominal*) existing, functioning, etc., at that time: *the then prime minister.*   [OE *thenne*]

thenar ('θiːnɑː) *n* **1** the palm of the hand. **2** the fleshy area of the palm at the base of the thumb.   [C17: via NL from Gk]

thence (ðɛns) *adv* **1** from that place. **2** Also: **thenceforth** ('ðɛns'fɔːθ). from that time or event; thereafter. **3** therefore.   [C13 *thannes,* from *thanne,* from OE *thanon*]

thenceforward ('ðɛns'fɔːwəd) *or* **thenceforwards** *adv* from that time or place on.

theo- *or before a vowel* **the-** *combining form.* indicating God or gods: *theology.*   [from Gk *theos* god]

theobromine (,θiːəʊ'brəʊmiːn, -mɪn) *n* a white crystalline alkaloid that occurs in tea and cacao: used to treat coronary heart disease and headaches.   [C18: from NL *theobroma* genus of trees, lit.: food of the gods]

theocentric (,θɪə'sɛntrɪk) *adj Theol.* having God as the focal point of attention.

theocracy (θɪ'ɒkrəsɪ) *n, pl* **theocracies. 1** government by a deity or by a priesthood. **2** a community under such government.
> ► '**theo,crat** *n* ► ,**theo'cratic** *adj*

theocrasy (θɪ'ɒkrəsɪ) *n* **1** a mingling into one of deities or divine attributes previously regarded as distinct. **2** the union of the soul with God in mysticism.   [C19: from Gk *theokrasia,* from THEO- + -*krasia* from *krasis* a blending]

Theocritus ★ (θɪ'ɒkrɪtəs) *n* ?310–?250 B.C., Greek poet, born in Syracuse.
> ► **The'ocritan** *or* **Theocritean** (θɪ,ɒkrɪ'tiːən) *adj, n*

theodicy (θɪ'ɒdɪsɪ) *n, pl* **theodicies.** the branch of theology concerned with defending the attributes of God against objections resulting from the existence of physical and moral evil.   [C18: coined by Leibnitz in F as *théodicée,* from THEO- + Gk *dikē* justice]
> ► **the,odi'cean** *adj*

theodolite (θɪ'ɒdə,laɪt) *n* a surveying instrument for measuring horizontal and vertical angles, consisting of a small tripod-mounted telescope. Also called (in the US and Canada): **transit.**   [C16: from NL *theodolitus,* from ?]
> ► **theodolitic** (θɪ,ɒdə'lɪtɪk) *adj*

Theodora ★ (,θɪə'dɔːrə) *n* ?500–548 A.D., Byzantine empress; wife and counsellor of Justinian I.

Theodorakis ★ (*Greek* θeɔðɔ'rakis) *n* **Mikis** ('mikis). born 1925, Greek composer: he wrote the music for the film *Zorba the Greek* (1965) and was imprisoned (1967–70) for opposing the military government.

Theodoric *or* **Theoderic** ★ (θɪ'ɒdərɪk) *n* called *the Great.* ?454–526 A.D., king and founder of the Ostrogothic kingdom.

Theodosius I ★ (,θɪə'dəʊsɪəs) *n* called *the Great.* ?346–395 A.D., Roman emperor of the Eastern Roman Empire (379–95) and of the Western Roman Empire (392–95).

theogony (θɪ'ɒgənɪ) *n, pl* **theogonies. 1** the origin and descent of the gods. **2** an account of this.   [C17: from Gk *theogonia*]
> ► **theogonic** (,θɪə'gɒnɪk) *adj* ► **the'ogonist** *n*

theol. *abbrev. for:* **1** theologian. **2** theological. **3** theology.

theologian (,θɪə'ləʊdʒɪən) *n* a person versed in or engaged in the study of theology.

theological (,θɪə'lɒdʒɪkᵊl) *adj* of, relating to, or based on theology.
> ► ,**theo'logically** *adv*

theological virtues *pl n* those virtues that are infused into man by a special grace of God, specifically faith, hope, and charity.

theologize *or* **theologise** (θɪ'ɒlə,dʒaɪz) *vb* **theologizes,**

★ **people and places**

theologizing, theologized *or* **theologises, theologising, theologised. 1** (*intr*) to speculate upon theological subjects or engage in theological study or discussion. **2** (*tr*) to render theological or treat from a theological point of view.
▶ **the,ologi'zation** *or* **the,ologi'sation** *n* ▶ **the'olo,gizer** *or* **the'olo,giser** *n*

theology (θɪ'ɒlədʒɪ) *n, pl* **theologies. 1** the systematic study of the existence and nature of the divine and its relationship to other beings. **2** the systematic study of Christian revelation concerning God's nature and purpose. **3** a specific system, form, or branch of this study. [C14: from LL *theologia*, from L]
▶ **the'ologist** *n*

theomachy (θɪ'ɒməkɪ) *n, pl* **theomachies.** a battle among the gods or against them. [C16: from Gk *theomakhia*, from THEO- + *makhē* battle]

theomancy ('θiːəʊ,mænsɪ) *n* divination or prophecy by an oracle or by people directly inspired by a god.

theomania (,θɪə'meɪnɪə) *n* religious madness, esp. when it takes the form of believing oneself to be a god.
▶ **,theo'mani,ac** *n*

theophany (θɪ'ɒfənɪ) *n, pl* **theophanies.** a visible manifestation of a deity to man. [C17: from LL *theophania*, from LGk, from THEO- + *phainein* to show]
▶ **theophanic** (,θɪə'fænɪk) *adj*

Theophrastus ★ (,θɪə'fræstəs) *n* ?372–?287 B.C., Greek Peripatetic philosopher.

theophylline (,θɪə'fɪliːn, -ɪn) *n* a white crystalline alkaloid that is an isomer of theobromine: it occurs in plants such as tea. [C19: from THEO(BROMINE) + PHYLLO- + -INE²]

theorem ('θɪərəm) *n* a statement or formula that can be deduced from the axioms of a formal system by means of its rules of inference. [C16: from LL *theōrēma*, from Gk: something to be viewed, from *theōrein* to view]
▶ **theorematic** (,θɪərə'mætɪk) *or* **theoremic** (,θɪə'rɛmɪk) *adj*

theoretical (,θɪə'rɛtɪk°l) *or* **theoretic** *adj* **1** of or based on theory. **2** lacking practical application or actual existence; hypothetical. **3** using or dealing in theory; impractical.
▶ **,theo'retically** *adv*

theoretician (,θɪərɪ'tɪʃən) *n* a student or user of the theory rather than the practical aspects of a subject.

theoretics (,θɪə'rɛtɪks) *n* (*functioning as sing or pl*) the theory of a particular subject.

theorize *or* **theorise** ('θɪə,raɪz) *vb* **theorizes, theorizing, theorized** *or* **theorises, theorising, theorised.** (*intr*) to produce or use theories; speculate.
▶ **'theorist** *n* ▶ **,theori'zation** *or* **,theori'sation** *n* ▶ **'theo-,rizer** *or* **'theo,riser** *n*

theory ('θɪərɪ) *n, pl* **theories. 1** a system of rules, procedures, and assumptions used to produce a result. **2** abstract knowledge or reasoning. **3** a conjectural view or idea: *I have a theory about that.* **4** an ideal or hypothetical situation (esp. in **in theory**). **5** a set of hypotheses related by logical or mathematical arguments to explain a wide variety of connected phenomena in general terms: *the theory of relativity.* **6** a nontechnical name for **hypothesis.** [C16: from LL *theōria*, from Gk: a sight, from *theōrein* to gaze upon]

theory of games *n* a mathematical theory concerned with the optimum choice of strategy in situations involving a conflict of interest. Also called: **game theory.**

theosophy (θɪ'ɒsəfɪ) *n* **1** any of various religious or philosophical systems claiming to be based on or to express an intuitive insight into the divine nature. **2** the system of beliefs of the Theosophical Society founded in 1875, claiming to be derived from the sacred writings of Brahmanism and Buddhism. [C17: from Med. L *theosophia*, from LGk; see THEO-, -SOPHY]
▶ **theosophical** (,θɪə'sɒfɪk°l) *or* **,theo'sophic** *adj* ▶ **the-'osophist** *n*

Thera ★ ('θɪərə) *n* a Greek island in the Aegean Sea, in the Cyclades: site of a Minoan settlement and of the volcano that ended Minoan civilization on Crete. Pop.: 7000 (latest est.). Also called: **Santoríni.** Modern Greek name: **Thíra.**

therapeutic (,θɛrə'pjuːtɪk) *adj* **1** of or relating to the treatment of disease; curative. **2** serving or performed to

maintain health: *therapeutic abortion.* [C17: from NL *therapeuticus*, from Gk, from *therapeuein* to minister to, from *theraps* an attendant]
▶ **,thera'peutically** *adv*

therapeutics (,θɛrə'pjuːtɪks) *n* (*functioning as sing*) the branch of medicine concerned with the treatment of disease.

therapy ('θɛrəpɪ) *n, pl* **therapies. a** the treatment of physical, mental, or social disorders or disease. **b** (*in combination*): *physiotherapy.* [C19: from NL *therapia*, from Gk *therapeia* attendance; see THERAPEUTIC]
▶ **'therapist** *n*

Theravada (,θɛrə'vɑːdə) *n* the southern school of Buddhism, the name preferred by Hinayana Buddhists. [from Pali: doctrine of the elders]

there (ðɛə) *adv* **1** in, at, or to that place, point, case, or respect: *we never go there; I agree with you there.* ◆ *pron* **2** used as a grammatical subject with some verbs, esp. *be*, when the true subject follows the verb: *there is a girl in that office.* ◆ *adj* **3** (*postpositive*) who or which is in that place or position: *that boy there did it.* **4 all there.** (*predicative*) of normal intelligence. **5 so there.** an exclamation that usually follows a declaration of refusal or defiance. **6 there you are.** an expression used when handing a person something requested or desired. **6b** an exclamation of triumph. ◆ *n* **7** that place: *near there.* ◆ *interj* **8** an expression of sympathy, as in consoling a child: *there, there, dear.* [OE *thǣr*]

> **USAGE NOTE** In correct usage, the verb should agree with the number of the subject in such constructions as *there is a man waiting* and *there are several people waiting.* However, where the subject is compound, it is common in speech to use the singular as in *there's a police car and an ambulance outside.*

thereabouts ('ðɛərə,baʊts) *or US* **thereabout** *adv* near that place, time, amount, etc.

thereafter (,ðɛər'ɑːftə) *adv* from that time on or after that time.

thereat (,ðɛər'æt) *adv Rare.* **1** at that point or time. **2** for that reason.

thereby (,ðɛə'baɪ, 'ðɛə,baɪ) *adv* **1** by that means; because of that. **2** *Arch.* thereabouts.

therefor (,ðɛə'fɔː) *adv Arch.* for this, that, or it.

therefore (,ðɛə,fɔː) *sentence connector.* **1** thus; hence: *those people have their umbrellas up; therefore, it must be raining.* **2** consequently; as a result.

therefrom (,ðɛə'frɒm) *adv Arch.* from that or there: *the roads that lead therefrom.*

therein (,ðɛər'ɪn) *adv Formal or law.* in or into that place, thing, etc.

thereinto (,ðɛər'ɪntuː) *adv Formal or law.* into that place, circumstance, etc.

thereof (,ðɛər'ɒv) *adv Formal or law.* **1** of or concerning that or it. **2** from or because of that.

thereon (,ðɛər'ɒn) *adv Arch.* thereupon.

Theresa ★ (tə'riːzə, *Spanish* te'resa) *n* See (Saint) **Teresa.**

Thérèse de Lisieux ★ (*French* terɛz də lizjø) *n* **Saint,** known as *the Little Flower of Jesus.* 1873–97, French Carmelite nun, noted for her autobiography, *The Story of a Soul* (1897). Feast day: Oct. 3.

thereto (,ðɛə'tuː) *adv* **1** *Formal or law.* to that or it. **2** *Obs.* in addition to that.

theretofore (,ðɛətʊ'fɔː) *adv Formal or law.* before that time; previous to that.

thereunder (,ðɛər'ʌndə) *adv Formal or law.* **1** (in documents, etc.) below that or it; subsequently in that; thereafter. **2** under the terms or authority of that.

thereupon (,ðɛərə'pɒn) *adv* **1** immediately after that; at that point. **2** *Formal or law.* upon that thing, point, subject, etc.

therewith (,ðɛə'wɪθ, -'wɪð) *or* **therewithal** *adv* **1** *Formal or law.* with or in addition to that. **2** a less common word for **thereupon** (sense 1). **3** *Arch.* by means of or on account of that.

Therezina ★ (*Portuguese* tere'zina) *n* the former name of Teresina.

therianthropic (ˌθɪərɪən'θrɒpɪk) *adj* **1** (of certain mythical creatures or deities) having a partly animal, partly human form. **2** of or relating to such creatures or deities. [C19: from Gk *thērion* wild animal + *anthrōpos* man]
▸ **therianthropism** (ˌθɪərɪ'ænθrəˌpɪzəm) *n*

theriomorphic (ˌθɪərɪəʊ'mɔːfɪk) *adj* (esp. of a deity) possessing or depicted in the form of a beast. [C19: from Gk *thēriomorphos*, from *thērion* wild animal + *morphē* shape]

therm (θɜːm) *n Brit.* a unit of heat equal to 100 000 British thermal units. One therm is equal to $1.055\ 056 \times 10^8$ joules. [C19: from Gk *thermē* heat]

thermae ('θɜːmiː) *pl n* public baths or hot springs, esp. in ancient Greece or Rome. [C17: from L, from Gk *thermai*, pl. of *thermē* heat]

thermal ('θɜːməl) *adj* **1** Also: **thermic**. of, caused by, or generating heat. **2** hot or warm: *thermal baths*. **3** (of garments) specially made so as to have exceptional heat-retaining qualities: *thermal underwear*. ◆ *n* **4** a column of rising air caused by local unequal heating of the land surface, and used by gliders and birds to gain height. **5** (*pl*) thermal garments, esp. underclothes.
▸ **'thermally** *adv*

thermal barrier *n* an obstacle to flight at very high speeds as a result of the heating effect of air friction. Also called: **heat barrier**.

thermal conductivity *n* a measure of the ability of a substance to conduct heat.

thermal efficiency *n* the ratio of the work done by a heat engine to the energy supplied to it.

thermal equator *n* an imaginary line round the earth running through the point on each meridian with the highest average temperature.

thermal imaging *n* the use of heat-sensitive equipment to detect or provide images of people or things.

thermalize *or* **thermalise** ('θɜːməˌlaɪz) *vb* **thermalizes, thermalizing, thermalized** *or* **thermalises, thermalising, thermalised**. *Physics*. to undergo or cause to undergo a process in which neutrons lose energy in a moderator and become thermal neutrons.
▸ ˌthermali'zation *or* ˌthermali'sation *n*

thermal neutrons *pl n* slow neutrons that are approximately in thermal equilibrium with a moderator.

thermal reactor *n* a nuclear reactor in which most of the fission is caused by thermal neutrons.

thermal shock *n* a fluctuation in temperature causing stress in a material. It often results in fracture, esp. in brittle materials such as ceramics.

thermion ('θɜːmɪən) *n Physics*. an electron or ion emitted by a body at high temperature.

thermionic (ˌθɜːmɪ'ɒnɪk) *adj* of, relating to, or operated by electrons emitted from materials at high temperatures: *a thermionic valve*.

thermionic current *n* an electric current produced between two electrodes as a result of electrons emitted by thermionic emission.

thermionic emission *n* the emission of electrons from very hot solids or liquids.

thermionics (ˌθɜːmɪ'ɒnɪks) *n* (*functioning as sing*) the branch of electronics concerned with the emission of electrons by hot bodies and with devices based on this effect.

thermionic valve *or esp. US & Canad.* **tube** *n* an electronic valve in which electrons are emitted from a heated rather than a cold cathode.

thermistor (θɜː'mɪstə) *n* a semiconductor device having a resistance that decreases rapidly with an increase in temperature. It is used for temperature measurement and control. [C20: from THERMO- + (RES)ISTOR]

Thermit ('θɜːmɪt) *or* **Thermite** ('θɜːmaɪt) *n Trademark*. a mixture of aluminium powder and a metal oxide, which when ignited produces great heat: used for welding and in incendiary bombs.

thermo- *or before a vowel* **therm-** *combining form*. related to, caused by, or measuring heat: *thermodynamics; thermophile*. [from Gk *thermos* hot, *thermē* heat]

thermobarograph (ˌθɜːməʊ'bærəˌɡrɑːf) *n* a device that simultaneously records the temperature and pressure of the atmosphere.

thermobarometer (ˌθɜːməʊbə'rɒmɪtə) *n* an apparatus that provides an accurate measurement of pressure by observation of the change in the boiling point of a fluid.

thermochemistry (ˌθɜːməʊ'kɛmɪstrɪ) *n* the branch of chemistry concerned with the study and measurement of the heat evolved or absorbed during chemical reactions.
▸ ˌthermo'chemical *adj* ▸ ˌthermo'chemist *n*

thermochromism (ˌθɜːməə'krəʊmɪzəm) *n* a phenomenon in which certain dyes made from liquid crystals change colour reversibly when their temperature is changed.
▸ 'thermoˌchromy *n* ▸ ˌthermo'chromic *adj*

thermocline ('θɜːməʊˌklaɪn) *n* a temperature gradient in a thermally stratified body of water, such as a lake.

thermocouple ('θɜːməʊˌkʌpᵊl) *n* **1** a device for measuring temperature consisting of a pair of wires of different metals or semiconductors joined at both ends. One junction is at the temperature to be measured, the second at a fixed temperature. The electromotive force generated depends upon the temperature difference. **2** a similar device with only one junction between two dissimilar metals or semiconductors.

thermodynamic (ˌθɜːməʊdaɪ'næmɪk) *or* **thermodynamical** *adj* **1** of or concerned with thermodynamics. **2** determined by or obeying the laws of thermodynamics.

thermodynamic equilibrium *n* the condition of a system in which the quantities that specify its properties, such as pressure, temperature, etc., all remain unchanged.

thermodynamics (ˌθɜːməʊdaɪ'næmɪks) *n* (*functioning as sing*) the branch of physical science concerned with the interrelationship and interconversion of different forms of energy.

thermodynamic temperature *n* temperature defined in terms of the laws of thermodynamics rather than of the properties of a real material: expressed in kelvins.

thermoelectric (ˌθɜːməʊɪ'lɛktrɪk) *or* **thermoelectrical** *adj* **1** of, relating to, used in, or operated by the conversion of heat energy to electrical energy. **2** of, relating to, used in, or operated by the conversion of electrical energy.

thermoelectric effect *n* another name for the **Seebeck effect**.

thermoelectricity (ˌθɜːməʊɪlɛk'trɪsɪtɪ) *n* **1** electricity generated by a thermocouple. **2** the study of the relationship between heat and electrical energy.

thermoelectron (ˌθɜːməʊɪ'lɛktrɒn) *n* an electron emitted at high temperature, as in a thermionic valve.

thermogenesis (ˌθɜːməʊ'dʒɛnɪsɪs) *n* the production of heat by metabolic processes.

thermogram ('θɜːməʊˌɡræm) *n* **1** *Med*. a picture produced by thermography, using film sensitive to infrared radiation. **2** the record produced by a thermograph.

thermograph ('θɜːməʊˌɡrɑːf, -ˌɡræf) *n* a type of thermometer that produces a continuous record of a fluctuating temperature.

thermography (θɜː'mɒɡrəfɪ) *n* **1** any writing, printing, or recording process involving the use of heat. **2** *Med*. the measurement and recording of heat produced by a part of the body: used in the diagnosis of tumours, esp. of the breast (**mammothermography**), which have increased blood supply and therefore generate more heat than normal tissue. See also **thermogram**.
▸ ther'mographer *n* ▸ thermographic (ˌθɜːməʊ'ɡræfɪk) *adj*

thermojunction (ˌθɜːməʊ'dʒʌŋkʃən) *n* a point of electrical contact between two dissimilar metals across which a voltage appears, the magnitude of which depends on the temperature of the contact and the nature of the metals.

★ people and places

hermolabile (ˌhɜːməʊˈleɪbɪl) *adj* easily decomposed or subject to a loss of characteristic properties by the action of heat.

hermoluminescence (ˌhɜːməʊˌluːmɪˈnɛsəns) *n* phosphorescence of certain materials or objects as a result of heating.

hermolysis (hɜːˈmɒlɪsɪs) *n* **1** *Physiol.* loss of heat from the body. **2** the dissociation of a substance as a result of heating.
▶ **thermolytic** (ˌhɜːməʊˈlɪtɪk) *adj*

hermomagnetic (ˌhɜːməʊmæɡˈnɛtɪk) *adj* of or concerned with the relationship between heat and magnetism, esp. the change in temperature of a body when it is magnetized or demagnetized.

hermometer (həˈmɒmɪtə) *n* an instrument used to measure temperature, esp. one in which a thin column of liquid, such as mercury, expands and contracts within a graduated sealed tube.
▶ **therˈmometry** *n*

hermonuclear (ˌhɜːməʊˈnjuːklɪə) *adj* **1** involving nuclear fusion. **2** involving thermonuclear weapons.

hermonuclear reaction *n* a nuclear fusion reaction occurring at a very high temperature: responsible for the energy produced in the sun, nuclear weapons, and fusion reactors.

hermophile (ˈhɜːməʊˌfaɪl) *or* **thermophil** (ˈhɜːməʊˌfɪl) *n* **1** an organism, esp. a bacterium or plant, that thrives under warm conditions. ◆ *adj* **2** thriving under warm conditions.
▶ ˌ**thermoˈphilic** *adj*

hermopile (ˈhɜːməʊˌpaɪl) *n* an instrument for detecting and measuring heat radiation or for generating a thermoelectric current. It consists of a number of thermocouple junctions.

hermoplastic (ˌhɜːməʊˈplæstɪk) *adj* **1** (of a material, esp. a synthetic plastic) becoming soft when heated and rehardening on cooling without appreciable change of properties. ◆ *n* **2** a synthetic plastic or resin, such as polystyrene, with these properties.

Thermopylae (hɜːˈmɒpɪˌliː) *n* (in ancient Greece) a narrow pass between the mountains and the sea linking Locris and Thessaly: scene of a famous battle (480 B.C.) in which an outnumbered Greek army delayed the advance of the Persians in their attempt to conquer Greece.

Thermos *or* **Thermos flask** (ˈhɜːməs) *n Trademark.* a type of stoppered vacuum flask used to preserve the temperature of its contents.

hermosetting (ˌhɜːməʊˈsetɪŋ) *adj* (of a material, esp. a synthetic plastic) hardening permanently after one application of heat and pressure.

hermosiphon (ˌhɜːməʊˈsaɪfən) *n* a system in which a coolant is circulated by convection caused by a difference in density between the hot and cold portions of the liquid.

hermosphere (ˈhɜːməˌsfɪə) *n* an atmospheric layer lying between the mesosphere and the exosphere.

hermostable (ˌhɜːməʊˈsteɪbᵊl) *adj* capable of withstanding moderate heat without loss of characteristic properties.

hermostat (ˈhɜːməˌstæt) *n* **1** a device that maintains a system at a constant temperature. **2** a device that sets off a sprinkler, etc., at a certain temperature.
▶ ˌ**thermoˈstatic** *adj* ▶ ˌ**thermoˈstatically** *adv*

hermostatics (ˌhɜːməˈstætɪks) *n* (*functioning as sing*) the branch of science concerned with thermal equilibrium.

hermotaxis (ˌhɜːməʊˈtæksɪs) *n* the directional movement of an organism in response to the stimulus of heat.
▶ ˌ**thermoˈtaxic** *adj*

hermotropism (ˌhɜːməʊˈtrəʊpɪzəm) *n* the directional growth of a plant in response to the stimulus of heat.
▶ ˌ**thermoˈtropic** *adj*

-thermy *n combining form.* indicating heat: *diathermy.* [from NL *-thermia,* from Gk *thermē*]
▶ **-thermic** *or* **-thermal** *adj combining form.*

theroid (ˈθɪərɔɪd) *adj* of, relating to, or resembling a beast. [C19: from Gk *thēroeidēs,* from *thēr* wild animal; see -OID]

Theroux ★ (θəˈruː) *n* **Paul** (**Edward**). born 1941, US writer. His novels include *The Mosquito Coast* (1981) and *My Other Life* (1996); travel writings include *The Great Railway Bazaar* (1975).

Thersites ★ (θəˈsaɪtiːz) *n* the ugliest and most evil-tongued fighter on the Greek side in the Trojan War, killed by Achilles.

thesaurus (θɪˈsɔːrəs) *n, pl* **thesauruses** *or* **thesauri** (-raɪ). **1** a book containing systematized lists of synonyms and related words. **2** a dictionary of selected words or topics. **3** *Rare.* a treasury. [C18: from L, Gk: TREASURE]

these (ðiːz) *determiner* **a** the form of **this** used before a plural noun: *these men.* **b** (*as pronoun*): *I don't much care for these.*

Theseus ★ (ˈθiːsɪəs) *n Greek myth.* a hero of Attica, noted for slaying the Minotaur and conquering the Amazons.
▶ **Thesean** (θɪˈsiːən) *adj*

Thesiger ★ (ˈθesɪdʒə) *n* **Wilfred** (**Patrick**). born 1910, British writer, whose books include *Arabian Sands* (1958) and *My Kenya Days* (1994).

thesis (ˈθiːsɪs) *n, pl* **theses** (-siːz). **1** a dissertation resulting from original research, esp. when submitted for a degree or diploma. **2** a doctrine maintained in argument. **3** a subject for a discussion or essay. **4** an unproved statement put forward as a premise in an argument. [C16: via LL from Gk: a placing, from *tithenai* to place]

Thespian (ˈθespɪən) *adj* **1** of or relating to Thespis. **2** (*usually not cap.*) of or relating to drama and the theatre; dramatic. ◆ *n* (*usually not cap.*) **3** *Often facetious.* an actor or actress.

Thespis ★ (ˈθespɪs) *n* 6th century B.C., Greek poet, regarded as the founder of tragic drama.

Thess. *Bible. abbrev. for* Thessalonians.

Thessalonian (ˌθesəˈləʊnɪən) *adj* **1** of or relating to ancient Thessalonica (modern Salonika). ◆ *n* **2** an inhabitant of ancient Thessalonica.

Thessaloníki ★ (*Greek* θesaloˈniki) *n* a port in NE Greece, in central Macedonia at the head of the **Gulf of Salonika** (an inlet of the Aegean): capital of the Roman province of Macedonia; university (1926). Pop.: 377 951 (1991). Latin name: **Thessalonica** (ˌθesəˈlɒnɪkə). English name: **Salonika** *or* **Salonica**.

Thessaly ★ (ˈθesəlɪ) *n* a region of E Central Greece, on the Aegean: an extensive fertile plain, edged with mountains. Pop.: 734 846 (1991). Area: 14 037 sq. km (5418 sq. miles). Modern Greek name: **Thessalía** (ˌθesaˈljia).
▶ **Thessalian** (θeˈseɪlɪən) *adj, n*

theta (ˈθiːtə) *n* the eighth letter of the Greek alphabet (Θ, θ). [C17: from Gk]

Thetford Mines ★ (ˈθetfəd) *n* a city in SE Canada, in S Quebec: asbestos industry. Pop.: 17 273 (1991).

Thetis ★ (ˈθiːtɪs) *n* one of the Nereids and mother of Achilles by Peleus.

theurgy (ˈθiːˌɜːdʒɪ) *n, pl* **theurgies**. **1** the intervention of a divine or supernatural agency in the affairs of man. **2** beneficent magic as taught by Egyptian Neoplatonists. [C16: from LL *theūrgia,* from LGk *theourgia* the practice of magic, from *theo-* THEO- + *-urgia,* from *ergon* work]
▶ **theˈurgic** *or* **theˈurgical** *adj* ▶ ˈ**theurgist** *n*

thew (θjuː) *n* **1** muscle, esp. if strong or well-developed. **2** (*pl*) muscular strength. [OE *thēaw*]
▶ ˈ**thewless** *adj* ▶ ˈ**thewy** *adj*

they (ðeɪ) *pron (subjective)* **1** refers to people or things other than the speaker or people addressed: *they fight among themselves.* **2** refers to people in general: *in Australia they have Christmas in the summer.* **3** refers to an indefinite antecedent such as *one, whoever,* or *anybody: if anyone objects, they can go.* [C12 *thei* from ON *their,* masc. nominative pl, equivalent to OE *thā*]

USAGE NOTE It was formerly considered correct to use *he, him,* or *his* after pronouns such as *everyone, no-one, anyone,* or *someone* as in *everyone did his best,* but it is now more common to use *they, them,* or *their,* and this use has become acceptable in all but the most formal contexts: *everyone did their best.*

★ people and places

they'd (ðeɪd) *contraction of* they would *or* they had.

they'll (ðeɪl) *contraction of* they will *or* they shall.

they're (ðɛə, ˈðeɪə) *contraction of* they are.

they've (ðeɪv) *contraction of* they have.

thi- *combining form.* a variant of **thio-**.

thiamine (ˈθaɪəˌmiːn, -mɪn) *or* **thiamin** (ˈθaɪəmɪn) *n* a white crystalline vitamin that occurs in the outer coat of rice and other grains. It forms part of the vitamin B complex: deficiency leads to nervous disorders and to the disease beriberi. Also called: **vitamin B₁, aneurin**. [C20: THIO- + (VIT)AMIN]

thiazine (ˈθaɪəˌziːn, -ˌzaɪn) *n* any of a group of organic compounds containing a ring system composed of four carbon atoms, a sulphur atom, and a nitrogen atom.

thiazole (ˈθaɪəˌzəʊl) *n* **1** a colourless liquid that contains a ring system composed of three carbon atoms, a sulphur atom, and a nitrogen atom. **2** any of a group of compounds derived from this substance that are used in dyes.

thick (θɪk) *adj* **1** of relatively great extent from one surface to the other: *a thick slice of bread.* **2a** (*postpositive*) of specific fatness: *ten centimetres thick.* **2b** (*in combination*): *a six-inch-thick wall.* **3** having a dense consistency: *thick soup.* **4** abundantly covered or filled: *a piano thick with dust.* **5** impenetrable; dense: *a thick fog.* **6** stupid, slow, or insensitive. **7** throaty or badly articulated: *a voice thick with emotion.* **8** (of accents, etc.) pronounced. **9** *Inf.* very friendly (esp. in **thick as thieves**). **10** a bit thick. *Brit.* unfair or excessive. ♦ *adv* **11** in order to produce something thick: *to slice bread thick.* **12** profusely; in quick succession (esp. in **thick and fast**). **13** lay it on thick. *Inf.* **13a** to exaggerate a story, etc. **13b** to flatter excessively. ♦ *n* **14** a thick piece or part. **15** the thick. the busiest or most intense part. **16 through thick and thin.** in good times and bad. [OE *thicce*]
  ▸ **'thickish** *adj* ▸ **'thickly** *adv*

thicken (ˈθɪkən) *vb* **1** to make or become thick or thicker. **2** (*intr*) to become more involved: *the plot thickened.*
  ▸ **'thickener** *n*

thickening (ˈθɪkənɪŋ) *n* **1** something added to a liquid to thicken it. **2** a thickened part or piece.

thicket (ˈθɪkɪt) *n* a dense growth of small trees, shrubs, and similar plants. [OE *thiccet*]

thickhead (ˈθɪkˌhɛd) *n* **1** a stupid or ignorant person; fool. **2** any of a family of Australian and SE Asian songbirds.
  ▸ **ˌthick'headed** *adj*

thickie *or* **thicky** (ˈθɪkɪ) *n, pl* **thickies**. *Brit. sl.* a variant of **thicko**.

thick-knee *n* another name for **stone curlew**.

thickness (ˈθɪknɪs) *n* **1** the state or quality of being thick. **2** the dimension through an object, as opposed to length or width. **3** a layer.

thicko (ˈθɪkəʊ) *n, pl* **thickos** *or* **thickoes**. *Brit. sl.* a slow-witted unintelligent person. Also: **thickie, thicky**.

thickset (ˌθɪk'sɛt) *adj* **1** stocky in build; sturdy. **2** densely planted or placed. ♦ *n* **3** a rare word for **thicket**.

thick-skinned *adj* insensitive to criticism or hints; not easily upset or affected.

thick-witted *or* **thick-skulled** *adj* stupid, dull, or slow to learn.
  ▸ **ˌthick-'wittedly** *adv* ▸ **ˌthick-'wittedness** *n*

thief (θiːf) *n, pl* **thieves** (θiːvz). a person who steals something from another. [OE *thēof*]
  ▸ **'thievish** *adj*

Thiers ★ (*French* tjɛr) *n* **Louis Adolphe** (lwi adɔlf). 1797–1877, French statesman, who became first president of the Third Republic (1871–73).

thieve (θiːv) *vb* **thieves, thieving, thieved**. to steal (someone's possessions). [OE *thēofian*, from *thēof* thief]
  ▸ **'thievery** *n* ▸ **'thieving** *adj*

thigh (θaɪ) *n* **1** the part of the leg between the hip and the knee in man. **2** the corresponding part in other vertebrates and insects. ♦ *Related adj*: **femoral**. [OE *thēh*]

thighbone (ˈθaɪˌbəʊn) *n* a nontechnical name for **femur**.

thimble (ˈθɪmbᵊl) *n* **1** a cap of metal, plastic, etc., used to protect the end of the finger when sewing. **2** any small metal cap resembling this. **3** *Naut.* a loop of metal having a groove at its outer edge for a rope or cable. [OE *thȳmel* thumbstall, from *thūma* thumb]

thimbleful (ˈθɪmbᵊlˌfʊl) *n* a very small amount, esp. of a liquid.

thimblerig (ˈθɪmbᵊlˌrɪg) *n* a game in which the operator rapidly moves about three inverted thimbles, often with sleight of hand, one of which conceals a token, the other player betting on which thimble the token is under. [C19: from THIMBLE + RIG (in obs. sense meaning a trick, scheme)]
  ▸ **'thimbleˌrigger** *n*

Thimbu (ˈθɪmbuː) *or* **Thimphu** ★ (ˈθɪmfuː) *n* the capital of Bhutan, in the west in the foothills of the E Himalayas: became the official capital in 1962. Pop.: 30 340 (1993 est.).

thin (θɪn) *adj* **thinner, thinnest**. **1** of relatively small extent from one side or surface to the other. **2** slim or lean. **3** sparsely placed; meagre: *thin hair.* **4** of low density: *a thin liquid.* **5** weak; poor: *a thin disguise.* **6** thin on the ground. few in number; scarce. ♦ *adv* **7** in order to produce something thin: *to cut bread thin.* ♦ *vb* **thins, thinning, thinned**. **8** to make or become thin or sparse. [OE *thynne*]
  ▸ **'thinly** *adv* ▸ **'thinness** *n*

thine (ðaɪn) *determiner Arch.* **a** (*preceding a vowel*) of or associated with you (thou): *thine eyes.* **b** (*as pronoun*): *thine is the greatest burden.* [OE *thīn*]

thin-film *adj* (of an electronic component, etc.) composed of one or more extremely thin layers of metal, semiconductor, etc.

thing (θɪŋ) *n* **1** an object, fact, affair, circumstance, or concept considered as being a separate entity. **2** any inanimate object. **3** an object or entity that cannot or need not be precisely named. **4** *Inf.* a person or animal: *you poor thing.* **5** an event or act. **6** a thought or statement. **7** *Law.* property. **8** a device, means, or instrument. **9** (*often pl*) a possession, article of clothing, etc. **10** *Inf.* a preoccupation or obsession (esp. in **have a thing about**). **11** an activity or mode of behaviour satisfying one's personality (esp. in **do one's (own) thing**). **12 make a thing of.** exaggerate the importance of. **13 the thing.** the latest fashion. [OE *thing* assembly]

thing-in-itself *n* (in the philosophy of Immanuel Kant) reality regarded apart from human knowledge and perception.

thingumabob *or* **thingamabob** (ˈθɪŋəməˌbɒb) *n Inf.* a person or thing the name of which is unknown, temporarily forgotten, or deliberately overlooked. Also: **thingumajig, thingamajig,** *or* **thingummy**. [C18: from THING, with humorous suffix]

think (θɪŋk) *vb* **thinks, thinking, thought**. **1** (*tr; may take a clause as object*) to consider, judge, or believe: *he thinks my ideas impractical.* **2** (*intr; often foll. by about*) to exercise the mind in order to make a decision; ponder. **3** (*intr*) to be capable of conscious thought: *man is the only animal that thinks.* **4** to remember; recollect. **5** (*intr*; foll. by *of*) to make the mental choice (of): *think of a number.* **6** (*may take a clause as object or an infinitive*) **6a** to expect; suppose. **6b** to be considerate enough (to do something): *he did not think to thank them.* **7** (*intr*) to focus the attention on being: *think big.* **8 think twice.** to consider carefully before deciding. ♦ *n* **9** *Inf.* a careful, open-minded assessment. **10** (*modifier*) *Inf.* characterized by or involving thinkers, thinking, or thought. ♦ *See also* **think over, think up**. [OE *thencan*]
  ▸ **'thinkable** *adj* ▸ **'thinker** *n*

thinking (ˈθɪŋkɪŋ) *n* **1** opinion or judgment. **2** the process of thought. ♦ *adj* **3** (*prenominal*) using or capable of using intelligent thought: *thinking people.* **4 put on one's thinking cap.** to ponder a matter or problem.

think over *vb* (*tr, adv*) to ponder or consider.

think-tank *n Inf.* a group of specialists commissioned to undertake intensive study and research into specified problems.

think up *vb* (*tr, adv*) to invent or devise.

thinner (ˈθɪnə) *n* (*often pl, functioning as sing*) a solvent, such as turpentine, added to paint or varnish to dilute it, reduce its opacity or viscosity, or increase its penetration.

thin-skinned *adj* sensitive to criticism or hints; easily upset or affected.

thio- *or before a vowel* **thi-** *combining form.* sulphur, esp. denoting the replacement of an oxygen atom with a sulphur atom: *thiol; thiosulphate.* [from Gk *theion* sulphur]

thiol ('θaɪɒl) *n* any of a class of sulphur-containing organic compounds with the formula RSH, where R is an organic group.

thionine ('θaɪəʊˌniːn, -ˌnaɪn) *or* **thionin** ('θaɪənɪn) *n* **1** a crystalline derivative of thiazine used as a violet dye to stain microscope specimens. **2** any of a class of related dyes. [C19: by shortening, from *ergothioneine*]

thiopentone sodium (ˌθaɪəʊˈpentəʊn) *or* **thiopental sodium** (ˌθaɪəʊˈpentæl) *n* a barbiturate drug used as an intravenous general anaesthetic. Also called: **Sodium Pentothal.**

thiophen ('θaɪəʊˌfen) *or* **thiophene** ('θaɪəʊˌfiːn) *n* a colourless liquid heterocyclic compound found in the benzene fraction of coal tar and manufactured from butane and sulphur.

thiosulphate (ˌθaɪəʊˈsʌlfeɪt) *n* any salt of thiosulphuric acid.

thiosulphuric acid (ˌθaɪəʊsʌlˈfjʊərɪk) *n* an unstable acid known only in solutions and in the form of its salts. Formula: $H_2S_2O_3$.

thiouracil (ˌθaɪəʊˈjʊərəsɪl) *n* a white crystalline water-insoluble substance with an intensely bitter taste, used in medicine to treat hyperthyroidism. [from THIO- + *uracil* (URO- + AC(ETIC) + -IL(E))]

thiourea (ˌθaɪəʊˈjʊərɪə) *n* a white crystalline substance used in photographic fixing, rubber vulcanization, and the manufacture of synthetic resins.

third (θɜːd) *adj (usually prenominal)* **1a** coming after the second in numbering, position, etc.; being the ordinal number of *three:* often written 3rd. **1b** (*as n*): *the third got a prize.* **2** rated, graded, or ranked below the second level. **3** denoting the third from lowest forward ratio of a gearbox in a motor vehicle. ◆ *n* **4a** one of three equal parts of an object, quantity, etc. **4b** (*as modifier*): *a third part.* **5** the fraction equal to one divided by three (1/3). **6** the forward ratio above second of a gearbox in a motor vehicle. **7a** the interval between one note and another three notes away from it counting inclusively along the diatonic scale. **7b** one of two notes constituting such an interval in relation to the other. **8** *Brit.* an honours degree of the third and usually the lowest class. Full term: **third class honours degree.** ◆ *adv* **9** Also: **thirdly.** in the third place. [OE *thirda,* var. of *thridda;* rel. to OFrisian *thredda,* OSaxon *thriddio*]
▶ 'thirdly *adv*

Third Age *n* the. old age, esp. when viewed as a period of opportunity for learning something new or for other new developments: *University of the Third Age.*

third class *n* **1** the class or grade next in value, quality, etc., to the second. ◆ *adj* (**third-class** *when prenominal*). **2** of the class or grade next in value, quality, etc., to the second. ◆ *adv* **3** by third-class transport, etc.

third degree *n Inf.* torture or bullying, esp. used to extort confessions or information.

third-degree burn *n Pathol.* the most severe type of burn, involving the destruction of both epidermis and dermis.

third dimension *n* the dimension of depth by which a solid object may be distinguished from a two-dimensional drawing or picture of it.

third eyelid *n* another name for **nictitating membrane.**

Third International *n* another name for **Comintern.**

third-line forcing *n* the deprecated practice of forcing a buyer to purchase a supply of a product that he does not want as a condition of supplying him with the product he does want.

third man *n Cricket.* **a** a fielding position on the off side near the boundary behind the batsman's wicket. **b** a fielder in this position.

Third Market *n Stock Exchange.* a new small market designed to meet the needs of young growing British companies for raising capital.

Third Order *n RC Church.* a religious society of laymen affiliated to one of the religious orders and following a mitigated form of religious rule.

third party *n* **1** a person who is involved by chance or only incidentally in a legal proceeding, agreement, or other transaction. ◆ *adj* **2** *Insurance.* providing protection against liability caused by accidental injury or death of other persons.

third person *n* a grammatical category of pronouns and verbs used when referring to objects or individuals other than the speaker or his addressee or addressees.

third-rate *adj* mediocre or inferior.

third reading *n* (in a legislative assembly) **1** *Brit.* the process of discussing the committee's report on a bill. **2** *US.* the final consideration of a bill.

Third World *n* the less economically and industrially advanced countries of Africa, Asia, and Latin America collectively. Also called: **developing world.**

Thirlmere ★ ('θɜːlmɪə) *n* a lake in NW England, in Cumbria in the Lake District: provides part of Manchester's water supply. Length: 6 km (4 miles).

thirst (θɜːst) *n* **1** a craving to drink, accompanied by a feeling of dryness in the mouth and throat. **2** an eager longing, craving, or yearning. ◆ *vb* (*intr*) **3** to feel a thirst. [OE *thyrstan,* from *thurst*]

thirsty ('θɜːstɪ) *adj* **thirstier, thirstiest. 1** feeling a desire to drink. **2** dry; arid. **3** (foll. by *for*) feeling an eager desire. **4** causing thirst.
▶ 'thirstily *adv* ▶ 'thirstiness *n*

thirteen ('θɜːˈtiːn) *n* **1** the cardinal number that is the sum of ten and three and is a prime number. **2** a numeral, 13, XIII, etc., representing this number. **3** something representing or consisting of 13 units. ◆ *determiner* **4a** amounting to thirteen. **4b** (*as pronoun*): *thirteen of them fell.* [OE *threotēne*]
▶ 'thir'teenth *adj, n*

thirteenth chord *n* a chord much used in jazz and pop, consisting of a major or minor triad upon which are superimposed the seventh, ninth, eleventh, and thirteenth above the root. Often shortened to **thirteenth.**

thirty ('θɜːtɪ) *n, pl* **thirties. 1** the cardinal number that is the product of ten and three. **2** a numeral, 30, XXX, etc., representing this number. **3** (*pl*) the numbers 30-39, esp. the 30th to the 39th year of a person's life or of a century. **4** the amount or quantity that is three times as big as ten. **5** something representing or consisting of 30 units. ◆ *determiner* **6a** amounting to thirty. **6b** (*as pronoun*): *thirty are broken.* [OE *thrītig*]
▶ 'thirtieth *adj, n*

Thirty-nine Articles *pl n* a set of formulas defining the doctrinal position of the Church of England, drawn up in the 16th century.

thirty-second note *n* the usual US and Canad. name for **demisemiquaver.**

thirty-twomo (ˌθɜːtɪˈtuːməʊ) *n, pl* **thirty-twomos.** a book size resulting from folding a sheet of paper into 32 leaves or 64 pages.

this (ðɪs) *determiner (used before a sing n)* **1a** used preceding a noun referring to something or someone that is closer: *look at this picture.* **1b** (*as pronoun*): *take this.* **2a** used preceding a noun that has just been mentioned or is understood: *this plan of yours won't work.* **2b** (*as pronoun*): *I first saw this on Sunday.* **3a** used to refer to something about to be said, read, etc.: *consider this argument.* **3b** (*as pronoun*): *listen to this.* **4a** the present or immediate: *this time you'll know better.* **4b** (*as pronoun*): *this being so, I was mistaken.* **5** *Inf.* an emphatic form of a or the[1]: *I saw this big brown bear.* **6 this and that.** various unspecified and trivial actions, matters, objects, etc. **7 with** (*or* **at**) **this.** after this. ◆ *adv* **8** used with adjectives and adverbs to specify a precise degree that is about to be mentioned: *go just this fast and you'll be safe.* [OE *thēs, thēos, this* (masc, fem, neuter sing)]

Thisbe ★ ('θɪzbɪ) *n* See **Pyramus and Thisbe.**

★ people and places

thistle ('θɪsᵊl) n **1** any of a genus of plants of the composite family, having prickly-edged leaves, dense flower heads, and feathery hairs on the seeds: the national emblem of Scotland. **2** any of various similar or related plants. [OE *thīstel*]
▸ **'thistly** adj

thistledown ('θɪsᵊl,daʊn) n the mass of feathery plumed seeds produced by a thistle.

thither ('ðɪðə) or **thitherward** adv Obs. or formal. to or towards that place; in that direction. [OE *thider*, var. of *thæder*, infl. by *hider* hither]

thitherto (,ðɪðə'tuː, 'ðɪðə,tuː) adv Obs. or formal. until that time.

thixotropic (,θɪksə'trɒpɪk) adj (of fluids and gels) having a reduced viscosity when stress is applied, as when stirred: *thixotropic paints*. [C20: from Gk *thixis* the act of touching + -TROPIC]
▸ **thixotropy** (θɪk'sɒtrəpɪ) n ▸ **thixotrope** ('θɪksə,trəʊp) n

tho' or **tho** (ðəʊ) conj, adv US or poetic. a variant spelling of **though.**

thole[1] (θəʊl) or **tholepin** ('θəʊl,pɪn) n a wooden pin or one of a pair, set upright in the gunwales of a rowing boat to serve as a fulcrum in rowing. [OE *tholl*]

thole[2] (θəʊl) vb tholes, tholing, tholed. **1** (tr) Scot. & N English dialect. to put up with; bear. **2** an archaic word for **suffer.** [OE *tholian*]

tholos ('θəʊlɒs) n, pl tholoi (-lɔɪ). a dry-stone beehive-shaped tomb associated with the Mycenaean culture of Greece from the 16th to the 12th centuries B.C. [C17: from Gk]

Thomas ★ ('tɒməs) n **1** Saint. Also called: **doubting Thomas.** one of the twelve apostles, who refused to believe in Christ's resurrection until he had seen his wounds (John 20:24–29). Feast day: July 3 or Dec. 21 or Oct. 6. **2** (French tɔma). **Ambroise** (ɑ̃brwaz). 1811–96, French composer of light operas, including *Mignon* (1866). **3 Dylan (Marlais)** ('dɪlən). 1914–53, Welsh poet, whose works include the play *Under Milk Wood* (1954). **4 (Philip) Edward**, pen name *Edward Eastaway*. 1878–1917, British poet; killed in World War I.

Thomas à Kempis ★ n See (Thomas à) **Kempis.**

Thomas Becket ★ n Saint. See (Saint Thomas) **Becket.**

Thomas of Woodstock ★ n 1355–97, youngest son of Edward III, who led opposition to his nephew Richard II (1386–89); died in prison.

Thomism ('təʊmɪzəm) n the system of philosophy and theology developed by Saint Thomas Aquinas in the 13th century.

Thompson ★ ('tɒmpsən, 'tɒmsən) n **1 Benjamin**, Count Rumford. 1753–1814, Anglo-American physicist, noted for his work on heat. **2 Daley.** born 1958, British athlete: Olympic decathlon champion (1980, 1984). **3 Emma.** born 1959, British actress: her films include *Howards End* (1991) and *The Winter Guest* (1997). **4 Francis.** 1859–1907, British poet, noted for his poem *The Hound of Heaven* (1893).

Thompson sub-machine-gun n Trademark. a .45 calibre sub-machine-gun. [C20: after John T. *Thompson* (1860–1940), US Army officer, its co-inventor]

Thomson ★ ('tɒmsən) n **1 Sir George Paget**, son of Joseph John Thomson. 1892–1975, British physicist, who discovered (1927) electron diffraction: shared the Nobel prize for physics (1937). **2 Sir Joseph John.** 1856–1940, British physicist, who discovered the electron (1897): Nobel prize for physics 1906. **3 Roy**, 1st Baron Thomson of Fleet. 1894–1976, British newspaper proprietor, born in Canada. **4 Virgil.** 1896–1989, US composer. His works include two operas, a cello concerto, and film music. **5 Sir William.** See (1st Baron) **Kelvin.**

-thon suffix forming nouns. indicating a large-scale event or operation of a specified kind: *telethon*. [C20: on the pattern of MARATHON]

Thonburi ★ (,tɒnbu'riː) n a city in central Thailand, part of Bangkok Metropolis on the Chao Phraya River; the national capital (1767–82).

thong (θɒŋ) n **1** a thin strip of leather or other material. **2** a whip or whiplash, esp. one made of leather. **3** US,

Canad., Austral., & NZ. the usual name for **flip-flop** (sense 5). [OE *thwang*]

Thor ★ (θɔː) n Norse myth. the god of thunder, depicted as wielding a hammer, emblematic of the thunderbolt. [OE *Thōr*, from ON *thōrr* THUNDER]

thoracic (θɔː'ræsɪk) adj of, near, or relating to the thorax.

thoracic duct n the major duct of the lymphatic system, beginning below the diaphragm and ascending in front of the spinal column to the base of the neck.

thoraco- or before a vowel **thorac-** combining form. thorax: *thoracotomy*.

thoracoplasty ('θɔːrəkəʊ,plæstɪ) n, pl thoracoplasties. **1** plastic surgery of the thorax. **2** surgical removal of several ribs or a part of them to permit the collapse of a diseased lung.

thorax ('θɔːræks) n, pl thoraxes or thoraces ('θɔːrə,siːz, θɔː'reɪsɪz). **1** the part of the human body enclosed by the ribs. **2** the corresponding part in other vertebrates. **3** the part of an insect's body between the head and abdomen. [C16: via L from Gk *thōrax* breastplate, chest]

Thoreau ★ ('θɔːrəʊ, θɔː'rəʊ) n Henry David. 1817–62, US writer, noted esp. for *Walden, or Life in the Woods* (1854) and *Civil Disobedience* (1849).

thorium ('θɔːrɪəm) n a silvery-white radioactive metallic element. It is used in electronic equipment and as a nuclear power source. Symbol: Th; atomic no.: 90; atomic wt.: 232.04. [C19: NL, THOR + -IUM]
▸ **'thoric** adj

thorium dioxide n a white powder used in incandescent mantles. Also called: **thoria.**

thorium series n a radioactive series that starts with thorium–232 and ends with lead–208.

thorn (θɔːn) n **1** a sharp pointed woody extension of a stem or leaf. Cf. **prickle** (sense 1). **2** any of various trees or shrubs having thorns, esp. the hawthorn. **3** a Germanic character of runic origin (þ) used in Icelandic to represent the sound of *th*, as in *thin*, *bath*. **4** this same character as used in Old and Middle English to represent this sound. **5** a source of irritation (esp. in **a thorn in one's side** or **flesh**). [OE]
▸ **'thornless** adj

Thorn ★ (German toːrn) n the German name for **Toruń.**

thorn apple n **1** a poisonous plant of the N hemisphere, having white funnel-shaped flowers and spiny fruits. US name: **jimson weed. 2** the fruit of certain types of hawthorn.

thornbill ('θɔːn,bɪl) n **1** any of various South American hummingbirds having a thornlike bill. **2** Also called: **thornbill warbler.** any of various Australasian wrens. **3** any of various other birds with thornlike bills.

Thorndike ★ ('θɔːn,daɪk) n **1 Edward Lee.** 1874–1949, US psychologist. **2 Dame Sybil.** 1882–1976, British actress.

thorny ('θɔːnɪ) adj thornier, thorniest. **1** bearing or covered with thorns. **2** difficult or unpleasant. **3** sharp.
▸ **'thornily** adv ▸ **'thorniness** n

thoron ('θɔːrɒn) n a radioisotope of radon that is a decay product of thorium. Symbol: Tn or ^{220}Rn; atomic no.: 86; half-life: 54.5s. [C20: from THORIUM + -ON]

thorough ('θʌrə) adj **1** carried out completely and carefully. **2** (prenominal) utter: *a thorough bore*. **3** painstakingly careful. [OE *thurh*]
▸ **'thoroughly** adv ▸ **'thoroughness** n

thorough bass (beɪs) n a bass part underlying a piece of concerted music. Also called: **basso continuo, continuo.** See also **figured bass.**

thoroughbred ('θʌrə,bred) adj **1** purebred. ♦ n **2** a pedigree animal; purebred. **3** a person regarded as being of good breeding.

Thoroughbred ('θʌrə,bred) n a British breed of horse the ancestry of which can be traced to English mares and Arab sires.

thoroughfare ('θʌrə,feə) n **1** a road from one place to another, esp. a main road. **2** way through; access, or passage: *no thoroughfare*.

thoroughgoing ('θʌrə,gəʊɪŋ) adj **1** extremely thorough.

★ people and places

2 (*usually prenominal*) absolute; complete: *thoroughgoing incompetence.*

thoroughpaced ('θʌrə,peɪst) *adj* **1** (of a horse) showing performing ability in all paces. **2** thoroughgoing.

thorp *or* **thorpe** (θɔ:p) *n Obs. except in place names.* a small village. [OE]

Thorpe ★ (θɔ:p) *n* **Jeremy.** born 1929, British politician; leader of the Liberal party (1967–76).

Thorshavn ★ (*Danish* 'tɔ:rshaun) *n* the capital of the Faeroe Islands, a port on the northernmost island. Pop.: 13 757 (1980).

Thorvaldsen *or* **Thorwaldsen** ★ (*Danish* 'tɔrvalsən) *n* **Bertel** ('bertəl). 1770–1884, Danish neoclassical sculptor.

those (ðəʊz) *determiner* the form of **that** used before a plural noun. [OE *thās*, pl. of THIS]

Thoth ★ (θəʊθ, təʊt) *n* (in Egyptian mythology) a moon deity, scribe of the gods and protector of learning and the arts.

thou[1] (ðaʊ) *pron* (*subjective*) **1** *Arch. or dialect.* refers to the person addressed: used mainly in familiar address. **2** (*usually cap.*) refers to God when addressed in prayer, etc. [OE *thū*]

thou[2] (ðaʊ) *n, pl* **thous** *or* **thou. 1** one thousandth of an inch. **2** *Inf.* short for **thousand.**

though (ðəʊ) *conj* (*subordinating*) **1** (sometimes preceded by *even*) despite the fact that: *though he tries hard, he always fails.* ◆ *adv* **2** nevertheless; however: *he can't dance; he sings well, though.* [OE *theah*]

thought (θɔ:t) *vb* **1** the past tense and past participle of **think.** ◆ *n* **2** the act or process of thinking. **3** a concept, opinion, or idea. **4** ideas typical of a particular time or place: *German thought in the 19th century.* **5** application of mental attention; consideration. **6** purpose or intention: *I have no thought of giving up.* **7** expectation: *no thought of reward.* **8** a small amount; trifle: *you could be a thought more enthusiastic.* **9** kindness or regard. [OE *thōht*]

thoughtful ('θɔ:tful) *adj* **1** considerate in the treatment of other people. **2** showing careful thought. **3** pensive; reflective.
▸ **'thoughtfully** *adv* ▸ **'thoughtfulness** *n*

thoughtless ('θɔ:tlɪs) *adj* **1** inconsiderate. **2** having or showing lack of thought.
▸ **'thoughtlessly** *adv* ▸ **'thoughtlessness** *n*

thought-out *adj* conceived and developed by careful thought: *a well thought-out scheme.*

thought transference *n Psychol.* another name for **telepathy.**

thousand ('θaʊzənd) *n* **1** the cardinal number that is the product of 10 and 100. **2** a numeral, 1000, 10³, M, etc., representing this number. **3** (*often pl*) a very large but unspecified number, amount, or quantity. **4** something representing or consisting of 1000 units. ◆ *determiner* **5a** amounting to a thousand. **5b** (*as pronoun*): *a thousand is hardly enough.* ◆ Related adj: **millenary.** [OE *thūsend*]
▸ **'thousandth** *adj, n*

Thousand Guineas *n* (*functioning as sing*), usually written **1,000 Guineas.** an annual horse race, restricted to fillies, run at Newmarket in England since 1814.

Thousand Island dressing *n* a salad dressing made from mayonnaise with ketchup, chopped gherkins, etc.

Thousand Islands ★ *pl n* a group of about 1500 islands on the border between the US and Canada, in the upper St Lawrence River: administratively divided between the US and Canada.
▸ **Thousand Island** *adj*

Thrace ★ (θreɪs) *n* **1** an ancient country in the E Balkan Peninsula: successively under the Persians, Macedonians, and Romans. **2** a region of SE Europe, corresponding to the S part of the ancient country: divided by the Maritsa River into **Western Thrace** (Greece) and **Eastern Thrace** (Turkey).

Thracian ('θreɪʃɪən) *n* **1** a member of an ancient Indo-European people who lived in Thrace. **2** the ancient language spoken by this people. ◆ *adj* **3** of or relating to Thrace, its inhabitants, or the extinct Thracian language.

thrall (θrɔ:l) *n* **1** Also: **thraldom** *or US* **thralldom** ('θrɔ:ldəm). the state or condition of being in the power of another person. **2** a person who is in such a state. **3** a person totally subject to some need, desire, appetite, etc. ◆ *vb* **4** (*tr*) to enslave or dominate. [OE *thræl* slave]

thrash (θræʃ) *vb* **1** (*tr*) to beat soundly, as with a whip or stick. **2** (*tr*) to defeat totally; overwhelm. **3** (*intr*) to beat or plunge about in a wild manner. **4** to sail (a boat) against the wind or tide or (of a boat) to sail in this way. **5** another word for **thresh.** ◆ *n* **6** the act of thrashing; beating. **7** *Inf.* a party. ◆ See also **thrash out.** [OE *threscan*]

thrasher[1] ('θræʃə) *n* another name for **thresher** (the shark).

thrasher[2] ('θræʃə) *n* any of various brown thrushlike American songbirds.

thrashing ('θræʃɪŋ) *n* a physical assault; flogging.

thrash metal *n* a type of very fast very loud rock music that combines elements of heavy metal and punk rock. Often shortened to **thrash.**

thrash out *vb* (*tr, adv*) to discuss fully or vehemently, esp. in order to come to an agreement.

thrasonical (θrə'sɒnɪk²l) *adj Rare.* bragging; boastful. [C16: from L *Thrasō* name of boastful soldier in *Eunuchus,* a play by Terence, from Gk *Thrasōn,* from *thrasus* forceful]
▸ **thra'sonically** *adv*

thrawn (θrɔ:n) *adj Scot. & N English dialect.* **1** crooked or twisted. **2** stubborn; perverse. [N English dialect, var. of *thrown,* from OE *thrāwan* to twist about; throw]

thread (θrɛd) *n* **1** a fine strand, filament, or fibre of some material. **2** a fine cord of twisted filaments, esp. of cotton, used in sewing, etc. **3** any of the filaments of which a spider's web is made. **4** any fine line, stream, mark, or piece. **5** the helical ridge on a screw, bolt, nut, etc. **6** a very thin seam of coal or vein of ore. **7** something acting as the continuous link or theme of a whole: *the thread of the story.* **8** the course of an individual's life believed in Greek mythology to be spun, measured, and cut by the Fates. ◆ *vb* **9** (*tr*) to pass (thread, film, tape, etc.) through (something). **10** (*tr*) to string on a thread: *she threaded the beads.* **11** to make (one's way) through or over (something). **12** (*tr*) to produce a screw thread. **13** (*tr*) to pervade: *hysteria threaded his account.* **14** (*intr*) (of boiling syrup) to form a fine thread when poured from a spoon. ◆ See also **threads.** [OE *thrǣd*]
▸ **'threader** *n* ▸ **'thread,like** *adj*

threadbare ('θrɛd,bɛə) *adj* **1** (of cloth, clothing, etc.) having the nap worn off so that the threads are exposed; worn out. **2** meagre or poor. **3** hackneyed: *a threadbare argument.* **4** wearing threadbare clothes; shabby.

thread mark *n* a mark put into paper money to prevent counterfeiting, consisting of a pattern of silk fibres.

Threadneedle Street ★ (,θrɛd'ni:d²l, 'θrɛd,ni:d²l) *n* a street in the City of London famous for its banks, including the Bank of England, known as **The Old Lady of Threadneedle Street.**

threads (θrɛdz) *pl n Sl.* clothes.

threadworm ('θrɛd,wɜ:m) *n* any of various nematodes, esp. the pinworm.

thready ('θrɛdɪ) *adj* **threadier, threadiest. 1** of or resembling a thread. **2** (of the pulse) barely perceptible; weak. **3** sounding thin, weak, or reedy.
▸ **'threadiness** *n*

threat (θrɛt) *n* **1** a declaration of the intention to inflict harm, pain, or misery. **2** an indication of imminent harm, danger, or pain. **3** a person or thing that is regarded as dangerous or likely to inflict pain or misery. [OE]

threaten ('θrɛt²n) *vb* **1** (*tr*) to be a threat to. **2** to be a menacing indication of (something); portend. **3** (when *tr,* may take a clause as object) to express a threat to (a person or people).
▸ **'threatening** *adj* ▸ **'threateningly** *adv*

three (θri:) *n* **1** the cardinal number that is the sum of two and one and is a prime number. **2** a numeral, 3, III, (iii), representing this number. **3** something representing or consisting of three units. **4** Also called: **three o'clock.** three hours after noon or midnight. ◆ *determiner* **5a** amounting to three. **5b** (*as pronoun*): *three were killed*. ◆ Related adjs.: **ternary, tertiary, treble, triple**. [OE *thrēo*]

three-card trick *n* a game in which players bet on which of three playing cards is the queen.

three-colour *adj* of or comprising a colour print or a photomechanical process in which a picture is reproduced by superimposing three prints from half-tone plates in inks corresponding to the three primary colours.

three-D *or* **3-D** *n* a three-dimensional effect.

three-decker *n* **1a** anything having three levels or layers. **1b** (*as modifier*): *a three-decker sandwich*. **2** a warship with guns on three decks.

three-dimensional *adj* **1** of, having, or relating to three dimensions. **2** simulating the effect of depth. **3** having volume. **4** lifelike.

threefold ('θriː,fəʊld) *adj* **1** equal to or having three times as many or as much; triple. **2** composed of three parts. ◆ *adv* **3** by or up to three times as many or as much.

three-legged race *n* a race in which pairs of competitors run with their adjacent legs tied together.

threepenny bit *or* **thrupenny bit** ('θrʌpnɪ, -ənɪ, 'θrɛp-) *n* a twelve-sided British coin valued at three old pence, obsolete since 1971.

three-phase *adj* (of an electrical circuit, etc.) having or using three alternating voltages of the same frequency, displaced in phase by 120°.

three-ply *adj* **1** having three layers or thicknesses. **2** (of wool, etc.) three-stranded.

three-point landing *n* an aircraft landing in which the main wheels and the nose or tail wheel touch the ground simultaneously.

three-point turn *n* a complete turn of a motor vehicle using forward and reverse gears alternately, and completed after only three movements.

three-quarter *adj* **1** being three quarters of something. **2** being of three quarters the normal length. ◆ *n* **3** *Rugby*. any of the four players between the fullback and the halfbacks.

three-ring circus *n US*. **1** a circus with three rings for simultaneous performances. **2** a situation of confusion, characterized by a bewildering variety of events or activities.

Three Rivers ★ *n* the English name for **Trois Rivières**.

three Rs *pl n* **the**. the three skills regarded as the fundamentals of education; reading, writing, and arithmetic. [from the humorous spelling *reading, 'riting,* and *'rithmetic*]

threescore ('θriː'skɔː) *determiner* an archaic word for **sixty**.

threesome ('θriːsəm) *n* **1** a group of three. **2** *Golf.* a match in which a single player playing his own ball competes against two others playing on the same ball. **3** any game, etc., for three people. **4** (*modifier*) performed by three.

thremmatology (,θrɛmə'tɒlədʒɪ) *n* the science of breeding domesticated animals and plants. [C19: from Gk *thremma* nursling + -LOGY]

threnody ('θrɛnədɪ, 'θriː-) *or* **threnode** ('θriːnəʊd, 'θrɛn-) *n, pl* **threnodies** *or* **threnodes**. an ode, song, or speech of lamentation, esp. for the dead. [C17: from Gk *thrēnōidia*, from *thrēnos* dirge + *ōidē* song]
▶ **threnodic** (θrɪ'nɒdɪk) *adj* ▶ **threnodist** ('θrɛnədɪst, 'θriː-) *n*

thresh (θrɛʃ) *vb* **1** to beat stalks of ripe corn, etc., either with a hand implement or a machine to separate the grain from the husks and straw. **2** (*tr*) to beat or strike. **3** (*intr; often foll. by about*) to toss and turn; thrash. [OE *threscan*]

thresher ('θrɛʃə) *n* **1** a person who threshes. **2** short for **threshing machine**. **3** any of a genus of large sharks occurring in tropical and temperate seas. They have a very long whiplike tail.

threshing machine *n* a machine for threshing crops.

threshold ('θrɛʃəʊld, 'θrɛʃ,həʊld) *n* **1** a sill, esp. one made of stone or hardwood, placed at a doorway. **2** any doorway or entrance. **3** the starting point of an experience, event, or venture. **4** *Psychol.* the point at which a stimulus is just perceived: *the threshold of consciousness.* **5a** a point at which something would stop, take effect, etc. **5b** (*as modifier*): *threshold price; threshold effect.* **6** the minimum intensity or value of a signal, etc., that will produce a response or specified effect. **7** (*modifier*) of a pay agreement, clause, etc., that raises wages to compensate for increases in the cost of living. ◆ Related adj: **liminal**. [OE *therscold*]

threshold agreement *n* an agreement between an employer and employees or their union to increase wages by a specified sum if inflation exceeds a specified level in a specified time.

threw (θruː) *vb* the past tense of **throw**.

thrice (θraɪs) *adv* **1** three times. **2** threefold. **3** *Arch.* greatly. [OE *thrīwa, thrīga*]

thrift (θrɪft) *n* **1** wisdom and caution in the management of money. **2** Also called: **sea pink**. any of a genus of perennial low-growing plants of Europe, W Asia, and North America, having narrow leaves and round heads of pink or white flowers. [C13: from ON: success; see THRIVE]
▶ **'thriftless** *adj* ▶ **'thriftlessly** *adv*

thrifty ('θrɪftɪ) *adj* **thriftier, thriftiest**. **1** showing thrift; economical or frugal. **2** *Rare.* thriving or prospering.
▶ **'thriftily** *adv* ▶ **'thriftiness** *n*

thrill (θrɪl) *n* **1** a sudden sensation of excitement and pleasure. **2** a situation producing such a sensation. **3** a trembling sensation caused by fear or emotional shock. **4** *Pathol.* an abnormal slight tremor. ◆ *vb* **5** to feel or cause to feel a thrill. **6** to tremble or cause to tremble; vibrate or quiver. [OE *thȳrlian* to pierce, from *thyrel* hole]
▶ **'thrilling** *adj*

thriller ('θrɪlə) *n* a book, film, play, etc., depicting crime, mystery, or espionage in an atmosphere of excitement and suspense.

thrips (θrɪps) *n, pl* **thrips**. any of various small slender-bodied insects typically having piercing mouthparts and feeding on plant sap. [C18: via NL from Gk: woodworm]

thrive (θraɪv) *vb* **thrives, thriving; thrived** *or* **throve; thrived** *or* **thriven** ('θrɪvⁿn). (*intr*) **1** to grow strongly and vigorously. **2** to do well; prosper. [C13: from ON *thrīfask* to grasp for oneself, from ?]

thro' *or* **thro** (θruː) *prep, adv Inf. or poetic*. variant spellings of **through**.

throat (θrəʊt) *n* **1a** that part of the alimentary and respiratory tracts extending from the back of the mouth to just below the larynx. **1b** the front part of the neck. **2** something resembling a throat, esp. in shape or function: *the throat of a chimney.* **3 cut one's (own) throat.** to bring about one's own ruin. **4 ram** *or* **force (something) down someone's throat.** to insist that someone listen to or accept (something). ◆ Related adjs.: **guttural, laryngeal**. [OE *throtu*]

throaty ('θrəʊtɪ) *adj* **throatier, throatiest**. **1** indicating a sore throat; hoarse: *a throaty cough.* **2** of or produced in the throat. **3** deep, husky, or guttural.
▶ **'throatily** *adv*

throb (θrɒb) *vb* **throbs, throbbing, throbbed**. (*intr*) **1** to pulsate or beat repeatedly, esp. with increased force. **2** (of engines, drums, etc.) to have a strong rhythmic vibration or beat. ◆ *n* **3** a throbbing, esp. a rapid pulsation as of the heart: *a throb of pleasure.* [C14: ? imit.]

throes (θrəʊz) *pl n* **1** a condition of violent pangs, pain, or convulsions: *death throes.* **2 in the throes of.** struggling with great effort with. [OE *thrāwu* threat]

thrombin ('θrɒmbɪn) *n Biochem.* an enzyme that acts on fibrinogen in blood causing it to clot. [C19: from THROMB(US) + -IN]

thrombocyte ('θrɒmbə,saɪt) *n* another name for **platelet**.
▶ **thrombocytic** (,θrɒmbə'sɪtɪk) *adj*

thromboembolism (,θrɒmbəʊ'ɛmbə,lɪzəm) *n* the obstruction of a blood vessel by a thrombus that has become detached from its original site.

thrombose ('θrɒmbəʊz) *vb* **thromboses, thrombosing, thrombosed.** to become or affect with a thrombus. [C19: back formation from THROMBOSIS]

thrombosis (θrɒm'bəʊsɪs) *n, pl* **thromboses** (-si:z). **1** the formation or presence of a thrombus. **2** *Inf.* short for **coronary thrombosis.** [C18: from NL, from Gk: curdling, from *thrombousthai* to clot, from *thrombos* THROMBUS]
► **thrombotic** (θrɒm'bɒtɪk) *adj*

thrombus ('θrɒmbəs) *n, pl* **thrombi** (-baɪ). a clot of coagulated blood that forms within a blood vessel or inside the heart, often impeding the flow of blood. [C17: from NL, from Gk *thrombos* lump, from ?]

throne (θrəʊn) *n* **1** the ceremonial seat occupied by a monarch, bishop, etc., on occasions of state. **2** the power or rank ascribed to a royal person. **3** a person holding royal rank. **4** (*pl; often cap.*) the third of the nine orders into which the angels are divided in medieval angelology. ◆ *vb* **thrones, throning, throned. 5** to place or be placed on a throne. [C13: from OF *trone*, from L *thronus*, from Gk *thronos*]

throng (θrɒŋ) *n* **1** a great number of people or things crowded together. ◆ *vb* **2** to gather in or fill (a place) in large numbers; crowd. **3** (*tr*) to hem in (a person); jostle. [OE *gethrang*]

throstle ('θrɒsᵊl) *n* **1** a poetic name for the **song thrush. 2** a spinning machine for wool or cotton in which the fibres are twisted and wound continuously. [OE]

throttle ('θrɒtᵊl) *n* **1** Also called: **throttle valve.** any device that controls the quantity of fuel or fuel and air mixture entering an engine. **2** an informal or dialect word for **throat.** ◆ *vb* **throttles, throttling, throttled.** (*tr*) **3** to kill or injure by squeezing the throat. **4** to suppress. **5** to control or restrict (a flow of fluid) by means of a throttle valve. [C14: *throtelen*, from *throte* THROAT]
► **'throttler** *n*

through (θru:) *prep* **1** going in at one side and coming out at the other side of: *a path through the wood.* **2** occupying or visiting several points scattered around in (an area). **3** as a result of; by means of. **4** *Chiefly US.* up to and including: *Monday through Friday.* **5** during: *through the night.* **6** at the end of; having completed. **7 through with.** having finished with (esp. when dissatisfied with). ◆ *adj* **8** (*postpositive*) having successfully completed some specified activity. **9** (on a telephone line) connected. **10** (*postpositive*) no longer able to function successfully in some specified capacity: *as a journalist, you're through.* **11** (*prenominal*) (of a route, journey, etc.) continuous or unbroken: *a through train.* ◆ *adv* **12** through some specified thing, place, or period of time. **13 through and through.** thoroughly; completely. [OE *thurh*]

through bridge *n Civil engineering.* a bridge in which the track is carried by the lower horizontal members.

throughout (θru:'aʊt) *prep* **1** right through; through the whole of (a place or a period of time): *throughout the day.* ◆ *adv* **2** through the whole of some specified period or area.

throughput ('θru:,pʊt) *n* the quantity of raw material or information processed or communicated in a given period, esp. by a computer.

throughway ('θru:,weɪ) *n US.* a thoroughfare, esp. a motorway.

throve (θrəʊv) *vb* a past tense of **thrive.**

throw (θrəʊ) *vb* **throws, throwing, threw, thrown.** (*mainly tr*) **1** (*also intr*) to project (something) through the air, esp. with a rapid motion of the arm. **2** (foll. by *in, on, onto,* etc.) to put or move suddenly, carelessly, or violently. **3** to bring to or cause to be in a specified state or condition, esp. suddenly: *the news threw them into a panic.* **4** to direct or cast (a shadow, light, etc.). **5** to project (the voice) so as to make it appear to come from other than its source. **6** to give or hold (a party). **7** to cause to fall or be upset: *the horse threw his rider.* **8a** to tip (dice) out onto a flat surface. **8b** to obtain (a specified number) in this way. **9** to shape (clay) on a potter's wheel. **10** to move (a switch or lever) to engage or disengage a mechanism. **11** to be subjected to (a fit). **12** to turn (wood, etc.) on a

lathe. **13** *Inf.* to baffle or astonish; confuse: *the question threw me.* **14** *Boxing.* to deliver (a punch). **15** *Wrestling.* to hurl (an opponent) to the ground. **16** *Inf.* to lose (a contest, etc.) deliberately. **17a** to play (a card). **17b** to discard (a card). **18** (of an animal) to give birth to (young). **19** to twist or spin (filaments) into thread. **20** *Austral. inf.* (often foll. by *at*) to mock or poke fun. **21 throw oneself at.** to strive actively to attract the attention or affection of. **22 throw oneself into.** to involve oneself enthusiastically in. **23 throw oneself on.** to rely entirely upon. ◆ *n* **24** the act or an instance of throwing. **25** the distance over which anything may be thrown: *a stone's throw.* **26** *Inf.* a chance or try. **27** an act or result of throwing dice. **28a** the eccentricity of a cam. **28b** the radial distance between the central axis of a crankshaft and the axis of a crankpin forming part of the shaft. **29** a decorative blanket or cover. **30** *Geol.* the vertical displacement of rock strata at a fault. **31** *Physics.* the deflection of a measuring instrument as a result of a fluctuation. ◆ *See also* **throwaway, throwback, throw in,** etc. [OE *thrāwan* to turn, torment]
► **'thrower** *n*

throwaway ('θrəʊə,weɪ) *adj* (*prenominal*) **1** said or done incidentally, esp. for rhetorical effect; casual: *a throwaway remark.* **2** designed to be discarded after use rather than reused, refilled, etc.: *a throwaway carton.* ◆ *n* **3** *Chiefly US & Canad.* a handbill. ◆ *vb* **throw away.** (*tr, adv*) **4** to get rid of; discard. **5** to fail to make good use of; waste.

throwback ('θrəʊ,bæk) *n* **1a** a person, animal, or plant that has the characteristics of an earlier or more primitive type. **1b** a reversion to such an organism. ◆ *vb* **throw back.** (*adv*) **2** (*intr*) to revert to an earlier or more primitive type. **3** (*tr;* foll. by *on*) to force to depend (on): *the crisis threw her back on her faith in God.*

throw in *vb* (*tr, adv*) **1** to add at no additional cost. **2** to contribute or interpose (a remark, argument, etc.). **3 throw in the sponge** (*or* **towel**). to give in; accept defeat. ◆ *n* **throw-in. 4** *Soccer, etc.* the method of putting the ball into play after it has gone into touch by throwing it to a team-mate.

thrown (θrəʊn) *vb* the past participle of **throw.**

throw off *vb* (*mainly tr, adv*) **1** to free oneself of; discard. **2** to produce or utter in a casual manner. **3** to escape from or elude. **4** to confuse or disconcert. **5** (*intr;* often foll. by *at*) *Austral. & NZ inf.* to deride or ridicule.

throw out *vb* (*tr, adv*) **1** to discard or reject. **2** to expel or dismiss, esp. forcibly. **3** to construct (something projecting or prominent). **4** to put forward or offer. **5** to utter in a casual or indirect manner. **6** to confuse or disconcert. **7** to give off or emit. **8** *Cricket.* (of a fielder) to put (the batsman) out by throwing the ball to hit the wicket. **9** *Baseball.* to make a throw to a team-mate who in turn puts out (a base runner).

throw over *vb* (*tr, adv*) to forsake or abandon; jilt.

throw together *vb* (*tr, adv*) **1** to assemble hurriedly. **2** to cause to become casually acquainted.

throw up *vb* (*adv, mainly tr*) **1** to give up; abandon. **2** to construct hastily. **3** to reveal; produce. **4** (*also intr*) *Inf.* to vomit.

thru (θru:) *prep, adv, adj Chiefly US.* a variant spelling of **through.**

thrum[1] (θrʌm) *vb* **thrums, thrumming, thrummed. 1** to strum rhythmically but without expression on (a musical instrument). **2** (*intr*) to drum incessantly: *rain thrummed on the roof.* ◆ *n* **3** a repetitive strumming. [C16: imit.]

thrum[2] (θrʌm) *n* **1a** any of the unwoven ends of warp thread remaining on the loom when the web has been removed. **1b** such ends of thread collectively. **2** a fringe or tassel of short unwoven threads. ◆ *vb* **thrums, thrumming, thrummed. 3** (*tr*) to trim with thrums. [C14: from OE]

thrush[1] (θrʌʃ) *n* any of a subfamily of songbirds, esp. those having a brown plumage with a spotted breast, such as the mistle thrush and song thrush. [OE *thrӯsce*]

thrush[2] (θrʌʃ) *n* **1** a fungal disease, esp. of infants, characterized by the formation of whitish spots. **2** a genital infection caused by the same fungus. **3** a softening of the frog of a horse's hoof characterized by inflammation and a thick foul discharge. [C17: from ?]

thrust (θrʌst) vb **thrusts, thrusting, thrust. 1** (tr) to push (someone or something) with force. **2** (tr) to force upon (someone) or into (some condition or situation): *they thrust responsibilities upon her.* **3** (tr; foll. by *through*) to pierce; stab. **4** (intr; usually foll. by *through* or *into*) to force a passage. **5** to make a stab or lunge at. ◆ n **6** a forceful drive, push, stab, or lunge. **7** a force, esp. one that produces motion. **8a** a propulsive force produced by the fluid pressure or the change of momentum of the fluid in a jet engine, rocket engine, etc. **8b** a similar force produced by a propeller. **9** a continuous pressure exerted by one part of an object, structure, etc., against another. **10** force, impetus, or drive. **11** the essential or most forceful part: *the thrust of the argument.* [C12: from ON *thrysta*]

thruster ('θrʌstə) n **1** a person or thing that thrusts. **2** a small rocket engine, esp. one used to correct the altitude or course of a spacecraft.

thrust fault n a fault in which the rocks on the lower side of an inclined fault plane have been displaced downwards; a reverse fault.

Thucydides ★ (θuːˈsɪdɪˌdiːz) n ?460–?395 B.C., Greek historian and politician, noted for his *History of the Peloponnesian War.*
▸ Thu,cydi'dean *adj*

thud (θʌd) n **1** a dull heavy sound. **2** a blow or fall that causes such a sound. ◆ vb **thuds, thudding, thudded. 3** to make or cause to make such a sound. [OE *thyddan* to strike]

thug (θʌg) n **1** a tough and violent man, esp. a criminal. **2** (sometimes cap.) (formerly) a member of an organization of robbers and assassins in India. [C19: from Hindi *thag* thief, from Sansk. *sthaga* scoundrel, from *sthagati* to conceal]
▸ 'thuggery n ▸ 'thuggish *adj*

thuja or **thuya** ('θuːjə) n any of a genus of coniferous trees of North America and East Asia, having scalelike leaves, small cones, and an aromatic wood. [C18: from NL, from Med. L *thuia*, ult. from Gk *thua* an African tree]

Thule ★ ('θjuːlɪ) n **1** Also called: **ultima Thule.** a region believed by ancient geographers to be the northernmost land in the inhabited world: sometimes thought to have been Iceland, Norway, or one of the Shetland Islands. **2** an Eskimo settlement in NW Greenland: a Danish trading post, founded in 1910, and US air force base.

thulium ('θjuːlɪəm) n a malleable ductile silvery-grey element. The radioisotope **thulium-170** is used as an electron source in portable X-ray units. Symbol: Tm; atomic no.: 69; atomic wt.: 168.93. [C19: NL, from THULE + -IUM]

thumb (θʌm) n **1** the first and usually shortest and thickest of the digits of the hand. **2** the corresponding digit in other vertebrates. **3** the part of a glove shaped to fit the thumb. **4 all thumbs.** clumsy. **5 thumbs down.** an indication of refusal or disapproval. **6 thumbs up.** an indication of encouragement or approval. **7 under someone's thumb.** at someone's mercy or command. ◆ vb **8** (tr) to touch, mark, or move with the thumb. **9** to attempt to obtain (a lift or ride) by signalling with the thumb. **10** (when intr, often foll. by *through*) to flip the pages of (a book, etc.) in order to glance at the contents. **11 thumb one's nose at.** to deride or mock, esp. by placing the thumb on the nose with fingers extended. [OE *thūma*]

thumb index n **1** a series of indentations cut into the fore-edge of a book to facilitate quick reference. ◆ vb **thumb-index. 2** (tr) to furnish with a thumb index.

thumbnail ('θʌmˌneɪl) n **1** the nail of the thumb. **2** (modifier) concise and brief: *a thumbnail sketch.*

thumbnut ('θʌmˌnʌt) n a wing nut.

thumb piano n another name for **mbira.**

thumbscrew ('θʌmˌskruː) n **1** an instrument of torture that pinches or crushes the thumbs. **2** a screw with projections on its head enabling it to be turned by the thumb and forefinger.

thumbstall ('θʌmˌstɔːl) n a protective sheathlike cover for the thumb.

thumbtack ('θʌmˌtæk) n the US and Canad. name fo **drawing pin.**

thump (θʌmp) n **1** the sound of a heavy solid body hitting a comparatively soft surface. **2** a heavy blow with the hand. ◆ vb **3** (tr) to strike or beat heavily; pound. **4** (intr) to throb, beat, or pound violently. [C16]
▸ 'thumper n

thumping ('θʌmpɪŋ) adj (prenominal) Sl. huge or excessive: *a thumping loss.*

Thun ★ (German tuːn) n **1** a town in central Switzerland in Bern canton on Lake Thun. Pop.: 36 700 (1990 est.). **2 Lake.** a lake in central Switzerland, formed by a widening of the Aar River. Length: about 17 km (11 miles). Width 3 km (2 miles). German name: **Thuner See.**

thunbergia (θʌnˈbɜːdʒɪə) n any of various climbing o dwarf plants of tropical and subtropical Africa and Asia [C19: after K. P. *Thunberg* (1743–1822), Swedish botanist]

thunder ('θʌndə) n **1** a loud cracking or deep rumbling noise caused by the rapid expansion of atmospheric gases which are suddenly heated by lightning. **2** any loud booming sound. **3** Rare. a violent threat or denunciation. **4 steal someone's thunder.** to lessen the effect o someone's idea or action by anticipating it. ◆ vb **5** tc make (a loud sound) or utter (words) in a manner suggesting thunder. **6** (intr; with *it* as subject) to be the case that thunder is being heard. **7** (intr) to move fast and heavily: *the bus thundered downhill.* **8** (intr) to utter vehement threats or denunciation; rail. [OE *thunor*]
▸ 'thundery *adj* ▸ 'thunderer n

Thunder Bay ★ n a port in central Canada, in Ontario on Lake Superior: formed in 1970 by the amalgamation of Fort William and Port Arthur; the head of the St Lawrence Seaway for Canada. Pop.: 113 746 (1991).

thunderbolt ('θʌndəˌbəʊlt) n **1** a flash of lightning accompanying thunder. **2** the imagined agency of destruction produced by a flash of lightning. **3** (in mythology) the destructive weapon wielded by several gods, esp. the Greek god Zeus. **4** something very startling.

thunderclap ('θʌndəˌklæp) n **1** a loud outburst of thunder. **2** something as violent or unexpected as a clap of thunder.

thundercloud ('θʌndəˌklaʊd) n a towering electrically charged cumulonimbus cloud associated with thunderstorms.

thunderhead ('θʌndəˌhed) n Chiefly US. the anvil-shaped top of a cumulonimbus cloud.

thundering ('θʌndərɪŋ) adj (prenominal) Sl. very great or excessive: *a thundering idiot.*

thunderous ('θʌndərəs) adj **1** threatening; angry. **2** resembling thunder, esp. in loudness.

thunderstorm ('θʌndəˌstɔːm) n a storm with thunder and lightning and usually heavy rain or hail.

thunderstruck ('θʌndəˌstrʌk) or **thunderstricken** ('θʌndəˌstrɪkən) adj **1** completely taken aback; amazed or shocked. **2** Rare. struck by lightning.

Thurber ★ ('θɜːbə) n James (Grover). 1894–1961, US humorist. He contributed many drawings and stories to the *New Yorker.*

Thurgau ★ (German 'tuːrgau) n a canton of NE Switzerland, on Lake Constance: annexed by the confederated Swiss states in 1460. Capital: Frauenfeld. Pop.: 220 335 (1995 est.). Area: 1007 sq. km (389 sq. miles). French name: **Thurgovie** (tyrgɔvi).

thurible ('θjʊərɪbᵊl) n another word for **censer.** [C15: from L *tūribulum* censer, from *tūs* incense]

Thuringia ★ (θjʊˈrɪndʒɪə) n a state of central Germany, formerly in East Germany. Pop.: 2 517 800 (1995 est.). German name: **Thüringen** ('tyːrɪŋən).
▸ Thu'ringian *adj, n*

Thuringian Forest ★ n a forested mountainous region in E central Germany, rising over 900 m (3000 ft); formerly in East Germany. German name: **Thüringer Wald** ('tyːrɪŋər 'valt).

Thurrock ★ ('θʌrək) n a unitary authority in SE England, in Essex. Pop.: 132 300 (1996 est.).

Thurs. abbrev. for Thursday.

★ people and places

Thursday ('θɜːzdɪ) *n* the fifth day of the week; fourth day of the working week. [OE *Thursdæg*, lit.: Thor's day]

Thursday Island ★ *n* an island in Torres Strait, between NE Australia and New Guinea: administratively part of Queensland, Australia. Area: 4 sq. km (1.5 sq. miles).

thus (ðʌs) *adv* **1** in this manner: *do it thus.* **2** to such a degree: *thus far and no further.* ◆ *sentence connector.* **3** therefore: *We have failed. Thus we have to take the consequences.* [OE]

Thutmose I ★ (θuːt'məusə, -'məus) *n* died *c.* 1500 B.C., king of Egypt of the 18th dynasty.

Thutmose III ★ *n* died *c.* 1450 B.C., king of Egypt of the 18th dynasty, who completed the conquest of Syria.

thuya ('θuːjə) *n* a variant spelling of **thuja**.

thwack (θwæk) *vb* **1** to beat, esp. with something flat. ◆ *n* **2a** a blow with something flat. **2b** the sound made by it. [C16: imit.]

thwart (θwɔːt) *vb* **1** to oppose successfully or prevent; frustrate. **2** *Obs.* to be or move across. ◆ *n* **3** an oarsman's seat lying across a boat. ◆ *adj* **4** passing or being situated across. ◆ *prep, adv* **5** *Obs.* across. [C13: from ON *thvert*, from *thverr* transverse]

thy (ðaɪ) *determiner (usually preceding a consonant) Arch. or Brit. dialect.* belonging to or associated in some way with you (thou): *thy goodness.* [C12: var. of THINE]

Thyestes ★ (θaɪ'estiːz) *n Greek myth.* son of Pelops and brother of Atreus, with whose wife he committed adultery. In revenge, Atreus killed Thyestes' sons and served them to their father at a banquet.
▶ **Thyestean** *or* **Thyestian** (θaɪ'estɪən, ˌθaɪe'stiːən) *adj*

thylacine ('θaɪləˌsaɪn) *n* an extinct or rare doglike carnivorous marsupial of Tasmania. Also called: **Tasmanian wolf.** [C19: from NL *thȳlacīnus*, from Gk *thulakos* pouch]

thyme (taɪm) *n* any of various small shrubs having a strong odour, small leaves, and white, pink, or red flowers. [C14: from OF *thym*, from L *thymum*, from Gk, from *thuein* to make a burnt offering]
▶ **'thymy** *adj*

-thymia *n combining form.* indicating a certain emotional condition, mood, or state of mind: *cyclothymia.* [NL, from Gk *thumos* temper]

thymine ('θaɪmiːn) *n* a white crystalline base found in DNA. [C19: from THYMIC (see THYMUS) + -INE²]

thymol ('θaɪmɒl) *n* a white crystalline substance obtained from thyme and used as a fungicide, antiseptic, etc. [C19: from THYME + -OL²]

thymus ('θaɪməs) *n, pl* **thymuses** *or* **thymi** (-maɪ). a glandular organ of vertebrates, consisting in man of two lobes situated below the thyroid. It atrophies with age and is almost nonexistent in the adult. [C17: from NL, from Gk *thumos* sweetbread]
▶ **'thymic** *adj*

thyratron ('θaɪrəˌtrɒn) *n Electronics.* a gas-filled tube that has three electrodes and can be switched between an 'off' state and an 'on' state. It has been superseded by the thyristor. [C20: orig. a trademark, from Gk *thura* door, valve + -TRON]

thyristor (θaɪ'rɪstə) *n* any of a group of semiconductor devices, such as the silicon-controlled rectifier, that can be switched between two states. [C20: from THYR(ATRON) + (TRANS)ISTOR]

thyroid ('θaɪrɔɪd) *adj* **1** of or relating to the thyroid gland. **2** of or relating to the largest cartilage of the larynx. ◆ *n* **3** See **thyroid gland.** **4** a preparation of the thyroid gland of certain animals, used to treat hypothyroidism. [C18: from NL *thyroīdēs*, from Gk *thureoeidēs*, from *thureos* oblong (lit.: door-shaped), from *thura* door]

thyroid gland *n* an endocrine gland of vertebrates, consisting in man of two lobes near the base of the neck. It secretes hormones that control metabolism and growth.

thyrotropin (ˌθaɪrəʊ'trəʊpɪn) *or* **thyrotrophin** *n* a hormone secreted by the pituitary gland: it stimulates the activity of the thyroid gland. [C20: from *thyro-* thyroid + -TROPE + -IN]

thyroxine (θaɪ'rɒksiːn, -sɪn) *or* **thyroxin** (θaɪ'rɒksɪn) *n* the principal hormone produced by the thyroid gland. [C19: from *thyro-* thyroid + OXY-² + -INE²]

thyrse (θɜːs) *or* **thyrsus** ('θɜːsəs) *n, pl* **thyrses** *or* **thyrsi** ('θɜːsaɪ). *Bot.* a type of inflorescence, occurring in the lilac and grape, in which the main branch is racemose and the lateral branches cymose. [C17: from F: THYRSUS]

thyrsus ('θɜːsəs) *n, pl* **thyrsi** (-saɪ). **1** *Greek myth.* a staff, usually one tipped with a pine cone, borne by Dionysus (Bacchus) and his followers. **2** a variant spelling of **thyrse.** [C18: from L, from Gk *thursos* stalk]

thyself (ðaɪ'self) *pron Arch.* **a** the reflexive form of *thou* or *thee.* **b** (intensifier): *thou, thyself, wouldst know.*

ti (tiː) *n Music.* a variant spelling of **te.**

Ti *the chemical symbol for* titanium.

Tia Juana ★ ('tɪə 'wɑːnə; *Spanish* 'tia 'xwana) *n* a variant spelling of **Tijuana.**

Tianjin ('tjen'dʒɪn), **Tientsin,** *or* **T'ien-ching** ★ *n* an industrial city in NE China, in Hebei province, on the Grand Canal, 51 km (32 miles) from the Yellow Sea: seat of Nankai University (1919). Pop.: 5 770 000 (1991 est.).

Tian Shan *or* **Tien Shan** ★ ('tjen'ʃɑːn) *n* a great mountain system of central Asia, in Kyrgyzstan and the Xinjiang Uygur Autonomous Region of W China, extending for about 2500 km (1500 miles). Highest peak: Pobeda Peak, 7439 m (24 406 ft). Russian name: **Tyan-Shan.**

tiara (tɪ'ɑːrə) *n* **1** a woman's semicircular jewelled headdress for formal occasions. **2** a high headdress worn by Persian kings in ancient times. **3** a headdress worn by the pope, consisting of a beehive-shaped diadem surrounded by three coronets. [C16: via L from Gk, of Oriental origin]
▶ **ti'araed** *adj*

Tiber ★ ('taɪbə) *n* a river in central Italy, rising in the Tuscan Apennines and flowing south through Rome to the Tyrrhenian Sea. Length: 405 km (252 miles). Ancient name: Tiberis ('tiːbəris). Italian name: Tevere.

Tiberias ★ (taɪ'bɪərɪˌæs) *n* **1** a resort in N Israel, on the Sea of Galilee: an important Jewish centre after the destruction of Jerusalem by the Romans. Pop.: 35 400 (1989 est.). **2** Lake. another name for the (Sea of) **Galilee.**

Tiberius ★ (taɪ'bɪərɪəs) *n* full name *Tiberius Claudius Nero Caesar Augustus.* 42 B.C.–37 A.D., Roman emperor (14–37 A.D.). He succeeded his father-in-law Augustus.

Tibesti *or* **Tibesti Massif** ★ (tɪ'bestɪ) *pl n* a mountain range of volcanic origin in NW Chad, in the central Sahara extending for about 480 km (300 miles). Highest peak: Emi Koussi, 3415 m (11 204 ft).

Tibet ★ (tɪ'bet) *n* an autonomous region of SW China: Europeans strictly excluded in the 19th century; invaded by China in 1950; rebellion (1959) against Chinese rule suppressed and the Dalai Lama fled to India; military rule imposed (1989–90) after demands for independence were made; consists largely of a vast high plateau between the Himalayas and Kunlun Mountains; formerly a theocracy and the centre of Lamaism. Capital: Lhasa. Pop.: 2 360 000 (1995 est.). Area: 1 221 601 sq. km (471 660 sq. miles). Chinese names: **Xizang Autonomous Region, Sitsang.**

Tibetan (tɪ'betªn) *adj* **1** of or characteristic of Tibet, its people, or their language. ◆ *n* **2** a native or inhabitant of Tibet. **3** the language of Tibet.

tibia ('tɪbɪə) *n, pl* **tibiae** ('tɪbɪˌiː) *or* **tibias. 1** the inner and thicker of the two bones of the human leg below the knee; shinbone. **2** the corresponding bone in other vertebrates. **3** the fourth segment of an insect's leg. [C16: from L; pipe]
▶ **'tibial** *adj*

Tibullus ★ (tɪ'bʌləs) *n* **Albius** ('ælbɪəs). ?54–?19 B.C., Roman elegiac poet.

Tibur ★ ('taɪbə) *n* the ancient name for **Tivoli.**

tic (tɪk) *n* spasmodic twitching of a particular group of muscles. [C19: from F, from ?]

tic douloureux ('tɪk ˌduːlə'ruː) *n* a condition of momentary stabbing pain along the trigeminal nerve. [C19: from F, lit.: painful tic]

Ticino ★ (*Italian* ti'tʃiːno) *n* **1** a canton in S Switzerland: predominantly Italian-speaking and Roman Catholic; mountainous. Capital: Bellinzona. Pop.: 302 131 (1995 est.). Area: 2810 sq. km (1085 sq. miles). German name: **Tessin. 2** a river in S central Europe, rising in S central Switzerland and flowing southeast and west to Lake Maggiore, then southeast to the River Po. Length: 248 km (154 miles).

tick¹ (tɪk) *n* **1** a recurrent metallic tapping or clicking sound, such as that made by a clock. **2** *Brit. inf.* a moment or instant. **3** a mark (✓) used to check off or indicate the correctness of something. **4** *Commerce.* the smallest increment by which a price can fluctuate in a commodity or financial futures market. ◆ *vb* **5** to produce a recurrent tapping sound or indicate by such a sound: *the clock ticked the minutes away.* **6** (when *tr*, often foll. by *off*) to mark or check with a tick. **7 what makes someone tick.** *Inf.* the basic drive or motivation of a person. ◆ See also **tick off, tick over.** [C13: from Low G *tikk* touch]

tick² (tɪk) *n* any of a large group of small parasitic arachnids typically living on the skin of warm-blooded animals and feeding on the blood, etc., of their hosts. [OE *ticca*]

tick³ (tɪk) *n* **1** the strong covering of a pillow, mattress, etc. **2** *Inf.* short for **ticking.** [C15: prob. from MDu. *tīke*]

tick⁴ (tɪk) *n Brit. inf.* account or credit (esp. in **on tick**). [C17: shortened from TICKET]

tick bird *n* another name for **oxpecker.**

ticker ('tɪkə) *n* **1** *Sl.* **1a** the heart. **1b** a watch. **2** a person or thing that ticks. **3** the US word for **tape machine.**

ticker tape *n* a continuous paper ribbon on which a tape machine prints current stock quotations.

ticket ('tɪkɪt) *n* **1a** a piece of paper, cardboard, etc., showing that the holder is entitled to certain rights, such as travel on a train or bus, entry to a place of public entertainment, etc. **1b** (*modifier*) concerned with the issue, sale, or checking of tickets: *a ticket collector.* **2** a piece of card, cloth, etc., attached to an article showing information such as its price, size, etc. **3** a summons served for a parking or traffic offence. **4** *Inf.* the certificate of competence issued to a ship's captain or an aircraft pilot. **5** *Chiefly US & NZ.* the group of candidates nominated by one party in an election; slate. **6** *Chiefly US.* the declared policy of a political party at an election. **7** *Brit. inf.* a certificate of discharge from the armed forces. **8** *Inf.* the right or appropriate thing: *that's the ticket.* **9 have (got) tickets on oneself.** *Austral. inf.* to be conceited. ◆ *vb* **tickets, ticketing, ticketed.** (*tr*) **10** to issue or attach a ticket or tickets to. [C17: from OF *etiquet*, from *estiquier* to stick on, from MDu. *steken* to stick]

ticket day *n Stock Exchange.* the day before settling day, when the stockbrokers are given the names of the purchasers.

ticket of leave *n* (formerly, in Britain) a permit allowing a convict (**ticket-of-leave man**) to leave prison, after serving only part of his sentence, with certain restrictions placed on him.

tick fever *n* any acute infectious febrile disease caused by the bite of an infected tick.

ticking ('tɪkɪŋ) *n* a strong cotton fabric, often striped, used esp. for mattress and pillow covers. [C17: from TICK³]

tickle ('tɪkᵊl) *vb* **tickles, tickling, tickled. 1** to touch or stroke, so as to produce pleasure, laughter, or a twitching sensation. **2** (*tr*) to excite pleasurably; gratify. **3** (*tr*) to delight or entertain (often in **tickle one's fancy**). **4** (*intr*) to itch or tingle. **5** (*tr*) to catch (a fish, esp. a trout) with the hands. **6 tickle pink** or **to death.** *Inf.* to please greatly. ◆ *n* **7** a sensation of light stroking or itching. **8** the act of tickling. **9** *Canad.* (in the Atlantic Provinces) a narrow strait. [C14]

tickler ('tɪklə) *n* **1** *Inf., chiefly Brit.* a difficult problem. **2** Also called: **tickler file.** *US.* a memorandum book. **3** a person or thing that tickles.

ticklish ('tɪklɪʃ) *adj* **1** sensitive to being tickled. **2** delicate or difficult. **3** easily upset or offended.
▸ 'ticklishly *adv* ▸ 'ticklishness *n*

tick off *vb* (*tr, adv*) **1** to mark with a tick. **2** *Inf., chiefly Brit.* to scold; reprimand.

tick over *vb* (*intr, adv*) **1** Also: **idle.** *Brit.* (of an engine) to run at low speed with the throttle control closed and the transmission disengaged. **2** to run smoothly without any major changes.

ticktack ('tɪk,tæk) *n* **1** *Brit.* a system of sign language, mainly using the hands, by which bookmakers transmit their odds to each other at race courses. **2** *US.* a ticking sound. [from TICK¹]

ticktock ('tɪk,tɒk) *n* **1** a ticking sound as made by a clock. ◆ *vb* **2** (*intr*) to make a ticking sound.

Ticonderoga ★ (,taɪkɒndə'rəʊgə) *n* a village in NE New York State, on Lake George: site of Fort Ticonderoga, scene of battles between the British and French (1758–59) and a strategic point in the War of American Independence.

tidal ('taɪdᵊl) *adj* **1** relating to, characterized by, or affected by tides. **2** dependent on the tide: *a tidal ferry.*
▸ 'tidally *adv*

tidal energy *n* energy obtained by harnessing tidal power.

tidal volume *n* **1** the volume of water associated with a rising tide. **2** *Physiol.* the amount of air passing into and out of the lungs during normal breathing.

tidal wave *n* **1** a name (not in technical usage) for **tsunami. 2** an unusually large incoming wave, often caused by high winds and spring tides. **3** a forceful and widespread movement in public opinion, action, etc.

tidbit ('tɪd,bɪt) *n* the usual US spelling of **titbit.**

tiddler ('tɪdlə) *n Brit. inf.* **1** a very small fish, esp. a stickleback. **2** a small child. [C19: from *tittlebat*, childish var. of STICKLEBACK, infl. by TIDDLY¹]

tiddly¹ ('tɪdlɪ) *adj* **tiddlier, tiddliest.** *Brit.* small; tiny. [C19: childish var. of LITTLE]

tiddly² ('tɪdlɪ) *adj Sl., chiefly Brit.* slightly drunk. [C19 (meaning: a drink): from ?]

tiddlywinks ('tɪdlɪ,wɪŋks) *n* (*functioning as sing*) a game in which players try to flick discs of plastic into a cup by pressing them with other larger discs. [C19: prob. from TIDDLY¹ + dialect *wink*, var. of WINCH¹]

tide (taɪd) *n* **1** the cyclic rise and fall of sea level caused by the gravitational pull of the sun and moon. There are usually two high tides and two low tides in each lunar day. **2** the current, ebb, or flow of water at a specified place resulting from these changes in level. **3** See **ebb** (sense 3) and **flood** (sense 3). **4** a widespread tendency or movement. **5** a critical point in time; turning point. **6** *Arch. except in combination.* a season or time: *Christmastide.* **7** *Arch.* a favourable opportunity. **8 the tide is in** (or **out**). the sea has reached its highest (or lowest) level. ◆ *vb* **tides, tiding, tided. 9** to carry or be carried with or as if with the tide. **10** (*intr*) to ebb and flow like the tide. [OE *tīd* time]
▸ 'tideless *adj*

tideland ('taɪd,lænd) *n US.* land between high-water and low-water marks.

tideline ('taɪd,laɪn) *n* the mark or line left by the tide when it retreats from its highest point.

tidemark ('taɪd,mɑːk) *n* **1** a mark left by the highest or lowest point of a tide. **2** *Chiefly Brit.* a mark showing a level reached by a liquid: *a tidemark on the bath.* **3** *Inf., chiefly Brit.* a dirty mark on the skin, indicating the extent to which someone has washed.

tide over *vb* (*tr, adv*) to help to get through (a period of difficulty, distress, etc.).

tide-rip *n* another word for **riptide** (sense 1).

tidewaiter ('taɪd,weɪtə) *n* (formerly) a customs officer who boarded and inspected incoming ships.

tidewater ('taɪd,wɔːtə) *n* **1** water that advances and recedes with the tide. **2** *US.* coastal land drained by tidal streams.

tideway ('taɪd,weɪ) *n* a strong tidal current or its channel, esp. the tidal part of a river.

tidings ('taɪdɪŋz) *pl n* information or news. [OE *tīdung*]

tidy ('taɪdɪ) *adj* **tidier, tidiest. 1** characterized by or indicat-

ing neatness and order. **2** *Inf.* considerable: *a tidy sum of money.* ◆ *vb* **tidies, tidying, tidied.** **3** (when *intr*, usually foll. by *up*) to put (things) in order; neaten. ◆ *n, pl* **tidies. 4a** a small container for odds and ends. **4b** sink tidy. a container to retain rubbish that might clog the plughole. **5** *Chiefly US & Canad.* an ornamental protective covering for the back or arms of a chair. [C13 (in the sense: timely, excellent): from TIDE + -Y¹]
▶ '**tidily** *adv* ▶ '**tidiness** *n*

tie (taɪ) *vb* **ties, tying, tied.** **1** (when *tr*, often foll. by *up*) to fasten or be fastened with string, thread, etc. **2** to make (a knot or bow) in (something). **3** (*tr*) to restrict or secure. **4** to equal (the score) of a competitor, etc. **5** (*tr*) *Inf.* to unite in marriage. **6** *Music.* **6a** to execute (two successive notes) as though they formed one note. **6b** to connect (two printed notes) with a tie. ◆ *n* **7** a bond, link, or fastening. **8** a restriction or restraint. **9** a string, wire, etc., with which something is tied. **10** a long narrow piece of material worn, esp. by men, under the collar of a shirt, tied in a knot close to the throat with the ends hanging down the front. US name: **necktie. 11a** an equality in score, attainment, etc., in a contest. **11b** the match or competition in which such a result is attained. **12** a structural member such as a tie beam or tie rod. **13** *Sport, Brit.* a match or game in an eliminating competition: *a cup tie.* **14** (*usually pl*) a shoe fastened by means of laces. **15** the US and Canad. name for **sleeper** (on a railway track). **16** *Music.* a slur connecting two notes of the same pitch indicating that the sound is to be prolonged for their joint time value. ◆ See also **tie in, tie up.** [OE *tīgan* to tie]

tie beam *n* a horizontal beam that serves to prevent two other structural members from separating, esp. one that connects two corresponding rafters in a roof or roof truss.

tie-break *or* **tie-breaker** *n* **1** *Tennis.* an extra game played to decide the result of a set when the score is 6–6. **2** any method of deciding quickly the result of a drawn contest, esp. an extra game, question, etc.

tie clasp *n* a clip which holds a tie in place against a shirt. Also called: **tie clip.**

tied (taɪd) *adj Brit.* **1** (of a public house, retail shop, etc.) obliged to sell only the beer, products, etc. of a particular producer: *a tied house; tied outlet.* **2** (of a house) rented out to the tenant for as long as he is employed by the owner. **3** (of a loan) bound by one nation to another on condition that the money is spent on goods or services provided by the lending nation.

tie-dyeing, tie-dye *or* **tie and dye** *n* a method of dyeing textiles to produce patterns by tying sections of the cloth together so that they will not absorb the dye.
▶ '**tie-,dyed** *adj*

tie in *vb* (*adv*) **1** to come or bring into a certain relationship; coordinate. ◆ *n* **tie-in. 2** a link, relationship, or coordination. **3** publicity material, a book, etc., linked to a film, etc. **4** *US.* **4a** a sale or advertisement offering products of which a purchaser must buy one or more in addition to his purchase. **4b** an item sold or advertised in this way. **4c** (*as modifier*): *a tie-in sale.*

tie line *n* a telephone line between two private branch exchanges or private exchanges that may or may not pass through a main exchange.

Tien Shan ★ ('tjen'ʃɑːn) *n* a variant transliteration of the Chinese name for the **Tian Shan.**

Tientsin ★ ('tjen'tsɪn) *n* a variant transliteration of the Chinese name for **Tianjin.**

tiepin ('taɪ,pɪn) *n* an ornamental pin of various shapes used to pin the two ends of a tie to a shirt.

Tiepolo ★ (*Italian* 'tjɛːpolo; *English* tiːˈpɛpə,ləʊ) *n* **Giovanni Battista** (dʒoˈvanni batˈtista). 1696–1770, Italian rococo painter.

tier¹ (tɪə) *n* **1** one of a set of rows placed one above and behind the other, such as theatre seats. **2a** a layer or level. **2b** (*in combination*): *a three-tier cake.* ◆ *vb* **3** to be or arrange in tiers. [C16: from OF *tire* rank, of Gmc origin]

tier² ('taɪə) *n* a person or thing that ties.

tierce (tɪəs) *n* **1** a variant of **terce. 2** the third of eight positions from which a parry or attack can be made in fencing. **3** (tɜːs). a sequence of three cards. **4** an obsolete measure of capacity equal to 42 wine gallons. [C15: from OF, fem of *tiers* third, from L *tertius*]

tiercel ('tɪəs°l) *n* a variant of **tercel.**

Tierra del Fuego ★ (*Spanish* 'tjɛrra ðel 'fweɣo) *n* an archipelago at the S extremity of South America, separated from the mainland by the Strait of Magellan: the west and south belong to Chile, the east to Argentina, and several islands are disputed. Area: 73 643 sq. km (28 434 sq. miles).

tie up *vb* (*adv*) **1** (*tr*) to bind securely with or as if with string, rope, etc. **2** to moor (a vessel). **3** (*tr; often passive*) to engage the attentions of. **4** (*tr; often passive*) to conclude (the organization of something). **5** to come or bring to a complete standstill. **6** (*tr*) to commit (funds, etc.) and so make unavailable for other uses. **7** (*tr*) to subject (property) to conditions that prevent sale, alienation, etc. ◆ *n* **tie-up. 8** a link or connection. **9** *Chiefly US & Canad.* a standstill. **10** *Chiefly US & Canad.* an informal term for **traffic jam.**

tiff (tɪf) *n* **1** a petty quarrel. **2** a fit of ill humour. ◆ *vb* **3** (*intr*) to have or be in a tiff. [C18: from ?]

tiffany ('tɪfənɪ) *n, pl* **tiffanies.** a sheer fine gauzy fabric. [C17 (in the sense: a fine dress worn on Twelfth Night): from OF *tifanie*, from ecclesiastical L *theophania* Epiphany]

Tiffany ★ ('tɪfənɪ) *n* **Louis Comfort.** 1848–1933, US Art-Nouveau craftsman, best known for creating the Favrile style of stained glass.

tiffin ('tɪfɪn) *n* (in India) a light meal, esp. at midday. [C18: prob. from obs. *tiffing*, from *tiff* to sip]

Tiflis ★ (tɪf'liːs) *n* transliteration of the Russian name for Tbilisi.

tig (tɪg) *n, vb* **tigs, tigging, tigged.** another word for **tag**² (senses 1, 4).

tiger ('taɪgə) *n* **1** a large feline mammal of forests in most of Asia, having a tawny yellow coat with black stripes. **2** a dynamic, forceful, or cruel person. **3a** a country, esp. in E Asia, that is achieving rapid economic growth. **3b** (*as modifier*): *a tiger economy.* [C13: from OF *tigre*, from L *tigris*, from Gk, of Iranian origin]
▶ '**tigerish** *or* '**tigrish** *adj*

Tiger ('taɪgə) *n* a variant of **TIGR.**

tiger beetle *n* any of a family of active predatory beetles, chiefly of warm dry regions, having powerful mandibles and long legs.

tiger cat *n* a medium-sized feline mammal of Central and South America, having a dark-striped coat.

tiger lily *n* a lily plant of China and Japan cultivated for its flowers, which have black-spotted orange petals.

tiger moth *n* any of various moths having wings that are conspicuously marked with stripes and spots.

tiger's-eye *or* **tigereye** ('taɪgər,aɪ) *n* a semiprecious golden-brown stone.

tiger shark *n* a voracious omnivorous requiem shark of tropical waters, having a striped or spotted body.

tiger snake *n* a highly venomous and aggressive Australian snake, usually with dark bands on the back.

tight (taɪt) *adj* **1** stretched or drawn so as not to be loose; taut. **2** fitting in a close manner. **3** held, made, fixed, or closed firmly and securely: *a tight knot.* **4a** of close and compact construction or organization, esp. so as to be impervious to water, air, etc. **4b** (*in combination*): *airtight.* **5** unyielding or stringent. **6** cramped or constricted. **7** mean or miserly. **8** difficult and problematic: *a tight fit.* **9** hardly profitable: *a tight bargain.* **10** *Econ.* **10a** (of a commodity) difficult to obtain. **10b** (of funds, money, etc.) difficult and expensive to borrow. **10c** (of markets) characterized by excess demand or scarcity. **11** (of a match or game) very close or even. **12** (of a team or group, esp. of a pop group) playing well together, in a disciplined coordinated way. **13** *Inf.* drunk. **14** *Inf.* (of a person) showing tension. ◆ *adv* **15** in a close, firm, or secure way. [C14: prob. var. of *thight*, from ON *thēttr* close]
▶ '**tightly** *adv* ▶ '**tightness** *n*

tightass ('taɪt,æs) *n Sl., chiefly US.* an inhibited or excessively self-controlled person.
▶ '**tight,assed** *adj*

tighten ('taɪtⁿn) *vb* to make or become tight or tighter.

tightfisted (,taɪt'fɪstɪd) *adj* mean; miserly.

tight head *n Rugby*. the prop on the hooker's right in the front row of a scrum. Cf. **loose head**.

tightknit (,taɪt'nɪt) *adj* **1** closely integrated: *a tightknit community*. **2** organized carefully.

tight-lipped *adj* **1** secretive or taciturn. **2** with the lips pressed tightly together, as through anger.

tightrope ('taɪt,rəʊp) *n* a rope stretched taut on which acrobats walk or perform balancing feats.
  ▸ **tightrope walker** *n*

tights (taɪts) *pl n* **1a** Also called: (US) **panty hose,** (Canad. and NZ) **pantyhose,** (Austral. and NZ) **pantihose.** a one-piece clinging garment covering the body from the waist to the feet, worn by women and also by acrobats, dancers, etc. **1b** *US & Canad*. Also called: **leotards.** a similar, tight-fitting garment worn instead of trousers by either sex. **2** a similar garment formerly worn by men, as in the 16th century with a doublet.

Tiglath-pileser I ★ ('tɪglæθpɪ'liːzə, -paɪ-) *n* king of Assyria (?1116–?1093 B.C.).

Tiglath-pileser III ★ *n* known as *Pulu*. died ?727 B.C., king of Assyria (745–727).

tiglic acid ('tɪglɪk) *n* a syrupy liquid or unsaturated carboxylic acid, found in croton oil and used in perfumery. [C19 *tiglic*, from NL *Croton tiglium* (the croton plant), from ?]

tigon ('taɪgən) *or* **tiglon** ('tɪglɒn) *n* the hybrid offspring of a male tiger and a female lion.

TIGR *abbrev.* for Treasury Investment Growth Receipts: a bond denominated in dollars and linked to US treasury bonds, the yield on which is taxed in the UK as income when it is cashed or redeemed. Also called: **Tiger.**

Tigré *or* **Tigray** ★ ('tiːgreɪ) *n* **1** an autonomous region of N Ethiopia, bordering on Eritrea: formerly a separate kingdom. Capital: Mekele. Pop.: 2 999 948 (1993 est.). Area: 53 498 sq. km (20 656 sq. miles). **2** a language of NE Ethiopia, belonging to the SE Semitic subfamily of the Afro-Asiatic family.

tigress ('taɪgrɪs) *n* **1** a female tiger. **2** a fierce, cruel, or wildly passionate woman.

tigridia (taɪ'grɪdɪə) *n* any of various bulbous plants of Mexico, Central America, and tropical S America. [C19: from Mod. L, from Gk *tigris* tiger (alluding to the spotted flowers of these plants)]

Tigris ★ ('taɪgrɪs) *n* a river in SW Asia, rising in E Turkey and flowing southeast through Baghdad to the Euphrates in SE Iraq, forming the delta of the Shatt-al-Arab, which flows into the Persian Gulf: part of a canal and irrigation system as early as 2400 B.C., with many ancient cities (including Nineveh) on its banks. Length: 1900 km (1180 miles).

Tihwa *or* **Tihua** ★ ('tiː'hwɑː) *n* a former name for **Urumchi.**

Tijuana (tiː'wɑːnə; *Spanish* ti'xwana) *or* **Tia Juana** ★ *n* a city and resort in NW Mexico, in Baja California. Pop.: 698 752 (1990).

tike (taɪk) *n* a variant spelling of **tyke.**

tiki ('tiːkiː) *n* a Maori greenstone neck ornament in the form of a fetus. Also called: **heitiki.** [from Maori *heitiki* figure worn round neck]

tikka ('tiːkə) *adj* (*immediately postpositive*) *Indian cookery.* (of meat, esp. chicken or lamb) marinated in spices and then dry-roasted, usually in a clay oven.

tilak ('tɪlək) *n, pl* **tilak** *or* **tilaks.** a coloured spot or mark worn by Hindus, esp. on the forehead, often indicating membership of a religious sect, caste, etc., or (in the case of a woman) marital status. [from Sansk. *tilaka*]

Tilburg ★ ('tɪlbɜːg; *Dutch* 'tɪlbyrx) *n* a city in the S Netherlands, in North Brabant: textile industries. Pop.: 163 383 (1994).

tilbury ('tɪlbərɪ, -brɪ) *n, pl* **tilburies.** a light two-wheeled horse-drawn open carriage, seating two people. [C19: prob. after the inventor]

Tilbury ★ ('tɪlbərɪ, -brɪ) *n* an area in Essex, on the River

Thames: extensive docks; principal container port of the Port of London.

tilde ('tɪldə) *n* the diacritical mark (~) placed over a letter to indicate a nasal sound, as in Spanish *señor*. [C19: from Sp., from L *titulus* title]

Tilden ★ ('tɪldⁿn) *n* **Bill,** full name *William Tatem Tilden,* known as *Big Bill*. 1893–1953, US tennis player: won the US singles championship (1920–25, 1929).

tile (taɪl) *n* **1** a thin slab of fired clay, rubber, linoleum, etc., used with others to cover a roof, floor, wall, etc. **2** a short pipe made of earthenware, plastic, etc., used with others to form a drain. **3** tiles collectively. **4** a rectangular block used as a playing piece in mah jong and other games. **5 on the tiles.** *Inf.* on a spree, esp. of drinking or debauchery. ◆ *vb* **tiles, tiling, tiled. 6** (*tr*) to cover with tiles. [OE *tīgele*, from L *tēgula*]
  ▸ **'tiler** *n*

tiling ('taɪlɪŋ) *n* **1** tiles collectively. **2** something made of or surfaced with tiles.

till¹ (tɪl) *conj, prep* short for **until.** Also (not standard): **'til.** [OE *til*]

> **USAGE NOTE** *Till* is a variant of *until* that is acceptable at all levels of language. *Until* is, however, often preferred at the beginning of a sentence in formal writing: *until his behaviour improves, he cannot become a member.*

till² (tɪl) *vb* (*tr*) **1** to cultivate and work (land) for the raising of crops. **2** to plough. [OE *tilian* to try, obtain]
  ▸ **'tillable** *adj* ▸ **'tiller** *n*

till³ (tɪl) *n* a box, case, or drawer into which money taken from customers is put, now usually part of a cash register. [C15 *tylle*, from ?]

till⁴ (tɪl) *n* a glacial deposit consisting of rock fragments of various sizes. The most common is boulder clay. [C17: from ?]

tillage ('tɪlɪdʒ) *n* **1** the act, process, or art of tilling. **2** tilled land.

tiller¹ ('tɪlə) *n Naut.* a handle fixed to the top of a rudderpost to serve as a lever in steering it. [C14: from Anglo-F *teiler* beam of a loom, from Med. L *tēlārium*, from L *tēla* web]
  ▸ **'tillerless** *adj*

tiller² ('tɪlə) *n* **1** a shoot that arises from the base of the stem in grasses. **2** a less common name for **sapling.** ◆ *vb* **3** (*intr*) (of a plant) to produce tillers. [OE *telgor* twig]

Till Eulenspiegel ★ ('tɪl 'ɔɪlən,ʃpiːgⁿl) *n* ?14th century, legendary German peasant, whose pranks became the subject of many tales.

Tilley ★ ('tɪlɪ) *n* **Vesta,** original name *Matilda Alice Powles*. 1864–1952, British music-hall entertainer.

Tillich ★ ('tɪlɪk) *n* **Paul Johannes.** 1886–1965, US Protestant theologian and philosopher, born in Germany. His works include *The Courage to Be* (1952) and *Systematic Theology* (1951–63).

Tilsit ★ ('tɪlzɪt) *n* the former name (until 1945) of **Sovetsk.**

tilt (tɪlt) *vb* **1** to incline or cause to incline at an angle. **2** (*usually intr*) to attack or overthrow (a person) in a tilt or joust. **3** (when *intr*, often foll. by *at*) to aim or thrust: *to tilt a lance.* **4** (*tr*) to forge with a tilt hammer. ◆ *n* **5** a slope or angle: *at a tilt.* **6** the act of tilting. **7** (esp. in medieval Europe) a jousting contest. **7b** a thrust with a lance or pole delivered during a tournament. **8** an attempt to win a contest. **9** See **tilt hammer. 10** (at) **full tilt.** at full speed or force. [OE *tealtian*]
  ▸ **'tilter** *n*

tilth (tɪlθ) *n* **1** the act or process of tilling land. **2** the condition of soil or land that has been tilled. [OE *tilthe*]

tilt hammer *n* a drop hammer with a heavy head; used in forging.

tiltyard ('tɪlt,jɑːd) *n* (formerly) an enclosed area for tilting.

Tim. *Bible. abbrev.* for Timothy.

Timaru ★ ('tɪmə,ruː) *n* a port and resort in S New Zealand, on E South Island. Pop.: 15 350 (1995 est.).

timbal *or* **tymbal** ('tɪmbªl) *n Music.* a type of kettledrum. [C17: from F *timbale*, from OF *tamballe*, (associated also with *cymbale* cymbal), from OSp. *atabal*, from Ar. *at-tabl* the drum]

timbale (tæmˈbɑːl) *n* **1** a mixture of meat, fish, etc., cooked in a mould lined with potato or pastry. **2** a straight-sided mould in which such a dish is prepared. [C19: from F: kettledrum]

timber ('tɪmbə) *n* **1a** wood, esp. when regarded as a construction material. Usual US and Canad. word: **lumber. 1b** (*as modifier*): *a timber cottage.* **2a** trees collectively. **2b** *Chiefly US.* woodland. **3** a piece of wood used in a structure. **4** *Naut.* a frame in a wooden vessel. ◆ *vb* **5** (*tr*) to provide with timbers. ◆ *sentence substitute.* **6** a lumberjack's shouted warning when a tree is about to fall. [OE] ▸ **'timbered** *adj* ▸ **'timbering** *n*

timber hitch *n* a knot used for tying a rope round a spar, log, etc., for haulage.

timber limit *n Canad.* **1** the area to which rights of cutting timber, granted by a government licence, are limited. **2** another term for **timber line.**

timber line *n* the altitudinal or latitudinal limit of normal tree growth. See also **tree line.**

timber wolf *n* a wolf with a grey brindled coat found in forested northern regions, esp. of North America.

timberyard ('tɪmbə,jɑːd) *n Brit., Austral., & NZ.* an establishment where timber, etc., is stored or sold. US and Canad. word: **lumberyard.**

timbre ('tɪmbə, 'tæmbə) *n* **1** *Phonetics.* the distinctive tone quality differentiating one vowel or sonant from another. **2** *Music.* tone colour or quality of sound. [C19: from F: note of a bell, from OF: drum, from Med. Gk *timbanon*, from Gk *tumpanon*]

timbrel ('tɪmbrəl) *n Chiefly biblical.* a tambourine. [C16: from OF; see TIMBRE]

Timbuktu ★ (,tɪmbʌkˈtuː) *n* **1** a town in central Mali, on the River Niger: terminus of a trans-Saharan caravan route; a great Muslim centre (14th–16th centuries). Pop.: 31 925 (1987). French name: **Tombouctou. 2** any distant or outlandish place: *from here to Timbuktu.*

time (taɪm) *n* **1** the continuous passage of existence in which events pass from a state of potentiality in the future, through the present, to a state of finality in the past. Related adj: **temporal. 2** *Physics.* a quantity measuring duration, usually with reference to a periodic process such as the rotation of the earth or the vibration of electromagnetic radiation emitted from certain atoms. Time is considered as a fourth coordinate required to specify an event. See **space-time continuum. 3** a specific point on this continuum expressed in hours and minutes: *the time is four o'clock.* **4** a system of reckoning for expressing time: *Greenwich Mean Time.* **5a** a definite and measurable portion of this continuum. **5b** (*as modifier*): *time limit.* **6a** an accepted period such as a day, season, etc. **6b** (*in combination*): *springtime.* **7** an unspecified interval; a while. **8** (*often pl*) a period or point marked by specific attributes or events: *the Victorian times.* **9** a sufficient interval or period: *have you got time to help me?* **10** an instance or occasion: *I called you three times.* **11** an occasion or period of specified quality: *have a good time.* **12** the duration of human existence. **13** the heyday of human life: *in her time she was a great star.* **14** a suitable moment: *it's time I told you.* **15** the expected interval in which something is done. **16** a particularly important moment, esp. childbirth or death: *her time had come.* **17** (*pl*) indicating a degree or amount calculated by multiplication with the number specified: *ten times three is thirty.* **18** (*often pl*) the fashions, thought, etc., of the present age (esp. in **ahead of one's time, behind the times**). **19** *Brit.* Also: **closing time.** the time at which bars, pubs, etc., are legally obliged to stop selling alcoholic drinks. **20** *Inf.* a term in jail (esp. in **do time**). **21a** a customary or full period of work. **21b** the rate of pay for this period. **22** Also: (esp. US): **metre. 22a** the system of combining beats or pulses in music into successive groupings by which the rhythm of the music is established. **22b** a specific system having a specific number of beats in each grouping or bar: *duple time.* **23** *Music.*

short for **time value. 24 against time.** in an effort to complete something in a limited period. **25 ahead of time.** before the deadline. **26 at one time. 26a** once; formerly. **26b** simultaneously. **27 at the same time. 27a** simultaneously. **27b** nevertheless; however. **28 at times.** sometimes. **29 beat time.** to indicate the tempo of a piece of music by waving a baton, hand, etc. **30 for the time being.** for the moment; temporarily. **31 from time to time.** at intervals; occasionally. **32 have no time for.** to have no patience with; not tolerate. **33 in good time. 33a** early. **33b** quickly. **34 in no time.** very quickly. **35 in one's own time. 35a** outside paid working hours. **35b** at one's own rate. **36 in time. 36a** early or at the appointed time. **36b** eventually. **36c** *Music.* at a correct metrical or rhythmic pulse. **37 keep time.** to observe correctly the accent or rhythmic pulse of a piece of music in relation to tempo. **38 make time. 38a** to find an opportunity. **38b** (often foll. by *with*) *US inf.* to succeed in seducing. **39 on time. 39a** at the expected or scheduled time. **39b** *US.* payable in instalments. **40 pass the time of day.** to exchange casual greetings (with an acquaintance). **41 time and again.** frequently. **42 time off.** a period when one is absent from work for a holiday, through sickness, etc. **43 time of one's life.** a memorably enjoyable time. **44 time out of mind.** from time immemorial. **45** (*modifier*) operating automatically at or for a set time: *time lock; time switch.* ◆ *vb* (*tr*) **46** to ascertain the duration or speed of. **47** to set a time for. **48** to adjust to keep accurate time. **49** to pick a suitable time for. **50** *Sport.* to control the execution or speed of (an action). ◆ *sentence substitute.* **51** the word called out by a publican signalling that it is closing time. [OE *tīma*]

time and a half *n* the rate of pay equalling one and a half times the normal rate, often offered for overtime work.

time and motion study *n* the analysis of industrial or work procedures to determine the most efficient methods of operation. Also: **time and motion, time study, motion study.**

time bomb *n* a bomb containing a timing mechanism that determines the time at which it will detonate.

time capsule *n* a container holding articles, documents, etc., representative of the current age, buried for discovery in the future.

time charter *n* the hire of a ship or aircraft for a specified period. Cf. **voyage charter.**

time clock *n* a clock which records, by punching or stamping **timecards** inserted into it, the time of arrival or departure of people, such as employees in a factory.

time-consuming *adj* taking up or involving a great deal of time.

time exposure *n* **1** an exposure of a photographic film for a relatively long period, usually a few seconds. **2** a photograph produced by such an exposure.

time-honoured *adj* having been observed for a long time and sanctioned by custom.

time immemorial *n* the distant past beyond memory or record.

timekeeper ('taɪm,kiːpə) *n* **1** a person or thing that keeps or records time. **2** an employee who maintains a record of the hours worked by the other employees. **3** an employee whose record of punctuality is of a specified nature: *a bad timekeeper.* ▸ **'time,keeping** *n*

time-lag *n* an interval between two connected events.

time-lapse photography *n* the technique of recording a very slow process on film by exposing single frames at regular intervals. The film is then projected at normal speed.

timeless ('taɪmlɪs) *adj* **1** unaffected or unchanged by time; ageless. **2** eternal. ▸ **'timelessly** *adv* ▸ **'timelessness** *n*

timely ('taɪmlɪ) *adj* **timelier, timeliest,** *adv* at the right or an opportune or appropriate time.

time machine *n* (in science fiction) a machine in which people or objects can be transported into the past or the future.

time-out *n Chiefly US & Canad.* **1** *Sport.* an interruption in play during which players rest, discuss tactics, etc. **2** a period of rest; break. **3** *Computing.* a condition that occurs when the amount of time a computer has been instructed to wait for another device to perform a task has expired, usually indicated by an error message. ◆ *vb* **time out. 4** (of a computer) to stop operating because of a timeout.

timepiece ('taɪm,piːs) *n* any of various devices, such as a clock, watch, or chronometer, which measure and indicate time.

timer ('taɪmə) *n* **1** a device for measuring, recording, or indicating time. **2** a switch or regulator that causes a mechanism to operate at a specific time. **3** a person or thing that times.

time-saving *adj* shortening the length of time required for an operation, activity, etc.
▶ **time-saver** *n*

timescale ('taɪm,skeɪl) *n* the span of time within which certain events occur or are scheduled in relation to any broader period of time.

time-served *adj* (of a craftsman or tradesman) having completed an apprenticeship; fully trained and competent.

timeserver ('taɪm,sɜːvə) *n* a person who compromises and changes his opinions, way of life, etc., to suit the current fashions.

time sharing *n* **1** a system of part ownership of a property for use as a holiday home whereby each participant owns the property for a particular period every year. **2** a system by which users at different terminals of a computer can, because of its high speed, apparently communicate with it at the same time.

time signal *n* an announcement of the correct time, esp. on radio or television.

time signature *n Music.* a sign usually consisting of two figures, one above the other, the upper figure representing the number of beats per bar and the lower one the time value of each beat; it is placed after the key signature.

Times Square ★ *n* a square formed by the intersection of Broadway and Seventh Avenue in New York City.

timetable ('taɪm,teɪb°l) *n* **1** a list or table of events arranged according to the time when they take place; schedule. ◆ *vb* **timetables, timetabling, timetabled. (tr) 2** to include in or arrange according to a timetable.

time value *n Music.* the duration of a note relative to other notes in a composition and considered in relation to the basic tempo.

time warp *n* an imagined distortion of the progress of time so that, for instance, events from the past may appear to be happening in the present.

timeworn ('taɪm,wɔːn) *adj* **1** showing the adverse effects of overlong use or of old age. **2** hackneyed; trite.

time zone *n* a region throughout which the same standard time is used. There are 24 time zones in the world, demarcated approximately by meridians at 15° intervals, an hour apart.

timid ('tɪmɪd) *adj* **1** easily frightened or upset, esp. by human contact; shy. **2** indicating shyness or fear. [C16: from L *timidus*, from *timēre* to fear]
▶ ti'**midity** *or* '**timidness** *n* ▶ '**timidly** *adv*

timing ('taɪmɪŋ) *n* the regulation of actions or remarks in relation to others to produce the best effect, as in music, the theatre, etc.

Timişoara ★ (*Romanian* timiˈʃwara) *n* a city in W Romania: formerly under Turkish and then Hapsburg rule, being allotted to Romania in 1920; scene of violence during the revolution of 1989. Pop.: 325 359 (1993 est.). Hungarian name: **Temesvár.**

timocracy (taɪˈmɒkrəsɪ) *n, pl* **timocracies. 1** a political system in which possession of property is a requirement for participation in government. **2** a political system in which love of honour is deemed the guiding principle of government. [C16: from OF *tymocracie*, ult. from Gk *timokratia*, from *timē* worth, honour, + -CRACY]

Timor ★ ('tiːmɔː, 'taɪ-) *n* an island in Indonesia in the Malay Archipelago, the largest and easternmost of the Lesser Sunda Islands: the east, together with an enclave on the NW coast, formed the Portuguese overseas province of Portuguese Timor until 1975, when it declared independence but was immediately invaded by Indonesia. In 1976 Indonesia formally annexed the east, the legality of this act being disputed by the UN. Area: 30 775 sq. km (11 883 sq. miles).

timorous ('tɪmərəs) *adj* **1** fearful or timid. **2** indicating fear or timidity. [C15: from OF *temoros*, from Med. L, from L *timor* fear, from *timēre* to be afraid]
▶ '**timorously** *adv* ▶ '**timorousness** *n*

Timor Sea ★ *n* an arm of the Indian Ocean between Australia and Timor. Width: about 480 km (300 miles).

Timoshenko ★ (ˌtɪməˈʃɛŋkəʊ; *Russian* timaˈʃɛnkə) *n* **Semyon Konstantinovich** (sɪˈmjɔn kənstanˈtinəvitʃ). 1895–1970, Soviet general in World War II.

Timothy ★ ('tɪməθɪ) *n New Testament.* **1 Saint.** a disciple of Paul, who became leader of the Christian community at Ephesus. Feast day: Jan. 26 or 22. **2** either of the two books addressed to him (in full **The First and Second Epistles of Paul the Apostle to Timothy**).

timothy grass *or* **timothy** *n* a perennial grass of temperate regions having erect stiff stems: grown for hay and pasture. [C18: apparently after a *Timothy Hanson*, who brought it to colonial Carolina]

timpani *or* **tympani** ('tɪmpənɪ) *pl n* (*sometimes functioning as sing*) a set of kettledrums. [from It., pl of *timpano* kettledrum, from L: TYMPANUM]
▶ '**timpanist** *or* '**tympanist** *n*

Timur *or* **Timour** ★ (tiːˈmʊə) *n* See **Tamerlane**.

tin (tɪn) *n* **1** a malleable silvery-white metallic element. It is used extensively in alloys, esp. bronze and pewter, and as a noncorroding coating for steel. Symbol: Sn; atomic no.: 50; atomic wt.: 118.69. Related adjs.: **stannic, stannous. 2** Also called (esp. US and Canad.): **can.** an airtight sealed container of thin sheet metal coated with tin, used for preserving and storing food or drink. **3** any container made of metallic tin. **4** Also called: **tinful.** the contents of a tin. **5** *Brit., Austral., & NZ.* galvanized iron: *a tin roof.* **6** any metal regarded as cheap or flimsy. **7** *Brit.* a loaf of bread with a rectangular shape. **8** *NZ.* a receptacle for home-baked biscuits, etc. (esp. in **fill her tins** to bake a supply of biscuits, etc.). ◆ *vb* **tins, tinning, tinned.** *(tr)* **9** to put (food, etc.) into a tin or tins; preserve in a tin. **10** to plate or coat with tin. **11** to prepare (a metal) for soldering or brazing by applying a thin layer of solder to the surface. [OE]

tinamou ('tɪnə,muː) *n* any of various birds of Central and South America, having small wings and a heavy body. [C18: via F from Carib *tinamu*]

Tinbergen ★ ('tɪn,bɜːgən) *n* **1 Jan** (jæn). 1903–94, Dutch economist: shared Nobel prize for economics 1969. **2** his brother, **Nikolaas** ('nɪkəlɑːs). 1907–88, British zoologist and a founder of ethology; Nobel prize for physiology or medicine 1973.

tin can *n* a metal food container, esp. when empty.

tinctorial (tɪŋkˈtɔːrɪəl) *adj* of or relating to colouring, staining, or dyeing. [C17: from L *tinctōrius*, from *tingere* to tinge]

tincture ('tɪŋktʃə) *n* **1** a medicinal extract in a solution of alcohol. **2** a tint, colour, or tinge. **3** a slight flavour, aroma, or trace. **4** a colour or metal used on heraldic arms. **5** *Obs.* a dye. ◆ *vb* **tinctures, tincturing, tinctured. 6** *(tr)* to give a tint or colour to. [C14: from L *tinctūra* a dyeing, from *tingere* to dye]

Tindal *or* **Tindale** ★ ('tɪnd°l) *n* variant spellings of (William) **Tyndale**.

tinder ('tɪndə) *n* **1** dry wood or other easily combustible material used for lighting a fire. **2** anything inflammatory or dangerous. [OE *tynder*]
▶ '**tindery** *adj*

tinderbox ('tɪndə,bɒks) *n* **1** a box used formerly for holding tinder, esp. one fitted with a flint and steel. **2** a person or thing that is particularly touchy or explosive.

tine (taɪn) *n* **1** a slender prong, esp. of a fork. **2** any of the sharp terminal branches of a deer's antler. [OE *tind*]
▶ '**tined** *adj*

★ people and places

tinea ('tɪnɪə) *n* any fungal skin disease, esp. ringworm. [C17: from L: worm]
▶ 'tineal *adj*

tinfoil ('tɪn,fɔɪl) *n* **1** thin foil made of tin or an alloy of tin and lead. **2** thin foil made of aluminium; used for wrapping foodstuffs.

ting (tɪŋ) *n* **1** a high metallic sound such as that made by a small bell. ◆ *vb* **2** to make or cause to make such a sound. [C15: imit.]

Ting ★ (tɪŋ) *n* **Samuel C(hao) C(hung).** born 1936, US physicist, who discovered the J/psi particle and shared (1976) the Nobel prize for physics.

ting-a-ling ('tɪŋə'lɪŋ) *n* the sound of a small bell.

tinge (tɪndʒ) *n* **1** a slight tint or colouring. **2** any slight addition. ◆ *vb* tinges, tingeing *or* tinging, tinged. (*tr*) **3** to colour or tint faintly. **4** to impart a slight trace to: *her thoughts were tinged with nostalgia.* [C15: from L *tingere* to colour]

tingle ('tɪŋgˀl) *vb* tingles, tingling, tingled. **1** (*usually intr*) to feel or cause to feel a prickling, itching, or stinging sensation of the flesh, as from a cold plunge. ◆ *n* **2** a sensation of tingling. [C14: ? a var. of TINKLE]
▶ 'tingler *n* ▶ 'tingling *adj* ▶ 'tingly *adj*

tin god *n* **1** a self-important person. **2** a person erroneously regarded as holy or venerable.

tin hat *n Inf.* a steel helmet worn by military personnel.

tinker ('tɪŋkə) *n* **1** (esp. formerly) a travelling mender of pots and pans. **2** a clumsy worker. **3** the act of tinkering. **4** *Scot. & Irish.* a Gypsy. ◆ *vb* **5** (*intr*; foll. by *with*) to play, fiddle, or meddle (with machinery, etc.), esp. while undertaking repairs. **6** to mend (pots and pans) as a tinker. [C13 *tinkere*, ?from *tink* tinkle, imit.]
▶ 'tinkerer *n*

tinker's damn *or* **cuss** *n Sl.* the slightest heed (esp. in **not give a tinker's damn** *or* **cuss**).

tinkle ('tɪŋkˀl) *vb* tinkles, tinkling, tinkled. **1** to ring with a high tinny sound like a small bell. **2** (*tr*) to announce or summon by such a ringing. **3** (*intr*) *Brit. inf.* to urinate. ◆ *n* **4** a high clear ringing sound. **5** the act of tinkling. **6** *Brit. inf.* a telephone call. [C14: imit.]
▶ 'tinkly *adj*

tin lizzie ('lɪzɪ) *n Inf.* an old or decrepit car.

tinned (tɪnd) *adj* **1** plated, coated, or treated with tin. **2** *Chiefly Brit.* preserved or stored in airtight tins. **3** coated with a layer of solder.

tinnitus (tɪ'naɪtəs) *n Pathol.* a ringing, hissing, or booming sensation in one or both ears, caused by infection of the ear, a side effect of certain drugs, etc. [C19: from L, from *tinnīre* to ring]

tinny ('tɪnɪ) *adj* tinnier, tinniest. **1** of or resembling tin. **2** cheap or shoddy. **3** (of a sound) high, thin, and metallic. **4** (of food or drink) flavoured with metal, as from a container. **5** *Austral. & NZ sl.* lucky. ◆ *n, pl* tinnies. **6** *Austral. sl.* a can of beer.
▶ 'tinnily *adv* ▶ 'tinniness *n*

tin-opener *n* a small tool for opening tins.

Tin Pan Alley ★ *n* **1** originally, a district in New York concerned with the production of popular music. **2** the commercial side of show business and pop music.

tin plate *n* **1** thin steel sheet coated with a layer of tin that protects the steel from corrosion. ◆ *vb* **tin-plate, tin-plates, tin-plating, tin-plated. 2** (*tr*) to coat with a layer of tin.

tinpot ('tɪn,pɒt) *adj* (*prenominal*) *Brit. inf.* **1** inferior, cheap, or worthless. **2** petty; unimportant.

tinsel ('tɪnsəl) *n* **1** a decoration consisting of a piece of string with thin strips of metal foil attached along its length. **2** a yarn or fabric interwoven with strands of glittering thread. **3** anything cheap, showy, and gaudy. ◆ *vb* **tinsels, tinselling, tinselled** *or US* **tinsels, tinseling, tinseled.** (*tr*) **4** to decorate with or as if with tinsel: *snow tinsels the trees.* **5** to give a gaudy appearance to. ◆ *adj* **6** made of or decorated with tinsel. **7** showily but cheaply attractive; gaudy. [C16: from OF *estincele* a spark, from L *scintilla*]
▶ 'tinselly *adj*

Tinseltown ★ ('tɪnsəl,taʊn) *n* an informal name for **Hol-**

lywood. [C20: from the insubstantial glitter of the film world]

tinsmith ('tɪn,smɪθ) *n* a person who works with tin or tin plate.

tin soldier *n* a miniature toy soldier, usually made of lead.

tinstone ('tɪn,stəʊn) *n* another name for **cassiterite.**

tint (tɪnt) *n* **1** a shade of a colour, esp. a pale one. **2** a colour that is softened by the addition of white. **3** a tinge. **4** a dye for the hair. **5** a trace or hint. **6** *Engraving.* uniform shading, produced esp. by hatching. ◆ *vb* **7** (*tr*) to colour or tinge. **8** (*intr*) to acquire a tint. [C18: from earlier *tinct*, from L *tingere* to colour]
▶ 'tinter *n*

Tintagel Head ★ (tɪn'tædʒəl) *n* a promontory in SW England, on the W coast of Cornwall: ruins of **Tintagel Castle**, legendary birthplace of King Arthur.

tintinnabulation (,tɪntɪ,næbjʊ'leɪʃən) *n* the act or an instance of the ringing or pealing of bells. [from L, from *tintinnāre* to tinkle, from *tinnīre* to ring]

Tintoretto ★ (,tɪntə'retəʊ; *Italian* tinto'retto) *n* **Il** (il). original name *Jacopo Robusti.* 1518–94, Italian painter of the Venetian school. His works include *Susanna bathing* (?1550) and the fresco cycle in the Scuola di San Rocco, Venice (from 1564).

tinware ('tɪn,weə) *n* objects made of tin plate.

tin whistle *n* another name for **penny whistle.**

tinworks ('tɪn,wɜːks) *n* (*functioning as sing or pl*) a place where tin is mined, smelted, or rolled.

tiny ('taɪnɪ) *adj* tinier, tiniest. very small. [C16 *tine*, from ?]
▶ 'tinily *adv* ▶ 'tininess *n*

-tion *suffix forming nouns.* indicating state, condition, action, process, or result: *election; prohibition.* [from OF, from L *-tiō, -tiōn-*]

tip¹ (tɪp) *n* **1** a narrow or pointed end of something. **2** the top or summit. **3** a small piece forming an end: *a metal tip on a cane.* ◆ *vb* tips, tipping, tipped. (*tr*) **4** to adorn or mark the tip of. **5** to cause to form a tip. [C15: from ON *typpa*]
▶ 'tipless *adj*

tip² (tɪp) *vb* tips, tipping, tipped. **1** to tilt or cause to tilt. **2** (usually foll. by *over* or *up*) to tilt or cause to tilt, so as to overturn or fall. **3** *Brit.* to dump (rubbish, etc.). **4 tip one's hat.** to raise one's hat in salutation. ◆ *n* **5** a tipping or being tipped. **6** *Brit.* a dump for refuse, etc. [C14: from ?]
▶ 'tipper *n*

tip³ (tɪp) *n* **1** a payment given for services in excess of the standard charge; gratuity. **2** a helpful hint or warning. **3** a piece of inside information, esp. in betting or investing. ◆ *vb* tips, tipping, tipped. **4** to give a tip to. [C18: ?from TIP⁴]
▶ 'tipper *n*

tip⁴ (tɪp) *vb* tips, tipping, tipped. (*tr*) **1** to hit or strike lightly. ◆ *n* **2** a light blow. [C13: ?from Low G *tippen*]

tip-off *n* **1** a warning or hint, esp. given confidentially and based on inside information. **2** *Basketball.* the act or an instance of putting the ball in play by the referee throwing it high between two opposing players. ◆ *vb* **tip off. 3** (*tr, adv*) to give a hint or warning to.

Tipperary ★ (,tɪpə'reərɪ) *n* a county of S Republic of Ireland, in Munster province; divided into the North Riding and South Riding: mountainous. County town: Clonmel. Pop.: 132 772 (1991). Area: 4255 sq. km (1643 sq. miles).

tipper truck *or* **lorry** *n* a truck or lorry the rear platform of which can be raised at the front end to enable the load to be discharged.

tippet ('tɪpɪt) *n* **1** a woman's fur cape for the shoulders. **2** the long stole of Anglican clergy worn during a service. **3** a long streamer-like part to a sleeve, hood, etc., esp. in the 16th century. [C14: ?from TIP¹]

Tippett ★ ('tɪpɪt) *n* **Sir Michael.** 1905–98, British composer, whose works include the oratorio *A Child of Our Time* (1941) and several operas.

tipple ('tɪpˀl) *vb* tipples, tippling, tippled. **1** to make a habit of taking (alcoholic drink), esp. in small quantities. ◆ *n*

2 alcoholic drink. [C15: back formation from obs. *tippler* tapster, from ?]
▶ **'tippler** *n*

tipstaff ('tɪpˌstɑːf) *n* **1** a court official. **2** a metal-tipped staff formerly used as a symbol of office. [C16 *tipped staff*]

tipster ('tɪpstə) *n* a person who sells tips on horse racing, the stock market, etc.

tipsy ('tɪpsɪ) *adj* **tipsier, tipsiest**. **1** slightly drunk. **2** slightly tilted or tipped; askew. [C16: from TIP²]
▶ **'tipsily** *adv* ▶ **'tipsiness** *n*

tipsy cake *n Brit.* a kind of trifle made from a sponge cake soaked with wine or sherry and decorated with almonds and crystallized fruit.

tiptoe ('tɪpˌtəu) *vb* **tiptoes, tiptoeing, tiptoed.** (*intr*) **1** to walk with the heels off the ground. **2** to walk silently or stealthily. ◆ *n* **3 on tiptoe. 3a** on the tips of the toes or on the ball of the foot and the toes. **3b** eagerly anticipating something. **3c** stealthily or silently. ◆ *adv* **4** on tiptoe. ◆ *adj* **5** walking or standing on tiptoe.

tiptop (ˌtɪp'top) *adj, adv* **1** at the highest point of health, excellence, etc. **2** at the topmost point. ◆ *n* **3** the best in quality. **4** the topmost point.

tip-up *adj* (*prenominal*) able to be turned upwards around a hinge or pivot: *a tip-up seat.*

TIR *abbrev. for* Transports Internationaux Routiers. [F: International Road Transport]

tirade (taɪ'reɪd) *n* a long angry speech or denunciation. [C19: from F, lit.: a pulling, from It. *tirata,* from *tirare* to pull, from ?]

Tiran ★ (tɪ'rɑːn) *n* **Strait of.** a strait between the Gulf of Aqaba and the Red Sea. Length: 16 km (10 miles). Width: 8 km (5 miles).

Tirana (tɪ'rɑːnə) *or* **Tiranë** ★ (*Albanian* ti'ranə) *n* the capital of Albania, in the central part 32 km (20 miles) from the Adriatic: founded in the early 17th century by Turks; became capital in 1920; the country's largest city and industrial centre. Pop.: 251 000 (1991).

tire¹ (taɪə) *vb* **tires, tiring, tired.** **1** (*tr*) to reduce the energy of, esp. by exertion; weary. **2** (*tr; often passive*) to reduce the tolerance of; bore or irritate: *I'm tired of the children's chatter.* **3** (*intr*) to become wearied or bored; flag. [OE *tēorian,* from ?]
▶ **'tiring** *adj*

tire² (taɪə) *n, vb* the US spelling of **tyre.**

tired ('taɪəd) *adj* **1** weary; fatigued. **2** no longer fresh; hackneyed. **3 tired and emotional.** *Euphemistic.* drunk.
▶ **'tiredness** *n*

Tiree ★ (taɪ'riː) *n* an island off the W coast of Scotland, in the Inner Hebrides. Pop.: 1054 (latest est.). Area: 78 sq. km (30 sq. miles).

tireless ('taɪəlɪs) *adj* unable to be tired.
▶ **'tirelessly** *adv* ▶ **'tirelessness** *n*

Tiresias ★ (taɪ'riːsɪˌæs) *n Greek myth.* a blind soothsayer of Thebes, who revealed to Oedipus that the latter had murdered his father and married his mother.

tiresome ('taɪəsəm) *adj* boring and irritating.
▶ **'tiresomely** *adv* ▶ **'tiresomeness** *n*

tirewoman ('taɪəˌwumən) *n, pl* **tirewomen.** an obsolete term for a lady's maid. [C17: from *tire* (obs.) to ATTIRE]

Tirgu Mureş ★ (*Romanian* 'tirgu 'mureʃ) *n* a city in central Romania: manufacturing and cultural centre. Pop.: 165 502 (1993 est.).

Tirich Mir ★ ('tɪərɪtʃ 'mɪə) *n* a mountain in N Pakistan: highest peak of the Hindu Kush. Height: 7690 m (25 230 ft).

tiring room ('taɪərɪŋ) *n Arch.* a dressing room.

tiro ('taɪrəu) *n, pl* **tiros.** a variant spelling of **tyro.**

Tirol ★ (tɪ'rəul, 'tɪrəul; *German* ti'roːl) *n* a variant spelling of **Tyrol.**
▶ **Tirolese** (ˌtɪrə'liːz) *or* ˌ**Tiro'lean** *adj, n*

Tirpitz ★ (*German* 'tɪrpɪts) *n* **Alfred von** ('alfreːt fɔn). 1849–1930, German admiral: as secretary of state for the Imperial Navy (1897–1916), he created the modern German navy.

Tiruchirapalli (ˌtɪrətʃɪrə'pʌlɪ, tɪˌruːtʃɪ'rɑːpəlɪ) *or* **Trichinopoly** ★ *n* an industrial city in S India, in central Tamil Nadu on the Cauvery River: dominated by a rock fortress 83 m (273 ft) high. Pop.: 387 223 (1991).

Tirunelveli ★ (ˌtɪru'nelvəlɪ) *n* a city in S India, in Tamil Nadu: site of St Francis Xavier's first preaching in India; textile manufacturing. Pop.: 135 825 (1991).

'tis (tɪz) *Poetic or dialect. contraction of* it is.

Tisa ★ ('tisa) *n* the Slavonic and Romanian name for the **Tisza.**

tisane (tɪ'zæn) *n* an infusion of leaves or flowers. [C19: from F, from L *ptisana* barley water]

Tishri *Hebrew.* (tɪʃ'riː) *n* (in the Jewish calendar) the seventh month of the year according to biblical reckoning and the first month of the civil year, falling in September and October. [C19: from Heb.]

Tisiphone ★ (tɪ'sɪfənɪ) *n Greek myth.* one of the three Furies; the others are Alecto and Megaera.

Tissot ★ ('tiːsəu; *French* tiso) *n* **James Joseph Jacques.** 1836–1902, French painter, who worked in England.

tissue ('tɪsjuː, 'tɪʃuː) *n* **1** a part of an organism consisting of a large number of cells having a similar structure and function: nerve tissue. **2** a thin piece of soft absorbent paper used as a disposable handkerchief, towel, etc. **3** See **tissue paper. 4** an interwoven series: *a tissue of lies.* **5** a woven cloth, esp. of a light gauzy nature. ◆ *vb* **tissues, tissuing, tissued.** (*tr*) **6** to decorate or clothe with tissue or tissue paper. [C14: from OF *tissu* woven cloth, from *tistre* to weave, from L *texere*]

tissue culture *n* **1** the growth of small pieces of animal or plant tissue in a sterile controlled medium. **2** the tissue produced.

tissue paper *n* very thin soft delicate paper used to wrap breakable goods, as decoration, etc.

Tisza ★ (*Hungarian* 'tisɔ) *n* a river in S central Europe, rising in the W Ukraine and flowing west, forming part of the border between the Ukraine and Romania, then southwest across Hungary into Yugoslavia to join the Danube north of Belgrade. Slavonic and Romanian name: **Tisa.**

tit¹ (tɪt) *n* any of numerous small active Old World songbirds, esp. the bluetit, great tit, etc. They have a short bill and feed on insects and seeds. [C16: ? imit., applied to small animate or inanimate objects]

tit² (tɪt) *n* **1** *Sl.* a female breast. **2** a teat or nipple. **3** *Derog.* a young woman. **4** *Taboo sl.* a despicable or unpleasant person. [OE *titt*]

Tit. *Bible. abbrev. for* Titus.

titan ('taɪt³n) *n* a person of great strength or size. [after TITAN]

Titan ('taɪt³n) *or* (*fem*) **Titaness** *n Greek myth.* **1** any of a family of primordial gods, the sons and daughters of Uranus (sky) and Gaea (earth). **2** any of the offspring of the children of Uranus and Gaea.
▶ **Titanesque** (ˌtaɪtə'nesk) *adj*

Titania ★ (tɪ'tɑːnɪə) *n* **1** (in medieval folklore) the queen of the fairies and wife of Oberon. **2** (in classical antiquity) a poetic epithet used of Circe, Diana, Latona, or Pyrrha.

titanic (taɪ'tænɪk) *adj* possessing or requiring colossal strength: *a titanic battle.*

titanium (taɪ'teɪnɪəm) *n* a strong malleable white metallic element, which is very corrosion-resistant. It is used in the manufacture of strong lightweight alloys, esp. aircraft parts. Symbol: Ti; atomic no.: 22; atomic wt.: 47.88. [C18: NL; see TITAN, -IUM]

titanium dioxide *n* a white powder used chiefly as a pigment. Formula: TiO_2. Also called: **titanium oxide, titanic oxide, titania.**

titbit ('tɪtˌbɪt) *or esp. US* **tidbit** *n* **1** a tasty small piece of food; dainty. **2** a pleasing scrap of anything, such as scandal. [C17: ?from dialect *tid* tender, from ?]

titchy *or* **tichy** ('tɪtʃɪ) *adj* **titchier, titchiest** *or* **tichier, tichiest.** *Brit. sl.* very small; tiny. [C20: from *tich* or *titch* a small person, from *Little Tich,* stage name of Harry Relph (1867–1928), E actor noted for his small stature]

★ people and places

titfer ('tɪtfə) *n Brit. sl.* a hat. [from rhyming slang *tit for tat*]

tit for tat *n* an equivalent given in return or retaliation; blow for blow. [C16: from earlier *tip for tap*]

tithe (taɪð) *n* **1** (*often pl*) a tenth part of produce, income, or profits, contributed for the support of the church or clergy. **2** any levy, esp. of one tenth. **3** a tenth or a very small part of anything. ♦ *vb* **tithes, tithing, tithed. 4** (*tr*) **4a** to exact or demand a tithe from. **4b** to levy a tithe upon. **5** (*intr*) to pay a tithe or tithes. [OE *teogoth*]
▶ 'tithable *adj*

tithe barn *n* a large barn where, formerly, the agricultural tithe of a parish was stored.

Tithonus ★ (tɪ'θəʊnəs) *n Greek myth.* the son of Laomedon of Troy who was loved by the goddess Eos. She asked that he be made immortal but forgot to ask that he be made eternally young. When he aged she turned him into a grasshopper.

titi ('tiːtiː) *n, pl* **titis.** any of a genus of small New World monkeys of South America, having beautifully coloured fur and a long nonprehensile tail. [via Sp. from Aymara, lit.: little cat]

Titian ★ ('tɪʃən) *n* original name *Tiziano Vecellio.* ?1490–1576, Italian painter of the Venetian school.
▶ ,Titian'esque *adj*

Titian red *n* a reddish-yellow colour, as in the hair colour in many of the works of Titian.

Titicaca ★ (*Spanish* titi'kaka) *n* **Lake.** a lake between S Peru and W Bolivia, in the Andes: the highest large lake in the world; drained by the Desaguadero River flowing into Lake Poopó. Area: 8135 sq. km (3141 sq. miles). Altitude: 3809 m (12 497 ft). Depth: 370 m (1214 ft).

titillate ('tɪtɪ,leɪt) *vb* **titillates, titillating, titillated.** (*tr*) **1** to arouse or excite pleasurably. **2** to cause a tickling or tingling sensation in, esp. by touching. [C17: from L *titillāre*]
▶ 'titil,lating *adj* ▶ ,titil'lation *n*

titivate *or* **tittivate** ('tɪtɪ,veɪt) *vb* **titivates, titivating, titivated** *or* **tittivates, tittivating, tittivated.** to smarten up; spruce up. [C19: earlier *tidivate*, ? based on TIDY & CULTIVATE]
▶ ,titi'vation *or* ,titti'vation *n*

titlark ('tɪt,lɑːk) *n* another name for **pipit**, esp. the meadow pipit. [C17: from TIT¹ + LARK¹]

title ('taɪt²l) *n* **1** the distinctive name of a work of art, musical or literary composition, etc. **2** a descriptive name or heading of a section of a book, speech, etc. **3** See title page. **4** a name or epithet signifying rank, office, or function. **5** a formal designation, such as *Mr.* **6** an appellation designating nobility. **7** *Films.* **7a** short for subtitle. **7b** written material giving credits in a film or television programme. **8** *Sport.* a championship. **9** *Law.* **9a** the legal right to possession of property, esp. real property. **9b** the basis of such right. **9c** the documentary evidence of such right: *title deeds.* **10a** any customary or established right. **10b** a claim based on such a right. **11** a definite spiritual charge or office in the church as a prerequisite for ordination. **12** *RC Church.* a titular church. ♦ *vb* **titles, titling, titled. 13** (*tr*) to give a title to. [C13: from OF, from L *titulus*]

title deed *n* a document evidencing a person's legal right or title to property, esp. real property.

titleholder ('taɪt²l,həʊldə) *n* a person who holds a title, esp. a sporting championship.

title page *n* the page in a book that gives the title, author, publisher, etc.

title role *n* the role of the character after whom a play, etc., is named.

titmouse ('tɪt,maʊs) *n, pl* **titmice.** another name for **tit¹**. [C14: *titemous*, from *tite* (see TIT¹) + MOUSE]

Tito ★ ('tiːtəʊ) *n* **Marshal.** original name *Josip Broz.* 1892–1980, Yugoslav statesman, who led the communist guerrilla resistance to German occupation during World War II; prime minister (1945–53) and president (1953–80).

Titograd ★ (*Serbo-Croat* 'tɪtəgraːd) *n* the former name (1946–92) of **Podgorica.**

titrate ('taɪtreɪt) *vb* **titrates, titrating, titrated.** (*tr*) to measure the volume or the concentration of (a solution) by titration. [C19: from F *titrer;* see TITRE]
▶ ti'tratable *adj*

titration (taɪ'treɪʃən) *n* an operation in which a measured amount of one solution is added to a known quantity of another solution until the reaction between the two is complete. If the concentration of one solution is known, that of the other can be calculated.

titre *or US* **titer** ('taɪtə) *n* the concentration of a solution as determined by titration. [C19: from F *titre* proportion of gold or silver in an alloy, from OF *title* TITLE]

titter ('tɪtə) *vb* (*intr*) **1** to snigger, esp. derisively or in a suppressed way. ♦ *n* **2** a suppressed laugh, chuckle, or snigger. [C17: imit.]
▶ 'titterer *n* ▶ 'tittering *adj*

tittle ('tɪt²l) *n* **1** a small mark in printing or writing, esp. a diacritic. **2** a jot; particle. [C14: from Med. L *titulus* label, from L: title]

tittle-tattle *n* **1** idle chat or gossip. ♦ *vb* **tittle-tattles, tittle-tattling, tittle-tattled. 2** (*intr*) to chatter or gossip.
▶ 'tittle-,tattler *n*

tittup ('tɪtəp) *vb* **tittups, tittupping, tittupped** *or US* **tittups, tittuping, tittuped. 1** (*intr*) to prance or frolic. ♦ *n* **2** a caper. [C18 (in the sense: a horse's gallop): prob. imit.]

titubation (,tɪtjʊ'beɪʃən) *n Pathol.* a disordered gait characterized by stumbling or staggering, often caused by a lesion of the cerebellum. [C17: from L *titubātiō*, from *titubāre* to reel]

titular ('tɪtjʊlə) *adj* **1** of, relating to, or of the nature of a title. **2** in name only. **3** bearing a title. **4** *RC Church.* designating any of certain churches in Rome to whom cardinals or bishops are attached as their nominal incumbents. ♦ *n* **5** the bearer of a title. **6** the bearer of a nominal office. [C18: from F *titulaire*, from L *titulus* title]

Titus ★ ('taɪtəs) *n* **1** *New Testament.* **1a** a Greek disciple and helper of Saint Paul. Feast day: Jan. 26 or Aug. 25. **1b** the book written to him (in full **The Epistle of Paul the Apostle to Titus**). **2** full name *Titus Flavius Sabinus Vespasianus.* ?40–81 A.D., Roman emperor (78–81 A.D.).

Tiu ★ ('tiːuː) *n* (in Anglo-Saxon mythology) the god of war and the sky. Norse counterpart: **Tyr.**

Tivoli ★ ('tɪvəlɪ; *Italian* 'tiːvoli) *n* a town in central Italy, east of Rome: a summer resort in Roman times; contains the Renaissance Villa d'Este and the remains of Hadrian's Villa. Pop.: 55 030 (1990). Ancient name: **Tibur.**

tizzy ('tɪzɪ) *n, pl* **tizzies.** *Inf.* a state of confusion or excitement. Also called: **tizz, tiz-woz.** [C19: from ?]

Tjirebon *or* **Cheribon** ★ ('tʃɪərə,bɒn) *n* a port in S central Indonesia, on N Java on the Java Sea: scene of the signing of the **Tjirebon Agreement** of Indonesian independence (1946) by the Netherlands. Pop.: 245 307 (1990).

T-junction *n* a road junction in which one road joins another at right angles but does not cross it.

TKO *Boxing. abbrev. for* technical knockout.

Tl *the chemical symbol for* thallium.

Tlaxcala ★ (*Spanish* tlas'kala) *n* **1** a state of S central Mexico: the smallest Mexican state; formerly an Indian principality, the chief Indian ally of Cortés in the conquest of Mexico. Capital: Tlaxcala. Pop.: 883 630 (1995 est.). Area: 3914 sq. km (1511 sq. miles). **2** a city in E central Mexico, capital of Tlaxcala state: the church of San Francisco (founded 1521 by Cortés) is the oldest in the Americas. Pop.: 25 000 (1990 est.). Official name: **Tlaxcala de Xicohténcatl.**

Tlemcen ★ (*French* tlɛmsɛn) *n* a city in NW Algeria: capital of an Arab kingdom from the 12th to the late 14th century. Pop.: 107 632 (1987).

Tm *the chemical symbol for* thulium.

TM *abbrev. for* transcendental meditation.

tmesis (tə'miːsɪs) *n* interpolation of a word or words between the parts of a compound word, as in *every-blooming-where.* [C16: via L from Gk, lit.: a cutting, from *temnein* to cut]

TN *abbrev. for* Tennessee.

★ people and places

TNT *n* 2,4,6-trinitrotoluene; a yellow solid: used chiefly as a high explosive.

T-number *or* **T number** *n Photog.* a function of the f-number of a lens that takes into account the light transmitted by the lens. [from *T(otal Light Transmission) Number*]

to (tuː; *unstressed* tʊ, tə) *prep* **1** used to indicate the destination of the subject or object of an action: *he climbed to the top.* **2** used to mark the indirect object of a verb: *telling stories to children.* **3** used to mark the infinitive of a verb: *he wanted to go.* **4** as far as; until: *working from Monday to Friday.* **5** used to indicate equality: *16 ounces to the pound.* **6** against; upon; onto: *put your ear to the wall.* **7** before the hour of: *five minutes to four.* **8** accompanied by: *dancing to loud music.* **9** as compared with, as against: *the score was eight to three.* **10** used to indicate a resulting condition: *they starved to death.* ◆ *adv* **11** towards a fixed position, esp. (of a door) closed. [OE *tō*]

toad (təʊd) *n* **1** any of a group of amphibians similar to frogs but more terrestrial, having a drier warty skin. **2** a loathsome person. [OE *tādige*, from ?]
▸ **'toadish** *adj*

toadfish ('təʊd,fɪʃ) *n, pl* **toadfish** *or* **toadfishes.** any of various spiny-finned marine fishes of tropical and temperate seas.

toadflax ('təʊd,flæks) *n* a perennial plant having narrow leaves and spurred two-lipped yellow-orange flowers. Also called: **butter-and-eggs.**

toad-in-the-hole *n Brit. & Austral.* a dish made of sausages baked in a batter.

toadstone ('təʊd,stəʊn) *n* an intrusive volcanic rock occurring in limestone. [C18: ?from a supposed resemblance to a toad's spotted skin]

toadstool ('təʊd,stuːl) *n* (*not in technical use*) any basidiomycetous fungus with a capped spore-producing body that is poisonous. Cf. **mushroom.**

toady ('təʊdɪ) *n, pl* **toadies. 1** Also: **toadeater.** a person who flatters and ingratiates himself in a servile way; sycophant. ◆ *vb* **toadies, toadying, toadied. 2** to fawn on and flatter (someone). [C19: shortened from *toadeater,* orig. a quack's assistant who pretended to eat toads, hence a flatterer]
▸ **'toadyish** *adj* ▸ **'toadyism** *n*

Toamasina ★ (*Portuguese* tōuma'sinə) *n* a port in E Madagascar, on the Indian Ocean: the country's chief commercial centre. Pop.: 127 441 (1993). Former name (until 1979): **Tamatave.**

to and fro *adv,* **to-and-fro** *adj* **1** back and forth. **2** here and there.
▸ **'toing and 'froing** *n*

toast[1] (təʊst) *n* **1a** sliced bread browned by exposure to heat. **1b** (*as modifier*): *a toast rack.* ◆ *vb* **2** (*tr*) to brown under a grill or over a fire: *to toast cheese.* **3** to warm or be warmed: *to toast one's hands by the fire.* [C14: from OF *toster,* from L *tōstus* parched, from *torrēre* to dry with heat]

toast[2] (təʊst) *n* **1** a tribute or proposal of health, success, etc., given to a person or thing and marked by people raising glasses and drinking together. **2** a person or thing honoured by such a tribute or proposal. **3** (esp. formerly) an attractive woman to whom such tributes are frequently made. ◆ *vb* **4** to propose or drink a toast to (a person or thing). **5** (*intr*) to add vocal effects to a prerecorded track: *a disc-jockey technique.* [C17 (in the sense: a lady to whom the company is asked to drink): from TOAST[1], from the idea that the name of the lady would flavour the drink like a piece of spiced toast]
▸ **'toaster** *n*

toaster ('təʊstə) *n* a device, esp. an electrical device, for toasting bread.

toastmaster ('təʊst,mɑːstə) *n* a person who introduces speakers, proposes toasts, etc., at public dinners.
▸ **'toast,mistress** *fem n*

toasty *or* **toastie** ('təʊstɪ) *n, pl* **toasties.** a toasted sandwich.

Tob. *abbrev. for* Tobit.

tobacco (tə'bækəʊ) *n, pl* **tobaccos** *or* **tobaccoes. 1** any of a

genus of plants having mildly narcotic properties, one species of which is cultivated as the chief source of commercial tobacco. **2** the leaves of certain of these plants dried and prepared for snuff, chewing, or smoking. [C16: from Sp. *tabaco,* ?from Taino: leaves rolled for smoking, assumed by the Spaniards to be the name of the plant]

tobacco mosaic virus *n* the virus that causes mosaic disease in tobacco and related plants: its discovery provided the first evidence of the existence of viruses. Abbrev.: **TMV.**

tobacconist (tə'bækənɪst) *n Chiefly Brit.* a person or shop that sells tobacco, cigarettes, pipes, etc.

Tobago ★ (tə'beɪgəʊ) *n* an island in the SE Caribbean, northeast of Trinidad: ceded to Britain in 1814; joined with Trinidad in 1888 as a British colony; part of the independent republic of Trinidad and Tobago. Pop.: 46 400 (1990).
▸ **Tobagonian** (ˌtəʊbəˈgəʊnɪən) *adj, n*

-to-be *adj* (*in combination*) about to be; future: *a mother-to-be; the bride-to-be.*

Tobey ★ ('təʊbɪ) *n* **Mark.** 1890–1976, US painter. Influenced by Chinese calligraphy, he devised a style of improvisatory abstract painting called "white writing".

Tobit ★ ('təʊbɪt) *n Old Testament.* **1** a pious Jew who was released from blindness through the help of the archangel Raphael. **2** a book of the Apocrypha relating this story.

toboggan (tə'bɒgən) *n* **1** a light wooden frame on runners used for sliding over snow and ice. **2** a long narrow sledge made of a thin board curved upwards at the front. ◆ *vb* **toboggans, tobogganing, tobogganed.** (*intr*) **3** to ride on a toboggan. [C19: from Canad. F, of Amerind origin]
▸ **to'bogganer** *or* **to'bogganist** *n*

Tobol ★ (*Russian* ta'bɔl) *n* a river in central Asia, rising in N Kazakhstan and flowing northeast to join the Irtysh River in Russia. Length: about 1300 km (800 miles).

Tobolsk ★ (*Russian* ta'bɔljsk) *n* a town in central Asia, at the confluence of the Irtysh and Tobol Rivers: the chief centre for the early Russian colonization of Siberia. Pop.: 83 000 (1988 est.).

Tobruk ★ (tə'brʊk, təʊ-) *n* a small port in NE Libya, in E Cyrenaica on the Mediterranean coast road: scene of severe fighting in World War II: taken from the Italians in the British in January 1941, from the British by the Germans in June 1942, and finally taken by the British in November 1942.

toby ('təʊbɪ) *n, pl* **tobies.** *NZ.* a water stopcock at the boundary of a street and house section.

toby jug *n* a beer mug or jug in the form of a stout seated man wearing a three-cornered hat and smoking a pipe. Also called: **toby.** [C19: from the familiar form of the name *Tobias*]

Tocantins ★ (*Portuguese* tokã'tĩs) *n* **1** a state of N Brazil, created from the northern part of Goiás state in 1988. Capital: Palmas. Pop.: 1 007 000 (1995 est.). Area: 278 421 sq. km (107 499 sq. miles). **2** a river in E Brazil, rising in S central Goiás state and flowing generally north to the Pará River. Length: about 2700 km (1700 miles).

toccata (tə'kɑːtə) *n* a rapid keyboard composition for organ, harpsichord, etc., usually in a rhythmically free style. [C18: from It., lit.: touched, from *toccare* to play (an instrument)]

Toc H ('tɒk 'eɪtʃ) *n* a society formed after World War I to encourage Christian comradeship. [C20: from the obs. telegraphic code for *T.H.,* initials of *Talbot House,* Poperinge, Belgium, the original headquarters of the society]

Tocharian *or* **Tokharian** (tɒ'kɑːrɪən) *n* **1** a member of an Asian people who lived in the Tarim Basin until around 800 A.D. **2** the language of this people, known from records in a N Indian script of the 7th and 8th centuries A.D. [C20: ult. from Gk *Tokharoi,* from ?]

tocopherol (tɒ'kɒfə,rɒl) *n* any of a group of fat-soluble alcohols that occur in wheat-germ oil, lettuce, egg yolk,

---

★ people and places

etc. Also called: **vitamin E**. [C20: from *toco-*, from Gk *tokos* offspring + *-pher-*, from *pherein* to bear + -OL[1]]

Tocqueville ★ ('təʊkvɪl, 'tɒk-; *French* tɔkvil) *n* **Alexis Charles Henri Maurice Clérel de** (aleksi ʃarl ᾶri mɔris klerεl də). 1805–59, French political writer. His works include *L'Ancien régime et la révolution* (1856).

tocsin ('tɒksɪn) *n* **1** an alarm or warning signal, esp. one sounded on a bell. **2** an alarm bell. [C16: from F, from OF *toquassen*, from OProvençal, from *tocar* to touch + *senh* bell, from L *signum*]

tod (tɒd) *n* **on one's tod**. *Brit. sl*. on one's own. [C19: rhyming sl. *Tod Sloan/alone*, after *Tod* Sloan, a jockey]

today (tə'deɪ) *n* **1** this day, as distinct from yesterday or tomorrow. **2** the present age. ◆ *adv* **3** during or on this day. **4** nowadays. [OE *tō dæge*, lit.: on this day]

Todd ★ (tɒd) *n* Baron **Alexander Robertus**. 1907–97, British chemist, noted for his work on nucleic acids: Nobel prize for chemistry 1957.

toddle ('tɒd²l) *vb* **toddles, toddling, toddled.** (*intr*) **1** to walk with short unsteady steps, as a child. **2** (foll. by *off*) *Jocular*. to depart. **3** (foll. by *round, over*, etc.) *Jocular*. to stroll. ◆ *n* **4** the act or an instance of toddling. [C16 (Scot. & N English): from ?]

toddler ('tɒdlə) *n* a young child, usually between the ages of one and two and a half.

toddy ('tɒdɪ) *n, pl* **toddies. 1** a drink made from spirits, esp. whisky, hot water, sugar, and usually lemon juice. **2** the sap of various palm trees used as a beverage. [C17: from Hindi *tārī* juice of the palmyra palm, from *tār* palmyra palm, from Sansk. *tāra*]

to-do (tə'duː) *n, pl* **to-dos.** a commotion, fuss, or quarrel.

toe (təʊ) *n* **1** any one of the digits of the foot. **2** the corresponding part in other vertebrates. **3** the part of a shoe, etc., covering the toes. **4** anything resembling a toe in shape or position. **5 on one's toes**. alert. **6 tread on someone's toes**. to offend a person, esp. by trespassing on his field of responsibility. ◆ *vb* **toes, toeing, toed**. **7** (*tr*) to touch, kick, or mark with the toe. **8** (*tr*) to drive (a nail, etc.) obliquely. **9** (*intr*) to walk with the toes pointing in a specified direction: *to toe inwards*. **10 toe the line** *or* **mark**. to conform to expected attitudes, standards, etc. [OE *tā*]

toe and heel *n* a technique used by racing drivers on sharp bends, in which the brake and accelerator are operated simultaneously by the toe and heel of the right foot.

toecap ('təʊ,kæp) *n* a reinforced covering for the toe of a boot or shoe.

toed (təʊd) *adj* **1** having a part resembling a toe. **2** fixed by nails driven in at the foot. **3** (*in combination*) having a toe or toes as specified: *five-toed; thick-toed*.

toehold ('təʊ,həʊld) *n* **1** a small foothold to facilitate climbing. **2** any means of gaining access, support, etc. **3** a wrestling hold in which the opponent's toe is held and his leg twisted.

toe-in *n* a slight forward convergence given to the wheels of motor vehicles to improve steering.

toenail ('təʊ,neɪl) *n* **1** a thin horny translucent plate covering part of the surface of the end joint of each toe. **2** *Carpentry*. a nail driven obliquely. ◆ *vb* **3** (*tr*) *Carpentry*. to join (beams) by driving nails obliquely.

toerag ('təʊ,ræg) *n Brit. sl*. a contemptible or despicable person. [C20: orig., a beggar, tramp: from the rags wrapped round their feet]

toey ('təʊɪ) *adj Austral. sl*. nervous and restless; anxious.

toff (tɒf) *n Brit. sl*. a well-dressed or upper-class person, esp. a man. [C19: ? var. of TUFT, nickname for a titled student at Oxford University, wearing a cap with a gold tassel]

toffee *or* **toffy** ('tɒfɪ) *n, pl* **toffees** *or* **toffies. 1** a sweet made from sugar or treacle boiled with butter, nuts, etc. **2 for toffee**. (preceded by *can't*) *Inf*. to be incompetent at: *he can't sing for toffee*. [C19: var. of earlier *taffy*]

toffee-apple *n* an apple fixed on a stick and coated with a thin layer of toffee.

toffee-nosed *adj Sl., chiefly Brit*. pretentious or supercilious; used esp. of snobbish people.

toft (tɒft) *n Brit. history*. **1** a homestead. **2** a homestead and its arable land. [OE]

tofu ('təʊ,fuː) *n* unfermented soya-bean curd, a food with a soft cheeselike consistency. [from Japanese]

tog[1] (tɒg) *Inf*. ◆ *vb* **togs, togging, togged**. **1** (often foll. by *up* or *out*) to dress oneself, esp. in smart clothes. ◆ *n* **2** See **togs**. [C18: ?from obs. cant *togemans* coat, from L *toga* TOGA + *-mans*, from ?]

tog[2] (tɒg) *n* **a** a unit of thermal resistance used to measure the power of insulation of a fabric, garment, quilt, etc. **b** (*as modifier*): *tog-rating*. [C20: arbitrary coinage from TOG[1] (n)]

toga ('təʊgə) *n* **1** a garment worn by citizens of ancient Rome, consisting of a piece of cloth draped around the body. **2** a robe of office. [C16: from L]
► **togaed** ('təʊgəd) *adj*

together (tə'gεðə) *adv* **1** with cooperation and interchange between constituent elements, members, etc.: *we worked together*. **2** in or into contact with each other: *to stick papers together*. **3** in or into one place; with each other: *the people are gathered together*. **4** at the same time. **5** considered collectively: *all our wages put together couldn't buy that car*. **6** continuously: *working for eight hours together*. **7** closely or compactly united or held: *water will hold the dough together*. **8** mutually or reciprocally: *to multiply seven and eight together*. **9** *Inf*. organized: *to get things together*. ◆ *adj* **10** *Sl*. self-possessed, competent, and well-organized. **11 together with**. (*prep*) in addition to. [OE *tōgædre*]

USAGE NOTE See at **plus**.

togetherness (tə'gεðənɪs) *n* a feeling of closeness or affection from being united with other people.

toggery ('tɒgərɪ) *n Inf*. clothes; togs.

toggle ('tɒg²l) *n* **1** a peg or rod at the end of a rope, chain, or cable, for fastening by insertion through an eye in another rope, chain, etc. **2** a bar-shaped button inserted through a loop for fastening. **3** a toggle joint or a device having such a joint. ◆ *vb* **toggles, toggling, toggled**. **4** (*tr*) to supply or fasten with a toggle. [C18: from ?]

toggle joint *n* a device consisting of two arms pivoted at a common joint and at their outer ends and used to apply pressure by straightening the angle between the two arms.

toggle switch *n* **1** an electric switch having a projecting lever that is manipulated in a particular way to open or close a circuit. **2** a computer device used to turn a feature on or off.

Togliatti ★ (ˌtɒlɪ'ætɪ) *n* a city in W central Russia, on the Volga River: automobile industry: renamed in honour of Palmiro Togliatti (1893–1964), an Italian communist. Pop.: 702 000 (1995 est.). Former name (until 1964): **Stavropol**. Russian name: **Tol'yatti**.

Togo[1] ★ ('təʊgəʊ) *n* a republic in West Africa, on the Gulf of Guinea: became French Togoland (a League of Nations mandate) after the division of German Togoland in 1922; independent since 1960. Official language: French. Religion: animist majority. Currency: franc. Capital: Lomé. Pop.: 4 736 000 (1997). Area: 56 700 sq. km (20 900 sq. miles).
► **Togolese** (ˌtəʊgə'liːz) *adj, n*

Togo[2] ★ ('təʊgəʊ) *n* Marquis **Heihachiro** (ˌheɪhɑː'tʃiːrəʊ). 1847–1934, Japanese admiral, who commanded the fleet in the war with Russia (1904–05).

Togoland ★ ('təʊgəʊˌlænd) *n* a former German protectorate in West Africa on the Gulf of Guinea: divided in 1922 into the League of Nations mandates of British Togoland (west) and French Togoland (east); the former joined Ghana in 1957; the latter became independent as Togo in 1960.
► **Togo,lander** *n*

togs (tɒgz) *pl n Inf*. **1** clothes. **2** *Austral., NZ, & Irish*. a swimming costume. [from TOG[1]]

toheroa (ˌtəʊə'rəʊə) *n* a large edible bivalve mollusc of New Zealand with a distinctive flavour. [from Maori]

★ people and places

tohunga ('tɒhʊŋə) *n NZ.* a Maori priest, the repository of traditional lore.

toil[1] (tɔɪl) *n* **1** hard or exhausting work. ◆ *vb (intr)* **2** to labour. **3** to progress with slow painful movements. [C13: from Anglo-F *toiler* to struggle, from OF *toeillier* to confuse, from L *tudiculāre* to stir, ult. from *tundere* to beat]
▶ 'toiler *n*

toil[2] (tɔɪl) *n* **1** (*often pl*) a net or snare. **2** *Arch.* a trap for wild beasts. [C16: from OF *toile*, from L *tēla* loom]

toile (twɑːl) *n* **1** a transparent linen or cotton fabric. **2** a garment of exclusive design made up in cheap cloth so that alterations can be made. [C19: from F, from L *tēla* a loom]

toilet ('tɔɪlɪt) *n* **1** another word for **lavatory**. **2** *Old-fashioned.* the act of dressing and preparing oneself. **3** *Old-fashioned.* a dressing table. **4** *Rare.* costume. **5** the cleansing of a wound, etc., after an operation or childbirth. [C16: from F *toilette* dress, from TOILE]

toilet paper *or* **tissue** *n* thin absorbent paper, often wound in a roll round a cardboard cylinder (**toilet roll**), used for cleaning oneself after defecation or urination.

toiletry ('tɔɪlɪtrɪ) *n, pl* **toiletries.** an object or cosmetic used in making up, dressing, etc.

toilet set *n* a matching set consisting of a hairbrush, comb, mirror, and clothes brush.

toilette (twɑːˈlɛt) *n* another word for **toilet** (sense 2). [C16: from F; see TOILET]

toilet water *n* a form of liquid perfume lighter than cologne.

toilsome ('tɔɪlsəm) *or* **toilful** *adj* laborious.
▶ 'toilsomely *adv* ▶ 'toilsomeness *n*

toitoi ('tɔɪtɔɪ) *n* a tall New Zealand grass with feathery seed-heads. [from Maori]

Tojo ★ ('təʊdʒəʊ) *n* **Hideki** ('hiːdɛˌkiː). 1885–1948, Japanese soldier and statesman; minister of war (1940–41) and premier (1941–44); hanged as a war criminal.

tokamak ('təʊkəˌmæk) *n Physics.* a toroidal reactor used in thermonuclear experiments, in which strong axial magnetic fields keep the plasma from contacting the external walls. [C20: from Russian acronym, from *to(roidál'naya) kám(era s) ak(siál'nym magnitnym pólem)*, toroidal chamber with magnetic field]

Tokay (təʊˈkeɪ) *n* **1** a sweet wine made near Tokaj, Hungary. **2** a variety of grape used to make this. **3** a similar wine made elsewhere.

Tokelau Islands ★ ('təʊkəˌlaʊ) *pl n* an island group in the South Pacific composed of three atolls, Nukunono, Atafu, and Fakaofo, which in 1948 was included within the territorial boundaries of New Zealand. Pop.: 1577 (1991). Area: about 11 sq. km (4 sq. miles).

token ('təʊkən) *n* **1** an indication, warning, or sign of something. **2** a symbol or visible representation of something. **3** something that indicates authority, proof, etc. **4** a metal or plastic disc, such as a substitute for currency for use in slot machines. **5** a memento. **6** a gift voucher that can be used as payment for goods of a specified value. **7** (*modifier*) as a matter of form only; nominal: *a token increase in salary.* ◆ *vb* **8** (*tr*) to act or serve as a warning or symbol of; betoken. [OE *tācen*]

tokenism ('təʊkəˌnɪzəm) *n* the practice of making only a token effort or doing no more than the minimum, esp. in order to comply with a law.
▶ 'toke,nist *adj*

token money *n* coins having greater face value than the value of their metal content.

token strike *n* a brief strike intended to convey strength of feeling on a disputed issue.

token vote *n* a Parliamentary vote of money in which the amount quoted is not binding.

tokoloshe (ˌtɒkɒˈlɒʃ, -ˈlɒʃɪ) *n* (in Bantu folklore) a malevolent mythical manlike animal. Also called: **tikoloshe**. [from Xhosa *uthikoloshe*]

toktokkie ('tɒkˌtɒkɪ) *n* a large S. African beetle. [from Afrik., from Du. *tokken* to tap]

Tokugawa Iyeyasu ★ (ˌtəʊkuːˈgɑːwə ˌiːjerˈjɑːsuː) *n* See (Tokugawa) **Iyeyasu**.

Tokyo ★ ('təʊkjəʊ, -kɪˌəʊ) *n* the capital of Japan, a port on SE Honshu on **Tokyo Bay** (an inlet of the Pacific): part of the largest conurbation in the world (the Tokyo-Yukohama metropolitan area) of over 25 million people; major industrial centre and the chief cultural centre of Japan. Pop.: 7 966 195 (1995).

tolbooth ('təʊlˌbuːθ, -ˌbuːð, 'tɒl-) *n* **1** *Chiefly Scot.* a town hall. **2** a variant spelling of **tollbooth.**

tolbutamide (tɒlˈbjuːtəˌmaɪd) *n* a synthetic crystalline compound used in the treatment of diabetes to lower blood glucose levels. [C20: from TOL(UENE) + BUT(YRIC ACID) + AMIDE]

told (təʊld) *vb* **1** the past tense and past participle of **tell**[1]. ◆ *adj* **2** See **all told.**

tole (təʊl) *n* enamelled or lacquered metal ware, popular in the 18th century. [from F *tôle* sheet metal, from F (dialect): table, from L *tabula* table]

Toledo ★ *n* **1** (tɒˈleɪdəʊ; *Spanish* toˈleðo). a city in central Spain, on the River Tagus: capital of Visigothic Spain, and of Castile from 1087 to 1560; famous for steel and swords since the first century. Pop.: 63 560 (1991). Ancient name: **Toletum** (təˈliːtəm). **2** (təˈliːdəʊ). an inland port in NW Ohio, on Lake Erie: one of the largest coal-shipping ports in the world; transportation and industrial centre; university (1872). Pop.: 322 550 (1994 est.). **3** a fine-tapered sword or sword blade.

tolerable ('tɒlərəbᵊl) *adj* **1** able to be tolerated; endurable. **2** permissible. **3** *Inf.* fairly good.
▶ ,tolera'bility *n* ▶ 'tolerably *adv*

tolerance ('tɒlərəns) *n* **1** the state or quality of being tolerant. **2** capacity to endure something, esp. pain or hardship. **3** the permitted variation in some characteristic of an object or workpiece. **4** the capacity to endure the effects of a poison or other substance, esp. after it has been taken over a prolonged period.

tolerant ('tɒlərənt) *adj* **1** able to tolerate the beliefs, actions, etc., of others. **2** permissive. **3** able to withstand extremes. **4** exhibiting tolerance to a drug.
▶ 'tolerantly *adv*

tolerate ('tɒləˌreɪt) *vb* **tolerates, tolerating, tolerated.** (*tr*) **1** to treat with indulgence or forbearance. **2** to permit. **3** to be able to bear; put up with. **4** to have tolerance for (a drug, etc.). [C16: from L *tolerāre* to sustain]

toleration (ˌtɒləˈreɪʃən) *n* **1** the act or practice of tolerating. **2** freedom to hold religious opinions that differ from the established religion of a country.
▶ ,toler'ationist *n*

Tolima ★ (*Spanish* toˈlima) *n* a volcano in W Colombia, in the Andes. Height: 5215 m (17 110 ft).

Tolkien ★ ('tɒlkiːn) *n* **J(ohn) R(onald) R(euel).** 1892–1973, British writer, born in South Africa. He is best known for *The Hobbit* (1937), *The Lord of the Rings* (1954–55), and the posthumous *Silmarillion* (1977).

toll[1] (təʊl) *vb* **1** to ring slowly and recurrently. **2** (*tr*) to summon or announce by tolling. **3** *US & Canad.* to decoy (game, esp. ducks). ◆ *n* **4** the act or sound of tolling. [C15: ? rel. to OE *-tyllan*, as in *fortyllan* to attract]

toll[2] (təʊl, tɒl) *n* **1a** an amount of money levied, esp. for the use of certain roads, bridges, etc. **1b** (*as modifier*): *toll road; toll bridge.* **2** loss or damage incurred through a disaster, etc.: *the war took its toll of the inhabitants.* **3** (formerly) the right to levy a toll. [OE *toln*]

tollbooth *or* **tolbooth** ('təʊlˌbuːθ, -ˌbuːð, 'tɒl-) *n* a booth or kiosk at which a toll is collected.

tollgate ('təʊlˌgeɪt, 'tɒl-) *n* a gate across a toll road or bridge at which travellers must pay.

tollhouse ('təʊlˌhaʊs, 'tɒl-) *n* a small house at a tollgate occupied by a toll collector.

tollie ('tɒlɪ) *n, pl* **tollies.** *S. African.* a castrated calf. [C19: from Xhosa *ithole* calf on which the horns have begun to appear]

Tolstoy ★ ('tɒlstɔɪ; *Russian* talˈstɔj) *n* **Leo,** Russian name *Count Lev Nikolayevich Tolstoy.* 1828–1910, Russian writer; his novels include *War and Peace* (1865–69) and *Anna Karenina* (1875–77).

Toltec ('tɒltɛk) *n, pl* **Toltecs** *or* **Toltec. 1** a member of a Central American Indian people who dominated the valley of Mexico until they were overrun by the Aztecs. ◆ *adj also* **Toltecan. 2** of or relating to this people.

tolu (tɒ'luː) *n* an aromatic balsam obtained from a South American tree. [C17: after *Santiago de Tolu*, Colombia, from which it was exported]

Toluca ★ (*Spanish* to'luka) *n* **1** a city in S central Mexico, capital of Mexico state, at an altitude of 2640 m (8660 ft). Pop.: 327 865 (1990). Official name: **Toluca de Lerdo** (de 'lerðo). **2 Nevado de** (ne'βaðo de). a volcano in central Mexico, in Mexico state near Toluca: crater partly filled by a lake. Height: 4577 m (15 017 ft).

toluene ('tɒljuˌiːn) *n* a colourless volatile flammable liquid obtained from petroleum and coal tar and used as a solvent and in the manufacture of many organic chemicals. [C19: from TOLU + -ENE, since it was previously obtained from tolu]

toluic acid (tɒ'luːɪk) *n* a white crystalline derivative of toluene used in synthetic resins and as an insect repellent. [C19: from TOLU(ENE) + -IC]

toluidine (tɒ'ljuːˌdiːn) *n* an amine derived from toluene, used in making dyes. [C19: from TOLU(ENE) + -IDE + -INE²]

tom (tɒm) *n* **a** the male of various animals, esp. the cat. **b** (*as modifier*): *a tom turkey.* **c** (*in combination*): *a tomcat.* [C16: special use of the short form of *Thomas*, applied to any male, often implying a common or ordinary type of person, etc.]

tomahawk ('tɒməˌhɔːk) *n* a fighting axe with a stone or iron head, used by the North American Indians. [C17: from Algonquian *tamahaac*]

tomato (tə'mɑːtəʊ) *n, pl* **tomatoes. 1** a South American plant widely cultivated for its red fleshy many-seeded fruits. **2** the fruit of this plant, eaten in salads, as a vegetable, etc. [C17 *tomate*, from Sp., from Nahuatl *tomatl*]

tomb (tuːm) *n* **1** a place, esp. a vault beneath the ground, for the burial of a corpse. **2** a monument to the dead. **3 the tomb.** a poetic term for death. [C13: from OF *tombe*, from LL *tumba* burial mound, from Gk *tumbos*]

tombac ('tɒmbæk) *n* any of various alloys containing copper and zinc: used for making cheap jewellery, etc. [C17: from F, from Du. *tombak*, from Malay *tambâga* copper, apparently from Sansk. *tāmraka*, from *tāmra* dark coppery red]

Tombaugh ★ ('tɒmbɔː) *n* **Clyde William.** 1906–97, US astronomer, who discovered (1930) Pluto.

tombola (tɒm'bəʊlə) *n Brit.* a type of lottery, esp. at a fête, in which tickets are drawn from a revolving drum. [C19: from It., from *tombolare* to somersault]

Tombouctou ★ (tōbuktu) *n* the French name for **Timbuktu.**

tomboy ('tɒmˌbɔɪ) *n* a girl who acts or dresses in a boyish way, liking rough outdoor activities.
▶ 'tom,boyish *adj* ▶ 'tom,boyishly *adv*

tombstone ('tuːmˌstəʊn) *n* another word for **gravestone.**

Tom Collins *n* a long drink consisting of gin, lime or lemon juice, sugar, and soda water.

Tom, Dick, and (or) Harry *n* an ordinary, undistinguished, or common person (esp. in **every Tom, Dick, and Harry; any Tom, Dick, or Harry**).

tome (təʊm) *n* **1** a large weighty book. **2** one of the several volumes of a work. [C16: from F, from L *tomus* section of larger work, from Gk *tomos* a slice, from *temnein* to cut]

-tome *n combining form.* indicating an instrument for cutting: *osteotome.* [from Gk *tomē* a cutting, *tomos* a slice, from *temnein* to cut]

tomentum (tə'mentəm) *n, pl* **tomenta** (-tə). **1** a covering of downy hairs on leaves and other plant parts. **2** a network of minute blood vessels occurring in the human brain. [C17: NL, from L: stuffing for cushions]
▶ to'mentose *adj*

tomfool (ˌtɒm'fuːl) *n* **a** a fool. **b** (*as modifier*): *tomfool ideas.*
▶ ˌtom'foolishness *n*

tomfoolery (ˌtɒm'fuːlərɪ) *n, pl* **tomfooleries. 1** foolish behaviour. **2** utter nonsense; rubbish.

tommy ('tɒmɪ) *n, pl* **tommies.** (*often cap.*) *Brit. inf.* a private

in the British Army. [C19: orig. *Thomas Atkins*, name representing typical private in specimen forms]

Tommy gun *n* an informal name for **Thompson sub-machine-gun.**

tommyrot ('tɒmɪˌrɒt) *n* utter nonsense.

tomography (tə'mɒgrəfɪ) *n* a technique used to obtain an X-ray photograph of a plane section of the human body or some other object. [C20: from Gk *tomē* a cutting + -GRAPHY]

tomorrow (tə'mɒrəʊ) *n* **1** the day after today. **2** the future. ◆ *adv* **3** on the day after today. **4** at some time in the future. [OE *tō morgenne*, from *to* on + *morgenne*, dative of *morgen* morning]

Tomsk ★ (*Russian* tɒmsk) *n* a city in central Russia: formerly an important gold-mining town and administrative centre for a large area of Siberia; university (1888); engineering industries. Pop.: 470 000 (1995 est.).

Tom Thumb ★ *n* **1 General,** stage name of *Charles Stratton.* 1838–83, US midget, exhibited in P. T. Barnum's circus. **2** a dwarf; midget. [after *Tom Thumb*, the tiny hero of several English folk tales]

tomtit ('tɒmˌtɪt) *n Brit.* any of various tits, esp. the bluetit.

tom-tom *n* a drum usually beaten with the hands as a signalling instrument. [C17: from Hindi *tamtam*, imit.]

-tomy *n combining form.* indicating a surgical cutting of a specified part or tissue: *lobotomy.* [from Gk *-tomia*]

ton¹ (tʌn) *n* **1** Also called: **long ton.** *Brit.* a unit of weight equal to 2240 pounds or 1016.046 909 kilograms. **2** Also called: **short ton, net ton.** *US & Canad.* a unit of weight equal to 2000 pounds or 907.184 kilograms. **3** See **metric ton, tonne.** a unit of weight equal to 1000 kilograms. **4** Also called: **freight ton, measurement ton.** a unit of volume or weight used for charging or measuring freight in shipping. It is usually equal to 40 cubic feet, 1 cubic metre, or 1000 kilograms. **5** Also called: **displacement ton.** a unit used for measuring the displacement of a ship, equal to 35 cubic feet of sea water or 2240 pounds. **6** Also called: **register ton.** a unit of internal capacity of ships equal to 100 cubic feet. ◆ *adv* **7** tons. (*intensifier*): *the new flat is tons better than the old one.* [C14: var. of TUN]

ton² (tʌn) *n Sl., chiefly Brit.* a score or achievement of a hundred, esp. a hundred miles per hour, as on a motorcycle. [C20: special use of TON¹ applied to quantities of one hundred]

tonal ('təʊn°l) *adj* **1** of or relating to tone. **2** of or utilizing the diatonic system; having an established key. **3** (of an answer in a fugue) not having the same melodic intervals as the subject, so as to remain in the original key.
▶ 'tonally *adv*

tonality (təʊ'nælɪtɪ) *n, pl* **tonalities. 1** *Music.* **1a** the presence of a musical key in a composition. **1b** the system of major and minor keys prevalent in Western music. **2** the overall scheme of colours and tones in a painting.

Tonbridge ★ ('tʌnˌbrɪdʒ) *n* a market town in SE England, in SW Kent on the River Medway. Pop.: 34 260 (1991).

tondo ('tɒndəʊ) *n, pl* **tondi** (-diː). a circular easel painting or relief carving. [C19: from It.: a circle, shortened from *rotondo* round]

tone (təʊn) *n* **1** sound with reference to quality, pitch, or volume. **2** short for **tone colour. 3** *US & Canad.* another word for **note** (sense 10). **4** an interval of a major second; whole tone. **5** Also called: **Gregorian tone.** any of several plainsong melodies or other chants used in the singing of psalms. **6** *Linguistics.* any of the pitch levels or pitch contours at which a syllable may be pronounced, such as high tone, falling tone, etc. **7** the quality or character of a sound: *a nervous tone of voice.* **8** general aspect, quality, or style. **9** high quality or style: *to lower the tone of a place.* **10** the quality of a given colour, as modified by mixture with white or black; shade; tint. **11** *Physiol.* **11a** the normal tension of a muscle at rest. **11b** the natural firmness of the tissues and normal functioning of bodily organs in health. **12** the overall effect of the colour values and gradations of light and dark in a picture. **13** *Photog.* a colour of a particular area on a negative or positive that can be distinguished from surrounding areas.

♦ *vb* **tones, toning, toned. 14** (*intr; often foll. by with*) to be of a matching or similar tone (to). **15** (*tr*) to give a tone to or correct the tone of. **16** (*tr*) *Photog.* to soften or change the colour of the tones of (a photographic image). ♦ See also **tone down, tone up.** [C14: from L *tonus*, from Gk *tonos* tension, tone, from *teinein* to stretch]
▶ '**toneless** *adj* ▶ '**tonelessly** *adv*

tone arm *n* another name for **pick-up.**

tone colour *n* the quality of a musical sound that is conditioned or distinguished by the upper partials or overtones present in it.

tone-deaf *adj* unable to distinguish subtle differences in musical pitch.
▶ **tone deafness** *n*

tone down *vb* (*adv*) to moderate or become moderated in tone: *to tone down an argument.*

tone language *n* a language, such as Chinese, in which differences in tone may make differences in meaning.

toneme ('təʊniːm) *n Linguistics.* a phoneme that is distinguished from another phoneme only by its tone. [C20]
▶ to'**nemic** *adj*

tone poem *n* another term for **symphonic poem.**

toner ('təʊnə) *n* **1** a person or thing that tones. **2** a cosmetic preparation that is applied to produce a desired effect, such as to reduce the oiliness of the skin. **3** *Photog.* a chemical solution that softens or alters the tones of a photographic image. **4** a powdered chemical used in photocopying machines, which adheres to electrostatically charged areas of a plate or roller and is then transferred onto the paper to form the copy.

tone row *or* **series** *n Music.* a group of notes having a characteristic pattern that forms the basis of the musical material in a serial composition, esp. one consisting of the twelve notes of the chromatic scale.

tone up *vb* (*adv*) to make or become more vigorous, healthy, etc.

tong (tɒŋ) *n* (formerly) a secret society of Chinese Americans. [C20: from Chinese (Cantonese) *t'ong* meeting place]

tonga ('tɒŋgə) *n* a light two-wheeled vehicle used in rural areas of India. [C19: from Hindi *tāṅgā*]

Tonga ★ ('tɒŋə, 'tɒŋgə) *n* a kingdom occupying an archipelago of more than 150 volcanic and coral islands in the SW Pacific, east of Fiji: inhabited by Polynesians; became a British protectorate in 1900 and gained independence in 1970; a member of the Commonwealth. Official languages: Tongan and English. Religion: Christian majority. Currency: pa'anga. Capital: Nuku'alofa. Pop.: 101 300 (1997). Area: 750 sq. km (290 sq. miles). Also called: **Friendly Islands.**
▶ '**Tongan** *adj, n*

Tongchak (ˌtɒŋ'tʃæk) *n* the former name for **Chondokyo.**

tongs (tɒŋz) *pl n* a tool for grasping or lifting, consisting of a hinged, sprung, or pivoted pair of arms or levers, joined at one end. Also called: **pair of tongs.** [pl. of OE *tange*]

tongue (tʌŋ) *n* **1** a movable mass of muscular tissue attached to the floor of the mouth in most vertebrates. It is used in tasting, eating, and (in man) speaking. Related adj: **lingual. 2** an analogous organ in invertebrates. **3** the tongue of certain animals used as food. **4** a language, dialect, or idiom: *the English tongue.* **5** the ability to speak: *to lose one's tongue.* **6** a manner of speaking: *a glib tongue.* **7** utterance or voice (esp. in **give tongue**). **8** anything which resembles a tongue in shape or function. **9** a promontory or spit of land. **10** a flap of leather on a shoe. **11** *Music.* the reed of an oboe or similar instrument. **12** the clapper of a bell. **13** the harnessing pole of a horse-drawn vehicle. **14** a projection on a machine part that serves as a guide for assembly, etc. **15** a projecting strip along an edge of a board that is made to fit a groove in another board. **16 hold one's tongue.** to keep quiet. **17 on the tip of one's tongue.** about to come to mind. **18 with (one's) tongue in (one's) cheek.** with insincere or ironical intent. ♦ *vb* **tongues, tonguing, tongued. 19** to articulate (notes on a wind instrument) by tonguing. **20** (*tr*) to lick, feel, or touch with the tongue. **21** (*tr*) to provide

(a board) with a tongue. **22** (*intr*) (of a piece of land) to project into a body of water. [OE *tunge*]
▶ '**tongueless** *adj* ▶ '**tongue,like** *adj*

tongue-and-groove joint *n* a joint made between two boards by means of a tongue along the edge of one board that fits into a groove along the edge of the other board.

tongued (tʌŋd) *adj* **1** having a tongue or tongues. **2** (*in combination*) having a manner of speech as specified: *sharp-tongued.*

tongue-lash *vb* (*tr*) to reprimand severely; scold.
▶ '**tongue-,lashing** *n, adj*

tongue-tie *n* a congenital condition in which the tongue has restricted mobility as the result of an abnormally short fraenum.

tongue-tied *adj* **1** speechless, esp. with embarrassment or shyness. **2** having a condition of tongue-tie.

tongue twister *n* a sentence or phrase that is difficult to articulate clearly and quickly, such as *Peter Piper picked a peck of pickled pepper.*

tonguing ('tʌŋɪŋ) *n* a technique of playing (any nonlegato passage) on a wind instrument by obstructing and uncovering the air passage through the lips with the tongue.

tonic ('tɒnɪk) *n* **1** a medicinal preparation that improves the functioning of the body or increases the feeling of wellbeing. **2** anything that enlivens or strengthens. **3** Also called: **tonic water.** a mineral water, usually carbonated and containing quinine and often mixed with gin or other alcoholic drinks. **4** *Music.* **4a** the first degree of a major or minor scale and the tonal centre of a piece composed in a particular key. **4b** a key or chord based on this. ♦ *adj* **5** serving to enliven and invigorate: *a tonic wine.* **6** of or relating to a tone or tones. **7** *Music.* of the first degree of a major or minor scale. **8** of or denoting the general effect of colour and light and shade in a picture. **9** *Physiol.* of or affecting normal muscular or bodily tone: *a tonic spasm.* [C17: from NL *tonicus*, from Gk *tonikos* concerning tone, from *tonos* TONE]
▶ '**tonically** *adv*

tonic accent *n* **1** emphasis imparted to a note by virtue of its having a higher pitch. **2** (*in some languages*) an accent in which emphatic syllables are pronounced on a higher musical pitch.

tonicity (təʊ'nɪsɪtɪ) *n* **1** the condition or quality of being tonic. **2** another name for **tonus.**

tonic sol-fa *n* a method of teaching music, by which syllables are used as names for the notes of the major scale in any key.

tonight (tə'naɪt) *n* **1** the night or evening of this present day. ♦ *adv* **2** in or during the night or evening of this day. **3** *Obs.* last night. [OE *tōniht*]

toning table *n* an exercise table, parts of which move mechanically for a set time in order to exercise specific parts of the body of the person lying on it.

tonka bean ('tɒŋkə) *n* **1** a tall tree of tropical America. **2** the seeds of this tree, used in the manufacture of perfumes, snuff, etc. [C18: prob. from Tupi *tonka*]

Tonkin ('tɒn'kɪn) *or* **Tongking** ★ ('tɒŋ'kɪŋ) *n* **1** a former state of N French Indochina (1883–1946), on the Gulf of Tonkin: forms the largest part of N Vietnam. **2 Gulf of.** an arm of the South China Sea, bordered by N Vietnam, the Leizhou Peninsula of SW China, and Hainan Island. Length: about 500 km (300 miles).

Tonle Sap ★ ('tɒnlɪ 'sæp) *n* a lake in W central Cambodia, linked with the Mekong River by the **Tonle Sap River.** Area: (dry season) about 2600 sq. km (1000 sq. miles); (rainy season) up to 10 000 sq. km (3860 sq. miles).

tonnage *or* **tunnage** ('tʌnɪdʒ) *n* **1** the capacity of a merchant ship expressed in tons. **2** the weight of the cargo of a merchant ship. **3** the total amount of shipping of a port or nation. **4** a duty on ships based either on their capacity or their register tonnage. [C15: from OF, from *tonne* barrel]

tonne (tʌn) *n* a unit of mass equal to 1000 kg or 2204.6 pounds. Also called (not in technical use): **metric ton.** [from F]

★ people and places

tonneau ('tɒnəu) *n, pl* **tonneaus** *or* **tonneaux** (-nəu, -nəuz). **1** a detachable cover to protect empty passenger seats in an open vehicle. **2** *Rare.* the part of an open car in which the rear passengers sit. [C20: from F: special type of vehicle body, from OF *tonnel* cask, from *tonne* tun]

tonometer (təu'nɒmɪtə) *n* **1** an instrument for measuring the pitch of a sound, esp. one consisting of a set of tuning forks. **2** any of various types of instrument for measuring pressure or tension, such as the blood pressure, vapour pressure, etc. [C18: from Gk *tonos* TONE + -METER]
  ▸ **tonometric** (ˌtɒnə'mɛtrɪk, ˌtəu-) *adj*

tonsil ('tɒnsəl) *n* either of two small masses of lymphatic tissue situated one on each side of the back of the mouth. [C17: from L *tōnsillae* (pl) tonsils, from ?]
  ▸ **'tonsillar** *adj*

tonsillectomy (ˌtɒnsɪ'lɛktəmɪ) *n, pl* **tonsillectomies.** surgical removal of the tonsils.

tonsillitis (ˌtɒnsɪ'laɪtɪs) *n* inflammation of the tonsils.
  ▸ **tonsillitic** (ˌtɒnsɪ'lɪtɪk) *adj*

tonsorial (tɒn'sɔːrɪəl) *adj Often facetious.* of barbering or hairdressing. [C19: from L *tōnsōrius* concerning shaving, from *tondēre* to shave]

tonsure ('tɒnʃə) *n* **1** (in certain religions and monastic orders) **1a** the shaving of the head or the crown of the head only. **1b** the part of the head left bare by shaving. ◆ *vb* **tonsures, tonsuring, tonsured. 2** (*tr*) to shave the head of. [C14: from L *tōnsūra* a clipping, from *tondēre* to shave]
  ▸ **'tonsured** *adj*

tontine ('tɒntiːn, tɒn'tiːn) *n* an annuity scheme by which several subscribers accumulate and invest a common fund out of which they receive an annuity that increases as subscribers die until the last survivor takes the whole. [C18: from F, after Lorenzo *Tonti*, Neapolitan banker who devised the scheme]

ton-up *Brit. inf.* ◆ *adj* (*prenominal*) **1** (esp. of a motorcycle) capable of speeds of a hundred miles per hour or more. **2** liking to travel at such speeds: *a ton-up boy.* ◆ *n* **3** a person who habitually rides at such speeds.

tonus ('təunəs) *n* the normal tension of a muscle at rest; tone. [C19: from L, from Gk *tonos* TONE]

too (tuː) *adv* **1** as well; in addition; also: *can I come too?* **2** in or to an excessive degree: *I have too many things to do.* **3** extremely: *you're too kind.* **4** *US & Canad. inf.* indeed: used to reinforce a command: *you will too do it!* [OE *tō*]

USAGE NOTE See at **very.**

took (tuk) *vb* the past tense of **take.**

tool (tuːl) *n* **1a** an implement, such as a hammer, saw, or spade, that is used by hand. **1b** a power-driven instrument; machine tool. **1c** (*in combination*): *a toolkit.* **2** the cutting part of such an instrument. **3** any of the instruments used by a bookbinder to impress a design on a book cover. **4** anything used as a means of achieving an end. **5** a person used to perform dishonourable or unpleasant tasks for another. **6** a necessary medium for or adjunct to one's profession: *numbers are the tools of the mathematician's trade.* ◆ *vb* **7** to work, cut, or form (something) with a tool. **8** (*tr*) to decorate (a book cover) with a bookbinder's tool. **9** (*tr; often foll. by up*) to furnish with tools. [OE *tōl*]
  ▸ **'tooler** *n*

tooling ('tuːlɪŋ) *n* **1** any decorative work done with a tool, esp. a design stamped onto a book cover, etc. **2** the selection, provision, and setting up of tools for a machining operation.

tool-maker *n* a person who specializes in the production or reconditioning of precision tools, cutters, etc.
  ▸ **'tool-ˌmaking** *n*

tool pusher *n* a foreman who supervises drilling operations on an oil rig.

toolroom ('tuːlˌruːm, -rum) *n* a room, such as in a machine shop, where tools are made, stored, etc.

toot (tuːt) *vb* **1** to give or cause to give (a short blast, hoot,

or whistle). ◆ *n* **2** the sound made by or as if by a horn, whistle, etc. **3** *Sl.* any drug for snorting, esp. cocaine. **4** *US & Canad. sl.* a drinking spree. **5** *Austral. sl.* a lavatory. [C16: from MLow G *tuten*, imit.]
  ▸ **'tooter** *n*

tooth (tuːθ) *n, pl* **teeth** (tiːθ). **1** any of various bonelike structures set in the jaws of most vertebrates and used for biting, tearing, or chewing. Related adj: **dental. 2** any of various similar structures in invertebrates. **3** anything resembling a tooth in shape, prominence, or function: *the tooth of a comb.* **4** any of the indentations on the margin of a leaf, petal, etc. **5** any of the projections on a gear, sprocket, rack, etc. **6** taste or appetite (esp. in **sweet tooth**). **7 long in the tooth.** old or ageing. **8 tooth and nail.** with ferocity and force. ◆ *vb* (tuːð, tuːθ). **9** (*tr*) to provide with a tooth or teeth. **10** (*intr*) (of two gearwheels) to engage. [OE *tōth*]
  ▸ **'toothless** *adj* ▸ **'tooth,like** *adj*

toothache ('tuːθ,eɪk) *n* a pain in or about a tooth. Technical name: **odontalgia.**

toothbrush ('tuːθ,brʌʃ) *n* a small brush, usually with a long handle, for cleaning the teeth.

toothed (tuːθt) *adj* **a** having a tooth or teeth. **b** (*in combination*): *sabre-toothed; six-toothed.*

toothed whale *n* any of a suborder of whales having simple teeth and feeding on fish, smaller mammals, etc.: includes dolphins and porpoises.

toothpaste ('tuːθ,peɪst) *n* a paste used for cleaning the teeth, applied with a toothbrush.

toothpick ('tuːθ,pɪk) *n* a small sharp sliver of wood, plastic, etc., used for extracting pieces of food from between the teeth.

tooth powder *n* a powder used for cleaning the teeth, applied with a toothbrush.

tooth shell *n* another name for the **tusk shell.**

toothsome ('tuːθsəm) *adj* of delicious or appetizing appearance, flavour, or smell.

toothwort ('tuːθ,wɜːt) *n* **1** a European plant having scaly stems and pinkish flowers and a rhizome covered with toothlike scales. **2** any of a genus of North American or Eurasian plants having rhizomes covered with toothlike projections.

toothy ('tuːθɪ) *adj* **toothier, toothiest.** having or showing numerous, large, or projecting teeth: *a toothy grin.*
  ▸ **'toothily** *adv* ▸ **'toothiness** *n*

tootle ('tuːtᵊl) *vb* **tootles, tootling, tootled. 1** to toot or hoot softly or repeatedly. ◆ *n* **2** a soft hoot or series of hoots. [C19: from TOOT]
  ▸ **'tootler** *n*

Toowoomba ★ (tə'wumbə) *n* a city in E Australia, in SE Queensland: agricultural and industrial centre. Pop.: 75 000 (latest est.).

top¹ (tɒp) *n* **1** the highest or uppermost part of anything: *the top of a hill.* **2** the most important or successful position: *the top of the class.* **3** the part of a plant that is above ground: *carrot tops.* **4** a thing that forms or covers the uppermost part of anything, esp. a lid or cap. **5** the highest degree or point: *at the top of his career.* **6** the most important person. **7** the best part of anything. **8** the loudest or highest pitch (esp. in **top of one's voice**). **9** another name for **top gear** (sense 1). **10** *Cards.* the highest card of a suit in a player's hand. **11** *Sport.* **11a** a stroke that hits the ball above its centre. **11b** short for **topspin. 12** a platform around the head of a lower mast of a sailing vessel. **13** a garment, esp. for a woman, that extends from the shoulders to the waist or hips. **14 off the top of one's head.** with no previous preparation; extempore. **15 on top of. 15a** in addition to. **15b** *Inf.* in complete control of (a difficult situation, etc.). **16 over the top. 16a** over the parapet or leading edge of a trench. **16b** over the limit; lacking restraint or a sense of proportion. **17 the top of the morning.** a morning greeting regarded as characteristic of Irishmen. ◆ *adj* **18** of, relating to, serving as, or situated on the top. ◆ *vb* **tops, topping, topped.** (*mainly tr*) **19** to form a top on (something): *to top a cake with cream.* **20** to remove the top of or from. **21** to reach or pass the top of. **22** to be at the top of: *he tops the team.* **23** to exceed or surpass. **24** *Sl.* to kill, esp. by hanging. **25** (*also intr*) *Sport.* **25a** to hit (a ball) above the centre. **25b** to make (a stroke) by hitting the ball in this way. **26 top and tail. 26a** to trim off the ends of (fruit or vegetables) before cooking them. **26b** to wash a baby's face and bottom without immersion in a bath. ◆ See also **top off, top out, tops, top up.** [OE *topp*]

top[2] (top) *n* **1** a toy that is spun on its pointed base. **2 sleep like a top.** to sleep very soundly. [OE, from ?]

topaz ('təʊpæz) *n* **1** a hard glassy mineral consisting of a silicate of aluminium and fluorine in crystalline form. It is yellow, pink, or colourless, and is a valuable gemstone. **2 oriental topaz.** a yellowish-brown variety of sapphire. **3 false topaz.** another name for **citrine. 4a** a yellowish-brown colour, as in some varieties of topaz. **4b** (*as adj*): *topaz eyes*. **5** either of two South American hummingbirds. [C13: from OF *topaze*, from L *topazus*, from Gk *topazos*]

top boot *n* a high boot, often with a decorative or contrasting upper section.

top brass *n* (*functioning as pl*) *Inf*. the most important or high-ranking officials or leaders.

topcoat ('tɒpˌkəʊt) *n* an outdoor coat worn over a suit, etc.

top dog *n Inf*. the leader or chief of a group.

top dollar *n Inf*. the highest level of payment.

top drawer *n* people of the highest standing, esp. socially (esp. in **out of the top drawer**).

top dressing *n* a surface application of some material, such as fertilizer.
▶ **'top-ˌdress** *vb* (*tr*)

tope[1] (təʊp) *vb* **topes, toping, toped.** to consume (alcoholic drink) as a regular habit, usually in large quantities. [C17: from F *toper* to keep an agreement, from Sp. *topar* to take a bet; prob. because a wager was generally followed by a drink]
▶ **'toper** *n*

tope[2] (təʊp) *n* a small grey shark of European coastal waters. [C17: from ?]

topee or **topi** ('təʊpiː, -piː) *n, pl* **topees** or **topis.** another name for **pith helmet.** [C19: from Hindi *topī* hat]

Topeka ★ (təˈpiːkə) *n* a city in E central Kansas, capital of the state, on the Kansas River: university (1865). Pop.: 120 646 (1994 est.).

Top End ★ *n* the. *Austral*. the northern part of the Northern Territory.

top-flight *adj* of superior or excellent quality.

topgallant (ˌtɒpˈgælənt; *Naut*. təˈgælənt) *n* **1** a mast on a square-rigger above a topmast or an extension of a topmast. **2** a sail set on a yard of a topgallant mast. **3** (*modifier*) of or relating to a topgallant.

top gear *n* **1** Also called: **top.** the highest forward ratio of a gearbox in a motor vehicle. **2** the highest speed, greatest energy, etc.

top hat *n* a man's hat with a tall cylindrical crown and narrow brim, often made of silk, now worn for some formal occasions.

top-hat scheme *n Inf*. a pension scheme for the senior executives of an organization.

top-heavy *adj* **1** unstable through being overloaded at the top. **2** *Finance*. characterized by too much debt capital in relation to revenue or profit; overcapitalized.

Tophet or **Topheth** ★ ('təʊfet) *n Old Testament*. a place in the valley immediately to the southwest of Jerusalem; the Shrine of Moloch, where human sacrifices were offered. [from Heb. *Tōpheth*]

tophus ('təʊfəs) *n, pl* **tophi** (-faɪ). a deposit of sodium urate in the ear or surrounding a joint: a diagnostic of gout. [C16: from L, var. of *tōfus* TUFA, TUFF]

topi[1] ('təʊpiː, -piː) *n, pl* **topis.** another name for **pith helmet.** [C19: from Hindi: hat]

topi[2] ('təʊpi) *n, pl* **topi** or **topis.** a glossy brown African antelope. [C19: from Swahili]

topiary ('təʊpɪərɪ) *adj* **1** of, relating to, or characterized by the trimming or training of trees or bushes into artificial decorative shapes. ◆ *n, pl* **topiaries. 2a** topiary work. **2b** a topiary garden. **3** the art of topiary. [C16: from F

topiaire, from L *topia* decorative garden work, from Gk *topion* little place, from *topos* place]
▶ **'topiarist** *n*

topic ('tɒpɪk) *n* **1** a subject or theme of a speech, book, etc. **2** a subject of conversation. [C16: from L *topica* translating Gk *ta topika*, lit.: matters relating to commonplaces, title of a treatise by Aristotle, from *topoi*, pl. of *topos* place]

topical ('tɒpɪk°l) *adj* **1** of, relating to, or constituting current affairs. **2** relating to a particular place; local. **3** of or relating to a topic or topics. **4** (of a drug, ointment, etc.) for application to the body surface; local.
▶ **topicality** (ˌtɒpɪˈkælɪtɪ) *n* ▶ **'topically** *adv*

topknot ('tɒpˌnɒt) *n* **1** a crest, tuft, chignon, etc., on top of the head. **2** any of several European flatfishes.

topless ('tɒplɪs) *adj* **1** having no top. **2a** denoting a costume which has no covering for the breasts. **2b** wearing such a costume.

top-level *n* (*modifier*) of, involving, or by those on the highest level of influence or authority: *top-level talks*.

toplofty ('tɒpˌlɒftɪ) *adj Inf*. haughty or pretentious.
▶ **'top,loftiness** *n*

topmast ('tɒpˌmɑːst; *Naut*. 'tɒpməst) *n* the mast next above a lower mast on a sailing vessel.

topmost ('tɒpˌməʊst) *adj* at or nearest the top.

top-notch ('tɒpˈnɒtʃ) *adj Inf*. excellent; superb.
▶ **'top-'notcher** *n*

topo- or before a vowel **top-** *combining form*. indicating place or region: *topography*. [from Gk *topos* place]

top off *vb* (*tr, adv*) to finish or complete, esp. with some decisive action.

topography (təˈpɒgrəfɪ) *n, pl* **topographies. 1** the study or detailed description of the surface features of a region. **2** the detailed mapping of the configuration of a region. **3** the land forms or surface configuration of a region. **4** the surveying of a region's surface features. **5** the study or description of the configuration of any object.
▶ **to'pographer** *n* ▶ **topographic** (ˌtɒpəˈgræfɪk) or **topo-'graphical** *adj*

topological group *n Maths*. a group, such as the set of all real numbers, that constitutes a topological space and in which multiplication and inversion are continuous.

topological space *n Maths*. a set *S* with an associated family of subsets τ that is closed under set union and finite intersection.

topology (təˈpɒlədʒɪ) *n* **1** the branch of mathematics concerned with generalization of the concepts of continuity, limit, etc. **2** a branch of geometry describing the properties of a figure that are unaffected by continuous distortion. **3** *Maths*. a family of subsets of a given set *S*, such that *S* is a topological space. **4** the study of the topography of a given place. **5** the anatomy of any specific bodily area, structure, or part.
▶ **topologic** (ˌtɒpəˈlɒdʒɪk) or **topo'logical** *adj* ▶ **topo'logically** *adv* ▶ **to'pologist** *n*

Topolski ★ (tɒˈpɒlskɪ) *n* **Feliks** ('fiːlɪks). 1907–89, British painter, born in Poland; best known for his sketches and murals, esp. for *Memoir of the Century* (1975–89).

top out *vb* (*adv*) to place the highest part of a building in position.

topper ('tɒpə) *n* **1** an informal name for **top hat. 2** a person or thing that tops or excels.

topping ('tɒpɪŋ) *n* **1** something that tops something else, esp. a sauce or garnish for food. ◆ *adj* **2** high or superior in rank, degree, etc. **3** *Brit. sl*. excellent; splendid.

topple ('tɒp°l) *vb* **topples, toppling, toppled. 1** to tip over or cause to tip over, esp. from a height. **2** (*intr*) to lean precariously or totter. [C16: frequentative of TOP[1] (vb)]

tops (tɒps) *Sl*. ◆ *n* **1 the tops.** a person or thing of top quality. ◆ *adj* **2** (*postpositive*) excellent.

topsail ('tɒpˌseɪl; *Naut*. 'tɒpsəl) *n* a square sail carried on a yard set on a topmast.

top-secret *adj* classified as needing the highest level of secrecy and security.

topside ('tɒpˌsaɪd) *n* **1** the uppermost side of anything. **2** *Brit. & NZ*. a lean cut of beef from the thigh containing

★ people and places

no bone. **3** (*often pl*) **3a** the part of a ship's sides above the water line. **3b** the parts of a ship above decks.

top slicing *n* the act or process of using a specific part of a sum of money for a special purpose, such as assessing a taxable gain.

topsoil ('top,sɔil) *n* the surface layer of soil.

topspin ('top,spin) *n Tennis, etc.* a spin imparted to make a ball bounce or travel exceptionally far, high, or quickly.

topsy-turvy ('topsi'tɜ:vi) *adj* **1** upside down. **2** in a state of confusion. ◆ *adv* **3** in a topsy-turvy manner. ◆ *n* **4** a topsy-turvy state. [C16: prob. from *tops*, pl. of TOP[1] + obs. *tervy* to turn upside down]

top up *vb* (*tr, adv*) *Brit.* **1** to raise the level of (a liquid, powder, etc.) in (a container), usually bringing it to the brim of the container. **2a** to increase the benefits from (an insurance scheme), esp. to increase a pension when a salary rise enables higher premiums to be paid. **2b** to add money to (a loan, bank account, etc.) in order to keep it at a constant or acceptable level. ◆ *n* **top-up. 3a** an amount added to something in order to raise it to or maintain it at a desired level. **3b** (*as modifier*): *a top-up loan; a top-up policy.*

toque (təuk) *n* **1** a woman's small round brimless hat. **2** a chef's tall white hat. **3** *Canad.* a variant spelling of **tuque** (sense 2). **4** a small plumed hat popular in the 16th century. [C16: from F, from OSp. *toca* headdress, prob. from Basque *tauka* hat]

tor (tɔ:) *n* a high hill, esp. a bare rocky one. [OE *torr*]

Torah ('təurə) *n* **1a** the Pentateuch. **1b** the scroll on which this is written. **2** the whole body of traditional Jewish teaching, including the Oral Law. [C16: from Heb.: precept, from *yārāh* to instruct]

Torbay ★ (,tɔ:'bei) *n* **1** a resort and unitary authority in SW England, in Devon, formed in 1968 by the amalgamation of Torquay with two neighbouring coastal towns. Pop.: 102 576 (1991). **2** Also: **Tor Bay.** an inlet of the English Channel on the coast of SW England, near Torquay.

torc (tɔ:k) *n* a variant of **torque** (sense 1).

torch (tɔ:tʃ) *n* **1** a small portable electric lamp powered by batteries. US and Canad. word: **flashlight. 2** a wooden or tow shaft dipped in wax or tallow and set alight. **3** anything regarded as a source of enlightenment, guidance, etc. **4** any apparatus with a hot flame for welding, brazing, etc. **5 carry a torch for.** to be in love with, esp. unrequitedly. ◆ *vb* **6** (*tr*) to set fire to, esp. deliberately as an act of arson. [C13: from OF *torche* handful of twisted straw, from Vulgar L *torca* (unattested), from L *torquēre* to twist]

torchbearer ('tɔ:tʃ,beərə) *n* **1** a person or thing that carries a torch. **2** a person who leads or inspires.

torchère (tɔ:'ʃɛə) *n* a tall stand for holding a candelabrum. [C20: from F, from *torche* TORCH]

torchier *or* **torchiere** ('tɔ:tʃiə) *n* a standing lamp with a bowl for casting light upwards. [C20: from TORCHÈRE]

torch song *n* a sentimental song, usually sung by a woman. [C20: from *to carry a torch for* (*someone*)]
▶ **torch singer** *n*

tore (tɔ:) *vb* the past tense of **tear**[2].

toreador ('torɪə,dɔ:) *n* a bullfighter. [C17: from Sp., from *torear* to take part in bullfighting, from *toro* a bull, from L *taurus*]

torero (tɒ'rɛərəu) *n, pl* **toreros.** a bullfighter, esp. one who fights on foot. [C18: from Sp., from LL *taurārius*, from L *taurus* a bull]

Torfaen ★ (tɔ:'væn) *n* a county borough of SE Wales, created in 1996 from part of Gwent. Administrative centre: Pontypool. Pop.: 90 527 (1996 est.). Area: 290 sq. km (112 sq. miles).

toric lens ('torik) *n* a lens used to correct astigmatism, having one of its surfaces shaped like part of a torus so that its focal lengths are different in different meridians.

torii ('tɔ:rɪ,i:) *n, pl* **torii.** a gateway at the entrance to a Shinto temple. [C19: from Japanese, lit.: a perch for birds]

Torino ★ (tɒ'ri:no) *n* the Italian name for **Turin.**

torment *vb* (tɔ:'mɛnt). (*tr*) **1** to afflict with great pain, suffering, or anguish; torture. **2** to tease or pester in an annoying way. ◆ *n* ('tɔ:mɛnt). **3** physical or mental pain. **4** a source of pain, worry, annoyance, etc. [C13: from OF, from L *tormentum*, from *torquēre*]
▶ **tor'mented** *adj* ▶ **tor'menting** *adj, n* ▶ **tor'mentor** *n*

tormentil ('tɔ:məntɪl) *n* a perennial plant of Europe and W Asia, having yellow flowers, and an astringent root used in medicine, tanning, and dyeing. [C15: from OF *tormentille*, from Med. L *tormentilla*, from L *tormentum* agony; from its use in relieving pain]

torn (tɔ:n) *vb* **1** the past participle of **tear**[2]. **2 that's torn it.** *Brit. sl.* an unexpected event or circumstance has upset one's plans. ◆ *adj* **3** split or cut. **4** divided or undecided, as in preference: *torn between staying and leaving.*

tornado (tɔ:'neidəu) *n, pl* **tornadoes** *or* **tornados. 1** a violent storm with winds whirling around a small area of extremely low pressure, usually characterized by a dark funnel-shaped cloud causing damage along its path. **2** a small but violent squall or whirlwind. **3** any violently active or destructive person or thing. [C16: prob. alteration of Sp. *tronada* thunderstorm (from *tronar* to thunder, from L *tonāre*) through infl. of *tornar* to turn, from L *tornāre* to turn in a lathe]
▶ **tornadic** (tɔ:'nædɪk) *adj*

toroid ('tɔ:rɔid) *n* **1** *Geom.* a surface generated by rotating a closed plane curve about a coplanar line that does not intersect the curve. **2** the solid enclosed by such a surface. See also **torus.**
▶ **to'roidal** *adj*

Toronto ★ (tə'rontəu) *n* a city in S central Canada, capital of Ontario, on Lake Ontario: the major industrial centre of Canada; two universities. Pop. (city): 635 395 (1991); (metropolitan area): 4 338 400 (1995).
▶ **,Toron'tonian** *adj, n*

torpedo (tɔ:'pi:dəu) *n, pl* **torpedoes. 1** a cylindrical self-propelled weapon carrying explosives that is launched from aircraft, ships, or submarines and follows an underwater path to hit its target. **2** *Obs.* a submarine mine. **3** *US & Canad.* a firework with a percussion cap. **4** an electric ray. ◆ *vb* **torpedoes, torpedoing, torpedoed.** (*tr*) **5** to attack or hit (a ship, etc.) with one or a number of torpedoes. **6** to destroy or wreck: *to torpedo the administration's plan.* [C16: from L: crampfish (whose electric discharges can cause numbness), from *torpēre* to be inactive]
▶ **tor'pedo-,like** *adj*

torpedo boat *n* (formerly) a small high-speed warship designed to carry out torpedo attacks.

torpedo tube *n* the tube from which a torpedo is discharged from submarines or ships.

torpid ('tɔ:pid) *adj* **1** apathetic; sluggish. **2** (of a hibernating animal) dormant. **3** unable to move or feel. [C17: from L *torpidus*, from *torpēre* to be numb]
▶ **tor'pidity** *n* ▶ **'torpidly** *adv*

torpor ('tɔ:pə) *n* a state of torpidity. [C17: from L: inactivity, from *torpēre* to be motionless]

Torquay ★ (,tɔ:'ki:) *n* a town and resort in SW England, in S Devon: administratively part of Torbay since 1968.

torque (tɔ:k) *n* **1** a necklace or armband made of twisted metal. **2** any force that causes rotation. [C19: from L *torquēs* necklace & *torquēre* to twist]

torque converter *n* a device for the transmission of power in which an engine-driven impeller transmits its momentum to a fluid held in a sealed container, which in turn drives a rotor. Also called: **hydraulic coupling.**

Torquemada ★ (*Spanish* tɔrke'maða) *n* Tomás de (to'mas de). 1420–98, Spanish Dominican monk. As first Inquisitor-General of Spain (1483–98), he had 2000 heretics burnt.

torques ('tɔ:kwi:z) *n* a distinctive band of hair, feathers, skin, or colour around the neck of an animal; a collar. [C17: from L: necklace, from *torquēre* to twist]
▶ **torquate** ('tɔ:kwit, -kweit) *adj*

torque wrench *n* a type of wrench with a gauge attached to indicate the torque applied.

torr (tɔː) *n, pl* **torr**. a unit of pressure equal to one milli-metre of mercury (133.322 newtons per square metre). [C20: after E. TORRICELLI]

Torrance ★ ('tɒrəns) *n* a city in SW California, south-west of Los Angeles: developed rapidly with the discov-ery of oil. Pop.: 138 219 (1994 est.).

Torre del Greco ★ (*Italian* 'torre del 'greːko) *n* a city in SW Italy, in Campania near Vesuvius on the Bay of Na-ples: damaged several times by eruptions. Pop.: 100 688 (1992).

torrefy ('tɒrɪˌfaɪ) *vb* **torrefies, torrefying, torrefied.** (*tr*) to dry (drugs, ores, etc.) by heat. [C17: from F *torréfier*, from L *torrefacere*, from *torrēre* to parch + *facere* to make]
▸ **torrefaction** (ˌtɒrɪˈfækʃən) *n*

Torrens ★ ('tɒrənz) *n* **Lake.** a shallow salt lake in E central South Australia, about 8 m (25 ft) below sea level. Area: 5776 sq. km (2230 sq. miles).

Torrens title *n Austral.* legal title to land based on re-cord of registration rather than on title deeds. [from Sir Robert Richard *Torrens* (1814–84), who introduced the system as premier of South Australia in 1857]

torrent ('tɒrənt) *n* **1** a fast or violent stream, esp. of water. **2** an overwhelming flow of thoughts, words, sound, etc. [C17: from F, from L *torrēns* (n), from *torrēns* (adj) burning, from *torrēre* to burn]
▸ **torrential** (tɒˈrɛnʃəl) *adj*

Torreón ★ (*Spanish* tɔrreˈɔn) *n* an industrial city in N Mexico, in Coahuila state. Pop.: 439 436 (1990).

Torres Strait ★ ('tɒrɪz, 'tɒr-) *n* a strait between NE Aus-tralia and S New Guinea, linking the Arafura Sea with the Coral Sea. Width: about 145 km (90 miles).

Torricelli ★ (ˌtɒrɪˈtʃɛlɪ) *n* **Evangelista** (evandʒeˈlista). 1608–47, Italian physicist who invented the barometer.

Torricellian tube (ˌtɒrɪˈsɛlɪən) *n* a vertical glass tube partly evacuated and partly filled with mercury, used to measure atmospheric pressure. [C17: after E. TORRICELLI]

torrid ('tɒrɪd) *adj* **1** so hot and dry as to parch or scorch. **2** arid or parched. **3** highly charged emotionally: *a torrid love scene.* [C16: from L *torridus*, from *torrēre* to scorch]
▸ **tor'ridity** *or* **'torridness** *n* ▸ **'torridly** *adv*

Torrid Zone *n Rare.* that part of the earth's surface lying between the tropics of Cancer and Capricorn.

torsion ('tɔːʃən) *n* **1a** the twisting of a part by application of equal and opposite torques. **1b** the condition of twist and shear stress produced by a torque on a part or com-ponent. **2** a twisting or being twisted. [C15: from OF, from Medical L *torsiō* griping pains, from L *torquēre* to twist, torture]
▸ **'torsional** *adj* ▸ **'torsionally** *adv*

torsion balance *n* an instrument used to measure small forces, esp. electric or magnetic forces, by the tor-sion they produce in a thin wire.

torsion bar *n* a metal bar acting as a torsional spring.

torsk (tɔːsk) *n, pl* **torsks** *or* **torsk.** a food fish of northern coastal waters. Usual US name: **cusk.** [C17: of Scand. origin]

torso ('tɔːsəʊ) *n, pl* **torsos** *or* **torsi** (-sɪ). **1** the trunk of the human body. **2** a statue of a nude human trunk, esp. without the head or limbs. [C18: from It.: stalk, stump, from L: THYRSUS]

tort (tɔːt) *n Law.* a civil wrong or injury arising out of an act or failure to act, independently of any contract, for which an action for damages may be brought. [C14: from OF, from Med. L *tortum*, lit.: something twisted, from L *torquēre* to twist]

torte (tɔːt) *n* a rich cake usually decorated or filled with cream, fruit, etc. [C16: ult. ?from LL *tōrta* a round loaf, from ?]

Tortelier ★ (*French* tɔrtəlje) *n* **Paul** (pɔl). 1914–90, French cellist.

torticollis (ˌtɔːtɪˈkɒlɪs) *n Pathol.* an abnormal position of the head, usually with the neck bent to one side. [C19: NL, from L *tortus* twisted (from *torquēre* to twist) + *collum* neck]

tortilla (tɔːˈtiːə) *n Mexican cookery.* a kind of thin pancake made from corn meal. [C17: from Sp.: a little cake, from *torta* a round cake, from LL]

tortoise ('tɔːtəs) *n* **1** any of a family of herbivorous rep-tiles having a heavy dome-shaped shell and clawed limbs. **2** a slow-moving person. **3** another word for **testudo.** [C15: prob. from OF *tortue* (infl. by L *tortus* twisted), from Med. L *tortūca*, from LL *tartarūcha* coming from Tartarus (in the underworld), from Gk *tartaroukhos*; from belief that the tortoise originated in the under-world]

tortoiseshell ('tɔːtəsˌʃɛl) *n* **1** the horny yellow-and-brown mottled shell of the hawksbill turtle: used for making ornaments, jewellery, etc. **2** a similar synthetic substance. **3** a breed of domestic cat having black, cream, and brownish markings. **4** any of several butter-flies having orange-brown wings with black markings. **5a** a yellowish-brown mottled colour. **5b** (*as adj*): *a tor-toiseshell décor.* **6** (*modifier*) made of tortoiseshell.

Tortola ★ (tɔːˈtəʊlə) *n* an island in the NE Caribbean, in the Leeward Islands group: chief island of the British Virgin Islands. Pop.: 13 568 (1991). Area: 62 sq. km (24 sq. miles).

tortricid ('tɔːtrɪsɪd) *n* any of a family of moths, the larvae of which live in leaves, which they roll or tie together. [C19: from NL *Tortrīcidae*, from *tortrix*, fem. of *tortor*, lit.: twister, from the leaf-rolling of the larvae, from *torquēre* to twist]

Tortuga ★ (tɔːˈtuːgə) *n* an island in the Caribbean, off the NW coast of Haiti: haunt of pirates in the 17th century. Area: 180 sq. km (70 sq. miles). French name: **La Tortue** (la tɔrty).

tortuous ('tɔːtjʊəs) *adj* **1** twisted or winding. **2** devious or cunning. **3** intricate.
▸ **tortuosity** (ˌtɔːtjʊˈɒsɪtɪ) *n* ▸ **'tortuously** *adv* ▸ **'tortuous-ness** *n*

torture ('tɔːtʃə) *vb* **tortures, torturing, tortured.** (*tr*) **1** to cause extreme physical pain to, esp. to extract information, etc.: *to torture prisoners.* **2** to give mental anguish to. **3** to twist into a grotesque form. ◆ *n* **4** physical or mental anguish. **5** the practice of torturing a person. **6** a cause of mental agony. [C16: from LL *tortūra* a twisting, from *torquēre* to twist]
▸ **'torturer** *n* ▸ **'torturous** *adj* ▸ **'torturously** *adv*

> **USAGE NOTE** The adjective *torturous* is some-times confused with *tortuous*. One speaks of a *tor-turous* experience, i.e. one that involves pain or suffering, but of a *tortuous* road, i.e. one that winds or twists.

Toruń ★ (*Polish* 'tɔrunj) *n* an industrial city in N Poland, on the River Vistula: developed around a castle that was founded by the Teutonic Knights in 1230; under Prus-sian rule (1793–1919). Pop.: 203 800 (1995 est.). Ger-man name: **Thorn.**

torus ('tɔːrəs) *n, pl* **tori** (-raɪ). **1** a large convex moulding semicircular in cross section, esp. one used on the base of a column. **2** *Geom.* a ring-shaped surface generated by rotating a circle about a coplanar line that does not in-tersect the circle. **3** *Bot.* another name for **receptacle** (sense 2). [C16: from L: a swelling, from ?]
▸ **toric** ('tɒrɪk) *adj*

Tory ('tɔːrɪ) *n, pl* **Tories. 1** a member or supporter of the Conservative Party in Great Britain or Canada. **2** a mem-ber of the English political party that opposed the exclu-sion of James, Duke of York from the royal succession (1679–80). Tory remained the label for conservative in-terests until they gave birth to the Conservative Party in the 1830s. **3** an American supporter of the British cause; loyalist. Cf. **Whig. 4** (*sometimes not cap.*) an ultraconserva-tive or reactionary. ◆ *adj* **5** of, characteristic of, or relat-ing to Tories. **6** (*sometimes not cap.*) ultraconservative or reactionary. [C17: from Irish *tōraidhe* outlaw, from MIrish *tōir* pursuit]
▸ **'Toryish** *adj* ▸ **'Toryism** *n*

tosa ('təʊsə) *n* a large dog, usually red in colour, that is a cross between a mastiff and a Great Dane: originally de-veloped for dog-fighting; it is not recognized as a breed by kennel clubs outside Japan. [C20: from the name of a province of Japan]

★ people and places

Toscana ★ (tos'ka:na) *n* the Italian name for **Tuscany**.

Toscanini ★ (ˌtɒskə'ni:nɪ) *n* **Arturo** (*Italian* ar'tu:ro). 1867–1957, Italian conductor.

tosh (tɒʃ) *n Sl., chiefly Brit.* nonsense; rubbish. [C19: from ?]

toss (tɒs) *vb.* **1** (*tr*) to throw lightly, esp. with the palm of the hand upwards. **2** to fling or be flung about, esp. in an agitated or violent way: *a ship tosses in a storm.* **3** to discuss or put forward for discussion in an informal way. **4** (*tr*) (of a horse, etc.) to throw (its rider). **5** (*tr*) (of an animal) to butt with the head or the horns and throw into the air. **6** (*tr*) to shake or disturb. **7** to toss up a coin with (someone) in order to decide something. **8** (*intr*) to move away angrily or impatiently. ◆ *n* **9** an abrupt movement. **10** a rolling or pitching motion. **11** the act or an instance of tossing. **12** the act of tossing up a coin. See **toss up**. **13** a fall from a horse. [C16: of Scand. origin]

tosser ('tɒsə) *n Brit. sl.* a stupid or despicable person. [C20: probably from TOSS OFF (to masturbate)]

toss off *vb* (*adv*) **1** (*tr*) to perform, write, etc., quickly and easily. **2** (*tr*) to drink at one draught. **3** (*intr*) *Brit. taboo.* to masturbate.

toss up *vb* (*adv*) **1** to spin (a coin) in the air in order to decide between alternatives by guessing which side will fall uppermost. ◆ *n* **toss-up**. **2** an instance of tossing up a coin. **3** *Inf.* an even chance or risk.

tot[1] (tɒt) *n* **1** a young child; toddler. **2** *Chiefly Brit.* a small amount of anything. **3** a small measure of spirits. [C18: ? short for *totterer*; see TOTTER]

tot[2] (tɒt) *vb* **tots, totting, totted**. (usually foll. by *up*) *Chiefly Brit.* to total; add. [C17: shortened from TOTAL or from L *totum* all]

total ('təʊt[ə]l) *n* **1** the whole, esp. regarded as the complete sum of a number of parts. ◆ *adj* **2** complete; absolute. **3** (*prenominal*) being or related to a total. ◆ *vb* **totals, totalling, totalled** or *US* **totals, totaling, totaled**. **4** (when *intr*, sometimes foll. by *to*) to amount: *to total six pounds.* **5** (*tr*) to add up. **6** (*tr*) *Sl.* to kill or destroy. [C14: from OF, from Med. L *tōtālis*, from L *tōtus* all]
▶ **'totally** *adv*

total football *n* an attacking style of play, popularized by the Dutch national team of the 1970s, in which there are no fixed positions and every outfield player can join in the attack.

total internal reflection *n Physics.* the complete reflection of a light ray at the boundary of two media, when the ray is in the medium with greater refractive index.

totalitarian (təʊˌtælɪ'teərɪən) *adj* **1** of, denoting, relating to, or characteristic of a dictatorial one-party state that regulates every realm of life. ◆ *n* **2** a person who advocates or practises totalitarian policies.
▶ **toˌtali'tarianism** *n*

totality (təʊ'tælɪtɪ) *n, pl* **totalities**. **1** the whole amount. **2** the state of being total.

totalizator ('təʊtˌlaɪˌzeɪtə), **totalizer** or **totalisator, totaliser** *n* **1** a system of betting on horse races in which the aggregate stake, less tax, etc., is paid out to winners in proportion to their stake. **2** the machine that records bets in this system and works out odds, pays out winnings, etc. ◆ *US and Canad. term:* **pari-mutuel**.

total quality management *n* an approach to the management of an organization that integrates the needs of customers with a deep understanding of the technical details, costs, and human-resource relationships of the organization. *Abbrev.:* **TQM**.

totaquine ('təʊtəˌkwiːn, -ˌkwɪn) *n* a mixture of quinine and other alkaloids derived from cinchona bark, used as a substitute for quinine in treating malaria. [C20: from NL *tōtaquīna*, from TOTA(L) + Sp. *quina* cinchona bark; see QUININE]

totara ('təʊtərə) *n* a tall coniferous forest tree of New Zealand with durable wood.

tote[1] (təʊt) *Inf.* ◆ *vb* **totes, toting, toted**. **1** (*tr*) to carry, convey, or drag. ◆ *n* **2** the act of or an instance of toting. **3** something toted. [C17: from ?]
▶ **'toter** *n*

tote[2] (təʊt) *n* (usually preceded by *the*) *Inf.* short for **totalizator**.

tote bag *n* a large handbag or shopping bag.

totem ('təʊtəm) *n* **1** (in some societies, esp. among North American Indians) an object, animal, plant, etc., symbolizing a clan, family, etc., often having ritual associations. **2** a representation of such an object. [C18: from Ojibwa *nintōtēm* mark of my family]
▶ **totemic** (təʊ'tɛmɪk) *adj* ▶ **'totem,ism** *n*

totem pole *n* a pole carved or painted with totemic figures set up by certain North American Indians as a tribal symbol, etc.

tother or **t'other** ('tʌðə) *adj, n Arch. or dialect.* the other. [C13 *the tother*, by mistaken division from *thet other* (*thet*, from OE *thæt*, neuter of THE[1])]

totipalmate (ˌtəʊtɪ'pælmɪt, -ˌmeɪt) *adj* (of certain birds) having all four toes webbed. [C19: from L *tōtus* entire + *palmate*, from *palmātus* shaped like a hand, from *palma* PALM[1]]

totter ('tɒtə) *vb* (*intr*) **1** to move in an unsteady manner. **2** to sway or shake as if about to fall. **3** to be failing, unstable, or precarious. ◆ *n* **4** the act or an instance of tottering. [C12: ?from OE *tealtrian* to waver, & MDu. *touteren* to stagger]
▶ **'totterer** *n* ▶ **'tottery** *adj*

totting ('tɒtɪŋ) *n Brit.* the practice of searching through rubbish for usable or saleable items. [C19: from ?]

toucan ('tuːkən) *n* any of a family of tropical American fruit-eating birds having a large brightly coloured bill and a bright plumage. [C16: from F, from Port. *tucano*, from Tupi *tucana*, prob. imit. of its cry]

touch (tʌtʃ) *n* **1** the sense by which the texture and other qualities of objects can be experienced when they come in contact with a part of the body surface, esp. the tips of the fingers. *Related adj:* **tactile**. **2** the quality of an object as perceived by this sense; feel; feeling. **3** the act or an instance of something coming into contact with the body. **4** a gentle push, tap, or caress. **5** a small amount; hint: *a touch of sarcasm.* **6** a noticeable effect; influence: *the house needed a woman's touch.* **7** any slight stroke or mark. **8** characteristic manner or style. **9** a detail of some work: *she added a few finishing touches to the book.* **10** a slight attack, as of a disease. **11** a specific ability or facility. **12** the state of being aware of a situation or in contact with someone. **13** the state of being in physical contact. **14** a trial or test (esp. in **put to the touch**). **15** *Rugby, soccer, etc.* the area outside the touchlines, beyond which the ball is out of play (esp. in **in touch**). **16** a scoring hit in fencing. **17** an estimate of the amount of gold in an alloy as obtained by use of a touchstone. **18** the technique of fingering a keyboard instrument. **19** the quality of the action of a keyboard instrument with regard to the ease with which the keys may be depressed. **20** *Sl.* **20a** the act of asking for money, often by devious means. **20b** money received. **20c** a person asked for money in this way. ◆ *vb* **21** (*tr*) to cause or permit a part of the body to come into contact with. **22** (*tr*) to tap, feel, or strike. **23** to come or cause to come into contact with. **24** (*intr*) to be in contact. **25** (*tr; usually used with a negative*) to take hold of (a person or thing), esp. in violence. **26** to be adjacent to (each other). **27** (*tr*) to move or disturb by handling. **28** (*tr*) to have an effect on. **29** (*tr*) to produce an emotional response in. **30** (*tr*) to affect; concern. **31** (*tr; usually used with a negative*) to partake of, eat, or drink. **32** (*tr; usually used with a negative*) to handle or deal with: *I wouldn't touch that business.* **33** (when *intr*, often foll. by *on*) to allude (to) briefly or in passing. **34** (*tr*) to tinge or tint slightly: *brown hair touched with gold.* **35** (*tr*) to spoil slightly: *blackfly touched the flowers.* **36** (*tr*) to mark, as with a brush or pen. **37** (*tr*) to compare to in quality or attainment. **38** (*tr*) to reach or attain: *he touched the high point in his career.* **39** (*intr*) to dock or stop briefly: *the ship touches at Tenerife.* **40** (*tr*) *Sl.* to ask for a loan or gift of money from. ◆ See also **touchdown, touch off, touch up**. [C13: from *tochier*, from Vulgar L *toccāre* (unattested) to strike, prob. imit. of a tapping sound]
▶ **'touchable** *adj* ▶ **'toucher** *n*

touch and go *adj* (**touch-and-go** when prenominal) risky or critical.

touchdown ('tʌtʃ,daʊn) *n* **1** the moment at which a landing aircraft or spacecraft comes into contact with the landing surface. **2** *Rugby.* the act of placing or touching the ball on the ground behind the goal line, as in scoring a try. **3** *American football.* a scoring play worth six points, achieved by being in possession of the ball in the opposing team's end zone. Abbrev.: **TD.** ◆ *vb* **touch down.** (*intr, adv*) **4** (of an aircraft, etc.) to land. **5** *Rugby.* to place the ball behind the goal line, as when scoring a try.

touché (tu:'ʃeɪ) *interj* **1** an acknowledgment of a scoring hit in fencing. **2** an acknowledgment of the striking home of a remark, witty reply, etc. [from F, lit.: touched]

touched (tʌtʃt) *adj* (*postpositive*) **1** moved to sympathy or emotion. **2** showing slight insanity.

touchhole ('tʌtʃ,həʊl) *n* a hole in the breech of early cannon and firearms through which the charge was ignited.

touching ('tʌtʃɪŋ) *adj* **1** evoking or eliciting tender feelings. ◆ *prep* **2** on the subject of; relating to.
▸ **'touchingly** *adv*

touch judge *n* one of the two linesmen in rugby.

touchline ('tʌtʃ,laɪn) *n* either of the lines marking the side of the playing area in certain games, such as rugby.

touchmark ('tʌtʃ,mɑ:k) *n* a maker's mark stamped on pewter objects.

touch-me-not *n* an impatiens with yellow spurred flowers and seed pods that burst open at a touch when ripe. Also called: **noli-me-tangere.**

touch off *vb* (*tr, adv*) **1** to cause to explode, as by touching with a match. **2** to cause (a disturbance, violence, etc.) to begin.

touchpaper ('tʌtʃ,peɪpə) *n* paper soaked in saltpetre for lighting fireworks or firing gunpowder.

touchstone ('tʌtʃ,stəʊn) *n* **1** a criterion or standard. **2** a hard dark stone that is used to test gold and silver from the streak they produce on it.

touch-tone *adj* of or relating to a telephone dialling system in which each dialling button pressed generates a different pitch, which is transmitted to the exchange.

touch-type *vb* **touch-types, touch-typing, touch-typed.** (*intr*) to type without looking at the keyboard.
▸ **'touch-,typist** *n*

touch up *vb* (*tr, adv*) **1** to put extra or finishing touches to. **2** to enhance, renovate, or falsify by putting extra touches to. **3** *Brit. sl.* to touch or caress (someone).

touchwood ('tʌtʃ,wʊd) *n* something, esp. dry wood or fungus material, used as tinder. [C16: TOUCH (in the sense: to kindle) + WOOD]

touchy ('tʌtʃɪ) *adj* **touchier, touchiest. 1** easily upset or irritated. **2** extremely risky. **3** easily ignited.
▸ **'touchily** *adv* ▸ **'touchiness** *n*

touchy-feely ('tʌtʃɪ,fi:lɪ) *adj Inf.,* sometimes *derog.* sensitive and caring.

tough (tʌf) *adj* **1** strong or resilient; durable. **2** not tender. **3** hardy and fit. **4** rough or pugnacious. **5** resolute or intractable. **6** difficult or troublesome to do or deal with: *a tough problem.* **7** *Inf.* unfortunate or unlucky: *it's tough on him.* ◆ *n* **8** a rough, vicious, or pugnacious person. ◆ *adv* **9** *Inf.* violently, aggressively, or intractably: *to treat someone tough.* ◆ *vb* (*tr*) **10** *Sl.* to stand firm, hold out against (a difficulty or difficult situation) (esp. in **tough it out**). [OE *tōh*]
▸ **'toughly** *adv* ▸ **'toughness** *n*

toughen ('tʌfən) *vb* to make or become tough or tougher.
▸ **'toughener** *n*

tough love *n* the practice of taking a stern attitude towards a relative or friend suffering from an addiction, etc., to help the addict overcome the problem.

tough-minded *adj* practical, unsentimental, or intractable.
▸ **,tough-'mindedness** *n*

Toul ★ (tu:l) *n* a town in NE France: a leading episcopal see in the Middle Ages. Pop.: 17 406 (1982).

Toulon ★ (*French* tulɔ̃) *n* a fortified port and naval base in SE France, on the Mediterranean: naval arsenal developed by Henry IV and Richelieu, later fortified by Vauban. Pop.: 170 167 (1990).

Toulouse ★ (tu:'lu:z) *n* a city in S France, on the Garonne River: scene of severe religious strife in the early 13th and mid-16th centuries; university (1229). Pop.: 365 933 (1990). Ancient name: **Tolosa** (tə'ləʊsə).

Toulouse-Lautrec ★ (*French* tuluzlotrɛk) *n* Henri (**Marie Raymond**) **de** (ɑ̃ri də). 1864–1901, French painter and lithographer, noted esp. for his posters, etc., depicting life in Montmartre, Paris.

toupee ('tu:peɪ) *n* a hairpiece worn by men to cover a bald place. [C18: apparently from F *toupet* forelock, from OF *toup* top, of Gmc origin]

tour (tʊə) *n* **1** an extended journey visiting places of interest along the route. **2** *Mil.* a period of service, esp. in one place. **3** a short trip, as for inspection. **4** a trip made by a theatre company, orchestra, etc., to perform in several places. **5** an overseas trip made by a cricket or rugby team, etc., to play in several places. ◆ *vb* **6** to make a tour of (a place). [C14: from OF: a turn, from L *tornus* a lathe, from Gk *tornos*]

touraco *or* **turaco** ('tʊərə,kəʊ) *n, pl* **touracos** *or* **turacos.** any of a family of brightly coloured crested African birds. [C18: of West African origin]

Touraine ★ (*French* turen) *n* a former province of NW central France: at its height in the 16th century as an area of royal residences, esp. along the Loire. Chief town: Tours.

Tourane ★ (tu:'rɑ:n) *n* the former name of **Da Nang.**

Tourcoing ★ (*French* turkwɛ̃) *n* a town in NE France: textile manufacturing. Pop.: 93 765 (1990).

tour de force *French.* (tur də fɔrs) *n, pl* **tours de force** (tur). a masterly or brilliant stroke, creation, effect, or accomplishment. [lit.: feat of skill or strength]

Touré ★ ('tʊəreɪ) *n* (**Ahmed**) **Sékou** ('seɪku:). 1922–84, president of the Republic of Guinea (1958–84).

tourer ('tʊərə) *n* a large open car with a folding top, usually seating a driver and four passengers. Also called (esp. US): **touring car.**

tourism ('tʊərɪzəm) *n* tourist travel, esp. when regarded as an industry.

tourist ('tʊərɪst) *n* **1a** a person who travels for pleasure, usually sightseeing and staying in hotels. **1b** (*as modifier*): *tourist attractions.* **2** a person on an excursion or sightseeing tour. **3** a member of a touring team. **4** Also called: **tourist class.** the lowest class of accommodation on a passenger ship or aircraft. ◆ *adj* **5** of or relating to tourist accommodation.
▸ **tour'istic** *adj*

touristy ('tʊərɪstɪ) *adj Inf.,* often *derog.* abounding in or designed for tourists.

tourmaline ('tʊəmə,li:n) *n* any of a group of hard glassy minerals of variable colour consisting of a complex silicate of boron and aluminium in crystalline form: used in jewellery and optical and electrical equipment. [C18: from G *Turmalin,* from Sinhalese *toramalli* carnelian]

Tournai ★ (*French* turnɛ) *n* a city in W Belgium, in Hainaut province on the River Scheldt: under several different European rulers until 1814. Pop.: 68 086 (1995 est.). Flemish name: **Doornik.**

tournament ('tʊənəmənt) *n* **1** a sporting competition in which contestants play a series of games to determine an overall winner. **2** a meeting for athletic or other sporting contestants: *an archery tournament.* **3** *Medieval history.* a martial sport or contest in which mounted combatants fought for a prize. [C13: from OF *torneiement,* from *torneier* to fight on horseback, lit.: to turn, from the constant wheeling round of the combatants; see TOURNEY]

tournedos ('tʊənə,dəʊ) *n, pl* **tournedos** (-,dəʊz). a thick round steak of beef. [from F, from *tourner* to TURN + *dos* back]

Tourneur ★ ('tɜ:nə) *n* **Cyril.** ?1575–1626, English dramatist; author of *The Atheist's Tragedy* (1611).

tourney ('tʊənɪ, 'tɔ:-) *Medieval history.* ◆ *n* **1** a knightly tournament. ◆ *vb* **2** (*intr*) to engage in a tourney. [C13 from OF *torneier,* from Vulgar L *torniāre* (unattested) to

★ people and places

turn constantly, from L *tornāre* to TURN (in a lathe); see TOURNAMENT].

tourniquet ('tʊənɪˌkeɪ) *n Med.* any device for constricting an artery of the arm or leg to control bleeding. [C17: from F: device that operates by turning, from *tourner* to TURN]

tour operator *n* a person or company that specializes in providing package holidays.

Tours ★ (*French* tur) *n* a town in W central France, on the River Loire: nearby is the scene of the defeat of the Arabs in 732, which ended the advance of Islam in W Europe. Pop.: 133 403 (1990).

tousle ('taʊzᵊl) *vb* **tousles, tousling, tousled.** (*tr*) **1** to tangle, ruffle, or disarrange. **2** to treat roughly. ◆ *n* **3** a disorderly, tangled, or rumpled state. **4** a dishevelled or disordered mass, esp. of hair. [C15: from Low G *tūsen* to shake]

Toussaint L'Ouverture ★ (*French* tusɛ̃ luvɛrtyr) *n* Pierre Dominique (pjɛr dɔminik). ?1743–1803, Haitian revolutionary, who was made governor by the French Revolutionary government (1794); when Napoleon I proclaimed the re-establishment of slavery he was arrested; died in prison in France.

tout (taʊt) *vb* **1** to solicit (business, customers, etc.) or hawk (merchandise), esp. in a brazen way. **2** (*intr*) **2a** to spy on racehorses being trained in order to obtain information for betting purposes. **2b** to sell such information or to take bets, esp. in public places. ◆ *n* **3** a person who touts. **4** Also: **ticket tout.** a person who sells tickets for a heavily booked event at inflated prices. [C14 (in the sense: to peer, look out): rel. to OE *tȳtan* to peep out]
▸ 'touter *n*

tout à fait *French.* (tut a fɛ) *adv* completely.

tout de suite *French.* (tud sɥit) *adv* at once.

tout le monde *French.* (tu lə mɔ̃d) *n* all the world; everyone.

tovarisch, tovarich, *or* **tovarish** (tə'vɑːrɪʃ) *n* comrade: a term of address. [from Russian]

tow¹ (təʊ) *vb* **1** (*tr*) to pull or drag (a vehicle, boat, etc.), esp. by means of a rope or cable. ◆ *n* **2** the act or an instance of towing. **3** the state of being towed (esp. in **in tow, on tow**). **4** something towed. **5** something used for towing. **6 in tow.** in one's charge or under one's influence. **7** short for **ski tow.** [OE *togian*]
▸ 'towable *adj* ▸ 'towage *n*

tow² (təʊ) *n* the coarse and broken fibres of hemp, flax, jute, etc., prepared for spinning. [OE *tōw*]
▸ 'towy *adj*

toward *adj* **1** *Now rare.* in progress; afoot. **2** *Obs.* about to happen; imminent. **3** *Obs.* promising or favourable. ◆ *prep* (tə'wɔːd, tɔːd). **4** a variant of **towards.** [OE *tōweard*]

towards (tə'wɔːdz, tɔːdz) *prep* **1** in the direction or vicinity of: *towards London.* **2** with regard to: *her feelings towards me.* **3** as a contribution or help to: *money towards a new car.* **4** just before: *towards noon.* ◆ Also: **toward.**

towbar ('təʊˌbɑː) *n* a rigid metal bar or frame used for towing vehicles.

towboat ('təʊˌbəʊt) *n* another word for **tug** (sense 4).

tow-coloured *adj* pale yellow; flaxen.

towel ('taʊəl) *n* **1** a piece of absorbent cloth or paper used for drying things. **2 throw in the towel.** See **throw in** (sense 3). ◆ *vb* **towels, towelling, towelled** *or US* **towels, toweling, toweled.** **3** (*tr*) to dry or wipe with a towel. **4** (*tr*; often foll. by *up*) *Austral. sl.* to assault or beat (a person). [C13: from OF *toaille*, of Gmc origin]

towelling ('taʊəlɪŋ) *n* an absorbent fabric used for making towels, bathrobes, etc.

tower ('taʊə) *n* **1** a tall, usually square or circular structure, sometimes part of a larger building and usually built for a specific purpose. **2** a place of defence or retreat. **3 tower of strength.** a person who gives support, comfort, etc. ◆ *vb* **4** (*intr*) to be or rise like a tower; loom. [C12: from OF *tur*, from L *turris*, from Gk]

Tower Hamlets ★ *n* a borough of E Greater London, on the River Thames: contains the main part of the East

End. Pop.: 159 000 (1994 est.). Area: 20 sq. km (8 sq. miles).

towering ('taʊərɪŋ) *adj* **1** very tall; lofty. **2** outstanding, as in importance or stature. **3** (*prenominal*) very intense: *a towering rage.*

Tower of London ★ *n* a fortress in the City of London, on the River Thames: begun 1078; later extended and used as a palace, the main state prison, and now as a museum containing the crown jewels.

towhead ('təʊˌhɛd) *n* **1** a person with blond or yellowish hair. **2** a head of such hair. [from TOW² (flax)]
▸ ˌtow'headed *adj*

towhee ('taʊˌhiː, 'təʊ-) *n* any of various North American brownish-coloured sparrows. [C18: imit.]

towline ('təʊˌlaɪn) *n* another name for **towrope.**

town (taʊn) *n* **1** a densely populated urban area, typically smaller than a city and larger than a village. **2** a city, borough, or other urban area. **3** (in the US) a territorial unit of local government that is smaller than a county; township. **4** the nearest town or commercial district. **5** London or the chief city of an area. **6** the inhabitants of a town. **7 go to town. 7a** to make a supreme or unrestricted effort. **7b** *Austral. & NZ inf.* to lose one's temper. **8 on the town.** seeking out entertainments and amusements. [OE *tūn* village]
▸ 'townish *adj*

town clerk *n* **1** (in Britain until 1974) the secretary and chief administrative officer of a town or city. **2** (in the US) the official who keeps the records of a town.

town crier *n* (formerly) a person employed to make public announcements in the streets.

Townes ★ (taʊnz) *n* Charles Hard. born 1915, US physicist; his research led to the invention of the laser; shared the Nobel prize for physics 1964.

town gas *n* coal gas manufactured for domestic and industrial use.

town hall *n* the chief building in which municipal business is transacted, often with a hall for public meetings.

town house *n* **1** a terraced house in an urban area, esp. a fashionable one. **2** a person's town residence as distinct from his country residence.

townie ('taʊnɪ) *or* **townee** (taʊ'niː) *n Inf., often disparaging.* a permanent resident in a town, esp. as distinct from country dwellers or students.

townland ('taʊnlænd) *n Irish.* a division of land of various sizes.

town planning *n* the comprehensive planning of the physical and social development of a town. US term: **city planning.**

townscape ('taʊnskeɪp) *n* **1** a view of an urban scene. **2** an extensive area of urban development.

Townshend ★ ('taʊnzɛnd) *n* Charles, 2nd Viscount, nicknamed *Turnip Townshend.* 1674–1738, English politician and agriculturist.

township ('taʊnʃɪp) *n* **1** a small town. **2** (in the Scottish Highlands) a small crofting community. **3** (in the US and Canada) a territorial area, esp. a subdivision of a county: often organized as a unit of local government. **4** (in Canada) a land-survey area, usually 36 square miles (93 square kilometres). **5** (formerly, in South Africa) a planned urban settlement of Black Africans or Coloured people. **6** *English history.* **6a** any of the local districts of a large parish. **6b** the parish itself.

townsman ('taʊnzmən) *n, pl* **townsmen. 1** an inhabitant of a town. **2** a person from the same town as oneself.
▸ 'townsˌwoman *fem n*

townspeople ('taʊnzˌpiːpᵊl) *or* **townsfolk** ('taʊnzˌfəʊk) *pl n* the inhabitants of a town; citizens.

Townsville ★ ('taʊnzvɪl) *n* a port in E Australia, in NE Queensland on the Coral Sea: centre of a vast agricultural and mining hinterland. Pop.: 124 900 (1995 est.).

towpath ('təʊˌpɑːθ) *n* a path beside a canal or river, used by people or animals towing boats. Also called: **towing path.**

towrope ('təʊˌrəʊp) *n* a rope or cable used for towing a vehicle or vessel. Also called: **towline.**

tox-, toxic- *or before a consonant* **toxo-, toxico-** *combining form.* indicating poison: *toxaemia*. [from L *toxicum*]

toxaemia *or US* **toxemia** (tɒkˈsiːmɪə) *n* **1** a condition characterized by the presence of bacterial toxins in the blood. **2** the condition in pregnancy of pre-eclampsia or eclampsia.
▶ **tox'aemic** *or US* **tox'emic** *adj*

toxic ('tɒksɪk) *adj* **1** of or caused by a toxin or poison. **2** harmful or deadly. [C17: from Medical L *toxicus*, from L *toxicum* poison, from Gk *toxikon* (*pharmakon*) (poison) used on arrows, from *toxon* arrow]
▶ **'toxically** *adv* ▶ **toxicity** (tɒkˈsɪsɪtɪ) *n*

toxicant ('tɒksɪkənt) *n* **1** a toxic substance; poison.
♦ *adj* **2** poisonous; toxic. [C19: from Med. L *toxicāre* to poison]

toxicology (ˌtɒksɪˈkɒlədʒɪ) *n* the branch of science concerned with poisons, their effects, antidotes, etc.
▶ **toxicological** (ˌtɒksɪkəˈlɒdʒɪkⁿl) *or* ˌtoxico'logic *adj*
▶ ˌtoxi'cologist *n*

toxic shock syndrome *n* a potentially fatal condition in women, characterized by fever, stomachache, a painful rash, and a drop in blood pressure, that is caused by staphylococcal blood poisoning, commonly from a retained tampon.

toxin ('tɒksɪn) *n* **1** any of various poisonous substances produced by microorganisms that stimulate the production of neutralizing substances (antitoxins) in the body. **2** any other poisonous substance of plant or animal origin.

toxin-antitoxin *n* a mixture of a toxin and antitoxin. The diphtheria toxin-antitoxin was formerly used for immunization.

toxocariasis (ˌtɒksəkəˈraɪəsɪs) *n* the infection of humans with the larvae of a genus of roundworms, *Toxocara*, of dogs and cats.

toxoid ('tɒksɔɪd) *n* a toxin that has been treated to reduce its toxicity and is used in immunization to stimulate production of antitoxins.

toxophilite (tɒkˈsɒfɪˌlaɪt) *Formal.* ♦ *n* **1** an archer. ♦ *adj* **2** of archery. [C18: from *Toxophilus*, the title of a book (1545) by Ascham, designed to mean: a lover of the bow, from Gk *toxon* bow + *philos* loving]
▶ **tox'ophily** *n*

toxoplasmosis (ˌtɒksəʊplæzˈməʊsɪs) *n* a protozoal disease characterized by jaundice and convulsions.
▶ ˌtoxo'plasmic *adj*

toy (tɔɪ) *n* **1** an object designed to be played with. **2a** something that is a nonfunctioning replica of something else, esp. a miniature one. **2b** (*as modifier*): *a toy guitar*. **3** any small thing of little value; trifle. **4a** something small or miniature, esp. a miniature variety of a breed of dog. **4b** (*as modifier*): *a toy poodle*. ♦ *vb* **5** (*intr*; usually foll. by *with*) to play, fiddle, or flirt. [C16 (in the sense: amorous dalliance): from ?]

Toyama ★ ('təʊjɑːˌmɑː) *n* a city in central Japan, on W Honshu on **Toyama Bay** (an inlet of the Sea of Japan): chemical and textile centre. Pop.: 325 303 (1995).

toy boy *n* the much younger male lover of an older woman.

Toynbee ★ ('tɔɪnbɪ) *n* **1** Arnold. 1852–83, British economist and social reformer. **2** his nephew, **Arnold Joseph.** 1889–1975, British historian; author of *A Study of History* (1934–61).

TPI *abbrev. for* tax and price index: a measure of the increase in taxable income needed to compensate for an increase in retail prices.

TQM *abbrev. for* total quality management.

tr *abbrev. for* treasurer.

tr. *abbrev. for:* **1** transitive. **2** translated. **3** translator. **4** *Music.* trill. **5** trustee.

trabeated ('treɪbɪˌeɪtɪd) *or* **trabeate** ('treɪbɪɪt, -ˌeɪt) *adj Archit.* constructed with horizontal beams as opposed to arches. [C19: back formation from *trabeation*, from L *trabs* a beam]

trabecula (trəˈbɛkjʊlə) *n, pl* **trabeculae** (-ˌliː). *Anat., bot.* any of various rod-shaped structures that support other organs. [C19: via NL from L: a little beam, from *trabs* beam]
▶ **tra'becular** *or* **tra'beculate** *adj*

Trabzon ('trɑːbzɒːn) *or* **Trebizond** ★ *n* a port in NE Turkey, on the Black Sea: founded as a Greek colony in the 8th century B.C. at the terminus of an important trade route from central Europe to Asia. Pop.: 145 400 (1994 est.).

trace[1] (treɪs) *n* **1** a mark or other sign that something has been in a place. **2** a scarcely detectable amount or characteristic. **3** a footprint or other indication of the passage of an animal or person. **4** any line drawn by a recording instrument or a record consisting of a number of such lines. **5** something drawn, such as a tracing. **6** *Chiefly US.* a beaten track or path. ♦ *vb* **traces, tracing, traced.** **7** (*tr*) to follow, discover, or ascertain the course or development of (something). **8** (*tr*) to track down and find, as by following a trail. **9** to copy (a design, map, etc.) by drawing over the lines visible through a superimposed sheet of transparent paper. **10** (*tr*; often foll. by *out*) **10a** to draw or delineate a plan or diagram of. **10b** to outline or sketch (an idea, etc.). **11** (*tr*) to decorate with tracery. **12** (usually foll. by *back*) to follow or be followed to source; date back: *his ancestors trace back to the 16th century*. [C13: from F *tracier*, from Vulgar L *tractiāre* (unattested), from L *tractus*, from *trahere*]
▶ **'traceable** *adj* ▶ ˌtracea'bility *or* 'traceableness *n*
▶ **'traceably** *adv*

trace[2] (treɪs) *n* **1** either of the two side straps that connect a horse's harness to the swingletree. **2** *Angling.* a length of nylon or, formerly, gut attaching a hook or fly to a line. **3 kick over the traces.** to escape or defy control. [C14 *trais*, from OF *trait*, ult. from L *trahere* to drag]

trace element *n* any of various chemical elements, such as iron, manganese, zinc, copper, and iodine, that occur in very small amounts in organisms and are essential for many physiological and biochemical processes.

trace fossil *n* the fossilized remains of a track, trail, footprint, burrow, etc., of an organism.

tracer ('treɪsə) *n* **1** a person or thing that traces. **2** a projectile that can be observed when in flight by the burning of chemical substances in its base. **3** *Med.* any radioactive isotope introduced into the body to study metabolic processes, etc., by following its progress with a gamma counter or other detector. **4** an investigation to trace missing cargo, mail, etc.

tracer bullet *n* a round of small arms ammunition containing a tracer.

tracery ('treɪsərɪ) *n, pl* **traceries. 1** a pattern of interlacing ribs, esp. as used in the upper part of a Gothic window, etc. **2** any fine pattern resembling this.
▶ **'traceried** *adj*

trachea (trəˈkiːə) *n, pl* **tracheae** (-ˈkiːiː). **1** *Anat., zool.* the tube that conveys inhaled air from the larynx to the bronchi. **2** any of the tubes in insects and related animals that convey air from the spiracles to the tissues. [C16: from Med. L, from Gk *trakheia*, shortened from (*artēria*) *trakheia* rough (artery), from *trakhus* rough]
▶ **tra'cheal** *or* **tra'cheate** *adj*

tracheitis (ˌtreɪkɪˈaɪtɪs) *n* inflammation of the trachea.

tracheo- *or before a vowel* **trache-** *combining form.* denoting the trachea.

tracheotomy (ˌtrækɪˈɒtəmɪ) *n, pl* **tracheotomies.** surgical incision into the trachea, as performed when the air passage has been blocked.

trachoma (trəˈkəʊmə) *n* a chronic contagious disease of the eye caused by a species of chlamydia: a severe form of conjunctivitis that can result in scarring and blindness. [C17: from NL, from Gk *trakhōma* roughness, from *trakhus* rough]
▶ **trachomatous** (trəˈkɒmətəs) *adj*

trachyte ('treɪkaɪt, 'træ-) *n* a light-coloured fine-grained volcanic rock. [C19: from F, from Gk *trakhutēs*, from *trakhus* rough]

tracing ('treɪsɪŋ) *n* **1** a copy made by tracing. **2** the act of making a trace. **3** a record made by an instrument.

track (træk) *n* **1** the mark or trail left by something that has passed by. **2** any road or path, esp. a rough one. **3** a

rail or pair of parallel rails on which a vehicle, such as a locomotive, runs. **4** a course of action, thought, etc.: *don't start on that track again!* **5** a line of motion or travel, such as flight. **6** an endless band on the wheels of a tank, tractor, etc., to enable it to move across rough ground. **7a** a course for running or racing. **7b** (*as modifier*): *track events*. **8** *US & Canad.* **8a** sports performed on a track. **8b** track and field events as a whole. **9** a path on a magnetic recording medium, esp. magnetic tape, on which music or speech is recorded. **10** any of a number of separate sections in the recording on a record, CD, or cassette. **11** the distance between the points of contact with the ground of a pair of wheels, as of a motor vehicle. **12 keep** (*or* **lose**) **track of.** to follow (or fail to follow) the passage, course, or progress of. **13 off the track.** away from what is correct or true. **14 on the track of.** on the scent or trail of; pursuing. ◆ *vb* **15** to follow the trail of (a person, animal, etc.). **16** to follow the flight path of (a satellite, etc.) by picking up signals transmitted or reflected by it. **17** *US railways.* **17a** to provide with a track. **17b** to run on a track of (a certain width). **18** (of a camera or camera-operator) to follow (a moving object) while operating. **19** to follow a track through (a place): *to track the jungles*. **20** (*intr*) (of the pick-up, stylus, etc., of a record player) to follow the groove of a record. ◆ See also **tracks.** [C15: from OF *trac*, prob. of Gmc origin]
▶ **'tracker** *n*

track down *vb* (*tr, adv*) to find by tracking or pursuing.

tracker dog *n* a dog specially trained to search for missing people.

track event *n* a competition in athletics, such as relay running or sprinting, that takes place on a running track.

tracking ('trækɪŋ) *n* **1** the act or process of following something or someone. **2** *Electrical engineering.* a leakage of electric current between two insulated points caused by dirt, carbon particles, moisture, etc.

tracking shot *n* a camera shot in which the cameraman follows a specific person or event in the action.

tracking station *n* a station that can use a radio or radar beam to follow the path of an object in space or in the atmosphere.

tracklaying ('træk,leɪɪŋ) *adj* also **tracked.** (of a vehicle) having an endless jointed metal band around the wheels.

track record *n Inf.* the past record of the accomplishments and failures of a person, business, etc.

track rod *n* the rod connecting the two front wheels of a motor vehicle.

tracks (træks) *pl n* **1** (*sometimes sing*) marks, such as footprints, etc., left by someone or something that has passed. **2 in one's tracks.** on the very spot where one is standing. **3 make tracks.** to leave or depart. **4 make tracks for.** to go or head towards.

track shoe *n* either of a pair of light running shoes fitted with steel spikes for better grip.

tracksuit ('træk,suːt) *n* a warm suit worn by athletes, etc., esp. during training.

tract[1] (trækt) *n* **1** an extended area, as of land. **2** *Anat.* a system of organs, glands, etc., that has a particular function: *the digestive tract.* **3** *Arch.* an extended period of time. [C15: from L *tractus* a stretching out, from *trahere* to drag]

tract[2] (trækt) *n* a treatise or pamphlet, esp. a religious or moralistic one. [C15: from L *tractātus* TRACTATE]

tractable ('træktəb⁰l) *adj* **1** easily controlled or persuaded. **2** readily worked; malleable. [C16: from L *tractābilis*, from *tractāre* to manage, from *trahere* to draw]
▶ ,tracta'bility *or* 'tractableness *n* ▶ 'tractably *adv*

Tractarianism (træk'tɛərɪəˌnɪzəm) *n* another name for the **Oxford Movement.** [after the series of tracts, *Tracts for the Times* published between 1833 and 1841, in which the principles of the movement were presented]
▶ **Trac'tarian** *n, adj*

tractate ('trækteɪt) *n* a treatise. [C15: from L *tractātus*, from *tractāre* to handle; see TRACTABLE]

traction ('trækʃən) *n* **1** the act of drawing or pulling, esp. by motive power. **2** the state of being drawn or pulled. **3**

Med. the application of a steady pull on a limb, etc., using a system of weights and pulleys or splints. **4** adhesive friction, as between a wheel of a motor vehicle and the road. [C17: from Med. L *tractiō*, from L *tractus* dragged, from *trahere* to drag]
▶ 'tractional *adj* ▶ **tractive** ('træktɪv) *adj*

traction engine *n* a steam-powered locomotive used, esp. formerly, for drawing heavy loads along roads or over rough ground.

traction load *n Geol.* the solid material that is carried along the bed of a river.

tractor ('træktə) *n* **1** a motor vehicle with large rear wheels or endless belt treads, used to pull heavy loads, esp. farm machinery. **2** a short vehicle with a driver's cab, used to pull a trailer, as in an articulated lorry. [C18: from LL: one who pulls, from *trahere* to drag]

Tracy ★ ('treɪsɪ) *n* **Spencer.** 1900–67, US film actor. His films include *Captains Courageous* (1937), *Adam's Rib* (1949), and *Inherit the Wind* (1960).

trad (træd) *n* **1** *Chiefly Brit.* traditional jazz. ◆ *adj* **2** short for **traditional.**

trade (treɪd) *n* **1** the act or an instance of buying and selling goods and services. **2** a personal occupation, esp. a craft requiring skill. **3** the people and practices of an industry, craft, or business. **4** exchange of one thing for something else. **5** the regular clientele of a firm or industry. **6** amount of custom or commercial dealings; business. **7** a specified market or business: *the tailoring trade.* **8** an occupation in commerce, as opposed to a profession. ◆ *vb* **trades, trading, traded. 9** (*tr*) to buy and sell (merchandise). **10** to exchange (one thing) for another. **11** (*intr*) to engage in trade. **12** (*intr*) to deal or do business (with). ◆ See also **trade-in, trade on.** [C14 (in the sense: track, hence, a regular business)]
▶ 'tradable *or* 'tradeable *adj*

trade agreement *n* a commercial treaty between two or more nations.

trade association *n* an association of organizations in the same trade formed to further their collective interests, esp. in negotiating with governments, trade unions, etc.

trade cycle *n* the recurrent fluctuation between boom and depression in the economic activity of a capitalist country.

trade discount *n* a sum or percentage deducted from the list price of a commodity allowed to a retailer or by one enterprise to another in the same trade.

traded option *n Stock Exchange.* an option that can itself be bought and sold on a stock exchange. Cf. **traditional option.**

trade down *vb* (*intr, adv*) to sell a large or relatively expensive house, car, etc., and replace it with a smaller or less expensive one.

trade gap *n* the amount by which the value of a country's visible imports exceeds that of visible exports; an unfavourable balance of trade.

trade-in *n* **1a** a used article given in part payment for the purchase of a new article. **1b** a transaction involving such part payment. **1c** the valuation put on the article traded in. ◆ *vb* **trade in. 2** (*tr, adv*) to give (a used article) as part payment for a new article.

trademark ('treɪd,mɑːk) *n* **1a** the name or other symbol used by a manufacturer or dealer to distinguish his products from those of competitors. **1b Registered Trademark.** one that is officially registered and legally protected. **2** any distinctive sign or mark of the presence of a person or animal. ◆ *vb* (*tr*) **3** to label with a trademark. **4** to register as a trademark.

trade name *n* **1** the name used by a trade to refer to a commodity, service, etc. **2** the name under which a commercial enterprise operates in business.

trade-off *n* an exchange, esp. as a compromise.

trade on *vb* (*intr, prep*) to exploit or take advantage of: *he traded on her endless patience.*

trade plate *n* a numberplate attached temporarily to a vehicle by a dealer, etc., before the vehicle has been registered.

trader ('treɪdə) n **1** a person who engages in trade. **2** a vessel regularly employed in trade. **3** Stock Exchange, US. a member who operates mainly on his own account.

trade reference n a reference in which one trader gives his opinion as to the credit worthiness of another trader in the same trade, esp. to a supplier.

tradescantia (ˌtrædes'kænʃɪə) n any of a genus of plants widely cultivated for their striped variegated leaves. [C18: NL, after John Tradescant (1608–62), E botanist]

Trades Council n (in Britain) an association of the different trade unions in one town or area.

trade secret n a secret formula, technique, process, etc., known and used to advantage by only one manufacturer.

tradesman ('treɪdzmən) n, pl **tradesmen**. **1** a man engaged in trade, esp. a retail dealer. **2** a skilled worker.
  ▸ '**trades,woman** fem n

tradespeople ('treɪdz,pi:pᵊl) or **tradesfolk** ('treɪdz,fəʊk) pl n Chiefly Brit. people engaged in trade, esp. shopkeepers.

Trades Union Congress n the major association of British trade unions, which includes all the larger unions. Abbrev.: **TUC**

trade union or **trades union** n an association of employees formed to improve their incomes and working conditions by collective bargaining.
  ▸ **trade unionism** or **trades unionism** n ▸ **trade unionist** or **trades unionist** n

trade up vb (intr, adv) to sell a small or relatively inexpensive house, car, etc., and replace it with a larger or more expensive one.

trade wind (wɪnd) n a wind blowing obliquely towards the equator either from the northeast in the N hemisphere or the southeast in the S hemisphere, between latitudes 30° N and S. [C17: from to blow trade to blow steadily in one direction, from trade in the obs. sense: a track]

trading estate n Chiefly Brit. a large area in which a number of commercial or industrial firms are situated. Also called: **industrial estate**.

trading post n a general store in an unsettled or thinly populated region.

tradition (trə'dɪʃən) n **1** the handing down from generation to generation of customs, beliefs, etc. **2** the body of customs, thought, etc., belonging to a particular country, people, family, or institution over a long period. **3** a specific custom or practice of long standing. **4** Christianity. a doctrine regarded as having been established by Christ or the apostles though not contained in Scripture. **5** (often cap.) Judaism. a body of laws regarded as having been handed down from Moses orally. **6** the beliefs and customs of Islam supplementing the Koran. **7** Law, chiefly Roman & Scots. the act of formally transferring ownership of movable property. [C14: from L trāditiō a handing down, surrender, from trādere to give up, transmit, from TRANS- + dāre to give]
  ▸ tra'ditionless adj

traditional (trə'dɪʃᵊnᵊl) adj **1** of, relating to, or being a tradition. **2** of the style of jazz originating in New Orleans, characterized by collective improvisation by a front line of trumpet, trombone, and clarinet.
  ▸ tra'ditionally adv

traditionalism (trə'dɪʃənᵊ,lɪzəm) n **1** the doctrine that all knowledge originates in divine revelation and is perpetuated by tradition. **2** adherence to tradition, esp. in religion.
  ▸ tra'ditionalist n, adj ▸ tra,ditional'istic adj

traditional logic n the logic of the late Middle Ages, derived from Aristotelian logic, and concerned esp. with the study of the syllogism.

traditional option n Stock Exchange. an option that once purchased cannot be resold. Cf. **traded option**.

traduce (trə'dju:s) vb **traduces, traducing, traduced**. (tr) to speak badly or maliciously of. [C16: from L trādūcere to lead over, disgrace]
  ▸ tra'ducement n ▸ tra'ducer n

Trafalgar ★ (trə'fælgə; Spanish trafal'γar) n Cape. a cape

on the SW coast of Spain, south of Cádiz: scene of the decisive naval battle (1805) in which the French and Spanish fleets were defeated by the English under Nelson.

traffic ('træfɪk) n **1a** the vehicles coming and going in a street, town, etc. **1b** (as modifier): traffic lights. **2** the movement of vehicles, people, etc., in a particular place or for a particular purpose: sea traffic. **3** (usually foll. by with) dealings or business. **4** trade, esp. of an illicit kind: drug traffic. **5** the aggregate volume of messages transmitted through a communications system in a given period. **6** Chiefly US. the number of customers patronizing a commercial establishment in a given time period. ◆ vb **traffics, trafficking, trafficked**. (intr) **7** (often foll. by in) to carry on trade or business, esp. of an illicit kind. **8** (usually foll. by with) to have dealings. [C16: from OF trafique, from Olt. traffico, from trafficare to engage in trade]
  ▸ 'trafficker n

trafficator ('træfɪ,keɪtə) n (formerly) an illuminated arm on a motor vehicle raised to indicate a left or right turn.

traffic calming n the use of a series of devices, such as bends and humps in the road, to slow down traffic, esp. in residential areas.

traffic island n a raised area in the middle of a road designed as a guide for traffic flow and to provide a stopping place for pedestrians crossing.

traffic jam n a number of vehicles so obstructed that they can scarcely move.

traffic light or **signal** n one of a set of coloured lights at crossroads or junctions, to control the flow of traffic.

traffic pattern n a pattern of permitted lanes in the air around an airport to which an aircraft is restricted.

traffic warden n Brit. a person who is appointed to supervise road traffic and report traffic offences.

Trafford ★ ('træfəd) n a unitary authority in NW England, in Greater Manchester. Pop.: 218 100 (1994 est.). Area: 106 sq. km (41 sq. miles).

tragacanth ('trægə,kænθ) n **1** any of various spiny plants that yield a substance that is made into a gum. **2** the gum obtained from these plants, used in the manufacture of pills and lozenges and in calico printing. [C16: from F tragacante, from L tragacantha goat's thorn, from Gk, from tragos goat + akantha thorn]

tragedian (trə'dʒi:dɪən) or (fem) **tragedienne** (trə,dʒi:dɪ'ɛn) n **1** an actor who specializes in tragic roles. **2** a writer of tragedy.

tragedy ('trædʒɪdɪ) n, pl **tragedies**. **1** a play in which the protagonist falls to disaster through the combination of a personal failing and circumstances with which he cannot deal. **2** any dramatic or literary composition dealing with serious or sombre themes and ending with disaster. **3** the branch of drama dealing with such themes. **4** the unfortunate aspect of something. **5** a shocking or sad event; disaster. [C14: from OF tragédie, from L tragoedia, from Gk, from tragos goat + ōidē song; ?from the goat-satyrs of Peloponnesian plays]

tragic ('trædʒɪk) or (less commonly) **tragical** adj **1** of, relating to, or characteristic of tragedy. **2** mournful or pitiable.
  ▸ 'tragically adv

tragic flaw n the failing of character in a tragic hero.

tragic irony n the use of dramatic irony in a tragedy so that the audience is aware that a character's words or actions will bring about a tragic or fatal result, while the character himself is not.

tragicomedy (ˌtrædʒɪ'kɒmɪdɪ) n, pl **tragicomedies**. **1** a drama in which aspects of both tragedy and comedy are found. **2** an event or incident having both comic and tragic aspects. [C16: from F, ult. from LL tragicōmoedia]
  ▸ ,tragi'comic or ,tragi'comical adj

tragopan ('trægə,pæn) n any of a genus of pheasants of S and SE Asia, having brightly coloured fleshy processes on the head. [C19: via L from Gk, from tragos goat + PAN]

tragus ('treɪgəs) n, pl **tragi** (-dʒaɪ). the fleshy projection that partially covers the entrance to the external ear.

★ people and places

[C17: from LL, from Gk *tragos* hairy projection of the ear, lit.: goat]

Traherne ★ (trə'hɜːn) *n* **Thomas.** 1637–74, English mystical writer. His prose works include *Centuries of Meditations.*

trail (treɪl) *vb* **1** to drag, stream, or permit to drag or stream along a surface, esp. the ground. **2** to make (a track) through (a place). **3** to follow or hunt (an animal or person) by following marks or tracks. **4** (when *intr*, often foll. by *behind*) to lag or linger behind (a person or thing). **5** (*intr*) (esp. of plants) to extend or droop over or along a surface. **6** (*intr*) to be falling behind in a race: *the favourite is trailing at the last fence.* **7** (*tr*) to tow (a caravan, etc.) behind a motor vehicle. **8** (*tr*) to carry (a rifle) at the full length of the right arm in a horizontal position, with the muzzle to the fore. **9** (*intr*) to move wearily or slowly. **10** (*tr*) (on television or radio) to advertise (a future programme) with short extracts. ♦ *n* **11** a print, mark, or scent made by a person, animal, or object. **12** the act or an instance of trailing. **13** a path, track, or road, esp. one roughly blazed. **14** something that trails behind or trails in loops or strands. **15** the part of a towed gun carriage and limber that connects the two when in movement and rests on the ground as a partial support when unlimbered. [C14: from OF *trailler* to tow, from Vulgar L *tragulāre* (unattested), from L *trāgula* dragnet, from *trahere* to drag]

trail away *or* **off** *vb* (*intr*, *adv*) to make or become fainter, quieter, or weaker. Cf. **leading edge.**

trailblazer ('treɪl,bleɪzə) *n* **1** a leader or pioneer in a particular field. **2** a person who blazes a trail.
▶ 'trail,blazing *adj*, *n*

trailer ('treɪlə) *n* **1** a road vehicle, usually two-wheeled, towed by a motor vehicle: used for transporting boats, etc. **2** the rear section of an articulated lorry. **3** a series of short extracts from a film, used to advertise it in a cinema or on television. **4** a person or thing that trails. **5** the US and Canad. name for **caravan** (sense 1).

trailing edge *n* the rear edge of a propeller blade or aerofoil. Cf. **leading edge.**

train (treɪn) *vb* **1** (*tr*) to guide or teach (to do something), as by subjecting to various exercises or experiences. **2** (*tr*) to control or guide towards a specific goal: *to train a plant up a wall.* **3** (*intr*) to do exercises and prepare for a specific purpose. **4** (*tr*) to improve or curb by subjecting to discipline: *to train the mind.* **5** (*tr*) to focus or bring to bear (on something): *to train a telescope on the moon.* ♦ *n* **6** a line of coaches or wagons coupled together and drawn by a railway locomotive. **7** a sequence or series: *a train of disasters.* **8** a procession of people, vehicles, etc., travelling together, such as one carrying equipment in support of a military operation. **9** a series of interacting parts through which motion is transmitted: *a train of gears.* **10** a fuse or line of gunpowder to an explosive charge, etc. **11** something drawn along, such as the long back section of a dress that trails along the floor. **12** a retinue or suite. [C14: from OF *trahiner*, from Vulgar L *tragīnāre* (unattested) to draw]
▶ 'trainable *adj*

trainband ('treɪn,bænd) *n* a company of English militia from the 16th to the 18th century. [C17: altered from *trained band*]

trainbearer ('treɪn,beərə) *n* an attendant who holds up the train of a dignitary's robe or bride's gown.

trainee (treɪ'niː) *n* **a** a person undergoing training. **b** (*as modifier*): *a trainee journalist.*

trainer ('treɪnə) *n* **1** a person who trains athletes. **2** a piece of equipment employed in training, such as a simulated aircraft cockpit. **3** a person who schools racehorses. **4** (*pl*) another name for **training shoes.**

training ('treɪnɪŋ) *n* **1a** the process of bringing a person, etc., to an agreed standard of proficiency, etc., by practice and instruction. **1b** (*as modifier*): *training college.* **2 in training. 2a** undergoing physical training. **2b** physically fit. **3 out of training.** physically unfit.

Training Agency *n* (in Britain) an organization established in 1989 to replace the Training Commission; it provides training and retraining for adult workers and operates the Youth Training Scheme, in England and Wales working through the local Training and Enterprise Councils (TECs) and in Scotland through the Local Enterprise Companies (LECs) set up in 1990.

training shoes *pl n* **1** running shoes for sports training, esp. in contrast to studded or spiked shoes worn for the sport itself. **2** shoes in the style of those used for sports training. ♦ Also called: **trainers.**

train oil *n* whale oil obtained from blubber. [C16: from earlier *train* or *trane*, from MLow G *trān*, or MDu. *traen* tear, drop]

train spotter *n* **1** a person who collects the numbers of railway locomotives. **2** *Inf.* a person who is obsessed with trivial details, esp. of a subject generally considered uninteresting.

traipse *or* **trapes** (treɪps) *Inf.* ♦ *vb* **traipses, traipsing, traipsed** *or* **trapeses, trapesing, trapesed.** **1** (*intr*) to walk heavily or tiredly. ♦ *n* **2** a long or tiring walk; trudge. [C16: from ?]

trait (treɪt, treɪ) *n* **1** a characteristic feature or quality distinguishing a particular person or thing. **2** *Rare.* a touch or stroke. [C16: from F, from OF: a pulling, from L *tractus*, from *trahere* to drag]

traitor ('treɪtə) *n* a person who is guilty of treason or treachery, in betraying friends, country, a cause, etc. [C13: from OF *traitour*, from L *trāditor*, from *trādere* to hand over]
▶ 'traitorous *adj* ▶ 'traitress *fem n*

Trajan ★ ('treɪdʒən) *n* Latin name *Marcus Ulpius Traianus.* ?53–117 A.D., Roman emperor (98–117).

trajectory (trə'dʒɛktərɪ) *n*, *pl* **trajectories. 1** the path described by an object moving in air or space, esp. the curved path of a projectile. **2** *Geom.* a curve that cuts a family of curves or surfaces at a constant angle. [C17: from L *trājectus* cast over, from *trāicere* to throw across]

Tralee ★ (trə'liː) *n* a market town in SW Republic of Ireland, county town of Kerry, near **Tralee Bay** (an inlet of the Atlantic). Pop.: 17 200 (1991).

tram (træm) *n* **1** Also called: **tramcar.** an electrically driven public transport vehicle that runs on rails let into the surface of the road. US and Canad. names: **streetcar, trolley car.** **2** a small vehicle on rails for carrying loads in a mine; tub. [C16 (in the sense: shaft of a cart): prob. from Low G *traam* beam]
▶ 'tramless *adj*

tramline ('træm,laɪn) *n* **1** (*often pl*) Also called: **tramway.** the tracks on which a tram runs. **2** the route taken by a tram. **3** (*often pl*) the outer markings along the sides of a tennis or badminton court.

trammel ('træməl) *n* **1** (*often pl*) a hindrance to free action or movement. **2** Also called: **trammel net.** a fishing net in three sections, the two outer nets having a large mesh and the middle one a fine mesh. **3** *Rare.* a fowling net. **4** *US.* a shackle for a horse. **5** a device for drawing ellipses consisting of a flat sheet having a cruciform slot in which run two pegs attached to a beam. **6** (*sometimes pl*) a beam compass. **7** a device set in a fireplace to support cooking pots. ♦ *vb* **trammels, trammelling, trammelled** *or US* **trammels, trammeling, trammeled.** **8** to hinder or restrain. **9** to catch or ensnare. [C14: from OF *tramail* three-mesh net, from LL *trēmaculum*, from L *trēs* three + *macula* mesh in a net]

tramontane (trə'mɒnteɪn) *adj* **1** being or coming from the far side of the mountains, esp. from the other side of the Alps as seen from Italy. ♦ *n* **2** an inhabitant of a tramontane country. **3** Also called: **tramontana.** a cold dry wind blowing south or southwest from the mountains in Italy and the W Mediterranean. [C16: from It. *tramontano*, from L *trānsmontānus*, from TRANS- + *montānus*, from *mōns* mountain]

tramp (træmp) *vb* **1** (*intr*) to walk long and far; hike. **2** to walk heavily or firmly across or through (a place). **3** (*intr*) to wander about as a vagabond or tramp. **4** (*tr*) to traverse on foot, esp. laboriously or wearily. **5** (*intr*) to tread or trample. ♦ *n* **6** a person who travels around on foot, living by begging or doing casual work. **7** a long hard walk; hike. **8** a heavy or rhythmic tread. **9** the sound of heavy treading. **10** a merchant ship that does not run on

a regular schedule but carries cargo wherever the shippers desire. **11** *Sl.*, *chiefly US & Canad.* a prostitute or promiscuous girl or woman. [C14: prob. from MLow G *trampen*]
▸ **'trampish** *adj*

tramper ('træmpə) *n NZ.* a person who tramps, or walks long distances, in the bush.

tramping ('træmpɪŋ) *n NZ.* **1** the leisure activity of walking in the bush. **2** (*as modifier*): *tramping boots.*

trample ('træmp°l) *vb* **tramples, trampling, trampled.** (when *intr*, usually foll. by *on*, *upon*, or *over*) **1** to stamp or walk roughly (on). **2** to encroach (upon) so as to violate or hurt. ◆ *n* **3** the action or sound of trampling. [C14: frequentative of TRAMP]
▸ **'trampler** *n*

trampoline ('træmpəlɪn, -ˌliːn) *n* **1** a tough canvas sheet suspended by springs or cords from a frame, used by acrobats, gymnasts, etc. ◆ *vb* **trampolines, trampolining, trampolined. 2** (*intr*) to exercise on a trampoline. [C18: via Sp. from It. *trampolino*, from *trampoli* stilts, of Gmc origin]
▸ **'trampoliner** or **'trampolinist** *n*

trance (trɑːns) *n* **1** a hypnotic state resembling sleep. **2** any mental state in which a person is unaware of the environment, characterized by loss of voluntary movement, rigidity, and lack of sensitivity to external stimuli. **3** a dazed or stunned state. **4** a state of ecstasy or mystic absorption so intense as to cause a temporary loss of consciousness at the earthly level. **5** *Spiritualism.* a state in which a medium can supposedly be controlled by an intelligence from without as a means of communication with the dead. ◆ *vb* **trances, trancing, tranced. 6** (*tr*) to put into or as into a trance. [C14: from OF *transe*, from *transir* to faint, from L *trānsīre* to go over]
▸ **'trance,like** *adj*

tranche (trɑːnʃ) *n* an instalment or portion, esp. of a loan or share issue. [F, lit.: slice]

trannie or **tranny** ('trænɪ) *n*, *pl* **trannies.** *Inf.*, *chiefly Brit.* a transistor radio.

tranquil ('træŋkwɪl) *adj* calm, peaceful, or quiet. [C17: from L *tranquillus*]
▸ **'tranquilly** *adv*

tranquillity or *US* (*sometimes*) **tranquility** (træŋ-'kwɪlɪtɪ) *n* a state of calm or quietude.

tranquillize, tranquillise, or *US* **tranquilize** ('træŋkwɪˌlaɪz) *vb* **tranquillizes, tranquillizing, tranquillized; tranquillises, tranquillising, tranquillised,** or *US* **tranquilizes, tranquilizing, tranquilized.** to make or become calm or calmer.
▸ ˌtranquilli'zation, ˌtranquilli'sation, or *US* ˌtranquili-'zation *n*

tranquillizer, tranquilliser, or *US* **tranquilizer** ('træŋkwɪˌlaɪzə) *n* **1** a drug that calms a person. **2** anything that tranquillizes.

tranquillo (ˌtræŋ'kwiːləʊ) *adj Music.* calm; tranquil. [It.]

trans. *abbrev. for:* **1** transaction. **2** transferred. **3** transitive. **4** translated. **5** translator. **6** transport(ation). **7** transverse.

trans- *prefix* **1** across, beyond, crossing, on the other side: *transatlantic.* **2** changing thoroughly: *transliterate.* **3** transcending: *transubstantiation.* **4** transversely: *transect.* **5** (*often in italics*) indicating that a chemical compound has a molecular structure in which two identical groups or atoms are on opposite sides of a double bond: *trans*-butadiene. [from L *trāns* across, through, beyond]

transact (træn'zækt) *vb* to do, conduct, or negotiate (business, a deal, etc.). [C16: from L *trānsactus*, from *trānsigere*, lit.: to drive through]
▸ **trans'actor** *n*

transactinide (træns'æktɪˌnaɪd) *n* any artificially produced element with an atomic number greater than 103. [C20]

transaction (træn'zækʃən) *n* **1** something that is transacted, esp. a business deal. **2** a transacting or being transacted. **3** (*pl*) the records of the proceedings of a society, etc.
▸ **trans'actional** *adj*

transalpine (trænz'ælpaɪn) *adj* (*prenominal*) **1** situated in or relating to places beyond the Alps, esp. from Italy. **2** passing over the Alps.

Transalpine Gaul ★ *n* (in the ancient world) that part of Gaul northwest of the Alps.

transaminase (trænz'æmɪˌneɪz, -ˌneɪs) *n Biochem.* an enzyme that catalyses the transfer of an amino group from one molecule, esp. an amino acid, to another, esp. a keto acid, in the process of **transamination.**

transatlantic (ˌtrænzət'læntɪk) *adj* **1** on or from the other side of the Atlantic. **2** crossing the Atlantic.

Transcaucasia ★ (ˌtrænskɔː'keɪzjə) *n* a region of central Asia, south of the Caucasus Mountains between the Black and Caspian Seas in Georgia, Azerbaijan, and Armenia: a constituent republic of the Soviet Union from 1918 until 1936.
▸ ˌTranscau'casian *adj*, *n*

transceiver (træn'siːvə) *n* a device which transmits and receives radio or electronic signals. [C20: from TRANS(MITTER) + (RE)CEIVER]

transcend (træn'sɛnd) *vb* **1** to go above or beyond (a limit, expectation, etc.), as in degree or excellence. **2** (*tr*) to be superior to. [C14: from L *trānscendere* to climb over]

transcendent (træn'sɛndənt) *adj* **1** exceeding or surpassing in degree or excellence. **2** (in the philosophy of Kant) beyond or before experience. **3** *Theol.* (of God) having existence outside the created world. **4** free from the limitations inherent in matter. ◆ *n* **5** *Philosophy.* a transcendent thing.
▸ **tran'scendence** or **tran'scendency** *n* ▸ **tran'scendently** *adv*

transcendental (ˌtrænsɛn'dɛnt°l) *adj* **1** transcendent, superior, or surpassing. **2** (in the philosophy of Kant) **2a** (of a judgment or logical deduction) being both synthetic and a priori. **2b** of or relating to knowledge of the presuppositions of thought. **3** *Philosophy.* beyond our experience of phenomena, although not beyond potential knowledge. **4** *Theol.* supernatural or mystical. **5** *Maths.* **5a** (of a number or quantity) not being a root of any polynomial with rational coefficients. **5b** (of a function) not capable of expression in terms of a finite number of arithmetical operations.
▸ ˌtranscen'dentally *adv*

transcendentalism (ˌtrænsɛn'dɛntəˌlɪzəm) *n* **1a** any system of philosophy, esp. that of Kant, holding that the key to knowledge of the nature of reality lies in the critical examination of the processes of reason on which depends the nature of experience. **1b** any system of philosophy, esp. that of Emerson, that emphasizes intuition as a means to knowledge or the importance of the search for the divine. **2** vague philosophical speculation. **3** the state of being transcendental. **4** something, such as thought or language, that is transcendental.
▸ ˌtranscen'dentalist *n*, *adj*

transcendental meditation *n* a technique, based on Hindu traditions, for relaxing and refreshing the mind and body through the silent repetition of a mantra.

transcontinental (ˌtrænzkɒntɪ'nɛnt°l) *adj* **1** crossing a continent. **2** on or from the far side of a continent.
▸ ˌtransconti'nentally *adv*

transcribe (træn'skraɪb) *vb* **transcribes, transcribing, transcribed.** (*tr*) **1** to write, type, or print out fully from speech, notes, etc. **2** to transliterate or translate. **3** to make an electrical recording of (a programme or speech) for a later broadcast. **4** *Music.* to rewrite (a piece of music) for an instrument or medium other than that originally intended; arrange. **5** *Computing.* **5a** to transfer (information) from one storage device to another. **5b** to transfer (information) from a computer to an external storage device. [C16: from L *trānscrībere*]
▸ **tran'scribable** *adj* ▸ **tran'scriber** *n*

transcript ('trænskrɪpt) *n* **1** a written, typed, or printed copy or manuscript made by transcribing. **2** *Chiefly US & Canad.* an official record of a student's school progress. **3** any reproduction or copy. [C13: from L *trānscriptum*, from *trānscrībere* to transcribe]

transcriptase (trænˈskrɪpteɪz) *n* See **reverse transcriptase**.

transcription (trænˈskrɪpʃən) *n* **1** the act or an instance of transcribing or the state of being transcribed. **2** something transcribed. **3** a representation in writing of the actual pronunciation of a speech sound, word, etc., using phonetic symbols.
▸ tran'scriptional *or* tran'scriptive *adj*

transducer (trænzˈdjuːsə) *n* any device, such as a microphone or electric motor, that converts one form of energy into another. [C20: from L *trānsdūcere* to lead across]

transect *vb* (trænˈsɛkt). (*tr*) **1** to cut or divide crossways. ◆ *n* (ˈtrænsɛkt). **2** a sample strip of land used to monitor plant distribution, animal populations, or some other feature, within a given area. [C17: from L TRANS- + *secāre* to cut]
▸ tran'section *n*

transept (ˈtrænsɛpt) *n* either of the two wings of a cruciform church at right angles to the nave. [C16: from Anglo-L *trānseptum*, from L TRANS- + *saeptum* enclosure]
▸ tran'septal *adj*

trans-fatty acid *n* a polyunsaturated fatty acid that has been converted from the cis-form by hydrogenation: used in the manufacture of margarine.

transfer *vb* (trænsˈfɜː), **transfers, transferring, transferred. 1** to change or go or cause to change or go from one thing, person, or point to another. **2** to change (buses, trains, etc.). **3** *Law.* to make over (property, etc.) to another; convey. **4** to displace (a drawing, design, etc.) from one surface to another. **5** (of a football player) to change clubs or (of a club, manager, etc.) to sell or release (a player) to another club. **6** to leave one school, college, etc., and enrol at another. **7** to change (the meaning of a word, etc.), esp. by metaphorical extension. ◆ *n* (ˈtrænsfɜː). **8** the act, process, or system of transferring, or the state of being transferred. **9** a person or thing that transfers or is transferred. **10** a design or drawing that is transferred from one surface to another. **11** *Law.* the passing of title to property or other right from one person to another; conveyance. **12** any document or form effecting or regulating a transfer. **13** *Chiefly US & Canad.* a ticket that allows a passenger to change routes. [C14: from L *trānsferre*, from TRANS- + *ferre* to carry]
▸ trans'ferable *or* trans'ferrable *adj* ▸ transference (ˈtrænsfərəns) *n*

transferable vote *n* a vote that is transferred to a second candidate indicated by the voter if the first is eliminated from the ballot.

transferee (ˌtrænsfəˈriː) *n* **1** *Property law.* a person to whom property is transferred. **2** a person who is transferred.

transfer fee *n* a sum of money paid by one football club to another for a transferred player.

transferrin (trænsˈfɜːrɪn) *n Biochem.* any of a group of blood proteins that transport iron. [C20: from TRANS- + FERRO- + -IN]

transfer RNA *n Biochem.* any of several soluble forms of RNA of low molecular weight, each of which transports a specific amino acid to a ribosome during protein synthesis.

transfiguration (ˌtrænsfɪɡjuˈreɪʃən) *n* a transfiguring or being transfigured.

Transfiguration (ˌtrænsfɪɡjuˈreɪʃən) *n* **1** *New Testament.* the change in the appearance of Christ that took place before three disciples (Matthew 17:1–9). **2** the Church festival held in commemoration of this on Aug. 6.

transfigure (trænsˈfɪɡə) *vb* **transfigures, transfiguring, transfigured.** (*usually tr*) **1** to change or cause to change in appearance. **2** to become or cause to become more exalted. [C13: from L *trānsfigūrāre*, from TRANS- + *figūra* appearance]
▸ trans'figurement *n*

transfinite number (trænsˈfaɪnaɪt) *n* a cardinal or ordinal number used in the comparison of infinite sets for which several types of infinity can be classified.

transfix (trænsˈfɪks) *vb* **transfixes, transfixing, transfixed** *or* **transfixt.** (*tr*) **1** to render motionless, esp. with horror or

shock. **2** to impale or fix with a sharp weapon or other device. [C16: from L *trānsfīgere* to pierce through]
▸ transfixion (trænsˈfɪkʃən) *n*

transform *vb* (trænsˈfɔːm). **1** to alter or be altered in form, function, etc. **2** (*tr*) to convert (one form of energy) to another form. **3** (*tr*) *Maths.* to change the form of (an equation, etc.) by a mathematical transformation. **4** (*tr*) to change (an alternating current or voltage) using a transformer. ◆ *n* (ˈtrænsˌfɔːm). **5** *Maths.* the result of a mathematical transformation. [C14: from L *trānsformāre*]
▸ trans'formable *adj* ▸ trans'formative *adj*

transformation (ˌtrænsfəˈmeɪʃən) *n* **1** a change or alteration, esp. a radical one. **2** a transforming or being transformed. **3** *Maths.* **3a** a change in position or direction of the reference axes in a coordinate system without an alteration in their relative angle. **3b** an equivalent change in an expression or equation resulting from the substitution of one set of variables by another. **4** *Physics.* a change in an atomic nucleus to a different nuclide as the result of the emission of either an alpha-particle or a beta-particle. **5** *Linguistics.* another word for **transformational rule. 6** an apparently miraculous change in the appearance of a stage set.
▸ ˌtransfor'mational *adj*

transformational grammar *n* a grammatical description of a language making essential use of transformational rules.

transformational rule *n Generative grammar.* a rule that converts one phrase marker into another. Taken together, these rules convert the deep structures of sentences into their surface structures.

transformer (trænsˈfɔːmə) *n* **1** a device that transfers an alternating current from one circuit to one or more other circuits, usually with a change of voltage. **2** a person or thing that transforms.

transfuse (trænsˈfjuːz) *vb* **transfuses, transfusing, transfused.** (*tr*) **1** to permeate or infuse. **2a** to inject (blood, etc.) into a blood vessel. **2b** to give a transfusion to (a patient). [C15: from L *trānsfundere* to pour out]
▸ trans'fuser *n* ▸ trans'fusible *or* trans'fusable *adj*
▸ trans'fusive *adj*

transfusion (trænsˈfjuːʒən) *n* **1** a transfusing. **2** the injection of blood, blood plasma, etc., into the blood vessels of a patient.

transgenic (trænzˈdʒɛnɪk) *adj* (of an animal or plant) containing genetic material artificially transferred from another species.

transgress (trænzˈɡrɛs) *vb* **1** to break (a law, etc.). **2** to go beyond or overstep (a limit). [C16: from L *trānsgredī*, from TRANS- + *gradī* to step]
▸ trans'gressive *adj* ▸ trans'gressor *n*

transgression (trænzˈɡrɛʃən) *n* **1** a breach of a law, etc.; sin or crime. **2** a transgressing.

tranship (trænˈʃɪp) *vb* **tranships, transhipping, transhipped.** a variant spelling of **transship.**

transhumance (trænsˈhjuːməns) *n* the seasonal migration of livestock to suitable grazing grounds. [C20: from F, from *transhumer* to change one's pastures, from Sp. *trashumar*, from L TRANS- + *humus* ground]
▸ trans'humant *adj*

transient (ˈtrænzɪənt) *adj* **1** for a short time only; temporary or transitory. ◆ *n* **2** a transient person or thing. [C17: from L *trānsiēns* going over, from *trānsīre* to pass over]
▸ 'transiently *adv* ▸ 'transience *or* 'transiency *n*

transistor (trænˈzɪstə) *n* **1** a semiconductor device, having three or more terminals attached to electrode regions, in which current flowing between two electrodes is controlled by a voltage or current applied to one or more specified electrodes. The device has replaced the valve in most circuits since it is much smaller and works at a much lower voltage. **2** *Inf.* a transistor radio. [C20: orig. a trademark, from TRANSFER + RESISTOR, from the transfer of electric signals across a resistor]

transistorize *or* **transistorise** (trænˈzɪstəˌraɪz) *vb* **transistorizes, transistorizing, transistorized** *or* **transistorises, transistorising, transistorised. 1** to convert to the use or manufacture of transistors and other solid-state components. **2** (*tr*) to equip with transistors and other solid-state components.

transit ('trænsɪt, 'trænz-) *n* **1a** the passage or conveyance of goods or people. **1b** (*as modifier*): *a transit visa*. **2** a change or transition. **3** a route. **4** *Astron*. **4a** the passage of a celestial body or satellite across the face of a larger body as seen from the earth. **4b** the apparent passage of a celestial body across the meridian. **5 in transit**. while being conveyed; during passage. ♦ *vb* **6** to make a transit through or over (something). [C15: from L *trānsitus* a going over, from *trānsīre* to pass over]

transit camp *n* a camp in which refugees, soldiers, etc., live temporarily.

transit instrument *n* an astronomical instrument used to time the transit of a star, etc., across the meridian.

transition (træn'zɪʃən) *n* **1** change or passage from one state or stage to another. **2** the period of time during which something changes. **3** *Music*. **3a** a movement from one key to another; modulation. **3b** a linking passage between two divisions in a composition; bridge. **4** a style of architecture in the late 11th and early 12th centuries, characterized by late Romanesque forms combined with early Gothic details. **5** *Physics*. a change in the configuration of an atomic nucleus, involving either a change in energy level or a transformation to another element or isotope. **6** a sentence, passage, etc., that links sections of a written work. [C16: from L *transitio*; see TRANSIENT] ▸ **tran'sitional** *adj* ▸ **tran'sitionally** *adv*

transition element *or* **metal** *n Chem.* any element belonging to one of three series of elements with atomic numbers between 21 and 30, 39 and 48, and 57 and 80. They have an incomplete penultimate electron shell and tend to form complexes.

transition temperature *n* the temperature at which a sudden change of physical properties occurs.

transitive ('trænsɪtɪv) *adj* **1** *Grammar*. **1a** denoting an occurrence of a verb when it requires a direct object or denoting a verb that customarily requires a direct object: *"to find" is a transitive verb*. **1b** (*as n*): *these verbs are transitives*. **2** *Logic, maths*. having the property that if one object bears a relationship to a second object that also bears the same relationship to a third object, then the first object bears this relationship to the third object: *if x = y and y = z then x = z.* ♦ Cf. **intransitive**. [C16: from LL *trānsitīvus*, from L *trānsitus* a going over; see TRANSIENT] ▸ **'transitively** *adv* ▸ **transi'tivity** *or* **'transitiveness** *n*

transitory ('trænsɪtərɪ, -trɪ) *adj* of short duration; transient or ephemeral. [C14: from Church L *trānsitōrius* passing, from L *trānsitus* a crossing over] ▸ **'transitoriness** *n*

transit theodolite *n* a theodolite the telescope of which can be rotated completely about its horizontal axis.

Trans-Jordan ★ *n* the former name (1922–49) of **Jordan.** ▸ **Trans-Jor'danian** *adj, n*

Transkei ★ (træn'skaɪ) *n* a former Bantu homeland in South Africa: the largest of South Africa's Bantu homelands and the first Bantu self-governing territory (1963); reintegrated into South Africa in 1994. Capital: Umtata. ▸ **Trans'keian** *adj, n*

transl. *abbrev. for:* **1** translated. **2** translator.

translate (træns'leɪt, trænz-) *vb* **translates, translating, translated. 1** to express or be capable of being expressed in another language. **2** (*intr*) to act as translator. **3** (*tr*) to express or explain in simple or less technical language. **4** (*tr*) to interpret or infer the significance of (gestures, symbols, etc.). **5** (*tr*) to transform or convert: *to translate hope into reality*. **6** to transfer from one place or position to another. **7** (*tr*) *Theol*. to transfer (a person) from one place or plane of existence to another, as from earth to heaven. **8** (*tr*) *Maths, physics*. to move (a figure or body) laterally, without rotation, dilation, or angular displacement. [C13: from L *trānslātus* carried over, from *trānsferre* to TRANSFER] ▸ **trans'latable** *adj* ▸ **trans'lator** *n*

translation (træns'leɪʃən, trænz-) *n* **1** something that is or has been translated. **2** a translating or being translated. **3** *Maths*. a transformation in which the origin of a coordinate system is moved to another position so that each axis retains the same direction. ▸ **trans'lational** *adj*

transliterate (trænz'lɪtəˌreɪt) *vb* **transliterates, transliterating, transliterated.** (*tr*) to transcribe (a word, etc.) into corresponding letters of another alphabet. [C19: TRANS- + -*literate*, from L *lĭttera* letter] ▸ **translite'ration** *n* ▸ **trans'liter,ator** *n*

translocation (ˌtrænzləʊ'keɪʃən) *n* **1** *Genetics*. the transfer of one part of a chromosome to another part of the same or a different chromosome. **2** *Bot*. the transport of minerals, sugars, etc., in solution within a plant. **3** a movement from one position or place to another.

translucent (trænz'luːs³nt) *adj* allowing light to pass through partially or diffusely; semitransparent. [C16: from L *trānslūcēre* to shine through] ▸ **trans'lucence** *or* **trans'lucency** *n* ▸ **trans'lucently** *adv*

translunar (trænz'luːnə) *or* **translunary** (trænz-'luːnərɪ) *adj* **1** lying beyond the moon. **2** unworldly or ethereal.

transmigrate (ˌtrænzmaɪ'greɪt) *vb* **transmigrates, transmigrating, transmigrated.** (*intr*) **1** to move from one place, state, or stage to another. **2** (of souls) to pass from one body into another at death. ▸ **transmi'gration** *n* ▸ **trans'migratory** *adj*

transmission (trænz'mɪʃən) *n* **1** the act or process of transmitting. **2** something that is transmitted. **3** the extent to which a body or medium transmits light, sound, etc. **4** the transference of motive force or power. **5** a system of shafts, gears, etc., that transmits power, esp. the arrangement of such parts that transmits the power of the engine to the driving wheels of a motor vehicle. **6** the act or process of sending a message, picture, or other information by means of radio waves, electrical signals, light signals, etc. **7** a radio or television broadcast. [C17: from L *trānsmissiō* a sending across] ▸ **trans'missible** *adj* ▸ **trans'missive** *adj*

transmission density *n Physics*. a measure of the extent to which a substance transmits light or other electromagnetic radiation.

transmission line *n* a coaxial cable, waveguide, etc., that transfers electrical signals from one location to another.

transmissivity (ˌtrænzmɪ'sɪvɪtɪ) *n Physics*. a measure of the ability of a material to transmit radiation.

transmit (trænz'mɪt) *vb* **transmits, transmitting, transmitted. 1** (*tr*) to pass or cause to go from one place or person to another; transfer. **2** (*tr*) to pass on or impart (a disease, etc.). **3** (*tr*) to hand down to posterity. **4** (*tr; usually passive*) to pass (an inheritable characteristic) from parent to offspring. **5** to allow the passage of (particles, energy, etc.): *radio waves are transmitted through the atmosphere*. **6a** to send out (signals) by means of radio waves or along a transmission line. **6b** to broadcast (a radio or television programme). **7** (*tr*) to transfer (a force, motion, etc.) from one part of a mechanical system to another. [C14: from L *trānsmittere* to send across] ▸ **trans'mittable** *adj* ▸ **trans'mittal** *n*

transmittance (trænz'mɪt³ns) *n* **1** the act of transmitting. **2** Also called: **transmission factor**. *Physics*. a measure of the ability of anything to transmit radiation, equal to the ratio of the transmitted flux to the incident flux.

transmitter (trænz'mɪtə) *n* **1** a person or thing that transmits. **2** the equipment used for generating and amplifying a radio-frequency carrier, modulating the carrier with information, and feeding it to an aerial for transmission. **3** the microphone in a telephone that converts sound waves into audio-frequency electrical signals. **4** a device that converts mechanical movements into coded electrical signals transmitted along a telegraph circuit. **5** a substance released by nerve endings that transmits impulses across synapses.

transmogrify (trænz'mɒgrɪˌfaɪ) *vb* **transmogrifies, transmogrifying, transmogrified.** (*tr*) *Jocular*. to change or trans-

form into a different shape, esp. a grotesque or bizarre one. [C17: from ?]
▸ **trans‚mogrifi'cation** *n*

transmontane (‚trænzmɒn'teɪn) *adj, n* another word for **tramontane**.

transmutation (‚trænzmju:'teɪʃən) *n* 1 the act or an instance of transmuting. 2 the change of one chemical element into another by a nuclear reaction. 3 the attempted conversion, by alchemists, of base metals into gold or silver.
▸ **‚transmu'tational** *or* **trans'mutative** *adj*

transmute (trænz'mju:t) *vb* **transmutes, transmuting, transmuted**. (*tr*) 1 to change the form, character, or substance of. 2 to alter (an element, metal, etc.) by alchemy. [C15: via OF from L *trānsmūtāre* to shift, from TRANS- + *mūtāre* to change]
▸ **trans‚muta'bility** *n* ▸ **trans'mutable** *adj*

transnational (trænz'næʃənəl) *adj* extending beyond the boundaries, etc., of a single nation.

transoceanic (trænz‚əʊʃɪ'ænɪk) *adj* 1 on or from the other side of an ocean. 2 crossing an ocean.

transom ('trænsəm) *n* 1 a horizontal member across a window. 2 a horizontal member that separates a door from a window over it. 3 the usual US name for **fanlight. 4** *Naut.* **4a** a surface forming the stern of a vessel. **4b** any of several transverse beams used for strengthening the stern of a vessel. [C14: earlier *traversayn*, from OF *traversin*, from TRAVERSE]
▸ **'transomed** *adj*

transonic (træn'sɒnɪk) *adj* of or relating to conditions when travelling at or near the speed of sound.

transparency (træns'pærənsɪ) *n, pl* **transparencies. 1** Also called: **transparence.** the state of being transparent. **2** Also called: **slide.** a positive photograph on a transparent base, usually mounted in a frame or between glass plates. It can be viewed by means of a slide projector.

transparent (træns'pærənt) *adj* 1 permitting the uninterrupted passage of light; clear. 2 easy to see through, understand, or recognize; obvious. 3 permitting the free passage of electromagnetic radiation. 4 candid, open, or frank. [C15: from Med. L *trānspārēre* to show through, from L TRANS- + *pārēre* to appear]
▸ **trans'parently** *adv* ▸ **trans'parentness** *n*

transpire (træn'spaɪə) *vb* **transpires, transpiring, transpired. 1** (*intr*) to come to light; be known. 2 (*intr*) *Inf.* to happen or occur. **3** *Physiol.* to give off or exhale (water or vapour) through the skin, a mucous membrane, etc. 4 (of plants) to lose (water), esp. through the stomata of the leaves. [C16: from Med. L *trānspīrāre*, from L TRANS- + *spīrāre* to breathe]
▸ **transpiration** (‚trænspə'reɪʃən) *n* ▸ **tran'spiratory** *adj*

> **USAGE NOTE** It is often maintained that *transpire* should not be used to mean happen or occur, as in *the event transpired late in the evening*, and that the word is properly used to mean become known, as in *it transpired later that the thief had been caught*. The word is, however, widely used in the former sense, esp. in spoken English.

transplant *vb* (træns'plɑ:nt). 1 (*tr*) to remove or transfer (esp. a plant) from one place to another. 2 (*intr*) to be capable of being transplanted. 3 *Surgery.* to transfer (an organ or tissue) from one part of the body or from one person to another. ◆ *n* ('træns‚plɑ:nt). 4 *Surgery.* **4a** the procedure involved in such a transfer. **4b** the organ or tissue transplanted.
▸ **trans'plantable** *adj* ▸ **‚transplan'tation** *n*

transponder (træn'spɒndə) *n* 1 a type of radio or radar transmitter-receiver that transmits signals automatically when it receives predetermined signals. 2 the receiver and transmitter in a communications satellite, relaying signals back to earth. [C20: from TRANSMITTER + RESPONDER]

transport *vb* (træns'pɔ:t). (*tr*) 1 to carry or cause to go from one place to another, esp. over some distance. 2 to

deport or exile to a penal colony. 3 (*usually passive*) to have a strong emotional effect on. ◆ *n* ('træns‚pɔ:t). **4a** the business or system of transporting goods or people. **4b** (*as modifier*): *a modernized transport system.* 5 *Brit.* freight vehicles generally. **6a** a vehicle used to transport goods or people, esp. troops. **6b** (*as modifier*): *a transport plane.* 7 a transporting or being transported. 8 ecstasy, rapture, or any powerful emotion. 9 a convict sentenced to be transported. [C14: from L *trānsportāre*, from TRANS- + *portāre* to carry]
▸ **trans'portable** *adj* ▸ **trans'porter** *n*

transportation (‚trænspɔ:'teɪʃən) *n* 1 a means or system of transporting. 2 the act of transporting or the state of being transported. 3 (esp. formerly) deportation to a penal colony.

transport café ('træns‚pɔ:t) *n Brit.* an inexpensive eating place on a main route, used mainly by long-distance lorry drivers.

transpose (træns'pəʊz) *vb* **transposes, transposing, transposed. 1** (*tr*) to alter the positions of; interchange, as words in a sentence. 2 *Music.* to play (notes, music, etc.) in a different key from that originally intended. 3 (*tr*) *Maths.* to move (a term) from one side of an equation to the other with a corresponding reversal in sign. [C14: from OF *transposer*, from L *trānspōnere* to remove]
▸ **trans'posable** *adj* ▸ **trans'posal** *n* ▸ **trans'poser** *n*
▸ **transposition** (‚trænspə'zɪʃən) *n*

transposing instrument *n* a musical instrument, esp. a horn or clarinet, pitched in a key other than C major, but whose music is written down as if its basic scale were C major.

transposon (træns'pəʊzɒn) *n Genetics.* a fragment of bacterial nucleic acid that can move from one site in a chromosome to another site in the same or a different chromosome and thus alter the genetic constitution of the bacterium. [C20: TRANSPOS(E) + -ON]

transputer (træns'pju:tə) *n Computing.* a type of fast powerful microchip that is the equivalent of a 32-bit microprocessor with its own RAM facility. [C20: from TRANS(ISTOR) + (COM)PUTER]

transsexual *or* **transexual** (trænz'seksjʊəl) *n* 1 a person who completely identifies with the opposite sex. 2 a person who has undergone medical procedures to alter sexual characteristics to those of the opposite sex.

transship (træns'ʃɪp) *or* **tranship** *vb* **transships, transshipping, transshipped** *or* **tranships, transhipping, transhipped.** to transfer or be transferred from one vessel or vehicle to another.
▸ **trans'shipment** *or* **tran'shipment** *n*

transubstantiation (‚trænsəb‚stænʃɪ'eɪʃən) *n* 1 (esp. in Roman Catholic theology) **1a** the doctrine that the whole substance of the bread and wine changes into the substance of the body and blood of Christ when consecrated in the Eucharist. **1b** the mystical process by which this is believed to take place during consecration. Cf. **consubstantiation.** 2 a substantial change; transmutation.
▸ **‚transub‚stanti'ationalist** *n*

transude (træn'sju:d) *vb* **transudes, transuding, transuded.** (of a fluid) to ooze or pass through interstices, pores, or small holes. [C17: from NL *trānsūdāre*, from L TRANS- + *sūdāre* to sweat]
▸ **transudation** (‚trænsju'deɪʃən) *n*

transuranic (‚trænzju'rænɪk), **transuranian** (‚trænzju'reɪnɪən), *or* **transuranium** *adj* 1 (of an element) having an atomic number greater than that of uranium. 2 of or having the behaviour of transuranic elements. [C20]

Transvaal ★ ('trænzvɑ:l) *n* a former province of NE South Africa: colonized by the Boers after the Great Trek (1836); became a British colony in 1902; joined South Africa in 1910; replaced by new administrative regions in 1994; the world's chief gold producer. Capital: Pretoria.
▸ **'Trans‚vaaler** *n* ▸ **Trans'vaalian** *adj*

transversal (trænz'vɜ:s²l) *n* 1 *Geom.* a line intersecting two or more other lines. ◆ *adj* 2 a less common word for **transverse.**
▸ **trans'versally** *adv*

★ people and places

transverse (trænz'vɜːs) adj 1 crossing from side to side; athwart; crossways. ◆ n 2 a transverse piece or object. [C16: from L trānsversus, from trānsvertere to turn across] ▸ trans'versely adv

transverse colon n Anat. the part of the large intestine passing transversely in front of the liver and stomach.

transverse wave n a wave, such as an electromagnetic wave, that is propagated in a direction perpendicular to the displacement of the transmitting field or medium.

transvestite (trænz'vestaɪt) n a person who seeks sexual pleasure from wearing clothes of the opposite sex. [C19: from G Transvestit, from TRANS- + L vestītus clothed, from vestīre to clothe] ▸ trans'vestism or trans'vestitism n

Transylvania ★ (ˌtrænsɪl'veɪnɪə) n a region of central and NW Romania: belonged to Hungary from the 11th century until 1918; restored to Romania in 1947.

Transylvanian Alps ★ (ˌtrænsɪl'veɪnɪən) pl n a mountain range in S Romania; a SW extension of the Carpathian Mountains. Highest peak: Mount Negoiu, 2548 m (8360 ft).

trap[1] (træp) n 1 a mechanical device or enclosed place or pit in which something, esp. an animal, is caught or penned. 2 any device or plan for tricking a person or thing into being caught unawares. 3 anything resembling a trap or prison. 4 a fitting for a pipe in the form of a U-shaped or S-shaped bend that contains standing water to prevent the passage of gases. 5 any similar device. 6 a device that hurls clay pigeons into the air to be fired at by trapshooters. 7 Greyhound racing. any one of a line of boxlike stalls in which greyhounds are enclosed before the start of a race. 8 See trap door. 9 a light two-wheeled carriage. 10 a slang word for mouth. 11 Golf. an obstacle or hazard, esp. a bunker. 12 (pl) Jazz sl. percussion instruments. 13 (usually pl) Austral. sl. a policeman. ◆ vb traps, trapping, trapped. 14 to catch, take, or pen in or as if in a trap. 15 (tr) to ensnare by trickery; trick. 16 (tr) to provide (a pipe) with a trap. 17 to set traps in (a place), esp. for animals. [OE træppe] ▸ 'trap,like adj

trap[2] (træp) vb traps, trapping, trapped. (tr; often foll. by out) to dress or adorn. ◆ See also traps. [C11: prob. from OF drap cloth]

trap[3] (træp) or **traprock** ('træp,rɒk) n 1 any fine-grained often columnar dark igneous rock, esp. basalt. 2 any rock in which oil or gas has accumulated. [C18: from Swedish trappa stair (from its steplike formation)]

Trapani ★ (Italian 'traːpani) n a port in S Italy, in NW Sicily: Carthaginian naval base, ceded to the Romans after the First Punic War. Pop.: 72 840 (1990).

trap door n a door or flap flush with and covering an opening, esp. in a ceiling.

trap-door spider n any of various spiders that construct a silk-lined hole in the ground closed by a hinged door of earth and silk.

trapes (treɪps) vb, n a less common spelling of traipse.

trapeze (trə'piːz) n a free-swinging bar attached to two ropes, used by circus acrobats, etc. [C19: from F trapèze, from NL; see TRAPEZIUM]

trapezium (trə'piːzɪəm) n, pl trapeziums or trapezia (-zɪə). 1 Chiefly Brit. a quadrilateral having two parallel sides of unequal length. Usual US and Canad. name: trapezoid. 2 Chiefly US & Canad. a quadrilateral having neither pair of sides parallel. [C16: via LL from Gk trapezion, from trapeza table] ▸ tra'pezial adj

trapezius (trə'piːzɪəs) n, pl trapeziuses. either of two flat triangular muscles that rotate the shoulder blades. [C18: from NL trapezius (musculus) trapezium-shaped (muscle)]

trapezoid ('træpɪ,zɔɪd) n 1 a quadrilateral having neither pair of sides parallel. 2 the usual US and Canad. name for trapezium. [C18: from NL trapezoidēs, from LGk trapezoeidēs trapezium-shaped, from trapeza table]

trapper ('træpə) n a person who traps animals, esp. for their furs or skins.

trappings ('træpɪŋz) pl n 1 the accessories and adorn-

ments that symbolize a condition, office, etc.: the trappings of success. 2 ceremonial harness for a horse or other animal. [C16: from TRAP[2]]

Trappist ('træpɪst) n a a member of a branch of the Cistercian order of Christian monks, which originated at La Trappe in France in 1664. They are noted for their rule of silence. b (as modifier): a Trappist monk.

traps (træps) pl n belongings; luggage. [C19: prob. shortened from TRAPPINGS]

trapshooting ('træp,ʃuːtɪŋ) n the sport of shooting at clay pigeons thrown up by a trap. ▸ 'trap,shooter n

trash (træʃ) n 1 foolish ideas or talk; nonsense. 2 Chiefly US & Canad. useless or unwanted matter or objects; rubbish. 3 a literary or artistic production of poor quality. 4 Chiefly US & Canad. a poor or worthless person or a group of such people. 5 bits that are broken or lopped off, esp. the trimmings from trees or plants. 6 the dry remains of sugar cane after the juice has been extracted. ◆ vb 7 to remove the outer leaves and branches from (growing plants, esp. sugar cane). 8 Sl. to attack or destroy (someone or something) wilfully or maliciously. [C16: from ?]

trashy ('træʃɪ) adj trashier, trashiest. cheap, worthless, or badly made. ▸ 'trashily adv ▸ 'trashiness n

Trasimene ★ ('træzɪ,miːn) n Lake. a lake in central Italy, in Umbria: the largest lake in central Italy; scene of Hannibal's victory over the Romans in 217 B.C. Area: 128 sq. km (49 sq. miles). Italian name: Trasimeno. Also called: (Lake) Perugia.

trass (træs) n a volcanic rock used to make a hydraulic cement. [C18: from Du. tras, tarasse, from It. terrazza worthless earth; see TERRACE]

trattoria (ˌtrætə'rɪə) n an Italian restaurant. [C19: from It., from trattore innkeeper, from F traiteur, from OF tretier to TREAT]

trauma ('trɔːmə) n, pl traumata (-mətə) or traumas. 1 Psychol. a powerful shock that may have long-lasting effects. 2 Pathol. any bodily injury or wound. [C18: from Gk: a wound] ▸ traumatic (trɔː'mætɪk) adj ▸ trau'matically adv

traumatize or **traumatise** ('trɔːmə,taɪz) vb traumatizes, traumatizing, traumatized or traumatises, traumatising, traumatised. 1 (tr) to wound or injure (the body). 2 to subject or be subjected to mental trauma. ▸ ,traumati'zation or ,traumati'sation n

travail ('træveɪl) Literary. ◆ n 1 painful or excessive labour or exertion. 2 the pangs of childbirth; labour. ◆ vb 3 (intr) to suffer or labour painfully, esp. in childbirth. [C13: from OF travaillier, from Vulgar L tripaliāre (unattested) to torture, from LL trepālium instrument of torture, from L tripālis having three stakes]

Travancore ★ (ˌtrævən'kɔː) n a former princely state of S India which joined with Cochin in 1949 to form Travancore-Cochin: part of Kerala state since 1956.

travel ('træv'l) vb travels, travelling, travelled or US travels, traveling, traveled. (mainly intr) 1 to go, move, or journey from one place to another. 2 (tr) to go, move, or journey through or across (an area, region, etc.). 3 to go, move, or cover a distance. 4 to go from place to place as a salesman. 5 (esp. of perishable goods) to withstand a journey. 6 (of light, sound, etc.) to be transmitted or move. 7 to progress or advance. 8 Basketball. to take an excessive number of steps while holding the ball. 9 (of part of a mechanism) to move in a fixed path. 10 Inf. to move rapidly. ◆ n 11a the act of travelling. 11b (as modifier): a travel brochure. Related adj: itinerant. 12 (usually pl) a tour or journey. 13 the distance moved by a mechanical part, such as the stroke of a piston. 14 movement or passage. [C14 travaillen to make a journey, from OF travaillier to TRAVAIL]

travel agency or **bureau** n an agency that arranges and negotiates flights, holidays, etc., for travellers. ▸ travel agent n

travelled or US **traveled** ('træv'ld) adj having experienced or undergone much travelling.

traveller ('trævələ, 'trævlə) n 1 a person who travels, esp.

habitually. **2** See **travelling salesman. 3** a part of a mechanism that moves in a fixed course. **4** *Austral.* a swagman.

traveller's cheque *n* a cheque sold by a bank, etc., to the bearer, who signs it on purchase and can cash it abroad by signing it again.

traveller's joy *n* a ranunculaceous Old World climbing plant having white flowers and heads of feathery plumed fruits; wild clematis.

travelling people *or* **folk** *pl n* (*sometimes caps.*) *Brit.* Gypsies or other itinerant people: a term used esp. by such people of themselves.

travelling salesman *n* a salesman who travels within an assigned territory in order to sell merchandise or to solicit orders for the commercial enterprise he represents by direct personal contact with customers.

travelling wave *n* **a** a wave carrying energy away from its source. **b** (*as modifier*): *a travelling-wave aerial.*

travelogue *or* US (*sometimes*) **travelog** ('træv°log) *n* a film, lecture, or brochure on travels and travelling.

Traven ('treɪvən) *n* **B(en)**, original name *Albert Otto Max Feige.* ?1882–1969, US novelist, born in Germany and living in Mexico from 1920. His novels include *The Treasure of Sierra Madre* (1934).

Travers ★ ('trævəz) *n* **Ben(jamin).** 1886–1980, British dramatist, noted for such farces as *Rookery Nook* (1926) and *Plunder* (1928).

traverse ('trævɜːs, trə'vɜːs) *vb* **traverses, traversing, traversed. 1** to pass or go over or back and forth over (something); cross. **2** (*tr*) to go against; oppose. **3** to move sideways or crosswise. **4** (*tr*) to extend or reach across. **5** to turn (an artillery gun) laterally or (of an artillery gun) to turn laterally. **6** (*tr*) to examine carefully. **7** (*tr*) *Law.* to deny (an allegation). **8** *Mountaineering.* to move across (a face) horizontally. ♦ *n* **9** something being or lying across, such as a transom. **10** a gallery or loft inside a building that crosses it. **11** an obstruction. **12** a protective bank or other barrier across a trench or rampart. **13** a railing, screen, or curtain. **14** the act or an instance of traversing or crossing. **15** *Mountaineering.* the act or an instance of moving horizontally across a face. **16** a path or road across. **17** *Naut.* the zigzag course of a vessel tacking frequently. **18** *Law.* the formal denial of a fact alleged in the opposite party's pleading. **19** *Surveying.* a survey consisting of a series of straight lines, the length of each and the angle between them being measured. ♦ *adj* **20** being or lying across; transverse. [C14: from OF *traverser*, from LL *trānsversāre*, from L *trānsversus* TRANSVERSE]
▸ **tra'versal** *n* ▸ **'traverser** *n*

travertine ('trævətɪn) *n* a porous rock consisting of calcium carbonate, used for building. [C18: from It. *travertino* (infl. by *tra-* TRANS-), from L *lapis Tīburtīnus* Tiburtine stone, from *Tīburs* the district around Tibur (now Tivoli)]

travesty ('trævɪstɪ) *n, pl* **travesties. 1** a farcical or grotesque imitation; mockery. ♦ *vb* **travesties, travestying, travestied.** (*tr*) **2** to make or be a travesty of. [C17: from F *travesti* disguised, from *travestir* to disguise, from It. *travestire*, from *tra-* TRANS- + *vestire* to clothe]

travois (trə'vɔɪ) *n, pl* **travois** (-'vɔɪz). **1** *History.* a sled formerly used by the Plains Indians of North America, consisting of two poles joined by a frame and pulled by an animal. **2** *Canad.* a similar sled used for dragging logs. [from Canad. F, from F *travail* beam, from L *trabs*]

trawl (trɔːl) *n* **1** Also called: **trawl net.** a large net, usually in the shape of a sock or bag, drawn at deep levels behind special boats (trawlers). **2** Also called: **trawl line.** a long line to which numerous shorter hooked lines are attached, suspended between buoys. **3** the act of trawling. ♦ *vb* **4** to catch (fish) with a trawl net or trawl line. **5** (*intr*; foll. by *for*) to seek or gather (information, etc.) from a wide variety of sources. [C17: from MDu. *traghelen* to drag, from L *trāgula* dragnet; see TRAIL]

trawler ('trɔːlə) *n* **1** a vessel used for trawling. **2** a person who trawls.

tray (treɪ) *n* **1** a thin flat board or plate of metal, plastic, etc., usually with a raised edge, on which things can be carried. **2** a shallow receptacle for papers, etc., sometimes forming a drawer in a cabinet or box. [OE *trieg*]

treacherous ('trɛtʃərəs) *adj* **1** betraying or likely to betray faith or confidence. **2** unstable, unreliable, or dangerous.
▸ **'treacherously** *adv* ▸ **'treacherousness** *n*

treachery ('trɛtʃərɪ) *n, pl* **treacheries. 1** the act or an instance of wilful betrayal. **2** the disposition to betray. [C13: from OF *trecherie*, from *trechier* to cheat]

treacle ('triːk°l) *n* **1** Also called: **black treacle**, (US and Canad.) **molasses.** *Brit.* a dark viscous syrup obtained during the refining of sugar. **2** *Brit.* another name for **golden syrup. 3** anything sweet and cloying. [C14: from OF *triacle*, from L *thēriaca* antidote to poison]
▸ **'treacly** *adj*

tread (trɛd) *vb* **treads, treading, trod; trodden** *or* **trod. 1** to walk or trample in, on, over, or across (something). **2** (when intr. foll. by *on*) to crush or squash by or as if by treading. **3** (*intr*; sometimes foll. by *on*) to subdue or repress. **4** (*tr*) to do by walking or dancing: *to tread a measure.* **5** (*tr*) (of a male bird) to copulate with (a female bird). **6 tread lightly.** to proceed with delicacy or tact. **7 tread water.** to stay afloat in an upright position by moving the legs in a walking motion. ♦ *n* **8** a manner or style of walking, dancing, etc.: *a light tread.* **9** the act of treading. **10** the top surface of a step in a staircase. **11** the outer part of a tyre or wheel that makes contact with the road, esp. the grooved surface of a pneumatic tyre. **12** the part of a rail that wheels touch. **13** the part of a shoe that is generally in contact with the ground. [OE *tredan*]
▸ **'treader** *n*

treadle ('trɛd°l) *n* **1** a lever operated by the foot to drive a machine. ♦ *vb* **treadles, treadling, treadled. 2** to work (a machine) with a treadle. [OE *tredel*, from *trǣde* something firm, from *tredan* to tread]

treadmill ('trɛd,mɪl) *n* **1** Also called: **treadwheel.** (formerly) an apparatus turned by the weight of men or animals climbing steps on the periphery of a cylinder or wheel. **2** a dreary round or routine. **3** an exercise machine that consists of a continuous moving belt on which to walk or jog.

treas. *abbrev. for:* **1** treasurer. **2** treasury.

treason ('triːz°n) *n* **1** betrayal of one's sovereign or country, esp. by attempting to overthrow the government. **2** any treachery or betrayal. [C13: from OF *traïson*, from L *trāditiō* a handing over; see TRADITION]
▸ **'treasonable** *or* **'treasonous** *adj* ▸ **'treasonably** *adv*

treasure ('trɛʒə) *n* **1** wealth and riches, usually hoarded, esp. in the form of money, precious metals, or gems. **2** a thing or person that is highly prized or valued. ♦ *vb* **treasures, treasuring, treasured.** (*tr*) **3** to prize highly as valuable, rare, or costly. **4** to store up and save; hoard. [C12: from OF *tresor*, from L *thēsaurus* anything hoarded, from Gk *thēsauros*]

treasure hunt *n* a game in which players act upon successive clues to find a hidden prize.

treasurer ('trɛʒərə) *n* a person appointed to look after the funds of a society, company, city, or other governing body.
▸ **'treasurership** *n*

Treasurer ('trɛʒərə) *n* (in Australia) the minister of finance.

treasure-trove *n* **1** *Brit. Law.* valuable articles, such as coins, etc., found hidden and of unknown ownership. **2** any valuable discovery. [C16: from Anglo-F *tresor trové* treasure found, from OF *tresor* TREASURE + *trover* to find]

treasury ('trɛʒərɪ) *n, pl* **treasuries. 1** a storage place for treasure. **2** the revenues or funds of a government, private organization, or individual. **3** a place where funds are kept and disbursed. **4** a person or thing regarded as a valuable source of information. **5** a collection of highly valued poems, etc.; anthology. **6** Also: **treasure house.** a source of valuable items: *a treasury of information.* [C13: from OF *tresorie*, from *tresor* TREASURE]

Treasury ('trɛʒərɪ) *n* (in various countries) the government department in charge of finance.

Treasury Bench *n* (in Britain) the front bench to the right of the Speaker in the House of Commons, traditionally reserved for members of the Government.

treasury note *n* a note issued by a government treasury and generally receivable as legal tender for any debt.

treat (tri:t) *n* **1** a celebration, entertainment, gift, or feast given for or to someone and paid for by another. **2** any delightful surprise or specially pleasant occasion. **3** the act of treating. ◆ *vb* **4** (*tr*) to deal with or regard in a certain manner: *she treats school as a joke*. **5** (*tr*) to apply treatment to. **6** (*tr*) to subject to a process or to the application of a substance. **7** (often foll. by *to*) to provide (someone) (with) as a treat. **8** (*intr*; usually foll. by *of*) to deal (with), as in writing or speaking. **9** (*intr*) to discuss settlement; negotiate. [C13: from OF *tretier*, from L *tractāre* to manage, from *trahere* to drag]
▸ **'treatable** *adj* ▸ **'treater** *n*

treatise ('tri:tɪz) *n* a formal work on a subject, esp. one that deals systematically with its principles and conclusions. [C14: from Anglo-F *tretiz*, from OF *tretier* to TREAT]

treatment ('tri:tmənt) *n* **1** the application of medicines, surgery, etc., to a patient. **2** the manner of handling a person or thing, as in a literary or artistic work. **3** the act, practice, or manner of treating. **4 the treatment.** *Sl.* the usual manner of dealing with a particular type of person (esp. in **give someone the (full) treatment**).

treaty ('tri:tɪ) *n*, *pl* **treaties**. **1a** a formal agreement between two or more states, such as an alliance or trade arrangement. **1b** the document in which such a contract is written. **2** any pact or agreement. **3** an agreement between two parties concerning the purchase of property at a price privately agreed between them. [C14: from OF *traité*, from Med. L *tractātus*, from L: discussion, from *tractāre* to manage; see TREAT]

treaty port *n History.* (in China, Japan, and Korea) a city, esp. a port, in which foreigners, esp. Westerners, were allowed by treaty to conduct trade.

Trebizond ★ ('trɛbɪˌzɒnd) *n* a variant of **Trabzon.**

treble ('trɛbəl) *adj* **1** threefold; triple. **2** of or denoting a soprano voice or part or a high-pitched instrument. ◆ *n* **3** treble the amount, size, etc. **4** a soprano voice or part or a high-pitched instrument. **5** the highest register of a musical instrument. **6** the high-frequency response of an audio amplifier, esp. in a record player or tape recorder. **7a** the narrow inner ring on a dartboard. **7b** a hit on this ring. ◆ *vb* **trebles, trebling, trebled. 8** to make or become three times as much. [C14: from OF, from L *triplus* threefold]
▸ **'trebly** *adv, adj*

treble chance *n* a method of betting in football pools in which the chances of winning are related to the number of draws and the number of home and away wins forecast by the competitor.

treble clef *n Music.* the clef that establishes G a fifth above middle C as being on the second line of the staff. Symbol: 𝄞

trebuchet ('trɛbjuˌʃɛt) or **trebucket** ('tri:ˌbʌkɪt) *n* a large medieval siege engine consisting of a sling on a pivoted wooden arm set in motion by the fall of a weight. [C13: from OF, from *trebuchier* to stumble, from *tre-* TRANS- + *-buchier*, from *buc* trunk of the body, of Gmc origin]

trecento (treɪ'tʃɛntəu) *n* the 14th century, esp. with reference to Italian art and literature. [C19: shortened from It. *mille trecento* one thousand three hundred]
▸ **tre'centist** *n*

tree (tri:) *n* **1** any large woody perennial plant with a distinct trunk giving rise to branches. Related adj: **arboreal. 2** any plant that resembles this. **3** a wooden post, bar, etc. **4** See **family tree, shoetree, saddletree. 5** *Chem.* a treelike crystal growth. **6** a branching diagrammatic representation of something. **7 at the top of the tree.** in the highest position of a profession, etc. **8 up a tree.** *US & Canad. inf.* in a difficult situation; trapped or stumped. ◆ *vb* **trees, treeing, treed.** (*tr*) **9** to drive or force up a tree. **10** to stretch on a shoetree. [OE *treo*]
▸ **'treeless** *adj* ▸ **'treelessness** *n* ▸ **'tree,like** *adj*

Tree ★ (tri:) *n* Sir **Herbert Beerbohm.** 1853–1917, British actor and theatre manager; half-brother of Sir Max Beerbohm. He was noted for his lavish productions of Shakespeare.

tree creeper *n* any of a family of small songbirds of the N hemisphere, having a slender downward-curving bill. They creep up trees to feed on insects.

tree diagram *n* a diagram in which relationships are represented by lines and nodes having other lines branching off from them.

tree fern *n* any of numerous large tropical ferns having a trunklike stem.

tree frog *n* any of various arboreal frogs of SE Asia, Australia, and America.

treehopper ('tri:ˌhɒpə) *n* any of a family of insects which live among trees and have a large hoodlike thoracic process curving backwards over the body.

tree kangaroo *n* any of several arboreal kangaroos of New Guinea and N Australia, having hind legs and forelegs of a similar length.

tree line *n* the zone, at high altitudes or high latitudes, beyond which no trees grow. Trees growing between the timber line and the tree line are typically stunted.

treen ('tri:ən) *adj* **1** made of wood; wooden. ◆ *n* **2** dishes and other utensils made of wood. [OE *trēowen*, from *trēow* tree]
▸ **'treen,ware** *n*

treenail or **trenail** ('tri:neɪl, 'trɛnəl) *n* a dowel used for pinning planks or timbers together.

tree of heaven *n* another name for **ailanthus.**

tree shrew *n* any of a family of small arboreal mammals of SE Asia having large eyes and resembling squirrels.

tree sparrow *n* **1** a small European weaverbird similar to the house sparrow but having a brown head. **2** a small North American finch.

tree surgery *n* the treatment of damaged trees by filling cavities, applying braces, etc.
▸ **tree surgeon** *n*

tree toad *n* a less common name for **tree frog.**

tree tomato *n* **1** an arborescent shrub of South America bearing red egg-shaped edible fruit. **2** the fruit of this plant. ◆ Also called: **tamarillo.**

tref (treɪf) *adj Judaism.* ritually unfit to be eaten. [Yiddish, from Heb. *terēphāh*, lit.: torn (i.e., animal meat torn by beasts), from *tāraf* to tear]

trefoil ('trɛfɔɪl) *n* **1** any of a genus of leguminous plants having leaves divided into three leaflets. **2** any of various related plants having similar leaves. **3** a flower or leaf having three lobes. **4** *Archit.* an ornament in the form of three arcs arranged in a circle. [C14: from Anglo-F *trifoil*, from L *trifolium* three-leaved herb]
▸ **'trefoiled** *adj*

trek (trɛk) *n* **1** a long and often difficult journey. **2** *S. African.* a journey or stage of a journey, esp. a migration by ox wagon. ◆ *vb* **treks, trekking, trekked. 3** (*intr*) to make a trek. [C19: from Afrik., from MDu. *trekken* to travel]

trellis ('trɛlɪs) *n* **1** a structure of latticework, esp. one used to support climbing plants. ◆ *vb* (*tr*) **2** to interweave (strips of wood, etc.) to make a trellis. **3** to provide or support with a trellis. [C14: from OF *treliz* fabric of open texture, from LL *trilīcius* woven with three threads, from L TRI- + *līcium* thread]
▸ **'trellis,work** *n*

trematode ('trɛmaˌtəud, 'tri:-) *n* any of a class of parasitic flatworms, which includes the flukes. [C19: from NL *Trematoda*, from Gk *trēmatōdēs* full of holes, from *trēma* hole]

tremble ('trɛmbəl) *vb* **trembles, trembling, trembled.** (*intr*) **1** to vibrate with short slight movements; quiver. **2** to shake involuntarily, as with cold or fear; shiver. **3** to experience fear or anxiety. ◆ *n* **4** the act or an instance of trembling. [C14: from OF *trembler*, from Med. L *tremulāre*, from L *tremulus* quivering, from *tremere* to quake]
▸ **'trembling** *adj* ▸ **'trembly** *adj*

trembler ('trɛmblə) *n* a device that vibrates to make or break an electrical circuit.

trembles ('trɛmbəlz) *n* (*functioning as sing*) a disease of cattle and sheep characterized by trembling.

trembling poplar *n* another name for **aspen.**

tremendous (trɪˈmɛndəs) *adj* **1** vast; huge. **2** *Inf.* very exciting or unusual. **3** *Inf.* (intensifier): *a tremendous help*. **4** *Arch.* terrible or dreadful. [C17: from L *tremendus* terrible, lit.: that is to be trembled at, from *tremere* to quake]
► treˈmendously *adv* ► treˈmendousness *n*

tremolo (ˈtrɛməˌləʊ) *n, pl* **tremolos.** *Music.* **1** (in playing the violin, cello, etc.) the rapid reiteration of a note or notes to produce a trembling effect. **2** (in singing) a fluctuation in pitch. **3** a device, as on an organ, that produces a tremolo effect. [C19: from It.: quavering, from Med. L *tremulāre* to TREMBLE]

tremor (ˈtrɛmə) *n* **1** an involuntary shudder or vibration. **2** any trembling movement. **3** a vibrating or trembling effect, as of sound or light. **4** a minor earthquake. ◆ *vb* **5** (*intr*) to tremble. [C14: from L: a shaking, from *tremere* to tremble]
► ˈtremorous *adj*

tremulous (ˈtrɛmjʊləs) *adj* **1** vibrating slightly; quavering; trembling. **2** showing or characterized by fear, anxiety, excitement, etc. [C17: from L *tremulus*, from *tremere* to shake]
► ˈtremulously *adv* ► ˈtremulousness *n*

trenail (ˈtriːneɪl, ˈtrɛnˀl) *n* a variant spelling of **treenail.**

trench (trɛntʃ) *n* **1** a deep ditch. **2** a ditch dug as a fortification, having a parapet of earth. ◆ *vb* **3** to make a trench in (a place). **4** (*tr*) to fortify with a trench. **5** to slash or be slashed. **6** (*intr;* foll. by *on* or *upon*) to encroach or verge. [C14: from OF *trenche* something cut, from *trenchier* to cut, from L *truncāre* to cut off]

trenchant (ˈtrɛntʃənt) *adj* **1** keen or incisive: *trenchant criticism*. **2** vigorous and effective: *a trenchant foreign policy*. **3** distinctly defined. **4** *Arch. or poetic.* sharp. [C14: from OF *trenchant* cutting, from *trenchier* to cut; see TRENCH]
► ˈtrenchancy *n* ► ˈtrenchantly *adv*

Trenchard ★ (ˈtrɛntʃɑːd) *n* **Hugh Montague**, 1st Viscount. 1873–1956, British air marshal, who established the RAF as a fully independent service. As commissioner of the Metropolitan Police (1931–35) he founded the police college at Hendon.

trench coat *n* a belted waterproof coat resembling a military officer's coat.

trencher (ˈtrɛntʃə) *n* **1** (esp. formerly) a wooden board on which food was served or cut. **2** Also called: **trencher cap.** a mortarboard. [C14 *trenchour* knife, plate for carving on, from OF *trencheoir*, from *trenchier* to cut; see TRENCH]

trencherman (ˈtrɛntʃəmən) *n, pl* **trenchermen.** a person who enjoys food; hearty eater.

trench fever *n* an acute infectious disease characterized by fever and muscular aches and pains and transmitted by lice.

trench foot *n* a form of frostbite affecting persons standing for long periods in cold water.

trench mortar *or* **gun** *n* a portable mortar used in trench warfare to shoot projectiles at a high trajectory over a short range.

trench warfare *n* a type of warfare in which opposing armies face each other in entrenched positions.

trend (trɛnd) *n* **1** general tendency or direction. **2** fashion; mode. ◆ *vb* **3** (*intr*) to take a certain trend. [OE *trendan* to turn]

trendsetter (ˈtrɛndˌsɛtə) *n* a person or thing that creates, or may create, a new fashion.
► ˈtrendˌsetting *adj*

trendy (ˈtrɛndɪ) *Brit. inf.* ◆ *adj* **trendier, trendiest.** **1** consciously fashionable. ◆ *n, pl* **trendies. 2** a trendy person.
► ˈtrendily *adv* ► ˈtrendiness *n*

Trengganu *or* **Terengganu** ★ (trɛŋˈɡɑːnuː, tɛrɛŋ-) *n* a state of E Peninsular Malaysia, on the South China Sea: under Thai suzerainty until becoming a British protectorate in 1909; joined the Federation of Malaya in 1948; an isolated forested region; mainly agricultural. Capital: Kuala Trengganu. Pop.: 752 030 (1993 est.). Area: 13 020 sq. km (5027 sq. miles).

Trent ★ (trɛnt) *n* **1** a river in central England, rising in Staffordshire and flowing generally northeast into the Humber: the chief river of the Midlands. Length: 270 km (170 miles). **2** Also: **Trient.** the German name for **Trento.**

trente et quarante (*French* trɑ̃t e karɑ̃t) *n Cards.* another name for **rouge et noir.** [C17: F, lit.: thirty and forty; from the rule that forty is the maximum number that may be dealt and the winning colour is the one closest to thirty-one]

Trentino-Alto Adige ★ (trɛnˈtiːnəʊˈɑːltəʊ ˈɑːdɪˌdʒeɪ) *n* a region of N Italy: consists of the part of the Tyrol south of the Brenner Pass, ceded by Austria after World War I. Pop.: 903 598 (1994 est.). Area: 13 613 sq. km (5256 sq. miles). Former name (until 1947): **Venezia Tridentina.**

Trento ★ (*Italian* ˈtrɛnto) *n* a city in N Italy, in Trentino-Alto Adige region on the Adige River: Roman military base; seat of the Council of Trent. Pop.: 103 063 (1994 est.). Latin name: **Tridentum.** German name: **Trent.**

Trenton ★ (ˈtrɛntən) *n* a city in W New Jersey, capital of the state, on the Delaware River: settled by English Quakers in 1679; scene of the defeat of the British by Washington (1776) during the War of American Independence. Pop.: 84 441 (1994 est.).

trepan (trɪˈpæn) *n* **1** *Surgery.* an instrument resembling a carpenter's brace and bit formerly used to remove circular sections of bone from the skull. **2** a tool for cutting out circular blanks or for making grooves around a fixed centre. ◆ *vb* **trepans, trepanning, trepanned.** (*tr*) **3** to cut (a hole or groove) with a trepan. **4** *Surgery.* another word for **trephine.** [C14: from Med. L *trepanum* rotary saw, from Gk *trupanon* auger, from *trupan* to bore, from *trupa* a hole]
► trepanation (ˌtrɛpəˈneɪʃən) *n*

trepang (trɪˈpæŋ) *n* any of various large sea cucumbers of tropical Oriental seas, the body walls of which are used as food by the Japanese and Chinese. [C18: from Malay *těripang*]

trephine (trɪˈfiːn) *n* **1** a surgical sawlike instrument for removing circular sections of bone esp. from the skull. ◆ *vb* **trephines, trephining, trephined. 2** (*tr*) to remove a circular section of bone from (esp. the skull). [C17: from F *tréphine*, from obs. E *trefine* TREPAN, allegedly from L *trēs fīnēs*, lit.: three ends]
► trephination (ˌtrɛfɪˈneɪʃən) *n*

trepidation (ˌtrɛpɪˈdeɪʃən) *n* **1** a state of fear or anxiety. **2** a condition of quaking or palpitation, esp. one caused by anxiety. [C17: from L *trepidātiō*, from *trepidāre* to be in a state of alarm]

trespass (ˈtrɛspəs) *vb* (*intr*) **1** (often foll. by *on* or *upon*) to go or intrude (on the property, privacy, or preserves of another) with no right or permission. **2** *Law.* to commit trespass. **3** *Arch.* (often foll. by *against*) to sin or transgress. ◆ *n* **4** *Law.* **4a** any unlawful act committed with force, which causes injury to another person, his property or his rights. **4b** a wrongful entry upon another's land. **5** an intrusion on another's privacy or preserves. **6** a sin or offence. [C13: from OF *trespas* a passage, from *trespasser* to pass through, ult. from L *passus* a PACE¹]
► ˈtrespasser *n*

tress (trɛs) *n* **1** (*often pl*) a lock of hair, esp. a long lock of woman's hair. **2** a plait or braid of hair. ◆ *vb* (*tr*) **3** to arrange in tresses. [C13: from OF *trece*, from ?]
► ˈtressy *adj*

trestle (ˈtrɛsˀl) *n* **1** a framework in the form of a horizontal member supported at each end by a pair of splayed legs, used to carry scaffold boards, a table top, etc. **2a** a framework of timber, metal, or reinforced concrete that is used to support a bridge or ropeway. **2b** a bridge constructed of such frameworks. [C14: from OF *trestel*, ult. from L *trānstrum* transom]

trestlework (ˈtrɛsˀlˌwɜːk) *n* an arrangement of trestles, esp. one that supports a bridge.

trevally (trɪˈvælɪ) *n, pl* **trevallies.** *Austral. & NZ.* any of various food and game fishes of the genus *Caranx*. [C19: prob. alteration of *cavally*, from *cavalla* species of tropical fish, from Sp. *caballa* horse]

Trevelyan ★ (trɪˈvɛljən, -ˈvɪl-) *n* **1 George Macaulay**. 1876–1962, British historian, noted for his *English Social History* (1944). **2** his father, Sir **George Otto**. 1838–1928, British historian.

Trèves ★ (trɛv) *n* the French name for **Trier.**

Trevino ★ (trə'viːnəʊ) *n* **Lee**. born 1939, US professional golfer: winner of the US Open Championship (1968; 1971) and the British Open Championship (1971; 1972).

Treviso ★ (*Italian* tre'viːzo) *n* a city in N Italy, in Veneto region: agricultural market centre. Pop.: 84 066 (1990).

Trevithick ★ (trə'vɪθɪk) *n* **Richard**. 1771–1833, British engineer, who built the first steam-driven passenger train.

trews (truːz) *pl n Chiefly Brit*. close-fitting trousers of tartan cloth. [C16: from Scot. Gaelic *triubhas*, from OF *trebus*]

trey (treɪ) *n* any card or dice throw with three spots. [C14: from OF *treis* three, from L *trēs*]

tri- *prefix* **1** three or thrice: *triaxial; trigon; trisect*. **2** occurring every three: *trimonthly*. [from L *trēs*, Gk *treis*]

triable ('traɪəb°l) *adj* **1** subject to trial in a court of law. **2** *Rare*. able to be tested.

triacid (traɪ'æsɪd) *adj* capable of reacting with three molecules of a monobasic acid.

triad ('traɪæd) *n* **1** a group of three; trio. **2** *Chem*. an atom, element, group, or ion that has a valency of three. **3** *Music*. a three-note chord consisting of a note and its third and fifth above it. **4** an aphoristic literary form used in medieval Welsh and Irish literature. [C16: from LL *trias*, from Gk]
▸ tri'adic *adj* ▸ 'triadism *n*

Triad ('traɪæd) *n* any of several Chinese secret societies, esp. one involved in criminal activities, such as drug trafficking.

triage ('traɪɪdʒ) *n* **1** the action of sorting casualties, patients, etc. according to priority. **2** the allocating of limited resources on a basis of expediency rather than moral principles. [C18: from F; see TRY, -AGE]

trial ('traɪəl, traɪl) *n* **1a** the act or an instance of trying or proving; test or experiment. **1b** (*as modifier*): *a trial run*. **2** *Law*. **2a** the judicial examination and determination of the issues in a civil or criminal cause by a competent tribunal. **2b** the determination of an accused person's guilt or innocence after hearing evidence and the judicial examination of the issues involved. **2c** (*as modifier*): *trial proceedings*. **3** an effort or attempt to do something. **4** trouble or grief. **5** an annoying or frustrating person or thing. **6** (*often pl*) a competition for individuals: *sheepdog trials*. **7** a motorcycling competition in which the skills of the riders are tested over rough ground. **8 on trial. 8a** undergoing trial, esp. before a court of law. **8b** being tested, as before a commitment to purchase. ♦ *vb* **trials**, **trialling**, **trialled**. **9** to test or make experimental use of (something): *the idea has been trialled in several schools*. [C16: from Anglo-F, from *trier* to TRY]
▸ 'trialling *n*

trial and error *n* a method of discovery, solving problems, etc., based on practical experiment and experience rather than on theory: *he learned to cook by trial and error*.

trial balance *n Book-keeping*. a statement of all the debit and credit balances in the ledger of a double-entry system, drawn up to test their equality.

triallist *or* **trialist** ('traɪəlɪst, 'traɪlɪst) *n* **1** a person who takes part in a competition, esp. a motorcycle trial. **2** *Sport*. a person who takes part in a preliminary match or heat held to determine selection for an event, a team, etc.

triangle ('traɪˌæŋɡ°l) *n* **1** *Geom*. a three-sided polygon that can be classified by angle, as in an acute triangle, or by side, as in an equilateral triangle. **2** any object shaped like a triangle. **3** any situation involving three parties or points of view. **4** *Music*. a percussion instrument consisting of a sonorous metal bar bent into a triangular shape, beaten with a metal stick. **5** a group of three. [C14: from L *triangulum* (n), from *triangulus* (adj), from TRI- + *angulus* corner]
▸ **triangular** (traɪ'æŋɡjʊlə) *adj*

triangle of forces *n Physics*. a triangle whose sides represent the magnitudes and directions of three forces in equilibrium.

triangulate *vb* (traɪ'æŋɡjʊˌleɪt), **triangulates**, **triangulating**, **triangulated**. (*tr*) **1a** to survey by the method of triangula-

tion. **1b** to calculate trigonometrically. **2** to divide into triangles. **3** to make triangular. ♦ *adj* (traɪ'æŋgjʊlɪt, -ˌleɪt). **4** marked with or composed of triangles.
▸ tri'angulately *adv*

triangulation (traɪˌæŋɡjʊ'leɪʃən) *n* a method of surveying in which an area is divided into triangles, one side (the base line) and all angles of which are measured and the lengths of the other lines calculated trigonometrically.

triangulation station *n* a point on a hilltop, etc., used for triangulation by a surveyor.

Triassic (traɪ'æsɪk) *adj* **1** of or formed in the first period of the Mesozoic era. ♦ *n* **2 the**. Also called: **Trias**. the Triassic period or rock system. [C19: from L *trias* triad, from the three subdivisions]

triathlon (traɪ'æθlɒn) *n* an athletic contest in which each athlete competes in three different events, swimming, cycling, and running. [C20: from TRI- + Gk *athlon* contest]
▸ tri'athlete *n*

triatomic (ˌtraɪə'tɒmɪk) *adj Chem*. having three atoms in the molecule.

tribade ('trɪbɑːd) *n* a lesbian who practises tribadism. [C17: from L *tribas*, from Gk *tribein* to rub]

tribadism ('trɪbədɪzəm) *n* a lesbian practice in which one partner lies on top of the other and simulates the male role in heterosexual intercourse.

tribalism ('traɪbəˌlɪzəm) *n* **1** the state of existing as a tribe. **2** the customs and beliefs of a tribal society. **3** loyalty to a tribe.
▸ 'tribalist *n, adj* ▸ ˌtribal'istic *adj*

tribasic (traɪ'beɪsɪk) *adj* **1** (of an acid) containing three replaceable hydrogen atoms in the molecule. **2** (of a molecule) containing three monovalent basic atoms or groups.

tribe (traɪb) *n* **1** a social division of a people, esp. of a preliterate people, defined in terms of common descent, territory, culture, etc. **2** an ethnic or ancestral division of ancient cultures, esp.: **2a** one of the political divisions of the Roman people. **2b** any of the 12 divisions of ancient Israel, each of which was believed to be descended from one of the 12 patriarchs. **3** *Inf*. **3a** a large number of persons, animals, etc. **3b** a specific class or group of persons. **3c** a family, esp. a large one. **4** *Biol*. a taxonomic group that is a subdivision of a subfamily. [C13: from L *tribus*]
▸ 'tribal *adj*

tribesman ('traɪbzmən) *n, pl* **tribesmen**. a member of a tribe.

tribo- *combining form*. indicating friction: *triboelectricity*. [from Gk *tribein* to rub]

triboelectricity (ˌtraɪbəʊɪlek'trɪsɪtɪ, -ˌiːlek-) *n* electricity generated by friction.

tribology (traɪ'bɒlədʒɪ) *n* the study of friction, lubrication, and wear between moving surfaces.

triboluminescence (ˌtraɪbəʊˌluːmɪ'nesəns) *n* luminescence produced by friction, such as the emission of light when certain crystals are crushed.
▸ ˌtribo ̩lumi'nescent *adj*

tribrach ('traɪbræk, 'trɪb-) *n* a metrical foot of three short syllables. [C16: from L *tribrachys*, from Gk, from TRI- + *brakhus* short]

tribromoethanol (traɪˌbrəʊməʊ'eθəˌnɒl) *n* a soluble white crystalline compound with a slight aromatic odour, used as a general anaesthetic.

tribulation (ˌtrɪbjʊ'leɪʃən) *n* **1** a cause of distress. **2** a state of suffering or distress. [C13: from OF, from Church L *trībulātiō*, from L *trībulāre* to afflict, from *trībulum* a threshing board, from *terere* to rub]

tribunal (traɪ'bjuːn°l, trɪ-) *n* **1** a court of justice. **2** (in England) a special court, convened by the government to inquire into a specific matter. **3** a raised platform containing the seat of a judge. [C16: from L *tribūnus* TRIBUNE[1]]

tribune[1] ('trɪbjuːn) *n* **1** (in ancient Rome) **1a** an officer elected by the plebs to protect their interests. **1b** a senior military officer. **2** a person who upholds public rights. [C14: from L *tribunus*, prob. from *tribus* tribe]
▸ **tribunate** ('trɪbjʊnɪt) *or* 'tribuneship *n*

★ people and places

tribune[2] ('trɪbjuːn) *n* **1a** the apse of a Christian basilica that contains the bishop's throne. **1b** the throne itself. **2** a gallery or raised area in a church. **3** *Rare.* a raised platform; dais. [C17: via F from It. *tribuna*, from Med. L *tribūna*, var. of L *tribūnal* TRIBUNAL]

tributary ('trɪbjʊtərɪ) *n, pl* **tributaries**. **1** a stream, river, or glacier that feeds another larger one. **2** a person, nation, or people that pays tribute. ◆ *adj* **3** (of a stream, etc.) feeding a larger stream. **4** given or owed as a tribute. **5** paying tribute.
▶ **'tributarily** *adv*

tribute ('trɪbjuːt) *n* **1** a gift or statement made in acknowledgment, gratitude, or admiration. **2** a payment by one ruler or state to another, usually as an acknowledgment of submission. **3** the obligation to pay tribute. [C14: from L *tribūtum*, from *tribuere* to grant (orig.: to distribute among the tribes), from *tribus* tribe]

trice (traɪs) *n* a moment; instant (esp. in **in a trice**). [C15 (in *at* or in *a trice*, in the sense: at one tug): apparent substantive use of *trice* to haul up, from MDu. *trīse* pulley]

tricentenary (ˌtraɪsɛn'tiːnərɪ) *or* **tricentennial** (ˌtraɪsɛn'tɛnɪəl) *adj* **1** of a period of 300 years. **2** of a 300th anniversary. ◆ *n, pl* **tricentenaries** *or* **tricentennials**. **3** an anniversary of 300 years.

triceps ('traɪsɛps) *n, pl* **tricepses** (-sɛpsɪz) *or* **triceps**. any muscle having three heads, esp. the one that extends the forearm. [C16: from L, from TRI- + *caput* head]

trichiasis (trɪ'kaɪəsɪs) *n Pathol.* an abnormal position of the eyelashes that causes irritation when they rub against the eyeball. [C17: via LL from Gk *trikhiasis*, from *thrix* a hair]

trichina (trɪ'kaɪnə) *n, pl* **trichinae** (-niː). a parasitic nematode worm occurring in the intestines of pigs, rats, and man and producing larvae that form cysts in skeletal muscle. [C19: from NL, from Gk *trikhinos* relating to hair, from *thrix* a hair]
▶ **trichinous** ('trɪkɪnəs) *adj*

Trichinopoly ★ (ˌtrɪkɪ'nɒpəlɪ) *n* another name for **Tiruchirapalli**.

trichinosis (ˌtrɪkɪ'nəʊsɪs) *n* a disease characterized by nausea, fever, diarrhoea, and swelling of the muscles, caused by ingestion of pork infected with trichina larvae. [C19: from NL TRICHINA]

trichloride (traɪ'klɔːraɪd) *n* any compound that contains three chlorine atoms per molecule.

tricho- *or before a vowel* **trich-** *combining form.* indicating hair or a part resembling hair: *trichocyst*. [from Gk *thrix* (genitive *thrikhos*) hair]

trichology (trɪ'kɒlədʒɪ) *n* the branch of medicine concerned with the hair and its diseases.
▶ **tri'chologist** *n*

trichomoniasis (ˌtrɪkəʊmə'naɪəsɪs) *n* inflammation of the vagina caused by infection with parasitic protozoa. [C19: NL]

trichopteran (traɪ'kɒptərən) *n* **1** any insect of the order *Trichoptera*, which comprises the caddis flies. ◆ *adj* **2** Also: **trichopterous** (trɪ'kɒptərəs). of or belonging to the order *Trichoptera*. [C19: from NL *Trichoptera*, lit.: having hairy wings, from Gk *thrix* a hair + *pteron* wing]

trichosis (trɪ'kəʊsɪs) *n* any abnormal condition or disease of the hair. [C19: via NL from Gk *trikhōsis* growth of hair]

trichotomy (traɪ'kɒtəmɪ) *n, pl* **trichotomies**. **1** division into three categories. **2** *Theol.* the division of man into body, spirit, and soul. [C17: prob. from NL *trichotomia*, from Gk *trikhotomein* to divide into three]
▶ **trichotomic** (ˌtrɪkə'tɒmɪk) *or* **tri'chotomous** *adj*

trichroism ('traɪkrəʊˌɪzəm) *n* a property of biaxial crystals as a result of which they show a difference in colour when viewed along three different axes. [C19: from Gk *trikhroos* three-coloured, from TRI- + *khrōma* colour]

trichromatic (ˌtraɪkrəʊ'mætɪk) *or* **trichromic** (traɪ'krəʊmɪk) *adj* **1** involving the combination of three primary colours. **2** of or having normal colour vision. **3** having or involving three colours.
▶ **tri'chroma,tism** *n*

trick (trɪk) *n* **1** a deceitful or cunning action or plan. **2a** a

mischievous, malicious, or humorous action or plan; joke. **2b** (*as modifier*): *a trick spider*. **3** an illusory or magical feat. **4** a simple feat learned by an animal or person. **5** an adroit or ingenious device; knack: *a trick of the trade*. **6** a habit or mannerism. **7** a turn of duty. **8** *Cards.* a batch of cards containing one from each player, usually played in turn and won by the player or side that plays the card with the highest value. **9 can't take a trick.** *Austral. sl.* to be consistently unsuccessful or unlucky. **10 do the trick.** *Inf.* to produce the desired result. **11 how's tricks?** *Sl.* how are you? **12 turn a trick.** *Sl.* (of a prostitute) to gain a customer. ◆ *vb* **13** (*tr*) to defraud, deceive, or cheat (someone). ◆ *See also* **trick out.** [C15: from OF *trique*, from *trikier* to deceive, ult. from L *trīcārī* to play tricks]

trick cyclist *n* **1** a cyclist who performs tricks, such as in a circus. **2** a slang term for **psychiatrist**.

trickery ('trɪkərɪ) *n, pl* **trickeries**. the practice or an instance of using tricks.

trickle ('trɪkəl) *vb* **trickles, trickling, trickled**. **1** to run or cause to run in thin or slow streams. **2** (*intr*) to move gradually: *the crowd trickled away*. ◆ *n* **3** a thin, irregular, or slow flow of something. **4** the act of trickling. [C14: ? imit.]
▶ **'trickling** *adj*

trickle charger *n* a small mains-operated battery charger, esp. one used by car owners.

trickle-down *adj* of or concerning the theory that granting concessions such as tax cuts to the rich will benefit all levels of society by stimulating the economy.

trick or treat *sentence substitute.* *Chiefly US & Canad.* a customary cry used by children at Halloween when they call at houses in disguise, indicating that they want a present of sweets, apples, or money and, if refused, will play a trick on the householder.

trick out *or* **up** *vb* (*tr, adv*) to dress up; deck out: *tricked out in frilly dresses*.

trickster ('trɪkstə) *n* a person who deceives or plays tricks.

tricksy ('trɪksɪ) *adj* **tricksier, tricksiest**. **1** playing tricks habitually; mischievous. **2** crafty or difficult to deal with.
▶ **'tricksiness** *n*

tricky ('trɪkɪ) *adj* **trickier, trickiest**. **1** involving snags or difficulties. **2** needing careful handling. **3** sly; wily: *a tricky dealer*.
▶ **'trickily** *adv* ▶ **'trickiness** *n*

triclinic (traɪ'klɪnɪk) *adj* of the crystal system characterized by three unequal axes, no pair of which are perpendicular.

triclinium (traɪ'klɪnɪəm) *n, pl* **triclinia** (-ɪə). (in ancient Rome) **1** an arrangement of three couches around a table for reclining upon while dining. **2** a dining room. [C17: from L, from Gk *triklinion*, from TRI- + *klinē* a couch]

tricolour *or US* **tricolor** ('trɪkələ, 'traɪˌkʌlə) *adj also* **tricoloured** *or US* **tricolored** ('traɪˌkʌləd). **1** having or involving three colours. ◆ *n* **2** (*often cap.*) the French flag, having three stripes in blue, white, and red. **3** any flag, badge, etc., with three colours.

tricorn ('traɪkɔːn) *n also* **tricorne**. **1** a cocked hat with the brim turned up on three sides. ◆ *adj also* **tricornered**. **2** having three horns or corners. [C18: from L *tricornis*, from TRI- + *cornu* horn]

tricot ('trɪkəʊ, 'triː-) *n* **1** a thin rayon or nylon fabric knitted or resembling knitting, used for dresses, etc. **2** a type of ribbed dress fabric. [C19: from F, from *tricoter* to knit, from ?]

tricuspid (traɪ'kʌspɪd) *Anat.* ◆ *adj also* **tricuspidal**. **1** having three points, cusps, or segments: *a tricuspid tooth; a tricuspid valve*. ◆ *n* **2** a tooth having three cusps.

tricycle ('traɪsɪkəl) *n* a three-wheeled cycle, esp. one driven by pedals.
▶ **'tricyclist** *n*

trident ('traɪdənt) *n* a three-pronged spear. [C16: from L *tridēns* three-pronged, from TRI- + *dēns* tooth]

Trident ('traɪdənt) *n* a type of US submarine-launched ballistic missile with independently targetable warheads.

tridentate (traɪˈdɛnteɪt) or **tridental** adj having three prongs, teeth, or points.

Tridentine (traɪˈdɛntaɪn) adj **1a** History. of the Council of Trent in the 16th century. **1b** in accord with Tridentine doctrine: Tridentine mass. ◆ n **2** an orthodox Roman Catholic. [C16: from Med. L Tridentīnus, from Tridentum TRENT]

Tridentum ★ (traɪˈdɛntəm) n the Latin name for **Trento**.

tried (traɪd) vb the past tense and past participle of **try**.

triella (traɪˈɛlə) n a cumulative bet on horses in three specified races.

triennial (traɪˈɛnɪəl) adj **1** relating to, lasting for, or occurring every three years. ◆ n **2** a third anniversary. **3** a triennial period, thing, or occurrence. [C17: from L TRIENNIUM]
▶ tri'ennially adv

triennium (traɪˈɛnɪəm) n, pl **trienniums** or **triennia** (-nɪə). a period or cycle of three years. [C19: from L, from TRI- + annus a year]

Trient ★ (triˈent) n the German name for **Trento**. Also: **Trent**.

trier (ˈtraɪə) n a person or thing that tries.

Trier ★ (German triːr) n a city in W Germany, in the Rhineland-Palatinate on the Moselle River: ancient capital of a Celto-Germanic tribe (the **Treveri**); an early centre of Christianity, ruled by archbishops until the 18th century; wine trade; Roman remains. Pop.: 98 750 (1991). Latin name: **Augusta Treverorum** (auˈguːstə ˌtrɛvəˈrəʊrəm). French name: **Trèves**.

Trieste ★ (triːˈɛst; Italian triˈɛste) n **1** a port in NE Italy, capital of Friuli-Venezia Giulia region, on the **Gulf of Trieste** at the head of the Adriatic Sea: under Austrian rule (1382–1918); capital of the Free Territory of Trieste (1947–54); important transit port for central Europe. Pop.: 226 707 (1994 est.). Slovene and Serbo-Croat name: **Trst. 2 Free Territory of.** a former territory on the N Adriatic: established by the UN in 1947; most of the N part passed to Italy and the remainder to Yugoslavia in 1954.

trifacial (traɪˈfeɪʃəl) adj another word for **trigeminal**.

trifecta (traɪˈfɛktə) n Austral. a form of betting in which punters select first-, second-, and third-place winners in the correct order.

trifid (ˈtraɪfɪd) adj divided or split into three parts or lobes. [C18: from L trifidus, from TRI- + findere to split]

trifle (ˈtraɪf°l) n **1** a thing of little or no value or significance. **2** a small amount; bit: a trifle more enthusiasm. **3** Brit. a cold dessert made with sponge cake spread with jam or fruit, soaked in sherry, covered with custard and cream. ◆ vb **trifles, trifling, trifled. 4** (intr; usually foll. by with) to deal (with) as if worthless; dally: to trifle with a person's affections. **5** to waste (time) frivolously. [C13: from OF trufle mockery, from trufler to cheat]
▶ 'trifler n

trifling (ˈtraɪflɪŋ) adj **1** insignificant or petty. **2** frivolous or idle.
▶ 'triflingly adv

trifocal adj (traɪˈfəʊk°l). **1** having three focuses. **2** having three focal lengths. ◆ n (traɪˈfəʊk°l, ˈtraɪˌfəʊk°l). **3** (pl) glasses that have trifocal lenses.

triforium (traɪˈfɔːrɪəm) n, pl **triforia** (-rɪə). an arcade above the arches of the nave, choir, or transept of a church. [C18: from Anglo-L, apparently from L TRI- + foris a doorway; from the fact that each bay had three openings]

trifurcate (ˈtraɪfɜːkɪt, -ˌkeɪt) or **trifurcated** adj having three branches or forks. [C19: from L trifurcus, from TRI- + furca a fork]

trig (trɪg) Arch. or dialect. ◆ adj **1** neat or spruce. ◆ vb **trigs, trigging, trigged. 2** to make or become trim or spruce. [C12 (orig.: trusty): from ON]
▶ 'trigly adv ▶ 'trigness n

trig. abbrev. for: **1** trigonometrical. **2** trigonometry.

trigeminal (traɪˈdʒɛmɪn°l) adj Anat. of or relating to the trigeminal nerve. [C19: from L trigeminus triplet, from TRI- + geminus twin]

trigeminal nerve n either one of the fifth pair of cranial nerves, which supply the muscles of the mandible and maxilla. Their ophthalmic branches supply the area around the orbit of the eye, the nasal cavity, and the forehead.

trigeminal neuralgia n Pathol. another name for **tic douloureux**.

trigger (ˈtrɪgə) n **1** a small lever that activates the firing mechanism of a firearm. **2** a device that releases a spring-loaded mechanism. **3** any event that sets a course of action in motion. ◆ vb (tr) **4** (usually foll. by off) to give rise (to); set off. **5** to fire or set in motion by or as by pulling a trigger. [C17 tricker, from Du. trekker, from trekken to pull]

triggerfish (ˈtrɪgəˌfɪʃ) n, pl **triggerfish** or **triggerfishes**. any of a family of fishes of tropical and temperate seas. They have erectile spines in the first dorsal fin.

trigger-happy adj Inf. **1** tending to resort to the use of firearms or violence irresponsibly. **2** tending to act rashly.

triglyceride (traɪˈglɪsəˌraɪd) n any ester of glycerol and one or more carboxylic acids, in which each glycerol molecule has combined with three carboxylic acid molecules.

triglyph (ˈtraɪglɪf) n Archit. a stone block in a Doric frieze, having three vertical channels. [C16: via L from Gk trigluphos, from TRI- + gluphē carving]

trigonal (ˈtrɪgən°l) adj **1** triangular. **2** of the crystal system characterized by three equal axes that are equally inclined and not perpendicular to each other. [C16: via L from Gk trigōnon triangle]

trigonometric function n any of a group of functions of an angle expressed as a ratio of two of the sides of a right-angled triangle containing the angle. The group includes sine, cosine, tangent, etc.

trigonometry (ˌtrɪgəˈnɒmɪtrɪ) n the branch of mathematics concerned with the properties of trigonometric functions and their application to the determination of the angles and sides of triangles: used in surveying, navigation, etc. [C17: from NL trigōnometria, from Gk trigōnon triangle]
▶ **trigonometric** (ˌtrɪgənəˈmɛtrɪk) or ˌtrigono'metrical adj

trig point n an informal name for **triangulation station**. [from trigonometric]

trigraph (ˈtraɪˌgrɑːf) n a combination of three letters used to represent a single speech sound or phoneme, such as eau in French beau.

trihedral (traɪˈhiːdrəl) adj **1** having three plane faces. ◆ n **2** a figure formed by the intersection of three lines in different planes.

trihedron (traɪˈhiːdrən) n, pl **trihedrons** or **trihedra** (-drə). a figure determined by the intersection of three planes.

trike (traɪk) n short for **tricycle**.

trilateral (traɪˈlætərəl) adj having three sides.

trilby (ˈtrɪlbɪ) n, pl **trilbies**. a man's soft felt hat with an indented crown. [C19: after Trilby, the heroine of a dramatized novel (1893) of that title by George Du Maurier]

trilingual (traɪˈlɪŋgwəl) adj **1** able to speak three languages fluently. **2** expressed or written in three languages.
▶ tri'lingualism n

trilithon (traɪˈlɪθɒn) or **trilith** (ˈtraɪlɪθ) n a structure consisting of two upright stones with a third placed across the top, as at Stonehenge. [C18: from Gk]
▶ trilithic (traɪˈlɪθɪk) adj

trill (trɪl) n **1** Music. a rapid alternation between a principal note and the note above it. **2** a shrill warbling sound, esp. as made by some birds. **3** the articulation of an (r) sound produced by the rapid vibration of the tongue or the uvula. ◆ vb **4** to sound, sing, or play (a trill or with a trill). **5** (tr) to pronounce an (r) sound by the production of a trill. [C17: from It. trillo, from trillare, apparently from MDu. trillen to vibrate]

trillion (ˈtrɪljən) n **1** the number represented as one followed by twelve zeros (10^{12}); a million million. **2** (formerly, in Britain) the number represented as one followed by eighteen zeros (10^{18}); a million million million. ◆ determiner **3** (preceded by a or a numeral)

★ **people and places**

amounting to a trillion. [C17: from F, on the model of *million*]
▶ 'trillionth *n, adj*

trillium ('trɪlɪəm) *n* any of a genus of herbaceous plants of Asia and North America, having a whorl of three leaves at the top of the stem with a single white, pink, or purple three-petalled flower. [C18: from NL, modification by Linnaeus of Swedish *trilling* triplet]

trilobate (traɪ'ləʊbeɪt, 'traɪlə,beɪt) *adj* (esp. of a leaf) consisting of or having three lobes or parts.

trilobite ('traɪlə,baɪt) *n* any of various extinct marine arthropods abundant in Palaeozoic times, having a segmented exoskeleton divided into three parts. [C19: from NL *Trilobītēs*, from Gk *trilobos* having three lobes]
▶ **trilobitic** (,traɪlə'bɪtɪk) *adj*

trilogy ('trɪlədʒɪ) *n, pl* **trilogies. 1** a series of three related works, esp. in literature, etc. **2** (in ancient Greece) a series of three tragedies performed together. [C19: from Gk *trilogia*]

trim (trɪm) *adj* **trimmer, trimmest. 1** neat and spruce in appearance. **2** slim; slender. **3** in good condition. ◆ *vb* **trims, trimming, trimmed.** (*mainly tr*) **4** to put in good order, esp. by cutting or pruning. **5** to shape and finish (timber). **6** to adorn or decorate. **7** (sometimes foll. by *off* or *away*) to cut so as to remove: *to trim off a branch.* **8** to cut down to the desired size or shape. **9a** *Naut.* (*also intr*) to adjust the balance of (a vessel) or (of a vessel) to maintain an even balance, by distribution of ballast, cargo, etc. **9b** (*also intr*) to adjust (a vessel's sails) to take advantage of the wind. **10** to balance (an aircraft) before flight by adjusting the position of the load or in flight by the use of trim tabs, fuel transfer, etc. **11** (*also intr*) to modify (one's opinions, etc.) for expediency. **12** *Inf.* to thrash or beat. **13** *Inf.* to rebuke. ◆ *n* **14** a decoration or adornment. **15** the upholstery and decorative facings of a car's interior. **16** proper order or fitness; good shape. **17** a haircut that neatens but does not alter the existing hairstyle. **18** *Naut.* **18a** the general set and appearance of a vessel. **18b** the difference between the draught of a vessel at the bow and at the stern. **18c** the fitness of a vessel. **18d** the position of a vessel's sails relative to the wind. **19** dress or equipment. **20** *US.* window-dressing. **21** the attitude of an aircraft in flight when the pilot allows the main control surfaces to take up their own positions. **22** material that is trimmed off. **23** decorative mouldings, such as architraves, picture rails, etc. [OE *trymman* to strengthen]
▶ 'trimly *adv* ▶ 'trimness *n*

Trim ★ (trɪm) *n* the county town of Meath, Republic of Ireland; 12th-century castle, medieval cathedral; textiles and machinery. Pop.: 18 120 (1991).

trimaran ('traɪmə,ræn) *n* a vessel, usually of shallow draught, with two hulls flanking the main hull. [C20: from TRI- + (CATA)MARAN]

Trimble ★ ('trɪmbəl) *n* (William) David. born 1944, Northern Irish politician; First Minister of Northern Ireland from 1998; awarded Nobel peace prize 1998 for his role in Northern Irish peace negotiations.

trimer ('traɪmə) *n* a polymer or a molecule of a polymer consisting of three identical monomers.

trimerous ('trɪmərəs) *adj* **1** having parts in groups of three. **2** having three parts.

trimester (traɪ'mɛstə) *n* **1** a period of three months. **2** (in some US and Canad. universities or schools) any of the three academic sessions. [C19: from F *trimestre*, from L *trimēstris* of three months]
▶ **tri'mestral** *or* **tri'mestrial** *adj*

trimeter ('trɪmɪtə) *Prosody.* ◆ *n* **1** a verse line consisting of three metrical feet. ◆ *adj* **2** designating such a line.

trimethadione (,traɪmɛθə'daɪəʊn) *n* a crystalline compound with a camphor-like odour, used in the treatment of epilepsy.

trimetric projection (traɪ'mɛtrɪk) *n* a geometric projection, used in mechanical drawing, in which the three axes are at arbitrary angles, often using different linear scales.

trimmer ('trɪmə) *n* **1** a beam attached to truncated joists in order to leave an opening for a staircase, chimney, etc. **2** a machine for trimming timber. **3** a variable ca-

pacitor of small capacitance used for making fine adjustments, etc. **4** a person who alters his opinions on the grounds of expediency. **5** a person who fits out motor vehicles.

trimming ('trɪmɪŋ) *n* **1** an extra piece used to decorate or complete. **2** (*pl*) usual or traditional accompaniments: *roast turkey with all the trimmings.* **3** (*pl*) parts that are cut off.

trimolecular (,traɪmə'lɛkjʊlə) *adj Chem.* of, formed from, or involving three molecules.

trimonthly (traɪ'mʌnθlɪ) *adj, adv* every three months.

trimorphism (traɪ'mɔːfɪzəm) *n* **1** *Biol.* the property exhibited by certain species of having or occurring in three different forms. **2** the property of certain minerals of existing in three crystalline forms.

Trinacria ★ (trɪ'neɪkrɪə, traɪ-) *n* the Latin name for **Sicily.**
▶ **Tri'nacrian** *adj*

trinary ('traɪnərɪ) *adj* **1** made up of three parts; ternary. **2** going in threes. [C15: from LL *trīnārius* of three sorts, from L *trīnī* three each, from *trēs* three]

Trincomalee ★ (,trɪŋkəʊmə'liː) *n* a port in NE Sri Lanka, on the **Bay of Trincomalee** (an inlet of the Bay of Bengal); British naval base until 1957. Pop.: 51 000 (latest est.).

trine (traɪn) *n* **1** *Astrol.* an aspect of 120° between two planets. **2** anything comprising three parts. ◆ *adj* **3** of or relating to a trine. **4** threefold; triple. [C14: from OF *trin*, from L *trīnus* triple, from *trēs* three]
▶ 'trinal *adj*

Trinidad ★ ('trɪnɪ,dæd) *n* an island in the West Indies, off the NE coast of Venezuela: colonized by the Spanish in the 17th century and ceded to Britain in 1802; joined with Tobago in 1888 as a British colony; now part of the independent republic of Trinidad and Tobago. Pop.: 1 184 106 (1990).
▶ ,Trini'dadian *adj, n*

Trinidad and Tobago ★ *n* an independent republic in the Caribbean, occupying the two southernmost islands of the Lesser Antilles: became a British colony in 1888 and gained independence in 1962; became a republic in 1976; a member of the Commonwealth. Official language: English. Religion: Christian majority, with a large Hindu minority. Currency: Trinidad and Tobago dollar. Capital: Port of Spain. Pop.: 1 276 000 (1997). Area: 5128 sq. km (1980 sq. miles).

Trinitarian (,trɪnɪ'tɛərɪən) *n* **1** a person who believes in the doctrine of the Trinity. ◆ *adj* **2** of or relating to the doctrine of the Trinity or those who uphold it.
▶ ,Trini'tarian,ism *n*

trinitroglycerine (traɪ,naɪtrəʊ'glɪsərɪn) *n* the full name for **nitroglycerine.**

trinitrotoluene (traɪ,naɪtrəʊ'tɒlju,iːn) *or* **trinitrotoluol** (traɪ,naɪtrəʊ'tɒlju,ɒl) *n* the full name for **TNT.**

trinity ('trɪnɪtɪ) *n, pl* **trinities. 1** a group of three. **2** the state of being threefold. [C13: from OF *trinite*, from LL *trīnitās*, from L *trīnus* triple]

Trinity ('trɪnɪtɪ) *n Christian theol.* the union of three persons, the Father, Son, and Holy Spirit, in one Godhead.

Trinity Brethren *pl n* the members of Trinity House.

Trinity House *n* an association that provides lighthouses, buoys, etc., around the British coast.

Trinity Sunday *n* the Sunday after Whit Sunday.

Trinity term *n* the summer term at the Inns of Court and certain universities.

trinket ('trɪŋkɪt) *n* **1** a small or worthless ornament or piece of jewellery. **2** a trivial object; trifle. [C16: ? from earlier *trenket* little knife, via OF, from L *truncāre* to lop]

trinomial (traɪ'nəʊmɪəl) *adj* **1** consisting of three terms. ◆ *n* **2** *Maths.* a polynomial consisting of three terms, such as $ax^2 + bx + c$. **3** *Biol.* the three-part name of an organism that incorporates its genus, species, and subspecies. [C18: TRI- + *-nomial* on the model of *binomial*]

trio ('triːəʊ) *n, pl* **trios. 1** a group of three. **2** *Music.* **2a** a group of three singers or instrumentalists or a piece of music composed for such a group. **2b** a subordinate section in a scherzo, minuet, etc. [C18: from It., ult. from L *trēs* three]

triode ('traɪəʊd) *n* **1** an electronic valve having three electrodes, a cathode, an anode, and a grid. **2** any electronic device having three electrodes. [C20: TRI- + ELECTRODE]

trioecious *or* **triecious** (traɪ'iːʃəs) *adj* (of a plant species) having male, female, and hermaphrodite flowers in three different plants. [C18: from NL *trioecia*, from Gk TRI- + *oikos* house]

triolein (traɪ'əʊlɪn) *n* a naturally occurring glyceride of oleic acid, found in fats and oils.

triolet ('triːəʊ,lɛt) *n* a verse form of eight lines, having the first line repeated as the fourth and seventh and the second line as the eighth, rhyming a b a a a b a b. [C17: from F: a little TRIO]

trioxide (traɪ'ɒksaɪd) *n* any oxide that contains three oxygen atoms per molecule.

trip (trɪp) *n* **1** an outward and return journey, often for a specific purpose. **2** any journey. **3** a false step; stumble. **4** any slip or blunder. **5** a light step or tread. **6** a manoeuvre or device to cause someone to trip. **7** Also called: **tripper.** any catch on a mechanism that acts as a switch. **8** *Inf.* a hallucinogenic drug experience. **9** *Inf.* any stimulating, profound, etc., experience. ♦ *vb* **trips, tripping, tripped. 10** (often foll. by *up*, or when *intr*, by *on* or *over*) to stumble or cause to stumble. **11** to make or cause to make a mistake. **12** (*tr*; often foll. by *up*) to trap or catch in a mistake. **13** (*intr*) to go on a short journey. **14** (*intr*) to move or tread lightly. **15** (*intr*) *Inf.* to experience the effects of a hallucinogenic drug. **16** (*tr*) to activate a mechanical trip. [C14: from OF *triper* to tread, of Gmc origin]

tripartite (traɪ'pɑːtaɪt) *adj* **1** divided into or composed of three parts. **2** involving three participants. **3** (esp. of leaves) consisting of three parts formed by divisions extending almost to the base.
▸ **tri'partitely** *adv*

tripe (traɪp) *n* **1** the stomach lining of an ox, cow, etc., prepared for cooking. **2** *Inf.* something silly; rubbish. [C13: from OF, from ?]

triphammer ('trɪp,hæmə) *n* a power hammer that is raised or tilted by a cam and allowed to fall under gravity.

triphibious (traɪ'fɪbɪəs) *adj* (esp. of military operations) occurring on land, at sea, and in the air. [C20: from TRI- + (AM)PHIBIOUS]

triphthong ('trɪfθɒŋ, 'trɪp-) *n* **1** a composite vowel sound during the articulation of which the vocal organs move from one position through a second, ending in a third, as in *fire*. **2** a trigraph representing such a composite vowel sound. [C16: via NL from Med. Gk *triphthongos*, from TRI- + *phthongos* sound]
▸ **triph'thongal** *adj*

tripinnate (traɪ'pɪnɪt, -eɪt) *adj* (of a leaf) having pinnate leaflets that are bipinnately arranged.

triplane ('traɪ,pleɪn) *n* an aeroplane having three wings arranged one above the other.

triple ('trɪpᵊl) *adj* **1** consisting of three parts; threefold. **2** (of musical time or rhythm) having three beats in each bar. **3** three times as great or as much. ♦ *n* **4** a threefold amount. **5** a group of three. ♦ *vb* **triples, tripling, tripled. 6** to increase threefold; treble. [C16: from L *triplus*]
▸ **'triply** *adv*

triple A *n Mil.* anti-aircraft artillery. [referring to the abbrev. AAA]

triple jump *n* an athletic event in which the competitor has to perform successively a hop, a step, and a jump in continuous movement.

triple point *n Chem.* the temperature and pressure at which the three phases of a substance are in equilibrium.

triplet ('trɪplɪt) *n* **1** a group or set of three similar things. **2** one of three offspring born at one birth. **3** *Music.* a group of three notes played in a time value of two, four, etc. **4** *Chem.* a state of a molecule or free radical in which there are two unpaired electrons. [C17: from TRIPLE, on the model of *doublet*]

Triplex ('trɪplɛks) *n Brit. trademark.* a laminated safety glass, as used in car windows.

triplicate *adj* ('trɪplɪkɪt). **1** triple. ♦ *vb* ('trɪplɪ,keɪt), tripli-

cates, triplicating, triplicated. **2** to multiply or be multiplied by three. ♦ *n* ('trɪplɪkɪt). **3a** a group of three things. **3b** one of such a group. **4 in triplicate.** written out three times. [C15: from L *triplicāre* to triple]
▸ **,tripli'cation** *n*

triploid ('trɪplɔɪd) *adj* **1** having or relating to three times the haploid number of chromosomes: *a triploid organism*. ♦ *n* **2** a triploid organism. [C19: from Gk *tripl(oos)* triple + (HAPL)OID]

tripod ('traɪpɒd) *n* **1** a three-legged stand to which a camera, etc., can be attached to hold it steady. **2** a stand or table having three legs.
▸ **tripodal** ('trɪpədᵊl) *adj*

tripoli ('trɪpəlɪ) *n* a lightweight porous siliceous rock used in a powdered form as a polish. [C17: after TRIPOLI, in Libya or in Lebanon]

Tripoli ★ ('trɪpəlɪ) *n* **1** the capital and chief port of Libya, in the northwest on the Mediterranean: founded by Phoenicians in about the 7th century B.C.; the only city that has survived of the three (Oea, Leptis Magna, and Sabratha) that formed the African Tripolis ("three cities"); fishing and manufacturing centre. Pop.: 591 062 (1988 est.). Ancient name: **Oea** ('iːə). Arabic name: **Tarabulus el Gharb. 2** a port in N Lebanon, on the Mediterranean: the second largest town in Lebanon; taken by the Crusaders in 1109 after a siege of five years; oil-refining and manufacturing centre. Pop.: 240 000 (1991 est.). Ancient name: **Tripolis.** Arabic name: **Tarabulus esh Sham.**

Tripolitania ★ (,trɪpəlɪ'teɪnɪə) *n* the NW part of Libya: established as a Phoenician colony in the 7th century B.C.; taken by the Turks in 1551 and became one of the Barbary states; under Italian rule from 1912 until World War II.
▸ **,Tripoli'tanian** *adj, n*

tripos ('traɪpɒs) *n Brit.* the final honours degree examinations at Cambridge University. [C16: from L *tripūs*, infl. by Gk noun ending -*os*]

tripper ('trɪpə) *n* **1** *Chiefly Brit.* a tourist. **2** another word for **trip** (sense 7). **3** any device that causes a trip to operate.

trippy ('trɪpɪ) *adj* **trippier, trippiest.** *Inf.* suggestive of or resembling the effect produced by a hallucinogenic drug.

triptane ('trɪpteɪn) *n* a liquid hydrocarbon used in aviation fuel. [C20: shortened & altered from *trimethylbutane*]

Triptolemus ★ (trɪp'tɒlɪməs) *n Greek myth.* a favourite of Demeter, sent by her to teach men agriculture.

triptych ('trɪptɪk) *n* **1** a set of three pictures or panels, usually hinged so that the two wing panels fold over the larger central one: often used as an altarpiece. **2** a set of three hinged writing tablets. [C18: from Gk *triptukhos*, from TRI- + *ptux* plate]

triptyque (trɪp'tiːk) *n* a customs permit for the temporary importation of a motor vehicle. [C20: from F: TRIPTYCH (from its three sections)]

Tripura ★ ('trɪpʊrə) *n* a state of NE India: formerly a princely state, ruled by the Maharajahs for over 1300 years; became a union territory in 1956 and a state in 1972; extensive jungles. Capital: Agartala. Pop.: 3 055 000 (1994 est.). Area: 10 486 sq. km (4051 sq. miles).

tripwire ('trɪp,waɪə) *n* a wire that activates a trap, mine, etc., when tripped over.

trireme ('traɪriːm) *n* an ancient Greek galley with three banks of oars on each side. [C17: from L *trirēmis*, from TRI- + *rēmus* oar]

trisect (traɪ'sɛkt) *vb* (*tr*) to divide into three parts, esp. three equal parts. [C17: TRI- + -*sect* from L *secāre* to cut]
▸ **trisection** (traɪ'sɛkʃən) *n*

trishaw ('traɪ,ʃɔː) *n* another name for **rickshaw** (sense 2). [C20: from TRI- + RICKSHAW]

triskelion (trɪ'skɛlɪ,ɒn) *n, pl* **triskelia** (trɪ'skɛlɪə). a symbol consisting of three bent limbs or lines radiating from a centre. [C19: from Gk *triskelēs* three-legged]

Trismegistus ★ (,trɪsmɪ'dʒɪstəs) *n* See **Hermes Trismegistus.**

★ people and places

trismus ('trɪzməs) *n Pathol.* the state of being unable to open the mouth because of sustained contractions of the jaw muscles, caused by tetanus. Nontechnical name: **lockjaw.** [C17: from NL, from Gk *trismos* a grinding]

Tristan ('trɪstən) *or* **Tristram ★** ('trɪstrəm) *n* (in medieval romance) the nephew of King Mark of Cornwall who fell in love with his uncle's bride, Iseult, after they mistakenly drank a love potion.

Tristan da Cunha ★ ('trɪstən də 'kuːnjə) *n* a group of four small volcanic islands in the S Atlantic: comprises the main island of Tristan and the uninhabited islands of Gough, Inaccessible, and Nightingale; discovered in 1506 by the Portuguese admiral Tristão da Cunha; annexed to Britain in 1816; population evacuated for two years after the volcanic eruption of 1961. Pop.: 313 (1988). Area: about 100 sq. km (40 sq. miles).

triste (triːst) *adj* an archaic word for **sad.** [from F]

trisyllable (traɪ'sɪləb°l) *n* a word of three syllables.
► **trisyllabic** (ˌtraɪsɪ'læbɪk) *adj*

trite (traɪt) *adj* hackneyed; dull: *a trite comment.* [C16: from L *trītus* worn down, from *terere* to rub]
► **'tritely** *adv* ► **'triteness** *n*

tritheism ('traɪθɪˌɪzəm) *n Theol.* belief in three gods, esp. in the Trinity as consisting of three distinct gods.
► **'tritheist** *n, adj*

triticum ('trɪtɪkəm) *n* any of a genus of cereal grasses which includes the wheats. [C19: L, lit.: wheat, prob. from *tritum*, supine of *terere* to grind]

tritium ('trɪtɪəm) *n* a radioactive isotope of hydrogen. Symbol: T or ³H; half-life: 12.5 years. [C20: NL, from Gk *tritos* third]

triton¹ ('traɪt°n) *n* any of various chiefly tropical marine gastropod molluscs having large spiral shells. [C16: via L from Gk *tritōn*]

triton² ('traɪton) *n Physics.* a nucleus of an atom of tritium, containing two neutrons and one proton. [C20: from TRIT(IUM) + -ON]

Triton ★ ('traɪt°n) *n Greek myth.* a sea god depicted as having the upper parts of a man with a fish's tail.

tritone ('traɪˌtəun) *n* a musical interval consisting of three whole tones.

triturate ('trɪtjuˌreɪt) *vb* **triturates, triturating, triturated. 1** (*tr*) to grind or rub into a fine powder or pulp. ♦ *n* **2** the powder or pulp resulting from this. [C17: from LL *trītūrāre* to thresh, from L *trītūra* a threshing, from *terere* to grind]
► **ˌtritu'ration** *n*

triumph ('traɪəmf) *n* **1** the feeling of exultation and happiness derived from a victory or major achievement. **2** the act or condition of being victorious; victory. **3** (in ancient Rome) a procession held in honour of a victorious general. ♦ *vb* (*intr*) **4** (often foll. by *over*) to win a victory or control: *to triumph over one's weaknesses.* **5** to rejoice over a victory. **6** to celebrate a Roman triumph. [C14: from OF *triumphe*, from L *triumphus*, from OL *triumpus*]
► **triumphal** (traɪ'ʌmfəl) *adj*

triumphant (traɪ'ʌmfənt) *adj* **1** experiencing or displaying triumph. **2** exultant through triumph.
► **tri'umphantly** *adv*

triumvir (traɪ'ʌmvə) *n, pl* **triumvirs** *or* **triumviri** (-vɪˌriː). (esp. in ancient Rome) a member of a triumvirate. [C16: from L: one of three administrators, from *trium virōrum* of three men, from *trēs* three + *vir* man]
► **tri'umviral** *adj*

triumvirate (traɪ'ʌmvɪrɪt) *n* **1** (in ancient Rome) a board of three officials jointly responsible for some task. **2** joint rule by three men. **3** any group of three men associated in some way. **4** the office of a triumvir.

triune ('traɪjuːn) *adj* constituting three in one, esp. the three persons in one God of the Trinity. [C17: TRI- + -*une*, from L *ūnus* one]
► **tri'unity** *n*

trivalent (traɪ'veɪlənt, 'trɪvələnt) *adj Chem.* **1** having a valency of three. **2** having three valencies. ♦ Also: **tervalent.**
► **tri'valency** *n*

Trivandrum ★ (trɪ'vændrəm) *n* a city in S India, capital of Kerala, on the Malabar Coast: made capital of the kingdom of Travancore in 1745; University of Kerala (1937). Pop.: 524 006 (1991).

trivet ('trɪvɪt) *n* **1** a stand, usually three-legged and metal, on which cooking vessels are placed over a fire. **2** a short metal stand on which hot dishes are placed on a table. **3 as right as a trivet.** in perfect health. [OE *trefet* (infl. by OE *thrifēte* having three feet), from L *tripēs* having three feet]

trivia ('trɪvɪə) *n* (*functioning as sing or pl*) petty details or considerations; trifles; trivialities. [from NL, pl of L *trivium* junction of three roads]

trivial ('trɪvɪəl) *adj* **1** of little importance; petty or frivolous: *trivial complaints.* **2** ordinary or commonplace; trite: *trivial conversation.* **3** *Biol., chem.* denoting the common name of an organism or substance. **4** *Biol.* denoting the specific name of an organism in binomial nomenclature. [C15: from L *triviālis* belonging to the public streets, common, from *trivium* junction of three roads]
► **'trivially** *adv* ► **'trivialness** *n*

triviality (ˌtrɪvɪ'ælɪtɪ) *n, pl* **trivialities. 1** the state or quality of being trivial. **2** something, such as a remark, that is trivial.

trivialize *or* **trivialise** ('trɪvɪəˌlaɪz) *vb* **trivializes, trivializing, trivialized** *or* **trivialises, trivialising, trivialised.** (*tr*) to cause to seem trivial or more trivial; minimize.
► **ˌtriviali'zation** *or* **ˌtriviali'sation** *n*

trivium ('trɪvɪəm) *n, pl* **trivia** (-ɪə). (in medieval learning) the arts of grammar, rhetoric, and logic. Cf. **quadrivium.** [C19: from Med. L, from L: crossroads]

-trix *suffix forming nouns.* indicating a feminine agent, corresponding to nouns ending in -*tor: executrix.* [from L]

t-RNA *abbrev.* for transfer RNA.

Troas ★ ('trəuæs) *n* the region of NW Asia Minor surrounding the ancient city of Troy. Also called: **the Troad** ('trəuæd).

Trobriand Islands ★ ('trəubrɪˌænd) *pl n* a group of coral islands in the Solomon Sea, north of the E part of New Guinea: part of Papua New Guinea. Area: about 440 sq. km (170 sq. miles).
► **Trobriand Islander** *n*

trocar ('trəukɑː) *n* a surgical instrument for removing fluid from bodily cavities. [C18: from F *trocart*, lit.: with three sides, from *trois* three + *carre* side]

trochal ('trəuk°l) *adj Zool.* shaped like a wheel. [C19: from Gk *trokhos* wheel]

trochanter (trəu'kæntə) *n* **1** any of several processes on the upper part of the vertebrate femur, to which muscles are attached. **2** the third segment of an insect's leg. [C17: via F from Gk *trokhantēr*, from *trekhein* to run]

troche (trəuʃ) *n Med.* another name for **lozenge** (sense 1). [C16: from F *trochisque*, from LL *trochiscus*, from Gk *trokhiskos* little wheel, from *trokhos* wheel]

trochee ('trəukiː) *n* a metrical foot of two syllables, the first long and the second short. [C16: via L from Gk *trokhaios pous*, lit.: a running foot, from *trekhein* to run]
► **trochaic** (trəu'keɪɪk) *adj*

trochlea ('trɒklɪə) *n, pl* **trochleae** (-lɪˌiː). any bony or cartilaginous part with a grooved surface over which a bone, etc., may slide or articulate. [C17: from L, from Gk *trokhileia* a sheaf of pulleys]

trochlear nerve ('trɒklɪə) *n* either one of the fourth pair of cranial nerves, which supply the superior oblique muscle of the eye.

trochoid ('trəukɔɪd) *n* **1** the curve described by a fixed point on the radius of a circle as the circle rolls along a straight line. ♦ *adj also* **trochoidal. 2** rotating about a central axis. **3** *Anat.* (of a structure or part) resembling or functioning as a pivot or pulley. [C18: from Gk *trokhoeidēs* circular, from *trokhos* wheel]

trod (trɒd) *vb* the past tense and a past participle of **tread.**

trodden ('trɒd°n) *vb* a past participle of **tread.**

trode (trəud) *vb Arch.* a past tense of **tread.**

troglodyte ('trɒgləˌdaɪt) *n* **1** a cave dweller, esp. of prehistoric times. **2** *Inf.* a person who lives alone and appears eccentric. [C16: via L from Gk *trōglodutēs* one who enters caves, from *trōglē* hole + *duein* to enter]
► **troglodytic** (ˌtrɒglə'dɪtɪk) *adj*

trogon ('trəʊgɒn) *n* any of an order of birds of tropical regions of America, Africa, and Asia, having a brilliant plumage and long tail. See also **quetzal** (sense 1). [C18: from NL, from Gk *trōgōn*, from *trōgein* to gnaw]

troika ('trɔɪkə) *n* **1** a Russian vehicle drawn by three horses abreast. **2** three horses harnessed abreast. **3** a triumvirate. [C19: from Russian, from *troe* three]

Troilus ★ ('trɔɪləs, 'trəʊɪləs) *n Greek myth.* the youngest son of King Priam and Queen Hecuba, slain at Troy. In medieval romance he is portrayed as the lover of Cressida.

Trois Rivières ★ (*French* trwɑ rivjer) *n* a port in central Canada, in Quebec on the St Lawrence River: one of the world's largest centres of newsprint production. Pop. (metropolitan area): 136 300 (1991). English name: **Three Rivers.**

Trojan ('trəʊdʒən) *n* **1** a native or inhabitant of ancient Troy. **2** a person who is hard-working and determined. ◆ *adj* **3** of or relating to ancient Troy or its inhabitants.

Trojan Horse *n* **1** *Greek myth.* the huge wooden hollow figure of a horse left outside Troy by the Greeks and dragged inside by the Trojans. The men concealed inside it opened the city to the final Greek assault. **2** a trap intended to undermine an enemy. **3** *Computing.* a bug inserted into a program or system designed to be activated after a certain time or a certain number of operations.

troll[1] (trəʊl) *vb* **1** *Angling.* **1a** to draw (a baited line, etc.) through the water. **1b** to fish (a stretch of water) by trolling. **1c** to fish (for) by trolling. **2** to roll or cause to roll. **3** *Arch.* to sing (a refrain, chorus, etc.) in a loud hearty voice. **4** (*intr*) *Brit. inf.* to walk or stroll. ◆ *n* **5** a trolling. **6** *Angling.* a bait or lure used in trolling. [C14: from OF *troller* to run about]
▶ **'troller** *n*

troll[2] (trəʊl) *n* (in Scandinavian folklore) one of a class of supernatural creatures that dwell in caves or mountains and are depicted either as dwarfs or as giants. [C19: from ON: demon]

trolley ('trɒlɪ) *n* **1** a small table on casters used for conveying food, etc. **2** *Chiefly Brit.* a wheeled cart or stand used for moving heavy items, such as shopping in a supermarket or luggage at a railway station. **3** *Brit.* (in a hospital) a bed mounted on casters and used for moving patients who are unconscious, etc. **4** *Brit.* See **trolleybus. 5** *US & Canad.* See **trolley car. 6** a device that collects the current from an overhead wire, third rail, etc., to drive the motor of an electric vehicle. **7** a pulley or truck that travels along an overhead wire in order to support a suspended load. **8** *Chiefly Brit.* a low truck running on rails, used in factories, mines, etc. **9** a truck, cage, or basket suspended from an overhead track or cable for carrying loads in a mine, etc. [C19: prob. from TROLL[1]]

trolleybus ('trɒlɪˌbʌs) *n* an electrically driven public-transport vehicle that does not run on rails but takes its power from two overhead wires.

trolley car *n* a US and Canad. name for **tram** (sense 1).

trollius ('trəʊlɪəs) *n* another name for **globeflower.** [from G *Trollblume* globeflower]

trollop ('trɒləp) *n* **1** a promiscuous woman, esp. a prostitute. **2** an untidy woman; slattern. [C17: ?from G dialect *Trolle* prostitute]
▶ **'trollopy** *adj*

Trollope ★ ('trɒləp) *n* **Anthony.** 1815–82, British novelist. His novels include *Barchester Towers* (1857), *Phineas Redux* (1874), and *The Prime Minister* (1876).

trombone (trɒm'bəʊn) *n* a brass instrument, a low-pitched counterpart of the trumpet, consisting of a tube the effective length of which is varied by means of a U-shaped slide. [C18: from It., from *tromba* a trumpet, from OHG *trumba*]
▶ **trom'bonist** *n*

trommel ('trɒməl) *n* a revolving cylindrical sieve used to screen crushed ore. [C19: from G: a drum]

trompe (trɒmp) *n* an apparatus for supplying the blast of air in a forge, consisting of a thin column down which water falls, drawing in air through side openings. [C19: from F, lit.: trumpet]

trompe l'oeil (*French* trɔ̃p lœj) *n, pl* **trompe l'oeils** (trɔ̃p lœj). **1** a painting, etc., giving a convincing illusion of reality. **2** an effect of this kind. [from F, lit.: deception of the eye]

Tromsø ★ ('trɒmsəʊ; *Norwegian* 'trumsø) *n* a port in N Norway, on a small island between Kvaløy and the mainland: fishing and sealing centre. Pop.: 51 218 (1990).

-tron *suffix forming nouns.* **1** indicating a vacuum tube. **2** indicating an instrument for accelerating atomic particles. [from Gk, suffix indicating instrument]

tronc (trɒŋk) *n* a pool into which waiters, etc., pay their tips for later distribution to staff by a **tronc master,** according to agreed percentages. [C20: from F: collecting box]

Trondheim ★ ('trɒnˌhaɪm; *Norwegian* 'trɔnhɛim) *n* a port in central Norway, on **Trondheim Fjord** (an inlet of the Norwegian Sea): national capital until 1380; seat of the Technical University of Norway. Pop.: 143 746 (1996). Former name (until the 16th century and from 1930 to 1931): **Nidaros.**

tronk (trɒŋk) *n S. African inf.* a prison. [Afrik.]

troop (truːp) *n* **1** a large group or assembly. **2** a subdivision of a cavalry squadron or artillery battery of about platoon size. **3** (*pl*) armed forces; soldiers. **4** a large group of Scouts comprising several patrols. ◆ *vb* **5** (*intr*) to gather, move, or march in or as if in a crowd. **6** (*tr*) *Mil.,* *chiefly Brit.* to parade (the colour or flag) ceremonially. [C16: from F *troupe,* from *troupeau* flock, of Gmc origin]

trooper ('truːpə) *n* **1** a soldier in a cavalry regiment. **2** *US & Austral.* a mounted policeman. **3** *US.* a state policeman. **4** a cavalry horse. **5** *Inf., chiefly Brit.* a troopship.

troopship ('truːpˌʃɪp) *n* a ship used to transport military personnel.

tropaeolum (trəʊ'piːələm) *n, pl* **tropaeolums** or **tropaeola** (-lə). any of a genus of garden plants, esp. the nasturtium. [C18: from NL, from L *tropaeum* TROPHY; from the shield-shaped leaves and helmet-shaped flowers]

trope (trəʊp) *n* a word or expression used in a figurative sense. [C16: from L *tropus* figurative use of a word, from Gk *tropos* style, turn]

-trope *n combining form.* indicating a turning towards, development in the direction of, or affinity to: *heliotrope.* [from Gk *tropos* a turn]

trophic ('trɒfɪk) *adj* of nutrition. [C19: from Gk *trophikos,* from *trophē* food, from *trephein* to feed]

tropho- *or before a vowel* **troph-** *combining form.* indicating nourishment or nutrition: *trophozoite.* [from Gk *trophē* food, from *trephein* to feed]

trophoblast ('trɒfəˌblæst) *n* a membrane that encloses the embryo of mammals and absorbs nourishment from the uterine fluids.

trophozoite (ˌtrɒfə'zəʊaɪt) *n* the form of a sporozoan protozoan, esp. of certain parasites, in the feeding stage.

trophy ('trəʊfɪ) *n, pl* **trophies. 1** an object such as a silver cup that is symbolic of victory in a contest, esp. a sporting contest; prize. **2** a memento of success, esp. one taken in war or hunting. **3** (in ancient Greece and Rome) a memorial to a victory, usually consisting of captured arms raised on the battlefield or in a public place. **4** an ornamental carving that represents a group of weapons, etc. [C16: from F *trophée,* from L *tropaeum,* from Gk *tropaion,* from *tropē* a turning, defeat of the enemy]

-trophy *n combining form.* indicating a certain type of nourishment or growth: *dystrophy.* [from Gk *-trophia,* from *trophē* nourishment]
▶ **-trophic** *adj combining form.*

tropic ('trɒpɪk) *n* **1** (*sometimes cap.*) either of the parallel lines of latitude at about 23½°N (**tropic of Cancer**) and 23½°S (**tropic of Capricorn**) of the equator. **2 the tropics.** (*often cap.*) that part of the earth's surface between the tropics of Cancer and Capricorn. **3** *Astron.* either of the two parallel circles on the celestial sphere having the same latitudes and names as the lines on the earth. ◆ *adj* **4** tropical. [C14: from LL *tropicus* belonging to a turn, from Gk *tropikos,* from *tropos* a turn; from the belief that the sun turned back at the solstices]

-tropic *adj combining form.* turning or developing in response to a certain stimulus: *heliotropic*. [from Gk *tropos* a turn]

tropical ('trɒpɪkᵊl) *adj* **1** situated in, used in, characteristic of, or relating to the tropics. **2** (of weather) very hot, esp. when humid. **3** of a trope.
 ▸ ˌtropiˈcality *n* ▸ 'tropically *adv*

tropicbird ('trɒpɪkˌbɜːd) *n* any of various tropical aquatic birds having long tail feathers and a white plumage with black markings.

tropism ('trəʊpɪzəm) *n* the response of an organism, esp. a plant, to an external stimulus by growth in a direction determined by the stimulus. [from Gk *tropos* a turn]
 ▸ ˌtropisˈmatic *adj*

-tropism *or* **-tropy** *n combining form*. indicating a tendency to turn or develop in response to a stimulus: *phototropism*. [from Gk *tropos* a turn]

tropo- *combining form*. indicating change or a turning: *tropophyte*. [from Gk *tropos* a turn]

tropopause ('trɒpəˌpɔːz) *n Meteorol*. the plane of discontinuity between the troposphere and the stratosphere, characterized by a sharp change in the lapse rate.

troposphere ('trɒpəˌsfɪə) *n* the lowest atmospheric layer, about 18 kilometres (11 miles) thick at the equator to about 6 km (4 miles) at the Poles, in which air temperature decreases normally with height at about 6.5°C per km.
 ▸ **tropospheric** (ˌtrɒpəˈsfɛrɪk) *adj*

-tropous *adj combining form*. indicating a turning away: *anatropous*. [from Gk *-tropos* concerning a turn]

troppo¹ ('trɒpəʊ) *adv Music*. too much; excessively. See **non troppo**. [It.]

troppo² ('trɒpəʊ) *adj Austral. sl*. mentally affected by a tropical climate.

Trossachs ★ ('trɒsəks) *n* (*functioning as pl or sing*) **the**. **1** a narrow wooded valley in central Scotland, between Loch Achray and Loch Katrine: made famous by Sir Walter Scott's descriptions. **2** (popularly) the area extending northwards from Loch Ard and Aberfoyle to Lochs Katrine, Achray, and Venachar.

trot (trɒt) *vb* **trots, trotting, trotted**. **1** to move or cause to move at a trot. ◆ *n* **2** a gait of a horse in which diagonally opposite legs come down together. **3** a steady brisk pace. **4** (in harness racing) a race for horses that have been trained to trot fast. **5** *Chiefly Brit*. a small child. **6** *US sl*. a student's crib. **7 on the trot**. *Inf*. **7a** one after the other: *to read two books on the trot*. **7b** busy, esp. on one's feet. **8 the trots**. *Inf*. **8a** diarrhoea. **8b** *NZ*. trotting races. ◆ See also **trot out**. [C13: from OF *trot*, from *troter* to trot, of Gmc origin]

Trot (trɒt) *n Inf*. a follower of Trotsky; Trotskyist.

troth (trəʊθ) *n Arch*. **1** a pledge of fidelity, esp. a betrothal. **2** truth (esp. in **in troth**). **3** loyalty; fidelity. [OE *trēowth*]

trotline ('trɒtˌlaɪn) *n Angling*. a long line suspended across a stream, river, etc., to which shorter hooked and baited lines are attached.

trot out *vb* (*tr, adv*) *Inf*. to bring forward, as for approbation or admiration, esp. repeatedly.

Trotsky *or* **Trotski** ★ ('trɒtskɪ) *n* **Leon**, original name *Lev Davidovich Bronstein*. 1879–1940, Russian revolutionary and a leader of the November Revolution (1917); as commissar of foreign affairs (1917–24), he created the Red Army. He was ousted by Stalin after Lenin's death and deported; assassinated by a Stalinist agent.

Trotskyism ('trɒtskɪˌɪzəm) *n* Trotsky's theory of communism, in which he called for immediate worldwide revolution by the proletariat.
 ▸ 'Trotskyist *or* 'Trotskyˌite *n, adj*

trotter ('trɒtə) *n* **1** a horse that is specially trained to trot fast. **2** (*usually pl*) the foot of certain animals, esp. of pigs.

troubadour ('truːbəˌdʊə) *n* any of a class of lyric poets who flourished principally in Provence and N Italy from the 11th to the 13th century, writing chiefly on courtly love. [C18: from F, from OProvençal *trobador*, from *trobar* to write verses, ? ult. from L *tropus* TROPE]

trouble ('trʌbᵊl) *n* **1** a state of mental distress or anxiety. **2** a state of disorder or unrest: *industrial trouble*. **3** a condition of disease, pain, or malfunctioning: *liver trouble*. **4** a

cause of distress, disturbance, or pain. **5** effort or exertion taken to do something. **6** liability to suffer punishment or misfortune (esp. in **be in trouble**): *he's in trouble with the police*. **7** a personal weakness or cause of annoyance: *his trouble is he's too soft*. **8** political unrest. **9** the condition of an unmarried girl who becomes pregnant (esp. in **in trouble**). ◆ *vb* **troubles, troubling, troubled**. **10** (*tr*) to cause trouble to. **11** (*intr*; usually with a negative and foll. by *about*) to put oneself to inconvenience; be concerned: *don't trouble about me*. **12** (*intr*; usually with a negative) to take pains; exert oneself. **13** (*tr*) to cause inconvenience or discomfort to. **14** (*tr*; *usually passive*) to agitate or make rough: *the seas were troubled*. **15** (*tr*) *Caribbean*. to interfere with. [C13: from OF *troubler*, from Vulgar L *turbulāre* (unattested), from LL *turbidāre*, ult. from *turba* commotion]
 ▸ 'troubler *n*

troublemaker ('trʌbᵊlˌmeɪkə) *n* a person who makes trouble, esp. between people.
 ▸ 'trouble,making *adj, n*

troubleshooter ('trʌbᵊlˌʃuːtə) *n* a person who locates the cause of trouble and removes or treats it.
 ▸ 'trouble,shooting *n, adj*

troublesome ('trʌbᵊlsəm) *adj* **1** causing trouble. **2** characterized by violence; turbulent.
 ▸ 'troublesomeness *n*

troublous ('trʌbləs) *adj Arch. or literary*. unsettled; agitated.
 ▸ 'troublously *adv*

trough (trɒf) *n* **1** a narrow open container, esp. one in which food or water for animals is put. **2** a narrow channel, gutter, or gulley. **3** a narrow depression, as between two waves. **4** *Meteorol*. an elongated area of low pressure. **5** a single or temporary low point; depression. **6** *Physics*. the portion of a wave in which the amplitude lies below its average value. **7** *Econ*. the lowest point of the trade cycle. [OE *trōh*]

trounce (traʊns) *vb* **trounces, trouncing, trounced**. (*tr*) to beat or defeat utterly; thrash. [C16: from ?]

troupe (truːp) *n* **1** a company of actors or other performers, esp. one that travels. ◆ *vb* **troupes, trouping, trouped**. **2** (*intr*) (esp. of actors) to move or travel in a group. [C19: from F; see TROOP]

trouper ('truːpə) *n* **1** a member of a troupe. **2** a dependable worker or associate.

trouser ('traʊzə) *n* (*modifier*) of or relating to trousers: *trouser buttons*.

trousers ('traʊzəz) *pl n* a garment shaped to cover the body from the waist to the ankles or knees with separate tube-shaped sections for both legs. [C17: from earlier *trouse*, var. of TREWS, infl. by DRAWERS]

trousseau ('truːsəʊ) *n, pl* **trousseaux** *or* **trousseaus** (-səʊz). the clothes, linen, etc., collected by a bride for her marriage. [C19: from OF, lit.: a little bundle; see TRUSS]

trout (traʊt) *n, pl* **trout** *or* **trouts**. any of various game fishes, mostly of fresh water in northern regions. They are related to the salmon but are smaller and spotted. [OE *trūht*, from LL *tructa*, from Gk *trōktēs* sharp-toothed fish]

trouvère (truːˈvɛə) *n* any of a group of poets of N France during the 12th and 13th centuries who composed chiefly narrative works. [C19: from F, from OF *troveor*, from *trover* to compose]

trove (trəʊv) *n* See **treasure-trove**.

trow (trəʊ) *vb Arch*. to think, believe, or trust. [OE *trēow*]

Trowbridge ★ ('trəʊˌbrɪdʒ) *n* a market town in SW England, administrative centre of Wiltshire: woollen manufacturing. Pop.: 29 334 (1991).

trowel ('traʊəl) *n* **1** any of various small hand tools having a flat metal blade attached to a handle, used for scooping or spreading plaster or similar materials. **2** a similar tool with a curved blade used by gardeners for lifting plants, etc. ◆ *vb* **trowels, trowelling, trowelled** *or US* **trowels, troweling, troweled**. **3** (*tr*) to use a trowel on. [C14: from OF *truele*, from L *trulla* a scoop, from *trua* a stirring spoon]

Troy ★ (trɔɪ) *n* any of nine ancient cities in NW Asia Minor, each of which was built on the ruins of its predecessor. The seventh was the site of the Trojan War (mid-13th century B.C.). Greek name: **Ilion**. Latin name: **Ilium**.

Troyes ★ *(French* trwa) *n* an industrial city in NE France: became prosperous through its great fairs in the early Middle Ages. Pop.: 59 271 (1990).

troy weight *or* **troy** (troɪ) *n* a system of weights used for precious metals and gemstones, based on the grain. 24 grains = 1 pennyweight; 20 pennyweights = 1 (troy) ounce; 12 ounces = 1 (troy) pound. [C14: after TROYES, where first used]

trs *Printing. abbrev. for* transpose.

Trst ★ (trst) *n* the Slovene and Serbo-Croat name for **Trieste.**

truant ('truːənt) *n* **1** a person who is absent without leave, esp. from school. ◆ *adj* **2** being or relating to a truant. ◆ *vb* **3** (*intr*) to play truant. [C13: from OF: vagabond, prob. of Celtic origin]
▶ 'truancy *n*

truce (truːs) *n* **1** an agreement to stop fighting, esp. temporarily. **2** temporary cessation of something unpleasant. [C13: from pl of OE *treow* trow]

Trucial States ★ ('truːʃəl) *pl n* a former name (until 1971) of the **United Arab Emirates.** Also called: **Trucial Sheikdoms, Trucial Oman, Trucial Coast.**

truck[1] (trʌk) *n* **1** *Brit.* a vehicle for carrying freight on a railway; wagon. **2** another name (esp. US, Canad., Austral., and NZ) for **lorry. 3** Also called: **truckload.** the amount carried by a truck. **4** a frame carrying two or more pairs of wheels attached under an end of a railway coach, etc. **5** *Naut.* a disc-shaped block fixed to the head of a mast having holes for receiving halyards. **6** any wheeled vehicle used to move goods. ◆ *vb* **7** to convey (goods) in a truck. **8** (*intr*) *Chiefly US & Canad.* to drive a truck. [C17: ? shortened from *truckle* a small wheel]

truck[2] (trʌk) *n* **1** commercial goods. **2** dealings (esp. in **have no truck with**). **3** commercial exchange. **4** *Arch.* payment of wages in kind. **5** miscellaneous articles. **6** *Inf.* rubbish. **7** *US & Canad.* vegetables grown for market. ◆ *vb* **8** *Arch.* to exchange (goods); barter. **9** (*intr*) to traffic or negotiate. [C13: from OF *troquer* (unattested) to barter, equivalent to Med. L *trocare*, from ?]

trucker ('trʌkə) *n Chiefly US & Canad.* **1** a lorry driver. **2** a person who arranges for the transport of goods by lorry.

truck farm *n US & Canad.* a market garden.
▶ **truck farmer** *n* ▶ **truck farming** *n*

truckie ('trʌkɪ) *n Austral. & NZ inf.* a truck driver.

trucking ('trʌkɪŋ) *n Chiefly US & Canad.* the transportation of goods by lorry.

truckle ('trʌkᵊl) *vb* **truckles, truckling, truckled.** (*intr;* usually foll. by *to*) to yield weakly; give in. [C17: from obs. *truckle* to sleep in a truckle bed]
▶ **'truckler** *n*

truckle bed *n* a low bed on wheels, stored under a larger bed. [C17: from *truckle* small wheel, ult. from L *trochlea* sheaf of a pulley]

truck system *n* a system during the early years of the Industrial Revolution of forcing workers to accept payment of wages in kind.

truculent ('trʌkjʊlənt) *adj* **1** defiantly aggressive, sullen, or obstreperous. **2** *Arch.* savage, fierce, or harsh. [C16: from L *truculentus,* from *trux* fierce]
▶ **'truculence** *or* **'truculency** *n* ▶ **'truculently** *adv*

Trudeau ★ ('truːdəu) *n* **Pierre Elliott.** born 1919, Canadian statesman; Liberal prime minister (1968–79; 1980–84).

trudge (trʌdʒ) *vb* **trudges, trudging, trudged. 1** (*intr*) to walk or plod heavily or wearily. **2** (*tr*) to pass through or over by trudging. ◆ *n* **3** a long tiring walk. [C16: from ?]
▶ **'trudger** *n*

trudgen ('trʌdʒən) *n* a type of swimming stroke that uses overarm action, as in the crawl, and a scissors kick. [C19: after John *Trudgen,* E swimmer, who introduced it]

true (truː) *adj* **truer, truest. 1** not false, fictional, or illusory; factual; conforming with reality. **2** (*prenominal*) real; not synthetic. **3** faithful and loyal. **4** conforming to a required standard, law, or pattern: *a true aim.* **5** exactly in tune. **6** (of a compass bearing) according to the earth's geographical rather than magnetic poles: *true north.* **7**

Biol. conforming to the typical structure of a designated type. **8** *Physics.* not apparent or relative. ◆ *n* **9** correct alignment (esp. in **in true, out of true**). ◆ *adv* **10** truthfully; rightly. **11** precisely or unswervingly. ◆ *vb* **trues, truing, trued. 12** (*tr*) to adjust so as to make true. [OE *triewe*]
▶ **'trueness** *n*

true bill *n* (formerly in Britain; now US) the endorsement made on a bill of indictment by a grand jury certifying it to be supported by sufficient evidence to warrant a trial.

true-blue *adj* **1** unwaveringly or staunchly loyal. ◆ *n* **true blue. 2** *Chiefly Brit.* a staunch royalist or Conservative.

true-life *adj* directly comparable to reality: *a true-life story.*

truelove ('truːˌlʌv) *n* **1** someone truly loved; sweetheart. **2** another name for **herb Paris.**

truelove knot *or* **true-lovers' knot** *n* a complicated bowknot that is hard to untie, symbolizing ties of love.

Trueman ★ ('truːmən) *n* **Fred(die),** full name *Frederick Sewards Trueman.* born 1931, English cricketer, a fast bowler for Yorkshire and England.

true north *n* the direction from any point along a meridian towards the North Pole. Also called: **geographic north.** Cf. **magnetic north.**

true rib *n* any of the upper seven pairs of ribs in man.

true time *n* the time shown by a sundial.

Truffaut ★ *(French* tryfo) *n* **François** (frɑ̃swa). 1932–84, French New Wave film director. His films include *Jules et Jim* (1961) and *Le Dernier Métro* (1980).

truffle ('trʌfᵊl) *n* **1** any of various edible subterranean European fungi. They have a tuberous appearance and are regarded as a delicacy. **2** Also called: **rum truffle.** *Chiefly Brit.* a sweet resembling this fungus in shape, flavoured with chocolate or rum. [C16: from F *truffe,* from OProvençal *trufa,* ult. from L *tūber*]

trug (trʌg) *n* a long shallow basket for carrying flowers, fruit, etc. [C16: ? var. of TROUGH]

trugo ('truːgəu) *n Austral.* a game similar to croquet, originally improvised in Victoria from the rubber discs used as buffers on railway carriages. [from *true go,* when the wheel is hit between the goalposts]

truism ('truːɪzəm) *n* an obvious truth; platitude.
▶ **tru'istic** *adj*

Trujillo ★ *(Spanish* tru'xixo) *n* a city in NW Peru: founded 1535; university (1824); centre of a district producing rice and sugar cane. Pop.: 627 553 (1995).

Truk Islands ★ (trʌk) *pl n* a group of islands in the W Pacific, in the E Caroline Islands: administratively part of the US Trust Territory of the Pacific Islands from 1947; became self-governing in 1979 as part of the Federated States of Micronesia; consists of 11 chief islands; a major Japanese naval base during World War II. Pop.: 52 870 (1994). Area: 130 sq. km (50 sq. miles).

trull (trʌl) *n Arch.* a prostitute; harlot. [C16: from G *Trulle*]

truly ('truːlɪ) *adv* **1** in a true, just, or faithful manner. **2** (*intensifier*): *a truly great man.* **3** indeed; really.

Truman ★ ('truːmən) *n* **Harry S.** 1884–1972, US Democratic statesman; 33rd president of the US (1945–53). He approved the dropping of atomic bombs on Japan (1945) and involved the US in the Korean War.

trumeau (tru'məu) *n, pl* **trumeaux** (-'məuz). *Archit.* a section of a wall or pillar between two openings. [from F]

trump[1] (trʌmp) *n* **1** Also called: **trump card. 1a** any card from the suit chosen as trumps. **1b** this suit itself; trumps. **2** a decisive or advantageous move, resource, action, etc. **3** *Inf.* a fine or reliable person. ◆ *vb* **4** to play a trump card (on a suit, or a particular card of a suit, that is not trumps). **5** (*tr*) to outdo or surpass. ◆ See also **trumps, trump up.** [C16: var. of TRIUMPH]

trump[2] (trʌmp) *n Arch. or literary.* **1** a trumpet or the sound produced by one. **2 the last trump.** the final trumpet call on the Day of Judgment. [C13: from OF *trompe,* from OHG *trumpa* trumpet]

trumpery ('trʌmpərɪ) *n, pl* **trumperies. 1** foolish talk or actions. **2** a useless or worthless article; trinket. ◆ *adj* **3**

★ people and places

useless or worthless. [C15: from OF *tromperie* deceit, from *tromper* to cheat]

trumpet ('trʌmpɪt) n **1** a valved brass instrument of brilliant tone consisting of a narrow tube ending in a flared bell. **2** any similar instrument, esp. a straight instrument used for fanfares, signals, etc. **3** a loud sound such as that of a trumpet, esp. when made by an animal. **4** an eight-foot reed stop on an organ. **5** something resembling a trumpet in shape. **6** short for **ear trumpet**. **7 blow one's own trumpet**. to boast about one's own skills or good qualities. ◆ vb **trumpets, trumpeting, trumpeted**. **8** to proclaim or sound loudly. [C13: from OF *trompette* a little TRUMP²]

trumpeter ('trʌmpɪtə) n **1** a person who plays the trumpet, esp. one whose duty it is to play fanfares, signals, etc. **2** any of three birds of South America, having a rounded body, long legs, and a glossy blackish plumage. **3** (*sometimes cap.*) a breed of domestic fancy pigeon with a long ruff. **4** a large silvery-grey Australian marine food and game fish that grunts when taken from the water.

trumpeter swan n a large swan of W North America, having a white plumage and black bill.

trumps (trʌmps) pl n **1** (*sometimes sing*) Cards. any one of the four suits that outranks all the other suits for the duration of a deal or game. **2 turn up trumps**. (of a person) to bring about a happy or successful conclusion, esp. unexpectedly.

trump up vb (tr, adv) to invent (a charge, accusation, etc.) so as to deceive.

truncate vb (trʌŋ'keɪt, 'trʌŋkeɪt), **truncates, truncating, truncated**. **1** (tr) to shorten by cutting. ◆ adj ('trʌŋkeɪt). **2** cut short; truncated. **3** Biol. having a blunt end. [C15: from L *truncāre* to lop]
► **trun'cation** n

truncated (trʌŋ'keɪtɪd) adj **1** (of a cone, prism, etc.) having an apex or end removed by a plane intersection. **2** shortened by or as if by cutting off; truncate.

truncheon ('trʌntʃən) n **1** Chiefly Brit. a club or cudgel carried by a policeman. **2** a baton of office. [C16: from OF *tronchon* stump, from L *truncus* trunk; see TRUNCATE]

trundle ('trʌnd°l) vb **trundles, trundling, trundled**. **1** to move heavily on or as if on wheels: *the bus trundled by*. ◆ n **2** a trundling. **3** a small wheel or roller. [OE *tryndel*]

trundle bed n a less common word for **truckle bed**.

trundler ('trʌndlə) n NZ. **1** a trolley for shopping or one for golf clubs. **2** a child's pushchair.

trunk (trʌŋk) n **1** the main stem of a tree. **2** a large strong case or box used to contain clothes, etc., when travelling and for storage. **3** the body excluding the head, neck, and limbs; torso. **4** the elongated nasal part of an elephant. **5** the US and Canad. name for **boot**¹ (sense 2). **6** the main stem of a nerve, blood vessel, etc. **7** Naut. a watertight boxlike cover within a vessel, such as one used to enclose a centreboard. **8** an enclosed duct or passageway for ventilation, etc. **9** (*modifier*) of a main road, railway, etc., in a network: *a trunk line*. ◆ See also **trunks**. [C15: from OF *tronc*, from L *truncus*, from *truncus* (adj) lopped]

trunk call n Chiefly Brit. a long-distance telephone call.

trunk curl n another name for **sit-up**.

trunkfish ('trʌŋk,fɪʃ) n, pl **trunkfish** or **trunkfishes**. any of a family of fishes having the body encased in bony plates.

trunk hose n a man's puffed-out breeches reaching to the thighs and worn with tights in the 16th century.

trunking ('trʌŋkɪŋ) n **1** Telecomm. the cables that take a common route through a telephone exchange building. **2** plastic housing used to conceal wires, etc.; casing. **3** the delivery of goods over long distances, esp. by road vehicles to local distribution centres.

trunk line n **1** a direct link between two telephone exchanges or switchboards that are a considerable distance apart. **2** the main route or routes on a railway.

trunk road n Brit. a main road, esp. one that is suitable for heavy vehicles.

trunks (trʌŋks) pl n **1** a man's garment worn for swimming, extending from the waist to the thigh. **2** shorts worn for some sports. **3** Chiefly Brit. men's underpants with legs that reach midthigh.

trunnion ('trʌnjən) n one of a pair of coaxial projections attached to opposite sides of a container, cannon, etc., to provide a support about which it can turn. [C17: from OF *trognon* trunk]

Truro ★ ('truərəʊ) n a market town in SW England, administrative centre of Cornwall. Pop.: 18 966 (1991).

truss (trʌs) vb (tr) **1** (sometimes foll. by *up*) to tie, bind, or bundle. **2** to bind the wings and legs of (a fowl) before cooking. **3** to support or stiffen (a roof, bridge, etc.) with structural members. **4** Med. to supply or support with a truss. ◆ n **5** a structural framework of wood or metal used to support a roof, bridge, etc. **6** Med. a device for holding a hernia in place, typically consisting of a pad held in position by a belt. **7** a cluster of flowers or fruit growing at the end of a single stalk. **8** Naut. a metal fitting fixed to a yard at its centre for holding it to a mast. **9** another name for **corbel**. **10** a bundle or pack. **11** Chiefly Brit. a bundle of hay or straw, esp. one having a fixed weight of 36, 56, or 60 pounds. [C13: from OF *trousse*, from *trousser*, apparently from Vulgar L *torciāre* (unattested), from *torca* (unattested) a bundle]

trust (trʌst) n **1** reliance on and confidence in the truth, worth, reliability, etc., of a person or thing; faith. Related adj: **fiducial**. **2** a group of commercial enterprises combined to control the market for any commodity. **3** the obligation of someone in a responsible position. **4** custody, charge, or care. **5** a person or thing in which confidence or faith is placed. **6** commercial credit. **7a** an arrangement whereby a person to whom the legal title to property is conveyed (the trustee) holds such property for the benefit of those entitled to the beneficial interest. **7b** property that is the subject of such an arrangement. Related adj: **fiduciary**. **8** (in the British National Health Service) a self-governing hospital, group of hospitals, or other body providing health-care services, which operates as an independent commercial unit within the NHS. **9** (*modifier*) of or relating to a trust or trusts. ◆ vb **10** (tr; may take a clause as object) to expect, hope, or suppose. **11** (when tr, may take an infinitive; when intr, often foll. by *in* or *to*) to place confidence in (someone to do something); rely (upon). **12** (tr) to consign for care. **13** (tr) to allow (someone to do something) with confidence in his or her good sense or honesty. **14** (tr) to extend business credit to. [C13: from ON *traust*]
► **'trustable** adj ► **'truster** n

trust account n **1** Also called: **trustee account**. a savings account deposited in the name of a trustee who controls it during his lifetime, after which the balance is payable to a prenominated beneficiary. **2** property under the control of a trustee or trustees.

trustee (trʌ'stiː) n **1** a person to whom the legal title to property is entrusted. **2** a member of a board that manages the affairs of an institution or organization.

trustee in bankruptcy n a person entrusted with the administration of a bankrupt's affairs and with realizing his assets for the benefit of the creditors.

trustee investment n Stock Exchange. an investment in which trustees are authorized to invest money belonging to a trust fund.

trusteeship (trʌ'stiːʃɪp) n **1** the office or function of a trustee. **2a** the administration or government of a territory by a foreign country under the supervision of the **Trusteeship Council** of the United Nations. **2b** (*often cap.*) any such dependent territory; trust territory.

trustful ('trʌstfʊl) or **trusting** adj characterized by a tendency or readiness to trust others.
► **'trustfully** or **'trustingly** adv

trust fund n money, securities, etc., held in trust.

trust territory n (*sometimes cap.*) another name for **trusteeship** (sense 2b).

trustworthy ('trʌst,wɜːðɪ) adj worthy of being trusted; honest, reliable, or dependable.
► **'trust,worthily** adv ► **'trust,worthiness** n

trusty ('trʌstɪ) adj **trustier, trustiest**. **1** faithful or reliable. ◆ n, pl **trusties**. **2** a trustworthy convict given special privileges.
► **'trustily** adv ► **'trustiness** n

truth (truːθ) n **1** the quality of being true, genuine, actual,

or factual. **2** something that is true as opposed to false. **3** a proven or verified fact, principle, etc.: *the truths of astronomy*. **4** (*usually pl*) a system of concepts purporting to represent some aspect of the world: *the truths of religion*. **5** fidelity to a standard or law. **6** faithful reproduction or portrayal. **7** honesty. **8** accuracy, as in the setting of a mechanical instrument. **9** loyalty. ◆ Related adjs: **veritable, veracious**. [OE *trīewth*]
▸ **'truthless** *adj*

truth drug *or* **serum** *n Inf*. any of various drugs supposed to have the property of making people tell the truth, as by relaxing them.

truthful ('truːθfʊl) *adj* **1** telling the truth; honest. **2** realistic: *a truthful portrayal of the king*.
▸ **'truthfully** *adv* ▸ **'truthfulness** *n*

truth-function *n Logic*. a function that determines the truth-value of a complex sentence solely in terms of the truth-values of the component sentences without reference to their meaning.

truth set *n Logic, maths*. the set of values that satisfy an open sentence, equation, inequality, etc., having no unique solution. Also called: **solution set**.

truth table *n* **1** a table, used in logic, indicating the truth-value of a compound statement for every truth-value of its component propositions. **2** a similar table, used in transistor technology, to indicate the value of the output signal of a logic circuit for every value of input signal.

truth-value *n Logic*. either of the values, true or false, that may be taken by a statement.

try (traɪ) *vb* **tries, trying, tried**. **1** (when *tr, may take an infinitive*, sometimes with *to* replaced by *and*) to make an effort or attempt. **2** (*tr; often foll. by out*) to sample, test, or give experimental use to (something). **3** (*tr*) to put strain or stress on: *he tries my patience*. **4** (*tr; often passive*) to give pain, affliction, or vexation to. **5a** to examine and determine the issues involved in (a cause) in a court of law. **5b** to hear evidence in order to determine the guilt or innocence of (an accused). **6** (*tr*) to melt (fat, lard, etc.) in order to separate out impurities. ◆ *n, pl* **tries**. **7** an experiment or trial. **8** an attempt or effort. **9** *Rugby*. the act of an attacking player touching the ball down behind the opposing team's goal line. **10** *American football*. an attempt made after a touchdown to score an extra point, as by kicking a goal. ◆ See also **try on, try out**. [C13: from OF *trier* to sort, from ?]

> **USAGE NOTE** The use of *and* instead of *to* after *try* is very common, but should be avoided in formal writing: *we must try to prevent* (not *try and prevent*) *this happening*.

trying ('traɪɪŋ) *adj* upsetting, difficult, or annoying.
▸ **'tryingly** *adv*

trying plane *n* a plane with a long body for planing the edges of long boards. Also called: **try plane**.

try on *vb* (*tr, adv*) **1** to put on (a garment) to find out whether it fits, etc. **2 try it on**. *Inf*. to attempt to deceive or fool someone. ◆ *n* **try-on**. **3** *Brit. inf*. something done to test out a person's tolerance, etc.

try out *vb* (*adv*) **1** (*tr*) to test or put to experimental use. **2** (when *intr*, usually foll. by *for*) *US & Canad*. (of an athlete, actor, etc.) to undergo a test or to submit (an athlete, actor, etc.) to a test in order to determine suitability for a place in a team, an acting role, etc. ◆ *n* **tryout**. **3** *Chiefly US & Canad*. a trial or test, as of an athlete or actor.

trypanosome ('trɪpənəˌsəʊm) *n* any parasitic flagellate protozoan that lives in the blood of vertebrates and causes sleeping sickness and certain other diseases. [C19: from NL *Trypanosoma*, from Gk *trupanon* borer + *sōma* body]

trypanosomiasis (ˌtrɪpənəsəˈmaɪəsɪs) *n* any infection of an animal or human with a trypanosome.

trypsin ('trɪpsɪn) *n* a digestive enzyme in the pancreatic juice: it catalyses the hydrolysis of proteins to peptides. [C19 *tryp-*, from Gk *tripsis* a rubbing, from *tribein* to rub +

-IN; from the fact that it was orig. produced by rubbing the pancreas with glycerine]
▸ **tryptic** ('trɪptɪk) *adj*

tryptophan ('trɪptəˌfæn) *n* an essential amino acid; a component of proteins necessary for growth. [C20: from *trypt(ic)*, from TRYPSIN + *-o-* + *-phan*, var. of -PHANE]

trysail ('traɪˌseɪl; *Naut*. 'traɪs°l) *n* a small fore-and-aft sail set on a sailing vessel in foul weather to help keep her head to the wind.

try square *n* a device for testing or laying out right angles, usually consisting of a metal blade fixed at right angles to a wooden handle.

tryst (trɪst, traɪst) *n Arch. or literary*. **1** an appointment to meet, esp. secretly. **2** the place of such a meeting or the meeting itself. [C14: from OF *triste* lookout post, apparently from ON]

Tsana ★ ('tsɑːnə) *n* **Lake**. another name for (Lake) **Tana**.

tsar *or* **czar** (zɑː) *n* **1** (until 1917) the emperor of Russia. **2** a tyrant; autocrat. **3** *Inf*. a person in authority. [C17: from Russian *tsar*, via Gothic *kaisar* from L: CAESAR]
▸ **'tsardom** *or* **'czardom** *n*

tsarevitch *or* **czarevitch** ('zɑːrəvɪtʃ) *n* a son of a Russian tsar, esp. the eldest son. [from Russian *tsarevich*, from TSAR + *-evich*, masc. patronymic suffix]

tsarevna *or* **czarevna** (zɑːˈrevnə) *n* **1** a daughter of a Russian tsar. **2** the wife of a Russian tsarevitch. [from Russian, from TSAR + *-evna*, fem. patronymic suffix]

tsarina, czarina (zɑːˈriːnə) *or* **tsaritsa, czaritza** (zɑːˈrɪtsə) *n* the wife of a Russian tsar; Russian empress. [from It., Sp. *czarina*, from G *Czarin*]

tsarism *or* **czarism** ('zɑːrɪzəm) *n* a system of government by a tsar.
▸ **'tsarist** *or* **'czarist** *n, adj*

Tsaritsyn ★ (*Russian* tsa'ritsɨn) *n* a former name (until 1925) of **Volgograd**.

TSE (in Canada) *abbrev. for* Toronto Stock Exchange.

Tselinograd ★ (*Russian* tsəlʲinaˈɡrat) *n* a former name (1961–94) of **Akmola**.

tsetse fly *or* **tzetze fly** ('tsetsɪ) *n* any of various bloodsucking African dipterous flies which transmit various diseases, esp. sleeping sickness. [C19: via Afrik. from Tswana]

T-shirt *or* **tee-shirt** *n* a lightweight simple garment for the upper body, usually short-sleeved. [from T-shape formed when laid out flat]

Tshombe ★ ('tʃɒmbɪ) *n* Moise (məʊˈiːz). 1919–69, Congolese statesman. He led the secession of Katanga (1960) from the newly independent Congo; exiled in 1963, he returned as premier of the Congo (1964–65); died in exile.

Tsinan ★ ('tsiːˈnæn) *n* a variant transliteration of the Chinese name for **Jinan**.

Tsinghai ★ ('tsɪŋˈhaɪ) *n* **1** a variant transliteration of the Chinese name for **Qinghai**. **2** a variant transliteration of the Chinese name for **Koko Nor**.

Tsingtao ★ ('tsɪŋˈtaʊ) *n* a variant transliteration of the Chinese name for **Qingdao**.

Tsingyuan ('tsɪŋˈjwɑːn) *or* **Ch'ing-yüan** ★ *n* the former name of **Baoding**.

Tsitsihar ★ ('tsɪtsɪˌhɑː) *n* a variant transliteration of the Chinese name for **Qiqihar**.

tsotsi ('tsɒtsɪ) *n, pl* **tsotsis**. *S. African inf*. a Black street thug or gang member; wide boy. [C20: ?from Nguni *tsotsa* to dress flashily]

tsp. *abbrev. for* teaspoon.

T-square *n* a T-shaped ruler used for drawing horizontal lines and to support set squares when drawing vertical and inclined lines.

T-stop *n* a setting of the lens aperture on a camera calibrated photometrically and assigned a T-number.

Tsugaru Strait ★ ('tsuɡɑˌru) *n* a channel between N Honshu and S Hokkaido islands, Japan. Width: about 30 km (20 miles).

tsunami (tsuˈnɑːmɪ) *n, pl* **tsunamis** *or* **tsunami**. a large, often destructive sea wave produced by a submarine earth-

| ★ people and places |

quake, subsidence, or volcanic eruption. [from Japanese, from *tsu* port + *nami* wave]

sushima ★ ('tsuːʃiːˌmɑː) *n* a group of five rocky islands between Japan and South Korea, in the Korea Strait: administratively part of Japan; scene of a naval defeat for the Russians (1905) during the Russo-Japanese war. Pop.: 50 810 (1980). Area: 698 sq. km (269 sq. miles).

sutsugamushi disease (ˌtsutsʊɡəˈmuʃɪ) *n* one of the five major groups of acute infectious rickettsial diseases affecting man, common in Asia. It is transmitted by the bite of mites. [from Japanese, from *tsutsuga* disease + *mushi* insect]

swana ('tswɑːnə) *n* **1** (*pl* **Tswana** *or* **Tswanas**) a member of a mixed Negroid and Bushman people of southern Africa, living chiefly in Botswana. **2** the language of this people.

T *abbrev. for:* **1** teetotal. **2** teetotaller. **3** telegraphic transfer: a method of sending money abroad by cabled transfer between banks. **4** Tourist Trophy (annual motorcycle races held in the Isle of Man). **5** tuberculin-tested.

TL *abbrev. for:* **1** transistor transistor logic: a method of constructing electronic logic circuits. **2** through-the-lens: denoting a system of light metering in cameras.

U *abbrev. for* trade union.

u. *abbrev. for* Tuesday.

uamotu Archipelago ★ (ˌtuːəˈmaʊtuː) *n* a group of about 80 coral islands in the S Pacific, in French Polynesia. Pop.: 11 793 (1983). Area: 860 sq. km (332 sq. miles). Also called: **Low Archipelago, Paumotu Archipelago.**

uatara (ˌtuːəˈtɑːrə) *n* a lizard-like reptile occurring on certain islands near New Zealand. [C19: from Maori, from *tua* back + *tara* spine]

ub (tʌb) *n* **1** a low wide open container, typically round: used in a variety of domestic and industrial situations. **2** a small plastic or cardboard container of similar shape for ice cream, margarine, etc. **3** another word (esp. US) for **bath** (sense 1). **4** Also called: **tubful.** the amount a tub will hold. **5** a clumsy slow boat or ship. **6a** a small vehicle on rails for carrying loads in a mine. **6b** a container for lifting coal or ore up a mine shaft. ◆ *vb* **tubs, tubbing, tubbed. 7** *Brit. inf.* to wash (oneself) in a tub. **8** (*tr*) to keep or put in a tub. [C14: from MDu. *tubbe*]
▶ **'tubbable** *adj* ▶ **'tubber** *n*

uba ('tjuːbə) *n, pl* **tubas** *or* **tubae** (-biː). **1** a valved brass instrument of bass pitch, in which the bell points upwards and the mouthpiece projects at right angles. **2** a powerful reed stop on an organ. [L]

ubal ('tjuːbᵊl) *adj* **1** of or relating to a tube. **2** of, relating to, or developing in a Fallopian tube.

Tubal-cain ★ ('tjuːbᵊlˌkeɪn) *n Old Testament.* a son of Lamech, said in Genesis 4:22 to be the first craftsman in metals.

ubby ('tʌbɪ) *adj* **tubbier, tubbiest. 1** plump. **2** shaped like a tub.
▶ **'tubbiness** *n*

ube (tjuːb) *n* **1** a long hollow cylindrical object, used for the passage of fluids or as a container. **2** a collapsible cylindrical container of soft metal or plastic closed with a cap, used to hold viscous liquids or pastes. **3** *Anat.* **3a** short for **Eustachian tube** or **Fallopian tube. 3b** any hollow cylindrical structure. **4** (*sometimes cap.*) *Brit.* **4a the tube.** an underground railway system, esp. that in London. US and Canad. equivalent: **subway. 4b** the tunnels through which the railway runs. **5** *Electronics.* **5a** another name for **valve** (sense 3). **5b** See **electron tube, cathode-ray tube, television tube. 6** *Sl., chiefly US.* a television set. **7** *Austral. sl.* a bottle or can of beer. **8** *Surfing.* the cylindrical passage formed when a wave breaks and the crest tips forward. ◆ *vb* **tubes, tubing, tubed.** (*tr*) **9** to supply with a tube. **10** to convey in a tube. **11** to shape like a tube. [C17: from L *tubus*]
▶ **'tubeless** *adj*

tube foot *n* any of numerous tubular outgrowths of most echinoderms that are used for locomotion, to aid ingestion of food, etc.

tubeless tyre *n* a pneumatic tyre in which the outer

casing makes an airtight seal with the rim of the wheel so that an inner tube is unnecessary.

tuber ('tjuːbə) *n* **1** a fleshy underground stem or root. **2** *Anat.* a raised area; swelling. [C17: from L *tūber* hump]

tubercle ('tjuːbᵊl) *n* **1** any small rounded nodule or elevation, esp. on the skin, on a bone, or on a plant. **2** any small rounded pathological lesion, esp. one characteristic of tuberculosis. [C16: from L *tūberculum* a little swelling]

tubercle bacillus *n* a rodlike bacterium that causes tuberculosis.

tubercular (tjuːˈbɜːkjʊlə) *adj also* **tuberculous. 1** of or symptomatic of tuberculosis. **2** of or relating to a tubercle. **3** characterized by the presence of tubercles. ◆ *n* **4** a person with tuberculosis.

tuberculate (tjuːˈbɜːkjʊlɪt) *adj* covered with tubercles.
▶ **tuˌbercuˈlation** *n*

tuberculin (tjuːˈbɜːkjʊlɪn) *n* a sterile liquid prepared from cultures of attenuated tubercle bacillus and used in the diagnosis of tuberculosis.

tuberculin-tested *adj* (of milk) produced by cows that have been certified as free of tuberculosis.

tuberculosis (tjuːˌbɜːkjʊˈləʊsɪs) *n* a communicable disease caused by infection with the tubercle bacillus, most frequently affecting the lungs. [C19: from NL]

tuberose ('tjuːbəˌrəʊz) *n* a perennial Mexican agave plant having a tuberous root and fragrant white flowers. [C17: from L *tūberōsus* full of lumps; from its root]

tuberous ('tjuːbərəs) *or* **tuberose** ('tjuːbəˌrəʊs) *adj* **1** (of plants) forming, bearing, or resembling a tuber or tubers. **2** *Anat.* of or having warty protuberances or tubers. [C17: from L *tūberōsus* full of knobs]

tube worm *n* any of various worms that construct and live in a tube of sand, lime, etc.

tubifex ('tjuːbɪˌfɛks) *n, pl* **tubifex** *or* **tubifexes.** any of a genus of small reddish freshwater worms. [C19: from NL, from L *tubus* tube + *facere* to make]

tubing ('tjuːbɪŋ) *n* **1** tubes collectively. **2** a length of tube. **3** a system of tubes. **4** fabric in the form of a tube.

Tübingen ★ (*German* 'tyːbɪŋən) *n* a town in SW Germany, in Baden-Württemberg: university (1477). Pop.: 76 040 (1989 est.).

Tubman ★ ('tʌbmən) *n* **William Vacanarat Shadrach** (vəˈkænəˌræt ˈʃædræk). 1895–1971, Liberian statesman; president of Liberia (1944–71).

tub-thumper *n* a noisy, violent, or ranting public speaker.
▶ **'tub-ˌthumping** *adj, n*

Tubuai Islands ★ (ˌtuːbuːˈaɪ) *pl n* a chain of small islands extending about 1400 km (850 miles) in the S Pacific, in French Polynesia; discovered by Captain Cook in 1777; annexed by France in 1880. Pop.: 6509 (1988). Area: 173 sq. km (67 sq. miles). Also called: **Austral Islands.**

tubular ('tjuːbjʊlə) *adj* **1** Also: **tubiform** ('tjuːbɪˌfɔːm). having the form of a tube or tubes. **2** of or relating to a tube or tubing.

tubular bells *pl n* a set of long tubes of brass tuned for use in an orchestra and struck with a mallet to simulate the sound of bells.

tubule ('tjuːbjuːl) *n* any small tubular structure, esp. in an animal body. [C17: from L *tubulus* a little TUBE]

TUC (in Britain) *abbrev. for* Trades Union Congress.

tuck (tʌk) *vb* **1** (*tr*) to push or fold into a small confined space or concealed place or between two surfaces. **2** (*tr*) to thrust the loose ends or sides of (something) into a confining space, so as to make neat and secure. **3** to make a tuck or tucks in (a garment). **4** (*usually tr*) to draw together, contract, or pucker. ◆ *n* **5** a tucked object or part. **6** a pleat or fold in a part of a garment, usually stitched down. **7** the part of a vessel where the planks meet at the sternpost. **8** *Brit. inf.* **8a** food, esp. cakes and sweets. **8b** (*as modifier*): *a tuck box.* **9** a position of the body, as in certain dives, in which the legs are bent with the knees drawn up against the chest and tightly

clasped. ◆ See also **tuck away, tuck in.** [C14: from OE *tūcian* to torment]

tuck away *vb* (*tr, adv*) *Inf.* **1** to eat (a large amount of food). **2** to store, esp. in a place difficult to find.

tucker[1] ('tʌkə) *n* **1** a person or thing that tucks. **2** a detachable yoke of lace, linen, etc., often white, worn over the breast, as of a low-cut dress. **3** *Austral. & NZ. old-fashioned* an informal word for **food**.

tucker[2] ('tʌkə) *vb* (*tr; often passive; usually foll. by out*) *Inf., chiefly US & Canad.* to weary or tire.

tucker-bag *or* **tuckerbox** ('tʌkə,bɒks) *n Austral. old-fashioned sl.* a bag or box in which food is carried or stored.

tucket ('tʌkɪt) *n Arch.* a flourish on a trumpet. [C16: from OF *toquer* to sound (on a drum)]

tuck in *vb* (*adv*) **1** (*tr*) Also: **tuck into.** to put to bed and make snug. **2** (*tr*) to thrust the loose ends or sides of (something) into a confining space: *tuck the blankets in.* **3** (*intr*) Also: **tuck into.** *Inf.* to eat, esp. heartily. ◆ *n* **tuck-in. 4** *Brit. inf.* a meal, esp. a large one.

tuck shop *n Chiefly Brit.* a shop, esp. one near a school, where cakes and sweets are sold.

Tucson ★ ('tuːsɒn) *n* a city in SE Arizona, at an altitude of 700m (2400 ft): resort and seat of the University of Arizona (1891). Pop.: 434 726 (1994 est.).

Tucumán ★ (*Spanish* tuku'man) *n* a city in NW Argentina: scene of the declaration (1816) of Argentinian independence from Spain; university (1914). Pop.: 642 473 (1992 est.).

-tude *suffix forming nouns.* indicating state or condition: *plenitude.* [from L *-tūdō*]

Tudor ('tjuːdə) *n* **1** an English royal house (1485–1603), consisting of Henry VII, Henry VIII, Edward VI, Mary I, and Elizabeth I, descended from a Welsh squire, **Owen Tudor** (died 1461). ◆ *adj* **2** denoting a style of architecture of this period, characterized by half-timbered houses.

Tues. *abbrev. for* Tuesday.

Tuesday ('tjuːzdɪ) *n* the third day of the week; second day of the working week. [OE *tīwesdæg*]

tufa ('tjuːfə) *n* a porous rock formed of calcium carbonate deposited from springs. [C18: from It. *tufo*, from LL *tōfus*]
▸ **tufaceous** (tjuː'feɪʃəs) *adj*

tuff (tʌf) *n* a hard volcanic rock consisting of consolidated fragments of lava. [C16: from OF *tuf*, from It. *tufo*; see TUFA]
▸ **tuffaceous** (tʌ'feɪʃəs) *adj*

tuffet ('tʌfɪt) *n* a small mound or low seat. [C16: alteration of TUFT]

tuft (tʌft) *n* **1** a bunch of feathers, grass, hair, etc., held together at the base. **2** a cluster of threads drawn tightly through upholstery, a quilt, etc., to secure the padding. **3** a small clump of trees or bushes. **4** (formerly) a gold tassel on the cap worn by titled undergraduates at English universities. ◆ *vb* **5** (*tr*) to provide or decorate with a tuft or tufts. **6** to form or be formed into tufts. **7** to secure with tufts. [C14: ?from OF *tufe*, of Gmc origin]
▸ **'tufted** *adj* ▸ **'tufty** *adj*

tufted duck *n* a European lake-dwelling duck, the male of which has a black plumage with white underparts and a long black drooping crest.

tug (tʌg) *vb* **tugs, tugging, tugged. 1** (when *intr*, sometimes foll. by *at*) to pull or drag with sharp or powerful movements. **2** (*tr*) to tow (a vessel) by means of a tug. ◆ *n* **3** a strong pull or jerk. **4** Also called: **tugboat.** a boat with a powerful engine, used for towing barges, ships, etc. **5** a hard struggle or fight. [C13: rel. to OE *tēon* to TOW[1]]
▸ **'tugger** *n*

Tugela ★ (tuː'geɪlə) *n* a river in E South Africa, rising in the Drakensberg where it forms the **Tugela Falls,** 856 m (2810 ft) high, before flowing east to the Indian Ocean: scene of battles during the Zulu War (1879) and the Boer War (1899–1902). Length: about 500 km (312 miles).

tug-of-love *n* a conflict over custody of a child between divorced parents or between natural parents and foster or adoptive parents.

tug-of-war *n* **1** a contest in which two people or teams pull opposite ends of a rope in an attempt to drag the opposition over a central line. **2** any hard struggle between two factions.

tui ('tuːiː) *n, pl* **tuis.** a New Zealand songbird with white feathers at the throat. Also called: **parson bird.** [from Maori]

tuition (tjuː'ɪʃən) *n* **1** instruction, esp. that received individually or in a small group. **2** the payment for instruction, esp. in colleges or universities. [C15: from OF *tuicion,* from L *tuitiō* a guarding, from *tuērī* to watch over]
▸ **tu'itional** *adj*

Tula ★ (*Russian* 'tulə) *n* an industrial city in W central Russia. Pop.: 532 000 (1995 est.).

tularaemia *or US* **tularemia** (,tuːlə'riːmɪə) *n* an infectious disease of rodents, transmitted to man by infected ticks or flies or by handling contaminated flesh. [C19/20: from NL, from *Tulare,* county in California where first observed]
▸ **,tula'raemic** *or US* **,tula'remic** *adj*

tulip ('tjuːlɪp) *n* **1** any of various spring-blooming bulb plants having long broad pointed leaves and single showy bell-shaped flowers. **2** the flower or bulb. [C17: from NL *tulipa,* from Turkish *tülbend* turban, which the opened bloom was thought to resemble]

tulip tree *n* Also called: **tulip poplar.** a North American tree having tulip-shaped greenish-yellow flowers and long conelike fruits. **2** any of various other trees with tulip-shaped flowers, such as the magnolia.

tulipwood ('tjuːlɪp,wʊd) *n* **1** the light soft wood of the tulip tree, used in making furniture and veneer. **2** any of several woods having streaks of colour.

Tull ★ (tʌl) *n* **Jethro** ('dʒɛθrəʊ). 1674–1741, English agriculturalist, who invented the seed drill.

Tullamore ★ (,tʌlə'mɔː:) *n* the county town of Offaly, Republic of Ireland; food processing and brewing. Pop.: 8484 (1986).

tulle (tjuːl) *n* a fine net fabric of silk, rayon, etc. [C19: from F, from *Tulle,* city in S central France, where first manufactured]

Tully ★ ('tʌlɪ) *n* the former English name for (Marcus Tullius) Cicero.

Tulsa ★ ('tʌlsə) *n* a city in NE Oklahoma, on the Arkansas River: a major oil centre; two universities. Pop.: 374 851 (1994 est.).

tumble ('tʌmbəl) *vb* **tumbles, tumbling, tumbled. 1** to fall or cause to fall, esp. awkwardly, precipitately, or violently. **2** (*intr; usually foll. by about*) to roll or twist, esp. in playing. **3** (*intr*) to perform leaps, somersaults, etc. **4** to move in a heedless or hasty way. **5** (*tr*) to polish (gemstones) in a tumbler. **6** (*tr*) to disturb, rumple, or toss around. ◆ *n* **7** a tumbling. **8** a fall or toss. **9** an acrobatic feat, esp. a somersault. **10** a state of confusion. **11** a confused heap or pile. ◆ See also **tumble to.** [OE *tumbian*]

tumbledown ('tʌmbəl,daʊn) *adj* falling to pieces; dilapidated; crumbling.

tumble dryer *or* **tumble drier** *n* a machine that dries wet laundry by rotating it in warmed air inside a metal drum. Also called: **tumbler dryer, tumbler.**

tumbler ('tʌmblə) *n* **1a** a flat-bottomed drinking glass with no handle or stem. **1b** Also called: **tumblerful.** its contents. **2** a person who performs somersaults and other acrobatic feats. **3** another name for **tumble dryer. 4** a box or drum rotated so that the contents (usually gemstones) become smooth and polished. **5** the part of a lock that retains or releases the bolt and is moved by the action of a key. **6** a lever in a gunlock that receives the action of the mainspring when the trigger is pressed and thus forces the hammer forwards. **7** a part that moves a gear in a train of gears into and out of engagement.

tumbler switch *n* a small electrical switch incorporating a spring, widely used in lighting.

tumble to *vb* (*intr, prep*) *Inf.* to understand; become aware of: *she tumbled to his plan quickly.*

tumbleweed ('tʌmbəl,wiːd) *n* any of various densely branched American and Australian plants that break off

---

★ people and places

near the ground on withering and are rolled about by the wind.

umbrel or **tumbril** ('tʌmbrəl) n **1** a farm cart, esp. one that tilts backwards to deposit its load. A cart of this type was used to take condemned prisoners to the guillotine during the French Revolution. **2** (formerly) a covered cart used to carry ammunition, tools, etc. [C14 *tumberell* ducking stool, from Med. L *tumbrellum*, from OF *tumberel* dump cart, ult. of Gmc origin]

umefacient (,tjuːmɪ'feɪʃənt) adj producing or capable of producing swelling: *a tumefacient drug.* [C16: from L *tumefacere* to cause to swell]

umefy ('tjuːmɪ,faɪ) vb **tumefies, tumefying, tumefied.** to make or become tumid; swell or puff up. [C16: from F *tuméfier,* from L *tumefacere*]
▸ ,tume'faction n

umescent (tjuː'mɛsənt) adj swollen or becoming swollen. [C19: from L *tumescere* to begin to swell, from *tumēre*]
▸ tu'mescence n

umid ('tjuːmɪd) adj **1** enlarged or swollen. **2** bulging. **3** pompous or fulsome in style. [C16: from L *tumidus,* from *tumēre* to swell]
▸ tu'midity or 'tumidness n ▸ 'tumidly adv

ummy ('tʌmɪ) n, pl **tummies.** an informal or childish word for **stomach.** Also called: **tum.**

ummy tuck n Inf. the surgical removal of abdominal fat and skin for cosmetic purposes.

umour or US **tumor** ('tjuːmə) n Pathol. **a** any abnormal swelling. **b** a mass of tissue formed by a new growth of cells. [C16: from L, from *tumēre* to swell]
▸ 'tumorous adj

umult ('tjuːmʌlt) n **1** a loud confused noise, as of a crowd; commotion. **2** violent agitation or disturbance. **3** great emotional agitation. [C15: from L *tumultus,* from *tumēre* to swell up]

umultuous (tjuː'mʌltjʊəs) adj **1** uproarious, riotous, or turbulent. **2** greatly agitated, confused, or disturbed. **3** making a loud or unruly disturbance.
▸ tu'multuously adv ▸ tu'multuousness n

umulus ('tjuːmjʊləs) n, pl **tumuli** (-lɪː). Archaeol. (no longer in technical usage) another word for **barrow**². [C17: from L: a hillock, from *tumēre* to swell up]

un (tʌn) n **1** a large beer cask. **2** a measure of capacity, usually equal to 252 wine gallons. ◆ vb **tuns, tunning, tunned. 3** (tr) to put into or keep in tuns. [OE *tunne*]

una¹ ('tjuːnə) n, pl **tuna** or **tunas.** another name for **tunny** (sense 1). [C20: from American Sp., from Sp. *atún,* from Ar. *tūn,* from L *thunnus* tunny, from Gk]

una² ('tjuːnə) n any of various tropical American prickly pear cacti. [C16: via Sp. from Taino]

unable or **tuneable** ('tjuːnəbᵊl) adj able to be tuned.

Tunbridge Wells ★ ('tʌn,brɪdʒ) n a town and resort in SE England, in SW Kent: chalybeate spring discovered in 1606. Pop.: 60 272 (1991). Official name: **Royal Tunbridge Wells.**

undra ('tʌndrə) n a vast treeless zone lying between the ice cap and the timber line of North America and Eurasia and having a permanently frozen subsoil. [C19: from Russian, from Lapp *tundar* hill]

une (tjuːn) n **1** a melody, esp. one for which harmony is not essential. **2** the condition of producing accurately pitched notes, intervals, etc. (esp. in **in tune, out of tune**). **3** accurate correspondence of pitch and intonation between instruments (esp. in **in tune, out of tune**). **4** the correct adjustment of a radio, television, etc., with respect to the required frequency. **5** a frame of mind; mood. **6 call the tune.** to be in control of the proceedings. **7 change one's tune.** to alter one's attitude or tone of speech. **8 to the tune of.** Inf. to the amount or extent of. ◆ vb **tunes, tuning, tuned. 9** to adjust (a musical instrument) to a certain pitch. **10** to adjust (a note, etc.) so as to bring it into harmony or concord. **11** (tr) to adapt or adjust (oneself); attune. **12** (tr; often foll. by up) to make fine adjustments to (an engine, machine, etc.) to obtain optimum performance. **13** Electronics. to adjust (one or more circuits) for

resonance at a desired frequency. ◆ See also **tune in, tune up.** [C14: var. of TONE]
▸ 'tuner n

tuneful ('tjuːnful) adj **1** having a pleasant tune; melodious. **2** producing a melody or music.
▸ 'tunefully adv ▸ 'tunefulness n

tune in vb (adv; often foll. by to) **1** to adjust (a radio or television) to receive (a station or programme). **2** Sl. to make or become more aware, knowledgeable, etc. (about).

tuneless ('tjuːnlɪs) adj having no melody or tune.
▸ 'tunelessly adv ▸ 'tunelessness n

tune up vb (adv) **1** to adjust (a musical instrument) to a particular pitch. **2** to tune (instruments) to a common pitch. **3** (tr) to adjust (an engine) in (a car, etc.) to improve performance. ◆ n **tune-up. 4** adjustments made to an engine to improve its performance.

tung oil (tʌŋ) n a fast-drying oil obtained from the seeds of an Asian tree, used in paints, varnishes, etc. [partial translation of Chinese *yu t'ung* tung tree oil, from *yu* oil + *t'ung* tung tree]

tungsten ('tʌŋstən) n a hard malleable ductile greyish-white element. It is used in lamp filaments, electrical contact points, X-ray targets, and, alloyed with steel, in high-speed cutting tools. Symbol: W; atomic no.: 74; atomic wt.: 183.85. Also called: **wolfram.** [C18: from Swedish *tung* heavy + *sten* stone]

tungsten lamp n a lamp in which light is produced by a tungsten filament heated to incandescence by an electric current. Sometimes small amounts of a halogen, such as iodine, are added to improve the intensity (**tungsten-halogen lamp**).

tungsten steel n any of various hard steels containing tungsten and traces of carbon.

Tungting or **Tung-t'ing** ★ (,tʊŋ'tɪŋ) n a variant transliteration of the Chinese name for the **Dongting.**

Tungusic (tʊŋ'gʊsɪk) n a branch or subfamily of the Altaic family of languages, some of which are spoken in NE Asia.

Tunguska ★ (Russian tun'guskə) n any of three rivers in Russia, in central Siberia, all tributaries of the Yenisei: the **Lower** (Nizhnyaya) **Tunguska,** 2690 km (1670 miles) long; the **Stony** (Podkamennaya) **Tunguska,** 1550 km (960 miles) long; the **Upper** (Verkhnyaya) **Tunguska,** which is the lower course of the Angara.

tunic ('tjuːnɪk) n **1** any of various hip-length or knee-length garments, such as the loose sleeveless garb worn in ancient Greece or Rome, the jacket of some soldiers, or a woman's hip-length garment, worn with a skirt or trousers. **2** a covering, lining, or enveloping membrane of an organ or part. **3** Also called: **tunicle.** a short vestment worn by a bishop or subdeacon. [OE *tunice* (unattested except in the accusative case), from L *tunica*]

tunicate ('tjuːnɪkɪt, -,keɪt) n **1** any of various minute primitive marine animals having a saclike unsegmented body enclosed in a cellulose-like outer covering. ◆ adj also **tunicated. 2** (esp. of a bulb) having concentric layers of tissue. [C18: from L *tunicātus* clad in a TUNIC]

tuning ('tjuːnɪŋ) n Music. **1** a set of pitches to which the open strings of a guitar, violin, etc., are tuned. **2** the accurate pitching of notes and intervals by a choir, orchestra, etc.; intonation.

tuning fork n a two-pronged metal fork that when struck produces a pure note of constant specified pitch. It is used to tune musical instruments and in acoustics.

Tunis ★ ('tjuːnɪs) n the capital and chief port of Tunisia, in the northeast on the **Gulf of Tunis** (an inlet of the Mediterranean): dates from Carthaginian times, the ruins of ancient Carthage lying to the northeast; university (1960). Pop.: 674 100 (1994).

Tunisia ★ (tjuː'nɪzɪə, -'nɪsɪə) n a republic in N Africa, on the Mediterranean: settled by the Phoenicians in the 12th century B.C.; made a French protectorate in 1881 and gained independence in 1955. It consists chiefly of the Sahara in the south, a central plateau, and the Atlas Mountains in the north. Exports include petroleum, phosphates, and iron ore. Official language: Arabic;

★ people and places

French is also widely spoken. Official religion: Muslim. Currency: dinar. Capital: Tunis. Pop.: 9 218 000 (1997). Area: 164 150 sq. km (63 380 sq. miles).
▸ **Tu'nisian** *adj, n*

tunnage ('tʌnɪdʒ) *n* a variant spelling of **tonnage**.

tunnel ('tʌn°l) *n* **1** an underground passageway, esp. one for trains or cars. **2** any passage or channel through or under something. ◆ *vb* **tunnels, tunnelling, tunnelled** *or US* **tunnels, tunneling, tunneled. 3** (*tr*) to make or force (a way) through or under (something). **4** (*intr*; foll. by *through, under,* etc.) to make or force a way (through or under something). [C15: from OF *tonel* cask, from *tonne* tun, from Med. L *tonna* barrel, of Celtic origin]
▸ **'tunneller** *or US* **'tunneler** *n*

tunnel diode *n* an extremely stable semiconductor diode, having a very narrow highly doped p-n junction, in which electrons travel across the junction by means of the tunnel effect. Also called: **Esaki diode.**

tunnel effect *n Physics.* the phenomenon in which an object, usually an elementary particle, tunnels through a potential barrier even though it does not have sufficient energy to surmount it.

tunnel vision *n* **1** a condition in which peripheral vision is greatly restricted. **2** narrowness of viewpoint resulting from concentration on a single idea, opinion, etc.

tunny ('tʌnɪ) *n, pl* **tunnies** *or* **tunny. 1** Also called: **tuna.** any of a genus of large marine spiny-finned fishes, chiefly of warm waters. They are important food fishes. **2** any of various similar and related fishes. [C16: from OF *thon,* from OProvençal *ton,* from L *thunnus,* from Gk]

tup (tʌp) *n* **1** *Chiefly Brit.* a male sheep; ram. **2** the head of a pile-driver or steam hammer. ◆ *vb* **tups, tupping, tupped. 3** (*tr*) (of a ram) to mate with (a ewe). [C14: from ?]

Tupamaro (,tu:pə'mɑ:rəʊ) *n, pl* **Tupamaros.** any of a group of Marxist urban guerrillas in Uruguay. [C20: after *Tupac Amaru,* 18th-century Peruvian Indian who led a rebellion against the Spaniards]

tupelo ('tju:pɪ,ləʊ) *n, pl* **tupelos. 1** any of several gum trees of the southern US. **2** the light strong wood of any of these trees. [C18: from Creek *ito opilwa,* from *ito* tree + *opilwa* swamp]

Tupi (tu:'pi:) *n* **1** (*pl* **Tupis** *or* **Tupi**) a member of a South American Indian people of Brazil and Paraguay. **2** their language.
▸ **Tu'pian** *adj*

tupik ('tu:pək) *n Canad.* a tent of seal or caribou skin used for shelter by the Inuit in summer. [from Eskimo]

Tupolev ★ (*Russian* 'tupəlɪf) *n* **Andrei Nikolaievich** (an'drjej nika'lajɪvitʃ). 1888–1972, Soviet engineer, who designed the first supersonic passenger aircraft.

tuppence ('tʌpəns) *n Brit.* a variant spelling of **twopence**.
▸ **'tuppenny** *adj*

Tupperware ('tʌpəweə) *n Trademark.* a range of plastic containers used for storing food. [C20: *Tupper,* US manufacturing company + WARE¹]

Tupungato ★ (*Spanish* tupuŋ'gato) *n* a mountain on the border between Argentina and Chile, in the Andes. Height: 6550 m (21 484 ft).

tuque (tu:k) *n Canad.* **1** a knitted cap with a long tapering end. **2** Also called: **toque.** a close-fitting knitted hat often with a tassel or pompom. [C19: from Canad. F, from F: TOQUE]

turaco ('tʊərə,kəʊ) *n, pl* **turacos.** a variant spelling of **touraco.**

Turanian (tju'reɪnɪən) *n, adj* another name for **Ural-Altaic.**

turban ('tɜ:b°n) *n* **1** a man's headdress, worn esp. by Muslims, Hindus, and Sikhs, made by swathing a length of linen, silk, etc., around the head or around a caplike base. **2** a woman's brimless hat resembling this. **3** any headdress resembling this. [C16: from Turkish *tülbend,* from Persian *dulband*]
▸ **'turbaned** *adj*

turbary ('tɜ:bərɪ) *n, pl* **turbaries. 1** land where peat or turf is cut. **2** the legal right to cut peat for fuel on a common.

[C14: from OF *turbarie,* from Med. L *turbāria,* from *turba* peat]

turbellarian (,tɜ:bɪ'leərɪən) *n* **1** any of a class of flatworms having a ciliated epidermis and a simple life cycle. ◆ *adj* **2** of or belonging to this class of flatworms. [C19: from NL *Turbellāria,* from L *turbellae* (pl) bustle, from *turba* brawl, referring to the swirling motion created in the water]

turbid ('tɜ:bɪd) *adj* **1** muddy or opaque, as a liquid clouded with a suspension of particles. **2** dense, thick, or cloudy: *turbid fog.* **3** in turmoil or confusion. [C17: from L *turbidus,* from *turbāre* to agitate, from *turba* crowd]
▸ **tur'bidity** *or* **'turbidness** *n* ▸ **'turbidly** *adv*

turbinate ('tɜ:bɪnɪt, -,neɪt) *or* **turbinal** ('tɜ:bɪn°l) *adj also* **turbinated. 1** *Anat.* of any of the scroll-shaped bones on the walls of the nasal passages. **2** shaped like a spiral or scroll. **3** shaped like an inverted cone. ◆ *n* **4** a turbinate bone. **5** a turbinate shell. [C17: from L *turbō* spinning top]
▸ **,turbi'nation** *n*

turbine ('tɜ:bɪn, -baɪn) *n* any of various types of machine in which the kinetic energy of a moving fluid, as water, steam, air, etc., is converted into mechanical energy by causing a bladed rotor to rotate. [C19: from F, from L *turbō* whirlwind, from *turbāre* to throw into confusion]

turbine blade *n* any of a number of bladelike vanes assembled around the periphery of a turbine rotor to guide the steam or gas flow.

turbit ('tɜ:bɪt) *n* a crested breed of domestic pigeon. [C17: from L *turbō* spinning top, from the bird's shape]

turbo- *combining form.* of, relating to, or driven by a turbine: *turbofan.*

turbocharger ('tɜ:bəʊ,tʃɑ:dʒə) *n* a centrifugal compressor which boosts the intake pressure of an internal-combustion engine, driven by an exhaust-gas turbine fitted to the engine's exhaust manifold.

turbofan (,tɜ:bəʊ'fæn) *n* **1** a type of bypass engine in which a large fan driven by a turbine forces air rearwards around the exhaust gases in order to increase the propulsive thrust. **2** an aircraft driven by turbofans. **3** the fan in such an engine.

turbogenerator (,tɜ:bəʊ'dʒɛnə,reɪtə) *n* an electrical generator driven by a steam turbine.

turbojet (,tɜ:bəʊ'dʒɛt) *n* **1** a turbojet engine. **2** an aircraft powered by turbojet engines.

turbojet engine *n* a gas turbine in which the exhaust gases provide the propulsive thrust to drive an aircraft.

turboprop (,tɜ:bəʊ'prɒp) *n* **1** an aircraft propulsion unit where a propeller is driven by a gas turbine. **2** an aircraft powered by turboprops.

turbosupercharger (,tɜ:bəʊ'su:pə,tʃɑ:dʒə) *n Obs.* a supercharging device for an internal-combustion engine, consisting of a turbine driven by the exhaust gases.

turbot ('tɜ:bət) *n, pl* **turbot** *or* **turbots. 1** a European flatfish having a speckled scaleless body covered with tubercles. It is highly valued as a food fish. **2** any of various similar or related fishes. [C13: from OF *tourbot,* from Med. L *turbō,* from L: spinning top, from a fancied similarity in shape]

turbulence ('tɜ:bjʊləns) *n* **1** a state or condition of confusion, movement, or agitation. **2** *Meteorol.* instability in the atmosphere causing gusty air currents and cumulonimbus clouds.

turbulent ('tɜ:bjʊlənt) *adj* **1** being in a state of turbulence. **2** wild or insubordinate; unruly. [C16: from L *turbulentus,* from *turba* confusion]
▸ **'turbulently** *adv*

turd (tɜ:d) *n Taboo.* **1** a piece of excrement. **2** *Sl.* a contemptible person or thing. [OE *tord*]

tureen (tə'ri:n) *n* a large deep usually rounded dish with a cover, used for serving soups, stews, etc. [C18: from F *terrine* earthenware vessel, from *terrin* made of earthenware, from Vulgar L *terrīnus* (unattested), from L *terra* earth]

turf (tɜ:f) *n, pl* **turfs** *or* **turves. 1** the surface layer of fields and pastures, consisting of earth containing a dense growth of grasses with their roots; sod. **2** a piece cut from this layer. **3 the turf. 3a** a track where horse races are run. **3b** horse racing as a sport or industry. **4** an area of knowledge or influence: *he's on home turf when it comes to music.* **5** another word for **peat.** ◆ *vb* **6** (*tr*) to cover with pieces of turf. ◆ See also **turf out.** [OE]

urf accountant *n Brit.* a formal name for a **bookmaker.**

urfman ('tɜːfmən) *n, pl* **turfmen.** *Chiefly US.* a person devoted to horse racing.

urf out *vb* (*tr, adv*) *Brit. inf.* to throw out or dismiss; eject.

urgenev ★ (*Russian* tur'gjenɪf) *n* **Ivan Sergeyevich** (i'van sɪr'gjejrvitʃ). 1818–83, Russian writer. His novels include *Fathers and Sons* (1862) and his plays include *A Month in the Country* (1890).

urgescent (tɜː'dʒɛsᵊnt) *adj* becoming or being swollen; inflated; tumid.
▶ **tur'gescence** *n*

urgid ('tɜːdʒɪd) *adj* **1** swollen and distended. **2** (of language) pompous; bombastic. [C17: from L *turgidus,* from *turgēre* to swell]
▶ **tur'gidity** *or* **'turgidness** *n* ▶ **'turgidly** *adv*

urgor ('tɜːgə) *n* the normal rigid state of a cell, caused by pressure of the cell contents against the cell wall or membrane. [C19: from LL: a swelling, from L *turgēre* to swell]

urin ★ (tjʊə'rɪn) *n* a city in NW Italy, capital of Piedmont region, on the River Po: became capital of the Kingdom of Sardinia in 1720; first capital (1861–65) of united Italy; university (1405); a major industrial centre, producing most of Italy's cars. Pop.: 945 551 (1994 est.). Italian name: **Torino.**

uring ★ ('tjʊərɪŋ) *n* **Alan Mathison.** 1912–54, British mathematician, who was responsible for formal description of abstract automata.

uring machine *n* a hypothetical universal computing machine able to modify its original instructions by reading, erasing, or writing a new symbol on a moving tape that acts as its program. [C20: after A. M. TURING]

urion ('tʊərɪən) *n* a scaly shoot produced by many aquatic plants: it detaches from the parent plant and remains dormant until the following spring. [C17: from F *turion,* from L *turio* shoot]

urishcheva ★ (*Russian* tu'riʃtʃəvə) *n* **Ludmilla** (lʊd'mɪlə). born 1952, Soviet gymnast: world champion 1970, 1972, and 1974.

urk (tɜːk) *n* **1** a native, inhabitant, or citizen of Turkey. **2** a native speaker of any Turkic language. **3** *Obs., derog.* a brutal or domineering person. See also **Young Turk.**

urk. *abbrev. for:* **1** Turkey. **2** Turkish.

urkana ★ (tɜː'kɑːnə) *n* **Lake.** a long narrow lake in E Africa, in the Great Rift Valley. Area: 7104 sq. km (2743 sq. miles). Former name: (Lake) **Rudolf.**

urkestan *or* **Turkistan** ★ (,tɜːkɪ'stɑːn) *n* an extensive region of central Asia between Siberia in the north and Tibet, India, Afghanistan, and Iran in the south: formerly divided into **West (Russian) Turkestan** (also called Soviet Central Asia), which includes Turkmenistan, Uzbekistan, Tajikistan, and Kyrgyzstan and the S part of Kazakhstan, and **East (Chinese) Turkestan,** consisting of the Xinjiang Uygur Autonomous Region.
▶ **,Turke'stani** *adj, n*

urkey ('tɜːkɪ) *n, pl* **turkeys** *or* **turkey. 1** a large bird of North America, having a bare wattled head and neck and a brownish plumage. The male has a fan-shaped tail. A domesticated variety is bred for its flesh. **2** *Inf.* something, esp. a film or theatrical production, that fails. **3** See **cold turkey. 4** talk turkey. *Sl., chiefly US & Canad.* to discuss frankly and practically. [C16: shortened from *Turkey cock* (*hen*), used at first to designate the African guinea fowl (apparently because the bird was brought through Turkish territory), later applied by mistake to the American bird]

urkey ★ ('tɜːkɪ) *n* a republic in W Asia and SE Europe, between the Black Sea, the Mediterranean, and the Aegean: one of the oldest inhabited regions of the world; the centre of the Ottoman Empire; became a republic in 1923. The major Asian part, consisting mainly of an arid plateau, is separated from European Turkey by the

Bosporus, Sea of Marmara, and Dardanelles. Official language: Turkish; Kurdish and Arabic minority languages. Religion: mostly Muslim. Currency: lira. Capital: Ankara. Pop.: 63 528 000 (1997). Area: 780 576 sq. km (301 380 sq. miles).

turkey buzzard *or* **vulture** *n* a New World vulture having a naked red head.

turkey cock *n* **1** a male turkey. **2** an arrogant person.

turkey nest *n Austral.* a small earth dam adjacent to, and higher than, a larger earth dam, to feed water by gravity to a cattle trough, etc.

Turkey red *n* **1a** a moderate or bright red colour. **1b** (*as adj*): *a Turkey-red fabric.* **2** a cotton fabric of a bright red colour.

Turki ('tɜːkɪ) *adj* **1** of or relating to the Turkic languages. **2** of or relating to speakers of these languages. ◆ *n* **3** these languages collectively.

Turkic ('tɜːkɪk) *n* a branch of the Altaic family of languages, including Turkish, Tatar, etc., members of which are found from Turkey to NE China, esp. in Soviet central Asia.

Turkish ('tɜːkɪʃ) *adj* **1** of Turkey, its people, or their language. ◆ *n* **2** the official language of Turkey, belonging to the Turkic branch of the Altaic family.

Turkish bath *n* **1** a type of bath in which the bather sweats freely in hot dry air, is then washed, often massaged, and has a cold plunge or shower. **2** (*sometimes pl*) an establishment where such a bath is obtainable.

Turkish coffee *n* very strong black coffee.

Turkish delight *n* a jelly-like sweet flavoured with flower essences, usually cut into cubes and covered in icing sugar.

Turkish towel *n* a rough loose-piled towel.

Turkmenistan ★ (,tɜːkmɛnɪ'stɑːn) *n* a republic in central Asia; the area has been occupied by a succession of empires; a Turkmen state was established in the 15th century but was gradually conquered by Russia; in 1918 it became a Soviet republic and gained independence in 1991: deserts, including the **Kara Kum,** cover most of the region. Official language: Turkmen. Religion: believers are mainly Muslim. Currency: manat. Capital: Ashkhabad. Pop.: 4 695 000 (1997). Area: 488 100 sq. km (186 400 sq. miles). Also called: **Turkmenia** (tɜːk'miːnɪə).

Turks and Caicos Islands ★ *pl n* a United Kingdom overseas territory in the Caribbean, southeast of the Bahamas: consists of the eight **Turks Islands,** separated by the **Turks Island Passage** from the Caicos group, which has six main islands. Capital: Grand Turk. Pop.: 14 000 (1993 est.). Area: 430 sq. km (166 sq. miles).

Turk's-cap lily *n* any of several cultivated lilies that have brightly coloured flowers with reflexed petals.

Turk's-head *n* an ornamental turban-like knot.

Turku ★ (*Finnish* 'turku) *n* a city and port in SW Finland, on the Gulf of Bothnia: capital of Finland until 1812. Pop.: 164 744 (1996 est.). Swedish name: **Åbo.**

turmeric ('tɜːmərɪk) *n* **1** a tropical Asian plant, *Curcuma longa,* having yellow flowers and an aromatic underground stem. **2** the powdered stem of this plant, used as a condiment and as a yellow dye. [C16: from OF *terre merite,* from Med. L *terra merita,* lit.: meritorious earth, name applied for obscure reasons to curcuma]

turmeric paper *n Chem.* paper impregnated with turmeric used as a test for alkalis and for boric acid.

turmoil ('tɜːmɔɪl) *n* violent or confused movement; agitation; tumult. [C16: ?from TURN + MOIL]

turn (tɜːn) *vb* **1** to move around an axis: *to turn a knob.* **2** (sometimes foll. by *round*) to change or cause to change positions by moving through an arc of a circle: *he turned the chair to face the light.* **3** to change or cause to change in course, direction, etc. **4** to go or pass to the other side of (a corner, etc.). **5** to assume or cause to assume a rounded, curved, or folded form: *the road turns here.* **6** to reverse or cause to reverse position. **7** (*tr*) to perform or do by a rotating movement: *to turn a somersault.* **8** (*tr*) to shape or cut a thread in (a workpiece) by rotating it on a lathe against a cutting tool. **9** (when *intr,* foll. by *into* or *to*) to change or convert or be changed or converted. **10**

(foll. by *into*) to change or cause to change in nature, character, etc.: *the frog turned into a prince*. **11** (*copula*) to change so as to become: *he turned nasty*. **12** to cause (foliage, etc.) to change colour or (of foliage, etc.) to change colour. **13** to cause (milk, etc.) to become rancid or sour or (of milk, etc.) to become rancid or sour. **14** to change or cause to change in subject, trend, etc.: *the conversation turned to fishing*. **15** to direct or apply or be directed or applied: *he turned his attention to the problem*. **16** (*intr*; usually foll. by *to*) to appeal or apply (to) for help, advice, etc. **17** to reach, pass, or progress beyond in age, time, etc.: *she has just turned twenty*. **18** (*tr*) to cause or allow to go: *to turn an animal loose*. **19** (*tr*) to affect or be affected with nausea. **20** to affect or be affected with giddiness: *my head is turning*. **21** (*tr*) to affect the mental or emotional stability of (esp. in **turn** (**someone's**) **head**). **22** (*tr*) to release from a container. **23** (*tr*) to render into another language. **24** (usually foll. by *against* or *from*) to transfer or reverse (one's) loyalties, affections, etc.). **25** (*tr*) to cause (an enemy agent) to become a double agent working for one's own side. **26** (*tr*) to bring (soil) from lower layers to the surface. **27** to blunt (an edge) or (of an edge) to become blunted. **28** (*tr*) to give a graceful form to: *to turn a compliment*. **29** (*tr*) to reverse (a cuff, collar, etc.). **30** (*intr*) *US*. to be merchandised as specified: *shirts are turning well this week*. **31** *Cricket*. to spin (the ball) or (of the ball) to spin. **32 turn a trick.** *Sl.* (of a prostitute) to gain a customer. **33 turn one's hand to.** to undertake (something practical). ◆ *n* **34** a turning or being turned. **35** a movement of complete or partial rotation. **36** a change of direction or position. **37** direction or drift: *his thoughts took a new turn*. **38** a deviation from a course or tendency. **39** the place, point, or time at which a deviation or change occurs. **40** another word for **turning** (sense 1). **41** the right or opportunity to do something in an agreed order or succession: *now it's George's turn*. **42** a change in nature, condition, etc.: *his illness took a turn for the worse*. **43** a period of action, work, etc. **44** a short walk, ride, or excursion. **45** natural inclination: *a speculative turn of mind*. **46** distinctive form or style: *a neat turn of phrase*. **47** requirement, need, or advantage: *to serve someone's turn*. **48** a deed that helps or hinders someone. **49** a twist, bend, or distortion in shape. **50** *Music*. a melodic ornament that makes a turn around a note, beginning with the note above, in a variety of sequences. **51** a short theatrical act. **52** *Stock Exchange, Brit.* the difference between a market maker's bid and offer prices, representing the market maker's profit. **53** *Inf.* a shock or surprise. **54 by turns.** one after another; alternately. **55 turn and turn about.** one after another; alternately. **56** to a turn. to the proper amount; perfectly. ◆ See also **turn down, turn in,** etc. [OE *tyrnian*, from OF *torner*, from L *tornāre* to turn in a lathe, from *tornus* lathe, from Gk *tornos* dividers]
▸ 'turner *n*

turnabout ('tɜːnəˌbaʊt) *n* **1** the act of turning so as to face a different direction. **2** a change or reversal of opinion, attitude, etc.

turnaround ('tɜːnəˌraʊnd) *n* **1a** the act or process in which a ship, aircraft, etc., unloads at the end of a trip and reloads for the next trip. **1b** the time taken for this. **2** the total time taken by a vehicle in a round trip. **3** a complete reversal of a situation.

turnbuckle ('tɜːnˌbʌkᵊl) *n* an open mechanical sleeve usually having a swivel at one end and a thread at the other to enable a threaded wire or rope to be tightened.

turncoat ('tɜːnˌkəʊt) *n* a person who deserts one cause or party for the opposite faction.

turncock ('tɜːnˌkɒk) *n* (formerly) an official employed to turn on the water for the mains supply.

turn down *vb* (*tr, adv*) **1** to reduce (the volume or brightness) of (something). **2** to reject or refuse. **3** to fold down (a collar, sheets, etc.). ◆ *adj* **turndown. 4** (*prenominal*) designed to be folded down.

Turner ★ ('tɜːnə) *n* **Joseph Mallord William.** 1775–1851, British landscape painter.

turn in *vb* (*adv*) *Inf.* **1** (*intr*) to go to bed for the night. **2** (*tr*) to hand in; deliver. **3** (*tr*) to give up or conclude (something). **4** (*tr*) to record (a score, etc.). **5 turn in on oneself.** to become preoccupied with one's own problems.

turning ('tɜːnɪŋ) *n* **1** a road, river, or path that turns off the main way. **2** the point where such a way turns off. **3** a bend in a straight course. **4** an object made on a lathe. **5** the process or skill of turning objects on a lathe. **6** (*pl*) the waste produced in turning on a lathe.

turning circle *n* the smallest circle in which a vehicle can turn.

turning point *n* **1** a moment when the course of events is changed. **2** a point at which there is a change in direction or motion.

turnip ('tɜːnɪp) *n* **1** a widely cultivated plant of the cabbage family with a large yellow or white edible root. **2** the root of this plant, which is eaten as a vegetable. [C16: from earlier *turnepe*, ?from TURN (indicating its rounded shape) + *nepe*, from L *nāpus* turnip]

turnkey ('tɜːnˌkiː) *n* **1** *Arch.* a keeper of the keys, esp. in a prison; warder or jailer. ◆ *adj* **2** denoting a project, as in civil engineering, in which a single contractor has responsibility for the complete job from the start to the time of installation or occupancy.

turn off *vb* **1** (*intr*) to leave (a road, etc.). **2** (*intr*) (of a road, etc.) to deviate from (another road, etc.). **3** (*tr, adv*) to cause (something) to cease operating by turning a knob, pushing a button, etc. **4** (*tr*) *Inf.* to cause (a person, etc.) to feel dislike or distaste for (something): *this music turns me off*. **5** (*tr, adv*) *Brit. inf.* to dismiss from employment. ◆ *n* **turn-off. 6** a road or other way branching off from the main thoroughfare. **7** *Inf.* a person or thing that elicits dislike or distaste.

turn on *vb* **1** (*tr, adv*) to cause (something) to operate by turning a knob, etc. **2** (*intr, prep*) to depend or hinge on: *the success of the party turns on you*. **3** (*prep*) to become hostile or to retaliate: *the dog turned on the children*. **4** (*tr, adv*) *Inf.* to produce (charm, tears, etc.) suddenly or automatically. **5** (*tr, adv*) *Sl.* to arouse emotionally or sexually. **6** (*intr, adv*) *Sl.* to take or become intoxicated by drugs. **7** (*tr, adv*) *Sl.* to introduce (someone) to drugs. ◆ *n* **turn-on. 8** *Sl.* a person or thing that causes emotional or sexual arousal.

turn out *vb* (*adv*) **1** (*tr*) to cause (something, esp. a light) to cease operating by or as if by turning a knob, etc. **2** (*tr*) to produce by an effort or process. **3** (*tr*) to dismiss, discharge, or expel. **4** (*tr*) to empty the contents of, esp. in order to clean, tidy, or rearrange. **5** (*copula*) to prove to be as specified. **6** to end up; result: *it all turned out well*. **7** (*tr*) to fit with clothes: *that woman turns her children out well*. **8** (*intr*) to assemble or gather. **9** (of a soldier) to parade or to call (a soldier) to parade. **10** (*intr*) *Inf.* to get out of bed. **11** (*intr*; foll. by *for*) *Inf.* to make an appearance, esp. in a sporting competition: *he was asked to turn out for Liverpool*. ◆ *n* **turnout. 12** the body of people appearing together at a gathering. **13** the quantity or amount produced. **14** an array of clothing or equipment.

turn over *vb* (*adv*) **1** to change or cause to change position, esp. so as to reverse top and bottom. **2** to start (an engine), esp. with a starting handle, or (of an engine) to start or function correctly. **3** to shift or cause to shift position, as by rolling from side to side. **4** (*tr*) to deliver; transfer. **5** (*tr*) to consider carefully. **6** (*tr*) **6a** to sell and replenish (stock in trade). **6b** to transact business and so generate gross revenue of (a specified sum). **7** (*tr*) to invest and recover (capital). **8** (*tr*) *Sl.* to rob. ◆ *n* **turnover. 9a** the amount of business transacted during a specified period. **9b** (*as modifier*): *a turnover tax*. **10** the rate at which stock in trade is sold and replenished. **11** a change or reversal of position. **12** a small pastry case filled with fruit, jam, etc. **13a** the number of workers employed by a firm in a given period to replace those who have left. **13b** the ratio between this number and the average number of employees during the same period. **14** *Banking*. the amount of capital funds loaned on call during a specified period. ◆ *adj* **turnover. 15** (*prenominal*) designed to be turned over.

turnpike ('tɜːnˌpaɪk) *n* **1** *History*. **1a** a barrier set across a road to prevent passage until a toll had been paid. **1b** a road on which a turnpike was operated. **2** an obsolete word for **turnstile. 3** *US*. a motorway for use of which a toll is charged. [C15: from TURN + PIKE²]

turnround ('tɜːnˌraʊnd) *n* another word for **turnaround.**

urnspit ('tɜːn,spɪt) *n* **1** (formerly) a servant or small dog whose job was to turn a spit. **2** a spit that can be so turned.

urnstile ('tɜːn,staɪl) *n* a mechanical barrier with arms that are turned to admit one person at a time.

urnstone ('tɜːn,stəʊn) *n* a shore bird, related to the plovers and sandpipers, that lifts up stones in search of food.

urntable ('tɜːn,teɪb°l) *n* **1** the circular platform that rotates a gramophone record while it is being played. **2** a circular platform used for turning locomotives and cars. **3** the revolvable platform on a microscope on which specimens are examined.

urntable ladder *n* Brit. a power-operated extending ladder mounted on a fire engine. US and Canad. name: **aerial ladder**.

urn to *vb* (*intr*, *adv*) to set about a task.

urn up *vb* (*adv*) **1** (*intr*) to arrive or appear. **2** to find or be found, esp. by accident. **3** (*tr*) to increase the flow, volume, etc., of. ◆ *n* **turn-up**. **4** (*often pl*) Brit. the turned-up fold at the bottom of some trouser legs. US, Canad. and Austral. name: **cuff**. **5** *Inf.* an unexpected or chance occurrence.

urpentine ('tɜːp°n,taɪn) *n* **1** Also called: **gum turpentine**. any of various oleoresins obtained from various coniferous trees and used as the main source of commercial turpentine. **2** a sticky oleoresin that exudes from the terebinth tree. **3** Also called: **oil of turpentine, spirits of turpentine**. a colourless volatile oil distilled from turpentine oleoresin. It is used as a solvent for paints and in medicine. **4** Also called: **turpentine substitute, white spirit**. (*not in technical usage*) any one of a number of thinners for paints and varnishes, consisting of fractions of petroleum. Related adj: **terebinthine**. ◆ *vb* **turpentines, turpentining, turpentined**. (*tr*) **5** to treat or saturate with turpentine. [C14 *terebentyne*, from Med. L, from L *terebinthīna* turpentine, from *terebinthus* the turpentine tree]

urpentine tree *n* **1** a tropical African tree yielding a hard dark wood and a useful resin. **2** either of two Australian evergreen trees that yield resin.

urpeth ('tɜːpɪθ) *n* **1** an East Indian plant having roots with purgative properties. **2** the root of this plant or the drug obtained from it. [C14: from Med. L *turbithum*, ult. from Ar. *turbid*]

Turpin ★ ('tɜːpɪn) *n* Dick. 1706–39, British highwayman.

urpitude ('tɜːpɪ,tjuːd) *n* base character or action; depravity. [C15: from L *turpitūdō* ugliness, from *turpis* base]

urps (tɜːps) *n* (*functioning as sing*) Brit. short for **turpentine** (sense 3).

urquoise ('tɜːkwɔɪz, -kwɑːz) *n* **1** a greenish-blue fine-grained mineral consisting of hydrated copper aluminium phosphate. It is used as a gemstone. **2a** the colour of turquoise. **2b** (*as adj*): *a turquoise dress*. [C14: from OF *turqueise* Turkish (stone)]

urret ('tʌrɪt) *n* **1** a small tower that projects from the wall of a building, esp. a castle. **2a** a self-contained structure, capable of rotation, in which weapons are mounted, esp. in tanks and warships. **2b** a similar structure on an aircraft. **3** (on a machine tool) a turret-like steel structure with tools projecting radially that can be indexed round to bring each tool to bear on the work. [C14: from OF *torete*, from *tor* tower, from L *turris*]
► 'turreted *adj*

urret lathe *n* another name for **capstan lathe**.

turtle[1] ('tɜːt°l) *n* **1** any of various aquatic reptiles, esp. those having a flattened shell enclosing the body and flipper-like limbs adapted for swimming. **2 turn turtle**. to capsize. [C17: from F *tortue* TORTOISE (infl. by TURTLE[2])]

turtle[2] ('tɜːt°l) *n* an archaic name for **turtledove**. [OE *turtla*, from L *turtur*, imit.]

turtleback ('tɜːt°l,bæk) *n* an arched projection over the upper deck of a ship for protection in heavy seas.

turtledove ('tɜːt°l,dʌv) *n* **1** any of several Old World doves having a brown plumage with speckled wings and a long dark tail. **2** a gentle or loving person. [see TURTLE[2]]

turtleneck ('tɜːt°l,nɛk) *n* a round high close-fitting neck on a sweater or the sweater itself.

turves (tɜːvz) *n* a plural of **turf**.

Tuscan ('tʌskən) *adj* **1** of or relating to Tuscany, its inhabitants, or their dialect of Italian. **2** of or denoting one of the five classical orders of architecture: characterized by a column with an unfluted shaft and a capital and base with mouldings but no decoration. ◆ *n* **3** a native or inhabitant of Tuscany. **4** any of the dialects of Italian spoken in Tuscany.

Tuscany ★ ('tʌskənɪ) *n* a region of central Italy, on the Ligurian and Tyrrhenian Seas: corresponds roughly to ancient Etruria; a region of numerous small states in medieval times; united in the 15th and 16th centuries under Florence; united with the rest of Italy in 1861. Capital: Florence. Pop.: 3 528 225 (1994 est.). Area: 22 990 sq. km (8876 sq. miles). Italian name: **Toscana**.

tusche (tʊʃ) *n* a substance used in lithography for drawing the design and as a resist in silk-screen printing and lithography. [from G, from *tuschen* to touch up with colour, from F *toucher* to touch]

Tusculum ★ ('tʌskjʊləm) *n* an ancient city in Latium near Rome.
► 'Tusculan *adj*

tush (tʌʃ) *interj* Arch. an exclamation of disapproval or contempt. [C15: imit.]

tusk (tʌsk) *n* **1** a pointed elongated usually paired tooth in the elephant, walrus, and certain other mammals. **2** a tusklike tooth or part. **3** a sharp pointed projection. ◆ *vb* **4** to stab, tear, or gore with the tusks. [OE *tūsc*]
► **tusked** *adj*

tusker ('tʌskə) *n* any animal with long tusks.

tusk shell *n* any of various burrowing seashore molluscs that have a long narrow tubular shell open at both ends.

Tussaud ★ (French tyso) *n* **Marie** (mari). 1760–1850, Swiss modeller in wax, who founded a permanent waxworks exhibition in London.

tussis ('tʌsɪs) *n* the technical name for a **cough**. See **pertussis**. [L: cough]
► 'tussive *adj*

tussle ('tʌs°l) *vb* **tussles, tussling, tussled**. **1** (*intr*) to fight or wrestle in a vigorous way. ◆ *n* **2** a vigorous fight; scuffle; struggle. [C15]

tussock ('tʌsək) *n* **1** a dense tuft of vegetation, esp. of grass. **2** Austral. & NZ. **2a** short for **tussock grass**. **2b** the country where tussock grass grows. [C16: from ?]
► 'tussocky *adj*

tussock grass *n* any of several pasture grasses.

tussore (tu'sɔː, 'tʌsə), **tusser** ('tʌsə), or (*Chiefly US*) **tussah** ('tʌsə) *n* **1** Also called: **wild silk**. a coarse silk obtained from an oriental silkworm. **2** the silkworm producing this. [C17: from Hindi *tasar* shuttle, from Sansk. *tasara* a wild silkworm]

tut (tʌt) *interj, n, vb* **tuts, tutting, tutted**. short for **tut-tut**.

Tutankhamen (,tuːtən'kɑːmɛn, -mən) or **Tutankhamun** ★ (,tuːtənkɑː'muːn) *n* king (1361–1352 B.C.) of the 18th dynasty of Egypt. His tomb near Luxor, discovered in 1922, contained a wealth of material objects.

tutelage ('tjuːtɪlɪdʒ) *n* **1** the act or office of a guardian or tutor. **2** instruction or guidance, esp. by a tutor. **3** the condition of being under the supervision of a guardian or tutor. [C17: from L *tūtēla* a caring for, from *tuērī* to watch over]

tutelary ('tjuːtɪlərɪ) or **tutelar** ('tjuːtɪlə) *adj* **1** invested with the role of guardian or protector. **2** of or relating to a guardian. ◆ *n, pl* **tutelaries** or **tutelars**. **3** a tutelary person, deity, etc.

tutor ('tjuːtə) *n* **1** a teacher, usually instructing individual pupils. **2** (at universities, colleges, etc.) a member of staff responsible for the teaching and supervision of a certain number of students. ◆ *vb* **3** to act as a tutor to (someone). **4** (*tr*) to act as guardian to. [C14: from L: a watcher, from *tuērī* to watch over]
► 'tutorage or 'tutorship *n*

tutorial (tjuː'tɔːrɪəl) *n* **1** a period of intensive tuition given by a tutor to an individual student or to a small group of students. ◆ *adj* **2** of or relating to a tutor.

tutsan ('tʌtsən) *n* a woodland shrub of Europe and W Asia, having yellow flowers and reddish-purple fruits. [C15: from OF *toute-saine* (unattested), lit.: all healthy]

tutti ('tutɪ) *adj, adv Music.* to be performed by the whole orchestra, choir, etc. [C18: from It., pl of *tutto* all, from L *tōtus*]

tutti-frutti ('tu:tɪ'fru:tɪ) *n* **1** (pl **tutti-fruttis**) an ice cream or a confection containing small pieces of candied or fresh fruits. **2** a preserve of chopped mixed fruits. **3** a flavour like that of many fruits combined. [from It., lit.: all the fruits]

tut-tut ('tʌt'tʌt) *interj* **1** an exclamation of mild reprimand, disapproval, or surprise. ◆ *vb* **tut-tuts, tut-tutting, tut-tutted. 2** (*intr*) to express disapproval by the exclamation of "tut-tut". ◆ *n* **3** the act of tut-tutting.

tutty ('tʌtɪ) *n* impure zinc oxide used as a polishing powder. [C14: from OF *tutie*, from Ar. *tūtiyā*, prob. from Persian, from Sansk. *tuttha*]

tutu ('tu:tu:) *n* a very short skirt worn by ballerinas, made of projecting layers of stiffened material. [from F, changed from the nursery word *cucu* backside, from L *cūlus* the buttocks]

Tutu ★ ('tu:tu:) *n* **Desmond.** born 1931, South African clergyman, noted for his opposition to apartheid: Anglican Bishop of Johannesburg (1984–86); Archbishop of Cape Town (1986–96); Nobel peace prize 1984.

Tutuila ★ (,tu:tu:'i:lə) *n* the largest island of American Samoa, in the SW Pacific. Chief town and port: Pago Pago. Pop.: 30 500 (latest est.). Area: 135 sq. km (52 sq. miles).

Tutuola ★ ('tu:tu:,əʊlə) *n* **Amos.** 1920–97, Nigerian writer: his books include *The Palm-Wine Drinkard* (1952).

Tuva Republic ★ ('tu:və) *n* a constituent republic of S Russia: mountainous. Capital: Kizyl. Pop.: 308 000 (1995 est.). Area: 170 500 sq. km (65 800 sq. miles). Also called: **Tuvinian Autonomous Republic.**

Tuvalu ★ (,tu:və'lu:) *n* a country in the SW Pacific, comprising a group of nine coral islands: established as a British protectorate in 1892. From 1915 until 1975 the islands formed part of the British colony of the Gilbert and Ellice Islands; achieved full independence in 1978: a special member of the Commonwealth. Languages: English and Tuvaluan. Religion: mostly Christian. Currency: Australian dollar; Tuvalu dollars are also used. Capital: Funafuti. Pop.: 10 300 (1997). Area: 26 sq. km (10 sq. miles). Former names: **Lagoon Islands, Ellice Islands.** ► ,Tuva'luan *adj, n*

tu-whit tu-whoo (tə'wɪt tə'wu:) *interj* an imitation of the sound made by an owl.

tuxedo (tʌk'si:dəʊ) *n, pl* **tuxedos.** the usual US and Canad. name for **dinner jacket.** [C19: after a country club in *Tuxedo Park*, New York]

Tuxtla Gutiérrez ★ (*Spanish* 'tustla gu'tjerreθ) *n* a city in SE Mexico, capital of Chiapas state: agricultural trading centre. Pop.: 289 626 (1990).

tuyère ('twi:ɛə, 'twaɪə) *or* **twyer** ('twaɪə) *n* a water-cooled nozzle through which air is blown into a cupola, blast furnace, or forge. [C18: from F, from *tuyau* pipe, from OF *tuel*, prob. of Gmc origin]

TV *abbrev. for* television.

TVEI (in Britain) *abbrev. for* technical and vocational educational initiative: a national educational scheme in which pupils gain practical experience in technology and industry often through work placement.

Tver (*Russian* tvjerj) *n* a city in central Russia, at the confluence of the Volga and Tversta Rivers: chief port of the upper Volga, linked by canal with Moscow. Pop.: 454 000 (1994 est.). Former name (1932–91): **Kalinin.**

TVP *abbrev. for* textured vegetable protein: protein from soya beans or other vegetables spun into fibres and flavoured: used esp. as a substitute for meat.

TVR *abbrev. for* television rating: a measurement of the popularity of a TV programme based on a survey.

TVRO *abbrev. for* television receive only: an antenna and associated apparatus for reception from a broadcasting satellite.

twaddle ('twɒdəl) *n* **1** silly, trivial, or pretentious talk or writing. ◆ *vb* **twaddles, twaddling, twaddled. 2** (*intr*) to talk or write in a silly or pretentious way. [C16 *twattle*, var. of *twittle* or *tittle*] ► 'twaddler *n*

twain (tweɪn) *determiner, n* an archaic word for **two.** [OE *twēgen*]

Twain ★ (tweɪn) *n* **Mark,** pen name of *Samuel Langhorne Clemens.* 1835–1910, US novelist, author of *The Adventures of Tom Sawyer* (1876) and *The Adventures of Huckleberry Finn* (1885).

twang (twæŋ) *n* **1** a sharp ringing sound produced by or as if by the plucking of a taut string. **2** the act of plucking a string to produce such a sound. **3** a strongly nasal quality in a person's speech. ◆ *vb* **4** to make or cause to make a twang. **5** to strum (music, a tune, etc.). **6** to speak with a nasal voice. **7** (*intr*) to be released or move with a twang: *the arrow twanged away.* [C16: imit.] ► 'twangy *adj*

'twas (twɒz; *unstressed* twəz) *Poetic or dialect. contraction of* it was.

twat (twæt, twɒt) *n Taboo sl.* **1** the female genitals. **2** a foolish person. [from ?]

twayblade ('tweɪ,bleɪd) *n* any of various orchids having a basal pair of unstalked leaves arranged opposite each other. [C16: translation of Med. L *bifolium* having two leaves, from obs. *tway* two + BLADE]

tweak (twi:k) *vb* (*tr*) **1** to twist or pinch with a sharp or sudden movement. **2** *Inf.* to make a minor alteration. ◆ *n* **3** a tweaking. **4** *Inf.* a minor alteration. [OE *twiccian*]

twee (twi:) *adj Brit. inf.* excessively sentimental, sweet, or pretty. [C19: from *tweet*, mincing or affected pronunciation of *sweet*] ► 'tweely *adv*

tweed (twi:d) *n* **1** a thick woollen cloth produced originally in Scotland. **2** (*pl*) clothes made of this. **3** (*pl*) *Austral. inf.* trousers. [C19: prob. from *tweel*, Scot. var. of TWILL, infl. by TWEED]

Tweed ★ (twi:d) *n* a river in SE Scotland and NE England, flowing east and forming part of the border between Scotland and England, then crossing into England to enter the North Sea at Berwick. Length: 156 km (97 miles).

Tweeddale ★ ('twi:d,deɪl) *n* another name for **Peeblesshire.**

Tweedledum and Tweedledee (,twi:dəl'dʌm, ,twi:dəl'di:) *n* any two persons or things that differ only slightly from each other; two of a kind. [C19: from the proverbial names of HANDEL and the rival musician Buononcini. The names were popularized by Lewis Carroll's use of them in *Through the Looking Glass* (1872)]

Tweedsmuir ★ ('twi:dz,mjʊə) *n* **Baron.** title of (John) **Buchan.**

tweedy ('twi:dɪ) *adj* **tweedier, tweediest. 1** of, made of, or resembling tweed. **2** showing a fondness for a hearty outdoor life, usually associated with wearers of tweeds.

'tween (twi:n) *Poetic or dialect. contraction of* between.

'tween deck *or* **decks** *n Naut.* a space between two continuous decks of a vessel.

tweet (twi:t) *interj* **1** an imitation of the thin chirping sound made by small birds. ◆ *vb* **2** (*intr*) to make this sound. [C19: imit.]

tweeter ('twi:tə) *n* a loudspeaker used in high-fidelity systems for the reproduction of high audio frequencies. It is usually employed in conjunction with a woofer. [C20: from TWEET]

tweezers ('twi:zəz) *pl n* a small pincer-like instrument for handling small objects, plucking out hairs, etc. Also called: **pair of tweezers, tweezer** (esp. US). [C17: pl of *tweeze* (on the model of *scissors*, etc.), from *tweeze* case of instruments, from F *étuis*, from OF *estuier* to preserve, ult. from L *studēre* to care about]

Twelfth Day *n* Jan. 6, the twelfth day after Christmas and the feast of the Epiphany.

★ people and places

welfth man n a reserve player in a cricket team.

welfth Night n **a** the evening of Jan. 5, the eve of Twelfth Day. **b** the evening of Twelfth Day itself.

welve (twelv) n **1** the cardinal number that is the sum of ten and two. **2** a numeral, 12, XII, etc., representing this number. **3** something representing or consisting of 12 units. **4** Also called: **twelve o'clock.** noon or midnight. ◆ determiner **5a** amounting to twelve. **5b** (as pronoun): twelve have arrived. ◆ Related adj: **duodecimal.** [OE twelf]
▸ **twelfth** adj, n

welve-inch n a gramophone record 12 inches in diameter and played at 45 revolutions per minute, usually containing an extended remix of a single.

welvemo ('twelvməʊ) n, pl **twelvemos.** Bookbinding. another word for **duodecimo.**

welvemonth ('twelv,mʌnθ) n Chiefly Brit. an archaic or dialect word for a **year.**

welve-tone adj of or denoting the type of serial music which uses as musical material a tone row formed by the 12 semitones of the chromatic scale. See **serialism.**

wenty ('twentɪ) n, pl **twenties. 1** the cardinal number that is the product of ten and two. **2** a numeral, 20, XX, etc., representing this number. **3** something representing or consisting of 20 units. ◆ determiner **4a** amounting to twenty: twenty questions. **4b** (as pronoun): to order twenty.
▸ **twentieth** adj, n [OE twēntig]

wenty-six counties pl n the counties of the Republic of Ireland.

wenty-twenty adj Med. (of vision) being of normal acuity: usually written 20/20.

twere (twɜː; unstressed twə) Poetic or dialect. contraction of it were.

werp or **twirp** (twɜːp) n Inf. a silly, weak-minded, or contemptible person. [C20: from ?]

wibill or **twibil** ('twaɪ,bɪl) n **1** a mattock with a blade shaped like an adze at one end and like an axe at the other. **2** Arch. a double-bladed battle-axe. [OE, from twi-double + bill sword]

wice (twaɪs) adv **1** two times; on two occasions or in two cases. **2** double in degree or quantity: twice as long. [OE twiwa]

Twickenham ★ ('twɪkənəm) n a former town in SE England, on the River Thames: part of the Greater London borough of Richmond-upon-Thames since 1965; contains the English Rugby Football Union ground.

twiddle ('twɪdəl) vb **twiddles, twiddling, twiddled. 1** (when intr, often foll. by with) to twirl or fiddle (with), often in an idle way. **2 twiddle one's thumbs.** to do nothing; be unoccupied. **3** (intr) to turn, twirl, or rotate. **4** (intr) Rare. to be occupied with trifles. ◆ n **5** an act or instance of twiddling. [C16: prob. a blend of TWIRL + FIDDLE]
▸ **twiddler** n

twig[1] (twɪg) n **1** any small branch or shoot of a tree. **2** something resembling this, esp. a minute branch of a blood vessel. [OE twigge]
▸ **twiggy** adj

twig[2] (twɪg) vb **twigs, twigging, twigged.** Brit. inf. **1** to understand (something). **2** to find out or suddenly comprehend (something): he hasn't twigged yet. [C18: ?from Scot. Gaelic tuig I understand]

twilight ('twaɪ,laɪt) n **1** the soft diffused light occurring when the sun is just below the horizon, esp. following sunset. **2** the period in which this light occurs. **3** any faint light. **4** a period in which strength, importance, etc., are waning. **5** (modifier) **5a** of or relating to the period towards the end of the day: the twilight shift. **5b** of or relating to the final phase of a particular era: the twilight days of the Bush presidency. **5c** denoting irregularity and obscurity: a twilight existence. [C15: lit.: half light (between day and night), from OE twi- half + LIGHT[1]]
▸ **twilit** ('twaɪ,lɪt) adj

Twilight of the Gods n another term for **Götterdämmerung.**

twilight sleep n Med. a state of partial anaesthesia in which the patient retains a slight degree of consciousness.

twilight zone n **1** any indefinite or transitional condition or area. **2** an inner-city area where houses have become dilapidated.

twill (twɪl) adj **1** (in textiles) of a weave in which the yarns are worked to produce an effect of parallel diagonal lines or ribs. ◆ n **2** any fabric so woven. ◆ vb **3** (tr) to weave in this fashion. [OE twilic having a double thread]

'twill (twɪl) Poetic or dialect. contraction of it will.

twin (twɪn) n **1a** either of two persons or animals conceived at the same time. **1b** (as modifier): a twin brother. See also **identical** (sense 3), **fraternal** (sense 3). **2a** either of two persons or things that are identical or very similar. **2b** (as modifier): twin carburettors. **3** Also called: **macle.** a crystal consisting of two parts each of which has a definite orientation to the other. ◆ vb **twins, twinning, twinned. 4** to pair or be paired together; couple. **5** (intr) to bear twins. **6** (intr) (of a crystal) to form into a twin. **7a** (tr) to create a reciprocal relation between (two towns in different countries); pair (a town) with another in a different country. **7b** (intr) (of a town) to be paired in a town in a different country. [OE twinn]
▸ **'twinning** n

twin bed n one of a pair of matching single beds.

twine (twaɪn) n **1** string made by twisting together fibres of hemp, cotton, etc. **2** a twining. **3** something produced or characterized by twining. **4** a twist, coil, or convolution. **5** a knot or tangle. ◆ vb **twines, twining, twined. 6** (tr) to twist together; interweave. **7** (tr) to form by or as if by twining. **8** (when intr, often foll. by around) to wind or cause to wind, esp. in spirals. [OE twīn]
▸ **'twiner** n

twin-engined adj (of an aeroplane) having two engines.

twinge (twɪndʒ) n **1** a sudden brief darting or stabbing pain. **2** a sharp emotional pang. ◆ vb **twinges, twinging, twinged. 3** to have or cause to have a twinge. [OE twengan to pinch]

twinkle ('twɪŋkəl) vb **twinkles, twinkling, twinkled.** (mainly intr) **1** to emit or reflect light in a flickering manner; shine brightly and intermittently; sparkle. **2** (of the eyes) to sparkle, esp. with amusement or delight. **3** Rare. to move about quickly. ◆ n **4** a flickering brightness; sparkle. **5** an instant. [OE twinclian]
▸ **'twinkler** n

twinkling ('twɪŋklɪŋ) or **twink** (twɪŋk) n a very short time; instant; moment. Also called: **twinkling of an eye.**

Twins (twɪnz) pl n the. the constellation Gemini, the third sign of the zodiac.

twin-screw adj (of a vessel) having two propellers.

twinset ('twɪn,set) n Brit. a matching jumper and cardigan.

twin town n a town that has civic associations, such as reciprocal visits and cultural exchanges, with a foreign town.

twin-tub n a type of washing machine that has two revolving drums, one for washing and the other for spin-drying.

twirl (twɜːl) vb **1** to move around rapidly and repeatedly in a circle. **2** (tr) to twist, wind, or twiddle, often idly: she twirled her hair around her finger. **3** (intr; often foll. by around or about) to turn suddenly to face another way. ◆ n **4** a rotating or being rotated; whirl or twist. **5** something wound around or twirled; coil. **6** a written flourish. [C16: ? a blend of TWIST + WHIRL]
▸ **'twirler** n

twirp (twɜːp) n a variant spelling of **twerp.**

twist (twɪst) vb **1** to cause (one end or part) to turn or (of one end or part) to turn in the opposite direction from another; coil or spin. **2** to distort or be distorted. **3** to wind or twine. **4** to force or be forced out of the natural form or position. **5** to change for the worse in character, meaning, etc.; pervert: she twisted the statement. **6** to revolve; rotate. **7** (tr) to wrench with a turning action. **8** (intr) to follow a winding course. **9** (intr) to squirm, as with pain. **10** (intr) to dance the twist. **11** (tr) Brit. inf. to cheat; swindle. **12 twist someone's arm.** to persuade or co-

erce someone. ◆ *n* **13** a twisting. **14** something formed by or as if by twisting. **15** a decisive change of direction, aim, meaning, or character. **16** (in a novel, play, etc.) an unexpected event, revelation, etc. **17** a bend: *a twist in the road*. **18** a distortion of the original shape or form. **19** a jerky pull, wrench, or turn. **20** a strange personal characteristic, esp. a bad one. **21** a confused tangle made by twisting. **22** a twisted thread used in sewing where extra strength is needed. **23 the twist.** a dance popular in the 1960s, in which dancers vigorously twist the hips. **24** a loaf or roll made of pieces of twisted dough. **25** a thin sliver of peel from a lemon, lime, etc., twisted and added to a drink. **26a** a cigar made by twisting three cigars around one another. **26b** chewing tobacco made in the form of a roll by twisting the leaves together. **27** *Physics*. torsional deformation or shear stress or strain. **28** *Brit., chiefly US & Canad*. spin given to a ball in various games. **29 round the twist.** *Brit. sl.* mad; eccentric. [OE]
▸ 'twisty *adj*

twist drill *n* a drill bit having two helical grooves running from the point along the shank to clear swarf and cuttings.

twister ('twɪstə) *n* **1** *Brit*. a swindling or dishonest person. **2** a person or thing that twists. **3** *US & Canad*. an informal name for **tornado**. **4** a ball moving with a twisting motion.

twist grip *n* a handlebar control in the form of a ratchet-controlled rotating grip.

twit[1] (twɪt) *vb* **twits, twitting, twitted. 1** (*tr*) to tease, taunt, or reproach, often in jest. ◆ *n* **2** *US & Canad. inf.* a nervous or excitable state. **3** *Rare*. a reproach; taunt. [OE ætwītan, from æt against + wītan to accuse]

twit[2] (twɪt) *n Inf., chiefly Brit*. a foolish or stupid person; idiot. [C19: from TWIT[1] (orig. in the sense: a person given to twitting)]

twitch (twɪtʃ) *vb* **1** to move in a jerky spasmodic way. **2** (*tr*) to pull (something) with a quick jerky movement. **3** (*intr*) to hurt with a sharp spasmodic pain. ◆ *n* **4** a sharp jerking movement. **5** a mental or physical twinge. **6** a sudden muscular spasm, esp. one caused by a nervous condition. **7** a loop of cord used to control a horse by drawing it tight about its upper lip. [OE *twiccian* to pluck]

twitcher ('twɪtʃə) *n* **1** a person or thing that twitches. **2** *Inf*. a bird-watcher who tries to spot as many rare varieties as possible.

twitch grass *n* another name for **couch grass**. Sometimes shortened to **twitch.** [C16: var. of QUITCH GRASS]

twite (twaɪt) *n* a N European finch with a brown streaked plumage. [C16: imit. of its cry]

twitter ('twɪtə) *vb* **1** (*intr*) (esp. of a bird) to utter a succession of chirping sounds. **2** (*intr*) to talk or move rapidly and tremulously. **3** (*intr*) to giggle. **4** (*tr*) to utter in a chirping way. ◆ *n* **5** a twittering sound. **6** the act of twittering. **7** a state of nervous excitement (esp. in **in a twitter**). [C14: imit.]
▸ 'twitterer *n* ▸ 'twittery *adj*

'twixt or **twixt** (twɪkst) *Poetic or dialect. contraction of* betwixt.

two (tuː) *n* **1** the cardinal number that is the sum of one and one. **2** a numeral, 2, II, (ii), etc., representing this number. **3** something representing or consisting of two units. **4** Also called: **two o'clock.** two hours after noon or midnight. **5 in two.** in or into two parts. **6 put two and two together.** to make an inference from available evidence, esp. an obvious inference. **7 that makes two of us.** the same applies to me. ◆ *determiner* **8a** amounting to two: *two nails*. **8b** (*as pronoun*): *he bought two*. ◆ Related adjs: **binary, double, dual.** [OE *twā* (fem)]

two-by-four *n* **1** a length of untrimmed timber with a cross section that measures 2 inches by 4 inches. **2** a trimmed timber joist with a cross section that measures 1½ inches by 3½ inches.

twoccing or **twocking** ('twɒkɪŋ) *n Brit. sl.* the act of breaking into a motor vehicle and driving it away. [C20: from *T(aking) W(ithout) O(wner's) C(onsent)*, the legal offence with which car thieves may be charged]
▸ 'twoccer or 'twocker *n*

two-dimensional *adj* **1** of or having two dimensions. **2** having an area but not enclosing any volume. **3** lacking in depth.

two-edged *adj* **1** having two cutting edges. **2** (esp. of a remark) having two interpretations, such as *she looks nice when she smiles*.

two-faced *adj* deceitful; hypocritical.

twofold ('tuːˌfəʊld) *adj* **1** equal to twice as many or twice as much. **2** composed of two parts. ◆ *adv* **3** doubly.

two-handed *adj* **1** requiring the use of both hands. **2** ambidextrous. **3** requiring the participation or cooperation of two people.

two-pack *adj* (of a paint, filler, etc.) supplied as two separate components, for example a base and a catalyst, that are mixed together immediately before use.

twopence or **tuppence** ('tʌpəns) *n Brit*. **1** the sum of two pennies. **2** (*used with a negative*) something of little value (in **not care** or **give twopence**). **3** a former British silver coin.

twopenny or **tuppenny** ('tʌpənɪ) *adj Chiefly Brit*. **1** Also: **twopenny-halfpenny.** cheap or tawdry. **2** (intensifier): *a twopenny damn*. **3** worth two pence.

two-phase *adj* (of an electrical circuit, device, etc.) generating or using two alternating voltages of the same frequency, displaced in phase by 90°.

two-piece *adj* **1** consisting of two separate parts, usually matching, as of a garment. ◆ *n* **2** such an outfit.

two-ply *adj* **1** made of two thicknesses, layers, or strands. ◆ *n, pl* **two-plies. 2** a two-ply wood, knitting yarn, etc.

Two Sicilies ★ *pl n* **the.** a former kingdom of S Italy, consisting of the kingdoms of Sicily and Naples (1061–1860).

two-sided *adj* **1** having two sides or aspects. **2** controversial; debatable.

twosome ('tuːsəm) *n* **1** two together, esp. two people. **2** a match between two people.

two-step *n* **1** an old-time dance in duple time. **2** a piece of music composed for or in the rhythm of this dance.

two-stroke *adj* (of an internal-combustion engine) whose piston makes two strokes for every explosion. US and Canad. word: **two-cycle.**

Two Thousand Guineas *n* (*functioning as sing*), *usually written* **2000 Guineas. the.** an annual horse race run at Newmarket since 1809.

two-time *vb* **two-times, two-timing, two-timed.** *Inf.* to deceive (someone, esp. a lover) by carrying on a relationship with another.
▸ ˌtwo-'timer *n*

two-tone *adj* **1** of two colours or two shades of the same colour. **2** (esp. of sirens, car horns, etc.) producing or consisting of two notes.

'twould (twʊd) *Poetic or dialect. contraction of* it would.

two-up *n Chiefly Austral*. a illegal gambling game in which two coins are tossed or spun.

two-way *adj* **1** moving, permitting movement, or operating in either of two opposite directions. **2** involving two participants. **3** involving reciprocal obligation or mutual action. **4** (of a radio, telephone, etc.) allowing communications in two directions using both transmitting and receiving equipment.

two-way mirror *n* a half-silvered sheet of glass that functions as a mirror when viewed from one side but is translucent from the other.

TX *abbrev. for* Texas.

-ty[1] *suffix of numerals*. denoting a multiple of ten: *sixty; seventy*. [from OE *-tig*]

-ty[2] *suffix forming nouns*. indicating state, condition, or quality: *cruelty*. [from OF *-te, -tet*, from L *-tās, -tāt-*]

Tyan-Shan ★ ('tjanˈʃan) *n* transliteration of the Russian name for the **Tian Shan.**

Tyburn ★ ('taɪbɜːn) *n* (formerly) a place of execution in London, on the River Tyburn.

Tyche ★ ('taɪkɪ) *n Greek myth*. the goddess of fortune. Roman counterpart: **Fortuna.**

tychism ('taɪkɪzəm) *n Philosophy*. the theory that chance

★ people and places

is an objective reality at work in the universe. [from Gk *tukhē* chance]

ycoon (taɪˈkuːn) *n* **1** a businessman of great wealth and power. **2** an archaic name for a **shogun**. [C19: from Japanese *taikun*, from Chinese *ta* great + *chün* ruler]

yke *or* **tike** (taɪk) *n* **1** a dog, esp. a mongrel. **2** *Inf.* a small or cheeky child. **3** *Brit. dialect.* a rough ill-mannered person. **4** *Brit. sl. often offens.* a person from Yorkshire. **5** *Austral. sl., offens.* a Roman Catholic. [C14: from ON *tík* bitch]

Tyler ★ (ˈtaɪlə) *n* **1** John. 1790–1862, US statesman; tenth president of the US (1841–45). **2** Wat (wɒt). died 1381, English leader of the Peasants' Revolt (1381).

ylopod (ˈtaɪləʊˌpɒd) *n* a mammal having padded, rather than hoofed, digits, such as camels and llamas. [C19: from NL, from Gk *tulos* knob *or* *tulē* cushion + -POD]

Tylor ★ (ˈtaɪlə) *n* Sir **Edward Burnett**. 1832–1917, British anthropologist, noted for his *Primitive Culture* (1871).

tympan (ˈtɪmpən) *n* **1** a membrane stretched over a frame or cylinder. **2** *Printing.* packing interposed between the platen and the paper to be printed in order to provide an even impression. **3** *Archit.* another name for **tympanum**. [OE *timpana*, from L; see TYMPANUM]

tympani (ˈtɪmpənɪ) *pl n* a variant spelling of **timpani**.

tympanic bone (tɪmˈpænɪk) *n* the part of the temporal bone that surrounds the auditory canal.

tympanic membrane *n* the thin membrane separating the external ear from the middle ear. It transmits vibrations, produced by sound waves, to the cochlea. Nontechnical name: **eardrum**.

tympanites (ˌtɪmpəˈnaɪtiːz) *n* distension of the abdomen caused by an accumulation of gas in the intestinal or peritoneal cavity. Also called: **meteorism, tympany**. [C14: from LL, from Gk *tumpanitēs* concerning a drum, from *tumpanon* drum]
▸ **tympanitic** (ˌtɪmpəˈnɪtɪk) *adj*

tympanitis (ˌtɪmpəˈnaɪtɪs) *n* inflammation of the eardrum.

tympanum (ˈtɪmpənəm) *n, pl* **tympanums** *or* **tympana** (-nə). **1a** the cavity of the middle ear. **1b** another name for **tympanic membrane**. **2** any diaphragm resembling that in the middle ear in function. **3** *Archit.* **3a** the recessed space bounded by the cornices of a pediment, esp. one that is triangular in shape. **3b** the recessed space bounded by an arch and the lintel of a doorway or window below it. **4** *Music.* a tympan or drum. **5** a scoop wheel for raising water. [C17: from L, from Gk *tumpanon* drum]
▸ **tympanic** (tɪmˈpænɪk) *adj*

Tyndale, Tindal, *or* **Tindale** ★ (ˈtɪndᵊl) *n* **William**. ?1492–1536, English Protestant and humanist, who translated the New Testament (1525), the Pentateuch (1530), and the Book of Jonah (1531) into English. He was burnt at the stake as a heretic.

Tyndall ★ (ˈtɪndᵊl) *n* John. 1820–93, Irish physicist, noted for his work on the radiation of heat by gases, the transmission of sound through the atmosphere, and the scattering of light.

Tyndall effect *n* the phenomenon in which light is scattered by particles of matter in its path. [C19: after John TYNDALL]

Tyndareus ★ (tɪnˈdæriəs) *n Greek myth.* a Spartan king; the husband of Leda.

Tyne ★ (taɪn) *n* a river in N England, flowing east to the North Sea. Length: 48 km (30 miles).

Tyne and Wear ★ *n* a metropolitan county of NE England, administered since 1986 by the unitary authorities of Newcastle upon Tyne, North Tyneside, Gateshead, South Tyneside, and Sunderland.

Tynemouth ★ (ˈtaɪnˌmaʊθ) *n* a port in NE England, in Tyne and Wear at the mouth of the River Tyne: includes the port and industrial centre of North Shields; fishing, ship-repairing, and marine engineering. Pop.: 20 716 (1991).

Tyneside ★ (ˈtaɪnˌsaɪd) *n* the conurbation on the banks of the Tyne from Newcastle to the coast.

Tynwald (ˈtɪnwəld, ˈtaɪn-) *n* **the**. the Parliament of the Isle of Man. [C15: from ON *thingvollr*, from *thing* assembly + *vollr* field]

typ., typo., *or* **typog.** *abbrev. for:* **1** typographer. **2** typographic(al). **3** typography.

typal (ˈtaɪpᵊl) *adj* a rare word for **typical**.

type (taɪp) *n* **1** a kind, class, or category, the constituents of which share similar characteristics. **2** a subdivision of a particular class; sort: *what type of shampoo do you use?* **3** the general form, plan, or design distinguishing a particular group. **4** *Inf.* a person who typifies a particular quality: *he's the administrative type.* **5** *Inf.* a person, esp. of a specified kind: *he's a strange type.* **6a** a small block of metal or more rarely wood bearing a letter or character in relief for use in printing. **6b** such pieces collectively. **7** characters printed from type; print. **8** *Biol.* the taxonomic group the characteristics of which are used for defining the next highest group. **8b** (*as modifier*): *a type genus.* **9** See **type specimen. 10** the characteristic device on a coin. **11** *Chiefly Christian theol.* a figure, episode, or symbolic factor resembling some future reality in such a way as to foreshadow or prefigure it. ◆ *vb* **types, typing, typed. 12** to write (copy) on a typewriter. **13** (*tr*) to be a symbol of; typify. **14** (*tr*) to decide the type of. **15** (*tr*) *Med.* to determine the blood group of (a blood sample). **16** (*tr*) *Chiefly Christian theol.* to foreshadow or serve as a symbol of (some future reality). [C15: from L *typus* figure, from Gk *tupos* image, from *tuptein* to strike]

-type *n combining form.* **1** type or form: *archetype.* **2** printing type or photographic process: *collotype.* [from L *-typus*, from Gk *-typos*, from *tupos* TYPE]

typecast (ˈtaɪpˌkɑːst) *vb* **typecasts, typecasting, typecast.** (*tr*) to cast (an actor) in the same kind of role continually, esp. because of his physical appearance or previous success in such roles.

typeface (ˈtaɪpˌfeɪs) *n* another name for **face** (sense 14).

type founder *n* a person who casts metallic printer's type.
▸ **type foundry** *n*

type metal *n Printing.* an alloy of tin, lead, and antimony, from which type is cast.

typescript (ˈtaɪpˌskrɪpt) *n* **1** a typed copy of a document, etc. **2** any typewritten material.

typeset (ˈtaɪpˌset) *vb* **typesets, typesetting, typeset.** (*tr*) *Printing.* to set (textual matter) in type.

typesetter (ˈtaɪpˌsetə) *n* **1** a person who sets type; compositor. **2** a typesetting machine.

type specimen *n Biol.* the original specimen from which a description of a new species is made.

typewrite (ˈtaɪpˌraɪt) *vb* **typewrites, typewriting, typewrote, typewritten.** to write by means of a typewriter; type.
▸ **'type,writing** *n*

typewriter (ˈtaɪpˌraɪtə) *n* a keyboard machine for writing mechanically in characters resembling print.

typhlitis (tɪfˈlaɪtɪs) *n* inflammation of the caecum. [C19: from NL, from Gk *tuphlon* the caecum, from *tuphlos* blind]
▸ **typhlitic** (tɪfˈlɪtɪk) *adj*

Typhoeus ★ (taɪˈfiːəs) *n Greek myth.* the son of Gaea and Tartarus who had a hundred dragon heads, which spurted fire, and a bellowing many-tongued voice. He created the whirlwinds and fought with Zeus before the god hurled him beneath Mount Etna.
▸ **Ty'phoean** *adj*

typhoid (ˈtaɪfɔɪd) *Pathol.* ◆ *adj also* **typhoidal. 1** resembling typhus. ◆ *n* **2** short for **typhoid fever**. [C19: from TYPHUS + -OID]

typhoid fever *n* an acute infectious disease characterized by high fever, spots, abdominal pain, etc. It is caused by a bacillus ingested with food or water.

Typhon ★ (ˈtaɪfɒn) *n Greek myth.* a monster and one of the whirlwinds: later confused with his father Typhoeus.

typhoon (taɪˈfuːn) *n* a violent tropical storm or cyclone, esp. in the China Seas and W Pacific. [C16: from Chinese *tai fung* great wind; infl. by Gk *tuphōn* whirlwind]
▸ **typhonic** (taɪˈfɒnɪk) *adj*

typhus (ˈtaɪfəs) *n* any one of a group of acute infectious

rickettsial diseases characterized by high fever, skin rash, and severe headache. Also called: **typhus fever**. [C18: from NL *tȳphus*, from Gk *tuphos* fever]
▶ **'typhous** *adj*

typical ('tɪpɪkªl) *adj* **1** being or serving as a representative example of a particular type; characteristic. **2** considered to be an example of some undesirable trait: *that is typical of you!* **3** of or relating to a representative specimen or type. **4** conforming to a type. **5** *Biol.* having most of the characteristics of a particular taxonomic group. [C17: from Med. L *typicālis*, from LL *typicus* figurative, from Gk *tupikos*, from *tupos* TYPE]
▶ **'typically** *adv* ▶ **'typicalness** *or* ,**typi'cality** *n*

typify ('tɪpɪ,faɪ) *vb* **typifies, typifying, typified**. (*tr*) **1** to be typical of; characterize. **2** to symbolize or represent completely, by or as if by a type. [C17: from L *typus* TYPE]
▶ ,**typifi'cation** *n*

typist ('taɪpɪst) *n* a person who types, esp. for a living.

typo ('taɪpəʊ) *n, pl* **typos**. *Inf.* a typographical error. Also called (*Brit.*): **literal**.

typographer (taɪ'pɒgrəfə) *n* **1** a person skilled in typography. **2** a compositor.

typography (taɪ'pɒgrəfɪ) *n* **1** the art, craft, or process of composing type and printing from it. **2** the planning, selection, and setting of type for a printed work.
▶ **typographical** (,taɪpə'græfɪkªl) *or* ,**typo'graphic** *adj* ▶ ,**typo'graphically** *adv*

typology (taɪ'pɒlədʒɪ) *n* **1** the study of types in archaeology, biology, etc. **2** *Christian theol.* the doctrine that symbols for events, figures, etc., in the New Testament can be found in the Old Testament.
▶ **typological** (,taɪpə'lɒdʒɪkªl) *adj* ▶ **ty'pologist** *n*

Tyr *or* **Tyrr** ★ (tjʊə, tɪə) *n Norse myth.* the god of war, son of Odin. Anglo-Saxon counterpart: **Tiu**.

tyrannical (tɪ'rænɪkªl) *or* **tyrannic** *adj* characteristic of or relating to a tyrant or to tyranny; oppressive.
▶ **ty'rannically** *adv*

tyrannicide (tɪ'rænɪ,saɪd) *n* **1** the killing of a tyrant. **2** a person who kills a tyrant.

tyrannize *or* **tyrannise** ('tɪrə,naɪz) *vb* **tyrannizes, tyrannizing, tyrannized** *or* **tyrannises, tyrannising, tyrannised**. (when *intr*, often foll. by *over*) to rule or exercise power (over) in a cruel or oppressive manner.
▶ **'tyran,nizer** *or* **'tyran,niser** *n*

tyrannosaurus (tɪ,rænə'sɔːrəs) *or* **tyrannosaur** (tɪ-'rænə,sɔː) *n* any of various large carnivorous two-footed dinosaurs common in North America in Upper Jurassic and Cretaceous times. [C19: from NL, from Gk *turannos* tyrant + -SAUR]

tyranny ('tɪrənɪ) *n, pl* **tyrannies**. **1a** government by a tyrant; despotism. **1b** oppressive and unjust government by more than one person. **2** arbitrary, unreasonable, or despotic behaviour or use of authority. **3** a tyrannical act. [C14: from OF *tyrannie*, from Med. L *tyrannia*, from L *tyrannus* TYRANT]
▶ **'tyrannous** *adj*

tyrant ('taɪrənt) *n* **1** a person who governs oppressively, unjustly, and arbitrarily; despot. **2** any person who exercises authority in a tyrannical manner. [C13: from OF *tyrant*, from L *tyrannus*, from Gk *turannos*]

tyre *or US* **tire** ('taɪə) *n* **1** a rubber ring placed over the rim of a wheel of a road vehicle to provide traction and reduce road shocks, esp. a hollow inflated ring (**pneumatic tyre**) consisting of a reinforced outer casing enclosing an inner tube. **2** a metal band or hoop attached to the rim of a wooden cartwheel. [C18: var. of C15 *tire*, prob. from archaic var. of ATTIRE]

Tyre *or* **Tyr** ★ ('taɪə) *n* a port in S Lebanon, on the Mediterranean: founded about the 15th century B.C.; for centuries a major Phoenician seaport, famous for silks and its Tyrian-purple dye; now a small market town. Pop. 70 000 (1991 est.). Arabic name: **Sur**.
▶ **Tyrian** ('tɪrɪən) *adj, n*

Tyrian purple *n* **1** a deep purple dye obtained from certain molluscs and highly prized in antiquity. **2a** a vivid purplish-red colour. **2b** (*as adj*): *a Tyrian-purple robe*.

tyro *or* **tiro** ('taɪrəʊ) *n, pl* **tyros** *or* **tiros**. a novice or beginner. [C17: from L *tīrō* recruit]

Tyrol *or* **Tirol** ★ (tɪ'rəʊl, 'tɪrəʊl; *German* ti'roːl) *n* a mountainous state of W Austria: passed to the Hapsburgs in 1363; S part transferred to Italy in 1919. Capital: Innsbruck. Pop.: 654 753 (1994 est.). Area: 12 648 sq. km (4883 sq. miles).
▶ **Tyrolese** (,tɪrə'liːz) *or* ,**Tyro'lean** *adj, n*

Tyrone ★ (tɪ'rəʊn) *n* a historic county of W Northern Ireland, occupying almost a quarter of the total area of Northern Ireland.

tyrosinase (,taɪrəʊsɪ'neɪz) *n* an enzyme that is a catalyst in the conversion of tyrosine to the pigment melanin.

tyrosine ('taɪrə,siːn, -sɪn, 'tɪrə-) *n* an amino acid that is a precursor of the hormones adrenaline and thyroxine and of the pigment melanin. [C19: from Gk *turos* cheese + -INE²]

tyrothricin (,taɪrəʊ'θraɪsɪn) *n* an antibiotic, obtained from a soil bacterium: applied locally for the treatment of ulcers and abscesses. [C20: from NL *Tyrothrix* (genus name), from Gk *turos* cheese + *thrix* hair]

Tyrr ★ (tjʊə, tɪə) *n* a variant spelling of **Tyr**.

Tyrrhenian Sea ★ (tɪ'riːnɪən) *n* an arm of the Mediterranean between Italy and the islands of Corsica, Sardinia, and Sicily.

Tyson ★ ('taɪsªn) *n* Mike. born 1966, US boxer, world heavyweight champion (1986–90; 1996): jailed for rape (1992–95).

Tyumen ★ (*Russian* tju'mjenj) *n* a port in S central Russia, on the Tura River: one of the oldest Russian towns in Siberia; industrial centre with nearby oil and natural gas reserves. Pop.: 494 000 (1995 est.).

tzar (zɑː) *n* a less common spelling of **tsar**.

Tzara ★ (*French* dzara; *Romanian* tsa'ra) *n* Tristan (*French* tristã) original name *Samuel Rosenstock*. 1896–1963, French poet, born in Romania; the founder of Dada.

tzatziki (tsæt'sɪkɪ) *n* a Greek dip made from yogurt, chopped cucumber, and mint. [C20: from Mod. Gk]

Tzekung ('tse'kʊŋ) *or* **Tzu-kung** ★ ('tsu:'kʊŋ) *n* a variant transliteration of the Chinese name for **Zigong**.

tzetze fly ('tsetsɪ) *n* a variant spelling of **tsetse fly**.

Tzigane (tsɪ'gɑːn, sɪ-) *n* **a** a Gypsy, esp. a Hungarian one. **b** (*as modifier*): *Tzigane music*. [C19: via F from Hungarian *czigány* Gypsy, from ?]

Tzu-po ('tsu:'pəʊ) *or* **Tzepo** ('tse'pəʊ) *n* a variant transliteration of the Chinese name for **Zibo**.

★ people and places

Uu

u or **U** (juː) n, pl **u's**, **U's**, or **Us**. **1** the 21st letter and fifth vowel of the English alphabet. **2** any of several speech sounds represented by this letter, as in *mute, cut*, or *minus*. **3a** something shaped like a U. **3b** (*in combination*): *a U-bolt*.

U *symbol for:* **1** united. **2** unionist. **3** university. **4** (in Britain) **4a** universal (used to describe a category of film certified as suitable for viewing by anyone). **4b** (*as modifier*): *a U certificate film.* **5** *Chem.* uranium. **6** *Biochem.* uracil. ◆ *adj* **7** *Brit. inf.* (esp. of language habits) characteristic of or appropriate to the upper class.

U. *abbrev. for:* **1** *Maths.* union. **2** unit. **3** united. **4** university. **5** upper.

UAE *abbrev. for* United Arab Emirates.

UAR *abbrev. for* United Arab Republic.

UB40 n (in Britain) **1** a registration card issued by the Department of Employment to a person registering as unemployed. **2** *Inf.* a person registered as unemployed.

Ubangi ★ (juːˈbæŋɡɪ) n a river in central Africa, flowing west and south, forming the border between the Democratic Republic of the Congo and the Central African Republic and the Republic of the Congo, into the River Congo. Length: (with the Uele) 2250 km (1400 miles). French name: **Oubangui.**

Ubangi-Shari ★ n a former name (until 1958) of the **Central African Republic.**

U-bend n a U-shaped bend in a pipe that traps water in the lower part of the U and prevents the escape of noxious fumes; trap.

uberrima fides (juˈbɛrɪmə ˈfaɪdiːz) n another name for **utmost good faith.** [L: utmost good faith]

ubiety (juːˈbaɪɪtɪ) n the condition of being in a particular place. [C17: from L *ubī* where + *-ety*, on the model of *society*]

Ubiquitarian (juːˌbɪkwɪˈtɛərɪən) n **1** a member of the Lutheran church who holds that Christ is no more present in the elements of the Eucharist than elsewhere, as he is present in all places at all times. ◆ *adj* **2** denoting or holding this belief. [C17: from L *ubīque* everywhere] ▸ **u,biqui'tarian,ism** n

ubiquitous (juːˈbɪkwɪtəs) *adj* having or seeming to have the ability to be everywhere at once. [C14: from L *ubīque* everywhere, from *ubī* where] ▸ **u'biquitously** *adv* ▸ **u'biquity** n

U-boat n a German submarine, esp. in World Wars I and II. [from G *U-Boot*, short for *Unterseeboot*, lit.: undersea boat]

UBR *abbrev. for* uniform business rate.

u.c. *Printing. abbrev. for* upper case.

UCAS (ˈjuːkæs) n (in Britain) *acronym for* Universities and Colleges Admission Service.

UCATT (in Britain) *abbrev. for* Union of Construction, Allied Trades and Technicians.

Ucayali ★ (*Spanish* ukaˈjali) n a river in E Peru, flowing north into the Marañón above Iquitos. Length: 1600 km (1000 miles).

UCCA (ˈʌkə) n (formerly, in Britain) *acronym for* Universities Central Council on Admissions.

Uccello ★ (*Italian* utˈtʃɛllo) n **Paolo** (ˈpaːolo). 1397–1475, Florentine painter noted for three paintings of *The Battle of San Romano, 1432* (1456–60).

UDA *abbrev. for* Ulster Defence Association.

Udaipur ★ (uːˈdaɪpʊə, ˈuːdaɪˌpʊə) n **1** Also called: **Mewar.** a former state of NW India: became part of Rajasthan in 1947. **2** a city in NW India, in S Rajasthan. Pop.: 308 571 (1991).

udal (ˈjuːdᵊl) n *Law.* a form of freehold possession of land existing in northern Europe before the introduction of the feudal system and still used in Orkney and Shetland. [C16: Orkney & Shetland dialect, from ON *othal*]

UDC (in Britain) *abbrev. for* Urban District Council.

udder (ˈʌdə) n the large baglike mammary gland of cows, sheep, etc., having two or more teats. [OE *ūder*]

UDI *abbrev. for* Unilateral Declaration of Independence.

Udine ★ (*Italian* ˈuːdine) n a city in NE Italy, in Friuli-Venezia Giulia region: partially damaged in an earthquake in 1976. Pop.: 98 872 (1990).

UDM (in Britain) *abbrev. for* Union of Democratic Mineworkers.

Udmurt Republic ★ (ˈʊdmʊət) n a constituent republic of W central Russia, in the basin of the middle Kama. Capital: Izhevsk. Pop.: 1 641 000 (1995 est.). Area: 42 100 sq. km (16 250 sq. miles).

udometer (juːˈdɒmɪtə) n another term for **rain gauge.** [C19: from F, from L *ūdus* damp]

UDR *abbrev. for* Ulster Defence Regiment.

UEFA (juːˈeɪfə, ˈjuːfə) n *acronym for* Union of European Football Associations.

Uele ★ (ˈweɪlə) n a river in central Africa, rising near the border between the Democratic Republic of the Congo and Uganda and flowing west to join the Bomu River and form the Ubangi River. Length: about 1100 km (700 miles).

uey (ˈjuːɪ) n, pl **ueys.** *Austral. sl.* a U-turn.

Ufa ★ (*Russian* uˈfa) n a city in W central Russia, capital of the Bashkir Republic: university (1957). Pop.: 1 094 000 (1995 est.).

Uffizi ★ (juːˈfɪtsɪ) n an art gallery in Florence; built by Giorgio Vasari in the 16th century and opened as a museum in 1765: contains chiefly Italian Renaissance paintings.

UFO (*sometimes* ˈjuːfəʊ) *abbrev. for* unidentified flying object.

ufology (ˌjuːˈfɒlədʒɪ) n the study of UFOs. ▸ **u'fologist** n

Uganda ★ (juːˈɡændə) n a republic in E Africa: British protectorate established in 1894–96; gained independence in 1962 and became a republic in 1963; a member of the Commonwealth. It consists mostly of a savanna plateau with part of Lake Victoria in the southeast and mountains in the southwest, reaching 5109 m (16 763 ft) in the Ruwenzori Range. Official language: English; Swahili, Luganda, and Luo are also widely spoken. Religion: chiefly Christian. Currency: Ugandan shilling. Capital: Kampala. Pop.: 20 605 000 (1997). Area: 235 886 sq. km (91 076 sq. miles). ▸ **U'gandan** *adj, n*

Ugaritic (ˌuːɡəˈrɪtɪk) n **1** an extinct Semitic language of N Syria. ◆ *adj* **2** of or relating to this language. [C19: after *Ugarit* (modern name: Ras Shamra), an ancient Syrian city-state]

UGC (in Britain) *abbrev. for* University Grants Committee.

ugh (ʊx, ʊh, ʌx) *interj* an exclamation of disgust, annoyance, or dislike.

UGLI (ˈʌɡlɪ) n, pl **UGLIS** or **UGLIES.** *Trademark.* a large juicy yellow-skinned citrus fruit of the Caribbean: a cross between a tangerine, grapefruit, and orange. Also called: **UGLI fruit.** [C20: prob. an alteration of UGLY, from its wrinkled skin]

uglify (ˈʌɡlɪˌfaɪ) *vb* **uglifies, uglifying, uglified.** to make or become ugly or more ugly. ▸ **,uglifi'cation** n

ugly (ˈʌɡlɪ) *adj* **uglier, ugliest. 1** of unpleasant or unsightly appearance. **2** repulsive or displeasing: *war is ugly.* **3** ominous or menacing: *an ugly situation.* **4** bad-tempered or

sullen: *an ugly mood.* [C13: from ON *uggligr* dreadful, from *ugga* fear]
► **'uglily** *adv* ► **'ugliness** *n*

ugly duckling *n* a person or thing, initially ugly or unpromising, that changes into something beautiful or admirable. [from *The Ugly Duckling* by Hans Christian Andersen]

Ugrian ('u:grɪən, 'ju:-) *adj* **1** of or relating to a subdivision of the Turanian people, who include the Samoyeds and Magyars. ◆ *n* **2** a member of this group. **3** another word for **Ugric**. [C19: from ORussian *Ugre* Hungarians]

Ugric ('u:grɪk, 'ju:-) *n* **1** one of the two branches of the Finno-Ugric family of languages, including Hungarian and some languages of NW Siberia. ◆ *adj* **2** of or relating to this group of languages or their speakers.

UHF *Radio. abbrev. for* ultrahigh frequency.

uh-huh ('ʌhʌ) *sentence substitute. Inf.* a less emphatic variant of **yes.**

uhlan ('u:la:n) *n History.* a member of a body of lancers first employed in the Polish army and later in W European armies. [C18: via G from Polish *ulan*, from Turkish *ōlan* young man]

Uhland (German 'u:lant) *n* **Johann Ludwig** (jo'han 'lu:tvɪç). 1787–1862, German romantic poet, esp. of lyrics and ballads.

UHT *abbrev. for* ultra-heat-treated (milk or cream).

uhuru (u'hu:ru:) *n* (esp. in E Africa) **1** national independence. **2** freedom. [C20: from Swahili]

Uigur *or* **Uighur** ('wi:guə) *n* **1** (*pl* **Uigur, Uigurs** *or* **Uighur, Uighurs**) a member of a Mongoloid people of NW China and adjacent parts of central Asia. **2** the language of this people, belonging to the Turkic branch of the Altaic family.
► **Ui'gurian, Ui'ghurian** *or* **Ui'guric, Ui'ghuric** *adj*

uillean pipes ('u:lɪən) *pl n* bagpipes developed in Ireland and operated by squeezing bellows under the arm. Also called: **Irish pipes, union pipes.** [C19: Irish *píob uilleann*, from *píob* pipe + *uileann* genitive sing of *uille* elbow]

Uinta Mountains ★ (ju'ɪntə) *pl n* a mountain range in NE Utah: part of the Rocky Mountains. Highest peak: Kings Peak, 4123 m (13 528 ft).

uitlander ('eɪt,landə, -,læn-) *n* (*sometimes cap.*) *S. African.* a foreigner. [C19: Afrik.: outlander]

Ujiji (u:'dʒi:dʒi) *n* a town in W Tanzania, on Lake Tanganyika: a former slave and ivory centre; the place where Stanley found Livingstone in 1871; merged with the town of Kigoma in the 1960s.

Ujjain ★ (u:'dʒeɪn) *n* a city in W central India, in Madhya Pradesh: one of the seven sacred cities of the Hindus; a major agricultural trade centre. Pop.: 362 266 (1991).

Ujung Pandang ★ ('u:dʒʊŋ pæn'dæŋ) *n* a port in central Indonesia, on SW Sulawesi: an important native port before Portuguese (16th century) and Dutch (17th century) control; capital of Dutch East Indonesia (1946–49); a major Indonesian distribution and transshipment port. Pop.: 913 916 (1990). Also called: **Makasar, Makassar, Macassar.**

UK *abbrev. for* United Kingdom.

ukase (ju:'keɪz) *n* **1** (in imperial Russia) an edict of the tsar. **2** a rare word for **edict.** [C18: from Russian *ukaz*, from *ukazat* to command]

UKCC *abbrev. for* United Kingdom Central Council for Nursing, Midwifery, and Health Visiting.

Ukr. *abbrev. for* Ukraine.

Ukraine ★ (ju:'kreɪn) *n* **the.** a republic in SE Europe, on the Black Sea and the Sea of Azov: from the 7th to 9th centuries the area was part of the Rurik kingdom and was subsequently part of the empires of the Mongols, Lithuania, Poland, and Russia; it was one of the four republics that originally formed the Soviet Union in 1922; became fully independent in 1991; consists chiefly of lowlands; mainly agricultural but has rich mineral resources. Official language: Ukrainian. Religion: believers are mainly Christian. Currency: hryvna. Capital: Kiev. Pop.: 50 668 000 (1997). Area 603 700 sq. km (231 990 sq. miles).

Ukrainian (ju:'kreɪnɪən) *adj* **1** of or relating to the Ukraine its people, or their language. ◆ *n* **2** the official language of the Ukraine: an East Slavonic language closely related to Russian. **3** a native or inhabitant of the Ukraine.

ukulele *or* **ukelele** (,ju:kə'leɪlɪ) *n* a small four-stringed guitar, esp. of Hawaii. [C19: from Hawaiian, lit.: jumping flea]

Ulan Bator ★ (u'la:n 'ba:tɔ:) *n* the capital of Mongolia, in the N central part: developed in the mid-17th century around the Da Khure monastery, residence until 1924 of successive "living Buddhas" (third in rank of Buddhist Lamaist leaders), and main junction of caravan routes across Mongolia; university (1942); industrial and commercial centre. Pop.: 680 000 (1994 est.). Former name (until 1924): **Urga.** Chinese name: **Kulun.**

Ulanova ★ (Russian u'lanəvə) *n* **Galina** (**Sergeyevna**) (ga'linə). 1910–98, Russian ballet dancer, who performed with the Leningrad Kirov ballet (1928–44) and the Moscow Bolshoi Ballet (1944–62).

Ulan-Ude ★ (u'la:n'u:de) *n* an industrial city in SE Russia capital of the Buryat Republic: an important rail junction. Pop.: 366 000 (1995 est.). Former name (until 1934): **Verkhne-Udinsk.**

Ulbricht ★ (German 'ʊlbrɪçt) *n* **Walter** ('valtər). 1893–1973, East German statesman; largely responsible for the establishment and development of East German communism.

ulcer ('ʌlsə) *n* **1** a disintegration of the surface of the skin or a mucous membrane resulting in an open sore that heals very slowly. **2** a source or element of corruption or evil. [C14: from L *ulcus*]

ulcerate ('ʌlsə,reɪt) *vb* **ulcerates, ulcerating, ulcerated.** to make or become ulcerous.
► **,ulce'ration** *n* ► **'ulcerative** *adj*

ulcerous ('ʌlsərəs) *adj* **1** relating to or characterized by ulcers. **2** being or having a corrupting influence.
► **'ulcerously** *adv*

-ule *suffix forming nouns.* indicating smallness: *globule.* [from L *-ulus,* dim. suffix]

Uleåborg ★ ('u:lio,bɔrjə) *n* the Swedish name for **Oulu.**

ulema ('u:lɪmə) *n* **1** a body of Muslim scholars or religious leaders. **2** a member of this body. [C17: from Ar. *'ulama* scholars, from *'alama* to know]

-ulent *suffix forming adjectives.* abundant or full of: *fraudulent.* [from L *-ulentus*]

ullage ('ʌlɪdʒ) *n* **1** the volume by which a liquid container falls short of being full. **2a** the quantity of liquid lost from a container due to leakage or evaporation. **2b** (in customs terminology) the amount of liquid remaining in a container after such loss. [C15: from OF *ouillage* filling of a cask, from *ouil* eye, from L *oculus* eye]

Ullswater ★ ('ʌlz,wɔ:tə) *n* a lake in NW England, in Cumbria in the Lake District. Length: 12 km (7.5 miles).

Ulm ★ (German ʊlm) *n* an industrial city in S Germany, in Baden-Württemberg on the Danube: a free imperial city (1155–1802). Pop.: 115 123 (1995 est.).

ulna ('ʌlnə) *n, pl* **ulnae** (-ni:) *or* **ulnas. 1** the inner and longer of the two bones of the human forearm. **2** the corresponding bone in other vertebrates. [C16: from L: elbow]
► **'ulnar** *adj*

ulnar nerve *n* a nerve situated along the inner side of the arm and passing close to the surface of the skin near the elbow.

ulotrichous (ju:'lɒtrɪkəs) *adj* having woolly or curly hair. [C19: from NL *Ulotrichī* (classification applied to humans having this type of hair), from Gk *oulothrix* from *oulos* curly + *thrix* hair]

ulster ('ʌlstə) *n* a man's heavy double-breasted overcoat with a belt or half-belt. [C19: from ULSTER]

Ulster ★ ('ʌlstə) *n* **1** a former kingdom and province of Ireland: passed to the English Crown in 1461; confiscated land given to English and Scottish Protestant settlers in the 17th century, giving rise to serious long-term conflict; partitioned in 1921, six counties forming Northern Ireland and three counties joining the Republic of Ireland. **2** an informal name for **Northern Ireland.**

★ people and places

Ulster Defence Association n (in Northern Ireland) a Loyalist paramilitary organization. Abbrev.: **UDA**.

Ulster Democratic Unionist Party n a Northern Irish political party advocating the maintenance of the Union with Great Britain.

Ulsterman ('ʌlstəmən) n, pl **Ulstermen**. a native or inhabitant of Ulster.
▶ **'Ulster,woman** fem n

Ulster Unionist Council n a Northern Irish political party advocating the maintenance of the Union with Great Britain.

ult. abbrev. for: **1** ultimate(ly). **2** ultimo.

ulterior (ʌl'tɪərɪə) adj **1** lying beneath or beyond what is revealed or supposed: ulterior motives. **2** succeeding, subsequent, or later. **3** lying beyond a certain line or point. [C17: from L: further, from ulter beyond]
▶ **ul'teriorly** adv

ultima ('ʌltɪmə) n the final syllable of a word. [from L: the last]

ultimate ('ʌltɪmɪt) adj **1** conclusive in a series or process; final: an ultimate question. **2** the highest or most significant: the ultimate goal. **3** elemental, fundamental, or essential. **4** most extreme: the ultimate abuse of human rights. **5** final or total: the ultimate cost. ◆ n **6** the most significant, highest, or greatest thing. [C17: from LL ultimāre to come to an end, from L ultimus last, from ulter distant]
▶ **'ultimately** adv ▶ **'ultimateness** n

ultima Thule ★ ('θju:lɪ) n **1** a region believed by ancient geographers to be the northernmost land. **2** any distant or unknown region. **3** a remote goal or aim. [L: the most distant Thule]

ultimatum (,ʌltɪ'meɪtəm) n, pl **ultimatums** or **ultimata** (-tə). **1** a final communication by a party setting forth conditions on which it insists, as during negotiations on some topic. **2** any final or peremptory demand and proposal. [C18: from NL, neuter of ultimatus ULTIMATE]

ultimo ('ʌltɪ,məʊ) adv Now rare except when abbreviated in formal correspondence. in or during the previous month: a letter of the 7th ultimo. Abbrev.: **ult**. [C16: from L ultimō in the last]

ultimogeniture (,ʌltɪməʊ'dʒɛnɪtʃə) n Law. a principle of inheritance whereby the youngest son succeeds to the estate of his ancestor. [C19: ultimo- from L ultimus last + LL genitūra a birth]

ultra ('ʌltrə) adj **1** extreme or immoderate, esp. in beliefs or opinions. ◆ n **2** an extremist. [C19: from L: beyond, from ulter distant]

ultra- prefix **1** beyond or surpassing a specified extent, range, or limit: ultramicroscopic. **2** extreme or extremely: ultramodern. [from L ultrā beyond]

ultracentrifuge (,ʌltrə'sɛntrɪ,fju:dʒ) n Chem. a high-speed centrifuge used to separate colloidal solutions.

ultraconservative (,ʌltrəkən'sɜ:vətɪv) adj **1** highly reactionary. ◆ n **2** a reactionary person.

ultra-distance n (modifier) Athletics. covering a distance in excess of 30 miles, often as part of a longer race or competition: an ultra-distance runner.

ultrafiche ('ʌltrə,fi:ʃ) n a sheet of film, usually the size of a filing card, that is similar to a microfiche but has a much larger number of microcopies. [C20: from ULTRA- + F fiche small card]

ultrahigh frequency (,ʌltrə,haɪ) n a radio-frequency band or radio frequency lying between 3000 and 300 megahertz. Abbrev.: **UHF**.

ultraism ('ʌltrə,ɪzəm) n extreme philosophy, belief, or action.
▶ **'ultraist** n, adj

ultramarine (,ʌltrəmə'ri:n) n **1** a blue pigment obtained by powdering natural lapis lazuli or made synthetically: used in paints, printing ink, plastics, etc. **2** a vivid blue colour. ◆ adj **3** of the colour ultramarine. **4** from across the seas. [C17: from Med. L ultramarinus, from ultrā beyond + mare sea; so called because the lapis lazuli from which the pigment was made was imported from Asia]

ultramicroscope (,ʌltrə'maɪkrə,skəʊp) n a microscope used for studying colloids, in which the sample is illumi-

nated from the side and colloidal particles are seen as bright points on a dark background.

ultramicroscopic (,ʌltrə,maɪkrə'skɒpɪk) adj **1** too small to be seen with an optical microscope. **2** of or relating to an ultramicroscope.

ultramodern (,ʌltrə'mɒdən) adj extremely modern.
▶ ,ultra'modernism n ▶ ,ultra'modernist n ▶ ,ultra,modern'istic adj

ultramontane (,ʌltrəmɒn'teɪn) adj **1** on the other side of the mountains, esp. the Alps, from the speaker or writer. **2** of or relating to a movement in the Roman Catholic Church which favours the centralized authority and influence of the pope as opposed to local independence. ◆ n **3** a person from beyond the mountains, esp. the Alps. **4** a member of the ultramontane party of the Roman Catholic Church.

ultramundane (,ʌltrə'mʌndeɪn) adj extending beyond the world, this life, or the universe.

ultranationalism (,ʌltrə'næʃnə,lɪzəm) n extreme devotion to one's own nation.
▶ ,ultra'national adj ▶ ,ultra'nationalist adj, n

ultrashort (,ʌltrə'ʃɔ:t) adj (of a radio wave) having a wavelength shorter than 10 metres.

ultrasonic (,ʌltrə'sɒnɪk) adj of, concerned with, or producing waves with the same nature as sound waves but frequencies above audio frequencies.
▶ ,ultra'sonically adv

ultrasonics (,ʌltrə'sɒnɪks) n (functioning as sing) the branch of physics concerned with ultrasonic waves. Also called: **supersonics**.

ultrasound ('ʌltrə,saʊnd) n ultrasonic waves at frequencies above the audible range (above about 20 kHz), used in cleaning metallic parts, echo sounding, medical diagnosis and therapy, etc.

ultrasound scanner n a device used to examine an internal bodily structure by the use of ultrasonic waves, esp. for the diagnosis of abnormality in a fetus.

ultrastructure ('ʌltrə,strʌktʃə) n the minute structure of an organ, tissue, or cell, as revealed by microscopy.

ultraviolet (,ʌltrə'vaɪəlɪt) n **1** the part of the electromagnetic spectrum with wavelengths shorter than light but longer than X-rays; in the range 0.4×10^{-6} and 1×10^{-8} metres. ◆ adj **2** of, relating to, or consisting of radiation lying in the ultraviolet: ultraviolet radiation; ultraviolet spectroscopy. Abbrev.: **UV**.

ultraviolet astronomy n the study of radiation from celestial sources in the wavelength range 91.2 to 320 nanometres.

ultra vires ('vaɪri:z) adv, adj (predicative) Law. beyond the legal power of a person, corporation, agent, etc. [L, lit.: beyond strength]

ultravirus (,ʌltrə'vaɪrəs) n a virus small enough to pass through the finest filter.

ululate ('ju:lju,leɪt) vb **ululates, ululating, ululated**. (intr) to howl or wail, as with grief. [C17: from L ululāre to howl, from ulula screech owl]
▶ **'ululant** adj ▶ **,ulu'lation** n

Uluru ★ (,u:lə'ru:) n the world's largest monolith, in the Northern Territory of Australia. Height: 330 m (1100 ft). Base circumference: 9 km (5.6 miles). Former name: **Ayers Rock**.

Ulyanovsk ★ (Russian ulj'janəfsk) n the former name (1924–91) of **Simbirsk**.

Ulysses ★ ('ju:lɪ,si:z, ju:'lɪsi:z) n the Latin name of **Odysseus**.

Umar ★ ('u:ma:) n a variant transliteration of the Arabic name for **Omar**.

Umayyad ★ (u:'maɪjæd) n a variant spelling of **Omayyad**.

umbel ('ʌmbᵊl) n a racemose inflorescence, characteristic of umbelliferous plants, in which the flowers arise from the same point in the main stem and have stalks of the same length, to give a cluster with the youngest flowers at the centre. [C16: from L umbella a sunshade, from umbra shade]
▶ **umbellate** ('ʌmbɪlɪt, -,leɪt) or **umbellar** (ʌm'bɛlə) adj
▶ **umbellule** (ʌm'bɛlju:l) n

umbelliferous (ˌʌmbɪˈlɪfərəs) *adj* of or belonging to a family of herbaceous plants and shrubs, typically having hollow stems, divided or compound leaves, and flowers in umbels: includes fennel, parsley, carrot, and parsnip. [C17: from NL, from L *umbella* sunshade + *ferre* to bear]
▶ um'bellifer *n*

umber (ˈʌmbə) *n* **1** any of various natural brown earths containing ferric oxide together with lime and oxides of aluminium, manganese, and silicon. **2** any of the dark brown to greenish-brown colours produced by this pigment. **3** *Obs.* shade. ◆ *adj* **4** of, relating to, or stained with umber. [C16: from F (*terre d'*)*ombre* or It. (*terra di*) *ombra* shadow (earth), from L *umbra* shade]

Umberto I ★ (*Italian* umˈbɛrto) *n* 1844–1900, king of Italy (1878–1900); son of Victor Emmanuel II: assassinated at Monza.

umbilical (ʌmˈbɪlɪkᵊl, ˌʌmbɪˈlaɪkᵊl) *adj* **1** of, relating to, or resembling the umbilicus or the umbilical cord. **2** in the region of the umbilicus: *an umbilical hernia.*

umbilical cord *n* **1** the long flexible tubelike structure connecting a fetus with the placenta. **2** any flexible cord, tube, or cable, as between an astronaut walking in space and his spacecraft.

umbilicate (ʌmˈbɪlɪkɪt, -ˌkeɪt) *adj* **1** having an umbilicus. **2** having a central depression: *an umbilicate leaf.* **3** shaped like a navel, as some bacterial colonies.
▶ um,bili'cation *n*

umbilicus (ʌmˈbɪlɪkəs, ˌʌmbɪˈlaɪkəs) *n*, *pl* **umbilici** (-ˈbɪlɪˌsaɪ, -bɪˈlaɪsaɪ). **1** *Biol.* a hollow or navel-like structure, such as the cavity at the base of a gastropod shell. **2** *Anat.* a technical name for the **navel**. [C18: from L: navel, centre]

umble pie (ˈʌmbᵊl) *n* See **humble pie** (sense 1).

umbles (ˈʌmbᵊlz) *pl n* See **numbles**.

umbo (ˈʌmbəʊ) *n*, *pl* **umbones** (ʌmˈbəʊniːz) *or* **umbos. 1** *Bot., anat.* a small hump, prominence, or convex area, as in certain mushrooms, bivalve molluscs, and the outer surface of the eardrum. **2** a large projecting central boss on a shield, esp. on a Saxon shield. [C18: from L: projecting piece]
▶ **umbonate** (ˈʌmbənɪt, -ˌneɪt), **umbonal** (ˈʌmbənᵊl), *or* **umbonic** (ʌmˈbɒnɪk) *adj*

umbra (ˈʌmbrə) *n*, *pl* **umbrae** (-briː) *or* **umbras. 1** a region of complete shadow resulting from the obstruction of light by an opaque object, esp. the shadow cast by the moon onto the earth during a solar eclipse. **2** the darker inner region of a sunspot. [C16: from L: shade]
▶ 'umbral *adj*

umbrage (ˈʌmbrɪdʒ) *n* **1** displeasure or resentment; offence (in **give** *or* **take umbrage**). **2** the foliage of trees, considered as providing shade. **3** *Rare.* shadow or shade. [C15: from OF, from L *umbrāticus* relating to shade, from *umbra* shade]

umbrageous (ʌmˈbreɪdʒəs) *adj* **1** shady or shading. **2** *Rare.* easily offended.

umbrella (ʌmˈbrelə) *n* **1** a portable device used for protection against rain, snow, etc., and consisting of a light canopy supported on a collapsible metal frame mounted on a central rod. **2** the flattened cone-shaped body of a jellyfish. **3** a protective shield or screen, esp. of aircraft or gunfire. **4** anything that has the effect of a protective screen, general cover, or organizing agency. [C17: from It. *ombrella*, dim. of *ombra* shade; see UMBRA]
▶ um'brella-ˌlike *adj*

umbrella pine *n* another name for **stone pine**.

umbrella stand *n* an upright rack or stand for umbrellas.

umbrella tree *n* **1** a North American magnolia having long leaves clustered into an umbrella formation at the ends of the branches and having unpleasant-smelling white flowers. **2** Also called: **umbrella bush.** any of various trees or shrubs having umbrella-shaped leaves or growing in an umbrella-like cluster.

Umbria ★ (ˈʌmbrɪə; *Italian* ˈumbrja) *n* a mountainous region of central Italy, in the valley of the Tiber. Pop.: 819 172 (1994 est.). Area: 8456 sq. km (3265 sq. miles).

Umbrian (ˈʌmbrɪən) *adj* **1** of or relating to Umbria, its inhabitants, or the ancient language once spoken there. **2** of or relating to a Renaissance school of painting that included Raphael. ◆ *n* **3** a native or inhabitant of Umbria. **4** an extinct language of ancient S Italy.

umfazi (ˌumˈfɑːzɪ) *n S. African.* a Black married woman [from Bantu]

umiak *or* **oomiak** (ˈuːmɪˌæk) *n* a large open boat made of stretched skins, used by Eskimos. [C18: from Eskimo boat for the use of women]

umlaut (ˈumlaut) *n* **1** the mark (¨) placed over a vowel in some languages, such as German, indicating modification in the quality of the vowel. **2** (esp. in Germanic languages) the change of a vowel within a word brought about by the assimilating influence of a vowel or semivowel in a preceding or following syllable. [C19: G from *um* around (in the sense of changing places) + *Laut* sound]

umlungu (ˌumˈluŋgu) *n S. African.* a White man: used esp. as a term of address. [from Bantu]

umpire (ˈʌmpaɪə) *n* **1** an official who rules on the playing of a game, as in cricket. **2** a person who rules on or judges disputes between contesting parties. ◆ *vb* **umpires, umpiring, umpired. 3** to act as umpire in (a game, dispute, or controversy). [C15: by mistaken division from *noumpere*, from OF *nomper* not one of a pair, from *nom-* non- not + *per* equal]

umpteen (ˌʌmpˈtiːn) *determiner Inf.* **a** very many: *umpteen things to do.* **b** (*as pronoun*): *umpteen of them came.* [C20 from *umpty* a great deal (?from *-enty* as in *twenty*) + *-teen*]
▶ ˌump'teenth *n, adj*

Umtali ★ (umˈtɑːlɪ) *n* the former name (until 1982) of Mutare.

Umtata ★ (umˈtɑːtə) *n* a city in SE South Africa. Pop. 80 000 (latest est.).

UN *abbrev.* for United Nations.

un-[1] *prefix* (*freely used with adjectives, participles, and their derivative adverbs and nouns: less frequently used with certain other nouns*) not; contrary to; opposite of: *uncertain; untidiness; unbelief; untruth.* [from OE *on-, un-*]

un-[2] *prefix forming verbs.* **1** denoting reversal of an action or state: *uncover; untangle.* **2** denoting removal from, release or deprivation: *unharness; unthrone.* **3** (intensifier): *unloose.* [from OE *un-, on-*]

'un *or* **un** (ən) *pron* a spelling of **one** intended to reflect a dialectal or informal pronunciation: *that's a big 'un.*

unable (ʌnˈeɪbᵊl) *adj* (*postpositive; foll. by to*) lacking the necessary power, ability, or authority (to do something); not able.

unaccented (ˌʌnækˈsɛntɪd) *adj* not stressed or emphasized in pronunciation.

unaccountable (ˌʌnəˈkaʊntəbᵊl) *adj* **1** allowing of no explanation; inexplicable. **2** extraordinary: *an unaccountable fear of heights.* **3** not accountable or answerable to.
▶ ˌunac,counta'bility *n* ▶ ˌunac'countably *adv*

unaccustomed (ˌʌnəˈkʌstəmd) *adj* **1** (foll. by *to*) not used (to): *unaccustomed to pain.* **2** not familiar.
▶ ˌunac'customedness *n*

una corda (ˈuːnə ˈkɔːdə) *adj, adv Music.* (of the piano) to be played with the soft pedal depressed. [It., lit.: one string; the pedal moves the mechanism so that only one string of the three tuned to each note is struck by the hammer]

unadopted (ˌʌnəˈdɒptɪd) *adj* **1** (of a child) not adopted **2** *Brit.* (of a road, etc.) not maintained by a local authority.

unadvised (ˌʌnədˈvaɪzd) *adj* **1** rash or unwise. **2** not having received advice.
▶ ˌunadvisedly (ˌʌnədˈvaɪzɪdlɪ) *adv* ▶ ˌunad'visedness *n*

unaffected[1] (ˌʌnəˈfɛktɪd) *adj* unpretentious, natural, or sincere.
▶ ˌunaf'fectedly *adv* ▶ ˌunaf'fectedness *n*

unaffected[2] (ˌʌnəˈfɛktɪd) *adj* not affected.

Unalaska Island ★ (ˌuːnəˈlæskə) *n* a large volcanic is-

★ people and places

land in SW Alaska, in the Aleutian Islands. Length: 120 km (75 miles). Greatest width: about 40 km (25 miles).

nalienable (ʌnˈeɪljənəbᵊl) *adj Law*. a variant of **inalienable**.

n-American *adj* 1 not in accordance with the aims, ideals, customs, etc., of the US. 2 against the interests of the US.
► ˌun-Aˈmericanism *n*

namuno ★ (*Spanish* unaˈmuno) *n* **Miguel de** (miˈɣel de). 1864–1936, Spanish philosopher and writer.

nanimous (juːˈnænɪməs) *adj* 1 in complete agreement. 2 characterized by complete agreement: *a unanimous decision.* [C17: from L, from *ūnus* one + *animus* mind]
► uˈnanimously *adv* ► unanimity (ˌjuːnəˈnɪmɪtɪ) *n*

napproachable (ˌʌnəˈprəʊtʃəbᵊl) *adj* 1 discouraging intimacy, friendliness, etc.; aloof. 2 inaccessible. 3 not to be rivalled.
► ˌunapˈproachableness *n* ► ˌunapˈproachably *adv*

nappropriated (ˌʌnəˈprəʊprɪˌeɪtɪd) *adj* 1 not set aside for specific use. 2 *Accounting*. designating that portion of the profits of a business enterprise that is retained in the business and not withdrawn by the proprietor. 3 (of property) not having been taken into any person's possession or control.

napt (ʌnˈæpt) *adj* 1 (*usually postpositive; often foll. by for*) not suitable or qualified; unfitted. 2 mentally slow. 3 (*postpositive; may take an infinitive*) not disposed or likely (to).
► unˈaptly *adv* ► unˈaptness *n*

narm (ʌnˈɑːm) *vb* a less common word for **disarm**.

narmed (ʌnˈɑːmd) *adj* 1 without weapons. 2 (of animals and plants) having no claws, prickles, spines, thorns, or similar structures.

nassailable (ˌʌnəˈseɪləbᵊl) *adj* 1 not able to be attacked. 2 undeniable or irrefutable.
► ˌunasˈsailableness *n* ► ˌunasˈsailably *adv*

nassuming (ˌʌnəˈsjuːmɪŋ) *adj* modest or unpretentious.
► ˌunasˈsumingly *adv* ► ˌunasˈsumingness *n*

nattached (ˌʌnəˈtætʃt) *adj* 1 not connected with any specific thing, body, group, etc. 2 not engaged or married. 3 (of property) not seized or held as security.

navailing (ˌʌnəˈveɪlɪŋ) *adj* useless or futile.
► ˌunaˈvailingly *adv*

navoidable (ˌʌnəˈvɔɪdəbᵊl) *adj* 1 unable to be avoided. 2 *Law*. not capable of being declared null and void.
► ˌunaˌvoidaˈbility *or* ˌunaˈvoidableness *n* ► ˌunaˈvoidably *adv*

naware (ˌʌnəˈweə) *adj* 1 (*postpositive*) not aware or conscious (of): *unaware of the danger he ran across the road.*
◆ *adv* 2 a variant of **unawares**.
► ˌunaˈwareness *n*

nawares (ˌʌnəˈweəz) *adv* 1 without prior warning or plan: *she caught him unawares.* 2 without knowing: *he lost it unawares.*

nbacked (ʌnˈbækt) *adj* 1 (of a book, chair, etc.) not having a back. 2 bereft of support, esp. on a financial basis. 3 not supported by bets.

nbalance (ʌnˈbæləns) *vb* **unbalances, unbalancing, unbalanced**. (*tr*) 1 to upset the equilibrium or balance of. 2 to disturb the mental stability of (a person or his mind).
◆ *n* 3 imbalance or instability.

nbalanced (ʌnˈbælənst) *adj* 1 lacking balance. 2 irrational or unsound; erratic. 3 mentally disordered or deranged. 4 biased; one-sided: *unbalanced reporting.* 5 (in double-entry book-keeping) not having total debit balances equal to total credit balances.

nbar (ʌnˈbɑː) *vb* **unbars, unbarring, unbarred**. (*tr*) 1 to take away a bar or bars from. 2 to unfasten bars, locks, etc., from (a door); open.

nbearable (ʌnˈbeərəbᵊl) *adj* not able to be borne or endured.
► unˈbearably *adv*

nbeatable (ʌnˈbiːtəbᵊl) *adj* unable to be defeated or outclassed; surpassingly excellent.

nbeaten (ʌnˈbiːtᵊn) *adj* 1 having suffered no defeat. 2 not worn down; untrodden. 3 not mixed or stirred by beating: *unbeaten eggs.*

unbecoming (ˌʌnbɪˈkʌmɪŋ) *adj* 1 unsuitable or inappropriate, esp. through being unattractive: *an unbecoming hat.* 2 (when *postpositive*, usually foll. by *of* or an object) not proper or seemly (for): *manners unbecoming a lady.*
► ˌunbeˈcomingly *adv* ► ˌunbeˈcomingness *n*

unbeknown (ˌʌnbɪˈnəʊn) *adv* (*sentence modifier;* foll. by *to*) without the knowledge (of a person): *unbeknown to him she had left the country.* Also (esp. Brit.): **unbeknownst**. [C17: from arch. *beknown* known]

unbelief (ˌʌnbɪˈliːf) *n* disbelief or rejection of belief.

unbelievable (ˌʌnbɪˈliːvəbᵊl) *adj* unable to be believed; incredible.
► ˌunbeˌlievaˈbility *n* ► ˌunbeˈlievably *adv*

unbeliever (ˌʌnbɪˈliːvə) *n* a person who does not believe, esp. in religious matters.

unbelieving (ˌʌnbɪˈliːvɪŋ) *adj* 1 not believing; sceptical. 2 proceeding from or characterized by scepticism.
► ˌunbeˈlievingly *adv*

unbend (ʌnˈbend) *vb* **unbends, unbending, unbent**. 1 to release or be released from the restraints of formality and ceremony. 2 *Inf.* to relax (the mind) or (of the mind) to become relaxed. 3 to straighten out from an originally bent shape. 4 (*tr*) *Naut.* 4a to remove (a sail) from a stay, mast, etc. 4b to untie (a rope, etc.) or cast (a cable) loose.

unbending (ʌnˈbendɪŋ) *adj* 1 rigid or inflexible. 2 characterized by sternness or severity: *an unbending rule.*
► unˈbendingly *adv* ► unˈbendingness *n*

unbent (ʌnˈbent) *vb* 1 the past tense and past participle of **unbend**. ◆ *adj* 2 not bent or bowed. 3 not compelled to give way by force.

unbidden (ʌnˈbɪdᵊn) *adj* 1 not ordered or commanded; voluntary or spontaneous. 2 not invited or asked.

unbind (ʌnˈbaɪnd) *vb* **unbinds, unbinding, unbound**. (*tr*) 1 to set free from restraining bonds or chains. 2 to unfasten or make loose (a bond, etc.).

unblessed (ʌnˈblest) *adj* 1 deprived of blessing. 2 cursed or evil. 3 unhappy or wretched.
► unblessedness (ʌnˈblesɪdnɪs) *n*

unblushing (ʌnˈblʌʃɪŋ) *adj* immodest or shameless.
► unˈblushingly *adv*

unbolt (ʌnˈbəʊlt) *vb* (*tr*) 1 to unfasten a bolt of (a door). 2 to undo (the nut) on a bolt.

unbolted (ʌnˈbəʊltɪd) *adj* (of grain, meal, or flour) not sifted.

unborn (ʌnˈbɔːn) *adj* 1 not yet born or brought to birth. 2 still to come in the future: *the unborn world.*

unbosom (ʌnˈbuzəm) *vb* (*tr*) to relieve (oneself) of (secrets, etc.) by telling someone. [C16: from UN-² + BOSOM (in the sense: seat of the emotions)]

unbounded (ʌnˈbaʊndɪd) *adj* having no boundaries or limits.
► unˈboundedly *adv* ► unˈboundedness *n*

unbowed (ʌnˈbaʊd) *adj* 1 not bowed or bent. 2 free or unconquered.

unbridled (ʌnˈbraɪdᵊld) *adj* 1 with all restraints removed. 2 (of a horse) wearing no bridle.
► unˈbridledly *adv* ► unˈbridledness *n*

unbroken (ʌnˈbrəʊkən) *adj* 1 complete or whole. 2 continuous or incessant. 3 undaunted in spirit. 4 (of animals, esp. horses) not tamed; wild. 5 not disturbed or upset: *the unbroken quiet of the afternoon.* 6 (of a record, esp. at sport) not improved upon.
► unˈbrokenly *adv* ► unˈbrokenness *n*

unbundling (ʌnˈbʌndlɪŋ) *n Commerce*. the takeover of a large conglomerate with a view to retaining the core business and selling off some of the subsidiaries to help finance the takeover.

unburden (ʌnˈbɜːdᵊn) *vb* (*tr*) 1 to remove a load or burden from. 2 to relieve or make free (one's mind, oneself, etc.) of a worry, trouble, etc., by revelation or confession.

unbutton (ʌnˈbʌtᵊn) *vb* to undo by unfastening (the buttons) of (a garment).

unbuttoned (ʌnˈbʌtᵊnd) *adj* 1 with buttons not fastened. **2** *Inf.* uninhibited; unrestrained: *hours of unbuttoned self-revelation.*

uncalled-for (ˌʌnˈkɔːldfɔː) *adj* unnecessary or unwarranted.

uncanny (ʌnˈkænɪ) *adj* **1** characterized by apparently supernatural wonder, horror, etc. **2** beyond what is normal: *uncanny accuracy.*
▸ un**'cannily** *adv* ▸ un**'canniness** *n*

uncap (ʌnˈkæp) *vb* **uncaps, uncapping, uncapped. 1** (*tr*) to remove a cap or top from (a container): *to uncap a bottle.* **2** to remove a cap from (the head).

uncared-for (ˌʌnˈkɛədfɔː) *adj* not cared for; neglected.

unceremonious (ˌʌnsɛrɪˈməʊnɪəs) *adj* without ceremony; informal, abrupt, rude, or undignified.
▸ ˌunceremoniously *adv* ▸ ˌuncereˈmoniousness *n*

uncertain (ʌnˈsɜːtᵊn) *adj* **1** not able to be accurately known or predicted: *the issue is uncertain.* **2** (when *postpositive*, often foll. by *of*) not sure or confident (about): *he was uncertain of the date.* **3** not precisely determined or decided: *uncertain plans.* **4** not to be depended upon: *an uncertain vote.* **5** liable to variation; changeable: *the weather is uncertain.* **6 in no uncertain terms. 6a** unambiguously. **6b** forcefully.
▸ un**'certainly** *adv*

uncertainty (ʌnˈsɜːtᵊntɪ) *n, pl* **uncertainties. 1** Also: **uncertainness.** the state or condition of being uncertain. **2** an uncertain matter, contingency, etc.

uncertainty principle *n* **the.** the principle that energy and time or position and momentum, cannot both be accurately measured simultaneously. Also called: **Heisenberg uncertainty principle, indeterminacy principle.**

uncharted (ʌnˈtʃɑːtɪd) *adj* (of a physical or nonphysical region or area) not yet mapped, surveyed, or investigated: *uncharted waters; the uncharted depths of the mind.*

unchartered (ʌnˈtʃɑːtəd) *adj* **1** not authorized by charter; unregulated. **2** unauthorized, lawless, or irregular.

USAGE NOTE Care should be taken not to use *unchartered* where *uncharted* is meant: *uncharted* (not *unchartered*) *territory.*

---

unchristian (ʌnˈkrɪstʃən) *adj* **1** not in accordance with the principles or ethics of Christianity. **2** non-Christian or pagan.
▸ un**'christianly** *adv*

unchurch (ʌnˈtʃɜːtʃ) *vb* (*tr*) **1** to excommunicate. **2** to remove church status from (a building).

uncial (ˈʌnsɪəl) *adj* **1** of, relating to, or written in majuscule letters, as used in Greek and Latin manuscripts of the third to ninth centuries, that resemble modern capitals, but are characterized by much greater curvature. ◆ *n* **2** an uncial letter or manuscript. [C17: from LL *unciālēs litterae* letters an inch long, from L *unciālis*, from *uncia* one twelfth, inch]
▸ **'uncially** *adv*

uncinate (ˈʌnsɪnɪt, -ˌneɪt) *adj Biol.* shaped like a hook: *the uncinate process of the ribs of certain vertebrates.* [C18: from L *uncinātus*, from *uncīnus* a hook, from *uncus*]

uncircumcised (ʌnˈsɜːkəmˌsaɪzd) *adj* **1** not circumcised. **2** not Jewish; gentile. **3** spiritually unpurified.
▸ ˌuncircumˈcision *n*

uncivil (ʌnˈsɪvəl) *adj* **1** lacking civility or good manners. **2** an obsolete word for **uncivilized.**
▸ **uncivility** (ˌʌnsɪˈvɪlɪtɪ) *n* ▸ un**'civilly** *adv*

uncivilized *or* **uncivilised** (ʌnˈsɪvɪˌlaɪzd) *adj* **1** (of a tribe or people) not yet civilized, esp. not having developed a written language. **2** lacking culture or sophistication.
▸ un**'civil,izedness** *or* un**'civil,isedness** *n*

unclad (ʌnˈklæd) *adj* having no clothes on; naked.

unclasp (ʌnˈklɑːsp) *vb* **1** (*tr*) to unfasten the clasp of (something). **2** to release one's grip (upon an object).

uncle (ˈʌŋkᵊl) *n* **1** a brother of one's father or mother. **2** the husband of one's aunt. **3** a term of address sometimes used by children for a male friend of their parents.

4 *Sl.* a pawnbroker. ◆ Related adj: **avuncular.** [C13: from OF *oncle*, from L *avunculus*]

unclean (ʌnˈkliːn) *adj* lacking moral, spiritual, or physical cleanliness.
▸ un**'cleanness** *n*

uncleanly[1] (ʌnˈkliːnlɪ) *adv* in an unclean manner.

uncleanly[2] (ʌnˈklɛnlɪ) *adj* characterized by an absence of cleanliness.
▸ un**'cleanliness** *n*

Uncle Sam (sæm) *n* a personification of the government of the United States. [C19: apparently a humorous interpretation of the letters stamped on army supply boxes during the War of 1812: *US*]

Uncle Tom (tɒm) *n Inf., derog.* a Black person whose behaviour towards White people is regarded as servile [C20: after the main character of H. B. Stowe's novel *Uncle Tom's Cabin* (1852)]
▸ **'Uncle 'Tom,ism** *n*

unclose (ʌnˈkləʊz) *vb* **uncloses, unclosing, unclosed. 1** to open or cause to open. **2** to come or bring to light.

unclothe (ʌnˈkləʊð) *vb* **unclothes, unclothing, unclothed** *or* **unclad.** (*tr*) **1** to take off garments from; strip. **2** to uncover or lay bare.

uncoil (ʌnˈkɔɪl) *vb* to unwind or become unwound; untwist.

uncomfortable (ʌnˈkʌmftəbᵊl) *adj* **1** not comfortable. **2** feeling or causing discomfort or unease; disquieting.
▸ un**'comfortableness** *n* ▸ un**'comfortably** *adv*

uncommitted (ˌʌnkəˈmɪtɪd) *adj* not bound or pledged to a specific opinion, course of action, or cause.

uncommon (ʌnˈkɒmən) *adj* **1** outside or beyond normal experience, etc. **2** in excess of what is normal: *an uncommon liking for honey.* ◆ *adv* **3** an archaic word for **uncommonly** (sense 2).
▸ un**'commonness** *n*

uncommonly (ʌnˈkɒmənlɪ) *adv* **1** in an uncommon or unusual manner or degree; rarely. **2** (intensifier): *you're uncommonly friendly.*

uncommunicative (ˌʌnkəˈmjuːnɪkətɪv) *adj* disinclined to talk or give information or opinions.
▸ ˌuncomˈmunicatively *adv* ▸ ˌuncomˈmunicativeness *n*

uncompromising (ʌnˈkɒmprəˌmaɪzɪŋ) *adj* not prepared to give ground or to compromise.
▸ un**'compro,misingly** *adv*

unconcern (ˌʌnkənˈsɜːn) *n* apathy or indifference.

unconcerned (ˌʌnkənˈsɜːnd) *adj* **1** lacking in concern or involvement. **2** untroubled.
▸ **unconcernedly** (ˌʌnkənˈsɜːnɪdlɪ) *adv*

unconditional (ˌʌnkənˈdɪʃənᵊl) *adj* without conditions or limitations; total: *unconditional surrender.*
▸ ˌuncon**'ditionally** *adv*

unconditioned (ˌʌnkənˈdɪʃənd) *adj* **1** *Psychol.* characterizing an innate reflex and the stimulus and response that form parts of it. **2** *Metaphysics.* unrestricted by conditions; absolute. **3** without limitations.
▸ ˌuncon**'ditionedness** *n*

unconformable (ˌʌnkənˈfɔːməbᵊl) *adj* **1** not conformable or conforming. **2** (of rock strata) consisting of a series of recent strata resting on different, much older rocks.
▸ ˌuncon,formaˈbility *or* ˌuncon**'formableness** *n* ▸ ˌuncon**'formably** *adv* ▸ ˌuncon**'formity** *n*

unconscionable (ʌnˈkɒnʃənəbᵊl) *adj* **1** unscrupulous or unprincipled: *an unconscionable liar.* **2** immoderate or excessive: *unconscionable demands.*
▸ un**'conscionably** *adv*

unconscious (ʌnˈkɒnʃəs) *adj* **1** lacking normal sensory awareness of the environment; insensible. **2** not aware of one's actions, behaviour, etc.: *unconscious of his bad manners.* **3** characterized by lack of awareness or intention: *an unconscious blunder.* **4** coming from or produced by the unconscious: *unconscious resentment.* ◆ *n* **5** *Psychoanal.* the part of the mind containing instincts, impulses, images, and ideas that are not available for direct examination.
▸ un**'consciously** *adv*

unconstitutional (ˌʌnkɒnstɪˈtjuːʃənˀl) *adj* at variance with or not permitted by a constitution.
  ▸ ˌunconstiˌtutionˈality *n*

unconventional (ˌʌnkənˈvɛnʃənˀl) *adj* not conforming to accepted rules or standards.
  ▸ ˌunconˌventionˈality *n* ▸ ˌunconˈventionally *adv*

uncool (ʌnˈkuːl) *adj Sl.* **1** unsophisticated; unfashionable. **2** excitable; tense; not cool.

uncork (ʌnˈkɔːk) *vb* (*tr*) **1** to draw the cork from (a bottle, etc.). **2** to release or unleash (emotions, etc.).

uncountable (ʌnˈkaʊntəbˀl) *adj* **1** too many to be counted; innumerable. **2** *Linguistics.* denoting a noun that does not refer to an isolable object. See **mass noun**.

uncounted (ʌnˈkaʊntɪd) *adj* **1** unable to be counted; innumerable. **2** not counted.

uncouple (ʌnˈkʌpˀl) *vb* **uncouples, uncoupling, uncoupled. 1** to disconnect or unfasten or become disconnected or unfastened. **2** (*tr*) to set loose; release.

uncouth (ʌnˈkuːθ) *adj* lacking in good manners, refinement, or grace. [OE *uncūth*, from UN-[1] + *cūth* familiar]
  ▸ unˈcouthly *adv* ▸ unˈcouthness *n*

uncover (ʌnˈkʌvə) *vb* **1** (*tr*) to remove the cover, cap, top, etc., from. **2** to reveal or disclose: *to uncover a plot.* **3** to take off (one's head covering), esp. as a mark of respect.

uncovered (ʌnˈkʌvəd) *adj* **1** not covered; revealed or bare. **2** not protected by insurance, security, etc. **3** with hat off, as a mark of respect.

UNCTAD *abbrev.* for United Nations Conference on Trade and Development.

unction (ˈʌŋkʃən) *n* **1** *Chiefly RC & Eastern Churches.* the act of anointing with oil in sacramental ceremonies, in the conferring of holy orders. **2** excessive suavity or affected charm. **3** an ointment or unguent. **4** anything soothing. [C14: from L *unctiō* an anointing, from *ungere* to anoint]
  ▸ ˈunctionless *adj*

unctuous (ˈʌŋktjʊəs) *adj* **1** slippery or greasy. **2** affecting an oily charm. [C14: from Med. L *unctuōsus*, from L *unctum* ointment, from *ungere* to anoint]
  ▸ unctuosity (ˌʌŋktjʊˈɒsɪtɪ) *or* ˈunctuousness *n* ▸ ˈunctuously *adv*

uncut (ʌnˈkʌt) *adj* **1** (of a book) not having the edges of its pages trimmed or slit. **2** (of a gemstone) not cut and faceted. **3** not abridged.

undamped (ʌnˈdæmpt) *adj* **1** (of an oscillating system) having unrestricted motion; not damped. **2** not repressed, discouraged, or subdued.

undaunted (ʌnˈdɔːntɪd) *adj* not put off, discouraged, or beaten.
  ▸ unˈdauntedly *adv* ▸ unˈdauntedness *n*

undecagon (ʌnˈdɛkəˌɡɒn) *n* a polygon having eleven sides. [C18: from L *undecim* eleven + -GON]

undeceive (ˌʌndɪˈsiːv) *vb* **undeceives, undeceiving, undeceived.** (*tr*) to reveal the truth to (someone previously misled or deceived).
  ▸ ˌundeˈceivable *adj* ▸ ˌundeˈceiver *n*

undecidability (ˌʌndɪˌsaɪdəˈbɪlɪtɪ) *n, pl* **undecidabilities.** *Maths, logic.* the condition of not being open to formal proof or disproof by logical deduction from the axioms of a system.

undecided (ˌʌndɪˈsaɪdɪd) *adj* **1** not having made up one's mind. **2** (of an issue, problem, etc.) not agreed or decided upon.
  ▸ ˌundeˈcidedly *adv* ▸ ˌundeˈcidedness *n*

undeniable (ˌʌndɪˈnaɪəbˀl) *adj* **1** unquestionably or obviously true. **2** of unquestionable excellence: *a man of undeniable character.* **3** unable to be resisted or denied.
  ▸ ˌundeˈniableness *n* ▸ ˌundeˈniably *adv*

under (ˈʌndə) *prep* **1** directly below; on, to, or beneath the underside or base of: *under one's feet.* **2** less than: *under forty years.* **3** lower in rank than: *under a corporal.* **4** subject to the supervision, jurisdiction, control, or influence of. **5** subject to (conditions); in (certain circumstances). **6** within a classification of: *a book under theology.* **7** known by: *under an assumed name.* **8** planted with: *a field under corn.* **9** powered by: *under sail.* **10** *Astrol.* during the period

that the sun is in (a sign of the zodiac): *born under Aries.*
  ◆ *adv* **11** below; to a position underneath something. [OE]

under- *prefix* **1** below or beneath: *underarm; underground.* **2** of lesser importance or lower rank: *undersecretary.* **3** insufficient or insufficiently: *underemployed.* **4** indicating secrecy or deception: *underhand.*

underachieve (ˌʌndərəˈtʃiːv) *vb* **underachieves, underachieving, underachieved.** (*intr*) to fail to achieve a performance appropriate to one's age or talents.
  ▸ ˌunderaˈchievement *n* ▸ ˌunderaˈchiever *n*

underact (ˌʌndərˈækt) *vb Theatre.* to play (a role) without adequate emphasis.

underage (ˌʌndərˈeɪdʒ) *adj* below the required or standard age, esp. below the legal age for voting or drinking.

underarm (ˈʌndərˌɑːm) *adj* **1** (of a measurement) extending along the arm from wrist to armpit. **2** *Cricket, tennis, etc.* denoting a style of throwing, bowling, or serving in which the hand is swung below shoulder level. **3** below the arm. ◆ *adv* **4** in an underarm style.

underbelly (ˈʌndəˌbɛlɪ) *n, pl* **underbellies. 1** the part of an animal's belly nearest to the ground. **2** a vulnerable or unprotected part, aspect, or region.

underbid (ˌʌndəˈbɪd) *vb* **underbids, underbidding, underbid. 1** (*tr*) to submit a bid lower than that of (others). **2** (*tr*) to submit an excessively low bid for. **3** *Bridge.* to bid (one's hand) at a lower level than the strength of the hand warrants: *he underbid his hand.*

underbidder (ˌʌndəˈbɪdə) *n* **1** the person who makes the highest bid below the top bidder, esp. in an auction. **2** a person who underbids.

underbody (ˈʌndəˌbɒdɪ) *n, pl* **underbodies.** the underpart of a body, as of an animal or motor vehicle.

underbred (ˌʌndəˈbrɛd) *adj* of impure stock; not thoroughbred.
  ▸ ˌunderˈbreeding *n*

underbuy (ˌʌndəˈbaɪ) *vb* **underbuys, underbuying, underbought. 1** to buy (stock in trade) in amounts lower than required. **2** (*tr*) to buy at a price below that paid by (others). **3** (*tr*) to pay a price less than the true value for.

undercapitalise *or* **undercapitalise** (ˌʌndəˈkæpɪtəˌlaɪz) *vb* **undercapitalises, undercapitalizing, undercapitalized** *or* **undercapitalises, undercapitalising, undercapitalised.** to provide or issue capital for (a commercial enterprise) in an amount insufficient for efficient operation.

undercarriage (ˈʌndəˌkærɪdʒ) *n* **1** Also called: **landing gear.** the assembly of wheels, shock absorbers, struts, etc., that supports an aircraft on the ground and enables it to take off and land. **2** the framework that supports the body of a vehicle, carriage, etc.

undercharge (ˌʌndəˈtʃɑːdʒ) *vb* **undercharges, undercharging, undercharged. 1** to charge too little for something. **2** (*tr*) to load (a gun, cannon, etc.) with an inadequate charge.

underclass (ˈʌndəˌklɑːs) *n* a class beneath the usual social scale consisting of the most disadvantaged people, such as the long-term unemployed.

underclothes (ˈʌndəˌkləʊðz) *pl n* a variant of **underwear.** Also called: **underclothing.**

undercoat (ˈʌndəˌkəʊt) *n* **1** a coat of paint or other substance applied before the top coat. **2** a coat worn under an overcoat. **3** *Zool.* another name for **underfur.** ◆ *vb* **4** (*tr*) to apply an undercoat to (a surface).

undercover (ˌʌndəˈkʌvə) *adj* done or acting in secret: *undercover operations.*

undercroft (ˈʌndəˌkrɒft) *n* an underground chamber, such as a church crypt, often with a vaulted ceiling. [C14: from *croft* a vault, cavern, ult. from L *crypta* CRYPT]

undercurrent (ˈʌndəˌkʌrənt) *n* **1** a current that is not apparent at the surface or lies beneath another current. **2** an opinion, emotion, etc., lying beneath apparent feeling or meaning. Also called: **underflow.**

undercut *vb* (ˌʌndəˈkʌt) **undercuts, undercutting, undercut. 1** to charge less than (a competitor) in order to obtain trade. **2** to cut away the under part of (something). **3** *Golf, tennis, etc.* to hit (a ball) in such a way as to impart backspin. ◆ *n* (ˈʌndəˌkʌt). **4** the act of cutting underneath. **5** a part that is cut away underneath. **6** a tenderloin of beef. **7** *Forestry, chiefly US & Canad.* a notch cut in a tree trunk, to ensure a clean break in felling. **8** *Tennis, golf, etc.* a stroke that imparts backspin to the ball.

underdevelop (ˌʌndədɪˈvɛləp) *vb* (*tr*) *Photog.* to process (a film, plate, or paper) in developer for less than the required time, or at too low a temperature, or in an exhausted solution.

underdeveloped (ˌʌndədɪˈvɛləpt) *adj* **1** immature or undersized. **2** relating to societies in which both the surplus capital and the social organization necessary to advance are lacking. **3** *Photog.* (of a film, etc.) processed in developer for less than the required time.

underdog (ˈʌndəˌdɒg) *n* **1** the losing competitor in a fight or contest. **2** a person in adversity or a position of inferiority.

underdone (ˌʌndəˈdʌn) *adj* insufficiently or lightly cooked.

underdressed (ˌʌndəˈdrɛst) *adj* wearing clothes that are not elaborate or formal enough for a particular occasion.

underemployed (ˌʌndərɪmˈplɔɪd) *adj* not fully or adequately employed.

underestimate *vb* (ˌʌndərˈɛstɪˌmeɪt), **underestimates, underestimating, underestimated.** (*tr*) **1** to make too low an estimate of: *he underestimated the cost.* **2** to think insufficiently highly of: *to underestimate a person.* ◆ *n* (ˌʌndərˈɛstɪmɪt). **3** too low an estimate.
▸ ˌunderˌestiˈmation *n*

> **USAGE NOTE** *Underestimate* is sometimes wrongly used where *overestimate* is meant: *the importance of his work cannot be overestimated* (not *cannot be underestimated*).

underexpose (ˌʌndərɪkˈspəʊz) *vb* **underexposes, underexposing, underexposed.** (*tr*) **1** *Photog.* to expose (a film, plate, or paper) for too short a period or with insufficient light so as not to produce the required effect. **2** (*often passive*) to fail to subject to appropriate or expected publicity.
▸ ˌunderexˈposure *n*

underfeed (ˌʌndəˈfiːd) *vb* **underfeeds, underfeeding, underfed.** (*tr*) **1** to give too little food to. **2** to supply (a furnace, engine, etc.) with fuel from beneath.

underfelt (ˈʌndəˌfɛlt) *n* thick felt laid between floorboards and carpet to increase insulation.

underfloor (ˈʌndəˌflɔː) *adj* situated beneath the floor: *underfloor heating.*

underfoot (ˌʌndəˈfʊt) *adv* **1** underneath the feet; on the ground. **2** in a position of subjugation. **3** in the way.

underfur (ˈʌndəˌfɜː) *n* the layer of dense soft fur occurring beneath the outer coarser fur in certain mammals, such as the otter and seal. Also called: **undercoat.**

undergarment (ˈʌndəˌgɑːmənt) *n* any garment worn under the visible outer clothes, usually next to the skin.

undergird (ˌʌndəˈgɜːd) *vb* **undergirds, undergirding, undergirded** *or* **undergirt.** (*tr*) to strengthen or reinforce by passing a rope, cable, or chain around the underside of (an object, load, etc.). [C16: from UNDER- + GIRD¹]

underglaze (ˈʌndəˌgleɪz) *adj* **1** *Ceramics.* applied to pottery or porcelain before the application of glaze. ◆ *n* **2** a pigment, etc., applied in this way.

undergo (ˌʌndəˈgəʊ) *vb* **undergoes, undergoing, underwent, undergone.** (*tr*) to experience, endure, or sustain: *to undergo a change of feelings.* [OE]
▸ ˈunderˌgoer *n*

undergraduate (ˌʌndəˈgrædjʊɪt) *n* a person studying in a university for a first degree. Sometimes shortened to **undergrad.**

underground *adj* (ˈʌndəˌgraʊnd), *adv* (ˌʌndəˈgraʊnd). **1** occurring, situated, used, or going below ground level: *an underground explosion.* **2** secret; hidden: *underground activities.* ◆ *n* (ˈʌndəˌgraʊnd). **3** a space or region below ground level. **4a** a movement dedicated to overthrowing a government or occupation forces, as in the European countries occupied by the German army in World War II. **4b** (*as modifier*): *an underground group.* **5** (often preceded by *the*) an electric passenger railway operated in underground tunnels. US and Canad. equivalent: **subway.** (usually preceded by *the*) **6a** any avant-garde, experimental, or subversive movement in popular art, films, music, etc. **6b** (*as modifier*): *the underground press.*

underground railroad *n* (*often cap.*) (in the pre-Civil War US) the system established by abolitionists to aid escaping slaves.

undergrowth (ˈʌndəˌgrəʊθ) *n* small trees, bushes, ferns, etc., growing beneath taller trees in a wood or forest.

underhand (ˈʌndəˌhænd) *adj also* **underhanded. 1** clandestine, deceptive, or secretive. **2** *Sport.* another word for **underarm.** ◆ *adv* **3** in an underhand manner or style.

underhanded (ˌʌndəˈhændɪd) *adj* another word for **underhand** or **short-handed.**

underhung (ˌʌndəˈhʌŋ) *adj* **1** (of the lower jaw) projecting beyond the upper jaw; undershot. **2** (of a sliding door, etc.) supported at its lower edge by a track or rail.

underlay *vb* (ˌʌndəˈleɪ), **underlays, underlaying, underlaid.** (*tr*) **1** to place (something) under or beneath. **2** to support by something laid beneath. **3** to achieve the correct printing pressure all over (a forme block) or to bring (a block) up to type height by adding material, such as paper, beneath it. ◆ *n* (ˈʌndəˌleɪ). **4** a lining, support, etc., laid underneath something else. **5** *Printing.* material such as paper, used to underlay a forme or block. **6** felt, rubber, etc., laid beneath a carpet to increase insulation and resilience.

underlie (ˌʌndəˈlaɪ) *vb* **underlies, underlying, underlay, underlain.** (*tr*) **1** to lie or be placed under or beneath. **2** to be the foundation, cause, or basis of: *careful planning underlies all our decisions.* **3** to be the root or stem from which (a word) is derived: *"happy" underlies "happiest".*
▸ ˈunderˌlier *n*

underline (ˌʌndəˈlaɪn) *vb* **underlines, underlining, underlined.** (*tr*) **1** to put a line under. **2** to state forcibly; emphasize.

underlinen (ˈʌndəˌlɪnən) *n* underclothes, esp. when made of linen.

underling (ˈʌndəlɪŋ) *n* a subordinate or lackey.

underlying (ˌʌndəˈlaɪɪŋ) *adj* **1** concealed but detectable: *underlying guilt.* **2** fundamental; basic. **3** lying under. **4** *Finance.* (of a claim, liability, etc.) taking precedence; prior.

undermentioned (ˈʌndəˌmɛnʃənd) *adj* mentioned below or subsequently.

undermine (ˌʌndəˈmaɪn) *vb* **undermines, undermining, undermined.** (*tr*) **1** (of the sea, wind, etc.) to wear away the bottom or base of (land, cliffs, etc.). **2** to weaken gradually or insidiously: *insults undermined her confidence.* **3** to tunnel or dig beneath.
▸ ˌunderˈminer *n*

undermost (ˈʌndəˌməʊst) *adj* **1** being the furthest under; lowest. ◆ *adv* **2** in the lowest place.

underneath (ˌʌndəˈniːθ) *prep, adv* **1** under; beneath. ◆ *adj* **2** lower. ◆ *n* **3** a lower part, surface, etc. [OE *underneothan*, from UNDER + *neothan* below]

undernourish (ˌʌndəˈnʌrɪʃ) *vb* (*tr*) to deprive of or fail to provide with nutrients essential for health and growth.
▸ ˌunderˈnourishment *n*

underpants (ˈʌndəˌpænts) *pl n* a man's undergarment covering the body from the waist or hips to the thighs or ankles. Often shortened to **pants.**

underpass (ˈʌndəˌpɑːs) *n* **1** a section of a road that passes under another road, railway line, etc. **2** another word for **subway** (sense 1).

underpay (ˌʌndəˈpeɪ) *vb* **underpays, underpaying, underpaid.** to pay (someone) insufficiently.
▸ ˌunderˈpayment *n*

underpin (ˌʌndəˈpɪn) *vb* **underpins, underpinning, underpinned.** (*tr*) **1** to support from beneath, esp. by a prop, while avoiding damaging or weakening the superstructure: *to underpin a wall.* **2** to give corroboration, strength, or support to.

underpinning (ˈʌndəˌpɪnɪŋ) n a structure of masonry, concrete, etc., placed beneath a wall to provide support.

underplay (ˌʌndəˈpleɪ) vb 1 to play (a role) with restraint or subtlety. 2 to achieve (an effect) by deliberate lack of emphasis. 3 (intr) Cards. to lead or follow suit with a lower card when holding a higher one.

underprivileged (ˌʌndəˈprɪvɪlɪdʒd) adj lacking the rights and advantages of other members of society; deprived.

underproduction (ˌʌndəprəˈdʌkʃən) n Commerce. production below full capacity or below demand.

underproof (ˌʌndəˈpruːf) adj (of a spirit) containing less than 57.1 per cent alcohol by volume.

underquote (ˌʌndəˈkwəʊt) vb **underquotes, underquoting, underquoted. 1** to offer for sale (securities, goods, or services) at a price lower than the market price. 2 (tr) to quote a price lower than that quoted by (another).

underrate (ˌʌndəˈreɪt) vb **underrates, underrating, underrated.** (tr) to underestimate.

underscore (ˌʌndəˈskɔː) vb **underscores, underscoring, underscored.** (tr) 1 to draw or score a line or mark under. 2 to stress or reinforce.

undersea (ˈʌndəˌsiː) adj, adv also **underseas** (ˌʌndəˈsiːz). below the surface of the sea.

underseal (ˈʌndəˌsiːl) Brit. ◆ n 1 a coating of a tar, etc., applied to the underside of a motor vehicle to retard corrosion. ◆ vb 2 (tr) to apply a coating of underseal to (a vehicle).

undersecretary (ˌʌndəˈsɛkrətrɪ) n, pl **undersecretaries. 1** (in Britain) **1a** any of various senior civil servants in certain government departments. **1b** short for **undersecretary of state:** any of various high officials subordinate only to the minister in charge of a department. **2** (in the US) a high government official subordinate only to the secretary in charge of a department.

undersell (ˌʌndəˈsɛl) vb **undersells, underselling, undersold. 1** to sell for less than the usual price. 2 (tr) to sell at a price lower than that of (another seller). 3 (tr) to advertise (merchandise) with moderation or restraint.
▶ ˌunderˈseller n

undersexed (ˌʌndəˈsɛkst) adj having weaker sex urges or responses than is considered normal.

undershirt (ˈʌndəˌʃɜːt) n the US and Canad. name for **vest** (sense 1).

undershoot (ˌʌndəˈʃuːt) vb **undershoots, undershooting, undershot. 1** (of a pilot) to cause (an aircraft) to land short of (a runway) or (of an aircraft) to land in this way. 2 to shoot a projectile so that it falls short of (a target).

undershorts (ˈʌndəˌʃɔːts) pl n another word for **shorts** (sense 2).

undershot (ˈʌndəˌʃɒt) adj 1 (of the lower jaw) projecting beyond the upper jaw; underhung. 2 (of a water wheel) driven by a flow of water that passes under the wheel rather than over it.

underside (ˈʌndəˌsaɪd) n the bottom or lower surface.

undersigned (ˈʌndəˌsaɪnd) n 1 **the.** the person or persons who have signed at the foot of a document, statement, etc. ◆ adj 2 having signed one's name at the foot of a document, statement, etc.

undersized (ˌʌndəˈsaɪzd) adj of less than usual size.

underskirt (ˈʌndəˌskɜːt) n any skirtlike garment worn under a skirt or dress; petticoat.

underslung (ˌʌndəˈslʌŋ) adj suspended below a supporting member, esp. (of a motor vehicle chassis) suspended below the axles.

understand (ˌʌndəˈstænd) vb **understands, understanding, understood. 1** (may take a clause as object) to know and comprehend the nature or meaning of: I understand you. 2 (may take a clause as object) to realize or grasp (something): he understands your position. 3 (tr; may take a clause as object) to assume, infer, or believe: I understand you are thinking of marrying. 4 (tr) to know how to translate or read: can you understand Spanish? 5 (tr; may take a clause as object; often passive) to accept as a condition or proviso: it is understood that children must be kept quiet. 6 (tr) to be

sympathetic to or compatible with: we understand each other. [OE understandan]
▶ ˌunderˈstandable adj ▶ ˌunderˈstandably adv

understanding (ˌʌndəˈstændɪŋ) n 1 the ability to learn, judge, make decisions, etc. 2 personal opinion or interpretation of a subject: my understanding of your predicament. 3 a mutual agreement or compact, esp. an informal or private one. 4 Chiefly Brit. an unofficial engagement to be married. 5 **on the understanding that.** providing. ◆ adj 6 sympathetic, tolerant, or wise towards people. 7 possessing judgment and intelligence.
▶ ˌunderˈstandingly adv

understate (ˌʌndəˈsteɪt) vb **understates, understating, understated. 1** to state (something) in restrained terms, often to obtain an ironic effect. 2 to state that (something, such as a number) is less than it is.
▶ ˌunderˈstatement n

understeer (ˌʌndəˈstɪə) vb (intr) (of a vehicle) to turn less sharply, for a particular movement of the steering wheel, than anticipated.

understood (ˌʌndəˈstʊd) vb 1 the past tense and past participle of **understand.** ◆ adj 2 implied or inferred. 3 taken for granted.

understudy (ˈʌndəˌstʌdɪ) vb **understudies, understudying, understudied. 1** (tr) to study (a role or part) so as to be able to replace the usual actor or actress if necessary. 2 to act as understudy to (an actor or actress). ◆ n, pl **understudies. 3** an actor or actress who studies a part so as to be able to replace the usual actor or actress if necessary. 4 anyone who is trained to take the place of another in case of need.

undertake (ˌʌndəˈteɪk) vb **undertakes, undertaking, undertook, undertaken.** (tr) 1 to contract to or commit oneself to (something) or (to do something): to undertake a job. 2 to attempt; agree to start. 3 to take (someone) in charge. 4 to promise.

undertaker (ˈʌndəˌteɪkə) n a person whose profession is the preparation of the dead for burial or cremation and the management of funerals; funeral director.

undertaking (ˈʌndəˌteɪkɪŋ) n 1 a task, venture, or enterprise. 2 an agreement to do something. 3 the business of an undertaker.

underthings (ˈʌndəˌθɪŋz) pl n girls' or women's underwear.

underthrust (ˈʌndəˌθrʌst) n Geol. a reverse fault in which the rocks on the lower surface of a fault plane have moved under the relatively static rocks on the upper surface.

undertone (ˈʌndəˌtəʊn) n 1 a quiet or hushed tone of voice. 2 an underlying suggestion in words or actions: his offer has undertones of dishonesty.

undertow (ˈʌndəˌtəʊ) n 1 the seaward undercurrent following the breaking of a wave on the beach. 2 any strong undercurrent flowing in a different direction from the surface current.

undertrick (ˈʌndəˌtrɪk) n Bridge. a trick by which a declarer falls short of making his or her contract.

undervalue (ˌʌndəˈvæljuː) vb **undervalues, undervaluing, undervalued.** (tr) to value at too low a level or price.
▶ ˌunderˌvaluˈation n ▶ ˌunderˈvaluer n

undervest (ˈʌndəˌvɛst) n Brit. another name for **vest** (sense 1).

underwater (ˌʌndəˈwɔːtə) adj 1 being, occurring, or going under the surface of the water, esp. the sea: underwater exploration. 2 Naut. below the water line of a vessel. ◆ adv 3 beneath the surface of the water.

under way adj (postpositive) 1 in progress; in operation: the show was under way. 2 Naut. in motion.

underwear (ˈʌndəˌwɛə) n clothing worn under the outer garments, usually next to the skin.

underweight (ˌʌndəˈweɪt) adj weighing less than is average, expected, or healthy.

underwent (ˌʌndəˈwɛnt) vb the past tense of **undergo.**

underwhelm (ˌʌndəˈwɛlm) vb (tr) to make no positive impact on; disappoint. [C20: orig. a humorous coinage based on *overwhelm*]
▶ ˌunderˈwhelming adj

underwing ('ʌndə,wɪŋ) n **1** the hind wing of an insect. **2** See **red underwing, yellow underwing.**

underwood ('ʌndə,wʊd) n a less common word for **undergrowth.**

underworld ('ʌndə,wɜːld) n **1a** criminals and their associates. **1b** (as modifier): underworld connections. **2** Greek & Roman myth. the regions below the earth's surface regarded as the abode of the dead. **3** the antipodes.

underwrite ('ʌndə,raɪt, ,ʌndə'raɪt) vb **underwrites, underwriting, underwrote, underwritten.** (tr) **1** Finance. to undertake to purchase at an agreed price any unsold portion of (a public issue of shares, etc.). **2** to accept financial responsibility for (a commercial project or enterprise). **3** Insurance. **3a** to sign and issue (an insurance policy) thus accepting liability. **3b** to insure (a property or risk). **3c** to accept liability up to (a specified amount) in an insurance policy. **4** to write (words, a signature, etc.) beneath (other written matter). **5** to support.

underwriter ('ʌndə,raɪtə) n **1** a person or enterprise that underwrites public issues of shares, bonds, etc. **2a** a person or enterprise that underwrites insurance policies. **2b** an employee or agent of an insurance company who determines the premiums payable.

undesirable (,ʌndɪ'zaɪərəb°l) adj **1** not desirable or pleasant; objectionable. ◆ n **2** a person or thing considered undesirable.
▶ ,unde,sira'bility or ,unde'sirableness n ▶ ,unde'sirably adv

undetermined (,ʌndɪ'tɜːmɪnd) adj **1** not yet resolved; undecided. **2** not known or discovered.

undies ('ʌndɪz) pl n Inf. women's underwear.

undine ('ʌndiːn) n any of various female water spirits. [C17: from NL undina, from L unda a wave]

undisputed world champion n Boxing. a boxer who holds the World Boxing Association and the World Boxing Council world championship titles simultaneously.

undistributed (,ʌndɪ'strɪbjutɪd) adj **1** Logic. (of a term) referring only to some members of the class designated by the term, as doctors in some doctors are overworked. **2** Business. (of a profit) not paid in dividends to the shareholders of a company but retained to help finance its trading.

undo (ʌn'duː) vb **undoes, undoing, undid, undone.** (mainly tr) **1** (also intr) to untie, unwrap, or open or become untied, unwrapped, etc. **2** to reverse the effects of. **3** to cause the downfall of.

undoing (ʌn'duːɪŋ) n **1** ruin; downfall. **2** the cause of downfall: drink was his undoing.

undone[1] (ʌn'dʌn) adj not done or completed; unfinished.

undone[2] (ʌn'dʌn) adj **1** ruined; destroyed. **2** unfastened; untied.

undoubted (ʌn'daʊtɪd) adj beyond doubt; certain or indisputable.
▶ un'doubtedly adv

undreamed (ʌn'driːmd) or **undreamt** (ʌn'drɛmt) adj (often foll. by of) not thought of, conceived, or imagined.

undress (ʌn'drɛs) vb **1** to take off clothes from (oneself or another). **2** (tr) to strip of ornamentation. **3** (tr) to remove the dressing from (a wound). ◆ n **4** partial or complete nakedness. **5** informal or normal working clothes or uniform.

undressed (ʌn'drɛst) adj **1** partially or completely naked. **2** (of an animal hide) not fully processed. **3** (of food, esp. salad) not prepared with sauce or dressing.

Undset ★ (Norwegian 'unset) n **Sigrid** ('sigri). 1882–1949, Norwegian novelist, best known for her trilogy Kristin Lavransdatter (1920–22): Nobel prize for literature 1928.

undue (ʌn'djuː) adj **1** excessive or unwarranted. **2** unjust, improper, or illegal. **3** (of a debt, bond, etc.) not yet payable.

USAGE NOTE The use of undue in sentences such as there is no cause for undue alarm is redundant and should be avoided.

---

undulant ('ʌndjʊlənt) adj Rare. resembling waves; undulating.
▶ 'undulance n

undulant fever n another name for **brucellosis.** [C19 so called because the fever symptoms are intermittent]

undulate vb ('ʌndjʊ,leɪt), **undulates, undulating, undulated.** **1** to move or cause to move in waves or as if in waves. **2** to have or provide with a wavy form or appearance. ◆ adj ('ʌndjʊlɪt, -,leɪt). **3** having a wavy or rippled appearance, margin, or form: an undulate leaf. [C17: from L from unda a wave]
▶ 'undu,lator n ▶ 'undulatory adj

undulation (,ʌndjʊ'leɪʃən) n **1** the act or an instance of undulating. **2** any wave or wavelike form, line, etc.

unduly (ʌn'djuːlɪ) adv excessively.

undying (ʌn'daɪɪŋ) adj unending; eternal.
▶ un'dyingly adv

unearned (ʌn'ɜːnd) adj **1** not deserved. **2** not yet earned.

unearned income n income from property, investment, etc., comprising rent, interest, and dividends.

unearth (ʌn'ɜːθ) vb (tr) **1** to dig up out of the earth. **2** to reveal or discover, esp. by exhaustive searching.

unearthly (ʌn'ɜːθlɪ) adj **1** ghostly; eerie: unearthly screams. **2** heavenly; sublime: unearthly music. **3** ridiculous or unreasonable (esp. in **unearthly hour**).
▶ un'earthliness n

uneasy (ʌn'iːzɪ) adj **1** (of a person) anxious; apprehensive. **2** (of a condition) precarious: an uneasy truce. **3** (of a thought, etc.) disquieting.
▶ un'ease n ▶ un'easily adv ▶ un'easiness n

uneatable (ʌn'iːtəb°l) adj (of food) not fit or suitable for eating, esp. because it is rotten or unattractive.

uneconomic (,ʌniːkə'nɒmɪk, ,ʌnɛkə-) adj not economic; not profitable.

uneconomical (,ʌniːkə'nɒmɪk°l, -ɛkə-) adj not economical; wasteful.

unemployable (,ʌnɪm'plɔɪəb°l) adj unable or unfit to keep a job.
▶ ,unem,ploya'bility n

unemployed (,ʌnɪm'plɔɪd) adj **1a** without remunerative employment; out of work. **1b** (as collective n; preceded by the): the unemployed. **2** not being used; idle.

unemployment (,ʌnɪm'plɔɪmənt) n **1** the condition of being unemployed. **2** the number of unemployed workers, often as a percentage of the total labour force.

unemployment benefit n (in Britain, formerly) a regular payment to a person who is out of work: replaced by jobseeker's allowance in 1996. Informal term: **dole.**

unequal (ʌn'iːkwəl) adj **1** not equal in quantity, size, rank, value, etc. **2** (foll. by to) inadequate; insufficient. **3** not evenly balanced. **4** (of character, quality, etc.) irregular; inconsistent. **5** (of a contest, etc.) having competitors of different ability.

unequalled or US **unequaled** (ʌn'iːkwəld) adj not equalled; unrivalled; supreme.

unequivocal (,ʌnɪ'kwɪvək°l) adj not ambiguous; plain.
▶ ,une'quivocally adv ▶ ,une'quivocalness n

unerring (ʌn'ɜːrɪŋ) adj **1** not missing the mark or target. **2** consistently accurate; certain.
▶ un'erringly adv ▶ un'erringness n

UNESCO (juː'nɛskəʊ) n acronym for United Nations Educational, Scientific, and Cultural Organization.

uneven (ʌn'iːvən) adj **1** (of a surface, etc.) not level or flat. **2** spasmodic or variable. **3** not parallel, straight, or horizontal. **4** not fairly matched: an uneven race. **5** Arch. not equal.
▶ un'evenly adv ▶ un'evenness n

uneventful (,ʌnɪ'vɛntfʊl) adj ordinary, routine, or quiet.
▶ ,une'ventfully adv ▶ ,une'ventfulness n

unexampled (,ʌnɪg'zɑːmp°ld) adj without precedent or parallel.

unexceptionable (,ʌnɪk'sɛpʃənəb°l) adj beyond criticism or objection.
▶ ,unex'ceptionably adv

★ people and places

unexceptional (ˌʌnɪkˈsɛpʃənᵊl) *adj* **1** usual, ordinary, or normal. **2** subject to or allowing no exceptions. ▸ ˌunexˈceptionally *adv*

unexcited (ˌʌnɪkˈsaɪtɪd) *adj* **1** not aroused to pleasure, interest, agitation, etc. **2** (of an atom, molecule, etc.) remaining in its ground state.

unexpected (ˌʌnɪkˈspɛktɪd) *adj* surprising or unforeseen. ▸ ˌunexˈpectedly *adv* ▸ ˌunexˈpectedness *n*

unfailing (ʌnˈfeɪlɪŋ) *adj* **1** not failing; unflagging. **2** continuous. **3** sure; certain. ▸ unˈfailingly *adv* ▸ unˈfailingness *n*

unfair (ʌnˈfɛə) *adj* **1** characterized by inequality or injustice. **2** dishonest or unethical. ▸ unˈfairly *adv* ▸ unˈfairness *n*

unfaithful (ʌnˈfeɪθful) *adj* **1** not true to a promise, vow, etc. **2** not true to a wife, husband, lover, etc., esp. in having sexual intercourse with someone else. **3** inaccurate; untrustworthy: *unfaithful copy*. **4** *Obs.* not having religious faith. ▸ unˈfaithfully *adv* ▸ unˈfaithfulness *n*

unfamiliar (ˌʌnfəˈmɪljə) *adj* **1** not known or experienced; strange. **2** (*postpositive*; foll. by *with*) not familiar. ▸ unfamiliarity (ˌʌnfəˌmɪlɪˈærɪtɪ) *n* ▸ unˌfaˈmiliarly *adv*

unfasten (ʌnˈfɑːsᵊn) *vb* to undo, untie, or open or become undone, untied, or opened.

unfathered (ʌnˈfɑːðəd) *adj* **1** having no known father. **2** of unknown or uncertain origin.

unfathomable (ʌnˈfæðəməbᵊl) *adj* **1** incapable of being fathomed; immeasurable. **2** incomprehensible. ▸ unˈfathomableness *or US* unˈfathomably *adv*

unfavourable *or US* **unfavorable** (ʌnˈfeɪvərəbᵊl) *adj* not favourable; adverse or inauspicious. ▸ unˈfavourably *or US* unˈfavorably *adv*

unfazed (ʌnˈfeɪzd) *adj Inf.* not disconcerted; unperturbed.

Unfederated Malay States ★ (ʌnˈfɛdəˌreɪtɪd) *pl n* a former group of native states in the Malay Peninsula that became British protectorates between 1885 and 1909. All except Brunei joined the Malayan Union (later Federation of Malaya) in 1946. Brunei joined the Federation of Malaysia in 1963.

unfeeling (ʌnˈfiːlɪŋ) *adj* **1** without sympathy; callous. **2** without physical feeling or sensation. ▸ unˈfeelingly *adv* ▸ unˈfeelingness *n*

unfinished (ʌnˈfɪnɪʃt) *adj* **1** incomplete or imperfect. **2** (of paint, polish, varnish, etc.) without an applied finish; rough. **3** (of fabric) unbleached or not processed.

unfit (ʌnˈfɪt) *adj* **1** (*postpositive*; often foll. by *for*) unqualified, incapable, or incompetent: *unfit for military service*. **2** (*postpositive*; often foll. by *for*) unsuitable or inappropriate: *the ground was unfit for football*. **3** in poor physical condition. ◆ *vb* unfits, unfitting, unfitted. **4** (*tr*) *Rare.* to render unfit. ▸ unˈfitly *adv* ▸ unˈfitness *n*

unfix (ʌnˈfɪks) *vb* (*tr*) **1** to unfasten, detach, or loosen. **2** to unsettle or disturb.

unflappable (ʌnˈflæpəbᵊl) *adj Inf.* hard to upset; calm; composed. ▸ unˌflappaˈbility *n* ▸ unˈflappably *adv*

unfledged (ʌnˈflɛdʒd) *adj* **1** (of a young bird) not having developed adult feathers. **2** immature and undeveloped.

unflinching (ʌnˈflɪntʃɪŋ) *adj* not shrinking from danger, difficulty, etc. ▸ unˈflinchingly *adv*

unfold (ʌnˈfəʊld) *vb* **1** to open or spread out or be opened or spread out from a folded state. **2** to reveal or be revealed: *the truth unfolds*. **3** to develop or expand or be developed or expanded. ▸ unˈfolder *n*

unfortunate (ʌnˈfɔːtʃənɪt) *adj* **1** causing or attended by misfortune. **2** unlucky or unhappy: *an unfortunate character*. **3** regrettable or unsuitable: *an unfortunate speech*. ◆ *n* **4** an unlucky person. ▸ unˈfortunately *adv*

unfounded (ʌnˈfaʊndɪd) *adj* **1** (of ideas, allegations,

etc.) baseless; groundless. **2** not yet founded or established. ▸ unˈfoundedly *adv* ▸ unˈfoundedness *n*

unfranked income (ʌnˈfræŋkt) *n* any income from an investment that does not qualify as franked investment income.

unfreeze (ʌnˈfriːz) *vb* **unfreezes, unfreezing, unfroze, unfrozen.** **1** to thaw or cause to thaw. **2** (*tr*) to relax governmental restrictions on (wages, prices, credit, etc.) or on the manufacture or sale of (goods, etc.).

unfriended (ʌnˈfrɛndɪd) *adj Now rare.* without a friend or friends; friendless.

unfriendly (ʌnˈfrɛndlɪ) *adj* **unfriendlier, unfriendliest.** **1** not friendly; hostile. **2** unfavourable or disagreeable. ◆ *adv* **3** *Rare.* in an unfriendly manner. ▸ unˈfriendliness *n*

unfrock (ʌnˈfrɒk) *vb* (*tr*) to deprive (a person in holy orders) of ecclesiastical status.

unfunded debt (ʌnˈfʌndɪd) *n* a short-term floating debt not represented by bonds.

unfurl (ʌnˈfɜːl) *vb* to unroll, unfold, or spread out or be unrolled, unfolded, or spread out from a furled state.

ungainly (ʌnˈgeɪnlɪ) *adj* **ungainlier, ungainliest.** **1** lacking grace when moving. **2** difficult to move or use; unwieldy. [C17: from UN-¹ + obs. or dialect *gainly* graceful] ▸ unˈgainliness *n*

Ungaretti ★ (*Italian* uŋɡaˈretti) *n* **Giuseppe** (dʒuˈzɛppe). 1888–1970, Italian poet, best known for his collection of war poems *Allegria di naufragi* (1919).

Ungava ★ (uŋˈɡeɪvə, -ˈɡɑː-) *n* a sparsely inhabited region of NE Canada, in N Quebec east of Hudson Bay: part of the Labrador peninsula: rich mineral resources. Area: 911 110 sq. km (351 780 sq. miles).

ungodly (ʌnˈɡɒdlɪ) *adj* **ungodlier, ungodliest.** **1a** wicked, sinful. **1b** (*as collective n*; preceded by *the*): *the ungodly*. **2** *Inf.* unseemly; outrageous (esp. in **an ungodly hour**). ▸ unˈgodliness *n*

ungovernable (ʌnˈɡʌvənəbᵊl) *adj* not able to be disciplined, restrained, etc.: *an ungovernable temper*. ▸ unˈgovernableness *n* ▸ unˈgovernably *adv*

ungual (ˈʌŋɡwəl) *adj* **1** of, relating to, or affecting the fingernails or toenails. **2** of or relating to an unguis. [C19: from L *unguis* nail]

unguarded (ʌnˈɡɑːdɪd) *adj* **1** unprotected; vulnerable. **2** open; frank. **3** incautious. ▸ unˈguardedly *adv* ▸ unˈguardedness *n*

unguent (ˈʌŋɡwənt) *n* a less common name for an **ointment**. [C15: from L, from *unguere* to anoint]

unguiculate (ʌŋˈɡwɪkjʊlɪt, -ˌleɪt) *adj* **1** (of mammals) having claws or nails. **2** (of petals) having a clawlike base. ◆ *n* **3** an unguiculate mammal. [C19: from NL *unguiculātus*, from L *unguiculus*, dim. of *unguis* nail]

unguis (ˈʌŋɡwɪs) *n, pl* **ungues** (-ɡwiːz). **1** a nail, claw, or hoof, or the part of the digit giving rise to it. **2** the clawlike base of a petal. [C18: from L]

ungulate (ˈʌŋɡjʊlɪt, -ˌleɪt) *n* any of a large group of mammals all of which have hooves: divided into odd-toed ungulates (see **perissodactyl**) and even-toed ungulates (see **artiodactyl**). [C19: from LL *ungulātus* having hooves, from *ungula* hoof]

unhallowed (ʌnˈhæləʊd) *adj* **1** not consecrated or holy: *unhallowed ground*. **2** sinful.

unhand (ʌnˈhænd) *vb* (*tr*) *Arch. or literary.* to release from the grasp.

unhappy (ʌnˈhæpɪ) *adj* **unhappier, unhappiest.** **1** not joyful; sad or depressed. **2** unfortunate or wretched: *an unhappy fellow*. **3** tactless or inappropriate: *an unhappy remark*. ▸ unˈhappily *adv* ▸ unˈhappiness *n*

UNHCR *abbrev.* for United Nations High Commissioner for Refugees.

unhealthy (ʌnˈhɛlθɪ) *adj* **unhealthier, unhealthiest.** **1** characterized by ill health; sick. **2** unwholesome of, conducive to, or resulting from ill health: *an unhealthy complexion*. **3** morbid or unwholesome. **4** *Inf.* dangerous; risky. ▸ unˈhealthily *adv* ▸ unˈhealthiness *n*

unheard (ʌnˈhɜːd) *adj* **1** not heard; not perceived by the ear. **2** not listened to: *his warning went unheard*. **3** *Arch.* unheard-of.

unheard-of *adj* **1** previously unknown: *an unheard-of actress*. **2** without precedent: *an unheard-of treatment*. **3** highly offensive: *unheard-of behaviour*.

unhinge (ʌnˈhɪndʒ) *vb* unhinges, unhinging, unhinged. (*tr*) **1** to remove (a door, etc.) from its hinges. **2** to derange or unbalance (a person, his mind, etc.). **3** to disrupt or unsettle (a process or state of affairs).

unholy (ʌnˈhəʊlɪ) *adj* unholier, unholiest. **1** not holy or sacred. **2** immoral or depraved. **3** *Inf.* outrageous or unnatural: *an unholy alliance*.
▸ un'holiness *n*

unhook (ʌnˈhʊk) *vb* **1** (*tr*) to remove (something) from a hook. **2** (*tr*) to unfasten the hook of (a dress, etc.). **3** (*intr*) to become unfastened or be capable of unfastening: *the dress wouldn't unhook*.

unhorse (ʌnˈhɔːs) *vb* unhorses, unhorsing, unhorsed. (*tr*) **1** (*usually passive*) to knock or throw from a horse. **2** to overthrow or dislodge, as from a powerful position.

unhouseled (ʌnˈhaʊzəld) *adj Arch.* not having received the Eucharist. [C16: from *un-* + obs. *housel* to administer the sacrament, from OE *hūsl* (n), *hūslian* (vb), from ?]

uni (ˈjuːnɪ) *n Inf.* short for **university**.

uni- *combining form.* consisting of, relating to, or having only one: *unilateral*. [from L *ūnus* one]

Uniat (ˈjuːnɪˌæt) *or* **Uniate** (ˈjuːnɪt, -ˌeɪt) *adj* **1** designating any of the Eastern Churches that retain their own liturgy but submit to papal authority. ♦ *n* **2** a member of one of these Churches. [C19: from Russian *uniyat*, from Polish *unja* union, from LL *ūniō*; see UNION]
▸ 'Uni,atism *n*

uniaxial (ˌjuːnɪˈæksɪəl) *adj* **1** (esp. of plants) having an unbranched main axis. **2** (of a crystal) having only one direction along which double refraction of light does not occur.

unicameral (ˌjuːnɪˈkæmərəl) *adj* of or characterized by a single legislative chamber.
▸ ˌuni'cameralism *n* ▸ ˌuni'cameralist *n* ▸ ˌuni'camerally *adv*

UNICEF (ˈjuːnɪˌsɛf) *n acronym for* United Nations Children's Fund (formerly, United Nations International Children's Emergency Fund).

unicellular (ˌjuːnɪˈsɛljʊlə) *adj* (of organisms, such as protozoans and certain algae) consisting of a single cell.
▸ ˌuniˌcellu'larity *n*

unicorn (ˈjuːnɪˌkɔːn) *n* **1** an imaginary creature usually depicted as a white horse with one long spiralled horn growing from its forehead. **2** *Old Testament.* a two-horned animal: mistranslation in the Authorized Version of the original Hebrew. [C13: from OF, from L *ūnicornis* one-horned, from *ūnus* one + *cornu* a horn]

unicycle (ˈjuːnɪˌsaɪkʰl) *n* a one-wheeled vehicle driven by pedals, esp. one used in a circus, etc. Also called: **monocycle**. [from UNI- + CYCLE, on the model of TRICYCLE]
▸ 'uniˌcyclist *n*

unidirectional (ˌjuːnɪdɪˈrɛkʃənʰl) *adj* having, moving in, or operating in only one direction.

UNIDO (juːˈniːdəʊ) *n acronym for* United Nations Industrial Development Organization.

Unification Church *n* a religious sect founded in 1954 by Sun Myung Moon (born 1920), S Korean industrialist and religious leader.

unified field theory *n* any theory capable of describing in one set of equations the properties of gravitational fields, electromagnetic fields, and strong and weak nuclear interactions. No satisfactory theory has yet been found. See also **grand unified theory**.

uniform (ˈjuːnɪˌfɔːm) *n* **1** a prescribed identifying set of clothes for the members of an organization, such as soldiers or schoolchildren. **2** a single set of such clothes. **3** a characteristic feature of some class or group. ♦ *adj* **4** unchanging in form, quality, etc.: *a uniform surface*. **5** alike or like: *a line of uniform toys*. ♦ *vb* (*tr*) **6** to fit out (a body of soldiers, etc.) with uniforms. **7** to make

uniform. [C16: from L *ūniformis*, from *ūnus* one + *formae* shape]
▸ 'uni,formly *adv* ▸ 'uni,formness *n*

Uniform Business Rate *n* a local tax in the UK paid by businesses, based on a local valuation of their premises and a rate fixed by central government that applies throughout the country. Abbrev.: **UBR**.

uniformitarianism (ˌjuːnɪˌfɔːmɪˈtɛərɪəˌnɪzəm) *n* the concept that the earth's surface was shaped in the past by gradual processes, such as erosion, and by small sudden changes, such as earthquakes, rather than by sudden divine acts, such as Noah's flood.
▸ ˌuniˌformi'tarian *n, adj*

uniformity (ˌjuːnɪˈfɔːmɪtɪ) *n, pl* uniformities. **1** a state or condition in which everything is regular, homogeneous, or unvarying. **2** lack of diversity or variation.

unify (ˈjuːnɪˌfaɪ) *vb* unifies, unifying, unified. to make or become one; unite. [C16: from Med. L *ūnificāre*, from L *ūnus* one + *facere* to make]
▸ 'uniˌfiable *adj* ▸ ˌunifi'cation *n* ▸ 'uniˌfier *n*

unilateral (ˌjuːnɪˈlætərəl) *adj* **1** of, having, affecting, or occurring on only one side. **2** involving or performed by only one party of several: *unilateral disarmament*. **3** *Law* (of contracts, obligations, etc.) made by, affecting, or binding one party only. **4** *Bot.* having or designating parts situated or turned to one side of an axis.
▸ ˌuni'lateralism *n* ▸ ˌuni'laterally *adv*

Unilateral Declaration of Independence *n* a declaration of independence made by a dependent state without the assent of the protecting state. Abbrev.: **UDI**.

Unimak Island ★ (ˈjuːnɪˌmæk) *n* an island in SW Alaska, in the Aleutian Islands. Length: 113 km (70 miles).

unimpeachable (ˌʌnɪmˈpiːtʃəbʰl) *adj* unquestionable as to honesty, truth, etc.
▸ ˌunim'peachably *adv*

unimproved (ˌʌnɪmˈpruːvd) *adj* **1** not improved or made better. **2** (of land) not cleared, drained, cultivated, etc. **3** neglected; unused: *unimproved resources*.

unincorporated business (ˌʌnɪnˈkɔːpəˌreɪtɪd) *n* a privately owned business, often owned by one person who has unlimited liability as the business is not legally registered as a company.

uninterested (ʌnˈɪntrɪstɪd) *adj* indifferent.
▸ un'interestedly *adv* ▸ un'interestedness *n*

USAGE NOTE See at **disinterested**.

union (ˈjuːnjən) *n* **1** the condition of being united, the act of uniting, or a conjunction formed by such an act. **2** an association, alliance, or confederation of individuals or groups for a common purpose, esp. political. **3** agreement or harmony. **4** short for **trade union**. **5** the act or state of marriage or sexual intercourse. **6** a device on a flag representing union, such as another flag depicted in the top left corner. **7** a device for coupling pipes. **8** (*often cap.*) **8a** an association of students at a university or college formed to look after the students' interests. **8b** the building or buildings housing the facilities of such an organization. **9** *Maths.* a set containing all members of two given sets. Symbol: ∪ (in 19th-century England) a number of parishes united for the administration of poor relief. **11** *Textiles.* a piece of cloth or fabric consisting of two different kinds of yarn. **12** (*modifier*) of or related to a union, esp. a trade union. [C15: from Church L *ūniō* oneness, from L *ūnus* one]

Union (ˈjuːnjən) *n* **the. 1** *Brit.* **1a** the union of England and Wales from 1543. **1b** the union of the English and Scottish crowns (1603–1707). **1c** the union of England and Scotland from 1707. **1d** the political union of Great Britain and Ireland (1801–1920). **1e** the union of Great Britain and Northern Ireland from 1921. **2** *US.* **2a** the United States of America. **2b** the northern states of the US during the Civil War. **2c** (*as modifier*): *Union supporters*.

union catalogue *n* a catalogue listing every publication held at cooperating libraries.

Union flag *n* the national flag of the United Kingdom, being a composite design composed of Saint George's Cross (England), Saint Andrew's Cross (Scotland), and Saint Patrick's Cross (Ireland). Often called: **Union Jack**.

unionism ('ju:njə,nɪzəm) *n* **1** the principles of trade unions. **2** adherence to the principles of trade unions. **3** the principle or theory of any union.
▶ '**unionist** *n, adj*

Unionist ('ju:njənɪst) *n* **1** (*sometimes not cap.*) **1a** (before 1920) a supporter of the Union of all Ireland and Great Britain. **1b** (since 1920) a supporter of Union between Britain and Northern Ireland. **2** a supporter of the US federal Union, esp. during the Civil War. ◆ *adj* **3** of, resembling, or relating to Unionists.
▶ '**Union,ism** *n*

Unionist Party *n* (formerly, in Northern Ireland) the major Protestant political party, closely identified with the Union with Britain. See also **Ulster Democratic Unionist Party, Ulster Unionist Council**.

unionize *or* **unionise** ('ju:njə,naɪz) *vb* **unionizes, unionizing, unionized** *or* **unionises, unionising, unionised**. **1** to organize (workers) into a trade union. **2** to join or cause to join a trade union. **3** (*tr*) to subject to the rules or codes of a trade union.
▶ ,**unioni'zation** *or* ,**unioni'sation** *n*

Union Jack *n* a common name for **Union flag**.

Union of South Africa ★ *n* the former name (1910–61) of the (Republic of) **South Africa**.

Union of Soviet Socialist Republics ★ *n* the official name of the former **Soviet Union**.

union pipes *pl n* another name for **uillean pipes**.

union shop *n* (formerly) an establishment whose employment policy is governed by a contract between employer and a trade union permitting the employment of nonunion labour only on the condition that such labour joins the union within a specified time period.

unipolar (,ju:nɪ'pəʊlə) *adj* **1** of, concerned with, or having a single magnetic or electric pole. **2** (of a nerve cell) having a single process. **3** (of a transistor) utilizing charge carriers of one polarity only, as in a field-effect transistor.
▶ **unipolarity** (,ju:nɪpəʊ'lærɪtɪ) *n*

unique (ju:'ni:k) *adj* **1** being the only one of a particular type. **2** without equal or like. **3** *Inf.* very remarkable. **4** *Maths.* **4a** leading to only one result: *the sum of two integers is unique*. **4b** having precisely one value: *the unique positive square root of 4 is 2*. [C17: via F from L *ūnicus* unparalleled, from *ūnus* one]
▶ **u'niquely** *adv* ▶ **u'niqueness** *n*

USAGE NOTE *Unique* is normally taken to describe an absolute state, i.e. one that cannot be qualified; thus something is either *unique* or *not unique*; it cannot be *rather unique* or *very unique*. However since *unique* is sometimes used informally to mean very remarkable or unusual and this makes it possible to use comparatives or intensifiers with it, although many people object to this use.

---

unisex ('ju:nɪ,sɛks) *adj* of or relating to clothing, a hairstyle, hairdressers, etc., that can be worn or used by either sex. [C20: from UNI- + SEX]

unisexual (,ju:nɪ'sɛksjʊəl) *adj* **1** of one sex only. **2** (of some organisms) having either male or female reproductive organs but not both.
▶ ,**uni,sexu'ality** *n* ▶ **uni'sexually** *adv*

unison ('ju:nɪs³n) *n* **1** *Music.* **1a** the interval between two sounds of identical pitch. **1b** (*modifier*) played or sung at the same pitch: *unison singing*. **2** complete agreement (esp. in **in unison**). [C16: from LL *ūnisonus*, from UNI- + *sonus* sound]
▶ **u'nisonous, u'nisonal,** *or* **u'nisonant** *adj*

UNISON ('ju:nɪs³n) *n* (in Britain) a trade union representing local government, health-care, and other workers: formed in 1993 by the amalgamation of COHSE, NALGO, and NUPE.

unit ('ju:nɪt) *n* **1** a single undivided entity or whole. **2** any

group or individual, esp. when regarded as a basic element of a larger whole. **3** a mechanical part or assembly of parts that performs a subsidiary function: *a filter unit*. **4** a complete system or establishment that performs a specific function: *a production unit*. **5** a subdivision of a larger military formation. **6** a standard amount of a physical quantity, such as length, mass, etc., multiples of which are used to express magnitudes of that physical quantity: *the second is a unit of time*. **7** the amount of a drug, vaccine, etc., needed to produce a particular effect. **8** a standard measure used in calculating alcohol intake and its effect. **9** the digit or position immediately to the left of the decimal point. **10** (*modifier*) having or relating to a value of one: *a unit vector*. **11** *NZ*. a self-propelled railcar. **12** *Austral. & NZ*. short for **home unit**. [C16: back formation from UNITY, ? on the model of *digit*]

unitarian (,ju:nɪ'tɛərɪən) *n* **1** a supporter of unity or centralization in politics. ◆ *adj* **2** of or relating to unity or centralization.

Unitarian (,ju:nɪ'tɛərɪən) *n* **1** a person who believes that God is one being and rejects the doctrine of the Trinity. **2** a member of the Church (**Unitarian Church**) that embodies this system of belief. ◆ *adj* **3** of or relating to Unitarians or Unitarianism.
▶ ,**Uni'taria,nism** *n*

unitary ('ju:nɪtərɪ, -trɪ) *adj* **1** of a unit or units. **2** based on or characterized by unity. **3** individual; whole.

unitary authority *n* (in Britain) a district administered by a single tier of local government.

unit character *n Genetics.* a character inherited as a single unit and dependent on a single gene.

unit cost *n* the actual cost of producing one article.

unite[1] (ju:'naɪt) *vb* **unites, uniting, united**. **1** to make or become an integrated whole or a unity. **2** to join, unify or be unified in purpose, action, beliefs, etc. **3** to enter or cause to enter into an association or alliance. **4** to adhere or cause to adhere; fuse. **5** (*tr*) to possess (qualities) in combination or at the same time: *he united charm with severity*. [C15: from LL *ūnīre*, from *ūnus* one]

unite[2] ('ju:naɪt, ju:'naɪt) *n* an English gold coin of the Stuart period, originally worth 20 shillings. [C17: from obs. *unite* joined, from the union of England & Scotland (1603)]

united (ju:'naɪtɪd) *adj* **1** produced by two or more persons or things in combination or from their union or amalgamation: *a united effort*. **2** in agreement. **3** in association or alliance.
▶ **u'nitedly** *adv* ▶ **u'nitedness** *n*

United Arab Emirates ★ *pl n* a group of seven emirates in SW Asia, on the Persian Gulf: consists of Abu Dhabi, Dubai, Sharjah, Ajman, Umm al Qaiwain, Ras el Khaimah, and Fujairah; a former British protectorate; became fully independent in 1971; consists mostly of flat desert, with mountains in the east; rich petroleum resources. Official language: Arabic. Official religion: Muslim. Currency: dirham. Capital: Abu Dhabi. Pop.: 2 580 000 (1997). Area: 83 600 sq. km (32 300 sq. miles). Former name (until 1971): **Trucial States**. Abbrev.: **UAE**.

United Arab Republic ★ *n* the official name (1958–71) of **Egypt**.

United Arab States ★ *pl n* a federation (1958–61) between the United Arab Republic and Yemen.

United Empire Loyalist *n Canad. history.* an American colonist who settled in Canada during or after the War of American Independence because of loyalty to the British Crown.

United Kingdom ★ *n* a kingdom of NW Europe, consisting chiefly of the island of Great Britain together with Northern Ireland: became the world's leading colonial power in the 18th century: the first country to undergo the Industrial Revolution. It became the **United Kingdom of Great Britain and Northern Ireland** in 1921, after the rest of Ireland became autonomous as the Irish Free State. Primarily it is a trading nation; a member of the European Union. Official language: English; Gaelic, Welsh, and other minority languages. Religion: Christian majority. Currency: pound sterling. Capital: London. Pop.: 58 919 000 (1997). Area: 244 110 sq. km (94 251 sq. miles). Abbrev.: **UK**. See also **Great Britain**.

★ people and places

United Kingdom overseas territory ★ *n* any of the territories that are governed by the UK but lie outside the British Isles; many were formerly British **crown colonies**: includes Bermuda, Falkland Islands, Gibraltar, and Montserrat.

United Nations *n* (*functioning as sing or pl*) an international organization of independent states, with its headquarters in New York City, that was formed in 1945 to promote peace and international cooperation and security. Abbrev.: **UN**.

United Provinces ★ *pl n* **1** a Dutch republic (1581–1795) formed by the union of the seven northern provinces of the Netherlands, which were in revolt against their suzerain, Philip II of Spain. **2** short for **United Provinces of Agra and Oudh**: the former name of **Uttar Pradesh**.

United States of America ★ (*functioning as sing or pl*) *n* a federal republic mainly in North America consisting of 50 states and the District of Columbia: colonized principally by the English and French in the 17th century, the native Indians being gradually defeated and displaced; 13 colonies under British rule made the Declaration of Independence in 1776 and became the United States after the War of American Independence. The northern states defeated the South in the Civil War (1861–65). It is the world's most productive industrial nation; agriculture is also significant. It participated reluctantly in World Wars I and II but since then has played a major role in international affairs. It consists generally of the Rocky Mountains in the west, the Great Plains in the centre, the Appalachians in the east, deserts in the southwest, and coastal lowlands and swamps in the southeast. Language: predominantly English; Spanish is widely spoken, also many Native American and other minority languages. Religion: Christian majority. Currency: dollar. Capital: Washington, D.C. Pop.: 267 839 000 (1997). Area: 9 518 323 sq. km (3 675 031 sq. miles). Often shortened to: **United States**. Abbrevs.: **US**, **USA**.

unitive ('juːnɪtɪv) *adj* **1** tending to unite or capable of uniting. **2** characterized by unity.

unitize *or* **unitise** ('juːnɪˌtaɪz) *vb* **unitizes, unitizing, unitized** *or* **unitises, unitising, unitised**. (*tr*) *Finance*. to convert (an investment trust) into a unit trust.
▶ ˌuniti'zation *or* ˌuniti'sation *n*

unit-linked policy *n* a life-assurance policy the benefits of which are directly in proportion to the number of units purchased on the policyholder's behalf.

unit of account *n* **1** *Econ*. the function of money that enables the user to keep accounts, value transactions, etc. **2** a monetary denomination used for accounting purposes, etc., but not necessarily corresponding to any real currency: *the ECU is the unit of account of the European Monetary Fund*. **3** the unit of currency of a country.

unit price *n* a price for foodstuffs, etc., stated or shown as the cost per unit, as per pound, per kilogram, per dozen, etc.

unit pricing *n* a system of pricing foodstuffs, etc., in which the cost of a single unit is shown to enable shoppers to see the advantage of buying multipacks.

unit trust *n Brit*. an investment trust that issues units for public sale, the holders of which are creditors and not shareholders with their interests represented by a trust company independent of the issuing agency. US and Canad. equivalent: **mutual fund**.

unity ('juːnɪtɪ) *n, pl* **unities**. **1** the state or quality of being one; oneness. **2** the act, state, or quality of forming a whole from separate parts. **3** something whole or complete that is composed of separate parts. **4** mutual agreement; harmony or concord: *the participants were no longer in unity*. **5** uniformity or constancy: *unity of purpose*. **6** *Maths*. **6a** the number or numeral one. **6b** a quantity assuming the value of one: *the area of the triangle was regarded as unity*. **6c** the element of a set producing no change in a number following multiplication. **7** any one of the three principles of dramatic structure by which the action of a play should be limited to a single plot (unity of action), a single location (unity of place), and a single day (unity of time). [C13: from OF *unité*, from L *ūnitās*, from *ūnus* one]

Univ. *abbrev. for* University.

univalent (ˌjuːnɪ'veɪlənt, juː'nɪvələnt) *adj* **1** (of a chromosome during meiosis) not paired with its homologue. **2** *Chem*. another word for **monovalent**.
▶ ˌuni'valency *n*

univalve ('juːnɪˌvælv) *Zool*. ♦ *adj* **1** relating to or possessing a mollusc shell that consists of a single piece (valve). ♦ *n* **2** a gastropod mollusc.

universal (ˌjuːnɪ'vɜːs^əl) *adj* **1** of or typical of the whole of mankind or of nature. **2** common to or proceeding from all in a particular group. **3** applicable to or affecting many individuals, conditions, or cases. **4** existing or prevailing everywhere. **5** applicable or occurring throughout or relating to the universe: *a universal constant*. **6** (esp. of a language) capable of being used and understood by all. **7** embracing or versed in many fields of knowledge, activity, interest, etc. **8** *Machinery*. designed or adapted for a range of sizes, fittings, or uses. **9** *Logic*. (of a statement or proposition) affirming or denying something about every member of a class, as in *all men are wicked*. Cf. **particular** (sense 6). **10** *Arch*. entire; whole. ♦ *n* **11** *Philosophy*. a general term or concept or the type such a term signifies. **12** *Logic*. a universal proposition, statement, or formula. **13** a characteristic common to every member of a particular culture or to every human being.

> **USAGE NOTE** The use of *more universal* as in *his writings have long been admired by fellow scientists, but his latest book should have more universal appeal* is acceptable in modern English usage.

universal class *or* **set** *n* (in Boolean algebra) the class containing all points and including all other classes.

universal gas constant *n* another name for **gas constant**.

universalism (ˌjuːnɪ'vɜːsəˌlɪzəm) *n* **1** a universal feature or characteristic. **2** another word for **universality**.

Universalism (ˌjuːnɪ'vɜːsəˌlɪzəm) *n* a system of religious beliefs maintaining that all men are predestined for salvation.
▶ ˌUni'versalist *n, adj*

universality (ˌjuːnɪvɜː'sælɪtɪ) *n* the state or quality of being universal.

universalize *or* **universalise** (ˌjuːnɪ'vɜːsəˌlaɪz) *vb* **universalizes, universalizing, universalized** *or* **universalises, universalising, universalised**. (*tr*) to make universal.
▶ ˌuniˌversali'zation *or* ˌuniˌversali'sation *n*

universal joint *or* **coupling** *n* a form of coupling between two rotating shafts allowing freedom of movement in all directions.

universally (ˌjuːnɪ'vɜːsəlɪ) *adv* everywhere or in every case: *this principle applies universally*.

universal motor *n* an electric motor capable of working on either direct current or single-phase alternating current at approximately the same speed and output.

universal time *n* **1** (from 1928) name adopted internationally for Greenwich Mean Time (measured from Greenwich midnight), now split into several slightly different scales, one of which (UT1) is used by astronomers Abbrev.: **UT**. **2** Also called: **universal coordinated time**. an internationally agreed system for civil timekeeping introduced in 1960 and redefined in 1972 as an atomic timescale. Available from broadcast signals, it has a second equal to the International Atomic Time (TAI) second, the difference between UTC and TAI being an integral number of seconds with leap seconds inserted when necessary to keep it within 0.9 seconds of UT1 Abbrev.: **UTC**.

universe ('juːnɪˌvɜːs) *n* **1** *Astron*. the aggregate of all existing matter, energy, and space. **2** human beings collectively. **3** a province or sphere of thought or activity. [C16: from F, from L *ūniversum* the whole world, from *ūniversus* all together, from UNI- + *vertere* to turn]

universe of discourse *n Logic*. the complete range of objects, relations, ideas, etc., that are expressed or implied in a discussion.

university (ˌjuːnɪ'vɜːsɪtɪ) *n, pl* **universities**. **1** an institution of higher education having authority to award bachelors' and higher degrees, usually having research facilities. **2** the buildings, members, staff, or campus of a university. [C14: from OF, from Med. L *universitās* group of scholars, from LL: guild, body of men, from L: *whole*]

UNIX ('juːnɪks) *n Trademark.* a multi-user operating system found on many types of computer.

unjust (ʌn'dʒʌst) *adj* not in accordance with accepted standards of fairness or justice; unfair.
▸ **un'justly** *adv* ▸ **un'justness** *n*

unkempt (ʌn'kɛmpt) *adj* **1** (of the hair) uncombed; dishevelled. **2** ungroomed; slovenly: *unkempt appearance.* [OE *uncembed;* from UN-[1] + *cembed*, p.p. of *cemban* to comb]
▸ **un'kemptly** *adv* ▸ **un'kemptness** *n*

unkind (ʌn'kaɪnd) *adj* lacking kindness; unsympathetic or cruel.
▸ **un'kindly** *adv* ▸ **un'kindness** *n*

unknowing (ʌn'nəʊɪŋ) *adj* **1** not knowing; ignorant. **2** (*postpositive*; often foll. by *of*) unaware (of).
▸ **un'knowingly** *adv*

unknown (ʌn'nəʊn) *adj* **1** not known, understood, or recognized. **2** not established, identified, or discovered: *an unknown island.* **3** not famous: *some unknown artist.* ◆ *n* **4** an unknown person, quantity, or thing. **5** *Maths.* a variable the value of which is to be discovered by solving an equation; a variable in a conditional equation.
▸ **un'knownness** *n*

Unknown Soldier *or* **Warrior** *n* (in various countries) an unidentified soldier who has died in battle and for whom a tomb is established as a memorial to the other unidentified dead of the nation's armed forces.

unlace (ʌn'leɪs) *vb* **unlaces, unlacing, unlaced.** (*tr*) **1** to loosen or undo the lacing of (shoes, etc.). **2** to unfasten or remove garments, etc., of (oneself or another) by or as if by undoing lacing.

unlawful assembly (ʌn'lɔːfʊl) *n Law.* a meeting of three or more people with the intent of carrying out any unlawful purpose.

unlay (ʌn'leɪ) *vb* **unlays, unlaying, unlaid.** (*tr*) to untwist (a rope or cable) to separate its strands.

unleaded (ʌn'lɛdɪd) *adj* **1** (of petrol) containing a reduced amount of tetraethyl lead, in order to reduce environmental pollution. ◆ *n* **2** petrol containing a reduced amount of tetraethyl lead.

unlearn (ʌn'lɜːn) *vb* **unlearns, unlearning, unlearnt** *or* **unlearned** (-'lɜːnd). to try to forget (something learnt) or to discard (accumulated knowledge).

unlearned (ʌn'lɜːnɪd) *adj* ignorant or untaught.
▸ **un'learnedly** *adv*

unlearnt (ʌn'lɜːnt) *or* **unlearned** (ʌn'lɜːnd) *adj* **1** denoting knowledge or skills innately present and therefore not learnt. **2** not learnt or taken notice of: *unlearnt lessons.*

unleash (ʌn'liːʃ) *vb* (*tr*) **1** to release from or as if from a leash. **2** to free from restraint.

unleavened (ʌn'lɛvənd) *adj* (of bread, etc.) made from a dough containing no yeast or leavening.

unless (ʌn'lɛs) *conj* (*subordinating*) except under the circumstances that; except on the condition that: *they'll sell it unless he hears otherwise.* [C14 *onlesse,* from *on* ON + *lesse* LESS]

unlettered (ʌn'lɛtəd) *adj* uneducated; illiterate.

unlike (ʌn'laɪk) *adj* **1** not alike; dissimilar or unequal; different. ◆ *prep* **2** not like; not typical of: *unlike his father he lacks intelligence.*
▸ **un'likeness** *n*

unlikely (ʌn'laɪklɪ) *adj* not likely; improbable.
▸ **un'likeliness** *or* **un'likeli,hood** *n*

unlimber (ʌn'lɪmbə) *vb* **1** (*tr*) to disengage (a gun) from its limber. **2** to prepare (something) for use.

unlimited (ʌn'lɪmɪtɪd) *adj* **1** without limits or bounds: *unlimited knowledge.* **2** not restricted, limited, or qualified: *unlimited power.*
▸ **un'limitedly** *adv* ▸ **un'limitedness** *n*

unlisted (ʌn'lɪstɪd) *adj* **1** not entered on a list. **2** the US and Canad. word for **ex-directory.**

Unlisted Securities Market *n* a market on the London Stock Exchange for trading in shares of smaller companies, who do not wish to comply with the requirements for a full listing. Abbrev.: **USM.**

unload (ʌn'ləʊd) *vb* **1** to remove a load or cargo from (a ship, lorry, etc.). **2** to discharge (cargo, freight, etc.). **3** (*tr*) to relieve of a burden or troubles. **4** (*tr*) to give vent to (anxiety, troubles, etc.). **5** (*tr*) to get rid of or dispose of (esp. surplus goods). **6** (*tr*) to remove the charge of ammunition from (a firearm).
▸ **un'loader** *n*

unlock (ʌn'lɒk) *vb* **1** (*tr*) to unfasten (a lock, door, etc.). **2** (*tr*) to release or let loose. **3** (*tr*) to provide the key to: *unlock a puzzle.* **4** (*intr*) to become unlocked.
▸ **un'lockable** *adj*

unlooked-for (ˌʌn'lʊktfɔː) *adj* unexpected; unforeseen.

unloose (ʌn'luːs) *or* **unloosen** *vb* **unlooses, unloosing, unloosed** *or* **unloosens, unloosening, unloosened.** (*tr*) **1** to set free; release. **2** to loosen or relax (a hold, grip, etc.). **3** to unfasten or untie.

unlovely (ʌn'lʌvlɪ) *adj* unpleasant in appearance or character.
▸ **un'loveliness** *n*

unlucky (ʌn'lʌkɪ) *adj* **1** characterized by misfortune or failure: *an unlucky chance.* **2** ill-omened; inauspicious: *an unlucky date.* **3** regrettable; disappointing.
▸ **un'luckily** *adv* ▸ **un'luckiness** *n*

unmake (ʌn'meɪk) *vb* **unmakes, unmaking, unmade.** (*tr*) **1** to undo or destroy. **2** to depose from office or authority. **3** to alter the nature of.

unman (ʌn'mæn) *vb* **unmans, unmanning, unmanned.** (*tr*) **1** to cause to lose courage or nerve. **2** to make effeminate. **3** to remove the men from.

unmanly (ʌn'mænlɪ) *adj* **1** not masculine or virile. **2** ignoble, cowardly, or dishonourable. ◆ *adv* **3** *Arch.* in an unmanly manner.
▸ **un'manliness** *n*

unmanned (ʌn'mænd) *adj* **1** lacking personnel or crew: *an unmanned ship.* **2** (of aircraft, spacecraft, etc.) operated by automatic or remote control. **3** uninhabited.

unmannered (ʌn'mænəd) *adj* **1** without good manners; rude. **2** without mannerisms.

unmannerly (ʌn'mænəlɪ) *adj* **1** lacking manners; discourteous. ◆ *adv* **2** *Arch.* rudely; discourteously.
▸ **un'mannerliness** *n*

unmask (ʌn'mɑːsk) *vb* **1** to remove (the mask or disguise) from (someone or oneself). **2** to appear or cause to appear in true character.
▸ **un'masker** *n*

unmeaning (ʌn'miːnɪŋ) *adj* **1** having no meaning. **2** showing no intelligence; vacant: *an unmeaning face.*
▸ **un'meaningly** *adv* ▸ **un'meaningness** *n*

unmeet (ʌn'miːt) *adj Literary or arch.* unsuitable.
▸ **un'meetly** *adv* ▸ **un'meetness** *n*

unmentionable (ʌn'mɛnʃənəbᵊl) *adj* **a** unsuitable or forbidden as a topic of conversation. **b** (*as n*): *the unmentionable.*
▸ **un'mentionableness** *n* ▸ **un'mentionably** *adv*

unmentionables (ʌn'mɛnʃənəbᵊlz) *pl n Chiefly humorous.* underwear.

unmerciful (ʌn'mɜːsɪfʊl) *adj* **1** showing no mercy; relentless. **2** extreme or excessive.
▸ **un'mercifully** *adv* ▸ **un'mercifulness** *n*

unmindful (ʌn'maɪndfʊl) *adj* (*usually postpositive* and foll. by *of*) careless or forgetful.
▸ **un'mindfully** *adv* ▸ **un'mindfulness** *n*

unmissable (ʌn'mɪsəbᵊl) *adj* (of a film, television programme, etc.) so good that it should not be missed.

unmistakable *or* **unmistakeable** (ˌʌnmɪs'teɪkəbᵊl) *adj* not mistakable; clear or unambiguous.
▸ ˌ**unmis'takably** *adv* ▸ ˌ**unmis'takeably** *adv*

unmitigated (ʌn'mɪtɪˌgeɪtɪd) *adj* **1** not diminished in intensity, severity, etc. **2** (*prenominal*) (intensifier): *an unmitigated disaster.*
▸ **un'miti,gatedly** *adv*

unmoral (ʌn'mɒrəl) adj outside morality; amoral.
  ▸ **un'morality** (ˌʌnmə'rælɪtɪ) n ▸ **un'morally** adv

unmurmuring (ʌn'mɜːmərɪŋ) adj not complaining.

unmuzzle (ʌn'mʌzəl) vb **unmuzzles, unmuzzling, unmuzzled.**
  (tr) **1** to take the muzzle off (a dog, etc.). **2** to free from
  control or censorship.

unnatural (ʌn'nætʃərəl) adj **1** contrary to nature; abnormal. **2** not in accordance with accepted standards of behaviour or right and wrong: *unnatural love*. **3** uncanny;
  supernatural: *unnatural phenomena*. **4** affected or forced:
  an unnatural manner. **5** inhuman or monstrous: *an unnatural crime*.
  ▸ **un'naturally** adv ▸ **un'naturalness** n

unnecessary (ʌn'nesɪsərɪ) adj not necessary.
  ▸ **un'necessarily** adv ▸ **un'necessariness** n

unnerve (ʌn'nɜːv) vb **unnerves, unnerving, unnerved.** (tr) to
  cause to lose courage, strength, confidence, self-control,
  etc.

unnumbered (ʌn'nʌmbəd) adj **1** countless; innumerable. **2** not counted or assigned a number.

UNO abbrev. for United Nations Organization.

unoccupied (ʌn'ɒkjʊˌpaɪd) adj **1** (of a building) without
  occupants. **2** unemployed or idle. **3** (of an area or country) not overrun by foreign troops.

unofficial (ˌʌnə'fɪʃəl) adj **1** not official or formal: *an unofficial engagement*. **2** not confirmed officially: *an unofficial
  report*. **3** (of a strike) not approved by the strikers' trade
  union.
  ▸ ˌ**unof'ficially** adv

unorganized or **unorganised** (ʌn'ɔːgəˌnaɪzd) adj **1**
  not arranged into an organized system, structure, or
  unity. **2** (of workers) not unionized. **3** nonliving; inorganic.

unowned (ʌn'əʊnd) adj **1** unacknowledged. **2** without
  an owner.

unpack (ʌn'pæk) vb **1** to remove the packed contents of
  (a case, trunk, etc.). **2** (tr) to take (something) out of a
  packed container. **3** (tr) to unload: *to unpack a mule*.
  ▸ **un'packer** n

unpaged (ʌn'peɪdʒd) adj (of a book) having no page
  numbers.

unparalleled (ʌn'pærəˌleld) adj unmatched; unequalled.

unparliamentary (ˌʌnpɑːlə'mentərɪ) adj not consistent
  with parliamentary procedure or practice.
  ▸ ˌ**unparlia'mentarily** adv ▸ ˌ**unparlia'mentariness** n

unpeg (ʌn'peg) vb **unpegs, unpegging, unpegged.** (tr) **1** to remove the peg from, esp. to unfasten. **2** to allow (prices,
  etc.) to rise and fall freely.

unpeople (ʌn'piːpəl) vb **unpeoples, unpeopling, unpeopled.**
  (tr) to empty of people.

unperson ('ʌnpɜːsˀn) n a person whose existence is officially denied or ignored.

unpick (ʌn'pɪk) vb (tr) **1** to undo (the stitches) of (a piece
  of sewing). **2** to unravel or undo (a garment, etc.).

unpin (ʌn'pɪn) vb **unpins, unpinning, unpinned.** (tr) **1** to remove a pin or pins from. **2** to unfasten by removing
  pins.

unpleasant (ʌn'plezˀnt) adj not pleasant or agreeable.
  ▸ **un'pleasantly** adv ▸ **un'pleasantness** n

unplugged (ʌn'plʌgd) adj (of a performer or performance of popular music) using acoustic rather than
  electric instruments: *Eric Clapton unplugged; an unplugged
  version of the song*.

unplumbed (ʌn'plʌmd) adj **1** unfathomed; unsounded.
  2 not understood in depth. **3** (of a building) having no
  plumbing.

unpolled (ʌn'pəʊld) adj **1** not included in an opinion
  poll. **2** not having voted. **3** *Arch*. unshorn.

unpopular (ʌn'pɒpjʊlə) adj not popular with an individual or group of people.
  ▸ **unpopularity** (ˌʌnpɒpjʊ'lærɪtɪ) n ▸ **un'popularly** adv

unpractical (ʌn'præktɪkˀl) adj another word for **impractical**.
  ▸ ˌ**unpracti'cality** n ▸ **un'practically** adv

unpractised or US **unpracticed** (ʌn'præktɪst) adj
  without skill, training, or experience. **2** not used or don‹
  often or repeatedly. **3** not yet tested.

unprecedented (ʌn'presɪˌdentɪd) adj having no prece‹
  dent; unparalleled.
  ▸ **un'prece,dentedly** adv

unprejudiced (ʌn'predʒʊdɪst) adj not prejudiced or bi‹
  ased; impartial.
  ▸ **un'prejudicedly** adv

unprincipled (ʌn'prɪnsɪpˀld) adj lacking moral princi‹
  ples; unscrupulous.
  ▸ **un'principledness** n

unprintable (ʌn'prɪntəbˀl) adj unsuitable for printing
  for reasons of obscenity, libel, etc.
  ▸ **un'printableness** n ▸ **un'printably** adv

unprofessional (ˌʌnprə'feʃənˀl) adj **1** contrary to the ac‹
  cepted code of conduct of a profession. **2** amateur. **3** no‹
  belonging to or having the required qualifications for ‹
  profession.
  ▸ ˌ**unpro'fessionally** adv

unprotected sex n an act of sexual intercourse o‹
  sodomy performed without the use of a condom thu‹
  involving the risk of sexually transmitted diseases.

unputdownable (ˌʌnpʊt'daʊnəbˀl) adj (esp. of a novel
  so gripping as to be read at one sitting.

unqualified (ʌn'kwɒlɪˌfaɪd) adj **1** lacking the necessar‹
  qualifications. **2** not restricted or modified: *an unquali‹
  fied criticism*. **3** (*usually prenominal*) (intensifier): *an un‹
  qualified success*.
  ▸ **un'quali,fiable** adj

unquestionable (ʌn'kwestʃənəbˀl) adj **1** indubitable o‹
  indisputable. **2** not admitting of exception: *an unques‹
  tionable ruling*.
  ▸ **un,questiona'bility** n ▸ **un'questionably** adv

unquestioned (ʌn'kwestʃənd) adj **1** accepted withou‹
  question. **2** not admitting of doubt or question: *unques‹
  tioned power*. **3** not questioned or interrogated.

unquiet (ʌn'kwaɪət) *Chiefly literary*. ◆ adj **1** character‹
  ized by disorder or tumult: *unquiet times*. **2** anxious; un‹
  easy. ◆ n **3** a state of unrest.
  ▸ **un'quietly** adv ▸ **un'quietness** n

unquote (ʌn'kwəʊt) interj **1** an expression used paren‹
  thetically to indicate that the preceding quotation is fin‹
  ished. ◆ vb **unquotes, unquoting, unquoted.** **2** to close (‹
  quotation), esp. in printing.

unravel (ʌn'rævˀl) vb **unravels, unravelling, unravelled** or US
  unravels, unraveling, unraveled. **1** (tr) to reduce (something
  knitted or woven) to separate strands. **2** (tr) to explain o‹
  solve: *the mystery was unravelled*. **3** (intr) to become unrav‹
  elled.

unreactive (ˌʌnrɪ'æktɪv) adj (of a substance) not readily
  partaking in chemical reactions.

unread (ʌn'red) adj **1** (of a book, etc.) not yet read. **2** (of a
  person) having read little.

unreadable (ʌn'riːdəbˀl) adj **1** illegible; undecipherable.
  2 difficult or tedious to read.
  ▸ **un,reada'bility** or **un'readableness** n

unready (ʌn'redɪ) adj **1** not ready or prepared. **2** slow or
  hesitant to see or act.
  ▸ **un'readily** adv ▸ **un'readiness** n

unreal (ʌn'rɪəl) adj **1** imaginary or fanciful or seemingly
  so: *an unreal situation*. **2** having no actual existence or
  substance. **3** insincere or artificial.
  ▸ **unreality** (ˌʌnrɪ'ælɪtɪ) n ▸ **un'really** adv

unreason (ʌn'riːzˀn) n **1** irrationality or madness. **2**
  something that lacks or is contrary to reason. **3** lack of
  order; chaos.

unreasonable (ʌn'riːznəbˀl) adj **1** immoderate: *unrea‹
  sonable demands*. **2** refusing to listen to reason. **3** lacking
  judgment.
  ▸ **un'reasonableness** n ▸ **un'reasonably** adv

unreasoning (ʌn'riːzənɪŋ) adj not controlled by reason;
  irrational.
  ▸ **un'reasoningly** adv

unregenerate (ˌʌnrɪ'dʒenərɪt) adj also **unregenerated.** **1**

★ people and places

unrepentant; unreformed. **2** obstinately adhering to one's own views. ◆ *n* **3** an unregenerate person.
▸ ˌunre'generacy *n* ▸ ˌunre'generately *adv*

unrelenting (ˌʌnrɪ'lentɪŋ) *adj* **1** refusing to relent or take pity. **2** not diminishing in determination, speed, effort, force, etc.
▸ ˌunre'lentingly *adv* ▸ ˌunre'lentingness *n*

unreligious (ˌʌnrɪ'lɪdʒəs) *adj* **1** another word for **irreligious. 2** secular.
▸ ˌunre'ligiously *adv*

unremitting (ˌʌnrɪ'mɪtɪŋ) *adj* never slackening or stopping; unceasing; constant.
▸ ˌunre'mittingly *adv* ▸ ˌunre'mittingness *n*

unreserved (ˌʌnrɪ'zɜːvd) *adj* **1** without reserve; having an open manner. **2** without reservation. **3** not booked or bookable.
▸ unreservedly (ˌʌnrɪ'zɜːvɪdlɪ) *adv* ▸ ˌunre'servedness *n*

unrest (ʌn'rest) *n* **1** a troubled or rebellious state of discontent. **2** an uneasy or troubled state.

unriddle (ʌn'rɪdᵊl) *vb* **unriddles, unriddling, unriddled.** (*tr*) to solve or puzzle out. [C16: from UN-² + RIDDLE¹]
▸ un'riddler *n*

unrig (ʌn'rɪg) *vb* **unrigs, unrigging, unrigged. 1** (*tr*) to strip (a vessel) of standing and running rigging. **2** *Arch. or dialect.* to undress (someone or oneself).

unrighteous (ʌn'raɪtʃəs) *adj* **1a** sinful; wicked. **1b** (*as collective n; preceded by the*): *the unrighteous.* **2** not fair or right; unjust.
▸ un'righteously *adv* ▸ un'righteousness *n*

unrip (ʌn'rɪp) *vb* **unrips, unripping, unripped.** (*tr*) **1** to rip open. **2** *Obs.* to reveal; disclose.

unripe (ʌn'raɪp) *or* **unripened** *adj* **1** not fully matured. **2** not fully prepared or developed; not ready.
▸ un'ripeness *n*

unrivalled *or US* **unrivaled** (ʌn'raɪvᵊld) *adj* having no equal; matchless.

unroll (ʌn'rəʊl) *vb* **1** to open out or unwind (something rolled, folded, or coiled) or (of something rolled, etc.) to become opened out or unwound. **2** to make or become visible or apparent, esp. gradually; unfold.

unruffled (ʌn'rʌfᵊld) *adj* **1** unmoved; calm. **2** still: *the unruffled seas.*
▸ un'ruffledness *n*

unruly (ʌn'ruːlɪ) *adj* **unrulier, unruliest.** disposed to disobedience or indiscipline.
▸ un'ruliness *n*

UNRWA ('ʌnrə) *n acronym for* United Nations Relief and Works Agency.

unsaddle (ʌn'sædᵊl) *vb* **unsaddles, unsaddling, unsaddled. 1** to remove the saddle from (a horse, mule, etc.). **2** (*tr*) to unhorse.

unsaddling enclosure *n* the area at a racecourse where horses are unsaddled after a race and often where awards are given to owners, trainers, and jockeys.

unsafe (ʌn'seɪf) *adj* **1** not safe; perilous. **2** (of a criminal conviction) based on inadequate or false evidence.

unsaid (ʌn'sed) *adj* not said or expressed; unspoken.

unsaturated (ʌn'sætʃəˌreɪtɪd) *adj* **1** not saturated. **2** (of a chemical compound, esp. an organic compound) containing one or more double or triple bonds and thus capable of undergoing addition reactions. **3** (of a fat, esp. a vegetable fat) containing a high proportion of fatty acids having double bonds.
▸ ˌunsatu'ration *n*

unsavoury *or US* **unsavory** (ʌn'seɪvərɪ) *adj* **1** objectionable or distasteful: *an unsavoury character.* **2** disagreeable in odour or taste.
▸ un'savoury *or US* un'savorily *adv* ▸ un'savouriness *or US* un'savoriness *n*

unsay (ʌn'seɪ) *vb* **unsays, unsaying, unsaid.** (*tr*) to retract or withdraw (something said or written).

unscathed (ʌn'skeɪðd) *adj* not harmed or injured.

unscramble (ʌn'skræmbᵊl) *vb* **unscrambles, unscrambling, unscrambled.** (*tr*) **1** to resolve from confusion or disorder-

liness. **2** to restore (a scrambled message) to an intelligible form.
▸ un'scrambler *n*

unscrew (ʌn'skruː) *vb* **1** (*tr*) to remove a screw from (an object). **2** (*tr*) to loosen (a screw, lid, etc.) by rotating, usually in an anticlockwise direction. **3** (*intr*) (esp. of an engaged threaded part) to become loosened or separated.

unscripted (ʌn'skrɪptɪd) *adj* (of a speech, play, etc.) not using or based on a script.

unscrupulous (ʌn'skruːpjʊləs) *adj* without scruples; unprincipled.
▸ un'scrupulously *adv* ▸ un'scrupulousness *n*

unseal (ʌn'siːl) *vb* (*tr*) **1** to remove or break the seal of. **2** to free (something concealed or closed as if sealed): *to unseal one's lips.*

unsealed (ʌn'siːld) *adj Austral. & NZ.* (of a road) surfaced with road metal not bound by bitumen or other sealant.

unseam (ʌn'siːm) *vb* (*tr*) to open or undo the seam of.

unseasonable (ʌn'siːzənəbᵊl) *adj* **1** (esp. of the weather) inappropriate for the season. **2** untimely; inopportune.
▸ un'seasonableness *n* ▸ un'seasonably *adv*

unseat (ʌn'siːt) *vb* (*tr*) **1** to throw or displace from a seat, saddle, etc. **2** to depose from office or position.

unseeded (ʌn'siːdɪd) *adj* (of players in various sports) not assigned to a preferential position in the preliminary rounds of a tournament.

unseemly (ʌn'siːmlɪ) *adj* **1** not in good style or taste. **2** *Obs.* unattractive. ◆ *adv* **3** *Rare.* in an unseemly manner.
▸ un'seemliness *n*

unseen (ʌn'siːn) *adj* **1** not observed or perceived; invisible. **2** (of passages of writing) not previously seen or prepared. ◆ *n* **3** *Chiefly Brit.* a passage, not previously seen, that is presented to students for translation.

unselfish (ʌn'selfɪʃ) *adj* not selfish; generous.
▸ un'selfishly *adv* ▸ un'selfishness *n*

unsettle (ʌn'setᵊl) *vb* **unsettles, unsettling, unsettled. 1** (*usually tr*) to change or become changed from a fixed or settled condition. **2** (*tr*) to confuse or agitate (emotions, the mind, etc.).
▸ un'settlement *n*

unsettled (ʌn'setᵊld) *adj* **1** lacking order or stability: *an unsettled era.* **2** unpredictable: *an unsettled climate.* **3** constantly changing or moving from place to place: *an unsettled life.* **4** (of controversy, etc.) not brought to an agreed conclusion. **5** (of debts, law cases, etc.) not disposed of.
▸ un'settledness *n*

unsex (ʌn'seks) *vb* (*tr*) *Chiefly literary.* to deprive (a person) of the attributes of his or her sex, esp. to make a woman more callous.

unshapen (ʌn'ʃeɪpᵊn) *adj* **1** having no definite shape; shapeless. **2** deformed; misshapen.

unsheathe (ʌn'ʃiːð) *vb* **unsheathes, unsheathing, unsheathed.** (*tr*) to draw or pull out (something, esp. a weapon) from a sheath.

unship (ʌn'ʃɪp) *vb* **unships, unshipping, unshipped. 1** to be or cause to be unloaded, discharged, or disembarked from a ship. **2** (*tr*) *Naut.* to remove from a regular place: *to unship oars.*

unsighted (ʌn'saɪtɪd) *adj* **1** not sighted. **2** not having a clear view. **3** (of a gun) not equipped with a sight.
▸ un'sightedly *adv*

unsightly (ʌn'saɪtlɪ) *adj* unpleasant or unattractive to look at; ugly.
▸ un'sightliness *n*

unskilful *or US* **unskillful** (ʌn'skɪlfʊl) *adj* lacking dexterity or proficiency.
▸ un'skilfully *or US* un'skillfully *adv* ▸ un'skilfulness *or US* un'skillfulness *n*

unskilled (ʌn'skɪld) *adj* **1** not having or requiring any special skill or training: *an unskilled job.* **2** having no skill; inexpert.

unsling (ʌn'slɪŋ) *vb* **unslings, unslinging, unslung.** (*tr*) **1** to remove or release from a slung position. **2** to remove slings from.

unsnap (ʌnˈsnæp) vb **unsnaps, unsnapping, unsnapped.** (tr) to unfasten (the snap or catch) of (something).

unsnarl (ʌnˈsnɑːl) vb (tr) to free from a snarl or tangle.

unsociable (ʌnˈsəʊʃəbˀl) adj **1** (of a person) disinclined to associate or fraternize with others. **2** unconducive to social intercourse: *an unsociable neighbourhood.*
▶ un,socia'bility *or* un'sociableness *n*

unsocial (ʌnˈsəʊʃəl) adj **1** not social; antisocial. **2** (of the hours of work of certain jobs) falling outside the normal working day.

unsophisticated (ˌʌnsəˈfɪstɪˌkeɪtɪd) adj **1** lacking experience or worldly wisdom. **2** marked by a lack of refinement or complexity: *an unsophisticated machine.* **3** unadulterated or genuine.
▶ ,unso'phisti,catedly *adv* ▶ ,unso'phisti,catedness *or* ,unso,phisti'cation *n*

unsound (ʌnˈsaʊnd) adj **1** diseased or unstable: *of unsound mind.* **2** unreliable or fallacious: *unsound advice.* **3** lacking strength or firmness: *unsound foundations.* **4** of doubtful financial or commercial viability: *an unsound enterprise.*
▶ un'soundly *adv* ▶ un'soundness *n*

unsparing (ʌnˈspeərɪŋ) adj **1** not sparing or frugal; lavish. **2** showing harshness or severity.
▶ un'sparingly *adv* ▶ un'sparingness *n*

unspeakable (ʌnˈspiːkəbˀl) adj **1** incapable of expression in words: *unspeakable ecstasy.* **2** indescribably bad or evil. **3** not to be uttered: *unspeakable thoughts.*
▶ un'speakableness *n* ▶ un'speakably *adv*

unstable (ʌnˈsteɪbˀl) adj **1** lacking stability, fixity, or firmness. **2** disposed to temperamental or psychological variability. **3** (of a chemical compound) readily decomposing. **4** *Physics.* **4a** (of an elementary particle) having a very short lifetime. **4b** spontaneously decomposing by nuclear decay: *an unstable nuclide.* **5** *Electronics.* (of an electrical circuit, etc.) having a tendency to self-oscillation.
▶ un'stableness *n* ▶ un'stably *adv*

unsteady (ʌnˈstedɪ) adj **1** not securely fixed: *an unsteady foothold.* **2** (of behaviour, etc.) erratic. **3** without regularity: *an unsteady rhythm.* **4** (of a manner of walking, etc.) precarious or staggering, as from intoxication.
▶ un'steadily *adv* ▶ un'steadiness *n*

unstep (ʌnˈstep) vb **unsteps, unstepping, unstepped.** (tr) *Naut.* to remove (a mast) from its step.

unstick (ʌnˈstɪk) vb **unsticks, unsticking, unstuck.** (tr) to free or loosen (something stuck).

unstop (ʌnˈstɒp) vb **unstops, unstopping, unstopped.** (tr) **1** to remove the stop or stopper from. **2** to free from any stoppage or obstruction. **3** to draw out the stops on (an organ).
▶ un'stoppable *adj* ▶ un'stoppably *adv*

unstopped (ʌnˈstɒpt) adj **1** not obstructed or stopped up. **2** *Phonetics.* denoting a speech sound for whose articulation the closure is not complete. **3** *Prosody.* (of verse) having the sense of the line carried over into the next. **4** (of an organ pipe or a string on a musical instrument) not stopped.

unstriated (ˌʌnstraɪˈeɪtɪd) adj (of muscle) composed of elongated cells that do not have striations; smooth.

unstring (ʌnˈstrɪŋ) vb **unstrings, unstringing, unstrung.** (tr) **1** to remove the strings of. **2** (of beads, etc.) to remove from a string. **3** to weaken emotionally (a person or his nerves).

unstriped (ʌnˈstraɪpt) adj (esp. of smooth muscle) not having stripes; unstriated.

unstructured (ʌnˈstrʌktʃəd) adj **1** without formal structure or systematic organization. **2** without a preformed shape; (esp. of clothes) loose; untailored.

unstrung (ʌnˈstrʌŋ) adj **1** emotionally distressed; unnerved. **2** (of a stringed instrument) with the strings detached.

unstuck (ʌnˈstʌk) adj **1** freed from being stuck, glued, fastened, etc. **2 come unstuck.** to suffer failure or disaster.

unstudied (ʌnˈstʌdɪd) adj **1** natural. **2** (foll. by *in*) without knowledge or training.

unsubstantial (ˌʌnsəbˈstænʃəl) adj **1** lacking weight or firmness. **2** (of an argument) of doubtful validity. **3** of no material existence.
▶ ,unsub,stanti'ality *n* ▶ ,unsub'stantially *adv*

unsung (ʌnˈsʌŋ) adj **1** not acclaimed or honoured: *unsung deeds.* **2** not yet sung.

unsuspected (ˌʌnsəˈspektɪd) adj **1** not under suspicion. **2** not known to exist.
▶ ,unsus'pectedly *adv* ▶ ,unsus'pectedness *n*

unswerving (ʌnˈswɜːvɪŋ) adj not turning aside; constant.

untangle (ʌnˈtæŋgˀl) vb **untangles, untangling, untangled.** (tr) **1** to free from a tangled condition. **2** to free from confusion.

untaught (ʌnˈtɔːt) adj **1** without training or education. **2** attained or achieved without instruction.

untenable (ʌnˈtɛnəbˀl) adj **1** (of theories, etc.) incapable of being maintained or vindicated. **2** unable to be maintained against attack.
▶ un,tena'bility *or* un'tenableness *n* ▶ un'tenably *adv*

Unter den Linden ★ (German ˈʊntər deːn ˈlɪndən) *n* the main street of Berlin, formerly in East Berlin, extending to the Brandenburg Gate.

Unterwalden ★ (German ˈʊntərˌvaldən) *n* a canton of central Switzerland, on Lake Lucerne: consists of the demicantons of **Nidwalden** (east) and **Obwalden** (west). Capitals: (Nidwalden) Stans; (Obwalden) Sarnen. Pop. (Nidwalden) 35 983 (1995 est.); (Obwalden) 30 958 (1995 est.). Areas: (Nidwalden) 274 sq. km (107 sq. miles); (Obwalden) 492 sq. km (192 sq. miles).

unthinkable (ʌnˈθɪŋkəbˀl) adj **1** not to be contemplated out of the question. **2** unimaginable; inconceivable. **3** unreasonable; improbable.
▶ un'thinkably *adv*

unthinking (ʌnˈθɪŋkɪŋ) adj **1** lacking thoughtfulness; inconsiderate. **2** heedless; inadvertent. **3** not thinking or able to think.
▶ un'thinkingly *adv* ▶ un'thinkingness *n*

unthread (ʌnˈθrɛd) vb (tr) **1** to draw out the thread or threads from (a needle, etc.). **2** to disentangle.

unthrone (ʌnˈθrəʊn) vb **unthrones, unthroning, unthroned.** (tr) a less common word for **dethrone**.

untidy (ʌnˈtaɪdɪ) adj **untidier, untidiest.** **1** not neat; slovenly. ◆ vb **untidies, untidying, untidied.** **2** (tr) to make untidy.
▶ un'tidily *adv* ▶ un'tidiness *n*

untie (ʌnˈtaɪ) vb **unties, untying, untied.** **1** to unfasten or free (a knot or something that is tied) or (of a knot, etc.) to become unfastened. **2** (tr) to free from constraint or restriction.

until (ʌnˈtɪl) conj (subordinating) **1** up to (a time) that: *he laughed until he cried.* **2** (used with a negative) before (a time or event): *until you change, you can't go out.* ◆ prep **3** (often preceded by *up*) in or throughout the period before: *he waited until six.* **4** (used with a negative) earlier than; before: *he won't come until tomorrow.* [C13 *untill;* see TILL[1]]

> **USAGE NOTE** The use of *until such time as* (as in *industrial action will continue until such time as our demands are met*) is unnecessary and should be avoided: *industrial action will continue until our demands are met.* See also **till**[1].

untimely (ʌnˈtaɪmlɪ) adj **1** occurring before the expected, normal, or proper time: *an untimely death.* **2** inappropriate to the occasion, time, or season: *his joking at the funeral was most untimely.* ◆ adv **3** prematurely or inopportunely.
▶ un'timeliness *n*

unto (ˈʌntuː) prep *Arch.* to. [C13: from ON]

untogether (ˌʌntəˈgɛðə) adj *Sl.* incompetent or badly organized; mentally or emotionally unstable.

untold (ʌnˈtəʊld) adj **1** incapable of description: *untold suffering.* **2** incalculably great in number or quantity: *untold thousands.* **3** not told.

★ people and places

untouchable (ʌnˈtʌtʃəbʰl) *adj* **1** lying beyond reach. **2** above reproach, suspicion, or impeachment. **3** unable to be touched. ✦ *n* **4** a member of the lowest class in India, whom those of the four main castes were formerly forbidden to touch.
▶ un,toucha'bility *n*

untoward (,ʌntəˈwɔːd) *adj* **1** characterized by misfortune or annoyance. **2** not auspicious; unfavourable. **3** unseemly. **4** out of the ordinary; out of the way. **5** *Arch.* perverse. **6** *Obs.* awkward.
▶ ,unto'wardly *adv* ▶ ,unto'wardness *n*

untrue (ʌnˈtruː) *adj* **1** incorrect or false. **2** disloyal. **3** diverging from a rule, standard, or measure; inaccurate.
▶ un'truly *adv*

untruss (ʌnˈtrʌs) *vb* **1** (*tr*) to release from or as if from a truss; unfasten. **2** *Obs.* to undress.

untruth (ʌnˈtruːθ) *n* **1** the state or quality of being untrue. **2** a statement, etc., that is not true.

untruthful (ʌnˈtruːθful) *adj* **1** (of a person) given to lying. **2** diverging from the truth.
▶ un'truthfully *adv* ▶ un'truthfulness *n*

untuck (ʌnˈtʌk) *vb* to become or cause to become loose or not tucked in: *to untuck the blankets.*

untutored (ʌnˈtjuːtəd) *adj* **1** without formal education. **2** lacking sophistication or refinement.

unused *adj* **1** (ʌnˈjuːzd). not being or never having been made use of. **2** (ʌnˈjuːst). (*postpositive*; foll. by *to*) not accustomed or used (to something).

unusual (ʌnˈjuːʒʊəl) *adj* uncommon; extraordinary: *an unusual design.*
▶ un'usually *adv*

unutterable (ʌnˈʌtərəbʰl) *adj* incapable of being expressed in words.
▶ un'utterableness *n* ▶ un'utterably *adv*

unvarnished (ʌnˈvɑːnɪʃt) *adj* not elaborated upon or glossed; plain and direct: *the unvarnished truth.*

unveil (ʌnˈveɪl) *vb* **1** (*tr*) to remove the cover from, esp. in the ceremonial unveiling of a monument, etc. **2** to remove the veil from (one's own or another person's face). **3** (*tr*) to make (something concealed) known or public.

unveiling (ʌnˈveɪlɪŋ) *n* **1** a ceremony involving the removal of a veil covering a statue, etc., for the first time. **2** the presentation of something, esp. for the first time.

unvoice (ʌnˈvɔɪs) *vb* **unvoices, unvoicing, unvoiced.** (*tr*) *Phonetics.* **1** to pronounce without vibration of the vocal cords. **2** Also: **devoice.** to make (a voiced speech sound) voiceless.

unvoiced (ʌnˈvɔɪst) *adj* **1** not expressed or spoken. **2** articulated without vibration of the vocal cords; voiceless.

unwaged (ʌnˈweɪdʒd) *adj* of or denoting a person who is not receiving pay because of being unemployed or working in the home.

unwarrantable (ʌnˈwɒrəntəbʰl) *adj* incapable of vindication or justification.
▶ un'warrantableness *n* ▶ un'warrantably *adv*

unwarranted (ʌnˈwɒrəntɪd) *adj* **1** lacking justification or authorization. **2** another word for **unwarrantable.**

unwary (ʌnˈwɛərɪ) *adj* lacking caution or prudence.
▶ un'warily *adv* ▶ un'wariness *n*

unwearied (ʌnˈwɪərɪd) *adj* **1** not abating or tiring. **2** not fatigued; fresh.
▶ un'weariedly *adv* ▶ un'weariedness *n*

unweighed (ʌnˈweɪd) *adj* **1** (of quantities purchased, etc.) not measured for weight. **2** (of statements, etc.) not carefully considered.

unwell (ʌnˈwɛl) *adj* (*postpositive*) not well; ill.

unwept (ʌnˈwɛpt) *adj* **1** not wept for or lamented. **2** *Rare.* (of tears) not shed.

unwholesome (ʌnˈhəʊlsəm) *adj* **1** detrimental to physical or mental health: *an unwholesome climate.* **2** morally harmful: *unwholesome practices.* **3** indicative of illness, esp. in appearance. **4** (esp. of food) of inferior quality.
▶ un'wholesomeness *n*

unwieldy (ʌnˈwiːldɪ) *adj* **1** too heavy, large, or awkwardly shaped to be easily handled. **2** ungainly; clumsy.
▶ un'wieldily *adv* ▶ un'wieldiness *n*

unwilled (ʌnˈwɪld) *adj* not intentional; involuntary.

unwilling (ʌnˈwɪlɪŋ) *adj* **1** reluctant. **2** performed or said with reluctance.
▶ un'willingly *adv* ▶ un'willingness *n*

unwind (ʌnˈwaɪnd) *vb* **unwinds, unwinding, unwound.** **1** to slacken, undo, or unravel or cause to slacken, undo, or unravel. **2** (*tr*) to disentangle. **3** to make or become relaxed: *he finds it hard to unwind.*
▶ un'windable *adj*

unwise (ʌnˈwaɪz) *adj* lacking wisdom or prudence.
▶ un'wisely *adv* ▶ un'wiseness *n*

unwish (ʌnˈwɪʃ) *vb* (*tr*) **1** to retract or revoke (a wish). **2** to desire (something) not to be or take place.

unwitting (ʌnˈwɪtɪŋ) *adj* (*usually prenominal*) **1** not knowing or conscious. **2** not intentional; inadvertent. [OE *unwitende*, from UN-[1] + *witting*, present participle of *witan* to know]
▶ un'wittingly *adv* ▶ un'wittingness *n*

unwonted (ʌnˈwəʊntɪd) *adj* **1** out of the ordinary; unusual. **2** (*usually foll. by to*) *Arch.* unaccustomed; unused.
▶ un'wontedly *adv*

unworldly (ʌnˈwɜːldlɪ) *adj* **1** not concerned with material values or pursuits. **2** lacking sophistication; naive. **3** not of this earth or world.
▶ un'worldliness *n*

unworthy (ʌnˈwɜːðɪ) *adj* **1** (often foll. by *of*) not deserving or worthy. **2** (often foll. by *of*) beneath the level considered befitting (to): *that remark is unworthy of you.* **3** lacking merit or value. **4** (of treatment) not warranted.
▶ un'worthily *adv* ▶ un'worthiness *n*

unwound (ʌnˈwaʊnd) *vb* the past tense and past participle of **unwind.**

unwrap (ʌnˈræp) *vb* **unwraps, unwrapping, unwrapped.** to remove the covering or wrapping from (something) or (of something wrapped) to have the covering come off.

unwritten (ʌnˈrɪtʰn) *adj* **1** not printed or in writing. **2** effective only through custom.

unwritten law *n* the law based upon custom, usage, and judicial decisions, as distinguished from the enactments of a legislature, orders or decrees in writing, etc.

unyoke (ʌnˈjəʊk) *vb* **unyokes, unyoking, unyoked.** **1** to release (an animal, etc.) from a yoke. **2** (*tr*) to set free; liberate. **3** (*tr*) to disconnect or separate.

unzip (ʌnˈzɪp) *vb* **unzips, unzipping, unzipped.** to unfasten the zip of (a garment, etc.) or (of a zip or garment with a zip) to become unfastened: *her skirt unzipped as she sat down.*

up (ʌp) *prep* **1** indicating movement from a lower to a higher position: *climbing up a mountain.* **2** at a higher or further level or position in or on: *a shop up the road.* ✦ *adv* **3** (*often particle*) to an upward, higher, or erect position, esp. indicating readiness for an activity: *up and doing something.* **4** (*particle*) indicating intensity or completion of an action: *he tore up the cheque.* **5** to the place referred to or where the speaker is: *the man came up and asked me.* **6a** to a more important place: *up to London.* **6b** to a more northerly place: *up to Scotland.* **6c** (of a member of some British universities) to or at university. **6d** in a particular part of the country: *up north.* **7** above the horizon: *the sun is up.* **8** appearing for trial: *up before the magistrate.* **9** having gained: *ten pounds up on the deal.* **10** higher in price: *coffee is up again.* **11** raised (for discussion, etc.): *the plan was up for consideration.* **12** taught: *well up in physics.* **13** (*functioning as imperative*) get, stand, etc., up: *up with you!* **14** *Inf.* over; finished. **14b** doomed to die. **15** *up with. (functioning as imperative)* wanting the beginning or continuation of: *up with the monarchy!* **16** **something's up.** *Inf.* something strange is happening. **17** **up against. 17a** touching. **17b** having to cope with: *look what we're up against now.* **18** **up for.** as a candidate or applicant for: *he's up for re-election again.* **19** **up to. 19a** devising or scheming: *she's up to no good.* **19b** dependent or incumbent upon: *the decision is up to you.* **19c** equal to (a challenge, etc.) or capable of (doing, etc.): *are you up to playing in the final?* **19d** as far as: *up to his waist in mud.* **19e** as many as: *up to two years' waiting time.* **19f** comparable with: *not up to your normal standard.* **20** **up top.** *Inf.* in the head or mind. **21** **up yours.** *Sl.* a vulgar expression of contempt or refusal. **22 what's up?** *Inf.* **22a** what is the matter? **22b** what is happening? ◆ *adj* **23** (*predicative*) of a high or higher position. **24** (*predicative*) out of bed: *the children aren't up yet.* **25** (*prenominal*) of or relating to a train or trains to a more important place or one regarded as higher: *the up platform.* **26** (*predicative*) over or completed: *their time was up.* **27** (*predicative*) beating one's opponent by a specified amount: *a goal up.* ◆ *vb* **ups, upping, upped. 28** (*tr*) to increase or raise. **29** (*intr*; foll. by *and* with a verb) *Inf.* to do (something) suddenly, etc.: *she upped and married someone else.* ◆ *n* **30** a high point (esp. in **ups and downs**). **31** *Sl.* another word (esp. US) for **upper** (sense 8). **32 on the up and up. 32a** trustworthy or honest. **32b** *Brit.* on the upward trend or movement: *our firm's on the up and up.* [OE *upp*]

> **USAGE NOTE**   The use of *up* before *until* is redundant and should be avoided: *the talks will continue until* (not *up until*) *23rd March.*

UP *abbrev. for:* **1** United Press. **2** Uttar Pradesh.

up- *prefix* up, upper, or upwards: *uproot; upmost; upthrust; upgrade; uplift.*

up-anchor *vb* (*intr*) *Naut.* to weigh anchor.

up-and-coming *adj* promising continued or future success; enterprising.

up-and-down *adj* **1** moving or formed alternately upwards and downwards. ◆ *adv, prep* **up and down. 2** backwards and forwards (along).

up-and-over *adj* (of a door, etc.) opened by being lifted and moved into a horizontal position.

up-and-under *n Rugby League.* a high kick forwards followed by a charge to the place where the ball lands.

Upanishad (uːˈpʌnɪʃəd) *n Hinduism.* any of a class of the Sanskrit sacred books probably composed between 400 and 200 B.C. and embodying the mystical and esoteric doctrines of ancient Hindu philosophy. [C19: from Sansk. *upanisad* a sitting down near something]

upas (ˈjuːpəs) *n* **1** a large tree of Java having whitish bark and poisonous milky sap. **2** the sap of this tree, used as an arrow poison. ◆ Also called: **antiar.** [C19: from Malay: poison]

upbeat (ˈʌpˌbiːt) *n* **1** *Music.* **1a** a usually unaccented beat, esp. the last in a bar. **1b** the upward gesture of a conductor's baton indicating this. ◆ *adj* **2** *Inf.* marked by cheerfulness or optimism.

upbraid (ʌpˈbreɪd) *vb* (*tr*) **1** to reprove or reproach angrily. **2** to find fault with. [OE *upbregdan*]
  ▸ **up'braider** *n* ▸ **up'braiding** *n*

upbringing (ˈʌpˌbrɪŋɪŋ) *n* the education of a person during his formative years.

upcast (ˈʌpˌkɑːst) *n* **1** material cast or thrown up. **2** a ventilation shaft through which air leaves a mine. **3** *Geol.* (in a fault) the section of strata that has been displaced upwards. ◆ *adj* **4** directed or thrown upwards. ◆ *vb* **upcasts, upcasting, upcast. 5** (*tr*) to throw or cast up.

upcountry (ʌpˈkʌntrɪ) *adj* **1** of or coming from the interior of a country or region. ◆ *n* **2** the interior part of a region or country. ◆ *adv* **3** towards, in, or into the interior part of a country or region.

update *vb* (ʌpˈdeɪt), **updates, updating, updated.** (*tr*) **1** to bring up to date. ◆ *n* (ˈʌpˌdeɪt). **2** the act of updating or something that is updated.
  ▸ **up'dateable** *adj* ▸ **up'dater** *n*

Updike ★ (ˈʌpˌdaɪk) *n* **John** (**Hoyer**). born 1932, US writer. His novels include *Rabbit, Run* (1960), *Couples* (1968), *Rabbit is Rich* (1982), *Rabbit at Rest* (1990), and *Toward the End of Time* (1998).

updraught *or US* **updraft** (ˈʌpˌdrɑːft) *n* an upward movement of air or other gas.

upend (ʌpˈɛnd) *vb* **1** to turn or set or become turned or set on end. **2** (*tr*) to affect or upset drastically.

upfront (ˈʌpˈfrʌnt) *adj* **1** open and frank. ◆ *adv, adj* **2** (of money) paid out at the beginning of a business arrangement.

upgrade *vb* (ʌpˈgreɪd), **upgrades, upgrading, upgraded.** (*tr*) to assign or promote (a person or job) to a higher professional rank or position. **2** to raise in value, importance, esteem, etc. **3** to improve (a breed of livestock) by crossing with a better strain. ◆ *n* (ˈʌpˌgreɪd). **4** *US & Canad.* an upward slope. **5 on the upgrade.** improving or progressing as in importance, status, health, etc.
  ▸ **up'grader** *n*

upheaval (ʌpˈhiːvˀl) *n* **1** a strong, sudden, or violent disturbance, as in politics. **2** *Geol.* another word for **uplift** (sense 7).

upheave (ʌpˈhiːv) *vb* **upheaves, upheaving, upheaved** *or* **uphove. 1** to heave or rise upwards. **2** *Geol.* to thrust (land) upwards or (of land) to be thrust upwards. **3** (*tr*) to throw into disorder.

upheld (ʌpˈhɛld) *vb* the past tense and past participle of **uphold.**

uphill (ˈʌpˈhɪl) *adj* **1** inclining, sloping, or leading upwards. **2** requiring protracted effort: *an uphill task.* ◆ *adv* **3** up an incline or slope. **4** against difficulties. ◆ *n* **5** a rising incline.

uphold (ʌpˈhəʊld) *vb* **upholds, upholding, upheld.** (*tr*) **1** to maintain or defend against opposition. **2** to give moral support to. **3** *Rare.* to support physically. **4** to lift up.
  ▸ **up'holder** *n*

upholster (ʌpˈhəʊlstə) *vb* (*tr*) to fit (chairs, sofas, etc.) with padding, springs, webbing, and covering.
  ▸ **up'holstery** *n*

upholsterer (ʌpˈhəʊlstərə) *n* a person who upholsters furniture as a profession. [C17: from *upholster* small furniture dealer]

upkeep (ˈʌpˌkiːp) *n* **1** the act or process of keeping something in good repair, esp. over a long period. **2** the cost of maintenance.

upland (ˈʌplənd) *n* **1** an area of high or relatively high ground. ◆ *adj* **2** relating to or situated in an upland.

uplift *vb* (ʌpˈlɪft). (*tr*) **1** to raise; lift up. **2** to raise morally, spiritually, etc. **3** *Scot. & NZ.* to collect; pick up (goods, documents, etc.). ◆ *n* (ˈʌpˌlɪft). **4** the act, process, or result of lifting up. **5** the act or process of bettering moral, social, or cultural conditions, etc. **6** (*modifier*) designating a brassiere for lifting and supporting the breasts: *an uplift bra.* **7** the process or result of land being raised to a higher level, as during a period of mountain building.
  ▸ **up'lifter** *n* ▸ **up'lifting** *adj*

uplighter (ˈʌpˌlaɪtə) *n* a lamp or wall light designed or positioned to cast its light upwards.

up-market *adj* relating to commercial products, services, etc., that are relatively expensive and of superior quality.

upmost (ˈʌpˌməʊst) *adj* another word for **uppermost.**

Upolu ★ (uːˈpəʊluː) *n* an island in the SW central Pacific, in Western Samoa. Chief town: Apia. Pop.: 112 228 (1986). Area: 1114 sq. km (430 sq. miles).

upon (əˈpɒn) *prep* **1** another word for **on. 2** indicating a position reached by going up: *climb upon my knee.* **3** imminent for: *the weekend was upon us again.* [C13: from UP + ON]

upper (ˈʌpə) *adj* **1** higher or highest in relation to physical position, wealth, rank, status, etc. **2** (*cap. when part of a name*) lying farther upstream, inland, or farther north: *the upper valley of the Loire.* **3** (*cap. when part of a name*) *Geol., archaeol.* denoting the late part or division of a period, system, etc.: *Upper Palaeolithic.* **4** *Maths.* (of a limit or bound) greater than or equal to one or more numbers or variables. ◆ *n* **5** the higher of two objects, people, etc. **6** the part of a shoe above the sole, covering the upper surface of the foot. **7 on one's uppers.** destitute. **8** *Sl.* any of various drugs having a stimulant effect.

upper atmosphere *n Meteorol.* that part of the atmosphere above the troposphere, esp. at heights that cannot be reached by balloon.

Upper Austria ★ *n* a state of N Austria: first divided from Lower Austria in 1251. Capital: Linz. Pop.: 1 383 620 (1994 est.). Area: 11 978 sq. km (4625 sq. miles). German name: **Oberösterreich.**

★ people and places

Upper Burma ★ *n* the inland regions of Burma, in the north of the country.

Upper Canada ★ *n* **1** *History*. (from 1791–1841) the official name of the region of Canada lying southwest of the Ottawa River and north of the lower Great Lakes. Cf. **Lower Canada**. **2** (esp. in E Canada) another name for **Ontario**.

upper case *Printing*. ◆ *n* **1** the top half of a compositor's type case in which capital letters, reference marks, and accents are kept. ◆ *adj* (**upper-case** *when prenominal*). **2** of or relating to capital letters kept in this case and used in the setting or production of printed or typed matter.

upper chamber *n* another name for an **upper house**.

upper class *n* **1** the class occupying the highest position in the social hierarchy, esp. the aristocracy. ◆ *adj* (**upper-class** *when prenominal*). **2** of or relating to the upper class.

upper crust *n Inf*. the upper class.

uppercut ('ʌpə,kʌt) *n* **1** a short swinging upward blow with the fist delivered at an opponent's chin. ◆ *vb* **uppercuts, uppercutting, uppercut**. **2** to hit (an opponent) with an uppercut.

Upper Egypt ★ *n* one of the four main administrative districts of Egypt: extends south from Cairo to the Sudan.

upper hand *n* the. the position of control (esp. in **have** *or* **get the upper hand**).

upper house *n* (*often cap.*) one of the two houses of a bicameral legislature.

uppermost ('ʌpə,məʊst) *adj also* **upmost**. **1** highest in position, power, importance, etc. ◆ *adv* **2** in or into the highest position, etc.

Upper Palatinate ★ *n* See **Palatinate**.

Upper Peninsula ★ *n* a peninsula in the northern US between Lakes Superior and Michigan, constituting the N part of the state of Michigan.

upper regions *pl n* the. *Chiefly literary*. the sky; heavens.

Upper Silesia ★ *n* a region of SW Poland, formerly ruled by Germany: coalmining and other heavy industry.

Upper Tunguska ★ *n* See **Tunguska**.

Upper Volta ★ ('vɒltə) *n* the former name (until 1984) of **Burkina-Faso**.

upper works *pl n Naut*. the parts of a vessel above the water line when fully laden.

uppish ('ʌpɪʃ) *adj Brit. inf*. another word for **uppity** (sense 1). [C18: from UP + -ISH]
▸ **'uppishly** *adv* ▸ **'uppishness** *n*

uppity ('ʌpɪtɪ) *adj Inf*. **1** snobbish, arrogant, or presumptuous. **2** offensively self-assertive. [from UP + fanciful ending, ? infl. by -ITY]

Uppsala *or* **Upsala** ★ ('ʌpsɑ:lə) *n* a city in E central Sweden: the royal headquarters in the 13th century; Gothic cathedral (the largest in Sweden) and Sweden's oldest university (1477). Pop.: 101 337 (1996 est.).

upraise (ʌp'reɪz) *vb* **upraises, upraising, upraised**. (*tr*) *Chiefly literary*. to lift up; elevate.
▸ **up'raiser** *n*

uprear (ʌp'rɪə) *vb* (*tr*) to lift up; raise.

upright ('ʌp,raɪt) *adj* **1** vertical or erect. **2** honest or just.
◆ *adv* **3** vertically. ◆ *n* **4** a vertical support, such as a stake or post. **5** short for **upright piano**. **6** the state of being vertical.
▸ **'up,rightly** *adv* ▸ **'up,rightness** *n*

upright piano *n* a piano which has a rectangular vertical case.

uprise *vb* (ʌp'raɪz), **uprises, uprising, uprose, uprisen**. **1** (*tr*) to rise up. ◆ *n* ('ʌp,raɪz). **2** another word for **rise** (senses 23, 24).
▸ **up'riser** *n*

uprising ('ʌp,raɪzɪŋ, ʌp'raɪzɪŋ) *n* **1** a revolt or rebellion. **2** *Arch*. an ascent.

uproar ('ʌp,rɔ:) *n* a commotion or disturbance characterized by loud noise and confusion.

uproarious (ʌp'rɔ:rɪəs) *adj* **1** causing or characterized by an uproar. **2** extremely funny. **3** (of laughter, etc.) loud and boisterous.
▸ **up'roariously** *adv* ▸ **up'roariousness** *n*

uproot (ʌp'ru:t) *vb* (*tr*) **1** to pull up by or as if by the roots. **2** to displace (a person or persons) from native or habitual surroundings. **3** to remove or destroy utterly.
▸ **up'rooter** *n*

uprush ('ʌp,rʌʃ) *n* an upward rush, as of consciousness.

upsadaisy ('ʌpsə'deɪzɪ) *interj* a variant spelling of **upsydaisy**.

Upsala ★ ('ʌpsɑ:lə) *n* a variant spelling of **Uppsala**.

ups and downs *pl n* alternating periods of good and bad fortune, high and low spirits, etc.

upscale ('ʌp,skeɪl) *adj Inf*. of or for the upper end of an economic or social scale; up-market.

upset *vb* (ʌp'sɛt), **upsets, upsetting, upset**. (*mainly tr*) **1** (*also intr*) to tip or be tipped over; overturn or spill. **2** to disturb the normal state or stability of: *to upset the balance of nature*. **3** to disturb mentally or emotionally. **4** to defeat or overthrow, usually unexpectedly. **5** to make physically ill: *seafood always upsets my stomach*. **6** to thicken or spread (the end of a bar, etc.) by hammering. ◆ *n* ('ʌp,sɛt). **7** an unexpected defeat or reversal, as in a contest or plans. **8** a disturbance or disorder of the emotions, body, etc. ◆ *adj* (ʌp'sɛt). **9** overturned or capsized. **10** emotionally or physically disturbed or distressed. **11** disordered; confused. **12** defeated or overthrown. [C14 (in the sense: to erect; C19 in the sense: to overthrow)]
▸ **up'setter** *n* ▸ **up'setting** *adj* ▸ **up'settingly** *adv*

upset price *n Chiefly Scot., US, & Canad*. the lowest price acceptable for something that is for sale, esp. a house. Cf. **reserve price**.

upshot ('ʌp,ʃɒt) *n* **1** the final result; conclusion; outcome. **2** *Archery*. the final shot in a match. [C16: from UP + SHOT[1]]

upside ('ʌp,saɪd) *n* the upper surface or part.

upside down *adj* **1** (*usually postpositive*; **upside-down** *when prenominal*) turned over completely; inverted. **2** (**upside-down** *when prenominal*) *Inf*. confused; topsy-turvy: *an upside-down world*. ◆ *adv* **3** in an inverted fashion. **4** in a chaotic manner. [C16: var., by folk etymology, of earlier *upsodown*]

upside-down cake *n* a sponge cake baked with fruit at the bottom, and inverted before serving.

upsides (,ʌp'saɪdz) *adv Inf., chiefly Brit*. (foll. by *with*) equal or level (with), as through revenge.

upsilon ('ʌpsɪ,lɒn) *n* **1** the 20th letter in the Greek alphabet (Y or υ), a vowel transliterated as *y* or *u*. **2** a heavy short-lived subatomic particle produced by bombarding beryllium nuclei with high-energy protons. [C17: from Med. Gk *u psilon* simple *u*, name adopted for graphic *u* to avoid confusion with graphic *oi*, since pronunciation was the same for both in LGk]

upskill ('ʌp,skɪl) *vb* (*tr*) *NZ*. to improve a person's aptitude for work by additional training.

upstage ('ʌp'steɪdʒ) *adv* **1** on, at, or to the rear of the stage. ◆ *adj* **2** of or relating to the back half of the stage. **3** *Inf*. haughty. ◆ *vb* **upstages, upstaging, upstaged**. (*tr*) **4** to move upstage of (another actor), thus forcing him to turn away from the audience. **5** *Inf*. to draw attention to oneself (from someone else). **6** *Inf*. to treat haughtily.

upstairs ('ʌp'stɛəz) *adv* **1** up the stairs; to or on an upper floor. **2** *Inf*. to or into a higher rank or office. ◆ *n* (*functioning as sing or pl*) **3a** an upper floor. **3b** (*as modifier*): *an upstairs room*. **4** *Brit. inf., old-fashioned*. the masters and mistresses of a household collectively, esp. of a large house.

upstanding (ʌp'stændɪŋ) *adj* **1** of good character. **2** upright and vigorous in build. **3 be upstanding**. **3a** (in a court of law) a direction to all persons present to rise to their feet before the judge enters or leaves the court. **3b** (at a formal dinner) a direction to all persons present to rise to their feet for a toast.

upstart ('ʌp,stɑ:t) *n* **1a** a person, group, etc., that has risen suddenly to a position of power. **1b** (*as modifier*): *an upstart family*. **2a** an arrogant person. **2b** (*as modifier*): *his upstart ambition*.

upstate ('ʌp'steɪt) *US.* ◆ *adj, adv* **1** towards, in, or relating to the outlying or northern sections of a state. ◆ *n* **2** the outlying, esp. northern, sections of a state.
▶ **'up'stater** *n*

upstream ('ʌp'striːm) *adv, adj* **1** in or towards the higher part of a stream; against the current. Cf. **downstream.** **2** (in the oil industry) of or for any of the stages prior to oil production, such as exploration or research.

upstretched (ʌp'stretʃt) *adj* (esp. of the arms) stretched or raised up.

upstroke ('ʌp,strəʊk) *n* **1a** an upward stroke or movement, as of a pen or brush. **1b** the mark produced by such a stroke. **2** the upward movement of a piston in a reciprocating engine.

upsurge *vb* (ʌp'sɜːdʒ), **upsurges, upsurging, upsurged. 1** (*intr*) *Chiefly literary.* to surge up. ◆ *n* ('ʌp,sɜːdʒ). **2** a rapid rise or swell.

upsweep *n* ('ʌp,swiːp). **1** a curve or sweep upwards. ◆ *vb* (ʌp'swiːp), **upsweeps, upsweeping, upswept. 2** to sweep, curve, or brush or be swept, curved, or brushed upwards.

upswing ('ʌp,swɪŋ) *n* **1** *Econ.* a recovery period in the trade cycle. **2** an upward swing or movement or any increase or improvement.

upsy-daisy ('ʌpsɪ'deɪzɪ) *or* **upsadaisy** *interj* an expression, usually of reassurance, uttered as when someone, esp. a child, stumbles or is being lifted up. [C18 *up-a-daisy*, irregularly formed from UP (adv)]

uptake ('ʌp,teɪk) *n* **1** a pipe, shaft, etc., that is used to convey smoke or gases, esp. one that connects a furnace to a chimney. **2** lifting up. **3** the act of accepting something on offer. **4 quick** (*or* **slow**) **on the uptake.** *Inf.* quick (or slow) to understand or learn.

upthrow ('ʌp,θrəʊ) *n* *Geol.* the upward movement of rocks on one side of a fault plane relative to rocks on the other side.

upthrust ('ʌp,θrʌst) *n* **1** an upward push or thrust. **2** *Geol.* a violent upheaval of the earth's surface.

uptight (ʌp'taɪt) *adj Inf.* **1** displaying tense repressed nervousness, irritability, or anger. **2** unable to give expression to one's feelings.

uptime ('ʌp,taɪm) *n Commerce.* time during which a machine, such as a computer, actually operates.

up-to-date *adj* **a** modern or fashionable: *an up-to-date magazine.* **b** (*predicative*): *the magazine is up to date.*
▶ **'up-to-'dateness** *n*

uptown ('ʌp'taʊn) *US & Canad.* ◆ *adj, adv* **1** towards, in, or relating to some part of a town that is away from the centre. ◆ *n* **2** such a part of a town, esp. a residential part.
▶ **'up'towner** *n*

upturn *vb* (ʌp'tɜːn). **1** to turn or cause to turn over or upside down. **2** (*tr*) to create disorder. **3** (*tr*) to direct upwards. ◆ *n* ('ʌp,tɜːn). **4** an upward trend or improvement. **5** an upheaval.

UPVC *abbrev. for* unplasticized polyvinyl chloride. See also **PVC.**

upward ('ʌpwəd) *adj* **1** directed or moving towards a higher point or level. ◆ *adv* **2** a variant of **upwards.**
▶ **'upwardly** *adv* ▶ **'upwardness** *n*

upwardly mobile *adj* (of a person or social group) moving or aspiring to move to a higher social class or status.

upward mobility *n* movement from a lower to a higher economic and social status.

upwards ('ʌpwədz) *or* **upward** *adv* **1** from a lower to a higher place, level, condition, etc. **2** towards a higher level, standing, etc.

upwind ('ʌp'wɪnd) *adv* **1** into or against the wind. **2** towards or on the side where the wind is blowing; windward. ◆ *adj* **3** going against the wind: *the upwind leg of the course.* **4** on the windward side.

Ur ★ (ɜː) *n* an ancient city of Sumer located on a former channel of the Euphrates.

uracil ('jʊərəsɪl) *n Biochem.* a pyrimidine present in all living cells, usually in a combined form, as in RNA. [C20: from URO- + ACETIC + -ILE]

uraemia *or US* **uremia** (jʊ'riːmɪə) *n Pathol.* the accumulation of waste products, normally excreted in the urine in the blood. [C19: from NL, from Gk *ouron* urine + *haima* blood]
▶ u'raemic *or US* u'remic *adj*

uraeus (jʊ'riːəs) *n, pl* **uraeuses.** the sacred serpent represented on the headdresses of ancient Egyptian kings and gods. [C19: from NL, from Gk *ouraios,* from Egyptian *uræasp*]

Ural ★ ('jʊərəl; *Russian* u'ral) *n* a river in central Russia, rising in the S Ural Mountains and flowing south to the Caspian Sea. Length: 2534 km (1575 miles).

Ural-Altaic *n* **1** a postulated group of related languages consisting of the Uralic and Altaic families of languages. ◆ *adj* **2** of or relating to this group of languages, characterized by agglutination and vowel harmony.

Uralic (jʊ'rælɪk) *or* **Uralian** (jʊ'reɪlɪən) *n* **1** a superfamily of languages consisting of the Finno-Ugric family together with Samoyed. See also **Ural-Altaic.** ◆ *adj* **2** of or relating to these languages.

Ural Mountains *or* **Urals** ★ *pl n* a mountain system in W central Russia, extending over 2000 km (1250 miles) from the Arctic Ocean towards the Aral Sea: forms part of the geographical boundary between Europe and Asia: one of the richest mineral areas in the world, with many associated major industrial centres. Highest peak: Mount Narodnaya, 1894 m (6214 ft).

uranalysis (,jʊərə'nælɪsɪs) *n, pl* **uranalyses** (-,siːz). *Med.* a variant spelling of **urinalysis.**

uranide ('jʊərə,naɪd) *n* any element having an atomic number greater than that of protactinium.

uranism ('jʊərənɪzəm) *n Rare.* homosexuality (esp. male homosexuality). [C20: from G *Uranismus,* from Gk *ouranios* heavenly, i.e. spiritual]

uranium (jʊ'reɪnɪəm) *n* a radioactive silvery-white metallic element of the actinide series. It occurs in several minerals including pitchblende and is used chiefly as a source of nuclear energy by fission of the radioisotope **uranium-235.** Symbol: U; atomic no.: 92; atomic wt.: 238.03; half-life of most stable isotope, ^{238}U: 4.51×10^9 years. [C18: from NL, from URANUS²; from the fact that the element was discovered soon after the planet]

uranium series *n Physics.* a radioactive series that starts with uranium-238 and proceeds by radioactive decay to lead-206.

urano- *combining form.* denoting the heavens: *uranography.* [from Gk *ouranos*]

uranography (,jʊərə'nɒgrəfɪ) *n* the branch of astronomy concerned with the description and mapping of the stars, galaxies, etc.
▶ ,ura'nographer *n* ▶ uranographic (,jʊərənə'græfɪk) *adj*

Uranus¹ ★ (jʊ'reɪnəs, 'jʊərənəs) *n Greek myth.* the personification of the sky, who, as a god, ruled the universe and fathered the Titans and Cyclopes; overthrown by his son Cronus.

Uranus² ★ (jʊ'reɪnəs, 'jʊərənəs) *n* the seventh planet from the sun, sometimes visible to the naked eye. [C19: from L *Uranus,* from Gk *Ouranos* heaven]

urate ('jʊəreɪt) *n* any salt or ester of uric acid.
▶ uratic (jʊ'rætɪk) *adj*

urban ('ɜːbªn) *adj* **1** of, relating to, or constituting a city or town. **2** living in a city or town. ◆ Cf. **rural.** [C17: from L *urbānus,* from *urbs* city]

Urban II ★ ('ɜːbªn) *n* original name *Odo* or *Udo.* ?1042–99, French ecclesiastic; pope (1088–99). He inaugurated the First Crusade at the Council of Clermont (1095).

urban area *n* (in population censuses) a city area considered as the inner city plus built-up environs, irrespective of local body administrative boundaries.

urban district *n* **1** (in England and Wales from 1888 to 1974 and Northern Ireland from 1898 to 1973) an urban division of an administrative county with an elected council in charge of housing and environmental services. **2** (in the Republic of Ireland) any of 49 medium-sized towns with their own elected councils.

urbane (ɜː'beɪn) *adj* characterized by elegance or sophistication. [C16: from L *urbānus* of the town; see URBAN]
▶ ur'banely *adv* ▶ ur'baneness *n*

★ people and places

urban guerrilla *n* a guerrilla who operates in a town or city, engaging in terrorism, kidnapping, etc.

urbanism ('ɜ:bə,nɪzəm) *n Chiefly US.* **a** the character of city life. **b** the study of this.

urbanite ('ɜ:bə,naɪt) *n* a resident of an urban community; city dweller.

urbanity (ɜ:'bænɪtɪ) *n*, *pl* **urbanities. 1** the quality of being urbane. **2** (*usually pl*) civilities or courtesies.

urbanize *or* **urbanise** ('ɜ:bə,naɪz) *vb* **urbanizes, urbanizing, urbanized** *or* **urbanises, urbanising, urbanised.** (*tr*) (*usually passive*) **a** to make (esp. a predominantly rural area or country) more industrialized and urban. **b** to cause the migration of an increasing proportion of (rural dwellers) into cities.
▸ ,urbani'zation *or* ,urbani'sation *n*

urban myth *or* **legend** *n* a story, esp. one with a shocking or amusing ending, related as having actually happened, usually to someone vaguely connected with the teller.

urban renewal *n* the process of redeveloping dilapidated or no longer functional urban areas.

urbi et orbi *Latin.* ('ɜ:bɪ ɛt 'ɔ:bɪ) *adv RC Church.* to the city and the world: a phrase qualifying the solemn papal blessing.

urceolate ('ɜ:sɪəlɪt, -,leɪt) *adj Biol.* shaped like an urn or pitcher: *an urceolate corolla.* [C18: via NL from L *urceolus,* dim. of *urceus* a pitcher]

urchin ('ɜ:tʃɪn) *n* **1** a mischievous roguish child, esp. one who is young, small, or raggedly dressed. **2** See **sea urchin.** **3** *Arch., dialect.* a hedgehog. **4** *Obs.* an elf or sprite. [C13 *urchon,* from OF *heriçon,* from L *ēricius* hedgehog]

Urdu ('ʊədu:, 'ɜ:-) *n* an official language of Pakistan, also spoken in India. The script derives primarily from Persia. It belongs to the Indic branch of the Indo-European family of languages, being closely related to Hindi. [C18: from Hindustani (*zabāni*) *urdū* (language of the) camp, from Persian *urdū* camp, from Turkish *ordū*]

-ure *suffix forming nouns.* **1** indicating act, process, or result: *seizure.* **2** indicating function or office: *legislature; prefecture.* [from F, from L *-ūra*]

urea ('jʊərɪə) *n* a white water-soluble crystalline compound, produced by protein metabolism and excreted in urine. A synthetic form is used as a fertilizer and animal feed. Formula: $CO(NH_2)_2$. [C19: from NL, from F *urée,* from Gk *ouron* urine]
▸ u'real *or* u'reic *adj*

urea-formaldehyde resin *n* any one of a class of rigid odourless synthetic materials that are made from urea and formaldehyde and are used in electrical fittings, adhesives, laminates, and finishes for textiles.

ureide ('jʊərɪ,aɪd) *n Chem.* **1** any of a class of organic compounds derived from urea by replacing one or more of its hydrogen atoms by organic groups. **2** any of a class of derivatives of urea and carboxylic acids, in which one or more of the hydrogen atoms have been replaced by acid radical groups.

-uret *suffix of nouns.* formerly used to form the names of binary chemical compounds. [from NL *-uretum*]

ureter (jʊ'ri:tə) *n* the tube that conveys urine from the kidney to the urinary bladder or cloaca. [C16: via NL from Gk *ourētēr,* from *ourein* to urinate]
▸ u'reteral *or* ureteric (,jʊərɪ'tɛrɪk) *adj*

urethane ('jʊərɪ,θeɪn) *or* **urethan** ('jʊərɪ,θæn) *n* short for **polyurethane.** [C19: from URO- + ETHYL + -ANE]

urethra (jʊ'ri:θrə) *n*, *pl* **urethrae** (-θri:) *or* **urethras.** the canal that in most mammals conveys urine from the bladder out of the body. In human males it also conveys semen. [C17: via LL from Gk *ourēthra,* from *ourein* to urinate]
▸ u'rethral *adj*

urethritis (,jʊərɪ'θraɪtɪs) *n* inflammation of the urethra. [C19: from NL, from LL URETHRA]
▸ urethritic (,jʊərɪ'θrɪtɪk) *adj*

urethroscope (jʊ'ri:θrə,skəʊp) *n* a medical instrument for examining the urethra. [C20: see URETHRA, -SCOPE]
▸ urethroscopic (ju,ri:θrə'skɒpɪk) *adj* ▸ urethroscopy (,jʊərɪ'θrɒskəpɪ) *n*

uretic (jʊ'rɛtɪk) *adj* of or relating to the urine. [C19: via LL from Gk *ourētikos,* from *ouron* urine]

Urey ★ ('jʊərɪ) *n* **Harold Clayton.** 1893–1981, US chemist, who discovered deuterium (1932), and worked on methods of separating isotopes: Nobel prize for chemistry 1934.

Urfa ★ ('ɜ:fə) *n* a city in SE Turkey: market centre. Pop.: 357 900 (1994 est.). Ancient name: **Edessa.**

Urga ★ ('ɜ:gə) *n* the former name (until 1924) of **Ulan Bator.**

urge (ɜ:dʒ) *vb* **urges, urging, urged.** (*tr*) **1** to plead, press, or move (someone to do something): *we urged him to surrender.* **2** (*may take a clause as object*) to advocate or recommend earnestly and persistently: *to urge the need for safety.* **3** to impel, drive, or hasten onwards: *he urged the horses on.* ◆ *n* **4** a strong impulse, inner drive, or yearning. [C16: from L *urgēre*]

urgent ('ɜ:dʒənt) *adj* **1** requiring or compelling speedy action or attention: *the matter is urgent.* **2** earnest and persistent. [C15: via F from L *urgent-, urgens,* present participle of *urgēre* to URGE]
▸ urgency ('ɜ:dʒənsɪ) *n* ▸ 'urgently *adv*

-urgy *n combining form.* indicating technology concerned with a specified material: *metallurgy.* [from Gk *-urgia,* from *ergon* work]

Uri ★ (*German* 'u:rɪ) *n* one of the original three cantons of Switzerland, in the centre of the country: mainly German-speaking and Roman Catholic. Capital: Altdorf. Pop.: 35 933 (1995 est.). Area: 1075 sq. km (415 sq. miles).

-uria *n combining form.* indicating a diseased or abnormal condition of the urine: *pyuria.* [from Gk *-ouria,* from *ouron* urine]
▸ -uric *adj combining form.*

Uriah ★ (jʊ'raɪə) *n Old Testament.* a Hittite officer, who was killed in battle on instructions from David so that he could marry Uriah's wife Bathsheba (II Samuel 11).

uric ('jʊərɪk) *adj* of, concerning, or derived from urine. [C18: from URO- + -IC]

uric acid *n* a white odourless tasteless crystalline product of protein metabolism, present in the blood and urine. Formula: $C_5H_4N_4O_3$.

uridine ('jʊərɪ,di:n) *n Biochem.* a nucleoside present in all living cells in a combined form, esp. in RNA. [C20: from URO- + -IDE + -INE²]

urinal (jʊ'raɪn°l, 'jʊərɪ-) *n* **1** a sanitary fitting, esp. one fixed to a wall, used by men for urination. **2** a room containing urinals. **3** any vessel for holding urine prior to its disposal.

urinalysis (,jʊərɪ'nælɪsɪs) *n*, *pl* **urinalyses** (-,si:z). *Med.* chemical analysis of the urine to test for the presence of disease.

urinary ('jʊərɪnərɪ) *adj* **1** *Anat.* of or relating to urine or to the organs and structures that secrete and pass urine. ◆ *n*, *pl* **urinaries. 2** a reservoir for urine.

urinary bladder *n* a distensible membranous sac in which the urine excreted from the kidneys is stored.

urinate ('jʊərɪ,neɪt) *vb* **urinates, urinating, urinated.** (*intr*) to excrete or void urine.
▸ ,uri'nation *n* ▸ 'urinative *adj*

urine ('jʊərɪn) *n* the pale yellow slightly acid fluid excreted by the kidneys, containing waste products removed from the blood. It is stored in the urinary bladder and discharged through the urethra. [C14: via OF from L *ūrīna*]

urinogenital (,jʊərɪnəʊ'dʒenɪt°l) *adj* another word for **urogenital.**

URL *abbrev. for* uniform resource locator: a standardized address of a location on the Internet.

Urmia ★ ('ɜ:mɪə) *n Lake.* a shallow lake in NW Iran, at an altitude of 1300 m (4250 ft): the largest lake in Iran, varying in area from 4000–6000 sq. km (1500–2300 sq. miles) between autumn and spring.

Urmston ★ ('ɜ:mstən) *n* a town in NW England, in Salford, in Greater Manchester. Pop.: 41 804 (1991).

urn (ɜ:n) *n* **1** a vaselike receptacle or vessel, esp. a large bulbous one with a foot. **2** a vase used as a receptacle for

the ashes of the dead. **3** a large vessel, usually of metal, with a tap, used for making and holding tea, coffee, etc. [C14: from L *ūrna*]
▶ **'urn,like** *adj*

urnfield ('ɜːn,fiːld) *n* **1** a cemetery full of individual cremation urns. ◆ *adj* **2** (of a number of Bronze Age cultures) characterized by cremation in urns, which began in E Europe about the second millennium B.C.

uro- *or before a vowel* **ur-** *combining form.* indicating urine or the urinary tract: *urogenital; urology.* [from Gk *ouron* urine]

urogenital (,jʊərəʊ'dʒɛnɪt°l) *or* **urinogenital** *adj* of or relating to the urinary and genital organs and their functions. Also: **genitourinary**.

urogenital system *or* **tract** *n Anat.* the urinary tract and reproductive organs.

urolith ('jʊərəʊlɪθ) *n Pathol.* a calculus in the urinary tract.
▶ ,**uro'lithic** *adj*

urology (jʊ'rɒlədʒɪ) *n* the branch of medicine concerned with the study and treatment of diseases of the urogenital tract.
▶ **urologic** (,jʊərə'lɒdʒɪk) *adj* ▶ **u'rologist** *n*

uropygial gland (,jʊərə'pɪdʒɪəl) *n* a gland, situated at the base of the tail in most birds, that secretes oil used in preening.

uropygium (,jʊərə'pɪdʒɪəm) *n* the hindmost part of a bird's body, from which the tail feathers grow. [C19: via NL from Gk *ouropugion,* from *oura* tail + *pugē* rump]
▶ ,**uro'pygial** *adj*

uroscopy (jʊ'rɒskəpɪ) *n Med.* examination of the urine. See also **urinalysis**.
▶ **uroscopic** (,jʊərə'skɒpɪk) *adj* ▶ **u'roscopist** *n*

Ursa Major ('ɜːsə 'meɪdʒə) *n, Latin genitive* **Ursae Majoris** ('ɜːsiː məˈdʒɔːrɪs). an extensive conspicuous constellation in the N hemisphere. The seven brightest stars form the **Plough**. Also called: the **Great Bear**, the **Bear**. [L: greater bear]

Ursa Minor ('ɜːsə 'maɪnə) *n, Latin genitive* **Ursae Minoris** ('ɜːsiː mɪˈnɔːrɪs). a small faint constellation, the brightest star of which is the Pole Star. Also called: the **Little Bear**, the **Bear**. [L: lesser bear]

ursine ('ɜːsaɪn) *adj* of, relating to, or resembling a bear or bears. [C16: from L *ursus* a bear]

Ursprache *German.* ('uːrʃpraːxə) *n* any hypothetical extinct and unrecorded language reconstructed from groups of related recorded languages. For example, Indo-European is an Ursprache reconstructed by comparison of the Germanic group, Latin, Sanskrit, etc. [from *ur-* primeval + *Sprache* language]

Ursula ★ ('ɜːsjʊlə) *n Saint.* a legendary British princess of the fourth or fifth century A.D., said to have been martyred together with 11 000 virgins by the Huns at Cologne. Feast day: Oct. 21.

Ursuline ('ɜːsjʊ,laɪn) *n* **1** a member of an order of nuns devoted to teaching in the Roman Catholic Church: founded in 1537 at Brescia. ◆ *adj* **2** of or relating to this order. [C16: after St Ursula, patron saint of St Angela Merici, who founded the order]

Urtext *German.* ('uːrtɛkst) *n* **1** the earliest form of a text as established by linguistic scholars as a basis for variants in later texts still in existence. **2** an edition of a musical score showing the composer's intentions without later editorial interpolation. [from *ur-* original + TEXT]

urticaceous (,ɜːtɪ'keɪʃəs) *adj* of or belonging to a family of plants having small flowers and, in many species, stinging hairs: includes the nettles and pellitory. [C18: via NL from L *urtīca* nettle, from *ūrere* to burn]

urticaria (,ɜːtɪ'kɛərɪə) *n* a skin condition characterized by the formation of itchy red or whitish raised patches, usually caused by an allergy. Nontechnical names: **hives**, **nettle rash**. [C18: from NL, from L *urtīca* nettle]

urtication (,ɜːtɪ'keɪʃən) *n* **1** a burning or itching sensation. **2** another name for **urticaria**.

Uru. *abbrev. for* Uruguay.

Uruapan ★ (*Spanish* uˈrwapan) *n* a city in SW Mexico, in

Michoacán state: agricultural trading centre. Pop 187 623 (1990).

Uruguay ★ ('jʊərə,gwaɪ) *n* a republic in South America on the Atlantic: Spanish colonization began in 1624 followed by Portuguese settlement in 1680; revolted against Spanish rule in 1820 but was annexed by the Portuguese to Brazil; gained independence in 1825. consists mainly of rolling grassy plains, low hills, and plateaus. Official language: Spanish. Religion: Roman Catholic. Currency: peso. Capital: Montevideo. Pop 3 185 000 (1997). Area: 176 215 sq. km (68 037 sq miles).
▶ ,**Uru'guayan** *adj, n*

Urumchi (uːˈruːmtʃɪ), **Urumqi**, *or* **Wu-lu-mu-ch'i** ★ *n* a city in NW China, capital of Xinjiang Uygur Autonomous Region: trading centre on a N route between China and central Asia. Pop.: 1 160 000 (1991 est.). Former name: **Tihwa**.

Urundi ★ (uˈrʊndɪ) *n* the former name (until 1962) of Burundi.

urus ('jʊərəs) *n, pl* **uruses**. another name for the **aurochs**. [C17: from *ūrus,* of Gmc origin]

urushiol ('uːrʊʃɪ,ɒl, uːˈruː-) *n* a poisonous pale yellow liquid occurring in poison ivy and the lacquer tree. [from Japanese *urushi* lacquer + -OL²]

us (ʌs) *pron (objective)* **1** refers to the speaker or writer and another person or other people: *don't hurt us.* **2** refers to all people or people in general: *this table shows us the tides.* **3** an informal word for **me**: *give us a kiss!* **4** a formal word for **me** used by editors, monarchs, etc. [OE *ūs*]

USAGE NOTE See at **me**¹.

US *or* **U.S.** *abbrev. for* United States.

USA *abbrev. for:* **1.** Also: **U.S.A.** United States of America. **2** United States Army.

usable *or* **useable** ('juːzəb°l) *adj* able to be used.
▶ ,**usa'bility** *or* ,**usea'bility** *n*

USAF *abbrev. for* United States Air Force.

usage ('juːsɪdʒ, -zɪdʒ) *n* **1** the act or a manner of using; use; employment. **2** constant use, custom, or habit. **3** something permitted or established by custom or practice. **4** what is actually said in a language, esp. as contrasted with what is prescribed. [C14: via OF from L *ūsus* USE (n)]

usance ('juːzəns) *n Commerce.* the period of time permitted by commercial usage for the redemption of foreign bills of exchange. [C14: from OF, from Med. L *ūsantia,* from *ūsāre* to USE]

USDAW ('ʌsdɔː) *n* (in Britain) *acronym for* Union of Shop, Distributive, and Allied Workers.

use *vb* (juːz), **uses, using, used.** (*tr*) **1** to put into service or action; employ for a given purpose: *to use a spoon to stir with.* **2** to make a practice or habit of employing; exercise: *he uses his brain.* **3** to behave towards in a particular way, esp. for one's own ends: *he uses people.* **4** to consume, expend, or exhaust: *the engine uses very little oil.* **5** to partake of (alcoholic drink, drugs, etc.) or smoke (tobacco, marijuana, etc.). ◆ *n* (juːs). **6** the act of using or the state of being used: *the carpet wore out through constant use.* **7** the ability or permission to use. **8** the occasion to use: *I have no use for this paper.* **9** an instance or manner of using. **10** usefulness; advantage: *it is of no use to complain.* **11** custom; habit: *long use has inured him to it.* **12** the purpose for which something is used; end. **13** *Christianity.* a distinctive form of liturgical or ritual observance, esp. one that is traditional. **14** the enjoyment of property, land, etc., by occupation or by deriving revenue from it. **15** *Law.* the beneficial enjoyment of property the legal title to which is held by another person as trustee. **16** **have no use for. 16a** to have no need of. **16b** to have a contemptuous dislike for. **17 make use of. 17a** to employ; use. **17b** to exploit (a person). ◆ See also **use up**. [C13: from OF *user,* from L *ūsus* having used, from *ūtī* to use]

used (juːzd) *adj* second-hand: *used cars.*

used to (juːst) *adj* **1** accustomed to: *I am used to hitchhik* ing. ◆ vb (tr) 2 (takes an infinitive or implied infinitive) used as an auxiliary to express habitual or accustomed actions, states, etc., taking place in the past but not continuing into the present: *I used to fish here every day.*

> **USAGE NOTE** The most common negative form of *used to* is *didn't used to* (or *didn't use to*), but in formal contexts *used not to* is preferred.

useful ('ju:sfʊl) *adj* **1** able to be used advantageously, beneficially, or for several purposes. **2** *Inf.* commendable or capable: *a useful term's work.*
  ► 'usefully *adv* ► 'usefulness *n*

useless ('ju:slɪs) *adj* **1** having no practical use or advantage. **2** *Inf.* ineffectual, weak, or stupid: *he's useless at history.*
  ► 'uselessly *adv* ► 'uselessness *n*

user ('ju:zə) *n* **1** *Law.* **1a** the continued exercise, use, or enjoyment of a right, esp. in property. **1b** a presumptive right based on long-continued use: *right of user.* **2** (*often in combination*) a person or thing that uses: *a road-user.* **3** *Inf.* a drug addict.

user-friendly *adj* (**user friendly** *when postpositive*) easy to familiarize oneself with, understand, or use.

use up *vb* (*tr, adv*) **1** to finish (a supply); consume completely. **2** to exhaust; wear out.

Ushant ★ ('ʌʃənt) *n* an island off the NW coast of France, at the tip of Brittany: scene of naval battles in 1778 and 1794 between France and Britain. Area: about 16 sq. km (6 sq. miles). French name: **Ouessant**.

Ushas ★ ('u:ʃəs) *n* the Hindu goddess of the dawn.

usher ('ʌʃə) *n* **1** an official who shows people to their seats, as in a church or theatre. **2** a person who acts as doorkeeper, esp. in a court of law. **3** (in England) a minor official charged with maintaining order in a court of law. **4** an officer responsible for preceding persons of rank in a procession. **5** *Brit., obs.* a teacher. ◆ *vb* (*tr*) **6** to conduct or escort, esp. in a courteous or obsequious way. **7** (*usually foll. by in*) to be a precursor or herald (of). [C14: from OF *huissier* doorkeeper, from Vulgar L *ustiārius* (unattested), from L *ostium* door]

usherette (ˌʌʃə'rɛt) *n* a woman assistant in a cinema, etc., who shows people to their seats.

Usk ★ (ʌsk) *n* a river in SE Wales, flowing southeast and south to the Bristol Channel. Length: 113 km (70 miles).

Üsküb ★ ('uskuːb) *n* the Turkish name (1392–1913) for **Skopje**.

Üsküdar ★ (ˌuːskuː'dɑː) *n* a town in NW Turkey, across the Bosporus from Istanbul: formerly a terminus of caravan routes from Syria and Asia; base of the British army in the Crimean War. Pop.: 261 141 (1980). Former name: **Scutari**.

USM *Stock Exchange. abbrev. for* unlisted securities market.

USN *abbrev. for* United States Navy.

Usnach *or* **Usnech** ★ ('ʊʃnəx) *n* (in Irish legend) the father of Naoise.

USP *abbrev. for* unique selling proposition: a characteristic of a product that can be used in advertising to differentiate it from its competitors.

Uspallata Pass ★ (ˌuːspə'lɑːtə; *Spanish* uspa'ʎata) *n* a pass over the Andes in S South America, between Mendoza (Argentina) and Santiago (Chile). Height: 3840 m (12 600 ft). Also called: **La Cumbre**.

usquebaugh ('ʌskwɪˌbɔː) *n* **1** *Irish.* the former name for whiskey. **2** *Scot.* the former name for whisky. [C16: from Irish Gaelic *uisce beathadh* or Scot. Gaelic *uisge beatha* water of life]

USS *abbrev. for:* **1** United States Senate. **2** United States Ship.

USSR *abbrev. for* (the former) Union of Soviet Socialist Republics.

Ussuri ★ (*Russian* ussu'ri) *n* a river in E central Asia, flowing north, forming part of the Chinese border with Russia, to the Amur River. Length: about 800 km (500 miles).

Ústí nad Labem ★ (*Czech* 'u:stji: nad 'labɛm) *n* a port in the Czech Republic, on the Elbe River: textile and chemical industries. Pop.: 118 000 (1993).

Ustinov ★ ('ju:stɪˌnɒf) *n* Sir **Peter** (**Alexander**). born 1921, British stage and film actor, director, dramatist, and raconteur.

Ust-Kamenogorsk ★ (*Russian* ustjkəmɪnə'gɔrsk) *n* a city in E Kazakhstan: centre of a zinc-, lead-, and copper-mining area. Pop.: 326 300 (1995 est.).

Ustyurt *or* **Ust Urt** ★ (*Russian* us'tjurt) *n* an arid plateau in central Asia, between the Caspian and Aral seas in SW Kazakhstan and Uzbekistan. Area: about 238 000 sq. km (92 000 sq. miles).

usual ('ju:ʒəl) *adj* **1** of the most normal, frequent, or regular type: *that's the usual sort of application to send.* ◆ *n* **2** ordinary or commonplace events (esp. in **out of the usual**). **3** **the usual.** *Inf.* the habitual or usual drink, etc. [C14: from LL *ūsuālis* ordinary, from L *ūsus* USE]
  ► 'usually *adv* ► 'usualness *n*

usufruct ('ju:sjuˌfrʌkt) *n* the right to use and derive profit from a piece of property belonging to another, provided the property itself remains undiminished and uninjured in any way. [C17: from LL *ūsūfrūctus*, from L *ūsus* use + *frūctus* enjoyment]
  ► ˌusu'fructuary *n, adj*

Usumbura ★ (ˌuːzəm'buərə) *n* the former name of **Bujumbura**.

usurer ('ju:ʒərə) *n* a person who lends funds at an exorbitant rate of interest.

usurp (ju:'zɜːp) *vb* to seize or appropriate (land, a throne, etc.) without authority. [C14: from OF, from L *ūsūrpāre* to take into use, prob. from *ūsus* use + *rapere* to seize]
  ► ˌusur'pation *n* ► u'surper *n*

usury ('ju:ʒərɪ) *n, pl* **usuries. 1** the practice of loaning money at an exorbitant rate of interest. **2** an unlawfully high rate of interest. **3** *Obs.* moneylending. [C14: from Med. L, from L *ūsūra* usage, from *ūsus* USE]
  ► **usurious** (ju:'ʒuərɪəs) *adj*

USW *Radio. abbrev. for* ultrashort wave.

ut (ʌt, uːt) *n Music.* the syllable used in the fixed system of solmization for the note C. [C14: from L *ut*; see GAMUT]

UT *abbrev. for:* **1** universal time. **2** Utah.

Utah ★ ('ju:tɔː, 'ju:tɑː) *n* a state of the western US: settled by Mormons in 1847; situated in the Great Basin and the Rockies, with the Great Salt Lake in the northwest. Capital: Salt Lake City. Pop.: 2 000 494 (1996 est.). Area: 212 628 sq. km (82 096 sq. miles). Abbrev.: **UT**.
  ► **Utahan** (ju:'tɔːən, -'tɑːən) *adj, n*

Utamaro ★ (ˌuːtə'mɑːrəʊ) *n* **Kitagawa** (ˌkiːtə'gɑːwə), original name *Kitagawa Nebsuyoshi*. 1753–1806, Japanese master of wood-block prints, noted esp. for his portraits of women.

UTC *abbrev. for* universal time coordinated. See **universal time**.

ute (ju:t) *n Austral. & NZ inf.* short for **utility truck**.

utensil (ju:'tɛnsəl) *n* an implement, tool, or container for practical use: *writing utensils.* [C14 *utensele*, via OF from L *ūtēnsilia* necessaries, from *ūtēnsilis* available for use, from *ūtī* to use]

uterine ('ju:təˌraɪn) *adj* **1** of, relating to, or affecting the uterus. **2** (of offspring) born of the same mother but not the same father.

uterus ('ju:tərəs) *n, pl* **uteri** ('ju:təˌraɪ). **1** *Anat.* a hollow muscular organ lying within the pelvic cavity of female mammals. It houses the developing fetus. Nontechnical name: **womb**. **2** the corresponding organ in other animals. [C17: from L]

Utgard ★ ('ʊtgɑːd, 'uːt-) *n Norse myth.* one of the divisions of Jotunheim, land of the giants, ruled by Utgard-Loki.

Utgard-Loki ★ *n Norse myth.* the giant king of Utgard.

Uther ('ju:θə) *or* **Uther Pendragon** ★ *n* (in Arthurian legend) a king of Britain and father of Arthur.

Utica ★ ('ju:tɪkə) *n* an ancient city on the N coast of Africa, northwest of Carthage.

utilidor (ju:'tɪlədə; *Canad.* -ˌdɒr) *n Canad.* above-ground insulated casing for pipes carrying water, etc., in permafrost regions.

utilitarian (juːˌtɪlɪˈtɛərɪən) *adj* **1** of or relating to utilitarianism. **2** designed for use rather than beauty. ◆ *n* **3** a person who believes in utilitarianism.

utilitarianism (juːˌtɪlɪˈtɛərɪəˌnɪzəm) *n Ethics.* **1** the doctrine that the morally correct course of action consists in the greatest good for the greatest number, that is, in maximizing the total benefit resulting, without regard to the distribution of benefits and burdens. **2** the theory that the criterion of virtue is utility.

utility (juːˈtɪlɪtɪ) *n, pl* **utilities. 1a** the quality of practical use; usefulness. **1b** (*as modifier*): *a utility fabric.* **2** something useful. **3a** a public service, such as the bus system. **3b** (*as modifier*): *utility vehicle.* **4** *Econ.* the ability of a commodity to satisfy human wants. Cf. **disutility. 5** *Austral.* short for **utility truck. 6** *Computing.* a piece of software that performs a routine task. [C14: from OF *utelite*, from L *ūtilitās* usefulness, from *ūtī* to use]

utility function *n Econ.* a function relating specific goods and services in an economy to individual preferences.

utility player *n Sport.* a player who is capable of playing competently in any of several positions.

utility room *n* a room with equipment for domestic work like washing and ironing.

utility truck *n Austral. & NZ.* a small truck with an open body and low sides, often with a removable tarpaulin cover; pick-up truck.

utilize *or* **utilise** (ˈjuːtɪˌlaɪz) *vb* **utilizes, utilizing, utilized** *or* **utilises, utilising, utilised.** (*tr*) to make practical or worthwhile use of.
▸ ˈuti,lizable *or* ˈuti,lisable *adj* ▸ ˌutiliˈzation *or* ˌutiliˈsation *n* ▸ ˈuti,lizer *or* ˈuti,liser *n*

utmost (ˈʌtˌməʊst) *or* **uttermost** *adj* (*prenominal*) **1** of the greatest possible degree or amount: *the utmost degree.* **2** at the furthest limit: *the utmost town on the peninsula.* ◆ *n* **3** the greatest possible degree, extent, or amount: *he tried his utmost.* [OE *ūtemest*, from *ūte* out + -*mest* MOST]

utmost good faith *n* a principle used in insurance contracts, legally obliging all parties to reveal to the others any information that might influence the others' decision to enter into the contract. [from L *uberrima fides*]

Utopia (juːˈtəʊpɪə) *n* (*sometimes not cap.*) any real or imaginary society, place, state, etc., considered to be perfect or ideal. [C16: from NL *Utopia* (coined by Sir Thomas More in 1516 as the title of his book that described an imaginary island representing the perfect society), lit.: no place, from Gk *ou* not + *topos* a place]

Utopian (juːˈtəʊpɪən) (*sometimes not cap.*) ◆ *adj* **1** of or relating to a perfect or ideal existence. ◆ *n* **2** an idealistic social reformer.
▸ Uˈtopianism *n*

Utrecht ★ (*Dutch* ˈyːtrɛxt; *English* ˈjuːtrɛkt) *n* **1** a province of the W central Netherlands. Capital: Utrecht. Pop.: 1 063 460 (1995). Area: 1362 sq. km (526 sq. miles). **2** a city in the central Netherlands, capital of Utrecht province: scene of the signing (1579) of the **Union of Utrecht** (the foundation of the later kingdom of the Netherlands) and of the **Treaty of Utrecht** (1713), ending the War of the Spanish Succession. Pop.: 234 106 (1994).

utricle (ˈjuːtrɪkᵊl) *n* **1** *Anat.* the larger of the two parts of the membranous labyrinth of the internal ear. Cf. **saccule. 2** *Bot.* the bladder-like one-seeded indehiscent fruit of certain plants. [C18: from L *ūtriculus*, dim. of *ūter* bag]
▸ uˈtricular *adj*

utriculitis (juːˌtrɪkjʊˈlaɪtɪs) *n* inflammation of the inner ear.

Utrillo ★ (*French* ytrijo) *n* **Maurice** (mɔris). 1883–1955, French painter, esp. of Parisian street scenes.

Uttar Pradesh ★ (ˈʊtə ˈprɑːdɛʃ) *n* a state of N India: the most populous state; originated in 1877 with the merging of Agra and Oudh as the United Provinces; the states of Rampur, Benares, and Tehri-Garhwal were added in

1949; lies mostly on the Upper Ganges plain but rises over 7500 m (25 000 ft) in the Himalayas in the northwest; agricultural. Capital: Lucknow. Pop.: 150 695 000 (1994 est.). Area: 294 413 sq. km (113 673 sq. miles).

utter[1] (ˈʌtə) *vb* **1** to give audible expression to (something): *to utter a growl.* **2** *Criminal law.* to put into circulation (counterfeit coin, forged banknotes, etc.). **3** (*tr*) to make publicly known; publish: *to utter slander.* [C14: prob. orig. a commercial term, from MDu. *ūteren* (modern Du. *uiteren*) to make known]
▸ ˈutterable *adj* ▸ ˈutterableness *n* ▸ ˈutterer *n*

utter[2] (ˈʌtə) *adj* (*prenominal*) (intensifier): *an utter fool; the utter limit.* [C15: from OE *utera* outer, comp. of *ūte* out (adv)]
▸ ˈutterly *adv*

utterance (ˈʌtərəns) *n* **1** something uttered, such as a statement. **2** the act or power of uttering or ability to utter.

utter barrister *n Law.* the full title of a barrister who is not a Queen's Counsel.

uttermost (ˈʌtəˌməʊst) *adj, n* a variant of **utmost.**

U-turn *n* **1** a turn made by a vehicle in the shape of a U, resulting in a reversal of direction. **2** a complete change in direction of political policy, etc.

UV *abbrev. for* ultraviolet.

UV-A *or* **UVA** *abbrev. for* ultraviolet radiation with a range of 320-380 nanometres.

uvarovite (uːˈvɑːrəˌvaɪt) *n* an emerald-green garnet found in chromium deposits. [C19: from G *Uvarovit*; after Count Sergei *Uvarov* (1785–1855), Russian author & statesman]

UV-B *or* **UVB** *abbrev. for* ultraviolet radiation with a range of 280-320 nanometres.

uvea (ˈjuːvɪə) *n* the part of the eyeball consisting of the iris, ciliary body, and choroid. [C16: from Med. L *ūvea*, from L *ūva* grape]
▸ ˈuveal *adj*

UVF *abbrev. for* Ulster Volunteer Force.

uvula (ˈjuːvjʊlə) *n, pl* **uvulas** *or* **uvulae** (-ˌliː). a small fleshy flap of tissue that hangs in the back of the throat and is an extension of the soft palate. [C14: from Med. L, lit.: a little grape, from L *ūva* a grape]

uvular (ˈjuːvjʊlə) *adj* **1** of or relating to the uvula. **2** *Phonetics.* articulated with the uvula and the back of the tongue, such as the (r) sound of Parisian French. ◆ *n* **3** a uvular consonant.

Uxbridge ★ (ˈʌksˌbrɪdʒ) *n* a town in SE England, part of the Greater London borough of Hillingdon since 1965; chiefly residential.

Uxmal ★ (*Spanish* uzˈmal) *n* an ancient ruined city in SE Mexico, in Yucatán: capital of the later Maya empire.

uxorial (ʌkˈsɔːrɪəl) *adj* of or relating to a wife: *uxorial influence.* [C19: from L *uxor* wife]
▸ uxˈorially *adv*

uxoricide (ʌkˈsɔːrɪˌsaɪd) *n* **1** the act of killing one's wife. **2** a man who kills his wife. [C19: from L *uxor* wife + -CIDE]
▸ ux,oriˈcidal *adj*

uxorious (ʌkˈsɔːrɪəs) *adj* excessively attached to or dependent on one's wife. [C16: from L *uxōrius* concerning a wife, from *uxor* wife]
▸ uxˈoriously *adv* ▸ uxˈoriousness *n*

Uzbek (ˈʊzbɛk, ˈʌz-) *n* **1** (*pl* **Uzbeks** *or* **Uzbek**) a member of a Mongoloid people of Uzbekistan. **2** the language of this people.

Uzbekistan ★ (ˌʊzbɛkɪˈstɑːn, ˌʌz-) *n* a republic in central Asia: annexed by Russia in the 19th century, it became a separate Soviet Socialist republic in 1924, gaining independence in 1991; mining, textile, and chemical industries are important. Official language: Uzbek. Religion: believers are mainly Muslim. Currency: sum. Capital: Tashkent. Pop.: 23 664 000 (1997). Area: 449 600 sq. km (173 546 sq. miles).

Vv

v _or_ **V** (viː) _n, pl_ **v's, V's,** _or_ **Vs. 1** the 22nd letter of the English alphabet. **2** a speech sound represented by this letter, usually a voiced fricative, as in _vote._ **3a** something shaped like a V. **3b** (_in combination_): _a V neck._

v _symbol. for:_ **1** _Physics._ velocity. **2** specific volume (of a gas).

V _symbol for:_ **1** _Chem._ vanadium. **2** (in transformational grammar) verb. **3** volume (capacity). **4** volt. **5** victory. ◆ **6** the Roman numeral for five.

v. _abbrev. for:_ **1** ventral. **2** verb. **3** verse. **4** verso. **5** (_usually italic_) versus. **6** very. **7** vide [L: see]. **8** volume.

V. _abbrev. for:_ **1** Venerable. **2** (in titles) Very. **3** (in titles) Vice. **4** Viscount.

V-1 _n_ a robot bomb invented by the Germans in World War II: used esp. to bombard London. Also called: **doodlebug, buzz bomb, flying bomb.** [from G _Vergeltungswaffe_ revenge weapon]

V-2 _n_ a rocket-powered ballistic missile invented by the Germans in World War II: used esp. to bombard London. [see V-1]

V6 _n_ a car or internal-combustion engine having six cylinders arranged in the form of a V.

V8 _n_ a car or internal-combustion engine having eight cylinders arranged in the form of a V.

VA _abbrev. for:_ **1** Vicar Apostolic. **2** (Order of) Victoria and Albert. **3** volt-ampere. **4** Virginia.

Va. _abbrev. for_ Virginia.

Vaal ★ (vɑːl) _n_ a river in South Africa, rising in the Drakensberg and flowing west across the country to join the Orange River. Length: 1160 km (720 miles).

Vaasa ★ (_Finnish_ 'vɑːsɑ) _n_ a port in W Finland, on the Gulf of Bothnia: the provisional capital of Finland (1918); textile industries. Pop.: 55 089 (1994). Former name: **Nikolainkaupunki.**

vac (væk) _n Brit. inf._ short for **vacation.**

vacancy ('veɪkənsɪ) _n, pl_ **vacancies. 1** the state or condition of being vacant or unoccupied; emptiness. **2** an unoccupied post or office: _we have a vacancy in the accounts department._ **3** an unoccupied room in a hotel, etc.: _the manager put up the "No Vacancies" sign._ **4** lack of thought or intelligent awareness. **5** _Obs._ idleness or a period spent in idleness.

vacant ('veɪkənt) _adj_ **1** without any contents; empty. **2** (_postpositive; foll. by of_) devoid (of something specified). **3** having no incumbent: _a vacant post._ **4** having no tenant or occupant: _a vacant house._ **5** characterized by or resulting from lack of thought or intelligent awareness. **6** (of time, etc.) not allocated to any activity: _it is pleasant to have a vacant hour in one's day._ **7** spent in idleness or inactivity: _a vacant life._ [C13: from L _vacāre_ to be empty] ▸ 'vacantly _adv_

vacant possession _n_ ownership of an unoccupied house or property, any previous owner or tenant having departed.

vacate (vəˈkeɪt) _vb_ **vacates, vacating, vacated.** (_mainly tr_) **1** to cause (something) to be empty, esp. by departing from or abandoning it: _to vacate a room._ **2** (_also intr_) to give up the tenure, possession, or occupancy of (a place, post, etc.). **3** _Law._ **3a** to cancel. **3b** to annul. ▸ va'catable _adj_

vacation (vəˈkeɪʃən) _n_ **1** _Chiefly Brit._ a period of the year when the law courts or universities are closed. **2** another word (esp. US. and Canad.) for **holiday** (sense 1). **3** the act of departing from or abandoning property, etc. ◆ _vb_ **4** (_intr_) US. & Canad. to take a holiday. [C14: from L _vacātiō_ freedom, from _vacāre_ to be empty] ▸ va'cationer _or_ va'cationist _n_

vaccinate ('væksɪ,neɪt) _vb_ **vaccinates, vaccinating, vacci-**

nated. to inoculate (a person) with vaccine so as to produce immunity against a specific disease. ▸ 'vacci,nator _n_

vaccination (,væksɪ'neɪʃən) _n_ **1** the act of vaccinating. **2** the scar left following inoculation with a vaccine.

vaccine ('væksiːn) _n Med._ **1** a suspension of dead, attenuated, or otherwise modified microorganisms for inoculation to produce immunity to a disease by stimulating the production of antibodies. **2** a preparation of the virus of cowpox inoculated in humans to produce immunity to smallpox. **3** (_modifier_) of or relating to vaccination or vaccinia. **4** _Computing._ software designed to detect and remove computer viruses from a system. [C18: from NL _variolae vaccīnae_ cowpox, title of medical treatise (1798) by Edward Jenner, from L _vacca_ a cow] ▸ 'vaccinal _adj_

vaccinia (væk'sɪnɪə) _n_ a technical name for **cowpox.** [C19: NL, from L _vaccīnus_ of cows]

vacherin _French._ (vaʃrɛ̃) _n_ a dessert consisting of a meringue shell filled with whipped cream, ice cream, fruit, etc. [also in France a kind of cheese, from F _vache_ cow, from L _vacca_]

vacillate ('væsɪ,leɪt) _vb_ **vacillates, vacillating, vacillated.** (_intr_) **1** to fluctuate in one's opinions. **2** to sway from side to side physically. [C16: from L _vacillāre_ to sway, from ?] ▸ ,vacil'lation _n_ ▸ 'vacil,lator _n_

vacua ('vækjuə) _n_ a plural of **vacuum.**

vacuity (væ'kjuːɪtɪ) _n, pl_ **vacuities. 1** the state or quality of being vacuous. **2** an empty space or void. **3** a lack or absence of something specified: _a vacuity of wind._ **4** lack of normal intelligence or awareness. **5** a statement, saying, etc., that is inane or pointless. **6** (in customs terminology) the difference in volume between the actual contents of a container and its full capacity. [C16: from L _vacuitās_ empty space, from _vacuus_ empty]

vacuole ('vækju,əʊl) _n Biol._ a fluid-filled cavity in a cell. [C19: from F, lit.: little vacuum, from L VACUUM] ▸ vacuolar (,vækju'əʊlə) _adj_

vacuous ('vækjuəs) _adj_ **1** empty. **2** bereft of ideas or intelligence. **3** characterized by or resulting from vacancy of mind: _a vacuous gaze._ **4** indulging in no useful mental or physical activity. [C17: from L _vacuus_ empty] ▸ 'vacuously _adv_

vacuum ('vækjʊəm) _n, pl_ **vacuums** _or_ **vacua. 1** a region containing no free matter; in technical contexts now often called: **free space. 2** a region in which gas is present at a low pressure. **3** the degree of exhaustion of gas within an enclosed space: _a perfect vacuum._ **4** a feeling of emptiness: _his death left a vacuum in her life._ **5** short for **vacuum cleaner. 6** (_modifier_) of, containing, producing, or operated by a low gas pressure: _a vacuum brake._ ◆ _vb_ **7** to clean (something) with a vacuum cleaner. [C16: from L: empty space, from _vacuus_ empty]

vacuum cleaner _n_ an electrical household appliance used for cleaning floors, carpets, etc., by suction. ▸ **vacuum cleaning** _n_

vacuum distillation _n_ distillation in which the liquid distilled is enclosed at a low pressure in order to reduce its boiling point.

vacuum flask _n_ an insulating flask that has double walls, usually of silvered glass, with an evacuated space between them. It is used for maintaining substances at high or low temperatures. Also called: **Thermos.**

vacuum gauge _n_ any of a number of instruments for measuring pressures below atmospheric pressure.

vacuum-packed _adj_ packed in an airtight container or packet under low pressure in order to maintain freshness, prevent corrosion, etc.

vacuum pump _n_ a pump for producing a low gas pressure.

vacuum tube or **valve** n the US. and Canad. name for valve (sense 3).

VAD abbrev. for **1** Voluntary Aid Detachment. ◆ n **2** a member of this organization.

vade mecum ('vɑːdɪ 'meɪkʊm) n a handbook or other aid carried on the person for immediate use when needed. [C17: from L, lit.: go with me]

Vadodara ★ (wə'dəʊdərə) n a city in W India, in SE Gujarat: textile manufacturing. Pop.: 1 031 346 (1991). Former name (until 1976): **Baroda**.

vadose ('veɪdəʊs) adj of, designating, or derived from water occurring above the water table: vadose deposits. [C19: from L vadōsus full of shallows, from vadum a ford]

Vaduz ★ (German fa'dʊts) n the capital of Liechtenstein, in the Rhine valley: an old market town, dominated by a medieval castle, residence of the prince of Liechtenstein. Pop.: 5067 (1995 est.).

vagabond ('væɡə,bɒnd) n **1** a person with no fixed home. **2** an idle wandering beggar or thief. **3** (modifier) of or like a vagabond. [C15: from L vagābundus wandering, from vagārī to roam, from vagus VAGUE]
▶ 'vaga,bondage n

vagal ('veɪɡ°l) adj Anat. of, relating to, or affecting the vagus nerve: vagal inhibition.

vagary ('veɪɡərɪ, və'ɡeərɪ) n, pl vagaries. an erratic notion or action. [C16: prob. from L vagārī to roam; cf. L vagus VAGUE]

vagina (və'dʒaɪnə) n, pl vaginas or vaginae (-niː). **1** the canal in most female mammals that extends from the cervix of the uterus to an external opening between the labia minora. **2** Anat., biol. any sheath or sheathlike structure. [C17: from L: sheath]
▶ vag'inal adj

vaginate ('vædʒɪnɪt, -,neɪt) adj (esp. of plant parts) sheathed: a vaginate leaf.

vaginectomy (,vædʒɪ'nektəmɪ) n, pl vaginectomies. **1** surgical removal of all or part of the vagina. **2** surgical removal of part of the serous sheath surrounding the testis and epididymis.

vaginismus (,vædʒɪ'nɪzməs) n painful spasm of the vagina. [C19: from NL, from VAGINA, + -ismus; see -ISM]

vaginitis (,vædʒɪ'naɪtɪs) n inflammation of the vagina.

vagotomy (væ'ɡɒtəmɪ) n, pl vagotomies. surgical division of the vagus nerve, performed to limit gastric secretion in patients with severe peptic ulcers. [C19: from VAG(US) + -TOMY]

vagotonia (,veɪɡə'təʊnɪə) n pathological overactivity of the vagus nerve, affecting various bodily functions controlled by this nerve. [C19: from VAG(US) + -tonia, from L tonus tension, TONE]

vagrancy ('veɪɡrənsɪ) n, pl vagrancies. **1** the state or condition of being a vagrant. **2** the conduct or mode of living of a vagrant.

vagrant ('veɪɡrənt) n **1** a person of no settled abode, income, or job; tramp. ◆ adj **2** wandering about. **3** of or characteristic of a vagrant or vagabond. **4** moving in an erratic fashion; wayward. **5** (of plants) showing straggling growth. [C15: prob. from OF waucrant (from wancrer to roam, of Gmc origin), but also infl. by OF vagant vagabond, from L vagārī to wander]
▶ 'vagrantly adv

vague (veɪɡ) adj **1** (of statements, meaning, etc.) imprecise: vague promises. **2** not clearly perceptible or discernible: a vague idea. **3** not clearly established or known: a vague rumour. **4** (of a person or his expression) absentminded. [C16: via F from L vagus wandering, from ?]
▶ 'vaguely adv ▶ 'vagueness n

vagus or **vagus nerve** ('veɪɡəs) n, pl vagi ('veɪdʒaɪ) or vagus nerves. the tenth cranial nerve, which supplies the heart, lungs, and viscera. [C19: from L vagus wandering]
▶ 'vagal adj

vail (veɪl) Obs. ◆ vb (tr) **1** to lower (something, such as a weapon), esp. as a sign of deference. **2** to remove (the hat, etc.) as a mark of respect. ◆ n **3** a tip. [C14 valen, from obs. avalen, from OF avaler to let fall, from L ad vallem, lit.: to the valley, i.e., down]

vain (veɪn) adj **1** inordinately proud of one's appearance, possessions, or achievements. **2** given to ostentatious display. **3** worthless. **4** senseless or futile. ◆ n **5** in vain. fruitlessly. [C13: via OF from L vānus]
▶ 'vainly adv ▶ 'vainness n

vainglory (,veɪn'ɡlɔːrɪ) n **1** boastfulness or vanity. **2** ostentation.
▶ ,vain'glorious adj

vair (veə) n **1** a fur, probably Russian squirrel, used to trim robes in the Middle Ages. **2** a fur used on heraldic shields, conventionally represented by white and blue skins in alternate lines. [C13: from OF: of more than one colour, from L varius variegated]

Vaisya ('vaɪsjə, 'vaɪʃjə) n the third of the four main Hindu castes, the traders. [C18: from Sansk., lit.: settler, from viś settlement]

Valais ★ (French vale) n a canton of S Switzerland: includes the entire valley of the upper Rhône and the highest peaks in Switzerland; produces a quarter of Switzerland's hydroelectricity. Capital: Sion. Pop.: 269 341 (1995 est.). Area: 5231 sq. km (2020 sq. miles). German name: **Wallis**.

valance ('væləns) n a short piece of drapery hung along a shelf or bed to hide structural detail. [C15: ? after VALENCE, noted for its textiles]
▶ 'valanced adj

Valdai Hills ★ (vɑːl'daɪ) pl n a region of hills and plateaus in NW Russia, between Moscow and Saint Petersburg. Greatest height: 346 m (1135 ft).

Valdemar I ★ (Danish 'valdəmar) n a variant spelling of **Waldemar I.**

Val-de-Marne ★ (French valdəmarn) n a department of N France, in Île-de-France region. Capital: Créteil. Pop.: 1 233 964 (1994 est.). Area: 244 sq. km (95 sq. miles).

Valdivia¹ ★ (Spanish bal'diβja) n a port in S Chile, on the **Valdivia River** about 19 km (12 miles) from the Pacific: developed chiefly by German settlers in the 1850s; university (1954). Pop.: 119 431 (1995 est.).

Valdivia² ★ (Spanish bal'diβja) n **Pedro de** ('peðro de). ?1500–54, Spanish soldier; conqueror of Chile.

Val-d'Oise ★ (French valdwaz) n a department of N France, in Île-de-France region. Capital: Pontoise. Pop.: 1 102 804 (1994 est.). Area: 1249 sq. km (487 sq. miles).

vale¹ (veɪl) n a literary word for **valley**. [C13: from OF val, from L vallis valley]

vale² Latin. ('vɑːleɪ) sentence substitute. farewell; goodbye.

valediction (,vælɪ'dɪkʃən) n **1** the act or an instance of saying goodbye. **2** any valedictory statement, etc. [C17: from L valedīcere, from valē farewell + dīcere to say]

valedictory (,vælɪ'dɪktərɪ) adj **1** saying goodbye. **2** of or relating to a farewell or an occasion of farewell. ◆ n, pl valedictories. **3** a farewell address or speech.

valence ('veɪləns) n Chem. **1** another name (esp. US. and Canad.) for **valency**. **2** the phenomenon of forming chemical bonds.

Valence ★ (French valɑ̃s) n a town in SE France, on the River Rhône. Pop.: 63 437 (1990).

Valencia ★ (Spanish ba'lenθja) n **1** a port in E Spain, capital of Valencia province, on the Mediterranean: the third largest city in Spain; capital of the Moorish kingdom of Valencia (1021–1238); university (1501). Pop.: 764 293 (1994 est.). Latin name: **Valentia** (və'lentɪə). **2** a region and former kingdom of E Spain, on the Mediterranean. **3** a city in N Venezuela: one of the two main industrial centres in Venezuela. Pop.: 903 621 (1990).

Valenciennes¹ (,vælənsɪ'en) n a flat bobbin lace typically having scroll and floral designs and originally made of linen. [after VALENCIENNES², where orig. made]

Valenciennes² ★ (French valɑ̃sjen) n a town in N France, on the River Escaut: a coal-mining and heavy industrial centre. Pop.: 39 276 (1990).

valency ('veɪlənsɪ) or esp. US. & Canad. **valence** n, pl valencies or valences. Chem. a property of atoms or groups equal to the number of atoms of hydrogen that the atom or group could combine with or displace in forming compounds. [C19: from L valentia strength, from valēre to be strong]

valency electron n *Chem.* an electron in the outer shell of an atom, responsible for forming chemical bonds.

Valens ★ ('veɪlenz) n ?328–378 A.D., emperor of the Eastern Roman Empire (364–378); appointed by his elder brother Valentinian I, emperor of the Western Empire.

valentine ('vælən,taɪn) n **1** a card or gift expressing love or affection, sent, often anonymously, on Saint Valentine's Day. **2** a sweetheart selected for such a greeting.

Valentine ★ ('vælən,taɪn) n **Saint.** 3rd century A.D., Christian martyr, associated by historical accident with the custom of sending valentines; bishop of Terni. Feast day: Feb. 14.

Valentinian I (,vælən'tɪnɪən) or **Valentinianus I** ★ (,vælən,tɪnɪ'eɪnəs) n 321–375 A.D., emperor of the Western Roman Empire (364–375); appointed his brother Valens to rule the Eastern Empire.

Valentinian II or **Valentinianus II** ★ n 371–392 A.D., emperor of the Western Roman Empire (375–392), reigning jointly with his half brother Gratian until 383.

Valentinian III or **Valentinianus III** ★ n ?419–455 A.D., emperor of the Western Roman Empire (425–455). His government lost Africa to the Vandals.

Valentino ★ (,vælən'tiːnəʊ) n **Rudolph,** original name *Rodolpho Guglielmi di Valentina d'Antonguolla.* 1895–1926, US. silent-film actor, born in Italy. His films include *The Sheik* (1921).

Vale of Glamorgan ★ n a county borough of S Wales, created in 1996 from parts of South Glamorgan and Mid Glamorgan. Administrative centre: Barry. Pop.: 119 200 (1996 est.). Area: 295 sq. km (114 sq. miles).

Valera ★ (və'lɛərə, -'lɪərə) n See (Eamon) **de Valera.**

valerian (və'lɛərɪən) n **1** Also called: **allheal.** a Eurasian plant having small white or pinkish flowers and a medicinal root. **2** a sedative drug made from the dried roots of this plant. [C14: via OF from Med. L *valeriana* (*herba*) (herb) of *Valerius,* unexplained L personal name]

Valerian ★ (və'lɛərɪən) n Latin name *Publius Licinius Valerianus.* died 260 A.D., Roman emperor (253–260): renewed persecution of the Christians; defeated by the Persians.

valeric (və'lɛrɪk, -'lɪərɪk) adj of, relating to, or derived from valerian.

valeric acid n another name for **pentanoic acid.**

Valéry ★ (French valeri) n **Paul** (pɒl). 1871–1945, French poet and essayist; author of *La Jeune Parque* (1917) and *Album de vers anciens 1890–1900* (1920).

valet ('vælɪt, 'væleɪ) n **1** a manservant who acts as personal attendant to his employer, looking after his clothing, serving his meals, etc. **2** a manservant who attends to the requirements of patrons in a hotel, etc.; steward. ◆ vb **valets, valeting, valeted. 3** to act as a valet for (a person). **4** (tr) to clean the bodywork and interior of (a car) as a professional service. [C16: from OF *vaslet* page, from Med. L *vassus* servant]

valeta or **veleta** (və'liːtə) n a ballroom dance in triple time. [from Sp.: weather vane]

valet de chambre French. (vale də ʃɑ̃brə) n, pl **valets de chambre** (vale də ʃɑ̃brə). the full French term for **valet** (sense 1).

valet parking n a system at hotels, airports, etc., in which patrons' cars are parked by a steward.

Valetta ★ (və'letə) n a variant spelling of **Valletta.**

valetudinarian (,vælɪ,tjuːdɪ'nɛərɪən) or **valetudinary** (,vælɪ'tjuːdɪnərɪ) n, pl **valetudinarians** or **valetudinaries. 1** a person who is chronically sick. **2** a hypochondriac. ◆ adj **3** relating to or resulting from poor health. **4** being a valetudinarian. [C18: from L *valētūdō* state of health, from *valēre* to be well] ▶ ,vale,tudi'narianism n

valgus ('vælgəs) adj *Pathol.* twisted away from the midline of the body. [C19: from L: bow-legged]

Valhalla (væl'hælə), **Walhalla, Valhall** (væl'hæl, 'vælhæl), or **Walhall** ★ n *Norse myth.* the great hall of Odin where warriors who die as heroes in battle dwell eternally. [C18: from ON, from *valr* slain warriors + *höll* HALL]

valiant ('væljənt) adj **1** courageous or intrepid. **2** marked by bravery or courage: *a valiant deed.* [C14: from OF, from *valoir* to be of value, from L *valēre* to be strong] ▶ 'valiantly adv

valid ('vælɪd) adj **1** having some foundation; based on truth. **2** legally acceptable: *a valid licence.* **3a** having legal force. **3b** having legal authority. **4** having some force or cogency: *a valid point in a debate.* **5** *Logic.* (of an inference or argument) having premises and a conclusion so related that if the premises are true, the conclusion must be true. [C16: from L *validus* robust, from *valēre* to be strong] ▶ **validity** (və'lɪdɪtɪ) n ▶ 'validly adv

validate ('vælɪ,deɪt) vb **validates, validating, validated.** (tr) **1** to confirm or corroborate. **2** to give legal force or official confirmation to. ▶ ,vali'dation n

valine ('veɪliːn) n an essential amino acid: a component of proteins. [C19: from VAL(ERIC ACID) + -INE²]

valise (və'liːz) n a small overnight travelling case. [C17: via F from It. *valigia,* from ?]

Valium ('vælɪəm) n *Trademark.* a preparation of the drug diazepam used as a tranquillizer.

Valkyrie, Walkyrie (væl'kɪərɪ, 'vælkɪərɪ), or **Valkyr** ★ ('vælkɪə) n *Norse myth.* any of the beautiful maidens who serve Odin and ride over battlefields to claim the dead heroes and take them to Valhalla. [C18: from ON *Valkyrja,* from *valr* slain warriors + *köri* to CHOOSE] ▶ **Val'kyrian** adj

Valladolid ★ (Spanish baʎaðo'lið) n **1** a city in NW Spain: residence of the Spanish court in the 16th century; university (1346). Pop.: 328 365 (1991). **2** the former name (until 1828) of Morelia.

vallation (və'leɪʃən) n **1** the act or process of building fortifications. **2** a wall or rampart. [C17: from LL *vallātiō,* from L *vallum* rampart]

vallecula (və'lekjulə) n, pl **valleculae** (-,liː). **1** *Anat.* any of various natural depressions or crevices. **2** *Bot.* a groove or furrow. [C19: from LL: little valley, from L *vallis* valley]

Valle d'Aosta ★ (Italian 'valle da'ɔsta) n an autonomous region of NW Italy: under many different rulers until passing to the house of Savoy in the 11th century; established as an autonomous region in 1944. Capital: Aosta. Pop.: 118 239 (1994 est.). Area: 3263 sq. km (1260 sq. miles).

Valletta or **Valetta** ★ (və'letə) n the capital of Malta, on the NE coast: founded by the Knights Hospitallers, after the victory over the Turks in 1565; became a major naval base after Malta's annexation by Britain (1814). Pop.: 9129 (1995 est.).

valley ('vælɪ) n **1** a long depression in the land surface, usually containing a river, formed by erosion or by movements in the earth's crust. **2** the broad area drained by a single river system: *the Thames valley.* **3** any elongated depression resembling a valley. [C13: from OF *valee,* from L *vallis*]

Valley Forge ★ n an area in SE Pennsylvania, northwest of Philadelphia: winter camp (1777–78) of Washington and the American Revolutionary Army.

Valley of Ten Thousand Smokes ★ n a volcanic region of SW Alaska, formed by the massive eruption of Mount Katmai in 1912; jets of steam issue from vents up to 45 m (150 ft) across.

Vallombrosa ★ (Italian vallom'brɔːsa) n a village and resort in central Italy, in Tuscany region: 11th-century Benedictine monastery.

vallum ('væləm) n *Archaeol.* a Roman rampart or earthwork.

Valois[1] ★ (French valwa) n a historic region and former duchy of N France.

Valois[2] ★ (French valwa) n a royal house of France, ruling from 1328 to 1589.

Valois[3] ★ ('vælwɑː) n Dame **Ninette de** (niː'net də). original name *Edris Stannus.* born 1898, British ballet dancer and choreographer, born in Ireland: a founder of the Vic-Wells Ballet Company (1931), which under her direction became the Royal Ballet (1956).

Valona ★ (vəˈləʊnə) n another name for **Vlorë**.

valonia (vəˈləʊnɪə) n the acorn cups and unripe acorns of the Eurasian oak, used in tanning, dyeing, and making ink. [C18: from It. *vallonia*, ult. from Gk *balanos* acorn]

valorize or **valorise** (ˈvæləˌraɪz) vb **valorizes, valorizing, valorized** or **valorises, valorising, valorised.** (tr) to fix an artificial price for (a commodity) by governmental action. [C20: back formation from *valorization;* see VALOUR]
► ˌvaloriˈzation or ˌvaloriˈsation n

valour or US **valor** (ˈvælə) n courage or bravery, esp. in battle. [C15: from LL *valor*, from *valēre* to be strong]
► ˈvalorous adj

Valparaíso ★ (Spanish balparaˈiso) n a port in central Chile, on a wide bay of the Pacific: the third largest city and chief port of Chile; two universities. Pop.: 282 168 (1995 est.).

valse French. (vals) n another word for **waltz**.

valuable (ˈvæljʊəbᵊl) adj 1 having considerable monetary worth. 2 of considerable importance or quality: *valuable information.* 3 able to be valued. ♦ n 4 (usually pl) a valuable article of personal property, esp. jewellery.
► ˈvaluably adv

valuate (ˈvæljʊˌeɪt) vb **valuates, valuating, valuated.** US. another word for **value** (senses 10, 12) or **evaluate.**
► ˈvaluˌator n

valuation (ˌvæljʊˈeɪʃən) n 1 the act of valuing, esp. a formal assessment of the worth of property, jewellery, etc. 2 the price arrived at by the process of valuing: *I set a high valuation on technical ability.*
► ˌvaluˈational adj

value (ˈvæljuː) n 1 the desirability of a thing, often in respect of some property such as usefulness or exchangeability. 2 an amount, esp. a material or monetary one, considered to be a fair exchange in return for a thing: *the value of the picture is £10 000.* 3 satisfaction: *value for money.* 4 precise meaning or significance. 5 (pl) the moral principles or accepted standards of a person or group. 6 Maths. a particular magnitude, number, or amount: *the value of the variable was 7.* 7 Music. short for **time value.** 8 (in painting, drawing, etc.) a gradation of tone from light to dark. 8b the relation of one of these elements to another or to the whole picture. 9 Phonetics. the quality of the speech sound associated with a written character representing it: *"g" has the value* (dʒ) *in English "gem".* ♦ vb **values, valuing, valued.** (tr) 10 to assess or estimate the worth, merit, or desirability of. 11 to have a high regard for, esp. in respect of worth, usefulness, merit, etc. 12 (foll. by at) to fix the financial or material worth of (a unit of currency, work of art, etc.). [C14: from OF, from *valoir*, from L *valēre* to be worth]
► ˈvalued adj ► ˈvalueless adj ► ˈvaluer n

value added n the difference between the total revenues of a firm, industry, etc., and its total purchases from other firms, industries, etc.

value-added tax n (in Britain) the full name for **VAT.**

valued policy n an insurance policy in which the amount payable in the event of a valid claim is agreed upon between the company and the policyholder when the policy is issued and is not related to the actual value of a loss.

value judgment n a subjective assessment based on one's own values or those of one's class.

Valuer General n Austral. a state official who values properties for rating purposes.

valuta (vəˈluːtə) n Rare. the value of one currency in terms of its exchange rate with another. [C20: from It., lit.: VALUE]

valvate (ˈvælveɪt) adj 1 furnished with a valve or valves. 2 Bot. 2a taking place by means of valves: *valvate dehiscence.* 2b (of petals) having the margins touching but not overlapping.

valve (vælv) n 1 any device that shuts off, starts, regulates, or controls the flow of a fluid. 2 Anat. a flaplike structure in a hollow organ, such as the heart, that controls the one-way passage of fluid through that organ. 3 Also called: **tube.** an evacuated electron tube containing a cathode, anode, and, usually, one or more additional control electrodes. When a positive potential is applied to the anode, it produces a one-way flow of current. 4 Zool. any of the separable pieces that make up the shell of a mollusc. 5 Music. a device on some brass instruments by which the effective length of the tube may be varied to enable a chromatic scale to be produced. 6 Bot. any of the several parts that make up a dry dehiscent fruit, esp. a capsule. [C14: from L *valva* a folding door]
► ˈvalveless adj ► ˈvalveˌlike adj

valve-in-head engine n the US name for **overhead-valve engine.**

valvular (ˈvælvjʊlə) adj 1 of, relating to, operated by, or having a valve or valves. 2 having the shape or function of a valve.

valvulitis (ˌvælvjʊˈlaɪtɪs) n inflammation of a bodily valve, esp. a heart valve. [C19: from NL *valvula* dim. of VALVE + -ITIS]

vamoose (vəˈmuːs) vb **vamooses, vamoosing, vamoosed.** (intr) Sl., chiefly US. to leave a place hurriedly; decamp. [C19: from Sp. *vamos* let us go, from L *vādere* to go, walk rapidly]

vamp¹ (væmp) Inf. ♦ n 1 a seductive woman who exploits men by use of her sexual charms. ♦ vb 2 to exploit (a man) in the fashion of a vamp. [C20: short for VAMPIRE]

vamp² (væmp) n 1 something patched up to make it look new. 2 the reworking of a story, etc. 3 an improvised accompaniment. 4 the front part of the upper of a shoe. ♦ vb 5 (tr; often foll. by up) to make a renovation of. 6 to improvise (an accompaniment) to (a tune). [C13: from OF *avantpié* the front part of a shoe (hence, something patched), from *avant-* fore- + *pié* foot, from L *pēs*]

vampire (ˈvæmpaɪə) n 1 (in European folklore) a corpse that rises nightly from its grave to drink the blood of the living. 2 See **vampire bat.** 3 a person who preys mercilessly upon others. [C18: from F, from G, from Magyar]
► vampiric (væmˈpɪrɪk) adj ► ˈvampirism n

vampire bat n a bat of tropical regions of Central and South America, having sharp incisor and canine teeth and feeding on the blood of birds and mammals.

van¹ (væn) n 1 short for **caravan** (sense 1). 2 a motor vehicle for transporting goods, etc., by road. 3 Brit. a closed railway wagon in which the guard travels, for transporting goods, etc.

van² (væn) n short for **vanguard.**

van³ (væn) n Tennis, chiefly Brit. short for **advantage** (sense 3).

van⁴ (væn) n 1 any device for winnowing corn. 2 Arch. a wing. [C17: var. of FAN¹]

Van ★ (vɑːn) n 1 a city in E Turkey, on Lake Van. Pop.: 194 600 (1994 est.). 2 **Lake.** a salt lake in E Turkey, at an altitude of 1650 m (5400 ft): fed by melting snow and glaciers. Area: 3737 sq. km (1433 sq. miles).

vanadium (vəˈneɪdɪəm) n a toxic silvery-white metallic element used in steel alloys and as a catalyst. Symbol: V; atomic no.: 23; atomic wt.: 50.94. [C19: NL, from ON *Vanadis*, epithet of the goddess Freya + -IUM]

Van Allen ★ (væn ˈælən) n James Alfred. born 1914, US physicist, noted for his use of satellites to investigate cosmic radiation in the upper atmosphere.

Van Allen belt ★ n either of two regions of charged particles above the earth, the inner one extending from 2400 to 5600 kilometres above the earth and the outer one from 13 000 to 19 000 kilometres. [C20: after its discoverer, J. A. VAN ALLEN]

Vanbrugh ★ (ˈvænbrə) n Sir John. 1664–1726, English dramatist and baroque architect. His comedies include *The Relapse* (1697) and *The Provok'd Wife* (1697). As an architect, he is noted for Blenheim Palace.

Van Buren ★ (væn ˈbjʊərən) n Martin. 1782–1862, US Democratic statesman; 8th president of the US (1837–41).

Vancouver¹ ★ (vænˈkuːvə) n 1 an island of SW Canada, off the SW coast of British Columbia: separated from the Canadian mainland by the Strait of Georgia and Queen Charlotte Sound, and from the US mainland by Juan de Fuca Strait; the largest island off the W coast of North

America. Chief town: Victoria. Pop.: 461 573 (1981). Area: 32 137 sq. km (12 408 sq. miles). **2** a city in SW Canada, in SW British Columbia: Canada's chief Pacific port, named after Captain George Vancouver: university (1908). Pop. (metropolitan area): 1 826 800 (1995). **3 Mount.** a mountain on the border between Canada and Alaska, in the St Elias Mountains. Height: 4785 m (15 700 ft).

Vancouver² ★ (væn'kuːvə) *n* Captain **George.** 1757–98, British navigator, noted for his exploration of the Pacific coast of North America (1792–94).

V and A (in Britain) *abbrev. for* Victoria and Albert Museum.

vandal ('vændˀl) *n* a person who deliberately causes damage to personal or public property. [C17: from VANDAL, from L *Vandallus*, of Gmc origin]

Vandal ('vændˀl) *n* a member of a Germanic people that raided Roman provinces in the 3rd and 4th centuries A.D. before devastating Gaul, conquering Spain and N Africa, and sacking Rome.
▸ **Vandalic** (væn'dælɪk) *adj*

vandalism ('vændə,lɪzəm) *n* the deliberate destruction caused by a vandal or an instance of such destruction.
▸ ,vandal'istic *adj*

vandalize *or* **vandalise** ('vændə,laɪz) *vb* **vandalizes, vandalizing, vandalized** *or* **vandalises, vandalising, vandalised.** (*tr*) to destroy or damage (something) by an act of vandalism.

Van de Graaff generator ('væn də ,grɑːf) *n* a device for producing high electrostatic potentials, consisting of a hollow metal sphere on which a charge is accumulated from a continuous moving belt of insulating material: used in particle accelerators. [C20: after R. J. *Van de Graaff* (1901–67), US physicist]

Vanderbilt ★ ('vændəbɪlt) *n* **Cornelius,** known as *Commodore Vanderbilt.* 1794–1877, US steamship and railway magnate and philanthropist.

Van der Post ★ (,væn də 'pɒst) *n* Sir **Laurens.** 1906–96, South African novelist and travel writer.

van der Waals ★ (*Dutch* vɑn dər 'waːls) *n* **Johannes Diderik** (joːˈhɑnəs 'diːdərik). 1837–1923, Dutch physicist, noted for his equations of state: Nobel prize for physics in 1910.

van der Weyden ★ (*Dutch* vɑn dər 'wejdə) *n* **Rogier** (roːˈxiːr). ?1400–64, Flemish painter, esp. of religious works and portraits.

Van Diemen Gulf ★ (væn 'diːmən) *n* an inlet of the Timor Sea in N Australia, in the Northern Territory.

Van Diemen's Land ★ (væn 'diːmənz) *n* the former name (1642–1855) of **Tasmania.**
▸ ,Vande'monian *n, adj*

Van Dyck *or* **Vandyke** ★ (væn 'daɪk) *n* Sir **Anthony.** 1599–1641, Flemish painter; court painter to Charles I of England (1632–41).

Vandyke beard ('vændaɪk) *n* a short pointed beard. Often shortened to **Vandyke.**

Vandyke collar *or* **cape** *n* a large white collar with several very deep points. Often shortened to **Vandyke.**

vane (veɪn) *n* **1** Also called: **weather vane.** a flat plate or blade of metal mounted on a vertical axis in an exposed position to indicate wind direction. **2** any one of the flat blades or sails forming part of the wheel of a windmill. **3** any flat or shaped plate used to direct fluid flow, esp. in a turbine, etc. **4** a fin or plate fitted to a projectile or missile to provide stabilization or guidance. **5** *Ornithol.* the flat part of a feather. **6** *Surveying.* **6a** a sight on a quadrant or compass. **6b** the movable marker on a levelling staff. [OE *fana*]
▸ **vaned** *adj*

Vänern ★ (*Swedish* 'veːnərn) *n* **Lake.** a lake in SW Sweden: the largest lake in Sweden and W Europe; drains into the Kattegat. Area: 5585 sq. km (2156 sq. miles).

van Eyck ★ (væn 'aɪk; *Dutch* vɑn 'ɛjk) *n* **Jan** (jɑn). died 1441, Flemish painter; founder of the Flemish school of painting. His most famous work is the altarpiece *The Adoration of the Lamb,* in Ghent, in which he may have been assisted by his brother **Hubert** ('hyːbərt), died ?1426.

Van Gogh ★ (væn 'ɡɒx; *Dutch* vɑn 'xɔx) *n* **Vincent** (vɪn'sɛnt). 1853–90, Dutch postimpressionist painter, noted for his landscapes and portraits.

vanguard ('væn,ɡɑːd) *n* **1** the leading division or units of a military force. **2** the leading position in any movement or field, or the people who occupy such a position. [C15: from OF *avant-garde,* from *avant-* fore- + *garde* GUARD]

vanilla (və'nɪlə) *n* **1** any of a genus of tropical climbing orchids having spikes of large fragrant flowers and long fleshy pods containing the seeds (beans). **2** the pod or bean of certain of these plants, used to flavour food, etc. **3** a flavouring extract prepared from vanilla beans and used in cooking. ◆ *adj* **4** flavoured with or as with vanilla: *vanilla ice cream.* **5** *Sl.* ordinary or conventional: *a vanilla kind of guy.* [C17: from NL, from Sp. *vainilla* pod, from *vaina,* from L *vāgīna* sheath]
▸ va'nillic *adj*

vanillin ('vænɪlɪn, və'nɪlɪn) *n* a white crystalline aldehyde found in vanilla and many natural balsams and resins. It is a by-product of paper manufacture and is used as a flavouring and in perfumes.

Vanir ★ ('vɑːnɪə) *pl n Norse myth.* a race of ancient gods often locked in struggle with the Aesir. The most notable of them are Njord and his children Frey and Freya. [from ON *Vanr,* a fertility god]

vanish ('vænɪʃ) *vb* (*intr*) **1** to disappear, esp. suddenly or mysteriously. **2** to cease to exist. **3** *Maths.* to become zero. [C14 *vanissen,* from OF *esvanir,* from L *ēvānēscere* to evaporate, from *ē-* EX-¹ + *vānēscere* to vanish, from *vānus* empty]
▸ 'vanisher *n*

vanishing cream *n* a cosmetic cream that is colourless once applied, used as a foundation for powder or as a cleansing cream.

vanishing point *n* **1** the point to which parallel lines appear to converge in the rendering of perspective, usually on the horizon. **2** a point at which something disappears.

vanity ('vænɪtɪ) *n, pl* **vanities. 1** the state or quality of being vain. **2** ostentation occasioned by ambition or pride. **3** an instance of being vain or something about which one is vain. **4** the state or quality of being valueless or futile. [C13: from OF, from L *vānitās* emptiness, from *vānus* empty]

vanity bag, case, *or* **box** *n* a woman's small bag or hand case used to carry cosmetics, etc.

vanity unit *n* a hand basin built into a wooden Formica-covered or tiled top, usually with a built-in cupboard below it. Also called (trademark): **Vanitory unit.**

vanquish ('væŋkwɪʃ) *vb* (*tr*) **1** to defeat or overcome in a battle, contest, etc. **2** to defeat in argument or debate. **3** to conquer (an emotion). [C14 *vanquisshen,* from OF *venquis,* from *veintre* to overcome, from L *vincere*]
▸ 'vanquishable *adj* ▸ 'vanquisher *n*

vantage ('vɑːntɪdʒ) *n* **1** a state, position, or opportunity affording superiority or advantage. **2** superiority or benefit accruing from such a position, etc. **3** *Tennis.* short for **advantage** (sense 3). [C13: from OF *avantage* ADVANTAGE]

vantage point *n* a position or place that allows one an overall view of a scene or situation.

van't Hoff ★ (*Dutch* vɑnt 'hɔf) *n* **Jacobus Hendricus** (jaˈkoːbys hɛnˈdriːkys). 1852–1911, Dutch physical chemist: founded stereochemistry with his theory of the asymmetric carbon atom: Nobel prize for chemistry 1901.

Vanua Levu ★ (vɑːˈnuːə 'levuː) *n* the second largest island of Fiji: mountainous. Area: 5535 sq. km (2137 sq. miles).

Vanuatu ★ ('vænuː,ætuː) *n* a republic comprising a group of islands in the W Pacific, W of Fiji: a condominium under Anglo-French joint rule from 1906; attained partial autonomy in 1978 and full independence in 1980; a member of the Commonwealth. Its economy is based chiefly on copra. Official languages: Bislama; French; English. Religion: Christian majority. Currency: vatu. Capital: Vila (on Efate). Pop.: 176 300 (1997). Area: about 14 760 sq. km (5700 sq. miles). Official name: **Republic of Vanuatu.** Former name (until 1980): **New Hebrides.**

vanward ('vænwəd) *adj, adv* in or towards the front.

vapid ('væpɪd) *adj* **1** bereft of strength, sharpness, flavour, etc. **2** boring or dull. [C17: from L *vapidus*]
▸ va'**pidity** *n* ▸ '**vapidly** *adv*

vapor ('veɪpə) *n* the US spelling of **vapour**.

vaporescence (,veɪpə'resəns) *n* the production or formation of vapour.
▸ ,vapor'**escent** *adj*

vaporetto (,veɪpə'retəu) *n, pl* **vaporetti** (-tɪ) *or* **vaporettos**. a steam-powered passenger boat, as used on the canals in Venice. [It., from *vapore* a steamboat]

vaporific (,veɪpə'rɪfɪk) *adj* **1** producing, causing, or tending to produce vapour. **2** of, concerned with, or having the nature of vapour. **3** tending to become vapour; volatile. [C18: from NL *vaporificus*, from L *vapor* steam + *facere* to make]

vaporimeter (,veɪpə'rɪmɪtə) *n* an instrument for measuring vapour pressure, used to determine the volatility of oils.

vaporize *or* **vaporise** ('veɪpə,raɪz) *vb* **vaporizes, vaporizing, vaporized** *or* **vaporises, vaporising, vaporised**. **1** to change or cause to change into vapour or into the gaseous state. **2** to evaporate or disappear or cause to evaporate or disappear, esp. suddenly. **3** to destroy or be destroyed by turning into a gas as a result of the extreme heat generated by a nuclear explosion.
▸ ,vapori'**zation** *or* ,vapori'**sation** *n*

vaporizer *or* **vaporiser** ('veɪpə,raɪzə) *n* **1** a substance that vaporizes or a device that causes vaporization. **2** *Med.* a device that produces steam or atomizes medication for inhalation.

vaporous ('veɪpərəs) *adj* **1** resembling or full of vapour. **2** lacking permanence or substance. **3** given to foolish imaginings.
▸ **vaporosity** (,veɪpə'rɒsɪtɪ) *n* ▸ '**vaporously** *adv*

vapour *or US* **vapor** ('veɪpə) *n* **1** particles of moisture or other substance suspended in air and visible as clouds, smoke, etc. **2** a gaseous substance at a temperature below its critical temperature. **3** a substance that is in a gaseous state at a temperature below its boiling point. **4 the vapours.** *Arch.* a depressed mental condition believed originally to be the result of vaporous exhalations from the stomach. ◆ *vb* **5** to evaporate or cause to evaporate. **6** (*intr*) to make vain empty boasts. [C14: from L *vapor*]
▸ '**vapourer** *or US* '**vaporer** *n* ▸ '**vapourish** *or US* '**vaporish** *adj* ▸ '**vapour-,like** *or US* '**vapor-,like** *adj* ▸ '**vapoury** *or US* '**vapory** *adj*

vapour density *n* the ratio of the density of a gas or vapour to that of hydrogen at the same temperature and pressure.

vapour lock *n* a stoppage in a pipe carrying a liquid caused by a bubble of gas, esp. in the pipe feeding the carburettor of an internal-combustion engine.

vapour pressure *n Physics*. the pressure exerted by a vapour in equilibrium with its solid or liquid phase at a particular temperature.

vapour trail *n* a visible trail left by an aircraft flying at high altitude or through supercold air caused by the deposition of water vapour in the engine exhaust as minute ice crystals.

Var ★ (*French* var) *n* **1** a department of SE France, in Provence-Alpes-Côte d'Azur region. Capital: Toulon. Pop.: 866 747 (1994 est.). Area: 6023 sq. km (2349 sq. miles). **2** a river in SE France, flowing southeast and south to the Mediterranean near Nice. Length: about 130 km (80 miles).

var. *abbrev. for:* **1** variable. **2** variant. **3** variation. **4** variety. **5** various.

varactor ('veə,ræktə) *n* a semiconductor diode that acts as a voltage-dependent capacitor, being operated with a reverse bias. [C20: prob. a blend of *variable reactor*]

Varah ★ ('vɑːrə) *n* (**Edward**) **Chad.** born 1911, British Anglican clergyman, who founded (1953) the Samaritans counselling service.

Varanasi ★ (və'rɑːnəsɪ) *n* a city in NE India, in SE Uttar Pradesh on the River Ganges: probably dates from the 13th century B.C.; an early centre of Aryan philosophy and religion; a place of pilgrimage for Hindus, Jains, Sikhs, and Buddhists, with many ghats along the Ganges; seat of the Banaras Hindu University (1916), India's leading university, and the Sanskrit University (1957). Pop.: 929 270 (1991). Former names: **Benares, Banaras**.

Vardar ★ (*Serbo-Croat* 'vardar) *n* a river in S Europe, rising in W Macedonia and flowing northeast, then south past Skopje into Greece, where it enters the Aegean at Thessaloníki. Length: about 320 km (200 miles).

varec ('værɛk) *n* **1** another name for **kelp. 2** the ash obtained from kelp. [C17: from F, from ON *wrek* (unattested); see WRECK]

Varese ★ (*Italian* va'reːse) *n* a historic city in N Italy, in Lombardy near Lake Varese. Pop.: 88 018 (1990).

Varèse ★ (və'rɛz) *n* **Edgar(d)**. 1883–1965, US composer, born in France. His works include *Ionisation* (1931) and *Poème électronique* (1958).

Vargas ★ (*Portuguese* 'vargas) *n* **Getúlio Dornelles** (ʒe'tulju dur'neləs). 1883–1954, Brazilian statesman; president (1930–45; 1951–54).

Vargas Llosa ★ (*Spanish* 'barɣas 'ʎosa) *n* (**Jorge**) **Mario** (**Pedro**). born 1936, Peruvian novelist. His novels include *The City and the Dogs* (1963) and *The Notebooks of Don Rigoberto* (1998).

variable ('veərɪəbᵊl) *adj* **1** liable to or capable of change: *variable weather*. **2** (of behaviour, emotions, etc.) lacking constancy. **3** *Maths.* having a range of possible values. **4** (of a species, etc.) liable to deviate from the established type. **5** (of a wind) varying in direction and intensity. **6** (of an electrical component or device) designed so that a characteristic property, such as resistance, can be varied. ◆ *n* **7** something that is subject to variation. **8** *Maths.* **8a** an expression that can be assigned any of a set of values. **8b** a symbol, esp. *x*, *y*, or *z*, representing an unspecified member of a class of objects, numbers, etc. **9** *Logic.* a symbol, esp. *x*, *y*, or *z*, representing any member of a class of entities. **10** *Computing.* a named unit of storage that can be changed to any of a set of specified values during execution of a program. **11** *Astron.* See **variable star. 12** a variable wind. **13** (*pl*) a region where variable winds occur. [C14: from L *variābilis* changeable, from *variāre* to diversify]
▸ ,varia'**bility** *or* '**variableness** *n* ▸ '**variably** *adv*

variable cost *n* a cost that varies directly with output.

variable-geometry *or* **variable-sweep** *adj* denoting an aircraft in which the wings are hinged to give the variable aspect ratio colloquially known as a **swing-wing**.

variable star *n* any star that varies considerably in brightness, either irregularly or in regular periods. **Intrinsic variables**, in which the variation is a result of internal changes, include novae and pulsating stars.

variance ('veərɪəns) *n* **1** the act of varying or the quality, state, or degree of being divergent. **2** an instance of diverging; dissension. **3 at variance. 3a** (often foll. by *with*) (of facts, etc.) not in accord. **3b** (of persons) in a state of dissension. **4** *Statistics*. a measure of dispersion; the square of the standard deviations. **5** a difference or discrepancy between two steps in a legal proceeding, esp. between a statement and the evidence given to support it. **6** *Chem.* the number of degrees of freedom of a system, used in the phase rule.

variant ('veərɪənt) *adj* **1** liable to or displaying variation. **2** differing from a standard or type: *a variant spelling*. ◆ *n* **3** something that differs from a standard or type. **4** *Statistics*. another word for **variate**. [C14: via OF from L, from *variāre* to diversify, from *varius* VARIOUS]

variate ('veərɪt) *n Statistics*. a random variable or a numerical value taken by it. [C16: from L *variāre* to VARY]

variation (,veərɪ'eɪʃən) *n* **1** the act, process, condition, or result of changing or varying. **2** an instance of varying or the amount, rate, or degree of such change. **3** something that differs from a standard or convention. **4** *Music.* a repetition of a musical theme in which the rhythm, harmony, or melody is altered or embellished. **5** *Biol.* a marked deviation from the typical form or function. **6** *Astron.* any deviation from the mean motion or orbit of a planet, satellite, etc. **7** another word for **magnetic declination. 8** *Ballet.* a solo dance.
▸ ,vari'**ational** *adj*

★ people and places

varicella (ˌværɪˈsɛlə) *n* the technical name for **chickenpox**. [C18: NL, irregular dim. of VARIOLA]
▸ ˌvariˈcellar *adj*

varices (ˈværɪˌsiːz) *n* the plural of **varix**.

varico- *or before a vowel* **varic-** *combining form.* indicating a varix or varicose veins: *varicotomy.* [from L *varix, varic-* distended vein]

varicoloured *or US* **varicolored** (ˈvɛərɪˌkʌləd) *adj* having many colours.

varicose (ˈværɪˌkəus) *adj* of or resulting from varicose veins: *a varicose ulcer.* [C18: from L *varicōsus,* from VARIX]

varicose veins *pl n* a condition in which the superficial veins, esp. of the legs, become knotted and swollen.

varicosis (ˌværɪˈkəusɪs) *n Pathol.* any condition characterized by distension of the veins. [C18: from NL, from L: VARIX]

varicosity (ˌværɪˈkɒsɪtɪ) *n, pl* **varicosities**. *Pathol.* 1 the state, condition, or quality of being varicose. 2 an abnormally distended vein.

varicotomy (ˌværɪˈkɒtəmɪ) *n, pl* **varicotomies**. surgical excision of a varicose vein.

varied (ˈvɛərɪd) *adj* 1 displaying or characterized by variety; diverse. 2 modified or altered: *the amount may be varied.* 3 varicoloured; variegated.
▸ ˈvariedly *adv*

variegate (ˈvɛərɪˌgeɪt) *vb* **variegates, variegating, variegated.** (*tr*) to alter the appearance of, esp. by adding different colours. [C17: from LL, from L *varius* diverse, VARIOUS + *agere* to make]
▸ ˌvarieˈgation *n*

variegated (ˈvɛərɪˌgeɪtɪd) *adj* 1 displaying differently coloured spots., streaks, etc. 2 (of foliage) having pale patches.

varietal (vəˈraɪətʲl) *adj* 1 of, characteristic of, designating, or forming a variety, esp. a biological variety. ◆ *n* 2 a wine labelled with the name of the grape from which it is pressed.
▸ vaˈrietally *adv*

variety (vəˈraɪɪtɪ) *n, pl* **varieties.** 1 the quality or condition of being diversified or various. 2 a collection of unlike things, esp. of the same general group. 3 a different form or kind within a general category: *varieties of behaviour.* 4a *Taxonomy.* a race whose distinct characters do not justify classification as a separate species. 4b *Horticulture, stockbreeding.* a strain of animal or plant produced by artificial breeding. 5a entertainment consisting of a series of short unrelated acts, such as comedy turns, songs, etc. 5b (*as modifier*): *a variety show.* [C16: from L *varietās,* from VARIOUS]

varifocal (ˌvɛərɪˈfəukʲl) *adj* 1 *Optics.* having a focus that can vary. 2 relating to a lens that is gradated to permit any length of vision between near and distant.

varifocals (ˌvɛərɪˈfəukʲlz) *pl n* a pair of spectacles with varifocal lenses.

variform (ˈvɛərɪˌfɔːm) *adj* varying in form or shape.
▸ ˈvariˌformly *adv*

variola (vəˈraɪələ) *n* the technical name for **smallpox**. [C18: from Med. L: disease marked by little spots, from L *varius* spotted]
▸ vaˈriolar *adj*

variole (ˈvɛərɪˌəul) *n* any of the rounded masses that make up the rock variolite. [C19: from F, from Med. L; see VARIOLA]

variolite (ˈvɛərɪəˌlaɪt) *n* any basic igneous rock containing rounded bodies (varioles). [C18: from VARIOLA, referring to the pockmarked appearance of the rock]
▸ **variolitic** (ˌvɛərɪəˈlɪtɪk) *adj*

variometer (ˌvɛərɪˈɒmɪtə) *n* 1 an instrument for measuring variations in a magnetic field. 2 *Electronics.* a variable inductor consisting of a movable coil mounted inside and connected in series with a fixed coil.

variorum (ˌvɛərɪˈɔːrəm) *adj* 1 containing notes by various scholars or various versions of the text. ◆ *n* 2 an edition or text of this kind. [C18: from L *ēditiō cum notīs variōrum* edition with the notes of various commentators]

various (ˈvɛərɪəs) *determiner* 1 several different: *he is an authority on various subjects.* ◆ *adj* 2 of different kinds, though often within the same general category: *his disguises are many and various.* 3 (*prenominal*) relating to a collection of separate persons or things: *the various members of the club.* 4 displaying variety; many-sided: *his various achievements.* [C16: from L *varius* changing]
▸ ˈvariously *adv* ▸ ˈvariousness *n*

varistor (vəˈrɪstə) *n* a two-electrode semiconductor device having a voltage-dependent nonlinear resistance. [C20: a blend of *variable resistor*]

Varityper (ˈvɛərɪˌtaɪpə) *n Trademark.* a justifying typewriter used to produce copy in various type styles.

varix (ˈvɛərɪks) *n, pl* **varices.** *Pathol.* **a** a tortuous dilated vein. **b** a similar condition affecting an artery or lymphatic vessel. [C15: from L]

varlet (ˈvɑːlɪt) *n Arch.* 1 a menial servant. 2 a knight's page. 3 a rascal. [C15: from OF, var. of *vallet* VALET]
▸ ˈvarletry *n*

varmint (ˈvɑːmɪnt) *n Inf.* an irritating or obnoxious person or animal. [C16: dialect var. of *varmin* VERMIN]

varna (ˈvɑːnə) *n* any of the four Hindu castes; Brahman, Kshatriya, Vaisya, or Sudra. [from Sansk.: class]

Varna ★ (*Bulgarian* ˈvarna) *n* a port in NE Bulgaria, on the Black Sea: founded by Greeks in the 6th century B.C.; under the Ottoman Turks (1391–1878). Pop.: 301 421 (1996 est.). Former name (1949–56): **Stalin.**

varnish (ˈvɑːnɪʃ) *n* 1 a preparation consisting of a solvent, a drying oil, and usually resin, rubber, etc., for application to a surface where it yields a hard glossy, usually transparent, coating. 2 a similar preparation consisting of a substance, such as shellac, dissolved in a volatile solvent, such as alcohol. It hardens to a film on evaporation of the solvent. 3 the sap of certain trees used to produce such a coating. 4 a smooth surface, coated with or as with varnish. 5 an artificial, superficial, or deceptively pleasing manner, covering, etc. 6 *Chiefly Brit.* another word for **nail polish.** ◆ *vb* (*tr*) 7 to cover with varnish. 8 to give a smooth surface to, as if by painting with varnish. 9 to impart a more attractive appearance to. [C14: from OF, from Med. L *veronix* sandarac, resin, from Med. Gk *berenikē,* ?from Gk *Berenikē,* city in Cyrenaica, Libya where varnishes were used]
▸ ˈvarnisher *n*

varnish tree *n* any of various trees, such as the lacquer tree, yielding substances used to make varnish or lacquer.

Varro ★ (ˈværəu) *n* **Marcus Terentius** (ˈmɑːkəs təˈrɛntɪəs). 116–27 B.C., Roman scholar and satirist.

varsity (ˈvɑːsɪtɪ) *n, pl* **varsities.** *Brit., S. African, & NZ inf.* short for **university.**

Varuna ★ (ˈværunə, ˈvʌ-) *n Hinduism.* the ancient sky god, later the god of the waters and rain-giver. In earlier traditions he was also the all-seeing divine judge.

varus (ˈvɛərəs) *adj Pathol.* turned inwards towards the midline of the body. [C19: from L: crooked, bent]

varve (vɑːv) *n Geol.* a band of sediment deposited in glacial lakes, consisting of a light layer and a dark layer deposited at different seasons. [C20: from Swedish *varv* layer, from *varva,* from ON *hverfa* to turn]

vary (ˈvɛərɪ) *vb* **varies, varying, varied.** 1 to undergo or cause to undergo change or modification in appearance, character, form, etc. 2 to be different or cause to be different; be subject to change. 3 (*tr*) to give variety to. 4 (*intr*; foll. by *from*) to differ, as from a convention, standard, etc. 5 (*intr*) to change in accordance with another variable: *her mood varies with the weather.* [C14: from L, from *varius* VARIOUS]
▸ ˈvarying *adj*

vas (væs) *n, pl* **vasa** (ˈveɪsə). *Anat., zool.* a vessel or tube that carries a fluid. [C17: from L: vessel]

Vasari ★ (vəˈsɑːrɪ; *Italian* vaˈzaːri) *n* **Giorgio** (ˈdʒɔrdʒo). 1511–74, Italian architect, painter, and art historian, noted for his *Lives of the Most Excellent Italian Architects, Painters, and Sculptors* (1550; 1568).

Vasco da Gama ★ (ˈvæskəʊ də ˈɡɑːmə) *n* See (Vasco da) Gama.

vascular (ˈvæskjʊlə) *adj Biol., anat.* of, relating to, or having vessels that conduct and circulate liquids: *a vascular bundle.* [C17: from NL *vāsculāris*, from L *vāsculum*, dim. of *vās* vessel]
▸ **vascularity** (ˌvæskjʊˈlærɪtɪ) *n* ▸ **ˈvascularly** *adv*

vascular bundle *n* a longitudinal strand of vascular tissue in the stems and leaves of higher plants.

vascular tissue *n* tissue of plants occurring as a continuous system throughout the plant: it conducts water, mineral salts, and synthesized food, and provides mechanical support. Also called: **conducting tissue.**

vas deferens (ˈvæs ˈdefəˌrenz) *n, pl* **vasa deferentia** (ˈveɪsə ˌdefəˈrenʃɪə). *Anat.* the duct that conveys spermatozoa from the epididymis to the urethra. [C16: from NL, from L *vās* vessel + *deferēns*, present participle of *deferre* to bear away]

vase (vɑːz) *n* a vessel used as an ornament or for holding cut flowers. [C17: via F from L *vās* vessel]

vasectomy (væˈsektəmɪ) *n, pl* **vasectomies.** surgical removal of all or part of the vas deferens, esp. as a method of contraception.

Vaseline (ˈvæsɪˌliːn) *n* a trademark for **petrolatum.**

Vashti ★ (ˈvæʃtaɪ) *n Old Testament.* the wife of the Persian king Ahasuerus: deposed for refusing to display her beauty before his guests (Esther 1–2). Douay spelling: **Vasthi.**

vaso- *or before a vowel* **vas-** *combining form.* **1** indicating a blood vessel: *vasodilator.* **2** indicating the vas deferens: *vasectomy.* [from L *vās* vessel]

vasoactive (ˌveɪzəʊˈæktɪv) *adj* affecting the diameter of blood vessels: *vasoactive peptides.*

vasoconstrictor (ˌveɪzəʊkənˈstrɪktə) *n* a drug, agent, or nerve that causes narrowing of the walls of blood vessels.

vasodilator (ˌveɪzəʊdaɪˈleɪtə) *n* a drug, agent, or nerve that can cause dilation of the walls of blood vessels.

vasoinhibitor (ˌveɪzəʊɪnˈhɪbɪtə) *n* any of a group of drugs that reduce or inhibit the action of the vasomotor nerves.

vasomotor (ˌveɪzəʊˈməʊtə) *adj* (of a drug, nerve, etc.) relating to or affecting the diameter of blood vessels.

vasopressin (ˌveɪzəʊˈpresɪn) *n* a hormone secreted by the pituitary gland. It increases the reabsorption of water by the kidney tubules and increases blood pressure by constricting the arteries. Also called: **antidiuretic hormone.** [from *Vasopressin*, a trademark]

vasopressor (ˈveɪzəʊˌpresə) *Med.* ◆ *adj* **1** causing an increase in blood pressure by constricting the arteries. ◆ *n* **2** a substance that has such an effect.

vassal (ˈvæsˀl) *n* **1** (in feudal society) a man who entered into a relationship with a lord to whom he paid homage and fealty in return for protection and often a fief. **2a** a person, nation, etc., in a subordinate or dependent position relative to another. **2b** (*as modifier*): *vassal status.* ◆ *adj* **3** of or relating to a vassal. [C14: via OF from Med. L *vassallus*, from *vassus* servant, of Celtic origin]
▸ **ˈvassalage** *n*

vast (vɑːst) *adj* **1** unusually large in size, degree, or number. **2** (*prenominal*) (intensifier): *in vast haste.* ◆ *n* **3 the vast.** *Chiefly poetic.* immense or boundless space. [C16: from L *vastus* deserted]
▸ **ˈvastly** *adv* ▸ **ˈvastness** *n*

Västerås ★ (*Swedish* vestərˈɔːs) *n* a city in central Sweden, on Lake Mälar: Sweden's largest inland port; site of several national parliaments in the 16th century. Pop.: 123 728 (1996 est.).

vasty (ˈvɑːstɪ) *adj* **vastier, vastiest.** an archaic or poetic word for **vast.**

vat (væt) *n* **1** a large container for holding or storing liquids. **2** *Chem.* a preparation of reduced vat dye. ◆ *vb* **vats,**

vatting, vatted. 3 (*tr*) to place, store, or treat in a vat. [OE *fæt*]

VAT (*sometimes* væt) (in Britain) *abbrev. for* value-added tax: a tax levied on the difference between the cost of materials and the selling price of a commodity or service.

vat dye *n* a dye, such as indigo, that is applied by first reducing it to its base, which is soluble in alkali, and then regenerating the insoluble dye by oxidation in the fibres of the material.
▸ **ˈvat-ˌdyed** *adj*

vatic (ˈvætɪk) *adj Rare.* of, relating to, or characteristic of a prophet; oracular. [C16: from L *vātēs* prophet]

Vatican ★ (ˈvætɪkən) *n* **1a** the palace of the popes in Rome, which includes administrative offices and is attached to the basilica of St Peter's. **1b** (*as modifier*): *the Vatican Council.* **2a** the authority of the Pope and the papal curia. **2b** (*as modifier*): *a Vatican edict.* [C16: from L *Vāticānus mons* Vatican hill, on the western bank of the Tiber, of Etruscan origin]

Vatican City ★ *n* an independent state forming an enclave in Rome, with extraterritoriality over 12 churches and palaces in Rome: the only remaining Papal State; independence recognized by the Italian government in 1929; contains St Peter's Basilica and Square and the Vatican; the spiritual and administrative centre of the Roman Catholic Church. Languages: Italian and Latin. Currency: lira. Pop.: 1000 (1997 est.). Area: 44 hectares (109 acres). Italian name: **Città del Vaticano.** Also called: **the Holy See.**

Vättern ★ (*Swedish* ˈvetərn) *n Lake.* a lake in S central Sweden: the second largest lake in Sweden; linked to Lake Vänern by the Göta Canal; drains into the Baltic. Area: 1912 sq. km (738 sq. miles).

Vaucluse ★ (*French* voklyz) *n* a department of SE France, in Provence–Alpes–Côte d'Azur region. Capital: Avignon. Pop.: 487 338 (1994 est.). Area: 3578 sq. km (1395 sq. miles).

Vaud ★ (*French* vo) *n* a canton of SW Switzerland: mountainous in the southeast; chief Swiss producer of wine. Capital: Lausanne. Pop.: 602 099 (1995 est.). Area: 3209 sq. km (1240 sq. miles). German name: **Waadt.**

vaudeville (ˈvəʊdəvɪl, ˈvɔː-) *n* **1** *Chiefly US & Canad.* variety entertainment consisting of short acts such as acrobatic turns, song-and-dance routines, etc. Brit. name: **music hall. 2** a light or comic theatrical piece interspersed with songs and dances. [C18: from F, from *vaudevire* satirical folk song, shortened from *chanson du vau de Vire* song of the valley of Vire, a district in Normandy]
▸ **ˌvaudeˈvillian** *n, adj*

Vaudois (ˈvəʊdwɑː) *pl n, sing* **Vaudois. 1** another name for the **Waldenses. 2** the inhabitants of Vaud.

Vaughan ★ (vɔːn) *n* **1 Henry.** 1622–95, Welsh mystic poet, best known for his *Silex Scintillans* (1650; 1655). **2** Dame **Janet (Maria).** 1899–1993, British doctor: helped set up Britain's first National Blood Transfusion Service (1939): Principal of Somerville College, Oxford (1945–67). **3** Sarah **(Lois).** 1924–90, US jazz vocalist and pianist.

Vaughan Williams ★ (ˈwɪljəmz) *n* Ralph. 1872–1958, British composer, who wrote operas, symphonies, hymns, and choral music.

vault¹ (vɔːlt) *n* **1** an arched structure that forms a roof or ceiling. **2** a room, esp. a cellar, having an arched roof down to floor level. **3** a burial chamber, esp. when underground. **4** a strongroom for the storage of valuables. **5** an underground room used for the storage of wine, food, etc. **6** *Anat.* any arched or domed bodily cavity or space: *the cranial vault.* **7** something suggestive of an arched structure, as the sky. ◆ *vb* **8** (*tr*) to furnish with or as if with an arched roof. **9** (*tr*) to construct in the shape of a vault. **10** (*intr*) to curve in the shape of a vault. [C14 *vaute*, from OF, from Vulgar L *volvita* (unattested) a turn, prob. from L *volvere* to roll]

vault² (vɔːlt) *vb* **1** to spring over (an object), esp. with the aid of a long pole or with the hands resting on the object. **2** (*intr*) to do, achieve, or attain something as if by a leap: *he vaulted to fame.* ◆ *n* **3** the act of vaulting. [C16:

from OF *voulter* to turn from It. *voltare*, from Vulgar L *volvitāre* (unattested) to turn, leap; see VAULT[1]]
▶ **'vaulter** *n*

vaulting[1] ('vɔːltɪŋ) *n* one or more vaults in a building or such structures considered collectively.

vaulting[2] ('vɔːltɪŋ) *adj* (*prenominal*) **1** excessively confident: *vaulting arrogance*. **2** used to vault: *a vaulting pole*.

vaunt (vɔːnt) *vb* **1** (*tr*) to describe, praise, or display (one's success, possessions, etc.) boastfully. **2** (*intr*) *Rare or literary*. to brag. ◆ *n* **3** a boast. [C14: from OF, from LL *vānitāre*, from L *vānus* VAIN]
▶ **'vaunter** *n*

Vauxhall ★ ('vɒks,hɔːl) *n* a district in London, on the south bank of the Thames.

vavasor ('vævə,sɔː) *or* **vavasour** ('vævə,suə) *n* (in feudal society) the noble or knightly vassal of a baron or great lord who also has vassals himself. [C13: from OF *vavasour*, ?from Med. L *vassus vassōrum* vassal of vassals]

vb *abbrev. for* verb.

VC *abbrev. for:* **1** Vice-chairman. **2** Vice Chancellor. **3** Vice Consul. **4** Victoria Cross.

V-chip *n* a device within a television set that allows the set to be programmed not to receive transmissions that have been classified as containing sex, violence, or obscene language.

VCR *abbrev. for* video cassette recorder.

VD *abbrev. for* venereal disease.

V-Day *n* a day nominated to celebrate victory, as in V-E Day or V-J Day in World War II.

VDQS *abbrev. for* vins délimités de qualité supérieure: on a bottle of French wine, indicates that it contains high-quality wine from an approved regional vineyard: the second highest French wine classification. Cf. **AOC**, *vin de pays*.

VDU *Computing. abbrev. for* visual display unit.

ve *contraction of* have: *I've; you've.*

veal (viːl) *n* the flesh of the calf used as food. [C14: from OF *veel*, from L *vitellus*, dim. of *vitulus* calf]

vealer ('viːlə) *n US, Canad., & Austral.* a calf bred for veal.

vector ('vɛktə) *n* **1** *Maths.* a variable quantity, such as force, that has magnitude and direction and can be resolved into components that are odd functions of the coordinates. **2** *Maths.* an element of a vector space. **3** Also called: **carrier.** *Pathol.* an organism, esp. an insect, that carries a disease-producing microorganism from one host to another. **4** Also called: **cloning vector.** *Genetics.* an agent, such as a bacteriophage or a plasmid, by means of which a fragment of foreign DNA is inserted into a host cell to produce a gene clone in genetic engineering. **5** the course or compass direction of an aircraft. ◆ *vb* (*tr*) **6** to direct or guide (a pilot, aircraft, etc.) by directions transmitted by radio. **7** to alter the direction of (the thrust of a jet engine) as a means of steering an aircraft. [C18: from L: carrier, from *vehere* to convey]
▶ **vectorial** (vek'tɔːrɪəl) *adj*

vector field *n* a region of space under the influence of some vector quantity, such as magnetic field strength, in which each point can be described by a vector.

vector product *n* the product of two vectors that is a pseudovector, whose magnitude is the product of the magnitudes of the given vectors and the sine of the angle between them. Its axis is perpendicular to the plane of the given vectors.

vector sum *n* a vector whose length and direction are represented by the diagonal of a parallelogram whose sides represent the given vectors.

Veda ('veɪdə) *n* any or all of the most ancient sacred writings of Hinduism, esp. the Rig-Veda, Yajur-Veda, Sama-Veda, and Atharva-Veda. [C18: from Sansk.: knowledge]

vedalia (vɪ'deɪlɪə) *n* an Australian ladybird introduced elsewhere to control the scale insect, which is a pest of citrus fruits. [C20: from NL]

Vedanta (vɪ'dɑːntə) *n* one of the six main philosophical schools of Hinduism, expounding the monism regarded as implicit in the Veda in accordance with the doctrines

of the Upanishads. [C19: from Sansk., from VEDA + *ánta* end]
▶ **Ve'dantic** *adj* ▶ **Ve'dantist** *n*

V-E Day *n* the day marking the Allied victory in Europe in World War II (May 8, 1945).

vedette (vɪ'dɛt) *n* **1** *Naval.* a small patrol vessel. **2** *Mil.* a mounted sentry posted forward of a formation's position. [C17: from F, from It. *vedetta* (infl. by *vedere* to see), from earlier *veletta*, ?from Sp., from L *vigilāre*]

Vedic ('veɪdɪk) *adj* **1** of or relating to the Vedas or the ancient form of Sanskrit in which they are written. ◆ *n* **2** the classical form of Sanskrit; the language of the Vedas.

veer (vɪə) *vb* **1** to alter direction (of). **2** (*intr*) to change from one position, opinion, etc., to another. **3** (*intr*) (of the wind) to change direction clockwise in the northern hemisphere and anticlockwise in the southern. ◆ *n* **4** a change of course or direction. [C16: from OF *virer*, prob. of Celtic origin]

veg (vɛdʒ) *n Inf.* a vegetable or vegetables.

Vega[1] ('viːgə) *n* the brightest star in the constellation Lyra and one of the most conspicuous in the N hemisphere. [C17: from Med. L, from Ar. (*al nasr*) *al wāqi*, lit.: the falling (vulture), i.e. the constellation Lyra]

Vega[2] ★ ('veɪgə; *Spanish* 'beɣa) *n* See **Lope de Vega**.

vegan ('viːgən) *n* a person who uses no animal products.

vegeburger *or* **veggieburger** ('vɛdʒɪ,bɜːgə) *n* a flat cake of chopped seasoned vegetables and pulses that is grilled or fried and often served in a bread roll.

Vegemite ('vɛdʒɪ,maɪt) *n Austral. & NZ trademark.* a yeast extract used as a spread, flavouring for stews, etc.

vegetable ('vɛdʒtəbʲl, 'vɛdʒətəbʲl) *n* **1** any of various herbaceous plants having parts that are used as food, such as peas, potatoes, cauliflower, and onions. **2** *Inf.* a person who has lost control of his mental faculties, limbs, etc., as from an injury, mental disease, etc. **3** a dull inactive person. **4** (*modifier*) consisting of or made from edible vegetables: *a vegetable diet*. **5** (*modifier*) of, characteristic of, derived from, or consisting of plants or plant material: *the vegetable kingdom*. **6** *Rare.* any member of the plant kingdom. [C14 (adj): from LL *vegetābilis*, from *vegetāre* to enliven, from L *vegēre* to excite]

vegetable butter *n* any of a group of vegetable fats having the consistency of butter.

vegetable ivory *n* the hard whitish material obtained from the endosperm of the ivory nut: used to make buttons, ornaments, etc.

vegetable marrow *n* **1** a plant, probably native to America but widely cultivated for its oblong green striped fruit which is eaten as a vegetable. **2** the fruit of this plant. Often shortened to **marrow**.

vegetable oil *n* any of a group of oils that are obtained from plants.

vegetable oyster *n* another name for **salsify** (sense 1).

vegetable silk *n* any of various silky fibres obtained from the seed pods of certain plants.

vegetable wax *n* any of various waxes that occur on parts of certain plants, esp. the trunks of certain palms, and prevent loss of water.

vegetal ('vɛdʒɪtʲl) *adj* **1** of or characteristic of vegetables or plant life. **2** vegetative. [C15: from LL *vegetāre* to quicken]

vegetarian (,vɛdʒɪ'tɛərɪən) *n* **1** a person who advocates or practises the exclusion of meat and fish, and sometimes eggs, milk, and cheese from the diet. ◆ *adj* **2** *Cookery.* strictly, consisting of vegetables and fruit only, but often including milk, cheese, eggs, etc.
▶ **,vege'tarianism** *n*

vegetate ('vɛdʒɪ,teɪt) *vb* **vegetates, vegetating, vegetated.** (*intr*) **1** to grow like a plant. **2** to lead a life characterized by monotony, passivity, or mental inactivity. [C17: from LL *vegetāre* to invigorate]

vegetation (,vɛdʒɪ'teɪʃən) *n* **1** plant life as a whole, esp. the plant life of a particular region. **2** the process of vegetating.
▶ **,vege'tational** *adj*

vegetative ('vɛdʒɪtətɪv) *adj* **1** of or concerned with plant

life or plant growth. **2** (of reproduction) characterized by asexual processes. **3** of or relating to functions such as digestion and circulation rather than sexual reproduction. **4** (of a style of living, etc.) unthinking or passive.
▸ **'vegetatively** adv

veggie ('vɛdʒɪ) n, adj an informal word for **vegetarian**.

veg out vb **vegges, vegging, vegged**. (intr, adv) Sl., chiefly US. to relax in an inert, passive way; vegetate: vegging out in front of the television.

vehement ('vi:mənt) adj **1** marked by intensity of feeling or conviction. **2** (of actions, gestures, etc.) characterized by great energy, vigour, or force. [C15: from L vehemēns ardent]
▸ **'vehemence** n ▸ **'vehemently** adv

vehicle ('vi:ɪk°l) n **1** any conveyance in or by which people or objects are transported, esp. one fitted with wheels. **2** a medium for the expression or communication of ideas, power, etc. **3** Pharmacol. a therapeutically inactive substance mixed with the active ingredient to give bulk to a medicine. **4** Also called: **base.** a painting medium, such as oil, in which pigments are suspended. **5** (in the performing arts) a play, etc., that enables a particular performer to display his talents. [C17: from L vehiculum, from vehere to carry]
▸ **vehicular** (vɪ'hɪkjʊlə) adj

Veii ★ ('vi:jaɪ) n an ancient Etruscan city, northwest of Rome: destroyed by the Romans in 396 B.C.

veil (veɪl) n **1** a piece of more or less transparent material, usually attached to a hat or headdress, used to conceal or protect a woman's face and head. **2** part of a nun's headdress falling round the face onto the shoulders. **3** something that covers, conceals, or separates: a veil of reticence. **4** the veil. the life of a nun in a religious order. **5** take the veil. to become a nun. **6** Also called: **velum.** Bot. a membranous structure, esp. the thin layer of cells covering a young mushroom. ◆ vb **7** (tr) to cover, conceal, or separate with or as if with a veil. **8** (intr) to wear or put on a veil. [C13: from Norman F veile, from L vēla, pl of vēlum a covering]
▸ **'veiler** n ▸ **'veil-,like** adj

veiled (veɪld) adj **1** disguised: a veiled insult. **2** (of sound, tone, the voice, etc.) not distinct.
▸ **veiledly** ('veɪlɪdlɪ) adv

veiling ('veɪlɪŋ) n a veil or the fabric used for veils.

vein (veɪn) n **1** any of the tubular vessels that convey oxygen-depleted blood to the heart. Cf. **pulmonary vein, artery** (sense 1). **2** any of the hollow branching tubes that form the supporting framework of an insect's wing. **3** any of the vascular bundles of a leaf. **4** a clearly defined mass of ore, mineral, etc. **5** an irregular streak of colour or alien substance in marble, wood, or other material. **6** a distinctive trait or quality in speech, writing, character, etc.: a vein of humour. **7** a temporary attitude or temper: the debate entered a frivolous vein. ◆ vb (tr) **8** to diffuse over or cause to diffuse over in streaked patterns. **9** to fill, furnish, or mark with or as if with veins. [C13: from OF, from L vēna]
▸ **'veinless** adj ▸ **'vein,like** adj ▸ **'veiny** adj

veining ('veɪnɪŋ) n a pattern or network of veins or streaks.

veinlet ('veɪnlɪt) n any small vein or venule.

velamen (və'leɪmən) n, pl **velamina** (-'læmɪnə). **1** the thick layer of dead cells that covers the aerial roots of certain orchids. **2** Anat. another word for **velum**. [C19: from L: veil, from vēlāre to cover]

velar ('vi:lə) adj **1** of or attached to a velum: velar tentacles. **2** Phonetics. articulated with the soft palate and the back of the tongue, as in (k) or (ŋ). [C18: from L, from vēlum VEIL]

Velázquez (Spanish be'laθkeθ) or **Velásquez** ★ (Spanish be'laskeθ) n Diego Rodríguez de Silva y ('djeɣo rɔ'ðriɣeθ de 'silβa i). 1599–1660, Spanish painter, noted for his royal portraits.

Velcro ('velkrəʊ) n Trademark. a fastening consisting of two strips of nylon fabric, one having tiny hooked threads and the other a coarse surface, that form a strong bond when pressed together.

veld or **veldt** (felt, velt) n elevated open grassland in Southern Africa. See also **bushveld, highveld.** [C19: from Afrik., from earlier Du. veldt FIELD]

veldskoen ('felt,skʊn, 'velt-) n an ankle-length boot o soft but strong rawhide. [from Afrik., lit.: field shoe]

veleta (və'li:tə) n a variant spelling of **valeta**.

veliger ('velɪdʒə) n the free-swimming larva of many molluscs, having a rudimentary shell and a ciliated velum used for feeding and locomotion. [C19: from NL from VEL(UM) + -GER(OUS)]

Vellore ★ (və'lɔ:) n a town in SE India, in NE Tamil Nadu medical centre. Pop.: 175 061 (1991).

vellum ('veləm) n **1** a fine parchment prepared from the skin of a calf, kid, or lamb. **2** a work printed or written or vellum. **3** a creamy coloured heavy paper resembling vellum. ◆ adj **4** made of or resembling vellum. [C15 from OF, from velin of a calf, from veel VEAL]

veloce (vɪ'ləʊtʃɪ) adj, adv Music. to be played rapidly [from It., from L vēlōx quick]

velocipede (vɪ'lɒsɪ,pi:d) n an early form of bicycle, esp one propelled by pushing along the ground with the feet. [C19: from F, from L vēlōx swift + pēs foot]
▸ **ve'loci,pedist** n

velocity (vɪ'lɒsɪtɪ) n, pl **velocities**. **1** speed of motion o operation; swiftness. **2** Physics. a measure of the rate o motion of a body expressed as the rate of change of it position in a particular direction with time. **3** Physics (not in technical usage) another word for **speed** (sense 3) [C16: from L vēlōcitās, from vēlōx swift]

velocity of circulation n Econ. the average number o times a unit of money is used in a given time, esp. calcu lated as the ratio of the total money spent in that time t the total amount of money in circulation.

velocity of light n a nontechnical name for **speed o light**.

velodrome ('vi:lə,drəʊm, 'vel-) n an arena with a banke track for cycle racing. [C20: from F vélodrome, from vélo (from L vēlōx swift) + -DROME]

velour or **velours** (və'lʊə) n any of various fabrics with velvet-like finish, used for upholstery, clothing, etc [C18: from OF, from OProvençal velos velvet, from L from villus shaggy hair]

velouté (və'lu:teɪ) n a rich white sauce or soup mad from stock, egg yolks, and cream. [from F, lit.: velvety from OF velous; see VELOUR]

Velsen ★ (Dutch 'velsə) n a port in the W Netherlands, i North Holland at the mouth of the canal connectin Amsterdam with the North Sea: fishing and heavy in dustrial centre. Pop.: 63 617 (1994).

velum ('vi:ləm) n, pl **vela** (-lə). **1** Zool. any of various mem branous structures. **2** Anat. any of various veil-like bodil structures, esp. the soft palate. **3** Bot. another word fo **veil** (sense 6). [C18: from L: veil]

velure (və'lʊə) n velvet or a similar fabric. [C16: from OF, from velous; see VELOUR]

velutinous (və'lu:tɪnəs) adj covered with short dens soft hairs. [C19: from NL velūtīnus like velvet]

velvet ('velvɪt) n **1a** a fabric of silk, cotton, nylon, etc. with a thick close soft pile. **1b** (as modifier): velvet curtains **2** anything with a smooth soft surface. **3a** smoothness **3b** (as modifier): a velvet night. **4** the furry covering of th newly formed antlers of a deer. **5** Sl., chiefly US. **5a** gam bling winnings. **5b** a gain. **6 on velvet**. Sl. in a condition o ease, advantage, or wealth. **7** velvet glove. gentlenes often concealing strength or determination (esp. in a **iron hand in a velvet glove**). [C14 veluet, from OF, from vel hairy, from Vulgar L villutus (unattested), from L villu shaggy hair]
▸ **'velvet-,like** adj ▸ **'velvety** adj

velveteen (,velvɪ'ti:n) n **1** a cotton fabric resembling ve vet with a short thick pile, used for clothing, etc. **2** (p trousers made of velveteen.

Velvet Underground ★ n the. US avant-garde roc group in New York City (formed in 1965; disintegrate 1969–72; reformed for a tour in 1993). See also (Lo Reed.

Ven. abbrev. for Venerable.

vena ('vi:nə) *n, pl* **venae** (-ni:). *Anat.* a technical word for **vein**. [C15: from L *vēna* VEIN]

vena cava ('keɪvə) *n, pl* **venae cavae** ('keɪvi:). either one of two large veins that convey oxygen-depleted blood to the heart. [L: hollow vein]

venal ('vi:n°l) *adj* **1** easily bribed or corrupted: *a venal magistrate*. **2** characterized by corruption or bribery. [C17: from L *vēnālis*, from *vēnum* sale] ▸ **ve'nality** *n* ▸ **'venally** *adv*

venation (vi:'neɪʃən) *n* **1** the arrangement of the veins in a leaf or in the wing of an insect. **2** such veins collectively. ▸ **ve'national** *adj*

vend (vend) *vb* **1** to sell or be sold. **2** to sell (goods) for a living. [C17: from L *vendere*, from *vēnum dare* to offer for sale]

vendace ('vendeɪs) *n, pl* **vendaces** *or* **vendace**. either of two small whitefish occurring in lakes in Scotland and NW England. [C18: from NL *vandēsius*, from OF *vandoise*, prob. of Celtic origin]

vendee (ven'di:) *n Chiefly law.* a person to whom something, esp. real property, is sold.

Vendée ★ (*French* vãde) *n* a department of W France, in Pays-de-la-Loire region: scene of the **Wars of the Vendée**, a series of peasant-royalist insurrections (1793–95) against the Revolutionary government. Capital: La Roche-sur-Yon. Pop.: 524 069 (1994 est.). Area: 7016 sq. km (2709 sq. miles).

vendetta (ven'detə) *n* **1** a private feud, originally between Corsican or Sicilian families, in which the relatives of a murdered person seek vengeance by killing the murderer or some member of his family. **2** any prolonged feud. [C19: from It., from L *vindicta*, from *vindicāre* to avenge] ▸ **ven'dettist** *n*

vendible ('vendəb°l) *adj* **1** saleable or marketable. ▸ *n* **2** (*usually pl*) *Rare.* a saleable object. ▸ **vendi'bility** *n*

vending machine *n* a machine that automatically dispenses consumer goods such as cigarettes or food, when money is inserted.

Vendôme ★ (*French* vãdom) *n* **Louis Joseph de** (lwi ʒoʒɛf də). 1654–1712, French marshal, noted for his command during the War of the Spanish Succession (1701–14).

vendor ('vendɔ:) *or* **vender** ('vendə) *n* **1** *Chiefly law.* a person who sells something, esp. real property. **2** another name for **vending machine**.

vendor placing *n Finance.* a method of financing the purchase of one company by another in which the purchasing company pays for the target company in its own shares, on condition that the vendor places these shares with investors for cash payment.

veneer (vɪ'nɪə) *n* **1** a thin layer of wood, plastic, etc., with a decorative or fine finish that is bonded to the surface of a less expensive material, usually wood. **2** a superficial appearance: *a veneer of gentility*. **3** any facing material that is applied to a different backing material. ▸ *vb* (*tr*) **4** to cover (a surface) with a veneer. **5** to conceal (something) under a superficially pleasant surface. [C17: from G *furnieren* to veneer, from OF *fournir* to FURNISH] ▸ **ve'neerer** *n*

veneering (vɪ'nɪərɪŋ) *n* material used as veneer or a veneered surface.

venepuncture ('venɪ,pʌŋktʃə) *n* a variant spelling of **venipuncture**.

venerable ('venərəb°l) *adj* **1** (esp. of a person) worthy of reverence on account of great age, religious associations, character, etc. **2** (of inanimate objects) hallowed on account of age or historical or religious association. **3** *RC Church.* a title bestowed on a deceased person when the first stage of his canonization has been accomplished. **4** *Church of England.* a title given to an archdeacon. [C15: from L *venerābilis*, from *venerārī* to venerate] ▸ **venera'bility** *or* **'venerableness** *n* ▸ **'venerably** *adv*

venerate ('venə,reɪt) *vb* **venerates, venerating, venerated.** (*tr*) **1** to hold in deep respect. **2** to honour in recognition of

qualities of holiness, excellence, etc. [C17: from L *venerārī*, from *venus* love] ▸ **'vener,ator** *n*

veneration (,venə'reɪʃən) *n* **1** a feeling or expression of awe or reverence. **2** the act of venerating or the state of being venerated.

venereal (vɪ'nɪərɪəl) *adj* **1** of or infected with venereal disease. **2** (of a disease) transmitted by sexual intercourse. **3** of or involving the genitals. **4** of or relating to sexual intercourse or erotic desire. [C15: from L *venereus*, from *venus* sexual love, from VENUS[1]]

venereal disease *n* another name for **sexually transmitted disease**. Abbrev.: **VD.**

venereology (vɪ,nɪərɪ'ɒlədʒɪ) *n* the branch of medicine concerned with the study and treatment of venereal disease. ▸ **ve,nere'ologist** *n*

venery[1] ('venərɪ, 'vi:-) *n Arch.* the pursuit of sexual gratification. [C15: from Med. L *veneria*, from L *venus* love, VENUS[1]]

venery[2] ('venərɪ, 'vi:-) *n* the art, sport, lore, or practice of hunting, esp. with hounds; the chase. [C14: from OF *venerie*, from *vener* to hunt, from L *vēnārī*]

venesection ('venɪ,sekʃən) *n* surgical incision into a vein. [C17: from NL *vēnae sectiō*; see VEIN, SECTION]

Venetia ★ (vɪ'ni:ʃə) *n* **1** the area of ancient Italy between the lower Po valley and the Alps: later a Roman province. **2** the territorial possessions of the medieval Venetian republic that were at the head of the Adriatic and correspond to the present-day region of Veneto and a large part of Friuli-Venezia Giulia.

Venetian (vɪ'ni:ʃən) *adj* **1** of, relating to, or characteristic of Venice or its inhabitants. ▸ *n* **2** a native or inhabitant of Venice. **3** See **Venetian blind.**

Venetian blind *n* a window blind consisting of a number of horizontal slats whose angle may be altered to let in more or less light.

Venetian red *n* **1** natural or synthetic ferric oxide used as a red pigment. **2a** a moderate to strong reddish-brown colour. **2b** (*as adj*): *a Venetian-red coat.*

Veneto ★ (*Italian* 've:neto) *n* a region of NE Italy, on the Adriatic: mountainous in the north with a fertile plain in the south, crossed by the Rivers Po, Adige, and Piave. Capital: Venice. Pop.: 4 415 309 (1994 est.). Area: 18 377 sq. km (7095 sq. miles). Also called: **Venezia-Euganea** (ve'nɛttsja eu'ga:nea).

Venez. *abbrev. for* Venezuela.

Venezia ★ (ve'nɛttsja) *n* the Italian name for **Venice**.

Venezia Giulia ★ (*Italian* 'dʒu:lja) *n* a former region of NE Italy at the N end of the Adriatic: divided between Yugoslavia and Italy after World War II; now divided between Italy and Slovenia.

Venezia Tridentina ★ (*Italian* triden'ti:na) *n* the former name (until 1947) of **Trentino-Alto Adige.**

Venezuela ★ (,venɪ'zweɪlə) *n* **1** a republic in South America, on the Caribbean: colonized by the Spanish in the 16th century; independence from Spain declared in 1811 and won in 1819 after a war led by Simón Bolívar. It contains Lake Maracaibo and the northernmost chains of the Andes in the northwest, the Orinoco basin in the centre, and the Guiana Highlands in the south. Exports petroleum, iron ore, and coffee. Official language: Spanish. Religion: Roman Catholic. Currency: bolívar. Capital: Caracas. Pop.: 22 777 000 (1994 est.). Area: 912 050 sq. km (352 142 sq. miles). **2 Gulf of.** an inlet of the Caribbean in NW Venezuela: continues south as Lake Maracaibo. ▸ **,Vene'zuelan** *adj, n*

vengeance ('vendʒəns) *n* **1** the act of or desire for taking revenge. **2 with a vengeance.** (intensifier): *he's a coward with a vengeance.* [C13: from OF, from *venger* to avenge, from L *vindicāre* to punish]

vengeful ('vendʒful) *adj* **1** desiring revenge. **2** characterized by or indicating a desire for revenge. **3** inflicting or taking revenge: *with vengeful blows.* ▸ **'vengefully** *adv*

venial ('vi:nɪəl) *adj* easily excused or forgiven: *a venial* *error.* [C13: via OF from LL *veniālis,* from L *venia* forgiveness]

▸ ˌveni'ality *n* ▸ 'venially *adv*

venial sin *n Christian theol.* a sin regarded as involving only a partial loss of grace.

Venice ★ ('vɛnɪs) *n* a port in NE Italy, capital of Veneto region, built on over 100 islands and mud flats in the **Lagoon of Venice** (an inlet of the **Gulf of Venice** at the head of the Adriatic): united under the first doge in 697 A.D.; became an independent republic and a great commercial and maritime power, defeating Genoa, the greatest rival, in 1380; contains the Grand Canal and about 170 smaller canals, providing waterways for city transport. Pop.: 306 439 (1994 est.). Italian name: **Venezia.** Related adj: **Venetian.**

venin ('vɛnɪn) *n* any of the poisonous constituents of animal venoms. [C20: from F *ven(in)* poison + -IN]

venipuncture *or* **venepuncture** ('vɛnɪˌpʌŋktʃə) *n Med.* the puncturing of a vein, esp. to take a sample of venous blood or inject a drug.

venison ('vɛnɪzˀn, -sˀn) *n* the flesh of a deer, used as food. [C13: from OF *venaison,* from L *vēnātiō* hunting, from *vēnārī* to hunt]

Venite (vɪ'naɪtɪ) *n* **1** the opening word of the 95th psalm, an invitatory prayer at matins. **2** a musical setting of this. [L: come ye]

Venizélos ★ (*Greek* vɛni'zɛlɔs) *n* **Eleutherios** (ˌɛlɛf'θɛrjɔs). 1864–1936, Greek statesman: prime minister (1910–15; 1917–20; 1924; 1928–32; 1933).

Venlo *or* **Venloo** ★ (*Dutch* 'vɛnloː) *n* a city in the SE Netherlands, in Limburg on the Maas River. Pop.: 63 820 (1988 est.).

Venn diagram (vɛn) *n Maths, logic.* a diagram in which mathematical sets or terms of a categorial statement are represented by overlapping circles within a boundary representing the universal set, so that all possible combinations of the relevant properties are represented by the various distinct areas in the diagram. [C19: after John *Venn* (1834–1923), Brit. logician]

venom ('vɛnəm) *n* **1** a poisonous fluid secreted by such animals as certain snakes and scorpions and usually transmitted by a bite or sting. **2** malice; spite. [C13: from OF, from L *venēnum* poison, love potion]

▸ 'venomous *adj* ▸ 'venomously *adv* ▸ 'venomousness *n*

venose ('viːnəʊs) *adj* **1** having veins; venous. **2** (of a plant) covered with veins or similar ridges. [C17: via L *vēnōsus,* from *vēna* a VEIN]

venosity (vɪ'nɒsɪtɪ) *n* **1** an excessive quantity of blood in the venous system or in an organ or part. **2** an unusually large number of blood vessels in an organ or part.

venous ('viːnəs) *adj* **1** *Physiol.* of or relating to the blood circulating in the veins. **2** of or relating to the veins. [C17: see VENOSE]

vent[1] (vɛnt) *n* **1** a small opening for the escape of fumes, liquids, etc. **2** the shaft of a volcano through which lava and gases erupt. **3** the external opening of the urinary or genital systems of lower vertebrates. **4** a small aperture at the breech of old guns through which the charge was ignited. **5 give vent to.** to release (an emotion, idea, etc.) in an outburst. ♦ *vb* (*mainly tr*) **6** to release or give expression or utterance to (an emotion, etc.): *he vents his anger on his wife.* **7** to provide a vent for or make vents in. **8** to let out (steam, etc.) through a vent. [C14: from OF *esventer* to blow out, from EX-[1] + *venter,* from Vulgar L *ventāre* (unattested), from L *ventus* wind]

vent[2] (vɛnt) *n* **1** a vertical slit at the back or both sides of a jacket. ♦ *vb* **2** (*tr*) to make a vent or vents in (a jacket). [C15: from OF *fente* slit, from *fendre* to split, from L *findere* to cleave]

venter ('vɛntə) *n Anat., zool.* **1a** the belly or abdomen of vertebrates. **1b** a protuberant structure or part, such as the belly of a muscle. **2** *Bot.* the swollen basal region of an archegonium. **3** *Law.* the womb. [C16: from L]

ventilate ('vɛntɪˌleɪt) *vb* **ventilates, ventilating, ventilated.** (*tr*) **1** to drive foul air out of (an enclosed area). **2** to provide with a means of airing. **3** to expose (a question, grievance, etc.) to public discussion. **4** *Physiol.* to oxygenate (the blood). [C15: from L *ventilāre* to fan, from *ventulus,* dim. of *ventus* wind]

▸ 'ventilable *adj* ▸ ˌventi'lation *n*

ventilator ('vɛntɪˌleɪtə) *n* **1** an opening or device, such as a fan, used to ventilate a room, building, etc. **2** *Med.* a machine that maintains a flow of air into and out of the lungs of a patient unable to breathe normally.

ventral ('vɛntrəl) *adj* **1** relating to the front part of the body. **2** of or situated on the upper or inner side of a plant organ, esp. a leaf, that is facing the axis. [C18: from L *ventrālis,* from *venter* abdomen]

▸ 'ventrally *adv*

ventral fin *n* **1** another name for **pelvic fin. 2** any unpaired median fin situated on the undersurface of fishes.

ventricle ('vɛntrɪkˀl) *n Anat.* **1** a chamber of the heart that receives blood from the atrium and pumps it to the arteries. **2** any one of the four main cavities of the vertebrate brain. **3** any of various other small cavities in the body. [C14: from L *ventriculus,* dim. of *venter* belly]

▸ ven'tricular *adj*

ventricose ('vɛntrɪˌkəʊs) *adj* **1** *Bot., zool., anat.* having a swelling on one side: *the ventricose corolla of many labiate plants.* **2** another word for **corpulent.** [C18: from NL, from L *venter* belly]

ventriculus (vɛn'trɪkjʊləs) *n, pl* **ventriculi** (-ˌlaɪ). **1** *Zool.* **1a** the midgut of an insect, where digestion takes place. **1b** the gizzard of a bird. **2** another word for **ventricle.** [C18: from L, dim. of *venter* belly]

ventriloquism (vɛn'trɪləˌkwɪzəm) *or* **ventriloquy** *n* the art of producing vocal sounds that appear to come from another source. [C18: from L *venter* belly + *loquī* to speak]

▸ ventriloquial (ˌvɛntrɪ'ləʊkwɪəl) *adj* ▸ ˌventri'loquially *adv* ▸ ven'triloquist *n* ▸ ven'trilo,quize *or* ven'trilo,quise *vb*

Ventris ★ ('vɛntrɪs) *n* **Michael George Francis.** 1922–56, British cryptographer, who deciphered the Linear B script.

venture ('vɛntʃə) *vb* **ventures, venturing, ventured. 1** (*tr*) to expose to danger: *he ventured his life.* **2** (*tr*) to brave the dangers of (something): *I'll venture the seas.* **3** (*tr*) to dare (to do something): *does he venture to object?* **4** (*tr; may take a clause as object*) to express in spite of possible criticism: *I venture that he is not that honest.* **5** (*intr;* often foll. by *out, forth,* etc.) to embark on a possibly hazardous journey, etc.: *to venture forth upon the high seas.* ♦ *n* **6** an undertaking that is risky or of uncertain outcome. **7** a commercial undertaking characterized by risk of loss as well as opportunity for profit. **8** something hazarded or risked in an adventure. **9 at a venture.** at random. [C15: var. of *aventure* ADVENTURE]

▸ 'venturer *n*

venture capital *n* another name for **risk capital.**

Venture Scout *or* **Venturer** *n Brit.* a person aged 16–20 who is a member of the senior branch of the Scouts.

venturesome ('vɛntʃəsəm) *or* **venturous** ('vɛntʃərəs) *adj* **1** willing to take risks; daring. **2** hazardous.

Venturi ★ (vɛn'tjʊərɪ) *n* **Robert.** born 1925, US architect, a pioneer of the postmodernist style. His writings include *Complexity and Contradiction in Architecture* (1966).

Venturi tube (vɛn'tjʊərɪ) *n Physics.* a device for measuring or controlling fluid flow, consisting of a tube so constricted that the pressure differential produced by fluid flowing through the constriction gives a measure of the rate of flow. [C19: after G. B. *Venturi* (1746–1822), It. physicist]

venue ('vɛnjuː) *n* **1** *Law.* **1a** the place in which a cause of action arises. **1b** the place fixed for the trial of a cause. **1c** the locality from which the jurors must be summoned. **2** a meeting place. **3** any place where an organized gathering, such as a rock concert, is held. [C14: from OF, from *venir* to come, from L *venīre*]

venule ('vɛnjuːl) *n* **1** *Anat.* any of the small branches of a vein that receives oxygen-depleted blood from the capillaries and returns it to the heart via the venous system. **2** any of the branches of a vein in an insect's wing. [C19: from L *vēnula,* dim. of *vēna* VEIN]

★ people and places

Venus[1] ★ ('vi:nəs) *n* the Roman goddess of love. Greek counterpart: **Aphrodite.**

Venus[2] ★ ('vi:nəs) *n* one of the inferior planets and the second nearest to the sun, visible as a bright morning or evening star.
  ▶ **Venusian** (vɪ'nju:zɪən) *n, adj*

Venusberg ★ ('vi:nəs,bɜ:g; *German* 've:nʊsbɛrk) *n* a mountain in central Germany: contains caverns that, according to medieval legend, housed the palace of the goddess Venus.

Venus's-flytrap *or* **Venus flytrap** *n* an insectivorous plant having hinged two-lobed leaves that snap closed when the sensitive hairs on the surface are touched.

Venus's looking glass *n* a purple-flowered plant of Europe, W Asia, and N Africa.

veracious (ve'reɪʃəs) *adj* **1** habitually truthful or honest. **2** accurate. [C17: from L *vērax*, from *vērus* true]
  ▶ **ve'raciously** *adv* ▶ **ve'raciousness** *n*

veracity (ve'ræsɪtɪ) *n, pl* **veracities. 1** truthfulness or honesty, esp. when consistent or habitual. **2** accuracy. **3** a truth. [C17: from Med. L *vērācitās*, from L *vērax*; see VERACIOUS]

Veracruz ★ (,verə'kru:z; *Spanish* bera'kruθ) *n* **1** a state of E Mexico, on the Gulf of Mexico: consists of a hot humid coastal strip with lagoons, rising rapidly inland to the central plateau and Sierra Madre Oriental. Capital: Jalapa. Pop.: 6 734 545 (1995 est.). Area: 72 815 sq. km (28 114 sq. miles). **2** the chief port of Mexico, in Veracruz state on the Gulf of Mexico. Pop.: 438 821 (1990).

veranda *or* **verandah** (və'rændə) *n* **1** a porch or portico, sometimes partly enclosed, along the outside of a building. **2** *NZ.* a continuous overhead canopy that gives shelter to pedestrians. [C18: from Port. *varanda* railing]

veratrine ('verə,tri:n) *or* **veratrin** ('verətrɪn) *n* a white poisonous mixture obtained from sabadilla, consisting of various alkaloids: formerly used in medicine as a counterirritant. [C19: from L *vērātrum* hellebore + -INE[2]]

verb (vɜ:b) *n* **1** (in traditional grammar) any of a large class of words that serve to indicate the occurrence or performance of an action, the existence of a state, etc. Such words as *run, make, do*, etc., are verbs. **2** (in modern descriptive linguistic analysis) **2a** a word or group of words that functions as the predicate of a sentence or introduces the predicate. **2b** (*as modifier*): *a verb phrase.*
  ♦ Abbrev.: **vb, v.** [C14: from L *verbum* word]

verbal ('vɜ:b°l) *adj* **1** of, relating to, or using words: *merely verbal concessions.* **2** oral rather than written: *a verbal agreement.* **3** verbatim; literal: *an almost verbal copy.* **4** *Grammar.* of or relating to verbs or a verb. ♦ See also **verbals.**
  ▶ **'verbally** *adv*

verbalism ('vɜ:bə,lɪzəm) *n* **1** a verbal expression; phrase or word. **2** an exaggerated emphasis on the importance of words. **3** a statement lacking real content.

verbalist ('vɜ:bəlɪst) *n* **1** a person who deals with words alone, rather than facts, ideas, etc. **2** a person skilled in the use of words.

verbalize *or* **verbalise** ('vɜ:bə,laɪz) *vb* **verbalizes, verbalizing, verbalized** *or* **verbalises, verbalising, verbalised. 1** to express (an idea, etc.) in words. **2** to change (any word) into a verb or derive a verb from (any word). **3** (*intr*) to be verbose.
  ▶ **,verbali'zation** *or* **,verbali'sation** *n*

verbal noun *n* a noun derived from a verb, such as *smoking* in the sentence *smoking is bad for you.*

verbals ('vɜ:b°lz) *pl n Sl.* a criminal's admission of guilt on arrest.

verbascum (vɜ:'bæskəm) *n* any of a genus of hairy plants, mostly biennial, having spikes of yellow, purple, or red flowers. [L: mullein]

verbatim (vɜ:'beɪtɪm) *adv, adj* using exactly the same words; word for word. [C15: from Med. L: word by word, from L *verbum* word]

verbena (vɜ:'bi:nə) *n* **1** any of a genus of plants of tropical and temperate America, having red, white, or purple fragrant flowers: much cultivated as garden plants. **2** any of various similar plants, esp. the lemon verbena. [C16: via Med. L, from L: sacred bough used by the priest in religious acts]

verbiage ('vɜ:bɪɪdʒ) *n* the excessive and often meaningless use of words. [C18: from F, from OF *verbier* to chatter, from *verbe* word, from L *verbum*]

verbose (vɜ:'bəʊs) *adj* using or containing an excess of words, so as to be pedantic or boring. [C17: from L, from *verbum* word]
  ▶ **ver'bosely** *adv* ▶ **verbosity** (vɜ:'bɒsɪtɪ) *n*

verboten *German.* (fɛr'bo:tən) *adj* forbidden.

verb phrase *n Grammar.* a constituent of a sentence that contains the verb and any direct and indirect objects but not the subject.

Vercelli ★ (*Italian* ver'tʃelli) *n* a city in NW Italy, in Piedmont: an ancient Ligurian and later Roman city; has an outstanding library of manuscripts (notably the *Codex Vercellensis*, dating from the 10th century). Pop.: 50 313 (1990).

Vercingetorix ★ (,vɜ:sɪn'dʒetərɪks) *n* died ?45 B.C., Gallic chieftain and hero, executed for leading a revolt against the Romans under Julius Caesar (52 B.C.).

verdant ('vɜ:d°nt) *adj* **1** covered with green vegetation. **2** (of plants, etc.) green in colour. **3** unsophisticated; green. [C16: from OF, from *verdoyer* to become green, from OF *verd* green, from L *viridis*]
  ▶ **'verdancy** *n* ▶ **'verdantly** *adv*

verd antique (vɜ:d) *n* **1** a dark green mottled impure variety of serpentine marble. **2** any of various similar marbles or stones. [C18: from F, from It. *verde antico* ancient green]

Verde ★ (vɜ:d) *n* **Cape.** a cape in Senegal, near Dakar: the westernmost point of Africa. See also **Cape Verde.**

Verdi ★ ('veədɪ; *Italian* 'verdi) *n* **Giuseppe** (dʒu'zeppe). 1813–1901, Italian composer of operas, esp. *Rigoletto* (1851), *Il Trovatore* (1853), *La Traviata* (1853), and *Aïda* (1871).

verdict ('vɜ:dɪkt) *n* **1** the findings of a jury on the issues of fact submitted to it for examination and trial. **2** any decision or conclusion. [C13: from Med. L *vērdictum*, from L *vērē dictum* truly spoken, from *vērus* true + *dīcere* to say]

verdigris ('vɜ:dɪgrɪs) *n* **1** a green or bluish patina formed on copper, brass, or bronze. **2** a green or blue crystalline substance obtained by the action of acetic acid on copper and used as a fungicide and pigment. [C14: from OF *vert de Grice* green of Greece]

Verdun ★ (*French* verdœ; *English* 'veədʌn) *n* a fortified town in NE France, on the Meuse: scene of the longest and most severe battle (1916) of World War I, in which the French repelled a German offensive. Pop.: 23 430 (1990). Ancient name: **Verodunum** (,verə'dju:nəm).

verdure ('vɜ:dʒə) *n* **1** flourishing green vegetation or its colour. **2** a condition of freshness or healthy growth. [C14: from OF *verd* green, from L *viridis*]
  ▶ **'verdured** *adj*

Vereeniging ★ (fə'ri:nɪkɪŋ, və-) *n* a city in E South Africa: scene of the signing (1902) of the treaty ending the Boer War. Pop.: 60 584 (1985).

verge[1] (vɜ:dʒ) *n* **1** an edge or rim; margin. **2** a limit beyond which something occurs: *on the verge of ecstasy.* **3** *Brit.* a grass border along a road. **4** *Archit.* the edge of the roof tiles projecting over a gable. **5** *English legal history.* **5a** the area encompassing the royal court that is subject to the jurisdiction of the Lord High Steward. **5b** a rod or wand carried as a symbol of office or emblem of authority, as in the Church. ♦ *vb* **verges, verging, verged. 6** (*intr;* foll. by *on*) to be near (to): *to verge on chaos.* **7** (when *intr,* sometimes foll. by *on*) to serve as the edge of (something): *this narrow strip verges the road.* [C15: from OF, from L *virga* rod]

verge[2] (vɜ:dʒ) *vb* **verges, verging, verged.** (*intr;* foll. by *to* or *towards*) to move or incline in a certain direction. [C17: from L *vergere*]

verger ('vɜ:dʒə) *n Chiefly Church of England.* **1** a church official who acts as caretaker and attendant. **2** an official who carries the verge or rod of office before a bishop or dean in ceremonies and processions. [C15: from OF, from *verge*, from L *virga* rod, twig]

Vergil ★ ('vɜːdʒɪl) *n* a variant spelling of **Virgil**.

verglas ('veəglɑː) *n, pl* **verglases** (-glɑː, -glɑːz). a thin film of ice on rock. [from OF *verre-glaz*, from *verre* glass + *glaz* ice]

veridical (vɪ'rɪdɪk°l) *adj* **1** truthful. **2** *Psychol.* of revelations in dreams, etc., that appear to be confirmed by subsequent events. [C17: from L, from *vērus* true + *dīcere* to say]
> ve̩ri̩di'cality *n* ► ve'ridically *adv*

veriest ('verɪɪst) *adj Arch.* (intensifier): *the veriest coward.*

verification (ˌverɪfɪ'keɪʃən) *n* **1** establishment of the correctness of a theory, fact, etc. **2** evidence that provides proof of an assertion, theory, etc.
> 'verifi̩catory *adj*

verify ('verɪˌfaɪ) *vb* **verifies, verifying, verified.** (*tr*) **1** to prove to be true; confirm. **2** to check or determine the correctness or truth of by investigation, etc. **3** *Law.* to substantiate or confirm (an oath). [C14: from OF, from Med. L *vērificāre*, from L *vērus* true + *facere* to make]
> 'veri̩fiable *adj* ► 'veri̩fiably *adv* ► 'veri̩fier *n*

verily ('verɪlɪ) *adv* (*sentence modifier*) *Arch.* in truth; truly: *verily, thou art a man of God.* [C13: from VERY + -LY²]

verisimilar (ˌverɪ'sɪmɪlə) *adj* probable; likely. [C17: from L, from *vērus* true + *similis* like]

verisimilitude (ˌverɪsɪ'mɪlɪˌtjuːd) *n* **1** the appearance or semblance of truth or reality. **2** something that merely seems to be true or real, such as a doubtful statement. [C17: from L, from *vērus* true + *similitūdō* SIMILITUDE]

verism ('vɪərɪzəm) *n* extreme naturalism in art or literature. [C19: from It. *verismo*, from *vero* true, from L *vērus*]
> 'verist *n, adj* ► ve'ristic *adj*

verismo (vɛ'rɪzməʊ) *n Music.* a school of composition that originated in Italian opera towards the end of the 19th century, drawing its themes from real life. [C19: from It.; see VERISM]

veritable ('verɪtəb°l) *adj* (*prenominal*) (intensifier; *usually qualifying a word used metaphorically*): *he's a veritable swine!* [C15: from OF, from *vérité* truth; see VERITY]
> 'veritableness *n* ► 'veritably *adv*

vérité ('verɪːˌteɪ; *French* verite) *adj* involving a high degree of realism or naturalism: *a vérité look at David Bowie.* See also **cinéma vérité**. [F, lit.: truth]

verity ('verɪtɪ) *n, pl* **verities. 1** the quality or state of being true, real, or correct. **2** a true statement, idea, etc. [C14: from OF from L *vērĭtās*, from *vērus* true]

verjuice ('vɜːˌdʒuːs) *n* **1** the acid juice of unripe grapes, apples, or crab apples, formerly much used in making sauces, etc. **2** *Rare.* sourness or sharpness of temper, looks, etc. [C14: from OF *vert jus* green (unripe) juice]

Verkhne-Udinsk ★ (*Russian* 'vjɛrxnɪʊ'djinsk) *n* the former name (until 1934) of **Ulan-Ude.**

verkrampte (fə'kramtə) *n* (in South Africa during apartheid) **a** an Afrikaner Nationalist violently opposed to the end of apartheid and to liberalism in general. **b** (*as modifier*): *verkrampte politics.* [C20: from Afrik. (adj), lit.: restricted]

Verlaine ★ (*French* verlɛn) *n* **Paul** (pɔl). 1844–96, French poet. His verse includes *Poèmes saturniens* (1866) and *Romances sans paroles* (1874).

verligte (fə'ləxtə) *n* (in South Africa during apartheid) **a** a follower of any liberal White political party. **b** (*as modifier*): *verligte politics.* [C20: from Afrik. (adj), lit.: enlightened]

Vermeer ★ (veə'mɪə; *Dutch* vər'meːr) *n* **Jan** (jɑn). full name *Jan van der Meer van Delft.* 1632–75, Dutch genre painter.

vermeil ('vɜːmeɪl) *n* **1** gilded silver, bronze, or other metal, used esp. in the 19th century. **2a** vermilion. **2b** (*as adj*): *vermeil shoes.* [C15: from OF, from LL *vermiculus* insect (of the genus *Kermes*) or the red dye prepared from it, from L: little worm]

vermi- *combining form.* worm: *vermicide; vermiform; vermifuge.* [from L *vermis* worm]

vermicelli (ˌvɜːmɪ'sɛlɪ, -'tʃɛlɪ) *n* **1** very fine strands of pasta, used in soups. **2** tiny chocolate strands used to coat cakes, etc. [C17: from It.: little worms, from *verme*, from L *vermis*]

vermicide ('vɜːmɪˌsaɪd) *n* any substance used to kill worms.
> ˌvermi'cidal *adj*

vermicular (vɜː'mɪkjʊlə) *adj* **1** resembling the form, motion, or tracks of worms. **2** of worms or wormlike animals. [C17: from Med. L, from L *vermiculus*, dim. of *vermis* worm]
> ver'miculate *adj* ► ver̩micu'lation *n*

vermiculite (vɜː'mɪkjuˌlaɪt) *n* any of a group of micaceous minerals consisting mainly of hydrated silicate of magnesium, aluminium, and iron: on heating they expand and in this form are used in heat and sound insulation. [C19: from VERMICUL(AR) + -ITE¹]

vermiform ('vɜːmɪˌfɔːm) *adj* resembling a worm.

vermiform appendix *n* a wormlike pouch extending from the lower end of the caecum in some mammals. Also called: **appendix.**

vermifuge ('vɜːmɪˌfjuːdʒ) *n* any drug or agent able to destroy or expel intestinal worms.
> vermifugal (ˌvɜːmɪ'fjuːg°l) *adj*

vermilion (və'mɪljən) *n* **1a** a bright red to reddish-orange colour. **1b** (*as adj*): *a vermilion car.* **2** mercuric sulphide, esp. when used as a bright red pigment; cinnabar. [C13: from OF *vermeillon*, from *vermeil*, from L *vermiculus*, dim. of *vermis* worm]

vermin ('vɜːmɪn) *n* **1** (*functioning as pl*) small animals collectively, esp. insects and rodents, that are troublesome to man, domestic animals, etc. **2** (*pl* **vermin**) an unpleasant person. [C13: from OF, from L *vermis* worm]
> 'verminous *adj*

vermis ('vɜːmɪs) *n, pl* **vermes** (-miːz). *Anat.* the middle lobe connecting the two halves of the cerebellum. [C19: via NL from L: worm]

Vermont ★ (vɜː'mɒnt) *n* a state in the northeastern US: crossed from north to south by the Green Mountains; bounded on the east by the Connecticut River and by Lake Champlain in the northwest; mainly agricultural. Capital: Montpelier. Pop.: 588 654 (1996 est.). Area: 24 887 sq. km (9609 sq. miles). Abbrevs.: **Vt.** or (with zip code) **VT**
> Ver'monter *n*

vermouth ('vɜːməθ) *n* any of several wines containing aromatic herbs. [C19: from F, from G *Wermut* WORMWOOD (absinthe)]

vernacular (və'nækjʊlə) *n* **1** the. the commonly spoken language or dialect of a particular people or place. **2** a local style of architecture, in which ordinary houses are built: *a true English vernacular.* ◆ *adj* **3** relating to or in the vernacular. **4** designating or relating to the common name of an animal or plant. **5** built in the local style of ordinary houses. [C17: from L *vernāculus* belonging to a household slave, from *verna* household slave]
> ver'nacularly *adv*

vernal ('vɜːn°l) *adj* **1** of or occurring in spring. **2** *Poetic.* of or characteristic of youth. [C16: from L, from *vēr* spring]
> 'vernally *adv*

vernal equinox *n* See at **equinox.**

vernal grass *n* any of a genus of Eurasian grasses, such as **sweet vernal grass**, having the fragrant scent of coumarin.

vernalize *or* **vernalise** ('vɜːnəˌlaɪz) *vb* **vernalizes, vernalizing, vernalized** *or* **vernalises, vernalising, vernalised.** to shorten the period between sowing and flowering in (plants), esp. by subjection of the seeds to low temperatures before planting.
> ˌvernali'zation *or* ˌvernali'sation *n*

vernation (vɜː'neɪʃən) *n* the way in which leaves are arranged in the bud. [C18: from NL, from L *vernāre* to be springlike, from *vēr* spring]

Verne ★ (vɜːn; *French* vern) *n* **Jules** (ʒyl). 1828–1905, French writer, esp. of science fiction, such as *Twenty Thousand Leagues under the Sea* (1870).

vernier ('vɜːnɪə) *n* **1** a small movable scale running paral-

★ people and places

lel to the main graduated scale in certain measuring instruments, such as theodolites, used to obtain a fractional reading of one of the divisions on the main scale. **2** (*modifier*) relating to or fitted with a vernier: *a vernier scale*. [C18: after Paul *Vernier* (1580–1637), F mathematician, who described the scale]

vernissage (ˌvɜːnɪˈsɑːʒ) *n* a preview or the opening on the first day of an exhibition of paintings. [F, from *vernis* VARNISH]

Vernoleninsk ★ (*Russian* vɪrnəlɪˈnjiːnsk) *n* the former name of **Nikolayev**.

Verny ★ (*Russian* ˈvjɛrnɪj) *n* a former name (until 1927) of **Alma-Ata**.

Verona ★ (vəˈrəʊnə; *Italian* veˈroːna) *n* a city in N Italy, in Veneto on the Adige River: strategically situated at the junction of major routes between Italy and N Europe; became a Roman colony (89 B.C.); under Austrian rule (1797–1866); Roman remains. Pop.: 256 756 (1994 est.).
► **Veronese** (ˌvɛrəˈniːz) *adj, n*

Veronal (ˈvɛrənʰl) *n* a trademark for **barbitone**.

Veronese ★ (*Italian* veroˈneːse) *n* **Paolo** (ˈpaːolo), original name *Paolo Cagliari* or *Caliari*. 1528–88, Italian painter of the Venetian school. His works include *The Marriage at Cana* (1563) and *The Feast of the Levi* (1573).

veronica[1] (vəˈrɒnɪkə) *n* any plant of a genus, including the speedwells, of temperate and cold regions, having small blue, pink, or white flowers and flattened notched fruits. [C16: from Med. L, ?from the name *Veronica*]

veronica[2] (vəˈrɒnɪkə) *n Bullfighting*. a pass in which the matador slowly swings the cape away from the charging bull. [from Sp., from the name *Veronica*]

Verrazano or **Verrazzano** ★ (*Italian* verraˈtsaːno) *n* **Giovanni da** (dʒoˈvanni da). ?1485–?1528, Florentine navigator; the first European to sight what was to become New York (1524).

Verrocchio ★ (vəˈrəʊkɪˌəʊ; *Italian* verˈrɔkkjo) *n* **Andrea del** (anˈdrɛːa del). 1435–88, Italian sculptor, painter, and goldsmith of the Florentine school.

verruca (vɛˈruːkə) *n*, *pl* **verrucae** (-siː) or **verrucas. 1** *Pathol.* a wart, esp. one growing on the hand or foot. **2** *Biol.* a wartlike outgrowth. [C16: from L: wart]

verrucose (ˈvɛruˌkəʊs) or **verrucous** (ˈvɛrukəs, veˈruːkəs) *adj Bot.* covered with warty processes. [C17: from L *verrūcōsus* full of warts, from *verrūca* a wart]
► **verrucosity** (ˌvɛruˈkɒsɪtɪ) *n*

Versace ★ (*Italian* verˈsatʃe) *n* **Gianni** (*Italian* ˈdʒani). 1946–97, Italian fashion designer.

Versailles ★ (vɛəˈsaɪ, -ˈseɪlz; *French* vɛrsɑj) *n* a city in N central France, near Paris: site of an elaborate royal residence built for Louis XIV; seat of the French kings (1682–1789). Pop.: 87 789 (1990).

versant (ˈvɜːsʰnt) *n* **1** the side or slope of a mountain or mountain range. **2** the slope of a region. [C19: from F, from *verser* to turn, from L *versāre*]

versatile (ˈvɜːsəˌtaɪl) *adj* **1** capable of or adapted for many different uses, skills, etc. **2** variable. **3** *Bot.* (of an anther) attached to the filament by a small area so that it moves freely in the wind. **4** *Zool.* able to turn forwards and backwards. [C17: from L *versātilis* moving around, from *versāre* to turn]
► **'versa,tilely** *adv* ► **versatility** (ˌvɜːsəˈtɪlɪtɪ) *n*

verse (vɜːs) *n* **1** (not in technical usage) a stanza of a poem. **2** poetry as distinct from prose. **3a** a series of metrical feet forming a rhythmic unit of one line. **3b** (*as modifier*): *verse line*. **4** a specified type of metre or metrical structure: *iambic verse*. **5** one of the series of short subsections into which most of the writings in the Bible are divided. **6** a poem. ◆ *vb* **verses, versing, versed. 7** a rare word for **versify**. [OE *vers*, from L *versus* furrow, lit.: a turning (of the plough), from *vertere* to turn]

versed (vɜːst) *adj* (*postpositive*; foll. by *in*) thoroughly knowledgeable (about), acquainted (with), or skilled (in).

versed sine *n* a trigonometric function equal to one minus the cosine of the specified angle. [C16: from NL, from SINE[1] + *versus*, from *vertere* to turn]

versicle (ˈvɜːsɪkʰl) *n* **1** a short verse. **2** a short sentence recited or sung by a minister and responded to by his con-

gregation. [C14: from L *versiculus* a little line, from *versus* VERSE]

versicolour or *US* **versicolor** (ˈvɜːsɪˌkʌlə) *adj* of variable or various colours. [C18: from L *versicolor*, from *versāre* to turn + *color* COLOUR]

versification (ˌvɜːsɪfɪˈkeɪʃən) *n* **1** the technique or art of versifying. **2** the form or metrical composition of a poem. **3** a metrical version of a prose text.

versify (ˈvɜːsɪˌfaɪ) *vb* **versifies, versifying, versified. 1** (*tr*) to render (something) into verse. **2** (*intr*) to write in verse. [C14: from OF, from L, from *versus* VERSE + *facere* to make]
► **'versi,fier** *n*

version (ˈvɜːʃən) *n* **1** an account of a matter from a certain point of view, as contrasted with others: *his version of the accident is different from the policeman's*. **2** a translation, esp. of the Bible, from one language into another. **3** a variant form of something. **4** an adaptation, as of a book or play into a film. **5** *Med.* manual turning of a fetus to correct an irregular position within the uterus. [C16: from Med. L *versiō* a turning, from L *vertere* to turn]
► **'versional** *adj*

vers libre *French.* (vɛr librə) *n* (in French poetry) another term for **free verse**.

verso (ˈvɜːsəʊ) *n*, *pl* **versos. 1a** the back of a sheet of printed paper. **1b** the left-hand pages of a book, bearing the even numbers. Cf. **recto** (sense 2). **2** the side of a coin opposite to the obverse. [C19: from NL *versō foliō* the leaf having been turned, from L *vertere* to turn + *folium* leaf]

verst (vɛəst, vɜːst) *n* a unit of length, used in Russia, equal to 1.067 kilometres (0.6629 miles). [C16: from F or G, from Russian *versta* line]

versus (ˈvɜːsəs) *prep* **1** (esp. in a competition or lawsuit) against. Abbrev.: **v.**, (esp. *US*) **vs. 2** in contrast with. [C15: from L: turned (in the direction of), opposite, from *vertere* to turn]

vertebra (ˈvɜːtɪbrə) *n*, *pl* **vertebrae** (-briː) or **vertebras.** one of the bony segments of the spinal column. [C17: from L: joint of the spine, from *vertere* to turn]
► **'vertebral** *adj* ► **'vertebrally** *adv*

vertebral column *n* another name for **spinal column.**

vertebrate (ˈvɜːtɪˌbreɪt, -brɪt) *n* **1** any animal of a subphylum characterized by a bony skeleton and a well-developed brain: the group contains fishes, amphibians, reptiles, birds, and mammals. ◆ *adj* **2** of or belonging to this subphylum.

vertebration (ˌvɜːtɪˈbreɪʃən) *n* the formation of vertebrae or segmentation resembling vertebrae.

vertex (ˈvɜːtɛks) *n*, *pl* **vertexes** or **vertices. 1** the highest point. **2** *Maths.* **2a** the point opposite the base of a figure. **2b** the point of intersection of two sides of a plane figure or angle. **2c** the point of intersection of a pencil of lines or three or more planes of a solid figure. **3** *Anat.* the crown of the head. [C16: from L: highest point, from *vertere* to turn]

vertical (ˈvɜːtɪkʰl) *adj* **1** at right angles to the horizon; upright: *a vertical wall*. **2** extending in a perpendicular direction. **3** directly overhead. **4** *Econ.* of or relating to associated or consecutive, though not identical, stages of industrial activity: *vertical integration*. **5** of or relating to the vertex. **6** *Anat.* of or situated at the top of the head (vertex). ◆ *n* **7** a vertical plane, position, or line. **8** a vertical post, pillar, etc. [C16: from LL *verticālis*, from L VERTEX]
► **ˌverti'cality** *n* ► **'vertically** *adv*

vertical angles *pl n Geom.* the pair of equal angles between a pair of intersecting lines.

vertical mobility *n Sociol.* the movement of individuals or groups to positions in society that involve a change in class, status, and power.

vertices (ˈvɜːtɪˌsiːz) *n* a plural of **vertex** (in technical and scientific senses only).

verticil (ˈvɜːtɪsɪl) *n Biol.* a circular arrangement of parts about an axis, esp. leaves around a stem. [C18: from L *verticillus* whorl (of a spindle), from VERTEX]
► **ver'ticillate** *adj*

vertiginous (vɜːˈtɪdʒɪnəs) *adj* **1** of, relating to, or having

vertigo. 2 producing dizziness. **3** whirling. **4** changeable; unstable. [C17: from L *vertīginōsus*, from VERTIGO]
  ► ver'tiginously *adv*

vertigo ('vɜːtɪgəʊ) *n, pl* **vertigoes** *or* **vertigines** (vɜː-'tɪdʒɪ,niːz). *Pathol.* a sensation of dizziness resulting from a disorder of the sense of balance. [C16: from L: a whirling round, from *vertere* to turn]

vertu (vɜː'tuː) *n* a variant spelling of **virtu**.

Vertumnus (vɜː'tʌmnəs) *or* **Vortumnus** ★ *n* a Roman god of gardens, orchards, and seasonal change. [from L, from *vertere* to turn, change]

Verulamium ★ (ˌvɛrʊ'leɪmɪəm) *n* the Latin name of Saint Albans.

vervain ('vɜːveɪn) *n* any of several plants of the genus *Verbena*, having square stems and long slender spikes of purple, blue, or white flowers. [C14: from OF *verveine*, from L *verbēna* sacred bough]

verve (vɜːv) *n* great vitality and liveliness. [C17: from OF: garrulity, from L *verba* words, chatter]

vervet ('vɜːvɪt) *n* a variety of a South African guenon monkey having dark hair on the hands and feet and a reddish patch beneath the tail. [C19: from F, from *vert* green]

Verwoerd ★ (fə'vʊt, feə'vʊət) *n* Hendrik Frensch ('hendrɪk frens). 1901–66, South African statesman, born in the Netherlands: prime minister of South Africa (1958–66) and the principal architect of the apartheid system: assassinated.

very ('vɛrɪ) *adv* **1** (intensifier) used to add emphasis to adjectives that are able to be graded: *very good; very tall.* ◆ *adj* (*prenominal*) **2** (intensifier) used with nouns preceded by a definite article or possessive determiner, in order to give emphasis to the significance or relevance of a noun in a particular context, or to give exaggerated intensity to certain nouns: *the very man I want to see; the very back of the room.* **3** (intensifier) used in metaphors to emphasize the applicability of the image to the situation described: *he was a very lion in the fight.* **4** *Arch.* genuine: *the very living God.* [C13: from OF *verai* true, from L *vērax*, from *vērus*]

> **USAGE NOTE** In strict usage adverbs of degree such as *very, too, quite, really,* and *extremely* are used only to qualify adjectives: *he is very happy; she is too sad.* By this rule, these words should not be used to qualify past participles that follow the verb *to be,* since they would then be technically qualifying verbs. With the exception of certain participles, such as *tired* or *disappointed,* that have come to be regarded as adjectives, all other past participles are qualified by adverbs such as *much, greatly, seriously,* or *excessively: he has been much* (not *very*) *inconvenienced; she has been excessively* (not *too*) *criticized.*

very high frequency *n* a radio-frequency band or radio frequency lying between 30 and 300 megahertz. Abbrev.: **VHF.**

Very light ('vɛrɪ) *n* a coloured flare fired from a special pistol (**Very pistol**) for signalling at night, esp. at sea. [C19: after Edward W. *Very* (1852–1910), US naval ordnance officer]

very low frequency *n* a radio-frequency band or radio frequency lying between 3 and 30 kilohertz. Abbrev.: **VLF.**

Vesalius ★ (vɪ'seɪlɪəs) *n* Andreas (*Dutch* an'dreːas). 1514–64, Flemish anatomist, noted for his *De Humani Corporis fabrica* (1543).

vesica ('vɛsɪkə) *n, pl* **vesicae** (-ˌsiː). *Anat.* a technical name for **bladder** (sense 1). [C17: from L: bladder, sac, blister]
  ► 'vesical *adj* ► vesiculate (ve'sɪkjuˌleɪt, -lɪt) *vb, adj*

vesicant ('vɛsɪkənt) *or* **vesicatory** ('vɛsɪˌkeɪtərɪ) *n, pl* **vesicants** *or* **vesicatories. 1** any substance that causes blisters. ◆ *adj* **2** acting as a vesicant. [C19: see VESICA]

vesicate ('vɛsɪˌkeɪt) *vb* **vesicates, vesicating, vesicated.** to blister. [C17: from NL *vēsīcāre*; see VESICA]
  ► ˌvesi'cation *n*

vesicle ('vɛsɪkᵊl) *n* **1** *Pathol.* **1a** any small sac or cavity, esp. one containing serous fluid. **1b** a blister. **2** *Geol.* a rounded cavity within a rock. **3** *Bot.* a small bladder-like cavity occurring in certain seaweeds. **4** any small cavity or cell. [C16: from L *vēsīcula*, dim. of VESICA]
  ► **vesicular** (ve'sɪkjulə) *adj*

Vespasian ★ (ve'speɪʒɪən) *n* Latin name *Titus Flavius Sabinus Vespasianus.* 9–79 A.D., Roman emperor (69–79), who consolidated Roman rule, esp. in Britain and Germany.

vesper ('vɛspə) *n* **1** an evening prayer, service, or hymn. **2** *Arch.* evening. **3** (*modifier*) of or relating to vespers. ◆ See also **vespers.** [C14: from L: evening, the evening star]

vespers ('vɛspəz) *n* (*functioning as sing*) **1** *Chiefly RC Church.* the sixth of the seven canonical hours of the divine office. **2** another word for **evensong** (sense 1).

vespertine ('vɛspəˌtaɪn) *adj* **1** *Bot., zool.* appearing, opening, or active in the evening: *vespertine flowers.* **2** occurring in the evening or (esp. of stars) setting in the evening.

vespiary ('vɛspɪərɪ) *n, pl* **vespiaries.** a nest or colony of social wasps or hornets. [C19: from L *vespa* a wasp, on the model of *apiary*]

vespid ('vɛspɪd) *n* **1** any of a family of hymenopterous insects, including the common wasp. ◆ *adj* **2** of or belonging to this family. [C19: from NL, from L *vespa* a wasp]
  ► 'vespine *adj*

Vespucci ★ (ve'spuːtʃɪ) *n* Amerigo (ame'riːgo), Latin name *Americus Vespucius.* ?1454–1512, Florentine navigator in the New World (1499–1500; 1501–02), after whom America was named.

vessel ('vɛsᵊl) *n* **1** any object used as a container, esp. for a liquid. **2** a passenger or freight-carrying ship, boat, etc. **3** *Anat.* a tubular structure that transports such body fluids as blood and lymph. **4** *Bot.* a tubular element of xylem tissue transporting water. **5** *Rare.* a person regarded as a vehicle for some purpose or quality. [C13: from OF, from LL *vascellum* urn, from L *vās* vessel]

vest (vest) *n* **1** an undergarment covering the body from the shoulders to the hips, made of cotton, nylon, etc. Austral. equivalent: **singlet.** US and Canad. equivalent: **undershirt. 2** *US, Canad., & Austral.* a waistcoat. **3** *Obs.* any form of dress. ◆ *vb* **4** (*tr;* foll. by *in*) to place or settle (power, rights, etc., in): *power was vested in the committee.* **5** (*tr;* foll. by *with*) to bestow or confer (on): *the company was vested with authority.* **6** (usually foll. by *in*) to confer (a right, title, etc., upon) or (of a right, title, etc.) to pass (to) or devolve (upon). **7** (*tr*) to clothe. **8** (*intr*) to put on clothes, ecclesiastical vestments, etc. [C15: from OF *vestir* to clothe, from L *vestīre*, from *vestis* clothing]

vesta ('vɛstə) *n* a short friction match, usually of wood. [C19: after VESTA]

Vesta ★ ('vɛstə) *n* the Roman goddess of the hearth and its fire. In her temple a perpetual flame was tended by the vestal virgins. Greek counterpart: **Hestia.**

vestal ('vɛstᵊl) *adj* **1** chaste or pure. **2** of or relating to the Roman goddess Vesta. ◆ *n* **3** a chaste woman, esp. a nun.

vestal virgin *n* (in ancient Rome) one of the virgin priestesses whose lives were dedicated to Vesta and to maintaining the sacred fire in her temple.

vested ('vɛstɪd) *adj Property law.* having a present right to the immediate or future possession and enjoyment of property.

vested interest *n* **1** *Property law.* an existing right to the immediate or future possession and enjoyment of property. **2** a strong personal concern in a state of affairs, etc. **3** a person or group that has such an interest.

vestiary ('vɛstɪərɪ) *n, pl* **vestiaries.** *Obs.* a room for storing clothes or dressing in, such as a vestry. [C17: from LL *vestiārius,* from *vestis* clothing]

vestibule ('vɛstɪˌbjuːl) *n* **1** a small entrance hall or anteroom. **2** any small bodily cavity at the entrance to a passage or canal. [C17: from L *vestibulum*]

vestige ('vɛstɪdʒ) *n* **1** a small trace; hint: *a vestige of truth.*

★ people and places

2 *Biol.* an organ or part of an organism that is a small nonfunctioning remnant of a functional organ in an ancestor. [C17: via F from L *vestīgium* track]
▶ **ves'tigial** *adj*

Vestmanaeyjar ★ (*Icelandic* 'vɛstmanaɛijar) *n* a group of islands off the S coast of Iceland: they include the island of Surtsey (emerged 1963) and the volcano Helgafell (erupted 1974). Pop.: 4888 (1994). English name: **Vestmann Islands** ('vɛstmən).

vestment ('vɛstmənt) *n* **1** a garment or robe, esp. one denoting office, authority, or rank. **2** any of various ceremonial garments worn by the clergy at religious services, etc. [C13: from OF *vestiment*, from L *vestīmentum*, from *vestīre* to clothe]
▶ **vestmental** (vɛst'mɛntˀl) *adj*

vest-pocket *n* (*modifier*) *Chiefly US.* small enough to fit into a waistcoat pocket.

vestry ('vɛstrɪ) *n, pl* **vestries.** **1** a room in or attached to a church in which vestments, sacred vessels, etc., are kept. **2** a room in or attached to some churches, used for Sunday school, etc. **3a** *Church of England.* a meeting of all the members of a parish or their representatives, to transact the official and administrative business of the parish. **3b** the parish council. [C14: prob. from OF *vestiarie;* see VEST]
▶ **'vestral** *adj*

vestryman ('vɛstrɪmən) *n, pl* **vestrymen.** a member of a church vestry.

vesture ('vɛstʃə) *Arch.* ◆ *n* **1** a garment or something that seems like a garment: *a vesture of cloud.* ◆ *vb* **vestures, vesturing, vestured.** **2** (*tr*) to clothe. [C14: from OF, from *vestir*, from L *vestīre*, from *vestis* clothing]
▶ **'vestural** *adj*

Vesuvius ★ (vɪ'suːvɪəs) *n* a volcano in SW Italy, on the Bay of Naples: first recorded eruption in 79 A.D., which destroyed Pompeii, Herculaneum, and Stabiae; numerous eruptions since then. Average height: 1220 m (4003 ft). Italian name: **Vesuvio** (ve'zuːvjo).

vet[1] (vɛt) *n* **1** short for **veterinary surgeon.** ◆ *vb* **vets, vetting, vetted.** **2** (*tr*) *Chiefly Brit.* to make a prior examination and critical appraisal of (a person, document, etc.): *the candidates were well vetted.* **3** to examine or treat (an animal).

vet[2] (vɛt) *n US & Canad.* short for **veteran** (senses 2, 3).

vet. *abbrev. for:* **1** veteran. **2** veterinarian. **3** veterinary. ◆ Also (for senses 2, 3): **veter.**

vetch (vɛtʃ) *n* **1** any of various climbing plants having pinnate leaves, typically blue or purple flowers, and tendrils on the stems. **2** any of various similar and related plants, such as the kidney vetch. **3** the beanlike fruit of any of these plants. [C14 *fecche*, from OF *veche*, from L *vicia*]

vetchling ('vɛtʃlɪŋ) *n* any of various tendril-climbing plants, mainly of N temperate regions, having winged or angled stems and showy flowers. See also **sweet pea.**

veteran ('vɛtərən) *n* **1a** a person or thing that has given long service in some capacity. **1b** (*as modifier*): *veteran firemen.* **2** a soldier who has seen considerable active service. **3** *US & Canad.* a person who has served in the military forces. [C16: from L, from *vetus* old]

veteran car *n Brit.* a car constructed before 1919, esp. one constructed before 1905. Cf. **classic car, vintage car.**

veterinary ('vɛtərɪnərɪ) *adj* of or relating to veterinary medicine. [C18: from L *veterīnārius*, from *veterīnae* draught animals]

veterinary medicine *or* **science** *n* the branch of medicine concerned with the health of animals and the treatment of injuries or diseases that affect them.

veterinary surgeon *n Brit.* a person qualified to practise veterinary medicine. US and Canad. term: **veterinarian.**

veto ('viːtəʊ) *n, pl* **vetoes. 1** the power to prevent legislation or action proposed by others: *the presidential veto.* **2** the exercise of this power. ◆ *vb* **vetoes, vetoing, vetoed.** (*tr*) **3** to refuse consent to (a proposal, esp. a government bill). **4** to prohibit, ban, or forbid: *her parents vetoed her trip.* [C17: from L: I forbid, from *vetāre* to forbid]
▶ **'vetoer** *n*

vex (vɛks) *vb* (*tr*) **1** to anger or annoy. **2** to confuse; worry. **3** *Arch.* to agitate. [C15: from OF *vexer*, from L *vexāre* to jolt (in carrying), from *vehere* to convey]
▶ **'vexer** *n* ▶ **'vexing** *adj*

vexation (vɛk'seɪʃən) *n* **1** the act of vexing or the state of being vexed. **2** something that vexes.

vexatious (vɛk'seɪʃəs) *adj* **1** vexing or tending to vex. **2** vexed. **3** *Law.* (of a legal action or proceeding) instituted without sufficient grounds, esp. so as to cause annoyance to the defendant.
▶ **vex'atiously** *adv*

vexed (vɛkst) *adj* **1** annoyed, confused, or agitated. **2** much debated (esp. in **a vexed question**).
▶ **vexedly** ('vɛksɪdlɪ) *adv*

vexillology (ˌvɛksɪ'lɒlədʒɪ) *n* the study and collection of information about flags. [C20: from L *vexillum* flag + -LOGY]
▶ **ˌvexil'lologist** *n*

vexillum (vɛk'sɪləm) *n, pl* **vexilla** (-lə). **1** *Ornithol.* the vane of a feather. **2** Also called: **standard.** *Bot.* the largest petal of a papilionaceous flower. [C18: from L: banner, ?from *vēlum* sail]
▶ **'vexillate** *adj*

VF *abbrev. for* video frequency.

VFA (in Australia) *abbrev. for* Victorian Football Association.

vg *abbrev. for* very good.

VG *abbrev. for* Vicar General.

VGA *abbrev. for* video graphics array: a computing standard for spatial and colour resolution.

VHF *or* **vhf** *Radio. abbrev. for* very high frequency.

VHS *Trademark. abbrev. for* video home system: a video cassette recording system using ½″ magnetic tape.

VI *abbrev. for:* **1** Vancouver Island. **2** Virgin Islands.

v.i. *abbrev. for* vide infra (see **vide**).

via ('vaɪə) *prep* by way of; by means of; through: *to London via Paris.* [C18: from L *viā*, from *via* way]

viable ('vaɪəbˀl) *adj* **1** capable of becoming actual, etc.: *a viable proposition.* **2** (of seeds, eggs, etc.) capable of normal growth and development. **3** (of a fetus) having reached a stage of development at which further development can occur independently of the mother. [C19: from F, from *vie* life, from L *vīta* life]
▶ **ˌvia'bility** *n*

Via Dolorosa ★ ('viːə ˌdɒlə'rəʊsə) *n* the route followed by Christ from the place of his condemnation to Calvary for his crucifixion. [L, lit.: sorrowful road]

viaduct ('vaɪəˌdʌkt) *n* a bridge, esp. for carrying a road or railway across a valley, etc. [C19: from L *via* way + *dūcere* to bring, on the model of *aqueduct*]

Viagra (vaɪ'ægrə, viː-) *n Trademark.* a drug that allows increased blood flow to the penis; used to treat impotence in men.

vial ('vaɪəl) *n* a less common variant of **phial.** [C14 *fiole*, from OF, ult. from Gk *phialē*; see PHIAL]

via media *Latin.* ('vaɪə 'miːdɪə) *n* a compromise between two extremes.

viand ('vɪənd) *n* **1** a type of food, esp. a delicacy. **2** (*pl*) provisions. [C14: from OF, ult. from L *vīvenda* things to be lived on, from *vivere* to live]

Viareggio ★ (*Italian* viaˈreddʒo) *n* a town and resort in W Italy, in Tuscany on the Ligurian Sea. Pop.: 50 310 (1987 est.).

viatical (vaɪ'ætɪkˀl) *adj* **1** of or denoting a road or a journey. **2** *Bot.* (of a plant) growing by the side of a road. [C19: from L *viāticus* belonging to a journey + -AL]

viatical settlement *n* the purchase by a charity of a life assurance policy owned by a person with only a short time to live, to enable that person to use the proceeds during his or her lifetime. See also **death futures.**

viaticum (vaɪ'ætɪkəm) *n, pl* **viatica** (-kə) *or* **viaticums. 1** *Christianity.* Holy Communion as administered to a person dying or in danger of death. **2** *Rare.* provisions or a travel allowance for a journey. [C16: from L, from *viāticus* belonging to a journey, from *via* way]

vibes (vaɪbz) *pl n* **1** *Inf.* short for **vibraphone**. **2** *Sl.* short for **vibrations**.

Viborg ★ *n* **1** ('viːbɔrj). the Swedish name for **Vyborg**. **2** (*Danish* 'viːbɒr). a town in N central Denmark, in Jutland: formerly a royal town and capital of Jutland. Pop.: 29 455 (1990).

vibraculum (vaɪ'brækjʊləm) *n, pl* **vibracula** (-lə). *Zool.* any of the specialized bristle-like polyps in certain bryozoans, the actions of which prevent parasites from settling on the colony. [C19: from NL, from L *vibrāre* to brandish]

vibrant ('vaɪbrənt) *adj* **1** characterized by or exhibiting vibration. **2** giving an impression of vigour and activity. **3** caused by vibration; resonant. [C16: from L *vibrāre* to agitate]
▶ **'vibrancy** *n* ▶ **'vibrantly** *adv*

vibraphone ('vaɪbrə,fəʊn) *n* a percussion instrument consisting of a set of metal bars placed over tubular metal resonators, which are made to vibrate electronically.
▶ **'vibra,phonist** *n*

vibrate (vaɪ'breɪt) *vb* **vibrates, vibrating, vibrated. 1** to move or cause to move back and forth rapidly. **2** (*intr*) to oscillate. **3** to resonate or cause to resonate. **4** (*intr*) to waver. **5** *Physics.* to undergo or cause to undergo an oscillatory process, as of an alternating current. **6** (*intr*) *Rare.* to respond emotionally; thrill. [C17: from L *vibrāre*]
▶ **vibratile** ('vaɪbrə,taɪl) *adj* ▶ **vi'brating** *adj* ▶ **vibratory** ('vaɪbrətərɪ) *adj*

vibration (vaɪ'breɪʃən) *n* **1** the act or an instance of vibrating. **2** *Physics.* **2a** a periodic motion about an equilibrium position, such as in the propagation of sound. **2b** a single cycle of such a motion. **3** the process or state of vibrating or being vibrated.
▶ **vi'brational** *adj*

vibrations (vaɪ'breɪʃənz) *pl n* *Sl.* **1** instinctive feelings supposedly influencing human communication. **2** a characteristic atmosphere felt to be emanating from places or objects.

vibrato (vɪ'brɑːtəʊ) *n, pl* **vibratos**. *Music.* **1** a slight, rapid, and regular fluctuation in the pitch of a note produced on a stringed instrument by a shaking movement of the hand stopping the strings. **2** an oscillatory effect produced in singing by fluctuation in breath pressure or pitch. [C19: from It., from L *vibrāre* to VIBRATE]

vibrator (vaɪ'breɪtə) *n* **a** a device for producing a vibratory motion, such as one used in massage. **b** such a device with a vibrating part or tip, used as a dildo.

vibrissa (vaɪ'brɪsə) *n, pl* **vibrissae** (-siː). (*usually pl*) **1** any of the bristle-like sensitive hairs on the face of many mammals; a whisker. **2** any of the specialized bristle-like feathers around the beak in certain insectivorous birds. [C17: from L, prob. from *vibrāre* to shake]
▶ **vi'brissal** *adj*

viburnum (vaɪ'bɜːnəm) *n* **1** any of various temperate and subtropical shrubs or trees having small white flowers and berry-like red or black fruits. **2** the dried bark of several species of this tree, sometimes used in medicine. [C18: from L: wayfaring tree]

Vic. *Austral. abbrev. for* Victoria (the state).

vicar ('vɪkə) *n* **1** *Church of England.* **1a** (in Britain) a clergyman appointed to act as priest of a parish from which, formerly, he did not receive tithes but a stipend. **1b** a clergyman who acts as assistant to or substitute for the rector of a parish at Communion. **2** *RC Church.* a bishop or priest representing the pope and exercising a limited jurisdiction. **3** Also called: **lay vicar, vicar choral.** *Church of England.* a member of a cathedral choir appointed to sing certain parts of the services. [C13: from OF, from L *vicārius* (n) a deputy, from *vicārius* (adj) VICARIOUS]
▶ **vicarial** (vɪ'kɛərɪəl) *adj* ▶ **vi'cariate** *n* ▶ **'vicarly** *adj*

vicarage ('vɪkərɪdʒ) *n* the residence or benefice of a vicar.

vicar apostolic *n RC Church.* a titular bishop having jurisdiction in missionary countries.

vicar general *n, pl* **vicars general.** an official, usually a layman, appointed to assist the bishop of a diocese in discharging his administrative or judicial duties.

vicarious (vɪ'kɛərɪəs, vaɪ-) *adj* **1** undergone at second hand through sympathetic participation in another's experiences. **2** undergone or done as the substitute for another: *vicarious punishment.* **3** delegated: *vicarious authority.* **4** taking the place of another. [C17: from L *vicārius* substituted, from *vicis* interchange]
▶ **vi'cariously** *adv* ▶ **vi'cariousness** *n*

Vicar of Bray ★ (breɪ) *n* a vicar (Simon Aleyn) appointed to the parish of Bray in Berkshire during Henry VIII's reign who changed his faith to Catholic when Mary I was on the throne and back to Protestant when Elizabeth I succeeded and so retained his living.

Vicar of Christ *n RC Church.* the pope when regarded as Christ's earthly representative.

vice[1] (vaɪs) *n* **1** an immoral, wicked, or evil habit, action, or trait. **2** frequent indulgence in immoral or degrading practices. **3** a specific form of pernicious conduct, esp. prostitution or sexual perversion. **4** an imperfection in character, conduct, etc.: *smoking is his only vice.* **5** a bad trick or disposition, as of horses, dogs, etc. [C13: via OF from L *vitium* a defect]

vice[2] *or US* (*often*) **vise** (vaɪs) *n* **1** an appliance for holding an object while work is done on it, usually having a pair of jaws. ◆ *vb* **2** (*tr*) to grip (something) with or as if with a vice. [C15: from OF *vis* a screw, from L *vītis* vine, plant with spiralling tendrils (hence the later meaning)]

vice[3] (vaɪs) *adj* **1a** (*prenominal*) serving in the place of. **1b** (*in combination*): *viceroy.* ◆ *n* **2** *Inf.* a person who serves as a deputy to another. [C18: from L, from *vicis* interchange]

vice[4] ('vaɪsɪ) *prep* instead of; as a substitute for. [C16: from L, ablative of *vicis* change]

vice admiral *n* a commissioned officer of flag rank in certain navies, junior to an admiral and senior to a rear admiral.

vice-chairman *n, pl* **vice-chairmen.** a person who deputizes for a chairman and serves in his place during his absence.
▶ **vice-'chairmanship** *n*

vice chancellor *n* **1** the chief executive or administrator at some British universities. **2** (in the US) a judge in courts of equity subordinate to the chancellor. **3** (formerly in England) a senior judge of the court of chancery who acted as assistant to the Lord Chancellor. **4** a person serving as the deputy of a chancellor.
▶ **vice-'chancellorship** *n*

vicegerent (,vaɪs'dʒɛrənt) *n* **1** a person appointed to exercise all or some of the authority of another. **2** *RC Church.* the pope or any other representative of God or Christ on earth, such as a bishop. ◆ *adj* **3** invested with or characterized by delegated authority. [C16: from NL, from VICE[3] + L *gerere* to manage]
▶ **vice'gerency** *n*

vicennial (vɪ'sɛnɪəl) *adj* **1** occurring every 20 years. **2** lasting for a period of 20 years. [C18: from LL *vīcennium* period of twenty years, from L *vīciēs* twenty times + *-ennium*, from *annus* year]

Vicenza ★ (*Italian* vi'tʃɛntsa) *n* a city in NE Italy, in Veneto: home of the architect Andrea Palladio and site of some of his finest works. Pop.: 108 013 (1994 est.).

vice president *n* an officer ranking immediately below a president and serving as his deputy. A vice president takes the president's place during his absence or incapacity, after his death, and in certain other circumstances. Abbrev.: **VP.**
▶ **vice-'presidency** *n*

viceregal (,vaɪs'riːgəl) *adj* **1** of or relating to a viceroy. **2** *Chiefly Austral. & NZ.* of or relating to a governor or governor general.
▶ **vice'regally** *adv*

vicereine (,vaɪs'reɪn) *n* **1** the wife of a viceroy. **2** a female viceroy. [C19: from F, from VICE[3] + *reine* queen, from L *rēgīna*]

viceroy ('vaɪsrɔɪ) *n* a governor of a colony, country, or province who acts for and rules in the name of his sovereign or government. Related adj: **viceregal.** [C16: from F, from VICE[3] + *roy* king, from L *rex*]
▶ **'viceroyship** *or* ,**vice'royalty** *n*

---

vice squad *n* a police division to which is assigned the enforcement of gaming and prostitution laws.

vice versa ('vaɪsɪ 'vɜːsə) *adv* the other way around. [C17: from L: relations being reversed, from *vicis* change + *vertere* to turn]

Vichy ★ (*French* viʃi; *English* 'viːʃi) *n* a town and spa in central France, on the River Allier: seat of the collaborationist government under Marshal Pétain (1940–44); mineral waters bottled for export. Pop.: 28 048 (1990). Latin name: **Vicus Calidus** ('viːkəs 'kælɪdəs).

vichyssoise (*French* viʃiswaz) *n* a thick soup made from leeks, potatoes, chicken stock, and cream, usually served chilled. [F, from (*crème*) *vichyssoise* (*glacée*) (ice-cold cream) from Vichy]

vichy water *n* **1** (*sometimes cap.*) a mineral water from springs at Vichy in France, reputed to be beneficial to health. **2** any sparkling mineral water resembling this.

vicinage ('vɪsɪnɪdʒ) *n Now rare.* **1** the residents of a particular neighbourhood. **2** a less common word for **vicinity**. [C14: from OF *vicenage*, from *vicin* neighbouring, from L *vīcīnus*]

vicinal ('vɪsɪnᵊl) *adj* **1** neighbouring. **2** (esp. of roads) of or relating to a locality. [C17: from L *vīcīnālis* nearby, from *vīcīnus*, from *vīcus* a neighbourhood]

vicinity (vɪ'sɪnɪtɪ) *n, pl* **vicinities. 1** a surrounding area; neighbourhood. **2** the fact or condition of being close in space or relationship. [C16: from L, *vīcīnus* neighbouring, from *vīcus* village]

vicious ('vɪʃəs) *adj* **1** wicked or cruel: *a vicious thug.* **2** characterized by violence or ferocity: *a vicious blow.* **3** *Inf.* unpleasantly severe; harsh: *a vicious wind.* **4** characterized by malice: *vicious lies.* **5** (esp. of dogs, horses, etc.) ferocious. **6** characterized by or leading to vice. **7** invalidated by defects; unsound: *a vicious inference.* [C14: from OF, from L *vitiōsus* full of faults, from *vitium* defect]
▸ **'viciously** *adv* ▸ **'viciousness** *n*

vicious circle *n* **1** Also: **vicious cycle.** a situation in which an attempt to resolve one problem creates new problems that lead back to the original situation. **2** *Logic.* **2a** a form of reasoning in which a conclusion is inferred from premises the truth of which cannot be established independently of that conclusion. **2b** an explanation given in terms that cannot be understood independently of that which was to be explained.

vicissitude (vɪ'sɪsɪ,tjuːd) *n* **1** variation or mutability in nature or life, esp. successive alternation from one condition or thing to another. **2** a variation in circumstance, fortune, etc. [C16: from L *vicissitūdō*, from *vicis* change]
▸ **vi,cissi'tudinous** *adj*

Vicksburg ★ ('vɪks,bɜːg) *n* a city in W Mississippi, on the Mississippi River: site of one of the most decisive campaigns (1863) of the American Civil War, in which the Confederates were besieged for nearly seven weeks before capitulating. Pop.: 20 908 (1990).

Vicky ★ ('vɪkɪ) *n* professional name of *Victor Weisz.* 1913–66, British political cartoonist, born in Germany.

Vico ★ ('vɪkəʊ; *Italian* 'viːko) *n* **Giovanni Battista** (dʒoˈvanni batˈtista). 1668–1744, Italian philosopher, noted for his *Scienza Nuova* (1721).

victim ('vɪktɪm) *n* **1** a person or thing that suffers harm, death, etc.: *victims of tyranny.* **2** a person who is tricked or swindled. **3** a living person or animal sacrificed in a religious rite. [C15: from L *victima*]

victimize or **victimise** ('vɪktɪ,maɪz) *vb* **victimizes, victimizing, victimized** or **victimises, victimising, victimised.** (*tr*) **1** to punish or discriminate against unfairly. **2** to make a victim of.
▸ **,victimi'zation** or **,victimi'sation** *n* ▸ **'victim,izer** or **'victim,iser** *n*

victimology (,vɪktɪ'mɒlədʒɪ) *n* the study of the psychological effects experienced by the victims of crime.
▸ **,victi'mologist** *n*

victor ('vɪktə) *n* **1a** a person, nation, etc., that has defeated an adversary in war, etc. **1b** (*as modifier*): *the victor army.* **2** the winner of any contest, conflict, or struggle. [C14: from L, from *vincere* to conquer]

Victor Emmanuel II ★ ('vɪktə) *n* 1820–78, king of

Sardinia-Piedmont (1849–78) and first king of Italy from 1861.

Victor Emmanuel III ★ *n* 1869–1947, last king of Italy (1900–46): dominated after 1922 by Mussolini: abdicated.

victoria (vɪk'tɔːrɪə) *n* **1** a light four-wheeled horse-drawn carriage with a folding hood, two passenger seats, and a seat in front for the driver. **2** Also called: **victoria plum.** *Brit.* a large sweet variety of plum, red and yellow in colour. [C19: both after Queen **Victoria**]

Victoria[1] ★ (vɪk'tɔːrɪə) *n* **1** a state of SE Australia: part of New South Wales colony until 1851; semiarid in the northwest, with the Great Dividing Range in the centre and east and the Murray River along the N border. Capital: Melbourne. Pop.: 4 533 300 (1996 est.). Area: 227 620 sq. km (87 884 sq. miles). **2 Lake.** Also called: **Victoria Nyanza.** a lake in East Africa, in Tanzania, Uganda, and Kenya, at an altitude of 1134 m (3720 ft): the largest lake in Africa and second largest in the world; drained by the Victoria Nile. Area: 69 485 sq. km (26 828 sq. miles). **3** a port in SW Canada, capital of British Columbia, on Vancouver Island: founded in 1843 by the Hudson's Bay Company; made capital of British Columbia in 1868; university (1963). Pop.: 287 897 (1991). **4** the capital of the Seychelles, a port on NE Mahé. Pop.: 25 000 (1993 est.). **5** a region in S China, on N Hong Kong Island: financial centre; university (1911). Pop.: 595 000 (latest est.). **6 Mount.** a mountain in SE Papua New Guinea: the highest peak of the Owen Stanley Range. Height: 4073 m (13 363 ft).

Victoria[2] ★ *n* **1** (vɪk'tɔːrɪə). 1819–1901, queen of the United Kingdom (1837–1901) and empress of India (1876–1901). She married Prince Albert of Saxe-Coburg-Gotha (1840). **2** (*Spanish* bik'torja). **Tomás Luis de** (to'mas lwis də). ?1548–1611, Spanish composer of motets and masses.

Victoria[3] ★ (vɪk'tɔːrɪə) *n* the Roman goddess of victory. Greek counterpart: **Nike.**

Victoria and Albert Museum ★ *n* a museum of the fine and applied arts in London, originating from 1856 and given its present name and site in 1899. Abbrev.: **V and A.**

Victoria Cross *n* the highest decoration for gallantry in the face of the enemy awarded to the British and Commonwealth armed forces: instituted in 1856 by Queen Victoria.

Victoria Day *n* the Monday preceding May 24: observed in Canada as a national holiday in commemoration of the birthday of Queen Victoria.

Victoria Desert ★ *n* See **Great Victoria Desert.**

Victoria Falls ★ *pl n* a waterfall on the border between Zimbabwe and Zambia, on the Zambezi River. Height: about 108 m (355 ft). Width: about 1400 m (4500 ft).

Victoria Island ★ *n* a large island in the Canadian Arctic: part of the Northwest Territories. Area: about 212 000 sq. km (82 000 sq. miles).

Victoria Land ★ *n* a section of Antarctica, largely in the Ross Dependency on the Ross Sea.

Victorian (vɪk'tɔːrɪən) *adj* **1** of or characteristic of Queen Victoria or the period of her reign. **2** exhibiting the characteristics popularly attributed to the Victorians, esp. prudery, bigotry, or hypocrisy. Cf. **Victorian values.** **3** of or relating to Victoria (the state or any of the cities). ◆ *n* **4** a person who lived during the reign of Queen Victoria. **5** an inhabitant of Victoria (the state or any of the cities).
▸ **Vic'torian,ism** *n*

Victoriana (vɪk,tɔːrɪ'ɑːnə) *pl n* objects, ornaments, etc., of the Victorian period.

Victoria Nile ★ *n* See **Nile.**

Victorian values *pl n* the qualities of enterprise and initiative, the importance of the family, and the development of charitable voluntary work considered to characterize the Victorian sense 2).

victorious (vɪk'tɔːrɪəs) *adj* **1** having defeated an adversary: *the victorious nations.* **2** of, indicative of, or characterized by victory: *a victorious conclusion.*
▸ **vic'toriously** *adv*

★ people and places

victory ('vɪktərɪ) *n, pl* **victories. 1** final and complete superiority in a war. **2** a successful military engagement. **3** a success attained in a contest or struggle or over an opponent, obstacle, or problem. **4** the act of triumphing or state of having triumphed. [C14: from OF *victorie*, from L *victōria*, from *vincere* to subdue]

Victory ★ ('vɪktərɪ) *n* another name (in English) for the Roman goddess **Victoria** or the Greek **Nike.**

victory roll *n* a rolling aircraft manoeuvre made by a pilot to announce or celebrate the shooting down of an enemy plane.

victual ('vɪtʲl) *vb* **victuals, victualling, victualled** *or US* **victuals, victualing, victualed.** to supply with or obtain victuals. See also **victuals.** [C14: from OF *vitaille*, from LL *victuālia* provisions, from L *victus* sustenance, from *vīvere* to live] ▸ **'victual-less** *adj*

victualler ('vɪtlə) *n* **1** a supplier of victuals, as to an army. **2** *Brit.* a licensed purveyor of spirits. **3** a supply ship, esp. one carrying foodstuffs.

victuals ('vɪtʲlz) *pl n* (*sometimes sing*) food or provisions.

vicuña (vɪ'kuːnjə) *or* **vicuna** (vɪ'kjuːnə, -'kuːnjə) *n* **1** a tawny-coloured cud-chewing Andean mammal similar to the llama. **2** the fine light cloth made from the wool obtained from this animal. [C17: from Sp., from Quechuan *wikúña*]

vid (vɪd) *n Inf.* short for **video** (sense 4).

Vidal ★ (viː'dæl) *n Gore.* born 1925, US novelist and essayist. His novels include *Burr* (1974), *Lincoln* (1984), and *The Season of Conflict* (1996).

vide ('vaɪdɪ) (used to direct a reader to a specified place in a text, another book, etc.) refer to, see (often in **vide ante** (see before), **vide infra** (see below), **vide supra** (see above), etc.) Abbrev.: **v., vid.** [C16: from L]

videlicet (vɪ'diːlɪˌsɛt) *adv* namely: used to specify items, etc. Abbrev.: **viz.** [C15: from L]

video ('vɪdɪəʊ) *adj* **1** relating to or employed in the transmission or reception of a televised image. **2** of, concerned with, or operating at video frequencies. ♦ *n, pl* **videos. 3** the visual elements of a television broadcast. **4** a film recorded on a video cassette. **5** short for **video cassette, video cassette recorder. 6** *US.* an informal name for **television.** ♦ *vb* **videos, videoing, videoed. 7** to record (a television programme, etc.) on a video cassette recorder. [C20: from L *vidēre* to see, on the model of AUDIO]

video cassette *n* a cassette containing video tape.

video cassette recorder *n* a tape recorder for vision and sound signals using magnetic tape in closed plastic cassettes: used for recording and playing back television programmes and films. Often shortened to **video** or **video recorder.**

videodisc ('vɪdɪəʊˌdɪsk) *n* another name for **optical disk.**

video frequency *n* the frequency of a signal conveying the image and synchronizing pulses in a television broadcasting system. It lies in the range from about 50 hertz to 8 megahertz.

video game *n* any of various games that can be played by using an electronic control to move graphical symbols on the screen of a visual display unit.

video jockey *n* a person who introduces and plays videos, esp. of pop songs, on a television programme.

video nasty *n, pl* **nasties.** a film, usually specially made for video, that is explicitly horrific and pornographic.

videophone ('vɪdɪəˌfəʊn) *n* a telephonic device through which there is both verbal and visual communication.

video recorder *n* short for **video cassette recorder.**

video tape *n* **1** magnetic tape used mainly for recording the sound and vision signals of a television programme or film for subsequent transmission. ♦ *vb* **video-tape, video-tapes, video-taping, video-taped. 2** to record (a programme, etc.) on video tape.

video tape recorder *n* a tape recorder for visual signals and usually accompanying sound, using magnetic tape on open spools: used in television broadcasting.

Videotex ('vɪdɪəʊˌtɛks) *n Trademark.* an information system that displays information from a distant computer on a television screen. See also **Teletext, Viewdata.**

videotext ('vɪdɪəʊˌtɛkst) *n* a means of providing a written or graphical representation of computerized information on a television screen.

vidicon ('vɪdɪˌkɒn) *n* a small television camera tube, used in closed-circuit television and outside broadcasts, in which incident light forms an electric charge pattern on a photoconductive surface. [C20: from VID(EO) + ICON(OSCOPE)]

vie (vaɪ) *vb* **vies, vying, vied.** (*intr;* foll. by *with* or *for*) to contend for superiority or victory (with) or strive in competition (for). [C15: prob. from OF *envier* to challenge, from L *invītāre* to INVITE] ▸ **'vier** *n* ▸ **'vying** *adj, n*

Vienna ★ (vɪ'ɛnə) *n* the capital and the smallest state of Austria, in the northeast on the River Danube: seat of the Hapsburgs (1278-1918); residence of the Holy Roman Emperor (1558-1806); withstood sieges by Turks in 1529 and 1683; political and cultural centre in the 18th and 19th centuries, associated with many composers; university (1365). Pop.: 1 595 768 (1994 est.). Area: 1075 sq. km (415 sq. miles). German name: **Wien.** ▸ **Viennese** (ˌvɪə'niːz) *adj, n*

Vienne ★ (*French* vjen) *n* **1** a department of W central France, in Poitou-Charentes region. Capital: Poitiers. Pop.: 388 701 (1994 est.). Area: 7044 sq. km (2747 sq. miles). **2** a town in SE France, on the River Rhône: extensive Roman remains. Ancient name: **Vienna. 3** a river in SW central France, flowing west and north to the Loire below Chinon. Length: over 350 km (200 miles).

Vientiane ★ (ˌvjɛntɪ'ɑːn) *n* the administrative capital of Laos, in the south near the border with Thailand: capital of the kingdom of Vientiane from 1707 until taken by the Thais in 1827. Pop.: 442 000 (1990 est.).

Vierwaldstättersee ★ (fiːr'valtʃtetərˌzeː) *n* the German name for (Lake) **Lucerne.**

vies (fɪs) *adj S. African sl.* angry, furious, or disgusted. [Afrik.]

Vietnam (ˌvjɛt'næm) *or* **Viet Nam ★** *n* a republic in SE Asia: an ancient empire, conquered by France in the 19th century; occupied by Japan (1940–45) when the Communist-led Vietminh began resistance operations that were continued against restored French rule after 1945. In 1954 the country was divided along the 17th parallel, establishing North Vietnam (under the Vietminh) and South Vietnam (under French control), the latter becoming the independent **Republic of Vietnam** in 1955. From 1959 the country was dominated by war between the Communist Vietcong, supported by North Vietnam, and the South Vietnamese government; increasing numbers of US forces were brought to the aid of the South Vietnamese army until a peace agreement (1973) led to the withdrawal of US troops; further fighting led to the eventual defeat of the South Vietnamese government in March 1975 and in 1976 an elected National Assembly proclaimed the reunification of the country. Official language: Vietnamese. Religion: Buddhist majority. Currency: dong. Capital: Hanoi. Pop.: 75 124 000 (1997). Area: 331 041 sq. km (127 816 sq. miles). Official name: **Socialist Republic of Vietnam.** ▸ ˌVietna'mese *adj, n*

vieux jeu *French.* (vjø ʒø) *adj* old-fashioned. [lit.: old game]

view (vjuː) *n* **1** the act of seeing or observing. **2** vision or sight, esp. range of vision: *the church is out of view.* **3** a scene, esp. of a fine tract of countryside: *the view from the top was superb.* **4** a pictorial representation of a scene, such as a photograph. **5** (*sometimes pl*) opinion: *my own view on the matter differs from yours.* **6** (foll. by *to*) a desired end or intention: *he has a view to securing further qualifications.* **7** a general survey of a topic, subject, etc. **8** visual aspect or appearance: *they look the same in outward view.* **9** a sight of a hunted animal before or during the chase. **10** in view of. taking into consideration. **11** on view. exhibited to the public gaze. **12** take a dim *or* poor view of. to regard (something) with disfavour. **13** with a view to. **13a** with the intention of. **13b** in anticipation or hope of. ♦ *vb* **14** (*tr*) to look at. **15** (*tr*) to consider in a specified manner: *they view Communism with horror.* **16** (*tr*) to examine or inspect carefully: *to view the accounts.* **17** (*tr*) to contem-

plate: *to view the difficulties*. **18** to watch (television). **19** (*tr*) to sight (a hunted animal) before or during the chase. [C15: from OF, from *veoir* to see, from L *vidēre*]
▸ **'viewable** *adj*

Viewdata ('vju:,deɪtə) *n Trademark*. an interactive form of Videotext that sends information from a distant computer along telephone lines, enabling shopping, booking theatre and airline tickets, and banking transactions to be conducted from the home.

viewer ('vju:ə) *n* **1** a person who views something, esp. television. **2** any optical device by means of which something is viewed, esp. one used for viewing photographic transparencies.

viewfinder ('vju:,faɪndə) *n* a device on a camera, consisting of a lens system, enabling the user to see what will be included in his photograph.

view halloo *interj* a huntsman's cry uttered when the quarry is seen breaking cover or shortly afterwards.

viewing ('vju:ɪŋ) *n* **1** the act of watching television. **2** television programmes collectively: *late-night viewing*.

viewless ('vju:lɪs) *adj* **1** (of windows, etc.) not affording a view. **2** having no opinions. **3** *Poetic*. invisible.

viewpoint ('vju:,pɔɪnt) *n* **1** the mental attitude that determines a person's judgments. **2** a place from which something can be viewed.

Vigée-Lebrun ★ (*French* viʒeləbrœ̃) *n* (**Marie Louise**) **Élisabeth** (elizabet). 1755–1842, French painter, noted for her portraits of women.

vigesimal (vaɪ'dʒɛsɪməl) *adj* **1** relating to or based on the number 20. **2** taking place or proceeding in intervals of 20. **3** twentieth. [C17: from L *vīgēsimus*, var. (infl. by *vīgintī* twenty) of *vīcēsimus* twentieth]

vigia ('vɪdʒɪə) *n Naut.* a navigational hazard marked on a chart although its existence and nature has not been confirmed. [C19: from Sp. *vigía* reef, from L *vigilāre* to keep watch]

vigil ('vɪdʒɪl) *n* **1** a purposeful watch maintained, esp. at night, to guard, observe, pray, etc. **2** the period of such a watch. **3** *RC Church, Church of England.* the eve of certain major festivals, formerly observed as a night spent in prayer. [C13: from OF, from Med. L *vigilia* watch preceding a religious festival, from L, from *vigil* alert, from *vigēre* to be lively]

vigilance ('vɪdʒɪləns) *n* **1** the fact, quality, or condition of being vigilant. **2** the abnormal state or condition of being unable to sleep.

vigilance committee *n* (in the US) a self-appointed body of citizens organized to maintain order, etc., where an efficient system of courts does not exist.

vigilant ('vɪdʒɪlənt) *adj* keenly alert to or heedful of trouble or danger. [C15: from L *vigilāns*, from *vigilāre* to be watchful; see VIGIL]
▸ **'vigilantly** *adv*

vigilante (,vɪdʒɪ'læntɪ) *n* **1** a self-appointed protector of public order. **2** *US.* a member of a vigilance committee. [C19: from Sp., from L *vigilāre* to keep watch]

vigilantism (,vɪdʒɪ'læntɪzəm) *n US.* the methods, conduct, attitudes, etc., associated with vigilantes, esp. militancy or bigotry.

Vigil Mass *n RC Church.* a Mass held on Saturday evening, attendance at which fulfils one's obligation to attend Mass on Sunday.

vigneron ('vi:njərɒn; *French* viɲrɔ̃) *n* a person who grows grapes for winemaking. [F, from *vigne* vine]

vignette (vɪ'njet) *n* **1** a small illustration placed at the beginning or end of a book or chapter. **2** a short graceful literary essay or sketch. **3** a photograph, drawing, etc., with edges that are shaded off. **4** any small endearing scene, view, etc. ◆ *vb* **vignettes, vignetting, vignetted.** (*tr*) **5** to finish (a photograph, etc.) with a fading border in the form of a vignette. **6** to portray in or as in a vignette. [C18: from F, lit.: little vine; with reference to the vine motif frequently used in embellishments to a text]
▸ **vi'gnettist** *n*

Vignola ★ (*Italian* viɲ'ɲɔːla) *n* **Giacomo Barozzi da** ('dʒaːkomo ba'rɔttsi da). 1507–73, Italian architect.

Vigny ★ (*French* viɲi) *n* **Alfred Victor de** (alfred viktɔr də).

1797–1863, French writer, whose work includes *Poèmes antiques et modernes* (1826), the novel *Cinq-Mars* (1826), and the play *Chatterton* (1835).

Vigo ★ ('vi:gəʊ; *Spanish* 'biɣo) *n* a port in NW Spain, in Galicia on **Vigo Bay** (an inlet of the Atlantic): site of a British and Dutch naval victory (1702) over the French and Spanish. Pop.: 275 580 (1988).

vigoro ('vɪgə,rəʊ) *n Austral.* a ball game combining elements of cricket and baseball. [C20: from VIGOUR]

vigorous ('vɪgərəs) *adj* **1** endowed with bodily or mental strength or vitality. **2** displaying, characterized by, or performed with vigour: *vigorous growth*.
▸ **'vigorously** *adv*

vigour *or US* **vigor** ('vɪgə) *n* **1** exuberant and resilient strength of body or mind. **2** substantial effective energy or force: *the vigour of the tempest*. **3** forcefulness: *I was surprised by the vigour of her complaints*. **4** the capacity for survival or strong healthy growth in a plant or animal. **5** the most active period or stage of life, manhood, etc. [C14: from OF, from L *vigor*, from *vigēre* to be lively]

Viipuri ★ ('vi:puri) *n* the Finnish name for **Vyborg.**

Vijayawada ★ (,vi:dʒaɪə'wɑ:də) *n* a town in SE India, in E central Andra Pradesh on the Krishna River: Hindu pilgrimage centre. Pop.: 701 827 (1991). Former name: **Bezwada.**

Viking ('vaɪkɪŋ) *n* (*sometimes not cap.*) **1** Also called: **Norseman, Northman.** any of the Danes, Norwegians, and Swedes who raided by sea most of N and W Europe from the 8th to the 11th centuries. **2** (*modifier*) of, relating to, or characteristic of a Viking or Vikings: *a Viking ship*. [C19: from ON *vīkingr*, prob. from *vīk* creek, sea inlet + *-ingr* (see -ING[3])]

vile (vaɪl) *adj* **1** abominably wicked; shameful or evil. **2** morally despicable; ignoble: *vile accusations*. **3** disgusting to the senses or emotions; foul: *a vile smell*. **4** tending to humiliate or degrade: *only slaves would perform such vile tasks*. **5** unpleasant or bad: *vile weather*. [C13: from OF *vil*, from L *vīlis* cheap]
▸ **'vilely** *adv* ▸ **'vileness** *n*

vilify ('vɪlɪ,faɪ) *vb* **vilifies, vilifying, vilified.** (*tr*) to revile with abusive language; malign. [C15: from LL, from L *vīlis* worthless + *facere* to make]
▸ **vilification** (,vɪlɪfɪ'keɪʃən) *n* ▸ **'vili,fier** *n*

vilipend ('vɪlɪ,pend) *vb* (*tr*) *Rare.* **1** to treat or regard with contempt. **2** to speak slanderously of. [C15: from LL, from L *vīlis* worthless + *pendere* to esteem]
▸ **'vili,pender** *n*

villa ('vɪlə) *n* **1** (in ancient Rome) a country house, usually consisting of farm buildings and residential quarters around a courtyard. **2** a large country residence. **3** *Brit.* a detached or semidetached suburban house. [C17: via It. from L]

Villa ★ ('vi:ə; *Spanish* 'biʎa) *n* **Francisco** (fran'sisko), called *Pancho Villa*, original name *Doroteo Arango*. ?1877–1923, Mexican revolutionary leader.

Villach ★ (*German* 'fɪlax) *n* a city in S central Austria, on the Drava River: nearby hot mineral springs. Pop.: 54 640 (1991).

village ('vɪlɪdʒ) *n* **1** a small group of houses in a country area, larger than a hamlet. **2** the inhabitants of such a community collectively. **3** an incorporated municipality smaller than a town in various parts of the US and Canada. **4** (*modifier*) of or characteristic of a village: *a village green*. [C15: from OF, from *ville* farm, from L: VILLA]
▸ **'villager** *n*

Villahermosa ★ (*Spanish* biʎaer'mosa) *n* a town in E Mexico, capital of Tabasco state: university (1959). Pop.: 261 231 (1990). Former name: **San Juan Bautista.**

villain ('vɪlən) *n* **1** a wicked or malevolent person. **2** (in a novel, play, etc.) the main evil character and antagonist to the hero. **3** *Often jocular.* a rogue. **4** *Obs.* an uncouth person; boor. [C14: from OF *vilein* serf, from LL *vīllānus* worker on a country estate, from L: VILLA]
▸ **'villainess** *fem n*

villainous ('vɪlənəs) *adj* **1** of, like, or appropriate to a villain. **2** very bad or disagreeable: *a villainous climate*.
▸ **'villainously** *adv* ▸ **'villainousness** *n*

villainy ('vɪlənɪ) n, pl **villainies. 1** vicious behaviour or action. **2** an evil or criminal act or deed. **3** the fact or condition of being villainous.

Villa-Lobos ★ ('vi:lɑ:'ləʊbɒs, 'vɪlə-; Portuguese 'vilja-'lɒbuʃ) n **Heitor** (ej'tor). 1887–1959, Brazilian composer.

villanelle (ˌvɪlə'nɛl) n a verse form of French origin consisting of 19 lines arranged in five tercets and a quatrain. [C16: from F, from It. villanella, from villano rustic]

-ville n and adj combining form. Sl., chiefly US. (denoting) a place, condition, or quality with a character as specified: dragsville; squaresville.

villein ('vɪlən) n (in medieval Europe) a peasant bound to his lord, to whom he paid dues and services in return for his land. [C14: from OF vilein serf; see VILLAIN]
▶ **'villeinage** n

Villeneuve ★ (French vilnœv) n **Pierre Charles Jean Baptiste Silvestre de** (pjɛr ʃarl ʒɑ̃ batist silvɛstrə də). 1763–1806, French admiral, defeated by Nelson at the Battle of Trafalgar (1805).

Villeurbanne ★ (French vijœrban) n a town in E France: an industrial suburb of E Lyons. Pop.: 119 848 (1990).

Villiers ★ ('vɪləz, 'vɪljəz) n **George.** See (Dukes of) **Buckingham.**

Villiers de l'Isle Adam ★ (French vilje də lil adɑ̃) n **August, Comte de** (ɔgyst, kɔ̃t də). 1838–89, French poet and dramatist. His works include Contes cruels (1883) and the play Axel (1885).

villiform ('vɪlɪˌfɔːm) adj having the form of a villus or a series of villi. [C19: from NL villiformis, from L villus shaggy hair + -FORM]

Villon ★ (French vijɔ̃) n **1 François** (frɑ̃swa). born 1431, French poet. His poems include Le Petit testament (?1456), Le Grand testament (1461), and many ballades and rondeaux. He disappeared after banishment in 1463. **2 Jacques** (ʒak), real name Gaston Duchamp. 1875–1963, French cubist painter.

villus ('vɪləs) n, pl **villi** ('vɪlaɪ). (usually pl) **1** Zool., anat. any of the numerous finger-like projections of the mucous membrane lining the small intestine of many vertebrates. **2** any similar membranous process. **3** Bot. any of various hairlike outgrowths. [C18: from L: shaggy hair]
▶ **villosity** (vɪ'lɒsɪtɪ) n ▶ **'villous** adj

Vilnius or **Vilnyus** ★ ('vɪlnɪʊs) n capital of Lithuania: passed to Russia in 1795; under Polish rule (1920–39); university (1578). Pop.: 575 700 (1995). Russian name: **Vilna** ('vilnə). Polish name: **Wilno.**

vim (vɪm) n Sl. exuberant vigour and energy. [C19: from L, from vīs; rel. to Gk is strength]

Viminal ★ ('vɪmɪnºl) n one of the seven hills on which ancient Rome was built. [from L Vīminālis Collis the Viminal Hill, from vīminālis of osiers, from vīmen an osier, referring to the willow grove on the hill]

vimineous (vɪ'mɪnɪəs) adj Bot. having, producing, or resembling long flexible shoots. [C17: from L vīmineus made of osiers, from vīmen flexible shoot]

vina ('vi:nə) n a stringed musical instrument, esp. of India, related to the sitar. [C18: from Hindi bīnā, from Sansk. vīnā]

vinaceous (vaɪ'neɪʃəs) adj **1** of, relating to, or containing wine. **2** having a colour suggestive of red wine. [C17: from LL vīnāceus, from L vīnum wine]

Viña del Mar ★ (Spanish 'biɲa ðel 'mar) n a city and resort in central Chile, just north of Valparaíso on the Pacific: the second largest city of Chile. Pop.: 322 220 (1995 est.).

vinaigrette (ˌvɪneɪ'grɛt) n **1** Also called: **vinaigrette sauce.** a salad dressing made from oil and vinegar with seasonings; French dressing. **2** Also called: **vinegarette.** a small decorative bottle or box with a perforated top, used for holding smelling salts, etc. [C17: from F, from vinaigre VINEGAR]

Vincennes ★ (French vɛ̃sɛn; English vɪn'sɛnz) n a suburb of E Paris: 14th-century castle. Pop.: 45 000 (latest est.).

Vincent de Paul ★ ('vɪnsənt də 'pɔːl; French vɛ̃sɑ̃ də pɔl) n **Saint.** ?1581–1660, French Roman Catholic priest, who founded two charitable orders, the Lazarists (1625) and the Sisters of Charity (1634). Feast day: Sept. 27.

Vincent's angina or **disease** n an ulcerative bacterial infection of the mouth, esp. involving the throat and tonsils. [C20: after J. H. Vincent (died 1950), F bacteriologist]

Vinci ★ ('vɪntʃɪ) n See **Leonardo da Vinci.**

vincible ('vɪnsɪbºl) adj Rare. capable of being defeated. [C16: from L vincibilis, from vincere to conquer]
▶ ˌ**vinci'bility** n

vincristine (vɪn'krɪsti:n) n an alkaloid used to treat leukaemia, derived from the tropical shrub Madagascar periwinkle. [C20: from NL Vinca genus name of the plant + L crista crest + -INE²]

vinculum ('vɪŋkjʊləm) n, pl **vincula** (-lə). **1** a horizontal line drawn above a group of mathematical terms, used as an alternative to parentheses in mathematical expressions, as in $x + \overline{y - z}$, which is equivalent to $x + (y - z)$. **2** Anat. any bandlike structure, esp. one uniting two or more parts. [C17: from L: bond, from vincīre to bind]

vindaloo (ˌvɪndə'lu:) n, pl **vindaloos.** a type of very hot Indian curry. [C20: ? from Port. vin d'alho wine and garlic sauce]

vin de pays French. (vɛ̃ də pei) n, pl **vins de pays** (vɛ̃ də pei). the third highest French wine classification: indicates that the wine meets certain requirements concerning area of production, strength, etc. Also called: **vin du pays.** Abbrev.: **VDP.** Cf. **AOC, VDQS.** [lit.: local wine]

Vindhya Pradesh ★ ('vɪndjə) n a former state of central India: merged with the reorganized Madhya Pradesh in 1956.

Vindhya Range or **Mountains** ★ n a mountain range in central India: separates the Ganges basin from the Deccan, marking the limits of northern and peninsular India. Greatest height: 1113 m (3651 ft).

vindicable ('vɪndɪkəbºl) adj capable of being vindicated; justifiable.
▶ ˌ**vindica'bility** n

vindicate ('vɪndɪˌkeɪt) vb **vindicates, vindicating, vindicated.** (tr) **1** to clear from guilt, blame, etc., as by evidence or argument. **2** to provide justification for: his promotion vindicated his unconventional attitude. **3** to uphold or defend (a cause, etc.): to vindicate a claim. [C17: from L vindicāre, from vindex claimant]
▶ **'vindiˌcator** n ▶ **'vindiˌcatory** adj

vindication (ˌvɪndɪ'keɪʃən) n **1** the act of vindicating or the condition of being vindicated. **2** a fact, evidence, etc., that serves to vindicate a claim.

vindictive (vɪn'dɪktɪv) adj **1** disposed to seek vengeance. **2** characterized by spite or rancour. **3** English law. (of damages) in excess of the compensation due to the plaintiff and imposed in punishment of the defendant. [C17: from L vindicta revenge, from vindicāre to VINDICATE]
▶ **vin'dictively** adv ▶ **vin'dictiveness** n

vin du pays French. (vɛ̃ du pei) n, pl **vins du pays.** a variant of **vin de pays.**

vine (vaɪn) n **1** any of various plants, esp. the grapevine, having long flexible stems that creep along the ground or climb by clinging to a support by means of tendrils, leafstalks, etc. **2** the stem of such a plant. [C13: from OF, from L vīnea vineyard, from vīnum wine]
▶ **'viny** adj

Vine ★ (vaɪn) n **Barbara.** See (Ruth) **Rendell.**

vinedresser ('vaɪnˌdrɛsə) n a person who prunes, tends, or cultivates grapevines.

vinegar ('vɪnɪgə) n **1** a sour-tasting liquid consisting of impure dilute acetic acid, made by fermentation of beer, wine, or cider. It is used as a condiment or preservative. **2** sourness or peevishness of temper, speech, etc. [C13: from OF, from vin WINE + aigre sour, from L acer]
▶ **'vinegarish** adj ▶ **'vinegary** adj

Vineland ★ ('vaɪnlənd) n a variant spelling of **Vinland.**

vinery ('vaɪnərɪ) n, pl **vineries. 1** a hothouse for growing grapes. **2** another name for a **vineyard. 3** vines collectively.

vineyard ('vɪnjəd) n a plantation of grapevines, esp. where wine grapes are produced. [OE wīngeard; see VINE, YARD²]

★ people and places

vingt-et-un *French.* (vɛ̃teœ̃) *n* another name for **pontoon**[2]. [lit.: twenty-one]

vinho verde (ˌviːnjəʊ ˈvɜːdɪ) *n* any of a variety of light sharp-tasting wines made from early-picked grapes of NW Portugal. [Port., lit.: green (or young) wine]

vini- *or before a vowel* **vin-** *combining form.* indicating wine: *viniculture.* [from L *vīnum*]

viniculture (ˈvɪnɪˌkʌltʃə) *n* the process or business of growing grapes and making wine.
▶ ˌvini'cultural *adj* ▶ ˌvini'culturist *n*

viniferous (vɪˈnɪfərəs) *adj* wine-producing.

Vinland (ˈvɪnlənd) *or* **Vineland** ★ *n* the stretch of the E coast of North America visited by Leif Ericson and other Vikings from about 1000.

Vinnitsa ★ (*Russian* ˈvinnitsə) *n* a city in the central Ukraine: passed from Polish to Russian rule in 1793. Pop.: 388 000 (1996 est.).

vino (ˈviːnəʊ) *n, pl* **vinos.** an informal word for **wine.** [jocular use of It. or Sp. *vino*]

vin ordinaire *French.* (vɛ̃ ɔrdinɛr) *n, pl* **vins ordinaires** (vɛ̃z ɔrdinɛr). cheap table wine, esp. French.

vinosity (vɪˈnɒsɪtɪ) *n* the distinctive and essential quality and flavour of wine. [C17: from LL *vīnōsitas*, from L *vīnōsus* VINOUS]

vinous (ˈvaɪnəs) *adj* **1** of or characteristic of wine. **2** indulging in or indicative of indulgence in wine. [C17: from L, from *vīnum* WINE]

vintage (ˈvɪntɪdʒ) *n* **1** the wine obtained from a harvest of grapes, esp. in an outstandingly good year. **2** the harvest from which such a wine is obtained. **3a** the harvesting of wine grapes. **3b** the season of harvesting these grapes or for making wine. **4** a time of origin: *a car of Edwardian vintage.* **5** *Inf.* a group of people or objects of the same period: *a fashion of last season's vintage.* ◆ *adj* **6** (of wine) of an outstandingly good year. **7** representative of the best and most typical: *vintage Shakespeare.* **8** of lasting interest and importance; classic: *vintage films.* **9** old-fashioned; dated. [C15: from OF *vendage* (infl. by *vintener* VINTNER), from L *vindēmia*, from *vīnum* WINE, grape + *dēmere* to take away]

vintage car *n Chiefly Brit.* an old car, esp. one constructed between 1919 and 1930. Cf. **classic car, veteran car.**

vintager (ˈvɪntɪdʒə) *n* a grape harvester.

vintner (ˈvɪntnə) *n* a wine merchant. [C15: from OF *vinetier*, from Med. L, from L *vīnētum* vineyard]

vinyl (ˈvaɪnɪl) *n* **1** (*modifier*) of or containing the monovalent group of atoms $CH_2:CH-$: *vinyl chloride.* **2** (*modifier*) of or made of a vinyl resin: *a vinyl raincoat.* **3** any vinyl resin or plastic, esp. PVC. **4** (collectively) conventional records made of vinyl as opposed to compact discs. [C19: from VINI- + -YL]

vinyl acetate *n* a colourless volatile liquid unsaturated ester that polymerizes readily in light and is used for making polyvinyl acetate.

vinyl chloride *n* a colourless flammable gaseous unsaturated compound made by the chlorination of ethylene and used as a refrigerant and in the manufacture of PVC.

vinyl resin *or* **polymer** *n* any one of a class of thermoplastic materials, esp. PVC and polyvinyl acetate, made by polymerizing vinyl compounds.

viol (ˈvaɪəl) *n* any of a family of stringed musical instruments that preceded the violin family, consisting of a fretted fingerboard, a body like that of a violin but having a flat back and six strings, played with a curved bow. [C15: from OF *viole*, from OProvençal *viola*; see VIOLA[1]]

viola[1] (vɪˈəʊlə) *n* **1** a bowed stringed instrument, the alto of the violin family; held beneath the chin when played. **2** any of various instruments of the viol family, such as the viola da gamba. [C18: from It., prob. from O Provençal]

viola[2] (ˈvaɪələ, vaɪˈəʊ-) *n* any of various temperate perennial herbaceous plants, the flowers of which have showy irregular petals, white, yellow, blue, or mauve in colour. [C15: from L: violet]

viola clef (vɪˈəʊlə) *n* another term for **alto clef.**

viola da gamba (vɪˈəʊlə də ˈgæmbə) *n* the second largest and lowest member of the viol family. [C18: from It., lit.: viol for the leg]

viola d'amore (vɪˈəʊlə dæˈmɔːrɪ) *n* an instrument of the viol family having no frets, seven strings, and a set of sympathetic strings. [C18: from It., lit.: viol of love]

violate (ˈvaɪəˌleɪt) *vb* **violates, violating, violated.** (*tr*) **1** to break, disregard, or infringe (a law, agreement, etc.). **2** to rape or otherwise sexually assault. **3** to disturb rudely or improperly. **4** to treat irreverently or disrespectfully: *he violated a sanctuary.* [C15: from L *violāre* to do violence to, from *vīs* strength]
▶ 'violable *adj* ▶ ˌvio'lation *n* ▶ 'vioˌlator *or* 'vioˌlater *n*

violence (ˈvaɪələns) *n* **1** the exercise or an instance of physical force, usually effecting or intended to effect injuries, destruction, etc. **2** powerful, untamed, or devastating force: *the violence of the sea.* **3** great strength of feeling, as in language, etc. **4** an unjust, unwarranted, or unlawful display of force. **5** do violence to. **5a** to inflict harm upon: *they did violence to the prisoners.* **5b** to distort the sense or intention of: *the reporters did violence to my speech.* [C13: via OF from L *violentia* impetuosity, from *violentus* VIOLENT]

violent (ˈvaɪələnt) *adj* **1** marked or caused by great physical force or violence: *a violent stab.* **2** (of a person) tending to the use of violence, esp. in order to injure or intimidate others. **3** marked by intensity of any kind: *a violent clash of colours.* **4** characterized by an undue use of force. **5** caused by or displaying strong or undue mental or emotional force. [C14: from L *violentus*, prob. from *vīs* strength]
▶ 'violently *adv*

violent storm *n* a wind of force 11 on the Beaufort scale, reaching speeds of 64 to 72 mph.

violet (ˈvaɪəlɪt) *n* **1** any of various temperate perennial herbaceous plants of the genus *Viola*, such as the **sweet** (or **garden**) **violet**, having mauve or bluish flowers with irregular showy petals. **2** any other plant of the genus *Viola*, such as the wild pansy. **3** any of various similar but unrelated plants, such as the African violet. **4a** any of a group of colours that have a purplish-blue hue. They lie at one end of the visible spectrum. **4b** (*as adj*): *a violet dress.* **5** a dye or pigment of or producing these colours. **6** violet clothing: *dressed in violet.* [C14: from OF *violete* a little violet, from L *viola* violet]

violin (ˌvaɪəˈlɪn) *n* a bowed stringed instrument, the highest member of the violin family, consisting of a fingerboard, a hollow wooden body with waisted sides, and a sounding board connected to the back by means of a soundpost that also supports the bridge. It has two f-shaped sound holes cut in the belly. [C16: from It. *violino* a little viola, from VIOLA[1]]

violinist (ˌvaɪəˈlɪnɪst) *n* a person who plays the violin.

violist[1] (vɪˈəʊlɪst) *n* a person who plays the viola.

violist[2] (ˈvaɪəlɪst) *n* a person who plays the viol.

Viollet-le-Duc ★ (*French* vjɔlɛlədyk) *n* Eugène Emmanuel (øʒɛn ɛmanɥɛl). 1814–79, French architect and leader of the Gothic Revival in France.

violoncello (ˌvaɪələnˈtʃɛləʊ) *n, pl* **violoncellos.** the full name for **cello.** [C18: from It., from *violone* large viol + *-cello*, dim. suffix]
▶ ˌviolon'cellist *n*

VIP *abbrev. for* very important person.

viper (ˈvaɪpə) *n* **1** any of a family of venomous Old World snakes having hollow fangs in the upper jaw that are used to inject venom. **2** any of various other snakes, such as the horned viper. **3** a malicious or treacherous person. [C16: from L *vīpera*, ?from *vīvus* living + *parere* to bear, referring to a tradition that the viper was viviparous]

viperous (ˈvaɪpərəs) *or* **viperish** *adj* **1** Also: **viperine** (ˈvaɪpəˌraɪn) of or resembling a viper. **2** malicious.

viper's bugloss *n* **1** Also called (US): **blueweed.** a Eurasian weed, having blue flowers and pink buds. **2** a related plant that has purple flowers and is naturalized in Australia and New Zealand. Also called: (Austral.) **Paterson's curse, Salvation Jane.**

virago (vɪˈrɑːgəʊ) n, pl **viragoes** or **viragos. 1** a loud, violent, and ill-tempered woman. **2** Arch. a strong or warlike woman. [OE, from L: a manlike maiden, from vir a man]
▸ viˈrago-ˌlike adj

viral (ˈvaɪrəl) adj of or caused by a virus.

Virchow ★ (German ˈfɪrço) n Rudolf Ludwig Karl (ˈruːdɔlf ˈluːtvɪç karl). 1821–1902, German pathologist, considered the founder of modern (cellular) pathology.

virelay (ˈvɪrɪˌleɪ) n an old French verse form, rarely used in English, having stanzas of short lines with two rhymes throughout and two opening lines recurring at intervals. [C14: from OF virelai, prob. from vireli (associated with lai LAY⁴), word used as a refrain]

Viren ★ (ˈvɪərən) n Lasse (ˈlæsɪ). born 1949, Finnish distance runner: winner of the 5000 m and the 10 000 m in the 1972 and 1976 Olympic Games.

vireo (ˈvɪrɪəʊ) n, pl **vireos.** any of a family of insectivorous American songbirds having an olive-grey back with pale underparts. [C19: from L: a bird, prob. a greenfinch; cf. virēre to be green]

vires (ˈvaɪriːz) n the plural of **vis.**

virescent (vɪˈrɛsˀnt) adj greenish or becoming green. [C19: from L virescere, from virēre to be green]
▸ viˈrescence n

virgate¹ (ˈvɜːgɪt, -geɪt) adj long, straight, and thin; rod-shaped: virgate stems. [C19: from L virgātus made of twigs, from virga a rod]

virgate² (ˈvɜːgɪt, -geɪt) n Brit. an obsolete measure of land area, usually taken as 30 acres. [C17: from Med. L virgāta (terrae) a rod's measurement (of land), from L virga rod; translation of OE gierd landes a yard of land]

Virgil or **Vergil** ★ (ˈvɜːdʒɪl) n Latin name Publius Vergilius Maro. 70–19 B.C., Roman poet, whose works include the Eclogues (42–37), the Georgics (37–30), and his masterpiece the Aeneid (30–19).
▸ Virˈgilian or Verˈgilian adj

virgin (ˈvɜːdʒɪn) n **1** a person, esp. a woman, who has never had sexual intercourse. **2** an unmarried woman who has taken a religious vow of chastity. **3** any female animal that has never mated. **4** a female insect that produces offspring by parthenogenesis. ◆ adj (usually prenominal) **5** of, suitable for, or characteristic of a virgin or virgins. **6** pure and natural, uncorrupted or untouched: virgin purity. **7** not yet cultivated, explored, exploited, etc., by man: virgin territories. **8** being the first or happening for the first time. **9** (of a metal) made from an ore rather than from scrap. **10** occurring naturally in a pure and uncombined form: virgin silver. [C13: from OF virgine, from L virgō virgin]

Virgin¹ ★ (ˈvɜːdʒɪn) n **1** the. See **Virgin Mary. 2** a statue or other artistic representation of the Virgin Mary.

Virgin² (ˈvɜːdʒɪn) n the. the constellation Virgo, the sixth sign of the zodiac.

virginal¹ (ˈvɜːdʒɪnˀl) adj **1** of, characterized by, or maintaining a state of virginity; chaste. **2** extremely pure or fresh. [C15: from L virgīnālis maidenly, from virgō virgin]
▸ ˈvirginally adv

virginal² (ˈvɜːdʒɪnˀl) n (often pl) a smaller version of the harpsichord, but oblong in shape, having one manual and no pedals. [C16: prob. from L virgīnālis VIRGINAL¹, ? because it was played largely by young ladies]
▸ ˈvirginalist n

Virgin Birth n the doctrine that Jesus Christ was conceived by the intervention of the Holy Spirit so that Mary remained a virgin.

virgin forest n a forest in its natural state, before it has been explored or exploited by man.

Virginia ★ (vəˈdʒɪnɪə) n a state of the eastern US, on the Atlantic: site of the first permanent English settlement in North America; consists of a low-lying deeply indented coast rising inland to the Piedmont plateau and the Blue Ridge Mountains. Capital: Richmond. Pop.: 6 675 451 (1996 est.). Area: 103 030 sq. km (39 780 sq. miles). Abbrevs.: **Va.** or (with zip code) **VA**
▸ Virˈginian adj, n

Virginia Beach ★ n a city and resort in SE Virginia, on the Atlantic. Pop.: 430 295 (1994 est.).

Virginia creeper n a woody vine of North America, having tendrils with adhesive tips, bluish-black berry-like fruits, and compound leaves that turn red in autumn: widely planted for ornament.

Virginia stock n a Mediterranean plant cultivated for its white and pink flowers.

Virgin Islands ★ pl n a group of about 100 small islands (14 inhabited) in the Caribbean, east of Puerto Rico: discovered by Columbus (1493); consists of the British Virgin Islands in the east and the Virgin Islands of the United States in the west and south. Pop.: 17 000 (1993 est.). Area: 497 sq. km (192 sq. miles).

Virgin Islands of the United States ★ pl n a territory of the US in the Caribbean, consisting of islands west and south of the British Virgin Islands: purchased from Denmark in 1917 for their strategic importance. Capital: Charlotte Amalie. Pop.: 101 809 (1990). Area: 344 sq. km (133 sq. miles). Former name: **Danish West Indies.**

virginity (vəˈdʒɪnɪtɪ) n **1** the condition or fact of being a virgin. **2** the condition of being untouched, unused, etc.

virginium (vəˈdʒɪnɪəm) n Chem. a former name for **francium.**

Virgin Mary ★ n Mary, the mother of Christ. Also called: the **Virgin.**

virgin's-bower n any of several American varieties of clematis.

virgin soil n **1** soil that has not been cultivated before. **2** a person or thing that is as yet undeveloped.

virgin wool n wool that is being processed or woven for the first time.

Virgo (ˈvɜːgəʊ) n, Latin genitive **Virginis** (ˈvɜːdʒɪnɪs). **1** Astron. a large constellation on the celestial equator. **2** Astrol. Also called: the **Virgin.** the sixth sign of the zodiac. The sun is in this sign between about Aug. 23 and Sept. 22. [C14: from L]

virgo intacta (ˈvɜːgəʊ ɪnˈtæktə) n a girl or woman whose hymen is unbroken. [L, lit.: untouched virgin]

virgule (ˈvɜːgjuːl) n Printing. another name for **solidus.** [C19: from F: comma, from L virgula dim. of virga rod]

viridescent (ˌvɪrɪˈdɛsˀnt) adj greenish or tending to become green. [C19: from LL viridescere, from L viridis green]
▸ ˌviriˈdescence n

viridian (vɪˈrɪdɪən) n a green pigment comprising a hydrated form of chromic oxide. [C19: from L viridis green]

viridity (vɪˈrɪdɪtɪ) n **1** the quality or state of being green. **2** innocence, youth, or freshness. [C15: from L viridītās, from viridis green]

virile (ˈvɪraɪl) adj **1** of or having the characteristics of an adult male. **2** (of a male) possessing high sexual drive and capacity for sexual intercourse. **3** of or capable of copulation or procreation. **4** strong, forceful, or vigorous. [C15: from L virīlis manly, from vir a man; rel. to OE wer man]
▸ virility (vɪˈrɪlɪtɪ) n

virilism (ˈvɪrɪˌlɪzəm) n Med. the abnormal development in a woman of male secondary sex characteristics.

virology (vaɪˈrɒlədʒɪ) n the branch of medicine concerned with the study of viruses.
▸ virological (ˌvaɪrəˈlɒdʒɪkˀl) adj

virtu or **vertu** (vɜːˈtuː) n **1** a taste or love for curios or works of fine art. **2** such objects collectively. **3** the quality of being appealing to a connoisseur (esp. in **articles of virtu; objects of virtu**). [C18: from It. virtù; see VIRTUE]

virtual (ˈvɜːtʃʊəl) adj **1** having the essence or effect but not the appearance or form of: a virtual revolution. **2** Physics. being or involving a virtual image: a virtual focus. **3** Computing. of or relating to virtual storage: virtual memory. **4** of or relating to a computer technique by which a person, wearing a headset or mask, has the experience of being in an environment created by the computer, and of interacting with and causing changes within it. [C14: from Med. L virtuālis effective, from L virtūs VIRTUE]
▸ ˌvirtuˈality n

★ people and places

virtual image *n* an optical image formed by the apparent divergence of rays from a point, rather than their actual divergence from a point.

virtually ('vɜːtʃʊəlɪ) *adv* in effect though not in fact; practically; nearly.

virtual reality *n* a computer-generated environment that, to the person experiencing it, closely resembles reality. Abbrev.: **VR**. See also **virtual** (sense 4).

virtual storage *or* **memory** *n* a computer system in which the size of the memory is increased by transferring sections of a program from a large capacity backing store, such as a disk, into the smaller core memory as they are required.

virtue ('vɜːtjuː) *n* **1** the quality or practice of moral excellence or righteousness. **2** a particular moral excellence: *the virtue of tolerance*. **3** any of the cardinal virtues (prudence, justice, fortitude, and temperance) or theological virtues (faith, hope, and charity). **4** any admirable quality or trait. **5** chastity, esp. in women. **6** *Arch.* an effective, active, or inherent power. **7** **by** *or* **in virtue of.** by reason of. **8** **make a virtue of necessity.** to acquiesce in doing something unpleasant with a show of grace because one must do it in any case. [C13 *vertu*, from OF, from L *virtūs* manliness, courage]

virtuoso (ˌvɜːtjʊˈəʊzəʊ, -səʊ) *n, pl* **virtuosos** *or* **virtuosi** (-siː). **1** a consummate master of musical technique and artistry. **2** a person who has a masterly or dazzling skill or technique in any field of activity. **3** a connoisseur or collector of art objects. **4** (*modifier*) showing masterly skill or brilliance: *a virtuoso performance*. [C17: from It.: skilled, from LL *virtuōsus* good, virtuous]
  ▸ **virtuosic** (ˌvɜːtjʊˈɒsɪk) *adj* ▸ ˌvirtuˈosity *n*

virtuous ('vɜːtjʊəs) *adj* **1** characterized by or possessing virtue or moral excellence. **2** (of women) chaste.
  ▸ 'virtuously *adv*

virulent ('vɪrʊlənt) *adj* **1a** (of a microorganism) extremely infective. **1b** (of a disease) having a violent effect. **2** extremely poisonous, injurious, etc. **3** extremely bitter, hostile, etc. [C14: from L *vīrulentus* full of poison, from *vīrus* poison]
  ▸ 'virulence *or* 'virulency *n* ▸ 'virulently *adv*

virus ('vaɪrəs) *n, pl* **viruses**. **1** any of a group of submicroscopic entities consisting of a single nucleic acid surrounded by a protein coat and capable of replication only within the cells of animals and plants. **2** *Inf.* a disease caused by a virus. **3** any corrupting or infecting influence. **4** *Computing.* an unauthorized program that inserts itself into a computer system, and then propagates itself to other computers via networks or disks; when activated it interferes with the operation of the computer. [C16: from L: slime, poisonous liquid]

vis *Latin.* (vɪs) *n, pl* **vires.** power, force, or strength.

visa ('viːzə) *n, pl* **visas. 1** an endorsement in a passport or similar document, signifying that the document is in order and permitting its bearer to travel into or through the country of the government issuing it. ♦ *vb* **visas, visaing, visaed. 2** (*tr*) to enter a visa into (a passport). [C19: via F from L: things seen, from *vīsus*, p.p. of *vidēre* to see]

visage ('vɪzɪdʒ) *n Chiefly literary.* **1** face or countenance. **2** appearance. [C13: from OF: aspect, from *vis* face, from L *vīsus* appearance]

visaged *adj* (*in combination*) having a visage as specified: *flat-visaged.*

Visakhapatnam ★ (vɪˌsɑːkəˈpʌtnəm) *n* a variant spelling of **Vishakhapatnam.**

vis-à-vis (ˌviːzɑːˈviː) *prep* **1** in relation to. **2** face to face with. ♦ *adv, adj* **3** face to face; opposite. ♦ *n, pl* **vis-à-vis. 4** a person or thing that is situated opposite to another. **5** a person who corresponds to another in office, capacity, etc. [C18: F, from *vis* face]

Visayan Islands ★ *pl n* a group of seven large and several hundred small islands in the central Philippines. Chief islands: Negros and Panay. Pop.: 13 041 000 (1990). Area: about 61 000 sq. km (23 535 sq. miles). Spanish name: **Bisayas.**

Visby ★ (*Swedish* 'viːsbyː) *n* a port in SE Sweden, on NW Gotland Island in the Baltic: an early member of the Hanseatic League and major N European commercial centre in the Middle Ages. Pop.: 57 110 (1990).

Visc. *abbrev. for* Viscount *or* Viscountess.

viscacha (vɪsˈkætʃə) *n* a gregarious burrowing rodent of southern South America, similar to but larger than the chinchillas. [C17: from Sp., from Quechuan *wiskácha*]

viscera ('vɪsərə) *pl n, sing* **viscus. 1** *Anat.* the large internal organs of the body collectively, esp. those in the abdominal cavity. **2** (less formally) the intestines; guts. [C17: from L: entrails, pl of *viscus* internal organ]

visceral ('vɪsərəl) *adj* **1** of or affecting the viscera. **2** characterized by instinct rather than intellect.
  ▸ 'viscerally *adv*

viscid ('vɪsɪd) *adj* **1** cohesive and sticky. **2** (esp. of a leaf) covered with a sticky substance. [C17: from LL *viscidus* sticky, from L *viscum* mistletoe, birdlime]
  ▸ **vis'cidity** *n*

Visconti ★ (*Italian* vis'konti) *n* **1** the ruling family of Milan from 1277 to 1447. **2 Luchino** (lu'kiːno), real name *Luchino Visconti de Modrone.* 1906–76, Italian film director; films include *Ossessione* (1942), *The Leopard* (1963), and *Death in Venice* (1970).

viscose ('vɪskəʊs) *n* **1a** a viscous orange-brown solution obtained by dissolving cellulose in sodium hydroxide and carbon disulphide. It can be converted back to cellulose by an acid, as in the manufacture of rayon and Cellophane. **1b** (*as modifier*): *viscose rayon.* **2** rayon made from this material. [C19: from LL *viscōsus* full of birdlime, sticky, from *viscum* birdlime]

viscosity (vɪsˈkɒsɪtɪ) *n, pl* **viscosities. 1** the state or property of being viscous. **2** *Physics.* **2a** the extent to which a fluid resists a tendency to flow. **2b** Also called: **absolute viscosity.** a measure of this resistance, measured in newton seconds per metre squared. Symbol: η

viscount ('vaɪkaʊnt) *n* **1** (in the British Isles) a nobleman ranking below an earl and above a baron. **2** (in various countries) a son or younger brother of a count. **3** (in medieval Europe) the deputy of a count. [C14: from OF, from Med. L, from LL *vice-* VICE[3] + *comes* COUNT[2]]
  ▸ 'viscountcy *or* 'viscounty *n*

viscountess ('vaɪkaʊntɪs) *n* **1** the wife or widow of a viscount. **2** a woman who holds the rank of viscount in her own right.

viscous ('vɪskəs) *adj* **1** (of liquids) thick and sticky. **2** having viscosity. [C14: from LL *viscōsus;* see VISCOSE]
  ▸ 'viscously *adv*

viscus ('vɪskəs) *n* the singular of **viscera.**

vise (vaɪs) *n, vb* **vises, vising, vised.** *US.* a variant spelling of **vice[2].**

Viseu ★ (*Portuguese* vi'zeu) *n* a city in N central Portugal: 12th-century cathedral. Pop.: 20 590 (1991).

Vishakhapatnam (vɪˌʃɑːkəˈpʌtnəm), **Visakhapatnam,** *or* **Vizagapatam** ★ *n* a port in E India, in NE Andhra Pradesh on the Bay of Bengal: shipbuilding and oil-refining industries. Pop.: 752 037 (1991).

Vishinsky ★ (*Russian* vi'ʃinskij) *n* a variant spelling of (Andrei Yanuaryevich) **Vyshinsky.**

Vishnu ★ ('vɪʃnuː) *n Hinduism.* the Pervader or Sustainer, originally a solar deity occupying a secondary place in the Hindu pantheon, later the saviour appearing in many incarnations. [C17: from Sansk. *Viṣṇu,* lit.: the one who works everywhere]
  ▸ 'Vishnuism *n*

visibility (ˌvɪzɪ'bɪlɪtɪ) *n* **1** the condition or fact of being visible. **2** clarity of vision or relative possibility of seeing. **3** the range of vision: *visibility is 500 yards.*

visible ('vɪzɪb°l) *adj* **1** capable of being perceived by the eye. **2** capable of being perceived by the mind: *no visible dangers.* **3** available: *the visible resources.* **4** of or relating to the balance of trade: *visible transactions.* [C14: from L *vīsibilis,* from *vidēre* to see]
  ▸ 'visibly *adv*

visible balance *n* another name for **balance of trade.**

visible radiation *n* electromagnetic radiation that causes the sensation of sight; light.

vision ('vɪʒən) *n* **1** the act, faculty, or manner of perceiving with the eye; sight. **2a** the image on a television screen. **2b** (*as modifier*): *vision control.* **3** the ability or an instance of great perception, esp. of future developments: *a man of vision.* **4** mystical or religious experience of seeing some supernatural event, person, etc.: *the vision of St John of the Cross.* **5** that which is seen, esp. in such a mystical experience. **6** (*sometimes pl*) a vivid mental image produced by the imagination: *he had visions of becoming famous.* **7** a person or thing of extraordinary beauty. [C13: from L *vīsiō* sight, from *vidēre* to see]

visionary ('vɪʒənərɪ) *adj* **1** marked by vision or foresight: *a visionary leader.* **2** incapable of being realized or effected. **3** (of people) characterized by idealistic or radical ideas, esp. impractical ones. **4** given to having visions. **5** of, of the nature of, or seen in visions. ♦ *n, pl* **visionaries.** **6** a visionary person.

vision mixer *n Television.* **1** the person who selects and manipulates the television signals from cameras, film, etc., to make the composite programme. **2** the equipment used for vision mixing.

visit ('vɪzɪt) *vb* **visits, visiting, visited. 1** to go or come to see (a person, place, etc.). **2** to stay with (someone) as a guest. **3** to go or come to (an institution, place, etc.) for the purpose of inspecting or examining. **4** (*tr*) (of a disease, disaster, etc.) to afflict. **5** (*tr*; foll. by *upon* or *on*) to inflict (punishment, etc.). **6** (often foll. by *with*) *US & Canad. inf.* to chat (with someone). ♦ *n* **7** the act or an instance of visiting. **8** a stay as a guest. **9** a professional or official call. **10** a formal call for the purpose of inspection or examination. **11** *International law.* the right of an officer of a belligerent state to stop and search neutral ships in war to verify their nationality and ascertain whether they carry contraband. **12** *US & Canad. inf.* a chat. [C13: from L *vīsitāre* to go to see, from *vīsere* to examine, from *vidēre* to see]
▶ 'visitable *adj*

visitant ('vɪzɪtənt) *n* **1** a ghost; apparition. **2** a visitor or guest, usually from far away. **3** Also called: **visitor.** a migratory bird that is present in a particular region only at certain times: *a summer visitant.* [C16: from L *vīsitāns*, from *vīsitāre*; see VISIT]

visitation (,vɪzɪ'teɪʃən) *n* **1** an official call or visit for the purpose of inspecting or examining an institution. **2** a visiting of punishment or reward from heaven. **3** any disaster or catastrophe: *a visitation of the plague.* **4** an appearance or arrival of a supernatural being. **5** *Inf.* an unduly prolonged social call.

Visitation (,vɪzɪ'teɪʃən) *n* **1a** the visit made by the Virgin Mary to her cousin Elizabeth (Luke 1:39–56). **1b** the Church festival commemorating this, held on July 2. **2** a religious order of nuns, the **Order of the Visitation,** founded in 1610 and dedicated to contemplation.

visiting card *n Brit.* a small card bearing the name and usually the address of a person, esp. for giving to business or social acquaintances.

visiting fireman *n US inf.* a visitor whose presence is noticed because he is important, impressive, etc.

visitor ('vɪzɪtə) *n* **1** a person who pays a visit. **2** another name for **visitant** (sense 3).

visitor centre *n* another term for **interpretive centre.**

visitor's passport *n* (in Britain) a passport, valid for one year, that can be purchased from post offices. It grants entry to certain countries, usually for a restricted period of time. Also called: **British Visitor's Passport.**

Vislinsky Zaliv ★ (*Russian* vis'linski 'za:lif) *n* a transliteration of the Russian name for **Vistula** (sense 2).

visor *or* **vizor** ('vaɪzə) *n* **1** a transparent flap on a helmet that can be pulled down to protect the face. **2** a piece of armour fixed or hinged to the helmet to protect the face. **3** another name for **peak** (on a cap). **4** a small movable screen used as protection against glare from the sun, esp. one attached above the windscreen of a motor vehicle. **5** *Arch. or literary.* a mask or any other means of disguise. [C14: from Anglo-F *viser,* from OF *visiere,* from *vis* face; see VISAGE]
▶ 'visored *or* 'vizored *adj*

vista ('vɪstə) *n* **1** a view, esp. through a long narrow avenue of trees, buildings, etc., or such a passage or avenue

itself. **2** a comprehensive mental view of a distant time or a lengthy series of events. [C17: from It., from *vedere* to see, from L *vidēre*]
▶ 'vistaed *adj*

Vistula ★ ('vɪstjʊlə) *n* **1** a river in central and N Poland, rising in the Carpathian Mountains and flowing generally north and northwest past Warsaw and Torun, then northeast to enter the Baltic via an extensive delta region. Length: 1090 km (677 miles). Polish name: **Wisla.** German name: **Weichsel. 2 Lagoon.** a shallow lagoon on the SW coast of the Baltic Sea, between Danzig and Kaliningrad, crossed by the border between Poland and Russia. German name: **Frisches Haff.** Polish name: **Wislany Zalew.** Russian name: **Vislinsky Zaliv.**

visual ('vɪʒʊəl, -zjʊ-) *adj* **1** of, done by, or used in seeing: *visual powers.* **2** another word for **optical. 3** capable of being seen; visible. **4** of, occurring as, or induced by a mental image. ♦ *n* **5** a sketch to show the proposed layout of an advertisement, as in a newspaper. **6** (*often pl*) a photograph, film, or other display material. [C15: from LL *visuālis,* from L *vīsus* sight, from *vidēre* to see]
▶ 'visually *adv*

visual aids *pl n* devices, such as films, videos, slides, models, and blackboards, that display in visual form material to be understood or remembered.

visual display unit *n Computing.* a device that displays characters or graphics representing data in a computer memory. It usually has a keyboard for the input of information or inquiries. Abbrev.: **VDU.**

visual field *n* the whole extent of the image falling on the retina when the eye is fixed on a given point.

visualize *or* **visualise** ('vɪʒʊə,laɪz) *vb* **visualizes, visualizing, visualized** *or* **visualises, visualising, visualised.** to form a mental image of (something incapable of being viewed or not at that moment visible).
▶ ,visuali'zation *or* ,visuali'sation *n*

visual magnitude *n Astron.* the magnitude of a star as determined by visual observation.

visual purple *n* another name for **rhodopsin.**

visual violet *n* another name for **iodopsin.**

visual yellow *n* another name for **retinene.**

vital ('vaɪt°l) *adj* **1** essential to maintain life: *the lungs perform a vital function.* **2** forceful, energetic, or lively: *a vital person.* **3** of, having, or displaying life: *a vital organism.* **4** indispensable or essential: *books vital to this study.* **5** of great importance: *a vital game.* ♦ *n* **6** (*pl*) the bodily organs, such as the brain, liver, heart, lungs, etc., that are necessary to maintain life. **7** (*pl*) the essential elements of anything. [C14: via OF from L *vītālis,* from *vīta* life]
▶ 'vitally *adv*

vital capacity *n Physiol.* the volume of air that can be exhaled from the lungs after the deepest possible breath has been taken.

vital force *n* (esp. in early biological theory) a hypothetical force, independent of physical and chemical forces, regarded as being the causative factor of the evolution of living organisms.

vitalism ('vaɪtə,lɪzəm) *n* the philosophical doctrine that the phenomena of life cannot be explained in purely mechanical terms because there is something immaterial which distinguishes living from inanimate matter.
▶ 'vitalist *n, adj* ▶ ,vital'istic *adj*

vitality (vaɪ'tælɪtɪ) *n, pl* **vitalities. 1** physical or mental vigour, energy, etc. **2** the power or ability to continue in existence, live, or grow: *the vitality of a movement.*

vitalize *or* **vitalise** ('vaɪtə,laɪz) *vb* **vitalizes, vitalizing, vitalized** *or* **vitalises, vitalising, vitalised.** (*tr*) to make vital, living, or alive.
▶ ,vitali'zation *or* ,vitali'sation *n*

vital staining *n* the technique of treating living cells and tissues with dyes that do not immediately kill them, facilitating observation under a microscope.

vital statistics *pl n* **1** quantitative data concerning human life or the conditions affecting it, such as the death rate. **2** *Inf.* the measurements of a woman's bust, waist, and hips.

vitamin ('vɪtəmɪn, 'vaɪ-) *n* any of a group of substances

that are essential, in small quantities, for the normal functioning of metabolism in the body. They cannot usually be synthesized in the body but they occur naturally in certain foods. [C20 *vit-* from L *vīta* life + *-amin* from AMINE; so named by Casimir FUNK, who believed the substances to be amines]
▸ ˌvitaˈminic *adj*

vitamin A *n* **1** Also called: **vitamin A₁, retinol.** a fat-soluble yellow unsaturated alcohol occurring in green and yellow vegetables, butter, egg yolk, and fish-liver oil. It is essential for the prevention of night blindness and the protection of epithelial tissue. **2** Also called: **vitamin A₂.** a vitamin that occurs in the tissues of freshwater fish and has a function similar to that of vitamin A₁.

vitamin B *n, pl* **B vitamins.** any of the vitamins in the vitamin B complex.

vitamin B complex *n* a large group of water-soluble vitamins occurring esp. in liver and yeast: includes thiamine (**vitamin B₁**), riboflavin (**vitamin B₂**), nicotinic acid, pyridoxine (**vitamin B₆**), pantothenic acid, biotin, choline, folic acid, and cyanocobalamin (**vitamin B₁₂**). Sometimes shortened to **B complex.**

vitamin C *n* another name for **ascorbic acid.**

vitamin D *n, pl* **D vitamins.** any of the fat-soluble vitamins, including calciferol (**vitamin D₂**) and cholecalciferol (**vitamin D₃**), occurring in fish-liver oils, milk, butter, and eggs: used in the treatment of rickets.

vitamin E *n* another name for **tocopherol.**

vitamin G *n* another name (esp. US and Canad.) for **riboflavin.**

vitamin H *n* another name (esp. US and Canad.) for **biotin.**

vitamin K *n, pl* **K vitamins.** any of the fat-soluble vitamins, including phylloquinone (**vitamin K₁**) and the menaquinones (**vitamin K₂**), which are essential for the normal clotting of blood.

vitamin P *n, pl* **P vitamins.** any of a group of water-soluble crystalline substances occurring mainly in citrus fruits, blackcurrants, and rose-hips: they regulate the permeability of the blood capillaries.

Vitebsk ★ (*Russian* 'vitɪpsk) *n* a city in NE Belarus: a port on the western Dvina river. Pop.: 365 000 (1996 est.).

vitellin (vɪ'tɛlɪn) *n Biochem.* a phosphoprotein that is the major protein in egg yolk. [C19: from VITELLUS + -IN]

vitelline membrane (vɪ'tɛlɪn) *n Zool.* a membrane that surrounds a fertilized ovum and prevents the entry of other spermatozoa.

vitellus (vɪ'tɛləs) *n, pl* **vitelluses** or **vitelli** (-laɪ) *Zool., rare.* the yolk of an egg. [C18: from L, lit.: little calf, later: yolk of an egg, from *vitulus* calf]

vitiate ('vɪʃɪˌeɪt) *vb* **vitiates, vitiating, vitiated.** (*tr*) **1** to make faulty or imperfect. **2** to debase or corrupt. **3** to destroy the force or legal effect of (a deed, etc.). [C16: from L *vitiāre* to injure, from *vitium* a fault]
▸ ˌvitiˈation *n* ▸ 'vitiˌator *n*

viticulture ('vɪtɪˌkʌltʃə) *n* **1** the science, art, or process of cultivating grapevines. **2** the study of grapes and the growing of grapes. [C19: *viti-*, from L *vītis* vine]
▸ ˌvitiˈculturist *n*

Viti Levu ★ ('viːtɪ 'levuː) *n* the largest island of Fiji: mountainous. Chief town (and capital of the state): Suva. Pop.: 340 561 (1986). Area: 10 386 sq. km (4010 sq. miles).

Vitoria[1] ★ (*Spanish* bi'torja) *n* a city in NE Spain: scene of Wellington's decisive victory (1813) over Napoleon's forces in the Peninsular War. Pop.: 258 243 (1991).

Vitoria[2] ★ (*Spanish* bi'torja) *n* **Francisco de** (fran'θisko de). ?1486–1546, Spanish theologian, sometimes considered the father of international law.

Vitória ★ (vɪ'tɔːrɪə; *Portuguese* vi'tɔrja) *n* a port in E Brazil, capital of Espírito Santo state, on an island in the Bay of Espírito Santo. Pop.: 144 143 (1980).

vitreous ('vɪtrɪəs) *adj* **1** of or resembling glass. **2** made of or containing glass. **3** of or relating to the vitreous humour or vitreous body. [C17: from L *vitreus* made of glass, from *vitrum* glass]
▸ 'vitreously *adv*

vitreous humour *or* **body** *n* a transparent gelatinous substance that fills the interior of the eyeball between the lens and the retina.

vitrescence (vɪ'trɛsəns) *n* **1** the quality or condition of being or becoming vitreous. **2** the process of producing a glass or turning a crystalline material into glass.
▸ vi'trescent *adj*

vitrify ('vɪtrɪˌfaɪ) *vb* **vitrifies, vitrifying, vitrified.** to convert or be converted into glass or a glassy substance. [C16: from F, from L *vitrum* glass]
▸ 'vitriˌfiable *adj* ▸ vitrification (ˌvɪtrɪfɪ'keɪʃən) *n*

vitrine ('vɪtriːn) *n* a glass display case or cabinet for works of art, curios, etc. [C19: from F, from *vitre* pane of glass, from L *vitrum* glass]

vitriol ('vɪtrɪˌɒl) *n* **1** another name for **sulphuric acid. 2** any one of a number of sulphate salts, such as ferrous sulphate (iron(II) sulphate; **green vitriol**), copper sulphate (**blue vitriol**), or zinc sulphate (**white vitriol**). **3** speech, writing, etc., displaying vituperation or bitterness. [C14: from Med. L *vitriolum*, from LL, from L *vitrum* glass, referring to the glossy appearance of the sulphates]

vitriolic (ˌvɪtrɪ'ɒlɪk) *adj* **1** (of a strong acid) highly corrosive. **2** severely bitter or caustic.

vitriolize *or* **vitriolise** ('vɪtrɪəˌlaɪz) *vb* **vitriolizes, vitriolizing, vitriolized** *or* **vitriolises, vitriolising, vitriolised.** (*tr*) **1** to convert into or treat with vitriol. **2** to injure with vitriol.
▸ ˌvitrioli'zation *or* ˌvitrioli'sation *n*

Vitruvius Pollio ★ (vɪ'truːvɪəs 'pɒlɪˌəʊ) *n* **Marcus** ('mɑːkəs). 1st century B.C., Roman architect, noted for his treatise *De architectura.*
▸ Vi'truvian *adj*

vittle ('vɪtᵊl) *n, vb* **vittles, vittling, vittled.** an obsolete or dialect spelling of **victual.**

vituperate (vɪ'tjuːpəˌreɪt) *vb* **vituperates, vituperating, vituperated.** to berate or rail (against) abusively; revile. [C16: from L *vituperāre* to blame, from *vitium* a defect + *parāre* to make]
▸ viˌtuper'ation *n* ▸ vi'tuperˌator *n*

viva[1] ('viːvə) *interj* long live; up with (a specified person or thing). [C17: from It., lit.: may (he) live! from *vivere* to live, from L *vīvere*]

viva[2] ('vaɪvə) *Brit.* ♦ *n* **1** an oral examination. ♦ *vb* **vivas, vivaing, vivaed.** (*tr*) **2** to examine orally. [shortened from VIVA VOCE]

vivace (vɪ'vɑːtʃɪ) *adj, adv Music.* to be performed in a brisk lively manner. [C17: from It., from L *vīvax* vigorous, from *vīvere* to live]

vivacious (vɪ'veɪʃəs) *adj* full of high spirits and animation. [C17: from L *vīvax* lively; see VIVACE]
▸ vi'vaciously *adv* ▸ vi'vaciousness *n*

vivacity (vɪ'væsɪtɪ) *n, pl* **vivacities.** the quality or condition of being vivacious.

Vivaldi ★ (vɪ'vældɪ) *n* **Antonio** (an'tɔːnjo). ?1675–1741, Italian composer, noted for his *The Four Seasons* (1725).

vivarium (vaɪ'veərɪəm) *n, pl* **vivariums** *or* **vivaria** (-ɪə). a place where live animals are kept under natural conditions for study, etc. [C16: from L: enclosure where live fish or game are kept, from *vīvus* alive]

viva voce ('vaɪvə 'vəʊtʃɪ) *adv, adj* **1** by word of mouth. ♦ *n, vb* **viva-voce, viva-voces, viva-voceing, viva-voced. 2** the full form of **viva**[2]. [C16: from Med. L, lit.: with living voice]

vive (viːv) *interj* long live; up with (a specified person or thing). [from F]

Vivian ★ ('vɪvɪən) *n* (in Arthurian legend) the mistress of Merlin, sometimes identified with the **Lady of the Lake.**

vivid ('vɪvɪd) *adj* **1** (of a colour) very bright; intense. **2** brilliantly coloured: *vivid plumage.* **3** conveying to the mind striking realism, freshness, or trueness to life: *a vivid account.* **4** (of a memory, etc.) remaining distinct in the mind. **5** (of the imagination, etc.) prolific in the formation of lifelike images. **6** uttered, operating, or acting with vigour. **7** full of life or vitality: *a vivid personality.* [C17: from L *vīvidus* animated, from *vīvere* to live]
▸ 'vividly *adv* ▸ 'vividness *n*

vivify ('vɪvɪˌfaɪ) *vb* **vivifies, vivifying, vivified.** (*tr*) **1** to bring

to life; animate. **2** to make more vivid or striking. [C16: from LL *vīvificāre*, from L *vīvus* alive + *facere* to make]
▸ ˌvivifiˈcation *n*

viviparous (vɪˈvɪpərəs) *adj* **1** (of most mammals) giving birth to living offspring that develop within the uterus of the mother. **2** (of seeds) germinating before separating from the parent plant. **3** (of plants) producing bulbils or young plants instead of flowers. [C17: from L, from *vīvus* alive + *parere* to bring forth]
▸ viviparity (ˌvɪvɪˈpærɪtɪ) *or* viˈviparousness *n* ▸ viˈviparously *adv*

vivisect (ˈvɪvɪˌsɛkt, ˌvɪvɪˈsɛkt) *vb* to subject (an animal) to vivisection. [C19: back formation from VIVISECTION]
▸ ˈviviˌsector *n*

vivisection (ˌvɪvɪˈsɛkʃən) *n* the act or practice of performing experiments on living animals, involving cutting into or dissecting the body. [C18: from vivi-, from L *vīvus* living + SECTION, as in DISSECTION]
▸ ˌviviˈsectional *adj*

vivisectionist (ˌvɪvɪˈsɛkʃənɪst) *n* a person who practises or advocates vivisection as being useful to science.

vivo (ˈviːvəʊ) *adj, adv Music.* (*in combination*) with life and vigour: *allegro vivo.* [It.: lively]

vixen (ˈvɪksən) *n* **1** a female fox. **2** a quarrelsome or spiteful woman. [C15 *fixen*; rel. to OE *fyxe*, fem. of FOX]
▸ ˈvixenish *adj* ▸ ˈvixenly *adv, adj*

Viyella (vaɪˈɛlə) *n Trademark.* a soft fabric made of wool and cotton.

viz *abbrev. for* videlicet.

Vizagapatam ★ (vɪˌzægəˈpʌtəm) *n* a variant spelling of **Vishakhapatnam.**

vizard (ˈvɪzəd) *n Arch. or literary.* a means of disguise. [C16: var. of VISOR]
▸ ˈvizarded *adj*

vizier (vɪˈzɪə) *n* a high official in certain Muslim countries, esp. in the former Ottoman Empire. [C16: from Turkish *vezīr*, from Ar. *wazīr* porter, from *wazara* to bear a burden]
▸ viˈzierate *n* ▸ viˈzierial *adj* ▸ viˈziership *n*

vizor (ˈvaɪzə) *n* a variant spelling of **visor.**

vizsla (ˈvɪʒlə) *n* a breed of Hungarian hunting dog with a smooth rusty-gold coat. [C20: after *Vizsla*, town in Hungary]

VJ *abbrev. for* video jockey.

V-J Day *n* the day marking the Allied victory over Japan in World War II (Aug. 15, 1945).

VL *abbrev. for* Vulgar Latin.

Vlaardingen ★ (*Dutch* ˈvlaːrdɪŋə) *n* a port in the W Netherlands, in South Holland west of Rotterdam: the third largest port in the Netherlands. Pop.: 73 820 (1994).

Vladikavkaz ★ (*Russian* vlədikafˈkas) *n* a city in S Russia, capital of the North Ossetian Republic on the N slopes of the Caucasus. Pop.: 312 000 (1995 est.). Former names: **Dzaudzhikau** (1944–54); **Ordzhonikidze** *or* **Orjonikidze** (1954–91).

Vladimir[1] ★ (*Russian* vlaˈdimir) *n* a city in W central Russia: capital of the principality of Vladimir until the court transferred to Moscow in 1328. Pop.: 339 000 (1995 est.).

Vladimir[2] ★ (ˈvlædɪˌmɪə; *Russian* vlaˈdimir) *n* **Saint,** called *the Great.* ?956–1015, grand prince of Kiev (980–1015); first Christian ruler of Russia. Feast day: July 15.

Vladivostok ★ (ˌvlædɪˈvɒstɒk; *Russian* vlədivasˈtɔk) *n* a port in SE Russia, on the Sea of Japan: terminus of the Trans-Siberian Railway; the main Russian Pacific naval base since 1872 and chief Russian port in the Far East; university (1956). Pop.: 632 000 (1995 est.).

Vlaminck ★ (*French* vlamɛ̃k) *n* **Maurice de** (mɔrɪs də). 1876–1958, French Fauvist painter.

vlei (fleɪ, vleɪ) *n S. African.* an area of low marshy ground, esp. one that feeds a stream. [C19: from Afrik.]

VLF *or* **vlf** *Radio. abbrev. for* very low frequency.

Vlissingen ★ (ˈvlɪsɪŋə) *n* the Dutch name for **Flushing.**

Vlorë (*Albanian* ˈvlorə) *or* **Vlonë** ★ (*Albanian* ˈvlonə) *n* a port in SW Albania, on the **Bay of Vlorë**: under Turkish

rule from 1462 until Albanian independence was declared here in 1912. Pop.: 76 000 (1991 est.). Ancient name: **Avlona.** Also called: **Valona.**

Vltava ★ (*Czech* ˈvltava) *n* a river in the Czech Republic, rising in the Bohemian Forest and flowing generally southeast and then north to the River Elbe near Melnik. Length: 434 km (270 miles). German name: **Moldau.**

V neck *n* **a** a neck on a garment that comes down to a point, resembling the shape of the letter V. **b** a sweater with such a neck.
▸ **'V-ˌneck** *or* **'V-ˌnecked** *adj*

voc. *or* **vocat.** *abbrev. for* vocative.

vocab (ˈvəʊkæb) *n* short for **vocabulary.**

vocable (ˈvəʊkəb°l) *n* any word, either written or spoken, regarded as a sequence of letters or spoken sounds. [C16: from L *vocābulum* a designation, from *vocāre* to call]
▸ ˈvocably *adv*

vocabulary (vəˈkæbjʊlərɪ) *n, pl* **vocabularies. 1** a listing, either selective or exhaustive, containing the words and phrases of a language, with meanings or translations into another language. **2** the aggregate of words in the use or comprehension of a specified person, class, etc. **3** all the words contained in a language. **4** a range of symbols or techniques constituting a means of communication or expression, as any of the arts or crafts: *a wide vocabulary of textures and colours.* [C16: from Med. L *vocābulārium*, from L *vocābulum* VOCABLE]

vocal (ˈvəʊk°l) *adj* **1** of or designed for the voice: *vocal music.* **2** produced or delivered by the voice: *vocal noises.* **3** connected with the production of the voice: *vocal organs.* **4** frequently disposed to outspoken speech, criticism, etc.: *a vocal minority.* **5** full of sound or voices: *a vocal assembly.* **6** endowed with a voice. **7** *Phonetics.* **7a** of or relating to a speech sound. **7b** of or relating to a voiced speech sound, esp. a vowel. ◆ *n* **8** a piece of jazz or pop music that is sung. **9** a performance of such a piece of music. [C14: from L *vōcālis* possessed of a voice, from *vōx* voice]
▸ **vocality** (vəʊˈkælɪtɪ) *n* ▸ ˈvocally *adv*

vocal cords *pl n* either of two pairs of membranous folds in the larynx. The upper pair (**false vocal cords**) are not concerned with vocal production; the lower pair (**true vocal cords**) can be made to vibrate and produce sound when air from the lungs is forced over them.

vocalic (vəʊˈkælɪk) *adj Phonetics.* of, relating to, or containing a vowel or vowels.

vocalise (ˌvəʊkəˈliːz) *n* a musical passage sung upon one vowel usually as an exercise to develop flexibility and control of pitch and tone.

vocalism (ˈvəʊkəˌlɪzəm) *n* **1** the exercise of the voice, as in singing or speaking. **2** *Phonetics.* **2a** a voiced speech sound, esp. a vowel. **2b** a system of vowels as used in a language.

vocalist (ˈvəʊkəlɪst) *n* a singer, esp. one who regularly appears with a jazz band or pop group.

vocalize *or* **vocalise** (ˈvəʊkəˌlaɪz) *vb* **vocalizes, vocalizing, vocalized** *or* **vocalises, vocalising, vocalised. 1** to express with or use the voice. **2** (*tr*) to make vocal or articulate. **3** (*tr*) *Phonetics.* to articulate (a speech sound) with voice. **4** another word for **vowelize. 5** (*intr*) to sing a melody on a vowel, etc.
▸ ˌvocaliˈzation *n* *or* ˌvocaliˈsation *n* ▸ ˈvocalˌizer *or* ˈvocalˌiser *n*

vocal score *n* a musical score with voice parts in full and orchestral parts in the form of a piano transcription.

vocation (vəʊˈkeɪʃən) *n* **1** a specified profession or trade. **2a** a special urge or predisposition to a particular calling or career, esp. a religious one. **2b** such a calling or career. [C15: from L *vocātiō*, from *vocāre* to call]

vocational (vəʊˈkeɪʃən°l) *adj* **1** of or relating to a vocation or vocations. **2** of or relating to applied educational courses concerned with skills needed for an occupation, trade, or profession.

vocational guidance *n* a guidance service based on psychological tests and interviews to find out what career may best suit a person.

vocative (ˈvɒkətɪv) *Grammar.* ◆ *adj* **1** denoting a case of nouns, in some inflected languages, used when the referent of the noun is being addressed. ◆ *n* **2a** the vocative case. **2b** a vocative noun or speech element.   [C15: from L *vocātīvus cāsus* the calling case, from *vocāre* to call]

voces ('vəʊsiːz) *n* the plural of **vox**.

vociferate (vəʊ'sɪfəˌreɪt) *vb* **vociferates, vociferating, vociferated.** to exclaim or cry out about (something) clamorously or insistently.   [C17: from L *vōciferārī*, from *vōx* voice + *ferre* to bear]
  ▶ **vo,cifer'ation** *n*

vociferous (vəʊ'sɪfərəs) *adj* **1** characterized by vehemence or noisiness: *vociferous protests*. **2** making an outcry: *a vociferous mob*.
  ▶ **vo'ciferously** *adv* ▶ **vo'ciferousness** *n*

vocoder ('vəʊˌkəʊdə) *n Music.* a type of synthesizer that uses the human voice as an oscillator.

vodka ('vɒdkə) *n* an alcoholic drink originating in Russia, made from grain, potatoes, etc., usually consisting only of rectified spirit and water.   [C19: from Russian, dim. of *voda* water]

voe (vəʊ) *n* (in Orkney and Shetland) a small bay or narrow creek.   [C17: from ON *vagr*]

voetsek ('fʊtsɛk, 'vʊt-) *interj S. African sl.* an expression of dismissal or rejection.   [C19: Afrik., from Du. *voort se ek* forward, I say, commonly applied to animals]

voetstoets *or* **voetstoots** ('fʊtstʊts, 'vʊt-) *S. African.* ◆ *adj* **1** denoting a sale in which the vendor is freed from all responsibility for the condition of the goods being sold. ◆ *adv* **2** without responsibility for the condition of the goods sold.   [from Afrik. *voetstoots* as it is]

Vogel ★ ('vəʊgªl) *n* Sir **Julius.** 1835–99, New Zealand statesman; prime minister (1873–75; 1876).

vogue (vəʊg) *n* **1** the popular style at a specified time (esp. in **in vogue**). **2** a period of general or popular usage or favour: *the vogue for such dances is over*. ◆ *adj* **3** (*usually prenominal*) fashionable: *a vogue word*.   [C16: from F: a rowing fashion, from OIt., from *vogare* to row, from ?]
  ▶ **'voguish** *adj*

vogueing ('vəʊgɪŋ) *n* a dance style of the late 1980s, in which a fashion model's movements and postures are imitated in a highly stylized manner.   [C20: from *Vogue* magazine]

voice (vɔɪs) *n* **1** the sound made by the vibration of the vocal cords, esp. when modified by the tongue and mouth. **2** the natural and distinctive tone of the speech sounds characteristic of a particular person. **3** the condition, quality, or tone of such sounds: *a hysterical voice*. **4** the musical sound of a singing voice, with respect to its quality or tone: *she has a lovely voice*. **5** the ability to speak, sing, etc.: *he has lost his voice*. **6** a sound resembling or suggestive of vocal utterance: *the voice of hard experience*. **7** written or spoken expression, as of feeling, opinion, etc. (esp. in **give voice to**). **8** a stated choice, wish, or opinion: *to give someone a voice in a decision*. **9** an agency through which is communicated another's purpose, etc.: *such groups are the voice of our enemies*. **10** *Music.* **10a** musical notes produced by vibrations of the vocal chords at various frequencies and in certain registers: *a tenor voice*. **10b** (in harmony) an independent melodic line or part: *a fugue in five voices*. **11** *Phonetics.* the sound characterizing the articulation of several speech sounds, including all vowels or sonants, that is produced when the vocal cords are set in vibration by the breath. **12** *Grammar.* a category of the verb that expresses whether the relation between the subject and the verb is that of agent and action, action and recipient, or some other relation. **13 in voice.** in a condition to sing or speak well. **14 with one voice.** unanimously. ◆ *vb* **voices, voicing, voiced.** (*tr*) **15** to give expression to: *to voice a complaint*. **16** to articulate (a speech sound) with voice. **17** *Music.* to adjust (a wind instrument or organ pipe) so that it conforms to the correct standards of tone colour, pitch, etc.   [C13: from OF *voiz*, from L *vōx*]
  ▶ **'voicer** *n*

voice box *n* **1** another word for the **larynx**. **2** Also called: **talkbox.** an electronic guitar attachment with a tube into the player's mouth to modulate the sound vocally.

voiced (vɔɪst) *adj* **1** declared or expressed by the voice. **2**

(*in combination*) having a voice as specified: *loud-voiced*. **3** *Phonetics.* articulated with accompanying vibration of the vocal cords: *in English* (b) *is a voiced consonant*.

voice input *n* the control and operation of computer systems by spoken commands.

voiceless ('vɔɪslɪs) *adj* **1** without a voice. **2** not articulated: *voiceless misery*. **3** silent. **4** *Phonetics.* articulated without accompanying vibration of the vocal cords: *In English* (p) *is a voiceless consonant*.
  ▶ **'voicelessly** *adv*

voice mail *n* an electronic system for the transfer and storage of telephone messages, which can then be dealt with by the user at his or her convenience.

voice-over *n* the voice of an unseen commentator heard during a film, etc.

voiceprint ('vɔɪsˌprɪnt) *n* a graphic representation of a person's voice recorded electronically, usually having time plotted along the horizontal axis and the frequency of the speech on the vertical axis.

void (vɔɪd) *adj* **1** without contents. **2** not legally binding: *null and void*. **3** (of an office, house, etc.) unoccupied. **4** (*postpositive;* foll. by *of*) destitute or devoid: *void of resources*. **5** useless: *all his efforts were rendered void*. **6** (of a card suit or player) having no cards in a particular suit: *his spades were void*. ◆ *n* **7** an empty space or area: *the huge desert voids of Asia*. **8** a feeling or condition of loneliness or deprivation. **9** a lack of any cards in one suit: *to have a void in spades*. ◆ *vb* (*mainly tr*) **10** to make ineffective or invalid. **11** to empty (contents, etc.) or make empty of contents. **12** (*also intr*) to discharge the contents of (the bowels or urinary bladder).   [C13: from OF, from Vulgar L *vocītus* (unattested), from L *vacuus*, from *vacāre* to be empty]
  ▶ **'voidable** *adj* ▶ **'voider** *n*

voidance ('vɔɪdªns) *n* **1** an annulment, as of a contract. **2** the condition of being vacant, as an office, benefice, etc. **3** the act of voiding or evacuating.   [C14: var. of AVOIDANCE]

voile (vɔɪl) *n* a light semitransparent fabric of silk, rayon, cotton, etc., used for dresses, scarves, shirts, etc.   [C19: from F: VEIL]

Voiotia ★ (*Greek* vjɔ'tiːa) *n* a department of E central Greece: corresponds to ancient Boeotia and part of ancient Phocis. Pop.: 134 108 (1991). Area: 3173 sq. km (1225 sq. miles). Modern Greek name: **Boeotia.**

Vojvodina *or* **Voivodina** ★ (*Serbo-Croat* 'vɔjvɒdɪna) *n* a region of NE Yugoslavia, in N Serbia: stripped of its previously autonomous status in 1990 after ethnic unrest. Capital: Novi Sad. Pop.: 2 114 000 (1995 est.). Area: 22 489 sq. km (8683 sq. miles).

vol. *abbrev. for:* **1** volcano. **2** volume. **3** volunteer.

volant ('vəʊlənt) *adj* **1** (*usually postpositive*) *Heraldry.* in a flying position. **2** *Rare.* flying or capable of flight.   [C16: from F, from *voler* to fly, from L *volāre*]

volar ('vəʊlə) *adj Anat.* of or relating to the palm of the hand or the sole of the foot.   [C19: from L *vola* hollow of the hand, palm, sole of the foot]

volatile ('vɒləˌtaɪl) *adj* **1** (of a substance) capable of readily changing from a solid or liquid form to a vapour. **2** (of persons) disposed to caprice or inconstancy. **3** (of circumstances) liable to sudden change. **4** lasting only a short time: *volatile business interests*. **5** *Computing.* (of a memory) not retaining stored information when the power supply is cut off. ◆ *n* **6** a volatile substance.   [C17: from L *volātīlis* flying, from *volāre* to fly]
  ▶ **'volatileness** *or* **volatility** (ˌvɒlə'tɪlɪtɪ) *n*

volatilize *or* **volatilise** (vɒ'lætɪˌlaɪz) *vb* **volatilizes, volatilizing, volatilized** *or* **volatilises, volatilising, volatilised.** to change or cause to change from a solid or liquid to a vapour.
  ▶ **vo'lati,lizable** *or* **vo'lati,lisable** *adj* ▶ **vo,latiliz'ation** *or* **vo,latilis'ation** *n*

vol-au-vent (*French* vɔlovɑ̃) *n* a very light puff pastry case filled with a savoury mixture in a sauce.   [C19: from F, lit.: flight in the wind]

volcanic (vɒl'kænɪk) *adj* **1** of, produced by, or characterized by the presence of volcanoes: *a volcanic region*. **2** sug-

gestive of or resembling an erupting volcano: *a volcanic era*.
▶ **vol'canically** *adv* ▶ **volcanicity** (ˌvɒlkə'nısıtı) *n*

volcanic glass *n* any of several glassy volcanic igneous rocks, such as obsidian.

volcanism ('vɒlkəˌnızəm) *or* **vulcanism** *n* those processes collectively that result in the formation of volcanoes and their products.

volcano (vɒl'keınəʊ) *n, pl* **volcanoes** *or* **volcanos**. **1** an opening in the earth's crust from which molten lava, rock fragments, ashes, dust, and gases are ejected from below the earth's surface. **2** a mountain formed from volcanic material ejected from a vent in a central crater. [C17: from It., from L *Volcānus* Vulcan, Roman god of fire and metalworking, whose forges were believed to be responsible for volcanic rumblings]

Volcano Islands ★ *pl n* a group of three volcanic islands in the W Pacific, about 1100 km (700 miles) south of Japan: the largest is Iwo Jima, taken by US forces in 1945 and returned to Japan in 1968. Area: about 28 sq. km (11 sq. miles). Japanese name: **Kazan Retto**.

volcanology (ˌvɒlkə'nɒlədʒı) *or* **vulcanology** *n* the study of volcanoes and volcanic phenomena.
▶ **volcanological** (ˌvɒlkənə'lɒdʒık'l) *or* ˌ**vulcano'logical** *adj*

vole (vəʊl) *n* any of various small rodents, mostly of Eurasia and North America, having a stocky body, short tail, and inconspicuous ears. [C19: short for *volemouse*, from ON *vollr* field + *mus* MOUSE]

Volga ★ ('vɒlgə) *n* a river in W Russia, rising in the Valdai Range and flowing through a chain of small lakes to the Rybinsk Reservoir and south to the Caspian Sea through Volgograd: the longest river in Europe. Length: 3690 km (2293 miles).

Volgograd ★ (*Russian* vəlga'grat; *English* 'vɒlgəˌgræd) *n* a port in SW Russia, on the River Volga: scene of a major engagement (1918) during the civil war and again in World War II (1942–43), in which the German forces were defeated; major industrial centre. Pop.: 1 003 000 (1995 est.). Former names: **Tsaritsyn** (until 1925), **Stalingrad** (1925–61).

volitant ('vɒlıtənt) *adj* **1** flying or moving about rapidly. **2** capable of flying. [C19: from L *volitāre* to flit, from *volāre* to fly]

volition (və'lıʃən) *n* **1** the act of exercising the will: *of one's own volition*. **2** the faculty of conscious choice, decision, and intention. **3** the resulting choice or resolution. [C17: from Med. L *volitiō*, from L *vol-* as in *volō* I will, present stem of *velle* to wish]
▶ **vo'litional** *adj*

volitive ('vɒlıtıv) *adj* of, relating to, or emanating from the will.

Volk (fɒlk) *n S. African.* the Afrikaner people. [from Afrik., from Du.]

Volksraad ('fɒlksˌrɑːt) *n* (formerly, in South Africa) the Legislative Assemblies of the Transvaal and Orange Free State republics. [from Afrik., from Du. *volks* people's + *raad* council]

volley ('vɒlı) *n* **1** the simultaneous discharge of several weapons, esp. firearms. **2** the projectiles or missiles so discharged. **3** a burst of oaths, protests, etc., occurring simultaneously or in rapid succession. **4** *Sport.* a stroke, shot, or kick at a moving ball before it hits the ground. **5** *Cricket.* the flight of such a ball or the ball itself. ◆ *vb* **6** to discharge (weapons, etc.) in or as if in a volley or (of weapons, etc.) to be discharged. **7** (*tr*) to utter vehemently. **8** (*tr*) *Sport.* to strike or kick (a moving ball) before it hits the ground. [C16: from F *volée* a flight, from *voler* to fly, from L *volāre*]
▶ **'volleyer** *n*

volleyball ('vɒlıˌbɔːl) *n* **1** a game in which two teams hit a large ball back and forth over a high net with their hands. **2** the ball used in this game.

Vologda (*Russian* 'vɒlǝgdǝ) *n* an industrial city in W central Russia. Pop.: 299 000 (1995 est.).

Vólos ★ (*Greek* 'vɒlɒs) *n* a port in E Greece, in Thessaly on the **Gulf of Volos** (an inlet of the Aegean): the third largest port in Greece. Pop.: 70 000 (latest est.).

volplane ('vɒlˌpleın) *vb* **volplanes, volplaning, volplaned.** **1** (*intr*) (of an aircraft) to glide without engine power. ◆ *n* **2** a glide by an aircraft. [C20: from F *vol plané* a gliding flight]

vols. *abbrev. for* volumes.

Volsung ★ ('vɒlsʊŋ) *n* **1** a great hero of Norse and Germanic legend and poetry who gave his name to a race of warriors; father of Sigmund and Signy. **2** any member of his family.

volt[1] (vəʊlt) *n* the derived SI unit of electric potential; the potential difference between two points on a conductor carrying a current of 1 ampere, when the power dissipated between these points is 1 watt. Symbol: V [C19: after Count Alessandro VOLTA]

volt[2] *or* **volte** (vɒlt) *n* **1** a circle executed in dressage. **2** a leap made in fencing to avoid an opponent's thrust. [C17: from F, from It. *volta*, ult. from L *volvere* to turn]

volta ('vɒltə; *Italian* 'vɔlta) *n, pl* **volte** (*Italian* -te). **1** an Italian dance popular during the 16th and 17th centuries. **2 Lake.** a piece of music for or in the rhythm of this dance. [C17: from It.: turn; see VOLT[2]]

Volta[1] ★ ('vɒltə) *n* **1** a river in W Africa, formed by the confluence of the **Black Volta** and the **White Volta** in central Ghana: flows south to the Bight of Benin: the chief river of Ghana. Length: 480 km (300 miles); (including the Black Volta) 1600 km (1000 miles). **2 Lake.** an artificial lake in Ghana, extending 408 km (250 miles) upstream from the **Volta River Dam** on the Volta River: completed in 1966. Area: 8482 sq. km (3275 sq. miles).

Volta[2] ★ ('vəʊltə; *Italian* 'vɔlta) *n* Count **Alessandro** (ales-'sandro). 1745–1827, Italian physicist, who invented the voltaic pile (1800) and an electroscope.

voltage ('vəʊltıdʒ) *n* an electromotive force or potential difference expressed in volts.

voltaic (vɒl'teıık) *adj* another word for **galvanic** (sense 1).

voltaic cell *n* another name for **primary cell**.

voltaic couple *n Physics.* a pair of dissimilar metals in an electrolyte with a potential difference between the metals resulting from chemical action.

voltaic pile *n* an early form of battery consisting of a pile of paired plates of dissimilar metals, such as zinc and copper, each pair being separated from the next by a pad moistened with an electrolyte.

Voltaire ★ (vɒl'teə, vəʊl-; *French* vɔltɛr) *n* pseudonym of *François Marie Arouet*. 1694–1778, French writer, noted for his outspoken belief in liberty. His major works include *Lettres philosophiques* (1734) and the satire *Candide* (1759).
▶ **Vol'tairean** *or* **Vol'tairian** *adj, n*

voltameter (vɒl'tæmıtə) *n* a device for measuring electric charge.
▶ **voltametric** (ˌvɒltə'mɛtrık) *adj*

voltammeter (ˌvəʊlt'æmˌmiːtə) *n* a dual-purpose instrument that can measure both potential difference and electric current, usually in volts and amperes respectively.

volt-ampere ('vəʊlt'æmpeə) *n* the product of the potential in volts across an electrical circuit and the resultant current in amperes.

Volta Redonda ★ (*Portuguese* 'vɔltə rə'dõdə) *n* a city in SE Brazil, in Rio de Janeiro state on the Paraíba River: founded in 1941; site of South America's largest steelworks. Pop.: 219 988 (1991).

volte-face ('vɒlt'fɑːs) *n, pl* **volte-face. 1** a reversal, as in opinion. **2** a change of position so as to look, lie, etc., in the opposite direction. [C19: from F, from It., from *volta* turn + *faccia* face]

voltmeter ('vəʊltˌmiːtə) *n* an instrument for measuring potential difference or electromotive force.

Volturno ★ (*Italian* vol'turno) *n* a river in S central Italy, flowing southeast and southwest to the Tyrrhenian Sea: scene of a battle (1860) during the wars for Italian unity, in which Garibaldi defeated the Neapolitans; German line of defence during World War II. Length: 175 km (109 miles).

voluble ('vɒljʊb'l) *adj* **1** talking easily and at length. **2** *Arch.* easily turning or rotating. **3** *Rare.* (of a plant) twin-

★ people and places

ing or twisting. [C16: from L *volūbilis* turning readily, from *volvere* to turn]
▶ ˌvolu'bility or 'volubleness *n* ▶ 'volubly *adv*

volume ('vɒljuːm) *n* **1** the magnitude of the three-dimensional space enclosed within or occupied by an object, geometric solid, etc. **2** a large mass or quantity: *the volume of protest.* **3** an amount or total: *the volume of exports.* **4** fullness of sound. **5** the control on a radio, etc., for adjusting the intensity of sound. **6** a bound collection of printed or written pages; book. **7** any of several books either bound in an identical format or part of a series. **8** the complete set of issues of a periodical over a specified period, esp. one year. **9** *History.* a roll of parchment, etc. **10 speak volumes.** to convey much significant information. [C14: from OF, from L *volūmen* a roll, from *volvere* to roll up]

volumetric (ˌvɒlju'mɛtrɪk) *adj* of, concerning, or using measurement by volume: *volumetric analysis.*
▶ ˌvolu'metrically *adv*

volumetric analysis *n Chem.* quantitative analysis of liquids or solutions by comparing the volumes that react with known volumes of standard reagents, usually by titration.

voluminous (və'luːmɪnəs) *adj* **1** of great size, quantity, or extent. **2** (of writing) consisting of or sufficient to fill volumes. [C17: from LL *volūminōsus* full of windings, from *volūmen* VOLUME]
▶ **voluminosity** (vəˌluːmɪ'nɒsɪtɪ) *n* ▶ vo'luminously *adv*

Völund ★ ('vølund) *n* the Scandinavian name of **Wayland.**

voluntarism ('vɒləntəˌrɪzəm) *n* **1** *Philosophy.* the theory that the will rather than the intellect is the ultimate principle of reality. **2** a doctrine or system based on voluntary participation in a course of action. **3** another name for **voluntaryism.**
▶ 'voluntarist *n, adj*

voluntary ('vɒləntərɪ) *adj* **1** performed, undertaken, or brought about by free choice or willingly: *a voluntary donation.* **2** (of persons) serving or acting in a specified function without compulsion or promise of remuneration: *a voluntary social worker.* **3** done by, composed of, or functioning with the aid of volunteers: *a voluntary association.* **4** exercising or having the faculty of willing: *a voluntary agent.* **5** spontaneous: *voluntary laughter.* **6** *Law.* **6a** acting or done without legal obligation, compulsion, or persuasion. **6b** made without payment or recompense: *a voluntary conveyance.* **7** (of the muscles of the limbs, neck, etc.) having their action controlled by the will. **8** maintained by the voluntary actions or contributions of individuals and not by the state: *voluntary schools.* ◆ *n, pl* **voluntaries. 9** *Music.* a composition or improvisation, usually for organ, played at the beginning or end of a church service. [C14: from L *voluntārius*, from *voluntās* will, from *velle* to wish]
▶ 'voluntarily *adv*

voluntary arrangement *n Law.* a procedure enabling an insolvent company to come to an arrangement with its creditors and resolve its financial problems, often in compliance with a court order.

voluntaryism ('vɒləntərɪˌɪzəm) or **voluntarism** *n* the principle of supporting churches, schools, and various other institutions by voluntary contributions rather than with state funds.
▶ 'voluntaryist or 'voluntarist *n*

voluntary retailer *n* another name for **symbol retailer.**

volunteer (ˌvɒlən'tɪə) *n* **1a** a person who performs or offers to perform voluntary service. **1b** (*as modifier*): *a volunteer system.* **2** a person who freely undertakes military service. **3a** a plant that grows from seed that has not been deliberately sown. **3b** (*as modifier*): *a volunteer plant.* ◆ *vb* **4** to offer (oneself or one's services) for an undertaking by choice and without request or obligation. **5** (*tr*) to perform, give, or communicate voluntarily: *to volunteer help.* **6** (*intr*) to enlist voluntarily for military service. [C17: from F, from L *voluntārius*; see VOLUNTARY]

voluptuary (və'lʌptjʊərɪ) *n, pl* **voluptuaries. 1** a person devoted to luxury and sensual pleasures. ◆ *adj* **2** of or furthering sensual gratification or luxury. [C17: from LL *voluptuārius* delightful, from L *voluptās* pleasure]

voluptuous (və'lʌptjʊəs) *adj* **1** relating to, characterized by, or consisting of pleasures of the body or senses. **2** devoted or addicted to sensual indulgence or luxurious pleasures. **3** sexually alluring, esp. through shapeliness or fullness: *a voluptuous woman.* [C14: from L *voluptuōsus* full of gratification, from *voluptās* pleasure]
▶ vo'luptuously *adv* ▶ vo'luptuousness *n*

volute ('vɒljuːt, və'luːt) *n* **1** a spiral or twisting turn, form, or object. **2** Also called: **helix.** a carved ornament, esp. as used on an Ionic capital, that has the form of a spiral scroll. **3** any of the whorls of the spirally coiled shell of a snail or similar gastropod mollusc. **4** any of a family of tropical marine gastropod molluscs having a spiral shell with beautiful markings. ◆ *adj also* **voluted** (və'luːtɪd). **5** having the form of a volute; spiral. [C17: from L *volūta* spiral decoration, from *volūtus*, from *volvere* to roll up]
▶ vo'lution *n*

vomer ('vəʊmə) *n* the thin flat bone forming part of the separation between the nasal passages in mammals. [C18: from L: ploughshare]

vomit ('vɒmɪt) *vb* **vomits, vomiting, vomited. 1** to eject (the contents of the stomach) through the mouth as the result of involuntary muscular spasms of the stomach and oesophagus. **2** to eject or be ejected forcefully. ◆ *n* **3** the matter ejected in vomiting. **4** the act of vomiting. **5** an emetic. [C14: from L *vomitāre* to vomit repeatedly, from *vomere* to vomit]
▶ 'vomiter *n*

vomitory ('vɒmɪtərɪ) *adj* **1** Also: **vomitive** ('vɒmɪtɪv). causing vomiting; emetic. ◆ *n, pl* **vomitories. 2** a vomitory agent. **3** Also called: **vomitorium** (ˌvɒmɪ'tɔːrɪəm). a passageway in an ancient Roman amphitheatre that connects an outside entrance to a tier of seats.

von Braun ★ (vɒn 'braʊn, fɒn) *n* **Wernher** ('vɜːnə). 1912–77, US rocket engineer, born in Germany, where he designed the V-2 missile used in World War II.

von Euler ★ (*German* fɒn 'ɔɪlər) *n* See (Ulf von) **Euler.**

von Laue ★ (*German* fɒn 'laʊə) *n* See (Max Theodor Felix von) **Laue.**

Vonnegut ★ ('vɒnɪɡʌt) *n* **Kurt.** born 1922, US novelist. His works include *Slaughterhouse Five* (1969) and *Timequake* (1997).

von Rundstedt ★ (*German* fɒn 'rʊntʃtɛt) *n* See (Karl Rudolf Gerd von) **Rundstedt.**

von Sternberg ★ (vɒn 'stɜːnˌbɜːɡ; *German* fɒn 'ʃtɛrnbɛrk) *n* **Joseph** ('jɔːzɛf), real name *Jonas Sternberg.* 1894–1969, US film director, born in Austria.

von Stroheim ★ (vɒn 'strəʊˌhaɪm, 'ʃtrəʊ-; fɒn) *n* **Erich** ('erɪk; *German* 'eːrɪç), real name *Hans Erich Maria Stroheim von Nordenwall.* 1885–1957, US film director and actor, born in Austria.

voodoo ('vuːduː) *n, pl* **voodoos. 1** Also called: **voodooism.** a religious cult involving witchcraft, common in Haiti and other Caribbean islands. **2** a person who practises voodoo. **3** a charm, spell, or fetish involved in voodoo worship. ◆ *adj* **4** relating to or associated with voodoo. ◆ *vb* **voodoos, voodooing, voodooed. 5** (*tr*) to affect by or as if by the power of voodoo. [C19: from Louisiana F *voudou*, ult. of West African origin]
▶ 'voodooist *n*

voorkamer ('fʊəˌkɑːmə) *n S. African.* the front room of a house. [Afrik., from Du. *voor* fore + *kamer* chamber]

voorskot ('fʊəˌskɒt) *n S. African.* advance payment made to a farmer for crops. Cf. **agterskot.** [C20: Afrik., from *voor* before + *skot* shot, payment]

Voortrekker ('fʊəˌtrɛkə) *n* (in South Africa) **1** one of the original Afrikaner settlers of the Transvaal and the Orange Free State who migrated from the Cape Colony in the 1830s. **2** a member of the Afrikaner youth movement founded in 1931. [C19: from Du., from *voor-* FORE- + *trekken* to TREK]

voracious (və'reɪʃəs) *adj* **1** devouring or craving food in great quantities. **2** very eager or unremitting in some activity: *voracious reading.* [C17: from L *vorāx*, from *vorāre* to devour]
▶ **voracity** (vɒ'ræsɪtɪ) or **vo'raciousness** *n*

Vorarlberg ★ (*German* 'foːrarlbɛrk) *n* a mountainous

state of W Austria. Capital: Bregenz. Pop.: 342 461 (1994 est.). Area: 2601 sq. km (1004 sq. miles).

Voronezh ★ (*Russian* va'rɔnɪʃ) *n* a city in W Russia: engineering and chemical industries; university (1918). Pop.: 908 000 (1995 est.).

Voroshilovgrad ★ (*Russian* vərəʃilaw'grat) *n* the former name (1935–91) of **Lugansk**.

Voroshilovsk ★ (*Russian* vərə'ʃilafsk) *n* the former name (1940–44) of **Stavropol**.

-vorous *adj combining form*. feeding on or devouring: *carnivorous*. [from L *-vorus*; rel. to *vorāre* to swallow up]
▶ **-vore** *n combining form*.

Vorster ★ ('fɔːstə, 'vɔː-) *n* **Balthazar Johannes,** known as **John.** 1915–83, South African statesman; Nationalist prime minister (1966–78); president (1978).

vortex ('vɔːtɛks) *n*, *pl* **vortexes** *or* **vortices** (-tɪˌsiːz). 1 a whirling mass or motion of liquid, gas, flame, etc., such as the spiralling movement of water around a whirlpool. 2 any activity or way of life regarded as irresistibly engulfing. [C17: from L: a whirlpool]
▶ **vortical** ('vɔːtɪkˀl) *adj*

vorticella (ˌvɔːtɪ'sɛlə) *n*, *pl* **vorticellae** (-liː). any of a genus of protozoans consisting of a goblet-shaped ciliated cell attached to the substratum by a long contractile stalk. [C18: from NL, lit.: a little eddy, from VORTEX]

vorticism ('vɔːtɪˌsɪzəm) *n* an art movement in England combining the techniques of cubism with the concern for the problems of the machine age evinced in futurism. [C20: referring to the "vortices" of modern life on which the movement was based]
▶ **vorticist** *n*

Vortumnus ★ (vɔː'tʌmnəs) *n* a variant spelling of **Vertumnus**.

Vosges ★ (*French* voʒ) *n* 1 a mountain range in E France, west of the Rhine valley. Highest peak: 1423 m (4672 ft). 2 a department of NE France, in Lorraine region. Capital: Épinal. Pop.: 385 376 (1994 est.). Area: 5903 sq. km (2302 sq. miles).

vostro account ('vɒstrəʊ) *n* a bank account held by a foreign bank with a British bank, usually in sterling. Cf. **nostro account**.

votary ('vəʊtərɪ) *n*, *pl* **votaries**, *also* **votarist**. 1 *RC Church, Eastern Churches*. a person, such as a monk or nun, who has dedicated himself or herself to religion by taking vows. 2 a devoted adherent of a religion, cause, etc. ◆ *adj* 3 ardently devoted to the worship of God or a saint. [C16: from L *vōtum* a vow, from *vovēre* to vow]
▶ **votaress** *fem n*

vote (vəʊt) *n* 1 an indication of choice, opinion, or will on a question, such as the choosing of a candidate: *10 votes for Jones*. 2 the opinion of a group of persons as determined by voting: *it was put to the vote*. 3 a body of votes or voters collectively: *the Jewish vote*. 4 the total number of votes cast. 5 the ticket, ballot, etc., by which a vote is expressed. 6a the right to vote; franchise. 6b a person regarded as the embodiment of this right. 7 a means of voting, such as a ballot. 8 *Chiefly Brit*. a grant or other proposition to be voted upon. ◆ *vb* **votes, voting, voted.** 9 (when *tr*, takes a clause as object or an infinitive) to express or signify (one's preference or will) (for or against some question, etc.): *to vote by ballot*. 10 (*intr*) to declare oneself as being (something or in favour of something) by exercising one's vote: *to vote socialist*. 11 (*tr*; foll. by *into* or *out of*, etc.) to appoint or elect (a person to or from a particular post): *he was voted out of office*. 12 (*tr*) to determine the condition of in a specified way by voting: *the court voted itself out of existence*. 13 (*tr*) to authorize or allow by voting: *vote us a rise*. 14 (*tr*) *Inf*. to declare by common opinion: *the party was voted a failure*. [C15: from L *vōtum* a solemn promise, from *vovēre* to vow]
▶ **votable** *or* **voteable** *adj*

vote down *vb* (*tr*, *adv*) to decide against or defeat in a vote: *the bill was voted down*.

vote of no confidence *n Parliament*. a vote on a motion put by the Opposition censuring an aspect of the Government's policy; if the motion is carried the Government is obliged to resign. Also called: **vote of censure**.

voter ('vəʊtə) *n* a person who can or does vote.

voting machine *n* (esp. in the US) a machine at a polling station that voters operate to register their votes and that mechanically or electronically counts all votes cast.

votive ('vəʊtɪv) *adj* 1 given or dedicated in fulfilment of or in accordance with a vow. 2 *RC Church*. having the nature of a voluntary offering: *a votive Mass*. [C16: from L *vōtīvus* promised by a vow, from *vōtum* a vow]

vouch (vaʊtʃ) *vb* 1 (*intr*; usually foll. by *for*) to give personal assurance: *I'll vouch for his safety*. 2 (when *tr*, usually takes a clause as object; when *intr*, usually foll. by *for*) to furnish supporting evidence (for) or function as proof (of). 3 (*tr*) *Arch*. to cite (authors, principles, etc.) in support of something. [C14: from OF *vocher* to summon, ult. from L *vocāre* to call]

voucher ('vaʊtʃə) *n* 1 a document serving as evidence for some claimed transaction, as the receipt or expenditure of money. 2 *Brit*. a ticket or card serving as a substitute for cash: *a gift voucher*. 3 a person or thing that vouches for the truth of some statement, etc. [C16: from Anglo-F, noun use of OF *voucher* to summon; see VOUCH]

vouchsafe (ˌvaʊtʃ'seɪf) *vb* **vouchsafes, vouchsafing, vouchsafed.** (*tr*) 1 to give or grant or condescend to give or grant: *she vouchsafed no reply*. 2 (*may take a clause as object or an infinitive*) to agree, promise, or permit, often graciously or condescendingly: *he vouchsafed to come yesterday*. [C14 *vouchen sauf*; see VOUCH, SAFE]

voussoir (vuː'swɑː) *n* a wedge-shaped stone or brick that is used with others to construct an arch or vault. [C18: from F, from Vulgar L *volsōrium* (unattested), ult. from L *volvere* to turn, roll]

vow (vaʊ) *n* 1 a solemn or earnest pledge or promise binding the person making it to perform a specified act or behave in a certain way. 2 a solemn promise made to a deity or saint, by which the promiser pledges himself to some future act or way of life. 3 **take vows**. to enter a religious order and commit oneself to its rule of life by the vows of poverty, chastity, and obedience. ◆ *vb* 4 (*tr*; *may take a clause as object or an infinitive*) to pledge, promise, or undertake solemnly: *he vowed to return*. 5 (*tr*) to dedicate or consecrate to God or a saint. 6 (*tr*; usually takes a clause as object) to assert or swear emphatically. 7 (*intr*) *Arch*. to declare solemnly. [C13: from OF *vou*, from L *vōtum*; see VOTE]
▶ **'vower** *n*

vowel ('vaʊəl) *n* 1 *Phonetics*. a voiced speech sound whose articulation is characterized by the absence of obstruction in the vocal tract, allowing the breath stream free passage. The timbre of a vowel is chiefly determined by the position of the tongue and the lips. 2 a letter or character representing a vowel. [C14: from OF, from L *vocālis littera* vowel, from *vocālis*, from *vox* voice]
▶ **'vowel-ˌlike** *adj*

vowel gradation *n* another name for **ablaut**. See **gradation** (sense 5).

vowelize *or* **vowelise** ('vaʊəˌlaɪz) *vb* **vowelizes, vowelizing, vowelized** *or* **vowelises, vowelising, vowelised.** (*tr*) to mark the vowel points in (a Hebrew word or text).
▶ ˌvoweliˈzation *or* ˌvoweliˈsation *n*

vowel mutation *n* another name for **umlaut**.

vowel point *n* any of several marks or points placed above or below consonants, esp. those evolved for Hebrew or Arabic, in order to indicate vowel sounds.

vox (vɒks) *n*, *pl* **voces**. a voice or sound. [L: voice]

vox pop *n* interviews with members of the public on a radio or television programme. [C20: shortened from VOX POPULI]

vox populi ('pɒpjuˌlaɪ) *n* the voice of the people; popular or public opinion. [L]

voyage ('vɔɪɪdʒ) *n* 1 a journey, travel, or passage, esp. one to a distant land or by sea or air. ◆ *vb* **voyages, voyaging, voyaged.** 2 to travel over or traverse (something): *we will voyage to Africa*. [C13: from OF *veiage*, from L *viāticum* provision for travelling, from *via* way]
▶ **'voyager** *n*

voyage charter *n* the hire of a ship or aircraft for a specific number of voyages. Cf. **time charter**.

voyageur (ˌvɔɪə'dʒɜː) *n* (in Canada) a woodsman, guide, trapper, boatman, or explorer, esp. in the North. [C19: F: traveller, from *voyager* to VOYAGE]

voyeur (vwaɪ'ɜː) *n* a person who obtains sexual pleasure from the observation of people undressing, having intercourse, etc. [C20: F, lit.: one who sees, from *voir* to see, from L *vidēre*]
▶ vo'yeurism *n* ▶ ˌvoyeur'istic *adj*

VP *abbrev. for:* **1** verb phrase. **2** Vice President.

VPL *Jocular abbrev. for* visible panty line.

VR *abbrev. for:* **1** variant reading. **2** Victoria Regina. [L: Queen Victoria] **3** virtual reality.

V. Rev. *abbrev. for* Very Reverend.

Vries ★ (vriːs) *n* See (Hugo) **De Vries.**

vrou (frəu) *n S. African.* an Afrikaner woman, esp. a married woman. [from Afrik., from Du.]

vrystater ('freɪˌstɑːtə) *n S. African.* a native inhabitant of the Free State, esp. one who is White. [from Afrik., from Du. *vrij* free + *staat* state]

vs *abbrev. for* versus.

VS *abbrev. for* Veterinary Surgeon.

v.s. *abbrev. for* vide supra (see **vide**).

V-sign *n* **1** (in Britain) an offensive gesture made by sticking up the index and middle fingers with the palm of the hand inwards. **2** a similar gesture with the palm outwards meaning victory or peace.

VSO *abbrev. for:* **1** very superior old: used to indicate that a brandy, port, etc., is between 12 and 17 years old. **2** (in Britain) Voluntary Service Overseas: an organization that sends young volunteers to use and teach their skills in developing countries.

VSOP *abbrev. for* very special (*or* superior) old pale: used to indicate that a brandy, port, etc., is between 20 and 25 years old.

Vt. *or* **VT** *abbrev. for* Vermont.

VTOL ★ ('viːtɒl) *n* vertical takeoff and landing; a system in which an aircraft can take off and land vertically. Cf. **STOL.**

VTR *abbrev. for* video tape recorder.

V-type engine *n* a type of internal-combustion engine having two cylinder blocks attached to a single crankcase, the angle between the two blocks forming a V.

Vuelta Abajo ★ (*Spanish* 'bwelta a'βaxo) *n* a region of W Cuba: famous for its tobacco.

vug (vʌg) *n Mining.* a small cavity in a rock or vein, usually lined with crystals. [C19: from Cornish *vooga* cave]
▶ 'vuggy *adj*

Vuillard ★ (*French* vɥijar) *n* **Jean Édouard** (ʒɑ̃ edwar). 1868–1940, French painter and lithographer.

Vulcan ★ ('vʌlkən) *n* the Roman god of fire and metalworking. Greek counterpart: **Hephaestus.**
▶ **Vulcanian** (vʌl'keɪnɪən) *adj*

vulcanian (vʌl'keɪnɪən) *adj Geol.* of or relating to a volcanic eruption characterized by the explosive discharge of gases, fine ash, and viscous lava that hardens in the crater. [C17: after VULCAN]

vulcanism ('vʌlkəˌnɪzəm) *n* a variant spelling of **volcanism.**

vulcanite ('vʌlkəˌnaɪt) *n* a hard usually black rubber produced by vulcanizing natural rubber with sulphur. It is used for electrical insulators, etc. Also called: **ebonite.**

vulcanize *or* **vulcanise** ('vʌlkəˌnaɪz) *vb* **vulcanizes, vulcanizing, vulcanized** *or* **vulcanises, vulcanising, vulcanised.** (*tr*) **1** to treat (rubber) with sulphur under heat and pressure to improve elasticity and strength or to produce a hard substance such as vulcanite. **2** to treat (substances other than rubber) by a similar process in order to improve their properties.
▶ ˌvulcani'zation *or* ˌvulcani'sation *n*

vulcanology (ˌvʌlkə'nɒlədʒɪ) *n* a variant spelling of **volcanology.**

Vulg. *abbrev. for* Vulgate.

vulgar ('vʌlgə) *adj* **1** marked by lack of taste, culture, delicacy, manners, etc.: *vulgar language.* **2** (*often cap.; usually prenominal*) denoting a form of a language, esp. of Latin, current among common people, esp. at a period when the formal language is archaic. **3** *Arch.* of or current among the great mass of common people. [C14: from L *vulgāris*, from *vulgus* the common people]
▶ 'vulgarly *adv*

vulgar fraction *n* another name for **simple fraction.**

vulgarian (vʌl'geərɪən) *n* a vulgar person, esp. one who is rich or has pretensions to good taste.

vulgarism ('vʌlgəˌrɪzəm) *n* **1** a coarse, crude, or obscene expression. **2** a word or phrase found only in the vulgar form of a language.

vulgarity (vʌl'gærɪtɪ) *n, pl* **vulgarities.** **1** the condition of being vulgar; lack of good manners. **2** a vulgar action, phrase, etc.

vulgarize *or* **vulgarise** ('vʌlgəˌraɪz) *vb* **vulgarizes, vulgarizing, vulgarized** *or* **vulgarises, vulgarising, vulgarised.** (*tr*) **1** to make commonplace or vulgar. **2** to make (something little known or difficult to understand) widely known or popular among the public.
▶ ˌvulgari'zation *or* ˌvulgari'sation *n*

Vulgar Latin *n* any of the dialects of Latin spoken in the Roman Empire other than classical Latin.

vulgate ('vʌlgeɪt, -gɪt) *n Rare.* **1** a commonly recognized text or version. **2** the vernacular.

Vulgate ('vʌlgeɪt, -gɪt) *n* **a** (from the 13th century onwards) the fourth-century Latin version of the Bible produced by Jerome. **b** (*as modifier*): *the Vulgate version.* [C17: from Med. L, from LL *vulgāta editiō* popular version (of the Bible), from L *vulgāre* to make common]

vulnerable ('vʌlnərəb'l) *adj* **1** capable of being physically or emotionally wounded or hurt. **2** open to temptation, censure, etc. **3** *Mil.* exposed to attack. **4** *Bridge.* (of a side who have won one game towards rubber) subject to increased bonuses or penalties. [C17: from LL, from L *vulnerāre* to wound, from *vulnus* a wound]
▶ ˌvulnera'bility *n* ▶ 'vulnerably *adv*

vulnerary ('vʌlnərərɪ) *Med.* ◆ *adj* **1** of or used to heal a wound. ◆ *n, pl* **vulneraries.** **2** a vulnerary drug or agent. [C16: from L *vulnerārius* from *vulnus* wound]

vulpine ('vʌlpaɪn) *adj* **1** of, relating to, or resembling a fox. **2** crafty, clever, etc. [C17: from L *vulpīnus* foxlike, from *vulpēs* fox]

vulture ('vʌltʃə) *n* **1** any of various very large diurnal birds of prey of Africa, Asia, and warm parts of Europe, typically having broad wings and soaring flight and feeding on carrion. **2** any similar bird of North, Central, and South America. **3** a person or thing that preys greedily and ruthlessly on others, esp. the helpless. [C14: from OF *voltour*, from L *vultur*]
▶ **vulturine** ('vʌltʃəˌraɪn) *or* **'vulturous** *adj*

vulva ('vʌlvə) *n, pl* **vulvae** (-viː) *or* **vulvas.** the external genitals of human females, including the labia, mons veneris, clitoris, and the vaginal orifice. [C16: from L: covering, womb, matrix]
▶ 'vulvar *adj*

vulvitis (vʌl'vaɪtɪs) *n* inflammation of the vulva.

vv *abbrev. for* vice versa.

vv. *abbrev. for:* **1** versus. **2** *Music.* volumes.

Vyatka ★ (*Russian* 'vjatkə) *n* the former name (1780–1934) of **Kirov¹.**

Vyborg ★ (*Russian* vi'bərk) *n* a port in NW Russia, at the head of **Vyborg Bay** (an inlet of the Gulf of Finland): belonged to Finland (1918–40). Pop.: 80 000 (1988 est.). Finnish name: **Viipuri.** Swedish name: **Viborg.**

Vyshinsky *or* **Vishinsky** ★ (*Russian* vi'ʃinskij) *n* **Andrei Yanuaryevich** (an'drjej jənu'arjivitʃ). 1883–1954, Soviet statesman; foreign minister (1949–53). He was public prosecutor (1935–38) at the Stalin show trials.

Ww

w *or* **W** ('dʌbªl,juː) *n, pl* **w's, W's,** *or* **Ws. 1** the 23rd letter of the English alphabet. **2** a speech sound represented by this letter, usually a bilabial semivowel, as in *web*.

W *symbol for:* **1** *Chem.* tungsten. [from NL *wolframium*, from G *Wolfram*] **2** watt. **3** West. **4** women's (size). **5** *Physics.* work.

w. *abbrev. for:* **1** week. **2** weight. **3** *Cricket.* **3a** wide. **3b** wicket. **4** width. **5** wife. **6** with.

W. *abbrev. for:* **1** Wales. **2** Welsh.

WA *abbrev. for:* **1** Washington (state). **2** Western Australia.

WAAAF (formerly) *abbrev. for* Women's Auxiliary Australian Air Force.

WAAC (wæk) *n* (formerly) **1** *acronym for* Women's Army Auxiliary Corps. **2** Also called: **Waac.** a member of this corps.

Waadt ★ (vat) *n* the German name for **Vaud.**

WAAF (wæf) *n* (formerly) **1** *acronym for* Women's Auxiliary Air Force. **2** Also called: **Waaf.** a member of this force.

Waal ★ (*Dutch* waːl) *n* a river in the central Netherlands: the S branch of the Lower Rhine. Length: 84 km (52 miles).

Wabash ★ ('wɔːbæʃ) *n* a river in the E central US, rising in W Ohio and flowing west and southwest to join the Ohio River in Indiana. Length: 764 km (475 miles).

wabble ('wɒbªl) *vb* **wabbles, wabbling, wabbled,** *n* a variant spelling of **wobble.**

Wace ★ (weɪs) *n* **Robert.** born ?1100, Anglo-Norman poet; author of the *Roman de Brut* and *Roman de Rou.*

wacke ('wækə) *n Obs.* any of various soft earthy rocks derived from basalt. [C18: from G: rock, gravel, basalt]

wacko ('wækəʊ) *Inf.* ◆ *adj* **1** mad or eccentric. ◆ *n, pl* **wackos. 2** a mad or eccentric person. [C20: back formation from WACKY]

wacky ('wækɪ) *adj* **wackier, wackiest.** *Sl.* eccentric or unpredictable. [C19 (in dialect sense: a fool): from WHACK (hence, a *whacky*, a person who behaves as if he had been whacked on the head)]
▸ **'wackily** *adv* ▸ **'wackiness** *n*

wad (wɒd) *n* **1** a small mass or ball of fibrous or soft material, such as cotton wool, used esp. for packing or stuffing. **2a** a plug of paper, cloth, leather, etc., pressed against a charge to hold it in place in a muzzle-loading cannon. **2b** a disc of paper, felt, etc., used to hold in place the powder and shot in a shotgun cartridge. **3** a roll or bundle of something, esp. of banknotes. ◆ *vb* **wads, wadding, wadded. 4** to form (something) into a wad. **5** (*tr*) to roll into a wad or bundle. **6** (*tr*) **6a** to hold (a charge) in place with a wad. **6b** to insert a wad into (a gun). **7** (*tr*) to pack or stuff with wadding. [C14: from LL *wadda*]

Wadai ★ (waː'daɪ) *n* a former independent sultanate of NE central Africa: now the E part of Chad.

Waddenzee ★ (*Dutch* 'wɑdənzeː) *n* the part of the North Sea between the Dutch mainland and the West Frisian Islands.

wadding ('wɒdɪŋ) *n* **1a** any fibrous or soft substance used as padding, stuffing, etc. **1b** a piece of this. **2** material for wads used in cartridges or guns.

waddle ('wɒdªl) *vb* **waddles, waddling, waddled.** (*intr*) **1** to walk with short steps, rocking slightly from side to side. ◆ *n* **2** a swaying gait or motion. [C16: prob. frequentative of WADE]
▸ **'waddler** *n* ▸ **'waddling** *adj*

waddy ('wɒdɪ) *n, pl* **waddies. 1** a heavy wooden club used as a weapon by native Australians. ◆ *vb* **waddies, waddying, waddied. 2** (*tr*) to hit with a waddy. [C19: from Abor., ? based on E WOOD]

wade (weɪd) *vb* **wades, wading, waded. 1** to walk with the feet immersed in (water, a stream, etc.). **2** (*intr*; often foll. by *through*) to proceed with difficulty: *to wade through a*

book. **3** (*intr*; foll. by *in* or *into*) to attack energetically. ◆ *n* **4** the act or an instance of wading. [OE *wadan*]
▸ **'wadable** *or* **'wadeable** *adj*

Wade ★ (weɪd) *n* **(Sarah) Virginia.** born 1945, British tennis player: Wimbledon champion 1977.

wader ('weɪdə) *n* **1** a person or thing that wades. **2** Also called: **wading bird.** any of various long-legged birds, esp. herons, storks, etc., that live near water and feed on fish, etc. **3** a Brit. name for **shore bird.**

waders ('weɪdəz) *pl n* long waterproof boots, sometimes extending to the chest like trousers, worn by anglers.

wadi *or* **wady** ('wɒdɪ) *n, pl* **wadies.** a watercourse in N Africa and Arabia, dry except in the rainy season. [C19: from Ar.]

Wadi Halfa ★ ('wɒdɪ 'hælfə) *n* a town in the N Sudan that was partly submerged by Lake Nasser: an important archaeological site.

Wad Medani ★ (waːd mɪ'dɑːniː) *n* a town in the E Sudan, on the Blue Nile: headquarters of the Gezira irrigation scheme. Pop.: 218 714 (1993).

wafer ('weɪfə) *n* **1** a thin crisp sweetened biscuit, served with ice cream, etc. **2** *Christianity.* a thin disc of unleavened bread used in the Eucharist. **3** *Pharmacol.* an envelope of rice paper enclosing a medicament. **4** *Electronics.* a large single crystal of semiconductor material, such as silicon, on which numerous integrated circuits are manufactured and then separated. **5** a small thin disc of adhesive material used to seal letters, etc. ◆ *vb* **6** (*tr*) to seal or fasten with a wafer. [C14: from OF *waufre*, from MLow G *wāfel*]
▸ **'wafery** *adj*

waffle[1] ('wɒfªl) *n* **a** a crisp golden-brown pancake with deep indentations on both sides. **b** (*as modifier*): *waffle iron.* [C19: from Du. *wafel* (earlier *wæfel*), of Gmc origin]

waffle[2] ('wɒfªl) *Inf., chiefly Brit.* ◆ *vb* **waffles, waffling, waffled. 1** (*intr*; often foll. by *on*) to speak or write in a vague and wordy manner. ◆ *n* **2** vague and wordy speech or writing. [C19: from ?]
▸ **'waffling** *adj, n*

waft (wɑːft, wɒft) *vb* **1** to carry or be carried gently on or as if on the air or water. ◆ *n* **2** the act or an instance of wafting. **3** something, such as a scent, carried on the air. **4** *Naut.* (formerly) a signal flag hoisted furled to signify various messages depending on where it was flown. [C16 (in obs. sense: to convey by ship): back formation from C15 *wafter* a convoy vessel, from MDu. *wachter* guard]

wag[1] (wæg) *vb* **wags, wagging, wagged. 1** to move or cause to move rapidly and repeatedly from side to side or up and down. **2** to move (the tongue) or (of the tongue) to be moved rapidly in talking, esp. in gossip. **3** to move (the finger) or (of the finger) to be moved from side to side, in or as in admonition. **4** *Sl.* to play truant (esp. in **wag it**). ◆ *n* **5** the act or an instance of wagging. [C13: from OE *wagian* to shake]

wag[2] (wæg) *n* a humorous or jocular person; wit. [C16: from ?]
▸ **'waggish** *adj*

wage (weɪdʒ) *n* **1** (*often pl*) payment in return for work or services, esp. that made to workers on a daily, hourly, weekly, or piecework basis. Cf. **salary. 2** (*pl*) *Econ.* the portion of the national income accruing to labour as earned income, as contrasted with the unearned income accruing to capital in the form of rent, interest, and dividends. **3** (*often pl*) recompense, return, or yield. ◆ *vb* **wages, waging, waged.** (*tr*) **4** to engage in. [C14: from OF *wagier* to pledge, from *wage*, of Gmc origin]
▸ **'wageless** *adj*

wage differential *n* the difference in wages between workers with different skills in the same industry or be-

★ people and places

tween those with comparable skills in different industries or localities.

wage earner *n* **1** a person who works for wages. **2** the person who earns money to support a household by working.

wage freeze *n* a statutory restriction on wage increases.

wage indexation *n* a linking of wage rises to increases in the cost of living usually in order to maintain real wages during periods of high inflation.

wager ('weɪdʒə) *n* **1** an agreement to pay an amount of money as a result of the outcome of an unsettled matter. **2** an amount staked on the outcome of such an event. **3 wager of battle.** (in medieval Britain) a pledge to do battle to decide guilt or innocence by single combat. **4 wager of law.** *English legal history.* a form of trial in which the accused offered to make oath of his innocence, supported by the oaths of 11 of his neighbours declaring their belief in his statements. ◆ *vb* **5** (when *tr, may take a clause as object*) to risk or bet (something) on the outcome of an unsettled matter. [C14: from Anglo-F *wageure* a pledge, from OF *wagier* to pledge; see WAGE]
▸ **'wagerer** *n*

wages council *n* (formerly, in Britain) a statutory body empowered to fix minimum wages in an industry; abolished in 1994.

wage slave *n Ironical.* a person dependent on a wage or salary.

wagga ('wɒɡə) *n Austral.* a blanket or bed covering of sacks stitched together. [C19: after WAGGA WAGGA]

Wagga Wagga ★ ('wɒɡə 'wɒɡə) *n* a city in SE Australia, in New South Wales on the Murrumbidgee River: agricultural trading centre. Pop.: 50 380 (1986).

waggle ('wæɡ°l) *vb* **waggles, waggling, waggled. 1** to move or cause to move with a rapid shaking or wobbling motion. ◆ *n* **2** a rapid shaking or wobbling motion. [C16: from WAG¹]
▸ **'waggly** *adj*

waggon ('wæɡən) *n* a variant spelling (esp. Brit.) of **wagon.**

wag-n-bietjie ('va:x°n,bɪkɪ) *n S. African.* any of various thorn bushes or trees. [from Afrik. *wag* wait + *n* a + *bietjie* bit]

Wagner ★ ('va:gnə) *n* **(Wilhelm) Richard** ('rɪçart). 1813–83, German composer noted for his cycle of four music dramas, *The Ring of the Nibelung* (1876). His other operas include *Tannhäuser* (1845; revised 1861), *Tristan and Isolde* (1865), and *Parsifal* (1882).

Wagnerian (va:g'nɪərɪən) *adj* **1** of or suggestive of the dramatic musical compositions of Richard Wagner, their massive scale, dramatic and emotional intensity, etc. ◆ *n also* **Wagnerite** ('va:gnə,raɪt). **2** a follower or disciple of the music or theories of Richard Wagner.

Wagner-Jauregg ★ (German 'va:gnər'jaurɛk) *n* **Julius** ('ju:lius). 1857–1940, Austrian psychiatrist and neurologist; a pioneer of the use of fever therapy in the treatment of mental disorders. Nobel prize for physiology or medicine 1927.

wagon *or* **waggon** ('wæɡən) *n* **1** any of various types of wheeled vehicles, ranging from carts to lorries, esp. a vehicle with four wheels drawn by a horse, tractor, etc., and used for carrying heavy loads. **2** *Brit.* a railway freight truck, esp. an open one. **3** an obsolete word for **chariot. 4 on** (*or* **off**) **the wagon.** *Inf.* abstaining (*or* no longer abstaining) from alcohol. [C16: from Du. *wagen* WAIN]
▸ **'wagonless** *or* **'waggonless** *adj*

wagoner *or* **waggoner** ('wæɡənə) *n* a person who drives a wagon.

wagonette *or* **waggonette** (,wæɡə'nɛt) *n* a light four-wheeled horse-drawn vehicle with two lengthwise seats facing each other behind a crosswise driver's seat.

wagon-lit (French vagɔ̃li) *n, pl* **wagons-lits** (vagɔ̃li). **1** a sleeping car on a European railway. **2** a compartment on such a car. [C19: from F, from *wagon* railway coach + *lit* bed]

wagonload *or* **waggonload** ('wæɡən,ləud) *n* the load that is or can be carried by a wagon.

wagon train *n* a supply train of horses and wagons, esp. one going over rough terrain.

wagon vault *n* another name for **barrel vault.**

Wagram ★ (German 'va:gram) *n* a village in NE Austria: scene of the defeat of the Austrians by Napoleon in 1809.

wagtail ('wæɡ,teɪl) *n* any of various passerine songbirds of Eurasia and Africa, having a very long tail that wags when the bird walks.

Wahhabi *or* **Wahabi** (wə'hɑ:bɪ) *n, pl* **Wahhabis** *or* **Wahabis.** a member of a strictly conservative Muslim sect founded in the 18th century.
▸ **Wah'habism** *or* **Wa'habism** *n*

wahine (wɑ:'hi:nɪ) *n* **1** NZ. a Maori woman. **2** a Polynesian woman. [from Maori & Hawaiian]

wahoo (wɑ:'hu:, 'wɑ:hu:) *n, pl* **wahoos.** a large fast-moving food and game fish of tropical seas. [from ?]

wah-wah ('wɑ:,wɑ:) *n* **1** the sound made by a trumpet, cornet, etc., when the bell is alternately covered and uncovered. **2** an electronic attachment for an electric guitar, etc., that simulates this effect. [C20: imit.]

waif (weɪf) *n* **1** a person, esp. a child, who is homeless, friendless, or neglected. **2** anything found and not claimed, the owner being unknown. [C14: from Anglo-Norman, var. of OF *gaif,* from ON]
▸ **'waif,like** *adj*

Waikaremoana ★ (waɪ'kɒrəməu,ɑ:nə) *n* **Lake.** a lake in the North Island of New Zealand in a dense bush setting. Area: about 55 sq. km (21 sq. miles).

Waikato ★ ('waɪ,kɑ:təu) *n* the longest river in New Zealand, flowing northwest across North Island to the Tasman Sea. Length: 350 km (220 miles).

Waikiki ★ ('waɪkɪ,ki:, ,waɪkɪ'ki:) *n* a resort area in Hawaii, on SE Oahu: a suburb of Honolulu.

wail (weɪl) *vb* **1** (*intr*) to utter a prolonged high-pitched cry, as of grief or misery. **2** (*intr*) to make a sound resembling such a cry: *the wind wailed in the trees.* **3** (*tr*) to lament, esp. with mournful sounds. ◆ *n* **4** a prolonged high-pitched mournful cry or sound. [C14: from ON]
▸ **'wailer** *n*

Wailing Wall ★ *n* another name for **Western Wall.**

wain (weɪn) *n Chiefly poetic.* a farm wagon or cart. [OE *wægn*]

wainscot ('weɪnskət) *n* **1** Also called: **wainscoting** *or* **wainscotting.** a lining applied to the walls of a room, esp. one of wood panelling. **2** the lower part of the walls of a room, esp. when finished in a material different from the upper part. **3** fine-quality oak used as wainscot. ◆ *vb* **4** (*tr*) to line (a wall of a room) with a wainscot. [C14: from MLow G *wagenschot,* ?from *wagen* WAGON + *schot* planking]

wainwright ('weɪn,raɪt) *n* a person who makes wagons.

waist (weɪst) *n* **1** *Anat.* the constricted part of the trunk between the ribs and hips. **2** the part of a garment covering the waist. **3** the middle part of an object that resembles the waist in narrowness or position. **4** the middle part of a ship. **5** the middle section of an aircraft fuselage. **6** the constriction between the thorax and abdomen in wasps and similar insects. [C14: from ?]
▸ **'waistless** *adj*

waistband ('weɪst,bænd) *n* an encircling band of material to finish and strengthen a skirt or trousers at the waist.

waistcoat ('weɪs,kəut) *n* **1** a man's sleeveless waistlength garment worn under a suit jacket, usually buttoning up the front. **2** a similar garment worn by women. ◆ US and Canad. name: **vest.**
▸ **'waist,coated** *adj*

waistline ('weɪst,laɪn) *n* **1** a line around the body at the narrowest part of the waist. **2** the intersection of the bodice and the skirt of a dress, etc., or the level of this.

wait (weɪt) *vb* **1** (when *intr,* often foll. by *for, until,* or *to*) to stay in one place or remain inactive in expectation (of something). **2** to delay temporarily or be temporarily delayed: *that work can wait.* **3** (when *intr,* usually foll. by *for*) (of things) to be ready or at hand; be in store (for a person): *supper was waiting for them when they got home.* **4** (*intr*) to act as a waiter or waitress. ◆ *n* **5** the act or an instance of waiting. **6** a period of waiting. **7** (*pl*) *Rare.* a band of musicians who go around the streets, esp. at Christmas, singing and playing carols. **8 lie in wait.** to prepare an ambush (for someone). ◆ See also **wait on, wait up.** [C12: from OF *waitier*]

wait-a-bit *n* any of various mainly tropical plants having sharp hooked thorns.

Waitangi Day (waɪˈtʌŋiː) *n* the national day of New Zealand (Feb. 6), commemorating the signing of the **Treaty of Waitangi** (1840) by Maori chiefs and a representative of the British Government. The treaty provided the basis for the British annexation of New Zealand.

Waite ★ (weɪt) *n* **Terry,** full name *Terence Hardy Waite.* born 1939, British special envoy to the Archbishop of Canterbury, who negotiated the release of Western hostages held in the Middle East before (1987) being taken hostage himself in Lebanon: released in 1991.

waiter (ˈweɪtə) *n* **1** a man whose occupation is to serve at table, as in a restaurant. **2** an attendant at the London stock exchange or Lloyd's who carries messages: the modern equivalent of waiters who performed these duties in the 17th-century London coffee houses in which these institutions originated. **3** a person who waits. **4** a tray or salver.

waiting game *n* the postponement of action or decision in order to gain the advantage.

waiting list *n* a list of people waiting to obtain some object, treatment, status, etc.

waiting room *n* a room in which people may wait, as at a railway station, doctor's or dentist's surgery, etc.

wait on *vb* (*intr, prep*) **1** to serve at the table of. **2** to act as an attendant to. ◆ *sentence substitute.* **3** *Austral. & NZ.* stop! hold on! ◆ Also (for senses 1, 2): **wait upon.**

waitress (ˈweɪtrɪs) *n* **1** a woman who serves at table, as in a restaurant. ◆ *vb* (*intr*) **2** to act as a waitress.

wait up *vb* (*intr, adv*) to delay going to bed in order to await some event.

waive (weɪv) *vb* **waives, waiving, waived.** (*tr*) **1** to set aside or relinquish: *to waive one's rights.* **2** to refrain from enforcing or applying (a law, penalty, etc.). **3** to defer. [C13: from OF *weyver*, from *waif* abandoned; see WAIF]

waiver (ˈweɪvə) *n* **1** the voluntary relinquishment, expressly or by implication, of some claim or right. **2** the act or an instance of relinquishing a claim or right. **3** a formal statement in writing of such relinquishment. [C17: from OF *weyver* to relinquish]

Wajda ★ (*Polish* ˈvajda) *n* **Andrei** or **Andrzej** (ˈandʒɛj). born 1926, Polish film director. His films include *Ashes and Diamonds* (1958) and *Ring of the Crowned Eagle* (1993).

Wakayama ★ (ˌwækəˈjɑːmə) *n* an industrial city in S Japan, on S Honshu. Pop.: 393 951 (1995).

wake[1] (weɪk) *vb* **wakes, waking, woke, woken. 1** (often foll. by *up*) to rouse or become roused from sleep. **2** (often foll. by *up*) to rouse or become roused from inactivity. **3** (*intr;* often foll. by *to* or *up to*) to become conscious or aware: *at last he woke up to the situation.* **4** (*intr*) to be or remain awake. ◆ *n* **5** a watch or vigil held over the body of a dead person during the night before burial. **6** (in Ireland) festivities held after a funeral. **7** the patronal or dedication festival of English parish churches. **8** a solemn or ceremonial vigil. **9** (*usually pl*) an annual holiday in various towns in Northern England, when the local factories close. [OE *wacian*]

▶ ˈwaker *n*

wake[2] (weɪk) *n* **1** the waves or track left by a vessel or other object moving through water. **2** the track or path

left by anything that has passed: *wrecked houses in the wake of the hurricane.* [C16: of Scand. origin]

Wakefield ★ (ˈweɪkˌfiːld) *n* **1** a city in N England, in West Yorkshire: important since medieval times as an agricultural and textile centre. Pop.: 73 955 (1991). **2** a unitary authority in N England, in West Yorkshire. Pop.: 317 300 (1994 est.). Area: 333 sq. km (129 sq. miles).

wakeful (ˈweɪkfʊl) *adj* **1** unable or unwilling to sleep. **2** sleepless. **3** alert.

▶ ˈwakefully *adv* ▶ ˈwakefulness *n*

Wake Island ★ *n* an atoll in the N central Pacific: claimed by the US in 1899; developed as a civil and naval air station in the late 1930s. Area: 8 sq. km (3 sq. miles).

wakeless (ˈweɪklɪs) *adj* (of sleep) unbroken.

waken (ˈweɪkən) *vb* to rouse or be roused from sleep or some other inactive state.

wake-robin *n* any of a genus of North American herbaceous plants having a whorl of three leaves and three-petalled solitary flowers.

wake-up *n* **a wake-up to.** *Austral. sl.* fully alert to (a person, thing, action, etc.).

Waksman ★ (ˈwæksmən) *n* **Selman Abraham.** 1888–1973, US microbiologist, born in Russia. He discovered streptomycin: Nobel prize for physiology or medicine 1952.

Walachia or **Wallachia** ★ (wɒˈleɪkɪə) *n* a former principality of SE Europe: a vassal state of the Ottoman Empire from the 15th century until its union with Moldavia in 1859, subsequently forming present-day Romania.

▶ Waˈlachian or Walˈlachian *n, adj*

Wałbrzych ★ (*Polish* ˈvaʊbʒix) *n* an industrial city in SW Poland. Pop.: 140 000 (1995 est.). German name: **Waldenburg.**

Walcheren ★ (*Dutch* ˈwalxərə) *n* an island in the SW Netherlands, in the Scheldt estuary: administratively part of Zeeland province; suffered severely in World War II, when the dykes were breached, and again in the floods of 1953. Area: 212 sq. km (82 sq. miles).

Walcott ★ (ˈwɔːlkət) *n* **Derek (Alton).** born 1930, St Lucian poet and playwright, whose works include the long poem *Omeros* (1990) and *The Bounty* (1997); Nobel prize for literature 1992.

Waldemar I or **Valdemar I** ★ (ˈvældɪˌmɑː) *n* known as *Waldemar the Great.* 1131–82, king of Denmark (1157–82). He conquered the Wends (1169) and established the hereditary rule of his line.

Waldenburg ★ (ˈvaldənburk) *n* the German name for **Wałbrzych.**

Waldenses (wɒlˈdɛnsiːz) *pl n* the members of a small sect founded as a reform movement within the Roman Catholic Church by Peter Waldo, a merchant of Lyons, in the late 12th century.

▶ Walˈdensian *n, adj*

Waldheim ★ (*German* ˈvalthaɪm) *n* **Kurt** (kʊrt). born 1918, Austrian diplomat; secretary-general of the United Nations (1972–81); president of Austria (1986–92).

waldo (ˈwɔːldəʊ) *n, pl* **waldos, waldoes.** a gadget for manipulating objects by remote control. [C20: after *Waldo* F. Jones, an inventor, in a science-fiction story by Robert Heinlein]

Waldorf salad ★ (ˈwɔːldɔːf) *n* a salad of diced apples, celery, and walnuts mixed with mayonnaise.

waldsterben (ˈwɔːldˌstɜːbən) *n* *Ecology.* the symptoms of tree decline in central Europe from the 1970s, considered to be caused by atmospheric pollution. [C20: from G *Wald* forest + *sterben* to die]

wale (weɪl) *n* **1** the raised mark left on the skin after the stroke of a rod or whip. **2** the weave or texture of a fabric, such as the ribs in corduroy. **3** *Naut.* a ridge of planking along the rail of a ship. ◆ *vb* **wales, waling, waled. 4** (*tr*) to raise a wale or wales on by striking. **5** to weave with a wale. [OE *walu* weal]

Wales ★ (weɪlz) *n* a principality that is part of the United Kingdom, in the west of Great Britain; conquered by the English in 1282; parliamentary union with England took place in 1536: the creation of a separate Welsh Assembly with limited power was approved by an extremely narrow margin in 1997. It consists mainly of moorlands and mountains and has an economy that is chiefly agricultural, with an industrial and former coal-mining area in the south. Capital: Cardiff. Pop.: 2 811 865 (1991). Area: 20 768 sq. km (8017 sq. miles). Welsh name: **Cymru**. Medieval Latin name: **Cambria**.

Wałęsa ★ (væ'wensə) *n* **Lech** (leç). born 1943, Polish statesman; president (1990–95); leader of the independent trade union Solidarity (1980–90); Nobel peace prize 1983.

Walfish Bay ★ ('wɔːlfɪʃ) *n* a variant spelling of **Walvis Bay**.

Walhalla (wæl'hælə, væl-) *or* **Walhall** ★ (wæl'hæl, væl-) *n* variants of **Valhalla**.

walk (wɔːk) *vb* **1** (*intr*) to move along or travel on foot at a moderate rate; advance in such a manner that at least one foot is always on the ground. **2** (*tr*) to pass through, on, or over on foot, esp. habitually. **3** (*tr*) to cause, assist, or force to move along at a moderate rate: *to walk a dog*. **4** (*tr*) to escort or conduct by walking: *to walk someone home*. **5** (*intr*) (of ghosts, spirits, etc.) to appear or move about in visible form. **6** (*intr*) to follow a certain course or way of life: *to walk in misery*. **7** (*tr*) to bring into a certain condition by walking: *I walked my shoes to shreds*. **8** to disappear or be stolen: *Where's my pencil? It seems to have walked*. **9** **walk it**. to win easily. **10** **walk on air**. to be delighted or exhilarated. **11** **walk tall**. *Inf*. to have self-respect or pride. **12** **walk the streets**. **12a** to be a prostitute. **12b** to wander round a town, esp. when looking for work or when homeless. ◆ *n* **13** the act or an instance of walking. **14** the distance or extent walked. **15** a manner of walking; gait. **16** a place set aside for walking; promenade. **17** a chosen profession or sphere of activity (esp. in **walk of life**). **18a** an arrangement of trees or shrubs in widely separated rows. **18b** the space between such rows. **19** an enclosed ground for the exercise or feeding of domestic animals, esp. horses. **20** *Chiefly Brit*. the route covered in the course of work, as by a tradesman or postman. **21** a procession; march: *Orange walk*. **22** *Obs*. the section of a forest controlled by a keeper. ◆ See also **walk away**, **walk into**, etc. [OE *wealcan*]
▶ **'walkable** *adj*

walkabout ('wɔːkə,baut) *n* **1** a periodic nomadic excursion into the Australian bush made by a native Australian. **2** an occasion when celebrities, royalty, etc., walk among and meet the public. **3** **go walkabout**. *Austral*. **3a** to wander through the bush. **3b** *Inf*. to be lost or misplaced. **3c** *Inf*. to lose one's concentration.

walk away *vb* (*intr, adv*) **1** to leave, esp. disregarding someone else's distress. **2** **walk away with**. to achieve or win easily.

walker ('wɔːkə) *n* **1** a person who walks. **2** Also called: **baby walker**. a tubular frame on wheels or casters to support a baby learning to walk. **3** a similar support for walking, often with rubber feet, for use by disabled or infirm people.

Walker ★ ('wɔːkə) *n* **Alice Malsenior**. born 1944, US writer: her novels include *The Color Purple* (1982) and *Possessing the Secret of Joy* (1992).

walkie-talkie *or* **walky-talky** (,wɔːkɪ'tɔːkɪ) *n, pl* **walkie-talkies**. a small combined radio transmitter and receiver that can be carried around by one person: widely used by the police, medical services, etc.

walk-in *adj* **1** (of a cupboard) large enough to allow a person to enter and move about in. **2** (of a flat or house) in a suitable condition for immediate occupation.

walking papers *pl n Sl.*, chiefly US & Canad. notice of dismissal.

walking stick *n* **1** a stick or cane carried in the hand to assist walking. **2** the usual US name for **stick insect**.

walk into *vb* (*intr, prep*) to meet with unwittingly: *to walk into a trap*.

Walkman ('wɔːkmən) *n Trademark*. a small portable cassette player with headphones.

walk off *vb* **1** (*intr*) to depart suddenly. **2** (*tr, adv*) to get rid of by walking: *to walk off an attack of depression*. **3** **walk (a person) off his** *or* **her feet**. to make (a person) walk so fast or far that he or she is exhausted. **4** **walk off with**. **4a** to steal. **4b** to win, esp. easily.

walk-on *n* **a** a small part in a play or theatrical entertainment, esp. one without any lines. **b** (*as modifier*): *a walk-on part*.

walk out *vb* (*intr, adv*) **1** to leave without explanation, esp. in anger. **2** to go on strike. **3** **walk out on**. *Inf*. to abandon or desert. **4** **walk out with**. *Brit*., *obs*. or *dialect*. to court or be courted by. ◆ *n* **walkout**. **5** a strike by workers. **6** the act of leaving a meeting, conference, etc., as a protest.

walkover ('wɔːk,əuvə) *n* **1** *Inf*. an easy or unopposed victory. **2** *Horse racing*. **2a** the running or walking over the course by the only contestant entered in a race at the time of starting. **2b** a race won in this way. ◆ *vb* **walk over**. (*intr, mainly prep*) **3** (*also adv*) to win a race by a walkover. **4** *Inf*. to beat (an opponent) conclusively or easily.

walk socks *pl n NZ*. knee-length, usually woollen, stockings.

walk through *Theatre*. ◆ *vb* **1** (*tr*) to act or recite (a part) in a perfunctory manner, as at a first rehearsal. ◆ *n* **walk-through**. **2** a rehearsal of a part.

walkway ('wɔːk,weɪ) *n* **1** a path designed and sometimes landscaped for pedestrian use. **2** a passage or path, esp. one for walking over machinery, connecting buildings, etc.

Walkyrie ★ (væl'kɪərɪ, 'vælkɪərɪ) *n* a variant spelling of **Valkyrie**.

wall (wɔːl) *n* **1a** a vertical construction made of stone, brick, wood, etc., with a length and height much greater than its thickness, used to enclose, divide, or support. **1b** (*as modifier*): *wall hangings*. Related adj: **mural**. **2** (*often pl*) a structure or rampart built to protect and surround a position or place for defensive purposes. **3** *Anat*. any lining, membrane, or investing part that encloses or bounds a bodily cavity or structure: *abdominal wall*. Technical name: **paries**. Related adj: **parietal**. **4** anything that suggests a wall in function or effect: *a wall of fire*. **5** **drive** (*or* **push**) **to the wall**. to force into an awkward situation. **6** **go to the wall**. *Inf*. to be ruined. **7** **go** (*or* **drive**) **up the wall**. *Sl*. to become (*or* cause to become) crazy or furious. **8** **have one's back to the wall**. to be in a difficult situation. ◆ *vb* (*tr*) **9** to protect, provide, or confine with or as if with a wall. **10** (often foll. by *up*) to block (an opening) with a wall. **11** (often foll. by *in* or *up*) to seal by or within a wall or walls. [OE *weall*, from L *vallum* palisade, from *vallus* stake]
▶ **walled** *adj* ▶ **'wall-less** *adj*

wallaby ('wɒləbɪ) *n, pl* **wallabies** *or* **wallaby**. any of various herbivorous marsupials of Australia and New Guinea, similar to but smaller than kangaroos. [C19: from Abor. *wolabā*]

Wallaby ('wɒləbɪ) *n, pl* **Wallabies**. a member of the international rugby football team of Australia.

Wallace ★ ('wɒlɪs) *n* **1 Alfred Russel**. 1823–1913, British naturalist, whose theory of natural selection influenced Charles Darwin. **2 Edgar**. 1875–1932, British crime novelist. **3** Sir **Richard**. 1818–90, British art collector. His bequest to the nation forms the Wallace Collection, London. **4** Sir **William**. ?1272–1305, Scottish patriot, who defeated the army of Edward I of England at Stirling (1297), was routed at Falkirk (1298), and later executed.

Wallace's line *n* the hypothetical boundary between the Oriental and Australasian zoogeographical regions, which runs through Indonesia and SE of the Philippines. [C20: after A. R. WALLACE]

Wallachia ★ (wɒ'leɪkɪə) *n* a variant spelling of **Walachia**.

wallah *or* **walla** ('wɒlə) *n* (*usually in combination*) *Inf*. a person involved with or in charge of (a specified thing): *the book wallah*. [C18: from Hindi *-wālā* from Sansk. *pāla* protector]

wallaroo (,wɒlə'ruː) *n, pl* **wallaroos** *or* **wallaroo**. a large stocky Australian kangaroo of rocky or mountainous regions. [C19: from Abor. *wolarū*]

Wallasey ★ ('wɒləsɪ) *n* a town in NW England, in Wirral, in Merseyside near the mouth of the River Mersey, opposite Liverpool. Pop.: 60 895 (1991).

wall bars *pl n* a series of horizontal bars attached to a wall and used in gymnastics.

wallboard ('wɔːl,bɔːd) *n* a thin board made of materials, such as compressed wood fibres or gypsum plaster, between stiff paper, and used to cover walls, partitions, etc.

wall creeper *n* a pink-and-grey woodpecker-like songbird of Eurasian mountain regions.

walled plain *n* any of the largest of the lunar craters, having diameters between 50 and 300 kilometres.

Wallenberg ★ (*Swedish* 'valənbærj) *n* **Raoul** (rɑːˈuːl). 1912–?, Swedish diplomat, who helped (1944–45) thousands of Hungarian Jews to escape from the Nazis: arrested (1945) by the Soviets and presumed to have died in prison.

Waller ★ ('wɒlə) *n* **1 Edmund.** 1606–87, English poet and politician, known for his poem *Go, Lovely Rose.* **2 Fats,** real name *Thomas Waller.* 1904–43, US jazz pianist and singer.

wallet ('wɒlɪt) *n* **1** a small folding case, usually of leather, for holding paper money, documents, etc. **2** *Arch.,* chiefly *Brit.* a rucksack or knapsack. [C14: of Gmc origin]

walleye ('wɔːl,aɪ) *n, pl* **walleyes** or **walleye.** **1** a divergent squint. **2** opacity of the cornea. **3** an eye having a white or light-coloured iris. **4** Also called: **walleyed pike.** a North American pikeperch valued as a food and game fish. [back formation from earlier *walleyed,* from ON *vagleygr,* from *vage* ? a film over the eye + *-eygr* -eyed, from *auga* eye; infl. by WALL]
► **'wall,eyed** *adj*

wallflower ('wɔːl,flauə) *n* **1** Also called: **gillyflower.** a cruciferous plant of S Europe, grown for its clusters of yellow, orange, brown, red, or purple fragrant flowers and naturalized on old walls, cliffs, etc. **2** *Inf.* a person who stays on the fringes of a dance or party on account of lacking a partner or being shy.

Wallis[1] ★ ('valıs) *n* the German name for **Valais.**

Wallis[2] ★ ('wɒlɪs) *n* Sir **Barnes (Neville).** 1887–1979, British aeronautical engineer. He designed the airship R100, the Wellesley and Wellington bombers, and the bouncing bomb (1943).

Wallis and Futuna Islands ★ ('wɒlɪs; fuːˈtjuːnə) *pl n* a French overseas territory in the SW Pacific, west of Samoa. Capital: Mata-Utu. Pop.: 14 400 (1993 est.). Area: 367 sq. km (143 sq. miles).

wall of death *n* (at a fairground) a giant cylinder round the inside vertical walls of which a motorcyclist rides.

Walloon (wɒˈluːn) *n* **1** a member of a French-speaking people living chiefly in S Belgium and adjacent parts of France. **2** the French dialect of Belgium. ◆ *adj* **3** of or characteristic of the Walloons or their dialect. [C16: from OF *Wallon,* from Med. L: foreigner, of Gmc origin]

Walloon Brabant ★ *n* a province of central Belgium, formed in 1995. Pop.: 336 505 (1995 est.). Area: 1091 sq. km (421 sq. miles).

wallop ('wɒləp) *vb* **wallops, walloping, walloped. 1** (*tr*) *Inf.* to beat soundly; strike hard. **2** (*tr*) *Inf.* to defeat utterly. **3** (*intr*) (of liquids) to boil violently. ◆ *n* **4** *Inf.* a hard blow. **5** *Inf.* the ability to hit powerfully, as of a boxer. **6** *Inf.* a forceful impression. **7** *Brit. sl.* beer. [C14: from OF *waloper* to gallop, from OF *galoper,* from ?]

walloper ('wɒləpə) *n* **1** a person or thing that wallops. **2** *Austral. sl.* a policeman.

walloping ('wɒləpɪŋ) *Inf.* ◆ *n* **1** a thrashing. ◆ *adj* **2** (intensifier): *a walloping drop in sales.*

wallow ('wɒləu) *vb* (*intr*) **1** (esp. of certain animals) to roll about in mud, water, etc., for pleasure. **2** to move about with difficulty. **3** to indulge oneself in possessions, emotion, etc.: *to wallow in self-pity.* ◆ *n* **4** the act or an instance of wallowing. **5** a muddy place where animals wallow. [OE *wealwian* to roll (in mud)]
► **'wallower** *n*

wallpaper ('wɔːl,peɪpə) *n* **1** paper usually printed or embossed with designs for pasting onto walls and ceilings. **2** *Computing.* a picture or pattern on a computer screen

between and behind program icons and windows. ◆ *vb* **3** to cover (a surface) with wallpaper.

wall pepper *n* a small Eurasian plant having yellow flowers and acrid-tasting leaves.

wall plate *n* a horizontal timber member placed along the top of a wall to support the ends of joists, rafters, etc., and distribute the load.

wallposter ('wɔːl,pəustə) *n* (in China) a bulletin or political message painted in large characters on a wall.

wall rocket *n* any of several yellow-flowered European cruciferous plants that grow on old walls and in waste places.

wall rue *n* a delicate fern that grows in rocky crevices and walls in North America and Eurasia.

Wallsend ★ ('wɔːlz,end) *n* a town in NE England, in North Tyneside on the River Tyne: situated at the E end of Hadrian's Wall. Pop.: 45 280 (1991).

Wall Street ★ *n* a street in lower Manhattan, New York, where the Stock Exchange and major banks are situated, regarded as the embodiment of American finance.

wall-to-wall *adj* **1** (esp. of carpeting) completely covering a floor. **2** *Inf.* nonstop; widespread: *wall-to-wall sales.*

wally ('wɒlɪ) *n, pl* **wallies.** *Sl.* a stupid person. [C20: shortened from the name *Walter*]

walnut ('wɔːl,nʌt) *n* **1** any of a genus of deciduous trees of America, SE Europe, and Asia. They have aromatic leaves and flowers in catkins and are grown for their edible nuts and for their wood. **2** the nut of any of these trees, having a wrinkled two-lobed seed and a hard wrinkled shell. **3** the wood of any of these trees, used in making furniture, etc. **4** a light yellowish-brown colour. ◆ *adj* **5** made from the wood of a walnut tree: *a walnut table.* **6** of the colour walnut. [OE *walh-hnutu,* lit.: foreign nut]

Walpole ★ ('wɔːl,pəul) *n* **1 Horace,** 4th Earl of Orford. 1717–97, British writer, noted for his novel *The Castle of Otranto* (1764). **2** his father, Sir **Robert,** 1st Earl of Orford. 1676–1745, British Whig statesman. As first lord of the Treasury and Chancellor of the Exchequer (1721–42) he was effectively Britain's first prime minister.

Walpurgis Night (væl'puəgɪs) *n* the eve of May 1, believed in German folklore to be the night of a witches' sabbath on the Brocken, in the Harz Mountains. [C19: translation of G *Walpurgisnacht,* the eve of the feast day of St Walpurga, 8th-cent. abbess in Germany]

walrus ('wɔːlrəs, 'wɒl-) *n, pl* **walruses** or **walrus.** a mammal of northern seas, having a tough thick skin, upper canine teeth enlarged as tusks, and coarse whiskers, and feeding mainly on shellfish. [C17: prob. from Du., of Scand. origin]

walrus moustache *n* a long thick moustache drooping at the ends.

Walsall ★ ('wɔːlsɔːl) *n* **1** an industrial town in central England, in the West Midlands. Pop.: 174 739 (1991). **2** a unitary authority in central England, in the West Midlands. Pop.: 263 900 (1994 est.). Area: 106 sq. km (41 sq. miles).

Walsingham[1] ★ ('wɔːlsɪŋəm) *n* a village in E England, in Norfolk: remains of a medieval priory; site of the shrine of Our Lady of Walsingham.

Walsingham[2] ★ ('wɔːlsɪŋəm) *n* Sir **Francis.** ?1530–90, English statesman; secretary of state (1573–90) to Elizabeth I.

Walter ★ *n* **1** (*German* 'valtər). **Bruno** ('bruːno), real name *Bruno Walter Schlesinger.* 1876–1962, US conductor, born in Germany. **2** ('wɔːltə). **John.** 1739–1812, British publisher; founded *The Daily Universal Register* (1785), which in 1788 became *The Times.*

Waltham Forest ★ ('wɔːlθəm) *n* a borough of NE Greater London. Pop.: 221 800 (1994 est.). Area: 40 sq. km (15 sq. miles).

Walton ★ ('wɔːltⁿn) *n* **1 Ernest Thomas Sinton.** 1903–95, Irish physicist: produced the first transmutation of a nucleus (1932) with Sir John Cockcroft, with whom he shared the Nobel prize for physics 1951. **2 Izaak** ('aɪzək). 1593–1683, English writer, best known for *The Compleat Angler* (1653; enlarged 1676). **3** Sir **William (Turner).** 1902–

★ people and places

83, British composer. His works include *Façade* (1923), the *Viola Concerto* (1929), and the oratorio *Belshazzar's Feast* (1931).

waltz (wɔːls) *n* **1** a ballroom dance in triple time in which couples spin around as they progress round the room. **2** a piece of music composed for or in the rhythm of this dance. ◆ *vb* **3** to dance or lead (someone) in or as in a waltz. **4** (*intr*) to move in a sprightly and self-assured manner. **5** (*intr*) *Inf.* to succeed easily. **6 waltz Matilda** *Austral.* See **Matilda**. [C18: from G *Walzer*, from MHG *walzen* to roll]

waltzer (ˈwɔːlsə) *n* **1** a person who waltzes. **2** a fairground roundabout on which people are spun round and moved up and down as it revolves.

Walvis Bay (ˈwɔːlvɪs) *or* **Walfish Bay** ★ *n* a port in Namibia, on the Atlantic: covers an area of 1124 sq. km (434 sq. miles) with its hinterland, formed an exclave of South Africa (1977–94); chief port of Namibia and rich fishing centre. Pop.: 23 000 (1992 est.).

wampum (ˈwɒmpəm) *n* (formerly) money used by North American Indians, made of cylindrical shells strung or woven together. Also called: **peag, peage**. [C17: of Amerind origin, short for *wampumpeag*, from *wampompeag*, from *wampan* light + *api* string + *-ag* pl. suffix]

wan (wɒn) *adj* **wanner, wannest**. **1** unnaturally pale, esp. from sickness, grief, etc. **2** suggestive of ill health, unhappiness, etc. **3** (of light, stars, etc.) faint or dim. [OE *wann* dark]
▸ **ˈwanly** *adv* ▸ **ˈwanness** *n*

Wanchüan *or* **Wan-ch'uan** ★ (ˌwæntʃʊˈɑːn) *n* a former name of **Zhangjiakou**.

wand (wɒnd) *n* **1** a slender supple stick or twig. **2** a thin rod carried as a symbol of authority. **3** a rod used by a magician, etc. **4** *Inf.* a conductor's baton. **5** *Archery.* a marker used to show the distance at which the archer stands from the target. [C12: from ON *vöndr*]

wander (ˈwɒndə) *vb* (*mainly intr*) **1** (*also tr*) to move or travel about, in, or through (a place) without any definite purpose or destination. **2** to proceed in an irregular course. **3** to go astray, as from a path or course. **4** (of thoughts, etc.) to lose concentration. **5** to think or speak incoherently or illogically. ◆ *n* **6** the act or an instance of wandering. [OE *wandrian*]
▸ **ˈwanderer** *n* ▸ **ˈwandering** *adj, n*

wandering albatross *n* a large albatross having a very wide wingspan and a white plumage with black wings.

wandering Jew *n* any of several related creeping or trailing plants of tropical America, such as tradescantia.

Wandering Jew ★ *n* (in medieval legend) a character condemned to roam the world eternally because he mocked Christ on the day of the Crucifixion.

wanderlust (ˈwɒndəˌlʌst) *n* a great desire to travel and rove about. [from G *Wanderlust*, lit.: wander desire]

wanderoo (ˌwɒndəˈruː) *n, pl* **wanderoos**. a macaque monkey of India and Sri Lanka, having black fur with a ruff of long greyish fur on each side of the face. [C17: from Sinhalese *vanduru* monkeys, lit.: forest-dwellers]

wandoo (wɒnˈduː) *n* a eucalyptus tree of W Australia, having white bark and durable wood. [from Abor.]

Wandsworth ★ (ˈwɒnzwəθ) *n* a borough of S Greater London, on the River Thames. Pop.: 266 600 (1994 est.). Area: 35 sq. km (13 sq. miles).

wane (weɪn) *vb* **wanes, waning, waned**. (*intr*) **1** (of the moon) to show a gradually decreasing portion of illuminated surface, between full moon and new moon. **2** to decrease gradually in size, strength, power, etc. **3** to draw to a close. ◆ *n* **4** a decrease, as in size, strength, power, etc. **5** the period during which the moon wanes. **6** a drawing to a close. **7** a rounded surface or defective edge of a plank, where the bark was. **8 on the wane**. in a state of decline. [OE *wanian* (vb)]
▸ **ˈwaney** *or* **ˈwany** *adj*

Wanganui ★ (ˌwɒŋəˈnuːɪ) *n* a port in New Zealand, on SW North Island: centre for a dairy-farming and sheep-rearing district. Pop.: 42 200 (1995 est.).

wangle (ˈwæŋɡ⁰l) *Inf.* ◆ *vb* **wangles, wangling, wangled**. **1** (*tr*) to use devious methods to get or achieve (some-

thing) for (oneself or another): *he wangled himself a salary increase*. **2** to manipulate or falsify (a situation, etc.). ◆ *n* **3** the act or an instance of wangling. [C19: orig. printers' sl., ? a blend of WAGGLE & dialect *wankle* wavering, from OE *wancol*]
▸ **ˈwangler** *n*

Wanhsien *or* **Wan-Hsien** ★ (ˈwænˈʃjen) *n* a variant transliteration of the Chinese name for **Wanxian**.

wanigan *or* **wannigan** (ˈwɒnɪɡən) *n Canad.* **1** a lumberjack's chest or box. **2** a cabin, caboose, or houseboat. [C19: from Algonquian]

wank (wæŋk) *Taboo sl.* ◆ *vb* **1** (*intr*) to masturbate. ◆ *n* **2** an instance of wanking. [from ?]

wankel engine (ˈwæŋk°l) *n* a type of rotary internal-combustion engine without reciprocating parts. It consists of a curved triangular-shaped piston rotating in an elliptical combustion chamber. [C20: after Felix *Wankel* (1902–88), G engineer who invented it]

wanker (ˈwæŋkə) *n Sl.* **1** *Taboo.* a person who wanks; masturbator. **2** *Derog.* a worthless fellow.

Wankie ★ (ˈwɑːŋkɪ) *n* the former name (until 1982) of **Hwange**.

wannabe *or* **wannabee** (ˈwɒnəˌbiː) *n Inf.* **a** a person who desires to be, or be like, something or someone else. **b** (*as modifier*): *a wannabe film star*. [C20: phonetic shortening of *want to be*]

Wanne-Eickel ★ (German ˈvanəˌaikəl) *n* an industrial town in W Germany, in North Rhine-Westphalia on the Rhine-Herne Canal: formed in 1926 by the merging of two townships. Pop.: 98 800 (latest est.).

want (wɒnt) *vb* **1** (*tr*) to feel a need or longing for: *I want a new hat*. **2** (when *tr, may take a clause as object or an infinitive*) to wish, need, or desire (something or to do something): *he wants to go home*. **3** (*intr; usually used with a negative and often foll. by for*) to be lacking or deficient (in something necessary or desirable): *the child wants for nothing*. **4** (*tr*) to feel the absence of: *lying on the ground makes me want my bed*. **5** (*tr*) to fall short by (a specified amount). **6** (*tr*) *Chiefly Brit.* to have need of or require (doing or being something): *your shoes want cleaning*. **7** (*intr*) to be destitute. **8** (*tr; often passive*) to seek or request the presence of: *you're wanted upstairs*. **9** (*tr; takes an infinitive*) *Inf.* should or ought (to do something): *you don't want to go out so late*. ◆ *n* **10** the act or an instance of wanting. **11** anything that is needed, desired, or lacked: *to supply someone's wants*. **12** a lack, shortage, or absence: *for want of common sense*. **13** the state of being in need: *the state should help those in want*. **14** a sense of lack; craving. [C12 (vb, in the sense: it is lacking), C13 (n): from ON *vanta* to be deficient]
▸ **ˈwanter** *n*

want ad *n Inf.* a classified advertisement in a newspaper, magazine, etc., for something wanted, such as property or employment.

wanting (ˈwɒntɪŋ) *adj* (*postpositive*) **1** lacking or absent. **2** not meeting requirements or expectations: *you have been found wanting*.

wanton (ˈwɒntən) *adj* **1** dissolute, licentious, or immoral. **2** without motive, provocation, or justification: *wanton destruction*. **3** maliciously and unnecessarily cruel. **4** unrestrained: *wanton spending*. **5** *Arch. or poetic.* playful or capricious. **6** *Arch.* (of vegetation, etc.) luxuriant. ◆ *n* **7** a licentious person, esp. a woman. ◆ *vb* **8** (*intr*) to behave in a wanton manner. [C13 *wantowen* (in the obs. sense: unruly): from *wan-* (prefix equivalent to UN-¹) + *-towen*, from OE *togen* brought up, from *tēon* to bring up]
▸ **ˈwantonly** *adv* ▸ **ˈwantonness** *n*

Wanxian, Wanhsien, *or* **Wan-Hsien** ★ (ˈwænˈʃjen) *n* an inland port in central China, in E Sichuan province, on the Yangtze River. Pop.: 156 823 (1990 est.).

wapentake (ˈwɒpənˌteɪk, ˈwæp-) *n English legal history.* a subdivision of certain shires or counties, esp. in the Midlands and North of England, corresponding to the hundred in other shires. [OE *wǣpen(ge)tæc*]

wapiti (ˈwɒpɪtɪ) *n, pl* **wapitis**. a large North American deer with large much-branched antlers, now also found in New Zealand. [C19: of Amerind origin, lit.: white deer, from *wap* (unattested) white; from the animal's white tail and rump]

war (wɔː) *n* **1** open armed conflict between two or more parties, nations, or states. Related adj: **belligerent** (see sense 2). **2** a particular armed conflict: *the 1973 war in the Middle East.* **3** the techniques of armed conflict as a study, science, or profession. **4** any conflict or contest: *the war against crime.* **5** (*modifier*) of, resulting from, or characteristic of war: *war damage; a war story.* **6 in the wars.** *Inf.* (esp. of a child) hurt or knocked about, esp. as a result of quarrelling and fighting. ♦ *vb* **wars, warring, warred. 7** (*intr*) to conduct a war. [C12: from ONorthern F *werre* (var. of OF *guerre*), of Gmc origin]

War. *abbrev. for* Warwickshire.

Warangal ★ (ˈwʌrəngəl) *n* a city in S central India, in N Andhra Pradesh: capital of a 12th-century Hindu kingdom. Pop.: 447 657 (1991).

waratah (ˈwɒrətə) *n Austral.* a shrub having dark green leaves and clusters of crimson flowers. [from Abor.]

Warbeck ★ (ˈwɔːbɛk) *n* **Perkin** (ˈpɜːkɪn). ?1474–99, Flemish impostor, pretender to the English throne. Professing to be Richard, Duke of York, he led an unsuccessful rising against Henry VII (1497): executed.

warble[1] (ˈwɔːbᵊl) *vb* **warbles, warbling, warbled. 1** to sing (words, songs, etc.) with trills, runs, and other embellishments. **2** (*tr*) to utter in a song. ♦ *n* **3** the act or an instance of warbling. [C14: via OF *werbler*, of Gmc origin]

warble[2] (ˈwɔːbᵊl) *n Vet. science.* **1** a small lumpy abscess under the skin of cattle caused by the larvae of the warble fly. **2** a hard lump of tissue on a horse's back, caused by prolonged friction of a saddle. [C16: from ?]

warble fly *n* any of a genus of hairy beelike dipterous flies, the larvae of which produce warbles in cattle.

warbler (ˈwɔːblə) *n* **1** a person or thing that warbles. **2** a small active passerine songbird of the Old World having a cryptic plumage and slender bill, that is an arboreal insectivore. **3** a small bird of an American family, similar to the Old World songbird but often brightly coloured.

Warburg ★ (*German* ˈvaːrburk) *n* **Otto** (**Heinrich**) (ˈɔto). 1883–1970, German biochemist and physiologist: Nobel prize for physiology or medicine (1931) for his work on respiratory enzymes.

war correspondent *n* a journalist who reports on a war from the scene of action.

war crime *n* a crime committed in wartime in violation of the accepted customs, such as ill-treatment of prisoners, etc.
▸ **war criminal** *n*

war cry *n* **1** a rallying cry used by combatants in battle. **2** a cry, slogan, etc., used to rally support for a cause.

ward (wɔːd) *n* **1** (in many countries) one of the districts into which a city, town, parish, or other area is divided for administration, election of representatives, etc. **2a** a room in a hospital, esp. one for patients requiring similar kinds of care: *a maternity ward.* **2b** (*as modifier*): *ward maid.* **3** one of the divisions of a prison. **4** an open space enclosed within the walls of a castle. **5** *Law.* Also called: **ward of court.** a person, esp. a minor or one legally incapable of managing his own affairs, placed under the control or protection of a guardian or of a court. **6** the state of being under guard or in custody. **7** a means of protection. **8a** an internal ridge or bar in a lock that prevents an incorrectly cut key from turning. **8b** a corresponding groove cut in a key. ♦ *vb* **9** (*tr*) *Arch.* to guard or protect. ♦ See also **ward off.** [OE *weard* protector]
▸ ˈ**wardless** *adj*

Ward ★ (wɔːd) *n* **1** Mrs **Humphry**, married name of *Mary Augusta Arnold.* 1851–1920, British novelist. Her novels include *Robert Elsmere* (1888) and *The Case of Richard Meynell* (1911). **2** Sir **Joseph George.** 1856–1930, New Zealand statesman; prime minister (1906–12; 1928–30).

-ward *suffix.* **1** (*forming adjectives*) indicating direction towards: *a backward step.* **2** (*forming adverbs*) a variant and the usual US and Canad. form of **-wards.** [OE *-weard* towards]

war dance *n* a ceremonial dance performed before

going to battle or after victory, esp. by certain North American Indian peoples.

warden (ˈwɔːdᵊn) *n* **1** a person who has the charge or care of something, esp. a building, or someone. **2** a public official, esp. one responsible for the enforcement of certain regulations: *traffic warden.* **3** a person employed to patrol a national park or a safari park. **4** *Chiefly US & Canad.* the chief officer in charge of a prison. **5** *Brit.* the principal of any of various universities or colleges. **6** See **churchwarden** (sense 1). [C13: from OF *wardein,* from *warder* to guard, of Gmc origin]

warder (ˈwɔːdə) *or* (*fem*) **wardress** *n* **1** *Chiefly Brit.* an officer in charge of prisoners in a jail. **2** a person who guards or has charge of something. [C14: from Anglo-F *wardere,* from OF *warder* to guard, of Gmc origin]

ward heeler *n US politics, disparaging.* a party worker who canvasses votes and performs chores for a political boss. Also called: **heeler.**

ward off *vb* (*tr, adv*) to turn aside or repel.

Wardour Street ★ (ˈwɔːdə) *n* **1** a street in Soho where many film companies have their London offices: formerly noted for shops selling antiques and mock antiques. **2** Also: **Wardour Street English.** affectedly archaic speech or writing.

wardrobe (ˈwɔːdrəʊb) *n* **1** a tall closet or cupboard, with a rail or hooks on which to hang clothes. **2** the total collection of articles of clothing belonging to one person. **3a** the collection of costumes belonging to a theatre or theatrical company. **3b** (*as modifier*): *wardrobe mistress.* [C14: from OF *warderobe,* from *warder* to guard + *robe* ROBE]

wardrobe trunk *n* a large upright rectangular travelling case, usually opening longitudinally, with one side having a hanging rail, the other having drawers or compartments.

wardroom (ˈwɔːˌdruːm, -ˌrʊm) *n* **1** the quarters assigned to the officers (except the captain) of a warship. **2** the officers of a warship collectively, excepting the captain.

-wards *or* **-ward** *suffix forming adverbs.* indicating direction towards: *a step backwards.* Cf. **-ward.** [OE *-weardes* towards]

wardship (ˈwɔːdʃɪp) *n* the state of being a ward.

ware[1] (wɛə) *n* (*often in combination*) **1** (*functioning as sing*) articles of the same kind or material: *silverware.* **2** porcelain or pottery of a specified type: *jasper ware.* ♦ See also **wares.** [OE *waru*]

ware[2] (wɛə) *vb Arch.* another word for **beware.** [OE *wær.* See AWARE, BEWARE]

warehouse *n* (ˈwɛəˌhaʊs). **1** a place where goods are stored prior to their use, distribution, or sale. **2** See **bonded warehouse. 3** *Chiefly Brit.* a large commercial, esp. wholesale, establishment. ♦ *vb* (ˈwɛəˌhaʊz, -ˌhaʊs), **warehouses, warehousing, warehoused. 4** (*tr*) to store or place in a warehouse, esp. a bonded warehouse.
▸ ˈ**ware**ˌ**houseman** *n*

warehousing (ˈwɛəˌhaʊzɪŋ) *n Business.* an attempt to gain a significant stake in a company without revealing the identity of the purchaser by buying small quantities of shares in the name of nominees.

wares (wɛəz) *pl n* **1** articles of manufacture considered as being for sale. **2** any talent or asset regarded as a saleable commodity.

warfare (ˈwɔːˌfɛə) *n* **1** the act, process, or an instance of waging war. **2** conflict or strife.

warfarin (ˈwɔːfərɪn) *n* a crystalline insoluble compound, used to kill rodents and, in the form of its sodium salt, as a medical anticoagulant. [C20: from the patent owners *W*(*isconsin*) *A*(*lumni*) *R*(*esearch*) *F*(*oundation*) + (COUM)ARIN]

war game *n* **1** a notional tactical exercise for training military commanders, in which no military units are actually deployed. **2** a game in which model soldiers are used to create battles, esp. past battles, in order to study tactics.

warhead (ˈwɔːˌhɛd) *n* the part of the fore end of a missile or projectile that contains explosives.

Warhol ★ (ˈwɔːhəʊl) *n* **Andy,** real name *Andrew Warhola.* ?1926–87, US pop artist and film maker.

★ people and places

warhorse ('wɔː,hɔːs) n **1** a horse used in battle. **2** Inf. a veteran soldier or politician.

Warks abbrev. for Warwickshire.

Warley ★ ('wɔːlɪ) n an industrial town in W central England, in Sandwell, in the West Midlands: formed in 1966 by the amalgamation of Smethwick, Oldbury, and Rowley Regis. Pop.: 145 542 (1991).

warlike ('wɔː,laɪk) adj **1** of, relating to, or used in war. **2** hostile or belligerent. **3** fit or ready for war.

warlock ('wɔː,lɒk) n a man who practises black magic. [OE wǣrloga oath breaker, from wǣr oath + -loga liar, from lēogan to lie]

Warlock ★ ('wɔː,lɒk) n **Peter**, real name Philip Arnold Heseltine. 1894–1930, British composer. His works include song cycles and the Capriol Suite (1926) for strings.

warlord ('wɔː,lɔːd) n a military leader of a nation or part of a nation: the Chinese warlords.

Warlpiri ('walpiri) n an Aboriginal language of central Australia.

warm (wɔːm) adj **1** characterized by or having a moderate degree of heat. **2** maintaining or imparting heat: a warm coat. **3** having or showing ready affection, kindliness, etc.: a warm personality. **4** lively or passionate: a warm debate. **5** cordial or enthusiastic: warm support. **6** quickly or easily aroused: a warm temper. **7** (of colours) predominantly red or yellow in tone. **8** (of a scent, trail, etc.) recently made. **9** near to finding a hidden object or guessing facts, as in children's games. **10** Inf. uncomfortable or disagreeable, esp. because of the proximity of danger. ◆ vb **11** (sometimes foll. by up) to make or become warm or warmer. **12** (when intr, often foll. by to) to make or become excited, enthusiastic, etc. (about): he warmed to the idea of buying a new car. **13** (intr; often foll. by to) to feel affection, kindness, etc. (for someone): I warmed to her mother from the start. ◆ n Inf. **14** a warm place or area: come into the warm. ◆ See also **warm up**. [OE wearm]
▸ 'warmer n ▸ 'warmish adj ▸ 'warmly adv ▸ 'warmness n

warm-blooded adj **1** ardent, impetuous, or passionate. **2** (of birds and mammals) having a constant body temperature, usually higher than the temperature of the surroundings. Technical term: **homoiothermic**.
▸ ,warm-'bloodedness n

warm-down n light exercises performed to aid recovery from strenuous physical activity.

war memorial n a monument, usually an obelisk or cross, to those who die in a war, esp. those from a particular locality.

warm front n Meteorol. the boundary between a warm air mass and the cold air above which it is rising, at a less steep angle than at the cold front.

warm-hearted adj kindly, generous, or readily sympathetic.
▸ ,warm-'heartedly adv ▸ ,warm-'heartedness n

warming pan n a pan, often of copper and having a long handle, filled with hot coals and formerly drawn over the sheets to warm a bed.

warmonger ('wɔː,mʌŋgə) n a person who fosters warlike ideas or advocates war.
▸ 'war,mongering n

warmth (wɔːmθ) n **1** the state, quality, or sensation of being warm. **2** intensity of emotion: he denied the accusation with some warmth. **3** affection or cordiality.

warm up vb (adv) **1** to make or become warm or warmer. **2** (intr) to exercise immediately before a game, contest, or more vigorous exercise. **3** (intr) to get ready for something important; prepare. **4** to run (an engine, etc.) until the working temperature is attained, or (of an engine, etc.) to undergo this process. **5** to make or become more animated: the party warmed up when Tom came. **6** to reheat (already cooked food) or (of such food) to be reheated. ◆ n **warm-up**. **7** the act or an instance of warming up. **8** a preparatory exercise routine.

warn (wɔːn) vb **1** to notify or make (someone) aware of danger, harm, etc. **2** (tr; often takes a negative and an infinitive) to advise or admonish (someone) as to action, conduct, etc.: I warn you not to do that again. **3** (takes a clause as

object or an infinitive) to inform (someone) in advance: he warned them that he would arrive late. **4** (tr; usually foll. by away, off, etc.) to give notice to go away, be off, etc. [OE wearnian]
▸ 'warner n

warning ('wɔːnɪŋ) n **1** a hint, intimation, threat, etc., of harm or danger. **2** advice to beware or desist. **3** an archaic word for **notice** (sense 6). ◆ adj **4** (prenominal) intended or serving to warn: a warning look.
▸ 'warningly adv

War of American Independence n the conflict following the revolt of the North American colonies against British rule, particularly on the issue of taxation. Hostilities began in 1775 when British and American forces clashed at Lexington and Concord. Articles of Confederation agreed in the Continental Congress in 1777 provided for a confederacy to be known as the United States of America. The war was effectively ended with the surrender of the British at Yorktown in 1781 and peace was signed at Paris in Sept. 1783. Also called: **American Revolution** or **Revolutionary War.**

warp (wɔːp) vb **1** to twist or cause to twist out of shape, as from heat, damp, etc. **2** to turn or cause to turn from a true, correct, or proper course. **3** to pervert or be perverted. **4** Naut. to move (a vessel) by hauling on a rope fixed to a stationary object ashore or (of a vessel) to be moved thus. **5** (tr) to flood (land) with water from which alluvial matter is deposited. ◆ n **6** the state or condition of being twisted out of shape. **7** a twist, distortion, or bias. **8** a mental or moral deviation. **9** the yarns arranged lengthways on a loom, forming the threads through which the weft yarns are woven. **10** Naut. a rope used for warping a vessel. **11** alluvial sediment deposited by water. [OE wearp a throw]
▸ 'warpage n ▸ 'warped adj ▸ 'warper n

war paint n **1** painted decoration of the face and body applied by certain North American Indians before battle. **2** Inf. finery or regalia. **3** Inf. cosmetics.

warpath ('wɔː,pɑːθ) n **1** the route taken by North American Indians on a warlike expedition. **2 on the warpath. 2a** preparing to engage in battle. **2b** Inf. in a state of anger.

warplane ('wɔː,pleɪn) n any aircraft designed for and used in warfare.

warrant ('wɒrənt) n **1** anything that gives authority for an action or decision; authorization. **2** a document that certifies or guarantees, such as a receipt for goods stored in a warehouse, a licence, or a commission. **3** Law. an authorization issued by a magistrate allowing a constable or other officer to search or seize property, arrest a person, or perform some other specified act. **4** (in certain armed services) the official authority for the appointment of warrant officers. **5** a security that functions as a stock option by giving the owner the right to buy ordinary shares in a company at a specified date, often at a specified price. ◆ vb (tr) **6** to guarantee the quality, condition, etc., of (something). **7** to give authority or power to. **8** to attest to the character, worthiness, etc., of. **9** to guarantee (a purchaser of merchandise) against loss of, damage to, or misrepresentation concerning the merchandise. **10** Law. to guarantee (the title to an estate or other property). **11** to declare confidently. [C13: from Anglo-F, var. of OF guarant, from guarantir to guarantee, of Gmc origin]
▸ 'warrantable adj ▸ ,warranta'bility n ▸ 'warrantably adv ▸ 'warranter n

warrantee (,wɒrən'tiː) n a person to whom a warranty is given.

warrant officer n an officer in certain armed services who holds a rank between those of commissioned and noncommissioned officers. In the British army the rank has two classes: regimental sergeant major and company sergeant major.

Warrant of Fitness n NZ. a six-monthly certificate required for motor vehicles certifying mechanical soundness.

warrantor ('wɒrən,tɔː) n an individual or company that provides a warranty.

warrant sale n Scots Law. a sale of someone's personal

belongings or household effects that have been seized to meet unpaid debts.

warranty ('wɒrəntɪ) *n, pl* **warranties. 1** *Property law.* a covenant, express or implied, by which the vendor of real property vouches for the security of the title conveyed. **2** *Contract law.* an express or implied term in a contract collateral to the main purpose, such as an undertaking that goods contracted to be sold shall meet specified requirements as to quality, etc. **3** *Insurance law.* an undertaking by the party insured that the facts given regarding the risk are as stated. [C14: from Anglo-F *warantie*, from *warantir* to warrant, var. of OF *guarantir*; see WARRANT]

warren ('wɒrən) *n* **1** a series of interconnected underground tunnels in which rabbits live. **2** a colony of rabbits. **3** an overcrowded area or dwelling. **4** *Chiefly Brit.* an enclosed place where small game animals or birds are kept, esp. for breeding. [C14: from Anglo-F *warenne*, of Gmc origin]

Warren ★ ('wɒrən) *n* a city in SE Michigan, northeast of Detroit. Pop.: 142 625 (1994 est.).

warrigal ('wɒrɪgæl) *Austral.* ♦ *n* **1** a dingo. ♦ *adj* **2** untamed or wild. [C19: from Abor.]

Warrington ★ ('wɒrɪŋtən) *n* an industrial town and unitary authority in NW England, in N Cheshire on the River Mersey: dates from Roman times. Pop. (urban area): 188 000 (1995 est.). Area: 176 sq. km (68 sq. miles).

warrior ('wɒrɪə) *n* **a** a person engaged in, experienced in, or devoted to war. **b** (*as modifier*): *a warrior nation.* [C13: from OF *werreieor*, from *werre* WAR]

Warsaw ★ ('wɔːsɔː) *n* the capital of Poland, in the E central part on the River Vistula: became capital at the end of the 16th century; almost completely destroyed in World War II as the main centre of the Polish resistance movement; rebuilt within about six years; university (1818); situated at the junction of important trans-European routes. Pop.: 1 640 700 (1995 est.). Polish name: **Warszawa** (var'ʃava).

Warsaw Pact *n* a military treaty and association of E European countries (1955–91).

warship ('wɔːˌʃɪp) *n* a vessel armed, armoured, and otherwise equipped for naval warfare.

Wars of the Roses *pl n* the struggle for the throne in England (1455-85) between the House of York (symbolized by the white rose) and the House of Lancaster (symbolized by the red rose).

wart (wɔːt) *n* **1** *Pathol.* any firm abnormal elevation of the skin caused by a virus. **2** *Bot.* a small rounded outgrowth. **3 warts and all.** with all blemishes evident. [OE *weart(e)*]
▶ 'warty *adj*

Warta ★ (*Polish* 'varta) *n* a river in Poland, flowing generally north and west across the whole W Polish Plain to the River Oder. Length: 808 km (502 miles).

Wartburg ★ (*German* 'vartburk) *n* a medieval castle in central Germany, in Thuringia southwest of Eisenach; residence of Luther (1521–22) when he began his German translation of the New Testament.

warthog ('wɔːthɒg) *n* a wild pig of S and E Africa, having heavy tusks, wartlike protuberances on the face, and a mane of coarse hair.

wartime ('wɔːˌtaɪm) *n* **a** a period or time of war. **b** (*as modifier*): *wartime conditions.*

war whoop *n* the yell or howl uttered, esp. by North American Indians, while making an attack.

Warwick[1] ★ ('wɒrɪk) *n* a town in central England, administrative centre of Warwickshire, on the River Avon: 14th-century castle: the university of Warwick (1965) is in Coventry. Pop.: 22 476 (1991).

Warwick[2] ★ ('wɒrɪk) *n* **Earl of,** title of *Richard Neville,* known as *the Kingmaker.* 1428–71, English statesman. During the Wars of the Roses, he fought first for the Yorkists, securing the throne (1461) for Edward IV, and then for the Lancastrians, restoring Henry VI (1470). He was killed at Barnet by Edward IV.

Warwickshire ★ ('wɒrɪkˌʃɪə, -ʃə) *n* a county of central England: until 1974, when the West Midlands metropolitan county was created, it contained one of the most highly industrialized regions in the world, centred on

Birmingham. Administrative centre: Warwick. Pop.: 496 300 (1994 est.). Area: 1981 sq. km (765 sq. miles).

wary ('weərɪ) *adj* **warier, wariest. 1** watchful, cautious, or alert. **2** characterized by caution or watchfulness. [C16: from VOUCHE² + -Y¹]
▶ 'warily *adv* ▶ 'wariness *n*

was (wɒz; *unstressed* wəz) *vb* (used with *I, he, she, it,* and with singular nouns) **1** the past tense (indicative mood) of **be. 2** *Not standard.* a form of the subjunctive mood used in place of *were,* esp. in conditional sentences: *if the film was to be with you, would you be able to process it?* [OE *wæs,* from *wesan* to be]

Wasatch Range ★ ('wɔːsætʃ) *n* a mountain range in the W central US, in N Utah and SE Idaho. Highest peak: Mount Timpanogos, 3581 m (11 750 ft).

wash (wɒʃ) *vb* **1** to apply water or other liquid, usually with soap, to (oneself, clothes, etc.) in order to cleanse. **2** (*tr;* often foll. by *away, from, off,* etc.) to remove by the application of water or other liquid and usually soap: *she washed the dirt from her clothes.* **3** (*intr*) to be capable of being washed without damage or loss of colour. **4** (of an animal such as a cat) to cleanse (itself or another animal) by licking. **5** (*tr*) to cleanse from pollution or defilement. **6** (*tr*) to make wet or moist. **7** (often foll. by *away,* etc.) to move or be moved by water: *the flood washed away the bridge.* **8** (esp. of waves) to flow or sweep against or over (a surface or object), often with a lapping sound. **9** to form by erosion or be eroded: *the stream washed a ravine in the hill.* **10** (*tr*) to apply a thin coating of paint, metal, etc., to. **11** (*tr*) to separate (ore, etc.) from (gravel, etc.) by immersion in water. **12** (*intr; usually used with a negative*) *Inf., chiefly Brit.* to admit of testing or proof: *your excuses won't wash.* ♦ *n* **13** the act or process of washing. **14** a quantity of articles washed together. **15** a preparation or thin liquid used as a coating or in washing: *a thin wash of paint.* **16** *Med.* **16a** any medicinal lotion for application to a part of the body. **16b** (*in combination*): *an eyewash.* **17a** the technique of making wash drawings. **17b** See **wash drawing. 18** the erosion of soil by the action of flowing water. **19** a mass of alluvial material transported and deposited by flowing water. **20** land that is habitually washed by tidal or river waters. **21** the disturbance in the air or water produced at the rear of an aircraft, boat, or other moving object. **22** gravel, earth, etc., from which valuable minerals may be washed. **23** waste liquid matter or liquid refuse, esp. as fed to pigs. **24** an alcoholic liquid resembling strong beer, resulting from the fermentation of wort in the production of whisky. **25 come out in the wash.** *Inf.* to become known or apparent in the course of time. ♦ See also **wash down, wash out, wash up.** [OE *wæscan, waxan*]

Wash ★ (wɒʃ) *n* **the.** a shallow inlet of the North Sea on the E coast of England, between Lincolnshire and Norfolk.

Wash. *abbrev. for* Washington.

washable ★ ('wɒʃəb³l) *adj* (esp. of fabrics or clothes) capable of being washed without deteriorating.
▶ ˌwasha'bility *n*

wash-and-wear *adj* (of fabrics, garments, etc.) requiring only light washing, short drying time, and little or no ironing.

washbasin ('wɒʃˌbeɪs³n) *n* **1** Also called: **washbowl.** a basin or bowl for washing the face and hands. **2** Also called: **wash-hand basin.** a bathroom fixture with taps, used for washing the face and hands.

washboard ('wɒʃˌbɔːd) *n* **1** a board having a surface, usually of corrugated metal, on which, esp. formerly, clothes were scrubbed. **2** such a board used as a rhythm instrument played with the fingers in skiffle, country-and-western music, etc. **3** *Naut.* a vertical planklike shield fastened to the gunwales of a boat to prevent water from splashing over the side.

washcloth ('wɒʃˌklɒθ) *n* **1** another term for **dishcloth. 2** the US and Canad. word for **face cloth.**

washday ('wɒʃˌdeɪ) *n* a day on which clothes and linen are washed.

wash down *vb* (*tr, adv*) **1** to wash completely, esp. from

★ people and places

top to bottom. **2** to take drink with or after (food or another drink).

wash drawing *n* a pen-and-ink drawing that has been lightly brushed over with water to soften the lines.

washed out *adj* (**washed-out** *when prenominal*). **1** faded or colourless. **2** exhausted, esp. when being pale in appearance.

washed up *adj* (**washed-up** *when prenominal*). *Inf., chiefly US, Canad., & NZ.* no longer hopeful, etc.: *our hopes for the new deal are all washed up.*

washer ('wɒʃə) *n* **1** a person or thing that washes. **2** a flat ring or drilled disc of metal used under the head of a bolt or nut. **3** any flat ring of rubber, felt, metal, etc., used to provide a seal under a nut or in a tap or valve seat. **4** See **washing machine**. **5** *Austral.* a face cloth; flannel.

washerwoman ('wɒʃə,wʊmən) *or* (*masc*) **washerman** *n, pl* **washerwomen** *or* **washermen**. a person who washes clothes for a living.

washery ('wɒʃərɪ) *n, pl* **washeries**. a plant at a mine where water or other liquid is used to remove dirt from a mineral, esp. coal.

wash-hand basin *n* another name for **washbasin** (sense 2).

wash house *n* (formerly) an outbuilding in which clothes were washed.

washing ('wɒʃɪŋ) *n* **1** articles that have been or are to be washed together on a single occasion. **2** something, such as gold dust, that has been obtained by washing. **3** a thin coat of something applied in liquid form.

washing machine *n* a mechanical apparatus, usually powered by electricity, for washing clothing, linens, etc.

washing powder *n* powdered detergent for washing fabrics.

washing soda *n* crystalline sodium carbonate, esp. when used as a cleansing agent.

Washington[1] ★ ('wɒʃɪŋtən) *n* **1** a state of the northwestern US, on the Pacific: consists of the Coast Range and the Olympic Mountains in the west and the Columbia Plateau in the east. Capital: Olympia. Pop.: 5 532 939 (1996 est.). Area: 172 416 sq. km (66 570 sq. miles). Abbrevs.: **Wash.** or (with zip code) **WA**   **2** Also called: **Washington, DC.** the capital of the US, coextensive with the District of Columbia and situated near the E coast on the Potomac River: site chosen by President Washington in 1790; contains the White House and the Capitol; a major educational and administrative centre. Pop.: 567 094 (1994 est.). **3** a town in Tyne and Wear: designated a new town in 1964. Pop.: 56 848 (1991). **4 Mount.** a mountain in N New Hampshire, in the White Mountains: the highest peak in the northeast US; noted for extreme weather conditions. Height: 1917 m (6288 ft). **5 Lake.** a lake in W Washington, forming the E boundary of the city of Seattle: linked by canal with Puget Sound. Length: about 32 km (20 miles). Width: 6 km (4 miles).
▶ **Washingtonian** (,wɒʃɪŋ'təʊnɪən) *adj, n*

Washington[2] ★ ('wɒʃɪŋtən) *n* **1 Booker T(aliaferro).** 1856–1915, US Black educationalist and writer. **2 George.** 1732–99, US general and statesman; first president of the US (1789–97). He presided over the convention at Philadelphia (1787) that formulated the constitution of the US and elected him president.

washing-up *n Brit.* **1** the washing of dishes, cutlery, etc., after a meal. **2** dishes and cutlery waiting to be washed up. **3** (*as modifier*): *a washing-up machine.*

wash out *vb* (*adv*) **1** (*tr*) to wash (the inside of something) so as to remove (dirt). **2** Also: **wash off.** to remove or be removed by washing: *grass stains don't wash out easily.* ♦ *n* **washout. 3** *Geol.* **3a** erosion of the earth's surface by the action of running water. **3b** a narrow channel produced by this. **4** *Inf.* **4a** a total failure or disaster. **4b** an incompetent person.

washroom ('wɒʃ,ruːm, -,rʊm) *n US & Canad.* a euphemism for **lavatory.**

washstand ('wɒʃ,stænd) *n* a piece of furniture designed to hold a basin, etc., for washing the face and hands.

washtub ('wɒʃ,tʌb) *n* a tub or large container used for washing anything, esp. clothes.

wash up *vb* (*adv*) **1** *Chiefly Brit.* to wash (dishes, cutlery, etc.) after a meal. **2** (*intr*) *US & Canad.* to wash one's face and hands. ♦ *n* **washup. 3** *Austral.* the end, outcome of a process: *in the washup, three were elected.*

washy ('wɒʃɪ) *adj* **washier, washiest. 1** overdiluted, watery, or weak. **2** lacking intensity or strength.
▶ **'washiness** *n*

wasn't ('wɒzᵊnt) *contraction of* was not.

wasp (wɒsp) *n* **1** a social hymenopterous insect, such as the **common wasp,** having a black-and-yellow body and an ovipositor specialized for stinging. **2** any of various solitary hymenopterans, such as the digger wasp and gall wasp. [OE *wæsp*]
▶ **'wasp,like** *adj* ▶ **'waspy** *adj* ▶ **'waspily** *adv*
▶ **'waspiness** *n*

Wasp *or* **WASP** (wɒsp) *n* (in the US) *acronym for* White Anglo-Saxon Protestant: a person descended from N European, usually Protestant stock, forming a group often considered the most dominant, privileged, and influential in American society.

waspish ('wɒspɪʃ) *adj* **1** relating to or suggestive of a wasp. **2** easily annoyed or angered.
▶ **'waspishly** *adv*

wasp waist *n* a very slender waist, esp. one that is tightly corseted.
▶ **'wasp-,waisted** *adj*

wassail ('wɒseɪl) *n* **1** (formerly) a toast or salutation made to a person at festivities. **2** a festivity when much drinking takes place. **3** alcoholic drink drunk at such a festivity, esp. spiced beer or mulled wine. ♦ *vb* **4** to drink the health of (a person) at a wassail. **5** (*intr*) to go from house to house singing carols at Christmas. [C13: from ON *ves heill* be in good health]
▶ **'wassailer** *n*

Wassermann test *or* **reaction** ('wæsəmən) *n Med.* a diagnostic test for syphilis. [C20: after August von *Wassermann* (1866–1925), G bacteriologist]

wast (wɒst; *unstressed* wəst) *vb Arch. or dialect.* (used with the pronoun *thou* or its relative equivalent) a singular form of the past tense (indicative mood) of **be.**

wastage ('weɪstɪdʒ) *n* **1** anything lost by wear or waste. **2** the process of wasting. **3** reduction in size of a workforce by retirement, etc. (esp. in **natural wastage**).

USAGE NOTE   *Waste* and *wastage* are to some extent interchangeable, but many people think that *wastage* should not be used to refer to loss resulting from human carelessness, inefficiency, etc.: *a waste* (not *a wastage*) *of time/money/effort,* etc.

---

waste (weɪst) *vb* **wastes, wasting, wasted. 1** (*tr*) to use, consume, or expend thoughtlessly, carelessly, or to no avail. **2** (*tr*) to fail to take advantage of: *to waste an opportunity.* **3** (when *intr*, often foll. by *away*) to lose or cause to lose bodily strength, health, etc. **4** to exhaust or become exhausted. **5** (*tr*) to ravage. **6** (*tr*) *Sl.* to murder or kill. ♦ *n* **7** the act of wasting or state of being wasted. **8** a failure to take advantage of something. **9** anything unused or not used to full advantage. **10** anything or anyone rejected as useless, worthless, or in excess of what is required. **11** garbage, rubbish, or trash. **12** a land or region that is devastated or ruined. **13** a land or region that is wild or uncultivated. **14** *Physiol.* **14a** the useless products of metabolism. **14b** indigestible food residue. **15** *Law.* reduction in the value of an estate caused by act or neglect, esp. by a life tenant. ♦ *adj* **16** rejected as useless, unwanted, or worthless. **17** produced in excess of what is required. **18** not cultivated, inhabited, or productive: *waste land.* **19a** of or denoting the useless products of metabolism. **19b** of or denoting indigestible food residue. **20** destroyed, devastated, or ruined. **21 lay waste.** to devastate or destroy. [C13: from Anglo-F, from L *vastāre* to lay waste, from *vastus* empty]

wasted ('weɪstɪd) *adj* **1** not taken advantage of: *a wasted opportunity.* **2** unprofitable: *wasted effort.* **3** enfeebled and emaciated: *a thin wasted figure.* **4** *Sl.* showing signs of habitual drug abuse.

★ people and places

wasteful ('weɪstful) adj **1** tending to waste or squander. **2** causing waste or devastation.
▶ 'wastefully adv ▶ 'wastefulness n

wasteland ('weɪst,lænd) n **1** a barren or desolate area of land. **2** a region, period in history, etc., that is considered spiritually, intellectually, or aesthetically barren or desolate.

wastepaper ('weɪst,peɪpə) n paper discarded after use.

wastepaper basket or **bin** n an open receptacle for paper and other dry litter. Usual US and Canad. word: **wastebasket**.

waste pipe n a pipe to take excess or used water away, as from a sink to a drain.

waster ('weɪstə) n **1** a person or thing that wastes. **2** a ne'er-do-well; wastrel.

wasting ('weɪstɪŋ) adj (prenominal) reducing the vitality, strength, or robustness of the body: a wasting disease.
▶ 'wastingly adv

wasting asset n an unreplaceable business asset of limited life, such as an oil well.

wastrel ('weɪstrəl) n **1** a wasteful person; spendthrift; prodigal. **2** an idler or vagabond.

Wast Water ★ (wɒst) n a lake in NW England, in Cumbria in the Lake District. Length: 5 km (3 miles).

wat (wɑːt) n a Thai Buddhist monastery or temple. [Thai, from Sansk. vāta enclosure]

watap (wæ'tɑːp, wɑː-) n a stringy thread made by North American Indians from the roots of various conifers and used for weaving and sewing. [C18: from Canad. F, from Cree watapiy]

watch (wɒtʃ) vb **1** to look at or observe closely or attentively. **2** (intr; foll. by for) to wait attentively. **3** to guard or tend (something) closely or carefully. **4** (intr) to keep vigil. **5** (tr) to maintain an interest in: to watch the progress of a child at school. **6 watch it!** be careful! ◆ n **7a** a small portable timepiece, usually worn strapped to the wrist (a **wristwatch**) or in a waistcoat pocket. **7b** (as modifier): a watch spring. **8** a watching. **9** a period of vigil, esp. during the night. **10** (formerly) one of a set of periods into which the night was divided. **11** Naut. **11a** any of the periods, usually of four hours, during which part of a ship's crew are on duty. **11b** those officers and crew on duty during a specified watch. **12** the period during which a guard is on duty. **13** (formerly) a watchman or band of watchmen. **14 on the watch**. on the lookout. ◆ See also **watch out**. [OE wæccan (vb), wæcce (n)]
▶ 'watcher n

-watch suffix of nouns. indicating a regular television programme or newspaper feature on the topic specified: Crimewatch.

watchable ('wɒtʃəb³l) adj **1** capable of being watched. **2** interesting, enjoyable, or entertaining: a watchable television documentary.

watchcase ('wɒtʃ,keɪs) n a protective case for a watch, generally of metal such as gold or silver.

watch chain n a chain used for fastening a pocket watch to the clothing. See also **fob**[1].

Watch Committee n Brit. history. a local government committee responsible for the efficiency of the local police force.

watchdog ('wɒtʃ,dɒg) n **1** a dog kept to guard property. **2a** a person or group that acts as a protector against inefficiency, etc. **2b** (as modifier): a watchdog committee.

watch fire n a fire kept burning at night as a signal or for warmth and light by a person keeping watch.

watchful ('wɒtʃful) adj **1** vigilant or alert. **2** Arch. not sleeping.
▶ 'watchfully adv ▶ 'watchfulness n

watch-glass n **1** a curved glass disc that covers the dial of a watch. **2** a similarly shaped piece of glass used in laboratories for evaporating small samples of a solution, etc.

watchmaker ('wɒtʃ,meɪkə) n a person who makes or mends watches.
▶ 'watch,making n

watchman ('wɒtʃmən) n, pl **watchmen**. **1** a person employed to guard buildings or property. **2** (formerly) a man employed to patrol or guard the streets at night.

watch night n (in Protestant churches) **1a** the night of December 24, during which a service is held to mark the arrival of Christmas Day. **1b** the night of December 31, during which a service is held to mark the passing of the old year. **2** the service held on either of these nights.

watch out vb (intr, adv) to be careful or on one's guard.

watchstrap ('wɒtʃ,stræp) n a strap of leather, cloth, etc., attached to a watch for fastening it around the wrist. Also called (US and Canad.): **watchband**.

watchtower ('wɒtʃ,tauə) n a tower on which a sentry keeps watch.

watchword ('wɒtʃ,wɜːd) n **1** another word for **password**. **2** a rallying cry or slogan.

water ('wɔːtə) n **1** a clear colourless tasteless odourless liquid that is essential for plant and animal life and constitutes, in impure form, rain, oceans, rivers, lakes, etc. Formula: H_2O. Related adj: **aqueous**. **2a** any body or area of this liquid, such as a sea, lake, river, etc. **2b** (as modifier): water sports; a water plant. Related adj: **aquatic**. **3** the surface of such a body or area: fish swam below the water. **4** any form or variety of this liquid, such as rain. **5** See **high water, low water**. **6** any of various solutions of chemical substances in water: ammonia water. **7** Physiol. **7a** any fluid secreted from the body, such as sweat, urine, or tears. **7b** (usually pl) the amniotic fluid surrounding a fetus in the womb. **8** a wavy lustrous finish on some fabrics, esp. silk. **9** Arch. the degree of brilliance in a diamond. **10** excellence, quality, or degree (in **of the first water**). **11** Finance. capital stock issued without a corresponding increase in paid-up capital. **12** (modifier) Astrol. of or relating to the three signs of the zodiac Cancer, Scorpio, and Pisces. **13 hold water**. to prove credible, logical, or consistent: the alibi did not hold water. **14 make water. 14a** to urinate. **14b** (of a boat, etc.) to let in water. **15 pass water**. to urinate. **16 water under the bridge**. events that are past and done with. ◆ vb **17** (tr) to sprinkle, moisten, or soak with water. **18** (tr; often foll. by down) to weaken by the addition of water. **19** (intr) (of the eyes) to fill with tears. **20** (intr) (of the mouth) to salivate, esp. in anticipation of food (esp. in **make one's mouth water**). **21** (tr) to irrigate or provide with water: to water the land. **22** (intr) to drink water. **23** (intr) (of a ship, etc.) to take in a supply of water. **24** (tr) Finance. to raise the par value of (issued capital stock) without a corresponding increase in the real value of assets. **25** (tr) to produce a wavy lustrous finish on (fabrics, esp. silk). ◆ See also **water down**. [OE wæter]
▶ 'waterer n ▶ 'waterless adj

water bag n a bag, sometimes made of skin, leather, etc., but in Australia usually canvas, for carrying water.

water bailiff n an official responsible for enforcing laws on shipping and fishing.

water bear n another name for a **tardigrade**.

water bed n a waterproof mattress filled with water.

water beetle n any of various beetles that live most of the time in freshwater ponds, rivers, etc.

water bird n any aquatic bird, including the wading and swimming birds.

water biscuit n a thin crisp plain biscuit, usually served with butter or cheese.

water blister n a blister containing watery or serous fluid, without any blood or pus.

water boatman n any of various aquatic bugs having a flattened body and oarlike hind legs, adapted for swimming.

waterborne ('wɔːtə,bɔːn) adj **1** floating or travelling on water. **2** (of a disease, etc.) transported or transmitted by water.

waterbuck ('wɔːtə,bʌk) n any of a genus of antelopes of swampy areas of Africa, having long curved ridged horns.

water buffalo or **ox** n a member of the cattle tribe of swampy regions of S Asia, having widely spreading back-curving horns. Domesticated forms are used as draught animals.

water bug n any of various heteropterous insects

★ people and places

adapted to living in the water or on its surface, esp. any of the **giant water bugs** of North America, India, and southern Africa, which have flattened hairy legs.

water butt *n* a barrel for collecting rainwater, esp. from a drainpipe.

water cannon *n* an apparatus for pumping water through a nozzle at high pressure, used in quelling riots.

Water Carrier *or* **Bearer** *n* **the.** the constellation Aquarius, the 11th sign of the zodiac.

water chestnut *n* **1** a floating aquatic plant of Asia, having four-pronged edible nutlike fruits. **2 Chinese water chestnut.** a Chinese plant with an edible succulent corm. **3** the corm of the Chinese water chestnut, used in Oriental cookery.

water clock *or* **glass** *n* any of various devices for measuring time that use the escape of water as the motive force.

water closet *n* **1** a lavatory flushed by water. **2** a small room that has a lavatory. ◆ Usually abbreviated to **WC.**

watercolour *or US* **watercolor** ('wɔːtəˌkʌlə) *n* **1** water-soluble pigment bound with gum arabic, applied in transparent washes and without the admixture of white pigment in the lighter tones. **2a** a painting done in watercolours. **2b** (*as modifier*): *a watercolour masterpiece.* **3** the art or technique of painting with such pigments.
▶ 'water,colourist *or US* 'water,colorist *n*

water-cool *vb* (*tr*) to cool (an engine, etc.) by a flow of water circulating in an enclosed jacket.
▶ 'water-,cooled *adj*

water cooler *n* a device for cooling and dispensing drinking water.

watercourse ('wɔːtəˌkɔːs) *n* **1** a stream, river, or canal. **2** the channel, bed, or route along which this flows.

watercraft ('wɔːtəˌkrɑːft) *n* **1** a boat or ship or such vessels collectively. **2** skill in handling boats or in water sports.

watercress ('wɔːtəˌkrɛs) *n* an Old World cruciferous plant of clear ponds and streams, having pungent leaves that are used in salads and as a garnish.

water cure *n Med.* a nontechnical name for **hydropathy** or **hydrotherapy.**

water cycle *n* the circulation of the earth's water, in which water evaporates from the sea into the atmosphere, where it condenses and falls as rain or snow, returning to the sea by rivers.

water diviner *n Brit.* a person able to locate the presence of water, esp. underground, with a divining rod.

water down *vb* (*tr, adv*) **1** to dilute or weaken with water. **2** to modify, esp. so as to omit anything unpleasant or offensive: *to water down the truth.*
▶ ,watered-'down *adj*

waterfall ('wɔːtəˌfɔːl) *n* a cascade of falling water where there is a vertical or almost vertical step in a river.

water flea *n* any of numerous minute freshwater crustaceans which swim by means of hairy branched antennae. See also **daphnia.**

Waterford ★ ('wɔːtəfəd) *n* **1** a county of S Republic of Ireland, in Munster province on the Atlantic: mountainous in the centre and in the northwest. County town: Waterford. Pop.: 91 624 (1991). Area: 1838 sq. km (710 sq. miles). **2** a port in S Republic of Ireland, county town of Co. Waterford: famous glass industry; fishing. Pop.: 40 345 (1991).

waterfowl ('wɔːtəˌfaʊl) *n* **1** any aquatic freshwater bird, esp. any species of the family Anatidae (ducks, geese, and swans). **2** such birds collectively.

waterfront ('wɔːtəˌfrʌnt) *n* the area of a town or city alongside a body of water, such as a harbour or dockyard.

water gap *n* a deep valley in a ridge, containing a stream.

water gas *n* a mixture of hydrogen and carbon monoxide produced by passing steam over hot carbon, used as a fuel and raw material.

water gate *n* **1** a gate in a canal, etc., that can be opened

or closed to control the flow of water. **2** a gate through which access may be gained to a body of water.

Watergate ('wɔːtəˌgeɪt) *n* **1** an incident during the 1972 US presidential campaign, when agents employed by the re-election organization of President Richard Nixon were caught breaking into the Democratic Party headquarters in the Watergate building, Washington, DC. The political scandal was exacerbated by attempts to conceal the fact that White House officials had approved the burglary, and eventually forced the resignation of President Nixon. **2** any similar public scandal, esp. involving politicians or a possible cover-up.

water gauge *n* an instrument that indicates the presence or the quantity of water in a tank, reservoir, or boiler feed. Also called: **water glass.**

water glass *n* **1** a viscous syrupy solution of sodium silicate in water: used as a protective coating for cement and a preservative, esp. for eggs. **2** another name for **water gauge.**

water gum *n* any of several Australian gum trees that grow in swampy ground and beside creeks and rivers.

water hammer *n* a sharp concussion produced when the flow of water in a pipe is suddenly blocked.

water hen *n* another name for **gallinule.**

water hole *n* **1** a depression, such as a pond or pool, containing water, esp. one used by animals as a drinking place. **2** a source of drinking water in a desert.

Waterhouse ★ ('wɔːtəˌhaʊs) *n* **1** Alfred. 1830–1905, British architect of the Gothic Revival. **2** George Marsden. 1824–1906, New Zealand statesman, born in England: prime minister (1872–73). **3** Keith. born 1929, British writer: best known for the novel *Billy Liar* (1959).

water hyacinth *n* a floating aquatic plant of tropical America, having showy bluish-purple flowers and swollen leafstalks. It forms dense masses in rivers, ponds, etc.

water ice *n* an ice cream made from a frozen sugar syrup flavoured with fruit juice or purée.

watering can *n* a container with a handle and a spout with a perforated nozzle used to sprinkle water over plants.

watering hole *n* **1** a pool where animals drink; water hole. **2** *Facetious sl.* a pub.

watering place *n* **1** a place where drinking water for people or animals may be obtained. **2** *Brit.* a spa. **3** *Brit.* a seaside resort.

water jacket *n* a water-filled envelope surrounding a machine or part for cooling purposes, esp. the casing around the cylinder block of a pump or internal-combustion engine.

water jump *n* a ditch or brook over which athletes or horses must jump in a steeplechase or similar contest.

water level *n* **1** the level reached by the surface of a body of water. **2** the water line of a boat or ship.

water lily *n* any of various aquatic plants of temperate and tropical regions, having large leaves and showy flowers that float on the surface of the water.

water line *n* **1** a line marked at the level around a vessel's hull to which the vessel will be immersed when afloat. **2** a line marking the level reached by a body of water.

waterlogged ('wɔːtəˌlɒgd) *adj* **1** saturated with water. **2** (of a vessel still afloat) having taken in so much water as to be unmanageable.

Waterloo ★ (ˌwɔːtə'luː) *n* **1** a small town in central Belgium, in Walloon Brabant province south of Brussels: battle (1815) fought nearby in which British and Prussian forces under the Duke of Wellington and Blücher routed the French under Napoleon. Pop.: 17 800 (latest est.). **2** a total or crushing defeat (esp. in **meet one's Waterloo**).

water main *n* a principal supply pipe in an arrangement of pipes for distributing water.

waterman ('wɔːtəmən) *n, pl* **watermen.** a skilled boatman.
▶ 'waterman,ship *n*

watermark ('wɔːtəˌmɑːk) *n* **1** a mark impressed on paper during manufacture, visible when the paper is held up to the light. **2** another word for **water line**. ◆ *vb* (*tr*) **3** to mark (paper) with a watermark.

water meadow *n* a meadow that remains fertile by being periodically flooded by a stream.

watermelon ('wɔːtə,mɛlən) *n* **1** an African melon widely cultivated for its large edible fruit. **2** the fruit of this plant, which has a hard green rind and sweet watery reddish flesh.

water meter *n* a device for measuring the quantity or rate of water flowing through a pipe.

water milfoil *n* any of various pond plants having feathery underwater leaves and inconspicuous flowers.

water mill *n* a mill operated by a water wheel.

water moccasin *n* a large dark grey venomous snake of swamps in the southern US. Also called: **cottonmouth**.

water nymph *n* any fabled nymph of the water, such as the Naiad, Nereid, or Oceanid of Greek mythology.

water of crystallization *n* water present in the crystals of certain compounds. It is chemically combined in a specific amount but can often be easily expelled.

water ouzel *n* another name for **dipper** (the bird).

water paint *n* any water-based paint, such as an emulsion or an acrylic paint.

water pipe *n* **1** a pipe for water. **2** another name for **hookah**.

water pistol *n* a toy pistol that squirts a stream of water or other liquid.

water plantain *n* any of a genus of marsh plants of N temperate regions and Australia, having clusters of small white or pinkish flowers and broad pointed leaves.

water polo *n* a game played in water by two teams of seven swimmers in which each side tries to throw or propel an inflated ball into the opponents' goal.

water power *n* **1** the power latent in a dynamic or static head of water as used to drive machinery, esp. for generating electricity. **2** a source of such power, such as a drop in the level of a river, etc.

waterproof ('wɔːtə,pruːf) *adj* **1** not penetrable by water. Cf. **water-repellent, water-resistant**. ◆ *n* **2** *Chiefly Brit.* a waterproof garment, esp. a raincoat. ◆ *vb* (*tr*) **3** to make (a fabric, etc.) waterproof.

water purslane *n* a marsh plant of temperate and warm regions, having reddish stems and small reddish flowers.

water rail *n* a large Eurasian rail of swamps, ponds, etc., having a long red bill.

water rat *n* **1** any of several small amphibious rodents, esp. the water vole or the muskrat. **2** any of various amphibious rats of New Guinea, the Philippines, and Australia.

water rate *n* a charge made for the public supply of water.

water-repellent *adj* (of fabrics, garments, etc.) having a finish that resists the absorption of water.

water-resistant *adj* (esp. of fabrics) designed to resist but not entirely prevent the penetration of water.

Waters ★ ('wɔːtəz) *n* **Muddy**, real name *McKinley Morganfield*. 1915–83, US blues guitarist and songwriter.

water scorpion *n* a long-legged aquatic insect that breathes by means of a long spinelike tube that projects from the rear of the body and penetrates the surface of the water.

watershed ('wɔːtə,ʃɛd) *n* **1** the dividing line between two adjacent river systems, such as a ridge. **2** an important period or factor that serves as a dividing line.

waterside ('wɔːtə,saɪd) *n* **a** the area of land beside a body of water. **b** (*as modifier*): *waterside houses*.

watersider ('wɔːtə,saɪdə) *n* *Austral. & NZ.* a dock labourer.

water-ski *n* **1** a type of ski used for planing or gliding over water. ◆ *vb* **water-skis, water-skiing, water-skied** or **water-ski'd. 2** (*intr*) to ride over water on water-skis while holding a rope towed by a speedboat. ► 'water-,skier *n* ► 'water-,skiing *n*

water snake *n* any of various snakes that live in or near water, esp. any of a genus of harmless North American snakes.

water softener *n* **1** any substance that lessens the hardness of water, usually by precipitating calcium and magnesium ions. **2** an apparatus that is used to remove chemicals that cause hardness.

water spaniel *n* either of two large curly-coated breeds of spaniel (the Irish and the American), which are used for hunting waterfowl.

water splash *n* a place where a stream runs over a road.

water sports *pl n* sports, such as swimming or windsurfing, that take place in or on water.

waterspout ('wɔːtə,spaut) *n* **1** *Meteorol.* **1a** a tornado occurring over water that forms a column of water and mist. **1b** a sudden downpour of heavy rain. **2** a pipe or channel through which water is discharged.

water table *n* **1** the level below which the ground is saturated with water. **2** a string course that has a moulding designed to throw rainwater clear of the wall below.

water thrush *n* either of two North American warblers having brownish backs and striped underparts and occurring near water.

watertight ('wɔːtə,taɪt) *adj* **1** not permitting the passage of water either in or out: *a watertight boat*. **2** without loopholes: *a watertight argument*. **3** kept separate from other subjects or influences.

water tower *n* ('tauə) *n* a reservoir or storage tank mounted on a tower-like structure so that water can be distributed at a uniform pressure.

water vapour *n* water in the gaseous state, esp. when due to evaporation at a temperature below the boiling point.

water vole *n* a large amphibious vole of Eurasian river banks. Also called: **water rat**.

water wagtail *n* another name for **pied wagtail**.

waterway ('wɔːtə,weɪ) *n* a river, canal, or other navigable channel used as a means of travel or transport.

waterweed ('wɔːtə,wiːd) *n* any of various weedy aquatic plants.

water wheel *n* **1** a simple water-driven turbine consisting of a wheel having vanes set axially across its rim, used to drive machinery. **2** a wheel with buckets attached to its rim for raising water from a stream, pond, etc.

water wings *pl n* an inflatable rubber device shaped like a pair of wings, which is placed under the arms of a person learning to swim.

waterworks ('wɔːtə,wɜːks) *n* **1** (*functioning as sing*) an establishment for storing, purifying, and distributing water for community supply. **2** (*functioning as pl*) a display of water in movement, as in fountains. **3** (*functioning as pl*) *Brit. inf., euphemistic.* the urinary system. **4** (*functioning as pl*) *Inf.* crying; tears.

waterworn ('wɔːtə,wɔːn) *adj* worn smooth by the action or passage of water.

watery ('wɔːtərɪ) *adj* **1** relating to, containing, or resembling water. **2** discharging or secreting water or a waterlike fluid. **3** tearful; weepy. **4** insipid, thin, or weak.

Watford ★ ('wɒtfəd) *n* a town in SE England, in SW Hertfordshire: printing. Pop.: 113 080 (1991).

Watling Island ★ ('wɒtlɪŋ) *n* another name for **San Salvador Island**.

Watson ★ ('wɒtsən) *n* **1 James Dewey.** born 1928, US biologist, who contributed to the discovery of the helical structure of DNA: shared the Nobel prize for physiology or medicine 1962. **2 John Broadus.** 1878–1958, US psychologist; a leading exponent of behaviourism. **3 John Christian.** 1867–1941, Australian statesman, born in Chile: prime minister (1904). **4 Tom**, full name *Thomas Sturges Watson.* born 1949, US golfer.

Watson-Watt ★ ('wɒtsən'wɒt) *n* Sir **Robert Alexander.** 1892–1973, Scottish physicist, who helped to develop radar.

watt (wɒt) *n* the derived SI unit of power, equal to 1 joule per second; the power dissipated by a current of 1 am-

★ people and places

pere flowing across a potential difference of 1 volt. Symbol: W [C19: after J. WATT]

Watt ★ (wɒt) *n* **James.** 1736–1819, Scottish engineer. His improvements to the steam engine led to the use of steam power in industry.

wattage ('wɒtɪdʒ) *n* **1** power, esp. electric power, measured in watts. **2** the power rating, measured in watts, of an electrical appliance.

Watteau ★ ('wɒtəu; *French* vato) *n* **Jean-Antoine** (ʒɑ̃ ɑ̃twan). 1684–1721, French painter, esp. of *fêtes champêtres*.

Wattenscheid ★ (*German* 'vatənʃait) *n* an industrial town in NW Germany, in North Rhine-Westphalia east of Essen. Pop.: 81 200 (latest est.).

watt-hour *n* a unit of energy equal to a power of one watt operating for one hour.

wattle ('wɒtᵊl) *n* **1** a frame of rods or stakes interwoven with twigs, branches, etc., esp. when used to make fences. **2** the material used in such a construction. **3** a loose fold of skin, often brightly coloured, hanging from the neck or throat of certain birds, lizards, etc. **4** any of various chiefly Australian acacia trees having spikes of small brightly coloured flowers and flexible branches. ◆ *vb* **wattles, wattling, wattled.** (*tr*) **5** to construct from wattle. **6** to bind or frame with wattle. **7** to weave or twist (branches, twigs, etc.) into a frame. ◆ *adj* **8** made of, formed by, or covered with wattle. [OE *watol*]
▶ **'wattled** *adj*

wattle and daub *n* a form of wall construction consisting of interwoven twigs plastered with a mixture of clay, water, and sometimes chopped straw.

wattmeter ('wɒt,miːtə) *n* a meter for measuring electric power in watts.

Watts ★ (wɒts) *n* **1 George Frederick.** 1817–1904, British painter and sculptor. **2 Isaac.** 1674–1748, English hymn-writer.

Waugh ★ (wɔː) *n* **Evelyn (Arthur St John)** ('iːvlɪn). 1903–66, British novelist. His novels include *Decline and Fall* (1928), *A Handful of Dust* (1934), *Brideshead Revisited* (1945), and the World War II trilogy *Sword of Honour* (1952–61).

waul *or* **wawl** (wɔːl) *vb* (*intr*) to cry or wail plaintively like a cat. [C16: imit.]

wave (weɪv) *vb* **waves, waving, waved. 1** to move or cause to move freely to and fro: *the banner waved in the wind*. **2** (*intr*) to move the hand to and fro as a greeting. **3** to signal or signify by or as if by waving something. **4** (*tr*) to direct to move by or as if by waving something: *he waved me on*. **5** to form or be formed into curves, undulations, etc. **6** (*tr*) to set waves in (the hair). ◆ *n* **7** one of a sequence of ridges or undulations that moves across the surface of a body of a liquid, esp. the sea. **8 the waves.** the sea. **9** any undulation on or at the edge of a surface reminiscent of a wave in the sea: *a wave across the field of corn*. **10** anything that suggests the movement of a wave, as by a sudden rise: *a crime wave*. **11** a widespread movement that advances in a body: *a wave of settlers*. **12** the act or an instance of waving. **13** *Physics*. an energy-carrying disturbance propagated through a medium or space by a progressive local displacement of the medium or a change in its physical properties, but without any overall movement of matter. **14** *Physics*. a graphical representation of a wave obtained by plotting the magnitude of the disturbance against time at a particular point in the medium or space. **15** a prolonged spell of some particular type of weather: *a heat wave*. **16** an undulating curve or series of curves or loose curls in the hair. **17 make waves.** to cause trouble; disturb the status quo. [OE *wafian* (vb); C16 (n) changed from earlier *wāwe*, prob. from OE *wǣg* motion]
▶ **'waveless** *adj* ▶ **'wave,like** *adj*

waveband ('weɪv,bænd) *n* a range of wavelengths or frequencies used for a particular type of radio transmission.

wave-cut platform *n* a flat surface at the base of a cliff formed by erosion by waves.

wave down *vb* (*tr, adv*) to signal with a wave to (a driver or vehicle) to stop.

wave energy *n* energy obtained by harnessing wave power.

wave equation *n* *Physics*. a partial differential equation describing wave motion.

waveform ('weɪv,fɔːm) *n* *Physics*. the shape of the graph of a wave or oscillation obtained by plotting the value of some changing quantity against time.

wavefront ('weɪv,frʌnt) *n* *Physics*. a surface associated with a propagating wave and passing through all points in the wave that have the same phase.

wave function *n* *Physics*. a mathematical function of position and sometimes time, used in wave mechanics to describe the state of a physical system. Symbol: ψ

waveguide ('weɪv,gaɪd) *n* *Electronics*. a solid rod of dielectric or a hollow metal tube, usually of rectangular cross section, used as a path to guide microwaves.

wavelength ('weɪv,leŋθ) *n* **1** the distance, measured in the direction of propagation, between two points of the same phase in consecutive cycles of a wave. Symbol: λ **2** the wavelength of the carrier wave used by a particular broadcasting station. **3 on someone's** (*or* **the same**) **wavelength.** *Inf.* having similar views, feelings, or thoughts (as someone else).

wavelet ('weɪvlɪt) *n* a small wave.

Wavell ★ ('weɪvᵊl) *n* **Archibald (Percival)**, 1st Earl. 1883–1950, British field marshal. During World War II he was commander in chief in the Middle East (1939–41), commander in chief in India (1941–43), and viceroy of India (1943–47).

wave mechanics *n* (*functioning as sing*) *Physics*. the formulation of quantum mechanics in which the behaviour of systems, such as atoms, is described in terms of their wave functions.

wave number *n* *Physics*. the reciprocal of the wavelength of a wave.

waver ('weɪvə) *vb* (*intr*) **1** to be irresolute; hesitate between two possibilities. **2** to become unsteady. **3** to fluctuate. **4** to move back and forth or one way and another. **5** (of light) to flicker or flash. ◆ *n* **6** the act or an instance of wavering. [C14: from ON *vafra* to flicker]
▶ **'waverer** *n* ▶ **'waveringly** *adv*

wave theory *n* **1** the theory proposed by Huygens that light is transmitted by waves. **2** any theory that light or other radiation is transmitted as waves. ◆ Cf. **corpuscular theory.**

wavey ('weɪvɪ) *n* *Canad.* a snow goose or other wild goose. Also called: **wawa.** [via Canad. F from Algonquian (Cree *wehwew*)]

wavy ('weɪvɪ) *adj* **wavier, waviest. 1** abounding in or full of waves. **2** moving or proceeding in waves. **3** (of hair) set in or having waves.
▶ **'wavily** *adv* ▶ **'waviness** *n*

wax[1] (wæks) *n* **1** any of various viscous or solid materials of natural origin: characteristically lustrous, insoluble in water, and having a low softening temperature, they consist largely of esters of fatty acids. **2** any of various similar substances, such as paraffin wax, that have a mineral origin and consist largely of hydrocarbons. **3** short for **beeswax** *or* **sealing wax. 4** *Physiol.* another name for **cerumen. 5** a resinous preparation used by shoemakers to rub on thread. **6** any substance or object that is pliable or easily moulded: *he was wax in their hands*. **7** (*modifier*) made of or resembling wax: *a wax figure*. ◆ *vb* **8** (*tr*) to coat, polish, etc., with wax. [OE *weax*]
▶ **'waxer** *n*

wax[2] (wæks) *vb* (*intr*) **1** to become larger, more powerful, etc. **2** (of the moon) to show a gradually increasing portion of illuminated surface, between new moon and full moon. **3** to become: *to wax eloquent*. [OE *weaxan*]

wax[3] (wæks) *n* *Brit. inf., old-fashioned*. a fit of rage or temper: *he's in a wax today*. [from ?]

waxberry ('wæksbərɪ) *n, pl* **waxberries.** the waxy fruit of the wax myrtle or the snowberry.

waxbill ('wæks,bɪl) *n* any of various chiefly African finchlike weaverbirds having a brightly coloured bill and plumage.

wax cloth *n* **1** another name for **oilcloth. 2** (formerly) another name for **linoleum.**

waxen ('wæksən) *adj* **1** made of, treated with, or covered with wax. **2** resembling wax in colour or texture.

waxeye ('wæks,aɪ) *n* a small New Zealand bird with a white circle around its eye. Also called: **silver-eye, blighty**.

wax flower *n Austral.* any of a genus of shrubs having waxy pink-white five-petalled flowers.

wax light *n* a candle or taper of wax.

wax myrtle *n* a shrub of SE North America, having evergreen leaves and a small berry-like fruit with a waxy coating. Also called: **bayberry, candleberry, waxberry**.

wax palm *n* **1** a tall Andean palm tree having pinnate leaves that yield a resinous wax used in making candles. **2** another name for **carnauba** (sense 1).

wax paper *n* paper treated or coated with wax or paraffin to make it waterproof.

waxplant ('wæks,plɑːnt) *n* a climbing shrub of E Asia and Australia, having fleshy leaves and clusters of small waxy white pink-centred flowers.

waxwing ('wæks,wɪŋ) *n* any of a genus of gregarious passerine songbirds having red waxy wing tips and crested heads.

waxwork ('wæks,wɜːk) *n* **1** an object reproduced in wax, esp. as an ornament. **2** a life-size lifelike figure, esp. of a famous person, reproduced in wax. **3** (*pl; functioning as sing or pl*) a museum or exhibition of wax figures.

waxy[1] ('wæksɪ) *adj* **waxier, waxiest. 1** resembling wax in colour, appearance, or texture. **2** made of, covered with, or abounding in wax. ► 'waxily *adv* ► 'waxiness *n*

waxy[2] ('wæksɪ) *adj* **waxier, waxiest.** *Brit. inf., old-fashioned.* bad-tempered or irritable; angry.

way (weɪ) *n* **1** a manner, method, or means: *a way of life.* **2** a route or direction: *the way home.* **3a** a means or line of passage, such as a path or track. **3b** (*in combination*): *waterway.* **4** space or room for movement or activity (esp. in **make way, in the way, out of the way**). **5** distance, usually distance in general: *you've come a long way.* **6** a passage or journey: *on the way.* **7** characteristic style or manner: *I did it my way.* **8** (*often pl*) habit: *he has some offensive ways.* **9** an aspect of something; particular: *in many ways he was right.* **10a** a street in or leading out of a town. **10b** (*cap. when part of a street name*): *Icknield Way.* **11** something that one wants in a determined manner (esp. in **get** *or* **have one's** (**own**) **way**). **12** the experience or sphere in which one comes into contact with things (esp. in **come one's way**). **13** *Inf.* a state or condition, usually financial or concerning health (esp. in **in a good** (*or* **bad**) **way**). **14** *Inf.* the area or direction of one's home: *drop in if you're ever over my way.* **15** movement of a ship or other vessel. **16** a guide along which something can be moved, such as the surface of a lathe along which the tailstock slides. **17** (*pl*) the wooden or metal tracks down which a ship slides to be launched. **18** a course of life including experiences, conduct, etc.: *the way of sin.* **19 by the way.** incidentally. **20 by way of. 20a** via. **20b** serving as: *by way of introduction.* **20c** in the state or condition of: *by way of being an artist.* **21 each way.** (of a bet) laid on a horse, dog, etc., to win or gain a place. **22 give way. 22a** to collapse or break down. **22b** to yield. **23 give way to. 23a** to step aside for or stop for. **23b** to give full rein to (emotions, etc.). **24 go out of one's way.** to take considerable trouble or inconvenience oneself. **25 have a way with.** to have such a manner or skill as to handle successfully. **26 have it both ways.** to enjoy two things that would normally be mutually exclusive. **27 in a way.** in some respects. **28 in no way.** not at all. **29 lead the way. 29a** to go first. **29b** to set an example. **30 make one's way. 30a** to proceed or advance. **30b** to achieve success in life. **31 on the way out.** *Inf.* **31a** becoming unfashionable, etc. **31b** dying. **32 out of the way. 32a** removed or dealt with so as to be no longer a hindrance. **32b** remote. **32c** unusual and sometimes improper. **33 see one's way (clear).** to find it possible and be willing (to do something). **34 under way.** having started moving or making progress. ♦ *adv* **35** *Inf.* **35a** at a considerable distance or extent: *way over yonder.* **35b** very far: *they're way up the mountain.* **36** *Inf.* by far; considerably: *way better.* [OE *weg*]

waybill ('weɪ,bɪl) *n* a document attached to goods in transit specifying their nature, point of origin, and destination as well as the route to be taken and the rate to be charged.

wayfarer ('weɪ,fɛərə) *n* a person who goes on a journey. ► 'way,faring *n, adj*

wayfaring tree *n* a shrub of Europe and W Asia, having white flowers and berries that turn from red to black.

Wayland *or* **Wayland Smith** ★ ('weɪlənd) *n* a smith, artificer, and king of the elves in European folklore. Scandinavian name: **Völund.** German name: **Wieland.**

waylay (weɪ'leɪ) *vb* **waylays, waylaying, waylaid.** (*tr*) **1** to lie in wait for and attack. **2** to await and intercept unexpectedly. ► **way'layer** *n*

wayleave ('weɪ,liːv) *n* access to property granted by a landowner for payment, for example to allow a contractor access to a building site.

waymark ('weɪ,mɑːk) *n* a symbol or signpost marking the route of a footpath. ► 'way,marked *adj*

Wayne ★ (weɪn) *n* **John,** real name *Marion Michael Morrison.* 1907–79, US film actor, esp. in Westerns.

way-out *adj Inf.* **1** extremely unconventional or experimental. **2** excellent or amazing.

-ways *suffix forming adverbs.* indicating direction or manner: *sideways.* [OE *weges,* lit.: of the way, from *weg* way]

ways and means *pl n* **1** the revenues and methods of raising the revenues needed for the functioning of a state or other political unit. **2** the methods and resources for accomplishing some purpose.

wayside ('weɪ,saɪd) *n* **1a** the side or edge of a road. **1b** (*modifier*) situated by the wayside: *a wayside inn.* **2 fall by the wayside.** to cease or fail to continue doing something: *of the nine starters, three fell by the wayside.*

wayward ('weɪwəd) *adj* **1** wanting to have one's own way regardless of others. **2** capricious, erratic, or unpredictable. [C14: changed from *awayward* turned or turning away] ► 'waywardly *adv* ► 'waywardness *n*

wayworn ('weɪ,wɔːn) *adj Rare.* worn or tired by travel.

Waziristan ★ (wə,zɪərɪ'stɑːn) *n* a mountainous region of N Pakistan, on the border with Afghanistan.

wb *abbrev. for:* **1** water ballast. **2** Also: **W/B, WB.** waybill. **3** westbound.

Wb *Physics. symbol for* weber.

WBA *abbrev. for* World Boxing Association.

WBC *abbrev. for* World Boxing Council.

WBU *abbrev. for* World Boxing Union.

WC *abbrev. for:* **1** Also: **wc.** water closet. **2** (in London postal code) West Central.

WD *abbrev. for:* **1** War Department. **2** Works Department.

we (wiː) *pron* (*subjective*) **1** refers to the speaker or writer and another person or other people: *we should go now.* **2** refers to all people or people in general: *the planet on which we live.* **3** a formal word for **I** used by editors or other writers, and formerly by monarchs. **4** *Inf.* used instead of *you* with a tone of condescension or sarcasm: *how are we today?* [OE *wē*]

WEA (in Britain) *abbrev. for* Workers' Educational Association.

weak (wiːk) *adj* **1** lacking in physical or mental strength or force. **2** liable to yield, break, or give way: *a weak link in a chain.* **3** lacking in resolution or firmness of character. **4** lacking strength, power, or intensity: *a weak voice.* **5** lacking strength in a particular part: *a team weak in defence.* **6a** not functioning as well as is normal: *weak eyes.* **6b** easily upset: *a weak stomach.* **7** lacking in conviction, persuasiveness, etc.: *a weak argument.* **8** lacking in political or strategic strength: *a weak state.* **9** lacking the usual, full, or desirable strength of flavour: *weak tea.* **10** *Grammar.* **10a** denoting or belonging to a class of verbs, in Germanic languages, whose conjugation relies on inflectional endings rather than internal vowel gradation, as *look, looks, looking, looked.* **10b** belonging to any part-of-speech class, in any of various languages, whose inflections follow the more regular of two possible patterns. Cf. **strong** (sense 13). **11** (of a syllable) not accented or

★ people and places

stressed. **12** (of an industry, market, securities, etc.) falling in price or characterized by falling prices. [OE *wāc* soft, miserable]
▶ ˈweakish *adj*

weaken (ˈwiːkən) *vb* to become or cause to become weak or weaker.
▶ ˈweakener *n*

weak interaction *n Physics.* an interaction between elementary particles that is responsible for certain decay processes, operates at distances less than about 10^{-15} metres, and is 10^{12} times weaker than the strong interaction. Also called: **weak nuclear interaction** *or* **force**.

weak-kneed *adj Inf.* yielding readily to force, intimidation, etc.
▶ ˌweak-ˈkneedly *adv*

weakling (ˈwiːklɪŋ) *n* a person or animal that is lacking in strength or weak in constitution or character.

weakly (ˈwiːklɪ) *adj* **weaklier, weakliest. 1** sickly; feeble.
◆ *adv* **2** in a weak or feeble manner.

weak-minded *adj* **1** lacking in stability of mind or character. **2** another word for **feeble-minded.**
▶ ˌweak-ˈmindedly *adv* ▶ ˌweak-ˈmindedness *n*

weakness (ˈwiːknɪs) *n* **1** a being weak. **2** a failing, as in a person's character. **3** a self-indulgent liking: *a weakness for chocolates.*

weal[1] (wiːl) *n* a raised mark on the skin produced by a blow. Also called: **welt.** [C19: var. of WALE, infl. in form by WHEAL]

weal[2] (wiːl) *n Arch.* prosperity or wellbeing (now esp. in **the public weal, the common weal**). [OE *wela*]

weald (wiːld) *n Brit. arch.* open or forested country. [OE]

Weald ★ (wiːld) *n* **the.** a region of SE England, in Kent, Surrey, and Sussex between the North Downs and the South Downs: formerly forested.

wealth (welθ) *n* **1** a large amount of money and valuable material possessions. **2** the state of being rich. **3** a great profusion: *a wealth of gifts.* **4** *Econ.* all goods and services with monetary or productive value. [C13 *welthe*, from WEAL[2]]

wealth tax *n* a tax on personal property.

wealthy (ˈwelθɪ) *adj* **wealthier, wealthiest. 1** possessing wealth; rich. **2** of or relating to wealth. **3** abounding: *wealthy in friends.*
▶ ˈwealthily *adv* ▶ ˈwealthiness *n*

wean[1] (wiːn) *vb (tr)* **1** to cause (a child or young mammal) to replace mother's milk by other nourishment. **2** (usually foll. by *from*) to cause to desert former habits, pursuits, etc. [OE *wenian* to accustom]

wean[2] (weɪn) *n Scot. & N English dialect.* a child. [? short form of WEANLING, or a contraction of *wee ane*]

weaner (ˈwiːnə) *n* **1** a person or thing that weans. **2** a pig that has just been weaned and weighs less than 40 kg. **3** *Austral. & NZ.* a lamb, pig, or calf in the year in which it is weaned.

weanling (ˈwiːnlɪŋ) *n* a child or young animal recently weaned. [C16: from WEAN[1] + -LING[1]]

weapon (ˈwepən) *n* **1** an object or instrument used in fighting. **2** anything that serves to get the better of an opponent: *his power of speech was his best weapon.* **3** any part of an animal that is used to defend itself, to attack prey, etc., such as claws or a sting. [OE *wæpen*]
▶ ˈweaponed *adj* ▶ ˈweaponless *adj*

weaponry (ˈwepənrɪ) *n* weapons regarded collectively.

wear[1] (weə) *vb* **wears, wearing, wore, worn. 1** *(tr)* to carry or have (a garment, etc.) on one's person as clothing, ornament, etc. **2** *(tr)* to carry or have on one's person habitually: *she wears a lot of red.* **3** *(tr)* to have in one's aspect: *to wear a smile.* **4** *(tr)* to display, show, or fly: *a ship wears its colours.* **5** to deteriorate or cause to deteriorate by constant use or action. **6** to produce or be produced by constant rubbing, scraping, etc.: *to wear a hole in one's trousers.* **7** to bring or be brought to a specified condition by constant use or action: *to wear a tyre smooth.* **8** *(intr)* to submit to constant use or action in a specified way: *his suit wears well.* **9** *(tr)* to harass or weaken. **10** (when *intr*, often foll. by *on*) (of time) to pass or be passed slowly. **11** *(tr) Brit. inf.* to accept: *Larry won't wear that argument.* ◆ *n*

12 the act of wearing or state of being worn. **13a** anything designed to be worn: *leisure wear.* **13b** (*in combination*): *nightwear.* **14** deterioration from constant or normal use. **15** the quality of resisting the effects of constant use. ◆ See also **wear down, wear off, wear out.** [OE *werian*]
▶ ˈwearer *n*

wear[2] (weə) *vb* **wears, wearing, wore, worn.** *Naut.* to tack by gybing instead of by going through stays. [C17: from earlier *weare*, from ?]

Wear ★ (wɪə) *n* a river in NE England, rising in NW Durham and flowing southeast then northeast to the North Sea at Sunderland. Length: 105 km (65 miles).

wearable (ˈweərəbˀl) *adj* suitable for wear or able to be worn.
▶ ˌwearaˈbility *n*

wear and tear *n* damage, depreciation, or loss resulting from ordinary use.

wear down *vb (adv)* **1** to consume or be consumed by long or constant wearing, rubbing, etc. **2** to overcome or be overcome gradually by persistent effort.

wearing (ˈweərɪŋ) *adj* causing fatigue or exhaustion; tiring.
▶ ˈwearingly *adv*

wearisome (ˈwɪərɪsəm) *adj* causing fatigue or annoyance; tedious.
▶ ˈwearisomely *adv*

wear off *vb (adv)* **1** *(intr)* to decrease in intensity gradually: *the pain will wear off in an hour.* **2** to disappear or cause to disappear gradually through exposure, use, etc.

wear out *vb (adv)* **1** to make or become unfit or useless through wear. **2** *(tr)* to exhaust or tire.

weary (ˈwɪərɪ) *adj* **wearier, weariest. 1** tired or exhausted. **2** causing fatigue or exhaustion. **3** caused by or suggestive of weariness: *a weary laugh.* **4** (*postpositive; often foll. by of* or *with*) discontented or bored. ◆ *vb* **wearies, wearying, wearied. 5** to make or become weary. **6** to make or become discontented or impatient. [OE *wērig*]
▶ ˈweariless *adj* ▶ ˈwearily *adv* ▶ ˈweariness *n* ▶ ˈwearying *adj* ▶ ˈwearyingly *adv*

weasand (ˈwiːzənd) *n* a former name for the **trachea.** [OE *wǣsend, wāsend*]

weasel (ˈwiːzˀl) *n, pl* **weasels** *or* **weasel. 1** any of various small predatory mammals, such as the **European weasel,** having reddish-brown fur, an elongated body and neck, and short legs. **2** *Inf.* a sly or treacherous person. [OE *weosule, wesle*]
▶ ˈweaselly *adj*

weasel out *vb* **weasels, weaselling, weaselled** *or US* **weasels, weaseling, weaseled.** (*intr, adv*) *Inf., chiefly US & Canad.* **1** to go back on a commitment. **2** to evade a responsibility, esp. in a despicable manner.

weasel words *pl n Inf.* intentionally evasive or misleading speech; equivocation. [C20: from the weasel's supposed ability to suck an egg out of its shell without seeming to break the shell]

weather (ˈweðə) *n* **1a** the day-to-day meteorological conditions, esp. temperature, cloudiness, and rainfall, affecting a specific place. **1b** (*modifier*) relating to the forecasting of weather: *a weather ship.* **2 make heavy weather. 2a** *Naut.* to roll and pitch in heavy seas. **2b** (foll. by *of*) *Inf.* to carry out with difficulty or unnecessarily great effort. **3 under the weather.** *Inf.* not in good health. ◆ *adj* **4** (*prenominal*) on or at the side or part towards the wind: *the weather anchor.* Cf. **lee** (sense 2). ◆ *vb* **5** to expose or be exposed to the action of the weather. **6** to undergo or cause to undergo changes, such as discoloration, due to the action of the weather. **7** *(intr)* to withstand the action of the weather. **8** (when *intr*, foll. by *through*) to endure (a crisis, danger, etc.). **9** *(tr)* to slope (a surface, such as a roof) so as to throw rainwater clear. **10** *(tr)* to sail to the windward of: *to weather a point.* [OE *weder*]
▶ ˈweatherer *n*

weather-beaten *adj* **1** showing signs of exposure to the weather. **2** tanned or hardened by exposure to the weather.

weatherboard (ˈweðəˌbɔːd) *n* a timber board, with a groove (rabbet) along the front of its top edge and along

the back of its lower edge, that is fixed horizontally with others to form an exterior covering on a wall or roof.
▶ **'weather,boarding** n

weather-bound adj (of a vessel, aircraft, etc.) delayed by bad weather.

weathercock ('wɛðə,kɒk) n **1** a weather vane in the form of a cock. **2** a person who is fickle or changeable.

weathered ('wɛðəd) adj **1** affected by exposure to the action of the weather. **2** (of rocks and rock formations) eroded, decomposed, or otherwise altered by the action of wind, frost, etc. **3** (of a sill, roof, etc.) having a sloped surface so as to allow rainwater to run off.

weather eye n **1** the vision of a person trained to observe changes in the weather. **2** Inf. an alert or observant gaze. **3 keep one's weather eye open.** to stay on the alert.

weatherglass ('wɛðə,glɑːs) n any of various instruments, esp. a barometer, that measure atmospheric conditions.

weather house n a model house, usually with two human figures, one that comes out to foretell bad weather and one that comes out to foretell good weather.

weathering ('wɛðərɪŋ) n the mechanical and chemical breakdown of rocks by the action of rain, snow, etc.

weatherly ('wɛðəlɪ) adj (of a sailing vessel) making very little leeway when close-hauled, even in a stiff breeze.
▶ **'weather,liness** n

weatherman ('wɛðə,mæn) n, pl **weathermen.** Inf. a person who forecasts the weather, esp. one who works in a meteorological office.

weather map or **chart** n a chart showing weather conditions, compiled from simultaneous observations taken at various weather stations.

weatherproof ('wɛðə,pruːf) adj **1** designed or able to withstand exposure to weather without deterioration. ◆ vb **2** (tr) to render (something) weatherproof.

weather station n one of a network of meteorological observation posts where weather data is recorded.

weather strip n a thin strip of compressible material, such as spring metal, felt, etc., that is fitted between the frame of a door or window and the opening part to exclude wind and rain. Also called: **weatherstripping.**

weather vane n a vane designed to indicate the direction in which the wind is blowing.

weather window n a limited interval when weather conditions can be expected to be suitable for a particular project.

weather-wise adj **1** skilful in predicting weather conditions. **2** skilful in predicting trends in opinion, reactions, etc.

weatherworn ('wɛðə,wɔːn) adj another word for **weather-beaten.**

weave (wiːv) vb **weaves, weaving, wove** or **weaved; woven** or **weaved. 1** to form (a fabric) by interlacing (yarn, etc.), esp. on a loom. **2** (tr) to make or construct by such a process: to weave a shawl. **3** to construct by interlacing (cane, twigs, etc.). **4** (of a spider) to make (a web). **5** (tr) to construct by combining separate elements into a whole. **6** (tr; often foll. by in, into, through, etc.) to introduce: to weave factual details into a fiction. **7** to create (a way, etc.) by moving from side to side: to weave through a crowd. **8 get weaving.** Inf. to hurry. ◆ n **9** the method or pattern of weaving or the structure of a woven fabric: an open weave. [OE wefan]

weaver ('wiːvə) n **1** a person who weaves, esp. as a means of livelihood. **2** short for **weaverbird.**

weaverbird ('wiːvə,bɜːd) or **weaver** n any of a family of small Old World passerine songbirds, having a short thick bill and a dull plumage and building covered nests: includes the house sparrow and whydahs.

web (wɛb) n **1** any structure, fabric, etc., formed by or as if by weaving or interweaving. **2** a mesh of fine tough threads built by a spider from a liquid secreted from its spinnerets and used to trap insects. **3** a similar network of threads spun by certain insect larvae, such as the silkworm. **4** a fabric, esp. one in the process of being woven. **5** a membrane connecting the toes of some aquatic birds or the digits of such aquatic mammals as the otter. **6** the vane of a bird's feather. **7** a thin piece of metal, esp. one

connecting two thicker parts as in an H-beam or an I-beam. **8a** a continuous strip of paper as formed on a paper machine or fed from a reel into some printing presses. **8b** (as modifier): web offset. **9a** (often cap.; preceded by the) short for **World Wide Web. 9b** (as modifier): web pages. **10** any structure, construction, etc., that is intricately formed or complex: a web of intrigue. ◆ vb **webs, webbing, webbed. 11** (tr) to cover with or as if with a web. **12** (tr) to entangle or ensnare. **13** (intr) to construct a web. [OE webb]
▶ **'webless** adj

Webb ★ (wɛb) n **Sidney (James),** Baron Passfield. 1859–1947, British economist and Fabian socialist. He and his wife (**Martha) Beatrice** (née Potter), 1858–1943, British writer, collaborated in The History of Trade Unionism (1894), helped found the London School of Economics (1895), and started the New Statesman (1913).

webbed (wɛbd) adj **1** (of the feet of certain animals) having the digits connected by a thin fold of skin. **2** having or resembling a web.

webbing ('wɛbɪŋ) n **1** a strong fabric of hemp, cotton, jute, etc., woven in strips and used under springs in upholstery or for straps, etc. **2** the skin that unites the digits of a webbed foot.

webby ('wɛbɪ) adj **webbier, webbiest.** of, relating to, resembling, or consisting of a web.

weber ('veɪbə) n the derived SI unit of magnetic flux; the flux that, when linking a circuit of one turn, produces in it an emf of 1 volt as it is reduced to zero at a uniform rate in one second. Symbol: Wb [C20: after W. E. WEBER]

Weber ★ (German 've:bər) n **1** Baron **Carl Maria Friedrich Ernst von** (karl maˈriːa ˈfriːdrɪç ɛrnst fɔn). 1786–1826, German composer. His operas include Der Freischütz (1821) and Oberon (1826). **2 Ernst Heinrich** (ɛrnst 'haɪnrɪç). 1795–1878, German physiologist. **3 Max** (maks). 1864–1920, German economist, known for The Protestant Ethic and the Spirit of Capitalism (1904–05). **4 Wilhelm Eduard** ('vɪlhɛlm 'eːduart), brother of Ernst Heinrich Weber. 1804–91, German physicist, who investigated electricity and magnetism.

Webern ★ (German 've:bərn) n **Anton von** ('antoːn fɔn). 1883–1945, Austrian composer; pupil of Schoenberg, whose twelve-tone technique he adopted.

webfoot ('wɛb,fʊt) n **1** Zool. a foot having the toes connected by folds of skin. **2** Anat. a foot having an abnormal membrane connecting adjacent toes.

web-footed or **web-toed** adj (of certain animals) having webbed feet that facilitate swimming.

website ('wɛb,saɪt) n a group of connected pages on the World Wide Web containing information on a particular subject.

Webster ★ ('wɛbstə) n **1 Daniel.** 1782–1852, US politician. **2 John.** ?1580–?1625, English dramatist, noted for his tragedy The Duchess of Malfi (?1613). **3 Noah.** 1758–1843, US lexicographer, known for his American Dictionary of the English Language (1828).

webwheel ('wɛb,wiːl) n **1** a wheel containing a plate or web instead of spokes. **2** a wheel of which the rim, spokes, and centre are in one piece.

wed (wɛd) vb **weds, wedding, wedded** or **wed. 1** to take (a person of the opposite sex) as a husband or wife; marry. **2** (tr) to join (two people) in matrimony. **3** (tr) to unite closely. [OE weddian]
▶ **'wedded** adj

we'd (wiːd; unstressed wɪd) contraction of we had or we would.

Wed. abbrev. for Wednesday.

Weddell Sea ★ ('wɛdᵊl) n an arm of the S Atlantic in Antarctica.

wedding ('wɛdɪŋ) n **1a** the act of marrying or the celebration of a marriage. **1b** (as modifier): wedding day. **2** the anniversary of a marriage (in such combinations as silver wedding or diamond wedding).

wedding breakfast n the meal usually served after a wedding ceremony or just before the bride and bridegroom leave for their honeymoon.

wedding cake n a rich fruit cake, with one, two, or

more tiers, covered with almond paste and decorated with royal icing, which is served at a wedding reception.

wedding ring *n* a band ring with parallel sides, typically of precious metal, worn to indicate married status.

Wedekind ★ (*German* 'veːdəkɪnt) *n* **Frank** (fraŋk). 1864–1918, German dramatist; plays include *The Awakening of Spring* (1891) and *Pandora's Box* (1904).

wedge (wedʒ) *n* **1** a block of solid material, esp. wood or metal, that is shaped like a narrow V in cross section and can be pushed or driven between two objects or parts of an object in order to split or secure them. **2** any formation, structure, or substance in the shape of a wedge. **3** something such as an idea, action, etc., that tends to cause division. **4** a shoe with a wedge heel. **5** *Golf.* a club, a No. 10 iron with a face angle of more than 50°, used for bunker or pitch shots. **6** (formerly) a body of troops formed in a V-shape. **7 thin end of the wedge.** anything unimportant in itself that implies the start of something much larger. ◆ *vb* **wedges, wedging, wedged. 8** (*tr*) to secure with or as if with a wedge. **9** to squeeze or be squeezed like a wedge into a narrow space. **10** (*tr*) to force apart or divide with or as if with a wedge. [OE *wecg*]
▶ 'wedge,like *adj* ▶ 'wedgy *adj*

wedge heel *n* a raised shoe heel with the heel and sole forming a solid block.

wedge-tailed eagle *n* a large brown Australian eagle having a wedge-shaped tail. Also called: **eaglehawk,** (Inf.) **wedgie.**

Wedgwood[1] ('wedʒwud) *n* **1** *Trademark.* pottery produced at the Wedgwood factories, esp. such pottery having applied classical decoration in white on a blue or other coloured ground. ◆ *adj* **2** relating to or characteristic of such pottery: *Wedgwood blue.*

Wedgwood[2] ★ ('wedʒwud) *n* **Josiah.** 1730–95, British potter, who founded the Wedgwood pottery works near Stoke-on-Trent in Staffordshire.

wedlock ('wedlɒk) *n* **1** the state of being married. **2 born or conceived out of wedlock.** born or conceived when one's parents are not legally married. [OE *wedlāc*, from *wedd* pledge + *-lāc*, suffix denoting activity, ?from *lāc* game]

Wednesday ('wenzdɪ) *n* the fourth day of the week; third day of the working week. [OE *Wōdnes dæg* Woden's day, translation of L *mercurii dies* Mercury's day]

wee[1] (wiː) *adj* very small; tiny; minute. [C13: from OE *wǣg* weight]

wee[2] (wiː) *Inf., chiefly Brit.* ◆ *n* **1a** the act or an instance of urinating. **1b** urine. ◆ *vb* **wees, weeing, weed. 2** (*intr*) to urinate. ◆ Also: **wee-wee.** [from ?]

weed (wiːd) *n* **1** any plant that grows wild and profusely, esp. one that grows among cultivated plants, depriving them of space, food, etc. **2** *Sl.* **2a the weed.** tobacco. **2b** marijuana. **3** *Inf.* a thin or unprepossessing person. **4** an inferior horse, esp. one showing signs of weakness. ◆ *vb* **5** to remove (useless or troublesome plants) from (a garden, etc.). [OE *weod*]
▶ 'weeder *n* ▶ 'weedless *adj*

weedkiller ('wiːd,kɪlə) *n* a substance, usually a chemical or hormone, used for killing weeds.

weed out *vb* (*tr, adv*) to separate out, remove, or eliminate (anything unwanted): *to weed out troublesome students.*

weeds (wiːdz) *pl n* a widow's black mourning clothes. Also called: **widow's weeds.** [C16: pl of *weed* (OE *wǣd, wēd*) a band worn in mourning]

weedy ('wiːdɪ) *adj* **weedier, weediest. 1** full of or containing weeds: *weedy land.* **2** (of a plant) resembling a weed in straggling growth. **3** *Inf.* thin or weakly in appearance.

week (wiːk) *n* **1** a period of seven consecutive days, esp. one beginning with Sunday. Related adj: **hebdomadal. 2** a period of seven consecutive days beginning from or including a specified day: *a week from Wednesday.* **3** the period of time within a week devoted to work. ◆ *adv* **4** *Chiefly Brit.* seven days before or after a specified day: *I'll visit you Wednesday week.* [OE *wice, wicu*]

weekday ('wiːk,deɪ) *n* any day of the week other than Sunday and, often, Saturday.

weekend *n* (,wiːk'end) **1a** the end of the week, esp. the

period from Friday night until the end of Sunday. **1b** (*as modifier*): *a weekend party.* ◆ *vb* ('wiːk,end). **2** (*intr*) *Inf.* to spend or pass a weekend.

weekends (,wiːk'endz) *adv Inf.* at the weekend, esp. regularly or during every weekend.

weekly ('wiːklɪ) *adj* **1** happening or taking place once a week or every week. **2** determined or calculated by the week. ◆ *adv* **3** once a week or every week. ◆ *n, pl* **weeklies. 4** a newspaper or magazine issued every week.

weeknight ('wiːk,naɪt) *n* the evening or night of a weekday.

Weelkes ★ (wiːlks) *n* **Thomas.** ?1575–1623, English composer of madrigals.

ween (wiːn) *vb Arch.* to think or imagine (something). [OE *wēnan*]

weeny ('wiːnɪ) *adj* **weenier, weeniest.** *Inf.* very small; tiny. [C18: from WEE[1] with the ending *-ny* as in TINY]

weenybopper ('wiːnɪ,bɒpə) *n Inf.* a child of about 8 to 12 years who is a keen follower of pop music. [C20: formed on the model of TEENYBOPPER, from WEENY]

weep (wiːp) *vb* **weeps, weeping, wept. 1** to shed (tears). **2** (*tr;* foll. by *out*) to utter, shedding tears. **3** (when *intr,* foll. by *for*) to lament (for something). **4** to exude (drops of liquid). **5** (*intr*) (of a wound, etc.) to exude a watery fluid. ◆ *n* **6** a spell of weeping. [OE *wēpan*]

weeper ('wiːpə) *n* **1** a person who weeps, esp. a hired mourner. **2** something worn as a sign of mourning.

weeping ('wiːpɪŋ) *adj* (of plants) having slender hanging branches.
▶ 'weepingly *adv*

weeping willow *n* a Chinese willow tree having long hanging branches.

weepy ('wiːpɪ) *Inf.* ◆ *adj* **weepier, weepiest. 1** liable or tending to weep. ◆ *n, pl* **weepies. 2** a sentimental film or book.
▶ 'weepily *adv* ▶ 'weepiness *n*

weever ('wiːvə) *n* a small marine fish having venomous spines around the gills and the dorsal fin. [C17: from OF *wivre* viper, ult. from L *vīpera* VIPER]

weevil ('wiːvɪl) *n* any of numerous beetles, many having elongated snouts, that are pests, feeding on plants and plant products. [OE *wifel*]
▶ 'weevily *adj*

wee-wee *n, vb* a variant of **wee**[2].

w.e.f. *abbrev. for* with effect from.

weft (weft) *n* the yarn woven across the width of the fabric through the lengthways warp yarn. Also called: **filling, woof.** [OE]

Wegener ★ (*German* 'veːgənər) *n* **Alfred** ('alfreːt). 1880–1930, German meteorologist.

Weichsel ★ ('vaiksəl) *n* the German name for the **Vistula** (sense 1).

weigela (waɪ'giːlə, -'dʒiː-) *n* a shrub of an Asian genus having clusters of showy bell-shaped flowers. [C19: from NL, after C. E. *Weigel* (1748–1831), G physician]

weigh[1] (wei) *vb* **1** (*tr*) to measure the weight of. **2** (*intr*) to have weight: *she weighs more than her sister.* **3** (*tr;* often foll. by *up*) to apportion according to weight. **4** (*tr*) to consider carefully: *to weigh the facts of a case.* **5** (*intr*) to be influential: *his words weighed little with the jury.* **6** (*intr;* often foll. by *on*) to be oppressive (to). **7 weigh anchor.** to raise a vessel's anchor or (of a vessel) to have its anchor raised preparatory to departure. ◆ See also **weigh down, weigh in,** etc. [OE *wegan*]
▶ 'weighable *adj* ▶ 'weigher *n*

weigh[2] (wei) *n* **under weigh.** a variant spelling of **under way.** [C18: var. due to the infl. of phrases such as *to weigh anchor*]

weighbridge ('wei,brɪdʒ) *n* a machine for weighing vehicles, etc., by means of a metal plate set into a road.

weigh down *vb* (*adv*) to press (a person, etc.) down by or as if by weight: *his troubles weighed him down.*

weigh in *vb* (*intr, adv*) **1a** (of a boxer or wrestler) to be weighed before a bout. **1b** (of a jockey) to be weighed after, or sometimes before, a race. **2** *Inf.* to contribute, as in a discussion, etc.: *he weighed in with a few sharp com-*

ments. ◆ *n* **weigh-in. 3** the act of checking a competitor's weight, as in boxing, racing, etc.

weight (weɪt) *n* **1** a measure of the heaviness of an object; the amount anything weighs. **2** *Physics.* the vertical force experienced by a mass as a result of gravitation. **3** a system of units used to express weight: *troy weight.* **4** a unit used to measure weight: *the kilogram is the weight used in the metric system.* **5** any mass or heavy object used to exert pressure or weigh down. **6** an oppressive force: *the weight of cares.* **7** any heavy load: *the bag was such a weight.* **8** the main force; preponderance: *the weight of evidence.* **9** importance; influence: *his opinion carries weight.* **10** *Statistics.* one of a set of coefficients assigned to items of a frequency distribution that are analysed in order to represent the relative importance of the different items. **11** *Printing.* the apparent blackness of a printed typeface. **12 pull one's weight.** *Inf.* to do one's full or proper share of a task. **13 throw one's weight around.** *Inf.* to act in an overauthoritarian manner. ◆ *vb* (*tr*) **14** to add weight to. **15** to burden or oppress. **16** to add importance, value, etc., to (one side rather than another). **17** *Statistics.* to attach a weight or weights to. [OE *wiht*]
▸ **'weighter** *n*

weighted average *n Statistics.* a result produced by a technique designed to give recognition to the importance of certain factors when compiling the average of a group of values.

weighting ('weɪtɪŋ) *n* **1** a factor by which some quantity is multiplied in order to make it comparable with others. **2** an allowance paid to compensate for higher living costs: *a London weighting.*

weightlessness ('weɪtlɪsnɪs) *n* a state in which an object has no actual weight (because it is in space and unaffected by gravitational attraction) or no apparent weight (because the gravitational attraction equals the centripetal force and the object is in free fall).
▸ **'weightless** *adj*

weightlifting ('weɪt,lɪftɪŋ) *n* the sport of lifting barbells of specified weights in a prescribed manner.
▸ **'weight,lifter** *n*

weight training *n* physical exercise involving lifting weights, either heavy or light weights, as a way of improving muscle performance.

weight watcher *n* a person who tries to lose weight, esp. by dieting.

weighty ('weɪtɪ) *adj* **weightier, weightiest. 1** having great weight. **2** important. **3** causing worry.
▸ **'weightily** *adv* ▸ **'weightiness** *n*

weigh up *vb* (*tr, adv*) to make an assessment of (a person, situation, etc.); judge.

Weihai *or* **Wei-hai** ★ ('weɪ'haɪ) *n* a port in NE China, in NE Shandong on the Yellow Sea: leased to Britain as a naval base (1898–1930). Pop.: 128 888 (1990 est.). Also called: **Weihaiwei** (,weɪ'haɪ,weɪ).

Weil ★ (*French* vaɪl) *n* **Simone** (simɔn). 1909–43, French philosopher, whose works include *Waiting for God* (1951) and *Notebooks* (1956).

Weill ★ (vaɪl) *n* **Kurt** (kurt). 1900–50, German composer, in the US from 1935. He wrote the music for Brecht's *The Rise and Fall of the City of Mahagonny* (1927) and *The Threepenny Opera* (1928).

Weil's disease (vaɪlz) *n* another name for **leptospirosis.** [named after Adolf **Weil** (1848–1916), G physician]

Weimar ★ (*German* 'vaɪmar) *n* a city in E central Germany, in Thuringia; a cultural centre in the 18th and early 19th century; scene of the adoption (1919) of the constitution of the Weimar Republic. Pop.: 59 100 (1991).

Weimaraner ('vaɪmə,rɑːnə, 'waɪmə,rɑː-) *n* a breed of hunting dog, having a short grey coat and short tail. [C20: after WEIMAR, where the breed was developed]

Weinberg ★ ('waɪnbɜːg) *n* **Steven.** born 1933, US physicist, who shared the Nobel prize for physics (1979) with Sheldon Glashow and Abdus Salam for his role in formulating the electroweak theory.

weir (wɪə) *n* **1** a low dam that is built across a river to raise the water level, divert the water, or control its flow. **2** a

series of traps or enclosures placed in a stream to catch fish. [OE *wer*]

Weir ★ (wɪə) *n* **Peter.** born 1944, Australian film director: his films include *The Last Wave* (1977), *Witness* (1985), *Dead Poets Society* (1989), and *The Truman Show* (1998).

weird (wɪəd) *adj* **1** suggestive of or relating to the supernatural; eerie. **2** strange or bizarre. **3** *Arch.* of or relating to fate or the Fates. ◆ *n* **4** *Arch., chiefly Scot.* **4a** fate or destiny. **4b** one of the Fates. [OE (ge)*wyrd* destiny]
▸ **'weirdly** *adv* ▸ **'weirdness** *n*

weirdo ('wɪədəʊ) *or* **weirdie** ('wɪədɪ) *n, pl* **weirdos** *or* **weirdies.** *Inf.* a person who behaves in a bizarre or eccentric manner.

Weismannism ('vaɪsmən,ɪzəm) *n* the theory that all inheritable characteristics are transmitted by the reproductive cells and that characteristics acquired during the lifetime of the organism are not inherited. [C19: after August **Weismann** (1834–1914), G biologist]

Weisshorn ★ ('vaɪs,hɔːn) *n* a mountain in S Switzerland, in the Pennine Alps. Height: 4505 m (14 781 ft).

Weissmuller ★ ('waɪs,mʌlə) *n* **John Peter,** known as *Johnny.* 1904–84, US swimmer and film actor, who won Olympic gold medals in 1924 and 1928 and played the title role in the early Tarzan films.

Weizmann ★ ('waɪtsmən, 'waɪz-) *n* **Chaim** ('xaɪm). 1874–1952, Israeli statesman, born in Russia. A Zionist, he was responsible for securing the Balfour Declaration (1917); first president of Israel (1949–52).

weka ('wɛkə) *n* a nocturnal flightless bird of New Zealand. Also called: **Maori hen, wood hen.** [from Maori]

welch (wɛlʃ) *vb* a variant spelling of **welsh.**

Welch (wɛlʃ) *adj, n* an archaic spelling of **Welsh.**

welcome ('wɛlkəm) *adj* **1** gladly and cordially received or admitted: *a welcome guest.* **2** bringing pleasure: *a welcome gift.* **3** freely permitted or invited: *you are welcome to call.* **4** under no obligation (only in such phrases as **you're welcome,** as conventional responses to thanks). ◆ *sentence substitute.* **5** an expression of cordial greeting. ◆ *n* **6** the act of greeting or receiving a person or thing; reception: *the new theory had a cool welcome.* **7 wear out** *or* **overstay one's welcome.** to come more often or stay longer than is pleasing. ◆ *vb* **welcomes, welcoming, welcomed.** (*tr*) **8** to greet the arrival of (guests, etc.) cordially. **9** to receive or accept, esp. gladly. [C12: changed (through infl. of WELL¹) from OE *wilcuma* (agent *n* referring to a welcome guest), *wilcume* (a greeting of welcome), from *wil* WILL² + *cuman* to come]
▸ **'welcomely** *adv* ▸ **'welcomer** *n*

weld¹ (wɛld) *vb* **1** (*tr*) to unite (pieces of metal or plastic), as by softening with heat and hammering or by fusion. **2** to bring or admit of being brought into close union. ◆ *n* **3** a joint formed by welding. [C16: altered from obs. *well* to melt, weld]
▸ **'weldable** *adj* ▸ **,welda'bility** *n* ▸ **'welder** *or* **'weldor** *n*

weld² (wɛld), **wold,** *or* **woald** (wəʊld) *n* a yellow dye obtained from the plant dyer's rocket. [C14: from Low G]

Weld ★ (wɛld) *n* **Sir Frederick Aloysius.** 1823–91, New Zealand statesman, born in England: prime minister (1864–65).

Weldon ★ ('wɛldən) *n* **Fay.** born 1931, British novelist and dramatist. Her novels include *Life and Loves of a She-Devil* (1984) and *Nobody Likes Me!* (1997).

welfare ('wɛl,fɛə) *n* **1** health, happiness, prosperity, and wellbeing in general. **2a** financial and other assistance given to people in need. **2b** (*as modifier*): *welfare services.* **3** Also called: **welfare work.** plans or work to better the social or economic conditions of various underprivileged groups. **4 on welfare.** *Chiefly US & Canad.* in receipt of financial aid from a government agency or other source. [C14: from *wel fare*; see WELL¹, FARE]

welfare economics *n* (*functioning as sing*) the aspects of economic theory concerned with the welfare of society and priorities to be observed in the allocation of resources.

welfare state *n* a system in which the government undertakes the chief responsibility for providing for the social and economic security of its population, usually through unemployment insurance, old age pensions, and other social-security measures.

welkin ('wɛlkɪn) *n Arch.* the sky, heavens, or upper air. [OE *wolcen, welcen*]

Welkom ★ ('wɛlkəm, 'vɛl-) *n* a town in central South Africa. Pop.: 230 000 (latest est.).

well[1] (wɛl) *adv* **better, best. 1** (*often used in combination*) in a satisfactory manner: *the party went very well.* **2** (*often used in combination*) in a skilful manner: *she plays the violin well; a well-chosen example.* **3** in a correct or careful manner: *listen well to my words.* **4** in a prosperous manner: *to live well.* **5** (*usually used with auxiliaries*) suitably; fittingly: *you can't very well say that.* **6** intimately: *I knew him well.* **7** in a kind or favourable manner: *she speaks well of you.* **8** fully: *to be well informed.* **9** by a considerable margin: *let me know well in advance.* **10** (preceded by *could, might,* or *may*) indeed: *you may well have to do it yourself.* **11** *Inf.* (intensifier): *well safe.* **12 all very well.** used ironically to express discontent, dissent, etc. **13 as well. 13a** in addition; too. **13b** (preceded by *may* or *might*) with equal effect: *you might as well come.* **14 as well as.** in addition to. **15 (just) as well.** preferable or advisable: *it would be just as well if you paid me now.* **16 leave well (enough) alone.** to refrain from interfering with something that is satisfactory. **17 well and good.** used to indicate calm acceptance, as of a decision. **18 well up in.** well acquainted with (a particular subject); knowledgeable about. ◆ *adj* (*usually postpositive*) **19** (when *prenominal, usually used with a negative*) in good health: *I'm very well, thank you; he's not a well man.* **20** satisfactory or pleasing. **21** prudent; advisable: *it would be well to make no comment.* **22** prosperous or comfortable. **23** fortunate: *it is well that you agreed to go.* ◆ *interj* **24a** an expression of surprise, indignation, or reproof. **24b** an expression of anticipation in waiting for an answer or remark. ◆ *sentence connector.* **25** an expression used to preface a remark, gain time, etc.: *well, I don't think I will come.* [OE *wel*]

well[2] (wɛl) *n* **1** a hole or shaft bored into the earth to tap a supply of water, oil, gas, etc. **2** a natural pool where ground water comes to the surface. **3a** a cavity, space, or vessel used to contain a liquid. **3b** (*in combination*): *an inkwell.* **4** an open shaft through the floors of a building, such as one used for a staircase. **5** a deep enclosed space in a building or between buildings that is open to the sky. **6** a bulkheaded compartment built around a ship's pumps for protection and ease of access. **7** (in England) the open space in the centre of a law court. **8** an abundant source: *he is a well of knowledge.* ◆ *vb* **9** to flow or cause to flow upwards or outwards: *tears welled from her eyes.* [OE *wella*]

we'll (wiːl) *contraction of* we will *or* we shall.

well-advised *adj* (**well advised** *when postpositive*). **1** acting with deliberation or reason. **2** well thought out: *a well-advised plan.*

well-affected *adj* (**well affected** *when postpositive*). favourably disposed (towards); steadfast or loyal.

Welland Canal ★ ('wɛlənd) *n* a canal in S Canada, in Ontario, linking Lake Erie to Lake Ontario: part of the St Lawrence Seaway, with eight locks. Length: 44 km (28 miles). Also called: **Welland Ship Canal.**

well-appointed *adj* (**well appointed** *when postpositive*). well equipped or furnished.

wellaway ('wɛlə'weɪ) *interj Arch.* woe! alas! [OE, from *wei lā wei,* var. of *wā lā wā,* lit.: woe! lo woe]

well-balanced *adj* (**well balanced** *when postpositive*). **1** having good balance or proportions. **2** sane or sensible.

wellbeing ('wɛl'biːŋ) *n* the condition of being contented, healthy, or successful; welfare.

well-bred *adj* (**well bred** *when postpositive*). **1** Also: **well-born.** of respected or noble lineage. **2** indicating good breeding: *well-bred manners.* **3** of good thoroughbred stock: *a well-bred spaniel.*

well-chosen *adj* (**well chosen** *when postpositive*). carefully selected to produce a desired effect; apt: *a few well-chosen words.*

well-connected *adj* (**well connected** *when postpositive*). having influential or important relatives or friends.

well-disposed *adj* (**well disposed** *when postpositive*). inclined to be sympathetic, kindly, or friendly.

well-done *adj* (**well done** *when postpositive*). **1** (of food, esp. meat) cooked thoroughly. **2** made or accomplished satisfactorily.

well dressing *n* the decoration of wells with flowers, etc.: a traditional annual ceremony of great antiquity in some parts of Britain, originally associated with the cult of water deities.

Welles ★ (wɛlz) *n* (**George**) **Orson** ('ɔːsⁿn). 1915–85, US film director and actor. His *Citizen Kane* (1941) and *The Magnificent Ambersons* (1942) are regarded as film classics.

Wellesley ★ ('wɛlzlɪ) *n* **1 Arthur.** See (1st Duke of) **Wellington. 2** his brother, **Richard Colley,** Marquis Wellesley. 1760–1842, British administrator: governor general of Bengal (1797–1805).

well-favoured *adj* (**well favoured** *when postpositive*). good-looking.

well-formed formula *n Logic.* a group of logical symbols that makes sense; a logical sentence.

well-found *adj* (**well found** *when postpositive*). furnished or supplied with all or most necessary things.

well-founded *adj* (**well founded** *when postpositive*). having good grounds: *well-founded rumours.*

well-groomed *adj* (**well groomed** *when postpositive*). having a tidy pleasing appearance.

well-grounded *adj* (**well grounded** *when postpositive*). **1** well instructed in the basic elements of a subject. **2** another term for **well-founded.**

wellhead ('wɛl,hɛd) *n* **1** the source of a well or stream. **2** a source, fountainhead, or origin.

well-heeled *adj* (**well heeled** *when postpositive*). *Inf.* rich; prosperous; wealthy.

wellies ('wɛlɪz) *pl n Brit. inf.* Wellington boots.

well-informed *adj* (**well informed** *when postpositive*). **1** having knowledge about a great variety of subjects: *he seems to be a well-informed person.* **2** possessing reliable information on a particular subject.

Wellingborough ★ ('wɛlɪŋbərə, -brə) *n* a town in central England in Northamptonshire. Pop.: 41 602 (1991).

Wellington[1] ★ ('wɛlɪŋtən) *n* **1** an administrative district, formerly a province, of New Zealand, on SW North Island: major livestock producer in New Zealand. Capital: Wellington. Pop.: 413 100 (1995 est.). Area: 28 153 sq. km (10 870 sq. miles). **2** the capital city of New Zealand. Its port, historically Port Nicholson, on **Wellington Harbour** has a rail-ferry link between the North and South Islands; university (1899). Pop.: 331 100 (1995 est.).

Wellington[2] ★ ('wɛlɪŋtən) *n* **1st Duke of,** title of *Arthur Wellesley.* 1769–1852, British soldier and statesman; prime minister (1828–30). He commanded the British forces against the French in the Peninsular War (1808–14) and routed Napoleon at Waterloo (1815).

Wellington boots *pl n* **1** Also called: **gumboots.** *Brit.* knee-length or calf-length rubber boots, worn esp. in wet conditions. Often shortened to **wellingtons, wellies. 2** military leather boots covering the front of the knee but cut away at the back to allow easier bending of the knee. [C19: after the 1st Duke of WELLINGTON]

wellingtonia (,wɛlɪŋ'təʊnɪə) *n* a giant Californian coniferous tree, often reaching 90 metres high. Also called: **big tree, sequoia.** [C19: after the 1st Duke of WELLINGTON]

well-intentioned *adj* (**well intentioned** *when postpositive*). having benevolent intentions, usually with unfortunate results.

well-knit *adj* (**well knit** *when postpositive*). strong, firm, or sturdy.

well-known *adj* (**well known** *when postpositive*). **1** widely known; famous; celebrated. **2** known fully or clearly.

well-mannered *adj* (**well mannered** *when postpositive*). having good manners; polite.

well-meaning *adj* (**well meaning** *when postpositive*). having or indicating good intentions, usually with unfortunate results.

well-nigh *adv Arch. or poetic.* nearly; almost: *it's well-nigh three o'clock.*

well-off *adj* (**well off** *when postpositive*). **1** in a comfortable or favourable position or state. **2** financially well provided for; moderately rich.

well-oiled *adj* (**well oiled** *when postpositive*). *Inf.* drunk.

well-preserved *adj* (**well preserved** *when postpositive*). **1** kept in a good condition. **2** continuing to appear youthful: *she was a well-preserved old lady*.

well-read ('wel'red) *adj* (**well read** *when postpositive*). having read widely and intelligently; erudite.

well-rounded *adj* (**well rounded** *when postpositive*). **1** rounded in shape or well developed: *a well-rounded figure*. **2** full, varied, and satisfying: *a well-rounded life*.

Wells[1] ★ (welz) *n* a city in SW England, in Somerset: 12th-century cathedral. Pop.: 9763 (1991).

Wells[2] ★ (welz) *n* **1 Henry.** 1805–78, US businessman, who founded (1852) with William Fargo the express mail service Wells, Fargo and Company. **2 H(erbert) G(eorge).** 1866–1946, British writer. His science fiction includes *The Time Machine* (1895) and *War of the Worlds* (1898). His novels include *Tono-Bungay* (1909) and *Ann Veronica* (1909).

well-spoken *adj* (**well spoken** *when postpositive*). **1** having a clear, articulate, and socially acceptable accent and way of speaking. **2** spoken satisfactorily or pleasingly.

wellspring ('wel,sprɪŋ) *n* **1** the source of a spring or stream. **2** a source of abundant supply.

well-stacked *adj* (**well stacked** *when postpositive*). *Sl.* (of a woman) of voluptuous proportions.

well sweep *n* a device for raising buckets from and lowering them into a well, consisting of a long pivoted pole, the bucket being attached to one end by a long rope.

well-tempered *adj* (**well tempered** *when postpositive*). (of a musical scale or instrument) conforming to the system of equal temperament. See **temperament** (sense 4).

well-thought-of *adj* respected.

well-thumbed *adj* (**well thumbed** *when postpositive*). (of a book) having the pages marked from frequent turning.

well-to-do *adj* moderately wealthy.

well-turned *adj* (**well turned** *when postpositive*). **1** (of a phrase, etc.) apt and pleasing. **2** having a pleasing shape: *a well-turned leg*.

well-upholstered *adj* (**well upholstered** *when postpositive*). *Inf.* (of a person) fat.

well-wisher *n* a person who shows benevolence or sympathy towards a person, cause, etc.
▶ 'well-,wishing *adj, n*

well-woman *n, pl* **well-women**. *Social welfare.* **a** a woman who attends a health-service clinic for preventive monitoring, health education, etc. **b** (*as modifier*): *well-woman clinic*.

well-worn *adj* (**well worn** *when postpositive*). **1** so much used as to be affected by wear: *a well-worn coat*. **2** hackneyed: *a well-worn phrase*.

welly ('welɪ) *n* **1** (*pl* **wellies**) *Inf.* Also called: **welly boot**. a Wellington boot. **2** *Sl.* energy, concentration, or commitment (esp. in **give it some welly**).

Wels ★ (*German* vɛls) *n* an industrial city in N central Austria, in Upper Austria. Pop.: 52 594 (1991).

welsh *or* **welch** (welʃ) *vb* (*intr; often foll. by on*) **1** to fail to pay a gambling debt. **2** to fail to fulfil an obligation. [C19: from ?]
▶ 'welsher *or* 'welcher *n*

Welsh (welʃ) *adj* **1** of, relating to, or characteristic of Wales, its people, their language, or their dialect of English. ◆ *n* **2** a language of Wales, belonging to the S Celtic branch of the Indo-European family. **3 the Welsh.** (*functioning as pl*) the natives or inhabitants of Wales. [OE *Wēlisc, Wælisc*]

Welsh corgi *n* another name for **corgi**.

Welsh dresser *n* a sideboard with drawers and cupboards below and open shelves above.

Welsh harp *n* a type of harp in which the strings are arranged in three rows.

Welshman ('welʃmən) *or* (*fem*) **Welshwoman** *n, pl* **Welshmen** *or* **Welshwomen**. a native or inhabitant of Wales.

Welsh poppy *n* a perennial W European plant with large yellow flowers.

Welsh rabbit *n* a savoury dish consisting of melted cheese sometimes mixed with milk, seasonings, etc., on hot buttered toast. Also called: **Welsh rarebit, rarebit**. [C18: a fanciful coinage; *rarebit* is a later folk-etymological var.]

Welsh terrier *n* a wire-haired breed of terrier with a black-and-tan coat.

welt (welt) *n* **1** a raised or strengthened seam in a garment. **2** another word for **weal**[1]. **3** (in shoemaking) a strip of leather, etc., put in between the outer sole and the inner sole and upper. ◆ *vb* (*tr*) **4** to put a welt in (a garment, etc.). **5** to beat soundly. [C15: from ?]

welter ('weltə) *vb* (*intr*) **1** to roll about, writhe, or wallow. **2** (esp. of the sea) to surge, heave, or toss. **3** to lie drenched in a liquid, esp. blood. ◆ *n* **4** a confused mass; jumble. [C13: from MLow G, MDu. *weltern*]

welterweight ('weltə,weit) *n* **1a** a professional boxer weighing 140–147 pounds (63.5–66.5 kg). **1b** an amateur boxer weighing 63.5–67 kg (140–148 pounds). **2a** a professional wrestler weighing 155–165 pounds (71–75 kg). **2b** an amateur wrestler weighing 69–74 kg (151–161 pounds).

Welwyn Garden City ★ ('welɪn) *n* a town in SE England, in Hertfordshire: established (1920) as a planned industrial and residential town. Pop.: 42 087 (1991).

Wembley ★ ('wemblɪ) *n* part of the Greater London borough of Brent: site of the English national soccer stadium.

wen[1] (wen) *n* **1** *Pathol.* a sebaceous cyst, esp. one occurring on the scalp. **2** a large overcrowded city (esp. London, **the great wen**). [OE *wenn*]

wen[2] (wen) *n* a rune having the sound of Modern English *w*. [OE *wen, wyn*]

Wenceslaus *or* **Wenceslas** ★ ('wensɪsləs) *n* **1** 1361–1419, Holy Roman Emperor (1378–1400) and, as **Wenceslaus IV**, king of Bohemia (1378–1419). **2 Saint**, known as *Good King Wenceslas*. ?907–929, duke of Bohemia (?925–29); patron saint of the Czech Republic. Feast day: Sept. 28.

wench (wentʃ) *n* **1** a girl or young woman: now used facetiously. **2** *Arch.* a female servant. **3** *Arch.* a prostitute. ◆ *vb* (*intr*) **4** *Arch.* to frequent the company of prostitutes. [OE *wencel* child, from *wancol* weak]
▶ 'wencher *n*

wend (wend) *vb* to direct (one's course or way); travel. [OE *wendan*]

Wend (wend) *n* (esp. in medieval European history) a member of the Slavonic people who inhabited the area between the Rivers Saale and Oder, in central Europe, in the early Middle Ages. Also called: **Sorb**.

wendigo ('wendɪ,gəʊ) *n Canad.* **1** (*pl* **wendigos**) (among Algonquian Indians) an evil spirit or cannibal. **2** (*pl* **wendigo** *or* **wendigos**) another name for **splake**. [from Algonquian: evil spirit or cannibal]

Wendy house ('wendɪ) *n* a small model house for children to play in. [C20: after the house built for *Wendy*, the girl in J. M. Barrie's play *Peter Pan* (1904)]

wensleydale ('wenzlɪ,deɪl) *n* **1** a type of white cheese with a flaky texture. **2** a breed of sheep with long woolly fleece. [after *Wensleydale*, North Yorkshire]

went (went) *vb* the past tense of **go**. [C15: p.t. of WEND used as p.t. of *go*]

wentletrap ('wentl,træp) *n* a marine gastropod mollusc having a long pointed pale-coloured longitudinally ridged shell. [C18: from Du. *winteltrap* spiral shell, from *wintel*, earlier *windel*, from *wenden* to wind + *trap* a step]

Wentworth ★ ('wentwəθ) *n* **1 Thomas.** See (Earl of) Strafford. **2 William Charles.** 1790–1872, Australian explorer and statesman, who was a member of the party that first crossed the Blue Mountains in 1813 and was later a leader in the movement for self-government in New South Wales.

Wenzhou, Wen-chou, *or* **Wenchow** ★ ('wen'tʃuː) *n* a port in SE China, in Zhejiang province: noted for its historic buildings. Pop.: 401 871 (1990 est.).

★ people and places

wept (wɛpt) *vb* the past tense and past participle of **weep.**

were (wɜ:; *unstressed* wə) *vb* the plural form of the past tense (indicative mood) of **be** and the singular form used with *you*. It is also used as a subjunctive, esp. in conditional sentences. [OE *wērun, wæron* p.t. pl of *wesan* to be]

> **USAGE NOTE** *Were*, as a remnant of the past subjunctive in English, is used in formal contexts in clauses expressing hypotheses (*if he were to die, she would inherit everything*), suppositions contrary to fact (*if I were you, I would be careful*), and desire (*I wish he were there now*). In informal speech, however, *was* is often used instead.

we're (wɪə) *contraction of* we are.

weren't (wɜ:nt) *contraction of* were not.

werewolf ('wɪə,wʊlf, 'weə-) *n, pl* **werewolves.** a person fabled in folklore and superstition to have been changed into a wolf by being bewitched or said to be able to assume wolf form at will. [OE *werewulf,* from *wer* man + *wulf* wolf]

wergild, weregild ('wɜ:,gɪld, 'weə-), *or* **wergeld** ('wɜ:,gɛld, 'weə-) *n* the price set on a man's life in Anglo-Saxon and Germanic law, to be paid as compensation by his slayer. [OE *wergeld,* from *wer* man + *gield* tribute]

Werner ★ (*German* 'vɛrnə) *n* **1 Abraham Gottlob** ('aːbrəham 'ɡɔtloːp). 1749–1817, German geologist. **2 Alfred** ('alfreːt). 1866–1919, Swiss chemist, born in Germany: Nobel prize for chemistry (1913) for his work on inorganic complexes.

wert (wɜ:t; *unstressed* wət) *vb Arch. or dialect.* (used with the pronoun *thou* or its relative equivalent) a singular form of the past tense (indicative mood) of **be.**

Weser ★ (*German* 'veːzər) *n* a river in NW Germany: flows northwest to the North Sea at Bremerhaven and is linked by the Mittelland Canal to the Ems, Rhine, and Elbe waterways. Length: 477 km (196 miles).

Wesermünde ★ (*German* veːzər'myndə) *n* the former name (until 1947) of **Bremerhaven.**

Wesker ★ ('weskə) *n* **Arnold.** born 1932, British dramatist, whose plays include *Roots* (1959), *Chips With Everything* (1962), and *Break My Heart* (1997).

weskit ('weskɪt) *n* an informal name for **waistcoat.**

Wesley ★ ('wezlɪ) *n* **1 Charles.** 1707–88, British Methodist preacher and writer of hymns. **2** his brother, **John.** 1703–91, British preacher, who founded Methodism.

Wesleyan ('wezlɪən) *adj* **1** of or deriving from John Wesley. **2** of or characterizing Methodism, esp. in its original form. ◆ *n* **3** a follower of John Wesley. **4** a member of the Methodist Church.
> ▸ '**Wesleyan,ism** *n*

Wessex ★ ('wesɪks) *n* **1** an Anglo-Saxon kingdom in S and SW England that became the most powerful English kingdom by the 10th century A.D. **2a** (in Thomas Hardy's works) the southwestern counties of England, esp. Dorset. **2b** (*as modifier*): *Wessex Poems.*

west (wɛst) *n* **1** the direction along a parallel towards the sunset, at 270° clockwise from north. **2 the west.** (*often cap.*) any area lying in or towards the west. Related adjs.: **Hesperian, Occidental. 3** (*usually cap.*) *Cards.* the player or position at the table corresponding to west on the compass. ◆ *adj* **4** situated in, moving towards, or facing the west. **5** (esp. of the wind) from the west. ◆ *adv* **6** in, to, or towards the west. **7 go west.** *Inf.* **7a** to be lost or destroyed. **7b** to die. [OE]

West[1] (wɛst) *n* **the. 1** the western part of the world contrasted historically and culturally with the East or Orient. **2** (formerly) the non-Communist countries of Europe and America contrasted with the Communist states of the East. **3** (in the US) that part of the US lying approximately to the west of the Mississippi. **4** (in the ancient and medieval world) the Western Roman Empire and, later, the Holy Roman Empire. ◆ *adj* **5** of or denoting the western part of a specified country, area, etc.

West[2] ★ (wɛst) *n* **1 Benjamin.** 1738–1820, US painter, in England from 1763. **2 Mae.** 1892–1980, US film actress. **3**

Dame **Rebecca**, real name *Mrs Cicily Isabel Andrews* (née *Fairfield*). 1892–1983, British novelist.

West Atlantic ★ *n* the W part of the Atlantic Ocean, esp. the N Atlantic around North America.

West Bank ★ *n* **the.** an autonomous Palestinian region in the Middle East on the W bank of the River Jordan, comprising the hills of Judaea and Samaria and part of Jerusalem: formerly part of Palestine: became part of Jordan after the ceasefire of 1949: occupied by Israel since the 1967 Arab-Israeli War. The provision of the Camp David Agreement that the West Bank should be granted a degree of Palestinian autonomy was re-established in 1993 by a peace treaty between Israel and the Palestinian Liberation Organization. Negotiations to determine the final status of the region have continued. Pop.: 1 122 900 (1994). Area: 5879 sq. km (2270 sq. miles).

West Bengal ★ *n* a state of E India, on the Bay of Bengal: formed in 1947 from the Hindu area of Bengal; additional territories added in 1950 (Cooch Behar), 1954 (Chandernagor), and 1956 (part of Bihar); mostly lowlying and crossed by the Hooghly River. Capital: Calcutta. Pop.: 73 600 000 (1994 est.). Area: 88 752 sq. km (34 260 sq. miles).

West Berkshire ★ *n* a unitary authority in S England. Pop.: 143 700 (1996 est.).

West Berlin ★ *n* (formerly) the part of Berlin under US, British, and French control.
> ▸ **West Berliner** *n, adj*

westbound ('west,baʊnd) *adj* going or leading towards the west.

West Bromwich ★ ('brɒmɪdʒ, -ɪtʃ) *n* a town in central England, in Sandwell, in the West Midlands: industrial centre. Pop.: 146 386 (1991).

west by north *n* one point on the compass north of west.

west by south *n* one point on the compass south of west.

West Country ★ *n* **the.** the southwest of England, esp. Cornwall, Devon, and Somerset.

West Dunbartonshire ★ *n* a council area of W central Scotland, formed in 1996. Capital: Dumbarton. Pop.: 95 760 (1996 est.). Area: 162 sq. km (63 sq. miles).

West End ★ *n* **the.** a part of W central London containing the main shopping and entertainment areas.

westering ('westərɪŋ) *adj Poetic.* moving towards the west: *the westering star.*

Westerlies ('westəlɪz) *pl n Meteorol.* the prevailing winds blowing from the west on the poleward sides of the horse latitudes, often bringing depressions and anticyclones.

westerly ('westəlɪ) *adj* **1** of, relating to, or situated in the west. ◆ *adv, adj* **2** towards or in the direction of the west. **3** (esp. of the wind) from the west. ◆ *n, pl* **westerlies. 4** a wind blowing from the west.
> ▸ '**westerliness** *n*

western ('westən) *adj* **1** situated in or facing the west. **2** going or directed to or towards the west. **3** (of a wind, etc.) coming from the west. **4** native to the west. **5** *Music.* See **country and western.**
> ▸ '**western,most** *adj*

Western ('westən) *adj* **1** of or characteristic of the West as opposed to the Orient. **2** of or characteristic of North America and western Europe. **3** of or characteristic of the western states of the US. ◆ *n* **4** (*often not cap.*) a film, book, etc., concerned with life in the western states of the US, esp. during the era of exploration.

Western Australia ★ *n* a state of W Australia: mostly an arid undulating plateau, with the Great Sandy Desert, Gibson Desert, and Great Victoria Desert in the interior; settlement concentrated in the southwest; rich mineral resources. Capital: Perth. Pop.: 1 755 500 (1996 est.). Area: 2 527 636 sq. km (975 920 sq. miles).

Western Church *n* **1** the part of Christendom that derives its liturgy, discipline, and traditions principally from the patriarchate of Rome. **2** the Roman Catholic Church, sometimes together with the Anglican Communion of Churches.

★ people and places

westerner ('wɛstənə) *n* (*sometimes cap.*) a native or inhabitant of the west of any specific region.

Western Ghats ★ *pl n* a mountain range in W peninsular India, parallel to the Malabar coast of the Arabian Sea. Highest peak: Anai Mudi, 2695 m (8841 ft).

western hemisphere *n* (*often caps.*) **1** that half of the globe containing the Americas, lying to the west of the Greenwich or another meridian. **2** the lands contained in this, esp. the Americas.

Western Isles ★ *n* (*functioning as sing or pl*) **1** an island authority in W Scotland, consisting of the Outer Hebrides; created in 1975. Administrative centre: Stornoway. Pop.: 31 834 (1996 est.). Area: 2900 sq. km (1120 sq. miles). **2** Also called: **Western Islands.** another name for the **Hebrides.**

westernize *or* **westernise** ('wɛstə,naɪz) *vb* **westernizes, westernizing, westernized** *or* **westernises, westernising, westernised.** (*tr*) to influence or make familiar with the customs, practices, etc., of the West.
▸ ,westerni'zation *or* ,westerni'sation *n*

Western Ocean ★ *n* (formerly) another name for the **Atlantic Ocean.**

Western Roman Empire *n* the westernmost of the two empires created by the division of the later Roman Empire, esp. after its final severance from the Eastern Roman Empire (395 A.D.). Also called: **Western Empire.**

Western Sahara ★ *n* a disputed region of NW Africa, on the Atlantic: mainly desert; rich phosphate deposits; a Spanish overseas province from 1958 to 1975; partitioned in 1976 between Morocco and Mauritania who faced growing resistance from the Polisario Front, an organization aiming for the independence of the region as the Democratic Saharan Arab Republic. Mauritania renounced its claim in 1979 and its territory was taken over by Morocco. Attempts by the UN to resolve the dispute have failed. Pop.: 214 000 (1993 est.). Area: 266 000 sq. km (102 680 sq. miles). Former name (until 1975): **Spanish Sahara.**

Western Samoa ★ *n* See **Samoa** (sense 1).

Western Wall ★ *n* a wall in Jerusalem, the last extant part of the Temple of Herod, held sacred by Jews as a place of prayer and pilgrimage. Also called: **Wailing Wall.**

Westfalen ★ (vɛst'faːlən) *n* the German name for **Westphalia.**

West Flanders ★ *n* a province of W Belgium: the country's chief agricultural province. Capital: Bruges. Pop.: 1 121 135 (1995 est.). Area: 3132 sq. km (1209 sq. miles).

West Germany ★ *n* a former republic in N central Europe, on the North Sea: established in 1949 from the zones of Germany occupied by the British, Americans, and French after the defeat of Nazi Germany; a member of the European Community; reunited with East Germany in 1990. Official name: **Federal Republic of Germany.** See also **Germany.**
▸ **West German** *adj, n*

West Glamorgan ★ *n* a former county in S Wales, formed in 1974 from part of Glamorgan and the county borough of Swansea: replaced in 1996.

West Hartlepool ★ ('hɑːtlɪ,puːl) *n* a former town in NE England, in Co. Durham: part of Hartlepool since 1967.

West Indies ★ ('ɪndɪz) *pl n* an archipelago off Central America, extending over 2400 km (1500 miles) in an arc from the peninsula of Florida to Venezuela, separating the Caribbean Sea from the Atlantic: consists of the Greater Antilles, the Lesser Antilles, and the Bahamas; largest island is Cuba. Area: over 235 000 sq. km (91 000 sq. miles). Also called: the **Caribbean.**

westing ('wɛstɪŋ) *n Navigation.* movement, deviation, or distance covered in a westerly direction, esp. as expressed in the resulting difference in longitude.

West Irian ★ *n* the English name for **Irian Jaya.**

West Lothian ★ *n* a council area and historic county of central Scotland; part of Lothian region (1975–96). Administrative centre: Livingston. Pop.: 150 770 (1996 est.). Area: 425 sq. km (164 sq. miles).

Westm. *abbrev. for* Westminster.

Westmeath ★ (,wɛst'miːð) *n* a county of N central Republic of Ireland, in Leinster province: mostly low-lying, with many lakes and bogs. County town: Mullingar. Pop.: 61 880 (1991). Area: 1764 sq. km (681 sq. miles).

West Midlands ★ *n* (*functioning as sing or pl*) a metropolitan county of central England, administered since 1996 by the unitary authorities of Wolverhampton, Walsall, Dudley, Sandwell, Birmingham, Solihull, and Coventry. Area: 899 sq. km (347 sq. miles).

Westminster ★ ('wɛst,mɪnstə) *n* **1** Also called: **City of Westminster.** a borough of Greater London, on the River Thames: contains the Houses of Parliament, Westminster Abbey, and Buckingham Palace. Pop.: 190 100 (1991 est.) Area: 22 sq. km (8 sq. miles). **2** the Houses of Parliament at Westminster.

Westminster Abbey ★ *n* a Gothic church in London: site of a Benedictine monastery (1050–65); scene of the coronations of almost all English monarchs since William I.

Westmorland ★ ('wɛstmələnd, 'wɛsmə-) *n* (until 1974) a county of NW England, now part of Cumbria.

west-northwest *n* **1** the point on the compass or the direction midway between west and northwest, 292° 30′ clockwise from north. ◆ *adj, adv* **2** in, from, or towards this direction.

Weston standard cell ('wɛstən) *n* a primary cell used as a standard of emf: consists of a mercury anode and a cadmium amalgam cathode in an electrolyte of saturated cadmium sulphate. [C20: from a trademark]

Weston-super-Mare ★ ('wɛstən,suːpə'mɛə, -,sjuː-) *n* a town and resort in SW England, in North Somerset on the Bristol Channel. Pop.: 69 372 (1991).

West Pakistan ★ *n* the former name (until the end of 1971) of **Pakistan.**

Westphalia ★ (wɛst'feɪlɪə) *n* a historic region of NW Germany, now mostly in the state of North Rhine-Westphalia. German name: **Westfalen.**
▸ **West'phalian** *adj, n*

West Prussia ★ *n* a former province of NE Prussia, on the Baltic: assigned to Poland in 1945. German name: **Westpreussen** ('vɛstprɔʏsən).

West Riding ★ *n* (until 1974) an administrative division of Yorkshire, now in West Yorkshire, North Yorkshire, Cumbria, and Lancashire.

west-southwest *n* **1** the point on the compass or the direction midway between southwest and west, 247° 30′ clockwise from north. ◆ *adj, adv* **2** in, from, or towards this direction.

West Sussex ★ *n* a county of SE England, comprising part of the former county of Sussex. Administrative centre: Chichester. Pop.: 714 100 (1989 est.). Area: 1989 sq. km (768 sq. miles).

West Virginia ★ *n* a state of the eastern US: part of Virginia until the outbreak of the American Civil War (1861); consists chiefly of the Allegheny Plateau; bounded on the west by the Ohio River; coal-mining. Capital: Charleston. Pop.: 1 825 754 (1996 est.). Area: 62 341 sq. km (24 070 sq. miles). Abbrevs.: **W. Va.** or (with zip code) **WV**
▸ **West Virginian** *adj, n*

westward ('wɛstwəd) *adj* **1** moving, facing, or situated in the west. ◆ *adv* **2** Also: **westwards.** towards the west. ◆ *n* **3** the westward part, direction, etc.
▸ **'westwardly** *adj, adv*

Westwood ★ ('wɛst,wʊd) *n* Vivienne (**Isabel**). born 1941, British fashion designer.

West Yorkshire ★ *n* a metropolitan county of N England, administered since 1986 by the unitary authorities of Bradford, Leeds, Calderdale, Kirklees, and Wakefield. Area: 2039 sq. km (787 sq. miles).

wet (wɛt) *adj* **wetter, wettest. 1** moistened, covered, saturated, etc., with water or some other liquid. **2** not yet dry or solid: *wet varnish.* **3** rainy: *wet weather.* **4** employing a liquid, usually water: *a wet method of chemical analysis.* **5** *Chiefly US & Canad.* permitting the free sale of alcoholic beverages: *a wet state.* **6** *Brit. inf.* feeble or foolish. **7 wet behind the ears.** *Inf.* immature or inexperienced. ◆ *n* **8** wetness or moisture. **9** rainy weather. **10** *Brit. inf.* a feeble or

---

foolish person. **11** (*often cap.*) *Brit. inf.* a Conservative politician who is not a hardliner. **12** *Chiefly US & Canad.* a person who advocates free sale of alcoholic beverages. **13 the wet.** *Austral.* (in northern and central Australia) the rainy season. ◆ *vb* **wets, wetting, wet** *or* **wetted. 14** to make or become wet. **15** to urinate on (something). **16** (*tr*) *Dialect.* to prepare (tea) by boiling or infusing.   [OE *wæt*]
▸ **'wetly** *adv* ▸ **'wetness** *n* ▸ **'wettable** *adj* ▸ **'wetter** *n*
▸ **'wettish** *adj*

wet-and-dry-bulb thermometer *n* another name for **psychrometer.**

wet blanket *n Inf.* a person whose low spirits or lack of enthusiasm have a depressing effect on others.

wet cell *n* a primary cell in which the electrolyte is a liquid.

wet dream *n* an erotic dream accompanied by an emission of semen.

wet fly *n Angling.* an artificial fly designed to float or ride below the water surface.

wether ('wɛðə) *n* a male sheep, esp. a castrated one.   [OE *hwæther*]

wetland ('wɛtlənd) *n* (*sometimes pl*) **a** an area of marshy land, esp. considered as part of an ecological system. **b** (*as modifier*): *wetland species.*

wet look *n* a shiny finish such as that given to certain clothing and footwear materials.

wet nurse *n* **1** a woman hired to suckle the child of another. ◆ *vb* **wet-nurse, wet-nurses, wet-nursing, wet-nursed.** (*tr*) **2** to act as a wet nurse to (a child). **3** *Inf.* to attend with great devotion.

wet pack *n Med.* a hot or cold damp sheet or blanket for wrapping around a patient.

wet rot *n* **1** a state of decay in timber caused by various fungi. The hyphal strands of the fungus are seldom visible, and affected timber turns dark brown. **2** any of the fungi causing this decay.

wet suit *n* a close-fitting rubber suit used by skin-divers, yachtsmen, etc., to retain body heat.

Wetterhorn ★ (*German* 'vɛtər,hɔrn) *n* a mountain in S Switzerland, in the Bernese Alps. Height: 3701 m (12 143 ft).

wetting agent *n Chem.* any substance added to a liquid to lower its surface tension and thus increase its ability to spread across or penetrate a solid.

we've (wiːv) *contraction of* we have.

Wexford ★ ('wɛksfəd) *n* **1** a county of SE Republic of Ireland, in Leinster province on the Irish Sea: the first Irish county to be colonized from England; mostly low-lying and fertile. County town: Wexford. Pop.: 102 069 (1991). Area: 2352 sq. km (908 sq. miles). **2** a port in SE Republic of Ireland, county town of Co. Wexford: sacked by Oliver Cromwell in 1649. Pop.: 9540 (1991).

Weymouth ★ ('weɪməθ) *n* a port and resort in S England, in Dorset on the English Channel: administratively part of the borough of **Weymouth and Melcombe Regis.** Pop. (with Melcombe Regis): 53 235 (1991).

wf *Printing. abbrev. for* wrong fount.

WFF *Logic. abbrev. for* well-formed formula.

WFTU *abbrev. for* World Federation of Trade Unions.

W. Glam *abbrev. for* West Glamorgan.

whack ★ (wæk) *vb* (*tr*) **1** to strike with a sharp resounding blow. **2** (*usually passive*) *Brit. inf.* to exhaust completely. ◆ *n* **3** a sharp resounding blow or the noise made by such a blow. **4** *Inf.* a share or portion. **5** *Inf.* a try or attempt (esp. in **have a whack at**). **6 out of whack.** *Inf.* out of order; unbalanced: *the whole system is out of whack.*   [C18: ? var. of THWACK, ult. imit.]
▸ **'whacker** *n*

whacking ('wækɪŋ) *Inf., chiefly Brit.* ◆ *adj* **1** enormous. ◆ *adv* **2** (intensifier): *a whacking big lie.*

whacky ('wækɪ) *adj* **whackier, whackiest.** *US sl.* a variant spelling of **wacky.**

whale[1] (weɪl) *n, pl* **whales** *or* **whale. 1** any of the larger cetacean mammals, excluding dolphins, porpoises, and narwhals. They have flippers, a streamlined body, and a horizontally flattened tail and breathe through a blow-

hole on the top of the head. **2 a whale of a** *Inf.* an exceptionally large, fine, etc., example of a (person or thing). [OE *hwæl*]

whale[2] (weɪl) *vb* **whales, whaling, whaled.** (*tr*) to beat or thrash soundly.   [C18: var. of WALE]

whaleboat ('weɪl,bəʊt) *n* a narrow boat from 20 to 30 feet long having a sharp prow and stern, formerly used in whaling. Also called: **whaler.**

whalebone ('weɪl,bəʊn) *n* **1** Also called: **baleen.** a horny elastic material forming numerous thin plates that hang from the upper jaw in the toothless (whalebone) whales and strain plankton from water entering the mouth. **2** a strip of this substance, used in stiffening corsets, etc.

whalebone whale *n* any whale belonging to a cetacean suborder having a double blowhole and strips of whalebone between the jaws instead of teeth: includes the rorquals, right whales, and the blue whale.

whale oil *n* oil obtained either from the blubber of whales (train oil) or the head of the sperm whale (sperm oil).

whaler ('weɪlə) *n* **1** Also called (US): **whaleman.** a person employed in whaling. **2** a vessel engaged in whaling. **3** *Austral. obs.* a tramp or sundowner. **4** an aggressive shark of Australian coastal waters.

whale shark *n* a large spotted whalelike shark of warm seas, that feeds on plankton and small animals.

whaling ('weɪlɪŋ) *n* the work or industry of hunting and processing whales for food, oil, etc.

wham (wæm) *n* **1** a forceful blow or impact or the sound produced by it. ◆ *vb* **whams, whamming, whammed. 2** to strike or cause to strike with great force.   [C20: imit.]

whammy ('wæmɪ) *n, pl* **whammies.** *Inf.* **1** something which has great, often negative impact: *a double whammy of falling demand and rising prices.* **2** an evil spell or curse: *she believed he had put the whammy on her.*   [C20: WHAM + -Y[2]]

whanau ('fɑːnaʊ) *n NZ.* a family, esp. an extended family.   [Maori]

whang (wæŋ) *vb* **1** to strike or be struck so as to cause a resounding noise. ◆ *n* **2** the resounding noise produced by a heavy blow. **3** a heavy blow.   [C19: imit.]

Whangarei ★ (,wɑːŋɑːˈreɪ) *n* a port in New Zealand, the northernmost city of North Island. Pop.: 44 800 (1994).

whangee (wæŋˈiː) *n* **1** a tall woody grass of an Asian genus, grown for its stems. **2** a cane or walking stick made from the stem of this plant.   [C19: prob. from Chinese (Mandarin) *huangli,* from *huang* yellow + *li* bamboo cane]

whare ('wɔːrɪ; *Maori* 'fɔre) *n NZ.* **1** a Maori hut or dwelling place. **2** any simple dwelling place.   [from Maori]

wharepuni ('fɔre,puni) *n NZ.* in a Maori community, a lofty carved building that is used as a guesthouse.   [from Maori WHARE + *puni* company]

wharf (wɔːf) *n, pl* **wharves** (wɔːvz) *or* **wharfs. 1** a platform built parallel to the waterfront at a harbour or navigable river for the docking, loading, and unloading of ships. ◆ *vb* (*tr*) **2** to moor or dock at a wharf. **3** to store or unload on a wharf.   [OE *hwearf* heap]

wharfage ('wɔːfɪdʒ) *n* **1** facilities for ships at wharves. **2** a charge for use of a wharf. **3** wharves collectively.

wharfie ('wɔːfɪ) *n Austral. & NZ.* a wharf labourer; docker.

wharfinger ('wɔːfɪndʒə) *n* an owner or manager of a wharf.   [C16: prob. alteration of *wharfager*]

Wharton ★ ('wɔːt⁽ə⁾n) *n* **Edith** (**Newbold**). 1862–1937, US novelist; author of *The House of Mirth* (1905) and *Ethan Frome* (1911).

wharve (wɔːv) *n* a wooden disc or wheel on a shaft serving as a flywheel or pulley.   [OE *hweorfa,* from *hweorfan* to revolve]

what (wɒt; *unstressed* wət) *determiner* **1a** used with a noun in requesting further information about the identity or categorization of something: *what job does he do?* **1b** (*as pron*): *what is her address?* **1c** (*used in indirect questions*): *tell me what he said.* **2a** (*the person, thing, persons, or things*) that: *we photographed what animals we could see.* **2b** (*as pron*): *bring me what you've written.* **3** (*intensifier; used in exclamations*): *what a good book!* ◆ *adv* **4** in what respect? to what degree?: *what do you care?* **5 what about.** what do you think, know, etc., concerning? **6 what for. 6a** for what purpose? why? **6b** *Inf.* a punishment or reprimand (esp. in **give (a person) what for). 7 what have you.** someone or something unknown or unspecified: *cars, motorcycles, or what have you.* **8 what if. 8a** what would happen if? **8b** what difference would it make if? **9 what matter.** what does it matter? **10 what's what.** *Inf.* the true state of affairs. [OE *hwæt*]

> **USAGE NOTE** The use of *are* in sentences such as *what we need are more doctors* is common, although many people think *is* should be used: *what we need is more doctors.*

whatever (wɒt'ɛvə, wət-) *pron* **1** everything or anything that: *do whatever he asks you to.* **2** no matter what: *whatever he does, he is forgiven.* **3** *Inf.* an unknown or unspecified thing or things: *take a hammer, chisel, or whatever.* **4** an intensive form of *what*, used in questions: *whatever can he have said to upset her so much?* ◆ *determiner* **5** an intensive form of *what*: *use whatever tools you can get hold of.* ◆ *adj* **6** (*postpositive*) absolutely; whatsoever: *I saw no point whatever in continuing.*

whatnot ('wɒt,nɒt) *n* **1** Also called: **what-d'you-call-it.** *Inf.* a person or thing the name of which is unknown or forgotten. **2** *Inf.* unspecified assorted material. **3** a portable stand with shelves for displaying ornaments, etc.

whatsit ('wɒtsɪt), **whatsitsname,** (*masc*) **whatshisname,** *or* (*fem*) **whatshername** *n Inf.* a person or thing the name of which is unknown or forgotten.

whatsoever (,wɒtsəʊ'ɛvə) *adj* **1** (*postpositive*) at all: used as an intensifier with indefinite pronouns and determiners such as *none, anybody,* etc. ◆ *pron* **2** an archaic word for **whatever.**

whaup (hwɔːp) *n Chiefly Scot.* a popular name for the **curlew.** [C16: rel. to OE *huilpe*, ult. imit. of the bird's cry]

wheal (wiːl) *n* a variant spelling of **weal**[1].

wheat (wiːt) *n* **1** any of a genus of grasses, native to the Mediterranean region and W Asia but widely cultivated, having erect flower spikes and light brown grains. **2** the grain of any of these grasses, used in making flour, pasta, etc. ◆ See also **durum.** [OE *hwǣte*]

wheatbelt ('wiːt,bɛlt) *n* an area in which wheat is the chief agricultural product.

wheatear ('wiːt,ɪə) *n* a small northern songbird having a pale grey back, black wings and tail, white rump, and pale brown underparts. [C16: back formation from *wheatears* (wrongly taken as pl), prob. from WHITE + ARSE]

wheaten ('wiːtⁿn) *adj* **1** made of the grain or flour of wheat. **2** of a pale yellow colour.

wheat germ *n* the vitamin-rich embryo of the wheat kernel.

wheatmeal ('wiːt,miːl) *n* **a** a brown flour intermediate between white flour and wholemeal flour. **b** (*as modifier*): *a wheatmeal loaf.*

Wheatstone bridge ('wiːtstən) *n* a device for determining the value of an unknown resistance by comparison with a known standard resistance. [C19: after Sir Charles *Wheatstone* (1802–75), Brit. physicist and inventor]

whee (wiː) *interj* an exclamation of joy, etc.

wheedle ('wiːdᵊl) *vb* **wheedles, wheedling, wheedled. 1** to persuade or try to persuade (someone) by coaxing words, flattery, etc. **2** (*tr*) to obtain thus: *she wheedled some money out of her father.* [C17: ?from G *wedeln* to wag one's tail, from OHG *wedil, wadil* tail]
► 'wheedler *n* ► 'wheedling *adj* ► 'wheedlingly *adv*

wheel (wiːl) *n* **1** a solid disc, or a circular rim joined to a hub by spokes, that is mounted on a shaft about which it can turn, as in vehicles. **2** anything like a wheel in shape or function. **3** a device consisting of or resembling a wheel: *a steering wheel; a water wheel.* **4** (usually preceded by *the*) a medieval torture in which the victim was tied to a wheel and then had his limbs struck and broken by an iron bar. **5** short for **wheel of fortune** or **potter's wheel. 6** the

act of turning. **7** a pivoting movement of troops, ships, etc. **8** a type of firework coiled to make it rotate when let off. **9** a set of short rhyming lines forming the concluding part of a stanza. **10** *US & Canad.* an informal word for **bicycle. 11** *Inf., chiefly US & Canad.* a person of great influence (esp. in **big wheel). 12 at the wheel. 12a** driving or steering a vehicle or vessel. **12b** in charge. ◆ *vb* **13** to turn or cause to turn on or as if on an axis. **14** (when *intr*, sometimes foll. by *about* or *around*) to move or cause to move on or as if on wheels; roll. **15** (*tr*) to perform with or in a circular movement. **16** (*tr*) to provide with a wheel or wheels. **17** (*intr*; often foll. by *about*) to change direction. **18 wheel and deal.** *Inf.* to operate free of restraint, esp. to advance one's own interests. ◆ See also **wheels.** [OE *hweol, hweowol*]

wheel and axle *n* a simple machine for raising weights in which a rope unwinding from a wheel is wound onto a cylindrical drum or shaft coaxial with or joined to the wheel to provide mechanical advantage.

wheel animalcule *n* another name for **rotifer.**

wheelbarrow ('wiːl,bærəʊ) *n* a simple vehicle for carrying small loads, typically being an open container supported by a wheel at the front and two legs behind.

wheelbase ('wiːl,beɪs) *n* the distance between the front and back axles of a motor vehicle.

wheelchair ('wiːl,tʃeə) *n* special chair on large wheels, for use by invalids or others for whom walking is impossible or inadvisable.

wheel clamp *n* a device fixed onto one wheel of an illegally parked car in order to immobilize it. The driver has to pay to have it removed.

wheeled (wiːld) *adj* **a** having a wheel or wheels. **b** (*in combination*): *four-wheeled.*

wheeler ('wiːlə) *n* **1** Also called: **wheel horse.** a horse or other draught animal nearest the wheel. **2** (*in combination*) something equipped with a specified sort or number of wheels: *a three-wheeler.* **3** a person or thing that wheels.

Wheeler ★ ('wiːlə) *n* **1 John Archibald.** born 1911, US physicist, noted for his work on nuclear fission and the development (1949–51) of the hydrogen bomb. **2** Sir (**Robert Eric) Mortimer.** 1890–1976, British archaeologist, noted for his excavations in the Indus Valley and at Maiden Castle in Dorset.

wheeler-dealer *n Inf.* a person who wheels and deals.

wheel horse *n* **1** another word for **wheeler** (sense 1). **2** *US & Canad.* a person who works steadily or hard.

wheelhouse ('wiːl,haʊs) *n* another term for **pilot house.**

wheelie ('wiːlɪ) *n* a manoeuvre on a bicycle or motorbike in which the front wheel is raised off the ground.

wheelie bin *or* **wheely bin** *n* a large container for rubbish, esp. one used by a household, mounted on wheels so that it can be moved more easily.

wheel lock *n* **1** a gunlock formerly in use in which the firing mechanism was activated by sparks produced by friction between a small steel wheel and a flint. **2** a gun having such a lock.

wheel of fortune *n* (in mythology and literature) a revolving device spun by a deity selecting random changes in the affairs of man.

wheels (wiːlz) *pl n* **1** the main directing force behind an organization, movement, etc.: *the wheels of government.* **2** an informal word for **car. 3 wheels within wheels.** a series of intricately connected events, plots, etc.

wheel window *n* another name for **rose window.**

wheel wobble *n* an oscillation of the front wheels of a vehicle caused by a defect in the steering gear, unbalanced wheels, etc.

wheelwright ('wiːl,raɪt) *n* a person who makes or mends wheels as a trade.

wheeze (wiːz) *vb* **wheezes, wheezing, wheezed. 1** to breathe or utter (something) with a rasping or whistling sound. **2** (*intr*) to make or move with a noise suggestive of wheezy breathing. ◆ *n* **3** a husky, rasping, or whistling sound or breathing. **4** *Brit. sl.* a trick, idea, or plan. **5** *Inf.* a hackneyed joke or anecdote. [C15: prob. from ON *hvǣsa* to hiss]

★ people and places

▶ **'wheezer** n ▶ **'wheezy** adj ▶ **'wheezily** adv ▶ **'wheezi-ness** n

whelk[1] (wɛlk) n a marine gastropod mollusc of coastal waters and intertidal regions, having a strong snail-like shell. [OE *weoloc*]

whelk[2] (wɛlk) n a raised lesion on the skin; wheal. [OE *hwylca*, from ?]
▶ **'whelky** adj

whelm (wɛlm) vb (tr) Arch. to engulf entirely; over-whelm. [C13 *whelmen* to turn over, from ?]

whelp (wɛlp) n 1 a young offspring of certain animals, esp. of a wolf or dog. 2 Disparaging. a youth. 3 Jocular. a young child. 4 Naut. any of the ridges, parallel to the axis, on the drum of a capstan to keep a rope, etc., from slipping. ◆ vb 5 (of an animal or, disparagingly, a woman) to give birth to (young). [OE *hwelp(a)*]

when (wɛn) adv 1a at what time? over what period?: *when is he due?* 1b (used in indirect questions): *ask him when he's due.* 2 say when. to state when an action is to be stopped or begun, as when someone is pouring a drink. ◆ conj 3 (subordinating) at a time at which; just as; after: *I found it easy when I tried.* 4 although: *he drives when he might walk.* 5 considering the fact that: *how did you pass the exam when you hadn't worked for it?* ◆ pron 6 at which (time); over which (period): *an age when men were men.* ◆ n 7 a question as to the time of some occurrence. [OE *hwanne, hwænne*]

> **USAGE NOTE** *When* should not be used loosely as a substitute for *in which* after a noun which does not refer to a period of time: *paralysis is a condition in which* (not *when*) *parts of the body cannot be moved.*

whenas (wɛn'æz) conj Arch. 1a when; whenever. 1b inasmuch as; while. 2 although.

whence (wɛns) Arch. or formal. ◆ adv 1 from what place, cause, or origin? ◆ pron 2 (subordinating) from what place, cause, or origin. [C13 *whannes*, adv. genitive of OE *hwanon*]

> **USAGE NOTE** The expression *from whence* should be avoided, since *whence* already means from which place: *the tradition whence* (not *from whence*) *such ideas flowed.*

whencesoever (ˌwɛnssəʊ'ɛvə) conj (subordinating), adv Arch. from whatever place, cause, or origin.

whenever (wɛn'ɛvə) conj 1 (subordinating) at every or any time that; when: *I laugh whenever I see that.* ◆ adv also **when ever.** 2 no matter when: *it'll be here, whenever you decide to come for it.* 3 Inf. at an unknown or unspecified time: *I'll take it if it comes today, tomorrow, or whenever.* 4 an intensive form of *when*, used in questions: *whenever did he escape?*

whensoever (ˌwɛnsəʊ'ɛvə) conj, adv Rare. an intensive form of **whenever.**

whenua (fɛn'uə) n NZ. land. [Maori]

where (wɛə) adv 1a in, at, or to what place, point, or position?: *where are you going?* 1b (used in indirect questions): *I don't know where they are.* ◆ pron 2 in, at, or to which (place): *the hotel where we spent our honeymoon.* ◆ conj 3 (subordinating) in the place at which: *where we live it's always raining.* ◆ n 4 a question as to the position, direction, or destination of something. [OE *hwær, hwār(a)*]

> **USAGE NOTE** It was formerly considered incorrect to use *where* as a substitute for *in which* after a noun which did not refer to a place or position, but this use has now become acceptable: *we have a situation where/in which no further action is needed.*

whereabouts ('wɛərəˌbaʊts) adv 1 at what approximate place; where: *whereabouts are you?* ◆ n 2 (functioning as

sing or pl) the place, esp. the approximate place, where a person or thing is.

whereas (wɛər'æz) conj 1 (coordinating) but on the other hand: *I like to go swimming whereas Sheila likes to sail.* ◆ sentence connector. 2 (in formal documents) it being the case that; since.

whereat (wɛər'æt) Arch. ◆ adv 1 at or to which place. ◆ sentence connector. 2 upon which occasion.

whereby (wɛə'baɪ) pron by or because of which: *the means whereby he took his life.*

wherefore ('wɛəˌfɔː) n 1 (usually pl) an explanation or reason (esp. in **the whys and wherefores**). ◆ adv 2 Arch. why? ◆ sentence connector. 3 Arch. or formal. for which reason: used in legal preambles.

wherefrom (wɛə'frɒm) Arch. ◆ adv 1 from what or where? whence? ◆ pron 2 from which place; whence.

wherein (wɛər'ɪn) Arch. or formal. ◆ adv 1 in what place or respect? ◆ pron 2 in which place, thing, etc.

whereof (wɛər'ɒv) Arch. or formal. ◆ adv 1 of what or which person or thing? ◆ pron 2 of which (person or thing): *the man whereof I speak is no longer alive.*

whereon (wɛər'ɒn) Arch. ◆ adv 1 on what thing or place? ◆ pron 2 on which thing, place, etc.

wheresoever (ˌwɛəsəʊ'ɛvə) conj (subordinating), adv, pron Rare. an intensive form of **wherever.**

whereto (wɛə'tuː) Arch. or formal. ◆ adv 1 towards what (place, end, etc.)? ◆ pron 2 to which. ◆ Also (archaic): **whereunto.**

whereupon (ˌwɛərə'pɒn) sentence connector. at which; at which point; upon which.

wherever (wɛər'ɛvə) pron 1 at, in, or to every place or point which; where: *wherever she went, he would be there.* ◆ conj 2 (subordinating) in, to, or at whatever place: *wherever we go the weather is always bad.* ◆ adv also **where ever.** 3 no matter where: *I'll find you, wherever you are.* 4 Inf. at, in, or to an unknown or unspecified place: *I'll go anywhere to escape: London, Paris, or wherever.* 5 an intensive form of *where*, used in questions: *wherever can they be?*

wherewith (wɛə'wɪθ, -'wɪð) Arch. or formal. ◆ pron 1 (often foll. by an infinitive) with or by which: *the pen wherewith I write.* 2 something with which: *I have not wherewith to buy my bread.* ◆ adv 3 with what? ◆ sentence connector. 4 with or after that; whereupon.

wherewithal n ('wɛəwɪðˌɔːl). 1 the **wherewithal.** necessary funds, resources, or equipment: *these people lack the wherewithal for a decent existence.* ◆ pron (ˌwɛəwɪð'ɔːl). 2 a less common word for **wherewith.**

wherry ('wɛrɪ) n, pl **wherries.** 1 any of certain kinds of half-decked commercial boats. 2 a light rowing boat. [C15: from ?]
▶ **'wherryman** n

whet (wɛt) vb **whets, whetting, whetted.** (tr) 1 to sharpen, as by grinding or friction. 2 to increase (the appetite, desire, etc.); stimulate. ◆ n 3 the act of whetting. 4 a person or thing that whets. [OE *hwettan*]
▶ **'whetter** n

whether ('wɛðə) conj 1 (subordinating) used to introduce an indirect question or a clause after a verb expressing or implying doubt or choice: *he doesn't know whether she's in Britain or whether she's gone to France.* 2 (coordinating) either: *any man, whether liberal or conservative, would agree with me.* 3 **whether or no.** in any case: *he will be here tomorrow, whether or no.* 4 **whether...or.** if on the one hand...or even if on the other hand: *you'll eat that, whether you like it or not.* [OE *hwæther, hwether*]

whetstone ('wɛtˌstəʊn) n 1 a stone used for sharpening edged tools, knives, etc. 2 something that sharpens.

whew (hwjuː) interj an exclamation or sharply exhaled breath expressing relief, delight, etc.

whey (weɪ) n the watery liquid that separates from the curd when milk is clotted, as in making cheese. [OE *hwæg*]

wheyface ('weɪˌfeɪs) n 1 a pale bloodless face. 2 a person with such a face.
▶ **'whey,faced** adj

which (wɪtʃ) determiner 1a used with a noun in requesting that its referent be further specified, identified, or distinguished: *which house did you buy?* **1b** (*as pron*): *which did you find?* **1c** (*used in indirect questions*): *I wondered which apples were cheaper.* **2a** whatever of a class; whichever: *bring which car you want.* **2b** (*as pron*): *choose which of the cars suits you.* ◆ *pron* **3** used in relative clauses with inanimate antecedents: *the house, which is old, is in poor repair.* **4** as; and that: used in relative clauses with verb phrases or sentences as their antecedents: *he died of cancer, which is what I predicted.* **5 the which.** an archaic form of **which** often used as a sentence connector.   [OE *hwelc, hwilc*]

whichever (wɪtʃˈɛvə) *determiner* **1a** any (one, two, etc., out of several): *take whichever car you like.* **1b** (*as pron*): *choose whichever appeals to you.* **2a** no matter which (one or ones): *whichever card you pick you'll still be making a mistake.* **2b** (*as pron*): *it won't make any difference, whichever comes first.*

whichsoever (ˌwɪtʃsəʊˈɛvə) *pron* an archaic or formal word for **whichever.**

whicker (ˈwɪkə) *vb* (*intr*) (of a horse) to whinny or neigh; nicker.   [C17: imit.]

whidah (ˈwɪdə) *n* a variant spelling of **whydah.**

whiff (wɪf) *n* **1** a passing odour. **2** a brief gentle gust of air. **3** a single inhalation or exhalation from the mouth or nose. ◆ *vb* **4** to puff or waft. **5** (*tr*) to sniff or smell. **6** (*intr*) *Brit. sl.* to stink.   [C16: imit.]

whiffle (ˈwɪf³l) *vb* **whiffles, whiffling, whiffled. 1** (*intr*) to think or behave in an erratic or unpredictable way. **2** to blow or be blown fitfully or in gusts. **3** (*intr*) to whistle softly.   [C16: frequentative of WHIFF]

whiffletree (ˈwɪf³l,triː) *n Chiefly US.* another word for **swingletree.**   [C19: var. of WHIPPLETREE]

Whig (wɪg) *n* **1** a member of the English political party that opposed the succession to the throne of James, Duke of York (1679–80), on the grounds that he was a Catholic. Standing for a limited monarchy, the Whigs later represented the desires of industrialists and Dissenters for political and social reform, and provided the core of the Liberal Party. **2** (in the US) a supporter of the War of American Independence. Cf. **Tory. 3** a member of the American political party that opposed the Democrats from about 1834 to 1855 and represented propertied and professional interests. **4** *History.* a 17th-century Scottish Presbyterian, esp. one in rebellion against the Crown. ◆ *adj* **5** of, characteristic of, or relating to Whigs.   [C17: prob. from *whiggamore*, one of a group of 17th-cent. Scottish rebels who joined in an attack on Edinburgh known as the *whiggamore raid*; prob. from Scot. *whig* to drive (from ?) + *more* horse]
▶ ˈ**Whiggery** or ˈ**Whiggism** *n* ▶ ˈ**Whiggish** *adj*

while (waɪl) *conj also* **whilst. 1** (*subordinating*) at the same time that: *please light the fire while I'm cooking.* **2** (*subordinating*) all the time that: *I stay inside while it's raining.* **3** (*subordinating*) in spite of the fact that: *while I agree about his brilliance I still think he's rude.* **4** (*coordinating*) whereas; and in contrast: *houses are expensive, while flats are cheap.* ◆ *prep, conj* **5** *Scot. & N English dialect.* another word for **until:** *you'll have to wait while Monday.* ◆ *n* **6** (*usually used in adverbial phrases*) a period or interval of time: *once in a long while.* **7** trouble or time (esp. in **worth one's while**): *it's hardly worth your while to begin work today.*   [OE *hwīl*]

while away *vb* (*tr, adv*) to pass (time) idly and usually pleasantly.

whiles (waɪlz) *Arch. or dialect.* ◆ *adv* **1** at times; occasionally. ◆ *conj* **2** while; whilst.

whilom (ˈwaɪləm) *Arch.* ◆ *adv* **1** formerly; once. ◆ *adj* **2** (*prenominal*) one-time; former.   [OE *hwīlum*, dative pl of *hwīl* while]

whilst (waɪlst) *conj Chiefly Brit.* another word for **while** (senses 1–4).   [C13: from WHILES + *-t* as in *amidst*]

whim (wɪm) *n* **1** a sudden, passing, and often fanciful idea; impulsive or irrational thought. **2** a horse-drawn winch formerly used in mining to lift ore or water.   [C17: from C16 *whim-wham*, from ?]

whimbrel (ˈwɪmbrəl) *n* a small European curlew with a striped head.   [C16: from dialect *whimp* or from WHIMPER, from its cry]

whimper (ˈwɪmpə) *vb* **1** (*intr*) to cry, sob, or whine softly or intermittently. **2** to complain or say (something) in a whining plaintive way. ◆ *n* **3** a soft plaintive whine.   [C16: from dialect *whimp*, imit.]
▶ ˈ**whimperer** *n* ▶ ˈ**whimpering** *n, adj* ▶ ˈ**whimperingly** *adv*

whimsical (ˈwɪmzɪk³l) *adj* **1** spontaneously fanciful or playful. **2** given to whims; capricious. **3** quaint, unusual, or fantastic.
▶ **whimsicality** (ˌwɪmzɪˈkælɪtɪ) *n* ▶ ˈ**whimsically** *adv*

whimsy or **whimsey** (ˈwɪmzɪ) *n, pl* **whimsies** or **whimseys. 1** a capricious idea or notion. **2** light or fanciful humour. **3** something quaint or unusual. ◆ *adj* **whimsier, whimsiest. 4** quaint, comical, or unusual, often in a tasteless way.   [C17: from WHIM]

whin[1] (wɪn) *n* another name for **gorse.**   [C11: from ON]

whin[2] (wɪn) *n* short for **whinstone.**   [C14 *quin*, from ?]

whinchat (ˈwɪn,tʃæt) *n* an Old World songbird having a mottled brown-and-white plumage with pale cream underparts.   [C17: from WHIN[1] + CHAT]

whine (waɪn) *n* **1** a long high-pitched plaintive cry or moan. **2** a continuous high-pitched sound. **3** a peevish complaint, esp. one repeated. ◆ *vb* **whines, whining, whined. 4** to make a whine or utter in a whine.   [OE *hwīnan*]
▶ ˈ**whiner** *n* ▶ ˈ**whining** or ˈ**whiny** *adj* ▶ ˈ**whiningly** *adv*

whinge (wɪndʒ) *vb* **whinges, whingeing, whinged.** (*intr*) **1** to cry in a fretful way. **2** to complain. ◆ *n* **3** a complaint. [from Northern var. of OE *hwinsian* to whine]
▶ ˈ**whingeing** *n, adj* ▶ ˈ**whinger** *n*

whinny (ˈwɪnɪ) *vb* **whinnies, whinnying, whinnied.** (*intr*) **1** (of a horse) to neigh softly or gently. **2** to make a sound resembling a neigh, such as a laugh. ◆ *n, pl* **whinnies. 3** a gentle or low-pitched neigh.   [C16: imit.]

whinstone (ˈwɪn,stəʊn) *n* any dark hard fine-grained rock, such as basalt.   [C16: from WHIN[2] + STONE]

whip (wɪp) *vb* **whips, whipping, whipped. 1** to strike (a person or thing) with several strokes of a strap, rod, etc. **2** (*tr*) to punish by striking in this manner. **3** (*tr;* foll. by *out, away,* etc.) to pull, remove, etc., with sudden rapid motion: *to whip out a gun.* **4** (*intr;* foll. by *down, into, out of,* etc.) *Inf.* to come, go, etc., in a rapid sudden manner: *they whipped into the bar for a drink.* **5** to strike or be struck as if by whipping: *the tempest whipped the surface of the sea.* **6** (*tr*) to bring, train, etc., forcefully into a desired condition. **7** (*tr*) *Inf.* to overcome or outdo. **8** (*tr;* often foll. by *on, out,* or *off*) to drive, urge, compel, etc., by or as if by whipping. **9** (*tr*) to wrap or wind (a cord, thread, etc.) around (a rope, cable, etc.) to prevent chafing or fraying. **10** (*tr*) (in fly-fishing) to cast the fly repeatedly onto (the water) in a whipping motion. **11** (*tr*) (in sewing) to join, finish, or gather with whipstitch. **12** to beat (eggs, cream, etc.) with a whisk or similar utensil to incorporate air. **13** (*tr*) to spin (a top). **14** (*tr*) *Inf.* to steal: *he whipped her purse.* ◆ *n* **15** a device consisting of a lash or flexible rod attached at one end to a stiff handle and used for driving animals, inflicting corporal punishment, etc. **16** a whipping stroke or motion. **17** a person adept at handling a whip, as a coachman, etc. **18** (in a legislative body) **18a** a member of a party chosen to organize and discipline the members of his faction. **18b** a call issued to members of a party, insisting with varying degrees of urgency upon their presence or loyal voting behaviour. **18c** (in the Brit. Parliament) a schedule of business sent to members of a party each week. Each item on it is underlined to indicate its importance: three lines means that the item is very important and every member must attend and vote according to the party line. **19** an apparatus for hoisting, consisting of a rope, pulley, and snatch block. **20** any of a variety of desserts made from egg whites or cream beaten stiff. **21** See **whipper-in. 22** flexibility, as in the

shaft of a golf club, etc. ◆ See also **whip-round, whip up, whips.** [C13: ?from MDu. *wippen* to swing]
► '**whip**,**like** *adj* ► '**whipper** *n*

whip bird *n Austral.* any of several birds having a whistle ending in a note sounding like the crack of a whip.

whipcord ('wɪp,kɔːd) *n* **1** a strong worsted or cotton fabric with a diagonally ribbed surface. **2** a closely twisted hard cord used for the lashes of whips, etc.

whip graft *n Horticulture.* a graft made by inserting a tongue cut on the sloping base of the scion into a slit on the sloping top of the stock.

whip hand *n* (usually preceded by *the*) **1** (in driving horses) the hand holding the whip. **2** advantage or dominating position.

whiplash ('wɪp,læʃ) *n* a quick lash or stroke of a whip or like that of a whip.

whiplash injury *n Med. inf.* any injury to the neck resulting from a sudden thrusting forwards and snapping back of the unsupported head. Technical name: **hyperextension-hyperflexion injury.**

whipper-in *n, pl* **whippers-in.** a person employed to assist the huntsman managing the hounds.

whippersnapper ('wɪpə,snæpə) *n* an insignificant but pretentious or cheeky person, often a young one. Also called: **whipster.** [C17: prob. from *whipsnapper* a person who snaps whips, infl. by earlier *snippersnapper*, from ?]

whippet ('wɪpɪt) *n* a small slender breed of dog similar to a greyhound. [C16: from ?; ? based on *whip it!* move quickly!]

whipping ('wɪpɪŋ) *n* **1** a thrashing or beating with a whip or similar implement. **2** cord or twine used for binding or lashing. **3** the binding formed by wrapping a rope, etc., with cord or twine.

whipping boy *n* a person of little importance who is blamed for the errors, incompetence, etc., of others, esp. his superiors; scapegoat. [C17: orig. referring to a boy who was educated with a prince and who received punishment for any faults committed by the prince]

whippletree ('wɪpᵊl,triː) *n* another name for **swingletree.** [C18: apparently from WHIP]

whippoorwill ('wɪpʊ,wɪl) *n* a nightjar of North and Central America, having a dark plumage with white patches on the tail. [C18: imit. of its cry]

whip-round *Inf., chiefly Brit.* ◆ *n* **1** an impromptu collection of money. ◆ *vb* **whip round. 2** (*intr, adv*) to make such a collection.

whips (wɪps) *pl n* (often foll. by *of*) *Austral. inf.* a large quantity: *I've got whips of cash at the moment.*

whipsaw ('wɪp,sɔː) *n* **1** any saw with a flexible blade, such as a bandsaw. ◆ *vb* **whipsaws, whipsawing, whip-sawed; whipsawed** *or* **whipsawn.** (*tr*) **2** to saw with a whipsaw. **3** *US.* to defeat in two ways at once.

whip scorpion *n* any of an order of nonvenomous arachnids, typically resembling a scorpion but lacking a sting.

whip snake *n* any of several long slender fast-moving nonvenomous snakes.

whipstitch ('wɪp,stɪtʃ) *n* a sewing stitch passing over an edge.

whipstock ('wɪp,stɒk) *n* a whip handle.

whip up *vb* (*tr, adv*) **1** to excite; arouse: *to whip up a mob; to whip up discontent.* **2** *Inf.* to prepare quickly: *to whip up a meal.*

whir *or* **whirr** (wɜː) *n* **1** a prolonged soft swish or buzz, as of a motor working or wings flapping. **2** a bustle or rush. ◆ *vb* **whirs** *or* **whirrs, whirring, whirred.** **3** to make or cause to make a whir. [C14: prob. from ON; see WHIRL]

whirl (wɜːl) *vb* **1** to spin, turn, or revolve or cause to spin, turn, or revolve. **2** (*intr*) to turn around or away rapidly. **3** (*intr*) to have a spinning sensation, as from dizziness, etc. **4** to move or drive or be moved or driven at high speed. ◆ *n* **5** the act or an instance of whirling; swift rotation or a rapid whirling movement. **6** a condition of confusion or giddiness: *her accident left me in a whirl.* **7** a swift round, as of events, meetings, etc. **8** a tumult; stir. **9** *Inf.* a brief trip, dance, etc. **10 give (something) a whirl.** *Inf.* to attempt

or give a trial to (something). [C13: from ON *hvirfla* to turn about]
► '**whirler** *n* ► '**whirling** *adj* ► '**whirlingly** *adv*

whirligig ('wɜːlɪ,gɪg) *n* **1** any spinning toy, such as a top. **2** another name for **merry-go-round. 3** anything that whirls about, spins, or moves in a circular or giddy way: *the whirligig of social life.* [C15 *whirlegigge*, from WHIRL + GIG¹]

whirlpool ('wɜːl,puːl) *n* **1** a powerful circular current or vortex of water. **2** something resembling a whirlpool in motion or the power to attract into its vortex.

whirlwind ('wɜːl,wɪnd) *n* **1** a column of air whirling around and towards a more or less vertical axis of low pressure, which moves along the land or ocean surface. **2a** a motion or course resembling this, esp. in rapidity. **2b** (*as modifier*): *a whirlwind romance.* **3** an impetuously active person.

whirlybird ('wɜːlɪ,bɜːd) *n* an informal word for **helicopter.**

whish (wɪʃ) *n, vb* a less common word for **swish.**

whisht (hwɪʃt) *or* **whist** *Arch. or dialect, esp. Scot.* ◆ *interj* **1** hush! be quiet! ◆ *adj* **2** silent or still. [C14: cf. HIST]

whisk (wɪsk) *vb* **1** (*tr;* often foll. by *away* or *off*) to brush, sweep, or wipe off lightly. **2** (*tr*) to move, carry, etc., with a light or rapid sweeping motion: *the taxi whisked us to the airport.* **3** (*intr*) to move, go, etc., quickly and nimbly: *to whisk downstairs for a drink.* **4** (*tr*) to whip (eggs, etc.) to a froth. ◆ *n* **5** the act of whisking. **6** a light rapid sweeping movement. **7** a utensil for whipping eggs, etc. **8** a small brush or broom. **9** a small bunch or bundle, as of grass, straw, etc. [C14: from ON *visk* wisp]

whisker ('wɪskə) *n* **1** any of the stiff sensory hairs growing on the face of a cat, rat, or other mammal. Technical name: **vibrissa. 2** any of the hairs growing on a man's face, esp. on the cheeks or chin. **3** (*pl*) that part of it growing on the sides of the face. **4** (*pl*) *Inf.* a moustache. **5** *Chem.* a very fine filamentary crystal having greater strength than the bulk material. **6** a person or thing that whisks. **7** a narrow margin or small distance: *he escaped death by a whisker.* [see WHISK]
► '**whiskered** *or* '**whiskery** *adj*

whiskey ('wɪskɪ) *n* the usual Irish and US spelling of **whisky.**

whiskey sour *n US.* a mixed drink of whisky and lime or lemon juice, sometimes sweetened.

whisky ('wɪskɪ) *n, pl* **whiskies.** a spirit made by distilling fermented cereals, which is matured and often blended. [C18: shortened from *whiskybae*, from Scot. Gaelic *uisge beatha*, lit.: water of life; see USQUEBAUGH]

whisky-jack *n Canad.* another name for **Canada jay.**

whisky mac *n Brit.* a drink consisting of whisky and ginger wine.

whisper ('wɪspə) *vb* **1** to speak or utter (something) in a soft hushed tone, esp. without vibration of the vocal cords. **2** (*intr*) to speak secretly or furtively, as in promoting intrigue, gossip, etc. **3** (*intr*) (of leaves, trees, etc.) to make a low soft rustling sound. **4** (*tr*) to utter or suggest secretly or privately: *to whisper treason.* ◆ *n* **5** a low soft voice: *to speak in a whisper.* **6** something uttered in such a voice. **7** a low soft rustling sound. **8** a trace or suspicion. **9** *Inf.* a rumour. [OE *hwisprian*]
► '**whisperer** *n*

whispering campaign *n* the organized diffusion of defamatory rumours to discredit a person, group, etc.

whispering gallery *n* a gallery or dome with acoustic characteristics such that a sound made at one point is audible at distant points.

whist¹ (wɪst) *n* a card game for four in which the two sides try to win the balance of the 13 tricks: forerunner of bridge. [C17: ? changed from WHISK, referring to the sweeping up or whisking up of the tricks]

whist² (hwɪst) *interj, adj* a variant of **whisht.**

whist drive *n* a social gathering where whist is played: the winners of each hand move to different tables to play the losers of the previous hand.

whistle ('wɪsᵊl) *vb* **whistles, whistling, whistled.** **1** to produce (shrill or flutelike sounds), as by passing breath through a narrow constriction most easily formed by the pursed lips. **2** (*tr*) to signal or command by whistling or blowing a whistle: *the referee whistled the end of the game*. **3** (of a kettle, train, etc.) to produce (a shrill sound) caused by the emission of steam through a small aperture. **4** (*intr*) to move with a whistling sound caused by rapid passage through the air. **5** (of animals, esp. birds) to emit (a shrill sound) resembling human whistling. **6 whistle in the dark**. to try to keep up one's confidence in spite of fear. ♦ *n* **7** a device for making a shrill high-pitched sound by means of air or steam under pressure. **8** a shrill sound effected by whistling or blowing a whistle. **9** a whistling sound, as of a bird, bullet, the wind, etc. **10** a signal, etc., transmitted by or as if by a whistle. **11** the act of whistling. **12** an instrument, usually made of metal, that is blown down its end to produce a tune, signal, etc. **13 blow the whistle**. (usually foll. by *on*) *Inf*. **13a** to inform (on). **13b** to bring a stop (to). **14 clean as a whistle**. perfectly clean or clear. **15 wet one's whistle**. *Inf*. to take an alcoholic drink. ♦ See also **whistle for, whistle up**. [OE *hwistlian*]

whistle-blower *n Inf*. a person who informs on someone or puts a stop to something.

whistle for *vb* (*intr, prep*) *Inf*. to seek or expect in vain.

whistler ('wɪslə) *n* **1** a person or thing that whistles. **2** *Radio*. an atmospheric disturbance picked up by radio receivers, caused by the electromagnetic radiation produced by lightning. **3** any of various birds having a whistling call, such as certain Australian flycatchers. **4** any of various North American marmots.

Whistler ★ ('wɪslə) *n* **James Abbott McNeill**. 1834–1903, US painter, living in Europe: best known for his portraits.

whistle stop *n* **1** *US & Canad*. **1a** a minor railway station where trains stop only on signal. **1b** a small town having such a station. **2a** a brief appearance in a town, esp. by a political candidate. **2b** (*as modifier*): *a whistle-stop tour*.

whistle up *vb* (*tr, adv*) to call or summon (a person or animal) by whistling.

whit (wɪt) *n* (*usually used with a negative*) the smallest particle; iota; jot: *he has changed not a whit*. [C15: prob. var. of WIGHT]

Whit (wɪt) *n* **1** See **Whitsuntide**. ♦ *adj* **2** of or relating to Whitsuntide.

Whitaker ★ ('wɪtəkə) *n* Sir **Frederick**. 1812–91, New Zealand statesman, born in Britain: prime minister (1863–64; 1882–83).

Whitbread ★ ('wɪt,brɛd) *n* **Fatima**. born 1961, British javelin thrower.

Whitby ★ ('wɪtbɪ) *n* a fishing port and resort in NE England, in E North Yorkshire at the mouth of the River Esk: an important ecclesiastical centre in Anglo-Saxon times; site of an abbey founded in 656. Pop.: 13 640 (1991).

white (waɪt) *adj* **1** having no hue, owing to the reflection of all or almost all incident light. **2** (of light, such as sunlight) consisting of all the colours of the spectrum or produced by certain mixtures of primary colours, as red, green, and blue. **3** comparatively white or whitish-grey or having parts of this colour: *white clover*. **4** (of an animal) having pale-coloured or white skin, fur, or feathers. **5** bloodless or pale, as from pain, emotion, etc. **6** (of hair, etc.) grey, usually from age. **7** benevolent or without malicious intent: *white magic*. **8** colourless or transparent: *white glass*. **9** capped with or accompanied by snow: *a white Christmas*. **10** blank, as an unprinted area of a page. **11** (of coffee or tea) with milk or cream. **12** (of wine) made from pale grapes or from black grapes separated from their skins. **13** denoting flour, or bread made from flour, that has had part of the grain removed. **14** *Physics*. having or characterized by a continuous distribution of energy, wavelength, or frequency: *white noise*. **15** *Inf*. honourable or generous. **16** *Poetic or arch*. having a fair complexion; blond. **17 bleed white**. to deprive slowly of resources. ♦ *n* **18** a white colour. **19** the condition of being white; whiteness. **20** the white or lightly coloured part of something. **21** (usually preceded by *the*) the viscous fluid that surrounds the yolk of a bird's egg, esp. a hen's egg; albumen. **22** *Anat*. the white part (sclera) of the eyeball. **23** any of various butterflies having white wings with scanty black markings. **24** *Chess, draughts*. **24a** a white or light-coloured piece or square. **24b** the player playing with such pieces. **25** anything that has or

is characterized by a white colour, such as a white paint or white clothing. **26** *Inf*. white wine: *a bottle of white*. **27** *Archery*. the outer ring of the target, having the lowest score. ♦ *vb* **whites, whiting, whited. 28** *Obs*. to make or become white. ♦ See also **white out, whites**. [OE *hwīt*]
► **'whitely** *adv* ► **'whiteness** *n* ► **'whitish** *adj*

White[1] (waɪt) *n* **1** a member of the Caucasoid race. **2** a person of European ancestry. ♦ *adj* **3** denoting or relating to a White or Whites.

White[2] ★ (waɪt) *n* **1** Gilbert. 1720–93, British clergyman and naturalist, noted for his *Natural History and Antiquities of Selborne* (1789). **2** Jimmy. born 1962, British snooker player. **3** Patrick (Victor Martindale). 1912–90, Australian novelist: his works include *Voss* (1957) and *A Fringe of Leaves* (1976): Nobel prize for literature 1973.

white admiral *n* a butterfly of Eurasia having brown wings with white markings.

white ant *n* another name for **termite**.

whitebait ('waɪt,beɪt) *n* **1** the young of herrings, sprats, etc., cooked and eaten whole as a delicacy. **2** any of various small silvery fishes. [C18: from its formerly having been used as bait]

whitebeam ('waɪt,biːm) *n* a N temperate tree having leaves that are densely hairy on the undersurface and hard timber.

white blood cell *n* a nontechnical name for **leucocyte**.

whitecap ('waɪt,kæp) *n* a wave with a white broken crest.

white cedar *n* either of two coniferous trees of North America, having scalelike leaves.

white clover *n* a Eurasian clover plant with rounded white flower heads: cultivated as a forage plant.

white coal *n* water, esp. when flowing and providing a potential source of usable power.

white-collar *adj* of or designating nonmanual and usually salaried workers employed in professional and clerical occupations.

white currant *n* a cultivated N temperate shrub having small rounded white edible berries.

whitedamp ('waɪt,dæmp) *n* a mixture of poisonous gases, mainly carbon monoxide, occurring in coal mines.

whited sepulchre *n* a hypocrite. [allusion to Matthew 23:27]

white dwarf *n* one of a large class of small faint stars of enormous density, thought to mark the final stage in the evolution of a sun-like star.

white elephant *n* **1** a rare albino variety of the Indian elephant, regarded as sacred in parts of S Asia. **2** a possession that is unwanted by its owner. **3** a rare or valuable possession the upkeep of which is very expensive.

White Ensign *n* the ensign of the Royal Navy and the Royal Yacht Squadron, having a red cross on a white background with the Union Jack at the upper corner of the vertical edge alongside the hoist.

white-eye *n* a songbird of Africa, Australia, New Zealand, and Asia, having a greenish plumage with a white ring around each eye.

white feather *n* **1** a symbol or mark of cowardice. **2 show the white feather**. to act in a cowardly manner. [from the belief that a white feather in a gamecock's tail was a sign of a poor fighter]

Whitefield ★ ('waɪt,fiːld) *n* **George**. 1714–70, British Methodist preacher, who separated from the Wesleys (?1741) because of his Calvinistic views.

whitefish ('waɪt,fɪʃ) *n, pl* **whitefish** or **whitefishes**. a food fish typically of deep cold lakes of the N hemisphere, having large silvery scales and a small head.

white fish *n* (in the Brit. fishing industry) any edible marine fish or invertebrate excluding herrings but including trout, salmon, and all shellfish.

white flag *n* a white flag or a piece of white cloth hoisted to signify surrender or request a truce.

white flour *n* flour that consists substantially of the starchy endosperm of wheat, most of the bran and the germ having been removed by the milling process.

★ people and places

whitefly ('waɪt,flaɪ) *n, pl* **whiteflies.** any of a family of insects typically having a body covered with powdery wax. Many are pests of greenhouse crops.

white friar *n* a Carmelite friar, so called because of the white cloak that forms part of the habit of this order.

white gold *n* any of various white lustrous hardwearing alloys containing gold together with platinum and palladium and sometimes smaller amounts of silver, nickel, or copper.

white goods *pl n* **1** household linen such as sheets, towels, tablecloths, etc. **2** large household appliances, such as refrigerators or cookers.

Whitehall ★ (,waɪt'hɔːl) *n* **1** a street in London stretching from Trafalgar Square to the Houses of Parliament: site of the main government offices. **2** the British Government.

Whitehead ★ ('waɪt,hɛd) *n* **Alfred North.** 1861–1947, British mathematician, who collaborated with Bertrand Russell in *Principia Mathematica* (1910–13).

white heat *n* **1** intense heat characterized by emission of white light. **2** *Inf.* a state of intense excitement or activity.

white hope *n Inf.* a person who is expected to bring honour or glory to his group, team, etc.

Whitehorse ★ ('waɪt,hɔːs) *n* a town in NW Canada: capital of the Yukon Territory. Pop.: 22 884 (1995 est.).

white horse *n* **1** the outline of a horse carved into the side of a chalk hill, usually dating to the Neolithic, Bronze, or Iron Ages. **2** (*usually pl*) a wave with a white broken crest.

white-hot *adj* **1** at such a high temperature that white light is emitted. **2** *Inf.* in a state of intense emotion.

White House ★ *n* **the. 1** the official Washington residence of the president of the US. **2** the US presidency.

white knight *n* a champion or rescuer, esp. a person or organization that rescues a company from financial difficulties, an unwelcome takeover bid, etc.

white-knuckle *adj* causing or experiencing fear or anxiety: *a white-knuckle fairground ride.*

white lead (lɛd) *n* **1** a white solid usually regarded as a mixture of lead carbonate and lead hydroxide; basic lead carbonate: used in paint and in making putty and ointments for the treatment of burns. **2** either of two similar white pigments based on lead sulphate or lead silicate.

white leg *n* another name for **milk leg.**

white lie *n* a minor or unimportant lie, esp. one uttered in the interests of tact or politeness.

white light *n* light that contains all the wavelengths of visible light at approximately equal intensities, as in sunlight.

white-livered *adj* **1** lacking in spirit or courage. **2** pallid and unhealthy in appearance.

White man's burden *n* the supposed duty of the White race to bring education and Western culture to the non-White inhabitants of their colonies.

white matter *n* the whitish tissue of the brain and spinal cord, consisting mainly of nerve fibres covered with a protective white fatlike substance.

white meat *n* any meat that is light in colour, such as veal or the breast of turkey.

white metal *n* any of various alloys, such as Babbitt metal, used for bearings.

white meter *n Brit.* an electricity meter used to record the consumption of off-peak electricity.

White Mountains ★ *pl n* **1** a mountain range in the US, chiefly in N New Hampshire: part of the Appalachians. Highest peak: Mount Washington, 1917 m (6288 ft). **2** a mountain range in the US, in E California and SW Nevada. Highest peak: White Mountain, 4342 m (14 246 ft).

whiten ('waɪtᵊn) *vb* to make or become white or whiter. ► **'whitener** *n* ► **'whitening** *n*

White Nile ★ *n* See **Nile.**

white noise *n* sound or electrical noise that has a relatively wide continuous range of frequencies of uniform intensity.

white oak *n* a large oak tree of E North America, having pale bark, leaves with rounded lobes, and heavy light-coloured wood.

white out *vb* (*adv*) **1** (*intr*) to lose or lack daylight visibility owing to snow or fog. **2** (*tr*) to create or leave white spaces in (printed or other matter). ◆ *n* **whiteout. 3** a polar atmospheric condition consisting of lack of visibility and sense of distance and direction due to a uniform whiteness of a heavy cloud cover and snow-covered ground, which reflects almost all the light it receives.

white paper *n* (*often caps.*) an official government report in any of a number of countries, which sets out the government's policy on a matter that is or will come before Parliament.

white pepper *n* a condiment, less pungent than black pepper, made from the husked dried beans of the pepper plant.

white pine *n* a North American coniferous tree having blue-green needle-like leaves, hanging brown cones, and rough bark.

white poplar *n* **1** Also called: **abele.** a Eurasian tree having leaves covered with dense silvery-white hairs. **2** another name for **tulipwood** (sense 1).

white rose *n English history.* an emblem of the House of York.

White Russia ★ *n* another name for **Belarus.** ► **White Russian** *adj, n*

whites (waɪts) *pl n* **1** household linen or cotton goods, such as sheets. **2** white or off-white clothing, such as that worn for playing cricket.

white sale *n* a sale of household linens at reduced prices.

white sauce *n* a thick sauce made from flour, butter, seasonings, and milk or stock.

White Sea ★ *n* an almost landlocked inlet of the Barents Sea on the coast of NW Russia. Area: 90 000 sq. km (34 700 sq. miles).

white settler *n* a well-off incomer to a district who takes advantage of what it has to offer without regard to the local inhabitants. [C20: from earlier colonial sense]

white slave *n* a girl or woman forced or sold into prostitution. ► **white slavery** *n* ► **,white-'slaver** *n*

white spirit *n* a colourless liquid obtained from petroleum and used as a substitute for turpentine.

white spruce *n* a N North American spruce tree with grey bark.

white squall *n* a violent highly localized weather disturbance at sea, in which the surface of the water is whipped into white spray by the winds.

whitethorn ('waɪt,θɔːn) *n* another name for **hawthorn.**

whitethroat ('waɪt,θrəʊt) *n* either of two Old World warblers having a greyish-brown plumage with a white throat and underparts.

white tie *n* **1** a white bow tie worn as part of a man's formal evening dress. **2a** formal evening dress for men. **2b** (*as modifier*): *a white-tie occasion.*

white trash *n Disparaging.* **a** poor White people living in the US, esp. the South. **b** (*as modifier*): *white-trash culture.*

White Volta ★ *n* a river in W Africa, rising in N Burkina-Faso flowing southwest and south to join the Black Volta in central Ghana and form the Volta River. Length: about 885 km (550 miles).

whitewall ('waɪt,wɔːl) *n* a pneumatic tyre having white sidewalls.

whitewash ('waɪt,wɒʃ) *n* **1** a substance used for whitening walls and other surfaces, consisting of a suspension of lime or whiting in water. **2** *Inf.* deceptive or specious words or actions intended to conceal defects, gloss over failings, etc. **3** *Inf.* a defeat in a sporting contest in which the loser is beaten in every match, game, etc. in a series. ◆ *vb* (*tr*) **4** to cover with whitewash. **5** *Inf.* to conceal, gloss over, or suppress. **6** *Inf.* to defeat (an opponent or opposing team) by winning every match in a series. ► **'white,washer** *n*

white water *n* **1** a stretch of water with a broken foamy surface, as in rapids. **2** light-coloured sea water, esp. over shoals or shallows.

white whale *n* a small white toothed whale of northern waters. Also called: **beluga**.

whitewood ('waɪt,wʊd) *n* **1** any of various trees with light-coloured wood, such as the tulip tree, basswood, and cottonwood. **2** the wood of any of these trees.

whitey *or* **whity** ('waɪtɪ) *n, pl* **whiteys** *or* **whities**. *Chiefly US.* (used contemptuously by Black people) a White man or White men collectively.

whither ('wɪðə) *Arch. or poetic.* ◆ *adv* **1** to what place? **2** to what end or purpose? ◆ *conj* **3** to whatever place, purpose, etc. [OE *hwider, hwæder;* Mod. E form infl. by HITHER]

whithersoever (,wɪðəsəʊ'evə) *adv, conj Arch. or poetic.* to whichever place.

whiting[1] ('waɪtɪŋ) *n* **1** an important gadoid food fish of European seas, having a dark back with silvery sides and underparts. **2** any of various similar fishes. [C15: ?from OE *hwītling*]

whiting[2] ('waɪtɪŋ) *n* white chalk that has been ground and washed, used in making whitewash, metal polish, etc. Also called: **whitening**.

Whitlam ★ ('wɪtləm) *n* **(Edward) Gough** (gɒf). born 1916, Australian Labor statesman: prime minister (1972–75).

Whitley Bay ★ ('wɪtlɪ) *n* a resort in NE England, in North Tyneside on the North Sea. Pop.: 33 335 (1991).

whitlow ('wɪtləʊ) *n* any pussy inflammation of the end of a finger or toe. [C14: changed from *whitflaw,* from WHITE + FLAW[1]]

Whitman ★ ('wɪtmən) *n* **Walt(er)**. 1819–92, US poet, whose work is collected in *Leaves of Grass* (1855 and subsequent enlarged editions).

Whitney[1] ★ ('wɪtnɪ) *n* **Mount**. a mountain in E California: the highest peak in the Sierra Nevada Mountains and in continental US (excluding Alaska). Height: 4418 m (14 495 ft).

Whitney[2] ★ ('wɪtnɪ) *n* **Eli**. 1765–1825, US inventor of a mechanical cotton gin (1793).

Whitsun ('wɪts°n) *n* **1** short for **Whitsuntide**. ◆ *adj* **2** of or relating to Whit Sunday or Whitsuntide.

Whitsunday (,hwɪt'sʌndɪ, ,wɪt-) *n* (in Scotland) May 15, one of the four quarter days.

Whit Sunday *n* the seventh Sunday after Easter, observed as a feast in commemoration of the descent of the Holy Spirit on the apostles. Also called: **Pentecost**. [OE *hwīta sunnandæg* white Sunday, prob. after the ancient custom of wearing white robes at or after baptism]

Whitsuntide ('wɪts°n,taɪd) *n* the week that begins with Whit Sunday, esp. the first three days.

Whittier ★ ('wɪtɪə) *n* **John Greenleaf**. 1807–92, US poet and humanitarian: a leading campaigner in the antislavery movement. His poems include *Snow-Bound* (1866).

Whittington ★ ('wɪtɪŋtən) *n* **Richard**, known as *Dick*. died 1423, English merchant, three times mayor of London. According to legend, he walked to London at the age of 13 with his cat.

whittle ('wɪt°l) *vb* **whittles, whittling, whittled**. **1** to cut or shave strips or pieces from (wood, a stick, etc.), esp. with a knife. **2** (*tr*) to make or shape by paring or shaving. **3** (*tr;* often foll. by *away, down,* etc.) to reduce, destroy, or wear away gradually. [C16: var. of C15 *thwittle* large knife, ult. from OE *thwitan* to cut]

Whittle ★ ('wɪt°l) *n* Sir **Frank**. 1907–96, British engineer, who invented the jet engine for aircraft: flew first British jet aircraft (1941).

whity ('waɪtɪ) *n, pl* **whities**. **1** *Inf.* a variant spelling of **whitey**. ◆ *adj* **2a** whitish in colour. **2b** (*in combination*): *whity-brown.*

whizz *or* **whiz** (wɪz) *vb* **whizzes, whizzing, whizzed**. **1** to make or cause to make a loud humming or buzzing sound. **2** to move or cause to move with such a sound. **3** (*intr*) *Inf.* to move or go rapidly. ◆ *n, pl* **whizzes**. **4** a loud humming or buzzing sound. **5** *Inf.* Also: **wizz**. a person who is extremely skilful at some activity. **6** a slang word for **amphetamine**. [C16: imit.]

whizz-bang *or* **whiz-bang** *n* **1** a World War I shell that travelled at such high velocity that the sound of its flight was heard only an instant before the sound of its explosion. **2** a type of firework that jumps around emitting a whizzing sound and occasional bangs.

whizz kid, whiz kid, *or* **wiz kid** *n Inf.* a person who is pushing, enthusiastic, and outstandingly successful for his or her age. [C20: from WHIZZ, ? infl. by WIZARD]

whizzy ('wɪzɪ) *adj* **whizzier, whizziest**. *Inf.* using sophisticated technology to produce vivid effects: *a whizzy new computer game.*

who (hu:) *pron* **1** which person? what person? used in direct and indirect questions: *he can't remember who did it; who met you?* **2** used to introduce relative clauses with antecedents referring to human beings: *the people who lived here have left.* **3** the one or ones who; whoever: *bring who you want.* [OE *hwā*]

USAGE NOTE See at **whom**.

Who ★ (hu:) *n* **the**. British rock group (mid-1960s–1983), originally comprising Roger Daltrey (born 1944; vocals), Pete Townshend (born 1945; guitar), John Entwistle (born 1944; bass guitar), and Keith Moon (1947–78; drums). Their recordings include "My Generation" (1965) and *Tommy* (1969).

WHO *abbrev. for* World Health Organization.

whoa (wəʊ) *interj* a command used esp. to horses to stop or slow down. [C19: var. of HO]

who-does-what *adj* (of a dispute, strike, etc.) relating to the separation of kinds of work performed by different trade unions.

whodunnit *or* **whodunit** (hu:'dʌnɪt) *n Inf.* a novel, play, etc., concerned with a crime, usually murder.

whoever (hu:'evə) *pron* **1** any person who: *whoever wants it can have it.* **2** no matter who: *I'll come round tomorrow, whoever may be here.* **3** an intensive form of *who,* used in questions: *whoever could have thought that?* **4** *Inf.* an unspecified person: *give those to Cathy or whoever.*

whole (həʊl) *adj* **1** containing all the component parts necessary to form a total; complete: *a whole apple.* **2** constituting the full quantity, extent, etc. **3** uninjured or undamaged. **4** healthy. **5** having no fractional or decimal part; integral: *a whole number.* **6** designating a relationship by descent from the same parents; full: *whole brothers.* **7 out of whole cloth**. *US & Canad. inf.* entirely without a factual basis. ◆ *adv* **8** in an undivided or unbroken piece: *to swallow a plum whole.* ◆ *n* **9** all the parts, elements, etc., of a thing. **10** an assemblage of parts viewed together as a unit. **11** a thing complete in itself. **12 as a whole**. considered altogether; completely. **13 on the whole**. **13a** taking all things into consideration. **13b** in general. [OE *hāl, hæl*]
► '**wholeness** *n*

whole blood *n* blood for transfusion from which none of the elements has been removed.

wholefood ('həʊl,fu:d) *n* (*sometimes pl*) **a** food that has been refined or processed as little as possible and is eaten in its natural state, such as brown rice, wholemeal flour, etc. **b** (*as modifier*): *a wholefood restaurant.*

wholehearted (,həʊl'hɑ:tɪd) *adj* done, acted, given, etc., with total sincerity, enthusiasm, or commitment.
► ,**whole'heartedly** *adv*

whole hog *n Sl.* the whole or total extent (esp. in **go the whole hog**).

wholemeal ('həʊl,mi:l) *adj Brit.* (of flour, bread, etc.) made from the entire wheat kernel. Also called (esp. US and Canad.): **whole-wheat**.

whole milk *n* milk from which no constituent has been removed.

whole note *n* the usual US and Canad. name for **semibreve**.

whole number *n* **1** an integer. **2** a natural number.

wholesale ('həʊl,seɪl) *n* **1** the business of selling goods to retailers in larger quantities than they are sold to final consumers but in smaller quantities than they are pur-

---

★ **people and places**

chased from manufacturers. Cf. **retail** (sense 1). ◆ *adj* **2** of or engaged in such business. **3** made, done, etc., on a large scale or without discrimination. ◆ *adv* **4** on a large scale or without discrimination. ◆ *vb* **wholesales, wholesaling, wholesaled. 5** to sell (goods) at wholesale.
▶ 'whole,saler *n*

wholesale price index *n* an indicator of price changes in the wholesale market.

wholesome ('həʊlsəm) *adj* **1** conducive to health or physical wellbeing. **2** conducive to moral wellbeing. **3** characteristic or suggestive of health or wellbeing, esp. in appearance. [C12: from WHOLE (healthy) + -SOME¹]
▶ 'wholesomely *adv* ▶ 'wholesomeness *n*

whole tone *or US & Canad.* **whole step** *n* an interval of two semitones. Often shortened to **tone.**

whole-tone scale *n* either of two scales produced by commencing on one of any two notes a chromatic semitone apart and proceeding upwards or downwards in whole tones for an octave.

whole-wheat *adj* another term (esp. US and Canad.) for **wholemeal.**

who'll (huːl) *contraction of* who will *or* who shall.

wholly ('həʊllɪ) *adv* **1** completely, totally, or entirely. **2** without exception; exclusively.

whom (huːm) *pron* the objective form of *who,* used when *who* is not the subject of its own clause: *whom did you say you had seen? he can't remember whom he saw.* [OE *hwām,* dative of *hwā* who]

> **USAGE NOTE** It was formerly considered correct to use *whom* whenever the objective form of *who* was required. This is no longer thought to be necessary and the objective form *who* is now commonly used, even in formal writing: *there were several people there who he had met before. Who* cannot be used directly after a preposition – the preposition is usually displaced, as in *the man (who) he sold his car to.* In formal writing *whom* is preferred in sentences like these: *the man to whom he sold his car.* There are some types of sentence in which *who* cannot be used: *the refugees, many of whom were old and ill, were allowed across the border.*

whomever (huːm'ɛvə) *pron* the objective form of *whoever: I'll hire whomever I can find.*

whoop (wuːp) *vb* **whoops, whooping, whooped. 1** to utter (speech) with loud cries, as of excitement. **2** (huːp). *Med.* to cough convulsively with a crowing sound. **3** (of certain birds) to utter (a hooting cry). **4** (*tr*) to urge on or call with or as if with whoops. **5** (wʊp, wuːp). **whoop it up.** *Inf.* **5a** to indulge in a noisy celebration. **5b** *Chiefly US.* to arouse enthusiasm. ◆ *n* **6** a loud cry, esp. one expressing excitement. **7** (huːp). *Med.* the convulsive crowing sound made during whooping cough. [C14: imit.]

whoopee *Inf.* ◆ *interj* (wʊ'piː). **1** an exclamation of joy, excitement, etc. ◆ *n* ('wʊpiː). **2 make whoopee. 2a** to engage in noisy merrymaking. **2b** to make love.

whoopee cushion *n* a joke cushion that emits a sound like the breaking of wind when someone sits on it.

whooper *or* **whooper swan** ('wuːpə) *n* a large Old World swan having a black bill with a yellow base and a noisy whooping cry.

whooping cough ('huːpɪŋ) *n* an acute infectious disease characterized by coughing spasms that end with a shrill crowing sound on inspiration. Technical name: **pertussis.**

whoops (wʊps) *interj* an exclamation of surprise or of apology.

whoosh *or* **woosh** (wuʃ) *n* **1** a hissing or rushing sound. ◆ *vb* **2** (*intr*) to make or move with such a sound.

whop (wɒp) *Inf.* ◆ *vb* **whops, whopping, whopped. 1** (*tr*) to strike, beat, or thrash. **2** (*tr*) to defeat utterly. **3** (*intr*) to drop or fall. ◆ *n* **4** a heavy blow or the sound made by such a blow. [C14: var. of *wap,* ? imit.]

whopper ('wɒpə) *n Inf.* **1** anything uncommonly large of its kind. **2** a big lie. [C18: from WHOP]

whopping ('wɒpɪŋ) *adj Inf.* uncommonly large.

whore (hɔː) *n* **1** a prostitute or promiscuous woman: often a term of abuse. ◆ *vb* **whores, whoring, whored.** (*intr*) **2** to be or act as a prostitute. **3** (of a man) to have promiscuous sexual relations, esp. with prostitutes. **4** (often foll. by *after*) to seek that which is immoral, idolatrous, etc. [OE *hōre*]
▶ 'whoredom *n* ▶ 'whorish *adj*

whorehouse ('hɔːˌhaʊs) *n* another word for **brothel.**

whoremonger ('hɔːˌmʌŋgə) *n* a person who consorts with whores; lecher. Also called: **whoremaster.**
▶ 'whore,mongery *n*

whoreson ('hɔːsən) *Arch.* ◆ *n* **1** a bastard. **2** a scoundrel; wretch. ◆ *adj* **3** vile or hateful.

whorl (wɜːl) *n* **1** *Bot.* a radial arrangement of petals, stamens, leaves, etc., around a stem. **2** *Zool.* a single turn in a spiral shell. **3** anything shaped like a coil. [C15: prob. var. of *wherville* whirl, infl. by Du. *worvel*]
▶ 'whorled *adj*

whortleberry ('wɜːtˀlˌbɛrɪ) *n, pl* **whortleberries. 1** Also called: **bilberry, blaeberry, huckleberry.** a small Eurasian ericaceous shrub with greenish-pink flowers and edible sweet blackish berries. **2** the fruit of this shrub. **3 bog whortleberry.** a related plant of mountain regions, having pink flowers and black fruits. [C16: SW English dialect var. of *hurtleberry,* from ?]

who's (huːz) *contraction of* who is *or* who has.

whose (huːz) *determiner* **1a** of whom? belonging to whom? used in direct and indirect questions: *I told him whose fault it was; whose car is this?* **1b** (*as pron*): *whose is that?* **2** of whom; of which: used as a relative pronoun: *a house whose windows are broken; a man whose reputation has suffered.* [OE *hwæs,* genitive of *hwā* who & *hwæt* what]

whoso ('huːsəʊ) *pron* an archaic word for **whoever.**

whosoever (ˌhuːsəʊ'ɛvə) *pron* an archaic or formal word for **whoever.**

who's who *n* a book or list containing the names and short biographies of famous people.

why (waɪ) *adv* **1a** for what reason?: *why are you here?* **1b** (*used in indirect questions*): *tell me why you're here.* ◆ *pron* **2** for or because of which: *there is no reason why he shouldn't come.* ◆ *n, pl* **whys. 3** (*usually pl*) the cause of something (esp. in **the whys and wherefores**). ◆ *interj* **4** an introductory expression of surprise, indignation, etc.: *why, don't be silly!* [OE *hwī*]

Whyalla ★ (waɪ'ælə) *n* a port in S South Australia, on Spencer Gulf: iron and steel and shipbuilding industries. Pop.: 25 526 (1991).

whydah *or* **whidah** ('wɪdə) *n* any of various predominantly black African weaverbirds, the males of which grow very long tail feathers in the breeding season. Also called: **whydah bird, whidah bird, widow bird.** [C18: after a town in Benin in W Africa]

WI *abbrev. for:* **1** West Indian. **2** West Indies. **3** Wisconsin. **4** (in Britain) Women's Institute.

Wicca ('wɪkə) *n* the cult or practice of witchcraft. [C20 revival of OE *wicca* witch]
▶ 'Wiccan *n, adj*

Wichita ★ ('wɪtʃɪˌtɔː) *n* a city in S Kansas, on the Arkansas River: the largest city in the state; two universities. Pop.: 310 236 (1994 est.).

wick¹ (wɪk) *n* **1** a cord or band of loosely twisted or woven fibres, as in a candle, that supplies fuel to a flame by capillary action. **2 get on (someone's) wick.** *Brit. sl.* to cause irritation to (someone). [OE *weoce*]

wick² (wɪk) *n Arch.* a village or hamlet. [OE *wīc;* rel. to *-wich* in place names]

Wick ★ (wɪk) *n* a town in N Scotland, in Highland, at the head of **Wick Bay** (an inlet of the North Sea). Pop.: 7681 (1991).

wicked ('wɪkɪd) *adj* **1a** morally bad. **1b** (*as collective n; preceded by the*): *the wicked.* **2** mischievous or roguish in a playful way: *a wicked grin.* **3** causing injury or harm. **4** troublesome, unpleasant, or offensive. **5** *Sl.* very good. [C13: from dialect *wick,* from OE *wicca* sorcerer, *wicce* witch]
▶ 'wickedly *adv* ▶ 'wickedness *n*

wicker ('wɪkə) n 1 a slender flexible twig or shoot, esp. of willow. 2 short for **wickerwork**. ◆ adj 3 made of, consisting of, or constructed from wicker. [C14: from ON]

wickerwork ('wɪkə,wɜːk) n a a material consisting of woven wicker. b (as modifier): a wickerwork chair.

wicket ('wɪkɪt) n 1 a small door or gate, esp. one that is near to or part of a larger one. 2 Chiefly US. a small window or opening in a door, esp. one fitted with a grating or glass pane. 3 a small sluicegate. 4a Cricket. either of two constructions, 22 yards apart, consisting of three stumps stuck in the ground with two wooden bails resting on top, at which the batsman stands. 4b the strip of ground between these. 4c a batsman's turn at batting or the period during which two batsmen bat. 4d the act or instance of a batsman being got out: the bowler took six wickets. 5 keep wicket. to act as a wicketkeeper. 6 on a good, sticky, etc., wicket. Inf. in an advantageous, awkward, etc., situation. [C18: from OF wiket]

wicketkeeper ('wɪkɪt,kiːpə) n Cricket. the player on the fielding side positioned directly behind the wicket.

wickiup, wikiup, or **wickyup** ('wɪki,ʌp) n US & Canad. a crude shelter made of brushwood or grass and having an oval frame, esp. of a kind used by nomadic Native Americans now in the Oklahoma area. [C19: of Amerind origin]

Wickliffe or **Wiclif** ★ ('wɪklɪf) n variant spellings of (John) **Wycliffe**.

Wicklow ★ ('wɪkləu) n 1 a county of E Republic of Ireland, in Leinster province on the Irish Sea: consists of a coastal strip rising inland to the **Wicklow Mountains**; mainly agricultural, with several resorts. County town: Wicklow. Pop.: 97 265 (1991). Area: 2025 sq. km (782 sq. miles). 2 a port in E Republic of Ireland, county town of Co. Wicklow. Pop.: 5850 (1991).

widdershins ('wɪdə,ʃɪnz) adv Chiefly Scot. a variant spelling of **withershins**.

wide (waɪd) adj 1 having a great extent from side to side. 2 spacious or extensive. 3a (postpositive) having a specified extent, esp. from side to side: two yards wide. 3b (in combination): extending throughout: nationwide. 4 remote from the desired point, mark, etc.: your guess is wide of the mark. 5 (of eyes) opened fully. 6 loose, full, or roomy: wide trousers. 7 exhibiting a considerable spread: a wide variation. 8 Phonetics. another word for **lax** (sense 4) or **open** (sense 32). ◆ adv 9 over an extensive area: to travel far and wide. 10 to the full extent: he opened the door wide. 11 far from the desired point, mark, etc. ◆ n 12 (in cricket) a bowled ball that is outside the batsman's reach and scores a run for the batting side. [OE wīd]
▶ 'widely adv ▶ 'wideness n ▶ 'widish adj

wide-angle lens n a lens system on a camera that has a small focal length and therefore can cover an angle of view of 60° or more.

wide-awake adj (wide awake when postpositive). 1 fully awake. 2 keen, alert, or observant. ◆ n 3 Also called: **wide-awake hat**. a hat with a low crown and very wide brim.

wide-body adj (of an aircraft) having a wide fuselage, esp. wide enough to contain three rows of seats abreast.

wide boy n Brit. sl. a man who is prepared to use unscrupulous methods to progress or make money.

wide-eyed adj innocent or credulous.

widen ('waɪdᵊn) vb to make or become wide or wider.
▶ 'widener n

wide-open adj (wide open when postpositive). 1 open to the full extent. 2 (postpositive) exposed to attack; vulnerable. 3 uncertain as to outcome. 4 US inf. (of a town or city) lax in the enforcement of certain laws, esp. those relating to the sale of alcohol, gambling, etc.

wide receiver n American football. a player whose function is to catch long passes from the quarterback.

widespread ('waɪd,sprɛd) adj 1 extending over a wide area. 2 accepted by or occurring among many people.

widgeon ('wɪdʒən) n a variant spelling of **wigeon**.

widget ('wɪdʒɪt) n Inf. any small mechanism or device, the name of which is unknown or temporarily forgotten. [C20: changed from GADGET]

Widnes ★ ('wɪdnɪs) n a town in NW England, in N Cheshire on the River Mersey: chemical industry. Pop.: 57 162 (1991).

widow ('wɪdəu) n 1 a woman whose husband has died, esp. one who has not remarried. 2 (with a modifier) Inf. a woman whose husband frequently leaves her alone while he indulges in a sport, etc.: a golf widow. 3 Printing. a short line at the end of a paragraph, esp. one that occurs as the top line of a page or column. 4 (in some card games) an additional hand or set of cards exposed on the table. ◆ vb (tr; usually passive) 5 to cause to become a widow. 6 to deprive of something valued. [OE widuwe]
▶ 'widowhood n

widow bird n another name for **whydah**.

widower ('wɪdəuə) n a man whose wife has died and who has not remarried.

widow's cruse n an endless or unfailing source of supply. [allusion to I Kings 17:16]

widow's mite n a small contribution by a person who has very little. [allusion to Mark 12:43]

widow's peak n a V-shaped point in the hairline in the middle of the forehead. [from the belief that it presaged early widowhood]

width (wɪdθ) n 1 the linear extent or measurement of something from side to side. 2 the state or fact of being wide. 3 a piece or section of something at its full extent from side to side: a width of cloth. 4 the distance across a rectangular swimming bath, as opposed to its length. [C17: from WIDE + -TH¹, analogous to BREADTH]

Wieland¹ ★ ('viːlant) n the German name for **Wayland**.

Wieland² ★ (German 'viːlant) n Christoph Martin ('krɪstɔf 'martiːn). 1733–1813, German writer, noted for his verse epic Oberon (1780).

wield (wiːld) vb (tr) 1 to handle or use (a weapon, tool, etc.). 2 to exert or maintain (power or authority). [OE wieldan, wealdan]
▶ 'wieldable adj ▶ 'wielder n

wieldy ('wiːldɪ) adj wieldier, wieldiest. easily handled, used, or managed.

Wien¹ ★ (viːn) n the German name for **Vienna**.

Wien² ★ (German viːn) n Wilhelm ('vɪlhɛlm). 1864–1928, German physicist, who studied black-body radiation: Nobel prize for physics 1911.

wiener ('wiːnə) or **wienerwurst** ('wiːnə,wɜːst) n US & Canad. a kind of smoked sausage, similar to a frankfurter. [C20: shortened from G Wiener Wurst Viennese sausage]

Wiener ★ ('wiːnə) n Norbert ('nɔːbət). 1894–1964, US mathematician, who developed cybernetics.

Wiener Neustadt ★ (German 'viːnər 'nɔyʃtat) n a city in E Austria, in Lower Austria. Pop.: 35 268 (1991).

Wiener schnitzel ('viːnə 'ʃnɪtsəl) n a thin escalope of veal, fried in breadcrumbs. [G: Viennese cutlet]

Wiesbaden ★ (German 'viːsbaːdən) n a city in W Germany, capital of Hesse state: a spa resort since Roman times. Pop.: 266 081 (1995 est.). Latin name: **Aquae Mattiacorum** ('ækwiː ,mætjə'kəurəm).

Wiesel ★ ('viːzəl) n Elie. born 1928, US human rights campaigner: noted for his documentaries of wartime atrocities against the Jews; Nobel peace prize 1986.

Wiesenthal ★ ('viːzən,taːl) n Simon. born 1908, Austrian investigator of Nazi war crimes.

wife (waɪf) n, pl wives. 1 a man's partner in marriage; a married woman. Related adj: **uxorial**. 2 an archaic or dialect word for **woman**. 3 take to wife. to marry (a woman). [OE wīf]
▶ 'wifehood n ▶ 'wifely adj

wig (wɪg) n 1 an artificial head of hair, either human or synthetic, worn to disguise baldness, as part of a theatrical or ceremonial dress, as a disguise, or for adornment. ◆ vb wigs, wigging, wigged. (tr) 2 Brit. sl. to berate severely. [C17: shortened from PERIWIG]
▶ 'wigged adj ▶ 'wigless adj

Wig. abbrev. for Wigtownshire.

Wigan ★ ('wɪgən) n 1 an industrial town in NW England, in Greater Manchester: former coal-mining centre. Pop.: 85 819 (1991). 2 a unitary authority in NW England, in

Greater Manchester. Pop.: 310 000 (1994 est.). Area: 199 sq. km (77 sq. miles).

wigeon *or* **widgeon** ('wɪdʒən) *n* **1** a Eurasian duck of marshes, swamps, etc., the male of which has a reddish-brown head and chest and grey-and-white back and wings. **2 American wigeon.** Also called: **baldpate.** a similar bird of North America, the male of which has a white crown. [C16: from ?]

wigging ('wɪgɪŋ) *n Brit. sl.* a reprimand.

wiggle ('wɪgᵊl) *vb* **wiggles, wiggling, wiggled. 1** to move or cause to move with jerky movements, esp. from side to side. ◆ *n* **2** the act of wiggling. [C13: from MLow G, MDu. *wiggelen*]
▶ **'wiggler** *n* ▶ **'wiggly** *adj*

wight (waɪt) *n Arch.* a human being. [OE *wiht;* rel. to OFrisian *āwet* something]

Wight ★ (waɪt) *n* **Isle of.** an island and county of S England in the English Channel. Administrative centre: Newport. Pop.: 124 600 (1994 est.). Area: 380 sq. km (147 sq. miles).

Wigner ★ ('wɪgnə) *n* **Eugene Paul.** 1902–95, US physicist, born in Hungary; noted for his work on nuclear physics: shared the Nobel prize for physics 1963.

Wigtownshire ★ ('wɪgtən,ʃɪə, -ʃə) *n* (until 1975) a county of SW Scotland, now part of Dumfries and Galloway.

wigwag ('wɪg,wæg) *vb* **wigwags, wigwagging, wigwagged. 1** to move (something) back and forth. **2** to communicate with (someone) by means of a flag semaphore. ◆ *n* **3a** a system of communication by flag semaphore. **3b** the message signalled. [C16: from obs. *wig,* prob. short for WIGGLE + WAG¹]
▶ **'wig,wagger** *n*

wigwam ('wɪg,wæm) *n* **1** any dwelling of the North American Indians, esp. one made of bark, rushes, or skins spread over a set of arched poles lashed together. **2** a similar structure for children. [from *wīkwām* (of Amerind origin), lit.: their abode]

Wilberforce ★ ('wɪlbə,fɔːs) *n* **William.** 1759–1833, British politician, who secured the abolition of the slave trade (1807) and slavery (1833) in the British Empire.

wilco ('wɪlkəʊ) *interj* an expression in signalling, telecommunications, etc., indicating that a message just received will be complied with. [C20: abbrev. for *I will comply*]

wild (waɪld) *adj* **1** (of animals) living independently of man; not domesticated or tame. **2** (of plants) growing in a natural state; not cultivated. **3** uninhabited; desolate: *a wild stretch of land.* **4** living in a savage or uncivilized way: *wild tribes.* **5** lacking restraint or control: *wild merriment.* **6** of great violence: *a wild storm.* **7** disorderly or chaotic: *wild talk.* **8** dishevelled; untidy: *wild hair.* **9** in a state of extreme emotional intensity: *wild with anger.* **10** reckless: *wild speculations.* **11** random: *a wild guess.* **12** (*postpositive;* foll. by *about*) *Inf.* intensely enthusiastic: *I'm wild about my new boyfriend.* **13** (of a card, such as a joker in some games) able to be given any value the holder pleases. **14 wild and woolly. 14a** rough; barbarous. **14b** (of theories, plans, etc.) not fully thought out. ◆ *adv* **15** in a wild manner. **16 run wild. 16a** to grow without cultivation or care: *the garden has run wild.* **16b** to behave without restraint: *he has let his children run wild.* ◆ *n* **17** (*often pl*) a desolate or uninhabited region. **18 the wild. 18a** a free natural state of living. **18b** the wilderness. [OE *wilde*]
▶ **'wildish** *adj* ▶ **'wildly** *adv* ▶ **'wildness** *n*

wild boar *n* a wild pig of parts of Europe and central Asia, having a pale grey to black coat and prominent tusks.

wild brier *n* another name for **wild rose.**

wild card *n* **1** See **wild** (sense 13). **2** *Sport.* a player or team that has not qualified for a competition but is allowed to take part, at the organizers' discretion, after all the regular places have been taken. **3** an unpredictable element in a situation. **4** *Computing.* a symbol that can represent any character or group of characters, as in a filename.

wild carrot *n* an umbelliferous plant of temperate regions, having clusters of white flowers and hooked fruits. Also called: **Queen Anne's lace.**

wildcat ('waɪld,kæt) *n, pl* **wildcats** *or* **wildcat. 1** a wild European cat that resembles the domestic tabby but is larger and has a bushy tail. **2** any of various other felines, such as the lynx and the caracal. **3** *US & Canad.* another name for **bobcat. 4** *Inf.* a savage or aggressive person. **5** an exploratory drilling for petroleum or natural gas. **6** (*modifier*) *Chiefly US.* involving risk, esp. financially or commercially unsound: *a wildcat project.* ◆ *vb* **wildcats, wildcatting, wildcatted. 7** (*intr*) to drill for petroleum or natural gas in an area having no known reserves.
▶ **'wild,catter** *n* ▶ **'wild,catting** *n, adj*

wildcat strike *n* a strike begun by workers spontaneously or without union approval.

wild cherry *n* another name for **gean.**

wild dog *n* another name for **dingo.**

Wilde ★ (waɪld) *n* **Oscar (Fingal O'Flahertie Wills).** 1854–1900, Irish writer, whose works include the play *The Importance of Being Earnest* (1895), the novel *The Picture of Dorian Gray* (1891), and *The Ballad of Reading Gaol* (1898), relating his experiences while serving a prison sentence for homosexuality.

wildebeest ('wɪldɪ,biːst, 'vɪl-) *n, pl* **wildebeests** *or* **wildebeest.** another name for **gnu.** [C19: from Afrik., lit.: wild beast]

wilder ('wɪldə) *vb Arch.* **1** to lead or be led astray. **2** to bewilder or become bewildered. [C17: from ?]

Wilder ★ ('waɪldə) *n* **1 Billy,** real name *Samuel Wilder.* born 1906, US film director, born in Austria. His films include *The Lost Weekend* (1945), *Some Like it Hot* (1959), and *Buddy Buddy* (1981). **2 Thornton.** 1897–1975, US writer. His works include the novel *The Bridge of San Luis Rey* (1927) and the play *The Skin of Our Teeth* (1942).

wilderness ('wɪldənɪs) *n* **1** a wild uninhabited uncultivated region. **2** any desolate area. **3** a confused mass or collection. **4 a voice (crying) in the wilderness.** a person, group, etc., making a suggestion or plea that is ignored. [OE *wildēornes,* from *wildēor* wild beast + -NESS]

Wilderness ★ ('wɪldənɪs) *n* **the.** the barren regions to the south and east of Palestine, esp. those in which the Israelites wandered before entering the Promised Land and in which Christ fasted for 40 days and nights.

wild-eyed *adj* glaring in an angry, distracted, or wild manner.

wildfire ('waɪld,faɪə) *n* **1** a highly flammable material, such as Greek fire, formerly used in warfare. **2a** a raging and uncontrollable fire. **2b** anything that is disseminated quickly (esp. in **spread like wildfire**). **3** another name for **will-o'-the-wisp.**

wild flower *n* **1** any flowering plant that grows in an uncultivated state. **2** the flower of such a plant.

wildfowl ('waɪld,faʊl) *n* **1** any bird that is hunted by man, esp. any duck or similar aquatic bird. **2** such birds collectively.
▶ **'wild,fowler** *n* ▶ **'wild,fowling** *adj, n*

wild-goose chase *n* an absurd or hopeless pursuit, as of something unattainable.

wilding ('waɪldɪŋ) *n* **1** an uncultivated plant or a cultivated plant that has become wild. **2** a wild animal. ◆ Also called: **wildling.**

wildlife ('waɪld,laɪf) *n* wild animals and plants collectively: a term used esp. of fauna.

wild pansy *n* a Eurasian plant of the violet family having purple, yellow, and pale mauve spurred flowers. Also called: **heartsease, love-in-idleness.**

wild parsley *n* any of various uncultivated umbelliferous plants that resemble parsley.

wild rice *n* an aquatic North American grass with dark-coloured edible grain.

wild rose *n* any of numerous roses, such as the dogrose and sweetbrier, that grow wild and have flowers with only one whorl of petals.

wild rubber *n* rubber obtained from uncultivated rubber trees.

wild silk *n* **1** silk produced by wild silkworms. **2** a fabric made from this, or from short fibres of silk designed to imitate it.

★ people and places

wild type *n Biol.* the typical form of a species of organism resulting from breeding under natural conditions.

Wild West ★ *n* the western US during its settlement, esp. with reference to its frontier lawlessness.

wildwood ('waɪld,wʊd) *n Arch.* a wood or forest growing in a natural uncultivated state.

wile (waɪl) *n* **1** trickery, cunning, or craftiness. **2** (*usually pl*) an artful or seductive trick or ploy. ◆ *vb* **wiles, wiling, wiled. 3** (*tr*) to lure, beguile, or entice. [C12: from ON *vel* craft]

wilful *or US* **willful** ('wɪlful) *adj* **1** intent on having one's own way; headstrong or obstinate. **2** intentional: *wilful murder*.
▶ **'wilfully** *or US* **'willfully** *adv* ▶ **'wilfulness** *or US* **'willfulness** *n*

Wilhelm I ★ ('vɪlhɛlm) *n* the German name for **William I** (sense 3).

Wilhelm II ★ *n* the German name for **William II** (sense 2).

Wilhelmina I ★ (,wɪlə'miːnə; *Dutch* wɪlhɛl'miːna:) *n* 1880–1962, queen of the Netherlands from 1890 until her abdication (1948) in favour of her daughter Juliana.

Wilhelmshaven ★ (*German* vɪlhɛlms'haːfən) *n* a port and resort in NW Germany, in Lower Saxony: founded in 1853; was the chief German North Sea naval base until 1945; a major oil port. Pop.: 91 150 (1991).

Wilhelmstrasse ★ (*German* 'vɪlhɛlmʃtraːsə) *n* **1** a street in the centre of Berlin, where the German foreign office and other government buildings were situated until 1945. **2** Germany's ministry of foreign affairs until 1945.

Wilkes ★ (wɪlks) *n* **1 Charles.** 1798–1877, US explorer of Antarctica. **2 John.** 1727–97, British politician, who was expelled from the House of Commons for writing scurrilous articles about the government. He became a champion of parliamentary reform.

Wilkes Land ★ *n* a region in Antarctica south of Australia, on the Indian Ocean.

Wilkins ★ ('wɪlkɪnz) *n* **1 Sir George Hubert.** 1888–1958, Australian polar explorer and aviator. **2 Maurice Hugh Frederick.** born 1916, British biochemist, born in New Zealand: shared the Nobel prize 1962 for his work on the structure of DNA.

will[1] (wɪl) *vb past* **would.** (takes an infinitive without *to* or an implied infinitive) used as an auxiliary. **1** (esp. with *you, he, she, it, they,* or a noun as subject) to make the future tense. Cf. **shall** (sense 1). **2** to express resolution on the part of the speaker: *I will buy that radio if it's the last thing I do.* **3** to indicate willingness or desire: *will you help me with this problem?* **4** to express commands: *you will report your findings to me tomorrow.* **5** to express ability: *this rope will support a load.* **6** to express probability or expectation: *that will be Jim telephoning.* **7** to express customary practice or inevitability: *boys will be boys.* **8** (with the infinitive always implied) to express desire: usually in polite requests: *stay if you will.* **9 what you will.** whatever you like. [OE *willan*]

> USAGE NOTE   See at **shall.**

will[2] (wɪl) *n* **1** the faculty of conscious and deliberate choice of action. Related adj: **voluntary. 2** the act or an instance of asserting a choice. **3a** the declaration of a person's wishes regarding the disposal of his property after his death. **3b** a document in which such wishes are expressed. **4** desire; wish. **5** determined intention: *where there's a will there's a way.* **6** disposition towards others: *he bears you no ill will.* **7 at will.** at one's own desire or choice. **8 with a will.** heartily; energetically. **9 with the best will in the world.** even with the best of intentions. ◆ *vb* (*mainly tr; often takes a clause as object or an infinitive*) **10** (*also intr*) to exercise the faculty of volition in an attempt to accomplish (something): *he willed his wife's recovery from her illness.* **11** to give (property) by will to a person, society, etc.: *he willed his art collection to the nation.* **12** (*also intr*) to order or decree: *the king wills that you shall die.* **13** to choose or prefer: *wander where you will.* [OE *willa*]
▶ **'willer** *n*

willed (wɪld) *adj* (*in combination*) having a will as specified: *weak-willed.*

Willemstad ★ (*Dutch* 'wɪləmstɑt) *n* the capital of the Netherlands Antilles, a port on the SW coast of Curaçao: important for refining Venezuelan oil. Pop.: 197 019 (1993 est.).

willet ('wɪlɪt) *n* a large American shore bird having a grey plumage with black-and-white wings. [C19: imit. of its call]

willful ('wɪlful) *adj* the US spelling of **wilful.**

William ★ ('wɪljəm) *n* **1** known as *William the Lion.* ?1143–1214, king of Scotland (1165–1214). **2 Prince,** title *Prince William of Wales,* born 1982, elder son of the Prince and Princess of Wales.

William I ★ *n* **1** known as *William the Conqueror.* ?1027–1087, duke of Normandy (1035–87) and king of England (1066–87). He invaded England in 1066, defeating Harold II at Hastings. In 1085 he ordered the Domesday Book to be compiled. **2** known as *William the Silent.* 1533–84, prince of Orange and count of Nassau: led the revolt of the Netherlands against Spain (1568–76) and became first stadholder of the United Provinces of the Netherlands (1579–84); assassinated. **3** German name *Wilhelm I.* 1797–1888, king of Prussia (1861–88) and first emperor of Germany (1871–88).

William II ★ *n* **1** known as *William Rufus.* ?1056–1100, king of England (1087–1100); son of William the Conqueror: killed by an arrow while hunting in the New Forest. **2** German name *Kaiser Wilhelm.* 1859–1941, German emperor and king of Prussia (1888–1918): forced to abdicate at the end of World War I.

William III ★ *n* known as *William of Orange.* 1650–1702, stadholder of the Netherlands (1672–1702) and king of Great Britain and Ireland (1689–1702): ruled jointly with his wife Mary II until her death in 1694.

William IV ★ *n* known as the *Sailor King.* 1765–1837, king of the United Kingdom and of Hanover (1830–37), succeeding his brother George IV; the third son of George III.

Williams ★ ('wɪljəmz) *n* **1 Hank,** real name *Hiram Williams.* 1923–53, US country singer and songwriter. **2 John.** born 1941, Australian classical guitarist, living in Britain. **3 J(ohn) P(eter) R(hys).** born 1949, Welsh Rugby Union player. A fullback, he played for Wales (1969–79; 1980–81) and the British Lions (1971–77). **4 Ralph Vaughan.** See (Ralph) **Vaughan Williams. 5 Tennessee.** real name *Thomas Lanier Williams.* 1912–83, US dramatist. His plays include *The Glass Menagerie* (1944), *A Streetcar Named Desire* (1947), and *Cat on a Hot Tin Roof* (1955). **6 William Carlos** ('kɑːləs). 1883–1963, US poet. His works include *Paterson* (1946–58).

Williamsburg ★ ('wɪljəmz,bɜːg) *n* a city in SE Virginia: the capital of Virginia (1693–1779); the restoration of large sections of the colonial city was begun in 1926. Pop.: 11 530 (1990).

Williamson ★ ('wɪljəmsən) *n* **1 Henry.** 1895–1977, British novelist, best known for *Tarka the Otter* (1927) and other animal stories. **2 Malcolm.** born 1931, Australian composer, living in Britain: Master of the Queen's Music since 1975. His works include operas and music for children.

William the Conqueror ★ *n* See **William I** (sense 1).

willies ('wɪlɪz) *pl n* **the.** *Sl.* nervousness, jitters, or fright (esp. in **give** (*or* **get**) **the willies**). [C20: from ?]

willing ('wɪlɪŋ) *adj* **1** favourably disposed or inclined; ready. **2** cheerfully compliant. **3** done, given, accepted, etc., freely or voluntarily.
▶ **'willingly** *adv* ▶ **'willingness** *n*

Willis ★ ('wɪlɪs) *n* **Norman (David).** born 1933, British trade-union leader; general secretary of the Trades Union Congress (1984–93).

williwaw ('wɪlɪ,wɔː) *n US & Canad.* **1** a sudden strong gust of cold wind blowing offshore from a mountainous coast, as in the Strait of Magellan. **2** a state of great turmoil. [C19: from ?]

will-o'-the-wisp (,wɪlədə'wɪsp) *n* **1** Also called: **friar's lantern, ignis fatuus, jack-o'-lantern.** a pale flame or phosphorescence sometimes seen over marshy ground at night. It is believed to be due to the spontaneous combustion of methane originating from decomposing organic matter. **2** a person or thing that is elusive or allures and misleads. [C17: from *Will*, short for *William* + *wisp*, in former sense of a twist of hay burning as a torch]

willow ('wɪləʊ) *n* **1** any of a large genus of trees and shrubs, such as the weeping willow and osiers of N temperate regions, which have graceful flexible branches and flowers in catkins. **2** the whitish wood of certain of these trees. **3** something made of willow wood, such as a cricket bat. [OE *welig*]

willowherb ('wɪləʊˌhɜːb) *n* **1** any of various temperate and arctic plants having narrow leaves and terminal clusters of pink, purplish, or white flowers. **2** short for **rosebay willowherb** (see **rosebay**).

willow pattern *n* **a** a pattern incorporating a willow tree, river, bridge, and figures, typically in blue on a white ground, used on porcelain, etc. **b** (*as modifier*): *a willow-pattern plate.*

Willow South ★ *n* a city in S Alaska, about 113 km (70 miles) northwest of Anchorage: chosen as the site of the projected new state capital in 1976.

willowy ('wɪləʊɪ) *adj* **1** slender and graceful. **2** flexible or pliant. **3** covered or shaded with willows.

willpower ('wɪlˌpaʊə) *n* **1** the ability to control oneself and determine one's actions. **2** firmness of will.

Wills ★ (wɪlz) *n* **1** Helen Newington, married names *Helen Wills Moody Roark*. 1905–97, US tennis player: Wimbledon singles champion eight times between 1927 and 1938. **2** William John. 1834–61, British explorer: Robert Burke's deputy in an expedition on which both men died after crossing Australia.

willy[1] ('wɪlɪ) *n, pl* **willies**. *Brit. inf.* a childish or jocular term for **penis**.

willy[2] ('wɪlɪ) *n Austral. sl.* a sudden loss of temper; fit: *to throw a willy.*

willy-nilly ('wɪlɪ'nɪlɪ) *adv* **1** whether desired or not. ◆ *adj* **2** occurring or taking place whether desired or not. [OE *wile hē, nyle hē*, lit.: will he or will he not]

willy wagtail *n* a black-and-white flycatcher found in Australasia and parts of Asia, having white feathers over the brows.

willy-willy ('wɪlɪˌwɪlɪ) *n, pl* **willy-willies**. *Austral.* a small sometimes violent upward-spiralling cyclone or dust storm. [from Abor.]

Wilmington ★ ('wɪlmɪŋtən) *n* a port in N Delaware, on the Delaware River: industrial centre. Pop.: 71 529 (1990).

Wilno ★ ('viːlnɔ) *n* the Polish name for **Vilnius**.

Wilson ★ ('wɪlsən) *n* **1** Alexander. 1766–1813, Scottish ornithologist in the US. **2** Sir Angus (Frank Johnstone). 1913–91, British writer, whose novels include *Anglo-Saxon Attitudes* (1956) and *No Laughing Matter* (1967). **3** Charles Thomson Rees. 1869–1959, British physicist, who invented the cloud chamber: shared the Nobel prize for physics 1927. **4** Edmund. 1895–1972, US critic noted esp. for *Axel's Castle* (1931). **5** (James) Harold, Baron Wilson of Rievaulx. 1916–95, British Labour statesman; prime minister (1964–70; 1974–76). **6** Richard. 1714–82, Welsh landscape painter. **7** (Thomas) Woodrow. 1856–1924, US Democratic statesman; 28th president of the US (1913–21). He led the US into World War I in 1917. Although he secured the formation of the League of Nations, the US Senate refused to join it: Nobel peace prize 1919.

wilt[1] (wɪlt) *vb* **1** to become or cause to become limp or drooping: *insufficient water makes plants wilt.* **2** to lose or cause to lose courage, strength, etc. ◆ *n* **3** the act of wilting or state of becoming wilted. **4** any of various plant diseases characterized by permanent wilting. [C17: ? var. of *wilk* to wither, from MDu. *welken*]

wilt[2] (wɪlt) *vb Arch. or dialect.* (used with the pronoun *thou* or its nearest equivalent) a singular form of the present tense (indicative mood) of **will**[1].

Wilton ('wɪltən) *n* a kind of carpet with a close velvet pile of cut loops. [after *Wilton*, town in Wiltshire, where first made]

Wilts (wɪlts) *abbrev. for* Wiltshire.

Wiltshire ★ ('wɪltʃə, -ˌʃɪə) *n* a county of S England, consisting mainly of chalk uplands, with Salisbury Plain in the south and the Marlborough Downs in the north, includes Swindon unitary authority; prehistoric remains (at Stonehenge and Avebury). Administrative centre: Trowbridge. Pop.: 586 300 (1994 est.). Area: 3481 sq. km (1344 sq. miles).

wily ('waɪlɪ) *adj* **wilier, wiliest.** sly or crafty.
▶ 'wiliness *n*

wimble ('wɪmbᵊl) *n* **1** any of a number of hand tools used for boring holes. ◆ *vb* **wimbles, wimbling, wimbled.** **2** to bore (a hole) with a wimble. [C13: from MDu. *wimmel* auger]

Wimbledon ★ ('wɪmbᵊldən) *n* part of the Greater London borough of Merton: headquarters of the All England Lawn Tennis Club since 1877 and the site of the annual international tennis championships.

wimp (wɪmp) *n Inf.* a feeble ineffective person. [C20: from ?]
▶ 'wimpish *or* 'wimpy *adj*

WIMP (wɪmp) *n acronym for*: **1** windows, icons, menus (*or* mice), pointers: denoting a type of user-friendly screen display used on small computing. **2** *Physics*. weakly interacting massive particle.

wimple ('wɪmpᵊl) *n* **1** a piece of cloth draped around the head to frame the face, worn by women in the Middle Ages and still worn by some nuns. ◆ *vb* **wimples, wimpling, wimpled.** *Arch.* **2** (*tr*) to cover with or put a wimple on. **3** (esp. of a veil) to lie or cause to lie in folds or pleats. [OE *wimpel*]

wimp out *vb* (*intr, adv*) *Sl.* to fail to do or complete something through fear or lack of conviction.

win (wɪn) *vb* **wins, winning, won.** **1** (*intr*) to achieve first place in a competition. **2** (*tr*) to gain (a prize, first place, etc.) in a competition. **3** (*tr*) to succeed in or gain (something) with an effort: *we won recognition.* **4** to gain victory or triumph in (a battle, argument, etc.). **5** (*tr*) to earn (a living, etc.) by work. **6** (*tr*) to capture: *the Germans never won Leningrad.* **7** (when *intr*, foll. by *out, through,* etc.) to reach with difficulty (a desired position) or become free, loose, etc., with effort: *the boat won the shore.* **8** (*tr*) to gain (the sympathy, loyalty, etc.) of someone. **9** (*tr*) to persuade (a woman, etc.) to marry one. **10** (*tr*) to extract (ore, coal, etc.) from a mine or (metal or other minerals) from ore. **11 you can't win.** *Inf.* an expression of resignation after an unsuccessful attempt to overcome difficulties. ◆ *n* **12** *Inf.* a success, victory, or triumph. **13** profit; winnings. ◆ See also **win over.** [OE *winnan*]
▶ 'winnable *adj*

wince[1] (wɪns) *vb* **winces, wincing, winced.** **1** (*intr*) to start slightly, as with sudden pain; flinch. ◆ *n* **2** the act of wincing. [C18 (earlier C13) meaning: to kick): via OF *wencier, guenchir* to avoid, of Gmc origin]
▶ 'wincer *n* ▶ 'wincingly *adv*

wince[2] (wɪns) *n* a roller for transferring pieces of cloth between dyeing vats. [C17: var. of WINCH[1]]

winceyette (ˌwɪnsɪ'ɛt) *n Brit.* a plain-weave cotton fabric with slightly raised two-sided nap. [from Scot. *wincey*, prob. altered from *woolsey* in *linsey-woolsey*, a fabric made of linen & wool]

winch[1] (wɪntʃ) *n* **1** a windlass driven by a hand- or power-operated crank. **2** a hand- or power-operated crank by which a machine is driven. ◆ *vb* **3** (*tr*; often foll. by *up* or *in*) to pull or lift using a winch. [OE *wince* pulley]

winch[2] (wɪntʃ) *vb* (*intr*) an obsolete word for **wince**[1].

Winchester ★ ('wɪntʃɪstə) *n* a city in S England, administrative centre of Hampshire: a Romano-British town; Saxon capital of Wessex; 11th-century cathedral; site of **Winchester College** (1382), English public school. Pop.: 36 121 (1991).

Winchester rifle ('wɪntʃɪstə) *n Trademark.* a breech-loading lever-action repeating rifle. Often shortened to **Winchester.** [C19: after O. F. *Winchester* (1810–80), US manufacturer]

Winckelmann ★ (German 'vɪŋkəlman) *n* **Johann Joachim** (jo'han 'joːaxɪm). 1717–68, German archaeologist and art historian.

wind[1] ('wɪnd) n 1 a current of air, sometimes of considerable force, moving generally horizontally from areas of high pressure to areas of low pressure. 2 *Chiefly poetic.* the direction from which a wind blows, usually a cardinal point of the compass. 3 air artificially moved, as by a fan, pump, etc. 4 a trend, tendency, or force: *the winds of revolution.* 5 *Inf.* a hint; suggestion: *we got wind that you were coming.* 6 something deemed insubstantial: *his talk was all wind.* 7 breath, as used in respiration or talk: *you're just wasting wind.* 8 (often used in sports) the power to breathe normally: *his wind is weak.* 9 *Music.* 9a a wind instrument or wind instruments considered collectively. 9b (*often pl*) the musicians who play wind instruments in an orchestra. 9c (*modifier*) of or composed of wind instruments: *a wind ensemble.* 10 an informal name for **flatus. 11** the air on which the scent of an animal is carried to hounds or on which the scent of a hunter is carried to his quarry. **12 between wind and water. 12a** the part of a vessel's hull below the water line that is exposed by rolling or by wave action. **12b** any particularly susceptible point. **13 break wind.** to release intestinal gas through the anus. **14 get** *or* **have the wind up.** *Inf.* to become frightened. **15 how** *or* **which way the wind blows** *or* **lies.** what appears probable. **16 in the teeth** (*or* **eye**) **of the wind.** directly into the wind. **17 in the wind.** about to happen. **18 into the wind.** against the wind or upwind. **19 off the wind.** *Naut.* away from the direction from which the wind is blowing. **20 on the wind.** *Naut.* as near as possible to the direction from which the wind is blowing. **21 put the wind up.** *Inf.* to frighten or alarm. **22 raise the wind.** *Brit. inf.* to obtain the necessary funds. **23 sail close** *or* **near to the wind.** to come near the limits of danger or indecency. **24 take the wind out of someone's sails.** to disconcert or deflate someone. ♦ *vb* (*tr*) **25** to cause (someone) to be short of breath: *the blow winded him.* **26a** to detect the scent of. **26b** to pursue (quarry) by following its scent. **27** to cause (a baby) to bring up wind after feeding. **28** to expose to air, as in drying, etc. [OE]
▸ **'windless** *adj*

wind[2] ('waɪnd) *vb* **winds, winding, wound. 1** (often foll. by *around, about,* or *upon*) to turn or coil (string, cotton, etc.) around some object or point or (of string, etc.) to be turned, etc., around some object or point: *he wound a scarf around his head.* **2** (*tr*) to cover or wreathe by or as if by coiling, wrapping, etc.: *we wound the body in a shroud.* **3** (*tr;* often foll. by *up*) to tighten the spring of (a clockwork mechanism). **4** (*tr;* foll. by *off*) to remove by uncoiling or unwinding. **5** (*usually intr*) to move or cause to move in a sinuous, spiral, or circular course: *the river winds through the hills.* **6** (*tr*) to introduce indirectly or deviously: *he is winding his own opinions into the report.* **7** (*tr*) to cause to twist or revolve: *he wound the handle.* **8** (*tr;* usually foll. by *up* or *down*) to move by cranking: *please wind up the window.* ♦ *n* **9** the act of winding or state of being wound. **10** a single turn, bend, etc.: *a wind in the river.* ♦ See also **wind down, wind up.** [OE *windan*]
▸ **'windable** *adj*

wind[3] (waɪnd) *vb* **winds, winding, winded** *or* **wound.** (*tr*) *Poetic.* to blow (a note or signal) on (a horn, bugle, etc.). [C16: special use of WIND[2]]

windage ('wɪndɪdʒ) *n* **1a** a deflection of a projectile as a result of the effect of the wind. **1b** the degree of such deflection. **2** the difference between a firearm's bore and the diameter of its projectile. **3** *Naut.* the exposed part of the hull of a vessel responsible for wind resistance.

windbag ('wɪnd,bæg) *n* **1** *Sl.* a voluble person who has little of interest to communicate. **2** the bag in a set of bagpipes, which provides a continuous flow of air to the pipes.

windblown ('wɪnd,bləʊn) *adj* **1** blown by the wind. **2** (of trees, shrubs, etc.) growing in a shape determined by the prevailing winds.

wind-borne *adj* (esp. of plant seeds or pollen) transported by wind.

windbound ('wɪnd,baʊnd) *adj* (of a sailing vessel) prevented from sailing by an unfavourable wind.

windbreak ('wɪnd,breɪk) *n* a fence, line of trees, etc., serving as a protection from the wind by breaking its force.

windburn ('wɪnd,bɜːn) *n* irritation of the skin caused by prolonged exposure to winds of high velocity.

Windcheater ('wɪnd,tʃiːtə) *n Aust. trademark.* a warm jacket, usually with a close-fitting knitted neck, cuffs, and waistband.

wind chest (wɪnd) *n* a box in an organ in which air from the bellows is stored under pressure before being supplied to the pipes or reeds.

wind-chill ('wɪnd-) *n* **a** the serious chilling effect of wind and low temperature: measured on a scale that runs from hot to fatal to life. **b** (*as modifier*): *wind-chill factor.*

wind cone (wɪnd) *n* another name for **windsock.**

wind down (waɪnd) *vb* (*adv*) **1** (*tr*) to lower or move down by cranking. **2** (*intr*) (of a clock spring) to become slack. **3** (*intr*) to diminish gradually in power; relax.

winded ('wɪndɪd) *adj* **1** out of breath, as from strenuous exercise. **2** (*in combination*) having breath or wind as specified: *broken-winded; short-winded.*

winder ('waɪndə) *n* **1** a person or device that winds. **2** an object, such as a bobbin, around which something is wound. **3** a knob or key used to wind up a clock, watch, or similar mechanism. **4** any plant that twists itself around a support. **5** a step of a spiral staircase. Cf. **flyer** (sense 4).

Windermere ★ ('wɪndə,mɪə) *n Lake.* a lake in NW England, in Cumbria in the SE part of the Lake District: the largest lake in England. Length: 17 km (10.5 miles).

windfall ('wɪnd,fɔːl) *n* **1** a piece of unexpected good fortune, esp. financial gain. **2** something blown down by the wind, esp. a piece of fruit.

windfall tax *n* a tax levied on an organization considered to have made excessive profits, esp. a privatized utility company that has exploited a natural monopoly.

wind farm *n* a large group of wind-driven generators for electricity supply.

windflower ('wɪnd,flaʊə) *n* any of various anemone plants, such as the wood anemone.

wind gauge (wɪnd) *n* **1** another name for **anemometer. 2** a scale on a gun sight indicating the amount of deflection necessary to allow for windage. **3** *Music.* a device for measuring the wind pressure in the bellows of an organ.

wind harp (wɪnd) *n* a less common name for **aeolian harp.**

Windhoek ★ ('vɪnt,hʊk, 'vɪnt-) *n* the capital of Namibia, in the centre, at an altitude of 1654 m (5428 ft): formerly the capital of German South West Africa. Pop.: 161 000 (1992 est.).

windhover ('wɪnd,hʊvə) *n Brit.* a dialect name for a **kestrel.**

winding ('waɪndɪŋ) *n* **1** a curving or sinuous course or movement. **2** anything that has been wound or wrapped around something. **3** a particular manner or style in which something has been wound. **4** a curve, bend, or complete turn in wound material, a road, etc. **5** (*often pl*) devious thoughts or behaviour: *the tortuous windings of political argumentation.* **6** one or more turns of wire forming a continuous coil through which an electric current can pass, as used in transformers, generators, etc. ♦ *adj* **7** curving; sinuous: *a winding road.*
▸ **'windingly** *adv*

winding sheet *n* a sheet in which a corpse is wrapped for burial; shroud.

winding-up *n* the process of finishing or closing something, esp. the process of closing down a business.

wind instrument (wɪnd) *n* any musical instrument sounded by the breath, such as the woodwinds and brass instruments of an orchestra.

windjammer ('wɪnd,dʒæmə) *n* a large merchant sailing ship.

windlass ('wɪndləs) *n* **1** a machine for raising weights by winding a rope or chain upon a barrel or drum driven by a crank, motor, etc. ♦ *vb* **2** (*tr*) to raise or haul (a weight, etc.) by means of a windlass. [C14: from ON *vindáss,* from *vinda* to WIND[2] + *ass* pole]

windlestraw ('wɪnd°l,strɔː) *n Irish, Scot., & English dialect.* the dried stalk of any of various grasses. [OE windelstrēaw, from windel basket, from windan to wind + strēaw straw]

wind machine (wɪnd) n a machine used, esp. in the theatre, to produce a wind or the sound of wind.

windmill ('wɪnd,mɪl, 'wɪn,mɪl) n **1** a machine for grinding or pumping driven by a set of adjustable vanes or sails that are caused to turn by the force of the wind. **2** the set of vanes or sails that drives such a mill. **3** Also called: **whirligig**. Brit. a toy consisting of plastic or paper vanes attached to a stick in such a manner that they revolve like the sails of a windmill. **4** an imaginary opponent or evil (esp. in **tilt at** or **fight windmills**). ◆ vb **5** to move or cause to move like the arms of a windmill.

window ('wɪndəʊ) n **1** a light framework, made of timber, metal, or plastic, that contains glass or glazed opening frames and is placed in a wall or roof to let in light or air or to see through. Related adj: **fenestral**. **2** an opening in the wall or roof of a building that is provided to let in light or air or to see through. **3** short for **windowpane**. **4** the area behind a glass window in a shop used for display. **5** any opening or structure resembling a window in function or appearance, such as the transparent area of an envelope revealing an address within. **6** an opportunity to see or understand something usually unseen: a window on the workings of Parliament. **7** a period of unbooked time in a diary, schedule, etc. **8** short for **launch window** or **weather window**. **9** Physics. a region of the spectrum in which a medium transmits electromagnetic radiation. **10** an area of a VDU display that can be manipulated separately from the rest of the display area. **11** (modifier) of or relating to a window or windows: a window ledge. ◆ vb **12** (tr) to furnish with or as if with windows. [C13: from ON vindauga, from vindr WIND[1] + auga eye]

window box n a long narrow box, placed on or outside a windowsill, in which plants are grown.

window-dresser n a person employed to design and build up a display in a shop window.

window-dressing n **1** the ornamentation of shop windows, designed to attract customers. **2** the pleasant aspect of an idea, etc., which is stressed to conceal the real nature.

windowpane ('wɪndəʊ,peɪn) n a sheet of glass in a window.

window sash n a glazed window frame, esp. one that opens.

window seat n **1** a seat below a window, esp. in a bay window. **2** a seat beside a window in a bus, train, etc.

window-shop vb **window-shops**, **window-shopping**, **window-shopped**. (intr) to look at goods in shop windows without intending to buy.
▶ 'window-,shopper n ▶ 'window-,shopping n

windowsill ('wɪndəʊ,sɪl) n a sill below a window.

windpipe ('wɪnd,paɪp) n a nontechnical name for **trachea** (sense 1).

Wind River Range ★ (wɪnd) n a mountain range in W Wyoming: one of the highest ranges of the central Rockies. Highest peak: Gannet Peak, 4202 m (13 785 ft).

wind rose (wɪnd) n a diagram with radiating lines showing the frequency and strength of winds from each direction affecting a specific place.

windrow ('wɪnd,rəʊ, 'wɪn,rəʊ) n **1** a long low ridge or line of hay or a similar crop, designed to achieve the best conditions for drying or curing. **2** a line of leaves, snow, dust, etc., swept together by the wind.

Windscale ★ ('wɪnd,skeɪl) n the former name of Sellafield.

windscreen ('wɪnd,skriːn) n Brit. the sheet of flat or curved glass that forms a window of a motor vehicle, esp. the front window. US and Canad. name: **windshield**.

windscreen wiper n Brit. an electrically operated blade with a rubber edge that wipes a windscreen clear of rain, snow, etc. US and Canad. name: **windshield wiper**.

windshield ('wɪnd,ʃiːld) n the US and Canad. name for **windscreen**.

windsock ('wɪnd,sɒk) n a truncated cone of textile mounted on a mast so that it is free to rotate about a ver-

tical axis: used, esp. at airports, to indicate the local wind direction. Also called: **air sock, drogue, wind sleeve, wind cone.**

Windsor[1] ★ ('wɪnzə) n **1** a town in S England, in Berkshire on the River Thames, linked by bridge with Eton: site of **Windsor Castle**, residence of English monarchs since its founding by William the Conqueror; **Old Windsor**, royal residence in the time of Edward the Confessor, is 3 km (2 miles) southeast. Pop.: 30 136 (1991). Official name: **New Windsor**. **2** a city in SE Canada, in S Ontario on the Detroit River opposite Detroit: motor-vehicle manufacturing; university (1963). Pop.: 191 435 (1991).

Windsor[2] ★ ('wɪnzə) n **1** the official name of the British royal family from 1917. **2 Duke of**. the title of **Edward VIII** from 1937.

Windsor and Maidenhead ★ n a unitary authority in SE England. Pop.: 141 500 (1996).

Windsor chair n a simple wooden chair, popular in England and America from the 18th century, usually having a shaped seat, splayed legs, and a back of many spindles.

Windsor knot n a wide triangular knot, produced by making extra turns in tying a tie.

windstorm ('wɪnd,stɔːm) n a storm consisting of violent winds.

wind-sucking n a harmful habit of horses in which the animal arches its neck and swallows a gulp of air.
▶ 'wind,sucker n

windsurfing ('wɪnd,sɜːfɪŋ) n the sport of riding on water using a surfboard steered and propelled by an attached sail.

windswept ('wɪnd,swept) adj open to or swept by the wind.

wind tunnel (wɪnd) n a chamber for testing the aerodynamic properties of aircraft, aerofoils, etc., in which a current of air can be maintained at a constant velocity.

wind up (waɪnd) vb (adv) **1** to bring to or reach a conclusion: he wound up the proceedings. **2** (tr) to tighten the spring of (a clockwork mechanism). **3** (tr; usually passive) Inf. to make nervous, tense, etc.: he was all wound up before the big fight. **4** (tr) to roll (thread, etc.) into a ball. **5** an informal word for **liquidate** (sense 2). **6** (intr) Inf. to end up (in a specified state): you'll wind up without any teeth. **7** (tr) Brit. sl. to tease (someone). ◆ n **wind-up. 8** the act of concluding. **9** the end.

windward ('wɪndwəd) Chiefly naut. ◆ adj **1** of, in, or moving to the quarter from which the wind blows. ◆ n **2** the windward point. **3** the side towards the wind. ◆ adv **4** towards the wind. ◆ Cf. **leeward**.

Windward Islands ★ pl n **1** a group of islands in the SE Caribbean, in the Lesser Antilles: consists of the French Overseas Department of Martinique and the independent states of Grenada, St Lucia, and St Vincent and the Grenadines. French name: **Iles du Vent**. **2** a group of islands in S Pacific, in French Polynesia in the W Society Archipelago: Moorea, Maio (Tubuai Manu), and Mehetia and Tetiaroa. Pop.: 140 341 (1988).

Windward Passage ★ n a strait in the Caribbean, between E Cuba and NW Haiti. Width: 80 km (50 miles).

windy ('wɪndɪ) adj **windier**, **windiest**. **1** of, resembling, or relating to wind; stormy. **2** swept by or open to powerful winds. **3** marked by or given to prolonged and often boastful speech: windy orations. **4** void of substance. **5** an informal word for **flatulent**. **6** Sl. frightened.
▶ 'windily adv ▶ 'windiness n

wine (waɪn) n **1a** an alcoholic drink produced by the fermenting of grapes with water and sugar. **1b** (as modifier): the wine harvest. **1c** an alcoholic drink produced in this way from other fruits, flowers, etc.: elderberry wine. **2a** a dark red colour, sometimes with a purplish tinge. **2b** (as adj): wine-coloured. **3** anything resembling wine in its intoxicating or invigorating effect. **4 new wine in old bottles**. something new added to or imposed upon an old or established order. ◆ vb **wines, wining, wined. 5** (intr) to drink wine. **6 wine and dine**. to entertain or be entertained with wine and fine food. [OE wīn, from L vīnum]
▶ 'wineless adj

wine bar *n* a bar in a restaurant, etc., or an establishment that specializes in serving wine and usually food.

winebibber ('waɪn,bɪbə) *n* a person who drinks a great deal of wine.
> ▶ 'wine,bibbing *n*

wine box *n* wine sold in a carton with a tap for pouring.

wine cellar *n* 1 a place, such as a dark cool cellar, where wine is stored. 2 the stock of wines stored there.

wine cooler *n* 1 a bucket-like vessel containing ice in which a bottle of wine is placed to be cooled. 2 the full name for **cooler** (sense 3).

wine gallon *n Brit.* a former unit of capacity equal to 231 cubic inches.

wineglass ('waɪn,glɑːs) *n* 1 a glass drinking vessel, typically having a small bowl on a stem, with a flared foot. 2 Also called: **wineglassful.** the amount that such a glass will hold.

wine grower *n* a person engaged in cultivating vines in order to make wine.
> ▶ wine growing *n*

wine palm *n* any of various palm trees, the sap of which is used, esp. when fermented, as a drink. Also called: **toddy palm.**

winepress ('waɪn,prɛs) *n* any equipment used for squeezing the juice from grapes in order to make wine.

winery ('waɪnərɪ) *n, pl* **wineries.** *Chiefly US & Canad.* a place where wine is made.

wineskin ('waɪn,skɪn) *n* the skin of a sheep or goat sewn up and used as a holder for wine.

wing (wɪŋ) *n* 1 either of the modified forelimbs of a bird that are covered with large feathers and specialized for flight in most species. 2 one of the organs of flight of an insect, consisting of a membranous outgrowth from the thorax containing a network of veins. 3 either of the organs of flight in certain other animals, esp. the forelimb of a bat. 4a a half of the main supporting surface on an aircraft, confined to one side of it. 4b the full span of the main supporting surface on both sides of an aircraft. 5 an organ, structure, or apparatus resembling a wing. 6 anything suggesting a wing in form, function, or position, such as a sail of a windmill or a ship. 7 *Bot.* 7a either of the lateral petals of a sweetpea or related flower. 7b any of various outgrowths of a plant part, esp. the process on a wind-dispersed fruit or seed. 8 a means or cause of flight or rapid motion; flight: *fear gave wings to his feet.* 9 *Brit.* the part of a car body that surrounds the wheels. US and Canad. name: **fender.** 10 *Soccer, hockey, etc.* 10a either of the two sides of the pitch near the touchline. 10b a player stationed in such a position; winger. 11 a faction or group within a political party or other organization. See also **left wing, right wing.** 12 a part of a building that is subordinate to the main part. 13 (*pl*) the space offstage to the right or left of the acting area in a theatre. 14 **in** or **on the wings**. ready to step in when needed. 15 either of the two pieces that project forwards from the sides of some chair backs. 16 (*pl*) an insignia in the form of stylized wings worn by a qualified aircraft pilot. 17 a tactical formation in some air forces, consisting of two or more squadrons. 18 any of various flattened organs or extensions in lower animals, esp. when used in locomotion. 19 **clip (someone's) wings. 19a** to restrict (someone's) freedom. **19b** to thwart (someone's) ambitions. 20 **on the wing.** 20a flying. 20b travelling. 21 **on wings.** flying or as if flying. 22 **spread** or **stretch one's wings.** to make full use of one's abilities. 23 **take wing. 23a** to lift off or fly away. **23b** to depart in haste. 23c to become joyful. 24 **under one's wing.** in one's care. ◆ *vb* (*mainly tr*) 25 (*also intr*) to make (one's way) swiftly on or as if on wings. 26 to shoot or wound (a bird, person, etc.) superficially, in the wing or arm, etc. 27 to cause to fly or move swiftly: *to wing an arrow.* 28 to provide with wings. [C12: from ON]
> ▶ **winged** *adj* ▶ 'wingless *adj* ▶ 'wing,like *adj*

Wingate ★ ('wɪn,geɪt) *n* **Orde Charles** (ɔːd) 1903–44, British soldier. During World War II he organized the Chindits in Burma: died in an air crash.

wing beat or **wing-beat** *n* a complete cycle of moving the wing by a bird when flying.

wing-case *n* the nontechnical name for **elytron.**

wing chair *n* an easy chair having wings on each side of the back.

wing collar *n* a stiff turned-up shirt collar worn with the points turned down over the tie.

wing commander *n* an officer holding commissioned rank in certain air forces, such as the Royal Air Force: junior to a group captain and senior to a squadron leader.

wing covert *n* any of the covert feathers of the wing of a bird, occurring in distinct rows.

wingding ('wɪŋ,dɪŋ) *n Sl., chiefly US & Canad.* 1 a noisy lively party or festivity. 2 a real or pretended fit or seizure. [C20: from ?]

winge (wɪndʒ) *vb, n Austral.* a variant spelling of **whinge.**

winger ('wɪŋə) *n Soccer, hockey, etc.* a player stationed on the wing.

wing loading *n* the total weight of an aircraft divided by its wing area.

wingman ('wɪŋmæn) *n pl* **wingmen.** a player in the wing position in Australian Rules.

wing nut *n* a threaded nut tightened by hand by means of two flat lugs or wings projecting from the central body. Also called: **butterfly nut.**

wingspan ('wɪŋ,spæn) or **wingspread** ('wɪŋ,sprɛd) *n* the distance between the wing tips of an aircraft, bird, etc.

wing tip *n* the outermost edge of a wing.

wink (wɪŋk) *vb* 1 (*intr*) to close and open one eye quickly, deliberately, or in an exaggerated fashion to convey friendliness, etc. 2 to close and open (an eye or the eyes) momentarily. 3 (*tr*; foll. by *away, back*, etc.) to force away (tears, etc.) by winking. 4 (*tr*) to signal with a wink. 5 (*intr*) (of a light) to gleam or flash intermittently. ◆ *n* 6 a winking movement, esp. one conveying a signal, etc., or such a signal. 7 an interrupted flashing of light. 8 a brief moment of time. 9 *Inf.* the smallest amount, esp. of sleep. 10 **tip the wink.** *Brit. inf.* to give a hint. [OE *wincian*]

wink at *vb* (*intr, prep*) to connive at; disregard: *the authorities winked at corruption.*

winker ('wɪŋkə) *n* 1 a person or thing that winks. 2 *Dialect or US & Canad. sl.* an eye. 3 another name for **blinker**¹ (sense 1).

winkle ('wɪŋkəl) *n* 1 See **periwinkle**¹. ◆ *vb* **winkles, winkling, winkled.** 2 (*tr*; usually foll. by *out, out of*, etc.) *Inf., chiefly Brit.* to extract or prise out. [C16: shortened from PERIWINKLE¹]

winkle-pickers *pl n* shoes or boots with very pointed narrow toes.

Winnebago ★ (,wɪnɪ'beɪgəʊ) *n* **Lake.** a lake in E Wisconsin, fed and drained by the Fox river: the largest lake in the state. Area: 557 sq. km (215 sq. miles).

winner ('wɪnə) *n* 1 a person or thing that wins. 2 *Inf.* a person or thing that seems to win or succeed.

winning ('wɪnɪŋ) *adj* 1 (of a person, character, etc.) charming or attractive: *a winning smile.* 2 gaining victory: *the winning goal.* ◆ *n* 3 a shaft or seam of coal. 4 (*pl*) money, prizes, or valuables won, esp. in gambling.
> ▶ 'winningly *adv* ▶ 'winningness *n*

winning gallery *n Real Tennis.* the gallery farthest from the net on either side of the court, into which any shot played wins a point.

winning opening *n Real Tennis.* the grille or winning gallery, into which any shot played wins a point.

winning post *n* the post marking the finishing line on a racecourse.

Winnipeg ★ ('wɪnɪ,pɛg) *n* 1 a city in S Canada, capital of Manitoba at the confluence of the Assiniboine and Red Rivers: University of Manitoba (1877) and University of Winnipeg (1871). Pop.: 616 790 (1991). 2 **Lake.** a lake in S Canada, in Manitoba: drains through the Nelson River into Hudson Bay. Area: 23 553 sq. km (9094 sq. miles).
> ▶ 'Winni,pegger *n*

Winnipeg couch *n Canad.* a couch with no arms or back, opening out into a double bed.

Winnipegosis ★ (,wɪnɪpə'gəʊsɪs) *n* **Lake.** a lake in S

★ people and places

Canada, in W Manitoba. Area: 5400 sq. km (2086 sq. miles).

winnow ('wɪnəʊ) *vb* **1** to separate (grain) from (chaff) by means of a wind or current of air. **2** (*tr*) to examine in order to select the desirable elements. **3** (*tr*) *Rare.* to blow upon; fan. ◆ *n* **4a** a device for winnowing. **4b** the act or process of winnowing. [OE *windwian*]
▸ **'winnower** *n*

wino ('waɪnəʊ) *n, pl* **winos.** *Inf.* a down-and-out who habitually drinks cheap wine.

win over *vb* (*tr, adv*) to gain the support or consent of (someone). Also: **win round.**

winsome ('wɪnsəm) *adj* charming; winning; engaging: *a winsome smile.* [OE *wynsum*, from *wynn* joy + *-sum* -SOME[1]]
▸ **'winsomely** *adv*

Winston-Salem ★ ('wɪnstən'seɪləm) *n* a city in N central North Carolina: formed in 1913 by the uniting of Salem and Winston; a major tobacco manufacturing centre. Pop.: 155 128 (1994 est.).

winter ('wɪntə) *n* **1a** (*sometimes cap.*) the coldest season of the year, between autumn and spring, astronomically from the December solstice to the March equinox in the N hemisphere and at the opposite time of year in the S hemisphere. **1b** (*as modifier*): *winter pasture.* **2** the period of cold weather associated with the winter. **3** a time of decline, decay, etc. **4** *Chiefly poetic.* a year represented by this season: *a man of 72 winters.* ◆ Related adj: **hibernal.** ◆ *vb* **5** (*intr*) to spend the winter in a specified place. **6** to keep or feed (farm animals, etc.) during the winter or (of farm animals) to be kept or fed during the winter. [OE]
▸ **'winterer** *n* ▸ **'winterless** *adj*

winter aconite *n* a small Old World herbaceous plant cultivated for its yellow flowers, which appear early in spring.

winter cherry *n* **1** a Eurasian plant cultivated for its ornamental inflated papery orange-red calyx. **2** the calyx of this plant. ◆ See also **Chinese lantern.**

winter garden *n* **1** a garden of evergreen plants. **2** a conservatory in which flowers are grown in winter.

wintergreen ('wɪntə,gri:n) *n* **1** any of a genus of evergreen ericaceous shrubs, esp. a subshrub of E North America, which has white bell-shaped flowers and edible red berries. **2** oil of wintergreen. an aromatic compound, formerly made from this and various other plants but now synthesized: used medicinally and for flavouring. **3** any of a genus of plants, such as **common wintergreen,** of temperate and arctic regions, having rounded leaves and small pink globose flowers. **4** chickweed wintergreen. a plant of N Europe and N Asia belonging to the primrose family, having white flowers and leaves arranged in a whorl. [C16: from Du. *wintergroen* or G *Wintergrün*]

winterize or **winterise** ('wɪntə,raɪz) *vb* **winterizes, winterizing, winterized** or **winterises, winterising, winterised.** (*tr*) *US & Canad.* to prepare (a house, car, etc.) to withstand winter conditions.
▸ **,winteri'zation** or **,winteri'sation** *n*

winter jasmine *n* a jasmine shrub widely cultivated for its winter-blooming yellow flowers.

winter solstice *n* the time at which the sun is at its southernmost point in the sky (northernmost point in the S hemisphere) appearing at noon at its lowest altitude above the horizon. It occurs about December 22 (June 21 in the S hemisphere).

winter sports *pl n* sports held in the open air on snow or ice, esp. skiing.

Winterthur ★ (German 'vɪntərtu:r) *n* an industrial town in NE central Switzerland, in Zürich canton: has the largest technical college in the country. Pop.: 88 168 (1994).

wintertime ('wɪntə,taɪm) *n* the winter season. Also (archaic): **wintertide.**

winterweight ('wɪntə,weɪt) *adj* (of clothes) suitably heavy and warm for wear in the winter.

winter wheat *n* a type of wheat that is planted in the autumn and is harvested the following summer.

wintry ('wɪntrɪ) or **wintery** ('wɪntərɪ) *adj* **wintrier, wintri-**

est. **1** (esp. of weather) of or characteristic of winter. **2** lacking cheer or warmth; bleak.
▸ **'wintrily** *adv* ▸ **'wintriness** or **'winteriness** *n*

winy ('waɪnɪ) *adj* **winier, winiest.** having the taste or qualities of wine; heady.

wipe (waɪp) *vb* **wipes, wiping, wiped.** (*tr*) **1** to rub (a surface or object) lightly, esp., with a cloth, hand, etc., as in removing dust, water, etc. **2** (usually foll. by *off, away, from, up,* etc.) to remove by or as if by rubbing lightly: *he wiped the dirt from his hands.* **3** to eradicate or cancel (a thought, memory, etc.). **4** to erase (a recording) from (a tape). **5** to apply (oil, etc.) by wiping. **6** *Austral. inf.* to abandon or reject (a person). **7 wipe the floor with (someone).** *Inf.* to defeat (someone) decisively. ◆ *n* **8** the act or an instance of wiping. **9** *Dialect.* a sweeping blow. [OE *wīpian*]

wipe out *vb* (*adv*) **1** (*tr*) to destroy completely. **2** (*tr*) *Inf.* to kill. **3** (*intr*) to fall off a surfboard. ◆ *n* **wipeout. 4** an act or instance of wiping out. **5** the interference of one radio signal by another so that reception is impossible.

wiper ('waɪpə) *n* **1** any piece of cloth, such as a handkerchief, etc., used for wiping. **2** a cam rotated to allow a part to fall under its own weight, as used in stamping machines, etc. **3** See **windscreen wiper. 4** *Electrical engineering.* a movable conducting arm that makes contact with a row or ring of contacts.

wire ('waɪə) *n* **1** a slender flexible strand or rod of metal. **2** a cable consisting of several metal strands twisted together. **3** a flexible metallic conductor, esp. one made of copper, usually insulated, and used to carry electric current in a circuit. **4** (*modifier*) of, relating to, or made of wire: *a wire fence.* **5** anything made of wire, such as wire netting. **6** a long continuous wire or cable connecting points in a telephone or telegraph system. **7** *Old-fashioned.* an informal name for **telegram** or **telegraph. 8** *US & Canad. horse racing.* the finishing line on a racecourse. **9** a snare made of wire for rabbits and similar animals. **10 get in under the wire.** *Inf., chiefly US & Canad.* to accomplish something with little time to spare. **11 get one's wires crossed.** *Inf.* to misunderstand. **12 pull wires.** *Chiefly US & Canad.* to exert influence behind the scenes; pull strings. ◆ *vb* **wires, wiring, wired.** (*mainly tr*) **13** (*also intr*) to send a telegram to (a person or place). **14** to send (news, a message, etc.) by telegraph. **15** to equip (an electrical system, circuit, or component) with wires. **16** to fasten or furnish with wire. **17** to snare with wire. **18** *US. inf.* to set about (something, esp. food) with enthusiasm. [OE *wīr*]
▸ **'wire,like** *adj*

wire brush *n* a brush having wire bristles, used for cleaning metal, esp. for removing rust, or for brushing against cymbals.

wire cloth *n* a mesh or netting woven from fine wire, used in window screens, strainers, etc.

wiredraw ('waɪə,drɔ:) *vb* **wiredraws, wiredrawing, wiredrew, wiredrawn.** to convert (metal) into wire by drawing through successively smaller dies.

wire-gauge *n* **1** a flat plate with slots in which standard wire sizes can be measured. **2** a standard system of sizes for measuring the diameters of wires.

wire gauze *n* a stiff meshed fabric woven of fine wires.

wire grass *n* any of various grasses that have tough wiry roots or rhizomes.

wire-guided *adj* (of a missile) able to be controlled in mid-flight by signals passed along a wire connecting the missile to the firer's control device.

wire-haired *adj* (of an animal) having a rough wiry coat.

wireless ('waɪəlɪs) *n, vb Chiefly Brit.* another word for **radio.**

wireless telegraphy *n* another name for **radiotelegraphy.**

wireless telephone *n* another name for **radiotelephone.**
▸ **wireless telephony** *n*

wire netting *n* a net made of wire, often galvanized, that is used for fencing, etc.

wirepuller ('waɪə,pʊlə) *n Chiefly US & Canad.* a person who uses private or secret influence for his own ends.
▸ **'wire,pulling** *n*

wire recorder *n* an early type of magnetic recorder in which sounds were recorded on a thin steel wire magnetized by an electromagnet.
▸ **wire recording** *n*

wire service *n Chiefly US & Canad.* an agency supplying news, etc., to newspapers, radio, and television stations, etc.

wiretap ('waɪə,tæp) *vb* **wiretaps, wiretapping, wiretapped. 1** (*intr*) to make a connection to a telegraph or telephone wire in order to obtain information secretly. **2** (*tr*) to tap (a telephone) or the telephone of (a person).
▸ **'wire,tapper** *n*

wire wheel *n* a wheel in which the rim is held to the hub by wire spokes, esp. one used on a sports car.

wire wool *n* a mass of fine wire used for cleaning and scouring.

wirework ('waɪə,wɜːk) *n* **1** functional or decorative work made of wire. **2** objects made of wire, esp. netting.

wireworks ('waɪə,wɜːks) *n* (*functioning as sing or pl*) a factory where wire or articles of wire are made.

wireworm ('waɪə,wɜːm) *n* the wormlike larva of various beetles, which feeds on the roots of many plants and is a serious pest.

wiring ('waɪərɪŋ) *n* **1** the network of wires used in an electrical system, device, or circuit. ◆ *adj* **2** used in wiring.

Wirral ★ ('wɪrəl) *n* **the. 1** a peninsula in NW England between the estuaries of the Rivers Mersey and Dee. **2** a unitary authority in NW England, in Merseyside. Pop.: 333 100 (1994 est.). Area: 158 sq. km (61 sq. miles).

wiry ('waɪərɪ) *adj* **wirier, wiriest. 1** (of people or animals) slender but strong in constitution. **2** made of or resembling wire, esp. in stiffness: *wiry hair.* **3** (of a sound) produced by or as if by a vibrating wire.
▸ **'wirily** *adv* ▸ **'wiriness** *n*

wis (wɪs) *vb Arch.* to know or suppose (something). [C17: a form derived from *iwis*, (from OE *gewiss* certain), mistakenly interpreted as *I wis* I know, as if from OE *witan* to know]

Wis. *abbrev. for* Wisconsin.

Wisbech ★ ('wɪzbiːtʃ) *n* a town in E England, in N Cambridgeshire: market-gardening. Pop.: 24 981 (1991).

Wisconsin ★ (wɪs'kɒnsɪn) *n* **1** a state of the N central US, on Lake Superior and Lake Michigan: consists of an undulating plain, with uplands in the north and west; over 168 m (550 ft) above sea level along the shore of Lake Michigan. Capital: Madison. Pop.: 5 159 795 (1996 est.). Area: 141 061 sq. km (54 464 sq. miles). Abbrevs.: **Wis.** or (with zip code) **WI. 2** a river in central and SW Wisconsin, flowing south and west to the Mississippi. Length: 692 km (430 miles).
▸ **Wis'consin,ite** *n*

Wisden ★ ('wɪzdən) *n* **John.** 1826–84, English cricketer; publisher of *Wisden Cricketers' Almanack,* which first appeared in 1864.

wisdom ('wɪzdəm) *n* **1** the ability or result of an ability to think and act utilizing knowledge, experience, understanding, common sense, and insight. **2** accumulated knowledge or enlightenment. **3** *Arch.* a wise saying or wise sayings. ◆ Related adj: **sagacious.** [OE *wīsdōm*]

wisdom tooth *n* **1** any of the four molar teeth, one at the back of each side of the jaw, that are the last of the permanent teeth to erupt. Technical name: **third molar. 2 cut one's wisdom teeth.** to arrive at the age of discretion.

wise[1] (waɪz) *adj* **1** possessing, showing, or prompted by wisdom or discernment. **2** prudent; sensible. **3** shrewd; crafty: *a wise plan.* **4** well-informed; erudite. **5** informed or knowing (esp. in **none the wiser**). **6** (*postpositive*; often foll. by *to*) *Sl.* in the know, esp. possessing inside information (about). **7** *Arch.* possessing powers of magic. **8 be** *or* **get wise.** (often foll. by *to*) *Inf.* to be or become aware or informed (of something). **9 put wise.** (often foll. by *to*) *Sl.* to inform or warn (of). ◆ *vb* **wises, wising, wised. 10** See **wise up.** [OE *wīs*]
▸ **'wisely** *adv* ▸ **'wiseness** *n*

wise[2] (waɪz) *n Arch.* way, manner, fashion, or respect (esp. in **any wise, in no wise**). [OE *wīse* manner]

-wise *adv combining form.* **1** indicating direction or man-

ner: *clockwise; likewise.* **2** with reference to: *businesswise.* [OE *-wisan;* see WISE[2]]

wiseacre ('waɪz,eɪkə) *n* **1** a person who wishes to seem wise. **2** a wise person: often used facetiously or contemptuously. [C16: from MDu. *wijsseggher* soothsayer. See WISE[1], SAY]

wisecrack ('waɪz,kræk) *Inf.* ◆ *n* **1** a flippant gibe or sardonic remark. ◆ *vb* (*intr*) **2** to make a wisecrack.
▸ **'wise,cracker** *n*

wise guy *n Inf.* a person who is given to making conceited, sardonic, or insolent comments.

Wiseman ★ ('waɪzmən) *n* **Nicholas Patrick Stephen.** 1802–65, British cardinal; first Roman Catholic archbishop of Westminster (1850–65).

wisent ('wiːzˀnt) *n* another name for **European bison.** See **bison** (sense 2). [G, from OHG *wisunt* BISON]

wise up *vb* (*adv*) *Sl., chiefly US & Canad.* (often foll. by *to*) to become or cause to become aware or informed (of).

wish (wɪʃ) *vb* **1** (when *tr,* takes a clause as object or an infinitive; when *intr,* often foll. by *for*) to want or desire (something, often that which cannot be or is not the case): *I wish I lived in Italy.* **2** (*tr*) to feel or express a desire or hope concerning the future or fortune of: *I wish you well.* **3** (*tr*) to desire or prefer to be as specified. **4** (*tr*) to greet as specified: *he wished us good afternoon.* ◆ *n* **5** the expression of some desire or mental inclination: *to make a wish.* **6** something desired or wished for: *he got his wish.* **7** (*usually pl*) expressed hopes or desire, esp. for someone's welfare, health, etc. **8** (*often pl*) *Formal.* a polite order or request. ◆ See also **wish on.** [OE *wȳscan*]
▸ **'wisher** *n*

wishbone ('wɪʃ,bəʊn) *n* the V-shaped bone above the breastbone in most birds consisting of the fused clavicles. [C17: from the custom of two people breaking apart the bone after eating: the person with the longer part makes a wish]

wishful ('wɪʃful) *adj* having wishes or characterized by wishing.
▸ **'wishfully** *adv* ▸ **'wishfulness** *n*

wish fulfilment *n* (in Freudian psychology) any successful attempt to fulfil a wish stemming from the unconscious mind, whether in fact, in fantasy, or by disguised means.

wishful thinking *n* the erroneous belief that one's wishes are in accordance with reality.
▸ **wishful thinker** *n*

wish on *vb* (*tr, prep*) to hope that (someone or something) should be imposed (on someone); foist: *I wouldn't wish my cold on anyone.*

wishy-washy ('wɪʃɪ,wɒʃɪ) *adj Inf.* **1** lacking in substance, force, colour, etc. **2** watery; thin.

Wisła ★ ('viswa) *n* the Polish name for **Vistula** (sense 1).

Wislany Zalew ★ (*Polish* viʃ'laːni 'zaːlɛf) *n* the Polish name for the **Vistula** (sense 2).

Wismar ★ (*German* 'vɪsmar) *n* a port in NE Germany, on an inlet of the Baltic: shipbuilding industries. Pop.: 54 470 (1991).

wisp (wɪsp) *n* **1** a thin, light, delicate, or fibrous piece or strand, such as a streak of smoke or a lock of hair. **2** a small bundle, as of hay or straw. **3** anything slender and delicate: *a wisp of a girl.* **4** a mere suggestion or hint. **5** a flock of birds, esp. snipe. [C14: var. of *wips,* from ?]
▸ **'wisp,like** *adj* ▸ **'wispy** *adj*

wist (wɪst) *vb Arch.* the past tense and past participle of **wit**[2].

wisteria (wɪ'stɪərɪə) *n* any twining woody climbing plant of the genus *Wisteria,* of E Asia and North America, having blue, purple, or white flowers in large drooping clusters. [C19: from NL, after Caspar *Wistar* (1761–1818), US anatomist]

wistful ('wɪstful) *adj* sadly pensive, esp. about something yearned for.
▸ **'wistfully** *adv* ▸ **'wistfulness** *n*

wit[1] (wɪt) *n* **1** the talent or quality of using unexpected associations between contrasting or disparate words or ideas to make a clever humorous effect. **2** speech or writing showing this quality. **3** a person possessing, show-

★ people and places

ing, or noted for such an ability. **4** practical intelligence (esp. in **have the wit to**). **5** *Arch.* mental capacity or a person possessing it. ◆ See also **wits**. [OE *witt*]

wit² (wɪt) *vb* **wits, witting, wot, wist. 1** *Arch.* to be or become aware of (something). **2 to wit.** that is to say; namely (used to introduce statements, as in legal documents). [OE *witan*]

witan ('wɪtⁿn) *n* (in Anglo-Saxon England) **1** an assembly of higher ecclesiastics and important laymen that met to counsel the king on matters such as judicial problems. **2** the members of this assembly. ◆ Also called: **witenagemot.** [OE *witan*, pl. of *wita* wise man]

witblits ('vɪt,blɪts) *n S. African.* alcoholic drink illegally distilled. [from Afrik. *wit* white + *blits* lightning]

witch¹ (wɪtʃ) *n* **1** a person, usually female, who practises or professes to practise magic or sorcery, esp. black magic, or is believed to have dealings with the devil. **2** an ugly or wicked old woman. **3** a fascinating or enchanting woman. ◆ *vb* (*tr*) **4** a less common word for **bewitch.** [OE *wicca*]
▸ 'witch,like *adj*

witch² (wɪtʃ) *n* a flatfish of N Atlantic coastal waters, having a narrow greyish-brown body marked with tiny black spots: related to the plaice, flounder, etc. [C19: ?from WITCH¹, from the appearance of the fish]

witchcraft ('wɪtʃ,krɑːft) *n* **1** the art or power of bringing magical or preternatural power to bear on the act or practice of attempting to do so. **2** the influence of magic or sorcery. **3** fascinating or bewitching influence or charm.

witch doctor *n* a man in certain societies, esp. preliterate ones, who appears to possess magical powers, used esp. to cure sickness but also to harm people. Also called: **shaman, medicine man.**

witch-elm *n* a variant spelling of **wych-elm.**

witchery ('wɪtʃərɪ) *n, pl* **witcheries. 1** the practice of witchcraft. **2** magical or bewitching influence or charm.

witches'-broom *n* a dense abnormal growth of shoots on a tree or other woody plant, usually caused by parasitic fungi.

witchetty grub ('wɪtʃɪtɪ) *n* the wood-boring edible caterpillar of an Australian moth. Also: **witchetty, witchety.** [C19 *witchetty*, from Abor.]

witch hazel *or* **wych-hazel** *n* **1** any of a genus of trees and shrubs of North America, having ornamental yellow flowers and medicinal properties. **2** an astringent medicinal solution containing an extract of the bark and leaves of one of these shrubs, applied to treat bruises, inflammation, etc.

witch-hunt *n* a rigorous campaign to expose dissenters on the pretext of safeguarding the public welfare.
▸ 'witch-,hunting *n, adj*

witching ('wɪtʃɪŋ) *adj* **1** relating to or appropriate for witchcraft. **2** *Now rare.* bewitching.
▸ 'witchingly *adv*

witching hour *n* **the. the** hour at which witches are supposed to appear, usually midnight.

witenagemot (,wɪtɪnəgɪ'məut) *n* another word for **witan.** [OE *witena*, genitive pl of *wita* councillor + *gemōt* meeting]

with (wɪð, wɪθ) *prep* **1** using; by means of: *he killed her with an axe.* **2** accompanying; in the company of: *the lady you were with.* **3** possessing; having: *a man with a red moustache.* **4** concerning or regarding: *be patient with her.* **5** in spite of: *with all his talents, he was still humble.* **6** used to indicate a time or distance by which something is away from something else: *with three miles to go, he collapsed.* **7** in a manner characterized by: *writing with abandon.* **8** caused or prompted by: *shaking with rage.* **9** often used with a verb indicating a reciprocal action or relation between the subject and the preposition's object: *agreeing with me.* **10 with it.** *Inf.* **10a** fashionable; in style. **10b** comprehending what is happening or being said. **11 with that.** after that. [OE]

withal (wɪ'ðɔːl) *adv* **1** *Literary.* as well. **2** *Arch.* therewith. ◆ *prep* **3** (*postpositive*) an archaic word for **with.** [C12: from WITH + ALL]

withdraw (wɪð'drɔː) *vb* **withdraws, withdrawing, withdrew,**

withdrawn. 1 (*tr*) to take or draw back or away; remove. **2** (*tr*) to remove from deposit or investment in a bank, etc. **3** (*tr*) to retract or recall (a promise, etc.). **4** (*intr*) to retire or retreat: *the troops withdrew.* **5** (*intr*; often foll. by *from*) to depart (from): *he withdrew from public life.* **6** (*intr*) to detach oneself socially, emotionally, or mentally. [C13: from WITH (in the sense: away from) + DRAW]
▸ with'drawer *n*

withdrawal (wɪð'drɔːəl) *n* **1** an act or process of withdrawing. **2** the period a drug addict goes through following abrupt termination in the use of narcotics, usually characterized by physical and mental symptoms (**withdrawal symptoms**). **3** Also called: **withdrawal method, coitus interruptus.** the deliberate withdrawing of the penis from the vagina before ejaculation, as a method of contraception.

withdrawing room *n* an archaic term for **drawing room.**

withdrawn (wɪð'drɔːn) *vb* **1** the past participle of **withdraw.** ◆ *adj* **2** unusually reserved or shy. **3** secluded or remote.

withe (wɪθ, wɪð, waɪð) *n* **1** a strong flexible twig, esp. of willow, suitable for binding things together; withy. **2** a band or rope of twisted twigs or stems. ◆ *vb* **withes, withing, withed. 3** (*tr*) to bind with withes. [OE *withthe*]

wither ('wɪðə) *vb* **1** (*intr*) (esp. of a plant) to droop, wilt, or shrivel up. **2** (*intr*; often foll. by *away*) to fade or waste: *all hope withered away.* **3** (*intr*) to decay or disintegrate. **4** (*tr*) to cause to wilt or lose vitality. **5** (*tr*) to abash, esp. with a scornful look. [C14: ? var. of WEATHER (vb)]
▸ 'witherer *n* ▸ 'withering *adj* ▸ 'witheringly *adv*

withers ('wɪðəz) *pl n* the highest part of the back of a horse, behind the neck between the shoulders. [C16: short for *widersones*, from *wider* with + *-sones*, ? var. of SINEW]

withershins ('wɪðə,ʃɪnz) *or* **widdershins** *adv Chiefly Scot.* in the direction contrary to the apparent course of the sun; anticlockwise. [C16: from MLow G *wedder-sinnes*, from MHG, lit.: opposite course, from *wider* against + *sinnes*, genitive of *sin* course]

withhold (wɪð'həuld) *vb* **withholds, withholding, withheld. 1** (*tr*) to keep back: *he withheld his permission.* **2** (*tr*) to hold back; restrain. **3** (*intr*; usually foll. by *from*) to refrain or forbear.
▸ with'holder *n*

within (wɪ'ðɪn) *prep* **1** in; inside; enclosed or encased by. **2** before (a period of time) has elapsed: *within a week.* **3** not differing by more than (a specified amount) from: *live within your means.* ◆ *adv* **4** *Formal.* inside; internally.

without (wɪ'ðaut) *prep* **1** not having: *a traveller without much money.* **2** not accompanied by: *he came without his wife.* **3** not making use of: *it is not easy to undo screws without a screwdriver.* **4** (foll. by a verbal noun or noun phrase) not, while not, or after not: *she can sing for two minutes without drawing breath.* **5** *Arch.* on the outside of: *without the city walls.* ◆ *adv* **6** *Formal.* outside.

withstand (wɪð'stænd) *vb* **withstands, withstanding, withstood. 1** (*tr*) to resist. **2** (*intr*) to remain firm in endurance or opposition.
▸ with'stander *n*

withy ('wɪðɪ) *n, pl* **withies.** a variant spelling of **withe** (senses 1, 2). [OE *wīdig(e)*]

witless ('wɪtlɪs) *adj* lacking wit, intelligence, or sense.
▸ 'witlessly *adv* ▸ 'witlessness *n*

witling ('wɪtlɪŋ) *n Arch.* a person who thinks himself witty.

witness ('wɪtnɪs) *n* **1** a person who has seen or can give first-hand evidence of some event. **2** a person or thing giving or serving as evidence. **3** a person who testifies, esp. in a court of law, to events or facts within his own knowledge. **4** a person who attests to the genuineness of a document, signature, etc., by adding his own signature. **5 bear witness to. 5a** to give written or oral testimony to. **5b** to be evidence or proof of. ◆ *Related adj:* **testimonial.** ◆ *vb* **6** (*tr*) to see, be present at, or know at first hand. **7** (*tr*) to give evidence of. **8** (*tr*) to be the scene or setting of: *this field has witnessed a battle.* **9** (*intr*) to testify, esp. in a court of law, to events within a person's own knowledge. **10** (*tr*) to attest to the genuineness of (a

document, etc.) by adding one's own signature. [OE *witnes,* from *witan* to know + -NESS]
▸ 'witnesser *n*

witness box *or esp. US* **witness stand** *n* the place in a court of law in which witnesses stand to give evidence.

wits (wits) *pl n* (*sometimes sing*) the ability to reason and act, esp. quickly (esp. in **have one's wits about one**). **2** (*sometimes sing*) right mind, sanity (esp. in **out of one's wits**). **3 at one's wits' end.** at a loss to know how to proceed. **4 live by one's wits.** to gain a livelihood by craftiness rather than by hard work.

Witt ★ (wit) *n* **Johan de** (joː'hɑn). 1625–72, Dutch statesman; chief minister of the United Provinces of the Netherlands (1653–72).

-witted *adj* (*in combination*) having wits or intelligence as specified: *slow-witted; dim-witted.*

Wittenberg ★ (*German* 'vɪtənbɛrk; *English* 'wɪtˀn,bɜːg) *n* a city in E Germany, on the River Elbe: Martin Luther, as a philosophy teacher at Wittenberg university, began the Reformation here in 1517 by nailing his 95 theses to the doors of a church. Pop.: 87 000 (1991).

witter ('wɪtə) *vb* (*intr*; often foll. by *on*) *Inf.* to chatter or babble pointlessly or at unnecessary length. [C20: ?from obs. *whitter* to warble, twitter]

Wittgenstein ★ ('vɪtɡənˌʃtaɪn, -ˌstaɪn) *n* **Ludwig Josef Johann** ('luːtvɪç 'joːzɛf jo'hɑn). 1889–1951, British philosopher, born in Austria. His principal works were the *Tractatus Logico-Philosophicus* (1921) and *Philosophical Investigations* (1953).

Wittgensteinian ('vɪtɡənˌʃtaɪnɪən, -ˌstaɪnɪən) *adj* (of a philosophical position or argument) derived from or related to the work of Wittgenstein and esp. the later work in which he attacks essentialism and stresses the open texture and variety of the use of ordinary language.

witticism ('wɪtɪˌsɪzəm) *n* a clever or witty remark. [C17: from WITTY; coined by Dryden (1677) by analogy with *criticism*]

witting ('wɪtɪŋ) *adj Rare.* **1** deliberate; intentional. **2** aware.
▸ 'wittingly *adv*

witty ('wɪtɪ) *adj* **wittier, wittiest. 1** characterized by clever humour or wit. **2** *Arch.* or *dialect.* intelligent.
▸ 'wittily *adv* ▸ 'wittiness *n*

Witwatersrand ★ (wɪt'wɔːtəzˌrænd; *Afrikaans* vət'vɑːtərs'rant) *n* a rocky ridge in NE South Africa: contains the richest gold deposits in the world, also coal and manganese; chief industrial centre of the region is Johannesburg. Height: 1500–1800 m (5000–6000 ft). Also called: **the Rand, the Reef.**

wive (waɪv) *vb* **wives, wiving, wived.** *Arch.* **1** to marry (a woman). **2** (*tr*) to supply with a wife. [OE *gewīfian,* from *wīf* wife]

wivern ('waɪvən) *n* a less common spelling of **wyvern.**

wives (waɪvz) *n* **1** the plural of **wife. 2 old wives' tale.** a superstitious tradition, occasionally one that contains an element of truth.

wiz (wɪz) *n, pl* **wizzes.** *Inf.* a variant spelling of **whizz** (sense 5).

wizard ('wɪzəd) *n* **1** a male witch or a man who practises or professes to practise magic or sorcery. **2** a person who is outstandingly clever in some specified field. **3** *Computing.* a program that guides a user through a complex task. ♦ *adj* **4** *Inf.,* chiefly *Brit.* superb; outstanding. **5** of or relating to a wizard or wizardry. [C15: var. of *wissard,* from WISE[1] + -ARD]
▸ 'wizardly *adj*

wizardry ('wɪzədrɪ) *n* the art, skills, and practices of a wizard, sorcerer, or magician.

wizen ('wɪzˀn) *vb* **1** to make or become shrivelled. ♦ *adj* **2** a variant of **wizened.** [OE *wisnian*]

wizened ('wɪzˀnd) *or* **wizen** *adj* shrivelled, wrinkled, or dried up, esp. with age.

wk *abbrev. for:* **1** (*pl* **wks**) week. **2** work.

wkly *abbrev. for* weekly.

w.l. *or* **WL** *abbrev. for* water line.

WMO *abbrev. for* World Meteorological Organization.

WNW *symbol for* west-northwest.

WO *abbrev. for:* **1** War Office. **2** Warrant Officer. **3** wireless operator.

woad (wəud) *n* **1** a European cruciferous plant, formerly cultivated for its leaves, which yield a blue dye. **2** the dye obtained from this plant, used esp. by the ancient Britons as a body dye. [OE *wād*]

wobbegong ('wɒbɪˌɡɒn) *n* any of various sharks of Australian waters, having a richly patterned brown-and-white skin. [from Abor.]

wobble ('wɒbˀl) *vb* **wobbles, wobbling, wobbled. 1** (*intr*) to move or sway unsteadily. **2** (*intr*) to shake: *her voice wobbled with emotion.* **3** (*intr*) to vacillate with indecision. **4** (*tr*) to cause to wobble. ♦ *n* **5** a wobbling movement or sound. [C17: var. of *wabble,* from Low G *wabbeln*]
▸ 'wobbler *n*

wobble board *n Austral.* a piece of fibreboard used as a rhythmic musical instrument, producing a characteristic sound when flexed.

wobbly ('wɒblɪ) *adj* **wobblier, wobbliest. 1** shaky, unstable, or unsteady. ♦ *n* **2 throw a wobbly.** *Sl.* to become suddenly very agitated or angry.
▸ 'wobbliness *n*

Wodehouse ★ ('wud,haus) *n* **Sir P(elham) G(renville).** 1881–1975, US author, born in England. His humorous novels of upper-class life in England include the *Psmith* and *Jeeves* series.

Woden *or* **Wodan** ★ ('wəudˀn) *n* the foremost Anglo-Saxon god. Norse counterpart: **Odin.** [OE *Wōden;* related to ON *thinn,* OHG *Wuotan,* G *Wotan;* see WEDNESDAY]

wodge (wɒdʒ) *n Brit. inf.* a thick lump or chunk cut or broken off something. [C20: alteration of WEDGE]

woe (wəu) *n* **1** *Literary.* intense grief. **2** (*often pl*) affliction or misfortune. **3 woe betide (someone).** misfortune will befall (someone): *woe betide you if you arrive late.* ♦ *interj* **4** Also: **woe is me.** *Arch.* an exclamation of sorrow or distress. [OE *wā, wǣ*]

woebegone ('wəubɪˌɡɒn) *adj* sorrowful or sad in appearance. [C14: from a phrase such as *me is wo begon* woe has beset me]

woeful ('wəufˀl) *adj* **1** expressing or characterized by sorrow. **2** bringing or causing woe. **3** pitiful; miserable: *a woeful standard of work.*
▸ 'woefully *adv* ▸ 'woefulness *n*

WOF (in New Zealand) *abbrev. for* Warrant of Fitness.

wog[1] (wɒg) *n Brit. sl., derog.* a person who is not White. [prob. from GOLLIWOG]

wog[2] (wɒg) *n Austral. sl.* any ailment or disease, such as influenza, a virus infection, etc. [C20: from ?]

woggle ('wɒgˀl) *n* the ring of leather through which a Scout neckerchief is threaded. [C20: from ?]

Wöhler ★ (*German* 'vøːlər) *n* **Friedrich** ('friːdrɪç). 1800–82, German chemist, who proved that organic compounds could be synthesized from inorganic compounds.

wok (wɒk) *n* a large metal Chinese cooking pot having a curved base like a bowl: used esp. for stir-frying. [from Chinese (Cantonese)]

woke (wəuk) *vb* the past tense of **wake**[1].

woken ('wəukən) *vb* the past participle of **wake**[1].

Woking ★ ('wəukɪŋ) *n* a town in S England, in central Surrey: mainly residential. Pop.: 98 138 (1991).

Wokingham ★ ('wəu,kɪŋəm) *n* a unitary authority in S England, in Berkshire. Pop.: 142 400 (1996 est.).

wokka board ('wɒkə) *n Austral.* another name for **wobble board.**

wold[1] (wəuld) *n Chiefly literary.* a tract of open rolling country, esp. upland. [OE *weald* bush]

wold[2] (wəuld) *n* a variant of **weld**[2].

Wolds ★ (wəuldz) *pl n* **the.** a range of chalk hills in NE England: consists of the **Yorkshire Wolds** to the north, separated from the **Lincolnshire Wolds** by the Humber estuary.

wolf (wulf) *n, pl* **wolves. 1** a predatory canine mammal which hunts in packs and was formerly widespread in North America and Eurasia but is now less common. Re-

★ people and places

lated adj: **lupine. 2** any of several similar and related canines, such as the red wolf and the coyote (**prairie wolf**). **3** the fur of any such animal. **4** a voracious or fiercely cruel person or thing. **5** *Inf.* a man who habitually tries to seduce women. **6** Also called: **wolf note.** *Music.* **6a** an unpleasant sound produced in some notes played on the violin, etc., owing to resonant vibrations of the belly. **6b** an out-of-tune effect produced on keyboard instruments accommodated esp. to the system of mean-tone temperament. **7 cry wolf.** to give a false alarm. **8 have** *or* **hold a wolf by the ears.** to be in a desperate situation. **9 keep the wolf from the door.** to ward off starvation or privation. **10 lone wolf.** a person or animal who prefers to be alone. **11 wolf in sheep's clothing.** a malicious person in a harmless or benevolent disguise. ◆ *vb* **12** (*tr*; often foll. by *down*) to gulp (down). **13** (*intr*) to hunt wolves. [OE *wulf*]
▶ **'wolfish** *adj* ▶ **'wolf,like** *adj*

Wolf ★ *n* **1** (*German* vɔlf). **Friedrich August** (ˈfriːdrɪç ˈaʊɡust). 1759–1824, German classical scholar, who suggested that the Homeric poems, esp. the *Iliad*, are products of an oral tradition. **2** (*German* vɔlf). **Hugo** (ˈhuːɡo). 1860–1903, Austrian composer, esp. of songs, including the *Italienisches Liederbuch* and the *Spanisches Liederbuch*. **3** (wʊlf). Howlin'. See **Howlin' Wolf.**

Wolf Cub *n Brit.* the former name for **Cub Scout.**

Wolfe ★ (wʊlf) *n* **1 James.** 1727–59, British soldier, who commanded the capture of Quebec, in which he was killed. **2 Thomas** (**Clayton**). 1900–38, US novelist, noted for his autobiographical fiction, esp. *Look Homeward, Angel* (1929).

wolffish (ˈwʊlf,fɪʃ) *n, pl* **wolffish** *or* **wolffishes.** a large northern deep-sea fish. It has large sharp teeth and no pelvic fins and is used as a food fish. Also called: **catfish.**

wolfhound (ˈwʊlf,haʊnd) *n* the largest breed of dog, used formerly to hunt wolves.

Wolfit ★ (ˈwʊlfɪt) *n* **Sir Donald.** 1902–68, British stage actor and manager.

wolfram (ˈwʊlfrəm) *n* another name for **tungsten.** [C18: from G, orig. ?from the proper name *Wolfram*, used pejoratively of tungsten because it was thought inferior to tin]

wolframite (ˈwʊlfrə,maɪt) *n* a black to reddish-brown mineral, a compound of tungsten, iron, and manganese: it is the chief ore of tungsten.

Wolfram von Eschenbach ★ (*German* ˈvɔlfram fɔn ˈeʃənbax) *n* died ?1220, German poet: author of the epic *Parzival*, incorporating the story of the Grail.

wolfsbane (ˈwʊlfs,beɪn) *or* **wolf's bane** *n* any of several poisonous N temperate plants of the ranunculaceous genus *Aconitum* having hoodlike flowers.

Wolfsburg ★ (*German* ˈvɔlfsbʊrk) *n* a city in N central Germany, in Lower Saxony: founded in 1938; motor-vehicle industry. Pop.: 126 965 (1995 est.).

wolf spider *n* a spider which chases its prey to catch it. Also called: **hunting spider.**

wolf whistle *n* **1** a whistle made by a man to express admiration of a woman's appearance. ◆ *vb* **wolf-whistle, wolf-whistles, wolf-whistling, wolf-whistled. 2** (when *intr*, sometimes foll. by *at*) to make such a whistle (at someone).

Wollongong ★ (ˈwʊlən,gɒŋ) *n* a city in E Australia, in E New South Wales on the Pacific: an early centre of dairy farming; now a coal-mining and heavy industrial centre. Pop.: 249 500 (1993).

Wollstonecraft ★ (ˈwʊlstən,krɑːft) *n* **Mary.** 1759–97, British writer, author of *A Vindication of the Rights of Woman* (1792); wife of William Godwin and mother of Mary Shelley.

Wolof (ˈwɒlɒf) *n* **1** (*pl* **Wolof** *or* **Wolofs**) a member of a Negroid people of W Africa living chiefly in Senegal. **2** the language of this people, belonging to the Niger-Congo family.

Wolsey ★ (ˈwʊlzɪ) *n* **Thomas.** ?1475–1530, English cardinal; archbishop of York (1514–30); lord chancellor (1515–29). He dominated Henry VIII's policies but failed to obtain papal consent to the annulment of the king's marriage: arrested for high treason (1530) but died before his trial.

Wolverhampton ★ (ˌwʊlvəˈhæmptən) *n* **1** a town in W central England, in the West Midlands: iron and steel foundries. Pop.: 257 943 (1991). **2** a unitary authority in W central England, in the West Midlands. Pop.: 245 100 (1994 est.). Area: 69 sq. km (27 sq. miles).

wolverine (ˈwʊlvə,riːn) *n* a large musteline mammal of northern forests of Eurasia and North America having dark very thick water-resistant fur. Also called: **glutton.** [C16 *wolvering*, from WOLF + -ING³ (later altered to -*ine*)]

wolves (wʊlvz) *n* the plural of **wolf.**

woman (ˈwʊmən) *n, pl* **women. 1** an adult female human being. **2** (*modifier*) female or feminine: *a woman politician*. **3** women collectively. **4** (usually preceded by *the*) feminine nature or feelings: *babies bring out the woman in him*. **5** a female servant or domestic help. **6** a man considered as having supposedly female characteristics, such as meekness. **7** *Inf.* a wife or girlfriend. **8 the little woman.** *Brit. inf., old-fashioned.* one's wife. **9 woman of the streets.** a prostitute. ◆ *vb* (*tr*) **10** *Obs.* to make effeminate. [OE *wīfmann, wimman*]
▶ **'womanless** *adj* ▶ **'woman-,like** *adj*

womanhood (ˈwʊmən,hʊd) *n* **1** the state or quality of being a woman or being womanly. **2** women collectively.

womanish (ˈwʊmənɪʃ) *adj* **1** having qualities regarded as unsuitable to a man. **2** of or suitable for a woman.
▶ **'womanishly** *adv* ▶ **'womanishness** *n*

womanize *or* **womanise** (ˈwʊmə,naɪz) *vb* **womanizes, womanizing, womanized** *or* **womanises, womanising, womanised. 1** (*intr*) (of a man) to indulge in casual affairs with women. **2** (*tr*) to make effeminate.
▶ **'woman,izer** *or* **'woman,iser** *n*

womankind (ˈwʊmən,kaɪnd) *n* the female members of the human race; women collectively.

womanly (ˈwʊmənlɪ) *adj* **1** possessing qualities, such as warmth, attractiveness, etc., generally regarded as typical of a woman. **2** of or belonging to a woman.

womb (wuːm) *n* **1** the nontechnical name for **uterus. 2** a hollow space enclosing something. **3** a place where something is conceived: *the Near East is the womb of western civilization*. **4** *Obs.* the belly. [OE *wamb*]
▶ **wombed** *adj* ▶ **'womb,like** *adj*

wombat (ˈwɒmbæt) *n* a burrowing herbivorous Australian marsupial having short limbs, a heavy body, and coarse dense fur. [C18: from Abor.]

women (ˈwɪmɪn) *n* the plural of **woman.**

womenfolk (ˈwɪmɪn,fəʊk) *pl n* **1** women collectively. **2** a group of women, esp. the female members of one's family.

Women's Institute *n* (in Britain and Commonwealth countries) a society for women interested in engaging in craft and cultural activities.

Women's Liberation *n* a movement directed towards the removal of attitudes and practices that preserve inequalities based upon the assumption that men are superior to women. Also called: **women's lib.**

Women's Movement *n* a grass-roots movement of women concerned with women's liberation. See **Women's Liberation.**

won (wʌn) *vb* the past tense and past participle of **win.**

wonder (ˈwʌndə) *n* **1** the feeling excited by something strange; a mixture of surprise, curiosity, and sometimes awe. **2** something that causes such a feeling, such as a miracle. **3** (*modifier*) exciting wonder by virtue of spectacular results achieved, feats performed, etc.: *a wonder drug*. **4 do** *or* **work wonders.** to achieve spectacularly fine results. **5 nine days' wonder.** a subject that arouses general surprise or public interest for a short time. **6 no wonder.** (*sentence connector*) (I am) not surprised at all (that): *no wonder he couldn't come*. **7 small wonder.** (*sentence connector*) (I am) hardly surprised (that): *small wonder he couldn't make it tonight*. ◆ *vb* (when *tr*, may take a clause as object) **8** (when *intr*, often foll. by *about*) to indulge in speculative inquiry: *I wondered about what she said*. **9** (when *intr*, often foll. by *at*) to be amazed (at something): *I wonder at your impudence*. [OE *wundor*]
▶ **'wonderer** *n*

Wonder ★ ('wʌndə) n **Stevie**. real name *Steveland Judkins Morris*. born 1950, US singer and songwriter. His recordings include *Up-Tight* (1966), *Songs in the Key of Life* (1976), and "I Just Called to Say I Love You" (1985).

wonderful ('wʌndəful) adj **1** exciting a feeling of wonder. **2** extremely fine; excellent.
▸ 'wonderfully adv

wonderland ('wʌndə,lænd) n **1** an imaginary land of marvels or wonders. **2** an actual place or scene of great or strange beauty or wonder.

wonderment ('wʌndəmənt) n **1** rapt surprise; awe. **2** puzzled interest. **3** something that excites wonder.

wonderwork ('wʌndə,wɜːk) n something done or made that excites wonder.
▸ 'wonder-,worker n ▸ 'wonder-,working n, adj

wondrous ('wʌndrəs) *Arch. or literary*. ◆ adj **1** exciting wonder; marvellous. ◆ adv **2** (intensifier): *wondrous cold*.
▸ 'wondrously adv ▸ 'wondrousness n

wonky ('wɒŋkɪ) adj **wonkier, wonkiest**. *Brit. sl*. **1** unsteady. **2** askew. **3** liable to break down. [C20: var. of dialect *wanky*, from OE *wancol*]

Wŏnsan ★ ('wɒn'sæn) n a port in SE North Korea, on the Sea of Japan: oil refineries. Pop.: 274 000 (1987).

wont (wəunt) adj **1** (*postpositive*) accustomed (to doing something): *he was wont to come early*. ◆ n **2** a manner or action habitually employed by or associated with someone (often in **as is my wont, as is his wont**, etc.). ◆ vb **3** (when *tr*, *usually passive*) to become or cause to become accustomed. [OE *gewunod*, p.p. of *wunian* to be accustomed to]

won't (wəunt) *contraction of* will not.

wonted ('wəuntɪd) adj **1** (*postpositive*) accustomed (to doing something). **2** (*prenominal*) usual: *she is in her wonted place*.

woo (wuː) vb **woos, wooing, wooed**. **1** to seek the affection, favour, or love of (a woman) with a view to marriage. **2** (*tr*) to seek after zealously: *to woo fame*. **3** (*tr*) to beg or importune (someone). [OE *wōgian*, from ?]
▸ 'wooer n ▸ 'wooing n

wood (wud) n **1** the hard fibrous substance consisting of xylem tissue that occurs beneath the bark in trees, shrubs, and similar plants. **2** the trunks of trees that have been cut and prepared for use as a building material. **3** a collection of trees, shrubs, grasses, etc., usually dominated by one or a few species of tree: usually smaller than a forest: *an oak wood*. Related adj: **sylvan**. **4** fuel; firewood. **5** *Golf*. **5a** a long-shafted club with a wooden head, used for driving. **5b** (*as modifier*): *a wood shot*. **6** *Tennis, etc.* the frame of a racket: *he hit a winning shot off the wood*. **7** one of the biased wooden bowls used in the game of bowls. **8** *Music*. short for **woodwind**. **9 from the wood**. (of a beverage) from a wooden container rather than a metal or glass one. **10 out of the wood** *or* **woods**. clear of or safe from dangers or doubts: *we're not out of the wood yet*. **11 see the wood for the trees**. (*used with a negative*) to obtain a general view of a situation without allowing details to cloud one's analysis: *he can't see the wood for the trees*. **12** (*modifier*) made of, employing, or handling wood: *a wood fire*. **13** (*modifier*) dwelling in or situated in a wood: *a wood nymph*. ◆ vb **14** (*tr*) to plant a wood upon. **15** to supply or be supplied with firewood. ◆ See also **woods**. [OE *widu, wudu*]

Wood ★ (wud) n Sir **Henry (Joseph)**. 1869–1944, British conductor, who founded the Promenade Concerts in London.

wood alcohol n another name for **methanol**.

wood anemone n any of several woodland anemone plants having finely divided leaves and solitary white flowers. Also called: **windflower**.

wood avens n another name for **herb bennet**.

woodbine ('wuːd,baɪn) n **1** a honeysuckle of Europe, SW Asia, and N Africa, having fragrant yellow flowers. **2** *US*. another name for **Virginia creeper**. **3** *Austral. sl.* an Englishman.

wood block n a small rectangular flat block of wood that is laid with others as a floor surface.

woodcarving ('wud,kɑːvɪŋ) n **1** the act of carving wood. **2** a work of art produced by carving wood.
▸ 'wood,carver n

woodchuck ('wud,tʃʌk) n a North American marmot having coarse reddish-brown fur. Also called: **groundhog**. [C17: by folk etymology from Cree *otcheck* fisher]

woodcock ('wud,kɒk) n an Old World game bird resembling the snipe but larger and with shorter legs and neck.

woodcraft ('wud,krɑːft) n *Chiefly US & Canad*. **1** ability and experience in matters concerned with living in a forest. **2** ability or skill at woodwork, carving, etc.

woodcut ('wud,kʌt) n **1** a block of wood with a design, illustration, etc., from which prints are made. **2** a print from a woodcut.

woodcutter ('wud,kʌtə) n **1** a person who fells trees or chops wood. **2** a person who makes woodcuts.
▸ 'wood,cutting n

wooded ('wudɪd) adj **1** covered with or abounding in woods or trees. **2** (*in combination*) having wood of a specified character: *a soft-wooded tree*.

wooden ('wudᵊn) adj **1** made from or consisting of wood. **2** awkward or clumsy. **3** bereft of spirit or animation: *a wooden expression*. **4** obstinately unyielding: *a wooden attitude*. **5** mentally slow or dull. **6** not highly resonant: *a wooden thud*.
▸ 'woodenly adv

wood engraving n **1** the art of engraving pictures or designs on wood by incising them with a burin. **2** a block of wood so engraved or a print taken from it.
▸ **wood engraver** n

woodenhead ('wudᵊn,hed) n *Inf*. a dull, foolish, or unintelligent person.
▸ ,wooden'headed adj ▸ ,wooden'headedness n

Wooden Horse n another name for the **Trojan Horse** (sense 1).

wooden spoon n a booby prize, esp. in sporting contests.

woodgrouse ('wud,graus) n another name for **capercaillie**.

woodland ('wudlənd) n **a** land that is mostly covered with woods or dense growths of trees and shrubs. **b** (*as modifier*): *woodland fauna*.
▸ 'woodlander n

woodlark ('wud,lɑːk) n an Old World lark similar to but slightly smaller than the skylark.

woodlouse ('wud,laus) n, pl **woodlice** (-,laɪs). any of various small terrestrial isopod crustaceans having a flattened segmented body and occurring in damp habitats.

woodman ('wudmən) n, pl **woodmen**. **1** a person who looks after and fells trees used for timber. **2** another word for **woodsman**.

woodnote ('wud,nəut) n a natural musical note or song, like that of a wild bird.

wood nymph n one of a class of nymphs fabled to inhabit the woods, such as a dryad.

woodpecker ('wud,pekə) n a climbing bird, such as the **green woodpecker**, having a brightly coloured plumage and strong chisel-like bill with which it bores into trees for insects.

wood pigeon n a large Eurasian pigeon having white patches on the wings and neck. Also called: **ringdove, cushat**.

woodpile ('wud,paɪl) n a pile or heap of firewood.

wood preservative n a coating applied to timber as a protection against decay, insects, weather, etc.

wood pulp n **1** wood that has been ground to a fine pulp for use in making newsprint and other cheap forms of paper. **2** finely pulped wood that has been digested by a chemical, such as caustic soda: used in making paper.

woodruff ('wudrʌf) n any of several plants, esp. the sweet woodruff of Eurasia, which has small sweet-scented white flowers and whorls of narrow fragrant leaves used to flavour wine and liqueurs and in perfumery. [OE *wudurofe*, from WOOD + *rōfe*]

woods (wudz) pl n **1** closely packed trees forming a forest or wood, esp. a specific one. **2** another word for **back-**

★ people and places

woods (sense 2). **3** the woodwind instruments in an orchestra.

Woods[1] ★ *n* Lake of the. See **Lake of the Woods**.

Woods[2] ★ (wʊdz) *n* **Tiger**, real name *Eldrick Woods*. born 1975, US golfer.

woodscrew ('wʊd,skruː) *n* a metal screw that tapers to a point so that it can be driven into wood by a screwdriver.

woodshed ('wʊd,ʃɛd) *n* a small outbuilding where firewood, garden tools, etc., are stored.

woodsman ('wʊdzmən) *n, pl* **woodsmen**. a person who lives in a wood or who is skilled in woodcraft. Also called: **woodman**.

wood sorrel *n* a Eurasian plant having trifoliate leaves, an underground creeping stem, and white purple-veined flowers.

wood spirit *n* Chem. another name for **methanol**.

Woodstock ★ ('wʊdstɒk) *n* a town in New York State, the site of a large rock festival in August 1969. Pop.: 1870 (1990).

wood tar *n* any tar produced by the destructive distillation of wood.

wood warbler *n* **1** a European woodland warbler with a dull yellow plumage. **2** another name for the **American warbler**. See **warbler** (sense 3).

Woodward ★ ('wʊdwəd) *n* **R(obert) B(urns)**. 1917–79, US chemist. For his work on the synthesis of quinine, strychnine, cholesterol, and other organic compounds he won the Nobel prize for chemistry 1965.

woodwind ('wʊd,wɪnd) *Music.* ◆ *adj* **1** of or denoting a type of wind instrument, formerly made of wood but now often made of metal, such as the flute. ◆ *n* **2** (*functioning as pl*) woodwind instruments collectively.

woodwork ('wʊd,wɜːk) *n* **1** the art or craft of making things in wood. **2** components made of wood, such as doors, staircases, etc.

woodworking ('wʊd,wɜːkɪŋ) *n* **1** the process of working wood. ◆ *adj* **2** of, relating to, or used in woodworking.
▸ '**wood,worker** *n*

woodworm ('wʊd,wɜːm) *n* **1** any of various insect larvae that bore into wooden furniture, beams, etc., esp. the larvae of the furniture beetle and the deathwatch beetle. **2** the condition caused in wood by any of these larvae.

woody ('wʊdɪ) *adj* **woodier, woodiest**. **1** abounding in or covered with forest or woods. **2** connected with, belonging to, or situated in a wood. **3** consisting of or containing wood or lignin: *woody tissue; woody stems*. **4** resembling wood in hardness or texture.
▸ '**woodiness** *n*

woodyard ('wʊd,jɑːd) *n* a place where timber is cut and stored.

woody nightshade *n* a scrambling woody Eurasian plant, having purple flowers and producing poisonous red berry-like fruits. Also called: **bittersweet**.

woof[1] (wuːf) *n* **1** the crosswise yarns that fill the warp yarns in weaving; weft. **2** a woven fabric or its texture. [OE ōwef, from ō-, ?from ON, + wef web (see WEAVE); modern form infl. by WARP]

woof[2] (wuf) *interj* **1** an imitation of the bark or growl of a dog. ◆ *vb* **2** (*intr*) (of dogs) to bark.

woofer ('wuːfə) *n* a loudspeaker used in high-fidelity systems for the reproduction of low audio frequencies.

woofter ('wuftə, 'wuːf-) *n* Derog. sl. a male homosexual. [C20: altered from *poofter*; see POOF]

Wookey Hole ★ ('wʊkɪ həʊl) *n* a village in SW England, in Somerset, near Wells: noted for the nearby limestone cave in which prehistoric remains have been found. Pop.: 1000 (latest est.).

wool (wʊl) *n* **1** the outer coat of sheep, yaks, etc., which consists of short curly hairs. **2** yarn spun from the coat of sheep, etc., used in weaving, knitting, etc. **3a** cloth or a garment made from this yarn. **3b** (*as modifier*): *a wool dress*. **4** any of certain fibrous materials: *glass wool; steel wool*. **5** Inf. short thick curly hair. **6** a tangled mass of soft fine hairs that occurs in certain plants. **7** keep one's wool

on. *Brit. inf.* to keep one's temper. **8** pull the wool over someone's eyes. to deceive or delude someone.   [OE *wull*]
▸ '**wool-,like** *adj*

wool clip *n* Austral. & NZ. the total amount of wool shorn from a particular flock in one year.

Woolf ★ (wulf) *n* **1 Leonard Sidney**. 1880–1969, British publisher and political writer. **2** his wife, **Virginia**. 1882–1941, British novelist. Her novels include *Mrs. Dalloway* (1925), *To the Lighthouse* (1927), and *The Waves* (1931).

wool fat *or* **grease** *n* another name for **lanolin**.

woolfell ('wʊl,fɛl) *n* Obs. the skin of a sheep or similar animal with the fleece still attached.

woolgathering ('wʊl,gæðərɪŋ) *n* idle or absent-minded daydreaming.

woolgrower ('wʊl,grəʊə) *n* a person who keeps sheep for their wool.
▸ '**wool,growing** *n*

woolled (wʊld) *adj* **1** (of animals) having wool. **2** (*in combination*) having wool as specified: *coarse-woolled*.

woollen *or US* **woolen** ('wʊlən) *adj* **1** relating to or consisting partly or wholly of wool. ◆ *n* **2** (*often pl*) a garment or piece of cloth made wholly or partly of wool, esp. a knitted one.

Woolley ★ ('wʊlɪ) *n* Sir (**Charles**) **Leonard**. 1880–1960, British archaeologist, noted for his excavations at Ur in Mesopotamia (1922–34).

woolly *or US* (*sometimes*) **wooly** ('wʊlɪ) *adj* **woollier, woolliest** *or US* (*sometimes*) **woolier, wooliest**. **1** consisting of, resembling, or having the nature of wool. **2** covered or clothed in wool or something resembling it. **3** lacking clarity or substance: *woolly thinking*. **4** Bot. covered with long soft whitish hairs: *woolly stems*. ◆ *n, pl* **woollies** *or US* (*sometimes*) **woolies**. **5** (*often pl*) a garment, such as a sweater, made of wool or something similar.
▸ '**woollily** *adv* ▸ '**woolliness** *n*

woolly bear *n* the caterpillar of any of various tiger moths, having a dense covering of soft hairs.

woolpack ('wʊl,pæk) *n* **1** the cloth wrapping used to pack a bale of wool. **2** a bale of wool.

woolsack ('wʊl,sæk) *n* **1** a sack containing or intended to contain wool. **2** (in Britain) the seat of the Lord Chancellor in the House of Lords, formerly made of a large square sack of wool.

woolshed ('wʊl,ʃɛd) *n* Austral. & NZ. a large building in which sheepshearing takes place.

wool stapler *n* a person who sorts wool into different grades or classifications.

Woolworth ★ ('wʊlwəθ) *n* **Frank Winfield** ('wɪn,fiːld). 1852–1919, US merchant; founder of an international chain of department stores selling inexpensive goods.

woomera *or* **womera** ('wʊmərə) *n* Austral. a type of notched stick used by native Australians to increase leverage and propulsion in the throwing of a spear.   [from Abor.]

Woomera ★ ('wʊmərə) *n* a town in South Australia: site of the Long Range Weapons Establishment. Pop.: 1660 (latest est.).

Woop Woop ('wuːp ˌwuːp) *n* Austral. Sl. a jocular name for any backward or remote town or district.

Wootton ★ ('wʊtᵊn) *n* **Barbara** (**Frances**), Baroness of Abinger. 1897–1988, British economist and social scientist.

woozy ('wuːzɪ) *adj* **woozier, wooziest**. Inf. **1** dazed or confused. **2** experiencing dizziness, nausea, etc.   [C19: ? a blend of *woolly* + *muzzy* or *dizzy*]
▸ '**woozily** *adv* ▸ '**wooziness** *n*

wop (wɒp) *n Sl., derog.* a member of a Latin people, esp. an Italian.   [C20: prob. from It. dialect *guappo* dandy, from Sp. *guapo*]

Worcester ★ ('wʊstə) *n* **1** a cathedral city in W central England, the administrative centre of Hereford and Worcester on the River Severn: scene of the battle (1651) in which Charles II was defeated by Cromwell. Pop.: 82 661 (1991). **2** an industrial city in central Massachusetts: Clark University (1887). Pop.: 165 387 (1994 est.). **3** a town in S South Africa. Pop.: 60 324 (1990).

★ people and places

Worcester sauce *or* **Worcestershire sauce** *n* a commercially prepared piquant sauce, made from a basis of soy sauce, with vinegar, spices, etc.

Worcestershire ★ ('wʊstə,ʃɪə, -ʃə) *n* a former county of W central England, since 1974 part of Hereford and Worcester.

Worcs *abbrev. for* Worcestershire.

word (wɜːd) *n* **1** one of the units of speech or writing that is the smallest isolable meaningful element of the language, although linguists would analyse these further into morphemes. **2** an instance of vocal intercourse; chat, talk, or discussion: *to have a word with someone.* **3** an utterance or expression, esp. a brief one: *a word of greeting.* **4** news or information: *he sent word that he would be late.* **5** a verbal signal for action; command: *when I give the word, fire!* **6** an undertaking or promise: *he kept his word.* **7** an autocratic decree; order: *his word must be obeyed.* **8** a watchword or slogan, as of a political party: *the word now is "freedom".* **9** *Computing.* a set of bits used to store, transmit, or operate upon an item of information in a computer. **10 as good as one's word.** doing what one has undertaken to do. **11 at a word.** at once. **12 by word of mouth.** orally rather than by written means. **13 in a word.** briefly or in short. **14 my word! 14a** an exclamation of surprise, annoyance, etc. **14b** *Austral.* an exclamation of agreement. **15 of one's word.** given to or noted for keeping one's promises: *I am a man of my word.* **16 put in a word** *or* **good word for.** to make favourable mention of (someone); recommend. **17 take someone at his** *or* **her word.** to assume that someone means, or will do, what he or she says: *when he told her to go, she took him at his word and left.* **18 take someone's word for it.** to accept or believe what someone says. **19 the last word. 19a** the closing remark of a conversation or argument, esp. a remark that supposedly settles an issue. **19b** the latest or most fashionable design, make, or model: *the last word in bikinis.* **19c** the finest example (of some quality, condition, etc.): *the last word in luxury.* **20 the word.** the proper or most fitting expression: *cold is not the word for it, it's freezing!* **21 upon my word! 21a** *Arch.* on my honour. **21b** an exclamation of surprise, annoyance, etc. **22 word for word.** (of a report, etc.) using exactly the same words as those employed in the situation being reported; verbatim. **23 word of honour.** a promise; oath. **24** (*modifier*) of, relating to, or consisting of words. ◆ *vb* **25** (*tr*) to state in words, usually specially selected ones; phrase. ◆ See also **words.** [OE]
▸ **'wordless** *adj* ▸ **'wordlessly** *adv*

Word (wɜːd) *n* **the. 1** *Christianity.* the 2nd person of the Trinity. **2** Scripture, the Bible, or the Gospels as embodying or representing divine revelation. Often called: **the Word of God.** [translation of Gk *logos*, as in John 1:1]

-word *n combining form.* (preceded by *the* and an initial letter) a euphemistic way of referring to a word by its first letter because it is considered unmentionable by the user: *the C-word* (meaning cancer).

wordage ('wɜːdɪdʒ) *n* words considered collectively, esp. a quantity of words.

word association *n* an early method of psychoanalysis in which the patient thinks of the first word that comes into consciousness on hearing a given word. In this way it was claimed that aspects of the unconscious could be revealed before defence mechanisms intervene.

word blindness *n* the nontechnical name for **alexia** and **dyslexia.**
▸ **'word-,blind** *adj*

wordbook ('wɜːd,bʊk) *n* a book containing words, usually with their meanings.

word deafness *n* loss of ability to understand spoken words, esp. as the result of a cerebral lesion. Also called: **auditory aphasia.**

word game *n* any game involving the formation, discovery, or alteration of a word or words.

wording ('wɜːdɪŋ) *n* **1** the way in which words are used to express a statement, report, etc., esp. a written one. **2** the words themselves.

word order *n* the arrangement of words in a phrase, clause, or sentence.

word-perfect *or US* **letter-perfect** *adj* **1** correct in every detail. **2** (of a speaker, actor, etc.) knowing one's speech, role, etc., perfectly.

wordplay ('wɜːd,pleɪ) *n* verbal wit based on the meanings of words; puns, repartee, etc.

word processing *n* the composition of documents using a computer system to input, edit, store, and print.

word processor *n* **a** a computer program that performs word processing. **b** a computer system designed for word processing.

words (wɜːdz) *pl n* **1** the text of a part of an actor, etc. **2** the text of a song, as opposed to the music. **3** angry speech (esp. in **have words with someone**). **4 eat** *or* **swallow one's words.** to retract a statement. **5 for words.** (preceded by *too* and an adj *or* adv) indescribably; extremely: *the play was too funny for words.* **6 have no words for.** to be incapable of describing. **7 in other words.** expressing the same idea but differently. **8 in so many words.** explicitly or precisely. **9 of many** (*or* few) **words.** (not) talkative. **10 put into words.** to express in speech or writing. **11 say a few words.** to give a brief speech. **12 take the words out of someone's mouth.** to say exactly what someone else was about to say. **13 words fail me.** I am too happy, sad, amazed, etc., to express my thoughts.

word square *n* a puzzle in which the player must fill a square grid with words that read the same across as down.

Wordsworth ★ ('wɜːdz,wəθ) *n* **1 Dorothy.** 1771–1855, British writer, whose *Journals* are noted for their descriptions of nature. **2** her brother, **William.** 1770–1850, British Lake poet. His works include *Lyrical Ballads* (1798, 1800), to which Coleridge contributed, and the autobiographical poem *The Prelude* (completed in 1805; revised thereafter and published posthumously).
▸ **Wordsworthian** (,wɜːdz'wɜːðɪən) *adj, n*

word wrapping *n Computing.* the automatic shifting of a word at the end of a line to a new line in order to keep within preset margins.

wordy ('wɜːdɪ) *adj* **wordier, wordiest.** using or containing an excess of words: *a wordy document.*
▸ **'wordily** *adv* ▸ **'wordiness** *n*

wore (wɔː) *vb* the past tense of **wear**[1] and **wear**[2].

work (wɜːk) *n* **1** physical or mental effort directed towards doing or making something. **2** paid employment at a job or a trade, occupation, or profession. **3** a duty, task, or undertaking. **4** something done, made, etc., as a result of effort or exertion: *a work of art.* **5** another word for **workmanship** (sense 3). **6** the place, office, etc., where a person is employed. **7a** decoration, esp. of a specified kind. **7b** (*in combination*): *wirework.* **8** an engineering structure such as a bridge, building, etc. **9** *Physics.* the transfer of energy expressed as the product of a force and the distance through which its point of application moves in the direction of the force. **10** a structure, wall, etc., built or used as part of a fortification system. **11 at work. 11a** at one's job or place of employment. **11b** in action; operating. **12 make short work of.** *Inf.* to dispose of very quickly. **13** (*modifier*) of, relating to, or used for work: *work clothes; a work permit; a work song.* ◆ *vb* **14** (*intr*) to exert effort in order to do, make, or perform something. **15** (*intr*) to be employed. **16** (*tr*) to carry on operations, activity, etc., in (a place or area): *that salesman works Yorkshire.* **17** (*tr*) to cause to labour or toil: *he works his men hard.* **18** to operate or cause to operate, esp. properly or effectively: *to work a lathe; that clock doesn't work.* **19** (*tr*) to till or cultivate (land). **20** to handle or manipulate or be handled or manipulated: *to work dough.* **21** to shape or process or be shaped or processed: *to work copper.* **22** to reach or cause to reach a specific condition, esp. gradually: *the rope worked loose.* **23** (*intr*) to move in agitation: *his face worked with anger.* **24** (*tr;* often foll. by *up*) to provoke or arouse: *to work someone into a frenzy.* **25** (*tr*) to effect or accomplish: *to work one's revenge.* **26** to make (one's way) with effort: *he worked his way through the crowd.* **27** (*tr*) to make or decorate by hand in embroidery, tapestry, etc.: *she was working a sampler.* **28** (*intr*) (of liquids) to ferment, as in brewing. **29** (*tr*) *Inf.* to manipulate or exploit to one's own advantage. ◆ See also **work in, work off,** etc., **works.** [OE *weorc* (n), *wircan, wyrcan* (vb)]
▸ **'workless** *adj*

workable ('wɜːkəb°l) *adj* **1** practicable or feasible. **2** able to be worked.
▶ ,worka'bility *or* 'workableness *n*

workaday ('wɜːkə,deɪ) *adj* (*usually prenominal*) **1** being a part of general human experience; ordinary. **2** suitable for working days; everyday or practical.

workaholic (,wɜːkə'hɒlɪk) *n* **a** a person obsessively addicted to work. **b** (*as modifier*): *workaholic behaviour*. [C20: from WORK + -HOLIC, coined in 1971 by US author Wayne Oates]

workbag ('wɜːk,bæg) *n* a container for implements, tools, or materials, esp. sewing equipment. Also called: **work basket, workbox.**

workbench ('wɜːk,bentʃ) *n* a heavy table at which work is done by a carpenter, mechanic, toolmaker, etc.

workbook ('wɜːk,bʊk) *n* **1** an exercise book used for study, esp. with spaces for answers. **2** a book of instructions for some process. **3** a book in which is recorded all work done or planned.

work camp *n* a camp set up for young people who voluntarily do manual work on a worthwhile project.

workday ('wɜːk,deɪ) *n* **1** the usual US and Canad. term for **working day.** ◆ *adj* **2** another word for **workaday.**

worked (wɜːkt) *adj* made or decorated with evidence of workmanship; wrought, as with embroidery or tracery.

worked up *adj* excited or agitated.

worker ('wɜːkə) *n* **1** a person or thing that works, usually at a specific job: *a research worker.* **2** an employee, as opposed to an employer or manager. **3** a manual labourer working in a manufacturing industry. **4** any other member of the working class. **5** a sterile female member of a colony of bees, ants, or wasps that forages for food, cares for the larvae, etc.

worker director *n* (in certain British companies) an employee of a company chosen by his or her fellow workers to represent their interests on the board of directors. Also called: **employee director.**

worker-priest *n* a Roman Catholic priest who has employment in a secular job to be more in touch with the problems of the laity.

work ethic *n* a belief in the moral value of work.

workfare ('wɜːk,feə) *n* a scheme under which the government of a country requires unemployed people to do community work or undergo job training in return for social-security payments. [C20: from WORK + (WEL)FARE]

workforce ('wɜːk,fɔːs) *n* **1** the total number of workers employed by a company on a specific job, project, etc. **2** the total number of people who could be employed: *the country's workforce is growing.*

work function *n Physics.* the minimum energy required to transfer an electron from a point within a solid to a point just outside its surface. Symbol: ϕ or Φ

work-harden *vb* (*tr*) to increase the strength or hardness of (a metal) by a mechanical process, such as tension, compression, or torsion.

workhorse ('wɜːk,hɔːs) *n* **1** a horse used for nonrecreational activities. **2** *Inf.* a person who takes on the greatest amount of work in a project.

workhouse ('wɜːk,haʊs) *n* **1** (formerly in England) an institution maintained at public expense where able-bodied paupers did unpaid work in return for food and accommodation. **2** (in the US) a prison for petty offenders serving short sentences at manual labour.

work in *vb* (*adv*) **1** to insert or become inserted: *she worked the patch in carefully.* **2** (*tr*) to find space for: *I'll work this job in during the day.* ◆ *n* **work-in. 3** a form of industrial action in which a factory that is to be closed down is occupied and run by its workers.

working ('wɜːkɪŋ) *n* **1** the operation or mode of operation of something. **2** the act or process of moulding something pliable. **3** a convulsive or jerking motion, as from excitement. **4** (*often pl*) a part of a mine or quarry that is being or has been worked. **5** a record of the steps by which the solution of a problem, calculation, etc., is obtained: *all working is to be submitted to the examiners.* ◆ *adj* (*prenominal*) **6** relating to or concerned with a person or thing that works: *a working man.* **7** concerned

with, used in, or suitable for work: *working clothes.* **8** (of a meal or occasion) during which business discussions are carried on: *a working lunch.* **9** capable of being operated or used: *a working model; in working order.* **10** adequate for normal purposes: *a working majority; a working knowledge of German.* **11** (of a theory, etc.) providing a basis, usually a temporary one, on which operations or procedures may be carried out.

working bee *n NZ.* a voluntary group doing a job for charity.

working capital *n* **1** *Accounting.* current assets minus current liabilities. **2** current or liquid assets. **3** that part of the capital of a business enterprise available for operations.

working class *n* **1** Also called: **proletariat.** the social stratum, usually of low status, that consists of those who earn wages, esp. as manual workers. ◆ *adj* **working-class. 2** of, relating to, or characteristic of the working class.

working day *or esp. US & Canad.* **workday** *n* **1** a day on which work is done, esp. for an agreed or stipulated number of hours in return for a salary or wage. **2** the part of the day allocated to work. **3** (*often pl*) *Commerce.* any day of the week except Sunday, public holidays, and, in some cases, Saturday.

working drawing *n* a scale drawing of a part that provides a guide for manufacture.

working memory *n Psychol.* the current contents of consciousness.

working party *n* **1** a committee established to investigate a problem, question, etc. **2** a group of soldiers or prisoners assigned to perform a manual task or duty.

working week *or esp. US & Canad.* **workweek** *n* the number of hours or days in a week allocated to work.

work-in-progress *n Book-keeping.* the value of work begun but not completed, as shown in a profit-and-loss account.

workload ('wɜːk,ləʊd) *n* the amount of work to be done, esp. in a specified period.

workman ('wɜːkmən) *n, pl* **workmen. 1** a man who is employed in manual labour or who works an industrial machine. **2** a craftsman of skill as specified: *a bad workman.*

workmanlike ('wɜːkmən,laɪk) *or* (*less commonly*) **workmanly** *adj* appropriate to or befitting a good workman.

workmanship ('wɜːkmənʃɪp) *n* **1** the art or skill of a workman. **2** the art or skill with which something is made or executed. **3** the degree of art or skill exhibited in the finished product. **4** the piece of work so produced.

workmate ('wɜːk,meɪt) *n* a person who works with another; fellow worker.

work of art *n* **1** a piece of fine art, such as a painting or sculpture. **2** something that may be likened to a piece of fine art, esp. in beauty, intricacy, etc.

work off *vb* (*tr, adv*) **1** to get rid of or dissipate, as by effort: *he worked off some of his energy by digging the garden.* **2** to discharge (a debt) by labour rather than payment.

work on *vb* (*intr, prep*) to persuade or influence or attempt to persuade or influence.

work out *vb* (*adv*) **1** (*tr*) to achieve or accomplish by effort. **2** (*tr*) to solve or find out by reasoning or calculation: *to work out an answer; to work out a sum.* **3** (*tr*) to devise or formulate: *to work out a plan.* **4** (*intr*) to prove satisfactory: *did your plan work out?* **5** (*intr*) to happen as specified: *it all worked out well.* **6** (*intr*) to take part in physical exercise, as in training. **7** (*tr*) to remove all the mineral in (a mine, etc.) that can be profitably exploited. **8** (*intr; often foll. by to or at*) to reach a total: *your bill works out at a pound.* ◆ *n* **workout. 9** a session of physical exercise, esp. for training or to keep oneself fit.

work over *vb* **1** (*tr, adv*) to do again; repeat. **2** (*intr, prep*) to examine closely and thoroughly. **3** (*tr, adv*) *Sl.* to assault or thrash.

workpeople ('wɜːk,piːp°l) *pl n* the working members of a population.

workroom ('wɜːk,ruːm, -,rʊm) *n* **1** a room in which

work, usually manual labour, is done. **2** a room in a house set aside for a hobby.

works (wɜːks) *pl n* **1** (*often functioning as sing*) a place where a number of people are employed, such as a factory. **2** the sum total of a writer's or artist's achievements, esp. when considered together: *the works of Shakespeare*. **3** the deeds of a person, esp. virtuous or moral deeds: *works of charity*. **4** the interior parts of the mechanism of a machine, etc.: *the works of a clock*. **5 the works.** *Sl.* **5a** full or extreme treatment. **5b** a very violent physical beating: *to give someone the works*.

works council *n Chiefly Brit.* **1** a council composed of both employer and employees convened to discuss matters of common interest concerning a factory, plant, business policy, etc. **2** a body representing the workers of a plant, factory, etc., elected to negotiate with the management about working conditions, wages, etc. ♦ Also called: **works committee**.

worksheet ('wɜːkˌʃiːt) *n* **1** a sheet of paper used for the rough draft of a problem, design, etc. **2** a piece of paper recording work in progress.

workshop ('wɜːkˌʃɒp) *n* **1** a room or building in which manufacturing or other forms of manual work are carried on. **2** a room in a private dwelling, school, etc., set aside for crafts. **3** a group of people engaged in study or work on a creative project or subject: *a music workshop*.

workshy ('wɜːkˌʃaɪ) *adj* not inclined to work.

Worksop ★ ('wɜːksɒp) *n* a town in N central England, in N Nottinghamshire. Pop.: 37 247 (1991).

work station *n* an area in an office where one person works.

work-study *n* an examination of ways of finding the most efficient method of doing a job.

worktable ('wɜːkˌteɪbªl) *n* **a** any table at which writing, sewing, or other work may be done. **b** (in English cabinetwork) a small elegant table fitted with sewing accessories.

worktop ('wɜːkˌtɒp) *n* a surface in a kitchen, often of heat-resistant plastic, used for food preparation.

work-to-rule *n* **1** a form of industrial action in which employees adhere strictly to all the working rules laid down by their employers, with the deliberate intention of reducing the rate of working. ♦ *vb* **work to rule. 2** (*intr*) to decrease the rate of working by this means.

work up *vb* **1** (*tr, adv*) to arouse the feelings of; excite. **2** (*tr, adv*) to cause to grow or develop: *to work up a hunger*. **3** to move or cause to move gradually upwards. **4** (*tr, adv*) to manipulate or mix into a specified object or shape. **5** (*tr, adv*) to gain skill at (a subject). **6** (*adv*) (foll. by *to*) to develop gradually or progress (towards): *working up to a climax*.

world (wɜːld) *n* **1** the earth as a planet, esp. including its inhabitants. **2** mankind; the human race. **3** people generally; the public: *in the eyes of the world*. **4** social or public life: *to go out into the world*. **5** the universe or cosmos; everything in existence. **6** a complex united whole regarded as resembling the universe. **7** any star or planet, esp. one that might be inhabited. **8** (*often cap.*) a division or section of the earth, its history, or its inhabitants: *the Ancient World; the Third World*. **9** an area, sphere, or realm considered as a complete environment: *the animal world*. **10** any field of human activity or way of life or those involved in it: *the world of television*. **11** a period or state of existence: *the next world*. **12** the total circumstances and experience of an individual that make up his life: *you have shattered my world*. **13** a large amount, number, or distance: *worlds apart*. **14** worldly or secular life, ways, or people. **15 bring into the world. 15a** (of a midwife, doctor, etc.) to deliver (a baby). **15b** to give birth to. **16 come into the world.** to be born. **17 for all the world.** in every way; exactly. **18 for the world.** (*used with a negative*) for any inducement, however great. **19 in the world.** (intensifier; *usually used with a negative*): *no-one in the world can change things.* **20 man** (*or* **woman**) **of the world.** a man (*or* woman) experienced in social or public life. **21 not long for this world.** nearing death. **22 on top of the world.** *Inf.* elated or very happy. **23 out of this world.** *Inf.* wonderful; excellent. **24 set**

the world on fire. to be exceptionally or sensationally successful. **25 the best of both worlds.** the benefits from two different ways of life, philosophies, etc. **26 think the world of.** to be extremely fond of or hold in very high esteem. **27 world of one's own.** a state of mental detachment from other people. **28 world without end.** forever. **29** (*modifier*) of or concerning most or all countries; worldwide: *world politics*. **30** (*in combination*) throughout the world: *world-famous*. [OE w(e)orold, from *wer* man + *ald* age, life]

World Bank *n* an international cooperative organization established in 1945 to assist economic development, esp. of backward nations, by the advance of loans guaranteed by member governments. Officially called: **International Bank for Reconstruction and Development.**

world-beater *n* a person or thing that surpasses all others in its category; champion.

world-class *adj* of or denoting someone with a skill or attribute that puts him or her in the highest class in the world: *a world-class swimmer*.

World Court *n* another name for **International Court of Justice.**

World Cup *n* an international competition held between national teams in various sports, most notably association football.

worldling ('wɜːldlɪŋ) *n* a person who is primarily concerned with worldly matters.

worldly ('wɜːldlɪ) *adj* **worldlier, worldliest. 1** not spiritual; mundane or temporal. **2** Also: **worldly-minded.** absorbed in material things. **3** Also: **worldly-wise.** versed in the ways of the world; sophisticated.
▸ **'worldliness** *n*

world music *n* popular music of various ethnic origins and styles.

world power *n* a state that possesses sufficient power to influence events throughout the world.

world-shaking *adj* of enormous significance.

World Trade Organization *n* an international body concerned with promoting and regulating trade between its member states; established in 1995 as a successor to GATT.

World War I *n* the war (1914–18), fought mainly in Europe and the Middle East, in which the Allies (principally France, Russia, Britain, Italy after 1915, and the US after 1917) defeated the Central Powers (principally Germany, Austria-Hungary, and Turkey). Also called: **First World War, Great War.**

World War II *n* the war (1939–45) in which the Allies (principally Britain, the Soviet Union, and the US) defeated the Axis powers (principally Germany, Italy, and Japan). Britain and France declared war on Germany (Sept. 3, 1939) as a result of the German invasion of Poland (Sept. 1, 1939). Italy entered the war on June 10, 1940 shortly before the collapse of France (armistice signed June 22, 1940). On June 22, 1941 Germany attacked the Soviet Union and on Dec. 7, 1941 the Japanese attacked the US at Pearl Harbor. On Sept. 8, 1943 Italy surrendered, the war in Europe ending on May 7, 1945 with the unconditional surrender of the Germans. The Japanese capitulated on Aug. 14, 1945. Also called: **Second World War.**

world-weary *adj* no longer finding pleasure in living.
▸ **'world-ˌweariness** *n*

worldwide ('wɜːldˈwaɪd) *adj* applying or extending throughout the world; universal.

World Wide Web *n Computing.* a vast network of linked hypertext files, stored on computers throughout the world, that can provide a computer user with information on a huge variety of subjects. Abbrev.: **WWW.**

worm (wɜːm) *n* **1** any of various invertebrates, esp. the annelids (earthworms, etc.), nematodes (roundworms), and flatworms, having a slender elongated body. **2** any of various insect larvae having an elongated body, such as the silkworm and wireworm. **3** any of various unrelated animals that resemble annelids, nematodes, etc., such as the glow-worm and shipworm. **4** a gnawing or insinuating force or agent that torments or slowly eats away. **5** a wretched or spineless person.

★ people and places

6 anything that resembles a worm in appearance or movement. **7** a shaft on which a helical groove has been cut, as in a gear arrangement in which such a shaft meshes with a toothed wheel. **8** a spiral pipe cooled by air or flowing water, used as a condenser in a still. **9** *Computing.* a program that duplicates itself many times in a network and prevents its destruction. It often carries a logic bomb or virus. ◆ *vb* **10** to move, act, or cause to move or act with the slow sinuous movement of a worm. **11** (foll. by *in, into, out of,* etc.) to make (one's way) slowly and stealthily; insinuate (oneself). **12** (*tr*; often foll. by *out of* or *from*) to extract (information, etc.) by persistent questioning. **13** (*tr*) to free from worms. ◆ See also **worms.** [OE *wyrm*]
▸ 'wormer *n* ▸ 'worm,like *adj*

WORM ('wɜːm) *n Computing.* acronym for write once read many times: an optical disk which enables users to store data but not change it.

wormcast ('wɜːm,kɑːst) *n* a coil of earth or sand that has been excreted by a burrowing earthworm or lugworm.

worm-eaten *adj* **1** eaten into by worms: *a worm-eaten table.* **2** decayed; rotten. **3** old-fashioned; antiquated.

worm gear *n* **1** a device consisting of a threaded shaft (**worm**) that mates with a gear-wheel (**worm wheel**) so that rotary motion can be transferred between two shafts at right angles to each other. **2** Also called: **worm wheel.** a gear-wheel driven by a threaded shaft or worm.

wormhole ('wɜːm,həul) *n* a hole made by a worm in timber, plants, etc.
▸ 'worm,holed *adj*

worms (wɜːmz) *n* (*functioning as sing*) any disease or disorder, usually of the intestine, characterized by infestation with parasitic worms.

Worms ★ (wɜːmz; *German* vɔrms) *n* a city in SW Germany, in Rhineland-Palatinate on the Rhine: famous as the seat of imperial diets, notably that of 1521, before which Luther defended his doctrines in the presence of Charles V; river port and manufacturing centre with a large wine trade. Pop.: 77 430 (1991).

worm's eye view *n* a view seen from below or from a more lowly or humble point.

wormwood ('wɜːm,wud) *n* **1** Also called: **absinthe.** any of various plants of a chiefly N temperate genus, esp. a European plant yielding a bitter extract used in making absinthe. **2** something that embitters, such as a painful experience. [C15: changed (through infl. of WORM & WOOD) from OE *wormōd, wermōd*]

wormy ('wɜːmɪ) *adj* **wormier, wormiest. 1** worm-infested or worm-eaten. **2** resembling a worm in appearance, ways, or condition. **3** (of wood) having irregular small tunnels bored into it and tracked over its surface, made by worms. **4** low or grovelling.
▸ 'worminess *n*

worn (wɔːn) *vb* **1** the past participle of **wear¹** and **wear².** ◆ *adj* **2** affected, esp. adversely, by long use or action: *a worn suit.* **3** haggard; drawn. **4** exhausted; spent.
▸ 'wornness *n*

worn-out *adj* (**worn out** *when postpositive*). **1** worn or used until threadbare, valueless, or useless. **2** exhausted; very weary.

worriment ('wʌrɪmənt) *n Inf., chiefly US.* anxiety or the trouble that causes it; worry.

worrisome ('wʌrɪsəm) *adj* **1** causing worry; vexing. **2** tending to worry.
▸ 'worrisomely *adv*

worrit ('wʌrɪt) *vb* (*tr*) *Dialect.* to tease or worry. [prob. var. of WORRY]

worry ('wʌrɪ) *vb* **worries, worrying, worried. 1** to be or cause to be anxious or uneasy, esp. about something uncertain or potentially dangerous. **2** (*tr*) to disturb the peace of mind of; bother: *don't worry me with trivialities.* **3** (*intr*; often foll. by *along* or *through*) to proceed despite difficulties. **4** (*intr*; often foll. by *away*) to struggle or work: *to worry away at a problem.* **5** (*tr*) (of a dog, wolf, etc.) to lacerate or kill by biting, shaking, etc. **6** (when *intr*, foll. by *at*) to bite, tear, or gnaw (at) with the teeth: *a dog worrying a bone.* **7** (*tr*) to touch or poke repeatedly and idly. **8 not to**

worry. *Inf.* you need not worry. ◆ *n, pl* **worries. 9** a state or feeling of anxiety. **10** a person or thing that causes anxiety. **11** an act of worrying. [OE *wyrgan*]
▸ 'worried *adj* ▸ 'worriedly *adv* ▸ 'worrying *adj* ▸ 'worryingly *adv*

worry beads *pl n* a string of beads that when fingered or played with supposedly relieves nervous tension.

worryguts ('wʌrɪ,gʌts) *n* (*functioning as sing*) *Inf.* a person who worries, esp. about insignificant matters.

worse (wɜːs) *adj* **1** the comparative of **bad¹. 2** none the **worse for.** not harmed by (adverse events or circumstances). **3 the worse for wear.** shabby or worn. **3b** a slang term for **drunk. 4 worse luck!** *Inf.* unhappily; unfortunately. **5 worse off.** (*postpositive*) in a worse, esp. a worse financial, condition. ◆ *n* **6** something that is worse. **7 for the worse.** into a less desirable or inferior state or condition: *a change for the worse.* ◆ *adv* **8** in a more severe or unpleasant manner. **9** in a less effective or successful manner. [OE *wiersa*]

worsen ('wɜːs³n) *vb* to grow or cause to grow worse.

worship ('wɜːʃɪp) *vb* **worships, worshipping, worshipped** *or US* **worships, worshiping, worshiped. 1** (*tr*) to show profound religious devotion and respect to; adore or venerate (God or any person or thing considered divine). **2** (*tr*) to be devoted to and full of admiration for. **3** (*intr*) to have or express feelings of profound adoration. **4** (*intr*) to attend services for worship. ◆ *n* **5** religious adoration or devotion. **6** the formal expression of religious adoration; rites, prayers, etc. **7** admiring love or devotion. [OE *weorthscipe*]
▸ 'worshipper *n*

Worship ('wɜːʃɪp) *n Chiefly Brit.* (preceded by *Your, His,* or *Her*) a title used to address or refer to a mayor, magistrate, etc.

worshipful ('wɜːʃɪpful) *adj* **1** feeling or showing reverence or adoration. **2** (*often cap.*) *Chiefly Brit.* a title used to address or refer to various people or bodies of distinguished rank.
▸ 'worshipfully *adv* ▸ 'worshipfulness *n*

worst (wɜːst) *adj* **1** the superlative of **bad¹.** ◆ *adv* **2** in the most extreme or bad manner or degree. **3** least well, suitably, or acceptably. **4** (*in combination*) in or to the smallest degree or extent; least: *worst-loved.* ◆ *n* **5 the worst.** the least good or most inferior person, thing, or part in a group, narrative, etc. **6** (often preceded by *at*) the most poor, unpleasant, or unskilled quality or condition: *television is at its worst these days.* **7** the greatest amount of damage or wickedness of which a person or group is capable: *the invaders came and did their worst.* **8** the weakest effort or poorest achievement that a person or group is capable of making: *the applicant did his worst at the test because he did not want the job.* **9 at worst. 9a** in the least favourable interpretation or view. **9b** under the least favourable conditions. **10 come off worst** *or* **get the worst of it.** to enjoy the least benefit from an issue or be defeated in it. **11 if the worst comes to the worst.** if all the more desirable alternatives become impossible or if the worst possible thing happens. ◆ *vb* **12** (*tr*) to get the advantage over; defeat or beat. [OE *wierrest*]

worsted ('wustɪd) *n* **1** a closely twisted yarn or thread made from combed long-staple wool. **2** a fabric made from this, with a hard smooth close-textured surface and no nap. **3** (*modifier*) made of this yarn or fabric: *a worsted suit.* [C13: after *Worstead,* a district in Norfolk]

wort (wɜːt) *n* **1** (*in combination*) any of various unrelated plants, esp. ones formerly used to cure diseases: *liverwort.* **2** the sweet liquid made from warm water and ground malt, used to make a malt liquor. [OE *wyrt* root]

worth (wɜːθ) *adj* (governing a noun with prepositional force) **1** worthy of; meriting or justifying: *it's not worth discussing.* **2** having a value of: *the book is worth £30.* **3 for all one is worth.** to the utmost. **4 worth one's weight in gold.** extremely helpful, kind, etc. ◆ *n* **5** high quality; excellence. **6** value; price. **7** the amount of something of a specified value: *five pounds' worth of petrol.* [OE *weorth*]

Worthing ★ ('wɜːðɪŋ) *n* a resort in S England, in West Sussex on the English Channel. Pop.: 95 732 (1991).

worthless ('wɜːθlɪs) *adj* **1** without value or usefulness. **2** without merit; good-for-nothing.
▶ 'worthlessly *adv* ▶ 'worthlessness *n*

worthwhile (ˌwɜːθ'waɪl) *adj* sufficiently important, rewarding, or valuable to justify time or effort spent.

worthy ('wɜːðɪ) *adj* **worthier, worthiest. 1** (*postpositive; often foll. by of* or an infinitive) having sufficient merit or value (for something or someone specified); deserving. **2** having worth, value, or merit. ◆ *n, pl* **worthies. 3** *Often facetious.* a person of merit or importance.
▶ 'worthily *adv* ▶ 'worthiness *n*

wot (wɒt) *vb Arch. or dialect.* (used with *I, she, he, it,* or a singular noun) a form of the present tense (indicative mood) of **wit**[2].

Wotan ★ ('vəʊtɑːn, 'vɔː-) *n* the supreme god in Germanic mythology. Norse counterpart: **Odin**.

would (wʊd; *unstressed* wəd) *vb* (takes an infinitive without *to* or an implied infinitive) used as an auxiliary: **1** to form the past tense or subjunctive mood of **will**[1]. **2** (with *you, he, she, it, they,* or a noun as subject) to indicate willingness or desire in a polite manner: *would you help me, please?* **3** to describe a past action as being accustomed or habitual: *every day we would go for walks.* **4** I wish: *would that he were here.*

USAGE NOTE See at **should**.

would-be *adj* (*prenominal*) **1** *Usually derog.* wanting or professing to be: *a would-be politician.* **2** intended to be.

wouldn't ('wʊd°nt) *contraction of* would not.

wouldst (wʊdst) *vb Arch. or dialect.* (used with the pronoun *thou* or its relative equivalent) a singular form of the past tense of **will**[1].

Woulfe bottle (wʊlf) *n Chem.* a bottle with more than one neck, used for passing gases through liquids. [C18: after Peter *Woulfe* (?1727–1803), Brit. chemist]

wound[1] (wuːnd) *n* **1** any break in the skin or an organ or part as the result of violence or a surgical incision. **2** any injury or slight to the feelings or reputation. ◆ *vb* **3** to inflict a wound or wounds upon (someone or something). [OE *wund*]
▶ 'wounding *adj* ▶ 'woundingly *adv*

wound[2] (waʊnd) *vb* the past tense and past participle of **wind**[2] and **wind**[3].

wounded ('wuːndɪd) *adj* **1a** suffering from wounds; injured, esp. in a battle or fight. **1b** (*as collective n*; preceded by *the*): *the wounded.* **2** (of feelings) damaged or hurt.

woundwort ('wuːndˌwɜːt) *n* **1** any of various plants, such as field woundwort, having purple, scarlet, yellow, or white flowers and formerly used for dressing wounds. **2** any of various other plants used in this way.

wove (wəʊv) *vb* a past tense of **weave**.

woven ('wəʊv°n) *vb* a past participle of **weave**.

wove paper *n* paper with a very faint mesh impressed on it by the paper-making machine.

wow[1] (waʊ) *interj* **1** an exclamation of admiration, amazement, etc. ◆ *n* **2** *Sl.* a person or thing that is amazingly successful, attractive, etc. ◆ *vb* **3** (*tr*) *Sl.* to arouse great enthusiasm in. [C16: orig. Scot.]

wow[2] (waʊ, wəʊ) *n* a slow variation or distortion in pitch that occurs at very low audio frequencies in sound-reproducing systems. See also **flutter** (sense 12). [C20: imit.]

wowser ('waʊzə) *n Austral. & NZ sl.* **1** a fanatically puritanical person. **2** a teetotaller. [C20: from E dialect *wow* to complain]

wp *abbrev. for* word processor.

wpb *abbrev. for* wastepaper basket.

WPC (in Britain) *abbrev. for* woman police constable.

wpm *abbrev. for* words per minute.

WRAAC *abbrev. for* Women's Royal Australian Army Corps.

WRAAF *abbrev. for* Women's Royal Australian Air Force.

WRAC (in Britain) *abbrev. for* Women's Royal Army Corps.

wrack[1] *or* **rack** (ræk) *n* **1** collapse or destruction (esp. in **wrack and ruin**). **2** something destroyed or a remnant of such. [OE *wræc* persecution, misery]

USAGE NOTE The use of the spelling *wrack* rather than *rack* in sentences such as *she was wracked by grief* or *the country was wracked by civil war* is very common but is thought by many people to be incorrect.

wrack[2] (ræk) *n* **1** seaweed or other marine vegetation that is floating in the sea or has been cast ashore. **2** any of various seaweeds, such as serrated wrack. [C14 (in the sense: a wrecked ship): from MDu. *wrak* wreckage; the term corresponds to OE *wræc* WRACK[1]]

WRAF (in Britain) *abbrev. for* Women's Royal Air Force.

wraith (reɪθ) *n* **1** the apparition of a person living or thought to be alive, supposed to appear around the time of his death. **2** any apparition. [C16: Scot., from ?]
▶ 'wraith,like *adj*

Wran (ræn) *n* a member of the Women's Royal Australian Naval Service.

Wrangel Island ★ ('ræŋg°l) *n* an island in the Arctic Ocean, off the coast of NE Russia: administratively part of Russia; mountainous and mostly tundra. Area: about 7300 sq. km (2800 sq. miles).

Wrangell ★ ('ræŋg°l) *n Mount.* a mountain in S Alaska, in the W Wrangell Mountains. Height: 4269 m (14 005 ft).

Wrangell Mountains ★ *pl n* a mountain range in SE Alaska, extending into the Yukon, Canada. Highest peak: Mount Blackburn, 5037 m (16 523 ft).

wrangle ('ræŋg°l) *vb* **wrangles, wrangling, wrangled. 1** (*intr*) to argue, esp. noisily or angrily. **2** (*tr*) to encourage, persuade, or obtain by argument. **3** (*tr*) *Western US & Canad.* to herd (cattle or horses). ◆ *n* **4** a noisy or angry argument. [C14: from Low G *wrangeln*]

wrangler ('ræŋglə) *n* **1** one who wrangles. **2** *Western US & Canad.* a herder; cowboy. **3** a person who handles or controls animals involved in the making of a film or television programme. **4** *Brit.* (at Cambridge University) a candidate who has obtained first-class honours in part II of the mathematics tripos. Formerly, the wrangler with the highest marks was called the **senior wrangler**.

WRANS *abbrev. for* Women's Royal Australian Naval Service. See also **Wran**.

wrap (ræp) *vb* **wraps, wrapping, wrapped.** (*mainly tr*) **1** to fold or wind (paper, cloth, etc.) around (a person or thing) so as to cover. **2** (often foll. by *up*) to fold paper, etc., around to fasten securely. **3** to surround or conceal by surrounding. **4** to enclose, immerse, or absorb: *wrapped in joy.* **5** to fold, wind, or roll up. **6** to complete the filming of (a motion picture or television programme). **7** (*intr;* often foll. by *about, around,* etc.) to be or become wound or extended. **8** (often foll. by *up*) Also: **rap.** *Austral. inf.* to praise (someone). ◆ *n* **9** a garment worn wrapped around the body, esp. the shoulders, such as a shawl or cloak. **10a** the end of a working day during the filming of a motion picture or television programme. **10b** the completion of filming of a motion picture or television programme. **11** *Chiefly US.* wrapping or a wrapper. **12 keep under wraps.** to keep secret. **13 take the wraps off.** to reveal. **14** Also: **rap.** *Austral. inf.* a commendation. [C14: from ?]

wrapover ('ræpˌəʊvə) *or* **wrapround** *adj* **1** (of a garment, esp. a skirt) not sewn up at one side, but worn wrapped round the body and fastened so that the open edges overlap. ◆ *n* **2** such a garment.

wrapped (ræpt) *vb* **1** the past tense and past participle of **wrap. 2 wrapped up in.** *Inf.* **2a** completely absorbed or engrossed in. **2b** implicated or involved in. ◆ *adj* **3** *Austral. inf.* a variant spelling of **rapt**[2].

wrapper ('ræpə) *n* **1** the cover, usually of paper or cellophane, in which something is wrapped. **2** a dust jacket of a book. **3** the firm tobacco leaf forming the outermost portion of a cigar. **4** a loose negligee or dressing gown.

★ people and places

wrapping ('ræpɪŋ) *n* the material used to wrap something.

wraparound ('ræp,raʊnd) *or* **wraparound** *adj* **1** made so as to be wrapped round something: *a wraparound skirt.* **2** surrounding, curving round, or overlapping. **3** curving round in one continuous piece: *a wraparound windscreen.* ◆ *n* **4** *Printing.* a flexible plate of plastic, metal, or rubber that is made flat but used wrapped round the plate cylinder of a rotary press. **5** another name for **wrapover.**

wrap up *vb* (*adv*) **1** (*tr*) to fold paper around. **2** to put warm clothes on. **3** (*intr; usually imperative*) *Sl.* to be silent. **4** (*tr*) *Inf.* **4a** to settle the final details of. **4b** to make a summary of.

wrasse (ræs) *n* a marine food fish of tropical and temperate seas, having thick lips, strong teeth, and usually a bright coloration. [C17: from Cornish *wrach*]

wrath (rɒθ) *n* **1** angry, violent, or stern indignation. **2** divine vengeance or retribution. **3** *Arch.* a fit of anger or an act resulting from anger. [OE *wrǣththu*]

Wrath ★ (rɒθ, rɔːθ) *n* **Cape.** a promontory at the NW extremity of the Scottish mainland.

wrathful ('rɒθfʊl) *adj* **1** full of wrath; raging or furious. **2** resulting from or expressing wrath.
▶ '**wrathfully** *adv* ▶ '**wrathfulness** *n*

wreak (riːk) *vb* (*tr*) **1** to inflict (vengeance, etc.) or to cause (chaos, etc.): *to wreak havoc on the enemy.* **2** to express or gratify (anger, hatred, etc.). **3** *Arch.* to take vengeance for. [OE *wrecan*]
▶ '**wreaker** *n*

USAGE NOTE   See at **wrought.**

---

wreath (riːθ) *n, pl* **wreaths** (riːðz, riːθs). **1** a band of flowers or foliage intertwined into a ring, usually placed on a grave as a memorial or worn on the head as a garland or a mark of honour. **2** any circular or spiral band or formation. **3** (*loosely*) any floral design placed on a grave as a memorial. [OE *wrǣth, wrǣd*]
▶ '**wreath.like** *adj*

wreathe (riːð) *vb* **wreathes, wreathing, wreathed. 1** to form into or take the form of a wreath by intertwining or twisting together. **2** (*tr*) to decorate with wreaths. **3** to move or cause to move in a twisting way: *smoke wreathed up to the ceiling.* [C16: ? back formation from *wrēthen,* from OE *writhen,* p.p. of *writhan* to writhe]

wreck (rɛk) *vb* **1** to involve in or suffer disaster or destruction. **2** (*tr*) to cause the wreck of (a ship). ◆ *n* **3a** the accidental destruction of a ship at sea. **3b** the ship so destroyed. **4** *Maritime law.* goods cast ashore from a wrecked vessel. **5** a person or thing that has suffered ruin or dilapidation. **6** Also called: **wreckage.** the remains of something that has been destroyed. **7** Also called: **wreckage.** the act of wrecking or the state of being wrecked. [C13: from ON]
▶ '**wrecking** *n, adj*

wrecked (rɛkt) *adj Sl.* in a state of intoxication, stupor, or euphoria, induced by drugs or alcohol.

wrecker ('rɛkə) *n* **1** a person or thing that ruins or destroys. **2** *Chiefly US & Canad.* a person whose job is to demolish buildings or dismantle cars. **3** (*formerly*) a person who lures ships to destruction to plunder the wreckage. **4** a US and Canad. name for a breakdown van.

wrecking bar *n* a short crowbar, forked at one end and slightly angled at the other to make a fulcrum.

Wrekin ★ ('riːkɪn) *n* **the.** an isolated hill in the English Midlands in Shropshire. Height: 400 m (1335 ft).

wren (rɛn) *n* **1** any small brown passerine songbird of a chiefly American family (in Britain **wren,** in the US and Canada **winter wren**). They have a slender bill and feed on insects. **2** any of various similar birds, such as the Australian warblers, New Zealand wrens, etc. [OE *wrenna, werna*]

Wren[1] (rɛn) *n Inf.* (in Britain and certain other nations) a member of the Women's Royal Naval Service. [C20: from the abbrev. *WRNS*]

Wren[2] ★ (rɛn) *n* Sir **Christopher.** 1632–1723, English architect. He designed St Paul's Cathedral and over 50 other London churches after the Great Fire.

wrench (rɛntʃ) *vb* **1** to give (something) a sudden or violent twist or pull, esp. so as to remove (something) from that to which it is attached: *to wrench a door off its hinges.* **2** (*tr*) to twist suddenly so as to sprain (a limb). **3** (*tr*) to give pain to. **4** (*tr*) to twist from the original meaning or purpose. **5** (*intr*) to make a sudden twisting motion. ◆ *n* **6** a forceful twist or pull. **7** an injury to a limb, caused by twisting. **8** sudden pain caused esp. by parting. **9** a parting that is difficult or painful to make. **10** a distorting of the original meaning or purpose. **11** a spanner, esp. one with adjustable jaws. See also **torque wrench.** [OE *wrencan*]

wrest (rɛst) *vb* (*tr*) **1** to take or force away by violent pulling or twisting. **2** to seize forcibly by violent or unlawful means. **3** to obtain by laborious effort. **4** to distort in meaning, purpose, etc. ◆ *n* **5** the act or an instance of wresting. **6** *Arch.* a small key to tune a piano or harp. [OE *wrǣstan*]
▶ '**wrester** *n*

wrestle ('rɛsˀl) *vb* **wrestles, wrestling, wrestled. 1** to fight (another person) by holding, throwing, etc., without punching with the closed fist. **2** (*intr*) to participate in wrestling. **3** (when *intr,* foll. by *with* or *against*) to fight with (a person, problem, or thing): *wrestle with one's conscience.* **4** (*tr*) to move laboriously, as with wrestling movements. ◆ *n* **5** the act of wrestling. **6** a struggle or tussle. [OE *wrǣstlian*]
▶ '**wrestler** *n*

wrestling ('rɛslɪŋ) *n* any of certain sports in which the contestants fight each other according to various rules governing holds and usually forbidding blows with the closed fist. The principal object is to overcome the opponent either by throwing or pinning him to the ground or by causing him to submit.

wrest pin *n* (on a piano, harp, etc.) a pin, embedded in the **wrest plank,** around which one end of a string is wound: it may be turned by means of a tuning key to alter the tension of the string.

wretch (rɛtʃ) *n* **1** a despicable person. **2** a person pitied for his misfortune. [OE *wrecca*]

wretched ('rɛtʃɪd) *adj* **1** in poor or pitiful circumstances. **2** characterized by or causing misery. **3** despicable; base. **4** poor, inferior, or paltry. **5** (*prenominal*) (intensifier qualifying something undesirable): *a wretched nuisance.*
▶ '**wretchedly** *adv* ▶ '**wretchedness** *n*

Wrexham ★ ('rɛksəm) *n* **1** a town in N Wales: seat of the Roman Catholic bishopric of Wales (except Glamorganshire); formerly noted for coal-mining. Pop.: 40 614 (1991). **2** a county borough in NE Wales, formed in 1996. Pop.: 123 400 (1996 est.). Area: 500 sq. km (193 sq. miles).

wrick (rɪk) *n* **1** a sprain or strain. ◆ *vb* **2** (*tr*) to sprain or strain.

wrier *or* **wryer** ('raɪə) *adj* the comparative of **wry.**

wriest *or* **wryest** ('raɪɪst) *adj* the superlative of **wry.**

wriggle ('rɪgˀl) *vb* **wriggles, wriggling, wriggled. 1** to make or cause to make twisting movements. **2** (*intr*) to progress by twisting and turning. **3** (*intr; foll. by into* or *out of*) to manoeuvre oneself by clever or devious means: *wriggle out of an embarrassing situation.* ◆ *n* **4** a wriggling movement or action. **5** a sinuous marking or course. [C15: from MLow G]
▶ '**wriggler** *n* ▶ '**wriggly** *adj*

wright (raɪt) *n* (*now chiefly in combination*) a person who creates, builds, or repairs something specified: *a playwright; a shipwright.* [OE *wryhta, wyrhta*]

Wright ★ (raɪt) *n* **1 Frank Lloyd.** 1869–1959, US architect, whose designs include the Guggenheim Museum, New York (1943). **2 Joseph,** known as *Wright of Derby.* 1734–97, British painter. **3 Joseph.** 1855–1930, British philologist; editor of *The English Dialect Dictionary* (1898–1905). **4 Judith (Arundel).** born 1915, Australian poet and conservationist. **5 Wilbur** (1867–1912) and his brother, **Orville** (1871–1948), US aviation pioneers, who designed and flew the first powered aircraft (1903).

wring (rɪŋ) *vb* **wrings, wringing, wrung. 1** (*often foll. by out*) to twist and compress to squeeze (a liquid) from (cloth,

---

★ people and places

etc.). **2** (*tr*) to twist forcibly: *wring its neck.* **3** (*tr*) to clasp and twist (one's hands), esp. in anguish. **4** (*tr*) to distress: *wring one's heart.* **5** (*tr*) to grip (someone's hand) vigorously in greeting. **6** (*tr*) to obtain as by forceful means: *wring information out of.* **7 wringing wet.** soaking; drenched. ◆ *n* **8** an act or the process of wringing. [OE *wringan*]

wringer ('rɪŋə) *n* another name for **mangle**² (sense 1).

wrinkle¹ ('rɪŋkᵊl) *n* **1** a slight ridge in the smoothness of a surface, such as a crease in the skin as a result of age. ◆ *vb* **wrinkles, wrinkling, wrinkled. 2** to make or become wrinkled, as by crumpling, creasing, or puckering. [C15: back formation from *wrinkled*, from OE *gewrinclod*, p.p. of *wrinclian* to wind around] ▷ **'wrinkly** *adj*

wrinkle² ('rɪŋkᵊl) *n Inf.* a clever or useful trick, hint, or dodge. [OE *wrenc* trick]

wrinklies ('rɪŋklɪz) *pl n Inf., derog.* old people.

wrist (rɪst) *n* **1** *Anat.* the joint between the forearm and the hand. Technical name: **carpus. 2** the part of a sleeve or glove that covers the wrist. **3** *Machinery.* **3a** See **wrist pin. 3b** a joint in which a wrist pin forms the pivot. [OE]

wristband ('rɪst,bænd) *n* **1** a band around the wrist, esp. one attached to a watch or forming part of a long sleeve. **2** a sweatband around the wrist.

wristlet ('rɪstlɪt) *n* a band or bracelet worn around the wrist.

wrist pin *n* **1** a cylindrical boss or pin attached to the side of a wheel parallel with the axis, esp. one forming a bearing for a crank. **2** the US and Canad. name for **gudgeon pin.**

wristwatch ('rɪst,wɒtʃ) *n* a watch worn strapped around the wrist.

wristy ('rɪstɪ) *adj* (of a player's style of hitting the ball in cricket, tennis, etc.) with much movement of the wrist.

writ (rɪt) *n* **1** a document under seal, issued in the name of the Crown or a court, commanding the person to whom it is addressed to do or refrain from doing some specified act. **2** *Arch.* a piece of writing: *Holy Writ.* [OE]

write (raɪt) *vb* **writes, writing, wrote, written. 1** to draw or mark (symbols, words, etc.) on a surface, usually paper, with a pen, pencil, or other instrument. **2** to describe or record (ideas, experiences, etc.) in writing. **3** to compose (a letter) or correspond regularly with (a person, organization, etc.). **4** (*tr; may take a clause as object*) to say or communicate by letter: *he wrote that he was on his way.* **5** (*tr*) *Inf., chiefly US & Canad.* to send a letter to (a person, etc.). **6** to write (words) in cursive as opposed to printed style. **7** (*tr*) to be sufficiently familiar with (a specified style, language, etc.) to use it in writing. **8** to be the author or composer of (books, music, etc.). **9** (*tr*) to fill in the details for (a document, form, etc.). **10** (*tr*) to draw up or draft. **11** (*tr*) to produce by writing: *he wrote ten pages.* **12** (*tr*) to show clearly: *envy was written all over his face.* **13** (*tr*) to spell or inscribe. **14** (*tr*) to ordain or prophesy: *it is written.* **15** (*intr*) to produce writing as specified. **16** *Computing.* to record (data) in a location in a storage device. **17** (*tr*) See **underwrite** (sense 3a). ◆ See also **write down, write in,** etc. [OE *wrītan* (orig.: to scratch runes into bark)] ▷ **'writable** *adj*

write down *vb* (*adv*) **1** (*tr*) to set down in writing. **2** (*tr*) to harm or belittle by writing about (a person) in derogatory terms. **3** (*intr; foll. by to or for*) to write in a simplified way to a supposedly less cultured readership. **4** (*tr*) *Accounting.* to decrease the book value of (an asset). ◆ *n* **write-down. 5** *Accounting.* a reduction made in the book value of an asset.

write in *vb* (*tr*) **1** to insert in (a document, form, etc.) in writing. **2** (*adv*) to write a letter to a company, institution, etc. **3** (*adv*) *US.* to vote for (a person not on a ballot) by inserting his name.

write off *vb* (*tr, adv*) **1** *Accounting.* **1a** to cancel (a bad debt or obsolete asset) from the accounts. **1b** to consider (a transaction, etc.) as a loss or set off (a loss) against revenues. **1c** to depreciate (an asset) by periodic charges. **1d** to charge (a specified amount) against gross profits as depreciation of an asset. **2** to cause or acknowledge the complete loss of. **3** to dismiss from consideration. **4** to send a written order (for something): *she wrote off for a brochure.* **5** *Inf.* to damage (something, esp. a car) beyond

repair. ◆ *n* **write-off. 6** *Accounting.* **6a** the act of cancelling a bad debt or obsolete asset from the accounts. **6b** the bad debt or obsolete asset cancelled. **6c** the amount cancelled against gross profits, corresponding to the book value of the bad debt or obsolete asset. **7** *Inf.* something damaged beyond repair, esp. a car.

write out *vb* (*tr, adv*) **1** to put into writing or reproduce in full form in writing. **2** to exhaust (oneself or one's creativity) by excessive writing. **3** to remove (a character) from a television or radio series.

writer ('raɪtə) *n* **1** a person who writes books, articles, etc., esp. as an occupation. **2** the person who has written something specified. **3** a person who is able to write or write well. **4** a scribe or clerk. **5** a composer of music. **6 Writer to the Signet.** (in Scotland) a member of an ancient society of solicitors, now having the exclusive privilege of preparing crown writs.

writer's cramp *n* a muscular spasm or temporary paralysis of the muscles of the thumb and first two fingers caused by prolonged writing.

write up *vb* (*tr, adv*) **1** to describe fully, complete, or bring up to date in writing: *write up a diary.* **2** to praise or bring to public notice in writing. **3** *Accounting.* **3a** to place an excessively high value on (an asset). **3b** to increase the book value of (an asset) in order to reflect more accurately its current worth in the market. ◆ *n* **write-up. 4** a published account of something, such as a review in a newspaper or magazine.

writhe (raɪð) *vb* **writhes, writhing, writhed. 1** to twist or squirm in or as if in pain. **2** (*intr*) to move with such motions. **3** (*intr*) to suffer acutely from embarrassment, revulsion, etc. ◆ *n* **4** the act of writhing. [OE *wrīthan*] ▷ **'writher** *n*

writing ('raɪtɪŋ) *n* **1** a group of letters or symbols written or marked on a surface as a means of communicating. **2** short for **handwriting. 3** anything expressed in letters, esp. a literary composition. **4** the work of a writer. **5** literary style, art, or practice. **6** written form: *give it to me in writing.* **7** (*modifier*) related to or used in writing: *writing ink.* **8 writing on the wall.** a sign or signs of approaching disaster. [sense 8: allusion to Daniel 5:5]

writing desk *n* a piece of furniture with a writing surface and drawers and compartments for papers, etc.

writing paper *n* paper sized to take writing ink and used for letters and other manuscripts.

writ of execution *n Law.* a writ ordering that a judgment be enforced.

written ('rɪtᵊn) *vb* **1** the past participle of **write.** ◆ *adj* **2** taken down in writing; transcribed: *written evidence.*

WRNS *abbrev. for* Women's Royal Naval Service. See also **Wren.**

Wrocław ★ (*Polish* 'vrɔtswaf) *n* an industrial city in SW Poland, on the River Oder: passed to Austria (1527) and to Prussia (1741); returned to Poland in 1945. Pop.: 642 900 (1995 est.). German name: **Breslau.**

wrong (rɒŋ) *adj* **1** not correct or truthful: *the wrong answer.* **2** acting or judging in error: *you are wrong to think that.* **3** (*postpositive*) immoral; bad: *it is wrong to cheat.* **4** deviating from or unacceptable to correct or conventional laws, usage, etc. **5** not intended or wanted: *the wrong road.* **6** (*postpositive*) not working properly; amiss: *something is wrong with the engine.* **7** (of a side, esp. of a fabric) intended to face the inside so as not to be seen. **8 get on the wrong side of.** *Inf.* to come into disfavour with. **9 go down the wrong way.** (of food) to pass into the windpipe instead of the gullet. ◆ *adv* **10** in the wrong direction or manner. **11 get wrong. 11a** to fail to understand properly. **11b** to fail to provide the correct answer to. **12 go wrong. 12a** to turn out other than intended. **12b** to make a mistake. **12c** (of a machine, etc.) to cease to function properly. **12d** to go astray morally. ◆ *n* **13** a bad, immoral, or unjust thing or action. **14** *Law.* **14a** an infringement of another person's rights, rendering the offender liable to a civil action: *a private wrong.* **14b** a violation of public rights and duties, affecting the community as a whole and actionable at the instance of the Crown: *a public wrong.* **15 in the wrong.** mistaken or guilty. ◆ *vb* (*tr*) **16** to

---

★ people and places

treat unjustly. **17** to malign or misrepresent. [OE *wrang* injustice]
▶ 'wronger *n* ▶ 'wrongly *adv* ▶ 'wrongness *n*

wrongdoer ('rɒŋ,duːə) *n* a person who acts immorally or illegally.
▶ 'wrong,doing *n*

wrong-foot *vb* (*tr*) **1** *Tennis, etc.* to play a shot in such a way as to cause (one's opponent) to be off balance. **2** to take by surprise so as to place in an embarrassing or disadvantageous situation.

wrongful ('rɒŋful) *adj* unjust or illegal.
▶ 'wrongfully *adv* ▶ 'wrongfulness *n*

wrong-headed *adj* **1** constantly wrong in judgment. **2** foolishly stubborn; obstinate.
▶ ,wrong-'headedly *adv* ▶ ,wrong-'headedness *n*

wrong number *n* a telephone number wrongly connected or dialled in error, or the person so contacted.

wrote (rəʊt) *vb* the past tense of **write**.

wroth (rəʊθ, rɒθ) *adj Arch. or literary.* angry; irate. [OE *wrāth*]

wrought (rɔːt) *vb* **1** *Arch.* a past tense and past participle of **work**. ◆ *adj* **2** *Metallurgy.* shaped by hammering or beating. **3** (*often in combination*) formed, fashioned, or worked as specified: *well-wrought.* **4** decorated or made with delicate care. [C16: var. of *worht*, from OE *geworht*, p.p. of (*ge*)*wyrcan* to work]

> **USAGE NOTE** *Wrought* is sometimes used as if it were the past tense and past participle of *wreak* as in *the hurricane wrought havoc in coastal areas.* Many people think this use is incorrect.

wrought iron *n* **a** a pure form of iron having a low carbon content: often used for decorative work. **b** (*as modifier*): *wrought-iron gates.*

wrought-up *adj* agitated or excited.

wrung (rʌŋ) *vb* the past tense and past participle of **wring**.

WRVS *abbrev. for* Women's Royal Voluntary Service.

wry (raɪ) *adj* wrier, wriest *or* wryer, wryest. **1** twisted, contorted, or askew. **2** (of a facial expression) produced or characterized by contorting of the features. **3** drily humorous; sardonic. **4** warped, misdirected, or perverse. ◆ *vb* wries, wrying, wried. **5** (*tr*) to twist or contort. [C16: from dialect *wry* to twist, from OE *wrīgian* to turn]
▶ 'wryly *adv* ▶ 'wryness *n*

wrybill ('raɪ,bɪl) *n* a New Zealand plover, having its bill deflected to one side enabling it to search for food beneath stones.

wryneck ('raɪ,nɛk) *n* **1** either of two cryptically coloured Old World woodpeckers, which do not drum on trees. **2** another name for **torticollis**. **3** *Inf.* a person who has a twisted neck.

WSW *symbol for* west-southwest.

wt. *abbrev. for* weight.

WTO *abbrev. for* World Trade Organization.

Wuchang *or* **Wu-ch'ang** ★ ('wuː'tʃæŋ) *n* a former city of E central China: now a part of Wuhan.

Wuhan ★ ('wuː'hæn) *n* a city in SE China, in Hubei province, at the confluence of the Han and Yangtze Rivers: formed in 1950 by the union of the cities of Hanyang, Hankou, and Wuchang (the Han Cities); port and industrial centre; university (1913). Pop.: 3 750 000 (1990 est.).

Wuhsien ★ ('wuː'ʃjen) *n* another name for **Suzhou**.

Wuhu ★ ('wuː'huː) *n* a port in E China, in E Anhui province on the Yangtze River. Pop.: 425 740 (1990 est.).

Wu-lu-mu-ch'i ★ ('wuː'luː'muː'tʃiː) *n* a variant of **Urumchi**.

wunderkind ('wʌndə,kɪnd; *German* 'vʊndər,kɪnt) *n*, *pl* wunderkinds *or* wunderkinder (*German* -,kɪndər). **1** a child prodigy. **2** a person who is extremely successful in his field while still young. [C20: from G *Wunderkind*, lit.: wonder child]

Wuppertal ★ (*German* 'vʊpərtaːl) *n* a city in W Germany, in North Rhine-Westphalia state on the **Wupper River** (a Rhine tributary): formed in 1929 from the amalgamation of the towns of Barmen and Elberfeld and other smaller towns; textile centre. Pop.: 383 776 (1995 est.).

wurst (wɜːst, wʊəst, vʊəst) *n* a sausage, esp. of a type made in Germany, Austria, etc. [from G *Wurst*, lit.: something rolled]

Württemberg ★ ('vɜːtəm,bɜːg; *German* 'vyrtəmberk) *n* a historic region and former state of S Germany; now part of the German state of Baden-Württemberg.

Würzburg ★ ('vɜːts,bɜːg; *German* 'vyrtsbʊrk) *n* a city in S central Germany, in NW Bavaria on the River Main: university (1582). Pop.: 127 946 (1995 est.).

wuss (wʊs) *or* **wussy** ('wʊsɪ) *n*, *pl* wusses *or* wussies. *Sl.*, *chiefly US.* a feeble or effeminate person. [C20: ?from PUSSY[1] (cat)]

wuthering ('wʌðərɪŋ) *adj N English dialect.* **1** (of a wind) blowing strongly with a roaring sound. **2** (of a place) characterized by such a sound. [var. of *whitherin*, from *whither* blow, from ON *hvithra*]

Wutsin ★ ('wuː'tsɪn) *n* the former name (until 1949) of **Zhangzhou**.

Wuxi, Wusih, *or* **Wu-hsi** ★ ('wuː'ʃiː, -'siː) *n* a city in E China, in S Jiangsu province on the Grand Canal: textile industry. Pop.: 826 833 (1990 est.).

WV *abbrev. for* West Virginia.

W. Va. *abbrev. for* West Virginia.

WW1 *abbrev. for* World War One.

WW2 *abbrev. for* World War Two.

WWF *abbrev. for* Worldwide Fund for Nature.

WWW *abbrev. for* World Wide Web.

WY *or* **Wy.** *abbrev. for* Wyoming.

Wyatt ★ ('waɪət) *n* **1 James.** 1746–1813, British architect; a pioneer of the Gothic Revival. **2 Sir Thomas.** ?1503–42, English poet at the court of Henry VIII.

wych-elm *or* **witch-elm** ('wɪtʃ,elm) *n* **1** a Eurasian elm tree, having a rounded shape, longish pointed leaves, clusters of small flowers, and winged fruits. **2** the wood of this tree. [C17: from OE *wice*]

Wycherley ★ ('wɪtʃəlɪ) *n* **William.** ?1640–1716, English dramatist. His comedies include *The Country Wife* (1675) and *The Plain Dealer* (1676).

Wycliffe *or* **Wyclif** ★ ('wɪklɪf) *n* **John.** ?1330–84, English religious reformer. A precursor of the Reformation, he instigated the first translation of the Bible into English. His followers were called Lollards. Also: **Wiclif, Wickliffe.**
▶ 'Wycliffism *or* 'Wyclifism *n* ▶ 'Wyclif,fite *or* 'Wyclif,ite *n, adj*

Wye ★ (waɪ) *n* a river in E Wales and W England, rising in Powys and flowing southeast into England, then south to the Severn estuary. Length: 210 km (130 miles).

Wykeham ★ ('wɪkəm) *n* **William of.** 1324–1404, English prelate, who founded New College, Oxford, and Winchester College: chancellor of England (1367–71; 1389–91); bishop of Winchester (1367–1404).

wynd (waɪnd) *n Scot.* a narrow lane or alley. [C15: from the stem of WIND[2]]

Wyndham ★ ('wɪndəm) *n* **John,** pseudonym of *John Wyndham Parkes Lucas Beynon Harris.* 1903–69, British science-fiction writer. His works include *The Day of the Triffids* (1951) and *The Midwich Cuckoos* (1957).

Wyo. *abbrev. for* Wyoming.

Wyoming ★ (waɪ'əʊmɪŋ) *n* a state of the western US: consists largely of ranges of the Rockies in the west and north, with part of the Great Plains in the east and several regions of hot springs. Capital: Cheyenne. Pop.: 481 400 (1996 est.). Area: 253 597 sq. km (97 914 sq. miles). Abbrevs.: **Wyo., Wy.,** or (with zip code) **WY**
▶ Wy'oming,ite *n*

WYSIWYG ('wɪzɪ,wɪg) *n, adj Computing. acronym for* what you see is what you get: referring to what is displayed on the screen being the same as what will be printed out.

wyvern *or* **wivern** ('waɪvən) *n* a heraldic beast having a serpent's tail and a dragon's head and a body with wings and two legs. [C17: var. of earlier *wyver*, from OF, from L *vīpera* VIPER]

Xx

x *or* **X** (εks) *n, pl* **x's, X's,** *or* **Xs. 1** the 24th letter of the English alphabet. **2** a speech sound sequence represented by this letter, pronounced as *ks* or *gz* or, in initial position, *z,* as in *xylophone.*

x *symbol for:* **1** *Commerce, finance, etc. ex.* **2** *Maths.* the *x*-axis or a coordinate measured along the *x*-axis in a Cartesian coordinate system. **3** *Maths.* an algebraic variable. **4** multiplication.

X 1a (in Britain, formerly) indicating a film that may not be publicly shown to anyone under 18. Since 1982 replaced by symbol 18. **1b** (*as modifier*): *an X film.* **2** denoting any unknown, unspecified, or variable factor, number, person, or thing. **3** (on letters, cards, etc.) denoting a kiss. **4** (on ballot papers, etc.) indicating choice. **5** (on examination papers, etc.) indicating error. **6** for Christ; Christian. [from the Gk letter khi (X), first letter of *Khristos* Christ] ◆ **7** *the Roman numeral for* ten. See **Roman numerals.**

xanthein (ˈzænθɪɪn) *n* the soluble part of the yellow pigment that is found in the cell sap of some flowers.

xanthene (ˈzænθiːn) *n* a yellowish crystalline compound used as a fungicide.

xanthic (ˈzænθɪk) *adj* **1** of, containing, or derived from xanthic acid. **2** *Bot., rare.* having a yellow colour.

xanthic acid *n* any of a class of sulphur-containing acids.

xanthine (ˈzænθiːn, -θaɪn) *n* **1** a crystalline compound found in urine, blood, certain plants, and certain animal tissues. Formula: $C_5H_4N_4O_2$. **2** any of three substituted derivatives of xanthine, which act as stimulants and diuretics.

Xanthippe (zænˈθɪpɪ) *or* **Xantippe** ★ (zænˈtɪpɪ) *n* **1** the wife of Socrates, proverbial as scolding and quarrelsome. **2** any nagging, peevish, or irritable woman.

xantho- *or before a vowel* **xanth-** *combining form.* indicating yellow: *xanthophyll.* [from Gk *xanthos* yellow]

xanthochroism (zænˈθɒkrəʊˌɪzəm) *n* a condition in certain animals, esp. aquarium goldfish, in which all skin pigments other than yellow and orange disappear. [C19: from Gk *xanthokhro(os)* yellow-skinned + -ISM]

xanthoma (zænˈθəʊmə) *n Pathol.* the presence in the skin of fatty yellow or brownish plaques or nodules, esp. on the eyelids, caused by a disorder of lipid metabolism.

xanthophyll *or esp.* US **xanthophyl** (ˈzænθəʊfɪl) *n* any of a group of yellow carotenoid pigments occurring in plant and animal tissue.
  ▸ ˌxanthoˈphyllous *adj*

xanthous (ˈzænθəs) *adj* of, relating to, or designating races with yellowish hair and a light complexion.

Xanthus ★ (ˈzænθəs) *n* the chief city of ancient Lycia in SW Asia Minor: source of some important antiquities.
  ▸ ˈXanthian *adj*

Xavier ★ (ˈzeɪvɪə, ˈzæv-; *Spanish* xaˈβjer) *n* **Saint Francis,** known as the *Apostle of the Indies.* 1506–52, Spanish missionary, who was a founder of the Jesuit society (1534) and preached in Goa, Ceylon, the East Indies, and Japan. Feast day: Dec. 3.

x-axis *n* a reference axis, usually horizontal, of a graph or two- or three-dimensional Cartesian coordinate system along which the *x*-coordinate is measured.

X-chromosome *n* the sex chromosome that occurs in pairs in the diploid cells of the females of many animals, including humans, and as one of a pair with the Y-chromosome in those of males. Cf. **Y-chromosome.**

Xe *the chemical symbol for* xenon.

xebec, zebec, *or* **zebeck** (ˈziːbɛk) *n* a small three-masted Mediterranean vessel with both square and lateen sails, formerly used by Algerian pirates and later used for commerce. [C18: earlier *chebec* from F, ult. from

Ar. *shabbāk;* present spelling infl. by Catalan *xabec,* Sp. *xabeque* (now *jabeque*)]

Xenakis ★ (zɛˈnɑːkɪs; *Greek* ksɛˈnakis) *n* **Yannis** (ˈjanis). born 1922, Greek composer, born in Romania. He is noted for his musical use of computing.

xeno- *or before a vowel* **xen-** *combining form.* indicating something strange, different, or foreign: *xenogamy.* [from Gk *xenos* strange]

Xenocrates ★ (zɛˈnɒkrəˌtiːz) *n* ?396–314 B.C., Greek Platonic philosopher.
  ▸ **Xenocratic** (ˌzɛnəˈkrætɪk) *adj*

xenogamy (zɛˈnɒgəmɪ) *n Bot.* another name for **cross-fertilization.**
  ▸ xeˈnogamous *adj*

xenogeneic (ˌzɛnəʊdʒɪˈneɪɪk) *adj* Med. derived from an individual of a different species: *a xenogeneic tissue graft.*

xenoglossia (ˌzɛnəˈglɒsɪə) *n* an ability claimed by some mediums, clairvoyants, etc., to speak a language with which they are unfamiliar. [C20: from Gk, from XENO- + *glossa* language]

xenolith (ˈzɛnəlɪθ) *n* a fragment of rock differing in origin, composition, structure, etc., from the igneous rock enclosing it.
  ▸ ˌxenoˈlithic *adj*

xenon (ˈzɛnɒn) *n* a colourless odourless gaseous element occurring in trace amounts in air; formerly considered inert, it is now known to form compounds and is used in radio valves, stroboscopic and bactericidal lamps, and bubble chambers. Symbol: Xe; atomic no.: 54; atomic wt.: 131.30. [C19: from Gk: something strange]

Xenophanes ★ (zɛˈnɒfəˌniːz) *n* ?570–?480 B.C., Greek philosopher and poet.

xenophile (ˈzɛnəˌfaɪl) *n* a person who likes foreigners or things foreign. [C19: from Gk, from XENO- + -PHILE]

xenophobia (ˌzɛnəˈfəʊbɪə) *n* hatred or fear of foreigners or strangers or of their politics or culture. [C20: from Gk, from XENO- + -PHOBIA]
  ▸ ˈxenoˌphobe *n* ▸ ˌxenoˈphobic *adj*

Xenophon ★ (ˈzɛnəfən) *n* 431–?355 B.C., Greek general and historian; a disciple of Socrates. He accompanied Cyrus the Younger against Artaxerxes II and, after Cyrus' death (401), led his army to the Black Sea, as described in his *Anabasis.* His other works include *Hellenica,* a history of Greece, and the *Memorabilia, Apology,* and *Symposium,* which contain recollections of Socrates.

Xeres ★ (*Spanish* ˈxerɛθ) *n* the former name of **Jerez.**

xeric (ˈzɪərɪk) *adj Ecology.* of, relating to, or growing in dry conditions.
  ▸ ˈxerically *adv*

xero- *or before a vowel* **xer-** *combining form.* indicating dryness: *xeroderma.* [from Gk *xēros* dry]

xeroderma (ˌzɪərəʊˈdɜːmə) *or* **xerodermia** (ˌzɪərəʊˈdɜːmɪə) *n Pathol.* **1** any abnormal dryness of the skin as the result of diminished secretions from the sweat or sebaceous glands. **2** another name for **ichthyosis.**
  ▸ xeroˈdermatic (ˌzɪərəʊdəˈmætɪk) *or* ˌxeroˈdermatous *adj*

xerography (zɪˈrɒgrəfɪ) *n* a photocopying process in which an electrostatic image is formed on a selenium plate or cylinder. The plate or cylinder is dusted with a resinous powder, which adheres to the charged regions, and the image is then transferred to a sheet of paper on which it is fixed by heating.
  ▸ xeˈrographer *n* ▸ xerographic (ˌzɪərəˈgræfɪk) *adj*
  ▸ ˌxeroˈgraphically *adv*

xerophilous (zɪˈrɒfɪləs) *adj* (of plants or animals) adapted for growing or living in dry surroundings.
  ▸ xerophile (ˈzɪərəʊˌfaɪl) *n* ▸ xeˈrophily *n*

xerophthalmia (ˌzɪərɒfˈθælmɪə) *n Pathol.* excessive dry-

ness of the cornea and conjunctiva, caused by a deficiency of vitamin A. Also called: **xeroma** (zɪ'rəumə).
  ► ,xeroph'thalmic *adj*

xerophyte ('zɪərə,faɪt) *n* a xerophilous plant, such as a cactus.
  ► **xerophytic** (,zɪərə'fɪtɪk) *adj* ► **xero'phytically** *adv*
  ► 'xero,phytism *n*

Xerox ('zɪərɒks) *n* **1** *Trademark.* **1a** a xerographic copying process. **1b** a machine employing this process. **1c** a copy produced by this process. ◆ *vb* **2** to produce a copy of (a document, illustration, etc.) by this process.

Xerxes I ★ ('zɜːksiːz) *n* ?519–465 B.C., king of Persia (485–465). He led his forces to victory against Greece at Thermopylae (480) but his fleet was defeated at Salamis (480) and his army at Plataea (479).

Xhosa ('kɔːsə) *n* **1** (*pl* **Xhosa** or **Xhosas**) a member of a cattle-rearing Negroid people of southern Africa, living chiefly in W South Africa. **2** the language of this people, belonging to the Bantu group and characterized by several clicks in its sound system.
  ► 'Xhosan *adj*

xi (zaɪ, saɪ, ksi:) *n, pl* **xis**. the 14th letter in the Greek alphabet (Ξ, ξ).

Xi, Hsi, or **Si** ★ (ʃiː) *n* a river in S China, rising in Yünnan province and flowing east to the Canton delta on the South China Sea: the main river system of S China. Length: about 1900 km (1200 miles).

Xia Gui or **Hsia Kuei** ★ ('ʃjɑː 'kweɪ) *n* ?1180–1230, Chinese landscape painter of the Sung dynasty; noted for his misty mountain landscapes in ink monochrome.

Xiamen ★ (,ʃjɑː'men) *n* a variant transliteration of the Chinese name for **Amoy**.

Xi An, Hsian, or **Sian** ★ (ʃjɑːn) *n* an industrial city in central China, capital of Shaanxi province: capital of China for 970 years at various times between the 3rd century B.C. and the 10th century A.D.; seat of the Northwestern University (1937). Pop.: 2 760 000 (1991 est.). Former name: **Siking**.

Xiang, Hsiang, or **Siang** ★ (ʃjɑːŋ) *n* **1** a river in SE central China, rising in NE Guangxi Zhuang and flowing northeast and north to Dongting Lake. Length: about 1150 km (715 miles). **2** a river in S China, rising in SE Yünnan and flowing east to the Hongxiu (the upper course of the Xi River). Length: about 800 km (500 miles).

Xiangtan or **Siangtan** ★ ('ʃjɑːŋ'tɑːn) *n* a city in S central China, in NE Hunan on the Xiang River: centre of a region noted for tea production. Pop.: 441 968 (1990 est.).

Ximenes or **Ximenez** ★ (*Spanish* xi'menes; *English* 'zɪmɪ,ni:z) *n* See (Francisco) **Jiménez de Cisneros**.

Xingú ★ (*Portuguese* ʃiŋ'gu) *n* a river in central Brazil, rising on the Mato Grosso plateau and flowing north to the Amazon delta, with over 650 km (400 miles) of rapids in its middle course. Length: 1932 km (1200 miles).

Xining, Hsining, or **Sining** ★ ('ʃiː'nɪŋ) *n* a city in W China, capital of Qinghai province, at an altitude of 2300 m (7500 ft). Pop.: 551 776 (1990 est.).

Xinjiang Uygur ('ʃɪn'dʒjæŋ 'wiːɡuə) or **Sinkiang-Uighur Autonomous Region** ★ *n* an administrative division of NW China: established in 1955 for the Uigur ethnic minority, with autonomous subdivisions for other small minorities; produces over half China's wool and contains valuable mineral resources. Capital: Urumqi. Pop.: 16 320 000 (1995 est.). Area: 1 646 799 sq. km (635 829 sq. miles).

xiphisternum (,zɪfɪ'stɜːnəm) *n, pl* **xiphisterna** (-nə). *Anat., zool.* the cartilaginous process forming the lowermost part of the breastbone (sternum). Also called: **xiphoid, xiphoid process**. [C19: from Gk *xiphos* sword + STERNUM]

xiphoid ('zɪfɔɪd) *adj* **1** *Biol.* shaped like a sword. **2** of or relating to the xiphisternum. ◆ *n* **3** Also called: **xiphoid process**. another name for **xiphisternum**. [C18: from NL, from Gk, from *xiphos* sword + *eidos* form]

Xizang Autonomous Region ★ ('ʃiː'zæŋ) *n* the Pinyin transliteration of the Chinese name for **Tibet**.

Xmas ('ɛksməs, 'krɪsməs) *n Inf.* short for **Christmas**. [C18: from symbol X for Christ + -MAS]

Xochimilco ★ (*Spanish* xotʃi'miko) *n* a town in central Mexico, on Lake Xochimilco: noted for its floating gardens. Pop.: 271 020 (1990).

X-rated *adj* **1** (formerly, in Britain) (of a film) considered suitable for viewing by adults only. **2** *Inf.* involving bad language, violence, or sex: *an X-rated conversation*.

X-ray or **x-ray** *n* **1a** electromagnetic radiation emitted when matter is bombarded with fast electrons. X-rays have wavelengths shorter than that of ultraviolet radiation, that is less than about 1×10^{-8} metres. Below about 1×10^{-11} metres they are often called gamma radiation or bremsstrahlung. **1b** (*as modifier*): *X-ray astronomy*. **2** a picture produced by exposing photographic film to X-rays: used in medicine as a diagnostic aid as parts of the body, such as bones, absorb X-rays and so appear as opaque areas on the picture. ◆ *vb* (*tr*) **3** to photograph (part of the body, etc.) using X-rays. **4** to treat or examine by means of X-rays. [C19: partial translation of G *X-Strahlen* (from *Strahl* ray), coined by W. K. ROENTGEN in 1895]

X-ray astronomy *n* the branch of astronomy concerned with the detection and measurement of X-rays emitted by certain celestial bodies, such as X-ray stars.

X-ray binary *n* a binary star that is an intense source of X-rays and is composed of a normal star in close orbit with a white dwarf, neutron star, or black hole.

X-ray crystallography *n* the study and practice of determining the structure of a crystal by passing a beam of X-rays through it and observing and analysing the diffraction pattern produced.

X-ray tube *n* an evacuated tube containing a metal target onto which is directed a beam of electrons at high energy for the generation of X-rays.

Xuan-tong ★ ('ʃwɑːn'tʊŋ) *n* the Pinyin transliteration of the title as emperor of China of (Henry) **Pu-yi**.

Xuthus ★ ('zuːθəs) *n Greek myth.* a son of Hellen, regarded as an ancestor of the Ionian Greeks through his son Ion.

Xuzhou ('ʃuː'dʒəu), **Hsü-chou,** or **Süchow** ★ *n* a city in N central China, in NW Jiangsu province: scene of a decisive battle (1949) in which the Communists defeated the Nationalists. Pop.: 805 695 (1990 est.).

xylem ('zaɪləm, -lɛm) *n* a plant tissue that conducts water and mineral salts from the roots to all other parts, provides mechanical support, and forms the wood of trees and shrubs. [C19: from Gk *xulon* wood]

xylene ('zaɪliːn) *n* an aromatic hydrocarbon existing in three isomeric forms, all three being colourless flammable volatile liquids used as solvents and in the manufacture of synthetic resins, dyes, and insecticides. Formula: $(CH_3)_2C_6H_4$. Systematic name: **dimethyl benzene**.

xylo- or before a vowel **xyl-** *combining form*. **1** indicating wood: *xylophone*. **2** indicating xylene: *xylidine*. [from Gk *xulon* wood]

xylocarp ('zaɪlə,kɑːp) *n Bot.* a fruit, such as a coconut, having a hard woody pericarp.
  ► ,xylo'carpous *adj*

xylograph ('zaɪlə,grɑːf) *n* **1** an engraving in wood. **2** a print taken from a wood block. ◆ *vb* **3** (*tr*) to print (a design, illustration, etc.) from a wood engraving.
  ► **xylography** (zaɪ'lɒgrəfɪ) *n*

Xylonite ('zaɪlənaɪt) *n Trademark.* a thermoplastic of the cellulose nitrate type.

xylophagous (zaɪ'lɒfəgəs) *adj* (of certain insects, crustaceans, etc.) feeding on or living within wood.

xylophone ('zaɪlə,fəun) *n Music.* a percussion instrument consisting of a set of wooden bars of graduated length. It is played with hard-headed hammers.
  ► **xylophonic** (,zaɪlə'fɒnɪk) *adj* ► **xylophonist** (zaɪ'lɒfənɪst) *n*

xylose ('zaɪləuz, -ləus) *n* a white crystalline sugar found in wood and straw. It is extracted by hydrolysis with acids and used in dyeing, tanning, and in foods for diabetics.

xyster ('zɪstə) *n* a surgical instrument for scraping bone; surgical rasp or file. [C17: via NL from Gk: tool for scraping, from *xuein* to scrape]

★ people and places

Yy

y *or* **Y** (waɪ) *n, pl* **y's, Y's,** *or* **Ys. 1** the 25th letter of the English alphabet. **2** a speech sound represented by this letter, usually a semivowel, as in *yawn*, or a vowel, as in *symbol* or *shy*. **3** something shaped like a Y.

y *Maths. symbol for:* **1** the *y*-axis or a coordinate measured along the *y*-axis in a Cartesian coordinate system. **2** an algebraic variable.

Y *symbol for:* **1** any unknown or variable factor, number, or thing. **2** *Chem.* yttrium.

y. *abbrev. for* year.

-y¹ *or* **-ey** *suffix forming adjectives.* **1** (*from nouns*) characterized by; consisting of; filled with; resembling: *sunny; sandy; smoky; classy.* **2** (*from verbs*) tending to; acting or existing as specified: *leaky; shiny.* [from OE *-ig, -æg*]

-y², **-ie,** *or* **-ey** *suffix of nouns. Inf.* **1** denoting smallness and expressing affection and familiarity: *a doggy; Jamie.* **2** a person or thing concerned with or characterized by being: *a groupie; a goalie; a fatty.* [C14: from Scot. *-ie, -y,* familiar suffix orig. in names]

-y³ *suffix forming nouns.* **1** (*from verbs*) indicating the act of doing what is indicated by the verbal element: *inquiry.* **2** (*esp. with combining forms of Greek, Latin, or French origin*) indicating state, condition, or quality: *geography; jealousy.* [from OF *-ie,* from L *-ia*]

Y2K *n Inf.* another name for the year 2000 A.D. (esp. referring to the millennium bug). [C20: Y(EAR) + 2 + K (in the sense: thousand)]

yabby *or* **yabbie** ('jæbɪ) *Austral.* ♦ *n, pl* **yabbies. 1** a small edible freshwater crayfish. **2** a saltwater prawn used as bait; nipper. ♦ *vb* **yabbies, yabbying, yabbied. 3** (*intr*) to fish for yabbies. [from Abor.]

Yablonovy Mountains ★ (*Russian* 'jablənəvij) *pl n* a mountain range in Russia, in Siberia. Highest peak: 1680 m (5512 ft). Also called: **Yablonoi Mountains** ('jɑ:blə,nɔɪ).

yacht (jɒt) *n* **1** a vessel propelled by sail or power, used esp. for pleasure cruising, racing, etc. ♦ *vb* **2** (*intr*) to sail or cruise in a yacht. [C16: from obs. Du. *jaghte,* short for *jahtschip,* from *jagen* to chase + *schip* ship]
  ▸ **'yachting** *n, adj*

yachtie ('jɒtɪ) *n Austral. & NZ inf.* a yachtsman; sailing enthusiast.

yachtsman ('jɒtsmən) *or* (*fem*) **yachtswoman** *n, pl* **yachtsmen** *or* **yachtswomen.** a person who sails a yacht or yachts.
  ▸ **'yachtsmanship** *n*

yack (jæk) *n, vb* a variant spelling of **yak**².

yackety-yak ('jækɪtɪ'jæk) *n Sl.* noisy, continuous, and trivial talk or conversation. [imit.]

yaffle ('jæf°l) *n* another name for **green woodpecker** (see **woodpecker**). [C18: imit. of its cry]

Yafo ★ ('jɑːfɔː) *n* transliteration of the Hebrew name for **Jaffa** (sense 1).

Yagi aerial ('jɑːgɪ, 'jægɪ) *n* a directional aerial, used esp. in television and radio astronomy, consisting of three or more elements lying parallel to each other, the principal direction of radiation being along the line of the centres. [C20: after Hidetsugu *Yagi* (1886–1976), Japanese engineer]

yah (jɑː, jɛə) *sentence substitute.* **1** an informal word for **yes.** ♦ *interj* **2** an exclamation of derision or disgust.

Yahata ★ ('jɑːhɑː,tɑː) *n* a variant of **Yawata.**

yahoo (jə'huː) *n, pl* **yahoos.** a crude, brutish, or obscenely coarse person. [C18: from a race of brutish creatures resembling men in Jonathan Swift's *Gulliver's Travels* (1726)]
  ▸ **ya'hoo,ism** *n*

Yahweh ('jɑːweɪ) *or* **Yahveh** ('jɑːveɪ) *n Old Testament.* a vocalization of the Tetragrammaton. [from Heb., from YHVH, with conjectural vowels; see also JEHOVAH]

Yahwism ('jɑːwɪzəm) *or* **Yahvism** ('jɑːvɪzəm) *n* the use of the name Yahweh, esp. in parts of the Old Testament, as the personal name of God.

Yahwist ('jɑːwɪst) *or* **Yahvist** ('jɑːvɪst) *n Bible.* **the.** the conjectured author or authors of the earliest sources of the Pentateuch in which God is called *Yahweh* throughout.
  ▸ **Yah'wistic** *or* **Yah'vistic** *adj*

yak¹ (jæk) *n* an ox of Tibet having long shaggy hair. [C19: from Tibetan *gyag*]

yak² (jæk) *Sl.* ♦ *n* **1** noisy, continuous, and trivial talk. ♦ *vb* **yaks, yakking, yakked. 2** (*intr*) to chatter or talk in this way. [C20: imit.]

yakka, yakker, *or* **yacker** ('jækə) *n Austral. & NZ inf.* work. [C19: from Abor.]

Yakut Republic ★ (jæ'kʊt) *n* the former name of the **Sakha Republic.**

Yakutsk ★ (*Russian* jɪ'kutsk) *n* a port in E Russia, capital of the Sakha Republic, on the Lena River. Pop.: 192 000 (1995 est.).

Yale lock (jeɪl) *n Trademark.* a type of cylinder lock using a flat serrated key. [C19: after L. *Yale* (1821–68), US inventor]

Yalta ★ (*Russian* 'jaltə) *n* a port and resort in the S Ukraine, in the Crimea on the Black Sea: scene of a conference (1945) between Churchill, Roosevelt, and Stalin, who met to plan the final defeat and occupation of Nazi Germany. Pop.: 89 000 (1988 est.).

Yalu ★ ('jɑː,luː) *n* a river in E Asia, rising in N North Korea and flowing southwest to Korea Bay, forming a large part of the border between North Korea and NE China. Length: 806 km (501 miles).

yam (jæm) *n* **1** any of various twining plants of tropical and subtropical regions, cultivated for their edible tubers. **2** the starchy tuber of any of these plants, eaten as a vegetable. **3** *Southern US.* the sweet potato. [C17: from Port. *inhame,* ult. of W African origin]

Yamagata ★ (,jæmə'gɑːtə) *n* Prince **Aritomo** (,ærɪ'təʊməʊ). 1838–1922, Japanese soldier and politician. As war minister (1873) and chief of staff (1878), he modernized Japan's military system. He was premier (1889–93; 1898).

Yamasaki ★ (,jæmə'sɑːkɪ) *n* **Minoru.** 1912–86, US architect. His buildings include St Louis Airport, Missouri (1953–55) and the World Trade Center, New York (1970–77).

yammer ('jæmə) *Inf.* ♦ *vb* **1** to utter or whine in a complaining manner. **2** to make (a complaint) loudly or persistently. ♦ *n* **3** a yammering sound. **4** nonsense; jabber. [OE *geōmrian* to grumble]
  ▸ **'yammerer** *n*

Yamoussoukro ★ (,jæmuːˈsuːkrəʊ) *n* the capital of the Côte d'Ivoire, in the S centre of the country. It replaced Abidjan as capital in 1983. Pop.: 100 000 (1989 est.).

Yanan ('jænˈæn) *or* **Yenan** ★ *n* a city in NE China, in N Shaanxi province: political and military capital of the Chinese Communists (1935–49). Pop.: 113 277 (1990 est.). Also called: **Fushih.**

Yang¹ (jæŋ) *n* See **Yin and Yang.**

Yang² ★ (jæŋ) *n* **Chen Ning** ('tʃen 'nɪŋ). born 1922, US physicist, born in China: with Tsung-Dao Lee he showed that parity is not always conserved; shared the Nobel prize for physics 1957.

Yangon ★ (,jæŋˈgɒn) *n* the capital and chief port of Myanmar (formerly Burma): an industrial city and transport centre; dominated by the gold-covered Shwe Dagon pagoda, 112 m (368 ft) high. Pop.: 2 500 000 (latest est.). Former name (until 1989): **Rangoon.**

Yangtze ★ ('jæŋtsɪ, 'jæŋktsɪ) *n* the longest river in

China, rising in SE Qinghai province and flowing east to the East China Sea near Shanghai: a major commercial waterway in one of the most densely populated areas of the world. Length: 5528 km (3434 miles). Also called: **Yangtze Jiang, Chang Jiang, Chang.**

Yanina ★ ('jɑːnɪnə) n a variant spelling of **Ioánnina.**

yank (jæŋk) vb **1** to pull with a sharp movement; tug. ◆ n **2** a jerk. [C19: from ?]

Yank (jæŋk) n **1** a slang word for an **American. 2** US inf. short for **Yankee.**

Yankee ('jæŋkɪ) or (inf.) **Yank** n **1** Often disparaging. a native or inhabitant of the US; American. **2** a native or inhabitant of New England. **3** a native or inhabitant of the Northern US, esp. a Northern soldier in the Civil War. **4** Finance. a bond issued in the US by a foreign borrower. ◆ adj **5** of, relating to, or characteristic of Yankees. [C18: ?from Du. Jan Kees John Cheese, derisive nickname of Du. settlers for English colonists in Connecticut]

Yankee Doodle n **1** an American song, popularly regarded as a characteristically national melody. **2** another name for **Yankee.**

Yantai ('jæn'taɪ), **Yentai,** or **Yen-t'ai** ★ n a port in E China, in NE Shandong. Pop.: 452 127 (1990 est.). Also called: **Chefoo.**

Yaoundé or **Yaunde** ★ (French jaunde) n the capital of Cameroon, in the southwest: University of Cameroon (1962). Pop.: 800 000 (1992 est.).

yap (jæp) vb **yaps, yapping, yapped.** (intr) **1** (of a dog) to bark in quick sharp bursts; yelp. **2** Inf. to talk at length in an annoying or stupid way; jabber. ◆ n **3** a high-pitched or sharp bark; yelp. **4** Sl. annoying or stupid speech; jabber. **5** Sl., chiefly US. a derogatory word for **mouth.** [C17: imit.]
► 'yapper n ► 'yappy adj

Yap ★ (jɑːp, jæp) n a group of four main islands in the W Pacific, in the W Caroline Islands: administratively a district of the US Trust Territory of the Pacific Islands from 1947; became self-governing in 1979 as part of the Federated States of Micronesia; important Japanese naval base in World War II. Pop.: 11 128 (1994). Area: 101 sq. km (39 sq. miles).

yapok (jə'pɒk) n an amphibious nocturnal opossum of Central and South America. Also called: **water opossum.** [C19: after Oyapok, a river flowing between French Guiana & Brazil]

Yapurá ★ (japu'ra) n the Spanish name for **Japurá.**

Yaqui ★ (Spanish 'jaki) n a river in NW Mexico, rising near the border with the US and flowing south to the Gulf of California. Length: about 676 km (420 miles).

yarborough ('jɑːbərə, -brə) n Bridge, whist. a hand of 13 cards in which no card is higher than nine. [C19: supposedly after the second Earl of Yarborough (d. 1897), said to have bet a thousand to one against its occurrence]

yard[1] (jɑːd) n **1** a unit of length equal to 3 feet and defined in 1963 as exactly 0.9144 metre. **2** a cylindrical wooden or hollow metal spar, slung from a mast of a vessel, and used for suspending a sail. [OE gierd rod, twig]

yard[2] (jɑːd) n **1** a piece of enclosed ground, often adjoining or surrounded by a building or buildings. **2a** an enclosed or open area used for some commercial activity, for storage, etc.: a builder's yard. **2b** (in combination): a shipyard. **3** a US and Canad. word for **garden** (sense 1). **4** an area having a network of railway tracks and sidings, used for storing rolling stock, making up trains, etc. **5** US & Canad. the winter pasture of deer, moose, and similar animals. **6** NZ. short for **stockyard.** [OE geard]

Yard (jɑːd) n the. Brit. inf. short for **Scotland Yard.**

yardage[1] ('jɑːdɪdʒ) n a length measured in yards.

yardage[2] ('jɑːdɪdʒ) n **1** the use of a railway yard for cattle. **2** the charge for this.

yardarm ('jɑːd‚ɑːm) n Naut. the two tapering outer ends of a ship's yard.

yard grass n an Old World perennial grass with prostrate leaves, growing as a troublesome weed on open ground, yards, etc.

Yardie ('jɑːdɪ) n a member of a Black criminal syndicate originally based in Jamaica. [origin unknown]

yard of ale n **1** the beer or ale contained in a narrow horn-shaped drinking glass. **2** such a drinking glass itself.

yardstick ('jɑːd‚stɪk) n **1** a measure or standard used for comparison. **2** a graduated stick, one yard long, used for measurement.

Yarkand ★ (‚jɑː'kænd) n another name for **Shache.**

Yarmouth ★ ('jɑːməθ) n short for **Great Yarmouth.**

yarmulke ('jɑːməlkə) n Judaism. a skullcap worn by Orthodox male Jews at all times and by others during prayer. [from Yiddish, from Ukrainian & Polish yarmulka cap, prob. from Turkish yağmurluk raincoat, from yağmur rain]

yarn (jɑːn) n **1** a continuous twisted strand of natural or synthetic fibres, used in weaving, knitting, etc. **2** Inf. a long and often involved story, usually of incredible or fantastic events. **3 spin a yarn.** Inf. **3a** to tell such a story. **3b** to make up a series of excuses. ◆ vb **4** (intr) to tell such a story or stories. [OE gearn]

yarn-dyed adj (of fabric) dyed while still in yarn form, before being woven.

Yaroslavl ★ (Russian jɪra'slavlj) n a city in W Russia, on the River Volga: a major trading centre since early times and one of the first industrial centres in Russia; textile industries. Pop.: 629 000 (1995 est.).

yarran ('jæran) n a small hardy tree of inland Australia: useful as fodder and for firewood. [from Abor.]

Yarra River ★ ('jæra) n a river in SE Australia, rising in the Great Dividing Range and flowing west and southwest through Melbourne to Port Phillip Bay. Length: 250 km (155 miles).

yarrow ('jærəʊ) n any of several plants of the composite family of Eurasia, having finely dissected leaves and flat clusters of white flower heads. Also called: **milfoil.** [OE gearwe]

yashmak or **yashmac** ('jæʃmæk) n the face veil worn by Muslim women when in public. [C19: from Ar.]

yataghan ('jætəgən) n a Turkish sword with a curved blade. [C19: from Turkish yatağan]

Yathrib ★ ('jæθrɪb) n the ancient Arabic name for **Medina.**

Yaunde ★ (French jaunde) n a variant spelling of **Yaoundé.**

yaup (jɔːp) vb, n a variant spelling of **yawp.**
► 'yauper n

Yavarí ★ (jaβa'ri) n the Spanish name for **Javari.**

yaw (jɔː) vb **1** (intr) (of an aircraft, etc.) to turn about its vertical axis. **2** (intr) (of a ship, etc.) to deviate temporarily from a straight course. **3** (tr) to cause (an aircraft, ship, etc.) to yaw. ◆ n **4** the movement of an aircraft, etc., about its vertical axis. **5** the deviation of a vessel from a straight course. [C16: from ?]

Yawata ('jɑːwɑː‚tɑː) or **Yahata** ★ n a former city in Japan, on N Kyushu: merged with Moji, Kokura, Tobata, and Wakamatsu in 1963 to form **Kitakyushu.**

yawl (jɔːl) n **1** a two-masted sailing vessel with a small mizzenmast aft of the rudderpost. **2** a ship's small boat, usually rowed by four or six oars. [C17: from Du. jol or MLow G jolle, from ?]

yawn (jɔːn) vb **1** (intr) to open the mouth wide and take in air deeply, often as in involuntary reaction to sleepiness or boredom. **2** (tr) to express or utter while yawning. **3** (intr) to be open wide as if threatening to engulf (someone or something): the mine shaft yawned below. ◆ n **4** the act or an instance of yawning. [OE gionian]
► 'yawner n ► 'yawning adj ► 'yawningly adv

yawp (jɔːp) n Dialect US & Canad. inf. ◆ vb (intr) **1** to yawn, esp. audibly. **2** to shout, cry, or talk noisily. **3** to bark or yowl. ◆ n **4** a shout, bark, or cry. **5** a noisy, foolish, or raucous utterance. [C15 yolpen, prob. imit.]
► 'yawper n

yaws (jɔːz) n (usually functioning as sing) an infectious disease of tropical climates characterized by red skin eruptions. [C17: of Carib origin]

y-axis n a reference axis of a graph or two- or three-dimensional Cartesian coordinate system along which the y-coordinate is measured.

Yazd (jɑːzd) *or* **Yezd** ★ *n* a city in central Iran: a major centre of silk weaving. Pop.: 275 298 (1991).

Yb *the chemical symbol for* ytterbium.

YC (in Britain) *abbrev. for* Young Conservative.

Y-chromosome *n* the sex chromosome that occurs as one of a pair with the X-chromosome in the diploid cells of the males of many animals, including humans. Cf. **X-chromosome.**

yclept (ɪ'klept) *adj Obs.* having the name of; called. [OE *gecleopod*, p.p. of *cleopian* to call]

Y connection *n Electrical engineering.* a three-phase star connection.

yd *or* **yd.** *abbrev. for* yard (measure).

YDT (in Canada) *abbrev. for* Yukon Daylight Time.

ye[1] (jiː, *unstressed* jɪ) *pron* **1** *Arch. or dialect.* refers to more than one person including the person addressed. **2** Also: **ee** (iː). *Dialect.* refers to one person addressed: *I tell ye.* [OE *gē*]

ye[2] (ðiː, *spelling pron* jiː) *determiner* a form of **the**[1], used as a supposed archaism: *ye olde oake.* [from a misinterpretation of *the* as written in some ME texts. The runic letter thorn (þ, representing *th*) was incorrectly transcribed as *y* because of a resemblance in their shapes]

yea (jeɪ) *sentence substitute.* **1** a less common word for **aye** (yes). ◆ *adv* **2** (*sentence modifier*) *Arch. or literary.* indeed; truly: *yea, though they spurn me, I shall prevail.* [OE *gēa*]

yeah (jɛə) *sentence substitute.* an informal word for **yes.**

yean (jiːn) *vb* (of a sheep or goat) to give birth to (offspring). [OE *geēanian*]

yeanling ('jiːnlɪŋ) *n* the young of a goat or sheep.

year (jɪə) *n* **1** the period of time, the **calendar year,** containing 365 days or in a **leap year** 366 days. It is divided into 12 calendar months, and reckoned from January 1 to December 31. **2** a period of twelve months from any specified date. **3** a specific period of time, usually occupying a definite part or parts of a twelve-month period, used for some particular activity: *a school year.* **4** Also called: **astronomical year, tropical year.** the period of time, the **solar year,** during which the earth makes one revolution around the sun, measured between two successive vernal equinoxes: equal to 365.242 19 days. **5** the period of time, the **sidereal year,** during which the earth makes one revolution around the sun, measured between two successive conjunctions of a particular star: equal to 365.256 36 days. **6** the period of time, the **lunar year,** containing 12 lunar months and equal to 354.3671 days. **7** the period of time taken by a planet to complete one revolution around the sun. **8** (*pl*) age, esp. old age: *a man of his years should be more careful.* **9** (*pl*) time: *in years to come.* **10** a group of pupils or students, who are taught or study together. **11** the **year dot.** *Inf.* as long ago as can be remembered. **12 year in, year out.** regularly or monotonously, over a long period. ◆ Related adj: **annual.** [OE *gear*]

USAGE NOTE In writing spans of years, it is important to choose a style that avoids ambiguity. The practice adopted in this dictionary is, in four-figure dates, to specify the last two digits of the second year if it falls within the same century as the first: *1801–08; 1850–51; 1899–1901.* In writing three-figure B.C. dates, it is advisable to give both dates in full: *159–156* B.C., not *159–56* B.C. unless of course the span referred to consists of 103 years rather than three years. It is also advisable to specify B.C. or A.D. in years under 1000 unless the context makes this self-evident.

---

yearbook ('jɪə,bʊk) *n* an almanac or other reference book published annually and containing details of events of the previous year.

yearling ('jɪəlɪŋ) *n* **1** the young of any of various animals, including the antelope and buffalo, between one and two years of age. **2** a thoroughbred racehorse counted as being one year old until the second January 1 following its birth. **3a** a bond intended to mature after one year. **3b** (*as modifier*): *yearling bonds.* ◆ *adj* **4** being a year old.

yearlong ('jɪə'lɒŋ) *adj* throughout a whole year.

yearly ('jɪəlɪ) *adj* **1** occurring, done, appearing, etc., once a year or every year; annual. **2** lasting or valid for a year; annual: *a yearly fee.* ◆ *adv* **3** once a year; annually.

yearn (jɜːn) *vb* (*intr*) **1** (usually foll. by *for* or *after* or an infinitive) to have an intense desire or longing (for). **2** to feel tenderness or affection. [OE *giernan*]
► '**yearner** *n* ► '**yearning** *n, adj* ► '**yearningly** *adv*

year of grace *n* any year of the Christian era, as from the presumed date of Christ's birth.

year-round *adj* open, in use, operating, etc., throughout the year.

yeast (jiːst) *n* **1** any of various single-celled fungi which reproduce by budding and are able to ferment sugars: a rich source of vitamins of the B complex. **2** a commercial preparation containing yeast cells and inert material such as meal, used in raising dough for bread or for fermenting beer, whisky, etc. **3** a preparation containing yeast cells, used to treat diseases caused by vitamin B deficiency. **4** froth or foam, esp. on beer. ◆ *vb* **5** (*intr*) to froth or foam. [OE *giest*]
► '**yeastless** *adj* ► '**yeast,like** *adj*

yeasty ('jiːstɪ) *adj* **yeastier, yeastiest. 1** of, resembling, or containing yeast. **2** fermenting or causing fermentation. **3** tasting of or like yeast. **4** insubstantial or frivolous. **5** restless, agitated, or unsettled. **6** covered with or containing froth or foam.
► '**yeastily** *adv* ► '**yeastiness** *n*

Yeats ★ (jeɪts) *n* **1** Jack Butler. 1871–1957, Irish painter. **2** his brother **W(illiam) B(utler).** 1865–1939, Irish poet and dramatist. His collections of verse include *The Tower* (1928) and his plays include *Cathleen ni Houlihan* (1902). He was a founder of the Irish National Theatre Company at the Abbey Theatre in Dublin: Nobel prize for literature 1923.

yegg (jeg) *n Sl., chiefly US.* a burglar or safe-breaker. [C20: ?from the surname of a burglar]

Yeisk, Yeysk, *or* **Eisk** ★ (*Russian* jejsk) *n* a port and resort in SW Russia, on the Sea of Azov. Pop.: 86 300 (1991 est.).

Yekaterinburg *or* **Ekaterinburg** ★ (*Russian* jɪkətrimˈburk) *n* a city in NW Russia, in the Ural Mountains: scene of the execution (1918) of Nicholas II and his family; university (1920); one of the largest centres of heavy engineering in Russia. Pop.: 1 280 000 (1995 est.). Former name (1924–91): **Sverdlovsk.**

Yekaterinodar *or* **Ekaterinodar** ★ (*Russian* jɪkətɪrinaˈdar) *n* the former name (until 1920) of **Krasnodar.**

Yekaterinoslav *or* **Ekaterinoslav** ★ (*Russian* jɪkətɪrinaˈslaf) *n* the former name (1787–96, 1802–1926) of **Dnepropetrovsk.**

Yelisavetgrad *or* **Elisavetgrad** ★ (*Russian* jɪlizaˈvjetgrət) *n* the former name (until 1924) of **Kirovograd.**

Yelisavetpol *or* **Elisavetpol** ★ (*Russian* jɪlizaˈvjetpəlj) *n* the former name (until 1920) of **Kirovabad.**

Yelizaveta Petrovna ★ (*Russian* jɪlizaˈvjetə pɪˈtrɔvnə) *n* See **Elizabeth**[2] (sense 3).

yell (jel) *vb* **1** to shout, scream, cheer, or utter in a loud or piercing way. ◆ *n* **2** a loud piercing inarticulate cry, as of pain, anger, or fear. **3** *US & Canad.* a rhythmic cry, used in cheering in unison. [OE *giellan*]
► '**yeller** *n*

yellow ('jeləʊ) *n* **1** any of a group of colours such as that of a lemon or of gold, which vary in saturation but have the same hue. Yellow is the complementary colour of blue. Related adj: **xanthous. 2** a pigment or dye of or producing these colours. **3** yellow cloth or clothing: *dressed in yellow.* **4** the yolk of an egg. **5** a yellow ball in snooker, etc. ◆ *adj* **6** of the colour yellow. **7** yellowish in colour or having parts or marks that are yellowish. **8** having a yellowish skin; Mongoloid. **9** *Inf.* cowardly or afraid. **10** offensively sensational, as a cheap newspaper (esp. in **yellow press**). ◆ *vb* **11** to make or become yellow. ◆ See also **yellows.** [OE *geolu*]
► '**yellowish** *adj* ► '**yellowly** *adv* ► '**yellowness** *n* ► '**yellowy** *adj*

★ people and places

yellow-belly n, pl **yellow-bellies**. a slang word for **coward**.
▶ **'yellow-,bellied** adj

yellow belly n Austral. any of several freshwater food fishes with yellow underparts.

yellow bile n Arch. one of the four bodily humours, choler.

yellow card n Soccer. a card of a yellow colour displayed by a referee to indicate that a player has been officially cautioned for some offence.

yellow fever n an acute infectious disease of tropical and subtropical climates, characterized by fever, haemorrhages, vomiting, and jaundice: caused by a virus transmitted by the bite of a certain mosquito. Also called: **yellow jack**.

yellowhammer ('jɛləʊ,hæmə) n a European bunting, having a yellowish head and body and brown-streaked wings and tail. [C16: from ?]

yellow jack n 1 Pathol. another name for **yellow fever**. 2 another name for **quarantine flag**. 3 any of certain large yellowish food fishes of warm and tropical Atlantic waters.

yellow jersey n (in the Tour de France) a yellow jersey awarded as a trophy to the cyclist with the fastest time in each stage of the race.

yellow journalism n the type of journalism that relies on sensationalism to attract readers. [C19: ? shortened from Yellow Kid journalism, referring to the Yellow Kid, a cartoon (1895) in the New York World, a newspaper having a reputation for sensationalism]

Yellowknife ★ ('jɛləʊ,naɪf) n a city in N Canada, capital of the Northwest Territories on Great Slave Lake. Pop.: 15 179 (1991).

yellow line n Brit. a yellow line painted along the edge of a road indicating vehicle waiting restrictions.

yellow metal n 1 a type of brass having about 60 per cent copper and 40 per cent zinc. 2 another name for **gold**.

Yellow Pages pl n Trademark. a classified telephone directory or section of one, often on yellow paper, that lists subscribers by the business or service they provide.

yellow peril n the power or alleged power of Asiatic peoples, esp. the Chinese, to threaten or destroy White or Western civilization.

Yellow River ★ n the second longest river in China, rising in SE Qinghai and flowing east, south, and east again to the Gulf of Bohai south of Tianjin; it has changed its course several times in recorded history. Length: about 4350 km (2700 miles). Chinese name: **Hwang Ho**.

yellows ('jɛləʊz) n (functioning as sing) 1 any of various fungal or viral diseases of plants, characterized by yellowish discoloration and stunting. 2 Vet. science. another name for **jaundice**.

Yellow Sea ★ n a shallow arm of the Pacific between Korea and NE China. Area: about 466 200 sq. km (180 000 sq. miles). Chinese name: **Hwang Hai**.

yellow spot n Anat. another name for **macula lutea**.

Yellowstone ★ ('jɛləʊ,stəʊn) n a river rising in N Wyoming and flowing north through Yellowstone National Park, then east to the Missouri. Length: 1080 km (671 miles).

Yellowstone Falls ★ pl n a waterfall in NW Wyoming, in Yellowstone National Park on the Yellowstone River.

Yellowstone National Park ★ n a national park in the NW central US, mostly in NW Wyoming: the oldest and largest national park in the US, containing unusual geological formations and geysers. Area: 8956 sq. km (3458 sq. miles).

yellow streak n Inf. a cowardly or weak trait.

yellow underwing n any of several species of noctuid moths, the hind wings of which are yellow with a black bar.

yellowwood ('jɛləʊ,wʊd) n 1 any of several leguminous trees of the southeastern US, having clusters of white flowers and yellow wood yielding a yellow dye. 2 Also called: **West Indian satinwood**. a rutaceous tree of the West Indies, with smooth hard wood. 3 any of several other

trees with yellow wood, esp. a conifer of southern Africa the wood of which is used for furniture and building. 4 the wood of any of these trees.

yelp (jɛlp) vb (intr) 1 (esp. of a dog) to utter a sharp or high-pitched cry or bark, often indicating pain. ◆ n 2 a sharp or high-pitched cry or bark. [OE gielpan to boast]
▶ **'yelper** n

Yeltsin ★ ('jɛltsɪn) n **Boris** (**Nicolayevich**). born 1931, Russian politician: president of the Russian Soviet Federative Socialist Republic (1990–91); president of Russia from 1991.

Yemen ★ ('jɛmən) n a republic in SW Arabia, on the Red Sea and the Gulf of Aden: formed in 1990 from the union of North Yemen and South Yemen; in 1994 the northern region won a civil war against the south: consists of arid coastal lowlands, rising to fertile upland valleys and mountains in the W and to the Hadhramaut plateau in the SE: the N and E contains part of the Great Sandy Desert. Official language: Arabic. Official religion: Muslim. Currency: riyal. Capital: San'a. Pop.: 16 496 000 (1997). Area (including territory claimed by Yemen along the undemarcated eastern border with Saudi Arabia): 472 099 sq. km (182 278 sq. miles). Official name: **Yemen Republic**.
▶ **'Yemeni** adj, n

yen[1] (jɛn) n, pl **yen**. the standard monetary unit of Japan. [C19: from Japanese en, from Chinese yüan dollar]

yen[2] (jɛn) Inf. ◆ n 1 a longing or desire. ◆ vb **yens**, **yenning**, **yenned**. 2 (intr) to yearn. [?from Chinese yǎn a craving]

Yenan ★ ('jɛn'æn) n a variant transliteration of the Chinese name for **Yanan**.

Yenisei or **Yenisey** ★ (,jɛnɪ'seɪ; Russian jɪni'sjej) n a river in central Russia, in central Siberia, formed by the confluence of two headstreams in the Tuva Republic: flows west and north to the Arctic Ocean; the largest river in volume in Russia. Length: 4129 km (2566 miles).

Yantai or **Yen-t'ai** ★ ('jɛn'taɪ) n a variant transliteration of the Chinese name for **Yantai**.

yeoman ('jəʊmən) n, pl **yeomen**. 1 History. 1a a member of a class of small freeholders who cultivated their own land. 1b an attendant or lesser official in a royal or noble household. 2 (in Britain) another name for **yeoman of the guard**. 3 (modifier) characteristic of or relating to a yeoman. 4 a petty officer or noncommissioned officer in the Royal Navy or Marines in charge of signals. [C15: ?from yongman young man]

yeomanly ('jəʊmənlɪ) adj 1 of, relating to, or like a yeoman. 2 having the virtues attributed to yeomen, such as staunchness, loyalty, and courage. ◆ adv 3 in a yeomanly manner.

yeoman of the guard n a member of the ceremonial bodyguard (**Yeomen of the Guard**) of the British monarch.

yeomanry ('jəʊmənrɪ) n 1 yeomen collectively. 2 (in Britain) a volunteer cavalry force, organized in 1761 for home defence: merged into the Territorial Army in 1907.

yep (jɛp) sentence substitute. an informal word for **yes**.

yerba or **yerba maté** ('jɜːbə) n another name for **maté**. [from Sp. yerba maté herb maté]

Yerevan ★ (Russian jɪrɪ'van) n the capital of Armenia: founded in the 8th century B.C.; a main focus of trade routes since ancient times; industrial centre; university. Pop.: 1 226 000 (1994 est.). Also called: **Erevan** or **Erivan**.

Yerwa-Maiduguri ★ ('jɜːwə,maɪdʊ'guːrɪ) n another name for **Maiduguri**.

yes (jɛs) sentence substitute. 1 used to express affirmation, consent, agreement, or approval or to answer when one is addressed. 2 used to signal someone to speak or keep speaking, enter a room, or do something. ◆ n 3 an answer or vote of yes. 4 (often pl) a person who votes in the affirmative. [OE gēse, from iā sīe may it be]

yeshiva (jə'ʃiːvə; Hebrew jə'ʃiːva) n, pl **yeshivahs** or **yeshivoth** (Hebrew -vɔt). 1 a traditional Jewish school devoted chiefly to the study of the Talmud. 2 a school run by Orthodox Jews for children of primary school age, provid-

---

★ people and places

ing both religious and secular instruction. [from Heb. *yĕshībhāh* a seat, hence, an academy]

Yeşil Irmak ★ (jɛˈʃiːl ɪəˈmɑːk) *n* a river in N Turkey, flowing northwest to the Black Sea. Length: 418 km (260 miles). Ancient name: **Iris.**

Yeşilköy ★ (jɛˈʃil‚kœi) *n* the Turkish name for **San Stefano.**

yes man *n* a servile, submissive, or acquiescent subordinate, assistant, or associate.

yester (ˈjɛstə) *adj Arch.* of or relating to yesterday: *yester sun.* [OE *geostror*]

yester- *prefix* indicating a period of time before the present one: *yesteryear.* [OE *geostran*]

yesterday (ˈjɛstədɪ, -‚deɪ) *n* **1** the day immediately preceding today. **2** (*often pl*) the recent past. ◆ *adv* **3** on or during the day before today. **4** in the recent past.

yesteryear (ˈjɛstə‚jɪə) *Formal or literary.* ◆ *n* **1** last year or the past in general. ◆ *adv* **2** during last year or the past in general.

yestreen (jɛˈstriːn) *adv Scot.* yesterday evening. [C14: from YEST(E)R- + E(V)EN²]

yet (jɛt) *sentence connector.* **1** nevertheless; still; in spite of that: *I want to and yet I haven't the courage.* ◆ *adv* **2** (*usually used with a negative or interrogative*) so far; up until then or now: *they're not home yet; is it teatime yet?* **3** (*often preceded by just; usually used with a negative*) now (as contrasted with later): *we can't stop yet.* **4** (*often used with a comparative*) even; still: *yet more old potatoes for sale.* **5** eventually in spite of everything: *we'll convince him yet.* **6** **as yet.** so far; up until then or now. [OE *gēta*]

yeti (ˈjɛtɪ) *n* another term for **abominable snowman.** [C20: from Tibetan]

Yevtushenko ★ (‚jɛvtuːˈʃɛŋkəʊ; *Russian* jɪftuˈʃɛnkə) *n* Yevgeny Aleksandrovich (jɪvˈgjenij alɪkˈsandrəvitʃ). born 1933, Russian poet. His poetry includes *Babi Yar* (1962), *Bratsk Station* (1966), and *Farewell to Red Banner* (1992).

yew (juː) *n* **1** any coniferous tree of the Old World and North America having flattened needle-like leaves, fine-grained elastic wood, and cuplike red waxy cones resembling berries. **2** the wood of any of these trees, used to make bows for archery. **3** *Archery.* a bow made of yew. [OE *īw*]

Yeysk ★ (*Russian* jejsk) *n* a variant spelling of **Yeisk.**

Yezd ★ (jɛzd) *n* a variant of **Yazd.**

Y-fronts *pl n Trademark.* boys' or men's underpants having a front opening within an inverted Y shape.

Yggdrasil *or* **Ygdrasil** (ˈɪgdrəsɪl) *n Norse myth.* the ash tree that was thought to bind together earth, heaven, and hell with its roots and branches. [ON (prob. meaning: Uggr's horse), from *Uggr* a name of Odin, from *yggr, uggr* frightful + *drasill* horse, from ?]

YHA *abbrev. for* Youth Hostels Association.

YHVH *or* **YHWH** *Bible.* the letters of the **Tetragrammaton.**

Yibin (ˈjiːˈbɪn) *or* **I-pin** ★ *n* a port in S central China, in Sichuan province: a commercial centre. Pop.: 241 019 (1990 est.).

Yichang (ˈjiːˈtʃæŋ), **Ichang,** *or* **I-ch'ang** ★ *n* a port in S central China, in Hubei province on the Yangtze River 1600 km (1000 miles) from the East China Sea: head of navigation of the Yangtze. Pop.: 371 601 (1990 est.).

yid (jɪd) *n Sl.* a derogatory word for a **Jew.** [C20: prob. from *Yiddish*, from MHG *Jude* JEW]

Yiddish (ˈjɪdɪʃ) *n* **1** a language spoken as a vernacular by Jews in Europe and elsewhere by Jewish emigrants, usually written in the Hebrew alphabet. It is a dialect of High German with an admixture of words of Hebrew, Romance, and Slavonic origin. ◆ *adj* **2** in or relating to this language. [C19: from G *jüdisch*, from *Jude* JEW]

Yiddisher (ˈjɪdɪʃə) *adj* **1** in or relating to Yiddish. **2** Jewish. ◆ *n* **3** a speaker of Yiddish; Jew.

yield (jiːld) *vb* **1** to give forth or supply (a product, result, etc.), esp. by cultivation, labour, etc.; produce or bear. **2** (*tr*) to furnish as a return: *the shares yielded three per cent.* **3** (*tr; often foll. by up*) to surrender or relinquish, esp. as a result of force, persuasion, etc. **4** (*intr; sometimes foll. by to*) to give way, submit, or surrender, as through force or

persuasion: *she yielded to his superior knowledge.* **5** (*intr; often foll. by to*) to agree; comply; assent: *he eventually yielded to their request for money.* **6** (*tr*) to grant or allow; concede: *to yield right of way.* ◆ *n* **7** the result, product, or amount yielded. **8** the profit or return, as from an investment or tax. **9** the annual income provided by an investment. **10** the energy released by the explosion of a nuclear weapon expressed in terms of the amount of TNT necessary to produce the same energy. **11** *Chem.* the quantity of a specified product obtained in a reaction or series of reactions. [OE *gieldan*]
▶ **'yieldable** *adj* ▶ **'yielder** *n*

yielding (ˈjiːldɪŋ) *adj* **1** compliant, submissive, or flexible. **2** pliable or soft: *a yielding material.*

yield point *n* the stress at which an elastic material under increasing stress ceases to behave elastically; the elongation becomes greater than the increase in stress.

Yin and Yang (jɪn) *n* two complementary principles of Chinese philosophy: Yin is negative, dark, and feminine, Yang is positive, bright, and masculine. [from Chinese *yin* dark + *yang* bright]

Yinchuan, **Yin-ch'uan,** *or* **Yinchwan** ★ (ˈjɪnˈtʃwɑːn) *n* a city in N central China, capital of the Ningxia Hui AR, on the Yellow River. Pop.: 356 652 (1990 est.).

Yingkou *or* **Yingkow** ★ (ˈjɪŋˈkaʊ) *n* a port in NE China, in SW Liaoning province: a major shipping centre for Manchuria. Pop.: 421 589 (1990 est.).

yippee (jɪˈpiː) *interj* an exclamation of joy, pleasure, anticipation, etc.

yips (jɪps) *pl n* **the.** *Inf.* (in sport) nervous twitching or tension that destroys concentration. [C20: from ?]

-yl *suffix forming nouns.* (in chemistry) indicating a group or radical: *methyl.* [from Gk *hulē* wood]

ylang-ylang (ˈiːlæŋˈiːlæŋ) *n* **1** an aromatic Asian tree with fragrant greenish-yellow flowers yielding a volatile oil. **2** the oil obtained from this tree, used in perfumery. [C19: from Tagalog *ilang-ilang*]

ylem (ˈaɪləm) *n* the original matter from which the basic elements are said to have been formed following the explosion postulated in the big-bang theory of cosmology. [ME, from OF *ilem*, from L *hȳlē* stuff, from Gk *hulē* wood]

YMCA *abbrev. for* Young Men's Christian Association.

Ymir (ˈiːmɪə) *or* **Ymer** ★ (ˈiːmə) *n Norse myth.* the first being and forefather of the giants. He was slain by Odin and his brothers, who made the earth from his flesh, the water from his blood, and the sky from his skull.

-yne *suffix forming nouns.* denoting an organic chemical containing a triple bond: *alkyne.* [alteration of -INE²]

yo (jəʊ) *sentence substitute.* an expression used as a greeting, to attract someone's attention, etc. [C20: of unknown origin]

yob (jɒb) *or* **yobbo** (ˈjɒbəʊ) *n, pl* **yobs** *or* **yobbos.** *Brit. sl.* an aggressive and surly youth, esp. a teenager. [C19: ? back sl. for BOY]
▶ **'yobbery** *n* ▶ **'yobbish** *adj*

yodel (ˈjəʊdə¹l) *n* **1** an effect produced in singing by an abrupt change of register from the chest voice to falsetto, esp. in folk songs of the Swiss Alps. ◆ *vb* **yodels, yodelling, yodelled** *or US* **yodels, yodeling, yodeled.** **2** to sing (a song) in which a yodel is used. [C19: from G *jodeln*, imit.]
▶ **'yodeller** *n*

yoga (ˈjəʊgə) *n* (*often cap.*) **1** a Hindu system of philosophy aiming at the mystical union of the self with the Supreme Being in a state of complete awareness and tranquillity through certain physical and mental exercises. **2** any method by which such awareness and tranquillity are attained, esp. a course of related exercises and postures. [C19: from Sansk.: a yoking, from *yunakti* he yokes]
▶ **yogic** (ˈjəʊgɪk) *adj*

yogh (jɒg) *n* **1** a character (ȝ) used in Old and Middle English to represent a palatal fricative very close to the semivowel sound of Modern English *y.* **2** this same character as used in Middle English for both the voiced and voiceless palatal fricatives; when final or in a closed syllable in

★ people and places

medial position the sound approached that of German *ch* in *ich*, as in *knyʒt* (knight). [C14: ?from *yok* yoke, from the letter's shape]

yogi ('jəʊgɪ) *n, pl* **yogis** *or* **yogin** (-gɪn). a person who is a master of yoga.

yogurt *or* **yoghurt** ('jəʊgət, jɒg-) *n* a thick custard-like food prepared from milk curdled by bacteria, often sweetened and flavoured with fruit. [C19: from Turkish *yoğurt*]

Yogyakarta (,jəʊgjɑː'kɑːtɑː, ,jɒg-), **Jogjakarta, Jokjakarta,** *or* **Djokjakarta** ★ *n* a city in S Indonesia, in central Java: seat of government of Indonesia (1946–49); university (1949). Pop.: 412 392 (1990).

yo-heave-ho (,jəʊhiːv'həʊ) *interj* a cry formerly used by sailors while pulling or lifting together in rhythm.

yohimbine (jəʊ'hɪmbiːn) *n* an alkaloid found in the bark of a West African tree and used in medicine. [C19: from Bantu *yohimbé* a tropical African tree + -INE¹]

yo-ho-ho *interj* **1** an exclamation to call attention. **2** another word for **yo-heave-ho**.

yoicks (haɪk; *spelling pron* jɔɪks) *interj* a cry used by fox-hunters to urge on the hounds.

yoke (jəʊk) *n, pl* **yokes** *or* **yoke**. **1** a wooden frame, usually consisting of a bar with an oxbow at either end, for attaching to the necks of a pair of draught animals, esp. oxen, so that they can be worked as a team. **2** something resembling a yoke in form or function, such as a frame fitting over a person's shoulders for carrying buckets. **3** a fitted part of a garment, esp. around the neck, shoulders, and chest or around the hips, to which a gathered, pleated, flared, or unfitted part is attached. **4** an oppressive force or burden: *under the yoke of a tyrant.* **5** a pair of oxen or other draught animals joined by a yoke. **6** a part that secures two or more components so that they move together. **7** (in the ancient world) a symbolic yoke, consisting of two upright spears with a third lashed across them, under which conquered enemies were compelled to march, esp. in Rome. **8** a mark, token, or symbol of slavery, subjection, or suffering. **9** *Now rare.* a link, tie, or bond: *the yoke of love.* ◆ *vb* **yokes, yoking, yoked. 10** (*tr*) to secure or harness (a draught animal) to (a plough, vehicle, etc.) by means of a yoke. **11** to join or be joined by means of a yoke; couple, unite, or link. [OE *geoc*]

yokel ('jəʊkᵊl) *n Disparaging.* (used chiefly by townspeople) a person who lives in the country, esp. one who appears to be simple and old-fashioned. [C19: ?from dialect *yokel* green woodpecker]

Yokohama ★ (,jəʊkəʊ'hɑːmə) *n* a port in central Japan, on SE Honshu on Tokyo Bay: a major port and the country's second largest city situated in the largest and most populous industrial region of Japan. Pop.: 3 307 408 (1995).

Yokosuka ★ (,jəʊkəʊ'suːkə) *n* a port in Japan, in SE Honshu: a major naval base with shipbuilding industries. Pop.: 432 202 (1995).

yolk (jəʊk) *n* **1** the substance in an animal ovum that nourishes the developing embryo. **2** a greasy substance in the fleece of sheep. [OE *geoloca,* from *geolu* yellow] ▸ **'yolky** *adj*

yolk sac *n Zool.* the membranous sac that is attached to the surface of the embryos of birds, reptiles, and some fishes, and contains yolk.

Yom Kippur (jɒm 'kɪpə; *Hebrew* jɔm ki'pur) *n* an annual Jewish day of fasting, on which prayers of penitence are recited in the synagogue. Also called: **Day of Atonement.** [from Heb., from *yōm* day + *kippūr* atonement]

yomp (jɒmp) *vb* (*intr*) to walk or trek laboriously, esp. over difficult terrain. [C20: mil. sl., from ?]

yon (jɒn) *determiner* **1** *Chiefly Scot. & N English.* an archaic or dialect word for **that**: *yon man.* **1b** (*as pronoun*): *yon's a fool.* **2** a variant of **yonder.** [OE *geon*]

yond (jɒnd) *Obs. or dialect.* ◆ *adj* **1** the farther, more distant. ◆ *determiner* **2** a variant of **yon.**

yonder ('jɒndə) *adv* **1** at, in, or to that relatively distant place; over there. ◆ *determiner* **2** being at a distance, either within view or as if within view: *yonder valleys.* [C13: from OE *geond* yond]

yoni ('jəʊnɪ) *n Hinduism.* **1** the female genitalia, regarded as a divine symbol of sexual pleasure and matrix of generation. **2** an image of these as an object of worship. [C18: from Sanskrit, lit.: vulva]

Yonkers ★ ('jɒŋkəz) *n* a city in SE New York State, near New York City on the Hudson River. Pop.: 183 490 (1994 est.).

yonks (jɒŋks) *pl n Inf.* a very long time; ages: *I haven't seen him for yonks.* [C20: from ?]

Yonne ★ (*French* jɒn) *n* **1** a department of N central France, in Burgundy region. Capital: Auxerre. Pop.: 330 794 (1994 est.). Area: 7461 sq. km (2910 sq. miles). **2** a river in N France, flowing generally northwest to the Seine at Montereau. Length: 290 km (180 miles).

yoo-hoo ('juː,huː) *interj* a call to attract a person's attention.

YOP (jɒp) *n* (formerly, in Britain) **a** *acronym for* Youth Opportunities Programme. **b** (*as modifier*): *a YOP scheme.*

yore (jɔː) *n* **1** time long past (now only in **of yore**). ◆ *adv* **2** *Obs.* in the past; long ago. [OE *geāra,* genitive pl of *gēar* year]

york (jɔːk) *vb* (*tr*) *Cricket.* to bowl (a batsman) by pitching the ball under or just beyond the bat. [C19: back formation from YORKER]

York¹ ★ (jɔːk) *n* **1** a walled city in NE England, in North Yorkshire, on the River Ouse: the military capital of Roman Britain; capital of the N archiepiscopal province of Britain since 625, with a cathedral (the Minster) begun in 1154; noted for its cycle of medieval mystery plays; university (1963). Pop.: 104 100 (1994 est.). Latin name: **Eboracum. 2** a unitary authority in NE England, in North Yorkshire. Pop.: 124 100 (1996 est.). Area: 272 sq. km (105 sq. miles). **3 Cape.** a cape in NE Australia, in Queensland at the N tip of Cape York Peninsula, extending into Torres Strait: the northernmost point of Australia.

York² ★ (jɔːk) *n* **1** the English royal house, a branch of the Plantagenet line, that reigned from 1461 to 1485. **2 Alvin C(ullum).** 1887–1964, US soldier and hero of World War I. **3 Prince Andrew, Duke of.** born 1960, second son of Elizabeth II of Great Britain and Northern Ireland. He married (1986) Miss Sarah Ferguson; they separated in 1992; their first daughter, Princess Beatrice of York, was born in 1988 and their second, Princess Eugenie of York, in 1990.

Yorke Peninsula ★ (jɔːk) *n* a peninsula in South Australia, between Spencer Gulf and St Vincent Gulf: mainly agricultural with several coastal resorts.

yorker ('jɔːkə) *n Cricket.* a ball bowled so as to pitch just under or just beyond the bat. [C19: prob. after the *Yorkshire* County Cricket Club]

yorkie ('jɔːkɪ) *n* short for **Yorkshire terrier.**

Yorkist ('jɔːkɪst) *English history.* ◆ *n* **1** a member or adherent of the royal House of York, esp. during the Wars of the Roses. ◆ *adj* **2** of, belonging to, or relating to the supporters or members of the House of York.

Yorks (jɔːks) *abbrev. for* Yorkshire.

Yorkshire ★ ('jɔːk,ʃɪə, -ʃə) *n* a historic county of N England: it was the largest English county, divided administratively into East, West, and North Ridings. In 1974 it was divided into the new counties of North, West, and South Yorkshire. The East Riding of Yorkshire was reinstated as a county in 1996.

Yorkshire Dales ★ *pl n* the valleys of the rivers flowing from the Pennines in W Yorkshire: chiefly Airedale, Ribblesdale, Teesdale, Swaledale, Nidderdale, Wharfedale, and Wensleydale; tourist area. Also called: **the Dales.**

Yorkshire pudding ('jɔːk,ʃɪə) *n Chiefly Brit.* a light puffy baked pudding made from a batter of flour, eggs, and milk, traditionally served with roast beef.

Yorkshire terrier *n* a very small breed of terrier with a long straight glossy coat of steel-blue and tan. Also called: **yorkie.**

Yorktown ★ ('jɔːk,taʊn) *n* a village in SE Virginia: scene of the surrender (1781) of the British under Cornwallis to the Americans under Washington at the end of the War of American Independence.

★ people and places

Yoruba ('jɒrubə) *n* **1** (*pl* **Yorubas** *or* **Yoruba**) a member of a Negroid people of W Africa, living chiefly in the coastal regions of SW Nigeria. **2** the language of this people.
▸ **'Yoruban** *adj*

Yosemite Falls ★ (jəu'sɛmɪtɪ) *pl n* a series of waterfalls in central California, in the Yosemite National Park, with a total drop of 770 m (2525 ft): includes the **Upper Yosemite Falls**, 436 m (1430 ft) high, and the **Lower Yosemite Falls**, 98 m (320 ft) high.

Yosemite National Park ★ *n* a national park in central California, in the Sierra Nevada Mountains: contains the **Yosemite Valley**, at an altitude of about 1200 m (4000 ft), with sheer walls rising about another 1200 m (4000 ft). Area: 3061 sq. km (1182 sq. miles).

Yoshihito ★ (,jɒʃɪ'hiːtəu) *n* See **Taisho**.

Yoshkar-Ola ★ (*Russian* jaʃ'kara'la) *n* a city in Russia, capital of the Mari El Republic. Pop.: 251 000 (1995 est.).

you (juː; *unstressed* ju) *pron* (*subjective or objective*) **1** refers to the person addressed or to more than one person including the person or persons addressed: *you know better; the culprit is among you.* **2** refers to an unspecified person or people in general: *you can't tell the boys from the girls.* ◆ *n* **3** *Inf.* the personality of the person being addressed: *that hat isn't really you.* **4 you know what** *or* **who.** a thing or person that the speaker does not want to specify. [OE *ēow*, dative & accusative of *gē* ye]

USAGE NOTE See at **me**¹.

---

you'd (juːd; *unstressed* jud) *contraction of* you had *or* you would.

you'll (juːl; *unstressed* jul) *contraction of* you will *or* you shall.

young (jʌŋ) *adj* **younger** ('jʌŋgə), **youngest** ('jʌŋgɪst). **1a** having lived, existed, or been made or known for a relatively short time: *a young country.* **1b** (*as collective n;* preceded by *the*): *the young.* **2** youthful or having qualities associated with youth; vigorous or lively. **3** of or relating to youth: *in my young days.* **4** having been established or introduced for a relatively short time: *a young member.* **5** in an early stage of progress or development; not far advanced: *the day was young.* **6** (*often cap.*) of or relating to a rejuvenated group or movement or one claiming to represent the younger members of the population: *Young Socialists.* ◆ *n* **7** (*functioning as pl*) offspring, esp. young animals: *a rabbit with her young.* **8 with young.** (of animals) pregnant. [OE *geong*]
▸ **'youngish** *adj*

Young ★ (jʌŋ) *n* **1 Brigham** ('brɪgəm). 1801–77, US Mormon leader, who led the Mormon migration to Utah and founded Salt Lake City (1847). **2 Edward.** 1683–1765, English poet and dramatist, noted for his *Night Thoughts on Life, Death, and Immortality* (1742–45). **3 Lester.** 1909–59, US saxophonist and clarinettist. **4 Neil.** born 1945, Canadian rock guitarist, singer, and songwriter. His albums include *Sleeps with Angels* (1994). **5 Thomas.** 1773–1829, British physicist, physician, and Egyptologist. He helped to establish the wave theory of light by his experiments on optical interference and assisted in deciphering the Rosetta Stone.

young blood *n* young, fresh, or vigorous new people, ideas, attitudes, etc.

Young Fogey *n* a young person who adopts the conservative values of an older generation.

young lady *n* a girlfriend; sweetheart.

youngling ('jʌŋlɪŋ) *n Literary.* **a** a young person, animal, or plant. **b** (*as modifier*): *a youngling brood.* [OE *geongling*]

young man *n* a boyfriend; sweetheart.

young offender institution *n* (in Britain) a place where offenders aged 15 to 21 may be detained and given training, instruction, and work. Former names: **borstal, youth custody centre.**

Young Pretender ★ *n* See (Charles Edward) **Stuart.**

Young's modulus *n* a modulus of elasticity, applicable to the stretching of a wire, etc., equal to the ratio of the applied load per unit area of cross section to the increase in length per unit length. [after Thomas YOUNG]

youngster ('jʌŋstə) *n* **1** a young person; child or youth. **2** a young animal, esp. a horse.

Youngstown ★ ('jʌŋz,taun) *n* a city in NE Ohio: a major centre of steel production: university (1908). Pop.: 91 775 (1994 est.).

Young Turk *n* **1** a progressive, revolutionary, or rebellious member of an organization, political party, etc. **2** a member of an abortive reform movement in the Ottoman Empire.

younker ('jʌŋkə) *n* **1** *Arch. or literary.* a young man; lad. **2** *Obs.* a young gentleman or knight. [C16: from Du. *jonker*, from MDu. *jonc* young]

your (jɔː, juə; *unstressed* jə) *determiner* **1** of, belonging to, or associated with you: *your nose; your house.* **2** belonging to or associated with an unspecified person or people in general: *the path is on your left heading north.* **3** *Inf.* used to indicate all things or people of a certain type: *your part-time worker is a problem.* [OE *eower*, genitive of *gē* ye]

you're (jɔː; *unstressed* jə) *contraction of* you are.

yours (jɔːz, juəz) *pron* **1** something or someone belonging to or associated with you. **2** your family: *greetings to you and yours.* **3** used in conventional closing phrases at the end of a letter: *yours sincerely; yours faithfully.* **4 of yours.** belonging to or associated with you.

yourself (jɔː'sɛlf, juə-) *pron, pl* **yourselves. 1a** the reflexive form of *you.* **1b** (intensifier): *you yourself control your fate.* **2** (*preceded by a copula*) your usual self: *you're not yourself.*

yours truly *pron* an informal term for *I* or *me.* [from the closing phrase of letters]

youth (juːθ) *n, pl* **youths** (juːðz). **1** the quality or condition of being young, immature, or inexperienced: *his youth told against him in the contest.* **2** the period between childhood and maturity. **3** the freshness, vigour, or vitality characteristic of young people. **4** any period of early development. **5** a young person, esp. a young man or boy. **6** young people collectively: *youth everywhere is rising in revolt.* [OE *geogoth*]

Youth ★ (juːθ) *n* **Isle of.** an island in the NW Caribbean, south of Cuba: administratively part of Cuba from 1925. Chief town: Nueva Gerona. Pop.: 73 319 (1990 est.). Area: 3061 sq. km (1182 sq. miles). Former name: **Isle of Pines.** Spanish name: **Isla de la Juventud** ('izla ðe la xuβen'tuð).

youth club *n* a centre providing leisure activities for young people.

youthful ('juːθful) *adj* **1** of, relating to, possessing, or characteristic of youth. **2** fresh, vigorous, or active: *he's surprisingly youthful for his age.* **3** in an early stage of development: *a youthful culture.* **4** Also: **young.** (of a river, valley, or land surface) in the early stage of the cycle of erosion, characterized by steep slopes, lack of flood plains, and V-shaped valleys.
▸ **'youthfully** *adv* ▸ **'youthfulness** *n*

youth hostel *n* one of an organization of inexpensive lodging places for people travelling cheaply. Often shortened to **hostel.**

Youth Training Scheme *n* (formerly, in Britain) a scheme, run by the Training Agency, to provide vocational training for unemployed 16–17-year-olds. Abbrev.: **YTS.**

you've (juːv; *unstressed* juv) *contraction of* you have.

yowl (jaul) *vb* **1** to express with or produce a loud mournful wail or cry; howl. ◆ *n* **2** a wail or howl. [C13: from ON *gaula*]
▸ **'yowler** *n*

yo-yo ('jəujəu) *n, pl* **yo-yos. 1.** a toy consisting of a spool attached to a string, the end of which is held while it is repeatedly spun out and reeled in. **2** *Sl., chiefly US.* a silly or insignificant person. ◆ *vb* **yo-yos, yo-yoing, yo-yoed.** (*intr*) to change repeatedly from one position to another; fluctuate. [from Filipino *yo yo* come come, a weapon consisting of a spindle attached to a thong]

Ypres ★ (*French* iprə) *n* a town in W Belgium, in W Flanders province near the border with France: scene of many sieges and battles, esp. in World War I, when it

---

was completely destroyed. Pop.: 21 400 (1991 est.). Flemish name: **Ieper.**

Ypsilanti (ˌɪpsɪˈlæntɪ), **Hypsilantis,** or **Hypsilantes** ★ n **1 Alexander** (ˌalekˈsander). 1792–1828, Greek patriot, who led an unsuccessful revolt against the Turks (1821). **2** his brother, **Demetrios** (ðimitriˈɔs). 1793–1832, Greek revolutionary leader; commander in chief of Greek forces (1828–30) during the war of independence.

yr abbrev. for: **1** (pl **yrs**) year. **2** younger. **3** your.

yrs abbrev. for: **1** years. **2** yours.

Yser ★ (French izer) n a river in NW central Europe, rising in N France and flowing through SW Belgium to the North Sea: scene of battles in World War I. Length: 77 km (48 miles).

Yseult ★ (ɪˈsuːlt) n a variant spelling of **Iseult.**

Yssel ★ (ˈaɪsᵊl) n a variant spelling of **IJssel.**

YST (in Canada) abbrev. for Yukon Standard Time.

YT abbrev. for Yukon Territory.

YTS (in Britain) abbrev. for Youth Training Scheme.

ytterbia (ɪˈtɜːbɪə) n another name for **ytterbium oxide.** [C19: NL; see YTTERBIUM]

ytterbium (ɪˈtɜːbɪəm) n a soft malleable silvery element of the lanthanide series of metals that is used to improve the mechanical properties of steel. Symbol: Yb; atomic no.: 70; atomic wt.: 173.04. [C19: NL, after Ytterby, Swedish quarry where discovered]

ytterbium oxide n a weakly basic hygroscopic substance used in certain alloys and ceramics.

yttria (ˈɪtrɪə) n another name for **yttrium oxide.** [C19: NL; see YTTERBIUM]

yttrium (ˈɪtrɪəm) n a silvery metallic element used in various alloys, in lasers, and as a catalyst. Symbol: Y; atomic no.: 39; atomic wt.: 88.90. [C19: NL; see YTTERBIUM]

yttrium metal n Chem. any one of a group of elements including yttrium and the related lanthanides.

yttrium oxide n a colourless or white insoluble solid used in incandescent mantles.

yuan (ˈjuːˈæn) n, pl **yuan**. the standard monetary unit of China. [from Chinese yüan round object; see YEN[1]]

Yüan[1] ★ (ˈjuːˈæn) n the imperial dynasty of China from 1279 to 1368.

Yüan[2] (ˈjuːˈæn) or **Yüen** ★ (ˈjuːˈɛn) n a river in SE central China, rising in central Guizhou province and flowing northeast to Lake Tungting. Length: about 800 km (500 miles).

Yuan Tan (ˈjuːˈæn ˈtæn) n an annual Chinese festival marking the Chinese New Year. It can last over three days and includes the exchange of gifts, firework displays, and dancing.

Yucatán ★ (ˌjuːkəˈtɑːn; Spanish jukaˈtan) n **1** a state of SE Mexico, occupying the N part of the Yucatán peninsula. Capital: Mérida. Pop.: 1 555 733 (1995 est.). Area: 39 340 sq. km (15 186 sq. miles). **2** a peninsula of Central America between the Gulf of Mexico and the Caribbean, including the Mexican states of Campeche, Yucatán, and Quintana Roo, and part of Belize: is centre of Mayan civilization from about 100 B.C. to the 18th century. Area: about 181 300 sq. km (70 000 sq. miles).

Yucatán Channel ★ n a channel between W Cuba and the Yucatán peninsula.

yucca (ˈjʌkə) n any of a genus of liliaceous plants of tropical and subtropical America, having stiff lancelike leaves and spikes of white flowers. [C16: from American Sp. yuca, ult. from Amerind]

yuck or **yuk** (jʌk) interj Sl. an exclamation indicating contempt, dislike, or disgust.

yucky or **yukky** (ˈjʌkɪ) adj **yuckier, yuckiest** or **yukkier, yukkiest.** Sl. disgusting; nasty.

Yugo. abbrev. for Yugoslavia.

Yugoslav or **Jugoslav** (ˈjuːgəʊˌslɑːv) n **1** a native or inhabitant of Yugoslavia. **2** (not in technical use) another name for **Serbo-Croat** (the language). ◆ adj **3** of, relating to, or characteristic of Yugoslavia or its people.

Yugoslavia or **Jugoslavia** ★ (ˌjuːgəʊˈslɑːvɪə) n **1** Federal Republic of Yugoslavia. a country, comprising Serbia

and Montenegro, that was formed in 1991, but has not been internationally recognized, mainly because of Serbia's role in the civil war in Bosnia-Herzegovina. It is mainly mountainous and rugged, with the fertile Danube-Sava Basin in the northeast. **2** a former country in SE Europe, on the Adriatic: established in 1918 from the independent states of Serbia and Montenegro, and regions that until World War I had belonged to Austria-Hungary (Croatia, Slovenia, and Bosnia-Herzegovina); the name was changed from Kingdom of Serbs, Croats, and Slovenes to Yugoslavia in 1929; German invasion of 1941–44 was resisted chiefly by a Communist group led by Tito, who declared a people's republic in 1945; it became the Socialist Federal Republic of Yugoslavia in 1963; in 1991, following political crises, Croatia, Slovenia, and Bosnia-Herzegovina declared independence, followed by Macedonia in 1992.
► ˌYugoˈslavian or ˌJugoˈslavian adj, n

Yukawa ★ (juˈkɑːwə) n **Hideki** (ˈhiːdɛkɪ). 1907–81, Japanese nuclear physicist, who predicted (1935) the existence of mesons: Nobel prize for physics 1949.

Yukon ★ (ˈjuːkɒn) n **the.** a territory of NW Canada, on the Beaufort Sea, between the Northwest Territories and Alaska: arctic and mountainous, reaching 6050 m (19 850 ft) at Mount Logan, Canada's highest peak; mineral resources. Capital: Whitehorse. Pop.: 30 100 (1995 est.). Area: 536 327 sq. km (207 076 sq. miles). Abbrev.: **YT.**
► ˈYukoner n

Yukon River ★ n a river in NW North America, rising in NW Canada on the border between the Yukon Territory and British Columbia: flows northwest into Alaska, US, and then southwest to the Bering Sea; navigable for about 2850 km (1775 miles) to Whitehorse. Length: 3185 km (1979 miles).

yulan (ˈjuːlæn) n a Chinese magnolia that is often cultivated for its showy white flowers. [C19: from Chinese, from yu a gem + lan plant]

yule (juːl) n (sometimes cap.) Literary, arch., or dialect. **a** Christmas or the Christmas season. **b** (in combination): yuletide. [OE geōla, orig. a pagan feast lasting 12 days]

yule log n a large log of wood traditionally used as the foundation of a fire at Christmas.

yummy (ˈjʌmɪ) Sl. ◆ interj **1** Also: **yum-yum.** an exclamation indicating pleasure or delight, as in anticipation of delicious food. ◆ adj **yummier, yummiest. 2** delicious, delightful, or attractive. [C20: from yum-yum, imit.]

Yünnan ★ (juːˈnæn) n a province of SW China: consists mainly of a plateau broken in the southeast by the Red and Black Rivers, with mountains in the west, rising over 5500 m (18 000 ft); large deposits of tin, lead, zinc, and coal. Capital: Kunming. Pop.: 39 390 000 (1995 est.). Area: 436 200 sq. km (168 400 sq. miles).

yuppie or **yuppy** (ˈjʌpɪ) (sometimes cap.) ◆ n **1** an affluent young professional person. ◆ adj **2** typical of or reflecting the values characteristic of yuppies. [C20: from y(oung) u(rban) or up(wardly mobile) p(rofessional) + -IE]
► ˈyuppiedom n

yuppie disease or **flu** n Inf., sometimes considered offens. any of a number of debilitating long-lasting viral disorders associated with stress, such as chronic fatigue syndrome, whose symptoms include muscle weakness, chronic tiredness, and depression.

yuppify (ˈjʌpɪˌfaɪ) vb **yuppies, yuppifying, yuppified.** (tr) to make yuppie in nature.
► ˌyuppifiˈcation n

Yurev ★ (Russian ˈjurjɪf) n the former name (11th century until 1918) of **Tartu.**

yurt (jʊət) n a circular tent consisting of a framework of poles covered with felt or skins, used by Mongolian and Turkic nomads of E and central Asia. [from Russian yurta, of Turkic origin]

Yuzovka ★ (Russian ˈjuzəfkə) n a former name (1872 until after the Revolution) of **Donetsk.**

Yvelines ★ (French ivlin) n a department of N France, in Île de France region. Capital: Versailles. Pop.: 1 363 068 (1994 est.). Area: 2271 sq. km (886 sq. miles).

YWCA abbrev. for Young Women's Christian Association.

★ people and places

Zz

z or **Z** (zɛd; *US* ziː) *n, pl* **z's, Z's,** or **Zs. 1** the 26th and last letter of the English alphabet. **2** a speech sound represented by this letter. **3a** something shaped like a Z. **3b** (*in combination*): *a Z-bend in a road.*

z *Maths. symbol for:* **1** the z-axis or a coordinate measured along the z-axis in a Cartesian or cylindrical coordinate system. **2** an algebraic variable.

Z *symbol for:* **1** any unknown, variable, or unspecified factor, number, person, or thing. **2** *Chem.* atomic number. **3** *Physics.* impedance. **4** zone.

z. *abbrev. for:* **1** zero. **2** zone.

Zaandam ★ (*Dutch* zaːnˈdɑm) *n* a former town in the W Netherlands, in North Holland: an important shipbuilding centre in the 17th century. It became part of Zaanstad in 1974.

Zaanstad ★ (*Dutch* zaːnˈtjtat) *n* a port in the W Netherlands, in North Holland: formed (1974) from Zaandam, Koog a/d Zaan, Zaandijk, Wormerveer, Krommenie, Westzaan, and Assendelft; food and machinery industries. Pop.: 132 508 (1994).

zabaglione (ˌzæbəˈljəʊnɪ) *n* a light foamy dessert made of egg yolks, sugar, and marsala, whipped together and served warm in a glass. [It.]

Zabrze ★ (*Polish* ˈzabʒɛ) *n* a city in SW Poland: a Prussian and German town from 1742 until 1945, when it passed to Poland; industrial centre in a coal-mining region. Pop.: 201 800 (1995 est.). German name: **Hindenburg**.

Zacatecas ★ (*Spanish* θakaˈtekas) *n* **1** a state of N central Mexico, on the central plateau: rich mineral resources. Capital: Zacatecas. Pop.: 1 336 348 (1995 est.). Area: 75 040 sq. km (28 973 sq. miles). **2** a city in N central Mexico, capital of Zacatecas state: silver mines. Pop.: 100 051 (1990).

Zacharias (ˌzækəˈraɪəs), **Zachariah** (ˌzækəˈraɪə), or **Zachary** ★ (ˈzækərɪ) *n New Testament.* John the Baptist's father, who underwent a temporary period of dumbness for his lack of faith (Luke 1).

Zacynthus ★ (zəˈsɪnθəs, -ˈkɪn-) *n* the Latin name for **Zante**.

zaffer or **zaffre** (ˈzæfə) *n* impure cobalt oxide, used to impart a blue colour to enamels. [C17: from It. *zaffera*]

Zagazig (ˈzægəˌzɪg) or **Zaqaziq** ★ *n* a city in NE Egypt, in the Nile Delta: major cotton market. Pop.: 287 000 (1992 est.).

Zagreb ★ (ˈzɑːgrɛb) *n* the capital of Croatia, on the River Sava; university (1874); industrial centre. Pop.: 867 717 (1991). German name: **Agram**.

Zagreus ★ (ˈzægrɪəs) *n Greek myth.* a young god whose cult came from Crete to Greece, where he was identified with Dionysus. The son of Zeus by either Demeter or Persephone, he was killed by the Titans at the behest of Hera.

Zagros Mountains ★ (ˈzægrɒs) *pl n* a mountain range in S Iran: has Iran's main oilfields in its W central foothills. Highest peak: Zard Kuh, 4548 m (14 920 ft).

zaibatsu (ˈzaɪbætˈsuː) *n* (*functioning as sing or pl*) the group or combine comprising a few wealthy families that controls industry, business, and finance in Japan. [from Japanese, from *zai* wealth + *batsu* family, person of influence]

Zaïre ★ (zɑːˈɪə) *n* **1** the former name (1971–97) of the (Democratic Republic of the) **Congo** (sense 2). **2** (formerly) the Zaïrian name for the (River) **Congo**.
▶ **Za'irian** or **Zaïr'ese** *adj, n*

Zákinthos ★ (ˈzakinˌθɒs) *n* transliteration of the Modern Greek name for **Zante**.

zakuski or **zakouski** (zæˈkʊskɪ) *pl n, sing* **zakuska** or **zakouska** (-kə). *Russian cookery.* hors d'oeuvres, consisting of tiny open sandwiches spread with caviar, smoked sausage, etc., or a cold dish such as radishes in sour cream, all usually served with vodka. [Russian, from *zakusit'* to have a snack]

Zama ★ (ˈzɑːmə) *n* the name of several ancient cities in N Africa, including the one near the site of Scipio's decisive defeat of Hannibal (202 B.C.).

Zambezi or **Zambese** ★ (zæmˈbiːzɪ) *n* a river in S central and E Africa, rising in NW Zambia and flowing across E Angola back into Zambia, continuing south to the Caprivi Strip of Namibia, then east forming the Zambia–Zimbabwe border, and finally crossing Mozambique to the Indian Ocean: the fourth longest river in Africa. Length: 2740 km (1700 miles).
▶ **Zam'bezian** *adj*

Zambia ★ (ˈzæmbɪə) *n* a republic in southern Africa: an early site of human settlement; controlled by the British South Africa Company by 1900 and unified as Northern Rhodesia in 1911; made a British protectorate in 1924; part of the Federation of Rhodesia and Nyasaland (1953–63), gaining independence as a member of the Commonwealth in 1964; important mineral exports, esp. copper. Official language: English. Religion: Christian majority, also animist. Currency: kwacha. Capital: Lusaka. Pop.: 9 350 000 (1997). Area: 752 617 sq. km (290 587 sq. miles). Former name (until 1964): **Northern Rhodesia**.
▶ **Zambian** *adj, n*

Zamboanga ★ (ˌzæmbəʊˈæŋɡə) *n* a port in the Philippines, on SW Mindanao on Basilan Strait: founded by the Spanish in 1635; tourist centre, with fisheries. Pop.: 464 466 (1994 est.).

zambuck or **zambuk** (ˈzæmbʌk) *n Austral. & NZ inf.* a first-aid attendant at a sports event. [from name of a proprietary ointment]

Zamenhof ★ (*Polish* ˈzamɛnxɔf) *n* **Lazarus Ludwig** (laˈzarus ˈludvik). 1859–1917, Polish oculist; invented Esperanto.

Zamora ★ (*Spanish* θaˈmora) *n* a city in NW central Spain, on the Douro River. Pop.: 58 560 (1980).

Zamyatin ★ (*Russian* zaˈmjatin) *n* **Yevgenii Ivanovich** (jɪvˈɡjenij ɪˈvanəvitʃ). 1884–1937, Russian writer, in Paris from 1931, whose works include the novel *We* (1924).

Zante ★ (ˈzæntɪ) *n* an island in the Ionian Sea, off the W coast of Greece: southernmost of the Ionian Islands; traditionally belonged to Ulysses, king of Ithaca. Pop.: 32 557 (1991). Area: 402 sq. km (155 sq. miles). Latin name: **Zacynthus**. Ancient Greek name: **Zakynthos** (zəˈkuːnθɒs). Modern Greek name: **Zákinthos**.

ZANU (ˈzɑːnuː) *n acronym for* Zimbabwe African National Union.

zany (ˈzeɪnɪ) *adj* **zanier, zaniest. 1** comical in an endearing way; imaginatively funny or comical, esp. in behaviour. ◆ *n, pl* **zanies. 2** a clown or buffoon, esp. one in old comedies who imitated other performers with ludicrous effect. **3** a ludicrous or foolish person. [C16: from It. *zanni*, from dialect *Zanni*, nickname for *Giovanni* John; one of the traditional names for a clown]
▶ **'zanily** *adv* ▶ **'zaniness** *n*

Zanzibar ★ (ˌzænzɪˈbɑː) *n* an island in the Indian Ocean, off the E coast of Africa: settled by Persians and Arabs from the 7th century onwards; became a flourishing trading centre for slaves, ivory, and cloves; made a British protectorate in 1890, becoming independent within the Commonwealth in 1963 and a republic in 1964; joined with Tanganyika in 1964 to form the United Republic of Tanzania. Pop.: 444 000 (1994 est.).
▶ **Zanzi'bari** *adj, n*

zap (zæp) *Sl.* ◆ *vb* **zaps, zapping, zapped. 1** (*tr*) to attack, kill, or destroy, as with a sudden bombardment. **2** (*intr*) to move quickly. **3** (*tr*) *Computing*. **3a** to clear from the screen. **3b** to erase. **4** (*intr*) *Television*. to change channels rapidly by remote control. ◆ *n* **5** energy, vigour, or pep.

★ people and places

◆ *interj* **6** an exclamation used to express sudden or swift action. [C20: imit.]

Zapata ★ (zə'paːtə; *Spanish* θa'pata) *n* **Emiliano** (emi-'ljano). ?1877–1919, Mexican guerrilla leader.

zapateado *Spanish.* (ˌθapateˈaðo) *n, pl* -**dos** (-ðos). a Spanish dance with stamping and very fast footwork. [from *zapatear* to tap with the shoe, from *zapato* shoe]

Zaporozhye ★ (*Russian* zəpa'rɔzje) *n* a city in the E Ukraine, on the Dnieper River: developed as a major industrial centre following the construction in 1932 of the Dnieper hydroelectric station. Pop.: 882 000 (1996 est.). Former name (until 1921): **Aleksandrovsk**.

Zappa ★ ('zæpə) *n* **Frank.** 1940–93, US rock musician, songwriter, and producer: leader of the Mothers of Invention.

zappy ('zæpɪ) *adj* **zappier, zappiest.** *Sl.* full of energy; zippy.

ZAPU ('zæpuː) *n acronym for* Zimbabwe African People's Union.

Zaqaziq ★ ('zækəˌzɪk) *n* a variant of **Zagazig**.

Zaragoza ★ (*Spanish* θaraˈɣoθa) *n* a city in NE Spain, on the River Ebro: Roman colony established 25 B.C.; under Moorish rule (714–1118); capital of Aragon (12th–15th centuries); twice besieged by the French during the Peninsular War and captured (1809); university (1474). Pop.: 596 080 (1986). Pre-Roman name: **Salduba**. Latin name: **Caesaraugusta**. English name: **Saragossa**.

Zarathustra ★ (ˌzærəˈθuːstrə) *n* the Avestan name of **Zoroaster**.
▶ ˌ**Zaraˈthustrian** *or* ˌ**Zaraˈthustric** *adj, n*

zareba *or* **zareeba** (zəˈriːbə) *n* (in northern E Africa, esp. formerly) **1** a stockade or enclosure of thorn bushes around a village or camp site. **2** the area so protected or enclosed. [C19: from Ár. *zarībah* cattlepen, from *zarb* sheepfold]

zarf (zɑːf) *n* (esp. in the Middle East) a holder, usually ornamental, for a hot coffee cup. [from Ar.: container]

Zaria ★ ('zɑːrɪə) *n* a city in N central Nigeria: former capital of a Hausa state; agricultural trading centre; university (1962). Pop.: 369 800 (1995 est.).

Zarqa ★ ('zɑːkə) *n* the second largest town in Jordan, northeast of Amman. Pop.: 344 524 (1994).

zarzuela (zɑːˈzweɪlə) *n* **1** a type of Spanish vaudeville or operetta, usually satirical in nature. **2** a seafood stew. [from Sp., after *La Zarzuela*, the palace near Madrid where such vaudeville was first performed (1629)]

Zátopek ★ (*Czech* 'zaːtɔpɛk) *n* **Emil** ('emil). born 1922, Czech runner; winner of the 5000 and 10 000 metres and the marathon at the 1952 Olympic Games in Helsinki.

z-axis *n* a reference axis of a three-dimensional Cartesian coordinate system along which the *z*-coordinate is measured.

ZB station *n* (in New Zealand) a radio station of a commercial network.

Z chart *n Statistics.* a chart often used in industry and constructed by plotting on it three series: monthly, weekly, or daily data, the moving annual total, and the cumulative total dating from the beginning of the current year.

Zea ★ ('tseːa) *n* the Italian name for **Keos**.

zeal (ziːl) *n* fervent or enthusiastic devotion, often extreme or fanatical in nature, as to a religious movement, political cause, ideal, or aspiration. [C14: from LL *zēlus*, from Gk *zēlos*]

Zealand ★ ('ziːlənd) *n* the largest island of Denmark, separated from the island of Funen by the Great Belt and from S Sweden by the Sound. Chief town: Copenhagen. Pop.: 2 000 254 (1988 est.). Area: 7016 sq. km (2709 sq. miles). Danish name: **Sjælland**. German name: **Seeland**.

zealot ('zɛlət) *n* an immoderate, fanatical, or extremely zealous adherent to a cause, esp. a religious one. [C16: from LL *zēlōtēs*, from Gk, from *zēloun* to be zealous, from *zēlos* zeal]
▶ '**zealotry** *n*

Zealot ('zɛlət) *n* any of the members of an extreme Jew-

ish sect or political party that resisted all aspects of Roman rule in Palestine in the 1st century A.D.

zealous ('zɛləs) *adj* filled with or inspired by intense enthusiasm or zeal; ardent; fervent.
▶ '**zealously** *adv* ▶ '**zealousness** *n*

Zeami *or* **Seami** ★ (siːˈɑːmɪ) *n* **Motokiyo** (ˌməʊtəʊˈkiːəʊ). 1363–1443, Japanese No dramatist.

zebec *or* **zebeck** ('ziːbɛk) *n* variant spellings of **xebec**.

Zebedee ★ ('zɛbɪˌdiː) *n New Testament.* the father of the apostles James and John (Matthew 4:21).

zebra ('ziːbrə, 'zɛbrə) *n, pl* **zebras** *or* **zebra**. any of several mammals of the horse family, such as the common zebra of southern and eastern Africa, having distinctive black-and-white striped hides. [C16: via It. from OSp.: wild ass, prob. from Vulgar L *eciferus* (unattested) wild horse, from L *equiferus*, from *equus* horse + *ferus* wild]
▶ '**zebrine** ('ziːbraɪn, 'zɛb-) *or* '**zebroid** *adj*

Zebra ('ziːbrə, 'zɛbrə) *n Finance.* a noninterest-paying bond in which the accrued income is taxed annually rather than on redemption. Cf. **zero** (sense 10). [C20: from *zero-coupon bond*]

zebra crossing *n Brit.* a pedestrian crossing marked on a road by broad alternate black and white stripes. Once on the crossing the pedestrian has right of way.

zebra finch *n* any of various Australasian songbirds with zebra-like markings.

zebrawood ('zebrəˌwʊd, 'ziː-) *n* **1** a tree of tropical America, Asia, and Africa, yielding striped hardwood used in cabinetwork. **2** any of various other trees or shrubs having striped wood. **3** the wood of any of these trees.

zebu ('ziːbuː) *n* a domesticated ox having a humped back, long horns, and a large dewlap: used in India and E Asia as a draught animal. [C18: from F *zébu*, ? of Tibetan origin]

Zebulun ★ ('zɛbjʊlən, zəˈbjuː-) *n Old Testament.* **1** the sixth son whom Leah bore to Jacob: one of the 12 patriarchs of Israel (Genesis 30:20). **2** the tribe descended from him. **3** the territory of this tribe, lying in lower Galilee to the north of Mount Carmel and to the east of the coastal plain. Douay spelling: **Zabulon** ('zæbjʊlən, zəˈbjuː-).

Zech. *Bible. abbrev. for* Zechariah.

Zechariah ★ (ˌzɛkəˈraɪə) *n* **1** *Old Testament.* **1a** a Hebrew prophet of the late 6th century B.C. **1b** the book containing his oracles, which are chiefly concerned with the renewal of Israel after the exile as a national, religious, and messianic community with the restored Temple and rebuilt Jerusalem as its centre. Douay spelling: **Zacharias. 2** a variant spelling of **Zachariah**. See **Zacharias**.

zed (zɛd) *n* the British spoken form of the letter z. [C15: from OF *zede*, via LL from Gk *zēta*]

Zedekiah ★ (ˌzɛdəˈkaɪə) *n Old Testament.* the last king of Judah, who died in captivity at Babylon. Douay spelling: **Sedecias** (ˌsɛdəˈkaɪəs).

zedoary ('zɛdəʊərɪ) *n* the dried rhizome of a tropical Asian plant, used as a stimulant and a condiment. [C15: from Med. L *zedoaria*, from Ar. *zadwār*, of Persian origin]

zee (ziː) *n* the US word for **zed** (letter z).

Zeebrugge ★ (*Flemish* 'zeːbryxə; *English* 'ziːˌbrʊgə) *n* a port in NW Belgium, in W Flanders on the North Sea: linked by canal with Bruges; German submarine base in World War I.

Zeeland ★ (*Dutch* 'zeːlɑnt; *English* 'ziːlənd) *n* a province of the SW Netherlands: consists of a small area on the mainland together with a number of islands in the Scheldt estuary; mostly below sea level. Capital: Middelburg. Pop.: 365 846 (1995). Area: 1787 sq. km (690 sq. miles).
▶ '**Zeelander** *n*

Zeeman effect ('ziːmən) *n* the splitting of a spectral line of a substance into several closely spaced lines when the substance is placed in a magnetic field. [C20: after Pieter *Zeeman* (1865–1943), Du. physicist]

Zeffirelli ★ (ˌzɛfɪˈrɛlɪ; *Italian* dzeffɪˈrɛlli) *n* **Franco** ('franko). born 1923, Italian stage and film director and designer, noted for his work in opera.

★ people and places

zein ('ziːɪn) n a protein occurring in maize and used in the manufacture of plastics, paper coatings, adhesives, etc. [C19: from NL *zēa* maize, from L: a kind of grain, from Gk *zeia* barley]

Zeist ★ (zaɪst; *Dutch* zɛjst) n a city in the central Netherlands, near Utrecht. Pop.: 59 258 (1994).

Zeitgeist *German.* ('tsaɪt,gaɪst) n the spirit, attitude, or general outlook of a specific time or period, esp. as it is reflected in literature, philosophy, etc. [G, lit.: time spirit]

Zen (zen) *Buddhism.* n **1** a Japanese school, of 12th-century Chinese origin, teaching that contemplation of one's essential nature to the exclusion of all else is the only way of achieving pure enlightenment. **2** (*modifier*) of or relating to this school: *Zen Buddhism.* [from Japanese, from Chinese *ch'an* religious meditation, from Pali *jhāna*, from Sansk. *dhyāna*]
▸ **'Zenic** adj ▸ **'Zenist** n

zenana (zɛ'nɑːnə) n (in the East, esp. in Muslim and Hindu homes) part of a house reserved for the women and girls of a household. [C18: from Hindi *zanāna*, from Persian, from *zan* woman]

Zend (zend) n **1** a former name for **Avestan**. **2** short for **Zend-Avesta**. **3** an exposition of the Avesta in the Middle Persian language (Pahlavi). [C18: from Persian *zand* commentary, exposition; used specifically of the MPersian commentary on the Avesta, hence of the language of the Avesta itself]
▸ **'Zendic** adj

Zend-Avesta (,zɛndə'vɛstə) n the Avesta together with the traditional interpretive commentary known as the Zend, esp. as preserved in the Avestan language among the Parsees. [from Avestan, representing *Avesta'-va-zend* Avesta with interpretation]

Zener diode ('ziːnə) n a semiconductor diode that exhibits a sharp increase in reverse current at a well-defined reverse voltage: used as a voltage regulator. [C20: after C. M. *Zener* (1905–93), US physicist]

zenith ('zɛnɪθ) n **1** *Astron.* the point on the celestial sphere vertically above an observer. **2** the highest point; peak; acme: *the zenith of someone's achievements.* [C17: from F *cenith*, from Med. L, from OSp. *zenit*, based on Ar. *samt*, as in *samt arrās* path over one's head]
▸ **'zenithal** adj

zenithal projection n a type of map projection in which part of the earth's surface is projected onto a plane tangential to it, either at one of the poles (**polar zenithal**), at the equator (**equatorial zenithal**), or between (**oblique zenithal**).

Zenobia ★ (zɪ'nəʊbɪə) n 3rd century A.D., queen of Palmyra (?267–272), who was captured by the Roman emperor Aurelian.

Zeno of Citium ★ ('ziːnəʊ əv 'sɪtɪəm) n ?336–?264 B.C., Greek philosopher, who founded the Stoic school in Athens.

Zeno of Elea ★ n ?490–?430 B.C., Greek Eleatic philosopher; disciple of Parmenides.

zeolite ('ziːə,laɪt) n **1** any of a large group of glassy secondary minerals consisting of hydrated aluminium silicates of calcium, sodium, or potassium: formed in cavities in lava flows and plutonic rocks. **2** any of a class of similar synthetic materials used in ion exchange and as selective absorbents. [C18: from *zeo-*, from Gk *zein* to boil + *-LITE*; from the swelling that occurs under the blowpipe]
▸ **zeolitic** (,ziːə'lɪtɪk) adj

Zeph. *Bible. abbrev.* for Zephaniah.

Zephaniah ★ (,zɛfə'naɪə) n *Old Testament.* **1** a Hebrew prophet of the late 7th century B.C. **2** the book containing his oracles, which are chiefly concerned with the approaching judgment by God upon the sinners of Judah. Douay spelling: **Sophonias** (,sɒfə'naɪəs).

zephyr ('zɛfə) n **1** a soft or gentle breeze. **2** any of several delicate soft yarns, fabrics, or garments, usually of wool. [C16: from L *zephyrus*, from Gk *zephuros* the west wind]

Zephyrus ★ ('zɛfərəs) n *Greek myth.* the god of the west wind.

zeppelin ('zɛpəlɪn) n (*sometimes cap.*) a large cylindrical rigid airship built from 1900 to carry passengers and used in World War I for bombing and reconnaissance. [C20: after Count von ZEPPELIN]

Zeppelin ★ (*German* 'tsɛpəliːn) n Count **Ferdinand von** ('ferdinant fɔn). 1838–1917, German aeronautical pioneer, who designed and manufactured airships (zeppelins).

Zermatt ★ (*German* tsɛr'mat) n a village and resort in S Switzerland, in Valais canton at the foot of the Matterhorn: cars are banned from the area. Pop.: 4200 (1989 est.).

zero ('zɪərəʊ) n, pl **zeros** or **zeroes**. **1** the symbol 0, indicating an absence of quantity or magnitude; nought. Former name: **cipher. 2** the integer denoted by the symbol 0; nought. **3** the cardinal number between +1 and –1. **4** nothing; nil. **5** a person or thing of no significance; nonentity. **6** the lowest point or degree: *his prospects were put at zero.* **7** the line or point on a scale of measurement from which the graduations commence. **8a** the temperature, pressure, etc., that registers a reading of zero on a scale. **8b** the value of a variable, such as temperature, obtained under specified conditions. **9** *Maths.* **9a** the cardinal number of a set with no members. **9b** the identity element of addition. **10** *Finance.* Also called: **zero-coupon bond.** a bond that pays no interest, the equivalent being paid in its redemption value. Cf. **Zebra.** ◆ adj **11** having no measurable quantity, magnitude, etc. **12** *Meteorol.* **12a** (of a cloud ceiling) limiting visibility to 15 metres (50 feet) or less. **12b** (of horizontal visibility) limited to 50 metres (165 feet) or less. ◆ vb **zeros** or **zeroes**, **zeroing**, **zeroed**. **13** (*tr*) to adjust (an instrument, apparatus, etc.) so as to read zero or a position taken as zero. ◆ determiner **14** *Inf.*, chiefly US. no (thing) at all: *this job has zero interest.* ◆ See also **zero in.** [C17: from It., from Med. L *zephirum*, from Ar. *sifr* empty]

zero gravity n the state or condition of weightlessness.

zero hour n **1** *Mil.* the time set for the start of an attack or the initial stage of an operation. **2** *Inf.* a critical time, esp. at the commencement of an action.

zero in vb (*adv*) **1** (often foll. by *on*) to bring (a weapon) to bear (on a target), as while firing repeatedly. **2** (*intr;* foll. by *on*) *Inf.* to bring one's attention to bear (on a problem, etc.). **3** (*intr;* foll. by *on*) *Inf.* to converge (upon): *the police zeroed in on the site of the crime.*

zero option n (in international nuclear arms negotiations) an offer to remove all shorter-range nuclear missiles or, in the case of the **zero-zero option** all intermediate-range nuclear missiles, if the other side will do the same.

zero-rated adj denoting goods on which the buyer pays no value-added tax although the seller can claim back any tax he has paid.

zero stage n a solid-propellant rocket attached to a liquid-propellant rocket to provide greater thrust at lift-off.

zeroth ('zɪərəʊθ) adj denoting a term in a series that precedes the term otherwise regarded as the first term. [C20: from ZERO + -TH²]

zero tolerance n the policy of applying laws or penalties to even minor infringements of a code in order to reinforce its overall importance.

zest (zɛst) n **1** invigorating or keen excitement or enjoyment: *a zest for living.* **2** added interest, flavour, or charm; piquancy: *her presence gave zest to the party.* **3** something added to give flavour or relish. **4** the peel or skin of an orange or lemon, used as flavouring in drinks, etc. ◆ vb **5** (*tr*) to give flavour, interest, or piquancy to. [C17: from F *zeste* peel of citrus fruits used as flavouring, from ?]
▸ **'zestful** adj ▸ **'zestfully** adv ▸ **'zestfulness** n ▸ **'zesty** adj

zeta ('ziːtə) n the sixth letter in the Greek alphabet (Z, ζ). [from Gk]

ZETA ('ziːtə) n a torus-shaped apparatus formerly used for research on controlled thermonuclear reactions. [C20: from *z(ero-)e(nergy) t(hermonuclear) a(pparatus)*]

Zetland ★ ('zɛtlənd) n the official name (until 1974) of Shetland.

zeugma ('zjuːgmə) n a figure of speech in which a word is used to modify or govern two or more words although appropriate to only one of them or making a different

★ people and places

sense with each, as in *Mr Pickwick took his hat and his leave* (Charles Dickens). [C16: via L from Gk: a yoking, from *zeugnunai* to yoke]
▸ **zeugmatic** (zjuːgˈmætɪk) *adj*

Zeus ★ (zjuːs) *n* the supreme god of the ancient Greeks, who became ruler of gods and men after he dethroned his father Cronus and defeated the Titans. He was the husband of his sister Hera and father by her and others of many gods, demigods, and mortals. He wielded thunderbolts and ruled the heavens, while his brothers Poseidon and Hades ruled the sea and the underworld respectively. Roman counterpart: **Jupiter**.

Zeuxis ★ (ˈzjuːksɪs) *n* late 5th century B.C., Greek painter.

Zhangjiakou (ˈdʒæŋˈdʒjækəu), **Changchiakow,** or **Changchiak'ou** ★ *n* a city in NE China, in NW Hebei province: a military centre, controlling the route to Mongolia, under the Ming and Manchu dynasties. Pop.: 529 136 (1990 est.). Former names: **Wanchüan, Kalgan**.

Zhangzhou (ˈdʒæŋˈdʒəu), **Changchow,** or **Ch'ang-chou** ★ *n* **1** a city in E China, in S Jiangsu province, on the Grand Canal: also known as **Wutsin** until 1949, when the 7th-century name was officially readopted. Pop.: 531 470 (1990 est.). **2** a city in SE China, in S Fujian province on the Saikoe River. Pop.: 181 424 (1990 est.). Former name: **Lungki**.

Zhdanov ★ (*Russian* ˈʒdanəf) *n* the former name (1948–91) for **Mariupol**.

Zhejiang (ˈdʒɛˈdʒjæŋ) or **Chekiang** ★ *n* a province of E China: mountainous and densely populated. Capital: Hangzhou. Pop.: 42 940 000 (1995 est.). Area: 102 000 sq. km (39 780 sq. miles).

Zhengzhou (ˈdʒʌŋˈdʒəu), **Chengchow,** or **Cheng-chou** ★ *n* a city in E central China, capital of Henan province. Pop.: 1 710 000 (1991 est.).

Zhitomir ★ (*Russian* ʒiˈtɒmir) *n* a city in the central Ukraine. Pop.: 301 000 (1996 est.).

Zhivkov ★ (*Bulgarian* ˈʒifkof) *n* **Todor** (ˈtɔdor). 1911–98, Bulgarian statesman; prime minister (1962–71); president (1971–89).

zho (zəu) *n* a variant spelling of **zo**.

Zhou ★ (dʒəu) *n* the Pinyin transliteration of the Chinese name for **Chou**.

Zhou En Lai ★ (en laɪ) *n* the Pinyin transliteration of the Chinese name for **Chou En-lai**.

Zhu De ★ (ˈdʒuː ˈdeɪ) *n* the Pinyin transliteration of the Chinese name for **Chu Teh**.

Zhu Jiang (ˈdʒuː ˈdʒjæŋ), **Chu Chiang,** or **Chu Kiang** ★ *n* a river in SE China, in S Guangdong province, flowing southeast from Canton to the South China Sea. Length: about 177 km (110 miles). Also called: **Canton River, Pearl River**.

Zhukov ★ (*Russian* ˈʒukəf) *n* **Georgi Konstantinovich** (ɡrˈɔrɡij kənstanˈtinəvitʃ). 1896–1974, Soviet marshal. In World War II, he broke the sieges of Stalingrad and Leningrad (1942–43) and later captured Warsaw and Berlin; minister of defence (1955–57).

Zia ul Haq ★ (ˈzɪə ʊl ˈhak) *n* **Mohammed** (məuˈhæmɪd). 1924–88, Pakistani general: president (1978–88), following the overthrow (1977) of Z. A. Bhutto by a military coup: killed in an air crash, possibly through sabotage.

zibeline (ˈzɪbəˌlaɪn, -lɪn) *n* **1** a sable or the fur of this animal. **2** a thick cloth made of wool or other animal hair, having a long nap and a dull sheen. ◆ *adj* **3** of, relating to, or resembling a sable. [C16: from F, from OIt. *zibellino*, ult. of Slavonic origin]

zibet (ˈzɪbɪt) *n* a large civet of S and SE Asia, having tawny fur marked with black spots and stripes. [C16: from Med. L *zibethum*, from Ar. *zabād* civet]

Zibo (ˈziːˈbɔː), **Tzu-po,** or **Tzepo** ★ *n* a city in NE China, in Shandong province. Pop.: 2 460 000 (1991 est.).

zidovudine (zaɪˈdɒvjuˌdiːn) *n* a drug that prolongs life and alleviates symptoms among some AIDS sufferers. Also called: **AZT**.

Ziegfeld ★ (ˈziːɡˌfɛld) *n* **Florenz** (ˈflɒrənz). 1869–1932, US theatrical producer, noted for his series of extravagant revues (1907–31), known as the Ziegfeld Follies.

ziff (zɪf) *n Austral. inf.* a beard. [C20: from ?]

ziggurat (ˈzɪɡuˌræt) *n* a type of rectangular temple tower or tiered mound erected by the Sumerians, Akkadians, and Babylonians in Mesopotamia. [C19: from Assyrian *ziqqurati* summit]

Zigong (ˈziːˈɡuŋ), **Tzekung,** or **Tzu-kung** ★ *n* an industrial city in W central China, in Sichuan. Pop.: 393 184 (1990 est.).

zigzag (ˈzɪɡˌzæɡ) *n* **1** a line or course characterized by sharp turns in alternating directions. **2** one of the series of such turns. **3** something having the form of a zigzag. ◆ *adj* **4** (*usually prenominal*) formed in or proceeding in a zigzag. **5** (of a sewing machine) capable of producing stitches in a zigzag. ◆ *adv* **6** in a zigzag manner. ◆ *vb* **zigzags, zigzagging, zigzagged. 7** to proceed or cause to proceed in a zigzag. **8** (*tr*) to form into a zigzag. [C18: from F, from G *zickzack*, from *Zacke* point]

zigzagger (ˈzɪɡˌzæɡə) *n* **1** a person or thing that zigzags. **2** an attachment on a sewing machine for sewing zigzag stitches, as for joining two pieces of material.

zilch (zɪltʃ) *n Sl.* **1** nothing. **2** *US & Canad. sport.* nil. [C20: from ?]

zillion (ˈzɪljən) *Inf.* ◆ *n, pl* **zillions** or **zillion. 1** (*often pl*) an extremely large but unspecified number, quantity, or amount: *zillions of flies in this camp.* ◆ *determiner* **2** amounting to a zillion: *a zillion different problems.* [C20: coinage after MILLION]

Zilpah ★ (ˈzɪlpə) *n Old Testament.* Leah's maidservant, who bore Gad and Asher to Jacob (Genesis 30:10–13).

Zimbabwe ★ (zɪmˈbɑːbwɪ, -weɪ) *n* **1** a country in SE Africa, formerly a self-governing British colony founded in 1890 by the British South Africa Company, which administered the country until a self-governing colony was established in 1923; joined with Northern Rhodesia (now Zambia) and Nyasaland (now Malawi) as the Federation of Rhodesia and Nyasaland from 1953 to 1963; made a unilateral declaration of independence under the leadership of Ian Smith in 1965 on the basis of White minority rule; proclaimed a republic in 1970; in 1976 the principle of Black majority rule was accepted and in 1978 a transitional government was set up; gained independence in 1980 following the Lancaster House Conference (1979–80); a member of the Commonwealth. Official language: English. Religion: Christian majority. Currency: Zimbabwe dollar. Capital: Harare. Pop: 11 423 000 (1997). Area: 390 622 sq. km (150 820 sq. miles). Former names: **Southern Rhodesia** (until 1964), **Rhodesia** (1964–79). **2** a ruined fortified settlement in Zimbabwe, which at its height, in the 15th century, was probably the capital of an empire covering SE Africa.
▸ **Zim'babwean** *n, adj*

Zimmer (ˈzɪmə) *n Trademark.* Also: **Zimmer frame**. another name for **walker** (sense 3).

zinc (zɪŋk) *n* **1** a brittle bluish-white metallic element that is a constituent of several alloys, e.g. brass and nickel-silver, and is used in die-casting, galvanizing metals, and in battery electrodes. Symbol: Zn; atomic no.: 30; atomic wt.: 65.37. **2** *Inf.* corrugated galvanized iron. [C17: from G *Zink*, ?from *Zinke* prong, from its jagged appearance in the furnace]
▸ **'zincic, 'zincous,** or **'zincoid** *adj* ▸ **'zincky, 'zincy,** or **'zinky** *adj*

zinc blende *n* another name for **sphalerite**.

zinc chloride *n* a white soluble poisonous granular solid used in manufacturing parchment paper and vulcanized fibre and in preserving wood. It is also a soldering flux, embalming agent, and medical astringent and antiseptic.

zincite (ˈzɪŋkaɪt) *n* a red or yellow mineral consisting of zinc oxide in hexagonal crystalline form. It occurs in metamorphosed limestone.

zincography (zɪŋˈkɒɡrəfɪ) *n* the art or process of etching on zinc to form a printing plate.
▸ **zincograph** (ˈzɪŋkəˌɡrɑːf) *n* ▸ **zin'cographer** *n*

zinc ointment *n* a medicinal ointment consisting of zinc oxide, petrolatum, and paraffin, used to treat certain skin diseases.

zinc oxide *n* a white insoluble powder used as a pigment in paints (**zinc white** or **Chinese white**), cosmetics, glass, and printing inks. It is an antiseptic and astringent and is used in making zinc ointment. Formula: ZnO. Also called: **flowers of zinc**.

zinc sulphate *n* a colourless soluble crystalline substance used as a mordant, in preserving wood and skins, and in the electrodeposition of zinc. Also called: **zinc vitriol**.

zine (ziːn) *n Inf.* a magazine or fanzine.

zing (zɪŋ) *n Inf.* **1** a short high-pitched buzzing sound, as of a bullet or vibrating string. **2** vitality; zest. ♦ *vb* **3** (*intr*) to make or move with or as if with a high-pitched buzzing sound. [C20: imit.]
▶ ˈzingy *adj*

zinjanthropus (zɪnˈdʒænθrəpəs) *n* a type of australopithecine, remains of which were discovered in the Olduvai Gorge in Tanzania in 1959. [C20: NL, from Ar. *Zinj* East Africa + Gk *anthrōpos* man]

zinnia (ˈzɪnɪə) *n* any of a genus of annual or perennial plants of the composite family, of tropical and subtropical America, having solitary heads of brightly coloured flowers. [C18: after J. G. *Zinn* (d. 1759), G botanist]

Zinoviev ★ (*Russian* ziˈnɒvjɪf) *n* **Grigori Yevseevich** (griˈɡɔːrij jɪfˈsjejɪvɪtʃ), original name *Ovsel Gershon Aronov Radomyslsky*. 1883–1936, Soviet politician: executed. He was the alleged author of the 'Zinoviev letter' urging British Communists to revolt, publication of which helped to defeat (1924) the first Labour Government.

Zinovievsk ★ (*Russian* ziˈnɒvjɪfsk) *n* a former name (1924–36) for **Kirovograd**.

Zion (ˈzaɪən) or **Sion** ★ *n* **1** the hill on which the city of Jerusalem stands. **2** *Judaism.* **2a** the ancient Israelites of the Bible. **2b** the modern Jewish nation. **2c** Israel as the national home of the Jewish people. **3** *Christianity.* heaven regarded as the city of God and the final abode of his elect.

Zionism (ˈzaɪəˌnɪzəm) *n* **1** a political movement for the establishment and support of a national homeland for Jews in Palestine, now concerned chiefly with the development of the modern state of Israel. **2** a policy or movement for Jews to return to Palestine from the Diaspora.
▶ ˈZionist *n, adj* ▶ ˌZionˈistic *adj*

zip (zɪp) *n* **1a** Also called: **zip fastener**. a fastening device operating by means of two parallel rows of metal or plastic teeth on either side of a closure that are interlocked by a sliding tab. US and Canad. term: **zipper**. **1b** (*modifier*) having such a device: *a zip bag*. **2** a short sharp whizzing sound, as of a passing bullet. **3** *Inf.* energy; vigour; vitality. **4** *US sl.* nothing. **5** *Sport, US & Canad. sl.* nil. ♦ *vb* **zips**, **zipping**, **zipped**. **6** (*tr*; often foll. by *up*) to fasten (clothing, etc.) with a zip. **7** (*intr*) to move with a zip: *the bullet zipped past.* **8** (*intr*; often foll. by *along, through*, etc.) to hurry; rush. [C19: imit.]

zip code *n* the US equivalent of **postcode**. [C20: from *z(one) i(mprovement) p(lan)*]

zip gun *n US & Canad. sl.* a crude home-made pistol, esp. one powered by a spring or rubber band.

zipper (ˈzɪpə) *n* the US and Canad. word for **zip** (sense 1a).

zippy (ˈzɪpɪ) *adj* **zippier**, **zippiest**. *Inf.* full of energy; lively.

zircalloy (zɜːkˈælɔɪ) *n* an alloy of zirconium containing small amounts of tin, chromium, and nickel. It is used in pressurized-water reactors.

zircon (ˈzɜːkɒn) *n* a reddish-brown, grey, green, blue, or colourless hard mineral consisting of zirconium silicate: it is used as a gemstone and a refractory. [C18: from G *Zirkon*, from F *jargon*, via It. & Ar., from Persian *zargūn* golden]

zirconium (zɜːˈkəʊnɪəm) *n* a greyish-white metallic element, occurring chiefly in zircon, that is exceptionally corrosion-resistant and has low neutron absorption. It is used as a coating in nuclear and chemical plants, as a deoxidizer in steel, and alloyed with niobium in superconductive magnets. Symbol: Zr; atomic no.: 40; atomic wt.: 91.22. [C19: from NL; see ZIRCON]
▶ zirconic (zɜːˈkɒnɪk) *adj*

zirconium oxide *n* a white amorphous powder that is

insoluble in water and highly refractory, used as a pigment for paints, a catalyst, and an abrasive.

Ziska (ˈzɪskə) or **Žižka** ★ (*Czech* ˈʒiʃka) *n* **Jan** (jan). ?1370–1424, Bohemian soldier, who successfully led the Hussite rebellion (1420–24) against emperor Sigismund.

zit (zɪt) *n Sl.* a pimple. [from ?]

zither (ˈzɪðə) *n* a plucked musical instrument consisting of numerous strings stretched over a resonating box, a few of which may be stopped on a fretted fingerboard. [C19: from G, from L *cithara*, from Gk *kithara*]
▶ ˈzitherist *n*

Zlatoust ★ (*Russian* zləˈtaʊst) *n* a town in W Russia, on the Ay river: one of the chief metallurgical centres of the Urals. Pop.: 203 000 (1995 est.).

zloty (ˈzlɒtɪ) *n, pl* **zlotys** or **zloty**. the standard monetary unit of Poland. [from Polish: golden, from *zlyoto* gold]

Zn the chemical symbol for zinc.

zo, zho, or **dzo** (zəʊ) *n, pl* **zos, zhos, dzos** or **zo, zho, dzo.** a Tibetan breed of cattle, developed by crossing the yak with common cattle. [C20: from Tibetan]

zo- *combining form.* a variant of **zoo-** before a vowel.

-zoa *suffix forming plural proper nouns.* indicating groups of animal organisms: *Metazoa*. [from NL, from Gk *zōia*, pl. of *zōion* animal]

Zoan ★ (ˈzəʊæn) *n* the Biblical name for **Tanis**.

zodiac (ˈzəʊdɪˌæk) *n* **1** an imaginary belt extending 8° either side of the ecliptic, which contains the 12 **zodiacal constellations** and within which the moon and planets appear to move. It is divided into 12 equal areas, called **signs of the zodiac**, each named after the constellation which once lay in it. **2** *Astrol.* a diagram, usually circular, representing this belt and showing the symbols, illustrations, etc., associated with each of the 12 signs of the zodiac, used to predict the future. [C14: from OF *zodiaque*, from L *zōdiacus*, from Gk *zōidiakos* (*kuklos*) (circle) of signs, from *zōidion* animal sign, from *zōion* animal]
▶ zodiacal (zəʊˈdaɪəkəl) *adj*

zodiacal constellation *n* any of the 12 constellations after which the signs of the zodiac are named: Aries, Taurus, Gemini, Cancer, Leo, Virgo, Libra, Scorpio, Sagittarius, Capricorn, Aquarius, or Pisces.

zodiacal light *n* a very faint cone of light in the sky, visible in the east just before sunrise and in the west just after sunset.

Zoffany ★ (ˈzɒfənɪ) *n* **John** or **Johann** ?1733–1810, British portrait painter, born in Germany.

Zog I ★ (zɒg) *n* 1895–1961, king of Albania (1928–39), formerly prime minister (1922–24) and president (1925–28).

zoic (ˈzəʊɪk) *adj* **1** relating to or having animal life. **2** *Geol.* (of rocks, etc.) containing fossilized animals. [C19: from NL, from Gk *zōion* animal]

-zoic *adj and n combining form.* indicating a geological era: *Palaeozoic.* [from Gk *zōē* life + -IC]

Zola ★ (ˈzəʊlə; *French* zɔla) *n* **Émile** (emil). 1840–1902, French novelist, noted for *Les Rougon-Macquart* (1871–93), a cycle of 20 novels that includes *Nana* (1880), *Germinal* (1885), and *La Terre* (1887). He defended Dreyfus in his pamphlet *J'accuse* (1898).

Zollverein *German.* (ˈtsɔlferaɪn) *n* the customs union of German states organized in the early 1830s under Prussian auspices. [C19: from *Zoll* tax + *Verein* union]

Zomba ★ (ˈzɒmbə) *n* a city in S Malawi: the capital of Malawi until 1971. Pop.: 62 700 (1994 est.).

zombie or **zombi** (ˈzɒmbɪ) *n, pl* **zombies** or **zombis. 1** a person who is or appears to be lifeless, apathetic, or totally lacking in independent judgment; automaton. **2** a supernatural spirit that reanimates a dead body. **3** a corpse brought to life in this manner. [from W African *zumbi* good-luck fetish]

zonation (zəʊˈneɪʃən) *n* arrangement in zones.

zone (zəʊn) *n* **1** a region, area, or section characterized by some distinctive feature or quality. **2** an area subject to a particular political, military, or government function, use, or jurisdiction: *a demilitarized zone.* **3** (*often cap.*) *Geog.* one of the divisions of the earth's surface, esp. divided

★ people and places

into latitudinal belts according to temperature. See **Torrid Zone, Frigid Zone, Temperate Zone. 4** *Geol.* a distinctive layer or region of rock, characterized by particular fossils (**zone fossils**), etc. **5** *Ecology.* an area, esp. a belt of land, having a particular flora and fauna determined by the prevailing environmental conditions. **6** *Maths.* a portion of a sphere between two parallel planes intersecting the sphere. **7** *Sport.* **7a** a period during which a competitor is performing particularly well: *Hingis is in the zone at the moment.* **7b** (*modifier*) of or relating to competitive performance that depends on the mood or state of mind of the participant: *a zone player.* **8** *Arch. or literary.* a girdle or belt. **9** *NZ.* a section on a transport route; fare stage. **10** *NZ.* a catchment area for a specific school. ♦ *vb* **zones, zoning, zoned.** (*tr*) **11** to divide into zones, as for different use, jurisdiction, activities, etc. **12** to designate as a zone. **13** to mark with or divide into zones. [C15: from L *zōna* girdle, climatic zone, from Gk *zōnē*]
▶ **'zonal** *adj* ▶ **'zonated** *adj* ▶ **'zoning** *n*

zone refining *n* a technique for producing solids of extreme purity, esp. for use in semiconductors. The material, in the form of a bar, is melted in one small region that is passed along the solid. Impurities concentrate in the melt and are moved to the end of the bar.

zonetime ('zəʊn,taɪm) *n* the standard time of the time zone in which a ship is located at sea, each zone extending 7½° to each side of a meridian.

zonked (zɒŋkt) *adj Sl.* **1** incapacitated by drugs or alcohol. **2** exhausted. [C20: imit.]

zonk out (zɒŋk) *vb* (*intr, adv*) *Sl.* to fall asleep, esp. from physical exhaustion or the effects of alcohol or drugs.

zoo (zuː) *n, pl* **zoos.** a place where live animals are kept, studied, bred, and exhibited to the public. Formal term: **zoological garden.** [C19: shortened from *zoological gardens* (orig. those in London)]

zoo- *or before a vowel* **zo-** *combining form.* indicating animals: *zooplankton.* [from Gk *zōion* animal]

zoogeography (,zəʊədʒɪ'ɒɡrəfɪ) *n* the branch of zoology concerned with the geographical distribution of animals.
▶ **,zooge'ographer** *n* ▶ **zoogeographic** (,zəʊə,dʒɪə'ɡræfɪk) *or* **,zoo,geo'graphical** *adj* ▶ **,zoo,geo'graphically** *adv*

zoography (zəʊ'ɒɡrəfɪ) *n* the branch of zoology concerned with the description of animals.
▶ **zo'ographer** *n* ▶ **zoographic** (,zəʊə'ɡræfɪk) *or* **,zoo'graphical** *adj*

zooid ('zəʊɔɪd) *n* **1** any independent animal body, such as an individual of a coelenterate colony. **2** a motile cell or body, such as a gamete, produced by an organism.
▶ **zo'oidal** *adj*

zool. *abbrev. for:* **1** zoological. **2** zoology.

zoolatry (zəʊ'ɒlətrɪ) *n* **1** (esp. in ancient or primitive religions) the worship of animals as the incarnations of certain deities, etc. **2** extreme or excessive devotion to animals, particularly domestic pets.
▶ **zo'olatrous** *adj*

zoological garden *n* the formal term for **zoo.**

zoology (zəʊ'ɒlədʒɪ, zuː-) *n, pl* **zoologies. 1** the study of animals, including their classification, structure, physiology, and history. **2** the biological characteristics of a particular animal or animal group. **3** the fauna characteristic of a particular region.
▶ **zoological** (,zəʊə'lɒdʒɪk°l, ,zuːə-) *adj* ▶ **zo'ologist** *n*

zoom (zuːm) *vb* **1** to make or cause to make a continuous buzzing or humming sound. **2** to move or cause to move with such a sound. **3** (*intr*) to move very rapidly; rush: *we zoomed through town.* **4** to cause (an aircraft) to climb briefly at an unusually steep angle, or (of an aircraft) to climb in this way. **5** (*intr*) (of prices) to rise rapidly. ♦ *n* **6** the sound or act of zooming. **7** See **zoom lens.** [C19: imit.]

zoom in *or* **out** *vb* (*intr, adv*) *Photog., films, television.* to increase or decrease rapidly the magnification of the image of a distant object by means of a zoom lens.

zoom lens *n* a lens system that allows the focal length of a camera lens to be varied continuously without altering the sharpness of the image.

zoomorphism (,zəʊə'mɔːfɪzəm) *n* **1** the conception or

representation of deities in the form of animals. **2** the use of animal forms or symbols in art, etc.
▶ **,zoo'morphic** *adj*

-zoon *n combining form.* indicating an individual animal or an independently moving entity derived from an animal: *spermatozoon.* [from Gk *zōion* animal]

zoophilism (zəʊ'ɒfɪ,lɪzəm) *n* the tendency to be emotionally attached to animals.
▶ **zoophile** ('zəʊə,faɪl) *n*

zoophobia (,zəʊə'fəʊbɪə) *n* an unusual or morbid dread of animals.
▶ **zoophobous** (zəʊ'ɒfəbəs) *adj*

zoophyte ('zəʊə,faɪt) *n* any animal resembling a plant, such as a sea anemone.
▶ **zoophytic** (,zəʊə'fɪtɪk) *or* **,zoo'phytical** *adj*

zooplankton (,zəʊə'plæŋktən) *n* the animal constituent of plankton, which consists mainly of small crustaceans and fish larvae.

zoospore ('zəʊə,spɔː) *n* an asexual spore of some algae and fungi that moves by means of flagella.
▶ **,zoo'sporic** *or* **zoosporous** (zəʊ'ɒspərəs, ,zəʊə'spɔːrəs) *adj*

zoosterol (zəʊ'ɒstə,rɒl) *n* any of a group of animal sterols, such as cholesterol.

zootechnics (,zəʊə'tɛknɪks) *n* (*functioning as sing*) the science concerned with the domestication and breeding of animals.

zootomy (zəʊ'ɒtəmɪ) *n* the branch of zoology concerned with the dissection and anatomy of animals.
▶ **zootomic** (,zəʊə'tɒmɪk) *or* **,zoo'tomical** *adj* ▶ **,zoo-'tomically** *adv* ▶ **zo'otomist** *n*

zootoxin (,zəʊə'tɒksɪn) *n* a toxin, such as snake venom, that is produced by an animal.

zoot suit (zuːt) *n Sl.* a man's suit consisting of baggy tapered trousers and a long jacket with wide padded shoulders, popular esp. in the 1940s. [C20: from ?]

zoril *or* **zorille** (zə'rɪl) *n* a skunklike African mammal, having a long black-and-white coat. [C18: from F, from Sp. *zorrillo* a little fox, from *zorro* fox]

Zoroaster ★ (,zɒrəʊ'æstə) *n* ?628–?551 B.C., Persian prophet; founder of Zoroastrianism. Avestan name: **Zarathustra.**

Zoroastrian (,zɒrəʊ'æstrɪən) *adj* **1** of or relating to Zoroastrianism. ♦ *n* **2** an adherent of Zoroastrianism.

Zoroastrianism (,zɒrəʊ'æstrɪən,ɪzəm) *or* **Zoroastrism** *n* the dualistic religion founded by the Persian prophet Zoroaster in the late 7th or early 6th century B.C. and set forth in the sacred writings of the Zend-Avesta. It is based on the concept of a continuous struggle between Ormazd (or Ahura Mazda), the god of creation, light, and goodness, and his archenemy, Ahriman, the spirit of evil and darkness.

Zorrilla y Moral ★ (*Spanish* θɒ'rriʎa i mo'ral) *n* **José** (xo'se). 1817–93, Spanish poet and dramatist, noted for his romantic plays, esp. *Don Juan Tenorio* (1844).

zoster ('zɒstə) *n Pathol.* short for **herpes zoster.** [C18: from L: shingles, from Gk *zōster* girdle]

Zouave (zuː'ɑːv, zwɑːv) *n* **1** (formerly) a member of a body of French infantry composed of Algerian recruits noted for their dash, hardiness, and colourful uniforms. **2** a member of any body of soldiers wearing a similar uniform, esp. a volunteer in such a unit of the Union Army in the American Civil War. [C19: from F, from *Zwāwa*, tribal name in Algeria]

Zoug ★ (zug) *n* the French name for **Zug.**

zouk (zuːk) *n* a style of dance music that combines African and Latin American rhythms and uses electronic instruments and modern studio technology. [C20: from West Indian Creole *zouk* to have a good time]

zounds (zaʊndz) *or* **swounds** (zwaʊndz, zaʊndz) *interj Arch.* a mild oath indicating surprise, indignation, etc. [C16: euphemistic shortening of *God's wounds*]

Zr the chemical symbol for zirconium.

Zsigmondy ★ (*German* 'ʃɪɡmɒndɪ) *n* **Richard Adolf** ('rɪçart 'aːdɔlf). 1865–1929, German chemist, born in Austria, noted for his introduction (1903) of the ultramicroscope: Nobel prize for chemistry 1925.

★ people and places

zucchetto (tsuˈkɛtəʊ, suː-, zuː-) *n*, *pl* **zucchettos**. *RC Church.* a small round skullcap worn by certain ecclesiastics and varying in colour according to the rank of the wearer, the Pope wearing white, cardinals red, bishops violet, and others black. [C19: from It., from *zucca* a gourd, from LL *cucutia*, prob. from L *cucurbita*]

zucchini (tsuˈkiːnɪ, zuː-) *n*, *pl* **zucchini** or **zucchinis**. *Chiefly US, Canad., & Austral.* another name for **courgette**. [It., pl of *zucchino* a little gourd, from *zucca* gourd; see ZUCCHETTO]

Zug ★ (*German* tsuːk) *n* **1** a canton of N central Switzerland: the smallest Swiss canton; mainly German-speaking and Roman Catholic; joined the Swiss Confederation in 1352. Capital: Zug. Pop.: 90 412 (1995 est.). Area: 239 sq. km (92 sq. miles). **2** a town in N central Switzerland, the capital of Zug canton, on Lake Zug. Pop.: 21 467 (1990). **3 Lake.** a lake in N central Switzerland, in Zug and Schwyz cantons. Area: 39 sq. km (15 sq. miles). French name: **Zoug**.

Zugspitze ★ (ˈtsuɡˌʃpɪtsə) *n* a mountain peak in S Germany in the Bavarian Alps, on the Austrian border: the highest peak in Germany. Height: 2963 m (9721 ft).

zugzwang (*German* ˈtsuːktsvaŋ) *Chess.* ◆ *n* **1** a position in which one player can move only with loss or severe disadvantage. ◆ *vb* **2** (*tr*) to manoeuvre (one's opponent) into a zugzwang. [from G, from *Zug* a pull + *Zwang* force]

Zuider Zee or **Zuyder Zee** ★ (ˈzaɪdə ˈziː; *Dutch* ˈzœidər ˈzeː) *n* a former inlet of the North Sea in the N coast of the Netherlands: sealed off from the sea by a dam in 1932, dividing it into the Waddenzee and the freshwater IJsselmeer, with several large areas under reclamation.

Zuidholland ★ (zœitˈhɔlɑnt) *n* the Dutch name for **South Holland**.

Zukerman ★ (ˈzukəmən) *n* **Pinchas.** born 1948, Israeli violinist.

Zulu (ˈzuːlu, -luː) *n* **1** (*pl* **Zulus** or **Zulu**) a member of a tall Negroid people of SE Africa, who became dominant during the 19th century due to a warrior-clan system organized by the powerful leader, Shaka. **2** the language of this people. [from Zulu *amaZulu* people of the sky]

Zululand ★ (ˈzuːluˌlænd, ˈzuːluː-) *n* a region of E South Africa, on the Indian Ocean; roughly corresponds to the Kwazulu/Natal region. Chief town: Eshowe. Pop.: 3 422 140 (1983). Area: 26 838 sq. km (10 362 sq. miles).

Zungaria (zʌŋˈɡɛərɪə) *n* a variant transliteration of **Junggar Pendi**.

Zuñi (ˈzuːnjiː, ˈsuː-) *n* **1** (*pl* **Zuñis** or **Zuñi**) a member of a North American Indian people of W New Mexico. **2** the language of this people.
▶ **ˈZuñian** *adj*, *n*

Zurbarán ★ (*Spanish* θurβaˈran) *n* **Francisco de** (franˈθisko de). 1598–1664, Spanish Baroque painter, esp. of religious subjects.

Zürich ★ (ˈzjʊərɪk; *German* ˈtsyːrɪç) *n* **1** a canton of NE Switzerland: mainly Protestant and German-speaking. Capital: Zürich. Pop.: 1 168 567 (1995 est.). Area: 1729 sq. km (668 sq. miles). **2** a city in NE Switzerland, the capital of Zürich canton, on Lake Zürich: the largest city and industrial centre in Switzerland; centre of the Swiss Reformation; financial centre. Pop.: 342 872 (1995 est.). **3 Lake.** a lake in N Switzerland, mostly in Zürich canton. Area: 89 sq. km (34 sq. miles).

Zuyder Zee ★ (ˈzaɪdə ˈziː; *Dutch* ˈzœidər ˈzeː) *n* a variant spelling of **Zuider Zee**.

Zweig ★ (*German* tsvaik) *n* **1 Arnold** (ˈarnɔlt). 1887–1968, German novelist, noted for his war novel *The Case of Sergeant Grischa* (1927). **2 Stefan** (ˈʃtɛfan). 1881–1942, Austrian writer.

Zwickau ★ (*German* ˈtsvɪkau) *n* a city in E Germany: Anabaptist movement founded here (1521); coal-mining and industrial centre. Pop.: 104 921 (1995 est.).

zwieback (ˈzwiːˌbæk; *German* ˈtsviːbak) *n* a small type of rusk, which has been baked first as a loaf, then sliced and toasted. [G: twice-baked]

Zwingli ★ (*German* ˈtsvɪŋli) *n* **Ulrich** (ˈulrɪç) or **Huldreich** (ˈhultraiç). 1484–1531, Swiss leader of the Reformation, based in Zürich.

Zwinglian (ˈzwɪŋliən, ˈtsvɪŋ-) *n* **1** an upholder of the religious doctrines or movement of Zwingli. ◆ *adj* **2** of or relating to Zwingli, his religious movement, or his doctrines.

zwitterion (ˈtsvɪtərˌaɪən) *n Chem.* an ion that carries both a positive and a negative charge. [C20: from G *Zwitter* bisexual + ION]

Zwolle ★ (*Dutch* ˈzwɔlə) *n* a town in the central Netherlands, capital of Overijssel province. Pop.: 99 139 (1994).

Zworykin ★ (ˈzwɔːrɪkɪn) *n* **Vladimir Kosma** (ˈvlædimɪə ˈkɒsmə). 1889–1982, US physicist and television pioneer, born in Russia. He developed the first practical television camera.

zygapophysis (ˌzɪɡəˈpɒfɪsɪs, ˌzaɪɡə-) *n*, *pl* **zygapophyses** (-ˌsiːz). *Anat., zool.* one of several processes on a vertebra that articulates with the corresponding process on an adjacent vertebra. [from Gk ZYG- + *apophusis* a sideshoot]

zygo- or *before a vowel* **zyg-** *combining form.* indicating a pair or a union: *zygodactyl; zygospore*. [from Gk *zugon* yoke]

zygodactyl (ˌzaɪɡəʊˈdæktɪl, ˌzɪɡə-) *adj also* **zygodactylous**. **1** (of the feet of certain birds) having the first and fourth toes directed backwards and the second and third forwards. ◆ *n* **2** a zygodactyl bird.

zygoma (zaɪˈɡəʊmə, zɪ-) *n*, *pl* **zygomata** (-mətə). another name for **zygomatic arch**. [C17: via NL from Gk, from *zugon* yoke]
▶ **zygomatic** (ˌzaɪɡəʊˈmætɪk, ˌzɪɡ-) *adj*

zygomatic arch *n* the slender arch of bone that forms a bridge between the cheekbone and the temporal bone on each side of the skull of mammals. Also called: **zygoma**.

zygomatic bone *n* either of two bones, one on each side of the skull, that form part of the side wall of the eye socket and part of the zygomatic arch; cheekbone.

zygomorphic (ˌzaɪɡəʊˈmɔːfɪk, ˌzɪɡ-) or **zygomorphous** *adj* (of a flower) capable of being cut in only one plane so that the two halves are mirror images.

zygomycete (ˌzaɪɡəʊˈmaɪsiːt) *n* any of a phylum of fungi that reproduce sexually by means of zygospores. The group includes various moulds.
▶ **ˌzygomyˈcetous** *adj*

zygophyte (ˈzaɪɡəʊˌfaɪt, ˈzɪɡ-) *n* a plant, such as an alga, that reproduces by means of zygospores.

zygospore (ˈzaɪɡəʊˌspɔː, ˈzɪɡ-) *n* a thick-walled sexual spore formed from the zygote of some fungi and algae.
▶ **ˌzygoˈsporic** *adj*

zygote (ˈzaɪɡəʊt, ˈzɪɡ-) *n* **1** the cell resulting from the union of an ovum and a spermatozoon. **2** the organism that develops from such a cell. [C19: from Gk *zugōtos* yoked, from *zugoun* to yoke]
▶ **zygotic** (zaɪˈɡɒtɪk, zɪ-) *adj* ▶ **zyˈgotically** *adv*

zymase (ˈzaɪmeɪs) *n* a mixture of enzymes that is obtained as an extract from yeast and ferments sugars.

zymo- or *before a vowel* **zym-** *combining form.* indicating fermentation: *zymology*. [from Gk *zumē* leaven]

zymogen (ˈzaɪməʊˌdʒɛn) *n Biochem.* any of a group of compounds that are inactive precursors of enzymes.

zymology (zaɪˈmɒlədʒɪ) *n* the chemistry of fermentation.
▶ **zymologic** (ˌzaɪməʊˈlɒdʒɪk) or **ˌzymoˈlogical** *adj* ▶ **zyˈmologist** *n*

zymolysis (zaɪˈmɒlɪsɪs) *n* the process of fermentation. Also called: **zymosis**.

zymosis (zaɪˈməʊsɪs) *n*, *pl* **zymoses** (-siːz). **1** *Med.* **1a** any infectious disease. **1b** the developmental process or spread of such a disease. **2** another name for **zymolysis**.

zymotic (zaɪˈmɒtɪk) *adj* **1** of, relating to, or causing fermentation. **2** relating to or caused by infection; denoting or relating to an infectious disease.
▶ **zyˈmotically** *adv*

zymurgy (ˈzaɪmɜːdʒɪ) *n* the branch of chemistry concerned with fermentation processes in brewing, etc.

★ people and places

Guide to the Text

Headword

bugle² ('bjuːgᵊl) *n* any of several Eurasian plants having small blue or white flowers. [C13: from LL *bugula*, from ?]

bugle³ ('bjuːgᵊl) *n* a tubular glass or plastic bead sewn onto clothes for decoration. [C16: from ?]

Pronunciation

bugloss ('bjuːglɒs) *n* any of various hairy Eurasian plants having clusters of blue flowers. [C15: from L, from Gk *bouglôssos* ox-tongued]

bugong ('buːgɒŋ) *n* another name for **bogong**.

buhl (buːl) *adj, n* a variant spelling of **boulle**.

Inflected forms

build (bɪld) *vb* **builds, building, built**. **1** to make, construct, or form by joining parts or materials: *to build a house*. **2** (*tr*) to order the building of: *the government builds most of our hospitals.* **3** (foll. by *on* or *upon*) to base; found: *his theory was not built on facts.* **4** (*tr*) to establish and develop: *it took ten years to build a business.* **5** (*tr*) to make in a particular way or for a particular purpose: *the car was not built for speed.* **6** (*intr*; often foll. by *up*) to increase in intensity. ◆ *n* **7** physical form, figure, or proportions: *a man with an athletic build.* [OE *byldan*]

Part of speech   Grammatical information

builder ('bɪldə) *n* a person who builds, esp. one who contracts for and supervises the construction or repair of buildings.

Definition

building ('bɪldɪŋ) *n* **1** something built with a roof and walls. **2** the act, business, occupation, or art of building houses, boats, etc.

building society *n* a cooperative banking enterprise financed by deposits on which interest is paid and from which mortgage loans are advanced on homes and real property; many now offer a range of banking services.

build up *vb* (*adv*) **1** (*tr*) to construct gradually, systematically, and in stages. **2** to increase, accumulate, or strengthen, esp. by degrees: *the murmur built up to a roar.* **3** (*tr*) to improve the health or physique of (a person). **4** (*intr*) to prepare for or gradually approach a climax. ◆ *n* **build-up. 5** progressive increase in number, size, etc.: *the build-up of industry.* **6** a gradual approach to a climax. **7** extravagant publicity or praise, esp. in the form of a campaign. **8** *Mil.* the process of attaining the required strength of forces and equipment.

Subject-field label

built (bɪlt) *vb* the past tense and past participle of **build**.

built-in *adj* **1** made or incorporated as an integral part: *a built-in cupboard.* **2** essential; inherent. ◆ *n* **3** *Austral.* a built-in cupboard.

Sense number

built-in obsolescence *n* See **planned obsolescence**.

built-up *adj* **1** having many buildings (esp. in **built-up area**). **2** increased by the addition of parts: *built-up heels.*

Buitenzorg ★ (*Dutch* 'bœitənzɔrx) *n* the former name of **Bogor**.

Bujumbura ★ (ˌbuːdʒəmˈbuərə) *n* the capital of Burundi, a port at the NE end of Lake Tanganyika. Pop.: 300 000 (1994 est.). Former name: **Usumbura**.

Bukavu ★ (buːˈkɑːvuː) *n* a port in E Democratic Republic of the Congo (formerly Zaire), on Lake Kivu: commercial and industrial centre. Pop.: 201 569 (1994 est.). Former name (until 1966): **Costermansville**.

Bukhara *or* **Bokhara** ★ (buˈxɑːrə) *n* **1** a city in S Uzbekistan: capital of the former emirate of Bukhara. Pop.: 236 000 (1993 est.). **2** a former emirate of central Asia: a powerful kingdom and centre of Islam; became a territory of the Soviet Union (1920) and was divided between the former Uzbek, Tajik, and Turkmen SSRs.

Bukovina *or* **Bucovina** ★ (ˌbuːkəˈviːnə) *n* a region of E central Europe, part of the NE Carpathians: the north was seized by the Soviet Union (1940) and later became part of the Ukraine; the south remained Romanian.

Bulawayo ★ (ˌbuləˈweɪəu) *n* a city in SW Zimbabwe founded (1893) on the site of the kraal of Lobengula, the last Matabele king; the country's main industrial centre. Pop.: 620 936 (1992).

bulb (bʌlb) *n* **1** a rounded organ of vegetative reproduction in plants such as the tulip and onion: a flattened stem bearing a central shoot surrounded by fleshy nutritive inner leaves and thin brown outer leaves. **2** a plant, such as a hyacinth or daffodil, that grows from a bulb. **3** See **light bulb**. **4** any bulb-shaped thing. [C16: from L *bulbus*, from Gk *bolbos* onion]

Cross-reference

▶ **'bulbous** *adj*

x